American Universities and Colleges

American

Universities

and

Colleges

Seventeenth Edition

Produced in Collaboration with the
American Council on Education

VOLUME 1

 AMERICAN COUNCIL ON EDUCATION
PRAEGER
Series on Higher Education

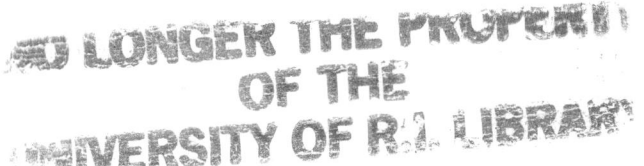

First published in 2006
Praeger Publishers, 88 Post Road West, Westport, CT 06881
An imprint of Greenwood Publishing Group, Inc.
www.Praeger.com

ISBN (Set): 0-275-98745-0

ISBN Vol. 1: 0-275-98746-9

ISBN Vol. 2: 0-275-98747-7

Printed in the United States of America

∞ The paper used in this book complies with the Permanent Paper Standard issued by the National Information Standards Organization (Z39.48-1984).

Contents of Volume 1

Contents of Volume 2

Foreword and Acknowledgments

American Universities and Colleges has been serving higher education since 1928. The American Council on Education's first edition of the directory included 401 institutions; this seventeenth edition includes detailed descriptions of more than 1,900 colleges and universities, all accredited institutions of higher education offering a baccalaureate or higher degree. The increase in the number of U.S. colleges and universities, and in the diversity of programs they offer, has greatly enriched the higher education enterprise. At the same time, it has added to the complexity of this directory. To help the directory's users navigate this complexity, we have included numerous indices that guide readers to specific institutional, degree, and accreditation information.

Many persons contributed to the preparation of this work, but without the cooperation and goodwill of the nation's college and university officials and their staffs, who supplied most of the information on which the institutional data are based, the publication of this directory would not be possible. In this edition, the data for all institutional exhibits (Part III) were collected and compiled by Modoc Press, Inc., Santa Monica, California.

Several individuals merit special thanks. Jacqueline King, director of ACE's Center for Policy Analysis, assisted greatly with the development of the survey instrument used to collect institutional data for the book. Eugene Anderson, associate director in the Center, and Natasha Janson, graduate research intern and a doctoral candidate at The College of William and Mary, revised the "Structure of Higher Education" and "Government and Higher Education" sections of Part I. Ken Von Alt of the Council's Publications Department provided updates to the accreditation and abbreviation information included in the book. Wendy Bresler, ACE's director of publications, provided project oversight. Special thanks are due Susan Slesinger, Greenwood Publishing Group's executive editor of the ACE/Praeger Series on Higher Education, who has been a source of professional guidance and support.

The American Council on Education is pleased to provide you with this latest edition of our first, and still one of our most important, publications.

BENJAMIN F. QUILLIAN
Senior Vice President
American Council on Education

Notes on Institutional Exhibits

Part III of this book includes more than 1,900 individual entries on degree-granting baccalaureate-or-above institutions and units thereof that are accredited or recognized candidates for accreditation by one of the eight regional agencies. Each institution's description also includes its regional, professional, and institutional accreditation. Those fields in which programs offering specific areas of the profession for accreditation are also indicated. For information on specialized professional accrediting agencies, see Part II of this book.

The information in Part III was prepared largely from data supplied by the institutions themselves in questionnaires sent to all degree-granting regionally accredited colleges and universities. In addition, information was gleaned from other available sources. The institutions which did not return questionnaires have exhibits prepared from data provided by the National Center for Education Statistics IPED Integrated Post-Secondary Education Database, college catalogs, and other institutional sources.

Unless noted, data are for the 2004-05 academic years. Changes in addresses, chief executive officers, and admissions officers up to 2004 are also reflected in the exhibits.

The material throughout Part III was prepared in as set a format as possible to augment comparison of data not only among exhibits in this edition but also to earlier editions of American Universities and Colleges. However, the variety of high education in America defies formulas, and the exhibits reflect diversity as well as similarity. Whenever possible, qualifications offered by the institutions appear (for example, estimates are so labeled). For the most part, negative information has been omitted. However, exhibits report if institutions conduct no summer sessions, offer no financial aid, especially for foreign students, have no campus housing, or do not permit cars on campus grounds.

Omission of sections from institutional descriptions may indicate negative information, data withheld, or unavailable or irrelevant material.

Institution Description. Institutions were asked to provide summary views—control, enrollment, degrees awarded, general relation to statewide coordinating bodies and governing boards, and membership in consortia oriented toward providing student services.

Accreditation. Regional, specialized, and institutional accreditation is noted.

History. Institutions were asked to provide brief histories followed, where available, by referrals to the best and most comprehensive institutional history available.

Institutional Structure. Institutions were asked to offer a summary view of their governing structure and composition. They were asked to list the number and type of members of the governing board and the number of administrators and faculty in the institution as well as the title of the academic governance body. Faculty represented by collective bargaining agents were so designated.

Calendar. This section indicates the institution's primary calendar system (semester, quarter, etc.) and whether or not summer session is available. It notes the months freshmen may enter and tells when degrees are offered and when commencement occurs.

Characteristics of Freshmen. Institutions were asked to offer information on the entering class (usually freshmen, but sometimes students at other levels in, for example, professional or upper-division-only schools). Institutions were further asked to specify average secondary school rank, SAT or ACT scores if appropriate, and to note number of Merit Scholars attending, number of applicants accepted, number of accepted applicants enrolling, number of freshmen graduating within five years.

Admission. Institutions were asked to describe both admission procedures and requirements. Procedures include the type of admission plan (rolling or standard) and the earliest and latest possible application dates, as well as information about the existence of early decision and early acceptance policies. Under the rolling admissions plan, applications are processed as received and the applicants notified when the processing is completed. Early decisions belong to the more traditional admissions plan and provide for a notification of acceptance for highly qualified students in advance of usual admissions notification date. Early acceptance pertains to a policy whereby such students may be admitted at the end of their junior year in high school. Institutions were asked to provide requirements common to their entering class (usually freshmen) as a whole. Requirements are distinguished from recommendations in information on number and distribution of secondary school units, secondary school class standing, GPA, and entrance examinations. Transfer student admission requirements could also be mentioned in this category.

Degree Requirements. Institutions were asked to indicate the levels of degrees for which they were reporting requirements and to list only common requirements. Special requirements often appear in the supplemental exhibits for complex institutions with separate units. Often credit, GPA, and residence requirements are reported as ranges rather than single figures. Institutions were asked to indicate whether students could fulfill requirements through achievement test, and whether exit examinations, chapel attendance, physical education , or ROTC were required. Finally, institutions were asked to describe their grading systems. In the case of regionally accredited graduate or professional schools, the degree requirements given, like the admission requirements, were those pertaining to programs entered directly following the baccalaureate.

Distinctive Educational Programs. Institutions were asked to report academic offerings such as work-experience programs, including cooperative education and internships; flexible meeting places and schedules, including off-campus centers, weekend and evening classes; accelerated degree plans; dual and joint degree programs involving two institutions and two degrees; double-degree programs where one institution awards two degrees; cooperative degree programs where two units or institutions offer one degree; external degree programs and continuing education curricula; special facilities for using telecommunications in the classroom; interdepartmental and interdisciplinary programs; study abroad; and many other programs.

ROTC. Institutions were asked to specify whether ROTC was available, whether it was required, and whether it was offered cooperatively with another institution.

Degrees Conferred. Institutions were asked to report degrees at the baccalaureate, master's, and doctoral degree levels in agriculture and natural resources, architecture and environmental design, area studies, biological sciences, business and management, communications, computer and information sciences, education, engineering, fine and applied arts, health professions, home economics, law, letters, library science, mathematics, military sciences, physical sciences, psychology, public affairs and services, social science, theology, interdisciplinary students, and other professions. Institutions listed in addition the number of degrees awarded at the associate level in arts and sciences; in science- or engineering-related organized occupational programs in data-processing, health services, and paramedical, mechanical and engineering, and natural science technologies, and in other occupational programs in business and commerce, and public service-related technologies. Finally, they were asked to report any intermediate degrees—formal recognitions for programs between master's and doctorates which are in essence the doctoral degree without the dissertation.

Fees and Other Expenses. Institutions were asked to provide tuition figures for 2004-05. They were also asked to provide information on fees and room and board.

Financial Aid. Institutions were asked to give the reasons for awarding their undergraduate scholarships, grants, and loans and their graduate fellowships (excluding first-professional awards). They were also asked to report figures on the number of recipients, the total funds awarded, and the range of awards for their undergraduate scholarships, grants, loans, and college-assigned jobs; and for their graduate fellowships (also excluding first-professional) and grants, teaching and research assistantships, and other college-assigned jobs. They were requested to provide similar information on federal and state aid received by their students.

Departments and Teaching Staff. Institutions were asked to list by department and rank those members of the teaching and research staff (including those with released time) who were employed on a full-time basis and whose major regular assignment was instruction. They were also asked to list part-time teachers who taught less than full time; however, that status was defined by the individual institutions. In complex institutions with separately defined units such as divisions, schools, or colleges,

total faculty figures appear in the main exhibits, with the departmental breakdown available in the descriptions of the individual unit.

Enrollment. Institutions were asked to report their total student enrollment, divided into full-and part-time students at the undergraduate, first professional, and graduate levels. They were also asked to list unclassified students who take courses for credit but are not degree candidates, and numbers of transfer students.

Characteristics of Student Body. In this section, institutions were asked to provide data on ethnic/racial makeup of the student body as well as the age distribution.

International Students. In this section, institutions were asked to provide information on nonresident aliens in attendance as well as the number of students from various world areas. They were also requested to indicate the availability and extent of the programs, scholarships, fellowships, and loans especially designated for foreign students.

Student Life. Institutions were asked to indicate the presence and nature (particularly whether the dormitories were single-sex or coed) of institutionally provided housing and to describe the availability of married-student housing. They were asked to specify what kinds of intercollegiate athletics were available for men and women; and what kinds of student publications, radio, and television activities were possible. Institutions were asked whether their campus had special regulations regarding cars or residence halls hours. And they were asked to provide information about their medical services, campus transportation systems, and (if appropriate) learning resources centers. Finally, they were asked to characterize the surrounding community as to population and availability of mass transportation.

Publications. If appropriate, institutions were asked to provide information about their scholarly journals and university presses.

Library Collections. Institutions were asked to provide figures on their current collections of volumes, government document collections, microforms, audiovisual materials, and periodical subscriptions. They were also asked to describe their three most important special collections.

Buildings and Grounds. Institutions were asked to report their campus area, grounds, and equipment, the buildings completed since 1999, the buildings currently being constructed, and the number of buildings.

Chief Executive Officer. The chief executive and admissions officers are, whenever possible, those who held the position in 2004.

Accreditation in Higher Education

Accreditation is a system for recognizing educational institutions and professional programs affiliated with those institutions for a level of performance, integrity, and quality which entitles them to the confidence of the educational community and the public they serve. In the United States this recognition is extended primarily through nongovernmental, voluntary institutional or professional associates. These groups establish criteria for recognition, arrange site visits, and evaluate those institutions and professional programs that desire recognition status; they approve for recognition those which meet their criteria.

Institutional accreditation is granted by the accrediting commissions of associations of schools and colleges, which collectively serve most of the institutions chartered or licensed in the United Sates and its possessions. These commissions and associations accredit total operating units only.

Specialized accreditation of professional schools and programs is granted by commissions on accreditation set up by national professional organizations in such areas as business, dentistry, engineering, and law. Each of these groups has its distinctive definitions of eligibility, criteria for accreditation and operating procedures, but all have undertaken accreditation activities, primarily to provide quality assurances concerning the educational preparation of members of the profession.

USES OF ACCREDITATION

In most other countries the establishment and maintenance of educational standards are the responsibility of a central government bureau. In the United States, however, public authority in education is constitutionally reserved to the states. The system of voluntary nongovernmental evaluation called accreditation has evolved to promote both regional and national approaches to the determination of educational quality.

While accreditation is basically a private, nonvoluntary process, accrediting decisions are used as a consideration in many official actions: federal funding agencies consider accreditation as an important factor in determining eligibility for financial assistance; scholarship commissions and philanthropic foundations frequently limit their grants to accredited institutions or programs of study; employers rely on the accredited status of institutions when evaluating credentials; school counselors use the decisions in advising students about colleges and programs; college and university officials depend on them to assess and award academic credit; and potential students need them for assurance that a college or university has met minimum requirements for educational quality. In addition, these decisions are useful to faculty and staff in their efforts to develop comprehensive educational goals. In many professions, eligibility for certification or licensure is limited to graduates of accredited institutions. Finally, the public is protected from unqualified graduates who may have been inadequately prepared for professional practice.

The accrediting process is also useful in helping institutions maintain high educational standards and improve quality. The accrediting bodies provide counsel to both established and developing institutions and protect them from both external and internal encroachments that might jeopardize their educational effectiveness and academic freedom.

The accrediting process is continuously evolving. The trend has been from quantitative to qualitative criteria, from the early days of simple checklists to an increasing interest and emphasis on measuring the outcomes of educational experiences.

The process begins with the institutional or programmatic self-study, a comprehensive effort to measure progress according to previously accepted objected. The self-study considers the interests of a broad cross-section of constituencies—students, faculty administrators, alumni, trustees, and in some circumstances, the local community. The resulting report is reviewed by the appropriate accrediting commission and serves as the basis for evaluation by a site-visit team from the accrediting group. The site-visit team normally consists of professional educators (faculty and administrators), specialists selected according to the nature of the institution and members representing specific public interests. The visiting team considers the institution or program according to the dimensions of the self-study and adds judgments based on its own expertise and its external perspective. The evaluation team completes a report, which is reviewed by the institution or program for factual accuracy. The original self-study, the team report and any response the institution or program may wish to make are forwarded to an accreditation review committee. The review body uses these materials as the basis for action regarding the accreditation status of the institution or program. Negative actions may be appealed according to established procedures of the accrediting body.

Accrediting bodies reserve the right to review member institutions or programs at any time for cause. They also reserve the right to review any substantive changes, such as an expansion from undergraduate to graduate offerings. In this way accrediting bodies hold their member institutions and programs continually accountable to their educational peers, to the constituencies they serve, and to the public interest.

Historically and currently, accreditation at the postsecondary level may be said to foster excellence in postsecondary education through the development of uniform national criteria and guidelines for assessing educational effectiveness; to encourage improvement through continuous self-study and review; and to assure the educational community, the general public, and other agencies or organizations that an institution or program has clearly defined and appropriate objectives, maintains conditions under which their achievement can reasonably be expected, appears in fact to be accomplishing them substantially, and can be expected to continue to do so.

Accrediting bodies do not rank or grade institutions; they either accredit or decline to accredit them. Most commissions, however, do specify a definite term for which their accreditation is valid, five years usually being the maximum for initial accreditation and ten years for reaccredidation. Many accrediting bodies award candidate status to developing or newly applying institutions, which satisfy eligibility requirements and that present evidence of sound planning, adequate implementation resources, and potential for meeting stated goals within a reasonable period of time.

This status, designed for postsecondary institutions and programs that may or may not be fully operational, usually is granted for a two-year term. If progress is being made, candidacy can be extended for up to six years. Institutions or programs that show serious weakness in one or more areas, but which at the same time show firm potential for remedying the deficiencies, may be placed in a probationary status. Accreditation continues, but generally for a sharply reduced term, and an interim report or extra site visit is generally required.

ACCREDITING ORGANIZATIONS

Eight regional commissions in six geographic areas cover all parts of the nation and grant total institutional accreditations. These associations are: Commission on Higher Education, Middle States Association of Colleges and Schools, 3624 Market Street, Philadelphia, Pennsylvania 19104 (Delaware, District of Columbia, Maryland, New Jersey, New York, Pennsylvania, Puerto Rico, Virgin Islands), Commission on Institutions of Higher Education, New England Association of Schools and Colleges and Commission on Technical and Career Institutions, New England Association of Schools and Colleges, 209 Burlington Road, Bedford, Massachusetts 01730-1433 (Connecticut, Maine, Massachusetts, New Hampshire, Rhode Island, Vermont); Commission on Institutions of Higher Education, North Central Association of Colleges and Schools, 30 N. LaSalle Street, Suite 2400, Chicago, Illinois 60602 (Arizona, Arkansas, Colorado, Illinois, Indiana, Iowa, Kansas, Michigan, Minnesota, Missouri, Nebraska, New Mexico, North Dakota, Ohio, Oklahoma, South Dakota, West Virginia, Wisconsin, Wyoming); Commission on Colleges, Northwest Association of Schools and Colleges, 11130 NE 33rd Place, Suite 120, Bellevue, Washington 98004 (Alaska, Idaho, Montana, Nevada, Oregon, Utah, Washington); Commission on Colleges, Southern Association of Colleges and Schools, 1866 Southern Lane, Decatur, Georgia 30033-4097 (Alabama, Florida, Georgia, Kentucky, Louisiana, Mississippi, North Carolina, South Carolina, Tennessee, Texas, Virginia), Accrediting Commission for Senior Colleges and Universities, Western Association of Schools and Colleges, c/o Mills College, Box 9990, Oakland, California 94613 (American Samoa, California, Guam, Hawaii, Trust Territory of the Pacific); and Accrediting Commission for Community and Junior Colleges, Western Association of Schools and Colleges, 3402 Mendocino Avenue, Santa Rosa, California 95403 (American Samoa, California, Guam, Hawaii, Trust Territory of the Pacific.)

Eight associations accredit total institutions on a national scale. These are: Commission on Accreditation, Accrediting Association of Bible Colleges, 5890 S. Semoran Boulevard, Orlando, FL 32822; Board of Commissioners, Accrediting Bureau of Health Education Schools, 2700 South Quincy Street, Suite 210, Arlington, VA 22206; Accrediting Commission for Career Schools/Colleges of Technology, 2101 Wilson Boulevard, Arlington, VA 22201; Accrediting Council for Independent Colleges and Schools, 750 First Street, NE, Suite 980, Washington, DC 20002; Accreditation Commission, Association of Advanced Rabbinical and Talmudic Schools, 175 Fifth Avenue, Suite 711, New York, NY 10010; Commission on Accrediting, The Association of Theological Schools in the United States and Canada, 10 Summit Park Drive, Pittsburgh, PA 15275-1103; Commission on Occupational Education, Council on Occupational Education, 41 Perimeter Center East, NE, Suite 640, Atlanta, GA 30346; and Accrediting Commission, Distance Education and Training Council, 1601 – 18th Street, NW, Washington, DC 20009.

Finally, forty-one national associations offer recognized specialized and professional accreditation for programs or other academic units within an institution, or for free-standing single purpose institutions. It is thus possible that a large number of accrediting bodies may be involved in a single institution, usually a university with a variety of professional programs. However, for most degree-granting institutions, the basic accreditation remains institutional (and usually regional) accreditation upon which virtually all other accreditation is built.

RELATIONSHIP OF ACCREDITATION TO THE STATES

Before the organization of voluntary accrediting associations, state departments of education and state universities were faced with the necessity of judging the quality of the educational programs of collegiate institutions within their state. The statutory responsibilities of the states for licensing public school teachers required the development of systems of state approval of teacher preparation institutions. The Board of Regents of the University of the State of New York was the first state agency to develop machinery for the approval of courses of study in teacher education, as well as in the liberal arts and many other specialized areas. The majority of the state agencies did not begin accrediting until after the first decade of the present century; and to a great extent, they have continued to limit their accrediting activities to approval of teacher education programs.

Accrediting activities by state universities in nearly every instance had their origin in relations with secondary schools. These accrediting activities related to the admissions of secondary school graduates to the universities on the basis of certification of the secondary schools rather than entrance examinations given to the applicants. Most of the state universities, however, have abandoned the practice of accrediting other institutions of higher education and now rely upon the accredited status given through the institutions accrediting associations.

THE RECOGNITION OF ACCREDITING BODIES

The Council for Higher Education Accreditation (CHEA) is the successor structure for the nongovernmental recognition of accrediting bodies. It replaces the Council on Postsecondary Accreditation (COPA), which dissolved on December 31, 1993, and its successor, the Commission on Recognition of Postsecondary Accreditation (CORPA) which dissolved on December 31, 1996.

The Council for Higher Education Accreditation (CHEA) is a non-profit organization of colleges and universities. Established in 1996, CHEA serves as a national advocate for voluntary self-regulation through accreditation. CHEA serves students and their families, colleges and universities, sponsoring bodies, governments, and employers by promoting academic quality through formal recognition of higher education accrediting bodies. CHEA recognizes, coordinates, and periodically reviews the work of its recognized accrediting bodies and the appropriateness of existing or proposed accrediting bodies and their activities through its granting of recognition.

RELATIONSHIP OF ACCREDITATION WITH THE FEDERAL GOVERNMENT

Although the federal government does not accredit any educational activities, the Veterans Readjustment Act of 1952, which provided for federal assistance to veterans for their education, charged the former United States Commissioner of Education with the responsibility of publishing a list of nationally recognized accrediting agencies, which he determined to be reliable authorities for determining the quality of training offered by educational institutions. In 1968, the Accreditation and Institutional Eligibility Staff and an associated internal advisory committee were established in United States Office of Education to administer the commissioner's review process for accrediting agencies being used to establish institutional eligibility for several other educational acts.

Congressional authorization for federal involvement in nongovernmental accreditation has traditionally been limited to the establishment of an institution's eligibility to apply for funds from federal programs and the maintenance of records of accrediting status by the Secretary of Education to implement the processes of legislation.

THE TRIAD

As the system presently functions, there is a need for the federal government to establish eligibility for its funds, as there is a need for the states to charter educational institutions within their jurisdictions. The voluntary sector, represented by the accrediting organizations, serves as a bridge between the federal and state roles in education.

Thus, a three-part structure for accreditation has been created. This three-part structure has been termed a "triad" for eligibility. The triad consists of the states, which grant institutional charter of licenses to operate; the accrediting bodies, which provide an educational assessment of institutions and programs; and the federal government, which provides funding for some activities related to student aid and education.

INFORMATION ON ACCREDITED INSTITUTIONS AND ACCREDITATION

The American Council on Education annually publishes Accredited Institutions of Postsecondary Education, which can be ordered from Greenwood Publishing Group, 88 Post Road West, Westport, CT 06881, 1-800-225-5800, www.greenwood.com. Each accrediting body recognized by CHEA publishes a list of accredited institutions or programs.

REFERENCES

Astin, Alexander W., Bowen, Howard R., and Chambers, Charles M. *Evaluating Educational Quality.* Washington, DC: Council on Postsecondary Accreditation, 1979.

Casey, Robert J. and Harris, John W. *Accountability in Higher Education.* Washington, DC: Council on Postsecondary Accreditation, 1979.

Finkin, Matthew W. *Federal Reliance on Educational Accreditation: The Scope of Administrative Discretion.* Washington, DC: Council on Postsecondary Accreditation, 1978.

Fisk, Robert S. and Duryea, E.D. *Academic Collective Bargaining and Regional Accreditation.* Washington, DC: Council on Postsecondary Accreditation, 1980.

Harcleroad, Fred F. *Voluntary Organizations in America and the Development of Educational Accreditation.* Washington, DC: Council on Postsecondary Accreditation, 1980.

Kaplin, William A. *Accrediting Agencies' Legal Responsibilities: In Pursuit of the Public Interest.* Washington, DC: Council on Postsecondary Accreditation, 1981.

Kuhns, Eileen and Martorana, S.V. *Toward Academic Quality Off-Campus: Monitoring Requirements of Institutional Accrediting Bodies and the States for Off-Campus, Military Base, and Study Abroad Programs.* Washington, DC: Council on Postsecondary Accreditation, 1984.

Lenn, Marjorie Peace. "The US Accreditation System," *Quality Assurance in International Higher Education.* The Falmer Press, London and Washington, DC: 1992.

Selden, William K. and Porter, Harry V. *Accreditation: Its Purposes and Uses.* Washington, DC: Council on Postsecondary Accreditation, 1979.

Abbreviations and Definitions

The following sections define many of the terms and abbreviations that readers will encounter in Part III.

DEGREES

B.A.	Bachelor of Arts
B.D.	Bachelor of Divinity
B.F.A.	Bachelor of Fine Arts
B.S.	Bachelor of Science
D.B.	Bachelor of Divinity
D.C.	Doctor of Chiropractic
D.D.	Doctor of Divinity
D.D.S.	Doctor of Dental Science or Doctor of Dental Surgery
D.M.D.	Doctor of Dental Medicine
D.O.	Doctor of Osteopathy
D.P.	Doctor of Podiatry
D.Pharm.	Doctor of Pharmacy
D.V.M.	Doctor of Veterinary Medicine
J.D.	Doctor of Jurisprudence
L.H.D.	Doctor of Humanities
Litt.D.	Doctor of Letters
LL.B.	Bachelor of Laws
LL.D.	Doctor of Laws
M.A.	Master of Arts
M.B.A.	Master of Business Administration
M.D.	Doctor of Medicine
M.Div.	Master of Divinity
M.F.A.	Master of Fine Arts
M.S.	Master of Science
M.S.W.	Master of Social Work or Master of Social Welfare
O.D.	Doctor of Optometry
Ph.B.	Bachelor of Philosophy
Ph.D.	Doctor of Philosophy
Ph.G.	Graduate in Pharmacy

OTHER ABBREVIATIONS

AAC&U	Association of American Colleges and Universities
AACC	American Association of Community Colleges
AACN	American Association of Colleges of Nursing
AACRAO	American Association of Collegiate Registrars and Admissions Officers
AACTE	American Association of Colleges for Teacher Education
AAHE	American Association for Higher Education
AALS	Association of American Law Schools
AAMC	Association of American Medical Colleges
AARTS	Association of Advanced Rabbinical and Talmudic Schools
AASCU	American Association of State Colleges and Universities
AAU	Association of American Universities
AAUP	American Association of University Professors
ABHE	Association for Biblical Higher Education (formerly AABC)
ABHES	Accrediting Bureau of Health Education Schools
ACCSCT	Accrediting Commission for Career Schools/Colleges of Technology
ACCT	Association of Community College Trustees
ACCU	Association of Catholic Colleges and Universities
ACE	American Council on Education
ACICS	Accrediting Council for Independent Schools and Colleges
ACPA	American College Personnel Association
ACT	American College Testing
ADEA	American Dental Education Association
AGB	Association of Governing Boards of Universities and Colleges
AHC	Association of Academic Health Centers
AJCU	Association of Jesuit Colleges and Universities
APPA	Association of Higher Education Facilities Officers
ASEE	American Society for Engineering Education
ATS	Association of Theological Schools in the United States
CASE	Council for Advancement and Support of Education
CB	The College Board
CCA	Career College Association
CCCU	Council for Christian Colleges & Universities
CGS	Council of Graduate Schools
CHEA	Council for Higher Education Accreditation
CIC	Council for Independent Colleges
COE	Council for Opportunity in Education
COGR	The Council on Governmental Relations
CUPA-HR	College and University Professional Association for Human Resources
DELC	Distance Education and Learning Council
EDUCAUSE	EDUCAUSE
ETS	Educational Testing Service
HACU	Hispanic Association of Colleges and Universities
MSA	Middle States Association of Colleges and Schools
NACAC	National Association of College Admission Counseling
NACUA	National Association of College and University Attorneys
NACUBO	National Association of College and University Business Officers
NAFEO	National Association for Equal Opportunity in Higher Education
NAFSA	NAFSA: Association of International Educators
NAICU	National Association of Independent Colleges and Universities
NASFAA	National Association of Student Financial Aid Administrators
NASPA	National Association of Student Personnel Administrators

NASULGC	National Association of State Universities and Land-Grant Colleges
NAWE	NAWE: Advancing Women in Higher Education
NCA	North Central Association of Colleges and Schools
NCAA	National Collegiate Athletic Association
NCURA	National Council of University Research Administrators
NEASC	New England Association of Schools and Colleges
NWCCU	Northwest Commission of Colleges and Universities (formerly NASC)
SACS	Southern Association of Colleges and Schools
UCEA	University Continuing Education Association
UNCF	United Negro College Fund
WASC	Western Association of Schools and Colleges
WCC	Women's College Coalition
WHES	Business-Higher Education Forum

DEFINITIONS

Administrators—institutional staff members with administrative responsibilities who teach no more than one class per term and who have titles such as dean of instruction, academic dean, dean of faculty, dean of students, librarian, registrar, coach, etc.

Audiovisual Materials—teaching and learning aids that are neither books nor microforms, that are interpreted through hearing and/or sight, and that require special equipment to use. Audiovisual materials include motion pictures, records and tapes, filmstrips, slides, transparencies, videotapes, and the like.

Branch Campus—a relatively permanent unit of an institution that offers and organized program(s) of work requiring at least two years of study (as opposed to merely courses) located in a community beyond a reasonable commuting distance from the main campus or parent institution.

Calendar—the system by which an institution divides its year into periods for instruction. The most common systems include those based on semesters, trimesters, and quarters.

Cluster College—a group of institutions, located within close proximity to each other, that cooperate in providing educational programs and other facilities to students in all institutions forming the aggregate. Cluster colleges cooperate more closely than institutions in a consortium.

Continuing Education—instruction other than that offered in the regular campus academic program. Examples include evening or weekend colleges or correspondence courses. These programs often are designed to serve the special needs of learners such as part-time or fully employed students.

Cooperative Education—a program in which a student alternates between periods of full-time study and full-time employment in a related field. Typically, five years are required to complete a bachelor's degree under this plan.

Early Admission—the practice of admitting students who have not yet completed high school—usually students of exceptional ability who have completed their junior year.

External-Degree Program—a system of study that grants credit for courses at institutions other than that offering the degree; that often counts as extrainstitutional learning; and that often emphasizes off-campus, self-directed study.

First-Professional Degree—signifies completion of academic requirements for a selected profession based on a program requiring at least two academic years of postsecondary study. First-professional degrees include architecture; dentistry; medicine; optometry; osteopathic medicine; pharmacy; podiatry or podiatric medicine (including chiropody); veterinary medicine; chiropractic; law; general; theological professions, general.

4-1-4—a semester system that consists of two terms, each about 16 weeks long, divided by one-month term during which students participate in intensive short courses, independent study, employment, or other educational activities.

Free University—programs—usually operating without credit, grades, or attendance constraints—set up by students and faculty for discussion of issues and subjects not necessarily typical of those covered in other postsecondary courses.

Full-Time Instructional Faculty—those members of the instructional/research staff (including those with released time) who are employed on a full-time basis and whose major regular assignment is instruction. The group includes department heads (if they have no other administrative title and hold faculty rank) but does not include administrators with titles such as dean of instruction, academic dean, dean of faculty, dean of students, librarian, registrar, coach, etc., even though they may devote part of their time to classroom instruction.

Honors Program—any special program for highly capable students that offers the opportunity for educational enrichment, independent study, acceleration, or some combination of these activities.

Independent Study—an arrangement that allows students to complete some of their college program by studying on their own rather than by attending scheduled classes and completing standard assignments. Typically, students plan these programs in consultation with a faculty advisor or committee, who evaluates their progress.

Institutional System—a complex comprising two or more separately organized or independently complete postsecondary units under the control or supervision of a single administrative body (Compare **Multicampus Institution**.)

Intermediate Degree—a formal recognition (degree or certificate) for a program between the master's degree and the doctorate, which is essence is the terminal degree without the dissertation. Examples are Master of Philosophy, Candidate in Philosophy, etc.

Internships—short-term, supervised work experiences, usually related to a student's major field of study, for which the student earns academic credit.

Learning Resource Center—a specially designed study area where individual students or groups are provided with study supplies and equipment, usually including books, programmed materials, and audiovisual supplies.

Main Campus—the most important unit in an institution that is made up of one or more branch campuses. The main campus (sometimes called the parent institution) usually houses the core, primary, or most comprehensive program and is usually also the location of the central administrative office.

Microforms—books, periodicals, and other materials that have been photographically reduced in size for storage, protection, and inexpensive publication. These materials must be read with the aid of enlarging equipment.

Minority Group—Any racial, religious, ethnic, or social aggregation of people who have suffered some discrimination due to bias. IPEDS surveys (formerly HEGIS) suggest the following five racial/ethnic groups as minority categories: Black, non-Hispanic; American

Indian or Alaskan Native; Asian or Pacific Islander; Hispanic; and under the heading White, non-Hispanic, Middle Eastern. For purposes of this questionnaire, women are not considered a minority group.

Multicampus Institution—an organization that resembles an institutional system but is unequivocally designated as a single body organized according to one of the following specifications: (1) an institution having two or more administratively equal campuses responsible to a central governing structure (that may or may not be located on one of the campuses) or (2) an institution having a main campus with one or more branch campuses. (Compare **Institutional System.**)

Open Admissions—policy of admitting high school graduates and other adults generally without regard to conventional academic qualifications. Virtually all applicants with high school diplomas or the equivalent are accepted.

Organized Occupational Program—a course of study consisting of an integrated series of required and elective courses designed to prepare students for employment in a job or cluster of occupations. Programs are science- or engineering-related in areas of data processing technologies, health services and paramedical technologies, mechanical and engineering technologies, or natural science technologies. Other nonscience- and nonengineering related programs are in business and commerce technologies, and public service-related technologies. Completion requires at least one but less than four years of full-time attendance, or the equivalent in part-time attendance, and culminates in formal recognition that the student has completed an organized program.

Part-Time Instruction Faculty—those members of the instruction/research staff who are employed to teach less than—and are paid for less than—a full-time course level, however defined by the institution.

Post-Baccalaureate—graduate study beyond the bachelor's degree including that toward the first-professional (see definition), master's, intermediate (see definition), and doctoral awards.

Quarter—an academic calendar period of about 11 weeks. Each academic year is made up of four quarters, but students can make normal academic progress by attending three quarters annually.

Rolling Admissions Plan—an admissions procedure by which the college considers each student's application as soon as all required materials have been received and reviewed. Colleges following this practice usually notify applicants of admissions decisions continuously over several months in contrast to other institutions that announce all decisions simultaneously.

Semester—a period of about 17-18 weeks that makes up half of the usual academic year at institutions following this calendar system.

Sponsored Research—projects funded by extra-institutional financial sources, such as government or industry.

Student Services—systems and facilities provided to contribute to student well-being outside the context of formal academic instruction. Student services are provided by counseling centers, financial aid programs, student health systems (unless operated as a self-supporting enterprise), registrar's procedures, and admissions offices.

Telecourses—televised courses, taken for credit, that are broadcast on public or cable stations that can be viewed in the home or on campus.

Terminal Degree—one that represents the highest formal academic recognition or certificate available to an individual in a given field.

3-3—a calendar system in which the academic year is divided into three terms with students enrolled in three courses per term.

Trimester—an academic calendar period of about 15 weeks. Three trimesters make up each academic year, but students can make normal academic progress by attending two terms annually.

Unclassified Students—students who take courses for credit but are not candidates for a degree or other formal award.

Upper Division Only—Institution that has no freshman or sophomore postsecondary program. Students complete lower division studies at other institutions before entering the upper division institution to earn their bachelor's degree.

Weekend College—a program that allows students to take a complete course of study by attending classes only on weekends. These programs generally are restricted to a few areas of study and require more than the traditional number of years to complete.

I

Higher Education in the United States

The Structure of Higher Education

Higher education is the general term for all programs of instruction customarily undertaken after the completion of the secondary school training, also commonly referred to as postsecondary education. Diversity, size, and steady change distinguish higher education in the United States. In the absence of a national agency for central educational direction, such as a ministry of education, each institution or formal administrative grouping of institutions has been developed according to its own conception of service and excellence. The U.S. Department of Education does not operate as ministries of education do in other nations. Rather, the Department primarily gathers data, distributes financial aid to students, and funds for research and development; it exercises only weak control over educational policy and curriculum.

A college's local and regional environment and the source and extent of its financial support combine to determine its form. Similarities in colleges may be related directly to similarities in these formative influences. The most cursory examination of the institutional exhibits in Part III, however, would support the remark of a university president that "the outstanding characteristic of the American system of higher education is that it is not a system at all." Control is widely dispersed.

1. Opening Fall Enrollment, by Gender and Matriculation Status, 2001

Institutional Category	Men	Women	Total enrollment	Full-time	Part-time
All institutions	6,960,815	8,967,172	15,927,987	9,447,502	6,480,485
Four-year institutions	4,285,615	5,391,793	9,677,408	7,073,011	2,604,397
Two-year institutions	2,675,200	3,575,379	6,250,579	2,374,491	3,876,088

SOURCE: U.S. Department of Education, National Center for Education Statistics, Integrated Postsecondary Education Data System (IPEDS) Fall 2001 Enrollment survey. Washington, GPO.

The patterns of evolution reflect responses to needs rather than planned development. Statewide master plans to guide the development of higher education within states are attempts to control and direct the evolution of institutions in categories that were historically determined and that antedate the planning program.

The second major attribute of American higher education is its size. The nation generally believes that all individuals should have the opportunity to develop themselves to their highest potential. Consequently, there is widespread feeling that it is the "right" of every interested and capable secondary school graduate to continue some sort of training beyond the secondary level. Such an attitude has led to an enrollment pattern different from that of any other developed nation. Approximately 45 percent of all 18- to 24-year old high school graduates in the U.S. were enrolled in colleges or universities in 2002.[1]

The recent history of American higher education reveals a quickening of the traditional patterns of change and development. After 1960, population growth and the increasing percentage of college-age students seeking instruction in a variety of programs caused rapid growth, development, and change. The willingness of government and private groups to give additional financial support led to expansion, diversification, and experimentation in higher education. Although colleges and universities have faced increased competition for funds in recent years, most have begun to look to other sources of revenue to support their programs rather than scaling back operations. Community and vocational colleges are now well established; liberal arts colleges are sending larger numbers of their students on to professional and graduate schools; most teachers' colleges and some special-purpose state schools have evolved into arts and sciences colleges; major universities have become research centers while continuing to perform their traditional educational roles.

2. Higher Education Degree-Granting Institutions, by Type, Control, and Size, Fall 2001

Control of institutions and size of enrollment	All Institutions	Universities	Other Four-year	Two-Year
All institutions	4,074	152	2,152	1,770
Under 1,000	1634	0	875	759
1,000-4,999	1533	6	909	618
5,000-9,999	456	12	227	217
10,000-19,999	298	52	115	131
20,000-29,999	110	53	21	36
30,000 or more	43	29	5	9
Public institutions	1,688	103	516	1,069
Under 1,000	187	0	54	133
1,000-4,999	736	1	191	544
5,000-9,999	366	1	149	216
10,000-19,999	256	27	98	131
20,000-29,999	102	47	19	36
30,000 or more	41	27	5	9
Private institutions	2,386	49	1636	701
Under 1,000	1,447	0	821	626
1,000-4,999	797	5	718	74
5,000-9,999	90	11	78	1
10,000-19,999	42	25	17	0
20,000-29,999	8	6	2	0
30,000 or more	2	2	0	0

SOURCE: U.S. Department of Education, National Center for Education Statistics, Digest of Education Statistics, 2003. Washington, GPO.

3. Earned Degrees Conferred, by Level, Selected Years

Year	All Degrees Conferred	Associate Degrees	Bachelor's Degrees	Master's Degrees	First Professional Degrees	Doctorate Degrees
1997-98*	2,297,733	558,555	1,184,406	430,164	78,598	46,010
1998-99*	2,322,759	559,954	1,200,303	439,986	78,439	44,077
1999-2000	2,384,729	564,933	1,237,875	457,056	80,057	44,808
2000-01	2,416,123	578,865	1,244,171	468,476	79,707	44,904
2001-02	2,494,009	595,133	1,291,900	482,118	80,698	44,160
Projection						
2002-03	2,588,700	662,000	1,311,000	492,000	80,400	43,300
2003-04	2,623,600	660,000	1,333,000	502,000	84,400	44,200
2004-05	2,659,400	669,000	1,352,000	506,000	87,800	44,600
2005-06	2,719,100	675,000	1,397,000	513,000	89,100	45,000
2006-07	2,743,400	676,000	1,413,000	519,000	90,100	45,300
2007-08	2,764,900	681,000	1,425,000	522,000	91,300	45,600
2008-09	2,788,900	684,000	1,441,000	526,000	92,200	45,700
2009-10	2,812,800	688,000	1,456,000	530,000	92,900	45,900
2010-11	2,836,800	692,000	1,469,000	536,000	93,600	46,200
2011-12	2,869,200	696,000	1,488,000	544,000	94,600	46,600
2012-13	2,907,200	699,000	1,509,000	556,000	95,900	47,300

NOTES: *Due to rounding, details may not add to totals. Numbers for 1997-98 and 1998-99 have been revised from previously published figures.
SOURCE: U.S. Department of Education, National Center for Education Statistics, Digest of Education Statistics, 2003, andProjections of Education Statistics to 2013. Washington: GPO.

THE BROAD STRUCTURAL COMPONENTS

Coordinating Bodies. The number of public colleges and universities governed wholly or in part by coordinating boards increased dramatically in the 1960s and early 1970s. Some boards, whether elected or appointed, govern senior institutions only, while others include all institutions in a state; others act to coordinate data gathering or serve as a convening authority on state higher education problems. In some states, there are statewide coordinating boards for single institutions or groups of institutions. Parallel to the growth of statutory superboards was the rise of voluntary consortia of institutions-public and private-to promote the exchange of faculty and students and to avoid the duplication of facilities or library materials.

Types of Institutions. Although any classification of American higher education involves some arbitrary judgments, it is useful to distinguish certain general types of institutions. An analysis of fall enrollment for 2001 is shown in Table 1. Information on the number of institutions is provided in Table 2.

The official name of an institution is frequently an unreliable guide to its actual structure or function. Some institutions called "university" offer no degree beyond the bachelor's degree (for example, Denison University). Others entitled "university" offer first-professional and master's degrees but have no doctoral program (for example, Colgate University). On the other hand, some institutions that are called "colleges" offer regular doctoral programs (for example, Boston College). Furthermore, several technical institutes have developed the characteristics of a general university, having large doctoral programs offering training in fields other than the physical sciences (for example, Massachusetts Institute of Technology).

The University. Many universities place considerable emphasis on graduate instruction; they confer advanced degrees in a variety of liberal arts and professional fields and strongly emphasize research. This definition is not very precise, however, and is open to various interpre-

tations. In popular usage, a university often is defined as an institution offering doctoral programs in a variety of fields.

Because of its size and its emphasis on scholarship and research, the university has had a formative influence on American higher education. Its components are, typically, an undergraduate college and a cluster of graduate and professional schools. Graduate schools stress research training in an academic discipline; professional schools emphasize the development and application of theory in such fields as law, medicine, engineering, and business. A mere count of institutions with graduate schools is a misleading guide to their relative productivity of earned doctorates, however. The number of earned degrees conferred is shown in Table 3 and the most prevalent disciplines of advanced degrees are reported in Table 4.

The Liberal Arts College. Liberal arts colleges place their principal emphasis on a program of general undergraduate education. The distinction between the university and the liberal arts colleges is not always clear, however. Because many of today's universities began as liberal arts colleges (Harvard, Columbia, and Yale, for example), they continue to place great emphasis on the undergraduate college within the university structure. Four-year liberal arts colleges concentrate on programs leading to the bachelor's degree. Academic disciplines usually are broken into departments, responsible to a dean of the college, rather than into semiautonomous schools (larger structural units are more common in universities). Since the 1960s, many liberal arts colleges have increased their emphasis on preparing students for advanced work in graduate and professional fields.

The Community and Junior College. Community and junior colleges are institutions offering two-year programs of study beyond the secondary school level. There are two basic curricula: transfer and terminal. The first type enables the student to take in his or her own community the first two years of work leading to the bachelor's degree, thereby reducing educational costs. Such programs also relieve the

4. Number and Ranking by Discipline of Graduate and First-Professional Degrees, 2001-02

Disciplines	Master's		Doctorate		First Professional	
	Number	Rank	Number	Rank	Number	Rank
Biological sciences/ life sciences			4,489	3		
Business	120,785	2	1,158	9		
Chiropractic					3,284	6
Computer and information sciences	16,113	6				
Dentistry					4,239	5
Education	136,579	1	6,967	1		
Engineering	26,015	4	5,195	2		
English language and literature	7,268	10	1,446	7		
Health professions/ related sciences	43,644	3	3,523	6		
Law					38,981	1
Medicine					15,237	2
Optometry					1,280	9
Osteopathic medicine					2,416	7
Pharmacy					7,076	3
Physical sciences			3,800			
Podiatry					474	10
Psychology	14,888	7	4,341	4		
Public administration	25,448	5				
Social sciences/history	14,112	8	3,902	5		
Theological and religious studies			1,355	8	5,195	4
Veterinary medicine					2,289	8
Visual and performing arts	11,595	9	1,114	10		

Source: U.S. Department of Education, National Center for Education Statistics, Integrated Postsecondary Education Data System (IPEDS), Fall 2002 survey. Washington: GPO.

pressure for admission on the senior colleges and universities, and may permit them to give more attention to upper division and graduate education. Terminal programs usually lead to the Associate in Arts or Associate in Science degree, indicating that the student has completed a unit of recognized academic work. The emphasis in such programs is vocational, enabling the student to become proficient in one of a wide variety of semiprofessional and technical areas.

The Upper Level Institution. A small number of institutions offer academic programs solely for students who have completed the first two years of college study elsewhere. In some instances, these institutions offer graduate programs as well.

State Colleges and Universities. State colleges and universities offer comprehensive programs attuned to the needs of their states. The teachers college as an identifiable category-an institution emphasizing the preparation of teachers and administrators for elementary and secondary schools-has virtually disappeared. Former teachers colleges have broadened their functions and assumed the characteristics of liberal arts colleges or small universities. Most universities have schools of education, and most liberal arts colleges have programs in teacher education that meet certification requirements.

Separately Organized Professional Schools. This category includes schools offering programs directed toward one or more fields of specialization that are not attached to a liberal arts college or university. Included in this group are specialized technological institutions, federally financed service academies, theological schools, and schools of fine arts.

Vocational and Adult Education. Within universities-especially land-grant universities-vocational education programs are designed to combine general education and training in such areas as agriculture, trade, and industry. More emphasis now is given to theoretical preparation in these fields than to practical training, to allow students to keep pace with changing technology.

Outside the academic community, the federal government has on occasion become involved in programs to upgrade the skills of workers displaced by the application of science and technology. These efforts have made continuing vocational education-both within and outside of existing school structures-an important part of postsecondary education in this country. Budgetary restrictions have limited these effects in recent years, however.

Vocational education is especially characteristic of community and junior colleges. Some states have vocational training institutes as part of their public colleges; in other state institutions, job-related education at various levels is an integral part of the curriculum. In addition, rising demand for updated skills training has resulted in a wide array of evening, weekend, summer, and other programs in adult education.

Besides adults who take courses as a leisure time activity, demand for further training also has come from professionals who, in rapidly expanding and changing fields, require formal refresher work; adults who, having never entered college before or having left it before completing a degree, now wish to complete a degree; and younger students who prefer the pacing and focus of typically part-time adult education programs over the conventional full-time, campus-oriented degree programs. Since these students make up a growing segment of higher education enrollment, institutions have begun to devise new organizational arrangements that more closely link the institution's traditional academic programs and its extension activities.

Proprietary Institutions. Most proprietary institutions (for-profit institutions) provide vocational training, however there are an increasing number of four-year proprietary institutions offering bachelor's and even graduate degrees. In addition, many business corporations operate

5. Number of Institutions of Higher Education, by Type, Control, and State, 2002-03

State	Total	Universities*			Other Four-Year		Two-Year	
		Public	Private		Public	Private	Public	Private
Alaska	8	0	0		3	2	2	1
California	400	8	4		25	172	111	80
Hawaii	20	1	0		2	7	7	3
Oregon	57	2	0		7	27	17	4
Washington	78	2	0		9	27	34	6
Pacific	**563**	**13**	**4**		**46**	**235**	**171**	**94**
Colorado	76	2	1		11	26	15	21
Idaho	14	1	0		3	5	3	2
Montana	22	0	0		6	4	11	1
Nevada	14	1	0		1	3	4	5
Utah	25	2	1		3	5	5	9
Wyoming	9	1	0		0	0	7	1
Mountain	**160**	**7**	**2**		**24**	**43**	**45**	**39**
Illinois	175	4	3		8	89	48	23
Indiana	99	2	1		12	43	15	26
Iowa	62	2	0		1	36	15	8
Kansas	60	2	0		7	21	26	4
Michigan	109	4	0		11	59	29	6
Minnesota	113	1	0		10	39	41	22
Missouri	119	1	2		12	59	19	26
Nebraska	38	1	0		6	15	7	9
North Dakota	22	0	0		7	4	9	2
Ohio	179	5	1		14	67	42	50
South Dakota	27	0	0		9	12	5	1
Wisconsin	68	2	1		11	32	18	4
Midwest	**1071**	**24**	**8**		**108**	**476**	**274**	**181**
Alabama	75	3	0		15	17	29	11
Arkansas	46	1	0		9	10	23	3
Delaware	10	1	0		1	4	3	1
District of Columbia	16	0	5		2	9	0	0
Florida	161	4	1		8	79	28	41
Georgia	124	3	1		16	37	55	12
Kentucky	79	2	0		6	26	29	16
Louisiana	87	1	1		14	12	47	12
Maryland	63	2	1		11	27	16	6
Mississippi	41	3	0		6	11	17	4
North Carolina	126	2	1		14	43	59	7
South Carolina	63	2	0		10	23	21	7
Tennessee	89	2	1		7	46	13	20
Virginia	100	4	0		10	46	24	16
West Virginia	37	1	0		11	10	3	12
South	**1117**	**31**	**11**		**140**	**400**	**367**	**168**
Arizona	71	2	0		3	21	20	25
New Mexico	43	2	0		5	13	20	3
Oklahoma	53	2	0		12	17	15	7
Texas	200	6	2		36	53	67	36
Southwest	**367**	**12**	**2**		**56**	**104**	**122**	**71**
Connecticut	45	1	1		9	17	12	5
Maine	32	1	0		7	11	7	6
Massachusetts	119	1	7		14	70	16	11
New Hampshire	25	1	0		4	13	4	3
New Jersey	57	1	1		13	19	19	4
New York	310	6	9		35	158	39	63
Pennsylvania	257	3	3		42	93	23	93
Rhode Island	13	1	1		1	8	1	1
Vermont	27	1	0		4	17	1	4
Northeast	**885**	**16**	**22**		**129**	**406**	**122**	**190**
U.S. Service Schools	**5**	**0**	**0**		**5**	**0**	**0**	**0**
Total	**4168**	**103**	**49**		**508**	**1664**	**1101**	**743**

NOTE: *Universities include doctoral extensive insitutions committed to graduate education through the doctorate and which award 50 or more doctorate degrees per year across at least 15 disciplines.

SOURCE: U.S. Department of Education, National Center for Education Statistics, Digest of Education Statistics, 2003. Washington: GPO.

major in-house professional training programs at a level of sophistication comparable to higher education. Xerox, Holiday Inn, IBM, and American Telephone and Telegraph are among the corporations prominent in this regard.

See Table 5 for a breakdown in the number of higher education institutions by state and region.

Faculty. The role of faculty members in administrative matters varies from institution to institution. Most, however, exert considerable influence in the appointment and promotion of colleagues, the conferring of tenure, curriculum, the admission and evaluation of students, and institutional planning and budgeting. Through departmental organizations, faculty senates, committees, and in some institutions collective bargaining units, faculty members can express their views on these issues.

In 2001, there were 1.1 million faculty members employed in degree granting institutions in higher education; approximately 55 percent were employed full time.[2] In Fall 2003, the average academic salary for a full professor at a private university was $79,519; at a public university, the figure was $76,609. Many faculty earn additional income through writing and consulting projects. At institutions that had tenure systems, 34 percent of the men and 22 percent of the women were tenured.[3]

Students. Until recently, student involvement in the administration of universities generally was limited to matters affecting their social or extracurricular activities. In the late 1960s, however, a number of institutions made provisions to allow students to participate in many administrative bodies that formerly were the provinces of faculty and administrators.

Students in the 2004-05 academic year paid an average charge for tuition, fees, and room and board of $11,354 at public four-year institutions and of $27,516 at private four-year colleges and universities.[4] Undergraduate tuition and fees for the academic year 2003-04 at sample universities were wide-ranging. Tuition and fees were $9,274 at the main campus of the University of Pittsburg and $2,466 at the University of Texas Pan American, both public four year institutions. Tuition and fees were $2,685 at Central Maine Community College, a public two year institution, and $26,223 at Villanova University, a four year private not-for-profit institution.[5]

6. Voluntary Support for Degree-Granting Institutions of Higher Education, by Source of Support (in millions of dollars)

	1997-98		1998-99		1990-2000		2000-01	
	Amount	Percentage	Amount	Percentage	Amount	Percentage	Amount	Percentage
Total Voluntary Support	$18,400	100.0	$20,400	100.0	$23,200	100.0	$24,200	100.0
Alumni	5,500	29.9	5,930	29.1	6,800	29.3	6,830	28.2
Other individuals	4,500	24.5	4,810	23.6	5,420	23.4	5,200	21.5
Corporations	3,250	17.7	3,610	17.7	4,150	17.9	4,350	18.0
Foundations	3,800	20.7	4,530	22.2	5,080	21.9	6,000	24.8
Religious organizations	300	1.6	330	1.6	370	1.6	370	1.5
Other	1,050	5.7	1,190	5.8	1,380	5.9	1,450	6.0

NOTE: Numbers for 1997-98 have been revised from previously published figures.
SOURCE: Council for Aid to Education, Voluntary Support of Education, various years. New York: CAE.

7. Current Fund Revenue of Institutions of Higher Education, by Source and Institutional Control, Selected Years (in millions of dollars)

	1997-98	1998-99	1999-00	2000-01					
				Total All Institutions	Percent Distribution All Institutions	Total Public Institutions	Percent Distribution Public Institutions	Total Private Not-For-Profit Institutions	Percent Distribution Private Institutions
Total current fund revenue	$2,328,118.3	$2,406,504.4	$2,788,234.7	$2,588,197.1	100.0	$1,766,452.2	100.0	$821,744.9	100.0
Tuition and fees	525,572.7	554,720.6	587,774.2	632,377.2	24.4	319,196.1	18.1	313,181.1	38.1
Federal government	257,009.8	271,765.2	291,439.4	331,229.9	12.8	197,449.7	11.2	133,780.2	16.3
State governments	500,684.1	531,772.9	574,873.1	640,719.5	24.8	628,958.9	35.6	11,760.6	1.4
Local governments	57,994.6	60,921.5	66,202.2	75,608.0	2.9	70,524.3	4.0	5,083.7	0.6
Private gifts, grants, and contracts	193,686.5	210,060.8	239,777.7	248,076.3	9.6	89,483.2	5.1	158,593.1	19.3
Endowment income	231,989.9	196,940.8	389,336.8	-22,503.4	-0.9	13,519.9	0.8	-36,023.3	-4.4
Sales and services	470,828.4	491,118.7	532,579.6	575,877.6	22.3	382,501.3	21.7	193,376.3	23.5
Other sources*	90,352.4	89,203.9	106,251.9	106,811.9	4.1	64,818.7	3.7	41,993.2	5.1

*For years 1996-97, includes Federal governmet monies and Hospital monies for the private not-for-profit institutions
NOTE: Details may not sum to totals due to rounding.
SOURCE: U.S. Department of Education, National Center for Education Statistics, Digest of Education Statistics, 2003, Washington: GPO.

8a. Current Fund Expenditures of Institutions of Higher Education, by Purpose, Selected Years (in millions of dollars)

	Academic Year				
	1996-97	*1997-98*	*1998-99*	*1999-2000*	*2000-01*
Total current fund expenditures	**$192,828.3**	**$202,146.9**	**$216,055.3**	**$233,880.7**	**$255,969.8**
Educational and general expenditures	149,605.8	160,165.1	170,845.1	182,516.4	200,814.7
Instruction	61,399.3	65,554.3	69,482.0	73,228.4	79,431.7
Research	19,410.9	20,683.3	22,087.2	24,381.0	27,057.5
Public service	7,319.1	7,784.0	8,285.7	8,868.8	9,854.6
Academic support	14,530.2	16,018.8	17,537.7	18,598.8	20,696.2
Student services	10,607.4	11,515.2	12,348.3	13,325.0	14,494.2
Institutional support	19,440.5	20,981.7	22,632.4	24,354.0	26,778.6
Plant operation and maintenance	8,265.3	8,572.7	8,953.00	9,710.4	10,973.6
Scholarships and fellowships	5,554.4	5,947.6	6,417.8	6,785.4	7,766.2
Net grant aid to students	1,529.5	1,297.7	1,222.6	1,180.9	1,176.2
Mandatory transfers	1,549.3	1,809.8	1,878.3	2,083.6	2,585.9
Auxiliary enterprises	19,110.7	20,517.6	21,594.4	22,748.4	25,388.0
Hospitals	12,111.6	19,359.9	20,317.0	21,950.9	23,401.8
Independent operations (FFRDC)	259.0	2,104.4	3,298.8	3,287.6	3,913.8
Other*	11,741.2	--	--	3,377.7	2,451.5
	Public Institutions				
Total current fund expenditures	**$125,428.7**	**$132,846.2**	**$140,538.6**	**$152,324.9**	**$170,344.8**
Educational and general expenditures	101,026.6	106,740.9	113,594.4	122,708.6	136,612.7
Instruction	40,272.9	42,149.9	44,300.2	47,215.8	51,824.4
Research	12,708.4	13,415.4	14,308.2	15,999.1	18,031.8
Public service	5,697.5	6,111.0	6,764.3	7,421.8	8,381.3
Academic support	9,587.8	10,280.5	11,188.6	12,087.8	13,328.0
Student services	6,177.2	6,611.2	7,053.2	7,636.5	8,377.0
Institutional support	11,213.9	11,842.8	12,730.7	13,768.1	15,344.5
Plant operation and maintenance	8,265.3	8,572.7	8,953.00	9,710.4	10,973.6
Scholarships and fellowships	5,554.4	5,947.6	6,417.8	6,785.4	7,766.2
Mandatory transfers	1,549.3	1,809.8	1,878.3	2,083.6	2,585.9
Auxiliary enterprises	12,031.6	12,819.0	13,566.9	14,448.4	16,377.1
Hospitals	12,111.6	12,964.1	13,058.1	14,057.1	16,146.4
Independent operations (FFRDC)	259.0	322.3	319.2	533.9	779.2
Other current expenditures	#	#	#	577.0	429.4
	Private Not-For-Profit Institutions				
Total current fund expenditures	**$67,399.6**	**$69,300.7**	**$75,516.7**	**$81,555.8**	**$85,625.0**
Educational and general expenditures	48,579.2	53,424.2	57,250.7	59,807.8	64,202.00
Instruction	21,126.4	23,404.4	25,181.8	26,012.6	27,607.3
Research	6,702.5	7,267.9	7,779.0	8,381.9	9,025.7
Public service	1,621.6	1,673.0	1,521.4	1,447.0	1,473.3
Academic support	4,942.4	5,738.3	6,349.1	6,511.0	7,368.2
Student services	4,430.2	4,904.0	5,295.1	5,688.5	6,117.2
Institutional support	8,226.6	9,138.9	9,901.7	10,585.9	11,434.1
Net grant aid to students	1,529.5	1,297.7	1,222.6	1,180.9	1,176.2
Auxiliary enterprises	7,079.1	7,698.6	8,027.5	8,300.0	9,010.90
Hospitals	--	6,395.8	7,258.90	7,893.80	7,255.40
Independent operations (FFRDC)	--	1,782.1	2,979.60	2,753.70	3,134.60
Other	11,741.2	--	--	2,800.70	2,022.10

-- Not available
\# Not applicable
* May include "Plant Operation and Maintenance" for the private no-for-profit institutions as this item is not separated for these institutions.
NOTE: Detail may not sum to totals due to rounding.
SOURCE: U.S. Department of Education, National Center for Education Statistics, Digest of Education Statistics, 2003. Washington: GPO.

Among students who began their college careers in the fall of 2003, one-third cited financial assistance as a "very important reason" for selecting their freshman college. Almost half (47 percent) reported chances were "very good" he/she would get a job to help pay for college expenses.

Students' choice of colleges also is becoming increasingly influenced by the extent to which graduates of the school are seen as marketable. The percent of freshman who selected a college because "This college has a very good academic reputation" reached 55% percent in 2003. Similarly, 13 percent choose a school because of "rankings in national magazines."

Seventy-three percent of the college freshman in Fall 2003 planned to pursue a master's, doctorate, or first-professional degree. One-fourth of freshman hoped to earn a baccalaureate as their highest degree. Interest in elementary and secondary teaching rose to its highest point in more than two decades; one in ten 2003 college freshman planned a career in education, compared with a low of 5 percent in 1982. Other popular career choices were business (12 percent), medicine (12 percent), engineering (7 percent), and law (4 percent). [6]

Financial Sources. Income for educational and general purposes of institutions of higher education traditionally come from four principal sources: (1) philanthropic gifts, (2) student tuition and fees, (3) endowment earnings, and (4) state and federal government appropriations. The relative contribution and importance of each of these sources have varied considerably during the past 50 years.

In the past, philanthropic gifts have not provided a large percentage of the total operating income of higher education in the United States. Most donors have preferred to give their gifts for endowments or buildings rather than for support of current expenditures. Many institutions, however, now are giving more attention to this source of support for current programs, as their budgets have become tighter. Their efforts have resulted in substantial increases in gifts available for current purposes. In most colleges and universities, alumni and other interested persons are encouraged to contribute to an annual financial campaign whose proceeds are available for unrestricted purposes. These campaigns have attracted many donors whose relatively small annual gifts add up to a significant total. The success of such efforts is indicated by the fact that the amount of income from voluntary gifts and grants to higher education in 2000-01 was 24.2 billion. (See Table 6).

Endowment is held chiefly by privately controlled institutions, although a number of large state-controlled universities, such as the Universities of Texas and California, have large endowments. Endowment funds of significant size tend to be concentrated in a small number of colleges and universities.

With a few notable exceptions, almost all institutions of higher education, including state-supported schools, charge tuition. In 2000-01, institutions received 24 percent of their current-fund revenues from tuition and fees.

Government financial support for higher education comes from three major sources-local, state, and federal. The contribution of local governments to higher education has been small, except in such instances as the City University of New York, but state governments have continuously provided funds toward the creation and support of state universities and colleges. The federal government, which prior to World War II contributed relatively small sums of money, has become a substantial supporter of higher education through the appropriation of research grants and contracts and student financial aid.

Tables 7, 8a and 8b show the current fund revenues and expenditures of higher education institutions (public and private) by source and percentage of distribution.

NATIONAL ASSOCIATIONS OF HIGHER EDUCATION

In the United States, where the control and operation of education are decentralized, hundreds of voluntary education associations have

8b. Current Fund Expenditures of Institutions of Higher Education, 2000-01 (in millions of dollars)

	Amount all institutions	Percent Distribution All Institutions		Amount Public Institutions	Percent Distribution Public Institutions		Amount Private Institutions	Percent Distribution Private Institutions
Total current fund expenditures	$255,969.8	100.0		$170,344.8	100.0		$85,625.0	100.0
Educational and general expenditures	200,814.7	78.5		136,612.7	80.2		64,202.00	75.0
Instruction	79,431.7	31.0		51,824.4	30.4		27,607.3	32.2
Research	27,057.5	10.6		18,031.8	10.6		9,025.7	10.5
Public service	9,854.6	3.9		8,381.3	4.9		1,473.3	1.7
Academic support	20,696.2	8.1		13,328.0	7.8		7,368.2	8.6
Student services	14,494.2	5.7		8,377.0	4.9		6,117.2	7.1
Institutional support	26,778.6	10.5		15,344.5	9.0		11,434.1	13.4
Plant operation and maintenance	10,973.6	4.3		10,973.6	6.4		#	#
Scholarships and fellowships	7,766.2	3.0		7,766.2	4.6		#	#
Net grant aid to students	1,176.2	0.5		#	#		1,176.2	1.4
Mandatory transfers	2,585.9	1.0		2,585.9	1.5		#	#
Auxiliary enterprises	25,388.0	9.9		16,377.1	9.6		9,010.90	10.5
Hospitals	23,401.8	9.1		16,146.4	9.5		7,255.40	8.5
Independent operations (FFRDC)	3,913.8	1.5		779.2	0.5		3,134.60	3.7
Other*	2,451.5	0.1		429.4	0.3		2,022.10	2.4

Not applicable
* May include "Plant Operation and Maintenance" for the private no-for-profit institutions as this item is not separated for these institutions.
NOTE: Detail may not sum to totals due to rounding.
SOURCE: U.S. Department of Education, National Center for Education Statistics, Digest of Education Statistics, 2003. Washington: GPO.

been formed to provide direction, leadership, and assistance to members. Through such associations, members, whether institutional or individual, are able to cooperate in the formulation of educational policies and practices.

The Association of American Colleges and Universities, which seeks to promote higher education in the liberal arts, is one such organization. The Association of American Universities, with a membership of major universities, seeks to maintain high quality in graduate and professional education. The National Association of State Universities and Land-Grant Colleges, the American Association of State Colleges and Universities, and the American Association of Community Colleges all have as their major objective the development of their constituent memberships.

The American Association of University Professors was founded in 1915 to work with institutional associations in setting national standards for the profession. In the late 1960s, it began to assist association chapters in collective-bargaining and now shares with the American Federation of Teachers and the National Education Association the one-third of the professoriate that bargains collectively. Besides the unions, a wide array of disciplinary associations are concerned not only with intellectual issues but also with the interests of research scholars and teachers.

Of those associations whose membership is by institution, the largest is the American Council on Education (ACE). Its membership consists primarily of national and regional education associations and institutions of higher education. A major function is to serve as the principal nongovernmental coordinating body in higher education. It represents higher education with the federal government and convenes bodies to address higher education's salient issues. The Council also sponsors independent research projects and institutes for those involved in higher education.

[1] Source: U.S. Census Bureau: Current Population Survey Reports, *School Enrollment- Social and Economic Characteristics of Students, 2002.*

[2] Source: U.S. Department of Education, *Digest of Education Statistics, 2003*

[3] Source: U.S. Department of Education, *National Study of Postsecondary Faculty 04* (analysis by author).

[4] Source: College Board: *Trends in College Pricing 2004.*

[5] Source: U.S. Department of Education, Integrated Postsecondary Education Data System (analysis by author).

[6] Freshman data from the Cooperative Institutional Research Program, the American Council on Education, and the University of California, Los Angeles, *The American Freshman: National Norms for Fall 2003.*

Government and Higher Education

The federal government of the United States has never been empowered to exercise direct administrative or legal control over education in the states. It has, however, been influential in educational affairs and in recent decades has had a marked effect on the development of both public and private higher education. Today, federal aid is a reality involving billions of dollars distributed through a number of government agencies to a large percentage of the nation's education institutions for a variety of purposes.

HISTORICAL DEVELOPMENT

Federal aid to education is not a new concept; rather, it is one that has evolved over a long period of time. Even before the adoption of the Constitution, the Congress of the Confederation passed the Ordinance of 1785 providing that certain portions of land in each township be set aside for the support of local schools. The Northwest Ordinance (1787) contained a declaration that "Religion, morality and knowledge, being necessary to good government and the happiness of mankind, schools and the means of education should forever be encouraged."

During the first half of the 19th century, the growing interest of the government in education was reflected in a number of ways. In at least twenty states, congressional grants for "internal improvements" were used for educational purposes, and when in 1837 a surplus of $28 million was distributed to the states by the federal government, a number of the states devoted all or part of their share to education. More directly, this period witnessed the creation by the federal government of two national educational institutions, the Military Academy at West Point (1802) and the Naval Academy at Annapolis (1845). In addition, two basic themes permeated many of the public statements of the era: that education was absolutely essential to the successful operation of the new nation and that the government had a legitimate stake in, and therefore some responsibility for, providing that education.

It was during the Civil War, however, that perhaps the most significant single piece of federal legislation pertaining to higher education in the entire century was passed. The Morrill Act of 1862 was a landmark in the relationship of the federal government and higher education. Under that act, land grants were made available to the states, and revenues from the sale of these lands were to provide for the endowment and support of at least one college in each state whose principal objective should be: "without excluding other scientific and classical studies and including military tactics, to teach such branches of learning as are related to agriculture and the mechanic arts, in such manner as the legislatures of the States may respectively prescribe, in order to promote the liberal and practical education of the industrial classes in the several pursuits and professions in life." The land-grant institutions that were subsequently established were destined to become an important segment of American higher education. The Morrill Act not only provided for the creation of a new type of institution—one that was more pragmatic than the old in its approach to education and more responsible to the popular will—but also recognized the need for trained manpower to be a national concern and established the precedent for subsequent federal legislation in this field by not limiting federal aid to public institutions.

Other examples illustrate the continuing interest of the federal government in higher education since the Civil War. In 1867, Congress established the Bureau of Education to gather and disseminate information the Bureau of Education to gather and disseminate information about the state of education in the United States. During World War I, colleges and universities were widely used in the training of officer personnel. Even in the depression years of the 1930s, programs such as the National Youth Administration (NYA) pointed up the fact that the federal government could act directly in the field of higher education in the people wanted it to.

9. Federal Funds for Education and Related Activities: Fiscal Years 1998 to 2003 (in millions of dollars)

	1998	1999	2000	2001	2002	2003*
Total	**$76,909**	**$82,864**	**$85,944**	**$94,847**	**$109,362**	**$124,737**
Elementary/secondary education prog	37,486	39,938	43,791	48,530	52,754	59,656
Higher education programs	15,800	17,651	15,009	14,938	22,964	29,320
Other education programs	5,149	5,318	5,485	5,880	6,298	6,585
Research programs at universities and related institutions	18,475	19,957	21,660	25,498	27,346	29,177

NOTES: *Due to rounding, details may not add to totals. Figures for 2003 are estimated.
SOURCE: U.S. Department of Education, National Center for Education Statistics, Digest of Education Statistics, 2003. Washington: GPO.

10. Federal Funds for Education and Related Programs, by Agency and Level of Educational Activity or Program: Fiscal Years 2000 to 2003 (in thousands of dollars)

Agency, level of program or activity	2000	2001	2002	2003
Department of Education	**34,106,697**	**36,562,025**	**46,324,352**	**57,442,854**
Elementary/secondary education program	20,039,563	22,862,445	25,246,185	30,749,304
Higher education programs	10,727,315	9,840,748	17,056,188	22,706,436
Other education programs	3,223,355	3,293,355	3,396,823	3,435,182
Research programs at universities and related institutions	116,464	565,477	625,156	551,932
Department of Agriculture	**11,080,031**	**11,329,740**	**12,033,544**	**12,756,018**
Elementary/secondary education program	10,051,278	10,140,527	10,836,407	11,614,372
Higher education programs	30,676	82,437	88,764	93,626
Other education programs	444,477	454,576	469,373	472,720
Research programs at universities and related institutions	553,600	652,200	639,000	575,300
Department of Commerce	**114,575**	**134,654**	**130,660**	**90,100**
Higher education programs	3,800	3,954	4,160	4,200
Research programs at universities and related institutions	110,775	130,700	126,500	85,900
Department of Defense	**4,525,080**	**5,417,621**	**5,438,182**	**5,244,192**
Elementary/secondary education program	1,485,611	1,475,014	1,439,818	1,511,066
Higher education programs	1,147,759	1,299,169	1,485,552	1,569,079
Research programs at universities and related institutions	1,891,710	2,643,438	2,512,812	2,164,047
Department of Energy	**3,577,004**	**3,885,773**	**3,992,886**	**4,086,914**
Research programs at universities and related institutions	3,577,004	3,885,773	3,992,886	4,086,914
Department of Health and Human Services	**17,670,867**	**20,540,411**	**22,875,705**	**25,406,660**
Elementary/secondary education program	6,011,036	6,958,027	7,365,761	7,589,057
Higher education programs	954,190	1,360,554	1,567,367	1,698,087
Other education programs	214,000	243,000	276,200	307,900
Research programs at universities and related institutions	10,491,641	11,978,830	13,666,377	15,811,616
Department of Housing and Urban Development	**1,400**	**1,600**	**1,600**	**1,500**
Research programs at universities and related institutions	1,400	1,600	1,600	1,500
Department of Interior	**959,802**	**1,092,588**	**1,186,213**	**1,231,006**
Elementary/secondary education program	725,423	890,497	945,264	982,061
Higher education programs	187,179	149,391	185,849	205,545
Research programs at universities and related institutions	47,200	52,700	55,100	43,400
Department of Justice	**278,927**	**431,220**	**454,933**	**477,201**
Elementary/secondary education program	224,800	380,600	408,400	436,100
Other education programs	34,727	29,120	23,433	25,301
Research programs at universities and related institutions	19,400	21,500	23,100	15,800
Department of Labor	**4,696,100**	**5,193,100**	**5,865,100**	**6,082,500**
Elementary/secondary education program	4,683,200	5,189,000	5,859,000	6,071,000
Research programs at universities and related institutions	12,900	4,100	6,100	11,500
Department of State	**388,349**	**390,068**	**487,097**	**404,127**
Higher education programs	319,000	316,800	385,000	299,000
Other education programs	69,349	73,268	102,097	105,127
Department of Transportation	**117,054**	**153,682**	**162,208**	**135,259**
Elementary/secondary education program	188	215	400	635
Higher education programs	60,300	80,500	78,700	90,200
Other education programs	700	495	591	600
Research programs at universities and related institutions	55,866	72,472	82,517	43,824

10. Federal Funds for Education and Related Programs, by Agency and Level of Educational Activity or Program: Fiscal Years 2000 to 2003 (in thousands of dollars) *(continued)*

Agency, level of program or activity	2000	2001	2002	2003
Department of Treasury	83,000	88,000	163,000	195,000
Other education programs	83,000	88,000	163,000	195,000
Department of Veterans Affairs	1,577,374	1,802,342	2,122,289	2,653,341
Elementary/secondary education program	445,052	487,422	487,490	525,420
Higher education programs	1,132,322	1,314,920	1,634,799	2,127,921
Agency for International Development	332,500	488,600	521,500	570,500
Other education programs	299,000	452,000	480,000	526,000
Research programs at universities and related institutions	33,500	36,600	41,500	44,500
Appalachian Regional Commission	7,243	9,560	15,767	14,800
Elementary/secondary education program	2,588	5,922	6,522	6,900
Higher education programs	2,286	2,025	7,258	6,000
Other education programs	2,369	1,613	1,987	1,900
Barry Goldwater Scholarship and Excellence in Education Foundation	3,000	3,000	3,000	3,000
Higher education programs	3,000	3,000	3,000	3,000
Corporation for National Service	386,000	452,000	404,000	516,000
Other education programs	386,000	452,000	404,000	516,000
Environmental Protection Agency	98,900	125,400	163,900	171,600
Research programs at universities and related institutions	98,900	125,400	163,900	171,600
Estimated Education Share of Federal Aid to the District of Columbia	127,127	147,093	166,057	174,400
Elementary/secondary education program	115,230	133,490	152,560	160,500
Higher education programs	11,493	13,199	12,539	13,000
Other education programs	404	404	958	900
Federal Emergency Management Agency	14,894	23,778	8,376	8,600
Other education programs	14,894	23,778	8,376	8,600
Harry S. Truman Scholarship Fund	3,000	2,000	4,000	3,000
Higher education programs	3,000	2,000	4,000	3,000
Institute of American Indian and Alaskan Native Culture and Arts Development	2,000	4,000	4,000	5,000
Higher education programs	2,000	4,000	4,000	5,000
Institute of Museum and Library Services	166,000	172,000	219,000	171,000
Other education programs	166,000	172,000	219,000	171,000
James Madison Memorial Fellowship Foundation	7,000	3,000	2,000	2,000
Higher education programs	7,000	3,000	2,000	2,000
Japanese-United States Friendship Commission	3,000	3,000	3,000	3,000
Other education programs	3,000	3,000	3,000	3,000
Library of Congress	299,000	315,000	397,000	399,000
Other education programs	299,000	315,000	397,000	399,000
National Aeronautics and Space Administration	2,077,830	2,406,036	2,320,469	2,361,100
Other education programs	6,800	6,832	6,569	
Research programs at universities and related institutions	2,071,030	2,399,204	2,313,900	2,361,100

10. Federal Funds for Education and Related Programs, by Agency and Level of Educational Activity or Program: Fiscal Years 2000 to 2003 (in thousands of dollars) *(continued)*

Agency, level of program or activity	*2000*	*2001*	*2002*	*2003*
National Archives and Records Administration	**121,879**	**148,175**	**219,000**	**294,000**
Other education programs	121,879	148,175	219,000	294,000
National Commission on Libraries and Information Science	**2,000**	**1,000**	**2,000**	**2,000**
Other education programs	2,000	1,000	2,000	2,000
National Endowment for the Arts	**10,048**	**10,442**	**11,109**	**11,350**
Elementary/secondary education program	6,002	5,839	5,800	8,842
Other education programs	4,046	4,603	5,309	2,508
National Endowment for the Humanities	**100,014**	**105,709**	**97,731**	**106,093**
Elementary/secondary education program	812	1,063	511	413
Higher education programs	28,395	30,581	30,000	39,538
Other education programs	70,807	74,065	67,220	66,141
National Science Foundation	**2,955,244**	**3,338,936**	**3,491,851**	**3,642,115**
Higher education programs	389,000	432,000	415,000	454,000
Research programs at universities and related institutions	2,566,244	2,906,936	3,076,851	3,188,115
Nuclear Regulatory Commission	**12,200**	**12,100**	**10,700**	**12,900**
Research programs at universities and related institutions	12,200	12,100	10,700	12,900
Smithsonian Institute	**25,764**	**28,723**	**36,761**	**35,799**
Other education programs	25,764	28,723	36,761	35,799
United States Institute of Peace	**13,000**	**15,000**	**15,000**	**16,000**
Other education programs	13,000	15,000	15,000	16,000
Other agencies	300	9,100	7,500	6,645
Research programs at universities and related institutions	300	9,100	7,500	6,645
Total	**85,944,203**	**94,846,476**	**109,361,491**	**124,736,574**
Elementary/secondary education program	43,790,783	48,530,061	52,754,118	59,655,670
Higher education programs	15,008,715	14,938,278	22,964,177	29,319,632
Other education programs	5,484,571	5,880,007	6,297,697	6,584,678
Research programs at universities and related institutions	21,660,134	25,498,130	27,345,499	29,176,593

NOTES: Figures for 2003 are estimated. To the extent possible, amounts reported represent outlays rather than obligations. Details may not sum to totals because of rounding.
SOURCE: U.S. Department of Education, National Center for Education Statistics, Digest of Education Statistics, 2003. Washington: GPO.

RECENT DEVELOPMENTS

Although federal aid to higher education has been an evolving concept with a long history, a tremendous concentration of activity in this field has taken place during the past fifty years. The reasons for this intensified activity were tied directly to attempts as a nation to deal with perplexing new problems, both foreign and domestic, that emerged after World War II. On the domestic scene, the nation was faced with the immediate problem of dismantling the enormous war machine that had been created, and one of the most pressing questions concerned what might be done about the millions of servicemen who were being mustered out of the armed forces and returning to civilian pursuits. The colleges and universities played a significant role in helping to solve this problem, as they were later to respond to the government's need for specialized research services and still later to the government's antipoverty programs. In the realm of foreign affairs, other problems were to grow out of the altered position of the United States in the family of nations. The collapse of the Grand Alliance, the realignment of nations, the reluctance of our people to assume the burdens and responsibilities of world leadership, the beginning and sharpening of what was to become known as the Cold war, the shock of Sputnik and subsequent Russian successes in the space rate—all these were to coalesce in such a way as to lead to an entirely new relationship between the federal government and higher education, a relationship that would be vastly more complex, involve many more dollars, and in which direct contacts would be far more frequent and numerous than had been the case before.

This new and altered relationship grew directly out of a series of decision to use college and universities to help in solving the nation's most pressing problems and can be traced in the major pieces of educational legislation:

The G.I. Bill (1944). There was no real precedence in the American experience for this practical program aimed at encouraging veterans to begin or return to college. In 1949, the program's peak year, there were two and one-half million students enrolled in American colleges and universities under the G.I. Bill. So great was its success, not only with the individuals concerned but also with the institutions and with Congress, that it was subsequently extended to cover veterans of other conflicts. Clearly, the G.I. Bill helped forge a strong new bond between the government and institutions of higher education. In 1985, Congress enacted a new G.I. Bill (The Montgomery G.I. Bill) for individuals who initially entered active military duty on or after July 1, 1985.

National Science Foundation (NSF). Created in 1950, the NSF has played an important role in improving education in the sciences and in the distribution to colleges and universities of research funds made available by the federal government.

National Defense Education Act (1958). A landmark in federal legislation pertaining to higher education, this act included among its most important features the creation of a student loan program, support for intensified foreign language training, and the inauguration of a program of fellowship for graduate study.

College Housing Loan Program. Created as part of the Housing Act of 1950 and now transferred to the Higher Education Act, this program provided loan guarantees and direct loans for the construction of college housing facilities. New loan commitments of $29 million in 1993 were authorized from the program's revolving funds. No new loans have been made since 1993.

Higher Education Facilities Act (1963). In an effort to meet the demands of a rapidly growing student population for additional classrooms and laboratories, this legislation provided for grants as well as loan to institutions for the construction of graduate and undergraduate academic facilities.

Economic Opportunity Act (1964). Although designed primarily to combat poverty wherever it existed in the United States, this act directly affected higher education in a number of ways. It not only involved colleges and universities in the administration and operation of such programs as Head Start, Upward Bound, Vista, and Job Corps, but also made available a combination work-study program for economically deprived college students, which later was transferred to the Office of Education.

11. Research and Development in Colleges and Universities, Fiscal Years 2000-2003 (in millions of dollars)

	1999#	2000	2001	2002*	2003*
Total federal obligations for research, development, and R&D plant by all performers (federal intramural research, industrial firms, colleges and universities, and others)	$72,613.9	$74,077.0	$79,692.2	$91,113.8	$97,171.7
Research and Development					
by colleges and universities	14,959.1	16,815.1	19,587.9	21,343.6	23,055.2
by FFRDCs	3,896.5	4,053.2	4,617.7	4,669.2	4,834.5
Research					
by colleges and universities	13,203.8	16,015.9	18,657.1	20,330.5	22,228.9
by FFRDCs	2,554.1	2,773.2	3,096.3	3,410.0	3,478.2
Basic research					
by colleges and universities	9,107.1	10,056.7	11,792.2	12,737.1	14,024.2
by FFRDCs	1,565.5	1,674.0	1,762.1	1,969.3	1,984.3
Applied research					
by colleges and universities	4,096.7	5,959.2	6,864.9	7,593.4	8,204.7
by FFRDCs	988.6	1,099.2	1,334.2	1,440.8	1,493.9
Development					
by colleges and universities	1,755.3	799.3	930.8	1,013.1	826.4
by FFRDCs	1,342.3	1,279.9	1,521.4	1,259.2	1,356.3
R & D Plant Obligations					
by colleges and universities	141.2	213.5	284.7	318.8	370.1
by FFRDCs	615.5	613.8	615.9	560.1	556.5
Total					
by colleges and universities	43,263.20	49,859.70	58,117.6	63,336.50	68,709.50
by FFRDCs	10,962.50	11,493.3	12,947.60	13,308.60	13,703.70
Grand Total	54,225.7	61,353.00	71,065.20	76,645.10	82,413.20

NOTES: FFRDCs=Federally funded research and development centers administered by colleges and universities.
#Figures for 1999 have been revised from previously published figures.* Figures for 2002 and 2003 are estimated.
SOURCE: National Science Foundation, Federal Funds for Research and Development, various years.

12. Higher Education Appropriations by State

States	1990-91	1998-99*	1999-2000*	2000-01		% change over 1999-2000		2 yr % change over 1998-99		10-year Gain over 1990-91
Alabama	815,623	1,037,680	1,100,328	1,159,193		5.3%		11.7%		42.1%
Alaska	187,892	170,403	176,494	190,573		8.0%		11.8%		1.4%
Arizona	598,328	836,389	865,736	892,621		3.1%		6.7%		49.2%
Arkansas	328,904	556,659	605,216	618,127		2.1%		11.0%		87.9%
California	5,498,886	7,250,661	7,704,525	9,017,418		17.0%		24.4%		64.0%
Colorado	508,758	682,210	719,221	743,483		3.4%		9.0%		46.1%
Connecticut	522,573	623,692	696,108	710,339		2.0%		13.9%		35.9%
Delaware	117,429	164,115	175,621	185,840		5.8%		13.2%		58.3%
Florida	1,548,285	2,501,857	2,639,821	2,829,525		7.2%		13.1%		82.8%
Georgia	961,283	1,483,818	1,553,588	1,600,329		3.0%		7.9%		66.5%
Hawaii	290,925	322,258	341,986	339,030		-0.9%		5.2%		16.5%
Idaho	183,997	266,522	279,290	298,210		6.8%		11.9%		62.1%
Illinois	1,735,316	2,411,068	2,573,964	2,699,067		4.9%		11.9%		55.5%
Indiana	877,136	1,147,819	1,226,677	1,283,197		4.6%		11.8%		46.3%
Iowa	579,777	784,987	824,062	851,124		3.3%		8.4%		46.8%
Kansas	451,299	604,704	650,069	680,313		4.7%		12.5%		50.7%
Kentucky	609,228	888,700	925,506	1,001,625		8.2%		12.7%		64.4%
Louisiana	585,703	859,036	882,798	880,064		-0.3%		2.4%		50.3%
Maine	172,054	199,149	213,024	228,917		7.5%		14.9%		33.0%
Maryland	809,926	942,748	1,044,250	1,174,603		12.5%		24.6%		45.0%
Massachusetts	697,248	975,360	1,040,083	1,145,029		10.1%		17.4%		64.2%
Michigan	1,357,339	1,882,500	2,084,779	2,231,607		7.0%		18.5%		64.4%
Minnesota	1,007,656	1,239,394	1,286,427	1,349,137		4.9%		8.9%		33.9%
Mississippi	398,467	751,195	877,821	881,827		0.5%		17.4%		121.3%
Missouri	602,146	919,548	977,626	1,027,548		5.1%		11.7%		70.6%
Montana	116,648	129,929	138,477	141,688		2.3%		9.1%		21.5%
Nebraska	329,122	440,095	475,158	526,041		10.7%		19.5%		59.8%
Nevada	163,324	290,363	305,983	316,613		3.5%		9.0%		93.9%
New Hampshire	72,959	91,156	95,790	98,695		3.0%		8.3%		35.3%
New Jersey	1,071,239	1,453,937	1,541,633	1,670,911		8.4%		14.9%		56.0%
New Mexico	335,468	517,261	544,090	568,295		4.4%		9.9%		69.4%
New York	3,180,867	3,104,892	3,209,687	3,452,636		7.6%		11.2%		8.5%
North Carolina	1,484,279	2,149,972	2,270,323	2,398,489		5.6%		11.6%		61.6%
North Dakota	133,860	173,107	183,508	184,631		0.6%		6.7%		37.9%
Ohio	1,472,920	1,934,587	2,063,007	2,206,398		7.0%		14.1%		49.8%
Oklahoma	499,621	725,450	740,544	779,672		5.3%		7.5%		56.1%
Oregon	420,047	556,412	658,487	667,236		1.3%		19.9%		58.8%
Pennsylvania	1,395,732	1,773,094	1,876,807	2,005,364		6.8%		13.1%		43.7%
Rhode Island	115,738	143,100	152,110	162,842		7.1%		13.8%		40.7%
South Carolina	638,296	777,801	812,709	880,120		8.3%		13.2%		37.9%
South Dakota	90,618	125,882	130,345	134,803		3.4%		7.1%		48.8%
Tennessee	711,978	957,970	984,860	1,039,373		5.5%		8.5%		46.0%
Texas	2,579,342	3,527,867	4,072,434	4,029,799		-1.0%		14.2%		56.2%
Utah	305,233	489,173	511,096	543,691		6.4%		11.1%		78.1%
Vermont	56,810	59,173	63,378	67,753		6.9%		14.5%		19.3%
Virginia	1,068,485	1,299,919	1,481,579	1,629,776		10.0%		25.4%		52.5%
Washington	908,129	1,146,399	1,237,155	1,333,911		7.8%		16.4%		46.9%
West Virginia	275,672	362,261	362,750	387,432		6.8%		6.9%		40.5%
Wisconsin	843,543	1,040,341	1,074,474	1,170,122		8.9%		12.5%		38.7%
Wyoming	124,902	139,711	139,711	153,582		9.9%		9.9%		23.0%
TOTALS	39,841,010	52,912,324	56,591,115	60,568,619						
Weighted average percentages of change						**7.0%**		**14.4%**		**52.0%**

NOTE: *1999-2000 figures have been revised from previously published figures.
SOURCE: State Tax Appropriations to Higher Education, Fiscal Year 2001 (James Palmer & Sandra Gillilan, Center for the Study of Education Policy, Illinois State University, March 2001)

Higher Education Act (1965). The most comprehensive piece of higher education legislation in recent years, this important act established federal scholarships for needy undergraduate students and made provision for government insurance on private loans to students. In addition, it created special programs dealing with developing institutions, libraries, and community services. This legislation was comprehensively amended or reauthorized in 1968, 1972, 1976, 1980, 1986, 1992, and 1998. In 1972, the Basic Educational Opportunity Grant program (now called Pell Grants) was first authorized, and the Higher Education Facilities Act, the International Education Act, and parts of the National Defense Education Act were transferred to the Higher Education Act. In addition to this series of comprehensive legislative revisions, portions of the Higher Education Act have been amended by numerous other statues. In 1967, HEA was amended by the Education Professions Development Act to improve the quality of teaching. In 1978, the Middle Income Student Assistance Act modified the student aid provisions to allow middle-income as well as low-income students to qualify for federal assistance.

The Historically Black Colleges and Universities (HBCUs) Capital Financing program was authorized by the Higher Education Act Amendments of 1992 to provide HBCUs with private funds for repair, renovation, and construction projects.

The Student Loan Reform Act of 1993 authorized a new Federal Direct Student Loan (FDSL) program, recently renamed the William D. Ford Direct Loan program. This program is a new streamlined lending system that simplifies the process of obtaining and repaying loans for student and parent borrowers and provides borrowers with greater choice in repayment plans, including income contingency.

The Taxpayer Relief Act of 1997 authorized new tax credits (Hope scholarships and lifetime learning tax credits) and education individual retirement accounts (IRAs) for postsecondary education. The Hope scholarship, for freshman and sophomores, is worth up to $1,500 per years, while the lifetime learning tax credit provides up for $1,000 per year for part-time students, as well as full-time juniors, seniors, and graduate students. Taxpayers cannot claim both Hope and lifetime credits for the same student in the same year, and these credits are phased out at upper-income levels.

National Foundation on the Arts and Humanities Act (1965). This act was adopted to promote progress and scholarship in the arts and humanities. It authorized research, training, and the publication of scholarly works in the humanities.

National Sea Grant College and Program Act (1966). Authorized support to establish and operate sea grant college and programs for research and training related to the development and preservation of marine resources.

Health Manpower. Beginning in 1963, the Congress has enacted a series of laws to aid medical, dental, nursing, and other health schools and their students. This support, greatly expanded in 1971, was constrained by budget cuts in the 1980s, a pattern which continued in the 1990s. Although several new programs targeted at minority and disadvantaged students were initiated overall funding in this area has achieved no real growth.

Department of Education Organization Act (1979). A cabinet-level department of education was established for the first time in U.S. history. Functions from the old Department of Health, Education, and Welfare, four other departments, and the National Science Foundation were transferred to the new department.

Student Right-to-Know and Campus Security Act (1990). This act required institutions of higher education receiving federal assistance to provide certain information with respect to the graduation rates of student-athletes at such institutions. The Act also required the institution to certify that it has a campus security policy and to provide campus crime statistics upon request to students, parents, and prospective students.

National and Community Service Act of 1990. This act increased school and college-based community service opportunities and authorized the president's Points of Light Foundation. This legislation was amended in 1993 by the National Service Trust Act, which established a Corporation for National Service and provided education awards up to $4,725 per year for two years to persons 17 years of age or older who perform community service before, during, or after postsecondary education.

This brief legislative summary illustrates the fact that while the federal government has long been interested in higher education, it has been only during the relatively recent past that federal aid to higher education has begun to assume massive proportions.

DIMENSIONS OF FEDERAL AND STATE SUPPORT

Federal funds have been provided for a number of purposes: student aid, research and development, community service programs, construction of dormitories and academic facilities, purchase of instructional equipment and material, improvement of libraries, and assistance to developing institutions. In addition to supporting traditional areas of study, federal programs also have been specifically focused on international education, health education, teacher preparation, adult education, literary, and vocational education.

Tables 9-11 outline the extent of federal appropriations to education. Table 12 presents an analysis of appropriations of tax money by state legislative for the opening expense of postsecondary education institutions.

FEDERAL AID IN PERSPECTIVE

The following generalizations about the evolution of federal aid to higher education in the United States appear to be defensible:

1. The existing pattern of federal aid has not been the result of any carefully worked out plan. There has been no comprehensive or coordinated program at the federal level or any agency or organization that allows the federal government to deal with higher education in a consistent manner. The federal government has an estimated 500 programs that affect higher education in some fashion.

2. Federal support over the years has grown in response to real and identifiable needs. Each advance was related to a specific need (e.g., military needs or economic emergencies), and the definition of need has been steadily widened.

3. While federal aid has generally been in response to a specific need, there were, from the earliest days of the nation, expressions about the importance of education to the general welfare and recognition of the responsibility of government in fostering it. The use, expansions, and strengthening of the nation's resources (including our people), and the fact that our colleges and universities were a prime resource for accomplishing the objectives of government, were enunciated as a matter of national policy.

4. The federal government, from the very beginning, has included both public and private institutions in its programs. Congress has made no significant distinctions in its legislation between public and private higher education.

5. The use of federal funds for direct financial assistance to students developed as an outgrowth of the conviction that it was clearly in the national interest to provide each student the opportunity to seek the most advance education his abilities would allow and that none should be denied this opportunity because of financial need.

6. In 2004, the federal government provided 70 percent of all financial aid to students, including the value of loans insured. Another 5 percent was provided by the states, and 25 percent came from institutional and other sources. The largest single source of aid was the federally guaranteed student loan program, which provided nearly $63 billion to students, 49 percent of all available aid. Student loan volume has increased by 89 percent since 1994.

7. In addition to dramatic increases in student loan volume, federal grant aid to students has increased similarly in the past decade.

8. During the past decade federal aid has failed to keep pace with inflation. However, institutional aid has grown significantly over the same period.

9. The increasing volume of federal support has in large measure resulted from the fact that the government found it necessary to turn to the colleges and universities for educating manpower and new knowledge.

10. Federal aid evolved as a voluntary association between the government and institutions and was based on mutual self-interest. Institutions expected and received financial support to subsidize research projects; to construct classrooms, laboratories, and dormitories; to increase their capacity for public service; to broaden and enrich the curriculum; to provide more and better scholarship and loan funds for students; and generally to increase both their prestige and their effectiveness. The government expected and received a number of benefits. For example, it was able to get a large amount of its own work done through university research. It also wanted and received an increased supply of the trained manpower necessary to both the economic well-being and security of the nation. In addition, the government received assistance from the campus in fulfilling its commitments abroad, and while it is true that many of these programs were not necessarily formulated with the primary goal as an educational program, they became an established part of the federal-institutional relationship.

Federal aid, in the last analysis, came about as a matter of necessity rather than a matter of convenience, and it has grown to its present dimensions not only because of agreement that education directly services the national interest, but also because of a persistent belief that a strong educational establishment is an essential element of a national purpose. The result is a mosaic of programs rather than a seamless—and therefore vulnerable—plan.

II

Professional Education in the United States

Professional Education in the United States

Professional education in the United States is evaluated and accredited by independent commissions recognized by the Council for Higher Education Accreditation (CHEA). The majority of these commissions are also recognized by the U.S. Department of Education, Office of Postsecondary Education (Division of Eligibility and Agency Evaluation).

Nonregionally accredited, freestanding, independent schools that have specialized accreditation are briefly described in this section. Information on these schools can be obtained by contacting the accrediting agency at the address given.

Most commissions accredit their members through a process involving several steps. Before achieving full accreditation, applicant institutions are awarded prior status, which may be called by various names and carries different meanings: for example, some agencies call their candidates for accreditation "preaccredited," some say they are "provisionally accredited," some are "probationary," and some are accredited for a "reduced term", depending on the results of an evaluatory visit. The applying institutions or programs may or may not have been operating professional offerings and may or may not have graduated a class. For some agencies, candidate members almost always automatically become fully accredited; for others, candidacy brings tentative accreditation. Because of these inconsistencies, Part II of *American Universities and Colleges* lists only fully accredited, degree-granting institutions and programs.

REGIONAL ACCREDITING AGENCIES

Eight accrediting commissions operate in six distinct regions of the United States: New England, Middle States, North Central, Southern, Western, and Northwest. These regional commissions accredit entire institutions, as opposed to programs within institutions.

A ninth commission, the Interregional Accrediting Committee, is controlled by four regional commissions and exists to accredit a single institution: Western Governor's University in Utah.

Interregional Accrediting Committee (IRAC)

IRAC was created by four regional accrediting commissions: the Western Association of Schools and Colleges, Accrediting Commission for Senior Colleges and Universities; the Western Association of Schools and Colleges, Accrediting Commission for Community and Junior Colleges; the Northwestern Commission on Colleges and Universities; and the North Central Association of Colleges and Schools, Higher Learning Commission. IRAC's membership consists of three commissioners from each region and the executive directors of each participating commission.

IRAC is administered through the Northwestern Commission on Colleges and Universities.

Middle States Association of Colleges and Schools
Commission on Higher Education
Jean Avnet Morse, Executive Director
3624 Market Street
Philadelphia, PA 19104-2680
(215) 284-5000
(215) 662-5501
http://www.msache.org

Middle States Association of Colleges and Schools
Commission on Secondary Schools
Henry Cram, Executive Director
3624 Market Street
Philadelphia, PA 19104-2680
(215) 662-5603
(215) 662-0957
http://www.css-msa.org

North Central Association
Commission on Accreditation and School Improvement, Board of Trustees
Kenneth F. Gose, Executive Director
Arizona State University
PO Box 874705
Tempe, AZ 85287-4705
(800) 525-9517
(480) 965-8658
http://www.ncacasi.org

North Central Association of Colleges and Schools
The Higher Learning Commission
Steven D. Crow, Executive Director
30 North LaSalle Street, Suite 2400
Chicago, IL 60602-2504
(312) 263-0456
(312) 263-7462
http://www.ncahigherlearningcommission.org

New England Association of Schools and Colleges
Commission on Institutions of Higher Education
Barbara E. Brittingham, Interim Director
209 Burlington Road
Bedford, MA 01730-1433
(781) 271-0022
(781) 271-0950
http://www.neasc.org

New England Association of Schools and Colleges
Commission on Technical and Career Institutions
Paul Bento, Director
209 Burlington Road
Bedford, MA 01730-1433
(781) 271-0022
(781) 271-0950
http://www.neasc.org

Northwest Commission on Colleges and Universities
Sandra E. Elman, Executive Director
8060 165th Avenue, NE, Suite 100
Redmond, WA 98052
(425) 558-4224
(425) 376-0596
http://www.nwccu.org

Southern Association of Colleges and Schools
    Commission on Colleges
    Belle S. Wheelan, President
    1866 Southern Lane
    Decatur, GA 30033-4097
    (404) 679-4500
    (404) 679-4525
    http://www.sacscoc.org

Western Association of Schools and Colleges
    Accrediting Commission for Community and Junior Colleges
    Barbara A. Beno, Executive Director
    10 Commercial Boulevard, Suite 204
    Novato, CA 94949-6175
    (415) 506-0234
    (415) 506-0238
    http://www.accjc.org

Western Association of Schools and Colleges
    Accrediting Commission for Schools
    David E. Brown, Executive Director
    533 Airport Boulevard, Suite 200
    Burlingame, CA 94010
    (650) 696-1060
    (650) 696-1867
    http://www.wascweb.org

Western Association of Schools and Colleges
    Accrediting Commission for Senior Colleges and Universities
    Ralph A. Wolff, Executive Director
    985 Atlantic Avenue, Suite 100
    Alameda, CA 94501
    (510) 748-9001
    (510) 748-9797
    http://www.wascweb.org

PROFESSIONAL AND NATIONAL ACCREDITING AGENCIES

This section of *American Universities and Colleges* provides descriptions of the accrediting commissions in each professional field. All of the accrediting commissions listed here are recognized by either CHEA, the U.S. Department of Education, or both.

Not every professional discipline is represented by a specialized accrediting commission. For example, there is no recognized accreditor for English or physics. Professional accreditation for a program is usually held in addition to the institutional accreditation of the college or university, which covers all degrees and programs offered by the institution.

Art and Design

National Association of Schools of Art and Design
    Samuel Hope, Executive Director
    11250 Roger Bacon Drive, Suite 21
    Reston, VA 20190
    (703) 437-0700
    (703) 437-6312
    http://www.arts-accredit.org

The National Association of Schools of Art and Design (NASAD), organized in 1944, is composed of institutions and individuals committed to the highest goals and traditions in art and design education. Through its annual meeting, NASAD provides a forum for discussion of the broad considerations and aims of the field whose programs it accredits.

NASAD membership is open to all postsecondary institutions that offer educational programs in the visual arts.

Art studies are offered by many institutions for many purposes. Professional schools of art and design provide, either independently or as units within colleges or universities, highly specialized preparation

for careers in the visual arts or design. Generally in such schools, students earn two-thirds to three-fourths of their credits in studio credits, while earning baccalaureate or master's degrees in fine arts. The latter is the terminal degree in studio art.

Many departments of art and design offer visual art or design majors as components of humanities or liberal arts programs. These programs do not attempt to provide complete professional training for careers in the studio arts, but instead cultivate a broad understanding of art. Students in such programs generally earn from one-third to one-half of their credits in studio art and art history courses. Graduates with these majors may earn baccalaureate and master's degrees in art; some continue their studies for doctorates in fields such as art history, art education, and other nonstudio specialties.

The same institutions also offer programs in art education, in which graduates may earn certification to teach art in elementary and secondary schools.

In addition, there are art institutions for vocational training that provide training exclusively in the practical techniques of commercial art and design. After two or three years of work in such programs, students usually earn certificates.

Business and Accounting

AACSB International-The Association to Advance Collegiate Schools of Business
    Jerry E. Trapnell, *Executive Vice-President and Chief Accreditation Officer*
    777 South Harbour Island Boulevard, Suite 750
    Tampa, FL 33602-5730
    (813) 769-6500
    (813) 769-6559
    http://www.aacsb.edu

AACSB International-The Association to Advance Collegiate Schools of Business (AACSB) is a not-for-profit corporation of educational institutions, corporations, and other organizations devoted to the promotion and improvement of higher education in business administration and management.

Organized in 1916, AACSB is the premier accrediting agency for bachelor's, master's and doctoral degree programs in business administration and accounting. Its founding members include Columbia University, Cornell University, Dartmouth College, Harvard University, New York University, Northwestern University, The Ohio State University, Tulane University, University of California at Berkeley, University of Chicago, University of Illinois, University of Nebraska, University of Pennsylvania, University of Pittsburgh, The University of Texas, University of Wisconsin-Madison, and Yale University.

The growing membership outside the United States provides new opportunities and challenges for AACSB, as it expands its role as a source of information, training, and networking for management educators. In addition to its accreditation function, AACSB conducts an extensive array of development programs for faculty and administrators; engages in research and survey projects on topics specific to the field of management education; maintains relationships with disciplinary associations and other groups; interacts with the corporate community on a variety of projects and initiatives; and produces a wide variety of publications and special reports on trends and issues within management education. AACSB also maintains close relationships with its counterpart associations worldwide.

AACSB membership information, including a membership application, can be downloaded from http://www.aacsb.edu/members/joining.asp.

Association of Collegiate Business Schools and Programs
   Douglas Viehland, Executive Director
   7007 College Boulevard, Suite 420
   Overland Park, KS 66211
   (913) 339-9356
   (913) 339-6226
   http://www.acbsp.org

The Association of Collegiate Business Schools and Programs (ACBSP) is the leading specialized accreditation association for business education supporting, celebrating, and rewarding teaching excellence. ACBSP embraces the virtues of teaching excellence and emphasizes to students that it is essential to learn how to learn. ACBSP develops, promotes, and recognizes best practices that contribute to continuous improvement of business education and accredits qualified business programs.

ACBSP, founded in 1988, was created to fulfill a need for specialized accreditation by institutions of higher education with business schools and programs. That need was for business education accreditation based on the mission of the institution and of the respective unit; an accreditation that acknowledged and emphasized quality in teaching and learning outcomes.

There are approximately 2,400 U.S. institutions of higher education that have business administration, finance, management, and marketing programs. Economics also is often taught within a school or college of business, and is considered a sixth business-related field in such institutions.

In 1988, only 260 of those 2,400 institutions had their business schools and programs accredited, an accreditation administered by only one organization. Many of the remaining 2,140 institutions felt that an alternative organization with an accreditation philosophy more attuned to the missions of their institutions should be created to satisfy their business accreditation needs. Most of these remaining institutions pursued—and still pursue—excellence in teaching as their primary goal, as opposed to a heavy emphasis on research, and they wanted an accrediting organization that had this teaching emphasis reflected in its accreditation standards. ACBSP was created in response to that desire.

As of June 2005, ACBSP membership included 396 educational institutions as members, 293 of which have successfully achieved accreditation. In addition, ACBSP included 10 corporate and 12 emeritus members. Nearly 4,300 persons at these entities are individual members and receive benefits of membership.

Construction Education

American Council for Construction Education
   Board of Trustees
   Michael Holland, Executive Vice President
   1717 North Loop 1604 East, Suite 320
   San Antonio, TX 78232-1570
   (210) 495-6161
   (210) 495-6168
   http://www.acce-hq.org

The American Council for Construction Education (ACCE) has been accrediting construction education programs since 1976. Forty-five programs currently hold full ACCE accreditation.

Numerous colleges and universities currently offer programs leading to the associate and baccalaureate degrees in construction, construction management, construction science, and building construction. ACCE accredits only programs in regionally accredited postsecondary institutions that have graduated at least one class of construction education students. Approved curricula normally include work in basic sciences; humanities; mathematics; social sciences; business administration; fundamentals of structural, mechanical, and electrical systems; and construction methods, procedures, and management.

Applicants to construction programs should be graduates of accredited secondary schools. Typical construction programs begin with two years spent in studying general liberal arts and sciences, while the last two years are devoted to more specialized courses in the field.

Counseling

Association for Clinical Pastoral Education, Inc.
   Accreditation Commission
   Teresa E. Snorton, Executive Director
   1549 Clairmont Road, Suite 103
   Decatur, GA 30033-4611
   (404) 320-1472
   (404) 320-0849
   http://www.acpe.edu

The Association for Clinical Pastoral Education, Inc. (ACPE) is a professional association committed to advancing experience-based theological education for seminarians, clergy and lay persons of diverse cultures, ethnic groups, and faith traditions. It establishes standards, certifies supervisors, and accredits programs and centers in varied settings. ACPE programs promote the integration of personal history, faith tradition, and the behavioral sciences in the practice of spiritual care.

ACPE is recognized by the U.S. Department of Education to:

• Encourage creative response to the changing context of spiritual care in the communities they serve.

• Model professional competence, integrity, and high ethical standards.

• Sustain a welcoming organizational culture in which members are encouraged to learn and grow.

• Embrace diversity, collaboration, and accountability on a national and international level.

• Prophetically advocate for excellence in pastoral education and the practice of spiritual care.

Council for Accreditation of Counseling and Related Educational Programs
   Carol L. Bobby, Executive Director
   5999 Stevenson Avenue
   Alexandria, VA 22304-3302
   (703) 823-9800
   (703) 823-1581
   http://www.cacrep.org

The Council for Accreditation of Counseling and Related Educational Programs (CACREP) was created in 1981 to be the independent accrediting arm for the American Counseling Association, a membership organization for more than 50,000 practicing counselors. From its inception, CACREP has provided an effective measure of quality assurance for counselor preparation programs.

CACREP accredits master's degree programs in community counseling, community counseling with specializations in both career and gerontological counseling, marriage and family counseling therapy, mental health counseling, school counseling, and student affairs practice in higher education, as well as doctoral programs in counselor education and supervision. Institutions applying for CACREP program accreditation must be regionally accredited.

The prerequisites for admission to a master's degree program in counseling vary. Generally, several courses in psychology and good interpersonal skills are required. Students in CACREP-accredited programs are required to complete a 100-hour practicum and a 600-hour internship before graduating (900 hours for mental health counseling.)

Programs in marriage and family counseling/therapy and mental health counseling require 60 semester hours of graduate study. The programs in other counseling areas require 48 semester hours of graduate study.

Professional counselors must pass an exam to practice in the states. School counselors are certified through state boards of education. Voluntary national certification is available through the National Board for Certified Counselors.

Culinary

American Culinary Federation, Inc.
    Accrediting Commission
    Candace Childers, Accreditation Manager
    180 Center Place Way
    St. Augustine, FL 32095
    (904) 824-4468
    (904) 825-4758
    http://www.acfchefs.org

The American Culinary Federation, Inc. (ACF), founded in 1929, is a professional, not-for-profit organization for chefs. The principal goal of ACF is to promote a professional image of the American chef worldwide, through education among culinarians at all levels, from apprentices to the most accomplished certified master chefs of the culinary arts.

The Accrediting Commission of ACF, established in 1986, represents the educational needs of the culinary profession. Graduates of ACF-accredited programs can be assured that the American Culinary Federation guided the curriculum of their career choice.

ACF accreditation is voluntary and requires that curriculum, faculty, facilities, resources, support staff, and organizational structure all substantially meet the standards set by the Accrediting Commission. These standards, set by industry leaders in both culinary arts and culinary arts education, are monitored constantly for accuracy in the culinary profession. ACF does not endorse any one program as being better than another, but strives to assure prospective students that the minimum standards have been met or exceeded by the accredited programs.

Dance

National Association of Schools of Dance
    Samuel Hope, Executive Director
    11250 Roger Bacon Drive, Suite 21
    Reston, VA 20190
    (703) 437-0700
    (703) 437-6312
    http://www.arts-accredit.org

The National Association of Schools of Dance (NASD) was established in 1981 to develop a closer relationship among schools and programs of dance for the purposes of examining and improving practices and professional standards in dance education and training.

The general aims and objectives of NASD are: to establish a national forum to stimulate the understanding and acceptance of the educational disciplines inherent in the creative arts in higher education in the United States; to establish reasonable standards in which quantitative measurements have validity, as in matters of budget, faculty qualifications, faulty-student ratios, class time requirements, library and physical facilities; to foster the development of instruction of the highest quality while simultaneously encouraging varied and experimental approaches to the teaching of dance; to evaluate, through the processes of voluntary accreditation, schools of dance and programs of dance instruction in terms of their quality and the results they achieve, as judged by experienced examiners; to assure students and parents that accredited dance programs provide competent

teachers, adequate plant and equipment, and sound curricula, and that they are capable of attaining their stated objectives; to counsel and assist schools in developing their programs and to encourage self-evaluation and continuing studies toward improvement; to invite and encourage the cooperation of professional dance groups and individuals of reputation in the field of dance in the formulation of appropriate curricula and standards; and to establish a national voice to be heard in matters pertaining to dance, particularly as they would affect member schools and their stated objectives.

The main role of NASD is that of a specialized, professional accrediting agency. The accreditation process focuses upon two principal concerns: educational quality and institutional quality. The review of educational quality is made according to nationally recognized standards developed by NASD with the full participation of its member institutions and in consultation with various professional groups in the field of dance. Institutions are periodically reviewed to determine that they are providing the educational services they promise and whether their own stated operational procedures are being followed.

Dietetics

American Dietetic Association
    Commission on Accreditation for Dietetics Education
    Beverly E. Mitchell, Senior Director, Accreditation, Education Programs, and Student Operations
    120 South Riverside Plaza, Suite 2000
    Chicago, IL 60606-6995
    (312) 899-0040
    (312) 899-4817
    http://www.eatright.org/cade

The Commission on Accreditation for Dietetics Education (CADE) of the American Dietetic Association exists to serve the public by establishing and enforcing eligibility requirements and accreditation standards that ensure the quality and continued improvement of nutrition and dietetics education programs. CADE accredits coordinated baccalaureate and master's degree programs in dietetics that combine academic and clinical experience.

All coordinated dietetics programs, based in regionally accredited institutions, must be in compliance with the established CADE standards. Graduates who successfully complete the program may apply for active membership in the association and may take the registration examination for dietitians.

Education

American Academy for Liberal Education
    Jeffrey D. Wallin, President
    1710 Rhode Island Avenue, NW, 4th Floor
    Washington, DC 20036
    (202) 452-8611
    (202) 452-8620
    http://www.aale.org

The American Academy for Liberal Education (AALE), a national association, accredits institutions offering quality general education programs in the liberal arts that meet the educational, administrative, and financial criteria. AALE is unique in grounding the entire institutional or program accreditation process on a rigorous set of standards. Accreditation enables liberal arts institutions to participate in programs authorized under the Higher Education Act and other federal programs.

Accreditation by AALE signifies institutional integrity and a strong commitment to liberal education, certifying that an institution meets or exceeds the independently established education standards, requiring students to complete demanding core studies in the arts, sciences, and humanities taught by senior as well as junior faculty. Consequently, AALE's Education Standards provide stakeholders in higher education, including parents and prospective students, with a clear means for identifying curricula with a focused, well-articulated core of languages, history, mathematics, science, literature, philosophy, and other elements of a liberal education.

AALE is listed by the Secretary of the U.S. Department of Education as a recognized national accrediting agency for the accreditation and preaccreditation of institutions, as well as programs within institutions, that offer liberal arts degrees at the baccalaureate level.

Montessori Accreditation Council for Teacher Education
Commission on Accreditation
Gretchen Warner, Executive Director, MACTE Commission
506 Seventh Street
Racine, WI 53403
(262) 898-1846
(262) 898-1849
http://www.macte.org

The Montessori Accreditation Council for Teacher Education (MACTE) was created in 1991 through a merger of two previous groups: the Accrediting Association for Montessori Teacher Education (AAMTE), an outgrowth of an ad hoc committee of Montessori educators founded in 1987; and the Accreditation Council for Childhood Education Specialist Schools (ACCESS), which began accrediting Montessori teacher education institutions and programs in 1982.

MACTE is an autonomous, international, nonprofit postsecondary accrediting agency for Montessori teacher education programs. It accredits independent postsecondary institutions that offer comprehensive, in-residence certification courses and programs or departments located within institutions already accredited by another recognized agency. MACTE accreditation enables Montessori teacher education programs to participate in Title IV funding and in other federal programs.

The MACTE Commission currently accredits Montessori teacher education programs designed for these age levels:

• Infant and Toddler (birth–age 3)

• Early Childhood (ages 2 1/2–6)

• Elementary I or I–II (ages 6–9 or 6–12)

• Secondary I or II (ages 12–15 or 12–18)

Teacher Education Accreditation Council
Accreditation Committee
Frank B. Murray, President
One Dupont Circle, NW, Suite 320
Washington, DC 20036-0110
(202) 466-7236
(202) 466-7238
http://www.teac.org

The Teacher Education Accreditation Council (TEAC), founded in 1997, is a nonprofit organization dedicated to improving academic degree programs for professional educators—those who will teach and lead in schools, pre-K through grade 12. TEAC's goal is to support the preparation of competent, caring, and qualified professional educators. TEAC accredits undergraduate and graduate professional education programs in order to assure the public about the quality of college and university programs. The education program, not the college, school, department or other administrative unit of the institution, receives TEAC accreditation.

TEAC's entire accreditation process is built around the program's case that it prepares competent, caring, and qualified professional educators. TEAC requires the program to have evidence to support its

case, and the accreditation process examines and verifies the evidence. TEAC's membership represents education programs within a broad range of higher education institutions, from small liberal arts colleges to large research universities, and includes professional organizations. Affiliate membership is granted to institutions that support the TEAC agenda but do not wish to pursue accreditation for any of their programs, and it is granted similarly to agencies, organizations, or individuals.

Recognized by the Council for Higher Education Accreditation and by the U.S. Department of Education, TEAC is also a member of the Association of Specialized and Professional Accreditation, the American Council on Education, Association of Teacher Educators, and the National Association of State Directors of Teacher Education and Certification.

Engineering and Related Disciplines

Accreditation Board for Engineering and Technology, Inc.
Applied Science Accreditation Commission (ASAC)
Computing Accreditation Commission (CAC)
Engineering Accreditation Commission (EAC)
Technology Accreditation Commission (TAC)
George D. Peterson, Executive Director
111 Market Place, Suite 1050
Baltimore, MD 21202
(410) 347-7700
(410) 625-2238
http://www.abet.org

Accreditation by the Accreditation Board for Engineering and Technology, Inc. (ABET) is an assurance that a college or university program meets the quality standards established by the profession for which it prepares its students. For example, an accredited engineering program must meet the quality standards set by the engineering profession. An accredited computer science program must meet the quality standards set by the computing profession.

Accreditation in engineering and its many specialties is voluntary and is initiated at the request of the institution. ABET accredits postsecondary degree-granting programs housed within regionally accredited institutions. Only programs are accredited by ABET, not degrees, departments, colleges, or institutions.

Applied Science

The Applied Science Accreditation Commission (ASAC) of ABET accredited programs in health physics, industrial hygiene, industrial management, occupational health and safety, and surveying/geomatics at the baccalaureate and master's levels.

Computing

The Computing Accreditation Commission (CAC) of ABET accredits programs in computer science, information systems, and information technology at the baccalaureate level. There are approximately 248 accredited computing programs at 192 institutions.

Engineering

The Engineering Accreditation Commission (EAC) of ABET accredits first-professional degrees at either the basic baccalaureate or the advanced master's level, with the institutions determining which of their programs qualify for evaluation as first-professional.

Acceptable engineering curricula include work in basic sciences and mathematics beyond trigonometry; engineering sciences, analysis, design, and systems; and social sciences and humanities. ABET accredits only curricula that have graduated a class in engineering.

Although curricula in the basic fields of engineering are available in most ABET-accredited colleges, universities, and schools of engineering, some specialties are taught in relatively few institutions. Students wishing to specialize in small branches of the field should investigate curricula offered by specific schools before making application.

Secondary school academic work of generally high quality, which includes courses in mathematics and physical sciences, is required for admission to undergraduate engineering programs. The typical four-year engineering curriculum requires students to spend their first two years studying the basic sciences—mathematics, physics, and chemistry—and the humanities, social sciences, and English. Students devote their last two years chiefly to advanced study in science and to engineering courses relevant to their specialties.

Basic engineering programs require at least four years to complete. However, the intensity of the curricula, the sequential nature of many courses, and the prerequisites required force most students either to take overload schedules or to attend one or two summer sessions to finish in four years.

A few institutions offer five-year programs leading to the baccalaureate. In addition, most engineering schools participate in dual-degree programs with liberal arts colleges, in which students spend three years in the college and two in the engineering school, graduating with baccalaureates from both institutions. Many engineering schools operate transfer programs with associate-level institutions, allowing students to complete their first two years of study in the two-year college.

Engineering Technology

The Technology Accreditation Commission of ABET accredits associate and baccalaureate programs in engineering technology. The field combines scientific and engineering knowledge and methods with technical skills in support of engineering activities. The associate and baccalaureate degree programs have a wide range of objectives, but all aim to prepare graduates for immediate technical employment.

The curricula are technological in nature and lie beyond the scope of secondary school, differing in content and purpose from those programs in vocational schools and industrial technology, on the one hand, and in engineering colleges, on the other. Accredited programs in engineering technology take between two and four years to complete. Admission requirements usually include graduation from secondary school with courses in science and mathematics.

Accredited programs are offered in technical institutes, junior and community colleges, colleges of technology, proprietary schools, and a division of complex postsecondary institutions.

National Association of Industrial Technology
  Rick Coscarelli, Executive Director
  3300 Washtenaw Avenue, Suite 220
  Ann Arbor, MI 48104-4200
  (734) 677-0720
  (734) 677-0046
  http://www.nait.org

The National Association of Industrial Technology (NAIT) is recognized as the premier professional association responsible for the promotion of industrial technology in business, industry, education, and government.

Industrial technology is a field of study designed to prepare technical and management-oriented professionals for employment in business, industry, education, and government. Industrial technology is primarily involved with the management, operation, and maintenance of complex technological systems, while engineering and engineering technology are primarily involved with the design and installation of these systems.

Accrediting Commission of Career Schools and Colleges of Technology
  Elise Scanlon, Executive Director
  2101 Wilson Boulevard, Suite 302
  Arlington, VA 22201
  (703) 247-4212
  (703) 247-4533
  http://www.accsct.org

ACCSCT is a private, nonprofit, independent accrediting agency whose goal is maintaining educational quality in the career schools and colleges it accredits by striving to ensure academic excellence and ethical practices. ACCSCT is dedicated to the more than 360,000 students who annually pursue career education at its accredited institutions.

As an accrediting agency, ACCSCT is responsible for assuring that member institutions and their educational programs are capable of preparing students for their chosen careers. The accrediting process also assures students and the public that high standards of career education are being met.

Originally founded as the Accrediting Commission of the National Association of Trade and Technical Schools, the Commission was established as an independent body in 1993 to conform with the Higher Education Act Amendments of 1992. The resulting organization—ACCSCT—is recognized by the U.S. Department of Education as a national accrediting agency for private, postsecondary institutions offering occupational vocational programs.

ACCSCT member institutions teach accounting, computer programming and servicing, graphic arts, court reporting, cosmetology, auto repair, printing, acting, theater production, pet grooming, child care, respiratory therapy, taxidermy, welding, photography, airplane piloting, massage therapy, culinary arts, hotel and restaurant management, jewelry design, appliance repair, banking services and management, motion picture/TV/video production, air conditioning and heating ventilation, data processing, nursing, merchandising, drafting, and floral design.

Family and Consumer Sciences

American Association of Family and Consumer Sciences
  Council for Accreditation
  Karen S. Tucker, Executive Director
  400 North Columbus Street
  Alexandria, VA 22314
  (703) 706-4600
  (703) 706-4663
  www.aafcs.org

Founded in 1909, the American Association of Family and Consumer Sciences (AAFSC), formerly the American Home Economics Association, is as an educational and scientific organization dedicated to improving the quality and standards of individual and family life through education, research, cooperative programs, and public information.

AAFCS is the only national organization representing family and consumer sciences professionals across practice areas and content specializations. Our members provide guidance and practical knowledge about the things of everyday life, including human growth and development, personal behavior, housing and environment, food and nutrition, apparel and textiles, and resource management.

AAFCS accreditation is a status granted to family and consumer sciences units within colleges and universities that meet or exceed standards established by the AAFCS Council for Accreditation. The AAFCS Council for Accreditation has accredited many focused, academic, family and consumer sciences programs across the United States.

Marriage and Family Therapy

American Association for Marriage and Family Therapy
   Commission on Accreditation for Marriage and Family Therapy Education
   Jeff Hamon, Director of Accreditation Services
   112 South Alfred Street
   Alexandria, VA 22314-3061

   (703) 253-0457
   (703) 253-0508
   http://www.aamft.org

The Commission on Accreditation for Marriage and Family Therapy Education (COAMFTE) is a specialized body that accredits master's, doctoral, and postgraduate programs in marriage and family therapy. Since 1978, the COAMFTE has been recognized by the U.S. Department of Education as the national accrediting body for the field of marriage and family therapy.

The COAMFTE works cooperatively with its parent organization, the American Association for Marriage and Family Therapy (AAMFT), state licensing and certification boards, and the Association of Marital and Family Therapy Regulatory Boards (AMFTRB). Once a program has become accredited, it is required to submit annual reports demonstrating continued compliance.

Forestry

Society of American Foresters
   Commission on Accreditation
   Terry Clark, Associate Director of Science and Education
   5400 Grosvenor Lane
   Bethesda, MD 20814-2198
   (301) 897-8720
   (301) 897-3690
   http://www.safnet.org

The Society of American Foresters (SAF) is the scientific and professional organization that represents both public and private forestry professionals, from researchers, administrators, and educators to forestry technician and students. Forestry is the science, practice, and art of the effective management, use, and conversation of these resources. The science of forestry was established in the United States at the turn of the century, at a time when vast areas of forests had been cut down with little thought of the future.

Typical forestry curricula include general studies in the liberal arts and the biological, physical, and social sciences, with intensive professional coursework in subjects such as ecology, dendrology, mensuration, silviculture, forest resources economics, policy and administration, and resource management and use. Specialization is possible in such areas as recreation, timber, wildlife management, or wood technology.

SAF's Committee on Accreditation accredits professional forestry programs at the baccalaureate and master's levels in institutions whose forestry curricula meet the Standards and Procedures for Accrediting Institutions for the Teaching of Professional Forestry.

Institutions receiving accreditation have undergone a self-study, completed an onsite visitation, and comply with SAF accreditation standards addressing forestry program goals, objectives, and policies; curriculum, organization, and administration of the forestry program; faculty; students; parent institution support; physical resources and facilities; and research extension, continuing education, and public service. Forestry programs may become candidates for SAF accreditation if they are offered at an institution accredited by its regional commission on accreditation; have offered a professional forestry degree program for at least two years; and require, for completion of the professional degree, study in a curriculum meeting the criteria established by SAF.

Funeral Service

American Board of Funeral Service Education
   Committee on Accreditation
   George P. Connick, Executive Director
   38 Florida Avenue
   Portland, ME 04103
   (207) 878-6530
   (207) 797-7686
   http://www.abfse.org

The American Board of Funeral Service Education (ABFSE) serves as the national academic accreditation agency for college and university programs in funeral service and mortuary science education. Although its roots go back to the 1940s, the ABFSE became an autonomous agency in 1962. It is recognized by the U.S. Department of Education and the Council for Higher Education Accreditation (CHEA) as the sole accrediting agency for academic programs that prepare funeral service professionals.

The ABFSE is composed of representatives from each of the accredited academic programs, as well as representatives from two sponsoring agencies—the National Funeral Directors Association and the Conference of Funeral Service Examining Boards—along with members of the general public. Meetings are held each spring, and most work is carried out through a series of committees, including Accreditation, Scholarship, Curriculum, National Board Examination, and College and University Council.

The associate degree, or its credit hour equivalent, is required for graduation from one of the accredited academic programs. Students are also required to pass the National Board Examination and complete a one- or two-year apprenticeship to be eligible for licensure. Each state has its own specific licensing requirements.

Health Professions

Acupuncture and Oriental Medicine

Accreditation Commission for Acupuncture and Oriental Medicine
   Dort S. Bigg, Executive Director
   Maryland Trade Center 3
   7501 Greenway Center Drive, Suite 820
   Greenbelt, MD 20770
   (301) 313-0855
   (301) 313-0912
   http://www.acaom.org

The Accreditation Commission for Acupuncture and Oriental Medicine (ACAOM) was established in June 1982 by the Council of Colleges of Acupuncture and Oriental Medicine and the American Association of Oriental Medicine. As an independent body, ACAOM evaluates professional master's degree and master's level certificate and diploma programs in Oriental medicine. In evaluating these programs, which have concentrations in both acupuncture and herbal therapy, ACAOM seeks to determine the level of performance, integrity, and quality that evokes confidence in the educational community and the public whom these programs serve.

ACAOM establishes accreditation criteria, arranges site visits, evaluates those programs that desire accredited status, and publicly designates those that meet the established criteria. The accrediting process requires each program to examine its goals, activities, and outcomes; to consider the criticism and suggestions of a visiting team; to determine internal procedures for action on recommendations from ACAOM; and to maintain continuous self-study and improvement mechanisms.

Allied Health

Commission on Accreditation of Allied Health Education Programs
Kathleen Megivern, Executive Director
35 East Wacker Drive, Suite 1970
Chicago, IL 60601-2208
(312) 553-9355
(312) 553-9616
http://www.caahep.org

The Commission on Accreditation of Allied Health Education Programs (CAAHEP), is the largest programmatic/specialized accreditor in the health sciences field. In collaboration with its committees on accreditation, CAAHEP reviews and accredits more than 2,000 educational programs in 21 health science occupations across the United States and Canada.

CAAHEP is composed of 17 Committees on Accreditation. These committees do the day-to-day work of accreditation, reviewing programs in their specific professional area, and formulating recommendations which are then considered by the CAAHEP Board of Directors. The committees cover the fields of anesthesiologist assistant, athletic training, cardiovascular technology, cytotechnology, diagnostic medical sonography, electroneurodiagnostic technology, emergency medical services professions, exercise sciences, kinesiotherapy, medical assistants, medical illustrator, orthotic and prosthetic, perfusion, polysomnographic technologists, respiratory care, specialists in blood bank technology, surgical assisting, and surgical technology.

CAAHEP is recognized by the Council for Higher Education Accreditation (CHEA) for all accredited programs that result in an associate, baccalaureate, or master's degree, and by the U.S. Department of Education (USDE) for six Committees on Accreditation that perform a gatekeeper role for programs and/or student access to federal grants or loans. These committees are: Accreditation Committee Perfusion Education, Cytotechnology Programs Review Committee, Joint Review Committee on Education in Cardiovascular Technology, Joint Review Committee on Education in Diagnostic Medical Sonography, Joint Review Committee on Education in Electroneurodiagnostic Technology, and the Committee on Accreditation of Educational Programs for the Emergency Medical Services Professions.

American College of Nurse-Midwives
Division of Accreditation
Deanne Williams, Executive Director
8403 Colesville Road, Suite 1550
Silver Spring, MD 20910-6374
(240) 485-1800
(240) 485-1818
http://www.midwife.org

The American College of Nurse-Midwives (ACNM) is the professional organization for certified nurse-midwives and certified midwives. Founded in 1929 and incorporated in 1955, ACNM provides research, accredits midwifery education programs, administers and promotes continuing education programs, establishes clinical practice standards, and creates liaisons with state and federal agencies and members of Congress.

During the mid-1940s, the National Organization of Public Health Nurses (NOPHN) established a section for nurse-midwives. A few years later, when there was a general reorganization of the national nursing organizations, the NOPHN was absorbed into the American Nurse's Association (ANA) and the National League for Nursing (NLN), and there was no provision within these organizations for a recognizable entity of nurse-midwives. Instead, the nurse-midwives were assigned to the Maternal and Child Health–National League for Nursing Interdivisional Council, which encompassed the areas of obstetrics, pediatrics, orthopedics, crippled children, and school nurs-

ing. The membership and concerns of this council were simply too broad to serve as a forum or voice for nurse-midwifery. Ironically, even though nurse-midwives were in positions of leadership in maternal-child nursing educational, professional, and federal organizations pertaining to health care, they were usually not thought of as being nurse-midwives.

The mission of ACNM is to promote the health and well-being of women and infants within their families and communities through the development and support of the profession of midwifery as practiced by certified nurse-midwives and certified midwives. The philosophy inherent in the profession states that nurse-midwives believe every individual has the right to safe, satisfying health care with respect for human dignity and cultural variations.

Midwifery Education Accreditation Council
Mary Ann Baul, Executive Director
515 East Birch Avenue
Flagstaff, AZ 86001
(928) 214-0997
(928) 773-9694
http://www.meacschools.org

The Midwifery Education Accreditation Council (MEAC) was established as a nonprofit corporation in 1991 by the National Coalition of Midwifery Educators. The mission of MEAC is to promote quality education in midwifery by creating standards and criteria for the education of midwives that reflect the nationally recognized core competencies and guiding principles of midwifery care, as set by the Midwives Alliance of North America.

MEAC's standards for accreditation were developed by expert midwifery educators from a variety of midwifery education programs and institutions in the United States. Its scope of accrediting includes comprehensive midwifery preparation through various routes of education including:

- Freestanding schools or colleges of midwifery offering certificate and degree programs.

- Certificate and degree programs of midwifery within other public and private accredited institutions.

- Freestanding schools or institutions that offer distance courses and/or structured apprenticeships as part of the midwifery curriculum, leading to a certificate or degree in midwifery.

Council on Naturopathic Medical Education
Daniel Seitz, Executive Director
PO Box 323
Johnson, VT 05656
(802) 635-7090
(802) 635-7492
http://www.cnme.org

The mission of the Council on Naturopathic Medical Education (CNME) is to assure the public of high-quality naturopathic education by accrediting programs that voluntarily seek recognition and meet or exceed CNME's standards.

Founded in 1978, CNME is accepted as the programmatic accrediting agency for naturopathic medical education at the four-year naturopathic colleges and programs in the United States and Canada. The U.S. Secretary of Education recognizes CNME as the national accrediting agency for programs leading to the Doctor of Naturopathic Medicine (N.D. or N.M.D.) or Doctor of Naturopathy (N.D.) degree.

CNME also approves postdoctoral programs (i.e., residency programs) in naturopathic medicine, providing licensed naturopathic physicians with postgraduate training in naturopathic family care and other specialties. CNME is a member of the Association of

Specialized and Professional Accreditors (ASPA) and abides by ASPA's Code of Good Practice.

Commission on Opticianry Accreditation
   Tamara A.L. Halstead, Director of Accreditation
   8665 Sudley Road, #341
   Manassas, VA 20110
   (703) 940-9134
   (703) 940-9135
   http://www.coaccreditation.com

The Commission on Opticianry Accreditation (COA) is an autonomous organization officially incorporated to serve as an independent agency for the sole purpose of accrediting opticianry and ophthalmic laboratory technology programs in the United States and its territories.

COA is committed to the fair and thorough assessment of educational quality. As an accrediting agency, the goal of COA is to assist opticianry programs in producing well-trained, competent graduates, capable of providing quality, professional services to the public.

Chiropractic Education

Council on Chiropractic Education
   Commission on Accreditation
   Martha S. O'Connor, Executive Director
   8049 North 85th Way
   Scottsdale, AZ 85258-4321
   (480) 443-8877
   (480) 483-7333
   http://www.cce-usa.org

Doctors of chiropractic medicine serve as primary providers of health care through diagnosis and treatment or referral. Chiropractic concerns itself with the relationship of the structural and neurological aspects of the body as related to disease and restoration and preservation of health.

The Council on Chiropractic Education (CCE) accredits programs and institutions offering the doctor of chiropractic degree. Students applying for admission to an accredited chiropractic college must furnish proof of having completed 60 semester hours leading to a baccalaureate degree, which must include communication or language skills, psychology, social sciences or humanities, biological sciences, general or inorganic chemistry, organic chemistry, and physics. The curriculum of instruction leading to the doctor of chiropractic degree must total not less than 4,200 50-minute hours. Offerings must address at least the following subjects: anatomy; biochemistry; physiology; microbiology; pathology; public health; physical, clinical, and laboratory diagnosis; gynecology; obstetrics; pediatrics; geriatrics; dermatology; otolaryngology; diagnostic imaging procedures; psychology; nutrition/dietetics; biomechanics; orthopedics; first aid and emergency procedures; spinal analysis; principles and practice of chiropractic; adjustive techniques, research methods, and procedures; and professional practice ethics.

All states, including the District of Columbia and Puerto Rico, require the licensure of chiropractic practitioners. Licensure requirements vary among the states and may be obtained from individual state chiropractic licensing boards.

Clinical Laboratory Science

National Accrediting Agency for Clinical Laboratory Science
   Olive M. Kimball, Chief Executive Officer
   8410 West Bryn Mawr Avenue, Suite 670
   Chicago, IL 60631-3415
   (773) 714-8880
   (773) 714-8886
   http://www.naacls.org

The National Accrediting Agency for Clinical Laboratory Sciences (NAACLS) is committed to being the premier agency for accreditation and approval of educational programs in the clinical laboratory sciences and related health care disciplines through the involvement of expert volunteers and its dedication to public service.

NAACLS is dedicated to peer review as the foundation of accreditation and approval. The agency strives to prepare volunteer reviewers and to assist them in providing exemplary program analysis, based upon principles of honesty, fairness, objectivity, and integrity.

NAACLS demonstrates commitment to public service by setting standards for education programs of high quality in clinical laboratory sciences and related health professions. NAACLS will continue to be responsive to the needs of the public and the health care community.

Dentistry

American Dental Association
   Commission on Dental Accreditation
   Morris Robbins, Chair
   211 East Chicago Avenue, 18th Floor
   Chicago, IL 60611-2678
   (312) 440-2940
   (312) 440-2915
   http://www.ada.org

Dental accreditation for the first-professional degree, a practice begun in 1938 under the auspices of the Council on Dental Education, is now awarded by the Commission on Dental Accreditation. To be eligible for dental accreditation, schools must be part of regionally accredited colleges or universities and must meet the commission's standards for institutional effectiveness, educational program, faculty and staff, educational support services, patient care, and research.

Admission to an accredited dental school requires a minimum of two academic years of college. All dental schools require applicants to take the Dental Admission Test (DAT), an examination designed to test perceptual ability, reading comprehension, quantitative ability, and knowledge of biomedical sciences. Most schools ask that application be made through the American Association of Dental Schools Application Service (AADSAS). Although prospective students should contact individual schools directly concerning admissions requirements, prerequisite courses typically include biology, English, inorganic and organic chemistry, and physics.

Students work in two broad areas during the four years of study at the predoctoral level: the basic biomedical sciences, and then apply those sciences to the clinical dental sciences in order to deliver oral health care in all aspects of clinical dentistry. Successful students earn either Doctor of Dental Surgery (DDS) or Doctor of Dental Medicine (DMD) degrees, at the discretion of the institution. Those wishing to pursue advanced education must study one to four more years in advanced general dentistry or in one of the eight dental specialties recognized by the American Dental Association: dental public health, endodontics, oral and maxillofacial pathology, oral and maxillofacial surgery, orthodontics and dentofacial orthopedics, pediatric dentistry, peridontics, and prosthodontics. Advanced dental education is available through commission-accredited programs based in hospitals and educational facilities.

In addition to graduating from an accredited dental school, prospective dentists must pass a battery of written and clinical examinations to gain licensure to practice dentistry in any given state. The national, written examinations given by the Joint Commission on National Dental Examinations partially fulfill the written examination requirement. Clinical examinations are administered by individual state boards of dental examiners or by one of four regional testing agencies. Where available, applicants may apply for licensure in more than one state, by taking only one clinical examination.

Health Services Administration

Commission on Accreditation of Healthcare Management Education

  Pamela S. Jenness, Director of Accreditation Operations
  2000 14th Street North, Suite 780
  Arlington, VA 22201
  (703) 894-0960
  (703) 894-0941
  http://www.cahmeweb.org

In 1968, the Commission on Accreditation of Healthcare Management Education (CAHME), originally known as the Accrediting Commission on Graduate Education for Hospital Administration, was incorporated in the State of Illinois as the accrediting agency in the field of graduate education in hospital administration.

CAHME replaced an older approval program, conducted since 1948, employing criteria for membership in the association as a measure of academic quality. As the field of hospital administration gained professional stature, health care organizations sought administrators with master's degrees from approved programs. Consequently, a plan for a formalized accreditation program was submitted and accepted in 1970 by what was then the National Commission on Accrediting (NCA). In 1976, the organization's name was changed to reflect the broad spectrum of opportunities that exists within the profession of health administration. The name changed again in 2004.

CAHME has been granted formal recognition by the U.S. Department of Education (DOE) as the only organization to accredit master's-level health care management programs in the United States and Canada. The corporation is organized exclusively for educational and scientific purposes:

• To establish criteria for the conduct of graduate education for health services administration.

• To conduct survey programs that will encourage universities to maintain and improve educational offerings in health services administration.

• To determine compliance with the criteria.

• To make the findings of the Commission available to the public.

• To assume such other responsibilities and to conduct such other activities as are compatible with the operation of an educational accreditation program.

Programs accredited by CAHME are housed in different settings within the university, including schools of business, medicine, public health, public administration, allied health sciences, and graduate studies.

Medicine

Liaison Committee on Medical Education (Even Years Beginning July 1)

  Robert Eaglen, Assistant LCME Secretary
  Association of American Medical Colleges
  2450 N Street, NW
  Washington, DC 20037
  (202) 828-0596
  (202) 828-1125
  http://www.lcme.org

Liaison Committee on Medical Education (Odd Years Beginning July 1)

  Barbara Barzansky, Assistant LCME Secretary
  American Medical Association
  515 North State Street
  Chicago, IL 60610
  (312) 464-4933
  (312) 464-5830
  http://www.lcme.org

The Liaison Committee on Medical Education (LCME) is represented by ad hoc teams of evaluators who conduct onsite surveys of medical schools. Survey team members are a mix of basic science and clinical educators and practitioners. Members of the LCME and surveyors conducting field evaluations serve as voluntary peer evaluators. The activities of the LCME are administered by two Secretariats, at AMA headquarters in Chicago, IL, and at the offices of the AAMC in Washington, DC. Members of the LCME and its survey teams, excluding full- and part-time staff, serve the LCME without compensation.

The Department of Education recognizes the LCME for the accreditation of programs of medical education leading to the MD degree in institutions that are themselves accredited by regional accrediting associations. Institutional accreditation ensures that medical education takes place in a sufficiently rich environment to foster broad academic purposes.

Accreditation by the LCME confers eligibility for participation in federal student loan programs. Most state boards of licensure require that U.S. medical schools be accredited by the LCME, as a condition for licensure of their graduates and to determine the eligibility of U.S. students to take the United States Medical Licensing Examination (USMLE). Graduates of LCME-accredited schools are eligible for residency programs accredited by the Accreditation Council for Graduate Medical Education (ACGME).

Nuclear Medicine Technology

Joint Review Committee on Education in Radiologic Technology
  Joanne S. Greathouse, Chief Executive Officer
  20 North Wacker Drive, Suite 900
  Chicago, IL 60606-2901
  (312) 704-5300
  (312) 704-5304
  http://www.jrcert.org

The Joint Review Committee on Education in Radiologic Technology (JRCERT) promotes excellence in education and enhances the quality and safety of patient care through the accreditation of radiography and radiation therapy educational programs. JRCERT is recognized by the U.S. Department of Education to accredit these programs, as well as programs in the related disciplines of magnetic resonance and medical dosimetry.

Programs accredited by the JRCERT must demonstrate that they are in compliance with the relevant JRCERT accreditation standards: Standards for an Accredited Educational Program in Radiologic Sciences (radiography and radiation therapy), Standards for an Accredited Educational Program in Magnetic Resonance, or Standards for an Accredited Educational Program in Medical Dosimetry.

Joint Review Committee on Educational Programs in Nuclear Medicine Technology
  Elaine Cuklanz, Executive Director
  716 Black Point Road
  PO Box 1149
  Polson, MT 59860-1149
  (406) 883-0003
  (406) 883-0022
  http://www.jrcnmt.org

The Joint Review Committee on Educational Programs in Nuclear Medicine Technology (JRCNMT) is the nationally recognized accrediting agency for educational programs for nuclear medicine technologists. JRCNMT was formed in 1970 by the American College of Radiologists, the American Society for Medical Technology, the American Society of Clinical Pathologists, the American Society of Radiologic Technologists, the Society of Nuclear Medicine, and the Society of Nuclear Medicine Technologists.

JRCNMT and its sponsoring organizations cooperate to establish, maintain, and promote appropriate standards of quality for postsecondary educational programs in nuclear medicine technology in order to provide skilled, professional services to patients. Educational programs that meet or exceed these minimum standard are granted accredited status.

Nuclear medicine technologists perform a number of tasks in the areas of patient care, technical skills, and administration. When caring for patients, they acquire knowledge of the patients' medical histories in order to understand and relate to their illnesses, as well as pending diagnostic procedures for therapy. They also instruct patients before and during procedures, evaluate the satisfactory preparation of patients before commencing a procedure, and recognize emergency patient conditions and initiate life-saving first aid when appropriate.

Nuclear medicine technologists apply their knowledge of radiation physics and safety regulations to limit radiation exposure, prepare and administer radiopharmaceuticals, use radiation detection devices and other kinds of laboratory equipment that measure the quantity and distribution of radionuclides deposited in the patient or in a patient specimen, perform in vivo and in vitro diagnostic procedures, use quality control techniques as part of a quality assurance program covering all procedures and products in the laboratory, and participate in research projects.

Potential students must have graduated from high school or the equivalent and have acquired postsecondary competencies in human anatomy and physiology, physics, mathematics, medical terminology, oral and written communications, chemistry, and medical ethics. The professional curriculum, usually one year in length, includes patient care, nuclear physics, instrumentation and statistics, health physics, biochemistry, immunology, radiopharmacology, administration, radiation biology, clinical nuclear medicine, radionuclide therapy, and introduction to computer applications.

Nursing

Commission on Collegiate Nursing Education
   Jennifer L. Butlin, Director
   One Dupont Circle NW, Suite 530
   Washington, DC 20036-1120
   (202) 887-6791
   (202) 887-8476
   http://www.aacn.nche.edu/accreditation

Officially recognized by the U.S. Secretary of Education as a national accreditation agency, the Commission on Collegiate Nursing Education (CCNE) is an autonomous accrediting agency contributing to the improvement of the public's health. CCNE ensures the quality and integrity of baccalaureate and graduate education programs preparing effective nurses.

CCNE serves the public interest by assessing and identifying programs that engage in effective educational practices. As a voluntary, self-regulatory process, CCNE accreditation supports and encourages continuing self-assessment by nursing education programs and the continuing growth and improvement of collegiate professional education.

Accreditation by CCNE is intended to accomplish at least four general purposes:

• To hold nursing education programs accountable to the community of interest—the nursing profession, consumers, employers, higher education, students and their families—and to one another by ensuring that these programs have mission statements, goals, and outcomes that are appropriate for programs preparing individuals to enter the field of nursing.

• To evaluate the success of a nursing education program in achieving its mission, goals, and outcomes.

• To assess the extent to which a nursing education program meets accreditation standards.

• To inform the public of the purposes and values of accreditation and to identify nursing education programs that meet accreditation standards.

National League for Nursing Accreditation Commission, Inc.
   Barbara R. Grumet, Executive Director
   61 Broadway, 33rd Floor
   New York, NY 10006
   (212) 363-5555
   (212) 812-0390
   http://www.nlnac.org

The National League for Nursing Accrediting Commission (NLNAC) is responsible for the specialized accreditation of nursing education programs through the master's level. NLNAC has authority and accountability for carrying out the standards and criteria, accreditation processes, and the affairs, management, policy making, and general administration of the Commission.

Graduation from secondary school is required for admission to all schools of nursing. The baccalaureate program combines general education, with emphasis on the humanities and on biological, natural, and social sciences, with specialized training in the theory and practice of nursing. In addition, all accredited baccalaureate programs prepare students for public health nursing.

Graduate education in nursing combines a specialized study of a clinical area, such as maternal and child nursing or psychiatric nursing, with information and prepares students for a field of employment such as administration or teaching. A baccalaureate degree with an upper-division major in nursing is a prerequisite for master's level work in nursing. In addition, there are several schools that offer a generic master's in nursing.

All states and the District of Columbia require licensure of professional nurses. To obtain a license, a nurse must have credentials from a school approved by a state board of nursing and must pass a state board examination.

National Association of Nurse Practitioners in Women's Health
   Council on Accreditation
   Susan Wysocki, President
   505 C Street, NE-
   Washington, DC 20002
   (202) 543-9693
   (202) 543-9858
   http://www.npwh.org

The mission of the National Association of Nurse Practitioners in Women's Health (NPWH), founded in 1980, is to ensure the provision of quality health care to women of all ages by nurse practitioners. NPWH defines quality health care to be inclusive of an individual's physical, emotional, and spiritual needs.

NPWH is recognized by the U.S. Department of Education as the designated organization for the accreditation of women's health nurse practitioner programs. Graduates of NPWH-accredited programs are eligible for certification through the National Certification Corporation (NCC).

Nurse Anesthesia

American Association of Nurse Anesthetists
   Council on Accreditation of Nurse Anesthesia Educational Programs
   Francis Gerbasi, Director of Accreditation and Education
   222 South Prospect Avenue, Suite 304
   Park Ridge, IL 60068-4010
   (847) 692-7050
   (847) 692-6968-
   http://www.aana.com

Founded in 1931, the American Association of Nurse Anesthetists (AANA) is the professional association representing more than 30,000 Certified Registered Nurse Anesthetists (CRNA) nationwide. The AANA promulgates education, practice standards, and guidelines; and provides consultation to both private and governmental entities regarding nurse anesthetists and their practice. Today, the CRNA credential is well recognized as an indicator of quality and competence.

The AANA developed and implemented a certification program in 1945 and instituted mandatory recertification in 1978. It established a mechanism for accreditation of nurse anesthesia educational programs in 1952, and has been recognized by the U.S. Department of Education since 1955. In 1975, the AANA was a leader among professional organizations in the United States by forming autonomous multidisciplinary councils with public representation for performing the profession's certification, accreditation, and public interest functions.

Occupational Therapy

American Occupational Therapy Association
   Accreditation Council for Occupational Therapy Education
   Sue Graves, Senior Program Administrator in Accreditation
   4720 Montgomery Lane
   PO Box 31220
   Bethesda, MD 20824-1220
   (301) 652-2682
   (301) 652-7711
   http://www.aota.org

The American Occupational Therapy Association (AOTA) is the nationally recognized professional association for occupational therapists and occupational therapy assistants. These individuals work with people experiencing health problems—including stroke, spinal cord injuries, cancer, congenital conditions, developmental problems, and mental illness—in a wide range of practice settings including hospitals, nursing facilities, home health agencies, outpatient rehabilitation clinics, psychiatric facilities, and schools. The mission of the association is to support a professional community of members and to develop and preserve the viability and relevance of the profession. The organization serves the interest of the members, represents the profession to the public, and promotes access to occupational therapy.

ACOTE is committed to the establishment, promotion, and evaluation of standards of excellence in occupational therapy education. To this end, ACOTE leads in the development of effective collaborative partnerships with the communities of interest, both internal and external to the profession of occupational therapy, which are affected by its activities. ACOTE continually evaluates its functions to serve as a model for ethical, accountable, and efficient practices, and upholds its founders' commitment to the promotion of occupational therapy as the signal discipline that studies and uses purposeful and meaningful occupation as a therapeutic measure.

Council on Occupational Education
   Gary Puckett, Executive Director/President
   41 Perimeter Center East, NE, Suite 640
   Atlanta, GA 30346
   (800) 917-2081
   (770) 396-3790
   http://www.council.org

The Council on Occupational Education (COE), a national accrediting agency, is committed to ensuring quality and integrity in career and workforce development. COE is a nonprofit voluntary membership organization serving postsecondary education and training institutions, centers, and similar entities interested in the improvement of the workforce in the United States. COE is the successor to the Commission on Occupational Education Institutions, founded in 1971 as a regional accrediting agency of the Southern Association of Colleges and Schools.

The Council offers the following services:

• Peer evaluation for institutions seeking recognition from various oversight agencies and improvement of their programs.

• Professional development for management and instructional personnel.

• Information services for workforce development providers about standards, outcomes measurement, assessment designs, institutional effectiveness, and other quality assurance–related topics through workshops, seminars, and periodic publications.

• Program quality reviews for agencies, states, and institutions, under contractual agreements.

Optometry

American Optometric Association
   Accreditation Council on Optometric Education
   Joyce Urbeck, Administrative Director
   243 North Lindbergh Boulevard
   St. Louis, MO 63141-7881
   (314) 991-4100
   (314) 991-4101
   http://www.aoanet.org

The Council on Optometric Education (ACOE), established in 1898 by the American Optometric Association, accredits professional optometric degree programs, optometric technician programs, and postgraduate optometric residency programs. As part of the process of accrediting programs in the United States and Canada, ACOE informs schools and colleges of innovations in education, advises about experimentation in education, and encourages continuous self-study.

Doctors of optometry are the primary health care professionals for the eye. Optometrists examine, diagnose, treat, and manage diseases, injuries, and disorders of the visual system, the eye, and associated structures, as well as identify related systemic conditions affecting the eye.

An optometrist has completed pre-professional undergraduate education in a college or university and four years of professional education at a college of optometry, leading to the doctor of optometry (O.D.) degree. Some optometrists complete an optional residency in a specific area of practice.

All 50 states and the District of Columbia require that graduate optometrists be state-licensed. Because some states permit only graduates of specified schools of optometry to take these examinations, prospective optometrists should choose schools approved by the particular state board of optometry where they expect to practice.

Osteopathic Medicine

American Osteopathic Association
   Commission on Osteopathic College Accreditation
   Susan Sweet, Director
   Division of College Accreditation
   142 East Ontario Street
   Chicago, IL 60611-2864
   (312) 202-8000
   (312) 202-8200
   http://do-online.osteotech.org

The American Osteopathic Association's Commission on Osteopathic College Accreditation (COCA) is recognized by the U.S. Department of Education as the only accrediting agency for predoctoral osteopathic medical education in the United States. Accreditation by COCA means a college or school of osteopathic medicine has appropriately identified its mission, secured the resources necessary to accomplish that mission, shown evidence of accomplishing its mission, and demonstrated that it can be expected to continue to accomplish its mission in the future.

Practitioners of osteopathic medicine diagnose and treat diseases of the human body, paying particular attention to impairments in the musculoskeletal system. Traditionally, osteopathic physicians have experience in general practice and other primary care areas and become active members of community health care teams. Today, however, many become specialists. Osteopathic physicians emphasize manipulative therapy techniques but also perform surgery, provide drugs, and use other accepted methods of medical care.

Admission to accredited colleges of osteopathic medicine requires at least three years' undergraduate work at an accredited postsecondary institution or a baccalaureate degree. In practice, the majority of osteopathic students have earned baccalaureates before they begin their professional training. Applicants should prepare for admission by taking courses that include English, biology, physics, and organic and inorganic chemistry; psychology is recommended. Most schools require applicants to take the Medical College Admission Test (MCAT).

The four-year professional curriculum leading to the doctorate in osteopathy includes basic science courses such as human anatomy, microbiology, physiology, biochemistry, pharmacology, embryology, and histology, in addition to initial course in osteopathic practice and theory. Students devote most of their third and fourth years to practical training in both hospitals and clinics, thereby gaining comprehensive experience.

Most graduates serve a year's internship with an intern program approved by the American Osteopathic Association. Osteopathic physicians intending to specialize spend an additional one to five years in residency training.

All states require a license to practice as an osteopathic physician. In most cases, the license is transferable among states without reexamination.

Pharmacy

Accreditation Council for Pharmacy Education
Peter H. Vlasses, Executive Director
20 North Clark Street, Suite 2500
Chicago, IL 60602-5109
(312) 664-3575
(312) 664-4652
http://www.acpe-accredit.org

The Accreditation Council for Pharmacy Education (ACPE), established in 1932, is a national accreditor of pre-service pharmacy education. In 1975, its scope of activity was broadened to include the accreditation of providers of continuing pharmacy education.

ACPE is an autonomous and independent agency whose Board of Directors is derived from the American Association of Colleges of Pharmacy (AACP), the American Pharmacists Association (APhA), the National Association of Boards of Pharmacy (NABP), and the American Council on Education (ACE).

Physical Therapy

American Physical Therapy Association
Commission on Accreditation in Physical Therapy Education
Mary Jane Harris, Director
1111 North Fairfax Street
Alexandria, VA 22314-3229
(703) 684-2782
(703) 684-7343
http://www.apta.org

The mission of the Commission on Accreditation in Physical Therapy Education (CAPTE) is to serve the public by establishing and applying standards that ensure quality and continuous improvement in the entry-level preparation of physical therapists and physical therapist assistants and that reflect the evolving nature of education, research, and practice. In achieving its mission, CAPTE has adopted the principle that accreditation is a process of quality assessment pursued by academic programs using nationally agreed-upon criteria (standards), yet measured in the context of each program's and institution's individual mission.

Physical therapists plan and implement treatment programs for the care of patients disabled by illness, accident, or congenital defects, and administer tests and make evaluations that provide information about joint motion, muscle strength, and general functional ability necessary for performance of activities required for daily living. Physical therapists treat patients directly or supervise personnel in carrying out selected procedures. Therapy may include exercise, application of heat and electricity to relieve pain and stimulate motor activity, instruction in everyday actions, and use of assistive devices. Physical therapists work in hospitals, nursing homes, schools, and private offices, as well as in other settings such as universities, research centers, and industry.

Professional programs in physical therapy accredited by CAPTE are offered mostly in colleges or universities. The typical therapy program requires general education courses and professionally focused work in basic sciences, clinical medicine, physical therapy theory and techniques, and supervised clinical practice. At the professional level, students may elect to study a program culminating in a baccalaureate degree, a postbaccalaureate certificate, or a master's degree. All states require licensure of practicing physical therapists.

Physician's Assistant

Accreditation Review Commission on Education for the Physician Assistant, Inc.
John E. McCarty, Executive Director
12000 Findley Road, Suite 240
Duluth, GA 30097
(770) 476-1224
(770) 476-1738
http://www.arc-pa.org

The Accreditation Review Commission on Education for the Physician Assistant (ARC-PA) protects the interests of the public and the physician assistant profession by defining the standards for education and evaluating educational programs within the territorial United States to ensure their compliance with those standards.

The physician's assistant is academically and clinically prepared to provide health care services with the direction and responsible supervision of a doctor of medicine or osteopathy. Physician assistants make clinical decisions and provide a broad range of diagnostic, therapeutic, preventive, and health maintenance services. The clinical role of physician assistants includes primary and specialty care in medical and surgical practice settings. Physician assistant practice is centered on patient care and may include educational, research, and administrative activities. It is also characterized by clinical knowledge and skills in areas traditionally defined by family medicine, internal medicine, pediatrics, obstetrics, gynecology, surgery, and psychiatry/behavioral medicine. Physician assistants practice in ambulatory, emergency, inpatient, and long-term care settings and deliver health care services to diverse patient populations of all ages with a range of acute and chronic medical and surgical conditions.

Podiatry

American Podiatric Medical Association
    Council on Podiatric Medical Education
    Alan R. Tinkleman, Director
    9312 Old Georgetown Road
    Bethesda, MD 20814-1612
    (301) 581-9290
    (301) 571-4903
    http://www.apma.org/cpme

The accreditation authority of the Council on Podiatric Medical Education (CPME) extends to first-professional degree programs offered at independent colleges as well as to component schools within academic health centers or universities. When independent or free-standing colleges are reviewed, CPME functions as both a professional and institutional accrediting agency. In the case of free-standing professional schools, accreditation attests not only to the quality of the program and its relevance to professional practice but also to the quality of the institution in which the program is conducted.

The colleges of podiatric medicine accredited by CPME are classified as postsecondary nonprofit institutions offering educational programs leading to the first-professional degree. At present, seven colleges of podiatric medicine are accredited by CPME— five colleges are independent free-standing institutions, one is based within an academic health center, and one is based in a university. Six of the seven institutions are regionally accredited and the seventh is recognized by the State Education Department of the University of the State of New York.

Each of the accredited colleges offers the degree of Doctor of Podiatric Medicine (DPM). All accredited colleges of podiatric medicine are properly chartered and licensed to operate within the jurisdiction in which they are located, and all have appropriate authorization from state agencies to offer the degrees conferred. The degrees granted by accredited colleges of podiatric medicine are accepted by state licensing authorities in all 50 states, the District of Columbia, and Puerto Rico.

Public Health

Council on Education for Public Health
    Laura Rasar King, Executive Director
    800 Eye Street, NW, Suite 202
    Washington, DC 20001-3710
    (202) 789-1050
    (202) 789-1895
    http://www.ceph.org

The Council on Education for Public Health (CEPH) is an independent agency recognized by the U.S. Department of Education to accredit schools of public health as well as certain public health programs offered in settings other than schools of public health. These schools and programs prepare students for entry into careers in public health. The primary professional degree is the Master of Public Health (MPH), but other master's and doctoral degrees are offered as well.

The field of public health employs a variety of professionals who work to conserve both human and financial resources by attacking the causes and spread of disease by educating citizens about health hazards and healthful living and by attempting to ensure the adequacy and accessibility of health and medical care services for all persons.

Specialties basic to public health practice include epidemiology, biostatistics, environmental and occupational health sciences, community health education, and public health and health service administration. Other specialists work in areas such as maternal and child health, public health nursing, public health dentistry, and international health. Public health professionals work in both public and private settings: for example, they are employed by state and local health departments, federal health agencies, voluntary health agencies, research laboratories, educational institutions, and various service-delivery organizations.

Admissions requirements for graduate public health schools and programs usually include completion of a baccalaureate degree and, often, some work experience. Graduate study for the MPH, or its subspecialties, generally covers 18 months to two years, but students who hold prior professional degrees, such as those in dentistry, medicine, or veterinary medicine, may often complete the sequence in less time.

The MPH is usually the entry-level professional degree. Concentrations are often possible in one of several specialties. Academic degree programs with strong research focus often are offered in areas such as biostatistics, nutrition, or environmental health science. Admission to doctoral programs usually requires a first-professional degree in public health, dentistry, medicine, or veterinary medicine, or another relevant master's degree.

Rehabilitation Counseling

Council on Rehabilitation Education
    Commission on Standards and Accreditation
    Marv Kuehn, Executive Director
    1835 Rohlwing Road, Suite E
    Rolling Meadows, IL 60008
    (847) 394-1785
    (847) 394-2108
    http://www.core-rehab.org

The Council of Rehabilitation Education (CORE) has been the accrediting body for master's degree programs in rehabilitation counselor education since 1972. An independent organization, CORE promotes the effective delivery of rehabilitation services to individuals with disabilities. Graduates of programs accredited by CORE provide both public and private rehabilitation agencies with expert staff.

CORE's Commission on Standards and Accreditation evaluates rehabilitation counselor education programs through an institution's self-study document, outcome data, and a site visit, and makes recommendations to CORE. The outcome data result from the evaluation of the employers of graduates, graduates, and current students. To be eligible for evaluation by CORE, rehabilitation programs must be part of a regionally accredited postsecondary institution and have a coordinator who is a Certified Rehabilitation Counselor.

Speech-Language Pathology and Audiology

American Speech-Language-Hearing Association
    Council on Academic Accreditation in Audiology and Speech-Language Pathology
    Patrima L. Tice, Director of Credentialing
    10801 Rockville Pike
    Rockville, MD 20852
    (301) 897-5700
    (301) 571-0457
    http://www.asha.org

The American Speech-Language-Hearing Association (ASHA) is the professional, scientific, and credentialing association for more than 118,000 members and affiliates who are speech-language pathologists, audiologists, and speech, language, and hearing scientists in the United States and around the world. ASHA accredits graduate programs that provide entry-level professional preparation, offering prospective graduate students the assurance that the academic and clinical experiences offered by these programs meet ASHA's standards. The Council on Academic Accreditation in Audiology and Speech-Language Pathology (CAA) is recognized by the U.S. Department of Education and the Council for Higher Education Accreditation (CHEA) as the only accrediting body for graduate programs in speech-language pathology and/or audiology.

Speech-language pathologists and audiologists provide clinical services to children and adults who have communication problems. They work in a variety of settings, including schools, hospitals, community clinics, rehabilitation centers, and private practices. Graduate study in speech-language pathology and audiology is a prerequisite for the Certificates of Clinical Competence (CCC) awarded by ASHA, as well as licensure in most states. The requirements for the CCC include earning a graduate degree, completing a nine-month clinical fellowship, and passing a national examination. All graduate-level coursework and graduate clinical practicum required must have been initiated and completed in a CAA-accredited program.

Undergraduate/preprofessional training in speech-language pathology and audiology generally include studies in the liberal arts, physiology, physics, phonetics, and normal language development, as well as introductory courses in speech-language pathology and audiology. Elective courses in early childhood development and child psychology are helpful. The graduate curriculum includes courses in the nature, prevention, evaluation, and treatment of speech, language, and hearing disorders.

Interior Design

Foundation for Interior Design Education Research
   Kayem Dunn, Executive Director
   146 Monroe Center, NW, Suite 1318
   Grand Rapids, MI 49503-2822
   (616) 458-0400
   (616) 458-0460
   http://www.fider.org

The Foundation for Interior Design Education Research (FIDER) establishes and administers a voluntary plan for accreditation of interior design programs offered at institutions of higher education in the United States, its possessions, and Canada. FIDER was established in 1970 by the Interior Design Educators Council (IDEC), the American Institute of Interior Designers (AID), and the National Society of Interior Designers (NSID). AID and NSID merged in 1975 to form the American Society of Interior Designers (ASID).

By defining and maintaining standards for accreditation of postsecondary interior design programs, FIDER aims to foster professional excellence in the training of interior design students that will protect the public from incompetence in the field. FIDER accredits interior design programs for either three- or six-year periods in private and public associate-level colleges, in trade and technical schools, and in baccalaureate, professional, and graduate institutions. FIDER's specialized accreditation is the only one recognized by the profession through its principal design organization.

To be considered for FIDER accreditation, a postsecondary institution must be: institutionally accredited and require that its entering students have completed secondary schools or have the equivalent qualifications; be chartered and licensed to offer education leading to recognized degrees, diplomas, or certificates; and have graduated at least two classes prior to accreditation.

Journalism and Mass Communications

Accrediting Council on Education in Journalism and Mass Communication
   Susanne Shaw, Executive Director
   Stauffer-Flint Hall
   1435 Jayhawk Boulevard
   University of Kansas
   Lawrence, KS 66045-7575
   (785) 864-3973
   (785) 864-5225
   http://www.ku.edu/~acejmc

The Accrediting Council on Education in Journalism and Mass Communications (ACEJMC) represents educational and professional organizations in the field of journalism and mass communications and accredits baccalaureate and master's programs in these disciplines.

Graduate and undergraduate journalism programs in college and universities blend liberal arts and professional courses to meet the needs of the mass media. At accredited institutions, about 24 percent of the student's four-year program consists of journalism and communications courses. Other academic work is taken in liberal arts, including such fields as English, economics, history, political science, languages, literature, philosophy, psychology, sociology, and the natural sciences.

ACEJMC accredits programs in advertising, news-editorial, broadcast news, radio-TV-film, magazine, public relations, photojournalism, technical journalism, agricultural journalism, and home economics journalism. ACEJMC does not accredit programs leading to the Ph.D., which is considered a research, and not a professional, degree.

Landscape Architecture

American Society of Landscape Architects
   Landscape Architectural Accreditation Board
   Ronald C. Leighton, Director, Education and Academic Affairs
   636 I Street, NW
   Washington, DC 20001-3736
   (202) 898-2444
   (202) 898-1185
   http://www.asla.org

The Landscape Architecture Accreditation Board (LAAB) is the body within the American Society of Landscape Architects (ASLA) responsible for accrediting landscape architecture first-professional degree programs at the bachelor's or master's level. These programs adhere to a basic core of professional courses designated by the ASLA Council on Education Standards, although curricula may reflect specific varying geographical phenomena, faculty specialties, and institutional missions. The foundation courses include landscape design and construction and professional practice; basic engineering and surveying; agronomy, botany, horticulture, plants, and planting design; geology and hydrology; urban and regional planning; political and behavioral sciences; and graphic and verbal expression.

Landscape architects use their cultural and scientific knowledge and their concern for natural conservation and stewardship to design, plan, and manage land resources as well as to effectively arrange the natural and artificial elements that make up a landscape. Among other things, landscape architects design parks and gardens, and plan parkways, shopping areas, and recreational facilities. Landscape architecture is a broad field, overlapping the concerns of architecture, art, engineering, horticulture, planning, environmental psychology, and other fields.

Because landscape architecture affects public health, safety, and welfare, many states require the licensing or registration of landscape architects. Although requirements vary among states, candidates for landscape architecture licensing examinations usually must be graduates of accredited programs, as well as have two or more years of experience in the field.

Law

American Bar Association
   Office of the Consultant on Legal Education/Section of Legal
   Education and Admissions to the Bar
   John A. Sebert, Consultant on Legal Education, ABA
   321 North Clark Street, 21st Floor
   Chicago, IL 60610
   (312) 988-6738
   (312) 988-5681
   http://www.abanet.org/legaled/approvedlawschools/
   approved.html

When the American Bar Association (ABA) was organized in 1878, one of the first standing committees it named was the Committee on Legal Education and Admissions to the Bar. About the time of the ABA's founding, written bar examinations were just coming into use—though required by most states, the bar examination previously had been largely oral and informal. Thus, the two subjects of legal education and admissions to the bar were coupled from the ABA's founding and remain so today. It was at its 1893 Annual Meeting that the ABA created its first section, the Section of Legal Education and Admissions to the Bar.

Most students prepare for their law career with seven years' study—four at the undergraduate level and three in law school. Most law schools require a baccalaureate degree of their candidates, but some admit applicants with three years' postsecondary work. Although few law programs specify particular prelegal curricula, most require the Law School Admission Test (LSAT), and many ask that application be made through the Law School Data Assembly Service (LSDAS).

For many years, almost all law schools awarded the baccalaureate of laws as their first-professional degree, reserving the juris doctor (J.D.) for distinguished students. Although the preparation has not changed substantially, all schools now grant the J.D. instead of the bachelor of laws as the first-professional degree.

Librarianship

American Library Association
   Committee on Accreditation
   Karen O'Brien, Director
   50 East Huron Street
   Office for Accreditation
   Chicago, IL 60611-2795
   (312) 545-2432
   (312) 280-2433
   http://www.ala.org/accreditation.html

The American Library Association Committee on Accreditation (COA) is a standing committee responsible for the implementation of the accreditation of library and information studies programs. COA develops and formulates standards of education for library and information studies and policies and procedures for accreditation at the master's level.

Music

National Association of Schools of Music
   Samuel Hope, Executive Director
   11250 Roger Bacon Drive, Suite 21
   Reston, VA 20190
   (703) 437-0700
   (703) 437-6312
   http://www.arts-accredit.org

The National Association of Schools of Music (NASM), founded in 1924, is an organization of schools, conservatories, and colleges and universities with approximately 610 accredited institutional members. It establishes national standards for undergraduate and graduate degrees and other credentials.

NASM's major responsibilities are to set curricular standards and guidelines, to develop the profession's overall code of ethics, and to accredit educational programs in music. NASM also provides a forum for the discussion of issues related to music education by publishing books and reports for members and by convening an annual meeting.

Institutions wishing to be evaluated for NASM membership must submit institutional self-studies and undergo peer evaluation, which is accomplished through onsite visits followed by formal reports and review by NASM commissions.

Planning

American Institute of Certified Planners/Association of Collegiate
Schools of Planning
   Planning Accreditation Board
   Shonagh Merits, Executive Director
   122 South Michigan Avenue, Suite 1600
   Chicago, IL 60603
   (312) 334-1271
   (312) 334-1273
   http://www.netins.net/showcase/pab_fi66

The mission of the Planning Accreditation Board (PAB) is to evaluate and reach decisions regarding applications for academic accreditation and to discuss and propose appropriate policy changes to enhance the role of accreditation in furthering academic excellence. The PAB conducts the planning accreditation program for all planning programs in North America.

The planning accreditation program is a cooperative undertaking sponsored jointly by three organizations: the American Institute of Certified Planners (AICP), the Association of Collegiate Schools of Planning (ACSP), and the American Planning Association (APA). The planning accreditation program reflects an assumption that all parties to the planning enterprise practitioners, educators, students, elected officials, and citizens have a committed interest in achieving the highest standards in quality education.

Psychology

American Psychological Association
   Committee on Accreditation
   Susan F. Zlotlow, Director, Office of Program Consultation and
   Accreditation
   750 First Street, NE
   Washington, DC 20002-4242
   (202) 336-5979
   (202) 336-5978
   http://www.apa.org/ed/accred.html

The American Psychological Association (APA) is the largest scientific and professional organization representing psychology in the United States. With more than 159,000 members, APA is also the largest association of psychologists worldwide.

To be eligible for APA accreditation, doctoral programs in psychology must be part of regionally accredited institutions and must apply for accreditation. The Committee on Accreditation (COA) approves doctoral programs only in clinical, counseling, school, and combined professional and scientific psychology. It also accredits the one-year predoctoral internship programs offered in hospitals, clinics, and other facilities. (However, APA does not evaluate or accredit either undergraduate psychology programs or graduate programs in other fields of psychology.)

Although APA does not accredit programs at the undergraduate level, almost every postsecondary institution in the United States offers instruction in psychology. Some institutions make an undergraduate major in psychology a prerequisite for their graduate programs. All undergraduate preparation should include not only introductory work in psychology but also courses in the biological, physical, and social sciences; mathematics; and statistics. Doctoral programs require four to five years' additional work and usually include one year of internship or supervised work experience.

Clinical psychologists generally work in hospitals or other medical settings and are especially trained to investigate, evaluate, and treat people with behavioral disorders. Counseling psychologists, who often work in schools, hospitals, and other related health care settings, work with individuals to help foster personal development and avoid behavioral disorders. Often, through a focus on appropriate vocational choice, they work to increase social and personal effectiveness. School psychologists try to assist educational institutions in helping children grow emotionally, intellectually, and socially. School psychologists function as specialists in research and evaluation, as consultants offering in-service training to faculty, and as clinicians who treat children with educational or psychological difficulties. Psychologists with combined professional and scientific training are able to function in two or more areas.

Public Affairs and Administration

National Association of Schools of Public Affairs and Administration
Commission on Peer Review and Accreditation
Laurel L. McFarland, Managing Director
1120 G Street, NW, Suite 730
Washington, DC 20005
(202) 628-8965
(202) 626-4978
http://www.naspaa.org

The National Association of Schools of Public Affairs and Administration (NASPAA), founded in 1970, serves as a national and international resource for the promotion of excellence in education and training for public service. Its institutional membership includes U.S. university programs in public affairs, public policy, public administration, and public management.

NASPAA accreditation recognizes that a master's program in public affairs has gone through a rigorous process of voluntary peer review conducted by the Commission on Peer Review and Accreditation (COPRA), and has met NASPAA's Standards for Professional Master's Degree Programs in Public Affairs, Policy and Administration.

Recreation and Park Planning

National Recreation and Park Association/American Association for Leisure and Recreation
Council on Accreditation
Danielle Timmerman, Academic Affairs Program Manager
22377 Belmont Ridge Road
Ashburn, VA 20148-4501
(703) 858-0784
(703) 858-0794
http://www.nrpa.org

The Council on Accreditation (COA), formally established in 1974 and jointly sponsored by the National Recreation and Park Association and the American Association for Leisure and Recreation, conducts the process of accreditation for park, recreation, and leisure services curricula. COA meets twice annually to review accredited programs, revise and update the standards for accreditation and procedures for program review, and conduct business. The ten members are appointed by the two sponsoring organizations and include educators, practitioners, and a public representative.

COA accredits institutions offering a four-year curriculum in parks, recreation, and leisure services education. Programs range in size from very small—with a strong focus in general professional preparation—to large state institutions.

Social Work

Council on Social Work Education
Office of Social Work Accreditation and Educational Excellence
Dean Pierce, Director
1725 Duke Street, Suite 500
Alexandria, VA 22314-3457
(703) 683-8080
(703) 739-9048
http://www.cswe.org

The Council on Social Work Education (CSWE) accredits programs in social work in the United States. Graduation from an accredited program is a requirement for licensing or certification by many state licensing boards, for membership in the National Association of Social Workers, and for employment in many civil service and merit systems as well as in private social agencies. Many federal, state, and local agencies require that their social work personnel be graduates of CSWE-accredited institutions.

Social work education takes place in four-year undergraduate and two-year graduate programs in regionally accredited institutions, leading to degrees at the baccalaureate and master's levels. Undergraduate and graduate programs have different educational goals and produce different levels of knowledge and skills in professional practice.

The undergraduate program, built on and integrated with a liberal arts base, prepares students for entry into professional social work practice at a beginning level. The curriculum includes work in the humanities, social, behavioral, and biological sciences, as well as providing context in the areas of social work practice, social welfare policy and services, human behavior and social environment, and social research. Undergraduate programs also require educationally directed field experience to engage students in service activities that provide varied learning opportunities. Emphasizing a broad approach, baccalaureate programs aim to prepare students for general social work practice—under supervision—with individuals, groups, and communities.

Social work education at the master's level also is based upon a liberal arts perspective in combination with the required professional foundation. In addition, one or more concentrations provide graduates with advanced analytic and practice skills to enable them to function as responsible professional social workers; able to practice self-critically, accountably, and ultimately, autonomously. Schools of social work offer varied concentrations of specialized knowledge and practice skills that may include fields of service, work with particular population groups, or study of specific issues in major social problem areas. Concentrations also include practice roles and interventive modes such as direct practice, consultation, training, community organization, social planning, program planning and development, administration, policy analysis, and research.

Formal admission to undergraduate programs in social work occurs at the third year of study after completion of all foundation course requirements with a satisfactory GPA and evidence of capacity for meaningful involvement in service to others. Prospective master's students must have a baccalaureate degree in social work or in another field with a liberal arts perspective. Some graduate programs waive foundation course content or substitute advanced courses for students holding undergraduate degrees from accredited social work programs.

Teacher and School Service Personnel Education

National Council for Accreditation of Teacher Education
    Arthur E. Wise, President
    2010 Massachusetts Ave, NW, Suite 500
    Washington, DC 20036-1023
    (202) 466-7496
    (202) 296-6620
    http://www.ncate.org

The National Council for Accreditation of Teacher Education (NCATE), organized in 1954 by associations representing state departments and local boards of education and institutions of teacher education within the profession, has become one of the largest specialized accrediting agencies in the United States, accrediting professional education units at colleges and universities. The professional education unit is the school, college, or department within the institution that is primarily responsible for the preparation of teachers and other professional school personnel. All programs for the preparation of personnel who work in school settings from birth to grade 12 are included in the accreditation review.

NCATE is the teaching profession's mechanism to help establish high-quality teacher, specialist, and administrator preparation. Through the process of accreditation of schools, colleges and departments of education, NCATE works to make a difference in the quality of teaching, teachers, school specialists and administrators. NCATE accreditation certifies that an institution's education program meets national standards.

Any regionally accredited, degree-granting institution offering the baccalaureate or above, is eligible for accreditation by NCATE, provided that preconditions are met, which include being an equal opportunity employer and offering—in states with program approval processes—only state-approved programs.

Theater

National Association of Schools of Theatre
    Samuel Hope, Executive Director
    11250 Roger Bacon Drive, Suite 21
    Reston, VA 20190
    (703) 437-0700
    (703) 437-6312
    http://www.arts-accredit.org

The National Association of Schools of Theatre (NAST) was established in 1969 to improve educational practices and maintain high professional standards in theatre education. NAST accredits institutional programs at schools, conservatories, and colleges and universities.

Theatre is a profession requiring talent, knowledge, skill, and dedication. Employment depends almost entirely on demonstrated competence. Success is based primarily on work rather than on credentials. The primary purpose of schools of theatre is to help individual students turn talent, inspiration, creativity, and dedication into significant potential for service to the development of theatre culture in its multiple dimensions. Therefore, the focus of NAST's work is on issues of theatre content and educational substance as applied to the preparation of theatre professionals.

Rabbinical and Talmudic Education (National)

Theology

Association for Biblical Higher Education (National)
    Commission on Accreditation
    Larry McKinney, Executive Director
    5575 South Semoran Boulevard, Suite 26
    Orlando, FL 32822-1781
    (407) 207-0808
    (407) 207-0840
    http://abhe.gospelcom.net

The mission of the Association for Biblical Higher Education (ABHE) is to provide accreditation and services for institutions and programs of biblical higher education within Canada, the United States, and related territories.

The Association seeks to fulfill its mission by:

• Promoting excellence among institutions and programs of biblical higher education through the process of accreditation.

• Promoting cooperation among member and affiliate institutions and the larger higher education community.

• Promoting the distinctives of biblical higher education to the higher education community, the church, and society.

• Providing services that will stimulate excellence among administrators, board members, faculty, and students at member and affiliate institutions.

From the humble beginnings of the Missionary Training Institute (Nyack College) in New York City in 1882 to the launching of such schools as Moody Bible Institute in 1886 and Toronto Bible School (Master's University College & Seminary) in 1894, the Bible college movement has proliferated throughout North America.

More than 120 years after the first Bible school was started, there are more than 1,200 Bible schools and colleges in the United States and Canada. Many of these institutions have a relationship with ABHE, either through accreditation or affiliation. Most institutions of biblical higher education offer programs in biblical studies, pastoral ministry, Christian education, cross-cultural missions, and music. Many also provide programs in elementary and perhaps secondary education, youth ministries, urban ministries, and business administration. A few even offer specialized programs in such areas as deaf ministries, social work, aviation, and technology-oriented fields.

Association of Theological Schools in the United States and Canada
    Commission on Accrediting
    Daniel O. Aleshire, Executive Director
    10 Summit Park Drive
    Pittsburgh, PA 15275-1103
    (412) 788-6505
    (412) 788-6510
    http://www.ats.edu

The Association of Theological Schools in the United States and Canada (ATS) is a membership organization of more than 250 graduate schools that conduct post-baccalaureate professional and academic degree programs to educate persons for the practice of ministry and for teaching and research in the theological disciplines. Its mission is to promote the improvement and enhancement of theological schools to the benefit of communities of faith and the broader public.

Accreditation is conducted by the Board of Commissioners on behalf of the Commission on Accrediting. The Commission accredits institutions and approves degree programs offered by accredited schools. The Commission is recognized by the U.S. Department of Education and by the Council for Higher Education Accreditation (CHEA) for the accreditation of graduate, professional theological schools in the United States. The Commission, through its Board, works cooperatively with regional accrediting associations in the United States, other professional associations, state departments of education, and other allied organizations in Canada and the United States.

Transnational Association of Christian Colleges and Schools (National)
    Accreditation Commission
    Russell G. Fitzgerald, Executive Director
    PO Box 328
    Forest, VA 24551
    (434) 525-9539
    (434) 525-9538
    http://www.tracs.org

The Transnational Association of Christian Colleges and Schools (TRACS) is recognized as a national accrediting body for Christian institutions, colleges, universities, and seminaries in the United States and its territories. TRACS was established in 1979 to promote the welfare, interests, and development of postsecondary institutions, whose mission is characterized by a distinctly Christian purpose, as defined in our Foundational Standards.

TRACS encourages each affiliated institution to develop its own distinctives, while providing quality postsecondary education within the context of spiritual development. TRACS institutions place an emphasis on high academic standards as well as Christian values.

Rabbinical & Talmudic Education (National)

Association of Advanced Rabbinical and Talmudic Schools (National)
Bernard Fryshman, Executive Vice President
11 Broadway, Suite 405
New York, NY 10004-1392
(212) 363-1991
(212) 533-5335

The history of the association properly begins in 1944 when the heads of several world-renowned Eastern European centers of scholarship that had been destroyed in World War II escaped to the United Sates and met in New York City to establish a Council of Roshei Yeshivos, whose primary purpose was to enable the growth of Talmudic scholarship in the United States. In the years between 1944 and 1971, a number of new institutions were founded, and the first graduates of these schools began to take positions of leadership in the community.

In the summer of 1971, the Association of Advanced Rabbinical and Talmudic Schools (AARTS) entered the scene as the successor to the Council of Roshei Yeshivos. By 1973, an Accreditation Commission had been created, with the goal of improving the quality of the education offered by these schools, enabling advanced rabbinical and Talmudic education to take its place as part of the total spectrum of American higher education. AARTS began to accredit institutions of the summer of 1996.

An institution seeking accreditation status with AARTS must first submit an extensive self-study. The school is then visited by a team consisting of one Rosh Yeshiva (senior faculty member of an accredited institution) and two senior faculty members from conventional colleges and universities. The institution is evaluated as a whole, and the visiting team report is submitted to the Accreditation Commission, which then determines whether to grant preaccreditation or accreditation status to successful applicants. Preaccreditation status (correspondent or candidate) is for a limited time only.

Veterinary Medicine

American Veterinary Medical Association
Council on Education
Donald G. Simmons, Director of Education and Research
1931 North Meacham Road, Suite 100
Schaumburg, IL 60173-4360
(847) 925-8070
(847) 925-9329
http://www.avma.org

Accreditation by the AVMA Council on Education (COE) represents the highest standard of achievement for veterinary medical education in the United States. Institutions that earn accreditation confirm their commitment to quality and continuous improvement through a rigorous and comprehensive peer review. COE—composed of veterinarians elected by members of AVMA and appointed public members—accredits colleges of veterinary medicine whose programs meet its standards for finance, physical facilities, libraries, admissions, enrollments, curricula, clinical and learning resources, research, and continuing and postgraduate education. Accredited schools admit students to their four-year curricula for the doctor of veterinary medicine after two or more years of postsecondary education. Approved programs are taught in regionally accredited universities with hospitals available for the treatment of domestic animals.

Communications, chemistry, and humanities are generally prerequisites for admission to veterinary colleges, although requirements vary. Professional instruction, much of which occurs in laboratory and clinical settings, includes courses in anatomy, physiology, pharmacology, microbiology, parasitology, pathology, medicine preventive medicines, theriogenology, surgery, radiology, and other clinical specialties.

Veterinarians in private practice must pass state board examinations to obtain licenses. Graduates from accredited colleges of veterinary medicine are eligible to sit for state licensing examinations or to occupy most government, industrial, and academic veterinary positions. Graduates of nonaccredited overseas colleges may qualify to take these licensing examinations by earning the Educational Commission for Foreign Veterinary Graduates (ECVFG) competency equivalency certificate.

Vocational and Technical

Accrediting Council for Independent Colleges and Schools
Steven A. Eggland, Executive Director
750 First Street, NE, Suite 980
Washington, DC 20002-4241
(202) 336-6780
(202) 842-2593
http://www.acics.org

The Accrediting Council for Independent Colleges and Schools (ACICS) is a nongovernmental organization incorporated in the Commonwealth of Virginia, with offices maintained in the District of Columbia. It is an independent, national, institutional accrediting agency recognized by the U.S. Department of Education and the Council for Higher Education Accreditation (CHEA).

The scope of ACICS accreditation is directed at private, postsecondary institutions offering programs through the master's level that are designed to train and educate persons for careers or professions in which business applications, business concepts, supervisory or management techniques, or professional or business-related applications or disciplines support or constitute the career or professional activity.

ACICS accredits more than 600 institutions in the United States and abroad. More than 60 percent of these institutions are degree-granting colleges.

Council on Aviation Accreditation
Gary W. Kiteley, Executive Director
3410 Skyway Drive
Auburn, AL 36830
(334) 844-2431
(334) 844-2432
http://www.caaaccreditation.org

The Council on Aviation Accreditation (CAA) advances quality aviation education worldwide through accreditation and leadership. CAA is committed to its role as the world's leader in the advancement of aviation accreditation. This global commitment is integral to all organizational activities.

Established in 1988 at the Annual Meeting of the University Aviation Association (UAA) in Dallas, CAA initially functioned as a subsidiary of the UAA. However, operationally, CAA was an autonomous, legally chartered entity with directors and officers elected from within the organization, with formulated and published bylaws by which the organization is governed.

CAA accredits aviation programs at the associate and baccalaureate levels within institutions that are also accredited by a recognized, regional accreditor.

The stated goals of collegiate aviation accreditation are to:

• Stimulate collegiate aviation program excellence and self-improvement.

• Establish uniform minimum educational quality standards.

• Increase the credibility, integrity, and acceptance of collegiate aviation programs within institutions of higher education and all aspects of the aviation community, to include industry, government, and the public at large.

Distance Education and Training Council
Accrediting Commission
Michael P. Lambert, Executive Director
1601 Eighteenth Street, NW
Washington, DC 20009-2529
(202) 234-5100
(202) 332-1386
http://www.detc.org

The Distance Education and Training Council (formerly the National Home Study Council) has been the standard-setting agency for correspondence study and distance education institutions since it was established in 1926. Its purpose was, and still is today, "to foster and preserve high-quality, educationally sound, and widely accepted distance education and independent learning institutions."

The DETC Accrediting Commission (DETC-AC) was established in 1955 with the mission to promote, by means of standard-setting, evaluation, and consultation processes, the development and maintenance of high educational and ethical standards in education and training programs delivered through distance learning. The DETC-AC identifies and accredits distance education and training institutions that have attained and maintained the standards deemed necessary to operate at a high level of quality.

Recently, DETC has emerged as a leader in global distance learning with accredited members in Canada, Ireland, Japan, South Africa, the United Kingdom, and the United States. With its 75-plus years of history and its highly refined and federally recognized accreditation program, DETC offers distance learning institutions the most current, relevant, and practical services for the 21st century.

III

Universities and Colleges:
Institutional Exhibits

Alabama

Alabama Agricultural and Mechanical University

4107 Meridian Street
P.O. Box 1357
Normal, Alabama 35762
Tel: (256) 851-5000   **E-mail:** admissions@aamu.edu
Fax: (256) 851-5244   **Internet:** www.aamu.edu

Institution Description: Alabama Agricultural and Mechanical University is a state institution and land-grant college. *Enrollment:* 6,588. *Degrees awarded:* Baccalaureate, master's, doctorate.

Accreditation: *Regional:* SACS-Comm. on Coll. *Professional:* business, dietetics, engineering technology, family and consumer science, forestry, planning, rehabilitation counseling, social work, speech-language pathology, teacher education

History: Established as Huntsville Normal School and offered first instruction at postsecondary level 1875; changed name to State Normal and Industrial School at Huntsville 1878; changed name to The State Agricultural and Mechanical Institute for Negroes 1919; offered first instruction as 4-year college 1939; awarded first baccalaureate 1941; changed name to Alabama Agricultural and Mechanical College 1948; adopted present name 1969.

Institutional Structure: *Composition of institution:* 11 administrators. Academic affairs headed by Provost/Vice President for Academic Affairs. Management, business, and finances directed by vice president for business and finance. Full-time instructional faculty: 300.

Calendar: Semesters. Academic year Aug. to May. Formal commencements May, July.

Characteristics of Freshmen: 94% (1,167 students) submitted ACT scores. *25th percentile:* ACT Composite 16, ACT English 14, ACT Math 15. *75th percentile:* ACT Composite 19; ACT English 20; ACT Math 18.

46.7% of applicants admitted. 42.8% of accepted applicants enrolled. 32.6% of entering freshmen expected to graduate within 5 years. 62% of freshmen from Alabama. Freshmen from 27 states.

Admission: For fall acceptance, recommend application during first semester of senior year at secondary school. *Requirements:* Secondary school courses in English, history, and political science, mathematics, science (including biology). GED accepted. Minimum GPA 2.0. *Entrance tests:* College Board SAT or ACT Composite. *For transfer students:* 2.0 minimum GPA.

Degree Requirements: 2.0 GPA; final 2 semesters in residence.

Fulfillment of some degree requirements and exemption from some beginning courses possible by passing College Board CLEP Subject Examinations. *Grading system:* A–F; withdraw (carries time limit).

Distinctive Educational Programs: Cooperative education. Flexible meeting places and schedules, including off-campus centers and evening classes. Dual-degree programs in engineering with Tuskegee Institute, in various fields with Georgia Institute of Technology. Cooperative program with University of Tennessee Space Institute. Special facilities for using telecommunications in the classroom. Cross-registration with Athens State University, John C. Calhoun State Community College; Oakwood College, University of Alabama. *Other distinctive programs:* Continuing education.

ROTC: Army.

Degrees Conferred: 589 *baccalaureate.* Degrees awarded in top five disciplines: business, management, marketing, and related support 123; education 110; computer and information sciences support services 44; biological and biomedical sciences 40; social sciences 34. 262 *master's*; 5 *doctorate*; 8 *post-master's certificates* .

Fees and Other Expenses: *Full-time tuition per academic year 2004–05:* undergraduate in-state resident $4,420; out-of-state $8,320. *Room and board per academic year:* $4.770. *Books and supplies:* $1,800. *Other expenses:* $2,600.

Financial Aid: Institution has a Program Participation Agreement with the U.S. Department of Education for eligible students to receive Pell Grants and other federal aid.

Financial aid to full-time, first-time undergraduate students: 57% received federal grants averaging $1,597; 28% institutional grants averaging $2,778; 56% loans averaging $2,714.

Departments and Teaching Staff: Agribusiness *professors* 1, *associate professors* 4, *assistant professors* 5, *instructors* 0; life sciences 11, 14, 13, 4; community planning 1, 3, 3, 0; natural and physical sciences 15, 9, 8, 2; mathematics and computer sciences 2, 8, 11, 3; English and foreign languages 2, 3, 18, 8; behavioral science 4, 8, 14, 0; accounting 0, 3, 6, 0; management and marketing 3, 2, 6, 5; economics 4, 0, 4, 2; office system management 1, 2, 2, 0; curriculum and instruction 6, 15, 19, 2; counseling and special education 6, 8, 5, 0; engineering 1, 5, 3, 1; technology 2, 0, 10, 3. *Total instructional faculty:* 300.

Enrollment: Total enrollment 6,588. Undergraduate 5,326.

Characteristics of Student Body: *Ethnic/racial makeup:* Black non-Hispanic: 92.6%; American Indian or Alaska Native: 2%; Asian or Pacific Islander: .2%; White non-Hispanic: 3.3%.

International Students: Programs available to aid students whose native language is not English: social, cultural. Financial aid specifically designated for international students: scholarships and loans available.

Student Life: On-campus residence halls. *Special regulations:* Cars permitted; parking fee charged. *Special services:* Learning Resources Center. *Surrounding community:* Normal (population 1,500) is located 4 miles north of Huntsville (population 145,000).

Library Collections: 253,600 volumes. 160,000 government documents; 48,300 microforms units. 3,100 audiovisual materials; 2,070 current periodical subscriptions. Most important special collections include Black History Collection; Archival, Museum, and Historical; Coretta Scott King Award Children's Book Collection.

Buildings and Grounds: Campus area 200 acres.

Chief Executive Officer: Dr. John T. Gibson, President.

Address admission inquiries to Antonio Boyle, Director of Admissions.

Alabama State University

915 South Jackson Street
Montgomery, Alabama 36101-0271
Tel: (334) 229-4200   **E-mail:** admissions@alasu.edu
Fax: (334) 834-6861   **Internet:** www.alasu.edu

Institution Description: *Enrollment:* 6,024. *Degrees awarded:* Associate, baccalaureate, master's. Educational specialist certificate also awarded.

Academic offerings subject to approval by statewide coordinating bodies. Member of the consortium Alabama Center for Higher Education.

Accreditation: *Regional:* SACS-Comm. on Coll. *Professional:* business, music, occupational therapy, physical therapy, social work, teacher education

History: Established and chartered as State Normal School and University for Colored Students and Teachers 1874; changed name to Alabama Colored Peoples University 1887, to State Normal School for Colored Students 1889; offered first instruction at postsecondary level and became junior college 1920; became 4-year institution and changed name to State Teachers College 1929; awarded first degree (baccalaureate) 1931; changed name to Alabama State College for Negroes 1946, to Alabama State College 1954; adopted present name 1969.

Institutional Structure: *Governing board:* Alabama State University Board of Trustees. Representation: 12 trustees, governor of Alabama. 1 ex officio. 12 voting. *Composition of institution:* Administrators 25 men / 5 women. Academic affairs headed by vice president for academic affairs. Management/business/finances directed by vice president for fiscal affairs. Full-time instructional faculty 223. Academic governance body, Faculty Senate, meets an average of 12 times per year.

Calendar: Semesters. Academic year late Aug. to mid-May. Freshmen admitted Aug., Dec., Mar., June. Degrees conferred and formal commencements May, Aug. Summer session of 1 term from mid-June to early Aug.

Characteristics of Freshmen: 50.4% of applicants accepted. 20.5% of accepted applicants enrolled.

17% (212 students) submitted SAT scores; 75% (936 students) submitted ACT scores. *25th percentile*: SAT Verbal 350; SAT Math 140; ACT Composite 14; ACT English 12; ACT Math 12. *75th percentile*: SAT Verbal 457; SAT Math 447; ACT Composite 18; ACT English 18; ACT Math 20.

58% of freshmen from Alabama. Freshmen from 30 states and 3 foreign countries.

Admission: Rolling admissions plan. Apply no later than last day of registration. *Requirements:* Either graduation from secondary school with 3 units in English, 8 from among foreign languages, mathematics, natural sciences, social studies, or GED. *Entrance tests:* ACT Composite preferred; College Board accepted. *For transfer students:* 2.0 minimum GPA; from 4-year accredited institution maximum transfer credit limited only by residence requirement; from 2-year accredited institution 64 hours; correspondence/extension students 45 hours.

Advanced placement for postsecondary-level work completed in secondary school. College credit for extrainstitutional learning on basis of ACE *2006 Guide to the Evaluation of Educational Experiences in the Armed Services*. Tutoring available. Developmental courses offered in summer session and regular academic year; credit given.

Degree Requirements: *For all associate degrees:* 62 credit hours; last 24 hours in residence. *For all baccalaureate degrees:* 129 credit hours; last 30 hours in residence; comprehensives in individual fields of study; English proficiency examination. *For all undergraduate degrees:* 2.0 GPA; core curriculum. *Grading system:* A–F; withdraw (carries time limit).

Distinctive Educational Programs: Work experience programs. Flexible meeting places and schedules, including off-campus centers (at Selma, 50 miles away from main institution; Uniontown, 80 miles away; Birmingham, 100 miles away; Mobile, 180 miles away), weekend and evening classes. Facilities and programs for independent research, including honors programs, tutorials. *Other distinctive programs:* Continuing education. Public service component provides workshops, seminars, conferences for local community.

ROTC: Air Force in cooperation with Auburn University, Huntingdon College, Troy State University.

Degrees Conferred: 1 *associate;* 589 *baccalaureate;* 220 *master's;* 6 *post-master's certificate;* 1 *doctorate.* Bachelor's degrees awarded in top five disciplines: education 177; computer and information sciences and support services 85; business, management, marketing, and related support services 80; public administration and social service professions 43; communication, journalism, and related programs 36.

Fees and Other Expenses: *Full-time tuition per academic year 2004–05:* in-state resident $4,008; out-of-state student $8,016. *Books and supplies* $800. *Room and board per academic year:* $3,600. *Other expenses:* $2,310.

Financial Aid: Aid from institutionally generated funds is provided on the basis of academic merit, financial need, athletic ability. Institution has a Program Participation Agreement with the U.S. Department of Education for eligible students to receive Pell Grants and other federal aid.

Financial aid to full-time, first-time undergraduate students: 58% received federal grants averaging $3,057; 3% state/local grants averaging $1,806; 6% institutional grants averaging $3,855; 61% loans averaging $4,145.

Departments and Teaching Staff: *Total instructional faculty:* 223. 70% of full-time faculty hold doctorates. Student-to-faculty ratio: 18:1.

Enrollment: Total enrollment 6,024. Undergraduate 5,020. 13.4% of entering freshmen expected to graduate within five years.

Characteristics of Student Body: *Ethnic and racial makeup:* Black non-Hispanic: 95.5%; Hispanic: 2%; White non-Hispanic: 3.1%.

International Students: No programs available to aid students whose native language is not English. No financial aid specifically designated for international students.

Student Life: On-campus residence halls house 39% of student body. Residence halls for men only constitute 36% of such space, for women only 64%. Housing available for married students. *Intercollegiate athletics:* men only: baseball, basketball, cross-country, football, tennis, track. women only: basketball, tennis, track, volleyball. *Special regulations:* Registered cars permitted in designated areas only. Quiet hours. Residence hall visitation from noon to 10:30pm. *Special services:* Learning Resources Center, medical services. *Student publications: The Hornet,* a yearbook; *The Hornet Tribune,* a monthly newspaper. *Surrounding community:* Montgomery population 180,000. Birmingham, 100 miles from campus, is nearest metropolitan area. Served by mass transit bus system; airport 10 miles from campus.

Publications: *COBA Vanguard* (quarterly) first published in 1980.

Library Collections: 396,900 volumes. 2,559,000 microforms; 43,000 37,500 audiovisual materials; 1,307 current periodicals. Online catalog. Students have access to the Internet at no charge.

Most important holdings include Ollie L. Brown Afro-American Heritage Collection; E. D. Nixon Collections; Levi Watkins papers.

Buildings and Grounds: Campus area 9 acres.

Chief Executive Officer: Dr. Joe A. Lee, President. Address inquiries to Danielle Kennedy-Lamar, Director of Admissions.

Athens State University

300 North Beaty Street
Athens, Alabama 35611
Tel: (256) 233-8100   **E-mail:** admissions@athens.edu
Fax: (256) 233-8164   **Internet:** www.athens.edu

Institution Description: Athens State University is a state institution providing upper division degree study only. *Enrollment:* 2,535. *Degrees awarded:* Baccalaureate.

Accreditation: *Regional:* SACS-Comm. on Coll. *Professional:* teacher education

History: Established as Athens Female Academy 1822; chartered, changed name to Athens Female Institute of the Tennessee Annual Conference of the Methodist Church, and offered first instruction at postsecondary level 1843; awarded first degree (baccalaureate) 1846; changed name to Athens Female Institute 1872; changed name to Athens Female College 1889; became coeducational and changed name to Athens College 1931; became Athens State College 1975; became Athens State University 1998.

Institutional Structure: *Governing board:* Alabama State Board of Education. Extrainstitutional representation: 8 trustees, state governor. 1 ex officio. All voting. *Composition of institution:* Administrators 4 men. Academic affairs headed by dean of the college. Management/business/finances directed by business manager/treasurer. Academic governance body, Administrative Council (advised by faculty and academic councils), meets weekly. *Faculty representation:* Faculty served by collective bargaining agent, NEA, affiliated with Alabama Education Association.

Calendar: Semester. Academic year Sept. to Aug. Formal commencement May. Summer session of 1 term from June to Aug.

Characteristics of Freshmen: 100% of applicants accepted. 89% of accepted applicants enrolled. Entering freshmen from 10 states and 4 foreign countries.

Admission: Rolling admissions plan. For fall acceptance, apply as early as 1 year prior to enrollment, but not later than week of registration. *Requirements:* Graduation from accredited junior, community, or technical college or completion of 60 hours or equivalent work at accredited institution. Exceptions may be made on an individual basis. Minimum GPA 2.0. *For transfer students:* 2.0 GPA; from 2-year accredited institution 60 hours; correspondence/extension students 18 hours. College credit for USAFI/DANTES and for extrainstitutional learning on basis of ACE *2006 Guide to the Evaluation of Educational Experiences in the Armed Services*; portfolio, faculty assessments, personal interview.

Degree Requirements: 120 semester hours; 2.0 GPA; final 30 hours in residence; distribution requirements. Fulfillment of some degree requirements and exemption from some beginning courses possible by passing departmental examinations, College Board CLEP, AP. *Grading system:* A–F; withdraw (carries time limit).

Distinctive Educational Programs: Flexible meeting places and schedules, including off-campus center (at Huntsville, less than 30 miles from main institution), and evening and weekend classes. Interdepartmental/interdisciplinary programs in behavioral science, personnel psychology. Individual majors. Cross-registration with Alabama Agricultural and Mechanical University, Oakwood College, and University of Alabama in Huntsville.

ROTC: Army offered in cooperation with Alabama Agricultural and Mechanical University.

Degrees Conferred: 740 *baccalaureate.* Degrees conferred in top five disciplines: education 306; business, management, marketing, and related support services 211; computer and information sciences and support services 42; liberal arts and sciences, general studies, and humanities 35; security and protective services 33.

Fees and Other Expenses: *Full-time tuition per academic year:* resident $1,905, nonresident $3,660. *Room and board per academic year:* $4,800.

Financial Aid: Aid from institutionally generated funds is provided on the basis of academic merit, athletic ability, other. Institution has a Program Participation Agreement with the U.S. Department of Education for eligible students to receive Pell Grants and other federal aid.

Departments and Teaching Staff: Business *professors* 2, *associate professors* 4, *assistant professors* 8, *part-time faculty* 7; accounting 1, 0, 2, 0; art 0, 2, 0, 3; biology 1, 0, 1, 3; chemistry 0, 0, 2, 0; computer science 1, 3, 0, 5; education 6, 3, 12, 29; English 2, 0, 1, 2; history 0, 1, 1, 2; justice studies 1, 0, 0, 1; mathematics 2, 1, 1, 5; music 0, 0, 0, 4; physics 1, 1, 0, 1; political science 1, 1, 0, 0; psychology 1, 1, 2, 5; political science 1, 1, 0, 0; religion 1, 0, 0, 3.

Total instructional faculty 141. Degrees held by full-time instructional faculty: master's 34%; doctorate 66%.

Enrollment: Total enrollment 2,535.

Characteristics of Student Body: *Ethnic and racial makeup:* Black non-Hispanic: 10.7%; American Indian or Alaska Native: 2.7%; Asian or Pacific Islander: .6%; Hispanic: .6%; White non-Hispanic: 77.9%; unknown 7.5%.

International Students: 4 nonresident aliens enrolled (2 men, 2 women); 3 Asia, 1 Latin America. No program for students whose native language is not English. No scholarships or loans specifically designated for international students.

Student Life: On-campus residence halls house 8% of student body. Dormitories for men only constitute 63% of such space, for women only 36%. *Intercollegiate athletics:* Men only, baseball, basketball. *Special regulations:* Cars permitted without restrictions. Dormitory visitation in lounges from 11am to midnight Sun.–Wed., 11am to 1am Thurs.–Sat. *Student publications: The Athenian*, a weekly newspaper; *The Columns*, a yearbook; *The Gyre*, an annual literary magazine. *Surrounding community:* Athens 2004 population 15,000. Nashville (Tenn.), 96 miles from campus, is largest metropolitan area. Served by airport 25 miles from campus.

Library Collections: 95,000 volumes. 13,000 microforms; 1,215 audiovisual materials; 350 current periodical subscriptions.Students have access to online information retrieval services and the Internet.

Most important holdings include education, business, and Athens State University Archives.

Buildings and Grounds: Campus area 44 acres.

Chief Executive Officer: Dr. Jerry F. Bartlett, President. Address admission inquiries to Ms. Necedah Henderson, Supervisor of Admissions and Records.

Auburn University

Auburn University, Alabama 36849-5245

Tel: (334) 844-4000   **E-mail:** admissions@auburn.edu
Fax: (334) 844-4080   **Internet:** www.auburn.edu

Institution Description: Auburn University is a coeducational state institution. *Enrollment:* 22,928. *Degrees awarded:* Baccalaureate, master's, doctorate, first-professional (pharmacy, veterinary medicine).

Academic offerings subject to approval by statewide coordinating bodies. *Member of:* Oak Ridge Associated Universities; National Association of State Universities and Land Grant Colleges.

Accreditation: *Regional:* SACS-Comm. on Coll. *Professional:* accounting, art, audiology, business, clinical psychology, computer science, construction education, counseling, counseling psychology, engineering, family and consumer science, forestry, interior design, journalism, landscape architecture, marriage and family therapy, music, nursing, pharmacy, public administration, rehabilitation counseling, social work, speech-language pathology, teacher education, theatre, veterinary medicine

History: Established by Methodist Episcopal Church, South and chartered as East Alabama Male College 1856; offered first instruction at postsecondary level and awarded first degree 1859; instruction suspended from 1861 to 1866; control transferred to state and name changed to Alabama Agricultural and Mechanical College 1872, to Alabama Polytechnic Institute 1899; adopted present name 1960. *See* Charles Wesley Edwards, *Auburn Starts a Second Century* (Auburn: Auburn University, 1958) for further information.

Institutional Structure: *Governing board:* Board of Trustees of Auburn University. Extrainstitutional representation: 10 trustees (appointed by governor of Alabama), governor, state superintendent of education; institutional representation: 2 students (1 from each campus). 2 ex officio. 12 voting. *Composition of institution:* Administrators 217. Academic affairs headed by vice president. Management/business/finance directed by vice president. Full-time instructional faculty 1,146. Academic governance body, University Senate, meets an average of 12 times per year.

Calendar: Semester. Academic year Sept. to June. Summer session June to Aug.

Characteristics of Freshmen: 3,570 applicants accepted and enrolled.

29% (1,054 students) submitted SAT scores; 71% (2,539 students) submitted ACT scores. *25th percentile:* SAT Verbal 500; SAT Math 510; ACT Composite 22, ACT English 21, ACT Math 20. *75th percentile:* SAT Verbal 600, SAT Math 610; ACT Composite 26, ACT English 27, ACT Math 26.

55% of entering freshmen expected to graduate within 5 years; 61% of freshmen from Alabama. Freshmen from 43 states and 91 foreign countries.

Admission: Rolling admissions plan. For fall acceptance, apply as early as Sept. 1 of previous year, but not later than three weeks prior to enrollment. Early acceptance available. *Requirements:* Graduation from secondary school with 4 years of English, 3 mathematics, 3 science, 4 social studies required; 1 year foreign language and 1 additional year of each of science and social studies recommended. *Entrance tests:* College Board SAT or ACT Composite. *For transfer*

students: 2.5 minimum GPA on all college work attempted. If student was not eligible to enter Auburn upon high school graduation, must also present 48 quarter hours (32 semester hours) of college credit in standard academic courses including English, history, mathematics and science with a 2.5 cumulative GPA.

College credit and advanced placement for postsecondary-level work completed in secondary school, and for extrainstitutional learning on basis of *The 2006 Guide to the Evaluation of Educational Experiences in the Armed Services.*

Tutoring available. Limited number of noncredit developmental courses offered in summer session and regular academic year.

Degree Requirements: It is the responsibility of each student to become familiar with degree requirements, graduation requirements, and all other aspects of satisfactory academic progress. Each student is assigned an academic advisor to assist in planning course schedules and give advice on timely graduation planning. The ultimate responsibility for understanding and completing degree and graduation requirements lies with the student. Fulfillment of some degree requirements and exemption from some beginning courses possible by passing departmental examinations; College Board CLEP and other standardized tests. *Grading system:* A–F; pass-fail; withdraw (deadline after which pass-fail is appended to withdraw).

Distinctive Educational Programs: Work-experience programs. Accelerated degree programs. Preprofessional programs in dental hygiene, dentistry, law, medicine, occupational therapy, optometry, pharmacy, physical therapy, veterinary medicine. Honors programs. Study abroad in France, Spain, and by individual arrangement. Video-based Outreach Program available for graduate study in business and engineering. AU Study Abroad in France, Guatemala, Germany, Spain.

ROTC: Army, Navy, Air Force.

Degrees Conferred: 3,969 *baccalaureate* (B), 788 *master's* (M), 161 *doctorate* (D): agriculture 176 (B), 43 (M), 18 (D); architecture 102 (B), 14 (M); biological sciences 176 (B), 20 (M), 3 (D); business/marketing 1,140 (B), 20 (M), 3 (D); communications/communication technologies 169 (B); computer and information sciences 42 (B); education 328 (B), 175 (M), 36 (D); engineering 515 (B), 145 (M), 28 (D); foreign languages 39 (B), 6 (M); health professions 192 (B), 37 (M), 9 (D); home economics 175 (B), 11 (M), 2 (D); mathematics 16 (B), 13 (M), 6 (D); natural resources/environmental science 58 (B), 7 (M), 2 (D); philosophy, religion, theology 8 (B); physical sciences 15 (B), 10 (M), 11 (D); public administration 37 (B), 20 (M), 5 (D); psychology 150 (B), 12 (M), 4 (D); social sciences and history 295 (B), 93 (M), 5 (D); visual and performing arts 170 (B), 6 (M). *First-professional:* pharmacy 57; veterinary medicine 41.

Fees and Other Expenses: *Full-time tuition per academic year 2004–2005:* undergraduate resident in-district $4,610; out-of-district $4,610; out-of-state $13,830; nonresident alien $13,994. *Required fees:* $218. *Room and board per academic year:* $6,686.

Financial Aid: Aid from institutionally generated funds is provided on the basis of academic merit, financial need, athletic ability.

Financial aid to full-time, first-time undergraduate students: need-based scholarships/grants $17,466,032, self-help $31,595,417, parent loans $4,403,874, tuition waivers $3,464,573, athletic awards $1,644,945; non-need-based scholarships/grants $1,666,876, self-help $12,407,132.

Departments and Teaching Staff: *Total instructional faculty:* 1,177 full-time, 143 part-time. Student-to-faculty ratio: 16:1. Degrees held by full-time faculty: doctorate 1,091, master's 136, baccalaureate 19.

Enrollment: Total enrollment 22,928. Undergraduate full-time 8,838 men / 8,580 women, part-time 908m / 570; graduate full-time 800m / 760w, part-time 860m / 728w; first-professional full-time 252m / 502w, part-time 53m / 77w. *Transfer students:* 1,387.

Characteristics of Student Body: *Ethnic/racial makeup:* number of Black non-Hispanic: 1,414; American Indian or Alaska Native: 100; Asian or Pacific Islander: 290; Hispanic: 248; White non-Hispanic: 16,479; unknown 221. *Age distribution:* number under 18: 211; 18–19: 993; 20–21: 7,406; 22–24: 3,406; 25–29: 603; 30–34: 131; 35–39:: 70; 40–50: 45; 50–64: 15; 65 and over: 2.

International Students: 891 nonresident aliens enrolled fall 2004. Students from Europe, Asia, Central and South America, Africa, Canada, Australia, other. Programs available to aid students whose native language is not English: Social and cultural. English as a Second Language Program. No financial aid specifically designated for international students.

Student Life: On-campus residence halls house 20% of student body; residence halls for men only constitute 25% of such space, for women only 75%. 5% of student body live in university-owned apartments. 21% of men join and live in fraternities. Some home economics students live in cooperative facilities. Housing available for married students. *Intercollegiate athletics:* men only: baseball, basketball, football, golf, swimming, tennis, track, women only: basketball, golf, gymnastics, volleyball, swimming, tennis, track. *Special regulations:* Cars permitted on campus during normal class hours for seniors and graduate students only. Dormitory visitation hours set by residents in individual halls. *Special services:* Learning Resources Center, medical services. *Student publications, radio: The Auburn Plainsman*, a weekly newspaper; *The Circle*, a biannual literary magazine; *The Glomerata*, a yearbook; *The Tiger Cub*, an annual student handbook. Radio station WEGL broadcasts 84 hours per week. *Surrounding community:* Auburn population 30,000. Birmingham (AL) and Atlanta (GA), each 120 miles from campus, are nearest metropolitan areas. Served by airport 3 miles from campus.

Publications: *Southern Humanities Review* (quarterly) first published in 1967.

Library Collections: 2,767,765 volumes. 2,430,191 microforms; 629,038 audiovisual units. 5,887 current serials subscriptions (paper), 25 microform, 26,100 via electronic access; 6,780 recordings (audio/video). 164 student computer work stations. Access to information retrieval systems. Students have access to the Internet at no charge. Total 2004-05 budget for books, periodicals, audiovisual materials, microforms: $5,533,059.

Most important holdings include Alabama Special Collection (books by Alabamans and about Alabama); U.S. map repository; Aerospace History Collection; Civil War.

Buildings and Grounds: Campus are 1,871 acres.

Chief Executive Officer: Edward Richardson, Interim President.

Undergraduates address admission inquiries to Doyle Bickess, Director of Admissions and Records (bickecd@auburn.edu); Graduate students address inquiries to Dr. Stephen McFarland, Dean of Graduate School (mcfarsl@auburn.edu)

Auburn University at Montgomery

7300 University Drive
Montgomery, Alabama 36117-3596
Tel: (334) 244-3000   **E-mail:** auminfo@mickey.aum.edu
Fax: (334) 244-3762   **Internet:** www.aum.edu

Institution Description: Auburn University at Montgomery is a state institution. *Enrollment:* 5,123. *Degrees awarded:* Baccalaureate, master's.

Accreditation: *Regional:* SACS-Comm. on Coll. *Professional:* business, clinical lab scientist, nursing, nursing education, public administration, teacher education

History: Established 1967; chartered and offered first instruction at postsecondary level 1968; awarded first degree (baccalaureate) 1970.

Institutional Structure: *Composition of institution:* Administrators 30 men/27 women. Full-time faculty 186. Academic affairs headed by vice chancellor for academic and student affairs. Management/business/finances directed by vice chancellor for financial and administrative services. Academic governance body, Faculty Senate, meets monthly; Faculty Council meets an average of 4 times per year.

Calendar: Semesters. 2004–05 academic year Sept. to Aug. Freshmen admitted Sept., Jan., June. Degrees conferred June, Jan. Formal commencement at end of each semester.

Characteristics of Freshmen: 953 applicants; 98% of applicants accepted.

609 enrolled students submitted ACT scores. *25th percentile*: ACT English 17, ACT Math 15; ACT Composite 17. *75th percentile*: ACT Composite 24, ACT English 24, ACT Math 21.

96% of freshmen from Alabama. Freshmen from 17 states and 4 foreign countries.

Admission: Rolling admissions plan. For fall acceptance, apply as early as Oct. 1 of previous year, but not later than Sept. 1 of year of enrollment. Early acceptance available. *Requirements:* Either graduation from secondary school or GED. *Entrance tests:* ACT Composite. *For transfer students:* Minimum GPA 2.0; from 4-year accredited institution 96 semester hours maximum transfer credit; from 2-year accredited institution 66 semester hours.

College credit for extrainstitutional learning (life experience) on basis of ACE *2006 Guide to the Evaluation of Educational Experiences in the Armed Services.* Tutoring available. Developmental courses offered in summer session and regular academic year; credit given.

Degree Requirements: 120 semester hours; 2.0 GPA on a 4.0 scale; 30 hours in residence; core requirements. Fulfillment of some degree requirements and exemption from some beginning courses possible by passing College Board CLEP. *Grading system:* A–F; withdraw (carries time limit).

Distinctive Educational Programs: Work experience programs. Weekend and evening classes. Interdisciplinary programs in mass communications, international studies, and economics. Facilities and programs for independent research, including honors programs, tutorials.

ROTC: Army; Air Force in cooperation with Alabama State University, Troy State University at Montgomery, and Huntingdon College.

Degrees Conferred: 605 *baccalaureate*; 225 *master's*: Bachelor's degrees awarded in top five disciplines: business, management, marketing, and related support sciences 230; education 117; health professions and related clinical sciences 76; security and protective services 32; biological and biomedical sciences 25.

Fees and Other Expenses: *Full-time tuition per academic year 2004–05:* resident undergraduate student $4,460, nonresident $12,920. *Room per and board per academic year:* $4,890. *Books and supplies:* $600.

Financial Aid: Aid from institutionally generated funds is provided on the basis of academic merit. Direct lending program available. Institution has a Program Participation Agreement with the U.S. Department of Education for eligible students to receive Pell Grants and other federal aid.

Financial aid to full-time, first-time undergraduate students: need-based scholarships/grants totaling $5,519,986, self-help $14,551,426, parent loans $595,428, athletic awards $227,140; non-need-based schlarships/grants totaling $118,058, self-help $185,000, athletic awards $270,401.

Departments and Teaching Staff: *Total instructional faculty:* 327 (members of minority groups 36; women 153, men 174). Total with doctorate, first-professional, or other terminal degree: 177. Student to faculty ratio: 16:1.

Enrollment: Total enrollment 5,123. Undergraduate full-time 1,072 men, 1,794 women; part-time 493m / 981w; graduate full-time 74m / 161w, part-time 165m / 383w.

Characteristics of Student Body: *Ethnic/racial makeup:* number of Black non-Hispanic: 1,135; American Indian or Alaska Native: 18; Asian or Pacific Islander: 83; Hispanic: 46; White non-Hispanic: 2,204; unknown 74.

International Students: 40 nonresident aliens enrolled fall 2004. English as a second language program. No financial aid specifically designated for international students.

Student Life: On-campus residence halls house 11% of student body. Dormitories for both men and women constitute 100% of such space. *Intercollegiate athletics:* men only: basketball, baseball, soccer, tennis; women only: basketball, soccer, tennis. *Special regulations:* Cars permitted without restrictions. *Special services:* Learning center, counseling center, career development center, nursing care center, child development center, physically disabled student services and health insurance. *Student publications: Aumnibus,* a bimonthly newspaper; *Filibuster,* an annual literary magazine; *Aumanac,* annual handbook. *Surrounding community:* Montgomery population 218,760. Served by airport 20 miles from campus.

Library Collections: 320,000 volumes. Online catalog. 2,000 current serial subscriptions. 25,000 audio/video/compact disks. Students have access to the Internet at no charge.

Library is regional depository for government documents and also houses the University Archives; Southern Women Writers Collection; Congressman William L. Dickinson Paper; Senator Otis J. Goodwyn Papers.

Buildings and Grounds: Campus area 500 acres.

Chief Executive Officer: Guin A. Nance, Chancellor.

Address all admission inquiries to Valerie S. Crawford, Associate Director of Admissions.

Birmingham Southern College

900 Arkadelphia Road
Birmingham, Alabama 35254
Tel: (205) 226-4600   **E-mail:** admission@bsc.edu
Fax: (205) 226-4627   **Internet:** www.bsc.edu

Institution Description: Birmingham Southern College is a private liberal arts college affiliated with the United Methodist Church. *Enrollment:* 582 men / 799 women. *Degrees awarded:* Baccalaureate, master's.

Accreditation: *Regional:* SACS-Comm. on Coll. *Professional:* business, chemistry, music, teacher education

History: Southern University established and chartered 1856; offered first instruction at postsecondary level 1859; first degree (baccalaureate) awarded 1860. North Alabama Conference College chartered and offered first instruction 1898; first degree (baccalaureate) awarded 1899; name changed to Birmingham College 1906. Institutions merged to form Birmingham Southern College 1918. *See* Robert Corley and Samuel Stayer, *View from the Hilltop* (Birmingham: Birmingham Publishing Company, 1981) for further information.

Institutional Structure: *Governing board:* Birmingham-Southern College Board of Trustees. Extrainstitutional representation: 69 trustees (including 38 alumni). All voting. *Composition of institution:* Administrators 16 men / 22 women. Academic affairs headed by Provost. Management/business/finances directed by vice president for financial affairs. Full-time instructional faculty 124. Academic governance body, the faculty, meets an average of 9 times per year.

Calendar: Semesters. 2004–05 academic year Sept. to May. Freshmen admitted Aug., Feb., June. Degrees conferred and formal commencement May. Summer session of 2 terms from early June to early Aug.

Characteristics of Freshmen: 95% of applicants accepted. 38% of accepted applicants enrolled.

51% (188 students) submitted SAT scores; 90% (332 students) submitted ACT scores. *25th percentile*: SAT Verbal 550, SAT Math 540; ACT Composite 24, ACT English 24, ACT Math 23. *75th percentile*: SAT Verbal 670, SAT Math 640, ACT Composite 29, ACT English 30, ACT Math 28.

71% of freshmen from Alabama. Freshmen from 18 foreign countries.

Admission: Rolling admissions plan. For fall acceptance, apply as early as Sept. 1 of previous year, but not later than Aug. 15 of year of enrollment. Priority filing deadline is January 15. Early acceptance available after junior year of secondary school. *Requirements:* Either minimum GPA 3.0 or GED. *Entrance tests:* College board SAT or ACT Composite. *For transfer students:* 2.0 minimum GPA, 60 semester hours maximum transfer credit.

College credit for extrainstitutional learning (life experience) based on test results, portfolios or any other materials requested by faculty to make an evaluation. College credit and advanced placement for postsecondary-level work completed in secondary school. Tutoring available.

Degree Requirements: 128 credit hours plus 1 interim unit for each year enrolled; 2.0 GPA; 2 years in residence. Some requirements can be fulfilled by passing College Board CLEP. *Grading system:* A–F; pass-fail; pass; withdraw.

Distinctive Educational Programs: Work-experience programs. Flexible meeting places and schedules. Accelerated degree programs. Individual majors, interdisciplinary studies, and area studies. Facilities and programs for independent research. Tutorials. Study abroad in Africa, Asia, Australia, Europe, South America, and the Middle East. Student/Faculty Exchange Programs and cooperative programs in all continents.

ROTC: Army, Air Force offered in cooperation with University of Alabama at Birmingham; Air Force with Samford University.

Degrees Conferred: 236 *baccalaureate*; 14 *master's*. Bachelor's degrees conferred in top five disciplines: business, management, marketing, and related support services 49; multidisciplinary studies 34; visual and performing arts 22; social sciences 20; biological and biomedical sciences 18. Honorary degrees awarded 2004–05: Doctor of Laws 4.

Fees and Other Expenses: *Full-time tuition per academic year 2005–06:* $20,425. *Room per academic year:* $5,000. *Board per academic year:* $2,080 (on-campus meal plan). *Books and supplies:* $1,000.

Financial Aid: Aid from institutionally generated funds is awarded on the basis of academic merit, financial need, athletic ability, other considerations.

Scholarships/grants need-based $1,354,525; self-help $1,945,021; non-need-based scholarships/grants $15,211,724, self-help $3,055,129, parent loans, parent loans $1,523,958, tuition waivers $363,769; athletic awards $3,091,327.

Departments and Teaching Staff: *Total instructional faculty:* 124 (women 459, men 247; members of minority groups 2). Total with doctorate, first-professional, or other terminal degree 96. Student to faculty ratio: 12:1.

Enrollment: Total enrollment 1,453. Undergraduate full-time 563 men / 772 women, part-time 12m / 9w; graduate full-time 19m / 27w, part-time 19m / 32w.

Characteristics of Student Body: *Ethnic/racial makeup:* number of Black non-Hispanic: 79; American Indian or Alaska Native: 1; Asian or Pacific Islander: 36; Hispanic: 12; White non-Hispanic: 1,220; unknown: 6.

International Students: 2 nonresident aliens enrolled 2004.

Student Life: On-campus residence halls house 80% of student body. Residence halls for men constitute 48% of such space, for women 52%. 50% of men join and 7% live in fraternities. 20% of student body live off campus in apartments or with relatives. Housing available for married students upon request. *Intercollegiate athletics:* men only: baseball; women only: volleyball; men and women: basketball, cross-country, soccer, and tennis. *Special regulations:* Cars with decals permitted on campus in designated areas. Quiet hours from 8:00pm to 8:00am. *Special services:* Learning Resources Center, Health Services. *Student publications: The Hilltop News*, a weekly newspaper; *Southern Academic Review*, a scholarly journal for the Birmingham Southern College community; *Southern Accent*, a yearbook; *Quad*, a biannual literary magazine. *Surrounding community:* Birmingham metropolitan area population 848,000. Served by mass transit bus system; airport 10 miles from campus; passenger rail service 5 miles from campus.

Library Collections: 231,815 volumes. Online catalog. 965 current serial publications. 27,000 audio/video/compact disks; 175,100 microform units. Students have access to the Internet at no charge.

Buildings and Grounds: Campus area 188 acres. *New buildings:* Elton B. Stephens Science Center completed 2002; 6 new houses on Fraternity Row 2003.

Chief Executive Officer: Dr. David Pollick, President.

Address undergraduate admission inquiries to Sheri Salmon, Associate Vice President for Admissions Services; graduate inquiries to Tara Sudderth, Dean of Business and Graduate Programs.

Concordia College

1804 Green Street
Selma, Alabama 36701
Tel: (334) 874-5700   **E-mail:** rosborn@concordiaselma.edu
Fax: (334) 874-5755   **Internet:** www.concordiaselma.edu

Institution Description: *Enrollment:* 731. *Degrees awarded:* Baccalaureate.
Accreditation: SACS-Comm. on Coll.

History: Concordia College is a private institution affiliated with the Lutheran Church.

Calendar: Semesters. Academic year Aug. to May.

Characteristics of Freshmen: 14% of applicants submitted ACT scores. 100% of applicants accepted. 89% of freshmen from Alabama. Freshmen from 17 states and 6 foreign countries.

Admission: *Requirements:* Graduation from an accredited secondary school or GED.

Degree Requirements: *For all baccalaureate degrees:* Completion of prescribed courses.

Degrees Conferred: 19 *baccalaureate:* business/marketing 13; education 6.

Fees and Other Expenses: *Full-time tuition per academic year:* $6,000. *Room per academic year:* $1,600. *Board per academic year:* $1,000. *Required fees:* $174. *Other fees:* $265.

Financial Aid: Financial aid is generated on the basis of academic merit, financial need, athletic ability. Institution has a Program Participation Agreement with the U.S. Department of Education for eligible students to receive Pell Grants and other federal aid.

Financial aid to full-time, first-time undergraduate students: need-based scholarships/grants federal $1,968,893, state $141,114, institutional $532,157.

Departments and Teaching Staff: Art *professors* 0, *associate professors* 0, *assistant professors* 0, *instructors* 0, *part-time faculty* 1; biology 0, 1, 0, 0, 2; business 2, 0, 0, 0 5; chemistry, 0, 0, 0, 0, 1; computer/information science 0, 0, 1, 0, 2; early childhood education 0, 0, 1, 0, 5; elementary education 0, 2, 0, 0, 6; English 0, 3, 0, 0, 3; health/physical education 0, 1, 0, 0, 1; history/political science 0, 0, 0, 0, 1; mathematics 0, 0, 3, 0, 2; music 0, 0, 1, 0, 1; psychology 0, 0, 0, 0, 1; theology 2, 0, 0, 0, 0.

Total instructional faculty: 49 (31 women, 18 men; members of minority groups 34). Full-time faculty with highest degree a doctorate, first-professional, or other terminal degree: 12. Student-to-faculty ratio: 20:1.

Enrollment: Total enrollment 731. Full-time 285 men / 446 women, part-time 24m / 147w, *Transfer students:* in-state 17m / 40w; out-of-state 3m / 6w.

Characteristics of Student Body: *Ethnic/racial makeup:* number of Black non-Hispanic: 840; American Indian or Alaska Native: 1; Asian or Pacific Islander: 2; White non-Hispanic: 32. *Age distribution:* number under 18: 18; 18–19: 226; 20-21: 18; 22-24: 19; 25-29: 81; 30-34: 75; 35-39: 81; 40-49: 118; 50-64: 65; 65 and over: 19.

International Students: 27 nonresident aliens enrolled fall 2004. 2 students from Asia, 10 Central and South America 10, Africa 14. No programs available to aid students whose native language is not English. No financial aid specifically designated for international students.

Student Life: Residence halls available for student housing.

Library Collections: 60,000 volumes. Card catalog. Serial subscriptions. 5 computer work-stations. Students have access to the Internet at no charge. Total budget for books, periodicals, audiovisual materials, and microforms 2004–05: $60,000.

Chief Executive Officer: Dr. Julius Jenkins, President.

Address admission inquiries to Erenlyn Pickens, Director of Admissions.

Faulkner University

5345 Atlanta Highway
Montgomery, Alabama 36109-3378
Tel: (334) 386-7200   **E-mail:** kmack@faulkner.edu
Fax: (334) 386-7137   **Internet:** www.faulkner.edu

Institution Description: Faulkner University (formerly Alabama Christian College) is a private, independent, nonprofit institution affiliated with the Churches of Christ in Montgomery. The university has four satellite campuses located in Mobile, Birmingham, Florence, and Huntsville. *Enrollment:* 2,530. *Degrees awarded:* Associate, baccalaureate.

Accreditation: *Regional:* SACS-Comm. on Coll.

History: Established as Montgomery Bible College 1942; changed name to Alabama Christian College 1953; adopted present name 1985.

Institutional Structure: *Governing board:* Board of Trustees. 30 members. *Composition of institution:* Administrators president, 4 vice presidents including academic vice president, vice presidents for campus affairs, finance, and development. Full-time instructional faculty 75.

Calendar: Semesters. 2004–05 academic year Aug. 18 to July 24. Formal commencement May.

Characteristics of Freshmen: 20% (47 students) submitted SAT scores; 93% (235 students) submitted ACT scores. *25th percentile*: SAT Verbal 460, SAT Math 440; ACT Composite 18, ACT English 17, ACT Math 16. *75th percentile*: SAT Verbal 570, SAT Math 590, ACT Composite 22, ACT English 24, ACT Math 21.

23.8% of entering freshmen expected to graduate within five years. 72% of freshmen from Alabama.

Admission: *Requirements:* High school graduates with an ACT score of 16 regularly admitted; others admitted provisionally. Early application up to one year prior to enrollment encouraged.

Degree Requirements: *For all associate degrees:* 68–72 credit hours. *For all baccalaureate degrees:* 128–132 credit hours. *For all degrees:* 2.0 GPA; core curriculum.

Distinctive Educational Programs: Day and evening schedules for both traditional and adult students.

Degrees Conferred: 61 *associate*; 659 *baccalaureate*; 37 *master's*; 22 *first-professional*.

Fees and Other Expenses: *Full-time tuition per academic year:* $9,750. *Room and board per academic year:* $5,000. *Books and supplies:* $1,000. *Other expenses:* 2,400.

Financial Aid: Aid from institutionally generated funds is provided on the basis of academic merit, financial need, athletic ability, other criteria.

Financial aid to full-time, first-time undergraduate students: 43% received federal scholarships/grants averaging $3,619; 61% state/local grants averaging $683; 84% institutional grants averaging $4,036; 72% loans averaging $3,172.

Departments and Teaching Staff: *Total instructional faculty:* 58. Student-to-faculty ratio: 28:1. 67% hold terminal degrees.

Enrollment: Total enrollment 2,530. Undergraduate 2,248.

Characteristics of Student Body: *Ethnic/racial makeup:* Black non-Hispanic: 43.6%; American Indian or Alaska Native: .6%; Asian or Pacific Islander: .3%; Hispanic: .6%; White non-Hispanic: 53.6%; unknown: 1%.

International Students: 76 nonresident aliens enrolled in 2003. No programs available to aid students whose native language is not English. No financial aid specifically designated for international students.

Student Life: *Student publications: The Reporter, The Spire.*

Library Collections: 220,600 volumes. 1,450 audiovisual materials; 3,323 current periodical subscriptions. 170,000 microform items. Online catalog. Students have access to the Internet at no charge.

Most important special holdings include Restoration Collection (historical materials relating to Churches of Christ).

Buildings and Grounds: Campus area 92 acres.

Chief Executive Officer: Billy D. Hillyer, President.

Address admission inquiries to Keith Mock, Director of Admissions.

Heritage Christian University

3625 Helton Drive
Florence, Alabama 35630-9977
Tel: (256) 766-6610   **E-mail:** admit1@hcu.edu
Fax: (256) 760-0981   **Internet:** www.hcu.edu

Institution Description: Heritage Christian University, formerly named International Bible College (IBC), is a private institution affiliated with the Churches of Christ. *Enrollment:* 134. *Degrees awarded:* Associate, baccalaureate.

Accreditation: *Nonregional:* ABHE.

History: Heritage Christian University was organized in 1971. From its beginning, the college offered a four-year program of study emphasizing the biblical text and evangelism. Awarded first baccalaureate in 1972.

Institutional Structure: *Governing board:* Board of Directors through its "Constitution and By-Laws." Academic affairs headed by vice president for institutional advancement and dean of the college. Management/business/finances directed by vice president of institutional advancement.

Calendar: Semesters. Academic year is composed of fall-spring semesters and several summer sessions of two weeks duration.

Characteristics of Freshmen: 78% of applicants accepted. 62% of accepted applicants enrolled. 32% of entering freshmen graduate within 5 years.

Admission: *Requirements:* Completed application with health form; official high school transcript or GED or home schooling record. Three positive personal references; official transcripts from every college previously attended. International students must provide proof of adequate financial resources to complete for years of college study. Student must pass the Test of Adult Basic Education (TABE) exam, maintain satisfactory grades during enrollment at the college.

Students transferring from unaccredited institutions must complete 12 semester hours with a grade point average of 2.50 or above before any credit is awarded.

Degree Requirements: *For all baccalaureate degrees:* 128 semester hours with a GPA 2.00; 39 hours in Bible and Doctrine; 36 hours in general education; 29 hours in professional studies; 24 elective hours if a minor is not chosen (6–18 if a minor is chosen). At least 33 hours of the 128 required hours must be completed at the university. Of the 33 hours, 12 must be in the division of Bible and Doctrine.

A student may receive a maximum of 24 hours of credit through CLEP.

Distinctive Educational Programs: Accelerated College Education (ACE) program is designed for students who have already earned a baccalaureate degree in another discipline (arts or science). Distance Learning Video program is designed to meet the needs of adult students who wish to pursue an accredited Bible degree but are unable to study in Florence, Alabama.

Degrees Conferred: 3 *associate*; 13 *baccalaureate*: theology and ministerial studies; 3 *master's*: theology and ministerial studies.

Fees and Other Expenses: *Full-time tuition per academic year 2004–05:* $6,840. *Room and board per academic year:* $1,500. *Books and supplies:* $1,000. *Other expenses:* $2,100.

Financial Aid: Institution has a Program Participation Agreement with the U.S. Department of Education for eligible students to receive Pell Grants and other federal aid.

Departments and Teaching Staff: Bible *professors* 4, *part-time teachers* 11. *Total instructional faculty:* 15. Student-to-faculty ratio: 8:1. Degrees held by full-time faculty: doctorate 75%, master's 25%.

Enrollment: Total enrollment 134. Undergraduate enrollment 121 (90.9% men, 9.1% women).

Characteristics of Student Body: *Ethnic/racial makeup:* Black non-Hispanic: 10.7%; Hispanic: 2.5%; White non-Hispanic: 72.7%; unknown 5%.

International Students: 13 nonresident aliens enrolled fall 2004.

Student Life: The college provides on-campus housing units for 20 single students. On-campus apartments are available for married students. Extracurricular activities include Mission Club, Student Government Association, Student Ladies Association; Evangelism Workshop, Chapel Services. *Publications: Lamplighter* published quarterly; *The Sower,* a yearbook. *Surrounding community:* The adjacent cities of Sheffield, Tuscumbia, and Muscle Shoals combine with Florence to create a metropolitan area with a population of 131,000.

Library Collections: 34,500 volumes including bound books, serial backfiles, electronic documents, and govern documents not in separate collections. Card catalog. Current serial subscriptions: 270 paper. 150 recordings; 49 CD-ROMs. 10 computer work stations. Students have access to the Internet at no charge.

Buildings and Grounds: Campus area 44 acres. Bible Building contains administrative and faculty offices, classroom, auditorium, cafeteria; Alexandria Activities Building contains faculty offices; Overton Memorial Library; gymnasium, nursery.

Chief Executive Officer: Dennis H. Jones, President. Address admission inquiries to Bryan Collins, Director of Enrollment Services.

Huntingdon College

1500 East Fairview Avenue
Montgomery, Alabama 36106-2148
Tel: (334) 833-4497   **E-mail:** admis@huntingdon.edu
Fax: (334) 833-4347   **Internet:** www.huntingdon.edu

Institution Description: Huntingdon College is a coeducational liberal arts college related to the United Methodist Church. *Enrollment:* 660. *Degrees awarded:* Associate, baccalaureate.

Member of Association of Schools and Colleges of the United Methodist Church, National Association of Independent Colleges and Universities, National Association of Schools of Music, American Association of Colleges for Teacher Education, Cooperative Center for Study Abroad, Alabama Consortium for the Development of Higher Education, Marine Environmental Sciences Consortium, National Association of Intercollegiate Athletics.

Accreditation: *Regional:* SACS-Comm. on Coll. *Professional:* music

History: Established and chartered as Tuskegee Female College 1854; offered first instruction at postsecondary level and awarded first degree (baccalaureate) 1856; changed name to Alabama Conference Female College 1872; changed name to Woman's College of Alabama 1909; adopted present name 1935. *See* Rhoda Ellison, *History of Huntingdon College 1854–1954* (University, AL: University of Alabama Press, 1954) for further information.

Institutional Structure: *Governing board:* Board of Trustees. Extrainstitutional representation: 41 trustees. All voting. *Composition of institution:* Executive officers 7. Academic affairs headed by Vice President for Academic Affairs and Dean of the college. Management/business/finances directed by Vice President for Business and Finance. Full-time instructional faculty 48. Academic governance body meets monthly during school year.

Calendar: Semesters. 2005–06 academic year late August to mid-May. Freshmen admitted Aug., Jan., June. Degrees conferred and formal commencement May. Summer session of 2 terms from early June to mid-Aug.

Characteristics of Freshmen: 876 applicants; 63.4% admitted; 34.6% of admitted students enrolled.

20% (39 students) submitted SAT scores; 89% (171 students) submitted ACT scores. *25th percentile*: SAT Verbal 470, SAT Math 470; ACT Composite 22, ACT English 21, ACT Math 20. *75th percentile*: SAT Verbal 600, SAT Math 590; ACT Composite 25, ACT English 24, ACT Math 25.

56.5% of entering freshmen expected to graduate within five years. 63% of freshmen from Alabama. Freshmen from 13 states and 5 foreign countries.

Admission: Rolling admissions plan. For fall acceptance, apply as early as 1 year prior to enrollment, but not later than Aug. 20. Early acceptance available. *Requirements:* Either graduation from accredited secondary school or GED. Minimum GPA 2.25. *Entrance tests:* Minimum 20 ACT Composite with 20 in English or 830 SAT-1 combined with 490 TOEFL. *For transfer students:* 2.25 minimum GPA; from 4-year accredited institution maximum transfer credit limited only by residence requirement; from 2-year accredited institution 64 semester hours maximum transfer credit.

Advanced placement for postsecondary-level work completed in secondary school. Tutoring available. Noncredit developmental courses offered in regular academic year.

Degree Requirements: *For all associate degrees:* 66 credit hours. *For all baccalaureate degrees:* 124 credit hours; last 31 hours in residence. *For all undergraduate degrees:* 2.0 GPA; distribution requirements.

Fulfillment of some degree requirements possible by passing College Board CLEP, IB, or APP. *Grading system:* A–F; pass-no credit; withdraw (deadline after which pass-fail is appended to withdraw); incomplete (carries time limit).

Distinctive Educational Programs: The Liberal Arts Symposium, an interdisciplinary core curriculum, and personal choice in fulfilling other general education requirements are part of *The Huntingdon Plan*. The *Plan* is a set of comprehensive, meaningful learning experiences designed to allow flexibility while providing a broad education that is centered on values, and reinforces critical thinking skills. Cooperative Center for Study Abroad (United Kingdom, Australia, Hong Kong, South Africa); also study abroad in England, Scotland, Ireland, Italy, Spain, Peru, Belize, Caribbean Islands, Mexico, Germany, Austria, France.

ROTC: Army offered in cooperation with Auburn University in Montgomery. Air Force offered in cooperation with Alabama State University.

Degrees Conferred: 3 *associate;* 105 *baccalaureate.* Bachelor's degrees awarded in top five disciplines: biological and biomedical sciences 17; business, management, marketing, and related support 16; visual and performing arts 16; history 11; English language and literature/letters 10.

Fees and Other Expenses: *Full-time tuition per academic year 2004–05:* $15,360. *Room and board per academic year:* $6,000. *Books and supplies:* $900. *Other expenses:* $950.

Financial Aid: Aid from institutionally generated funds is awarded on the basis of academic merit, financial need, other considerations.

Financial aid to full-time, first-time undergraduates: includes: 27% received federal grants averaging $3,496; 71% state/local grants averaging $570; 100% institutional grants averaging $6,011; 70% loans averaging $3,125.

Departments and Teaching Staff: *Total instructional faculty:* 48. 60% hold doctorates. Student-to-faculty ratio: 13:1.

Enrollment: Total enrollment 660 (44.8%, 55.2% women).

Characteristics of Student Body: *Ethnic/racial makeup:* Black non-Hispanic: 9.5%; American Indian or Alaska Native: 1.1%; Asian or Pacific Islander: .8%; Hispanic: 8%; White non-Hispanic: 82.7%.

International Students: 21 nonresident aliens enrolled 2004. Cultural, social, and financial programs available to aid students whose native language is not English. 5 scholarships awarded annually to international students.

Student Life: On-campus residence halls house 65% of student body. More than 50 clubs, organizations, and honoraries. Student Government Association; 2 national fraternities and 3 national sororities. *Intercollegiate athletics:* men only: baseball, basketball, golf, soccer, tennis, track; women only: basketball, soccer, softball, tennis, track, volleyball; intramural and club sports for men and women. *Special services:* Student Development Center (Counseling, College Chaplain, Residential Life, Health Services, Student Programs, Leadership

Development), Academic Resource Center (Registrar, Placement, and Career Services, Academic Enrichment Program), Reading and Writing Lab. *Student publications: Bells and Pomegranates,* a yearbook; *The Gargoyle,* student newspaper; *The Prelude,* a literary magazine. *Surrounding community:* Metropolitan Montgomery population 275,000, Birmingham, 90 miles from campus; Atlanta, 170 miles from campus. Served by mass transit bus system; airport 8 miles from campus.

Library Collections: 102,100 volumes. Online catalog. Current serial subscriptions: 390 paper, 47,500 microform items; 8,000 recordings; 700 compact discs. All students have computers connected to college network and access to library. Students have free access to the Internet and online services.

Most important holdings include historical memorabilia, books, and artifacts detailing history of The United Methodist Church in Alabama from the early 19th century to the present; Alabama Collection; Autographed Book Collection.

Buildings and Grounds: Campus area 58 acres.

Chief Executive Officer: Rev. J. Cameron West, President.

Address admission inquiries to Christy C. Mehaffey, Director of Admissions.

Jacksonville State University

700 Pelham Road North
Jacksonville, Alabama 36265-1602
Tel: (256) 782-5781   **E-mail:** info@jsu.edu
Fax: (256) 782-5705   **Internet:** www.jsu.edu

Institution Description: Jacksonville State University is a state institution. *Enrollment:* 2,202 full-time, 2,728 part-time. *Degrees awarded:* Baccalaureate, master's.

Accreditation: *Regional:* SACS-Comm. on Coll. *Professional:* art, business, electronic technology, industrial technology, music, nursing, social work, teacher education, theatre

History: Established, chartered, and offered first instruction at postsecondary level 1883; became 4-year institution and changed name to State Teachers College 1929; awarded first degree (baccalaureate) 1931; changed name to Jacksonville State College 1957; adopted present name 1967.

Institutional Structure: *Governing board:* Representation: Board of Trustees comprised of 9 members and 2 ex officio. All voting. *Composition of institution:* Administrators 7 men / 2 women. Academic affairs headed by vice president of academic affairs. Full-time instructional faculty 300. Academic governance body, Jacksonville State University Faculty Senate, meets an average of 12 times per year.

Calendar: Semesters. Academic year Sept. to Aug. Freshmen admitted for all semesters. Degrees conferred and formal commencements Dec., May, Aug. 2005 summer session of 2 terms from June to Aug.

Characteristics of Freshmen: Mean ACT Composite scores men 20.5, women 20.1, class 20.3.

89% of applicants accepted. 59% of accepted applicants enrolled. 85% of freshmen from Alabama. Freshmen from 18 states.

Admission: Rolling admissions plan. For fall acceptance, apply as early as 6 months prior to enrollment, but not later than last day of registration. Early acceptance available. *Requirements:* Graduation from accredited secondary school. GED also accepted. *Entrance tests:* College Board SAT or ACT Composite. For foreign students minimum TOEFL score 500. *For transfer students:* C average; from 4-year accredited institution maximum transfer credit limited only by residence requirement; from 2-year accredited institution 64 hours; correspondence/extension students 12 hours.

College credit and advanced placement for postsecondary-level work completed in secondary school and for extrainstitutional learning on the basis of *The 2006 Guide to the Evaluation of Educational Experiences in the Armed Services.* Occupational Technology program allows up to 36 semester hours for nontraditional experiences.

Degree Requirements: It is the responsibility of each student to become familiar with degree requirements, graduation requirements, and other aspects of satisfactory academic progress. Each student is assigned an academic advisor to assist in planning course schedules and give advice on timely graduation planning. The ultimate responsibility for understanding and completing degree and graduation requirements lies with the student.

Fulfillment of some degree requirements possible by passing departmental examination, College Board CLEP, other standardized tests. *Grading system:* A–F.

Distinctive Educational Programs: Accelerated high school; dual enrollment; distance learning; Internet courses.

ROTC: Army.

Degrees Conferred: 1,081 *baccalaureate:* (B), 484 *master's:* (M): biological/life sciences 28 (B), 5 (M); business/marketing 161 (B), 35 (M); communications/communications technologies 16 (B); computer and information sciences 33 (B), 11 (M); education 347 (B), 346 (M); English 14 (B), 11 (M); health professions and related sciences 83 (B), 9 (M); home economics and vocational home economics 17 (B); liberal arts/general studies 16 (B), 3 (M); mathematics 4 (B), 2 (M); parks and recreation 17 (B); protective services/public administration 142 (B), 45 (M); psychology 35 (B), 10 (M); social sciences and history 68 (B), 5 (M); visual and performing arts 47 (B), 2 (M).

Fees and Other Expenses: *Full-time tuition per semester 2004–05:* undergraduate resident $4,040, nonresident $8,080. *Room per academic year:* $2,00. *Board per academic year:* $1,312. *Required fees:* $20.

Financial Aid: Aid from institutionally generated funds is provided on the basis of academic merit, athletic ability, financial need.

Financial aid to full-time, first-time undergraduate students: need-based scholarships/grants totaling $17,065,790, self-help $17,574,247; non-need-based scholarships/grants $22,488, self-help $13,710,682; athletic awards $1,567,852.

Departments and Teaching Staff: Art *professors* 6, *associate professors* 1, *assistant professors* 1, *instructors* 0, *part-time faculty:* 4; biology 7, 2, 4, 0, 1; communication 1, 1, 1, 2, 1; criminal justice 1, 3, 1, 1, 6; drama 3, 1, 0, 0, 0; dual enrollment 0, 0, 0, 0, 6; education 14, 11, 24, 5, 31; emergency management 0, 1, 1, 0, 5; English 5, 3, 3, 19, 9; family consumer science 0, 1, 1, 2, 2; finance 4, 7, 3, 2, 2; history 0, 0, 0, 0, 1; history and foreign languages 4, 1, 6, 3, 4; learning services 1, 0, 0, 4, 2; management 4, 7, 1, 2, 1; mathematics and computer sciences 6, 7, 3, 17, 3; music 5, 1, 6, 4, 12; nursing 1, 0, 3, 12, 5; physical and earth sciences 6, 6, 1, 2, 1; physical science 3, 1, 2, 0, 4; psychology 5, 0, 2, 1, 5; social work 3, 0, 2, 0, 0; sociology 3, 0, 2, 0, 0; technology 0, 0, 4, 2, 3.

Total instructional faculty: 412 (women 200, men 212; members of minority groups32). Total with doctorate, first-professional, or other terminal degree 220. Student to faculty ratio: 21:1. *Faculty development:* $1,208,888 in grants for research. 3 faculty members awarded sabbaticals 2004–05.

Enrollment: Total enrollment 8,930. Undergraduate full-time 2,397 men / 3,303 women, part-time 582m / 856w; graduate full-time 184m / 318w, part-time 406m / 884w.

Characteristics of Student Body: *Ethnic/racial makeup:* number of Black non-Hispanic: 1,573; American Indian or Alaska Native: 53; Asian or Pacific Islander: 70; Hispanic: 71; White non-Hispanic: 5,081; unknown 205. *Age distribution:* number under 18: 178; 18–19: 1,728; 20–21: 1,868; 22–24: 1,579; 25–29: 734; 30–34: 421; 35–39: 239; 40–49: 299; 50–64: 39; 65 and over: 3.

International Students: 229 nonresident aliens enrolled fall 2004. 41 students from Europe, 62 Asia, Central and South America 56, 51 Africa, 14 Canada, 5 Australia. Programs available to aid students whose native language is not English: Social, cultural. English as a Second Language Program. Financial aid specifically designated for international students: 20 scholarships available annually.

Student Life: On-campus residence halls house 19% of student body. Residence halls men only constitute 26% of such space, for women only 31%. University-operated off-campus housing available for married students. *Intercollegiate athletics:* men only: baseball, basketball, football, golf, tennis, rifle; women only: basketball, rifle, track, volleyball. *Special regulations:* Registered cars with decals permitted. *Special services:* Learning Resources Center, medical services. *Student publications, radio:* Weekly newspaper; yearbook. Radio station WLJS broadcasts 133 hours per week. *Surrounding community:* Jacksonville population 11,000. Birmingham, 80 miles from campus, is nearest metropolitan area. Served by airport 15 miles from campus; passenger rail service 10 miles from campus.

Library Collections: 674,818 volumes including bound books, serial backfiles, electronic documents, and government documents not in separate collections. Online catalog. Current serial subscriptions in paper and microform; 33,319 recordings; 136 computer work stations. Students have access to the Internet at no charge.

Most important special collection: The Alabama Collection; Harry Strange Collection; University Presidents' Papers.

Buildings and Grounds: Campus area 360 acres.

Chief Executive Officer: Dr. William A. Meehan, President.

Address undergraduate admission inquiries to Martha Mitchell, Director of Admissions (infor@jsu.edu); graduate inquires to Dr. William Carr, Dean of the College of Graduate Studies (graduate@jsu.edu).

Judson College

Bibb Street
P.O. Box 120
Marion, Alabama 36756
Tel: (334) 683-5100   **E-mail:** admissions@judson.edu
Fax: (334) 683-5147   **Internet:** www.judson.edu

Institution Description: Judson College is a private church-related (Southern Baptist) liberal arts college for women. *Enrollment:* 360 women. *Degrees awarded:* Baccalaureate. Academic offerings subject to approval by statewide coordinating bodies. Member of Alabama Consortium for the Development of Higher Education.

Accreditation: *Regional:* SACS-Comm. on Coll. *Professional:* music

History: Established as Judson Female Institute, 1838; offered first instruction at postsecondary level 1839; chartered 1841; awarded first degree (baccalaureate) and adopted present name 1904. *See* Louise Manly, *History of Judson College* (Atlanta: Foote and Davies Co., 1913) and Frances Dew Wells Hamilton and Elizabeth Crabtree, *Daughters of the Dream*for further information.

Institutional Structure: *Governing board:* Judson College Board of Trustees. Extrainstitutional representation: 38 trustees. 1 ex officio. 38 voting. *Composition of institution:* Administrators 2 men/3 women. Academic affairs headed by dean. Management/business/finances directed by business manager. Full-time instructional faculty 15 men / 15 women. Academic governance body, the faculty, meets an average of 10 times per year.

Calendar: Semesters. Academic year Sept. to June. Freshmen admitted Sept., Jan., May. Degrees conferred and formal commencement June.

Characteristics of Freshmen: 72% of applicants accepted. 27% of accepted applicants enrolled.

25th percentile: SAT Verbal 500, SAT Math 420; ACT Composite 90, ACT English 20, ACT Math 17. *75th percentile:* SAT Verbal 600, SAT Math 600; ACT Composite 23, ACT English 24, ACT Math 24.

42% of entering freshmen expected to graduate within 5 years. 88% of freshmen from Alabama. Freshmen from 6 states.

Admission: Rolling admissions plan. For fall acceptance apply no later than Aug. 15. *Requirements:* Either graduation from an accredited secondary school with 15 units which must include 12 academic, 4 of them in English; or GED. Graduates of nonaccredited secondary schools may be admitted by passing Judson examinations. *Entrance tests:* ACT Composite preferred; College Board SAT accepted. *For transfer students:* 2.0 minimum GPA.

College credit for extrainstitutional learning on basis of *The 2006 Guide to the Evaluation of Educational Experiences in the Armed Services,* portfolio and faculty assessments, personal interviews. College credit and advanced placement for postsecondary-level work completed in secondary school. Tutoring available.

Degree Requirements: 128 credit hours; 2.0 GPA; 32 semester hours, including 30 of the last 36 hours must be taken in residence; exit competency examination in writing; English language usage required of all first-year students; 1 semester hour physical education distribution requirements, including 9 semester hours English, 9 humanities and 7 hours in mathematics/science. Additional requirements depending on program followed. Some degree requirements can be met by passing College Board CLEP or institutional tests. *Grading system:* A–F.

Distinctive Educational Programs: Work-experience programs. Distance learning program. Accelerated degree program. Preprofessional programs in dentistry, law, medicine, pharmacy, physical therapy.

ROTC: Army in cooperation with Marion Military Institute.

Degrees Conferred: 63 *baccalaureate:* biological/life sciences 8, business/marketing 9; education 5; interdisciplinary studies 2; mathematics 2; philosophy/religion/theology 1; physical sciences 1; protective services/public administration 7; psychology 12; social sciences and history 4; visual and performing arts 5

Fees and Other Expenses: *Full-time tuition per academic year 2004–05:* $8,900. *Room and board per academic year:* $5,850. *Required fees:* $430.

Financial Aid: Aid from institutionally generated funds is provided on the basis of academic merit, financial need, athletic ability.

Financial aid to full-time, first-time undergraduate students: need-based scholarships/grants totaling $1,355,184, self-help $1,027,539, parent loans $163,564, tuition waivers $52,006, athletic awards $118,500; non-need-based scholarships/grants 4237,058, self-help $78,067, parent loans $81,717, tuition waivers $58,300, athletic awards $13,800.

Departments and Teaching Staff: Accounting *professors* 0, *associate professors* 0, *assistant professors* 0, *instructors* 1, *part-time faculty* 1; art 0, 1, 0, 0, 1; biology 1, 1, 0, 0; business 0, 0, 0, 1, 1; chemistry 1, 0, 0, 0, 0; criminal justice 0, 0, 1, 0, 0; education 0, 2, 3, 0, 0; equine science 0, 0, 1, 0, 0; fine and performing arts 0, 0, 0, 1, 0; history 0, 0, 1, 0, 0; journalism 0, 1, 0, 0, 0; mathematics

1, 0, 0, 1, 0; modern foreign language 1, 0, 1, 0, 0; music 2, 0, 1, 0, 0; physics 0, 0, 1, 0, 0; psychology 1, 0, 0, 1, 0; religion 0, 1, 0, 0, 0; web design 0, 0, 0, 2, 0.

Total instructional faculty: 31 (women 24, men 18; members of minority groups 2). Student-to-faculty ratio: 10:1. Total number with highest degree a doctorate, first-professional, or other terminal degree: 27.

Enrollment: Total enrollment 296 full-time; 64 part-time.

Characteristics of Student Body: *Ethnic/racial makeup:* number of Black non-Hispanic: 45; American Indian or Alaska Native: 1; Asian or Pacific Islander: 4; Hispanic: 3; White non-Hispanic: 200; unknown 2. *Age distribution:* number under 18: 5; 18–19: 114; 20–21: 110; 22–24: 28; 25–29: 21; 30–34: 29; 35–39: 18; 40–49: 26; 50–64: 7; 65 and over: 2.

International Students: 5 nonresident aliens enrolled fall 2004. 4 students from Central and South America; 1 Canada.

Student Life: On-campus residence halls house 60% of student body. 40% live at home. *Intercollegiate athletics:* basketball, tennis, volleyball. *Special regulations:* Curfews begin 1pm Sun.–Thurs., 1am Fri. and Sat. Quiet hours from 8pm to 9am. *Student publications: The Conversationalist,* a yearbook; *Scrimshaw,* an annual literary magazine; *The Triangle,* a newspaper published every 3 months. *Surrounding community:* Marion population 5,000. Birmingham, 75 miles from campus, is nearest metropolitan area.

Library Collections: 55,746 volumes. Online catalog. Current serial subscriptions: paper 330; microform 2,035; via electronic access 17,376. 7,248 recordings/tapes. 11 computer work stations. Students have access to the Internet at no charge.

Most important holdings include Judson Collection; J.I. Riddle Collection; Gwen Bristow Collection; Perry County and Marion history.

Buildings and Grounds: Campus area 80 acres. Renovation of Alumnae Auditorium and Jewett Building, Lowder Science building, Marian A. Tucker Hall.

Chief Executive Officer: David E. Potts, President.

Address admission inquiries to Michael Scotto, Director of Admissions (mscotto@judson.edu).

Miles College

5500 Myron Massey Boulevard
Fairfield, Alabama 35064

Tel: (205) 929-1000   **E-mail:** info@miles.edu
Fax: (205) 929-1453   **Internet:** www.miles.edu

Institution Description: Miles College is a private college affiliated with the Christian Methodist Episcopal Church. *Enrollment:* 1,660. *Degrees awarded:* Baccalaureate.

Member of Alabama Consortium for the Development of Higher Education.

Accreditation: *Regional:* SACS-Comm. on Coll. *Professional*: social work

History: Established as Miles Memorial College 1905; offered first instruction at postsecondary level 1907; chartered 1908; awarded first degree (baccalaureate) 1911; adopted present name 1911.

Institutional Structure: *Governing board:* Board of Trustees. Extrainstitutional representation: 22 trustees; institutional representation: president of the college, 1 full-time instructional faculty member, 1 student. 1 ex officio. All voting. *Composition of institution:* Academic affairs headed by vice president for academic affairs. Management/business/finances directed by vice president for administration and finance. Full-time instructional faculty 46.

Calendar: Semesters.

Admission: Rolling admissions plan. Apply no later than registration. *Requirements:* Open admissions for secondary school graduates; GED accepted. *Entrance tests:* ACT Composite. Tutoring available. Developmental courses offered during regular academic year; credit given.

Degree Requirements: 126 credit hours; 2.0 GPA; 32 hours in residence. *Grading system:* A–F; withdraw (deadline after which pass-fail is appended to withdraw).

Distinctive Educational Programs: Work-experience programs, including cooperative education, internships. Evening classes. Facilities and programs for independent research, including honors programs, tutorials, independent study. Cross-registration with University of Alabama in Birmingham.

Degrees Conferred: 219 *baccalaureate:* biological and life sciences 13, business management and administrative services 44, education 63, public administration and services 15, social sciences and history 12.

Fees and Other Expenses: *Full-time tuition per academic year 2004–05:* $5,668. *Room and board per academic year:* $5,074. *Books and supplies:* $875. *Other expenses:* $2,525.

Financial Aid: Aid from institutionally generated funds is provided on the basis of academic merit, financial need, other criteria.

Institution has a Program Participation Agreement with the U.S. Department of Education for eligible students to receive Pell Grants and other federal aid.

Financial aid to full-time, first-time undergraduate students: 87% received federal grants averaging $2,566; 64% state/local grants averaging $675; 55 institutional grants averaging $2,431; 90% loans averaging $2,947.

Departments and Teaching Staff: *Total instructional faculty:* 46. 50% of faculty hold doctorates. Student-faculty ratio: 30:1.

Enrollment: Total enrollment 1,660 (42.8% men, 57.2% women).

Characteristics of Student Body: *Ethnic/racial makeup:* Black non-Hispanic: 98.4%; White non-Hispanic: 1%; unknown .7%.

Student Life: On-campus residence halls, apartments and houses available for single and married students. *Surrounding community:* The college is located in the Birmingham metropolitan area.

Buildings and Grounds: Campus area 34 acres.

Chief Executive Officer: Dr. Albert J. Sloan, II, President. Address admission inquiries to Director of Admissions.

Oakwood College

7000 Adventist Boulevard, NW
Huntsville, Alabama 35896
Tel: (256) 726-7000
Fax: (256) 726-7154

Institution Description: Oakwood College is a private college affiliated with the General Conference of Seventh-day Adventists. *Enrollment:* 1,787. *Degrees awarded:* Associate, baccalaureate.

Accreditation: *Regional:* SACS-Comm. on Coll. *Professional*: teacher education

History: Established as Oakwood Industrial School 1896; changed name to Oakwood Manual Training School 1904; chartered 1907; offered first instruction at postsecondary level and changed name to Oakwood Junior College 1917; became senior college and adopted present name 1944; awarded first degree (baccalaureate) 1945. See Don Neufeld (ed.), *Seventh-day Adventist Encyclopedia* (Washington, D.C.: Review and Herald, 1976) for further information.

Institutional Structure: *Governing board:* The Board of Trustees. Extrainstitutional representation: 38 trustees; institutional representation: president of the college. 1 ex officio. 38 voting. *Composition of institution:* Administrators 13 men / 4 women. Academic affairs headed by dean of academic affairs. Management/business/finances directed by business manager. Full-time instructional faculty 96. Academic governance body, the faculty, meets an average of 9 times per year.

Calendar: Semesters. Academic year Sept. to June. Freshmen admitted Sept. Degrees conferred and formal commencement June. No summer session.

Characteristics of Freshmen: 1,011 applicants. 47.3% were admitted. 84.5% of admitted students enrolled.

58% (234 students) submitted SAT scores; 65% (262 students) submitted ACT scores. *25th percentile*: SAT Verbal 410, SAT Math 380; ACT Composite 16, ACT English 15, ACT Math 15. *75th percentile*: SAT Verbal 550, SAT Math 500; ACT Composite 21, ACT English 22, ACT Math 19.

Freshmen from 40 states and 21 foreign countries.

Admission: For fall acceptance, apply as early as completion of junior year of secondary school, but not later than 2 weeks before registration. Students are notified of acceptance during summer prior to enrollment. *Requirements:* Either graduation from secondary school with 3 units English, 2 mathematics, 2 science, 2 social studies; or GED. Recommend 2 additional units in a foreign language, 2 religion, 1 typing. Minimum GPA 2.0. *Entrance tests:* ACT Composite. For foreign students TOEFL. *For transfer students:* 2.0 GPA; from 4-year accredited institution 156 quarter hours maximum transfer credit; from 2-year accredited institution 96 hours.

College credit and advanced placement for postsecondary-level work completed in secondary school and for extrainstitutional learning (life experience) on basis of portfolio assessment.

Tutoring available. Developmental/remedial courses offered during regular academic year; credit given.

Degree Requirements: *For all associate degrees:* 60 semester hours. *For all baccalaureate degrees:* 128 semester hours; exit competency examination in writing. *For all degrees:* 2.0 GPA; 1 term in residence; weekly chapel attendance; 4 hours physical education; core requirements; attendance at commencement.

Fulfillment of some degree requirements and exemption from some beginning courses possible by passing institutional examinations, College Board CLEP, AP. *Grading system:* A–F; pass-fail; withdraw (carries time limit).

Distinctive Educational Programs: Work-experience programs. Evening classes. Dual-degree programs in architecture and in engineering with Tuskegee

Institute. Cooperative program in veterinary medicine through the consortium. Cross-registration with Alabama Agricultural and Mechanical University, Athens State College, and The University of Alabama at Huntsville. Interdepartmental program in general studies. Facilities and programs for independent research, including individual majors, tutorials. Credit transfer agreement with Home Study Institute, the extension division of the Associated Colleges of Seventh-day Adventists. Study abroad varies. Students may enroll at Oakwood for a master's program in education and/or religion offered by Andrews University.

Degrees Conferred: 16 *associate;* 350 *baccalaureate.* Bachelor's degrees awarded in top five disciplines: business, management, marketing, and related support services 70; education 36; biological and biomedical sciences 34, theology and ministerial studies 33, health professions and related clinical sciences 27.

Fees and Other Expenses: *Full-time tuition per academic year 2004–05:* $11,298. *Room and board per academic year:* $6,374. *Books and supplies:* $1,000.

Financial Aid: Aid from institutionally generated funds is awarded on the basis of academic merit, financial need.

Institution has a Program Participation Agreement with the U.S. Department of Education for eligible students to receive Pell Grants and other federal aid.

Financial aid to full-time, first-time undergraduate students: 47% received federal grants averaging $2,806; 36% state/local grants averaging $635; 71% institutional grants averaging $565; 66% loans to students averaging $5,313.

Departments and Teaching Staff: *Total instructional faculty:* 96. 54% of faculty hold doctorates. Student-to-faculty ratio: 16:1.

Enrollment: Total enrollment 1,797 (41.6% men, 58.4% women). 29.4% of entering freshmen expected to graduate within five years.

Characteristics of Student Body: *Ethnic/racial makeup:* Black non-Hispanic: 88.2%; American Indian or Alaska Native: .3%; Asian or Pacific Islander: .1%; Hispanic: .6%; White non-Hispanic: .6%; unknown 2.1%.

International Students: 143 nonresident aliens enrolled fall 2004.

Student Life: On-campus residence halls house 77% of student body. Residence halls for men only constitute 40% of such space, for women only 60%. 5% of student body live on campus in cooperative houses. All unmarried students are required to live on campus unless they live with parents or relatives in Huntsville. Housing available for married students. 90% of married students request institutional housing; 40% are so housed. *Special regulations:* Cars with decals permitted. Dress must be modest; jewelry not permitted. Curfews. Quiet hours. Residence hall visitation until 10pm Sun.–Thurs., until midnight Fri. and Sat. *Special services:* Learning Resources Center, medical services, buses to and from shopping centers. *Student publications, radio: Spreading Oak,* a biweekly newspaper. Radio station WOCG broadcasts 91 hours per week. *Surrounding community:* Huntsville population 145,000. Birmingham, 100 miles from campus, is nearest metropolitan area. Served by airport 10 miles from campus.

Library Collections: 125,400 volumes. 2,140 microform item; 630 periodical subscriptions; 4,815 recordings/tapes. Online catalog. Students have access to online information retrieval services and the Internet.

Most important holdings include Seventh-day Adventist Black History collection; collection of children's books; 5,000 volumes on black studies.

Buildings and Grounds: Campus area 1,185 acres.

Chief Executive Officer: Delbert W. Baker, President.

Address inquiries to Fred Pullins, Director of Enrollment Management.

Samford University

800 Lakeshore Drive
Birmingham, Alabama 35229
Tel: (205) 726-2011   **E-mail:** admiss@samford.edu
Fax: (205) 726-2171   **Internet:** www.samford.edu

Institution Description: Samford University is a private institution affiliated with the Baptist State Convention. *Enrollment:* 1,774 men / 2,642 women. *Degrees awarded:* Associate, baccalaureate, first-professional (law, pharmacy), master's, doctorate (divinity, education). Specialist certificates in education also awarded.

Member of Marine Environmental Sciences Consortium.

Accreditation: *Regional:* SACS-Comm. on Coll. *Professional:* athletic training, business, law, music, nursing, pharmacy, teacher education

History: Established as Howard College and chartered 1841; awarded first degree (baccalaureate) 1843; adopted present name 1965. *See* Thomas E. Corts, *Samford University At Its Sesquicentennial: Empowered to Bless,* (New York, Newcomen Society, 1991) and James F. Sulzby, Jr., *Toward a History of Samford University* (Birmingham: Samford University Press, 1986) for further information.

Institutional Structure: *Governing board:* Total active trustees, voting members, 43; total honorary trustees, nonvoting 4; total ex officio trustees nonvoting, 2; executive director-treasurer, Alabama Baptist State Convention; president Alabama Baptist State Convention. Full-time instructional faculty 243. Administrative staff: 38 men / 17 women.

Calendar: Semesters. 2004–2005 academic year June to May. Freshmen admitted Sept., Feb., June, July. Degrees conferred May, Aug. Formal commencement May. Summer session of 2 terms from June to Aug.

Characteristics of Freshmen: 88% of applicants accepted. 39% of accepted applicants enrolled.

53% (353 students) submitted SAT scores; 75% (499 students) submitted ACT scores. *25th percentile:* SAT Verbal 500, SAT I Math 510; ACT Composite 22, ACT English 22, ACT Math 20. *75th percentile:* SAT Verbal 620, SAT Math 610; ACT Composite 28, ACT English 29, ACT Math 26. 12 National Merit Scholars.

69% of entering freshmen expected to graduate within 5 years. 40% of freshmen from Alabama. Freshmen from 28 states and 5 foreign countries.

Admission: Rolling admissions plan with priority given for applications received by March 1. High school students may enroll as full-time first-year students one year or more before high school graduation. *Requirements:* Graduation from approved secondary school with 4 units English, 3 math, 3 science (2 of which is lab), 2 social studies, 2 history recommended, 2 foreign language. 2.5 minimum GPA from 4-year accredited institution. *For transfer students:* 2.5 minimum GPA; from 4-year accredited institution; 64 hours must be completed at Samford.

College credit for postsecondary-level work completed in secondary school. Tutoring available.

Degree Requirements: *For all associate degrees:* 64 credit hours. *For all baccalaureate degrees:* 128 credit hours; convocation attendance 8 times per semester; four 1-hour activities courses; general curriculum requirements. *For all undergraduate degrees:* 2.0 GPA on a 4.0 scale. In order to receive a first undergraduate degree, students must earn at least 50 percent of their total credits from Samford. At least 40 credits must be earned in junior-level and senior-level courses.

Fulfillment of some degree requirements and exemption from some beginning courses possible with Advanced Placement, scores of 50 or higher on CLEP credit and International Baccalaureate. *Grading system:* A–F; pass-fail; withdraw (carries time limit).

Distinctive Educational Programs: Accelerated program, cooperative (work-study) program, distance learning, double major, dual enrollment, exchange student program, Independent Study, honors program, internships, teacher certification program, study abroad in British Columbia, Czech Republic, Egypt, England, France, Germany, Italy, Jamaica, Kenya, Nicaragua, Peru Russia, Spain. Extension Division offers training for preachers and church leaders.

ROTC: Air Force in cooperation with Birmingham Southern College, University of Alabama in Birmingham. 4 Air Force commissions awarded in 2004.

Degrees Conferred: 626 *baccalaureate* (B); 140 *master's* (M): area and ethnic studies 3 (B); biological/life sciences 42 (B); business/marketing 120 (B); communications/communications technologies 51 (B); computer and information sciences 4 (B); education 53 (B), 46 (M), 13 (D); engineering and engineering technologies 11 (M); English 26 (B); foreign languages and literature 32 (B); health professions and related sciences 90 (B), 74 (M); home economics and vocational home economics 45 (B); interdisciplinary studies 2 (B); law/legal studies 5 (B), 9 (M); liberal arts/general studies 9 (B); mathematics 9 (B); parks and recreation 6 (B); philosophy/religion/theology 27 (B), 11 (M), 8 (D); physical sciences 3 (B); protective services/public administration 16 (B); psychology 28 (B); social sciences and history 65 (B); visual and performing arts 44 (B). *First professional:* pharmacy 112; law 158; theology 32.

Fees and Other Expenses: *Full-time tuition per academic year 2004–05:* $14,642; graduate varies by program. *Room per academic year:* $2,736. *Board per academic year:* $2,880.

Financial Aid: Aid from institutionally generated funds is provided on the basis of academic merit, financial need, athletic ability. Contact: Ann Campbell (apcampbe@samford.edu).

Financial aid to full-time, first-time undergraduate students: need-based scholarships/grants totaling $5,926,715, self-help $4,505,812, tuition waivers $458,135, athletic awards $893,183; non-need-based schlarships/grants $3,164,482; self-help $3,547,472; parent loans $5,763,144; tuition waivers $760,488; athletic awards $2,225,672. *Graduate aid:* 143 received federal and state-funded fellowships/grants totaling $30,637 (ranging from $108 to $175); 1,028 received federal and state-funded loans totaling $26,918,706 (ranging $2,318 to $3,150); 100 other college-assigned jobs totaling $84,020 (ranging from $52 to $5,385); 655 received other fellowships/grants totaling $3,479,780 (ranging from $21 to $31,920).

Departments and Teaching Staff: *Professors* 99, *associate professors* 68, *assistant professors* 81, *instructors* 22, *part-time faculty* 139.

Total instructional faculty: 406 (women 189, men 217; members of minority groups 34). Total with doctorate, first-professional, or other terminal degree: 258. Student to faculty ratio: 13:1. *Faculty development:* $22,000 in grants for research 2004: $22,000. 6 faculty members awarded sabbaticals 2004–05.

Enrollment: Total enrollment 4,416. Undergraduate full-time 944 men / 708 women; part-time 63m / 141w. First-professional full-time 594m / 549w, part-time 17m / 12w; graduate full-time 66m / 93w, part-time 90m / 139w. *Transfer students:* in-state into lower division 13m / 24w, upper division 2m / 22w; out-of-state into lower division 12m / 28w, upper division 4m / 5w.

Characteristics of Student Body: *Ethnic/racial makeup:* number of Black non-Hispanic: 180; American Indian or Alaska Native: 8; Asian or Pacific Islander: 20; Hispanic: 25; White non-Hispanic: 2,542; unknown 65. *Age distribution:* number under 18: 23; 18–19: 1,227; 22–24: 257; 25–29: 35; 35–39: 12; 40–49: 15; 50–64: 8.

International Students: 32 nonresident aliens enrolled fall 2004. 9 students from Europe, 7 Asia, 1 Latin America, 2 Africa, 2 Canada, 1 Australia, 10 other. No financial aid specifically designated for international students.

Student Life: On-campus residence halls house 65% of student body accommodating 1,860. Unmarried undergraduates 20 years of age and under are required to reside in university housing. Greek-housing on campus. *Intercollegiate athletics:* men: baseball, basketball, cross-country, football, golf, indoor track, tennis, track and field; women: basketball, cross-country, golf, indoor track, tennis, track and field, softball, soccer, volleyball. *Special regulations:* Required meal plan for campus residents; freshmen and sophomores required to live on campus; juniors may reside off campus with parental permission. Cars permitted on campus in designated areas only. Curfews. Quiet hours. *Special services:* Career Development Center, counseling services, Disability Support Services; Student Health Services. *Student publications, radio: The Samford Crimson,* a weekly newspaper; *Entre Nous,* two-issue set of publications (serves as yearbook); *Sojourn Magazine,* published each semester. Radio station WVSU broadcasts 24 hours per day. *Surrounding community:* Birmingham 2000 population 1,052,238. Airport 18 miles from campus; passenger rail service 10 miles from campus.

Library Collections: 607,761 volumes including bound books, serial backfiles, electronic documents, and government documents not in separate collections. Online catalog. Current serial subscriptions: 4,629 paper, microform 851,176, electronic 38,513. 5,680 recordings, 4,071 compact discs, 39 CD-ROM. 580 computer work stations. Students have access to the Internet at no charge. Total budget for books, periodicals, audiovisual materials, microforms 2004–05: $424,476.

Most important holdings include Baptist collection (books, periodicals, manuscripts); Irish Historical Sources (books, periodicals, microfilm); author collections (Masefield, Ruskin, Tennyson).

Buildings and Grounds: Campus area 178 acres. *New buildings:* Samford Science Center completed 2001; Recital Hall to be completed in 2006.

Chief Executive Officer: Dr. Thomas C. Corts, President.

Address admission inquiries to Phil Kimrey, Dean of Admission and Financial Aid (e-mail: admiss@samford.edu).

Howard College of Arts and Sciences

Degree Programs Offered: *Baccalaureate, Master's.*

Departments and Teaching Staff: *Professors* 36, *associate professors* 27, *assistant professors* 25, *instructors* 16, *part-time faculty* 51.

Total instructional faculty: 155.

Distinctive Educational Programs: Interdisciplinary core curriculum and programs in church recreation, communication, computer science, interior design, international business, law enforcement, public administration, public affairs, religious education, congregational studies, environmental management, environmental science and geographic information systems, language and world trade.

Enrollment: Total enrollment 1,003.

School of Business

Degree Programs Offered: *Baccalaureate, master's* in business administration; *master's* in accountancy.

Admission: MBA program requires completion of 3 years of work experience.

Departments and Teaching Staff: Business *professors* 6, *associate professors* 4, *assistant professors* 8, *instructors* 2, *part-time faculty* 6. Total instructional faculty: 27.

Distinctive Educational Programs: Joint M.B.A.-J.D. program with School of Law.

Enrollment: Total enrollment 432.

Orlean Bullard Beeson School of Education

Degree Programs Offered: *Baccalaureate, master's, doctorate* in education.

Departments and Teaching Staff: *Professors* 7, *associate professors* 8, *assistant professors* 7, *part-time faculty* 28. *Total instructional faculty:* 50.

Close cooperation between public school and faculty for laboratory-based field experience; professional portfolios during senior internship; Curriculum Materials Center with updated technology equipment; problem-based learning center; pre-physical therapy major; pre-med major emphasizing fitness, exercise, and nutrition; NATA approved athletic training major; laboratory experience and service learning included in human development and family studies and food service administration majors. Fifth-year master's degree program to enable students who hold a bachelor's degree in a non-teacher education field to become certified. London studies in all majors.

Enrollment: Total enrollment 685.

Beeson Divinity School

Degree Programs Offered: Master of Divinity, Master of Theological Studies, Doctor of Ministry.

Departments and Teaching Staff: *Professors* 8, *associate professors* 5, *assistant professors* 1, *part-time faculty* 4. *Total instructional faculty:* 18.

Enrollment: Total enrollment: 224.

Ida V. Moffett School of Nursing

Degree Programs Offered: *Associate, baccalaureate, master's.*

Admission: Freshmen: 2.5 GPA on a 4.0 scale; ACT 21 or SAT 1000 or NET 74%. Graduate: Admission to Samford University; Bachelor of Science in Nursing or Bachelor of Science with a major in Nursing from a National League for Nursing accredited program; undergraduate cumulative grade point average of at least 2.50 or above on 4.00 scale; Miller's Analogy Test score of 50 or GRE Composite of 1500 or 1000 on the GRE combined; one undergraduate course in basic statistics with a grade of C or better; one undergraduate course in nursing research with a grade of C or better; evidence of one year of successful nursing practice; evidence of current Alabama license to practice as a registered nurse; personal interview with a member of the Graduate faculty.

Departments and Teaching Staff: *Professors* 5, *associate professors* 5, *assistant professors* 15, *instructors* 1, *part-time faculty* 35. *Total instructional faculty:* 35.

Distinctive Educational Programs: Challenge opportunities for LPN/RN; experienced RN option. Graduate program consisting of MSN/Educator, MSN/Manager, MSN/Missionary, MSNMBA, MSN/FNP, and Post NSN/FNP.

Enrollment: Total enrollment: 333.

Cumberland School of Law

Degree Programs Offered: *First-professional.*

Admission: Baccalaureate degree, satisfactory LSAT score.

Degree Requirements: 90 credit hours, 2.0 GPA (on a 4.0 scale).

Departments and Teaching Staff: *Professors* 19, *associate professors* 4, *assistant professors* 3, *instructors* 1, *part-time faculty* 16. *Total instructional faculty:* 43. *Degrees held by full-time faculty:* Professional 100%.

Distinctive Educational Programs: Joint M.B.A.-J.D., M.Div.-J.D., M.Acc.-J.D., M.Acc.-J.D., M.S.-J.D. program with School of Graduate Studies.

Enrollment: Total enrollment 539.

School of Performing Arts

Degree Programs Offered: *Baccalaureate, master's.*

Departments and Teaching Staff: *Professors* 9, *associate professors* 3, *assistant professors* 6, *instructors* 2, *part-time faculty* 15. *Total instructional faculty:* 35.

Enrollment: Total enrollment 153.

School of Pharmacy

Degree Programs Offered: *First-professional.*

Admission: 2.0 GPA (on a 4.0 scale) in mathematics and science courses, 4 semesters pre-pharmacy curriculum.

Degree Requirements: 163 credit hours, 2.0 GPA, 24 months in residence.

Departments and Teaching Staff: *Professors* 9, *associate professors* 12, *assistant professors* 16, *part-time faculty* 1. *Total instructional faculty:* 38. 96% hold terminal degrees.

Enrollment: Total enrollment 588.

Southeastern Bible College

3001 Highway 280 East
Birmingham, Alabama 35243
Tel: (205) 970-9200   **E-mail:** info@sebc.edu
Fax: (205) 970-9207   **Internet:** www.sebc.edu

Institution Description: Southeastern Bible College is a private, independent, nonprofit college. *Enrollment:* 206. *Degrees awarded:* Associate, baccalaureate.

Accreditation: *National institutional:* ABHE. *Professional:* teacher education

History: Founded in 1933 as Birmingham School of the Bible; name changed and first degree awarded 1950.

Institutional Structure: *Governing board:* 16 trustees (extrainstitutional) and president of college. *Composition of institution:* Administrators 6 men. Administrative affairs directed by academic dean. Administration includes president, vice president for academics, vice president for business, dean of students, director of institutional effectiveness and research, director of development.

Calendar: Semesters plus 1 intersession. Academic year early Sept. to May. Freshmen admitted Aug., Jan. Degrees conferred and formal commencement in May.

Characteristics of Freshmen: ACT mean Composite scores men 19.2, women 20.5, class 19.9.

57% of applicants accepted. 44% of accepted applicants enrolled. 50% of entering freshmen expected to graduate within 5 years. 50% of freshmen from Alabama. Freshmen from 9 states and 4 foreign countries.

Admission: Rolling admissions plan. Apply as early as end of junior year in high school. *Requirements:* Graduation from secondary school or GED. *Entrance tests:* ACT or SAT required. *For transfer students:* students transferring from approved institutions will be given credit for courses equivalent to those offered by Southeastern Bible College; only courses with grade of C or above may be transferred.

College credit and advanced placement for postsecondary-level work completed in high school. Remedial English available and often required.

Degree Requirements: *For all baccalaureate degrees:* 127–157 credit hours; 2.0 GPA; minimum 30 hours in residence.

Limited credits accepted via CLEP, AP, correspondence. *Grading system:* A–F; withdraw (pass-fail).

Distinctive Educational Programs: Special audiovisual laboratory for Homiletics courses (12 semester hours available). Majors in Bible and elementary education only with emphases in church education, counseling, missions, music, youth ministry, and general studies.

Degrees Conferred: 27 *baccalaureate:* bible 21, education 6.

Fees and Other Expenses: *Tuition per academic year 2004–05:* $7,500. *Room and board per academic year:* $3,450. *Required fees:* $25. *Books and supplies:* $500.

Financial Aid: Aid from institutionally generated funds is provided on the basis of academic merit and financial need. Institution has a Program Participation Agreement with the U.S. Department of Education for eligible students to receive Pell Grants and other federal aid.

Departments and Teaching Staff: *Total instructional faculty:* 32. Total tenured faculty: 12. Student-to-faculty ratio: 16:2. Degrees held by full-time faculty: Doctorate 66%, master's 33%. 66% hold terminal degrees.

Enrollment: Total enrollment 206. Undergraduate full-time 117men / 89 women, part-time 38m / 12w.

Characteristics of Student Body: *Ethnic/racial makeup:* number of Black non-Hispanic: 41; Asian or Pacific Islander: 2; Hispanic: 2; White non-Hispanic: 209. *Age distribution:* number under 18: 1; 18–19: 40; 20–21 48; 22–24: 53; 25–29: 24; 30–34: 16; 35–39: 14; 40–49: 34; 50–64: 15; 65 and over: 1.

International Students: 2 nonresident aliens from Africa enrolled in fall 2004. No financial aid specifically designated for international students.

Student Life: On-campus residence halls house 30% of student body. Intramural sports. *Special regulations:* Student automobiles must be registered. Chapel attendance required. Dormitory hours regulated. *Special services:* Medical services. *Surrounding community:* The campus is located in a residential section of Birmingham. Served by mass transit bus system; airport 10 miles from campus; passenger rail service 5 miles from campus.

Library Collections: 35,000 volumes. Online and card catalogs. Current serial subscriptions: 194 paper. 18 CD-ROMs. 14 computer work stations.

Buildings and Grounds: Campus area 22 acres.

Chief Executive Officer: Dr. Donald Hawkins, President.

Address admission inquiries to John Patton, Director of Admissions (e-mail: jpatton@sebc.edu).

Southern Christian University

1200 Taylor Road
Montgomery, Alabama 36117
Tel: (334) 387-3877   **E-mail:** admitt@southernchristian.edu
Fax: (334) 387-3878   **Internet:** www.southernchristian.edu

Institution Description: *Enrollment:* 655. *Degrees awarded:* Baccalaureate, master's, doctorate. Certificates also awarded.

Accreditation: *Regional:* SACS-Comm. on Coll.

History: Established in 1967 by Rex A. Turner, Sr. as Alabama Christian School of Religion (ACSR); moved to its present location in 1989; offered first instruction at the third and fourth years of college and awarded a bachelor's degree; expanded curricular programs at ACSR in 1972 to to include a master's program; in 1977 the graduate curricula were expanded to include a three-year program terminating in a Master of Divinity degree; adopted present name in 1991; SCU began offering a Doctor of Ministry program in 1993.

Institutional Structure: *Governing board:* Board of Regents. Representation: 25 regents. *Composition of institution:* SCU is composed of three schools within the university: Dr. Rex Turner, Sr., School of theology; School of Religion; School of Human Services. Academic affairs headed by vice president for academic affairs and each school headed by a dean. Management/business/finances directed by business manager. Full-time instructional faculty 15.

Calendar: Semesters. Academic year late Aug. to late Apr. Degrees conferred each semester. Formal commencement May or June. Summer sessions from early May to mid-Aug.

Characteristics of Freshmen: 90% of applicants accepted. 50% of accepted applicants enrolled. 75% of entering students expected to graduate within 3 years. Students from 38 states and 2 foreign countries.

Admission: Rolling admission plan. *Requirements:* Verification of high school graduation or GED; at least two semesters of college; demonstrated proficiency in computer literacy.

Degree Requirements: For Bachelor of Arts, Bachelor of Science, Master of Science 2.0 GPA. All others 2.5 GPA. No residency requirements; all courses can be taken at a distance; general education requirements; courses required at SCU varies by program.

Fulfillment of some degree requirements possible by passing College Board CLEP; credit by examination; credit for lifetime learning; credit for military service.

Distinctive Educational Programs: All courses taught on campus can also be taken via distance learning. All courses are available online via interactive web instruction. Some courses are videotaped. Live video and audio is streamed over the Internet. SCU's EXCEL program for undergraduates allow students to receive credit for lifetime learning, enabling students to complete their degree at an accelerated rate.

Degrees Conferred: 8 *baccalaureate*; 33 *master's*. Baccalaureate degrees awarded in top two disciplines include: liberal arts and sciences, general studies, and humanities 65; theology and ministerial studies 47.

Fees and Other Expenses: *Full-time tuition per academic year:* $10,040. *Off-campus room and board:* $7,782. *Books and supplies:* $600. *Other expenses:* $1,474.

Financial Aid: Aid from institutionally generated funds is provided on the basis of academic merit, financial need, other criteria. A limited number of scholarships is available. Priority given to early applicants.

Institution has a Program Participation Agreement with the U.S. Department of Education to eligible students to receive Pell Grants and other federal aid.

Departments and Teaching Staff: *Total instructional faculty:* 50. *Degrees held by full-time faculty:* doctorate 68%. Student-to-faculty ratio: 7:1.

Enrollment: Total enrollment 655. Undergraduate 336 (54.5% men, 45.5%women).

Characteristics of Student Body: *Ethnic/racial makeup:* Black non-Hispanic: 24.1%; Hispanic: 2.1%; White non-Hispanic: 66.4%; unknown 7.4%.

Student Life: Southern Christian University is located in close proximity to many large apartment complexes. SCU students are typically older students.

Library Collections: 73,000 volumes including bound books, serial backfiles, electronic documents, and government documents not in separate collections. Online catalog. 120 current serial subscriptions; 500 microform titles; *First Search* program is available online giving students access to many databases, including the Library of Congress and ATLA index plus abstracts and full text of many sources. *Pro-Quest Religion Database* is also available online. SUC is a member of the *American Theological Users Group* (ATUG) that gives students access to the collections of 150 theological schools via an online database.

Buildings and Grounds: Campus area 9 acres. Modern building is adjacent to Interstate 85.

Chief Executive Officer: Dr. Rex A. Turner, Jr., President.

Address admissions inquiries to Rick Johnson, Director of Enrollment Management.

Spring Hill College

4000 Dauphin Street
Mobile, Alabama 36608-1791
Tel: (251) 380-4000 **E-mail:** admit@shc.edu
Fax: (251) 460-2186 **Internet:** www.shc.edu

Institution Description: Spring Hill College is a private college sponsored by the Society of Jesus, Roman Catholic Church. *Enrollment:* 1,427. *Degrees awarded:* Associate, baccalaureate; master's.

Member of Marine Environmental Science Consortium.

Accreditation: *Regional:* SACS-Comm. on Coll.

History: Established and offered first instruction at postsecondary level 1830; first degree (baccalaureate) awarded 1837. Spring Hill College is the third oldest Jesuit college and the first institution of higher education in Alabama. *See* Michael Kenny, *The Torch on the Hill* (New York: The American Press, 1931) for further information.

Institutional Structure: *Governing board:* Board of Trustees. Extrainstitutional representation: President of college, 5 Jesuits, 2 ex officio, 27 non-Jesuits. *Composition of institution:* Administrators 17 men/30 women. Academic affairs headed by the provost and vice president for academic affairs. Management/business/finances directed by vice president for finance. Full-time instructional faculty 69. Academic governance body, Faculty Assembly, meets an average of 6 times per year.

Calendar: Semesters. Academic year Aug. to May. Freshmen admitted Sept., Jan, June. Degrees conferred May, Aug. Formal commencement May. Summer session of 3 terms.

Characteristics of Freshmen: 80% of applicants accepted. 39% of accepted applicants enrolled.

39% (123 students) submitted SAT scores; 40% (281 students) submitted ACT scores. *25th percentile:* SAT Verbal 510, SAT Math 490; ACT Composite 21, ACT English 21, ACT Math 19. *75th percentile:* SAT Verbal 620, SAT Math 620; ACT Composite 27, ACT English 29, ACT Math 26.

61% of entering freshmen expected to graduate within 5 years. 38% of freshmen from Alabama. Freshmen from 26 states and 1 foreign country.

Admission: Rolling admissions plan. For fall acceptance, apply as early as Sept. 1 of previous year, but not later than July 1 of year of enrollment. Students are notified of acceptance within 1 month. *Requirements:* Either graduation from approved secondary school with 16 units which must include 4 English, 3 mathematics, 1 history, 3 science, 2 social science, and 3 academic electives; or GED. Counselor recommendation. 4 additional units (electives) recommended. Minimum GPA 2.0. *Entrance tests:* College Board SAT I or ACT Composite. *For transfer students:* All students 2.5 minimum GPA. Students from 4-year institution 96 semester hours maximum transfer credit; from 2-year institution 64 semester hours credit.

College credit and advanced placement for postsecondary-level work completed in secondary school and for satisfactory scores on ACT, College Board SAT, CLEP, APP. Advanced placement for extrainstitutional learning on basis of portfolio and faculty assessments. College credit for extrainstitutional learning on basis of *The 2006 Guide to the Evaluation of Educational Experiences in the Armed Services.* Tutoring available. Remedial courses offered in regular academic year and summer session; credit given.

Degree Requirements: 128 credit hours; 2.0 GPA; 24 of last 30 hours in residence, comprehensives in individual fields of study. Some degree requirements can be fulfilled by taking achievement tests for maximum credit of 30 semester hours. Exemption from most freshman courses possible by passing CLEP, offered 3rd week of every month. *Grading system:* A–F, pass-fail, withdraw (carries time limit).

Distinctive Educational Programs: Internships with approval of department chairman. Flexible meeting places and schedules. Weekend and evening classes. Accelerated degree programs. Dual-degree programs in engineering with Auburn University and the University of Alabama at Birmingham, University of Florida, Marquette University, and Texas A&M University. 3+3 bachelor's/master's dual-degree programs in physical science therapy and occupational therapy with Rockhurst University and Nova Southeastern University. Interdisciplinary program in humanities. Facilities and programs for independent research, individual majors, tutorials. Courses in marine environmental sciences through consortium. Government internships: Washington semester program in cooperation with American University (D.C.) and "Washington Winterim"(D.C.). Summer tour and study abroad in various countries in cooperation with the Cooperative Center for Study Abroad.

ROTC: Army and Air Force in cooperation with the University of South Alabama.

Degrees Conferred: 267 *baccalaureate* (B); 52 *master's* (M): biological/life sciences 23 (B); business/marketing 67 (B), 14 (M); communications/communication technologies 24 (B); education 28 (B), 15 (M); English 22 (B); foreign languages and literature 2 (B); health professions and related sciences 15 (B); interdisciplinary studies 14 (B); liberal arts/general studies 8 (B), 3 (M); mathematics 1 (B); philosophy/religion/theology 7 (B), 20 (M); psychology 29 (B); social sciences and history 12 (B); visual and performing arts 11 (B).

Fees and Other Expenses: *Full-time tuition per academic year 2004–05:* $19,658; graduate tuition varies by program. *Books and supplies:* $900. *Required fees:* $1,240. *Room and board per academic year:* $7,730.

Financial Aid: Aid from institutionally generated funds is provided on the basis of academic merit, financial need, athletic ability, other criteria. Institution has a Program Participation Agreement with the U.S. Department of Education for eligible students to receive Pell Grants and other federal aid.

Financial aid to full-time, first-time undergraduate students: need-based scholarships/grants totaling $9293,351, self-help $2,922,965, parent loans $427,455, athletic awards $466,757; non-need-based scholarships/grants $2,961,269, self-help $1,996,999, parent loans $1,694,071, athletic awards $695,178.

Departments and Teaching Staff: English *professors* 3, *associate professors* 2, *assistant professors* 3, *instructors* 1, *part-time faculty* 6; languages 1, 0, 1, 1, 5; philosophy 2, 1, 2, 0, 0; theology 4, 0, 2, 0, 6; biology 0, 3, 1, 0, 0; chemistry 0, 0, 2, 0, 2; mathematics 2, 0, 1, 0, 3; physics 1, 0, 0, 0, 0; history 2, 0, 2, 0, 4; political science 1, 1, 1, 0, 0; psychology 1, 2, 0, 0, 3; sociology 1, 0, 0, 0, 2; business 2, 3, 3, 1, 11; communication arts 1, 1, 0, 2, 3; fine arts 1, 1, 0, 1, 6; performing arts 0, 1, 0, 0, 1; teacher 1, 0, 3, 0, 5; nursing 1, 2, 2, 0, 2; interdisciplinary studies 0, 0, 0, 0, 3.

Total instructional faculty: 131 (women 55, men 76; members of minority groups 8). Total with doctorate, first-professional, or other terminal degree: 83. Student-to-faculty ratio: 13:1. *Faculty development:* 4 faculty members granted sabbaticals 2004–05.

Enrollment: Total enrollment 1,427. Full-time 1,040; part-time 337.

Characteristics of Student Body: *Ethnic/racial makeup:* number of Black non-Hispanic: 172; American Indian or Alaska Native: 10; Asian or Pacific Islander: 15; Hispanic: 72; White non-Hispanic: 895; unknown 32. *Age distribution:* number under 18: 9; 18–19: 56; 20–21: 403; 22–24: 99; 25–29: 47; 30–34: 42; 35–39: 28; 40–49: 38; 50–64: 27; 65 and over: 3.

International Students: 10 nonresident aliens enrolled fall 2004. 2 students from Europe, 1 Asia, 13 Latin America, 1 Africa. No programs available to aid students whose native language is not English. No financial aid specifically designated for international students.

Student Life: On-campus residence halls house 79% of student body. Residence halls for men only 12% of such space, for women only 19%. Coed residence halls and apartments constitute 69% of this space. 27% of men and women join fraternities/sororities. All single students must live on campus or with parents except in certain rare instances, and then only with approval of the vice president of student affairs/dean of students. *Intercollegiate athletics:* men only: baseball, basketball, soccer, tennis, golf, cross-country, swimming; women only: basketball, cross-country, golf, tennis, soccer, softball, swimming, basketball, volleyball. Men's rugby, lacrosse, coed crew (rowing), and coed ultimate frisbee are club sports. *Special regulations:* Cars permitted. *Special services:* Medical services. *Student publications, radio, television:* Springhillian, a weekly newspaper; *The Motley,* a biannual literary magazine; *The Torch,* school yearbook. WHIL, a professional full-range FM radio station, broadcasts 133 hours per week. *Surrounding community:* Mobile metropolitan area population 540,000. New Orleans, La., 150 miles from campus, is nearest metropolitan area. Served by mass transit bus system; airport 10 miles from campus.

Publications: Sources of information about Spring Hill College include the college's *Bulletin of Information, Spring Hill Alumni Magazine,* and the Admissions *Viewbook.*

Library Collections: 180,404 volumes. Online and card catalogs. Current serial subscriptions: 2,195 paper; 305,470 microform; 1,494 audiovisual materials; 12,506 e-books. Access to various online information retrieval services. Students have access to the Internet at no charge.

Most important holdings include rare book collection, Mobiliania, archives including Jesuit House materials and the personal papers of Father Steve Foley, S.J., and Father Abram Ryan.

Buildings and Grounds: Campus area 450 acres. Marie and John Burke Memorial Library completed 2004.

Chief Executive Officer: Rev. Gregory F. Lucey, S.J., President.

Undergraduates address admission inquiries to Steve Pochard, Dean of Admissions (spochard@shc.edu); graduate inquiries to Joyce Genz, Dean of Lifelong Leaning and Director of Graduate Programs (jgenz@shc.edu).

Stillman College

3601 Stillman Boulevard
Tuscaloosa, Alabama 35403
Tel: (205) 349-4240   **E-mail:** admissions@stillman.edu
Fax: (205) 366-8996   **Internet:** www.stillman.edu

Institution Description: Stillman College is a private, historically black, four-year institution affiliated with the Presbyterian Church (USA) and the College Fund/UNCF. *Enrollment:* 1,200. *Degrees awarded:* Baccalaureate.

Accreditation: *Regional:* SACS-Comm. on Coll. *Professional:* teacher education

History: Established as Tuscaloosa Institute 1876; incorporated as Stillman Institute 1895; became junior college 1937; became 4-year institution and adopted present name 1948; awarded first degree (baccalaureate) 1951.

Institutional Structure: *Governing board:* Board of trustees. Extrainstitutional representation: 30 trustees; institutional representation: president of the college. Academic affairs headed by vice president for academic affairs. Management/business/finances directed by vice president for business and finance. Full-time instructional faculty 36.

Calendar: Semesters.

Characteristics of Freshmen: 50.1% of applicants admitted. 33.1% admitted students enrolled full-time.

15% (54 students) submitted SAT scores; 68% (245 students) submitted ACT scores. *25th percentile:* SAT Verbal 310, SAT Math 320; ACT Composite 15, ACT English 15, ACT Math 15. *75th percentile:* SAT Verbal 420, SAT Math 430; ACT Composite 19, ACT English 17, ACT Math 19.

77% of freshmen from Alabama. Freshmen from 16 states. 29.9% of entering freshmen expected to graduate in five years.

Admission: Ongoing acceptance of applications. *Requirements:* Graduation from accredited secondary school or GED. Recommended units: 4 in English, 1 mathematics, 1 science. *Entrance tests:* ACT Composite or College Board SAT.

Degree Requirements: 124 credit hours; 2.0 GPA on 4.0 scale; final year in residence. *Grading system:* A–F; N (no credit), WP (withdrawn while passing), WF (withdrawn while failing); WD (withdrawn), W (administrative withdrawal).

Degrees Conferred: 172 *baccalaureate.* Degrees conferred in top five disciplines include: business management, marketing, and related support services 69; education 27; history 22; English language and literature/letters 18; biological and biomedical sciences 15.

Fees and Other Expenses: *Full-time tuition per academic year 2004–05:* $9,550. *Room and board per academic year:* $4,949. *Books and supplies:* $750. *Other expenses:* $1,675.

Financial Aid: Aid from institutionally generated funds is provided on the basis of academic merit, financial need. Institution has a Program Participation Agreement with the U.S. Department of Education for eligible students to receive Pell Grants and other federal aid.

Financial aid to first-time, full-time undergraduate students: 48% federal grants averaging $2,640; 49% state/local grants averaging $330; 58% institutional grants averaging $1,500; 59% loans averaging $2,265.

Departments and Teaching Staff: Business administration *professors* 1, *associate professors* 1, *assistant professors* 3, *instructors* 0, *part-time teachers* 12; education 2, 1, 1, 0, 2; physical education 2, 1, 1, 2; social sciences 3, 3, 0, 0, 2; English 3, 2, 6, 2, 0; communications 0, 2, 1, 0, 1; religion 0, 2, 0, 0, 0; fine arts 1, 2, 2, 0, 1; biology 3, 1, 2, 0, 1; chemistry 0, 1, 1, 0, 0; computer science 0, 0, 1, 0, 0; mathematics 0, 1, 3, 1, 0; physics 1, 0, 0, 0, 0.

Total instructional faculty: 52. 70% of faculty hold doctorates. Student-to-faculty ratio: 27:1.

Enrollment: Total enrollment 1,200 (46.8% men, 53.3% women).

Characteristics of Student Body: *Ethnic/racial makeup:* Black non-Hispanic: 97.6%; White non-Hispanic: 1.3%; Asian or Pacific Islander: .2%; Hispanic: .3%; unknown: .3%.

International Students: 35 nonresident aliens enrolled fall 2004. Programs available for students whose native language is not English: Social, cultural.

Student Life: On-campus residence halls and apartments available. Intramural sports. *Surrounding community:* Tuscaloosa population 76,000.

Library Collections: 113,200 volumes. 7,245 microforms; 3,550 audiovisual materials; 360 current periodical subscriptions. Access to online information retrieval services. Students have access to the Internet at no charge.

Most important holdings include African American Collection.

Buildings and Grounds: Campus area 100 acres.

Chief Executive Officer: Dr. Ernest McNealey, President.

Address admission inquiries to Mason Bonner, Director of Admissions.

Talladega College

627 West Battle Street
Talladega, Alabama 35160
Tel: (256) 362-0206   **E-mail:** admissions@talladega.edu
Fax: (256) 761-9206   **Internet:** www.talladega.edu

Institution Description: Talladega College is a private, nonprofit college affiliated with the United Church of Christ. *Enrollment:* 362. *Degrees awarded:* Baccalaureate.

Accreditation: *Regional:* SACS-Comm. on Coll. *Professional:* social work

History: Established as a primary school 1867; normal school training began 1868; incorporated 1869; chartered 1889; offered first instruction at postsecondary level 1890; first degree (baccalaureate) awarded 1895.

Institutional Structure: *Governing board:* Talladega College Board of Trustees. Extrainstitutional representation: 25 trustees (including 6 alumni), 2 emeritus members, 2 institutional representatives, 2 ex officio. 25 voting. *Composition of institution:* Administrators 3 male / 2 female. Academic affairs headed by provost/vice president for academic affairs. Management/business/financial affairs directed by vice president. Full-time instructional faculty 38. Academic governance body, the faculty, meets an average of 9 times per year.

Calendar: Semesters. Academic year Aug. to May. Freshmen admitted Aug., Jan., June. Degrees conferred and formal commencement May.

Characteristics of Freshmen: Mean ACT Composite class score 17.

23% of applicants accepted. 31% of accepted applicants enrolled. 56% of entering freshmen expected to graduate within 5 years. 59% of freshmen from Alabama. Freshmen from 13 states and 1 foreign country.

Admission: Rolling admissions plan. For fall acceptance, apply as early as beginning of junior year of secondary school, but not later than June 15. Early acceptance available. *Requirements:* Either graduation from approved secondary school with 4 units in English, 4 history, 4 mathematics, 4 science; or GED. Minimum GPA 2.0. Lowest acceptable secondary school class standing 40th percentile. *Entrance tests:* College Board SAT or ACT Composite. *For transfer students:* 2.0 minimum GPA; 60 hours maximum transfer credit.

College credit and advanced placement for postsecondary-level work completed in secondary school. Tutoring available. Developmental reading and writing courses offered.

Degree Requirements: 123 credit hours; 2.0 GPA in major; 2 years in residence; two 1-credit physical education courses during freshman year; general education requirements. *Grading system:* A–F; withdraw (carries time limit and deadline after which pass-fail is appended to withdraw); incomplete.

Distinctive Educational Programs: Flexible meeting places and schedules. Dual-degree programs in biomedical science with Meharry Medical College (TN); in engineering with Auburn University; in engineering, nursing, and veterinary medicine with Tuskegee Institute; in pharmacy with Florida Agricultural and Mechanical University. Cooperative programs in engineering, physics, and veterinary medicine through ACHE. Interdisciplinary courses in energy and politics, blacks in American society and culture. Honors programs. Individual majors. Tutorials.

ROTC: Army. Joint program with Jacksonville State University.

Degrees Conferred: 69 *baccalaureate:* biological/life sciences 12; business/marketing 14; communications/communication technologies 1; computer and information sciences 10; education 3; English 3; physical sciences 5; psychology 13; social sciences and history 6; visual and performing arts 2.

Fees and Other Expenses: *Full-time tuition per academic year 2004–05:* $6,720. *Room and board per academic year:* $4,420. *Required fees:* $408. *Books and supplies:* $1,000.

Financial Aid: Aid from institutionally generated funds is provided on the basis of academic merit, financial need, athletic ability. *Contact:* Michael Francois (mfrancois@talladega.edu). Institution has a Program Participation Agreement with the U.S. Department of Education for eligible students to receive Pell Grants and other federal aid.

Financial aid to full-time, first-time undergraduate students: need-based scholarships/grants totaling $1,191,559, self-help $941,226; non-need-based scholarships/grants totaling $804,331, self-help $440,257, parent loans $169,409, tuition waivers $64,120, athletic awards $79,468.

Departments and Teaching Staff: Art *professors* 0, *associate professors* 1, *assistant professors* 0, *instructors* 0, *part-time faculty* 0; biology 1, 0, 1, 0, 0; business administration 1, 0, 1, 0, 0; chemistry 2, 0, 0, 0, 0; communications 0, 2, 3, 0, 0; computer science 0, 0, 1, 0, 0; education 1, 1, 0, 0, 0; English 1, 0, 0, 0, 0; finance and economics 1, 0, 0, 0, 0; fine arts 1, 0, 0, 0, 0; foreign languages 0, 0, 0, 0, 1; history 0, 1, 0, 0, 0; humanistic studies 1, 0, 0, 0, 0; marketing 1, 0, 0, 0, 0; mathematics 0, 0, 0, 0, 1; music 0, 0, 1, 0, 0; philosophy 1, 0, 0, 0, 0; physical education 0, 0, 1, 0, 0; physics 0, 3, 0, 0, 0; psychology 0, 0, 0, 0, 1; public administration 1, 0, 0, 0, 0; social work 1, 0, 2, 0, 0; sociology 1, 0, 2, 0, 0.

Total instructional faculty: 45 (women 17, men 28; members of minority groups 32). Total with doctorate, first-professional, or other terminal degree 21. Student to faculty ratio: 8:1.

Enrollment: Total enrollment 362.

Characteristics of Student Body: *Ethnic/racial makeup:* number of Black non-Hispanic: 353; Hispanic: 1; White non-Hispanic: 1; unknown 7. *Age distribution:* number under 18: 7; 18–19: 109; 20–21: 125; 22–24: 40; 25–29: 46; 30–34: 15; 35–39: 2; 40–49: 1; 50–64: 2; 65 and over: 1.

International Students: 20 nonresident aliens enrolled fall 2004. No programs available for students whose native language is not English. No financial aid specifically designated for international students.

Student Life: On-campus residence halls house 71% of student body. 3 female and 2 male residence halls. *Intercollegiate athletics:* men only: basketball; women only: basketball. *Special regulations:* Cars permitted without restrictions. Quiet hours from 8pm to 8am. Residence hall visitation from 6pm to 10pm. *Special services:* Medical services. *Student publications: Amistad,* a yearbook; *The Talladega Student Star,* a student newspaper. *Surrounding community:* Talladega population 20,000. Birmingham, 60 miles from campus and Atlanta, 125 miles from campus, are nearest metropolitan areas. Served by airport 20 miles from campus; passenger rail service 20 miles from campus.

Library Collections: 127,158 volumes. Online and card catalogs. audiovisual materials; 100 current periodical subscriptions. Access to online information retrieval services and the Internet at no charge. 25 computer work stations.

Most important special holdings include archives collection; Schamburg Collection; Black Studies Collection.

Buildings and Grounds: Campus area 130 acres. Campus has been declared a National Historic Site by the U.S. Department of the Interior; Swayne Hall is a National Historic Landmark.

Chief Executive Officer: Dr. Oscar Prater, Interim President.

Address admission inquiries to Florence Sanders, Vice President for Student Affairs (fsanders@talladega.edu).

Troy State University

University Avenue
Troy, Alabama 36082
Tel: (334) 670-3100   **E-mail:** bstar@@trojan.troyst.edu
Fax: (334) 670-3774   **Internet:** www.troyst.edu

Institution Description: Troy State University is a public institution with branch campuses at Dothan and Montgomery. *Enrollment:* 17,613. *Degrees awarded:* Associate, baccalaureate, master's. Certificates, including specialist in education, also awarded.

Accreditation: *Regional:* SACS. *Professional:* accounting, athletic training, business, counseling, music, nursing, social work, teacher education

History: Established and chartered as Troy State Normal School and offered first instruction at postsecondary level 1887; awarded first degree (associate) 1889; changed name to Troy State Teachers College 1929, to Troy State College 1957; adopted present name 1967.

Institutional Structure: *Governing board:* Troy State University Board of Trustees. Representation: 10 trustees, including 1 non-voting student, Governor of Alabama. 2 ex officio. *Composition of institution:* Administrators 7 men / 1 woman. Academic affairs headed by Provost. Management/business/finances directed by Vice President for Financial Affairs. Full-time instructional faculty 209. Academic governance bodies, Academic and Graduate Councils, each meet an average of 12 times per year.

Calendar: Semesters. Academic year Aug. to May. Freshmen admitted Aug., Jan., and May. Degrees conferred and formal commencement Dec., May, and Aug. Summer session of 3 terms from June to Aug.

Characteristics of Freshmen: 4,073 applicants of which 67.5% admitted; 36.9% of admitted students enrolled full-time.

91% (921 students) submitted ACT scores. *25th percentile:* ACT Composite 17, ACT English 17, ACT Math 16. *75th percentile:* ACT Composite 23, ACT English 25, Math 22.

52.1% of entering freshmen expected to graduate within 5 years. 90% of freshmen from Alabama. Freshmen from 23 states and 16 foreign countries.

Admission: Rolling admissions plan. Early acceptance available. *Requirements:* Either graduation from accredited secondary school with 3 units English, 12 other academic units; or GED. Minimum grade average C. *Entrance tests:* College Board SAT or ACT Composite. For foreign students TOEFL. *For transfer students:* C average; from 2- or 4-year accredited institution.

College credit for postsecondary-level work completed in secondary school and for extrainstitutional learning basis of ACE *2006 Guide to the Evaluation of Educational Experiences in the Armed Services.* Tutoring available. Remedial course offered in summer session and regular academic year; credit given.

Degree Requirements: *For all associate degrees:* 60 semester hours; 30 hours, including 15 in major field, in residence. *For all undergraduate degrees:* 2.0 GPA on a 4.0 scale; general studies program.

Fulfillment of some baccalaureate degree requirements possible by passing departmental examinations, College Board CLEP. *Grading system:* A–F; withdraw; incomplete.

Distinctive Educational Programs: Flexible meeting places and schedules, including off-campus centers (at military bases in U.S. and in Europe and at Faulkner State Junior College), weekend and evening classes. Facilities for independent research, including honors programs, individual majors, tutorials. Accelerated degree programs. Distance learning; double major; English as a Second Language program; independent study; Teacher Certification Program.

ROTC: Air Force.

Degrees Conferred: 299 *associate;* 1,309 *baccalaureate;* 2,603 *master's.* Bachelor's degrees awarded in top five disciplines: business, management marketing, and related support services 443; security and protective services 174; education 140; computer and information sciences and support service 113; psychology 77.

Fees and Other Expenses: *Full-time tuition per academic year 2004–05:* in-state resident $4,162; out-of-state $8,012. *Room and board per academic year:* $4,812. *Books and supplies:* $860. *Other expenses:* $2,919.

Financial Aid: Aid from institutionally generated funds is provided on the basis of academic merit, athletic ability. Institution has a Program Participation Agreement with the U.S. Department of Education for eligible students to receive Pell Grants and other federal aid.

Financial aid to full-time, first-time undergraduate students: 33% federal grants averaging $2,964; 1% state/local grant worth $1,455; 39% institutional grants averaging $3,830; 55% loans averaging $2,603.

Departments and Teaching Staff: *Total instructional faculty:* 209. 146 faculty members hold doctorates. Student-to-faculty ratio: 17:1.

Enrollment: Total enrollment 17,613. Full-time 2,360 men / 3,895 women.

Characteristics of Student Body: *Ethnic/racial makeup:* Black non-Hispanic: 28.8%; American Indian or Alaska Native: .6%; Asian or Pacific Islander1.1%; Hispanic: 4%; White non-Hispanic: 56.6%; unknown: 6.2%.

International Students: 476 nonresident aliens enrolled fall 2004. English as a Second Language Program. Social and cultural programs available.

Student Life: On-campus residence halls house 30% of student body. Housing for available for married students. 20% of men join fraternities and 20% of women join sororities. *Intercollegiate athletics:* men only: basketball, golf, softball, tennis, track; women only: basketball, golf, softball, track, volleyball. *Special regulations:* Registered cars permitted without restrictions. *Special services:* Learning Resources Center, medical services. *Student publications: Palladium,* a yearbook; *Tropolitan,* a weekly newspaper. Television station WTSU broadcasts 10 hours per week. *Surrounding community:* Troy population 15,000. Montgomery, 50 miles from campus, is nearest metropolitan area. Served by airport 60 miles from campus.

Library Collections: 319,500 volumes. 1,362,100 microforms; 10,065 audiovisual materials; 4,190 current periodicals. Online and card catalogs. Students have access to the Internet at no charge.

Buildings and Grounds: Campus area 577 acres.

Chief Executive Officer: Dr. Jack Hawkins, Jr., Chancellor.

Undergraduates address admission inquiries to Buddy Starling, Dean of Enrollment Management (e-mail: bstar@trojan.troyst.edu); graduate inquiries to Brenda Campbell, Director of Graduate Admissions (e-mail: bcampbell@trojan.troyst.edu).

Troy State University Dothan

500 University Drive
Dothan, Alabama 36304
Tel: (334) 983-6556   **E-mail:** ariversjr@tsud.edu
Fax: (334) 983-6322   **Internet:** www.tsud.edu

Institution Description: Troy State University Dothan (TSUD), a member of the Troy State University System, is a nonprofit, state-assisted institution. TSUD is a comprehensive, coeducational, commuter university. A branch campus is located on the military base at Fort Rucker, and the Continuing Education Center is located at Northside Mall in Dothan. *Enrollment:* 1,998. *Degrees awarded:* Associate, baccalaureate, master's. Education Specialist also awarded.

Accreditation: *Regional:* SACS-Comm. on Coll. *Professional:* business, teacher education

History: Established as a resident center at Fort Rucker in 1961 and was named Troy State University at Fort Rucker in 1967; began offering classes in Dothan 1974; became Troy State University at Dothan/Fort Rucker 1975;

changed name to Troy State University at Dothan 1986; adopted present name 1996.

Institutional Structure: *Governing board:* Troy State University Board of Trustees. 9 members, 2 ex officio, 1 nonvoting student member. *Composition of institution:* 2 full-time administrators, 3 deans. Full-time instructional faculty 53.

Calendar: Semesters. Academic year Aug. to Aug. Applications continually accepted; quarterly admissions. Formal commencements at end of fall and spring semesters.

Characteristics of Freshmen: 2% submitted SAT scores; 100% submitted ACT scores. *25th percentile*: ACT Composite 20, ACT English 20, ACT Math 19. *75th percentile*: ACT Composite 24, ACT English 26, ACT Math 24.

66.5% of applicants accepted. 70.1% of accepted applicants enrolled. 99% of freshmen from Alabama.

Admission: *Requirements:* Unconditional admission for beginning freshmen. ACT or 910 SAT and a minimum GPA of 2.0 (4.0 scale). Official high school transcript with minimum of 23 Carnegie units, all in academic courses, including three or more units in English. Applicants who are 21 years of age or older not required to submit ACT/SAT for admission. Transfer students must be in good standing at last college attended and have an overall GPA of 2.0 (4.0 scale) on all college work attempted. Technical and remedial/developmental work is not considered in GPA. Unconditional admission to Graduate School requires a baccalaureate degree from an accredited four-year institution, and a minimum overall undergraduate GPA of 2.5 (4.0 scale) or a 3.0 average for the last 45 quarter hours. Students must also meet the unconditional requirements of the department program. Additional admissions statuses available.

Degree Requirements: *For baccalaureate degree:* 180 to 236 quarter hours; 90 quarter hours of tradition credits, 45 of which must have been completed at Troy State University Dothan; 20 quarter hours must be completed in residence. Junior college transfers must earn a minimum of 50% of all degree program hours with a senior college.

Distinctive Educational Programs: Highly flexible scheduling through day evening and weekend classes; interim and mini-term sessions; telecourses; workshops.

Degrees Conferred: *Baccalaureate* (B), *master's* (M): biological/life sciences 6 (B); business/marketing 103 (B), 30 (M); computer and information sciences 27 (B); education 27 (B), 50 (M), 18 (D); English 6 (B); mathematics 1 (B); physical sciences 1 (B), protective services/public administration 25 (B); psychology 27 (B), 14 (M); social sciences and history 16 (B), 1 (M)

Fees and Other Expenses: *Full-time tuition per academic year 2004–05:* undergraduate $3,850 resident, $7,700 nonresident; graduate resident $4,200; nonresident $8,400. *Required fees:* $312.

Financial Aid: Institution has a Program Participation Agreement with the U.S. Department of Education for eligible students to receive Pell Grants and other federal aid. Undergraduate need-based scholarships/grants: $2,098,393 (federal $2,088,393; state $10,000); self-help $10,177,334 (student loans $10,081,034; federal work-study $96,300).

Departments and Teaching Staff: College of Arts and Sciences *professors* 6, *associate professors* 7, *assistant professors* 2, *instructors* 7; *part-time faculty* 24; School of Business 6, 4, 7, 2, 15; School of Education 5, 4, 5, 4, 20.

Total instructional faculty: 116 (women 48, men 58; members of minority groups 70). Total with doctorate, first-professional, or other terminal degree: 58. Student to faculty ratio: 15:1.

Enrollment: Total enrollment 1,998. Undergraduate full-time 231 men / 521 women, part-time 267m / 519w; graduate full-time 19m / 71w, part-time 60m / 206. *Transfer students:* in-state 346; from out-of-state 30.

Characteristics of Student Body: *Ethnic/racial makeup:* number of Black non-Hispanic: 342; American Indian or Alaska Native: 16; Asian or Pacific Islander: 20; Hispanic: 34; White non-Hispanic: 1,089; unknown 37. *Age distribution:* number of 18–19: 107; 20–21: 224; 22–24: 287; 25–29: 316; 30–34: 231; 35–39: 130; 40–49: 194; 50–64: 67; 65 and over: 2.

International Students: No programs available to aid students whose native language is not English. No financial aid specifically designated for international students.

Student Life: Commuter institution with active student clubs, organizations, and honor societies. Student representation on Administrative Council, and most policy/procedure committees.

Library Collections: 102,968 volumes including bound books, serial backfiles, electronic documents, and government documents not in separate collections. Online catalog. Current serial subscriptions: 403 paper. 115 CD-ROMs. 8 computer work stations. Students have access to the Internet at no charge. Total budget for books, periodicals, audiovisual materials, microforms 2004–05: $155,000.

Most important special holdings include papers of Alabama Congressman Terry Everett; National Peanut Festival Collection; Dixie Railway Depot Reports.

Buildings and Grounds: Campus area 225 acres. Library and Technology Building completed 2002; Science Lab completed 2004.

Chief Executive Officer: Bob Willis, Interim Vice Chancellor.

Address undergraduate admission inquiries to Andrew Rivers, Coordinator of Undergraduate Admissions (ariversjr@tsud.edu); graduate inquiries to Reta Cordell, Director of Graduate Admissions (rcordell@tsud.edu).

Troy State University Montgomery

231 Montgomery Street
Montgomery, Alabama 36103-4419

Tel: (334) 241-9506   **E-mail:** frabe@tsum.edu
Fax: (334) 241-9714   **Internet:** www.tsum.edu

Institution Description: Troy State University Montgomery offers programs in education for working adults. *Enrollment:* 3,758. *Degrees awarded:* Associate, baccalaureate, master's.

Academic offers subject to approval by statewide coordinating bodies. Budget subject to approval by state governing boards.

Accreditation: *Regional:* SACS-Comm. on Coll. *Professional:* business

Calendar: Semesters.

Admission: *Requirements:* Graduation from secondary school with at least 7 units; C average accepted.

Degree Requirements: Completion of prescribed curriculum.

Distinctive Educational Programs: Classes conducted after working hours in various civilian and military facilities.

Degrees Conferred: 73 *associate:* 275 *baccalaureate*; 209 *master's*. Baccalaureate degrees awarded in top five disciplines include: business, management, marketing, and related support services 28; psychology 28; liberal arts and sciences, general studies, and humanities 24; computer and information sciences and support services 23, social sciences 16. 3 *post-master's certificates*.

Fees and Other Expenses: *Full-time tuition per academic year 2004–5:* in-state resident $3,920, out-of-state $7,770. *Books and supplies:* $860.

Financial Aid: Aid from institutionally generated funds is provided on the basis of academic merit, financial need. Institution has a Program Participation Agreement with the U.S. Department of Education for eligible students to receive Pell Grants and other federal aid.

Financial aid to full-time, first-time undergraduates: 36% received federal grants averaging $3,256 and 55% loans averaging $2,709.

Departments and Teaching Staff: *Total instructional faculty:* 37. Student-to-faculty ratio: 29:1.

Enrollment: Total enrollment 3,758. Full-time 1,155 men/ 1,513 women.

Characteristics of Student Body: *Ethnic/racial makeup:* Black non-Hispanic: 51.4%; American Indian or Alaska Native: .3%; Asian or Pacific Islander: 1.2%; Hispanic: 1%; White non-Hispanic: 45%; unknown: 1.2%.

Library Collections: 36,600 volumes including bound books, serial backfiles, electronic documents, and government documents not in separate collections. Online catalog. 9,170 audiovisual materials. 484 current serial subscriptions. Students have access to the Internet at no charge.

Chief Executive Officer: Dr. Cameron J. Martindale, President.

Address admission inquiries to Larry Hawkins, Director of Enrollment Management.

Tuskegee University

Old Montgomery Road
Tuskegee Institute, Alabama 36088

Tel: (334) 727-8500   **E-mail:** adm@tusk.edu
Fax: (334) 727-5750   **Internet:** www.tusk.edu

Institution Description: Tuskegee University is a private, independent, nonprofit institution of higher learning. Tuskegee University was the first black college to be designated as a Registered National Historic Landmark (April 2, 1966), and the first black college to be designated a National Historic Site (1974). *Enrollment:* 2,695. *Degrees awarded:* Baccalaureate, first-professional (veterinary medicine), master's. Specialist certificates in education also awarded.

Member of Alabama Center for Higher Education, Mississippi-Alabama Sea Grant Consortium.

Accreditation: *Regional:* SACS-Comm. on Coll. *Professional:* architecture, chemistry, dietetics, engineering, nursing, occupational therapy, social work, veterinary medicine

History: Established as Tuskegee Normal School 1881; incorporated 1893; offered first instruction at postsecondary level 1923; awarded first degree (baccalaureate) 1925; became Tuskegee Institute 1937; renamed Tuskegee University 1985. *See* Booker T. Washington, *Up From Slavery* [rev. ed.] (New York: Airmont, Inc., 1967) for further information.

Institutional Structure: *Governing board:* Tuskegee Institute Board of Trustees consisting of 25 members. The general officers include the president, provost, vice president for business and fiscal affairs, senior vice president for university advancement. The key internal campus bodies include a Faculty Senate, Staff Senate, and the Student Government Association.

Calendar: Semesters. Academic year Aug. to May. Freshmen admitted Aug., Jan., June. Degrees conferred May and end of summer term. Summer session June to Aug.

Characteristics of Freshmen: 68% of applicants accepted. 47% of accepted applicants enrolled.

25th percentile: SAT Verbal 390, SAT Math 380; ACT Composite 17. *75th percentile*: SAT Verbal 380, SAT Math 510; ACT Composite 20.

40% of entering freshmen expected to graduate within 5 years. 41% of freshmen from Alabama. Freshmen from 39 states and 15 foreign countries.

Admission: Rolling admissions plan. For fall acceptance, apply up by Mar. 15; for spring Oct. 15; for summer Apr. 1. Initial enrollment in nursing and veterinary medicine is restricted to fall semester. *Requirements:* Either graduation from secondary school with 3 units English, 3 mathematics, 2 science, 3 history-social studies; or GED. Additional units in English, foreign language, mathematics, science, social studies recommended. Minimum GPA 2.5 preferred; SAT of 900 and ACT of 18. GED minimum of 45 required for non-high school graduates. *For transfer students:* 2.0 minimum GPA; from 4-year accredited institution maximum transfer credit limited only by residence requirement; from 2-year accredited institution 2 years.

College credit and advanced placement for extrainstitutional learning on basis of *The 2006 Guide to the Evaluation of Educational Experiences in the Armed Services;* faculty assessment. Tutoring available. Noncredit developmental courses available.

Degree Requirements: *Undergraduate:* Variable number of credit hours depending on program pursued (average 130 credit hours); 2.0 GPA; 2 terms in residence; proficiency examination in English; 2 credit hours in physical education; liberal arts requirements. Comprehensives in individual fields of study for architecture, engineering, and nursing students.

Fulfillment of some degree requirements and exemption from some beginning courses possible by passing College Board CLEP. *Grading system:* A–F; pass-fail; satisfactory-unsatisfactory; incomplete.

Distinctive Educational Programs: Cooperative education. Dual-degree programs in engineering through ACHE and with Bethune-Cookman College (FL), College of the Virgin Islands, Stillman College, Rust College (MS). Cooperative baccalaureate in forestry with Auburn University, Iowa State University, North Carolina State University at Raleigh, University of Michigan, Virginia Polytechnic Institute and State University. Special facilities for using telecommunications in the classroom. Interdisciplinary program in Black studies. Preprofessional program in animal and poultry science. Facilities and programs for independent research, including honors programs, individual majors, tutorials. Regional veterinary medicine education plan provides training for students from 11 cooperating states. Minority Introduction to Engineering summer program for high school students. Intensive pre-engineering summer program.

ROTC: Army, 7 commissions awarded 2004; Air Force 7 commissions.

Degrees Conferred: 416 *baccalaureate (B),* 42 *master's* (M): agriculture 28 (B), 6 (M); architecture 13 (B); biological/life sciences 45 (B), 2 (M); computer and information sciences 9 (B); education 13 (B); engineering and engineering technologies 60 (B), 22 (M); English 18 (B), health professions and related sciences 22 (B); liberal arts/general studies 97 (B), 12 (M); psychology 29 (B); social sciences and history 18 (B) 52 *first-professional:* veterinary medicine.

Fees and Other Expenses: *Full-time tuition per academic year 2004–05:* $11,290. Contact the school for veterinary medicine tuition. *Room and board per academic year:* $5,940. *Books and supplies:* $755. *Required fees:* $300.

Financial Aid: Aid from institutionally generated funds is provided on the basis of academic merit, financial need, athletic ability.

Financial aid to full-time, first-time undergraduate students: need-based scholarships/grants totaling $5,738,363, self-help $9,780,348; non-need-based scholarships/grants totaling $2,338,453, self-help $7,735,003, parent loans $1,997,596, tuition waivers $4,247,550, athletic awards $899,553.

Departments and Teaching Staff: *Professors* 64, *associate professors* 63; *assistant professors* 73; *instructors* 28, *part-time faculty* 40. *Total instructional faculty:* 265 (women 44, men 1,697; members of minority groups 161). Total with doctorate, first-professional, or other terminal degree: 191. Student to faculty ratio: 12:1. 1 faculty member awarded sabbatical 2004–05.

Enrollment: Total enrollment 2,695. Undergraduate full-time 1,022 men / 1,329 women; part-time 74m / 55w. Graduate full-time 59m / 58w, part-time 23m / 19w.

Characteristics of Student Body: *Ethnic/racial makeup:* number of Black non-Hispanic: 1,834; American Indian or Alaska Native: 2; Asia or Pacific Islander: 2; Hispanic: 2; White non-Hispanic: 5; unknown: 621. *Age distribution:* number under 18: 5; 18–19: 515; 20–21: 890; 22–24: 890; 25–29: 125; 40–49: 5; 50–64: 2.

International Students: 97 nonresident aliens enrolled fall 2004. Social and cultural programs available to aid students whose native language is not English. No financial aid specifically designated for international students.

Student Life: On-campus residence halls house 51% of student body. Residence halls for men constitute 42% of such space, for women 58%. Housing available for married students. 90% of married students request institutional housing. 40% are so housed. *Intercollegiate athletics:* men only: baseball, basketball, football, golf, swimming, tennis, track; women only: basketball, swimming, tennis, track, volleyball. *Special regulations:* Cars with parking decal permitted on campus; fee charged. *Special services:* Learning Resources Center, medical services. *Student publication:* A monthly newspaper. *Surrounding community:* Tuskegee population 15,000. Atlanta (GA), 135 miles from campus, is nearest metropolitan area. Served by airport 2 miles from campus.

Publications: *Publisher:* Tuskegee Institute Press.

Library Collections: 310,000 volumes. Online and card catalogs. Access to online information retrieval services. Access to the Internet available at no charge.

Most important holdings include Washington Collection; General Daniel "Chappie" James Collection; George Washington Carver Papers; veterinary medicine.

Buildings and Grounds: Campus area 5,189 acres.

Chief Executive Officer: Dr. Benjamin F. Payton, President.

Address admission inquiries to Dr. Robert L. Lahey, Jr., Vice President and Director of Admissions (rhaney@tuskegee.edu).

United States Sports Academy

One Academy Drive
Daphne, Alabama 36526

Tel: (251) 626-3303   **E-mail:** info@sport.ussa.edu
Fax: (251) 626-3874   **Internet:** www.ussa.edu

Institution Description: The United States Sports Academy is a private professional institution offering undergraduate and graduate programs. *Enrollment:* 446. *Degrees awarded:* Baccalaureate, master's, doctorate.

Accreditation: *Regional:* SACS-Comm. on Coll.

Institutional Structure: *Governing board:* Board of Trustees. Academic affairs headed by president. Management/business/finances directed by business manager.

Calendar: Semesters.

Admission: *Requirements:* Baccalaureate degree from accredited institution.

Degree Requirements: Completion of prescribed curriculum.

Degrees Conferred: 23 *baccalaureate:* physical education, teaching, and coaching; 122 *master's*; 12 *doctorate*.

Fees and Other Expenses: *Undergraduate tuition and fees*: $13,200. Contact the academy for current graduate tuition, fees, and expenses.

Financial Aid: Institution has a Program Participation Agreement with the U.S. Department of Education for eligible students to receive Pell Grants and other federal aid.

Enrollment: Total enrollment 446 (73.5% men; 25.5% women).

International Students: No programs available to aid students whose native language is not English. No financial aid specifically designated for international students.

Chief Executive Officer: Dr. Thomas P. Rosandich, President.

Direct admission inquiries to Charles Cornwall, Dean, Student Services.

University of Alabama

739 University Boulevard
P.O. Box 870132
Tuscaloosa, Alabama 35487-0132

Tel: (205) 348-6010   **E-mail:** admissions@ua.edu
Fax: (205) 348-9046   **Internet:** www.ua.edu

Institution Description: *Enrollment:* 20,929. *Degrees awarded:* Baccalaureate, first-professional (law), master's, doctorate. Education specialist degree also awarded; teacher certification in specific programs.

Member of Oak Ridge Association, National Association of State Universities and Land Grant Colleges, Southeastern Universities Research Association, American Association of University Professors, Association of Research Libraries, National Association for Colleges and University Business Officers.

Accreditation: *Regional*: SACS-Comm. on Coll. *Professional*: accounting, art, athletic training, audiology, business, clinical psychology, computer science, dietetics, engineering, engineering technology, English language education, family and consumer science, interior design, journalism, law, librarianship, music, nursing, rehabilitation counseling, social work, speech-language pathology, teacher education, theatre

History: Established and chartered 1820; offered first instruction at postsecondary level 1831; awarded first degree (baccalaureate) 1832. *See* James B. Sellers, *History of the University of Alabama* (University: University of Alabama Press, 1953) for further information.

Institutional Structure: *Composition of institution:* Administrators 54 men / 39 women. Central administration: president, vice president for academic affairs and provost, and vice president for community affairs, financial affairs, research, student affairs, and university advancement. Instructional faculty 1,088. Academic governance body, The Faculty Senate of The University of Alabama, meets 9 times per year.

Calendar: Semesters. Academic year Sept. to May. Freshmen admitted Aug., Jan., June, July. Degrees conferred Dec., May, Aug. Summer session May-Aug.

Characteristics of Freshmen: 77% of applicants accepted. 48% of accepted applicants enrolled.

34.9% (1,176 students) submitted SAT scores; 86.9% (2,926 students) submitted ACT scores. *25th percentile*: SAT Verbal 490, SAT I Math 500; ACT Composite 21, ACT English 21, ACT Math 19. *75th percentile*: SAT Verbal 620, SAT Math 610; ACT Composite 26, ACT English 28, ACT Math 26.

22.8% of entering freshmen expected to graduate within 5 years. 57.3% of freshmen from Alabama. Freshmen from 47 states and 34 foreign countries.

Admission: Rolling admissions plan. Applications for admission accepted as early as one year prior to the anticipated date of enrollment. Admission standards are subject to change on an annual basis. Visit www.admissions.ua.edu for the most current information. *Requirements:* Applicants for freshman admission must submit official copies of their high school transcripts (3.0 cumulative grade point average) and either ACT (20) or SAT (950) scores. *For transfer students:* Transfer applicants: 2.0 (on a 4.0 scale) average of all college-level work attempted. Transfer credit is limited to 60 semester hour. Students who have attempted fewer than 24 semester hours (or 36 quarter hours) of collegiate work must also submit official copies of their ACT or SAT scores and high school records.

Degree Requirements: *Undergraduate:* 128 semester hours; 2.0 GPA on 4.0 scale; 32 hours in residence; core curriculum requirements.

Fulfillment of some degree requirements and exemption from some beginning courses possible by passing College Board CLEP, AP, other standardized tests. *Grading system:* A–F; pass-fail (with restrictions).

Distinctive Educational Programs: Alabama Shakespeare Festival; work-experience programs; cooperative education, internships, weekend and evening classes; facilities and programs for independent research; honors programs; independent study; Belser-Parton Reading Center; Intercampus Interactive Telecommunications System; Cartographic Laboratory; Center for Alcohol and Drug Education; Center for Business and Economic Research; Mineral Resource Institute; Quality University Extended Sight Telecourses (QUEST). Study abroad in Belgium, England, Germany, Japan, Korea. Summer study in China, Mexico, Russia. Programs vary. UA has sponsored programs in The Netherlands, Denmark, and Latvia. New College provides organized opportunity to develop and pursue unique, multidisciplinary degree programs.

ROTC: Army, Air Force. 30 commissions awarded 2004.

Degrees Conferred: 3,024 *baccalaureate* (B), 1,175 *master's* (M), 158 *doctorate* (D): area and ethnic studies 12 (B), 9 (M); biological/life sciences 82 (B), 5 (M), 9 (D); business/marketing 905 (B), 155 (M), 11 (D); communications/communication technologies 399 (B), 39 (M), 5 (D); computer and information sciences 27 (B), 22 (M), 4 (D); education 209 (B), 320 (M), 34 (D); engineering and engineering technologies 177 (B), 71 (M), 16 (D); English 60 (B), 24 (M), 8 (D); foreign languages and literature 27 (B), 9 (M), 1 (D); health professions and related sciences 221 (B), 136 (M); home economics and vocational home economics 218 (B), 38(M); law/legal studies 5 (M); library science 65 (M), 1 (D); mathematics 7 (B), 19 (M), 3 (D); parks and recreation 8 (D); philosophy/religion/theology 12 (B); physical sciences 23 (B), 15 (M), 16 (D); protective services/public administration 113 (B), 139 20 (M), 10 (D); psychology 118 (B), 27 (M), 17 (D); social sciences and history 186 (B), 40 (M), 9 (D); visual and performing arts 131 (B), 37 (M), 5 (D).

First-professional: 172 law. *Honorary degrees awarded 2003–04:* Doctor of Humane Letters 4.

Fees and Other Expenses: *Full-time tuition per academic year 2004–2005:* Resident $4,630, nonresident $12,664. *Room per academic year:* $2,982. *Board per academic year:* $1,752.

Financial Aid: Aid from institutionally generated funds is provided on the basis of academic merit, financial need, athletic ability, other criteria. *Contact:* Jeanetta Allen.

Financial aid to full-time, first-time undergraduate students: need-based scholarships/grants totaling $11,863,251, self-help $23,504,704; non-need-based scholarships/grants totaling $18,838,251, self-help $20,931,336, parent loans $7,248,144, tuition waivers $1,750,769, athletic awards $4,095,304. *Graduate aid:* 1,785 federal and state fellowships/grants totaling $24,416,225 (ranging from $399 to $18,500); 33 federal and state-funded loans totaling $250,004 (ranging from $2,532 to $9,872), 663 teaching assistantships totaling $6,630,000 (ranging from $8,000 to $10,000); 465 research assistantships totaling $4,650,000 (ranging from $8,000 to $10,000).

Departments and Teaching Staff: Arts and sciences *professors* 158, *associate professors* 93, *assistant professors* 91, *instructors* 44, *part-time faculty* 664; Commerce and Business Administration 43, 31, 11, 5, 20; Communication and Information Sciences 19, 10, 12, 10, 8; Continuing Studies 0, 0, 0, 0, 20; Education 19, 20, 31, 3, 18; English Language Institute 38, 40, 62, 14, 37; Engineering 20, 41, 28, 9, 7; Honors College 0, 0, 0, 1, 1; Human Environmental Sciences 11, 8, 12, 12, 17; Law 17, 24, 1, 3, 8, 34; Libraries 4, 13, 16, 3, 1; Nursing 4, 6, 8, 7, 6; Social Work 4, 7, 8, 4, 13.

Total instructional faculty: 1,088. Student-to-faculty ratio: 9:1. Degrees held by full-time faculty: doctorate 77%, master's 7%, baccalaureate 1%, professional 3%. 93% hold terminal degrees. *Faculty development:* $27,969,598 total grants for research. 35 faculty members awarded sabbaticals 2004–05.

Enrollment: Total enrollment 20,929. Undergraduate full-time 6,975 men / 7,880 women, part-time 785m / 928w; first-professional full-time 360m / 225w, part-time 16m / 6w; graduate full-time 933m / 1,051w, part-time 672m / 1,098w. *Transfer students:* in-state into lower division 408m / 347w, out-of-state 68m / 63w; in-state into upper division 213m / 198w, out-of-state 35m / 29w.

Characteristics of Student Body: *Ethnic/racial makeup:* number of Black non-Hispanic: 2,058; American Indian or Alaska Native: 105; Asian or Pacific Islander: 156; Hispanic: 189; White non-Hispanic: 13,737. *Age distribution:* number under 18: .9%; 18–19: 36 6%; 20–21: 34%; 22–24: 17%; 25–29: 4.8%; 30–34: 2%; 35–39: 1.5%; 40–49: 2%; 50–64: .8%; 65 and over: 1%.

International Students: 861 nonresident aliens enrolled fall 2004. 175 students from Europe, 541 Asia, 39 Latin America, 22 Africa, 22 Canada, 4 Australia, 1 New Zealand; 12 other. Programs to aid students whose native language is not English: Social, cultural, financial. English as a Second Language Program. No financial aid specifically designated for international students.

Student Life: On-campus residence halls house 24% of student body. Residence halls for men only constitute 40% of such space, for women only 60%. 19% of men join and 10% live in fraternities; 33% of women join and 12% live in sororities. 18% of undergraduate students affiliated with Greek organizations. Housing available for married students. 41% of students live on campus. *Intercollegiate athletics:* men: baseball, basketball, cross-country, football, golf, swimming and diving, indoor and outdoor track and field, tennis; women: basketball, cross-country, golf, gymnastics, soccer, softball, swimming and diving, indoor and outdoor track and field, tennis, volleyball. *Student publications, radio: Southern Historian*, an annual history journal; *Black Warrior Review*, a biannual literary magazine; *Corolla*, a yearbook; *Crimson White*, a newspaper published 4 times per week; *Dateline Alabama* datelinealabama.com, web magazine (weekly); WUAL-FM (90.7) radio (broadcasts 24/7); WVUA7-TV, a full-service commercial station operated as a community service and to train students. *Surrounding community:* Tuscaloosa population 83,376. Birmingham, 50 miles from campus, is nearest metropolitan area. Served by airport 62 12 miles from campus; passenger rail service 5 miles from campus.

Publications: *Alabama Heritage* (quarterly); *Alabama Law Review* (quarterly); *Alumna Alumni Magazine* (quarterly), *Journal of the Legal Profession* (annually); *Law and Psychology Review* (annually); *Black Warrior Review* (biannually); *Capstone Engineer* (biannually); *Communicator* (biannually); *Dialog* (bimonthly); *Executive* (biannually); *Southern Historian* (annually). University of Alabama Press publishes an average of 55 books and two journals.

Library Collections: 2,465,217 volumes. 936,546 government documents; 3,951,914 microforms; 523,749 audiovisual materials; 31,199 current periodical subscriptions. Access to numerous CD-ROM products; OCLC, RLIN, and various online information retrieval systems and locally mounted databases. Total 2004–05 materials expenditures $6,420,160. Collections include 14 digital collections and a wide array of electronic data bases, full-text e-journals, and e-books.

Most important special holdings include Confederate Imprints; Gorgas Family Papers; Shelby Iron Works Papers; T. P. Thompson Rare Books Collection (Louisiana); Wade Hall Collection of Southern America; 11 Senatorial and Congressional collections; Archive of American Minority Culture; over 100 manuscripts pertaining to nearly every aspect of the southern region.

Buildings and Grounds: Campus area 1,000 acres. *New buildings:* Alabama Institute for Manufacturing Excellence; Athletics Facility; Blount-Living-Learning Center; Bryant Hall Annex; Child Development Research Center;

Lakeside Residential Community; Riverside Community Residence Hall Complex; Russell Student Health Center; Shelby Hall-Instructional/Research Building; Student Recreation Center and Pool; University of Alabama School of Medicine, Tuscaloosa Campus; Varsity Soccer Complex; Varsity Tennis Stadium.

Chief Executive Officer: Dr. Robert E. Witt, President.

Undergraduates address admission inquiries to Mary K. Spiegel, Director, Office of Undergraduate Admissions (e-mail: admissions@us.edu).

University of Alabama at Birmingham

1530 3rd Avenue South
Birmingham, Alabama 35294
Tel: (205) 934-3254   **E-mail:** UndergradAdmit@uab.edu
Fax: (205) 934-3179   **Internet:** www.uab.edu

Institution Description: *Enrollment:* 16,693. *Degrees awarded:* Baccalaureate, first-professional (dentistry,medicine, optometry); master's, doctorate. Certificates also awarded.

Member of Gulf Universities Research Consortium and the consortium Oak Ridge Associated Universities.

Accreditation: *Regional:* SACS-Comm. on Coll. *Professional:* accounting, blood bank technology, business, clinical lab scientist, clinical psychology, dental assisting, dental hygiene, dental public health, dentistry, dietetics, endodontics, engineering, health information administration, medicine, music, nuclear medicine technology, nurse anesthesia education, nursing, nursing education, occupational therapy, optometry, pediatric dentistry, periodontics, physical therapy, physician assisting, psychology internship, public administration, public health, radiation therapy technology, radiography, rehabilitation counseling, respiratory therapy, social work, surgeon assisting, teacher education

History: Established and offered first instruction at postsecondary level 1966; awarded first degree (baccalaureate) 1970.

Institutional Structure: *Composition of institution:* Executive/administrative staff 133 men / 134 women. President serves a chief executive officer. Hospital and non-academic health affairs headed by director and chief executive officer of health system. University management and business headed by vice president for financial affairs and administration. Other administrators include vice president for planning and information management; vice president for student affairs; provost; vice president for development, alumni, and external relations; vice president for information technology; vice president for equity and diversity; vice president for research; senior vice president for medicine. Full-time instructional faculty 1,899. Academic governance body, UAB Faculty Senate, meets monthly.

Calendar: Semesters. Academic year mid-August to early May. Freshmen admitted all semesters. Summer session available.

Characteristics of Freshmen: 1,615 of applicants accepted. 1,043 applicants enrolled.

9% (142 students) submitted SAT scores; 87% (1,413 students) submitted ACT scores. *25th percentile:* ACT Composite 19, ACT English 19, ACT Math 18. *75th percentile:* ACT Composite 25, ACT English 23, ACT Math 24.

Admission: Rolling admissions plan. Call Admissions Office for admissions deadlines. Unconditional admission is granted to applicants who have a GPA of at least 2.0 (C) on high school academic subjects in grades 9–12, including a minimum 2.0 in English and mathematics courses, minimum ACT Composite score of 20, and a minimum of 12 Carnegie units in academic subjects, including 4 in English, 2 in mathematics, 2 in science, and 2 in social studies. *For transfer students:* requirements include a minimum overall grade average of C on all college work attempted.

Degree Requirements: *Undergraduate:* minimum total hours 128 semester hours; cumulative GPA of at least 2.0 (C) is necessary for graduation; Students must satisfy core curriculum requirements in English composition, mathematics, computer technology, foreign culture, western civilization, literature and the fine arts, science and technology, social/political/economic systems, ethical reasoning. At least 32 of the 128 semester hours required for graduation, including 24 of the last 32, must be taken at UAB. A minimum of 9 semester hours required for the major (at or above the 300-level) must be completed at UAB.

Fulfillment of some degree requirements possible by passing departmental examinations, College Board CLEP, AP. *Grading system:* A–F; pass; withdrawn passing; withdrawn failing.

Distinctive Educational Programs: Cooperative education. Honors program; early morning, evening, and weekend classes. Joint graduate programs with University of Alabama and University of Alabama in Huntsville offered in materials engineering, materials science, art history, educational leadership, and applied mathematics. Cooperative programs with U of A and U of A/Huntsville offered in civil and electrical engineering and anthropology. Unique program which combines the resources of an academic health center and an urban

research university. Study abroad in Barbados, Bahamas, Costa Rica, England, France, Israel, Italy, Mexico, Scotland.

ROTC: Army; Air Force in cooperation with Samford University. .

Degrees Conferred: 1,575 *baccalaureate* (B), 1,065 *master's* (M), 111 *doctorate* (D): area and ethnic studies 3 (B); biological/life sciences 10 (B), 12 (M), 54 (D); business/marketing 342 (B), 153 (M); communications/communication technologies 93 (B); computer and information sciences 54 (B), 35 (M), 2 (D); education 116 (B), 328 (M), 7 (D); engineering and engineering technologies 74 (B), 88 (M), 7 (D); English 22 (B), 13 (M); foreign languages and literature 9 (B); health professions and related sciences 235 (B), 370 (M), 20 (D); interdisciplinary studies 1 (D); liberal arts/general studies 4 (B); mathematics 6 (B), 6 (M), 2 (D); parks and recreation 15 (D); philosophy/religion/theology 27 (B); physical sciences 21 (B), 7 (D); protective services/public administration 111 (B), 35 (M); psychology 132 (B), 10 (M), 1 (D); social sciences and history 152 (B), 7 (M), 2 (D); visual and performing arts 71 (B), 1 (M).

257 first professional: dentistry 56, optometry 41, medicine 160. Honorary degree: 1 Doctor of Humane Letters.

Fees and Other Expenses: *Full-time tuition per academic year 2004–05:* undergraduate resident $3,840, out-of-state $9,600; graduate resident $3,888; out-of-state $9,720. *Required fees:* $822. *Room and board per academic year:* $8,743. *Books and supplies:* $900.

Financial Aid: Aid from institutionally generated funds is provided on the basis of academic merit, financial need, athletic ability. Institution has a Program Participation Agreement with the U.S. Department of Education for eligible students to receive Pell Grants and other federal aid.

Financial aid to full-time, first-time undergraduate students: need-based scholarships/grants totaling $11,606,591, self-help $23,547,549; non-need-based scholarships/grants totaling $4,472,949, self-help $9,161,024, parent loans $4,621,761, athletic awards $3,671,711.

Departments and Teaching Staff: *Professors* 216, *associate professors* 260, *assistant professors* 240, *instructors* 58, *part-time faculty* 103.

Total instructional faculty: 880 (women 334, men 546; members of minority groups 141). Total with doctorate, first-professional, or other terminal degree 772. Student to faculty ratio: 18:1. *Faculty development:* Total grants for research in 2004: $4,769,687.

Enrollment: Total enrollment 16,693. Undergraduates full-time 3,085 men / 4,910 women, part-time 1,429m / 2,017w; graduates full-time 917m / 1,311w; first-professional full-time 543m / 434w. *Transfer students:* 1,043 enrolled applicants.

Characteristics of Student Body: *Ethnic/racial makeup:* number of Black non-Hispanic: 3,682; American Indian or Alaska Native: 367; Asian or Pacific Islander: 367; Hispanic: 125; White non-Hispanic: 6,642; unknown 242. *Age distribution:* number under 18: 26; 18–19: 2,535; 20–21: 2,832; 22–24: 2,822; 25–29: 1,609; 30–34: 683; 35–39: 378; 40–49: 410; 50–64: 139; 65 and over: 7.

International Students: 1,009 nonresident aliens enrolled fall 2004. 72 students from Europe, 677 Asia, 70 Central and South America, 154 Africa, 24 Canada, 4 Australia, 1 New Zealand, 7 other. No programs available to aid students whose native language is not English. No financial aid specifically designated for international students.

Student Life: On-campus housing is used by 12% of the undergraduate student body. Approximately 6% of the undergraduate students join one of the 10 fraternity or 9 sorority groups on campus. *Intercollegiate athletics:* men only: baseball, basketball, football, golf, soccer, tennis; women only: basketball, cross-country, golf, rifle, soccer softball, synchronized swimming, tennis, track and field, volleyball. *Special regulations:* Registered cars with decals permitted in designated areas. *Special services:* Campus bus service, career resource library, career planning, academic and personal counseling, student development seminars, student placement, and handicapped services. *Student publications: Kaleidoscope,* a weekly newspaper; *Aura,* a literary publication; *Phoenix,* a nonfiction magazine; *Internal Organ,* a student newspaper for School of Nursing; *Contact,* a yearbook for School of Optometry; *Dentala,* a yearbook for School of Dentistry; *Progress Notes,* a yearbook for the School of Medicine. *Surrounding community:* UAB is located in the heart of Birmingham, Alabama's largest city. Cultural, social, and service opportunities are numerous. Convenient access to air, train, and bus services. Mass transit system available.

Publications: UAB publications include *UAB Magazine* and *UAB Insight.* Some schools may publish specific alumni magazines.

Library Collections: 1,257,166 volumes. 1,171,772 microforms; 4,409 audiovisual materials; 5,254 current periodicals. Online and card catalogs. 300 computer work stations. Students have access to the Internet at no charge.

Most important holdings include Reynolds Historical Library (over 10,000 items, including rare books); incunabula; medical mannequins; Pittman Collection on Endocrinology; Daniel Drake Collection; letters of William Osler, Louis Pasteur, Florence Nightingale, Oliver Wendell Holmes, Sr., Pierre Curie, George and Martha Washington; personal papers of George G. Wallace; extensive collection of Marcel Proust.

Buildings and Grounds: Campus area 250 acres. *New buildings:* Ryals Public Health Building; Stephens Performing Arts Center; Hoen Engineering Building; Facilities Administration Building; Lister Hill Library Addition; Volker Hall Addition.

Chief Executive Officer: Dr. Carol Z. Garrison, President.

Undergraduates address admission inquiries to Chenise Ryan, Admissions Director; graduate inquiries to Dr. James D. McClintock, Dean of Graduate School.

School of Arts and Humanities

Degree Programs Offered: *Baccalaureate* in African-American studies, art, communication studies, English, foreign language, music, philosophy, theater; *master's* in English, art history jointly with University of Alabama, information systems.

Departments and Teaching Staff: Total instructional faculty: 119.

School of Business

Degree Programs Offered: *Baccalaureate* in accounting, economics, finance, industrial distribution, information systems, management, marketing; *master's* in accounting, business administration; *doctorate* in administration/health services.

Admission: All undergraduates are designated as pre-business until they successfully complete certain required freshman and sophomore level courses and achieve a 2.0 GPA.

Degree Requirements: In addition to UAB general graduation requirements, all business students must maintain a 2.0 GPA in courses required for their major, and must earn a 2.0 for all business courses attempted for the degree.

Departments and Teaching Staff: Total instructional faculty: 57.

Distinctive Educational Programs: Center for Labor Education and Research, providing programs and research reports on labor union issues.

School of Dentistry

Degree Programs Offered: *First-professional* in dentistry.

Admission: *For first-professional degree:* 90 semester hours or equivalent from accredited college or university, including 16 chemistry, 12 biology, 8 physics, 6 mathematics; 30 nonscience courses; DAT.

Degree Requirements: *For first-professional degree:* Prescribed curriculum clinical experience, exit competency examinations.

Departments and Teaching Staff: Total instructional faculty: 111.

Distinctive Educational Programs: Joint first-professional-doctoral program in anatomy, biochemistry, biophysics, microbiology, pharmacology, physiology with Graduate School. Honors program for independent study in scientific areas. Summer research fellowship program for selected students.

School of Education

Degree Programs Offered: *Baccalaureate, master's* in arts education, elementary education, health education, high school education, physical education, special education; *baccalaureate* in music education; *baccalaureate, master's, doctorate* in early childhood education; *master's* in counseling, allied health, school psychology; *master's, doctorate* in educational leadership; *doctorate* in health education/promotion.

Admission: Admission to teacher education program requires completion of pre-education courses with 2.50 GPA; complete 48 semester hours in core, including math with 2.50 GPA; evidence of writing and speaking proficiency; complete Pre-TEP portfolio; negative TB test or chest x-ray; CPR training.

Departments and Teaching Staff: Total instructional faculty: 59.

School of Engineering

Degree Programs Offered: *Baccalaureate, master's* in civil engineering, electrical engineering, materials engineering, mechanical engineering; *master's, doctorate* in biomedical engineering; *doctorate* in environmental health engineering, materials engineering (joint program with University of Alabama); civil engineering, computer engineering (cooperative with University of Alabama), electrical engineering and mechanical engineering (cooperative programs with University of Alabama); materials science (joint interdisciplinary program with University of Alabama).

Admission: High school grads admissible with 21 ACT (970 SAT) and minimum high school GPA of 2.00/4.00; may be admitted to pre-engineering with 18-20 ACT (840-860 SAT) and high school GPA of 2.00/4.00..

Departments and Teaching Staff: Total instructional faculty: 60.

Distinctive Educational Programs: Continuing education degree program for professional development.

School of Health-Related Professions

Degree Programs Offered: *Baccalaureate* in cytotechnology, health information management; health sciences, medical technology, nuclear medicine technology, respiratory therapy, radiologic sciences, surgical physician assistant, *master's* in clinical lab sciences, clinical nutrition and dietetics, allied health sciences, health administration, health informatics, nurse anesthesia, occupational therapy; *doctorate* in administration/health services and nutrition sciences. Certificate (post-baccalaureate) in dietetic internship.

Distinctive Educational Programs: Health Extension Learning Program in cooperation with Alabama Cooperative Extension Service of Auburn University and Alabama Department of Public Health, providing information to rural public. Deaf Interpreter and Referral Center. Management training program for personnel in state residential and community-based facilities for the developmentally disabled.

School of Medicine

Degree Programs Offered: *First-professional.* Sub-baccalaureate certificate in emergency medical technician.

Admission: 90 semester hours credit including 8 semester hours general biology with zoology; 8 semester hours in general chemistry with lab; 8 semester hours organic chemistry with lab; 8 semester hours general physics with lab; 6 semester hours college mathematics, statistics, or computer science; 6 semester hours English; MCAT.

Degree Requirements: *For first-professional degree:* Prescribed 4-year curriculum, clinical experience, faculty evaluations.

Departments and Teaching Staff: *Professors* 218, *associate professors* 165, *assistant professors* 359, *instructors* 145, *part-time teachers* 73. *Total instructional faculty:* 923.5 FTE. *Degrees held by full-time instructional faculty:* 21.4% doctorate, 2.5% masters, 1.9% baccalaureate, 74.2% professional. 95.6% hold terminal degrees.

Distinctive Educational Programs: Joint first-professional/doctoral program in cooperation with Graduate School.

School of Natural Sciences and Mathematics

Degree Programs Offered: *Baccalaureate* in African-American studies, biology, chemistry, computer and information sciences, mathematics, natural science, physics; *master's* and *doctorate* in biology, chemistry, computer and information sciences, physics; *doctorate* in applied mathematics (joint interdisciplinary program with University of Alabama).

Departments and Teaching Staff: Total instructional faculty: 92.

School of Nursing

Degree Programs Offered: *Baccalaureate, master's, doctorate* in nursing.

Admission: New students are admitted into Pre-Nursing. Admission is competitive and requires (at a minimum): completion of pre-nursing curriculum and 65 semester hours with C or better in all courses; CPR certification and medical clearance.

Departments and Teaching Staff: Total instructional faculty: 45.

Distinctive Educational Programs: Interdisciplinary course in health care.

Enrollment: Total enrollment 519.

School of Optometry

Degree Programs Offered: *Master's, doctorate* in vision science; *first-professional* in optometry.

Admission: *For first-professional degree:* College-level prerequisites include English (2 semesters or 3 quarters), inorganic chemistry (2 semesters or 3 quarters), organic chemistry (1 semester or 2 quarters), physics (2 semesters or 2 quarters), mathematics (1 semester or 1 quarter in calculus, 1 semester or 1 quarter in statistics), biology (2 semesters or 3 quarters), psychology (2 semesters or 3 quarters), social and behavioral sciences (2 semesters or 2 quarters). OAT.

Departments and Teaching Staff: Total instructional faculty 57.

Distinctive Educational Programs: Rotating internship program. Joint first-professional-master's program in physiological optics or public health with Graduate School. Residency programs in family practice optometry, low vision rehabilitation, hospital-based optometry, contact lens practice. *Other distinctive programs:* Optometric training and service program of vision screening and referral services for preschool and school-age children, in cooperation with county school systems.

School of Public Health

Degree Programs Offered: *Master's* in public health, biostatistics; *doctorate* in biostatistics, environmental health engineering, environmental health sciences, epidemiology, health education/promotion, and public health.

Admission: Bachelor's degree with minimum 3.00 GPA; graduate admissions tests vary by department.

Departments and Teaching Staff: Total instructional faculty: 85.

School of Social and Behavioral Sciences

Degree Programs Offered: *Baccalaureate* in African-American studies, anthropology, criminal justice, economics, history, international studies, political science, psychology, social work, sociology; *master's* in anthropology (cooperative with University of Alabama), criminal justice, forensic science, history, psychology, public administration, sociology; *doctorate* in medical sociology, psychology.

Departments and Teaching Staff: Total instructional faculty: 86.

University of Alabama in Huntsville

301 Sparkman Drive
Huntsville, Alabama 35899

Tel: (256) 824-1000   **E-mail:** admitme@email.uah.edu
Fax: (256) 890-6120   **Internet:** www.uah.edu

Institution Description: *Enrollment:* 7,036. *Degrees awarded:* Baccalaureate, master's, doctorate. Certificates are also awarded.

Academic offering subject to approval by statewide coordinating bodies. Budget subject to approval by state governing boards.

Accreditation: *Regional:* SACS-Comm. on Coll. *Professional:* business, chemistry, computer science, engineering, music, nursing

History: Established as resident center for University of Alabama 1950; offered first instruction at postsecondary level (graduate) 1963; present name adopted 1966; began undergraduate program and awarded first degree (baccalaureate) 1968; became autonomous institution 1969. *See* James E. Ferguson III, *The University of Alabama in Huntsville: The Birth and Growth of a Modern University* (Huntsville: The University of Alabama in Huntsville, 1975) for further information.

Institutional Structure: *Composition of institution:* Academic affairs headed by provost and vice president for academic affairs. Management/business/finances directed by vice president for finance and administration. The remaining divisions of the university are headed by the senior/vice president for research, vice president for student affairs, vice president of university advancement. Full-time instructional faculty 271. Academic governance body, Faculty Senate, meets an average of 12 times per year.

Calendar: Semesters. Academic year Aug. to May. Freshmen admitted fall, spring, and summer. Degrees conferred and formal commencement May. Summer session from May to Aug.

Characteristics of Freshmen: 89% of applicants accepted. 43% of accepted applicants enrolled.

24% (164 students) submitted SAT scores; 90% (614 students) submitted ACT scores. *25th percentile:* SAT Verbal 520, SAT Math 530; ACT Composite 22, ACT English 22, ACT Math 21. *75th percentile:* SAT Verbal 638, SAT Math 640; ACT Composite 27, ACT English 28, ACT Math 27.

22% of entering freshmen expected to graduate within 5 years. 84% of freshmen from Alabama. Freshmen from 24 states and 9 foreign countries.

Admission: Rolling admissions plan. Apply as early as one year prior to enrollment, but not later than registration period. Early acceptance available. *Requirements:* Either graduation from accredited secondary school with 20 units which normally include 4 English, 3 mathematics, 1 biology, 3 history or social studies, 7 academic electives; or GED. For some divisions, chemistry, physics, and additional units mathematics recommended. *Entrance tests:* For foreign students TOEFL. *For transfer students:* 2.0 minimum GPA on 4.0 scale; from 4-year accredited institution maximum transfer credit limited only by residence requirement; from 2-year accredited institution 64 hours maximum transfer credit.

College credit and advanced placement for postsecondary-level work completed in secondary school. Tutoring available. Developmental courses offered in summer session and regular academic year; credit given.

Degree Requirements: *Undergraduate:* For all baccalaureate degrees: 128–140 credit hours; 32 hours in residence; general education requirements. Fulfillment of some degree requirements and exemption from some beginning courses possible by passing departmental examinations, College Board CLEP, AP. *Grading system:* A–F; pass-fail; withdraw (deadline after which pass-fail is appended to withdraw).

Distinctive Educational Programs: UAH offers students a variety of distinctive programs including cooperative education, honors program, internships, independent study, and supervised research. Academic programs include atmospheric science, global studies, web design, foreign languages, international trade, and optical engineering.

ROTC: Army in cooperation with Alabama Agricultural and Mechanical University.

Degrees Conferred: 810 *baccalaureate* (B); 379 *master's* (M); 34 *doctorate* (D): biological/life sciences 48 (B), 21 (M), 1 (D); business/marketing 240 (B), 71 (M); computer and information sciences 46 (B), 44 (M), 1 (D); education 15 (B); engineering and engineering technologies 164 (B), 125 (M), 25 (D); English 36 (B), 18 (M); foreign languages and literature 16 (B); health professions and related sciences 133 (B), 70 (D); mathematics 7 (B), 4 (M); philosophy/religion/theology 9 (B); physical sciences 11 (B), 13 (M), 5 (D); protective services/public administration 2 (M); psychology 24 (B), 4 (M); social sciences and history 37 (B), 5 (D); visual and performing arts 24 (B).

Fees and Other Expenses: *Full-time tuition per academic year 2004–05:* undergraduate resident $4,516, nonresident $9,518; graduate resident $5,646, nonresident $11,608. *Room and board per academic year:* $5,200. *Books and supplies:* $750.

Financial Aid: Aid from institutionally generated funds is provided on the basis of academic merit, financial need, athletic ability. Institution has a Program Participation Agreement with the U.S. Department of Education for eligible students to receive Pell Grants and other federal aid.

Financial aid to full-time, first-time undergraduate students: need-based scholarships/grants totaling $4,788,027, self-help $9,905,324, parent loans $1,098,365, athletic awards $196,895; non-need-based scholarships/grants totaling $2,172,079, athletic awards $967,308. *Graduate aid:* 13 federal and state-funded scholarships and grants totaling $21,141; 158 teaching assistantships totaling $1,632,967; 160 research assistantships totaling $1,264,414.

Departments and Teaching Staff: *Professors 76, associate professors 83, assistant professors 81, instructors 31; part-time faculty 188.*

Total instructional faculty: 459 (women 181, men 278; members of minority groups 60). Total with doctorate, first-professional, or other terminal degree 323. Student to faculty ratio: 16:1. *Faculty development:* $50 million in grants for research 2004. faculty members awarded sabbaticals in 2004–05.

Enrollment: Total enrollment 7,036. Full-time 4,579; part-time 2,457.

Characteristics of Student Body: *Ethnic/racial makeup:* number of Black non-Hispanic: 823; American Indian or Alaska Native: 12; Asian or Pacific Islander: 206; Hispanic: 101; White non-Hispanic: 4,113; unknown: 14. *Age distribution:* number under 18: 93; 18–19: 1,387; 20–21: 1,382; 22–24: 1,143; 25–29: 690; 30–34 357; 35–39: 177; 40–49: 224; 50–64: 67; 65 and over: 3.

International Students: 476 nonresident aliens enrolled fall 2004. 27 students from Europe, 334 Asia, 34 Latin America, 35 Africa, 21 Canada, 3 Australia, 12 other. Programs available to aid students whose native language is not English: Social. English as a Second Language courses. No financial aid specifically designated for international students.

Student Life: On-campus housing available. *Intercollegiate athletics:* men only: baseball, basketball, hockey, soccer, tennis; women only: basketball, soccer, softball, tennis, volleyball. *Special regulations:* Registered cars permitted. *Student publications: The Charger Chronicle*, a weekly newspaper; *TIC*, student literary magazine. *Surrounding community:* Huntsville population 175,000. Birmingham, 85 miles from campus, is nearest metropolitan area. Served by airport 10 miles from campus.

Library Collections: 327,663 volumes. Online and card catalogs. Current periodical subscriptions: paper 1,051; microform 584,267; via electronic access 38,513. 2,677 recordings; 983 CD-ROM. 204 computer work stations. Access to online information retrieval services. Students have access to the Internet at no charge.

Most important holdings include papers of Congressman Robert Jones; Fern Garth Family Papers; space and rocket collection including Willy Ley Memorial Collection; University Archives.

Buildings and Grounds: 354-acre campus. New buildings: University Fitness Center; North Campus residence hall; Library and Materials Science additions.

Chief Executive Officer: Dr. Frank A. Franz, President.

Address undergraduate admission inquiries to Ginger Reed, Director of Admissions; graduate inquiries to Kathy Biggs, Manager of Graduate Studies.

University of Mobile

5735 College Parkway
P.O. Box 13220
Mobile, Alabama 36663-0220
Tel: (251) 675-5990   **E-mail:** adminfo@umobile.edu
Fax: (251) 442-2523   **Internet:** www.umobile.edu

Institution Description: The University of Mobile, formerly known as Mobile College, is a private college affiliated with the Southern Baptist Church. *Enrollment:* 1,813. *Degrees awarded:* Associate, baccalaureate, master's.

Accreditation: *Regional:* SACS Comm. on Coll. *Professional:* music, nursing

History: Chartered 1961; offered first instruction at postsecondary level 1963; awarded first degree (baccalaureate) 1967; adopted present name 1993.

Institutional Structure: *Governing board:* Board of Trustees. Representation: 44 trustees; all voting. *Composition of institution:* Administrators 3 men / 2 women. Academic affairs headed by academic vice president. Full-time instructional faculty 89.

Calendar: Semesters. 2004–05 academic year late Aug. to late Apr.

Characteristics of Freshmen: 89% of applicants admitted. 47% of applicants admitted and enrolled.

15.3% submitted SAT scores; 82.7% submitted ACT scores.

38% of entering freshmen expected to graduate within 5 years. 80% of freshmen from Alabama. Freshmen from 19 states and 9 foreign countries.

Admission: Rolling admissions plan. *Requirements:* Graduation from secondary school or GED. *Entrance tests:* College Board SAT or ACT Composite.

Degree Requirements: *For all baccalaureate degrees:* 2.0 GPA; 128 semester hours; last 35 semester hours in residence. Church and community service required; general education requirements. *Grading system:* A–F.

Distinctive Educational Programs: Adult Degree Completion Program and Basic Core Program for adults returning to higher education.

ROTC: Army in cooperation with University of South Alabama. 1 commission awarded 2004.

Degrees Conferred: 100 *baccalaureate* (B); 50 *master's* (M): biological/life sciences 2 (B); business/marketing 30 (B), 14 (M); communications/communication technologies 8 (B); education 16 (B), 16 (M); English 1 (B); health professions and related sciences 10 (B), 47 (M); liberal arts/general studies 10 (B); natural resources/environmental science 1 (B); psychology 5 (B), social sciences and history 6 (B), visual and performing arts 4 (B).

Fees and Other Expenses: *Full-time tuition per academic year 2004–05:* Undergraduate $321 per semester hour; graduate $241 per semester hour. *Required fees:* $205 per year. *Room and board per academic year:* $5,300.

Financial Aid: Aid from institutionally generated funds is provided on the basis of academic merit, financial need, athletic ability. Institution has a Program Participation Agreement with the U.S. Department of Education for eligible students to receive Pell Grants and other federal aid.

Financial aid to full-time, first-time undergraduate students: need-based scholarships/grants totaling $4,689,921, self-help $3,686,076; non-need-based scholarships/grants totaling $2,467,203, self-help $3,776,434, parent loans $333,281, athletic awards $764,004.

Departments and Teaching Staff: *Professors* 24, *associate professors* 26, *assistant professors* 26, *instructors* 15, *part-time faculty* 75.

Total instructional faculty: 167 (women 479, men 42; members of minority groups 3). Total with doctorate, first-professional, or other terminal degree 54. Student to faculty ratio: 14:1.

Enrollment: Total enrollment 1,813. Undergraduate full-time 492 men / 809 women, part-time 93m / 238w; graduate full-time 12m / 57w, part-time 48m / 116w.

Characteristics of Student Body: *Ethnic/racial makeup:* number of Black non-Hispanic: 351; American Indian or Alaska Native: 33; Asian or Pacific Islander: 5; White non-Hispanic: 1,028; unknown 140. *Age distribution:* number under 18: 3; 18–19: 267; 20–21: 338; 22–24: 325; 25–29: 291; 30–34: 179; 35–39: 122; 40–49: 148; 50–64: 51; 65 and over: 2.

International Students: 56 nonresident aliens enrolled fall 2004. 26 students from Europe, 6 Asia, 7 Central and South America, 5 Africa, 6 Canada, 11 other. English as a Second Language Program. No financial aid specifically designated for international students.

Student Life: *Student activities:* Baptist Campus Ministries; Fellowship of Christian Athletes; Student Government Association; Campus Activities Board. Intramural sports. *Student publication: The Communicator. Surrounding community:* The campus is 10 miles from downtown Mobile.

Library Collections: 69,544 volumes. Online and card catalogs. Current serial subscriptions: 459 paper, 257 microform. 15 computer work stations. Students have access to the Internet at no charge. Total 2005–05 budget for books, periodicals, audiovisual materials, microforms: $183,500.

Most important special collections include the Alabama Collection; Delaney Collection; Southern Baptist Collection.

Buildings and Grounds: Campus area 830 acres. *New buildings:* Samford Hall (55 dormitory rooms) completed 2004.

Chief Executive Officer: Dr. Mark R. Foley, President.

Address undergraduate admission inquiries to Kris Nelson, Director of Admissions; graduate inquires to Kaye Brown, Dean of Graduate Programs.

University of Montevallo

Station 6392
Montevallo, Alabama 35115
Tel: (205) 665-6030   **E-mail:** admissions@montevallo.edu
Fax: (205) 665-6401   **Internet:** www.montevallo.edu

Institution Description: University of Montevallo is a state institution. *Enrollment:* 3,061. *Degrees awarded:* Baccalaureate, master's. Certificate in education also awarded.

New academic offerings subject to approval by statewide coordinating bodies. Member of Alabama Consortium for the Development of Higher Education.

Accreditation: *Regional:* SACS-Comm. on Coll. *Professional:* art, audiology, business, counseling, family and consumer science, music, social work, speech-language pathology, teacher education

History: Established as Alabama Girls' Industrial School 1896; changed name to Alabama College and awarded first degree (baccalaureate) in 1920s; men admitted as full-time students 1956; adopted present name 1969. *See* Lucille Griffith, *Alabama College 1896–1969* (Baton Rouge, LA: Thomas J. Moran's Sons, Inc., 1969) for further information.

Institutional Structure: *Governing board:* University of Montevallo Board of Trustees. Extrainstitutional representation: 11 trustees, state superintendent, governor of Alabama. Institutional representation: president of the university. 1 student (nonvoting). *Composition of institution:* Academic affairs headed by vice president for academic affairs. Management/business/finances directed by business manager and treasurer. Full-time instructional faculty 136. Academic governance body via elected Faculty Council and standing committees which include students.

Calendar: Semesters. Academic year Aug. to May. Freshmen admitted Aug., Jan., June, July. Degrees conferred and formal commencements May, Aug., Dec. Summer session from early June to mid-Aug.

Characteristics of Freshmen: 80% of applicants admitted. 50% of applicants admitted and enrolled.

95% submitted ACT scores. *25th percentile:* ACT Composite 24, ACT English 26, ACT Math 24. *75th percentile:* ACT Composite 19, ACT English 19, ACT Math 17.

43% of entering freshmen expected to graduate within 5 years. 90% of freshmen from Alabama.

Admission: Rolling admissions plan. Apply as early as 1 year prior to enrollment, but not later than 2 weeks before registration. Apply by end of junior year for early decision; need not limit application to University of Montevallo. Early acceptance available. *Requirements:* Either graduation from secondary school with 15 units which must include 3 English and no more than 4 vocational; or GED. 1–2 units mathematics recommended. Minimum GPA 2.0 on a 4.0 scale. *Entrance tests:* SAT or ACT. For foreign students TOEFL. *For transfer students:* 2.0 GPA on 4.0 scale; from 4-year accredited institution 100 semester hours maximum transfer credit; from 2-year accredited institution 65 hours.

College credit and advanced placement for postsecondary-level work completed in secondary school. College credit for extrainstitutional learning on the basis of *The 2006 Guide to the Evaluation of Educational Experiences in the Armed Services;* faculty assessment. Tutoring available. Noncredit developmental courses offered in summer session and regular academic year.

Degree Requirements: *Undergraduate:* 130 credit hours; 2.0 GPA on 4.0 scale; 24 hours in residence; 4 hours physical education; distribution requirements.

Fulfillment of some degree requirements and exemption from some beginning courses possible by passing College Board CLEP, AP. *Grading system:* A–F; withdraw (carries time limit); incomplete (carries time limit).

Distinctive Educational Programs: *For undergraduates:* Common general education program for all curricula. Writing across the curriculum. Accelerated degree programs. Dual-degree program in engineering with Auburn University. Preprofessional programs for medical fields and law. Special facilities in telecommunications and speech and hearing science. Honors program. Interdisciplinary program in international-intercultural studies. Travel and study abroad programs. *Available to all students:* Evening classes.

ROTC: Air Force offered in cooperation with Samford University; Army in cooperation with University of Alabama Birmingham. 1 commission awarded in 2004.

Degrees Conferred: 677 *baccalaureate* (B), 150 *master's* (M): biological/life sciences 11 (B); business/marketing 76 (B); communications/communication technologies 19 (B); education 59 (B), 126 (M); English 51 (B), 5 (M); foreign languages and literature 10 (B); health professions and related sciences 30 (B), 19 (M); home economics and vocational home economics 35 (B); mathematics 5 (B); parks and recreation 22 (B); physical sciences 3 (B); protective services/public administration 16 (B); psychology 23 (B); social sciences and history 55 (B); visual and performing arts 62 (B).

Fees and Other Expenses: *Full-time tuition per academic year 2004–05:* in-state resident undergraduate $5,190; out-of-state $10,380; graduate $4,416. *Required fees:* $284. *Room and board per academic year:* $3,850.

Financial Aid: Aid from institutionally generated funds is provided on the basis of academic merit, financial need, athletic ability, other criteria. Contact: Maria Parker, telephone (205) 665-6050.

Financial aid to full-time, first-time undergraduate students: need-based scholarships/grants $3,666,187, self-help $5,678,111; non-need-based scholarships/grants totaling $2,575,866, self-help $2,326,092, parent loans $438,596, tuition waivers $129,751, athletic awards $792,297.

Departments and Teaching Staff: *Professors* 97; *associate professors* 33; *assistant professors* 46; *instructors* 21; *part-time faculty:* 50.

Total instructional faculty: 247 (women 104, men 83; members of minority groups 14). Total with doctorate, first-professional, or other terminal degree 125. Student to faculty ratio: 17:1. 2 faculty members granted sabbaticals 2004–05.

Enrollment: Total enrollment: 3,061. Undergraduate full-time 750 men / 1,571 women, part-time 99m / 194w; graduate full-time 52m / 117w, part-time 59m / 188w.

Characteristics of Student Body: *Ethnic/racial makeup:* number of Black non-Hispanic: 343; American Indian or Alaska Native: 16; Asian or Pacific Islander: 22; Hispanic: 14; White non-Hispanic: 1,510; unknown 18. *Age distribution:* number under 18: 18; 18–19: 896; 20–21: 870; 22–24: 453; 25–29: 152; 30–34 72; 35–39: 41; 40–49: 40; 50–64: 20.

International Students: 49 nonresident aliens enrolled fall 2004. Students from Europe 19, Asia 4, Central and South America 7, Africa 5, Canada 7, other 1. No programs available to aid students whose native language is not English.. No financial aid specifically designated for international students.

Student Life: On-campus residence halls house 58% of student body. Halls for men only constitute 30% of such space, for women only 70%. Some students join and live in fraternities and sororities. *Intercollegiate athletics:* men only: baseball, basketball, golf; women only: basketball, volleyball. *Special regulations:* Cars displaying school registration sticker permitted. *Special services:* Harbert Composition Laboratory, Student Support Services Program. *Student publications: The Alabamian,* a semimonthly student newspaper; *The Fledgling,* an annual student handbook; *The Montage,* a yearbook; *The Tower,* an annual literary magazine. *Surrounding community:* Montevallo population 4,000. Birmingham, 25 miles from campus, is nearest metropolitan area. Served by airport 25 miles from campus.

Library Collections: 258,122 volumes. Online catalog. 363,500 microforms; 2,100 audiovisual materials; 847 045 current periodical subscriptions. 24 computer work stations. Access to online information retrieval systems. Students have access to the Internet at no charge.

Most important special holdings include History of City of Montevallo and Shelby County; publications and records of the university.

Buildings and Grounds: Campus area 200 acres. *New buildings:* Student Activity Center completed 2004.

Chief Executive Officer: Dr. Robert M. McChesney, President.

Address undergraduate admission inquiries to Mr. Lynn Gurganus, Director of Admissions; graduate inquiries to Dr. Terry Roberson, Dean, Graduate Office.

University of North Alabama

Wesleyan Avenue
Florence, Alabama 35632-0001
Tel: (256) 765-4221   **E-mail:** admissions@una.edu
Fax: (256) 765-4329   **Internet:** www.una.edu

Institution Description: University of North Alabama is a state institution. *Enrollment:* 2,535 men / 3,436 women. *Degrees awarded:* Baccalaureate, master's. Educational specialist also awarded.

Academic offering subject to approval by statewide coordinating bodies. Member of Marine Environmental Sciences Consortium.

Accreditation: *Regional:* SACS-Comm. on Coll. *Professional:* art, chemistry, music, nursing, social work, teacher education

History: Established when faculty and students of LaGrange College (established 1830) moved to Florence to open new institution 1854; incorporated by Methodist Church as Wesleyan University 1855; operations suspended 1862; facilities donated to state and institution reopened as Florence Normal School 1872; changed name to Florence State Teachers College and became 4-year institution 1929; awarded first degree (baccalaureate) 1931; changed name to Florence State College 1957, to Florence State University 1968; adopted present name 1974.

Institutional Structure: *Governing board:* Board of Trustees of the University of North Alabama. Representation: 11 trustees, including governor of Alabama, state superintendent of education; president of the university; 1 student, 3 ex officio. 11 voting. *Composition of institution:* Administrators 13 men / 1 women. Academic affairs headed by vice president for academic affairs and provost. Management/business/finances directed by vice president for business affairs. Full-time instructional faculty 203.

Calendar: Semesters. 2005–06 academic year Aug. 24 to May 13. Freshmen admitted Aug., Jan., June. Degrees conferred and formal commencements May, Dec. Summer session of 3 terms offered from early June to late July.

Characteristics of Freshmen: 80% of applicants accepted. 56% of accepted applicants enrolled.

97% of freshmen submitted ACT scores. *25th percentile*: ACT Composite 18, ACT English 18, ACT Math 17. *75th percentile*: Composite 23, ACT English 25, ACT Math 23.

31% of entering freshmen expected to graduate within 5 years; 79% of freshmen from Alabama. Freshmen from 15 states and 8 foreign countries.

Admission: Rolling admissions plan. Apply no later than day of registration. Early acceptance available. *Requirements:* Either graduation from accredited secondary school or GED. *Entrance tests:* ACT Composite. For foreign students TOEFL. *For transfer students:* must submit transcripts from all institutions previously attended; be eligible to return to last institution attended; must earn a minimum of 64 semester hours from University of North Alabama and/or other senior institution.

College credit and advanced placement for postsecondary-level work completed in secondary school, for USAFI, and for extrainstitutional learning on basis of *The 2006 Guide to the Evaluation of Educational Experiences in the Armed Services.* Tutoring available. Noncredit remedial courses offered in summer session and regular academic year.

Degree Requirements: *Undergraduate:* 128 semester hours; 2.0 GPA on 3.0 scale; 30 hours of upper division courses in residence; 2 hours physical education; distribution requirements; demonstrated proficiency in English.

Fulfillment of some degree requirements and exemption from some beginning courses possible by passing College Board CLEP, AP. *Grading system:* A–F; withdraw (deadline after which pass-fail is appended to withdraw).

Distinctive Educational Programs: *For undergraduates:* Preprofessional programs in agriculture, dentistry, forestry, law, medical technology, medicine, optometry, pharmacy, podiatry, and veterinary medicine. Study abroad in cooperation with various schools and by individual arrangement. *Available to all students:* Evening classes. Special facilities for using telecommunications in the classroom. Independent study.

Degrees Conferred: 849 *baccalaureate* (B); 195 *master's* (M): biological/life sciences 26 (B); business/marketing 242 (B), 86 (M); communications/communication technologies 65 (B); education 118 (B), 136 (M); English 22 (B), 3 (M); foreign languages and literature 8 (B); health professions and related sciences 132 (B); home economics and vocational home economics 30 (B); mathematics 13 (B); parks and recreation 22 (B), 3 (M); physical sciences 9 (B); protective services/public administration 11 (B), 3 (M); psychology 24 (B); social sciences and history 103 (B), 9 (M); visual and performing arts 25 (B).

Fees and Other Expenses: *Full-time tuition per academic year 2004–05:* undergraduate resident $3,528; nonresident $7,056. *Room and per academic year:* $4,140.

Financial Aid: Aid from institutionally generated funds is provided on the basis of academic merit, athletic ability, other criteria. Institution has a Program Participation Agreement with the U.S. Department of Education for eligible students to receive Pell Grants and other federal aid.

Financial aid to full-time, first-time undergraduate students: need-based scholarships/grants totaling $4,358,379; self-help $6,374,459, parent loans $434,993, tuition waivers $115,685, athletic $1,037,680; non-need-based scholarships/grants $3,270,818, self-help $55,393,163.

Departments and Teaching Staff: *Total instructional faculty:* 290 (women 163, men 128; members of minority groups 28). Total with doctorate, first-professional, or other terminal degree 167. Total whose highest degree is master's 123. Student to faculty ratio: 17:1.

Enrollment: Total enrollment 5,971. Undergraduate full-time 1,860 men / 2,440; part-time 364m / 536w; graduate full-time 65m / 70w, part-time 246m / 390w.

Characteristics of Student Body: *Ethnic/racial makeup:* number of Black non-Hispanic: 496; American Indian or Alaska Native: 83; Asian or Pacific Islander: 37; Hispanic: 411; White non-Hispanic: 3,865.

International Students: 344 nonresident aliens enrolled fall 2004. 127 students from Europe, 203 Asia, 10 Central and South America, 2 Africa, 4 Canada, 1 Australia. Programs available to aid students whose native language is not English: English as a Second Language Program. No financial aid specifically designated for international students.

Student Life: On-campus residence halls house 15% of student body. Dormitories for men only constitute 44% of such space, for women only 56%. 2.5% of men live in off-campus fraternities. 1% of women live in sorority housing. Housing available for married students. *Intercollegiate athletics:* men only: baseball, basketball, cross-country, football, golf, riflery, softball, tennis, volleyball; women only: basketball, volleyball. *Special regulations:* Cars with decals permitted in designated areas. Quiet hours. Dormitory visitation set by residents in individual halls. *Special services:* Learning Resources Center, medical services. *Student publications: Diorama,* a yearbook; *The Flor-Ala,* a weekly newspaper; *Lights and Shadows,* an annual literary magazine. *Surrounding community:* Florence population 37,000. Birmingham, 116 miles from campus, is nearest metropolitan area. Served by airport.

Library Collections: 371,123 volumes. 2,000 (est.) government documents; 1,047,732 microforms; 11,368 audiovisual materials; 3,540 current periodicals. Online and card catalogs. Students have access to the Internet at no charge.

Most important holdings include Congressman Flippo Papers and the Alabama Collection.

Buildings and Grounds: Campus area 100 acres. New buildings: Student Recreation Center; 7-story parking deck; 4 new cluster residence halls.

Chief Executive Officer: Dr. William G. Cale, Jr., President.

Address admission inquiries Office of Admissions.

University of South Alabama

307 North University Boulevard

Mobile, Alabama 36688-0002

Tel: (251) 460-6101   **E-mail:** admiss@usouthal.edu
Fax: (251) 460-7023   **Internet:** www.usouthal.edu

Institution Description: The University of South Alabama is a state institution. *Enrollment:* 13,340. *Degrees awarded:* Baccalaureate, master's, specialist certificate, doctorate, first-professional (medicine).

Academic offerings subject to approval by statewide coordinating agency.

Accreditation: *Regional:* SACS-Comm. on Coll. *Professional:* art, audiology, business, computer science, medicine, music, nursing, occupational therapy, physical therapy, physician assisting, radiography, speech-language pathology, teacher education

History: Established and chartered 1963; offered first instruction at postsecondary level 1964; awarded first degree (baccalaureate) 1967.

Institutional Structure: Governed by Board of Trustees composed of 17 members. The Governor of Alabama serves as president, ex officio, of the board, and the state superintendent of higher education serves as a member, ex officio. The following administrative officers report to the president: Senior Vice President for Academic Affairs, Vice President for Medical Affairs, Administrator of University Hospitals, Vice President for Business Affairs, Vice President for University Services, Vice President for Finance, Vice President for Student Services. Full-time instructional faculty: 689. Faculty Senate is primary representative body of the faculty and meets at least five times a year.

Calendar: Semesters. Academic year Aug. to May.

Characteristics of Freshmen: 94% of applicants accepted. 49% of accepted applicants enrolled.

92% submitted ACT scores. *25th percentile:* ACT Composite 20, ACT English 20, ACT Math 18. *75th percentile:* ACT Composite 25, ACT English 26, ACT Math 24.

27% of entering freshmen expected to graduate within 5 years. 78% of freshmen from Alabama. Freshmen from 44 states and 102 foreign countries.

Admission: Rolling admissions plan. For fall acceptance, apply up to Sept. 10. Early acceptance available. *Requirements:* Either graduation from accredited secondary school or GED. *Entrance tests:* College Board SAT or ACT Composite. For foreign students TOEFL. *For transfer students:* 2.0 minimum GPA; from 4-year accredited institution maximum transfer credit limited only by residence requirement; from 2-year accredited institution 96 quarter hours maximum transfer credit; for correspondence/extension students 48 hours.

College credit and advanced placement for postsecondary-level work completed in secondary school and for extrainstitutional learning as recommended in *The 2006 Guide to the Evaluation of Educational Experiences in the Armed Services.* Tutoring available. Developmental courses offered in all quarters. Credits earned in developmental courses are not counted in meeting degree requirements.

Degree Requirements: *Undergraduate:* 120 semester hours minimum; 2.0 GPA; 48 of upper division coursework must be complete in residence; minimum of 45 hours of general education requirements. *Grading system:* A–F;

Distinctive Educational Programs: Marine sciences, international studies, interdisciplinary program in personalized studies, concentrations in environmental science and meteorology.

ROTC: 6 Air Force and 12 Army commissions awarded in 2004.

Degrees Conferred: 1,303 *baccalaureate* (B), 575 *master's* (M), 11 *doctorate* (D): biological/life sciences 41 (B), 6 (M), 2 (D); business/marketing 247 (B), 67 (M); communications/communication technologies 83 (B), 6 (M); computer and information sciences 52 (B), 31 (M); education 201 (B), 224 (M), 5 (D); engineering and engineering technologies 79 (B), 53 (M); English 17 (B), 7 (M); foreign languages and literature 11 (B); health professions and related sciences 243 (B), 156 (M), 4 (D); interdisciplinary studies 11 (B); liberal arts/general studies 51 (B); mathematics 7 (B), 2 (M); parks and recreation 19 (B); philosophy/religion/theology 5 (b); physical sciences 30 (B), protective services/public administration 28 (B), 7 (M); psychology 55 (B), 10 (M); social sciences and history 81 (B), 6 (M); visual and performing arts 42 (B). *First-professional:* medicine 60.

Fees and Other Expenses: *Full-time tuition per academic year 2004–2005:*in-state undergraduate $3,810, graduate $2,880 (graduate fees are based on 6 hours per semester); out-of-state undergraduate $7,620, graduate $4,008. *Required fees:* $480. *Room per academic year:* $2,352. *Board per academic year:* $1,870. *Books and supplies:* $700.

Financial Aid: Aid from institutionally generated funds is provided on the basis of academic merit, financial need, athletic ability. Institution has a Program Participation Agreement with the U.S. Department of Education for eligible students to receive Pell Grants and other federal aid.

Financial aid to full-time, first-time undergraduate students: need-based scholarships/grants totaling $16,900,000, self-help $30,600,000, parent loans $380,000, athletic awards $1,700,000; non-need-based self-help $36,000,00.

Departments and Teaching Staff: *Professors* 199, *associate professors* 186, *assistant professors* 221, *instructors* 100, *part-time faculty* 275.

Total instructional faculty: 981 (women 459, men 247; members of minority groups 96). Total with doctorate, first-professional,or other terminal degree: 546. Student to faculty ratio: 15:1. *Faculty development:* $4,769,687 total grants for research in 2004.

Enrollment: Total enrollment 13,340 (full-time 9,653, part-time 3,687). Undergraduate full-time 3,077 men / 4,513 women, graduate full-time 568m / 1,239w, part-time 212m / 715w; first-professional full-time 142m / 114w.

Characteristics of Student Body: *Ethnic/racial makeup:* number of Black non-Hispanic: 1,829; American Indian or Alaska Native: 89; Asian or Pacific Islander: 165; Hispanic: 165; White non-Hispanic: 7,035; unknown: 465. *Age distribution:* number under 18: 122; 18–19: 2,294; 20–21: 2,531; 22–24: 2,236; 25–29: 1,465; 30–34 711; 35–39: 399; 40–49: 467; 50–64:135; 65 and over: 9.

International Students: 813 nonresident aliens enrolled fall 2004. 109 from Europe, 619 Asia, 99 Central and South America, 80 Africa, 25 Canada, other 47. Programs available to aid students whose native language is not English: Social, cultural. English as a Second Language program. No financial aid specifically designated for international students.

Student Life: On-campus residence halls house 18% of student body. Residence halls for both men and women constitute 100% of such space. Housing available for married students. *Intercollegiate athletics:* men: baseball, basketball, cross-country, golf, soccer, tennis, track; women: basketball, cross-country, golf, soccer, tennis, track, volleyball. *Special regulations:* Registered cars permitted without restriction. *Special services:* Medical services. *Student publications: Vanguard,* a weekly newspaper. *Surrounding community:* Mobile population 205,000. New Orleans (LA), 140 miles from campus, is nearest metropolitan area. Served by airport 5 miles from campus.

Library Collections: 548,847 volumes. 1,100,000 government documents; 790,000 microforms; 3,750 current periodicals. Online catalog. Access to online information retrieval services. Students have access to the Internet at no charge.

Buildings and Grounds: Main campus area 1,200 acres with 107 major buildings. Other facilities include three teaching hospitals, waterfront complex, and two off-campus theaters.

Chief Executive Officer: Dr. V. Gordon Moulton, President.

Address admission inquiries to Melissa Haab, Director of Admissions.

University of West Alabama

Station One
Livingston, Alabama 35470
Tel: (205) 652-3400   **E-mail:** admissions@univ.westal.edu
Fax: (205) 652-3708   **Internet:** www.univ.westal.edu

Institution Description: The University of West Alabama, formerly named Livingston University, is a state institution. *Enrollment: 2,372. Degrees awarded:* Associate, baccalaureate, master's.

Member of Alabama Marine Environmental Sciences Consortium.

Accreditation: *Regional:* SACS-Comm. on Coll. *Professional*: nursing, teacher education

History: Established and chartered as Livingston Female Academy 1835; received state grant, became Alabama Normal School, and offered first instruction at postsecondary level 1882; changed name to State Teachers College, Livingston, Alabama; awarded first degree (baccalaureate) 1931; changed name to Livingston State College 1957; became Livingston University 1967; adopted present name 1996.

Institutional Structure: *Governing board:* University of West Alabama Board of Trustees. Representation: 13 trustees (appointed by governor of Alabama), state superintendent of education, governor. 2 ex officio. All voting. *Composition of institution:* Administrators 19 men / 3 women. Academic affairs headed by provost. Management/business/finances directed by vice president for business affairs. Full-time instructional faculty 87. Academic governance body, University Senate, meets an average of 12 times per year.

Calendar: Semesters. Academic year mid-Aug. to early May. Freshmen admitted Aug., Jan., May. Degrees conferred and formal commencement May. Summer session of 3 terms from late May to early Aug.

Characteristics of Freshmen: 891 applicants of which 73.8% admitted; 51% of admitted students enrolled full-time.

1% (1 student) submitted SAT scores; 99% (263 students) submitted ACT scores. *25th percentile*: ACT Composite 14, ACT English 8, ACT Math 11. *75th percentile*: ACT Composite 22, ACT English 20, ACT Math 20.

22.9% of entering freshmen expected to graduate witin 5 years. 84% of freshmen from Alabama. Freshmen from 13 states and 2 foreign countries.

Admission: Rolling admissions plan. Apply as early as 1 year prior to enrollment, but not later than week of enrollment. Early acceptance available. *Requirements:* Either 15 units from a 4-year secondary school or 11 units from a 3-year secondary school which required for admission the completion of a 3-year junior high school program. Required units include 4 English, 1 mathematics, 1 science, 1 social studies. GED accepted. Minimum GPA 2.0. *Entrance tests:* College Board SAT or ACT Composite with acceptable score. (Minimum ACT Composite score of 19 for nursing students.) For foreign students TOEFL. *For transfer students:* 2.0 minimum GPA; from 4-year accredited institution maximum transfer credit limited only by residence requirements; from 2-year accredited institution 60 semester hours maximum; correspondence/extension students 30 semester hours.

College credit for postsecondary-level work completed in secondary school, for superior ACT scores, and for extrainstitutional learning basis of ACE *2006 Guide to the Evaluation of Educational Experiences in the Armed Services*.

Tutoring available. Developmental courses offered in summer session and regular academic year; credit given.

Degree Requirements: *For all associate degrees:* 60 semester hours (72 for nursing). *For all baccalaureate degrees:* 120 semester hours. *For all undergraduate degrees:* 2.0 GPA (2.2 for education degrees), exit proficiency in written and spoken English; distribution requirements. For education degrees, exit pro-

ficiency examinations: Alabama Initial Teacher Certification Test, comprehensives in individual fields of study, professional education area test.

Fulfillment of some degree requirements possible by passing College Board CLEP. *Grading system:* A–F; pass; withdraw (deadline after which pass-fail is appended to withdraw); incomplete (deadline after which A–F assigned).

Distinctive Educational Programs: *For undergraduates:* Dual-degree program in engineering with Auburn University. Preprofessional programs in allied health fields, dentistry, engineering, fisheries and wildlife management, forestry, law, medicine, pharmacy. *For graduate students:* Off-campus centers for education. Evening classes. *Available to all students:* Special facilities for using telecommunications in the classroom. *Other distinctive programs:* Special services for disadvantaged students. Servicemembers Opportunity College. Interdisciplinary master's program in education offered through Continuing Education.

Degrees Conferred: 47 *associate;* 238 *baccalaureate.* Bachelor's degrees awarded in top five disciplines: education 82; business, management, marketing, and related support services 61; health professions and related clinical sciences 15; social sciences 15; engineering technologies/technicians 14. 123 *master's*.

Fees and Other Expenses: *Full-time tuition per academic year 2004–05:* in-state undergraduate $4,196; out-of-state $7,922. *Room and board per academic year:* 3,388. *Books and supplies:* $900.

Financial Aid: Aid from institutionally generated funds is provided on the basis of academic merit, financial need, athletic ability, other criteria. Institution has a Program Participation Agreement with the U.S. Department of Education for eligible students to receive Pell Grants and other federal aid.

Financial aid to first-time, full-time undergraduate students include: 42% received federal grants averaging $3,266; 12% state/local grants averaging $1,335; 57% institutional grants averaging $1,785; 51% loans averaging $3,705.

Departments and Teaching Staff: *Total instructional faculty:* 87. 57 faculty members hold doctorates. Student-to-faculty ratio: 17:1.

Enrollment: Total enrollment 2,372. Undergraduate 1,692. 22.9% of entering freshmen expected to graduate within five years.

Characteristics of Student Body: *Ethnic/racial makeup:* Black non-Hispanic: 41.2%; American Indian or Alaska Native: .2%; Asian or Pacific Islander: .55; Hispanic: .4%; White non-Hispanic: 56.6%.

International Students: 19 nonresident aliens enrolled fall 2004. 2 students from Europe, 3 Asia, 6 Central and South America, 6 Africa, 2 Canada. No programs available to aid students whose native language is not English. No financial aid specifically designated for international students.

Student Life: On-campus residence halls house 36% of student body. Dormitories for men only constitute 17% of such space, for women only 26%. 3% of student body housed on campus in married student housing. *Intercollegiate athletics:* men only: baseball, basketball, cross-country, football; women only: basketball, softball, volleyball, cross-country. *Special regulations:* Registered cars permitted on campus in designated areas. *Special services:* Learning Resources Center, medical services. *Student publications: Livingston Life*, a weekly newspaper; *Paragon*, a yearbook. *Surrounding community:* Livingston population 3,500. Birmingham, 110 miles from campus, is nearest metropolitan area.

Library Collections: 135,000 volumes including bound books, serial backfiles, electronic documents, and government documents not in separate collections. Online catalog. Current serial subscriptions: 700 paper; 7,500 audiovisual materials. Students have access to the Internet at no charge.

Most important holdings include Ruby Pickens Tartt Collection of regional folklore, folk songs, and ring games from Sumter County, Alabama; University of West Alabama Archives; Sumter County Archival Collection.

Buildings and Grounds: Campus area 592 acres.

Chief Executive Officer: Dr. Richard D. Holland, President.

Address admission inquiries to Richard Hester, Director of Admissions.

Alaska

Alaska Bible College

Box 289
Glennallen, Alaska 99588-0289
Tel: (907) 822-3201   **E-mail:** info@akbible.edu
Fax: (907) 822-5027   **Internet:** www.akbible.edu

Institution Description: Alaska Bible College is a private, evangelical, non-denominational, nonprofit college. *Enrollment:* 61. *Degrees awarded:* Associate, baccalaureate. Certificates also awarded.

Accreditation: *Nonregional:* ABHE.

History: Established 1966 as Alaska Bible College. First baccalaureate degree awarded 1970.

Institutional Structure: *Governing board:* Board of Directors, 8 member board. A subsidiary corporation of SEND International of Alaska. *Composition of institution:* Administrators 6. Academic affairs headed by Academic Dean; business affairs headed by Business Manager; student affairs headed by Dean of Students; admissions headed by Dean of Admissions; development headed by Director of Development. Full-time instructional faculty 4.

Calendar: Semesters. Academic year Aug. to May. Freshmen admitted Aug., Jan. Degrees conferred and formal commencement May.

Characteristics of Freshmen: 24% of applicants accepted. 20% of accepted applicants enrolled. 60% of freshmen from Alaska. Freshmen from 5 states.

Admission: All application materials must be postmarked by July 1 for first semester and Dec. 11 for second semester. *Requirements:* High school graduation with 2.0 GPA or GED; ACT requested. *For transfer students:* minimum 2.0 GPA and SAT/ACT requested.

Degree Requirements: *For associate degree:* 22 credit hours in Bible; 30 credit hours in general education; 8 credit hours in ministry requirements. *For baccalaureate degree:* 40 credit hours in Bible; 36 credit hours in general education; 11 credit hours in ministry requirements; 28–33 credit hours in program studies; 2.0 GPA.

Distinctive Educational Programs: BA programs with a major in Bible and second major in Christian Education, Missions, Integrated Studies, or Pastoral Studies; terminal or preparatory for advanced degrees; AA program in Bible; certificate program in Bible.

Degrees Conferred: 2 *associate;* 7 *baccalaureate*: philosophy, religion, theology 7.

Fees and Other Expenses: *Full-time tuition per academic year 2005–06:* $5,720. *Required fees:* $425. *Room and board per academic year:* $5,720. *Books and supplies:* $500.

Financial Aid: Aid from institutional generated funds is provided on the basis of academic merit and financial need. Institution has a Program Participation Agreement with the U.S. Department of Education for eligible students to receive Pell Grants and other federal aid.

Departments and Teaching Staff: *Total instructional faculty:* 10 (women 2, men 8) Total with doctorate, first-professional, or other terminal degree: 2.

Enrollment: Total enrollment 61.

Characteristics of Student Body: *Ethnic/racial makeup:* number of American Indian or Alaska Native: 1; Asian or Pacific Islander: 3; White non-Hispanic: 56.

International Students: No programs available to aid students whose native language is not English. No financial aid specifically designated for international students.

Student Life: On-campus dormitory and married student housing. College maintains a 2-mile cross-country ski trail; weight lifting equipment. *Special regulations:* Students may have cars on campus if they have insurance for property and liability. *Surrounding community:* Glenallen population 800.

Library Collections: 27,000 volumes. 85 microforms. 100 audiovisual materials. 200 current periodical subscriptions. Students have access to the Internet.
Most important special holdings in the biblical field and Alaskana.

Chief Executive Officer: Steven J. Hostetter, President.

Address admission inquiries to Jackie Sands, Registrar (registrar@akbible.edu).

Alaska Pacific University

4101 University Drive
Anchorage, Alaska 99508
Tel: (907) 561-1266   **E-mail:** admissions@alaskapacific.edu
Fax: (907) 562-4276   **Internet:** www.alaskapacific.edu

Institution Description: Alaska Pacific University is a private institution affiliated with the United Methodist Church. *Enrollment:* 673. *Degrees awarded:* Associate, baccalaureate, master's. Certificates also awarded.

Accreditation: *Regional:* NWCCU.

History: Incorporated as Alaska Methodist University 1957; offered first instruction at postsecondary level 1960; adopted present name 1978.

Institutional Structure: *Governing board:* Alaska Pacific University Board of Trustees. Representation: 35 trustees. *Composition of institution:* Administrators 5 men / 2 women. Academic affairs headed by provost. Management/business/finances directed by business officer.

Calendar: Semesters. Academic year Sept. to May. Summer session mid-May to late Aug.

Characteristics of Freshmen: 52% of 13 enrolled students submitted SAT scores; 60% (15 students) submitted ACT scores. *25th percentile*: SAT Verbal 430, SAT Math 460; ACT Composite 17, ACT English 16, ACT Math 16. *75th percentile*: SAT Verbal 630, SAT Math 590; ACT Composite 26, ACT English 26, ACT Math 27.
48% of freshmen from Alaska. Freshmen from 9 states and 1 foreign country.

Admission: Rolling admissions plan. For fall acceptance, apply no later than May 15. Early acceptance available. *Requirements:* Either graduation from secondary school or GED. Minimum GPA 2.0. *Entrance tests:* College Board SAT or ACT Composite. For foreign students TOEFL. *For transfer students:* 2.0 minimum GPA; from 4-year accredited institution maximum transfer credit limited only by degree requirement; from 2-year accredited institution 60 hours maximum transfer credit.
College credit for postsecondary-level work completed in secondary school.

Degree Requirements: *For all associate degrees:* 64 semester hours; 3 hours physical education courses. *For all baccalaureate degrees:* 128 hours; 3 hours physical education courses. *For all undergraduate degrees:* 30 hours in residence; general education and practicum requirements.
Fulfillment of some degree requirements and exemption from some beginning courses possible by passing College Board CLEP, AP. *Grading system:* A–F; credit-no credit; withdraw; incomplete.

Distinctive Educational Programs: Study abroad in Japan, Mexico, China. School maintains 275-acre facility for research and recreation. Continuing education programs.

Degrees Conferred: 96 *baccalaureate*; 84 *master's*. Bachelor's degrees awarded in top five disciplines: business, management, marketing, and related support services 44; education 14; natural resources and conservation 12; public administration and social service professions 6; psychology 6.

Fees and Other Expenses: *Full-time tuition per academic year 2004–05:* $17,200. *Room and board per academic year:* $5,950. *Books and supplies:* $840. *Other expenses:* $1,100.

Financial Aid: Aid from institutionally generated funds is provided on the basis of financial need. Institution has a Program Participation Agreement with the U.S. Department of Education for eligible students to receive Pell Grants and other federal aid.
Financial aid to full-time, first-time undergraduate students: 30% received federal grants; 83% institutional grants; 74% loans.

Departments and Teaching Staff: *Professors* 7, *associate professors* 7, *assistant professors* 9, *instructors* 7. *Total instructional faculty:* 30. Degrees held by full-time instructional faculty: doctorate 70%; master's 30%.

Enrollment: Total enrollment 673. Undergraduate 478.

Characteristics of Student Body: *Ethnic/racial make-up:* Black non-Hispanic: 5%; American Indian or Alaska Native: 16.1%; Asian or Pacific Islander: 3,6%; Hispanic: 3.1%; White non-Hispanic: 68.6.

International Students: 40 nonresident aliens enrolled fall 2004. Programs available to aid students whose native language is not English: Social and cultural. English as a Second Language Program. Financial aid specifically designated for international students: Scholarships available annually.

Student Life: On-campus residence halls house 25% of student body. Housing available for married students. *Special services:* Medical services. *Surrounding community:* Anchorage population 250,000. Served by airport.

Library Collections: 760,500 volumes including bound books, serial backfiles, electronic documents, and government documents not in separate collections (consortium library). Online catalog. 3,400 current serial subscriptions. 1,035 audio/visual/CD's. Students have access to the Internet at no charge.

Buildings and Grounds: Campus area 275 acres.

Chief Executive Officer: Dr. Douglas M. North, President.

Address admission inquiries to Michael Warner, Director of Admissions.

Sheldon Jackson College

801 Lincoln
Sitka, Alaska 99835
Tel: (907) 747-5220   **E-mail:** admissions@sj-alaska.edu
Fax: (907) 747-2594   **Internet:** www.sj-alaska.edu

Institution Description: Sheldon Jackson College is a private, independent, nonprofit college affiliated with the Presbyterian Church (U.S.A.). *Enrollment:* 147. *Degrees awarded:* Associate, baccalaureate.

Academic offerings subject to approval by statewide coordinating bodies.

Accreditation: *Regional:* NWCCU.

History: Established 1878 as Sitka Training School; moved to present location 1882; became coeducational 1884; changed name to Sheldon Jackson Training School 1911; offered first instruction at postsecondary level 1944; awarded first degree (associate) 1946; adopted present name 1966; awarded first baccalaureate degree 1977.

Institutional Structure: *Governing board:* Board of Trustees of Sheldon Jackson College. Representation: 18 trustees, 5 clergy. 3 ex officio. Full-time instructional faculty 15. Academic governance body: Faculty and Academic Programs Committee.

Calendar: Semesters. Academic year Aug. to May. Degrees conferred and formal commencement May.

Characteristics of Freshmen: 65% of applicants accepted. 23% of applicants admitted and enrolled. 40% of entering freshmen graduate within 5 years. 59% of freshmen from Alaska. Freshmen from 11 states.

Admission: Rolling admissions plan. For fall acceptance, apply no later than July 1 of year of enrollment. Early acceptance available. *Requirements:* Either graduation from secondary school or GED. *For transfer students:* 2.0 minimum GPA; maximum transfer credit limited only by residence requirement.

College credit for extrainstitutional learning on basis of ACE *2006 Guide to the Evaluation of Educational Experiences in the Armed Services*; portfolio and faculty assessments. Tutoring available. Developmental courses offered during regular academic year; credit given.

Degree Requirements: *For all associate degrees:* 60 credit hours. *For all baccalaureate degrees:* 120 hours. *For all degrees:* 6 credit hours in communication, 12 humanities, 10 math/science, 9 social science, multicultural class. 2.0 GPA; 20 of last 30 credits in residence.

Fulfillment of some degree requirements possible by passing departmental examinations. *Grading system:* A–F; pass-no pass; withdraw; incomplete (carries time limit).

Distinctive Educational Programs: Internships; individualized majors; independent studies; service learning. Interdisciplinary program in humanities. Opportunities for study at Sheldon Jackson Museum which houses collection of native Alaskan artifacts dating from the 19th century.

Degrees Conferred: 17 *baccalaureate:* business/marketing 1; interdisciplinary studies 1; natural resources/environmental science 7; parks and recreation 4.

Fees and Other Expenses: *Full-time tuition per academic year 2004–05:* $10,000. *Required fees:* 250. *Room and board per academic year:* 7,300.

Financial Aid: Institution has a Program Participation Agreement with the U.S. Department of Education for eligible students to receive Pell Grants and other federal aid.

Financial aid to full-time, first-time undergraduate students: need-based scholarships/grants totaling $1,211,327, self-help $932,125, parent loans $50,069, tuition waivers $24,953.

Departments and Teaching Staff: Alaska Native Studies *professors* 0, *associate professors* 0, *assistant professors* 1, *instructors* 0, *part-time faculty* 2; art 0, 0, 0, 1, 0; business 1, 0, 0, 0, 1; education 0, 0, 2, 0, 4; English 0, 0, 2, 0, 0; environmental science 0, 1, 2, 0, 0; history 0, 1, 0, 0, 0; human services 0, 1, 0, 0, 1; humanities 0, 0, 0, 0, 3; mathematics 0, 0, 1, 1, 0; outdoor leadership 0, 0, 1, 0, 3; physical education 0, 0, 0, 0, 1; social science 0, 0, 0, 0, 1.

Total instructional faculty: 31 (women 16, men 13). Total with doctorate, first-professional, or other terminal degree: 9. Student to faculty ratio: 7:1. *Faculty development:* $100,000 in grants for research in 2004. faculty member awarded a sabbatical 2004.

Enrollment: Total enrollment 147. Full-time men 41 / women 94; part-time 6m / 5w.

Characteristics of Student Body: *Ethnic/racial makeup:* number of Black non-Hispanic: 7; American Indian or Alaska Native: 57; Hispanic: 7; White non-Hispanic: 93; unknown: 3. *Age distribution:* number under 18: 6; 18–19: 47; 20–21: 41; 22–24: 17; 25–29: 9; 30–34 9; 35–39: 8; 40–49: 8; 50–64: 2.

International Students: No programs available to aid students whose native language is not English.

Student Life: On-campus residence halls house 97% of student body. Residence halls for men only constitute 50% of such space, for women only 50%. Housing available for married students. *Special regulations:* Cars permitted for all except freshmen. *Special services:* Learning Resources Center. *Surrounding community:* Sitka population 8,000. Anchorage, 800 miles from campus is nearest metropolitan area. Served by airport 2 miles from campus.

Publications: Sources of information about Sheldon Jackson include *S.J.C. Adventures*, distributed to Presbyterian churches, alumni, friends of the college.

Library Collections: 46,265 volumes. Online and card catalogs. 10,000 Alaska state documents; 10,000 audiovisual materials; 142 current periodical subscriptions. 46 CD-ROM. Students have access to Internet at no charge. Total 2004–05 budget for books and materials: $39,996.

Most important holdings include C.L. Andrews Collection (materials on Alaska consisting of rare books, first editions, original periodicals, and maps from late 19th and early 20th century); Elbridge Warren Merrill Collection (969 original glass plates of photographs of Sitka and surrounding region between 1920 and 1940s, including scenery, natives, and buildings); the Stratton Library Collection of Alaska History (835 reference items, including rare books, first editions with emphasis on Sitka region).

Buildings and Grounds: Campus area 34 acres.

Chief Executive Officer: Dr. Arthur G. Cleveland, President.

Address inquiries to Rick Eber, Director of Admissions.

University of Alaska Anchorage

3211 Providence Drive
Anchorage, Alaska 99508
Tel: (907) 786-1800   **E-mail:** admissions@uaa.alaska.edu
Fax: (907) 786-4888   **Internet:** www.uaa.alsask.edu

Institution Description: The University of Alaska Anchorage (UAA) is comprised of 1 main and 4 community campuses (Kenai Peninsula College, Kodiak College, Matanuska-Susitna College, and Prince William Sound Community College). UAA is one of 3 major administrative units of the statewide system. *Enrollment:* 16,607. *Degrees awarded:* Baccalaureate, master's. Associate degrees are offered at the community campuses.

Accreditation: *Regional:* NWCCU. *Professional:* applied science, art, business, clinical lab technology, dental assisting, dental hygiene, engineering, journalism, medical assisting, nursing, social work

History: Established, offered first instruction at postsecondary level, and awarded first degree 1970.

Institutional Structure: *Composition of institution:* Administrators 16 men / 9 women. Academic Affairs headed by provost. Office of Student Affairs headed by Dean of Students. Management/business/finances directed by vice chancellor for administrative services. Governing bodies: APT Council, Classified Council, Faculty Senate, Graduate Affairs Board, Undergraduate Affairs Board. University Assembly meets an average of 10 times per year.

Calendar: Semesters. Academic year June to May. Freshmen and other transfer students admitted Aug., Jan., May. Formal commencement May. Two summer sessions.

Characteristics of Freshmen: 865 (56% of enrolled students) submitted SAT scores; 25% (384 students) submitted ACT scores. *25th percentile:* SAT Verbal I 440, SAT I Math 440; ACT Composite 18, ACT English 16, Math 18. *75th percentile:* SAT verbal 570, SAT Math 570; ACT Composite 24, ACT English 24, ACT Math 24.

91% of freshmen from Alaska. Students from 50 states and 35 foreign countries.

Admission: Rolling admissions plan; early acceptance available. Priority date Apr. 1 for financial aid. For fall acceptance to specific program, apply no later than mid-July. *Requirements:* Either graduation from accredited secondary school or GED. Minimum GPA 2.5. *Entrance tests:* College Board SAT or ACT Composite. For foreign students TOEFL. *For transfer students:* 2.0 minimum GPA; from 2-year accredited institution 72 credit hours maximum transfer credit; correspondence-extension students 32 hours.

College credit for postsecondary-level work completed in secondary school.

Degree Requirements: *Undergraduate:* 130 credit hours; 2.0 GPA; 30 of last 36 hours in residence; general education requirements.

Fulfillment of some degree requirements and exemption from some beginning courses possible by passing College Board CLEP, AP. *Grading system:* A–F; pass; withdraw (carries time limit); incomplete.

Distinctive Educational Programs: Evening classes. Postsecondary education programs for active duty military personnel and their dependents, DOD employees, and civilians at Alaska military bases. Certified Experience Credit. Credit for Prior Learning. Study abroad programs in Cologne (Germany), Avignon (France), Siena (Italy), London (England).

ROTC: Air Force.

Degrees Conferred: 705 *baccalaureate.* Degrees awarded in top five disciplines include: business, management, marketing, and related support services 163; health professions and related clinical sciences 136; psychology 62; social sciences 49; history 45. 241 *master's. Honorary degrees awarded 2004–5:* Doctor of Law 1, Doctor of Science 1.

Fees and Other Expenses: *Full-time tuition per academic year 2004=05:* resident $3,517, out-of-state $10,447. *Room and board per academic year:* $6,430. *Other expenses;* $1,761. *Books and supplies:* $965.

Financial Aid: Aid from institutionally generated funds provided on the basis of academic merit, financial need, athletic ability, other criteria. Institution has a Program Participation Agreement with the U.S. Department of Education for eligible students to receive Pell Grants and other federal aid.

Financial aid to full-time, first-time undergraduate students: 16% received federal grants averaging $3,128; 27% institutional grants averaging $2,993; 27% loans averaging $5,399.

Departments and Teaching Staff: *Professors* 113, *associate professors* 116, *assistant professors* 126, *instructors* 24, *part-time faculty* 247.

Total full-time instructional faculty: 390. Student-to-faculty ratio: 14:1. *Degrees held by full-time faculty:* 73.7% hold terminal degrees.

Enrollment: Total enrollment 16,607. Undergraduate 15,810. *Transfer students:* in-state 164; from out-of-state 766.

Characteristics of Student Body: *Ethnic/racial makeup:* Black non-Hispanic: 4.1%; American Indian or Alaska Native: 8.4%; Asian or Pacific Islander: 4.7%; Hispanic: 4.0%; White non-Hispanic: 71.7%; unknown: 4.7%.

International Students: 379 nonresident aliens enrolled fall 2004. Programs available to aid students whose native language is not English: Social, cultural. No financial aid specifically designated for international students.

Student Life: Apartment style on-campus housing. *Intercollegiate athletics:* men only: basketball, cross-country, hockey, nordic and alpine skiing, swimming; women only: basketball, cross-country, gymnastics, nordic and alpine skiing, volleyball. 78 clubs and organizations on campus. *Special regulations:* Paid parking permit areas. *Student publications: The Northern Light,* the student newspaper. Student-run radio station KRUA. *Surrounding community:* Anchorage population 260,000. Served by airport 6 miles from campus.

Library Collections: 677,000 volumes including bound books, serial backfiles, electronic documents, and government documents not in separate collections. Online catalog. 3,480 current periodical subscriptions. 8,7000 audio/video/CD units; 3,406 microform titles; 115 electronic titles. Students have access to online information retrieval services and the Internet.

Most important special collections include Alaskana Collection; government documents; manuscripts/records.

Buildings and Grounds: Campus area 428 acres.

Chief Executive Officer: Dr. Elaine P. Maimon, Chancellor.

Address all admission inquiries to Cecile Mitchell, Director of Enrollment Services.

University of Alaska Fairbanks

P.O. Box 757480
Fairbanks, Alaska 99775-7480
Tel: (907) 474-7500   **E-mail:** admissions@uaf.edu
Fax: (907) 474-6725   **Internet:** www.uaf.edu

Institution Description: *Enrollment:* 8,693. *Degrees awarded:* Baccalaureate, master's, doctorate.

Accreditation: *Regional:* NWCCU. *Professional:* accounting, business, computer science, engineering, forestry, journalism, music, social work, teacher education

History: Established 1917; awarded first instruction at postsecondary level 1922; awarded first degree 1923; adopted present name 1935.

Institutional Structure: *Composition of institution:* Administrators 46 men / 25 women. Academic affairs headed by provost. Management/business/finances directed by director of administrative services. Full-time instructional faculty 309. Academic governance body, Academic Council, meets an average of 15 times per year.

Calendar: Semesters. Academic year 2004–05 Sept. 2 to May 12. Freshmen admitted Sept., Dec., June. Degrees conferred June, Aug., Dec. Formal commencement May. Summer session from early June to mid-Aug.

Characteristics of Freshmen: 91% of applicants accepted. 61% of accepted applicants enrolled.

52% (494 students) submitted SAT scores; 33% (309 students) submitted ACT scores. *25th percentile:* SAT Verbal 450, SAT Math 450; ACT Composite 18, ACT English 16, ACT Math 16. *75th percentile:* SAT Verbal 610, SAT Math 590; ACT Composite 25, ACT English 24, ACT Math 24.

20% of entering freshmen expected to graduate within 5 years. 89% of freshmen from Alaska. Students from 35 states and 7 foreign countries.

Admission: Rolling admissions plan. For fall acceptance, apply no later than Aug. 1. Early acceptance available. *Requirements:* Either graduation from accredited secondary school or GED. *Entrance tests:* ACT Composite or SAT. For foreign students TOEFL. *For transfer students:* 2.0 minimum GPA.

College credit and advanced placement for postsecondary-level work completed in secondary school and for extrainstitutional learning on basis of ACE *2006 Guide to the Evaluation of Educational Experiences in the Armed Services.* Developmental courses offered during regular academic year.

Degree Requirements: *For all baccalaureate degrees:* 120 to 130 semester hours; 30 hours in residence. *For all associate degrees:* 60 semester hours; 15 in residence. All certificate programs require 30 semester hours; 15 in residence. *For all undergraduate degrees:* 2.0 GPA; general education requirements.

Fulfillment of some degree requirements and exemption from some beginning courses possible by passing College Board CLEP, AP, departmental examinations. *Grading system:* A–F; pass-fail; pass; withdraw (carries penalty, carries time limit); deferred; audit; credit-no credit; incomplete.

Distinctive Educational Programs: National Student Exchange Program. Interdepartmental programs in Asian studies, Northern studies. Individual majors. Study abroad Australia, Canada, Ecuador, England, Finland, Japan, Mexico, Norway, Russia, Sweden, Taiwan, Venezuela, and many locations in Europe.

ROTC: Army.

Degrees Conferred: 411 *baccalaureate* (B), 143 *master's* (M), 27 *doctorate* (D): area and ethnic studies 5 (B), 8 (M); biological/life sciences 40 (B), 9 (M), 3 (D); business/marketing 31 (B), 16 (M); communications/communication technologies 30 (B), 6 (M); computer and information sciences 12 (B), 2 (M); education 14 (B), 20 (M); engineering and engineering technologies 35 (B), 33 (M), 1 (D); English 17 (B), 15 (M); foreign languages and literature 11 (B); interdisciplinary studies 20 (B), 2 (M), 6 (D); liberal arts/general studies 5 (B); mathematics 12 (B), 6 (M); natural resources/environmental science 19 (B), 21 (M), 31 (D); philosophy/religion/theology 1 (B); physical sciences 33 (B), 19 (M), 5 (D); protective services/public administration 40 (B), 9 (D); psychology 24 (B), 9 (M); social sciences and history 42 (B), 5 (M), 2 (D); visual and performing arts 19 (B), 3 (D). *Honorary degrees awarded 2003–04:* Doctor of Laws 2, Doctor of Sciences 2.

Fees and Other Expenses: *Full-time tuition per academic year 2005–06:* undergraduate resident $3,480, nonresident $11,100; graduate resident $5,226, nonresident $9,384. *Required fees:* $1,244. *Room per academic year:* $2,990. *Board per academic year:* $2,590.

Financial Aid: Direct lending program available. Contact (e-mail: financial-aid.uaf.edu). Aid from institutionally generated funds is provided on the basis of academic merit, financial need, athletic ability. Institution has a Program Participation Agreement with the U.S. Department of Education for eligible students to receive Pell Grants and other federal aid.

Financial aid to full-time, first-time undergraduate students: need-based scholarships/grants totaling $3,359,628, self-help $10,692,298, parent loans $112,348, tuition waivers $106,575, athletic awards $76,930; non-need-based scholarships/grants totaling $2,170,094, self-help $3,902,711, parent loans $253,783, tuition waivers $297,628, athletic awards $431,397.

Departments and Teaching Staff: Branch campuses *professors* 8, *associate professors* 12, *assistant professors* 44, *instructors* 18, *part-time faculty* 83 education 0, 6, 11, 0, 3; engineering 12, 9, 9, 1, 0; fisheries and ocean science 3, 1, 0, 0, 0; liberal arts 19, 28, 40, 11, 0; management 6, 6, 5, 3, 1; natural resources and agriculture 2, 3, 3, 0, 0; research institutes 1, 1, 4, 1, 0; science and mathematics 18, 12, 10, 2, 0;

Total instructional faculty: 314 (women 117, men 197; members of minority groups 36). Student to faculty ratio: 18:1.

Enrollment: Total enrollment 8.693. Undergraduate full-time 1,696 men / 1,826 women, part-time 1,372m / 2,716w; graduate full-time 364m / 300w, part-time 159m / 260w. *Transfer students:* in-state 78m / 80w; out-of-state 104m / 184w.

Characteristics of Student Body: *Ethnic/racial makeup:* number of Black non-Hispanic: 215; American Indian or Alaska Native: 1,556; Asian or Pacific Islander: 196; Hispanic: 191; White non-Hispanic: 5,488. *Age distribution:* number under 18: 180; 18–19: 1,084; 20–21: 1,264; 22–24: 1,426; 25–29: 1,507; 30–34 824; 35–39: 1,009; 40–49: 1,062; 50–64: 794; 65 and over: 69.

14% of total student body attend summer sessions. Extension courses offered on campus. Correspondence courses are offered for both credit and noncredit.

International Students: 485 nonresident aliens enrolled fall 2004. 68 students from Europe, 54 Asia, 14 Central and South America, 72 Africa, 39 Canada, 1 Australia, 1 New Zealand, 301 other. English as a Second Language program offered to students whose native language is not English.

Student Life: On-campus residence halls house 26% of student body. Dormitories are coed. Some students housed on campus in college-owned apartments. *Special regulations:* Cars permitted without restrictions. *Special services:* Learning Resources Center, medical services, campus-wide shuttle bus service. *Student publications, radio, television: Sun Star,* a weekly newspaper. Radio stations KUAC and KUSA broadcast over 140 hours per week. TV station KUAC broadcasts 112 hours per week. *Surrounding community:* Fairbanks population over 70,000. Served by mass transit bus system. Airport 2 miles from campus; passenger rail service 5 miles from campus.

Publications: University press publishes numerous titles yearly.

Library Collections: 1,059,001 volumes including bound books, serial backfiles, electronic documents, and government documents not in separate collections. Online catalog. Current serial subscriptions: 3,000. 24,937 recordings. 46 computer work stations. Students have access to the Internet at no charge.

Most important holdings include Skinner Arctic Collection; Gruvening Papers; Bartlett Papers.

Buildings and Grounds: Campus area 2,250 acres. New buildings: West Ridge Research Building; Museum Extension.

Chief Executive Officer: Dr. Steve Jones, Chancellor.

Address admission inquiries to Nancy Dix, Director of Admissions.

University of Alaska Southeast

11120 Glacier Highway
Juneau, Alaska 99801
Tel: (907) 465-6547   **E-mail:** jyuas@acadi.alaska.edu
Fax: (907) 465-6395   **Internet:** uas.alaska.edu

Institution Description: *Enrollment:* 3,268. *Degrees awarded:* Associate, baccalaureate, master's. Postgraduate certificate awarded.

Accreditation: *Regional:* NWCCU.

History: Established as University of Alaska, Juneau and offered first instruction at postsecondary level 1956; awarded first degree 1967; adopted present name 1980.

Institutional Structure: *Composition of institution:* Administrators 13 men / 5 women. Academic affairs headed by chancellor. Management/business/finances directed by administration services. Full-time instructional faculty 83. Academic governance body, University of Alaska Juneau Assembly, meets an average of 4 times per year.

Calendar: Semesters. Academic year Sept. to May. Freshmen admitted Sept., Jan., June. Degrees conferred Apr., Aug., Dec. Formal commencement Apr. Summer session of 2 terms from early June to late July.

Admission: Rolling admissions plan. Early acceptance available. *Requirements:* Either graduation from accredited secondary school or GED. Approval by secondary school counselor or university official. *For transfer students:* 2.0 minimum GPA.

College credit and advanced placement for postsecondary level work completed in secondary school. For extrainstitutional learning college credit on basis of ACE *2006 Guide to the Evaluation of Educational Experiences in the Armed Services.* Tutoring available. Developmental/remedial courses offered during regular academic year; credit given.

Degree Requirements: *For all associate degrees:* 60 semester hours; 15 hours in residence. *For all baccalaureate degrees:* 130 semester hours; 30 hours in residence. *For all undergraduate degrees:* 2.0 GPA; general education requirements.

Fulfillment of some degree requirements and exemption from some beginning courses possible by passing College Board CLEP, AP, departmental examinations. *Grading system:* A–F; pass-fail; pass; withdraw (deadline after which pass-fail is appended to withdraw); deferred; audit, credit-no credit, incomplete; satisfactory-unsatisfactory.

Distinctive Educational Programs: Weekend and evening classes. Individual majors.

Degrees Conferred: 92 *baccalaureate.* Bachelor's degrees awarded in top five disciplines: liberal arts and sciences, general studies, and humanities 42; business, management, marketing, and related support sciences 32; biological and sciences 13, English language and literature/letters 2; natural resources and conservation 2; 77 *master's.*

Fees and Other Expenses: *Full-time tuition per academic year 2004–05:* $3,633 resident, out-of-state $10,563. *Room and board per academic year:* $5,807. *Books and supplies:* $622.

Financial Aid: Aid from institutionally generated funds is awarded on the basis of academic merit, financial need. Loans available to qualified applicants.

Financial aid to full-time, first-time undergraduate students: 29% received federal grants averaging $2,131; 25% institutional grants averaging $3,0764; 38% loans averaging $6,074.

Departments and Teaching Staff: *Total instructional faculty:* 83. Degrees held by full-time faculty: 39% hold terminal degrees.

Enrollment: Total enrollment 3,268. Undergraduate 3,126.

Characteristics of Student Body: *Ethnic/racial makeup:* Black non-Hispanic: 1%; American Indian or Alaska Native: 18.7%; Asian or Pacific Islander: 3.6%; Hispanic: 1.5%; White non-Hispanic: 63.9%; unknown: 9.4%.

International Students: 74 nonresident aliens enrolled fall 2004. Programs available to aid students whose native language is not English: English as a Second Language Program.

Student Life: On-campus residence halls house 1% of student body. Dormitories for men only constitute 50% of such space, for women only 50%. *Special services:* Learning Resources Center. *Surrounding community:* Juneau population 20,000. Seattle (WA), 700 miles from campus, is nearest metropolitan area. Served by mass transit bus system; airport 3 miles from campus.

Library Collections: 250,000 volumes. 1,500 periodicals. 2,000 audio/visual and CD's. On-line catalog. Students have access to online information retrieval services and the Internet.

Buildings and Grounds: Campus area 198 acres.

Chief Executive Officer: John Pugh, Chancellor.

Address admission inquiries to Barbara Carlson Burnett, Director of Admissions.

Arizona

American Indian College of the Assemblies of God

10020 North 15th Avenue
Phoenix, Arizona 85021
Tel: (602) 944-3335   **E-mail:** aicadm@aicag.edu
Fax: (602) 943-8299   **Internet:** www.acag.edu

Institution Description: The American Indian College of the Assemblies of God, formerly known as the American Indian Bible College is a private institution affiliated with the Assemblies of God Church. *Enrollment:* 66. *Degrees awarded:* Associate, baccalaureate.

Accreditation: *Regional:* NCA.

Calendar: Semesters. Academic year mid-Aug. to late Apr.

Characteristics of Freshmen: 6.7% (4 students) submitted SAT scores; 6.7% (4 students) submitted ACT scores. *25th percentile:* SAT Verbal 380, SAT Math 425; ACT Composite 15, ACT English 14, ACT Math 16. *75th percentile:* SAT Verbal 114, SAT Math 127; ACT Composite 15, ACT English 15, ACT Math 16.

Degree Requirements: Completion of prescribed curriculum.

Degrees Conferred: 3 *associate;* 11 *baccalaureate:* education 6, philosophy/religion/theology 5.

Fees and Other Expenses: *Full-time tuition per academic year:* $4,950. *Room and board per academic year:* $3,850. *Required fees:* $650. *Other fees:* $500.

Financial Aid: Aid from institutionally generated funds is provided on the basis of financial need. Institution has a Program Participation Agreement with the U.S. Department of Education for eligible students to receive Pell Grants and other federal aid.

Financial aid to full-time, first-time undergraduate students: need-based scholarships/grants totaling $295,484, self-help $20,550, tuition waivers $17,815; non-need-based scholarships/grants $500.

Departments and Teaching Staff: *Total instructional faculty:* 20 (8 full-time, 12 part-time). Student-to-faculty ratio: 5:1. 5 faculty members hold doctorates or other terminal degrees.

Enrollment: Total enrollment 66.

Characteristics of Student Body: *Ethnic/racial makeup:* number of Black non-Hispanic: 3; American Indian or Alaska Native: 48; Asian or Pacific Islander: 4; Hispanic: 4; White non-Hispanic: 10. *Age distribution:* number of 18–19: 10; 20–21: 15; 22–24: 17; 25–29: 11; 30–34 6; 35–39: 3; 40–49: 8.

International Students: 1 student from Africa. No programs to aid students whose native language is not English.

Library Collections: 15,000 volumes. 500 microform titles; 120 periodicals; 900 recordings and tapes. Access to online information retrieval systems.

Buildings and Grounds: New buildings: Cafeteria completed 2002; renovated chapel 2003.

Chief Executive Officer: James V. Comer, President.

Address admission inquiries to Sandy Ticeahkie, Director of Admissions.

Arizona State University at the Tempe Campus

P.O. Box 872803
Tempe, Arizona 85287-2803
Tel: (480) 965-9011   **E-mail:** ugradinq@.asu.edu
Fax: (480) 965-7788   **Internet:** www.asu.edu

Institution Description: Arizona State University at the Tempe Campus, formerly named Arizona State University Main, is a state institution. *Enrollment:* 49,171. *Degrees awarded:* Baccalaureate, master's, doctorate, first-professional (law).

Academic offerings subject to approval by statewide coordinating bodies. Budget subject to approval by state governing board.

Accreditation: *Regional:* NCA. *Professional:* accounting, art, audiology, business, clinical lab scientist, clinical psychology, computer science, construction education, counseling, counseling psychology, engineering, engineering technology, health services administration, interior design, journalism, landscape architecture, law, marriage and family therapy, music, nursing, planning, psychology internship, public administration, public health, recreation and leisure services, school psychology, social work, speech-language pathology

History: Established as Territorial Normal School 1885; chartered and offered first instruction at postsecondary level 1886; changed name to Arizona Territorial Normal School 1889, to Normal School of Arizona 1896, to Tempe Normal School of Arizona 1903, added senior level and changed name to Tempe State Teachers College 1929; to Arizona State College at Tempe 1945; became Arizona State University 1958; became Arizona State University Main 1996; adopted present name 2004. *See* Ernest J. Hopkins and Alfred Thomas, Jr., *The Arizona State University Story* (Phoenix: Southwest Publishing Company, 1960) for further information.

Institutional Structure: *Governing board:* Arizona Board of Regents. Representation: 8 regents, governor of Arizona, state superintendent of public instruction, 2 student regents. All voting. *Composition of institution:* Academic affairs headed by executive vice president and provost. Management/business/finances directed by executive vice president and chief financial officer. Full-time instructional faculty 1,778. Academic governance body, Faculty Senate, meets an average of 10 times per year.

Calendar: Semesters. 2004–05 academic year Aug. to May. Freshmen admitted Aug., Jan., summer. Degrees conferred and formal commencement May, Aug, Dec. Summer session of 3 terms from June to Aug.

Characteristics of Freshmen: 78% of freshmen applicants accepted. 38% of accepted freshmen applicants enrolled.

77.9% (5,565 students) submitted SAT scores; 45.4% (3,246 students) submitted ACT scores. *25th percentile:* SAT Verbal 490, SAT Math 500; ACT Composite 21, ACT English 19, ACT Math 20. *75th percentile:* SAT Verbal 600, SAT Math 620; ACT Composite 26, ACT English 26, ACT Math 27.

49% of entering freshmen expected to graduate within 5 years. 65% of freshmen from Arizona. Freshmen from 50 states and 38 foreign countries.

Admission: *Undergraduate admission:* Rolling admissions plan. Freshmen may apply as early as Sept. of year prior to enrollment. Transfer students may apply during their final term at their current institution. Admissions information must be received 30 days prior to the first day of classes. *Requirements:* Graduation from accredited secondary school with rank in the upper 25% of graduating class, or 3.0 GPA/4.0=A, or minimum ACT Composite score of 22 for in-state students, 24 for out-of-state students or minimum SAT combined score of 1040 for in-state students, 1110 for out-of-state students, and with the following coursework: 4 years of English, 3 years of mathematics, 2 years of laboratory science, 2 years of social science (including American history); or GED score of 500 or higher. Additional requirements for some programs. *Entrance tests:* SAT or ACT Composite. TOEFL for foreign students. *For transfer students:* 2.5 minimum GPA for out-of-state students, 2.0 minimum GPA for in-state residents; from 4-year accredited institution maximum transfer credit limited only by residency requirements; from 2-year accredited institution 64 semester hours; correspondence/extension students 30 hours.

College credit and advanced placement for postsecondary level work completed in secondary school and for USAFI-DANTES.

Graduate admission: Application deadlines: The Division of Graduate Studies should receive in one envelope the application for admission, application fee, two transcripts of all undergraduate and post baccalaureate work, and entrance test scores, if required by the program, at least two months before enrollment. Many programs have specific earlier deadlines, so applicants are urged to contact the academic unit. The Graduate College should receive materials from international students by mid-January for study in the fall semester and by mid-September for study in the spring semesters. *Requirements:* A bachelor's (or equivalent) or graduate degree from a college or university of recognized standing; generally a 3.0 GPA/4.0=A scale, or the equivalent, in the last two years of work leading to the bachelor's degree; and acceptance by the academic unit and Graduate College. *Entrance Tests:* Most programs require scores from an academic aptitude test such as the GRE, GMAT, or MAT; scores from the TOEFL are required for all international students. *Other Application materials:* some programs require letters of recommendation, statement of goals, and/or a portfolio.

Degree Requirements: *See* individual colleges below.

Distinctive Educational Programs: The Honors College draws its participants from all colleges within the university. Distinctive interdisciplinary undergraduate programs include among others, Women's Studies, Gerontology, Southeast Asian, East Asian, and Latin American Studies, and Engineering Interdisciplinary Studies. A strong Writing Across the Curriculum program is in place and internship opportunities, including legislative internships, are available in many disciplines. Graduate and/or undergraduate students participate in educational programs supported by numerous centers and institute, among which are the National Center for Electron Microscopy, a National Plant Science Center for the Study of Photosynthesis, the Center for Southeast Asian Studies, the Herberger Center for Design, the Services Marketing Center, and the Center for Medieval and Renaissance Studies. ASU participates in international exchange and study abroad programs in England, Israel, Italy, France, Germany, Japan, Macedonia, Mexico, Netherlands, Norway, Spain, Sweden, Thailand. ASU's Downtown Center, located in the heart of Phoenix, offers continuing education programs and is a major part of a rapidly growing College of Extended Education.

ROTC: Army, Air Force.

Degrees Conferred: 7,046 *baccalaureate* (B), 2,440 *master's* (M), 355 *doctorate* (D): architecture 112, (B), 21 (M), 3 (D); area and ethnic studies 25 (B); biological/life sciences 280 (B), 11 (M), 21 (D); business/marketing 1,300 (B), 637 (M); 6 (D); communications/communication technologies 672 (B), 16 (M), 8 (D); computer and information sciences 135 (B), 114 (M), 15 (D); education 611 (B), 499 (M); 59 (D); engineering and engineering technologies 508 (B), 372 (M), 71 (D); English 155 (B), 44 (M), 10 (D); foreign languages and literature 160 (B), 23 (M), 10 (D); health professions and related sciences 236 (B), 106 (M), 3 (D); home economics and vocational home economics 96 (B), 5 (M); interdisciplinary studies 623 (B), 18 (M); liberal arts/general studies 24 (B), 1 (M); mathematics 50 (B), 20 (M), 12 (D); parks and recreation 204 (B), 29 (M), 4 (D); philosophy/religion/theology 54 (B), 12 (M), 2 (D); physical sciences 47 (B), 22 (M), 18 (D); protective services/public administration 361 (B), 249 (M), 16 (D); psychology 366 (B), 18 (M), 25 (D); social sciences and history 637 (B), 64 (M), 31 (D); visual and performing arts 369 (B), 98 (M), 31 (D); other 1 (M). 169 *first-professional:* law.

Fees and Other Expenses: *Full-time tuition per academic year 2005–06:* resident undergraduate $3,973; out-of-state $12,828. *Mandatory fees:* $91. *Room per academic year:* $4,178. *Board per academic year:* $2,396.

Financial Aid: Aid from institutional generated funds is provided on the basis of academic merit, financial need, athletic ability. Institution has a Program Participation Agreement with the U.S. Department of Education for eligible students to receive Pell Grants and other federal aid.

Financial aid to full-time, first-time undergraduate students: need-based scholarships/grants totaling $59,959,557, self-help $69,221,157, parent loans $9,122,282, tuition waivers $620,082, athletic awards $1,294,327; non-need-based scholarships/grants totaling $24,527,597, self-help $30,237,896, parent loans $19,268,636, tuition waivers $1,703,172, athletic awards $4,069,949.

Departments and Teaching Staff: *Total full-time faculty* 2,184 (full-time 1,778, part-time 406; 876 women, 1,308 men). Student-to-faculty ratio: 22:1.

Degrees held by full-time faculty: doctorate, first-professional, or other terminal degree 1,593.

Enrollment: Total enrollment 49,171. Undergraduate full-time 15,302 men / 16,268 women, part-time 3,752m / 4,055w; first-professional full-time 302m / 259w, part-time 5m / 8w; graduate full-time 2,846m / 2,739w, part-time 1,506m / 2,129w.

Characteristics of Student Body: *Ethnic and racial makeup of degree-seeking undergraduates:* number of Black non-Hispanic: 1,414; American Indian or Alaska Native: 916; Asian or Pacific Islander: 2,051; Hispanic: 4,821; White non-Hispanic: 27,405; unknown: 640.

Age distribution: number under 18: 509; 18–19: 12,341; 20–21: 11,224; 22–24: 8,520; 25–29: 3,890; 30–34: 1,267; 35–39: 632; 40–49: 718; 50–64: 260; 65 and over: 12.

International Students: 1,130 nonresident aliens enrolled fall 2004. 269 students from Europe, 1,843 Asia, 205 Central and South America, 85 Africa, 121 Canada, 11 Australia, 2 New Zealand, other 243. English as a Second Language Program available.

Student Life: On-campus residence halls house 16% of student body. 5% of men join and live in fraternities; 3% of women join and live in sororities. Over 500 student clubs and organizations. *Intercollegiate athletics:* men only: archery, badminton, baseball, basketball, football, golf, gymnastics, swimming, tennis, track, wrestling; women only: archery, badminton, basketball, golf, gymnastics, softball, swimming, tennis, track, volleyball. *Special regulations:* Cars permitted in designated areas. *Special services:* Medical services, shuttle bus service between campus and parking areas. *Student publications, television, radio:* State

Press, a weekday daily newspaper; *Hayden's Ferry Review*, literary magazine; *Sun Devil Spark*, yearbook; public broadcasting television (KAET); student-run radio station (K-ASU). *Surrounding community:* Tempe population 160,000. Served by airport 5 miles from campus.

Publications: Contact each College separately for ASU's extensive publications list.

Library Collections: 3,593,677 volumes. 730,500 government documents. 5,500,000 microforms; 58,000 audiovisual materials. 32,001 current periodicals.

Most important holdings include solar energy archives; William Burroughs Archives; Alberto Pradeau Archives; Child Drama Collection; Patten Herbal Collection; Labriola Indian Education Collection.

Buildings and Grounds: Campus area 644 acres.

Chief Executive Officer: Dr. Michael M. Crow, President.

Undergraduates address admission inquiries to Timothy J. Desch, Director of Undergraduate Admissions; graduate inquiries to Graduate Admissions Office.

College of Architecture and Environmental Design

Degree Programs Offered: *Baccalaureate* in architectural studies, design science, environmental resources, industrial design, interior design, housing and urban development, landscape architecture, urban planning.

Degree Requirements: 120 semester hours, 30 hours in residence (12 semester credit hours immediately preceding graduation), 2.0 CGPA.

Departments and Teaching Staff: Total instructional faculty: 61.

Enrollment: Total enrollment: 2,094.

W. P. Carey School of Business

Degree Programs Offered: *Baccalaureate* in accountancy, purchasing and logistics management, real estate, computer information systems, economics, finance, management and marketing.

Admission: Admissions limited. Progression to upper division, professional programs requires 2.50 CGPA, 2.50 in all lower division business courses with a grade of C or better.

Degree Requirements: 120 semester hours, 24 in professional business courses taken after admission to the professional program, 2.00 CGPA in all business courses and for all courses in the major, 30 hours in residence (12 semester credit hours immediately preceding graduation).

Departments and Teaching Staff: Total instructional faculty: 194.

Distinctive Educational Programs: Interdisciplinary programs in Asian studies, Latin American studies, pre-law studies. Certificate in international business studies, certificate in quantitative business analysis, an opportunity to graduate with an honors degree from the college of business.

Enrollment: Total enrollment: 7,988.

College of Education

Degree Programs Offered: *Baccalaureate* in selected studies in education, early childhood education, elementary education, secondary education, and special education.

Degree Requirements: 120 hours, 2.50 CGPA and 2.50 in professional teacher preparation program with at least a C in each professional teacher preparation program course, directed field experiences during each of four semesters of program, including student teaching. 30 hours in residence (12 semester hours immediately preceding graduation).

Departments and Teaching Staff: Total instructional faculty: 132.

Enrollment: Total enrollment: 4,384. Undergraduate full-time 487 men, 1,839 women, part-time 100m / 260w; graduate full-time 204m / 260w, part-time 233m / 715w.

Ira A. Fulton School of Engineering

Degree Programs Offered: *Baccalaureate* in agribusiness, aeronautical engineering technology, aeronautical management technology, construction, electronics engineering technology, industrial technology, manufacturing engineering technology, engineering special studies, engineering interdisciplinary programs, bioengineering, chemical engineering, materials science and engineering, civil engineering, computer science, computer systems engineering, electrical engineering, industrial engineering, aerospace engineering, mechanical engineering.

Admission: Arizona residents require the following for admission. *For Agribusiness and Environmental Resources:* ACT Composite score of 22 or SAT combined score of 930; upper 50% of high school graduating class or transfer minimum GPA of 2.00. *For Construction:* ACT Composite score of 23 or SAT combined score of 1050; upper 50% of high school graduating class or transfer minimum GPA of 2.24. *For Technology:* ACT Composite score of 22 or SAT combined score of 930; upper 50% of high school graduating class or transfer minimum GPA of 2.25. *For Engineering:* ACT Composite score of 23 or SAT combined score of 1050; upper 25% of high school graduating class or transfer minimum GPA of 2.50. Nonresidents require the following for admission. *For Agribusiness and Environmental Resources:* ACT Composite of 24 or SAT combined score of 1010; TOEFL of 500; upper 25% of high school graduating class or transfer minimum GPA of 2.50. *For Construction:* ACT Composite score of 24 or SAT combined score of 1050; TOEFL of 550; upper 25% of high school graduating class or transfer minimum GPA of 2.50. *For Engineering:* ACT Composite of 24 or SAT combined score of 1050; TOEFL of 550; upper 25% of high school graduating class or transfer minimum GPA of 2.50. *For Technology:* ACT Composite score of 24 or SAT combined score of 1010; TOEFL of 500; upper 25% of high school graduating class or transfer GPA of 2.50.

Degree Requirements: 128 semester hours.

Departments and Teaching Staff: Total instructional faculty: 241.

Distinctive Educational Programs: Engineering Special and Interdisciplinary Programs in engineering mechanics. Geological engineering, manufacturing engineering, microelectronics manufacturing engineering, nuclear engineering science, premedical engineering, systems engineering.

Enrollment: Total enrollment: 6,191.

Walter Cronkite School of Journalism and Mass Communication

Degree Programs Offered: *Baccalaureate.*

Degree Requirements: 120 semester hours, 2.50 CGPA, 30 hours in residence (12 semester hours immediately preceding graduation).

Departments and Teaching Staff: Total instructional faculty: 26.

Enrollment: Total enrollment: 1,940. Undergraduate full-time 558 men / 1,063 women, part-time 77m / 162w. Graduate full-time 4m / 28w, part-time 17m / 31w.

The Katherine K. Herberger College of Fine Arts

Degree Programs Offered: *Baccalaureate* in art, dance, music, choral-general music, instrumental music, music therapy, performance, theatre, and theory and composition.

Degree Requirements: 120 semester hours, 2.00 GPA, with many professional programs requiring additional hours and higher GPAs; 30 hours in residence (12 semester credit hours immediately preceding graduation).

Departments and Teaching Staff: Total instructional faculty: 179.

Enrollment: Total enrollment: 2,554.

College of Liberal Arts and Sciences

Degree Programs Offered: *Baccalaureate* in anthropology, biology, botany, botany, chemistry, computer sciences, economics, English, exercise science/physical education, family resources and human development, Asian language, Chicana and Chicano studies, French, German, Italian, Russian, Spanish, geography, geology, history, humanities, mathematics, clinical laboratory sciences, microbiology, philosophy, physics, political science, psychology, religious studies, wildlife conservation biology, sociology, speech and hearing science, women's studies, zoology.

Degree Requirements: 120 credit hours, at least 50 in upper division, 2.00 CGPA. Program of study must be filed after the 87th credit hour. 30 hours in residence (12 semester credit hours immediately preceding graduation).

Departments and Teaching Staff: Total instructional faculty: 988.

Distinctive Educational Programs: Interdisciplinary studies with concentrations in health physics, Jewish studies. Certificate programs in museum studies, Russian and East European studies, Southeast Asian studies, women's studies, Center for Early Events in Photosynthesis.

Enrollment: Total enrollment: 14,537. Undergraduate full-time 3,947 men / 5,372 women; part-time 958m / 1,302w. Graduate full-time 682m / 928w; part-time 427m / 632w. Unclassified full-time 1m / 1w; part-time 152m / 135w.

College of Law

Degree Programs Offered: *Juris Doctor.*

Degree Requirements: 87 credit hours.

Departments and Teaching Staff: Total instructional faculty: 56.

Distinctive Educational Programs: Center for the Study of Law, Science and Technology; Indian Legal Program; Law School clinic with mediation and arbitration component.

Enrollment: Total enrollment: 591. First-professional full-time 302 men / 259 women, part-time 5m / 8w. Graduate full-time 5m / 9w, part-time 1m / 2w.

College of Nursing

Degree Programs Offered: *Baccalaureate.*

Degree Requirements: 120 credit hours, at least a "C" in all required prerequisite courses with a 2.5 GPA in prerequisite courses.

Departments and Teaching Staff: Total instructional faculty: 64.

Enrollment: Total enrollment: 1,332. Undergraduate full-time 65 men / 770 women, part-time 36m / 292w. Graduate full-time 5m / 83w, part-time 3m / 17w.

College of Public Programs

Degree Programs Offered: *Baccalaureate* in communication, broadcasting, journalism, justice studies, recreation.

Degree Requirements: 120 semester hours, 2.00 CGPA, 30 hours in residence (12 semester hours immediately preceding graduation).

Departments and Teaching Staff: Total instructional faculty: 74.

Enrollment: Total enrollment: 1,434. Undergraduate full-time 97 men / 376 women, part-time 37m / 89w. Graduate full-time 105m / 366w, part-time 93m / 267w; unclassified full-time 2m / 2w.

Division of Graduate Studies

Degree Programs Offered: *Master's* in architecture, building design, industrial design, interior design, environmental planning, business administration, accountancy, decision and information systems, health services administration, economics, educational media and computers, secondary education, special education, educational administration and supervision, social and philosophical foundations of education, higher and adult education, school library science, educational psychology, learning and instructional technology, counseling, counselor education, agribusiness, environmental resources, engineering science, bioengineering, chemical engineering, civil engineering, computer science, construction, electrical engineering, industrial engineering, aerospace engineering, mechanical engineering, art, dance, performance, theatre, laws, anthropology, botany, biological sciences, chemistry, English, teaching English as a second language, exercise science/physical education, family resources and human development, French, German, Spanish, geography, geology, history, mathematics, microbiology, philosophy, physics, political science, religious studies, sociology, zoology, nursing, communication, mass communication, recreation, public administration, justice studies, social work, curriculum and instruction, humanities, music, creative writing, music composition, music education, natural science, communication disorders, molecular and cellular biology, statistics, taxation, technology. *Doctorate* in business administration, economics, educational administration and supervision, higher and adult education, educational leadership and policy studies, counselor education, counseling psychology, educational psychology, learning and instructional technology, engineering science, bioengineering, chemical engineering, civil engineering, computer science, electrical engineering, industrial engineering, aerospace engineering, mechanical engineering, theatre, law, anthropology, botany, chemistry, English, Spanish, geography, geology, history, mathematics, microbiology, physics, political since, psychology, sociology, zoology, social work, communication, justice studies, public administration, science and engineering of materials, speech and hearing science, curriculum and instruction; environmental design and planning, music, exercise science, family science, molecular and cellular biology.

Departments and Teaching Staff: Faculty drawn from other colleges of the university.

Distinctive Educational Programs: Interdisciplinary programs in creative writing, exercise science, science and engineering of materials, statistics, speech and hearing science, humanities, public administration, justice studies.

Arizona State University at the West Campus

4701 West Thunderbird Road
Glendale, Arizona 85306

Tel: (602) 543-5500   **E-mail:** admissions@west.asu.edu
Fax: (602) 543-7012   **Internet:** www.west.asu.edu

Institution Description: Arizona State University at the West Campus is a unit of the Arizona State University system. *Enrollment:* 7,105. *Programs offered:* Baccalaureate, master's.

Academic offerings and budget subject to approval by state governing bodies.

Accreditation: *Regional:* NCA. *Professional:* accounting, business, recreation and leisure services, social work, nursing, social work, teacher education

History: Arizona State University West was separately accredited by the NCA in 1992.

Calendar: Academic year mid-Aug. to early May.

Characteristics of Freshmen: 631 applicants in fall 2004; 82.1% admitted; 46.8% admitted students enrolled full-time.

62% (245 students) submitted SAT scores; 42% (168 students) submitted ACT scores. *25th percentile*: SAT Verbal 450, SAT Math 450; ACT Composite 18, ACT English 17, ACT Math 18. *75th percentile*: SAT Verbal 570, SAT Math 560; ACT Composite 24, ACT English 24, ACT Math 24.

Degrees Conferred: 1,422 *baccalaureate* 321 *master's*. Baccalaureate degrees awarded in top five disciplines include: education 413; business, management, marketing, and related support services 381; psychology 106; security and protective services 93; communication, journalism, and related programs 89.

Fees and Other Expenses: *Full-time tuition per academic year 2004–05:* undergraduate in-state $4,064; out-of-state $12,919. *Books and supplies:* $838. *Room and board per academic year:* $6,574. *Other expenses:* $3,726.

Financial Aid: Aid from institutionally generated funds is provided on the basis of academic merit, financial need. Direct institutional lending program available. Institution has a Program Participation Agreement with the U.S. Department of Education for eligible students to receive Pell Grants and other federal aid.

Financial aid to full-time, first-time undergraduate students: 24% received federal grants averaging $3,016; 61% received institutional grants averaging $2,338; 20% loans averaging $2,939.

Departments and Teaching Staff: American studies *professors* 2, *associate professors* 6, *assistant professors* 4 *instructors* 4, *part-time teachers* 13; integrative studies 1, 1, 3, 2, 3; interdisciplinary studies/arts/performance 1, 3, 1, 3, 1; life sciences 2, 4, 3, 1, 5; social and behavioral sciences 1, 7, 6, 3, 10; women's studies 1, 1, 1, 0, 2; collaborative programs 0, 0, 0, 1, 0; education 5, 11, 17, 4, 63; gerontology 1, 0, 0, 0, 3; administration of justice 1, 2, 5, 2, 7; communication 0, 3, 7, 1, 3; recreation and tour management 2, 1, 1, 0, 4; social work 0, 1, 1, 4, 4; school of management 9, 15, 4, 10, 14.

Total instructional faculty: 301. Total tenured faculty: 81. Student-to-faculty ratio: 10:1.

Enrollment: Total enrollment 7,105. Undergraduate 5,751 (32.4% men, 67.6% women).

Characteristics of Student Body: *Ethnic and racial makeup:* Black non-Hispanic: 66.5%; American Indian or Alaskan Native: 2.1%; Asian or Pacific Islander: 3.9%, Hispanic: 17.9%; White non-Hispanic: 66.5%.

International Students: 575 nonresident aliens enrolled fall 2004. No programs available to aid students whose native language is not English. No scholarships specifically for international students.

Library Collections: 1,800,000 volumes including bound books, serial backfiles, electronic documents, and government documents not in separate collections. Online and card catalogs. Current serial subscriptions: paper, microform, electronic. 2,151 compact discs; 227 CD-ROMs. 90 computer work stations. Students have access to the Internet at no charge.

Most important special collection is the Jetro Collection.

Chief Executive Officer: Dr. Michael A. Crow, President.

Address admission inquiries to Thomas J. Cabot, Registrar.

DeVry University-Arizona

2149 West Dunlap Avenue
Phoenix, Arizona 85021-2995
Tel: (602) 870-0222   **E-mail:** admissions@devry.edu
Fax: (602) 331-1494   **Internet:** www.devry.edu

Institution Description: DeVry University-Arizona is a private institution that offers a hands-on technology-based curriculum in a variety of programs. *Enrollment:* 2,526. *Degrees offered:* Associate, baccalaureate, master's.

Accreditation: *Regional:* NCA.

History: The university in Phoenix opened in 1967 and is one of 66 other Devry locations in the United States and Canada.

Calendar: Semester. Academic year Sept. to May. Summer session.

Characteristics of Freshmen: 1,434 applicants for fall 2003 (1,034 men, 400 women). 62% of applicants admitted; 33.6% admitted and enrolled full-time; 12.7% part-time.

Admission: High school graduation with 2.0 GPA or GED. CLEP accepted for credit; ACT or SAT scores; interview required.

Degree Requirements: 25% of 48 to 154 credits required for the bachelor's degree must be completed at DeVry.

Distinctive Educational Programs: Computer information systems and electronics engineering technology are the largest programs offered.

Degrees Conferred: 109 *associate*; 645 *baccalaureate*. Bachelor's degrees awarded in top three disciplines: computer and information sciences and support services 324; engineering technologies/technicians 175; business, management,

marketing, and related support services 146. 124 *master's*. (Statistics for the 2003–04 academic year).

Fees and Other Expenses: *Full-time tuition per academic year 2004–05:* Tuition and fees $11,200. *Room and board:* (Off-campus) $9,620. *Books and supplies:* 41,200. *Other expenses:* $3,560.

Financial Aid: Aid from institutionally generated funds is provided on the basis of financial need. Institution has a Program Participation Agreement with the U.S. Department of Education for eligible students to receive Pell Grants and other federal aid.

Financial aid to full-time, first-time undergraduate students: 46% received federal grants averaging $2,505; 2% state/local grants; 12% institutional grants averaging $2,127; 78% loans averaging $5,339.

Enrollment: Total enrollment 2,526. Undergraduate 2,079 (76.2% men, 23.8% women).

Characteristics of Student Body: *Ethnic and racial makeup:* Black non-Hispanic: 6%, American Indian or Alaskan Native: 5.5%; Asian or Pacific Islander: 5.5%, Hispanic: 17.2%; White non-Hispanic: 63.4%; unknown 1.7%.

International Students: 26 nonresident aliens enrolled fall 2003. Students from Europe, Asia, Latin America, Africa, Canada. No programs available to aid students whose native language is not English. No financial aid specifically designated for international students.

Student Life: No on-campus housing.

Library Collections: 22,500 volumes. 730 current periodical subscriptions. Students have access to online database searching.

Buildings and Grounds: 18-acre campus.

Chief Executive Officer: James Dugan, Regional Vice President. Address admission inquiries to Director of Admissions.

Embry Riddle Aeronautical University

3200 Willow Creek Road
Prescott, Arizona 86301-3270
Tel: (800) 888-3728   **E-mail:** admit@pre/erau.edu
Fax: (520) 708-3740   **Internet:** www.embryriddle.edu

Institution Description: The Prescott campus is a branch of the Florida-based institution. *SEE* FLORIDA - Embry Riddle Aeronautical University. *Enrollment:* 1,669. *Degrees awarded:* Associate, baccalaureate.

Accreditation: *Regional:* SACS (parent institution). *Professional:* business, engineering

Calendar: Semesters. Aug. to Aug.

Characteristics of Freshmen: 80% of applicants accepted. 28% of accepted applicants enrolled. 48% of entering freshmen expected to graduate within 5 years. Freshmen from 37 states and 8 foreign countries.

Admission: *Requirements:* Graduation from an accredited secondary school or GED.

Degree Requirements: *For all associate degrees:* 60–81 credit hours. *For all baccalaureate degrees:* 120–138 credit hours.

Distinctive Educational Programs: The Extended Campus provides instruction through 124 teaching centers in the U.S. and Europe, through independent study and computerized instruction.

Degrees Conferred: 325 *baccalaureate*. Bachelor's degrees conferred in top five disciplines include transportation and materials moving 211, engineering 86, social sciences 14, multidisciplinary studies 14. 5 *master's*.

Fees and Other Expenses: *Full-time tuition per academic year 2004–05:* $22,820. *Room per academic year:* $3,580. *Board per academic year:* $2,936. *Required fees:* $670.

Financial Aid: Aid from institutionally generated funds is provided on the basis of academic merit, financial need. Institution has a Program Participation Agreement with the U.S. Department of Education for eligible students to receive Pell Grants and other federal aid.

Financial aid to full-time, first-time undergraduate students: need-based scholarships/grants totaling $11,272,616, self-help $15,427,831, parent loans $5,242,261, athletic awards $579,000.

Departments and Teaching Staff: Aeronautical science *professors* 1, *associate professors* 9, *assistant professors* 5, *instructors* 0, *part-time teachers* 5; arts and sciences 11, 10, 5, 1, 22; engineering 4, 11, 4, 0, 6.

Total instructional faculty: 106. Total faculty with doctorate, first-professional, or other terminal degree: 62. Student-to-faculty ratio: 17:1.

Enrollment: Total enrollment 1,668. Full-time 1,206 men / 261 women, part-time 141m / 29w. *Transfer students:* in-state 26; from out-of-state 118.

Characteristics of Student Body: *Ethnic/racial makeup:* number of Black non-Hispanic: 37, American Indian Alaskan Native: 15; Asian or Pacific Islander: 106; Hispanic: 107, White non-Hispanic: 1,140; unknown: 182.

International Students: 50 nonresident aliens enrolled fall 2004. Programs available to aid students whose native language is not English: English as a Second Language Program. No financial aid specifically designated for international students.

Student Life: *Student publications: Horizons,* newspaper.

Library Collections: 26,300 volumes including bound books, serial backfiles, electronic documents, and govern documents not in separate collections. Online catalog. 630 current serial subscriptions. Students have access to the Internet at no charge.

Most important special collections include aviation history; safety.

Chief Executive Officer: Dr. George Ebbs, President.

Address admission inquiries to Bill Thompson, Director of Enrollment Management.

Grand Canyon University

3300 West Camelback Road
Phoenix, Arizona 85017
Tel: (602) 249-3300   **E-mail:** admissions@gcu.edu
Fax: (602) 589-2895   **Internet:** www.gcu.edu

Institution Description: Grand Canyon University, formerly known as Grand Canyon College, is a private college. *Enrollment:* 7,001. *Degrees awarded:* Baccalaureate, master's.

Accreditation: *Regional:* NCA. *Professional:* business, nursing

History: Established in Prescott, chartered, incorporated, and offered first instruction at postsecondary level 1949; awarded first degree (baccalaureate) 1950; moved to present location 1951; adopted present name 1994.

Institutional Structure: *Governing board:* Member managed. Academic affairs headed by Chief Academic Officer. Business/finances directed by Chief Financial Officer. Total instructional faculty 66.

Calendar: Semesters (4-4 plan). Academic year late Aug. to May. Degrees conferred May and Aug. Formal commencement May. Summer session of 2 terms from mid-May to mid-Aug.

Characteristics of Freshmen: 63% of applicants accepted. 44% of entering freshmen expected to graduate within 5 years. 63% of freshmen from Arizona. Freshmen from 28 states.

Admission: Rolling admissions plan. Early acceptance available. *Requirements:* Either graduation from accredited secondary school or GED. Recommend 4 units in English, 3 mathematics (algebra, geometry, and 1 advanced mathematics unit), 2 science (1 laboratory), 2 social studies (1 American history), 6 academic electives. Lowest acceptable secondary school class standing 50th percentile. Provisional acceptance possible. *Entrance tests:* College Board SAT or ACT Composite. For foreign students minimum TOEFL score 500. *For transfer students:* From 2-year accredited institution 64 hours maximum transfer credit; correspondence students 30 hours; extension students 12 hours.

College credit and advanced placement for postsecondary level work completed in secondary school.

Degree Requirements: 128 credit hours; 2.0 GPA; 30 semester hours in residence (18 hours in upper division); for day students, chapel attendance 20 times per semester; general education requirements.

Fulfillment of some degree requirements and exemption from some beginning courses possible by passing College Board CLEP, APP. *Grading system:* A–F; withdraw; incomplete (carries time limit).

Distinctive Educational Programs: Practicums, internships, overseas study. Evening classes. Facilities and programs for independent research, honors program, independent study. Tommy Barnett School of Applied Ministry. Latin American Studies Program. American Studies Program in Washington, D.C.; Los Angeles Film Studies Center. Urban Education Program in Los Angeles. Neonatal Practitioner Program.

ROTC: Army, Air Force; both in cooperation with Arizona State University.

Degrees Conferred: 287 *baccalaureate*; 1,225 *master's.* Bachelor's degrees awarded in top five disciplines: health professions and related clinical sciences 80; business, management, marketing, and related support services 76; education 56; biological and biomedical sciences 25; visual and performing arts 21.

Fees and Other Expenses: *Full-time tuition per academic year 2005–06:* $9,750. *Room and board per academic year:* $7,130. *Books and supplies:* varies by course.

Financial Aid: Aid from institutionally generated funds is provided on the basis of academic merit, financial need, athletic ability, other. Institution has a Program Participation Agreement with the U.S. Department of Education for eligible students to receive Pell Grants and other federal aid. Financial aid available to qualified applicants in assistance packages (institutional, state, federal funds).

Departments and Teaching Staff: *Professors* 20, *associate professors* 12, *assistant professors* 21, *instructors* 13, *adjunct teachers* 278, *online faculty* 400.

Total instructional faculty: 744. Total tenured faculty: 21. Degrees held by full-time faculty: 53% hold terminal degrees.

Enrollment: Total enrollment: 7,001. Undergraduate 1,957.

Characteristics of Student Body: *Ethnic and racial makeup:* Black non-Hispanic: 1.3%, American Indian or Alaska Native: .4%; Asian or Pacific Islander: .6%, Hispanic: 2%; White non-Hispanic: 15%; unknown: 80.7%.

International Students: Students from Europe, Asia, Latin America, Africa, Canada, New Zealand, other. No financial programs specifically designated for international students.

Student Life: On-campus residence halls, apartments and married housing available. Curfews and quiet hours. *Special services:* Health Center on campus. *Intercollegiate athletics:* men: baseball, basketball, golf, soccer; women: basketball, golf, soccer, softball, tennis, volleyball, basketball. *Student publications: The Echoes*; *Surrounding community:* Phoenix metropolitan area populations 3,000,000. Served by mass transit system; airport 15 miles from campus.

Library Collections: 68,000 volumes. 111 paper journals; electronic/remote access collection; 56 electronic journals. Access to online information retrieval databases.

Most important holdings include Vera Butler collection (120 children's books dating from 1800s); Brantner Library of Recordings (700 78rpm and 1,500 33–1/3rpm albums of classical music); Robert I. Schattner Special Collections (870 special and rare books).

Buildings and Grounds: Campus area 90 acres.

Chief Executive Officer: Dr. Brent Richardson, President.

Address admission inquiries to Director of Admissions (admissions-ground@gcu.edu).

Northern Arizona University

P.O. Box 4132
Flagstaff, Arizona 86011-4132
Tel: (928) 523-5865   **E-mail:** admissions@nau.edu
Fax: (928) 523-0332   **Internet:** www.nau.edu

Institution Description: Northern Arizona University is a state institution. *Enrollment:* 19,147. *Degrees awarded:* Associate, baccalaureate, master's, doctorate. Specialist certificate in education also awarded.

Academic offerings subject to approval by statewide coordinating bodies. Budget subject to approval by state governing boards.

Accreditation: *Regional:* NCA. *Professional:* business, computer science, construction education, counseling, dental hygiene, engineering, engineering technology, forestry, music, nursing, nursing education, physical therapy, public health, recreation and leisure services, social work, speech-language pathology

History: Established as Northern Arizona Normal School and offered first instruction at postsecondary level 1899; chartered, changed name to Northern Arizona State and Teachers College, and became a 4-year institution 1925; awarded first degree (baccalaureate) 1927; changed name to Arizona State College at Flagstaff 1945; adopted present name 1966. *See* Melvin Hutchinson, *The Making of Northern Arizona University* (Flagstaff: Northland Press, 1971) for further information.

Institutional Structure: *Governing board:* Arizona Board of Regents. Representation: 9 regents, including 1 student (appointed by governor of Arizona); governor; superintendent of public instruction. 2 ex officio. 10 voting. *Composition of institution:* Administrators 80 men / 43 women. Academic affairs headed by provost. Management/business/finances directed by vice president for business affairs. Full-time instructional faculty 1,317. Academic governance body, Faculty Senate, meets an average of 9 times per year.

Calendar: Semesters. Academic year Aug. to May. Freshmen admitted Aug., Nov., Jan., June, July. Degrees conferred and formal commencement May, Dec. Summer session of 4 terms from May to Aug.

Characteristics of Freshmen: 2,382 applicants accepted. 1,522 accepted applicants enrolled.

68% (1,713 students) submitted SAT scores; 47% (1,184 students) submitted ACT scores. *25th percentile*: SAT Verbal 470, SAT Math 470; ACT Composite 19, ACT English 19, ACT Math 18. *75th percentile*: SAT Verbal 590, SAT Math 590; ACT Composite 25, ACT English 25, ACT Math 25.

75% of freshmen from Arizona. Freshmen from 50 states and 28 foreign countries.

Admission: Rolling admissions plan. For fall acceptance, apply as early as end of junior year of secondary school, but not later than July 15 of year of enrollment. *Requirements:* Either graduation from accredited secondary school or GED. Lowest acceptable secondary school class standing 50th percentile. *Entrance tests:* With secondary school class standing of less than 50th percentile, College Board SAT (combined score 930 for in-state residents, 1010 for out-of-state students) or ACT Composite (score of 22 for in-state, 24 for out-of-state). For foreign students, TOEFL. *For transfer students:* 2.0 minimum GPA; from 4-year accredited institution maximum transfer credit limited only by residence requirement; from 2-year accredited institution 63 semester hours; correspondence/extension students 30 hours.

College credit and advanced placement for postsecondary level work completed in secondary school; for extrainstitutional learning college credit on basis of ACE *2006 Guide to the Evaluation of Educational Experiences in the Armed Services* faculty assessment, and personal interview. Tutoring available.

Degree Requirements: *For all baccalaureate degrees:* 120 hours. *For all undergraduate degrees:* 2.0 GPA; 30 hours in residence; general education requirements. Higher GPA for some baccalaureate programs.

Fulfillment of some degree requirements and exemption from some beginning courses by passing departmental examinations. College Board CLEP, AP. *Grading system:* A–F; high pass-pass-fail; withdraw.

Distinctive Educational Programs: Work-experience programs, including internships, cooperative education. Evening classes. Cooperative baccalaureate in medical technology with approved hospitals. Interdisciplinary programs in American studies, environmental studies; area studies, including Asian studies, black studies, European studies, native American Indian studies, Southwest and Latin American studies. Preprofessional programs in dentistry, medicine, veterinary medicine. Facilities and programs for independent research, including honors programs, independent study. Institutionally sponsored study abroad in France, Great Britain, Spain, The Netherlands, Australia, Germany, Italy, Zimbabwe, Israel, Mexico, China, Sweden. *Other distinctive programs:* Continuing education. Bilingual-multicultural education program.

ROTC: Army, Air Force.

Degrees Conferred: 2,931 *baccalaureate*; 2,059 *master's*; 75 *doctorate.* Bachelor's degrees awarded in top five disciplines: education 641; business, management, marketing, and related support services 569; liberal arts and sciences, general studies, and humanities 216; visual and performing arts 181; social sciences 148.

Fees and Other Expenses: *Full-time tuition per academic year 2004–05:* undergraduate resident $3,983, out-of-state $12,503. *Room and board per academic year:* $5,785. *Required fees:* $90. *Books and supplies:* $800.

Financial Aid: Aid from institutionally generated funds is provided on the basis of academic merit, financial need, athletic ability. Institution has a Program Participation Agreement with the U.S. Department of Education for eligible students to receive Pell Grants and other federal aid.

Financial aid to full-time, first-time undergraduate students: need-based scholarships/grants totaling $24,442,211, self-help $36,254,164, parent loans $3,418,656, tuition waivers $5,008,725, athletic awards $1,296,797; non-need-based scholarships/grants $2,732,798, self-help $10,147,113, parent loans $2,375,482, tuition waivers $5,343,107, athletic awards $1,454,826.

Departments and Teaching Staff: *Total instructional faculty:* 1,317 (women 300, men 669). Total faculty with doctorate, first-professional, or other terminal degree: 781.

Enrollment: Total enrollment: 19,147. Undergraduate 13,333; graduate and professional students 5,814.

Characteristics of Student Body: *Ethnic and racial makeup:* number of Black non-Hispanic: 273, American Indian or Alaska Native: 997; Asian or Pacific Islander: 284, Hispanic: 1,440; White non-Hispanic: 9,824; unknown: 273.

International Students: 242 nonresident aliens enrolled fall 2004. Students from Europe, Asia, Latin America, Africa, Canada, Australia, New Zealand. Programs available to aid students whose native language is not English: Social, cultural, financial. English as a Second Language Program.

Student Life: On-campus residence halls house 44% of the undergraduate student body. *Intercollegiate athletics:* men only: basketball, cross-country, football, tennis, indoor and outdoor track and cross-country; women only: basketball, cross-country, tennis, indoor and outdoor track, volleyball, swimming/diving. *Special regulations:* Cars permitted with parking permits. *Special services:* Learning Assistance Center, Multicultural Student Center, Counseling and Testing Center, medical services, campus shuttle bus, Career Services. *Student publications, radio:* The Lumberjack, a weekly newspaper; *Pine Knots,* an annual literary magazine. Radio stations KNAU-FM, KRCK. *Surrounding community:* Flagstaff population 53,000. Phoenix, 140 miles from campus, is nearest metropolitan area. Served by airport, bus, and passenger rail service (each 1 mile from campus).

Library Collections: 645,000 volumes. 221,000 government documents; 370,500 microforms; 19,000 audiovisual materials. Students have access to online search services and the Internet.

Most important holdings include Arizona Resource Collection (history, geology, archaeology, political economy, culture, business and industry); The Emery Kolb Collection (early Grand Canyon photographer); The Norman Allerdice Collection (extremist literature); Raycroft Press Collection.

Buildings and Grounds: Campus area 738 acres.

Chief Executive Officer: Dr. John D. Haeger, President.

Undergraduates address admission inquiries to Susan J. McKinnon, Director of Admissions.

Prescott College

220 Grove Avenue
Prescott, Arizona 86301
Tel: (520) 778-2090   **E-mail:** rdpadmissions@prescott.edu
Fax: (520) 776-5137   **Internet:** www.prescott.edu

Institution Description: Prescott College (Prescott Center College until 1981) is a private, independent, nonprofit college. *Enrollment:* 1,024. *Degrees awarded:* Baccalaureate, master's.

Accreditation: *Regional:* NCA.

History: Established as Prescott College 1965; chartered and offered first instruction at postsecondary level 1966; first degree (baccalaureate) offered 1970; closed 1974; reopened as Prescott Center College 1975; adopted present name 1981.

Institutional Structure: *Governing board:* Prescott Center for Alternative Education, which represents the whole college. Extrainstitutional representation: 14directors; institutional representation: 1 full-time instructional faculty member, 1 student; 16 voting. *Composition of institution:* President, 2 deans, financial officer. Full-time instructional faculty 78. Academic governance body, Academic Council, meets an average of 10 times per year.

Calendar: Undergraduate programs under quarter system; master of arts program runs in semesters. 2004–05 academic year Sept. to May. Freshmen admitted Sept., Jan. Degrees conferred Dec., May. (Adult Degree Program on a rolling basis.) Formal commencement May. Summer session.

Characteristics of Freshmen: 74% of applicants accepted. 47% of accepted applicants enrolled.

Admission: Priority for filing dates of February 1 for fall enrollment and Sept. 1 for spring enrollment. After priority dates, applications considered on a rolling basis. Graduation from secondary school or GED, 2 letters of recommendation; interview strongly recommended. The Adult Degree Program offers bachelor of arts degree and Arizona Teacher Certification programs. Admission is based on a qualitative assessment of the student's potential for successful completion of the program, self-motivation, and ability to work independently. *For Master of Arts program:* The deadline for applying is June 1 for fall admission and Nov. 1 for spring admission.

Adult Degree Program offers college credit for extrainstitutional learning (life experience) on basis of faculty assessment.

Tutoring available.

Degree Requirements: 2 years in residence, writing and math proficiency documented through evaluation or course credit. ADP requirements: 1 year in residence; writing and math proficiency, documented through examination, faculty evaluation, or course credit.

Grading system: Transcript is record of achievement. Only work of C level or above is recorded. Letter grades A, B, or C are issued only at the request of the student. All other successfully completed work is recorded as credit.

Distinctive Educational Programs: Work-experience programs. Flexible meeting places and schedules, including weekend classes. External degree-programs with cooperating institutions in Network for Alternatives in Undergraduate and Teacher Education. Off-campus self-directed study exchange program may be contracted through Prescott. Interdisciplinary programs in environmental studies, human development, Southwest studies, humanities. Internships. All disciplines may be approached in interdisciplinary fashion. Students are self-directed in their program planning, using advisers for feedback and guidance. Interdisciplinary courses offered, but programs individualized. Adult Degree Program allows older students to incorporate learning from previous college and professional experiences into a program of study leading to the baccalaureate.

The Master of Arts Program is designed to meet the needs of adult students for highly individualized graduate study.

Degrees Conferred: 263 *baccalaureate*; 77 *master's.* Bachelor's degrees conferred in top five disciplines: education 110; psychology 35; natural resources and conservation 25; visual and performing arts 16; parks, recreation, leisure, and fitness studies.

Fees and Other Expenses: *Full-time tuition per 2004–05 academic year for full-time, first-time undergraduates:* $16,320. *Room and board:* (off-campus) $6,500. *Books and supplies:* $600. *Other expenses:* 3,200. Contact the college for graduate tuition.

Financial Aid: Aid from institutionally generated funds is provided on the basis of financial need, academic merit, and competency specialization. Institution has a Program Participation Agreement with the U.S. Department of Education for eligible students to receive Pell Grants and other financial aid.

Financial aid to full-time, first-time undergraduates: 9% received federal grants; 5% state/local grants; 14% institutional grants; 30% loans averaging $3,144.

Departments and Teaching Staff: *Total instructional faculty:* 82. Student-to-faculty ratio: 12:1.

Enrollment: Total enrollment 1,024. Undergraduate 807 (42.6%men, 57.4% women).

Characteristics of Student Body: *Ethnic and racial makeup:* Black non-Hispanic: 1.1%; American Indian or Alaskan Native: 2.9%; Asian or Pacific Islander: .7%; Hispanic: 4.5%; White non-Hispanic: 64.3%; unknown: .6%.

International Students: 5 nonresident aliens enrolled fall 2004. No programs available to aid students whose native language is not English.

Student Life: No on-campus housing. Prescott assists students in finding housing. *Special regulations:* Cars permitted without restrictions; time limit on parking. *Student publications:* A student newsletter, a quarterly alumni newsletter. *Surrounding community:* Prescott population 35,000. Phoenix, 100 miles from campus, is nearest metropolitan area. Served by airport 15 miles from campus.

Library Collections: 22,500 volumes. 270 periodical subscriptions. Online catalog. 30 computer work stations. Students have access to the Internet at no charge.

Most important special collections include The Vern Taylor Native: American Collection; Dr. and Mrs. J. Curtis Kovacs Mountaineering Collection.

Buildings and Grounds: Campus area 4 acres.

Chief Executive Officer: Daniel E. Garvey, President. Address admission to RDP Program inquiries to Timothy Robinson, Admissions Director; ADP/MAP inquiries to Abbey Carpenter, Admissions Director.

Southwestern College

2625 East Cactus Road
Phoenix, Arizona 85032
Tel: (602) 992-6101 **E-mail:** admissions@swcaz.edu
Fax: (602) 404-2159 **Internet:** www.swcaz.edu

Institution Description: Southwestern College, formerly known as Southwestern Conservative Baptist Bible College is a private college operated by the Conservative Baptist Association of America. *Enrollment:* 267. *Degrees awarded:* Associate, baccalaureate.

Accreditation: *Regional:* NCA. *Nonregional:* ABHE.

History: Founded 1960 as Southwestern Baptist Bible College; became Southwestern Conservative Baptist Bible College 1993; current name adopted in 2000..

Calendar: Semesters. Academic year late Aug. to early May. Freshmen admitted Aug. Degrees conferred May.

Characteristics of Freshmen: 190 applicants (90 men, 100 women). 51.6% of applicants admitted; 51.8% of admitted students enrolled full-time; 5.1% part-time. 81% of freshmen from Arizona. Freshmen from 8 states.

Admission: Rolling admissions plan. *Requirements:* Either graduation from accredited secondary school or GED.

Degree Requirements: Completion of prescribed curriculum.

Degrees Conferred: 3 *associate;* 57 *baccalaureate.* Bachelor's degrees awarded in top four disciplines: theology and ministerial studies 18; education 17; business, management, marketing, and related support 13; psychology 9.

Fees and Other Expenses: *Full-time tuition per academic year 2004–05:* $11,140. *Room and board:* $5,000. *Books and supplies:* $800. *Other expenses:* $3,460.

Financial Aid: Aid from institutionally generated funds is provided on the basis of academic merit, financial need, other criteria (children of missionaries and pastors).

Financial aid to full-time, first-time undergraduate students: 40% received federal grants averaging $1,800; 85% received institutional grants averaging $1,600; 68% loans averaging $2,800.

Departments and Teaching Staff: Biblical studies *professors* 0, *associate professors* 1, *assistant professors* 1, *instructors* 0, *part-time teachers* 0; general studies 0, 1, 0, 0, 0; elementary education 0, 0, 0, 0, 1; athletic 0, 0, 0, 1, 0; Bible 0, 0, 0, 0, 3; business 0, 0, 0, 0, 1; Christian ministries 0, 0, 0, 0, 5; computer science 0, 0, 0, 0, 1; music 0, 0, 0, 0, 2. *Total instructional faculty:* 28. Degrees held by full-time faculty: doctorate 33%, master's 67%. 33% hold terminal degrees.

Enrollment: Total enrollment 267.

Characteristics of Student Body: *Ethnic/racial makeup:* Black non-Hispanic: 7.5%; American Indian of Alaskan Native: .7%; Asian or Pacific Islander: .7%; Hispanic: 7.5%; White non-Hispanic: 85.4%; unknown: 2.2%.

International Students: 3 nonresident aliens enrolled fall 2004. 3 students from Europe. No programs available to aid students whose native language is not English. No financial aid specifically designated for international students.

Library Collections: 52,860 volumes including bound books, serial backfiles, electronic documents, and government documents not in separate collections. Current serial subscriptions: 278. 20,500 microforms; 2,700 audiovisual materials. Students have access to the Internet at no charge. Most important special collection is the Baptist History Collection.

Buildings and Grounds: Campus area 19 acres.

Chief Executive Officer: Dr. Brent D. Garrison, President.

Address admission inquiries to Pete L. Leonard, Director of Admissions.

Thunderbird-The Garvin School of International Management

15249 North 59th Avenue
Glendale, Arizona 85306-6000
Tel: (602) 978-7000 **E-mail:** admissions@t-bird.edu
Fax: (602) 978-8328 **Internet:** www.t-bird.edu

Institution Description: Thunderbird-The Garvin School of International Management is a private, independent, nonprofit institution. *Enrollment:* 1,357. *Degrees awarded:* Master's. Post-baccalaureate and post-master's certificates also awarded.

Accreditation: *Regional:* NCA. *Professional:* business

History: Established as American Institute for Foreign Trade, incorporated, and offered first instruction at postsecondary level 1946; first certificate awarded 1947; first degree (baccalaureate) awarded 1951; name changed to Thunderbird Graduate School of International Management 1968; present name adopted 2002.

Institutional Structure: *Governing board:* Board of Trustees. 31 trustees, including 6 alumni, and school president; 23 members of Board of Fellows; 4 members of Academic Board of Visitors. 30 voting members. *Composition of institution:* Administrators 15 men / 9 women. Academic affairs headed by academic vice president. Management/business/finances directed by executive vice president. Full-time instructional faculty 51 men / 20 women. Academic governance body, Faculty Senate, meets an average of 7 times per year.

Calendar: Trimesters. Academic year Sept. to May.

Characteristics of Freshmen: 82% of applicants accepted. 51% of accepted applicants enrolled. Entering students from 49 states and 59 foreign countries.

Admission: Rolling admissions plan. Apply approximately one year ahead of term of preference. *Requirements:* Minimum 3.0 GPA from undergraduate school, minimum GMAT score 500, 3 letters of recommendation. *Entrance tests:* For foreign students minimum TOEFL 450 (if education not in English), plus GMAT. *For transfer students:* 3.0 minimum GPA, 3 hours maximum transfer credit for work done in graduate standing.

Degree Requirements: 42 credit hours; 3.0 GPA; minimum of 3 terms in residence. Exemption from some courses possible by passing departmental tests, or on basis of College Board CLEP, transcript evidence confirming successful completion of equivalent courses at another institution, plus faculty assessment.

Grading system: A–F; pass-fail; withdraw (pass-fail appended to withdraw).

Distinctive Educational Programs: Dual-degree program with Arizona State University; Drury College in Springfield (MO); and Escuela Superior de Administracion y Direccion de Empresas (Spain). Study in Germany, France, Norway, Japan, Mexico, People's Republic of China, and Spain.

Degrees Conferred: 733 *master's:* international business/trade/commerce; 21 *post-baccalaureate certificates.*

Fees and Other Expenses: *Full-time tuition per term (fall, spring, summer):* $14,650. *Room:* $1,575 to $1,700 per term. *Board:* $675 per term. Other fees may apply.

Financial Aid: Aid from institutionally generated funds is provided on the basis of academic merit, financial need. A variety of financial aid plans available. Institution has a Program Participation Agreement with the U.S. Department of Education for eligible students to receive Pell Grants and other federal aid.

Departments and Teaching Staff: International studies *professors* 6, *associate professors* 5, *assistant professors* 0, *instructors* 0, *part-time teachers* 1; modern languages 8, 19, 5, 5, 7; world business 13, 9, 6, 0, 5.

Total instructional faculty: 91. Degrees held by full-time faculty: Doctorates 57%, master's 38%, baccalaureates 5%.

Enrollment: Total enrollment 1,357 (1,016 men; 341 women).

Characteristics of Student Body: *Ethnic/racial makeup:* Black non-Hispanic: .7%, American Indian or Alaskan Native: 2.4%; Asian or Pacific Islander: 2.4%; Hispanic: 3.1%; White non-Hispanic: 25% unknown 6%.

International Students: 853 international students enrolled 2004. Programs available to aid students whose native language is not English: English as a Second Language Program. No financial aid specifically designated for international students.

Student Life: On-campus residence halls for both men and women house 40% of student body. Off-campus housing and housing for married students available. 40% of married students request institutional housing; 30% are so housed. *Special regulations:* Registered cars permitted with registration. *Special services:* Medical services. *Student publications: Das Tor,* a weekly newspaper. *Surrounding community:* Phoenix metropolitan area population 1,750,000. Served by mass transit system; airport 25 miles from campus.

Library Collections: 100,000 volumes. 15,000 microforms; 211 audiovisual materials; 1,056 current periodical subscriptions. Students have access to online information retrieval services and the Internet.

Buildings and Grounds: Campus area 157 acres.

Chief Executive Officer: Dr. Angel Cabrera, President.

Address admission inquiries to Dean of Admissions.

University of Advancing Technology

2625 West Baseline Road
Tempe, Arizona 85283-1042
Tel: (602) 383-8228   **E-mail:** admissions@uat.edu
Fax: (602) 383-8250   **Internet:** www.uat.edu

Institution Description: The University of Advancing Technology (UAT), formerly known as the University of Advancing Computer Technology, is a private technical university offering associate, baccalaureate, and master degree programs in design, multimedia, software engineering and technology. *Enrollment:* 1,004.

Accreditation: *Nonregional:* ACICS.

History: Founded in 1983, UAT (formerly CAD Institute) has become one of the few educational institutions to emphasize computer technology such as the Internet, networks, animation, game design, interactive media, design, and computer programming in software demanded by industry.

Calendar: Trimesters. Academic year Sept. to Aug.

Admission: *Requirements:* High school graduation with GED minimum score of 500; SAT minimum of 500 verbal and 520 math; or ACT minimum of 21; successful completion of 15 credits from an accredited institution or four years satisfactory military service; interview required. Applicants for the Graduate College in Applied Technology must have either a bachelor's degree from an accredited institution, or GPA of 2.5/4.0 in undergraduate program or obtained a minimum score in the GRE General Test of 470 Verbal, 570 Quantitative, 540 Analytical.

Degree Requirements: *For all undergraduate degrees:* Satisfactory completion of each term of the prescribed program.

Distinctive Educational Programs: Programs of study in mechanical/industrial design, architectural/civil design, interior design, CAD, digital animation, game design, interactive media, web design, application development, computer programming, Internet administration, network engineering.

Degrees Conferred: 32*associate*; 144*baccalaureate.* Bachelor's degrees awarded in top three disciplines: communications technologies/technicians, and support services 72; engineering technologies/technicians 67; computer and information sciences and support services 5. 3 *master's.*

Fees and Other Expenses: Tuition per academic undergraduate $7,100; graduate $4,300.

Financial Aid: Aid from institutionally generated funds is provided on the basis of academic merit, financial need. Institution has a Program Participation Agreement with the U.S. Department of Education for eligible students to receive Pell Grants and other federal aid.

Financial aid to full-time, first-time undergraduate students: need-based scholarships/grants totaling $1,759,460, self-help $7,027,100, parent loans $2,532,000.

Departments and Teaching Staff: *Total instructional faculty:* 59 (26 full-time, 33 part-time). Total number with doctorate, first-professional, or other terminal degree: 7. Student-to-faculty ratio: 13:1.

Enrollment: Total enrollment 1,004. Undergraduate 896 men / 87 women; graduate 14m / 7w.

Characteristics of Student Body: *Ethnic/racial makeup:* number of Black non-Hispanic: 44; American Indian or Alaska Native: 8; Asian or Pacific Islander: 33; Hispanic: 52; White non-Hispanic: 644; unknown: 192. *Age distribution:* number of 18–19: 207; 20–21: 260; 22–24: 243; 25–29: 62; 30–34 66; 35–39: 33; 40–49: 17; 50–64: 3; 65 and over: 2.

International Students: No programs available to aid students whose native language is not English.

Publications: *The Journal of Advancing Technology,* a scholarly publication produced twice per year.

Buildings and Grounds: New campus completed in 1998 with state-of-the-art computer classrooms.

Chief Executive Officer: Dominic Pistillo, President.

Address admissions inquiries to Director of Admissions (e-mail: admissions@uat.edu).

University of Arizona

1401 East University
Tucson, Arizona 85721-0066
Tel: (520) 621-2211   **E-mail:** appinfo@arizona.edu
Fax: (520) 621-9323   **Internet:** www.arizona.edu

Institution Description: The University of Arizona is a state institution and land-grant college. *Enrollment:* 37,083. *Degrees awarded:* Baccalaureate, first-professional (law, medicine, pharmacy), master's, doctorate. Specialist certificates in education and nursing also given.

Academic offerings subject to approval by statewide coordinating bodies. Budget subject to approval by state governing boards.

Accreditation: *Regional:* NCA. *Professional:* accounting, art, audiology, business, clinical lab scientist, clinical psychology, dance, dietetics, engineering, journalism, landscape architecture, law, librarianship, medicine, music, nursing, nursing education, pharmacy, planning, psychology internship, public administration, public health, rehabilitation counseling, school psychology, speech-language pathology, theatre

History: Established and chartered 1885; offered first instruction at postsecondary level 1891; awarded first degree (baccalaureate) 1895. See Douglas Martin, *Lamp in the Desert* (Tucson: University of Arizona Press, 1960) for further information.

Institutional Structure: *Governing board:* Arizona Board of Regents. Representation: 8 regents, governor of Arizona, state superintendent of public instruction, 1 student regent. 2 ex officio. 10 voting. *Composition of institution:* Administrators 88 men / 67 women. Academic affairs headed by executive vice president. Management/business/finances directed by comptroller. Full-time instructional faculty 1,629. Academic governance body, Faculty Senate, meets an average of 10 times per year.

Calendar: Semesters. Academic year mid-Aug. to mid-May. Freshmen admitted Aug., Jan., June. Degrees conferred May, Aug., Dec. Formal commencements May, Dec. Summer session of 3 terms late May to mid-Aug.

Characteristics of Freshmen: 83.4% of applicants admitted; 28.1% admitted and enrolled full-time, 8.8% part-time.

83% (4,771 students) submitted SAT scores; 34% (2,066 students) submitted ACT scores. *25th percentile:* SAT Verbal 490, SAT Math 600; ACT Composite 21, ACT English 20, ACT Math 20. *75th percentile:* SAT Verbal 610, SAT Math 620; ACT Composite 26, ACT English 26, ACT Math 27.

45% of entering freshmen expected to graduate within 5 years. 57% of freshmen from Arizona. Freshmen from 50 states.

Admission: Rolling admissions plan. For fall acceptance, apply no later than one Apr. 1 for Priority Service Program. Final deadline is 1 month prior to registration. *Requirements:* Either graduation from accredited secondary school with 16 units which must include 4 units in English, 3 mathematics, 3 laboratory science, 2 social science, 2 foreign language, 1 fine arts. *Entrance tests:* College Board SAT or ACT Composite. For foreign students TOEFL. *For transfer students:* Out-of-state students 2.0 minimum GPA. From 4- and 2-year accredited institutions maximum transfer credit limited only by residence requirement; correspondence/extension students 60 credit hours.

Certain curricula require higher test scores and expanded entrance credentials. Contact the Office of Undergraduate Admission for details. Advanced placement for postsecondary-level work completed in secondary school.

Degree Requirements: 120–166 semester hours; 2.0 GPA; 30 hours in residence. Additional requirements vary with program.

Fulfillment of some degree requirements and exemption from some beginning courses possible by passing College Board CLEP, AP. *Grading system:* A–F; pass-fail; withdraw.

Distinctive Educational Programs: Evening classes. Interdisciplinary programs in applied mathematics, biomedical engineering, history and philosophy of science, statistics, and toxicology. Facilities and programs for independent research, including honors programs, individual majors, tutorials. Study abroad in England, Brazil, Costa Rica, Denmark, France, Germany, Greece, Italy, Japan, Spain. *Other distinctive programs:* Optical sciences, arid land studies, hydrology and water resources.

ROTC: Air Force, Army, Navy.

Degrees Conferred: 5,303 *baccalaureate*. Bachelor's degrees awarded in top five disciplines: business, management, marketing, and related support services;781; communication, journalism and related programs 540; education 491; social sciences 490; engineering 384. 1,478 *master's*, 398 *doctorate*, 304 *first-professional, post master's certificates* 8.

Fees and Other Expenses: *Full-time tuition per academic year 2004–05:* in-state resident $4,098, out-of-state $13,078. *Room and board:* $7,108. *Books and supplies:* $762. *Other expenses:* $2,924.

Financial Aid: Aid from institutionally generated funds is provided on the basis of academic merit, financial need, athletic ability, other considerations. Institution has a Program Participation Agreement with the U.S. Department of Education for eligible students to receive Pell Grants and other federal aid.

Financial aid to full-time, first-time undergraduate students: 24% received federal grants averaging $2,194; 1% state/local grant for $848; 34% institutional grants averaging $3,179; 31% loans averaging $3,422.

Departments and Teaching Staff: *Professors* 812, *associate professors* 505, *assistant professors* 469, *instructors/lecturers* 210, *part-time faculty* 428.

Total instructional faculty: 2,424. Total tenure track faculty: 1,568. Student-to-faculty ratio: 17.8:1. Degrees held by full-time faculty: doctorate 73.45%, master's 10.67%, baccalaureate .90%, professional 14.98%. 94.34% hold terminal degrees.

Enrollment: Total enrollment 37,083. Undergraduate 28,482 (46.9% men, 53.1% women).

Characteristics of Student Body: *Ethnic/racial makeup:* Black non-Hispanic: 3%; American Indian or Alaskan Native: 1.8%; Asian or Pacific Islander: 5.6%; Hispanic: 14.8%; White non-Hispanic: 86.3%.

International Students: 997 nonresident aliens enrolled fall 2003. Social and cultural programs available to aid students whose native language is not English. English as a Second Language Program. Financial aid specifically designated for international students.

Student Life: On-campus residence halls house 18% of undergraduate student body. Residence halls for men only constitute 27% of such space, for women only 27%. 15% of men join fraternities; 15% of women join sororities. Housing available for married students. *Intercollegiate athletics:* men only: baseball, basketball, cross-country, football, ice hockey, golf, lacrosse, rugby, soccer, swimming and diving, tennis, track, volleyball; women only: basketball, cross-country, golf, gymnastics, soccer, softball, swimming, tennis, track, volleyball. *Special regulations:* Cars permitted on campus in designated areas. *Special services:* Office of Minority Student Affairs; Student Resource Center; medical services. *Student publications, radio, television: Arizona Daily Wildcat*, a newspaper; *Desert*, a yearbook; *Student Handbook*, an annual publication; *Summer Wildcat*, a newspaper. Radio station KUAT-AM broadcasts from dawn to dusk. KUAT-FM (classical)broadcasts 24 hours a day; KUAZ-FM broadcasts 5AM to midnight (jazz and National Public Radio); TV station KUAT broadcasts 122 hours per week. *Surrounding community:* Tucson population 800,000. Served by mass transit bus system; airport 6 miles from campus; passenger rail service 2 miles from campus.

Library Collections: 4,920,178 volumes including bound books, serial backfiles, electronic documents, and government documents not in separate collections. Online and card catalogs. 26,700 current serial subscriptions. 5,992,440 microforms. 55,200 audiovisual materials. Students have access to the Internet at no charge.

Most important special collections include Thomas Wood Stevens Manuscript Collection; Udall Family Papers; A.E. Douglass Papers; Ansell Adams Papers; Edward Abbey Papers; Ed Weston Papers.

Buildings and Grounds: Campus area 355 acres.

Chief Executive Officer: Dr. Peter Likins, President.

Address admission inquiries to Dr. Lori Goldman, Director of Admissions; address first-professional inquiries to school or college of choice; graduate study inquiries to Dean of the Graduate College.

College of Agriculture

Degree Programs Offered: *Baccalaureate* in agricultural and biosystems engineering, agricultural and resource economics, agricultural education, agronomy, animal health science, animal sciences, entomology, fisheries science, food science, general agriculture, horticulture, landscape architecture, natural resource recreation, nutritional sciences, plant pathology, plant sciences, range management, soil and water science, watershed management, wildlife ecology.

Distinctive Educational Programs: Research and educational programs abroad, in Brazil, Ecuador, Israel, Mexico, Niger, the Philippines, Saudi Arabia, Turkey. Institutional and regional research facilities include Campbell Avenue Farm, Casa Grande Highway Farm, Citrus Branch Station, Cotton Research Center, Marana Farm, Mesa Branch Station, Mt. Lemmon Experimental Watershed, Safford Branch Station, Santa Rita Experimental Range, Yuma Branch

Station. Resource facilities include Center for Remote Sensing, Center for Quantitative Studies, Council for Environmental Studies.

College of Architecture

Degree Programs Offered: *Baccalaureate.*

College of Fine Arts

Degree Programs Offered: *Baccalaureate* in anthropology, astronomy, biochemistry, cellular and developmental biology, chemistry, classics, creative writing, ecology and evolutionary biology, economics, English, French, general biology, general studies, geography, geology, German, Greek, history, Italian, journalism, Latin, Latin American studies, linguistics, mathematics, Mexican American studies, microbiology, Oriental studies, philosophy, physics, political science, Portuguese, psychology, Romance languages, Russian, sociology, Spanish.

Distinctive Educational Programs: Cooperative program with American Graduate School of International Management prepares students for international careers. Interdisciplinary programs in American Indian studies, black studies, religious studies, women's studies. Study abroad in Cyprus, Egypt, Jerusalem, Jordan, Taiwan.

College of Humanities

Degree Programs Offered: *Baccalaureate* in art, art education, art history, composition, conducting, dance, drama, drama education, drama production, dramatic theory, general fine arts studies, jazz and contemporary media, music, music education, music theory, musicology, performance (keyboards, percussion, string, voice), radio-television, speech and hearing sciences, speech communication, studio art, theory and composition.

College of Science

Degree Programs Offered: *Baccalaureate* in astronomy, atmospheric sciences, biochemistry, chemistry, computer science, ecological and evolutionary biology, geosciences, mathematics, microbiology/immunology, molecular and cell biology, physics, planetary sciences, soil and water science; speech and hearing science, statistics.

College of Social and Behavioral Sciences

Degree Programs Offered: *Baccalaureate* in anthropology, communications, geography and regional development, history, journalism, library science, linguistics, Near East studies, philosophy, political science, sociology.

College of Business and Public Administration

Degree Programs Offered: *Baccalaureate* in business administration, public administration.

Distinctive Educational Programs: Division of Economics and Business Research conducts research on business and public sector issues and problems. *Other distinctive programs:* Yearly executive development conference through Institute of Industrial and Labor Relations.

College of Education

Degree Programs Offered: *Baccalaureate* in bilingual education, elementary education, instructional media and library services, postsecondary education, rehabilitation, secondary education, special education, student personnel services, supervision and administration.

College of Engineering and Mines

Degree Programs Offered: *Baccalaureate* in aerospace engineering, agricultural engineering, civil engineering, electrical engineering, engineering mathematics, engineering physics, industrial engineering, mechanical engineering, nuclear engineering, systems engineering.

Distinctive Educational Programs: Cooperative education. Engineering Experiment Station. Research programs in biophysics technology, digital image analysis, interactive computational mechanics, microelectronics, nuclear fuel cycles, nuclear reactor safety, plasma physics and nuclear fusion, solar energy.

College of Health Related Professions

Degree Programs Offered: *Baccalaureate* in health education, medical technology, occupational safety and health.

College of Law

Degree Programs Offered: *First-professional.*

Admission: Baccalaureate from accredited college or university, 3.0 GPA, LSAT.

Degree Requirements: 3-year curriculum, last 2 semesters in residence.

College of Medicine

Degree Programs Offered: *First-professional.*

Admission: 90 semester hours (30 upper division) from accredited college or university with 2 semesters each in English, general biology or zoology, general chemistry, organic chemistry, physics; MCAT.

Degree Requirements: 4-year curriculum, 2 years in residence.

College of Nursing

Degree Programs Offered: *Baccalaureate.*

College of Pharmacy

Degree Programs Offered: *First-professional.*

Admission: 31 semester hours in prepharmacy curriculum, including 1 unit algebra, 1 plane geometry, 1 trigonometry advanced algebra; PCAT.

Degree Requirements: 48 credit hours, 2.0 GPA, internship.

University of Phoenix

4615 East Elwood Street
Phoenix, Arizona 85040-1908
Tel: (480) 966-9577   **E-mail:** info@uph.edu
Fax: (480) 829-9030   **Internet:** www.uphx.edu

Institution Description: University of Phoenix (Institute for Professional Development until 1977) is a private institution, primarily for working adults, that offers upper division and graduate study only. *Enrollment:* 71,052 (all locations). *Degrees awarded:* Associate, baccalaureate, master's, doctorate.

Accreditation: *Regional:* NCA. *Professional:* counseling, nursing

History: Established and incorporated as Institute for Professional Development, and offered first instruction at postsecondary level 1976; adopted present name 1977; awarded first degree (baccalaureate) 1979. *See Staff of University of Phoenix, Self Study for North Central Association* (Phoenix: University of Phoenix Press, 1981) for further information.

Institutional Structure: *Governing board:* Board of Directors. Extrainstitutional representation: 5 directors; institutional representation: 3 administrators. All voting. *Composition of institution:* Administrators 12 men / 13 women. Academic affairs headed by provost/senior vice president of academic affairs. John Sperling School of Business headed by vice president of academic affairs. School of Education, Health, and Human Services headed by associate vice president of academic affairs. Academic Cabinet meets a minimum of twice a year.

Calendar: Semester credit system; 5-, 6, 11-week sessions throughout calendar year. Entering students admitted at any time. Degrees conferred monthly.

Characteristics of Freshmen: 95% of accepted applicants enrolled. 80% of entering students expected to graduate within 5 years.

Admission: Rolling admissions plan. Apply as early as 1 year prior to enrollment, but not later than 8 weeks prior to enrollment. *Requirements:* Either graduation from accredited secondary school or GED; minimum 2 years experience in occupation related to degree program. Minimum GPA 2.0. *Entrance tests:* For foreign students TOEFL. *For transfer students:* 2.0 minimum GPA; maximum transfer credit from 4-year accredited institution 69 semester hours in lower division courses, 24 hours in upper division; from 2-year accredited institution 66 hours.

College credit for extrainstitutional learning on basis of ACE *2006 Guide to the Evaluation of Educational Experiences in the Armed Services,* portfolio and faculty assessments.

Degree Requirements: *Undergraduate:* 120 semester hours; 2.0 GPA; 30 hours in residence; general education and core requirements. *Graduate:* requirements vary by program.

Fulfillment of some degree requirements possible by passing College Board CLEP. *Grading system:* A–F.

Distinctive Educational Programs: Weekend and evening classes. Accelerated degree programs. Special facilities for using telecommunications in the classroom. Independent study.

Degrees Conferred: 386 *associate*: 4,234 *baccalaureate.* Bachelor's degrees awarded in top five disciplines: business, management, marketing, and related support services 2,812; computer and information sciences and support services 1,073; health professions and related clinical sciences 341; public administration

and social service professions 6; security and protective services 1. 6,572 *master's*; 54 *doctorate*; 7 *post-baccalaureate certificates.*

Fees and Other Expenses: *Full-time undergraduate tuition per academic year 2004–05:* $13,200. *Books and supplies:* $400. Contact the university for current graduate tuition and fees.

Financial Aid: Institution has a Program Participation Agreement with the Department of Education for eligible students to receive Pell Grants and other federal aid.

Financial aid for full-time, first-time undergraduate students: 23% of students received federal grants averaging $667; 45% loans averaging $2,784. State/local and institutional grants may be available to qualifying students.

Departments and Teaching Staff: Faculty is composed of 125 full-time members and 8,000 part-time.

Enrollment: Total enrollment 71,052 (all locations).

Student Life: No on-campus housing. *Special services:* Learning Resources Center. *Surrounding community:* Phoenix population over 1.5 million.

Library Collections: Comprehensive Internet-accessible digital library holding 9.9 million full text documents.

Buildings and Grounds: The University of Phoenix locates campuses in visible areas within each city where it is approved to operate.

Chief Executive Officer: Dr. Laura Palmer Noone, President.

Address admission inquiries to University Services.

Western International University

9215 North Black Canyon Highway
Phoenix, Arizona 85021
Tel: (602) 943-2311   **E-mail:** admissions@wintu.edu
Fax: (602) 371-8637   **Internet:** www.wintu.edu

Institution Description: Western International University is a private institution. *Enrollment:* 2,138. *Degrees offered:* Associate, baccalaureate, master's.

Accreditation: *Regional:* NCA.

History: Founded 1978 to serve the adult community.

Calendar: Semester. Academic year Sept. to May.

Characteristics of Freshmen: 180 applicants for fall 2003 (99 men, 81 women). 60% of applicants admitted; 90.7% admitted and enrolled.

Admission: High school graduation with 2.0 GPA or GED.

CLEP and AP accepted for credit; major consideration is for special talent and leadership record.

Degree Requirements: 120 credit hours; completion of courses in a concentration, business core, and general curriculum; 2.0 GPA.

Degrees Conferred: 22 *associate*; 239 *baccalaureate*; 122 *master's.* Bachelor's degrees awarded in top five disciplines: business, management, marketing, and related support services 150; computer and information sources and support services 59; liberal arts and sciences, general studies, and humanities 25; security and protective services 5.

Fees and Other Expenses: *Full-time tuition per academic year 2004–05:* Tuition and fees vary by program and range from $18,300 to $38,430. *Books and supplies:* varies by program and range from $1,580 to $5,040. Contact the university for current rates.

Financial Aid: Aid from institutionally generated funds is provided on the basis of financial need. Financial aid packages available to qualified applicants (institutional, state, federal funds).

30% of students received federal grants; 22% received state/local grants; 43% loans.

Departments and Teaching Staff: *Part-time teachers* 85.

Total instructional faculty: 85. Degrees held by faculty: doctorate 55%, master's 45%. 55% hold terminal degrees.

Enrollment: Total enrollment 2,138. Undergraduate 1,665 (38.3% men, 61.7% women).

Characteristics of Student Body: *Ethnic and racial makeup:* Black non-Hispanic: 5.9%, American Indian or Alaskan Native: 1.1%; Asian or Pacific Islander: 1.5%; Hispanic: 13.2%; White non-Hispanic: 61%; unknown: 14.9%.

International Students: 38 nonresident aliens enrolled fall 2003. Students from Europe, Asia, Latin America, Africa, Canada. No programs available to aid students whose native language is not English. No financial aid specifically designated for international students.

Student Life: No on-campus housing.

Library Collections: 25,000 volumes. 50 microform titles; 370 current periodical subscriptions.

Buildings and Grounds: 4-acre campus.

Chief Executive Officer: Michael J. Seiden, President.

Address inquiries to Karen Janitell, Director of Enrollment.

Arkansas

Arkansas Baptist College

1600 Bishop Street

Little Rock, Arkansas 72202-6099

Tel: (501) 374-7856 **E-mail:** admissions@abaptcol

Fax: (501) 375-4257 **Internet:** www.abaptcol.edu

Institution Description: Arkansas Baptist College is a private institution affiliated with the American Baptists Churches, U.S.A. *Enrollment:* 375. *Degrees awarded:* Baccalaureate.

Member of the consortium Little Rock/North Little Rock Center for Postsecondary and Higher Education.

Accreditation: *Regional:* NCA. *Professional:* teacher education

History: Established 1884.

Institutional Structure: *Governing board:* Trustees of Arkansas Baptist College. Representation: 30 trustees. *Composition of institution:* 11 administrators. Academic affairs headed by academic dean. Management/business/finances directed by business manager and director of financial aid. Full-time instructional faculty 8.

Calendar: Semesters. Academic year Aug. to May. Summer session from early June to early Aug.

Admission: Rolling admissions plan. For fall acceptance, apply no later than 1 month prior to beginning of semester. *Requirements:* Either graduation from approved secondary school with 15 units which must include 3 English, 2 mathematics or science; or GED. Minimum GPA 1.5. *Entrance tests:* College Board SAT or ACT Composite. *For transfer students:* 2.0 minimum GPA.

Degree Requirements: 124 credit hours; 2.0 GPA; 30 hours in residence; 9 hours religion courses; general education requirements.

Grading system: A–F; credit-no credit; withdraw (deadline after which pass-fail is appended to withdraw); incomplete.

Distinctive Educational Programs: Interdisciplinary program in general studies. Independent study.

Degrees Conferred: 16 *baccalaureate:* public administration and social service professions 7: business management, marketing, and related support services 6; theology and ministerial studies, other 3.

Fees and Other Expenses: *Full-time tuition per academic year 2004–05:* $4,750. *Room and board per academic year:* $5,000. *Books and supplies:* $900. *Other expenses:* $5,000.

Financial Aid: Aid from institutionally generated funds is provided on the basis of academic merit, financial need. Institution has a Program Participation Agreement with the U.S. Department of Education for eligible students to receive Pell Grants and other federal aid.

Financial aid for full-time, first-time undergraduate students: 90% received federal grants averaging $4,050; 96% loans averaging $2,589.

Departments and Teaching Staff: Faculty members are unranked. *Total instructional faculty:* 15. Student-to-faculty ratio: 16:1.

Enrollment: Total enrollment: 375 (44.3% men, 56.7% women).

Characteristics of Student Body: *Ethnic/racial makeup:* Black non-Hispanic: 100%.

Student Life: On-campus housing available. *Surrounding community:* Little Rock metropolitan population 400,000.

Library Collections: 32,000 volumes. 10,000 microfilm items; 2,000 audiovisual materials. Students have access to online services and the Internet.

Chief Executive Officer: Dr. Israel R. Dunn, Jr., President. Address admission inquiries to Jamesetta Ballard, Director of Admissions/Enrollment.

Arkansas State University

P.O. Box 10

State University, Arkansas 72467

Tel: (870) 972-2100 **E-mail:** admissions@astate.edu

Fax: (870) 972-3465 **Internet:** www.astate.edu

Institution Description: Arkansas State University (ASU) is a state institution located in Jonesboro, Arkansas (State University AR is used for postal purposes although the campus is physically located in Jonesboro). ASU is associated with four 2-year institutions located in the state: Arkansas State University - Beebe; Arkansas State University - Mountain Home; Arkansas State University - Newport; and Arkansas State Technical Institute - Beebe. *Enrollment:* 10,508. *Degrees awarded:* Associate, baccalaureate, master's, doctorate. Education specialist certificates are also awarded.

Academic offerings subject to approval by statewide coordinating bodies. Budget subject to approval by state governing board.

Accreditation: *Regional:* NCA. *Professional:* art, athletic training, business, clinical lab scientist, counseling, engineering, journalism, music, nursing, physical therapy, physical therapy assisting, public administration, radiation therapy, radiography, rehabilitation counseling, social work, speech-language pathology, teacher education

History: Arkansas State University developed from one of four state agricultural schools that were established in 1909 by the Arkansas General Assembly. The institution opened as a vocational high school in 1910; reorganized as a junior college 1918; name changed to State Agricultural and Mechanical College in 1925; awarded first degrees (baccalaureate) 1931; changed name to Arkansas State College in 1933; graduate program leading to master of science in education was established in 1955; university status granted 1967 and name became Arkansas State University. Other graduate programs were later added including specialist degree programs in 1969 and a doctoral degree program in 1933. *See* Lee A. Dew, *The ASU Story 1909–1967* (State University: Privately printed, 1968) and Larry Ball and William Clements, *Voices From State* for further information.

Institutional Structure: *Governing board:* Board of Trustees. Representation: 5 trustees. All voting. *Composition of institution:* Administrators 39 men / 24 women. Chief Executive Officer: President of the University; Chief Academic Officer: Vice President for Academic Affairs; Chief Business Officer: Vice President for Finance and Administration; Chief Public Relations Officer: Vice President for University Advancement; Chief Governmental/Legislative Relations Officer: Executive Director of Governmental Relations. Full-time instructional faculty 621. Governance bodies: Faculty Senate, Staff Senate, Council of Academic Deans, President's Council, Student Government Association.

Calendar: Semesters. 2004–05 academic year mid-Aug. to early Aug. Freshmen admitted Aug., Jan., July. Degrees conferred with formal commencement May, Aug., Dec. Summer sessions from early June to mid-Aug.

Characteristics of Freshmen: 2,029 students admitted; 1,378 admitted and enrolled.

10% (139 students) submitted SAT scores; 90% (1,239 students) submitted ACT scores.

25th percentile: ACT Composite 17, ACT English 18, ACT Math 16; *75th percentile:* ACT Composite 24, ACT English 25, ACT Math 23.

15% of entering freshmen are expected to graduate within 5 years. 88% of freshmen from Arkansas. Freshmen from 21 states and 10 foreign countries.

Admission: Rolling admissions plan. Early acceptance available. *Requirements:* high school graduation; GED accepted. Recommended high school core courses: 4 units of English, 4 units mathematics (algebra, algebra I, geometry, advanced math course), 3 units natural science (biology, chemistry, physics; each with lab), 2 units of one foreign language, 3 units of social studies (American history, world history, civics or American government). Unconditional admission: GPA 2.5. ACT Composite score 19. Proof of immunization for measles, rubeola, and rubella. *Entrance exams:* ACT preferred. SAT and ASSET accepted. *Transfer student admission requirements:* 2.0 GPA required. Official transcript must be mailed directly to ASU from each institution previously attended. Immunization record required. May transfer no more than the maximum number of hours the student would be permitted to earn at ASU in a period comparable to that in which the transfer credit was earned.

College credit for postsecondary level work completed in secondary school. Tutoring available in selected subject areas. Noncredit developmental courses offered during regular academic year.

Degree Requirements: *For all associate degrees:* 62 credit hours; 2.0 GPA; 12 hours of last 18 hours must be in Arkansas State University work; 16 semester hours completed on the ASU-Jonesboro campus. *For all baccalaureate degrees:* 124 credit hours; 2.0 GPA; 18 of last 24 hours must be Arkansas State University work; 32 semester hours completed on the ASU-State University campus.

Fulfillment of some degree requirements and exemption from some beginning courses possible by passing institutional examinations, CLEP exams, or College Board Advanced Placement Tests. *Grading system:* A–F; withdraw. Maximum of 30 semester credit hours may be counted toward a degree.

Distinctive Educational Programs: Evening classes, web classes, and accelerated degree programs are available. Facilities and programs for independent research, including an Honors College, individual majors, and tutorials. Study abroad is available in 2 sites in Asia, 22 sites in Europe, and 1 site in the Middle East. There are semester and year-long programs abroad. Study abroad also offers summer study in Latin America and Europe.

ROTC: Army. 10 commissions awarded in 2004.

Degrees Conferred: 160 *associate.* 1,460 *baccalaureate* (B), 331 *master's* (M), 14 *doctorate* (D): agriculture 79 (B), 8 (M); biological/life sciences 54 (B), 7 (M); business/marketing 284 (B), 71 (M); communications/communication technologies 84 (B), 8 (M); computer and information sciences 78 (B), 9 (M); education 301 (B), 116 (M), 10 (D); engineering and engineering technologies 77 (B); English 31 (B), 15 (M); foreign languages and literature 3 (B); health professions and related sciences 152 (B), 43 (M); home economics and vocational home economics 7 (M); liberal arts/general studies 46 (B); mathematics 2 (B), 2 (M); natural resources/environmental science 6 (B), 4 (D); parks and recreation 28 (B), 2 (M); philosophy, religion, theology 7 (B); physical sciences 18 (B), 3 (M); protective services/public administration 52 (B), 6 (M); psychology 47 (B), 7 (M); social sciences and history 82 (B), 20 (M); visual and performing arts 29 (B), 7 (M). 32 *post-master's certificates.*

Fees and Other Expenses: *Full-time tuition per academic year 2004–05:* undergraduate in-state resident $4,305, out-of-state $10,395; graduate resident $3,060, out-of-state $7,740. *Room per academic year:* $4,000.

Financial Aid: Aid from institutionally generated funds is provided on the basis of academic merit, financial need, athletic ability, and other considerations. Institution has a Program Participation Agreement with the U.S. Department of Education for eligible students to receive Pell Grants and other federal aid.

Financial aid to full-time, first-time undergraduate students: need-based scholarships/grants totaling $25,386,982, self-help $22,612,077; non-need-based scholarships/grants $18,750,258, athletic awards $1,859,000.

Departments and Teaching Staff: Agriculture full-time *professors* 6, *associate professors* 5, *assistant professors* 3, *instructors* 2; business 4, 13, 12, 10; communications 5, 2, 4, 13; education 14, 17, 30, 22; engineering 3, 3, 3, 6; fine arts 13, 8, 12, 5; humanities/social science 21, 28, 21, 14; nursing and health 3, 10, 39, 5; sciences and mathematics 11, 15, 24, 18; other 2, 0, 2, 16.

Total instructional faculty: 621 (454 full-time, 167 part-time; 296 women, 325 men). Total number of faculty with doctorate, first-professional, or other terminal degree: 314. Student-to-faculty ration: 18:1. *Faculty development:* $3,373,308 in grants for research. 9 faculty members were awarded sabbaticals 2004–05.

Enrollment: Total enrollment 10,508. Undergraduate full-time 2,974 men / 4,289 women, part-time 765m / 1,234w; graduate full-time 146m / 209w, part-time 291m / 600w. *Transfer students:* In-state into lower division 93m / 204w, upper division 125m / 263w, graduate 108m / 214w; out-of-state into lower division 47m / 58w, upper division 39m / 41w, graduate 52m / 48w.

Characteristics of Student Body: *Ethnic/racial makeup:* number of Black non-Hispanic: 1,416; American Indian or Alaska Native: 34; Asian or Pacific Islander: 65; Hispanic: 80; White non-Hispanic: 7,409; unknown: 136. *Age distribution:* number under 18: 178; 18–19: 1,956; 20–21: 2,454; 22–24: 2,105; 25–29: 1,054; 30–34 619; 35–39: 357; 40–49: 416; 50–64: 112; 65 and over: 11.

42% of student body attend summer sessions. Distance learning courses offered for credit.

International Students: 181 nonresident aliens enrolled fall 2004. 13 students from Europe, 70 Asia, 21 Central and South America, 29 Africa, 13 Canada, 1 New Zealand, 6 other. Programs available to aid students whose native language is not English: English as a Second Language Program. No financial aid specifically designated for international students.

Student Life: Four single-sex, on-campus residence halls, an apartment complex, and married and graduate student housing are available. 16.4% of the student body resides in on-campus housing. *Special services:* Career Services Center, Counseling Center, Student Health Center, New Student Orientation,

International Student Services, Student Union. *Student publications, radio: The Herald,* a biweekly newspaper; *The Indian,* a yearbook. KASU radio station; ASU-TV station. *Student activities:* 200 social, academic, service, and honorary organizations are available. Twelve fraternities and nine sororities are represented on campus. Various minority and international associations are available. Men's intercollegiate athletics include baseball, basketball, cross-country, football, golf, and track. Women's intercollegiate athletics include basketball, cross-country, golf, soccer, tennis, track, and volleyball. Many intramural sports are also available for men's, women's, or coed teams, including archery, badminton, basketball, bowling, football, golf, racquetball, soccer, softball, swimming, table tennis, tennis, volleyball, and wallyball. *Surrounding community:* ASU is located halfway between the Mississippi River Valley and the Ozark Mountains on the slopes of Crowley's Ridge in Jonesboro, Arkansas. Memphis, Tennessee is the nearest metropolitan area and is 70 miles from campus. Memphis is served by an international airport.

Publications: *Affairs of State* published quarterly and mailed to all ASU graduates; *Campus News,* weekly faculty-staff newsletter; *ASU Undergraduate Bulletin, ASU Graduate Bulletin, ASU Independent Study-by-Mail Bulletin, Viewbook,* and *Voices.*

Library Collections: 586,176 volumes including bound books, serial backfiles, electronic documents, and government documents not in separate collections. Online and card catalogs. Current serial subscriptions: 1,675 paper, 53 5 electronic, 578,473 microform, 5,527 001 recordings. 77 computer work stations. Students have access to the Internet at no charge. Total budget for books, periodicals, audiovisual materials, microforms 2004–05: $1,328,890.

Most important special collections include the E.C. Gaithings Collection; Gieseck Collection; Judd Hill Collection.

Buildings and Grounds: Campus area 2,008 acres; 100 buildings. *New buildings:* Arkansas Biosciences completed 2004; Childhood Services 2002; College Park Club House 2000; Equine Arena 1999; Fowler Performing Arts Center 2000; Information and Technology 2001; Soccer Complex 2002; Student Health Center 2004; Student Union 2004; Track Facility 2003.

Chief Executive Officer: Dr. J. Leslie Wyatt, President.

Address admission inquiries to Paula Lynn, Director of Admissions. Graduate inquiries to Dr. Andrew Sustich, Dean of the Graduate School.

Arkansas Tech University

Russellville, Arkansas 72801-2222

Tel: (479) 968-0389   **E-mail:** tech.enroll@atu.edu
Fax: (479) 964-0522   **Internet:** www.atu.edu

Institution Description: Arkansas Tech University (Arkansas Polytechnic College until 1976) is a state institution. *Enrollment:* 6,483. *Degrees awarded:* Associate, baccalaureate, master's.

Academic offerings subject to approval by statewide coordinating bodies.

Accreditation: *Regional:* NCA. *Professional:* business, engineering, health information administration, medical assisting, music, nursing, recreation and leisure services, teacher education

History: Established as a Second District Agricultural School 1909; offered first instruction at postsecondary level 1921; changed name to Arkansas Polytechnic College, became 4-year institution, and awarded first degree (baccalaureate) 1925; changed to 2-year institution 1927; became 4-year institution again 1948; added master's program and adopted present name 1976.

Institutional Structure: *Governing board:* Arkansas Tech University Board of Trustees. Representation: 5 trustees. All voting. *Composition of institution:* Administrators 24 men / 25 women. Academic affairs headed by vice president of academic affairs. Management/business/finances directed by vice president for administration and finance. Full-time instructional faculty 240. Academic governance body, Faculty Senate, meets an average of 10 times per year.

Calendar: Semesters. 2004–05 academic year July to June. Freshmen admitted Aug., Jan., June, July. Degrees conferred and formal commencements May and December. Summer sessions of 2 terms from early June to early Aug.

Characteristics of Freshmen: 53% of applicants admitted; 49% of applicants admitted and enrolled.

1% (12 students) submitted SAT scores; 83% (1,216 students) submitted ACT scores *25th percentile:* SAT Verbal 420, SAT Math 440; ACT Composite 19, ACT English 19, ACT Math 17. *75th percentile:* SAT Verbal 530, SAT Math 530; ACT Composite 25, ACT English 27, ACT Math 25.

33.4% of entering freshmen expected to graduate within 5 years. 97% of freshmen from Arkansas.

Admission: *Requirements:* Completion of secondary school graduation requirements evidenced by submission of official transcript showing completion of the Tech Prep or College Prep curriculum to include class rank, date of graduation, and a minimum 2.0 grade point average from an Arkansas public secondary school or an accredited non-public secondary school; ACT Composite minimum score of 15.

College credit for extrainstitutional learning; college credit on basis of ACE *2006 Guide to the Evaluation of Educational Experiences in the Armed Services.* Tutoring available. Developmental/remedial courses offered in summer session and regular academic year; no degree credit given.

Degree Requirements: *For all associate degrees:* 62 semester hours. *For all baccalaureate degrees:* 124 hours; general education requirements. *For all undergraduate degrees:* 2.0 GPA; last 30 hours in residence. Fulfillment of some degree requirements possible by passing College Board CLEP. *Grading system:* A–F; withdraw (deadline after which pass-fail is appended to withdraw).

ROTC: Army offered in cooperation with the University of Central Arkansas.

Degrees Conferred: 16 *associate;* 777 *baccalaureate;* 139 *master's.*

Fees and Other Expenses: *Full-time tuition per 2004–05 academic year:* resident undergraduate: $4,158, out-of-state $8,316; graduate resident $3,912, out-of-state $7,824. *Room and board per academic year:* $3,841.

Financial Aid: Aid from institutionally generated funds is provided on the basis of academic merit, financial need, athletic ability, and other criteria. Institution has a Program Participation Agreement with the U.S. Department of Education for eligible students to receive Pell Grants and other federal aid.

Departments and Teaching Staff: *Total instructional faculty:* 367 (full-time 240, part-time 127). Student-to-faculty ratio: 19:1.

Enrollment: Total enrollment 6,483. Undergraduate full-time 2,463 men / 2,759 women, part-time 372m / 497w; graduate full-time 40m / 55w, part-time 85m / 212w.

Characteristics of Student Body: *Ethnic/racial makeup:* number of Black non-Hispanic: 257; American Indian or Alaska Native: 97; Asian or Pacific Islander: 59; Hispanic: 112; White non-Hispanic: 5,496.

Student Life: On-campus residence halls house 18.7% of student body. Residence halls for men only constitute 49% of such space, for women only 51%. Housing available for married students. *Intercollegiate athletics:* men only: baseball, basketball, football, golf, tennis; women only: basketball, volleyball. *Special regulations:* Cars permitted without restrictions. Quiet hours. Residence hall visitation from 7pm to 11pm. *Special services:* Learning Resources Center, medical services. *Student publications: Agricola,* a yearbook, *Arka-Tech,* a weekly newspaper. *Surrounding community:* Russellville 2000 population 25,000. Little Rock, 76 miles from campus, is nearest metropolitan area.

Library Collections: 259,372 volumes including bound books, serial backfiles, electronic documents, and government documents not in separate collections. Online catalog. Current serial subscriptions: 1,054 paper. 700 computer work stations. Students have access to the Internet at no charge.

Most important holdings include collections on Arkansiana, Americana, and recreation and park administration.

Buildings and Grounds: Campus area 518 acres. *New buildings:* Don Bryan Student Services Building; Summit Residence Hall; student apartments.

Chief Executive Officer: Dr. Robert C. Brown, President.

Undergraduate admission inquiries to Shauna H. Donnell, Director of Admissions. Graduate inquiries to Dr. Eldon Clary, Dean of Graduate Studies.

Central Baptist College

1501 College Avenue
Conway, Arkansas 72032

Tel: (501) 329-6872   **E-mail:** admissions@cbc.edu
Fax: (501) 329-2941   **Internet:** www.cbc.edu

Institution Description: Central Baptist College is a private, coeducational college affiliated with the Baptist Missionary Association of Arkansas. *Enrollment:* 198 men / 175 women. *Degrees awarded:* Associate, baccalaureate.

Accreditation: *Regional:* NCA.

History: Founded 1952.

Institutional Structure: Governing board.

Calendar: Semesters. 2004–05 academic year Aug. to May.

Characteristics of Freshmen: 98% (80 students) submitted ACT scores. Mean ACT Composite score 20.8.

67% of applicants accepted. 55% of accepted applicants enrolled. 65% of freshmen from Arkansas. Freshmen from 4 states and 1 foreign country.

Admission: *Requirements:* High school graduates with a C or better average; non-high school graduates with a minimum ACT score of 18 and 15 units of credit, including 3 English, 1 mathematics, 1 natural science, 2 social science, and not more than 2 activities.

Degree Requirements: 125 credit hours; 2.00 GPA.

Distinctive Educational Programs: Programs for Christian ministries, social services, music, business, organizational management, management information systems.

ROTC: Available through nearby institution.

Degrees Conferred: 22 *associate;* 41 *baccalaureate:* computer and information sciences 2; philosophy/religion/theology 11; psychology 7; visual and performing arts 1; other 20.

Fees and Other Expenses: *Full-time tuition per academic year 2004–05:* $7,176. *Required fees:* $500. *Room and board per academic year:* $4,560.

Financial Aid: Aid from institutionally generated funds is provided on the basis of academic merit, athletic ability, financial need. Institution has a Program Participation Agreement with the U.S. Department of Education for eligible students to receive Pell Grants and other federal aid.

Financial aid to full-time, first-time undergraduate students: need-based scholarships and grants totaling $1,205,173; self-help $1,027,203; non-need-based parent loans totaling $156,137; tuition waivers $245,210; athletic awards $87,467.

Departments and Teaching Staff: Business *professors* 0, *associate professors* 2; *assistant professors* 0, *instructors* 1, *part-time faculty* 19; English 0, 1, 1, 0, 3; general education 0, 1, 0, 0, 1; music 0, 1, 1, 0, 6; physical education 0, 1, 0, 0, 0; religion 2, 0, 0, 0, 3; science/mathematics 1, 0, 1, 1, 2; social science 1, 0, 2, 0, 2.

Total instructional faculty: 53 (full-time 17, part-time 36; women 20, men 33). Total number with doctorate, first-professional, or other terminal degree: 13. Student-to-faculty ratio: 13:1.

Enrollment: Total enrollment 373. Undergraduate full-time 175 men / 143 women, part-time 23m / 22w. *Transfer students:* in-state into lower division 28m / 15w; out-of-state 10m / 5w.

Characteristics of Student Body: *Ethnic/racial makeup:* number of Black non-Hispanic: 10; American Indian or Alaska Native: 2; Asian or Pacific Islander: 4; Hispanic: 5; White non-Hispanic: 320. *Age distribution:* number under 18: 1; 18–19: 131; 20–21: 79; 22–24: 55; 25–29: 24; 30–34: 23; 35–39: 23; 40–49: 28; 50–64: 7; 65 and over: 2.

International Students: 1 nonresident alien from Africa enrolled fall 2004. No programs available to aid students whose native language is not English. No financial aid specifically designated for international students.

Student Life: *Student publications:* Yearbook.

Library Collections: 56,009 volumes including bound books, serial backfiles, electronic documents, and government documents not in separate collections. Online catalog and card catalog. Current serial subscriptions: 276 paper, 46 microform. 3,775 via electronic access. 683 recordings; 344 compact discs; 50 CD-ROMs. Online and card catalogs. Students have access to the Internet at no charge. Total budget for books, periodicals, audiovisual materials, microforms 2004–05: $106,656.

Most important special holdings include minutes of the Baptist Missionary Association of Arkansas.

Buildings and Grounds: Campus area 11 acres.

Chief Executive Officer: Charles E. Attebery, President.

Address admission inquiries to Cory Calhoun, Director of Admissions.

Harding University

900 East Center
Searcy, Arkansas 72149

Tel: (501) 279-4400   **E-mail:** admissions@harding.edu
Fax: (501) 279-4129   **Internet:** www.@harding.edu

Institution Description: Harding University (Harding College until 1979) is a private university affiliated with the Church of Christ. *Enrollment:* 5,348. *Degrees awarded:* Baccalaureate, master's.

Accreditation: *Regional:* NCA. *Professional:* business, marriage and family therapy, music, nursing, social work, teacher education

History: Chartered in Morrilton as Arkansas Christian College, a junior college, 1919; offered first instruction at postsecondary level 1922; purchased assets of Harper College (in Kansas, established 1915), became 4-year college and changed name to Harding College 1924; awarded first degree (baccalaureate) 1925; moved to present location 1934; adopted present name 1979.

Institutional Structure: *Governing board:* Harding University Board of Trustees. Extrainstitutional representation: 24 trustees; institutional representation: president of the university. 1 ex officio. 24 voting. *Composition of institution:* Administrators 16 men / 1 woman. Academic affairs headed by vice president of academic affairs. Management/business/finances directed by vice president for finance. Full-time instructional faculty 215. Academic governance body, the faculty, meets an average of 10 times per year.

Calendar: Semester. 2004–05 academic year Aug. to May. Freshmen admitted Aug., Jan., June, July. Degrees conferred and formal commencements May, Aug., Dec. Summer session of 3 terms from mid-May to mid-Aug.

Characteristics of Freshmen: 60% of applicants admitted. 57% admitted and enrolled.

41% (400 students) submitted SAT scores; 73% (711 students) submitted ACT scores. *25th percentile*: SAT Verbal 496, SAT Math 480; ACT Composite 20, ACT English 20, ACT Math 19. *75th percentile*: SAT Verbal 640, SAT Math 610; ACT Composite 27, ACT English 28; ACT Math 26.

57% of entering freshmen expected to graduate within 5 years. 29% of freshmen from Arkansas. Freshmen from 50 states.

Admission: Rolling admissions plan. Apply no later than June 1 of year of enrollment. Early acceptance available. *Requirements:* Either graduation from accredited secondary school with 15 academic units must include 4 English, 3 mathematics, 2 science, 3 social studies, 3 from any academic area. For mathematics and science majors, recommend 4 additional units in college preparatory mathematics. Minimum GPA 2.0. *Entrance tests:* ACT Composite or SAT. *For transfer students:* 2.0 minimum GPA; from 4-year accredited institution 96 hours maximum transfer credit; from 2-year accredited institution 68 hours; correspondence/extension students 18 hours.

College credit and advanced placement for postsecondary level work completed in secondary school. For extrainstitutional learning (life experience) college credit on basis of faculty assessment, ACE *2006 Guide to the Evaluation of Educational Experiences in the Armed Services*, portfolio assessment. Developmental courses offered in summer session; credit given.

Degree Requirements: *For all associate degrees:* 64 credit hours; 2 kinesiology hours. *For all baccalaureate degrees:* 128 credit hours; 3 kinesiology courses; exit proficiency examination in writing for grades of less than B in English. *For all undergraduate degrees:* 2.0 GPA; 32 hours in residence; chapel; general education requirements; religion course each semester.

Fulfillment of some degree requirements and exemption from some beginning courses possible by passing departmental examinations, College Board CLEP, AP (score of 3), International Baccalaureate. *Grading system:* A–F; withdraw (carries time limit, deadline after which pass-fail is appended to withdraw).

Distinctive Educational Programs: Work-experience programs, including cooperative education, internships in missionary work. Evening classes. Dual-degree program in engineering with Georgia Institute of Technology, Louisiana Tech University, Stanford University (CA), University of Arkansas at Fayetteville, University of Missouri (Rolla). Cooperative baccalaureate in medical technology with affiliated hospitals. Interdisciplinary program in American studies offering academic training as well as seminars; observation tours; and lectures by industry, government, and community leaders. Preprofessional programs in agriculture, allied health, architecture. Individual majors. Institutionally sponsored study abroad in Italy (Harding owns a campus in Florence, Italy where 50 students from the main campus attend each semester). Study abroad also in Greece, Australia, and England. Small Business Institute provides students practical experience and community service. *Other distinctive programs:* Qualified secondary school seniors may enroll in college courses for credit.

ROTC: Army in cooperation with University of Central Arkansas.

Degrees Conferred: 753 *baccalaureate (B); 207 master's (M)*: area and ethnic studies 2 (B); biological/life sciences 16 (B); business/marketing 166 (B), 30 (M); communications/communication technologies 52 (B); computer and information sciences 81 (B); education 107 (B), 159 (M); English 22 (B); foreign languages and literature 6(B); health professions and related sciences 51 (B), 18 (M); home economics 28 (B); liberal arts/general studies 36 (B); mathematics 6; parks and recreation 19 (B); philosophy, religion, theology 57 (B); physical sciences 7 (B); protective services/public administration 25 (B); psychology 35 (B); social sciences and history 21 (B); visual and performing arts 35 (B).

Fees and Other Expenses: *Full-time tuition per academic year 2004–05:* $10,380. *Required fees:* $400. *Room and board per academic year:* $5,182.

Financial Aid: Institutional direct lending program available. Aid from institutionally generated funds is awarded on the basis of academic merit, financial need, athletic ability. Institution has a Program Participation Agreement with the U.S. Department of Education for eligible students to receive Pell Grants and other federal aid.

Financial aid to full-time, first-time undergraduate students: need-based scholarships/grants totaling $10,808,112, self-help $16,998,867, parent loans $2,762,009, tuition waivers $796,685, athletic awards $521,234; non-need-based scholarships and grants $5,919,579, self-help $3,367,771, parent loans $1,664,472, tuition waivers $744,430, athletic awards $808,791.

Departments and Teaching Staff: *Total instructional faculty:* 322 (full-time 215, part-time 107). Total number with doctorate, first-professional, or other terminal degree: 155. Student-to faculty ratio: 18:1.

Enrollment: Total enrollment 5,348. Undergraduate full-time 1,783 men / 2,079 women, part-time 91m / 84w; graduate full-time 96m / 159w, part-time 192m / 804w.

Characteristics of Student Body: *Ethnic/racial makeup:* number of Black non-Hispanic: 157; American Indian or Alaska Native: 35; Asian or Pacific Islander: 28; Hispanic: 50; White non-Hispanic: 3,519; unknown 16. *Age distribution:* number under 18: 322; 18–19: 1,697; 20–21: 1,417; 22–24: 668; 25–29: 96; 30–34 38; 35–39: 21; 40–49: 30; 50–64: 8. 35% of student body attend summer sessions.

International Students: 148 nonresident aliens enrolled fall 3004. 28 students from Europe, 23 Asia, 76 Central and South Latin America, 21 Africa, 19 Canada, 2 Australia, 13 other. Social and cultural programs available to aid students whose native language is not English. English as a Second Language Program.

Student Life: On-campus residence halls house 70% of student body. On-campus housing available for married students. 95% of married students request institutional housing; all are so housed. *Intercollegiate athletics:* men only: baseball, basketball, cross-country, football, golf, swimming, tennis, track; women only: basketball, cross-country, tennis, track and field, volleyball. *Special regulations:* Cars permitted without restrictions. Students must dress in a manner that is modest and consistent with Christian principles. Curfews and quiet hours. *Special services:* Medical services. *Student publications, radio:* Literary magazine published several times per year; weekly newspaper; yearbook. Radio station KHCA broadcasts 36 hours per week. *Surrounding community:* Searcy 2000 population 16,000. Little Rock, 40 miles from campus, is nearest metropolitan area. Served by airport 2 miles from campus.

Library Collections: 253,436 volumes including bound books, serial backfiles, electronic documents, and government documents not in separate collections. Online catalog. Current serial subscriptions: 16,879 paper, 251,230 microform, 8,281. Students have access to the Internet at no charge.

Most important holdings include G.C. Brewer Collection (personal library of influential writer and minister in Church of Christ); oral history collection; Miles-Williams Science History Collection.

Buildings and Grounds: Campus area 200 acres. *New buildings:* Pryor England Science Center completed 2004; Thornton Education Center 2005.

Chief Executive Officer: Dr. David B. Burks, President.

Address admission inquiries to Glenn Dillard, Director of Enrollment Management.

Harding University Graduate School of Religion

1000 Cherry Road
Memphis, Tennessee 38117
Tel: (901) 761-1353
Degree Programs Offered: *SEE* description of institution under TENNESSEE.

Henderson State University

1100 Henderson Street
Arkadelphia, Arkansas 71999-0001

Tel: (870) 230-5000	**E-mail:** hardwrvk@hsu.edu
Fax: (870) 230-5147	**Internet:** www.hsu.edu

Institution Description: Henderson State University (Henderson State College until 1975) is a state institution. *Enrollment:* 3,461. *Degrees awarded:* Associate, baccalaureate, master's.

Academic offerings subject to approval by statewide coordinating bodies. Member of Joint Education Consortium, Inc.

Accreditation: *Regional:* NCA. *Professional:* business, counseling, music, nursing, teacher education

History: Established by Methodist Conferences of Arkansas, chartered, and offered first instruction at postsecondary level 1890; awarded first degree (baccalaureate) 1894; changed name to Henderson College 1904, to Henderson Brown College 1911; became state institution and changed name to Henderson State Teachers College 1929, to Henderson State College 1967; adopted present name 1975. *See* John G. Hall, *Henderson State University, The Methodist Years, 1890–1929* (Arkadelphia: Henderson State University Alumni Association, 1975) for further information.

Institutional Structure: *Governing board:* Board of Trustees. Representation: 7 trustees. All voting. *Composition of institution:* Administrators 19 men / 19 women. Academic affairs headed by vice president for academic affairs. Management/business/finances directed by vice president for fiscal affairs. Full-time instructional faculty 99 men / 58 women. Academic governance body, University Academic Council, meets an average of 11 times per year.

Calendar: Semesters. 2004–05 academic year July to June. Freshmen admitted Aug., Jan., June, July. Degrees conferred May, Aug., Dec. Formal commencements May, Dec. Summer session of 2 terms from early June to mid-Aug.

Characteristics of Freshmen: 61% of applicants admitted. 37% admitted and enrolled.

7% (9 students) submitted SAT scores; 93% (538 students) submitted ACT scores. *25th percentile*: SAT Verbal 456, SAT Math 460; ACT Composite 19, ACT English 20, ACT Math 18. *75th percentile*: SAT Verbal 560, SAT Math 570; ACT Composite 25, ACT English 26, ACT Math 24.

38% of entering freshmen expected to graduate within 5 years. 52% of freshmen from Arkansas. Freshmen from 12 states and 6 foreign countries.

Admission: Rolling admissions plan. Apply anytime before, but no later than, last day of registration. Early acceptance available. *Unconditional admission:* Entering freshmen must have minimum ACT score of 19 or equivalent score on alternate exam, minimum high school GPA of 2.50, and if graduated from high school after May 1, 1997, must have completed college/technical prep core curriculum with minimum GPA of 2.00. *Conditional admission*: Entering freshmen must have graduated from high school or earned GED certificate and have GPA of 1.25 after 12 semester hours of coursework. If ACT score is below 16, they must apply for admission prior to July 15 and provide supplemental application materials by July 31 (Nov. 15/Nov. 30 for Spring semester). Material will be reviewed by admissions committee. Students may not enroll in upper division courses until all remedial requirements are met. *Entrance tests:* ACT Composite. *For transfer students:* From 4-year accredited institution 94 semester hours maximum transfer credit; from 2-year accredited institution 67 hours; correspondence/extension students 30 hours. Good standing at institution previously attended.

Advanced placement for postsecondary-level work completed in secondary school. College credit and advanced placement for extrainstitutional learning on basis of ACE *2006 Guide to the Evaluation of Educational Experiences in the Armed Services*. Tutoring available. Developmental courses offered during regular academic year; credit given.

Degree Requirements: *For all associate degrees:* 60 credit hours; 1 physical education course. *For all baccalaureate degrees:* 124 credit hours; 2–3 physical education courses. *For all undergraduate degrees:* 2.0 GPA; 2 semesters in residence; general education requirements.

Fulfillment of some degree requirements and exemption from some beginning courses possible by passing College Board CLEP. *Grading system:* A–F; credit-no credit.

Distinctive Educational Programs: Flexible meeting places and schedules, including off-campus centers and evening classes. Preprofessional programs in dentistry, engineering, medical technology, medicine, pharmacy. Facilities and programs for independent research, including honors programs, tutorials. *Other distinctive programs:* Continuing education; five-year program in aviation.

ROTC: Army in cooperation with Ouachita Baptist University.

Degrees Conferred: 456 *baccalaureate* (B); 102 *master's* (M): biological/life sciences 22 (B); business/marketing 86 (B), 23 (M); communications/communication technologies 9 (B); computer and information sciences 10 (B); education 114 (B), 45 (M); English 30 (B); foreign languages and literature 1 (B); home economics 14 (B); liberal arts/general studies 6 (M); mathematics 6 (B); parks and recreation 23 (B), 19 (M); physical sciences 8 (B); protective services/public administration 25 (B), 9 (M); psychology 28 (B); social sciences and history 37 (B); trade and industry 18 (B); visual and performing arts 29 (B); other 26.

Fees and Other Expenses: *Full-time tuition per academic year 2004–05:* $3,640, out-of-state $7,280; graduate resident $2,916, out-of-state $5,832. *Required fees:* $489. *Room and board per academic year:* $3,874.

Financial Aid: Aid from institutionally generated funds is provided on the basis of academic merit, financial need, other criteria. Institution has a Program Participation Agreement with the U.S. Department of Education for eligible students to receive Pell Grants and other federal aid.

Financial aid to full-time, first-time undergraduate students: need-based scholarships/grants $5,725,639, self-help $6,700,514; non-need-based scholarships and loans $4,213,564, self-help $3,979,143, parent loans $406,920, athletic awards $402,014.

Departments and Teaching Staff: *Total instructional faculty:* 218 (full-time 157, part-time 61; women 17, men 121). Total number with doctorate, first-professional, or other terminal degree: 199. Student-to-faculty ratio: 17:1. *Faculty development:* 5 faculty members awarded sabbaticals in 2004–05.

Enrollment: Total enrollment: 3,461. Undergraduate full-time 1,154 men / 1,514 women, part-time 122m / 216w. Graduate full-time 38m / 102w, part-time 77m / 208w. *Transfer students:* in-state into lower division 53m / 75w, out-of-state 10m / 13w; in-state into upper division 33m / 67w, out-of-state 22m / 19w; graduate school in-state 1m / 1w.

Characteristics of Student Body: *Ethnic/racial makeup:* number of Black non-Hispanic: 520; American Indian or Alaska Native: 21; Asian or Pacific Islander: 15; Hispanic: 35; White non-Hispanic: 2,354; unknown: 26. *Age distribution:* number under 18: 37; 18–19: 931; 20–21: 378; 22–24: 580; 25–29: 251; 30–34: 144; 35–39: 75; 40–49: 106; 50–64: 30; 65 and over: 3.

International Students: 81 nonresident aliens enrolled fall 2004. Programs available to aid students whose native language is not English: English as a Second Language Program.

Student Life: On-campus residence halls house 29% of student body. Residence halls for men constitute 44% of such space, for women 56%. *Intercollegiate athletics:* men only: baseball, basketball, football, swimming, tennis, track; women only: basketball, cross country, softball, swimming, tennis, volleyball. *Special regulations:* Registered cars permitted. Curfews. Quiet hours. Residence hall visitation from 6pm to 10:45pm. Sun.–Thurs., 6pm. to 12:45am Fri. and Sat. *Special services:* Learning Resources Center, medical services. *Student publications, radio: The Oracle*, a weekly newspaper; *The Star*, a yearbook. Radio station KSWH broadcasts 40 hours per week. *Surrounding community:* Arkadelphia population 10,000. Little Rock, Arkansas, 70 miles from campus, is nearest metropolitan area.

Library Collections: 260,443 volumes including bound books, serial backfiles, electronic documents, and government documents not in separate collections. Online card catalog. Current serial subscriptions in microform 214,922; via electronic access 19,384. Students have access to the Internet at no charge.

Most important holdings include Howard A. Dawson Memorial Collection; Arkansas History Collection.

Buildings and Grounds: Campus area 157 acres. *New buildings:* Arkansas Hall renovation completed 2004.

Chief Executive Officer: Dr. Charles D. Dunn, President.

Address undergraduate admission inquiries to Vikita Hardwick, Director of University Relations and Admissions; graduate inquiries to Missie Bell, Graduate School Office.

Hendrix College

1600 Washington Avenue
Conway, Arkansas 72032-3080

Tel: (501) 329-6811   **E-mail:** adm@hendrix.edu
Fax: (501) 450-1200   **Internet:** www.hendrix.edu

Institution Description: Hendrix College is a private college affiliated with the United Methodist Church. *Enrollment:* 1,049. *Degrees awarded:* Baccalaureate.

Accreditation: *Regional:* NCA. *Professional:* music, teacher education

History: Established in Altus as Central Collegiate Institute 1876; offered first instruction at postsecondary level 1881; purchased by Arkansas Methodist Conference and incorporated 1884; first degree (baccalaureate) awarded 1887, changed name to Hendrix College 1889; moved to present location 1890; merged with Henderson-Brown College to become Hendrix-Henderson College 1929; merged with Galloway Women's College and adopted present name 1933.

Institutional Structure: *Governing board:* Board of Trustees of Hendrix College. Extrainstitutional representation: 39 trustees of whom 12 are United Methodist Church members and 60% alumni; 1 life member. 3 ex officio, including bishop, college president, 1 church official. 39 voting members. *Composition of institution:* Administrators 4 men / 2 women. Academic affairs headed by provost. Management/business/finances directed by vice president for business and finance. Full-time instructional faculty 81. Academic governance body, the faculty, meets an average of 8 times per year.

Calendar: Semesters. Academic year Aug. to May. Freshmen admitted Aug., Jan. Degrees conferred and formal commencement May. No summer session.

Characteristics of Freshmen: 85% of applicants accepted. 29% of accepted applicants enrolled.

56% (166 students) submitted SAT scores; 80% (235 students) submitted ACT scores. *25th percentile*: SAT Verbal 590, SAT Math 560; ACT Composite 24, ACT English 25, ACT Math 22. *75th percentile*: SAT Verbal 700, SAT Math 670; ACT Composite 30, ACT English 33, ACT Math 28.

66% entering freshmen expected to graduate within 5 years. 58% of freshmen from Arkansas. Freshmen from 25 states and 1 foreign country.

Admission: Rolling admissions plan. For fall acceptance, apply as early as July of previous year; but not later than August of year of enrollment. *Requirements:* Either graduation from accredited secondary school or GED. Academic program in secondary school recommended. *Entrance tests:* College Board SAT or ACT Composite. *For transfer students:* 2.0 minimum GPA; 16 courses maximum transfer credit.

College credit and advanced placement for postsecondary level work completed in secondary school and for extrainstitutional learning college credit on basis of ACE *2006 Guide to the Evaluation of Educational Experiences in the Armed Services*.

Degree Requirements: *Undergraduate:* 32 courses; 2.0 GPA; 2 years in residence capstone experiences in individual fields of study. Course credits earned through CLEP, AP, or IB exams may be counted toward graduation although they may not be used to satisfy specific graduation requirements. *Grading system:* A–F; pass (1 course outside of major per semester); withdraw (carries time limit).

Distinctive Educational Programs: Flexible meeting places and schedules. Dual-degree program in engineering with Columbia University School of Engineering and Applied Science (NY), Washington University (MO), and Vanderbilt University (TN). Honors programs. Study abroad in England, France, Spain, Germany. Extensive undergraduate research; internships for academic credit available in most majors.

Degrees Conferred: 230 *baccalaureate:* biological sciences 32, business and management 10, education 7, fine and applied arts 7, foreign languages 8, letters 21, mathematics 12, physical sciences 18, psychology 32, social sciences 56, theology 15, interdisciplinary studies 7.

Fees and Other Expenses: *Full-time tuition per academic year 2005–06:* $21,336. *Room and board per academic year:* $6,010. *Books and supplies:* $900.

Financial Aid: Aid from institutionally generated funds is provided on the basis of academic merit, financial need, other criteria. nstitution has a Program Participation Agreement with the U.S. Department of Education for eligible students to receive Pell Grants and other federal aid.

Financial aid to full-time, first-time undergraduate students: need-based scholarships/grants $5,404,608, self-help $2,467,941, parent loans $574,834, tuition waivers $47,948; non-need-based scholarships/grants $4,210,683, self-help 942,314, parent loans $2,621,537, tuition waivers $247,880. *Graduate aid:* $72,723 in loans (5 awards ranging from $8,500 to $18,500); 1 work-study worth $500; 3 college assigned jobs averaging $1,500; 8 fellowships/grants totaling $52,499 (ranging from $2,000 to $16,510).

Departments and Teaching Staff: Art *professors* 0, *associate professors* 2, *assistant professors* 2, *part-time faculty* 2; biology 2, 2, 5, 0; chemistry 5, 2, 0, 0; business/economics 5, 0, 1, 3; English 4, 0, 1, 1; education 0, 1, 1, 2; foreign languages 2, 1, 5, 2; history 2, 2, 1, 0; kinesiology 2, 0, 1, 2; liberal studies 0, 0, 0, 1; mathematics/computer science 1, 2, 3, 1; music 2, 2, 1, 0; philosophy 1, 1, 1, 0; physics 3, 1, 0, 0; psychology 1, 2, 2, 0; religion 2, 1, 1, 0; sociology/anthropology 1, 1, 1, 0; theatre arts 2, 0, 1, 2.

Total instructional faculty: 100 (full-time 83, part-time 17; women 40, men 60). Total number with doctorate, first-professional, or other terminal degree: 54. Student-to-faculty ratio: 11:1. *Faculty development:* total grants to faculty for research 2003–04: $622,674. 10 faculty members awarded sabbaticals in 2004–05.

Enrollment: Total enrollment 1,049. Undergraduate 1,042.

Characteristics of Student Body: *Ethnic/racial makeup:* Black non-Hispanic: 4%, American Indian or Alaska Native: 1.6%; Asian or Pacific Islander: 3.1%; Hispanic: 2.8%; White non-Hispanic: 70.3%; unknown: 17.1%.

International Students: 12 nonresident aliens enrolled fall 2004. No programs available to aid students whose native language is not English. Financial aid specifically designated for international students: Variable number of undergraduate scholarships available annually.

Student Life: On-campus residence halls house 85% of student body. Halls for men constitute 42% of such space, for women only 38%, for both sexes 20%. 15% of student body live off campus. *Intercollegiate athletics:* men only: baseball. For women only: volleyball and softball. For men and women: basketball, cross country, golf, swimming and diving, soccer, tennis, track and field. *Special regulations:* Cars with decals permitted. Quiet hours established by each residence hall. Visitation hours established by each residence hall. *Student publications, radio: Profile,* a weekly newspaper; *Aonian,* an annual magazine; *Troubadour,* an annual. Radio station KHDX broadcasts 50 hours per week. *Surrounding community:* Conway population 40,000. Little Rock, 30 miles from campus, is nearest metropolitan area. Airport 35 miles from campus.

Library Collections: 256,714 volumes. 182,229 microforms; 1,170 audiovisual materials; 736 current periodical subscriptions. Students have access to online information retrieval services and the Internet.

Most important holdings include Hendrix College Archives; United Methodist Archives; Wilbur Mills Papers.

Buildings and Grounds: Campus area 40 acres.

Chief Executive Officer: Dr. J. Timothy Cloyd, President.

Address admission inquiries to Karen Foust, Vice President for Enrollment.

John Brown University

2000 West University Street
Siloam Springs, Arkansas 72761
Tel: (479) 524-9500   **E-mail:** dcrandall@jbu.edu
Fax: (479) 524-9548   **Internet:** www.jbu.edu

Institution Description: John Brown University is a private, independent, nonprofit Christian college. *Enrollment:* 1,947. *Degrees awarded:* Baccalaureate, master's.

Member of Christian College Coalition.

Accreditation: *Regional:* NCA. *Professional:* construction education, engineering, teacher education

History: Established and incorporated as Southwestern Collegiate Institute, a junior college, and offered first instruction at postsecondary level 1919; changed name to John E. Brown College 1920; awarded first degree (associate) 1921; reorganized to comprise John E. Brown College, Siloam School of the Bible (established 1920) and John E. Brown Vocational College (established 1920) and John E. Brown Vocational College (established 1934), added upper division program and adopted present name 1934; divisions merged into single unit 1948. *See* Earl R. Williams, *John Brown University: Its Founder and Its Founding* (Diss., University of Arkansas at Fayetteville, 1971) for further information.

Institutional Structure: *Governing board:* John Brown University Board of Trustees. Extrainstitutional representation: 28 trustees, including 15 alumni. All voting. *Composition of institution:* Administrators 6 men / 2 women. Academic affairs headed by vice president for academic affairs. Management/business/finances directed by vice president for finance and administration. Full-time instructional faculty 79. Academic governance body, Educational Policies Division, meets an average of 30 times per year.

Calendar: Semesters. 2004–05 academic year Aug. to May. Freshmen admitted Aug., Jan. Degrees conferred May, Dec. Formal commencement May, Dec. Summer session of from mid-May to early June.

Characteristics of Freshmen: 71% of applicants admitted. 46% admitted and enrolled.

37% (110 students) submitted SAT scores; 71% (209 students) submitted ACT scores. *25th percentile:* SAT Verbal 510, SAT Math 500; ACT Composite 21, ACT English 21, ACT Math 20. *75th percentile:* SAT Verbal 630, SAT Math 620; ACT Composite 28, ACT English 29, ACT Math 27.

60% of entering freshmen expected to graduate within 5 years. 25% of freshmen from Arkansas. Freshmen from 45 states and 27 foreign countries.

Admission: Application deadline June 1. *Requirements:* graduation from accredited high school or GED. Recommended 4 units English, 4 units mathematics, 3 science, 2 American history, and 5 units representing at least two additional subjects. Additional requirements specified for entrance in certain fields. Minimum standards include 2.5 cumulative high school GPA and 40th percentile on the SAT; two references from individuals assessing both academic and spiritual fit. *Entrance tests:* SAT or ACT Composite. *For transfer students:* 2.0 minimum GPA; from 4-year accredited institution 90 hours maximum transfer credit; from 2-year accredited institution 68 hours; correspondence/extension students 30 hours maximum.

College credit and advanced placement for postsecondary level work completed in secondary school and for extrainstitutional learning college credit on basis of ACE *2006 Guide to the Evaluation of Educational Experiences in the Armed Services.*

Developmental courses offered during regular academic year; credit given.

Degree Requirements: *For all associate degrees:* 62 credit hours; 2.0 GPA in major. *For all baccalaureate degrees:* 124 credit hours; 2.25 GPA in major; 4 hours physical education; comprehensives in individual fields of study. *For all degrees:* 2.0 GPA; 2 terms in residence; weekly chapel attendance; general education requirements; exit competency examinations in writing and mathematics.

Fulfillment of some degree requirements and exemption from some beginning courses possible by passing departmental and institutional examinations, College Board CLEP, APP. *Grading system:* A–F; satisfactory-unsatisfactory; withdraw (carries time limit); incomplete (carries time limit).

Distinctive Educational Programs: Environmental science, digital media, international business, corporate/community wellness management, engineering, Christian ministries, intercultural studies, construction management, broadcasting, teacher education, health science track including cadaver dissection. Writing-intensive core in the liberal arts. Nontraditional Bachelor of Science in Education for adult learners. Work-experience programs. Special telecommunications facilities. *Study abroad:* Latin American Studies (Costa Rica), Holy Land Studies (Jerusalem), Global Stewardship Study (Belize), Russian Studies (Moscow/Leningrad), Middle Eastern Studies (Cairo), Centre for Medieval and Renaissance Studies (Oxford), National Collegiate Honors Council Semesters.

ROTC: Army in cooperation with the University of Arkansas.

Degrees Conferred: 383 *baccalaureate* (B), 53 *master's* (M): biological and life sciences 10 (B); business/marketing 217 (B), 84 (M); communications/communication technologies 41 (B); education 25 (B); engineering/engineering technologies 15 (B); English 5, law/legal studies 2 (B); philosophy, religion, theology 18 (B), 8 (M); physical sciences 1 (B); psychology 5 (B); social sciences and history 28 (B); trade and industry 8 (B); visual and performing arts 12 (B); other 11 (M).

Fees and Other Expenses: *Full-time tuition per academic year 2004–05:* $13,724. *Required fees:* $710. *Room and board per academic year:* $5,326.

Financial Aid: Aid from institutionally generated funds is provided on the basis of academic merit, financial need, athletic ability. Institution has a Program Participation Agreement with the U.S. Department of Education for eligible students to receive Pell Grants and other federal aid.

Financial aid to full-time, first-time undergraduate students: scholarships/grants totaling $5,187,856, self-help $6,491,366, parent loans $1,326,266, tuition waivers $426,583, athletic awards $1,013,350; non-need-based scholarships/grants totaling $1,321,437, self-help $217,777, parent loans $152,000, athletic awards $49,974. *Graduate aid:* 42 federal and state-funded loans totaling $1,662,525 (ranging from $500 to $5,793); 41 fellowships/grants totaling $204,558 (ranging from $750 to $6,480).

Departments and Teaching Staff: *Professors* 24, *associate professors* 18, *assistant professors* 31, *instructors* 6, *part-time faculty* 27.

Total instructional faculty: 106 (79 full-time, 27 part-time; women 28, men 78). Total number with doctorate, first-professional, or other terminal degree: 57. Student-to-faculty ratio: 13:1. *Faculty development:* 3 faculty members awarded sabbaticals in 2004–05.

Enrollment: Total enrollment 1,947. Undergraduate full-time 840 men / 808 women, part-time 33m / 51w; graduate full-time 17m / 35w, part-time 77m / 86w. *Transfer students:* in-state into lower division 13m / 12w; out-of-state 20m / 23w; in-state into lower division 4w; upper division 1w.

Characteristics of Student Body: *Ethnic/racial makeup:* number of Black non-Hispanic: 47; American Indian or Alaska Native: 39; Asian or Pacific Islander: 29; Hispanic: 34; White non-Hispanic: 1,428; unknown 20. *Age distribution:* number under 18: 13; 18–19: 456; 20–21: 480; 22–24: 206; 25–29: 29; 30–34 122; 35–39: 86; 40–49: 121; 50–64: 27.

International Students: 115 nonresident aliens enrolled fall 2004. Programs available to aid students whose native language is not English: Social, cultural. English as a Second Language Program. Financial aid specifically designated for foreign students: 20 scholarships awarded annually (value of $84,000).

Student Life: On-campus residence halls house 61% of undergraduate student population. Dormitories for men only constitute 45% of such space, for women only 55%. Housing available for married students. 25% of married students request institutional housing; 20% are so housed. *Intercollegiate athletics:* men only: basketball, soccer, swimming and diving, tennis; women only: basketball, swimming and diving, tennis, volleyball. *Special regulations:* Cars permitted without restrictions. Quiet hours and dormitory visitation hours regulated by residence life office. *Special services:* Academic assistance center, advocate for students with disabilities, health services. *Student publications, radio: Threefold Advocate,* a weekly newspaper; *The Nesher,* a yearbook. Radio station KLRC broadcasts 24 hours per day; KARQ broadcasts 30 hours per week. Approximately six hours of television news, sports, and variety shows are broadcast weekly. *Surrounding community:* Siloam Springs population 9,300. Fayetteville/Springdale, 30 miles from campus, has population of 90,000. Tulsa (OK) is 90 miles from campus. Served by airports in Fayetteville and Tulsa.

Publications: Sources of information about John Brown University include *Campus Life Magazine; The Brown Bulletin* (published five times annually).

Library Collections: 1,25,000 volumes including bound books, serial backfiles, electronic documents, and government documents not in separate collections. Online catalog. Current serial subscriptions: paper 450; microform 250; via electronic access 6,000. 30 computer work stations. Students have access to the Internet at no charge.

Most important special collections include manuscripts and artifacts relating to the life of John E. Brown, Sr.; J. Vernon McGee Collection; Romig Juvenile Literature Collection.

Buildings and Grounds: Campus area 67 acres. *New buildings:* Bell Science Hall; Walker Student Center and Residence Hall; North Hall; Soderquist Business Center.

Chief Executive Officer: Dr. Charles W. Pollard, President.

Address admission inquiries to Donald E. Crandall, Vice President for Enrollment Management.

Lyon College

2300 Highland Road
Batesville, Arkansas 72501
Tel: (870) 793-9813   **E-mail:** admissions@lyon.edu
Fax: (870) 698-4622   **Internet:** www.lyon.edu

Institution Description: Lyon College, formerly known as Arkansas College, is a private, independent, nonprofit college affiliated with the Presbyterian Church (U.S.A.). *Enrollment:* 237 men / 250 women. *Degrees awarded:* Baccalaureate.

Accreditation: *Regional:* NCA. *Professional:* teacher education

History: Lyon College is the oldest private college in Arkansas still operating under its original charter. Since its founding as Arkansas College in 1872, the institution changed its name in 1994 to honor the service of the Frank Lyon, Sr. family of Little Rock.

Institutional Structure: *Governing board:* Lyon College Board of Trustees. Extrainstitutional representation: 40 members elected by the Synod of the Sun of the Presbyterian Church (U.S.A.), 3 clergy trustees elected by the Presbytery of Arkansas; 3 alumni trustees elected by the Lyon College Alumni Association, and the president of the college. Full-time instructional faculty 44. Academic governance body, Faculty Assembly, meets an average of 10 times per year.

Calendar: Semesters. 2004–05 academic year Aug. 25 to May 5. Freshmen admitted fall, spring, and summer terms. Degrees conferred and formal commencement in May. Summer terms in June and July.

Characteristics of Freshmen: 67% of applicants accepted. 46% of applicants enrolled.

16% (22 students) submitted SAT scores; 93% (131 students) submitted ACT scores. *25th percentile:* SAT Verbal 480, SAT Math 490; ACT Composite 21, ACT English 21, ACT Math 19. *75th percentile:* SAT Verbal 640, SAT Math 610; ACT Composite 28, ACT English 29, ACT Math 27. 61% of entering freshmen expected to graduate within 5 years. 82% of freshmen from Arkansas. Freshmen from 10 states and 1 foreign country.

Admission: Selective admission. Priority is given to applicants for the fall semester who apply by Jan. 15. *Requirements:* Admitted students will ordinarily have taken a college-preparatory curriculum in high school that includes at least 4 units in English, 3 units each of mathematics, sciences, and history/social studies; and 2 units of foreign language. *Entrance tests:* ACT or SAT Reasoning. *For transfer students:* 2.75 college GPA, lowest grade of C for a college course to be transferred for credit, minimum of 24 credit hours that must be complete at Lynn College to earn a bachelor's degree.

Degree Requirements: *Undergraduate:* 120 credit hours; successful completion of core curriculum and the requirements of at least one major; 2.0 cumulative GPA for all work taken at Lyon, and a 2.0 cumulative GPA in the major.

Grading system: A–F; pass-fail (for courses outside of core curriculum and major or minor field).

Distinctive Educational Programs: The Nichols International Studies program offers study-abroad opportunities to qualified juniors and seniors through semesters- and year-abroad programs; study-travel courses. Lyon has an academic honor system that is administered by an honor council consisting of students elected by their peers.

Degrees Conferred: 104 *baccalaureate:* biological/life sciences 24; business 23; computer and information sciences 5; English 1; mathematics 6; natural resources/environmental sciences 1; philosophy, religion, theology 1; physical sciences 3; psychology 15; social sciences and history 16; visual and performing arts 4.

Fees and Other Expenses: *Full-time tuition per academic year 2004–05:* $12,710. *Required fees:* $420. *Room and board per academic year:* $5,820.

Financial Aid: Aid from institutionally generated funds is provided on the basis of academic merit, financial need, athletic ability. Institution has a Program Participation Agreement with the U.S. Department of Education for eligible students to receive Pell Grants and other federal aid.

Financial aid to full-time, first-time undergraduate students: need-based scholarships/grants $3,156,162, self-help $1,464,215, parent loans $117,306, tuition waivers $77,341, athletic awards $270,804; non-need-based scholarships/grants $1,244,381, self-help $389,860, parent loans $291,884, tuition waivers $18,822, athletic awards $639,826.

Departments and Teaching Staff: *Professors* 10, *associate professors* 14, *assistant professors* 18, *instructors* 2, *part-time faculty* 15. *Total instructional faculty:* 59. Student-to-faculty ratio: 10:1. *Faculty development:* $62,000 in grants for research. 3 faculty members awarded sabbaticals 2004–05.

Enrollment: Total enrollment 511. Undergraduate full-time 237 men / 250 women, part-time 6m / 18w. Transfer students: in-state into lower division 14m / 9w, upper division 1m / 16w; out-of-state into lower division 9m / 2w, upper division 5m / 1w.

Characteristics of Student Body: *Ethnic/racial makeup:* number of Black non-Hispanic: 19; American Indian or Alaska Native: 8; Asian or Pacific Islander: 5; Hispanic: 8; White non-Hispanic: 437; unknown: 13. *Age distribution:* number under 18: 4; 18–19: 199; 20–21: 185; 22–24: 68; 25–29: 9; 30–34 15; 35–39: 15; 40–49: 13; 65 or over: 1.

International Students: 17 nonresident aliens enrolled fall 2004. 4 students from Europe, 3 Asia, 5 Central and South America, 1 Africa, 2 Canada, 2 New Zealand. No programs available to aid students whose native language is not English. No financial aid specifically designated for international students.

Student Life: Campus residence halls are grouped into three house systems, two with live-in faculty member who designs programs to integrate the academic and cocurricular aspects of campus life. *Student organizations:* More than 40 clubs, societies and special interest groups including pipe band, Highland dance ensemble, concert choir, concert band, Hyde Park Players (student theater group), Black Students' Association, campus religious organizations, Model U.N., 3 fraternities, 3 sororities. *Intercollegiate athletics:* TranSouth Conference (NAIA). *Sports activities:* men: baseball, basketball, cross-country, golf, tennis; women: basketball, cross-country, golf, tennis, volleyball. *Student publications: Highlander* (student newspaper), *Scot* (yearbook), *Wheelbarrow* (literary magazine). *Surrounding community:* Batesville population 10,000, is 90 miles north of Little Rock and 110 miles west of Memphis.

Publications: *Piper* (semiannual alumni magazine), *Tabloid* (semiannual alumni tabloid sheet), *Greensheet* (weekly online newsletter), *Teaching Matters @ Lynn College* (annual faculty accomplishments publication), *Cultural Events* (annual cultural events brochure).

Library Collections: 184,717 volumes including bound books, serial backfiles, electronic documents, and government documents not in separate collections. Online catalog. Current serial subscriptions: 646 paper, 17,118 via electronic access. 1,978 recordings; 1,032 compact discs; 117 CD-ROM. 16 computer work stations. Students have access to the Internet at no charge. Total 2004–05 budget for books and materials: $156,300.

Most important special holdings include Ozark Regional Studies Collection, John Quincy Wolf Collection, Craig Genealogy Collection.

Buildings and Grounds: Campus area 136 acres.

Chief Executive Officer: Dr. Walter B. Roettger, President.

Address admission inquiries to Danny Bardos, Vice President for Enrollment Services.

Ouachita Baptist University

410 Ouachita Street
Arkadelphia, Arkansas 71998-0001
Tel: (870) 245-5000   **E-mail:** admissions@obu.edu
Fax: (870) 245-5500   **Internet:** www.obu.edu

Institution Description: Ouachita Baptist University is a private institution affiliated with the Arkansas Baptist State Convention (Southern Baptist). *Enrollment:* 1,530. *Degrees awarded:* Associate, baccalaureate.

Accreditation: *Regional:* NCA. *Professional* : business, music, teacher education

History: Established and chartered as Ouachita Baptist College 1886; awarded first degree (baccalaureate) 1888.

Institutional Structure: *Governing board:* Board of Trustees. Representation: 24 trustees. All voting. *Composition of institution:* 10 administrators. Academic affairs headed by vice president. Management/business/finances directed by vice president for development. Full-time instructional faculty 118.

Calendar: Semesters. 2004–05 academic year Aug. to May. May term between spring and summer terms. Summer session of 2 terms during which a student may register for from 1 to 12 hours of coursework.

Characteristics of Freshmen: 1,096 applicants (488 men / 608 women). 87.2% of applicants admitted; 60.9% admitted students enrolled.

40% (153 students) submitted SAT scores; 66% (328 students) submitted ACT scores. *25th percentile*: SAT Verbal 460, SAT Math 470; ACT Composite 20, ACT English 20, ACT Math 19. *75th percentile*: SAT Verbal 590, SAT Math 590; ACT Composite 26, ACT English 28, ACT Math 26.

40.6% of entering freshmen expected to graduate within 5 years. 51% of freshmen from Arkansas. Freshmen from 33 states and 11 foreign countries.

Admission: Rolling admissions plan. *Requirements:* Completion of 16 units in college preparatory courses (graduation not required), or GED. *Entrance tests:* ACT or SAT. *For transfer students:* From 4-year accredited institution 104 hours maximum transfer credit; from 2-year accredited institution 64 hours; correspondence/extension students 12 hours.

Degree Requirements: *Undergraduate:* 128 credit hours; 2.0 GPA; 60 hours of residency required; weekly chapel attendance; Old and New Testament

courses. *Grading system:* A–F; pass-fail; withdraw (deadline after which pass-fail is appended to withdraw).

Distinctive Educational Programs: Cross-registration with Henderson State College. Dual-degree program in engineering with University of Arkansas, University of Southern California, Vanderbilt University (TN). Honors program for selected students who may pursue their search for knowledge through independent study and small group seminars. Exchange program with Seinan Gakuin University, Fukuoka, Japan.

Degrees Conferred: 2 *associate*; 328 *baccalaureate*. Bachelor's degrees awarded in top five disciplines: business, management, marketing, and related support services 52; theology and ministerial studies 46; biological and biomedical sciences 28; education 28; visual and performing arts 27.

Fees and Other Expenses: *Full-time tuition per academic year 2004–05:* $15,170. *Room and board per academic year:* $4,800. *Books and supplies:* $775. *Other expenses:* $2,250.

Financial Aid: Aid from institutionally generated funds is provided on the basis of academic merit, financial need, athletic ability. Institution has a Program Participation Agreement with the U.S. Department of Education for eligible students to receive Pell Grants and other federal aid.

Financial aid to full-time, first-time undergraduate students: 29% received federal grants averaging $2,897; 6% state/local grants averaging $1,335; 95% institutional grants averaging $7,879; 44% received loans averaging $3,029.

Departments and Teaching Staff: *Total instructional faculty:* 111. Student-to-faculty ratio: 13:1. Degrees held by full-time faculty: Doctorate 68%, master's 32%. 71% hold terminal degrees.

Enrollment: Total enrollment 1,530 (46% men, 54% women).

Characteristics of Student Body: *Ethnic and racial makeup:* Black non-Hispanic: 5.9%; American Indian or Alaska Native: .4%; Asian or Pacific Islander: .3%; Hispanic: .8%; White non-Hispanic: 88.8%.

International Students: 57 nonresident aliens enrolled fall 2004. Programs available to aid students whose native language is not English: Social, cultural. English as a Second Language Program. No financial aid specifically designated for international students.

Student Life: On-campus housing for single and married students available. *Intercollegiate athletics:* men only: football, basketball, baseball, volleyball, tennis, cross-country, swimming, golf; women only: basketball, volleyball, tennis. *Student publications: Ouachitonian,* a yearbook; *Signal,* a weekly newspaper; *Ripples,* a literary magazine. *Surrounding community:* Arkadelphia population 10,500. Little Rock; 65 miles from campus, is nearest metropolitan area.

Library Collections: 117,550 volumes including bound books, serial backfiles, electronic documents, and government documents not in separate collections. Online catalog. Current serial subscriptions: 1,067 periodicals; 3,159 audiovisual materials; 205,650 microforms. Students have access to the Internet at no charge.

Most important special collections include Senator John L. McClellan Papers; Arkansas Baptist History Collection; Clark County Historical Archives.

Buildings and Grounds: Campus area 60 acres.

Chief Executive Officer: Dr. Andrew Westmoreland, President.

Address admission inquiries to Judy Jones, Director of Admissions.

Philander Smith College

812 West 13th Street
Little Rock, Arkansas 72202-3799
Tel: (501) 375-9845   **E-mail:** admissions@philander.edu
Fax: (501) 370-5225   **Internet:** www.philander.edu

Institution Description: Philander Smith College is an independent, nonprofit institution affiliated with the United Methodist Church. *Enrollment:* 887. *Degrees awarded:* Baccalaureate.

Academic offerings subject to approval by statewide coordinating bodies.

Accreditation: *Regional:* NCA. *Professional:* business, social work, teacher education

History: Established as Walden Seminary and offered first instruction at postsecondary level 1877; adopted present name 1882; chartered 1883; awarded first degree (baccalaureate) 1888. See Delois Gibson, *A Historical Study of Philander Smith College 1877–1969* (Fayetteville: University of Arkansas, 1972) for further information.

Institutional Structure: *Governing board:* Philander Smith College Board of Trustees. Representation: 41 trustees, including 15 alumni, 5 administrators, 3 full-time instructional faculty members, 3 students. 8 ex officio. All voting. *Composition of institution:* Administrators 4 men / 12 women. Academic affairs headed by vice president for academic services. Management/business/finances directed by vice president for administration. Full-time instructional faculty 32. Academic governance body, the faculty, meets an average of 9 times per year.

Calendar: Semesters. Academic year Aug. to May. Freshmen admitted Aug., Jan., June, July. Degrees conferred and formal commencement May. Summer session of 2 terms from early June to early Aug.

Characteristics of Freshmen: Average secondary school rank men 48th percentile, women 50th percentile, class 49th percentile. 100% of applicants accepted. 54% of accepted applicants enrolled. 17.3% of entering freshmen expected to graduate within 5 years. 75% of freshmen from Arkansas.

Admission: Rolling admissions plan. For fall acceptance, apply no later than Aug. 1. Early acceptance available. *Requirements:* Either graduation from accredited secondary school with 16 units which must include 3 English; 2 from among foreign language, social studies, or science; 2 mathematics, 7 additional units with no more than 4 vocational; or GED. Minimum GPA 2.0. *Entrance tests:* College Board SAT or ACT Composite. *For transfer students:* 2.0 minimum GPA; from 2-year accredited institution 62 hours.

College credit and advanced placement for postsecondary level work completed in secondary school and for extrainstitutional learning college credit on basis of ACE *2006 Guide to the Evaluation of Educational Experiences in the Armed Services* and faculty assessment. Noncredit developmental/remedial courses offered during regular academic year.

Degree Requirements: 124 semester hours; 2.0 GPA; 2 terms in residence; 2 courses possible by passing College Board CLEP, APP. *Grading system:* A–F; withdraw (carries time limit, deadline after which pass-fail is appended to withdraw); incomplete; no credit.

Distinctive Educational Programs: Weekend and evening classes. Dual-degree program in engineering with Tuskegee Institute (AL).

ROTC: Army offered in cooperation with University of Central Arkansas.

Degrees Conferred: 128 *baccalaureate.* Bachelor's degrees awarded in top five disciplines: business,management, marketing, and related support services 64; education 15; social sciences 14; public administration and social service professions 9; biological and biomedical sciences 7.

Fees and Other Expenses: *Full-time tuition per academic year 2004–05:* $6,393. *Room and board per academic year:* $5,090. *Books and supplies:* $875.

Financial Aid: Philander Smith College offers a direct lending program. Aid from institutionally generated funds is awarded on the basis of academic merit, financial need, athletic ability. Institution has a Program Participation Agreement with the U.S. Department of Education for eligible students to receive Pell Grants and other federal aid.

Financial aid to full-time, first-time undergraduate students: 81% received federal grants averaging $3,595; 6% received state/local grants; 20% received institutional grants averaging $4,506; 60% received loans averaging $3,961.

Departments and Teaching Staff: *Total instructional faculty:* 32. Total tenured faculty: 8. Student-to-faculty ratio: 24:1. Degrees held by full-time faculty: doctorate 20%.

Enrollment: Total enrollment 887 (33.9% men, 66.1% women).

Characteristics of Student Body: *Ethnic/racial makeup:* Black non-Hispanic: 96.4%; Hispanic: .6%. White non-Hispanic: 1.2%; unknown: .1%.

International Students: 15 nonresident aliens enrolled fall 2003.

Student Life: On-campus residence halls house 17% of student body. Dormitories for men only constitute 49% of such space, for women only 51%. *Intercollegiate athletics:* For men and for women: basketball. *Special regulations:* Cars permitted without restrictions. Curfews. Quiet hours. Residence hall visitation from noon to 10:30pm. *Special services:* Learning Resources Center, medical services. *Student radio:* KPSC broadcasts 40 hours per week. *Surrounding community:* Little Rock metropolitan area population 400,000. Served by mass transit bus system; airport 8 miles from campus; passenger rail service 2.5 miles from campus.

Library Collections: 83,000 volumes. 170 microform items; 4,855 audiovisual materials; 370 current periodical subscriptions. Students have access to the Internet.

Most important holdings include juvenile collection.

Buildings and Grounds: Campus area 25 acres.

Chief Executive Officer: Dr. Julius S. Scott, President.

Address admission inquiries to Director of Enrollment Management.

Southern Arkansas University

100 East University
Magnolia, Arkansas 71754-9392
Tel: (870) 235-4000   **E-mail:** sjennings@saumag.edu
Fax: (870) 235-5005   **Internet:** www.saumag.edu

Institution Description: Southern Arkansas University (formerly Southern State College) is a state institution with a branch campus in East Camden. *Enrollment:* 3,008. *Degrees awarded:* Associate, baccalaureate, master's.

Academic offerings subject to approval by statewide coordinating bodies.

Accreditation: *Regional:* NCA. *Professional:* business, music, nursing, social work, teacher education

History: Established by Arkansas Legislature as a secondary-level Third District Agricultural School and chartered 1909; changed name to Agricultural and Mechanical College, Third District 1925; awarded first degree (associate) 1927; changed name to Southern State College 1951; added branch campus in Camden (formerly the Southwest Technical Institute), and in El Dorado, and adopted present name 1976. *See* Phillip Daniel Skelton, *A History of Southern Arkansas University from 1909 to 1976* (Diss., University of Mississippi, 1979) for further information.

Institutional Structure: *Governing board:* Board of Trustees, Southern Arkansas University. Representation: 5 trustees. All voting. *Composition of institution:* Administrators 14 men / 11 women. Academic affairs headed by vice president for academic affairs. Management/business/finances directed by vice president for finance and administration. Student Affairs headed by vice president for student affairs. Full-time instructional faculty 118. Academic governance body, Faculty, meets an average of 8 times per year.

Calendar: Semesters. 2004–05 year July 1 to June 30. Freshmen admitted Aug., Jan., June, July. Degrees conferred and formal commencements May, Aug., Dec. Summer session of 2 terms from early June to early Aug.

Characteristics of Freshmen: 81% of applicants accepted; 54% admitted and enrolled.

9% (94 students) submitted SAT scores; 98% (651 students) submitted ACT scores. *25th percentile:* ACT Composite 18, ACT English 18, ACT Math 18. *75th percentile:* ACT Composite 23, ACT English 25, ACT Math 23.

58% of entering freshmen expected to graduate within 5 years. 35% of freshmen from Arkansas. Freshmen from 17 states and 20 foreign countries.

Admission: Rolling and selective admissions plans. Apply no later than 1 week after registration. Early acceptance available. *Requirements:* Unconditional admission: graduate from an accredited high school (or GED) with a 19 ACT in English, Math, and reading. Conditional admission: graduation from an accredited high school and have an ACT Composite score of 16 or be in upper one fourth of the graduating class. A first-time freshman 25 years of age or older will be granted admissions regardless of ACT score or high school rank, but ACT is required for placement. A first-time freshman may successfully complete GED certification and have an ACT Composite score of 16. *Entrance tests:* ACT Composite of 16+ or upper one fourth of graduating class. *For transfer students:* From 4-year accredited institution maximum transfer credit limited only by residence requirement; from 2-year accredited institution 68 semester hours. Good standing at institution previously attended.

Tutoring available. Developmental courses offered in summer session and regular academic year.

Degree Requirements: *For all associate degrees:* 64–71 credit hours. *For all baccalaureate degrees:* 124–158 credit hours including general education curriculum. *For all undergraduate degrees:* 2.0 GPA (2.5 for BSE degree).

Fulfillment of some degree requirements possible by passing departmental examinations. College Board CLEP. *Grading system:* A–F; withdraw (carries penalty, time limit).

Distinctive Educational Programs: Evening classes. Special facilities for using telecommunications in the classroom. Individual majors. Honors College. Tutorials. Study abroad. *Other distinctive programs:* Continuing education program offers extension classes and conferences for certificates and enrichment. Bachelor's degree in applied studies for graduates of accredited community and junior colleges who have concentrations in technical or vocational skills.

Degrees Conferred: 52 *associate;* 429 *baccalaureate;* 49 *master's.* Bachelor's degrees awarded in top five disciplines: business, management, marketing, and related support services 129; education 71; agriculture, agriculture operations, and related sciences 38; security and protective services 31; biological and biomedical sciences 26.

Fees and Other Expenses: *Full-time undergraduate tuition per academic year 2004–05:* in-state resident $3,798, out-of-state $5,618. *Room and board per academic year:* $3,600. *Books and supplies:* $1,000.

Financial Aid: Aid from institutionally generated funds is provided on the basis of academic merit, financial need, athletic ability. Institution has a Program Participation Agreement with the U.S. Department of Education for eligible students to receive Pell Grants and other federal aid.

Financial aid to full-time, first-time undergraduate students: 60% received federal grants averaging $2,539; 7% state/local grants averaging $919; 81% institutional grants averaging $1,670; 40% loans averaging $2,110.

Departments and Teaching Staff: *Total instructional faculty* 183 (full-time 118, part-time 65; women 75, men 106). Student-to-faculty ratio: 19: Total tenured faculty: 61. Degrees held by full-time faculty: doctorates 53%.

Enrollment: Total enrollment 3,008. Undergraduate 2,804 (43.5% men, 56.5% women). 21% of entering freshmen expected to graduate within 5 years.

Characteristics of Student Body: *Ethnic/racial makeup:* Black non-Hispanic: 24.9%, American Indian or Alaska Native: .4%; Asian or Pacific Islander: .5%; Hispanic: 1.4%; White non-Hispanic: 68.2%. *Age distribution:* under 18:

71; 18–19: 853; 20–21: 746; 22–24: 577; 25–29: 193; 30–34: 121; 35–39: 62; 40–49: 72; 50–64: 43; 65 and over: 65.

International Students: 111 nonresident aliens enrolled fall 2004. No programs available to aid students whose native language is not English. No financial aid specifically designated for international students.

Student Life: On-campus residence halls house 43% of student body. Residence halls for men only constitute 55% of such space, for women only 45%. *Intercollegiate athletics:* men only: baseball, basketball, football, golf; women only: basketball, softball, tennis, volleyball; both sexes: cross-country, track and field. *Special regulations:* Cars must be registered. Quiet hours. Residence hall visitation hours set by residents in individual halls. *Special services:* Student Support Services, student health service. *Student publications: Bray,* a weekly newspaper; *Mulerider,* a yearbook. *Surrounding community:* Magnolia population 12,700. Dallas (TX), 242 miles from campus, is nearest metropolitan area.

Library Collections: 1,185,883 volumes. Online catalog. Current serial subscriptions: 528 paper, 377 microform, 13 via electronic access. 12,130 recordings. 2,001 compact discs; 61 CD-ROMs. 36 computer work stations. Students have access to the Internet at no charge. Total budget for books and materials: $385,000.

Most important special collection is the Arkansas Collection.

Buildings and Grounds: Campus area 781 acres. *New buildings:* Donald W. Reynolds Campus and Community Court completed 2004.

Chief Executive Officer: Dr. David F. Rankin, President.

Address admission inquiries to Sarah E. Jennings, Dean of Enrollment Services.

University of Arkansas at Fayetteville

200 Silas Hunt Hall
Fayetteville, Arkansas 72701
Tel: (479) 575-2000   **E-mail:** uafadmis@uark.edu
Fax: (479) 575-7515   **Internet:** www.uark.edu

Institution Description: The University of Arkansas at Fayetteville is the main campus of the University of Arkansas system. *Enrollment:* 17,269. *Degrees awarded:* Baccalaureate, first-professional, master's, doctorate.

Academic offerings subject to approval by statewide coordinating bodies. Budget subject to approval by state governing boards.

Accreditation: *Regional:* NCA. *Professional:* accounting, clinical psychology, counseling, engineering, family and consumer science, interior design, journalism, landscape architecture, law, music, nursing, nursing education, radiography, recreation and leisure services, rehabilitation counseling, social work, speech-language pathology, teacher education

History: Established as Arkansas Industrial University 1871; offered first instruction at postsecondary level 1872; awarded first degree (baccalaureate) 1876; adopted present name 1899. *See* Robert Leflar, *The First Hundred Years* (Fayetteville: University of Arkansas Foundation, 1972) for further information.

Institutional Structure: *Composition of institution:* Administrators 155 men / 12 women. Academic affairs headed by vice chancellor for academic affairs. Management/business/finances directed by vice chancellor for finance and administration. Student service directed by vice chancellor for student services. Public relations directed by associate vice chancellor for University Relations. Fund raising directed by associate vice chancellor for development. Alumni directed by associate vice chancellor for alumni. Academic governance bodies, Campus Faculty and Campus Council, meet an average of 2 and 4 times per year, respectively.

Calendar: Semesters. Academic year late Aug. to mid-May. Freshmen admitted Aug., Jan., May, June. Degrees conferred Dec., May, June. Formal commencement May. Summer session of 2 terms from mid-May to mid-Aug.

Characteristics of Freshmen: 5,89 applicants fall 2004 (2,785 men / 3,034 women). 78.5% of applicants admitted; 53.8% of admitted students enrolled full-time.

23% (582 students) submitted SAT scores; 93% (2,346 students) submitted ACT scores. *25th percentile:* SAT Verbal 510, SAT Math 510; ACT Composite 22, ACT English 23, ACT Math 21. *75th percentile:* SAT Verbal 650, SAT Math 650; ACT Composite 28, ACT English 29, ACT Math 27.

42.5% of entering freshmen expected to graduate in 5 years. 91% of freshmen from Arkansas. Freshmen from 49 states and 109 foreign countries.

Admission: Rolling admission after Feb. 15. Early acceptance available. *Requirements:* Either graduation from secondary school and either a 2.5 GPA or 18 or better on ACT (or SAT combined score of 770); course requirements in grades 9–12 include 4 English, 3 math (must include 1 year of algebra and 1 additional year of algebra, geometry, trigonometry, precalculus, or calculus), 3 natural sciences (must include 2 years chosen from biology, chemistry, and physics), 2 years of one foreign language (for students entering the Fulbright College

of Arts and Sciences); or GED. *Entrance tests:* ACT or SAT. *For transfer students:* 2.0 GPA; from 4-year accredited institution maximum transfer credit limited only by residence requirements; from 2-year accredited institution 68 credit hours maximum transfer credit; correspondence-extension students 12 hours.

College credit and advanced placement for postsecondary level work completed in secondary school.

Tutoring available. Developmental courses offered during regular academic year.

Degree Requirements: *For all baccalaureate degrees:* 124–132 credit hours; general education requirements; American history or civil government course; English composition and English competency requirement. *For all undergraduate degrees:* 2.0 GPA; 2 terms in residence; six hours of freshman composition.

Fulfillment of some degree requirements and exemption from some beginning courses possible by passing College Board CLEP, AP, other standardized tests. *Grading system:* A–F; pass-fail; withdraw (carries penalty, deadline after which pass-fail is appended to withdraw).

Distinctive Educational Programs: Flexible meeting places and schedules for graduate students, including four off-campus centers and evening classes. Accelerated degree programs. Interdisciplinary programs in agribusiness, agriengineering, agrijournalism, community planning, environmental science, industrial management, public administration. Facilities and programs for independent research, including honors programs, individual majors, tutorials. Study abroad in England, Japan, Greece, Italy, and other countries available. Cooperative Education project is designed to give students an opportunity to participate in a paid work experience directly related to their academic major.

ROTC: Army in cooperation with Northeastern Oklahoma State University; Air Force. 15 commissions awarded 2004–05.

Degrees Conferred: 2,194 *baccalaureate;* 833 *master's;* 12 *post-master's certificates;* 110 *doctorate;* 118 *first-professional.* Bachelor's degrees awarded in top five disciplines: business, management, marketing, and related support services 543; engineering 233; education 179; communication, journalism, and related programs 154; social sciences 105.

Fees and Other Expenses: *Full-time undergraduate tuition per academic year 2004–05:* in-state $15,135; out-of-state $12,425. *Room and board per academic year:* $5,927. *Books and supplies:* $892.

Financial Aid: Aid from institutionally generated funds is provided on the basis of academic merit, athletic ability. Institution has a Program Participation Agreement with the U.S. Department of Education for eligible students to receive Pell Grants and other federal aid.

Financial aid to full-time, first-time undergraduate students: 22% received federal grants averaging $3,156; 7% received state/local grants averaging $1,348; 56% institutional grants averaging $6 281; 335 loans averaging $3,391.

Departments and Teaching Staff: *Professors* 312, *associate professors* 227, *assistant professors* 177, *instructors* 81; *part-time faculty:* 50. *Total instructional faculty:* 847. Student-to-faculty ratio: 16.9:1. 91% of faculty hold terminal degrees.

Enrollment: Total enrollment: 17,269. Undergraduate 13,083 (50.8% men, 49.2% women). *Transfer students:* in-state into lower division 229 men / 314 women, out-of-state 62m / 45w; in-state into upper division 173m / 163w, out-of-state 19m / 21w; in-state into graduate schools 192m / 214w, out-of-state 181m / 160w.

Characteristics of Student Body: *Ethnic/racial makeup:* number of Black non-Hispanic: 697; American Indian or Alaska Native: 281; Asian or Pacific Islander: 369; Hispanic: 233; White non-Hispanic: 10,995; unknown: 289.

International Students: 532 nonresident aliens enrolled fall 2004. Programs available to aid students whose native language is not English: Social, cultural. English as a Second Language Program. Variable number of scholarships awarded annually; 166 totaling $1,508,471 awarded 2004–05.

Student Life: The majority of undergraduates live on-campus; off-campus accommodations available. Some students live in fraternity and sorority houses. Married student housing available. *Intercollegiate athletics:* men only: baseball, basketball, cross-country, football, golf, swimming, tennis, track; women only: basketball, swimming, diving, tennis, track, cross country, soccer. *Special regulations:* Cars permitted with parking stickers. Quiet hours. Residence hall visitation varies. *Special services:* Learning Resources Center, medical services, student development center, career planning and placement, tutoring services, Minority Affairs Office, Disabled Students Resource Center, Women's Resource Center, International Student Advising Office. *Student publications, radio-tv: The Arkansas Razorback,* a yearbook; *The Arkansas Traveler,* a biweekly newspaper; radio station KUAF; KRFA, a student-managed station available by cable. *Surrounding community:* Fayetteville population 58,000. Tulsa (OK), 90 miles from campus, is nearest metropolitan area. Served by airport 20 miles from campus (Northwest Arkansas Regional Airport).

Publications: *The Spectrum,* a weekly newspaper; *The University, The Guide for New Students,* a yearly handbook for new students; *The A Book,* a yearly student handbook. Alumni publications: *The Arkansas Alumnus,* published 5 times yearly and *The Razorback Report,* published 5 times yearly. College publications: *The Arkansas Engineer*, published by the College of Engineering; *The Arkansas Law Review*, published quarterly by the School of Law; *The Arkansas Business and Economic Review*, published quarterly by the College of Business Administration.

Library Collections: 1,714,085 volumes including bound books, serial backfiles, electronic documents, and government documents not in separate collections. Online catalog. Current serial subscriptions: 11,460 paper; 3,336,000 microforms; 29,800 audiovisual materials. Students have access to the Internet at no charge.

Most important special holdings include papers of Senator David Pryor, Senator Dale Bumpers; Judge Henry Woods Papers; "Mack" McLarty Papers; manuscript collections of J. William Fulbright, Joseph T. Robinson, and Edward Durrell Stone.

Buildings and Grounds: Campus area 345 acres. *New buildings:* Bev Lewis Center for Women's Athletics completed 2002; Intramural Sports Facilities 2002; Botany Greenhouse 2003; Pat Walker Student Health Center 2004; North Quad Accommodation 2004; Anthony Chapel-Garvan Woodland Gardens 2005.

Chief Executive Officer: Dr. John A. White, Chancellor.

Address undergraduate admission inquiries to Dawn Medley, Director of Admissions; graduate inquiries to Lynn Mosesso, Director of Graduate Admissions.

College of Arts and Sciences

Degree Programs Offered: *Baccalaureate:* anthropology, architectural studies, art, botany, chemistry, classical studies, communication, comparative literature, computer science, creative writing, criminal justice, drama, earth science, economics, English, environmental science, French, geography, geology, German, history, journalism, mathematics, microbiology, music, natural sciences, philosophy, physics, political science, psychology, public administration, secondary mathematics, social work, sociology, Spanish, statistics, translation, zoology; *master's, doctorate:* various fields.

Degree Requirements: Cumulative GPA of at least 2.0; no fewer than 30 hours of credits must be earned at the college and at least 24 of those hours must be numbered above 3000.

Distinctive Educational Programs: Urban studies program for majors in architecture, geography, political science, sociology. Curriculum in natural sciences for teachers. Interdepartmental programs in Asian, black studies. *See* School of Architecture.

College of Agriculture and Home Economics

Degree Programs Offered: *Baccalaureate, master's, doctorate:* agriculture, home economics.

Degree Requirements: 124 semester hours; minimum of 64 semester hours, including 30 semester hours in agriculture, at the University of Arkansas; GPA 2.0 on all work attempted.

School of Architecture

Degree Programs Offered: *Baccalaureate:* architecture, landscape architecture; *first-professional:* architecture; *master's:* community planning.

Admission: 30 hours general education work from accredited college or university, including 6 hours English composition, college algebra and trigonometry, introduction to environmental design, architectural communications, and first design studio; all of the above for landscape architecture plus at least 1 four-hour laboratory science course; 2.5 GPA.

Degree Requirements: *For baccalaureate:* 167 credit hours, 2.0 GPA, 36 months in residence (18 months in residence for transfer students).

Distinctive Educational Programs: Baccalaureate with major in architectural studies. Summer abroad in Europe.

College of Business Administration

Degree Programs Offered: *Baccalaureate:* accounting, business economics, data processing and quantitative finance, management (administrative, industrial, personnel), marketing, transportation, public administration; *master's, doctorate:* various fields.

Degree Requirements: *For baccalaureate:* 124 semester hours; minimum of 69 semester hours in economics and business administration courses; no less than 40% of total credits must be in approved subjects other than business administration.

Distinctive Educational Programs: Accounting-data processing major leading to a bachelor of science in business administration degree.

College of Education

Degree Programs Offered: *Baccalaureate:* adult education, art education, business and office education, dance education, educational administration, elementary education, health education, higher education, home economics education, industrial and technical education, instructional resources, teaching of the mildly handicapped, music education, physical education, secondary education, special education, speech pathology-audiology, vocational education. *Master's, doctorate:* various fields.

Degree Requirements: 124 semester hours of work with at least a 2.00 GPA on all work attempted. Teacher education majors are required by law to take the appropriate NTE tests and report the results prior to graduation.

College of Engineering

Degree Programs Offered: *Baccalaureate:* agricultural engineering, chemical engineering, civil engineering, computer science engineering, electrical engineering, engineering science, industrial engineering, mechanical engineering; *master's, doctorate:* various fields.

Degree Requirements: Minimum 32 semester hours of an appropriate combination of mathematics and basic sciences, 32 semester hours of engineering sciences, 16 semester hours of engineering design, and 16 semesters hours of humanities and social sciences; 2.0 GPA on all work completed.

School of Law

Degree Programs Offered: *First-professional.*

Admission: Baccalaureate from accredited college or university; LSAT.

Graduate Institute of Technology

Degree Programs Offered: *Master's, doctorate:* civil engineering, engineering science, industrial engineering, instrumental sciences, mechanical engineering.

University of Arkansas at Fort Smith

5210 Grand Avenue
P.O. Box 3649
Fort Smith, Arkansas 72913-3649
Tel: (479) 788-7000   **E-mail:** information@uafortsmith.edu
Fax: (479) 788-7016   **Internet:** www.uafortsmith.edu

Institution Description: The University of Arkansas at Fort Smith, formerly Westark College, is a public four-year institution. *Enrollment:* 6,631. *Degrees awarded:* Associate, baccalaureate. Certificates are also awarded.

Academic offerings subject to approval by statewide coordinating bodies.

Accreditation: *Regional:* NCA. *Professional:* dental hygiene, nursing, surgical technology

History: Established as Fort Smith Junior College in 1928; changed name to Westark College 1998; became a four-year university and adopted present name January 2002.

Institutional Structure: *Governing board:* University of Arkansas System Board of Trustees.

Calendar: Semesters. Academic year July to June. Formal commencement May. Summer sessions from early June to early August.

Characteristics of Freshmen: ACT Composite 25th percentile 18; 75th percentile 23.

Admission: Official final high school transcripts or copies of GED scores are required with the exception of those students taking courses while still in high school. An ACT score of 19 or above is required for reading, writing, and math. If scores are below the minimum, students are referred to the Adult Educaiton Center or Learning Assistance Center for additional skill building and are subject to the "Retest Policy." All degree-seeking students who place into development courses of reading, writing, or math must enroll in all required developmental coursework and are limited to 12 hours the first semester.

Degree Requirements: UA Fort Smith has adopted a "State Minimum Core" of 35 credit hours of general educaiton courses that are required of all baccalaureate and associate of arts degree candidates. All state institutions of higher education in Arkansas have a 35-hour minimum core requirement with specified hours in each academic area. A student must maintain a cumulative grade point average of 2.00 to maintain satisfactory academic progress.

Grading system: A-D, AU (audited), W (withdrew), IP (in-progress), F (failing).

Distinctive Educational Programs: UA Fort Smith offers hands-on, applied learning through innovative programs. Students find a variety of educational opportunities and are offered a wide selection of alternate delivery methods to meet the growing needs of a diverse student population: e-mail, web telecourses, evening and weekend courses, interactive video, and distance education options.

Degrees Conferred: 129 *baccalaureate*: business/marketing 47; communications/communication technologies 19; education 48; liberal arts/general studies 15.

Fees and Other Expenses: *Full-time tuition 2004–05:* in-district $1,740; in-state (out-of-district) $1,890; out-of-state $6,840. *Required fees:* $540.

Financial Aid: Aid from institutionally generated funds is provided on the basis of academic merit, athletic ability, financial need. Institution has a Program Participation Agreement with the U.S. Department of Education for eligible students to receive Pell Grants and other federal aid.

Financial aid to full-time, first-time undergraduate students: need-based scholarships/grants totaling $7,055,942, self-help $2,892,940; non-need-based scholarships/grants totaling $1,716,771, self-help $932,317; parent loans $39,679, tuition waivers $9,335, athletic awards $229,599.

Departments and Teaching Staff: *Total instructional faculty:* 333 (full-time 172, part-time 161; women 163, men 170). Total number with doctorate, first-professional, or other terminal degree: 63. Student-to-faculty ratio: 21:1.

Enrollment: Total enrollment: 6,623. Full-time 1,416 men / 2,366 women; part-time 1,215m / 1,626w. Transfer students: in-state into lower division 102m / 144w, out-of-state 43m / 71w.

Characteristics of Student Body: *Ethnic/racial makeup:* number of Black non-Hispanic: 273; American Indian or Alaska Native: 246; Asian or Pacific Islander: 272; Hispanic: 179; White non-Hispanic: 5,641. *Age distribution:* number under 18: 642; 18–19: 1.630; 20–21: 1,009; 22–24: 823; 25–29: 450; 30–34: 528; 35–39: 380; 40–49: 471; 50–64: 175; 65 and over: 55. 26% of student body attend summer sessions.

International Students: 12 nonresident aliens enrolled fall 2004.

Student Life: More than 40 organizations are active on campus, including academic, arts and culture, political, religious, and special interest clubs. The UA Fort Smith Lions compete in baseball, women;'s volleyball, and men's and women's basketball. Sebastian Commons Apartments are located next to campus.

Library Collections: 81,637 volumes including bound books, serial backfiles, electronic documents, and government documents not in separate collections. Online catalog. Current serial subscriptions: 406 paper and 14,144 via electronic access. 101 recordings, 455 compact discs; 109 CD-ROMs. 30 computer work stations. Students have access to the Internet at no charge.

Most important special collections are housed in the Pebley Historical and Cultural Center.

Buildings and Grounds: Twenty-one major buildings. *New buildings:* Health Sciences; Baldor Technology Center; Smith-Pendergraft Campus Center; Stubblefield Center.

Chief Executive Officer: Dr. Joel R. Stubblefield, Chancellor.

Address admission inquiries to Mandy Keyes, Director of Admissions.

University of Arkansas at Little Rock

2801 South University
Little Rock, Arkansas 72204-1099
Tel: (501) 569-3000   **E-mail:** admissions@ualr.edu
Fax: (501) 569-8915   **Internet:** www.ualr.edu

Institution Description: *Enrollment:* 11,757. *Degrees awarded:* Associate, baccalaureate, first-professional (law), master's. Educational specialist certificates also awarded.

Academic offerings subject to approval by statewide coordinating bodies. Budget subject to approval by state governing boards.

Accreditation: *Regional:* NCA. *Professional:* art, audiology, business, computer science, construction education, engineering technology, health services administration, journalism, law, music, nursing, public administration, social work, speech-language pathology, teacher education, theatre

History: Established and incorporated as Little Rock Junior College and offered first instruction at postsecondary level 1927; awarded first degree (associate) 1929; became 4-year institution and changed name to Little Rock University 1957; merged with University of Arkansas and adopted present name 1969.

Institutional Structure: *Composition of institution:* Administrators 27 men / 5 women. Academic affairs headed by vice chancellor and provost. Management/business/finances directed by vice chancellor for finance and administration. Instructional faculty 453. Academic governance body, The University of Arkansas at Little Rock Assembly, meets an average of 6 times per year.

Calendar: Semesters. Academic year Aug. to May. Freshmen admitted Aug., Jan., June, July. Degrees conferred and formal commencement May. Summer session of 2 terms.

Characteristics of Freshmen: 92% of applicants accepted. 62% of accepted applicants enrolled. 95% of freshmen from Arkansas. Freshmen from 37 states.

Admission: Rolling admissions plan. Early acceptance available. *Requirements:* Either graduation from accredited secondary school with 15 units or GED. Minimum GPA 2.0; minimum SAT. *Entrance tests:* College Board SAT or ACT Composite. *For transfer students:* 2.0 minimum GPA; from 4-year accredited institution maximum transfer credit limited only by residence requirement; from 2-year accredited institution 64 semester hours. Transfer credit also accepted for correspondence/extension students.

College credit and advanced placement for postsecondary level work completed in secondary school and for extrainstitutional learning college credit on basis of ACE *2006 Guide to the Evaluation of Educational Experiences in the Armed Services*; faculty assessment.

Tutoring available. Developmental courses offered in summer session and regular academic year; credit given.

Degree Requirements: *For all associate degrees:* 64 semester hours; 15 hours in residence. *For all baccalaureate degrees:* 124 hours; 30 hours in residence. The university has adopted a "State Minimum Core" of 35 credit hours of general educaiton courses that are required of all baccalaureate and associate of arts degree candidates. All state institutions of higher education in Arkansas have a 35-hour minimum core requirement with specified hours in each academic area. A student must maintain a cumulative grade point average of 2.00 to maintain satisfactory academic progress.

Grading system: A-D, AU (audited), W (withdrew), IP (in-progress), F (failing).

Fulfillment of some degree requirements and exemption from some beginning courses possible by passing departmental examinations; College Board CLEP, AP, other

Distinctive Educational Programs: Work-experience programs, including internships, cooperative education. Free University. Flexible meeting places and schedules, including more than 20 off-campus facilities in Little Rock area, weekend and evening classes. Accelerated degree programs. Cooperative baccalaureate and master's programs in communicative disorders with University of Arkansas at Fayetteville's Medical Center at Little Rock. Special facilities for using telecommunications in the classroom. Interdisciplinary program in liberal arts; study abroad Autonomous Universidad Guadalajara (Mexico) and University of Strasbourg (France). Individual majors. *Other distinctive program:* Continuing education.

ROTC: Army.

Degrees Conferred: 155 *associate;* 1,020 *baccalaureate;* 349 *master's;* 33 *doctorate;* 109 *first-professional.* Bachelor's degrees awarded in top five disciplines: business, management, marketing, and related support services 287; security and protective services 99; psychology 73; health professions and related clinical sciences 70; communication, journalism, and related programs 55.

Fees and Other Expenses: *Full-time tuition per academic year 2004–05:* in-state resident $3,535, out-of-state $8,642. Contact the university for current graduate tuition rates. *Room and board per academic year:* $2,950. *Books and supplies:* $750.

Financial Aid: Aid from institutionally generated funds is provided on the basis of academic merit, financial need, athletic ability, other criteria. Institution has a Program Participation Agreement with the U.S. Department of Education for eligible students to receive Pell Grants and other federal aid.

financial aid to full-time, first-time undergraduate students: 56% received federal grants averaging $2,400; 2% state/local grants averaging $2,716; 27% institutional grants averaging $3,060; 45% loans averaging $2,500.

Departments and Teaching Staff: *Total faculty (instruction, research, public service):* 653.

Enrollment: Total enrollment: 11,757. Undergraduate 9,330 (38.1% men; 61.9% women).

Characteristics of Student Body: *Ethnic/racial makeup:* Black non-Hispanic: 32.2%, American Indian or Alaska Native: .6%; Asian or Pacific Islander: 1.9%; Hispanic: 1.9%; White non-Hispanic: 60.5%; unknown: .1.6%.

International Students: 149 nonresident aliens enrolled fall 2004. Programs available to aid students whose native language is not English: English as a Second Language Program.

Student Life: One residence hall. *Intercollegiate athletics:* men only: baseball, basketball, golf, swimming, tennis, water polo; women only: basketball, swimming, tennis, volleyball. *Special regulations:* Cars with decals permitted; fee charged. *Special services:* Learning Resource Center, medical services. *Student publications: Equinox*, a biannual literary magazine; *UALR Forum*, a weekly newspaper. *Surrounding community:* Little Rock population 200,000. Memphis (TN), 135 miles from campus, is nearest metropolitan area. Served by mass transit bus system; airport 10 miles from campus.

Publications: *UALR Monograph Series*, first number published in 1978, last number published in 1981.

Library Collections: 394,780 volumes. 300,000 government documents; 692,000 microforms; 2,626 current periodical subscriptions. 8,000 audiovisual materials. Online catalog. Students have access to online information retrieval services and the Internet.

Most important holdings include Winthrop Rockefeller Papers; Fadjo Craven Arkansas Collection; Fletcher-Terry Family Collection. Educational Resources Information Center (ERIC) Collection; Library of American Civilization (ultrafiche); Library of English Literature (ultrafiche).

Buildings and Grounds: Campus area 150 acres.

Chief Executive Officer: Dr. Joel E. Anderson, Chancellor.

Address admission inquiries to John T. Noah, Director of Admissions.

University of Arkansas at Monticello

Highway 425 South
P.O. Box 3596
Monticello, Arkansas 71655-3596
Tel: (870) 367-6811   **E-mail:** admissions@uamont.edu
Fax: (870) 367-1923   **Internet:** www.uamont.edu

Institution Description: *Enrollment:* 2,875. *Degrees awarded:* Associate, baccalaureate, master's.

Academic offerings subject to approval by statewide coordinating bodies.

Accreditation: *Regional:* NCA. *Professional:* business, forestry, music, nursing, social work, teacher education

History: Established as Fourth District Agricultural School 1909; chartered 1910; changed name to Agricultural and Mechanical College and offered first instruction at postsecondary level 1923; changed name to Arkansas Agricultural and Mechanical College 1925; awarded first degree (baccalaureate) 1935; merged with University of Arkansas and adopted present name 1971.

Institutional Structure: *Composition of institution:* Administrators 7 men / 7 women. Academic affairs headed by vice chancellor for academic affairs. Management/business/finances directed by vice chancellor for business and finance. Full-time instructional faculty 116. Academic governance body, UAM Assembly, meets an average of 9 times per year.

Calendar: Semesters. Academic year Aug. to May. Freshmen admitted Aug., Jan., June, July. Degrees conferred May, Aug., Dec. Formal commencement May. Summer session of 2 terms from June to Aug.

Characteristics of Freshmen: 95% of applicants accepted. 65% of accepted applicants enrolled.

Mean ACT Composite scores men 18.5, women 18.4, class 18.4.

87% of freshmen from Arkansas. Freshmen from 6 states.

Admission: Rolling admissions plan. For fall acceptance apply as early as Jan. prior to enrollment, but no later than Aug. 17 of year of enrollment. Early acceptance available. *Requirements:* graduation from approved high school or 20 units, including 3 units English, 2 mathematics. *Entrance tests:* ACT Composite. For foreign students TOEFL. *For transfer students:* 2.0 minimum GPA, 94 semester hours maximum transfer credit.

College credit and advanced placement for postsecondary level work completed in secondary school and for extrainstitutional learning college credit on basis of ACE *2006 Guide to the Evaluation of Educational Experiences in the Armed Services.*

Tutoring available. Developmental courses offered during regular academic year; credit given.

Degree Requirements: *For all associate degrees:* 60–66 semester hours; 30 hours in residence. *For all baccalaureate degrees:* 124 hours; 30 hours in residence (24 with senior standing). *For all degrees:* 2.0 GPA; general education hours. The university has adopted a "State Minimum Core" of 35 credit hours of general educaiton courses that are required of all baccalaureate and associate of arts degree candidates. All state institutions of higher education in Arkansas have a 35-hour minimum core requirement with specified hours in each academic area. A student must maintain a cumulative grade point average of 2.00 to maintain satisfactory academic progress.

Grading system: A-D, AU (audited), W (withdrew), IP (in-progress), F (failing).

Fulfillment of some degree requirements and exemption from some beginning courses possible by passing departmental examinations. College Board CLEP.

Distinctive Educational Programs: Flexible meeting places and schedules and evening classes. Preprofessional programs in agriculture, engineering, medical science, pharmacy. Facilities and programs for independent research, including honors programs, tutorials.

Degrees Conferred: 140 *associate;* 275 *baccalaureate;* 51 *master's;* 5 *postbaccalaureate certificates.* Bachelor's degrees awarded in top five disciplines: business, management, marketing, and related support services 87; education

38; health professions and related clinical sciences 29; English language and literature/letters 14; agriculture, agriculture operations, and related sciences 14.

Fees and Other Expenses: *Full-time tuition per academic year 2004–05:* undergraduate in-state $3,625, out-of-state $7,195. *Room and board:* $3,104. *Books and supplies:* $800.

Financial Aid: Aid from institutionally generated funds is provided on the basis of academic merit, financial need, other criteria. Institution has a Program Participation Agreement with the U.S. Department of Education for eligible students to receive Pell Grants and other federal aid.

Financial aid to full-time, first-time undergraduate students: 83% received federal grants averaging $2,798; 18% state/local grants averaging $1,712; 34% institutional grants averaging $2,794; 38% loans averaging $3,030.

Departments and Teaching Staff: *Total instructional faculty:* 116. Total tenured faculty: 56. Degrees held by full-time faculty: Doctorates 60%, master's 37%, baccalaureates 4%, first-professional 1%.

Enrollment: Total enrollment: 2,875. Undergraduate 2,694 (40.5% men, 59.5% women).

Characteristics of Student Body: *Ethnic/racial makeup:* Black non-Hispanic: 27.5%, American Indian or Alaska Native: .6%; Asian or Pacific Islander: .6%; Hispanic: 1.5%; White non-Hispanic: 69.7%; unknown .3%.

International Students: 9 nonresident aliens enrolled fall 2004. No programs available to aid students whose native language is not English. No financial aid specifically designated for international students.

Student Life: On-campus residence halls house 30% of student body. Residence halls for men only constitute 60% of such space, for women only 40%. Housing available for married students. *Intercollegiate athletics:* men only: baseball, basketball, football, cross-country, track; women only: basketball, cross-country, track. *Special regulations:* Cars permitted without restrictions. Residence hall visitation from 12 noon to 10:30pm. Sun.–Thurs. and from 12 noon to 12 midnight Fri.–Sat. *Special services:* International Resource Center; writing laboratory; developmental programs in reading, mathematics, and English; comprehensive tutorial program. *Student publications: The Foliate Oak,* a literary magazine; *Boll Weevil,* a yearbook. *Surrounding community:* Monticello population 10,000. Little Rock (AR), 95 miles from campus, is nearest metropolitan area.

Library Collections: 146,000 volumes. 500 microform titles; 1,140 periodical subscriptions. Online catalog. Students have access to online information retrieval services and the Internet.

Most important holdings include Arkansas Collection; Forestry Collection. Library is depository for U.S. government documents.

Buildings and Grounds: Campus area 75 acres.

Chief Executive Officer: Dr. Jack Lassiter, Chancellor.

Address admission inquiries to Mary Whiting, Director of Admissions.

University of Arkansas at Pine Bluff

1200 North University Drive
Mail Slot 4789
Pine Bluff, Arkansas 71601
Tel: (870) 575-8000   **E-mail:** admissions@uapb.edu
Fax: (870) 543-8009   **Internet:** www.uapb.edu

Institution Description: *Enrollment:* 3,251. *Degrees awarded:* Associate, baccalaureate, master's.

Academic offerings subject to approval by state governing boards.

Accreditation: *Regional:* NCA. *Professional:* art, family and consumer science, industrial technology, music, nursing, social work, teacher education

History: Chartered 1873; established as Branch Normal College and offered first instruction at postsecondary level 1875; awarded first degree (baccalaureate) 1882; became junior college 1885; changed name to Arkansas Agricultural, Mechanical and Normal College 1928; became senior college 1929; merged with University of Arkansas and adopted present name 1972.

Institutional Structure: *Composition of institution:* Administrators 35 men / 12 women. Academic affairs headed by vice chancellor for academic affairs. Management/business/finances directed by vice chancellor for fiscal affairs. Instructional faculty 171. Academic governance body, Faculty Senate, meets an average of 4 times per year.

Calendar: Semesters. Academic year Aug. to May. Freshmen admitted Aug., Jan., June, July. Degrees conferred and formal commencement May. Summer session of 2 terms from June to Aug.

Characteristics of Freshmen: Mean ACT scores men 10.6, women 10.5, class 10.5. 23.4% of undergraduate students completed a degree within 5 years. Freshmen from 19 states and 6 foreign countries.

Admission: Rolling admissions plan. Early acceptance available. *Requirements:* Either graduation from accredited secondary school with 16 units which must include 3 English, 2 mathematics, 1 science, 1 U.S. history; or GED. *Entrance tests:* ACT Composite. For foreign students TOEFL. *For transfer students:* 2.0 minimum GPA; from 4-year accredited institution 90 hours maximum transfer credit; from 2-year accredited institution 60 hours; correspondence/extension students 30 hours.

College credit and advanced placement for postsecondary level work completed in secondary school. Tutoring available. Developmental courses offered in summer session and regular academic year; credit given.

Degree Requirements: *For all associate degrees:* 60 credit hours. *For all baccalaureate degrees:* 120 credit hours. *For all degrees:* 2.0 GPA; 30 hours in residence; 2 hours physical education; general education requirements. The university has adopted a "State Minimum Core" of 35 credit hours of general educaiton courses that are required of all baccalaureate and associate of arts degree candidates. All state institutions of higher education in Arkansas have a 35-hour minimum core requirement with specified hours in each academic area. A student must maintain a cumulative grade point average of 2.00 to maintain satisfactory academic progress.

Grading system: A-D, AU (audited), W (withdrew), IP (in-progress), F (failing).

Fulfillment of some degree requirements and exemption from some beginning courses possible by passing College Board CLEP.

Distinctive Educational Programs: Cooperative education. Weekend and evening classes. Dual-degree program in engineering with University of Arkansas at Fayetteville. Interdepartmental program in gerontology. Facilities for independent research, including honors programs, individual majors, tutorials.

ROTC: Army.

Degrees Conferred: 334 *baccalaureate*; 34 *master's.* Bachelor's degrees awarded in top five disciplines: business, management, marketing, and related support services 84; family and consumer sciences/human sciences 31; security and protective services 29, liberal arts and sciences, general studies, and humanities 29; English language and literature/letters 26.

Fees and Other Expenses: *Full-time tuition per academic year 2004–05:* in-state resident undergraduate $4,044, out-of-state $8,019. *Room and board per academic year:* $5,492. *Books and supplies:* $1,200.

Financial Aid: Aid from institutionally generated funds is awarded on the basis of academic merit, financial need, athletic ability. Institution has a Program Participation Agreement with the U.S. Department of Education for eligible students to receive Pell Grants and other federal aid.

Financial aid to full-time, first-time undergraduate students: 71% received federal grants averaging $3,220; 7% state/local grants averaging $932; 33% institutional grants averaging $2,770; 67% received loans averaging $2,630.

Departments and Teaching Staff: *Total instructional faculty:* 171. Total tenured faculty: 98. Degrees held by full-time faculty: 57% hold terminal degrees.

Enrollment: Total enrollment 3,251. Undergraduate 3,136 (45.2% men, 54.8% women).

Characteristics of Student Body: *Ethnic/racial makeup:* Black non-Hispanic: 95%; Asian or Pacific Islander: .2%; Hispanic: .1%; White non-Hispanic: 3.6%; unknown: 1%.

International Students: 33 nonresident aliens enrolled fall 2004.

Student Life: On-campus residence halls house 31% of student body. *Intercollegiate athletics:* men only: basketball, football, tennis, track; women only: basketball, volleyball. *Special regulations:* Cars permitted without restrictions. *Special services:* Learning Resources Center, medical services. *Student publication:* Arkansawer, a bimonthly newspaper. *Surrounding community:* Pine Bluff population 58,000. Little Rock, 42 miles from campus, is nearest metropolitan area. Served by mass transit bus system; airport 5 miles from campus.

Library Collections: 271,600 volumes. 9,000 government documents; 119,205 microform materials; 1,060 current periodicals; 4,300 recordings/tapes. Online catalog. Students have access to information retrieval services and the Internet.

Most important holdings include John M. Ross, Knox Nelson, and J. B. Watson Collections.

Buildings and Grounds: Campus area 318 acres.

Chief Executive Officer: Dr. Lawrence A. Davis, Jr., Chancellor.

Address admission inquiries to Erica Fulton, Director of Enrollment Management.

University of Arkansas for Medical Sciences

4301 West Markham Street
Mail Slot 601
Little Rock, Arkansas 72205

Tel: (501) 686-5454   **E-mail:** admissions@uams.edu
Fax: (501) 686-5905   **Internet:** www.uams.edu

Institution Description: The University of Arkansas for Medical Sciences includes the College of Health Related Professions, College of Medicine, College of Nursing, College of Pharmacy, and the Graduate School. *Enrollment:* 2,170. *Degrees awarded:* Associate, baccalaureate, first-professional, master's, doctorate.

Accreditation: *Regional:* NCA. *Professional*: clinical lab scientist, clinical pastoral education, cytotechnology, dental hygiene, diagnostic medical sonography, dietetics, health information technician, medicine, nuclear medicine technology, nursing, pharmacy, psychology internship, radiography, respiratory therapy, respiratory therapy technology, surgical technology

Calendar: Semesters. Academic year Aug. to May.

Admission: Varies by indivisual college.

Degree Requirements: Varies by individual college.

Degrees Conferred: 65 *associate;* 274 *baccalaureate;* 70 *master's;* 12 *doctorate;* 238 *first-professional.*

Fees and Other Expenses: *Full-time tuition per academic year 2004–05:* Contact the university for current tuition for undergraduate, graduate, and professional schools.

Financial Aid: Aid from institutionally generated funds is provided on the basis of academic merit, financial need. Institution has a Program Participation Agreement with the U.S. Department of Education for eligible students to receive Pell Grants and other federal aid.

Departments and Teaching Staff: *Total instructional faculty:* 703.

Enrollment: Total enrollment 2,170. Undergraduate 750 (17.3% men, 82.7% women).

Characteristics of Student Body: *Ethnic and racial makeup (undergraduate):* Black non-Hispanic: 13.6%, American Indian or Alaska Native: .8%; Asian or Pacific Islander: 1.5%; Hispanic: 2%; White non-Hispanic: 81.7%.

International Students: No programs available to aid students whose native language is not English. No financial aid specifically designated for international students.

Library Collections: 180,000 volumes. 42,000 microform units; 6,000 audiovisual materials (units); 1,567 current periodical subscriptions. Students have access to online information retrieval services and the Internet.

Chief Executive Officer: Dr. I. Dodd Wilson, Chancellor.

Address admission inquiries to individual colleges.

College of Health Related Professions

Degree Programs Offered: *Associate* in biomedical instrument technology, dental hygiene, emergency medical sciences, radiologic technology, respiratory therapy, surgical technology; *baccalaureate* in cytotechnology, dental hygiene, medical technology, nuclear medicine technology, radiologic technology; *master's* in various fields. Certificates are also awarded.

Admission: Contact specific program; requirements vary by program.

Degree Requirements: Completion of prescribed program.

College of Medicine

Degree Programs Offered: *First-professional* in medicine (M.D.).

Admission: Contact the college directly for requirements.

Degree Requirements: Completion of prescribed program.

College of Nursing

Degree Programs Offered: *Baccalaureate, master's* in nursing.

Admission: Contact the college directly for requirements.

Degree Requirements: Completion of prescribed program.

College of Pharmacy

Degree Programs Offered: *First-professional, master's* in pharmacy.

Admission: Contact the college directly for requirements.

Degree Requirements: Completion of prescribed program.

Graduate School

Degree Programs Offered: *Master's, doctorate.*
Admission: Contact the Graduate School directly for requirements.
Degree Requirements: Completion of prescribed program.
Departments and Teaching Staff: Faculty drawn from other colleges of the university.

University of Central Arkansas

201 Donaghey Avenue
Conway, Arkansas 72035-0001

Tel: (501) 450-5000   **E-mail:** admissions@ecom.uca.edu
Fax: (501) 450-5228   **Internet:** www.uca.edu

Institution Description: University of Central Arkansas (State College of Arkansas until 1975) is a state institution. *Enrollment:* 9,516. *Degrees awarded:* Associate, baccalaureate, master's. Specialist certificates in education also given.

Academic offerings subject to approval by statewide coordinating bodies. Budget subject to approval by state governing boards.

Accreditation: *Regional:* NCA. *Professional:* art, business, dietetics, music, nursing, occupational therapy, physical therapy, physical therapy assisting, speech-language pathology, teacher education, theatre

History: Established and chartered as the Arkansas State Normal School 1907; offered first instruction at postsecondary level 1908; awarded first degree (baccalaureate) 1920; changed name to Arkansas State Teachers College 1925, State College of Arkansas 1967; adopted present name 1975.

Institutional Structure: *Governing board:* Board of Trustees. Representation: 7 trustees. All voting. *Composition of institution:* Administrators 40 men / 7 women. Academic affairs headed by vice president for academic affairs. Management/business/finances directed by vice president for business affairs. Full-time instructional faculty 398. Academic governance body, Council of Deans, meets an average of 30 times per year.

Calendar: Semesters. Academic year late Aug. to mid-May. Freshmen admitted Aug., June, July. Degrees conferred and formal commencements May, Aug. Summer session of 2 terms from early June to mid-Aug.

Characteristics of Freshmen: 5,342 applicants (68.4% admitted; 60.7% enrolled).

1% (27 students) submitted SAT scores; 95% (2,129 students) submitted ACT scores. *25th percentile:* SAT Verbal 440, SAT Math 440; ACT Composite 20, ACT English 20, ACT Math 18. *75th percentile:* SAT Verbal 600, SAT Math 650; ACT Composite 26, ACT English 27, ACT Math 25.

Admission: Selective admissions policy for freshman class. Criteria: ACT score, high school GPA, high school rank, high school coursework, letters of recommendation, special talents, class diversity. Rolling admissions plan. For foreign students TOEFL. *For transfer students:* 2.0 minimum GPA; from 4-year accredited institution maximum transfer credit limited only by residence requirement; from 2-year accredited institution 60 hours; correspondence/extension students 30 hours.

Advanced placement for postsecondary-level work completed in secondary school. For extrainstitutional learning related to concentrations offered at Central Arkansas, college credit on basis of ACE *2006 Guide to the Evaluation of Educational Experiences in the Armed Services.* Tutoring available.

Degree Requirements: *For all associate degrees:* 62 credit hours; 2 physical education courses. *For all baccalaureate degrees:* 124 credit hours; 2 physical education courses. *For all undergraduate degrees:* 2.0 GPA; 24 of last 30 hours in residence; general education requirements.

Fulfillment of some degree requirements and exemption from some beginning courses possible by passing departmental examinations, College Board CLEP. *Grading system:* A–F; pass-fail; withdraw.

Distinctive Educational Programs: Weekend and evening classes. Cooperative baccalaureate programs in medical technology with Baptist Medical Center and Sparks Regional Center, and in radiography with Baptist Medical Center, Sparks Regional Medical Center, St. Vincent's Infirmary. Preprofessional programs in dental hygiene, dentistry, engineering, medicine, optometry, pharmacy, veterinary science. Facilities and programs for independent research, including honors programs, individual majors, tutorials. *Other distinctive programs:* UCA Honors College for academically superior students (60 freshmen per year); four-year program. Ed.S. degree in educational leadership. Study abroad in Mexico (intensive Spanish) and Montreal (intensive French).

ROTC: Army in cooperation with the University of Arkansas at Little Rock.

Degrees Conferred: 1,159 *baccalaureate*; 360 *master's*; 50 *doctorate*. Bachelor's degrees awarded in top five disciplines: business, management, marketing, and related support services 274; health professions and related clinical sciences

204; education 115, English language and literature/letters 101; social sciences 67.

Fees and Other Expenses: *Full-time undergraduate tuition per academic year 2004–05:* in-state resident $5,053, out-of-state $8,609. *Room and board per academic year:* $3,920. *Books and supplies:* $1,000.

Financial Aid: Aid from institutionally generated funds is provided on the basis of academic merit. Institution has a Program Participation Agreement with the U.S. Department of Education for eligible students to receive Pell Grants and other federal aid.

Financial aid to full-time, first-time undergraduate students: 39% received federal grants averaging $2,632; 8% state/local grants averaging $615; 53% institutional grants averaging $4,790; 49% loans averaging $2,969.

Departments and Teaching Staff: *Total instructional faculty:* 398. Total tenured faculty: 187. Student-to-faculty ratio: 18:1. Degrees held by full-time faculty: doctorate 68%.

Enrollment: Total enrollment 9,516. Undergraduate 8,580 (40.1% men, 59.9% women).

Characteristics of Student Body: *Ethnic/racial makeup:* Black non-Hispanic: 16.8%, American Indian or Alaska Native: .9%; Asian or Pacific Islander: 1.2%; Hispanic: 1.2%; White non-Hispanic: 75.2%.

International Students: 200 nonresident aliens enrolled fall 2004. Social and cultural programs available to aid students whose native language is not English. English as a Second Language Program. No financial aid specifically designated for international students.

Student Life: On-campus residence halls house 35% of student body. Dormitories for men only constitute 45% of such space, for women only 55%. *Intercollegiate athletics:* men only: baseball, basketball, football, swimming, track; women only: softball, track. *Special regulations:* Cars permitted with restrictions. *Special services:* Learning Resources Center, medical services. *Student publications, radio: Echo,* a weekly newspaper; *Scroll,* a yearbook. Radio station KUCA-FM and KCON-AM broadcast 126 hours per week. *Surrounding community:* Conway population 21,000. Little Rock 30 miles from campus.

Library Collections: 405,000 volumes. 867,000 microforms; 6,200 audiovisual materials; 2,000 periodicals. Online catalog. Students have access to the Internet at no charge.

Most important special holdings include W.C. and J.P. Faucette Papers; Arkansas Conservation Coalition Records; Arkansas Repertory Theater Records.

Buildings and Grounds: Campus area 260 acres.
Chief Executive Officer: Lu W. Hardin, President.
Address admission inquiries to Penny Hatfield, Director of Admissions.

University of the Ozarks

415 North College Avenue
Clarksville, Arkansas 72830

Tel: (479) 979-1421   **E-mail:** jdecker@ozarks.edu
Fax: (479) 979-1355   **Internet:** www.ozarks.edu

Institution Description: The University of the Ozarks is a private, nonprofit college affiliated with the United Presbyterian Church (U.S.A.). *Enrollment:* 284 men / 344 women. *Degrees awarded:* Associate, baccalaureate, master's.

Academic offering subject to approval by statewide coordinating bodies.

Accreditation: *Regional:* NCA. *Professional:* business, teacher education

History: Established by Cumberland Presbyterians as Cane Hill College and offered first instruction at postsecondary level 1834; awarded first degree (baccalaureate) 1856; moved to present location and changed name to Arkansas Cumberland College 1891; became The College of the Ozarks 1920; adopted present name 1987.

Institutional Structure: *Governing board:* Board of Trustees. Extrainstitutional representation: 33 trustees (including 6 alumni), 6 life-time trustees; institutional representation: College president, faculty member, 1 student government officer. 3 ex officio. 33 voting. *Composition of institution:* Administrators 6 men / 2 women. Academic affairs headed by vice president for academic affairs. Management/business/finances directed by business manager. Full-time instructional faculty 32 men / 11 women. Academic governance body, Academic Affairs Council, meets an average of 10 times per year.

Calendar: Semesters. 2004–05 academic year mid-Aug. to early May. Freshmen admitted Aug., Jan. Degrees conferred and formal commencement May. Summer session of 2 terms from late May to mid-July.

Characteristics of Freshmen: 18% (38 students) submitted SAT scores; 74% (155 students) submitted ACT scores. *25th percentile:* SAT Verbal 490, SAT Math 470; ACT Composite 18, ACT English 20, ACT Math 17. *75th percentile:* SAT Verbal 580, SAT Math 570; ACT Composite 26, ACT English 27, ACT Math 25.

53% of freshmen from Arkansas. Freshmen from 22 states and 22 foreign countries.

Admission: Admission is selective. Students are notified as applications are complete and minimum requirements are met. *Requirements:* Graduation from secondary school; GPA 2.0; minimum 18 on ACT. *For transfer students:* 2.0 GPA; 66 hours maximum transfer credit.

College credit for extrainstitutional learning on basis of ACE *2006 Guide to the Evaluation of Educational Experiences in the Armed Services* and work-experience program at University of the Ozarks; College Board AP. Tutoring available. Noncredit developmental courses offered during regular academic year.

Degree Requirements: *For all baccalaureate degrees:* 124 credit hours; 2.0 GPA; 30 hours in residence; 4 hours physical education or military science (students over 25 excused); general education requirements. *Grading system:* A–F; high pass—pass-fail; withdraw (deadline after which pass-fail is appended to withdraw).

Distinctive Educational Programs: Study abroad programs available.

Degrees Conferred: 69 *baccalaureate:* biological and life sciences 6, business 23, communications/communication technologies 4, education 13, English 2, liberal arts/general studies 6, mathematics 1, natural resources/environmental science 3, physical sciences 4, psychology 1, social sciences and history 2, visual and performing arts 4.

Fees and Other Expenses: *Full-time tuition per academic year 2004–05:* $12,902. *Required fees:* $410. *Room and board per academic year:* $4,880.

Financial Aid: Aid from institutionally generated funds is provided on the basis of academic merit, financial need, other criteria. Institution has a Program Participation Agreement with the U.S.Department of Education for eligible students to receive Pell Grants and other federal aid.

Departments and Teaching Staff: *Total instructional faculty:* 61 (43 full-time, 18 part-time; women 20, men 41). Total number with doctorate, first-professional, or other terminal degree: 37. Student-to-faculty ratio: 13:1.

Enrollment: Total enrollment 628. Undergraduate full-time 278 men / 318 women, part-time 6m / 26s.

Characteristics of Student Body: *Ethnic/racial makeup:* number of Black non-Hispanic: 13; American Indian or Alaska Native: 21; Asian or Pacific Islander: 12; Hispanic: 19; White non-Hispanic: 426.

International Students: 105 nonresident aliens enrolled fall 2004. No programs available to aid students whose native language is not English. No financial aid specifically designated for international students.

Student Life: On-campus residence halls house 60% of student body. Residence halls are men only, women only, and coed. Housing available for married students. *Intercollegiate athletics:* men only: baseball, basketball, cross-country, soccer, tennis; women only: basketball, cross-country, soccer, softball. *Special regulations:* Cars permitted without restrictions. *Special services:* Jones Learning Center, support program for students with learning disabilities. *Student publications: Aerie,* a yearbook; *Falstaff,* an annual literary magazine; *Mountain Eagle,* a monthly newspaper. *Surrounding community:* Clarksville population 7,500. Little Rock, 90 miles from campus, is nearest metropolitan area.

Library Collections: 70,000 volumes. Online catalog. Current serial subscriptions: 408 paper, 94 microform. 2,612 recordings; 20 compact discs. 16 computer work stations. Students have access to the Internet at no charge.

Buildings and Grounds: Campus area 60 acres. *New buildings:* Walker Hall, teacher education and communications building, completed 2003; Mabee Residence Hall completed 2001.

Chief Executive Officer: Dr. Rick Niece, President.

Address inquiries to James Decker, Director of Admissions.

Williams Baptist College

60 West Fulbright Avenue
Walnut Ridge, Arkansas 72476
Tel: (870) 886-6741   **E-mail:** admissions@wbcoll.edu
Fax: (870) 886-3924   **Internet:** www.wbcoll.edu

Institution Description: Williams Baptist College is a private institution affiliated with the Southern Baptist Convention. *Enrollment:* 653. *Degrees awarded:* Associate, baccalaureate.

Accreditation: *Regional:* NCA. *Professional:* teacher education

History: Formerly Southern Baptist College (two-year college); adopted present name 1990.

Institutional Structure: *Governing board:* Trustees of Williams Baptist College. Academic affairs headed by academic dean. Management/business/finances directed by business manager and director of financial aid. Full-time instructional faculty 28.

Calendar: Semesters. 2004–05 academic year Aug. to May. Summer session from early June to early Aug.

Characteristics of Freshmen: 443 applicants (187 men / 256 women). 71.6% of applicants admitted; 45.4% enrolled.

2% (3 students) submitted SAT scores; 98% (141 students) submitted ACT scores. *25th percentile:* SAT Verbal 440, SAT Math 400; ACT Composite 19, ACT English 19, ACT Math 17. *75th percentile:* SAT Verbal 600, SAT Math 550; ACT Composite 24, ACT English 26, ACT Math 23.

Admission: Rolling admissions plan. For fall acceptance, apply no later than 1 month prior to beginning of semester. *Requirements:* Either graduation from approved secondary school. *Entrance tests:* ACT. Foreign students TOEFL.

Degree Requirements: *For baccalaureate degree:* 124 credit hours; 2.0 GPA; 30 hours in residence; general requirements.

Grading system: A–F; credit-no credit; withdraw (deadline after which pass-fail is appended to withdraw); incomplete.

Distinctive Educational Programs: Coalition of Christian Colleges Programs; Oxford Summer School Program.

Degrees Conferred: 4 *associate:* 89 *baccalaureate.* Bachelor's degrees awarded in top five disciplines: education 44, theology and ministerial studies 13, business, management, marketing, and related support services 11; biological and biomedical sciences 8, psychology 5.

Fees and Other Expenses: *Full-time undergraduate tuition per academic year 2004–05:* $8,600. *Room and board per academic year:* $4,000. *Books and supplies:* $900.

Financial Aid: Aid from institutionally generated funds is provided on the basis of academic merit, athletic ability. Institution has a Program Participation Agreement with the U.S. Department of Education for eligible students to receive Pell Grants and other federal aid.

Financial aid to full-time, first-time undergraduate students: 55% received federal grants averaging $2,659; 24% state/local grants averaging $1,078; 96% institutional grants averaging $3,422; 71% loans averaging $2,234.

Departments and Teaching Staff: *Total instructional faculty:* 28. Total tenured faculty: 5. Student-to-faculty ratio: 18:1. Degrees held by full-time faculty: doctorate 50%, master's 50%. 50% hold terminal degrees.

Enrollment: Total enrollment 653 (44.4% men, 55.6% women).

Characteristics of Student Body: *Ethnic/racial makeup:* Black non-Hispanic: 3.2%, American Indian or Alaska Native: .5%; Hispanic: .8%; White non-Hispanic: 94.5%.

International Students: 20 nonresident aliens enrolled fall 2004. Variable scholarships specifically designated for undergraduate international students.

Student Life: On-campus housing available. *Surrounding community:* Walnut Ridge is a rural area located 125 miles north of Little Rock.

Library Collections: 68,000 volumes. Online catalog. Current serial subscriptions: 206 paper. 18,700 microform materials. Students have access to the Internet at no charge.

Buildings and Grounds: 180 acres.

Chief Executive Officer: Dr. Jerol B. Swaim, President.

Address admission inquiries to Angela Flippo, Vice President for Enrollment Management.

California

Academy of Art University

79 New Montgomery Street
San Francisco, California 94105
Tel: (415) 274-2000 **E-mail:** info@academyart.edu
Fax: (415) 274-8665 **Internet:** www.academyart.edu

Institution Description: The Academy of Art College is a private, independent college offering training in advertising, computer arts, fashion, fine arts, graphic design, illustration, interior design, motion pictures, photography, and product design. *Enrollment:* 6,761. *Degrees awarded:* Associate, baccalaureate, master's.

Accreditation: *Nonregional:* ACICS. *Professional:* art, interior design

History: The university was founded in 1929. The present name was adopted in 2002.

Calendar: Semesters. Summer session. Academic year from Sept. to May.

Characteristics of Freshmen: 52% of entering students expected to graduate within five years. 66% of entering students from California. Students from 45 states and 10 foreign countries.

Admission: *Requirements:* Graduation from an approved secondary school or GED; portfolio required for advanced placement; last 32 credits must be completed in residence.

Degree Requirements: B.F.A. program requires the completion of 132 units. M.F.A. program requires the completion of 63 units.

Distinctive Educational Programs: Associate of arts program added 1998.

Degrees Conferred: 85 *associate;* 785 *baccalaureate;* 208 *master's.* Bachelor's degrees awarded in top three disciplines: visual and performing arts 443; computer and information sciences and support services 287; business, management, marketing, and related support services 55.

Fees and Other Expenses: *Full-time tuition per academic year 2004–05:* $14,480. *Room and board per academic year:* $12,000. *Books and supplies:* $1,260. *Other expenses:* $2,430.

Financial Aid: Financial aid available for qualified applicants. Institution has a Program Participation Agreement with the U.S. Department of Education for eligible students to receive Pell Grants and other federal aid.

Financial aid to full-time, first-time undergraduate students: 24% received federal grants averaging $1,800; 8% state/local grants averaging $4,500; 46% averaging $1,798.

Departments and Teaching Staff: *Total instructional faculty:* 150. 80% hold terminal degrees. *Student-to-faculty ratio:* 18:1.

Enrollment: Total enrollment 6,761. Undergraduate 5,641 (51.9% men, 48.1% women).

Characteristics of Student Body: *Ethnic/racial makeup:* Black non-Hispanic: 31.5%; American Indian or Alaska Native: .3%; Asian or Pacific Islander: 13.1%; Hispanic: 6.4%; White non-Hispanic: 21.5; unknown: 27.9%. 40% of students attend summer sessions.

International Students: 1,026 nonresident aliens enrolled fall 2004. Students from Europe, Asia, Central and South America, Africa, Canada, Australia, New Zealand. Social programs available specifically for international students. English as a Second Language Program. No financial aid specifically designated for international students.

Student Life: Housing available for a limited number of students in Academy accommodations. Tutoring available; counseling; student exhibition galleries.

Library Collections: 30,000 volumes including bound books, serial backfiles, electronic documents, and government documents not in separate collections. Online catalog. Current serial subscriptions: 467 paper, 5 electronic. 371 CD-ROMs. 22 computer work stations. Students have access to the Internet at no charge.

Most important special collections include Slide Library supporting 10 disciplines with over 100,000 slides; videotape collection of 1,305 titles; design annuals collection.

Buildings and Grounds: Campus is located in downtown San Francisco in eleven buildings and galleries and one foundry in South San Francisco.

Chief Executive Officer: Elisa Stephens, President.

Address undergraduate admission inquiries to John Meurer, Vice President, Undergraduate Admissions; graduate inquiries to Sandra Weber, Vice President of Graduate Admissions.

Alliant International University - Los Angeles

1000 South Fremont Avenue
Alhambra, California 91803-1360
Tel: (626) 284-2777 **E-mail:** admissions@alliant.edu
Fax: (626) 284-0550 **Internet:** www.alliant.edu

Institution Description: Alliant International University was formerly named the California School of Professional Psychology. The school also has campuses in Fresno, San Francisco, and San Diego. *Enrollment:* 609. *Degrees awarded:* Master's, doctorate.

Accreditation: *Regional:* WASC-Sr. *Professional:* psychology internship

Institutional Structure: *Composition of institution:* The chief executive officer of the institution is the chancellor. The senior management team consists of the vice-chancellor for academic affairs; director of business affairs; director of human resources and risk management; director of student affairs; director of the library and information services. Four deans have oversight of day-to-day administration of the academic programs and professional training: Clinical PsyD Program; Clinical Ph.D. Program; Organizational Psychology Programs; Professional Field Training. Administrators: 8 men / 5 women.

Calendar: Semesters. Summer session of 1 term from mid-Aug. to mid-Sept.

Distinctive Educational Programs: Evening classes. Organizational psychology; ethnic minority, mental health emphasis, health psychology emphasis. The PsyD degree program in Executive Management and Leadership was initiated in 1996.

Degrees Conferred: 58 *master's:* psychology; 90 *doctorate:* psychology.

Fees and Other Expenses: *Full-time tuition per academic year:* $18,240. Contact the university for current tuition and fees.

Financial Aid: Aid from institutionally generated funds is provided on the basis of financial need. Institution has a Program Participation Agreement with the U.S. Department of Education for eligible students to receive Pell Grants and other federal aid.

Departments and Teaching Staff: Psychology *professors* 19, *associate professors* 13, *assistant professors* 7; *adjunct* 63, *core* 7.

Total full-time instructional faculty: 39. *Degrees held by full-time faculty:* Doctorate 100%.

Enrollment: Total enrollment 609 (men 20.9%, women 79.1%).

Characteristics of Student Body: *Ethnic/racial makeup:* Black non-Hispanic: 9%; American Indian or Alaska Native: .7%; Asian or Pacific Islander: 11.5%; Hispanic: 12.3%, White non-Hispanic: 46.6%; unknown: 18.9%.

International Students: 7 nonresident aliens enrolled fall 2004. No programs available to aid students whose native language is not English. No financial aid specifically designated for international students.

Student Life: No on-campus housing. *Special regulations:* Cars permitted without restrictions. *Special services:* Learning Resources Center. *Surrounding community:* Los Angeles population over 3,100,000. Served by mass transit bus system; airport 15 miles from campus; passenger rail service 3 miles from campus.

Library Collections: 30,000 volumes. 2,600 microforms; 650 audiovisual materials; 350 current periodical subscriptions. Access to online information retrieval services and the Internet.

Most important special collections include the Abbott Kaplan Collection of Fine and First Editions in Psychology.

Buildings and Grounds: The campus is located 6 miles from downtown Los Angeles and occupies a 38-acre complex.

Chief Executive Officer: Corina Espinoza, Assistant Vice President.

Address admission inquiries to Stephanie Byers-Bell, Director of Admissions.

Alliant International University - Fresno/Sacramento

5130 East Clinton Way

Fresno, California 93727-2014

Tel: (559) 456-2777   **E-mail:** admissions@alliant.edu
Fax: (559) 253-2267   **Internet:** www.alliant.edu

Institution Description: Alliant International University was formerly named the California School of Professional Psychology. It is a private, non-profit, professional graduate school offering three doctoral programs and one master's program. *Enrollment:* 358.

Accreditation: *Regional:* WASC-Sr. *Professional:* psychology internship

History: Founded 1969; first classes held on campuses in San Francisco and Los Angeles 1970; San Diego campus added 1972; Fresno campus founded 1973.

Institutional Structure: *Composition of institution:* Academic affairs headed by dean for academic affairs. Core instructional faculty of 21.

Calendar: Semesters. Two 15-week semesters; 3-week winter session and 5-week summer session.

Admission: *Requirements:* Bachelor's degree in psychology or must meet prerequisites: introduction to statistics, abnormal psychology, experimental psychology and/or one of learning theory, physiological psychology or tests and measurement or score at 80th percentile on the Advanced Psychology section of the GRE. No pre-entry class offered on the Fresno campus.

Degree Requirements: The doctorate is awarded to students who have completed: an acceptable doctoral/clinical dissertation; the equivalent of no less than 4 academic years of full-time attendance following admission at the graduate entry level, or three academic years following credit for prior graduate work; successful completion of a minimum of 120 units for the Doctor of Psychology, or 150 semester units for the Ph.D. For the Clinical Doctor of Philosophy program: 125 units; for the Forensic Doctor of Psychology program: 125 units; for the Master of Organizational Behavior Program: 40 units. *Grading system:* Credit-no credit.

Distinctive Educational Programs: Ecosystemic clinical child proficiency; ethnocultural mental health proficiency; general clinical proficiency.

Degrees Conferred: 22 *master's:* psychology; 53 *doctorate:* psychology.

Fees and Other Expenses: *Full-time tuition per academic year:* $18,240. Contact the university for current tuition and fees.

Financial Aid: Aid from institutionally generated funds is provided on the basis of financial need. Institution has a Program Participation Agreement with the U.S. Department of Education for eligible students to receive Pell Grants and other federal aid.

Departments and Teaching Staff: Clinical psychology *professors* 10.5, *associate professors* 3.5, *assistant professors* 1, *part-time teachers* 15; forensic 1, 1, 0, 1. *Total instructional faculty:* 21 FTE. *Degrees held by full-time faculty:* Doctorate 100%.

Enrollment: Total enrollment: 358 (men 21.8%, women 78.2%).

Characteristics of Student Body: *Ethnic/racial makeup:* Black non-Hispanic: 6.1%; American Indian or Alaska Native: 2.5%; Asian or Pacific Islander: 6.4%; Hispanic: 12.3%, White non-Hispanic: 61.2%.

International Students: No programs available to aid students whose native language is not English. No financial aid specifically designated for international students.

Student Life: *Special services:* Tutorial Program, Minority Mentoring Program. Psychological Services Center. Student Association. On-campus parking available. *Surrounding community:* Fresno metropolitan area population 475,000.

Library Collections: 30,000 volumes. 300 microform titles; 475 audiovisual materials; 253 current periodical subscriptions. Access to online information retrieval services and the Internet.

Most important special collections include clinical psychology; psychological test materials.

Buildings and Grounds: Moved to new campus in 1996; 43,000 square feet.

Chief Executive Officer: Gregory Timberlake, Assistant Vice President.

Address admissions inquiries to Director for Admissions.

Alliant International University - San Diego

10455 Pomerado Road

San Diego, California 92131-1799

Tel: (858) 271-4300   **E-mail:** admissions@alliant.edu
Fax: (858) 693-8562   **Internet:** www.alliant.edu

Institution Description: Alliant International University was formerly known as the California School of Professional Psychology. It merged with United States International University in 2002. *Enrollment:* 1,790. *Degrees awarded:* Master's, doctorate. Certificates also awarded.

Accreditation: *Regional:* WASC-Sr. *Professional:* clinical psychology

History: Established 1969; offered first instruction at postsecondary level 1972; chartered and awarded first degree (master's) 1974.

Institutional Structure: *Composition of institution:* Administrators 5 men / 4 women. Academic affairs headed by dean for academic and professional affairs. Management/business/finances directed by director, student services and director, business and administrative affairs. Core instructional faculty 16 men / 5 women. Academic governance body, Management-Faculty Leadership Committee, meets an average of 40 times per year.

Calendar: Quarters. Academic year Sept. to May. Degrees conferred May, July, Dec. Formal commencement May. Summer session early June to late July; summer pre-entry program sessions June to Aug.

Characteristics of Freshmen: Undergraduate applicants 373 (214 men, 159 women). 45% of applicants admitted; 24.4% of admitted students enrolled full-time.

Admission: Degree-seeking students accepted for fall entry only. Three entry levels: 4 years plus summers, 4 years, and 3 years. Minimum coursework requirements for each entry level. Prefer 3.0 undergraduate GPA but will consider applicants with graduate GPA above 3.0 or acceptable GRE scores.

Degree Requirements: Clinical program: For M.A. degree—60 semester units including required courses; for Ph.D.—minimum 120 semester units including required courses (minimum 90 units for 3 year entry). Industrial/organizational program: For M.A. degree—minimum 60 semester units including required courses plus one advanced seminar and a master's thesis (terminal degree only); for Ph.D.—minimum 120 semester units including required courses (minimum 90 units for 3 year entry).

Distinctive Educational Programs: Extended degree option with late afternoon and evening classes. Doctoral retraining—clinical and industrial/organizational programs. Double major in clinical and industrial/organizational psychology; double major in clinical and health psychology. California Psychological Services offers internship training to students and low-cost mental health care to the community.

Degrees Conferred: 116 *bachelor's;* 242 *master's:* clinical psychology; 125 *doctorate:* clinical psychology. Bachelor's degrees awarded in top five disciplines: business, management, marketing, and related support services 76; social sciences 13, liberal arts and sciences, general studies and humanities 12, psychology 9; education 2.

Fees and Other Expenses: *Full-time tuition per academic year:* $19,450. Contact the school for current tuition and fees. *Books and supplies:* $1,260. *Room and board per academic year:* $7,430.

Financial Aid: Aid from institutionally generated funds is awarded on the basis of financial need. Institution has a Program Participation Agreement with the U.S. Department of Education for eligible students to receive Pell Grants and other federal aid.

Financial aid to full-time, first-time undergraduate students: 65% received federal grants averaging $7,952; 29% state/local grants averaging $3,275; 91% institutional grants averaging $6,689; 55% loans averaging $5,743.

Departments and Teaching Staff: *Professors* 13, *associate professors* 5, *assistant professors* 6, *part-time teachers* 84. *Total instructional faculty:* 108. *Degrees held by full-time faculty:* Doctorate 100%.

Enrollment: Total enrollment: 1,790. Undergraduate 419.

Characteristics of Student Body: *Ethnic/racial makeup:* Black non-Hispanic: 12.4%; American Indian or Alaska Native: 16.6%; Asian or Pacific Islander: 7.4%; Hispanic: 18.6%, White non-Hispanic: 23.4%; unknown: 9.3%.

International Students: 114 nonresident aliens enrolled in undergraduate program 2004. No programs available to aid students whose native language is not English. *Financial aid specifically designated for international students:* Variable number of scholarships available annually.

Student Life: No on-campus housing. *Special regulations:* Cars permitted without restrictions. *Surrounding community:* San Diego population over 1 million. Served by airport 26 miles from campus; passenger rail service 9 miles from campus.

Library Collections: 191,600 volumes. 351,700 microforms; 3,100 audiovisual materials; 1,150 periodicals. Access to online information retrieval systems.

Buildings and Grounds: Campus area 60 acres.

Chief Executive Officer: Dr. Ramona Kunard, Director.

Address admission inquiries to Helen Bucheli, Director of Admissions.

Alliant International University - San Francisco Bay Area

One Beach Street, Suite
San Francisco, California 94133-1221

Tel: (415) 955-1000   **E-mail:** admissions@alliant.edu
Fax: (415) 955-2179   **Internet:** www.alliant.edu

Institution Description: Alliant International University was formerly named California School of Professional Psychology. Other campuses are located in Fresno, Los Angeles, and San Diego. *Enrollment:* 728. *Degrees awarded:* Master's, doctorate.

Accreditation: *Regional:* WASC-Sr. *Professional:* psychology internship

Institutional Structure: *Composition of institution:* Administrators 1 man / 2 women. Academic affairs headed by dean for academic and professional affairs. Management/business/finances directed by dean for student and administrative affairs. Instructional faculty core 12m / 13w. Academic governance body, Faculty Senate, meets an average of 11 times per year.

Distinctive Educational Programs: Weekend and evening classes. Tutorials.

Degrees Conferred: 3 *master's,* 108 *doctorate:* psychology.

Fees and Other Expenses: *Full-time tuition per academic year:* Contact the school for current tuition and fees.

Financial Aid: Aid from institutionally generated funds is provided on the basis of financial need, other criteria. Institution has a Program Participation Agreement with the U.S. Department of Education for eligible students to receive Pell Grants and other federal aid.

Departments and Teaching Staff: Clinical program *part-time professors* 107, masters program in organizational behavior 14, Center for Integrative Psychoanalytic Studies (CIPS) 6. *Total instructional faculty:* 127 part-time professors. *Total tenured faculty:* 25 core faculty on three-year rolling contracts renewed annually. *Degrees held by faculty:* doctorate 100%. 100% of faculty hold terminal degrees.

Enrollment: Total enrollment 728. (men 25.4%, women 74.6%).

Characteristics of Student Body: *Age distribution:* Average age 32 years.

International Students: No programs available to aid students whose native language is not English. No financial aid specifically designated for foreign students.

Student Life: No on-campus housing. *Surrounding community:* San Francisco is nearest metropolitan area. Served by mass transit bus and rail system, airport 25 miles from campus, passenger rail service 10 miles from campus.

Publications: *Cathexis* (biannually) first published in 1979.

Library Collections: 25,000 volumes. 300 microforms; 315 current periodical subscriptions.

Chief Executive Officer: Lewis Bundy, Assistant Vice President.

Address admission inquiries Ned Doherty, Director of Admissions.

American Baptist Seminary of the West

2606 Dwight Way
Berkeley, California 94704-3029

Tel: (510) 841-1905   **E-mail:** dschirer@absw.edu
Fax: (510) 841-2446   **Internet:** www.absw.edu

Institution Description: The American Baptist Seminary of the West is a founding and continuing member of the Graduate Theological Union in Berkeley, California. *Enrollment:* 80. *Degrees awarded:* Master's, doctorate, first-professional.

Accreditation: *National:* ATS. *Professional:* theology

History: Created by merger of Berkeley Baptist Divinity School (founded 1852) and the California Baptist Theological Seminary (founded 1944) in 1968.

Institutional Structure: *Composition of institution:* President. Academic affairs headed by vice president and dean of academic affairs.

Calendar: Semesters. Academic year Sept. to May.

Admission: *Requirements:* Bachelor's degree.

Degree Requirements: *For Master of Divinity:* 77 elective units; required curriculum. *For Master of Arts in Religion:* 48 semester units. *For Doctor of Ministry:* 8 courses plus a professional paper.

Distinctive Educational Programs: Through the Graduate Theological Union, a person may enroll in the master of arts, doctor of theology, or doctor of philosophy programs and may affiliate with the American Baptist Seminary of the West.

Degrees Conferred: 2 *master's;* 11 *first-professional* divinity/ministry.

Fees and Other Expenses: *Full-time tuition per academic year 2004–05:* Contact the institution for current tuition/fees. Off-campus housing only.

Financial Aid: Aid packages are developed on the basis of need, including grants, work–study, and loans. Institution has a Program Participation Agreement with the U.S. Department of Education for eligible students to receive Pell Grants and other federal aid.

Departments and Teaching Staff: *Total instructional faculty:* 15. 100% hold terminal degrees.

Enrollment: Total enrollment 80 (51.3% men, 48.8% women).

Characteristics of Student Body: *Ethnic/racial makeup:* Black non-Hispanic: 38.8%; Asian or Pacific Islander: 12.5%; Hispanic: 2.5%; White non-Hispanic: 20%; unknown: 13.8%.

International Students: 10 nonresident aliens enrolled fall 2004. Students from Europe, Asia, Africa. No programs available to aid students whose native language is not English.

Student Life: A limited number of studio, one- and two-bedroom apartments are available on the campus. *Surrounding community:* Berkeley is a major university center located across the bay from San Francisco.

Library Collections: Students have access to the library of the Graduate Theological Union Library in Berkeley. The collection numbers over 500,000 volumes.

Chief Executive Officer: Dr. Keith Russell, President.

Address admission inquiries to Anne Russell, Registrar.

American Conservatory Theater

30 Grant Avenue
San Francisco, California 94108-5800

Tel: (415) 439-2530   **E-mail:** admissions@act-sf.org
Fax: (415) 834-3210   **Internet:** www.act-sf.org

Institution Description: American Conservatory Theater is a private, independent, nonprofit institution. *Enrollment:* 48. *Degrees awarded:* Master's. Certificates also awarded.

Accreditation: *Regional:* WASC-Sr.

History: Established 1965.

Institutional Structure: *Governing board:* Board of Directors. 20 directors including Artistic Director, Managing Director; Conservatory Director; Associate Conservatory Director; Dean. *Composition of institution:* Academic affairs headed by dean. Full-time instructional faculty 11.

Calendar: Semesters. Academic year from mid-Sept. to early May.

Admission: Rolling admissions plan. Apply no later than Jan. 15 for Master of Fine Arts Program. May 1 for Summer Training Congress. Enrollment in Master of Fine Arts Program by audition only. *Requirements:* High school graduation; minimum age: 20.

Degree Requirements: 3-year curriculum. *Grading system:* Pass–fail.

Distinctive Educational Programs: Summer certificate program.

Degrees Conferred: 17 *master's:* visual and performing arts.

Fees and Other Expenses: *Full-time tuition per academic year 2004–05:* $14,207.

Financial Aid: Aid from institutionally generated funds is provided on the basis of academic merit, financial need. *Institutional funding for undergraduates:* 3 scholarships and grants totaling $12,000.

Federal and state funding for undergraduates: 5 scholarships and grants totaling $39,000 ($1,400 to $9,000); 10 loans worth $56,000; 8 work-study jobs worth $10,000. *For graduates:* 30 fellowships and grants totaling $163,000 ($2,000 to $16,000); 62 loans worth $668,000; 22 work-study jobs totaling $32,000.

Departments and Teaching Staff: Faculty members are unranked. *Full-time teachers* 11, *part-time teachers* 14.

Total instructional faculty: 25.

Enrollment: Total enrollment 48.

Characteristics of Student Body: *Ethnic/racial makeup:* number of Black non-Hispanic: 10; American Indian or Alaska Native: 1; Asian or Pacific Islander: 2; Hispanic: 2; White non-Hispanic: 49; unknown: 2.

International Students: 1 nonresident alien enrolled fall 2004. 1 student from Canada. No programs to aid students whose native language is not English.

Student Life: No on-campus housing. *Surrounding community:* San Francisco population 750,000.

Library Collections: 15,000 volumes. Card catalog.

Chief Executive Officer: Melissa Smith, Conservatory Director.

Address admission inquiries to Dr. Jack F. Sharrar, Director of Academic Affairs.

American Film Institute Conservatory

2021 North Western Avenue
Los Angeles, California 90027-1625
Tel: (323) 856-7714   **E-mail:** jackman@afionline.org
Fax: (323) 467-4578   **Internet:** www.afionline.org

Institution Description: The American Film Institute Conservatory, formerly known as the AFI Center for Advanced Film and Television Studies is an independent, national, nonprofit organization dedicated to advancing and preserving the art of the moving image. *Enrollment:* 298. *Degrees awarded:* Master of Fine Arts; Certificate of Attendance.

Accreditation: *Professional:* art

History: The Institute Center was created in 1967 by the National Endowment for the Arts.

Institutional Structure: Board Advisory Committee includes members of the AFT Board of Trustees, former Fellows of the conservatory, as well as other outstanding individuals from the film and television creative community.

Calendar: Academic year 2004–05: Sept. 12 to June 14.

Admission: Applications may be submitted to the First Year Program in the fields of cinematography, digital media, directing, editing, producing, production design, and screenwriting. An academic degree is desirable, but not mandatory, as a prerequisite. Applicants are expected to have a basic background in the arts and humanities and to be at least 21 years of age.

Degree Requirements: Completion of prescribed curriculum. Fellows are evaluated by the faculty on the quality of work completed; attendance in classes and commitment to work; professional attitude; creative potential. A bachelor's degree is required to receive a Master of Fine Arts degree after the successful completion of the Second Year Program.

Degrees Conferred: 88 *master of fine arts.*

Fees and Other Expenses: *Graduate tuition and fees per academic year:* $31,500.

Financial Aid: The Institute Center participates in the federally guaranteed student loan program. Institution has a Program Participation Agreement with the U.S. Department of Education for eligible students to receive Pell Grants and other federal aid.

Departments and Teaching Staff: *Total instructional faculty* 42.

Enrollment: Total enrollment 298 (70.1% men, 29.9% women).

Characteristics of Student Body: *Ethnic/racial makeup:* Black non-Hispanic: 8.7%; American Indian of Alaska Native: 9.3%; Asian or Pacific Islander: 4%; Hispanic: 4.7%; White non-Hispanic: 64.1%.

International Students: 54 nonresident aliens enrolled fall 2003. Students from Europe, Asia, Latin America, Africa, Canada, Australia. No programs available to aid students whose native language is not English. No financial aid specifically designated for international students.

Library Collections: 15,000 volumes. 100 current periodical subscriptions. Computer work stations available. Students have access to the Internet at no charge.

Numerous special collections including Martin Scorsese Collection, Robert Aldrich Collection, Charles K. Feldman Papers, Fritz Lang Collection.

Buildings and Grounds: 8-acre campus; 4 buildings.

Chief Executive Officer: Jean Firstenberg, Director.

Address admission inquiries to J.J. Jackman, Admissions Manager.

Antioch University Southern California

400 Corporate Pointe
Culver City, California 90230-7615
Tel: (310) 578-1080   **E-mail:** admisssions@antiochsc.edu
Fax: (310) 822-4824   **Internet:** www.antiochsc..edu

Institution Description: Antioch University Southern California is an independent institution that provides innovative graduate and undergraduate education for adults. The Antioch approach emphasizes: the development of the student as a whole person; the integration of academic and experiential learning; creative, critical, and independent thinking. *Degrees offered:* Baccalaureate, masters's.

Accreditation: *Regional:* NCA by virtue of Antioch University (Ohio).

History: Antioch University Southern California, established in 1972, is part of the Antioch University (Ohio) campus system. There are two locations in Southern California: SEE Los Angeles Branch in Culver City and the Santa Barbara Branch.

Chief Executive Officer: Lucy Ann Geiselman, President.

Antioch University - Los Angeles Branch

400 Corporate Pointe
Culver City, California 90230-7615
Tel: (310) 578-1080   **E-mail:** admisssions@antiochla.edu
Fax: (310) 822-4824   **Internet:** www.antiochla.edu

Institution Description: Antioch University Southern California is an independent institution that provides innovative graduate and undergraduate education for adults. Programs offered include Bachelor of Arts in Liberal Studies with concentrations in urban community and environment, liberal studies, business, child studies, psychology, and creative writing. *Degrees awarded:* Baccalaureate, masters's.

Accreditation: *Regional:* NCA by virtue of Antioch University (Ohio).

Calendar: Quarters. Formal commencement twice per year. Quarterly design portfolio shows for graduates.

Admission: Applicants are accepted on a quarterly (rolling) basis. *Requirements:* High school graduation or GED; interview.

Degree Requirements: Students must complete 112 quarter credits to be eligible for the associate degree and 192 quarter credits for the bachelor's degree; cumulative 2.0 GPA; passing grade for all coursework; completion of portfolio requirements.

Degrees Conferred: 57 *baccalaureate;* 161 *master's.* Bachelor's degrees awarded: liberal arts and sciences, general studies and humanities 57.

Fees and Other Expenses: Contact the university for current tuition, fees, and other costs.

Financial Aid: Institution has a Program Participation Agreement with the U.S. Department of Education for eligible students to receive Pell Grants and other federal aid.

Departments and Teaching Staff: The faculty's primary duties are to teach and advise, as well as to engage in the intellectual dialogue of their profession.

Enrollment: Total enrollment 631. Undergraduate 157 (men 21%, women 79%).

Characteristics of Student Body: *Ethnic/racial makeup:* Black non-Hispanic: 15.9%; American Indian or Alaska Native: 1.9%; Asian or Pacific Islander: 3.2%; Hispanic: 10.2%; White non-Hispanic: 66.9%; unknown: 1.9%.

Student Life: Off-campus apartments available. *Special services:* counseling; tutoring. *Surrounding community:* Culver City is located on the westside of the Los Angeles area. It is served by mass transit bus and train service. Los Angeles airport located five miles away.

Chief Executive Officer: Lucy Ann Geiselman, President.

Address admission inquiries to Kathie Rawding, Director of Admissions, Los Angeles campus.

Antioch University - Santa Barbara Branch

801 Garden Street
Santa Barbara, California 93101-1581
Tel: (805) 962-8179   **E-mail:** admisssions@antiochsb.edu
Fax: (310) 822-4824   **Internet:** www.antiochsb..edu

Institution Description: Antioch University Southern California is an independent institution that provides innovative graduate and undergraduate education for adults. Programs offered include Bachelor of Arts in Liberal Studies with concentrations in urban community and environment, liberal studies, business, child studies, psychology, and creative writing. *Degrees awarded:* Baccalaureate, masters's.

Accreditation: *Regional:* NCA by virtue of Antioch University (Ohio).

Calendar: Quarters. Formal commencement twice per year. Quarterly design portfolio shows for graduates.

Admission: Applicants are accepted on a quarterly (rolling) basis. *Requirements:* High school graduation or GED; interview.

Degree Requirements: Students must complete 112 quarter credits to be eligible for the associate degree and 192 quarter credits for the bachelor's degree; cumulative 2.0 GPA; passing grade for all coursework; completion of portfolio requirements.

Degrees Conferred: 44 *baccalaureate*; 81 *master's*. Bachelor's degrees awarded: liberal arts and sciences, general studies and humanities 44.

Fees and Other Expenses: Contact the university for current tuition, fees, and other costs.

Financial Aid: Institution has a Program Participation Agreement with the U.S. Department of Education for eligible students to receive Pell Grants and other federal aid.

Departments and Teaching Staff: The faculty's primary duties are to teach and advise, as well as to engage in the intellectual dialogue of their profession.

Enrollment: Total enrollment 289. Undergraduate 103 (men 25.2, women 74.8%).

Characteristics of Student Body: *Ethnic/racial makeup:* Black non-Hispanic: 4.99%; American Indian or Alaska Native: 1.9%; Asian or Pacific Islander: 5.8%; Hispanic: 11.7%; White non-Hispanic: 69.9%; unknown: 1.9%.

Student Life: Off-campus apartments available. *Special services:* counseling; tutoring. *Surrounding community:* Santa Barbara is located 100 miles northwest of Los Angeles and is served by AMTRAK and major airlines.

Chief Executive Officer: Lucy Ann Geiselman, President.

Address admission inquiries to Mary Ann Marwitz, Registrar, Santa Barbara campus.

Art Center College of Design

1700 Lida Street
Pasadena, California 91103
Tel: (626) 396-2000   **E-mail:** admissions@artcenter.edu
Fax: (626) 795-0578   **Internet:** www.artcenter.edu

Institution Description: Art Center College of Design is a private, independent, nonprofit college. *Enrollment:* 1,501. *Degrees awarded:* Baccalaureate, master's.

Accreditation: *Regional:* WASC-Sr. *Professional:* art

History: Established in Los Angeles as Art Center School and offered first instruction at postsecondary level 1930; incorporated 1932; awarded first degree (baccalaureate) 1950; adopted present name 1965; moved to present location 1976.

Institutional Structure: *Governing board:* Board of Trustees. Representation: 15 outside trustees, 2 administrators, and president of the college. 15 voting. *Composition of institution:* Administrators 14 men / 17 women. Academic affairs headed by chairman, academic studies. Management/business/finances directed by vice president and treasurer. *Faculty representation:* Full-time instructional faculty 57.

Calendar: Trimesters. Academic year Sept. to May. Freshmen admitted Sept., Feb., June. Degrees conferred and formal commencement May, Sept., Jan.

Characteristics of Freshmen: 450 applicants (264 men / 156 women). 32.4% of applicants accepted. 74.2% of admitted students enrolled full-time.

Admission: Rolling admissions plan. Apply as early as 6 months prior to enrollment. *Requirements:* Graduation from secondary school or GED. Portfolio. Minimum GPA 2.5 Lowest acceptable secondary school class standing 50th percentile. *Entrance tests:* College Board SAT or ACT composite. *For transfer students:* 2.5 GPA; 42 hours maximum transfer credit. Advanced placement on basis of portfolio assessment.

Degree Requirements: 159 credit hours; 2.5 GPA; 4 terms in residence, academic studies requirement. *Grading system:* A–F; withdraw (carries time limit).

Distinctive Educational Programs: *Distinctive programs:* Nondegree evening division.

Degrees Conferred: 361 *baccalaureate:* visual and performing arts 353, architecture and related services 8; 18 *master's*.

Fees and Other Expenses: *Full-time tuition per academic year 2004–2005:* $24,125. *Room and board per academic year:* $10,528.

Financial Aid: Aid from institutionally generated funds is provided on the basis of academic merit, financial need.

Financial aid to full-time, first-time undergraduate students: 29% received federal grants averaging $4,542; 11% state/local grants; 21% institutional grants; 40% loans averaging $20,670.

Departments and Teaching Staff: Faculty members are unranked. *Instructors* 72, *part-time teachers* 290.

Total instructional faculty: 126 FTE. *Degrees held by full-time faculty:* baccalaureate 98%, master's 15%, doctorate 5%. *Student-to-faculty ratio:* 9:1.

Enrollment: Total enrollment 1,501. Undergraduate 1,379 (men 28.2%, women 41.8%).

Characteristics of Student Body: *Ethnic/racial makeup:* Black non-Hispanic: 1.3%; American Indian or Alaska Native: .7%; Asian or Pacific Islander: 34.7%; Hispanic: 9.8%; White non-Hispanic: 38.4%.

International Students: Students from Europe, Asia, Latin America, Africa, Canada, Australia. Social and cultural programs available to aid students whose native language is not English. No financial aid specifically designated for international students.

Student Life: No on-campus housing. *Special regulations:* Registered cars with decal permitted. *Surrounding community:* Pasadena population 130,000. Los Angeles, 9 miles from campus, is nearest metropolitan area. Served by airport 15 miles from campus; passenger rail service 5 miles from campus.

Library Collections: 70,000 volumes. 60,000 slides; 350 current periodical subscriptions. Computer work stations available. Students have access to the Internet at no charge.

Most important holdings include fine arts, graphic design, photography-film collections.

Buildings and Grounds: Campus area 175 acres.

Chief Executive Officer: Richard Koshalek, President.

Address admission inquiries to Kit Baron, Director of Admissions.

Art Institute of California - Los Angeles

2900 31st Street
Santa Monica, California 90405-3035
Tel: (310) 752-4700   **E-mail:** ailaadm@aila.aii.edu
Fax: (310) 752-4708   **Internet:** www.aila.aii.edu

Institution Description: The Art Institute of California - Los Angeles is an institution for career preparation in the visual and culinary arts. The institute is a member of the Art Institutes System. Associate degree programs are offered in: culinary arts, graphic design, multimedia and web design, video production. Bachelor's degree programs include culinary management, game art and design, graphic art and design, media arts and animation. *Degrees offered:* Associate, baccalaureate.

Accreditation: *Nonregional:* ACICS. *Professional:* art, interior design

History: The institute is one of the Art Institutes with 31 locations throughout North America. The location in Santa Monica was opened in 1997.

Calendar: Each program is offered on a year-round basis, allowing students to continue working uninterrupted toward their degrees. Quarters. Formal commencement twice per year. Quarterly design portfolio shows for graduates.

Characteristics of Freshmen: 934 applicants (571 men / 363 women). 47.9% of applicants admitted. 85.8% of admitted students enrolled full-time.

Admission: Applicants are accepted on a quarterly (rolling) basis. *Requirements:* High school graduation or GED; interview.

Degree Requirements: Students must complete 112 quarter credits to be eligible for the associate degree and 192 quarter credits for the bachelor's degree; cumulative 2.0 GPA; passing grade for all coursework; completion of portfolio requirements.

Degrees Conferred: 263 *associate*; 153 *baccalaureate*. Bachelor's degrees awarded in top five disciplines: visual and performing arts 60, communications technologies/technicians and support services 52; computer and information sciences and support services 27; personal and culinary services 11; communication, journalism, and related programs 3.

Fees and Other Expenses: *Full-time tuition and fees per academic year 2004–05:* $23,872. *Books and supplies:* $1,680. *Room and board per academic year:* $11,168.

Financial Aid: Institution has a Program Participation Agreement with the U.S. Department of Education for eligible students to receive Pell Grants and other federal aid.

Financial aid to full-time, first-time undergraduate students: 53% received federal grants averaging $3,655; 27% state/local grants averaging $8,542; 59% institutional grants averaging $1,295; 87% loans averaging $10,643.

Departments and Teaching Staff: 50% of faculty hold terminal degrees. *Student-to-faculty ratio:* 16:1.

Enrollment: Total enrollment 1,939 (men 64.9%, women 35.1%).

Characteristics of Student Body: *Ethnic/racial makeup:* Black non-Hispanic: 7.9%; American Indian or Alaska Native: .1%; Asian or Pacific Islander: 13%; Hispanic: 29.2%; White non-Hispanic: 21.6%; unknown: 27.1%.

International Students: 194 nonresident aliens enrolled fall 2004. Social programs available for international students. English as a Second Language Program. No financial aid specifically designated for international students.

Student Life: Off-campus apartments available. *Special services:* counseling; tutoring; disability services;. A variety of student clubs available. *Surrounding community:* Los Angeles/Santa Monica served by mass transit bus and train system.

Library Collections: 10,000 volumes. 200 current periodical subscriptions. Computer work stations available.

Buildings and Grounds: Campus is located in Santa Monica, a seaside community of Los Angeles County.

Chief Executive Officer: Laura Soloff, President.

Address admission inquiries to Byron Chung, Director of Admissions.

Art Institute of California - San Francisco

1170 Market Street
San Francisco, California 94102-4908
Tel: (415) 865-0198   **E-mail:** aisfadm@aii.edu
Fax: (415) 863-6344   **Internet:** www.aisf.aii.edu

Institution Description: The Art Institute of California - San Francisco offers career-focused degree programs in advertising, graphic design, media arts and animation, game art and design, visual and game programming, interactive media design fashion design, fashion marketing and management, and interior design. The institute is one of the Art Institutes with 31 education institutions located throughout North America. *Degrees offered:* Associate, baccalaureate.

Accreditation: *Nonregional:* ACICS. *Professional:* art, interior design

History: The institute was established in 1998.

Calendar: Quarters. Formal commencement twice per year. Quarterly design portfolio shows for graduates.

Characteristics of Freshmen: 608 applicants (325 men / 283 women). 45.7% of applicants admitted. 91.4% of admitted students enrolled full-time.

Admission: Applicants are accepted on a quarterly (rolling) basis. *Requirements:* High school graduation or GED; interview.

Degree Requirements: Students must complete 112 quarter credits to be eligible for the associate degree and 192 quarter credits for the bachelor's degree; cumulative 2.0 GPA; passing grade for all coursework; completion of portfolio requirements.

Degrees Conferred: 23 *associate*; 55 *baccalaureate.* Bachelor's degrees awarded in top disciplines: visual and performing arts 52, communications technologies/technicians and support services 2; business, management, marketing, and related support services 1.

Fees and Other Expenses: *Full-time tuition and fees per academic year 2004–05:* $23,872. *Books and supplies:* $2,950. *Room and board per academic year:* $9,878.

Financial Aid: Institution has a Program Participation Agreement with the U.S. Department of Education for eligible students to receive Pell Grants and other federal aid.

Financial aid to full-time, first-time undergraduate students: 24% received federal grants averaging $11,439; 16% state/local grants averaging $2,431; 26% institutional grants averaging $1,843; 82% loans averaging $9,473.

Departments and Teaching Staff: *Total instructional faculty:* 108. 50% hold terminal degrees. *Student-to-faculty ratio:* 16:1.

Enrollment: Total enrollment 901 (men 61.4%, women 38.6%).

Characteristics of Student Body: *Ethnic/racial makeup:* Black non-Hispanic: 6.9%; American Indian or Alaska Native: .1%; Asian or Pacific Islander: 17.6%; Hispanic: 16.8%; White non-Hispanic: 36%; unknown: 20.4%.

International Students: 60 nonresident aliens enrolled fall 2004. Social programs available for international students. English as a Second Language Program. No financial aid specifically designated for international students.

Student Life: Off-campus apartments available. *Special services:* counseling; tutoring; disability services;. A variety of student clubs available. *Surrounding community:* served by mass transit bus and train system. *Student publication: Evolve,* published quarterly.

Library Collections: 8,000 volumes. 125 current periodical subscriptions. 5 computer work stations.

Buildings and Grounds: Campus is located in downtown San Francisco in buildings located in San Francisco's Civic Center neighborhood.

Chief Executive Officer: Charles Nagele, President.

Address admission inquiries to Daniel Cardenas, Director of Admissions.

Art Institute of California - San Diego

7650 Mission Valley Road
San Diego, California 92108-4423
Tel: (866) 275-2422   **E-mail:** aicadm@aicsd.aii.edu
Fax: (619) 291-3206   **Internet:** www.aicsd.aii.edu

Institution Description: The Art Institute of California - San Diego offers career-focused degree programs in advertising, graphic design, media arts and animation, game art and design, visual and game programming, interactive media design fashion design, fashion marketing and management, and interior design. *Degrees awarded:* Associate, baccalaureate.

Accreditation: *Nonregional:* ACICS. *Professional:* art, interior design

History: The institute is one of the Art Institutes with 31 education institutions located throughout North America.

Calendar: Quarters. Formal commencement twice per year. Quarterly design portfolio shows for graduates.

Admission: Applicants are accepted on a quarterly (rolling) basis. *Requirements:* High school graduation or GED; interview.

Degree Requirements: Students must complete 112 quarter credits to be eligible for the associate degree and 192 quarter credits for the bachelor's degree; cumulative 2.0 GPA; passing grade for all coursework; completion of portfolio requirements.

Degrees Conferred: 25 *associate*; 117 *baccalaureate.* Bachelor's degrees awarded in top disciplines: visual and performing arts 82; communication, journalism, and related programs 26; computer and information sciences and support services 9.

Fees and Other Expenses: *Full-time tuition and fees per academic year 2004–05:* $17,904. *Books and supplies:* $1,260. *Room and board per academic year:* $6,900.

Financial Aid: Institution has a Program Participation Agreement with the U.S. Department of Education for eligible students to receive Pell Grants and other federal aid.

Financial aid to full-time, first-time undergraduate students: 23% received federal grants averaging $2,912; 9% state/local grants averaging $8,073; 16% institutional grants averaging $1,561; 46% loans averaging $4,923.

Departments and Teaching Staff: 50% of faculty hold terminal degrees. *Student-to-faculty ratio:* 16:1.

Enrollment: Total enrollment 1,329 (men 58.2%, women 41.8%).

Characteristics of Student Body: *Ethnic/racial makeup:* Black non-Hispanic: 3.7%; American Indian or Alaska Native: .1%; Asian or Pacific Islander: 13.3%; Hispanic: 20.8%; White non-Hispanic: 46.9%; unknown: 10.3%.

International Students: 52 nonresident aliens enrolled fall 2004. Social programs available for international students. English as a Second Language Program. No financial aid specifically designated for international students.

Student Life: Off-campus apartments available. *Special services:* counseling; tutoring; disability services;. A variety of student clubs available. *Surrounding community:* San Diego served by mass transit bus system.

Library Collections: 12,000 volumes. 300 current periodical subscriptions. Computer work stations available.

Buildings and Grounds: Campus is located in the Mission Valley area of San Diego.

Chief Executive Officer: Bill Soulis, President.

Address admission inquiries to Sandy Park, Director of Admissions.

Azusa Pacific University

901 East Alosta Avenue
Azusa, California 91702-7000
Tel: (626) 969-3434   **E-mail:** admiss@apu.edu
Fax: (626) 969-7180   **Internet:** www.apu.edu

Institution Description: Azusa Pacific University (Azusa Pacific College until 1981) is a private, independent, nonprofit institution. *Enrollment:* 8,162. *Degrees awarded:* Associate, baccalaureate, master's, doctorate.

Accreditation: *Regional:* WASC-Sr. *Professional:* nursing, nursing education, physical therapy, social work, teacher education

History: Established and chartered as Training School for Christian Workers and offered first instruction at postsecondary level 1899; awarded first degree (baccalaureate) 1946; merged with Los Angeles Pacific College and changed name to Azusa Pacific College 1965; adopted present name 1981.

Institutional Structure: *Governing board:* Board of Directors of Azusa Pacific University. Extrainstitutional representation: 38 directors, including 1 alumnus. All voting. *Composition of institution:* Administrators 5 men. Academic affairs headed by vice president for academic affairs. Management/business/finances directed by vice president for financial affairs. *Faculty representation:* Full-time instructional faculty 289. Academic governance bodies, Council of Faculty and faculty as a whole, meet an average of 18 per year.

Calendar: Semesters (4-1-4 plan). Academic year Sept. to May. Freshmen admitted Sept., Jan., June, July. Degrees conferred and formal commencements May, Aug. Summer session of 2 terms from June to Aug.

Characteristics of Freshmen: 73% of applicants accepted. 44% of accepted applicants enrolled.

90% (791 students) submitted SAT scores; 37% (329 students) submitted ACT scores. *25th percentile*: SAT Verbal 500, SAT Math 500; ACT Composite 20. *75th percentile*: SAT Verbal 610, SAT Math 600; ACT Composite 26.

39% of entering freshmen expected to graduate within 5 years. 70% of freshmen from California. Freshmen from 36 state and 3 foreign countries.

Admission: Rolling admissions plan. For fall acceptance, apply as early as Sept. 1 of previous year, but not later than Aug. 15 of year of enrollment. Early acceptance available. *Requirements:* Either graduation from accredited secondary school with college preparatory curriculum or GED. Additional requirements for some programs. Minimum GPA 2.5 Lowest acceptable secondary school class standing 40th percentile. *Entrance tests:* College Board SAT or ACT Composite. *For transfer students:* 2.0 minimum GPA, 96 hours maximum transfer credit; from 2-year accredited institution 64 hours.

College credit and advanced placement for postsecondary-level work completed in secondary school. Tutoring available. Noncredit developmental courses offered during regular academic year.

Degree Requirements: *For all associate degrees:* 60 credit hours. *For all baccalaureate degrees:* 126 credit hours; chapel attendance 3 times weekly; 2 courses in physical education; 4 semesters of student ministry assignments; 8 religion courses. *For all undergraduate degrees:* 2.0 GPA; 2 terms in residence; distribution requirements.

Fulfillment of some degree requirements and exemption from some beginning courses possible by passing College Board CLEP, AP. *Grading system:* A–F; pass; withdraw; incomplete.

Distinctive Educational Programs: *For undergraduates:* Free university. Special facilities for using telecommunications in the classroom. *For graduate students:* Weekend classes. *Available to all students:* Paid internships available for business majors. Flexible meeting places and schedules, including off-campus centers, evening classes. Facilities and programs for independent research, including individual majors, tutorials. *Other distinctive programs:* Baccalaureate completion program in nursing for registered nurses. Associate degree students complete traditional college courses through prerecorded videotape Universal College Program.

Degrees Conferred: 1,041 *baccalaureate* (B), 1,227 *master's* (M), 22 *doctorate* (D): area and ethnic studies 16 (B); biological/life sciences 29 (B); business/marketing 243 (B), 92 (M); communications/communication technologies 85 (B); computer and information sciences 21 (B), 44 (M); education 17 (B), 911 (M); 3 (D); English 26 (B); foreign languages and literature 8 (B); liberal arts/general studies 313 (B); mathematics 10 (B); philosophy, religion, theology 59 (B), 53 (M), 2 (D); physical sciences 3 (B); protective services/public administration 15 (B); psychology 59 (B), 38 (M), 15 (D); social sciences and history 66 (B), 47 (M); visual and performing arts 61 (B), 5 (M). *First-professional:* theology 25.

Fees and Other Expenses: *Full-time tuition per academic year 2004–05:* $20,006 undergraduate; $450 per unit graduate. *Required fees:* $660. *Room and board per academic year:* $6,132.

Financial Aid: Aid from institutionally generated funds is provided on the basis of academic merit, financial need, athletic ability, other considerations. Institution has a Program Participation Agreement with the U.S. Department of Education for eligible students to receive Pell Grants and other federal aid.

Financial aid to full-time, first-time undergraduate students: need-based scholarships/grants totaling $22,657,338, self-help $14,408,702, parent loans $7,403,893, tuition waivers $1,536,510, athletic awards $1,541,005; non-need-based scholarships/grants totaling $2,633,846, self-help 2,040,750, parent loans $6,921,194.

Departments and Teaching Staff: *Professors* 38, *associate professors* 68, *assistant professors* 46, *instructors* 5, *part-time faculty* 132.

Total instructional faculty: 765 (full-time 289, part-time 526). Total number with doctorate, first-professional, or other terminal degree: 214. Student-to-faculty ratio: 15:1.

Enrollment: Total enrollment 8,162. Undergraduate full-time 1,337 men / 2,433 women, part-time 199m / 472w; graduate full-time 210m / 424w, part-time 473m / 1,951m; first-professional full-time 79m / 13, part-time 56m / 15w. *Transfer students:* in-state into lower division 80m / 122w, upper division 133m / 268w, graduate 33m / 66w; out-of-state into lower division 25m / 23w, upper division 8m / 13w, graduate 6m / 4w.

Characteristics of Student Body: *Ethnic/racial makeup:* number of Black non-Hispanic: 141; American Indian or Alaska Native: 15; Asian or Pacific Islander: 212; Hispanic: 515; White non-Hispanic: 3,254; unknown: 226. *Age distribution:* number under 18: 1; 18–19: 650; 20–21: 1,717; 22–24: 1,305; 25–29: 224; 30–34: 170, 35–39: 122; 40–49: 175; 50–64: 73.

International Students: 261 nonresident aliens enrolled fall 2004. Programs available to aid students whose native language is not English: Social, cultural, financial. English as a Second Language Program.

Student Life: On-campus residence halls house 58% of student body. Residence halls for men only constitute 50% of such space, for women only 50%. Housing available for married students. 30% of married students request institutional housing; 15% are so housed. *Intercollegiate athletics:* men only: baseball, basketball, cross-country, football, soccer, tennis, track; women only: basketball, cross-country, tennis, track, volleyball. *Special regulations:* Cars permitted without restrictions. Quiet hours begin 10pm Sun.–Thurs. *Special services:* Learning Resources Center, medical services, campus van and bus service. *Student publications: Clause,* a weekly newspaper; a yearbook. *Surrounding community:* Azusa population 30,000. Los Angeles, 55 miles from campus, is nearest metropolitan area. Served by mass transit bus system; airport 25 miles from campus; passenger rail service 40 miles from campus.

Library Collections: 185,000 volumes. 613,100 microform; 148,500 audiovisual materials; 1,800 periodicals. Online catalog. Students have access to online information retrieval systems and the Internet.

Most important holdings include Fullerton Collection (books and serials on the 19th century American West focusing on the California Gold Rush, overland journeys to the Pacific coast, and the fur trade); Francis J. Weber Collection (books on history of the Catholic Church in the U.S.); Clifford Drury Collection (books pertaining to the Protestant missionary in the West).

Buildings and Grounds: Campus area 60 acres.

Chief Executive Officer: Dr. Jon Wallace, President.

Address admission inquiries to Deana Porterfield, Associate Vice President for Enrollment.

Bethany College of the Assemblies of God

800 Bethany Drive
Scotts Valley, California 95066-2898

Tel: (831) 438-3800   **E-mail:** info@bethany.edu
Fax: (831) 438-4517   **Internet:** www.bethany.edu

Institution Description: Bethany College is a private college affiliated with the Assemblies of God. *Enrollment:* 597. *Degrees awarded:* Associate, baccalaureate, master's. Post-baccalaureate certificates also awarded.

Accreditation: *Regional:* WASC-Sr.

History: Established as Glad Tidings Bible Training School 1919; offered first instruction at postsecondary level 1921; incorporated 1922; changed name to Glad Tidings Bible Institute 1924; became Bethany Bible College 1955; awarded first degree (baccalaureate) 1956; adopted present name 1989.

Institutional Structure: *Governing board:* Board of Trustees of Bethany College, Scotts Valley. Extrainstitutional representation: 28 trustees; institutional representation: president of the college, 9 ex officio. All voting. *Composition of institution:* Administrators 1 woman / 13 men. Academic affairs headed by academic dean. Management/business/finances directed by vice president for business. Full-time instructional faculty 25. Academic governance body, Academic Governance Committee, meets an average of 4 times per year.

Calendar: Semesters. Academic year Aug. to May. Freshmen admitted Aug., Jan. Degrees conferred and formal commencement May. Summer session of 2 terms from early June to mid-July.

Characteristics of Freshmen: 434 applicants (172 men, 262 women). 59.2% admitted; 37.7% enrolled full-time.

58% (63 students) submitted SAT scores; 20% (22 students) submitted ACT scores. *25th percentile:* SAT I Verbal 443, AT I Math 435; ACT Composite 16, ACT English 17, ACT Math 15. *75th percentile:* SAT I Verbal 550, SAT I Math 540; ACT Composite 21, ACT English 21, ACT Math 20.

Admission: Rolling admissions plan. For fall acceptance, apply as early as 1 year prior to enrollment, but not later than Aug. 1 of year of enrollment. Early acceptance available. *Requirements:* Either graduation from accredited secondary school or GED. Minimum GPA 2.0. Christian conversion. *For transfer students:* 2.0 minimum GPA recommended; from 4-year accredited institution 100 credit hours maximum transfer credit; from 2-year accredited institution 62 hours; correspondence/extension students 15 hours.

College credit for extrainstitutional learning on basis of ACE *2006 Guide to the Evaluation of Educational Experiences in the Armed Services.*

Remedial English courses offered during regular academic year; credit given.

Degree Requirements: 124 credit hours; 2.0 GPA; 1 year in residence; daily chapel attendance; 2 terms physical education; distribution requirements.

Fulfillment of some degree requirements and exemption from some beginning courses possible by passing College Board CLEP. *Grading system:* A–F; pass-fail; withdraw; incomplete.

Distinctive Educational Programs: Evening classes. Interdisciplinary program leading to California teaching credential. External degree program.

Degrees Conferred: 2 *associate*; 85 *baccalaureate*; 3 *master's*; 13 *post-baccalaureate certificates.* Bachelor's degrees awarded in top five disciplines: theology and ministerial studies 31; social sciences 12; multidisciplinary studies 11; education 10; business, management, marketing, and related support services 6.

Fees and Other Expenses: *Full-time tuition per academic year 2004–05:* $13,830. *Room and board per academic year:* $5,940. *Books and supplies:* $1,260.

Financial Aid: Aid from institutionally generated funds is awarded on the basis of academic merit, other considerations. Institution has a Program Participation Agreement with the U.S. Department of Education for eligible students to receive Pell Grants and other federal aid.

Financial aid to full-time, first-time undergraduate students: 36% received federal grants averaging $3,366; 18% state/local grants averaging $8,688; 54% institutional grants averaging $4,444; 66% loans averaging $5,968.

Departments and Teaching Staff: *Professors* 8, *associate professors* 5, *assistant professors* 4, *instructors* 17, *part-time teachers* 38.

Total instructional faculty: 30 FTE. Degrees held by full-time faculty: doctorate 53%, master's 47%.

Enrollment: Total enrollment 597. Undergraduate 535 (30.3% men, 60.7% women).

Characteristics of Student Body: *Ethnic/racial makeup:* Black non-Hispanic: 9.5%; American Indian or Alaska Native: .7%; Asian or Pacific Islander: 3%; Hispanic: 14.2%; White non-Hispanic: 64.9%; unknown: 6.2%.

International Students: 8 nonresident aliens enrolled fall 2003. No programs to aid students whose native language is not English. No financial aid specifically designated for international students.

Student Life: On-campus residence halls house 71% of student body. Residence halls for men only constitute 47% of such space, for women only 53%. Housing available for married students. *Intercollegiate athletics:* men only: baseball, basketball, football; women only: softball, volleyball. *Special regulations:* Cars with decals permitted on campus in designated areas only. Curfews begin midnight Mon.–Thurs., 1am Fri.–Sun. Residence hall visitation until 11pm Mon.–Thurs., midnight Fri.–Sun. Visitation is limited to lobbies. *Special services:* Medical services. *Student publications: Dialog*, a biweekly newspaper; *Tidings*, a yearbook. *Surrounding community:* San Jose; 25 miles from campus, is nearest metropolitan area. Served by airport 25 miles from campus.

Library Collections: 65,000 volumes. 3,750 microforms, 3,000 audiovisual materials, 860 current periodical subscriptions. Students have access to online information retrieval services and the Internet.

Buildings and Grounds: Campus area 40 acres.

Chief Executive Officer: Dr. Maximo Rossi, Jr., President.

Address admission inquiries to Dr. Martin Harris, Vice President for Enrollment Management.

Biola University

13800 Biola Avenue
La Mirada, California 90639-0001
Tel: (562) 903-6000   **E-mail:** admissions@biola.edu
Fax: (562) 903-4709   **Internet:** www.biola.edu

Institution Description: Biola University is a private, independent, interdenominational institution comprised of the School of Arts and Sciences, School of Business, School of Continuing Studies, Rosemead School of Psychology, School of Intercultural Studies, and Talbot School of Theology. *Enrollment:* 5,370. *Degrees awarded:* Baccalaureate, first-professional (divinity), master's, doctorate.

Accreditation: *Regional:* WASC-Sr. *Professional:* art, business, clinical psychology, music, nursing, teacher education, theology

History: Established as the Bible Institute of Los Angeles, 1908; offered first instruction at postsecondary level and changed name to Biola Bible College 1947; awarded first degree (baccalaureate) 1951; changed name to Biola Schools and College, 1956, to Biola College 1972; became a university and adopted present name 1981.

Institutional Structure: *Governing board:* Board of Trustees. Extrainstitutional representation: 21 trustees, including 6 alumni; institutional representation: president of the university. 1 ex officio. All voting. *Composition of institution:* Administrators 70 men / 66 women. Academic affairs headed by provost and senior vice president for academic affairs. Management/business/finances directed by vice president for business and financial affairs. Full-time instructional faculty 177. Academic governance body, Department Chairman's Council, meets an average of 16 times per year.

Calendar: Semesters (4-1-4 plan). Academic year Aug. to May. Freshmen admitted Sept., Feb., June. Degrees conferred May, Dec. Summer session of 2 terms from late May to mid-July.

Characteristics of Freshmen: 78% of applicants admitted; 34% admitted and enrolled.

80% (644 students) submitted SAT scores; 25% (211 students) submitted ACT scores. *25th percentile:* SAT Verbal 510, SAT Math 500; ACT Composite 22. *75th percentile:* SAT Verbal 630, SAT Math 620; ACT Composite 27.

56% of freshmen from California. Freshmen from 29 states.

Admission: Rolling admissions plan. For fall acceptance, apply as early as Oct. 15 of previous year, but not later than June 1 of year of enrollment. *Requirements:* Either graduation from accredited secondary school with 16 units (12 in academic subjects which must include 3 English, 2 in a foreign language, 2 mathematics, 2 social studies, 1 laboratory science, and 2 in related areas; 4 units in academic electives); or GED. 2 additional units in foreign language recommended. Minimum GPA 2.8. Lowest acceptable secondary school class standing 50th percentile. All applicants must be evangelical Christians. *Entrance tests:* College Board SAT or ACT composite. For foreign students TOEFL. *For transfer students:* 2.5 minimum GPA; from 4-year accredited institution 100 hours maximum transfer credit; from 2-year accredited institution 70 hours; for extension students 30 hours; for correspondence students 12 hours. College credit and advanced placement for postsecondary-level work completed in secondary school; college credit for extrainstitutional learning on basis of ACE *2006 Guide to the Evaluation of Educational Experiences in the Armed Services.* Tutoring available. Noncredit remedial course available.

Degree Requirements: *For baccalaureate degrees:* 130–142 credit hours; 2.0 GPA; 30 hours in residence; chapel attendance 3 times per week; 4 units in physical education courses (waived if entering at age 21 or above); 30 units of Biblical studies or theology; general education requirements.

Fulfillment of some degree requirements and exemption from some beginning courses possible by passing departmental examinations, College Board CLEP, AP. *Grading system:* A–F; withdraw (deadline after which pass-fail is appended to withdraw).

Distinctive Educational Programs: Interdisciplinary programs in American studies, communication studies, intercultural studies. Study abroad in Australia, China, England, Egypt, Honduras, Israel, Mexico, Russia, Uganda. Student ministry program gives students in-service in a variety of outreach opportunities. *Other distinctive programs:* Credit and noncredit continuing education. Adult degree-completion program.

ROTC: Army offered in cooperation with University of California, Los Angeles; Air Force with University of Southern California and California State University, Long Beach.

Degrees Conferred: 690 *baccalaureate* (B); 254 *master's* (M); 39 *doctorate:* biological/life sciences 15 (B); business/marketing 136 (B); 30 (M); communications/communication technologies 96 (B); computer and information sciences 9 (B); education 61 (B); 50 (M); English 29 (B); foreign languages and literature 1 (B); health professions and related sciences 45 (B); liberal arts/general studies 14 (B); mathematics 3 (B); philosophy, religion, theology 101 (B), 152 (M), 19 (D); physical sciences 5 (B); psychology 65 (B), 22 (M), 20 (D); social sciences and history 61 (B); visual and performing arts 49 (B). 27 *first-professional:* theology/divinity.

Fees and Other Expenses: *Full-time tuition per academic year 2004–05:* undergraduate $20,932, graduate $6,516. *Room and board per academic year:* $6,800.

Financial Aid: Aid from institutionally generated funds is provided on the basis of academic merit, financial need, athletic ability, other criteria. Undergraduate need-based scholarships/grants: $20,539,969, self-help $10,767,294, parent loans $4,195,698, athletic awards $433,404; non-need-based scholarships/grants $1,132,886, self-help $2,470,279, athletic awards $129,515.

Departments and Teaching Staff: *Total instructional faculty:* 375 (full-time 177, part-time 198; women 45, men 130). Student-to-faculty ratio: 18:1. 150 faculty members hold terminal degrees.

Enrollment: Total enrollment 5,370. Undergraduate full-time 1,207 men / 1,957 women; graduate full-time 236m / 261w, part-time 518m / 413w; first-professional full-time 193m / 19w, part-time 123m / 12w. *Transfer students:* 225.

Characteristics of Student Body: *Ethnic/racial makeup:* number of Black non-Hispanic: 193; American Indian or Alaska Native: 21; Asian or Pacific Islander: 651; Hispanic: 457; White non-Hispanic: 3,571; unknown: 147.

International Students: 330 nonresident aliens enrolled fall 2004. English as a Second Language Program available.

Student Life: On-campus residence halls and apartments house 50% of student body. Dormitories for men only constitute 37% of such space, for women only 63%. *Intercollegiate athletics:* men only: baseball, basketball, cross-country, soccer, swimming and diving; track and field; women only: basketball, soccer, softball, swimming, tennis, track and field, volleyball. *Special regulations:* Registered cars permitted on campus. Modest, clean, conservative dress. *Special services:* Career and Learning Assistance Services, medical services. *Student publications, radio: Chimes*, a weekly newspaper. Radio station KBBK. *Surrounding community:* La Mirada population 42,000. Los Angeles; 25 miles from campus, is nearest metropolitan area. Served by airport and passenger rail service, each 25 miles from campus.

Publications: *Journal of Psychology and Theology,* an evangelical forum for the integration of psychology and theology; *Christian Education Journal.*

Library Collections: 279,560 volumes including bound books, serial backfiles, electronic documents, and government documents not in separate collections. Current serial subscriptions: 1,052 paper, 541,582 microform. 10,297 recordings; 110 compact discs. Online catalog. 50 computer work stations. Students have access to the Internet at no charge.

Most important special holdings include collections on Bible and theology; psychology; Evangelical Christianity. Total budget for books and materials 2004–05: $179,218.

Buildings and Grounds: Campus area 95 acres. *New buildings:* Biola Library completed Hope Hall (residence) 2003.

Chief Executive Officer: Dr. Clyde Cook, President.

Address undergraduate admission inquiries to Andre Stephens, Director of Undergraduate Admissions; graduate admission inquiries to Roy Allinson, Director of Graduate Admissions.

Brooks Institute of Photography

1321 Alameda Padre Serra
Santa Barbara, California 93103
Tel: (805) 966-3888   **E-mail:** admissions@brooks.edu
Fax: (805) 565-1386   **Internet:** www.brooks.edu

Institution Description: Brooks Institute of Photography is a private institution. *Enrollment:* 2,154. *Degrees awarded:* Baccalaureate, master's.

Accreditation: *Nonregional:* ACICS.

History: Established as Brooks Institute of Photography and offered first instruction at postsecondary level 1945; incorporated 1952; awarded first degree (baccalaureate) 1961.

Calendar: Trimesters. Freshmen admitted Jan., Mar., Apr., July, Sept., Oct. Degrees conferred and formal commencements Jan., Apr., July, Aug., Oct., Feb. No summer session.

Characteristics of Freshmen: 583 applicants (282 men; 301 women). 100% of applicants admitted. 40.7% of admitted students enrolled full-time.

Admission: Rolling admissions plan. *Requirements:* 9 semester hours in general education from an accredited college, including English and liberal arts. Minimum GPA 2.0. *For transfer students:* 2.0 minimum GPA; from 2- and 4-year accredited institutions, maximum transfer credit limited only by residence requirements.

Degree Requirements: 153 semester hours; 2.0 GPA; 15 hours in residence; graduate's exhibition; core requirements.

Fulfillment of some degree requirements and exemption from some beginning courses possible by passing College Board CLEP, AP.

College credit for extrainstitutional learning on basis of ACE *2006 Guide to the Evaluation of Educational Experiences in the Armed Guide,* portfolio and faculty assessments. *Grading system:* A–F; withdraw (carries time limit).

Distinctive Educational Programs: Internships. Weekend classes. Special facilities for using telecommunications in the classroom. Individual majors. Study abroad at Royal Melbourne Institute of Technology (Australia).

Degrees Conferred: 12 *associate;* 192 *baccalaureate;* 10 *master's.* Bachelor's degrees awarded in the following disciplines: visual and performing arts 178; communication, journalism, and related programs14.

Fees and Other Expenses: *Full-time tuition per academic year 2004–05:* $22,200. *Room and board per academic year:* $12,432 (off-campus). *Other expenses:* $8,628.

Financial Aid: Aid from institutionally generated funds is provided on the basis of academic merit, financial need.

Institution has a Program Participation Agreement with the U.S. Department of Education for eligible students to receive Pell Grants and other federal aid.

Financial aid to full-time, first-time undergraduate students: 25% received federal grants averaging $3,142; 9% state/local grants averaging $10,571; 61% loans averaging $6,013.

Departments and Teaching Staff: Faculty members are unranked. Still photography *instructors* 13, *part-time teachers* 0; general education 0, 12; motion picture 6, 0. *Total instructional faculty:* 31. Degrees held by full-time faculty: baccalaureate 58%, master's 26%.

Enrollment: Total enrollment 2,154. Undergraduate 2,065 (53.2% men, 46.8% women).

Characteristics of Student Body: *Ethnic/racial makeup:* Black non-Hispanic: .1.3%; Asian or Pacific Islander: 2.9%; Hispanic: 5.1%; White non-Hispanic: 52.2%; unknown: 35.2%.

International Students: 62 nonresident aliens enrolled fall 2003. No programs available to aid students whose native language is not English. No financial aid specifically designated for international students.

Student Life: No on-campus housing. *Surrounding community:* Santa Barbara population 85,000. Los Angeles, 100 miles from campus, is nearest metropolitan area. Served by mass transit bus system; airport 12 miles from campus; passenger rail service 3 miles from campus.

Library Collections: 10,000 volumes. Audiovisual materials; 200 current periodical subscriptions.

Most important holdings include a collection of photographic art and science publications. Entire collection relates to photography.

Buildings and Grounds: Campus area 31 acres.

Chief Executive Officer: Greg J. Strick, President.

Address admission inquiries to Ted Girgus, Vice President, Marketing and Admissions.

California Baptist University

8432 Magnolia Avenue
Riverside, California 92504
Tel: (951) 343-4212   **E-mail:** admissions@calbaptist.edu
Fax: (951) 343-4525   **Internet:** www.calbaptist.edu

Institution Description: California Baptist University, formerly named California Baptist College, is a four-year liberal arts institution affiliated with Southern Baptist General Convention. *Enrollment:* 2,905. *Degrees awarded:* Baccalaureate, master's.

Accreditation: *Regional:* WASC-Sr.

History: Established in El Monte and offered first instruction at postsecondary level 1950; chartered and awarded first degree (baccalaureate) 1954; moved to present location 1955; became California Baptist University in 1998. *See* O.T. Brown and L.E. Nelson, *It's a Great Day* (Riverside, CA: California Baptist College Press, 1970) for further information.

Institutional Structure: *Governing board:* Board of Trustees of California Baptist University. Representation: 36 trustees. All voting. *Composition of institution:* Administrators 6 men. Academic affairs headed by Provost and Vice president for Academic Affairs. Management/business/finances directed by Vice President for Finance and Administration. Full-time instructional faculty 88. Academic governance body, the faculty, meets an average of 8 times per year.

Calendar: Semesters (4-4-1 plan). Academic year July to June. Freshmen admitted Aug., Jan., May. Degrees conferred May, Aug., Dec. Formal commencement May. Summer sessions in May-June and July-Aug.

Characteristics of Freshmen: 734 applicants admitted; 421 admitted and enrolled.

68% (372 students) submitted SAT scores; 32% (178 students) submitted ACT scores. *25th percentile:* SAT Verbal 474, SAT Math 478; ACT Composite 18, ACT English 16, ACT Math 17. *75th percentile:* SAT Verbal 535, SAT Math 523; ACT Composite 19, ACT English 18, ACT Math 18.

53% of freshmen expected to graduate within 5 years. 95% of freshmen from California. Freshmen from 31 states and 15 foreign countries.

Admission: Rolling admissions plan. For fall acceptance, apply as early as 1 year but not later than 1 month prior to enrollment. Early acceptance available. *Requirements:* Either graduation from an accredited secondary school or GED. College preparatory curriculum recommended. Minimum GPA 2.5. *Entrance tests:* College Board SAT or ACT composite. For foreign students minimum TOEFL score 520. *For transfer students:* 2.5 minimum GPA, 100 hours maximum transfer credit; from 2-year accredited institution 70 hours; correspondence/extension students 24 hours.

College credit and advanced placement for postsecondary-level work completed in secondary school. For extrainstitutional learning college credit on basis of ACE *2006 Guide to the Evaluation of Educational Experiences in the Armed Services,* portfolio and faculty assessments, personal interview. Tutoring available. Developmental courses offered during regular academic year; credit given.

Degree Requirements: 124 credit hours; 2.0 GPA; 2 semesters in residence; 2 units physical education; English proficiency and distribution requirements.

Fulfillment of some degree requirements and exemption from some beginning courses possible by passing College Board CLEP, AP. *Grading system:* A–F; pass; withdraw (deadline after which pass-fail is appended to withdraw); incomplete (deadline after which A–F is assigned); credit; no credit.

Distinctive Educational Programs: Evening classes and accelerated degree completion programs; 26 baccalaureate majors and 7 master's degree programs in School of Behavioral Science, Business, Education, Christian Ministries, Music, Nursing, and the College of Arts and Sciences.

Degrees Conferred: 430 *baccalaureate* (B); 84 *master's* (M): biological/life sciences 2 (B); business/marketing 58 (B), 7 (M); communications/communication technologies 12 (B); computer and information sciences 18 (B); education 46 (M); English 23 (B), 4 (M); kinesiology 22 (B); liberal arts/general studies 156 (B); mathematics 3 (B); philosophy/religion/theology 22 (B); protective services/public administration 8 (B); psychology 71 (B), 27 (M); social sciences and history 25 (B); visual and performing arts 10 (B). 1 honorary degree awarded 2004: Doctor of Divinity.

Fees and Other Expenses: *Full-time tuition per academic year 2004–05:* undergraduate 16,250, graduate $7,506. *Required fees:* $1,220. *Room and board per academic year:* $6,310.

Financial Aid: Aid from institutionally generated funds is awarded on the basis of academic merit, financial need, athletic ability. Institution has a Program Participation Agreement with the U.S. Department of Education for eligible students to receive Pell Grants and other federal aid.

Financial aid to full-time, first-time undergraduate students: need-based scholarships/grants totaling $9,837,449, self-help $19,759,731, parent loans $940,435, tuition waivers $417,217, athletic awards $1,082,880; non-need-based scholarships/grants totaling $768,964, self-help $2,965,523, parent loans $403,043, tuition waivers $191,664, athletic awards $464,092. *Graduate aid:* 32 federal/state-funded scholarships/grants totaling $83,179; 862 federal/state-funded loans totaling $3,486,495;6 work-study jobs totaling $2,653.

Departments and Teaching Staff: *Professors 23, associate professors 19, assistant professors 46, part-time faculty 119. Total instructional faculty:* 207 (full-time 88, part-time 119; women 78, men 129). Total number with doctorate, first-professional, or other terminal degree: 125. Student-to-faculty ratio: 18:1. 2 faculty members awarded sabbaticals in 2004–05: 2.

Enrollment: Total enrollment 2,905. Undergraduate full-time 634 men / 1,180 women, part-time 147m / 282w; graduate full-time 51m / 158w, part-time 109m / 344w. *Transfer students:* in-state into lower division: 90m / 114w.

Characteristics of Student Body: *Ethnic/racial makeup:* number of Black non-Hispanic: 168; American Indian or Alaska Native: 30; Asian or Pacific Islander: 60; Hispanic: 361; White non-Hispanic: 1,335; unknown: 271. *Age distribution:* number under 18: 43; 18–19: 606; 20–21: 570; 22–24: 259; 25–29: 143; 30–34: 79, 35–39: 55; 40–49: 92; 50–64: 27. 13% of student body attend summer sessions.

International Students: 22 nonresident aliens enrolled fall 2004. 7 students from Europe, 7 Asia, 4 Central and South Latin America, 5 Africa, 2 Canada. No programs available to aid students whose native language is not English. No financial aid specifically designated for international students.

Student Life: On-campus residence halls and apartments house 45% of undergraduate population. Residence halls for men and women in separate buildings. Apartments available for married students and upper division and graduate students. *Intercollegiate athletics:* 7 men's and 7 women's varsity sports (NAIA). *Special regulations:* Cars permitted without restrictions. Quiet hours from 10pm to 7am Sun.–Fri., 1am to 7am Saturday. *Special services:* Medical services. *Student publications: Angelos*, a yearbook; *The Banner*, a biweekly newspaper. *Surrounding community:* Riverside population 249,000. Los Angeles 60 miles from campus. Served by mass transit bus system; international airport 20 miles from campus; passenger rail system 6 miles from campus.

Library Collections: 87,420 volumes including bound books, serial backfiles, electronic documents, and government documents not in separate collections. Online catalog. 428 current serial subscriptions; 50,990 microforms; 154 computer work stations. Online and card catalogs. Students have access to the Internet at no charge.

Most important holdings include Nie Wieder Holocaust Collection; Virginia M. Hyatt Memorial Alcove for Baptist Studies; P. Boyd Smith Hymnology Collection.

Buildings and Grounds: Campus area 83 acres.

Chief Executive Officer: Dr. Ronald L. Ellis, President.

Address undergraduate admission inquiries to Allen Johnson, Dean of Admissions; graduate admission inquiries to Gail Ronveaux, Director, Graduate Services.

California College of the Arts

5212 Broadway
Oakland, California 94618-1487
Tel: (510) 594-3600   **E-mail:** admissions@cca.edu
Fax: (415) 292-0439   **Internet:** www.cca.edu

Institution Description: California College of the Arts a private, independent, nonprofit institution offering programs in fine arts, design, and architecture. *Enrollment:* 1,484. *Degrees awarded:* Baccalaureate, master's.

Accreditation: *Regional:* WASC-Sr. *Professional:* art, interior design

History: The college was established in 1907.

Calendar: Semesters. Academic year Aug. to May. Students admitted Aug. Degrees conferred and formal commencement May.

Characteristics of Freshmen: 655 applicants (men 206, women 449). 80.6% of applicants admitted. 32.2% of admitted students enrolled full-time.

Admission: For fall acceptance, apply as early as July 1 of previous year, but not later than Apr. 1 of year of enrollment. *Requirements:* High school graduation; SAT or ACT. Essay, portfolio, and letters of recommendation are required.

Degree Requirements: Completion of required curriculum. Fulfillment of some degree requirements and exemption from some beginning courses possible by passing departmental examination.

Distinctive Educational Programs: Co-op programs in design are available. Cross-registration with Mills College and Holy Names College and University of San Francisco.

Degrees Conferred: 236 *baccalaureate;* 59 *master's.* Bachelor's degrees awarded: visual and performing arts 204; architecture and related services 25; precision production 7.

Fees and Other Expenses: *Full-time tuition per academic year 2004–05:* $24,640. *Books and supplies:* $1,300. *Room and board per academic year:* $8,230. *Other expenses:* $2,530.

Financial Aid: Aid from institutionally generated funds is provided on the basis of academic merit, financial need, other considerations.

Financial aid to full-time, first-time undergraduate students: 25% received federal grants averaging $3,745; 13% received state/local grants averaging $8,097; 91% institutional grants averaging $7,348; 55% loans averaging $3,590.

Departments and Teaching Staff: *Total instructional faculty:* 34. Total faculty with doctorate, first-professional, or other terminal degree: 63%.

Enrollment: Total enrollment 1,484. Undergraduate 1,295 (men 39.5%, women 60.5%).

Characteristics of Student Body: *Ethnic and racial makeup:* Black non-Hispanic: 1.7%; American Indian or Alaska Native: .5%; Asian or Pacific Islander: 10,8%; Hispanic: 8.7%; White non-Hispanic: 58%; unknown: 16.7%.

International Students: 83 nonresident aliens enrolled fall 2003. No programs available to aid students whose native language is not English. No financial aid specifically designated for international students.

Student Life: Campus housing for 225 students. *Special regulations:* Cars permitted without restrictions. *Special services:* Medical services.

Library Collections: 39,000 volumes. 550 audiovisual materials; 320 current periodical subscriptions. Access to online retrieval services and the Internet.

Buildings and Grounds: Campus area 4 acres.

Chief Executive Officer: Dr. Michael S. Roth, President.

Address undergraduate admission inquiries to Kate Wees, Director of Undergraduate Admissions; graduate inquiries to Lea Modigliani, Director of Graduate Admissions.

California Institute of the Arts

24700 McBean Parkway
Valencia, California 91355-2397
Tel: (661) 255-1050   **E-mail:** kyoung@indyl.calarts.edu
Fax: (661) 254-8352   **Internet:** www.calarts.edu

Institution Description: California Institute of the Arts is a private, independent, nonprofit institution. *Enrollment:* 1,327. *Degrees awarded:* Baccalaureate, master's. Certificates also awarded.

Accreditation: *Regional:* WASC-Sr. *Professional:* art, dance, music, theatre

History: Established as California Institute of the Arts by merger of Chouinard Art Institute (established 1921) and Los Angeles Conservatory of Music (established 1883); incorporated and offered first instruction at postsecondary level. Awarded first degrees (baccalaureate, master's) 1961.

Institutional Structure: *Governing board:* Board of Trustees. Extrainstitutional representation: 35 trustees; institutional representation: president of the college, 1 full-time instructional faculty member, 1 student, 1 staff representative. 1 ex officio. All voting. *Composition of institution:* Administrators 12 men / 10 women. Academic affairs headed by provost. Management/business/finances directed by vice president for administration. Full-time instructional faculty 95. Academic governance body, Academic Council, meets an average of 26 times per year.

Calendar: Semesters. Academic year Sept. to May. Freshmen admitted Sept., Dec. Degrees conferred May, Dec. Formal commencement May. No summer session.

Characteristics of Freshmen: 39% of applicants accepted. 49% of accepted applicants enrolled. 33% of freshmen from California. Freshmen from 29 states and 30 foreign countries.

Admission: For fall acceptance, apply Feb. 1. Students are notified of acceptance Apr.-May. Early acceptance available. *Requirements:* Either graduation from accredited secondary school or GED. Portfolio review in art and design, film and video; audition in dance, music, theatre. *Entrance tests:* For international students TOEFL. *For transfer students:* Transfer credit determined on individual basis.

College credit and advanced placement for postsecondary-level work completed in secondary school.

Degree Requirements: Degrees awarded on completion of 120 units of coursework, faculty reviews, artistic achievement; 1–4 years in residence; distribution requirements. *Grading system:* High pass-pass-low pass.

Distinctive Educational Programs: Interdisciplinary courses and self-designed interdisciplinary projects. Tutorials. Institutionally sponsored study abroad in Berlin, France (Paris and Nice), Glasgow, London. *Other distinctive programs:* Visiting artists program.

Degrees Conferred: 164 *baccalaureate:* visual and performing arts; 192 *master's:* visual and performing arts. 2 honorary Doctor of the Arts degrees awarded 2004.

Fees and Other Expenses: *Full-time tuition per academic year 2004–05:* $25,520. *Room per academic year:* $4,167. *Board per academic year:* $3,060. *Other fees:* $800.

Financial Aid: Aid from institutionally generated funds is awarded on basis of artistic merit, financial need. Institution has a Program Participation Agreement with the U.S. Department of Education for eligible students to receive Pell Grants and other federal aid.

Departments and Teaching Staff: Art *instructors* 17, *part-time teachers* 30; dance 5, 11; film 22, 45; music 24; 40; theatre 20; 25; critical studies 12, 24; library 5, 0. *Total instructional faculty:* 165 FTE.

Enrollment: Total enrollment 1,327. Undergraduate full-time 461 men / 366 women, part-time 4m / 6w; graduate full-time 241m / 247w, part-time 1m / 1w.

Characteristics of Student Body: *Ethnic/racial makeup:* number of Black non-Hispanic: 59; American Indian or Alaska Native: 9; Asian or Pacific Islander: 87; Hispanic: 89; White non-Hispanic: 537.

International Students: 54 nonresident aliens enrolled fall 2004. Programs available to aid students whose native language is not English: Social, cultural. English as a Second Language Program. Scholarships for both undergraduate and graduate qualifying international students.

Student Life: On-campus residence halls house 47% of student body. Residence halls for both sexes constitute 100% of such space. *Special regulations:* Cars permitted without restriction. *Special services:* Medical services. *Surrounding community:* Valencia and surrounding area population 250,000. Los Angeles, 35 miles from campus, is nearest metropolitan area.

Library Collections: 90,000 volumes 105,000 audiovisual materials, 700 current periodical subscriptions. 12,000 recordings; 2,500 compact discs; 150 CD-ROMS. Computer work stations available. Students have access to the Internet at no charge.

Most important holdings include film and video collection (1150 student, faculty, and commercial films, 3,300 videocassettes); music collection (17,500 performance scores and 13,200 records); exhibition catalog collection (12,500 catalogs of art exhibitions around the world).

Buildings and Grounds: Campus area 60 acres.

Chief Executive Officer: Dr. Steven D. Lavine, President.

Address admission inquiries to Carol Kim, Director of Enrollment Services.

California Institute of Integral Studies

1453 Mission Street
San Francisco, California 94103
Tel: (415) 575-6100   **E-mail:** info@ciis.edu
Fax: (415) 575-6105   **Internet:** www.ciis.edu

Institution Description: California Institute of Integral Studies (California Institute of Asian Studies until 1980) is a private, independent, nonprofit institution. *Enrollment:* 980. *Degrees awarded:* Master's, doctorate. Certificates also awarded.

Accreditation: *Regional:* WASC-Sr. *Professional:* clinical psychology

History: Established as the California Institute of Asian Studies, the educational branch of the Cultural Integration Fellowship, and chartered 1968; awarded first degree (doctorate) 1969; incorporated independently 1974; adopted present name 1980.

Institutional Structure: *Governing board:* Board of Trustees. Representation: 22 trustees (includes 1 core faculty, 1 staff, 1 student). *Composition of institution:* Administrators 49 women, 17 men. Academic affairs headed by academic dean. Management/business/finances directed by Director of Administration and Finance. Full-time (core) instructional faculty 57, Academic governance body, Faculty Council, meets an average of 10 times per year.

Calendar: Semesters. Academic year Sept. to May. Entering students admitted Oct., Jan., Mar. Degrees conferred and formal commencement June. Summer session of 1 term from July to Aug.

Admission: Rolling admissions plan. See www.ciis.edu/admission/deadlines for program specific deadlines. Baccalaureate from accredited college or university. Additional requirements for some programs. Minimum GPA 3.0 in upper division work. *Entrance tests:* for foreign students minimum TOEFL score 500. *For transfer students:* 3.0 minimum GPA, 12 quarter hours maximum transfer credit.

Degree Requirements: 36 units for Master of Arts; 60 units for Master of Arts in Counseling Psychology; 36 units for Ph.D. in Humanities; 90 units from Doctor of Psychology. *Grading system:* A–F; pass/not pass.

Distinctive Educational Programs: Flexible schedules, including weekend and evening classes. Interdisciplinary programs, cross-cultural (especially Asian-South Asian-Western) emphasis. Facilities and programs for independent study and research.

Degrees Conferred: 6 *master's;* 24 *doctorate.*

Fees and Other Expenses: *Full-time tuition per academic year 2004–05:* undergraduate $17,205, graduate $22,840. *Required fees:* $155. *Room and board per academic year:* varies (off-campus).

Financial Aid: Aid from institutionally generated funds is provided on the basis of academic merit, financial need, other considerations. Financial assistance is available in the form of Pell Grants, College Work-Study, Veterans Administration Benefits, National Direct Student Loans, Supplemental Education Opportunity Grants (SEOG), Stafford Loans, other federal aid programs. *Graduate aid:* 549 students received $10,385,000 (awards ranging from $500 to $31,000); 253 students had work-study jobs totaling $810,500 (ranging from $400 to $11,000); 42 students had teaching assistantships totaling $26,800; 7 students had research assistantships totaling $5,100.

Departments and Teaching Staff: *Professors* 28, *associate professors* 20, *assistant professors* 7, *part-time faculty* 70. *Total instructional faculty:* 125.

Enrollment: Total enrollment 980. Undergraduate full-time 8 men / 27 women, part-time 1m / 1w; graduate full-time 174m / 478w, part-time 58m / 238w.

Characteristics of Student Body: *Age distribution:* 22–24: 4%; 25–29: 18%; 30–34: 22%, 35–39: 19%; 40–49: 30%; 50–59: 6%; 60 and over: 1%.

International Students: 81 nonresident aliens enrolled fall 2004. 17 students from Europe, 30 Asia, 6 Central and South America, 1 Africa, 18 Canada, 2 Australia, 7 other. No programs available to aid students whose language is not English. 50 scholarships available annually for international students; 40 totaling $160,000 awarded 2004–05.

Student Life: No on-campus housing. Limited off-street parking, excellent public transportation. Active student association and student representation on program committees and Board of Trustees. *Special regulations:* Cars permitted without restrictions. *Student publications:* A weekly and a monthly newsletter. *Surrounding community:* San Francisco population 700,000. Served by mass transit bus system, airport 10 miles from campus, passenger rail service 1/2 mile from campus.

Publications: *Open Eye,* a biannual community newsletter; *twg: A Journal of Organizational Transformation; Inner Eye,* in-house newsletter also available online.

Library Collections: 38,000 volumes. 600 audiovisual materials; 210 current periodical subscriptions; 1,300 recordings; 50 compact discs. Students have access to online information retrieval services and the Internet.

Most important holdings include special collections of books, periodicals, manuscripts, personal papers, etc. relating to counseling and psychology, East/West comparative studies, Hinduism and Buddhism; Allen Watts Memorial Library.

Buildings and Grounds: Campus area 50,000 square feet.

Chief Executive Officer: Dr. Joseph Subbiondo, President.

Address admission inquiries to Greg Canada, Director of Admissions.

California Institute of Technology

1201 East California Boulevard
Pasadena, California 91125
Tel: (626) 395-6811   **E-mail:** ugadmissions@caltech.edu
Fax: (626) 795-1547   **Internet:** www.caltech.edu

Institution Description: California Institute of Technology is a private, independent institution. *Enrollment:* 2,172. *Degrees awarded:* Baccalaureate, master's, doctorate. Post-master's certificates also awarded.

Accreditation: *Regional:* WASC-Sr. *Professional:* engineering

History: Established and incorporated as Throop Polytechnic Institute 1891; offered first instruction at postsecondary level 1892; awarded first degree (baccalaureate) 1896; changed name to Throop College of Technology 1913, adopted present name 1920.

Institutional Structure: *Governing board:* Board of Trustees. Representation: 44 trustees, 1 administrator. All voting. *Composition of institution:* Academic affairs headed by vice president and provost, dean of the faculty. Management/business/finances directed by vice president for business and finance, treasurer. Full-time instructional faculty 310. Academic governance body, Faculty Board, meets an average of 9 times per year.

Calendar: Quarters. 2004–05 academic year Sept. to June. Freshmen admitted Sept. Degrees conferred and formal commencement June. No summer session.

Characteristics of Freshmen: 2,761 applicants (2,120 men, 241 women). 20.5% of applicants admitted; 36.6% admitted students enrolled full-time.

100% (207 students) submitted SAT scores. *25th percentile*: SAT Verbal 700, SAT Math 750; *75th percentile*: SAT Verbal 770, SAT Math 800.

30% of freshmen from California. Freshmen from 34 states and 8 foreign countries.

Admission: For fall acceptance, apply as early as Sept. 1 of previous year, but not later than Jan. 1 of year of enrollment. Students are notified of acceptance Apr. Apply by Nov. 1 for early decision; need not limit applications to Cal Tech. Early acceptance available. *Requirements:* Graduation from approved secondary school with units that must include 3 in English, 4 mathematics, 1 U.S. History, 1 chemistry, 1 physics, 5 additional academic units. *Entrance tests:* College Board SAT, 3 subject test. *For transfer students:* 3.0 GPA; 1 year calculus; 1 year calculus-based physics.

College credit and advanced placement for postsecondary-level work completed in secondary school.

Degree Requirements: 486 units (483 units in applied mathematics and mathematics options); 1.9 GPA; 2 years in residence; 3 quarters physical education courses; core curriculum requirements. *Grading system:* A–F; pass-fail; withdraw (carries time limit).

Distinctive Educational Programs: Evening classes. Dual-degree programs with Occidental College, Pomona College, Wesleyan University (CT); Grinnell College (IA); Bowdoin College (ME); Ohio Wesleyan University; Reed College (OR); Bryn Mawr College (PA); Whitman College (WV). Student exchange programs with Cambridge (England), Occidental College, Scripps College, and Art Center College of Design. Facilities and programs for independent research, including honors programs, individual majors, tutorials. *Other distinctive programs:* Graduate Aeronautical Laboratories. Palomar and Big Bear Solar Observatories. Environmental Quality Laboratory.

ROTC: Army offered in cooperation with University of California, Los Angeles; Air Force with University of Southern California.

Degrees Conferred: 208 *baccalaureate*; 156 *master's*; 2 *post-master's certificates*; 166 *doctorate*. Bachelor's degrees awarded in top five disciplines: engineering 81; physical sciences 63; biological and biomedical sciences 24; mathematics and statistics 21; computer and information sciences and support services 11.

Fees and Other Expenses: *Full-time tuition per academic year 2004–05:* $25,566. *Room and board per academic year:* $8,013. *Books and supplies:* $1,029. *Other expenses:* $3,803.

Financial Aid: Aid from institutionally generated funds is provided on the basis of academic merit, financial need. Institution has a Program Participation Agreement with the U.S. Department of Education for eligible students to receive Pell Grants and other federal aid.

Financial aid to full-time, first-time undergraduate students: 11% received federal grants averaging $5,735; 23% state/local grants averaging $3,404; 60 institutional grants averaging $17,228; 21% loans averaging $1,942.

Departments and Teaching Staff: Biology *professors* 26, *associate professors* 5, *assistant professors* 3, *instructors* 0, *part-time teachers* 1; chemistry and chemical engineering 25, 5, 2, 0, 1; engineering and applied science 53, 10, 9, 5, 3; geology and planetary science 23, 1, 5, 0, 1; humanities and social sciences 23, 11, 7, 4, 11; physics, mathematics and astronomy 58, 2, 4, 10, 0; other 0, 0, 0, 0, 1.

Total instructional faculty: 321 FTE. *Total tenured faculty:* 243. *Degrees held by full-time faculty:* Doctorate 95%, master's 100%. 95% hold terminal degrees.

Enrollment: Total enrollment 2,172 Undergraduate 891 (66.7% men, 33.3% women).

Characteristics of Student Body: *Ethnic and racial makeup:* Black non-Hispanic: 1.3%; American Indian or Alaska Native: .6%; Asian or Pacific Islander: 31.1%; Hispanic: 7.3%; White non-Hispanic: 51.4%; unknown: .8%.

International Students: 66 undergraduate nonresident aliens enrolled 2003. Programs available to aid students whose native language is not English: Social, cultural, and English as a Second Language Program.

Student Life: Most undergraduates reside in Institute-owned housing. Some 60% live in on-campus residence halls around which much of the social life revolves. Another 28% live in off-campus Institute housing including former single family dwellings and apartments. *Intercollegiate athletics:* men only: baseball, basketball, cross-country, fencing, golf, swimming, tennis, track, water

polo; women only: basketball, cross-country, fencing, swimming, tennis, track and field, volleyball. *Special regulations:* Cars permitted without restrictions. *Special services:* Medical services. *Student publications: The California Tech,* a weekly newspaper; a literary magazine; a yearbook. *Surrounding community:* Pasadena population 150,000. Los Angeles, 12 miles from campus, is nearest metropolitan area. Served by mass transit system, airports 12 and 35 miles from campus, passenger rail service 18 miles from campus.

Library Collections: 705,500 volumes including bound books, serial backfiles, electronic documents, and government documents not in separate collections. Online catalog. Current serial subscriptions: 3,000 paper, 550 electronic. 614,000 microforms; 3,500 recordings. Computer work stations available. Students have access to the Internet at no charge.

Most important holdings include Robert A. Millikan Collection; George E. Hale Collection; Theodore von Karman Collection; aeronautical technical reports; earthquake engineering.

Buildings and Grounds: Campus area 124 acres.

Chief Executive Officer: Dr. David Baltimore, President.

Address admission inquiries to Richard Bischoff, Director of Admissions.

California Lutheran University

60 West Olsen Road
Thousand Oaks, California 91360-2787

Tel: (805) 492-2411   **E-mail:** cluadm@callutheran.edu
Fax: (805) 492-3114   **Internet:** www.callutheran.edu

Institution Description: California Lutheran University is a private college affiliated with The Evangelical Lutheran Church in America. *Enrollment:* 2,920. *Degrees awarded:* Baccalaureate, master's.

Accreditation: *Regional:* WASC-Sr.

History: Established 1959; incorporated 1959; offered first instruction at postsecondary level 1961; first degree (baccalaureate) awarded 1964.

Institutional Structure: *Governing board:* Board of Regents. Extrainstitutional representation: 36 regents; institutional representation: 1 administrator, 1 full-time instructional faculty member, 1 student; 1 alumnus. 40 voting. *Composition of institution:* 35 men / 31 women. Academic affairs headed by vice president for academic affairs and dean of the college. Management/business/ finances directed by vice president for business and finance. Instructional faculty 100. Academic governance body, the faculty, meets an average of 9 times per year.

Calendar: Semesters (4-1-4 plan). Academic year Sept. to May. Freshmen admitted Sept., Jan., Feb., June, July. Degrees conferred May, Aug., Dec. Formal commencement May. Summer session of 2 terms from mid-June to mid-Aug.

Characteristics of Freshmen: 1,660 applicants (704 men, 956 women). 75.7% of applicants admitted. 35.2% admitted students enrolled full-time.

92% (369 students) submitted SAT scores; 35% (140 students) submitted ACT scores. *25th percentile:* SAT Verbal 480, SAT Math 500; ACT Composite 21, ACT English 20, ACT Math 19. *75th percentile:* SAT Verbal 590, SAT Math 600; ACT Composite 26, ACT English 25, ACT Math 25.

80% of freshmen from California. Freshmen from 23 states and 6 foreign countries.

Admission: Rolling admissions plan. For fall acceptance, apply as early as June 1 of previous year. Apply by Dec. 1 for early decision; need not limit application to California Lutheran. Early acceptance available. *Requirements:* Secondary school units recommended are 4 English, 2 in a foreign language, 2 mathematics, 2 science, 2 social studies, plus 2 to 4 additional academic units. GED accepted. Minimum 2.0 GPA. *Entrance tests:* College Board SAT or ACT composite. *For transfer students:* 2.0 minimum GPA overall and in last semester of full-time study, 97 semester hours maximum transfer credit (may not count toward major); from 2-year accredited institutions 70 hours maximum transfer credit; from 4-year accredited institutions 97 hours maximum transfer credit.

College credit for College Board CLEP and extrainstitutional learning on basis of ACE *2006 Guide to the Evaluation of Educational Experiences in the Armed Services,* portfolio assessment, work experience. Advanced placement for postsecondary-level work completed in secondary school, CLEP, faculty assessment. Tutoring available.

Degree Requirements: *For all baccalaureate degrees:* 127 credit hours; 2.0 GPA overall (2.25 in major); 30 hours in residence; core requirements in liberal arts; 3 credits in physical education. Degree credit and exemption from some beginning courses based on ACT; College Board SAT, CLEP, TSWE, education APP. Exemption from freshmen English also available through school's freshman English equivalency exam (offered before classes start) and the freshman English exam (offered during the year). Advanced placement, at discretion of department, in chemistry, English, history, languages, mathematics, physics.

Grading system: A–F; withdraw (deadline after which pass-fail appended to withdrawal); limited pass-no credit option.

Distinctive Educational Programs: *For undergraduates:* Flexible meeting places and schedules. Dual-degree program in engineering with Washington University (MO). Exchange program with Wagner College (NY). Individually arranged study abroad in France, The Netherlands, Mexico, elsewhere. Humanities tutorial. Mental health specialist program. *For graduate students:* Off-campus centers at Bakersfield, Los Angeles, North Hollywood, San Gabriel, Santa Barbara, Torrance, and Ventura. *Available to all students:* Work-experience programs (academic credit for undergraduates). Evening baccalaureate program for adults offering degrees in business administration, accounting, and computer science. Study abroad through Institute for American Universities (France) and Central College of Iowa Program (Austria, England, France, Wales, Spain, Mexico); Augsburg College Program (Mexico); and Norwegian Art School Exchange (Oslo). Semester abroad in Liberia. Facilities and programs for independent research. Interdepartmental and interdisciplinary programs. Some facilities for using telecommunications in the classroom. Course clusters.

Degrees Conferred: 484 *baccalaureate*; 276 *master's*. Bachelor's degrees awarded in top five disciplines: business, management, marketing, and related support services 127; communication, journalism, and related programs 50; liberal arts and sciences, general studies, and humanities 47, computer and information sciences and support services 47, psychology 44.

Fees and Other Expenses: *Full-time undergraduate tuition per academic year 2004–05:* $22,285. *Room and board per academic year:* $7,570. *Books and supplies:* $1,260. Contact the university for graduate tuition.

Financial Aid: Aid from institutionally generated funds is provided on the basis of academic merit, financial need, athletic ability, other criteria. Institution has a Program Participation Agreement with the U.S. Department of Education for eligible students to receive Pell Grants and other federal aid.

Financial aid to full-time, first-time undergraduate students: 14% received federal grants averaging $2,825; 16% state/local grants averaging $8,664; 90% institutional grants averaging $9,803; 61% loans averaging $3,719.

Departments and Teaching Staff: *Total instructional faculty:* 100. *Total tenured faculty:* 50. Degrees held by full-time faculty: doctorate 94%. Student-to-faculty ratio: 17:1.

Enrollment: Total enrollment 2,920. Undergraduate 1,920 (44.3% men, 55.7% women).

Characteristics of Student Body: *Ethnic/racial makeup:* Black non-Hispanic: 1.9%; American Indian or Alaska Native: .9%; Asian or Pacific Islander: 4.5%; Hispanic: 12.8%, White non-Hispanic: 67.1%; unknown: 10.7%.

International Students: 40 nonresident aliens enrolled fall 2004. Programs available for students whose native language is not English: English as a Second Language program. Financial aid specifically designated for undergraduate foreign students: Scholarships available annually.

Student Life: On-campus residence halls house 35% of student body and 66% of the undergraduates. *Intercollegiate athletics:* men only: baseball, cross country, football, tennis, track, volleyball, basketball, soccer; women only: tennis, track, cross country, basketball, softball, volleyball. *Special regulations:* Cars allowed with parking permit. Quiet hours from 7pm to 6am Sun.–Thurs. Residence hall visitation 10am to 11pm Sun.–Tours., 10am to 1am Fri. and Sat. *Special services:* Learning Resources Center, medical services. *Student publications, radio: The California Lutheran College Echo,* a weekly newspaper; *Kairos,* college yearbook; *Morning Glory,* an annual literary magazine. Radio station, KRLC-FM, broadcasts 105 hours per week. *Surrounding community:* Thousand Oaks population 150,000. Los Angeles; 50 miles from campus, is nearest metropolitan area. Served by mass transit system; airport 50 miles from campus; passenger rail service 25 miles from campus.

Library Collections: 120,000 volumes. 95,000 separate government documents collection; 27,000 microforms; 2,475 audiovisual materials; 610 current periodical subscriptions. Students have access to online information retrieval services and the Internet.

Most important special collection holds materials on Scandinavians and Lutherans in the West.

Buildings and Grounds: Campus area 285 acres.

Chief Executive Officer: Dr. Luther S. Luedtke, President.

Address admission inquiries to Director of Admissions.

California Maritime Academy

200 Maritime Academy Drive
P.O. Box 1392
Vallejo, California 94590-8181
Tel: (707) 654-1000   **E-mail:** enroll@csum.edu
Fax: (707) 649-1001   **Internet:** www.csum.edu

Institution Description: California Maritime Academy is a public institution in the California State University System. *Enrollment:* 698. *Degrees awarded:* Baccalaureate.

Accreditation: *Regional:* WASC-Sr. *Professional:* engineering technology, industrial technology

History: Established and chartered as California Nautical School 1929; offered first instruction at postsecondary level 1930; awarded first degree (baccalaureate) 1931; adopted present name 1972; became part of the California State University System in 1995.

Institutional Structure: *Governing board:* Board of Trustees, California State University. *Composition of institution:* Administrators 33 men / 7 women. Academic affairs headed by vice president. Management/business/finances directed by administrative officer. Academic governance body, Faculty Senate, meets an average of 10 times per year.

Calendar: Semesters. Academic year Aug. to July. Freshmen admitted Aug. Degrees conferred and formal commencement May. No summer session.

Characteristics of Freshmen: 652 applicants (447 men, 205 women). 23% of applicants admitted; 100 percent enrolled full-time.

94% (142 students) submitted SAT scores. *25th percentile:* SAT Verbal 500, SAT Math 500. *75th percentile:* SAT Verbal 580, SAT Math 600.

Admission: Rolling admissions plan. For fall acceptance, apply as early as Nov. 1 of year prior to enrollment, but no later than July 1 of year of enrollment. *Requirements:* Either graduation from secondary school with 4 units in English, 3 college preparatory mathematics, 1 physics or chemistry (with laboratory); or GED. Physical examination. Recommend having both physics and chemistry. *Entrance tests:* College Board SAT or ACT composite. *For transfer students:* 2.0 minimum GPA; must study at least 3 years at the academy.

College credit and advanced placement for postsecondary-level work completed in secondary school. College credit for extrainstitutional learning on basis of ACE *2006 Guide to the Evaluation of Educational Experiences in the Armed Services.*

Degree Requirements: 2.0 GPA; 9 terms in residence; completion of U.S. Coast Guard entry level license; exit competency examinations for U.S. Merchant Marine, Deck, or Engineering Officer. *Grading system:* A–F; pass-fail; pass; withdraw (carries time limit).

Distinctive Educational Programs: Work-experience programs. Special facilities for using telecommunications in the classroom. Training ship serving as floating laboratory. Deep water pier enclosing boat basin for power, sail, and row boats.

ROTC: NROTC available.

Degrees Conferred: 118 *baccalaureate:* transportation and materials moving 67; engineering technologies/technicians 26; engineering 24; business, management, marketing, and related support services 11.

Fees and Other Expenses: *Full-time tuition per academic year 2004–05:* in-state resident $3,240; out-of-state $13,410. *Room and board per academic year:* $7,030. *Books and supplies:* $1,260. *Other expenses:* $2,780.

Financial Aid: Aid from institutionally generated funds is provided on the basis of academic merit, financial need, athletic ability. Institution has a Program Participation Agreement with the U.S. Department of Education for eligible students to receive Pell Grants and other federal aid.

Financial aid to full-time, first-time undergraduate students: 12% received federal grants averaging $3,242; 22% state/local grants averaging $2,375; 28% institutional grants averaging $3,644; 41% loans averaging $3,858.

Departments and Teaching Staff: *Professors* 15, *associate professors* 9, *assistant professors* 14, *instructors* 32.

Total instructional faculty: 70. Total tenured faculty: 24. Student-to-faculty ratio: 12:1.

Enrollment: Total enrollment 698 (84.5% men, 15.5% women).

Characteristics of Student Body: *Ethnic/racial makeup:* Black non-Hispanic: 2.6%; American Indian or Alaska Native: 1.3%; Asian or Pacific Islander: 9.2%; Hispanic: 6%; White non-Hispanic: 51%; unknown: 26.2%.

International Students: 26 nonresident aliens enrolled fall 2003. English as a Second Language Program available to aid students whose native language is not English. No financial aid specifically designated for international students.

Student Life: On-campus residence halls house 100% of student body. *Intercollegiate athletics:* men and women: basketball, crew, soccer, water polo, volleyball. *Special regulations:* Merchant marine uniform required. Curfews. Quiet hours. Residence hall visitation hours. *Special services:* Learning Resources Center, medical services. *Student publications: Binnacle* (quarterly), *Hawsepipe* (annually). *Surrounding community:* Vallejo population 113,000. San Francisco, 32 miles from campus, is nearest metropolitan area. Served by mass transit bus system, airport 25 miles from campus, passenger rail service 10 miles from campus.

Library Collections: 25,000 volumes. Online catalog. 15,000 microforms; 225 current periodical subscriptions; access to online bibliographic retrieval systems. Computer work stations available.

Most important special collections are the Academy History Archives; Marine Engineering, Technology, and Transportation.

Buildings and Grounds: Campus area 70 acres.

Chief Executive Officer: Dr. William B. Eisenhardt, President.

Address admission inquiries to Chris Urzak, Director of Enrollment Services.

California Polytechnic State University, San Luis Obispo

San Luis Obispo, California 93407

Tel: (805) 756-1111   **E-mail:** admprosp@calpoly.edu
Fax: (805) 756-5400   **Internet:** www.calpoly.edu

Institution Description: *Enrollment:* 18,303. *Degrees awarded:* Baccalaureate, first-professional, master's.

Accreditation: *Regional:* WASC-Sr. *Professional:* architecture, art, business, computer science, construction education, counseling, engineering, engineering technology, forestry, industrial technology, journalism, landscape architecture, planning, recreation and leisure services

History: Established as California Polytechnic School, a vocational secondary school, 1901; became junior college and offered first instruction at postsecondary level 1927; added third year 1936; added fourth year 1940; awarded first degree (baccalaureate) 1942; changed name to California State Polytechnic College, San Luis Obispo 1947; adopted present name 1972. *See* Morris Eugene Smith, *A History of California State Polytechnic College, the First 50 Years, 1901–1951* (Ann Arbor, Mich.: University Microfilms, 1968).

Institutional Structure: *Composition of institution:* Administrators 95 men / 33 women. Academic affairs headed by vice president for academic affairs. Management/business/finances directed by director of business affairs. Full-time instructional faculty 654. Academic governance body, Academic Senate, meets an average of 10 times per year.

Calendar: Quarters. 2004–5 academic year Sept. to June. Freshmen admitted Sept., Jan., Mar., July. Degrees conferred June, Sept., Dec., Mar. Formal commencement June.

Characteristics of Freshmen: 21,794 applicants. 15.9% admitted; 81.7% enrolled full-time.

97% (2,976 students) submitted SAT scores. *25th percentile:* SAT Verbal 530, SAT Math 570; *75th percentile:* SAT Verbal 620, SAT Math 670.

Admission: For fall acceptance, apply as early as Nov. 1 of previous year, but not later than Nov. 30. Students are notified of acceptance beginning Mar. *Requirements:* High school graduation with English 4 years, math 3 years, history 1 year, science 1 year with lab; 2 years in same foreign language; visual and performing arts 1 year.

Degree Requirements: 2.0 GPA; completion of general education and breadth requirements. Computer literacy and math courses and a senior project are required. 186 to 263 quarter units required to graduate.

Distinctive Educational Programs: School offers college credit for extrainstitutional learning experience on basis of ACE *2006 Guide to the Evaluation of Educational Experiences in the Armed Services*; portfolio assessment. Tutoring available. Remedial courses offered during regular academic year; credit given. Work-experience programs. Evening classes. Special facilities for using telecommunications in the classroom. Interdisciplinary program in engineering science. Study abroad in England (London Study Program). The CSU International Program places students in 16 countries.

ROTC: Army.

Degrees Conferred: 4,677 *baccalaureate,* 534 *master's.* Bachelor's degrees awarded in top five disciplines: business, management, marketing, and related support services 1,206; engineering 793; agriculture, agriculture operations, and related sciences 513; social sciences 249; architecture and related services 240.

Fees and Other Expenses: *Undergraduate tuition/fees per academic year 2004–05:* California resident $3,974; out-of-state $14,144. *Room and board:* $7,939. *Books and supplies:* $1,260.

Financial Aid: Aid from institutionally generated funds is provided on the basis of academic merit, financial need, athletic ability, other criteria. Institution

has a Program Participation Agreement with the U.S. Department of Education for eligible students to receive Pell Grants and other federal aid.

Financial aid to full-time, first-time undergraduate students: 11% received federal grants averaging $3,089; 33% state/local grants averaging $2,050; 15% institutional grants averaging $2,566; 28% loans averaging $3,072.

Departments and Teaching Staff: *Total instructional faculty:* 654 full-time, 439 part-time. Student-to-faculty ratio: 20:1. Degrees held by full-time faculty: doctorate 477.

Enrollment: Total enrollment 18,303. Undergraduate 17,295 (55.8% men, 44.2% women).

Characteristics of Student Body: *Ethnic/racial makeup (undergraduate):* Black non-Hispanic: 1%; American Indian or Alaska Native: .8%; Asian or Pacific Islander: 11.1%; Hispanic: 9.5%; White non-Hispanic: 62.7%; unknown: 13.7%.

International Students: 208 nonresident aliens enrolled fall 2003.

Student Life: On-campus residence halls house 2,783 students. Residence halls for men and women constitute 100% of such space. Less than 1% of men and women live in fraternities and sororities. *Intercollegiate athletics:* Men only, baseball, basketball, cross-country, football, soccer, swimming, tennis, track, wrestling. Women only, basketball, cross-country, gymnastics, swimming, tennis, track, volleyball, softball. *Special regulations:* Cars with permit allowed. *Special services:* Learning Resources Center, medical services. *Student publications, radio: Mustang Daily,* a newspaper published 5 times per week. Radio station KCPR-FM broadcasts 168 hours per week; offers news, public affairs, and music programs. *Surrounding community:* San Luis Obispo population 35,000. Los Angeles, 200 miles from campus, is nearest metropolitan area. Served by airport and passenger rail service, each 5 miles from campus.

Library Collections: 1,207,000 volumes. 2,056,000 microforms; 37,500 audiovisual materials; 3,198 periodical subscriptions. Access to electronic databases and full-text files. Online catalog. Students have access to the Internet at no charge.

Most important holdings include Julia Morgan Collection; fine printing and graphic arts collection, architectural history collection.

Buildings and Grounds: Campus area 5,898 acres.

Chief Executive Officer: Dr. Warren J. Baker, President.

Address admission inquiries to Dr. Linda C. Dalton, Director, Enrollment Management.

California State Polytechnic University, Pomona

3801 West Temple Avenue
Pomona, California 91768

Tel: (909) 869-7659   **E-mail:** cppadmit@csupomona.edu
Fax: (909) 869-2418   **Internet:** www.csupomona.edu

Institution Description: *Enrollment:* 19,002. *Degrees awarded:* Baccalaureate, master's.

Accreditation: *Regional:* WASC-Sr. *Professional:* art, business, computer science, dietetics, engineering, engineering technology, landscape architecture, planning, veterinary technology

History: Established as Southern California branch of California State Polytechnic School 1938; awarded first degree (baccalaureate) 1957; established as independent state college 1966; adopted present name 1972.

Institutional Structure: Academic affairs headed by provost/vice president for academic affairs. Management/business/finances directed by director for business affairs. Full-time instructional faculty 369 men, 187 women. Academic governance body, The Senate, meets an average of 16 times per year.

Calendar: Quarters. Academic year mid-June to mid-June. Freshmen admitted Sept., Jan., Apr., June. Degrees conferred and formal commencement June.

Characteristics of Freshmen: 97% (1,886 students) submitted SAT scores; 16% (308 students) submitted ACT scores. *25th percentile:* SAT Verbal 430, SAT Math 470; ACT Composite 17, ACT English 16, ACT Math 18. *75th percentile:* SAT Verbal 550, SAT Math 600; ACT Composite 23, ACT English 23, ACT Math 25.

2,188 applicants admitted; 1,950 admitted students enrolled full-time. 43% of entering freshmen expected to graduate within 5 years.

Admission: Rolling admissions plan. Early acceptance available. For fall acceptance, students are encouraged to apply as early as possible in November of previous year.

Distinctive Educational Programs: Tutoring available; credit given for developmental courses offered during regular academic year. Cooperative education. Weekend and evening courses. Accelerated degree programs. Special facilities for using telecommunications in the classroom. Interdisciplinary programs in American studies, biotechnology, behavioral sciences, ethnic studies, liberal studies, social science. Preprofessional program in veterinary science. Facilities and programs for independent research. Programs in aerospace, animal science with Equine Research Center, architecture, agricultural biology, computer science, electrical engineering, engineering technology, fruit industries, land laboratory with reclamation research program, mechanical engineering, ornamental horticulture, other fields through School of Agriculture. *Other distinctive programs:* Small Business Development Center. Small Ruminant Center for teaching and research on sheep and goats.

ROTC: Army in cooperation with Claremont College; Air Force in cooperation with University of Southern California.

Degrees Conferred: 3,201 *baccalaureate* (B), 328 *master's* (M): agriculture 109 (B), 9 (M); architecture 205 (B), 36 (M); biological/life sciences 107 (B), 13 (M); business/marketing 947 (B), 70 (M); communications/communication technologies 62 (B); computer and information sciences 351 (B), 9 (M); education 1 (B), 82 (M); engineering and engineering technologies 478 (B), 54 (M); English 60 (B), 7 (M); foreign languages and literature 9 (B); health professions and related sciences 29 (B), 1 (M); home economics and vocational home economics 29 (B); interdisciplinary studies 58 (B); liberal arts/general studies 237 (B); mathematics 17 (B), 10 (M); parks and recreation 38 (B), 2 (M); philosophy/religion/theology 12 (B); physical sciences 25 (B), 4 (M); protective services/public 8 (M); psychology 106 (B), 8 (M); social sciences and history 184 (B), 15 (M); visual and performing arts 130 (B).

Fees and Other Expenses: *Full-time tuition per academic year 2004–05:* $226 per unit. *Required fees:* $2,832. *Room and board per academic year:* $7,212. Contact the university for graduate and out-of-state costs.

Financial Aid: Aid from institutionally generated funds is provided on the basis of academic merit, financial need, athletic ability, other criteria. Institution has a Program Participation Agreement with the U.S. Department of Education for eligible students to receive Pell Grants and other federal aid.

Financial aid to full-time, first-time undergraduate students: need-based scholarships/grants $38,263,709, self-help $30,874,287; non-need-based scholarships/grants $18,586,400, self-help $18,586,400; parent loans $1,261,105, athletic awards $429,120.

Departments and Teaching Staff: *Total instructional faculty:* 1,012 (full-time 556, part-time 456; 380 women, 632 men). Total faculty with doctorate, first-professional, or other terminal degree: 597. Student-to-faculty ratio: 23:1.

Enrollment: Total enrollment 19,002. Full-time 15,301; part-time 3,701.

Characteristics of Student Body: *Ethnic/racial makeup:* number of Black non-Hispanic: 606; American Indian or Alaska Native: 70; Asian or Pacific Islander: 5,563; Hispanic: 4,320; White non-Hispanic: 4,147; unknown: 701.

International Students: 548 nonresident aliens enrolled fall 2004. Programs available to aid students whose native language is not English: Social, cultural, financial; English as a Second Language Program.

Student Life: On-campus residence halls house 13% of student body. *Intercollegiate athletics:* men only: baseball, basketball, cross-country, soccer, tennis, track; women only: basketball, cross-county, soccer, softball, tennis, track, volleyball. *Special regulations:* Cars with decals permitted; $36 fee charged. Quiet hours. *Special services:* Learning Resources Center, medical services, transportation service between parking lots and inner campus. *Student publications: Opus,* a quarterly magazine; *Poly Post,* a biweekly newspaper. *Surrounding community:* Pomona population 95,000. Los Angeles; 30 miles from campus, is nearest metropolitan area. Served by mass transit bus system; airport 14 miles from campus; passenger rail service 6 miles from campus.

Library Collections: 758,700 volumes including bound books, serial backfiles, electronic documents, and government documents not in separate collections. Online catalog. Current serial subscriptions: paper, microform, electronic. 80 Computer work stations. Students have access to the Internet at no charge.

Most important holdings include W.K. Kellogg Arabian Horse collection; University Archives - Rose Fleet Collection; Wine and Wine Industry Collection; John Gill and Virginia Adair Modern Poetry Collections.

Buildings and Grounds: Campus area 1,437 acres. *New buildings:* Science Building completed 2000; Engineering Building 2003.

Chief Executive Officer: Dr. J. Michael Ortiz, President.

Address all undergraduate admission inquiries to Dr. George Bradshaw, Director of Admissions and Outreach; graduate inquiries to Dan Aseltine, Coordinator, International/Graduate Admissions.

California State University, Bakersfield

9001 Stockdale Highway
Bakersfield, California 93311-1099
Tel: (661) 664-2111   **E-mail:** admissions@csubak.edu
Fax: (661) 664-3131   **Internet:** www.csubak.edu

Institution Description: *Enrollment:* 7,755. *Degrees awarded:* Baccalaureate, master's.

Accreditation: *Regional:* WASC-Sr. *Professional:* business, nursing, nursing education, public administration, teacher education

History: Established and chartered as California State College, Kern County 1965; name changed to California State College, Bakersfield 1967; offered first instruction at postsecondary level and awarded first degree (baccalaureate) 1970; achieved university status 1988.

Institutional Structure: *Composition of institution:* Administrators 13 men / 1 woman. Academic affairs headed by vice president. Management/business/finances directed by business manager. Full-time instructional faculty 325. Academic governance body, Academic Senate, meets an average of 15 times per year.

Calendar: Quarters. Academic year Sept. to June. Freshmen admitted Sept., Jan., Mar., June. Degrees conferred June, Aug., Dec., Apr. Formal commencement June. Summer session of 2 terms.

Characteristics of Freshmen: 49% of applicants admitted; 17% admitted and enrolled. 73% (561 students) submitted SAT scores; 16% (122 students) submitted ACT scores. *25th percentile:* SAT Verbal 400, SAT Math ; 410; ACT Composite 15, ACT English 14, ACT Math 16. *75th percentile:* SAT Verbal 530, SAT Math 530; ACT Composite 21, ACT English 21, ACT Math 23.

29% of freshmen expected to graduate within 5 years. 98% of freshmen from California. Freshmen from 11 states and 8 foreign countries.

Admission: Rolling admissions plan. For fall acceptance, apply as early as Nov. of previous year. First-time freshmen applicants are required to be high school graduates, to have completed the 15-unit comprehensive pattern of college preparatory study with grades of C or better and to have a qualifiable eligibility index. The eligibility index is the combination of high school grade point average and test scores on either the ACT or SAT.

Degree Requirements: *For baccalaureate degree:* A minimum of 186 quarter units, including 60 upper division. A student must complete a minimum of 45 quarter units in resident study at CSUB. Each student must maintain a grade point average of 2.0 or better on all courses in which a letter grade is assigned. *For master's degree:* Most programs consist of a minimum of 45 quarter units. A minimum of 32 quarter units must be completed in resident study at CSUB.

Credit for courses by challenge examination, experiential learning credit, credit for externally developed tests, APP, CLEP, English equivalency examination, career-related internships, cooperative education, management internship program, departmental internships, Human Corp Program, independent study, individual study, cooperative research and directed research. CSUB participates in the National Student Exchange for a year or part of a year in study abroad; also participation in the International Student Exchange.

Degrees Conferred: 1,193 *baccalaureate* (B); 308 *master's* (M): biological and life sciences 34 (B); business/marketing 162 (B), 26 (M); communications/communication technologies 61 (B); education 57 (B), 174 (M); English 15 (B), 9 (M); foreign languages and literature 6 (B); health professions and related sciences 31 (B), 21 (M); interdisciplinary studies 1 (B); liberal arts/general studies 363 (B); mathematics 15 (B), 3 (M); natural resources/environmental science 22 (B); philosophy/religion,theology 15 (B); protective services/public administration 12 (B), 21 (M); psychology 93 (B), 10 (M); social sciences and history 40 (M); visual and performing arts 28 (B); other 248 (B), 4 (M).

Fees and Other Expenses: *Full-time tuition per academic year 2004–05:* undergraduate resident $2,334. graduate resident $2,820. *Required fees:* $127. *Room and board per academic year:* $5,035.

Financial Aid: Aid from institutionally generated funds is provided on the basis of academic merit, financial need, athletic ability, other considerations. Institution has a Program Participation Agreement with the U.S. Department of Education for eligible students to receive Pell Grants and other federal aid.

Undergraduate need-based scholarships/grants totaling $15,609,262, self-help $8,315,964; non-need-based scholarships/grants totaling $855,917, self-help $2,009,327, parent loans $199,985, tuition waivers $223,355, athletic awards $558,277.

Graduate aid: 770 students received federal grants ranging from $85 to $4,050; 1,048 loans ranging from $244 to $10,500; 110 fellowships/grants ranging from $50 to $7,500.

Departments and Teaching Staff: *Total instructional faculty:* 478 (325 full-time, 153 part-time; women 231, men 247). Total number with doctorate, first-professional, or other terminal degree: 238. Student-to-faculty ratio: 19:1.

Enrollment: Total enrollment 7,755. Undergraduate 5,768.

Characteristics of Student Body: *Ethnic and racial makeup:* number of Black non-Hispanic: 426; American Indian or Alaska Native: 78; Asian or Pacific Islander: 372; Hispanic: 2,055; White non-Hispanic: 2,368; unknown: 573. *Age distribution:* number of 18–19: 1,351; 20–21: 2,487; 22–24: 750; 25–29: 50; 30–34: 329; 35–39: 24; 40–49: 337; 50–64: 135.

International Students: 156 nonresident aliens enrolled fall 2004. Programs available to aid students whose native language is not English: Social, cultural. English as a Second Language Program. No financial aid specifically designated for international students.

Student Life: On-campus residence halls house 9% of student body. Dormitories for women only constitute 17% of such space, for both sexes 83%. *Intercollegiate athletics:* men only: basketball, soccer, tennis, track, wrestling; women only: tennis, track, volleyball. *Special regulations:* Cars with term parking stickers or 1 day permits allowed; fee charged. *Special services:* Learning Resources Center, medical services. *Student publications: The Runner*, a weekly newspaper. *Surrounding community:* Bakersfield population 135,000. Fresno, 107 miles from campus, is nearest metropolitan area. Served by mass transit bus system, airport 2 miles from campus, passenger rail service 10 miles from campus.

Library Collections: 450,874 volumes. 725,412 microforms; 2,683 sound recordings; 5,478 film and video materials; 3,168 serial subscriptions. Online catalog. Students have access to online information retrieval services and at no charge for access to the Internet. Total 2004–05 budget for books and materials $551,202.

Most important special collections include the California Odyssey Project; Harlan Hagen Collection.

Buildings and Grounds: Campus area 376 acres. *New buildings:* Raymond S. Dezenber Leadership Development Center opened 2002.

Chief Executive Officer: Dr. Horace Mitchell, President.

Address admission inquiries to Kendyl Magnuson, Associate Director, Admissions/Records.

California State University, Channel Islands

One University Drive
Camarillo, California 93012
Tel: (800) 542-4426   **E-mail:** info@csuci.edu
                                    Internet: www.csuci.edu

Institution Description: *Enrollment:* 1,560. *Degrees awarded:* Baccalaureate.

Accreditation: *Regional:* WASC-Sr.

History: California State University Channel Islands is the newest campus of the state university system. Placing students at the center of the educational experience, the university provides undergraduate and graduate education that facilitates learning within and across disciplines through integrative approaches, emphasizes experiential and service learning, and graduates students with multicultural and international perspectives.

Institutional Structure: *Composition of institution:* Academic affairs headed by vice president of academic affairs. Management/business/finances directed by vice president of business and administration.

Calendar: Semesters. Academic year Aug. to May. Freshmen admitted Aug., Jan. Degrees conferred May, July, Dec. Formal commencement May. Summer session from May to Aug.

Characteristics of Freshmen: 2,195 applicants (874 men, 1,321 women). 60.8% of applicants admitted. 16.6% of admitted students enrolled full-time.

81% (190 students) submitted SAT scores. *25th percentile*: SAT Verbal 450, SAT Math 460. *75th percentile*: SAT Verbal 560, SAT Math 570.

Admission: Rolling admissions plan. For fall acceptance, apply as early as Nov. of previous year, but not later than beginning of term. Early acceptance available.

Degree Requirements: *For baccalaureate degree:* 120 or more units, depending on program pursued. *For master's degree:* development and completion of an approved program of at least 30 units of 200/300-level courses; comprehensive examination.

Distinctive Educational Programs: International and national student exchange programs: Taiwan, Costa Rica, Ireland, Germany, Japan, Republic of China, Sweden, Mexico, Denmark, France, Israel, Italy, New Zealand, Canada, Spain, Zimbabwe, United Kingdom. Student Learning Center.

Degrees Conferred: 142 *baccalaureate.* Bachelor's degrees awarded in top five disciplines: liberal arts and sciences, general studies and humanities 69; business, management, marketing, and related support services 31; visual and performing arts 20; biological and biomedical sciences 8; English language and literature/letters 8.

Fees and Other Expenses: *Full-time fees per academic year 2004–05:* California resident $2,794, out-of-state $12964. *Room and board per academic year:* $8,800. *Books and supplies:* $1,260. *Other expenses:* $2,742.

Financial Aid: Aid from institutionally generated funds is provided on the basis of financial need, other considerations. Institution has a Program Participation Agreement with the U.S. Department of Education for eligible students to receive Pell Grants and other federal aid.

Enrollment: Total enrollment: 1,560. Undergraduate 1,375 (men 38.5%, women 61.5%).

Characteristics of Student Body: *Ethnic and racial makeup:* Black non-Hispanic: 1.7%; American Indian or Alaska Native: 1.2%, 184; Asian or Pacific Islander: 7.9%; Hispanic: 33.3%; White non-Hispanic: 49.4%; unknown: 16.6%.

International Students: 14 nonresident aliens enrolled fall 2004. Programs available to aid students whose native language is not English: Social, cultural. English as a Second Language. No financial aid available specifically for international students.

Student Life: On-campus residence halls. *Intercollegiate athletics:* men only: baseball, basketball, cross-country, football, soccer, track; women only: softball, basketball, cross-country, soccer, track, volleyball. *Special regulations:* Cars permitted without restrictions. *Special services:* Learning Resources Center, medical services.

Library Collections: Library resources are currently being built to accommodate the subject areas of the universities curricula.

Buildings and Grounds: Campus area occupies the site of a former state institutional hospital.

Chief Executive Officer: Dr. Richard R. Rush, President.

Address admission inquiries to Director of Admissions.

California State University, Chico

400 West First Street
Chico, California 95929-0722
Tel: (800) 542-4426   **E-mail:** info@csuchico.edu
Fax: (530) 898-6456   **Internet:** www.csuchico.edu

Institution Description: *Enrollment:* 15,516. *Degrees awarded:* Baccalaureate, master's. Certificates also awarded.

Accreditation: *Regional:* WASC-Sr. *Professional*: art, business, computer science, construction education, dietetics, engineering, industrial technology, journalism, music, nursing, nursing education, public administration, recreation and leisure services, social work, speech-language pathology

History: Established as Chico Normal School 1887; offered first instruction at postsecondary level 1889; awarded first degree (baccalaureate) 1891; changed name to Chico State Teachers College 1921, to Chico State College 1935; adopted present name 1972. *See* C. McIntosh, *Chico State College: The First 75 Years* (Chico: Chico State College, 1972) for further information.

Institutional Structure: *Composition of institution:* Administrators 72 men / 39 women. Academic affairs headed by vice president of academic affairs. Management/business/finances directed by vice president of business and administration. Full-time instructional faculty 615. Academic governance body, Academic Senate, meets an average of 14 times per year.

Calendar: Semesters. Academic year Aug. to May. Freshmen admitted Aug., Jan. Degrees conferred May, July, Dec. Formal commencement May. Summer session from May to Aug.

Characteristics of Freshmen: SAT or ACT scores are only required if high school GPA is less than 3.0. 93% (1,851 students) submitted SAT scores; 56% (516 students) submitted ACT scores. *25th percentile*: SAT Verbal 460, SAT Math 470; ACT Composite 19, ACT English 18, ACT Math 18. *75th percentile*: SAT Verbal 570, SAT Math 570; ACT Composite 24, ACT English 24, ACT Math 24.

83% of applicants accepted. 35% of accepted applicants enrolled. 40% of freshmen expected to graduate within 5 years. 97% of freshmen from California. Freshmen from 10 states and 16 foreign countries.

Admission: Rolling admissions plan. For fall acceptance, apply as early as Nov. of previous year, but not later than beginning of term. Early acceptance available.

Degree Requirements: *For baccalaureate degree:* 120 or more units, depending on program pursued. *For master's degree:* development and completion of an approved program of at least 30 units of 200/300-level courses; comprehensive examination.

Distinctive Educational Programs: Degree programs in agriculture, child development, environmental science, instructional technology, and mechatronics. College of Business's partnership with SAP America, Inc. in their University Alliance Program. School of the Arts; American Language and Culture Institute.

Cooperative and experiential education; internships; continuing education for professionals. Disabled Student Services. Minority Engineering Program. International and national student exchange programs: Taiwan, Costa Rica, Ireland, Germany, Japan, Republic of China, Sweden, Mexico, Denmark, France, Israel, Italy, New Zealand, Canada, Spain, Zimbabwe, United Kingdom. Student Learning Center.

Degrees Conferred: 3,093 *baccalaureate* ; 305 *master's*; 818 *post-bachelor certificates*: 34 *post-master's certificates*. Bachelor's degrees awarded in top five disciplines: business, management, marketing, and related support services 602; liberal arts and sciences, general studies, and humanities 367; visual and performing arts 340; social sciences 273; parks, recreation, leisure and fitness studies 208.

Fees and Other Expenses: *Full-time fees per academic year 2004–05:* California resident $3,154, out-of-state $13,324. *Room and board per academic year:* $8,730. *Books and supplies:* $1,250. *Other expenses:* $2,500.

Financial Aid: Aid from institutionally generated funds is provided on the basis of financial need, other considerations. Institution has a Program Participation Agreement with the U.S. Department of Education for eligible students to receive Pell Grants and other federal aid.

Financial aid to full-time, first-time undergraduate students: 245 received federal grants averaging $3,361; 33% state/local grants averaging $1,964; 24% institutional grants averaging $2,152; 33% loans averaging $2,569.

Departments and Teaching Staff: *Total instructional faculty:* 615. *Total tenured faculty* 545. *Degrees held by full-time faculty:* Doctorate 62%.

Enrollment: Total enrollment 15,516. Undergraduate 13,903; graduate and professional students 1,613.

Characteristics of Student Body: *Ethnic and racial makeup:* number of Black non-Hispanic: 258; American Indian or Alaska Native: 184; Asian or Pacific Islander: 712; Hispanic: 1,443; White non-Hispanic: 9,117; unknown: 1,859.

International Students: 330 nonresident aliens enrolled fall 2004. Programs available to aid students whose native language is not English: Social, cultural. English as a Second Language. No financial aid available specifically for international students.

Student Life: On-campus residence halls. *Intercollegiate athletics:* men only: baseball, basketball, cross-country, football, soccer, track; women only: softball, basketball, cross-country, soccer, track, volleyball. *Special regulations:* Cars permitted without restrictions. *Special services:* Learning Resources Center, medical services. *Student publications, radio: The Orion,* a weekly newspaper. Radio stations KCSC and KCHO broadcast a total of 168 hours per week. Over 200 student organizations available. *Surrounding community:* Chico population 50,000. Sacramento, 98 miles from campus, is nearest metropolitan area. Served by airport 6 miles from campus; passenger rail service adjacent to campus.

Library Collections: 948,700 volumes. 1,140,500 microforms; 22,965 audiovisual materials; 3,095 current periodical subscriptions. Online catalog. Students have access to online information retrieval services and access at no charge to the Internet.

Most important holdings include John Bidwell Collection; Northeastern California Historical Photograph Collection; Sacramento Valley Sugar Company Papers; Senator Clair Engle Collection.

Buildings and Grounds: Campus area 130 acres plus university farm of 734 acres.

Chief Executive Officer: Dr. Paul J. Zingg, President.

Address admission inquiries to John F. Swiney, Director of Admission.

California State University, Dominguez Hills

1000 East Victoria Street
Carson, California 90747

Tel: (310) 243-3532   **E-mail:** infor@csudh.edu
Fax: (310) 516-3870   **Internet:** www.csudh.edu

Institution Description: *Enrollment:* 13,613. *Degrees awarded:* Baccalaureate, master's. Certificates also awarded.

Member of Los Angeles Urban Consortium of Higher Education, Southern California Ocean Studies Consortium.

Accreditation: *Regional:* WASC-Sr. *Professional:* business, clinical lab scientist, computer science, music, nursing, occupational therapy, orthist/prothetist, public administration, teacher education, theatre

History: Established as California State College, Dominguez Hills and chartered 1960; offered first instruction at postsecondary level 1965; awarded first degree (baccalaureate) 1967; adopted present name 1977.

Institutional Structure: *Composition of institution:* Administrators 33 men / 10 women. Academic affairs headed by president. Management/business/finances directed by vice president, operations. Full-time instructional faculty

252. Academic governance body, Academic Senate, meets an average of 20 times per year.

Calendar: Semesters. Academic year Aug. to May. Freshmen admitted beginning of each semester. Degrees conferred at end of each semester and in summer. Formal commencement June.

Characteristics of Freshmen: 75% of applicants accepted. 74.7% of accepted applicants enrolled. 28.3% of entering freshmen expected to graduate within 5 years. 88% of freshmen from California.

25.6% (188 students) submitted SAT scores. *25th percentile:* SAT Verbal 360, SAT Math 370; ACT Composite 13, ACT English 12, ACT Math 15. *75th percentile:* SAT Verbal 470, SAT Math 480; ACT Composite 19, ACT English 19, ACT Math 19.

Admission: Rolling admissions plan. For fall acceptance, apply as early as Nov. 1 of previous year. Early decision available, must limit application to CSU, Dominguez Hills. Early acceptance available. Top one-third of high school graduates are eligible. Applicants with grade point averages above 3.10 (3.60 for nonresidents) are exempt for the test requirement.

Degree Requirements: 120 units or more as specified by the curricular requirements.

School offers college credit for extrainstitutional learning on basis of ACE *2006 Guide to the Evaluation of Educational Experiences in the Armed Services,* portfolio and faculty assessments. Tutoring available. Credit given for developmental courses offered in summer session and regular academic year.

Distinctive Educational Programs: Work-experience programs. Weekend and evening classes. Accelerated degree programs. Cooperative baccalaureate program in health sciences. External degree programs in humanities at various locations. Special facilities for using telecommunications in the classroom. Pre-professional programs in dentistry, medicine, optometry, osteopathy, pharmacy, podiatry, veterinary medicine. Facilities and programs for independent research, including individual majors, tutorials. Interdisciplinary programs in Afro-American studies, behavioral science, computer science, earth and marine sciences, East Asian/Asian-American studies, energy studies, health science, human services, labor studies, liberal studies, linguistics, medical technology, Mexican-American studies, psychobiology, recreation, religious studies.

ROTC: Army in cooperation with UCLA and CSU Long Beach; Air Force in cooperation with USC, UCLA, Loyola Marymount University.

Degrees Conferred: 1,836 *baccalaureate* (B); 1,074 *master's* (M): biological/life sciences 4 (B), 8 (M); business/marketing 31 (B), 121 (M); communications/communication technologies 74 (B); computer and information sciences 26 (M); education 539 (M); engineering and engineering technologies 24 (M); English 52 (B), 16 (M); foreign languages and literature 37 (B); health professions and related sciences 222 (B), 78 (M); home economics and vocational home economics 23 (M); interdisciplinary studies 3 (B), 1 (M); liberal arts/general studies 500 (B), 112 (M); parks and recreation 47 (B); philosophy/religion/theology 2 (B); physical sciences 10 (B); protective services/public administration 154 (B), 60 (M); psychology 111 (B), 81 (M); social sciences and history 288 (B), 11 (M); visual and performing arts 40 (B), 8 (M); other 40 (B), 8 (M).

Fees and Other Expenses: *Full-time undergraduate tuition per academic year 2004–05:* $2,704. *Books and supplies:* $1,260. *Room and board per academic year:* $7,180.

Financial Aid: Aid from institutionally generated funds is provided on the basis of financial need. Institution has a Program Participation Agreement with the U.S. Department of Education for eligible students to receive Pell Grants and other federal aid.

Undergraduate need-based scholarships/grants: $21,606,600; self-help $14,634,055; parent loans $76,917; athletic awards $174,176; non-need-based scholarships/grants $27,172; self-help $878,147; parent loans $36,150; athletic awards $32,927.

Departments and Teaching Staff: *Total instructional faculty:* 678 (full-time 252, part-time 426; women 360; men 318). Total number with doctorate, first-professional, or other terminal degree: 361. Student-to-faculty ratio: 22:1.

Enrollment: Total enrollment 13,613. Undergraduate full-time 1,793 men / 3,723 women 7,834; part-time 940m / 2,242w. Graduate full-time 447m / 1,075w; part-time 719m / 1,674w.

Characteristics of Student Body: *Ethnic/racial makeup:* number of Black non-Hispanic: 2,415; American Indian or Alaska Native: 53; Asian or Pacific Islander: 789; Hispanic: 3,150; White non-Hispanic: 1,204; unknown: 1. *Age distribution:* number under 18: 487; 18–19: 1,259, 20–21: 1,121; 22–24: 1,814; 25–29: 1536; 30–34: 874, 35–39: 594; 40–49: 512; 50–64: 348; 65 and over: 23.

International Students: 236 nonresident aliens enrolled fall 2004. No programs available to aid students whose native language is not English. Financial aid specifically designated for foreign students: loans available for international students.

Student Life: Apartments available for single and married students. *Intercollegiate athletics:* men only: baseball, basketball, cross-country, golf, soccer; women only: basketball, cross-country, softball, volleyball. *Special regulations:*

Cars permitted; parking permit each semester required. *Special services:* Medical services. *Student publications: Dominguez News,* a weekly newspaper; *Panorama,* a quarterly literary magazine. *Surrounding community:* Los Angeles population 3,500,000. Served by mass transit bus system; airport 13 miles from campus.

Library Collections: 396,500 volumes. 74,577 government documents; 640,802 microforms; 17,130 audiovisual materials; 4,740 periodicals. Online catalog. Students have access to online information retrieval services and the Internet.

Most important holdings include collections of Rancho San Pedro Historical Papers; Claudia Buckner Collection of American Bestsellers; California State University Archives.

Buildings and Grounds: Campus area 346 acres. *New buildings:* James L. Welch Hall completed 2002.

Chief Executive Officer: Dr. James E. Lyons, President.

Address admission inquiries to James Wood, Director of Admissions.

California State University, East Bay

25800 Carlos Bee Boulevard
Hayward, California 94542
Tel: (510) 885-3000   **E-mail:** info@csueastbay.edu
Fax: (510) 885-3816   **Internet:** www.csueastbay.edu

Institution Description: California State University, Hayward was renamed California State University, East Bay in 2004. *Enrollment:* 13,455. *Degrees awarded:* Baccalaureate, master's. Certificates also awarded.

Accreditation: *Regional:* WASC-Sr. *Professional:* art, business, music, nursing, public administration, speech-language pathology, teacher education

History: Established as Alameda County State College and chartered 1957; offered first instruction at postsecondary level 1959; awarded first degree (baccalaureate) 1961; changed name to California State College at Hayward 1963, to California State College, Hayward 1968; became California State University, Hayward 1972; adopted present name 2004.

Institutional Structure: *Composition of institution:* Administrators 31 men / 10 women. Academic affairs headed by Provost and Vice President, Academic Affairs. Management/business/finances directed by Vice President, Administration and Business Affairs. Student Services headed by Vice President, Student Services. Full-time instructional faculty 370. Academic governance body, Academic Senate, meets an average of 9 times per year.

Calendar: Quarters. Academic year late Sept. to mid-June. Freshmen admitted Sept., Dec., March, July. Formal commencement June.

Characteristics of Freshmen: 4,700 applicants (1,197 men, 2,903 women). 46% of applicants admitted; 31.2% admitted students enrolled full-time.

77% (533 students) submitted SAT scores. *25th percentile*: SAT Verbal 390, SAT Math 420. *75th percentile*: SAT Verbal 530, SAT Math 550.

23.1% of entering freshmen expected to graduate within 5 years. 84.6% of freshmen from California. Freshmen from 4 states and 19 foreign countries.

Admission: Rolling admissions plan. For fall acceptance, apply as early as Nov. 1 of previous year, but not later than beginning of quarter. Early acceptance available.

Degree Requirements: Minimum 120 more credits depending on curricular requirements. College credit for extrainstitutional learning on basis of ACE *2006 Guide to the Evaluation of Educational Experiences in the Armed Services.* Tutoring available. Limited credit given for remedial courses offered during regular academic year.

Distinctive Educational Programs: Flexible meeting places and schedules, including off-campus center (at Pleasant Hill; 30 miles away from main institution), weekend and evening classes. Cooperative work programs on a paid or volunteer basis available in many departments. Cross-registration with the University of California, Berkeley and with Chabot, Merritt, and Mills Colleges. Preprofessional programs in engineering, health sciences, theology. Interdepartmental or interdisciplinary programs in environmental studies, general studies, liberal studies, religious studies, urban studies, western heritage, women's studies. Study abroad through London Semester, London Summer Quarter, Middlesex Exchange with Middlesex Polytechnic in London, the Geneva Accord at the University of Geneva, Switzerland, International Programs at a foreign university or special program center. *Other distinctive programs:* Continuing education; credit given.

ROTC: Army, Navy, Air Force.

Degrees Conferred: 2,396 *baccalaureate*; 1,226 *master's.* Bachelor's degrees awarded in top five disciplines: business, management, marketing, and related support services 521; liberal arts and sciences, general studies, and humanities 329; social sciences 178; computer and information sciences and support services 169; health professions and related sciences 119.

Fees and Other Expenses: *Full-time tuition per academic year 2004–95:* in-state resident $2,706, out-of-state $12,876. *Books and supplies:* $1,260. *Room and board per academic year:* $6,423. *Other expenses:* $2,988.

Financial Aid: Aid from institutionally generated funds is provided on the basis of academic merit, financial need. Institution has a Program Participation Agreement with the U.S. Department of Education for eligible students to receive Pell Grants and other federal aid.

Financial aid to full-time, first-time undergraduate students: 36% received federal grants averaging $3,430; 33% state/local grants averaging $1,574; 37% institutional grants averaging $1,850; 15% loans averaging $2,557.

Departments and Teaching Staff: *Total instruction faculty:* 510 (full-time 374, part-time 136).

Enrollment: *Total enrollment:* 13,455. Undergraduate 9,685 (37.2% men, 62.8% women).

Characteristics of Student Body: *Ethnic/racial makeup:* Black non-Hispanic: 10.2%; American Indian or Alaska Native: .6%; Asian or Pacific Islander: 27.3%; Hispanic: 12%; White non-Hispanic: 23.9%; unknown: 20.2%. *Age distribution:* 17–21: 22.6%; 22–24: 24.2%; 25–29: 20.9%; 30–34: 12.6%, 35–39: 9.2%; 40–49: 8.2%; 50–59: 1.6%; 60 and over: 0.7%.

International Students: 571 nonresident aliens enrolled fall 2004. Programs available to aid students whose native language is not English: English as a Second Language Program. No financial programs specifically designated for international students.

Student Life: On-campus housing available. *Intercollegiate athletics:* men only: baseball, basketball, cross-country, football, soccer, swimming, tennis, track, water polo; women only: basketball, cross-country, gymnastics, softball, swimming, tennis, track, volleyball. Both sexes, badminton, judo. *Special regulations:* Cars permitted in designated areas. *Special services:* Learning Resources Center, medical services. *Student publications: Escape,* an annual magazine; *The Pioneer,* a biweekly newspaper. *Surrounding community:* Hayward population 95,000. Oakland, 12 miles from campus, is nearest metropolitan area. Served by mass transit bus and subway system; airport 12 miles from campus; passenger rail service 15 miles from campus.

Library Collections: 850,000 volumes. 700,000 microforms; 26,000 audiovisual materials. 1,900 periodicals subscriptions. Online catalog. Students have access to online information retrieval services and the Internet.

Most important holdings include Jensen Family Papers, collection of Bay Area poetry, Western U.S. fine press books.

Buildings and Grounds: Campus area 348 acres.

Chief Executive Officer: Dr. Norma S. Rees, President.

Address admission inquiries to Robert Strobel, Director of Admissions.

California State University, Fresno

5241 North Maple Avenue
Fresno, California 93740
Tel: (559) 278-4240   **E-mail:** info@csufresno.edu
Fax: (559) 278-4812   **Internet:** www.csufresno.edu

Institution Description: *Enrollment:* 22,342. *Degrees awarded:* Baccalaureate, master's.

Accreditation: *Regional:* WASC-Sr. *Professional:* athletic training, business, construction education, counseling, dietetics, engineering, environmental health, industrial technology, interior design, journalism, music, nursing, physical therapy, public administration, public health, recreation and leisure services, rehabilitation counseling, social work, speech-language pathology, teacher education, theatre

History: Established as Fresno State Normal School, chartered, and offered first instruction at postsecondary level 1911; awarded first degree (baccalaureate), changed name to Fresno State Teachers College and became 4-year institution 1921; changed name to Fresno State College 1935; adopted present name 1972.

Institutional Structure: *Composition of institution:* Administrators 84 men / 53 women. Academic affairs headed by vice president for academic affairs. Management/business/finances directed by director of budget and finance. Full-time tenured instructional faculty 681. Academic governance body, Academic Senate, meets an average of 12 times per year.

Calendar: Semesters. Academic year late Aug. to mid-May. Freshmen admitted Aug., Jan., May. Degrees conferred May, Aug., Dec. Formal commencement May. Summer session from late May to mid-Aug.

Characteristics of Freshmen: 10,401 applicants (4,593 men, 5,808 women). 69.7% admitted; 34.3% admitted and enrolled full-time.

86% (2,260 students) submitted SAT scores. *25th percentile*: SAT Verbal 400, SAT Math 420; *75th percentile*: SAT Verbal 530, SAT Math 550.

97% of freshmen from California. Freshmen from 42 states and 65 foreign countries.

Admission: Rolling admissions plan. For fall acceptance, apply as early as Nov. of previous year, but not later than Aug. of year of enrollment. Early acceptance available.

Degree Requirements: Minimum 124 semester units; academic major; general education requirements; specific course/skill requirements; minimum of 30 residence units; minimum of 40 upper division units; minimum of C average for units in major, all CSU Fresno units, and total units.

School offers college credit for extrainstitutional learning on basis of ACE *2006 Guide to the Evaluation of Educational Experiences in the Armed Services.* Tutoring and noncredit developmental and remedial courses available.

Distinctive Educational Programs: Work-experience programs. Flexible meeting places and schedules, including off-campus centers (at Visalia; 50 miles away from main institution) and evening classes. Special facilities for using telecommunications in the classroom. Interdisciplinary programs in Armenian studies; Asian studies, child development, Classical studies, computer science, gerontology, Latin American studies, liberal studies, Russian area studies, women's studies. Facilities and programs for independent research, including individual majors, tutorials. *Other distinctive programs:* Continuing education. Study abroad in Australia, Brazil, Canada, Chile, China, Costa Rica, Denmark, England, France, Germany, Israel, Italy, Japan, Malta, Mexico, New Zealand, Scotland, Spain, Sweden, Thailand, Taiwan.

ROTC: Army, Air Force.

Degrees Conferred: 2,922 *baccalaureate*; 563 *master's*; 2 *doctorate.* Bachelor's degrees awarded in top five disciplines: liberal arts and sciences, general studies, and humanities 616; business, management, marketing, and related support services 496; health professions and related clinical sciences 250; social sciences 236; psychology 163.

Fees and Other Expenses: *Full-time undergraduate tuition per academic year 2004–05:* in-state $2,704, out-of-state $12,874. *Books and supplies:* $1,260. *Other expenses:* $2,184.

Financial Aid: Institutional direct lending program available. Aid from institutionally generated funds is provided on the basis of financial need. Institution has a Program Participation Agreement with the U.S. Department of Education for eligible students to receive Pell Grants and other federal aid.

Financial aid to full-time, first-time undergraduate students: 42% received federal grants averaging $3,409; 48% state/local grants averaging $1,714; 48% institutional grants averaging $2,348; 19% loans averaging $2,536.

Departments and Teaching Staff: *Total instructional faculty:* 1,101 (full-time 681). Student-to-faculty ratio: 21:1.

Enrollment: Total enrollment 22,342. Undergraduate 18,708 (42.1% men, 57.9% women).

Characteristics of Student Body: *Ethnic/racial makeup:* Black non-Hispanic: 4.8%; American Indian or Alaska Native: .9%; Asian or Pacific Islander: 12.8%; Hispanic: 26.4%; White non-Hispanic: 36.2%.

International Students: 580 nonresident aliens enrolled fall 2004. Social and cultural programs available to aid students whose native language is not English. English as a Second Language Program. No financial aid programs specifically designated for international students.

Student Life: On-campus residence halls house 6% of student body. Dormitories for men only constitute 4% of such space, for women only 25%, for both sexes 71%. 8% of men live in fraternities; 4% of women live in sororities. *Intercollegiate athletics:* men: baseball, basketball, cross-country, football, golf, soccer, tennis, track, wrestling; women: basketball, cross-country, softball, swimming/diving, track and field, tennis, volleyball; both sexes: badminton. *Special regulations:* Cars permitted without restrictions. *Special services:* Learning Resources Center, medical services. *Student publications, radio: Daily Collegian, Insight, La Voz, Uhuru,* all newspapers. Radio station KFSR broadcasts 50 hours per week. *Surrounding community:* Fresno county metropolitan area population 850,000. Served by mass transit bus system; airport 6 miles from campus; passenger rail service 10 miles from campus.

Library Collections: 978,000 volumes. 1,207,500 microforms; 2,560 current periodicals. 71,500 audiovisual materials. Online catalog. Access to online information retrieval systems. Students have access to the Internet at no charge.

Most important holdings include Roy J. Woodward Memorial Library of California (on San Joaquin Valley and the Sierra Nevadas); Donald G. Larson Collection of International Fairs and Expositions, 1851–1940; manuscripts and printed materials about Credit Foncier of Topolobampo; American utopian colony in Mexico.

Buildings and Grounds: Campus area 330.

Chief Executive Officer: Dr. John D. Welty, President.

Address admission inquiries to Bernie Vinovrski, Director of Enrollment Services.

California State University, Fullerton

800 North State College Boulevard
Fullerton, California 92634-9480
Tel: (714) 278-2011   **E-mail:** arservicecenter@csufullerton.edu
Fax: (714) 278-2649   **Internet:** www.csufullerton.edu

Institution Description: California State University, Fullerton is a state institution. *Enrollment:* 32,744. *Degrees awarded:* Baccalaureate, master's.

Member of Southern California Ocean Studies Consortium, Desert Studies Consortium.

Accreditation: *Regional:* WASC-Sr. *Professional:* accounting, art, business, computer science, dance, engineering, journalism, music, nurse anesthesia education, nursing, nursing education, public administration, speech-language pathology, teacher education

History: Established and chartered as Orange County State College 1957; offered first instruction at postsecondary level 1959; awarded first degree (baccalaureate) 1960; changed name to Orange State College 1962, to California State College at Fullerton 1964; adopted present name 1972.

Institutional Structure: *Composition of institution:* Administrators 44 men / 33 women. Academic affairs headed by Vice President; Student Affairs headed by Vice President; Administration headed by Vice President; University Advancement headed by Vice President. Full-time instructional faculty 1,078.3 FTE. Academic governance body, Academic Senate, meets an average of 20 times per year.

Calendar: Semesters. Academic year Aug. to June. Freshmen admitted Sept., Feb. Degrees conferred June, Sept., Jan. Formal commencement May. Summer session of 12 weeks from early June to mid-Aug.

Characteristics of Freshmen: 97% (3,516 students) submitted SAT scores; 19% (704 students) submitted ACT scores. *25th percentile:* SAT Verbal 430, SAT Math 450; ACT Composite 17, ACT English 16, ACT Math 17. *75th percentile:* SAT Verbal 540, SAT Math 560; ACT Composite 22, ACT English 22, ACT Math 24.

13,446 applicants admitted; 36.27% admitted and enrolled. 98% of freshmen from California. Freshmen from 20 states and 17 foreign countries.

Admission: Rolling admissions plan. For fall acceptance, apply as early as Nov. 1 of previous year, but not later than registration period. Apply by end of junior year of secondary school for early decision; need not limit application to Fullerton. Early acceptance available.

Degree Requirements: *For baccalaureate degree:* minimum 120 semester units depending on major; minimum of 40 units must be upper division courses; completion of minimum of 30 semester hours in residence; 2.0 GPA or better. *For master's degree:* minimum of 30 approved semester units or more, as determined by the particular program, and of this total a minimum of 21 semester units in residence; 3.0 GPA or better; final evaluation required (thesis, project, comprehensive examination, or a combination of these).

Distinctive Educational Programs: Work-experience programs, including cooperative education, internships. Evening classes. Cooperative program in foreign languages and literature with University of California, Los Angeles. Special facilities for using telecommunications in the classroom. Interdisciplinary programs in American studies, Chicano studies, environmental studies, ethnic studies, Latin American studies, liberal studies, Russian and East European area studies. Facilities and programs for independent research, including honors programs, individual majors, tutorials. Study abroad in Australia, Brazil, Canada, Denmark, France, Germany, Israel, Italy, Japan, Mexico, New Zealand, Spain, Sweden, Taiwan, United Kingdom, Zimbabwe (all CSU Systemwide Programs); Russia, China, France, Japan, Mexico (CSU Fullerton Campus-Based Exchange Programs). *Other distinctive programs:* Center for Professional Development. Center for Economic Education. International Business Center. Institute for Early Childhood Education. Institute for Bilingual Studies. Laboratory for Phonetic Research. Speech and Hearing Clinic. Sport and Movement Institute. Institute for Community Research and Development. Institute of Geophysics. Tucker Wildlife Sanctuary.

ROTC: Army in cooperation with the Claremont Colleges.

Degrees Conferred: 5,636 *baccalaureate* (B); 1,242 *master's* (M): area and ethnic studies 74 (B), 7 (M); biological/life sciences 114 (B), 19 (M); business/marketing 1,261 (B), 163 (M); communications/communication technologies 677 (B), 47 (M); computer and information sciences 357 (B), 96 (M); education 506 (B), 461 (M); engineering and engineering technologies 53 (B), 47 (M); English 181 (B), 42 (M); foreign languages and literature 51 (B), 2 (M); health professions and related sciences 180 (B); 50 (M); interdisciplinary studies 29 (M); liberal arts/general studies 433 (B); mathematics 37 (B), 15 (M); parks and recreation 130 (B), 14 (M); philosophy, religion, theology 23 (B); physical sciences 27 (B), 15 (M); protective services/public administration 423 (B); 22 (M); psychology 263 (B), 100 (M); social sciences and history 508 (B), 77 (M); visual and performing arts 338 (B), 36 (M).

Fees and Other Expenses: *Fees per academic year 2004–05:* All full-time undergraduate in-state students pay a fee of $2,804 per year; out-of-state pay an additional $339 per unit; all full-time in-state graduate students pay a fee of $3,290 per year, out-of-state students pay an additional $339 per unit. *Room per academic year:* $5,813.

Financial Aid: Aid from institutionally generated funds is provided on the basis of academic merit, financial need, athletic ability. Financial assistance is available in the form of Pell Grants, College Work-Study, Veterans Administration Benefits, National Direct Student Loans, Supplemental Education Opportunity Grants (SEOG), Higher Education Assistance Loans (HEAL), Stafford Loans, other federal aid programs.

Departments and Teaching Staff: *Total instructional faculty:* 1,935 (full-time 319, part-time 1,216). Student-to-faculty ratio: 21:1. *Degrees held by full-time faculty:* doctorate 86.5%, master's 10.9%, baccalaureate 1.8%, professional 0.8%.

Enrollment: Total enrollment 32,744. Undergraduate 20,855.

Characteristics of Student Body: *Ethnic/racial makeup:* number of Black non-Hispanic: 845; American Indian or Alaska Native: 156; Asian or Pacific Islander: 6,104; Hispanic: 7,143; White non-Hispanic: 8,926; unknown: 2,998.

International Students: 1,056 nonresident aliens enrolled fall 2004. No programs available to aid students whose native language is not English. No financial aid specifically designated for international students.

Student Life: On-campus housing for 800 students. *Intercollegiate athletics:* men only: baseball, basketball, cross-country, soccer, wrestling; women only: basketball, cross-country, fencing, gymnastics, soccer, softball, tennis, volleyball. *Special regulations:* Cars permitted without restrictions. *Special services:* Handicapped student services, medical services, learning assistance resource center, women's center, center for internships and cooperative education, writing assistance center. *Student publications: Daily Titan,* a campus newspaper published 4 times a week during the academic year. *Surrounding community:* Fullerton is located in the Los Angeles metropolitan area (population 3,100,000). Served by mass transit bus system. Airport 17 miles from campus; passenger rail service 3 miles from campus.

Library Collections: 1,169,030 volumes. 342,864 government documents; 970,429 microforms; 42,870 audiovisual materials; 2,603 current periodical subscriptions. Online catalog. Students have access to online information retrieval services and the Internet.

Most important holdings include collections of science fiction manuscripts; history of cartography collection; Kerridge Angling Collection.

Buildings and Grounds: Campus area 225 acres. *New buildings:* Residence hall housing for 440 students completed 2003; major addition to Physical Education Building 2004.

Chief Executive Officer: Dr. Milton A. Gordon, President.
Address admission inquiries to Office of Admissions and Records.

California State University, Long Beach

1250 Bellflower Boulevard
Long Beach, California 90840
Tel: (562) 985-4111   **E-mail:** eslb@csulb.edu
Fax: (562) 985-4973   **Internet:** www.csulb.edu

Institution Description: *Enrollment:* 33,479. *Degrees awarded:* Baccalaureate, master's. Certificates also awarded.

Accreditation: *Regional:* WASC-Sr. *Professional:* art, audiology, business, computer science, dance, dietetics, engineering, engineering technology, English language education, family and consumer science, music, nursing, nursing education, phlebotomy, physical therapy, psychology internship, public administration, public health, radiation therapy, radiation therapy technology, recreation and leisure services, social work, speech-language pathology, teacher education, theatre

History: Established as Los Angeles-Orange County State College and offered first instruction at postsecondary level 1949; awarded first degree (baccalaureate) and changed name to Long Beach State College 1950; changed name to California State College, Long Beach 1968; adopted present name 1972. *See* Robert Breunig, *History of California State University, Long Beach* (Long Beach: California State University, 1979) for further information.

Institutional Structure: *Composition of institution:* Administrators 98 men / 94 women. Academic affairs headed by vice president for academic affairs. Management/business/finances directed by vice president for administration and finance. Total instructional faculty 1,877. Academic governance body, Academic Senate, meets an average of 16 times per year.

Calendar: Semesters. 2004–05 academic year Aug. 23 to May 27. Freshmen admitted Aug., Jan. Degrees conferred May, Dec. Formal commencement May. Summer session from early June to mid-Aug.

Characteristics of Freshmen: 97% (3,299 students) submitted SAT scores; 30% (1,027 students) submitted ACT scores. *25th percentile:* SAT Verbal 440, SAT Math 470; ACT Composite 17, ACT English 16, ACT Math 17. *75th percentile:* SAT Verbal 550, SAT Math 580; ACT Composite 23, ACT English 23, ACT Math 24.

39% of applicants admitted; 10.2% admitted and enrolled. 32% of entering freshmen expected to graduate within 5 years. 99% of freshmen from California. Freshmen from 23 states and 64 foreign countries.

Admission: Rolling admissions plan. Admission deadline for first-time freshmen Nov. 30. Students notified of acceptance on a rolling basis.

Degree Requirements: Completion of prescribed curriculum. School offers college credit for extrainstitutional learning on basis of ACE *2006 Guide to the Evaluation of Educational Experiences in the Armed Services.* Tutoring available. Credit given for developmental/remedial courses offered in summer session and regular academic year.

Distinctive Educational Programs: Work-experience programs and internships. Weekend and evening classes. Special facilities for using telecommunications in the classroom. Interdisciplinary programs in American studies; Asian studies, black studies, Chicano-Latino studies, women's studies. Facilities and programs for independent research, including honors programs for graduate students, individual majors, directed and independent study. Study abroad participation in CSU International Programs (16 countries) and CSULB Exchange Programs (14 countries).

ROTC: Army.

Degrees Conferred: 4,078 *baccalaureate* (B), 1,181 *master's* (M): area and ethnic studies 36 (B), 9 (M); biological and life sciences 139 (B), 15 (M); business 713 (B), 116 (M); communications/communication technologies 104 (B); computer and information science 38 (B), 41 (M); education 332 (B), 147 (M); engineering/engineering technologies 286 (B), 125 (M); English 250 (B), 47 (M); foreign languages and literature 63 (B), 21 (M); health professions and related sciences 296 (B), 107 (M); home economics 124 (B), 5 (M); liberal arts/general studies 56 (B); mathematics 19 (B), 11 (M); parks and recreation 147 (B), 42 (M); philosophy/religious studies/interdisciplinary 46 (B), 18 (M); physical sciences 24 (B), 6 (M); protective services/public administration 285 (B), 311 (M); psychology 380 (B), 68 (M); social sciences and history 402 (B), 44 (M); visual and performing arts 338 (B), 48 (M).

Fees and Other Expenses: *Full-time fees per academic year 2004–05:* undergraduate in-state $2,864, out-of-state $5,397; graduate in-state $3,446, out-of-state $6,780. *Room and board per academic year:* $6,530.

Financial Aid: Aid from institutionally generated funds is provided on the basis of academic merit, financial need, athletic ability. Institution has a Program Participation Agreement with the U.S. Department of Education for eligible students to receive Pell Grants and other federal aid.

Undergraduate need-based scholarships/grants totaling $55,500,000, self-help $37,500,000, parent loans $2,700,000; non-need-based scholarships/grants totaling $30,000, self-help $15,000,000, tuition waivers $425,000, athletic awards $1,300,000. *Graduate aid:* 1,028 fellowships and grants totaling $3,700,000; 2,149 loans totaling $25,000,000; 124 work-study jobs totaling $335,480.

Departments and Teaching Staff: *Total instructional faculty:* 1,846 (full-time 969, part-time 877; 844 women, 1,002 men). Total faculty with doctorate, first-professional, or other terminal degree: 1,070. Total tenured faculty: 623. Student-to-faculty ratio: 20:1. Degrees held by full-time faculty: Doctorate 80%, master's 18%, baccalaureate 2%.

Enrollment: Total enrollment 33,479. Undergraduate full-time 23,635; part-time 9,844.

Characteristics of Student Body: *Ethnic/racial makeup:* number of Black non-Hispanic: 1,577; American Indian or Alaska Native: 178; Asian or Pacific Islander: 4,342; Hispanic: 8,194, White non-Hispanic: 8,864; unknown: 2,701.

International Students: 1,324 nonresident aliens enrolled fall 2004. 207 students from Europe, 912 Asia, 57 Latin America, 27 Africa, 15 Canada, 2 Australia, other 336. Programs available to aid students whose native language is not English: Social, cultural. English as a Second Language Program. No financial aid specifically designated for international students.

Student Life: On-campus residence halls house 6.1% of student body. Dormitories are all coed. 7% of men join and 4% live in fraternity houses; 5% of women join and 3% live in sorority houses. *Intercollegiate athletics:* men only: baseball, basketball, cross-country, golf, track, volleyball, water polo; women only: basketball, cross-country, golf, soccer, softball, tennis, track, water polo, volleyball. *Special regulations:* Cars permitted without restrictions. *Special services:* Learning Resources Center, medical services. *Student publications: The Daily 49'er,* a newspaper; *The Union Daily,* a newspaper. *Surrounding community:* Long Beach population 450,000. Los Angeles, 17 miles from campus, is nearest metropolitan area. Served by mass transit bus system; airport 3 miles from campus.

Publications: *Critique: Southern California Public Policy and Administration* (quarterly) first published in 1976, *Current Business Prospectives* (quarterly) first published 1981, *The History Teacher* (quarterly) first published 1972; *The Journal of Criminal Justice* (annually) first published 1978.

Library Collections: 1,472,080 volumes including bound books, serial backfiles, electronic documents, and government documents not in separate collections. Online catalog. Current serial subscriptions of paper, microform, electronic 6,617. Microforms 1,427,206; audiovisual materials 34,609. Over 2,000 computer work stations. Students have access to the Internet at no charge.

Most important holdings include Dumond Collection on the abolitionist movement from 1810–1864; Dorothy Healey Collection on radical politics in Southern California; Samuel Taylor Coleridge Collection.

Buildings and Grounds: Campus area 322 acres. *New buildings:* Science Building completed 2002.

Chief Executive Officer: Dr. Robert C. Maxson, President.

Address admission inquiries to Thomas Enders, Assistant Vice President, Enrollment Services (e-mail: tenders@csulb.edu).

California State University, Los Angeles

5151 State University Drive
Los Angeles, California 90032
Tel: (323) 343-2000   **E-mail:** admission@calstatela.edu
Fax: (323) 343-6469   **Internet:** www.calstatela.edu

Institution Description: *Enrollment:* 20,307. *Degrees awarded:* Baccalaureate, master's. Certificates also awarded.

Accreditation: *Regional:* WASC-Sr. *Professional:* art, audiology, business, computer science, dance, dietetics, engineering, engineering technology, English language education, family and consumer science, music, nursing, nursing education, phlebotomy, physical therapy, psychology internship, public administration, public health, radiation therapy, radiation therapy technology, recreation and leisure services, social work, speech-language pathology, teacher education, theatre

History: Established as Los Angeles State College, chartered, and offered first instruction at postsecondary level 1947; awarded first degree (baccalaureate) 1948; changed name to Los Angeles State College of Applied Arts and Sciences 1949, California State College at Los Angeles 1964, California State College, Los Angeles 1968; adopted present name 1972.

Institutional Structure: *Composition of institution:* Administrators 59 men / 45 women. Academic affairs headed by vice president for academic affairs and provost. Management/business/finances directed by vice president for operations. Full-time instructional faculty 317 men / 249 women. Academic governance body, Academic Senate, meets an average of 35 times per year.

Calendar: Quarters. Academic year Sept. to June. Freshmen admitted Sept., Jan., Mar., June. Degrees conferred June, Sept., Dec., Mar. Formal commencement June. Summer quarter from June to Sept.

Characteristics of Freshmen: 11,551 applicants (4,194 men, 7,357 women). 45% of applicants admitted; 18% admitted and enrolled full-time. 98% of freshmen from California. Freshmen from 7 states and 13 foreign countries.

74% (858 students) submitted SAT scores; 10% (118 students) submitted ACT scores. *25th percentile:* SAT Verbal 380, SAT Math 400; ACT Composite 16, ACT English 14, ACT Math 16. *75th percentile:* SAT Verbal 490, SAT Math 520; ACT Composite 20, ACT English 20, ACT Math 21.

Admission: Rolling admissions plan. For fall quarter, apply as early as Nov. 1, but no later than Aug. 7; foreign students by Feb. 28. Apply by Nov 1 for early decision; need not limit application to California State University, Los Angeles. Early acceptance available.

College credit for extrainstitutional learning on basis of ACE *2006 Guide to the Evaluation of Educational Experiences in the Armed Services*, portfolio, faculty assessments, personal interviews, Peace Corps training, and active duty in the military. Tutoring available. Remedial courses offered during regular academic year; credit given.

Distinctive Educational Programs: Work-experience programs, including cooperative education, internships. Evening and weekend classes. Joint doctoral program in special education, and cooperative foreign language program with University of California, Los Angeles, Joint master's program in geology with California State University, Long Beach and Northridge. Interdisciplinary programs in health care management, Latin American studies, liberal studies, social science, urban education. Facilities and programs for independent research, including honors programs; individual majors. Study abroad in Australia, Brazil, Canada, Denmark, France, Germany, Italy, Israel, Japan, New Zealand, Mexico, Spain, Sweden, Taiwan, United Kingdom, Zimbabwe. *Other distinctive programs:* On-campus facilities include the Bilingual Center, Bureau of Business and Economic Research, Center for Japanese Studies, Center for Korean-American and Korean Studies, Center for the Study of Armament and Disarmament, Center for the Study of Business in Society, Institute for Retail Management,

Small Business Institute; Asian-American Resource Center, Center for Economic Education, Center for Counselor Renewal, Center for Information Resource Management, Center for the Study of Black on Black Crime, Chines Studies Center, Employment and Training Center for the Disabled, Southern California Child Abuse Prevention Training Center, World Trade Education Center, Writing Center, Pacific Rim Institute, Health Care Management Institute, Institute of Entrepreneurship, Edmund G. 'Pat' Brown Institute of Public Affairs, Center for Criminal Justice Studies, Center for Effective Teaching, Center for Excellence in Early Intervention, Center for Multicultural Education, Center for Technology Education, Center for the Study of Child Maltreatment and Family Violence, Engineering and Technology Center, Institute for Asian American and Pacific Asian Studies, Institute of Business Law, Institute of Nursing, Latin American Studies Center, Pacific Contemporary Music Center, Productivity Center, Edward R. Roybal Center for Applied Gerontology, Roger Wagner Center for Choral Studies.

ROTC: Army in cooperation with University of California, Los Angeles (UCLA). University of Southern California, Loyola Marymount University; Air Force in cooperation with University of California, Los Angeles (UCLA).

Degrees Conferred: 2,638 *baccalaureate*; 980 *master's*. Bachelor's degrees awarded in top five disciplines: business, management, marketing, and related support services 573; education 279; liberal arts and sciences, general studies, and humanities 248; computer and information sciences and support services 192; social sciences 185.

Fees and Other Expenses: *Full-time undergraduate tuition per academic year 2005–06:* in-state $3,035, out-of-state $11,171; graduate in-state $3,617, out-of-state $11,753. *Room and board per academic year:* $7,353. *Books and supplies:* $1,260. *Other expenses:* $2,664.

Financial Aid: Aid from institutionally generated funds is provided on the basis of academic merit, financial need, athletic ability. Institution has a Program Participation Agreement with the U.S. Department of Education for eligible students to receive Pell Grants and other federal aid.

Financial aid to full-time, first-time undergraduate students: need-based scholarships/grants totaling $42,501,114, self-help $14,625,068, parent loans $377,105, athletic awards $182,373. *Graduate aid:* 981 students received federal and state-funded grants totaling $2,192,990; 1,389 loans totaling $9,612,991; 161 fellowships and grants totaling $239,743.

Departments and Teaching Staff: *Total instructional faculty:* 1,041 (full-time 566, part-time 475; women 481, men 560). Total faculty with doctorate, first-professional, or other terminal degree: 690. Student-to-faculty ratio: 17:1. *Faculty development:* $30,220,666 in grants for research. 37 faculty members awarded sabbaticals 2004–05.

Enrollment: *Total enrollment:* 20,307. Undergraduate full-time 13,141, part-time 7,166. *Transfer students:* in-state into lower division 72 men / 103 women, upper division 708m / 1,050 w, graduate 42m / 110w; out-of-state into lower division 122m / 302w, upper division 257m / 308w, graduate 147m / 230w.

Characteristics of Student Body: *Ethnic/racial makeup:* Black non-Hispanic: 1,208; American Indian or Alaska Native: 59; Asian or Pacific Islander: 3,309; Hispanic: 6,944; White non-Hispanic: 1,648; unknown: 1,730. *Age distribution:* number under 18: 501; 18–19: 2,137, 20–21: 2,660; 22–24: 3,989; 25–29: 3,003; 30–34: 1,221, 35–39: 716; 40–49: 636; 50–64: 230; 65 and over: 15.

International Students: 210 nonresident aliens enrolled fall 2004. 25 students from Europe, 170 Asia, 93 Central and South America, 5 Africa, 4 Canada, 2 Australia, 1 New Zealand. Programs available to aid students whose native language is not English: English as a Second Language Program. No financial aid specifically designated for international students.

Student Life: On-campus housing available. *Intercollegiate athletics:* men only: baseball, basketball, cross-country, soccer, swimming, tennis, track, water polo; women only: basketball, cross-country, swimming, tennis, track, volleyball. *Special regulations:* Cars with permits allowed in designated lots. *Special services:* Learning Resources Center, medical services, intercampus minibus service. *Student publications: The Literary Gazette*, an annual literary magazine; *University Times*, a newspaper published 2 times per week, *Statement*, a literary magazine; *Perspectives: A Journal of History, The Looking Glass. Surrounding community:* Los Angeles. Served by mass transit bus system; airport 25 miles from campus; passenger rail service 10 miles from campus.

Publications: *California Anthropologist* (biannual) first published 1971, *Cal State L.A. Engineer* (quarterly) first published 1971, *Business Forum* (quarterly) first published 1975.

Library Collections: 1,156,919 volumes. Current serial subscriptions: 871 paper, 178 microform, 13,000 via electronic access. 1,807 recordings. 168 computer work stations. Online catalog. Students have access to online information retrieval services and the Internet.

Most important holdings include Perry R. Long Collection on Printing and Graphic Design; Roy Harris Collection of Musical Scores and Personal Papers; Edward R. Roybal Collection.

Buildings and Grounds: Campus area 175 acres.

Chief Executive Officer: Dr. James M. Rosser, President.

Address admission inquiries to Joan V. Woosley, Director of Admissions.

California State University, Monterey Bay

100 Campus Center
Seaside, California 93955-8001
Tel: (831) 582-3518   **E-mail:** Student_info_center@monterey.edu
Fax: (831) 582-3783   **Internet:** www.monterey.edu

Institution Description: California State University, Monterey Bay is part of the California State University System. *Enrollment:* 3,760. *Degrees awarded:* Baccalaureate, master's.

Accreditation: *Regional:* WASC-Sr.

History: The university was established in 1994 on the former Fort Ord Army Base. It opened for classes in 1995.

Institutional Structure: *Governing board:* Board of Trustees. Academic programs headed by provost and deans. Academic Senate several times each year.

Calendar: Semesters. Academic year Aug. to May.

Admission: Apply in Nov. for next fall terms and in Aug. for next spring terms. *Requirements:* High school graduation or GED; 2.0 GPA.; high school courses to include English 4 units, 2 foreign language, 1 history; 1 social studies, 3 mathematics, 1 science including 1 laboratory science.

Degree Requirements: *For all baccalaureate degrees:* Completion of general education and major area requirements; 124 units; language, technology, service learning and culture.

Distinctive Educational Programs: *For undergraduates:* Online liberal studies; degree completion partnerships with local community colleges.

Degrees Conferred: 490 *baccalaureate*; 25 *master's*. Bachelor's degrees awarded in top five disciplines: liberal arts and sciences, general studies, and humanities 176; computer and information sciences and support services 74; social sciences 65; business, management, marketing, and related support services 64; communication, journalism, and related programs 38.

Fees and Other Expenses: *Full-time undergraduate tuition per academic year 2004–05:* in-state resident $2,761, out-of-state $12,931. *Boom and board per academic year:* $8,254. *Books and supplies:* $1,260.

Financial Aid: Aid from institutionally generated funds is provided on the basis of academic merit, athletic ability, financial need, other criteria. Institution has a Program Participation Agreement with the U.S. Department of Education for eligible students to receive Pell Grants and other federal aid.

Financial aid to full-time, first-time undergraduate students: 34% received federal grants averaging $3,631; 31% state/local grants averaging $1,601; 33% institutional grants averaging $1,964; 50% loans averaging $2,819.

Departments and Teaching Staff: *Total instructional faculty:* 142.

Enrollment: *Total enrollment:* 3,760. Undergraduate 3,362 (41.8% men, 58.2% women).

Characteristics of Student Body: *Ethnic/racial makeup:* Black non-Hispanic: 4%; American Indian or Alaska Native: .9%; Asian or Pacific Islander: 5.9%; Hispanic: 27%; White non-Hispanic: 45.6%; unknown: 15.3%.

International Students: 40 nonresident aliens enrolled fall 2003. No programs to aid students whose native language is not English. No financial aid specifically designated for international students.

Student Life: Clubs and activities available for student participation; NAIA athletics. Campus is located 90 miles south of San Francisco.

Library Collections: 50,000 volumes including bound books, serial backfiles, electronic documents, and government documents not in separate collections. 1,250 audiovisual materials. Online catalog. Students have access to online information retrieval services and the Internet.

Buildings and Grounds: Campus of 1,400 acres. Development and renovation of former Fort Ord military base are ongoing activities.

Chief Executive Officer: Dr. Peter Smith, President.

Address admission inquiries to Alethea DeSoto, Director of Admissions.

California State University, Northridge

18111 Nordhoff Street
Northridge, California 91330
Tel: (818) 677-3700   **E-mail:** admissions@.csun.edu
Fax: (818) 677-3766   **Internet:** www.csun.edu

Institution Description: The university was founded in 1956. *Enrollment:* 33,426. *Degrees awarded:* Baccalaureate, master's. Academic offerings subject to approval by statewide coordinating bodies. Budget subject to approval by state governing boards.

Accreditation: *Regional:* WASC-Sr. *Professional:* applied science, art, athletic training, audiology, business, computer science, counseling, dietetics, engineering, environmental health, family and consumer science, interior design, journalism, music, nursing education, physical therapy, public health, radiography, recreation and leisure services, speech-language pathology, teacher education

History: Established as San Fernando Valley Campus of Los Angeles State College of Applied Arts and Sciences and offered first instruction at postsecondary level 1956; awarded first degree (baccalaureate) 1957; chartered as separate institution and changed name to San Fernando Valley State College 1958; adopted present name 1972.

Institutional Structure: *Composition of institution:* Administrators 97 men / 66 women. Academic affairs headed by vice president. Management/business/finances directed by vice president. Full-time instructional faculty 75. Academic governance body, Faculty Senate, meets an average of 6 to 8 times per academic year.

Calendar: Semesters. Academic Aug. to May. Freshmen admitted Sept., Jan. Degrees conferred and formal commencement Jan., May, Aug. Summer session from June to Aug.

Characteristics of Freshmen: 13,211 applicants (5,185 men, 8,026 women). 76.4% of applicants admitted; 34.9% of admitted students enrolled full-time.

88% (3,183 students) submitted SAT scores. *25th percentile:* SAT Verbal 400, SAT I Math 410. *75th percentile:* SAT Verbal 520, SAT Math 540.

Admission: Eligibility for freshman admission is governed in part by an eligibility index, computed on the basis of high school grades and results from standardized entrance examinations (SAT or ACT). California residents who have an index of at least 2800 (SAT) or 694 (ACT) qualify. Nonresidents must have an index of at least 2800 (ACT) or 842 (ACT). *Requirements:* Graduation from accredited secondary school with 4 years of college preparatory English, 3 years of college preparatory mathematics, 2 years of a foreign language, 1 year of history or government, 1 year of visual or performing arts, 1 year of laboratory science, 3 years of approved college preparatory electives.

College credit for extrainstitutional learning on basis of ACE *2006 Guide to the Evaluation of Educational Experiences in the Armed Services.* Tutoring available. Noncredit developmental courses offered in summer session and regular academic year.

Degree Requirements: Writing skills requirements; general education program; completion of requirements for major; Title V requirements in American History, the U.S. Constitution, and State and Local Government; distribution requirements; GPA of 2.0 in all areas: CSUN, overall, major, minor; completion of 30 units in residence, 24 of which must be completed in the upper division.

Distinctive Educational Programs: Flexible meeting places and schedules, including off-campus center (at Ventura, 45 miles away from main institution) and evening classes. Interdisciplinary programs in Afro-American studies, child development, earth sciences, environmental health, humanities, Mexican-American studies, urban studies, women's studies. Facilities and programs for independent research, including honors programs, individual majors. International Programs offers students the opportunity to continue their studies overseas for a full academic year while they remain enrolled at their home CSU campus; study in Australia, Brazil, Canada, Denmark, France, Germany, Israel, Italy, Japan, Korea, Mexico, New Zealand, Spain, Sweden, Taiwan, United Kingdom, Zimbabwe.

ROTC: Army, Navy in cooperation with University of California, Los Angeles; Air Force in cooperation with Loyola Marymount University, University of California, Los Angeles and University of Southern California.

Degrees Conferred: 4,944 *baccalaureate.* Bachelor's degrees awarded in top five disciplines: business, management, marketing, and related support services 1,172; social sciences 501; liberal arts and sciences, general studies and humanities 468; psychology 412; English language and literature/letters 364. 1,048 *master's.*

Fees and Other Expenses: *Full-time tuition per academic year 2004–05:* in-state resident undergraduate $2,778, out-of-state $12,948. *Books and supplies:* $1,200. *Room and board per academic year:* $8,216. *Other expenses:* $3,294.

Financial Aid: Aid from institutionally generated funds is provided on the basis of academic merit, financial need, athletic ability. Institution has a Program Participation Agreement with the U.S. Department of Education for eligible students to receive Pell Grants and other federal aid.

46% of undergraduate students received scholarships/grants averaging $3,303; 37% state/local grants averaging $1,545; 50% institutional grants averaging $2,210; 27% loans averaging $2,608.

Departments and Teaching Staff: *Total instructional faculty:* 1,735 (750 full-time, 985 part-time). Student-to-faculty ratio: 21:1. Degrees held by full-time faculty: doctorate 693.

Enrollment: Total enrollment 33,426. Undergraduate 26,065 (41.2% men, 58.8% women).

Characteristics of Student Body: *Ethnic and racial makeup:* Black non-Hispanic: 8%; American Indian or Alaska Native: .6%; Asian or Pacific Islander: 12%; Hispanic: 26.2%; White non-Hispanic: 29%; unknown: 20.7%.

International Students: 1,172 nonresident aliens enrolled fall 2003. Programs available to aid students whose native language is not English: Social, cultural. English as a Second Language Program. No financial programs specifically designated for international students.

Student Life: 5% of student body live on campus in an apartment complex. Some students join and live in fraternities and sororities. 1% of student body live off-campus in privately owned residence hall. *Intercollegiate athletics:* men: basketball, cross country, football, golf, soccer, swimming, track and field, volleyball, indoor tract; women: basketball, cross country, golf, soccer, softball, swimming, tennis, track and field, indoor track, volleyball. *Special regulations:* Cars with parking permits allowed. *Special services:* Learning Resources Center, medical services. *Student publications, radio: Daily Sundial,* a newspaper; *Scene,* a biannual magazine; an annual poetry collection. *Surrounding community:* Los Angeles area population approximately 7,500,000. Served by mass transit bus system; airport and passenger rail service each 25 miles from campus.

Library Collections: 1,274,000 volumes. 3,129,000 microforms; 18,000 audiovisual materials; 2,314 periodical subscriptions. Online catalog. Access to online information retrieval systems. Students have access to the Internet at no charge.

Most important special holdings include Human Sexuality Collection; Women in Music Collection; Jewish Federation Council and Community Relations Collections.

Buildings and Grounds: Campus area 355 acres.

Chief Executive Officer: Dr. Jerome, Koester, President.

Address admission inquiries to Eric Forbes, Director of Admissions and Records.

California State University, Sacramento

6000 J Street
Sacramento, California 95819
Tel: (916) 278-6011   **E-mail:** admissions@csus.edu
Fax: (916) 278-6664   **Internet:** www.csus.edu

Institution Description: *Enrollment:* 27,972. *Degrees awarded:* Baccalaureate, master's.

Accreditation: *Regional:* WASC-Sr. *Professional*: art, athletic training, audiology, business, computer science, construction education, engineering, engineering technology, interior design, music, nursing, nursing education, physical therapy, recreation and leisure services, rehabilitation counseling, social work, speech-language pathology, theatre

History: Chartered and offered first instruction at postsecondary level 1947; awarded first baccalaureate 1948.

Institutional Structure: *Composition of institution:* President; academic affairs headed by provost. Vice presidents head major areas including finance. Full-time instructional faculty 724.

Calendar: Semesters. Academic year Aug. to May.

Characteristics of Freshmen: 51% of applicants accepted. 19% of accepted applicants enrolled. 27% of freshmen expected to graduate within 5 years.

84% (1,975 students) submitted SAT scores; 22% (526 students) submitted ACT scores. *25th percentile:* SAT Verbal 410, SAT Math 440; ACT Composite 17, ACT English 15, ACT Math 17. *75th percentile*: SAT Verbal 530, SAT Math 560; ACT Composite 22, ACT English 22, ACT Math 23.

Admission: Rolling admissions plan. For fall acceptance, apply as early as Nov. 1 of previous year. Students are notified of acceptance by May 1st or within 2 weeks if notified thereafter.

Degree Requirements: Completion of prescribed curriculum; 124–140 semester units including 51 units in general education; GPA 2.0.

Distinctive Educational Programs: Internships. Interdisciplinary programs in Asian American studies, Chicano studies, ethnic studies, Native: American studies, Pan African studies. Cooperative education for engineering and computer science students; College Assistance Migrant Program. Programs offered in conjunction with the State Capitol: California Senate Fellows Program, California Assembly Fellows Program, California Executive Fellows Program.

Degrees Conferred: 4,557 *baccalaureate* (B); 963 *master's* (M):. architecture 36 (B); area and ethnic studies 19 (B); biological/life sciences 109 (B), 6 (M); business/marketing 988 (B), 81 (M); communications/communication technologies 411 (B), 10 (M); computer and information sciences 114 (B), 46 (M); education 260 (B), 312 (M); engineering and engineering technologies 209 (B), 74 (M); English 134 (B); 50 (M); foreign languages and literature 27 (B), 24

(M); health professions and related sciences 164 (B), 78 (M); home economics and vocational home economics 54 (B); interdisciplinary studies 54 (B), 1 (M); liberal arts/general studies 364 (B), 1 (M); mathematics 18 (B), 1 (M); natural resources/environmental science 31 (B); parks and recreation 159 (B), 23 (M); philosophy/religion/theology 27 (B); physical sciences 42 (B), 3 (M); protective services/public administration 437 (B), 179 (M); psychology 228 (B), 13 (M); social sciences and history 475 (B), 45 (M); visual and performing arts 197 (B), 16 (M).

Fees and Other Expenses: *Full-time tuition per academic year 2004–05:* in-state undergraduate $2,824, graduate $3,310; out-of-state undergraduate and graduate $13,480. *Required fees:* $490. *Room and board per academic year:* $6,374.

Financial Aid: Aid from institutionally generated funds is provided on the basis of academic merit, athletic ability, financial need, other criteria. Institution has a Program Participation Agreement with the U.S. Department of Education for eligible students to receive Pell Grants and other federal aid.

Financial aid to full-time, first-time undergraduate students: need-based scholarships/grants totaling $39,723,785, self-help $25,764,039, tuition waivers $840,244; non-need-based scholarships/grants totaling $5,000,000; student loans $14,899,138, parent loans $8,715,111. *Graduate aid:* 1,268 fellowships/grants totaling $2,629,184; 1,810 federal/state loans totaling $16,619,075; 84 work-study jobs totaling $174,278.

Departments and Teaching Staff: *Total instructional faculty:* 1,433 (720 full-time, 713 part-time; women 673, men 760). Total number with doctorate, first-professional, or other terminal degree 735. Student-to-faculty ratio: 22:1.

Enrollment: Total enrollment 27,972. Undergraduate full-time 7,279 men / 10,150 women, part-time 2,317m / 2,809w; graduate full-time 805m / 1,964w, part-time 918m / 1,730w. *Transfer students:* in-state into lower division 46m / 80w, upper division 1,225m / 1,642w, graduate 70m / 137w; out-of-state into lower division 7m / 5w, upper division 10m / 18w, graduate 1m / 1w.

Characteristics of Student Body: *Ethnic and racial makeup:* number of Black non-Hispanic: 1,320; American Indian or Alaska Native: 218; Asian or Pacific Islander: 4,292; Hispanic: 3,214; White non-Hispanic: 9,567; unknown: 3,601. *Age distribution:* number under 18: 961; 18–19: 4,270, 20–21: 5,212; 22–24: 6,743; 25–29: 3,007; 30–34: 976; 35–39: 488; 40–49: 652; 50–64: 233; 65 and over: 13.

International Students: 673 nonresident aliens enrolled fall 2004. 23 students from Europe, 274 Asia, 9 Central and South America, 14 Africa, 7 Canada, 3 Australia, 2 New Zealand, 1 other. Programs available to aid students whose native language is not English: Social, cultural. English as a Second Language Program. No financial aid specifically designated for international students.

Student Life: On-campus housing available. *Intercollegiate athletics:* men only: baseball, basketball, cross-country, football, golf, soccer, swimming, tennis, track and field, women only: basketball, cross-country, golf, gymnastics, softball, swimming, tennis, track and field, volleyball. *Special regulations:* Cars with permits allowed. *Special services:* Learning Skills Center, medical services, shuttle between parking areas and campus buildings for disabled students. *Surrounding community:* Sacramento 2000 population 407,018. Served by mass transit bus system.

Library Collections: 1,309,619 volumes. 3,761 current serial subscriptions; 2,373,502 microforms. Online and card catalogs. Students have access to the Internet at no charge.

Most important special collections include the California Underground Railroad Digital Archive; Japanese American Archival Collection; Tsakopoulos Hellenic Collection.

Buildings and Grounds: Campus area 300 acres.

Chief Executive Officer: Dr. Alexander Gonzalez, President.

Address admission inquiries to Emiliano Diaz, Director of Admissions.

California State University, San Bernardino

5500 State College Parkway
San Bernardino, California 92407-2397
Tel: (909) 880-5000   **E-mail:** admissions@csusb.edu
Fax: (909) 880-5903   **Internet:** www.csusb.edu

Institution Description: *Enrollment:* 16,927. *Degrees awarded:* Baccalaureate, master's. Certificates also awarded.

Accreditation: *Regional:* WASC-Sr. *Professional*: art, business, computer science, music, nursing, nursing education, public administration, rehabilitation counseling, social work

History: Established 1960; offered first instruction at postsecondary level 1965; awarded first degree (baccalaureate) 1967.

Institutional Structure: *Composition of institution:* Administrators 20 men / 2 women. Academic affairs headed by vice president for academic affairs. Management/business/finances directed by business manager. Full-time instructional faculty 241. Academic governance body, Faculty Senate, meets an average of 10 times per year.

Calendar: Quarters. Academic year Sept. to June. Freshmen admitted Sept., Jan., Mar., June. Degrees conferred June, Aug., Dec., Mar. Formal commencement June. Summer session of 2 terms from mid-June to mid-Aug.

Characteristics of Freshmen: 6,309 applicants (2,275 men / 4,034 women). 62.6% of applicants accepted; 33.8% of accepted applicants enrolled full-time. 30.4% of entering freshmen expected to graduate within 5 years. 90% of freshmen from California. Freshmen from 14 states and 9 foreign countries.

93% (1,287 students) submitted SAT scores. *25th percentile*: SAT Verbal 380, SAT Math 390. *75th percentile*: SAT Verbal 490, SAT Math 510.

Admission: Rolling admissions plan. For fall acceptance, apply as early as Nov. 1 of previous year, but not later than end of first week of classes.

Degree Requirements: Completion of curricular requirements for the degree program pursued. College credit for extrainstitutional learning (life experience) on basis of ACE *2006 Guide to the Evaluation of Educational Experiences in the Armed Services.* Tutoring available. Noncredit developmental and remedial courses offered during regular academic year.

Distinctive Educational Programs: Flexible meeting places and schedules, including off-campus centers (at Palm Springs, 100 miles away from main institution), weekend and evening classes. Interdisciplinary programs in American studies, environmental studies, ethnic studies, liberal studies, women's studies. Facilities and programs for independent research, including individual majors, tutorials, independent study. *Other distinctive programs:* Degree-granting continuing education. Servicemembers Opportunity College.

ROTC: Army in cooperation with Claremont Colleges; Air Force in cooperation with Loyola Marymount University, UCLA, and USC.

Degrees Conferred: 2,531 *baccalaureate*. Bachelor;s degrees awarded in top five disciplines: liberal arts and sciences, general studies and humanities 583; business, management, marketing, and related support services 575; social sciences 238; psychology 200; security and protective services 127. 795 *master's*: various disciplines.

Fees and Other Expenses: *Full-time tuition per academic year 2004–05:* in-state resident $2,906, out-of-state $13,076. *Books and supplies:* $1,260. *Room and board per academic year:* $8,206. *Other expenses:* $2,430.

Departments and Teaching Staff: *Total instructional faculty:* 241.

Enrollment: Total enrollment 16,927. Undergraduate 12,297 (34.8% men, 65.2% women).

Characteristics of Student Body: *Ethnic/racial makeup:* Black non-Hispanic: 17.7%; American Indian or Alaska Native: .8%; Asian or Pacific Islander: 7.2%; Hispanic: 30.4%; White non-Hispanic: 34.7%; unknown: 12.1%.

International Students: 381 nonresident aliens enrolled fall 2004. Programs available to aid students whose native language is not English: English for Foreign Students. No financial aid specifically designated for international students.

Student Life: On-campus residence halls house 10% of student body. Residence halls for men only constitute 40% of such space, for women only 40%, for both sexes 20%. *Special regulations:* Cars permitted without restrictions. *Special services:* Learning Resources Center, medical services. *Student publications: Pawprint,* a weekly newspaper; *Prickly Pear,* an annual literary magazine. *Surrounding community:* San Bernardino population 150,500. Los Angeles, 60 miles from campus, is nearest metropolitan area.

Library Collections: 762,000 volumes. 653,000 microforms, 1,658 periodicals; 16,000 audiovisual materials. Online catalog. Students have access to online information retrieval services and the Internet.

Most important holdings include collections on railroads and trains, and the Mojave Desert.

Chief Executive Officer: Dr. Albert K. Karnig, President.

Address admission inquiries to Dr. Robert McGowan, Director Enrollment Management.

California State University, San Marcos

333 South Twin Oaks Valley Road
San Marcos, California 92096
Tel: (760) 750-4000   **E-mail:** apply@csusm.edu
Fax: (760) 750-4030   **Internet:** www.csusm.edu

Institution Description: *Enrollment:* 7,777. *Degrees awarded:* Baccalaureate, master's.

Accreditation: *Regional:* WASC-Sr. *Professional:* business, teacher education

History: California State University, San Marcos, began enrollments in 1990.

Calendar: Semesters. Academic year late Aug. to late May.

Characteristics of Freshmen: 4,455 applicants (1,743 men, 2,712 women). 69.6% of applicants admitted; 22.2% of admitted students enrolled full-time. 94% (842 students) submitted SAT scores. *25th percentile*: SAT Verbal 430, SAT Math 440. *75th percentile*: SAT Verbal 540, SAT Math 560.

Admission: Rolling admissions plan. For fall acceptance, apply as early as Nov. 1 of previous year, but not later than end of first week of classes.

Degree Requirements: Completion of curricular requirements for the degree program pursued. College credit for extrainstitutional learning (life experience) on basis of ACE *2006 Guide to the Evaluation of Educational Experiences in the Armed Services.* Tutoring available. Noncredit developmental and remedial courses offered during regular academic year.

Degrees Conferred: 1,342 *baccalaureate*. Bachelor's degrees awarded in top five disciplines: business, management, marketing, and related support services 361; liberal arts and sciences, general studies and humanities 328; social sciences 166; psychology 97; communication, journalism, and related programs 92. 117 *master's*.

Fees and Other Expenses: *Full-time tuition per academic year:* in-state undergraduate $2,776; out-of-state $12,946. *Books and supplies:* $1,260. *Room and board per academic year:* $8,616. *Other expenses:* $3,204.

Financial Aid: Aid from institutionally generated funds is provided on the basis of academic merit, financial need, athletic ability, other criteria. Institution has a Program Participation Agreement with the U.S. Department of Education for eligible students to receive Pell Grants and other federal aid.

Financial aid to full-time, first-time undergraduate students: 24% received federal grants averaging $3,127; 27% state/local grants averaging $1,663; 22% institutional grants averaging $1,346; 10% loans averaging $2,579.

Departments and Teaching Staff: *Professors* 37, *associate professors* 58, *assistant professors* 72, *instructors* 10, *part-time faculty* 184. *Total instructional faculty:* 238 FTE. Total tenured faculty: 90. Degrees held by full-time faculty: doctorate 95%.

Enrollment: Total enrollment 7,777. Undergraduate 6,461 (39.8% men, 60.2% women).

Characteristics of Student Body: *Ethnic and racial makeup:* Black non-Hispanic: 2.8%; American Indian or Alaska Native: .9%; Asian or Pacific Islander: 10.2%; Hispanic: 19.4%; White non-Hispanic: 51%; unknown: 13.1%.

International Students: 174 nonresident aliens enrolled fall 2003. English as a Second Language Program. No financial aid specifically designated for international students.

Library Collections: 148,500 volumes including bound books, serial backfiles, electronic documents, and government documents not in separate collections. Online catalog. Current serial subscriptions: 1,871 paper. 755,500 microforms. 5,600 audiovisual materials. Computer work stations available. Students have access to the Internet at no charge.

Most important holdings include the Center for the Study of Books in Spanish for Children and Adolescents; World Music/Jazz CD Collection.

Buildings and Grounds: Campus area 305 acres. *New buildings:* Science Hall and Arts Complex completed 2002.

Chief Executive Officer: Dr. Karen S. Haynes, President.

Address admission inquiries to Dr. Karl Beeler, Director of Enrollment Management.

California State University, Stanislaus

801 West Monte Vista Avenue
Turlock, California 95382
Tel: (209) 667-3122   **E-mail:** outreach_help_desk@csustan.edu
Fax: (209) 667-3788   **Internet:** www.csustan.edu

Institution Description: *Enrollment:* 7,858. *Degrees awarded:* Baccalaureate, master's.

Accreditation: *Regional:* WASC-Sr. *Professional:* art, business, chemistry, music, nursing, nursing education, psychology internship, public administration, social work, teacher education, theatre

History: Established by state legislature 1957 and chartered as Stanislaus State College; offered first instruction at postsecondary level 1960; awarded first degree (baccalaureate) 1961; became California State University, Stanislaus 1985.

Institutional Structure: *Composition of institution:* Administrators 63. Academic affairs headed by provost/vice president for academic affairs. The vice president for business and finance is the chief financial officer and is responsible for business affairs, public safety, data processing, personnel, and plant operations. Full-time instructional faculty 264. Academic governance body, Academic Senate, meets an average of 10 times per year.

Calendar: Semesters (4-1-4 plan). Academic year Sept. to May. Freshmen admitted Sept., Jan., Feb. Degrees conferred May, July, Aug., Dec., Feb. Formal commencement May. Summer session of 2 terms from mid-June to mid-Aug.

Characteristics of Freshmen: 85.8% (641 students) submitted SAT scores; 27.2% (203 students) submitted ACT scores *25th percentile*: SAT Verbal 420, SAT Math 430; ACT Composite 18, ACT English 16, ACT Math 17. *75th percentile*: SAT Verbal 540, SAT Math 560; ACT Composite 23, ACT English 22, ACT Math 24.

83.8% of applicants accepted. 36.4% of accepted applicants enrolled. 38.7% of entering freshmen expected to graduate within 5 years. 98.3% of freshmen from California. Freshmen from 7 states and 13 foreign countries.

Admission: Rolling admissions plan. For fall acceptance, apply no later than May 1. Early acceptance available. Submission of ACT or SAT scores are urged. Submission is required only from undergraduates who have less than a 3.0 high school GPA or have a college preparatory subject deficiency; GED accepted.

Tutoring available. Noncredit developmental courses offered in summer session and regular academic year. Internships. Flexible meeting places and schedules, including off-campus centers, evening classes. Special facilities for using telecommunications in the classroom. Interdisciplinary programs in applied studies, cognitive studies, social sciences; interdisciplinary minor programs in environmental resources studies, ethnic studies, gender studies, gerontology, interpersonal studies, Latin American studies; Permaculture; student-designed interdepartmental majors available. Individual majors. Independent study. Institute for Archaeological Research studies archaeological and cultural resources in California, Montana, Nevada, Central Australia, and Africa. Institute for Cultural Resources provides information on regional heritage. Center for public Policy Studies works with area public officials and community groups.

Degrees Conferred: 1,387 *baccalaureate* (B), 182 *master's* (M): agriculture 1 (B); biological/life sciences 50 (B), 1 (M); business/marketing 240 (B), 29 (M); communications/communication technologies 71 (B); computer and information sciences 50 (B); education 21 (B); 40 (M); English 42 (B), 10 (M); foreign languages and literature 19 (B); health professions and related sciences 26 (B); interdisciplinary studies 2 (B), 4 (M); liberal arts/general studies 378 (B); mathematics 12 (B); parks and recreation 47 (B); philosophy, religion, theology 7 (B); physical sciences 12 (B); protective services/public administration 97 (B), 73 (M); psychology 102 (B), 19 (M); social sciences and history 175 (B), 6 (M); visual and performing arts 35 (B). 1 honorary degree awarded 2004: Doctor of Fine Arts.

Fees and Other Expenses: *Full-time tuition per academic year 2004–05:* $2,807 resident undergraduate, $3,293 graduate; out-of-state student: contact the university for current rates. *Room and board per academic year:* $6,522.

Financial Aid: Aid from institutionally generated funds is provided on the basis of academic merit, financial need, athletic ability. Institution has a Program Participation Agreement with the U.S. Department of Education for eligible students to receive Pell Grants and other federal aid.

Undergraduate need-based scholarships/grants totaling $14,070,860, self-help $9,703,207; non-need-based scholarships/grants totaling $721,953, parent loans $504,828, athletic awards $252,825. *Graduate aid:* 427 federal and state-funded fellowships/grants totaling $1,181,931; 585 federal and state-funded loans totaling $3,507,809; 4 work-study jobs totaling $11,500; 144 fellowships/grants totaling $338,561.

Departments and Teaching Staff: *Professors* 103, *associate professors* 62, *assistant professors* 66, *lecturers* 33, *part-time faculty* 193.

Total instructional faculty: 457 (264 full-time, 193 part-time; 214 women, 243 men). Total faculty with doctorate, first-professional, or other terminal degree: 255. Student-to-faculty ratio: 18:1. *Faculty development:* $93,064 total grants for research. 9 faculty members granted sabbaticals during 2004–05.

Enrollment: Total enrollment 7,858. Undergraduate full-time 1,494 men / 2,760 women, part-time 630m / 1,308w; graduate full-time 182m / 614m, part-time 269m / 601w. *Transfer students:* in-state into lower division 215m / 412w, into upper division 1,159m / 2,664w; out-of-state into lower division 14m / 21w, into upper division 59m / 93w.

Characteristics of Student Body: *Ethnic/racial makeup:* Black non-Hispanic: 203; American Indian or Alaska Native: 68; Asian or Pacific Islander: 685; Hispanic: 1,667; White non-Hispanic: 2,601; unknown: 886. *Age distribution:* number under 18: 10; 18–19: 1,219; 20–21: 1,364; 22–24: 1,713; 25–29: 232; 30–34: 367; 35–39: 257; 40–49: 321; 50–64: 102; 65 and over: 7.

International Students: 97 nonresident aliens enrolled fall 2004. 17 students from Europe, 39 Asia, 21 Central and South America, 5 Africa, 2 Canada, 13 other. English as a Second Language courses available. No financial aid specifically designated for international students.

Student Life: On-campus residence halls house 9% of student body. Residence halls for both men and women constitute 100% of such space. *Intercollegiate athletics:* men only: baseball, basketball, golf, soccer, track; women only: basketball, cross-country, indoor track, soccer, softball, track, volleyball. *Special regulations:* Cars with decals permitted. *Special services:* Learning Resources Center, medical services. *Student publications, radio:* The Signal, a weekly newspaper. Radio station KCSS broadcasts 84 hours per week. *Surrounding community:* Turlock population 65,000. San Francisco, 100 miles from campus, is nearest metropolitan area. Served by airport approximately 11 miles from campus; passenger rail service approximately 17.5 miles from campus.

Publications: *University Digest* (September through May) to faculty and staff; *Stanislaus Magazine* (Spring to Fall) to alumni, supporters, faculty and staff.

Library Collections: 359,626 volumes including bound books, serial backfiles, electronic documents, and government documents not in separate collections. Online and card catalogs. Current serial subscriptions: 1,446 paper, 1,300,671 microform, 3,693 via electronic access. 2,507 recordings; 1,397 compact discs; 403 CD-ROMs. 25 computer work stations. Students have access to the Internet at no charge. Total budget for books, periodicals, audiovisual materials, microforms 2004–05: $870,128.

Most important special holdings include Western Fine Press Books; Sayad Assyrian Theological Collection; Dias Photographic Collection.

Buildings and Grounds: Campus area 236 acres. *New buildings:* Bio-Ag Dome completed 2001; Mary Stuart Rogers Educational Services Gateway Building 2002; John Stuart Rogers Faculty Development Center 2003; Bernell and Flora Snider Music Recital Hall 2003; Biology Field Site Storage and Restrooms 2004; Residential Life Village III (with dining hall) 2004;

Chief Executive Officer: Dr. Marvalene Hughes, President.

Address undergraduate admission inquiries to Lisa Bernardo, Director, Admissions and Records; graduate inquiries to James Burns, Dean, Graduate School.

California Western School of Law

225 Cedar Street
San Diego, California 92101
Tel: (619) 239-0391   **E-mail:** admissions@cwsl.edu
Fax: (619) 685-2917   **Internet:** www.cwsl.edu

Institution Description: California Western School of Law is a private, independent law school. *Enrollment:* 977. *Degrees awarded:* First-professional (J.D., M.C.L.).

Accreditation: *Professional:* law

History: Founded as Balboa University Law School 1927; first law graduate 1931; closed from 1952–58; reopened 1958 as California Western University School of Law; gained professional accreditation 1962; became independent law school and adopted present name 1975.

Institutional Structure: *Governing board:* Extrainstitutional representation: 30 trustees; institutional representation: 1 administrator, ex officio; 2 faculty representative, ex officio. *Composition of institution:* Administrators 4 men / 4 women. Full-time instructional faculty 24 men / 26 women. Academic governance body, the faculty, meets monthly.

Calendar: Trimesters. Academic year early Sept. to late Apr. Entering students admitted Sept., Jan. Degrees conferred and formal commencement May, Dec. Summer trimester early May to late Aug.

Admission: The deadline for the fall class is April 1. The deadline for the spring class is Nov. 1. *Requirements:* Bachelor's degree; LSAT and LSDAS required; primary factors considered by admissions officers, in order of importance, are LSAT scores, GPA, advanced degrees, work experience, life experience, evidence of maturity.

Degree Requirements: 89 credits, including 45 required credits; 74 GPA; completion of perspective, practicum, and scholarly writing courses; residence requirements. *Grading system:* numerical scale 50–95.

Distinctive Educational Programs: Two year option: flexible trimester system allows students to begin school in either September or January, and to graduate in 2, 2½, or 3 years. *Other distinctive programs:* Practical legal education; areas of concentration in Child, Family and Elder Law, Creative Problem Solving, Criminal Justice Program, Intellectual Property, Telecommunications and Technology Regulation, International Law, Labor and Employment Law, International Law Program, California Innocence Project, Center for Creative Problem Solving, Institute of Health Law Studies, Muster of Comparative Law Program, LL.M in Trial Advocacy.

Degrees Conferred: 17 *master's:* law/legal studies; 248 *first-professional:* law. 3 *honorary degrees awarded:* Doctor of Laws.

Fees and Other Expenses: *Full-time tuition per academic year 2004–05:* $30,000. *Required fees:* $100 student activity fee.

Financial Aid: Aid from institutionally generated funds is provided on the basis of academic merit, financial need, other criteria.

4 federal and state-funded fellowships and grants totaling $9,950 (ranging from $575 to $4,725); 926 federal and state-funded loans totaling $19,640,399

(ranging from $8,500 to $22,500); 169 work-study jobs totaling $450,592 (ranging from $1,500 to $8,000); 17 outside scholarships totaling $63,850.

Departments and Teaching Staff: *Total instructional faculty:* 104 (full-time 50, part-time 54; women 47, men 57). Total faculty with doctorate, first-professional, or other terminal degree: 104. Student-to-faculty ratio: 19.5:1. 3 faculty members awarded sabbaticals 2004-05.

Enrollment: Total enrollment 977 (full-time 436 men / 401 women; part-time 55 men / 85w).

International Students: 24 nonresident aliens enrolled fall 2004. 7 students from Europe, 11 Asia, 2 Central and South America, 3 Canada, 1 Australia. Programs available to aid students whose native language is not English: Social, cultural. No financial aid specifically designated for international students.

Student Life: *Student publications: Commentary,* a bimonthly, student-edited newspaper; *Intramural sports:* basketball. *Special services:* Career Service Placement Office for career counseling, on- and off-campus interviewing. Diversity Services provides support for nontraditional and under-represented students. *Surrounding community:* California Western School of Law is located on the edge of downtown San Diego, the 7th largest city in the United States.

Publications: *Alumni Quarterly,* a quarterly publication written for California Western alumni; *Res Ipsa,* a new quarterly publication.

Library Collections: 313,598 volumes. Current serial subscriptions: 3,943 paper, 11 microform, 428 via electronic access. 1,198 recordings, 182 CD-ROM. Online catalog. 67 computer work stations. Students have access to the Internet at no charge.

Most important special collections include Creative Problem Solving; International Law; California Law.

Buildings and Grounds: Campus area 50,000 square feet. *New buildings:* Law Library completed 1999; renovation of classroom building 2001.

Chief Executive Officer: Dr. Steven R. Smith, Dean and President.

Address admission inquiries to Jean Whalen, Assistant Director of Admissions.

Chapman University

One University Drive
Orange, California 92866
Tel: (714) 997-6826   **E-mail:** admit@chapman.edu
Fax: (714) 997=6713   **Internet:** www.chapman.edu

Institution Description: Chapman University is a private, independent, non-profit college affiliated with the Christian Church (Disciples of Christ). *Enrollment:* 5,554. *Degrees awarded:* Associate, baccalaureate, master's.

Accreditation: *Regional:* WASC-Sr. *Professional:* athletic training, business, music, physical therapy, social work

History: Established at Woodland as Hesperian College, chartered, and offered first instruction at postsecondary level 1861; changed name to Berkeley Bible Seminary 1896, to California School of Christianity 1921; awarded first degree (baccalaureate) and changed name to California Christian College 1923; became Chapman College 1934; moved to present location 1954; changed name to Chapman University 1991. See Fredric S. Burgh and Lucy Parker, eds., *Chapman Remembers* (Orange: M.C. McInnis Printing and Publishing, 1969) for further information.

Institutional Structure: *Governing board:* Board of Trustees. Extrainstitutional representation: 35 trustees, 8 life trustees, 6 ex officio trustees (including president of the university, 6 clergy, president of Town and Gown, and president of Alumni Association). *Composition of institution:* Administrators 111 men / 126 women. Academic affairs headed by provost. Management/business/finances directed by vice president for finance. Total instructional faculty 536. Academic governance body, Faculty of Chapman University meets an average of 2 times per year.

Calendar: Semesters (4-1-4 plan). Academic year Aug. to Aug. Freshmen admitted Aug., Feb. Degrees conferred as earned. Formal commencement May. Summer session of 3 terms from early June to late Aug.

Characteristics of Freshmen: 53% of applicants admitted. 41.4% of admitted students enrolled full-time.

83.7% (695 students) submitted SAT scores; 37.6% (312 students) submitted ACT scores. *25th percentile:* SAT Verbal 539, SAT Math 543; ACT Composite 23, ACT English 22, ACT Math 21. *75th percentile:* SAT Verbal 652, SAT Math 655; ACT Composite 28, ACT English 29, ACT Math 28.

63% of entering freshmen expected expected to graduate within 5 years. 70% of freshmen from California. Freshmen from 39 states and 24 foreign countries.

Admission: Rolling admissions plan. Jan. 31 is the priority deadline for the following fall semester; Nov. 1 is deadline for the spring semester. Early acceptance available. *Requirements:* Either graduation from secondary school or GED. 11 academic units required with 2 units in composition or literature, 3

social studies, 2 mathematics (algebra and geometry), 2 foreign language, 2 science. Minimum GPA 2.5. *Entrance tests:* College Board SAT or ACT Composite. For foreign students minimum TOEFL, score 550. *For transfer students:* 2.0 minimum GPA, maximum transfer credit limited only by residence requirement. Tutoring available.

Degree Requirements: 124 semester hours; 36 credits earned in upper division coursework. 2.0 GPA; 32 semester hours in residence (18 of which must be in upper division courses; 12 of which must be completed in the student's major); 2 physical education courses; distribution requirements.

Fulfillment of some requirements and exemption from some beginning courses possible by passing departmental examinations, College Board CLEP, AP, 1B. *Grading system:* A–F; pass-fail; pass; withdraw; (deadline after which pass-fail is appended to withdraw); incomplete (carries time limit).

Distinctive Educational Programs: *For undergraduates:* Cooperative education and internships. Special facilities for using telecommunications in the classroom. Interdisciplinary programs, including ethnic studies, leadership seminars, peace studies. Honors programs. Exchange program with King Alfred's College in England. *Available to all students:* Evening classes. Facilities and programs for independent research, including individual majors and tutorials. *Other distinctive programs:* Continuing education. University College offer associate, baccalaureate, and master's programs at 14 campuses in California and Washington.

ROTC: Air Force offered in cooperation with Loyola Marymount University; Army with Cal Poly Pomona, Claremont Colleges. University of Southern California.

Degrees Conferred: 665 *baccalaureate* (B); 303 *master's* (M): biological/life sciences 22 (B); business/marketing 144 (B), 78 (M); communications/communication technologies 101 (B); computer and information sciences 9 (B); education 10 (B), 96 (M); English 25 (B), 15 (M); foreign languages and literature 2 (B); health professions and related sciences 8 (B), 23 (M); interdisciplinary studies 7 (B), 4 (M); law/legal studies 18 (B), 2 (M); liberal arts/general studies 35 (B); mathematics 3 (B); natural resources/environmental science 1 (B); parks and recreation 4 (B); philosophy/religion/theology 3 (B); physical sciences 5 (B); protective services/public administration 4 (B); psychology 36 (B), 36 (M); social sciences and history 46 (B), 1 (M); visual and performing arts 182 (B), 48 (M). 96 *first-professional:* law. Honorary degrees awarded 2003-04: Doctor of Arts 2, Doctor of Humane Arts 1.

Fees and Other Expenses: *Full-time tuition per academic year 2004–05:* $28,050 undergraduate; graduate $12,888. *Room and board per academic year:* $10,971. *Required fees:* $688.

Financial Aid: Aid from institutionally generated funds is awarded on the basis of academic merit, financial need, talent. Institution has a Program Participation Agreement with the U.S. Department of Education for eligible students to receive Pell Grants and other federal aid.

Financial aid to full-time, first-time undergraduate students: need-based scholarships/grants $30,796,643, self-help $11,782,848, parent loans $5,340,599, tuition waivers $320,210; non-need-based scholarships/grants $7,109,475, self-help $937,759, parent loans $1,706,867, tuition waivers $804,661.

Departments and Teaching Staff: *Professors* 63, *associate professors* 75, *assistant professors* 90, *instructors* 14, *part-time faculty* 293. *Total instructional faculty:* 535 (full-time 242, part-time 293; 231 women; 305 men). Total faculty with doctorate, first-professional, or other terminal degree 214. 80.3% hold terminal degrees. Student-to-faculty ratio: 14:1.

Enrollment: Total enrollment 5,554. Undergraduate full-time 3,520, part-time 213.

Characteristics of Student Body: *Ethnic/racial makeup:* number of Black non-Hispanic: 91; American Indian or Alaska Native: 23; Asian or Pacific Islander: 312; Hispanic: 390; White non-Hispanic: 2,409; unknown: 412. *Age distribution:* number under 18: 99; 18–19: 1,506, 20–21: 1,362; 22–24: 506; 25–29: 156; 30–34: 40; 35–39: 18; 40–49: 24; 50–64: 12.

International Students: 147 nonresident aliens enrolled fall 2004. 21 students from Europe, 101 Asia, 8 Central and South America, 5 Africa, 12 Canada, 2 Australia. Programs available to aid students whose native language is not English: Social; English as a Second Language program. No financial aid specifically designated for international students.

Student Life: On-campus residence halls house 41% of student body. Residence halls for both men and women constitute 100% of such space. 19% of student body housed on campus in apartments. 38% of students live on campus. Housing available for graduate and law students. *Intercollegiate athletics:* men only: baseball, basketball, cross-country, football, soccer, tennis, water polo, lacrosse; women only: basketball, soccer, softball, volleyball, cross-country, swimming, track and field, Lacrosse, tennis. Coed golf. *Special services:* Learning Resources Center, medical services. *Student publications, radio: Panther,* a weekly newspaper; KNAB broadcasts 20 hours per week. *Surrounding community:* Orange population 120,000. Los Angeles, 35 miles from campus is nearest metropolitan area. Served by mass transit bus system; airport 15 miles from campus.

Library Collections: 182,169 volumes. Electronic access to 38,909 serials. 18,099 recordings. 1,802 current periodical subscriptions. Online catalog. Students have access to online information retrieval services and the Internet. Total 2004–05 budget for materials and operations: $906,357.

Most important special holdings include the Albert Schweitzer Collection (books and papers); Disciples of Christ Collection; Charles C. Chapman Collection of Rare Books and Bibles; Roberta Dale Collection of California History.

Buildings and Grounds: Campus area 45 acres. *New buildings:* Leatherby Libraries; Interfaith Center/Wallace All Faiths Chapel; Oliphant Hall (School of Music); Aquatics Center.

Chief Executive Officer: Dr. James L. Doti, President.

Undergraduates address admission inquiries Michael Drummy, Director of Undergraduate Admissions; graduate inquiries to Director of Graduate Admissions.

Christian Heritage College

2100 Greenfield Drive
El Cajon, California 92019
Tel: (619) 441-2200   **E-mail:** cgcadn@adm.christianheritage.edu
Fax: (619) 440-0209   **Internet:** www.christianheritage.edu

Institution Description: Christian Heritage College is a private college affiliated with the Shadow Mountain Community Church. *Enrollment:* 558. *Degrees awarded:* Baccalaureate.

Accreditation: *Regional:* WASC-Sr.

History: Established and offered first instruction at postsecondary level 1970; awarded first degree (baccalaureate) 1973.

Institutional Structure: *Governing board:* Board of Trustees (24 members). Administrative Council (6 members). *Composition of institution:* Academic affairs headed by vice president for academic affairs. Management/business/ finances directed by director by Chief Financial Officer. Full-time instructional faculty 30.

Calendar: Semesters. 2004–05 academic year late Aug. to early May. Formal commencement May. Summer session of 1 term from late May to early Sept.

Characteristics of Freshmen: 240 applicants (92 men, 148 women). 65.8% of applicants admitted; 45.6% admitted students enrolled full-time.

78% (58 students) submitted SAT scores; 22% (16 students) submitted ACT scores. *25th percentile*: SAT Verbal 450, SAT Math 410; ACT Composite 16, ACT English 15, ACT Math 16. *75th percentile*: SAT Verbal 570, SAT Math 520; ACT Composite 21, ACT English 23, ACT Math 25.

35.4% of entering freshmen expected to graduate within five years. 80% of freshmen from California. Freshmen from 19 states and 3 foreign countries.

Admission: *Requirements:* Graduation from accredited secondary school or GED. *Entrance tests:* College Board SAT. For foreign students TOEFL.

Degree Requirements: 2.0 GPA; chapel attendance; general education program.

Fulfillment of some degree requirements possible by taking departmental examinations. *Grading system:* A–F; withdraw (deadline after which pass-fail is appended to withdraw).

Distinctive Educational Programs: *For undergraduates:* Independent study. Study abroad at the Institute for Holy Land Studies in Jerusalem.

ROTC: Army in affiliation with San Diego State University.

Degrees Conferred: 116 *baccalaureate.* Bachelor's degrees awarded in top five disciplines: multidisciplinary studies 29; family and consumer sciences/ human sciences 23; business, management, marketing, and related support services 18; theology and ministerial studies 9; education 8.

Fees and Other Expenses: *Full-time tuition per academic year 2004–05:* $14,840. *Room and board per academic year:* $5,990. *Books and supplies:* $1,260. *Other expenses:* $2,574.

Financial Aid: Financial aid to full-time, first-time undergraduate students; 38% received federal grants averaging $3,181; 22% state/local grants averaging $8,006; 84 institutional grants averaging $4,376; 61% loans averaging $5,777.

Departments and Teaching Staff: *Total instructional faculty:* 30. *Student-to-faculty ratio:* 17:1. *Degrees held by full-time faculty:* Doctorate 30%, master's 94%, baccalaureate 100%. 30% hold terminal degrees.

Enrollment: Total enrollment 558. Undergraduate 522 (38.3% men, 61.7% women).

Characteristics of Student Body: *Ethnic/racial makeup:* Black non-Hispanic: 7.1%; American Indian or Alaska Native: .6%; Asian or Pacific Islander: 3.3%; Hispanic: 11.1%; White non-Hispanic: 74.9%; unknown: 1.1%.

International Students: 11 nonresident aliens enrolled fall 2003. English as a Second Language Program offered. Financial aid available for international students.

Student Life: On-campus residence halls. *Special services:* Medical services. *Surrounding community:* San Diego 2005 population over 1 million.

Library Collections: 71,000 volumes including bound books, serial backfiles, electronic documents, and government documents not in separate collections. Online catalog. 250 current serial subscriptions. 2,830 recordings; 3,850 audiovisual materials. Computer work stations available. Students have access to the Internet at no charge.

Buildings and Grounds: Campus area 32 acres.

Chief Executive Officer: Dr. David P. Jeremiah, President.

Address admission inquiries to Misty Chapelle, Director of Admissions.

Church Divinity School of the Pacific

2451 Ridge Road
Berkeley, California 94709-1217
Tel: (510) 204-0700   **E-mail:** admissions@cdsp.edu
Fax: (510) 644-0712   **Internet:** www.cdsp.edu

Institution Description: Church Divinity School of the Pacific is a private institution affiliated with the Episcopal Church. *Enrollment:* 132. *Degrees awarded:* Master's, doctorate, first-professional.

Academic offerings subject to approval by statewide coordinating bodies. Member of the Consortium Graduate Theological Union.

Accreditation: *Regional:* WASC-Sr. *National:* ATS. *Professional:* theology

History: Established and offered first instruction at postsecondary level 1893; incorporated 1918. See Henry H. Shires, "History of the Church Divinity School of the Pacific," *Historical Magazine of the Protestant Episcopal Church*, XI:2 (June 1942), for further information.

Institutional Structure: *Governing board:* Board of Trustees. Extrainstitutional representation: 32 trustees; institutional representation: president of institution, 1 administrator, 1 full-time instructional faculty member; 3 alumni. 6 ex officio. All voting. *Composition of institution:* Administrators 4 men / 3 women. Academic affairs headed by dean and president. Management/business/ finances directed by business manager. Full-time instructional faculty 6 men / 5 women. Academic governance body, the faculty, meets an average of 18 times per year.

Calendar: Semesters. Academic year Sept. to May. Degrees conferred and formal commencement May.

Admission: *Requirements:* Baccalaureate from accredited college or university. *Entrance tests:* GRE.

Degree Requirements: *For first-professional degree:* Prescribed curriculum; 3 years in residence; distribution requirements.

Distinctive Educational Programs: *For graduate students:* Interdisciplinary programs in theology, religious studies, and various other fields. Facilities and programs for independent research, including tutorials. *Other distinctive programs:* Cross registration with consortium members.

Degrees Conferred: 20 *first-professional:* theology; 3 *doctorate:* ministry. 3 honorary degrees awarded 2004: Doctor of Humane Letters 2, Doctor of Divinity 1.

Fees and Other Expenses: *Full-time tuition per academic year 2004–05:* $11,760. *Room and board per academic year:* $5,830.

Financial Aid: Students demonstrating financial need receive up to 75% of tuition in grant-in-aid.

Departments and Teaching Staff: *Total instructional faculty:* 12.

Enrollment: Total enrollment 132.

International Students: 6 nonresident aliens enrolled fall 2004. 5 students from Asia, 1 Canada.

Student Life: On-campus residence halls house 50% of student body. 1 dormitory and 2 apartment buildings constitute 100% of such space. 50% of students live on campus. *Special regulations:* Cars permitted. *Surrounding community:* Berkeley population 120,000. Oakland, 1 mile from campus, is nearest metropolitan area. Served by mass transit bus and rail systems, airport 15 miles from campus, passenger rail service 7 miles from campus.

Library Collections: Students have access to the library of the Graduate Theological Union.

Buildings and Grounds: Campus area 5 acres.

Chief Executive Officer: Dr. Donn F. Morgan, President and Dean.

Address all admission inquiries to Kathleen Crisp, Director of Admissions and Recruitment.

Claremont McKenna College

500 East 9th Street
Claremont, California 91711
Tel: (909) 621-8088   **E-mail:** admission@mckenna.edu
Fax: (909) 621-8516   **Internet:** www.mckenna.edu

Institution Description: Claremont McKenna College (Claremont Men's College until 1981) is a private, independent, nonprofit college. *Enrollment:* 1,124. *Degrees awarded:* Baccalaureate.

Accreditation: *Regional:* WASC-Sr.

History: Established as Claremont Men's College 1946; became coeducational 1976; adopted present name 1981.

Institutional Structure: *Governing board:* Board of Trustees. Extrainstitutional representation: 40 voting trustees, 20 life trustees, 1 honorary trustee, 2 ex officio trustees; institutional representation: president of the college, chancellor of the college; 3 alumni, including president of the Alumni Association; president of the Parent's Association. 4 ex officio. All voting. *Composition of institution:* Administrators 16 men / 17 women. Academic affairs headed by dean of the faculty. Management/business/finances directed by treasurer. Full-time instructional faculty 125. Academic governance body, the faculty, meets an average of 8 times per year.

Calendar: Semesters. Academic year late Aug. to mid-May. Freshmen admitted Sept., Jan. Degrees conferred and formal commencement May. No summer session.

Characteristics of Freshmen: 27.7% of applicants accepted. 36.6% of accepted applicants enrolled. 89% (250 students) submitted SAT scores; 32% (90 students) submitted ACT scores. *25th percentile:* SAT Verbal 630, SAT Math 640; ACT Composite 28. *75th percentile:* SAT Verbal 720, SAT Math 720; ACT Composite 31.

90% of entering freshmen expected to graduate within 5 years. 11 National Merit Scholars.

Admission: For fall acceptance, apply as early as 1 year prior to enrollment, but not later than Jan. 15. of year of enrollment. Students are notified of acceptance April. Apply by Nov. 15 for early decision (first choice must be Claremont McKenna). Early acceptance available. *Requirements:* Graduation from accredited secondary school with 4 years English, 3 foreign language, 1 history, 3 (preferably 4) mathematics, 2 (preferably 3) science. Additional requirements for some programs. *Entrance tests:* College Board SAT. 3 Achievements recommended. For international students TOEFL. *For transfer students:* 16 semester courses maximum transfer credit. Transfer credit also accepted for extension students.

College credit and advanced placement for postsecondary-level work completed in secondary school. Tutoring available.

Degree Requirements: 32 semester course credits; 2.0 GPA; 2 years in residence; 1 semester English composition and literary analysis, 1 semester calculus, 2 semester courses in science 3 semester courses in social sciences, 2 semester courses in humanities, 3 semesters of a foreign language, 1 semester of civilization, a senior thesis, 3 semesters physical education.

Fulfillment of some degree requirements and exemption from some beginning courses possible by passing departmental examinations, or with International Baccalaureate. *Grading system:* A–F; pass-fail; withdraw.

Distinctive Educational Programs: *For undergraduates:* Internships. Accelerated degree programs. Dual-degree programs in business with University of Chicago (IL), in law with Columbia University (NY), in management-engineering with Stanford University, and in mathematics with The Claremont Graduate School. Interdisciplinary programs in international relations; American studies, Asian studies, Black studies, ethics, film studies, Latin American studies, legal studies, and management; the environment, economics, and politics. Special tutorial program in politics, philosophy, and economics in conjunction with the University of Buckingham in England. Facilities and programs for independent research, including honors programs, individual majors, tutorials, independent study. Study abroad through programs sponsored by or approved by the college in various countries, including Lugano, London, Durham, Freiburg, Vienna, Nantes, Paris, Madrid, Stockholm, Breukelen (The Netherlands), Dublin, Bogota, Lima, Hong Kong, and Tokyo. Semester in Washington (DC). Other distinctive programs include opportunities for research at various CMC research institutes.

ROTC: Army, Air Force in cooperation with the University of Southern California.

Degrees Conferred: 322 *baccalaureate:* area and ethnic studies 3, biological/life sciences 19, business/marketing 22, communications/communication technologies 1, computer and information sciences 1, engineering and engineering technologies 9, English 14, interdisciplinary studies 22, mathematics 4, natural resources/environmental science 4, philosophy/religion/theology 10, physical

sciences 4, psychology 33, social sciences and history 161, visual and performing arts 2.

Fees and Other Expenses: *Full-time tuition per academic year 2004–05:* $29,010. *Required fees:* $200. *Room and board per academic year:* $9,780.

Financial Aid: Aid from institutionally generated funds is provided on the basis of academic merit, financial need. Institution has a Program Participation Agreement with the U.S. Department of Education for eligible students to receive Pell Grants and other federal aid.

Financial aid to full-time, first-time undergraduate students: need-based scholarships/grants totaling $13,910,786, self-help $1,610,357; non-need-based scholarships/grants $705,738, self-help $2,682,986, parent loans $1,421,984.

Departments and Teaching Staff: Economics/accounting *professors* 10, *associate professors* 6, *assistant professors* 5, *instructors* 2, *part-time faculty* 0; government 12, 3, 4, 0, 3; history 3, 3, 3, 0, 1; literature 2, 4, 3, 0, 1; mathematics 4, 3, 2, 0, 1; modern languages 1, 1, 7, 1, 1; philosophy/religion 3, 2, 3, 0, 2; psychology 5, 2, 4, 0, 1; science 11, 6, 10, 0, 0.

Total instructional faculty: 135 (full-time 125, part-time 10; 41 women, 84 men). Total faculty with doctorate, first-professional, or other terminal degree 131. Student-to-faculty ratio: 8:1. Total faculty grants for research $150,000. 26 faculty members awarded sabbaticals 2004–05.

Enrollment: Total enrollment 1,124 (full-time 589 men / 535 women).

Characteristics of Student Body: *Ethnic/racial makeup:* number of Black non-Hispanic: 47; American Indian or Alaska Native: 5; Asian or Pacific Islander: 160; Hispanic: 123; White non-Hispanic: 654; unknown: 101. *Age distribution:* number under 18: 37; 18–19: 532, 20–21: 763; 22–24: 61; 25–29: 1.

International Students: 33 nonresident aliens enrolled fall 2004. Full-time 21 men / 12 women. 11 students from Europe, 17 Asia, Central and South America 1, 3 Canada, 1 Australia. No programs available to aid students whose native language is not English. No financial aid specifically designated for international students.

Student Life: On-campus facilities (residence halls and apartments) house 96% of student body; all residence halls are coed. *Intercollegiate athletics:* men only: baseball, basketball, cross-country, golf, swimming, tennis, track, water polo; women only: basketball, cross-country, soccer, softball, swimming, tennis, track, volleyball. *Special regulations:* Cars permitted without restrictions. *Special services:* Learning Resources Center, medical services. *Student publications:* A calendar of events, a newsletter, yearbook, newspaper.

Publications: *CMC Magazine, Inside CMC,* and various research institute publications.

Library Collections: 2,000,000 volumes including bound books, serial backfiles, electronic documents, and government documents not in separate collections. Online catalog. Current serial subscriptions: 4,310 paper, 590 electronic. 75 computer work stations. Students have access to the Internet at no charge.

Most important holdings include Philbrick Library of Dramatic Literature, Mason Collection of Western Americana, Herbert Hoover Collection of History of Science, William W. Clary Oxford Collection.

Buildings and Grounds: Campus area 50 acres. *New buildings:* Claremont Boulevard Building completed 2005.

Chief Executive Officer: Dr. Pamela Gann, President.

Address admission inquiries to Richard C. Vos, Dean of Admissions.

Claremont School of Theology

1325 North College Avenue
Claremont, California 91711
Tel: (909) 447-2500   **E-mail:** admissions@cst.edu
Fax: (909) 626-7062   **Internet:** www.cst.edu

Institution Description: Claremont School of Theology, formerly known as School of Theology at Claremont, is a private institution affiliated with the United Methodist Church, the Christian Church (Disciples of Christ), and the Episcopal Church. The Episcopal Theological School at Claremont, offering evening and weekend adult education, and the Disciples Seminary Foundation are both located on or near the Claremont campus. *Enrollment:* 478. *Degrees awarded:* Master's, doctorate, first-professional.

Accreditation: *Regional:* WASC-Sr. *National:* ATS. *Professional:* pastoral counseling, theology

History: Established in San Fernando as Maclay College of Theology, chartered, incorporated, and offered first instruction at postsecondary level 1885; awarded first degree (baccalaureate) 1888; moved to Los Angeles 1894; became part of University of Southern California 1922; became School of Religion of University of Southern California 1940; became separate institution, adopted present name, and moved to present location 1957.

Institutional Structure: *Governing board:* Board of Trustees. Extrainstitutional representation: representatives with vote total 42 including president;

president of alumni association; bishops of Cal-Pacific and Desert Southwest Conferences; chair of faculty policy committee; 2 student representatives. *Composition of institution:* Administrators 6 men / 2 women. Academic affairs headed by dean. Facilities/business management directed by vice president for campus management. Finances directed by vice president for financial affairs and CFO. Full-time instructional faculty 22. Academic governance body, the faculty, meets an average of 10 times per year.

Calendar: Semesters. Academic year early Sept. to mid-May. Entering students admitted Sept., Jan., June, July, Aug. Degrees conferred and formal commencement May. Summer session of 1 term from mid-May to mid-Aug.

Admission: Rolling admissions plan. For fall acceptance, apply no later than Apr. 1 of year of enrollment. Apply by Jan. 15 for Ph.D. programs. *Requirements:* Baccalaureate from accredited university or college. *Entrance tests:* For foreign students minimum TOEFL score 230 computer.

Degree Requirements: *For first-professional degrees:* 90 units; field education program; distribution requirements. *For master's degrees:* 54-60 units; research paper or project in area of concentration and oral examination. Additional requirements for some programs. *For first-professional and master's degrees:* 30 to 45 units in residence. *For doctor of ministry degree:* 32 units, project or thesis, field examination. *For Ph.D.:* 48 units, qualifying examination, dissertation, oral defense. *Grading system:* A–F; pass-fail, withdraw (carries time limit).

Distinctive Educational Programs: *For first-professional students:* Internships, including urban ministries and parish projects. *Available to all students:* Claremont Colleges. Facilities and programs for independent research, including individual majors and tutorials. Centers and institutes including Ancient Biblical Manuscript Center for Preservation and Research; The Robert and Francis Flaherty Study Center, Institute for Antiquity and Christianity; Center for Process Studies (philosophy espoused by Alfred North Whitehead in *Process and Reality*); Dead Sea Scrolls Project. *Other distinctive programs:* Asian American Ministries program.

Degrees Conferred: 23 *first-professional:* master of divinity; 18 *master's:* theology; 27 *doctorate:* theology.

Fees and Other Expenses: *Full-time tuition per academic year 2004–05:* $12,300 MA, M.Div; $14,160 Ph.D. *Required fees:* $200. Housing $480 to $1,335 per month.

Financial Aid: Aid from institutionally generated funds is provided on the basis of academic merit, financial need. *Graduate aid:* 174 federal and state-funded loans totaling $1,779,354 (ranging from $5,000 to $18,500); 23 work-study jobs totaling $66,342 (ranging from $500 to $4,000); 23 other college-assigned jobs totaling $48,906 (ranging from $500 to $4,000); 59 fellowships/grants totaling $243,433 (ranging from $500 to $25,000); 5 teaching assistantships at $2,000 each; 9 research assistantships totaling $13,992 (ranging from $500 to $2,000).

Departments and Teaching Staff: *Professors* 12, *associate professors* 8, *assistant professors* 1, *instructors* 1, *part-time faculty* 21. *Total instructional faculty:* 43 (full-time 22, part-time 21; minority groups 8; women 23, men 20). Total faculty with doctorate, first-professional, or other terminal degree: 21. 7 faculty members awarded sabbaticals 2004–05.

Enrollment: Total enrollment 478 (full-time 269, part-time 209).

Characteristics of Student Body: *Ethnic/racial makeup:* number of Black non-Hispanic: 52; American Indian or Alaska Native: 6; Asian or Pacific Islander: 86; Hispanic: 24; White non-Hispanic: 318.

International Students: 51 nonresident aliens enrolled fall 2004. 2 students from Europe, 41 Asia, 6 Africa, 2 other. No programs available to aid students whose native language is not English. Financial aid specifically designated for international students: 16 scholarships awarded annually; total of $60,147 awarded in 2004.

Student Life: On-campus apartments house 78% of student body. Housing available for married students. 45% of married students request institutional housing; 43% are so housed. *Special regulations:* Cars permitted without restrictions. *Student publications: Theology,* monthly student journal. *Surrounding community:* Claremont population 37,000. Los Angeles, 35 miles from campus, is nearest metropolitan area. Served by airport 9 miles from campus; passenger rail service 2 miles from campus.

Publications: *Perspective* (three times per year) for alumni and friends of the school, first published in 1957; *Process Studies* (quarterly) first published in 1971.

Library Collections: 191,879 volumes including bound books, serial backfiles, electronic documents, and government documents not in separate collections. Online catalog. Current serial subscriptions: 641 paper; 2,000 via electronic access. 158 recordings. 20 computer work stations. Students have access to the Internet at no charge. Total budget for books, periodicals, audiovisual materials, microforms 2004–05: $127,958.

Most important holdings include Tune Collection of Coptic Studies; Kirby Page Manuscripts/Personal Papers; Archives of the California Pacific Conference of the United Methodist Church (mid-1880-present).

Buildings and Grounds: Campus area 15 acres.

Chief Executive Officer: Dr. Philip A. Amerson, President.

Address admission inquiries to Janet Cromwell, Director of Admissions.

Claremont University Consortium

150 East Eighth Street
Claremont, California 91711-3190
Tel: (909) 621-8026
Fax: (909) 621-6517   **Internet:** www.cuc.claremont.edu

Institution Description: Claremont University Consortium includes five private undergraduate colleges and a graduate school located in adjoining campuses in Claremont, California. The six member colleges are The Claremont Graduate School, Claremont McKenna College, Harvey Mudd College, Pitzer College, Pomona College, and Scripps College. Each school is autonomous, but they share many academic programs and facilities, including a computer center and a central library.

Distinctive Educational Programs: Cross-registration. Accelerated degree program allows qualified seniors to begin master's degree while completing baccalaureate. Intercollegiate interdisciplinary programs in American; Asian, Black, Chicano, European, and Latin American studies, and in women's studies. Study abroad in England, France, Germany, China, Japan, Scotland, Switzerland, Greece, Israel, Sweden, and the Russia. Students at any Claremont college may participate in study abroad programs sponsored by another member of the consortium. Study at 70-acre biological field station. Affiliated centers and institutes for research, including Rancho Santa Ana Botanic Garden, California Institute of Public Affairs, School of Theology at Claremont.

Student Life: *Student publications, radio: The College,* a weekly news magazine. Radio station KSPC broadcasts 147 hours per week. *Surrounding community:* Claremont population 35,000. Los Angeles, 35 miles from campus, is nearest metropolitan area. Served by mass transit bus system; airport 10 miles from campus; passenger rail service 4 miles from campus.

Chief Executive Officer: Dr. Brenda Barham Hill, Chief Executive Officer.

Address admission inquiries to individual schools.

Cleveland Chiropractic College, Los Angeles

590 North Vermont Avenue
Los Angeles, California 90004-2196
Tel: (323) 660-6166   **E-mail:** L.A.Admissions@cleveland.edu
Fax: (323) 660-3190   **Internet:** www.clevelandchiropractic.edu

Institution Description: Cleveland Chiropractic College is a private, independent, nonprofit college. It is part of a multicampus system with the Cleveland Chiropractic College of Kansas City (MO). *Enrollment:* 490. *Degree awarded:* First-professional (chiropractic).

Accreditation: *Regional:* WASC-Sr. *Professional:* chiropractic education

History: Established as Ratledge Chiropractic College 1908; chartered 1911; awarded first degree (first-professional) 1912; subsumed by Cleveland Chiropractic College, Los Angeles and rechartered to present name 1950.

Institutional Structure: Board of Trustees. 13 members. All voting. *Composition of institution:* Administrators 6 men / 5 women.

Calendar: Trimesters. Academic year Sept. to Aug. Entering students admitted Sept., Jan., May. Degrees conferred and formal commencement Apr., Aug., Dec. Summer session May through Aug.

Characteristics of Freshmen: 81% of students expected from California, Students from 8 states and 1 foreign country.

Admission: Rolling admissions. Students should apply 9 months to 1 year in advance of term for which they wish to be considered. *Requirements:* 60 transferable semester units which must include 6 hours in English/communication skills, 3 social science, 12 additional social science or humanities, 3 general psychology, 6 biology, 6 general chemistry, 6 organic chemistry, 6 physics (all must include lab and be for science majors); minimum 2.50 GPA required. Applicants with baccalaureate degree preferred.

Degree Requirements: 90 semester units required to enter the professional doctoral program. College algebra required. BS liberal arts courses (other than science) must be transferred from other institutions; last 3 trimesters in residence; 2.00 GPA; clinic internship; competency exams.

Distinctive Educational Programs: Chiropractic program includes sports injury elective; elective available on cross cultural communications. Doctor seminars feature prominent guest speakers offering information on practice management techniques, business law, and communication skills. Small business training program is a year-long series of classes focusing on a particular aspect of starting up a small business.

Degrees Conferred: 49 *baccalaureate:* biological/life sciences; 82 *first-professional:* chiropractic.

Fees and Other Expenses: *Full-time tuition per academic year 2004–05:* undergraduate $4,992; graduate $14,177. *Required fees:* $135. No on-campus housing.

Financial Aid: Aid from institutionally generated funds is provided on the basis of academic merit. Undergraduate need-based scholarships/grants totaling $1,818,092, self-help $1.945.468; non-need-based self-help $608,000, parent loans $42,853. *Graduate aid:* 383 students received federal and state-funded loans totaling $11,089,122 (ranging from $2,625 to $31,000); 107 students had work-study jobs totaling $191,623 (ranging from $300 to $9,200).

Departments and Teaching Staff: *Professors* 10, *associate professors:* 10, *assistant professors* 6, *part-time faculty* 13.

Total instructional faculty: 39 (full-time 26, part-time 13; women 13, men 26). Student-to-faculty ratio: 9:1. Total number with doctorate, first-professional, or other terminal degree 30.

Enrollment: Total enrollment 490 (full-time 443, part-time 47).

Characteristics of Student Body: *Ethnic and racial makeup:* number of Black non-Hispanic: 8; Asian or Pacific Islander: 20; Hispanic: 22; White non-Hispanic: 43; unknown: 37. *Age distribution:* number of 18–19: 16; 20–21: 15; 22–24: 39; 25–29: 24; 30–34: 14; 35–39: 7; 40–49: 8; 50–64: 1.

International Students: 26 nonresident aliens enrolled fall 2004. Students from Europe, Asia, Canada. No social or cultural programs available for students whose native language is not English. No financial aid specifically designated for international students.

Student Life: Student Body Association; professional chiropractic associations; technique clubs. CCC-LA is primarily a commuter campus. Off-campus housing in surrounding communities is available. The college is located in the mid-Wilshire area of Los Angeles.

Publications: *In Touch*, a monthly publication; *Clevelander*, a quarterly; weekly student sports newsletter.

Library Collections: 23,618 volumes including bound books, serial backfiles, electronic documents, and government documents not in separate collections. Online catalog. Current serial subscriptions: 148 paper, 50 via electronic access. 139 CD-ROMs. 22 computer work stations. Students have access to the Internet at no charge.

Most important special holdings include chiropractic history archival collection.

Buildings and Grounds: Campus area 5 acres.

Chief Executive Officer: Carl S. Cleveland III, D.C., President.

Address admission inquiries to Melissa Denton, Director of Admissions.

Cogswell Polytechnical College

1175 Bordeaux Drive
Sunnyvale, California 94089
Tel: (408) 541-0100   **E-mail:** admissions@cogswell.edu
Fax: (408) 747-0764   **Internet:** www.cogswell.edu

Institution Description: Cogswell Polytechnical College is a private, independent, nonprofit institution. *Enrollment:* 387. *Degrees awarded:* Baccalaureate.

Accreditation: *Regional:* WASC-Sr. *Professional:* engineering technology

History: Established and chartered as Cogswell Polytechnical School 1887; changed name to Cogswell Polytechnical College and offered first instruction at postsecondary level 1930; awarded first degree (associate) 1952; awarded first baccalaureate degree 1971.

Institutional Structure: *Governing board:* Board of trustees of Cogswell Polytechnical College. 6 members. *Composition of institution:* Administrators 6 men / 5 women. Academic affairs headed Dean of Academic Affairs. Management/business/finances directed by Dean of Administration. Full-time instructional faculty 12 men / 3 women. Academic governance body, Academic Standards Committee, meets an average of 8 times per year.

Calendar: Trimesters. Academic year Sept. to Apr. Freshmen admitted Sept., Jan., May. Degrees conferred May, Aug., Dec. Formal commencement April.

Characteristics of Freshmen: 61 applicants (53 men / 8 women). 62.3% of applicants admitted; 76.3% enrolled full-time.

Average secondary school rank of freshmen men 70th percentile, women 80th percentile, class 15th percentile.

75% of entering freshmen expected to graduate within 5 years. 80% of freshmen from California. Freshmen from 7 states and 3 foreign countries.

Admission: Rolling admissions plan. Apply as early as one year, but no later than one month, prior to semester of enrollment. Students are notified of acceptance as soon as file complete. Early acceptance available. *Requirements:* Graduation from accredited secondary school with 3 units English and algebra I and II, geometry, trigonometry, chemistry, physics. Drafting and additional units in proposed field of concentration recommended. Minimum GPA 2.3. English proficiency examination. Receipt of short essay written by student. *Entrance tests:* For foreign students minimum TOEFL score 550 or acceptable score on other standardized test. *For transfer students:* 2.0 minimum GPA; from 4-year accredited institution 94 semester hours; from 2-year accredited institution 70 semester hours. Standardized test required in some cases.

Degree Requirements: *For all degrees:* 2.0 GPA. *For all baccalaureate degrees:* 130 semester credits; 36 in residence, 18 in major.

Fulfillment of some degree requirements and exemption from some beginning courses possible by passing departmental examinations, College Board CLEP, AP. *Grading system:* A–F, pass-fail.

Distinctive Educational Programs: *For undergraduates:* Branch campus in Seattle (WA). Evening classes. Interdisciplinary courses, including energy concepts, environmental design. Individual majors, tutorials. Open Learning Fire Service correspondence courses. Program in music engineering technology, computer engineering technology, electronic engineering technology.

ROTC: Offered in cooperation with University of Santa Clara.

Degrees Conferred: 68 *baccalaureate.* Bachelor's degrees awarded: communications technologies/technicians, and support services 42; security and protective services 14, engineering technologies/technicians 11, visual and performing arts 1.

Fees and Other Expenses: *Full-time tuition per academic year 2004–05:* $12,420. *Books and supplies:* $1,200. *Room and board per academic year:* $6,300.

Financial Aid: Aid from institutionally generated funds is provided on the basis of academic merit, financial need. Institution has a Program Participation Agreement with the U.S. Department of Education for eligible students to receive Pell Grants and other federal aid.

Financial aid to full-time, first-time undergraduate students: 10% received federal grants; 5% state/local grants; 62% loans.

Departments and Teaching Staff: *Total instructional faculty:* 55. Degrees held by full-time faculty: baccalaureate 6%, master's 60%, doctorate 33%.

Enrollment: Total enrollment 387 (87.9% men, 12.1% women).

Characteristics of Student Body: *Ethnic/racial makeup:* Black non-Hispanic: 3.9%; American Indian or Alaska Native: .8%; Asian or Pacific Islander: 15.5%; Hispanic: 7.8%; White non-Hispanic: 59.7%; unknown: 12.4%.

International Students: 7 nonresident aliens enrolled fall 2004. No programs available to aid students whose native language is not English. No financial aid specifically designated for international students.

Student Life: No on-campus housing. College assists students in finding off-campus housing. *Special services:* Learning Resources Center. *Surrounding community:* Served by mass transit bus and rail systems. Airport 15 miles from campus, passenger rail service 6 miles from campus.

Publications: *Cogswell Contact*, a bimonthly publication.

Library Collections: 14,000 volumes. 250 audiovisual materials; 125 current periodical subscriptions. Students have access to online information retrieval services and the Internet.

Most important holdings include collections of manufacturer's data manuals; music engineering technology; Cogswell Archives (1887–present).

Buildings and Grounds: Cogswell Polytechnical College occupies a single-story building on 4.6 acres surrounded by high-tech companies in the "Silicon Valley."

Chief Executive Officer: Dr. William H. Pickens, President.

Address admission inquiries to Patty Delrio, Director of Admissions.

Coleman College

7380 Parkway Drive
La Mesa, California 91942-1532
Tel: (619) 465-3990   **E-mail:** admissions@coleman.edu
Fax: (619) 463-0162   **Internet:** www.coleman.edu

Institution Description: Coleman College is a private, independent institution. *Enrollment:* 783.. *Degrees awarded:* Associate, baccalaureate, master's.

Accreditation: *Nonregional:* ACICS.

Institutional Structure: *Governing board:* Board of Directors.

Calendar: Quarters.

Admission: 39 applicants in fall 2004 (31 men / 8 women). 100% of applicants admitted; 93.3% enrolled full-time.

Degree Requirements: Completion of prescribed curriculum.

Degrees Conferred: 212 *associate*; 144 *baccalaureate*; 28 *master's*. Bachelor's degrees awarded in computer and information sciences and support services.

Fees and Other Expenses: *Full-time tuition per academic year 2004–05:* $16,368. *Room and board:* $6,482. *Other expenses:* $2,492.

Financial Aid: Aid from institutionally generated funds is provided on the basis of academic merit, financial need, other criteria. Institution has a Program Participation Agreement with the U.S. Department of Education for eligible students to receive Pell Grants and other federal aid.

Financial aid to full-time, first-time undergraduate students: 44% received federal grants averaging $3,753; 5% state/local grants; 80% loans averaging $9,328.

Departments and Teaching Staff: *Total instructional faculty:* 36.

Enrollment: Total enrollment 783. Undergraduate 749.

Characteristics of Student Body: *Ethnic/racial makeup:* Black non-Hispanic: 6.7%; American Indian or Alaska Native: 1.75; Asian or Pacific Islander: 9.3%; Hispanic: 12%; White non-Hispanic: 65.3%; unknown: 4.9%.

Library Collections: 35,000 volumes. 85 periodical subscriptions. Access to online information retrieval systems.

Chief Executive Officer: Paul Panesar, President.

Address admission inquiries to Debbie R. Coleman, Director of Admissions.

Columbia College Hollywood

18618 Oxnard Street
Tarzana, California 91356-1411

Tel: (818) 345-8414   **E-mail:** admissions@columbiacollege.edu
Fax: (213) 345-9053   **Internet:** www.columbiacollege.edu

Institution Description: Columbia College is a private, independent, nonprofit college. *Enrollment:* 170. *Degrees awarded:* Associate, baccalaureate.

Accreditation: *Nonregional:* ACCSCT.

History: Established and incorporated 1952; offered first instruction at postsecondary level 1953; awarded first degree 1955.

Institutional Structure: *Governing board:* Board of Trustees. Representation: 9 trustees. All ex officio. *Composition of institution:* Administrators 10 men / 4 women. Academic/administrative affairs headed by Director of Admissions. Management/business/finances directed by president.

Calendar: Quarters. Academic year is 3 quarters. Freshmen admitted Sept., Jan., Apr., July. Degrees conferred and formal commencement June.

Characteristics of Freshmen: 65% of entering freshmen expected to graduate within 5 years. 30% of freshmen are residents of California. Freshmen from 15 states and 8 foreign countries.

Admission: Rolling admissions plan. For fall acceptance, apply as early as 9 months prior to or as late as 30 days of first quarter of enrollment. *Requirements:* Either graduation from secondary school or GED. Minimum GPA 2.0. *For transfer students:* 2.0 minimum GPA; from 4-year accredited institution 96 credit hours maximum transfer credit; from 2-year accredited institution 45 hours.

Degree Requirements: *For all associate degrees:* 96 credit hours. *For all baccalaureate degrees:* 192 credit hours. *For all degrees:* 2.0 GPA. *Grading system:* A–F.

Distinctive Educational Programs: *For undergraduates:* Special facilities for using telecommunications in the classroom. Honors programs.

Degrees Conferred: 50 *baccalaureate:* visual and performing arts 50.

Fees and Other Expenses: *Full-time tuition per academic year 2005–06:* $11,400. *Production institutional fees:* $225. *Estimated lab fees:* $875.

Financial Aid: Aid from institutionally generated funds is provided on the basis of academic merit, financial need. Financial assistance is available in the form of Pell Grants, College Work-Study, Supplemental Education Opportunity Grants (SEOG), Stafford and Plus Loans, and other federal aid program. Veterans Administration Benefits available.

Departments and Teaching Staff: Broadcasting *part-time teachers* 36. *Total instructional faculty:* 36. Degrees held by full-time faculty: baccalaureates 75%, master's 20%, doctorates 5%.

Enrollment: Total enrollment 170.

Characteristics of Student Body: *Ethnic/racial makeup:* Black non-Hispanic: 34%; Asian or Pacific Islander: 4.2%; Hispanic: 6.9%; White non-Hispanic: 41%; unknown: 5.6%.

International Students: 49 nonresident aliens enrolled fall 2004. No programs available to aid students whose native language is not English. No financial aid specifically designated for foreign students.

Student Life: No on-campus housing. *Student publications:* Monthly student newsletter. *Surrounding community:* Los Angeles population over 3 million. Served by mass transit system; airport 10 miles from campus; passenger rail service 6 miles from campus.

Library Collections: 5,000 volumes. 40 current periodical subscriptions; wide-ranging screenplay and teleplay collection plus an extensive collection of audiovisual materials, including documentaries, industry seminars, and film scores.

Most important holdings include *Society of Motion Picture and Television Engineers Journal* 1910 to present; screenplay and teleplay collection.

Chief Executive Officer: Paul Lo, President.

Address admission inquiries to Carmen Munoz, Admissions Director.

Concordia University

1530 Concordia West
Irvine, California 92612-3299

Tel: (949) 854-8002   **E-mail:** admission@cui.edu
Fax: (949) 854-6854   **Internet:** www.cui.edu

Institution Description: Concordia University, formerly known as Christ College Irvine, is a private liberal arts college affiliated with The Lutheran Church-Missouri Synod. *Enrollment:* 1,834. *Degrees awarded:* Associate, baccalaureate, master's.

Accreditation: *Regional:* WASC-Sr.

History: Established and incorporated 1972; offered first instruction at postsecondary level 1976; awarded first degree (baccalaureate) 1980.

Institutional Structure: *Governing board:* Concordia University Board of Regents. Representation: 13 regents. All voting. *Composition of institution:* Administrators 7 men / 2 women. Academic affairs headed by provost. Full-time instructional faculty 76. Academic governance body, Concordia University Faculty, meets 8 times per year.

Calendar: Semesters. Academic year Aug. to May. Degrees conferred and commencement May. Summer session of 3 terms.

Characteristics of Freshmen: 67% of applicants admitted. 43% of admitted students enrolled full-time.

77% (182 students) submitted SAT scores; 23% (53 students) submitted ACT scores. *25th percentile:* SAT Verbal 450, SAT Math 450; ACT Composite 20. *75th percentile:* SAT Verbal 570, SAT Math 560; ACT Composite 21.

77% of freshmen from California. Freshmen from 24 states and 1 foreign country.

Admission: Rolling admissions plan. For fall acceptance, apply as early as June of previous year. Early acceptance available. *Requirements:* Either graduation from accredited secondary school with 3 units English, 3 mathematics (2 algebra and geometry), 2 science (biology and chemistry), 2 social studies (world and U.S. history); or GED. Minimum GPA 2.5. *Entrance tests:* College Board SAT minimum 900. For foreign students TOEFL. *For transfer students:* 2.3 minimum GPA.

College credit and advanced placement for postsecondary-level work completed in secondary school. Tutoring available.

Degree Requirements: *For baccalaureate degrees:* 128 credit hours; 2 units physical education activities; 2 units of applied music or ensemble, 2 units of practicum in any one subject field (after general education, program, major and minor requirements have been met) may be counted toward those 128 units. 32 semester hours in residence. *For all degrees:* 2.0 minimum GPA in major, minor, and program unless the program requirement is higher.

Fulfillment of some degree requirements and exemption from some beginning courses possible by passing departmental examinations, College Board CLEP. *Grading system:* A–F; withdraw (carries time limit); incomplete (carries time limit).

Distinctive Educational Programs: Internships. Evening classes. Special facilities for using telecommunications in the classroom. Interdisciplinary programs in evangelism, humanities. Facilities and programs for independent research, including honors programs, individual majors, tutorials, independent study. Institutionally sponsored study abroad. *Other distinctive programs:* Credit and noncredit continuing education program.

Degrees Conferred: 7 *associate;* 286 *baccalaureate:* (B), 64 *master's* (M): biological/life sciences 10 (B); business/marketing 53 (B), 14 (M); communications/communication technologies 13 (B); education 1 (B), 45 (M); liberal arts/general studies 102 (M); mathematics 1 (B); parks and recreation 11 (B); philosophy/religion/theology 26 (B), 5 (M); psychology 15 (B); social sciences and history 29 (B); visual and performing arts 12 (B).

Fees and Other Expenses: *Full-time tuition per academic year 2004–05:* $18,800. *Room per academic year:* $4,000. *Board per academic year:* meal plan/19 per week $2,670.

Financial Aid: Aid from institutionally generated funds is provided on the basis of academic merit, financial need, athletic ability, other criteria. Institution has a Program Participation Agreement with the U.S. Department of Education for eligible students to receive Pell Grants and other federal aid.

Undergraduate need-based scholarships/grants totaling $2,523,481, self-help $2,823,481, tuition waivers $65,697, athletic awards $657,101; non-need-based scholarships/grants totaling $2,074,310, self-help $3,420,090, parent loans $1,751,074, tuition waivers $165,761, athletic awards $407,154.

Departments and Teaching Staff: *Total instructional faculty:* 185 (full-time 76, part-time 109; women 77, men 108). Total faculty with doctorate, first-professional, or other terminal degree: 47. Student-to-faculty ratio: 15:1. 2 faculty members awarded sabbaticals in 2004–05.

Enrollment: Total enrollment 1,834. Undergraduate full-time 456 men/ 804 women, part-time 34m 73w; graduate full-time 93m / 172w, part-time 70m / 132w.

Characteristics of Student Body: *Ethnic/racial makeup:* number of Black non-Hispanic: 44; American Indian or Alaska Native: 11; Asian or Pacific Islander: 64; Hispanic: 61; White non-Hispanic: 919; unknown: 93. *Age distribution:* number under 18: 26; 18–19: 457, 20–21: 491; 22–24: 206; 25–29: 63; 35–39: 12; 40–49: 29; 50–64: 16.

International Students: 75 nonresident aliens enrolled in degree and nondegree programs in fall 204. Students from Asia, Canada, Europe. English as a Second Language program. No financial aid specifically designated for international students.

Student Life: On-campus residence halls house 75% of student body. *Intercollegiate athletics:* men only: baseball; women only: softball, volleyball; men and women: basketball, cross country, soccer, track. *Special regulations:* Cars with decals permitted; fee charged. Quiet hours schedule for residence hall visitation. *Special services:* Learning Resources Center, career center, medical services. *Student publications: Clearlight,* a yearbook; *Hilltop Herald,* published 8 times per year; *The Eagle,* a daily campus bulletin. *Surrounding community:* Irvine population 160,000. Los Angeles; 40 miles from campus, is nearest metropolitan area. Served by mass transit bus system; airport 4 miles from campus; passenger rail service 10 miles from campus.

Publications: Sources of information about the college include *Concordia Today,* a quarterly newsletter.

Library Collections: 85,432 volumes. Online catalog. Microforms 53,175; 3,692 audiovisual materials. 414 current serial subscriptions. Electronic reference sources services 20. 7 computer work stations. Students have access to the Internet at no charge.

Most important special holdings include 3,000 books and bound periodicals on Lutheran history and theology; foreign language Bible collection; curriculum and teacher resource library.

Buildings and Grounds: Campus area 70 acres.

Chief Executive Officer: Rev. Jacob Preus, S.T.M., President.

Address admission inquiries to Lori McDonald, Admission Director.

Dominican School of Philosophy and Theology

2401 Ridge Road
Berkeley, California 94709
Tel: (510) 849-2030   **E-mail:** admissions@dspt.edu
Fax: (510) 949-1372   **Internet:** www.dspt.edu

Institution Description: Dominican School of Philosophy and Theology (Saint Albert's College until 1978) is a private, nonprofit institution operated by the Western Dominican Province, Roman Catholic Church, providing upper division and graduate study only. It is a member of the Graduate Theological Union, which was created by 9 Protestant and Roman Catholic institutions to coordinate joint programs and award graduate degrees. *SEE* separate exhibit for Graduate Theological Union. *Enrollment:* 99. *Degrees awarded:* Baccalaureate, master's, first-professional. Certificates also awarded.

Accreditation: *Regional:* WASC-Sr. *Professional:* theology

History: Established as Saint Albert's College, chartered, and offered first instruction at postsecondary level 1932; awarded first degree (baccalaureate) 1936; adopted present name 1978.

Institutional Structure: *Governing board:* The Provincial Council of the Western Dominican Province. Extrainstitutional representation: 15 council members; institutional representation: president of the college. 2 ex officio. All voting. *Composition of institution:* Administrators 2 men / 1 woman. Academic affairs headed by president. Management/business/finances directed by business manager. Full-time instructional faculty 13 men. Academic governance body, the faculty, meets an average of 6 times per year.

Calendar: Semesters. Academic year Sept. to May.

Admission: Rolling admissions plan. *Requirements:* Associate degree or equivalent from accredited college or university. Minimum GPA 2.5. *For transfer students:* 2.5 minimum GPA.

Degree Requirements: *For baccalaureate degree:* 124 semester hours; 2.5 GPA; 3 terms in residence; distribution requirements. A–F; pass-fail; pass; withdraw; incomplete (carries time limit).

Distinctive Educational Programs: *For graduate students:* Field education programs. Double-degree program leading to master of divinity and master of arts in theology. Cooperative master's programs and cross-registration through Graduate Theological Union. Students may take courses at University of California, Berkeley. Study abroad by individual arrangement. *Available to all students:* tutorials.

Degrees Conferred: 5 *baccalaureate:* philosophy, theology, religion; 10 *master's;* 6 *first-professional.*

Fees and Other Expenses: *Full-time tuition per academic year:* $10,010 undergraduate; contact the school for first-professional and graduate study rates. *Books and supplies:* $1,020. *Off campus room and board:* $7,000.

Financial Aid: Aid from institutionally generated funds is provided on the basis of academic merit, financial need.

Financial assistance is available in the form of Pell Grants, Veterans Administration Benefits, Stafford Loans. *Federal funding:* loans averaging $8,666 each.

Departments and Teaching Staff: Philosophy and theology *professors* 6, *associate professors* 2, *assistant professors* 7, *part-time teachers* 12. *Total instructional faculty:* 27. Degrees held by full-time faculty: Professional 95%, doctorate 95%, master's 5%, baccalaureate 100%.

Enrollment: Total enrollment 99. Undergraduate 9.

Characteristics of Student Body: *Ethnic/racial makeup:* Asian or Pacific Islander: 11.1%; Hispanic: 33.3%; White non-Hispanic: 44.4%.

International Students: 10 nonresident aliens enrolled 2004. No programs available to aid students whose native language is not English. No financial aid specifically designated for international students.

Student Life: Residence halls house 25% of student body who are members of Dominican Order. *Special regulations:* Cars permitted without restrictions. *Surrounding community:* Berkeley, population over 100,000, is located within San Francisco metropolitan area. Served by mass transit subway system; airport 12 miles from campus, passenger rail service 5 miles from campus.

Library Collections: Library services provided through Graduate Theological Union.

Buildings and Grounds: Campus area 1 square block.

Chief Executive Officer: Rev. Michael Sweeney, O.P., President.

Address admission inquiries to Susan M. McGinnis Hardie, Director of Admissions/Recruitment.

Dominican University of California

50 Acacia Avenue
San Rafael, California 94901-2298
Tel: (415) 457-4440   **E-mail:** enroll@dominican.edu
Fax: (415) 485-3205   **Internet:** www.dominican.edu

Institution Description: Dominican University of California (formerly Dominican College of San Rafael) is an independent, Catholic, international, learning-centered university. *Enrollment:* 1,742. *Degrees awarded:* Baccalaureate, master's.

Accreditation: *Regional:* WASC-Sr. *Professional:* nursing, nursing education, occupational therapy

History: Incorporated as a women's college 1890; offered first instruction at postsecondary level 1912; awarded first degree (baccalaureate) 1917; established coeducational graduate division 1950; became coeducational 1971.

Institutional Structure: *Governing board:* Board of Trustees. Representation: 35 trustees. *Composition of institution:* Administrators 51. Academic affairs, finance/administration, enrollment management each headed by a vice president. Full-time instructional faculty: 43.

Calendar: Semesters. Academic year Aug. to May.

Characteristics of Freshmen: 2,426 applicants (693 men, 1,733 women). 50.9% of applicants admitted; 22.3% enrolled full-time.

88% (244 students) submitted SAT scores; 34% (95 students) submitted ACT scores. *25th percentile:* SAT Verbal 450, SAT Math 440; ACT Composite 18. *75th percentile:* SAT Verbal 570, SAT Math 560, ACT Composite 24.

43% of entering freshmen expected to graduate in 5 years. 88% of freshmen from California. Freshmen from 8 states and 3 foreign countries.

Admission: Rolling admissions plan. Priority admissions Feb. 1. *Requirements:* Graduation from accredited secondary school with 4 units in English, 2 foreign language, 1 algebra, 1 geometry, 1 history, 1 laboratory science, 4-5 additional units from among any of the above fields, 1-2 electives. Minimum GPA 2.5 for last 3 years of secondary school. *Entrance tests:* College Board SAT. For foreign students TOEFL. *For transfer students:* 2.0 minimum GPA; 2.5 GPA for nursing and physical therapy; maximum transfer credit limited only by residence requirement.

College credit and advanced placement for postsecondary-level work completed in secondary school. College credit for extrainstitutional learning (life experience) on basis of portfolio assessment.

Degree Requirements: 124 semester hours; 2.0 GPA; last 30 hours in residence; general education requirements.

Fulfillment of some degree requirements and exemption from some beginning courses possible by passing institutional examinations, College Board CLEP, AP, other standardized tests. *Grading system:* A–F; pass-fail; no credit.

Distinctive Educational Programs: Interdisciplinary programs. Study abroad programs in France and Italy. Electronic studies (E-Art or E-Commerce).

ROTC: Students with transportation may participate in Air Force ROTC at San Francisco State University, Army ROTC at the University of San Francisco, and Navy ROTC at the University of California, Berkeley.

Degrees Conferred: 201 *baccalaureate*; 119 *master's*; 118 *post-baccalaureate certificates*. Bachelor's degrees awarded in top five disciplines: health professions and related clinical sciences 58; business, management, marketing, and related support services 34; liberal arts and sciences, general studies and humanities 31; psychology 27; visual and performing arts 18.

Fees and Other Expenses: *Full-time tuition per academic year 2004–05:* $24,254. *Room and board per academic year:* $9,892. *Books and supplies:* $1,260.

Financial Aid: Aid from institutionally generated funds is provided on the basis of academic merit, financial need. Institution has a Program Participation Agreement with the U.S. Department of Education for eligible students to receive Pell Grants and other federal aid.

Financial aid to full-time, first-time undergraduate students: 34% received federal grants averaging $3,862; 27% state/local grants averaging $6,488; 92% institutional grants averaging $13,347; 75% loans averaging $4,380.

Departments and Teaching Staff: *Professors* 15, *associate professors* 9, *assistant professors* 18, *instructors* 1, *part-time teachers* 157. Total instructional faculty 95.3 FTE. Total tenured faculty: 8. Student-to-faculty ratio: 11.8:1. Degrees held by full-time faculty: doctorate 55.8%, master's 44.2%. 60.5% hold terminal degrees.

Enrollment: Total enrollment 1,742. Undergraduate 1,124 (214.7% men, 78.3% women).

Characteristics of Student Body: *Ethnic/racial makeup:* Black non-Hispanic: 8.9%; American Indian or Alaska Native: 1%; Asian or Pacific Islander: 13.4%; Hispanic: 12.7%; White non-Hispanic: 46.8%; unknown: 13.3%.

International Students: 44 nonresident aliens enrolled fall 2004. Social and cultural programs available to aid students whose native language is not English. English as a Second Language Program.

Student Life: On-campus housing. Students from a wide range of cultural and religious backgrounds. Small classes. The Dominican experience features such unique traditions such as Shield Day, the senior thesis, and a 4-year graduation guarantee. The campus is located in the San Francisco Bay area, just north of the Golden Gate Bridge. New recreation center completed spring 2000. *Student activities:* Student government, choir, Multicultural Club, Dominican Ambassadors. *Intercollegiate athletics:* Men's and women's basketball, soccer, and tennis; women's volleyball and softball. *Student publications: The Habit,* a student newspaper, *Tuxedo,* a literary magazine, and *Firebrand,* a yearbook.

Library Collections: 97,914 volumes including bound books, serial backfiles, electronic documents, and government documents not in separate collections. Online catalog. Current serial subscriptions: 425 paper, 70 microform, 13 electronic. 754 recordings; 193 compact discs; 217 CD-ROMs. 52 computer work stations. Students have access to the Internet at no charge.

Most important holdings include special collections on art history, music, English literature; Nimitz Collection (papers, pictures, writings of Chester William Nimitz); Pacific Basin Studies Collection (economics, politics, cross-cultural communication, business); Ansel Adams Collection; representative collection of fine press editions.

Buildings and Grounds: Campus area 80 acres. *New buildings:* Sister Samuel Conlan Recreation Center completed 2000.

Chief Executive Officer: Dr. Joseph R. Fink, President.

Address undergraduate admission inquiries to Art Criss, Director of Undergraduate Admissions; graduate inquiries to Loretta Corvello, Director of Graduate Admissions.

Fielding Graduate University

2112 Santa Barbara Street
Santa Barbara, California 93120
Tel: (800) 340-1099   **E-mail:** admissions@fielding.edu
Fax: (805) 689-9793   **Internet:** www.fielding.edu

Institution Description: Fielding Graduate University, formerly known as Fielding Institute, is a private, independent, nonprofit graduate school offering programs in human and organization development, clinical psychology, neuropsychotherapy, and educational leadership and change. Most Fielding programs combine face-to-face and online interaction. Some master's degrees, certificate programs, and custom and corporate programs are delivered exclusively online. *Enrollment:* 1.598. *Degrees awarded:* Master's, doctorate.

Accreditation: *Regional:* WASC-Sr. *Professional:* psychology internship

History: Established, incorporated, offered first instruction at postsecondary level, awarded first degree (doctorate) 1974.

Institutional Structure: *Governing board:* Board of trustees. Extrainstitutional representation: 20 trustees. *Composition of institution:* Administrators 2 men / 3 women. Programs directed by deans. Management/business/finances and academic affairs directed president, provost, chief financial officer.

Calendar: Year-round operation.

Admission: Applicants must have a bachelor's degree from a college or university that is accredited by one of the six regional accrediting associations recognized by the U.S. Department of Education. Degrees or academic records from schools outside of the U.S. and Canada must be evaluated for equivalency. Additional admission requirements vary according to the program.

Degree Requirements: *For doctorate:* Dissertation. *For all degrees:* Area core curriculum. For psychology degrees, training and internships. *Grading system:* A–C, pass.

Distinctive Educational Programs: Fielding Graduate University offers flexible study options and schedules that address the 21st-century needs of a global network of school practitioners. The Fielding learning model allows students to build on their individual backgrounds and areas of experience.

Degrees Conferred: 161 *master's:* psychology 28, social sciences 123; 86 *doctorate:* education 25, psychology 33, social sciences 28.

Fees and Other Expenses: *Full-time tuition per academic year 2004–05:* $16,980.

Financial Aid: Aid is provided on the basis of academic merit and financial need. Federal and state-funded loans awarded to 1,813 students.

Departments and Teaching Staff: *Total instructional faculty:* 108 (full-time 105, part-time 3; 48 women, 60 men). Total faculty with doctorate, first-professional, or other terminal degree: 108. Student-to-faculty ratio: 15:1.

Enrollment: Total enrollment 1,598 (full-time 1,589, part-time 39).

Library Collections: Fielding Graduate University has a virtual library, with an online library comprised of thousands of electronic books and dissertations, and several dozen online databases providing access to full-text articles from several thousand periodicals. Two full-time librarians are available to assist students and faculty in obtaining research resources.

Buildings and Grounds: The Fielding Graduate University administrative offices are located in Santa Barbara, California. Seminars, research, and other academic sessions are held at various locations throughout the country.

Chief Executive Officer: Judith L. Kuipers, President.

Address admissions inquiries to Director of Admissions.

Five Branches Institute

200 Seventh Avenue
Suite 115
Santa Cruz, California 95062
Tel: (831) 476-9424   **E-mail:** admissions@fivebranches.edu
Fax: (831) 476-8928   **Internet:** www.fivebranches.edu

Institution Description: Five Branches Institute, College of Traditional Chinese Medicine (TCM), provides college graduate students with a professional education in traditional Chinese medicine through classroom courses and clinical training that emphasizes acupuncture and herbology. *Enrollment:* 193.

Accreditation: *Professional:* acupuncture

History: The institute was founded in 1984.

Calendar: Semesters. Academic year Sept. to May.

Admission: Rolling admissions. *Requirements:* Statement of purpose, three letters of personal reference; original transcripts of all college coursework undertaken. All applicants must have the minimum education requirement of 60

semester units of general education from a nationally accredited college. *For transfer students:* Application procedure as above plus a catalog of the TCM college where studied previously.

Degree Requirements: Completion of specified courses. *Grading system:* Pass/fail.

Distinctive Educational Programs: Post-Graduate Study Abroad Program in China at Zhejiang Provincial TCM College and Shanghai TCM College.

Degrees Conferred: 55 *master's:* health professions and related clinical studies.

Fees and Other Expenses: *Tuition per academic year 2004–05:* Contact the school for current tuition and fees that are subject to change without notice.

Departments and Teaching Staff: *Core faculty:* 7; *auxiliary studies and modern science faculty:* 9; *adjunct faculty:* 7. *Total instructional faculty:* 23.

Enrollment: Total enrollment 193 (55 men, 138 women).

Characteristics of Student Body: *Ethnic/racial makeup:* Asian or Pacific Islander: 6,2%; Hispanic: 5.7%; White non-Hispanic: 73.6%; American Indian or Alaska Native: .5%.

International Students: 8 nonresident aliens enrolled 2004. No programs available to aid students whose native language is not English. No financial aid specifically designated for international students.

Student Life: Santa Cruz is a located in the northern Monterey Bay area of California. The institute is one block from Twin Lakes Beach near the mouth of the Bay.

Library Collections: 2,000 books and periodicals divided into over 20 subjects related to TCM, complementary medicine, modern science, and Asian Culture. Students enrolled at the institute may take advantage of the local University of California campus and join the library system for an annual membership fee.

Chief Executive Officer: Ron Zaidman, President.

Address admissions inquiries to Eleonor Mendelson, Admissions Director.

Franciscan School of Theology

1712 Euclid Avenue
Berkeley, California 94709
Tel: (510) 848-5232 **E-mail:** jdiaz@fst.edu
Fax: (510) 549-9466 **Internet:** www.fst.edu

Institution Description: Franciscan School of Theology is a private, independent, nonprofit institution affiliated with the Roman Catholic Church. The institution is a member of the Graduate Theological Union (GTU) which was created by 9 Protestant and Roman Catholic institutions to coordinate joint programs and award graduate degrees. *SEE* separate exhibit for Graduate Theological Union. *Enrollment:* 95. *Degrees awarded:* Master's, first-professional.

Accreditation: *Regional:* WASC-Sr. *Professional:* theology

History: Chartered as Mission Santa Barbara, an apostolic college, 1854; adopted secondary school and college seminary program 1896; secondary school and college became separate institutions 1910 and 1929, respectively; moved to present location and became participating school in Graduate Theological Union 1968.

Institutional Structure: *Governing board:* Board of Trustees. Representation: 8 trustees, members of the province of St. Barbara. *Composition of institution:* Administrators 1 man / 3 women. Academic affairs headed by president and academic dean. Full-time instructional faculty 8.

Calendar: Semesters. Academic year early Sept. to late May.

Admission: For fall acceptance, apply no later than April 1 for master of divinity and master of theological studies students; March 1 for master of arts students. *Requirements:* Baccalaureate from accredited college or university. For master of divinity program, 6 semester hours philosophy. *Entrance tests:* GRE. For foreign students TOEFL.

Degree Requirements: *For first-professional degree:* 96 semester units; 8 semesters in residence. *For master of theological studies degree:* 36 semester hours; 4 semesters in residence. *For master of pastoral ministry:* 48 semester hours; 4 semesters in residence. *For all degrees:* 3.0 GPA; core curriculum. *Grading system:* A–F.

Distinctive Educational Programs: *For graduate students:* Cooperative master's and doctoral program through consortium. Cross-registration through consortium. *Other distinctive programs:* Nondegree continuing education programs for students with first-professional degrees.

Degrees Conferred: 21 *master's,* 5 *first-professional:* theology and ministerial studies.

Fees and Other Expenses: *Full-time tuition per academic year:* $10,700. Contact the school for housing costs.

Financial Aid: Institution has a Program Participation Agreement with the U.S. Department of Education for eligible students to receive Pell Grants and other federal aid.

Departments and Teaching Staff: Church history *professors* 0, *assistant professors* 0, *part-time teachers* 2; liturgy 1, 0, 0; new testament 0, 1, 0; old testament 1, 0, 0; pastoral theology, phenomenology and religion 1, 0, 1; philosophical theology 1, 0, 1; religion and personality science 1, 1, 0; religion and society 0, 0, 2; rhetoric 0, 0, 1; systematic theology 2, 0, 0.
Total instructional faculty: 15. *Degrees held by faculty:* doctorates 100%.

Enrollment: Total enrollment 95.

Characteristics of Student Body: *Ethnic/racial makeup:* Asian or Pacific Islander: 15.8%; Hispanic: 13.7%; White non-Hispanic: 63.2%.

International Students: 7 nonresident aliens enrolled fall 2004. Students from Europe, Asia, Africa, Canada, Australia. No programs available to aid students whose language is not English. No financial aid specifically designated for international students.

Student Life: *Surrounding community:* Berkeley, population over 100,000, is located in San Francisco-Oakland metropolitan area.

Library Collections: Library services provided by Graduate Theological Union.

Chief Executive Officer: Dr. Mario Dicicco, President.

Address admission inquiries to Jonathan Diaz, Director of Recruitment.

Fresno Pacific University

1717 South Chestnut Avenue
Fresno, California 93702
Tel: (559) 453-2000 **E-mail:** ugadmis@fresno.edu
Fax: (559) 453-2007 **Internet:** www.fresno.edu

Institution Description: Fresno Pacific University, formerly Fresno Pacific College (Pacific College of Fresno until 1979) is a private college affiliated with Pacific District Conference of the Mennonite Brethren Churches. *Enrollment:* 2,305. *Degrees awarded:* Associate, baccalaureate, master's.

Accreditation: *Regional:* WASC-Sr.

History: Established as Pacific Bible Institute, chartered, and offered first instruction at postsecondary level 1944; awarded first degree 1949; changed name to Pacific College of Fresno 1960; became Fresno Pacific College 1979; awarded first baccalaureate degree 1965; adopted present name 1997.

Institutional Structure: *Governing board:* Fresno Pacific College Board of Trustees with 30 external members, 1 faculty, 1 student, 1 staff. External trustees: 18 selected by the Pacific District Conference of Mennonite Brethren Churches and 12 appointed by the Board. *Composition of institution:* Administrators 4 men / 1 woman. Academic affairs headed by academic vice president. Management/business/finances directed by director of finance and management. Full-time instructional faculty d64. Academic governance body, Faculty Session, meets an average of 20 times per year.

Calendar: Semesters. Academic year Aug. to May. Freshmen admitted year round. Formal commencement May, Dec.

Characteristics of Freshmen: 64% of applicants admitted; 34% of admitted students enrolled full-time. 81% (151 students) submitted SAT scores; 32% (59 students) submitted ACT scores. *25th percentile:* SAT Verbal 440, SAT Math 440; ACT Composite 17. *75th percentile:* SAT Verbal 570, SAT Math 570; ACT Composite 24.

95% of freshmen from California. Freshmen from 7 states and 2 foreign countries.

Admission: Rolling admissions plan. For fall acceptance, apply as early as March of previous year, but not later than July 31 of year of enrollment. Early acceptance available. *Requirements:* Either graduation from accredited secondary school with at least 15 units, 9 college preparatory; or GED. Recommend 4 years English, 2-3 mathematics, 2 social studies, 1 laboratory science, additional units in a foreign language. Minimum GPA 3.0. *Entrance tests:* For foreign students TOEFL. *For transfer students:* 2.0 minimum GPA; from 4-year accredited institution 45 semester units minimum transfer credit, 70 semester units maximum transfer credit.

College credit and advanced placement for postsecondary-level work completed in secondary school and for extrainstitutional learning on basis of ACE *2006 Guide to the Evaluation of Educational Experiences in the Armed Services.*

Degree Requirements: *For all associate degrees:* 60 semester hours. *For all baccalaureate degrees:* 124 hours with 45 hours in upper division. *For all degrees:* 2.0 GPA (2.0 GPA in major courses); distribution requirements; weekly convocation attendance.

Fulfillment of some degree requirements and exemption from some beginning courses possible by passing College Board CLEP, APP. *Grading system:* A–F, credit-no credit.

Distinctive Educational Programs: *For undergraduates:* Work-experience programs. Dual-degree program in law with San Joaquin College of Law. Interdisciplinary majors in humanities, liberal arts, Mexican-American studies, natural sciences, social science, urban studies, other programs by individual arrangement. Directed readings and independent study. Study abroad through Brethren Colleges Abroad in England, Wales, Costa Rica, France, Germany, Spain; through Latin American Studies Program of Christian College Coalition; through American Institute of Holy Land Studies in Israel. Additional study abroad by individual arrangement. *For graduate students:* Evening and weekend classes. *Available to all students:* Enrollment for courses at California State University, Fresno, and Mennonite Brethren Biblical Seminary.

Degrees Conferred: 2 *associate;* 309 *baccalaureate* (B); 141 *master's* (M): area and ethnic studies 1 (B); biological/life sciences 7 (B); business/marketing 99 (B), 8 (M); education 118 (B), 122 (M); English 7 (B); foreign languages and literature 1 (B); interdisciplinary studies 11 (M); mathematics 4 (B); philosophy/religion/theology 17 (B); physical sciences 2 (B), protective services/public administration 19 (B); psychology 12 (B); social sciences and history 12 (B), trade and industry 1 (B), visual and performing arts 9 (B).

Fees and Other Expenses: *Full-time tuition per academic year 2004–05:* undergraduate $19,430; graduate $10,665. *Required fees:* $334. *Room and board per academic year:* $5,946.

Financial Aid: Aid from institutionally generated funds is provided on the basis of academic merit, financial need, athletic ability. Institution has a Program Participation Agreement with the U.S. Department of Education for eligible students to receive Pell Grants and other federal aid.

Financial aid to full-time, first-time undergraduate students: need-based scholarships/grants totaling $12,496,813, self-help $6,020,024, parent loans $542,477, athletic awards $882,025; non-need-based scholarships/grants $805,845. *Graduate ad:* 59 students received federal and state funded fellowships and grants totaling $419,471 (ranging from $772 to $9,308); 393 received federal and state-funded loans totaling $3,454,349 (ranging from $109 to $17,448).

Departments and Teaching Staff: *Total instructional faculty:* 86 (full-time 71, part-time 15; 34 women, 52 men). Student-to-faculty ratio: 16:1. Total faculty with doctorate, first-professional, or other terminal degree: 57.

Enrollment: Total enrollment 2,305 (1,296 full-time, 1,009 part-time).

Characteristics of Student Body: *Ethnic/racial makeup:* number of Black non-Hispanic: 25; American Indian or Alaska Native: 14; Asian or Pacific Islander: 38; Hispanic: 149; White non-Hispanic: 560.

International Students: 39 nonresident aliens enrolled fall 2004. 9 students from Europe, 4 Asia, 12 Central and South America, 1 Africa, 2 Canada, 12 other. Programs available to aid students whose native language is not English: English as a Second Language Program. Financial aid specifically designated for international students: 6 scholarships totaling $46,503 awarded 2004.

Student Life: On-campus residence halls include a variety of living spaces for men, women, and some housing set aside for nontraditional students such as international students. Student population is 55% residential and 45% commuter. *Intercollegiate athletics:* co-ed cross-country, women's and men's basketball; women's volleyball; men's soccer. *Special regulations:* Freshmen are permitted to bring vehicles to campus. Parking permits are required for on-campus parking. Students are expected to live by a code of conduct consistent with the university's mission statement. *Student publications: Syrinx,* a bimonthly newspaper; *One Flew Over,* an annual literary magazine. *Surrounding community:* Fresno metropolitan area population 500,000. Served by mass transit bus system, airport 8 miles from campus, passenger rail service 6 miles from campus.

Publications: Sources of information about Fresno Pacific include *Pacific Magazine,* a Fresno Pacific University publication; *Christian Leader,* a denominational publication, and *Mennonite Weekly Review,* an inter-Mennonite publication.

Library Collections: 196,301 volumes including bound books, serial backfiles, electronic documents, and government documents not in separate collections. Online catalog. Current serial subscriptions: 1,500 paper, 5 microform., 14,102 via electronic access. 7,761 recordings; 580 compact discs; 29 CD-ROMs; 2,096 VCRs. 20 computer work stations. Students have access to the Internet at no charge.

Most important holdings include Center for Mennonite Brethren Studies (7,500 volumes, 175 periodicals, archives), special collection on Radical Reformation (1,000 volumes).

Buildings and Grounds: Campus area 42 acres. *New buildings:* Steinert Campus Center completed in 2003.

Chief Executive Officer: Dr. D. Merrill Ewert, President.

Address undergraduate admission inquiries to Ana Gonzales-Pina, Director of College Admissions; graduate inquiries to Director of Graduate Admissions.

Fuller Theological Seminary

135 North Oakland Avenue
Pasadena, California 91182
Tel: (626) 584-5200   **E-mail:** admissions@fuller.edu
Fax: (626) 584-5672   **Internet:** www.fuller.edu

Institution Description: Fuller Theological Seminary is a private, independent, nonprofit institution. *Enrollment:* 3,128. *Degrees awarded:* Master's, doctorate, first-professional.

Accreditation: *Regional:* WASC-Sr. *Professional:* clinical psychology, marriage and family therapy, theology

History: Established, chartered, and offered first instruction at postsecondary level 1947; awarded first degree (baccalaureate) 1950; incorporated 1951.

Institutional Structure: *Governing board:* Board of Trustees. Extrainstitutional representation: 32 trustees. institutional representation: president of the seminary; 2 alumni. All voting. *Composition of institution:* Administrators 68 men / 63 women. Academic affairs headed by president. Management/business/finances directed by director of business affairs. Full-time instructional faculty 49. Academic governance body, Joint Faculty, meets an average of 10 times per year.

Calendar: Quarters. Academic year Sept. to June. Freshmen admitted Sept., Jan., Mar., June. Degrees conferred Dec., Mar., June., Sept. Formal commencement June. Summer session of 1 term from late June to early Sept.

Admission: Rolling admissions plan. *Requirements:* Baccalaureate degree. *For transfer students:* 48 quarter hours maximum transfer credit.

Degree Requirements: *For first-professional degree:* 144 quarter hours; 2.0 GPA; 2 terms in residence. Fulfillment of some degree requirements possible by passing departmental examination in Biblical Greek and Biblical Hebrew. *Grading system:* A–C; pass-fail option; withdraw (carries time limit).

Distinctive Educational Programs: *For graduate students:* Required field experience internship for first-professional students. Weekend and evening classes. Special facilities for using telecommunications in the classroom. Facilities and programs for independent research, including individual majors, tutorials. Institutionally sponsored study abroad in Israel.

Degrees Conferred: 455 *master's;* 182 *doctorate;* 156 *first-professional.*

Fees and Other Expenses: *Full-time tuition per academic year:* $11, 952. Contact the seminary for current housing costs.

Financial Aid: Institution has a Program Participation Agreement with the U.S. Department of Education for eligible students to receive Pell Grants and other federal aid. Teaching assistantships available.

Departments and Teaching Staff: *Total instructional faculty:* 58 (full-time 48, part-time 10; 17 women, 41 men). Total faculty with doctorate, first-professional, or other terminal degree 57. Student-to-faculty ratio: 21:1. 20 faculty members awarded sabbaticals 2004.

Enrollment: Total enrollment 3,128 (full-time 1,121, part-time 2,007).

Characteristics of Student Body: *Ethnic/racial makeup:* Black non-Hispanic: 5.5%; American Indian or Alaska Native: .4%; Asian or Pacific Islander: 6%; Hispanic: 4.6%; White non-Hispanic: 57.1%; unknown: 5.6%.

International Students: 454 nonresident aliens enrolled fall 2004. English as a Second Language Program available. Variable number of scholarships available for qualified international students.

Student Life: On-campus residence halls house 4% of student body. Residence halls for both men and women constitute 100% of such space. Off-campus college-owned apartments also offer residence space. Housing available for married students. *Special regulations:* Cars permitted without restrictions. *Special services:* Learning Resources Center, medical services. *Surrounding community:* Pasadena population 125,000. Los Angeles, 15 miles from campus, is nearest metropolitan area. Served by mass transit bus system; airport 15 miles from campus; passenger rail service 2 miles from campus.

Library Collections: 256,809 volumes. Current serial subscriptions: 1,106 paper, 51,540 microform, 1,000 via electronic access. 43 computer work stations. Student have access to online information retrieval services and the Internet.

Buildings and Grounds: Campus area 6 square blocks.

Chief Executive Officer: Dr. Richard J. Mouw, President.

Address admission inquiries to Erwin Wong, Director of Admissions.

Golden Gate Baptist Theological Seminary

201 Seminary Drive
Mill Valley, California 94941-3197
Tel: (415) 380-1300   **E-mail:** admissions@ggbts.edu
Fax: (415) 380-1302   **Internet:** www.ggbts.edu

Institution Description: Golden Gate Baptist Theological Seminary is a private institution affiliated with the Southern Baptist Convention. Other branches are located in Brea, California; Portland, Oregon; Phoenix, Arizona; and Denver, Colorado. *Enrollment: 333. Degrees awarded:* First-professional (Master of Divinity, Master of Arts in Christian Education Master of Church Music), doctorate.

Accreditation: *Regional:* WASC-Sr. *Professional:* music, theology

History: Established in Oakland, incorporated, and offered first instruction at postsecondary level 1944; moved to Berkeley and awarded first degree 1949; moved to present location 1959.

Institutional Structure: *Governing board:* The Trustees, Golden Gate Baptist Theological Seminary. Extrainstitutional representation: 36 trustees. All voting. *Composition of institution:* Academic affairs headed by dean of academic affairs. Management/business/finances directed by vice president for business affairs. Academic governance body, the faculty, meets an average of 9 times per year.

Calendar: Semesters. Academic year Aug. to July. Degrees conferred and formal commencements May, Dec. In addition to basic calendar, two intensive terms: January and summer.

Admission: *Requirements:* Baccalaureate degree, transcript of any seminary training beyond college, church endorsement, short autobiography, references, recent photograph, health certificate. *Entrance tests:* Concept Mastery Test, California Psychological Inventory, English test, Theological School Inventory, all administered at orientation. *For transfer students:* Transfer credit available. Remedial courses offered during regular academic year.

Degree Requirements: *For first-professional degree:* 88 semester hours for M. Div., 66 hours M.A.C.E., 58 hours M.M.C.M., M.A.C.M. 40 hours, M.A.I.S. 49 hours. *For first-professional and master's degrees:* 1.75 GPA; last 9 hours in residence; distribution requirements.

Fulfillment of some degree requirements and exemption from some beginning courses possible by passing departmental examinations. *Grading system:* A–F; pass-fail.

Distinctive Educational Programs: *For graduate students:* Off-campus centers (at Brea, CA; Portland, OR; Phoenix, AZ; Denver, CO.). Ethnic language programs from Alaska to Tuscon, AZ. Independent study. Evening classes.

Degrees Conferred: 86 *first-professional:* master of divinity 75; other master's 11; 4 *master's:* theology/theological ministries.

Fees and Other Expenses: *Full-time tuition per academic year 2004–05:* Contact the seminary for current tuition and housing costs.

Financial Aid: Aid from institutionally generated funds is provided on the basis of academic merit, financial need, other criteria.

Departments and Teaching Staff: *Professors 9, associate professors 12, assistant professors 2, part-time teachers 61.*

Total instructional faculty: 109. 5% of full-time faculty hold terminal degrees.

Enrollment: Total enrollment 333.

Characteristics of Student Body: *Ethnic/racial makeup:* Black non-Hispanic: 3.6%; American Indian or Alaska Native: 6%; Asian or Pacific Islander: 27%; Hispanic: 4.2%; White non-Hispanic: 50.5%.

International Students: 45 nonresident aliens enrolled fall 2003. Programs available to aid students whose native language is not English: Social, cultural. English as a Second Language Program. No financial aid specifically designated for international students.

Student Life: On-campus residence halls and apartments house 55% of student body. *Special regulations:* Cars permitted for a fee. *Special services:* Medical services. *Surrounding community:* Mill Valley, population 13,000, is located within the San Francisco-Oakland metropolitan area. Served by mass transit bus system; airport 25 miles from campus.

Library Collections: 150,000 volumes. 5,000 microforms; 9,000 audiovisual materials; 790 current periodical subscriptions. Students have access to online information retrieval services and the Internet.

Most important special collections include Dr. Graves personal papers (first seminary president); Baptist History collection; archaeological collection.

Buildings and Grounds: Campus area 148 acres.

Chief Executive Officer: William O. Crews, Jr., President.

Address admission inquiries to Karen Robinson, Director of Admissions.

Golden Gate University

536 Mission Street
San Francisco, California 94105-2968
Tel: (415) 442-7000   **E-mail:** info@ggu.edu
Fax: (415) 495-2671   **Internet:** www.ggu.edu

Institution Description: Golden Gate University is a private, independent, nonprofit institution. *Degrees awarded:* Associate, baccalaureate, master's, doctorate, first-professional (law). Certificates also awarded. *Enrollment:* 4,299.

Accreditation: *Regional:* WASC-Sr. *Professional:* law

History: Established and offered first instruction at postsecondary level 1901; awarded first degree (first-professional) 1905; incorporated as Golden Gate College 1923; adopted present name 1972.

Institutional Structure: *Governing board:* Board of Trustees of Golden Gate University. Representation: 41 trustees, including president, plus 6 ex officio. *Composition of institution:* Administrators 44 men / 24 women. Academic affairs headed by president. Management/business/finances directed by vice president, finance and administration. Full-time instructional faculty 108. Academic governance body, Executive Council, meets an average of 24 times per year.

Calendar: Trimesters. Academic year from early Sept. to late Aug. Sept., Jan., May. Degrees conferred June, Mar., Dec. Formal commencement June.

Characteristics of Freshmen: 57% of applicants accepted. 32% of accepted applicants enrolled. 78% of freshmen expected to graduate within 5 years.

Admission: Rolling admissions plan. *Requirements:* Graduation from accredited or approved secondary school, or GED. Minimum GPA 2.0. *Entrance tests:* College Board SAT or ACT composite recommended. For foreign students TOEFL minimum score 525, satisfactory scores on ACT or SAT, or other standardized test. *For transfer students:* 2.0 minimum GPA; from 4-year accredited institution 99 semester credits maximum accepted for transfer; from 2-year institution 70 credits; for correspondence/extension students 24 credits.

College credit for postsecondary-level work completed in secondary school and for extrainstitutional learning on basis of ACE *2006 Guide to the Evaluation of Educational Experiences in the Armed Services*, USAFI/DANTES.

Tutoring available. Developmental and remedial courses offered in summer and regular academic year; credit given.

Degree Requirements: *For all associate degrees:* 12 credits in residence. *For all baccalaureate degrees:* 123 hours; 24 credits, including last 12, in residence. *For all undergraduate degrees:* 2.0 GPA; courses in Western civilization; distribution requirements.

Fulfillment of some degree requirements possible by passing departmental examinations, College Board CLEP, AP (score of 3). *Grading system:* A–F; credit-no credit (from some electives); withdraw (carries time limit); incomplete (carries time limit).

Distinctive Educational Programs: Work-experience programs, including cooperative education, internships. Flexible meeting places and schedules, including off-campus centers (at Los Altos, 38 miles from main institution; Sacramento, 75 miles; Walnut Creek, 20 miles; Santa Rosa; 50 miles; Monterey, 80 miles; Los Angeles, 400 miles; and at several U.S. military bases), evening and weekend classes. Special facilities for using telecommunications in the classroom. Facilities and programs for independent research, including honors programs, individual majors. Written and oral communications workshop programs. *Other distinctive programs:* Center for Professional Development offers seminars, conferences, and workshops for business professionals. Master's in business program for employees of selected corporations.

ROTC: Army, Navy in cooperation with University of California, Berkeley; Air Force with San Francisco State University.

Degrees Conferred: 4 *associate:* 238 *baccalaureate:* 968 *master's:* 21 *doctorate:* 426 *first-professional:* law. Bachelor's degrees awarded in top five disciplines: business, management, marketing, and related support services 160; computer and information sciences and support services 63; public administration and social service professions 9; liberal arts and sciences, general studies and humanities 4; social sciences 1.

Fees and Other Expenses: *Tuition per academic year 2004–05:* undergraduate $11,610; graduate: contact the university for current rates. *Room and board per academic year (off-campus):* $12,000. *Books and supplies:* $1,080. *Other expenses:* $3,000.

Financial Aid: Aid from institutionally generated funds is provided on the basis of academic merit, financial need. Institution has a Program Participation Agreement with the U.S. Department of Education for eligible students to receive Pell Grants and other federal aid.

Departments and Teaching Staff: *Professors 24, associate professors 44, assistant professors 4, visiting faculty 268. Total instructional faculty:* 222.5 FTE. 83% of faculty hold terminal degrees.

Enrollment: Total enrollment 4,299. Undergraduate 686 (46.9% men, 53.1% women).

International Students: 502 nonresident aliens enrolled fall 2003. Students from Europe, Asia, Central and South America, Africa, Canada. Programs available to aid students whose native language is not English: Social and cultural; English as a Second Language. No financial aid specifically designated for international students.

Student Life: No on-campus housing. *Student publications: The Gateway*, a newspaper. *Surrounding community:* San Francisco population 725,000. Served by mass transit bus and rail system, airport; passenger rail service a few blocks from campus.

Library Collections: 300,000 volumes. 715,000 microforms; 2,600 periodicals. Online catalog. Computer work stations available. Access to online information retrieval services.

Most important law library holdings include collections on taxation, labor law, individual rights.

Buildings and Grounds: Campus area 1 acre.

Chief Executive Officer: Dr. Phillip Friedman, President.

Address admission inquiries to Louis Riccardi, Registrar.

School of Law

Degree Programs Offered: *First-professional, master's.*

Admission: Baccalaureate from accredited college or university.

Degree Requirements: *See* general requirements. *For first-professional degree:* 84 credit hours, 2.0 GPA.

Departments and Teaching Staff: *Total instructional faculty:* 72.

Distinctive Educational Programs: Clinical programs. Internship and externship programs. Superior and Supreme Court clerkships. Joint-degree programs in business-law. Cross-registration with University of California, Davis; University of San Francisco; University of Santa Clara.

Graduate Theological Union

2400 Ridge Road
Berkeley, California 94709
Tel: (510) 649-2400   **E-mail:** gtuadm@gtu.edu
Fax: (510) 649-1417   **Internet:** www.gtu.edu

Institution Description: Graduate Theological Union is a private, independent, nonprofit institution which is also a consortium of 9 California theological schools (American Baptist Seminary of the West, Church Divinity School of the Pacific, Dominican School of Philosophy and Theology, Franciscan School of Theology, Jesuit School of Theology at Berkeley, Pacific Lutheran Theological Seminary, Pacific School of Religion, San Francisco Theological, Seminary Starr King School for the Ministry). The consortium offers a cooperative academic program with a faculty drawn from the participating schools. *Enrollment:* 264. *Degrees awarded:* Master's offered in cooperation with an affiliated school, doctorate. (Professional degrees are offered by participating schools).

Member of the consortium Regional Association of East Bay Colleges and Universities.

Accreditation: *Regional:* WASC-Sr. *Professional:* theology

History: Established, incorporated, and offered first instruction at post-secondary level 1962; awarded first degree (doctorate) 1967.

Institutional Structure: *Governing board:* The Board of Trustees. Extrainstitutional representation: 25 trustees, 9 representatives of boards of affiliated schools; institutional representation: 10 administrators (including president of the college, presidents of affiliated schools), 2 full-time instructional faculty members, 2 students, 1 alumni representative. 10 ex officio. 49 voting. *Composition of institution:* Administrators 2 man / 3 women. Academic affairs headed by dean. Finances directed by vice president for financial affairs. Academic governance body, the core doctoral faculty, meets an average of 5 times per year.

Calendar: Semesters. Academic year Sept. to May. Entering students admitted Sept., Feb. Degrees conferred May, Oct.

Admission: Ph.D./Th.D. applications must be postmarked no later than midnight Dec. 15 to be considered for admission in the fall of the following year. MA applications must be postmarked no later than midnight Mar. 1 or Sept. 10 for admission the following fall or spring semester, respectively. *Requirements:* Baccalaureate from an accredited college or university for MA applications. For Ph.D./Th.D. applications, also an MA in theology or religious studies or the equivalent. *Entrance tests:* TWE and TOEFL (500 minimum score), GRE (600 minimum score on verbal/quantitative). *For transfer students:* Only MA students and only up to one (1) semester of course work.

Degree Requirements: MA: 2 years in residence; 48 semester hours; distribution requirements; demonstrated proficiency in a modern foreign language; B

average on and A-F scale; thesis and an oral defense. PH.D./Th.D.:2 years in residence; languages, modern and ancient at demonstrated proficiency; comprehensive examination; dissertation and oral defense. *Grading system:* A-F; Pass/Fail; withdraw; incomplete (carries time limit).

Distinctive Educational Programs: *For graduate students:* Cooperative doctorate in Near Eastern religions and Jewish Studies with University of California, Berkeley. Interdisciplinary doctoral studies. Cross-registration through consortium. Centers for specialized study include: The Center for Ethics and Social Policy, The Center for the Study of Religion and Culture, The Center for Jewish Studies, The Institute of Buddhist Studies, The Center for Women and Religion, Pacific and Asian American Center for Theology and Strategies, The School of Applied Theology, The Center for Theology and Natural Sciences, patriarch Athenagoras Orthodox Institute.

Degrees Conferred: 5 *master's:* theology; 26 *doctorate:* theology.

Fees and Other Expenses: *Full-time tuition per academic year 2004–05:* $19,240.

Financial Aid: Aid from institutionally generated funds is awarded on the basis of academic merit, financial need. Institution has a Program Participation Agreement with the U.S. Department of Education for eligible students to receive Pell Grants and other federal aid.

Departments and Teaching Staff: *Total tenured faculty:* 77. 100% of faculty members hold terminal degrees.

Enrollment: Total enrollment 264 (46.2% men, 53.8% women).

Characteristics of Student Body: *Ethnic/racial makeup:* Black non-Hispanic: 3%; Asian or Pacific Islander: 4.5%; White non-Hispanic: 65.5%; unknown: 1.9%.

International Students: 61 nonresident aliens enrolled fall 2003.

Student Life: Apartment house available for student housing. Housing also available on campuses of affiliated schools. *Special regulations:* Cars permitted without restrictions; street parking has 2-hour limit. *Surrounding community:* Berkeley, population 115,000, is located in San Francisco-Oakland metropolitan area. Served by mass transit bus and subway system; airport 10 miles from campus; passenger rail service 5 miles from campus.

Library Collections: 415,000 volumes including bound books, serial backfiles, electronic documents, and government documents not in separate collections. Online catalog. Current serial subscriptions: paper, microform. 2,279 recordings; 209 compact discs; 16 CD-ROMs. Computer work stations available. Students have access to the Internet at no charge.

Most important holdings include New Religious Movements (3,000 books dealing with contemporary American cults; also periodicals, ephemera); manuscript and institutional archive collection.

Buildings and Grounds: Campus area 3 buildings.

Chief Executive Officer: Dr. James A. Donahue, President.

Address admission inquiries to Kathleen Kook, Assistant Dean for Admissions.

Harvey Mudd College

301 East 12th Street
Claremont, California 91711
Tel: (909) 621-8011   **E-mail:** admission@hmc.edu
Fax: (909) 621-8360   **Internet:** www.hmc.edu

Institution Description: Harvey Mudd College is a private, independent, nonprofit college. *Enrollment:* 721. *Degrees awarded:* Baccalaureate.

Accreditation: *Regional:* WASC-Sr. *Professional:* engineering

History: Established and chartered 1955; offered first instruction at postsecondary level 1957; awarded first degree (baccalaureate) 1959.

Institutional Structure: *Governing board:* Board of Trustees. Representation: 55 trustees. All voting. *Composition of institution:* Administrators 10 men / 6 women. Academic affairs headed by dean of the faculty. Management/business/finances directed by treasurer. Full-time instructional faculty 80. Academic governance body, the faculty, meets an average of 15 times per year.

Calendar: Semesters. Academic year Aug. to May. Freshmen admitted Sept. Degrees conferred and formal commencement May. No summer session.

Characteristics of Freshmen: 38% of applicants admitted; 10% of admitted students enrolled full-time.

100% (193 students) submitted SAT scores. *25th percentile:* SAT Verbal 610, SAT Math 710. *75th percentile:* SAT Verbal 730, SAT Math 800.

38 National Merit Scholars. 81% of freshmen expected to graduate within five years. 93% of freshmen from California. Freshmen from 33 states and 5 foreign countries.

Admission: For fall acceptance, apply as early as fall of previous year, but not later than Feb. 1. Students are notified of acceptance Apr. Apply by Dec. 1 for early decision; need not limit application to Harvey Mudd. Early acceptance available. *Requirements:* 4 units English, 4 college preparatory mathematics (recommend calculus), 1 chemistry or physics. Recommend 2 foreign language, 1 history. *Entrance tests:* College Board SAT, 3 Achievements which must include level 2 mathematics, English composition. Recommend 1 in physics or chemistry. *For transfer students:* Maximum transfer credit limited only by residence requirement. College credit and advanced placement for postsecondary-level work completed in secondary school. Tutoring available.

Degree Requirements: *For undergraduates:* 128 hours; 2.0 GPA; 2 years in residence; 3 physical education courses; distribution requirements. Additional requirements for some majors. Fulfillment of some degree requirements and exemption from some beginning courses possible by passing departmental examinations, College Board AP. *Grading system:* A–F; high pass-pass-fail (freshmen year only).

Distinctive Educational Programs: Fellowships awarded to cover costs of tuition, room and board. Facilities and programs for independent research, including honors programs, individual majors, directed reading. Preprofessional program in medicine. Study abroad by individual arrangement or through an extensive program at Pomona College and Scripps College. Exchange programs with Swarthmore College and Rensselaer Polytechnic Institute. Clinic programs in engineering, computer science, and mathematics offer real-world experience. *Other distinctive programs:* Clinic programs in engineering and mathematics offer real world experience. Qualified secondary school students may enroll for college courses; credit given. Budapest Semesters in Mathematics; Group Ecole Superieure D'Ingenieurs en Electrotechniue et Electronique (ESIEE); various programs with faculty approval.

ROTC: Air Force (5 commissions awarded 2004). Army available through Claremont McKenna College.

Degrees Conferred: 137 *baccalaureate*: biological/life sciences 13, computer and information sciences 35, engineering and engineering technology 59, English 1, interdisciplinary studies 16, philosophy/religion/theology 1, physical sciences 42, psychology 1, social sciences and history 5, visual and performing arts 3.

Fees and Other Expenses: *Full-time tuition per academic year 2004–05:* $29,553. *Room and board per academic year:* $9,485. *Required fees:* $684.

Financial Aid: Aid from institutionally generated funds is provided on the basis of financial need. Institution has a Program Participation Agreement with the U.S. Department of Education for eligible students to receive Pell Grants and other federal aid.

Financial aid to full-time, first-time undergraduate students: need-based scholarships/grants totaling $7,910,287, self-help $1,182,045; non-need-based scholarships/grants totaling $1,550,532, self-help $531,104, parent loans $1,953,009.

Departments and Teaching Staff: Biology *professors* 2, *associate professors* 2, *assistant professors* 2, *part-time faculty* 1; chemistry 7, 0, 4, 1; computer science 3, 1, 5, 0; engineering 9, 3, 4, 3; humanities and social sciences 4, 5, 3, 4; mathematics 6, 3, 3, 1; physics 7, 3, 2, 3.

Total instructional faculty: 91 (full-time 78, part-time 13; women 50, men 61). Total faculty with doctorate, first-professional, or other terminal degree: 87. Student-to-faculty ratio: 8:1. 11 faculty members awarded sabbaticals 2004.

Enrollment: Total enrollment 721 (503 men, 218 women).

Characteristics of Student Body: *Ethnic/racial makeup:* number of Black non-Hispanic: 8; American Indian or Alaska Native: 3; Asian or Pacific Islander: 131; Hispanic: 41; White non-Hispanic: 351; unknown: 159. *Age distribution:* number under 18: 44; 18–19: 45; 20–21: 302; 22–24: 26; 25–29: 2; 30–34: 1, 35–39: 1.

International Students: 28 nonresident aliens enrolled fall 2004. 3 students from Europe, 14 Asia, 1 Central and South America, 4 Africa, 1 Canada, 5 other. No programs available to aid students whose native language is not English. Financial aid specifically designated for international students: 15 scholarships awarded 2004–05 totaling $410,185.

Student Life: On-campus residence halls house 95% of student body. *Intercollegiate athletics:* men only: baseball, basketball, football, golf, soccer, swimming, tennis, track, wrestling, water polo; women only: basketball, tennis, track, volleyball. *Special regulations:* Cars permitted with proof of adequate insurance. Quiet hours. *Special services:* Medical services, counseling service, Honor Code, handicap accessibility. *Student publications: The Muddraker,* a biweekly newspaper; *Spectrum,* a yearbook; *Mudd Online,* a student online newspaper.

Library Collections: 2,406,548.volumes. Current periodical subscriptions: paper and microform 4,019; via electronic access 12,439. 248 computer work stations. Students have access to various information retrieval services and the Internet.

Most important holdings include Herbert Hoover Collection of Mining and Metallurgy; Norman Philbrick Library of Theatre and Dramatic Arts; Mason Collection of Western Americana; Carruthers Aviation Collection, William W. Clary Oxford Collection.

Buildings and Grounds: Campus area 30 acres. *New buildings:* Frederick and Susan Sontag Residence Hall completed 2004; Hoch-Shanahan Dining Commons 2005.

Chief Executive Officer: Dr. Jon C. Strauss, President.

Address admission inquiries to Deren Finks, Vice President and Dean of Admissions/Financial Aid.

Hebrew Union College - Jewish Institute of Religion

3077 University Avenue
Los Angeles, California 91007-3796
Tel: (213) 749-3424   **E-mail:** sgoodman@huc.edu
Fax: (213) 747-6128   **Internet:** www.huc.edu

Institution Description: Hebrew Union College - Jewish Institute of Religion is an institution offering upper division and graduate study only. It is a branch campus of an institution with four campuses located in Cincinnati, New York, Los Angeles, and Jerusalem (Israel). *Enrollment:* 110. *Degrees awarded:* Baccalaureate, first-professional (master of arts in Hebrew letters), master's, doctorate.

Accreditation: *Regional:* WASC-Sr.

History: Hebrew Union College established in Cincinnati (OH) 1875; merged with Jewish Institute of Religion (founded in New York 1922) 1950; Los Angeles branch chartered and offered first instruction at postsecondary level 1954; awarded first degree (baccalaureate) 1958. *See* Michael Myer, *Hebrew Union College - Jewish Institute of Religion at 100 Years,* Samuel Karff, ed. (Cincinnati: Hebrew College Press, 1976) for further information.

Institutional Structure: *Governing board:* Board of Governors. Extrainstitutional representation: 42 members; institutional representation: 4 administrators; 10 alumni. 4 ex officio. All voting. *Composition of institution:* Administrators 3 men / 4 women. Academic affairs headed by Dean. Management/business/finances directed by centralized business office in Cincinnati. Full-time instructional faculty 12. Academic governance body, Academic Council, meets an average of 5 times per year.

Calendar: Semester plus quadmester. Academic year Aug. to May. Entering students admitted Aug., Jan. Degrees conferred May, Aug. Formal commencement May. Summer session from mid-June to early Aug. in one program only.

Admission: For fall acceptance, apply as early as Oct. of previous year, but not later than Feb. 15 of year of enrollment. *Requirements:* For first-professional students, baccalaureate from accredited college or university, personal interview, including testing, to determine commitment to Reformed Judaism. *Entrance tests:* GRE.

Degree Requirements: *For first-professional degree:* 120 semester hours; passing GPA or C, depending on system chosen by student; entire program in residence, with first year spent in Jerusalem for intensive study in Hebrew; 3 rabbinic skills practicums; thesis, sermon delivery requirement; demonstrated proficiency in speech; *For all master's degrees:* 45 hours; 3.0 GPA; 1 year in residence; language requirement in Hebrew; thesis; distribution requirements. *Grading system:* P, C, or F.

Distinctive Educational Programs: Work-experience programs, including field experience, in-service rabbinical training. Dual-degree programs in social work with Washington University (MO). Joint master's program in Jewish communal service and Jewish (or Hebrew) education.

Degrees Conferred: 42 *master's:* education 11, philosophy/religion/theology 17, Jewis communal service 14; *first-professional:* rabbinical ordination 4.

Fees and Other Expenses: *Full-time tuition per academic year 2004–05:* $15,000. *Other fees:* health fee $394; activity fee $25.

Financial Aid: Aid from institutionally generated funds is awarded on the basis of financial need.

Departments and Teaching Staff: *Total instructional faculty:* 31 (full-time 14, part-time 17; 14 women, 17 men). Total faculty with doctorate, first-professional, or other terminal degree: 27. Student-to-faculty ratio: 4:1. 2 faculty members awarded sabbaticals 2004.

Enrollment: Total enrollment 110 (full-time 97, part-time 13).

International Students: 10 nonresident aliens enrolled fall 2004. 2 students from Europe, 2 Asia, 2 Central and South America, 1 Canada, 3 Australia. No programs available to aid students whose language is not English. Some financial aid specifically designated for international students.

Student Life: No on-campus housing. *Surrounding community:* Los Angeles population over 3,000,000. Served by mass transit bus system; airport 15 miles from campus; passenger rail service 5 miles from campus.

Publications: *Publisher:* Hebrew Union College Press located at parent institution.

Library Collections: 90,000 volumes. Card catalog. 280 current periodical subscriptions. 6 computer work stations. Students have access to the Internet at no charge.

Most important holdings include Judaica collection.

Buildings and Grounds: Campus area 5 acres.

Chief Executive Officer: Dr. Lewis Barth, Dean.

Address admission inquiries to S. Goodman, Director of Recruitment and Admissions.

Holy Names University

3500 Mountain Boulevard
Oakland, California 94619-1699
Tel: (510) 436-1000   **E-mail:** admissions@hnu.edu
Fax: (510) 436-1199   **Internet:** www.hnu.edu

Institution Description: Holy Names University is a private, independent, nonprofit Catholic college sponsored by the Sisters of the Holy Names of Jesus and Mary. *Enrollment:* 973. *Degrees awarded:* Baccalaureate, master's. Certificates also awarded.

Member of the consortium Regional Association of East Bay Colleges and Universities.

Accreditation: *Regional:* WASC-Sr. *Professional:* nursing

History: Established as Convent of Our Lady of the Sacred Heart in 1868; chartered 1880; became Convent and College of the Holy Names in 1908; first admitted secular students at junior college level in 1917 and to senior college in 1925; awarded first baccalaureate degree in 1926; graduates received California teaching credentials beginning in 1930; coeducational graduate division established in 1955; campus moved from Lake Merritt, Oakland, in 1957; became completely coeducational in 1971; added Weekend College in 1981, a weekend schedule to help working adults earn regular degrees. Achieved university status 2004.

Institutional Structure: *Governing board:* Board of Directors of Holy Names University. Maximum; 30 Directors; 2 ex officio; all members vote; all are extrainstitutional except the university president. *Composition of institution:* Administrators 3 men / 4 women. Undergraduate and graduate academic affairs headed by vice president for academic affairs. Management/business/finances directed by vice president of finance. Academic governance body, Faculty Senate, meets average of 16 times per year.

Calendar: Semesters. Academic year Aug. to May. Freshmen and transfers admitted Aug., Jan., June. Formal commencement May. Summer session June to Aug.

Characteristics of Freshmen: 76% (83 students) submitted SAT scores; 16% (17 students) submitted ACT scores. *25th percentile:* SAT Verbal 430, SAT Math 440; ACT Composite 17. *75th percentile:* SAT Verbal 520, SAT Math ; 540; ACT Composite 23.

75% of applicants accepted. 39% of accepted applicants enrolled. 51% of entering freshmen expected to graduate within 5 years. 78% of freshmen from California. Freshmen from 12 states and 7 foreign countries.

Admission: Rolling admissions plan. For fall acceptance, apply as early as June 1 of previous year, but not later than Aug. 1 of year of enrollment. Early acceptance available. *Requirements:* Either graduation from accredited secondary school with 4 units English, 2 foreign language, 3 mathematics, 1 history, 1 laboratory science, 1 advanced course in foreign language, laboratory science or mathematics, 5 academic electives; or GED. Minimum GPA 2.9. *Entrance tests:* College Board SAT. For foreign students TOEFL. *For transfer students:* 2.2 minimum GPA; from 4-year accredited institution 96 hours maximum transfer credit; from 2-year accredited institution 66 hours.

College credit and advanced placement for postsecondary-level work completed in secondary school. Member of Service Members' Opportunity Colleges.

Degree Requirements: 120 credit hours; 2.0 GPA; 24 hours of the last 30, including 12 in upper division courses, in residence; distribution requirements. General education requirements include interdisciplinary program, plus area courses, plus satisfaction of proficiency requirements (writing, speech, computer, math, language, critical thinking), plus senior seminar with research paper.

Fulfillment of some degree requirements and exemption from some beginning courses possible by passing College Board CLEP, AP. *Grading system:* A–F; pass-fail; withdraw (carries time limit); incomplete (carries time limit).

Distinctive Educational Programs: Emphasis on liberal arts with career preparation. Encouragement of double majors, supportive elective programs, internships. Self-designed majors can be approved. Interdisciplinary majors in international affairs, liberal studies, human services, humanistic studies. Laboratories for music, languages, computer, accounting; open to all students. Facilities and programs for independent study and research. Cross-registration on 6 nearby senior college campuses, and several community colleges, through a consortium. Exchange study at Anna Maria College (MA). Evening and weekend classes available. Preparatory Music department offers laboratory experience for music majors. Raskob Learning Institute facilities available for LD students. Communications disorders clinic for children. Degree-granting weekend college, with regular faculty as instructors, for working adults. Credit and non-credit continuing education program. Distinctive graduate programs: master's degree and certificate in Kodaly method of music education; master's degree and licensure preparation in pastoral counseling/marriage, family, child counseling; master's degree and certificate programs in Institute of Culture and Creation Spirituality. Study abroad for a semester or a year can be arranged through Dean of Academic Affairs. Accelerated degree program in business. Distance learning available for the BSN program. Three-year degree program.

Degrees Conferred: 130 *baccalaureate* (B), 88 *master's* (M): biological/life sciences 4 (B); business/marketing 22 (B), 12 (M); communications/communication technologies 2 (B); computer and information sciences 2 (B); education 10 (M); English 3 (B), 4 (M); foreign languages and literature 1 (B); health professions and related sciences 3 (B), 16 (M); liberal arts/general studies 16 (B); philosophy, religion, theology 6 (B), 28 (M); protective services/public administration 5 (B); psychology 17 (B), 11 (M); social sciences and history 8 (B); visual and performing arts 6 (B), 7 (M). 2 honorary degrees awarded 2004: Doctor of Humane Letters.

Fees and Other Expenses: *Full-time tuition per academic year 2004–05:* $21,400 undergraduate; $10,170 graduate. *Required fees:* $240. *Room and board per academic year:* $7,800. *Books and supplies:* $983.

Financial Aid: Aid from institutionally generated funds is provided on the basis of academic merit, financial need, athletic ability, other considerations Institution has a Program Participation Agreement with the U.S. Department of Education for eligible students to receive Pell Grants and other federal aid.

Financial aid to full-time, first-time undergraduate students: need-based scholarships/grants totaling $2,420,198, self-help $2,635,929; non-need-based scholarships/grants totaling $1,313,270, self-help $2,900,853, parent loans $761,086, athletic awards $811,230. *Graduate aid:* 115 federal/state-funded loans totaling $1,486,689; 7 fellowships/grants totaling $23,000.

Departments and Teaching Staff: Arts and humanities *professors* 4, *associate professors* 5, *assistant professors* 0, *part-time faculty* 25; business 0, 2, 0, 15; education 0, 2, 3, 14; mathematics/science 2, 3, 1, 10; music 0, 2, 0, 8; nursing 0, 1, 1, 7; social sciences 2, 4, 1, 11. *Total instructional faculty:* 123 (women 79, men 44). Total faculty with doctorate, first-professional, or other terminal degree: 68. Student-to-faculty ratio: 13:1.

Enrollment: Total enrollment 973. Undergraduate full-time 347, part-time 254.

Characteristics of Student Body: *Ethnic/racial makeup:* number of Black non-Hispanic: 193; American Indian or Alaska Native: 11; Asian or Pacific Islander: 57; Hispanic: 104; White non-Hispanic: 167; unknown: 79. *Age distribution:* number under 18: 12; 18–19: 128; 20–21: 92; 22–24: 68; 25–29: 67; 30–34: 57; 35–39: 53; 40–49: 108; 50–64: 56.

International Students: 30 nonresident aliens enrolled fall 2004. 9 students from Europe, 17 Asia, 9 Central and South America, 3 Africa, 7 Canada, 1 Australia. Programs available to aid students whose native language is not English: English as a Second Language Program. No financial aid specifically designated for international students.

Student Life: On-campus residence halls house 30% of the full-time undergraduate student body. *Intercollegiate athletics:* men only: basketball, cross-country, golf, soccer, volleyball; women only: basketball, cross-country, soccer, volleyball. *Special regulations:* Adequate parking for registered cars in designated areas, free permit required. Quiet hours in residence halls, 10:30pm to 8am Sun.–Thurs. *Special services:* Campus Ministry, includes students on the team. Student activities include drama (children's and adult theater), music ensembles, student government, academic and activity clubs. *Surrounding community:* Oakland population 412,000. Served by bus and rapid transit systems; Amtrak station; three international airports; Ports of Oakland and San Francisco. Variety of cultural activities and ocean/mountain sports within 1 to 4 hours traveling distance.

Publications: *H.N.C. Quarterly*, a magazine for alumni and friends.

Library Collections: 111,243 volumes. Online and card catalogs. 198 current serial subscriptions; 48,000 microforms; 9,000 government documents; 4,384 audiovisual materials. Students have access to online information retrieval services and the Internet. Total 2004–05 budget for materials: $63,693.

Most important holdings include Kodaly Music Collection (includes a special collection of international folk music).

Buildings and Grounds: Campus area 60 acres.

Chief Executive Officer: Dr. Rosemarie Nassif, SSND, President.

Undergraduates address admission inquiries to Muriad Dibbini, Director of Undergraduate Admissions; graduate inquiries to Dr. Annette Hoffman Marr, Director of Graduate Admissions.

Hope International University

2500 East Nutwood Avenue
Fullerton, California 92831
Tel: (714) 879-3901   **E-mail:** ug-admissions@hiu.edu
Fax: (714) 526-0231   **Internet:** www.hiu.edu

Institution Description: Hope International University, formerly named Pacific Christian College and later Hope International College, is a private, independent, nonprofit college affiliated with the Churches of Christ and Christian Churches. *Enrollment:* 1,275. *Degrees awarded:* Associate, baccalaureate, master's.

Accreditation: *Regional:* WASC-Sr.

History: Established and incorporated as Pacific Bible Seminary 1928; offered first instruction at postsecondary level 1929; awarded first degree (baccalaureate) 1932; became Pacific Christian College 1962; became Hope International College 1998; adopted present name 2002. *See* (Fullerton: Pacific Christian College, 1979) for further information.

Institutional Structure: *Governing board:* Hope International College Board of Directors. Extrainstitutional representation: 30 directors; institutional representation: president of the college. 1 ex officio. 30 voting. *Composition of institution:* Administrators 4 men / 3 women. Academic affairs headed by dean of the college. Management/business/finances directed by administrative vice president. Full-time instructional faculty 27. Academic governance body, Council for Academic Affairs, meets an average of 20 times per year.

Calendar: Semester (4-1-4 plan). Academic year mid-Aug. to late May. Freshmen admitted Sept., Feb., June. Degrees conferred May, Aug., Dec. Formal commencement May. Summer session from early to late June.

Characteristics of Freshmen: 94% of accepted applicants enrolled. 78% of accepted applicants enrolled.

25th percentile: SAT Verbal 46, SAT Math 470; ACT Composite 17, ACT English 15, ACT Math 16. *75th percentile:* SAT Verbal 560, SAT Math 570; ACT Composite 24, ACT English 24, ACT Math 24.

54% of entering freshmen expected to graduate within 5 years. 46% of freshmen from California. Freshmen from 16 states and 24 foreign countries.

Admission: Rolling admissions plan. For fall acceptance, apply as early as Jan., but not later than July. 1; for spring acceptance, Dec. 1. *Requirements:* Either graduation from accredited secondary school or GED. Minimum GPA 2.0. *Entrance tests:* College Board SAT or ACT composite. For foreign students minimum TOEFL score 500 undergraduate; 550 graduate. *For transfer students:* 2.0 minimum GPA; from 4-year accredited institution 90 semester hours maximum transfer credit; from 2-year accredited institution 60 hours.

College credit and advanced placement for postsecondary-level work completed in secondary school and for extrainstitutional learning on basis of ACE *2006 Guide to the Evaluation of Educational Experiences in the Armed Services* and faculty assessment. Tutoring available.

Degree Requirements: *For all associate degrees:* 64 credit hours; 1 term in residence. *For all baccalaureate degrees:* 124 hours; 2 terms in residence. *For all undergraduate degrees:* 2.0 GPA; convocation attendance required (twice weekly); distribution requirements.

Fulfillment of some degree requirements and exemption from some beginning courses possible by passing departmental examinations, College Board CLEP, APP. *Grading system:* A–F; credit-no credit; withdraw (deadline after which pass-fail is appended to withdraw); incomplete (deadline after which A–F is assigned).

Distinctive Educational Programs: *For undergraduates:* Work-experience programs. Off-campus centers (at varying locations in Orange County and Los Angeles County, each less than 30 miles away from main institution; Ventura county, 60 miles away; Sacramento, 350 miles away). Individually arranged interdisciplinary majors. Facilities and programs for independent research, including honors program and individual majors. Students may take courses at California State University, Fullerton. *For graduate students:* Cooperative master's program in management with Western State University College of Law of Orange County. *Available to all students:* Evening classes. *Other distinctive programs:* Degree-granting extension education program for adults. Annual 3-day Christian scholar lecture programs sponsored by the Thomas F. Staley Foundation (NY).

Degrees Conferred: 11 *associate;* 147 *baccalaureate:* business and management 51, communications 1, education 16, psychology 15, social sciences 36, theology 28; 28 *master's:* psychology 16, theology 12.

Fees and Other Expenses: *Full-time tuition per academic year 2004–05:* $16,100 undergraduate. Contact the university for current graduate tuition. *Required fees:* $200. *Room and board per academic year:* $5,202.

Financial Aid: Aid from institutionally generated funds is provided on the basis of academic merit, financial need. Institution has a Program Participation Agreement with the U.S. Department of Education for eligible students to receive Pell Grants and other federal aid.

Undergraduate aid: need-based scholarships/grants totaling $4,563,988, self-help $369,170, parent loans $256,415, tuition waivers $3,051; non-need-based scholarships/grants totaling $906,503, self-help $1,035,922, parent loans $457,907, tuition waivers $9,123.

Departments and Teaching Staff: *Total instructional faculty:* 155 (full-time 27, part-time 122; women 50, men 105). Total faculty with doctorate, first-professional, or other terminal degree 32. Student-to-faculty ratio: 15:1.

Enrollment: Total enrollment 1,275 (full-time 566, part-time 709).

Characteristics of Student Body: *Ethnic/racial makeup:* number of Black non-Hispanic: 85; American Indian or Alaska Native: 8; Asian or Pacific Islander 40; Hispanic: 192; White non-Hispanic: 590; unknown: 55.

International Students: 39 nonresident aliens enrolled fall 2004. No programs available to aid students whose native language is not English. No financial aid specifically designated for international students.

Student Life: On-campus residence halls house 50% of student body. Residence halls for men only constitute 40% of such space, for women only 60%. *Intercollegiate athletics:* men only: basketball, soccer, volleyball; women only: basketball, softball, volleyball. *Special regulations:* Cars permitted without restrictions. Quiet hours from 11pm to 7am. Residence hall visitation in designated lobbies 9am to 11pm. Medical services. *Student publications: The Lampas,* a yearbook; *News and Announcements,* a weekly news bulletin. *Surrounding community:* Fullerton population 110,000. Los Angeles, 20 miles from campus, is nearest metropolitan area. Served by mass transit bus system; airport 20 miles from campus; passenger rail service 4 miles from campus.

Publications: Sources of information about Hope International University include *The Bulletin,* a bimonthly publication sent to affiliate churches, faculty members, alumni and friends of the college.

Library Collections: 63,237 volumes. Electronic access to 10,647 periodicals. 1,000 microform titles; 4,300 audiovisual materials, 278 current periodical subscriptions (paper). 30 computer work stations. Online catalog.

Most important holdings include collection of over 2,000 books and historical materials on the 19th century Christian Church Restoration Movement in the U.S.; collection of approximately 15,000 books and bound periodicals about the Bible and Christian Church history.

Buildings and Grounds: Campus area 2 square blocks.

Chief Executive Officer: Dr. John Derry, President.

Address admission inquiries to Director of Admissions.

Humboldt State University

1 Harpst Street
Arcata, California 95521-8299
Tel: (707) 826-4402   **E-mail:** hsuinfo@laurel.humboldt.edu
Fax: (707) 826-6194   **Internet:** www.humboldt.edu

Institution Description: *Degrees awarded:* Baccalaureate, master's. *Enrollment:* 7,550.

Accreditation: *Regional:* WASC-Sr. *Professional:* art, engineering, forestry, music, nursing, nursing education, social work

History: Established and chartered as Humboldt State Normal School 1913; offered first instruction at postsecondary level 1914; awarded first degree (baccalaureate) 1918; changed name to Humboldt State Teachers College 1921, Humboldt State College 1935, California State University, Humboldt 1972; adopted present name 1974.

Institutional Structure: *Composition of institution:* Administrators 16. Academic affairs headed by vice president for academic affairs. Management/ business/finances directed by vice president for administrative affairs. Full-time instructional faculty 313. Academic governance body, Academic Senate, meets an average of 15 times per year.

Calendar: Semester. Academic year Aug. to May. Freshmen and transfer students admitted Aug. and Jan. Degrees conferred Aug., Dec., May. Formal commencement May. Summer extension only.

Characteristics of Freshmen:

63% of applicants accepted. 95% of accepted applicants enrolled.

25th percentile: SAT Verbal 470, SAT Math 470; ACT Composite 18. *75th percentile:* SAT Verbal 600, SAT Math 580; ACT Composite 25.

27% of entering freshmen expected to graduate within 5 years. 97% of freshmen from California.

Admission: Rolling admissions plan. For fall acceptance, apply as early as Nov. 1 of year prior to enrollment. Apply after junior year of secondary school for early decision. Need not limit application to Humboldt. Early acceptance available.

Degree Requirements: *Requirements:* Graduation for accredited secondary school.

College credit for extrainstitutional learning on basis of ACE *2006 Guide to the Evaluation of Educational Experiences in the Armed Services;* assessment of prior learning. Tutoring available. Noncredit developmental courses offered during regular academic year.

Distinctive Educational Programs: Sciences and natural resources programs including environmental resources engineering, environmental science, fisheries, marine biology, oceanography, and wildlife. Access to natural resource habitats for study and research. In addition to the sciences, Humboldt's fine arts, business, humanities, and behavioral and social studies have also earned national distinction. Interdisciplinary studies in language, women's studies, and Native American studies.

Degrees Conferred: 1,424 *baccalaureate;* 143 *master's.*

Fees and Other Expenses: *Full-time fees per academic year 2004–05:* undergraduate $2,860 resident, out-of-state $6,128; graduate resident $3,346, out-of-state $7,414. *Room and board per academic year:* $7,038.

Financial Aid: Aid from institutionally generated funds is provided on the basis of financial need. Institution has a Program Participation Agreement with the U.S. Department of Education for eligible students to receive Pell Grants and other federal aid.

Departments and Teaching Staff: *Professors* 154, *associate professors* 74, *assistant professors* 59, *lecturers* 293. *Full-time faculty:* 490. Student -to-faculty ratio: 19:1.

Enrollment: Total enrollment 7,550 (full-time 6,574, part-time 976).

Characteristics of Student Body: *Ethnic/racial makeup:* Black non-hispanic 2.8%; American Indian or Alaska Native: 2.3%; Asian or Pacific Islander: .6%; Hispanic: 7.8%; White non-Hispanic: 60.6%; unknown: 17.5%.

International Students: English as a Second Language Program available. No financial aid specifically designated for international students.

Student Life: On-campus residence halls house 20% of student body. Residence halls for both sexes constitute 100% of such space. *Intercollegiate athletics:* men and women: cross country, track and field, soccer, basketball. Men only: football. Women only: softball, crew. *Special regulations:* Registered cars with decals permitted. *Special services:* Learning Resources Center, medical services. *Student publications, radio: The Lumberjack,* a weekly newspaper; radio station KHSU broadcasts 70 hours per week. *Surrounding community:* Arcata population 12,500. San Francisco; 300 miles from campus, is nearest metropolitan area. Served by mass transit system; airport 8 miles from campus.

Publications: *Humboldt Stater,* alumni magazine.

Library Collections: 597,921 bound volumes. 400,419 government documents. 57 computer work stations. Students have access to the Internet at no charge.

Most important holdings include collections on natural resources; Northwest Coast history.

Buildings and Grounds: Campus area 145 acres.

Chief Executive Officer: Dr. Rollin C. Richmond, President.

Address admission inquiries to Scott Hagg, Admissions Director.

Humphreys College

6650 Inglewood Street
Stockton, California 95207-3896
Tel: (209) 478-0800   **E-mail:** admissions@humphreys.edu
Fax: (209) 478-8721   **Internet:** www.humphreys.edu

Institution Description: Humphreys College is a private institution offering programs in business. *Enrollment:* 759. *Degrees awarded:* Associate, baccalaureate, first-professional.

Accreditation: WASC-Sr.

History: Founded 1896 by John R. Humphreys; occupied various locations in downtown Stockton; moved to present location 1967.

Institutional Structure: Board of Trustees; 9 elected members.

Calendar: Quarters. Academic year begins in Sept. Summer session.

Admission: Open admissions. Early admissions plan.

Degree Requirements: *For baccalaureate degree:* 180 quarter units of which 56 must be in the major.

Distinctive Educational Programs: Students have access to local computer facilities.

Degrees Conferred: 11 *associate*; 32 *baccalaureate*; 12 *first-professional*: law. Bachelor's degrees awarded in top five disciplines: legal professions and studies 12; education 8; public administration and social service professions 6;

business, management, marketing, and related support services 4; liberal arts and sciences, general studies and humanities 1.

Fees and Other Expenses: *Tuition per academic year 2004–05:* $7,560. *Room and board per academic year:* $6,350. *Books and supplies:* $1,260. *Other expenses:* $2,430.

Financial Aid: Aid from institutionally generated funds is provided on the basis of academic merit, financial need. Institution has a Program Participation Agreement with the U.S. Department of Education for eligible students to receive Pell Grants and other federal aid.

Financial aid to full-time, first-time undergraduate students: 98% received federal grants averaging $4,050; 47% state/local grants averaging $9,447; 94% loans averaging $8,562.

Departments and Teaching Staff: *Total instructional faculty:* 39. *Degrees held by full-time instructional faculty:* Doctorate 2%, master's 50%, baccalaureate 48%.

Enrollment: Total enrollment 759. Undergraduate 692 (15% men, 85% women).

Characteristics of Student Body: *Ethnic and racial makeup:* Black non-Hispanic: 13.7%; American Indian or Alaska Native: 1.6%; Asian or Pacific Islander: 11.7%; Hispanic: 35.5%; White non-Hispanic: 37.3%; unknown: .1%.

International Students: No programs available to aid students whose native language is not English. No financial aid specifically designated for international students.

Student Life: Limited on-campus residence hall space available.

Library Collections: 25,000 volumes. 2,300 microforms; 976 audiovisual materials; 115 current periodical subscriptions. Access to online information retrieval services and the Internet.

Chief Executive Officer: Dr. Robert G. Humphreys, President.

Address admission inquiries to Santa Lopez, Director of Admissions.

ITT Technical Institute, San Diego

9680 Granite Ridge Drive
San Diego, California 92123-2662
Tel: (858) 571-8500   **E-mail:** admissions@itt-tech.edu
Fax: (858) 571-1277   **Internet:** www.itt-tech.edu

Institution Description: ITT Technical Institute is owned and operated by ITT Educational Services, Inc. of Indianapolis, Indiana. Other California locations include Anaheim, Hayward, Modesto-Stockton, Oxnard, Rancho Cordova, San Bernardino, Santa Clara, Sylmar, Torrance, West Covina. Programs may vary at these locations. Detailed information can be found on ITT's website: www.itt-tech.edu.

Accreditation: *Nonregional:* ACICS.

Calendar: Quarters.

Admission: The student must provide documented proof of his or her high school diploma or recognized equivalency certificate.

Degree Requirements: Student must attain an overall 2.0 cumulative grade point average for the entire program pursued; must successfully complete all courses specified in the catalog for the program.

Degrees Conferred: 255 *associate:* engineering/engineering technologies; 52 *baccalaureate:* engineering.

Fees and Other Expenses: *Full-time tuition per academic year 2004–05:* $13,548. *Room and board per academic year (off-campus):* $5,958.

Financial Aid: Aid from institutionally generated funds is provided on the basis of academic merit, financial need, other criteria. Institution has a Program Participation Agreement with the U.S. Department of Education for eligible students to receive Pell Grants and other federal aid.

Departments and Teaching Staff: *Instructors* 25, *part-time faculty* 11. *Total instructional faculty:* 28.7 FTE. *Degrees held by full-time faculty:* baccalaureate 41.8%, master's 31.4%.

Enrollment: Total enrollment 1,071 (88.6% men, 11.4% women).

Characteristics of Student Body: *Ethnic/racial makeup:* Black non-Hispanic: 10.8%; American Indian or Alaska Native: .7%; Asian or Pacific Islander: 13.8%; Hispanic: 39,6%; White non-Hispanic: 38,8%; unknown: 5.1%.

International Students: 95 nonresident aliens enrolled fall 2003. No programs available to aid students whose native language is not English.

Student Life: No on-campus housing; assistance in finding housing available.

Library Collections: 1,000 volumes. 25 current periodical subscriptions. Students have access to online information retrieval services and the Internet.

Chief Executive Officer: Robert Hammond, Director.

Address admissions inquiries to Director of Recruitment.

Jesuit School of Theology at Berkeley

1735 LeRoy Avenue
Berkeley, California 94709-1193
Tel: (510) 841-8804   **E-mail:** admissions@jstb.edu
Fax: (510) 841-8536   **Internet:** www.jstb.edu

Institution Description: Jesuit School of Theology at Berkeley is a private institution affiliated with the Society of Jesus, Roman Catholic Church. It is a member of the Graduate Theological Union, which was created by 9 Protestant and Roman Catholic institutions to coordinate joint programs and award graduate degrees. See separate exhibit for Graduate Theological Union. *Enrollment:* 175. *Degrees awarded:* First-professional (master of divinity, master of theological studies, master of theology, master of sacred theology, licentiate in sacred theology, master of arts-in conjunction with Graduate Theological Union, doctor of sacred theology). Certificates are also awarded.

Accreditation: *Regional:* WASC-Sr. *Professional:* theology

History: Established as Alma College, incorporated, and offered first instruction at postsecondary level 1934; awarded first degree (licentiate) 1935; affiliated with University of Santa Clara from 1957 to 1971; adopted present name 1969.

Institutional Structure: *Governing board:* Board of Members (policy-making body). Representation: 11 members. All voting. Board of Trustees (administrative body). Extrainstitutional representation: 17 trustees; institutional representation: 2 administrators, ex officio. All voting. *Composition of institution:* Administrators 3 men / 5 women. Academic affairs headed by dean. Management/business/finances directed by treasurer. Full-time instructional faculty 24. Academic governance body, Academic Council, meets an average of 8 times per year.

Calendar: Semesters. Academic year Sept. to May. Entering students admitted Sept., Jan., Feb. Degrees conferred as earned. Formal commencement May. Graduate Theological Union Cooperative Summer Session.

Admission: Rolling admissions plan. For fall acceptance, apply as early as 1 year prior to enrollment, but application suggested by Mar. 15. *Requirements:* Baccalaureate degree from accredited college or university. *Entrance tests:* GRE for master's degree programs. For foreign students TOEFL. *For transfer students:* Maximum transfer credit limited.

Degree Requirements: *For first-professional degree:* 78 semesters units; comprehensives; distribution requirements. *For graduate degrees:* range from 24 to 48 semester units; thesis. *Grading system:* A–F; pass-fail; withdraw (carries time limit); incomplete.

Distinctive Educational Programs: Field education for first-professional students throughout U.S. and abroad. Cluster colleges. Interdisciplinary programs, cross-registration, and cooperative master's program in theological studies through Graduate Theological Union. Tutorials. Students may take courses at University of California, Berkeley. *Other distinctive programs:* Continuing education programs. Institute for Spirituality and Worship.

Degrees Conferred: 12 *first-professional:* theological; 24 *master's:* theology; 1 *doctorate:* theology.

Fees and Other Expenses: *Full-time tuition per academic year 2004–05:* $11,200.

Financial Aid: Aid from institutionally generated funds is provided on the basis of academic merit, financial need, commitment to social justice. Institution has a Program Participation Agreement with the U.S. Department of Education for eligible students to receive Pell Grants and other federal aid.

Departments and Teaching Staff: *Total instructional faculty:* 24. Total tenured faculty: 10. Degrees held by full-time faculty: doctorate 88%, master's 8%, professional 4%. 100% of faculty members hold terminal degrees.

Enrollment: Total enrollment 175 (68.6% men, 31.4% women).

Characteristics of Student Body: *Ethnic/racial makeup:* Black non-Hispanic: 2.3%; Asian or Pacific Islander: 8%; Hispanic: 6.3%; White non-Hispanic: 49.7%; unknown: 1.7%.

International Students: 56 nonresident aliens enrolled fall 2003. No financial aid specifically designated for international students.

Student Life: *Surrounding community:* Berkeley, population 115,000 is located in San Francisco-Oakland metropolitan area. Served by mass transit bus; commuter train system; airport 15 miles from campus; passenger rail service 6 miles from campus.

Library Collections: Library services provided by Graduate Theological Union.

Buildings and Grounds: Campus area 1 square block.

Chief Executive Officer: Rev. Joseph P. Daoust, S.J., President.

Address admission inquiries to Linda Menes, Dean of Admissions

John F. Kennedy University

100 Ellinwood Way
Pleasant Hill, California 94523-4817
Tel: (925) 969-3300   **E-mail:** proginfo@jfku.edu
Fax: (925) 969-3399   **Internet:** www.jfku.edu

Institution Description: John F. Kennedy University is a private, independent, nonprofit institution providing undergraduate, graduate, professional, and doctoral study, primarily serving older students. *Enrollment:* 1,606. *Degrees awarded:* Baccalaureate, master's, doctorate, first-professional.

Member of the consortium Regional Association of East Bay Colleges and Universities.

Accreditation: *Regional:* WASC-Sr.

History: Established and incorporated 1964; offered first instruction at postsecondary level 1965; awarded first degree (baccalaureate) 1966.

Institutional Structure: *Governing board:* Board of Regents. Extrainstitutional representation: 31 regents; institutional representation: president of the university, 1 full-time instructional faculty member, 2 students; 1 alumnus. 1 ex officio. *Composition of institution:* Administrators 7 men / 6 women. Academic affairs headed by academic vice president. Management/business/finances directed by vice president of student services and administration. Full-time instructional faculty 32, adjunct faculty 748. Academic governance body, Faculty Senate, meets an average of 9 times per year.

Calendar: Quarters. Academic year July to June. Entering students admitted Oct., Jan., Apr., July (varies for some programs). Degrees conferred June, Sept., Dec., Mar. Formal commencement June. Summer session of 4 terms from late June to mid-Sept.

Admission: Rolling admissions for most programs. *Requirements:* 45 quarter hours of baccalaureate study. *Entrance tests:* For foreign students TOEFL. *For transfer students:* 2.0 minimum GPA; from 4-year accredited institution 144 quarter hours maximum transfer credit; from 2-year accredited institution 105 hours.

College credit for extrainstitutional learning (life experience) through faculty assessment.

Degree Requirements: *Undergraduate:* 180 quarter hours; 2.0 GPA; 36 of last 45 units in residence; distribution requirements; demonstrated proficiency in writing. *Graduate:* units vary; 3.0 GPA; residency requirement.

Fulfillment of some degree requirements and exemption from some beginning courses possible by passing College Board CLEP. *Grading system:* A–D; credit-no credit; withdraw; incomplete.

Distinctive Educational Programs: *For undergraduates:* Interdisciplinary programs in liberal arts, business, psychology. *For graduate students:* Programs in career development, education, fine arts, law, management, museum studies, psychology internship, studio arts. *Available to all students:* Weekend and evening classes. Facilities for independent research, including individual majors, tutorials. *Other distinctive programs:* Community Counseling Centers.

Degrees Conferred: 43 *baccalaureate:* 216 *master's;* 15 *doctorate;* 38 *first-professional.* Bachelor's degrees awarded in top disciplines: liberal arts and sciences, general studies and humanities 29; business, management, marketing, and related support services 8; psychology 6.

Fees and Other Expenses: *Full-time tuition per academic year 2004–05:* $14,656.

Financial Aid: Aid from institutionally generated funds is provided on the basis of financial need. Institution has a Program Participation Agreement with the U.S. Department of Education for eligible students to receive Pell Grants and other federal aid.

Departments and Teaching Staff: Full-time faculty 32, adjunct faculty 742. *Total instructional faculty:* 774. Student-to-faculty ratio: 12:1.

Enrollment: Total enrollment 1,606. Undergraduate 237 (23.2% men, 76.8% women).

Characteristics of Student Body: *Ethnic/racial makeup:* Black non-Hispanic: 8.9%; American Indian or Alaska Native: 1.3%; Asian or Pacific Islander: 8%; Hispanic: 4.6%; White non-Hispanic: 72.2%; unknown: 5.1%.

International Students: 12 nonresident aliens enrolled fall 2003. No programs available to aid students whose native language is not English. No financial aid programs specifically designated for international students.

Student Life: No on-campus housing. *Special regulations:* Cars permitted without restrictions. *Student publications: J.F.K. University Student Newspaper,* a bimonthly publication. *Surrounding community:* Orinda is located in the San Francisco-Oakland metropolitan area. Served by mass transit bus systems; airport 30 miles from campus; passenger rail service 20 miles from campus.

Library Collections: 90,000 volumes including bound books, serial backfiles, electronic documents, and government documents not in separate collections. Online catalog. Current serial subscriptions: 935 paper, 12 microform, 1,305 electronic. Students have access to the Internet at no charge.

Most important special holdings include Law Library; Career Planning Library; Business Library.

Buildings and Grounds: Leased locations in Orinda, Walnut Creek, Pleasant Hill, Oakland, Berkeley, Campbell, and Sunnyvale.

Chief Executive Officer: Dr. Steven A. Stargardter, President.

Address admission inquiries to K. Sue Duncan, Enrollment Services.

La Sierra University

4500 Riverwalk Parkway
Riverside, California 92515-8247

Tel: (951) 785-2000   **E-mail:** ivy@lasierra.edu
Fax: (951) 782-2901   **Internet:** www.lasierra.edu

Institution Description: La Sierra University is a private institution owned by the Seventh-day Adventist Church. *Enrollment:* 1,940. *Degrees awarded:* Baccalaureate, master's, doctorate.

Accreditation: WASC-Sr. *Professional:* music, social work

History: Established 1922 as La Sierra College; became Loma Linda University - La Sierra Campus 1967; became La Sierra University 1990.

Calendar: Quarters. Academic year Sept. to June. Summer session. Commencement June.

Characteristics of Freshmen: 1,399 applicants (1,399 men, 538 women). 51.7% of applicants accepted; 49.1% of admitted students enrolled full-time.

73% (263 students) submitted SAT scores; 41% (263 students) submitted ACT scores. *25th percentile:* SAT Verbal 430, SAT Math 430, ACT Composite 17, ACT English 15, ACT Math 16. *75th percentile:* SAT Verbal 550, SAT Math 560, ACT Composite 22, ACT English 21, ACT Math 22.

Admission: Rolling admissions plan. *Requirements:* graduation from accredited secondary school. *Entrance tests:* ACT preferred; SAT accepted.

Degree Requirements: *For baccalaureate degree:* 190 quarter hours; last 45 quarter hours in residence. *Grading system:* A–F; pass-fail.

Distinctive Educational Programs: English Language Institute; evening classes; external adult degree. Study abroad in Argentina, Austria, France, Spain.

Degrees Conferred: 180 *baccalaureate;* 57 *master's;* 9 *post-master's certificates;* 11 *first-professional.* Bachelor's degrees awarded in top five disciplines: business, management, marketing, and related support services51; biological and biomedical sciences 24; liberal arts and sciences, general studies and humanities 23; visual and performing arts 16; public administration and social services professions 12.

Fees and Other Expenses: *Full-time tuition per academic year 2004–05:* undergraduate $17,244; graduate tuition per unit (contact the university for current rate). *Room and board per academic year:* $4,902. *Books and supplies:* $1,260.

Financial Aid: Aid from institutionally generated funds is provided on the basis of academic merit, financial need, other considerations. Institution has a Program Participation Agreement with the U.S. Department of Education for eligible students to receive Pell Grants and other federal aid.

Departments and Teaching Staff: *Professors* 32, *associate professors* 28, *assistant professors* 33, *instructors* 3, *part-time faculty* 13.

Total instructional faculty: 100.33 FTE. Total tenured faculty 43. Degrees held by full-time faculty: doctorate 72%, master's 26%, professional 2%. 74% hold terminal degrees.

Enrollment: Total enrollment 1,940. Undergraduate 1,571.

Characteristics of Student Body: *Ethnic and racial makeup:* Black non-Hispanic: 9.4%; American Indian or Alaska Native: 1.5%; Asian or Pacific Islander: 17.3%; Hispanic: 21.3%; White non-Hispanic: 26.3%; unknown: 3.7%.

International Students: 324 nonresident aliens enrolled fall 2003. Programs available to aid students whose language is not English: English as a Second Language Program; social and cultural. No financial aid specifically designated for international students.

Student Life: Campus is located in a country setting on the edge of the city of Riverside; 50 miles east of Los Angeles.

Library Collections: 235,000 volumes. 340,000 audiovisual materials; 1,500 current periodical subscriptions. Students have access to online information retrieval services and the Internet.

Buildings and Grounds: Campus area 350 acres.

Chief Executive Officer: Dr. Lawrence T. Geraty, President.

Address admission inquiries Gene Edelbach, Vice President, Enrollment Services.

Life Pacific College

1100 Covina Boulevard
San Dimas, California 91773-3298

Tel: (909) 599-5433   **E-mail:** adm@lifepacific.edu
Fax: (909) 599-6690   **Internet:** www.lifepacific.edu

Institution Description: Life Pacific College, formerly named L.I.F.E. Bible College, is a private institution operated by the International Foursquare Gospel. *Enrollment:* 489. *Degrees awarded:* Associate, baccalaureate. Diplomas also awarded.

Accreditation: *Regional:* WASC-Sr. *Nonregional:* ABHE.

History: Founded 1923.

Calendar: Semesters. Academic year Aug. to May.

Characteristics of Freshmen: 68% (30 students) submitted SAT scores; 32% (14 students) submitted ACT scores. *25th percentile:* SAT Verbal 413, SAT Math 401; ACT Composite 15. *75th percentile:* SAT Verbal 608, SAT Math 510; ACT Composite 27.

49 National Merit Scholars. 93% of applicants admitted; 74% of admitted students enrolled full-time. 21% of entering freshmen expected to graduate within 5 years. 49% of freshmen from California. Freshmen from 14 states.

Admission: Rolling admissions plan. *Requirements:* High school diploma or GED; evidence of Christian character. *Entrance tests:* ACT or SAT. Deadline for applications for fall semester July 1; spring semester Dec. 1.

Degree Requirements: Completion of prescribed curriculum.

Distinctive Educational Programs: Day and evening classes. Distance learning associate degree program.

Degrees Conferred: 8 *associate;* 19 *baccalaureate:* Bible.

Fees and Other Expenses: *Full-time tuition per academic year 2004–05:* $9,750. *Room and board per academic year:* $5,000. *Required fees:* $350.

Financial Aid: Aid from institutionally generated funds is provided on the basis of academic merit and financial need. Institution has a Program Participation Agreement with the U.S. Department of Education for eligible students to receive Pell Grants and other federal aid.

Financial aid to full-time, first-time undergraduate students: need-based scholarships/grants totaling $1,103,816, self-help $1,587,420, parent loans $183,186; non-need-based scholarships/grants totaling $36,995, self-help $453,159, parent loans $143,708.

Departments and Teaching Staff: *Total instructional faculty:* 37 (full-time 13, part-time 24; women 9, men 28). Total faculty with doctorate, first-professional, or other terminal degree: 8. Student-to-faculty ratio: 19:1.

Enrollment: Total enrollment 489 (full-time 345, part-time 144).

Characteristics of Student Body: *Ethnic/racial makeup:* number of Black non-Hispanic: 28; American Indian or Alaska Native: 5; Asian or Pacific Islander: 25; Hispanic: 73; White non-Hispanic: 350; unknown: 6.

International Students: 2 nonresident aliens enrolled fall 2004. No programs available to aid students whose native language is not English. No financial aid specifically designated for international students.

Student Life: Student housing available. *Surrounding community:* Los Angeles is a major metropolitan area.

Library Collections: 40,022 volumes including bound books, serial backfiles, electronic documents, and government documents not in separate collections. Online catalog. Current serial subscriptions: 230 paper, 1,954 via electronic access. 172 recordings; 150 compact discs; 22 CD-ROMs. 13 computer work stations. Students have access to the Internet at no charge.

Most important special collections: Greek/Hebrew Language Helps; Archives of Life Bible College.

Chief Executive Officer: Rev. Dan Stewart, President.

Address admission inquiries to Linda Hibdon, Admissions Coordinator.

Life Chiropractic College - West

25001 Industrial Boulevard
Hayward, California 94545-2800

Tel: (510) 780-4500   **E-mail:** admissions@lifewest.edu
Fax: (510) 780-4525   **Internet:** www.lifewest.edu

Institution Description: Life Chiropractic College West is a private, independent, nonprofit college offering a first-professional degree in chiropractic. *Enrollment:* 519.

Accreditation: *National:* Council on Chiropractic Education. *Professional:* chiropractic education

History: Established 1976 as Pacific States Chiropractic College; adopted present name 1981 in agreement with Life University of Marietta, Georgia.

Institutional Structure: *Governing board:* Life Chiropractic College West Board of Regents. *Composition of institution:* 32 administrators.

Calendar: Quarters. Academic year Sept. to June. New classes admitted Jan., Apr., July, Oct. Academic year Sept. to June.

Characteristics of Freshmen: Average secondary school rank of entering students 70th percentile. 50% of applicants accepted. 48% of accepted applicants enrolled. 94% of entering students expected to graduate within 5 years. Students from 12 foreign countries.

Admission: Prerequisites for admission: minimum of 60 semester credits with at least a 2.5 GPA; minimum of 6 semester credits in biology (must be animal or human oriented); minimum of 6 semester credits in each of the following: physics, organic chemistry, inorganic chemistry; minimum 6 semester credits of English (composition or communicative skills); minimum of 3 semester credits of psychology; minimum of 15 semester credits in social sciences or humanities; all science prerequisite courses must contain a lab component, have been completed in two or more academic terms, and passed with a grade of C or better.

Degree Requirements: 12 quarters in residence; completion of prescribed curriculum; clinical internship.

Degrees Conferred: 164 *first-professional:* chiropractic.

Fees and Other Expenses: *Tuition per academic year 2004–05:* $15,480.

Financial Aid: Institution has a Program Participation Agreement with the U.S. Department of Education for eligible students to receive Pell Grants and other federal aid.

Departments and Teaching Staff: Chiropractic *professors* 7, *associate professors* 12, *assistant professors* 19, *instructors* 46 *part-time faculty* 15 FTE.

Total instructional faculty: 99. Total tenured faculty: 6. Degrees held by full-time faculty: doctorate 7%, master's 6%, professional 25%. 32% of faculty hold terminal degrees.

Enrollment: *Total enrollment:* 519 (59.9% men; 40.1% women).

Characteristics of Student Body: *Ethnic and racial makeup:* Black non-Hispanic: 1.5%; American Indian or Alaska Native: .8%; Asian or Pacific Islander: 11%; Hispanic: 6.6%; White non-Hispanic: 57.2%; unknown: 12.5%.

International Students: 54 nonresident aliens enrolled fall 2004. No programs available to aid students whose native language is not English.

Student Life: *Student activities:* Student Council sponsors various activity and athletics programs; social clubs; chiropractic-related clubs.

Library Collections: 15,000 monographs. 6,000 microforms; 1,400 audiovisual materials; 250 current periodical subscriptions. Access to OCLC, MEDLARS, MANTIS.

Most important special holdings include collections in manipulative medicine; chiropractic archives and history; musculoskeletal system.

Chief Executive Officer: Dr. Gerard W. Clum, President.

Address admission inquiries to Steve Eckstone, Director of Admissions and Recruitment.

Loma Linda University

Loma Linda, California 92350
Tel: (909) 558-1000   **E-mail:** admissions@llu.edu
Fax: (909) 558-0242   **Internet:** www.llu.edu

Institution Description: Loma Linda University is a private health sciences university affiliated with the Seventh-day Adventist Church. *Enrollment:* 3,501. *Degrees awarded:* Associate, baccalaureate, master's, doctorate, first-professional. Specialist certificates in dentistry and certificates in occupational therapy are also awarded.

Accreditation: *Regional:* WASC-Sr. *Professional:* clinical lab scientist, clinical pastoral education, clinical psychology, cytotechnology, dental hygiene, dentistry, diagnostic medical sonography, dietetics, endodontics, health information administration, marriage and family therapy, medicine, nuclear medicine technology, nursing, nursing education, occupational therapy, oral and maxillofacial surgery, periodontics, phlebotomy, physical therapy, physician assisting, public health, radiation therapy, radiography, respiratory therapy, social work, speech-language pathology, surgical technology

History: Established as Loma Linda Sanitarium School of Nursing 1905; chartered as College of Medical Evangelists and offered first instruction at postsecondary level 1909; awarded first degree (first-professional) 1914; adopted present name 1961; merged with La Sierra College (established 1922) 1967; La Sierra (Riverside) campus separated as La Sierra University in 1990. *SEE Seventh-day Adventist Encyclopedia* (Washington, DC: Review and Herald Press Publishing Association, 1976) for further information.

Institutional Structure: *Governing board:* Board of Trustees. Extrainstitutional representation: 23 trustees (including 4 alumni), 6 representatives of Gen-

eral Conference of Seventh-day Adventists, 1 representative of North American Division of Seventh-day Adventists, and the president of Adventist Health Systems/Loma Linda. Institutional representation: 1 administrator. 13 ex officio. All voting. *Composition of institution:* University-wide administrators: 1 woman / 4 men. Academic affairs headed by vice president for academic and research affairs. Management/business/finances directed by vice president for financial affairs. Full-time instructional faculty 735 men / 256 women. Academic governance bodies, Deans Council (meets an average of 48 times a year) and University Academic Affairs Committee (meets an average of 11 times per year).

Calendar: Quarters. Academic year Sept. to June. Students may be admitted any quarter. Degrees conferred at end of any quarter. Formal commencements My or June. Summer sessions from June to Sept.

Admission: Admission requirements vary from program to program; check with specific school.

Degree Requirements: Varies from program to program; contact the individual school. Weekly chapel attendance require in some years of all programs.

Fulfillment of some degree requirements possible by passing qualifying examinations. *Grading system:* A–F; withdraw (carries time limit); satisfactory-unsatisfactory; incomplete.

Distinctive Educational Programs: Flexible meeting places and schedules, including off-campus centers (in 6 regional areas of North America and several other countries), evening classes. Facilities and programs for independent research and independent study.

Degrees Conferred: 134 *associate;* 236 *baccalaureate;* 321 *master's;* 64 *doctorate;* 241 *first-professional:* 141 dentistry, 141 medicine.

Fees and Other Expenses: Undergraduate, graduate and professional school tuition varies from program to program; contact the school for current information.

Financial Aid: Aid from institutionally generated funds is awarded on the basis of academic merit, financial need. Institution has a Program Participation Agreement with the U.S. Department of Education for eligible students to receive Pell Grants and other federal aid.

Departments and Teaching Staff: *Total instructional faculty:* 1,991.

Enrollment: Total enrollment 3,501 (25.2% men, 74.8% women). Undergraduate 978.

Characteristics of Student Body: *Ethnic/racial makeup:* Black non-Hispanic: 6.7%; American Indian or Alaska Native: .5%; Asian or Pacific Islander: 22.9%; Hispanic: 18.8%; White non-Hispanic: 45.1%.

International Students: 207 nonresident aliens enrolled fall 2004.

English as a Second Language Program available. No financial aid specifically designated for international students.

Student Life: On-campus residence halls house 500 students. *Intramural athletics:* men's, women's, and co-ed football, volleyball, indoor soccer, basketball. *Special regulations:* Traditional conservative Christian values in dress and appearance emphasized. Curfews in women's dormitory. *Special services:* Learning Resources Center, medical services, bus transportation for local residents to and from university. *Student publications: Courier,* a monthly newspaper. *Surrounding community:* Loma Linda 2000 population 20,000.Los Angeles, 60 miles from campus, is nearest metropolitan area. Served by mass transit bus system; Ontario Airport 20 miles from campus; passenger rail service 6 miles from campus.

Publications: *SCOPE,* published quarterly; *TODAY* published biweekly.

Library Collections: 285,000 volumes. 65,908 audiovisual materials, 2,683 current periodical subscriptions. Online catalog. Students have access to online information retrieval systems and the Internet.

Most important holdings include collection on Seventh-day Adventist heritage and 19th-century health reform; Jerry and Shirley Pettis Papers; Edward A. Sutherland papers.

Buildings and Grounds: Campus area 234 acres.

Chief Executive Officer: Dr. Richard H. Hart, President.

Address admission inquiries to admissions office of appropriate school.

School of Allied Health Professions

Degree Programs Offered: *Associate* in medical radiography, occupational therapy, physical therapy, radiation therapy; *baccalaureate* in cytotechnology, nutrition and dietetics, health information administration, medical technology, occupational therapy, radiation technology, respiratory therapy; *master's* in physical therapy. Certificates also given.

Departments and Teaching Staff: *Total instructional faculty:* 251.

School of Dentistry

Degree Programs Offered: *Baccalaureate* in dental hygiene; *first-professional* in dentistry.

Admission: *For first-professional:* 90 semester hours from accredited college or university, manual dexterity examination, DAT; credentials must be processed through American Association of Dental Schools Admission Service.

Degree Requirements: *First-professional:* must be registered for full course load the entire junior and senior years; 2.0 GPA.

Departments and Teaching Staff: *Total instructional faculty:* 326.

School of Medicine

Degree Programs Offered: *First-professional* in medicine.

Admission: 85 semester hours from accredited college or university with units in English composition, general biology, general chemistry, general physics, organic chemistry; MCAT; credentials must be processed through AMCAS.

Degree Requirements: Must be registered for full-time course work during the entire junior and senior academic years; successful completion of National Board Examinations.

Departments and Teaching Staff: *Total instructional faculty:* 1,196.

School of Nursing

Degree Programs Offered: *Associate and baccalaureate.*

Departments and Teaching Staff: *Total instructional faculty:* 77.

School of Public Health

Degree Programs Offered: *Master's* in biostatistics, epidemiology, environmental health, health administration, health promotion and education, health science, international health, nutrition; *doctorate* in epidemiology, health education, nutrition, preventive care.

Departments and Teaching Staff: *Total instructional faculty:* 128.

Graduate School

Degree Programs Offered: *Master's* in dental specialties (endodontics, oral implantology, oral and maxillofacial surgery, orthodontics, and periodontics), family life education, marriage and family therapy, nursing, nutrition, paleontology, and speech-language pathology; *master's* and *doctorate* in anatomy, biochemistry, biology, microbiology, pharmacology, physiology.

Departments and Teaching Staff: *Total instructional faculty:* 13 full-time plus 201 faculty members drawn from other schools of the university.

Loyola Marymount University

One LMU Drive
Los Angeles, California 90045-2659
Tel: (310) 338-2700   **E-mail:** admissions@lmumail.lmu.edu
Fax: (310) 338-2797   **Internet:** www.lmu.edu

Institution Description: Loyola Marymount University (Loyola University of Los Angeles and Marymount College until 1973) is a private institution conducted by the Society of Jesus, Religious of the Sacred Heart of Mary, and the Sisters of St. Joseph of Orange, Roman Catholic Church. *Enrollment:* 8,652. *Degrees awarded:* Baccalaureate, master's, first-professional. Post-baccalaureate certificates also awarded.

Accreditation: *Regional:* WASC-Sr. *Professional:* business, dance, engineering, law, music, teacher education

History: Established by Vincentian Fathers as St. Vincent's College 1865; control assumed by Society of Jesus and name changed to Los Angeles College 1911; offered first instruction at postsecondary level 1914; renamed St. Vincent's College 1917; chartered as Loyola College of Los Angeles, incorporated, and awarded first degree (baccalaureate) 1918; changed name to Loyola University of Los Angeles 1930; affiliated with Marymount College (a women's college established by Religious of the Sacred Heart of Mary 1933) 1968; institutions merged and adopted present name 1973.

Institutional Structure: *Governing board:* Board of Trustees. Representation: 37 trustees, including a minimum of 7 members of the Society of Jesus, a minimum of 3 members of the Religious of the Sacred Heart of Mary and/or the Sisters of Saint Joseph of Orange, and the president of the university. *Composition of institution:* Administrators 24 men / 7 women. Academic affairs headed by academic vice president. Management/business/finances directed by vice president for business affairs.

Calendar: Semesters. Academic year Aug. to May. Freshmen admitted Aug., Feb., June. Degrees conferred May, Aug., Dec., Jan. Formal commencement May. Summer session from June to Aug.

Characteristics of Freshmen: 7,075 applicants (2,724 men / 4,351 women). 59.8% of applicants admitted; 32.9% admitted and enrolled full-time.

83% (1,117 students) submitted SAT scores; 16% (225 students) submitted ACT scores. *25th percentile:* SAT Verbal 530, SAT Math 640; ACT Composite 24. *75th percentile:* SAT Verbal 620, SAT Math ; 630; ACT Composite 28.

78% of freshmen from California. Freshmen from 26 states and 21 foreign countries.

Admission: Fall deadline for freshmen is Feb. 1 and July 2. for transfers. The spring deadline is Dec. 1. Freshmen candidates who provide all documents prior to Feb. 1 receive priority for acceptance, financial aid, and housing. *Requirements:* Graduation from accredited secondary school with 16 units in academic subjects, including 4 units in English, 3 in a foreign language, 3 mathematics, 3 social sciences, 2 science, 1 academic elective. Certain majors require additional mathematics. *Entrance tests:* College Board SAT or ACT Composite. For foreign students TOEFL. *For transfer students:* 2.75 minimum GPA for transfer from accredited institutions. The Admissions Office will make tentative evaluations of transfer credits. Deadline for transfer application July 1.

Degree Requirements: *Undergraduate:* 120–136 credit hours; 2.0 GPA; last 30 semester hours in residence; core curriculum with distribution requirements.

Fulfillment of some degree requirements and exemption from some beginning courses by passing departmental examinations, College Board CLEP, AP. *Grading system:* A–F; pass; withdraw (carries time limit).

Distinctive Educational Programs: University Honors Program. Visual, performing, and communications arts. Small Business Entrepreneurship Program; international business. Pre-health program in biology or chemistry. 'Encore' program for adults over 30 wishing to resume an interrupted educational program. Study abroad programs in Germany, England, Monaco, and Mexico; other locations are available through affiliated universities.

ROTC: Air Force available on campus; Army and Navy offered in cooperation with UCLA.

Degrees Conferred: 1,306 *baccalaureate;* 10 *post-baccalaureate certificates;* 498 *master's.* Bachelor's degrees awarded in top five disciplines: business, management, marketing, and related support services 388; visual and performing arts 172; communication, journalism, and related programs 156; social sciences 121; liberal arts and sciences, general studies and humanities 81.

Fees and Other Expenses: *Full-time tuition per academic year 2004–05:* $25,266 undergraduate; graduate study per credit (contact the university for current rate); Law School per academic year (contact the school for current rate). *Books and supplies:* $832. *Room and board per academic year:* $9,456.

Financial Aid: Aid from institutionally generated funds is provided on the basis of academic merit, financial need, athletic ability. Institution has a Program Participation Agreement with the U.S. Department of Education for eligible students to receive Pell Grants and other federal aid.

Financial aid to full-time, first-time undergraduate students: 23% received federal grants averaging $3,797; 20% state/local grants averaging $9,265; 46% institutional grants averaging $9,186; 60% loans averaging $11,283.

Departments and Teaching Staff: *Professors* 143, *associate professors* 84, *assistant professors* 79, *instructors* 2, *part-time faculty* 259.

Total instructional faculty: 355 FTE. Total tenured faculty: 211. Degrees held by full-time faculty: 86% hold terminal degrees.

Enrollment: Total enrollment 8,652. Undergraduate 5,700.

Characteristics of Student Body: *Ethnic and racial makeup:* Black non-Hispanic: 6.6%; American Indian or Alaska Native: .6%; Asian or Pacific Islander: 11.3%; Hispanic: 18.2%; White non-Hispanic: 52.4%; unknown: 8.9%.

International Students: 183 nonresident aliens enrolled fall 2004. Programs available to aid students whose native language is not English: Social, cultural. No financial aid specifically designated for international students.

Student Life: On-campus residence halls house 50% of undergraduates. *Intercollegiate athletics:* men only: baseball, basketball, crew, cross-country, soccer, tennis, volleyball; women only: basketball, crew, cross-country, swimming, tennis, volleyball. *Special services:* Learning Resources Center, medical services. *Student publications, radio: El Playano,* an annual literary magazine; *Inter-Com,* a daily news bulletin; *The Tower,* a yearbook; *The Los Angeles Loyolan,* a weekly newspaper. Radio station KXLU-AM serves the LMU campus; KXLU-FM serves a large portion of the Los Angeles area 24 hours a day all year. *Surrounding community:* Los Angeles population over 3 million. Served by mass transit bus system; airport 3 miles from campus.

Library Collections: 943,700 volumes. 1,560 microform units; 20,900 audiovisual materials. Computer work stations available. Students have access to the Internet at no charge.

Buildings and Grounds: Campus area 128 acres.

Chief Executive Officer: Rev. Robert B. Lawton, S.J., President.

Address admission inquiries to Matthew X. Fissinger, Director of Admissions.

College of Liberal Arts

Degree Programs Offered: *Baccalaureate* in area studies, foreign languages, interdisciplinary studies, letters, psychology, social sciences, theology; *master's* in area studies, education, interdisciplinary studies, letters, psychology, social sciences, theology.

Distinctive Educational Programs: Interdisciplinary programs in alcohol and drug studies, Afro-American studies, Chicano studies, European studies, humanities, Latin American studies, liberal studies, Los Angeles studies, urban studies, women's studies.

College of Business Administration

Degree Programs Offered: *Baccalaureate, master's* in business and management; *master's* in business and management.

Admission: *See* general requirements. Recommend 1 additional unit in intermediate algebra. Graduate requirements vary with program and level.

Degree Requirements: *See* general requirements. *For baccalaureate:* 120 credit hours. Graduate requirements vary.

College of Communication and Fine Arts

Degree Programs Offered: *Baccalaureate* in communications, fine and applied arts; *master's* in communication arts.

Admission: *See* general requirements. *For baccalaureate:* 120 credit hours. Graduate requirements vary.

College of Science and Engineering

Degree Programs Offered: *Baccalaureate* in engineering, mathematics, physical sciences; *master's* in computer and information sciences, engineering, mathematics, physical sciences.

Admission: *See* general requirements. Recommend 2 additional units in college preparatory mathematics and laboratory science. Graduate requirements vary with program and level.

Degree Requirements: *See* general requirements. *For baccalaureate* in engineering: 136 credit hours; in mathematics and science: 124 credit hours. Graduate requirements vary.

Distinctive Educational Programs: *For undergraduates:* Preprofessional program in allied health.

Loyola Law School

Degree Programs Offered: *First-professional.*

Admission: Baccalaureate from accredited university or college; LSAT.

Degree Requirements: *For first-professional:* 87 semester hours, 2.0 GPA, 18 months in residence.

The Master's College

21726 West Placerita Canyon Road
Santa Clarita, California 91321
Tel: (661) 259-3540   **E-mail:** enrollment@masters.edu
Fax: (661) 254-1998   **Internet:** www.masters.edu

Institution Description: The Master's College, formerly named Los Angeles Baptist College, is a private, independent, nonprofit college. *Enrollment:* 1,523. *Degrees awarded:* Associate, baccalaureate, master's. Diplomas also awarded.

Accreditation: *Regional:* WASC-Sr.

History: Established, chartered, and incorporated as Los Angeles Baptist Theological Seminary and offered first instruction at postsecondary level 1927; awarded first degree (first-professional) 1930; changed name to Los Angeles Baptist College and Seminary 1958; adopted present name 1985.

Institutional Structure: *Governing board:* Board of Trustees. Representation: 16 trustees. All voting. *Composition of institution:* Administrators 7 men. Academic affairs headed by vice president for academic affairs. President, provost, vice president for operations. Student affairs directed by vice president for student affairs. Seminary operations directed by vice president for operations. Full-time instructional faculty 76. Academic governance body, the faculty, meets monthly.

Calendar: Semesters. Academic year Aug. to May. Freshmen admitted Sept., Jan. Degrees conferred May, Dec. Formal commencement May. Winterterm and two post-sessions (summer).

Characteristics of Freshmen: 75% of applicants admitted; 65% of admitted students enrolled full-time.

74% (163 students) submitted SAT scores; 38% (83 students) submitted ACT scores. *25th percentile:* SAT Verbal 530, SAT Math 490; ACT Composite 21, ACT English 21, ACT Math 19. *75th percentile:* SAT Verbal 650, SAT Math 620; ACT Composite 27, CT English 29, ACT Math 26.

56% of entering freshmen expected to graduate within 5 years. 59% of freshmen from California. Students from 26 states and 5 foreign countries.

Admission: Rolling admissions plan. For fall acceptance, apply as early as Oct. of previous year, but not later than Aug. 15 of year of enrollment. *Requirements:* Either graduation from secondary school with 15 units which must include 4 in English, 3 mathematics, 2 science, 2 history; or GED. 2 additional units in a modern language recommended. Minimum GPA 2.75. *Entrance tests:* College Board SAT or ACT Composite. For foreign students TOEFL. *For transfer students:* 2.50 minimum GPA; from 4-year accredited institution 94 semester hours maximum transfer credit; from 2-year institution 70 hours, for correspondence/extension students 6 hours.

College credit and advanced placement for postsecondary-level work completed in secondary school; college credit for extrainstitutional learning on basis of ACE *2006 Guide to the Evaluation of Educational Experiences in the Armed Services.*

Tutoring available. Developmental/remedial course offered during regular academic year; credit given.

Degree Requirements: *For all baccalaureate degrees:* 122 hours; 2 semester hours physical education. *For all degrees:* 2.0 GPA; 2 terms in residence; demonstrated proficiency in English; general education requirements. *Grading system:* A–F.

Distinctive Educational Programs: Evening classes. Interdisciplinary program in women's ministries. Summer Overseas (short-term mission trips). IBEX - Israel Bible Extension (one semester course in Israel).

Degrees Conferred: 258 *baccalaureate:* biological/life sciences 8, business/marketing 56, communications/communication technologies 12, computer and information sciences 10, education 8, English 9, home economics and vocational home economics 7, liberal arts/general studies 37, mathematics 1, philosophy/religion/theology 84, social sciences and history 18, visual and performing arts 8. 77 *master's:* religion.

Fees and Other Expenses: *Full-time tuition per academic year 2004–05:* undergraduate $17,000; graduate $460 per unit. *Required fees:* $200. *Room and board per academic year:* $6,050.

Financial Aid: Aid from institutionally generated funds is provided on the basis of academic merit, financial need, athletic ability, other considerations. Institution has a Program Participation Agreement with the U.S. Department of Education for eligible students to receive Pell Grants and other federal aid.

Financial aid to full-time, first-time undergraduate students: need-based scholarships/grants totaling $5,810,634, self-help $3,550,813, parent loans $1,589,458, tuition waivers $343,051, athletic awards $421,249; non-need-bases scholarships/grants totaling $974,132, self-help $1,038,146, parent loans $1,346,922, tuition waivers $88,582; athletic awards $302,265.

Departments and Teaching Staff: Biblical studies *professors* 6, *associate professors* 8, *assistant professors* 0, *instructors* 0, *part-time faculty* 8; biological sciences 3, 1, 0, 1, 1; business administration 3, 1, 0, 1, 1; communication 2, 1, 0, 0, 3; education 0, 1, 2, 0, 3; English 1, 2, 1, 0, 0; history/political science 3, 1, .75, 0, 3; home economics 1, 0, 1.5, 0, 4; liberal studies/teacher education 3, 1, 0, 0, 6; mathematics 1, 1, 0, 0, 0; music 4, 1.5, 0, 0, 10.

Total instructional faculty: 159 (full-time 76, part-time 89; women 28, men 131). Total faculty with doctorate, first-professional, or other terminal degree: 82. Student-to-faculty ratio: 15:1. 1 faculty member awarded a sabbatical 2004. *Transfer students:* in-state 98, out-of-state 31.

Enrollment: Total enrollment 1,523 (full-time 1,120, part-time 403).

Characteristics of Student Body: *Ethnic/racial makeup:* number of Black non-Hispanic: 24; American Indian or Alaska Native: 9; Asian or Pacific Islander: 49; Hispanic: 81; White non-Hispanic: 929; unknown: 4. *Age distribution:* number under 18: 7; 18–19: 356, 20–21: 405; 22–24: 157; 25–29: 52; 30–34: 30; 35–39: 32, 40–49: 38; 50–64: 25; 65 and over: 1.

International Students: 38 nonresident aliens enrolled fall 2004. 15 students from Europe, 8 Asia, 6 Central and South America, 3 Africa, 3 Canada, 2 New Zealand, 1 other.

Student Life: On-campus residence halls house 75% of student body. Residence halls for men only constitute 45% of such space, for women only 55%. *Intercollegiate athletics:* men only: baseball, basketball, cross-country, soccer; women only: basketball, cross-country, tennis, volleyball. *Special regulations:* Cars permitted without restrictions. Curfews. Quiet hours. *Special services:* Medical services. *Student publications, radio:* A bimonthly sports report; webcast sporting events. *Surrounding community:* Santa Clarita population 163,000. Los Angeles; 40 miles from campus, is nearest metropolitan area.

Publications: *The Master's Current,* published 2 times per year.

Library Collections: 215,000 volumes including bound books, serial backfiles, electronic documents, and government documents not in separate collections. Online catalog. Current serial subscriptions: 446 paper, 7 microform,

10,652 electronic. 7,120 recordings; 4,170 compact discs; 2,950 CD-ROMs. 32 computer work stations. Students have access to the Internet at no charge.

Most important special collections include theology and the Los Angeles Baptist College Archives.

Buildings and Grounds: Campus area 110 acres. *New buildings:* Music Center Performance Hall completed 2003; C.W. Smith Residence Hall 2003; Campus Fitness Center 2001; Student Dining Center 2005.

Chief Executive Officer: Dr. John F. MacArthur, Jr. President.

Address admission inquiries to Yaphet Peterson, Director of Enrollment (e-mail: ypeterson@masters.edu).

Menlo College

1000 El Camino Real
Atherton, California 94027-4301
Tel: (800) 55-MENLO
Fax: (650) 543-4496

Institution Description: Menlo College is a private, independent, nonprofit college emphasizing management-oriented, liberal arts education. *Enrollment:* 749. *Degrees awarded:* Baccalaureate.

Accreditation: *Regional:* WASC-Sr.

History: Established as William Warren School, a military academy, 1915; incorporated as Menlo School and Junior College and offered first instruction at postsecondary level 1927; awarded first degree (associate) 1929; founded School of Business Administration and adopted present name 1949; became coeducational 1971; introduced second baccalaureate program 1983; converted junior college to four-year college 1986.

Institutional Structure: *Governing board:* Board of Trustees. Representation: 23 trustees. 19 voting. *Composition of institution:* Administrators 17. Academic affairs headed by provost and academic dean. Management/business/finances directed by vice president for finance and administration. Full-time instructional faculty 22. Academic governance body meets an average of 18 times per year.

Calendar: Semesters. Academic year Aug. to May. Freshmen admitted Sept., Jan., Feb., June. Degrees conferred May, Aug., Dec. Formal commencement May. Limited summer session.

Characteristics of Freshmen: 68% of applicants admitted. 27% of admitted students enrolled full-time.

81% (167 students) submitted SAT scores; 19% (39 students) submitted ACT scores. *25th percentile:* SAT Verbal 400, SAT Math 410; ACT Composite 16, ACT English 15, ACT Math 17. *75th percentile:* SAT Verbal 550, SAT Math 510; ACT Composite ; 22, ACT English 20, ACT Math 21.

60% of freshmen from California. Freshmen from 16 states and 13 foreign countries.

Admission: Rolling admissions plan. For fall acceptance, apply as early as Aug. of previous year, but not later than Aug. of year of enrollment. Foreign students apply no later than July 1. Apply by Dec. 1 for early decision; must limit application to Menlo. Early acceptance available. *Requirements:* Either graduation from accredited secondary school with minimum GPA of 2.0 in at least 12 academic units; or GED. *Entrance tests:* College Board SAT preferred; ACT composite accepted. For foreign students minimum TOEFL score 550. *For transfer students:* 2.0 minimum GPA; from 4-year accredited institution 94 units maximum transfer credit; from 2-year accredited institution 70 units.

College credit and placement awarded based on scores earned on the College Board's Advanced Placement Tests. Tutoring available.

Degree Requirements: *For all baccalaureate degrees:* 124 units and cumulative and professional 2.0 GPA; minimum 42 upper division units at Menlo.

Fulfillment of some degree requirements and exemption from some beginning courses possible by passing College Board CLEP, AP. *Grading system:* A–F; withdraw (carries time limit).

Distinctive Educational Programs: Menlo College offers the bachelor's degree in management, liberal arts, and mass communications.

Degrees Conferred: 98 *baccalaureate:* business/marketing 84; communications/communication technologies 9; liberal arts/general studies 5. Honorary degree awarded 2004: Doctor of Humane Letters.

Fees and Other Expenses: *Full-time tuition per academic year 2004–05:* $16,800. *Required fees:* $300. *Other fees:* $725. *Room and board per academic year:* $4,675.

Financial Aid: Aid from institutionally generated funds is provided on the basis of academic merit, financial need. Institution has a Program Participation Agreement with the U.S. Department of Education for eligible students to receive Pell Grants and other federal aid.

Financial aid to full-time, first-time undergraduate students: need-based scholarships/grants totaling $6,093,137, self-help $2,545,479, parent loans

$747,333; non-need-based scholarships/grants totaling $1,655,323, self-help $822,998, tuition waivers $46,000.

Departments and Teaching Staff: Management faculty 26, liberal arts faculty 33, mass communications faculty 6. *Total instructional faculty:* 65 (full-time 22, part-time 43; women 30, men 35). Total faculty with doctorate, first-professional, or other terminal degree: 31. Student-to-faculty ratio: 11.5:1. 1 faculty member awarded sabbatical 2004.

Enrollment: Total enrollment 749 (undergraduate 651, graduate 98).

Characteristics of Student Body: *Ethnic/racial makeup:* number of Black non-Hispanic: 60; American Indian or Alaska Native: 4; Asian or Pacific Islander: 98; Hispanic: 102; White non-Hispanic: 285; unknown: 123. *Age distribution:* number under 18: 1; 18–19: 251, 20–21: 205; 22–24: 161; 25–29: 80; 30–34: 17, 35–39: 7; 40–49: 5; 50–64: 2; 65 and over: 1.

International Students: 77 nonresident aliens enrolled fall 2004. 17 students from Europe, 43 Asia, 7 Central and South America, 5 Africa, 3 Canada, 1 Australia, 1 other. Programs available to aid students whose native language is not English: Social, cultural. English as a Second Language Program. Financial aid specifically designated for international students: 10-12 scholarships awarded annually.

Student Life: On-campus residence halls house 75% of student body. *Intercollegiate athletics:* men only: baseball, basketball, cross-country, football, golf, soccer, tennis, track, volleyball; women only: basketball, cross-country, softball, tennis, track, volleyball. *Special regulations:* Cars with permits allowed in designated areas. Quiet hours 11pm to 9am Sun.–Thur., after 1am Fri.–Sat. night. *Special services:* counseling. *Student publications: The Menlo Oak,* a biweekly newspaper. Radio station KMXX, TV station KMLO. *Surrounding community:* Atherton population 8,000. San Francisco; 30 miles from campus, is nearest metropolitan area. Served by mass transit bus and rail system; airport 20 miles from campus; passenger rail service 1/4 mile from campus.

Library Collections: 64,700 volumes. Online catalog. Current periodical subscriptions: 175 paper; 11,563 via electronic access. 100 compact discs; 25 CD-ROMs. 36 computer work stations. Students have access to the Internet at no charge.

Most important special collections include Alva H. Griffin Library of Management Essentials; Frank H. Tuban Memorial Tax Library; Historical Press of California.

Buildings and Grounds: Campus area 62 acres.

Chief Executive Officer: Carlos Lopez, President.

Address admission inquiries to Jennifer Munoz, Admission Operations Manager.

Mennonite Brethren Biblical Seminary

4824 East Butler Avenue
Fresno, California 93727
Tel: (559) 251-8628   **E-mail:** dsiegel@fresno.edu
Fax: (559) 251-7212   **Internet:** www.mbseminary.com

Institution Description: Mennonite Brethren Biblical Seminary is a private institution owned and operated by the General Conference of the Mennonite Brethren Churches. *Enrollment:* 179. *Degrees awarded:* Master's, first-professional.

Accreditation: *Regional:* WASC-Sr. *Professional:* theology

History: Established, chartered, and offered first instruction at graduate level 1955; awarded first degree (baccalaureate) 1957. *See* David Ewert, ed., *Called to Teach* (Fresno: Center for Mennonite Brethren Studies, 1980) and current catalog for further information.

Institutional Structure: *Governing board:* Board of Directors. Extrainstitutional representation: 15 directors; 1 representative from the executive of the General Conference of Mennonite Brethren Churches in North America. Institutional representation: president of the seminary, 1 full-time instructional faculty member, 1 student, 16 voting. Academic affairs headed by dean of academic affairs. Management/business/finances directed by president and executive administrator. Full-time instructional faculty 7 men / 2 women. Academic governance body, Faculty Council, meets an average of 10 times per year.

Calendar: Semesters. Academic year June to May. Freshmen admitted Sept., Jan., Feb. Degrees conferred and formal commencement May. Summer session of 1 term.

Admission: Rolling admissions plan. For fall acceptance, apply as early as 1 year, but not later than 4 weeks prior to enrollment. *Requirements:* Baccalaureate from accredited institution with 2 years course work in humanities, social sciences, natural sciences. Minimum GPA 2.5. *Entrance tests:* GRE (or TOEFL instead of GRE for non-English speaking applicants) for M.A. in Marriage/Family/Child Counseling. *For transfer students:* 2.5 GPA; maximum transfer credit from one degree to another is 30 units; other is limited only by residence requirement.

Degree Requirements: *For first-professional degrees:* 90 semester hours; 2.5 GPA; 30 hours in residence; core curriculum; generic M.Div. *For master of arts degree:* 60 semester hours; 2.5 GPA; 30 hours in residence. *Grading system:* A–F; pass-fail; withdraw (carries time limit).

Distinctive Educational Programs: *For graduate students:* Work-experience programs, including field education, internships. Evening classes. Cross-cultural Immersion.

ROTC: 17 *master's:* theology and ministerial studies; 16 *first-professional:* theology. .

Fees and Other Expenses: *Full-time tuition per academic year 2004–05:* $9.300. *Other fees:* $200.

Financial Aid: Aid from institutionally generated funds is provided on the basis of academic merit, financial need, other considerations.

Departments and Teaching Staff: Biblical studies *associate professors* 2, *assistant professors* 1; theological and historical 0, 1; practical studies 3, 0.

Total instructional faculty: 7. Student-to-faculty ratio: 10:1. Degrees held by full-time faculty: doctorate 72%, master's 28%. 72% hold terminal degrees.

Enrollment: Total enrollment 179 (56.4% men, 43.6% women).

Characteristics of Student Body: *Ethnic/racial makeup:* Black non-Hispanic: 4.5%; Asian or Pacific Islander: 3.9%; Hispanic: 8.9%; White non-Hispanic: 65.9%; unknown: 3.9%.

International Students: 23 nonresident aliens enrolled fall 2004. 4 students from Europe, 2 Asia, 2 Latin America, 15 Canada. Programs available to aid students whose native language is not English: Social, cultural, financial. English as a Second Language Program. Financial aid specifically designated for international students: Variable number of scholarships available annually.

Student Life: On-campus seminary-owned furnished apartments are available. *Special services:* Learning Resources Center, Missions Resource Center. *Student publications: Pipeline,* weekly student information newsletter. *Surrounding community:* Fresno population 460,000. Los Angeles and San Francisco, each about 200 miles from campus, are nearest metropolitan areas. Served by mass transit bus system, airport 4 miles from campus, passenger rail service 3 miles from campus.

Publications: *In Touch,* quarterly newspaper to pastors, supporters, and friends; *Direction,* a semi-scholarly journal, published by the Seminary and several other denominational schools/agencies.

Library Collections: 165,000 volumes including bound books, serial backfiles, electronic documents, and government documents not in separate collections. Online catalog. Current serial subscriptions: 2,115 paper, 5,000 microform. 6,000 recordings. Students have access to the Internet at no charge.

Most important special collection: Anabaptist-Mennonite History.

Buildings and Grounds: Campus area 5 acres.

Chief Executive Officer: Dr. James Holm, President.

Address admission inquiries to Devora Siegel, Director of Admissions.

Mills College

5000 MacArthur Boulevard
Oakland, California 94613
Tel: (510) 430-2255   **E-mail:** admission@mills.edu
Fax: (510) 430-33298   **Internet:** www.mills.edu

Institution Description: Mills College is a private, independent, nonprofit college for women. *Enrollment:* 1,256. Men are admitted to graduate programs. *Degrees awarded:* Baccalaureate, master's, doctorate.

Accreditation: *Regional:* WASC-Sr.

History: Established at Benicia as Young Ladies Seminary 1852; moved to present location 1871; incorporated 1877; chartered as Mills Seminary and College 1885; changed name to Mills College; offered first instruction at postsecondary level 1885; awarded first degree (baccalaureate) 1889; adopted present name 1911. *See* Rosalind A. Keep, *Fourscore and Ten Years Ago: A History of Mills College* (Oakland: Mills College, 1946) for further information.

Institutional Structure: *Governing board:* Board of Trustees of Mills College. Representation: 47 trustees, including 23 alumnae, president of the college. 1 ex officio. All voting. *Composition of institution:* Administrators 2 men / 9 women. Academic affairs headed by dean of the faculty. Management/business/finances directed by vice president and treasurer. Full-time instructional faculty 87 (35 men / 52 women). Academic governance body, The Faculty of Mills College, meets an average of 6 times per year.

Calendar: Semesters. Academic year Aug. to May. Freshmen admitted Sept., Jan. Degrees conferred May, Jan. Formal commencement May. No summer session.

Characteristics of Freshmen: 93% of applicants admitted. 29% of admitted students enrolled full-time.

89% (121 students) submitted SAT scores; 31% (42 students) submitted ACT scores. *25th percentile:* SAT Verbal 540, SAT Math 490, ACT Composite 19. *75th percentile:* SAT Verbal 670, SAT Math 610, ACT Composite 27.

77% of entering freshmen expected to graduate within 5 years. 63% of freshmen from California. Freshmen from 27 states and 3 foreign countries.

Admission: Merit Scholarship and international candidates, as well as those seeking financial aid, should apply by Feb. 15 for fall entrance and Nov. 1 for spring. For first-year students: early action deadline Nov. 15, regular decision for spring semesters Nov. 1; transfer students: California residents Mar. 2, out-of-state Apr. 2; transfer students for spring semester Nov. 1. *Requirements:* Either graduation from accredited secondary school or GED. Recommend college preparatory program with 4 units English, 2–4 foreign language (with at least 2 in one language), 2–4 social science, 3–4 mathematics, 2–4 laboratory science. Interview also recommended. Teacher, school, or employer recommendation forms are required. *Entrance tests:* College Board SAT or ACT composite; Achievement tests highly recommended. *For transfer students:* Up to 2 years of a normal course load are transferable. If fewer than 12 transferable units exist, or if the existing college GPA is lower than 3.0, or if the applicant is younger than 23, an SAT or ACT is required.

College credit and advanced placement for postsecondary-level work completed in secondary school.

Degree Requirements: *Undergraduate:* total 34 course credits, 8 in distribution requirements including the First Year Seminar and a cross/multicultural course; 12 course credits (including senior year) in residence; demonstrated proficiency in English composition.

Fulfillment of some degree requirements and exemption from some beginning courses possible by passing departmental examinations, College Board APP. *Grading system:* A–F; pass/no pass; withdraw (unofficial); incomplete (carries time limit).

Distinctive Educational Programs: *For undergraduates:* Interdisciplinary programs in political, legal, and economic analysis; American civilization; anthropology and sociology; biochemistry; child development; communication; fine arts, general studies; physical science; women's studies. Preprofessional program in allied health fields. Individual majors. Study abroad at various locations through programs of American University of Paris, Antioch University (OH), Beaver College (PA), Boston University (MA), Butler University (IN), Center for Cross-Cultural Study (Spain), Central University of Iowa, Council of International Exchange (CIEE), Denmark's International Study Program, Ehwa Women's University (Korea), Institute for American Universities (France); Kansai Gaidai (Japan), Marymount College (NY), New York University, Northern Illinois University, Salzburg College (Austria), Sarah Lawrence College (NY), School of International Training (VT), Syracuse University (NY), Tel Aviv University (Israel), University of Bath (England), Via Montpellier (France). Semester or year of exchange with University, (TN), Howard University (DC); Agnes Scott and Spelman Colleges (GA); Mount Holyoke, Wellesley, Simmons, and Wheaton Colleges (MA); Manhattanville, and Barnard,. Washington (DC) Semester at American University. Cross-registration with University of California, Berkeley and limited cross-registration with California College of Arts and Crafts; California State University, Hayward; College of Alameda; Holy Names, Merritt, and St. Mary's Colleges; Graduate Theological Seminary.

Available to all students: Internships. Facilities and programs for independent research, including tutorials, independent study. *Other distinctive programs:* English Center for International Women, an intensive, residential program in English as a second language, located on Mills College campus. Women's Leadership Institute sponsors visiting scholars lecture series and conferences. Postbaccalaureate pre-medical program; doctoral program in educational leadership.

Degrees Conferred: 194 *baccalaureate* (B), 155 *master's* (M), 1 *doctorate* (D): area and ethnic studies 21 (B); biological/life sciences 9 (B); business/marketing 3 (B), 13 (M); communications/communication technologies 8 (B); computer and information sciences 5 (B), 4 (M); education 52 (M), 1 (D); English 55 (B), 48 (M); foreign languages and literature 4 (B); home economics and vocational home economics 5 (B); interdisciplinary studies 2 (B); liberal arts/general studies 6 (B), 2 (M); mathematics 5 (B); philosophy/religion/theology 1 (B); physical sciences 3 (B); protective services/public administration 5 (B); psychology 17 (B); social sciences and history 35 (B); visual and performing arts 30 (B), 36 (M).

Fees and Other Expenses: *Full-time tuition per academic year 2004–05:* undergraduate $25,250, graduate (contact the college for current rates). *Required fees:* $1,835 for undergraduate. *Room and board per academic year:* $9,400.

Financial Aid: Aid from institutionally generated funds is awarded on the basis of academic merit, financial need. Institution has a Program Participation Agreement with the U.S. Department of Education for eligible students to receive Pell Grants and other federal aid.

Financial aid to full-time, first-time undergraduate students: need-based scholarships/grants totaling $9,688,325, self-help $5,031,670, parent loans

$833,763, tuition waivers $155,760; non-need-based scholarships/grants totaling $623,215, self-help $402,178, parent loans $123,293, tuition waivers $177,120. *Graduate aid:* 11 students received federal and state-funded fellowship/grants totaling $56,036; 203 federal and state-funded loans totaling $4,409,016; 4 work-study jobs totaling $2,521; 28 other college-assigned jobs (nonteaching, nonresearch) totaling $57,125; 59 other fellowships/grants totaling $1,108,259; 230 teaching assistantships totaling $1,147,500.

Departments and Teaching Staff: *Total instructional faculty:* 154 (full-time 87, part-time 67; women 107, men 47). Total faculty with doctorate, first-professional, or other terminal degree: 110. Student-to-faculty ratio: 11:1.

Enrollment: Total enrollment 1,256 (full-time 1,166, part-time 90).

Characteristics of Student Body: *Ethnic/racial makeup:* number of Black non-Hispanic: 68; American Indian or Alaska Native: 6; Asian or Pacific Islander: 66; Hispanic: 69; White non-Hispanic: 541; unknown: 175. *Age distribution:* number under 18: 17; 18–19: 225, 20–21: 229; 22–24: 99; 25–29: 69; 30–34: 51; 35–39: 28; 40–49: 29; 50–64: 11; 65 and over: 1.

International Students: 37 nonresident aliens enrolled fall 2004. Students from Europe, Asia, Central and South America, Canada. Programs available to aid students whose native language is not English: Social, cultural. No financial aid specifically designated for international students.

Student Life: On-campus residence halls house 79% of student body, including 12% of male graduate students. Residence halls for men only constitute 1% of such space, for women only 99%. 6% of student body live on campus in institutionally-owned and operated apartments. Housing available for married students. *Intercollegiate athletics:* basketball, crew, cross-country, soccer, tennis, volleyball. *Special regulations:* Cars permitted without restrictions. *Special services:* Medical services, limited van service (on campus at night, to and from University of California, Berkeley, during day). *Student publications: Crest,* a yearbook; *Mills College Student Handbook,* an annual publication; *Mills Weekly,* a weekly newspaper; *Walrus,* annual literary magazine. *Surrounding community:* San Francisco-Oakland metropolitan area population over 6 million. Served by mass transit system; airport 3.5 miles from campus; passenger rail service 2 miles from campus.

Library Collections: 241,140 volumes including bound books, serial backfiles, electronic documents, and government documents not in separate collections. Online catalog. Current serial subscriptions: 3,160 paper, 28,324 microforms. 2,500 via electronic access. 2,640 recordings. 267 computer work stations. Students have access to the Internet at no charge.

Most important holdings include Jane Bourne Parton Dance Collection (materials on ballet, ballroom, and modern dance from 16th century to present, including some rare books); Darius Milhaud Music Collection (scores and recordings of the music of the 20th-century French composer, including some manuscripts); Albert Bender Collection (approximately 1,000 books in literary first editions and printing history); Oakland Oral Histories; Aurelia Hnery Reinhardt Collection on Women's History.

Buildings and Grounds: Campus area 135 acres.

Chief Executive Officer: Dr. Janet L. Holmgren, President.

Address undergraduate admission inquiries to Julie Richardson, Vice President for Enrollment Management; graduate admission inquiries to Marianne Sheldon, Director of Graduate Studies.

Monterey Institute of International Studies

480 Pierce Street
Monterey, California 93940

Tel: (831) 647-4100   **E-mail:** admit@miis.edu
Fax: (831) 647-4199   **Internet:** www.miis.edu

Institution Description: The Monterey Institute of International Studies is a private, independent, nonprofit institution providing upper division and master's degree study only. *Enrollment:* 776. *Degrees awarded:* Baccalaureate, master's.

Accreditation: *Regional:* WASC. *Professional:* business

History: Established and chartered in 1955.

Institutional Structure: *Governing board:* Board of Trustees of Monterey Institute of International Studies. *Composition of institution:* Full-time instructional faculty 64. Academic governance body, Faculty Assembly, meets an average of 6 times per year.

Calendar: Semesters. Academic year Sept. to May. Degrees conferred May, Aug., Dec. Formal commencement Dec. and May. Summer semester mid-June to mid-Aug.

Admission: *Requirements:* Successful completion of 2 or more years of study at an accredited college or university. Minimum GPA 3.0. *Entrance tests:* GMAT required for graduate students. *For transfer students:* 3.0 minimum GPA, 2 years foreign language.

Degree Requirements: *Undergraduate:* 120 semester hours; 2.0 GPA; 1 year in residence; distribution requirements. *Graduate:* 32 to 64 units; 3.0 GPA.

Distinctive Educational Programs: Foreign study opportunities include programs in cooperation with U.S. colleges and foreign colleges and businesses. Custom Language Services Program offers intensive tutorials in many languages.

Degrees Conferred: 626 *baccalaureate:* social sciences and history; 313 *master's:* business 65, education 47; environmental science 28, foreign languages 61; public administration 17, social sciences and history 95.

Fees and Other Expenses: *Full-time tuition per academic year 2004–05:* $23,900.

Financial Aid: Institution has a Program Participation Agreement with the U.S. Department of Education for eligible students to receive Pell Grants and other federal aid.

Departments and Teaching Staff: *Total instructional faculty:* 64. 95% hold terminal degrees.

Enrollment: Total enrollment 776. Undergraduate 7 (57.1% men, 42.9% women); graduate 769.

Characteristics of Student Body: *Ethnic/racial makeup:* number of Black non-Hispanic: 15; Asian or Pacific Islander: 14; Hispanic: 15; White non-Hispanic: 313; unknown: 36.

International Students: 286 nonresident aliens enrolled fall 204. 42% of student body represent 51 counties. Social and cultural programs available to aid students whose native language is not English, including English as a Second Language Program.

Student Life: No on-campus housing. Campus newspaper; literary magazine. *Surrounding community:* Monterey population 35,000. San Jose, 70 miles from campus, is nearest metropolitan area. Served by mass transit bus system, airport 3 miles from campus, passenger rail service 20 miles from campus.

Library Collections: 80,000 volumes including bound books, serial backfiles, electronic documents, and government documents not in separate collections. Online catalog. Computer work stations available. Students have access to the Internet at no charge.

Buildings and Grounds: Small urban campus.

Chief Executive Officer: Dr. Steven J. Baker, President.

Address all admission inquiries to Dennis Johnson, Vice President for Enrollment.

Mount St. Mary's College

12001 Chalon Road
Los Angeles, California 90049-1599

Tel: (310) 954-4000   **E-mail:** admissions@msmc.la.edu
Fax: (310) 954-4019   **Internet:** www.msmc.la.edu

Institution Description: Mount St. Mary's College is a private, nonprofit institution conducted by the Los Angeles Province of the Sisters of St. Joseph of Carondelet, Roman Catholic Church. The school has 2 campuses, Chalon and Doheny. Baccalaureate programs are offered at Chalon, the main campus. Associate degree programs, as well as graduate and teacher credential programs, are offered at Doheny. A Doctor of Physical Therapy is also offered at the Doheny campus. *Enrollment:* 2,257. Men are admitted to the undergraduate music and nursing programs and to all graduate programs. *Degrees awarded:* Associate, baccalaureate, master's.

Accreditation: *Regional:* WASC-Sr. *Professional:* music, nursing, nursing education, physical therapy

History: Established, chartered, and offered first instruction at postsecondary level 1925; awarded first degree (baccalaureate) 1929; added graduate level 1932.

Institutional Structure: *Governing board:* Board of Trustees. Extrainstitutional representation: 14 trustees, including 2 regents; institutional representation: 1 administrator. 2 ex officio. All voting. *Composition of institution:* Administrators 9 men / 21 women Academic affairs headed by dean for academic development. Management/business/finances directed by director of business and finance. Full-time instructional faculty 102 FTE. Academic governance body, Faculty Assembly, meets an average of 5 times per year.

Calendar: Semesters. Academic year Aug. to May. Freshmen admitted Sept., Jan., Feb. Degrees conferred May, Aug., Dec. Formal commencement May. Summer session from mid-June to late July.

Characteristics of Freshmen: 87% (169 students) submitted SAT scores; 13% (25 students) submitted ACT scores. *25th percentile:* SAT Verbal 470, SAT Math 450. *75th percentile:* SAT Verbal 550, SAT Math 540.

96% of freshmen from California. Freshmen from 23 states.

Admission: Rolling admissions plan. For fall acceptance, apply as early as senior year in secondary school, but not later than Aug. 1. Students are notified of acceptance beginning Nov. 15. *Requirements:* For associate and baccalaureate programs, graduation from accredited secondary school. For baccalaureate, 4 units English; 2 in a foreign language; 1 each in algebra, geometry, government, U.S. history, laboratory science; an advanced course in a foreign language, mathematics, or science. Additional requirements for some programs. Minimum GPA 3.0 for baccalaureate. *Entrance tests:* College Board SAT or ACT composite. For foreign students, minimum TOEFL score 550. *For transfer students:* 2.25 minimum GPA; from 4-year accredited institution 105 hours maximum transfer credit; from 2-year accredited institutions 66 hours.

College credit for postsecondary-level work completed in secondary school and for extrainstitutional learning on basis of ACE *2006 Guide to the Evaluation of Educational Experiences in the Armed Services* and portfolio assessment. Tutoring available. Learning assistance program offered in summer session and regular academic year; credit given for some courses.

Degree Requirements: *For all associate degrees:* 60 credit hours. *For most baccalaureate degrees:* 124 hours; exit competency examinations or program in writing. *For all undergraduate degrees:* 2.0 GPA; last 24 units in residence. *Grading system:* A–F; credit-no credit; withdraw.

Fulfillment of some degree requirements possible by passing departmental examinations, College Board CLEP or AP.

Distinctive Educational Programs: *For undergraduates:* Work-experience programs. Off-campus centers for Evening College at various locations in Los Angeles area. Study abroad for semester or academic year. *For graduate students:* Weekend classes. *Available to all students:* Evening classes. Interdepartmental or interdisciplinary programs. Facilities and programs for independent research, including individual majors, tutorials. Off-campus study at Avila College (MO), The College of St. Catherine (MN), The College of Saint Rose (NY), Fontbonne College (MO), Regis College (MA).

Degrees Conferred: 147 *associate;* 307 *baccalaureate* (B), 51 *master's* (M): biological/life sciences 16 (B); business/marketing 37 (B); education 26 (B); 25 (M); English 16 (B); foreign languages and literature 1 (B); health professions and related sciences 84 (B), 10 (M); liberal arts/general studies 34 (B); mathematics 1 (B); philosophy, religion, theology 2 (B); psychology 32 (B), 6 (M); social sciences and history 47 (B); visual and performing arts 2 (B), 10 (M).

Fees and Other Expenses: *Full-time tuition per academic year 2005–06:* undergraduate $22,054; graduate study charged per unit (contact the college for current rate). *Required fees:* $770. *Room and board per academic year:* $8,492.

Financial Aid: Aid from institutionally generated funds is provided on the basis of academic merit, financial need. Institution has a Program Participation Agreement with the U.S. Department of Education for eligible students to receive Pell Grants and other federal aid.

Departments and Teaching Staff: *Total instructional faculty:* 287 (full-time 70, part-time 217; women 216, men 71). Total faculty with doctorate, first-professional, or other terminal degree: 71. Student-to-faculty ratio: 19:1.

Enrollment: Total enrollment 2,257 (full-time 1,634, part-time 623).

Characteristics of Student Body: *Ethnic/racial makeup:* number of Black non-Hispanic: 189; American Indian or Alaska Native: 11; Asian or Pacific Islander: 316; Hispanic: 832; White non-Hispanic: 268; unknown: 183.

International Students: 5 nonresident aliens enrolled fall 2004. No programs available to aid students whose native language is not English. No financial aid specifically designated for international students.

Student Life: On-campus residence halls house 50% of student body. Dormitories for women only constitute 97% of such space. *Special regulations:* Cars permitted without restrictions. Quiet hours from 10pm to 8am Mon.–Thurs., 9pm to 8am Sun. Residence hall visitation from 10am to midnight Mon.-Thurs., 10am to 2:00am Fri.–Sun. *Special services:* Learning Resources Center, medical services, shuttle bus service between the 2 campuses. *Student publications: The View,* a monthly newspaper; *Westwords,* a quarterly literary magazine. *Surrounding community:* Los Angeles metropolitan area population 7,500,000. Served by mass transit bus and rail systems; airport and passenger rail service each 20 miles from campus.

Library Collections: 160,000 volumes. 100 microform titles; 700 current periodical subscriptions. 3,125 audiovisual materials. Online catalog. Students have access to information retrieval services and the Internet.

Most important holdings include John Henry Neman Collection; Mills Sheet Music Collection.

Buildings and Grounds: Campus area 71 acres.

Chief Executive Officer: Dr. Jacqueline Powers Doud, President.

Address admission inquiries to Dean Kilgour, Director of Admissions.

National University

11255 North Torrey Pines Road
La Jolla, California 92037-1011

Tel: (800) 628-8648   **E-mail:** advisor@nu.edu
Fax: (858) 642-8709   **Internet:** www.nu.edu

Institution Description: National University is a private, independent, nonprofit institution focused on the working adult. The university is an affiliate of the National University System. *Enrollment:* 10,251 men / 15,433 women. *Degrees awarded:* Associate, baccalaureate, master's;. Certificates are also awarded.

Accreditation: *Regional:* WASC-Sr. *Professional:* business, nursing

History: Founded in 1971 to serve the needs of diverse group of students who were then labeled as nontraditional; offered instruction at postsecondary level 1971; awarded first degree (baccalaureate) 1972.

Institutional Structure: *Governing board:* Board of Trustees. Extrainstitutional representation: 25 trustees. Academic affairs headed by provost/vice president for academic affairs. Administration head by chancellor, lead by president and managed by eight vice presidents and 14 regional deans. Total instructional faculty 2,205.

Calendar: The university offers education through a one-course-per month format.

Characteristics of Freshmen: 71% of entering freshmen expected to graduate within 5 years. 94% of freshmen from California. Freshmen from 35 states and 76 foreign countries.

Admission: Rolling admissions plan. Qualified applicants can begin classes any month of the year, depending on course offerings at their chosen learning facility. Admission is based on the student's academic record at other institutions, test scores, interviews, professional experience, motivation, and educational objectives. *Requirements:* Graduation from an accredited secondary school or GED with a 2.0 GPA and interview with an admissions counselor. *Entrance tests:* English and math tests available. *For transfer students:* 2.0 minimum GPA; 135 quarter hours maximum transfer credit from a 4-year accredited institution; 103.5 quarter hours from a 2-year accredited institution; extension students 36 quarter hours of maximum transfer credit.

College credit and advanced placement for extrainstitutional learning on basis of ACE *2006 Guide to the Evaluation of Educational Experiences in the Armed Services,* portfolio, and faculty assessments. Tutoring available.

Degree Requirements: *For all associate degrees:* 90 quarter hours; 31.5 units in residence. *For all baccalaureate degrees:* 180 quarter hours with 45 units in residence. Graduate degrees require the completion of 45–54 quarter units. Students must earn a minimum of 40.5 quarter units at National University and complete half of the field of study and three-fourths of the area of specialization in residence.

Fulfillment of some degree requirements and exemption from some beginning courses possible by passing departmental examinations. College Board CLEP. *Grading system:* A–F; withdraw (carries time limit).

Distinctive Educational Programs: Campuses in 18 major metropolitan areas in California, including locations in San Diego, San Bernardino, Los Angeles, Ventura, Kern, Fresno, San Joaquin, Santa Clara, Sacramento, and Shasta counties.

ROTC: Army and Navy in cooperation with San Diego State University and the University of San Diego.

Degrees Conferred: 35 *associate;* 1,195 *baccalaureate* (B), 7,689 *master's* (M): business/marketing 320 (B); 403 (M); communications/communication technologies 4 (B); computer and information sciences 186 (B), 28 (M); education 6,813; engineering and engineering technologies 603 (M); English 2 (B); health professions and related sciences 5 (B), 5 (M); interdisciplinary studies 298 (B); law/legal studies 12 (B); liberal arts/general studies 100 (B); mathematics 12, physical sciences 1 (B); protective services/public administration 112 (B), 173 (M); psychology 100 (B), 201 (M); trade and industry 1 (B); visual and performing arts 1 (M).

Fees and Other Expenses: *Full-time tuition per academic year 2004–05:* undergraduate $7,960, graduate $10,125.

Financial Aid: Aid from institutionally generated funds is provided on the basis of academic merit, financial need.

Financial aid to full-time, first-time undergraduate students: need-based scholarships/grants totaling $5,371,743, self-help $36,593,095, parent loans $318,603. *Graduate aid:* 4,873 students received federal and state-funded loans totaling $78,875,795.

Departments and Teaching Staff: *Total instructional faculty:* 2,208 (full-time 210, part-time 1,995; women 1,018, men 1,187). Total faculty with doctorate, first-professional, or other terminal degree 720. Student-to-faculty ratio: 17:1.

Enrollment: Total enrollment 25,684. Undergraduate full-time, part-time 17,192.

Characteristics of Student Body: *Ethnic/racial makeup:* number of Black non-Hispanic: 754; American Indian or Alaska Native: 58; Asian or Pacific Islander: 509; Hispanic: 104; White non-Hispanic: 2,982; unknown: 354. *Age distribution:* number under 18: 6; 18–19: 138; 20–21: 458; 22–24: 928; 25–29: 1,521; 30–34: 1,070, 735–39: 715; 40–49: 818; 50–64: 165; 65 and over: 1.

International Students: 196 nonresident aliens enrolled fall 2004. Students from Europe, Asia, Central and South America, Africa, Canada. Social and cultural programs available to aid students whose native language is not English. English as a Second Language Program available. No financial aid specifically designated for international students.

Student Life: Classes are offered in an evening-based one-course-per month format. No on-campus housing.

Library Collections: 220,518 volumes including bound books, serial backfiles, electronic documents, and government documents not in separate collections. Online and card catalogs. Current serial subscriptions: 1,573 paper, 589 microform, 11,973 electronic. 96 computer work stations. Students have access to the Internet at no charge. Total budget for books, periodicals, audiovisual materials, microforms 2004–05: $2,248,877.

Most important holdings include collections in business, law, and education (adult learner).

Buildings and Grounds: In 2005, new centers opened in Camarillo (CA) and Ontario (CA).

Chief Executive Officer: Dr. Jerry C. Lee, President.

Address admission inquiries to Megan Magee, Association Regional Dean, San Diego.

Notre Dame de Namur University

1500 Ralston Avenue
Belmont, California 94002-1908

Tel: (650) 508-3500   **E-mail:** admiss@ndmu.edu
Fax: (650) 508-3736   **Internet:** www.ndmu.edu

Institution Description: Notre Dame de Namur University, formerly known as College of Notre Dame, is a private, independent, nonprofit college affiliated with the Sisters of Notre Dame de Namur, Roman Catholic Church. *Enrollment:* 1,798. *Degrees offered:* Baccalaureate, master's.

Accreditation: *Regional:* WASC-Sr. *Professional*: music

History: Established as a women's college 1851; chartered 1868; offered first instruction at postsecondary level 1916; awarded first degree (baccalaureate) 1953; became coeducational 1969.

Institutional Structure: *Governing board:* Governance Board. Extrainstitutional representation: 15 trustees, 12 regents; institutional representation: 1 administrator, 3 full-time instructional faculty members, 1 student. All voting. *Composition of institution:* Administrators 3 men / 4 women. Academic affairs headed by Dean of Academic Administration. Dean of Faculty and Graduate Dean. Management/business/finances directed by Vice President of Finance and Administrative Services. Full-time instructional faculty 44. Academic governance body, Curriculum Committee, meets an average of 8 times per year.

Calendar: Semesters. Academic year Aug. to May. Freshmen and transfers admitted on a rolling basis Aug., Jan. Degrees conferred May, Aug., Dec. Formal commencement May.

Characteristics of Freshmen: 706 applicants fall 2004 (234 men, 472 women). 84.1% of applicants admitted; 27.3% of admitted students enrolled full-time.

87% (143 students) submitted SAT scores; 26% (43 students) submitted ACT scores. *25th percentile*: SAT Verbal 440, SAT Math 440; ACT Composite 18. *75th percentile*: SAT Verbal 550, SAT Math 550; ACT Composite 200.

45.7% of entering freshmen freshmen expected to graduate within 5 years. 69% of freshmen from California. Freshmen from 13 states and 19 foreign countries.

Admission: Rolling admissions plan. For fall acceptance, apply as early as Sept. 1 of previous year, but not later than Aug. 1 of year of enrollment. *Requirements:* Graduation from accredited secondary school. Recommend 4 units English, 2–3 in a foreign language, 2–3 mathematics, 2 social studies, 1 fine arts, 1 laboratory science, 2 units of advanced coursework; Minimum GPA 2.5. *Entrance tests:* College Board SAT preferred; ACT composite accepted. For foreign students TOEFL or SAT. *For transfer students:* 2.0 minimum GPA, 90 semester hours maximum transfer credit; from accredited 2-year institution 78 hours.

College credit and advanced placement for postsecondary-level work completed in secondary school. Tutoring available.

Degree Requirements: *For all baccalaureate degrees:* 124 credit hours; 24 hours in residence. *For all undergraduate degrees:* 2.0 GPA; distribution requirements.

Fulfillment of some degree requirements and exemption from some beginning courses possible by passing departmental examinations, College Board CLEP, AP. *Grading system:* A–F; pass-not pass; incomplete (carries time limit).

Distinctive Educational Programs: Several specialized majors not generally available in the small college environment include interior design, art therapy, communications, studio art (BFA) and music performance; liberal studies; cooperative education internships; exchange program with SND colleges in Washington (DC) and Boston; study abroad opportunities, and intensive evening programs for employed adults.

Degrees Conferred: 257 *baccalaureate*; 230 *master's*. Bachelor's degrees awarded in top five disciplines: business, management, marketing, and related support services 89; liberal arts and sciences, general studies and humanities 37; public administration and social service professions 31; psychology 27; biological and biomedical sciences 17.

Fees and Other Expenses: *Full-time tuition per academic year 2004–05:* undergraduate $21.500. *Books and supplies:* $1,250. *Room and board per academic year:* $9,630.

Financial Aid: Aid from institutionally generated funds is provided on the basis of academic merit, financial need. Institution has a Program Participation Agreement with the U.S. Department of Education for eligible students to receive Pell Grants and other federal aid.

Financial aid to full-time, first-time undergraduate students: 33% received federal grants averaging $3,948; 21% state/local grants averaging $6,530; 78% institutional grants averaging $10,674; 66% loans averaging $4,184.

Departments and Teaching Staff: *Professors* 21, *associate professors* 22, *assistant professors* 16, *instructors* 2, *part-time teachers* 132.

Total full-time instructional faculty: 61. Total tenured faculty: 27. Degrees held by full-time faculty: doctorate 79%, master's 20%; professional 1%. 92% hold terminal degrees.

Enrollment: Total enrollment 1,798. Undergraduate 988 (32.5% men, 67.5% women).

Characteristics of Student Body: *Ethnic/racial makeup:* Black non-Hispanic: 6.7%; American Indian or Alaska Native: 1.2%; Asian or Pacific Islander: 14.2%; Hispanic: 17.4%, White non-Hispanic: 45.6%; unknown: 10.5%.

International Students: 43 nonresident aliens enrolled fall 2004. Programs available to aid students whose native language is not English: English as a Second Language Program. No financial aid specifically designated for international students.

Student Life: On-campus residence halls and apartments house 49% of student body. *Intercollegiate athletics:* men only: soccer; women only: softball, volleyball; men and women: cross-country, basketball, tennis. NCAA Division II, ranked in top ten in country. *Special regulations:* Cars permitted without restrictions. *Special services:* Medical services. *Student publications: Argonaut,* a bimonthly newspaper; *Cat's Feet,* a biannual literary magazine; *Surrounding community:* Belmont population 30,000. San Francisco; 25 miles from campus, is nearest metropolitan area. Served by mass transit system; airport 10 miles from campus; passenger rail service 1 mile from campus.

Publications: Sources of information about Notre Dame de Namur University can be found in the *NDMU News.*

Library Collections: 108,000 volumes. 69,000 microforms; 8,000 audiovisual materials; 750 current periodical subscriptions. Students have access to the Internet at no charge.

Most important holdings include Archives of Modern Christian Art; Californiana; Letters from Writers between World War I and World War II Collection.

Buildings and Grounds: Campus area 80 acres.

Chief Executive Officer: Dr. John B. Oblak, President.

Address admission inquiries to Richard Scaffidi, Director of Admissions.

Occidental College

1600 Campus Road
Los Angeles, California 90041-3392

Tel: (323) 259-2500   **E-mail:** admission@oxy.edu
Fax: (323) 341-2958   **Internet:** www.oxy.edu

Institution Description: Occidental College is a private, independent, nonprofit college. *Enrollment:* 1,858. *Degrees awarded:* Baccalaureate, master's.

Accreditation: *Regional:* WASC-Sr. *Professional*: chemistry

History: Established and incorporated as the Occidental University 1887; offered first instruction at postsecondary level 1888; awarded first degree (baccalaureate) 1893. *See* Andrew F. Rolle, *Occidental College: The First Seventy-*

Five Years—1887–1962 (Los Angeles: Anderson, Ritchie and Simon, 1962) for further information.

Institutional Structure: *Governing board:* Board of Trustees of Occidental College. Extrainstitutional representation: 30 trustees; institutional representation: president of the college; 5 alumni. 1 ex officio. 32 voting. *Composition of institution:* Administrators 13 men / 13 women. Academic affairs headed by dean of the faculty and vice president for academic affairs. Management/business/finances directed by executive vice president. Full-time instructional faculty 135. Academic governance body, Faculty of Occidental College, meets an average of 10 times per year.

Calendar: Semesters. Academic year Sept. to May. Freshmen admitted Aug. Degrees conferred June, July, Aug., Dec., Mar. Formal commencement June. Summer sessions from June to Aug.

Characteristics of Freshmen: 4,836 applicants (2,042 men, 2,794 women). 44.9% of applicants admitted; 22.9% of admitted students enrolled full-time.

84% (415 students) submitted SAT scores; 16% (81 students) submitted ACT scores. *25th percentile*: SAT Verbal 590, SAT Math 580; ACT Composite 27. *75th percentile*: SAT Verbal 690, SAT Math 670; ACT Composite 31.

77% of entering freshmen expected to graduate within 5 years. 60% of freshmen from California. Freshmen from 47 states and 45 foreign countries.

Admission: For fall acceptance, apply as early as Sept. of senior year, but not later than Jan. 15. Students are notified of acceptance Apr. For early decision, apply by Nov. 15 for Dec. 15 notification; must limit application to Occidental College. *Requirements:* Either graduation from accredited secondary school with 4 units English, 3 foreign language (preferably in 1 language), 3 mathematics, 3 social studies, 2 biological and physical sciences; or GED. *Entrance tests:* College Board SAT or ACT composite. For foreign students minimum TOEFL score 600. *For transfer students:* 3.0 minimum GPA, 18 courses maximum transfer credit.

College credit and advanced placement for postsecondary-level work completed in secondary school. Tutoring available.

Degree Requirements: *Undergraduate:* 128 credits; 2.0 GPA; 4 semesters in residence; core curriculum; demonstration of competence in a foreign language; satisfaction of writing proficiency requirement; comprehensives in individual fields of study.

Fulfillment of some degree requirements and exemption from some beginning courses possible by passing departmental examinations or College Board APP. *Grading system:* A–F; withdraw (carries deadline after which pass-fail is appended to withdraw); credit-no credit.

Distinctive Educational Programs: *For undergraduates:* Dual-degree programs in engineering with the California Institute of Technology and Columbia University (NY); in law with Columbia University. Interdepartmental/interdisciplinary programs in American studies; Asian studies, biochemistry, comparative literature, diplomacy and world affairs, geochemistry, geophysics, Hispanic/Latin American studies, religious studies, women's studies; the Collegium program (intensive study of an annually selected interdisciplinary topic). Facilities and programs for independent research, including honors programs, individual majors. Institutionally sponsored study abroad China, Costa Rica, England, France, Germany, Hungary, Italy, Japan, Mexico, Nepal, Russia, Spain, Taiwan, Turkey, and Zimbabwe. Competitive international fellowships available to support independent study projects. Cross-registration with California Institute of Technology, Art Center College of Design, and with institutions cooperating in Southern California Conference on International Studies. *Available to all students:* Facilities and programs for independent research, including tutorials, independent study, and independent study combined with field experience or academic internship.

ROTC: Army, Air Force offered in cooperation with University of California, Los Angeles; University of Southern California.

Degrees Conferred: 459 *baccalaureate*; 16 *master's*. Bachelor's degrees awarded in top five disciplines: social sciences 143; psychology 58; visual and performing arts 46; biological and biomedical sciences 39; English language and literature/letters 34.

Fees and Other Expenses: *Full-time tuition per academic year 2004–05:* $29,485. *Room and board per academic year:* $8,230. *Books and supplies:* $914. *Other expenses:* $1,596.

Financial Aid: Aid from institutionally generated funds is awarded on the basis of academic merit, financial need. Institution has a Program Participation Agreement with the U.S. Department of Education for eligible students to receive Pell Grants and other federal aid.

Financial aid to full-time, first-time undergraduate students: 25% received federal grants averaging $2,707; 19% state/local grants averaging $3,772; 66% institutional grants averaging $16,310; 52% loans averaging $3,579.

Departments and Teaching Staff: *Professors* 58, *associate professors* 41, *assistant professors* 30, *instructors* 12, *part-time faculty* 58.

Total instructional faculty: 199. Student-to-faculty ratio: 10:1. Degrees held by full-time faculty: Doctorate 92.8%, master's 6.5%, baccalaureate .7%. 97.1% hold terminal degrees.

Enrollment: Total enrollment 1,858. Undergraduate 1,840 (41.9% men, 58.1% women).

Characteristics of Student Body: *Ethnic/racial makeup:* Black non-Hispanic: 6.9%; American Indian or Alaska Native: 1.1%; Asian or Pacific Islander: 12.1%; Hispanic: 15.1%; White non-Hispanic: 54.5%; unknown: 6.2%.

International Students: 75 nonresident aliens enrolled 2003. Students from Europe, Asia, Africa, Canada, Mexico, Middle East. No programs to aid students whose native language is not English. No financial aid specifically designated for international students.

Student Life: On-campus residence halls house 70% of student body. Coed dormitories constitute 99% of such space, for women only 1%. 11% of men join and 5% live in fraternities; 11% of women join and 4% live in sororities. *Intercollegiate athletics:* men only: baseball, basketball, football, golf, soccer, swimming, tennis, track and cross-country, water polo; women only: basketball, golf, soccer, softball, swimming, tennis, track and field, cross-country, volleyball. *Special regulations:* Cars permitted without restrictions. Quiet hours from midnight to 7am. *Special services:* Medical services, shuttle bus to airport and to cultural and shopping centers. *Student publications: La Encina*, a yearbook; *The Occidental*, a weekly newspaper; *Surrounding community:* Los Angeles population over 3,000,000. Served by mass transit bus system; airport 25 miles from campus; passenger rail service 9 miles from campus.

Publications: Sources of information about Occidental include *Occidental College Magazine.*

Library Collections: 497,000 volumes. 318,600 government documents; 413,190 microforms. 17,500 audiovisual materials. 903 current serial subscriptions. Online catalog. Students have access to the Internet at no charge.

Most important holdings include Guymon Collection (17,000 British and American detective and mystery novels and related critical and historical works); Robinson Jeffers Collection (1,000 original manuscripts, galley proofs, letters, and books by and about Jeffers); Risdon Lincoln Collection (3,140 Lincoln and Civil War items, including books, pamphlets, and memorabilia of the period).

Buildings and Grounds: Campus area 120 acres.

Chief Executive Officer: Dr. Theodore Reed Mitchell, President.

Address admission inquiries to Vincent Cusio, Director of Admissions.

Otis College of Art and Design

9045 Lincoln Boulevard
Los Angeles, California 90045
Tel: (310) 665-6800   **E-mail:** admissions@otis.edu
Fax: (310) 665-6821   **Internet:** www.otis.edu

Institution Description: Otis College of Art and Design is a private, independent, nonprofit institution. *Degrees awarded:* Baccalaureate, master's. *Enrollment:* 1,043.

Accreditation: *Regional:* WASC-Sr. *Professional:* art

History: Established as part of the Art Division of the Los Angeles County Museum of History, Science and Art 1918; chartered and incorporated as Los Angeles County Art Institute 1947; offered first instruction at postsecondary level 1954; awarded first degree (master's) 1956; began upper division baccalaureate program 1965; began lower division baccalaureate program 1978; merged with Parsons School of Design and adopted name Otis Art Institute of Parson School of Design 1979; separated from the New School for Social Research and became and independent, private, nonprofit institution in 1994.

Institutional Structure: *Governing board:* Board of Trustees. *Composition of institution:* Administrators 16 men / 15 women. Academic affairs headed by vice president of academic affairs. Management/business/finances directed by vice president of administration and finance. Academic governance body, Academic Assembly, meets 9 times per year.

Calendar: Semesters. Academic year Aug. to May. Freshmen admitted Aug., Jan. Degrees conferred May, Jan. Formal commencement May. Limited summer session for January freshmen, summer session in continuing education.

Characteristics of Freshmen: 695 applicants. 406 students admitted; 121 students enrolled.

79% (96 students) submitted SAT scores; 10% (12 students) submitted ACT scores. *25th percentile*: SAT Verbal 420, SAT Math 440, ACT Composite 17. *75th percentile*: SAT Verbal 550; SAT Math 580; ACT Composite 22.

28% of entering freshmen expected to graduate within 5 years.

Admission: Rolling admissions plan. *Requirements:* Either graduation from accredited secondary school or GED; portfolio; essay required. *Entrance tests:* College Board SAT or ACT composite. For foreign students TOEFL. *For transfer students:* 2.5 minimum GPA; 63 semester hours maximum transfer credit. College credit and advanced placement for postsecondary-level work completed in secondary school.

Degree Requirements: *For all baccalaureate degrees:* 134 hours; art history requirement; liberal arts requirement. *For all degrees:* 2.0 GPA. 4 terms in residence. *Grading system:* A–F; W (withdrawal with no penalty); UW (withdrawal after deadline, equivalent to failing grade).

Distinctive Educational Programs: Cross-registration with consortium. Summer courses for college credit offered to high school students. Evening and weekend courses offered on credit and noncredit basis for part-time study.

Degrees Conferred: 172 *baccalaureate*; 11 *master's*.

Fees and Other Expenses: *Full-time tuition per academic year 2004–05:* $24,500. *Required fees:* $600.

Financial Aid: Aid from institutionally generated funds is provided on the basis of academic merit, financial need. Institution has a Program Participation Agreement with the U.S. Department of Education for eligible students to receive Pell Grants and other federal aid.

Financial aid to full-time, first-time undergraduate students: need-based scholarships/grants totaling $7,169,324, self-help $4,566,469, parent loans $1,604,644; non-need-based scholarships/grants totaling $378,108, self-help $315,400, parent loans $237,530.

Departments and Teaching Staff: *Total instructional faculty:* 235 (full-time 43, part-time 192; women 113, men 122). Student-to-faculty ratio: 8.36:1. Total faculty with doctorate, first-professional, or other terminal degree: 92.

Enrollment: *Total enrollment* 1,043. Undergraduate full-time 335 men / 653 women, part-time 3m / 6w; graduate full-time 9m / 24w, part-time 4m / 9w.

Characteristics of Student Body: *Ethnic/racial makeup:* number of Black non-Hispanic: 28; American Indian or Alaska Native: 7; Asian or Pacific Islander: 290; Hispanic: 124; White non-Hispanic: 320; unknown: 108.

International Students: 120 nonresident aliens enrolled fall 2004. Students from Europe, Asia, Central and South America, Canada. No programs available to aid students whose native language is not English. No financial aid specifically designated for international students.

Student Life: *Special regulations:* Cars with parking permit allowed. *Surrounding community:* Los Angeles population over 3,000,000. Served by mass transit bus system; Los Angeles International airport 2 miles from campus.

Publications: *Otis Magazine*, published annually.

Library Collections: 40,000 volumes. 75,000 audiovisual materials; 150 current periodical subscriptions. Online catalog. Computer work stations available.

Most important holdings include special collections of artist's books, rare and out-of print books.

Buildings and Grounds: The college has 3 campuses in the Los Angeles area.

Chief Executive Officer: Samuel Hoi, President.

Address admission inquiries to Marc D. Meredith, Director of Admissions.
billb

Pacific Graduate School of Psychology

935 East Meadow Drive
Palo Alto, California 94303
Tel: (650) 494-7477   **E-mail:** admissions@pgsp.edu
Fax: (650) 493-6147   **Internet:** www.pgsp.edu

Institution Description: Pacific Graduate School of Psychology is a private, independent, nonprofit institution. *Enrollment:* 332. *Degrees awarded:* Master's, doctorate.

Accreditation: *Regional:* WASC-Sr. *Professional*; clinical psychology

History: Established and incorporated 1975; offered first instruction at postsecondary level 1976; adopted present official name, Pacific Graduate School of Psychology, Professional Doctoral Studies, 1978; awarded first degree (doctorate) 1979.

Calendar: Academic year Sept. to Aug.

Admission: Application due Jan. 15 of year of enrollment for those who want to be considered for a PGSP fellowship. Applications received after that date are accepted and reviewed on a space available basis. *Requirements:* Baccalaureate in any field; prerequisites in abnormal psychology or personality theory; development psychology; physiological psychology; statistics; GRE; letters of reference and written statements.

Degree Requirements: 150 quarter hours; grade of pass or B- or above in courses; dissertation; oral and written comprehensive examinations; qualifying examination; 2,000 hours of internship. *Grading system:* A to B-.

Distinctive Educational Programs: *For graduate students:* Ph.D. in clinical psychology; Ph.D./J.D. program with Golden Gate University; Ph.D./MBA program with University of San Francisco McClaren School of Business; Forensic Psychology Graduate Proficiency certificate program.

Degrees Conferred: 67 *master's:* psychology; 43 *doctorate:* psychology.

Fees and Other Expenses: *Full-time tuition per academic year 2004–05:* $29,194.

Financial Aid: Aid from institutionally generated funds is provided on the basis of academic merit, financial need, other considerations. *Institutional funding for graduates:* 248 federal and state-funded loans totaling $6,398,915 (ranging from $8,500 to F$31,000), 51 federal and state-funded loans totaling $132,365 (ranging from $1,000 to $8,000); 35 teaching assistantships totaling $45,000 (ranging from $750 to $1,000); 11 research assistantships totaling $16,500 (ranging from $1,000 to $2,500).

Departments and Teaching Staff: Psychology *professors* 5, *associate professors* 4, *assistant professors* 5, *instructors* 14, *part-time faculty* 22.

Total instructional faculty: 50 (full-time 15, part-time 22; women 19, men 13). Total faculty with doctorate, first-professional, or other terminal degree 35.

Enrollment: Total enrollment 332. Graduate full-time 68 men / 240 women, part-time 3m / 21w.

Characteristics of Student Body: *Ethnic/racial makeup:* number of Black non-Hispanic: 17; American Indian or Alaska Native: 2; Asian or Pacific Islander: 42; Hispanic: 24; White non-Hispanic: 196; unknown: 38. *Age distribution:* number of 22–24: 46; 25–29: 29; 30–34: 71; 35–39: 33; 40–49: 32; 50–64: 12; 65 and over: 9.

International Students: 14 nonresident aliens enrolled fall 2004. 1 student from Europe, 4 Asia, 2 Central and South America, 1 Canada, 6 other. No programs available to aid students whose native language is not English. No financial aid specifically designated for international students.

Student Life: No on-campus housing. *Surrounding community:* San Francisco metropolitan area population over 3 million. Served by mass transit bus, train systems; airport 20 miles from campus; passenger rail service 1 mile from campus.

Library Collections: 8,303 volumes including bound books, serial backfiles, electronic documents, and government documents not in separate collections. Online catalog. Current serial subscriptions: 110 paper, 849 via electronic access. 10 computer work stations. Students have access to the Internet at no charge. Total budget for books, periodicals, audiovisual materials, microforms 2004–05: $55,000.

Most important special collections include psychological assessment materials; PGSP dissertations.

Buildings and Grounds: Campus area 23,200 square feet.

Chief Executive Officer: Dr. Allen Calvin, President.

Address admission inquiries to Nora Marquez, Registrar.

Pacific Lutheran Theological Seminary

2770 Marin Avenue
Berkeley, California 947081597
Tel: (510) 524-5264   **E-mail:** admissions@plts.edu
Fax: (510) 524-2408   **Internet:** www.plts.edu

Institution Description: Pacific Lutheran Theological Seminary is a privately supported graduate seminary of the Evangelical Lutheran Church in America. *Enrollment:* 151. *Degrees awarded:* Master's doctorate, first-professional.

Member of the Graduate Theological Union.

Accreditation: *Professional:* theology

History: Founded by the California and Pacific Synods of the United Lutheran Church in America; ownership by the Evangelical Lutheran Church in America (established in 1985).

Institutional Structure: *Governing board:* Board of Directors. 26 members.

Calendar: Semesters. Academic year Sept. to May.

Admission: *Requirements:* Baccalaureate from accredited college or university; 1 year of Greek required; approval of appropriate church body required for admission to candidacy for ordainment.

Degree Requirements: Completion of prescribed curriculum which varies for the various graduate programs offered.

Distinctive Educational Programs: Cross-registration with other theological schools through the Graduate Theological Union in Berkeley.

Degrees Conferred: 40 *master's;* 1 *doctorate:* theology. 12 *certificates*.

Fees and Other Expenses: *Full-time tuition and fees per academic year 2004–05:* $8,500. Contact the seminary for housing costs and other information.

Financial Aid: *Institutional funding:* Fellowships and grants available to qualifying students.

Departments and Teaching Staff: *Total instructional faculty:* 8.

Enrollment: Total enrollment 151. Full-time 158, part-time 13.

Characteristics of Student Body: *Ethnic/racial makeup:* Black non-Hispanic: 2%; Asian or Pacific Islander: 4.6%; Hispanic: .7%; White non-Hispanic: 86.8%.

International Students: 9 nonresident aliens enrolled fall 2003. Programs available to aid students whose native language is not English: Social, cultural. No financial aid specifically designated for international students.

Student Life: Residence hall and apartment housing available on-campus. *Surrounding community:* Berkeley is the site of the University of California and is located across the bay from San Francisco.

Library Collections: Students have access to the library of the Graduate Theological Union near the seminary.

Buildings and Grounds: Campus area 9 acres.

Chief Executive Officer: Dr. Ted F. Peters, President.

Address admission inquiries to Rev. Gregory Schaefer, Director of Admissions.

Pacific Oaks College

5 Westmoreland Place
Pasadena, California 911030-3592
Tel: (626) 397-1300   **E-mail:** admissions@pacificoaks.edu
Fax: (626) 685-2529   **Internet:** www.pacificoaks.edu

Institution Description: Pacific Oaks College is a Quaker-founded upper division and graduate college, focused on the needs of young children, their families, and those who service them. The college maintains sites in Pasadena and Oakland. *Enrollment:* 1,266. *Degrees awarded:* Baccalaureate, master's. Postgraduate certificates also awarded.

Accreditation: *Regional:* WASC-Sr.

History: Established as Pacific Oaks Friends School in 1945; incorporated 1947; offered first instruction at postsecondary level 1951; awarded first degree (baccalaureate) 1954; adopted present name 1961.

Institutional Structure: *Governing board:* Board of Trustees. Extrainstitutional representation: 28; institutional representation: president of the college; faculty representative, staff representative, Children's School staff representative, all ex officio. *Composition of institution:* Administrators 2 men / 4 women. Academic affairs headed by a provost; business/finance headed by chief financial officer. Full-time instructional faculty 24. Academic governance body: Faculty Senate.

Calendar: Semesters. Academic year early Aug. to July. Degrees conferred Dec., May, July. Formal commencement June.

Admission: Rolling admissions plan. Application deadlines: summer and fall priority (April 15) and final fall (June 1), spring (Oct. 1). *Requirements:* Minimum of 70 units of previous college work with C or better; 9 units oral and written expression (including English composition), 9 units of math and science; 9 units of social science including Introduction to Psychology and Introductory Sociology or Cultural Anthropology; 9 units humanities and the arts. *Entrance tests:* For Multiple Subject Teaching Credential Program, CBEST. For foreign students TOEFL. *For transfer students:* From 4-year accredited institution, maximum transfer credit limited only by residence requirement.

Degree Requirements: *Undergraduate:* 124 semester units; 30 semester units in residence; master of arts: 30 to 48 units, depending on major, all in residence; thesis. *Grading system:* narrative evaluations upon successful completion of course.

Distinctive Educational Programs: Focus on needs of young children and their families; social justice, social and political contexts of human development; community-based action research. Latino/a Family Studies specialization within Marriage, Family, Child Counseling degree. African American Family Studies specialization within Marriage, Family, Child Counseling degree.

Degrees Conferred: 95 *baccalaureate*; 161 *master's*.

Fees and Other Expenses: *Full-time tuition per academic year 2005–06:* undergraduate $16,320, graduate $10,880.

Financial Aid: Aid from institutionally generated funds is provided on the basis of financial need.

Financial aid to full-time, first-time undergraduate students: need-based scholarships/grants totaling $617,380, self-help $2,107,980, parent loans $29,000; non-need-based scholarships/grants totaling $800,000, self-help $800,000. *Graduate* aid: 183 students received federal and state-funded loans totaling $5,940,212 (ranging from $3,000 to $18,500), 18 students had work-study jobs totaling $37,520 (ranging from $1,000 to $5,000).

Departments and Teaching Staff: Human development faculty 19, marriage/family and child counseling 6, teacher education 4. *Total instructional faculty:* 29 (full-time 24, part-time 5; women 23, men 6). Total faculty with doctorate, first-professional, or other terminal degree: 15. Student-to-faculty ratio: 11:1. 3 faculty members awarded sabbaticals 2004.

Enrollment: Total enrollment 1,266.

Characteristics of Student Body: *Ethnic/racial makeup:* number of Black non-Hispanic: 26; American Indian or Alaska Native: 4; Asian or Pacific Islander: 12; Hispanic: 73; White non-Hispanic: 56; unknown: 36. *Age distribution:* number of 22–24: 27; 25–29: 49; 30–34: 40, 35–39: 23; 40–49: 40; 50–64: 29.

International Students: 3 nonresident aliens enrolled fall 2004. 1 student from Asia, 2 Canada. No programs available to aid students whose native language is not English. No scholarships specifically designated for international students.

Student Life: No on-campus housing. Career guidance, housing assistance, personal development workshops, services for students with disabilities, student government, thesis support groups. *Special regulations:* Cars permitted without restrictions. *Surrounding community:* Pasadena population 150,000, is located in Los Angeles county. Served by mass transit bus system.

Publications: *Connections,* quarterly institutional newsletter.

Library Collections: 32,580 volumes. 87 current periodical subscriptions (paper) plus electronic access to others. 10 computer work stations. Access to online information retrieval systems.

Most important holdings include Early Childhood and Development; Marriage, Family, and Child Counseling; Society of Friends (Quaker) Collection; 19th Century Children's Collection.

Buildings and Grounds: Campus area 2 acres. Pacific Oaks College has a main campus in Pasadena and additional site in and Oakland (CA). .

Chief Executive Officer: Dr. Carolyn H. Denham, President.

Address admission inquiries to Marsha Franker, Dean of Enrollment Management.

Pacific School of Religion

1798 Scenic Avenue
Berkeley, California 94709
Tel: (800) 999-0528   **E-mail:** admissions@psr.edu
Fax: (510) 845-8948   **Internet:** www.psr.edu

Institution Description: Pacific School of Religion is a private, independent, nonprofit, interdenominational institution. It is a member of the Graduate Theological Union (GTU) that was created by 9 Protestant and Roman Catholic institutions to coordinate joint programs and award graduate degrees. See separate exhibit for Graduate Theological Union. *Enrollment:* 263. *Degrees awarded:* First-professional (master of divinity), master's, doctorate. Certificates also given.

Accreditation: *Regional:* WASC-Sr. *Professional:* theology

History: Established as Pacific Theological Seminary 1866; offered first instruction at postsecondary level 1869; chartered and awarded first degree (first-professional) 1872; adopted present name 1916. *See* Harland E. Hogue, *Christian Seed in Western Soil* (Berkeley: Pacific School of Religion, 1965) for further information.

Institutional Structure: *Governing board:* Board of Trustees of Pacific School of Religion. 44 trustees maximum. All voting. *Composition of institution:* Administrators 3 men / 1 woman. Academic affairs headed by dean of faculty. Management/business/ finances directed by vice president for administration. Full-time instructional faculty 8 men / 9 women. Academic governance body, the faculty, meets an average of 16 times per year.

Calendar: Semesters with a 4-week January intersession. Academic year Sept. to May. Entering students admitted either semester. Degrees conferred once a year at May commencement. Cooperative summer session with nearby seminaries.

Admission: Rolling admissions plan. For fall acceptance, applications must be in and completed by March 1. For spring acceptance, applications must be in by Nov. 1 of that school year. *Requirements:* Baccalaureate degree from accredited college, university, or seminary. For master's program, minimum recommended GPA 3.0.

Degree Requirements: *For first-professional degree:* 81 units; 3.0 GPA; field education. *For master's degree:* Master of Divinity 81 semester units, 3.0 GPA; Master of Arts 48 semester units, 3.0 GPA overall with 3.5 in area of concentration, thesis; joint Master of Divinity/Master of Arts 105 semester units; Master of Theological Studies 48 semester units with 3.0 GPA. *For doctorate:* Doctor of Ministry, variable coursework, one semester residency, research project; Doctor of Theology and Doctor of Philosophy requirements set by GTU. *Grading system:* A–F; pass-fail.

Distinctive Educational Programs: Certificate programs in theological studies, ministry studies, sexuality and religion, advanced professional studies, special studies, field education, clinical pastoral education, relationships with: Center for Ethics and Social Policy, Pacific and Asian American Center for Theology and Strategies, Center for Jewish Studies, Center for Lesbian and Gay Studies, Center for the Arts, Religion, and Education. Cross registration at University of California Berkeley, Mills College, Holy Names College. Special reading courses, lay leadership and pastoral conferences, summer session courses, and January intensive courses.

Degrees Conferred: 16 *master's:* theology; 51 *first-professional:* theology; 6 *doctorate:* doctor of ministry.

Fees and Other Expenses: *Full-time tuition per academic year 2004–05:* $10,570 to $11,400 (depending on program). *Other fees:* $100. *Room and board per academic year:* $4,950.

Financial Aid: Aid from institutionally generated funds is provided on the basis of academic merit, financial need.

Institutional funding: 192 scholarships/grants totaling $850,693 ($4,000 to $8,100). 140 federal/state-funded fellowships/grants totaling $1,000,000 (ranging from $1,000 to $18,500); 37 work-study jobs totaling $91,625 (ranging from $1,000 to $3,000).

Departments and Teaching Staff: *Total instructional faculty:* 22 (9 women, 13 men). Total faculty with doctorate, first-professional, or other terminal degree: 22. 3 faculty members awarded sabbaticals 2004.

Enrollment: Total enrollment 263.

Characteristics of Student Body: *Ethnic/racial makeup:* number of Black non-Hispanic: 39; American Indian or Alaska Native: 3; Asian or Pacific Islander: 15; Hispanic: 5; White non-Hispanic: 172; unknown: 2.

International Students: 27 nonresident aliens enrolled fall 2004. No programs to aid students whose native language is not English. Some financial aid specifically designated for international students.

Student Life: On-campus housing includes: residence hall rooms; studio, 1, 2, and 3 bedroom apartments which house 135 students and their families. Special features include: pets permitted; parking spaces available for residents. *Student publications: Logos,* a weekly calendar. *Surrounding community:* PSR campus is one block north of the University of California, Berkeley; 15 miles from San Francisco. Served by mass transit bus system and BART subway system. Oakland airport 22 miles and AMTRAK 18 miles from campus

Library Collections: 650,000 volumes. 238,084 audiovisual materials and periodicals. Access to online information retrieval systems and the Internet.

Most important holdings include Bade Archeological Collection; Howell Bible Collection (rare Bibles, 15th to 18th centuries); Academy of American Franciscan History Library.

Buildings and Grounds: Campus area 8 acres.

Chief Executive Officer: Dr. William McKinney, President.

Address admission inquiries to Nicole Naffaa, Director of Recruitment and Admissions.

Pacific Union College

One Angwin Way
Angwin, California 94508-9707
Tel: (802) 862-7080   **E-mail:** admissions@puc.edu
Fax: (707) 965-6390   **Internet:** www.puc.edu

Institution Description: Pacific Union College is a private college affiliated with the Seventh-day Adventist Church. *Enrollment:* 1,543. *Degrees awarded:* Associate, baccalaureate, master's. Certificates also awarded.

Member of the consortium Adventist Colleges Abroad.

Accreditation: *Regional:* WASC-Sr. *Professional:* music, nursing, social work

History: Established and incorporated as Healdsburg College 1882; offered first instruction at postsecondary level 1884; awarded first degree (baccalaureate) 1889; adopted present name 1906.

Institutional Structure: *Governing board:* Pacific Union College Board of Trustees. Extrainstitutional representation: 23 trustees; institutional representation: president of the college. 1 ex officio. All voting. *Composition of institution:* Administrators 28 men / 14 women. Academic administration headed by vice president for academic administration. Management/business/finances directed by vice president for financial administration. Full-time instructional faculty 98. Academic governance body, Academic Council, meets an average of 12 times pr year.

Calendar: Quarters. Academic year Sept. to June. Freshmen admitted Sept., Jan., Mar., June. Degrees conferred June, Aug., Dec., March. Formal commencement June. Summer session of 1 term from mid-June to mid-Aug.

Characteristics of Freshmen: 1,941 applicants (752 men, 1,189 women). 35.4% of applicants admitted; 51.4% admitted students enrolled full-time.

68% (217 students) submitted SAT scores; 45% (143 students) submitted ACT scores. *25th percentile:* SAT Verbal 490, SAT Math 490; ACT Composite

18, ACT English 18, ACT Math 17. *75th percentile:* SAT Verbal 650, SAT Math 600; ACT Composite 25, ACT English 25, ACT Math 24.

Admission: Rolling admissions plan. For fall acceptance, apply as early as Oct. 15 of previous year, but not later than Sept. 15 of year of enrollment. Early acceptance available. *Requirements:* Either graduation from secondary school or GED. Recommend 4 units English, 3 science, 2 mathematics, 2 foreign language, 1–2 history. Minimum GPA 2.3. *Entrance tests:* ACT Composite. *For transfer students:* 2.0 minimum GPA; from 4-year accredited institution 156 quarter hours maximum transfer credit; from 2-year accredited institution 108 quarter hours; correspondence/extension students 18 quarter hours.

College credit and advanced placement for postsecondary-level work completed in secondary school and for extrainstitutional learning on basis of ACE *2006 Guide to the Evaluation of Educational Experiences in the Armed Services.*

Tutoring available. Developmental courses offered during regular academic year; credit given.

Degree Requirements: *For all associate degrees:* 90 quarter hours; 2 quarters, including last, in residence; 2 physical activity courses. *For all baccalaureate degrees:* 192 hours; 2.25 GPA in upper division major; 3 consecutive quarters of senior year in residence; distribution requirements; exit competency examinations; comprehensives in individual fields of study, Undergraduate Assessment Program Area Tests. *For all degrees:* 2.0 GPA; general education requirements; weekly chapel attendance.

Fulfillment of some degree requirements and exemption from some beginning courses possible by passing departmental examinations, College Board CLEP, AP. *Grading system:* A–F; pass-fail; withdraw (carries time limit); incomplete (carries time limit).

Distinctive Educational Programs: *For undergraduates:* Off-campus center at Albion, 120 miles away from main institution;. Individually designed interdisciplinary programs. Honors program. Study abroad at Argentina, Austria, France, Spain. Summer programs in Argentina, Austria, France, Italy, Spain. Adult Degree Completion Program. *Available to all students:* Evening classes and individual majors.

Degrees Conferred: 88 *associate;* 267 *baccalaureate;* 2 *master's.* Bachelor's degrees awarded in top five disciplines: business, management, marketing, and related support services 69; health professions and related clinical sciences 31; education 27; visual and performing arts 17; physical sciences 17.

Fees and Other Expenses: *Full-time tuition per academic year 2004–05:* $17,934. *Room and board per academic year:* $5,136. *Books and supplies:* $1,260. *Other expenses:* $3,204.

Financial Aid: Aid from institutionally generated funds is provided on the basis of academic merit, financial need. Institution has a Program Participation Agreement with the U.S. Department of Education for eligible students to receive Pell Grants and other federal aid.

Financial aid to full-time, first-time undergraduate students: 26% received federal grants averaging $4,111; 17% state/local grants averaging $8,492; 100% institutional grants averaging $6,174; 46% loans averaging $3,929.

Departments and Teaching Staff: *Total instructional faculty:* 98 (full-time 81, part-time 17; women 12, men 56). Degrees held by full-time faculty: doctorate 42%, master's 21%, baccalaureate 7%. 53% hold terminal degrees. Student-to-faculty ratio: 15:1.

Enrollment: Total enrollment 1,543 (full-time 1,387, part-time 156).

Characteristics of Student Body: *Ethnic/racial makeup:* number of Black non-Hispanic: 64; American Indian or Alaska Native: 9; Asian or Pacific Islander: 319; Hispanic: 171; White non-Hispanic: 656; unknown: 225.

International Students: 99 nonresident aliens enrolled fall 2004. Programs available available to aid students whose native language is not English: Social, cultural.

Student Life: On-campus residence halls house 70% of student body. Residence halls for men constitute 45% of such space, for women 55%. 99% of married students request institutional housing; 45% are so housed. *Special regulations:* Registered cars permitted without restrictions. Curfew from 10:30pm to 6am. Quiet hours for freshmen from 7:30pm to 9:30pm Sun.–Thurs. *Special services:* Learning Resources Center, medical services. *Student publications, radio: Campus Chronicle,* a weekly newspaper; *Diogenes Lantern,* a yearbook; *Funnybook,* an annual student-faculty directory; *Quicksilver,* an annual literary magazine. Radio station KPRN broadcasts 126 hours per week. *Surrounding community:* Angwin population 3,500. San Francisco, 70 miles from campus, is nearest metropolitan area. Served by airport 80 miles from campus; passenger rail service 70 miles from campus.

Library Collections: 137,200 volumes. 122,000 microform units; 5,400 audiovisual materials; 830 periodical subscriptions. Online catalog. Students have access to online information retrieval services and the Internet.

Most important special holdings include Pitcairn Islands Study Center; E.G. White Seventh-day Adventist Study Center.

Buildings and Grounds: Campus area 1,800 acres.

Chief Executive Officer: Dr. Richard C. Osborn, President.

Address admission inquiries to Sean Kootsey, Director of Enrollment Services.

Pardee RAND Graduate School of Policy Studies

1706 Main Street
Santa Monica, California 90406-2138
Tel: (310) 393-0411   **E-mail:** prgs@rand.org
Fax: (310) 451-6978   **Internet:** www.prgs.edu

Institution Description: The Pardee RAND Graduate School of Policy Studies is a private, independent, nonprofit institution. It is the world's leading producer of Ph.D.'s in policy analysis and combines analytic rigor with practical experience. Working with senior RAND mentors on policy research provides PRGS fellows with the interdisciplinary training that equips them to tackle the critical problems of t he day: justice, health, security, education, and poverty. *Enrollment:* 83. *Degrees awarded:* Master's, doctorate.

Accreditation: *Regional:* WASC-Sr.

History: Established, chartered, and offered first instruction at postsecondary level 1970; first degree (doctorate) awarded 1974.

Institutional Structure: *Governing board:* RAND Board of Trustees Committee for the Pardee RAND Graduate School. *Composition of institution:* Administrators 1 man / 1 woman. Academic affairs headed by dean. Management/business/finances directed by dean. Academic governance body, Board of Governors, meets an average of 3 times per year.

Calendar: Quarters. Academic year Sept. to June. Entering students admitted Sept. Degrees conferred and formal commencement when applicable.

Characteristics of Freshmen: 21% of applicants accepted. All accepted applicants enrolled. 30% of students from California. Students from 7 states.

Admission: For fall acceptance, apply as early as Dec. of previous year, but not later than Feb. 1. Students are notified of acceptance in Apr. Some late applications are considered. *Requirements:* Master's degree or equivalent; knowledge of physical or biological science, social science, and mathematics; recent research paper, study, or report. *Entrance tests:* GRE or equivalent standardized graduate-level examination.

Degree Requirements: 20 courses, comprising core courses, seminar workshops, on-the-job training in current RAND policy research projects; no credit for grade of C; 3 years in residence; doctoral dissertation; written and oral qualifying examinations. *Grading system:* A–F; pass-fail (at faculty discretion); incomplete (carries time limit).

Distinctive Educational Programs: Special facilities for using telecommunications is the classroom. Interdisciplinary programs, including housing studies, international economics, microeconomics, policy making, statistics, strategic assessment. Tutorials.

Degrees Conferred: 18 *master's:* public administration and social services programs.

Fees and Other Expenses: *Full-time tuition per academic year 2004–05:* $17,000.

Financial Aid: Aid from institutionally generated funds is provided on the basis of financial need. Institution has a Program Participation Agreement with the U.S. Department of Education for eligible students to receive Pell Grants and other federal aid.

Departments and Teaching Staff: *Total instructional faculty* 48. Student-to-faculty ratio: 1.125:1. Degrees held by faculty: doctorate 94%, master's 4%, baccalaureate 2%. 100% hold terminal degrees.

Enrollment: Total enrollment 83 (69.9% men; 30.1% women).

Characteristics of Student Body: *Ethnic/racial makeup:* Black non-Hispanic: 1.2%; Asian or Pacific Islander: 4.8%; Hispanic: 2.4%; White non-Hispanic: 45.8%.

International Students: 38 nonresident aliens enrolled fall 2003. Students from Europe, Asia, Central and South America, Africa. No programs to aid students whose native language is not English. No financial aid specifically designated for international students.

Student Life: No on-campus housing. *Special regulations:* Cars permitted without restrictions. *Special services:* Medical services. *Surrounding community:* Santa Monica, population 95,000, is located in the Los Angeles metropolitan area. Served by mass transit bus system; airport 8 miles from campus; passenger rail service 11 miles from campus.

Publications: Sources of information about The Pardee RAND Graduate School can be found on the school's website (www.prgs.edu).

Library Collections: 200,000 books; 250,000 reports; 20,000 bound periodicals; 2,000 subscriptions.

Most important holdings include Slavic and Oriental collection (8,000 monographs and 7,000 volumes of bound periodicals pertaining to all aspects of Slavic and Oriental countries).

Buildings and Grounds: Campus area 14 acres.

Chief Executive Officer: Dr. Robert Klitgaard, Dean.

Address admission inquiries to Maggie Clay, Registrar.

Patten University

2433 Coolidge Avenue
Oakland, California 94601
Tel: (510) 533-8300
Fax: (510) 534-4344

Institution Description: Patten University (Patten Bible College and Theological Seminary, until 1980 and Patten College until 2002) is an independent Christian college dedicated to providing a liberal arts education with a strong Biblical Studies emphasis. *Enrollment:* 653. *Degrees awarded:* Associate, baccalaureate, master's. Certificates also awarded,

Accreditation: *Regional:* WASC-Sr.

History: Established as Oakland Bible Institute and offered first instruction at postsecondary level 1944; incorporated 1945; changed name to Patten Bible College and Theological Seminary, Inc., 1966; awarded first degree (baccalaureate) 1969; became Patten College 1980 and in 2002 acquired university status.

Institutional Structure: *Governing board:* Patten University Board of Trustees. Representation: 16 regents. All voting. *Composition of institution:* Administrators 10 men / 8 women. Academic affairs headed by Academic Dean. Management/business/finances directed by Business Manager. Total instructional faculty 58.

Calendar: Semesters. Academic year Aug. to May. Freshmen admitted Aug., Jan. Degrees conferred and formal commencement May.

Characteristics of Freshmen: SAT recommended but not required. 95% of applicants accepted. 87% of accepted applicants enrolled. 94% of entering students from from California. Students from 3 states and 3 foreign countries.

Admission: Rolling admissions plan. For fall acceptance, apply no later than 2 weeks after beginning of term. Early acceptance available. *Requirements:* Either graduation from approved secondary school with 3 units English, 5 from among foreign language, mathematics, science, and social studies (with 2 units in 2 fields and 1 in a third field), 8 additional units; or GED. Strong Christian commitment required. Minimum GPA 2.0. *Entrance tests:* College Board SAT or ACT composite. *For transfer students:* 2.5 minimum GPA; from 4-year accredited institution 97 units maximum transfer credit; from 2-year accredited institution 64 units. TOEFL score 500.

College credit and advanced placement for postsecondary-level work completed in secondary school. Tutoring available. Noncredit developmental courses offered during regular academic year.

Degree Requirements: *For all associate degrees:* 63 units; 3 semesters of Christian service. *For all baccalaureate degrees:* 127 units; 6 semesters of Christian service; exit competency examination in Bible. *For all degrees:* 2.0 GPA; 2 terms in residence; daily chapel attendance. *Grading system:* A–F; withdraw (carries time limit); incomplete (carries time limit).

Distinctive Educational Programs: Christian service internships. Evening classes. Facilities and programs for independent research, including tutorials, directed study.

Degrees Conferred: 23 *associate;* 43 *baccalaureate;* 5 *master's.* Bachelor's degrees awarded in: business, management, marketing, and related support22; liberal arts and sciences, general studies and humanities 10; theology and ministerial studies 9.

Fees and Other Expenses: *Full-time tuition per academic year 2004–05:* $11,520. *Room and board per academic year:* $5,800. *Books and supplies:* $1,250. *Other expenses:* $1,818.

Financial Aid: Aid from institutionally generated funds is provided on the basis of academic merit, financial need, athletic ability. Institution has a Program Participation Agreement with the U.S. Department of Education for eligible students to receive Pell Grants and other federal aid.

Financial aid to full-time, first-time undergraduate students: 40% received federal grants averaging $3,039; 10% state/local grants; 13% institutional grants; 47% loans averaging $6,127.

Departments and Teaching Staff: Biblical studies *professors* 2, *associate professors* 2, *assistant professors* 2; *instructors* 0, *part-time faculty* 4; general studies 0, 3, 1, 1, 13; professional studies 1, 1, 2, 0, 16; credential program 1, 0, 0, 0, 9.

Total instructional faculty: 58. Degrees held by full-time faculty: doctorate 47%, master's 50%, baccalaureate 100%.

Enrollment: Total enrollment 653. Undergraduate 602 (51.5% men, 48.5% women).

Characteristics of Student Body: *Ethnic/racial makeup:* Black non-Hispanic: 15%; Asian or Pacific Islander: 25.1%; Hispanic: 8.6%; White non-Hispanic: 24.6%; unknown: 26.7%.

International Students: 50 nonresident aliens enrolled fall 2003. Programs available to aid students whose native language is not English: English as a Second Language Program. No financial aid specifically designated for international students.

Student Life: On-campus apartments house 20% of student body. Apartments for men only constitute 25% of such space, for women only 25%. 17% of student body live off campus in college-owned apartments and houses. *Special regulations:* Cars permitted in designated parking lots. *Special services:* Learning Resources Center. *Student publications: Patten Pages,* a weekly newspaper; yearbook. *Surrounding community:* Oakland population 360,000. Served by mass transit bus and rail systems; airport 5 miles from campus; passenger rail service 1 mile from campus.

Publications: Sources of information about Patten College include *The Trumpet Call*; alumni publication: *Oak Leaf*. radio station KFAX and television station KVOF.

Library Collections: 40,000 volumes. 580 audiovisual materials; 250 current periodical subscriptions. Computer work stations. Students have access to the Internet at no charge.

Most important holdings include collections of 10,000 religious materials, 6,000 biblical studies.

Buildings and Grounds: Campus area 6 acres.

Chief Executive Officer: Dr. Gary B. Moncher, President.

Address admission inquiries to Inez Bailey, Director of Admissions.

Pepperdine University

24255 Pacific Coast Highway
Malibu, California 90263
Tel: (310) 506-4000   **E-mail:** admission-seaver@pepperdine.edu
Fax: (310) 506-4861   **Internet:** www.pepperdine.edu

Institution Description: Pepperdine University is a private, independent, nonprofit institution affiliated with the Church of Christ. *Enrollment:* 7,919. *Degrees awarded:* Baccalaureate, master's, doctorate, first-professional (law). Certificates also awarded.

Accreditation: *Regional:* WASC-Sr. *Professional:* business, clinical psychology, law, music

History: Established and incorporated as George Pepperdine College and offered first instruction at postsecondary level 1937; awarded first degree (baccalaureate) 1938; changed name to Pepperdine College 1962; added first-professional and doctoral programs 1969; adopted present name 1971. *See* Bill Young, *Faith was His Fortune* and *The Legacy of Frank Roger Seaver* (Los Angeles: Pepperdine Press, 1976) for further information.

Institutional Structure: *Governing board:* Board of Regents. Representation: 50 regents. All voting. *Composition of institution:* Administrators 54 men / 8 women. Academic affairs headed by provost. Full-time instructional faculty 167. Academic governance body, Academic Council Credits Committee, meets monthly.

Calendar: Semesters. Academic year late Aug. to mid-Apr. Freshmen admitted Dec. and Apr. Degrees conferred and formal commencements Aug., Dec., Apr. Summer session of 3 terms from May to July.

Characteristics of Freshmen: 29% of applicants admitted. 12% of admitted students enrolled full-time.

91% (663 students) submitted SAT scores; 40% (289 students) submitted ACT scores. *25th percentile*: SAT Verbal 550, SAT Math 560; ACT Composite 24. *75th percentile*: SAT Verbal SAT 650, Math 660; ACT Composite 29.

33% of entering freshmen expected to graduate within five years. 52% of freshmen from California.

Admission: For fall acceptance, apply as early as 12 months no later than 5 months prior to enrollment. Students are notified of acceptance Dec., Apr. Apply by Nov. 15 for early action. *Requirements:* Either graduation from accredited secondary school with 4 units English and a college preparatory program normally including communication, foreign language, humanities, mathematics, science, social studies; or GED. *Entrance tests:* College Board SAT or ACT composite. For foreign students TOEFL (minimum score 550). *For transfer students:* 2.7 minimum GPA; from 4-year accredited institution maximum transfer credit limited only by residence requirement; from 2-year accredited institution 70 hours; correspondence/extension students 15 hours.

College credit for postsecondary-level work completed in secondary school. Advanced placement for extrainstitutional learning on basis of faculty assess-

ment, personal interview. Tutoring and noncredit developmental courses available.

Degree Requirements: *Undergraduate:* 128 credit hours; 2.0 GPA; last 28 units in residence (from business school, last 45 units); 14 convocations per semester; general education requirements.

Fulfillment of some degree requirements possible by passing departmental examinations, College Board CLEP. *Grading system:* A–F; pass-fail; withdraw (deadline after which passing is appended to withdraw).

Distinctive Educational Programs: Flexible meeting places and schedules, including off-campus centers (at various locations throughout California), weekend and evening classes. Independent study. Study abroad in Heidelberg, Germany; Florence, Italy; London, England; Lyon, France; Tokyo, Japan. Hong Kong. Honduras Medical Program; Foreign exchange programs in Buenos Aires (Argentina) and Canberra (Australia).

ROTC: Air Force in cooperation with University of California, Los Angeles and Loyola Marymount University; Army in cooperation with UCLA.

Degrees Conferred: 800 *baccalaureate* (B), 1,605 *master's* (M), 68 *doctorate* (D): area and ethnic studies 61 (B); biological/life sciences 23 (B); business/marketing 290 (B), 823 (M); communications/communication technologies 124 (B), 5 (M); computer and information sciences 8 (B); education 14 (B), 427 (M), 49 (D); foreign languages and literature 19 (B); law/legal studies 34 (M); liberal arts/general studies 41 (B); mathematics 4 (B); parks and recreation 17 (B); philosophy/religion/theology 19 (B), 17 (M); protective services/public administration 42 (M); psychology 49 (B), 243 (M), 19 (D); social sciences and history 96 (B), 14 (M); visual and performing arts 34 (B). 182 *first-professional:* law 180, theology 2.

Fees and Other Expenses: *Full-time tuition per academic year 2004–05:* $28,630. *Room and per academic year:* $8,640. *Required fees:* $90.

Financial Aid: Aid from institutionally generated funds is provided on the basis of academic merit, financial need, athletic ability, other criteria. Institution has a Program Participation Agreement with the U.S. Department of Education for eligible students to receive Pell Grants and other federal aid.

Financial aid to full-time, first-time undergraduate students: need-based scholarships/grants totaling $28,097,869, self-help $12,511,144, parent loans $7,208,910, tuition waivers $206,604, athletic awards $529,740; non-need-based scholarships/grants totaling $8,229,860, self-help $3,366,309, parent loans $3,857,850, tuition waivers $1,525,664, athletic awards $3,027,390.

Departments and Teaching Staff: *Total instructional faculty:* 743 (full-time 390, part-time 353; women 304, men 439). Total faculty with doctorate, first-professional, or other terminal degree: 689. Student-to-faculty ratio: 12:1.

Enrollment: Total enrollment 7,919. Undergraduate full-time 1,107 men / 1,544 women, part-time 280m / 270w; graduate full-time 789m / 961w, part-time 792m / 1,227; first-professional full-time 346m / 362w, part-time 20m / 21w.

Characteristics of Student Body: *Ethnic/racial makeup:* number of Black non-Hispanic: 249; American Indian or Alaska Native: 54; Asian or Pacific Islander: 573; Hispanic: 376; White non-Hispanic: 1,729; unknown: 224. *Age distribution:* number under 18: 17; 18–19: 986, 20–21: 1,325; 22–24: 431; 25–29: 136; 30–34: 109; 35–39: 77; 40–49: 78; 50–64: 21; 65 and over: 1.

International Students: 196 nonresident aliens enrolled fall 2004. 67 students from Europe, 196 Asia, 34 Central and South America, 14 Africa, 32 Canada, 5 Australia, 1 New Zealand, 56 other. No programs available to aid students whose native language is not English. No financial aid specifically designated for international students.

Student Life: On-campus residence halls. *Intercollegiate athletics:* men only: baseball, basketball, tennis, volleyball, water polo, cross-country, golf; women only: basketball, diving, soccer, tennis, volleyball, swimming, cross-country, golf. *Special regulations:* Cars permitted in designated areas. Quiet hours. *Special services:* Medical services. *Student publications, radio, television: The Expressionist,* an annual literary magazine; *The Graphic,* a weekly newspaper; *Impressions,* a yearbook; *The Oasis,* a news magazine published 3 times per year. Radio station KMBU-FM. TV station KMBU. *Surrounding community:* Malibu is located in the Los Angeles-Long Beach metropolitan area. Mass transit bus system; airport 27 miles from campus.

Library Collections: 920,440 volumes including bound books, serial backfiles, electronic documents, and government documents not in separate collections. Online catalog. Current serial subscriptions: 6,910 paper. 4,086 recordings; 1,401 compact discs and CD-ROMs. 170 computer work stations. Students have access to the Internet at no charge.

Most important holdings include Mynarsky Collection (19th-century French literature); collection on 19th century U.S. Restoration Movement; collection on 19th-century children's literature; The Pourlis Collection.

Buildings and Grounds: Campus area 830 acres. *New buildings:* Drescher Graduate Campus.

Chief Executive Officer: Dr. Andrew K. Benton, President.

Address undergraduate admission inquiries to Paul Long, Dean of Admissions; first-professional students to Director of Admissions, School of Law; graduate students to Director of Admissions, Graduate School of Education and Psychology; business students to Director of Admissions, School of Business and Management.

Seaver College

Degree Programs Offered: *Baccalaureate* in accounting, advertising; American studies, art, biology, broadcasting, business administration, chemistry, communication theory, computer science, economics, English, foreign languages, French, German, history, humanities, journalism, liberal arts, literature, mathematics, music, nutritional science, philosophy, physical education and kinesiology, political science, psychology, religion, social science, sociology, Spanish, speech communication, sports medicine, telecommunications, theater; *master's* in various fields.

Distinctive Educational Programs: Interdisciplinary programs in American studies, fine arts, humanities and human values. Individual majors. Study abroad in Germany. Off-campus study in Washington (D.C.) through social science division.

The George L. Graziadio School of Business and Management

Degree Programs Offered: *Baccalaureate* management; *master's* in business administration, international business, organization development, technology management; joint juris doctor/MBA; joint MBA/public policy.

Distinctive Educational Programs: Courses and degree programs offered at various off-campus centers in California and Hawaii.

School of Law

Degree Programs Offered: *First-professional;* master of dispute resolution; joint JD/MBA; joint JD/MPP (master of public policy); Joint MDR/MPP (master of dispute resolution and master of public policy).

Admission: LSAT.

Degree Requirements: 88 credit hours, 72 grade average, 90 weeks in residence.

Fees and Other Expenses: Contact the school for current tuition.

School of Public Policy

Degree Programs Offered: Master of public policy; joint juris doctor/master of public policy; joint master of dispute resolution/master of public policy.

Admission: GRE preferred, GMAT, LSAT,

Fees and Other Expenses: Contact the school for current tuition.

Graduate School of Education and Psychology

Degree Programs Offered: *Master's* in education, counseling psychology, educational computing; *master's* and *doctorate* in educational administration and psychology.

Pitzer College

1050 North Mills Avenue
Claremont, California 91711
Tel: (909) 621-8219   **E-mail:** admission@pitzer.edu
Fax: (909) 621-8770   **Internet:** www.pitzer.edu

Institution Description: Pitzer College is a private, independent, nonprofit college. *Enrollment:* 942. *Degrees awarded:* Baccalaureate.

Accreditation: *Regional:* WASC-Sr.

History: Established as a women's college, incorporated, and offered first instruction at postsecondary level 1963; awarded first degree (baccalaureate) 1965; became coeducational 1970.

Institutional Structure: *Governing board:* Pitzer College Board of Trustees. Extrainstitutional representation: 37 trustees, 7 Life Members; institutional representation: 1 administrator (President of Pitzer College), 7 alumni. 37 voting. *Composition of institution:* Administrators 7 men / 16 women. Academic affairs headed by dean of faculty. Management/business/finances directed by the Vice President for Administration/Treasurer. Total instructional faculty 61. Academic governance body, College Council, meets an average of 15 times per year.

Calendar: Semesters. Academic year late Aug. to mid-May. Freshmen admitted Sept., Jan. Degrees conferred May., Sept., Feb. Formal commencement May. No summer session.

Characteristics of Freshmen: 3,108 applicants (1,184 men, 1,924 women). 40.4% of applicants admitted; 17.5% of admitted students enrolled full-time. 56% of freshmen from California. Freshmen from 27 states.

Admission: Admission deadline Feb. 1. Apply by Dec. 1 for early action (early action candidates need not reply to an offer of admission before May 1). Early admission available for qualified juniors. *Requirements:* Graduation from an accredited secondary school or GED. Recommend 4 units English, 3 foreign language, 3 math, 3 natural science, 3 social science. *Entrance tests:* College Board SAT or ACT Composite. For foreign students TOEFL. *For transfer students:* 3.0 minimum GPA; 2 years maximum transfer credit.

Degree Requirements: 128 hours, 2.0 GPA; 4 semesters in residence; distribution requirements; comprehensives in some fields of study.

Fulfillment of some degree requirements and exemption from some beginning courses possible by passing College Board AP. *Grading system:* A–F; pass-fail; withdraw.

Distinctive Educational Programs: *For undergraduates:* Work-experience programs, including field work, internships. Evening classes. Dual-degree programs in business and economics and in mathematics with the Claremont Graduate School. Special facilities for using telecommunications in the classroom. Interdisciplinary programs in environmental studies, organizational studies, and other fields. Independent study; self-designed majors. Institutionally sponsored study abroad in over 100 sites throughout the world, including Pitzer-operated programs in Nepal, China, Zimbabwe, Italy, Wales, Turkey, and Guatemala. Off-campus study in U.S., including Washington (DC) semester, exchange program with Colby College (ME), and by individual arrangement. *Other distinctive programs:* Degree-granting New Resources program, primarily for older students. 7-year B.A./D.O. program in cooperation with Western University of Health Sciences in Pomona, California.

Degrees Conferred: 207 *baccalaureate.* Bachelor's degrees awarded in top five disciplines: social sciences 68; English language and literature/letters 28; 24 visual and performing arts 24; psychology 18; communication, journalism, and related programs 12.

Fees and Other Expenses: *Full-time tuition per academic year 2004–05:* $31,438. *Room and board per academic year:* $8,222. *Books and supplies:* $950. *Other expenses:* 1,250.

Financial Aid: Aid from institutionally generated funds is provided on the basis of academic merit, financial need. Institution has a Program Participation Agreement with the U.S. Department of Education for eligible students to receive Pell Grants and other federal aid.

Financial aid to full-time, first-time undergraduate students: 11% received federal grants averaging $4,677; 9% state/local grants averaging $5,259; 39% institutional grants averaging $15,004; 31% loans averaging $3,095.

Departments and Teaching Staff: *Professors* 33, *associate professors* 14, *assistant professors* 10, *instructors* 2, *part-time faculty* 5.

Total instructional faculty: 63.4 FTE. Student-to-faculty ratio: 13.4:1. Degrees held by full-time faculty: Doctorate 91%, master's 8%. 96% of faculty hold terminal degrees.

Enrollment: Total enrollment 942 (40.3% men, 59.7% women).

Characteristics of Student Body: *Ethnic/racial makeup:* Black non-Hispanic: 5.4%; American Indian or Alaska Native: 1.1%; Asian or Pacific Islander: 9.8%; Hispanic: 13%; White non-Hispanic: 44.6%.

International Students: 28 nonresident aliens enrolled fall 2003. Students from Europe, Asia, Central and South America, Africa, Canada. Programs available to aid students whose native language is not English: Social and cultural. English as a Second Language Program. No financial aid specifically designated for international students.

Student Life: On-campus residence halls house 85% of student body. *Intercollegiate athletics:* men only: baseball, basketball, football, golf, soccer, swimming, tennis, track and field, water polo; women only: basketball, cross-country, swimming, tennis, track and field, volleyball. Both sexes, badminton, fencing. *Special regulations:* Registered cars permitted without restrictions; parking limited. *Special services:* Counseling, health, ethnic centers (for Black and Chicano students), medical services. *Student publications:* A monthly newspaper and a yearbook published annually.

Library Collections: 2,280,000 volumes. 1,500,000 microforms; 17,000 audiovisual materials; 5,750 periodicals. Students have access to the Internet at no charge.

Most important special collections include Asian studies and religious studies.

Buildings and Grounds: Campus area 35 acres.

Chief Executive Officer: Dr. Laura Skandra Trombly, President.

Address admission inquiries to Art Stenmo, Director of Admissions.

Point Loma Nazarene University

3900 Lomaland Drive
San Diego, California 92106
Tel: (619) 849-2200   **E-mail:** discover@ptloma.edu
Fax: (619) 849-2579   **Internet:** www.ptloma.edu

Institution Description: Point Loma Nazarene University is a private college affiliated with the Church of the Nazarene. *Enrollment:* 3,219. *Degrees awarded:* Baccalaureate, master's.

Accreditation: *Regional:* WASC-Sr. *Professional:* nursing

History: Established in Los Angeles, chartered, and incorporated as Pacific Bible College 1902; moved to Pasadena, changed name to Pasadena University, and offered first instruction at postsecondary level 1910; awarded first degree (baccalaureate) 1912; changed name to Pasadena College 1915; moved to present location and changed name to Point Loma College 1973; became Point Loma Nazarene College 1983; adopted present name 1998. *See* Ronald Kirkemo's *For Zion's Sake* (Point Loma Press, 1992).

Institutional Structure: *Governing board:* Board of Trustees of Point Loma College: An Institution of the Church of the Nazarene. Representation: 40 trustees, including 1 alumnus, president of the college. 2 ex officio. All voting. *Composition of institution:* Administrators 16 men / 5 women. Academic affairs headed by vice president for academic affairs. Management/business/finances directed by vice president for financial affairs. Full-time instructional faculty 129. Academic governance body, the faculty, meets an average of 18 times per year.

Calendar: Semesters. Academic year Aug. to May. Freshmen admitted Aug., Jan., June, July. Degrees conferred and formal commencement May.

Characteristics of Freshmen: 1,768 applicants (567 men, 1,201 women). 65% of applicants admitted; 46.5% of admitted students enrolled full-time.

93% (497 students) submitted SAT scores; 34% (180 students) submitted ACT scores. *25th percentile*: SAT Verbal 520, SAT Math 530, ACT Composite 22. *75th percentile*: SAT Verbal 620, SAT Math 630, ACT Composite 27.

41.3% of entering freshmen expected to graduate within 5 years. 67% of freshmen from California. Freshmen from 22 states and 5 foreign countries.

Admission: Rolling admissions plan. For fall acceptance, apply as early as end of junior year of secondary school, but not later than July 1 of year of enrollment. *Requirements:* Either graduation from accredited secondary school with college preparatory units which normally include 4 English, 2 in a foreign language, 1 algebra, 1 geometry, 1 history, 1 laboratory science; or GED. Minimum GPA 2.5. *Entrance tests:* College Board SAT preferred; Basic ACT accepted. *For transfer students:* 2.0 minimum GPA; from 4-year accredited institution 104 semester quarter hours maximum transfer credit; from 2-year accredited institution 70 semester hours; correspondence/extension students 16 semester hours.

College credit and advanced placement for postsecondary-level work completed in secondary school. College credit for extrainstitutional learning on basis of ACE *2006 Guide to the Evaluation of Educational Experiences in the Armed Services.* Tutoring available. Developmental/remedial courses offered in summer session and regular academic year; credit given.

Degree Requirements: *Undergraduate:* 128 semester hours; 2.0 GPA; last 24 semester hours in residence; weekly chapel attendance; physical education; distribution requirements. For some degrees, comprehensives in individual fields of study.

Fulfillment of some degree requirements and exemption from some beginning courses possible by passing College Board AP, CLEP Subject Examinations. *Grading system:* A–F, pass-no credit; credit-no credit; withdrawn failing; incomplete (carries time limit).

Distinctive Educational Programs: *For undergraduates:* Business internships. Honors programs. *For graduate students:* Off-campus center at Pasadena (130 miles away from main institution). *Available to all students:* Evening classes. Special facilities for using telecommunications in the classroom. Independent field projects. Campus-based summer ministries.

ROTC: Army, Navy, Air force offered in cooperation with San Diego State University and University of San Diego.

Degrees Conferred: 501 *baccalaureate*; 91 *master's.* Bachelor's degrees awarded in top five disciplines: business, management, marketing, and related support services 86; liberal arts and sciences, general studies and humanities 68; psychology 46; health professions and related clinical sciences 45; communication, journalism, and related programs 39.

Fees and Other Expenses: *Full-time tuition per academic year 2004–05:* $19,040. *Books and supplies:* $1,260; *Room and board per academic year:* $6,940. *Other expenses:* $2,782.

Financial Aid: Aid from institutionally generated funds is provided on the basis of academic merit, financial need, athletic ability, other criteria. Institution

has a Program Participation Agreement with the U.S. Department of Education for eligible students to receive Pell Grants and other federal aid.

Departments and Teaching Staff: Art *professors* 1, *associate professors* 0, *assistant professors* 2, *instructors* 0; biology 3, 1, 1, 0; business 3, 4, 0, 0; chemistry 3, 0, 0, 0; communication studies 1, 1, 1, 1; education 5, 6, 4 1; history/political science 1, 2, 2, 0; human environmental science 1, 2, 0, 0; literature/journalism/languages 10, 1, 2, 2; mathematics/computer science 4, 3, 1, 0; music 3, 2, 2, 1; nursing 2, 3, 3, 0; philosophy/religion 4, 3, 1, 0; physical education 3, 0, 0, 0; physics/engineering 3, 0, 0, 0; psychology 1, 2, 1, 0; sociology 2, 1, 0, 0.

Total instructional faculty: 128.5 FTE. *Total tenured faculty:* 48. *Degrees held by full-time faculty:* Doctorate 61%, master's 37%. 65% hold terminal degrees.

Enrollment: Total enrollment 3,219. Undergraduate 2,375 (40.5% men, 59.5% women).

Characteristics of Student Body: *Ethnic/racial makeup:* Black non-Hispanic: 2%; American Indian or Alaska Native: .6%; Asian or Pacific Islander: 5%; Hispanic: 8.2%; White non-Hispanic: 82.9%.

International Students: 35 nonresident aliens enrolled fall 2003. Students from Europe, Asia, Latin America, Africa, Canada, Australia. Programs available to aid students whose native language is not English: Social and cultural. English as a Second Language Program. No financial aid specifically designated for international students.

Student Life: On-campus residence halls house 54% of student body. Residence halls for men only constitute 43% of such space, for women only 57%. *Intercollegiate athletics:* men only: baseball, basketball, golf, soccer, tennis, track; women only: basketball, tennis, track, volleyball. *Special regulations:* Registered cars permitted on campus in designated areas only. Residence hall closing at midnight Sun., 11pm Mon.–Thurs., 1am Fri.–Sat. Quiet hours from 7pm to 9pm, after 11pm. Residence hall visitation during open house. *Special services:* Learning Resources Center, medical services. *Student publications:* *The Mariner,* a yearbook; *The Mascot,* an annual student handbook; *The Point,* a weekly newspaper. *Surrounding community:* San Diego population over 1,000,000. Served by mass transit bus system; airport 5 miles from campus; passenger rail service 8 miles from campus.

Library Collections: 175,000 volumes. 55,000 microforms; 13,000 audiovisual materials; 615 current periodical subscriptions. Access to online information retrieval systems. Online catalog.

Most important special holdings include books, pamphlets, and periodicals pertaining to the 19th- and 20th-century holiness movement; 17th- and 18th-century books by Methodist theologians James Arminius and John Wesley and their followers.

Buildings and Grounds: Campus area 89 acres.

Chief Executive Officer: Dr. Bob Brower, President.

Address admission inquiries to Eric Groves, Director of Undergraduate Admissions; address graduate inquiries to John Burlison, Director of Graduate Admissions.

Pomona College

550 North College Avenue
Claremont, California 91711
Tel: (909) 621-8147   **E-mail:** registrar@pomona.edu
Fax: (909) 621-8671   **Internet:** www.pomona.edu

Institution Description: Pomona College is a private, independent, nonprofit college. *Enrollment:* 1,540. *Degrees awarded:* Baccalaureate.

Accreditation: *Regional:* WASC-Sr.

History: Established by General Association of Congregational Churches of Southern California and incorporated 1887; offered first instruction at postsecondary level 1888; awarded first degree (baccalaureate) 1894; ended church affiliation 1903. *See* E. Wilson Lyon, *The History of Pomona College* (Claremont: Pomona College, 1977) for further information.

Institutional Structure: *Governing board:* Board of Trustees. Extrainstitutional representation: 35 trustees; institutional representation: president of the college. 3 ex officio. All voting. *Composition of institution:* Administrators 5 men / 7 women. Academic affairs headed by vice president and dean of the college. Management/business/finances directed by vice president and treasurer. Total instructional faculty 161. Academic governance body, the faculty, meets an average of 9 times per year.

Calendar: Semesters. Academic year Aug. to May. Freshmen admitted Aug., Jan. Degrees conferred May, Sept., Dec. Formal commencement May. No summer session.

Characteristics of Freshmen: 19.7% of applicants admitted; 40.6% of admitted students enrolled full-time.

93% (365 students) submitted SAT scores; 20% (79 students) submitted ACT scores. *25th percentile*: SAT Verbal 690, SAT Math 680; ACT Composite 30,

ACT English 29, ACT Math 28. *75th percentile*: SAT Verbal 770, SAT Math 760; ACT Composite 34, ACT English 34, ACT Math 33.

89% of entering freshmen expected to graduate within 5 years. 33.2% of freshmen from California. Freshmen from 44 states and 9 foreign countries.

Admission: Application for freshman admission is due Jan. 2. Applicants will receive notification by mid-April. Two binding early decision opinions are available; the first has a deadline of Nov. 15 and the second has a deadline of Dec. 28. *Requirements:* 4 secondary school units in English, 3 mathematics, 2 each in science and social studies, 3 in a foreign language. *Entrance tests:* All applicants are required to submit results of the new SAT and two SAT subject exams or the ACT. Students for whom English is their second language must submit results of the TOEFL. *For transfer students:* Maximum of 16 courses (64 semester hours or 96 quarter hours).

College credit and advanced placement for postsecondary-level work completed in secondary school. Tutoring available.

Degree Requirements: 32 courses; 6.0 GPA (12-point scale); 4 semesters in residence; comprehensives, senior thesis, or other final exercise; 1 physical education activity; general education requirements include a Critical Inquiry Seminar, two writing intensive courses(one of which is the Critical Inquiry Seminar), one speaking-intensive course, and one course in each of ten intellectual skill areas (perception, analysis, and communication); and a demonstrated proficiency in a foreign language. *Grading system:* A–F; pass-no credit; withdraw (granted for approved withdrawals after the drop deadline).

Distinctive Educational Programs: Cross-enrollment opportunities within the Claremont Colleges Consortium. Dual-degree programs in engineering with Washington University in St. Louis and California Institute of Technology. Interdisciplinary program in public policy analysis. Facilities and programs for independent research, including individual majors, independent study, directed reading and research. 40 institutionally sponsored study abroad programs in Europe, South America, Africa, Australia, and Asia. Exchange programs with California Institute of Technology, Colby College (ME), Swarthmore College (PA). Smith College (MA), and Spelman College (GA). Washington (DC) internship program through Claremont McKenna College.

Degrees Conferred: 368 *baccalaureate:* area and ethnic studies 13, biological/life sciences 49, computer and information sciences 5, English 34, foreign languages and literature 12, interdisciplinary studies 69, liberal arts/general studies 1, mathematics 20, natural resources/environmental science 7, philosophy/religion/theology 20, physical sciences 8, psychology and cognitive science 19, social sciences and history 101, visual and performing arts 10. arts 12. *Honorary degrees awarded 2003–04:* Doctor of Law 1, Doctor of Letters 1, Doctor of Science 1.

Fees and Other Expenses: *Full-time tuition per academic year 2004–05:* $28,100. *Room per academic year:* $5,555. *Board per academic year:* $3,830. *Other fees:* $265.

Financial Aid: Aid from institutionally generated funds is provided on the basis of financial need. Institution has a Program Participation Agreement with the U.S. Department of Education for eligible students to receive Pell Grants and other federal aid.

Financial aid to full-time, first-time undergraduate students: need-based scholarships/grants totaling $19,283,000, self-help $3,400,000; non-need-based scholarships/grants totaling $588,000, parent loans $2,000,000.

Departments and Teaching Staff: *Professors* 69, *associate professors* 54, *assistant professors* 36, *instructors* 2, *part-time faculty* 60.

Total instructional faculty: 221 (full-time 161, part-time 60; women 103, men 118). Total faculty with doctorate, first-professional, or other terminal degree: 180. 38 faculty members were awarded sabbaticals in 2004–05.

Enrollment: Total enrollment 1,540. Full-time undergraduate 807 men / 714 women, part-time 5m / 6w; unclassified full-time 3m / 4w.

Characteristics of Student Body: *Ethnic and racial makeup:* number of Black non-Hispanic: 71; American Indian or Alaska Native: 5; Asian or Pacific Islander: 293; Hispanic: 151; White non-Hispanic: 808.

International Students: 31 nonresident aliens enrolled fall 2004. 8 students from Europe, 11 Asia, 3 Central and South Latin America, 4 Africa, 4 Canada, 1 New Zealand. No programs available to aid students whose native language is not English. Some financial aid specifically designated for international students.

Student Life: On-campus residence halls house 92% of student body. *Intercollegiate athletics:* men only: baseball, basketball, cross-country, football, golf, soccer, swimming, tennis, track, water polo; women only: basketball, cross-country, swimming, tennis, track, volleyball. *Special regulations:* Cars permitted without restrictions. *Special services:* Medical services; counseling services; Office of Black Student Affairs; Office of Chicano Student Affairs; Campus Security; Health Education Office. *Student publications: Metate,* a yearbook; *The Spectator,* a biannual literary magazine; *The Student Life,* a weekly newspaper; *Re-View,* a feminist newspaper. *Surrounding community:* Claremont is located approximately 35 miles east of Los Angeles at the foot of the San Gabriel Mountains. It is the home of the Claremont Colleges of which Pomona College

is the founding college. The area is served by mass transit bus and rail systems and nearby Ontario International Airport.

Library Collections: 1,975,000 volumes. 718,505 government documents; 1,304,065 microforms; 750 audiovisual materials; 5,750 current periodical subscriptions. Students have access online information retrieval services and the Internet. Online catalog.

Special collections include the Irving Wallace Collection; the MacPherson Collection (materials for the study of women); the Westergaard Collections (Scandinavia and the Baltic Area); Western Americana Collection; Philbrick Collection of Dramatic Literature and Theatre History; William W. Clary Oxford Collection.

Buildings and Grounds: Campus area 140 acres.

Chief Executive Officer: Dr. David W. Oxtoby, President.

Address admission inquiries to Bruce Poch, Dean of Admissions.

Saint Mary's College of California

1928 St. Mary's Road
Moraga, California 94575

Tel: (510) 631-4000 **E-mail:** smcadmit@stmarys-ca.edu
Fax: (510) 376-7193 **Internet:** www.stmarys-ca.edu

Institution Description: Saint Mary's College of California is a private institution affiliated with the Institute of the Brothers of the Christian Schools. *Enrollment:* 4,536. *Degrees awarded:* Associate, baccalaureate, master's. Certificates also awarded.

Member of Regional Association of East Bay Colleges and Universities.

Accreditation: *Regional:* WASC-Sr.

History: Established as Saint Mary's College by Archbishop of San Francisco 1863; offered first instruction at postsecondary level and came under the control of the Institute of the Brothers of the Christian Schools 1868; chartered and awarded first degree (baccalaureate) 1872; adopted present name 1938. *See* Ronald E. Isetti, F.S.C., *Called to the Pacific* (Moraga: Saint Mary's College of California, 1979) for further information.

Institutional Structure: *Governing board:* The Board of Trustees of Saint Mary's College of Moraga. Extrainstitutional representation: 12 trustees (including the Regional Provincial of the Christian Brothers); institutional representation: 3 trustees (including president of the college). 2 ex officio. 15 voting. *Composition of institution:* Administrators 24 men / 12 women. Academic affairs headed by academic vice president. Management/business/finances directed by vice president for business and finance. Full-time instructional faculty 198. Academic governance body, Faculty Assembly, meets an average of 9 times per year.

Calendar: Semesters (4-1-4 plan). Academic year Sept. to May. Freshmen admitted Sept. Degrees conferred May, Aug., Dec., Jan. Formal commencement May. Summer session of 1 term from late June to late July.

Characteristics of Freshmen: 2,779 applicants. 611 applicants admitted and enrolled.

90%% (503 students) submitted SAT scores; 10% (53 students) submitted ACT scores. *25th percentile*: SAT Verbal 500, SAT Math 490. *75th percentile*: SAT Verbal 590, SAT Math 600.

82% of freshmen from California. Freshmen from 22 states.

Admission: Rolling admissions plan. For fall acceptance, apply by Nov. 30 for early action; decision; need not limit application to St. Mary's. Early acceptance available. Final deadline Feb. 1. *Requirements:* Either graduation from accredited secondary school college preparatory curriculum, including: 2 years science, 2 foreign language, 4 English, 3 mathematics (1 algebra, 1 geometry), 1 U.S. history and civics; or GED. *Entrance tests:* College Board SAT or ACT composite. For foreign students TOEFL. *For transfer students:* 2.5 minimum GPA, from 4- and 2-year accredited institutions maximum transfer credit limited only by residency requirement.

College credit and advanced placement for postsecondary-level work completed in secondary school. Tutoring available.

Degree Requirements: *For all associate degrees:* 18 course credits; 2.0 GPA; 7 course credits in residence; 2 collegiate seminars, 1 religious studies, 6 area requirements in arts and letters, sciences, and social sciences. *For all baccalaureate degrees:* 36 course credits; 2.0 GPA (overall and in major); 9 course credits in residence; 4 collegiate seminars, 2 religious studies, 4 area requirements in liberal arts and sciences; demonstration of competency in written English.

Fulfillment of some degree requirements and exemption from some beginning courses possible by passing departmental examinations, College Board CLEP, APP. *Grading system:* A–F; pass-fail; withdraw (carries time limit).

Distinctive Educational Programs: Weekend and evening classes. Dual-degree program in engineering with Washington University (MO). Cooperative bachelor's degree program in nursing with Samuel Merritt School of Nursing (Oakland, CA). Multidisciplinary programs in American studies, cross-cultural studies, European studies, Latin American studies. Individual majors. Tutorials. Independent study. Study abroad in Belgium, England, France, Greece, Ireland, Italy; Mexico, Spain, South America (Argentina, Peru). Travel-study during January term. Study abroad may be individually arranged. Off-campus exchange programs during January term with participating colleges. Cross-registration through consortium. High Potential Program offers academic and other support services for economically and educationally disadvantaged students. Summer master's programs in health, physical education and recreation, and theology. *Other distinctive programs:* One-year paralegal program. External degree programs for working adults provide baccalaureate and master's completion through weekly workshops and individualized study. Credit and enrichment continuing education programs.

ROTC: Army and Air Force offered in cooperation with University of California, Berkeley.

Degrees Conferred: 804 *baccalaureate* (B); 265 *master's* (M); 3 *doctorate* (D): area and ethnic studies 4 (B); biological/life sciences 19 (B); business/marketing 396 (B), 131 (M); communications/communication technologies 67 (B); education 97 (M), 3 (D); engineering and engineering technologies 2 (B); English 31 (B), 14 (M); foreign languages and literature 4 (B); health professions and related sciences 30 (B), 3 (M); interdisciplinary studies 6 (B); law/legal studies 19 (B); liberal arts/general studies 33 (B), 1 (M); mathematics 2 (B); parks and recreation 20 (B), 7 (M); philosophy/religion/theology 18 (B); physical sciences 9 (B); psychology 65 (B), 12 (M); social sciences and history 73; visual and performing arts 16 (B).

Fees and Other Expenses: *Full-time tuition per academic year 2004–05:* $27,130 undergraduate; graduate tuition varies by program. *Room and board per academic year:* $10,100.

Financial Aid: Aid from institutionally generated funds is provided on the basis of financial need. Institution has a Program Participation Agreement with the U.S. Department of Education for eligible students to receive Pell Grants and other federal aid.

Financial aid to full-time, first-time undergraduate students: need-based scholarships/grants totaling $21,953,611, self-help $9,700,389, parent loans $664,516, tuition waivers $516,728, athletic awards $1,431,251; non-need-based scholarships/grants totaling $901,728, self-help $3,882,339, parent loans $3,882,939, tuition waivers $529,245, athletic awards $1,687,790.

Departments and Teaching Staff: *Total instructional faculty:* 571 (full-time 198, part-time 373; women 294, men 277). Total faculty with doctorate, first-professional, or other terminal degree: 92. Student-to-faculty ratio: 12:1.

Enrollment: Total enrollment 4,536. Undergraduate full-time 949 men / 1,508 women, part-time 315m / 558w; graduate full-time 224m / 293w, part-time 153m / 536w. *Transfer students:* in-state into upper division: 37m / 102w.

Characteristics of Student Body: *Ethnic/racial makeup:* number of Black non-Hispanic: 278; American Indian or Alaska Native: 31; Asian or Pacific Islander: 362; Hispanic: 632; White non-Hispanic: 2,255; unknown: 901. *Age distribution:* number under 18: 49: 18–19: 974; 20–21: 1,051; 22–24: 249; 25–29: 59; 30–34: 21; 35–39: 28; 40–49: 20; 50–64: 2; 65 and over: 1.

International Students: 77 nonresident aliens enrolled fall 2004. No programs available to aid students whose native language is not English. No financial aid specifically designated for international students.

Student Life: On-campus residence halls house 75% of student body. Residence halls for men constitute 11% of such space, for women 5%, for both sexes 84%. *Intercollegiate athletics:* men only: baseball, basketball, cross-country, golf, soccer, tennis; women only: basketball, softball, tennis, volleyball. *Special regulations:* Cars permitted in designated areas. Quiet hours. Residence hall visitation from 8am to 2am. *Special services:* Medical services. *Student publications, radio: The Gael,* a yearbook; *The Red and Blue,* official student directory; *The Saint Mary's Collegian,* a monthly newspaper. Radio station KSMC broadcasts 112 hours per week. *Surrounding community:* Moraga is located in the San Francisco-Oakland metropolitan area. Served by mass transit bus and commuter train systems; airport 35 miles from campus; passenger rail service 25 miles from campus.

Library Collections: 111,068 volumes. Current serial subscriptions: paper 13,012, 484,760 microform; 5,377 via electronic access. 250 computer work stations. Students have access to online information retrieval services and the Internet. Total 2004–05 budget for materials and operations: $604,106.

Most important holdings include collection of LaSallian Research Institute for the Study of Christian Spirituality; Californiana and Western Americana; Cardinal Newman Collection.

Buildings and Grounds: Campus area 95 acres. *New buildings:* Science Building completed 2000.

Chief Executive Officer: Dr. Ronald Gallagher, FSC, President.

Address admission inquiries to Dorothy Jones, Dean of Admissions.

St. Patrick's Seminary

320 Middlefield Road
Menlo Park, California 94025-3596
Tel: (650) 325-5621   **E-mail:** info@stpatricksseminary.org
Fax: (650) 322-0997   **Internet:** www.stpatricksseminary.org

Institution Description: St. Patrick's Seminary is a private institution affiliated with the Archdiocese of San Francisco, Roman Catholic Church. *Enrollment:* 85 men. *Degrees awarded:* Master's, first-professional (master of divinity)

Accreditation: *Regional:* WASC-Sr. *Professional:* theology

History: Established and chartered as St. Patrick's Seminary 1891; offered first instruction at postsecondary level 1898; awarded first degree (baccalaureate) 1902; changed name to St. Patrick's Seminary-Theologate 1924; adopted present name 1969.

Institutional Structure: *Governing board:* Board of Trustees of St. Patrick's Seminary. Representation: 15 trustees, including archbishop of San Francisco. 1 ex officio. All voting. *Composition of institution:* Administrators 5 men. Academic affairs headed by academic dean. Management/business/finances directed by Business Manager. Full-time instructional faculty 20 FTE. Academic governance body, Board of Trustees, meets an average of 4 times per year.

Calendar: Semesters. Academic year Aug. to May. Entering students admitted Sept. Degrees conferred May. No summer session.

Admission: Rolling admissions plan. For fall acceptance, apply as early as Feb., but not later than June. *Requirements:* Baccalaureate degree with 24 units of philosophy and 12 units of theology/religious education; personal interview; baptism and confirmation records, parents' marriage certificate. All candidates must be formally accepted by a diocese or religious order. *Entrance tests:* GRE or its equivalent. Psychometric tests administered by St. Patrick's. *For transfer students:* Transfer applications evaluated individually.

Degree Requirements: *For all first-professional degrees:* 2.0 GPA. *For all master's degrees:* 3.0 GPA; research thesis or supervised project; 16 additional units at master's level. *For all degrees:* first-professional: 113 credit hours (57 hours in residence); for Master of Arts: 30 credit hours (plus 6 units for thesis). daily chapel attendance; oral or written examinations in sacred scripture, dogmatic and moral theology. *Grading system:* A–F; withdraw (deadline after which pass-fail is appended to withdraw); incomplete (carries time limit).

Distinctive Educational Programs: *For graduate students:* Field education. For some courses, individually arranged independent research. Hispanic: studies program which included courses in Spanish language and culture, internships in the Spanish-speaking community and may involve study abroad in Guatemala, Mexico, elsewhere.

Degrees Conferred: 31 *master's:* theology; 33 *first-professional:* master of divinity.

Fees and Other Expenses: *Full-time tuition per academic year 2004–05:* $9,800. *Room and board per academic year:* $7,500. *Other fees:* $850.

Financial Aid: Aid from institutionally generated funds is awarded on basis of financial need. Institution has a Program Participation Agreement with the U.S. Department of Education for eligible students to receive Pell Grants and other federal aid.

Departments and Teaching Staff: Theology *professors* 5, *assistant professors* 3, *assistant professors* 1, *instructors* 4, *part-time faculty* 4.

Total instructional faculty: 25. Student-to-faculty ratio: 14:1. Degrees held by full-time faculty: Doctorate 64.2%, professional 35.7%, master's 85.7%.

Enrollment: Total enrollment 85.

Characteristics of Student Body: *Ethnic/racial makeup:* Black non-Hispanic: 1.2%; White non-Hispanic: 36.3%. *Age distribution:* 22–24: 11%; 25–29: 11%; 30–34: 25%; 35–39: 13%; 40–49: 8%; 50–59: 6%, 60–and over: 2.%.

International Students: English as a Second Language Program available.

Student Life: On-campus residence halls house 100% of full-time students. Dormitories for men only constitute 100% of such space. *Special regulations:* Cars permitted without restrictions. *Special services:* Learning Resources Center. *Surrounding community:* Menlo Park population 30,000. San Francisco, 31 miles from campus, is nearest metropolitan area. Served by airport 20 miles from campus; passenger rail service 3 miles from campus.

Library Collections: 111,250 volumes including bound books, serial backfiles, electronic documents, and government documents not in separate collections. Online catalog. Current serial subscriptions: 286 paper. 6 computer work stations. Students have access to the Internet.

Most important holdings include *Bibliotecha Sancti Francisci Archidioceseos* (1,612 volumes), consisting of library of first archbishop of San Francisco, Joseph S. Alemany, and historical papers, letters, and documents pertaining to archdiocese of San Francisco; Migne's *Patrologia Cursus Completus*, writings of the church fathers in Greek (161 volumes) and Latin (221 volumes); Duchaine Research Collection.

Buildings and Grounds: Campus area 47 acres.

Chief Executive Officer: Rev. Gerald Brown, S.S., President/Rector.

Address admission inquiries to Rev. James P. Oberle, S.S., Director of Admissions.

Samra University of Oriental Medicine

3000 South Robertson Boulevard
Los Angeles, California 90034

Tel: (310) 202-6444 **E-mail:** admissions@samra.edu
Fax: (310) 202-6007 **Internet:** www.samra.edu

Institution Description: Samra University of Oriental Medicine is a private, nonprofit corporation. *Degrees awarded:* Master's. *Enrollment:* 281.

Accreditation: *Professional:* acupuncture

Calendar: Quarters.

Degree Requirements: Completion of prescribed program.

Degrees Conferred: 61 *master's:* acupuncture.

Fees and Other Expenses: *Tuition per academic year 2004–05:* $5,760.

Financial Aid: Aid from institutionally generated funds is provided on the basis of academic merit, financial need. has a Program Participation Agreement with the U.S. Department of Education for eligible students to receive Pell Grants and other federal aid.

Departments and Teaching Staff: *Total instructional faculty:* 14. *Student-to-faculty ratio:* 20:1

Enrollment: Total enrollment 281 (58.4% men, 41.6% women).

International Students: 51 nonresident aliens enrolled fall 2004. Students from Europe, Asia, Central and South America, Canada. Programs available to aid students whose native language is not English: Some classes taught in Chinese and Korean. No financial aid specifically designated for international students.

Student Life: No on-campus housing.

Chief Executive Officer: Dr. Hyung Joo Park, President.

Address admission inquiries to Elizabeth Gomez, Registrar.

Samuel Merritt College

370 Hawthorne Avenue
Oakland, California 94609

Tel: (510) 869-6511 **E-mail:** admission@samuelmerritt.edu
Fax: (510) 869-6525 **Internet:** www.samuelmerrit.edu

Institution Description: The primary purpose of Samuel Merritt College is to prepare graduates in health-related disciplines to assume responsible roles as health care professionals and members of their communities. The California College of Podiatric Medicine merged with Samuel Merritt College in 2002. *Enrollment:* 896. *Degrees awarded:* Baccalaureate, master's, doctorate, first-professional. Post-master's certificates also awarded.

Accreditation: *Regional:* WASC. *Professional:* nurse anesthesia education, nursing, nursing education, occupational therapy, physical therapy, physician assisting, podiatry

History: Founded in 1909 as a hospital school of nursing.

Calendar: Semesters. Academic year early Sept. to late May. Degrees conferred and formal commencement May. Mandatory summer sessions for some graduate programs.

Characteristics of Freshmen: 120 applicants (8 men, 112 women). 55.8% of applicants admitted; 13.4l% admitted and enrolled full-time.

67% (6 students) submitted SAT scores; 22% (2 students) submitted ACT scores. *25th percentile:* SAT Verbal 483, SAT Math 496, ACT Composite 22. *75th percentile:* SAT Verbal 598, SAT Math 615, ACT Composite 23.

68% of entering freshmen expected to graduate within years. 100% of freshmen from California.

Admission: *Requirements:* Freshmen candidates are admitted directly into the BSN program for both fall and spring semesters; minimum GPA of 2.5 and SAT combined score of 920; strong college-preparatory curriculum with specific prerequisites. Master's program in nursing students must have a BSN, a current California RN license, and clinical practice experience. The Master of Physical Therapy program requires a baccalaureate degree; cumulative GPA for last 60 semester units of 2.8 and a cumulative science GPA of 2.6; minimum GRE composite score of 1500 and a minimum verbal score of 450; letter(s) of reference. The Master of Occupational Therapy program requires applicants to have a a baccalaureate degree; minimum cumulative GPA of 2.8 for last 60 semester units; GRE composite score of 1500 and a minimum verbal score of 450. Contact

the school for specific admission requirements for the Master of Science in Physical Therapy degree program. *For transfer students:* TOEFL score of 600.

Distinctive Educational Programs: The Bachelor of Science in Nursing degree is offered in conjunction with Saint Mary's College of California, a liberal arts college in Moraga, California.

Degrees Conferred: 75 *baccalaureate:* health professions and related sciences; 122 *master's:* health professions and related sciences; 65 *first-professional.*

Fees and Other Expenses: *Full-time tuition per academic year 2004–05:* undergraduate $23,768; graduate study charged per unit (contact the college for current rate). *Books and Supplies:* $1,260. *Room and board per academic year:* $10,055.

Financial Aid: Aid from institutionally generated funds is provided on the basis of academic merit, financial need. Institution has a Program Participation Agreement with the U.S. Department of Education for eligible students to receive Pell Grants and other federal aid.

Financial aid to full-time, first-time undergraduate students: 33% received federal grants; 20% state/local grants; 67% institutional grants; 73% received loans.

Departments and Teaching Staff: *Total instructional faculty:* 97. Degrees held by full-time faculty: 48% hold terminal degrees.

Enrollment: Total enrollment 896. Undergraduate 285 (7.4% men, 92.6% women).

Characteristics of Student Body: *Ethnic/racial makeup:* Black non-Hispanic: 12.3%; American Indian or Alaska Native: 1.8%; Asian or Pacific Islander: 23.2%; Hispanic: 14.4%; White non-Hispanic: 39.3%; unknown 9.1%.

International Students: 3 nonresident aliens enrolled fall 2003. No programs to aid students whose native language is not English.

Student Life: The Student Body Association, the California Nursing Students Association, and various associations for graduate students are actively involved in planning educational and social activities throughout the academic year. On-campus housing, computer center, student lounge, swimming pool, workout room, sundeck, and eating facilities are available to students. Secured parking is available on campus.

Library Collections: The John A Graziano Memorial Library contains the largest private health science literature and multimedia collection in the East Bay. 350 active journal subscriptions; access to online information retrieval systems.

Buildings and Grounds: Campus is located in the Summit Medical Center complex in Oakland, California.

Chief Executive Officer: Dr. Sharon L. Diaz, President.

Address admissions inquiries to Anne Seede, Director of Admissions.

San Diego State University

5500 Campanile Drive
San Diego, California 92182-8143

Tel: (619) 594-5200 **E-mail:** admission@sdsu.edu
Fax: (619) 594-1520 **Internet:** www.sdsu.edu

Institution Description: *Enrollment:* 32,936. *Degrees awarded:* Baccalaureate, master's, doctorate. Certificates also awarded.

Accreditation: *Regional:* WASC-Sr. *Professional:* accounting, applied science, art, athletic training, audiology, business, clinical psychology, computer science, dietetics, engineering, health services administration, nursing, nursing education, public administration, public health, recreation and leisure services, rehabilitation counseling, social work, speech-language pathology, teacher education, theatre

History: Established as San Diego State Normal School and chartered 1987; offered first instruction at postsecondary level 1898; changed name to San Diego State Teachers College 1921; awarded first degree (baccalaureate) 1923; changed name to San Diego State College 1935; adopted present name 1971.

Institutional Structure: *Composition of institution:* president, vice president for academic affairs, vice president for business affairs, vice president for student affairs, vice president for university advancement. Full-time instructional 919. Academic governance body, University Senate, meets an average of 9 times per year.

Calendar: Semesters. Academic year late Aug. to late May. Freshmen admitted to fall and spring semesters. Degrees conferred May, Aug., Dec. Formal commencement May. Summer session from May to Aug.

Characteristics of Freshmen: 29,128 applicants (11,972 men, 17,156 women).

49.6% of applicants admitted; 23.7% of admitted students enrolled full-time. 96% (3,600 students) submitted SAT scores. *25th percentile:* SAT Verbal 480, SAT Math 490. *75th percentile:* SAT Verbal 580, SAT Math 800.

26% of entering freshmen expected to graduate within 5 years. 96.3% of freshmen from California. Freshmen from 34 states and 15 foreign countries.

Admission: For fall acceptance, apply during Nov. of year prior to enrollment. Students are notified of acceptance beginning in Jan.

Degree Requirements: Completion of 124 units for graduation; 49 units of general education covering: arts/fine arts, humanities, mathematics, English (including composition); foreign languages, sciences (biological or physical); history, social science, communication, and critical thinking.

Distinctive Educational Programs: Special facilities for using telecommunications in the classroom. Interdisciplinary programs in American studies; Asian studies, child development, comparative literature, European studies, Latin American studies, liberal studies, linguistics, Russian and East European studies, social science. Preprofessional programs in dentistry, law, medicine, veterinary medicine. Honors programs. Study abroad in Australia, France, Germany, Japan, Mexico, The Netherlands, China, Spain, Taiwan, Turkey, United Kingdom. London Semester; Paris Semester. *Other distinctive programs:* Continuing education. Living Learning Center; Language Institute (for foreign students); Developmental Writing Program; General Mathematics Studies; Communications Clinic.

ROTC: Army, Air Force, Navy.

Degrees Conferred: 6,019 *baccalaureate*; 1,686 *master's*; 50 *doctorate*. Bachelor's degrees awarded in top five disciplines: business, management, marketing, and related support 1,216; social sciences 738; psychology 481; liberal arts and sciences, general studies and humanities 479; English language and literature/letters 400.

Fees and Other Expenses: *Full-time tuition per academic year 2004–05:* undergraduate resident $2,936; out-of-state $13,106 (contact the university for current graduate tuition and fees). *Books and supplies:* $1,260. *Room and board per academic year:* $8,787.

Financial Aid: Aid from institutionally generated funds is provided on the basis of academic merit, financial need, athletic ability, other criteria. Institution has a Program Participation Agreement with the U.S. Department of Education for eligible students to receive Pell Grants and other federal aid.

Financial aid to full-time, first-time undergraduate students: need-based scholarship/grants totaling $46,413,000, self-help $56,281,000, parent loans $33,000,000; non-need-based scholarships/grants totaling $5,258.000, self-help $16,426,000, parent loans $30,180,000, athletic awards $3,436,000.

Departments and Teaching Staff: *Total instructional faculty:* 1,580 (full-time 919, part-time 661; women 719, men 861). Total full-time faculty with doctorate, first-professional, or other terminal degree: 790.

Enrollment: Total enrollment 32,936. Undergraduate 26.853, graduate 6,083.

Characteristics of Student Body: *Ethnic/racial makeup:* Black non-Hispanic: 4.2%; American Indian or Alaska Native: .7%; Asian or Pacific Islander:15.5%; Hispanic: 19.2%; White non-Hispanic: 45.8%; unknown: 11.7%.

International Students: 779 nonresident aliens enrolled fall 2004. Students from Europe, Asia, Central and South America, Africa, Canada, Australia. Programs available to aid students whose native language is not English: Social, cultural. English as a Second Language Program. No financial aid specifically designated for international students.

Student Life: The 5 coeducational residence hall house 2,842 students; furnished student apartments house 560 students; 24 national fraternities; 18 national and 4 local sororities. *Intercollegiate athletics:* men only: baseball, basketball, football, golf, soccer, tennis, volleyball; women only: basketball, crew, cross-country, golf, soccer, softball, swimming, tennis, track and field, volleyball, water polo, indoor track. *Special regulations:* Registered cars permitted in designated areas only. *Special services:* Beyond the normal support assistance for student records, medical counseling, financial aid, and housing there exists the following distinctive services: low income and minority counseling, tutoring and advising; Ombudsman; student athlete academic assistance; learning resources center; new student programs, parent programs and parents advisory board; statewide student leadership retreat; student enrichment programs and lectures; 300+ clubs and organizations; New Hampshire exchange; social issues forums and teleconferences; classes in leadership development; leadership library and Student Assessment Center; biannual student opinion poll; Ethnic Mentor and Mentee program; "Quest for the Best" Vice President's award; community service programs. *Student publications, radio: Daily Aztec,* campus paper; *Student Life-lines,* quarterly; *Parenthetically Speaking,* parents newspaper; *Montezuma Life,* biannual literary magazine. Radio stations KPBS and KCR both broadcast 168 hours per week. TV station KPBS broadcasts 126 hours per week. *Surrounding community:* City of San Diego population 1.2 million. The campus is located on a hill above historic Mission Valley, 10 miles from the ocean. Air and rail transportation to the city with bus routes to the campus.

Library Collections: 1,342,740 volumes including bound books, serial backfiles, electronic documents, and government documents not in separate collections. Online catalog. 4,262,200 microforms; 3,500 recordings; 950 compact

discs; 12,615 CD-ROMs. 288 computer work stations. Students have access to the Internet at no charge.

Most important holdings include Zinner Collection on the History of Astronomy; early printed herbals; Calvert Norland Collection (natural sciences).

Buildings and Grounds: Campus area 283 acres.

Chief Executive Officer: Dr. Stephen L. Weber, President.

Address admission inquiries to Dr. Sandra Cook, Director of Admissions.

San Francisco Art Institute

800 Chestnut Street
San Francisco, California 94133-2299

Tel: (415) 749-7020   **E-mail:** admissions@cdmweb.sfai.edu
Fax: (415) 749-4590   **Internet:** www.sfai.edu

Institution Description: San Francisco Art Institute is a private, independent, nonprofit institution affiliated with University of California. *Enrollment:* 655. *Degrees awarded:* Baccalaureate, master's. Post-baccalaureate certificates also awarded.

Accreditation: *Regional:* WASC-Sr. *Professional:* art

History: Established as San Francisco Art Association 1871; offered first instruction at postsecondary level as School of Art and Design 1874; incorporated 1889; became affiliated with the University of California and changed name to Mark Hopkins Institute 1893; changed name to California School of Fine Arts 1916; awarded first degree (baccalaureate) 1954; adopted present official name, The College of the San Francisco Art Institute, 1961.

Institutional Structure: *Governing board:* Board of Trustees. Representation: 31 public trustees, 2 honorary trustees, 8 artist trustees; institutional representation: president of the institute, 4 full-time instructional faculty members (including chairman of faculty senate), 4 students (including chairman of student senate), chairman of artists committee, chairman of San Francisco Art Institute Council. 5 ex officio. *Composition of institution:* Administrators 7 women / 2 men. Academic affairs headed by dean of the college. Management/business/ finances directed by director of administration. Full-time instructional faculty 42. Academic governance body, Faculty Senate.

Calendar: Semesters. Academic year Sept. to May. Freshmen admitted Sept., Jan. Formal commencement May.Summer session of 2 terms from early June to late Aug.

Characteristics of Freshmen: 51% of freshmen from California. Freshmen from 14 states and 4 foreign countries.

Admission: Apply no later than Apr. 1 for early notification; thereafter, rolling admissions on basis of space availability. *Requirements:* Open admissions for graduates from accredited secondary school; GED accepted for applicants aged 21 years or older. *Entrance tests:* For foreign students TOEFL. *For transfer students:* Maximum transfer credit for studio courses limited by residence requirement; for liberal arts 20 hours; for art history 16 hours. Good standing at institution previously attended.

College credit and advanced placement for postsecondary-level work completed in secondary school.

Degree Requirements: *Undergraduate:* 120 semester units distributed among courses in letters and science, art history, studio major, and electives; final year in residence. Additional requirements vary according to major.

Fulfillment of some degree requirements and exemption from some beginning courses possible by passing College Board CLEP, AP. *Grading system:* Honors-pass-no credit; withdraw; incomplete (carries time limit).

Distinctive Educational Programs: Independent study. *Other distinctive programs:* Visiting artists program. Diego Rivera Gallery program provides students with curatorial experience and formal exhibition opportunities. Study abroad in England, The Netherlands, Germany, France, China, Canada, Japan, Italy, Czechoslovakia.

Degrees Conferred: 91 *baccalaureate*; 26 *post-baccalaureate certificates*; 97 *master's*. Bachelor's degrees awarded in top disciplines: visual and performing arts 85; multidisciplinary studies 6.

Fees and Other Expenses: *Full-time tuition per academic year 2004–05:* $24,240. *Books and supplies:* $1,800. *Room and board per academic year:* $9,450. *Other expenses:* $3,625.

Financial Aid: Scholarships and grants awarded on basis of academic merit, financial need. Institution has a Program Participation Agreement with the U.S. Department of Education for eligible students to receive Pell Grants and other federal aid.

Financial aid to full-time, first-time undergraduate students: 46% received federal grants averaging $3,211; 15% state/local grants; 70% institutional grants averaging $11,466; 65% loans averaging $3,244.

Departments and Teaching Staff: *Professors* 26, *associate professors* 11, *assistant professors* 2, *instructors* 3, *part-time* 81.

Total instructional faculty: 124. Degrees held by full-time faculty: Doctorate 5%, master's 82%. 58% hold terminal degrees.

Enrollment: Total enrollment 655. Undergraduate 407.

Characteristics of Student Body: *Ethnic/racial makeup:* Black non-Hispanic: 1.7%; American Indian or Alaska Native: 2.5%; Asian or Pacific Islander: 7.1%; Hispanic: 9.6%; White non-Hispanic: 72.7%.

International Students: 42 nonresident aliens enrolled fall 2003. *Programs available to aid students whose native language is not English:* English as a Second Language Program.

Student Life: No on-campus housing. *Surrounding community:* San Francisco population over: 700,000. Served by mass transit system; airport.

Library Collections: 31,000 volumes. 30,000 microforms; 60,000 slides; 210 current periodical subscriptions. Students have access to online information retrieval services and the Internet.

Buildings and Grounds: Campus is located in 1 building on 3 acres.

Chief Executive Officer: Chris Bratton, President and Dean.

Address admission inquiries to Michael Frendian, Vice President for Enrollment.

San Francisco Conservatory of Music

1201 Ortega Street
San Francisco, California 94122-4498
Tel: (415) 564-8086   **E-mail:** admit@sfcm.edu
Fax: (415) 759-3499   **Internet:** www.sfcm.edu

Institution Description: The San Francisco Conservatory of Music is a private, independent, nonprofit institution. *Enrollment:* 313. *Degrees awarded:* Baccalaureate, master's.

Accreditation: *Regional:* WASC-Sr. *Professional:* music

History: Established 1917; incorporated 1917; first instruction at postsecondary level 1922; first degree (Bachelor of Music) awarded 1950.

Institutional Structure: *Governing board:* Board of Trustees. Extrainstitutional representation: 38 trustees; institutional representation: 1 administrator. 1 ex officio. 39 voting. *Composition of institution:* Administrators 2 men / 4 women. Academic affairs headed by president. Management/business/finances directed by director of finance. Academic governance body, Academic Standards Committee, meets an average of 20 times per year.

Calendar: Semesters. Academic year Aug. to May. Freshmen admitted Sept., Jan. Degrees conferred May. Formal commencement May. No summer session.

Characteristics of Freshmen: 202 applicants (77 men, 125 women). 49.5% of applicants admitted; 69% of entering freshmen expected to graduate within 5 years. 30 freshmen from California. Freshmen from 10 states and 3 foreign countries.

Admission: Rolling admissions plan. For fall admission, apply by Feb. 15. Applications received after that date can only be accepted if vacancies still exist in the department. *Requirements:* Either graduation from secondary school with 3 years English or GED. Audition. 3 years foreign language recommended. Minimum GPA 2.0. *Entrance tests:* SAT or ACT composite. *For transfer students:* 2.0 minimum GPA, no maximum transfer credit.

College credit and advanced placement for postsecondary-level work completed in secondary school and for faculty assessment of audition and exam. Tutoring available. Remedial courses offered in regular academic year;credit given.

Degree Requirements: *For all baccalaureate degrees:* 130 credit hours; 2.0 GPA; 2 semesters in residence; recital. Some baccalaureate degree requirements can be fulfilled by taking College Board CLEP for maximum credit of 36 hours. *Grading system:* A–F; pass-fail; withdraw (carries time limit and deadline after which pass-fail is appended to withdraw).

Distinctive Educational Programs: Independent study. Our community service and chamber music programs provide students with extensive performance opportunities. Visiting artists give frequent master classes at the school.

Degrees Conferred: 36 *baccalaureate:* visual and performing arts; 62 *master's:* visual and performing arts; 12 *post-master's certificates.*

Fees and Other Expenses: *Full-time tuition per academic year 2004–05:* $25,850. *Books and supplies:* $950. *Room and board per academic year:* $8,100. *Other expenses:* $2,900.

Financial Aid: Aid from institutionally generated funds is provided on the basis of financial need, other criteria. Institution has a Program Participation Agreement with the U.S. Department of Education for eligible students to receive Pell Grants and other federal aid.

Financial aid to full-time, first-time undergraduate students: 38% received federal grants; 19 state/local grants; 78% institutional grants averaging $6,120; 47% loans averaging $1,275.

Departments and Teaching Staff: Faculty members are unranked. Music *instructors* 22, *part-time teachers* 41. Student-to-faculty ratio: 6:1. Degrees held by faculty: doctorate 30%, master's 30%, baccalaureate 10%, professional 10%. 30% hold terminal degrees.

Enrollment: Total enrollment 313. Undergraduate 157 (33.5% men, 46.5% women).

Characteristics of Student Body: *Ethnic/racial makeup:* Black non-Hispanic: 1.3%; Asian or Pacific Islander: 14%; Hispanic: 6.4%; White non-Hispanic: 57.3%; unknown: 3.2%.

International Students: 56 nonresident aliens enrolled fall 2004. Students from Europe, Asia, Central and South America, Africa, Canada, Australia, New Zealand. No programs available to aid students whose native language is not English. No financial aid specifically designated for international students.

Student Life: No on-campus housing. *Special services:* Limited medical services. *Surrounding community:* San Francisco population 700,000. Served by mass transit system, airport 15 miles from campus, passenger rail service 6 miles from campus.

Library Collections: 35,000 volumes. Online catalog. 78 current serial subscriptions. 17,000 recordings. Computer work stations available. Students have access to the Internet at no charge.

Special collection of guitar music and recordings; ethnomusicology; musical scores for performance (27,500).

Buildings and Grounds: Campus area under 1 square block. Facilities include classrooms, practice rooms, rehearsal spaces, library and listening room, bookstore, electronic music studio, lounges, and 333-seat performance hall. The extensive instrument collection includes 75 pianos.

Chief Executive Officer: Colin Muldock, President.

Address admission inquiries to Alexander Brose, Director of Admissions.

San Francisco State University

1600 Holloway Avenue
San Francisco, California 94132
Tel: (415) 338-1111   **E-mail:** ugadmit@sfsu.edu
Fax: (415) 338-2514   **Internet:** www.sfsu.edu

Institution Description: San Francisco State University is a multipurpose institution of higher education. *Enrollment:* 29,686. *Degrees awarded:* Baccalaureate, master's. Doctorate in education offered in cooperation with University of California, Berkeley. Certificates also awarded.

Member of Moss Landing Marine Consortium, San Francisco Consortium.

Accreditation: *Regional:* WASC-Sr. *Professional:* art, audiology, business, clinical lab scientist, computer science, counseling, dietetics, engineering, family and consumer science, journalism, music, nursing, nursing education, physical therapy, public health, recreation and leisure services, rehabilitation counseling, social work, speech-language pathology, teacher education, theatre

History: Established and chartered as San Francisco Normal School and offered first instruction at postsecondary level 1899; changed name to San Francisco State Teachers' College 1921, added upper division program 1923, awarded first degree (baccalaureate) 1924; changed name to San Francisco State College 1935; changed name to California State University, San Francisco, 1972; adopted present name 1974.

Institutional Structure: *Composition of institution:* Administrators 85 men / 60 women. Academic affairs headed by vice president for academic affairs. Management/business/finances directed by vice president for administration. Full-time instructional faculty 891 men / 608 women. Academic governance body, Academic Senate, meets an average of 16 times per year.

Calendar: Semesters. Academic year late Aug. to early June. Freshmen admitted Sept., Jan. Degrees conferred May, Aug, Jan. Formal commencement May. Summer session of overlapping terms early June to mid-Aug.

Characteristics of Freshmen: 15,325 applicants (5,453 men, 9,872 women). 64.9% of applicants admitted; 23% of admitted students enrolled full-time.

78% (1,961 students) submitted SAT scores. *25th percentile*: SAT Verbal 430, SAT Math 440. *75th percentile*: SAT Verbal 560, SAT Math 570.

24% of entering freshmen expected to graduate within 5 years. 97% of freshmen from California. Freshmen from 13 states and 8 foreign countries.

Admission: Rolling admissions plan. For fall acceptance, apply as early as Nov. 1 of previous year. For spring acceptance, apply as early as Aug. 1 of previous year. Application deadlines vary by major and program.

Degree Requirements: *For all undergraduate degrees:* 124-132 units; general education requirements; 30 units in residence; 2.0 GPA minimum; major requirements as designated by program; written English requirements; U.S. history and government requirement. *Grading system:* A–F; credit-no credit; withdrawal; incomplete.

Distinctive Educational Programs: School offers college credit for extrainstitutional learning on basis of ACE *2006 Guide to the Evaluation of Educational Experiences in the Armed Services*, portfolio assessment. Work-experience programs. Flexible meeting places and schedules, including off-campus center (in San Francisco) and evening classes. Special facilities for using telecommunications in the classroom. Interdisciplinary programs in American studies, creative arts, labor studies, liberal studies, museum studies, science, social science, urban studies. Preprofessional programs in allopathic and osteopathic medicine, dentistry, veterinary medicine, pharmacy, podiatry, related health professions, law business, physical therapy. Facilities and programs for independent research, including individual majors, tutorials. Off-campus study at Moss Landing Marine Laboratories, Sierra Nevada Field Campus, the Paul F. Romberg Tiburon Center for Environmental Studies. *Other distinctive programs:* Extended education, including extension and external degree, certificate, and other post-baccalaureate study programs. Study abroad in Australia, Brazil, Canada, Denmark, France, Germany, Israel, Italy, Japan, Mexico, New Zealand, China/Taiwan, Spain, Sweden, United Kingdom, Zimbabwe.

ROTC: Cross enrollment with other universities for Air Force, Army, and Navy.

Degrees Conferred: 4,574 *baccalaureate*; 1,714 *master's*; 17 *doctorate*. Bachelor's degrees awarded in top five disciplines: business, management, marketing, and related support services 1,175; visual and performing arts 389; social sciences 370; psychology 361; English language and literature/letters 328.

Fees and Other Expenses: *Full-time tuition per academic year:* $2,880 instate undergraduate; out-of-state $13,050. Contact the university for graduate tuition and fees. *Room and board per academic year:* $10,458. *Books and supplies:* $1,260. *Other expenses:* $3,534.

Financial Aid: Aid from institutionally generated funds is provided on the basis of academic merit, financial need. Institution has a Program Participation Agreement with the U.S. Department of Education for eligible students to receive Pell Grants and other federal aid.

Financial aid to full-time, first-time undergraduate students: 28% received federal grants averaging $3,550; 23% state/local grants averaging $1,544; 28% institutional grants averaging $1,698; 28% loans averaging $3,136.

Departments and Teaching Staff: Behavioral and social sciences *professors* 131, *associate professors* 14, *assistant professors* 26, *instructors* 3, *part-time lecturers* 44; business 71, 23, 4, 15, 66; creative arts 72, 18, 19, 8, 77; education 79, 28, 19, 12, 96; ethnic studies 13, 7, 3, 1, 40; health, physical education, recreation/leisure studies 18, 9, 2, 17, 29; humanities 107, 25, 19, 13, 49; science 106, 20, 14, 10, 60.

Total full-time instructional faculty: 1,112.3 FTE. Degrees held by full-time faculty: Doctorate 84.77%, master's 13.11%, baccalaureate 1.65%, professional .47%. 85.24% hold terminal degrees.

Enrollment: Total enrollment 29,686. Undergraduate 22,798 (41.1% men, 58.9% women).

Characteristics of Student Body: *Ethnic/racial makeup:* Black non-Hispanic: 6.1%; American Indian or Alaska Native: .9%; Asian or Pacific Islander: 31%; Hispanic: 12.8%; White non-Hispanic: 26.3%; unknown: 16.5%.

International Students: 1,459 undergraduate nonresident aliens enrolled 2003. Students from Europe, Asia, Latin America, Africa, Canada, Australia, New Zealand. Programs available to aid students whose native language is not English: Social and cultural. English as a Second Language Program. No financial aid specifically designated for international students.

Student Life: On-campus residence halls house 6% of student body. *Varsity athletics:* men only: baseball, basketball, cross-country, football, soccer, swimming, track and field, wrestling; women only: basketball, cross-country, soccer, softball, swimming and diving, track and field, volleyball. *Special regulations:* Cars permitted in designated parking lots; fee charged. *Special services:* Academic advising, academic and personal counseling, health services, disabled students office; offices for veterans, international students, re-entry students, and students over: 60. *Student publications, radio, television: Golden Gater,* published twice weekly; *Prism,* general interest magazine published twice each semester; *Transfer,* literary magazine published twice yearly in association with Creative Writing Department. Radio station KSFS. University television station SFSU Cable 35. *Surrounding community:* San Francisco population 750,800. Served by mass transit bus and rail system; airport 10 miles from campus; passenger rail service 15 miles from campus.

Library Collections: 780,500 volumes. 2,210,000 microforms; 72,500 audiovisual materials; Online catalog. Access electronically to 3,700 periodicals. Access to online information retrieval systems.

Most important special holdings include Frank V. de Bellis Collection (early Italian literature, music, and art); KQED Film Collection; Labor Archives Collection.

Buildings and Grounds: Campus area 100 acres.

Chief Executive Officer: Dr. Robert A. Corrigan, President.

Address admission inquiries to Admissions Office.

San Francisco Theological Seminary

2 Kensington Road
San Anselmo, California 94960
Tel: (415) 451-2800   **E-mail:** sftsinfo@sfts.edu
Fax: (415) 451-2852   **Internet:** www.sfts.edu

Institution Description: San Francisco Theological Seminary is a private, independent, nonprofit institution affiliated with the Presbyterian Church (U.S>A) and maintains a Southern California campus in Pasadena's First Presbyterian Church. It is a member of the Graduate Theological Union that was created by nine Protestant and Roman Catholic institutions to coordinate joint programs and award graduate degrees. See separate entry for Graduate Theological Union. *Enrollment:* 548. *Degrees awarded:* Master's, doctorate, first-professional.

Accreditation: *Regional:* WASC-Sr. *Professional:* theology

History: Established and offered first instruction at postsecondary level 1871; incorporated 1872; awarded first degree (first-professional) 1917. *See* Robert B. Coote and John S. Madsell, *San Francisco Theological Seminary, The Shaping of a Western School of the Church,* (First Presbyterian Church, San Anselmo, 1999).

Institutional Structure: *Governing board:* Board of Trustees. Representation: 50 trustees, including 1 alumni, 2 honorary, 2 life. 40 voting. *Composition of institution:* Administrators 14 men / 12 women Academic affairs headed by dean. Management/business/finances directed by business administrator. Full-time instructional faculty 23. Academic governance body, Faculty, meets 8 times per year.

Calendar: Semesters. Jan. term. Academic year Sept. to May. Entering students admitted Sept. Degrees conferred and formal commencement May. Summer session from June to Aug.

Admission: Rolling admissions plan. For fall acceptance, apply as early as 1 year prior to enrollment, but not later than May 15 of year of enrollment. *Requirements:* Baccalaureate degree from accredited college or university. Minimum GPA 3.0. *Entrance tests:* For foreign students TOEFL. *For transfer students:* From accredited theological school 3.0 minimum GPA, 36 units maximum transfer credit. Tutoring available. Noncredit remedial courses offered during regular academic year.

Degree Requirements: *For first-professional degrees:* 81 semester units; 2.0 GPA; 3 years in residence; distribution requirements; field education. *Grading system:* A–F; pass-fail; withdraw (carries time limit); incomplete.

Distinctive Educational Programs: Work-experience programs, including internships. Evening classes. Cooperative master's and doctoral programs and cross-registration through Graduate Theological Union. *Other distinctive programs:* Extension education programs, including advanced degree programs in pastoral studies.

Degrees Conferred: 13 *master's*; 20 *doctorate*; 40 *first-professional:* master of divinity.

Fees and Other Expenses: *Full-time tuition per academic year 2004–05:* $9,450. *Required fees:* $200. Housing $600 per semester.

Financial Aid: Aid from institutionally generated funds is provided on the basis of financial need.

Departments and Teaching Staff: *Total instructional faculty:* 24. Total faculty with doctorate, first-professional, or other terminal degree: 24. Student-to-faculty ratio: 10:1.

Enrollment: Total enrollment 548.

Characteristics of Student Body: *Ethnic/racial makeup:* Black non-Hispanic: 3%; American Indian or Native: Alaskan .2%; Asian or Pacific Islander: 10.4%; Hispanic: 3.5%; White non-Hispanic: 38.8%; unknown: 4.8%.

International Students: 112 nonresident aliens enrolled fall 2004. Students from Europe, Asia, Central and South America, Africa, Canada, Australia, New Zealand. No programs available to aid students whose native language is not English.

Student Life: On-campus residence halls house 70% of student body. 16% of student body live off campus in San Anselmo. 80% of married students request institutional housing; 72% are so housed. *Special regulations:* Cars permitted without restrictions. *Special services:* Van service to consortium schools. *Student publications: Overview,* an annual student handbook. *Surrounding community:* San Anselmo population 15,000. San Francisco, 20 miles from campus, is nearest metropolitan area. Served by mass transit bus system; airport 40 miles from campus.

Publications: Sources of information about San Francisco Theological Seminary include a quarterly journal, *Chimes,* distributed among students, alumni, and friends of the seminary.

Library Collections: Library service provided by Graduate Theological Union.

Buildings and Grounds: Campus area 22 acres.
Chief Executive Officer: Dr. Philip W. Butin, President.
Address admission inquiries to Office of Recruitment.

San Jose State University

One Washington Square
San Jose, California 95192-0031
Tel: (408) 924-1000   **E-mail:** admissions@sjsu.edu
Fax: (408) 924-1018   **Internet:** www.sjsu.edu

Institution Description: *Enrollment:* 29,044. *Degrees awarded:* Baccalaureate, master's.
Member of the consortium Moss Landing Marine Laboratories.

Accreditation: *Regional:* WASC-Sr. *Professional:* art, business, computer science, dance, dietetics, engineering, journalism, librarianship, music, nursing, nursing education, occupational therapy, planning, public administration, public health, recreation and leisure services, social work, speech-language pathology, teacher education

History: Established as Minns' Evening Normal School, a department of San Francisco School System, and offered first instruction at postsecondary level 1857; became state institution and changed name to California State Normal School 1862; changed name to San Jose State Teachers College, added upper division 1921; awarded first degree (baccalaureate) 1923; changed name to San Jose State College 1935, to California State University, San Jose 1972; adopted present name 1974. *See* Benjamin Gilbert and Charles Burdick, *Washington Square 1857–1979* (San Jose: San Jose State University, 1980) for further information.

Institutional Structure: *Composition of institution:* Administrators 46 men / 26 women. Academic affairs headed by academic vice president. Management/ business/finances directed by executive vice president. Full-time instructional faculty 736. Academic governance body, Academic Senate, meets an average of 20 times per year.

Calendar: Semesters. Academic year Aug. to May. Freshmen admitted Sept., Feb. Degrees conferred May, Aug., Dec. Formal commencement May. Summer session of 3 terms from early June to late Aug.

Characteristics of Freshmen: 13,078 applicants (6,425 men, 6,653 women). 51.9% of applicants admitted; 26.8% of admitted students enrolled full-time. 92% (1,836 students) submitted SAT scores. *25th percentile*: SAT Verbal 420, SAT Math 450. *75th percentile*: SAT Verbal 540, SAT Math 570. 97% of freshmen from California. Freshmen from 19 states and 27 foreign countries.

Admission: For fall acceptance, apply as early as Nov. of previous year, but not later than first day of classes. Students are notified of acceptance in Mar. Early acceptance available.

Degree Requirements: Minimum of 124 credits; completion of prescribed curriculum.

Distinctive Educational Programs: Credit granted for extrainstitutional learning on the basis of ACE *2006 Guide to the Evaluation of Educational Experiences in the Armed Services.* Tutoring available. Remedial courses offered in summer session and during regular academic year. Evening classes. External degree programs. Special facilities for using telecommunications in the classroom. Interdepartmental programs in child development, liberal studies, women's studies. Honors program. Individual majors.

ROTC: Army, Air Force.

Degrees Conferred: 3,854 *baccalaureate;* 2,066 *master's.* Bachelor's degree awarded in top five disciplines: business, management, marketing, and related support services 1,250; engineering 362; visual and performing arts 282; health professions and related clinical sciences 281; computer and information sciences and support services 272.

Fees and Other Expenses: *Full-time tuition per academic year:* $2,958 undergraduate resident, $13,128 out-of-state; contact the university for current graduate tuition and fees. *Room and board per academic year:* $8,136. *Books and supplies:* $1,260.

Financial Aid: Aid from institutionally generated funds is provided on the basis of academic merit, financial need, athletic ability. Institution has a Program Participation Agreement with the U.S. Department of Education for eligible students to receive Pell Grants and other federal aid.

Financial aid to full-time, first-time undergraduate students: 33% received federal grants averaging $3,241; 31% state/local grants averaging $1,652; 29 institutional grants averaging $2,051; 18% received loans averaging $2,587.

Departments and Teaching Staff: *Total instructional faculty:* 1,925 (full-time 791, par time 1,134). Student-to-faculty ratio: 17.20:1. Degrees held by full-time faculty: Doctorate 82.68%. 86.98% hold terminal degrees.

Enrollment: Total enrollment 29,044.

Characteristics of Student Body: *Ethnic/racial makeup:* Black non-Hispanic: 4.3%; American Indian or Alaska Native: .4%; Asian or Pacific Islander: 50.5%; Hispanic: 12.8%; White non-Hispanic: 21.6%; unknown: 14.2%.

International Students: 3,466 nonresident aliens enrolled fall 2003. Programs available to aid students whose native language is not English: English as a Second Language Program. No financial aid specifically designated for international students.

Student Life: On-campus residence halls house 7% of student body. Residence halls for men and women constitute 100% of such space. Fraternities, sororities, International House also offer residence space. Housing available for married students. 15% of students live on campus. *Intercollegiate athletics:* men only, baseball, basketball, football, soccer; women only: basketball, swimming, tennis, volleyball. *Special regulations:* Cars permitted in designated areas only. *Special services:* Learning Resources Center, medical services, shuttle bus system between north and south campuses. *Student publications, radio: Independent Weekly,* a newspaper; *The Reed,* a biannual magazine; *Spartan Daily,* a newspaper. Radio station KSJS broadcasts irregularly. *Surrounding community:* San Jose population 894,495. Served by mass transit bus system; airport 10 miles from campus; passenger rail service 5 miles from campus.

Publications: *San Jose Studies* (quarterly) first published in 1975.

Library Collections: 900,000 volumes. 215,000 government documents; 1,100,000 microforms; 4,500 periodicals. Access to online information retrieval systems.

Most important holdings include John Steinbeck Center Collection; Dr. Martin Luther King, Jr. Civil Rights Collection; Ira F. Brilliant Center for Beethoven Studies Collection.

Buildings and Grounds: Campus area 154 acres.
Chief Executive Officer: Dr. Donald Kassing, President.
Address admission inquiries to Marshall Rose, Vice President for Enrollment and Academic Services.

Santa Clara University

500 El Camino Real
Santa Clara, California 95053-0015
Tel: (408) 554-4000   **E-mail:** ugadmissions@scu.edu
Fax: (408) 554-6705   **Internet:** www.scu.edu

Institution Description: Santa Clara University is a private, independent, nonprofit institution affiliated with the Society of Jesus, Roman Catholic Church. *Enrollment:* 7,908. *Degrees awarded:* Baccalaureate, masters's, doctorate, first-professional (law).

Accreditation: *Regional:* WASC-Sr. *Professional:* accounting, business, engineering, law, music

History: Established as Santa Clara College and offered first instruction at postsecondary level 1851; chartered 1855; awarded first degree (baccalaureate) 1857; changed name to University of Santa Clara 1912; adopted present name recently. *See* Rev. Gerald McKevit, S.J., *The University of Santa Clara: A History 1851–1977* (Stanford: Stanford Press, 1979) and Giacomini, George Gerald McKevitt, S.J., *Serving the Intellect, Touching the Heart: A Portrait of Santa Clara University, 1851-2001,* (Santa Clara University, 2002) for further information.

Institutional Structure: *Governing board:* The President and Board of Trustees of Santa Clara College. Representation: 35 members. 2 ex officio. All voting. *Composition of institution:* Administrators 13 men / 8 women. Academic affairs headed by provost. Management/business/finances directed by vice president for business and finance. Full-time instructional faculty 423. Academic governance body, Faculty Senate, meets an average of 3 times per year.

Calendar: Quarters. Academic year Sept. to June. Freshmen admitted Sept., Jan., Mar. Degrees conferred June, Aug. Dec., Mar. Formal commencement June; for law school, May. Summer session of 2 terms from June to Sept.

Characteristics of Freshmen: 57% of applicants accepted. 27% of accepted applicants enrolled full-time. 95% (1,118 students) submitted SAT scores; 34% (395 students) submitted ACT scores. *25th percentile*: SAT Verbal 550, SAT Math 560, ACT Composite 24. *75th percentile*: SAT Verbal 640, SAT Math 660; ACT Composite 28.

2 National Merit Scholars. 83% of entering freshmen expected to graduate within 5 years. 63% of freshmen from California. Freshmen from 35 states and 11 foreign countries.

Admission: Modified rolling admissions plan. For fall acceptance, apply as early as July 1 of previous year, but not later than Jan. 15 of year of enrollment. Students are notified of acceptance beginning in Dec. of previous year. *Requirements:* Graduation from secondary school with 18 units which must include 4 English, 3 in a foreign language, 1 history, 2 laboratory science, 4 math. Additional requirements for some programs. *Entrance tests:* College Board SAT. For foreign students TOEFL. *For transfer students:* From 4-year accredited institution maximum transfer credit limited only by residence requirement; from 2-year accredited institution 88 quarter units.

College credit and advanced placement for postsecondary-level work completed in secondary school. Tutoring available.

Degree Requirements: *Undergraduate:* 175–193 quarter units; 2.0 GPA; 3 terms in residence; general education requirements which must include 3 religious studies courses. *Grading system:* A–F; pass-fail; withdraw (carries time limit).

Distinctive Educational Programs: Work-experience programs, including cooperative education, field work. Interdisciplinary programs. Facilities and programs for independent research, including honors programs, individual majors. Study abroad in Austria, England, France, Germany, Ireland, Italy, Russia, Spain, Japan, Singapore, Taiwan, China, Australia, Argentina, Brazil, Chile, Dominican Republic, South Korea, Vietnam, and other. *Other distinctive programs:* Continuing education includes professional and religious education, child and family research, international business and retail studies.

ROTC: Army offered in cooperation with San Jose State University. 12 commissions awarded 2004–05.

Degrees Conferred: 1,138 *baccalaureate* (B), 704 *master's* (M), 6 *doctorate* (D): agriculture 1 (M); biological/life sciences 31 (B); business/marketing 350 (B), 308 (M); communications/communication technologies 92 (B); education 75 (M); engineering and engineering technologies 135 (B), 240 (M), 6 (D); English 48 (B); foreign languages and literature 29 (B); interdisciplinary studies 43 (B); law/legal studies 14 (M); liberal arts/general studies 35 (B); mathematics 12 (B), 1 (M); natural resources/environmental science 4 (B); philosophy/religion/theology 39 (B), 12 (M); physical sciences 11 (B); psychology 95 (B), 53 (M); social sciences and history 74 (B); visual and performing arts 40 (B). 259 *first-professional:* law.

Fees and Other Expenses: *Full-time tuition per academic year 2005–06:* Undergraduate $28,899; graduate tuition $365 to $600 per unit (varies by program); law $31,980. *Room and board per academic year:* $10,032.

Financial Aid: Santa Clara University offers a direct lending program. Aid from institutionally generated funds is provided on the basis of academic merit, financial need, athletic ability. Institution has a Program Participation Agreement with the U.S. Department of Education for eligible students to receive Pell Grants and other federal aid.

Financial aid to full-time, first-time undergraduate students: need-based scholarships/grants totaling $33,208,397, self-help $7,604,833; non-need-based scholarships/grants totaling $9,648,773, self-help $5,445,005, parent loans $14,007,415, tuition waivers $1,866,192, athletic awards $2,689,386.

Graduate and Law School aid: 457 federal and state-funded fellowships/grants totaling $6,581,507; 1,201 federal and state-funded loans totaling $19,691,924; 30 work-study jobs worth $127,164; 21 other fellowships/grants totaling $556,500; 41 teaching assistantships totaling $378,209; 33 research assistantships totaling $250,776.

Departments and Teaching Staff: *Total instructional faculty:* 710 (full-time 423, part-time 287; member of minority groups 116; women 276, men 434). Total faculty with doctorate, first-professional, or other terminal degree: 535 Student-to-faculty ratio: 12.25:1. *Faculty development:* $1,334,536 total grants for research. 47 faculty members awarded sabbaticals 2004–05.

Enrollment: Total enrollment 7,908. Undergraduate full-time 1,915 men / 2,401 women, part-time 55m / 63w; first-professional full-time 464m/ 474w, part-time 32m / 39w; graduate full-time 306m / 291w, part-time 1,111m / 757w.

Characteristics of Student Body: *Ethnic and racial makeup:* number of Black non-Hispanic: 124; American Indian or Alaska Native: 24; Asian or Pacific Islander: 848; Hispanic: 586; White non-Hispanic: 2,489; unknown: 216. *Age distribution:* number under 18: 18; 18–19: 1,784; 20–21: 2,882; 22–24: 597; 25–29: 87; 30–34: 36; 35–39: 10; 40–49: 12; 50–64: 6.

International Students: 629 nonresident aliens enrolled fall 2004. No programs available to aid students whose native language is not English. No financial aid specifically designated for international students.

Student Life: On-campus residence halls house 44% of student body. . *Intercollegiate athletics:* men only: baseball, basketball, crew, cross-country, golf, outdoor track, soccer, tennis, water polo; women only: basketball, crew, cross-country, golf, outdoor track, soccer, softball, tennis, volleyball, water polo. *Special regulations:* Cars permitted in designated areas only. *Special services:* Drahmann Advising Center; medical services. *Student publications, radio: The Advocate,* a monthly law school newspaper; *The Santa Clara Review,* a quarterly literary magazine; *Redwood,* a yearbook; *The Santa Clara Law Review,* a quarterly journal; *The Santa Clara,* a weekly newspaper. Radio station KSCU. *Surrounding community:* Santa Clara population 107,000. Served by mass transit bus system; airport 3 miles from campus; passenger rail service less than 1 mile from campus.

Library Collections: 932,498 volumes. Online catalog. Current serial subscriptions: 7,996 paper; 260 microform; 810 via electronic access. 4,240 record-

ings. 205 computer work stations. Students have access to the Internet at no charge. Total budget for books and materials 2004–05: $3,507,721.

Most important holdings include rare book collection containing the Levertov Collection; California Room containing special California Fiction Collection; Clay M. Greene Manuscript Collection.

Buildings and Grounds: Campus area 104 acres. *New buildings:* Residential Learning Complex completed 2000; Facilities Building 2000; 21st Century Library Automated Retrieval System 2005.

Chief Executive Officer: Rev. Paul L. Locatelli, S.J., President.

Address undergraduate admission inquiries to Sanara Hayes, Dean of Undergraduate Admissions; direct graduate admission inquiries directly to School of Law, Graduate School of Business, or Graduate School of Engineering.

School of Law

Degree Programs Offered: *First-professional*; *Master of Laws* in Comparative and International Law; Intellectual Property; U.S. Law for Foreign Lawyers.

Admission: Graduation from accredited college or university; LSAT; LSDAS.

Degree Requirements: 86 credit hours, 2.3 GPA, 3 years in residence.

Departments and Teaching Staff: Law *professors* 26, *associate professors* 3, *assistant professors* 2, *instructors* 5, *part-time teachers* 23. *Total instructional faculty:* 59. Degrees held by full-time faculty: Doctorate 100%, baccalaureate 100%, professional 100%. 100% hold terminal degrees.

Distinctive Educational Programs: Internships and clinical practice programs. Study abroad in Australia, England, France, Germany, Japan, Hong Kong, Malaysia, Singapore, South Korea, Switzerland, Thailand, Vietnam. Joint J.D.-M.B.A. degree program; L.L.M. degree program. Juris Doctor/Master of Science in Taxation Combined Degree Program with San Jose State University. Cross-registration with Golden State University, University of California at Davis, University of San Francisco. Public interest law program with Golden State University, University of California, Hastings College of the Law.

Saybrook Graduate School and Research Center

450 Pacific Street
San Francisco, California 94133-4640
Tel: (415) 433-9200   **E-mail:** admissions@saybrook.edu
Fax: (415) 433-9271   **Internet:** www.saybrook.edu

Institution Description: Saybrook Graduate School and Research Center (formerly Saybrook Institute) is a private, independent, nonprofit institution offering external degree programs. All coursework is done off campus as independent study. *Enrollment:* 517. *Degrees awarded:* Master's, doctorate.

Accreditation: *Regional:* WASC-Sr.

History: Established 1970 as Humanistic Psychology Institute; chartered, incorporated, and offered first instruction at postsecondary level 1971; first degree (doctorate) awarded 1974; adopted present name 1982.

Institutional Structure: *Governing board:* Board of Trustees. Extrainstitutional representation: 15 trustees, including 1 alumnus. *Composition of institution:* Administrators 7 men / 8 women. Academic affairs headed by vice president; management headed by vice president of finance and operations. Full-time instructional faculty 11 men / 8 women. Academic governance body, the faculty, meets monthly.

Calendar: Semesters. Academic year Sept. to Aug. Students admitted Sept. and Mar.

Admission: Degree students begin studies in Sept. or Mar. Applications are received at all times of the year and individual admissions decisions will be rendered as quickly as possible after an application file is fully complete for Mar. or Sept. admission. *Requirements:* bachelor's degree from a regionally accredited institution is required for all applicants to the master's degree programs. Master's degree from a regionally accredited institution is required of all applicants to the doctoral degree programs. A 3.0 or higher GPA is highly recommended. *For transfer students:* Maximum of 12 graduate units/credits toward master's degree; maximum of 18 graduate units/credits toward a doctoral degree ("all-but-dissertation" candidates accepted). 31 units/credits may be transferred toward a doctoral program if entering

Degree Requirements: *For all master's degrees:* 25 units of coursework, and 6 units thesis/1 year minimum duration. *For all doctoral degrees:* 58 units of coursework, three 5,000 word candidacy essays, and 9 unit dissertation. Oral defense of candidacy essays and dissertation. 3-year minimum duration. All students required to two one-week residential conference per year which are located in the Bay area. *Grading system:* Pass.

Distinctive Educational Programs: Interdisciplinary doctorate in human sciences. Leadership and Organizational Inquiry master's program; Organization Systems Inquiry doctoral program.

Degrees Conferred: 21 *master's* (M); 30 *doctorate* (D): psychology 16 (M), 22 (D), other 5 (M), 8 (D).

Fees and Other Expenses: *Tuition per academic year:* Contact the institute for current tuition and fees.

Financial Aid: Aid from institutionally generated funds is provided on the basis of academic merit.

Departments and Teaching Staff: *Total instructional faculty:* 114. *Degrees held by full-time faculty:* doctorate 100%. All faculty members hold terminal degrees.

Enrollment: Total enrollment 517 (full-time 157 men / 349 women, part-time 4m / 7w).

Characteristics of Student Body: *Ethnic/racial makeup:* number of Black non-Hispanic: 25; American Indian or Native: Alaskan 5; Asian or Pacific Islander: 13; Hispanic: 13; White non-Hispanic: 286.

International Students: 13 nonresident aliens enrolled fall 2004. No programs available to aid students whose native language is not English. No financial aid specifically designated for international students.

Student Life: *Special services:* Learning Resources Center.

Publications: Sources of information about Humanistic Psychology Institute include *Perspectives*, a triennial magazine. *Saybrook Review* (biannual) first published 1978 as *HPI Review*.

Library Collections: 6,000 volumes. Online catalog. Access to 10,000 serials via electronic access. Students have access to the Internet at no charge.

Most important special collections include the Saybrook Online Catalog of Dissertations; Rollo May Collection.

Chief Executive Officer: Dr. Maureen O'Hara, President.

Address admission inquiries to Admissions Department.

Scripps College

1030 North Columbia Avenue
Claremont, California 91711
Tel: (909) 621-8149   **E-mail:** admission@scrippscollege.edu
Fax: (909) 607-7508   **Internet:** www.scrippscollege.edu

Institution Description: Scripps College is a private, independent, nonprofit college for women. *Enrollment:* 839. *Degrees awarded:* Baccalaureate.

Accreditation: *Regional:* WASC-Sr.

History: Established and chartered as Scripps College for Women 1926; offered first instruction at postsecondary level and adopted present name 1927; awarded first degree (baccalaureate) 1931.

Institutional Structure: *Governing board:* Scripps College Board of Trustees. Extrainstitutional representation: 37 trustees including 17 alumnae, 2 recent graduates, and 2 parents. 36 voting. 13 emeriti trustees. Composition of institution: senior administrators 2 men / 8 women. Academic affairs headed by dean of faculty. Management/business/finances directed by vice president of business affairs. Full-time instructional faculty 65. Academic governance body, Faculty Executive Committee, meets weekly during school year.

Calendar: Semesters. Academic year Sept. to May. Freshmen admitted Sept., Jan. Degrees conferred Oct., June. Formal commencement May. No summer session.

Characteristics of Freshmen: 48.75 of applicants admitted; 24% of applicants admitted and enrolled full-time.

94% (190 students) submitted SAT scores; 41% (84 students) submitted ACT scores. *25th percentile*: SAT Verbal 630, SAT Math 610; ACT Composite 26. *75th percentile*: SAT Verbal 740, SAT Math 700; ACT Composite 31.

83% of entering freshmen expected to graduate within 5 hears. 41% of freshmen from California. Freshmen from 28 states and 6 foreign countries.

Admission: For fall acceptance, apply as early as Sept. 1 of previous year, but not later than Feb. 1 of year of enrollment. Students are notified of acceptance Apr. 1. Early acceptance available. *Requirements:* Recommend either graduation from accredited secondary school with 20 units, including 4 in English, 4 foreign language, 4 mathematics, 4 laboratory science, 4 social science and history; or GED. Personal interview strongly recommended. *Entrance tests:* College Board SAT. Recommend 2 achievement tests (English composition and foreign language). For foreign students TOEFL. *For transfer students:* 3.0 minimum GPA; 16 semester courses maximum transfer credit.

College credit and advanced placement for postsecondary-level work completed in secondary school. Tutoring available.

Degree Requirements: 32 semester courses; 2.0 GPA; 2 years in residence; core courses in humanities, senior thesis, exhibit, or performance; demonstrated competence in a foreign language and in science. *Grading system:* A–F; pass-fail; withdraw (carries time limit).

Distinctive Educational Programs: *For undergraduates:* Internships. Evening classes. Accelerated degree programs with Claremont Graduate School in business administration, government, international relations, public policy studies, and religion; with Stanford University in engineering. Facilities and programs for independent research, including honors programs, individual majors, tutorials, independent study. Study abroad in France, Ecuador, Germany, Zimbabwe and in various locations through Claremont Colleges and other approved institutions. Washington (DC) semester at American University. United Nations semester with Drew University (NJ) Exchange program with California Institute of Technology. Cross-registration with other Claremont Colleges.

ROTC: Air Force in cooperation with Harvey Mudd College; Army in cooperation with Claremont McKenna College.

Degrees Conferred: 172 *baccalaureate:* area and ethnic studies 21, biological/life sciences 10, computer and information sciences 1, engineering and engineering technologies 3, English 14, foreign languages and literature 5, interdisciplinary studies 16, mathematics 2, natural resources/environmental science 1, philosophy/religion/theology 5, protective services/public administration 1, psychology 15, social sciences and history 48, visual and performing arts 29.

Fees and Other Expenses: *Full-time tuition per academic year 2004–05:* $28,860. *Required fees:* $140. *Room and board per academic year:* $9,000.

Financial Aid: Aid from institutionally generated funds is provided on the basis of financial need. Institution has a Program Participation Agreement with the U.S. Department of Education for eligible students to receive Pell Grants and other federal aid.

Financial aid to full-time, first-time undergraduate students: need-based scholarships/grants totaling $8,378,171, self-help $1,686,044; non-need-based scholarships/grants totaling $1,092,415, self-help $1,091,648, parent loans $1,396,584.

Departments and Teaching Staff: Anthropology *professors* 0, *associate professors* 1, *assistant professors* 1, *instructors* 0, *part-time faculty* 0; art 2, 1, 2, 0, 4; art history 1, 0, 1, 0, 1; classics 0, 0, 1, 0, 1; dance 2, 0, 0, 0, 2; economics 2, 0, 1, 0, 0; English 2, 1, 1, 0, 2; French 2,1, 0, 0, 0, German 1, 1, 0, 0, 0; Hispanic: studies 0, 3, 1, 1, 0; history 1, 3, 0, 1, 0; Italian 1, 0, 1, 0, 1; mathematics 0, 2, 0, 0, 0; music 2, 0, 2, 1, 6; philosophy 1, 2, 1, 0, 0; politics 1, 2, 1, 0, 0; psychology 1, 2, 1, 0, 1; religion 0, 0, 1, 0, 0; writing 0, 0, 1, 0, 6; science 5, 1, 2, 0, 0.

Total instructional faculty: 90 (full-time 65, part-time 25; women 57, men 33). Total faculty with doctorate, first-professional, or other terminal degree: 79. Student-to-faculty ratio: 10.9:1. 14 faculty members awarded sabbaticals 2003–04.

Enrollment: Total enrollment 839 (full-time 828, part-time 11).

Characteristics of Student Body: *Ethnic/racial makeup:* number of Black non-Hispanic: 26; Asian or Pacific Islander: 108; Hispanic: 49; White non-Hispanic: 488; unknown 137. *Age distribution:* number under 18: 12; 18–19: 362; 20–21: 374; 22–24: 64; 25–29: 7; 35–39: 1; 50–64: 2.

International Students: 10 nonresident aliens enrolled fall 2004. Financial aid specifically designated for international students: variable number of scholarships awarded annually; 4 scholarships totaling $79,160 were awarded 2004–05.

Student Life: 97% of student body resides in on-campus residence halls and upperclass apartments. *Intercollegiate athletics:* basketball, cross-country, soccer, softball, swimming, tennis, track, volleyball. *Special regulations:* Cars must be registered. Quiet hours. Residence hall visitation hours set by residents. *Special services:* Office of Black Student Affairs, Chicano Studies Center, Monsour Counseling Center, Baxter Medical Center, International Place, tutoring and continuing education. *Student publications: Guide to Student Life*, an annual information booklet, *La Semeuse*, a yearbook; *This Week @ Scripps*, literary magazine; student newspaper.

Library Collections: 2,406,548 volumes including bound books, serial backfiles, electronic documents, and government documents not in separate collections. Online catalog. Current serial subscriptions: paper and microform 4,019; via electronic access 12,289. 125 computer work stations. Students have access to the Internet at no charge. Total budget for books, periodicals, audiovisual materials, microforms 2004–05: $2,693,793.

Most important holdings include Ida Rust MacPherson Collection by and about women (including Stein collection); John I. Perkins collection of rare books; Scripps College Archives, including Ellen Browning Scripps papers. (All of the above at Denison Library).

Buildings and Grounds: 30 landscaped acres include intimate courtyards with over: a dozen fountains. The original buildings were designed in the California Mediterranean style by Gordon B. Kaufman, a noted Southern California architect, in collaboration with Edward Huntsman Trout as landscape architect. The campus, which is nationally recognized for its beauty, was placed on the National Register of Historic Places by the U.S. Department of the Interior in 1984. There are 8 residence halls, designed on the house system, each with its own living room and upstairs library. *New buildings:* Elizabeth Hubert Malott Commons completed in 2000; Performing Arts Center 2003.

Chief Executive Officer: Dr. Nancy Y. Bekavac, President.

Address admission inquiries to Patricia F. Goldsmith, Vice President of Admission and Financial Aid.

Simpson University

2211 College View Drive
Redding, California 96003-8606
Tel: (530) 224-5600   **E-mail:** admissions@simpsonuniversity.edu
Fax: (530) 224-4861   **Internet:** www.simpsonuniversity.edu

Institution Description: Simpson University, formerly Simpson College, is a private Christian college of liberal arts and professional studies, owned by The Christian and Missionary Alliance. *Enrollment:* 1,131. *Degrees awarded:* Associate, baccalaureate, master's.

Accreditation: *Regional:* WASC-Sr.

History: Established as Simpson Bible Institute in Seattle and offered first instruction at postsecondary level 1921; awarded first degree (baccalaureate) 1952; moved to San Francisco and changed name to Simpson Bible College 1955; adopted present name 1971; relocated to Redding 1989; achieved university status 2002. .

Institutional Structure: *Governing board:* Simpson University Board of Trustees. Extrainstitutional representation: 20 trustees; institutional representation: president of the college; 1 alumnus. 5 ex officio. 21 voting. *Composition of institution:* Administrators 8 men / 2 women. Academic affairs headed by provost. Management directed by chief operating officer; finances by chief financial officer. Full-time instructional faculty 40.

Calendar: Semesters. Academic year Sept. to Apr. Freshmen admitted Sept., Jan. Degrees conferred Apr., Aug., Dec. Formal commencement Apr., Oct. Summer session of 4 terms from May to Aug.

Characteristics of Freshmen: 60% of applicants accepted. 80% (155 students) submitted SAT scores; 26% (50 students) submitted ACT scores. *25th percentile*: SAT I Verbal 450, SAT Math 430; ACT Composite 18, ACT English 18, ACT Math 17. *75th percentile*: SAT Verbal 590, SAT Math 560; ACT Composite 23, ACT English 24, ACT Math 23.

11% of entering freshmen expected to graduate within 5 years. 80% of freshmen from California. Freshmen from 12 states and 2 foreign countries.

Admission: Rolling admissions plan. Apply before Aug. 15. *Requirements:* SAT/ACT scores at least in 50th percentile for applicant's ethnic group; academic GPA at least 2.00. Additional requirements: personal commitment to Jesus Christ; pastor's reference; academic reference. *For transfer students:* at least 2.0 in previous college work; SAT/ACT required if student has completed fewer than 30 satisfactory semester college credits.

College credit and advanced placement for postsecondary-level work completed in secondary school. College credit for extrainstitutional learning on basis of ACE *2006 Guide to the Evaluation of Educational Experiences in the Armed Services*, portfolio and faculty assessments, personal interviews.

Developmental courses offered during regular academic year; credit given.

Degree Requirements: *Undergraduate:* 124 credit hours; 2.0 GPA; 30 credits, including last 15, in residence; 66% chapel attendance; general education requirements; 8 semesters ministry practicum.

Fulfillment of some degree requirements possible by through CLEP, AP, or challenge examination. *Grading system:* A–F.

Distinctive Educational Programs: *For undergraduates:* Several ministry majors with internships as part of the program (youth ministry, church education, pastoral studies, general ministry, cross-cultural missions); individualized majors possible.

Degrees Conferred: 1 *associate:* 319 *baccalaureate*; 29 *master's:* education 21, theology 8. .

Fees and Other Expenses: *Full-time tuition and fees per academic year 2005–06:* undergraduate $17,000, graduate $15,500. *Room and board per academic year:* $5,900.

Financial Aid: Aid from institutionally generated funds is awarded on basis of academic merit, financial need. institution has a Program Participation Agreement with the U.S. Department of Education for eligible students to receive Pell Grants and other federal aid.

Financial aid to full-time, first-time undergraduate students: need-based scholarships/grants totaling $3,938,847, self-help $3,117,612; non-need-based scholarships/grants totaling $2,899,246, self-help $1,482,881, parent loans $1,706,973.

Departments and Teaching Staff: *Professors* 6, *associate professors* 8, *assistant professors* 26, *part-time faculty* 42. *Total instructional faculty:* 81 (full-time 40, part-time 42; member of minority groups 1; women 25, men 57). Total faculty with doctorate, first-professional, or other terminal degree: 36. Student-to-faculty ratio: 18:1. 1 faculty member awarded a sabbatical 2004.

Enrollment: Total enrollment 1,131. Undergraduate full-time 322 men / 601 women, part-time 14m / 14w; graduate full-time 22m / 71w, part-time 44m / 43w.

Characteristics of Student Body: *Ethnic/racial makeup:* number of Black non-Hispanic: 11; American Indian or Alaska Native: 6; Asian or Pacific Islander: 53; Hispanic: 35; White non-Hispanic: 718; unknown: 120.

International Students: 8 nonresident aliens enrolled fall 2004. No programs available to aid students whose native language is not English. Some financial aid programs specifically designated for international students.

Student Life: On-campus residence halls house 60% of student body. *Intercollegiate athletics:* men: basketball, soccer; women: basketball, softball, volleyball. *Special regulations:* Curfew; campus is tobacco-free, alcohol free, drug-free. Registered vehicles permitted without restrictions. *Special services:* Health center; on-campus counseling center. *Student publications:* yearbook; *The Slate*, student newspaper. *Surrounding community:* Redding population 86,000.

Library Collections: 87,203 volumes. 242,577 microforms, 2,270 recordings, 850 audiovisual materials. 292 current periodical subscriptions. Online catalog. 42 computer work stations. Students have access to the Internet at no charge. Total budget for books and materials 2004–05: $396,095.

Most important holdings include the A.B. Simpson Memorial Collection (denominational history); Weggland Art Collection.

Buildings and Grounds: 92-acre campus. *New buildings:* Bible and Theology Building; Morgan-Sharpe Residence Hall; Owen Student Services Center.

Chief Executive Officer: Dr. James M. Grant, President.

Address admission inquiries to Richard Luiz, Director of Enrollment Development.

Sonoma State University

1801 East Cotati Avenue
Rohnert Park, California 94928
Tel: (707) 664-2778   **E-mail:** admitme@sonoma.edu
Fax: (707) 664-2060   **Internet:** www.sonoma.edu

Institution Description: Sonoma State University is a unit of the California State University System. *Enrollment:* 7,448. *Degrees awarded:* Baccalaureate, master's.

Accreditation: *Regional:* WASC-Sr. *Professional:* art, business, counseling, music, nursing, teacher education

History: Established and chartered as Sonoma State College 1960; awarded first degree 1962; changed name to California State College, Sonoma 1972; adopted present name 1978.

Institutional Structure: *Composition of institution:* Administrators 17 men / 10 women. Academic affairs headed by academic vice president. Management/business/finances directed by vice president for administration and finance. Full-time instructional faculty 246. Academic governance body, Academic Senate, meets an average of 20 times per year.

Calendar: Semesters. Academic year late Aug. to late May. Freshmen admitted Sept., Jan., June. Degrees conferred June, Jan. Formal commencements May or June. Summer session of 5 terms from early June to early Aug.

Characteristics of Freshmen: 70% of applicants admitted. 19% of applicants admitted and enrolled full-time.

79% (1,068 students) submitted SAT scores; 21% (284 students) submitted ACT scores. *25th percentile*: SAT Verbal 470, SAT Math 470; ACT Composite 19. *75th percentile*: SAT Verbal 540, SAT Math 570; ACT Composite 24.

45% of entering freshmen expected to graduate within 5 years. 98% of freshmen from California. Freshmen from 9 states and 2 foreign countries.

Admission: Rolling admissions plan. For fall acceptance, apply as early as Nov. 1 of previous year, but not later than Aug. 15 of year of enrollment. Students are notified of acceptance beginning Mar. Early acceptance available. School offers college credit for extrainstitutional learning on basis of ACE *2006 Guide to the Evaluation of Educational Experiences in the Armed Services*. Tutoring available. Nondegree credit given for developmental/remedial courses offered during regular academic year.

Degree Requirements: *For baccalaureate degree:* 124 semester units (some majors require 132 semester units); GPA 2.00; writing competency as evidenced by Written English Proficiency Test administered in the junior year. *For master's degree:* minimum of 30 semester units; 3.00 GPA.

Distinctive Educational Programs: Work-experience programs, including internships. Weekend and evening classes. Special facilities for using telecommunications in the classroom. Interdisciplinary programs in American multicultural studies, environmental studies, gerontology, India studies, interdisciplinary studies, liberal studies, Mexican-American studies, Native: American studies, women's studies. Facilities and programs for individual majors, tutorials, special studies courses. Preprofessional programs in allied health fields. National student exchange program. Study abroad open to students with GPAs of 2.75 for France, Germany, Israel, Italy, Mexico, Canada (Quebec), Taiwan, Sweden, and Spain; to students with GPAs of 3.00 in Australia, Denmark (business), Japan, New Zealand, Peru, United Kingdom, and Zimbabwe. Distance Learning Program for M.S. in Nursing. Twenty-four hour assured computer access.

ROTC: Army, Navy, Air Force offered in cooperation with Reserved Officer's Training Corps at University of California, Berkeley.

Degrees Conferred: 1,431 *baccalaureate* (B), 222 *master's* (M): area and ethnic studies 40 (B); biological/life sciences 52 (B), 6 (M); business/marketing 302 (B), 21 (M); communications/communication technologies 76 (B); computer and information sciences 32 (B); education 38 (M); English 64 (B), 16 (M); foreign languages and literature 19 (B); health professions and related sciences 43 (B), 50 (M); interdisciplinary studies 10 (M); liberal arts/general studies 119 (B); mathematics 8 (B); resources/environmental natural science 61 (B); philosophy/religion/theology 15 (B); physical sciences 31 (B) protective services/public administration 7 (M); psychology 139 (B), 29 (M); social sciences and history 46 (B), 5 (M); other 384 (B), 40 (M).

Fees and Other Expenses: *Full-time tuition per academic year 2004–05:* California resident undergraduate $3,408, graduate $8,136 plus $3,894; out-of-state student undergraduate $8,136 plus $3,894. *Room and board per academic year:* $8,805.

Financial Aid: An institutional direct lending program is available. Aid from institutionally generated funds is awarded on the basis of academic merit, financial need. Institution has a Program Participation Agreement with the U.S. Department of Education for eligible students to receive Pell Grants and other federal aid.

Financial aid to full-time, first-time undergraduate students: need-based scholarships/grants totaling $8,603,694, self-help $10,783,432; non-need-based scholarships/grants totaling $1,821,483, self-help $4,730,131, parent loans $7,066,285, tuition waivers $40,408, athletic awards $183,005. *Graduate aid:* 320 students received federal and state-funded fellowships and grants totaling $947,249 (ranging from $200 to $4,050); 657 received federal and state-funded loans totaling $6,806,607 (ranging from $51 to $8,500); 32 students had work-study jobs totaling $86,249 (ranging from $1,000 to $5,000).

Departments and Teaching Staff: *Total instructional faculty:* 498 (241 full-time, 229 part-time; members of minority groups 76; women 247, men 251). Total faculty with doctorate, first-professional, or other terminal degree: 347. Student-to-faculty ratio: 24.66:1. 9 faculty members awarded sabbaticals 2004.

Enrollment: Total enrollment 7,448. Undergraduate full-time 2,157 men / 3,665 women, part-time 372m / 604w; graduate full-time 164m / 455w, part-time 157m / 403w. *Transfer students:* in-state 811, out-of-state 10.

Characteristics of Student Body: *Ethnic and racial makeup:* number of Black non-Hispanic: 122; American Indian or Alaska Native: 51; Asian or Pacific Islander: 178; Hispanic: 727; White non-Hispanic: 4,517; unknown 1,132. *Age distribution:* number under 18: 20; 18–19: 1,937; 20–21: 2,017; 22–24: 1,602; 25–29: 574; 30–34: 217; 35–39: 117; 40–49: 207; 50–64: 103; 65 and over: 4.

International Students: 91 nonresident aliens enrolled fall 2004. 12 students from Europe, 38 Asia, 3 Central and South Latin America, 11 Africa, 6 Canada, 1 New Zealand, 20 other. Programs available to aid students whose language is not English: Social and cultural. English as a Second Language Program. No financial aid specifically designated for international students.

Student Life: On-campus residence halls house 14% of student body. Residence halls (suites) and apartments for both men and women constitute 100% of such space. *Intercollegiate athletics:* men only: baseball, basketball, cross-country, gymnastics, soccer, tennis, track/field; women only: basketball, cross-country, soccer, tennis, track/field, volleyball. *Special regulations:* Cars permitted without restrictions. *Special services:* Tutorial Center, Intensive Learning Experience, Disability Resource Center, Student Health Center, Reentry Services, Learning Skills Services. *Student publications, radio:* Sonoma Mandala, a literary magazine; *Sonoma State Star*, a weekly newspaper. Radio station KSUN broadcasts 98 hours per week. *Surrounding community:* Rohnert Park population 40,000. San Francisco, 50 miles from campus, is nearest metropolitan area. Served by mass transit bus system and shuttle service to San Francisco airport.

Publications: *Sonoma Management Review* (biannually) first published 1979.

Library Collections: 700,000 volumes including bound books, serial backfiles, electronic documents, and government documents not in separate collections. Online catalog. Current serial subscriptions: 3,171 paper, 1,587,019 microforms, 40 electronic. 22,899 recordings; 1,730 compact discs; 317 CD-ROMs. 225 computer work stations. Students have access to the Internet at no charge.

Most important holdings include Women Artists Archives (more than 5,000 items including slides of women artists); miniature books and fine printing collection; Wallace Collection of Sonoma County maps, survey field books, and building plans; Lyman Collection of Celtic Literature; Jack London Collection.

Buildings and Grounds: Campus area 270 acres. *New buildings:* Jean and Charles Schulz Information Center completed 2000; new student apartments 2000.

Chief Executive Officer: Dr. Ruben Arminana, President.

Address admission inquiries to Troy Lyons, Director of Admissions.

Southern California College of Optometry

2575 Yorba Linda Boulevard
Fullerton, California 92831-1699
Tel: (714) 870-7226   **E-mail:** admissions@scco.edu
Fax: (714) 992-7878   **Internet:** www.scco.edu

Institution Description: Southern California College of Optometry is a private, independent, nonprofit institution. *Enrollment:* 378. *Degrees awarded:* First-professional.

Accreditation: *Regional:* WASC-Sr. *Professional:* optometry

History: Established 1904.

Institutional Structure: *Composition of institution:* 12 administrators. Academic affairs headed by dean. Management/business/finances directed by vice president for administration. Full-time instructional faculty 54. Academic governance bodies, administrative and curriculum committees, which advise the president, meet an average of 14 times per year.

Calendar: Quarters. Academic year Aug. to May. Freshmen admitted Aug. Degrees conferred and formal commencement May.

Admission: Rolling admissions plan. For fall acceptance, apply as early as Sept. 1 of previous year, but not later than March 15 of year of enrollment. *Requirements:* For first-professional degree: bachelor's degree from accredited institution which must include 6 hours English, 8 each biology, chemistry, and physics (all with laboratory), 6 psychology, 3 calculus, 3 microbiology (with laboratory), 3 statistics, 3 organic chemistry; OAT; interview. Tutoring available.

Degree Requirements: *For first-professional:* 229 quarter hours; 2.0 GPA; 12 terms in residence; prescribed curriculum; clinical proficiency in written and practical examinations; National Board of Examiners examination. *Grading system:* A–F; pass-fail; withdraw.

Distinctive Educational Programs: Work-experience programs. Weekend classes. Special facilities for using telecommunications in the classroom. Honors programs. Independent research.

Degrees Conferred: 96 *first-professional:* optometry.

Fees and Other Expenses: *Full-time tuition per academic year 2004–05:* $23,625. *Required fees:* $105.

Financial Aid: Aid from institutionally generated funds is provided on the basis of academic merit and financial need. Institution has a Program Participation Agreement with Department of Education for eligible students to receive Pell Grants and other federal aid.

Departments and Teaching Staff: Optometry *professors* 12, *associate professors* 6, *assistant professors* 16, *instructors* 4, *part-time faculty* 54. *Total instructional faculty:* 92. Degrees held by full-time faculty: 100% hold first-professional degrees. Student-to-faculty ratio: 4:1. 1 faculty member awarded a sabbatical 2004–05.

Enrollment: Total enrollment 378 (140 men / 238 women).

Characteristics of Student Body: *Ethnic/racial makeup:* number of Black non-Hispanic: 3; American Indian or Native: Alaskan 1; Asian or Pacific Islander: 209; Hispanic: 16; White non-Hispanic: 149.

International Students: 10 nonresident aliens enrolled fall 2004. 4 students from Asia, 6 Canada. No programs available to aid students whose native language is not English. No financial aid specifically designated for international students.

Student Life: *Special regulations:* Cars with parking pass permitted; fee charged. Appropriate professional attire required in clinics. *Student publications: Reflex,* a yearbook; *Scope,* a newspaper. *Surrounding community:* Fullerton population 110,000. Los Angeles, 20 miles from campus, is nearest metropolitan area. Served by mass transit bus system; airport 20 miles from campus; passenger rail service 5 miles from campus.

Library Collections: 17,000 volumes. 570 audiovisual materials, 35 microform titles, 300 current periodical subscriptions. 32 computer work stations.

Special historical eyeglass collection.

Buildings and Grounds: *New buildings:* Remodeled Eye Care Center and Student Center completed 2003.

Chief Executive Officer: Dr. Lesley L. Walls, President.

Address admission inquiries to Office of Admissions.

Southern California University of Health Sciences

16200 East Amber Valley Drive
P.O. Box 1166
Whittier, California 90604-1066
Tel: (562) 947-8755   **E-mail:** admissions@scuhs.edu
Fax: (502) 947-5724   **Internet:** www.scuhs.edu

Institution Description: Southern California University of Health Sciences, formerly named Los Angeles College of Chiropractic is a private, independent professional school. *Enrollment:* 685. *Degrees awarded:* First-professional (chiropractic), baccalaureate.

Accreditation: *Regional:* WASC-Sr. *Professional:* acupuncture, chiropractic education

History: Chartered 1911; offered first instruction at postsecondary level 1911; absorbed the Eclectic College of Chiropractic 1922; subsequently acquired Golden State College, College of Chiropractic Physicians and Surgeons, Southern California College of Chiropractic, Continental Chiropractic College, and the California College of Natural Healing Arts; acquired by The California Chiropractic Educational Foundation in late 1940s and new college established as Los Angeles College of Chiropractic; course of study expanded to four years in 1950; moved to Glendale 1950; purchased new Whittier campus 1981; present name adopted 2001.

Institutional Structure: *Governing board:* Board of Regents 22 (6 honorary members). Four administrative areas: Development and Alumni Affairs, Financial and Business Affairs, Institutional Studies, Postgraduate and Academic Affairs. Full-time instructional faculty 42.

Calendar: Trimesters. Academic year Sept. to Aug. Degrees conferred and formal commencement Dec., Apr. 1997 summer trimester May to Aug.

Characteristics of Freshmen: Institution has a Program Participation Agreement with the U.S. Department of Education for eligible students to receive Pell Grants and other federal aid.

66% of students from California. Students from 12 states and 4 foreign countries.

Admission: Applicants are encouraged to submit applications not less than 12 months prior to the starting date of the class to which they seek entrance. *Requirements:* Either graduation from accredited secondary school or present evidence of equivalent; completion of at least 90 semester or 135 quarter units leading to a baccalaureate degree in the arts and sciences; pre-chiropractic credits must be earned at an accredited institution; prerequisite courses taken in the biological sciences, general (inorganic) chemistry, organic chemistry, and physics must equal one academic year (not less than 6 semester units in each subject area); all preadmission courses must be completed with not less than a 2.50 cumulative GPA on a 4.0 scale. All new students are required to have a complete physical examination to completed during the first trimester of attendance and available through the college clinics. *Entrance tests:* For foreign students TOEFL with a score of 500.

Degree Requirements: *For Doctor of Chiropractic degree:* attained age 21; four academic years of resident study; completion of all courses in the curriculum; 2.0 GPA; clinical internship.

Grading system: A–F; I-incomplete; W-withdrew without credit; DS-dismissal; Z-advanced credit.

Degrees Conferred: 25 *master's:* health professions; 148 *first-professional:* chiropractic.

Fees and Other Expenses: *Full-time tuition and fees per trimester 2004–05:* $7,125.

Financial Aid: Aid from institutionally generated funds is provided on the basis of academic merit, financial need, other considerations. Institution has a Program Participation Agreement with the U.S. Department of Education for eligible students to receive Pell Grants and other federal aid.

Departments and Teaching Staff: *Total instructional faculty:* 103 (full-time 39, part-time 64). Total faculty with doctorate, first-professional, or other terminal degree: 94.

Enrollment: Total enrollment 685 (full-time 586, part-time 99).

International Students: No programs available to aid students whose native language is not English. No financial aid specifically designated for international students.

Student Life: No on-campus housing. *Special services:* Tutoring/counseling services, veteran's services, College Legal Clinic. *Surrounding community:* Whittier, a city of over: 71,000 residents, is located 14 miles southeast of Los Angeles. Served by mass transit bus system. Los Angeles International Airport is 20 miles west of the campus.

Library Collections: 27,220 volumes. Current periodical subscriptions: 512 paper; 64,636 microform. 50 computer work stations. Students have access to online information retrieval services and the Internet.

Special collections in Chiropractic History, Homeopathic Medicine, and Nutrition and Sports Medicine.

Buildings and Grounds: Campus area 38 acres.

Chief Executive Officer: Reed B. Phillips, President.

Address admission inquiries to Director of Admissions.

Southwestern University School of Law

675 South Westmoreland Avenue
Los Angeles, California 90005-3992
Tel: (213) 738-6700   **E-mail:** admissions@swlaw.edu
Fax: (213) 383-1688   **Internet:** www.swlaw.edu

Institution Description: Southwestern University School of Law is a private, independent, nonprofit, nonsectarian law school. *Enrollment:* 991. *Degrees awarded:* First-professional.

Accreditation: ABA. *Professional:* law

History: Founded as Southwestern College of Law 1911; chartered as Southwestern University 1913; first graduate 1915; fully accredited 1972.

Institutional Structure: *Governing board:* Extrainstitutional representation: 20 trustees; institutional representation: chief executive officer and chief financial officer. *Composition of institution:* Administrators 4 men / 11 women. Total instructional faculty 75.

Calendar: Semesters. Academic year Aug. to May Formal commencement May. Summer session from May to July.

Admission: Rolling admissions plan. First-year students accepted fall semester only. Suggested application deadlines are June 30 for the traditional programs. Applications are reviewed as completed. *Requirements:* Bachelor's degree from an accredited institution. Transfer students must be in good standing. *Entrance tests:* LSAT.

Degree Requirements: Minimum 87 semester units; passage of all required courses and an overall GPA of 2.0. *Grading system:* A–F.

Distinctive Educational Programs: SCALE (Southwestern's Conceptual Approach to Legal Education): alternative curriculum, two-calendar year, full-time day program of study which emphasizes conceptual learning and simulation training to facilitate the transition from classroom to law office. PLEAS (Part-time Legal Education Alternative at Southwestern): Four-year, part-time day program designed to accommodate those who have scheduling constraints due to child care responsibilities. Designated curriculum the first two years with a course load of 8–11 semester units to be taken thereafter. Traditional evening division. Study abroad programs in Argentina, Canada, Mexico.

Degrees Conferred: 253 *first-professional:* law (juris doctor).

Fees and Other Expenses: *Tuition per academic year 2004–05:* $25,600. Contact the school for off-campus housing costs.

Financial Aid: Aid from institutionally generated funds is provided on the basis of academic merit, financial need. Institution has a Program Participation Agreement with the U.S. Department of Education for eligible students to receive Pell Grants and other federal aid.

Departments and Teaching Staff: *Professors* 28, *associate professors* 14, *instructors* 3, *part-time faculty* 31. *Total instructional faculty* 75. Student-to-faculty ratio: 17:1. Degrees held by full-time faculty: Doctorate 10%, master's 36%, baccalaureate 93%, professional 100%.

Enrollment: Total enrollment 991 (48.7% men, 51.3% women).

Characteristics of Student Body: *Ethnic/racial makeup:* Black non-Hispanic: 5%; American Indian or Alaska Native: .7%; Asian or Pacific Islander: 19.3%; Hispanic: 11%; White non-Hispanic: 61.6%; unknown: 1.3%.

International Students: 11 nonresident aliens enrolled fall 2004. No programs available to aid students whose native language is not English. No financial aid specifically designated for international students.

Student Life: *Student publications: The Commentator,* a student newspaper. *Surrounding community:* Located in the commercial mid-Wilshire district of Los Angeles, in the midst of law firms and corporate headquarters, a short distance from state and federal court buildings. 20 minutes from beaches, 1 hour from mountain resorts. Near cultural and recreational facilities. Easy access to public transportation and freeways.

Publications: *Southwestern University Law Review.*

Library Collections: 415,000 volumes. 650,000 microforms; 1,100 audiovisual materials; Online catalog. 4,200 periodicals. Students have access to the Internet at no charge.

Special attention is given to the development of the collection in the area of tax law, freedom of information, and the law of the People's Republic of China. The library is a designated depository for California and federal government documents. The media center houses one of the largest multimedia collections in Southern California, including LEXIS and Westlaw Computer Assisted Legal Instruction terminals.

Buildings and Grounds: Southwestern's campus includes the historic Bullocks Wilshire Building which has been restored and renovated to accommodate the Law Library, large assembly and reception rooms, administrative offices, and dining facilities. Other additions to the campus include new tiered classrooms with state-of-the art technology, an easily accessible student services suite and a new student lounge.

Chief Executive Officer: Leigh H. Taylor, Dean.

Address admission inquiries to the Anne L. Wilson, Director of Admissions.

Stanford University

Stanford, California 94305-2060

Tel: (650) 723-2300   **E-mail:** undergrad.admissions@forsythe.stanford.edu

Fax: (650) 725-6847   **Internet:** www.stanford.edu

Institution Description: Stanford University is a private, independent, nonprofit institution. *Enrollment:* 18,836. *Degrees awarded:* Baccalaureate, master's, doctorate, first-professional (business, law, medicine).

Accreditation: *Regional:* WASC-Sr. *Professional:* business, counseling psychology, engineering, law, medicine, teacher education

History: Established and chartered under present official name Leland Stanford Junior University 1885; offered first instruction at postsecondary level 1891; awarded first degree (baccalaureate) 1892. *See* Karen Bartholomew, Claude Brineger, and Roxanne Nilan, *A Chronology of Stanford University and Its Founders,* (Stanford Historical Society, 2001) for further information.

Institutional Structure: *Governing board:* Stanford University is a trust with corporate powers under the laws of California. Under the provisions of the Founding Grant, the Board of Trustees, with a maximum membership of 35, is custodian of the endowment and all the properties. *Composition of institution:* Academic and budget affairs headed by vice president and provost. Management/business/finances directed by vice president for business and finance. Instructional faculty 1,783. Academic governance body, Senate of the Academic Council, meets an average of 16 times per year.

Calendar: Quarters; for law school, semesters. Academic year Sept. to June. Freshmen admitted Sept. Degrees conferred June, Oct., Jan., Apr. Formal Commencement June. Summer session of 2 terms from late June to late Aug.

Characteristics of Freshmen: 13% of applicants admitted. 66% of admitted applicants enrolled full-time.

97.5% (1,607 students) submitted SAT scores; 22.8% (377 students) submitted ACT scores. *25th percentile:* SAT Verbal 680, SAT Math 690; ACT Composite 29, ACT English 29, ACT Math 29. *75th percentile:* SAT Verbal 770, SAT Math 780; ACT Composite 34, ACT English 34, ACT Math 34.

90% of entering freshmen expected to graduate within 5 years. 40.3% of freshmen from California. Freshmen from 49 states and 47 foreign countries.

Admission: For fall acceptance, apply as early as beginning of senior year of secondary school, but not later than Dec. 15 of year of enrollment. Students are notified of acceptance Apr. 1. Early decision program deadline is Nov. 1 with notification by mid-December. *Requirements:* Graduation from accredited secondary school or GED. Recommend 4 years in English, 3 foreign language, 4 mathematics, 3 or 4 history, 3 laboratory science. *Entrance tests:* College Board SAT or ACT. *For transfer students:* 90 quarter units maximum transfer credit. College credit and advanced placement for postsecondary-level work completed in secondary school.

Tutoring available. Developmental courses offered in summer session and regular academic year; credit given.

Degree Requirements: *Undergraduate:* 180 quarter units; 9 quarters, including final one, in residence; general education, writing, and language requirements. Fulfillment of some degree requirements and exemption of some beginning courses possible by passing College Board AP. *Grading system:* A–NP; satisfactory/no credit; elective credit/no credit.

Distinctive Educational Programs: Off-campus centers (at Hopkins Marine Station, 100 miles away). Special facilities for using telecommunications in the classroom. Interdisciplinary programs. Facilities and programs for independent research, including honors programs, individual majors, tutorials. Study abroad programs in Australia, Austria, Chile, China, England, France, Japan, Israel, Italy, Germany, Spain. Undergraduate grant programs aid undergraduate participation in research.

ROTC: Army in cooperation with Santa Clara University; Air Force in cooperation with San Jose State University; Navy in cooperation with University of California, Berkeley.

Degrees Conferred: 1,713 *baccalaureate* (B); 2,011 *master's* (M); 625 *doctorate* (D): area and ethnic studies 65 (B), 20 (M); biological/life sciences 131 (B), 30 (M), 62 (D); business/marketing 444 (M), 19 (D); communications/communication technologies 33 (B), 35 (M), 4 (D); computer and information sciences 108 (B), 162 (M), 17 (D); education 161 (M), 37 (M); engineering and engineering technologies 259 (B), 801 (M), 206 (D); English 83 (B), 30 (M), 15 (D); foreign languages and literature 48 (B), 19 (M), 14 (D); health professions and related sciences 8 (M), 5 (D); interdisciplinary studies 238 (B), 4 (M), 6 (D); law/legal studies 38 (D); philosophy/religion/theology 26 (B), 12 (M), 5 (D); physical sciences 68 (B), 56 (M), 76 (D); protective services/public administration 21 (B); psychology 79 (B), 22 (M), 6 (D); social sciences and history 466 (B), 121 (M), 66 (D); visual and performing arts 42 (B), 22 (M), 17 (D). 266 *first-professional:* law 176; medicine 90.

Fees and Other Expenses: *Full-time tuition per academic year 2004–05:* $29,847. *Required fees:* $380 (freshmen only). *Room and board per academic year:* undergraduate $9,503, graduate $12,200.

Financial Aid: Aid from institutionally generated funds is awarded on basis of financial need, athletic ability. Institution has a Program Participation Agreement with the U.S. Department of Education for eligible students to receive Pell Grants and other federal aid.

Financial aid to full-time, first-time undergraduate students: need-based scholarships/grants totaling $71,959,047, self-help $13,831,096, athletic awards $804,317; non-need-based scholarships/grants totaling $8,563,652, self-help $2,148,099, parent loans $9,141,090, athletic awards $11,004,853.

Departments and Teaching Staff: *Total instructional faculty:* 1,031 (full-time 1,010, part-time 21; members of minority groups 157; women 219, men 812). Total faculty with doctorate, first-professional, or other terminal degree: 1,012. Student-to-faculty ratio: 7:1.

Enrollment: Total enrollment 18,836. Full-time 3,409 men / 3,097 women, part-time 21m / 28w; graduate full-time 3,649m /1,845w, part-time 3,125m / 2,648w; first-professional full-time 455m / 436w, part-time 58m / 65w.

Characteristics of Student Body: *Ethnic/racial makeup:* number of Black non-Hispanic: 698; American Indian or Alaska Native: 137; Asian or Pacific Islander: 1,581; Hispanic: 768; White non-Hispanic: 2,693; unknown 293. *Age distribution:* number under 18: 63; 18–19: 2,818; 20–21: 2,885; 22–24: 695; 25–29: 33; 30–34: 11; 35–39: 4; 40–49: 3; 50–64: 2; unknown: 41.

International Students: 3,948 nonresident aliens enrolled fall 2004. 829 students from Europe, 2,125 Asia, 238 Central and South America, 60 Africa, 295 Canada, 55 Australia, 19 New Zealand, 265 other. Social and cultural programs available for students whose native language is not English. No financial aid specifically designated for international students.

Student Life: On-campus residence halls house 94% of students enrolled at the home campus. Housing for graduate students consists of university-owned apartments, residences, and spaces in cooperative houses. About 52% of matriculated graduate students live on campus. *Intercollegiate athletics:* men only: baseball, basketball, football, gymnastics, soccer, swimming, tennis, track, volleyball; women only: basketball, field hockey, gymnastics, swimming, tennis, track, volleyball. *Special regulations:* Freshmen are not permitted to have cars on campus. *Special services:* Learning Resources Center, medical services, campus transportation. *Student publications, radio: Chapparal,* a magazine published irregularly; *Stanford Daily,* a newspaper. Radio station KZUS broadcasts 126 hours per week. *Surrounding community:* San Jose, 20 miles from campus, is nearest metropolitan area. Served by mass transit system; airport 25 miles from campus; passenger rail service 1 mile campus.

Publications: *Stanford Report,* published by the Stanford News Service, is a weekly newspaper. Numerous scholarly journals are published at Stanford. HighWire Press, part of the university's library, assists in the online publication of 186 scholarly journals, focusing on science, technology, and medicine.

Library Collections: 8 million volumes including bound books, serial backfiles, electronic documents, and government documents not in separate collections. Online catalog. 50,000 current serials; 281,011 cartographic holdings; 5.8 million microform holdings. Students have access to the Internet at no charge. Total budget for acquisitions $18 million annually.

Most important holdings include the John Steinbeck Collection; R. Buckminster Fuller Archive; historical archives of Apple Computer.

Buildings and Grounds: Campus area 8,180 acres. *New buildings:* James H. Clark Center; Center for Clinical Sciences; Graduate Community Center; Hewlett-Packard Science and Engineering Quadrangle. .

Chief Executive Officer: Dr. John L. Hennessy, President.

Undergraduates address admission inquiries to Dean of Admissions; first-professional students in law to Director of Admissions, Law School; medicine to Admissions Committee School of Medicine; graduate inquiries to Office of Graduate Admissions, business students to Director of Admissions, Graduate School of Business.

Starr King School for the Ministry

2441 Le Conte Avenue
Berkeley, California 94709
Tel: (510) 845-6232   **E-mail:** admissions@sksm.edu
Fax: (510) 845-6273   **Internet:** www.sksm.edu

Institution Description: Starr King School for the Ministry is a private seminary of the Unitarian Universalist religious denomination offering graduate theological training. *Enrollment:* 86. *Degrees awarded:* First-professional: master of divinity.

Member of the Graduate Theological Union.

Accreditation: *Nonregional:* ATS. *Professional:* theology

History: Established 1904.

Calendar: Semesters. Academic year Aug. to May.

Admission: *Requirements:* Baccalaureate from an accredited college or university; B average required; admission highly selective.

Degree Requirements: Completion of prescribed curriculum; professional competencies.

Distinctive Educational Programs: Three-year program for the development of religious leadership in congregations and communities (M.Div). Two-year program for the development of lay leaddership for social change (MASC). Two-year program focusing on the scholarly study of religion and preparation for further work at the doctoral level (M.A.) Free and open access to courses at other GTU-member schools and the nearby University of California, Berkeley.

Degrees Conferred: The seminary awards the Master of Divinity, Master of Arts in Religious Leadership for Social Change (MASC), Master of Arts.

Fees and Other Expenses: *Full-time tuition for the degree program 2004–05:* Contact the school for current information.

Departments and Teaching Staff: *Total instructional faculty:* 28 (5 full-time).

Enrollment: Total enrollment 86 (27 men, 58 women, 1 transgender).

Characteristics of Student Body: *Ethnic/racial makeup:* Black non-Hispanic: 4%; American Indian or Alaska Native 1%; Asian or Pacific Islander: 1%; Hispanic: 1%; White non-Hispanic: 77%; unknown: 15%.

Student Life: No on-campus housing. Some nearby GTU-member school housing available. *Surrounding community:* The SKSM campus is located in the midst of a university and seminary environment in Berkeley, two blocks from the University of California campus.

Library Collections: Students have access to the resources of the Graduate Theological Union Library.

Chief Executive Officer: Dr. Rebecca Parker, President.

Address admission inquiries to Becky Leyser, Dean of Students.

Thomas Jefferson School of Law

2121 San Diego Avenue
San Diego, California 92110
Tel: (619) 297-9700   **E-mail:** adm@tjsl.edu
Fax: (619) 294-4713   **Internet:** www.tjsl.edu

Institution Description: Thomas Jefferson School of Law, formerly known as Western State University College of Law of San Diego, is a private, independent law school that emphasizes an individualized approach to legal education. *Enrollment:* 835. *Degrees awarded:* First-professional (law).

Accreditation: *Regional:* WASC-Sr. *Professional:* law

Institutional Structure: *Composition of institution:* Administrators 5 men / 2 women. Academic affairs headed by dean and campus director. Management/business/finances directed by vice president of finance. Full-time instructional faculty 29.

Calendar: Semesters. Academic year late Aug. to late May.

Admission: Rolling admissions. LSAT, LSDAS required.

Degree Requirements: *Requirements:* 88 units for graduation.

Distinctive Educational Programs: Work experience programs. Flexible meeting places and schedules, including weekend and evening classes. Accelerated degree programs. Women's Law Institute. Honors program.

Degrees Conferred: 175 *first-professional:* law.

Fees and Other Expenses: *Full-time tuition per academic year 2004–05:* $26,800. Contact the school for current housing costs.

Financial Aid: All entering students with an LSAT score of 150 or higher automatically receive a partial or full scholarship for the first year. Partial and full tuition scholarships are awarded after the first year but are based on class

rank at the end of the prior year rather than LSAT score. Student loans and work-study funds are also available.

Departments and Teaching Staff: Law *professors 9, associate professors* 15, *part-time teachers* 5. *Total instructional faculty:* 29. Student-to-faculty ratio: 17.8:1. Degrees held by full-time faculty: Professional 100%.

Enrollment: Total enrollment 835 (58.7% men, 41.3% women).

Characteristics of Student Body: *Ethnic/racial makeup:* Black non-Hispanic: 3.1%; American Indian or Alaska Native: .2%; Asian or Pacific Islander: 7.8%; Hispanic: 8.1%; White non-Hispanic: 80.6%; unknown: .1%.

International Students: 2 nonresident aliens enrolled fall 2004. No programs available to aid students whose native language is not English. No financial aid specifically designated for foreign students.

Student Life: No on-campus housing. *Student publications: The Criminal Justice Journal,* published once per semester; *The Restater,* a newspaper published 3 times per semester. *Surrounding community:* San Diego population 1.2 million. Served by mass transit bus system; airport 3 miles from campus; passenger rail service 10 blocks from campus.

Library Collections: 220,000 volumes including bound books, serial back-files, electronic documents, and government documents not in separate collections. Online catalog. Current serial subscriptions: 4,462 paper, 10 microform. 1,572 recordings; 44 CD-ROMs. Computer work stations available. Students have access to the Internet at no charge.

Most important special holdings include collection on Anglo-American law; Thomas Jefferson Collection; U.S. Supreme Court Records, Briefs, and Argued Cases (microfilm).

Buildings and Grounds: The Law School occupies a modern 30,000 square foot facility in San Diego's Old Town.

Chief Executive Officer: Kenneth J. Vandevelde, Dean.

Address admission inquiries to Jennifer Keller, Assistant Dean of Admissions.

Thomas Aquinas College

10000 North Ojai Road
Santa Paula, California 93060
Tel: (800) 634-9797   **E-mail:** admissions@thomasaquinas.edu
Fax: (805) 525-9342   **Internet:** www.thomasaquinas.edu

Institution Description: Thomas Aquinas College is a private liberal arts college affiliated with the Roman Catholic Church, offering an integrated studies curriculum based upon the great books. *Enrollment:* 331, *Degrees awarded:* Baccalaureate.

Accreditation: *Regional:* WASC-Sr. *National:* American Academy for Liberal Education.

History: Established 1968; offered first instruction at postsecondary level 1971.

Institutional Structure: *Governing board:* Board of Governors with 29 members and 5 emeriti. 27 voting, 9 nonvoting. *Administration:* president, vice president for finance, vice president for development, dean, and assistant dean.

Calendar: Semesters. Academic year Aug. to May.

Characteristics of Freshmen: 82% of applicants admitted. 50% of applicants admitted and enrolled.

92% (96 students) submitted SAT scores; 12% (12 students) submitted ACT scores. *25th percentile:* SAT Verbal 610, SAT Math 570; ACT Composite 27, ACT English 28, ACT Math 24. *75th percentile:* SAT Verbal 750, SAT Math 670; ACT Composite 30, ACT English 34, ACT Math 28.

64% of entering freshmen are expected to graduate within 5 years. 42% of freshmen from California. Freshmen from 26 states and 5 foreign countries.

Admission: Rolling admissions. *Requirements:* Applicants evaluated individually on basis of SAT, ACT scores, secondary and postsecondary (if applicable) school records, written essays, and three reference letters. No specific requirements. College preparatory curriculum recommended.

Degree Requirements: 4-year prescribed curriculum; entire program in residence; 2.0 GPA; senior thesis. *Grading system:* A–F.

Distinctive Educational Programs: The Great Books Catholic liberal arts curriculum is what makes Thomas Aquinas College unique. The academic program is, essentially, a sustained and lively conversation with some of the best minds of the world. There are no textbooks used at the college. The works of Aristotle, St. Augustine, St. Thomas Aquinas, Dante, Shakespeare, Isaac Newton, Thomas Jefferson, and Albert Einstein are read, discussed, analyzed, and evaluated day in and day out. There are no classroom lectures. The faculty lead tutorials, seminars, and laboratories by which students get regular practice in the arts of language, logic, conversation, inquiry, argument, and mathematical demonstration.

Degrees Conferred: 71 *baccalaureate:* liberal arts.

Fees and Other Expenses: *Full-time tuition per academic year 2005–06:* $18,600. *Room and board per academic year:* $5,800.

Financial Aid: Aid from institutionally generated funds is provided on the basis of financial need. Institution has a Program Participation Agreement with the U.S. Department of Education for eligible students to receive Pell Grants and other federal aid.

Financial aid to full-time, first-time undergraduate students: need-based scholarships/grants totaling $2,124,596, self-help $1,242,922, parent loans $43,144, tuition waivers $5,550; non-need-based scholarships/grants totaling $59,331, self-help $202,118, parent loans $131,007, tuition waivers $41,700.

Departments and Teaching Staff: *Total instructional faculty:* 30 (full-time 29, part-time 1; members of minority groups 1; women 3, men 27). Total faculty with doctorate, first-professional, or other terminal degree: 21. Student-to-faculty ratio: 11:1.

Enrollment: Total enrollment 331 (161 men / 170 women).

Characteristics of Student Body: *Ethnic and racial makeup:* number of Black non-Hispanic: 1; American Indian or Alaska Native: 4; Asian or Pacific Islander: 9; Hispanic: 22; White non-Hispanic: 273. *Age distribution:* number under 18: 14; 18–19: 156; 20–21: 105; 22–24: 42; 25–29: 9; 30–34: 2; 35–39: 3.

International Students: 28 nonresident aliens enrolled fall 2004. 3 students from Europe, 1 Asia, 21 Canada, 2 Australia, 1 Philippines. No programs available to aid students whose native language is not English. No financial aid specifically designated for international students.

Student Life: All non-married students live in on-campus residence halls. Students are able to participate in a variety of social activities and intramural sports. *Surrounding community:* The college is situated in a rural area east of Ventura, between Santa Paula and Ojai. Ventura, nearest metropolitan area, is 20 miles away; Los Angeles 60 miles.

Library Collections: 59,500 volumes including bound books, serial backfiles, electronic documents, and government documents not in separate collections. Online catalog. Current serial subscriptions: 63 paper. 8,400 recordings; 495 compact discs; 390 CD-ROMs. 11 computer work stations. Students have access to the Internet at no charge.

Most important special collections include *Patrologia Latina, Graeca, Opera Omnia, St. Thomas Aquinas, and* St. Albert the Great Migne. Incunabula Book of Hours, many first editions and manuscripts.

Buildings and Grounds: Campus area 130 acres; bordered by Los Padres National Forest. *New buildings:* St. Peter and Paul Hall completed 2002; St. Monica Hall 2004.

Chief Executive Officer: Dr. Thomas E. Dillon, President.

Address admission inquiries to Jonathan P. Daly, Director of Admissions.

United States Naval Postgraduate School

1 University Circle
Monterey, California 94943-5001
Tel: (831) 656-2511   **E-mail:** provost@nps.navy.mil
Internet: www.nps.navy.mil

Institution Description: The Naval Postgraduate School is a federal institution primarily for graduate study but also offering upper division baccalaureate study. The majority of its students are members of the military. *Enrollment:* 1,746. *Degrees awarded:* Baccalaureate, master's, doctorate. Certificates also awarded.

Accreditation: *Regional:* WASC-Sr. *Professional:* business, engineering, public administration

History: Established, chartered as School of Marine Engineering at the Naval Academy at Annapolis, MD, and offered first instruction at postsecondary level 1909; changed name to Postgraduate Department of the Naval Academy 1912; changed name to United States Naval Postgraduate School 1921; awarded first degree (baccalaureate) 1947; moved to present location 1951; adopted present name 1968.

Institutional Structure: *Governing board:* Board of Advisors, Department of Navy. Extrainstitutional representation: 13 members. All voting. *Composition of institution:* Administrators 16 men. Academic affairs headed by the provost. Management/business/finances directed by resource manager/comptroller. Full-time instructional faculty 182 men / 11 women. Academic governance body, Faculty Council, meets an average of 12 times per year.

Calendar: Quarters. Academic year begins Oct. Entering students admitted Oct., Jan., Apr., July. Degrees conferred and formal commencements June, Sept., Dec., Mar. Students attend year-round classes.

Admission: Rolling admissions plan. *Requirements:* Baccalaureate degree from accredited institution (some exceptions for foreign students). Must be commissioned officer in U.S. armed services or sponsored by either a U.S. federal agency or a foreign government. Minimum GPA 2.2. *For transfer students:* 2.2 minimum GPA; maximum transfer credit limited only by residence requirement.

Degree Requirements: *For all master's degrees:* 32 quarter hours; 12 credits in residence. *For all engineering degrees:* 72 hours; 1 year in residence. *For all master's and engineer's degrees:* 3.0 GPA; thesis.

Fulfillment of some degree requirements and exemption from some beginning courses possible by passing departmental examinations. *Grading system:* A–D, X; pass-fail; withdraw; incomplete (carries time limit).

Distinctive Educational Programs: *For graduate students:* Interdisciplinary programs in command, control and communications; computers and intelligence (C4I) systems; electronic warfare; information systems and operations; product development in the 21st century and undersea warfare. Individual majors. *Other distinctive programs:* Distributed learning program. Six distributed learning degree programs (video-tele-education). Center for Civil Military Relations instructs international students. Defense Resources Management Education Center programs for military officers and defense officials of U.S. and cooperating foreign nations.

Degrees Conferred: 682 *master's* (M); 9 *doctorate* (D): area and ethnic studies 45 (M); business 148 (M); computer and information science 117 (M); engineering/engineering technologies 129 (M), 6 (D); mathematics 76 (M), 1 (D); military science and technology 138 (M), 1 (D); physical sciences 20 (M), 1 (D); other 9 (M). 6 *first-professional:* engineering.

Fees and Other Expenses: No tuition; only charge is for textbooks and related supplies.

Departments and Teaching Staff: *Total instructional faculty:* 200 tenure track; 30 military faculty.

Enrollment: *Total enrollment:* 1,746.

International Students: 250 nonresident aliens enrolled fall 2004. 76 students from Europe, 63 Asia, 25 Central and South America, 8 Africa, 2 Canada, 3 Australia, 73 other.

Student Life: The Combined Bachelor Housing at Herrmann Hall is designated as a transient only facility and does not house permanent party personnel. Single and geographic bachelor officers can be accommodated on a space-available basis for 30 days and may request and be granted an additional 30 days occupancy is space available. Housing Office. 78% of all students request family housing and are so housed. *Special regulations:* Cars permitted without restrictions. *Special services:* Medical services. *Surrounding community:* Monterey population 35,000. San Jose, 70 miles from campus, is nearest metropolitan area. Served by mass transit bus system; airport 2 miles from campus.

Library Collections: 300,000 volumes. 500,000 microforms, government documents and 1,300 current periodical subscriptions. 75 computer work stations. Students have access to the Internet at no charge.

Most important holdings include Christopher Buckley, Jr. Collection (8,000 volumes about U.S. and British navies and the sea); collection of 430,000 Department of Defense and defense contractors technical reports.

Buildings and Grounds: Campus area 613 acres.

Chief Executive Officer: Patrick W. Dunne, Rear Admiral, USN, Superintendent.

Address admission inquiries to Associate Provost for Instruction.

University of California, Berkeley

Berkeley, California 94720-5800
Tel: (510) 642-6000   **E-mail:** ouars@uclink.berkeley.edu
Fax: (510) 642-7333   **Internet:** www.berkeley.edu

Institution Description: *Enrollment:* 32,814. *Degrees awarded:* Baccalaureate, master's, doctorate, first-professional.

Member of the consortium Regional Association of East Bay Colleges and Universities.

Accreditation: *Regional:* WASC-Sr. *Professional:* business, clinical psychology, computer science, dietetics, engineering, forestry, health services administration, interior design, journalism, landscape architecture, law, optometry, planning, psychology internship, public health, social work

History: Incorporated as College of California, a private institution, 1855; offered first instruction at postsecondary level 1960; transferred control to state and changed name to University of California 1868; awarded first degree (baccalaureate) 1870; adopted present name 1952.

Institutional Structure: *Composition of institution:* Administrators 129 full-time, 18 part-time. Chief campus officer is the chancellor. Academic affairs headed by executive vice chancellor and provost. Business affairs directed by vice chancellor-business and administrative services. Academic staff: 1,046 men / 450 women. Full-time faculty 1,496. Academic governance body, Berkeley Division of the Academic Senate, meets an average of 4 times per year.

Calendar: Semesters. Academic year Aug. to May. Degrees conferred May, Aug., Dec. Formal commencement May. Summer session term from June to Aug.

Characteristics of Freshmen: 25% of applicants admitted; 41% of admitted students enrolled full-time.

99% (3,633 students) submitted SAT scores; 1% (14 students) submitted ACT scores. *25th percentile*: SAT Verbal 580, SAT Math 620. *75th percentile*: SAT Verbal 710, SAT Math 740.

65% of entering freshmen expected to graduate within 5 years. 93% of freshmen from California. Freshmen from 34 states and 30 foreign countries.

Admission: For fall semester acceptance, apply by Nov. 1-30. Applications for undergraduate admission are not accepted for the spring semester. *Requirements:* Graduation from secondary school with a minimum of 15 college-preparatory units, including 4 English, 2 foreign language, 3 mathematics, 2 history, 1 visual or performing arts, 2 laboratory science. *For transfer students:* students must have 60 transferable units and transfer as a junior. Preference is given to California community college transfers. Refer to *General Catalog* for further information. School offers college credit for extrainstitutional learning on basis of ACE *2006 Guide to the Evaluation of Educational Experiences in the Armed Services.* Tutoring available. Nondegree credit given for developmental/remedial courses offered during regular academic year.

Degree Requirements: *Undergraduate:* 120 semester credit hours; 2.0 GPA; after the completion of 90 units, at least the last 24 must be completed in residence in no fewer than 2 semesters; general education requirements. *Grading system:* A–F; pass-not passed; incomplete.

Distinctive Educational Programs: Work experience programs. Evening classes. Special facilities for using telecommunications in the classroom. Interdisciplinary programs in demography, energy and resources, ethnic studies, field studies program, health arts and sciences, health and medical sciences, interdepartmental studies program. Facilities and programs for independent research, including honors programs, individual majors, tutorials, independent study. Cross-registration for graduate students with Graduate Theological Union. Graduate exchange program with California State University, Sonoma; California State University, Hayward; Harvard University (MA); Mills College; Stanford University. Exchange Scholar Program with Brown, Chicago, Columbia, Cornell, Harvard, MIT, Pennsylvania, Princeton, and Yale. The University-wide Education Abroad Program has study centers at universities in Africa, People's Republic of China, Japan, India, Korea, Australia, Mexico, Austria, France, Germany, Hungary, Ireland, Italy, Norway, Portugal, Spain, Sweden, Russia, England, Israel, Egypt, Brazil, Peru.

ROTC: Army, Navy, Air Force.

Degrees Conferred: 6,850 *baccalaureate*; 1,896 *master's*; 775 *doctorate*; 394 *first-professional.* Bachelor's degrees awarded in top five disciplines: social sciences 1,384; engineering 812; biological and biomedical sciences 710; English language and literature/letters 455; multidisciplinary studies 447.

Fees and Other Expenses: *Full-time tuition per academic year 2004–05:* undergraduate resident $5,956; out-of-state $16,956; graduate resident $7,457, out-of-state $14,989; variable for graduate/first-professional programs. *Room and board per academic year:* $11,629.

Financial Aid: Aid from institutionally generated funds is awarded on the basis of academic merit, financial need, athletic ability. Institution has a Program Participation Agreement with the U.S. Department of Education for eligible students to receive Pell Grants and other federal aid.

Financial aid to full-time, first-time undergraduate students: need-based scholarships/grants totaling $103,465,332, self-help $43,854,418, parent loans $3,769,188, athletic awards $702,517; non-need-based scholarships/grants totaling $11,106,098, self-help $10,210,571, parent loans $21,295,094, athletic awards $3,787,765.

Departments and Teaching Staff: *Professors* 867, *associate professors* 269, *assistant professors* 242, *instructors* 118, *part-time faculty* 469. *Total instructional faculty:* 1,965 (full-time 1,496, part-time 469; minority groups 376; women 656, men 1,309). Student-to-faculty ratio: 15.5:1.

Enrollment: Total enrollment 32,814. Undergraduate full-time 30,295, part-time 2,519. *Transfer students:* undergraduate 843 men / 890 women.

Characteristics of Student Body: *Ethnic/racial makeup:* number of Black non-Hispanic: 833; American Indian or Alaska Native: 131; Asian or Pacific Islander: 9,390; Hispanic: 2,410; White non-Hispanic: 6,980; unknown 2,400. *Age distribution:* number under 18: 509; 18–19: 7,730; 20–21: 9,378; 22–24: 3,005, 25–29: 791; 30–34: 292; 35–39: 113; 40–49: 103; 50–64: 18; 65 and over: 3.

International Students: 2,537 nonresident aliens enrolled fall 2004. Programs available to aid students whose native language is not English: Social, cultural. English as a Second Language Program. No financial aid specifically designated for international students.

Student Life: On-campus residence halls house 35% of student body; 35% are housed in family student housing; 12% reside with parents or relatives; 35%

share an apartment or house in the community; 18% either live in the community alone, or with a spouse. *Intercollegiate athletics:* men only: baseball, basketball, crew, football, gymnastics, soccer, swimming, tennis, track, water polo; women only: basketball, crew, cross-country, field hockey, gymnastics, softball, swimming, tennis, track, volleyball. *Special regulations:* Registered cars permitted in designated areas only; fee charged. *Special services:* Student Learning Center (providing tutoring, learning skills assistance, and counseling), medical services, student legal services, Community Projects Office, Women's Resource Center, Career Planning and Placement, Child Care, Disabled Students' Program; shuttle bus service to and from Berkeley. *Student publications, radio:* Over 50 registered publications, including *Berkeley Fiction Review, Berkeley Science Review, California Engineer, California Voice, Onyx Express, Tennis Journal.* Radio station KALX broadcasts 24 hours per day. *Surrounding community:* Berkeley, population over: 100,000, is located in San Francisco/Oakland metropolitan area. Served by mass transit bus, rail, subway systems; airport and passenger rail service, each 20 miles from campus.

Library Collections: 8,112,936 volumes. Current serial subscriptions in paper, microform, and via electronic access. 61,900 recordings; 25,444 compact discs; 13,660 CD-ROMs. Over 500 computer work stations. Online catalog. Students have access to online information retrieval services and the Internet.

Most important holdings include collections of Western Americana (books, manuscripts, pictorial materials, microforms, newspapers, maps, covering especially the history of trans-Mississippi West to 1860); East Asian history and literature; Mark Twain's papers and manuscripts.

Buildings and Grounds: Campus area 1,290 acres.

Chief Executive Officer: Dr. Robert J. Birgeneam, Chancellor.

Undergraduates address admission inquiries to Undergraduate Admissions Office (120 Sproul Hall); first-professional students to School of Optometry (381 Minor Hall), School of Law (220 Boalt Hall); graduate students to Graduate Admissions Office (1 California Hall).

College of Letters and Science

Degree Programs Offered: *Baccalaureate, master's, doctorate* in various fields.

Departments and Teaching Staff: *Total instructional faculty:* 789.

Haas School of Business

Degree Programs Offered: *Baccalaureate, master's, doctorate.*

Departments and Teaching Staff: *Total instructional faculty:* 69.5.

College of Chemistry

Degree Programs Offered: *Baccalaureate, master's, doctorate* in chemical engineering, chemistry.

Departments and Teaching Staff: *Total instructional faculty:* 63.5.

Distinctive Educational Programs: Interdisciplinary programs. Research opportunities in Lawrence Berkeley Laboratory, Melvin Calvin Laboratory, Giauque Low Temperature Laboratory.

College of Engineering

Degree Programs Offered: *Baccalaureate, master's, doctorate, first-professional* in various fields.

Departments and Teaching Staff: *Total instructional faculty:* 217.4.

College of Environmental Design

Degree Programs Offered: *Baccalaureate, master's, doctorate, first-professional* in architecture.

Departments and Teaching Staff: *Total instructional faculty:* 56.3.

College of Natural Resources

Degree Programs Offered: *Baccalaureate, master's, doctorate, first-professional* in various fields.

Departments and Teaching Staff: *Total instructional faculty:* 36.13.

School of Law (Boalt Hall)

Degree Programs Offered: *First-professional, master's, doctorate.*

Admission: *For first-professional degree:* Baccalaureate from accredited college or university; LSAT.

Degree Requirements: *For first-professional degree:* 81 credit hours.

Departments and Teaching Staff: *Total instructional faculty:* 49.75.

School of Optometry

Degree Programs Offered: *Baccalaureate, master's, doctorate* in physiological optics; *first-professional* in optometry.

Admission: *For first-professional degree:* 90 semester hours from accredited college or university which must include 2 courses in English; 2 semesters biology or zoology with laboratory; 2 semesters general physics with laboratory; 1 semester analytic geometry combined with calculus; 1 course each in bacteriology or microbiology with laboratory, general chemistry with laboratory, human anatomy with laboratory, human physiology with laboratory, psychology, and statistics. OCAT.

Degree Requirements: *For first-professional degree:* 2.0 GPA, 2 years in residence.

Departments and Teaching Staff: *Total instructional faculty:* 18.

Graduate School of Education

Degree Programs Offered: *Master's, doctorate, first-professional.*
Departments and Teaching Staff: *Total instructional faculty:* 32,75.
Distinctive Educational Programs: Master's programs in English and comparative literature. Joint doctoral program in special education with San Francisco State University.

Graduate School of Journalism

Degree Programs Offered: *Master's, first-professional.*
Departments and Teaching Staff: *Total instructional faculty:* 12.5.

School of Information Management and Systems

Degree Programs Offered: *Doctorate, first-professional.*
Departments and Teaching Staff: *Total instructional faculty:* 10.

School of Public Health

Degree Programs Offered: *Master's, doctorate, first-professional* in applied behavioral e sciences, biostatistics, comparative pathology, environmental health sciences, epidemiology and biostatistics, health planning and policy, health services administration, immunology, maternal and child health, microbiology, nutrition, parasitology, public health education, public health nutrition.

Departments and Teaching Staff: *Total instructional faculty:* 46.5.
Distinctive Educational Programs: Joint master's of public health-M.B.A. with School of Business.

Richard and Rhoda Goodman School of Public Policy

Degree Programs Offered: *Master's, doctorate, first-professional.*
Departments and Teaching Staff: *Total instructional faculty:* 14.
Distinctive Educational Programs: Double-degree programs with School of Law (Boalt Hall), College of Engineering, Graduate School of Journalism.

School of Social Welfare

Degree Programs Offered: *Master's, doctorate, first-professional.*
Departments and Teaching Staff: *Total instructional faculty:* 16.

University of California, Davis

One Shields Avenue
Davis, California 95616-8678
Tel: (530) 752-1011　　**E-mail:** thinkucd@ucdavis.edu
Fax: (530) 752-6363　　**Internet:** www.ucdavis.edu

Institution Description: *Enrollment:* 29,402. *Degrees awarded:* Baccalaureate, master's, doctorate, first-professional (law, medicine, veterinary medicine).

Accreditation: *Regional:* WASC-Sr. *Professional:* business, clinical lab scientist, clinical pastoral education, computer science, engineering, landscape architecture, law, medicine, physician assisting, psychology internship, veterinary medicine

History: Established as University Farm, a 3-year institution, 1905; became 4-year degree-granting institution, offered first instruction at postsecondary level, changed name to College of Agricultural Branch at Davis, and awarded first degree (baccalaureate) 1922; changed name to College of Agriculture 1923; adopted present name 1959.

Institutional Structure: *Composition of institution:* Administrators 84 men / 19 women. Academic affairs headed by provost. Management/business/finances directed by vice chancellor of administration. Full-time instructional faculty

1,398. Academic governance body, Academic Senate, meets an average of 3–6 times per year.

Calendar: Quarters. Academic year late Sept. to mid-June. Freshmen admitted year round. Law School on semester system. Sept. Degrees conferred June, Sept., Dec., Mar. Formal commencement June. Summer sessions from mid-June to early Aug. and early Aug. to mid-Sept.

Characteristics of Freshmen: 32,530 applicants (14,661 m3n, 17,869 women). 58,8% of applicants admitted; 18% of admitted students enrolled full-time.

97% (4,687 students) submitted SAT scores; 32% (1,582 students) submitted ACT scores. *25th percentile:* SAT Verbal 510, SAT Math 560, ACT Composite 21, ACT English 19, ACT Math 22. *75th percentile:* SAT Verbal 630, SAT Math 670; ACT Composite 27, ACT English 27, ACT Math 29.

63% of entering freshmen expected to graduate within 5 years.

Admission: Applicants must meet standard University of California admission requirements.

Degree Requirements: *Undergraduate:* 180 quarter hours; 2.0 GPA; 1 year in residence; general education requirements. *Grading system:* A–F; pass-fail; withdraw (carries time limit).

Distinctive Educational Programs: Internships. Accelerated degree programs. Cooperative baccalaureate program in forestry with University of California, Berkeley. Special facilities for using telecommunications in the classroom. Interdepartmental programs in Afro-American and black studies; American studies, biological sciences, comparative literature, East Asian studies, international relations, linguistics, mass communication, medieval studies, Mexican-American studies; Asian American and Native: American studies, religious studies, women's studies. Facilities and programs for independent research, including honors programs, individual majors, tutorials. Opportunity to study abroad during junior year in Austria, Denmark, France, Germany, Hungary, Italy, Norway, Portugal, Spain, Sweden, United Kingdom, Ireland, Russia, Egypt, Israel, Hong Kong, India, Indonesia, Japan, China, Taiwan, Thailand, Ghana, Kenya, Togo, Brazil, Costa Rica, Ecuador, Mexico, Peru, Canada, Australia, New Zealand.

ROTC: Army.

Degrees Conferred: 5,608 *baccalaureate*; 810 *master's*; 375 *doctorate*; 395 *first-professional*. Bachelor's degrees awarded in top five discipline: social sciences 1,086; biological and biomedical sciences 960; engineering 557; agriculture, agriculture operations and related sciences 482; psychology 476.

Fees and Other Expenses: *Full-time tuition per academic year 2004–05:* undergraduate in-state resident $7,557, out-of-state $24,513. Contact the university for current graduate tuition and fees. *Books and supplies:* $1,145. *Room and board per academic year:* $10,234. *Other expenses:* $2,025.

Financial Aid: Institutional, federal, and state financial aid plans available. Aid from institutionally generated funds is provided on the basis of academic merit, financial need. Institution has a Program Participation Agreement with the U.S. Department of Education for eligible students to receive Pell Grants and other federal aid.

Financial aid to full-time, first-time undergraduate students: 22% received federal grants averaging $3,277; 37% state/local grants averaging $2,285; 50% institutional grants averaging $2,893; 33% loans averaging $3,427.

Departments and Teaching Staff: *Total instructional faculty:* 1,445. *Total tenured faculty:* 1,117. *Degrees held by full-time faculty:* Doctorate 98%.

Enrollment: Total enrollment 29,402. Undergraduate 23,472 (44.1% men, 55.9% women).

Characteristics of Student Body: *Ethnic/racial makeup:* Black non-Hispanic: 2.5%; American Indian or Alaska Native: .7%; Asian or Pacific Islander: 36.9%; Hispanic: 10.4%, White non-Hispanic: 41.4%; unknown 6.4%. *Age distribution:* 17–21: 60%; 22–24: 22%; 25–29: 9%; 30–44: 3%, 45–54: 1%.

International Students: 399 undergraduate nonresident aliens enrolled fall 2004. Programs available to aid students whose native language is not English: English as a Second Language Program. No financial aid specifically designated for international students.

Student Life: On-campus residence halls and married student apartments house 20% of student body. 13.5% of men join fraternities; 12.5% of women join sororities. *Intercollegiate athletics:* men only: baseball, basketball, football, golf, gymnastics, soccer, swimming, tennis, track, water polo, wrestling; women only: basketball, field hockey, gymnastics, softball, swimming, tennis, track, volleyball. *Special regulations:* Cars not permitted on core of campus. *Special services:* Learning Resources Center, medical services, campus transportation system, services for students with physical and learning disabilities. *Student publications, radio: The California Aggie, Student Viewpoint*, and *Third World Forum*, daily, annual, and weekly publications, respectively. Radio station KDVS broadcasts 168 hours per week. *Surrounding community:* Davis population 50,000. San Francisco, 72 miles from campus, is nearest metropolitan area. Served by airport and passenger rail service, each less than 1 mile from campus.

Library Collections: 3,181,000 volumes. 3.9 million microforms; 47,200 periodicals; 14,000 recordings/tapes. Online catalog. Students have access to online information retrieval services and the Internet.

Buildings and Grounds: Campus area 3,555 acres in main campus, 731 additional acres includes medical school and outlying agricultural project areas.

Chief Executive Officer: Dr. Larry N. Vanderhoef, Chancellor.

Undergraduates address admission inquiries to Director of Undergraduate Admissions; graduate and/or first-professional inquiries to Graduate Division.

University of California, Hastings College of the Law

200 McAllister Street
San Francisco, California 94102
Tel: (415) 565-4600   **E-mail:** admiss@uchastings.edu
Fax: (415) 565-4863   **Internet:** www.uchastings.edu

Institution Description: Hastings College of the Law, the law department of the University of California in San Francisco, is a state institution. *Enrollment:* 1,269. *Degrees awarded:* Master's, first-professional (law).

Accreditation: *Professional:* law

History: Founded 1878.

Institutional Structure: Hastings is governed by an 11-member Board of Directors. 10 members are appointed by the Governor of California and approved by the State Senate for 12-year terms, and one is a lineal descendant of its founder, Serranus Hastings, the first Chief Justice of California. The officers of the college are the Dean, who is the Chief Executive Officer, the Academic Dean, the General Counsel, and the Chief Financial Officer.

Calendar: Semesters. Academic year Aug. to May.

Admission: *Requirements:* Applicants for the first-professional degree of Juris Doctor must have earned a bachelor's degree from a college or university of approved standing; admittance on the basis of academic achievement, potential for law study, and potential for achievement in and contribution to the field of law, as evidenced by undergraduate grades, performance on the Law School Admissions Test, and evidence of skills, abilities, and other characteristics. All application materials must be submitted no later than Mar. 1 of the year in which admission is sought but may be submitted as early as the prior October.

Prior to enrollment, foreign student applicants for the L.L.M. degree must have or expect to receive a degree from a recognized law faculty outside the United States. Each applicant must complete an application, including an essay written in English, an official transcript, TOEFL score or its equivalent, and two letters of recommendation, at least of by a member of a law faculty. In general, applicants with a TOEFL score below 600 or its equivalent may not be admitted.

Degree Requirements: L.L.M, candidates are required to complete successfully at least 24 credit hours of classes, including a legal writing and research seminar and one first-year required course (contracts, torts, criminal law, property, or civil procedure). The Director of the L.L. M. Programs helps each student select courses that are tailored to his or her interests. An L.L.M. candidate may elect any course (except a clinic) with the consent of the L.L.M. Director and subject to any prerequisites determined by the instructor for the class. Students must receive a passing grade in all classes to obtain course credit and receive the degree.

Distinctive Educational Programs: As early as the 4th semester, enrollment is permitted in one of the clinics. Each clinic contains a class component and placement in a designated Bay Area law office(s). Current clinics are: Civil Justice (in-house), Immigrants' Rights (in-house), Criminal Practice, Environmental Law, Local Government Law, and Workers' Rights. As early as the 4th or 5th semester, enrollment is permitted in a judicial externship, which has a class component and placement as a law clerk for a Bay Area state or federal court judge. Course concentrations, exchange programs, and appellate advocacy (intramural and extramural moot court competitions).

Concentrations are offered in each of five separate subjects: public interest law, civil litigation, family law, international law, and tax. A special legislation clinic places students in Sacramento with individual legislators and the governor's office.

Degrees Conferred: 10 *master's:* law/legal studies; 396 *first-professional:* law.

Fees and Other Expenses: *Full-time costs per academic year 2004–05:* $18,750 resident; out-of-state student $30,950. *Other fees:* $2,169.

Financial Aid: Aid from institutionally generated funds is provided on the basis of financial need. *Graduate aid:* 17 students received federal and state-funded fellowships and grants totaling $222,470 (ranging from $13,000 to $13,735); 1,045 federal and state-funded loans totaling $21,347,535 (ranging from $5,000 to $24,500); 176 received work-study jobs worth $379,460 (ranging

from $1,83 to $6,800); 895 other fellowships and grants were awarded totaling $3,846,092 (ranging from $2,150 to $4,500).

Departments and Teaching Staff: *Professors* 49, *associate professors* 2, *assistant professors* 2, *part-time faculty* 183. *Total instructional faculty:* 236 (full-time 53, part-time 183; members of minority groups 67; women 99, men 137). Total faculty with doctorate, first-professional, or other terminal degree: 236. Student-to-faculty ratio: 22.7:1. Faculty received $577,650 in grants for research. 4 faculty members awarded sabbaticals 2004.

Enrollment: Total enrollment 1,269. Full-time 578, part-time 691.

International Students: 52 nonresident aliens enrolled fall 2004. 7 students from Europe, 12 Asia, 1 Central and South America, 2 Canada, 30 other. *Programs available to aid students whose native language is not English:* Social and cultural. *Financial aid available to qualified international students;* 10 scholarships available annually.

Student Life: Hastings offers quality student housing in a high-rise apartment building located within one block of the campus. McAllister Tower's 248 apartments include newly renovated efficiencies, studios, one-bedroom and a few two-bedroom apartments. The College also maintains a Housing Office that lists available off-campus housing.

Publications: Hastings has six student-run scholarly publications: *Hastings Communications and Entertainment Law Journal, Hastings Constitutional Law Quarterly, Hastings International and Comparative Law Review, Hastings Law Journal, Hastings West-Northwest Journal of Environmental Law and Policy,* and *Hastings Women's Law Journal.*

Library Collections: 433,575 volumes including bound books, serial backfiles, electronic documents, and government documents not in separate collections. Online catalog. Current serial subscriptions: 7,961 paper. 3,497 recordings. 75 computer work stations. Students have access to the Internet at no charge. Total budget for books and materials 2004–05: $1,128,339.

Most important special holdings include Roger J. Traynor Memorial Collection; Criminal Justice Collection; congressional documents; U.S. Law, Tax Law, U.S. and California Court Records and Briefs; International Law Collection.

Chief Executive Officer: Mary Kay Kane, Chancellor and Dean.

Address admission inquiries to Suzanne Carlson, Director of Enrollment Management; inquires regarding L.L.M. program to Pamela Serota, Coordinator of International Programs.

University of California, Irvine

Campus Drive
Irvine, California 92697-1425
Tel: (949) 824-5011   **E-mail:** oars@uci.edu
Fax: (949) 824-5451   **Internet:** www.uci.edu

Institution Description: *Enrollment:* 24,273. *Degrees awarded:* Baccalaureate, master's, doctorate, first-professional (medicine).

Accreditation: *Regional:* WASC-Sr. *Professional:* business, clinical lab scientist, engineering, medicine, planning, psychology internship

History: Established 1961; chartered 1962; offered first instruction 1965; awarded first degree (baccalaureate) 1968.

Institutional Structure: *Composition of institution:* Administrators 20 men / 6 women. Academic affairs headed by chancellor. Management/business/finances directed by vice chancellor of administrative and business services. Total instructional faculty 2,467. Academic governance body, Academic Senate, meets an average of 7 times per year.

Calendar: Quarters. Academic year Sept. to June. Freshmen admitted year round. Degrees conferred as earned. Formal commencement June. Summer session June to Sept.

Characteristics of Freshmen: 34,393 applicants (15,736 men, 18,657 women). 21.7% of applicants admitted; 21.7% of admitted students enrolled full-time.

99% (4,018 students) submitted SAT scores; 26% (1,075 students) submitted ACT scores. *25th percentile:* SAT Verbal 520, SAT Math 570; ACT Composite 22, ACT English 21, ACT Math 23. *75th percentile:* SAT Verbal 620, SAT Math 680; ACT Composite 27, ACT English 27, ACT Math 29.

48% of entering freshmen expected to graduate within 5 years. 84% of freshmen from California. Freshmen from 24 states and 14 foreign countries.

Degree Requirements: *Undergraduate:* 180 quarter hours; 2.0 GPA; last 3 quarters in residence; general education requirements; writing requirements. *Grading system:* A–F; high pass-pass-fail; withdraw (deadline after which pass-fail is appended to withdraw).

Distinctive Educational Programs: Work-experience programs, including cooperative education, field study. Weekend and evening classes. Special facilities for using telecommunications in the classroom. Interdisciplinary programs in applied ecology, criminal justice, human development, mental health. Facilities and programs for independent research, including honors programs, individual majors, tutorials. University Extension Program; ESL Extension Programs also provided. Study abroad available for upper division students with 3.0 cumulative GPA; while abroad, students can learn the language or history of the visiting country. 28 countries and 60 host institutions are available: Asia, Africa, Latin America, Europe, Middle East.

ROTC: Air Force, Navy.

Degrees Conferred: 4,633 *baccalaureate*; 907 *master's*; 187 *doctorate*; 95 *first-professional.* Bachelor's degrees awarded in top five disciplines: social sciences 1,416; biological and biomedical sciences 594; psychology 516; engineering 391; computer and information sciences and support services 388.

Fees and Other Expenses: *Full-time tuition per academic year 2004–05:* undergraduate in-state resident $6,895, out-of-state $23,851. Contact the university for current graduate resident/nonresident tuition and fees. *Room and board per academic year:* $6,768. *Books and supplies:* $1,524. *Other expenses:* $2,708.

Departments and Teaching Staff: *Total instructional faculty:* 2,467. *Degrees held by full-time faculty:* Doctorate 98%, master's 100%, baccalaureate 100%.

Enrollment: Total enrollment 24,273. Undergraduate 19,967 (49.5% men, 50.5% women).

Characteristics of Student Body: *Ethnic/racial makeup:* Black non-Hispanic: 2.2%; American Indian or Alaska Native: .4%; Asian or Pacific Islander: 50.4%; Hispanic: 11.5%; White non-Hispanic: 24.1%; unknown: 8.8%.

International Students: 519 undergraduate nonresident aliens enrolled 2004. Programs available to aid students whose native language is not English: Social, cultural. English as a Second Language Program. No financial aid specifically designated for international students.

Student Life: 12% of student body live in apartments. 18% of student body live in on-campus apartments. *Intercollegiate athletics:* men only: baseball, basketball, crew, soccer, swimming, tennis, track, water polo; women only: basketball, swimming, tennis, track. *Special regulations:* Cars permitted without restrictions. *Special services:* Learning Resources Center, medical services. *Student publications, radio: New University,* a weekly newspaper; *UC Insights,* an annual literary magazine. Radio station KUCI broadcasts 168 hours per week. *Surrounding community:* Irvine population 80,000. Los Angeles, 45 miles from campus, is nearest metropolitan area. Served by mass transit bus system; airport 2 miles from campus; passenger rail service 10 miles from campus.

Library Collections: 2,300,000 volumes. 2,584,000 microforms; 102,000 audiovisual materials; 17,500 periodicals; 12,000 recordings/tapes. Online catalog. Students have access to online information services and the Internet.

Most important special holdings include Dance Collection; Regional California History Collection.

Buildings and Grounds: Campus area 1,743 acres.

Chief Executive Officer: Dr. Michael Drake, Chancellor.

Address admission inquiries to Barbara Hamkkalo, Director of Enrollment Management.

University of California, Los Angeles

405 Hilgard Avenue
Los Angeles, California 90095
Tel: (310) 825-4321   **E-mail:** ugadm@saonet.ucla.edu
Fax: (310) 825-3101   **Internet:** www.ucla.edu

Institution Description: *Enrollment:* 37,563. *Degrees awarded:* Baccalaureate, master's, doctorate, first-professional (dentistry, law, medicine).

Graduate academic offerings subject to approval by statewide coordinating bodies. Budget subject to approval by state governing boards.

Accreditation: *Regional:* WASC-Sr. *Professional:* business, clinical pastoral education, clinical psychology, computer science, cytotechnology, dentistry, endodontics, engineering, health services administration, law, librarianship, maxillofacial prosthodontics, medicine, nursing, nursing education, periodontics, planning, psychology internship, public health, social work, theatre

History: On May 23, 1919, California Governor William D. Stephens signed Assembly Bill 626, transferring the Los Angeles State Normal School's 25-acre site on Vermont Avenue to the Regents of the University of California. The Southern Branch of the University of California opened on September 15, 1919, offering a 2-year program in undergraduate instruction to 250 students in letters and science and 1,125 students in the Teachers College; added 4-year Teachers College curriculum 1922; added 4-year Letters and Science curriculum and awarded first degree (baccalaureate) 1923; changed name to University of California at Los Angeles 1927, soon to be known as UCLA; authorized graduate work 1933; changed to present name University of California, Los Angeles 1958.

Institutional Structure: *Composition of institution:* Administrators 36 male / 16 female. The Chancellor serves as chief executive office, the executive vice chancellor serves as chief operation officer and the senior vice chancellor-academic affairs serves as chief academic officer. There are also 8 vice chancellors with responsibilities in the following areas: academic affairs, academic personnel, academic planning and budget, administration, legal affairs, research programs, student affairs, and university relations. There are 3 directors of the UCLA Medical Center Hospital Systems: director-medical center, director-neuropsychiatric hospital and Santa Monica Hospital; 2 provosts: provost-letters and science, and provost-medical sciences/dean-school of medicine. There are 10 other deans of professional schools and 4 deans of UCLA Extension, and the dean of International Studies and Overseas Programs. The Academic Senate is the academic governing body and meets periodically throughout the year.

Calendar: Quarters. Academic year Sept. to June. Degrees conferred Sept., Mar., Apr., June. Formal commencement June. Summer session offers more than 500 courses from approximately 60 UCLA departments in 6-, 8-, and 10-week sessions.

Characteristics of Freshmen: 44,981 freshmen applicants (20,207 men, 24,774 women). 23.5% of applicants admitted; 39.1% of admitted students enrolled full-time.

99% (3,699 students) submitted SAT scores; 28%% (1,039 students) submitted ACT scores. *25th percentile:* SAT Verbal 570, SAT Math 610; ACT Composite 24, ACT English 23, ACT Math 24. *75th percentile:* SAT Verbal 690, SAT Math 720; ACT Composite 30, ACT English 30, ACT Math 31.

97% of degree-seeking freshmen were in top tenth of high school graduating class.

Admission: Freshmen are admitted in fall quarter only. Admission is highly selective. Many elements are considered in the selection process, but the primary ones are: academic preparation; performance in courses completes; scores received on the standardized college tests; number of performance in honors and advance placement (AP) courses; depth and quality of senior-year coursework.

Transfer students: admitted at the junior-level (90–130 quarter units) in the fall and spring quarters. Primary elements in selection are: GPA on academic college courses; progress toward completion of the general education requirements; completion of prerequisite courses in the major. *Graduate students: See* individual school/college listing below.

Degree Requirements: *Undergraduate:* In all campus units, except the School of Engineering and Applied Science, students are required to earn a minimum of 180 units from all college level coursework for the bachelor's degree. A maximum of 208 units is allowed in the School of the Arts and Architecture, School of Nursing, and School of Theater, Film, and Television; in the College of Letters and Science a maximum of 216 units (228 for double majors and special programs) is allowed. In the School of Engineering and Applied Science, the minimum units allowed are between 180 and 201 (depending on the program); 213 maximum units are allowed. In addition to unit requirements there are three types of requirements which must be satisfied: (1) university requirements - Subject A or English as a Second Language (ESL), and American history and institutions; (2) college or school requirements (e.g., credit and scholarship, English composition, general education requirements); (3) department requirements (courses in preparation for the major and in satisfaction of the major). Minimum 2.0 GPA. *Grading system:* A–F; pass-fail; withdraw; incomplete; in progress. *Graduate: See* individual school/college listing. (See UCLA General Catalog for further details.)

Distinctive Educational Programs: *For undergraduates:* UCLA's national award-winning projects provide computer and technology support to undergraduates in a wide range of disciplines. These include, among others, Science Challenge, which offers advanced computer services and laboratories to undergraduates; virtual office hours; access to computers in laboratories and library dataline access; and specialized multimedia classrooms for humanities and social science courses. Powell Library houses advanced new classrooms and computer systems specifically for courses in the Humanities and Social Sciences. Freshman and sophomore programs include the Honors Collegium, which offers small, specially devised classes with an interdisciplinary emphasis; and the Professional School Seminar Program, featuring small classes taught by professional school faculty. The Student Research Program allows undergraduates to participate in a research project with a senior faculty member.

The Center of American Politics and Public Policy selects 20 to 30 undergraduates each fall and spring to participate in its Quarter in Washington, D.C. Program, combining UCLA courses with research and field experience. Honors and independent study courses and individually designed majors are also available. The Professional Schools Seminary Program allows undergraduates to enroll in undergraduate seminars taught by faculty from the professional schools (law, medicine, business, social welfare, architecture, etc.). The Education Abroad Program allows students to study abroad for transferable UC credit at distinguished universities throughout the world. Currently over: 85 universities and 33 countries participate.

Tutorial and counseling programs: College tutorial services; Academic Advancement Program; Freshman and Transfer Summer Program; Learning Resource Centers (Instructional Media Laboratory, Instructional Media Library, Language Laboratory). *International Programs:* The International Studies and Overseas Program (ISOP) office supports and coordinates international and foreign area studies; under its aegis are the Coleman African Studies Center, the Latin American Center, the Center for Russian and East European Studies, the Center for International and Strategic Affairs, and other programs. UCLA's overseas outreach also includes international exchange agreements with more than 50 institutions around the world. In addition, the Education Abroad Program offers study opportunities at more than 85 different universities in 33 countries.

Other distinctive programs: Field Studies Development; Extramural Programs and Opportunities. Eligible students may participate in special enrichment programs such as the Marine Biology Quarter on Catalina, the Diversified Liberal Arts Program which reduces course requirements for those going on to Credential Programs in teaching, and the Developmental Learning Program which includes field work in behavioral psychology.

ROTC: Army, Navy, Air Force. 15 Air Force, 17 Army, and 16 Navy commissions awarded 2004.

Degrees Conferred: 7,026 *baccalaureate*; 2,488 *master's*; 665 *doctorate*; 585 *first-professional*. Bachelor's degrees awarded in top area five disciplines: social sciences 1,799; psychology 917; biological and biomedical sciences 822; engineering 572; history 462.

Fees and Other Expenses: *Full-time tuition per academic year 2005–06:* undergraduate resident $6,141, out-of-state student $23,961; graduate students contact the university for current fees. *Required fees:* $344. *Room and board per academic year:* $11,928. *Books and supplies:* $1,452.

Financial Aid: Aid from institutionally generated funds is provided on the basis of academic merit, financial need, athletic ability, other criteria. Institution has a Program Participation Agreement with the U.S. Department of Education for eligible students to receive Pell Grants and other federal aid.

Financial aid to full-time, first-time undergraduate students: need-based scholarships/grants from state, institutional, external sources totaling $121,269,522, self-help (student loans, federal work-study state and other work-study) totaling $52,547,978, parent loans $3,966,621, athletic awards $2,057,236; non-need-based scholarships/grants totaling $10,313,495, self-help $8,967,876, parent loans $16,131,493, athletic awards $3,935,371.

Departments and Teaching Staff: *Professors* 3,111.4, *associate professors* 970.4, *assistant professors* 1,012.3, *instructors* 2,133.4. *Total instructional faculty:* 7,227.4. Student-to-faculty ratio: 19:1.

Enrollment: Total enrollment 37,583. Undergraduate full-time 10,349 men / 13.656 women, part-time 466m / 475w; graduate full-time 5,466m / 4,951w, part-time 213m / 141w; first-professional full-time 898m / 948w, no part-time. Total undergraduates: 24,946; graduate and first-professional 12,617. *Transfer students:* 13,679 applicants; 4,954 admitted applicants; 3,066 enrolled applicants.

Characteristics of Student Body: *Ethnic and racial makeup:* number of Black non-Hispanic: 829; American Indian or Alaska Native: 110; Asian or Pacific Islander: 9,337; Hispanic: 3,821; White non-Hispanic: 8,281; unknown: 1,600.

International Students: 2,100 nonresident aliens enrolled fall 2004. Students from Europe, Asia, Central and South America, Africa, Canada, Australia, New Zealand, and other countries. Programs available to aid students whose native language is not English: Social, cultural. English as a Second Language Program. Scholarships available to undergraduate international students.

Student Life: On-campus co-ed residence halls house 26% of student body (high-rise dorms and residence suites). Housing available for married students. *Intercollegiate athletics:* 10 men's teams: baseball, basketball, cross-country, football, golf, soccer, swimming, tennis, track and field, volleyball, water polo; 11 women's teams: basketball, cross-country, golf, gymnastics, soccer, softball, swimming, tennis, track and field, volleyball, water polo. The Center for Student Programming registers, assists, and provides information about UCLA's several hundred student organizations. Student government provides involvement opportunities. *Special regulations:* Limited on-campus parking for students. *Special services:* Learning Resources Center, medical services, shuttle bus service to off-campus housing and parking. *Student publications, radio: Daily Bruin,* newspaper; *Bruin Life,* a yearbook; *Al-Talib,* a news magazine for Muslim students; *Ha'Am,* Jewish student news magazine; *La Gente,* Chicano and Latino student newspaper; *Nommo,* news magazine for African American students; *Pacific Ties;* Asian student newspaper; *TenPercent,* gay and lesbian news magazine; and *Together,* news magazine about women's issues; *UCLA Community Directory.* Radio station KLA provides music, news, and sports. *Surrounding community:* Los Angeles population 3,640,000. Served by mass transit bus system; airport and passenger rail service each 10 miles from campus.

Publications: *Amerasia Journal; American Indian Culture and Research Journal; AZTLAN; Backdirt; CSE Report; Carte Italiane; Challenge, Chicano-Latino Law Review; Comitatus; Cross Currents; Epoche; Folkore and Mythol-*

ogy Studies; Iconomania; Issues in Applied Linguistics; Journal of Asian Culture; Journal of Latin American Lore, Journal of Legal Pluralism and Unofficial Law; Jusur; Media Scene; MESTER Journal; National Black Law Journal; New German Review; Pacific Review of Ethnomusicology; Paroles Gelees; Romance Linguistics and Literature Review; Selected Reports in Ethnomusicology; Strategies; SurFace; UCLA Business Forecast for the Nation and California; UCLA Cancer Trials; UCLA Entertainment Law Review; UCLA Folkore Annals; UCLA French Studies; UCLA Historical Journal; UCLA Journal of Dance Ethnology; UCLA Journal of Education; UCLA Journal of Environmental Law and Policy; UCLA Law Review; UCLA Librarian; UCLA Pacific Basin Law Journal; UCLA Undergraduate Science Journal; UCLA Women's Law Journal; Ufahamu. Other UCLA publications include: *African Studies Center Newsletter; American Freshmen; Annual UCLA Survey of Business School Computer Usage; California Human Resources Forecast; Evaluation Comment; GSE&IS Forum; The Guide to Life at UCLA; Hispanic: American Periodical Index; ISOP Intercom; Newsletter/Center for the Study of Women; Regulations for Thesis and Dissertation Preparation; Statistical Abstract of Latin America; UCLA Athletics Newsletter; UCLA Center for the Performing Arts; UCLA Dentistry; UCLA General Catalog; UCLA Latin American Studies; UCLA Law Magazine; UCLA Library News for the Faculty; UCLA Magazine; UCLA Medicine; UCLA Nursing; UCLA Public Health; UCLA Today; Ultra Cool Law Review.*

Library Collections: 8,265,200 volumes including bound books, serial backfiles, electronic documents, and government documents not in separate collections. Online catalog. 6,500,000 microform items. 4,100 CD-ROMs; 251,800 audiovisual materials; paper and electronic access to 79,200 serials/periodicals. Students have access to the Internet at no charge. Database searching available. Total budget for books and materials 2004–05: $15,222,163.

Most important holdings include manuscript collections of papers of Aldous Huxley, Henry Miller, Anais Nin, Jack Benny, and Dr. Ralph I. Bunche; the Ahmanson-Murphy Aldine and Early Italian Printing collections and the Michael Sadleir Collection of Nineteenth Century Fiction; Children's Book Collection; Walter H. Rubsamen Music Library includes musical scores and original manuscripts, recordings, and personal collections of composers such as Henry Mancini, Andre Previn, and Ernst Toch; Hoffberg collection of artists books; Walter Lantz archive.

Buildings and Grounds: Campus area 419 acres.

Chief Executive Officer: Dr. Albert Carnesale, Chancellor.

Undergraduates address admission inquiries to Vic Tran, Director of Undergraduate Admissions and Relations with Schools; graduate inquiries to Claudia Mitchell-Kernan, Dean of Graduate Division.

Anderson Graduate School of Management

Degree Programs Offered: *Master's, MBA, doctorate* in management.

Admission: B.A. from accredited 4-year college/university; matrix algebra and differential calculus; computer knowledge; GMAT.

Degree Requirements: *For MBA:* course requirements; field study. *For master's:* course requirements; thesis. *For doctorate:* course requirements; written qualifying exam; university oral qualifying exam; dissertation; final oral exam.

Fees and Other Expenses: Fees vary by program. Contact the school for details.

Enrollment: Total enrollment: 1,431.

College of Letters and Science

Degree Programs Offered: *Baccalaureate* in African languages, African Studies, Afro-American studies; American literature and culture, ancient Near Eastern civilizations, anthropology, applied geophysics, applied mathematics; Arabic; art history; Asian American studies, astronomy; astrophysics; atmospheric sciences; biochemistry; biological anthropology; biology; cell and molecular biology, chemistry; chemistry/materials science; Chicano studies; Chinese; classical civilization; cognitive science; communication studies; comparative literature; cybernetics; developmental studies; East Asian studies; earth sciences; economics/business; economics/international area studies; engineering geology, English; English/Greek; English/Latin; European studies, French; French and linguistics; general chemistry; general mathematics, general physics; geography; geography/ecosystems; geology; geology-engineering geology; geology-geochemistry; geology-nonrenewable natural resources; geology-paleobiology; geophysics-applied geophysics; geophysics and space physics; German; Greek; Hebrew; history; history/art history; Italian; Italian and special fields; Japanese; Jewish studies; Latin; Latin American studies; linguistics; linguistics and computer science; linguistics and East Asian Languages and cultures; linguistics and English; linguistics and French; Linguistics and Italian; mathematics; mathematics-applied science; mathematics/computer science; mathematics of computation; microbiology; Near Eastern studies; philosophy; physics; political science; Portuguese; psychobiology; psychology; religion; Russian linguistics; Scandinavian languages; Slavic languages and literatures;

sociology; Spanish; Spanish and linguistics; Spanish and Portuguese; *master's, doctorate* in various fields.

Admission: Contact the college for detailed requirements.

Degree Requirements: *For baccalaureate:* each student must meet university, college, and department requirements; completion of 180–216 units (depending on program); 2.0 GPA. *For master's:* minimum of 9 courses including 5 graduate courses; foreign language requirement; thesis or comprehensive examination. *For doctorate:* course requirements set by department; written oral examination; university oral qualifying examination; dissertation and final oral examination.

Enrollment: Total enrollment 23,593.

David Geffen School of Medicine at UCLA

Degree Programs Offered: *First-professional* in medicine; *doctorate* in biological chemistry, biomathematics, microbiology and immunology, experimental pathology, human genetics, molecular and medical pharmacology, neurobiology, neuroscience, physiology.

Admission: Requirements vary by degree program. Contact the school for detailed information.

Degree Requirements: Joint degree programs: M.D./Ph.D, MSTP; M.D./M.B.A.-Anderson Graduate School of Management; M.D./MPH-School of Public Health.

Fees and Other Expenses: Contact the school for details. School of Medicine is on the semester system.

Enrollment: Total enrollment: 971.

Graduate School of Education and Information Studies

Degree Programs Offered: *Master's, doctorate* in education, library and information science; *doctorate* in special education (joint program with California State University, Los Angeles).

Admission: Varies by program; contact the school for details.

Degree Requirements: *For master's:* course requirements (9 courses); thesis or comprehensive exam. *For doctorate:* course requirements; screening and oral exams; dissertation; final oral exam.

Fees and Other Expenses: Contact with the school for current fees.

Henry Samueli School of Engineering and Applied Science

Degree Programs Offered: *Baccalaureate* aerospace, biomedical engineering, chemical, and civil engineering; computer science; computer science and engineering; electrical engineering; materials engineering; mechanical engineering; *master's* in manufacturing engineering; *master's, doctorate* in biomedical engineering, chemical engineering; civil engineering; computer science; electrical engineering; materials science and engineering, aerospace engineering, mechanical engineering.

Admission: Contact the school for detailed requirements.

Degree Requirements: *For baccalaureate:* Completion of the minimum number of required units (180–201), depending on curriculum selected; general university requirements; school requirements for scholarship and senior residence (of the last 48 units, 36 must be earned in residence); 2.0 GPA.

Enrollment: Total enrollment: 3,782.

School of the Arts and Architecture

Degree Programs Offered: *Baccalaureate* in art, design/media arts, ethnomusicology, music, world arts and cultures; *master's* in architecture, art, culture and performance, dance, design/media arts, ethnomusicology, music; *doctorate* in architecture and urban design, ethnomusicology, music.

Admission: Contact each department for detailed requirements. Auditions, portfolios, evidence of creativity required.

Degree Requirements: *For baccalaureate:* Completion of the minimum number of required units (180–216) depending on curriculum selected; general university requirements; school requirements for scholarship and senior residence (of the last 45 units, 35 must be earned in residence) 2.0 GPA. *For graduate:* requirements vary by major; contact the department for detailed information.

Distinctive Educational Programs: Experiential Technologies Center; Center for Intercultural Performance.

Enrollment: Total enrollment 1,189.

School of Dentistry

Degree Programs Offered: *First-professional* in dental surgery (D.D.S.); *master of science and doctorate* in oral biology.

Admission: *For first-professional degree:* 90 semester hours undergraduate work at an accredited college or university which must include 6 hours English,

8 biology (with laboratory), 8 inorganic chemistry (with laboratory), 8 physics (with laboratory), 6 organic chemistry (with laboratory), 1 course in biological chemistry, 1 course introductory psychology; DAT.

Degree Requirements: *For first-professional degree:* 5,225 clock hours, 4 years in residence. *For master's:* course requirements of 36 units (17 at graduate level); thesis plan; final oral for thesis.

Enrollment: Total enrollment: 454.

School of Law

Degree Programs Offered: *Juris Doctor* (J.D.); *master of laws* (LL.M.). *Joint degree program:* J.D./M.B.A.; J.D./M.A. urban planning; J.D./M.A. American Indian studies; J.D./M.A., Ph.D., M.Ed., Ed.D. education; J.D./M.S.W. social welfare; J.D./M.P. Public Policy. Other programs may be arranged with the approval of the Law School.

Admission: *For first-professional degree:* Baccalaureate from an accredited college or university, LSAT. Students beginning their professional work are admitted only for the fall semester. UCLA offers a three-year, full-time course of study. Evening, summer, or part-time programs are not offered.

Degree Requirements: *For first-professional degree:* 87 credit hours, 6 semesters in residence. For transfer students 4 semesters in residence. *For LL.M:* 20 semester credits. Contact the school for SJD degree requirements.

Enrollment: Total enrollment: 926.

School of Nursing

Degree Programs Offered: *Baccalaureate, master's, doctorate* in nursing.

Admission: *For baccalaureate:* RN licensure, completion of 84 quarter units with grades of C or better in prerequisite courses, 4 Excelsior Exams, and overall GPA of 3.0; 3 letters of recommendation. *For MSN: BS degree in nursing; 3 prerequisite courses, RN licensure; 3 letters of recommendation. For Ph.D.:* RN licensure; 3 prerequisite courses; GRE, and 4 recommendations. .

Degree Requirements: *For baccalaureate:* completion of 76 to 88 unites in residence; minimum of 180 quarter units; overall GPA of 2.0; *For MN:* core courses plus additional coursework for each area of clinical specialization; comprehensive examination. *For Ph.D.:* completion of core, statistics, and cognate courses; written qualifying exam; university oral qualifying exam; dissertation, final oral exam.

Fees and Other Expenses: Professional fee charged to MSN students. Contact the school for details.

Enrollment: Total enrollment: 316.

School of Public Affairs

Degree Programs Offered: *Master of Public Policy, Master of Social Welfare, Master of Arts in Urban Planning; doctorate* in social welfare, urban planning.

Admission: Each department has specialized requirements. Contact the school for details.

Degree Requirements: For Master of Social Welfare: 76 units; field practicums. For Master of Public Policy and Master of Arts: 72 units; internship. Each department has specialized requirements for Ph.D. Contact the school for details.

Fees and Other Expenses: Contact the school for current fees.

Enrollment: Total enrollment: 475.

School of Public Health

Degree Programs Offered: *Master's* in preventative medicine and public health; *master's and doctorate* in biostatistics, environmental health sciences, epidemiology, health services, public health; *doctorate* in environmental science and engineering.

Admission: Each department has limitations and additional requirements. *See* UCLA catalog or contact the school for detailed information.

Degree Requirements: *For master's:* Requirements vary by degree program and department. *For doctorate:* Course requirements; qualifying exams; final oral exams.

Fees and Other Expenses: Contact the school for current tuition and additional professional fees.

School of Theater, Film, and Television

Degree Programs Offered: *Baccalaureate, master's, doctorate* in film and television, theater, moving image archive studies.

Admission: *For baccalaureate:* In addition to the University of California undergraduate admission requirements, departments in the School require supplementary material. Contact the School for detailed information. *For master's, doctorate:* Each department has specialized requirements.

Degree Requirements: *For baccalaureate:* university, school, unit, major, and scholarship requirements must be met; GPA 2.0; contact the School for detailed information. *For MA:* research tool; 9 courses; thesis or comprehensive exam. *For MFA:* 18 courses; comprehensive exam. *For doctorate:* foreign language requirement; courses; teaching experience; qualifying exams; university oral exam; final oral exam; dissertation.

Fees and Other Expenses: Contact the school for information regarding tuition and additional professional fees.

Distinctive Educational Programs: The UCLA School of Theater, Film, and Television is the only academic organization in the U.S. that offers professional training in the three interrelated disciplines of theater, film, and television within a single professional school.

Enrollment: Total enrollment: 923.

University of California, Riverside

900 University Avenue
Riverside, California 92521-4009
Tel: (951) 787-1012   **E-mail:** discover@ucr.edu
Fax: (951) 787-3800   **Internet:** www.ucr.edu

Institution Description: *Enrollment:* 17,104. *Degrees awarded:* Baccalaureate, master's, doctorate. Specialist and administration certificates also awarded.

Accreditation: business, biomedical, chemistry, engineering, psychology internship, teacher education

History: Citrus Experiment Station established by University of California in 1907 at Riverside. In 1954, College of Letters and Sciences founded as small undergraduate college. In 1961, Graduate Division founded. Established as Citrus Experimental Station, an agricultural research center, 1907; adopted present name, offered first instruction at postsecondary level, and awarded first degree (baccalaureate) 1954.

Institutional Structure: *Composition of institution:* Senior management and professionals: 111 men / 75 women. Academic affairs headed by executive vice chancellor. Management/business/finances directed by vice chancellor administration and vice chancellor academic planning and budget. Total faculty 835. Academic governance body, UC Riverside Division of the Academic Senate, meets an average of 3 times per year.

Calendar: Quarters. Academic year Sept. to June. Freshmen admitted Sept., Jan., Mar. Degrees conferred June, Aug., Dec., Mar. Formal commencement June.

Characteristics of Freshmen: 79% of applicants admitted. 19% of applicants admitted and enrolled.

99% (3,418 students) submitted SAT scores; 28% (953 students) submitted ACT scores. *25th percentile:* SAT Verbal 460, SAT Math 560; ACT Composite 18. *75th percentile:* SAT Verbal 570, SAT Math 630; ACT Composite 24.

60% of entering freshmen expected to graduate within 5 years. 99% of freshmen from California. Freshmen from 12 states and 7 foreign countries.

Admission: University of California admission requirements. Applicants who are UC eligible will be evaluated for selective admission under Comprehensive Review.

Degree Requirements: *Undergraduate:* 180 quarter units; 35 of last 45 units in residence; core curriculum; for art history majors, exit competency examination. *Grading system:* A–F; satisfactory-no credit; withdraw.

Distinctive Educational Programs: Biomedical Science program leading to 7 year M.D. jointly with UCLA; large undergraduate independent research program including research grants; work experience/internship programs; undergraduate business administration degree; interdisciplinary programs in law society; women's studies; Latin American studies; ethnic studies; Opportunity for study abroad at 100 host institutions in 32 countries.

ROTC: Air Force in cooperation with California State University, San Bernardino and Claremont-McKenna College; Army in cooperation with California State University, San Bernardino.

Degrees Conferred: 2,874 *baccalaureate*; 360 *master's*; 141 *doctorate*.

Fees and Other Expenses: *Full-time tuition per academic year 2004–05:* undergraduate resident $6,585, out-of-state $16,476; graduate contact the university for current fees. *Room and board per academic year:* $9,800.

Financial Aid: Aid from institutionally generated funds is provided on the basis of academic merit, financial need, athletic ability, other criteria. Institution has a Program Participation Agreement with the U.S. Department of Education for eligible students to receive Pell Grants and other federal aid.

Financial aid to full-time, first-time undergraduate students: need-based scholarships/grants totaling $71,451,513, self-help $34,305,044, parent loans $7,774,761, athletic awards $547,504; non-need-based scholarships/grants totaling $4,370,658, self-help $5,226,343, parent loans $11,457,343, athletic awards $1,090,204. *Graduate aid:* 1,018 students received $9,574,301 in federal and state-funded fellowships/grants; 495 received $5,136,963 federal and state-funded loans; 337 received $1,016,013 for college-assigned jobs; 183 received other fellowships/grants totaling $1,852,598; 914 teaching assistantships awarded totaling $13,140,351; 737 research assistantships were awarded totaling $11,191,046.

Departments and Teaching Staff: *Total instructional faculty:* 796 (full-time 647, part-time 149; members of minority groups 206; women 251, men 545). Total faculty with doctorate, first-professional, or other terminal degree: 780. Student-to-faculty ratio: 18:1. Faculty development: $82 million in grants for research in 2004.

Enrollment: Total enrollment 17,104. Undergraduate full-time 6,692 men / 7,958 women, part-time 307m / 232w; graduate full-time 1,001m / 928w, part-time 14m / 21w; first-professional: full-time 25m / 26w. *Transfer students:* 822 new undergraduate transfers.

Characteristics of Student Body: *Ethnic/racial makeup:* number of Black non-Hispanic: 996; American Indian or Alaska Native: 64; Asian or Pacific Islander: 6,289; Hispanic: 3,566; White non-Hispanic: 3,055; unknown 847. *Age distribution:* number of 307; 18–19: 6,573; 20–21: 3,255; 22–24: 2,248, 25–29: 444; 30–34: 137; 35–39: 45; 40–49: 58; 50–64: 19; 65 and over: 3.

International Students: 545 nonresident aliens enrolled fall 2004. Students from Europe, Asia, Central and South America, Africa, Canada, Australia. Programs available to aid students whose native language is not English: English as a Second Language Program. No financial aid specifically designated for international students.

Student Life: Most students live on campus in residence halls, apartments, or family housing. *Intercollegiate athletics:* (NCAA Division II) men only: basketball, baseball, cross-country, soccer, track, tennis, water polo; women only: basketball, cross-country, soccer, softball, tennis, track, volleyball. *Special regulations:* Cars permitted without restrictions. *Special services:* Learning Center, Student Health, Women's Resource, Campus Activities, Disabled, Veterans, Career Planning and Placement, Financial Aid, Chicano/Black/Native: American Programs; Asian Programs, Counseling Center, Children's Center, International Services. more than 200 student recreation, religious, academic, cultural and ethnic organizations, including fraternities and sororities. *Student publications, radio: Highlander,* campus newspaper; radio station KUCR. *Surrounding community:* :Inland Empire area of Southern California is one of the fastest growing in the nation. Riverside is a metropolitan area of 255,000 population. Ontario International Airport is 20 miles away. Near mountain skiing and desert resorts.

Publications: *Fiat Lux* published several times per year.

Library Collections: 2,305,526 volumes including bound books, serial backfiles, electronic documents, and government documents not in separate collections. Online catalog. Current serial subscriptions: 10,755 paper; 649 microform; 20,019 via electronic access. 12,427 recordings; 4,698 compact discs; 6,330 CD-ROM. 520 computer work stations. Students have access to the Internet at no charge. Total budget for books, periodicals, audiovisual materials, microforms 2004–05: $5,214,071.

Most important holdings include J. Lloyd Eaton Collection of Science Fiction; manuscripts of Thomas Hardy and Ezra Pound; Jonas/Schenker Collection of Music Theory; Rupert Costo Library of American Indian; B. Traven Collection.

Buildings and Grounds: Campus area 1,100 acres. *New buildings:* Science Library; Fine Arts; Chemistry Building; Entomology Building; Pentland Hills Resident Halls; Stonehaven Apartments.

Chief Executive Officer: Dr. France Cordova, Chancellor.

Undergraduates address admission inquiries to Emily Engel Schall, Director, Office of Immediate Outreach; graduate inquiries to Graduate Admissions.

University of California, San Diego

900 Gilman Drive
La Jolla, California 92093
Tel: (858) 534-2230   **E-mail:** admissionsinfo@ucsd.edu
Fax: (858) 534-6523   **Internet:** www.admissions.ucsd.edu

Institution Description: *Enrollment:* 24,105. *Degrees awarded:* Baccalaureate, master's, doctorate, first-professional (medicine).

Accreditation: *Regional:* WASC-Sr. *Professional:* engineering, medicine, nursing-midwifery, psychology internship

History: Established as Marine Biological Station of San Diego 1903; joined University of California system as Scripps Institution of Biological Research 1912; awarded first degree (doctorate) 1920; changed name to University of California Scripps Institution of Oceanography 1925; became general campus of University of California 1958; offered first instruction at postsecondary level (graduate only) and adopted present name 1960; offered undergraduate study

1964. *See* Verne A. Stadtman, ed., *The University of California, 1868–1968* (San Francisco: McGraw-Hill Book Co., 1970) for further information.

Institutional Structure: *Composition of institution:* Administrators (Executives) 31 men / 8 women. Academic affairs/management/business/finances directed by vice chancellors. Full-time instructional faculty 1,569 (1,195 men / 374 women). Academic governance body, Academic Senate, meets an average of 8 times per year.

Calendar: Quarters. Academic year Sept. to June. Freshmen admitted fall quarter only. Degrees conferred June, Aug., Dec., Mar. Formal commencement June.

Characteristics of Freshmen: 43,443 applicants (19,542 men, 23,901 women). 37.2% of applicants admitted; 22.3% of admitted students enrolled full-time.

99% (3,767 students) submitted SAT scores; 31% (1,202 students) submitted ACT scores. *25th percentile*: SAT Verbal 550, SAT Math 600; ACT Composite 23, ACT English 22, ACT Math 25. *75th percentile*: SAT Verbal 660, SAT Math 710; ACT Composite 29, ACT English 28, ACT Math 30.

93% of entering freshmen expected to graduate within 5 years. 98% of freshmen from California.

Admission: Applications accepted for the fall term only. Admission is extremely competitive. Freshmen must complete UC "a-f" high school course requirements; SAT or ACT; three SATI Subject Tests (writing, math, and optional subject). School offers college credit for extrainstitutional learning on basis of ACE *2006 Guide to the Evaluation of Educational Experiences in the Armed Services*. Tutoring available. Developmental courses offered for credit.

Degree Requirements: *Bachelor of Arts degree:* 180–184 credit hours; 2.0 GPA; *Bachelor of Science degree:* 192 credit hours; 2.0 GPA. Each candidate for the bachelor's degree must complete 36 of the final 45 units in residence. Additional requirements vary by program. *Grading system:* A–F; withdraw (carries time limit).

Distinctive Educational Programs: Work-experience programs. Some weekend and evening classes. Accelerated degree programs. Interdisciplinary programs. Facilities and programs for independent research, including honors programs, individual majors, tutorials. Five undergraduate colleges each with different general education requirements. Exchange programs with Dartmouth, Spelman, and Morehouse Colleges. *Other distinctive programs:* Continuing education. Study abroad programs in 33 countries.

Degrees Conferred: 4,131 *baccalaureate*; 784 *master's*; 161 *post-master's certificates*; 327 *doctorate*; 100 *first-professional*. Bachelor's degrees awarded in top five disciplines: social sciences 818; biological and biomedical sciences 661; engineering 462; psychology 338; visual and performing arts 266.

Fees and Other Expenses: *Full-time costs per academic year 2004–05:* undergraduate resident $6,651; out-of-state $23,807; graduate resident/nonresident and first-professional program tuition and fees vary, contact the school of interest for current information. *Room and board per academic year:* $8,996. *Books and supplies:* $1,407.

Financial Aid: Aid from institutionally generated funds is provided on the basis of academic merit, financial need. Institution has a Program Participation Agreement with the U.S. Department of Education for eligible students to receive Pell Grants and other federal aid.

Financial aid to full-time, first-time undergraduate students: 31% received federal grants averaging $3,530; 46% state/local grants averaging $2,481; 40% institutional grants averaging $2,282; 40% loans averaging $3,211.

Departments and Teaching Staff: *Total instructional faculty:* 1,569. *Degrees held by full-time faculty:* Doctorate 99%. 99% hold terminal degrees.

Enrollment: Total enrollment 24,105. Undergraduate 19,872.

Characteristics of Student Body: *Ethnic and racial makeup:* Black non-Hispanic: 1.2%; American Indian or Alaska Native: .4%; Asian or Pacific Islander: 39.6%; Hispanic: 10.2%; White non-Hispanic: 35.3%; unknown 10.3%.

International Students: 556 nonresident aliens enrolled fall 2003. Programs available to aid students whose native language is not English: English as a Second Language Program. No financial aid specifically designated for international students.

Student Life: On-campus residence halls house 37% of student body. 50% of married students request institutional housing and are so housed. *Intercollegiate athletics:* men only: baseball, basketball, crew, cross-country, fencing, soccer, swimming and diving, tennis, track and field, volleyball, water polo; women only: basketball, crew, cross-country, fencing, golf, soccer, softball, swimming and diving, tennis, track and field, volleyball, water polo. *Special regulations:* Cars permitted without restrictions. *Special services:* Learning Resources Center, medical services, bus service to and from university hospital. *Student publications, radio:* The Guardian, a biweekly newspaper; *The New Indicator*, a bimonthly newspaper; *The Koala*, a bimonthly humor newspaper; *The California Review*, a monthly paper; *Voz Fronteriza*, a monthly Chicano newspaper; *People's Voice*, a monthly Black Student Union newspaper; *L'Chayim*, a quarterly Jewish student newspaper; *Birdcage Review*, a quarterly literary magazine;

Sappho Speaks, a quarterly Lesbian and Gay newspaper; *Journal of Undergraduate Research*, a yearly student research journal; *Freshman Record*, an annual yearbook. Radio station KSDT broadcasts a wide range of music over: cable seven days a week. *Surrounding community:* San Diego population 1,200,000. Served by mass transit bus system; airport 12 miles from campus; passenger rail service 6 miles from campus

Library Collections: 2,881,000 volumes. 322,000 government documents; 2,020,000 microforms; 88,000 audiovisual materials; 24,990 periodicals. Online catalog. Students have access to online information retrieval services and the Internet.

Most important holdings include biomedicine collection; oceanography-marine biology collection; Kenneth Hill Collection on Pacific Voyages; Spanish Civil War Collection; Archive for New Poetry; Theodore Geisel (Dr. Seuss) Collection.

Buildings and Grounds: Campus area 1,950 acres.

Chief Executive Officer: Dr. Marye Anne Fox, Chancellor.

Undergraduates address admission inquiries to Director of Admissions and Outreach; graduate students to Graduate Coordinator (of each particular discipline).

University of California, San Francisco

513 Parnassus Avenue
San Francisco, California 94143-0244

Tel: (415) 476-9000   **E-mail:** admission@ucsf.edu
Fax: (415) 476-9634   **Internet:** www.ucsf.edu

Institution Description: *Enrollment:* 2,763. *Degrees awarded:* Baccalaureate, master's, doctorate, first-professional (dentistry, medicine, pharmacy). Post-baccalaureate certificates also awarded.

Member of the San Francisco Consortium on Higher Education and Urban Affairs.

Accreditation: *Regional:* WASC-Sr. *Professional:* clinical pastoral education, prosthodontics, dental hygiene, dental public health, dentistry, dietetics, endodontics, oral and maxillofacial surgery, nursing-midwifery, nursing, nursing education, oral pathology, periodontics, pharmacy, physical therapy, psychology internship

History: Established as Toland Medical Center, incorporated, offered first instruction at postsecondary level, and awarded first degree (first-professional) 1864; became a department of University of California 1873; changed name to University of California, San Francisco Medical Center 1958; adopted present name 1970.

Institutional Structure: *Composition of institution:* Administrators 24 men / 4 women. Academic affairs headed by senior vice chancellor. Management/business/finances directed by administrative vice chancellor. Instructional faculty 1,125 men / 459 women. Academic governance body, Academic Senate, meets an average of 3 times per year.

Calendar: Quarters. Academic year Sept. to June. Degrees conferred Sept., Jan., Mar., June. Formal commencement June. Summer session from mid-June to early Sept.

Admission: Students are admitted to all programs in the fall quarter. Application filing dates and financial aid procedures differ from those at other campuses. To obtain all the necessary information, contact the appropriate UCSF school at least 18 months in advance of enrollment. A solid background in the sciences is necessary preparation for education in the health sciences. Good grades and test scores are required for admission; however, a student's academic and career potential and willingness to work hard are also important considerations.

Degree Requirements: Completion of prescribed curriculum.

Distinctive Educational Programs: Off-campus centers are affiliated clinics in various locations throughout the state where students practice and take courses. *Other distinctive programs:* Continuing education programs in dentistry, medicine, nursing, and pharmacy for practicing professionals.

Degrees Conferred: 21 *baccalaureate*: health professions and related clinical services; 204 *master's*: 95 *doctorate*; 368 *first-professional*; 12 *post-baccalaureate certificates*.

Fees and Other Expenses: *Full-time tuition per academic year 2004–05:* Contact the university for current tuition and fees.

Financial Aid: Aid from institutionally generated funds is provided on the basis of financial need. Institution has a Program Participation Agreement with the U.S. Department of Education for eligible students to receive Pell Grants and other federal aid.

Departments and Teaching Staff: *Total instructional faculty:* 1,584.

Enrollment: Total enrollment 2,763. Undergraduate 26.

Characteristics of Student Body: *Ethnic/racial makeup:* Asian or Pacific Islander: 38.5%; White non-Hispanic: 50%; American Indian or Alaska Native: 3.8%; unknown: 7.7%.

Student Life: On-campus residence halls house 7% of student body. Houses and apartments for both men and women constitute 100% of such space. Professional fraternities also offer residence space. Additional accommodations are available for married students with dependent children. 14% of student body live on campus. *Special regulations:* Parking on campus for medical housestaff. *Special services:* Learning Resources Center, medical services, shuttle buses. *Student publications: Synapse,* weekly newspaper. *Surrounding community:* San Francisco population over: 700,000. Served by mass transit bus and subway system; airport 15 miles from campus; passenger rail service 3 miles from campus.

Publications: *UCSF Magazine* (quarterly), *UCSF Newsbreak* (biweekly, triweekly July, Aug., Dec.), *UCSF Annual Report.*

Library Collections: 950,000 volumes. 915,000 government documents; 425,000 microforms; 22,000 audiovisual materials; 2,400 current periodical subscriptions. Access to Medline and other computerized information retrieval services.

Most important holdings include History of Health Sciences Collection; Oriental Medicine Collection; California Health Sciences Collection.

Buildings and Grounds: Campus area 136 acres total (various locations).

Chief Executive Officer: Dr. J. Michael Bishop, President.

Address admission inquiries to Director of Student Admission.

School of Dentistry

Degree Programs Offered: *Baccalaureate* in dental hygiene; *first-professional* in dental surgery; *master's* in oral biology.

Admission: *For first-professional degree:* Completion of 135 quarter units or 90 semester units of college with a minimum of 30 quarter units or 20 semester units at a 4-year institution. Postsecondary units must include 8 quarter units English, 12 inorganic chemistry with laboratory, 8 organic chemistry with laboratory, 12 physics with laboratory, 12 biology or zoology with laboratory, 8 psychology, 16 social studies and/or humanities and/or foreign language. Additional recommended electives in biochemistry, embryology, comparative vertebrate science, statistics, genetics; DAT; AAD-SAS.

Degree Requirements: *For first-professional degree:* 190 quarter units, minimum grade average C, 4-year prescribed curriculum.

School of Medicine

Degree Programs Offered: *Baccalaureate* in physical therapy; *first-professional* in medicine. Master's and doctorate in various fields. Certificates given in exfoliate cytology.

Admission: *For first-professional degree:* 3 years college credit (135 quarter units or 90 semester units) which must include 1 year general chemistry with laboratory, 2 quarters organic chemistry, 1 year physics with laboratory, 1 year biology with laboratory including invertebrate zoology; 3.20 GPA; MCAT.

Degree Requirements: *See* general requirements. *For first-professional degree:* 4-year prescribed curriculum.

School of Nursing

Degree Programs Offered: *Baccalaureate, master's, doctorate.*

Admission: *For baccalaureate degree:* 10 quarter units anatomy/physiology with laboratory; 5 chemistry with laboratory; 8 freshman English; 8 U.S. history/U.S. government; 8 social sciences including sociology; 4 nutrition; 4 statistics; 8 additional biological or physical sciences; 8 humanities or social sciences; nursing diploma; ACT PEP in nursing; GRE.

School of Pharmacy

Degree Programs Offered: *First-professional* in pharmacy; *master's* in pharmaceutical chemistry; *doctorate* in pharmaceutical chemistry.

Admission: *For first-professional degree:* 90 quarter units including 8-10 quarter units freshman English; 1 year general chemistry with laboratory (15-16 units including quantitative analysis); 1 year physics with laboratory; mathematics including 2 calculus courses and analytic geometry; 1 year integrated course biology with laboratory including invertebrate and vertebrate zoology; 28 elective units. Minimum GPA 2.4 residents, 2.8 nonresidents.

Degree Requirements: *For first-professional degree:* 190 quarter units, 36 months in residence.

University of California, Santa Barbara

Santa Barbara, California 93106-2030

Tel: (805) 893-8000   **E-mail:** appinfo@sa.ucsb.edu
Fax: (805) 893-2676   **Internet:** www.ucsb.edu

Institution Description: *Enrollment: 21,026. Degrees awarded:* Baccalaureate, master's, doctorate.

Accreditation: *Regional:* WASC-Sr. *Professional:* computer science, dance, engineering, psychology internship

History: Established as Anna S. C. Blake Manual Training School, a private school, 1891; control transferred to city 1892; came under state jurisdiction as Santa Barbara Normal School of Manual Arts and Home Economics 1909; changed name to Santa Barbara Normal School 1919; offered first instruction at postsecondary level and changed name to Santa Barbara State Teachers College 1921, to Santa Barbara State College 1935; became part of university system as Santa Barbara College 1944; adopted present name 1958. *See* Robert L. Kelley, *Transformation: University of California, Santa Barbara 1909–1979* (Santa Barbara: Kimberly Press, 1981) for further information.

Institutional Structure: *Composition of institution:* Administrators 29 men/ 6 women. Academic affairs headed by and management/business/finances directed by the Vice Chancellor. Academic governance body, The Academic Senate, meets an average of 8 times per year.

Calendar: Quarters. Academic year Sept. to May. Freshmen admitted Sept., Jan., Mar., June. Degrees conferred June, Aug., Dec., Mar. Formal commencement June.

Characteristics of Freshmen: 53% of applicants admitted. 19,9% of applicants admitted and enrolled full-time.

84% (3,272 students) submitted SAT scores; 37% (1,425 students) submitted ACT scores. *25th percentile:* SAT Verbal 520, SAT Math 550; ACT Composite 21. *75th percentile:* SAT Verbal 640, SAT Math 660; ACT Composite 28.

75% of entering freshmen expected to graduate within 5 years. 94% of freshmen from California. Freshmen from 51 states and 10 foreign countries.

Admission: The University of California now allows applicants to apply to more than one campus of the system. Deadline for application Nov. 30 for fall admission; Notification of admission is sent Mar1-15. Applicants must accept admission by May 1. *Requirements:* Applicant must have high school graduation with 2 years of history, 4 English, 3 mathematics, 2 laboratory science, 2 of one foreign language, and 2 years of college preparatory elective courses. SAT or ACT and SATI tests are required for freshmen admission. TOEFL for foreign students; essay required.

Degree Requirements: 180 quarter hours, 2.0 GPA, 3 quarters in residence; general education requirements. *Grading system:* A–F; pass-fail.

Distinctive Educational Programs: Evening classes. Special facilities for using telecommunications in the classroom. Interdepartmental programs in African area studies, aquatic biology; Asian studies, classical archaeology, classical civilization, comparative literature, computer science, economics-mathematics, environmental studies, film studies; Hispanic: civilization, law and society, medieval studies, pharmacology, Renaissance studies, Russian area studies, social science. Facilities and programs for independent research, including honors programs, individual majors. College of Creative Studies, Global Peace and Security Program, Robotics Program in Engineering. Education Abroad Program (with students attending classes at more than 50 host universities in 27 countries), International Scholars, Robert Maynard Hutchins Center for the Study of Democratic Institutions.

ROTC: Army.

Degrees Conferred: 5,078 *baccalaureate* (B), 618 *master's* (M), 253 *doctorate* (D): area and ethnic studies 152 (B), 6 (M); biological/life sciences 339 (B), 14 (M), 21 (D); business/marketing 557 (B); communications/communication technologies 242 (B), 2 (M), 8 (D); computer and information sciences 108 (B), 37 (M), 7 (D); education 146 (M), 30 (D); engineering and engineering technologies 194 (B), 81 (M), 46 (D); English 243 (B), 9 (M), 6 (D); foreign languages and literature 198 (B), 34 (M), 10 (D); interdisciplinary studies 479 (B), 8 (M); law/legal studies 249 (B); mathematics 75 (B), 26 (M), 8 (D); natural resources/ environmental science 92 (B), 55 (M), 2 (D); philosophy/religion/theology 136 (B), 12 (M), 7 (D); physical sciences 103 (B), 43 (M), 31 (D); psychology 351 (B), 9 (M), 9 (D); social sciences and history 1,105 (B), 102 (M), 54 (D); visual and performing arts 450 (B), 34 (M), 14 (D).

Fees and Other Expenses: *Full-time tuition per academic year 2004–05:* undergraduate resident $6,995, out-of-state $23,451; contact the university for graduate tuition and fees. *Room and board per academic year:* $9,897. Other campus-based fees may be applicable.

Financial Aid: Institution has a Program Participation Agreement with the U.S. Department of Education for eligible students to receive Pell Grants and other federal aid.

Financial aid to full-time, first-time undergraduate students: need-based scholarships/grants totaling $55,543,330, self-help $29,462,407, parent loans $6,154,226, athletic awards $503,591; non-need-based scholarships/grants totaling $3,673,441, self-help $8,286,929, parent loans $19,431,172, athletic awards $1,421,837.

Departments and Teaching Staff: *Total instructional faculty:* 1,033 (full-time 903, part-time 130; members of minority groups 167; women 323, men 710). Total faculty with doctorate, first-professional, or other terminal degree: 45. Student-to-faculty ratio: 17:1.

Enrollment: Total enrollment 21,026 (full-time 20,408, part-time 618). Undergraduate full-time 7,758 men / 9,771 women, part-time 333m / 259w; graduate full-time 1,640m / 1,239w, part-time 18m /8w.

Characteristics of Student Body: *Ethnic/racial makeup:* number of Black non-Hispanic: 474; American Indian or Alaska Native: 139; Asian or Pacific Islander: 2,852; Hispanic: 3,102; White non-Hispanic: 9,508; unknown: 1,787.

International Students: 259 nonresident aliens enrolled fall 2004. No programs available to aid students whose native language is not English. No financial aid specifically designated for international students.

Student Life: College-owned/college-operated housing is available to undergraduates. Freshman applicants are given priority for college housing. Extensive intramural sports program. There are nineteen sororities on campus; eighteen fraternities. Thirty-seven campus-based religious organizations on campus. Over 450 registered campus organizations available. *Intercollegiate athletics:* men only: baseball, basketball, cross-country, football, gymnastics, swimming, tennis, track, volleyball, water polo; women only: basketball, cross-country, gymnastics, soccer, swimming, tennis, track, volleyball, water polo. *Special regulations:* Cars permitted in designated areas; fee charged. *Special services:* Learning Resources Center, medical services. *Student publications, radio: Collage,* an alternative newspaper published irregularly; *Daily Nexus,* a daily newspaper; *Discovery,* annual research journal; *Hustler's Handbook,* annual student handbook; *La Cumbre,* a yearbook; *Spectrum,* a biannual literary magazine. Radio station KCSB broadcasts 168 hours per week. *Surrounding community:* Santa Barbara population 100,000. Los Angeles, 100 miles from campus, is nearest metropolitan area. Served by mass transit bus system; airport 1 mile from campus; passenger rail service 7 miles from campus.

Publications: *Public Historian* (quarterly) first published 1978.

Library Collections: 3,228,557 volumes including bound books, serial backfiles, electronic documents, and government documents not in separate collections. Online catalog. 3,753,711 microforms; 306,334 audio items; 5,529 video units. Students have access to the Internet at no charge.

Most important holdings include Land SAT Satellite Imagery Collection; Wyles Collection (Civil War and westward expansion); Art Exhibition Collection.

Buildings and Grounds: Campus area 989 acres. *New buildings:* Manzanita Village Student Housing Complex completed 2002; Donald Bran Hall 2002.

Chief Executive Officer: Dr. Henry T. Yang, Chancellor.

Undergraduates address admission inquiries to Admissions Office; graduate inquiries to Graduate Division.

University of California, Santa Cruz

1156 High Street
Santa Cruz, California 95064

Tel: (831) 459-4008   **E-mail:** admissions@cats.ucsc.edu
Fax: (831) 459-4452   **Internet:** www.ucsc.edu

Institution Description: The University of California, Santa Cruz is a public research institution. *Enrollment:* 15,036. *Degrees awarded:* Baccalaureate, master's, doctorate. Post-baccalaureate certificates also awarded.

Accreditation: *Regional:* WASC-Sr. *Professional:* engineering, psychology internship

History: Established 1962; offered first instruction at postsecondary level 1965; awarded first degree (baccalaureate) 1967.

Institutional Structure: *Composition of institution:* 14 Senior Administrators headed by the Chancellor. The Campus Provost and Executive Vice Chancellor is in charge of academic affairs. Full-time instructional faculty 446. Academic governance body, Academic Senate, meets an average of 3 times per year.

Calendar: Quarters. Academic year Sept. to June. Freshmen admitted fall quarter only. Degrees conferred Dec., Mar., June, Aug. Formal commencement June. Summer session June to Aug.

Characteristics of Freshmen: 69.8% of applicants admitted. 13.2% of applicants admitted and enrolled full-time.

97.95% (3,001 students) submitted SAT scores; 28.63% (379 students) submitted ACT scores. *25th percentile:* SAT Verbal 520, SAT Math 530; ACT Composite 21. *75th percentile:* SAT Verbal 640, SAT Math 640; ACT Composite 27.

65% of entering freshmen expected to graduate within 5 years.

Degree Requirements: *Undergraduate:* 180 credit hours; 36 courses with grades of pass, or C or above on each; 3 quarters in residence; general education requirements in American history and institutions and in English composition; exit competency examinations-comprehensives in individual fields of study or senior thesis. *Grading system:* Letter grades are mandatory for entering students. These students can take no more than 25% of their course load on a pass or no pass basis. Performance evaluations are provided to each student in every class.

Distinctive Educational Programs: Work-experience programs, including internships, field education. Flexible meeting places and schedules, including evening classes. Dual-degree program in engineering with University of California, Berkeley. Exchange program with University of New Hampshire. Education Abroad Program. Special facilities for using telecommunications in the classroom. Interdisciplinary programs in American studies, East Asian studies, environmental studies, Latin American studies, modern society and social thought, psychobiology, western civilization, women's studies. Facilities and programs for independent research, including honors programs, individual majors, tutorials.

Degrees Conferred: 3,083 *baccalaureate;* 300 *master's;* 107 *doctorate.* Bachelor's degrees awarded in top five disciplines: social sciences 485; visual and performing arts 413; psychology 301; business, management, marketing, and related support services 276; biological and biomedical sciences 261. 31 *post-baccalaureate certificates.*

Fees and Other Expenses: *Full-time fees per academic year 2004–05:* undergraduate resident $7,023, out-of-state student $16,956; contact the university for current graduate fees. *Room and board per academic year:* $10,947.

Financial Aid: Aid from institutionally generated funds is provided on the basis of academic merit, financial need. Institution has a Program Participation Agreement with the U.S. Department of Education for eligible students to receive Pell Grants and other federal aid.

Financial aid to full-time, first-time undergraduate students: need-based scholarships/grants totaling $49,677,678, self-help $27,583,322, parent loans $1,071,100; non-need-based scholarship/grants totaling $3,086,541, self-help $6,137,377, parent loans $14,179,843, tuition waivers $8,164.

Departments and Teaching Staff: *Total instructional faculty:* 729 (full-time 533, part-time 196; members of minority groups 148; women 285, men 444). Total faculty with doctorate, first-professional, or other terminal degree: 714. Student-to-faculty ratio: 19.38:1.

Enrollment: Total enrollment 15,036. Full-time undergraduate 5,916 men / 7,067 women, part-time 353m / 358w; graduate full-time 600m / 655w, part-time 58m / 29w.

Characteristics of Student Body: *Ethnic/racial makeup:* number of Black non-Hispanic: 349; American Indian or Alaska Native: 122; Asian or Pacific Islander: 2,462; Hispanic: 1,960; White non-Hispanic: 7,077; unknown: 1,515.

International Students: 231 nonresident aliens enrolled fall 2004. Programs available to aid students whose native language is not English: English as a Second Language. No financial aid specifically designated for international students.

Student Life: 45% of all undergraduate students are housed in 10 residential colleges. Housing available for students with families. *Intercollegiate athletics:* men and women: basketball, soccer, swimming, tennis, volleyball, and waterpolo. Club sports: rugby, lacrosse, sailing, and ultimate frisbee. *Special regulations:* Cars must have parking permits. *Special services:* Learning Resources Center, Disability Resource Center, medical services, child care, re-entry services for older students, shuttle bus services, over: 100 student organizations. *Student publications, radio: Chinquapin,* an annual literary review; *City on a Hill Press,* a multicultural newspaper. Radio station KSZC broadcasts 24 hours daily. *Surrounding community:* Santa Cruz population 55,000. San Jose, 35 miles from campus, is nearest metropolitan area. Served by mass transit bus system; airport 35 miles from campus; passenger rail service 35 miles from campus.

Library Collections: 1,535,118 volumes including bound books, serial backfiles, electronic documents, and government documents not in separate collections. Online catalog. Current serial subscriptions: 21,924 paper, microform, electronic access. 14,151 recordings; 3,290 compact discs; 1,662 CD-ROMs. 151 computer work stations. Students have access to the Internet at no charge.

Most important holdings include Mary Lea Shane Archives of Lick Observatory; Norman and Charlotte Strouse Collection on 19th-century English essayist and historian Thomas Carlyle; Trianon Press Archive; Gregory Bateson Archive; Kenneth Patchen Archive.

Buildings and Grounds: Campus area 2,000 acres. *New buildings:* Bookstore and Graduate Commons 2002; Interdisciplinary Science Building 2004; Center for Adaptive Optics 2003; Engineering 2 Building 2004.

Chief Executive Officer: Dr. Denice D. Denton, Chancellor.

Address admission inquiries to Michael McCawley, Associate Director, Evaluation/Processing (e-mail: mikemc@cats.ucsc.edu).

University of Judaism

15600 Mulholland Drive
Bel Air, California 90077

Tel: (310) 476-9777   **E-mail:** admissions@uj.edu
Fax: (310) 472-2374   **Internet:** www.uj.edu

Institution Description: University of Judaism is a private institution affiliated with the Conservative Movement in American Judaism. *Enrollment:* 280. *Degrees awarded:* Baccalaureate, master's.

Accreditation: *Regional:* WASC-Sr.

History: Established, chartered, and offered first instruction at postsecondary level 1947; awarded first degree (baccalaureate) 1949.

Institutional Structure: *Governing board:* Board of Governors. Representation: 35 members. All voting. *Composition of institution:* Administrators 15 men / 7 women. Academic affairs headed by academic dean. Full-time instructional faculty 26, part-time 23. Academic governance body, faculty senate, meets an average of 12 times per year.

Calendar: Semesters. Academic year Sept. to May. Students admitted fall and spring. Degrees conferred and formal commencement June.

Characteristics of Freshmen: Mean SAT class scores 560 verbal, 550 mathematical. Mean ACT Composite class score 19.

91% of applicants accepted. 47% of accepted applicants enrolled. 67% of entering freshmen expected to graduate within 5 years. 52% of freshmen from California. Freshmen from 9 states and 2 foreign countries.

Admission: For fall acceptance, undergraduates must apply by Nov. 15 of previous year for early decision; Jan. 31 of year of enrollment for regular admission. Transfer students apply by April 15. For spring acceptance, apply by Oct. 15 of previous year for regular admission; transfer students by Nov. 1 of previous year. *Requirements:* Graduation from accredited secondary school. Minimum GPA 3.2; graduate students 3.0. *Entrance tests:* College Board SAT. *For transfer students:* 3.0 minimum GPA; 80 hours maximum transfer credit.

College credit for postsecondary-level work completed in secondary school and for extrainstitutional learning (life experience) on basis of faculty assessment. Tutoring available.

Degree Requirements: *For all associate degrees:* 67 credit hours. *For all baccalaureate degrees:* 126 hours. *For all undergraduate degrees:* 2.0 GPA; last 30 hours in residence; breadth requirements.

Fulfillment of some degree requirements possible by passing College Board AP. *Grading system:* A–F; pass-fail; withdraw (carries time limit).

Distinctive Educational Programs: Limited evening classes. Dual-degree programs in various fields with University of California, Los Angeles. Interdisciplinary program in Jewish and Western civilization. Tutorials. Study abroad in Israel and other countries. Strong emphasis in internships.

Degrees Conferred: 30 *baccalaureate* (B), 25 *master's* (M): area and ethnic studies 5 (B); biological/life sciences 10 (B); business/marketing 3 (B), 5 (M); communications/communication technologies 1 (B); education 3 (B), 15 (M); liberal arts and sciences, general studies and humanities3 (B); philosophy, religion, theology 5 (M); psychology 5 (B).

Fees and Other Expenses: *Full-time tuition per academic year 2004–05:* $18,840. *Room per academic year:* $5,478. *Board per academic year:* $5,082. *Required fees:* $430.

Financial Aid: Aid from institutionally generated funds is provided on the basis of academic merit, financial need, leadership ability.

Institutional funding for undergraduates: 73 scholarships and grants totaling $646,506 (ranging from $4,000 to $14,500). *For graduates:* 72 fellowships and grants totaling $650,000 (ranging from $1,000 to $14,500); 2 research assistantships worth $9,000.

Federal and state funding for undergraduates: 38 scholarships and grants totaling $166,695 (ranging from $400 to $12,545); 48 loans totaling $310,045 (ranging from $2,500 to $10,500); 45 work-study jobs totaling $85,000. *For graduates:* 68 loans totaling $708,575 (ranging from $3,000 to $18,500); 5 work-study jobs worth $10,000.

Departments and Teaching Staff: *Professors* 7, *assistant professors* 3, *instructors* 1, *part-time lecturers* 113.

Total instructional faculty: 67 FTE. Degrees held by full-time faculty: Doctorate 100%. 100% hold terminal degrees. Faculty development: $126,000 total grants for research.

Enrollment: Total enrollment 280.

Characteristics of Student Body: *Ethnic/racial makeup:* number of Black non_Hispanic: 6; American Indian or Alaskan Native: 1; Asian or Pacific Islander: 3; Hispanic: 6; White non-Hispanic: 189.

International Students: 5 nonresident aliens enrolled fall 2004. No programs available to aid students whose native language is not English. No financial aid specifically designated for international students.

Student Life: On-campus housing. 2 student governments; intramural athletics. *Special services:* Learning Resources Center. *Student publications: The Catalyst,* a newspaper; *Cymbals,* annual literary magazine. *Surrounding community:* Los Angeles population 3,100,000. Served by airport 10 miles from campus, passenger rail service 20 miles from campus.

Library Collections: 120,000 volumes including bound books, serial backfiles, electronic documents, and government documents not in separate collections. Online and card catalogs. Current serial subscriptions: 375 paper, 10 microform, 12 electronic. 7 CD-ROMs. 14 computer work stations. Students have access to the Internet at no charge.

Most important holdings include collection of rare Bibles; Judaica Collection.

Buildings and Grounds: Campus area 26 acres.

Chief Executive Officer: Dr. Robert Wexler, President.

Undergraduates address admission inquiries to Shoshana Kapnek, Director of Undergraduate Admissions; graduate inquiries to Saul Korin, Director of Graduate Admissions.

University of La Verne

1950 Third Street
La Verne, California 91750

Tel: (909) 593-3511   **E-mail:** admissions@ulv.edu
Fax: (909) 593-0965   **Internet:** www.ulv.edu

Institution Description: University of La Verne is a private, independent, nonprofit institution. *Enrollment:* 4,021. *Degrees awarded:* Associate, baccalaureate, first-professional (law), master's, doctorate.

Member of Inland Empire Academic Library Cooperative.

Accreditation: *Regional:* WASC.

History: Established as Lordsburg College, chartered, and offered first instruction at postsecondary level 1891; awarded first degree (baccalaureate) 1914; changed name to La Verne College 1917; adopted present name 1977.

Institutional Structure: *Governing board:* Board of Trustees of University of La Verne. Extrainstitutional representation: 39 trustees including 15 alumni, 1 honorary, 4 emeriti. Institutional representation: president of the university, 1 student, 1 faculty. *Composition of institution:* Administrators 37 men / 23 women (13% are members of minority groups). Academic affairs headed by academic vice president. Business/finances directed by vice president for business and finance. Full-time instructional faculty 120. Academic governance body, University Faculty, meets an average of 4 times per year.

Calendar: Semesters (4-1-4 plan). Academic year Sept. to May. Freshmen admitted Sept., Jan. Degrees conferred May, Dec. Formal commencement May.

Characteristics of Freshmen: 59% of applicants admitted. 23% of admitted applicants enrolled full-time.

96% (364 students) submitted SAT scores; 23% (86 students) submitted ACT scores. *25th percentile:* SAT Verbal 450, SAT Math 460; ACT Composite 18, ACT English 18, ACT Math 17. *75th percentile:* SAT Verbal 542, SAT Math 560; ACT Composite 23, ACT English 23, ACT Math 23.

45% of entering freshmen expected to graduate within 5 years. 7% of freshmen from California. Freshmen from 17 states.

Admission: Rolling admissions plan. For fall acceptance, the preferred application deadline is Feb. 1. *Requirements:* Freshmen: graduate from accredited secondary school with college preparatory coursework. SAT or ACT may be submitted. Transfer students: minimum 32 transferable units of credit from 4- or 2-year accredited institution, completion of college algebra and college writing. Study skills workshop available.

Degree Requirements: *For all associate degrees:* 60 credit hours; 16 hours in residence. *For all baccalaureate degrees:* 128 hours; 32 hours in residence. *For all undergraduate degrees:* 2.0 GPA; general education and core requirements. Fulfillment of some degree requirements and exemption from some beginning courses possible by passing departmental examinations, College Board CLEP, AP, other standardized tests. *Grading system:* A–F; pass-fail; withdraw (deadline after which pass-fail is appended to withdraw); incomplete (carries time limit).

Distinctive Educational Programs: *For undergraduates:* Honors Program, cluster colleges, interdisciplinary programs in over: 15 locations. Institutionally arranged internships in most fields. Work experience programs, including practicums and internships. *Other distinctive programs:* La Verne College Accelerated Program for Adults.

Degrees Conferred: 250 *baccalaureate*; 477 *master's*; 63 *doctorate*; 21 *first-professional*: law. Honorary Doctor of Humane Letters awarded 2004.

Fees and Other Expenses: *Full-time tuition per academic year:* $22,800 undergraduate, graduate varies by program. *Room and board per academic year:* $9,110.

Financial Aid: Aid from institutionally generated funds is provided on the basis of academic merit, financial need. Institution has a Program Participation Agreement with the U.S. Department of Education for eligible students to receive Pell Grants and other federal aid.

Financial aid to full-time, first-time undergraduate students: need-based scholarships/grants totaling $17,817,975, self-help $3,631,339; non-need-based scholarships/grants totaling $693,672, self-help $519,614, parent loans $1,646,943.

Departments and Teaching Staff: *Total instructional faculty:* 397 (full-time 183, part-time 214; members of minority groups 65; women 182, men 207). Total faculty with doctorate, first-professional, or other terminal degree: 154. Student-to-faculty ratio: 13:1.

Enrollment: Total enrollment 4,021. Undergraduate full-time 555 men / 999 women, part-time 40m / 56w, graduate full-time 348m / 649w, part-time 344m / 509w, first-professional full-time 115m / 97w, part-time 3m / 6w.

Characteristics of Student Body: *Ethnic/racial makeup:* number of Black non-Hispanic: 149; American Indian or Alaska Native: 11; Asian or Pacific Islander: 77; Hispanic: 615; White non-Hispanic: 594; unknown: 192. *Age distribution:* number under 18: 9; 18–19: 23; 20–21: 644; 22–24: 311; 25–29: 45; 30–34: 8; 35–39: 2; 40–49: 6; 50–64: 2.

International Students: 151 nonresident aliens enrolled fall 2004. Programs available to aid students whose native language is not English: English as a Second Language Program. Financial aid specifically designated for international students: Scholarships available to undergraduate international students.

Student Life: On-campus residence halls house 40% of student body. *Intercollegiate athletics:* men only: baseball, football; both men and women: basketball, soccer, swimming and diving, tennis, track, water polo. *Special regulations:* Cars permitted without restrictions. *Special services:* Medical services, First Generation Student Success Program, Learning Enhancement Center, Career Development. *Student publications, radio: The Campus Times,* a weekly newspaper; *La Verne Magazine* (biannually), *The Prism* (biannually). Radio station KULV broadcasts 50 hours per week. LVATV, local cable television produced by ULV students and faculty. *Surrounding community:* La Verne population 30,000. Los Angeles, 30 miles from campus, is nearest metropolitan area. Served by mass transit bus system; airport 15 miles from campus; passenger rail service 2 miles from campus.

Library Collections: 148,790 volumes including bound books, serial backfiles, electronic documents, and government documents not in separate collections. Online catalog. Current serial subscriptions: 11,585 paper, 2,727 microform, 2,476 via electronic access. Computer work stations available in computer labs. Students have access to the Internet at no charge.

Most important holdings include the Muir Collection (2,500 volumes on Brethren history with rare books, manuscripts, church documents); the Bunelle Collection of California History (600 volumes, including first and rare editions); mystery fiction collection; Law Library.

Buildings and Grounds: Campus area 32 acres. *New buildings:* New residence hall completed 2001.

Chief Executive Officer: Dr. Stephen C. Morgan, President.

Address admission inquiries to Ana Liza V. Zell, Dean of Undergraduate Admissions; graduate inquiries to Jo Nell Baker, Director, Graduate Student Services; law school inquiries to Alexis E. Thompson, Assistant Dean of Admissions, Law.

University of the Pacific

3601 Pacific Avenue
Stockton, California 95211-0197
Tel: (209) 946-2211   **E-mail:** admissions@pacific.edu
Fax: (209) 946-2413   **Internet:** www.pacific.edu

Institution Description: University of the Pacific is a private, nonsectarian institution formerly affiliated with the United Methodist Church. *Enrollment:* 6,268. *Degrees awarded:* Baccalaureate, master's, doctorate. first-professional (dentistry, pharmacy, law). Specialist certificates in education also awarded.

Accreditation: *Regional:* WASC-Sr. *Professional:* business, computer science, dentistry, engineering, law, music, pharmacy, physical therapy, speech-language pathology, teacher education

History: Established and chartered as California Wesleyan University 1851; offered first instruction at postsecondary level and changed name to University of the Pacific 1852; awarded first degree (baccalaureate) 1858; changed name to College of the Pacific 1911; readopted present name 1961.

Institutional Structure: *Governing board:* Board of Regents. Representation: 39 regents. All voting. *Composition of institution:* Administrators 29 men / 10 women. Academic affairs headed by academic vice president. Management/business/finances directed by financial vice president. Full-time instructional faculty 401. Academic governance body, Academic Council, meets an average of 10 times per year.

Calendar: Early semester. Academic year Aug. to May. Freshmen admitted Sept., Feb., June. Degrees conferred May, June, Aug., Dec. Formal commencement May. Summer sessions from late May to late Aug.

Characteristics of Freshmen: 95% (833 students) submitted SAT scores; 37% (523 students) submitted ACT scores. *25th percentile:* SAT Verbal 520, SAT Math 540; ACT Composite 22. *75th percentile:* SAT Verbal 620, SAT 660; ACT Composite 27.

64% of applicants admitted; 81% of admitted students enrolled full-time. 85% of students from California. Freshmen from 27 states and 12 foreign countries.

Admission: Rolling admissions plan. For fall acceptance, priority filing date is Feb. 15. Admissions deadline is Dec. 15. Early acceptance available. *Requirements:* Either graduation from accredited secondary school or GED. *Entrance tests:* College Board SAT preferred; ACT composite accepted. For foreign students TOEFL. *For transfer students:* 2.8 minimum GPA; from 4-year accredited institution 70 units maximum transfer credit.

College credit and advanced placement for postsecondary-level work completed in secondary school. College credit for extrainstitutional learning on basis of ACE *2006 Guide to the Evaluation of Educational Experiences in the Armed Services,* portfolio assessment.

Tutoring available. Developmental courses offered in summer session and regular academic year; credit given.

Degree Requirements: *Undergraduate:* 124 semester hours; 2.0 GPA; 32 of last 40 units in residence; general education requirements.

Fulfillment of some degree requirements and exemption from some beginning courses possible by passing College Board CLEP, AP. *Grading system:* A–F; pass-fail.

Distinctive Educational Programs: Work-experience programs, including cooperative education, internships, practicums. Weekend and evening classes. Accelerated degree programs. Joint first-professional-master's of business administration with McGeorge School of Law, Sacramento University. Doctoral program in physical therapy. Dental hygiene program. Interdisciplinary programs. Facilities and programs for independent research, including honors programs, individual majors. Study abroad in Austria, England, France, Spain, Germany.

Degrees Conferred: 650 *baccalaureate* (B), 158 *master's* (M), *doctorate* (D): area and ethnic studies 6 (B); biological/life sciences 99 (B), 5 (M); business/marketing 134 (B), 23 (M); communications/communication technologies 35 (B), 5 (M); computer and information sciences 11 (B); education 65 (B), 28 (M), 12 (D); engineering and engineering technologies 63 (B); English 19 (B); foreign languages and literature 2 (B); health professions and related sciences 21 (B), 55 (M), 26 (D); interdisciplinary studies 12 (B); law/legal studies 18 (M); liberal arts/general studies 12 (B); mathematics 6 (B); natural resources/environmental science 1 (B); parks and recreation 38 (B), 2 (M); philosophy/religion/theology 1 (B); physical sciences 7 (B), 1 (M); psychology 20 (B), 21 (M), 3 (M); social sciences and history 63 (B); visual and performing arts 35 (B). 601 *First-professional:* dentistry 146; pharmacy 199; law 256.

Fees and Other Expenses: *Full-time tuition per academic year 2004–05:* $25,658. *Required fees:* $430. *Room and board per academic year:* $8,478.

Financial Aid: Aid from institutionally generated funds is awarded on basis of academic merit, financial need, athletic ability, other criteria. Institution has a Program Participation Agreement with the U.S. Department of Education for eligible students to receive Pell Grants and other federal aid.

Undergraduate aid: need-based scholarships/grants $36,175,911, self-help $13,270,183, parent loans $5,735,147, tuition waivers $743,435, athletic awards $12,843,352; non-need-based scholarships/grants $3,124,759, self-help $802,147, parent loans $1,433,552, tuition waivers $7008,682, athletic awards $2,383,018. *Graduate aid:* 495 students received awards totaling $5,527,000 (ranging from $500 to $18,500); 48 students received a total of $115,200 for work-study jobs (ranging from $2,000 to $3,000); 152 fellowships/grants totaling $478,000 (ranging from $1,000 to $5,000); 118 teaching assistantships totaling $1,008,000 (ranging from $5,000 to $15,000).

Departments and Teaching Staff: *Total instructional faculty:* 656 (full-time 401, part-time 255; 239 women, 417 men). Total faculty with doctorate, first-professional, or other terminal degree: 554. Student-to-faculty ratio: 14:1. *Faculty development:* $472,490 in grants for research. 19 faculty members awarded sabbaticals 2004–05.

Enrollment: Total enrollment 6,268 (full-time 5,521, part-time 747).

Characteristics of Student Body: *Ethnic/racial makeup:* number of Black non-Hispanic: 104; American Indian or Alaska Native: 22; Asian or Pacific

Islander: 983; Hispanic: 336; White non-Hispanic: 1,595; unknown: 341. *Age distribution:* number under 18: 103; 18–19: 1,546; 20–21: 1,200; 22–24: 392; 25–29: 88; 30–34: 46m 35–39: 28; 40–49: 45; 50–64: 11.

International Students: 132 nonresident aliens enrolled fall 2004. Students from Europe, Asia, Central and South America, Africa, Canada, Australia, Middle East. Programs available to aid students whose native language is not English: Social and cultural. English as a Second Language Program. No financial aid specifically designated for international students.

Student Life: On-campus residence halls. *Intercollegiate athletics:* men only: baseball, basketball, golf, swimming, tennis, water polo; women only: basketball, cross-country, field hockey, soccer, softball, swimming, tennis, volleyball, water polo. More than 90 campus organizations, fraternities, sororities, intramural sports, club sports, and on-campus fitness center. *Special regulations:* Campus parking by permit only. *Special services:* Student Advising Center, Learning Resources Center, Retention Services Center, Disabled Student Services, medical services. *Student publications, radio: Pacifican,* a weekly newspaper. Radio stations KPAC, KUOP. *Surrounding community:* Stockton population 150,000. Sacramento, 30 miles from campus, is nearest metropolitan area. Served by mass transit bus system; airport 15 miles from campus; passenger rail service 5 miles from campus.

Library Collections: 282,313 volumes including bound books, serial backfiles, electronic documents, and government documents not in separate collections. Online catalog. Current serial subscriptions: paper 1,356; microform 701,325; via electronic access 10,894. 9,319 recordings; 4,000 compact discs. 90 computer work stations. Students have access to the Internet at no charge. Total budget for books, periodicals, audiovisual materials, microforms 2004–05: $810,500.

Most important special collections include John Muir Papers, Stuart Library of Western Americana; Lawton Harris Folk Dance Collection; Dave Brubeck Collection (manuscripts and papers).

Buildings and Grounds: Campus area 167 acres. *New buildings:* Brookside Hall; Monagan Hall; Fitness Center; Library Addition.

Chief Executive Officer: Dr. Donald DeRosa, President.

Address admission inquiries to Marc McGee, Director of Admissions.

University of Redlands

1200 East Colton Avenue
Redlands, California 92373-0999

Tel: (909) 793-2121   **E-mail:** admissions@redlands.edu
Fax: (909) 793-2029   **Internet:** www.redlands.edu

Institution Description: University of Redlands is a private, independent, nonprofit institution. *Enrollment:* 2,451. *Degrees awarded:* Baccalaureate, master's.

Accreditation: *Regional:* WASC-Sr. *Professional::* music, speech-language pathology, teacher education

History: Established and chartered 1907; offered first instruction at postsecondary level 1909; awarded first degree (baccalaureate) 1911. *See* Lawrence E. Nelson, *Redlands: Biography of a College* (Redlands: University of Redlands, 1958) for further information.

Institutional Structure: *Governing board:* University of Redlands Board of Trustees. Representation: 36 voting trustees. *Composition of institution:* president assisted by 4 vice presidents (finance and administration, dean of student life, university relations, academic affairs). Administrators 127. Full-time instructional faculty 206. Academic governance body, Academic Assembly, meets an average of 9 times per year.

Calendar: Semesters. (4-1-4 plan). Academic year Sep. to May. Freshmen admitted Sep., Feb. Degrees conferred and formal commencement May.

Characteristics of Freshmen: 75% of applicants admitted. 21% of applicants admitted and enrolled full-time.

75% (455 students) submitted SAT scores; 38% (232 students) submitted ACT scores. *25th percentile:* SAT Verbal 540, SAT Math 530; ACT Composite 22. *75th percentile:* SAT Verbal 640, SAT Math 630; ACT Composite 27.

67% of freshmen from California. Freshmen from 36 states and 6 foreign countries.

Admission: Rolling admissions plan. For fall acceptance, apply as early as Dec. 1 of previous year, but not later than May 1 of year of enrollment. acceptance available. *Requirements:* Graduation from an accredited secondary school. Recommend 4 years English; 2-3 years of foreign language, laboratory sciences, and social studies; 3 years of mathematics. . *Entrance tests:* College Board SAT or ACT composite. *For transfer students:* 2.5 minimum GPA; 66 semester hours maximum from a 2-year institution and 100 semester hours from a 4-year institution.

College credit and advanced placement for postsecondary-level work completed in secondary school. Tutoring available. Noncredit remedial courses offered during regular academic year.

Degree Requirements: *Arts and Sciences Program:* 128 credit hours; 2.0 GPA; last 32 units in residence; general education requirement of 42 semester credits; must complete all requirements within 4 years from the date of the first class meeting (may apply for a single 3-year extension). *Johnson Center Program:* graduation contract and descriptive evaluations. Fulfillment of some degree requirements and exemption from some beginning courses possible by passing departmental examinations, College Board AP. *Grading system:* 0.0 to 4.0 scale OR descriptive reports for courses taken in Johnston Center Program.

Distinctive Educational Programs: *College of Arts and Sciences* Johnston Center for Integrative Studies permits students to design individualized programs of study leading to B.A. or B.S. degree. Environmental Studies combine academic study with hands-on experience in analysis of real-world environmental problems, creative writing program, musical theater degree, interdisciplinary honors program. Study abroad in Austria and in over: 100 other approved programs in England, Scotland, France, Germany, Spain, Japan, China, and Singapore. *Whitehead College:* The University of Redlands School of Business and School of Education contain an array of full-time undergraduate and graduate programs designed for working adults. Flexible meeting places and schedules, evening and weekend classes, regional centers.

ROTC: Air Force and Army in cooperation with California State University, San Bernardino.

Degrees Conferred: 712 *baccalaureate* (B), 279 *master's* (M): area and ethnic studies 2 (B), biological/life sciences 15 (B); business/marketing 490 (B), 208 (M); computer and information sciences 1 (B); education 7 (B), 51 (M); English 15 (B); foreign languages and literature 3 (B); health professions and related sciences 9 (B), 20 (M); liberal arts/general studies 51 (B); mathematics 6 (B); natural resources/environmental science 7 (B); philosophy/religion/theology 2 (B), physical sciences 4 (B); psychology 24 (B); social sciences and history 46 (B); visual and performing arts 20 (B).

Fees and Other Expenses: *Full-time tuition per academic year 2004–05:*undergraduate $25,224; graduate varies by program. *Books and supplies:* $1,000. *Required fees:* $300. *Room per academic year:* $4,850. *Board per academic year:* $3,846.

Financial Aid: Aid from institutionally generated funds is provided on the basis of academic merit. Institution has a Program Participation Agreement with the U.S. Department of Education for eligible students to receive Pell Grants and other federal aid.

Financial aid to full-time, first-time undergraduate students: need-based scholarships/grants totaling $28,777,529, self-help $10,452,098, parent loans $2,261,173, tuition waivers $669,020; non-need-based scholarships/grants totaling $2,511,673, self-help $877,775, parent loans $697,396, tuition waivers $50,248. *Graduate aid:* fellowships and grants totaling $27,960; teaching assistantships totaling $87,381; research assistantships totaling $82,550.

Departments and Teaching Staff: *Total full-time instructional faculty:* 325 (full-time 163, part-time 162; members of minority groups 45; women 147, men 168). Total faculty with doctorate, first-professional, or other terminal degree: 186. Student-to-faculty ratio: 11:1.

Enrollment: Total enrollment 2,451.

Characteristics of Student Body: *Ethnic and racial makeup:* number of Black non-Hispanic: 46; American Indian or Alaska Native: 14; Asian or Pacific Islander: 133; Hispanic: 280; White non-Hispanic: 1,423; unknown 433. *Age distribution:* number under 18: 37; 18–19: 1,071; 20–21: 984; 22–24: 205; 25–29: 27; 30–34: 12; 35–39: 4; 40–49: 9; 50–64: 2; 65 and over: 1.

International Students: 17 nonresident aliens enrolled fall 2004. 4 students from Europe, 9 Asia, 2 Africa, 1 Canada, 1 Australia. No programs available to aid students whose native language is not English. No financial aid specifically designated for international students.

Student Life: On-campus residence halls house 73% of student body. 2% of men join fraternities; 1% of women join sororities. *Intercollegiate athletics:* men only: baseball, football, golf, hockey; women only: softball, volleyball. Men and women's programs: basketball, cross-country, diving, softball, swimming, soccer, tennis, track and field (outdoor), water polo. *Special regulations:* Cars permitted without restrictions. Quiet hours. *Special services:* Medical services. *Student publications, radio: Bulldog,* a weekly newspaper; *La Letra,* a yearbook. Radio station KUOR broadcasts 7 days per week. *Surrounding community:* Redlands population 66,000. Los Angeles, 65 miles from campus, is nearest metropolitan area. Served by mass transit bus system; airport 28 miles from campus; passenger rail service 10 miles from campus.

Library Collections: 262,893 volumes including bound books, serial backfiles, electronic documents, and government documents not in separate collections. Online catalog. Current serial subscriptions: 1,800 paper, 8,000 via electronic access. 1,875 recordings; 3,053 compact discs. Students have access to the Internet at no charge.

Most important holdings include Vernon and Helen Farquhar Collection of Californiana and the Southwest; Barney Childs Collection of Music; McNair Collection of Far Eastern Books; Irvine Foundation Map Collection; Hawaii-Pacific Collection; Ann Peppers Art Collection

Buildings and Grounds: Campus area 138 acres. *New buildings:* Stauffer Center for Science and Mathematics completed 2000; Brockton Avenue Student Apartments; Field House renovation and Fitness Center addition.

Chief Executive Officer: Dr. James R. Appleton, President.

Undergraduates address admission inquiries to Paul Driscoll, Dean of Admissions (e-mail: adpdrisc@redlands.edu); graduate inquiries for Communicative Disorders Program to Christopher Walker (e-mail: walker@redlands.edu); graduate Music Program to Donald Beckie (e-mail: beckie@redlands.edu).

University of San Diego

5998 Alcala Park
San Diego, California 92110-2492

Tel: (619) 260-4600   **E-mail:** admissions@sandiego.edu
Fax: (619) 260-6836   **Internet:** www.sandiego.edu

Institution Description: University of San Diego is a private, independent, nonprofit institution officially affiliated with the Roman Catholic Church. *Enrollment:* 7,486. *Degrees awarded:* Baccalaureate, master's, doctorate, first-professional (law). Certificates and specialist certificates in education also awarded.

Accreditation: *Regional:* WASC-Sr. *Professional:* business, engineering, law, marriage and family therapy, nursing, teacher education

History: Established and chartered as San Diego College for Women 1949; offered first instruction at postsecondary level 1952; awarded first degree (baccalaureate) 1954; merged with the University of San Diego College for Men and its coeducational law school and adopted present name 1972.

Institutional Structure: *Governing board:* Board of Trustees. Extrainstitutional representation: 36 trustees; institutional representation: 1 administrator. 1 ex officio. All voting. *Composition of institution:* Administrators 80 men / 128 women. President and four vice presidents: academic affairs and provost, administration and finance, student affairs, mission and university relations. Full-time instructional faculty 290. Academic governance body, University Senate, meets an average of 14 times per year.

Calendar: Semesters (4-1-4 plan; intersession and summer sessions optional). Academic year Sept. to May. Freshmen admitted Sept., Jan. Degrees conferred May, Aug., Jan. Formal commencement May. Summer session of 3 terms from June to Aug.

Characteristics of Freshmen: 66% of applicants admitted. 23% of applicants admitted and enrolled full-time.

86% (1,006 students) submitted SAT scores; 30% (355 students) submitted ACT scores. *25th percentile:* SAT Verbal 530, SAT Math 550; ACT Composite 23, ACT English 23, ACT Math 23. *75th percentile:* SAT Verbal 620, SAT Math 640; ACT Composite 28, ACT English 29, ACT Math 28.

72% of entering freshmen expected to graduate within 5 years. 58% of freshmen from California. Freshmen from 40 states and 7 foreign countries.

Admission: Admission is selective. Freshmen applicants must submit for fall semester no later that Jan. 5. Official high school transcript, official SAT or ACT scores, essay, letter of recommendation. The deadline for transfer applicants is Mar. 1. Transfer students must have completed at least 24 transferable semester units with a minimum GPA of 3.0 prior to matriculation.

Degree Requirements: *Undergraduate:* 124 semester units of credit with at least 48 units of upper division courses; 2.0 GPA; final 30 hours in residence; core curriculum requirements. Fulfillment of some degree requirements and exemption from some beginning courses possible by passing College Board CLEP, AP. *Grading system:* A–F; pass-fail; withdraw (carries time limit).

Distinctive Educational Programs: Internship and employment opportunities available on campus and in the San Diego community. Interdisciplinary study; honors program. Study abroad opportunities include Australia, Austria, Costa Rica, England, France, Germany, Ireland, Italy, Mexico, Japan, West Indies.

ROTC: Air Force and Army in cooperation with San Diego State University; 1 Air Force and 2 Army commissions awarded 2004; Navy/Marine units on campus; 27 Navy and 4 Marine commissions awarded 2004.

Degrees Conferred: 1,186 *baccalaureate;* 438 *master's;* 21 *doctorate.* Bachelor's degrees awarded in top five disciplines: business/marketing 434; communication/communication technologies 106; social sciences and history 208; liberal arts/general studies 70; biological/life sciences 63. 315 *first-professional:* law.

Fees and Other Expenses: *Full-time tuition per academic year 2004–05:* undergraduate $24,860, graduate $15,750. *Required fees:* $204 (undergraduate),

$136 (graduate). *Room and board per academic year:* undergraduate $11,260; graduate $8,334. Graduate housing apartments $9,800 per year.

Financial Aid: Aid from institutionally generated funds is provided on the basis of academic merit, financial need. Institution has a Program Participation Agreement with the U.S. Department of Education for eligible students to receive Pell Grants and other federal aid.

Financial aid to full-time, first-time undergraduate students: need-based scholarships/grants totaling $39,402,477, self-help $15,874,799, parent loans $11,203,882, tuition waivers $566,639, athletic awards $370,305; non-need-based scholarships/grants totaling $6,913,404, self-help $1,715,072, parent loans $3,289,904, tuition waivers $756,882, athletic awards $2,533,317.

Graduate aid: 44 federal and state-funded fellowships/grants totaling $230,778; 607 federal and state-funded loans totaling $9,029,767; 12 work-study jobs worth $124,198; 604 fellowships and grants totaling $2,534,466; 33 teaching assistantships totaling $71,332; 86 research assistantships worth $427,200.

Departments and Teaching Staff: *Professors* 110, *associate professors* 89, *assistant professors* 80, *instructors* 11; *part-time faculty* 315. *Total instructional faculty:* 605 (full-time 290, part-time 315; members of minority groups 99; women 298, men 307). Total faculty with doctorate, first-professional, or other terminal degree: 418. Student-to-faculty ratio: 16:1. *Faculty development:* Total grants to faculty for research: $13,661,114. 37 faculty members awarded sabbaticals 2004–05.

Enrollment: Total enrollment 7,486. Undergraduate full-time 1,880 men / 2,890 women, part-time 58m / 80w; graduate full-time 240m / 394w, part-time 373m / 541w; first-professional full-time 428m / 344w, part-time 138m / 120w. *Transfer students:* in-state into lower division 86m / 97w, upper division 41m / 43w; out-of-state into lower division 26m / 21w, upper division 11m / 10w.

Characteristics of Student Body: *Ethnic and racial makeup:* number of Black non-Hispanic: 96; American Indian or Alaska Native: 49; Asian or Pacific Islander: 353; Hispanic: 748; White non-Hispanic: 3,324; unknown 241. *Age distribution:* number under 18: 97; 18–19: 2,020; 20–21: 1,938; 22–24: 608; 25–29: 141; 30–34: 52; 35–39: 17; 40–49: 23; 50–64: 6. 24% of student body attend summer sessions.

International Students: 292 nonresident aliens enrolled fall 2004. 61 students from Europe, 68 Asia, 15 Central and South America, 10 Africa, 14 Canada, 25 other. No programs available to aid students whose native language is not English. No financial aid specifically designated for international students.

Student Life: 94% of freshmen and 49% of undergraduate student body live in on-campus housing. *Intercollegiate athletics:* men only: baseball, basketball, crew, cross-country, football, golf, soccer, tennis; women only: basketball, crew, cross-country, soccer, softball, swimming, tennis, volleyball. *Student activities:* Over 45 elected and selected student officers and directors. 65 student organizations, including multicultural groups, fraternities, and sororities. Emerging Leader and Leadership Minor programs. *Special regulations:* Cars permitted without restrictions. *Special services:* Counseling Center, Health Center. *Student publications: Alcala,* a yearbook; *Vista,* a weekly newspaper; *Asylum,* a monthly literary magazine. *Surrounding community:* San Diego population 1,300,000. Served by mass transit bus system; airport and passenger rail service.

Library Collections: 960,898 volumes. Current serial subscriptions: 5,785 paper, 766 microforms, 20,366 via electronic access. Online and card catalogs. 16,170 recordings; 2,011 compact discs; 754 CD-ROMs. 131 computer work stations. Students have access to online information retrieval services and the Internet. Total 2004–05 budget for materials and operations: $1,692,177.

Most important special holdings include liturgical music collection; Culligan Collection (personal papers).

Buildings and Grounds: Campus area 182 acres.

Chief Executive Officer: Dr. Mary E. Lyons, President.

Undergraduates address admission inquiries to Stephen Pultz, Director of Admissions; graduate inquiries to Carl Eging, Director of Admissions, School of Law.

School of Law

Degree Programs Offered: *First-professional; master's* in taxation, business and corporate law, international law, criminal law, comparative law. Graduation certificates also awarded.

Admission: *For first-professional degree:* Baccalaureate degree; LSAT.

Degree Requirements: *For first-professional degree:* 85 course credits and 96 residence units; written work requirement; 6 semesters full-time or 8 semesters and 1 summer session part-time in residence.

Departments and Teaching Staff: *Total instructional faculty:* 101. 100% hold terminal degrees.

Distinctive Educational Programs: Joint J.D.-M.B.A. program with School of Business Administration. Joint J.D.-master's program in International Relations. Summer programs in France, England, Mexico.

Enrollment: Total enrollment 1,114.

University of San Francisco

2130 Fulton Street
San Francisco, California 94117-1080
Tel: (415) 422-6563   **E-mail:** admissions@usfca.edu
Fax: (415) 422-2217   **Internet:** www.usfca.edu

Institution Description: University of San Francisco is a private institution affiliated with the Society of Jesus, Roman Catholic Church. *Enrollment:* 8,271. *Degrees awarded:* Baccalaureate, master's, doctorate, first-professional.

Accreditation: *Regional:* WASC-Sr. *Professional:* business, law, nursing, nursing education

History: Established as Saint Ignatius College 1855; chartered and offered first instruction at postsecondary level 1859; awarded first degree (baccalaureate) 1863; adopted present name 1930.

Institutional Structure: *Governing board:* University of San Francisco Board of Trustees. Extrainstitutional representation: 44 trustees; institutional representation: 2 administrators. 2 ex officio. All voting. *Composition of institution:* Academic affairs headed by provost; Management/business/finances directed by vice president of business and finance. Full-time instructional faculty 290. Academic governance body, Deans, meets regularly. *Faculty representation:* Faculty served by collective bargaining agent affiliated with an independent local union.

Calendar: Semesters. Academic year Aug. to May. Freshmen admitted Sept., Feb., June. Degrees conferred May, Aug., Dec. Formal commencement Dec., May. Summer session of 3 terms from early June to mid-Aug.

Characteristics of Freshmen: 4,782 applicants admitted. 1,316 admitted students enrolled full-time.

25th percentile: SAT Verbal 510, SAT Math 500; ACT Composite 21, ACT English 20, ACT Math 19. *75th percentile:* SAT Verbal 620, SAT Math 620; ACT Composite 26, ACT English 27, ACT Math 26.

63% of entering freshmen expected to graduate within 5 years. 68% of freshmen from California, Freshmen from 45 states and 15 foreign countries.

Admission: Early action deadline Dec. 1. Notification of early action applicants in January. Regular deadline for fall semester Feb. 15. *Requirements:* Either graduation from accredited secondary school with units which normally include 4 English, 2 in a foreign language, 3 social studies, 3 mathematics, 2 laboratory science, 6 academic electives; or GED. Additional requirements for some programs. Minimum GPA 3.0. *Entrance tests:* College Board SAT or ACT composite. For foreign students TOEFL. *For transfer students:* 2.0 minimum GPA; from 4-year accredited institution maximum transfer credit 45 units.

College credit for postsecondary-level work completed in secondary school. For extrainstitutional learning, college credit on basis of portfolio assessment, ACE 2006 Guide to the Evaluation of Educational Experiences in the Armed Services. Tutoring available.

Degree Requirements: *Undergraduate:* 128 semester hours; 2.0 GPA; 1½ years (45 units) in residence; general education requirements. *Grading system:* A–F; pass-fail; withdraw (carries time limit); satisfactory-unsatisfactory; audit.

Distinctive Educational Programs: Work-experience programs. Freshmen Seminar; College Success Programs. Weekend and evening classes. Facilities and programs for independent research, including honors programs, individual majors, tutorials. Overseas programs in Europe, Asia, Latin and South America. Student exchange program with Fordham University (NY).

ROTC: Army.

Degrees Conferred: 1,180 *baccalaureate* (B); 1,047 *master's* (M); 47 *doctorate:* architecture 6 (B); area and ethnic studies 2 (B), 19 (M); biological/life sciences 49 (B); business/marketing 389 (B), 312 (M); communications/communication technologies 83 (B); computer and information sciences 155 (B), 124 (M); education 58 (M), 4 (D); English 40 (B), 20 (M); foreign languages and literature 3 (B); health professions and related sciences 47 (B), 56 (M); law/legal studies 18 (B); mathematics 8 (B); natural resources/environmental science 12 (B), 59 (M); parks and recreation 20 (B), 23 (M); philosophy/religion/theology 20 (B), 23 (M); physical sciences 13 (B), 4 (M); protective services/public administration 39 (B), 69 (M); psychology 77 (B), 56 (M), 2 (D); social sciences and history 174 (B), 8 (M); visual and performing arts 41 (B). *First-professional:* law 206. 5 honorary degrees awarded 2003–04: Doctor of Humane Letters.

Fees and Other Expenses: *Full-time tuition per academic year 2004–05:* undergraduate $26,680; graduate and first-professional tuition rates vary, contact the school for current information. *Required fees:* $160. *Room per academic year:* $6,500. *Board per academic year:* $3,740.

Financial Aid: Aid from institutionally generated funds is provided on the basis of academic merit, financial need. Institution has a Program Participation Agreement with the U.S. Department of Education for eligible students to receive Pell Grants and other federal aid.

Financial aid to full-time, first-time undergraduate students: need-based scholarships/grants totaling $30,182,548, self-help $12,462,948, athletic awards $14,830; non-need-based scholarships/grants totaling $5,372,017, self-help $10,041,314, parent loans $13,459,467, tuition waivers $1,749,496, athletic awards $3,523,410.

Departments and Teaching Staff: *Total instructional faculty:* 820 (full-time 348, part-time 472; members of minority groups 130; women 377, men 443). Total faculty with doctorate, first-professional, or other terminal degree: 687. Student-to-faculty ratio: 14:1.

Enrollment: Total enrollment 8,271. Full-time 7,267, part-time 1,004.

Characteristics of Student Body: *Ethnic and social makeup:* number of Black non-Hispanic: 227; American Indian or Alaska Native: 15; Asian or Pacific Islander: 1,110; Hispanic: 574; White non-Hispanic: 1,599; unknown: 455. *Age distribution:* number under 18: 54; 18–19: 1,698; 20–21: 1,587; 22–24: 625; 25–29: 145; 30–34: 29; 35–39: 18; 40–49: 4; 50–64: 7; 65 and over: 1.

International Students: 635 nonresident aliens enrolled fall 2004. Programs available to aid students whose native language is not English: Social, cultural. English as a Second Language Program. No financial aid specifically designated for international students.

Student Life: On-campus residence halls house 40% of student body. Coed residences constitute 75% of such space with 25% for women only. Some fraternities, sororities and honor societies; a variety of other clubs and organizations. *Intercollegiate athletics:* men only: baseball, basketball, cross-country, golf, soccer, tennis; women only: basketball, cross-country, soccer, golf, tennis, volleyball; coed: riflery. *Special regulations:* Freshmen and sophomores under 21 are required to live on campus. Permits required for on-campus parking; parking is very limited. *Special services:* Learning and Writing Center; Academic Support Services; Services for learning disabled students; disability-related services. *Student publications, radio:* Foghorn, a weekly newspaper; Ignatian, a literary magazine. Radio stations KUSF-FM, KDNS-AM. *Surrounding community:* San Francisco population 715,000. Served by mass transit bus and subway system; airport 15 miles from campus; passenger rail service 5 miles from campus.

Library Collections: 1,411,445 volumes. Online catalog. 4,500 audiovisual materials; 3,200 current periodicals. 121 computer work stations. Students have access to online information retrieval services and the Internet.

Most important holdings include Sir Thomas More and Recusant Literature Collection; modern fine printing collection (emphasis on San Francisco Bay area); English and American literature collections (Eric Gill, Robert Graves, Richard LeGallienne, English 1890s, Robinson Jeffers).

Buildings and Grounds: Campus area 51 acres. *New buildings:* Dorraine Zief Law Library completed 2000; Malloy Hall 2004.

Chief Executive Officer: Dr. Stephen A. Priuett, S.J., President.

Address admission undergraduate admission inquiries to Michael Hughes, Director of Admissions; graduate inquiries to Anne McCormick, Director of Graduate Admission; law school inquiries to Alan Guerrero, Director of Law Admission.

College of Liberal Arts and Science

Degree Programs Offered: *Baccalaureate* in biology, chemistry, communication arts, computer engineering, computer science, economics, electronics physics, English, environmental science, fine arts, government, history, mathematics, modern languages and classics, philosophy, physical education, physics, psychology internship, psychological services, sociology, theology and religious studies; *master's* in biology, chemistry, computer science, economics, environmental management, theology and religious studies.

Distinctive Educational Programs: Preprofessional programs in medicine, health sciences, law. St. Ignatius Institute offers interdisciplinary program in Christian humanism and western civilization. The bachelor of fine arts program is offered in cooperation with the San Francisco Academy of Art College. Special programs in the humanities, study abroad, Judaic Studies. The Davies Forum explores values in modern society through lectures and seminars conducted by noted scholars. Certificate programs in Latin American Studies, Urban Studies, Western European Studies, fine arts, elementary and secondary teaching, and English as a Second Language. Special research facilities include the Institute for Asian and Pacific Studies, the Institute for Chemical Biology, the Lily Drake Cancer Research Institute, and laboratories for software engineering, radiation physics, biochemistry, and genetics research.

McLaren School of Business

Degree Programs Offered: *Baccalaureate* in accounting, business administration, finance, hospitality management, international business, marketing, *master's* in business administration, rehabilitative administration.

School of Nursing

Degree Programs Offered: *Baccalaureate* programs include accelerated option for 2nd baccalaureate students, RN accelerated; *master's* in nursing (MS) and *joint master's* (MSN/MBA).

Admission: *For master's:* GPA of 3.00; GRE, GMAT; 1 year experience as RN; BS in nursing programs.

Degree Requirements: *For master's:* 42 units for MS in nursing; 54 units for MS in nursing/MBA.

College of Professional Studies

Degree Programs Offered: *Baccalaureate* in applied economics, organizational behavior, information systems management, general studies, public administration; *master's* in human resources and organization behavior, health systems leadership, writing, and public administration.

School of Law

Degree Programs Offered: *First-professional.*

Admission: Baccalaureate from accredited institution; LSAT.

Degree Requirements: 82 credit hours, 2.0 GPA, 6 semesters in residence.

School of Education

Degree Programs Offered: *Master of Arts* in Counseling with emphasis in Marital and Family Therapy; Educational Counseling; Curriculum and Instruction; Multicultural Education; Teaching English as a Second Language; Educational Administration with California Preliminary Administrative Services Credential; Private School Administration. *Doctor of Education* in Counseling and Educational Psychology; Curriculum and Instruction; Multicultural Education; Organization and Leadership; Private School Administration. Teacher preparation program leading to California Credentials for Multiple Subject and Single Subject.

Distinctive Educational Programs: Institute for Catholic Educational Leadership; Center for Instruction and Technology.

University of Southern California

University Park
Los Angeles, California 90089-1455
Tel: (213) 740-2311   **E-mail:** admission@usc.edu
Fax: (213) 740-6364   **Internet:** www.usc.edu

Institution Description: University of Southern California is a private, independent, nonprofit institution. *Enrollment:* 32,160. *Degrees awarded:* Baccalaureate, master's, doctorate, first-professional (dentistry, law, medicine, pharmacy).

Accreditation: *Regional:* WASC-Sr. *Professional:* accounting, business, clinical psychology, dental hygiene, dentistry, dietetics, endodontics, engineering, health services administration, journalism, law, medicine, music, nurse anesthesia education, nursing, nursing education, occupational therapy, oral and maxillofacial surgery, periodontics, pharmacy, physical therapy, physician assisting, planning, psychology internship, public administration, public health, radiation therapy, radiography, social work

History: Established and incorporated under Methodist sponsorship and offered first instruction at postsecondary level 1880; awarded first degree (baccalaureate) 1884; ended religious affiliation 1929. *See* M.P. Servin and I.H. Wilson, *Southern California and its University* (Los Angeles: Ward Ritchie Press, 1969) for further information.

Institutional Structure: *Governing board:* Board of Trustees. Extrainstitutional representation: 44 trustees (including 26 alumni), 14 life trustees, 3 trustees emeriti; institutional representation: president of the university. 44 voting. *Composition of institution:* Administrators 36 men / 4 women. Academic affairs headed by provost. Management/business/finances directed by senior vice president for administration. Development and alumni affairs headed by senior vice president for university advancement. Total instructional faculty 2,918.

Calendar: Semesters. Trimesters for School of Dentistry. Academic year early Sept. to early May. Freshmen admitted for fall and spring term on a rolling basis. Degrees conferred May, Aug., Dec. Formal commencement May. Summer sessions from May to Aug.

Characteristics of Freshmen: 29,792 applicants (13,468 men, 16,324 women). 27% of applicants admitted; 34.5% of admitted students enrolled full-time.

83% (2,306 students) submitted SAT scores; 26% (720 students) submitted ACT scores. *25th percentile:* SAT Verbal 620, SAT Math 640, ACT Composite 27, ACT English 27, Math 27. *75th percentile:* SAT Verbal 710, SAT Math 730, ACT Composite 31, ACT English 32, ACT Math 32.

56% of entering freshmen expected to graduate within 5 years. 61% of freshmen from California. Freshmen from 30 states and 35 foreign countries.

Admission: Rolling admissions plan. For fall acceptance, apply as early as Sept. 1 of previous year, but not later than May 1 of year of enrollment; Early Action Admission filing deadline is Nov. 1; First Priority filing period ends Dec. 15. Application deadline for equal consideration is Feb. 1. *Requirements:* Either graduation from accredited secondary school which normally includes 4 units English, 2 foreign language, 2–4 mathematics, 3 social science, 1 laboratory science. Writing sample required. Additional requirements for some programs. Minimum GPA 2.7. *Entrance tests:* College Board SAT preferred; ACT Composite accepted. For foreign students: TOEFL. *For transfer students:* From 4-year accredited institution 2.0–3.0 minimum GPA, 80 semester hours maximum transfer credit; from 2-year accredited institution 2.5 minimum GPA, 70 hours maximum transfer credit.

College credit and advanced placement for postsecondary-level work completed in secondary school. Tutoring available. Noncredit developmental courses offered in summer session and regular academic year.

Degree Requirements: *Undergraduate:* 128 semester hours; 2.0 GPA; last 48 hours in residence; general education requirements. Additional requirements for some programs. Fulfillment of some degree requirements and exemption from some beginning courses possible by passing departmental examinations, College Board APP. *Grading system:* A–F (with plus/minus); pass-fail; withdraw (carries time limit).

Distinctive Educational Programs: Facilities and programs for independent research, including honors programs, individual majors. Cross-registration with Hebrew Union College-Jewish Institute of Religion and University of California, Los Angeles. Study abroad programs in Australia (Australian National University, Canberra); China (Fudan University, Shanghai); England (University of Kent, Canterbury; University of Sussex, Brighton; Semester in London); France (University of Paris; Semester in Paris); Germany (University of Freiburg); Israel (Tel Aviv University; Hebrew University, Jerusalem); Italy (Florence, Milan); Japan (Waseda University, Tokyo; Nanzan University, Nagoya); Kenya (Nairobi, Mombasa); Spain (Madrid); Zimbabwe (Harare). *Other distinctive programs:* Thematic Option: integrated core honors GE curriculum; professional undergraduate degree programs in: Annenberg School for Communication, architecture, business, cinema/TV, education, engineering, fine arts, gerontology, music, nursing, occupational therapy, public administration, safety and systems management, theatre, and urban and regional planning.

ROTC: Army, Navy, Air Force.

Degrees Conferred: 4,344 *baccalaureate*; 3,668 *master's*; 573 *doctorate*; 696 *first-professional*; 157 *post-baccalaureate certificates*; 67 *post-master's certificates*. Bachelor's degrees awarded in top five disciplines: business, management, marketing, and related support services 1,177; social sciences 588; visual and performing arts 550; communication, journalism, and related programs 429; engineering 302.

Fees and Other Expenses: *Full-time tuition per academic year 2004–05:* undergraduate $30,512. Contact the university for graduate and first-professional tuition and fees. *Room and board per academic year:* $8,998. *Books and supplies:* $644. *Other expenses:* $2,214.

Financial Aid: Aid from institutionally generated funds is provided on the basis of academic merit, financial need, athletic ability, other criteria. Institution has a Program Participation Agreement with the U.S. Department of Education for eligible students to receive Pell Grants and other federal aid.

Financial aid to full-time, first-time undergraduate students: 16% received federal grants averaging $4,283; 12% state/local grants averaging $8,865; 38% institutional grants averaging $16,016; 64% loans averaging $4,332.

Departments and Teaching Staff: *Total instructional faculty:* 2,408 (full-time 1,489, part-time 919; women 188, men 1,620; members of minority groups 512). Total faculty with doctorate, first-professional, or other terminal degree 1,834. Student-to-faculty ratio: 10:1.

Enrollment: Total enrollment 32,160. Undergraduate 16,381 (49.5% men, 50.5% women). *Transfer students:* 1,350 undergraduate (80% from California).

Characteristics of Student Body: *Ethnic/racial makeup:* number of Black non-Hispanic: 1,069; American Indian or Alaska Native: 122; Asian or Pacific Islander: 3,459; Hispanic: 2,136; White non-Hispanic: 7,809; unknown: 443. 60% of undergraduate student body under 21; 35% 24–25; 4% over 25.

International Students: 5,533 nonresident aliens enrolled fall 2004. 555 students from Europe, 4,174 Asia, 149 Central and South America, 49 Africa, 246 Canada, 28 Australia, 7 New Zealand, 325 other. Programs available to aid students whose native language is not English: Social, cultural. English a Second Language Program. No financial aid programs specifically designate funds for international students.

Student Life: On-campus residence halls and apartment halls house 20.2% of student body. Residence for men only constitute 2% of such space, for women only 2%; the balance of 96% for both sexes. 32% of undergraduate men join and

10% live in fraternities; 20% of undergraduate women join and 9% live in sororities. 33% of the graduate and undergraduate population live on or in the immediate campus neighborhood. Over 300 student clubs and organizations. *Intercollegiate athletics:* men only: baseball, basketball, crew, cross-country, football, golf, sailing, swimming, tennis, track, volleyball, water polo; women only: basketball, crew, cross-country, golf, swimming, tennis, track, volleyball. *Special services:* Learning Support Services, medical and counseling services; trams to parking lots, health sciences center and area points of interest. *Student publications: Daily Trojan,* a newspaper; *El Rodeo,* a yearbook; several magazines. *Surrounding community:* Los Angeles population over: 3 million. Served by mass transit bus system; airport 13 miles from campus; passenger rail service 5 miles from campus.

Publications: *Coranto,* an annual humanities journal; *MELUS* a quarterly, first published 1974, *Pacific Philosophical Quarterly* first published 1920, *Quarterly Review of Film Studies* first published 1976, *Studies in Comparative Communism* (quarterly) first published 1968, *Southern California Anthology,* (annual) literary journal.

Library Collections: 3,801,000 titles. 6,114,000 microforms; 250,000 government documents; 51,550 audiovisual materials; 30,355 serial subscriptions. Online catalog. Students have access to online information retrieval services and the Internet.

Most important holdings include a collection of California former governor Jerry Brown's papers from his time in office; American Literature Collection consisting of 60,000 titles, including Hamlin Garland's manuscripts; cinema archives consisting of 215 individual collections, including the major studios of Warner Brothers, Universal, Fox, and MGM; Hancock Collection of Natural History.

Buildings and Grounds: Campus area 155 acres.

Chief Executive Officer: Dr. Steven B. Sample, President.

Address admission inquiries to J. Michael Thompson, Dean of Admissions.

Annenberg School of Communications

Degree Programs Offered: *Master's* in communication management; *doctorate* in communication theory and research.

Admission: *For both degrees:* baccalaureate degree and GRE; international students must have baccalaureate equivalent, GRE, and TOEFL.

Degree Requirements: M.A: 28 units and comprehensive exam; Ph.D.: 60 units, preliminary paper, qualifying exam, dissertation.

School of Architecture

Degree Programs Offered: *First professional: masters* of architecture, landscape architecture, building science; master of architecture and master of urban and regional planning (joint degree).

Degree Requirements: 160 credit hours, 2.0 GPA, core curriculum.

School of Business Administration

Degree Programs Offered: *Baccalaureate* in accounting, business administration. *Master's* in accounting, business administration, business taxation, decision systems.

School of Cinema/Television

Degree Programs Offered: *Baccalaureate* in film-television production, critical studies, creative writing, still photography; *master's* in film-television production, critical studies, motion picture producing, screenwriting; *doctorate* in critical studies.

Departments and Teaching Staff: Many faculty members are drawn from the local and national film and television communities.

School of Dentistry

Degree Programs Offered: *Baccalaureate* in dental hygiene; *first-professional. Certificate programs* (post DDS) in endodontics, oral pathology, oral and maxillofacial surgery, orthodontics, pediatric dentistry, periodontology, and prosthodontics.

Admission: *For first-professional:* 60 semester hours from accredited college or university, including 6 English composition; 8 each (with laboratory) biology, inorganic chemistry, organic chemistry, physics; additional units in biochemistry, economics, or comparative anatomy; embryology; genetics; histology; physiology; psychology; sociology. DAT. AADSAS. Interview.

Degree Requirements: *For first-professional degree:* Eleven 14-week trimesters, prescribed curriculum.

School of Education

Degree Programs Offered: *Baccalaureate* in general studies; *master's* in teacher education, administration, counseling, curriculum, instructional technology, psychology, special education; *doctorate* in administration, counseling, curriculum, instructional technology, psychology, special education.

School of Engineering

Degree Programs Offered: *Baccalaureate* in aerospace engineering, applied mechanics, biomedical engineering, chemical engineering, civil engineering, computer science, electrical engineering, industrial and systems engineering, mechanical engineering, metallurgical engineering, petroleum engineering; *master's* in aerospace engineering, applied mechanics, civil engineering, chemical engineering, computer engineering, computer science engineering, construction engineering, electrical engineering, engineering management, environmental engineering, industrial and systems engineering, manufacturing engineering, materials science, mechanical engineering, ocean engineering, petroleum engineering. Professional engineer degree also awarded.

Distinctive Educational Programs: Cooperative education. Dual-degree program in cooperation with College of Letters, Arts, and Sciences.

School of Fine Arts

Degree Programs Offered: *Baccalaureate* in art history, fine arts, studio art.

Leonard Davis School of Gerontology

Degree Programs Offered: *Baccalaureate, master's, doctorate.*

The Graduate School

Degree Programs Offered: *Master's* in anatomy and cell biology, applied biometry/epidemiology, applied linguistics, applied mathematics, art history, art history-museum studies, biology, biometry, building science, chemistry, classics, communication arts and sciences, comparative literature, craniofacial biology, East Asian languages and cultures, economics, English, fine arts, French, geological sciences, German, history, industrial hygiene, international relations, journalism, linguistics, mathematics, occupational safety and health, occupational therapy, orthodontics, otology, pharmaceutical sciences, philosophy, physical education, physical therapy, physics, political economy and public policy, political science, public relations, regional science, religion, safety, Slavic languages and literatures, Spanish, speech science and technology, systems management, urban design; *doctorate* in aerospace engineering, anatomy, art history, biochemistry, biology, biomedical engineering, biometry, business administration, chemical engineering, chemistry, civil engineering, classics, communication, communication arts and sciences, comparative literature, computer engineering, computer science, craniofacial biology, economics, education, electrical engineering, English, French, geological sciences, German, history, industrial and systems engineering, international political science, library and information management, linguistics, materials science, mathematics, mechanical engineering, microbiology, molecular biology, music, pathology, pharmacology and nutrition, pharmaceutical sciences, philosophy, physical education, physical therapy, physics, physiology, political economy and public policy, psychology, public administration, religion, sociology, Spanish, special education, speech science and technology, urban and regional planning.

Departments and Teaching Staff: Faculty members are drawn from among the departments of the university.

Law Center

Degree Programs Offered: *First-professional;* paralegal certification program.

Admission: Baccalaureate from accredited college or university. LSAT. LSDAS.

Degree Requirements: 88 credit hours, 6 semesters in residence, core curriculum in first year.

Distinctive Educational Programs: Joint J.D.-M.B.A. program with Graduate School of Business Administration; J.D.-master's in business taxation with School of Accounting; J.D.-master's in public administration with Center for Public Affairs; J.D.-master's in economics with The Graduate School; J.D.-master's in social work with School of Social Work; J.D.-Ph.D. in social science with California Institute of Technology.

College of Letters, Arts, and Sciences

Degree Programs Offered: *Baccalaureate* in American studies, anthropology, astronomy, biological sciences, broadcast journalism, chemistry, classical civilization, classics, communication arts and sciences, comparative literature, drama, East Asian area studies, East Asian languages and cultures, economics, English, French-Italian, geological sciences, German, international relations, linguistics, mathematics, philosophy, physical education, physical sciences, physics, political science, Portuguese-Brazilian studies, print journalism, psychology, public relations, religion, Slavic languages and literatures, sociology, Spanish-Portuguese, sports information.

Distinctive Educational Programs: Resident Honors Program; Thematic Option; Psychobiology Program; Freshman Seminars; Freshman-only Program; interdisciplinary majors program; international study programs; Freshman Mentoring Program.

School of Medicine

Degree Programs Offered: *First-professional.*

Admission: 120 semester hours from accredited college or university, including 2 each (with laboratory) biology, general chemistry, organic chemistry, physics, and 1 of molecular biology (laboratory optional); 30 hours in social sciences, humanities, and English composition. Facility in principles of higher mathematics and basic statistics and in use of computers recommended; MCAT. AMCAS. Interview.

Degree Requirements: 38 weeks of prescribed curriculum in first years followed by 2 consecutive years of clerkships.

Distinctive Educational Programs: Joint M.D.-Ph.D. programs in anatomy and cell biology, biochemistry, pathology, pharmacology and nutrition, physiology and biophysics in cooperation with The Graduate School.

School of Music

Degree Programs Offered: *Baccalaureate* in performance, music, music education, music theory, jazz studies, composition, music history, composition with film scoring emphasis, recording arts; *master's* in performance, church music, choral music, jazz studies, conducting, music education, music history and literature, music theory, early music; *doctorate* in performance, church music, music education, choral music, composition.

Admission: Applications are accepted until a particular program is filled; applicant must submit a Music Supplemental application in addition to the university application; audition required (tapes accepted in lieu of a personal audition).

Degree Requirements: *For baccalaureate degree:* 128–134 units. *For master's degree:* 30 units; varying requirements depending on program (recitals, thesis, oral examination). *For doctorate:* 26–55 units depending on program.

School of Pharmacy

Degree Programs Offered: *First-professional; master's* in radiopharmacy.

Admission: 60 semester hours from accredited college or university, including 9 English composition, literature, and speech communication; 2 each (with laboratory) biology, inorganic chemistry, organic chemistry; 1 calculus; 12 social and behavioral science, including 1 general psychology; 6 humanities.

Degree Requirements: *For first-professional degree:* 204 credit hours, 2.4 GPA, 24 months in residence, 1,600 clock hours approved supervised practical experience.

Distinctive Educational Programs: Joint PharmD/PhD program in toxicology and pharmaceutical sciences with the Graduate School. dual PharmD/MBA in cooperation with the School of Business Administration.

School of Public Administration

Degree Programs Offered: *Baccalaureate* in public administration, public administration and planning; *master's* in public administration, health administration, public policy, international public administration; *doctorate* in public administration. Programs also offered in Washington, DC, and Sacramento, CA.

Admission: For baccalaureate programs, same process and requirements as University; rolling admissions basis; GRE scores required for domestic applicants (GMAT scores may substitute for GRE for some programs). Application deadlines for doctoral programs differ by Center. US Sacramento Center: 1201 J Street, Sacramento, CA 95814; Washington Public Affairs Center: 512 Tenth Street N.W., Washington, DC, 20004.

Degree Requirements: Varies by program.

School of Social Work

Degree Programs Offered: *Master's, doctorate.*

Distinctive Educational Programs: Joint J.D.-M.S.W. program with Law Center; M.S.W.-master's in public administration with Center for Public Affairs; M.S.W.-master's in gerontology with Leonard Davis School of Gerontology. Dual-degree program with Hebrew Union College-Jewish Institute of Religion.

School of Urban and Regional Planning

Degree Programs Offered: *Baccalaureate* in public administration and planning, planning and development; *master's* in planning, planning studies, real estate development; *doctorate* in planning.

Admission: For undergraduate program: High school graduation; 3.00 GPA; SAT 1050. For graduate program: GRE, GMAT or LSAT; 3.00 GPA. Real Estate Development Program requires 2 years work experience in real estate or related field.

Degree Requirements: Baccalaureate: 128 units; master's 32–40 units, depending on program; doctorate 40–60 units.

Division of Allied Health Sciences - Department of Nursing

Degree Programs Offered: *Baccalaureate* in nursing; *master's* in midwifery, family nurse practitioner, nursing administration.

Admission: 30 semester units from an accredited institution, including 6 units of English composition; anatomy with laboratory; physiology with laboratory; 1 semester of chemistry with lab; 6 social and behavioral science units including general psychology, general sociology, American history or political science and Western civilization.

Degree Requirements: 130 semester hours (60 units general education, 70 units nursing); 2.0 GPA; satisfactory completion of clinical and theory components.

University of West Los Angeles

1155 West Arbor Vitae
Inglewood, California 90301-2902
Tel: (310) 342-5200
Fax: (310) 342-5295

Institution Description: The University of West Los Angeles is a private, nonprofit institution comprised of a School of Law and a School of Paralegal Studies. *Enrollment:* 396. *Degrees awarded:* Baccalaureate, first-professional.

Accreditation: *Regional:* WASC-Sr. *Professional:* law

History: Established and awarded first degree (first-professional) 1966.

Institutional Structure: *Governing board:* Board of Trustees. Representation: 16 trustees. *Composition of institution:* Administrators 8 men / 2 women. Management/business/finances directed by comptroller. Full-time instructional faculty 7. Adjunct faculty 40.

Calendar: Trimesters for undergraduate; semesters for law school. Academic year Sept. to Aug. Entering students admitted Sept., Jan., Apr. Degrees conferred Dec., Apr., Aug. Formal commencement Aug. Summer session.

Admission: Rolling admissions plan. *Requirements:* For first-professional degree, baccalaureate from accredited college or university. Admission also possible by passing college equivalency examination and LSAT. *For transfer students:* Maximum transfer credit limited only by residence requirement of 45 units; good standing at institution previously attended.

Degree Requirements: Completion of prescribed courses.

Distinctive Educational Programs: Clinical internship program. Weekend and evening classes. Tutors, counselors, computer center. Mini law program on weekends.

Degrees Conferred: 6 *baccalaureate:* legal professions and studies; 55 *first-professional:* law.

Fees and Other Expenses: *Full-time tuition per academic year 2004–05:* $6,500. undergraduate; contact the university for current law school tuition and fees.

Financial Aid: Aid from institutionally generated funds is provided on the basis of academic merit, financial need. Institution has a Program Participation Agreement with the U.S. Department of Education for eligible students to receive Pell Grants and other federal aid.

Departments and Teaching Staff: *Total full-time instructional faculty:* 7. *Part time faculty:* 50. *Student-to-faculty ratio:* 30:1. 100% hold terminal degrees.

Enrollment: Total enrollment 396. Undergraduate 97.

Characteristics of Student Body: *Ethnic/racial makeup:* Black non-Hispanic: 44.3%; American Indian or Alaska Native: 2.1%; Asian or Pacific Islander: 8.2%; Hispanic: 13,4%; White non-Hispanic: 25.8%; unknown: 5.2%.

International Students: 1 undergraduate nonresident alien enrolled fall 2003.

Student Life: No on-campus housing available. *Special services:* Learning Resources Center. *Student publications:* Newspaper published 3 times per year. *Surrounding community:* Los Angeles population over: 3,000,000. Served by mass transit bus system; airport 8 miles from campus; passenger rail service 12 miles from campus.

Library Collections: 40,000 volumes. 250 current periodical subscriptions. Computer work stations available.

Chief Executive Officer: Robert W. Brown, President.

Address Law School admission inquiries to Lynda Freeman, Admissions Counselor; Paralegal Studies admission inquiries to Cynthia Moj.

Vanguard University of Southern California

55 Fair Drive
Costa Mesa, California 92626
Tel: (714) 556-3610   **E-mail:** admissions@vanguard.edu
Fax: (714) 957-9317   **Internet:** www.vanguard.edu

Institution Description: Vanguard University of Southern California (formerly Vanguard College of Southern California) is a private college affiliated with the Southern California District of the Assemblies of God. *Enrollment:* 2,195. *Degrees awarded:* Baccalaureate, master's.

Accreditation: *Regional:* WASC-Sr.

History: Established as Southern California Bible School and offered first instruction at postsecondary level 1920; chartered and changed name to Southern California Bible College 1939; awarded first degree (baccalaureate) 1941; became Southern California College 1959; renamed Vanguard College of Southern California 1998; adopted current name in 2002.

Institutional Structure: *Composition of institution:* Administrators 5 men. Academic affairs headed by vice president for academic affairs. Management/business/finances directed by vice president for business and finance. Total full-time faculty 70.

Calendar: Semesters. Academic year Aug. to May. Formal commencement May.

Characteristics of Freshmen: 80% of applicants admitted. 47% of admitted applicants enrolled full-time.

70% (252 students) submitted SAT scores; 24% (86 students) submitted ACT scores. *25th percentile:* SAT Verbal 450, SAT Math 430; ACT Composite 19, ACT English 18, ACT Math 17. *75th percentile:* SAT Verbal 570, SAT Math 560; ACT Composite 24, ACT English 24, ACT Math 24.

15% of entering freshmen expected to graduate within 5 years. 80% of freshmen from California.

Admission: Rolling admissions plan. *Requirements:* Either graduation from accredited secondary school or GED. Recommend 4 units English, 3 social studies, 2 mathematics, 2 science. *Entrance tests:* College Board SAT or ACT composite. For foreign students TOEFL score of 550. *For transfer students:* 2.0 minimum GPA; from 2-year accredited institution 70 hours maximum transfer credit; correspondence/extension students 24 hours; good standing at institution previously attended.

Degree Requirements: 124 credit hours with 40 in upper-level work; 2.0 GPA; last 24 credits in residence; regular chapel attendance; general education requirements; maintenance of good character and consistent Christian life. Fulfillment of some degree requirements possible by passing College Board CLEP, AP; exemption from some beginning courses possible by passing College Board AP. *Grading system:* A–F.

Distinctive Educational Programs: *For undergraduates:* Work-experience programs, including internships, practicums. Double majors. Individual studies programs.

Degrees Conferred: 402 *baccalaureate:* 70 *master's.*

Fees and Other Expenses: *Full-time tuition per academic year 2005–06:* $19,900. *Required fees:* $430. *Room and board per academic year:* $6,756.

Financial Aid: Aid from institutionally generated funds is provided on the basis of academic merit, financial need, athletic ability. Institution has a Program Participation Agreement with the U.S. Department of Education for eligible students to receive Pell Grants and other federal aid.

Financial aid to full-time, first-time undergraduate students: need-based scholarships/grants totaling $10,848,504, self-help $4,955,935, parent loans $618,822, tuition waivers $153,933, athletic awards $495,477; non-need-based scholarships/grants totaling $1,608,227, self-help $1,525,835, parent loans $888,259, tuition waivers $291,701, athletic awards $856,708.

Departments and Teaching Staff: *Total instructional faculty:* 146 (full-time 70, part-time 76; members of minority groups 36; women 62, men 84). Total faculty with doctorate, first-professional, or other terminal degree: 78. Student-to-faculty ratio: 17:1.

Enrollment: Total enrollment 2,195 (full-time 1,567, part-time 628).

Characteristics of Student Body: *Ethnic/racial makeup:* number of Black non-Hispanic: 72; American Indian or Alaska Native: 14; Asian or Pacific Islander: 82; Hispanic: 332; White non-Hispanic: 1,194; unknown: 92.

International Students: 13 nonresident aliens enrolled fall 2004. No programs available to aid students whose native language is not English.

Student Life: Students are expected to live on campus. 6 residence halls and campus apartments are available. Housing available for married students. *Intercollegiate athletics:* Baseball, basketball, cross-country, soccer, softball, tennis, track and field, volleyball. *Special regulations:* Registered cars with stickers permitted. *Special services:* Learning Resources Center, medical services, computer lab. *Student publications: Vanguard Voice,* student newspaper; yearbook. *Surrounding community:* Costa Mesa population 103,823. Los Angeles, 40 miles from campus, is nearest metropolitan area.

Library Collections: 142,393 volumes. Current serial subscriptions: 800 paper; 9,682 via electronic access. Students have access to the Internet at no charge.

Buildings and Grounds: Campus area 40 acres. *New buildings:* Heath Academic Center for Religion and Business completed 2004.

Chief Executive Officer: Dr. Murray W. Dempster, President.

Address undergraduate admission inquiries to Jennifer Purga, Director of Undergraduate Admissions; graduate inquiries to Rina Campbell, Director of Graduate Admissions.

Western State University College of Law

1111 North State College Boulevard
Fullerton, California 92831-3014
Tel: (714) 738-1000   **E-mail:** adm@wsulaw.edu
Fax: (714) 871-4806   **Internet:** www.wsulaw.edu

Institution Description: *Enrollment:* 497. *Degrees awarded:* First-professional.

Accreditation: *Regional:* WASC-Sr. *Professional:* law

Calendar: Semesters. Academic year Aug. to May.

Admission: LSAT required; 3 letters of recommendation advised.

Degree Requirements: 88 semester units with a minimum 2.00 grade point average.

Distinctive Educational Programs: Work experience programs. Flexible meeting places and schedules, including weekend and evening classes. Accelerated degree programs. Special facilities for using telecommunications in the classroom. Women's Law Institute. Honors programs. Study abroad in England (Cambridge) and China (Beijing).

Degrees Conferred: 111 *first-professional* law.

Fees and Other Expenses: *Full-time tuition per academic year 2004–05:* $25,200. *Other fees:* $140.

Financial Aid: Aid from institutionally generated funds is provided on the basis of academic merit, financial need. Institution has a Program Participation Agreement with the U.S. Department of Education for eligible students to receive Pell Grants and other federal aid.

Departments and Teaching Staff: Law *assistant professors* 33, *part-time teachers* 16. *Total instructional faculty:* 49. Student-to-faculty ratio: 20:1. Degrees held by full-time faculty: Professional 100%. 100% hold terminal degrees.

Enrollment: Total enrollment 497.

Characteristics of Student Body: *Ethnic/racial makeup:* Black non-Hispanic: 6.6%; American Indian Alaska Native: .4%; Asian or Pacific Islander: 20.3%; Hispanic: 13.9%; White non-Hispanic: 46.1%.

Student Life: No on-campus housing. Students live off-campus in apartment housing surrounding the college community. *Special regulations:* Cars must have decals; entering students must park in designated areas. *Student publications: Dictum,* a monthly newspaper; *Western State University International Law Journal* and *Western State University Law Review,* both published annually. *Surrounding community:* Fullerton population 150,000. Los Angeles, 35 miles from campus, is nearest metropolitan area. Served by mass transit bus system; airport 20 miles from campus; passenger rail service 3 miles from campus.

Library Collections: 100,000 volumes including bound books, serial backfiles, electronic documents, and government documents not in separate collections. Online catalog. Serial collections: 17,673 paper, 71,676 microform, 295 electronic. Students have access to the Internet at no charge.

Most important special holdings include collection on Anglo-American law.

Buildings and Grounds: Campus area 4 square blocks.

Chief Executive Officer: Dr. Maryann Jones, Dean/President.

Address admission inquiries to Gloria Switzer, Director of Admissions.

Western University of Health Sciences

College Plaza
309 East Second Street
Pomona, California 91766-1854
Tel: (909) 469-5340   **E-mail:** admissions@westernu.edu
Fax: (909) 469-5425   **Internet:** www.westernu.edu

Institution Description: Western University of Health Sciences, formerly known as the College of Osteopathic Medicine of the Pacific, is an independent, nonprofit academic health center. *Enrollment:* 1,681. *Degrees awarded:* Master's, doctorate, first-professional. Professional certificates also awarded.

Accreditation: *Regional:* WASC-Sr. *Professional:* nursing, osteopathy, pharmacy, physical therapy, physician assisting, surgeon assisting, veterinary medicine

History: Founded 1977; charter class admitted 1978 and graduated 1982; full accreditation granted 1982; joined with College of Allied Health Professions and College of Pharmacy to become Western University of Health Sciences in 1996.

Institutional Structure: *Governing board:* Board of Trustees comprised of 9 extrainstitutional members; president of college, ex officio. *Composition of institution:* Administrators 27 men / 20 women. Academic affairs headed by provost/executive vice president for academic affairs. Management/business/finance headed by executive vice president of finance and administration. Full-time instructional faculty 112. Academic governance body, faculty council, meets monthly.

Calendar: Semesters. Academic year Aug. to May. Formal commencement May.

Admission: Rolling admissions plan. *Requirements:* 90 semester hours or three-fourths of the credits required for a baccalaureate degree from an accredited college or university; 1 academic year or its equivalent in English, biology, physics, organic chemistry, inorganic chemistry and behavioral sciences; New Medical College Admission Test scores.

Degree Requirements: *For first-professional degree:* for Doctor of Osteopathic Medicine degree: 358 units; Doctor of Pharmacy 186 units; Master of Science in Pharmaceutical Sciences 40 units; Doctor of Veterinary Medicine 151 units; Master of Science in Health Sciences 34 units; Doctor of Physical Therapy: 142.5 units; Master of Science Physician Assistant 116 units; Master of Science in Nursing 65 units. *Grading system:* A–D; U (unsatisfactory), I (incomplete), CR (credit), W (withdrawal).

Distinctive Educational Programs: Doctor of Osteopathic Medicine, Primary Care Physician Assistant, Master of Physical Therapy, Doctor of Pharmacy, Master of Science in Health Professions Education, Master of Science in Nursing/Family Nurse Practitioner, Doctor of Veterinary Medicine.

Degrees Conferred: 147 *master's* health professions and related sciences. 276 *first-professional:* osteopathic medicine 178, pharmacy 88, physical therapy 10.

Fees and Other Expenses: *Full-time tuition per academic year:* varies by program; *see* institution's website for current tuition/fees.

Financial Aid: Aid from institutionally generated funds is provided on the basis of financial need and other considerations.

Financial aid to graduate students: 1,351 federal and state-funded loans totaling $47,079,015 (ranging from $2,500 to $15,167); 18 teaching fellowships totaling $593,916.

Departments and Teaching Staff: Allied health *professors* 2, *associate professors* 2, *assistant professors* 11, *instructors* 1, *part-time faculty* 1; nursing 1, 1, 4, 0, 6; osteopathic medicine 17, 7, 8, 1, 4; pharmacy 2, 10, 19, 0, 1; veterinary medicine 6, 10, 7, 1, 3.

Total instructional faculty: 129 (full-time 112, part-time 17; women 62, men 67). Total faculty with doctorate, first-professional, or other terminal degree: 117. Student-to-faculty ratio: 15:1.

Enrollment: Total full-time enrollment 1,681.

Characteristics of Student Body: 44 nonresident aliens enrolled fall 2004. 4 students from Europe, 39 Asia, 1 Canada.

International Students: No programs available to aid students whose native language is not English. No financial aid specifically designated for international students.

Student Life: *Surrounding community:* Pomona is located 35 miles east of Los Angeles, near the foothills of the San Gabriel Mountains. Served by mass transit bus system; near major east-west freeway; Ontario International Airport 15 miles from campus.

Library Collections: 22,986 volumes. Online catalog. 307 current serial subscriptions. 2,000 audiovisual materials. Students have access to online information retrieval services and the Internet.

Most important special holdings include rare and out-of-print osteopathic medicine books and journals.

Buildings and Grounds: All academic and administrative facilities of the college are located on College Plaza in Pomona.

Chief Executive Officer: Dr. Philip Pumerantz, President.

Address admission inquiries to Susan Hanson, Director of Admissions.

Westminster Seminary California

1725 Bear Valley Parkway
Escondido, California 92027-4128
Tel: (760) 480-8474
Fax: (760) 480-0252

Institution Description: Westminster Seminary California, formerly named Western Theological Seminary in California, is a private, independent, nonprofit seminary for graduate studies. *Enrollment:* 169. *Degrees awarded:* master's, first-professional.

Accreditation: *Regional:* WASC. *Institutional:* American Association of Theology Schools in the United States and Canada (ATS). *Professional:* theology

History: Chartered in 1979 as a branch of Westminster Theological Seminary (Philadelphia, PA); offered first instruction 1980; first degree (master's) awarded 1982; became separate institution in 1982; moved to current location 1984; adopted present name 2002.

Institutional Structure: *Governing board:* Western Seminary California Board of Trustees. *Extrainstitutional representation:* 18 trustees. All voting. *Composition of institution:* administrators 5 men / 2 women. Academic affairs headed by academic dean. Management/business/finances directed by vice president for administration. Full-time instructional faculty 11; adjunct and visiting faculty 9. Academic governance body, Westminster Faculty, meets an average of 10 times per year.

Calendar: Semesters (1-4-1-4 plan). Academic year July to May. Formal commencement May. Summer session July-Aug. Classes generally taught Tues.-Fri.

Admission: Rolling admissions plan. *Requirements:* B.A. or equivalent from approved institution; recommendations from a professor and a pastor. Successful completion of Greek and Hebrew placement exams given by the seminary, or taking language courses simultaneously with other coursework. M.Div requires successful completion of a 2-hour college-level public speaking course. Under special circumstances applicants lacking a B.A. who are over: 35 and have completed at least 30 semester hours of undergraduate study may be admitted. For students whose first language is not English, completion of the TOEFL with a score of 570 and 4.5 on TWE.

Degree Requirements: *For master of divinity degree:* 90 credit hours not including those needed to meet the language requirements in Greek and Hebrew; field education; GPA of 2.0 or better. *Master of arts in religion with Biblical emphasis:* 54 credit hours not including those needed to meet the language requirements in Greek and Hebrew; GPA of 2.0 or better. *Master of arts in religion, theological emphasis:* 54 credit hours not including those need to satisfy language requirements in Greek and Hebrew; GPA of 2.0 or better.

Degrees Conferred: 12 *master's:* theology; 17 *first-professional:* master of divinity.

Fees and Other Expenses: *Full-time tuition per academic year 2004–05:* $10,620.

Financial Aid: Institutional, federal, and state funding possibilities. Aid from institutionally generated funds is provided on the basis of financial need. 52 students received federal and state-funded loans totaling $618,000 (ranging from $3,000 to $18,500); 64 students received fellowships and grants totaling $71,000 (ranging from $500 to $2,000).

Departments and Teaching Staff: *Total instructional faculty:* 20 (full-time 11, part-time 9; member of minority groups 1; women 1, men 19). Total faculty with doctorate, first-professional, or other terminal degree: 16. 2 faculty members awarded sabbaticals 2004–05.

Enrollment: Total enrollment 169.

Characteristics of Student Body: *Ethnic/racial makeup:* Black non-Hispanic: .6%; Asian or Pacific Islander: 33.7%; Hispanic: 1.2%; White non-Hispanic: 59.8%. *Age distribution:* 22–24: 12.3%; 25–29: 19.5%; 30–34: 20.8%; 35–39: 19.5%; 40–49: 21.4%; 50–59: 5.2%, 60–and over: 1.3%.

International Students: 8 nonresident aliens enrolled fall 2004. 2 students from Europe, 2 Asia, 1 Central America, 1 Africa, 1 Canada, 1 other. No programs available to aid students whose native language is not English. Financial aid specifically designated for international students: Loans and scholarships available.

Student Life: On-campus housing. *Special regulations:* cars permitted without restriction. *Special services:* Christian bookstore on campus. *Surrounding*

community: Escondido has a population of over: 100,000; close to Los Angeles and San Diego.

Library Collections: 67,301 volumes. Online catalog. Current serial holdings: 247 paper; 52,239 microforms. 1,254 CD-ROMs. 6 computer work stations. Students have access to the Internet at no charge. Total budget for books and materials: $44,000.

Most important special holdings include Biblical studies; early American imprints (all Evans); early English books (STC I and STC II).

Chief Executive Officer: W. Robert Godfrey, President.

Address admission inquiries to Admissions Coordinator.

Westmont College

955 La Paz Road
Santa Barbara, California 93108-1089

Tel: (805) 565-6200   **E-mail:** admissions@westmont.edu
Fax: (805) 565-6234   **Internet:** www.westmont.edu

Institution Description: Westmont College is a private, nonprofit, interdenominational Christian college. *Enrollment:* 1,337. *Degrees awarded:* Baccalaureate.

Member of Christian College Consortium (CCC).

Accreditation: *Regional:* WASC-Sr.

History: Established, incorporated, and offered first instruction at postsecondary level 1937; awarded first degree (baccalaureate) 1941. *See* Lyle Hillegas, "A History of Westmont College" (Diss., Dallas Theological Seminary, 1964) for further information.

Institutional Structure: *Governing board:* Westmont College Board of Trustees. Representation: 30 trustees; 1 alumnus; 1 parent's council. All voting. *Composition of institution:* Administrators 40 men / 35 women. Academic affairs headed by provost. Management/business/finances directed by vice president for administration and finance. Full-time instructional faculty 89. Academic governance body, Faculty Senate, meets an average of 10 times per year.

Calendar: Semesters. Academic year Aug. to May. Freshmen orientation Aug., Jan. Degrees conferred May, Dec. Formal commencement May. Limited summer session begins in May.

Characteristics of Freshmen: 1,534 applicants (509 men, 1,125 women). 74.5% of applicants admitted; 29.6% of admitted students enrolled full-time.

90% (328 students) submitted SAT scores; 33% (118 students) submitted ACT scores. *25th percentile:* SAT Verbal 550, SAT Math 550; ACT Composite 24, ACT English 23, ACT Math 24. *75th percentile:* SAT Verbal 660, SAT Math 660; Composite 28, ACT English 29, ACT Math28.

66% of entering freshmen expected to graduate within 5 years. 64% of freshmen from California. Freshmen from 41 states and 12 foreign countries.

Admission: Freshmen applying for the fall semester must send completed application to the Admissions Office prior to the Mar. 1 Priority Application Filing Deadline. Early Action applications are due prior to Dec. 1. Early Action is for the fall semester only. Notifications for the fall are sent beginning Jan. 15. Evaluation is based on cumulative grade point average, results of either SAT or ACT, and an assessment of several personal areas: activities, leadership, and a desire to support the values of Westmont College. *Requirements:* Either graduation from accredited secondary school or GED. Recommend 16 units, including 4 English, 2 foreign language, 3 college preparatory mathematics, 2 laboratory science, 1 U.S. history or government. *For transfer students:* From 4-year accredited institution 2.0 minimum GPA, 104 hours maximum transfer credit; from 2-year accredited institution 2.5 minimum GPA, 64 hours.

College credit and advanced placement for postsecondary-level work completed in secondary school. Tutoring available.

Degree Requirements: 124 credit hours; 2.0 GPA; last year in residence; chapel attendance 3 times weekly; 4 hours physical education; distribution requirements; demonstrated proficiency in a foreign language.

Fulfillment of some degree requirements and exemption from some beginning courses possible by passing departmental examinations, College Board CLEP, AP. *Grading system:* A–F; honors-pass-no credit; withdraw (deadline after which pass-fail is appended to withdraw); incomplete (carries time limit).

Distinctive Educational Programs: Work-experience programs, internships. Evening classes. Interdisciplinary programs in fine arts, natural science, social science. Pre-engineering programs with Stanford, University of Washington (St. Louis). Facilities and programs for independent research, including honors programs, individual majors, tutorials. Institutionally sponsored study tours in Asia, Europe, Latin America; internships in Third World studies in Mexico. Through the Institute of Holy Land Studies, study abroad in Jerusalem. Foreign study also by individual arrangement. Summer Business Institute in Europe. Off-campus study in the U.S. includes urban semester internship program in San Francisco; semester in Washington (DC) through The American University or CCC;

exchange program with member institutions of CCC. *Other distinctive programs:* Fifth-year advanced studies program in teacher preparation.

ROTC: Army offered in cooperation with University of California, Santa Barbara.

Degrees Conferred: 305 *baccalaureate.* Degrees awarded in top five disciplines: social sciences 64; biological and biomedical sciences 37; communication, journalism, and related programs 35; English language and literature/letters 30; parks, recreation, leisure and fitness studies 25.

Fees and Other Expenses: *Full-time tuition and fees per academic year 2004–05:* $26,240. *Room and board per academic year:* $8,610. *Books and supplies:* $1,260. *Other expenses:* $2,430.

Financial Aid: Aid from institutionally generated funds is provided on the basis of academic merit, financial need, athletic ability. Institution has a Program Participation Agreement with the U.S. Department of Education for eligible students to receive Pell Grants and other federal aid.

Financial aid to full-time, first-time undergraduate students: need-based scholarships/grants totaling $8,710,687, self-help $4,298,840, parent loans $1,996,930, tuition waivers $334,561, athletic awards $274,266; non-need-based scholarships/grants totaling $2,930,267, self-help $1,073,029, parent loans $2,014,583, tuition waivers $574,219, athletic awards $334,348.

Departments and Teaching Staff: *Total instructional faculty:* 145 (full-time 89, part-time 56; women 58, men 87). Total full-time faculty with doctorate, first-professional, or other terminal degree: 78. Student-to-faculty ratio: 13:1.

Enrollment: Total enrollment 1,337. Undergraduate 1,331 (full-time 34.7% men, 65.3% women).

Characteristics of Student Body: *Ethnic/racial makeup:* Black non-Hispanic: 1.1%; American Indian or Alaska Native: 1.2%; Asian or Pacific Islander: 5.6%; Hispanic: 6.7%; White non-Hispanic: 92%; unknown: 2.6%.

International Students: 11 nonresident aliens enrolled fall 2003. Programs available to aid students whose native language is not English: social, cultural, financial.

Student Life: On-campus residence halls house 90% of student body. Residence halls for both sexes constitute 100% of such space. 10% of student body housed off campus in college-owned apartments. *Intercollegiate athletics:* men only: baseball, basketball, cross-country, soccer, tennis, track; women only: basketball, cross-country, soccer, tennis, track, volleyball. *Special regulations:* Registered cars permitted for all but freshmen. Quiet hours vary according to residence hall area. Visitation hours set by residents. *Special services:* Medical services, college-funded bus system. *Student publications: Citadel,* a yearbook; *Horizon,* a weekly newspaper; *Phoenix,* an annual literary magazine. *Surrounding community:* Santa Barbara population 150,000. Los Angeles, 90 miles from campus, is nearest metropolitan area. Served by mass transit bus system; airport 9 miles from campus; passenger rail service 4 miles from campus.

Publications: Sources of information about Westmont include an on-campus newsletter (*Intercom*) to faculty/staff; *La Paz,* alumni publication; *Westmont Monthly Magazine.*

Library Collections: 162,275 volumes including bound books, serial backfiles, electronic documents, and government documents not in separate collections. Online catalog. Current serial subscriptions: paper, microform, electronic. 6,305 recordings; 706 compact discs; 70 CD-ROMs. 100 computer work stations. Students have access to the Internet at no charge.

Most important special holdings include Christ and Culture Collection (1,000 books relating to Christian values and cultural concerns); 700 books, pamphlets, and tapes produced since 1976 by the American Enterprise Institute; 2,500 volumes of children's and young adult literature.

Buildings and Grounds: Campus area 140 acres.

Chief Executive Officer: Dr. Stan Gaede, President.

Address admission inquiries to Joyce Luy, Director of Admissions

Whittier College

13406 East Philadelphia Street
Whittier, California 90608

Tel: (562) 907-4200   **E-mail:** admission@whittier.edu
Fax: (562) 907-4242   **Internet:** www.whittier.edu

Institution Description: Whittier College is a private, independent, nonprofit college. *Enrollment:* 2,275. *Degrees awarded:* Baccalaureate, master's, first-professional.

Accreditation: *Regional:* WASC-Sr. *Professional:* law, social work

History: Established, chartered, and offered first instruction at postsecondary level 1901; awarded first degree (baccalaureate) 1904. *See* Charles W. Cooper, *Whittier: Independent College in California* (Los Angeles: The Ward Ritchie Press, 1967) for further information.

Institutional Structure: *Governing board:* Whittier College Board of Trustees. Extrainstitutional representation: 49 trustees; institutional representation: president of the college; vice president for college advancement, 1 alumnus, 1 ex officio. All voting. *Composition of institution:* Administrators 42 men / 49 women. Academic affairs headed by executive vice president and dean of faculty. Management/business/finances directed by vice president for finance and administration. Full-time instructional faculty 57 men / 31 women. Academic governance body, Faculty Meeting, meets an average of 30 times per year.

Calendar: Semesters (4-1-4 plan). Academic year Sept. to May. Freshmen admitted Sept. term only. Degrees conferred and formal commencement May. Summer session of 3 terms from early June to late Aug.

Characteristics of Freshmen: 1,957 applicants (925 men, 1,032 women). 79.3% of applicants admitted; 25.3% admitted and enrolled full-time.

95% (382 students) submitted SAT scores; 27% (109 students) submitted ACT scores. *25th percentile:* SAT Verbal 480, SAT Math 470; ACT Composite 19. *75th percentile:* SAT Verbal 590, SAT Math 590; ACT Composite 25.

70% of freshmen from California. Freshmen from 26 states and 8 foreign countries.

Admission: Freshman priority date Feb. 1 for fall acceptance. Apply by Dec. 1 for early decision. *Requirements:* Graduation from secondary school with 3 units English, 2 in a foreign language, 2 in mathematics, 1 history, 1 laboratory science. Personal interview recommended. *Entrance tests:* College Board SAT or ACT composite. For foreign students TOEFL. *For transfer students:* 2.5 minimum GPA recommended; from 4-year accredited institution 90 hours maximum transfer credit; from 2-year accredited institution 70 hours.

Advanced placement for postsecondary-level work completed in secondary school. Tutoring available.

Degree Requirements: *Undergraduate:* 120 credit hours; 2.0 GPA; 1 year in residence; course and distribution requirements.

Fulfillment of some degree requirements possible by scoring 4 or above on AP test. *Grading system:* A–C; credit-no credit; incomplete (carries time limit); letter of evaluation.

Distinctive Educational Programs: *For undergraduates:* Dual-degree program in engineering with Colorado State University, Dartmouth College, Columbia University, University of Southern California, Washington University. Interdisciplinary programs in child development, comparative cultures, environmental studies, Latin American studies, urban studies. Facilities for independent research, including honors programs, individual majors. Institutionally sponsored study abroad in Denmark, India, and 18 other countries under a consortium agreement with the University of Miami.

Degrees Conferred: 223 *baccalaureate.* Bachelor's degrees awarded in top five disciplines: business, management, marketing, and related support services 49; social sciences 47; psychology 35; English language and literature/letters 22; biological and biomedical sciences 15.

Fees and Other Expenses: *Full-time tuition per academic year 2004–05:* $24,468. *Books and supplies:* $656. *Room and board per academic year:* $7,698. *Other expenses:* $1,884.

Financial Aid: Aid from institutionally generated funds is awarded on basis of academic merit, financial need. Institution has a Program Participation Agreement with the U.S. Department of Education for eligible students to receive Pell Grants and other federal aid.

Financial aid to full-time, first-time undergraduate students: 26% received federal grants averaging $3,991; 18% state/local grants averaging $7,510; 775 institutional grants averaging $11,234; 60% loans averaging $6,326.

Departments and Teaching Staff: *Professors* 33, *associate professors* 15, *assistant professors* 36 *instructors* 9, *part-time teachers* 41.

Total instructional faculty 133. Total tenured faculty: 53. Degrees held by full-time faculty: Doctorate 76%, master's 100%, baccalaureate 100%. 90% hold terminal degrees.

Enrollment: Total enrollment 2,275. Undergraduate 1,203.

Characteristics of Student Body: *Ethnic/racial makeup:* Black non-Hispanic: 3.3%; American Indian or Alaska Native: 1.8%; Asian or Pacific Islander: 9.1%; Hispanic: 25.4%; White non-Hispanic: 46.2%; unknown: 9.1%.

International Students: 114 nonresident aliens enrolled fall 2003. Programs available to aid students whose native language is not English: Social, cultural. English as a Second Language Program. Financial aid specifically designated for international students: 30 to 40 scholarships available annually.

Student Life: On-campus residence halls house 63% of student body. *Intercollegiate athletics:* men only: baseball, basketball, cross-country, football, golf, soccer, swimming, tennis, track, volleyball, water polo, wrestling; women only: basketball, soccer, cross-country, softball, water polo, lacrosse, swimming, tennis, track, volleyball. *Special regulations:* Registered cars permitted without restrictions. *Special services:* Learning Resources Center, medical services, van service to airport. *Student publications: Quaker Campus,* a weekly newspaper; *Acropolis,* a yearbook. *Surrounding community:* Whittier population 80,000, is located within Los Angeles metropolitan area. Served by mass transit bus system; airport 25 miles from campus; passenger rail service 10 miles from campus.

Library Collections: 225,500 volumes. 34,500 microforms; 4,700 audiovisual materials; 700 current periodical subscriptions. Online catalog. Students have access to online information retrieval services and the Internet.

Most important holdings include John Greenleaf Whittier Collection (6,300 items including letters, inscribed 1st editions, furniture); Jessamyn West Collection (200 manuscripts of the American novelist and short story writer's work up to 1970, typewritten and in longhand; also copies of published works); Clifford and Susan Johnson Library of Quaker Literature (4,000 items, some dating back to the 17th century); Richard Nixon Collection; Society of Friends Collection.

Buildings and Grounds: Campus area 100 acres.

Chief Executive Officer: Dr. James A. Legoza, President.

Address admission inquiries to Lisa Meyer, Dean of Enrollment.

Whittier College School of Law

Degree Programs Offered: *First-professional* in law.

Admission: LSAT required; 3 letters of recommendation advised.

Degree Requirements: 87 credit hours; 2.0 GPA; 42 hours in residence.

Departments and Teaching Staff: *Total instructional faculty:* 28. *Degrees held by full-time faculty:* 23 professional degrees. 100% hold terminal degrees.

Distinctive Educational Programs: 4-year double-degree program leads to first-professional degree in law and master's in business administration.

William Jessup University

333 Sunset Boulevard
Rocklin, California 95765

Tel: (916) 577-2200   **E-mail:** admissions@jessup.edu
Fax: (916) 577-2203   **Internet:** www.jessup.edu

Institution Description: William Jessup University, formerly named San Jose Christian College, is a nondenominational institution that prepares Christians for leadership and service and society through Christian higher education, spiritual formation, and directed experiences. Major areas of study include Bible and theology, business management, Christian education, Christian leadership, counseling psychology, intercultural studies, management and ethics, music and worship, pastoral ministry, teacher education, and youth ministry. *Enrollment:* 436. *Degrees awarded:* Associate, baccalaureate. Post-baccalaureate certificates also awarded.

Accreditation: *Regional:* WASC-Sr. *Nonregional:* ABHE.

History: Founded 1939; moved to San Jose campus 1951; relocated to Rocklin CA and adopted present name 2004.

Institutional Structure: Board of Trustees of 19 members. Executive administration 5; full-time faculty 19. Academic governance body: Academic Senate.

Calendar: Semesters. Academic year Sept. to May.

Characteristics of Freshmen: 55% of applicants admitted and enrolled full-time. 79% (46 students) submitted SAT scores; 28% (16 students) submitted ACT scores. *25th percentile:* SAT Verbal 440, SAT Math 430; ACT Composite 18, ACT English 17, ACT Math 16. *75th percentile:* SAT Verbal 590, SAT Math 580; ACT Composite 23, ACT English 24, ACT Math 22.

Admission: Early action plan. *Requirements:* Graduation from accredited secondary school with a 2.0 GPA or GED; letter of introduction; personal and academic recommendations. *Entrance tests:* College Board SAT or ACT.

Degree Requirements: 128 units required for graduation, including 66 units of general education, 32 units of Bible and theology, and 30 units of student's prescribed major.

Distinctive Educational Programs: Adult Degree Completion Program; Post-Baccalaureate Teacher Education Certificate Program.

Degrees Conferred: 6 *associate;* 72 *baccalaureate:* business/marketing 21, philosophy/religion/theology 33, psychology 11, visual and performing arts 7.

Fees and Other Expenses: *Full-time tuition per academic year 2004–05:* $15,590. *Required fees:* $760. *Room and board per academic year:* $5,858.

Financial Aid: Aid from institutionally generated funds is provided on the basis of academic merit, financial need, other criteria. Institution has a Program Participation Agreement with the U.S. Department of Education for eligible students to receive Pell Grants and other federal aid.

Departments and Teaching Staff: *Total instructional faculty:* 86 (full-time 19, part-time 67; members of minority groups 11; women 22, men 64). Total faculty with doctorate, first-professional, or other terminal degree: 78. Student-to-faculty ratio: 10:1.

Enrollment: Total enrollment 436. Undergraduate full-time 141 men / 158 women, part-time 61m / 71w; graduate full-time 1m, part-time 1m / 3w.

Characteristics of Student Body: *Ethnic/racial makeup:* number of Black non-Hispanic: 38; American Indian or Alaska Native: 5; Asian or Pacific Islander: 29; Hispanic: 46; White non-Hispanic: 288; unknown: 19. *Age distri-*

bution: number under 18–19: 89; 20–21: 92; 22–24: 79; 25–29: 61; 30–34: 24; 35–39: 20; 40–49: 39; 50–64: 27.

International Students: 6 nonresident aliens enrolled fall 2004. 6 students from Asia. No programs available to aid students whose native language is not English. No financial aid specifically designated for international students.

Student Life: On-campus residence halls available.

Library Collections: 58,114 volumes. 198 serial subscriptions; 90 microform titles; 1,500 audiovisual materials. Online catalog. Students have access to online information retrieval services and the Internet.

Most important special collections include biblical commentaries and historical works and periodicals of the Restoration Movement.

Buildings and Grounds: Campus area 125 acres.

Chief Executive Officer: Dr. Bryce L. Jessup, President.

Address admission inquiries to Director of Admissions.

Wright Institute

2728 Durant Avenue
Berkeley, California 94704-1796
Tel: (510) 841-9230   **E-mail:** info@wrightinst.edu
Fax: (510) 841-0167   **Internet:** www.wrightinst.edu

Institution Description: The Wright Institute is a private, independent, nonprofit institution offering programs in professional psychology. *Enrollment:* 286. *Degrees awarded:* Doctorate.

Accreditation: *Regional:* WASC-Sr. *Professional:* psychology internship

History: Established 1969.

Institutional Structure: *Governing board:* Board of Trustees. Representation: 17 trustees. All voting. *Composition of institution:* 6 administrators. Academic affairs headed by dean of graduate school of psychology. Management/business/finances directed by business officer.

Calendar: Trimester. Academic year Sept. to June.

Admission: Rolling admissions plan. *Requirements:* Baccalaureate from accredited college or university.

Degree Requirements: 3–5 year program; dissertation.

Distinctive Educational Programs: Programs in social-clinical psychology and psycho-social development and education.

Degrees Conferred: 42 *master's:* clinical psychology; 41 *doctorate:* clinical psychology.

Fees and Other Expenses: *Full-time tuition per academic year 2004–05:* $28,000.

Financial Aid: Aid from institutionally generated funds is provided on the basis of academic merit. Institution has a Program Participation Agreement with the U.S. Department of Education for eligible students to receive Pell Grants and other federal aid.

Departments and Teaching Staff: Psychology *professors* 5, *part-time teachers* 36. *Total faculty:* 41 FTE. 100% hold terminal degrees.

Enrollment: Total enrollment 286 (24.8% men, 75.2% women).

Characteristics of Student Body: *Ethnic/racial makeup:* Black non-Hispanic: 8.7%; American Indian or Alaska Native: .7%; Asian or Pacific Islander: 5.6%; Hispanic: 5.2%; White non-Hispanic: 76.6%. *Age distribution:* 22–24: 2%, 25–29: 24%; 30–34: 25%; 35–39: 14%; 40–49: 24%; 50–59: 9%, 60–and over: 1%.

International Students: 9 nonresident aliens enrolled fall 2003. Students from Europe, Asia, Africa, Canada. No programs available to aid students whose native language is not English. No financial aid specifically designated for international students.

Student Life: *Surrounding community:* Berkeley population 125,000. Served by mass transit bus system; airport.

Chief Executive Officer: Dr. Peter Dybwad, President.

Address admission inquiries to Elizabeth Hertz, Director of Admissions.

Woodbury University

7500 Glenoaks Boulevard
Burbank, California 91510-7846
Tel: (818) 767-0888   **E-mail:** admissions@woodbury.edu
Fax: (818) 504-9320   **Internet:** www.woodbury.edu

Institution Description: Woodbury University is a private, independent, nonprofit institution. *Enrollment:* 1,446. *Degrees awarded:* Baccalaureate, master's.

Accreditation: *Regional:* WASC-Sr. *Professional:* business, interior design

History: Established as Woodbury Business College 1884; chartered and changed name to Woodbury College 1926; awarded first degree (baccalaureate) 1927; adopted present name 1974.

Institutional Structure: *Governing board:* Board of Trustees. Extrainstitutional representation: 24 trustees; institutional representation: president of the university; 2 trustees emeritus (nonvoting); 24 voting *Composition of institution:* Administrators 17 men / 6 women. Academic affairs headed by executive vice president for academic affairs/dean of faculty. Facilities management/business/finances directed by vice president, business affairs and controller. Full-time instructional faculty 40. Academic governance body, Faculty Association, meets quarterly.

Calendar: Semesters. Academic year Aug. to Aug. Freshmen admitted Sept., Jan., Mar., June. Degrees conferred and formal commencements June, Dec. Summer semester June to Aug.

Characteristics of Freshmen: 92% of students submitted SAT scores; 8 % of students submitted ACT scores. *25th percentile*: SAT Verbal 420, SAT Math 440. *75th percentile*: SAT Verbal 580, SAT Math 600.

70% of applicants accepted. 33% of accepted applicants enrolled. 87% of freshmen from California. Freshmen from 6 states and 3 foreign countries.

Admission: Rolling admissions plan. For fall acceptance, apply as early as senior year of secondary school. Early acceptance available. *Requirements:* Graduation from accredited secondary school or GED. *Entrance tests:* College Board SAT. *For transfer students:* 2.0 minimum GPA; from 4- and 2-year accredited institutions.

College credit and advanced placement for postsecondary-level work completed in secondary school. College credit for College Board AP (scores of 3 or higher), CLEP, DANTES, and on basis of ACE *2006 Guide to the Evaluation of Educational Experiences in the Armed Services.*

Degree Requirements: *Undergraduate:* 5-year bachelor's degree, 160 semester hours; 4-year bachelor's degree 120 to 128 semester hours (varies by major); 2.0 GPA; 45 unit residency requirement; general education requirements. *Grading system:* A–F. Graduate: MBA 36 semester hours; MA 30 semester hours; 30 unit residency requirement.

Distinctive Educational Programs: Professional degree programs in business, computer information systems, and architecture and design; internships; weekend college, and evening programs in business administration.

Degrees Conferred: 212 *baccalaureate* (B); 81 *master's* (M): architecture 74 (B); business/marketing 84 (B), 81 (M); communications/communication technologies 2 (B); computer and information sciences 12 (B); liberal arts/general studies 2 (B); psychology 11 (B); social sciences and history 2 (B); visual and performing arts 45 (B). Honorary Doctor of Letters awarded 2003–04.

Fees and Other Expenses: *Full-time tuition per academic year 2004–05:* $21,074 undergraduate; graduate and professional study vary in cost (contact the university for current rates). *Room and board per academic year:* $8,220. *Required fees:* $240.

Financial Aid: Aid from institutionally generated funds is provided on the basis of academic merit, financial need. Institution has a Program Participation Agreement with the U.S. Department of Education for eligible students to receive Pell Grants and other federal aid.

Financial aid to full-time, first-time undergraduate students: need-based scholarships/grants totaling $10,043,371, self-help $7,318,086, parent loans $1,578,519; non-need-based scholarships/grants totaling $771,333, self-help $1,225,101, tuition waivers $4,000. *Graduate aid:* 56 federal and state-funded loans totaling $785,280 (ranging from $4,500 to $18,500).

Departments and Teaching Staff: *Professors* 15, *associate professors* 13, *assistant professors* 12. *Total instructional faculty:* 221 (full-time 40, part-time 181; women 89, men 32). Total faculty with doctorate, first-professional, or other terminal degree: 97.

Enrollment: Total enrollment 1,146. Undergraduate full-time 420 men / 573 women, part-time 107 / 169w; graduate full-time 54m / 84w, part-time 18m / 21w.

Characteristics of Student Body: *Ethnic/racial makeup:* number of Black non-Hispanic: 82; American Indian or Alaska Native: 3; Asian or Pacific Islander: 49; Hispanic: 451; White non-Hispanic: 493; unknown 1. *Age distribution:* number under 18: 20; 18–19: 259; 20–21: 297; 22–24: 278; 25–29: 188; 30–34: 84; 35–39: 60; 40–49: 67; 50–64: 16.

International Students: 118 nonresident aliens enrolled fall 2004. 21 students from Europe, 81 Asia, 7 Central and South America, 3 Africa, 2 Canada, 1 Australia, 3 other. No programs to aid students whose native language is not English. No financial aid specifically designated for international students.

Student Life: On-campus limited housing available. Intramural sports. *Special regulations:* Cars permitted without restrictions. *Surrounding community:* Burbank population 100,000. Served by mass transit bus system; airport 2 miles from campus; passenger rail service 2 miles from campus; 15 minutes by car from downtown Los Angeles.

Library Collections: 66,654 volumes. Current serial subscriptions: paper 283; microform 22; via electronic access 33. 78 recordings; 78 compact discs; 120 CD-ROMs. 20 computer work stations. Students have access to online information retrieval services and the Internet. Total 2004–05 budget for materials and operations: $131,000.

Most important special holdings include John C. Hogan Law Collection; Senior Thesis Collection; Senior Papers Collection.

Buildings and Grounds: Campus area 23 acres.

Chief Executive Officer: Dr. Kenneth R. Nielson, President.

Address admission inquiries to Mario Diaz, Admissions Director.

Colorado

Adams State College

208 Edgemont Boulevard
Alamosa, Colorado 81102
Tel: (719) 587-7712   **E-mail:** ascadmit@adams.edu
Fax: (719) 587-7522   **Internet:** www.adams.edu

Institution Description: Adams State College is a state institution. *Degrees awarded:* Associate, baccalaureate, master's. *Enrollment:* 6,491 (includes graduate and professional students).

Budget subject to approval by The State Colleges in Colorado governing board.

Accreditation: *Regional:* NCA. *Professional:* counseling, music, teacher education

History: Established as State Normal School at Alamosa 1921; changed name to Adams State Normal School 1923; offered first instruction at postsecondary level 1925; awarded first degree (baccalaureate) 1926; changed name to Adams State Teachers College of Southern Colorado 1929; adopted present name 1945.

Institutional Structure: *Governing board:* Trustees of The State Colleges in Colorado. Representation: 9 trustees. *Composition of institution:* Administrators 29 men / 17 women. Academic affairs headed by vice president for academic affairs. Management/business/finances directed by vice president. Full-time instructional faculty 100 (women 41, men 59).

Calendar: Semesters. Academic year from Aug. to May. Summer terms from May to July.

Characteristics of Freshmen: 15% (61 students) submitted SAT scores; 89.4% (363 students) submitted ACT scores. *25th percentile:* SAT Verbal 420, SAT Math 410; ACT Composite 17, ACT English 16, ACT Math 16. *75th percentile:* SAT Verbal 560, SAT Math 540; ACT Composite 22, ACT English 22, ACT Math 22.

30% of freshmen expected to graduate within 5 years. 81% of freshmen from Colorado. Freshmen from 20 states and 1 foreign country.

Admission: To be considered for unconditional admission to the Bachelor of Arts (BA), Bachelor of Science (BS), or Associate of Arts (AA) degree programs, a student should meet two of the following three criteria: have a high school grade point average of 2.0 or above, a ranking in the upper two-thirds of his/her graduating class, and an average or above-average score on the ACT or SAT. Applicants should meet these criteria: (1) graduation from an accredited high school with a minimum of 15 secondary school units, grades 9 through 12; (2) of the 15 required units, 10 must be chosen from academic fields of English, foreign language, mathematics, science, and social studies., including not fewer than four units of English. Recommended units are as follows: English (4 units); mathematics (3 units), including algebra and a higher level mathematics class; laboratory science (2 units); social science (3 units); foreign language (2 units); and computer applications (1/2 unit). Prospective transfer students must have at least a C or 2.0 GPA to be unconditionally accepted for admission to ASC. In the case of repeated courses, honor points for grade point averages are compiled on the basis of performance in the repeated class. Recommended entrance test is ACT. For foreign students a minimum 550 TOEFL is required. For transfer students, 2.0 GPA; from 4-year accredited institutions students must complete at least 30 semester hours at ASC and in combination with accepted transfer credit must have at least 124 semester hours to graduate; from 2-year accredited institutions students must complete at least 60 semester hours at ASC and in combination with accepted transfer credit must have at least 124 semester hours to graduate. Electronic applications accepted.

Advanced placement examination of 3 and above are generally accepted for college credit by the academic deans. A limited number of developmental/remedial courses are offered.

Degree Requirements: *For all associate degrees:* 60 semester hours (including general education, advisor-guided electives, competency exams in writing and mathematics, at least 30 semester hours in residence; minimum 2.0 GPA). *For all baccalaureate degrees:* 120 semester hours (including general education, a major, electives, competency exams in writing and mathematics, at least 30 semester hours in residence, minimum 2.0 GPA).

Fulfillment of some degree requirements possible by passing departmental examinations, College Board APP, ACT English. Exemption from some beginning courses possible by passing College Board APP, ACT Mathematics. *Grading system:* A–F; pass-fail, satisfactory-unsatisfactory; withdraw.

Distinctive Educational Programs: Off-Campus Master of Arts degree programs in (a) elementary education with the University of Southern Colorado and Mesa State College, and (b) guidance and counseling with the University of Southern Colorado, Mesa State College, and Fort Lewis College. Field-based Master of Arts degrees in elementary education and secondary education with emphasis in art, business, English, mathematics, music, physical education, science, social studies, and liberal arts. Cooperative baccalaureate program in medical technology with affiliated hospitals. Preprofessional programs in dentistry, engineering, law, medicine, nursing, osteopathic medicine, pharmacy, physical therapy, veterinary medicine. Guaranteed transfer programs with the University of Colorado, Colorado State University, and Colorado School of Mines.

Degrees Conferred: 27 *associate;* 269 *baccalaureate* (B); 298 *master's* (M): biological and life sciences 19 (B); business 72 (B); computer and information science 2 (B); education 130 (M); English 20 (B); foreign languages and literature 5 (B); health professions and related sciences 15 (B); liberal arts/general studies 34 (B); mathematics 1 (B); physical sciences 8 (B); psychology 23 (B); visual and performing arts 16 (B), 5 (M); counseling 52 (M).

Fees and Other Expenses: *Full-time tuition per academic year 2004–05:* undergraduate resident $1,818, out-of-state student $7,510. Contact the university for current graduate tuition. *Required fees:* $784.50. *Room and board per academic year:* $9,240.

Financial Aid: Aid from institutionally generated funds is provided on the basis of academic merit, financial need, athletic ability, other considerations. Institution has a Program Participation Agreement with the U.S. Department of Education for eligible students to receive Pell Grants and other federal aid.

Financial aid to full-time, first-time undergraduate students: need-based federal scholarship/grants $3,076,422, state $903,502; non-need-based state scholarships/grants $318,052, institutional $541,317, external sources $888,688.

Departments and Teaching Staff: *Total instructional faculty:* 211 (full-time 100, part-time 111; women 120, men 91; members of minority groups 44). Total number with doctorate, first-professional, or other terminal degree: 85.

Enrollment: Total enrollment 6,491. Undergraduate full-time 766 men / 881 women, part-time 227m / 502w; graduate full-time 53m / 128w, part-time 876m / 3,058w.

Characteristics of Student Body: *Ethnic/racial makeup:* number of Black non-Hispanic: 126; American Indian or Alaska Native: 33; Asian or Pacific Islander: 640; Hispanic: 640; White non-Hispanic: 1,397; unknown: 163.

International Students: 10 nonresident aliens enrolled fall 2004.

Student Life: On-campus housing and food service is available for about 1,000 students. Over 40 clubs and organizations. *Intercollegiate athletics:* men: basketball, cross-country, football, golf, track and field (indoor and outdoor), wrestling; women: basketball, cross-country, softball, track and field (indoor and outdoor), volleyball. In 1995–96, ASC had 1 NAIA National Division II team championship; 26 National All-American honors, and 3 National Scholar-Athlete academic honors. *Surrounding community:* Alamosa population 7,000. Denver, 220 miles from campus, is nearest metropolitan area.

Library Collections: 478,334 books, serial backfiles, and government titles that are accessible through the library's catalog. Online catalog. Current serial subscriptions: 400. 705,547 microform units; 15,520 audiovisual materials. Computer work stations available. Students have access to the Internet at no charge.

Most important special collections include Woodward Law Room; Colorado Room; ASC Archives.

Buildings and Grounds: Campus area 97 acres.

Chief Executive Officer: Dr. Robert A. Wueste, President.

Address admission inquiries to Walter Roybal, Director of Admissions.

Colorado Christian University

8787 West Alameda Avenue
Lakewood, Colorado 80226
Tel: (303) 963-3000   **E-mail:** admissions@ccu.edu
Fax: (303) 963-3230   **Internet:** www.ccu.edu

Institution Description: Colorado Christian University, is a private, non-profit, interdenominational university of the Bible, arts and sciences and career education. *Enrollment:* 1,580. *Degrees awarded:* Associate, baccalaureate, master's.

Accreditation: *Regional:* NCA. *Professional:* teacher education

History: The university is the result of a merger in July 1985 between Rockmont College (established 1914) and Western Bible College (established 1948); in 1989 Colorado Christian College and Colorado Baptist University merged to become Colorado Christian University.

Institutional Structure: *Governing board:* Board of Trustees. Extrainstitutional representation: 23 trustees (president-ex officio); institutional representation: president of the university, chancellor of the university. All voting. *Composition of institution:* Administrators 41 men / 46 women. Academic affairs headed by vice president. Management/business/finances directed by vice president of finance/chief executive officer. Full-time instructional faculty 48.

Calendar: Semesters. Academic year Aug. to May. Formal commencement May. Summer session of two terms from June 1 to July 23.

Characteristics of Freshmen: 981 applicants (332 men, 649 women). 73.6% of applicants admitted. 36.7% of admitted students enrolled full-time.

34% (92 students) submitted SAT scores; 67% (181 students) submitted ACT scores. *25th percentile:* SAT Verbal 510, SAT Math 480; ACT Composite 21, ACT English 21, ACT Math 19. *75th percentile:* SAT Verbal 600, SAT Math 580; ACT Composite 26, ACT English 27, ACT Math 26.

24% of freshmen expected to graduate within 5 years.

Admission: Rolling admissions plan. *Requirements:* 19 credit units from accredited secondary school; GED accepted. *Entrance tests:* College Board SAT or ACT composite. For foreign students TOEFL. *For transfer students:* 2.0 minimum GPA.

College credit and advanced placement for postsecondary-level work completed in secondary school. College credit for academically-relevant life experience on basis of portfolio assessment.

Degree Requirements: *For all associate degrees:* 64 semester hours. *For all baccalaureate degrees:* 128 semester hours; chapel attendance. *For all undergraduate degrees:* 2.5 GPA cumulative average in major; 1 year of resident study; general education requirements; 3 semester hours math, 3 science. Fulfillment of some degree requirements possible by passing College Board CLEP, APP. *Grading system:* A–F; withdraw (carries time limit).

Distinctive Educational Programs: Cross-registration with some Denver area colleges. *Other distinctive programs:* Continuing education offering credit and noncredit courses, evening school, extension programs, other programs. Degree completion program.

Degrees Conferred: 11 *associate;* 471 *baccalaureate;* 52 *master's.* Bachelor's degrees awarded in to five disciplines: business, management, marketing, and related support services 188; computer and information sciences and support services 96; education 50; theology and ministerial studies 31; psychology 28.

Fees and Other Expenses: *Full-time tuition per academic year 2004–05:* $15,950. *Room and board per academic year:* $6,500. *Books and supplies:* $1,100.

Financial Aid: Aid from institutionally generated funds is provided on the basis of academic merit, financial need, athletic ability. Institution has a Program Participation Agreement with the U.S. Department of Education for eligible students to receive Pell Grants and other federal aid.

Financial aid to full-time, first-time undergraduate students: 29% received federal grants averaging $3,717; 87% institutional grants averaging $4,425; 61% loans averaging $2,944.

Departments and Teaching Staff: *Professors* 10, *associate professors* 10, *assistant professors* 27, *instructors* 10, *part-time teachers* 144. *Total full-time instructional faculty:* 48. Student-to-faculty ratio: 12:1. Degrees held by full-time faculty: Doctorate 50%, master's 44%, baccalaureate 2%, professional 4%. 54% of faculty hold terminal degrees.

Enrollment: Total enrollment 1,580. Undergraduate 1,459 (40.1% men, 59.9% women).

Characteristics of Student Body: *Ethnic/racial makeup:* Black non-Hispanic: 4%; American Indian or Alaska Native: 1.2%; Asian or Pacific Islander: 1.4%; Hispanic: 5.6%; White non-Hispanic: 76.8%; unknown: 10.4%.

International Students: 9 nonresident aliens enrolled fall 2003. No programs available to aid students whose native language is not English. No financial aid specifically designated for international students.

Student Life: *Intercollegiate athletics:* men and women: basketball, cross-country, soccer, tennis; women only: volleyball; men only: golf. Complete intramural sports for all students. *Special regulations:* Chapel required twice weekly. All freshmen required to live on campus, except married students, or students over 21 living with relatives. All students living on campus required to purchase meal service. *Surrounding community:* Denver metropolitan area population 1,800,000.

Library Collections: 58,000 volumes. Online catalog. 230,000 microforms; 4,000 audiovisual materials; 415 current periodical subscriptions. Students have access to the Internet at no charge.

Most important special holdings include Biblical Studies Collection; Hymnology Collection; titles in psychology/Christian counseling.

Buildings and Grounds: Campus area (Lakewood) 35 acres; Foothills Conference Center 50 acres.

Chief Executive Officer: Dr. Larry R. Donnithorne, President.

Address admission inquiries to Director of Admissions.

Colorado College

14 East Cache La Poudre Street
Colorado Springs, Colorado 80903
Tel: (719) 389-6000   **E-mail:** admissions@coloradocollege.edu
Fax: (719) 389-6282   **Internet:** www.coloradocollege.edu

Institution Description: The Colorado College is a private, independent, nonprofit college. *Enrollment:* 2,044. *Degrees awarded:* Baccalaureate, master's. Member of consortium Associated Colleges of the Midwest.

Accreditation: *Regional:* NCA.

History: Established, chartered, first instruction at postsecondary level 1874; first degree (baccalaureate) awarded 1882. *See* J. Juan Reid, *Colorado College—The First Century (1874–1974)* (Colorado Springs: Colorado College, 1979) for further information.

Institutional Structure: *Governing board:* Board of Trustees. Extrainstitutional representation: 25 trustees, including president of college and 4 alumni. 2 ex officio. All voting. *Composition of institution:* Senior staff 4 men / 6 women. Academic affairs headed by dean of the college. Management/business/finances directed by business manager and treasurer. Total instructional faculty 208. Academic governance body, the faculty, meets an average of 10 times per year.

Calendar: Semesters. Academic year Sept. to May. Freshmen admitted Sept., June. Degrees conferred Jan., Dec., Aug. Formal commencement June. Summer session from June to Aug.

Characteristics of Freshmen: 55% (322 students) submitted SAT scores; 45% (261 students) submitted ACT scores. *25th percentile:* SAT I Verbal 600, SAT I Math 610; ACT Composite 25, ACT English 25, ACT Math 24. *75th percentile:* SAT I Verbal 690, SAT I Math 690; ACT Composite 30, ACT English 31, ACT Math 29.

78% of entering freshmen expected to graduate within 5 years. 25% of freshmen from Colorado. Freshmen from 45 states and 16 foreign countries.

Admission: For fall acceptance, apply no later than mid-Feb. Students are notified of acceptance Apr. 1–15. *Requirements:* Either 16 secondary school units in academic subjects which normally include English, foreign languages, government, history, laboratory science, mathematics; or GED. Most accepted applicants present 16–18 units. *Entrance tests:* College Board SAT or ACT composite. College credit for postsecondary-level work completed in secondary school.

Noncredit developmental courses offered in summer session and regular academic year.

Degree Requirements: *Undergraduate:* 32 units; C- minimum grade average; last 2 terms in residence; 3 units each humanities, natural sciences, social sciences; 18 units outside of major department. For some degrees, comprehensive in field of study, thesis, GRE. *Grading system:* A–C; pass/no pass; excused grade after drop-add deadline.

Distinctive Educational Programs: *For undergraduates:* Work-experience programs. Cooperative program in art with Allegheny and Lake Forest Colleges at Whitney Museum of American Art (NY). Dual-degree programs in engineering with Columbia University (NY), Rensselaer Polytechnic Institute (NY), University of Southern California, Washington University (MO); in forestry with Duke University (NC); in law with Columbia University School of Law (NY); in medical technology and in nursing with Rush University (IL). Study abroad in France, Mexico, West Germany. Individually arranged study abroad with approval of Foreign Study Committee. Off-campus consortium programs: arts of Florence and London, Chinese studies, geology in the Rocky Mountains, India studies, Japan studies, Newberry Library program in the humanities, Oak Ridge science semester, studies in Latin American culture and society, tropical field research, urban education, urban studies, wilderness field station, women in management. Honors programs, individual majors, tutorials. Summer reading program. *Available to all students:* Summer session, which includes interdisciplinary institutes in cooperation with Knox College (IL) and Grinnell College (IA), Hanya Holm school of dance. Flexible meeting places and schedules. Interdepartmental/interdisciplinary programs, including urban planning-environmental studies, fine arts with drama concentration, history-philosophy, history-political science, liberal arts and sciences, medical technology, political economy, philosophy-political science. *Other distinctive programs:* Alumni/parent summer college.

ROTC: Army in cooperation with University of Colorado.

Degrees Conferred: 523 *baccalaureate*; 39 *master's*. Bachelor's degrees awarded in top five disciplines: social sciences 149; biological and biomedical sciences 83; English language and literature/letters 50; visual and performing arts 39; psychology 35.

Fees and Other Expenses: *Full-time tuition per academic year 2004–05:* $30,048. *Room and board per academic year:* $7,620. *Books and supplies:* $870.

Financial Aid: Aid from institutionally generated funds is provided on the basis of financial need. Institution has a Program Participation Agreement with the U.S. Department of Education for eligible students to receive Pell Grants and other federal aid.

Financial aid to full-time, first-time undergraduate students: need-based scholarships/grants $16,975,499, self-help $3,398,496, parent loans $550,568, tuition waivers $187,187, athletic awards $183,587; non-need-based scholarships/grants $3,333,210, self-help $1,576,212, parent loans $3,071,221, tuition waivers $967,353, athletic awards $892,026.

Departments and Teaching Staff: *Total instructional faculty:* 208 (full-time 171, part-time 37; women 68, men 103; members of minority groups 28). Total number with doctorate, first-professional, or other terminal degree: 160.

Enrollment: Total enrollment 2,044. Undergraduate full-time 938 men / 1,056 women, part-time 7m / 10w; graduate full-time 6m / full-time 27.

Characteristics of Student Body: *Ethnic/racial makeup:* number of Black non-Hispanic: 32; American Indian or Alaska Native: 26; Asian or Pacific Islander: 88; Hispanic: 137; White non-Hispanic: 1,587; unknown: 90.

International Students: 51 nonresident aliens enrolled fall 2004. Students from Europe, Asia, Central and South America, Africa, Canada. Programs available to aid students whose native language is not English: Social, cultural. Financial aid specifically designated for international students: Scholarships available annually.

Student Life: On-campus residence halls house 75% of student body. Residence halls for men constitute 10% of such space, for women 15%. 13% of men join and 8% live in fraternities. *Intercollegiate athletics:* men only: baseball, basketball, football, golf, hockey, lacrosse, soccer, swimming, tennis, track, skiing; women only: basketball, tennis, track, volleyball, soccer, swimming, skiing. *Special services:* Medical services. *Student publications, radio:* The Catalyst, a weekly newspaper; The Leviathan, a quarterly literary magazine; The Disparaging Eye, a journal of political, social and scientific thought. Radio station KRCC, an NPR station, broadcasts 24 hours a day. *Surrounding community:* Colorado Springs population 255,000. Denver, 75 miles from campus, is nearest metropolitan area. Served by mass transit bus system; airport 6 miles from campus; passenger rail service 75 miles from campus.

Publications: *The Colorado College Studies* (published irregularly), first published 1890, *The Colorado College Music Press* (irregularly), first published 1955.

Library Collections: 579,370 volumes. 301,000 government documents; 122,800 microforms; 2,190 audiovisual materials; 2,330 current periodicals. Online catalog. Students have access to online information retrieval services and the Internet.

Most important holdings include special collections of fine printed books, Western Americana, Helen Hunt Jackson Papers, Dickens Collection, Edmund van Diest Papers; autographs of British poets.

Buildings and Grounds: Campus area 90 acres.

Chief Executive Officer: Richard F. Celeste, President.

Address admission inquiries to Mark Hatch, Dean of Admissions and Financial Aid.

Colorado School of Mines

1500 Illinois Street
Golden, Colorado 80401-1843
Tel: (303) 273-3000   **E-mail:** admit@mines.edu
Fax: (303) 273-3278   **Internet:** www.mines.edu

Institution Description: Colorado School of Mines is a state institution. *Enrollment:* 3,660. *Degrees awarded:* Baccalaureate, master's, doctorate.

Accreditation: *Regional:* NCA. *Professional:* engineering, English language education

History: Established by Episcopal Church 1869; chartered as state institution, adopted present name, and offered first instruction at postsecondary level 1874; awarded first degree (baccalaureate) 1882.

Institutional Structure: *Governing board:* Board of Trustees of Colorado School of Mines. Extrainstitutional representation: 7 trustees, including 4 alumni; institutional representation: 1 student. 7 voting. *Composition of institution:* Academic affairs headed by vice president. Management/business/finances directed by vice president. Total instructional faculty 299. Academic governance body, the faculty, meets an average of 8 times per year.

Calendar: Semesters. Academic year Aug. to May. Freshmen admitted Aug., Jan., June. Degrees conferred May, June, Aug., Dec. Formal commencements May, Dec. Summer session of one term from late June to mid-Aug.

Characteristics of Freshmen: 58.9% (444 students) submitted SAT scores; 84.6% (638 students) submitted ACT scores. *25th percentile:* SAT Verbal 550, SAT Math 600; ACT Composite 25, ACT English 23, ACT Math 25. *75th percentile:* SAT Verbal 650, SAT Math 690; ACT Composite 29, ACT English 39, ACT Math 31.

15 National Merit Scholars. 85% of applicants admitted. 24% of admitted students enrolled full-time. 65% of entering freshmen expected to graduate within 5 years. 76.6% of freshmen from Colorado. Freshmen from 45 states and 62 foreign countries.

Admission: Rolling admissions plan. For fall acceptance, apply as early as Aug. 1 of senior year of secondary school, but not later than Aug. 10 of year of enrollment. *Requirements:* Freshmen must graduate from secondary school with 16 academic units: 2 algebra, 1 geometry, 1 advanced math (including trigonometry), 4 English, 2 history, 2 social science, 3 laboratory science, and 5 additional academic units. *Entrance tests:* College Board SAT or ACT composite. *For transfer students:* 2.5 minimum GPA; from 4-year accredited institution 110 semester hours maximum transfer credit; from 2-year accredited institution 60 hours. College credit and advanced placement for postsecondary-level work completed in secondary school. Tutoring available.

Degree Requirements: *Undergraduate:* 131–147 semester hours; 2.0 GPA; 4 semesters in residence; 4 physical education courses; prescribed course distribution in major fields. Fulfillment of some degree requirements and exemption from some beginning courses possible by passing College Board CLEP, AP. *Grading system:* A–F; withdraw (carries time limit), no credit.

Distinctive Educational Programs: *For undergraduates:* Cooperative education. Honors programs for Public Affairs in Engineering. Engineering Practices Introductory Course Sequence. International Studies.

ROTC: Army, Air Force.

Degrees Conferred: 544 *baccalaureate* (B), 130 *master's* (M), 44 *doctorate:* engineering and engineering technologies 440 (B), 125 (M); 30 (D); mathematics 69 (B), 7 (M), 1 (D); physical sciences 9 (B), 32 (M), 10 (D); social sciences and history 26 (B), 16 (M), 3 (D).

Fees and Other Expenses: *Full-time tuition per academic year 2004–05:* resident $6,336, nonresident $19,240. *Room and board per academic year:* $6,448. *Required fees:* $746.

Financial Aid: Aid from institutionally generated funds is provided on the basis of academic merit, financial need, athletic ability, other considerations. Institution has a Program Participation Agreement with the U.S. Department of Education for eligible students to receive Pell Grants and other federal aid.

Financial aid to full-time, first-time undergraduate students: need-based scholarships/grants totaling $7,550,000; self-help $560,000; athletic awards $630,000; non-need-based scholarships/grants totaling $2,140,000, self-help $2,700,000; athletic awards $350,000. *Graduate aid:* 24 fellowships and grants totaling $790,000; 151 teaching assistantships totaling $2,200,000; 236 research assistantships totaling $5,100,000.

Departments and Teaching Staff: *Total instructional faculty:* 299 (full-time 193, part-time 106; women 65, men 234; members of minority groups 25). Total number with doctorate, first-professional, or other terminal degree: 215. Student-to-faculty ratio: 15:1. 11 faculty members awarded sabbaticals 2004–05.

Enrollment: Total enrollment 3,660. Undergraduate full-time 2,132 men / 631 women, part-time 37m / 23w; graduate full-time 429m / 160w, part-time 143m / 55w.

Characteristics of Student Body: *Ethnic and racial makeup:* number of Black non-Hispanic: 39; American Indian or Alaska Native: 22; Asian or Pacific Islander: 148; Hispanic: 174; White non-Hispanic: 2,183; unknown: 182.

International Students: 95 nonresident aliens enrolled fall 2004.

Student Life: On-campus residence halls, Greek societies, and housing available for married students. *Intercollegiate athletics:* men only: baseball, basketball, football, lacrosse, wrestling; women only: basketball, volleyball; both sexes: golf, tennis, track, swimming, skiing. *Special regulations:* Cars permitted in designated areas. *Special services:* Medical services. *Student publications:* Hygrade, a literary magazine published each semester; The Oredigger, a weekly newspaper; *The Prospector*, a yearbook. *Surrounding community:* Golden, population 15,000, is located in Denver metropolitan area. Served by mass transit bus system.

Publications: *Colorado School of Mines Quarterly* first published in 1905.

Library Collections: 145,000 volumes. 260,000 government documents; 400,000 microforms; 2,000 current periodical subscriptions. Online catalog. Students have access to online information retrieval services and the Internet. Total 2004–05 budget for materials and operations: $2.7 million.

Most important holdings include Boettcher Collection; map collection; U.S. government documents.

Buildings and Grounds: Campus area 373 acres.

Chief Executive Officer: Dr. John U. Trefny, President.

Address admission inquiries to William Young, Director of Enrollment Management.

Colorado State University

102 Administration Building
Fort Collins, Colorado 80523-0100
Tel: (970) 491-1101   **E-mail:** admissions@colostate.edu
Fax: (970) 491-0501   **Internet:** www.colostate.edu

Institution Description: Colorado State University is a state institution and land-grant college. *Enrollment:* 26,801. *Degrees awarded:* Baccalaureate, first-professional (veterinary medicine), master's, doctorate.

Academic offerings subject to approval by statewide coordinating bodies. Budget subject to approval by state governing boards. Member of the consortium Western Interstate Commission for Higher Education.

Accreditation: *Regional:* NCA. *Professional:* applied science, business, construction education, counseling, counseling psychology, dietetics, engineering, environmental health, forestry, industrial technology, interior design, journalism, landscape architecture, marriage and family therapy, music, occupational therapy, psychology internship, recreation and leisure services, social work, teacher education, veterinary medicine

History: Established as Agricultural College of Colorado 1870; chartered 1877; offered first instruction at postsecondary level 1879; awarded first degree (baccalaureate) 1884; changed name to The Colorado State College of Agriculture and Mechanic Arts 1935, to Colorado Agricultural and Mechanical College 1951; adopted present name 1957. *See* James E. Hansen II, *Democracy's College in the Centennial State - A History of Colorado State University* (Fort Collins: Colorado State University, 1977) for further information.

Institutional Structure: *Governing board:* Colorado State University of one of three schools governed by the State Board of Agriculture. Representation: 9 members appointed by the governor of Colorado. Faculty and students each have one nonvoting representative to the Board. The President is assisted by five vice presidents: Academic, Student Affairs, Administrative Services, Research. 8 colleges house over 100 majors. The faculty is governed by Faculty Council.

Calendar: Semesters. Academic year Aug. to May. Freshmen and transfer students admitted to each session as space permits. Degrees conferred each term, but formal commencement offered only at the end of fall and spring semesters. Three summer sessions are offered: 4 week (mid-May to mid-June), 8 week (mid-June to beginning of August) and 12 week (mid-May to beginning of August).

Characteristics of Freshmen: 11,652 applicants (5,286 men, 6,336 women). 84% of applicants admitted. 42% of admitted students enrolled full-time.

46% (1,870 students) submitted SAT scores; 89% (3,621 students) submitted ACT scores. *25th percentile:* SAT Verbal 500, SAT Math 510; ACT Composite 22, ACT English 21, ACT Math 21. *75th percentile:* SAT Verbal 600, SAT Math 610; ACT Composite 26, ACT English 26, ACT Math 26.

25% of entering freshmen expected to graduate within 5 years. 79% of freshmen from Colorado. Freshmen from 50 states and 83 countries.

Admission: Applications are processed up to 14 months before the requested date of entrance. Admission for any term may close whenever CSU meets its enrollment limit. *Requirements:* freshmen applicants must have completed 18 high school units of which 15 are academic during the grades 9–12. Of the 15 academic units, 12 must include 4 units of English, 5 units of social science and natural science with a minimum of 2 from each, and 3 units of math, including 1 unit of algebra and 1 of geometry. Individual colleges may have additional requirements. *Entrance tests:* College Board SAT or ACT. TOEFL for foreign students. *For transfer students:* Students with 9 or fewer credits must include the same information as high school applicants. Students with 9 to 28 credits must include high school transcripts. Student with more than 28 semester credits should submit transcripts of all college work attempted.

Degree Requirements: *Undergraduate:* 128 credit hours; 2.0 GPA; 32 semester hours in residence; 2 credits in physical education or exercise concepts;

distribution, course, curriculum requirements. Additional requirements for some programs.

Fulfillment of some degree requirements and exemption from some beginning courses possible by passing departmental examinations, College Board CLEP, AP. *Grading system:* A–F; pass-fail; withdraw (carries time limit).

Distinctive Educational Programs: Work-experience programs. Weekend and evening classes. Special facilities for using telecommunications in the classroom. Facilities and programs for independent research, including honors programs, individual majors, tutorials. Study abroad and exchange programs in United Kingdom Czech Republic, Mexico, Hungary, Japan, New Zealand, a consortia of 10 Australian universities, and the International Student Exchange Program (worldwide). Other study abroad opportunities area available through a variety of U.S. sponsoring universities and private nonprofit organizations.

ROTC: Army, 9 commissions awarded 2004; Air Force; 35 commissions awarded 2004.

Degrees Conferred: 3,964 *baccalaureate;* 1,011 *master's;* 160 *doctorate;* 126 *first-professional:* veterinary medicine. Bachelor's degrees awarded in top five disciplines: business, management, marketing, and related support services 672; social sciences 295; family and consumer sciences/human sciences 278; agriculture, agriculture operations, and related sciences 273; biological and biomedical sciences 271.

Fees and Other Expenses: *Full-time tuition per academic year 2004–05:* undergraduate resident $3,790, out-of-state student $14,377. Contact the university for current graduate study fees and expenses. *Room and board per academic year:* $6,016. *Books and supplies:* $900.

Financial Aid: Aid from institutionally generated funds is provided on the basis of academic merit, financial need, athletic ability, other criteria. Institution has a Program Participation Agreement with the U.S. Department of Education for eligible students to receive Pell Grants and other federal aid.

Financial aid to full-time, first-time undergraduate students: need-based scholarships/grants totaling $24,293,669, self-help $38,898,613, parent loans $13,650,070, athletic awards $1,063,814; non-need-based scholarships/grants totaling $12,800,675, self-help $13,331,292, parent loans $11,017,847, athletic awards $2,457,259. *Graduate aid:* 1,806 students received federal and state-funded loans totaling $22,609,213; 137 obtained work-study jobs totaling $254,923; 501 teaching assistantships and 742 research assistantships awarded.

Departments and Teaching Staff: *Professors* 421, *associate professors* 254, *assistant professors* 182, *part-time faculty* 39. *Total instructional faculty:* 896 (full-time 857, part-time 39; c women 229, men 667; members of minority groups 98). Total faculty with doctorate, first-professional, or other terminal degree: 888. Student-to-faculty ratio: 18:1. *Faculty development:* 36 faculty members awarded sabbaticals 2004.

Enrollment: Total enrollment 26,201. Undergraduate full-time 9,407 men / 9,887 women, part-time 1,199m / 1,236w; graduate full-time 873m / 1,083 w, part-time 1,310m / 1,278w; first-professional full-time 17m / 421w.

Characteristics of Student Body: *Ethnic and racial makeup:* number of Black non-Hispanic: 312; American Indian or Alaska Native: 77; Asian or Pacific Islander: 416; Hispanic: 1,059; White non-Hispanic: 17,547; unknown: 414. *Age distribution:* under 18: 220; 18–19: 7,453; 20–21: 7,468; 22–24: 3,972; 25–29: 1,262; 30–34: 337; 35–39: 128; 40–49: 150; 50 and over: 60; not reported: 10.

International Students: 868 nonresident aliens enrolled fall 2004. 96 students from Europe, 617 Asia, 82 Central and South America; 40 Africa, 21 Canada, 8 Australia, other 4. Programs available to aid students whose native language is not English: Social, culture. Intensive English course available. No financial aid specifically designated for international students.

Student Life: Freshmen under 21 are required to live on campus. Coeducational residence halls house these students. Graduate and married student housing is also available. There are 20 national fraternities and 15 national sororities on campus. *Intercollegiate athletics:* men only: football, basketball, cross-country, golf, track; women only: basketball, cross-country, golf, softball, swimming/diving tennis, track and volleyball. *Special regulations:* On-campus students are permitted to have cars. *Special services:* Comprehensive health care facility on campus. *Student publications, radio:* The Rocky Mountain Collegian, a student newspaper published 5 days a week; Silver Spruce, a yearbook. Radio station KCSU. *Surrounding community:* Fort Collins population 100,000. Denver, 65 miles south of the campus, is the largest nearby metropolitan area.

Library Collections: 2,920,205 volumes including bound books, serial backfiles, electronic documents, and government documents not in separate collections. Online catalog. Current serial subscriptions: 16,505 paper, 11,937 via electronic access. 6,918 recordings; 7,559 compact discs. 431 computer work stations. Students have access to the Internet at no charge.

Most important holdings include collection on Germans from Russia (manuscripts, oral histories, books); Vietnam War Literature; Western novels; Imaginary Wars; Colorado Agriculture Archives; International Poster Collection.

Buildings and Grounds: The main campus covers 700 acres.

Chief Executive Officer: Dr. Larry E. Penley, President.

Address admission inquiries to Mary R. Ontiveros, Director of Admissions.

College of Agricultural Sciences

Degree Programs Offered: *Baccalaureate* in agricultural business, agricultural economics, agronomy, animal science, bioagricultural science, equine science, horticulture, landscape architecture, landscape horticulture, soil and crop sciences. *Master's* and *doctorate* in various fields.

College of Applied Human Sciences

Degree Programs Offered: *Baccalaureate* in human development and family studies, industrial sciences and technology education, construction management, vocational education, occupational therapy, physical education, textiles and clothing; *master's* and *doctorate* in various fields. *Teacher certification* also available in art, music and physical education for kindergarten, elementary and secondary levels; in English, French, German, Spanish, mathematics, biology, chemistry, geology, physics, social studies and speech for the secondary level; in business and office education, distributive education, technical education, trade and industrial education, vocational education and vocational home economics education for vocational secondary levels.

College of Liberal Arts

Degree Programs Offered: *Baccalaureate* in anthropology, art, economics, English, French, German, history, liberal arts, music, music therapy, performing arts, philosophy, political science, social sciences, sociology, Spanish, speech communication, technical journalism. *Master's* and *doctorate* in various fields.

College of Business

Degree Programs Offered: *Baccalaureate* in accounting, entrepreneurship, finance-real estate, information systems, management, marketing; *master's* in accounting, business administration, management, computer information systems, marketing.

Admission: Very selective for new freshmen and transfers. Contact the Office of Admissions for information.

College of Engineering

Degree Programs Offered: *Baccalaureate* in bioresource and agricultural engineering, chemical, civil, electrical, environmental engineering, mechanical engineering, engineering science; *master's* and *doctorate* in various fields.

College of Natural Resources

Degree Programs Offered: *Baccalaureate* in fishery biology, forestry, geology, landscape architecture, natural resources management, natural resource recreation and tourism, rangeland ecology, watershed science, wildlife biology. *Master's* and *doctorate* in various fields.

College of Natural Sciences

Degree Programs Offered: *Baccalaureate, master's,* and *doctorate* in biochemistry, biological science, botany, chemistry, computer science, mathematics, physical science, physics, psychology, statistics, zoology.

College of Veterinary Medicine and Biomedical Sciences

Degree Programs Offered: *Baccalaureate* in environmental health, microbiology; *first-professional* in veterinary medicine; *master's* and *doctorate* in various fields.

Admission: Consult advisers in Preveterinary Veterinary Advising Office for detailed admission requirements to the professional veterinary medicine program.

Degree Requirements: *For first-professional degree:* Prescribed 4-year curriculum, 2.0 GPA, complete program in residence.

Fees and Other Expenses: Contact the college for current tuition and fees.

Colorado State University - Pueblo

2200 Bonforte Boulevard
Pueblo, Colorado 81001-4901
Tel: (719) 549-2100   **E-mail:** info@colstate-pueblo.edu
Fax: (719) 549-2419   **Internet:** www.colstate-pueblo.edu

Institution Description: Colorado State University - Pueblo, formerly named the University of Southern Colorado, is a state institution. *Enrollment:* 5,835. *Degrees awarded:* Baccalaureate, master's.

Academic offerings subject to approval by statewide coordinating bodies. Budget subject to approval by state governing board, State Board of Agriculture. Member of Consortium of State Colleges in Colorado.

Accreditation: *Regional:* NCA. *Professional:* business, engineering, nursing, social work

History: Established as the Southern Colorado Junior College and offered first instruction at postsecondary level 1933; changed name to Pueblo Junior College (PJC) 1937. In 1951, PJC became the first accredited junior college in Colorado. PJC became Southern Colorado State College in 1963. In 1975, the Colorado General Assembly granted the institution university status, and the name University of Southern Colorado was adopted. The current name was adopted in 2003.

Institutional Structure: *Governing board:* State Board of Agriculture. Representation: 9 members (appointed by governor of Colorado), 3 full-time faculty members, 3 students. 9 voting. *Composition of institution:* Academic affairs headed by vice president for academic affairs. Management/business/finances directed by vice president for business and finance. Full-time instructional faculty 168. Academic governance body, Faculty Senate, meets an average of 8 times per year.

Calendar: Semesters. Academic year Aug. to May. Freshmen admitted Aug., Jan., June. Degrees conferred Aug., Dec., May. Formal commencement May, Dec. Multiple summer sessions from May through Aug.

Characteristics of Freshmen: 1,850 applicants (men 651, women 999). 93% of applicants admitted. 38.6% of admitted students enrolled full-time.

13% (92 students) submitted SAT scores; 86% (607 students) submitted ACT scores. *25th percentile:* SAT Verbal 420, SAT Math 420; ACT Composite 17, ACT English 16, ACT Math 16. *75th percentile:* SAT Verbal 520, SAT Math 560; ACT Composite 21, ACT English 22, ACT Math 21.

Admission: Rolling admissions plan. For fall acceptance, apply as early as 1 year prior to enrollment, but not later than July 21 of year of enrollment. Early acceptance available. *Requirements:* First time students whose high school grade point averages and SAT or ACT composite scores place them among the upper two-thirds of graduating seniors are eligible for admission. For foreign students TOEFL or other standardized test of English. *For transfer students:* 2.0 minimum GPA; from 4-year accredited institution 96 hours maximum transfer credit; from 2-year accredited institution 64 hours. College credit for postsecondary-level work completed in secondary school and for extrainstitutional learning on basis of ACE *2006 Guide to the Evaluation of Educational Experiences in the Armed Services.* Tutoring available. Noncredit remedial courses offered in summer session and regular academic year.

Degree Requirements: *For all associate degrees:* 62 credit hours; 2 semesters in residence. *For all baccalaureate degrees:* 128 credit hours; 2 semesters or 30 hours in residence. *For all undergraduate degrees:* 2.0 GPA; general education requirements; demonstrated proficiency in mathematics.

Fulfillment of some degree requirements and exemption from some beginning courses possible by passing departmental examinations, College Board CLEP, AP. *Grading system:* A–F; pass-fail; withdraw (deadline after which pass-fail is appended to withdraw).

Distinctive Educational Programs: Programs unique include Industrial Engineering, Auto Parts Service Management, and Facilities Management (BS degrees). Students are able to sit for the following certification programs attached to baccalaureate degree programs: Victimology (sociology); American Humanics (social work); Athletic Training (exercise science and health promotion); Wilderness Education Association Outdoor Leader (recreation); American Chemical Society (Chemistry). Work-experience programs, including cooperative education, internships. Off-campus center (at Peterson Air Force Base 45 miles away from main institution). Courses also offered at the United States Air Force Academy, 55 miles away, and at Fort Carson in Colorado Springs. Special facilities for using telecommunications in the classroom. Interdepartmental program in women's studies. Independent study.

Degrees Conferred: 796 *baccalaureate;* 32 *master's.* Bachelor's degrees awarded in top five disciplines: social sciences 179; business, management, marketing, and related support services 113; psychology 58; liberal arts and sciences, general studies and humanities 51; communication, journalism, and related programs 50.

Fees and Other Expenses: *Full-time tuition per academic year 2004–05:* undergraduate and graduate resident $3,190; out-of-state student $9,730. *Room and board per academic year:* $5,912. *Other expenses:* $3,312.

Financial Aid: Aid from institutionally generated funds is provided on the basis of academic merit, financial need, athletic ability. Institution has a Program Participation Agreement with the U.S. Department of Education for eligible students to receive Pell Grants and other federal aid.

Financial aid to full-time, first-time undergraduate students: 37% received federal grants averaging $2,615; 38% state/local grants averaging $1,742; 31% institutional grants averaging $1,446; 48% loans averaging $1,932.

Departments and Teaching Staff: Art/music *professors* 3, *associate professors* 5, *assistant professors* 1, *instructors* 4; biology 3, 4, 2, 1; business 3, 11, 5, 0; chemistry 2, 4, 3, 0; computer and information systems 1, 1, 5, 1; education 5, 1, 1, 0; engineering 1, 3, 2, 0; English 3, 3, 4, 4; foreign language 1, 2, 1, 0; mathematics 3, 5, 3, 0; mass communications 2, 3, 2, 0; nursing 2, 1, 2, 1; philosophy 2, 0, 1, 0; physics 1, 1, 0, 0; psychology 6, 3, 1, 1; recreation 1, 0, 1, 2; social sciences 6, 4, r, 0; social work 0, 4, 2, 0; technology 1, 6, 3, 0.

Total instructional faculty: 165 full-time, 99 part-time. Student-to-faculty ratio: 17:1. Degrees held by full-time faculty: doctorate 69.7%, master's 26.1%, baccalaureate 4.2%.

Enrollment: Total enrollment 5,835 (40.1% men, 59.9% women).

Characteristics of Student Body: *Ethnic/racial makeup:* Black non-Hispanic: 4.9%; American Indian or Alaska Native: 1.7%; Asian or Pacific Islander: 2%; Hispanic: 24.9%; White non-Hispanic 58.1%.

International Students: 119 nonresident aliens enrolled fall 2004. English as a Second Language Program available. Financial aid specifically designated for international students: Undergraduate scholarships available.

Student Life: On-campus residence halls house 10% of student body. *Intercollegiate athletics:* men only: baseball, basketball, tennis, track, wrestling; women only: basketball, softball, tennis, track, volleyball. *Special regulations:* Cars permitted without restrictions. *Special services:* Learning Resources Center, medical services. *Student publications, radio:* A weekly newspaper. Radio and TV stations KTSC each broadcast 60 hours per week; television programming includes preschool education. *Surrounding community:* Pueblo population 120,000. Colorado Springs; 40 miles from campus, is nearest metropolitan area. Served by mass transit bus system; airport 7 miles from campus.

Library Collections: 180,000 volumes including bound books, serial backfiles, electronic documents, and government documents not in separate collections. Online catalog. Current serial subscriptions: 1,330. 10,000 microform units. 16,800 video and audiovisual materials. Students have access to the Internet at no charge.

Most important holdings include O'Brien Western History Collection; Hopkins Black Cultural Collection.

Buildings and Grounds: Campus area 225 acres.

Chief Executive Officer: Dr. Ronald L. Applebaum, President.

Address admission inquiries to Joe Marshall, Director of Admissions/Records.

Colorado Technical University

4435 North Chestnut Street
Colorado Springs, Colorado 80907-3812

Tel: (719) 598-0200   **E-mail:** admission@colotechu.edu
Fax: (719) 598-3740   **Internet:** www.colotechu.edu

Institution Description: Colorado Technical University is a private, coeducational, commuter college. *Enrollment:* 1,904. *Degrees awarded:* Associate, baccalaureate, master's, doctorate.

Academic offerings subject to approval by statewide coordinating bodies.

Accreditation: *Regional:* NCA. *Professional:* engineering

History: Established and incorporated as Colorado Electronic Training Center and offered first instruction at postsecondary level 1965; changed name to Colorado Electronic Technical College 1966; awarded first degree (associate) and changed name to Colorado Technical College 1970; began baccalaureate programs 1972; began master's programs 1989; began doctoral programs and adopted present name 1995.

Institutional Structure: *Governing board:* Colorado Technical University Governing Board of Directors. Extrainstitutional representation: 10 directors; *Composition of institution:* Administrators: president, vice president for academic affairs, vice president of finance/CFO, director of human resources, 3 deans, 2 chancellors. Full-time instructional faculty 29 men / 5 women. Academic governance body, the faculty, meets an 4 times per year.

Calendar: Quarters. Academic year Oct. to Sept. Freshmen admitted Oct., Feb., Apr., July. Degrees conferred Sept., Dec., Mar., June. Summer term from July to Sept.

Characteristics of Freshmen: Average secondary school rank of freshmen men 85th percentile, women 90th percentile, class 87th percentile.

87% of applicants accepted.

60% of accepted applicants enrolled. 60% of entering freshmen expected to graduate within 5 years. 63% of freshmen from Colorado. Freshmen from 12 states and 4 foreign countries.

Admission: Rolling admissions plan. For fall acceptance, apply as early as one year prior to enrollment, but not later than 2 weeks before beginning of quarter. *Requirements:* Either graduation from accredited secondary school or GED. *For transfer students:* 2.0 GPA; maximum transfer credit limited only by residence requirement.

College credit and advanced placement for postsecondary-level work completed in secondary school. College credit for extrainstitutional learning on basis of ACE *2006 Guide to the Evaluation of Educational Experiences in the Armed Services* and portfolio assessment. Tutoring available. Noncredit remedial courses offered in summer session and regular academic year.

Degree Requirements: *For all associate degrees:* electronics technology 95 quarter hours; 30 hours in residence. *For baccalaureate degrees:* 178 to 199 quarter hours depending on program; 60 hours in residence. *For master's degrees:* 48 quarter hours; 40 hours residence; 3.0 GPA, distribution requirements. *For doctoral programs:* 32 hours of coursework; 32 hours research/dissertation.

Fulfillment of some degree requirements and exemption from some beginning courses possible by passing standard examinations, College Board CLEP, AP. *Grading system:* A–F; withdraw; incomplete (carries time limit).

Distinctive Educational Programs: Flexible meeting places and schedules. Evening and weekend classes.

ROTC: Army offered in cooperation with University of Colorado at Colorado Springs.

Degrees Conferred: 37 *associate;* 240 *baccalaureate;* 276 *master's;* 10 *doctorate.* Bachelor's degrees awarded in top four disciplines: computer and information sciences and support services 112; business, management, marketing, and related support services 61; engineering 51; engineering technologies/technicians 16.

Fees and Other Expenses: *Full-time tuition per academic year 2004–05:* $9,378. *Room and board per academic year:* $7,449. *Books and supplies:* $1,500. *Other expenses:* $3,378.

Financial Aid: Aid from institutionally generated funds is provided on the basis of academic merit, financial need. Institution has a Program Participation Agreement with the U.S. Department of Education for eligible students to receive Pell Grants and other federal aid.

Financial aid to full-time, first-time undergraduate students: 23% received federal grants; 17% state/local grants; 20% institutional grants; 47% loans averaging $5,163.

Departments and Teaching Staff: Engineering technology *professors* 7, *associate professors* 6, *part-time faculty* 12; computer science 8, 6; 20; management 3, 4, 26. *Total instructional faculty:* 92. Degrees held by full-time faculty: Doctorate 47%, master's 47%. 53% hold terminal degrees.

Enrollment: Total enrollment 1,904. Undergraduate 1,206 (70.1% men, 29.9% women).

Characteristics of Student Body: *Ethnic/racial makeup:* Black non-Hispanic: 10.8%; American Indian or Alaska Native: 1.1%; Asian or Pacific Islander: 3.6%; Hispanic: 5.8%; White non-Hispanic: 69.2%.

International Students: 33 nonresident aliens enrolled fall 2003. No programs available to aid students whose native language is not English. No financial aid specifically designated for international students.

Student Life: No on-campus housing. *Special regulations:* Cars permitted without restrictions. *Special services:* Learning Resources Center. *Surrounding community:* Colorado Springs population 400,000. Denver; 50 miles from campus, is nearest metropolitan area. Served by mass transit bus system; airport 12 miles from campus.

Library Collections: 33,000 volumes. 15,000 microforms; 400 audiovisual materials; 560 current periodical subscriptions. Students have access to online information retrieval services and the Internet.

Most important holdings include technical videocassette library; CD-ROM technical periodical indexes; logistics collection.

Buildings and Grounds: Campus area 3 acres.

Chief Executive Officer: David D. O'Donnell, President.

Address admission inquiries Ron Begora, Admissions Director.

Denver Seminary

3401 South University Boulevard
Englewood, Colorado 80110
Tel: (303) 761-2482   **E-mail:** admissions@densem.edu
Fax: (303) 761-8060   **Internet:** www.densem.edu

Institution Description: Denver Seminary, formerly named Denver Conservative Baptist Seminary, is a private institution affiliated with the Conservative Baptists. *Enrollment:* 706. *Degrees awarded:* First-professional (master of divinity), master's, doctorate. Certificates and diplomas also awarded.

Accreditation: *Regional:* NCA. *Professional:* counseling, theology

History: Established, chartered, incorporated as Conservative Baptists Theological Seminary, and offered first instruction at postsecondary level 1950; awarded first degree (first-professional) 1952; became Denver Conservative Baptist Seminary 1982; adopted present name 1998..

Institutional Structure: *Governing board:* Board of Trustees. Extrainstitutional representation: 48 trustees, including 11 alumni. All voting. *Composition of institution:* Administrators 5 men / 1 women. Academic affairs headed by academic dean. Management/business/finances directed by vice president for business affairs. Full-time instructional faculty 14. Academic governance body, the faculty, meets an average of 12–15 times per year.

Calendar: Semesters. Academic year Sept. to May. Entering students admitted Sept., Jan., June. Degrees conferred and formal commencement June. Summer session of 2 terms from June to Aug.

Admission: Rolling admissions plan. Apply no later than 3 weeks before registration. *Requirements:* Baccalaureate degree from a college or university in a preseminary program which must include 5–20 quarter hours English, 15–20 in a foreign language, 9 history, 9 philosophy, 9 social sciences, 6–9 Bible or religion, 6–9 natural sciences, 4 psychology. Provisional acceptance possible for students from nonaccredited institutions. Major in bible, history, philosophy, psychology or speech recommended. Minimum GPA 2.5. *Entrance tests:* GRE. For foreign students TOEFL. *For transfer students:* 2.5 minimum GPA; for first-professional degree 60 hours maximum transfer credit; for master's 30 hours. Noncredit remedial courses offered during regular academic year.

Degree Requirements: *For first-professional degree:* 92 semester hours; for master's degree 61 semester hours; exit competency examination in Greek. *For first-professional and master's degrees:* 2.0 on 4.0 scale; 30 credits in residence; chapel attendance 1 day per week; core curriculum; field education; exit competency examinations in Bible, English; doctrinal statement and oral examination. *Grading system:* A–F; withdraw (carries time limit).

Distinctive Educational Programs: Work-experience programs, including internships, field ministry. Special facilities for using telecommunications in the classroom. Honors programs. Study abroad in Israel at the Institute of Holy Land Studies. Independent study and extension courses through the Institute of Theological Studies. Off-campus study possible at Center for Judaic Studies, University of Denver. Extensive training and mentoring required for all students. *Other distinctive programs:* One-year diploma programs in theology, religious education. Summer master's degree program for staff leaders working with Conservative Baptist Home Mission Society's Campus Ambassador program.

Degrees Conferred: 26 *master's:* Bible/Biblical studies 5; pastoral counseling and specialized ministries 5; religious education 1; theology and religious vocations 9; youth ministry 6. *doctorate* 3; *first-professional:* master of divinity 36.

Fees and Other Expenses: *Full-time tuition per academic year:* $10,050.

Financial Aid: Aid from institutionally generated funds is awarded on the basis of financial need. Institution has a Program Participation Agreement with the U.S. Department of Education for eligible students to receive Pell Grants and other federal aid.

Departments and Teaching Staff: *Total instructional faculty:* 45. *Total tenured faculty:* 14.

Enrollment: Total enrollment 706 (men 63.7%, women 36.3%).

Characteristics of Student Body: *Ethnic/racial makeup:* Black non-Hispanic: 3.3%; American Indian or Alaska Native: .3%; Asian or Pacific Islander: 3.4%; Hispanic: 1.7%; White non-Hispanic: 83.1%; unknown: 2.5%.

International Students: 40 nonresident aliens enrolled fall 2003. Students from Europe, Asia, Central and South America, Africa, Canada, Australia, New Zealand. Social and Cultural programs available to aid students whose native language is not English. No financial aid specifically designated for international students.

Student Life: On-campus apartments house 35% of student body. 80% of married students request institutional housing; 76% are so housed. *Special regulations:* Cars with registration stickers permitted in designated parking areas. Students are asked to exercise Christian discretion in their dress. *Special ser-*

vices: Learning Resources Center. *Surrounding community:* Denver area population over 1,000,000. Served by mass transit bus system; airport 10 miles from campus; passenger rail service 6 miles from campus.

Library Collections: 165,000 volumes. 525 serial subscriptions. 6 computer work stations. Students have access to the Internet at no charge.

Buildings and Grounds: Campus area 12 acres.

Chief Executive Officer: Dr. G. Craig Williford, President.

Address admission inquiries to Robert Fomer, Vice President for Enrollment Management.

Fort Lewis College

1000 Rim Drive
Durango, Colorado 81301-3999
Tel: (970) 247-7184   **E-mail:** admission@fortlewis.edu
Fax: (970) 247-7179   **Internet:** www.fortlewis.edu

Institution Description: Fort Lewis College is a state institution. *Enrollment:* 4,190. *Degrees awarded:* Associate, baccalaureate. Academic offerings subject to approval by statewide coordinating bodies. Budget subject to approval by state governing boards.

Accreditation: *Regional:* NCA. *Professional:* business, music, teacher education

History: Established as Fort Lewis School and chartered 1911; offered first instruction at postsecondary level 1927; changed name to Fort Lewis A&M College 1948; awarded first degree (associate) 1952; adopted present name 1964. *See* Robert W. Delaney, *Blue Coats, Red Skins and Black Gowns* (Durango: Durango Herald, 1977) for further information.

Institutional Structure: *Governing board:* The State Board of Agriculture. Representation: 9 members (appointed by governor of Colorado); 3 full-time instructional faculty members; 1 student. 9 voting. *Composition of institution:* Administrators 25 men / 6 women. Academic affairs headed by vice president for academic affairs. Management/business/finances directed by director of budget and planning; business manager. Full-time instructional faculty 178. Academic governance body, the faculty, meets an average of 9 times per year.

Calendar: Trimesters. Academic year early Sept. to early May. Freshmen admitted Sept., Jan., Apr., June, July. Degrees conferred Apr., Aug. Formal commencement Apr. Summer session of 3 terms from late Apr. to early Aug.

Characteristics of Freshmen: 30% (298 students) submitted SAT scores; 89% (877 students) submitted ACT scores. *25th percentile:* SAT Verbal 470, SAT Math 450; ACT Composite 18, ACT English 17, ACT Math 17. *75th percentile:* SAT Verbal 570, SAT Math 560; ACT Composite 23, ACT English 23, ACT Math 23.

20% of entering freshmen expected to graduate within 5 years. 68% of freshmen from Colorado. Freshmen from 44 states and 11 foreign countries.

Admission: Rolling admissions plan. For fall acceptance, apply by Aug. 1. Early acceptance available. Students must meet 2 of the following 3 criteria: 2.5 GPA overall (on a 4.0 scale); ACT 19 or SAT 810; top two-thirds of graduating class. *Requirements:* Either graduation from secondary school with 15 units which must include 10 from among English, foreign languages, mathematics, science, social studies; or GED. *Entrance tests:* College Board SAT or ACT composite.

College credit and advanced placement for postsecondary-level work completed in secondary school. College credit for extrainstitutional learning on basis of ACE 2006 *Guide to the Evaluation of Educational Experiences in the Armed Services.* Tutoring available.

Degree Requirements: *For all associate degrees:* 64 credit hours. *For all baccalaureate degrees:* 120 credit hours. *For all undergraduate degrees:* 2.0 GPA; last 28 hours in residence; 2 physical activity courses; distribution requirements. Fulfillment of some degree requirements and exemption from some beginning courses possible by passing College Board CLEP, APP, other standardized tests.

Grading system: A–F; pass-fail; withdraw; incomplete (carries time limit).

Distinctive Educational Programs: Work-experience programs, including internships, practicums. Evening classes. Cooperative programs in agriculture, engineering, and forestry with Colorado State University. Interdisciplinary programs in humanities, physical science, Southwest studies. Facilities for independent research, including honors programs, individual majors. Institutionally sponsored study abroad in Japan and Mexico. Summer travel-study programs. *Other distinctive programs:* Continuing education program.

Degrees Conferred: 684 *baccalaureate.* Bachelor's degrees awarded in top five disciplines: business, management, marketing, and related support services133; social sciences 92; liberal arts and sciences, general studies and humanities 72; multi/interdisciplinary studies 65; psychology 62.

Fees and Other Expenses: *Full-time tuition per academic year 2004–05:* resident $2,270, nonresident $11,862. *Room and board per academic year:* $5,894. *Books and supplies:* $850.

Financial Aid: Aid from institutionally generated funds is provided on the basis of academic merit, financial need, athletic ability, other criteria. Institution has a Program Participation Agreement with the U.S. Department of Education for eligible students to receive Pell Grants and other federal aid.

Financial aid to full-time, first-time undergraduate students: need-based scholarships/grants totaling $6,435,143, self-help $9,381,790, parent loans $987,385, tuition waivers $753,000, athletic awards $11,373; non-need-based scholarships/grants totaling $9,494,453, self-help $4,356,402, parent loans $595,861, tuition waivers $8,102,011, athletic awards $237,633.

Departments and Teaching Staff: *Total instructional faculty:* 242 (full-time 178, part-time 64; women 119, men 123; members of minority groups 24). Total number with doctorate, first-professional, or other terminal degree: 138. *Faculty development:* $3,457,221 total grants for research. 6 faculty members awarded sabbaticals in 2004–05.

Enrollment: Total enrollment 4,190. Undergraduate full-time 1,977 men / 1,838 women; part-time 199m / 176w. *Transfer students:* 279.

Characteristics of Student Body: *Ethnic/racial makeup:* Black non-Hispanic: 42; American Indian or Alaska Native: 730; Asian or Pacific Islander: 36; Hispanic: 234; White non-Hispanic: 2,858; unknown: 226. *Age distribution:* number under 18: 60; 18–19: 1,454; 20–21: 1,203; 22–24: 870; 25–29: 340; 30–34: 131; 35–39: 61; 40–49: 70; 50–64: 27; 65 and over: 1.

International Students: 64 nonresident aliens enrolled fall 2004. 29 students from Europe, 31 Asia, 2 Central and South America, 1 Africa. No programs available to aid students whose native language is not English. No financial aid specifically designated for international students.

Student Life: On-campus residence halls house 37% of student body. Residence halls for men constitute 29% of such space, for women 26%, for both sexes 45%. 10% of married students request institutional housing; 1% are so housed. *Intercollegiate athletics:* men only: basketball, cross-country, football, golf, tennis, wrestling; women only: basketball, cross-country, softball, tennis, volleyball. *Special regulations:* Cars permitted without restrictions. Quiet hours 7pm to 6am Sun.–Thurs. *Special services:* Learning Resources Center, medical services. *Student publications, radio: Images,* an annual literary magazine; *Independent,* a newspaper published twice weekly. Radio station KDUR broadcasts 168 hours per week. *Surrounding community:* Durango 13,000. Albuquerque, New Mexico, 215 miles from campus, is nearest metropolitan area. Served by airport 14 miles from campus.

Library Collections: 182,000 volumes. Online catalog. Current serial subscriptions: 580 paper, 345,000 microform. 4,825 audiovisual materials. Students have access to online information retrieval services and the Internet.

Most important special holdings include the Center for Southwest Studies, a collection of rare manuscripts, documents, maps, photographs, as well as artifacts of the Southwest and the American Indian and 7,000 volumes of secondary works.

Buildings and Grounds: Campus area 300 acres.

Chief Executive Officer: Dr. Brad Bartel, President.

Address admission inquiries to Gretchen Foster, Admissions Director.

Iliff School of Theology

2201 South University Boulevard
Denver, Colorado 80210
Tel: (303) 744-1287   **E-mail:** admissions@iliff.edu
Fax: (303) 777-3387   **Internet:** www.iliff.edu

Institution Description: The Iliff School of Theology is a private institution affiliated with the United Methodist Church. *Enrollment:* 346. *Degrees awarded:* First-professional (master of divinity), master's, doctorate.

Accreditation: *Regional:* NCA. *Professional:* theology

History: Established 1892; offered first instruction at postsecondary level and awarded first degree (first-professional) 1893; chartered 1903.

Institutional Structure: *Governing board:* Board of Trustees of The Iliff School of Theology. Extrainstitutional representation: 41 trustees, including 2 church officials; institutional representation: president of the college; 11 alumni. All voting. *Composition of institution:* Administrators 3men / 1 woman. Academic affairs headed by dean. Management/business/finances directed by chief fiscal officer. Full-time instructional faculty 23. Academic governance body, Faculty Council, meets an average of 8 times per year.

Calendar: Quarters. Academic year Sept. to May. Entering students admitted Sept., Jan., Mar., June, July, Aug. Degrees conferred May, Aug. Formal commencement May. Summer session of 4 terms from June to Aug.

Admission: Rolling admissions plan. For fall acceptance, apply as early as one year, but not later than 6 weeks prior to enrollment. *Requirements:* Baccalaureate degree from accredited institution. Minimum GPA: 2.5 for M.Div. and MAR degrees; 3.0 for MA. Additional requirements for doctoral programs. *Entrance tests:* For international students TOEFL. *For transfer students:* 2.5 minimum GPA; maximum transfer credit limited only by residence requirement.

Degree Requirements: *For first-professional degrees:* 120 quarter hours; supervised, in-service career ministry field experience; divisional requirements to be met through coursework. *For master's degrees:* 80 hours. *For first-professional and master's degrees:* 2.0 GPA; 40 hours in residence; participation in personal and professional guidance and counseling programs; project, thesis, or field experience. *Grading system:* A–F, pass-fail; withdraw (carries time limit); incomplete (carries time limit).

Distinctive Educational Programs: *For first-professional students:* Cooperative program in divinity/religion and social work with University of Denver. Work experience programs, including internships and field experience. Evening classes. Cross-registration with University of Denver and Denver Seminary. A new D.Min. program was added in winter 2000. *Other distinctive programs:* Justice and Peace Studies; Urban Ministry Studies; Rural Ministry Studies; Anglican Studies Program. Joint doctoral program in religious and theological studies with University of Denver.

Degrees Conferred: 16 *master's:* theology; 11 *doctorate:* theology; 25 *first-professional:* master of divinity.

Fees and Other Expenses: *Full-time tuition per academic year:* $12,000.

Financial Aid: Aid from institutionally generated funds is awarded on basis of academic merit, financial need. Institution has a Program Participation Agreement with the U.S. Department of Education for eligible students to receive Pell Grants and other federal aid.

Departments and Teaching Staff: *Professors* 14, *associate professors* 4, *assistant professors* 6, *part-time faculty* 34. *Total instructional faculty:* 58. Total tenured faculty: 24. Student-to-faculty ratio: 11:1. Degrees held by full-time faculty: Doctorate 100%.

Enrollment: Total enrollment 346 (men 41.3%, women 58.7%).

Characteristics of Student Body: *Ethnic/racial makeup:* Black non-Hispanic: 6.4%; American Indian or Alaska Native: .6%; Asian or Pacific Islander: 1.7%; Hispanic: 2.6%; White non-Hispanic: 82.4%.

International Students: 22 nonresident aliens enrolled fall 2003. Students from Asia, Central and South America, Africa. English as a Second Language Program. Financial aid specifically designated for international students: variable number of scholarships available annually.

Student Life: On-campus apartments house 25% of student body. Housing available for married students. *Special regulations:* Cars permitted without restrictions. *Student publication:* Biweekly newspaper. *Surrounding community:* Denver area population over 1 million. Served by mass transit bus system; airport 30 miles from campus; passenger rail service 9 miles from campus.

Library Collections: 200,000 volumes including bound books, serial backfiles, electronic documents, and government documents not in separate collections. Online catalog. Current serial subscriptions: 850 paper, 5 microform. 2,415 recordings; 116 CD-ROMs. Computer work stations available. Students have access to the Internet at no charge.

Most important holdings include the Van Pelt Collection of hymnals; archives of the Rocky Mountain Conference of the United Methodist Church; archives of Iliff School of Theology.

Buildings and Grounds: Campus area 8 acres.

Chief Executive Officer: Dr. J. Phillip Wagaman, President.

Address admission inquiries to Carmen E. Baca, Registrar.

ITT Technical Institute

500 East 84th Avenue
Thornton, Colorado
Tel: (303) 288-4488   **E-mail:** admissions@itt-tech.edu
Fax: (303) 288-8166   **Internet:** www.itt-tech.edu

Institution Description: ITT Technical Institute is owned and operated by ITT Educational Services, Inc. of Indianapolis, Indiana.

Accreditation: *Nonregional:* ACICS.

Calendar: Quarters. Academic year begins Sept.

Characteristics of Freshmen: 211 applicants (181 men; 30 women). 55% of applicants admitted. 90.5% of admitted students enrolled full-time.

Admission: The student must provide documented proof of his or her high school diploma or recognized equivalency certificate.

Degree Requirements: Student must attain an overall 2.0 cumulative grade point average for the entire program pursued; must successfully complete all courses specified in the catalog for the program.

Degrees Conferred: 115 *associate:* mechanical and engineering technologies; 30 *baccalaureate:* engineering.

Fees and Other Expenses: *Full-time tuition per academic year 2004–05:* $13,548. *Room and board per academic year:* $5,958.

Financial Aid: Institution has a Program Participation Agreement with the U.S. Department of Education for eligible students to receive Pell Grants and other federal aid.

Financial aid to full-time, first-time undergraduate students: 40% received federal grants averaging $3,772; 1% institutional grant; 68% loans averaging $12,899.

Departments and Teaching Staff: Electronics and engineering technology *instructors* 9, *part-time faculty* 2; computer-aided drafting technology 4, 1; computer systems technology 8, 1.

Total instructional faculty: 24.

Enrollment: Total enrollment 540 (53.7% men, 16.3% women).

Characteristics of Student Body: *Ethnic/racial makeup:* Black non-Hispanic: 3.5%; American Indian or Alaska native: 2.8%; Asian or Pacific Islander: 3.5%; Hispanic: 22.2%; White non-Hispanic: 65.7%; unknown: 2.2%.

International Students: No programs to aid students whose native language is not English. No financial aid programs specifically designated for international students.

Library Collections: 2,000 volumes. 50 audiovisual materials; 50 current periodical subscriptions. Students have access to the Aurora Public Library and virtual sources.

Chief Executive Officer: Address admissions inquiries to Director of Recruitment.

Mesa State College

1100 North Avenue
Grand Junction, Colorado 81501
Tel: (970) 248-1020   **E-mail:** admissions@mesastate.edu
Fax: (970) 248-1076   **Internet:** www.mesastate.edu

Institution Description: *Enrollment:* 5,765. *Degrees awarded:* Associate, baccalaureate, master's. Certificates also awarded.

Academic offerings subject to approval by statewide coordinating bodies. Budget subject to approval by state governing boards. Member of the Consortium of State Colleges in Colorado.

Accreditation: *Regional:* NCA. *Professional:* nursing, nursing education, radiography

History: Established as Grand Junction State Junior College and offered first instruction at postsecondary level 1925; awarded first degree (associate) 1927; became Mesa College 1937; became 4-year institution 1974; adopted present name 1988.

Institutional Structure: *Governing board:* Trustees of the State College of Colorado. Representation: 9 trustees (appointed by governor of Colorado), 1 student. 8 voting. *Composition of institution:* Administrators 16 men/3 women. Academic affairs headed by vice president for academic affairs. Management/business/finances directed by vice president for business and finance. Full-time instructional faculty 201. Academic governance body, Faculty Senate, meets an average of 18 times per year.

Calendar: Semesters. Academic year Aug. to May. Freshmen admitted Aug., Jan., May, July. Degrees conferred May, Aug., Dec. Formal commencement May.

Characteristics of Freshmen: 3,000 applicants (1,413 men, 1,587 women). 81.4% of applicants admitted. 47.6% of admitted students enrolled full-time.

14% (179 students) submitted SAT scores; 88% (1,129 students) submitted ACT scores. *25th percentile:* SAT Verbal 430, SAT Math 430; ACT Composite 17, ACT English 16, ACT Math 16. *75th percentile:* SAT Verbal 570, SAT Math 560; ACT Composite 23, ACT English 22, ACT Math 23.

20% of entering freshmen expected to graduate within 5 years. 88% of freshmen from Colorado. Freshmen from 26 states.

Admission: Rolling admissions plan. For fall semester, apply no later than one month prior to beginning of term; spring/summer semesters no later than two weeks prior to beginning of term. *Requirements:* Freshmen applicants should have a grade point average of 2.50; a composite score of 19 on the ACT, or 860 combined on the SAT. GED (score of 45 or higher) accepted. Additional requirements for some programs. *Entrance tests:* SAT or ACT composite (ACT preferred). For foreign students TOEFL or demonstrated proficiency in English also required. *For transfer students:* 2.0 for 12 semester hours minimum GPA or associate degree.

Degree Requirements: *For all associate degrees:* 64–89 credit hours. *For all baccalaureate degrees:* 124–130 credit hours. *For all degrees:* 2.0 GPA; 2 terms in residence; 4 hours physical education requirements.

Fulfillment of some degree requirements and exemption from some beginning courses possible by passing departmental examinations. College Board CLEP. *Grading system:* A–F; withdraw (deadline after which pass-fail is appended to withdraw).

Distinctive Educational Programs: Work-experience programs. Evening classes. Accelerated degree programs. Special facilities for using telecommunications in the classroom. Facilities and programs for independent research, including individual majors, tutorials, independent study. Cross-registration through consortium. *Other distinctive programs:* Area vocational school provides training in technical skills. Continuing education program for credit and enrichment.

Degrees Conferred: 118 *associate;* 479 *baccalaureate;* 15 *master's.* Bachelor's degrees awarded in top five disciplines: business, management, marketing, and related support services 143; social sciences 43; psychology 39; health professions and related clinical sciences 35; parks, recreation, leisure, and fitness studies 32.

Fees and Other Expenses: *Full-time tuition per academic year 2004–05:* resident $2,724, out-of-state $9,010. *Room and board per academic year:* $6,501. *Books and supplies:* $1,186. *Other expenses:* $3,180.

Financial Aid: Aid from institutionally generated funds is provided on the basis of academic merit, financial need, athletic ability. Institution has a Program Participation Agreement with the U.S. Department of Education for eligible students to receive Pell Grants and other federal aid.

Financial aid to full-time, first-time undergraduate students: 28% received federal grants averaging $2,743; 16% state/local grants averaging $1,350; 15% institutional grants averaging $1,867; 50% loans averaging $2,116.

Departments and Teaching Staff: *Professors* 54, *associate professors* 36, *assistant professors* 66, *instructors* 45, *part-time faculty* 91.

Total instructional faculty: 231 FTE. Student-to-faculty ratio: 20:1. Degrees held by full-time faculty: Doctorate 76%, master's 25%, baccalaureate 2%. 76% hold terminal degrees.

Enrollment: Total enrollment 5,765. Undergraduate 5,699 (42.3% men, 57.7% women).

Characteristics of Student Body: *Ethnic/racial makeup:* Black non-Hispanic: 7.6%; American Indian or Alaska Native: 1.3%; Asian or Pacific Islander: 2%; Hispanic: 7.6%; White non-Hispanic: 82.9%; unknown: 4%.

International Students: 40 nonresident aliens enrolled fall 2003. Social and cultural programs available to aid students whose native language is not English. English as a Second Language Program. No financial aid specifically designated for international students.

Student Life: On-campus residence halls and apartments house 16% of student body. Dormitories for men only constitute 54% of such space, for women only 46%. 4% of student body live off-campus in college-owned apartments. Housing available for married students. *Intercollegiate athletics:* men only: baseball, basketball, football, tennis; women only: cross-country, basketball, golf, soccer, softball, tennis, volleyball. *Special regulations:* Registered cars permitted in designated areas only. *Special services:* Learning Resource Center, medical services. *Student publications, radio:* Criterion, a weekly newspaper; radio station KMSA broadcasts 136 hours per week. *Surrounding community:* Grand Junction population 38,000. Denver; 250 miles from campus, is nearest metropolitan area. Served by airport 3 miles from campus, passenger rail service 2 miles from campus.

Library Collections: 189,000 volumes. Online catalog. 60,000 government documents; 803,000 microforms; 1,035 current periodical subscriptions. Students have access to the Internet at no charge.

Most important special holdings include Colorado history; George Armstrong Custer Collection; Wayne Aspinall Collection.

Buildings and Grounds: Main campus area 42 acres.

Chief Executive Officer: Dr. Timothy Foster, President.

Address admission inquiries to Tyre Bush, Director of Admissions.

Metropolitan State College of Denver

1006 Eleventh Street
P.O. Box 173362
Denver, Colorado 80217-3362
Tel: (303) 556-3876   **E-mail:** admission@mscd.edu
Fax: (303) 556-3912   **Internet:** www.mscd.edu

Institution Description: Metropolitan State College of Denver is a state institution which shares a campus and facilities with the Community College of Denver-Auraria Campus and the University of Colorado at Denver. *Enrollment:* 20,261. *Degrees awarded:* Baccalaureate.

Academic offerings subject to approval by statewide coordinating bodies. Budget subject to approval by state governing boards. Member of Consortium of State Colleges in Colorado.

Accreditation: *Regional:* NCA. *Professional:* engineering, music, nursing, recreation and leisure services, social work, teacher education

History: Established as 2-year institution 1963; offered first instruction at postsecondary level 1965; became 4-year college and awarded first degree (associate) 1967.

Institutional Structure: *Governing board:* Trustees of the Consortium of State Colleges in Colorado. Representation: 7 trustees (appointed by governor of Colorado), 1 student. 1 ex officio. 7 voting. *Composition of institution:* Administrators 44 men / 43 women. Academic affairs headed by vice president for business and finance. Full-time instructional faculty 1,033. Academic governance body, Faculty Senate, meets an average of 12 times per year.

Calendar: Semesters. Academic year late Aug. to mid-May. Freshmen admitted Aug., Jan., June. Degrees conferred May, Aug., Dec. Formal commencement May.

Characteristics of Freshmen: 4,550 applicants (2,087 men, 2,453 women). 78.6% of applicants admitted. 44% of admitted students enrolled full-time.

9% (211 students) submitted SAT scores; 73% (1,707 students) submitted ACT scores. *25th percentile:* SAT Verbal 450, SAT Math 440; ACT Composite 17, ACT English 16, ACT Math 16. *75th percentile:* SAT Verbal 560, SAT Math 560; ACT Composite 23, ACT English 23, ACT Math 22.

Admission: Rolling admissions plan. Apply before classes begin. Early acceptance available. *Requirements:* First-time college students who are less than 20 years of age must meet two of the following three requirements to be eligible for admission: (1) 19 composite score on the ACT or 810 combined score on the SAT; (2) 2.50 cumulative high school GPA; (3) upper 2/3 high school class ranking. Students who do not meet these requirements will be considered on an individual basis. First-time college students who are 20 years of age or older must have graduated from an approved high school or have a GED certificate to be eligible for admission. *Entrance tests:* Recommend College Board SAT or ACT composite. For foreign students, TOEFL score of 500, affidavits of financial support and acceptable academic records. *For transfer students:* Applicants who have previously attended or are currently attending a college or university are expected to have a 2.00 GPA from each institution attended and be eligible to return. Applicants who do not meet these requirements must have official transcripts sent directly to the Office of Admissions and Records and make an appointment with an MSC admissions officer prior to submitting their application.

College credit and advanced placement for postsecondary-level work completed in secondary school. For extrainstitutional learning, college credit on basis of ACE *2006 Guide to the Evaluation of Educational Experiences in the Armed Services.* College credit and advanced placement on basis of portfolio and faculty assessments. Personal interviews required.

Tutoring available. Developmental courses offered in summer session and regular academic year; credit given.

Degree Requirements: 120–130 semester hours; 2.0 GPA; 2 semesters, including last 10 hours, in residence; distribution requirements. Fulfillment of some degree requirements and exemption from some beginning courses possible by passing departmental examinations, College Board CLEP, AP. *Grading system:* A–F; pass-fail; withdraw (permission of instructor required); incomplete (carries time limit).

Distinctive Educational Programs: Interdisciplinary major and minor programs, such as communications multi-major; holistic health and wellness multi-minor. Interdisciplinary programs in Afro-American studies, ethnic studies, women's studies, urban studies and bilingual Chicano studies. Internships and practicums, such as Colorado legislature internships, nursing practicums. Institutes: Intercultural Studies; Women's Studies; Entrepreneurship and Creativity. Cooperative education and off-campus programs. Weekend edition program. Honors program. "Freshmen Year" experience. Contract major and minor programs. Study abroad semester. Cross-registration through Consortium. Special facilities for using telecommunications in classes. Only teacher education program in Colorado located in urban setting.

ROTC: Army optional. Air force offered in cooperation with University of Colorado at Boulder.

Degrees Conferred: 2,182 *baccalaureate.* Bachelor's degrees awarded in top five disciplines: business, management, marketing, and related support services 510; multi/interdisciplinary studies 257, English language and literature/letters 187; security and protective services 137; visual and performing arts 119.

Fees and Other Expenses: *Full-time tuition per academic year 2004–05:* resident $3,768, out-of-state $10,510. *Room and board per academic year* $7,235. *Books and supplies:* $1,187. *Other expenses:* $1,620.

Financial Aid: Aid from institutionally generated funds is provided on the basis of academic merit, financial need, athletic ability. Institution has a Program Participation Agreement with the U.S. Department of Education for eligible students to receive Pell Grants and other federal aid.

Financial aid to full-time, first-time undergraduate students: 24% received federal grants averaging $2,909; 19% state/local grants averaging $3,407; 29% loans averaging $3,188.

Departments and Teaching Staff: Accounting *professors* 2, *associate professors* 2, *assistant professors* 5, *instructors* 2, *part-time faculty* 10; business education and communication 1, 2, 1, 1, 8; computer and management science 4, 6, 4, 3, 7; economics 5, 2, 3, 0, 8; finance 2, 5, 0, 0, 4; management 3, 6, 5, 0, 10; marketing 2, 1, 2, 0, 9; physical education and recreation 4, 2, 5, 0, 23; reading 3, 2, 1, 0, 5; education 7, 5, 5, 1, 27; aerospace science 3, 1, 3, 0, 8; civil engineering technology 5, 0, 1, 0, 3; mechanical/industrial technology and technology communication 5, 5, 1, 0, 6; electrical engineering technology 4, 2, 4, 0, 3; criminal justice 2, 2, 3, 0, 6; hosp/meet/and travel 1, 2, 0, 1, 6; human service 4, 3, 1, 0, 7; nursing/health care management 3, 5, 1, 0, 1; art 7, 3, 2, 0, 11; English/journalism 10, 7, 7, 2, 55; modern language 2, 7, 0, 0, 6; music 6, 1, 2, 0, 16; philosophy 2, 1, 1, 0, 3; speech 3, 2, 0, 0, 12; history 7, 4, 0, 0, 5; political science 3, 1, 1, 0, 2; psychology 12, 4, 0, 0, 5; sociology/anthropology 3, 4, 4, 0, 6; biology 8, 2, 1, 0, 5; chemistry 7, 3, 0, 0, 7; earth science 6, 1, 2, 0, 0; math science 11, 6, 7, 0, 32; physics 4, 2, 0, 0, 1.

Total instructional faculty: 386 full-time, 647 part-time. Student-to-faculty ratio: 20:1. Degrees held by full-time faculty: 353 faculty members hold terminal degrees.

Enrollment: Total enrollment 20,261 (men 43.6%, women 36.2%).

Characteristics of Student Body: *Ethnic/racial makeup:* Black non-Hispanic: 5.7%; American Indian or Alaska Native: 1%; Asian or Pacific Islander: 3.9%; Hispanic: 12.7%; White non-Hispanic: 70.2%; unknown: 5.5%.

International Students: 203 nonresident aliens enrolled fall 2004. *Programs available to aid students whose native language is not English:* English as a Second Language Program. No financial aid specifically designated for international students.

Student Life: No on-campus housing. *Intercollegiate athletics:* men only: baseball, basketball, soccer, tennis; women only: basketball, soccer, softball, tennis, volleyball; both sexes: swimming. *Special services:* Title IV TRIO programs, writing center, mathematics, tutorial program, reading instruction, freshman year program, child care center, parent education, comprehensive health clinic, campus recreation intramural program, student activities support, Lecture series. *Student publications: The Metropolitan,* a weekly newspaper; *Metrosphere,* a biannual magazine; student almanac. *Surrounding community:* Population approximately 1.8 million in the service area. Served by mass transit bus system; airport 10 miles from campus; passenger rail service 1/2 mile from campus.

Publications: *Metropolitan Magazine* for alumni.

Library Collections: 692,700 volumes. 1,054,000 microforms; 4,150 current periodicals; 17,000 video and audio units. Online catalog. Computer work stations available. Students have access to online information retrieval systems and the Internet.

Most important holdings include collections on public affairs, architecture and related areas of design.

Buildings and Grounds: Campus area 169 acres.

Chief Executive Officer: Dr. Raymond Kieft, President.

Address admission inquiries to William Hathaway-Clark, Director of Admissions.

Naropa University

2130 Arapahoe Avenue
Boulder, Colorado 80302-6697

Tel: (303) 444-0202   **E-mail:** admissions@naropa.edu
Fax: (303) 546-3583   **Internet:** www.naropa.edu

Institution Description: Naropa University is a private, nonprofit, nonsectarian liberal arts institution dedicated to advancing contemplative education, an approach to learning that integrates the best of Eastern and Western educational traditions. The university comprises undergraduate and graduate programs in the arts, education, environmental leadership, psychology, religious studies, as well as study-abroad programs. *Enrollment:* 1,206. *Degrees awarded:* Baccalaureate, master's.

Accreditation: *Regional:* NCA.

History: The university was established as Naropa Institute in 1974.

Institutional Structure: *Governing board:* Board of Trustees.

Calendar: Semesters. Academic year late Aug. to early May. Summer session from May to Aug.

Characteristics of Freshmen: 44% (24 students) submitted SAT scores; 19% (10 students) submitted ACT scores. *25th percentile:* SAT Verbal 543, SAT Math

545; ACT Composite 23. *75th percentile*: SAT Verbal 650, SAT Math 650; ACT Composite 31.

Admission: The Admissions Committee considers inquisitiveness and engagement with the world as well as previous academic achievement when making admission decisions. A student's statement of interest, interview, and letters of recommendation play important roles in the admissions process. SAT and ACT scores are not required, but are recommended.

Deadline for fall admission is Jan. 15, Oct. 15 for spring.

Degree Requirements: 120 credit hours with a cumulative GPA of at least 2.0; fulfillment of core requirements; earn the final 60 upper-division credit hours at Naropa. *Grading system:* C is the minimum grade a student may receive in required courses in the major and minor field of study; completion of the requirements for one of the majors and for one minor (except Interdisciplinary Studies majors); Naropa University entry/exit survey for assessment.

Distinctive Educational Programs: The educational philosophy of Naropa University offers students a highly individualized, experiential, and transformative learning path that engages students both academically and spiritually.

Degrees Conferred: 104 *baccalaureate* (B); 203 *master's* (M): education 2 (B), 7 (M); English 14 (B), 26 (M); home economics 1 (M); interdisciplinary studies 12 (B), 2 (M); liberal arts/general studies 26 (B); natural resources/environmental science 6 (B), 13 (M); parks and recreation 4 (B); philosophy/religion/theology 10 (B), 11 (M); psychology 33 (B), 112 (M); visual and performing arts 23 (B), 5 (M). 4 *first-professional*: master of divinity.

Fees and Other Expenses: *Full-time tuition per academic year 2005–06:* undergraduate $18,500, graduate $13,486. *Room and board per academic year:* $7,236.

Financial Aid: Aid from institutionally generated funds is provided on the basis of academic merit, financial need, athletic ability. Institution has a Program Participation Agreement with the U.S. Department of Education for eligible students to receive Pell Grants and other federal aid.

Financial aid to full-time, first-time undergraduate students: need-based scholarships/grants totaling $2,067,825, self-help $3,000,328, parent loans $921,657, tuition waivers $79,426; non-need-based self-help $115,457, parent loans $862,500.

Departments and Teaching Staff: *Total instructional faculty:* 298 (full-time 49, part-time 249; women 178, men 120). Total faculty with doctorate, first-professional, or other terminal degree: 128. Student-to-faculty ratio: 7:1.

Enrollment: Total enrollment 1,206 (418 men / 688 women).

Characteristics of Student Body: *Ethnic/racial makeup:* number of Black non-Hispanic: 7; American Indian or Alaska Native: 1; Asian or Pacific Islander: 9; Hispanic: 27; White non-Hispanic: 318; unknown: 78. *Age distribution:* number under 18: 2; 18–19: 49; 20–21: 100; 22–24: 137; 25–29: 94; 30–34: 31; 35–39: 12; 40–49: 12; 50–64: 8; 65 and over: 1.

International Students: 52 nonresident aliens enrolled fall 2004. 16 students from Europe, 17 Asia, 5 Central and South America, 1 Africa; 22 Canada, 2 Australia, 1 New Zealand. No programs available to aid students whose native language is not English.

Student Life: The majority of students live off-campus. Dormitory residence and apartment housing are available. *Student publications: naropa! Magazine*, a general interest publication distributed to alumni, faculty, staff, students, parents, and donors; *Bombay Gin*, a student literary magazine; *Tendril*, the university's diversity journal. *Community environment:* Boulder is a city of 10,000, nestled at the base of the Rocky Mountains 25 miles northwest of Denver. Hiking, skiing, and snowboarding are available in the nearby mountains.

Library Collections: The Allen Ginsberg Library is located on the Arapahoe campus. 27,500 volumes. Online catalog. 75 current serial subscriptions. 10,150 recordings. Computer work stations available. Students have access to the Internet at no charges.

Buildings and Grounds: The university is located on three campuses in central Boulder.

Chief Executive Officer: Dr. Thomas B. Coburn, President.

Address admission inquiries to Joshua Shalek, Admissions Office.

National Theatre Conservatory

1050 13th Street
Denver, Colorado 80204
Tel: (303) 623-0693   **E-mail:** admissions@denvercenter.org
Fax: (303) 446-4855   **Internet:** www.denvercenter.org

Institution Description: The National Theatre Conservatory (NTC) is part of the Denver Center Theater Company. The NTC offers a Master of Fine Arts in Acting; Certificate of Completion in Acting is also awarded. *Enrollment:* 23.

Accreditation: *Regional:* NCA.

History: In October 1984, the Denver Center Theatre Company (DCTC) and the American National Theatre and Academy (ANTA) joined together to establish the National Theatre Conservatory. The conservatory is the only educational institution of its kind chartered by Congress and represents a commitment to the arts by the United States government. The NTC is much more than the addition of a theatre school within the Denver Center's walls. It represents the transformation of the DCTC into a viable training ground for actors: a place where the skills of the acting company can be meshed with the skills of talented students. All third-year acting students join the DCTC company as apprentices.

Institutional Structure: *Composition of institution:* Artistic Director, Producing Director, Educational Programming Director, Registrar/Administrator, Librarian, Dean Emeritus, and heads of various departments. Full-time instructional faculty 11.

Calendar: Semesters.

Admission: DCTC accepts 8 students per academic year. Students must have a baccalaureate degree. Certificate students must have at least 90 quarter or 60 semester credit hours to be considered for admittance. Students admitted in Sept. only. Commencement late April. Students must apply by Jan. 31 for fall acceptance. Admission is by audition only. The NTC holds auditions in 6 U.S. cities in Feb.

Degree Requirements: Students must pass all classes and complete their thesis project to graduate. Grading is credit/no credit. Successful completion of the program enables students to be fully eligible for Actor's Equity Association membership.

Distinctive Educational Programs: The NTC fosters an ongoing relationship between its students and the artists of the DCTC. The classic master/apprenticeship relationship is designed to bring all students closer to the realization of their potential. The NTC provides an opportunity for third-year students to perform in an annual repertory every spring, as well as providing a graduate showcase in both New York and Los Angeles. Students receive training in vocal health from the professionals of the Wilbur James Gould Vice Research Center. Students also receive extensive training in acting before the camera in the studios of the Emmy award-winning Denver Center Media.

Fees and Other Expenses: Full tuition is provided to each student with a three-year living stipend which increases each year. Housing is located near the NTC. The NTC does not offer student housing.

Departments and Teaching Staff: *Total instructional faculty:* 11. 50% hold terminal degrees.

Enrollment: Total enrollment 23 (men 56.5%, women 43.5%).

Characteristics of Student Body: *Ethnic/racial makeup:* Black non-Hispanic: 17.4%; White non-Hispanic: 82.6%.

Library Collections: Students have access to the NTC library which has an extensive collection of theatre-related books, scripts, music scores, films, and videos.

Buildings and Grounds: The NTC is located in the historic Tramway building in downtown Denver. It is adjacent to the Denver Performing Arts Complex, one of the largest theatre complexes in the United States. All DCTC rehearsal facilities, design, and costume shops, classrooms, and administrative spaces are under one roof.

Chief Executive Officer: Lester Ward, President.

Address admission inquiries to Daniel Renner, Director.

Nazarene Bible College

1111 Academy Park Loop
Colorado Springs, Colorado 80910-3704
Tel: (719) 884-5000   **E-mail:** info@nbc.edu
Fax: (719) 884-5199   **Internet:** www.nbc.edu

Institution Description: Nazarene Bible College is a private, four-year, undergraduate professional school for ministers. It is affiliated with the Church of the Nazarene. *Enrollment:* 346 men / 189 women. *Degrees awarded:* Baccalaureate.

Accreditation: *National:* Association of Biblical Higher Education (ABHE). *Professional:* theology

History: The college was established in 1967.

Institutional Structure: *Governing board:* Representation: Nazarene Bible College Board of Trustees. 3 elected members from each of the 8 U.S. educational regions of the Church of the Nazarene plus the president.

Calendar: Trimesters. Academic year Aug. to May. Freshmen admitted fall, winter, spring.

Admission: Rolling admissions.

Degree Requirements: Associate of arts degree requires completion of a minimum of 64 semester hours; the baccalaureate degree a minimum of 128 semester hours.

Distinctive Educational Programs: All degree programs are offered through the online delivery system except Music and Christian Counseling. The college offers a strong schedule of courses in such a cycle that all courses necessary for degrees are offered each year. Students must have adequate computer equipment and sufficient skills to be able to receive instruction through this medium. The online program has equivalent curricula to the on-campus programs.

Degrees Conferred: 14 *associate* ; 47 *baccalaureate.*

Fees and Other Expenses: *Full-time tuition per academic year 2004–05:* $7,040. *Other fees:* $90 per term.

Financial Aid: Aid from institutionally generated funds is provided on the basis of academic merit, financial need.

Departments and Teaching Staff: *Total instructional faculty:* 15 (full-time 14, part-time 1; women 4, men 11; members of minority groups 1). Total faculty with doctorate, first-professional, or other terminal degree: 7.

Enrollment: Total enrollment 535 (full-time 136 men / 67 women, part-time 210 men / 122w).

Characteristics of Student Body: *Ethnic/racial makeup:* number of Black non-Hispanic: 17; American Indian or Alaska Native: 7; Asian or Pacific Islander: 5; Hispanic: 12; White non-Hispanic: 457; unknown: 34. *Age distribution:* number 18–19: 4; 20–21: 18; 22–24: 39; 25–29: 73; 30–34: 90; 35–39: 87; 40–49: 156; 50–64: 1.

International Students: 1 nonresident alien enrolled fall 2004.

Student Life: No on-campus housing. High profile is given to spiritual values, spiritual formation, and administerial skill development. Intramural sports. *Student publications: High Peaks,* yearbook; *NBCommunicator,* weekly campus newsletter.

Library Collections: 60,000 volumes including bound books, serial back-files, electronic documents, and government documents not in separate collections. Online catalog. Current serial subscriptions: 198 paper. 5,000 recordings. Computer work stations available. Students have access to the Internet at no charge.

Buildings and Grounds: Campus area 46 acres. *New buildings:* The Brand Center for Innovative Education completed in 2004 (houses the Online Education Department).

Chief Executive Officer: Hiram E. Sanders, President. Address admissions inquiries to Dr. Laurel Matson, Vice President for Enrollment and Student Development.

Regis University

3333 Regis Boulevard
Denver, Colorado 80221-1099

Tel: (303) 458-4100   **E-mail:** regisadm@regis.edu
Fax: (303) 964-5534   **Internet:** www.regis.edu

Institution Description: Regis University is a nonprofit institution affiliated with the Society of Jesus. *Enrollment:* 11,583. *Degrees offered:* Baccalaureate, master's.

Accreditation: *Regional:* NCA.

History: Established in 1877, Regis University, a Jesuit school, began as Las Vegas College in the New Mexico Territory. In 1884, the school moved to Colorado as the College of the Sacred Heart. The name was changed to Regis College in 1921, and the school received accreditation from North Central Association of Colleges and Universities. In 1979, programs were designed to meet the needs of working adults, offering both master's degrees and baccalaureate degrees. These adult programs are now incorporated into the School for Professional Studies (SPS), following a reorganization in 1991. At that time, Regis College and SPS, along with the School for Health Care Professions (nursing, physical therapy, health information management, health administration), all came under the umbrella of Regis University.

Institutional Structure: *Governing board:* Board of Trustees. Extrainstitutional representation: 29 trustees; institutional representation: 1 administrator. 1 ex officio. 29 voting. *Composition of institution:* Administrators 59 men / 53 women (8% are members of minority groups). Academic affairs headed by vice president of the college. Management/business/finances directed by vice president. Full-time instructional 128. *Faculty representation:* Faculty served by collective bargaining agent affiliated with AAUP.

Calendar: Semesters. Academic year Aug. to May. Regis College freshmen admitted each semester. School for the Professional Studies students may start at 12 different times throughout the year. Health Care students follow traditional semester enrollment. A variety of summer sessions available.

Characteristics of Freshmen: 1,607 applicants (men 655, women 952). 82.7% of applicants admitted. 30.3% of admitted students enrolled full-time.

55% (221 students) submitted SAT scores; 83% (335 students) submitted ACT scores. *25th percentile:* SAT Verbal 470, SAT Math 470; ACT Composite 20, ACT English 20, ACT Math 20. *75th percentile:* SAT Verbal 600, SAT Math 590; ACT Composite 26, ACT English 26, ACT Math 26.

53% of freshmen from Colorado. Freshmen from 23 states and 1 foreign country.

Admission: Rolling admissions plan. For fall acceptance, apply as early as junior year of secondary school, but not later than Aug. 15 of year of enrollment. Apply by Dec. 31 for early decision; need not limit application to Regis. Early acceptance available. *Requirements:* Either 15 academic units from grades 9–12 or GED. Recommend GPA 2.5. Essay required. *Entrance tests:* College Board SAT and 1 Achievement, or ACT composite. *For transfer students:* 2.0 GPA; 98 hours maximum transfer credit. *Adult student requirements:* 3 years of full-time work experience. College credit and advanced placement for postsecondary-level work completed in secondary school and for extrainstitutional learning on basis of ACE *2006 Guide to the Evaluation of Educational Experiences in the Armed Services,* portfolio, faculty assessments, PEP, CLEP. Tutoring available. Developmental/remedial courses offered days and evenings in summer session and regular academic year; credit given.

Degree Requirements: *For all baccalaureate degrees:* 128 credit hours; 30 hours in residence. *For all undergraduate degree:* 2.0 GPA.

Fulfillment of some degree requirements and exemption from some beginning courses possible by passing College Board CLEP. Adult programs offer opportunities for life experience credit through portfolio. *Grading system:* A–F; pass-fail; withdraw (carries time limit).

Distinctive Educational Programs: Undergraduate degree-completion programs for adults include: School for Professional Studies; School for Health Care Professions; Corporate Education; distance learning programs. Experiential Learning Program in Ireland; Service Learning in Mexico and Belize.

ROTC: Air Force offered in cooperation with University of Colorado at Boulder.

Degrees Conferred: 1,279 *baccalaureate;* 1,393 *master's;* 131 *post-baccalaureate certificates.* Bachelor's degrees awarded in top five disciplines: business, management, marketing, and related support services 518; health professions and related clinical sciences 236; computer and information sciences and support services 165; multi/interdisciplinary studies 149; communication, journalism, and related programs 68.

Fees and Other Expenses: *Full-time tuition per academic year 2004–05:* $22,200. *Room and board per academic year:* $7,870. *Books and supplies:* $1,187. *Other expenses:* $1,494.

Financial Aid: Aid from institutionally generated funds is provided on the basis of academic merit, financial need, other criteria. Institution has a Program Participation Agreement with the U.S. Department of Education for eligible students to receive Pell Grants and other federal aid.

Financial aid to full-time, first-time undergraduate students: 18% received federal grants averaging $4,384; 16% state/local grants averaging $7,424; 87% institutional grants averaging $8,155; 48% loans averaging $4,578.

Departments and Teaching Staff: Regis College *professors* 18, *associate professors* 25, *assistant professors* 20, *instructors* 0, *part-time faculty* 8; School for Professional Studies 0, 0, 0, 34, 296; School for Health Care Professions 0, 5, 15, 4, 1. *Total instructional faculty:* 425. *Total tenured faculty:* 48.

Enrollment: Total enrollment 11,583. Undergraduate 5,946.

Characteristics of Student Body: *Ethnic/racial makeup:* Black non-Hispanic: 4.3%; American Indian or Alaska Native: .5%; Asian or Pacific Islander: 3%; Hispanic: 7.8%; White non-Hispanic: 62.4%; unknown: 21%.

International Students: 69 undergraduate nonresident aliens enrolled fall 2003. Students from Europe, Asia, Central and South America, Africa, Canada. Programs available to aid students whose native is not English: English as a Second Language. No financial aid specifically designated for international students.

Student Life: On-campus residence halls for men and women house 45% of student body. *Intercollegiate athletics:* men only: baseball, basketball, golf, soccer, tennis; women only: basketball, soccer, softball, tennis, volleyball. *Special regulations:* Vehicle parking on campus by permit only. *Special services:* Learning Resources Center, medical services, Life Directions Center. *Student publications, radio: Highlander,* a bimonthly newspaper; *Reflections,* an annual literary magazine; *The Ranger,* a yearbook. Radio station KRCX broadcasts 35 hours per week; programs of student interest, music, sports. *Surrounding community:* Metropolitan Denver population 1,800,000. Served by mass transit bus system; airport 20 miles from campus; passenger rail service 4 miles from campus. Close proximity to major ski areas.

Publications: *Update,* a biweekly publication for faculty and staff; *Regis University Magazine,* published quarterly; *Annual Report* published yearly.

Library Collections: 421,000 volumes. 105,000 audiovisual materials; 3,980 850 periodicals. Computer work stations available. Modem ports/electricity available in all study tables, rooms, alcoves. 136,500 microform items. Online catalog. Students have access to online information retrieval services and the Internet.

Most important special collections include Jesuitica Book Collection; fine arts slide collection; Santos Collection.

Buildings and Grounds: Campus area 90 acres. Ten satellite campuses.

Chief Executive Officer: Michael J. Sheeran, S.J., President.

Address admission inquiries to Victor L. Davolt, Director of Admissions.

United States Air Force Academy

2304 Cadet Drive
Colorado Springs, Colorado 80840-5001
Tel: (719) 333-2520   **E-mail:** admissions@usafa.af.mil
Fax: (719) 333-3012   **Internet:** www.usafa.af.mil

Institution Description: United States Air Force Academy is a public, federal, four-year, coeducational, undergraduate college. *Enrollment:* 4,149. *Degrees awarded:* Baccalaureate.

Accreditation: *Regional:* NCA. *Professional:* business, computer science, engineering

History: Established 1954; offered first instruction at postsecondary level 1955; awarded first degree (baccalaureate) 1959; women first admitted in 1976. *See* Henry Fellerman, *The Official History of the United States Air Force Academy* (Colorado: United States Air Force Academy, 1954 [updated annually]), for further information.

Institutional Structure: *Governing board:* Board of Visitors. Extrainstitutional representation: 6 members appointed by the President of the United States; 4 members, including 2 members of the House Appropriations Committee, designated by the Speaker of the House; 3 members, including 2 members of the Senate Appropriations Committee, designated by the Vice President of the United States; 1 member designated by the chairman of the Senate Armed Services Committee; 1 designated by the chairman of the House Armed Services Committee. All voting. *Composition of institution:* Administrators 12 men (8% are members of minority groups). Academic affairs headed by dean of faculty. Management/business/finances directed by comptroller. Full-time instructional faculty 531. Academic governance body, Faculty Council, meets at least monthly.

Calendar: Semesters. Academic year Aug. to May. Freshmen admitted July. Formal commencement late May or early June. Summer session of 3 terms from June to Aug.

Characteristics of Freshmen: 12,591 applicants (men 9,471, women 3,120). 12.6% of applicants admitted. 80.4% of admitted students enrolled full-time.

62% (982 students) submitted SAT scores; 38% (601 students) submitted ACT scores. *25th percentile:* SAT Verbal 590, SAT Math 610; ACT Composite 26, ACT English 26, ACT Math 27. *75th percentile:* SAT Verbal 680, SAT Math 700; ACT Composite 32, ACT English 31, ACT Math 32.

Admission: Modified rolling admissions plan. For fall acceptance, apply as early as Feb. of junior year of secondary school, but not later than Jan. 31 of year of enrollment. Students are notified of acceptance Nov.–May. Apply by Nov. of senior year for early decision; need not limit application to U.S. Air Force Academy. Early acceptance available. *Requirements:* Recommend 15 secondary school units including 4 English, 3 foreign language, 4 mathematics, 4 social studies and electives; GED accepted. Nomination to Air Force Academy by specified official source. Candidate must be 17–22 years of age on July 1 of year of admission, unmarried with no dependent children, and U.S. citizen, except for limited quota of foreign students authorized by Congress. Course in computer literacy recommended. Lowest acceptable secondary school class standing 60th percentile. *Entrance tests:* College Board SAT or entire ACT battery of 4 tests, medical examination measuring physical and mental fitness.

College credit and advanced placement for postsecondary-level work completed in secondary school. Tutoring available. Remedial courses offered in summer session and during regular academic year; credit given.

Degree Requirements: 145 credit hours depending on major; 2.0 GPA; 4 years in residence; 4 years military training; 4 years physical education; physical fitness standards; Military Performance Average of 2.0; physical education average of 2.0; commitment to 6 years of military service; core requirements.

Fulfillment of some degree requirements and exemption from some beginning courses possible by passing departmental examinations, College Board CLEP, AP. *Grading system:* A–F; pass-fail; withdraw (deadline after which pass-fail is appended to withdraw); incomplete (carries time limit).

Distinctive Educational Programs: Special facilities for using telecommunications in the classroom. Interdepartmental/interdisciplinary majors in foreign studies, meteorology, sciences, operations research, and space operations. Facilities and programs for independent research, including honors programs, individual majors, tutorials. Exchange program with French, Chilean, Spanish, German, and Japanese Air Force Academies during fall semester of senior year. Periodic travel to service academies of allied countries. Interservice Exchange Program with United States Military, Naval, and Coast Guard Academies (in NY, MD, CT respectively during fall of junior year).

Degrees Conferred: 1,440 *baccalaureate.* Bachelor's degrees awarded in top five disciplines: engineering 337; business, management, marketing, and related support services 233; social sciences 132; psychology 91; biological and biomedical sciences 71.

Fees and Other Expenses: *Per academic year:* $2,500 deposit; cadets receive a monthly salary (deducted from this amount are monthly allotments to pay for uniforms, books, linens, activities, taxes, etc.)

Departments and Teaching Staff: *Professors* 42, *associate professors* 86, *assistant professors* 262, *instructors* 141. *Total instructional faculty:* 531. Student-to-faculty ratio: 7.9:1. Degrees held by full-time faculty: doctorate 55%, master's 41%, professional 4%. 55% hold terminal degrees.

Enrollment: Total enrollment 4,149 (3,410 men / 739 women).

Characteristics of Student Body: *Ethnic/racial makeup:* Black non-Hispanic: 5.1%; American Indian or Alaska Native: 1%; Asian or Pacific Islander: 5.4%; Hispanic: 6.1%, White non-Hispanic: 79.4%; unknown: 2%.

International Students: 46 nonresident aliens enrolled fall 2003. Students from Europe, Asia, Central and South America, Middle East. English as a Second Language Program available.

Student Life: On-campus residence halls house 100% of student body. Two on-campus coeducational residence halls house 100% of the student body. *Intercollegiate athletics:* men: baseball, basketball, cross-country, fencing, football, golf, gymnastics, ice hockey, lacrosse, rifle, soccer, swimming, tennis, track (indoor and outdoor), water polo, wrestling, volleyball; women: basketball, cross-country, fencing, gymnastics, rifle, soccer, swimming, tennis, track (indoor and outdoor), volleyball. *Special regulations:* Cars permitted for juniors and seniors. All students are required to live on campus. Prescribed Air Force uniforms worn daily. Curfews and study hours are in effect. The day ends at 11:30pm with the study hours beginning at 7am. *Special services:* Learning Resources Center, medical services. *Student publications, television:* DoDo, a humor magazine published irregularly; *Polaris,* a yearbook; *Basic Cadet Training (BCT) Yearbook; Contrails Calendar.* Closed circuit television station broadcasts 2 hours per week. *Surrounding community:* Academy is 8 miles from Colorado Springs. Population 485,000 in Colorado Springs metropolitan area. Denver is 65 miles from campus. Served by airport 20 miles from campus.

Publications: Sources of information about U.S. Air Force Academy include U.S. Air Force advertising program (including national advertisements, publications and films); Air Force Admission Liaison Offices throughout U.S.

Library Collections: 750,000 volumes including bound books, serial backfiles, electronic documents, and government documents not in separate collections. Online catalog. Current serial subscriptions: 1,800 paper. 4,597 recordings. 140 computer work stations. Students have access to the Internet at no charge.

Most important holdings include U.S. Air Force Academy Archives; Colonel Richard Gimbel Aeronautical History Library (6,000 prints depicting the evolution of aeronautics; 5,000 books dating from 1489, including 7 incunabulae; seals dating from 2,500 B.C.; memorabilia, manuscripts, letters); personal papers and manuscripts of Laurence S. Kuter, George O. Squire and numerous other military and aviation leaders (including photographic albums of Gen. James H. Doolittle); Stalag Luft III Collection; World War II/Korea/Vietnam POW Collections.

Buildings and Grounds: Campus area 18,455 acres.

Chief Executive Officer: Lt. Gen. Tad J. Oelstrom, Superintendent.

Address admission inquiries to Rolland Stoneman, Associate Director, Admissions/Selections.

University of Colorado at Boulder

17 UCB
Boulder, Colorado 80309-0017
Tel: (303) 492-1411   **E-mail:** apply@colorado.edu
Fax: (303) 492-7115   **Internet:** www.colorado.edu

Institution Description: *Enrollment:* 32,423. *Degrees awarded:* Baccalaureate, master's, doctorate, first-professional (law).

Accreditation: *Regional:* NCA. *Professional:* audiology, business, clinical psychology, engineering, English language education, journalism, law, music, psychology internship, speech-language pathology, teacher education

History: Established and chartered 1876; offered first instruction at postsecondary level 1877; awarded first degree 1882. *See* William E. Davis, *Glory Colorado* (Boulder: Pruett Press, 1965) for further information.

Institutional Structure: *Composition of institution:* Administrators 16 men / 4 women. Chancellor is chief executive. Vice chancellors direct academic affairs, student affairs, and administration. Full-time instructional faculty 1,140. Academic governance body, Boulder Faculty Assembly, meets an average of 9 times per year.

Calendar: Semesters. Academic year Aug. to May. Freshmen admitted Aug., Jan., June. Degrees conferred and formal commencement May, Aug., Dec. Summer session from early June to mid-Aug.

Characteristics of Freshmen: 19,360 applicants (3,807 men, 9,563 women). 84.8% of applicants admitted. 31% of admitted students enrolled full-time.

70% (3,590 students) submitted SAT scores; 74% (3,815 students) submitted ACT scores. *25th percentile:* SAT Verbal 530, SAT Math 550; ACT Composite 23, ACT English 22, 3ACT Math 23. *75th percentile:* SAT Verbal 630, SAT Math 650; ACT Composite 28, ACT English 28, ACT Math 28.

Admission: Rolling admissions plan. For summer and fall, the assured consideration deadline for completed applications is Feb. 15, and for spring, Nov. 15. *Requirements:* Either graduation from accredited secondary school with 15 units, or GED. Additional requirements, including specific secondary school units, SAT or ACT scores, and percentile rank vary according to program. *Entrance tests:* College Board SAT or ACT composite. *For transfer students:* From 4-year accredited institution 102 hours maximum transfer credit; from 2-year accredited institution 72 hours; for correspondence/extension students 60 hours. Minimum GPA and other requirements vary. College credit and advanced placement for postsecondary-level work completed in secondary school. Tutoring available.

Degree Requirements: *For baccalaureate degrees:* 120–128 semester hours; 2.0–2.25 GPA; 30 hours in residence. Additional requirements for some programs.

Fulfillment of some degree requirements and exemption from some beginning courses possible by passing College Board CLEP, APP. *Grading system:* A–F; pass-fail; withdraw (carries time limit).

Distinctive Educational Programs: Undergraduate Academy offers a range of special activities and individual advising for intellectually committed students. CU-Boulder's $11 million Integrated Teaching and Learning Laboratory provides hands-on, real-world learning experience for engineering students, teachers, and school-aged children in the community. The Mountain Research Station is one of the best known sites for alpine research in Facilities and programs for independent research, including honors programs, individual majors. Independent study. Study abroad in Canada, Czechoslovakia, Costa Rica, Denmark, Dominican Republic, Egypt, England, France, Hungary, Israel, Italy, Japan, Mexico, Poland, Spain, Germany, and several sites through the International Student Exchange Program. Research institutes, including Cooperative Institute for Research in Environmental Sciences (interdepartmental), Institute for Study of Arctic and Alpine Research, Institute for Behavioral Genetics, Institute of Cognitive Science, Institute for Behavioral Science, Laboratory for Atmospheric and Space Physics, Joint Institute for Laboratory Astrophysics (in cooperation with the National Bureau of Standards). The Chancellor's Leadership Program combines theoretical, historical, practical, and experiential knowledge in the study of leadership.

ROTC: Army, Navy, Air Force.

Degrees Conferred: 5,196 *baccalaureate*; 1,062 *master's*; 286 *doctorate*; 157 *first-professional*. Bachelor's degrees awarded in top five disciplines: social sciences 799; business, management, marketing, and related support services 786; communication, journalism, and related programs 574; psychology 421; engineering 363.

Fees and Other Expenses: *Full-time tuition per academic year 2004–05:* Undergraduate resident $4,431, out-of-state student $21,453. *Room and board per academic year:* $7,564. *Books and supplies:* $1,187.

Financial Aid: Institution has a Program Participation Agreement with the U.S. Department of Education for eligible students to receive Pell Grants and other federal aid.

Financial aid to full-time, first-time undergraduate students: 12% received federal grants averaging $4,083; 22% state/local grants averaging $2,759; 20% institutional grants averaging $2,767; 31% loans averaging $4,234.

Departments and Teaching Staff: *Professors* 457, *associate professors* 303, *assistant professors* 220, *instructors* 120, *part-time faculty* 236.

Total instructional faculty: 1,255. Student-to-faculty ratio: 13.7:1. 94% of faculty hold terminal degrees.

Enrollment: Total enrollment 32,423 (62.5% men, 47/5% women).

Characteristics of Student Body: *Ethnic/racial makeup:* Black non-Hispanic: 7.6%; American Indian or Alaska Native: .7%; Asian or Pacific Islander: 5.8%; Hispanic: 5.7%; White non-Hispanic: 78.9%; unknown: 6%.

International Students: 421 nonresident aliens enrolled fall 2003. Students from Europe, Asia, Central and South America, Africa, Canada, Australia, New Zealand. Programs available to aid students whose native language is not English: Social, cultural. English as a Second Language Program. No financial aid specifically designated for international students.

Student Life: On-and off-campus residence halls house both single students and married students. 13% of women join and many of them live in sorority houses; 10% of mean join and many live in fraternity houses. *Intercollegiate athletics:* men only: football, golf, track; women only: volleyball; both sexes: basketball, skiing, soccer, tennis; intramural sports program. *Special services:* Student academic support; Cultural Unite Student Center; Wardenburg Student Health Center; Student Recreation Center; Office of Services to Disabled Students and Learning Development Program; RTD bus pass program; University Memorial Center and CULine/Ralphie. *Student publications, radio: Colorado Daily*, daily newspaper, *Campus Press*, published twice per week; a yearbook. Radio station KUCB 1190 broadcasts from 7am to 1am 7 days a week. *Surrounding community:* Boulder population 110,000. Denver, 35 miles from campus, is nearest metropolitan area. Served by mass transit bus system; airport 45 miles from campus.

Publications: Arctic and Alpine Research, T'ang Studies; American Music Research Center Journal, Southwestern Lore, English Language Notes, On Stage Studies, University of Colorado Law Review, Tourism's Top Twenty.

Library Collections: 3,314,500 volumes including bound books, serial backfiles, electronic documents, and government documents not in separate collections. Online catalog. Current serial subscriptions: 24,000 paper and microform. 76,000 audiovisual materials. 1,700 computer work stations. Students have access to the Internet at no charge.

Most important holdings include Western Historical Collection, including Gary Hart papers; Rare Books Collection, including Epstein Children's Book Collection; Women Poets of the Romantic Period, Hart Mountaineering Collection; Tippit Photobook Collection.

Buildings and Grounds: Campus area 600 acres.

Chief Executive Officer: Dr. Richard L. Byyny, Chancellor.

Address admission inquiries to Barbara H. Schneider, Director of Admissions.

College of Arts and Sciences

Degree Programs Offered: *Baccalaureate* in African and Middle Eastern studies; American studies; anthropology; art education; art history; Asian studies; biology with education; Black studies; Central and Eastern European studies; chemistry; Chinese; classics; communication; communication disorders and speech service; dance; distribution studies; economics; English; environmental conservation; environmental population and organismic biology; fine arts; French; geography; geology; German; history; humanities; international affairs; Italian; Japanese; Latin American studies; linguistics; mathematics; molecular, cellular, and developmental biology; philosophy; physical education; physics; political science; psychology; recreation; religious studies; Russian; sociology; Spanish; studio art; theater.

Distinctive Educational Programs: Center for Interdisciplinary Studies.

College of Business and Administration

Degree Programs Offered: *Baccalaureate* in accounting, business education, computer information systems, finance, international business, marketing, minerals land management, organization management, personnel-human resources management, production and operation, transportation and traffic management; *master's* in business administration.

School of Education

Degree Programs Offered: *Baccalaureate* in elementary education, secondary education.

College of Engineering

Degree Programs Offered: *Baccalaureate* in aerospace engineering, applied mathematics, architectural engineering, chemical engineering, civil engineering, electrical engineering, electrical and computer science engineering, engineering physics, industrial engineering, mechanical engineering.

School of Journalism

Degree Programs Offered: *Baccalaureate* in advertising, news-editorial, broadcast news, broadcast productions management, media studies.

College of Music

Degree Programs Offered: *Baccalaureate* in music, music education.

School of Law

Degree Programs Offered: *First-professional.*

Admission: Baccalaureate from accredited college or university. LSAT.

Degree Requirements: 86 credit hours, 72 average (on 0-100 scale), 6 semesters in residence.

Distinctive Educational Programs: Legal Aid and Defender Programs provide students with practical experience as well as community service for low-income clients.

Graduate School

Degree Programs Offered: *Master's* in accounting, aerospace engineering, anthropology, applied mathematics, applied physics, art education, art history, astrophysics, basic science, biochemistry, chemical engineering, chemistry, civil engineering, classics, communication, communication disorders, comparative literature, computer science, dance, economics, education, electrical engineering, English, environmental population and organismic biology, finance, French, geography, geology, German, history, industrial engineering, Italian, journalism, linguistics, management science, marketing, mathematics, mechanical engineering, biology, music, music education, organization management, pharmaceutical sciences, philosophy, physical education, physics, political science, psychology, Russian and Slavic language and literature, sociology, Spanish, studio arts, telecommunications, theater; *doctorate* in aerospace engineering, anthropology, applied mathematics, applied physics, astrogeophysics, biochemistry, business administration, chemical engineering, chemical physics, chemistry, civil engineering, classics, communication, communication disorders and speech science, comparative literature, computer science, economics, education, electrical engineering, English, French, geography, geology, geophysics, German, history, linguistics, mathematics, mathematical physics, mechanical engineering, mechanics, music, musical arts, pharmaceutical sciences, philosophy, physics, political science, psychology, Slavic languages and literature, sociology, Spanish, theater. Specialist certificates in education also given.

Departments and Teaching Staff: Graduate school faculty drawn from Colleges of Arts and Sciences, Business, Engineering, Music, and Schools of Education, Journalism, Pharmacy.

University of Colorado at Colorado Springs

1420 Austin Bluffs Parkway
P.O. Box 7150
Colorado Springs, Colorado 80933-7150
Tel: (719) 262-3383   **E-mail:** admrecor@uccs.edu
Fax: (719) 262-3116   **Internet:** www.uccs.edu

Institution Description: University of Colorado at Colorado Springs is a state institution. *Enrollment:* 8,862. *Degrees awarded:* Baccalaureate, master's, doctorate.

Accreditation: *Regional:* NCA. *Professional:* business, computer science, counseling, engineering, nursing, nursing education, public administration, teacher education

History: Established, chartered, offered first instruction at postsecondary level, and awarded first degrees (baccalaureate, master's) 1965; known as University of Colorado - Colorado Springs Center until 1972 when present name was adopted.

Institutional Structure: *Composition of institution:* Campus administration consists of chancellor, vice chancellor for academic affairs, deans of schools and colleges, heads of various departments. Full-time instructional faculty 253. Academic governance body, Colorado Springs Faculty Assembly, meets an average of 9 times per year.

Calendar: Semesters. Academic year Aug. to May. Freshmen admitted Aug., Jan., June. Degrees conferred May, Aug., Dec. Formal commencement May. Summer session from early June to early Aug.

Characteristics of Freshmen: 69% of applicants accepted. 29% of accepted students admitted and enrolled full-time.

36% (370 students) submitted SAT scores; 41% (737 students) submitted ACT scores. *25th percentile:* SAT Verbal 480, SAT Math 470; ACT Composite 20, ACT Math 19. *75th percentile:* SAT Verbal 590, SAT Math 590; ACT Composite 25, ACT Math 26.

39% of entering freshmen expected to graduate within 5 years. 94% of freshmen from Colorado.

Admission: Rolling admissions plan. For fall acceptance, apply as early as Oct. of previous year, but not later than July 1 of year of enrollment. Early acceptance available. *Requirements:* Either graduation from accredited secondary school with 16 units which should include at least 4 units English, 3 units natural science, 4 units mathematics, 2 units social science, and 2 units foreign language; or GED. Additional requirements for individual programs. Lowest acceptable secondary school class standing 60th percentile. *Entrance tests:* College Board SAT or ACT Composite. For foreign students TOEFL. *For transfer students:* 2.5 minimum GPA; from 4-year accredited institution 102 hours maximum transfer credit; from 2-year accredited institution 72 hours; extension students 60 hours; for correspondence students 30 hours.

College credit and advanced placement for postsecondary-level work completed in secondary school. For extrainstitutional learning (life experience) college credit on basis of ACE *2006 Guide to the Evaluation of Educational Experiences in the Armed Services.* Tutoring available.

Degree Requirements: *Undergraduate:* 120–128 credit hours; 2.0 GPA; 30 hours in residence; additional requirements for individual programs. Fulfillment of some degree requirements and exemption from some beginning courses possible by passing College Board CLEP, APP. *Grading system:* A–F; high pass-pass-fail (for honors programs); pass-fail; withdraw (carries time limit).

Distinctive Educational Programs: Work-experience programs. Evening classes. Special facilities for using telecommunications in the classroom. Interdisciplinary programs in geography and applied earth sciences, geography and environmental studies. Preprofessional programs in allied health fields leading to degrees awarded by University of Colorado Health Science Center. Facilities and programs for independent research, including honors programs, individual majors, independent studies. Study abroad available through University of Colorado (Boulder campus) by individual arrangement. Semester-at-sea program. *Other distinctive programs:* Credit and non-credit continuing education. New Department of Geropsychology.

ROTC: Army.

Degrees Conferred: 950 *baccalaureate* (B), 436 *master's* (M), 4 *doctorate:* biological/life sciences 55 (B), 7 (M); business/marketing 174 (B), 130 (M); communications/communication technologies 113 (B); computer and information sciences 43 (B), 12 (M); education 149 (M); engineering and engineering technologies 53 (B), 38 (M), 4 (D); English 29 (B); foreign languages and literature 6 (B); health professions and related sciences 113 (B), 38 (M); interdisciplinary studies 6 (B); mathematics 10 (B); natural resources/environmental science 46 (B), 1 (M); philosophy/religion/theology 10 (B); physical sciences 20 (B), 2 (M); protective services/public administration 27 (M); psychology 113 (B), 8 (M); social sciences and history 137 (B), 19 (M); visual and performing arts 22 (B).

Fees and Other Expenses: *Full-time tuition per academic year 2004–05:* undergraduate resident $3,730, out-of-state $15,540; graduate tuition resident $2,274, out-of-state $7,754 (may vary across colleges offering the graduate programs). *Room per academic year:* $7,148.

Financial Aid: Aid from institutionally generated funds is provided on the basis of academic merit, financial need, athletic ability, other criteria. Institution has a Program Participation Agreement with the U.S. Department of Education for eligible students to receive Pell Grants and other federal aid.

Financial aid to full-time, first-time undergraduate students: need-based scholarships/grants totaling $10,704,038, self-help $21,347,732, parent loans $2,655,010, athletic awards $276,159; non-need-based self-help $148,455.

Departments and Teaching Staff: *Total instructional faculty:* 550 (full-time 296, part-time 254; women 272, men 278; members of minority groups 58). Total faculty with doctorate, first-professional, or other terminal degree: 361. Student-to-faculty ratio: 18:1.

Enrollment: Total enrollment 8,862. Undergraduate full-time 1,874 men / 1,860 women, part-time 599m / 900w; graduate full-time 290m / 275w, part-time 837m / 1,327w. Transfer students: in-state 486, out-of-state 114.

Characteristics of Student Body: *Ethnic and racial makeup:* number of Black non-Hispanic: 245; American Indian or Alaska Native: 60; Asian or Pacific Islander: 292; Hispanic: 540; White non-Hispanic: 4,764; unknown: 289. *Age distribution:* number under 18: 33; 18–19: 1,382; 20–21: 1,639; 22–24: 1,405, 25–29: 688; 30–34: 315; 35–39: 201; 40–49: 262; 50–64: 92; 65 and over: 2.

International Students: 94 nonresident aliens enrolled fall 2004. 14 students from Europe, 56 Asia, 9 Central and South America, 6 Africa, 10 Canada. No programs available to aid students whose native language is not English. No financial aid specifically designated for international students.

Student Life: On-campus housing for 600 students in private rooms or four-person suites. Off-campus housing assistance also available. *Intercollegiate athletics:* men only: basketball, cross-country, golf, soccer, tennis; women only: basketball, cross-country, softball, tennis, volleyball. *Special regulations:* Cars with parking permits allowed. *Special services:* Personal growth counseling and workshops, CU Opportunity Program, disabled students services, Women's Information Center, tutoring, career development and placement, veterans services. *Student publications:* A weekly newspaper, an annual literary magazine. *Surrounding community:* Colorado Springs population 300,000. Denver, 65 miles from campus, is nearest metropolitan area. Served by mass transit bus system; airport 12 miles from campus.

Library Collections: 414,343 volumes including bound books, serial backfiles, electronic documents, and government documents not in separate collections. Online catalog. Current serial subscriptions: 2,876 paper, 825 microform. 6,324 recordings. 245 computer work stations. Students have access to the Internet at no charge.

Buildings and Grounds: Campus area 400 acres. *New buildings:* Cragmore Hall renovation completed 2000; Alpine Village Apartments 2004; parking garage 2004.

Chief Executive Officer: Dr. Pamela Shockley-Zalabak, Chancellor.

Address admission inquiries to Steve Ellis, Director Admissions/Registrar.

University of Colorado at Denver and Health Sciences Center-Downtown Denver Campus

Denver, Colorado 80217-3364

Tel: (303) 556-5600   **E-mail:** admissions@cudenver.edu
Fax: (303) 556-4838   **Internet:** www.cudenver.edu

Institution Description: University of Colorado at Denver shares a campus and facilities with the Community College of Denver and Metropolitan State College of Denver. *Enrollment:* 7,051 full-time, 9,559 part-time. *Degrees awarded:* Baccalaureate, master's, doctorate.

Accreditation: *Regional:* NCA. *Professional:* architecture, business, chemistry, engineering, health services administration, landscape architecture, music, nursing, physical therapy, planning, public administration, teacher education

History: Established and offered first instruction at postsecondary level 1912; became University of Colorado at Denver and Health Sciences Center-Downtown Campus in 2004.

Institutional Structure: *Composition of institution:* Administrators 40 men / 53 women. Academic affairs headed by Vice Chancellor for Academic Affairs. Management/business/finances directed by Vice Chancellor for Administration and Finance. Full-time instructional faculty 286 men / 180 women. Academic governance body, Denver Campus Faculty Assembly, meets an average of 9 times per year.

Calendar: Semesters. Academic year June to May. Freshmen admitted Sept., Jan., June. Degrees conferred May, Dec, Aug. Formal commencement May. Summer session from June to Aug.

Characteristics of Freshmen: 72% of applicants admitted. 32% of admitted students enrolled full-time.

53% (248 students) submitted SAT scores; 94% (708 students) submitted ACT scores. *25th percentile:* SAT Verbal 475, SAT Math 470; ACT Composite 19, ACT English 19, ACT Math 18. *75th percentile:* SAT Verbal 590, SAT Math 590; ACT Composite 25, ACT English 24, ACT Math 25.

60% of entering freshmen expected to graduate within 5 years. 95% of freshmen from Colorado. Freshmen from 6 states.

Admission: Rolling admissions plan. For fall acceptance, apply as early as middle of junior year in secondary school, but not later than July 22 in year of enrollment. *Requirements:* Graduation from accredited secondary school with 16 units. GED accepted. Audition for music majors. Additional requirements for some programs. Requirements for first-time freshmen: High School Performance Index Score based on formula (high school percentile rank, SAT/ACT score, and GPA). *For transfer students:* Admission requirements based on GPA, institutional type and the number of credit hours transferred.

College credit and advanced placement for postsecondary-level work completed in secondary school. Advanced placement for extrainstitutional learning on basis of ACE *2006 Guide to the Evaluation of Educational Experiences in the Armed Services.*

Degree Requirements: *Undergraduate:* 120–136 semester hours; 2.0 GPA; last 30 hours in residence. Additional requirements vary with program. Fulfillment of some degree requirements and exemption from some beginning courses possible by passing College Board CLEP, APP. *Grading system:* A–F; pass-fail, withdraw (carries time limit).

Distinctive Educational Programs: Cooperative education. Off-campus centers at locations in the Denver area, weekend and evening classes. Accelerated degree programs. Joint baccalaureate in engineering and business administration. Special facilities for using telecommunications in the classroom. Inter-

departmental or interdisciplinary programs in basic studies, distributed studies, environmental science, ethnic studies, humanities, planning and community development, social sciences, urban studies. Facilities for independent research, including honors programs, individual majors, tutorials. International program offering studies in the social sciences, humanities, foreign languages, and international business. Study abroad in Italy, Russia, Germany, France, Australia, Mexico. Educational Opportunity Program provides academic and other support services for economically and educationally disadvantaged students. *Other distinctive programs:* Credit and noncredit continuing education programs. Tuition-free classes for senior citizens.

ROTC: Army and Air Force in cooperation with University of Colorado at Boulder.

Degrees Conferred: 1,387 *baccalaureate*; 1,576 *master's*; 33 *doctorate*: architecture 10 (M), 3 (D); biological/life sciences 91 (B), 4 (M); business/marketing 334 (B), 560 (M); communications/communication technologies 157 (B), 7 (M); computer and information sciences 61 (B), 113 (M), 18 (D); education 289 (M), 18 (D); engineering and engineering technologies 73 (B), 63 (M); English 53 (B), 63 (M); foreign languages and literature 28 (B); health professions and related sciences 6 (M); interdisciplinary 19 (B), 3 (M), 7 (D); liberal arts/general studies 15 (M); library science 59 (B); mathematics 13 (B), 11 (M), 3 (D); natural resources/environmental science 9 (M); philosophy/religion/theology 18 (B); physical sciences 20 (B), 6 (M); protective services/public administration 149 (M), 2 (D); psychology 136 (B), 71 (M); social sciences and history 273 (B), 77 (M); visual and performing arts 111 (B), 5 (M).

Fees and Other Expenses: *Full-time tuition per academic year 2004–05:* undergraduate resident $3,664, out-of-state $15,634; graduate resident $5,414, out-of-state $16,684. *Required fees:* $793.

Financial Aid: Aid from institutionally generated funds is provided on the basis of academic merit, financial need. Institution has a Program Participation Agreement with the U.S. Department of Education for eligible students to receive Pell Grants and other federal aid.

Financial aid to full-time, first-time undergraduate students: need-based scholarships/grants totaling $6,661,370, self-help $10,052,124, parent loans $184,097; non-need-based scholarships/grants totaling $598,275, self-help $3,086,769, parent loans $506,649. *Graduate aid:* 278 students received federal and state-funded fellowships/grants totaling $890,093 (ranging from $50 to $11,281); 1,822 loans totaling $15,511,530; 54 work-study jobs worth $222,709; 554 fellowships and grants totaling $1,171,728.

Departments and Teaching Staff: *Total instructional faculty:* 945 (full-time 443, part-time 501; women 387, men 558; members of minority groups 101). Total faculty with doctorate, first-professional, or other terminal degree: 581. Student-to-faculty ratio: 14:1.

Enrollment: Total enrollment 16,610. Undergraduate full-time 2,390 men / 2762 women, part-time 2,050m / 2,719w; graduate full-time 377m / 1022w, part-time 1,800m / 2,990w. *Transfer students:* in-state 1,126; out-of-state 203.

Characteristics of Student Body: *Ethnic and racial makeup:* number of Black non-Hispanic: 315; American Indian or Alaska Native: 84; Asian or Pacific Islander: 751; Hispanic: 776; White non-Hispani: 4,525; unknown: 568. *Age distribution:* number under 18: 44; 18–19: 1,427; 20–21: 1,712; 22–24: 1,767, 25–29: 1,180; 30–34: 561; 35–39: 241; 40–49: 250; 50–64: 73; 65 and over: 2.

International Students: 421 nonresident aliens enrolled fall 2004. 17 students from Europe, 27 Asia, 7 Central and South America, 6 Africa, 1 Australia. Programs available to aid students whose native language is not English: English as a Second Language Program. No financial aid specifically designated for international students.

Student Life: No on-campus housing. *Special services:* Learning Resources Center. *Student publications:* A weekly newspaper. *Surrounding community:* Denver area population 1,750,000. Served by mass transit bus system; airport 30 miles from campus; passenger rail service 1 mile from campus.

Library Collections: 720,830 volumes. Online catalog. Current serial subscriptions: 5,088 paper; 850 microform; 46,000 via electronic access. 13,027 recordings; 2,533 compact discs; 1,281 CD-ROMs. 151 computer work stations. Students have access to the Internet at no charge. Total 2004–05 budget for materials and operation: $1,888,826.

Most important holdings include Senator John Carroll collection; Professor Donald Sutherland collection; Minoru Wasui collection; National Municipal League Records; Lester Thorssen Rhetoric Collection.

Buildings and Grounds: Campus area 171 acres. *New buildings:* King Center for the Performing Arts completed in fall 2000.

Chief Executive Officer: Dr. James Shore, Chancellor. Address admission inquiries to Barbara Edwards, Director of Admissions.

University of Colorado at Denver and Health Sciences Center-Health Sciences Program

4200 East Ninth Avenue
Denver, Colorado 80262
Tel: (303) 372-0000   **E-mail:** admissions@uchsc.edu
Internet: www.uchsc.edu

Institution Description: The University of Colorado at Denver Health Sciences Center provides upper division baccalaureate, first-professional, and graduate degree study only. *Enrollment:* 2,419. *Degrees awarded:* Baccalaureate, first-professional (dentistry, medicine, nursing), master's, doctorate.

Accreditation: *Regional:* NCA. *Professional:* dentistry, medical assisting, medicine, nursing, physical therapy

History: Established as University of Colorado Medical Center 1882; offered first instruction at postsecondary level 1883; awarded first degree (first-professional) 1885; chartered 1876; adopted present name 2004.

Institutional Structure: *Composition of institution:* Administrators 31 men / 42 women. Academic affairs headed by chancellor. Management/business/finances directed by vice chancellor for administration. Academic governance body, Health Sciences Center faculty councils.

Calendar: Semesters (quarters for medical students). Academic year June to May. Degrees conferred May, Aug., Dec. Formal commencement May. Summer session of 1 term from early June to mid-Aug.

Admission: Admission requirements vary by program.

Distinctive Educational Programs: Tutorials. Statewide Educational Activities for Rural Colorado's Health program provides off-campus work experience and study for students as well as continuing professional education and community service at Alamosa, Grand Junction, Greeley, Pueblo and other areas.

Degrees Conferred: 201 *baccalaureate* (B), 183 *master's* (M), 60 *doctorate*: biological/life sciences 6 (B), 16 (M), 33 (D); health professions and related sciences 195 (B), 167 (M), 24 (D); interdisciplinary studies 3 (D). 235 *first-professional:* dentistry 40, pharmacy 82, medicine 113.

Fees and Other Expenses: *Tuition and fees per academic year 2004–05:* undergraduate in-state $6,360, out-of-state $21,600. Contact the university for current graduate tuition and fees; rates vary by program and for in-state/out-of-state students. *Required fees:* in-state student $212, out-of-state $720.

Financial Aid: Aid from institutionally generated funds is awarded on the basis of financial need. Institution has a Program Participation Agreement with the U.S. Department of Education for eligible students to receive Pell Grants and other federal aid.

Financial aid to full-time, first-time undergraduate students: need-based scholarships/grants totaling $329,000, self-help $3,478,000, parent loans $190,000; non-need-based scholarships/grants totaling $230,500, self-help $300,000. *Graduate aid:* 489 students received federal and state-funded fellowships/grants totaling $1,867,408; 1,528 received federal and state-funded loans totaling $35,223,359; 64 work-study jobs worth $554,059, 348 fellowships/grants totaling $1,202,234; 468 research assistantships totaling $1,701,027.

Departments and Teaching Staff: *Professors* 409, *associate professors* 424, *assistant professors* 579, *instructors* 517, *part-time faculty* 133. *Total instructional faculty:* 2,928 (2,523 full-time; 405 part-time; 1,686 women, 1,242 686 men; members of minority groups 346).

Enrollment: Total enrollment 2,919. Undergraduate full-time 34 men / 299 women, part-time 1m / 25w; graduate full-time 39m / 145w, part-time 182m / 554w; first-professional full-time 540m / 996w, part-time 96m/ 208w.

Characteristics of Student Body: *Ethnic/racial makeup:* number of Black non-Hispanic: 3; American Indian or Alaska Native: 4; Asian or Pacific Islander: 19; Hispanic: 23; White non-Hispanic: 285; unknown: 18. *Age distribution:* number 18–19: 1; 20–21: 38; 22–24: 87; 25–29: 95; 30–34: 71; 35–39: 28; 40–49: 28; 50–64: 11.

International Students: 56 nonresident aliens enrolled fall 2004. 6 students from Europe, 8 Asia, 2 Central and South America, 1 Africa, 1 Canada. No programs available to aid students whose native language is not English. No financial aid specifically designated for international students.

Student Life: No on-campus housing. *Special regulations:* Cars with parking permits allowed; monthly fee charged. *Special services:* Learning Resources Center, medical services. *Surrounding community:* Denver metropolitan area population over 1,500,000. Served by mass transit bus system; airport 5 miles from campus; passenger rail service 6 miles from campus.

Library Collections: 273,326 volumes. Online catalog. Current serial subscriptions: 480 paper, 1,600 via electronic access. 60 computer work stations. Students have access to online information retrieval services and the Internet. Total budget 2004–05 budget for books and materials: $1,318,689.

Most important holdings include history of medicine collection (6,000 volumes); Florence G. Strauss Complementary and Indigenous Medicine Collection.

Buildings and Grounds: Campus area 40 acres.

Chief Executive Officer: Dr. James H. Shore, Chancellor.

All admission contact information is program specific. *See* www.uchsc.edu for specific program information.

School of Dentistry

Degree Programs Offered: Provides upper division baccalaureate and first-professional degree study only. *Baccalaureate* in dental hygiene; *first-professional* in dentistry.

Admission: *For baccalaureate:* 60 semester hours of accredited college or university, with 2 semesters English, 2 general biology or zoology, 2 general chemistry with lab, 1 mathematics, 1 psychology, 1 public speaking, 1 sociology; Dental Hygiene Aptitude Test; personal interview. *For first-professional:* 90 semester hours at accredited college or university with 2 semesters English literature or humanities, 1 English composition, 2 general biology or zoology, 2 general chemistry, 2 general physics, 2 organic chemistry, 8 genetics; DAT; credentials assembled through AADSAS. Recommend baccalaureate.

Degree Requirements: *For baccalaureate:* 2,257 upper division clock hours. *For first-professional:* 4,461 clock hours. *For both degrees:* 12 months in residence; 2.5 GPA; prescribed curriculum.

Fees and Other Expenses: Contact the school for current tuition and fees.

School of Medicine

Degree Programs Offered: Provides upper division baccalaureate, first-professional and graduate degree study only. *Baccalaureate* in medical laboratory sciences; *first-professional* in medicine; *master's* in biochemistry, biometrics, biophysics and genetics, laboratory medicine, microbiology, pathology, pharmacology, physiology, child health associate, medical physics, physical therapy, radiation biology; *doctorate* in cell and developmental biology, anesthesiology, biochemistry, biometrics, biophysics and genetics, laboratory medicine, microbiology, pathology, pharmacology, physiology.

Admission: *For first-professional:* 120 semester hours at accredited college or university, which must include 6 English literature, 3 English composition; 8 each (with lab) biology or zoology, general chemistry, organic chemistry, physics; 6 college-level mathematics; MCAT.

Degree Requirements: *For first-professional:* 2 years in residence, must pass all required courses, 106 credit hours in prescribed curriculum in first 2 years; 10 quarters clerkships in final 2 years.

Fees and Other Expenses: Contact the school for current tuition.

Departments and Teaching Staff: *Total instructional faculty:* 817. FTE of part-time teachers 98. Degrees held by full-time faculty: Doctorate 33%, master's 6%, baccalaureate 2%, professional 59%. 92% hold terminal degrees.

Distinctive Educational Programs: Interdisciplinary institutes and centers for research, teaching, and patient care include Webb-Waring Lung Institute, John F. Kennedy Child Development Center, National Center for Child Abuse, Barbara Davis Childhood Diabetes Center, Eleanor Roosevelt Cancer Institute, Rocky Mountain Multiple Sclerosis Center. Cooperative master's in public administration with University of Colorado at Denver.

School of Nursing

Degree Programs Offered: Provides upper division baccalaureate and graduate study only. *Baccalaureate* in nursing; *master's* in nurse midwifery, women's health care nurse practitioner, family nurse practitioner, geriatric nurse practitioner, pediatric nurse practitioner, psychiatric mental health, clinical nurse specialist, public health nursing, health systems leadership, MS-MBS dual degree, pediatric special needs, health care informatics; *doctorate* in health experience of health, illness, and healing, environmental context and outcomes; *first-professional* in nursing.

Admission: *For baccalaureate:* 59 semester hours at accredited college or university with grade of 2.0 in each of the following: 3 English composition, 8 chemistry, 3 developmental psychology, 4–6 physiology, 3 anatomy, 3 cultural anthropology, 3 general psychology, 3 general sociology, 3 microbiology, 3 statistics, 6 humanities, 3 history, political science, or economics, 3 nutrition; overall 2.75 GPA.

For nursing master's: overall 3.0 GPA; preferred GRE score of 883.5; 1 elementary statistics course and 1 undergraduate research course with a grade of C or better; current RN licensure in Colorado. *For doctorate:* Graduate-level inferential statistics course and graduate-level nursing theory course. *For first-professional:* baccalaureate degree with overall 2.75 GPA; courses in: microbiology, anatomy, physiology with a grade of C or better and an introductory statistics course with a minimum grade of B.

Degree Requirements: *For baccalaureate:* 132 credit hours, 2.0 GPA; 30 semester hours in residence.

Fees and Other Expenses: Contact school for current tuition and fees.

School of Pharmacy

Degree Programs Offered: *Baccalaureate* in pharmacy; *first-professional* in pharmacy; *master's* in pharmaceutical sciences; *doctorate* in pharmaceutical sciences, toxicology.

Admission: Contact the school for specific admission requirements.

University of Denver

2199 South University Boulevard
Denver, Colorado 80208

Tel: (303) 871-2036   **E-mail:** admission@du.edu
Fax: (303) 871-3301   **Internet:** www.du.edu

Institution Description: University of Denver is a private, independent, non-profit institution. *Enrollment:* 9,808. *Degrees offered:* Baccalaureate, master's, doctorate, first-professional (law). Certificates also awarded.

Accreditation: *Regional:* NCA. *Professional:* art, business, clinical psychology, English language education, law, music, psychology internship, social work

History: Established and chartered as Colorado Seminary 1864; closed 1867; reopened, offered first instruction at postsecondary level, and adopted present name 1880; awarded first degree (baccalaureate) 1884.

Institutional Structure: *Governing board:* Board of Trustees with 25 voting members and 20 nonvoting honorary life members. *Composition of institution:* Administrators 10 men / 4 women. Academic affairs headed by provost. Management/business/finances directed by vice chancellor for business and financial affairs. Full-time instructional faculty 277 men / 125 women. Academic governance body, Faculty Senate, meets an average of 9 times per year.

Calendar: Quarters. Academic year Sept. to June. Freshmen admitted Sept., Jan., Mar., June. Degrees conferred June, Aug., Dec., Mar. Formal commencement June, Aug. Summer session of 9 weeks.

Characteristics of Freshmen: 64% (744 students) submitted SAT scores; 66% (752 students) submitted ACT scores. *25th percentile:* SAT I Verbal 510, SAT I Math 520; ACT Composite 22, ACT English 21, ACT Math 21. *75th percentile:* SAT I Verbal 630, SAT I Math 630; ACT Composite 27, ACT English 28, ACT Math 27.

Admission: Rolling admissions plan. For fall acceptance, apply as early as 1 year prior to enrollment, but not later than Mar. 1 of year of enrollment. Apply by Dec. 20 for early admission. *Requirements:* Either graduation from accredited secondary school or GED. Recommend 4 units English, 4 mathematics, 3 science, 4 social studies and history combined, 2 foreign language. Minimum GPA 3.0. *For transfer students:* 2.0 minimum GPA to be considered; average GPA 3.0; from 4-year accredited institution maximum transfer credit limited only by residence requirement; from 2-year accredited institution 90 quarter hours.

College credit and advanced placement for postsecondary-level work completed in secondary school. Tutoring available.

Degree Requirements: *Undergraduate:* 183–202 quarter hours depending on major and degree; 2.0 GPA (except BA in accounting which requires 2.5 GPA); 45 hours of UofD credit; core requirement.

Fulfillment of some degree requirements and exemption from some beginning courses possible by passing College Board CLEP or AP tests. *Grading system:* A–F.

ROTC: Army in cooperation with Metropolitan State College; Air Force in cooperation with the University of Colorado at Boulder.

Degrees Conferred: 931 *baccalaureate;* 1,224 *master's;* 98 *doctorate;* 364 *first-professional.*

Fees and Other Expenses: *Full-time tuition per academic year 2004–05:* $24,873. *Room and board per academic year:* $7,275. *Books and supplies:* $1,187.

Financial Aid: Aid from institutionally generated funds is provided on the basis of academic merit, financial need, athletic ability, fine arts talent. Institution has a Program Participation Agreement with the U.S. Department of Education for eligible students to receive Pell Grants and other federal aid.

Financial aid to full-time, first-time undergraduate students: need-based scholarships/grants totaling $25,522,544, self-help $11,099,761, parent loans $1,335,983, tuition waivers $369,131, athletic awards $541,727; non-need-based scholarships/grants totaling $11,488,444, self-help $2,803,259, parent loans $3,904,609, tuition waivers $1,347,973, athletic awards $4,349,972.

Departments and Teaching Staff: *Total instructional faculty:* 997 (full-time 463, part-time 534; full-time women 183, men 280; full-time members of minor-ity groups 62). Total full-time faculty with doctorate, first-professional, or other terminal degree: 429. Student-to-faculty ratio: 10:1.

Enrollment: Total enrollment 9,808. Undergraduate full-time 2,022 men / 2,184 women, part-time 97m / 366w; graduate full-time 703m / 1,122w, part-time 990m / 1,158w; first-professional full-time 573m / 557w, part-time 16m / 20w.

Characteristics of Student Body: *Ethnic and racial makeup:* number of Black non-Hispanic: 130; American Indian or Alaska Native: 45; Asian or Pacific Islander: 218; Hispanic: 325; White non-Hispanic: 3,742; unknown: 14.

International Students: 195 undergraduate nonresident aliens enrolled fall 2004. Programs to aid students whose native language is not English: Social, cultural. English as a Second Language Program.

Student Life: On-campus residence and apartment halls house over 30% of student body. Freshmen and sophomores are required to live on campus. Approximately 35% of undergraduate women join sororities and 11% live in sorority houses; 45% of men join fraternities and 20% live in fraternity houses. *Intercollegiate athletics:* men only: baseball, basketball, hockey, lacrosse, soccer, swimming, tennis; women only: basketball, gymnastics, soccer, swimming, tennis. *Special regulations:* Cars permitted without restrictions. *Student publications: Clarion,* a biweekly newspaper; *Kynewisbok,* a yearbook. *Surrounding community:* Denver metropolitan area population over 1.5 million. Served by mass transit bus system; airport 30 miles from campus; passenger rail service 6 miles from campus.

Publications: *Denver Quarterly,* published by the English Department; *Africa Today* and a Monograph Series published by the School of International Relations; *Denver University Law Review, Denver Journal of International Law and Policy, Tax Law Journal, Transportation Law Journal* published by the College of Law; curriculum materials from the Center for the Teaching of International Relations are published for pre-collegiate classrooms; newsletters from main academic units; *University of Denver News,* a quarterly university publication for alumni.

Library Collections: 1,268,928 volumes. 5,788 current serials; 970,022 microforms; 1,736 audiovisual units. Online catalog. Students have access to the Internet.

Most important special holdings include Solomon Schwayder Judaica Collection; Margaret Husled Culinary Collection; papers of Congressman Wayne Aspinall.

Buildings and Grounds: Campus area 125 acres.

Chief Executive Officer: Dr. Daniel L. Ritchie, Chancellor.

Address admission inquiries Thomas Willoughby, Vice Chancellor for Enrollment.

University of Northern Colorado

Carter 4000
Campus Box 59
Greeley, Colorado 80639

Tel: (970) 351-2881   **E-mail:** unc@mail.unco.edu
Fax: (970) 351-2984   **Internet:** www.unco.edu

Institution Description: University of Colorado is a state institution. *Enrollment:* 4,875 men / 8,281 women. *Degrees awarded:* Baccalaureate, master's, doctorate. Specialist in education also awarded.

Academic offerings subject to approval by statewide coordinating bodies. Budget subject to approval by university governing board.

Accreditation: *Regional:* NCA. *Professional:* accounting, athletic training, audiology, business, counseling, counseling psychology, dietetics, music, nursing, nursing education, public health, recreation and leisure services, rehabilitation counseling, psychology internship, speech-language pathology, teacher education

History: Established as State Normal School and offered first instruction at postsecondary level 1889; chartered 1890; awarded first degree (baccalaureate) 1891; changed name to Colorado State Teachers College 1911, to Colorado State College of Education 1935, to Colorado State College 1957; adopted present name 1970. *See* Robert Larson *Shaping Educational Change: The First Century of the University of Northern Colorado at Greeley* (University of Colorado Press, 1989) for further information.

Institutional Structure: *Governing board:* Board of Trustees. Extrainstitutional representation: 7 trustees; nonvoting institutional representatives: 1 full-time instructional faculty member and 1 student. *Composition of institution:* Administrators 64 men / 93 women. Academic affairs headed by vice president for academic affairs. Management/business/finances directed by vice president for finance and administration. Full-time instructional faculty 216 men / 196 women. Academic governance body, Faculty Senate, meets an average of 20 times per year.

Calendar: Semesters. Academic year Aug. to May. Freshmen admitted Aug., Jan., June. Degrees conferred and formal commencements Dec., May, Aug. Summer sessions from mid-May to mid-Aug.

Characteristics of Freshmen: 81% of applicants admitted. 43% of admitted students enrolled full-time.

% 29.6% (722 students) submitted SAT scores; 94% (2,291 students) submitted ACT scores. *25th percentile*: SAT Verbal 470, SAT Math 460; ACT Composite 19, ACT English 19, ACT Math 18. *75th percentile*: SAT Verbal 570, SAT Math 571; ACT Composite 24, ACT English 24, ACT Math24.

42% of entering freshmen expected to graduate within 5 years. 89% of freshmen from Colorado. Freshmen from 41 states and 32 foreign counties.

Admission: Rolling admissions plan. Apply as early as 1 year, but not later than 30 days, prior to registration. Early acceptance available. *Requirements:* Either graduation from accredited secondary school or GED with score of 55 or higher. Recommend 15 secondary school units: 4 units in English, 2 history/ social science, 2 natural sciences. Applicants must have completed 3 years of college preparatory mathematics, either 2 years of algebra or 1 year of algebra and 1 year of geometry. Applicants are expected to have a 2.9 high school GPA and a composite ACT score of 26 or SAT combined score of 970 . Applicants are considered on an individual basis and the institution may admit students based on other criteria. *For transfer students:* The admission standards are based on the grade point average from previous collegiate work, transfer hours, and high school record. Similar to the first-time freshman standards, the institution may admit students who do not meet the standards, but who meet other criteria; from 4-year accredited institution 90 semester hours or 135 quarter hours maximum transfer credit; from 2-year institution 60 semester hours or 90 quarter hours maximum transfer credit.

College credit and advanced placement for postsecondary-level work completed in secondary school. College credit for extrainstitutional learning on basis of ACE *2006 Guide to the Evaluation of Educational Experiences in the Armed Services.* Tutoring available.

Degree Requirements: *Undergraduate:* 120 semester hours; cumulative GPA 2.0. At least 40 semester hours in general education courses. Minimum of 30 semester hours earned at UNC, and 20 of last 30 hours must be earned on campus. Fulfillment of some degree requirements and exemption from some beginning courses possible by passing institutional examinations, departmental examinations, College Board CLEP, AP. *Grading system:* A–F; withdraw.

Distinctive Educational Programs: *For undergraduates:* "Life of the Mind" interdisciplinary program involving arts, sciences, humanities and social sciences. Individualized education program which includes independent study, research and tutorials. Interdisciplinary Studies program allows students to pursue a course of study tailored to their individual needs and interests. Honors Program which includes interdisciplinary courses, small group seminars and a thesis project. Preprofessional programs in engineering, health professions, and law. Study abroad (French, various locations in France; German, various locations in Germany; Spanish, various locations in Spain). *For graduate students:* Interdisciplinary Program allows students to develop innovative degree programs to meet individual needs. Graduate Internship Program provides students with on-the-job experiences under the supervision of experts. *Other distinctive programs:* National Student Exchange, International Student Exchange, and Oxford (England) Exchange Program. The University's Jazz Studies Program has received national recognition. UNC has been designated as the primary teacher education institution in Colorado and many programs are nationally recognized. Continuing Education Services offers courses and degree programs for professional educators and others.

ROTC: Air Force, Army.

Degrees Conferred: 1,960 *baccalaureate* (B), 637 *master's* (M), 13 *doctorate* (D): area and ethnic studies 9 (B); biological/life sciences 39 (B), 6 (M), 4 (D); business/marketing 287 (B); communications/communication technologies 181 (B), 10 (M); education 28 (B); 308 (M); 30 (D); English 58 (B), 14 (M); foreign languages and literature 32 (B), 13 (M); health professions and related sciences 199 (B), 67 (M), 2 (D); home economics and vocational home economics 2 (B), 7 (M); interdisciplinary studies 267 (B), 12 (M); mathematics 43 (B), 8 (M); parks and recreation 132 (B), 54 (M), 7 (D); philosophy/religion/theology 14 (B); physical sciences 51 (B), 8 (M); protective services/public administration 8 (B); psychology 152 (B), 84 (M), 13 (D); social sciences and history 300 (B), 12 (M); visual and performing arts 158 (B), 34 (M), 13 (D).

Fees and Other Expenses: *Full-time tuition per academic year 2004–05:* undergraduate resident $2,850, out-of-state $11,740; graduate resident $3,360, out-of-state $12,520. *Required fees:* $520. *Room and board per academic year:* $5,954.

Financial Aid: Aid from institutionally generated funds is provided on the basis of academic merit, financial need, athletic ability. Institution has a Program Participation Agreement with the U.S. Department of Education for eligible students to receive Pell Grants and other federal aid.

Financial aid to full-time, first-time undergraduate students: need-based scholarships/grants totaling $8,188,543, self-help $16,706,763; non-need-based scholarships/grants totaling $8,260,553, self-help $22,122,856, parent loans $31,790,033, athletic awards $685,412. *Graduate aid:* 329 federal and state-funded fellowships and grants totaling $921,058; 123 federal and state-funded loans totaling $218,900; 25 work-study jobs worth $46,386; 117 college assigned jobs worth $334,704; 114 fellowships/grants totaling $439,221; 309 teaching assistantships totaling $6,148,787; 426 research assistantships totaling $9,809,033.

Departments and Teaching Staff: *Professors* 161, *associate professors* 86, *assistant professors* 86, *instructors* 79, *lecturers* 79, *part-time faculty* 169. *Total instructional faculty:* 581 (full-time 412, part-time 169; women 292, men 285; members of minority groups 59). Total faculty with doctorate, first-professional, or other terminal degree: 367. Student-to-faculty ratio: 23:1. *Faculty development:* $8,873,303 in grants for research. 20 faculty members awarded sabbaticals 2004–05.

Enrollment: Total enrollment 13,156. Undergraduate full-time 3,817 men / 5,858 women, part-time 424m / 702; graduate full-time 295m / 711w, part-time 339m / 1,000w. *Transfer students:* in-state 755, out-of-state 150.

Characteristics of Student Body: *Ethnic and racial makeup:* number of Black non-Hispanic: 266; American Indian or Alaska Native: 129; Asian or Pacific Islander: 361; Hispanic: 867; White non-Hispanic: 8,474; unknown: 661. *Age distribution:* number under 18: 139; 18–19: 4,089; 20–21: 3,357; 22–24: 1,661; 25–29: 470; 30–34: 145; 35–39: 95; 40–49: 76; 50–64: 21.

International Students: 132 nonresident aliens enrolled fall 2004. 32 students from Europe, 93 Asia; 22 Central and South America, 6 Africa, 14 Canada, 1 Australia, 1 New Zealand, 23 other. Social and cultural programs available to aid students whose native language is not English. English as a Second Language program. Some financial aid specifically designated for international students.

Student Life: On-campus residence halls house 31% of student body. Residence halls for for women only 2%, coed facilities 98%. *Intercollegiate athletics:* men only: baseball, basketball, football, golf, tennis, track, wrestling; women only: basketball, golf, soccer, softball, swimming, tennis, track and field, volleyball. *Special regulations:* Cars permitted; fee charged. *Special services:* Learning Resources Center, medical services. *Student publications, radio:* Colorado North Review, a literary magazine published twice each year; *Mirror*, a tri-weekly newspaper. Opportunity is provided for student interns to work with full-time professional staff on station KJMC. *Surrounding community:* Greeley population 80,000. Served by airport 50 miles from campus, bus and shuttle service available from airport to Greeley.

Library Collections: 1,046,197 volumes including bound books, serial backfiles, electronic documents, and government documents not in separate collections. Online catalog. Current serial subscriptions: 3,417 n paper, microform, and electronic. 30,450 recordings. 782 computer work stations. Students have access to the Internet at no charge. Total budget for books and materials 2004–05: $1,740,413.

Most important holdings include James A. Michener Collection.

Buildings and Grounds: Campus area 236 acres.

Chief Executive Officer: Dr. Kay Norton, President.

Undergraduates address admission inquiries to Gary Gullickson, Director of Admissions; graduate inquiries to Graduate School.

Western State College of Colorado

210 Taylor Hall
College Heights
Gunnison, Colorado 81231
Tel: (970) 943-2120   **E-mail:** discover@western.edu
Fax: (970) 943-7069   **Internet:** www.western.edu

Institution Description: Western State College of Colorado is a state-supported institution located in a small community high in the Colorado Rockies. *Enrollment:* 2,410. *Degrees awarded:* Baccalaureate.

Accreditation: *Regional:* NCA. *Professional:* music, teacher education

History: Established as Colorado State Normal School 1901; offered first instruction at postsecondary level 1911; became 4-year institution 1920; awarded first degree (baccalaureate) 1921; adopted present name 1923.

Institutional Structure: *Governing board:* Board of Trustees for the Consortium of State Colleges in Colorado. Representation: 7 trustees (appointed by governor of Colorado), 1 student, 1 faculty. 7 voting. *Composition of institution:* Administrators 30. Academic affairs headed by vice president for academic affairs. Management/business/ finances directed by vice president for administration/finance; dean of students; director of development.

Calendar: Semesters. Academic year Aug. to May. 5-week summer terms.

Characteristics of Freshmen: 1,586 applicants (men 926, women 660). 85.1% of applicants admitted. 35.5% of admitted students enrolled full-time.

27% (135 students) submitted SAT scores; 88% (434 students) submitted ACT scores. *25th percentile*: SAT Verbal 440, SAT Math 460; ACT Composite 18, ACT English 17, ACT Math 17. *75th percentile*: SAT Verbal 550, SAT Math 550; ACT Composite 23, ACT English 22, ACT Math 23.

Admission: Early acceptance available. *Requirements:* Graduation from accredited secondary school with necessary units from English, mathematics, science, social studies. Admission decision based on evaluation of GPA, class rank, and ACT or SAT score. Home school or GED accepted. *Entrance tests:* ACT or SAT accepted. For foreign students, 550 TOEFL. *For transfer students:* Admission decision based on evaluation of GPA and coursework.

Degree Requirements: *Undergraduate:* 120 semester hours; 2.0 GPA overall and in major. 30 semester hours in residence; 39 in general education.

Fulfillment of some degree requirements and exemption from some beginning courses possible by passing College Board CLEP, other standardized tests. *Grading system:* A–F; withdraw (carries time limit).

Distinctive Educational Programs: Credit and non-credit continuing education and off-campus programs. Non-credit tuition-free program for senior citizens. Summer programs abroad in Puebla, Mexico (Spanish) and Prague.

Degrees Conferred: 429 *baccalaureate.* Bachelor's degrees awarded in top five disciplines: business, management, marketing, and related support services 135; parks, recreation, leisure, and fitness studies 60; visual and performing arts 45; social sciences 38; psychology 34.

Fees and Other Expenses: *Full-time tuition per academic year 2004–05:* undergraduate resident $2,763. *Books and supplies:* $1,000. *Other expenses:* $2,020. *Room and board per academic year:* $7,120.

Financial Aid: Aid from institutionally generated funds is provided on the basis of academic merit, financial need, athletic ability. Institution has a Program Participation Agreement with the U.S. Department of Education for eligible students to receive Pell Grants and other federal aid.

Financial aid to full-time, first-time undergraduate students: 23% received federal grants averaging $2,525; 23% state/local grants averaging $1,556; 27% institutional grants averaging $1,442; 52% loans averaging $3,589.

Departments and Teaching Staff: Art and technology *professors* 5, *associate professors* 1, *assistant professors* 2, *part-time faculty* 0; business and accounting 7, 2, 1, 1; communication arts and sociology 4, 3, 5, 0; computer science/mathematics 4, 1, 2, 0; education/geography 3, 1, 2, 0; history, economics, and political science 4, 2, 3, 0; kinesiology/recreation 1, 1, 5, 2; music 1, 0, 4, 0; modern language 6, 0, 2, 4; sciences 13, 2, 5, 0.

Total instructional faculty: 111. Student-to-faculty ratio: 19:1. Degrees held by full-time faculty: baccalaureates 1%, master's 30%, doctorates 54%, professional 15%. 72% of faculty hold terminal degrees.

Enrollment: Total enrollment 2,410 (59.4% men; 40.6% women).

Characteristics of Student Body: *Ethnic/racial makeup:* Black non-Hispanic: 1%; American Indian or Alaska Native: 1%; Asian or Pacific Islander: .9%; Hispanic: 5.6%; White non-Hispanic: 54.3%; unknown: 7.1%.

International Students: 17 nonresident aliens enrolled fall 2003. Students from Europe, Asia, Central and South America, Canada, Australia, New Zealand. Social programs available for students whose native language is not English. No financial aid specifically designated for international students.

Student Life: Approximately one-half of student body live on campus. Exceptional intramural program. *Intercollegiate athletics:* men only: basketball, cross-country, football, skiing (alpine and Nordic), track and field, wrestling; women only: basketball, cross-country, skiing (alpine and Nordic), track and field, volleyball. *Special services:* 60 clubs provide for varied interests and many leadership opportunities. *Student publications, radio: Top of the World*, a student newspaper; *The Curecanti*, a yearbook; *Mountain Thought Review*, a literary magazine. Campus radio station KWSB-FM. Student Government supports over 60 cultural, social, and environmental clubs. *Surrounding community:* Gunnison population 6,000. Denver, 210 miles from campus, is nearest metropolitan area.

Publications: Quarterly alumni newsletter (*Crimson & Slate*); biweekly newsletter for faculty and staff (*Western Watch*); quarterly newsletter for perspective students (*Western Exposure*).

Library Collections: 156,000 volumes. 317,500 government documents; 1,065,484 microforms; 5,000 audiovisual materials; 600 current periodical subscriptions. Access to computerized information retrieval systems.

Most important holdings include Western Colorado History Collection; Historical Gunnison Area Newspaper Collection; Public Land Law Review Commission (papers); Colorado newspapers.

Buildings and Grounds: 228-acre campus. 42 buildings on landscaped acres.

Chief Executive Officer: Dr. Jay Hellman, President.

Address admission inquiries to Tom Albers, Director of Admissions (e-mail: talbers@western.edu).

Connecticut

Albertus Magnus College

700 Prospect Street
New Haven, Connecticut 06511-1189
Tel: (203) 773-8550   **E-mail:** admissions@albertus.edu
Fax: (203) 785-8652   **Internet:** www.albertus.edu

Institution Description: Albertus Magnus College is a private institution affiliated with the Roman Catholic Church. *Enrollment:* 2,389. *Degrees awarded:* Associate, baccalaureate, master's.

Accreditation: *Regional:* NEASC.

History: Established 1925; incorporated 1925; first instruction at postsecondary level 1925; first degree (baccalaureate) awarded 1928.

Institutional Structure: *Governing board:* Board of Trustees of Albertus Magnus College. Extrainstitutional representation: 24 trustees; institutional representation: 1 administrator; 2 alumni. Total members 28; 27 voting (including 4 ex officio), 1 emeritus non-voting. *Composition of institution:* Administrators 2 women / 5 men. Full-time instructional faculty 27.

Calendar: Semesters. Academic year early Aug. to May. Freshmen admitted Sept., Jan. Degrees conferred May. Formal commencement May. Summer sessions from late May to early Aug.

Characteristics of Freshmen: 84.6% of applicants admitted. 29% of admitted students enrolled full-time.

96.3% (131 students) submitted SAT scores. Average secondary school rank of freshmen men 65th percentile, women 53rd percentile, class 59th percentile. Mean SAT scores men 461 verbal, 468 math; women 493 (v), 444 (m); class 477 (v), 456 (m).

60% entering freshmen expected to graduate within 5 years. 87% of freshmen from Connecticut. Freshmen from 12 states and 1 foreign country.

Admission: Rolling admissions plan. Early acceptance available. *Requirements:* 16 secondary school academic units which must include 4 college preparatory English; 2 foreign language, 1 history, 1 laboratory science, 2 mathematics recommended. Lowest acceptable secondary school class standing depends on type of program followed. *Entrance tests:* College Board SAT or ACT composite. *For transfer students:* Minimum GPA 2.0. Maximum transfer credit for all students from 4-year institutions 90 semester hours; from 2-year institutions 64 hours.

College credit for postsecondary-level work completed in secondary school. College Board CLEP, and for extrainstitutional learning on basis of ACE *2006 Guide to the Evaluation of Educational Experiences in the Armed Services*, portfolio assessment, and faculty assessment of challenge examinations. Noncredit developmental courses offered in regular academic year.

Degree Requirements: 2.0 GPA; 2 terms in residence; 2 physical education credits; CLEP exams offered monthly (21 credits can be earned by passing CLEP exams). *For all associate degrees:* 60 credit hours (21 can be earned by passing CLEP with score of 500 or better). *For all baccalaureate degrees:* 120–129 credit hours (45 with CLEP). *Grading system:* A–F, pass-fail, withdraw (pass-fail appended at midterm).

Distinctive Educational Programs: *Available to all students:* first year humanities program; general education program featuring departmental courses which identify stages in the process of inquiry and develop habits of mind associated with liberal learning; majors in art (BA and BFA), biology, business and economics, chemistry, English, classics, French, Italian, Spanish, history, mathematics, physical science, political science, psychology and sociology; interdepartmental majors in biology-chemistry, communications, general studies, humanities, Romance languages, social sciences; minors available in all departments, including drama, philosophy and religious studies; sophomore or junior academic semester or year abroad in approved American-college-sponsored programs; work-experience programs, including practicums, internships, work-study; For continuing education students, weekend and evening classes.

Degrees Conferred: 375 *baccalaureate* (B); 233 *master's* (M): biological/life sciences 4 (B); business/marketing 276 (B); 223 (M); communications/communication technologies 16 (B); computer and information sciences 9 (B); English 4 (B); liberal arts/general studies 3 (M); philosophy/religion/theology 2 (B); psychology 26 (B), 7 (M); social sciences and history 22 (B); visual and performing arts 6 (B).

Fees and Other Expenses: *Full-time tuition per academic year 2004–05:* $15,800. *Room and board per academic year:* $7,330.

Financial Aid: Aid from institutionally generated funds is provided on the basis of academic merit, financial need. Institution has a Program Participation Agreement with the U.S. Department of Education for eligible students to receive Pell Grants and other federal aid.

Departments and Teaching Staff: *Professors* 6, *associate professors* 13, *assistant professors* 13, *instructors* 2, *part-time faculty* 165. *Total instructional faculty:* 199 (women 75, men 126). Total faculty with doctorate, first-professional, or other terminal degree: 58. Student-to-faculty ratio: 15:1. 1 faculty members awarded a sabbatical 2004–05.

Enrollment: Total enrollment: 2,389. Undergraduate full-time 583 men / 1,326 women; graduate full-time 234m / 246w.

Characteristics of Student Body: *Ethnic and racial makeup:* number of Black non-Hispanic: 444; American Indian or Alaska Native: 6; Asian or Pacific Islander: 18; Hispanic: 170; White non-Hispanic: 1,153.

International Students: 6 nonresident aliens enrolled fall 2004. English as a Second Language Program available. No financial aid specifically designated for international students.

Student Life: On-campus residence halls house 47% of undergraduate students (co-ed). 5% of student body live off campus with approved families who offer room and board to students in exchange for services. *Intercollegiate athletics:* women: basketball, softball, volleyball, tennis; men: baseball, basketball, soccer, tennis. *Special regulations:* Registered cars permitted on campus in designated areas only. *Special services:* Medical services. *Student publications: Breakwater*, an annual literary magazine; *Prospect*, a college yearbook; *Silver Horn*, a college newspaper. *Surrounding community:* New Haven population 150,000. New York City, 75 miles from campus, is nearest metropolitan area. Served by city mass transit bus system; airport 10 miles from campus; passenger rail service 3 miles from campus.

Publications: *Albertus Announcer*, founded in 1984, is the college's publication for students, staff, and faculty.

Library Collections: 115,000 volumes including bound books, serial backfiles, electronic documents, and government documents not in separate collections. Online and card catalogs. Current serial subscriptions: 554 paper. Computer work stations available. Students have access to the Internet at no charge.

Most important holdings include Samuel F. Bemis Collection (archival material); Connecticut Collection (books); Louise Imogen Guiney Collection; Donald Grant Mitchell "Ik Marvel" Collection.

Buildings and Grounds: Campus area 50 acres. *New buildings:* Academic Center Building for Science, Technology, and the Arts.

Chief Executive Officer: Sr. Julia M. McNamara, Ph.D., President.

Address admission inquiries to Richard J. Locatte, Dean of Admissions and Financial Aid.

Central Connecticut State University

1615 Stanley Street
New Britain, Connecticut 06050-4010
Tel: (860) 832-3200   **E-mail:** admissions@ccsu.edu
Fax: (860) 832-2522   **Internet:** www.ccsu.edu

Institution Description: Central Connecticut State University is a state institution. *Enrollment:* 12,320. *Degrees awarded:* Baccalaureate, master's. Specialist certificates in education also awarded.

Academic offerings subject to approval by statewide coordinating bodies. Budget subject to approval by state governing boards.

Accreditation: *Regional:* NEASC. *Professional:* business, computer science, construction education, engineering, industrial technology, marriage and family therapy, nurse anesthesia education, nursing, nursing education, social work, teacher education

History: Established as New Britain Normal School, chartered, and offered first instruction at postsecondary level 1849; became 4-year institution and changed name to Teachers College of Connecticut 1933; awarded first degree (baccalaureate) 1934; changed name to Central Connecticut State College 1959; became Central Connecticut State University 1983. *See* Herbert E. Fowler, *A Century of Teacher Education in Connecticut* (New Britain: Teachers College of Connecticut, 1949) for further information.

Institutional Structure: *Governing board:* Board of Trustees for Connecticut State University. Representation: 16 trustees (14 appointed by governor of Connecticut, 2 students). 14 voting. The president of the state system is responsible for administration. Each campus of the 4 state universities is given a considerable amount of autonomy and functions under the leadership of a president. *Composition of institution:* Administrators 15 men / 10 women. Academic affairs headed by vice president for academic affairs. Management/business/finances directed by chief financial officer. Full-time instructional faculty 409. Academic governance body, Faculty Senate, meets an average of 18 times per year. *Faculty representation:* Faculty served by collective bargaining agent affiliated with AAUP.

Calendar: Semesters. Academic year Aug. to May. Freshmen admitted Aug., Jan. Degrees conferred May, Aug., Dec. Formal commencement May. Summer session from May to July.

Characteristics of Freshmen: 61% of applicants admitted. 41% of admitted students enrolled full-time.

99% (1,285 students) submitted SAT scores. *25th percentile*: SAT Verbal 470, SAT Math 470. *75th percentile*: SAT Verbal 560, SAT Math 570.

76% of entering freshmen expected to graduate within 5 years. 96% of freshmen from Connecticut. Freshmen from 15 states and 18 foreign countries.

Admission: Applications for fall admission may be submitted beginning in Oct. of the senior year of high school. Fall semester candidates are encouraged to apply by admission by May 1, and spring candidates before Nov. 1. *Requirements:* Either graduation from accredited secondary school with at least 13 units of college preparatory work: 4 English, 3 mathematics, 2 science (1 laboratory), 2 social studies (1 U.S. history); 2 foreign language. GED also considered. CLEP and AP credit possible for postsecondary work completed in high school. *Entrance tests:* College Board SAT. For foreign students TOEFL. *For transfer students:* 2.0 minimum GPA; official transcript sent from institution(s); hand-carried transcripts not accepted.

Degree Requirements: *Undergraduate:* 122–130 credit hours; 46 general education credits; 2.0 GPA; 45 semester hours in residence. *Graduate:* Approval of planned program of study, including a minimum of 30 credit hours of courses and either a master's thesis, a comprehensive examination, or other approved research project; minimum 3.0 GPA in all courses.

Grading system: A–F; pass-fail; withdraw (carries time limit).

Distinctive Educational Programs: Institutes for European and American Studies and Asian and American Studies; Institute for Business Studies; Center for Industrial and Engineering Technology. Study abroad in United Kingdom, Brazil, China, Costa Rica, Cyprus, France, Germany, Ghana, Jamaica, Japan, Korea, Mexico, Poland, Puerto Rico, Spain, Sweden.

Degrees Conferred: 1,474 *baccalaureate* (B), 690 *master's* (M): area and ethnic studies 1 (M); biological/life sciences 391 (B), 52 (M); communications/communication technologies 65 (B); computer and information sciences 35 (B), 38 (M); education 165 (B), 459 (M); engineering and engineering technologies 95 (B), 1 (M); English 74 (B), 4 (M); foreign languages and literature 15 (B), 10 (M); health professions and related sciences 28 (B), 32 (M); home economics and vocational home economics 13 (M); interdisciplinary studies 9 (B); mathematics 20 (B), 19 (M); parks and recreation 2 (B); philosophy/religion/theology 6 (B); physical sciences 15 (B), 14 (M); protective services/public administration 218(B), 10 (M); psychology 142 (B), 6 (M); social sciences and history 253 (B); trade and industry 12 (B); visual and performing arts 84 (B), 4 (M); other 9 (B).

Fees and Other Expenses: *Full-time tuition per academic year 2004–05:* undergraduate resident in-district $2,862, in-state out-of-district $4,294, out-of-state $9,264; graduate resident $3,666, out-of-state $9,934. *Room and board per academic year:* $7,036.

Financial Aid: Aid from institutionally generated funds is provided on the basis of academic merit, financial need, athletic ability. Institution has a Program Participation Agreement with the U.S. Department of Education for eligible students to receive Pell Grants and other federal aid.

Departments and Teaching Staff: *Total instructional faculty:* 884 (full-time 409, part-time 475; women 390, men 494; members of minority groups 95). Total faculty with doctorate, first-professional, or other terminal degree: 338. Student-to-faculty ratio: 19:1; 22 faculty members awarded sabbaticals 2004–05.

Enrollment: Total enrollment 12,320. Undergraduate full-time 3,558 men / 3,687 women, part-time 1,212m / 1,147w; graduate full-time 175m / 358w, part-time 823m / 1,360w.

Characteristics of Student Body: *Ethnic and racial makeup:* number of Black non-Hispanic: 756; American Indian or Alaska Native: 48; Asian or Pacific Islander: 264; Hispanic: 546; White non-Hispanic: 7,079; unknown: 749. *Age distribution:* number under 18: 193; 18–19: 2,362; 20–21: 462; 22–24: 1,740; 25–29: 555; 30–34: 104; 35–39: 121; 40–49: 37.

International Students: 289 nonresident aliens enrolled fall 2004. 92 students from Europe, 59 Asia; 18 Central and South America, 5 Africa; 25 Canada, 1 New Zealand, 18 other. Programs available to aid students whose native language is not English: Social and cultural. English as a Second Language Program. Some financial aid available for international students.

Student Life: On-campus residence halls house 30% of full-time undergraduate population. *Intercollegiate athletics:* 19 varieties of varsity sports; intramural sports. *Special services:* University counseling services, special student services for the differently abled; Women's Center, International Student Services, Veterans' affairs. *Student publications, radio: The Central Recorder,* a weekly newspaper; *Dial,* a yearbook; *Helix,* a biannual literary magazine; Radio station WFCS-FM broadcasts 140 hours per week. *Surrounding community:* New Britain population 76,000. Hartford, 9 miles from campus, is nearest metropolitan area. Served by mass transit bus system; airport 25 miles from campus; passenger rail service 5 miles from campus.

Library Collections: 620,000 volumes. 100,000 government documents; 46,580 microforms; 1,184 audiovisual titles; 2,928 current periodical subscriptions. 4,921 CD-ROMs. 265 computer work stations. Online catalog. Access to online information retrieval systems (fee-based). Students have access to the Internet.

Most important holdings include Connecticut Polish-American Archives and Manuscript Collection; Elihu Burritt Collection; Oriental Language Collection; Map Depository (30,000 sheets).

Buildings and Grounds: Campus area 294 acres. *New buildings:* Vance Academic Center completed 2000; Early Learning Center 2002; Energy Center 2003.

Chief Executive Officer: Dr. John W. Miller, President.

Address admission inquiries to Myrna Garcia-Bowen, Director of Recruitment and Admissions.

Charter Oak State College

55 Paul Manafort Drive
New Britain, Connecticut 06053-2142

Tel: (860) 832-3800   **E-mail:** info@charteroak.edu
Fax: (860) 832-3999   **Internet:** www.charteroak.edu

Institution Description: Charter Oak State College is the external degree program of the State of Connecticut functioning under the administration and degree-granting authority of the Board for State Academic Awards. *Enrollment:* 650 men / 943 women. *Degrees awarded:* Associate, baccalaureate.

Accreditation: *Regional:* NEASC.

History: Established as Board for State Academic Awards 1973; awarded first degree (associate) 1974; adopted present name 1992.

Institutional Structure: *Governing board:* Board for State Academic Awards. Extrainstitutional representation: 9 trustees. All voting. *Composition of institution:* Administrators 1 man / 3 women. Academic affairs headed by vice president of academic affairs. Management/business/finances directed by dean, finance and administration. Academic governance body, Core Consulting Faculty, meets an average of 15 times per year.

Calendar: Students may apply and enroll at any time during the year. Degrees conferred and formal commencement in June.

Characteristics of Freshmen: All applicants accepted; must have 9 completed semester hour credits.

Admission: *Requirements:* Open admissions. Degree candidate should be secondary school graduate, at least 16 years old. GED accepted. Other applicants encouraged to present evidence of proficiency in college-level work through course work or examination. *For transfer students:* No limit to transfer credit for courses acceptable toward a degree at an accredited institution.

College credit for extrainstitutional learning on basis of ACE *2006 Guide to the Evaluation of Educational Experiences in the Armed Services,* University of the State of New York Program on Noncollegiate Sponsored Instruction, and various examinations.

Degree Requirements: *For all associate degrees:* 60 credit hours. *For all baccalaureate degrees:* 120 credit hours. *For all degrees:* 2.0 GPA; distribution requirements. Fulfillment of some degree requirements possible by passing departmental examinations, College Board CLEP, AP, GRE, other standardized tests. *Grading system:* A–F.

Distinctive Educational Programs: Programs individually planned and interdisciplinary. Credit may be earned through programs of noncollegiate educational activity and assessment of prior learning.

Degrees Conferred: 60 *associate* arts or sciences; 439 *baccalaureate:* liberal arts/general studies.

Fees and Other Expenses: *Enrollment fee per academic year 2004–05:* in-state residents $925 enrollment fee, out-of-state students $1,190. *Tuition:* resident $145 per credit hour; nonresident $203 per credit.

Financial Aid: Aid from institutionally generated funds is provided on the basis of academic merit, financial need. Institution has a Program Participation Agreement with the U.S. Department of Education for eligible students to receive Pell Grants and other federal aid.

Financial aid to full-time, first-time undergraduate students: need-based scholarships/grants $219,442, self-help $52,986; non-need-based self-help $387,235.

Departments and Teaching Staff: Adjunct faculty establish degree requirements, review programs of individual candidates, appoint outside examiners in specific subjects when required, validate credits, and make recommendations to the Board for awarding degrees. *Total instructional faculty:* 48 (women 21, men 27; members of minority groups 3). Total faculty with doctorate, first-professional, or other terminal degree: 29. Student-to-faculty ratio: 8:1. 11 faculty members awarded sabbaticals 2004.

Enrollment: Total enrollment 1,637.

Characteristics of Student Body: *Ethnic/racial makeup:* number of Black non-Hispanic: 156; American Indian or Alaska Native: 17; Asian or Pacific Islander: 33; Hispanic: 86; White non-Hispanic: 1,081. *Age distribution:* 20–24: 4%; 25–29: 9%; 30–34: 12%; 35–39: 15%; 40–49: 195; 50–59: 19%; 60–64: 2%; 65 and over: 1%.

International Students: 1 nonresident alien enrolled fall 2004. No programs to aid students whose native language is not English.

Library Collections: All Charter Oak students permitted to use library services and facilities of institutions in the Connecticut public higher education system.

Chief Executive Officer: Dr. Merle W. Harris, President.

Address admission inquiries to Lori Pendleton, Admissions Office.

Connecticut College

270 Mohegan Avenue
New London, Connecticut 06320-4125
Tel: (860) 447-1911   **E-mail:** admit@conncoll.edu
Fax: (860) 439-2700   **Internet:** www.conncoll.edu

Institution Description: Connecticut College is a private, independent, nonprofit college. *Enrollment:* 1,905. *Degrees awarded:* Baccalaureate, master's.

Accreditation: *Regional:* NEASC.

History: Established and chartered as Connecticut College for Women 1911; offered first instruction at postsecondary level 1915; awarded first degree (baccalaureate) 1919; adopted present name and became coeducational 1969. *See* Irene Nye, *History of Connecticut College* (New York: J. J. Little and Ives, 1943) and *A History of Connecticut College* by Gertrude E. Noyes for further information.

Institutional Structure: *Governing board:* Board of Trustees. 35 members including President of College, President of Alumni Association, 3 alumni trustees, and 3 young alumni trustees. All voting. Administrators 19 men / 22 women (7% are members of minority groups; at dean's level and above; 18% are women). Academic governance body, voting members of the faculty, meets an average of 10 times per year.

Calendar: Semesters. Academic year Sept. to May. Freshmen admitted Sept., Jan., July. Degrees conferred and formal commencement May. Summer session of 1 term from late June to early Aug.

Characteristics of Freshmen: 34.4% applicants admitted. 32.1% of admitted students enrolled full-time.

53% (262 students) submitted SAT scores. *25th percentile:* SAT Verbal 530, SAT Math 620. *75th percentile:* SAT Verbal 700, SAT Math 700.

86% of entering freshmen expected to graduate within 5 years. 18% of freshmen from Connecticut. Freshmen from 46 states and 39 foreign countries.

Admission: For fall acceptance, apply no later than Jan. 15. Students are notified of acceptance April. Application deadline for Early Decision Round II Jan. 15 with notification mid-Feb. *Requirements:* Graduation from accredited secondary school with at least 4 years English, 3 years in one foreign language or 2 years in each of 2 foreign languages, 3 years mathematics, 1 year history, 1 year lab science. *Entrance tests:* Two SAT II subject (Achievement) tests or ACT required, TOEFL required for foreign students whose first language is not

English. *For transfer students:* 3.0 minimum GPA, 64 semester hours maximum transfer credit.

College credit and advanced placement for postsecondary-level work completed in secondary school and extrainstitutional learning on basis of ACE *2006 Guide to the Evaluation of Educational Experiences in the Armed Services.* Tutoring available.

Degree Requirements: *Undergraduate:* 130 semester hours; 2.0 GPA; 4 semesters in residence, including one semester senior year. Fulfillment of some degree requirements and exemption from some beginning courses possible by passing college-administered or standardized achievement tests. *Grading system:* A–F; pass-fail (for courses outside major or general education requirements); withdraw.

Distinctive Educational Programs: Four Academic Centers: Center for International Studies and the Liberal Arts, Center for Conservation Biology and Environmental Studies, Center for Community Challenges and Center for Arts and Technology. Additional programs include the National Theater Institute, Washington University Three-Two Program, Boston University College of Engineering Three-Two Program, Study Away involving 20 countries, Study Away-Teach Away, Honors and Individual Studies as well as funded student research and internship programs. *For graduate students:* Work-experience programs. *Available to all students:* Evening classes. Facilities and programs for independent research. Tutorials. *Other distinctive programs:* Teacher certification.

Degrees Conferred: 475 *baccalaureate:* architecture 12, area and ethnic studies 25, biological/life sciences 84, computer and information sciences 3, education 2, English 45, foreign languages and literature 14, home economics 9, interdisciplinary studies 1, mathematics 1, philosophy/religion,theology 21, physical sciences 7, psychology 39, social sciences and history 178, visual and performing arts 34; 6 *master's:* education 3, physical sciences 1, psychology 2.

Fees and Other Expenses: *Full-time comprehensive tuition/room and board:* $41,975.

Financial Aid: Aid from institutionally generated funds is provided on the basis of financial need. Institution has a Program Participation Agreement with the U.S. Department of Education for eligible students to receive Pell Grants and other federal aid.

Financial aid to full-time, first-time undergraduate students: need-based scholarships/grants totaling $16,661,678, self-help $3,528,654; non-need-based scholarships/grants totaling $212,948, self-help $1,272,103, parent loans $4,746,775, tuition waivers $83,200.

Departments and Teaching Staff: *Professors* 67, *associate professors* 32, *assistant professors* 34, *instructors* 19, *part-time faculty* 62. *Total instructional faculty:* 214 (full-time 152, part-time 62; women 89, men 125; members of minority groups 37). Total faculty with doctorate, first-professional, or other terminal degree: 152. Student-to-faculty ratio: 11:1. 29 faculty members awarded sabbaticals 2004–05.

Enrollment: Total enrollment 1,905. Undergraduate full-time 738 men / 1,089 women, part-time 24m / 43w.

Characteristics of Student Body: *Ethnic/racial makeup:* number of Black non-Hispanic: 72; American Indian or Alaska 5; Asian or Pacific Islander: 69; Hispanic: 81; White non-Hispanic: 1,353; unknown: 76. *Age distribution:* number under 18: 38; 18–19: 889; 20–21: 800; 22–24: 93; 25–29: 6; 30–34: 3; 35–39: 4; 40–49: 1.

International Students: 138 nonresident aliens enrolled fall 2004. 36 students from Europe, 31 Asia, 3 Central and South America, 12 Africa, 2 Canada, 1 Carbine, 2 Middle East. Social and cultural programs to aid students whose native language is not English. No financial aid specifically designated for international students.

Student Life: On-campus residence halls and cooperative facilities house 97% of student body. Residence halls for men and women constitute 100% of such space. *Intercollegiate athletics:* men only: basketball, cross country, diving, ice hockey, lacrosse, rowing (crew), sailing, soccer, squash, swimming, tennis, track and field; women only: basketball, cross-country, diving, field hockey, lacrosse, rowing (crew), sailing, soccer, squash, swimming, tennis, track and field, volleyball. 13 club sports are offered. *Special regulations:* Cars permitted on campus in accord with campus parking regulations. *Special services:* Medical services. *Student publications, radio: The College Voice,* a weekly newspaper; *Koine,* a yearbook; *CC: Connecticut College Magazine.* Radio station WCNI-FM broadcasts 18 hours per day during the academic year. *Surrounding community:* New London population 70,000. Boston New York City, each 100 miles from campus, are nearest metropolitan areas. Served by airport 6 miles from campus; passenger rail service 3 miles from campus.

Publications: The *Connecticut College Monographs* (published irregularly) first published 1941.

Library Collections: 911,456 volumes including bound books, serial backfiles, electronic documents, and government documents not in separate collections. Online catalog. Current serial subscriptions: 2,337 paper. 16,990 recordings. Computer work stations available. Students have access to the Internet at no charge.

Most important holdings include Eugene O'Neill manuscripts and first editions; Gildersleeve Collection of early children's literature and illustration; New London County history; William Meredith Collection; Frederick Irwin Collection.

Buildings and Grounds: Campus area 1 square mile.

Chief Executive Officer: Dr. Norman Fainstein, President.

Address admission inquiries to Martha Merrill, Dean of Admissions and Financial Aid.

Eastern Connecticut State University

83 Windham Street

Willimantic, Connecticut 06226

Tel: (860) 465-5000   **E-mail:** admissions@easternct.edu
Fax: (860) 465-5544   **Internet:** www.easternct.edu

Institution Description: Eastern Connecticut State University is a state institution. *Enrollment:* 5,156. *Degrees awarded:* Associate, baccalaureate, master's.

Academic offerings subject to approval by statewide coordinating bodies.

Accreditation: *Regional:* NEASC. *Professional:* social work

History: Established as Willimantic Normal School, a 2-year institution, chartered, and offered first instruction at postsecondary level 1889; became 3-year institution and changed name to Willimantic State Teachers College 1937; became 4-year institution and awarded first degree (baccalaureate) 1938; changed name to Willimantic State College 1959; adopted present name 1982.

Institutional Structure: *Governing board:* Board of Trustees for the Connecticut State University. Representation: 15 trustees, 1 student. All voting. *Composition of institution:* Administrators 60; management 22. Academic affairs headed by vice president for academic affairs. Management/business/finances directed by vice president for administrative affairs. Full-time instructional faculty 137. Academic governance body, University Senate, meets an average of 10 times per year. *Faculty representation:* Faculty served by collective bargaining agent affiliated with AAUP.

Calendar: Semesters. Academic year late Aug. to May. Freshmen admitted Aug., Jan. Degrees conferred and formal commencement May. Summer session of 3 terms from early June to early Aug.

Characteristics of Freshmen: 69% of applicants admitted. 44% of admitted students enrolled full-time.

100% (883 students) submitted SAT scores. *25th percentile:* SAT Verbal 460, SAT Math 460. *75th percentile:* SAT Verbal 560, SAT Math 560.

17% of entering freshmen are expected to graduate within 5 years. 89% of freshmen from Connecticut. Freshmen from 14 states and 1 foreign country.

Admission: Rolling admissions plan. For fall acceptance, apply as early as Oct. 1 of previous year, but not later than Aug. 1 of year of enrollment. Early acceptance available. *Requirements:* Either graduation from accredited secondary school with 4 units English, 2 in a foreign language, 2 mathematics, 2 science, 2 social studies; or GED. Lowest acceptable secondary school class standing 50th percentile. *Entrance tests:* College Board SAT. For foreign students TOEFL. *For transfer students:* 2.0 minimum GPA; from 4-year accredited institution 90 semester hours maximum transfer credit; from 2-year accredited institution 60 hours.

College credit and advanced placement for postsecondary-level work completed in secondary school. College credit for extrainstitutional learning on basis of ACE *2006 Guide to the Evaluation of Educational Experiences in the Armed Services*, portfolio and faculty assessments, personal interviews. Tutoring available. Noncredit developmental courses offered in summer session and regular academic year.

Degree Requirements: *For all associate degrees:* 60 semester hours minimum; 1 term in residence. *For all baccalaureate degrees:* 120 hours minimum; 30 semester hours in residence. *For all undergraduate degrees:* 2.0 GPA; distribution requirements.

Fulfillment of some degree requirements and exemption from some beginning courses possible by passing departmental examinations, College Board CLEP, AP, other standardized tests. *Grading system:* A–F; credit-no credit; withdraw (carries time limit).

Distinctive Educational Programs: *For undergraduates:* Internships. Weekend classes. Cooperative baccalaureate program in fine arts with University of Connecticut, and in library science with Southern Connecticut State College. Honors programs. *For graduate students:* Cooperative master's program in educational administration and supervision with Southern Connecticut State College. National Student Exchange program. International student exchange programs. *Available to all students:* Flexible meeting places and schedules, including off-campus centers (at East Hartford, Hartford, and Manchester, all less than 30 miles away from main institution), and evening classes. Accelerated degree programs. Special facilities for using telecommunications in the classroom. Interdepartmental programs in American studies, women's studies. Interdisciplinary program in environmental science. Facilities and programs for independent research, including individual majors, tutorials. Study abroad in Canada, Germany, Greece, Spain, United Kingdom; elsewhere by individual arrangement. *Other distinctive programs:* Center for Connecticut Studies seeks to improve the quality of instruction in the field of Connecticut history and culture. Students from other New England states may enroll in programs in applied social relations, environmental science, and Spanish at Eastern Connecticut through New England Regional Student Program.

ROTC: Army, Air Force offered in cooperation with University of Connecticut.

Degrees Conferred: 812 *baccalaureate:* biological/life sciences 15, business 111, communications/communication technologies 52, computer and information science 21, education 60, English 65, foreign languages and literature 8, interdisciplinary studies 11, liberal arts/general studies 56, mathematics 28, parks and recreation 23, physical sciences 12, protective services/public administration 45, psychology 111, social sciences and history 159, visual and performing arts 36. 105 *master's:* business/marketing 30, education 75.

Fees and Other Expenses: *Full-time tuition and fees per academic year 2004–05:* undergraduate resident $2,862, out-of-state $9,264; graduate resident $3,566, out-of-state $9,934. *Required fees:* $2,694 undergraduate, $508 graduate. *Room and board per academic year:* $7,256.

Financial Aid: Aid from institutionally generated funds is awarded on the basis of academic merit, financial need. Institution has a Program Participation Agreement with the U.S. Department of Education for eligible students to receive Pell Grants and other federal aid.

Financial aid to full-time, first-time undergraduate students: need-based scholarships/grants totaling $5,179,376, self-help $7,782,808; non-need-based scholarships/grants totaling $700,202, self-help $6,674,866, parent loans $2,281,832.

Departments and Teaching Staff: *Professors* 35, *associate professors* 45, *assistant professors* 74, *instructors* 9, *part-time faculty* 191. *Total instructional faculty:* 374 (full-time 183, part-time 191; women 159, men 215; members of minority groups 63). Total faculty with doctorate, first-professional, or other terminal degree: 225. Student-to-faculty ratio: 16:1.

Enrollment: Total enrollment 5,156. Undergraduate full-time 1,640 men / 2,060 women, part-time 424m / 596w. *Transfer students:* in-state 413, from out-of-state 67.

Characteristics of Student Body: *Ethnic and racial makeup:* number of Black non-Hispanic: 329; American Indian or Alaska Native: 18; Asian or Pacific Islander: 65; Hispanic: 193; White non-Hispanic: 3,889; unknown: 169. *Age distribution:* number under 18: 163; 18–19:1,208; 20–21: 1,372; 22–24: 815; 25–29: 268; 30–34: 137; 35–39: 127; 40–49: 234; 50–64: 78; 65 and over: 8.

International Students: 41 nonresident aliens enrolled fall 2004. 8 students from Europe, 16 Asia, 2 Central and South America, 8 Africa, 6 Canada, 7 other. No programs available for students whose native language is not English. No financial aid specifically designated for international students.

Student Life: On-campus residence halls house 50% of student body. Residence halls for both sexes constitute 100% of such space. *Intercollegiate athletics:* men only: baseball, basketball, cross-country, soccer, track; women only: basketball, cross-country, softball, track, volleyball. *Special regulations:* Cars permitted without restrictions. *Special services:* Learning Resources Center, medical services. *Student publications, radio: Campus Lantern*, a weekly newspaper; *Dimension*, a biannual literary journal; *Sustinet*, a yearbook. Radio station WECS broadcasts 126 hours per week. *Surrounding community:* Willimantic population 15,000. Boston (MA), 105 miles from campus, is nearest metropolitan area. Served by mass transit bus system.

Library Collections: 239,218 volumes. Current serial subscriptions: 1,729 paper. 3,396 recordings. Online catalog. Computer work stations available. Students have access to the Internet at no charge.

Most important collections include the Mead Collection (Latin American Studies); Connecticut Studies (in the Center for Connecticut Studies); Caribbean Collection.

Buildings and Grounds: Campus area 100 acres.

Chief Executive Officer: Dr. David G. Carter, President.

Address admission inquiries to Kimberly Crone, Director of Admissions.

Fairfield University

1073 North Benson Road
Fairfield, Connecticut 06430-5195
Tel: (203) 254-4000   **E-mail:** admis@fair1.fairfield.edu
Fax: (203) 254-4199   **Internet:** www.fairfield.edu

Institution Description: Fairfield University is a private, nonprofit Jesuit institution. *Enrollment:* 5,059. *Degrees awarded:* Baccalaureate, master's.

Accreditation: *Regional:* NEASC. *Professional:* business, counseling, engineering, marriage and family therapy, nursing, nursing education

History: Founded as Fairfield University with a preparatory school 1942; chartered as Fairfield University of Saint Robert Bellarmine 1945; offered first instruction at postsecondary level 1947; awarded first degree (baccalaureate) 1951.

Institutional Structure: *Governing board:* Board of Trustees. Representation: 36 members: 25% are Jesuits; 35% are alumni, and 8 trustees emeriti. All voting. *Composition of institution:* Administrators 123 men / 111 women. Academic affairs headed by academic vice president. Management/business/finances directed by vice president of finance. Full-time instructional faculty 292. Academic governance body, Academic Council, meets an average of 10 times per year.

Calendar: Semesters. Academic year Sep. to May. Freshmen admitted Sep. Degrees conferred May, Aug. Formal commencement May. Summer session of 2 terms from May to Aug.

Characteristics of Freshmen: 64% of applicants admitted; 19% of admitted students enrolled full-time.

95% (516 students) submitted SAT scores; 14% (120 students) submitted ACT scores. *25th percentile:* SAT Verbal 540, SAT Math 560; ACT Composite 26. *75th percentile:* SAT Verbal 630, SAT Math 650; ACT Composite 28.

18% of freshmen from Connecticut. Freshmen from 25 states and 7 foreign countries.

Admission: For fall acceptance, apply no later than Feb. 1. Apply by Nov. 15 for early decision; must limit application to Fairfield University. Early acceptance available. *Requirements:* Graduation from accredited secondary school with 4 units English, 3 language, 3 mathematics, 2 science, 3 history. Additional units for mathematics and science programs and nursing program recommended. Minimum grade average B. Lowest acceptable secondary school class standing 60th percentile. *Entrance tests:* College Board SAT and 3 Achievements or ACT composite. *For transfer students:* 2.6 minimum GPA; from 4- and 2-year accredited institutions 60 semester hours maximum transfer credit. Transfer credit also accepted for correspondence/extension students.

College credit or advanced placement for postsecondary-level work completed in secondary school.

Degree Requirements: *For all baccalaureate degrees:* 120 credit hours; 2.0 GPA; core curriculum in liberal arts.

Fulfillment of some degree requirements or exemption from some beginning courses possible by passing College Board CLEP, AP. *Grading system:* A–F; withdraw.

Distinctive Educational Programs: Evening classes. 3-2 engineering program with the University of Connecticut, R.P.I., and Columbia. Special facilities for using telecommunications in the classroom. Interdisciplinary programs in American studies, Latin American and Caribbean studies, Asian studies, international studies, Greek and Roman studies. Honors programs. Tutorials. Study abroad through university in Florence, Harlexton, and Wroxton as well as cooperative arrangements with other schools. School of Continuing Education. Fairfield University offers graduate programs in five schools: School of Business, School of Graduate Education and Applied Professions, School of Nursing, Master's in American Studies, Mathematics, Management of Technology from the School of Engineering.

Degrees Conferred: 996 *baccalaureate* (B), 292 *master's* (M): area and ethnic studies 3 (B), 5 (M); biological/life sciences 47 (B); business/marketing 345 (B), 80 (M); communications/communication technologies 95 (B); computer and information sciences 6 (B); education 111 (M); engineering and engineering technologies 29 (B), 73 (M); English 95 (B); foreign languages and literature 8 (B); health professions and related sciences 55 (B), 9 (M); home economics and vocational home economics 8 (B); liberal arts/general studies 6 (B); mathematics 23 (B), 6 (M); philosophy/religion/theology 10 (B); physical sciences 10 (B); psychology 73 (B); social sciences and history 68 (B); visual and performing arts 23 (B). *Honorary degrees awarded 2003–04:* Doctor of Laws 4.

Fees and Other Expenses: *Full-time tuition per academic year 2004–05:* $27,450 undergraduate; graduate $435-$550 per credit hour. *Required fees:* $485. *Room and board per academic year:* $9,270.

Financial Aid: Aid from institutionally generated funds is provided on the basis of academic merit, financial need, athletic ability. Institution has a Program Participation Agreement with the U.S. Department of Education for eligible students to receive Pell Grants and other federal aid.

Financial aid to full-time, first-time undergraduate students: need-based scholarships/grants totaling $18,269,418, self-help $7,511,800; non-need-based scholarships/grants totaling $6,264,235, self-help $8,74,823, parent loans $6,546,426, athletic awards $3,724,458.

Departments and Teaching Staff: College of Arts and Science *professors:* 49, *associate professors* 52, *assistant professors* 38, *instructors* 6, *part-time faculty* 109; Dolan School of Business 9; 20, 14, 0, 6; Engineering 1, 4, 0, 0; 20; Nursing 3, 3, 6, 0, 14; Graduate Education and Allied Professions 2, 9, 6, 0, 27. *Total instructional faculty:* 426 (women 187, men 239; members of minority groups 32). Total faculty with doctorate, first-professional, or other terminal degree: 271. Student-to-faculty ratio: 13:1. 19 faculty members awarded sabbaticals in 2004–05.

Enrollment: Total enrollment 5,059. Undergraduate full-time 1,413 men / 1,892 women, part-time 263m / 374w; graduate full-time 63m / 169w; part-time 316m / 570w. *Transfer students:* in-state into lower division 28; out-of-state into lower division 30.

Characteristics of Student Body: *Ethnic/racial makeup:* number of Black non-Hispanic: 95; American Indian or Alaska Native: 11; Asian or Pacific Islander: 124; Hispanic: 201; White non-Hispanic: 3,344; unknown: 102. *Age distribution:* number under 18: 90; 18–19: 1,657; 20–21: 1,530; 22–24: 226; 25–29: 91; 30–34: 66; 35–39: 55; 40–49: 122; 50–64: 42; 65 and over: 5.

International Students: 122 nonresident aliens enrolled fall 2004. 30 students from Europe, 44 Asia, 9 Central and South America, 3 Africa, 3 Canada, 1 New Zealand; 22 other. No programs available to aid students whose native language is not English. No financial aid specifically designated for international students.

Student Life: On-campus residence halls house 80% of student body, of which 15% live in on-campus townhouse apartments. All residence halls are coed. *Intercollegiate athletics:* men only: basketball, lacrosse, soccer, tennis, baseball, golf; women only: basketball, crew, field hockey, golf, lacrosse, soccer, softball, tennis, volleyball; both sexes: cross-country, swimming, club sports: fencing, men and women lacrosse, soccer, rugby, ski clubs, equestrian club, karate club. *Special regulations:* Registered cars permitted for all but freshmen. *Special services:* Medical services, shuttle bus from campus to town and train station. *Student publications, radio:* The Mirror, student-run weekly newspaper. Radio station WVOF broadcasts 135 hours per week. *Surrounding community:* Fairfield, a town of 55,000, is 50 miles from New York City. The passenger rail service to NYC is one mile from campus.

Publications: *Fairfield Now,* (quarterly) first published in 1978; *The Owl* (School of Engineering); *Forum,* a yearly published by the School of Business; *1073 North Benson* (replaces *Alumni News*); *Annual President's Report.*

Library Collections: 325,166 volumes including bound books, serial backfiles, electronic documents, and government documents not in separate collections. Online catalog. Current serial subscriptions: 1,993 paper. 2,742 compact discs; 497 CD-ROMs. 97 computer work stations. Students have access to the Internet at no charge.

Most important holdings include Small Pond Magazine Collection; Bibliography of American Literature; Landmarks of Science Collection; University Archives.

Buildings and Grounds: Campus area 200 acres. *New buildings:* Renovation to Science Building, Student Center, and Library completed 2002; Kelley Administration Building 2005.

Chief Executive Officer: Rev. Jeffrey P. Von Arx, S.J., President.

Undergraduates address admission inquiries to Karen Pellegrino, Director of Admission; graduate inquiries to Marianne Gumpper, Director of Graduate and Continuing Education.

Hartford Seminary

77 Sherman Street
Hartford, Connecticut 06105-2260
Tel: (860) 509-9500   **E-mail:** admission@hartsem.edu
Fax: (860) 509-9509   **Internet:** www.hartsem.edu

Institution Description: Hartford Seminary is a private, independent, nonprofit, interdenominational seminary. *Enrollment:* 147. *Degrees awarded:* Master's, doctorate.

Accreditation: *Regional:* NEASC. *Nonregional:* ATS. *Professional:* theology

History: Formed 1913 by a merger of three schools, Hartford Theological Seminary (established at Theological Institute of Connecticut 1834), Hartford School of Religious Education (established as the School of Christian Workers 1885, changed name to the Bible Normal College 1897, to The Hartford School of Religious Pedagogy 1903, and to The Hartford School of Religious Education 1913), and The John Stewart Kennedy School of Missions (established 1911), and incorporated as The Hartford Seminary Foundation; adopted present name 1981. *See* Curtis Manning Geer, *The Hartford Theological Seminary; 1834–1934* (Hartford: The Case, Lockwood and Brainard Co., 1934) for further information.

Institutional Structure: *Governing board:* Board of Trustees of Hartford Seminary. *Composition of institution:* Administrators 2 men / 4 women. Academic affairs headed by president. Management/business/finances directed by accounts manager. Full-time instructional faculty 14. Academic governance body, Academic Programs Committee, meets an average of 5 times per year.

Calendar: Semesters. Academic year Sept. to June. Entering students admitted Sept., Jan., June. Degrees conferred as earned. Summer session of 3 weeks in June. January intercession of 1 week.

Admission: Rolling admissions plan for M.A. Apply by May 1 for D.Min. *Requirements:* First-professional degree in divinity or equivalent required for D.Min. A baccalaureate from accredited college or university required for M.A.

Degree Requirements: For M.A., 48 credit hours; for D.Min., 36 credit hours, major written project, and oral evaluation; distribution requirements. *Grading system:* For M.A., A–F; for D.Min., high pass-fail; incomplete (carries time limit).

Distinctive Educational Programs: Evening classes. Most students are part-time. Nondegree Black Ministries Certificate Program; Hispanic: Ministries and Women's Leadership Institute. Graduate certificates for 18 credit hours in 7 concentrations.

Degrees Conferred: 21 *master's:* theology; 12 *doctorate:* theology.

Fees and Other Expenses: *Tuition per academic year 2004–05:* $10,120.

Financial Aid: Aid from institutionally generated funds is provided on the basis of academic merit and financial need.

Departments and Teaching Staff: Faculty members are unranked. *Professors* 15, *part-time faculty* 13. *Total instructional faculty:* 28. Degrees held by full-time faculty: Doctorate 100%. 100% hold terminal degrees.

Enrollment: Total enrollment 147. Graduate 10 men / 7 women; part-time 43m / 87w.

Characteristics of Student Body: *Ethnic/racial makeup:* number of Black non-Hispanic: 25; Asian or Pacific Islander: 3; Hispanic: 1; White non-Hispanic: 96.

International Students: 11 nonresident aliens enrolled 2004. No financial programs available to aid students whose native language is not English.

Student Life: Limited on-campus housing for international students. *Surrounding community:* Hartford is a metropolitan region of nearly one million people, midway between New York and Boston. Served by mass transit bus system; airport 15 miles from campus; passenger rail service 2 miles from campus.

Publications: *The Muslim World* (quarterly) first published in 1911; *Conversations in Religion and Theology; Reviews in Religion and Theology.*

Library Collections: 75,000 volumes. 325 paper serial subscriptions. 25 CD-ROMs. 10 computer work stations.

Most important holdings include over 1,200 Arabic manuscripts dating from the 9th century, primarily about Arab culture, literature, and religion; over 1,300 first and second editions of the *Arabian Nights*, primarily in Arabic, English, and Romance languages; Islam collection of 40,000 books and scholarly texts, primarily about Muslim law, philosophy, political history and religion; archival material regarding 18th century New England theology; Hartford Seminary Archives.

Buildings and Grounds: Campus area 1 square block.

Chief Executive Officer: Dr. Heidi Hadsell, President.

Address admission inquiries to Meg Wichser, Director of Enrollment Services.

Holy Apostles College and Seminary

33 Prospect Hill Road
Cromwell, Connecticut 06416-2005
Tel: (860) 632-3010   **E-mail:** admissions@holyapostles.edu
Fax: (860) 632-3030   **Internet:** www.holyapostles.edu

Institution Description: Holy Apostles College and Seminary (Holy Apostles Seminary College until 1972) is a private institution affiliated with Church Missionaries of the Holy Apostles, Roman Catholic Church, with college and seminary divisions primarily for older students. *Enrollment:* 246. Women are admitted to the college division only. *Degrees awarded:* Associate, baccalaureate, first-professional (master of divinity). Certificates also awarded.

Accreditation: *Regional:* NEASC.

History: Established as Holy Apostles Seminary, chartered, and incorporated 1956; offered first instruction at postsecondary level 1957; awarded first degree (baccalaureate) 1961; changed name to Holy Apostles Seminary College and first admitted laypersons and women 1970; adopted present name 1972.

Institutional Structure: *Governing board:* Board of Trustees. Representation: 21 trustees, including 13 Missionaries of the Holy Apostles (1 an administrator), 2 other church representatives, 6 laypersons. 10 ex officio. All voting. *Composition of institution:* Administrators 5 men / 2 women. Academic affairs headed by academic dean. Management/business/finances directed by director of business management. Full-time instructional faculty 20. Academic governance body, the faculty, meets an average of 4 times per year.

Calendar: Semesters. Academic year Aug. to May. Freshmen admitted Sept., Jan. Degrees conferred and formal commencement May. No summer session.

Characteristics of Freshmen: 60% of applicants accepted. 60% of accepted applicants enrolled. 75% of entering freshmen expected to graduate within 5 years. 40% of freshmen from Connecticut. Freshmen from 4 states and 1 foreign country.

Admission: Rolling admissions plan. For fall acceptance, apply as early as 1 year prior to enrollment, but not later than Aug. 1 of year of enrollment for seminarians, Aug. 15 for laypersons. *Requirements:* Either graduation from accredited secondary school or GED. Personal interview for all entering students; psychological assessment for seminarians. Recommended minimum—GPA 2.0. *For transfer students:* 2.0 minimum GPA; from 4-year accredited institution 75 semester hours maximum transfer credit; from 2-year accredited institution 60 hours.

College credit and advanced placement for postsecondary-level work completed in secondary school and for extrainstitutional learning on basis of ACE *2006 Guide to the Evaluation of Educational Experiences in the Armed Services*, portfolio, and faculty assessments. Tutoring available. Developmental courses offered during regular academic year; credit given.

Degree Requirements: *For all associate degrees:* 60 credit hours; 45 hours in residence. *For all baccalaureate degrees:* 120 credit hours; 30 hours in residence; daily chapel attendance for resident students. *For all undergraduate degrees:* 2.0 GPA; distribution requirements. For resident students, participation in work program. *For master's degrees:* 30 credits plus thesis or 39 credits without thesis, language and comprehensive exams. *For post-master's:* 30 credits plus a culminating paper.

Fulfillment of some degree requirements and exemption from some beginning courses possible by passing College Board CLEP. *Grading system:* A–F; pass-fail; withdraw (deadline after which pass-fail is appended to withdraw); incomplete (carries time limit).

Distinctive Educational Programs: *For undergraduates:* Off-campus center (at Bridgeport, 48 miles away from main institution). *Available to all students:* Field education. Evening classes. Facilities and programs for independent research, including tutorials and independent study.

Degrees Conferred: 5 *baccalaureate:* liberal arts/general studies 2, philosophy and religion 3; 7 *master's;* 10 *first-professional.*

Fees and Other Expenses: *Full-time tuition per academic year 2004–05:* $8,900. *Room and board per academic year:* $7,200.

Financial Aid: Aid from institutionally generated funds is awarded on basis of academic merit, financial need. Institution has a Program Participation Agreement with the U.S. Department of Education for eligible students to receive Pell Grants and other federal aid.

Financial aid to full-time, first-time undergraduate students: need-based scholarships/grants $16,000, self-help $10,500. *Graduate aid:* 30 federal loans totaling $125,921.

Departments and Teaching Staff: Faculty members are unranked. *Total instructional faculty:* 27. Degrees held by full-time faculty: 100% hold terminal degrees.

Enrollment: Total enrollment 246. Undergraduate full-time 8 men / 1 woman, part-time 10m / 10w; graduate full-time 16m / 6w, part-time 96m / 62w; first-professional full-time 57m.

Characteristics of Student Body: *Ethnic/racial makeup:* number of White non-Hispanic: 24; Hispanic: 2; unknown: 2.

International Students: 5 nonresident aliens enrolled fall 2004. 1 student from South America, 5 Canada.

Student Life: On-campus residence halls house 67% of student body. Residence halls for men constitute 100% of such space. *Special regulations:* Cars permitted without restrictions. Curfews begin 11:30pm. *Special services:* Medical services. *Surrounding community:* Cromwell population 11,000. Hartford; 22 miles from campus, is nearest metropolitan area. Served by mass transit bus and rail system; airport 37 miles from campus; passenger rail service 7 miles from campus.

Library Collections: 85,000 volumes. Online catalog. 250 current periodical subscriptions. Students have access to online information retrieval services and the Internet.

Most important special holdings include collections on theology and philosophy.

Buildings and Grounds: Campus area 39 acres.

Chief Executive Officer: V.Rev. Douglas L. Mosey, C.S.B., President/Rector.

Undergraduate laypersons address admission inquiries to Director of Admissions.

Lyme Academy College of Fine Arts

84 Lyme Street

Old Lyme, Connecticut 06371-2333

Tel: (860) 434-5232   **E-mail:** dsigmon@lymeacademy.edu
Fax: (860) 434-8725   **Internet:** www.lymeacademy.edu

Institution Description: The Lyme Academy College of Fine Arts is an intimate artistic community that attracts students who are most fully engaged when they are creating art, and who also want to be around people who love to draw, paint, and sculpt. *Enrollment:* 424. *Degrees awarded:* Baccalaureate. Three-year certificates and post-baccalaureate certificates are also awarded.

Accreditation: *Regional:* NEASC. *Nonregional:* NASAD. *Professional:* art

History: The college was founded in 1976. It centers around work in the studio, as well as work out in the natural surroundings of Old Lyme.

Institutional Structure: *Governing board:* Board of Trustees.

Calendar: Semesters. Freshmen admitted Sept., Jan. Degrees conferred and formal commencement May.

Characteristics of Freshmen: 34 applicants (25 men, 9 women). 100% of applicants admitted. 44.1% of admitted students enrolled full-time.

94% (16 students) submitted SAT scores. *25th percentile*: SAT I Verbal 400, SAT I Math 540. *75th percentile*: SAT I Verbal 620, SAT I Math 590.

Admission: Rolling admissions plan. A portfolio interview is required by the admissions office as well as two letters of recommendation, transcripts, SAT/ACT scores, and an essay on the student's commitment to fine art; campus visit highly recommended.

Degree Requirements: *For all baccalaureate degrees:* 120 credit hours; 30 hours in residence; 2.0 GPA; distribution requirements. *Grading system:* A–F; pass-fail; withdraw (deadline after which pass-fail is appended to withdraw); incomplete (carries time limit).

Degrees Conferred: 16 *baccalaureate:* visual and performing arts.

Fees and Other Expenses: *Full-time tuition per academic year 2004–05:* $15,312. *Room and board (off-campus) per academic year:* $7,740.

Financial Aid: Institution has a Program Participation Agreement with the U.S. Department of Education for eligible students to receive Pell Grants and other federal aid.

Financial aid to full-time, first-time undergraduate students: 75% of the college's degree-seeking students received financial assistance from federal, state, private, and Academy funds. Need-based aid is available only to U.S. citizens or eligible non-citizens.

Departments and Teaching Staff: Faculty members are unranked. 55% of faculty hold the Ph.D or MFA degrees. All faculty have high levels of achievement and expertise and all studio faculty are practicing artists in their chosen fields. Student-to-faculty ratio: 12:1.

Enrollment: Total enrollment: 424 (212 undergraduate, 90 degree, 122 continuing education). 68% women, 33% men.

Characteristics of Student Body: *Ethnic/racial makeup:* White non-Hispanic: 92.3%; Hispanic: 5.6%, American Indian or Alaska Native: .7%; unknown: .7%

International Students: 2 nonresident aliens enrolled fall 2004.

Student Life: All housing is off-campus. The Office of Student Services maintains an approved list of available nearby houses and apartments.

Library Collections: 11,527 volumes. 68 periodicals, 21,000 slides; 200 videos, 19 electronic resources.

Buildings and Grounds: The college is located on 47 acres overlooking the Lieutenant River. the campus is two hours from either New York or Boston.

Chief Executive Officer: Frederick S. Osborne, President.

Address admission inquiries to Debbie Sigmon, Director of Admissions.

Mitchell College

437 Pequot Avenue

New London, Connecticut 063203

Tel: (860) 701-5000   **E-mail:** admissions@mitchell.edu
Fax: (860) 701-5090   **Internet:** www.mitchell.edu

Institution Description: Mitchell College is a coeducational, private residential institution offering associate and bachelor degree programs in the liberal arts professional areas. The college is dedicated to providing a challenging education in a caring and cooperative environment for all students, including those with untapped potential and those with diagnosed learning disabilities. *Enrollment:* 742.

Accreditation: *Regional:* NEASC.

History: Mitchell College was founded in 1939.

Institutional Structure: *Governing board:* Board of Trustees.

Calendar: Semesters. Freshmen admitted Sept., Jan. Degrees conferred and formal commencement May.

Characteristics of Freshmen: 977 applicants (458 men, 519 women). 61.2% of applicants admitted; 37.8% of admitted students enrolled full-time.

88% (204 students) submitted SAT scores; 9% (22 students) submitted ACT scores. *25th percentile:* SAT I Verbal 350, SAT I Math 330; ACT Composite 15. *75th percentile:* SAT I Verbal 470, SAT I Math 450; ACT Composite 17.

Admission: Rolling admissions plan. SAT I or ACT required; GED accepted; 2.0 GPA; recommendation and personal statement required.

Degree Requirements: *For all baccalaureate degrees:* 120 credit hours; 30 hours in residence; 2.0 GPA (2.7 GPA for early Childhood); distribution requirements. *Grading system:* A–F; pass-fail; withdraw (deadline after which pass-fail is appended to withdraw); incomplete (carries time limit).

Degrees Conferred: 77 *associate*; 64 *baccalaureate*. Bachelor's degrees awarded in top five disciplines: business, management, marketing, and related support 19; liberal arts and sciences, general studies and humanities 13; security and protective services 10; parks, recreation, leisure, and fitness studies 7; family and consumer sciences/human sciences 7.

Fees and Other Expenses: *Full-time tuition per academic year 2004–05:* $19,030. *Books and supplies:* $1,000. *Room and board per academic year:* $8,680. *Other expenses:* $2,600.

Financial Aid: Institution has a Program Participation Agreement with the U.S. Department of Education for eligible students to receive Pell Grants and other federal aid.

Financial aid to full-time, first-time undergraduate students: 29% received federal grants averaging $3,000; 39% state/local grants averaging $2,649; 64% institutional grants averaging $5,783; 66% loans averaging $5,445.

Departments and Teaching Staff: *Total instructional faculty:* 24. 55% hold terminal degrees. Student-to-faculty ratio: 26:1.

Enrollment: Total enrollment: 742 (men 49.2%, women 50.8%).

Characteristics of Student Body: *Ethnic/racial makeup:* Black non-Hispanic: 11.3%; American Indian or Alaska Native: .3%; Asian or Pacific Islander: 6.3%; Hispanic: 6.6%; White non-Hispanic: 65.9%; unknown: 8.6%.

International Students: 6 nonresident aliens enrolled fall 2004.

Student Life: On-campus housing available for 450 students. Thirty-five activity groups available for student participation. No sororities or fraternities.

Library Collections: 45,000 volumes. 39,000 microforms; 50 audiovisual materials. 90 current periodical subscriptions. Computer work stations (1 for every 4 students). .

Buildings and Grounds: The college is located on a 65-acre campus on the shore of the Thames River where it meets Long Island Sound.

Chief Executive Officer: Dr. Mary Ellen Jukoski, President.

Address admission inquiries to Kimberly S. Hodges, Vice President for Enrollment Management.

Paier College of Art

20 Gorham Avenue

Hamden, Connecticut 06514-3902

Tel: (203) 287-3031   **E-mail:** admissions@paierart.com
Fax: (203) 287-3020   **Internet:** www.paierart.com

Institution Description: Paier College of Art is a private, independent, proprietary institution. *Enrollment:* 291. *Degrees awarded:* Baccalaureate. Diplomas and certificates also awarded.

Accreditation: *Nonregional:* ACCSCT.

History: Established as art school and offered first instruction 1946; chartered and awarded first degrees 1982; adopted present name 1981.

Institutional Structure: *Governing board:* Extrainstitutional representation: 4 directors; institutional representation: 2 directors/administrators. All voting. *Composition of institution:* Administrators 5 men / 1 woman. Academic affairs headed by director. Full-time instructional faculty 12.

Calendar: Semesters. Academic year mid-Aug. to mid-May. Students admitted Aug., Jan. Degrees conferred and formal commencement May. Summer session early July to early Aug.

Characteristics of Freshmen: 85% of applicants accepted. 60% of accepted applicants enrolled. Average secondary school rank of freshmen 53rd percentile. Mean SAT class score 418 verbal, 412 mathematical.

66% of entering freshmen expected to graduate within 5 years. 95% of freshmen from Connecticut. Freshmen from 10 states and 7 foreign countries.

Admission: Rolling admissions plan. Apply no later than one month prior to term. *Requirements:* Either graduation from secondary school or GED. *Entrance tests:* SAT or ACT. *For transfer students:* 2.0 minimum GPA; 68 hours maximum credit. Art portfolio and interview required.

Degree Requirements: *For associate degree:* 64 semester hours; 2.0 GPA. *For baccalaureate degree:* 130 semester hours; 2.0 GPA. *Grading system:* A–F; withdraw (deadline after which pass-fail is appended to withdraw).

Distinctive Educational Programs: Day and evening classes in fine arts, graphic design, illustration, interior design, and photography. Degree and diploma programs.

Degrees Conferred: 7 *associate*; 38 *baccalaureate:* architecture and related services 6; visual and performing arts 36.

Fees and Other Expenses: *Full-time tuition per academic year 2004–05:* $11,540. *Books and supplies:* $600. *Room and board* $3,500 (average); private housing and apartments near the campus offer accommodations for both male and female students.

Financial Aid: Aid from institutionally generated funds is provided on the basis of financial need. Institution has a Program Participation Agreement with the U.S. Department of Education for eligible students to receive Pell Grants and other federal aid.

Financial aid to full-time, first-time undergraduate students: 16% relieved federal grants; 38% state/local grants averaging $2,853; 58% loans averaging $2,788.

Departments and Teaching Staff: Academic studies *professors* 1, *part-time faculty* 2; photography 1, 2; interior design 1, 8; graphic design 2, 3; illustration 2, 3; fine art 3, 4; academics 1, 4. *Total instructional faculty:* 34. Degrees held by full-time faculty: Doctorate 10%, master's 30%, baccalaureate 90%, professional 100%.

Enrollment: Total enrollment 291 (40.5% men, 59.5% women).

Characteristics of Student Body: *Ethnic and racial makeup:* Black non-Hispanic: 3.1%; Asian or Pacific Islander: 1%; Hispanic: 3,8%; White non-Hispanic: 89.3%; unknown .1.4%.

International Students: 4 nonresident aliens enrolled fall 2004. No programs available to aid students whose native language is not English. No financial aid specifically designated for international students.

Student Life: All students are commuters. Student Association for social activities and exhibitions.

Library Collections: 15,000 volumes. 66,000 audiovisual materials; 70 current periodical subscriptions. Computer work stations available. Students have access to online information retrieval services and the Internet.

Buildings and Grounds: Campus area includes 3 classroom buildings and a library. Administration building 1 mile from campus.

Chief Executive Officer: Jonathan E. Paier, President.

Address admission inquiries to Maureen Depose, Registrar.

Post University

800 Country Club Road
Waterbury, Connecticut 06723-2540

Tel: (203) 596-4500   **E-mail:** admissions@post.edu
Fax: (203) 756-5810   **Internet:** www.post.edu

Institution Description: Post University (formerly Teikyo Post University) is a private, independent, nonprofit institution. *Enrollment:* 1,198. *Degrees awarded:* Associate, baccalaureate. Certificates also awarded.

Accreditation: *Regional:* NEASC.

History: Established as Mattoon School of Business in 1890; changed name to Post College 1931; became Post Junior College of Commerce 1939; changed name to Post Junior College 1962; incorporated 1965; awarded first degree (associate) 1967; added upper division curriculum and readopted name Post Col-

lege 1976; became affiliated with Teikyo University, Tokyo, Japan 1990; changed name to Teikyo Post University and began offering study abroad opportunities worldwide; ended affiliation with Teikyo Group in 2004 and became Post University.

Institutional Structure: *Governing board:* Post University, Inc. Board of Trustees. Extrainstitutional representation: 11 trustees. *Composition of institution:* Administrators 3 men / 1 woman. Full-time instructional faculty 31. Academic governance body, Post University Faculty Senate, meets an average of 10 times per year. *Faculty representation:* Faculty is served by collective bargaining agent, Post University Faculty Association.

Calendar: Semesters. Academic year Sept. to May. Freshmen admitted on a rolling basis. Degrees conferred May, Aug., Dec. Formal commencement May. Summer session from May to Aug.

Characteristics of Freshmen: 65% of applicants admitted. 21% of admitted students enrolled full-time.

71% (143 students) submitted SAT scores; 4% (8 students) submitted ACT scores.

68% of freshmen from Connecticut. Freshmen from 12 states and 15 foreign countries.

Admission: Rolling admissions plan. Apply as early as May 15 of junior year in secondary school, but not later than Aug. 31 of year of enrollment. Apply by Nov. 1 of senior year for early decision. Early acceptance available. *Requirements:* Either graduation from accredited secondary school with 16 academic units or GED. Minimum GPA 2.0. *Entrance tests:* College Board SAT. *For transfer students:* 2.0 minimum GPA, 90 hours maximum transfer credit; from 2-year accredited institution 60 credit hours.

Advanced placement for postsecondary-level work completed in secondary school. College credit for extrainstitutional learning on basis of various ACE *2006 Guide to the Evaluation of Educational Experiences in the Armed Services,* portfolio and faculty assessments, and personal interviews.

Tutoring available. Developmental courses offered during regular academic year; credit given. Academic scholarships available for freshmen and transfer students.

Degree Requirements: *For all associate degrees:* 60 credit hours; minimum 9 credits in major. *For all baccalaureate degrees:* 120 hours; minimum 15 credits in major; core requirements. *For all undergraduate degrees:* 2.0 GPA; 30 credits in residence.

Fulfillment of some degree requirements and exemption from some beginning courses possible by passing departmental examinations, College Board CLEP or APP. *Grading system:* A–F.

Distinctive Educational Programs: Accelerated degree programs including online an onground classes. Honors courses; certificate programs in accounting, legal studies, equine studies, early childhood education, human resources, and finance. Study abroad opportunities.

Degrees Conferred: 229 *baccalaureate:* agriculture 8, biological/life sciences 4, business/marketing 140, English 4, law/legal studies 12, liberal arts/general studies 21, protective services/public administration 23, psychology 13, social sciences and history 4.

Fees and Other Expenses: *Full-time tuition per academic year 2005–06:* $19,500. *Required fees:* $700. *Room and board per academic year:* $8,300.

Financial Aid: Aid from institutionally generated funds is awarded on the basis of athletic ability. Institution has a Program Participation Agreement with the U.S. Department of Education for eligible students to receive Pell Grants and other federal aid.

Financial aid to full-time, first-time undergraduate students: need-based scholarships/grants totaling $6,759,873, self-help $4,618,076, parent loans $872,495, athletic awards $325,000; non-need-based athletic awards $150,000.

Departments and Teaching Staff: Arts and sciences *professors* 8, *associate professors* 1, *assistant professors* 8, *instructors* 0, *part-time faculty* 47; business/professional studies 7, 2, 1, 3, 49. *Total instructional faculty:* 127 (full-time 31, part-time 96; women 53, men 74). Total faculty with doctorate, first-professional, or other terminal degree: 20. Student-to-faculty ratio: 14:1. 2 faculty members awarded sabbaticals 2004–o5.

Enrollment: Total enrollment 1,198. Full-time 312 men / 377 women, part-time 141m / 368w.

Characteristics of Student Body: *Ethnic/racial makeup:* number of Black non-Hispanic: 221; American Indian or Alaska Native: 5; Asian or Pacific Islander: 22; Hispanic: 129; White non-Hispanic: 740; unknown: 21. *Age distribution:* number under 18: 25; 18–19: 301; 20–21: 203; 22–24: 154; 25–29: 99; 30–34: 92; 35–39: 89; 40–49: 176; 50–64: 47; 65 and over: 5.

International Students: 60 nonresident aliens enrolled fall 2004. 8 students from Europe, 24 Asia, 2 Africa, 2 Canada, 24 other. Programs available to aid students whose native language is not English: Social, cultural. English as a Second Language Program. No financial aid specifically designated for international students

Student Life: On campus residence required in freshman year unless living with parents or guardian. Freshman housing guaranteed. Co-ed residence halls. 47% of full-time student body live in residence halls. NCAA Division II men's sports: baseball, basketball, golf, soccer, cross-country. NCAA Division II women's sports: basketball, softball, soccer, cross-country. Coed intercollegiate equine team. *Special services:* Learning Resources Center, medical services. *Surrounding community:* Waterbury population 110,000. New York City, 130 miles from campus, is nearest metropolitan area. Served by airport 10 miles from campus; passenger rail service 2.5 miles from campus.

Library Collections: 85,000 volumes including bound books, serial backfiles, electronic documents, and government documents not in separate collections. Online catalog. Current serial subscriptions: 500 paper; 75,158 microforms. 12 computer work stations. Students have access to the Internet at no charge. Total budget for books, periodicals, audiovisual materials, microforms 2004–05: $94,500.

Most important special collections include business materials; Zwicker Tax Institute Library; federal documents depository; Equine Management Collection; Beaufort Theater Collection; Japan Collection.

Buildings and Grounds: Campus area 65 acres. *New buildings:* Residence Hall for upper classmen completed 2004.

Chief Executive Officer: Dr. John Jay Detemple, President.

Address admission inquiries William Johnson, Associate Director of Admissions.

Quinnipiac College

275 Mount Carmel Avenue

Hamden, Connecticut 06518-1908

Tel: (203) 281-8200   **E-mail:** admissions@quinnipiac.edu
Fax: (203) 281-4703   **Internet:** www.quinnipiac.edu

Institution Description: Quinnipiac College is a private, independent, nonprofit college. *Enrollment:* 7,121. *Degrees awarded:* Baccalaureate, master's, first-professional (law). Certificates also awarded.

Accreditation: *Regional:* NEASC. *Professional:* clinical lab scientist, law, nursing, occupational therapy, physical therapy, physician assisting, radiography, respiratory therapy, veterinary technology

History: Established and incorporated as Connecticut College of Commerce in New Haven, and offered first instruction at postsecondary level 1929; awarded first degree (associate) 1930; changed name to Junior College of Commerce 1935; adopted present name and added senior level 1951; merged with Larson College 1952; moved to present location 1966; acquired University of Bridgeport School of Law 1992 and established as Quinnipiac College Law School on campus 1995.

Institutional Structure: *Governing board:* Board of trustees. Extrainstitutional representation: 24 trustees; institutional representation: 1 alumnus, 1 administrator, 3 full-time instructional faculty, 2 students. All voting. *Composition of institution:* Administrators 19 men / 7 women. Admissions and Financial Aid headed by vice president and dean of admissions; academic affairs headed by provost/vice president for academic affairs. Management/business/finances directed by vice president for finance and administration. Full-time instructional faculty 167. Academic governance body, College Senate, meets an average of 18 times per year. *Faculty representation:* Faculty is served by collective bargaining agent affiliated with AFT and Quinnipiac Faculty Federation, Local 3394.

Calendar: Semesters. Academic year Aug. to May. Freshmen admitted Aug., Jan., June. Degrees conferred May, Oct., Jan. Formal commencement May. Summer session of 2 terms from early June to early Aug.

Characteristics of Freshmen: 10,624 applicants (3,807 men, 6,617 women). 55% of applicants admitted; 22.8% of admitted students enrolled full-time.

98% (1,311 students) submitted SAT scores; 14% (186 students) submitted ACT scores. *25th percentile:* SAT I Verbal 510, SAT I Math 520; ACT Composite 21, ACT English 20, ACT Math 20. *75th percentile:* SAT I Verbal 590, SAT I Math 600; ACT Composite 25, ACT English 25, ACT Math 26.

78% of entering freshmen expected to graduate within 5 years. 30% of freshmen from Connecticut. Freshmen from 25 states and 18 foreign countries.

Admission: Rolling admissions plan for all programs except occupational and physical therapy. For fall acceptance, apply as early as Oct. 1 of previous year but not later than June 30 of year of enrollment. Students applying to occupational and physical therapy programs are notified of acceptance Feb.-Apr. Early acceptance available. *Requirements:* Graduation from approved secondary school with 16 units which must include 4 English, 3 mathematics, 2 history, 2 science, 5 college preparatory electives; or GED. For students applying to science programs, additional science units recommended. Lowest acceptable secondary school class standing 50th percentile. *Entrance tests:* College Board SAT or ACT composite. *For transfer students:* 2.0 minimum GPA; from 2-year accredited institutions 60 hours maximum transfer credit; from others, 75 hours.

College credit and advanced placement for postsecondary-level work completed in secondary school. College credit for advanced placement exams. Tutoring available through the Learning Center.

Degree Requirements: *For all undergraduate degrees:* 2.0 GPA; 3 terms in residence; 1 semester hour physical education. *For baccalaureate degree:* 120 hours; 2.0 minimum GPA during last 60 hours. *For associate degree:* 60 hours. Some degree requirements may be met and exemption from some beginning courses possible by passing College Board CLEP and institutional tests. *Grading system:* A–F; withdraw (carries time limit).

Distinctive Educational Programs: *For undergraduates:* Flexible meeting places and schedules. Special facilities for using telecommunications in the classroom for mass communication classes. Interdepartmental/interdisciplinary programs in psychobiology, information systems or chemistry and mathematics. Facilities for independent research, including honors programs, individual majors, tutorials, and independent study courses. Extensive internships and clinical experiences augment classroom experience. *Available to all students:* Evening classes. Interdepartmental/interdisciplinary program in health services administration. Hospital or health care internships in all health-related programs. Internships in accounting, information systems, international business. Articulation programs in chiropractic and podiatric medicine.

ROTC: Army and Air Force offered at nearby colleges.

Degrees Conferred: 6 *associate;* 1,217 *baccalaureate;* 399 *master's;* 7 *postbaccalaureate certificates.* Bachelor's degrees awarded top five disciplines: business, management, marketing, and related support services291; health professions and related clinical sciences 283; communication, journalism, and related programs 239; psychology 82; social sciences 67. *First-professional:* law 176.

Fees and Other Expenses: *Full-time tuition per academic year 2004–05:* undergraduate $22,500. graduate study charged per credit hour; contact the college for current professional tuition and fees. *Room and board per academic year:* $9,900. *Books and supplies:* $800.

Financial Aid: Aid from institutionally generated funds is provided on the basis of academic merit, financial need, athletic ability. Institution has a Program Participation Agreement with the U.S. Department of Education for eligible students to receive Pell Grants and other federal aid.

Financial aid to full-time, first-time undergraduate students: 11% received federal grants averaging $4,447; 12% state/local grants averaging $4,316; 68% institutional grants averaging $7,934; 83% loans averaging $4,159.

Departments and Teaching Staff: *Total instructional faculty:* 678. Degrees held by full-time faculty: Doctorate 65%; 78% hold terminal degrees. Student-to-faculty ratio: 23:1.

Enrollment: Total enrollment 7,121. Undergraduate 5,470 (38.5% men, 61.5% women).

Characteristics of Student Body: *Ethnic/racial makeup:* Black non-Hispanic: 2.2%; American Indian or Alaska Native: .2%; Asian or Pacific Islander: 2.1.%; Hispanic: 3.8%; White non-Hispanic: 83.7%; unknown: 7%.

International Students: 54 nonresident aliens enrolled fall 2004. Programs available to aid students whose native language is not English: social, cultural. Financial aid specifically designated for international students: scholarships available annually.

Student Life: On-campus residence halls house 70% of student body. Residence halls for women only constitute 10% of such space, for both sexes 90%. 10% of student body live off campus in private homes and apartments; 20% commute. *Intercollegiate athletics:* men only: baseball, basketball, cross-country, golf, hockey, lacrosse, soccer, tennis; women only: basketball, cross-country, field hockey, lacrosse, soccer, softball, tennis, volleyball. *Special regulations:* Cars permitted without restrictions. *Special services:* Learning Center, medical services. *Student publications, radio: Brave,* a yearbook; *Chronicle,* a biweekly publication. Radio station WQAQ-FM broadcasts 131 hours per week. *Surrounding community:* Hamden population 60,000. New Haven, 12 miles from campus, is nearest metropolitan area. Served by mass transit bus system; passenger rail service 12 miles from campus.

Library Collections: 305,000 volumes. 3,900 current periodicals; 9,100 microform items; 2,000 audiovisual units. Online catalog. Students have access to online information retrieval services and the Internet.

Buildings and Grounds: Campus area 200 acres.

Chief Executive Officer: Dr. John L. Lahey, President.

Address undergraduate admission inquiries to Joan Isaac Mohr, Vice President and Dean of Admissions; graduate inquiries to Scott Farber, Director of Graduate Admissions; Law School inquiries to John Noonan, Director of Law School Admissions.

Rensselaer at Hartford

275 Windsor Street

Hartford, Connecticut 06120-2991

Tel: (860) 548-2400   **E-mail:** adm-info@rh.edu

Fax: (860) 548-7823   **Internet:** www.rh.edu

Institution Description: Rensselaer at Hartford, formerly named the Hartford Graduate Center, is an independent, nonprofit institution affiliated with Rensselaer Polytechnic Institute. The Center maintains a branch campus at the University of Connecticut's Avery Point campus in Groton. *Enrollment:* 798. *Degrees awarded:* Master's.

Member of the Hartford Consortium.

Accreditation: *Regional:* MSA.

History: Established 1955; adopted current name 1997.

Institutional Structure: *Composition of institution:* Management/business/finances directed by vice president. Full-time instructional faculty 27 men / 8 women.

Calendar: Semesters. Academic year Sept. to April. Formal commencement June. Summer session from May to Aug.

Admission: Rolling admissions plan. For fall acceptance, apply no later than 30 days prior to beginning of class. *Requirements:* Baccalaureate from accredited college or university. Additional requirements for some programs. *Entrance tests:* GMAT/GRE; for foreign students TOEFL. *For transfer students:* 6 hours maximum transfer credit.

Degree Requirements: Minimum of 30 credit hours, 60 credit hours for M.B.A.; B average; 24 hours in residence. School of Engineering and Science: seminar or project. *Grading system:* A–F; withdraw; incomplete (carries time limit).

Distinctive Educational Programs: Cooperative master's program in biomedical engineering with Trinity College, including internships with affiliated hospitals and medical centers. Thesis option. Cross-registration through consortium. *Other distinctive programs:* 12-month Corporate Degree Program (M.S. in Management) for mid-career managers; computer science graduate certificate programs; engineering graduate certificate programs; weekend MBA program.

Degrees Conferred: 424 *master's:* business/marketing 312, computer and information sciences 50, engineering/engineering technologies 62.

Fees and Other Expenses: *Full-time tuition per academic year 2004–05:* $24,000.

Financial Aid: Aid from institutionally generated funds is provided on the basis of financial need. Institution has a Program Participation Agreement with the U.S. Department of Education for eligible students to receive Pell Grants and other federal aid. *Graduate aid:* 35 students received federal and state-funded loans totaling $400,000.

Departments and Teaching Staff: School of Engineering *professors:* 1, *associate professors* 2, *assistant professors* 1, *part-time faculty* 16; School of Management 6, 6, 3, 2; School of Computer Science 2, 2, 1, 10. *Total instructional faculty:* 52 (full-time 24, part-time 28; women 5, men 47; members of minority groups 7). Total faculty with doctorate, first-professional, or other terminal degree: 35. Student-to-faculty ratio: 16:1.

Enrollment: Total enrollment 798. Full-time 23 men / 16 women, part-time 576m / 191w.

International Students: 33 nonresident aliens enrolled fall 2004. No programs available to aid students whose native language is not English. No financial aid specifically designated for international students.

Student Life: No on-campus housing. *Surrounding community:* Hartford, metropolitan area population over 1 million. Served by mass transit bus system, airport, passenger rail service.

Publications: Bimonthly *Newsletter* mailed to students and graduates, first published 1970.

Library Collections: 30,000 volumes. 12,000 microforms; 55 audiovisual materials; 500 current periodical subscriptions. 20 computer work stations. Access to online information retrieval systems and the Internet.

Most important holdings include collections on Association for Computing Machinery (ACM); Institute of Electrical and Electronics Engineers (IEEE); 10-K and annual reports on selected companies.

Buildings and Grounds: Campus area of over 15 acres.

Chief Executive Officer: John A. Minosian, Vice President and Dean.

Address admission inquiries to Director of Admissions,

Sacred Heart University

5151 Park Avenue

Fairfield, Connecticut 06432-1000

Tel: (203) 371-7880   **E-mail:** enroll@sacredheart.edu

Fax: (203) 365-7852   **Internet:** www.sacredheart.edu

Institution Description: Sacred Heart University is a private, independent, nonprofit institution affiliated with the Roman Catholic Church. *Enrollment:* 5,730. *Degrees awarded:* Associate, baccalaureate, master's. Certificates also awarded.

Accreditation: *Regional:* NEASC. *Professional:* nursing, occupational therapy, physical therapy, respiratory therapy, social work

History: Established, incorporated, and offered first instruction at postsecondary level 1963; first degree (baccalaureate) awarded 1967.

Institutional Structure: *Governing board:* Board of Trustees. Extrainstitutional representation: 30 trustees. *Composition of institution:* Administrators 6 men / 1 woman. Academic affairs headed by academic vice president and provost. Management/business/finances directed by vice president for finance. Full-time instructional faculty 111. Academic governance body, Academic Council, meets an average of 10 times per year.

Calendar: Semesters. Academic year early Sept. to mid-May. Freshmen admitted Sept., Jan., June. Degrees conferred May, Aug., Dec. Formal commencement May. Summer session of 3 terms from May to Aug.

Characteristics of Freshmen: 4,971 applicants (2,001 men, 2,970 women). 71.2% of applicants admitted; 24.9% of admitted students enrolled full-time.

99% (867 students) submitted SAT scores; 14% (122 students) submitted ACT scores. *25th percentile:* SAT I Verbal 490, SAT I Math 490; ACT Composite 19, ACT English 19, ACT Math 19. *75th percentile:* SAT I Verbal 570, SAT I Math 580; ACT Composite 24, ACT English 24, ACT Math 24.

47% of entering freshmen expected to graduate within 5 years. 40% of freshmen from Connecticut. Freshmen from 26 states and 12 foreign countries.

Admission: For fall acceptance, apply as early as Oct. 1 of previous year, but not later than Mar. 1 of year of enrollment. Apply by Oct. 1 for Early Decision I or Dec. 1 for Early Decision II; need not limit application to Sacred Heart University. *Requirements:* Graduation from accredited secondary school with 4 units English, 2 foreign language, 3 history, 1 laboratory science, 3 mathematics. Minimum GPA 3.0. Lowest acceptable secondary school class standing 20th percentile. *Entrance tests:* College Board SAT. *For transfer students:* 2.5 GPA; from 4-year accredited institution 60 hours maximum transfer credit; from 2-year accredited institution 30 hours.

College credit for postsecondary-level work completed in secondary school.

Degree Requirements: *For all associate degrees:* 60 credit hours. *For all baccalaureate degrees:* 120 credit hours. *For all undergraduate degrees:* 2.0 GPA.

Grading system: A–F; withdraw.

Distinctive Educational Programs: *For undergraduates:* Accelerated degree programs. Honors programs. Institution-sponsored study abroad in various locations during summer; study abroad during regular academic year. *Available to all students:* Weekend and evening classes.

Degrees Conferred: 48 *associate;* 817 *baccalaureate;* 615 *master's;* 20 *postmaster's certificates.* Bachelor's degrees awarded in top five disciplines: business, management, marketing, and related support services 293; psychology 148; health professions and related clinical sciences 80; computer and information sciences and support services 52; communication, journalism, and related programs 34.

Fees and Other Expenses: *Full-time tuition per academic year 2004–05:* $21,990. *Room and board per academic year:* $9,280. *Books and supplies:* $700. *Other expenses:* $1,500.

Financial Aid: Aid from institutionally generated funds is provided on the basis of academic merit, financial need, athletic ability, other criteria. Institution has a Program Participation Agreement with the U.S. Department of Education for eligible students to receive Pell Grants and other federal aid.

Financial aid to full-time, first-time undergraduate students: 15% received federal grants averaging $3,347; 20% state/local grants averaging $3,283; 85% institutional grants averaging $6,117; 67% loans averaging $2,853.

Departments and Teaching Staff: *Professors* 22, *associate professors* 50, *assistant professors* 49, *instructors* 9. *Total instructional faculty:* 130. Student-to-faculty ratio: 17:1. 85% of faculty hold terminal degrees.

Enrollment: Total enrollment 5,730. Undergraduate: 4,049 (men 38.2%, women 61.8%).

Characteristics of Student Body: *Ethnic/racial makeup:* Black non-Hispanic: 6.5%; Asian or Pacific Islander: 1.5%; Hispanic: 5.7%; White non-Hispanic: 85.1%.

International Students: 69 nonresident aliens enrolled fall 2003. Programs available to aid students whose native language is not English: Social, cultural. English as a Second Language Program. No financial aid specifically designated for international students.

Student Life: Residence halls house 68% of undergraduate students. *Intercollegiate NCAA I athletics:* men's and women's baseball, basketball, bowling, crew, cross country, equestrian, field hockey, golf, ice hockey, lacrosse, soccer, softball, tennis, indoor and outdoor track and field, volleyball. *Special regulations:* Cars with parking stickers permitted on campus in designated areas only. *Special services:* Learning Resources Center. *Student publications, radio:* Spectrum, a monthly newspaper; *Prologue*, a yearbook; an annual literary magazine. Radio station WSHU broadcasts 98 hours per week. *Surrounding community:* Bridgeport population 150,000. New York City, 55 miles from campus, is nearest metropolitan area. Served by mass transit bus system; airport 10 miles from campus; passenger rail service 6 miles from campus.

Library Collections: 121,100 volumes. 770,000 microform units; 1,125 audiovisual materials; 4,570 periodicals. Access to online information retrieval systems.

Buildings and Grounds: Campus area 56 acres.

Chief Executive Officer: Dr. Anthony J. Cernera, President.

Address undergraduate admission inquiries to Karen N. Guastelle, Dean of Undergraduate Admissions; graduate inquiries to Alexis Haakonsen, Dean of Graduate Admissions.

Saint Joseph College

1678 Asylum Avenue
West Hartford, Connecticut 06117-2791

Tel: (860) 232-4571 **E-mail:** admissions@mercy.sjc.edu
Fax: (860) 233-5695 **Internet:** www.sjc.edu

Institution Description: Saint Joseph College is a private, independent, nonprofit college for women affiliated with the Sisters of Mercy, Roman Catholic Church. *Enrollment:* 1,836. Men are admitted to the McAuley Program (undergraduate Weekend College) and the Graduate School. *Degrees awarded:* Baccalaureate, master's. Certificates also awarded.

Member of Hartford Consortium for Higher Education.

Accreditation: *Regional:* NEASC. *Professional:* dietetics, marriage and family therapy, nursing, social work

History: Established, chartered, and incorporated as Mount Saint Joseph College 1925; offered first instruction at postsecondary level 1932; adopted present name 1935; awarded first degree (baccalaureate) 1936.

Institutional Structure: *Governing board:* Saint Joseph College Board of Trustees. Extrainstitutional representation: 28 trustees; institutional representation: 1 administrator; 1 alumna. 2 ex officio. 28 voting. *Composition of institution:* Administrators Council 1 man / 7 women. Academic affairs headed by President. Management/business/finances directed by treasurer. Full-time instructional faculty 23 men / 39 women. Academic governance body, Faculty Committee of the Whole, meets an average of 8 times per year.

Calendar: Semesters. Academic year early Sept. to mid-May. Degrees conferred at formal commencement in May. Summer session available.

Characteristics of Freshmen: 789 applicants. 69.7% of applicants admitted. 33.8% of admitted students enrolled full-time.

99% (185 students) submitted SAT scores; 1 student submitted ACT scores. *25th percentile:* SAT I Verbal 488, SAT I Math 475. *75th percentile:* SAT I Verbal 510, SAT I Math 480.

69% of entering freshmen expected to graduate within 5 years. 91% of freshmen from Connecticut. Freshmen from 5 states and 1 foreign country.

Admission: Rolling admissions plan. For fall acceptance, apply not later than June 1. Apply by Nov. 15 for early decision; must limit application to Saint Joseph. Early acceptance available. *Requirements:* Either graduation from accredited secondary school with 16 units in academic subjects including English, foreign languages, mathematics, natural sciences, social studies; or GED. Interview required. *Entrance tests:* College Board SAT. *For transfer students:* 2.5 minimum QPR (or GPA).

College credit and advanced placement for postsecondary-level work completed in secondary school. College credit for extrainstitutional learning (life experience) on basis of assessments by departments and dean.

Degree Requirements: 120–125 credit hours; 2.0 GPA; 60 credits in residence with final 24 credits earned at the college or in college-approved program; 2.0 GPA. Core curriculum: humanities, 21 credits; social science, 9 credits; natural science/math 8 credits; physical education 1 credit (2 semesters). Comprehensives in individual fields of study.

Fulfillment of some degree requirements possible through College Board CLEP, or Challenge Examinations. Fulfillment of some requirements and

exemption from some introductory courses possible by passing College Board AP. *Grading system:* A–F; pass-fail.

Distinctive Educational Programs: *For undergraduates:* Interdepartmental/interdisciplinary programs in American studies, biology/chemistry, classical studies, gerontology, humanities, performing arts, women's studies. Self-designed majors. Dual-degree program in engineering with George Washington University (DC). College approved language studies in several foreign countries. Evening classes available to all students. Facilities and programs for independent research, independent study projects, and computer usage. Off-campus internships available for most majors with various local corporations, government offices, private and public agencies, educational institutions, media, and state legislature. McAuley Program, an undergraduate Weekend College program for non-traditional students (male and female), with majors in Business Administration and American studies.

Degrees Conferred: 212 *baccalaureate*; 156 *master's*. Bachelor's degrees awarded in top five disciplines: health professions and related clinical sciences 43; psychology 37; family and consumer sciences/human sciences 32; public administration and social service professions 29; English language and literature/letters 13.

Fees and Other Expenses: *Full-time tuition per academic year 2004–05:* $21,370; contact the college for graduate tuition and fees. *Room and board per academic year:* $12,255. *Books and supplies:* $850.

Financial Aid: Aid from institutionally generated funds is provided on the basis of academic merit, financial need, other criteria. Institution has a Program Participation Agreement with the U.S. Department of Education for eligible students to receive Pell Grants and other federal aid.

Financial aid to full-time, first-time undergraduate students: 37% received federal grants averaging $2,673; 27% state/local grants averaging $2,522; 96% institutional grants averaging $10,759; 84% loans averaging $5,985.

Departments and Teaching Staff: *Total instructional faculty:* 137. Degrees held by full-time faculty: Doctorate 63%, master's 37%. 65% hold terminal degrees. Student-to-faculty ratio: 12:1.

Enrollment: Total enrollment 1,836. Undergraduate 1,193 (men 1.8%, women 98.2%).

Characteristics of Student Body: *Ethnic/racial makeup:* Black non-Hispanic: 13%; American Indian or Alaska Native: .3%; Asian or Pacific Islander: 1.7%; Hispanic: 7%; White non-Hispanic: 68.7%; unknown: .4%.

International Students: 12 nonresident aliens enrolled 2003. Programs available to aid students whose native language is not English: English as a Second Language Program. No financial aid specifically designated for international students.

Student Life: On-campus residence halls house 60% of student body. *Intercollegiate athletics:* women only: softball, volleyball. *Athletic facilities available:* tennis courts, platform-tennis court, all-weather metric track. *Special services:* Medical services, van service for off-campus activities. *Student publications:* Epilogue, a yearbook; *Interpretations*, an annual literary magazine; *Insight*, student published newspaper. *Surrounding community:* Campus is located in West Hartford, with close proximity to Hartford, the state capital, providing cultural and social opportunities. Within two hours by car to Boston and New York. Served by mass transit bus system, airport 15 miles from campus, train service 3 miles from campus.

Library Collections: 134,000 volumes. 5,900 microforms; 3,000 audiovisual materials; 558 current periodical subscriptions; 1,720 recordings/tapes. Online catalog. Students have access to online information retrieval services and the Internet.

Most important holdings include Curriculum Materials Center; Junior Book Collection; archives.

Buildings and Grounds: Campus area 84 acres.

Chief Executive Officer: Dr. Evelyn C. Lynch, President.

Address admission inquiries to Kimberly Manning, Director of Admissions.

Southern Connecticut State University

501 Crescent Street
New Haven, Connecticut 06515-0901

Tel: (203) 392-5200 **E-mail:** adminfo@scsu.ctstateu.edu
Fax: (203) 392-5727 **Internet:** www.scsu.ctstateu.edu

Institution Description: Southern Connecticut State University is a public institution. *Enrollment:* 12,143. *Degrees awarded:* Associate, baccalaureate, master's.

Academic offerings subject to approval by statewide coordinating bodies. Budget subject to approval by state governing boards.

Accreditation: *Regional:* NEASC. *Professional:* athletic training, audiology, computer science, counseling, librarianship, marriage and family therapy, nurse anesthesia education, nursing, nursing education, public health, social work, speech-language pathology

History: Established and chartered as New Haven Normal School and offered first instruction at postsecondary level 1893; third year added 1930; became New Haven State Teachers College, a 4-year college, and awarded first degree (baccalaureate) 1937; adopted present name 1959; awarded university status 1983. See *Southern Journal*, March 1983 (New Haven: Southern Connecticut State University, 1983) for further information.

Institutional Structure: *Governing board:* Board of Trustees for the State Colleges. Extrainstitutional representation: 14 trustees; institutional representation: 2 students. All voting. *Composition of institution:* Administrators 70 men / 40 women (8% are members of minority groups; at dean's level and above, 23% are women). Academic affairs headed by vice president for academic affairs. Management/business/finances directed by vice president for administrative affairs. Full-time instructional faculty 408. Academic governance body, Faculty Senate, meets an average of 16 times per year. *Faculty representation:* Faculty served by collective bargaining agent, AAUP.

Calendar: Semesters. Academic year Aug. to May. Freshmen admitted Sept., Jan., May, June. Degrees conferred and formal commencement May. Summer session early June to early Aug.

Characteristics of Freshmen: 4,969 applicants. 65.4% of applicants admitted; 43% of admitted students enrolled full-time.

96% (1,366 students) submitted SAT scores. *25th percentile*: SAT I Verbal 430, SAT I Math 430. *75th percentile*: SAT I Verbal 480, SAT I Math 470.

60% of entering freshmen expected to graduate within 5 years. 92% of freshmen from Connecticut. Freshmen from 11 states and 9 foreign countries.

Admission: Modified rolling admissions plan. For fall acceptance, apply as early as Oct. 1 of previous year, but not later than July 15 of year of enrollment. *Requirements:* Either graduation from accredited secondary school with 4 units in English, 3 mathematics, 2 science, 2 social science, or GED. Recommend 2 foreign language, 4 electives. Additional requirements for some majors. Minimum GPA 2.0. *Entrance tests:* College Board SAT. For foreign students, TOEFL may be required in addition to or in place of SAT. *For transfer students:* 2.0 minimum GPA; from 4-year accredited institution 90 hours maximum transfer credit, from 2-year accredited institution 61 hours.

College credit and advanced placement for postsecondary-level work completed in secondary school and for extrainstitutional learning on basis of departmental examinations. Tutoring available.

Degree Requirements: 122 credit hours; 2.0 GPA; 2 semesters in residence; 2 physical education courses; English composition and distribution requirements; exit competency examination in speech.

Fulfillment of some degree requirements and exemption from some beginning courses possible by passing departmental examination, College Board CLEP. *Grading system:* A–F; pass-fail; withdraw (carries time limit); incomplete (carries time limit).

Distinctive Educational Programs: *For undergraduates:* Work-experience programs. Dual-degree program in engineering with University of Connecticut. Honors programs. Cross-registration through the New England Regional Student Program and the State College Student Exchange. *For graduate students:* Dual-degree program in library science or instructional technology and law with University of Connecticut. Interdisciplinary master's program in urban studies. *Available to all students:* Evening classes. Special facilities for using telecommunications in the classroom. Interdisciplinary program in environmental studies. Institutionally sponsored summer travel and study tours to Africa, Asia, Europe, South America. *Other distinctive programs:* Free tuition for adults over 62 years of age. Continuing education.

ROTC: Army offered in cooperation with University of Bridgeport; Air Force in cooperation with University of Connecticut.

Degrees Conferred: 4 *associate;* 1,197 *baccalaureate;* 868 *master's;* 161 *post-master's certificates.* Bachelor's degrees awarded in top five disciplines psychology 193; education 145; business, management, marketing, and related support services 123, social sciences 119; communication, journalism, and related programs 108.

Fees and Other Expenses: *Full-time tuition per academic year 2004–05:* $5,622 in-state resident, $13,470 out-of-state. Contact the university for current graduate tuition and fees. *Room and board per academic year:* $7,275. *Books and supplies:* $1,200.

Financial Aid: Aid from institutionally generated funds is provided on the basis of financial need. Institution has a Program Participation Agreement with the U.S. Department of Education for eligible students to receive Pell Grants and other federal aid.

Financial aid to full-time, first-time undergraduate students: 22% received federal grants averaging $3,163; 16% state/local grants averaging $2,990; 13% institutional grants averaging $3,070; 54% loans averaging $5,702.

Departments and Teaching Staff: *Total instructional faculty:* 674. Degrees held by full-time faculty: Doctorate 60.7%, master's 38.6%, baccalaureate .7%. 67.5% hold terminal degrees. Student-to-faculty ratio: 17:1.

Enrollment: Total enrollment 12,143. Undergraduate 8,123 (men 39.8%, women 60.2%).

Characteristics of Student Body: *Ethnic/racial makeup:* Black non-Hispanic: 12.2%; American Indian or Alaska Native: .3%; Asian or Pacific Islander: 2.6%; Hispanic: 6.4%; White non-Hispanic: 69.6%; unknown: 7.4%.

International Students: 121 nonresident aliens enrolled. Programs available to aid students whose native language is not English: Social, cultural. English as a Second Language Program. No financial aid specifically designated for international students.

Student Life: On-campus residence halls house 32% of student body. All residence halls are coed. *Intercollegiate athletics:* men only: baseball, basketball, cross-country, football, golf, gymnastics, soccer, swimming, tennis, track, wrestling; women only: basketball, cross-country, field hockey, gymnastics, softball, swimming, tennis, track, volleyball. *Special regulations:* Cars permitted without restrictions. Quiet hours and residence hall visitation hours are set by the Board of Trustees. All residence halls are run by professional student personnel staff, 24 to 1 student-staff ratio. *Special services:* Learning Resources Center, medical services, Equal Opportunities Program, Handicapped Student Office, shuttle bus to and from parking lots during evening classes. *Student publications, radio, television:* Folio, an annual literary magazine; Laurel, a yearbook; Southern News, a weekly publication. Closed circuit radio station WSCB operates 50 hours per week. Closed circuit television station WVPC operates 50 hours per week. *Surrounding community:* New Haven population 150,000. New York City, 76 miles from campus, is nearest metropolitan area. Served by mass transit bus system; airport 6 miles from campus; passenger rail service 3 miles from campus.

Library Collections: 496,000 volumes. 149,000 government documents; 753,000 microforms; 4,700 audiovisual materials; 3,550 serial subscriptions. Online catalog. Students have access to online information retrieval services and the Internet.

Most important holdings include Caroline Sherwin Bailey Historical Children's Collection; Connecticut History Collection in the Early American textbooks; India Collection.

Buildings and Grounds: Campus area 162 acres.

Chief Executive Officer: Dr. Cheryl J. Norton, President.

Undergraduates address admission inquiries to Sharon B. Brennan, Director of Admissions; graduate inquiries to Dean of Graduate Studies.

Trinity College

300 Summit Street
Hartford, Connecticut 06106-3100
Tel: (860) 297-2180   **E-mail:** admissions.office@trincoll.edu
Fax: (860) 297-2287   **Internet:** www.trincoll.edu

Institution Description: Trinity College is a private, independent, nonprofit college. *Enrollment:* 2,373. *Degrees awarded:* Baccalaureate, master's.

Member of Hartford Consortium for Higher Education.

Accreditation: *Regional:* NEASC. *Professional:* engineering

History: Established and chartered as Washington College 1823; offered first instruction at postsecondary level 1824; awarded first degree 1828; adopted present name 1845; became coeducational 1969. See Glenn Weaver, *The History of Trinity College* (Hartford: Trinity College, 1967) for further information.

Institutional Structure: *Governing board:* Board of Trustees. Representation: 24 trustees, including 6 alumni, 1 administrator. 1 ex officio. All voting. *Composition of institution:* Administrators 9 men / 7 women Academic affairs headed by dean of the faculty. Management/business/finances directed by treasurer. Full-time instructional faculty 247. Academic governance body, the faculty, meets an average of 9 times per year.

Calendar: Semesters. Academic year Sept. to May. Freshmen admitted Sept. Degrees conferred and formal commencement May.

Characteristics of Freshmen: 40% of applicants admitted; 27% of admitted students enrolled full-time.

57% (325 students) submitted SAT scores; 14% (80 students) submitted ACT scores. *25th percentile*: SAT Verbal 600, SAT Math 610; ACT Composite 25. *75th percentile*: SAT Verbal 700, SAT Math 700; ACT Composite 29.

86% entering freshmen expected to graduate within 5 years. 18% of freshmen from Connecticut. Freshmen from 33 states and 12 foreign countries.

Admission: For fall acceptance, apply as early as Oct. 1 of senior year in secondary school, but not later than Jan. 15. Students are notified of acceptance Apr. Apply by Nov. 15 for early decision (option 1), or Jan. 1 (option 2); Jan. 1 for regular decision. Need not limit application to Trinity, but candidates must agree to attend if accepted. *Requirements:* Graduation from accredited secondary school with 4 units in English, 2 in a foreign language, 2 algebra, 1 plane geometry, 1 laboratory science, 1 history. Additional units in some areas recommended.

Entrance tests: College Board SAT and English Achievement or ACT composite. 3.0 minimum GPA; 20 courses maximum transfer credit.

College credit and advanced placement for postsecondary-level work completed in secondary school. Tutoring available.

Degree Requirements: 36 course credits; 4 GPA on 12.0 scale; 16 credits in residence; exit competency examinations—comprehensives in some fields of study; distribution requirements; proficiency requirements in writing and mathematics. All students must complete an interdisciplinary minor or its equivalent.

Fulfillment of some degree requirements and exemption from some beginning courses possible by passing College Board APP or United Kingdom "A" Level Certificate Examinations. *Grading system:* A–F; pass-fail; withdraw (carries time limit).

Distinctive Educational Programs: *For undergraduates:* Study internships. Accelerated degree programs. Dual-degree programs in engineering with the Hartford Graduate Center of Rensselaer Polytechnic Institute Cooperative program in music with the University of Hartford; in elementary education with St. Joseph College. Interdisciplinary programs in area studies, comparative literature, computer science, neuroscience, public policy, and women's studies, medieval and Renaissance studies; computer coordinate majors; student-designed interdisciplinary programs. Faculty-designed, nondepartmental courses. Guided Studies in Humanities, a 13-course program available to a limited number of entering freshmen. Independent study and various nontraditional programs involving study and research on- and off-campus, including Intensive Study, Open Semester, teaching assistantships in freshman seminar and other courses, student-taught courses. Study abroad in Rome at Trinity's Barbieri Center and at the Intercollegiate Center for Classical Studies; in England in cooperation with the University of East Anglia; in Greece at the American School of Classical Studies, Athens. Other study abroad through Institute of European Studies programs in Vienna, Austria; Durham and London, England; Nantes and Paris, France; Freiburg, Germany; Madrid, Spain. Study abroad also available through programs sponsored by other institutions. Off-campus study in U.S. through Twelve College Exchange Program; Mystic-Williams Maritime Studies Program; theater arts program at the National Theatre Institute of the Eugene O'Neill Theatre Center at Waterford; Trinity La Mama Performing Arts Program (NYC); Washington (DC) semester in cooperation with American University; may be individually arranged. Cross-registration with Wesleyan University. Individualized degree program for adult students. Joint-degree programs in American studies in cooperation with St. Joseph College and the University of Hartford, and in public policy studies with University of Connecticut School of Law. Master's program in liberal arts. Global learning sites in South Africa, Trinidad, Kathmandu. *Available to all students:* Evening classes. Cross-registration through the consortium.

ROTC: Army in cooperation with University of Connecticut.

Degrees Conferred: 493 *baccalaureate* (B), 36 *master's* (M): area and ethnic studies 34 (B), 4 (M); biological/life sciences 25 (B); computer and information sciences 28 (B); education 10 (B); engineering and engineering technologies 12 (B); English 46 (B), 5 (M); foreign languages and literature 27 (B); interdisciplinary studies 15 (B); mathematics 13 (B); natural resources/environmental science 2 (B); philosophy/religion/theology 21 (B); physical sciences 2 (B); protective services/public administration 8 (B); psychology 41 (B); social sciences and history 221 (B), 27 (M); visual and performing arts 37 (B). *Honorary degrees awarded 2003–04:* Doctor of Laws 2, Doctor of Letters 1, Doctor of Humane Letters 1.

Fees and Other Expenses: *Full-time tuition per academic year 2004–05:* $32,000 undergraduate, $9,600 graduate. *Required fees:* $1,630. *Room and board per academic year:* $8,590.

Financial Aid: Aid from institutionally generated funds is provided on the basis of financial need. Institution has a Program Participation Agreement with the U.S. Department of Education for eligible students to receive Pell Grants and other federal aid.

Financial aid to full-time, first-time undergraduate students: need-based scholarships/grants totaling $2,816,343, self-help $3,887,292; non-need-based scholarships/grants totaling $57,951, self-help $578,952, parent loans $5,385,837. *Graduate aid:* 11 fellowships and grants awarded totaling $20,550 (ranging from $400 to $6,600).

Departments and Teaching Staff: *Professors* 61, *associate professors* 65, *assistant professors* 42, *lecturers* 19, *part-time faculty* 58, *other* 3. *Total instructional faculty:* 248 (full-time 190, part-time 58; women 96, men 152; members of minority groups 38). Total faculty with doctorate, first-professional, or other terminal degree: 199. Student-to-faculty ratio: 10:1. *Faculty development:* $388,000 in grants for research.

Enrollment: Total enrollment 2,373. Undergraduate full-time 1,055 men / 993 women, part-time 70m / 135w; graduate full-time 3m, part-time 59m / 58w. *Transfer students:* in-state 88; from out-of-state 129.

Characteristics of Student Body: *Ethnic/racial makeup:* number of Black non-Hispanic: 109; American Indian or Alaska Native: 3; Asian or Pacific Islander: 125; Hispanic: 106; White non-Hispanic: 1,391; unknown: 480.

International Students: 39 nonresident aliens enrolled fall 2004. 13 students from Europe, 14 Asia, 7 Central and South America, 1 Africa, 2 Canada, 1 New Zealand, 1 other. Social and cultural programs available for students whose native language is not English. No financial aid specifically designated for international students.

Student Life: On-campus residence halls house 89% of student body. Residence halls for both men and women constitute 100% of such space. 15% of men join and 3% live in fraternities. 10% of women join sororities. *Intercollegiate athletics:* men only: baseball, basketball, crew, football, hockey, lacrosse, soccer, squash, swimming, tennis, track; women only: basketball, crew, field hockey, lacrosse, soccer, squash, swimming, tennis, track, volleyball. *Special regulations:* Cars permitted without restrictions for upperclass students; very limited usage allowed freshmen. *Special services:* Medical services, evening escort services provided by campus security. *Student publications: Trinity Review,* a biannual literary magazine; *Tripod,* a weekly newspaper; *Trincoll Journal,* (Internet 'zine); *Trinity Papers,* annual collection of student essays, fiction, poetry, and art. *Surrounding community:* Hartford population 150,000. Boston (MA) and New York (NY), both 125 miles from campus, are nearest metropolitan areas. Served by mass transit bus system, airport 20 miles from campus, passenger rail service 3 miles from campus.

Library Collections: 1,002,145 volumes. 1,939 current periodical subscriptions. Access to 12,000 journals via electronic access. 16,416 recordings; 8,615 compact discs; 80 CD-ROMs. 140 computer work stations. Students have access to the Internet at no charge. Total budget for books, periodicals, audiovisual materials, microforms 2004–05: $3,368,394.

Most important holdings include Watkinson Library (collection of 19th-century Americana consisting of 167,823 volumes); Enders Ornithology Collection (6,200 volumes); Moore Collection regarding the Far East (30,000 volumes).

Buildings and Grounds: Campus area 100 acres. *New buildings:* Admissions and Career Services Center completed 2001; Library and Information Technology Center 2004.

Chief Executive Officer: Dr. James F. Jones, Jr., President.

Address admission inquiries to Larry Dow, Dean of Admissions and Financial Aid; graduate inquiries to Denise Best, Director of Special Academic Programs.

United States Coast Guard Academy

15 Mohegan Avenue
New London, Connecticut 06320-8100
Tel: (800) 883-3724 **E-mail:** admissions@cga.uscg.mil
Fax: (860) 701-6700 **Internet:** www.cga.edu

Institution Description: The United States Coast Guard Academy is a federal institution. *Enrollment:* 994. *Degrees awarded:* Baccalaureate.

Accreditation: *Regional:* NEASC. *Professional:* engineering

History: Established by Congress as U.S. Revenue Cutter Service School of Instruction 1876; offered first instruction 1877; changed name to Revenue Cutter Academy 1914; adopted present name 1915; awarded first baccalaureate 1941.

Institutional Structure: The Academy is governed by a Board of Trustees whose purpose is to maintain cognizance of all programs at the Academy and to provide guidance and advice to the Superintendent of the USCG Academy and the Chief of Staff and the Commandant of the U.S. Coast Guard. The Dean of Academics is responsible for all educational programs administered by the Academic Division. Full-time instructional faculty 105.

Calendar: Semesters. Academic year Aug. to May. Formal commencement May. Summer session begins in May.

Characteristics of Freshmen: 21% of applicants admitted. 92% (283 students) submitted SAT scores; 40% (122 students) submitted ACT scores. *25th percentile:* SAT Verbal 580, SAT Math 620; ACT Composite 25, ACT English 26, ACT Math 26. *75th percentile:* SAT Verbal 670, SAT Math 680; ACT Composite 30, ACT English 30, ACT Math 30.

Admission: For fall acceptance, apply after May 1 of junior year of secondary school, but not later than Dec. 15 of senior year. *Requirements:* Graduation from accredited secondary school with 15 units which must include 3 English, 1 algebra, 1 plane geometry, 1 quadratics. Applicant must meet medical, physical, and aptitude requirements. *Entrance tests:* College Board SAT or ACT.

Advanced placement for postsecondary-level work completed in secondary school.

Degree Requirements: Pass at least 37 courses of 3 credits or greater and earn a minimum of 126 credits; pass every course in the core curriculum; accumulate at least 90 credits of coursework with grades of C or better, exclusive of physical education; complete the academic requirements for one of the majors as specified in the official *Catalog of Courses. Grading system:* A–F.

Distinctive Educational Programs: Facilities and programs for independent research, including honors programs.

Degrees Conferred: 210 *baccalaureate:* business 46, engineering/engineering technologies 81, mathematics 15, physical sciences 25, social sciences and history 43.

Fees and Other Expenses: Tuition is paid by the U.S. Government. *Other fees:* $3,000 at entrance.

Departments and Teaching Staff: *Total instructional faculty:* 134 (full-time 114, part-time 20; women 29, men 105; members of minority groups 10). Total faculty with doctorate, first-professional, or other terminal degree: 60. Student-to-faculty ratio: 10:1.

Enrollment: Total enrollment 994 (707 men / 287 women).

Characteristics of Student Body: *Ethnic/racial makeup:* number of Black non-Hispanic: 32; American Indian or Alaska 7; Asian or Pacific Islander: 44; Hispanic: 48; White non-Hispanic: 849. *Age distribution:* number under 18: 24; 18–19: 952; 20–21: 456; 22–24: 62.

International Students: 16 nonresident aliens enrolled fall 2004. 3 students from Europe, 2 Asia, 11 Central and South America. No Programs available to aid students whose native language is not English. No financial aid specifically designated for international students.

Student Life: Students required to live in on-campus housing. *Surrounding community:* New London population 76,000.

Library Collections: 140,000 volumes including bound books, serial backfiles, electronic documents, and government documents not in separate collections. Online catalog. Current serial subscriptions: 650 paper, 8 microform, 45 electronic. 7 computer work stations. Students have access to the Internet at no charge. Total budget for books, periodicals, audiovisual materials, microforms 2004–05: $300,000.

Most important special collection: Coast Guard History.

Chief Executive Officer: Rear Admiral James C. Van Sice, Superintendent.

Address admission inquiries to Director of Admissions.

University of Bridgeport

380 University Avenue
Bridgeport, Connecticut 06601
Tel: (203) 576-4000   **E-mail:** admit@bridgeport.edu
Fax: (203) 576-4941   **Internet:** www.bridgeport.edu

Institution Description: University of Bridgeport is a private, independent, nonprofit institution. *Enrollment:* 3,274. *Degrees awarded:* Associate, baccalaureate, master's, doctorate, first-professional (chiropractic).

Accreditation: *Regional:* NEASC. *Professional:* acupuncture, art, business, chiropractic education, dental hygiene, engineering, naturopathic medicine

History: Established and chartered as Junior College of Connecticut 1927; offered first instruction at postsecondary level 1928; first degree (associate) awarded 1929; chartered as University of Bridgeport 1947.

Institutional Structure: *Governing board:* Board of Trustees. Extrainstitutional representation: 30 trustees, 12 life trustees; institutional representation: 1 administrator; 7 alumni. 1 ex officio. 30 voting. *Composition of institution:* Administrators 19 men / 5 women. Academic affairs headed by provost/vice president of academic affairs. Management/business/finances directed by vice president of administration and finance, and treasurer. Full-time instructional faculty 88. Academic governance body, University Senate, meets an average of 12 times per year.

Calendar: Semesters. Academic year Sept. to May. Freshmen admitted May, June, July, Aug., Sept., Jan. Degrees conferred Aug., Dec., May. Formal commencement May. Summer session of 4 terms from May to Aug.

Characteristics of Freshmen: 76% of applicants admitted; 13% of admitted students enrolled full-time.

91% (233 students) submitted SAT scores; 6% (16 students) submitted ACT scores. *25th percentile:* SAT Verbal 380, SAT Math 380; ACT Composite 16, ACT English 15, ACT Math 18. *75th percentile:* SAT Verbal 500, SAT Math 520; ACT Composite 23, ACT English 22, ACT Math 22.

55% of entering freshmen expected to graduate within 5 years. 33% of freshmen from Connecticut. Freshmen from 17 states and 16 foreign countries.

Admission: Rolling admissions plan. For fall acceptance, apply as early as Aug. 1 of previous year, but not later than Aug. 15 of year of enrollment. Students are notified of acceptance beginning in Nov. Early acceptance available. *Requirements:* Graduation from accredited secondary school with 16 units which must include 4 English. GED or state secondary school equivalency may be accepted. Minimum GPA 2.0. *Entrance tests:* College Board SAT. *For transfer students:* Depending on desired program, 2.0–3.0 minimum GPA and 66–90 hours maximum transfer credit.

College credit for postsecondary-level work completed in secondary school. College credit and advanced placement for extrainstitutional learning (life experience) on basis of examination and review by faculty committee, portfolio assessment. Tutoring available. Developmental courses offered in summer session and regular academic year; credit given.

Degree Requirements: *For all baccalaureate degrees:* 120–135 credit hours; 30 hours in residence. *For all associate degrees:* 60–65 credit hours; residence requirement varies according to program. *For all undergraduate degrees:* 2.0 GPA.

Fulfillment of some degree requirements and exemption from some beginning courses possible by passing College Board English composition (score of 600), CLEP, AP. *Grading system:* A–F; pass-fail; withdraw.

Distinctive Educational Programs: *For undergraduates:* Honors programs. *Available to all students:* Work-experience programs. Flexible meeting places and schedules, including off-campus centers (at Stamford and Waterbury, less than 30 miles away from main institution and various other locations) and weekend and evening classes. Facilities and programs for independent research, including individual majors.

ROTC: Army offered in cooperation with University of Connecticut.

Degrees Conferred: 31 *associate* ; 182 *baccalaureate* (B), 656 *master's* (M); *doctorate* (D): architecture 2 (B); biological/life sciences 6 (B); business/marketing 51 (B), 121 (M); communications/communication technologies 3 (B); computer and information sciences 9 (B), 88 (M); education 296 (M), 7 (D); engineering and engineering technologies 2 (B), 75 (M); health professions and related sciences 2 (B), 2 (M), 21 (D); home economics and vocational home economics 74 (M); interdisciplinary studies 55 (B); liberal arts/general studies 1 (B); mathematics 2 (B); protective services/public administration 15 (B); psychology 12 (B); visual and performing arts 16 (B). *First-professional:* chiropractic 43.

Fees and Other Expenses: *Full-time tuition per academic year 2004–05:* $18,300 undergraduate; $16,720 graduate. *Required fees:* $1,225. *Room and board per academic year:* $8,400.

Financial Aid: Aid from institutionally generated funds is awarded on basis of academic merit, financial need, athletic ability. Institution has a Program Participation Agreement with the U.S. Department of Education for eligible students to receive Pell Grants and other federal aid.

Departments and Teaching Staff: *Professors* 24, *associate professors* 32, *assistant professors* 25, *instructors* 5, *part-time faculty* 259. *Total instructional faculty:* 347 (full-time 88, part-time 259; women 132, men 215; members of minority groups 52). Total faculty with doctorate, first-professional, or other terminal degree: 75. Student-to-faculty ratio: 11:1.

Enrollment: Total enrollment 3,274. Undergraduate full-time 455 men / 633 women, part-time 77m / 2093w; first-professional full-time 128m / 71w, part-time 2w; graduate full-time 350m / 445w, part-time 361m / 348w.

Characteristics of Student Body: *Ethnic/racial makeup:* number of Black non-Hispanic: 451; American Indian or Alaska Native: 2; Asian or Pacific Islander: 62; Hispanic: 184; White non-Hispanic: 405; unknown: 49. *Age distribution:* number under 18: 62; 18–19: 394; 20–21: 293; 22–24: 224; 25–29: 181; 30–34: 73; 35–39: 52; 40–49: 72; 50–64: 22; 65 and over: 1.

International Students: 221 nonresident aliens enrolled fall 2004. Students from Europe, Asia, Central and South America, Africa, Canada. Social and cultural programs available for students whose native language is not English. No financial aid specifically designated for international students.

Student Life: On-campus residence halls house 47% of student body; all are coed by floor. Fewer than 1% live in university-owned houses or apartments. *Intercollegiate athletics:* men: baseball, basketball, cross country, soccer; women: basketball, cross country, gymnastics, soccer, softball, swimming, volleyball. *Special regulations:* Cars with decals permitted on campus in designated areas only. Quiet hours from 8am to 8pm Sun.–Thur. *Special services:* Learning Resources Center, medical services, shuttle system transports students within campus and from campus to shopping areas, public transportation, and medical services. *Student publications: Alternatives* and *Groundswell,* annual literary magazines; *Wisterian,* a yearbook. *Surrounding community:* Bridgeport population 145,000. New York City, 60 miles from campus, is nearest metropolitan area. Served by mass transit bus system; airport 7 miles from campus; passenger rail service 1 mile from campus.

Publications: Sources of information about Bridgeport include a promotional film.

Library Collections: 275,000 volumes including bound books, serial backfiles, electronic documents, and government documents not in separate collections. Online catalog. Current serial subscriptions: 1,700. 1,051,139 microform units; 5,485 electronic. Students have access to the Internet at no charge.

Buildings and Grounds: Campus area 86 acres.

Chief Executive Officer: Neil Albert Salonen, President.

Address admission inquiries to Barbara L. Maryak, Director of Admissions.

School of Arts and Sciences

Degree Programs Offered: *Baccalaureate* in biology, English, literature, industrial design, interior design, graphic design, illustration, mathematics, music.

Admission: In addition to general requirements, portfolio assessment, audition, or interview required in some fields.

Degree Requirements: *See* general requirements. Graduate requirements vary.

Distinctive Educational Programs: Double majors. Individualized program of study for baccalaureate candidates in elective studies. Interdisciplinary programs, American civilization, early childhood education.

School of Business

Degree Programs Offered: *Baccalaureate* in accounting, business administration, computer applications and information systems, finance and banking, international business, marketing, management and industrial relations; *master's* in accounting, business economics, finance, international business, management and industrial relations, managerial information systems, marketing.

Admission: *See* general requirements. Graduate requirements vary with programs and levels.

Degree Requirements: *See* general requirements. General education requirements for baccalaureate. Graduate requirements vary.

Fones School of Dental Hygiene

Degree Programs Offered: *Associate, baccalaureate* in dental hygiene.

Admission: *See* general requirements. Graduate requirements vary with programs and levels.

Degree Requirements: *See* general requirements.

College of Chiropractic

Degree Programs Offered: *Doctorate* in chiropractic.

Nutrition Institute

Degree Programs Offered: *Baccalaureate* in medical technology; *master's* in human nutrition.

School of General Studies

Degree Programs Offered: *Associate, baccalaureate* in general studies.

School of Engineering

Degree Programs Offered: *Baccalaureate* in computer science, computer engineering (electrical, management, mechanical).

Admission: In addition to general requirements, 4 secondary school units mathematics; minimum combined College Board SAT score of 1,000; lowest acceptable secondary school standing upper 40% of class.

Degree Requirements: *See* general requirements.

Distinctive Educational Programs: Computer graphics facility. Special program to help disadvantaged youth pursue engineering degrees.

College of Nations

Degree Programs Offered: *Baccalaureate* in mass communications, world religions, social sciences, international political economy and diplomacy.

College of Naturopathic Medicine

Degree Programs Offered: *Doctorate* in naturopathic medicine.

University of Connecticut

Gulley Hall
352 Mansfield Road
Storrs, Connecticut 06269-2048
Tel: (860) 486-2000   **E-mail:** admissions@uconn.edu
Fax: (860) 486-1476   **Internet:** www.uconn.edu

Institution Description: University of Connecticut is a state institution with Schools of Law in Hartford and Social Work in West Hartford, Schools of Dental Medicine and Medicine at the University of Connecticut Health Center in Farmington, and regional campuses in Avery Point, Hartford, Stamford, Torrington,

and Waterbury. *Enrollment:* 22,694. *Degrees awarded:* Baccalaureate, first-professional (dentistry, law, medicine), master's, doctorate. Certificates also awarded.

Academic offerings subject to approval by statewide coordinating bodies.

Accreditation: *Regional:* NEASC. *Professional:* accounting, art, audiology, business, clinical psychology, cytogenetic technology, dentistry, dietetics, endodontics, engineering, English language education, landscape architecture, law, marriage and family therapy, music, nursing, periodontics, pharmacy, physical therapy, public administration, public health, recreation and leisure services, social work, speech-language pathology, teacher education, theatre

History: Established and chartered as Storrs Agricultural School and offered first instruction at postsecondary level 1881; changed name to Storrs Agricultural College 1893, to Connecticut Agricultural College 1899; awarded first degree (baccalaureate) 1914; changed name to Connecticut State College 1933; adopted present name 1939.

Institutional Structure: *Governing board:* Board of Trustees of the University of Connecticut. Extrainstitutional representation: 19 trustees, Governor of Connecticut, Commissioner of Agriculture, Commissioner of State Board of Education ex officio; institutional representation: 2 students; 2 alumni. All voting. *Composition of institution:* Administrators 63 men / 35 women. Academic affairs headed by vice president for academic affairs. Management/business/finances directed by vice president for finance and administration. Total instructional faculty 1,234. Academic governance body, University Senate, meets an average of 9 times per year. *Faculty representation:* Faculty of all schools except Schools of Law, Medicine, and Dental Medicine served by collective bargaining agent affiliated with AAUP.

Calendar: Semesters. Academic year early late Aug. to early May. Freshmen admitted Sept., Jan. Degrees conferred May, Aug., Dec. Formal commencement May. Summer sessions early late May to mid-Aug.

Characteristics of Freshmen: 50% of applicants admitted. 35% of applicants admitted and enrolled full-time.

98% (3,190 students) submitted SAT scores; 8% (263 students) submitted ACT scores. *25th percentile*: SAT Verbal 530, SAT Math 550; ACT Composite 22. *75th percentile*: SAT Verbal 630, SAT Math 640; ACT Composite 27.

24 National Merit Scholars. 68% of entering freshmen expected to graduate within 6 years. 70% of freshmen from Connecticut. Freshmen from 31 states and 10 foreign countries.

Admission: Rolling admissions plan. For fall acceptance, apply as early as Sept. 1 of previous year, but not later than Feb. 1 of year of enrollment. Early action program available. *Requirements:* Either graduation from approved secondary school with 16 units (15 college preparatory), including 4 English, 2 history or social science, 3 mathematics, 2 laboratory science, 2 foreign language (3 years strongly recommended); or State Equivalency Diploma. Additional requirements for some programs. *Entrance tests:* College Board SAT or ACT. *For transfer students:* 2.7 minimum GPA; maximum transfer credit varies according to program.

College credit and advanced placement for postsecondary-level work completed in secondary school. Tutoring available.

Degree Requirements: 120–155 credit hours; 2.0 GPA in all upper division courses; last 2 semesters in residence. Additional requirements for some programs. Fulfillment of some degree requirements and exemption from some beginning courses possible by passing College Board CLEP, AP. *Grading system:* A–F; pass-fail; withdraw (carries time limit).

Distinctive Educational Programs: Evening classes. Special facilities for using telecommunications in the classroom. Facilities and programs for independent research, including honors programs, individual majors. Study abroad in 28 countries including Argentina, Australia, Austria, Brazil, Canada, Chile, Costa Rica, Czech Republic, Denmark, Dominican Republic, England, France, Germany, Ghana, Hungary, Ireland, Israel, Italy, Japan, Mexico, The Netherlands, Poland, Portugal, Russia, Spain, Sweden, and Switzerland. *Other distinctive programs: See* each school or college.

ROTC: Army, Air Force.

Degrees Conferred: 3,673 *baccalaureate* (B), 1,111 *master's* (M), 257 *doctorate* (D): agriculture 95 (B), 17 (M), 7 (D); architecture 7 (B); area and ethnic studies 6 (B), 10 (M); biological/life sciences 210 (B), 52 (M), 45 (D); business/marketing 500 (B); 509 (M), 9 (D); communications/communication technologies 213 (B), 13 (M); computer and information sciences 13 (B), 8 (M); education 107 (B), 195 (M), 52 (D); engineering and engineering technologies 203 (B), 53 (M), 34 (D); English 213 (B), 18 (M), 8 (D); foreign languages and literature 40 (B), 17 (M), 8 (D); health professions and related sciences 250 (B), 96 (M); 22 (D); home economics and vocational home economics 246 (B), 10 (M), 2 (D); interdisciplinary studies 71 (B), 5 (M), 2 (D); liberal arts/general studies 291 (B); mathematics 32 (B), 39 (M), 7 (D); natural resources/environmental science 36 (B), 3 (M); parks and recreation 21 (B); philosophy/religion/theology 11 (B), 6 (D); physical sciences 33 (B); 20 (M), 18 (D); protective services/public administration 153 (M); psychology 274 (B), 16 (M), 23 (D); social sciences and history 672 (B), 48 (M); 18 (D); visual and performing arts 129 (B), 23 (M),

1 (D). 374 *first-professional:* dentistry 35, law 192, medicine 68, pharmacy 79. Honorary degrees awarded 2003–04: 2 Doctor of Science, 1 Doctor of Laws.

Fees and Other Expenses: *Full-time tuition per academic year 2004–05:* $6,096 undergraduate, $18,600 out-of-state; graduate resident $7,524, out-of-state $19,584. *Required fees:* $1,816 undergraduate, $1,446 graduate. *Room and board per academic year:* $7,848.

Financial Aid: Aid from institutionally generated funds is provided on the basis of academic merit, financial need, athletic ability. Institution has a Program Participation Agreement with the U.S. Department of Education for eligible students to receive Pell Grants and other federal aid.

Financial aid to full-time, first-time undergraduate students: need-based scholarships/grants totaling $3,196,097, self-help $28,170,108, parent loans $6,627,315, tuition waivers $925,406, athletic awards $217,446; non-need-based scholarships/grants totaling $8,979,271, self-help $17,529,318, parent loans $7,377,812, tuition waivers $2,105,367, athletic awards$4,361,757. *Graduate aid:* 349 students received $983,892 in federal and state-funded fellowships/grants; 1,038 received $12,761,334 in federal and state-funded loans; 169 received $370,626 for work-study jobs; 596 students received other fellowships/grants totaling $1,527,207; 2,465 teaching assistantships awarded totaling $29,673,500; 135 students received research assistantships totaling $498,179.

Departments and Teaching Staff: *Total instructional faculty:* 1,234 (full-time 922, part-time 312; women 403, men 831; members of minority groups 202). Total faculty with doctorate, first-professional, or other terminal degree: 1,151. Student-to-faculty ratio: 17:1.

Enrollment: Total enrollment 22,694. Undergraduate full-time 7,028 men / 7,815 women, part-time 519m / 389w; graduate full-time 1,504m / 1,774w, part-time 1,286m / 1,489w; first-professional full-time 313m / 359w, part-time 121m / 97w.

Characteristics of Student Body: *Ethnic/racial makeup:* number of Black non-Hispanic: 764; American Indian or Alaska Native: 49; Asian or Pacific Islander: 1,029; Hispanic: 688; White non-Hispanic: 11,704; unknown: 1,359. *Age distribution:* number under 18: 545; 18–19: 6,272; 20–21: 6,270; 22–24: 1,655; 25–29: 286; 30–34: 108; 35–39: 36; 40–49: 73; 50–64: 15.

International Students: 1,438 nonresident aliens enrolled fall 2004. Programs available to aid students whose native language is not English: Social, cultural. English as a Second Language Program. No financial aid specifically designated for international students.

Student Life: On-campus residence halls house 72% of full-time undergraduate student body at the Storrs campus. Housing available for graduate students and for married students. *Intercollegiate athletics:* men only: baseball, basketball, cross-country, football, hockey, soccer, swimming, tennis, track, golf; women only: basketball, cross-country, field hockey, gymnastics, soccer, softball, swimming, tennis, track, volleyball. *Special regulations:* Cars with permits allowed in designated parking areas; fee charged. *Special services:* Medical services, campus bus service. *Student publications, radio: Connecticut Daily Campus,* a newspaper; *Nutmeg,* a yearbook. Radio station WHUS. *Surrounding community:* Storrs population 15,000. Boston, 70 miles from campus, is nearest metropolitan area.

Library Collections: 2,403,349 volumes. 2,602,752 microforms; 5,946 audiovisual materials; 22,298 serial subscriptions. Online catalog. Students have access to online information retrieval services and the Internet.

Most important holdings include Charles Olson Archives; Geigel Puerto Rican Collections; Chilean Collections.

Buildings and Grounds: Total university (all campuses) including Health Center: 4,299 acres.

Chief Executive Officer: Dr. Philip E. Austin, President.

Address admission inquiries to Director of Admissions; first-professional inquiries to Admissions Office of the School of Law; graduate inquiries to Graduate Admissions.

College of Liberal Arts and Sciences

Degree Programs Offered: *Baccalaureate, master's, doctorate* in various fields.

Distinctive Educational Programs: Interdisciplinary programs in international studies, Judaic studies, Latin American language and area studies, medieval studies, Middle East language and area studies. Slavic and East European language and area studies, urban studies.

College of Agriculture and Natural Resources

Degree Programs Offered: *Baccalaureate, master's, doctorate.* Certificates also awarded.

Distinctive Educational Programs: 2-year vocational certificate program in agriculture through on-campus Ratcliffe Hicks School of Agriculture.

School of Allied Health Professions

Degree Programs Offered: *Baccalaureate, master's.* Certificates also awarded.

Distinctive Educational Programs: Articulated baccalaureates in sports physical therapy and clinical dietetics in sports fitness and wellness. CUP program in dietetics. Certificate and baccalaureates in medical cytogenetics and cytotechnology. Articulated physical therapy program for PTA's.

School of Business Administration

Degree Programs Offered: *Baccalaureate, master's, doctorate.*

Distinctive Educational Programs: Joint baccalaureate-M.B.A. programs with Schools of Engineering, Pharmacy, and Department of Mathematics. Joint M.B.A.-M.S.W. with School of Social Work; M.B.A.-master's in international studies with College of Liberal Arts and Sciences. Joint M.B.A.-J.D. with School of Law. Facilities include Center for Real Estate and Urban Economics, Center for Transnational Accounting and Financial Research, Center for Research and Development in Financial Services, Bureau of Utility Research.

School of Education

Degree Programs Offered: *Baccalaureate, master's, doctorate.* Specialist certificates also awarded.

School of Engineering

Degree Programs Offered: *Baccalaureate, master's, doctorate.*

Distinctive Educational Programs: Double majors are possible between any of the regular undergraduate programs and also with materials engineering.

School of Family Studies

Degree Programs Offered: *Master's.* Certificates also awarded.

Distinctive Educational Programs: Concentration in marital and family therapy. Certificate program in gerontology.

School of Fine Arts

Degree Programs Offered: *Baccalaureate, master's, doctorate.*

Distinctive Educational Programs: Joint baccalaureate programs with the School of Education leading to B.S. in Music Education; with the College of Liberal Arts and Sciences leading to a B.A. in Art History. In conjunction with the Department of Modern and Classical Languages, option to study Conservation and Restoration in the Study Abroad Program in Florence; through the Department of Art, semester exchange with the Nova Scotia College of Art and Design. Specialized concentrations within the programs include bronze casting (Department of Art); puppetry (Department of Dramatic Arts); psychomusicology and electronic music techniques (Department of Music). Facilities include the Atrium Gallery, the Design Center, the Yankee Foundry, the Harriet S. Jorgensen, Studio and Mobius Theaters, and Von Der Mehden Recital Hall.

School of Nursing

Degree Programs Offered: *Baccalaureate, master's.*

Distinctive Educational Programs: Work-study course for undergraduate students in summer between junior and senior year; perioperative-CHN experience offered; master's entry program; geriatric nurse practitioner program.

School of Pharmacy

Degree Programs Offered: *First-professional, master's, doctorate.*

Admission: *See* general requirements. 14 college preparatory units which must include 4 years English, 3 mathematics (2 algebra and 1 plane geometry or equivalent), 1 laboratory science. Recommend additional units laboratory science, 4 years mathematics. Admission to professional program in third college year requires minimum GPA and specified university courses or their equivalent.

Degree Requirements: *For first-professional:* 155 credit hours, minimum GPA, completion of professional program requirements.

Distinctive Educational Programs: Combined B.S. Pharm./M.B.A. program with School of Business Administration. Interdisciplinary doctorate in neurosciences in collaboration with psychology and biological sciences. Drug information residencies and post-Pharm.D. Fellowships in clinical research.

Extended and Continuing Education

Degree Programs Offered: *Baccalaureate.*

Admission: Associate degree or 60 semester credits from accredited institution; special application forms; admission essay; interview.

Degree Requirements: 60 credits beyond associate or freshman-sophomore level; general university requirements; completion of an individualized interdisciplinary plan of study.

Departments and Teaching Staff: Faculty located in the various schools and colleges.

School of Law

55 Elizabeth Street
Hartford, Connecticut 06105
Tel: (860) 241-4638
Degree Programs Offered: *First-professional.*

Admission: Baccalaureate from accredited college with courses that emphasize critical reasoning and writing.

Degree Requirements: 86 credit hours; 2.0 GPA; core requirements.

Distinctive Educational Programs: Dual-degree program in law and public policy studies with Trinity College, in law and library studies with Southern Connecticut State College. J.D./M.S.W. with the University of Connecticut School of Social Work; J.D./M.B.A. with the University of Connecticut School of Business Administration; J.D./M.P.A. with the University of Connecticut Graduate School.

School of Social Work

1798 Asylum Avenue
West Hartford, Connecticut 06117
Tel: (860) 241-4737
Degree Programs Offered: *Master's.*

Distinctive Educational Programs: Dual-degree programs have been developed with the University of Connecticut School of Law (J.D./M.S.W.), Business Administration (M.B.A./M.S.W.) and Medicine (M.P.H./M.S.W). A program of exchange courses has also been developed with Yale Divinity School (M.Div./M.S.W.).

University of Connecticut Health Center - School of Dental Medicine

263 Farmington Avenue
Farmington, Connecticut 06032
Tel: (860) 674-2808
Degree Programs Offered: *First-professional, master's, doctorate* administered through graduate school.

Admission: Baccalaureate from approved college or university with 1 year laboratory biology (including 1 semester zoology); 1 year each in inorganic chemistry, organic chemistry, physics; facility in English and mathematics; DAT.

Degree Requirements: 4 years in residence with first 2 years curriculum, 3rd year clerkship, 4th year in general dentistry program.

University of Connecticut Health Center - School of Medicine

263 Farmington Avenue
Farmington, Connecticut 06032
Tel: (860) 674-2102
Degree Programs Offered: *First-professional.* Master's, doctorate administered through graduate school.

Admission: Baccalaureate from approved college or university with 1 year each in biology or zoology, general chemistry, organic chemistry, physics, MCAT. Courses in English composition, literature recommended.

Degree Requirements: 4 years in residence with 2 years core curriculum, 1 year departmental clerkships, 1 year electives.

University of Hartford

200 Bloomfield Avenue
West Hartford, Connecticut 06117
Tel: (860) 768-4100   **E-mail:** admission@hartford.edu
Fax: (860) 768-4961   **Internet:** www.hartford.edu

Institution Description: University of Hartford is a private, independent, nonprofit institution. *Enrollment:* 7,246. *Degrees awarded:* Associate, baccalaureate, master's, doctorate. Certificates also awarded.

Member of the Greater Hartford Consortium.

Accreditation: *Regional:* NEASC. *Professional:* business, clinical psychology, dance, engineering, engineering technology, music, nursing, occupational therapy, physical therapy, public administration, radiography, respiratory therapy, teacher education

History: Chartered as University of Hartford by union of Hartford Art School (established 1877), Hillyer College (established 1879), and Hartt College of Music (established 1920), offered first instruction at postsecondary level, and awarded first degrees (associate, baccalaureate) 1957.

Institutional Structure: *Governing board:* Board of Regents. Extrainstitutional representation: 60 regents; institutional representation: 6 members. *Composition of institution:* Administrators 45 men / 46 women. Academic affairs headed by executive vice president. Management/business/finances directed by vice president for finance and administration. Full-time instructional faculty 319. Academic governance body, Faculty Senate, meets an average of 10 times per year.

Calendar: Semesters. Academic year Aug. to May. Freshmen admitted Sept., Jan., May. Degrees conferred May, Sept., Jan. Formal commencement May. Summer session of 2 terms from May to Aug.

Characteristics of Freshmen: 60% of applicants admitted. 16% of admitted students enrolled full-time.

95% (968 students) submitted SAT scores; 10% (97 students) submitted ACT scores. *25th percentile:* SAT Verbal 480, SAT Math 490; ACT Composite 19. *75th percentile:* SAT Verbal 480, SAT Math 580; ACT Composite 27.

14% of entering freshmen expected to graduate within 5 years. 20% of freshmen from Connecticut. Freshmen from 31 states and 22 foreign countries.

Admission: Modified rolling admissions plan. For fall acceptance, apply as early as Oct. 1 of previous year, but not later than Feb. 1 of year of enrollment for students requesting on-campus housing or financial aid. Students are notified of acceptance beginning Jan. *Requirements:* Graduation from accredited secondary school or GED. Music evaluation for applicants to Hartt School of Music; interview and portfolio review for Hartford Art School. Recommend 16 units with 4 English, 2 in a foreign language, 2 to 2.3 mathematics, 2 science, 2 social studies, academic electives. Minimum GPA 2.5. *Entrance tests:* College Board SAT or ACT composite. For foreign students TOEFL. *For transfer students:* From 4-year accredited institution 2.0 minimum GPA; from 2-year accredited institution 2.2 minimum GPA; maximum transfer credit limited by residence requirement.

College credit and advanced placement for postsecondary-level work completed in secondary school and for extrainstitutional learning on basis of ACE *2006 Guide to the Evaluation of Educational Experiences in the Armed Services,* faculty assessment. Tutoring available. Noncredit developmental courses offered.

Degree Requirements: Varies by major. *For associate degrees:* 60–67 credit hours. *For baccalaureate degrees:* 120–139 credit hours. *For all undergraduate degrees:* 2.0 GPA; 30 credits in residence.

Fulfillment of some degree requirements possible by passing College Board CLEP, AP. Exemption from some beginning courses possible by passing College Board AP. *Grading system:* A–F; pass-fail; withdraw (deadline after which pass-fail is appended to withdraw).

Distinctive Educational Programs: Cooperative education. Accelerated degree programs, individual contract and interdisciplinary majors, intercollege minors. Facilities and programs for independent research; all university curriculum, and acturial studies.

ROTC: Army in cooperation with University of Connecticut (Hartford), Air Force with University of Connecticut (Storrs).

Degrees Conferred: 911 *baccalaureate* (B); 407 *master's* (M); 53 *doctorate* (D): area and ethnic studies12 (B); biological/life sciences 11 (B), 2 (M); business/marketing 124 (B), 159 (M); communications/communication technologies 12 (M); computer and information sciences 65 (B); education 65 (B), 67 (M), 14 (D); engineering and engineering technologies 105 (B), 34 (M); English 19 (B); foreign languages and literature 3 (B); health professions and related sciences 86 (B), 55 (M); interdisciplinary studies 2 (B); law/legal studies 10 (B); liberal arts/general studies 15 (B); mathematics 4 (B); philosophy/religion/theology 1 (B); physical sciences 2 (B); protective services/public administration 17 (B); psychology 49 (B), 44 (M), 34 (D); social sciences and history 29 (B); visual and performing arts 196 (B), 34 (M), 5 (D).

Fees and Other Expenses: *Full-time tuition per academic year 2004–05:* undergraduate $22,290; graduate $8,550 (varies). *Required fees:* $1,190. *Room and board per academic year:* $8,996.

Financial Aid: Aid from institutionally generated funds is provided on the basis of academic merit, financial need, athletic ability, other criteria. Institution has a Program Participation Agreement with the U.S. Department of Education for eligible students to receive Pell Grants and other federal aid.

Financial aid to full-time, first-time undergraduate students: need-based scholarships/grants totaling $37,134,551, self-help $24,616,184, parent loans $9,864,611, tuition waivers $1,141,675, athletic awards $1,053,029; non-need-based scholarships/grants totaling $3,344,841, self-help $2,533,897, parent loans $2,533,897, tuition waivers $1,044,765, athletic awards $1,918,954. *Grad-*

uate aid: 48 fellowships/grants totaling $147,000 (ranging from $2,000 to $6,000); 61 teaching assistantships totaling $247,825 (ranging from $2,500 to $9,000); 55 research assistantships totaling $197,590 (ranging from $2,000 to $5,000).

Departments and Teaching Staff: *Professors* 75, *associate professors* 119; *assistant professors* 110, *instructors* 6, *part-time faculty* 436. *Total instructional faculty:* (full-time 319, part-time 425; women 313, men 431). Total full-time faculty with doctorate, first-professional, or other terminal degree: 260. Student-to-faculty ratio: 14:1. *Faculty development:* $3,173,997 in grants for research. 14 faculty members awarded sabbaticals 2004–05.

Enrollment: Total enrollment 7,246. Undergraduate full-time 2,278 men / 2,267 women, part-time 380m / 641w; graduate full-time 222m / 357w, part-time 431m / 670w.

Characteristics of Student Body: *Ethnic/racial makeup:* number of Black non-Hispanic: 551; American Indian or Alaska Native: 14; Asian or Pacific Islander: 131; Hispanic: 225; White non-Hispanic: 3,662; unknown: 821. *Age distribution:* number under 18: 177; 18–19: 2,220; 20–21: 1,799; 22–24: 519, 25–29: 184; 30–34: 129; 35–39: 131; 40–49: 240; 50–64: 81; 65 and over: 18.

International Students: 339 nonresident aliens enrolled fall 2004. 36 students from Europe, 230 Asia, 24 Central and South America, 13 Africa, 27 Canada, 1 other. Programs available to aid students whose native language is not English: Social and cultural. English as a Second Language Program. No financial aid specifically designated for international students.

Student Life: On-campus residences house 64% of full-time students. Townhouse-style housing available for upperclassmen. 13 Greek organizations; 54 student clubs and organizations. *Intercollegiate athletics:* men only: baseball, basketball, golf, lacrosse, soccer, tennis, track; women only: basketball, golf, soccer, softball, tennis, track, volleyball. Intramural athletics include 13 sports. *Special regulations:* Registered cars with decals permitted; fee charged. *Special services:* Counseling services, health services (with OB-GYN, orthopedic, and dental services), Office for International Student Services, student employment office, 12 Greek organizations, 70 student clubs and organizations, 3 religious and cultural centers (Newman, Hillel and Protestant). *Student publications, radio: Informer,* a weekly newspaper; yearbook. Radio station WWUH broadcasts 168 hours per week, station WSAM broadcasts 112 hours per week. *Surrounding community:* Hartford metropolitan area population over 800,000. Served by mass transit bus system; airport 12 miles from campus; passenger rail service 4 miles from campus.

Library Collections: 606,154 volumes including bound books, serial backfiles, electronic documents, and government documents not in separate collections. Online catalog. Current serial subscriptions: 2,121 paper, 1,326 via electronic access. 11,736 recordings; 7,441 compact discs. 100 computer work stations. Students have access to the Internet at no charge. Total 2004–05 budget for books and materials: $513,672.

Most important holdings include Black studies; Millie and Irving Bercowetz Judaica Collection, Arnold Franchetti Performance Collection; Elmer Nagy Collection.

Buildings and Grounds: Campus area 275 acres.

Chief Executive Officer: Dr. Walter Harrison, President.

Address admission inquiries to Richard Zeiser, Dean of Admissions.

Barney School of Business and Public Administration

Degree Programs Offered: *Baccalaureate* in accounting, economics and finance, entrepreneurial studies, insurance and finance, management, management information systems, marketing; *master's* in business administration, insurance, organizational behavior, professional accounting, taxation, joint MBA and master of engineering.

Distinctive Educational Programs: Accelerated masters in professional accounting, accelerated programming combining baccalaureate and master's degrees in 5 years of study; Center for Insurance Study, cooperative education, executive master's (weekend study) in business administration and professional accounting, international studies, minor in business administration; Tax Institute.

College of Arts and Sciences

Degree Programs Offered: *Associate* in biological sciences, communication, humanities, physical sciences, social sciences; *baccalaureate* in art history, biology, chemistry, chemistry/biology joint major, cinema, communication, computer science, criminal justice, drama, economics, English (literature), history, international languages and cultures, international studies, linguistics, mathematics, music, philosophy, physics, political economy, politics and gov-

ernment, professional and technical writing, psychology, sociology, theatre arts; *master's* in communication, biology, chemistry, clinical psychology, experimental psychology, neurosciences, school psychology; *doctorate* in clinical psychology.

Distinctive Educational Programs: An interdisciplinary all-university general education curriculum; double degrees; Greenburg Center for Jewish Studies; Humanities Center for Interdisciplinary Study in the Humanities, individual contract and interdisciplinary majors; pre-medical professional programs (dentistry, medicine, optometry, osteopathy, podiatry, veterinary); pre-law programs; study abroad programs.

College of Education, Nursing, and Health Professions

Degree Programs Offered: *Baccalaureate* in early childhood education, elementary education, human services, pre-chiropractic, pre-dental, health science, secondary education, special education, nursing, medical technology, occupational therapy, pre-optometry, radiologic technology/health science, respiratory therapy. *Master's* in education computing, nursing, physical therapy; *master's* and *sixth year certificate* in counseling, early childhood education, elementary education, secondary education, special education; *master's, sixth year certificate* and *C.A.G.S.* in administration and supervision.

Admission: Admission requirements vary according to major.

Degree Requirements: Degree requirements vary according to major.

Distinctive Educational Programs: Joint master's, 6th year certificate programs and doctoral programs with the Hartt School of Music. In-service training for teachers, including workshops, travel seminars, instructional institutes. University of Hartford/New England College of Optometry offer a combined program that prepares highly motivated students for a career in optometry. Students in this program can earn both the Bachelor of Science and Doctor of Optometry degrees in a 7-year period.

College of Engineering

Degree Programs Offered: *Baccalaureate* in civil, computer, electrical, and mechanical engineering; *master's* in engineering with specialties in civil, mechanical, and electrical engineering.

Distinctive Educational Programs: Cooperative education. Accelerated degree programs. Interdisciplinary studies in acoustics and music. Manufacturing option in mechanical engineering majors. Individualized contract majors. Pre-engineering program.

Hartford Art School

Degree Programs Offered: *Baccalaureate* in ceramics, drawing, experimental studio, design, illustration, painting, photography, printmaking, sculpture, video. *Master's* in ceramics, painting, photography, printmaking, sculpture.

Distinctive Educational Programs: Internships, independent study for advanced students, study abroad.

The Hartt School

Degree Programs Offered: *Baccalaureate* in composition, dance, jazz, music education, music history, music management, music production and technology, music theatre, performance, opera, theatre arts, theory; *master's* in composition, conducting, liturgical music, music, music history, music education, opera, performance, theory; *artist diploma* in performance; *graduate professional diploma* in performance, composition, conducting, opera; *certificate of advanced graduate study; doctorate* in music education, musical arts (composition, conducting education, performance).

Distinctive Educational Programs: Interdisciplinary program in management in cooperation with Austin Dunham Barney School of Business and Public Administration; in acoustics with College of Engineering. Hartt Opera-Theater. Performing organizations include symphony orchestra, concert jazz band, collegium musicum, chorale, madrigal singers. Institute of Contemporary American Music. Individualized contract majors. Kodaly Musical Training Institute (for music education).

Hillyer College

Degree Programs Offered: *Associate.*

Departments and Teaching Staff: *Professors* 14, *associate professors* 7, *assistant professors* 16, *instructors* 4, *part-time teachers* 31. *Total instructional faculty:* 31. 74% of faculty hold terminal degrees.

University of New Haven

300 Boston Post Road
West Haven, Connecticut 06516

Tel: (203) 932-7000   **E-mail:** adminfo@newhaven.edu
Fax: (203) 931-0756   **Internet:** www.newhaven.edu

Institution Description: University of New Haven is a private, independent, nonprofit institution. *Enrollment:* 4,386. *Degrees awarded:* Associate, baccalaureate, master's, doctorate.

Accreditation: *Regional:* NEASC. *Professional*: business, computer science, dental hygiene, engineering

History: Established by YMCA of New Haven as New Haven College, a 2-year branch of Northeastern University, and offered first instruction at postsecondary level 1920; first degree (associate) awarded 1924; incorporated as New Haven YMCA Junior College 1926; added senior level and changed name to New Haven College 1958; present name adopted 1970.

Institutional Structure: *Governing board:* Board of Governors. Extrainstitutional representation: 30 governors; institutional representation: 1 administrator, 2 full-time instructional faculty members, 3 students, 1 part-time faculty member; 1 alumni. 2 ex officio. 38 voting. *Composition of institution:* Administrators 11 men / 3 women. Academic affairs headed by provost. Management/business/finances directed by treasurer. Academic governance body, Faculty Senate, meets an average of 52 times per year.

Calendar: Semesters. Academic year Sept. to May.

Characteristics of Freshmen: 2,672 applicants. 72.2% of applicants admitted; 29.6% of admitted students enrolled full-time.

93% (550 students) submitted SAT scores. *25th percentile*: SAT I Verbal 450, SAT I Math 460. *75th percentile*: SAT I Verbal 560, SAT I Math 570.

78% of freshmen from Connecticut. Freshman from 28 states and 56 foreign countries.

Admission: Rolling admissions plan. For fall acceptance, apply no later than Aug. 15. Early acceptance available to students attending area secondary schools. *Requirements:* Either graduation from accredited secondary school with 15 units, including at least 9 academic; or GED. Engineering school applicants should present 4 units English; 2 algebra; 1 each in plane geometry, physics, and a second science; 1/2 trigonometry. Minimum GPA 2.0. *Entrance tests:* SAT, ACT composite, or UNH Placement Test. *For transfer students:* 2.0 minimum GPA, 90 hours maximum transfer credit (60 hours from 2-year institutions).

Advanced placement for extrainstitutional learning on basis of portfolio and faculty assessments, and ACE *2006 Guide to the Evaluation of Educational Experiences in the Armed Services.* College credit and advanced placement for postsecondary-level work completed in secondary school. Tutoring available. Remedial courses offered in summer session and regular academic year.

Degree Requirements: *For all undergraduate degrees:* 2.0 GPA; 30 hours in residence. *For all associate degrees:* 60 credit hours. *For all baccalaureate degrees:* 120 credit hours. Some degree requirements can be met by passing College Board ACH tests or departmental examinations. *Grading system:* A–F; withdraw; satisfactory-unsatisfactory (for noncredit courses only).

Distinctive Educational Programs: *For undergraduates:* Off-campus center (at Mitchell College campus, 65 miles away from main institution). Accelerated degree programs. Interdisciplinary programs in world music, forensic science. Honors programs. *For graduate students:* Off-campus centers (at Madison, New Haven, and Trumbull, less than 30 miles away from main institution; at Waterbury; 35 miles away; at Middletown; 40 miles away; at Greenwich, 60 miles away; at Danbury and Groton/New London, 65 miles away). Interdisciplinary programs in environmental engineering, community psychology. *Available to all students:* Flexible meeting places and schedules. Weekend and evening classes. Facilities and programs for independent research. Individual majors. *Other distinctive programs:* Criminal justice, aviation, environmental science, fire science, occupational safety and health.

Degrees Conferred: 57 *associate*; 418 *baccalaureate*; 736 *master's*; 1 *doctorate*; 92 *post-baccalaureate certificates*. Bachelor's degrees awarded in top five disciplines: security and protective services 149; business, management, marketing, and related support services 86; engineering 50; visual and performing arts 46; health professions and related clinical sciences 16.

Fees and Other Expenses: *Full-time tuition per academic year 2004–05:* $21,120. *Room and board per academic year:* $9,095. *Books and supplies:* $750. *Other expenses:* $1,500.

Financial Aid: Aid from institutionally generated funds is provided on the basis of academic merit, financial need, athletic ability. Institution has a Program Participation Agreement with the U.S.Department of Education for eligible students to receive Pell Grants and other federal aid.

Financial aid to full-time, first-time undergraduate students: 27% received federal grants averaging $3,426; 24% state/local grants averaging $4,386; 76% institutional grants averaging $8,800; 64% loans averaging $4,800.

Departments and Teaching Staff: School of: Arts and sciences *professors* 29, *associate professors* 9, *assistant professors* 11, *instructors and lecturers* 8; Business 14, 13, 15, 0; Engineering 21, 11, 5, 1; Public Safety 4, 9, 2, 2; Hotel, Restaurant Management, and Tourism 0, 2, 1, 2. *Total instructional faculty:* 323 FTE (includes part-time). Student-to-faculty ratio: 11:1. Degrees held by full-time faculty: Doctorate 80%, master's 10%. 88% hold terminal degrees.

Enrollment: Total enrollment 4,386. Undergraduate 2,627 (men 54.6%, women 46.4%).

Characteristics of Student Body: *Ethnic/racial makeup:* Black non-Hispanic: 10.4%; American Indian or Alaska Native: .6%; Asian or Pacific Islander: 1.8%; Hispanic: 5.9%; White non-Hispanic: 62.1%.

International Students: 162 nonresident aliens enrolled fall 2004. Social and cultural programs available to aid students whose native language is not English. English as a Second Language Program. No financial aid specifically designated for international students.

Student Life: On-campus residence halls house 54% of full-time student body; suite-style freshman residence hall; apartment-style for upperclassmen. *Intercollegiate athletics:* men only: baseball, basketball, cross-country, football, lacrosse, soccer, track; women only: baseball, basketball, cross-country, tennis, volleyball. *Special regulations:* Quiet hours from 11pm to 9am Mon.–Fri. Residence visitation limited Mon.–Fri. to hours between 8am and midnight. *Special services:* Learning Resources Center, medical services. *Student publications, radio:* The Chariot, a yearbook; *The News*, a weekly newspaper. Radio station WNHU broadcasts 154 hours per week. *Surrounding community:* West Haven population 55,000. New Haven, 3 miles from campus, is nearest metropolitan area. Served by mass transit bus system; airport 10 miles from campus; passenger rail service 5 miles from campus.

Publications: *Essays in Arts and Sciences* (annually) first published 1971.

Library Collections: 384,000 volumes including bound books, serial backfiles, electronic documents, and government documents not in separate collections. Online catalog. 1,320 current serial subscriptions; 541,000 microform units; 1,100 audiovisual materials. 30 computer work stations. Students have access to the Internet at no charge.

Most important special collections include the International Society of Fire Service Instructors Library; Lionel Bradford Collection of Forensic Sciences; Kaplan Collection of Economics.

Buildings and Grounds: Campus area 78 acres.

Chief Executive Officer: Dr. Steven Kaplan, President.

Address admission inquiries to James E. Shapiro, Director of Enrollment Management; graduate inquiries to Joseph Spellman, Director of Graduate Admissions.

Wesleyan University

70 Wyllys Avenue
Middletown, Connecticut 06459

Tel: (860) 685-2000   **E-mail:** admiss@wesleyan.edu
Fax: (860) 685-3001   **Internet:** www.wesleyan.edu

Institution Description: Wesleyan University is a private, independent, nonprofit institution. *Enrollment:* 3,217. *Degrees awarded:* Baccalaureate, master's, doctorate. Certificate of advanced study also awarded..

Member of Consortium on the Financing of Higher Education.

Accreditation: *Regional:* NEASC.

History: Established, chartered, offered first instruction at postsecondary level 1831; first degree (baccalaureate) awarded 1833. *See* David B. Potts, *Wesleyan University; 1831–1910: Collegiate Enterprise in New England* (Hanover NY: Wesleyan University Press, 1992) for further information.

Institutional Structure: *Governing board:* The Board of Trustees. Extrainstitutional representation: 2 trustees; institutional representation: 1 administrator; 28 alumni. All voting. *Composition of institution:* Academic affairs headed by vice president for academic affairs. Business/finances directed by vice president and treasurer. Full-time instructional faculty 273. Academic governance body, the faculty, meets an average of 6 times per year.

Calendar: Semesters. Academic year Sept. to May. Freshmen admitted Sept. Degrees conferred and formal commencement May.

Characteristics of Freshmen: 6,568 applicants (2,700 men, 3,868 women). 28.1% of applicants admitted; 39.6% of admitted students enrolled full-time.

95% (695 students) submitted SAT scores, *25th percentile*: SAT I Verbal 660, SAT I Math 650. *75th percentile*: SAT I Verbal 750, SAT I Math 740.

88% of entering freshmen expected to graduate within 5 years. 8% of freshmen from Connecticut. Freshmen from 38 states and 27 foreign countries.

Admission: For fall acceptance apply no later than Jan. 1. Students are notified of acceptance in April. Apply by Nov. 15 for early decision. *Requirements:* 3–4 secondary school units each in English, foreign languages, mathematics, science, social studies recommended. *Entrance tests:* College Board SAT I or ACT. *For transfer students:* minimum of 2 years at Wesleyan.

College credit for postsecondary-level work completed in secondary school. Tutoring available. Remedial courses offered; credit given.

Degree Requirements: For students entering in fall 2000 and beyond, the degree requirements are for 32 semester credits; 74% average; 6 semesters in residence; completion of concentration program. Some degree requirements can be fulfilled by passing achievement tests. *Grading system:* A–F; pass-fail; withdraw (carries time limit); descriptive reports.

Distinctive Educational Programs: Interdisciplinary programs; certificate programs in international relations and environmental studies; honors program; individualized majors; dual-degree programs in engineering with Columbia University (New York) and California Institute of Technology; Twelve College Exchange Program; first-year program with seminars and special initiatives; facilities and programs for independent research; individual and group tutorials; teaching and research apprenticeships; study abroad in Wesleyan-sponsored programs in France, Spain, Germany, Israel, Italy, Germany, Mexico, plus over 100 Wesleyan-approved programs throughout the world; intensive language program; master's programs in anthropology, astronomy, earth science, and psychology; master's and Ph.D. programs in biology, ethnomusicology, molecular biology and biochemistry, chemistry; concurrent baccalaureate/master's option; Certificates in Advanced Studies and Masters in Arts in Liberal Studies offered by the Graduate Liberal Studies Program.

Degrees Conferred: 704 *baccalaureate*; 115 *master's*; 2 *post-master's certificates*; 16 *doctorate*.

Fees and Other Expenses: *Full-time tuition and fees per academic year 2005–06:* $32,976; contact the university for current graduate tuition and fees. *Room per academic year:* $5,378. *Board per academic year:* $3,554. *Other fees:* $514.

Financial Aid: Aid from institutionally generated funds is provided on the basis of financial need. Institution has a Program Participation Agreement with the U.S. Department of Education for eligible students to receive Pell Grants and other federal aid.

Financial aid to full-time, first-time undergraduate students: need-based scholarships/grants totaling $28,641,118, self-help $8,119,476.

Departments and Teaching Staff: *Total instructional faculty :* 364 (women 147, men 217; members of minority groups 51). Total faculty with doctorate, first-professional, or other terminal degree: 51. Student-to-faculty ratio: 9:1.

Enrollment: Total enrollment 3,217. Undergraduate full-time 1,317 men / 1,449 women, part-time 4m / 7w; graduate full-time 106m / 102w, part-time 72m / 160w.

Characteristics of Student Body: *Ethnic and racial makeup:* number of Black non-Hispanic: 190; American Indian or Alaska Native: 13; Asian or Pacific Islander: 249; Hispanic: 200; White non-Hispanic: 1,702; unknown: 232.

International Students: 177 nonresident aliens enrolled fall 2004. English as a Second Language Program available. No financial aid specifically designated for international students.

Student Life: On-campus residence halls. Institutionally controlled housing. 99% of student body live on campus. *Intercollegiate athletics:* men only: baseball, basketball, crew, cross-country, football, golf, ice hockey, lacrosse, soccer, squash, swimming/diving, tennis, track/field, volleyball, wrestling; women only: basketball, crew, field hockey, ice hockey, lacrosse, soccer, softball, squash, swimming/diving, tennis, track/field. *Special regulations:* Cars permitted for all students. *Special services:* Medical services, evening escort service. *Student publications, radio: Argus,* a semiweekly newspaper; *Hermes,* a monthly publication; *Olla Podrida,* a yearbook; *The Ankh,* a student of color publication. Radio station WESU broadcasts 24 hours per day. *Surrounding community:* Middletown population 44,000. Hartford; 20 miles from campus, is nearest metropolitan area. Served by mass transit bus systems, airport 29 miles from campus, passenger rail service 8 miles from campus.

Library Collections: 1,386,575 volumes including bound books, serial backfiles, electronic documents, and government documents not in separate collections. Online catalog. Current serial subscriptions: 4,280. 43,800 audiovisual materials; 255,200 microform items; 16,952 recordings; 275 CD-ROMs. 145 computer work stations. Students have access to the Internet at no charge.

Most important holdings include George Davison Rare Book Collection; Henry Bacon Architectural Drawings; Hymnology Collection.

Buildings and Grounds: Campus area 170 acres.

Chief Executive Officer: Dr. Douglas J. Bennet, President.

Undergraduates address admission inquiries to Nancy Hargrave Meislahn, Director of Admissions; graduate inquiries to Marina Melendez, Director Graduate Student Services.

Western Connecticut State University

181 White Street
Danbury, Connecticut 06810-9972
Tel: (203) 837-8200   **E-mail:** admissions@wcsu.ctstateu.edu
Fax: (203) 837-8276   **Internet:** www.wcsu.ctstateu.edu

Institution Description: Western Connecticut State University is a state institution. *Enrollment:* 5,084. *Degrees awarded:* Associate, baccalaureate, master's. Academic offerings subject to approval by statewide coordinating bodies. Budget subject to approval by state governing boards.

Accreditation: *Regional:* NEASC. *Professional*: business, counseling, music, nursing, social work, teacher education

History: Established as Danbury State Normal School 1903; offered first instruction at postsecondary level 1904; added senior level 1933; changed name to Danbury State Teachers College 1937; awarded first degree (baccalaureate) 1938; changed name to Danbury State College 1959; became Western Connecticut State College 1967; attained university status and adopted present name 1983.

Institutional Structure: *Governing board:* Board of Trustees for the Connecticut State University. Extrainstitutional representation: 18 trustees; institutional representation: 1 student. All voting. *Composition of institution:* Administrators 25 men / 11 women. Academic affairs headed by vice president for academic affairs. Student affairs head by vice president for student and external affairs; alumni/institutional advancement/public relations headed by vice president for institutional advancement. Management/business/finances directed by vice president for administrative affairs. Full-time instructional faculty 106 men/ 72 women. Academic governance body, College Faculty Senate, meets an average of 8 times per year. *Faculty representation:* Faculty served by collective bargaining agent affiliated with AAUP.

Calendar: Semesters. Academic year early Sept. to late May. Freshmen admitted Sept., Jan., May. Degrees conferred May, Aug., Jan. Formal commencement May. Summer session from early June to early Aug.

Characteristics of Freshmen: 69% of applicants accepted. 31% of accepted applicants enrolled full-time.

83% (854 students) submitted SAT scores. *25th percentile:* SAT Verbal 450, SAT Math 450. *75th percentile*: SAT Verbal 540, SAT Math 550.

42% of entering freshmen expected to graduate within 5 years. 85% of freshmen from Connecticut. Freshmen from 10 states.

Admission: Rolling admissions plan with notification beginning Dec. 1. For fall acceptance, apply as early as Oct. 1 of previous year, but not later than Aug. 1 of year of enrollment. *Requirements:* Either graduation from accredited secondary school with 14 units which normally include 4 English, 2 foreign language, 3 mathematics, 3 social studies, 2 sciences; or GED. Minimum GPA 2.5. Lowest acceptable secondary school class standing 33rd percentile. *Entrance tests:* College Board SAT. For foreign students TOEFL. *For transfer students:* 2.0 minimum GPA; from 4-year accredited institution maximum transfer credit 90 hours; from 2-year accredited institution 60 hours maximum transfer credit.

College credit and advanced placement for postsecondary-level work completed in secondary school. College credit for extrainstitutional learning on basis of ACE 2006 *Guide to the Evaluation of Educational Experiences in the Armed Services.* Tutoring available.

Degree Requirements: *For all associate degrees:* 62 semester hours. *For all baccalaureate degrees:* 120–123 hours. *For all undergraduate degrees:* 2.0 GPA; 30 hours in residence; 2 hours physical education; general education requirements. *Grading system:* A–F; withdraw (deadline after which pass-fail is appended to withdraw).

Distinctive Educational Programs: Work-experience programs, including cooperative education, internships. Evening classes. Accelerated degree programs. Interdepartmental programs in Afro-American studies, biochemistry, environmental studies. Individual majors. Honors interdisciplinary bachelor degree program. Interactive Marketing program; Information Security Management program.

Degrees Conferred: 621 *baccalaureate* (B); 254 *master's* (M): area and ethnic studies 3 (B), biological/life sciences 9 (B), 5 (M); business/marketing 187 (B), 24 (M); communications/communication technologies 44 (B); computer and information sciences 8 (B); education 84 (B), 159 (M); English 15 (B), 10 (M); foreign languages and literature 2 (B); health professions and related sciences 22 (B), 21 (M); interdisciplinary studies 1 (B); liberal arts/general studies 14 (B); mathematics 12 (B), 4 (M); physical sciences 5 (B), 5 (M); protective services/public administration 77 (B), 5 (M); psychology 43 (B); social sciences and history 53 (B); 20 (M); visual and performing arts 42 (B), 5 (M).

Fees and Other Expenses: *Full-time tuition per academic year 2004–05:* undergraduate resident $3,010, out-of-state $9,744; graduate resident $3,750, out-of-state $10,449. *Required fees:* $2,671. *Room per academic year:* $3.950. *Board per academic year:* $2,940.

Financial Aid: Institutionally generated funds is provided on the basis of financial need. Institution has a Program Participation Agreement with the U.S. Department of Education for eligible students to receive Pell Grants and other federal aid.

Financial aid to full-time, first-time undergraduate students: need-based scholarships/grants totaling $4,505,526, self-help $6,090,001; non-need-based scholarships/grants totaling $3,614,558, self-help $4,744,500, parent loans $1,207,498, tuition waivers $401,786.

Departments and Teaching Staff: *Total instructional faculty:* 496 (women 216, men 280; members of minority groups 84). Total faculty with doctorate, first-professional, or other terminal degree: 168. Student-to-faculty 16.5:1. 8 faculty members awarded sabbaticals 2004–05.

Enrollment: Total enrollment 5,084. Undergraduate full-time 1,738 men / 2,135 women, part-time 553m / 711w; graduate full-time 29m / 68w, part-time 178m / 452.

Characteristics of Student Body: *Ethnic/racial makeup:* number of Black non-Hispanic: 289; American Indian or Alaska Native: 14; Asian or Pacific Islander: 82; Hispanic: 303; White non-Hispanic: 3,974; unknown: 362. *Age distribution:* number under 18: 221; 18–19:1,524; 20–21: 1,358; 22–24: 1,028; 25–29: 392; 30–34: 173; 35–39: 129; 40–49: 204; 50–64 78' 65 and over: 22.

International Students: 14 nonresidents enrolled fall 2004. Students from Europe, Asia, Central and South America, Africa, Canada. Programs available to aid students whose native language is not English: Social, cultural. English as a Second Language Program. No financial aid specifically designated for international students.

Student Life: On-campus residence halls house 24% of degree-seeking undergraduates. Residence halls for both men and women constitute 100% of such space. *Intercollegiate athletics:* men only: baseball, basketball, football, soccer, tennis; women only: basketball, cross-country, lacrosse, soccer, softball, swimming, tennis, volleyball. *Special regulations:* Cars permitted without restrictions. *Special services:* Child Care Center, Learning Resources Center, medical services. *Student publications: Conatus,* an annual literary magazine; *Echo,* a weekly newspaper; a yearbook. *Surrounding community:* Danbury population 61,000. White Plains (NY); 30 miles from campus, is nearest metropolitan area. Served by airport 30 miles from campus; passenger rail service .5 mile from campus.

Library Collections: 262,000 volumes including bound books, serial backfiles, electronic documents, and government documents not in separate collections. Online catalog. Current serial subscriptions: 1,273; 471,000 microform items; 8,700 audiovisual materials. 400 computer work stations. Students have access to the Internet at no charge.

Buildings and Grounds: Midtown campus 25 acres; Westside Campus area 365 acres.

Chief Executive Officer: Dr. James W. Schmotter, President.

Address admission inquiries to William Hawkins, Director of Admissions.

Yale University

105 Wall Street
Box 208229
New Haven, Connecticut 06520-8229

Tel: (203) 432-4771　　**E-mail:** admissions@yale.edu
Fax: (203) 432-9392　　**Internet:** www.yale.edu

Institution Description: Yale University is a private, independent, nonprofit institution. *Enrollment:* 11,471. *Degrees awarded:* Baccalaureate, first-professional (law, management, medicine, theology), master's, doctorate.

Member of Consortium on Financing Higher Education.

Accreditation: *Regional:* NEASC. *Professional:* architecture, business, clinical psychology, law, medicine, music, nursing-midwifery, nursing, nursing education, physician assisting, psychology internship, public health

History: Established and chartered as The Collegiate School, and offered first instruction at postsecondary level 1701; awarded first degree (baccalaureate) 1703; changed name to Yale College 1718; adopted present name 1887; became coeducational 1969. *See* Brooks Mather Kelley, *Yale: A History* (London: Yale University Press, 1974) for further information.

Institutional Structure: *Governing board:* President and Fellows of Yale University. Representation: 10 trustees, governor and lieutenant governor of Connecticut, president of the university, 6 alumni. 3 ex officio. All voting. *Composition of institution:* Academic affairs headed by president. Management/business/finances directed by provost. Full-time instructional faculty 1,540. Academic governance body, Faculties of Yale, meets 2 to 7 times per year.

Calendar: Semesters. Academic year Sept. to May. Freshmen admitted Sept. Degrees conferred May, Dec. Formal commencement May. No summer session.

Characteristics of Freshmen: 17,735 applicants (8,543 men, 9,192 women). 11.4% of applicants admitted. 67.2% of admitted students enrolled full-time.

98% (1,324 students) submitted SAT scores; 19% (264 students) submitted ACT scores. *25th percentile:* SAT I Verbal 690, SAT I Math 690; ACT Composite 30. *75th percentile:* SAT I Verbal 790, SAT I Math 790; ACT Composite 34.

Admission: For fall acceptance, apply as early as Sept. 1 of previous year, but not later than Dec. 31 of year prior to enrollment. Students are notified of acceptance in Apr. Early decision application deadline Nov. 1; notification mid-Dec; reply date by Feb. 1. *Requirements:* Rigorous high school program; recommend units from wide variety of subjects. *Entrance tests:* College Board SAT, 3 Achievements; or ACT. For foreign students TOEFL.

College credit and advanced placement for postsecondary-level work completed in secondary school. Tutoring available.

Degree Requirements: 36 semester courses; distribution requirements. Fulfillment of some degree requirements and exemption from some beginning courses possible by passing College Board AP, other standardized tests. *Grading system:* A–F; high pass-pass-fail; pass; withdraw (carries time limit).

Distinctive Educational Programs: Accelerated degree programs. Interdepartmental and interdisciplinary programs. Facilities and programs for independent research, including honors programs, individual majors, tutorials. Individually arranged study abroad.

ROTC: Available to qualified male and female college students through cross-enrollment in the U.S. Army ROTC program at Southern Connecticut University and at the University of Bridgeport, and in the U.S. Air Force ROTC program at the University of Connecticut.

Degrees Conferred: 1,339 *baccalaureate;* 1,309 *master's;* 332 *doctorate;* 3301 *post-master's certificate.* Bachelor's degrees awarded in top five disciplines: social sciences 321; history 181; biological and biomedical sciences 133; English language literature/letters 114; psychology 110. 367 *first-professional:* law, medicine, theology.

Fees and Other Expenses: *Full-time tuition per academic year 2004–05:* undergraduate $29,820. Graduate and professional schools tuition and fees vary; contact the school of choice for current information. *Room and board per academic year:* $9,030; graduate room and board varies by school.

Financial Aid: Aid from institutionally generated funds is provided on the basis of academic merit, financial need. Institution has a Program Participation Agreement with the U.S. Department of Education for eligible students to receive Pell Grants and other federal aid.

Financial aid to full-time, first-time undergraduate students: 10% received federal grants averaging $6,414; 3% state/local grants averaging $3,497; 40% institutional grants averaging $19,657; 19% loans averaging $2,950.

Departments and Teaching Staff: School faculties: Arts and Sciences 1,120; Architecture 43, Art 39, Divinity 44, Drama 46, Forestry and Environmental Studies 32, Law 101, Management 58, Medicine 1,702, Music 58, Nursing 87. *Total instructional faculty:* 3,330. Degrees held by full-time faculty: 96% hold terminal degrees.

Enrollment: Total enrollment 11,471. Undergraduate 5,354 (50.1% men, 49.9% women).

Characteristics of Student Body: *Ethnic and racial makeup:* Black non-Hispanic: 7.5%; American Indian or Alaska Native: .7%; Asian or Pacific Islander: 13.3%; Hispanic: 6%; White non-Hispanic: 51.2%; unknown: 12.6%.

International Students: 1,009 nonresident aliens enrolled fall 2003. Students from Europe, Asia, Central and South America, Africa, Canada, Australia, New Zealand. Programs available to aid students whose native language is not English: English as a Second Language Program.

Student Life: The residential college system divides the undergraduate population of about 5,100 into separate communities of 400 to 500 members, and enables Yale to offer both the vast resources of a major university and the intimacy of a small college environment. These colleges house 88% of the undergraduate student body. Housing available for married students. *Intercollegiate athletics:* men only: baseball, basketball, crew, cross-country, fencing, football, hockey, lacrosse, soccer, squash, swimming, tennis, track; women only: basketball, crew, cross-country, fencing, field hockey, gymnastics, lacrosse, soccer, squash, swimming, tennis, track. *Special regulations:* Cars permitted without restrictions. *Special services:* Medical services, campus transportation system. *Student publications, radio: Yale Banner,* a yearbook; *Yale Daily News; Yale Daily News Magazine; Yale Theater Magazine.* Radio station WYBC broadcasts 168 hours per week. *Student activities:* Students write for over 30 college publications. The freshman class have over 150 social, political, cultural, and special interest groups from which to choose. Over 40% of the student body volunteers in some aspect of community service. *Surrounding community:* New Haven population 130,000. New York City, 80 miles from campus, is nearest metropolitan area. Served by mass transit system; airport 50 miles from campus; passenger rail service 1 mile from campus.

Publications: *The Yale Review* (quarterly) first published in 1911.

Library Collections: 10.9 million volumes. Access to 60,700 periodicals; 6.5 million microform units. 216,000 audiovisual materials. Online catalog. Access to online information retrieval systems and the Internet.

Most important holdings include Beinecke rare book and manuscript library; manuscript and archives collection; historical medical library.

Buildings and Grounds: Campus area 260 acres.

Chief Executive Officer: Dr. Richard C. Levin, President.

Undergraduates address admission inquiries to Richard H. Shaw, Office of Undergraduate Admissions; first-professional and graduate students to individual schools of the university.

Yale College

Degree Programs Offered: *Baccalaureate* in African and African-American studies; American studies, anthropology, applied mathematics, applied physics, archaeology, architecture, art, astronomy and physics, biology, chemistry, Chinese, classical civilization, classics, comparative literature, computer science, computer science and mathematics, computer science and psychology; East Asian studies, economics, economics and mathematics, economics and political science, engineering and applied science, English, ethics/politics/economics, film studies, French, geology and geophysics, German, German studies, history of art, history of medicine, history of science, humanities, Italian, international studies, Japanese, Judaic studies, Latin American studies, linguistics, literature, mathematics, mathematics-engineering and applied science, mathematics and philosophy, mathematics and physics, molecular biophysics and biochemistry, music, Near Eastern languages and literature, philosophy, physics, physics and philosophy, political science, psychology, religious studies, Renaissance studies, Russian, Russian and Eastern European studies, scholars of the house, sociology, Spanish, theater studies, women's studies.

Divinity School

Degree Programs Offered: *First-professional* in theology; *master's* in religion, sacred theology.

Admission: *For first-professional degree:* Baccalaureate from accredited college or university. Coursework in English composition and literature, one or more foreign languages, history, philosophy, psychology, and social sciences recommended.

Degree Requirements: *For first-professional:* 72 credit hours, 2 years, including final year, in residence, minimum 12 hours per year with Divinity School faculty members, completion of program within 4 years.

Law School

Degree Programs Offered: *First-professional, master's,* and *doctorate.*

Admission: *For first-professional degree:* Baccalaureate from accredited college or university, LSAT, registration with LSDAS.

Degree Requirements: *For first-professional:* 82 credit hours, 6 terms in residence.

Distinctive Educational Programs: Intensive Semester Program. Master's program for non-lawyers provides familiarity with legal thought.

School of Medicine

Degree Programs Offered: *First-professional* in medicine; *master's* in epidemiology, public health; *doctorate* in epidemiology, public health. Graduate certificates in physician's assistance also given.

Admission: *For first-professional degree:* Minimum 3 academic years at approved college of arts and science or institute of technology with coursework in biology or zoology, general chemistry, organic chemistry, general physics; MCAT.

Degree Requirements: *For first-professional:* 4 years in residence, part I and II of the National Board of Medical Examiners examination.

School of Architecture

Degree Programs Offered: *Master's* in architecture, environmental design.

Distinctive Educational Programs: Combined master's program in public and private management and architecture with the School of Organization and Management.

School of Art

Degree Programs Offered: *Master of Fine Arts.*

Distinctive Educational Programs: Summer school of music and art at Norfolk, an 8-week session for currently enrolled juniors; credit given. Summer program in graphic design at Brissago, Switzerland, a 5-week session; credit given. Summer art courses taught in New Haven. Yale University Art Gallery. Yale Center for British Art, a public museum and research institute.

School of Drama

Degree Programs Offered: *Certificate, Master of Fine Arts/Drama, Doctor of Fine Arts* in acting, design, playwriting, and technical design and production.

Distinctive Educational Programs: Certificate program in drama for students without a baccalaureate who successfully complete 3-year program in acting, playwriting, design, or technical design and production. Upon completion of a recognized baccalaureate degree, the Certificate in Drama will be converted to the M.F.A. degree.

School of Forestry and Environmental Studies

Degree Programs Offered: *Master's, doctorate.*

Distinctive Educational Programs: Joint degree programs with the department of epidemiology and public health in the School of Medicine, the School of Law, the School of Organization and Management, and International Relations and International and Development Economics.

School of Music

Degree Programs Offered: *Master's, doctorate.* Certificate and Artist Diploma also awarded.

School of Nursing

Degree Programs Offered: *Master's.*

Distinctive Educational Programs: 3-year basic program for non-nurse college graduates; Doctor of 2m / 75w.

School of Management

Degree Programs Offered: *Master's* in public and private management (MPPM).

Distinctive Educational Programs: Joint degree programs with several other schools of the university.

Graduate School of Arts and Sciences

Degree Programs Offered: *Master's* and *doctorate* in various fields.

Admission: Applications for admission due January 2.

Delaware

Delaware State University

1200 North DuPont Highway
Dover, Delaware 19901
Tel: (302) 857-6060   **E-mail:** admissions@dsc.edu
Fax: (302) 857-6069   **Internet:** www.dsc.edu

Institution Description: Delaware State University, formerly named Delaware State College, is a state institution. *Enrollment:* 3,178. *Degrees awarded:* Baccalaureate, master's.

Academic offerings subject to approval by state department of public instruction. Budget subject to approval by state governing boards. Member of Middle Atlantic Consortium For Energy Research.

Accreditation: *Regional:* MSA/CHE. *Professional:* business, nursing, nursing education,social work, teacher education

History: Chartered and incorporated as State College for Colored Students 1891; offered first instruction at postsecondary level 1892; awarded first degree 1893.

Institutional Structure: *Governing board:* Board of Trustees of Delaware State College. Extrainstitutional representation: 11 trustees (including 1 alumnus); institutional representation 1 trustee (administrator). 1 ex officio. 11 voting. *Composition of institution:* Administrators 6. Academic affairs headed by vice president and dean of academic affairs. Management/business/finances directed by vice president for fiscal affairs and business manager. Total instructional faculty 157. Academic governance body, Faculty Senate, meets an average of 10 times per year. *Faculty representation:* Faculty served by collective bargaining agent affiliated with AAUP.

Calendar: Semesters. Academic year early Sept. to May. Freshmen admitted Sept., Jan., June. Degrees conferred and formal commencement May. Summer session of 3 terms from mid-May to early-Aug.

Characteristics of Freshmen: 3.458 applicants (1,389 men, 2,069 women). 55.8% of applicants admitted. 35.6% of admitted students enrolled.

81% (609 students) submitted SAT scores; 5% (44 students) submitted ACT scores. *25th percentile:* SAT I Verbal 360, SAT I Math 350; ACT Composite 13, ACT English 10, ACT Math 14. *75th percentile:* SAT I Verbal 460, SAT I Math 460; ACT Composite 17, ACT English 16, ACT Math 17.

Admission: Rolling admissions plan. For fall acceptance, apply as early as junior year of secondary school. *Requirements:* Either graduation from accredited secondary school with 4 units English, 2 mathematics, 2 science, 1 or 2 social studies, 5 or 6 in electives; or GED. Minimum GPA 2.0. *Entrance tests:* Achievement or ACT composite. *For transfer students:* 2.0 minimum GPA, maximum transfer credit from accredited institution limited only by residence requirement.

College credit for postsecondary-level work completed in secondary school and extrainstitutional learning on basis of ACE *2006 Guide to the Evaluation of Educational Experiences in the Armed Services.* Tutoring available. Noncredit learning skills courses offered during academic year.

Degree Requirements: 121 credit hours; 2.0 GPA; 30 semester hours in residence; 2 hours physical education; general education requirement. Fulfillment of degree requirements possible by passing College Board CLEP and APP. *Grading system:* A–F; withdraw (carries time limit); incomplete; satisfactory; unsatisfactory.

Distinctive Educational Programs: Work-experience programs in nursing, political science, psychology, social work, teaching, urban affairs. Off-campus centers (at Wilmington, 45 miles away from main institution; and at Dover Air Force Base, and other neighboring locations). Evening classes. 4- and 5-year dual-degree programs in engineering with University of Delaware. Interdepartmental/interdisciplinary programs in black studies. Master's degree programs in education (curriculum and instruction), special education, social work, business. Preprofessional programs in law and veterinary medicine. Facilities and programs for independent research. Honors programs. Individual majors. Tutorials. Summer institute prepares incoming students for engineering program.

Degrees Conferred: 419 *baccalaureate;* 90 *master's.* Bachelor's degrees awarded in top five disciplines: business, management, marketing, and related

support services 68; public administration and social service professions 41; social sciences 39; psychology 37; education 36.

Fees and Other Expenses: *Full-time tuition per academic year 2004–05:* $4,646 undergraduate resident, $10,303 out-of-state student. *Books and supplies:* $1,350. *Room and board per academic year:* $6,761.

Financial Aid: Aid from institutionally generated funds is provided on the basis of academic merit, financial need, athletic ability, other criteria. Institution has a Program Participation Agreement with the U.S. Department of Education for eligible students to receive Pell Grants and other federal aid.

Financial aid to full-time, first-time undergraduate students: 49% received federal grants averaging $3,093; 28% state/local grants averaging $3,185; 21% institutional grants averaging $3,971; 68% loans averaging $6,427.

Departments and Teaching Staff: Agriculture *professors* 3, *associate professors* 1, *assistant professors* 1, *instructors* 0, *part-time teachers* 1; airway science 0, 1, 1, 0, 0; art/art education 1, 1, 1, 1, 0; biology 3, 0, 5, 0, 3; chemistry 3, 3, 0, 0, 0; economics/business administration 3, 3, 10, 2, 0; education 1, 6, 2, 3, 1; English 1, 4, 8, 7, 2; foreign language 0, 1, 2, 1, 1; health and physical education 1, 1, 2, 2, 2; history and political science 2, 2, 4, 0, 0; home economics 1, 2, 1, 0, 0; mathematics 0, 1, 6, 1, 2; music 1, 2, 1, 2, 0; nursing 2, 4, 2, 0, 0; philosophy 0, 1, 1, 0, 0; physics 3, 0, 0, 1, 0; psychology 4, 4, 0, 0, 1; social work 0, 4, 2, 3, 0; sociology 0, 2, 2, 0, 0.

Total instructional faculty: 157. *Degrees held by full-time faculty:* Doctorate 53%, master's 40%, baccalaureate 7%. Student-to-faculty ratio: 12:1.

Enrollment: Total enrollment 3,178. Undergraduate 2,992 (men 41.7%, women 58.3%).

Characteristics of Student Body: *Ethnic/racial makeup:* Black non-Hispanic: 80.2%; American Indian or Alaska Native: .3%; Asian or Pacific Islander: .1.3%; Hispanic: 1.5%; White non-Hispanic: 80.2%; unknown: .2.7%.

International Students: 120 nonresident aliens enrolled fall 2004. No programs available to aid students whose native language is not English. No financial aid specifically designated for international students.

Student Life: On-campus residence halls house 45% of student body. Residence halls for men only constitute 45% of such space, for women only 55%. *Intercollegiate athletics:* men only: baseball, basketball, cross-country, football, track, wrestling; women only: basketball, cross-country, tennis, track, volleyball. *Special regulations:* Cars permitted without restrictions. Dormitory visitation from 4pm to 10:45pm Sun.–Thurs.; 8am to 2am Fri., Sat. *Special services:* Learning Resources Center, medical services. *Student publications, radio: Hornet,* monthly newspaper; *Statesman,* yearbook. Radio station WDSC. *Surrounding community:* Dover population 30,000. Philadelphia, 70 miles from campus, is nearest metropolitan area.

Library Collections: 201,550 volumes. 76,100 microforms; 3,060 periodical subscriptions; 13,660 audiovisual materials. Online catalog. Students have access to online information retrieval services and the Internet.

Most important special holdings include collections on Delaware; Black Americans.

Buildings and Grounds: Campus area 400 acres.

Chief Executive Officer: Dr. Allen L. Sessoms, President.

Address admission inquiries to Jimmy Arrington, Director of Admissions.

Goldey Beacom College

4701 Limestone Road
Wilmington, Delaware 19808
Tel: (302) 998-8814   **E-mail:** admissions@.gbc.edu
Fax: (302) 998-3467   **Internet:** www.gbc.edu

Institution Description: Goldey Beacom College is a private college. *Enrollment:* 1,185. *Degrees awarded:* Associate, baccalaureate. Certificates also awarded.

Accreditation: *Regional:* MSA/CHE. *Professional:* business

History: Goldey College established 1886. Beacom College established 1900. In 1951 the two colleges merged and became Goldey Beacom College.

Institutional Structure: *Governing board:* Board of Trustees; Extrainstitutional representation 25 trustees, 2 ex officio, all voting. *Composition of institution:* 4 vice presidents. Full-time instructional faculty 25.

Calendar: Semesters. Academic year early Sept. to late May. Freshmen admitted Sept., Feb. Formal commencement June. Summer session of 1 term from early June to mid-Aug.

Characteristics of Freshmen: 408 applicants. 57.1% of applicants admitted; 76% of admitted students enrolled full-time. Mean SAT scores 378 verbal, 424 mathematical. 51% of freshmen from Delaware. Freshmen from 10 states and 26 foreign countries.

Admission: Early acceptance available. *Requirements:* Graduation from secondary school or GED. Recommend business courses. *Entrance tests:* SAT for Bachelor of Science degrees. College Board Comparative Guidance and Placement Test. For foreign students TOEFL. *For transfer students:* 2.0 minimum GPA.

Advanced placement for postsecondary-level work completed in secondary school.

Degree Requirements: *For all associate degrees:* 66 credit hours. *For all baccalaureate degrees:* 126–129 credit hours. *For all undergraduate degrees:* 2.0 GPA; general education requirements. Fulfillment of some degree requirements possible by passing departmental examinations. *Grading system:* A–F; withdraw (deadline after which pass-fail is appended to withdraw).

Distinctive Educational Programs: Cooperative education and internships. Study abroad programs in England and France.

Degrees Conferred: 53 *associate;* 207 *baccalaureate*; 140 *master's.* Bachelor's degrees awarded in top two disciplines: business, management, marketing, and related support 178; computer and information sciences and support services 31.

Fees and Other Expenses: *Full-time tuition per academic year 2004–05:* $10,290. *Room and board per academic year:* $4,116. *Books and supplies:* $807.

Financial Aid: Aid from institutionally generated funds is provided on the basis of academic merit, financial need, athletic ability, other criteria. Institution has a Program Participation Agreement with the U.S. Department of Education for eligible students to receive Pell Grants and other federal aid.

Financial aid to full-time, first-time undergraduate students: 23% received federal grants averaging $2,619; 5% state/local grants averaging $954; 31% institutional grants averaging $2,170; 52% loans averaging $4,747.

Departments and Teaching Staff: *Professors* 5, *associate professors* 13, *assistant professors* 7, *part-time faculty* 40. *Total instructional faculty:* 65. Degrees held by full-time faculty: doctorate 20%, master's 80%.

Enrollment: Total enrollment 1,185. Undergraduate 1,019 (42.8% men, 57.2% women).

Characteristics of Student Body: *Ethnic/racial makeup:* Black non-Hispanic: 15.9%; Asian or Pacific Islander: 7.2%; Hispanic: 4%; White non-Hispanic: 42.3%; unknown: 30.3%.

International Students: 4 nonresident aliens enrolled fall 2004. Programs available to aid students whose native language is not English: Social. English as a Second Language Program. Some financial aid available for international students.

Student Life: On-campus residence halls. *Intercollegiate athletics:* Men's soccer; women's softball. Intramural softball, basketball, golf, football. *Special regulations:* Registered cars permitted without restrictions. *Special services:* Counseling and medical services available. Lifetime placement assistance. *Student publications: Communicator,* a newspaper; *The Key,* a yearbook; *International Student Association Newsletter. Surrounding community:* Wilmington population 100,000. Philadelphia and Baltimore nearest metropolitan areas.

Publications: *Reflections,* an alumni newsletter; *Graduate Survey,* employment statistics for graduates; *Career Spotlight,* Career Planning and Placement newsletter.

Library Collections: 48,000 volumes. 27,300 microforms; 1,200 audiovisual materials; 800 periodical subscriptions. Students have access to online information retrieval services and the Internet.

Emphasis of library collections placed on business subjects and computers due to specialized nature of college.

Chief Executive Officer: Mohammad Ilyas, President.

Address admission inquiries to Dean of Admissions.

University of Delaware

101 Hullhen Hall
Newark, Delaware 19716
Tel: (302) 831-2000   **E-mail:** admissions@udel.edu
Fax: (302) 831-6905   **Internet:** www.udel.edu

Institution Description: The University of Delaware is a privately-controlled, state-assisted institution. *Enrollment:* 19,058. *Degrees awarded:* Associate, baccalaureate, master's, doctorate.

Accreditation: *Regional:* MSA/CHE. *Professional:* accounting, athletic training, business, clinical psychology, dietetics, engineering, engineering technology, English language education, medical assisting, music, nursing, physical therapy, psychology internship, public administration, teacher education

History: Founded in 1743 and chartered as Newark College; offered first instruction at postsecondary level in 1833; awarded first degree in 1836; became land-grant college and changed name to Delaware College in 1876; established women's college in 1913; merged with women's college and adopted present name in 1921. See John A. Munroe, *The University of Delaware: A History* (Newark: University of Delaware Press, 1986) for further information.

Institutional Structure: *Governing board:* Board of Trustees. Extrainstitutional representation: 28 trustees, Governor of State of Delaware, master of state grange, president of state board of education. Institutional representation: President of the University. 4 ex-officio. All voting. *Composition of institution:* Academic affairs headed by provost. Management/business/finances directed by vice president and university treasurer. Instructional faculty 1,379. Academic governance body, Faculty Senate, meets an average of 12 times per year. Faculty *Faculty representation:* faculty served by collective bargaining agent affiliated with AAUP.

Calendar: Semesters. Academic year Sept. to May. Summer session of three terms (two day, one evening) from June to Aug. 5-week winter session begins in Jan.

Characteristics of Freshmen: 45% of applicants admitted; 35% of admitted students enrolled full-time.

99.5% (3,438 students) submitted SAT scores; 9,4% (325 students) submitted ACT scores. *25th percentile:* SAT Verbal 540, SAT Math 560; ACT Composite 24, ACT English 28, ACT Math 29. *75th percentile:* SAT Verbal 630, SAT Math 630; ACT Composite 28, ACT English 28, ACT Math 29.

54% of entering freshmen expected to graduate within 5 years. 30% of freshmen from Delaware. Freshmen from 39 states and 34 foreign countries.

Admission: For fall acceptance, apply by Jan. 15. Applicants are notified of acceptance beginning in mid-March. Early acceptance available. *Requirements:* Graduation from an accredited secondary school. Require 4 years English, 2 or more years foreign language, 3 years mathematics, 3 years science (at least 2 laboratory), academic electives; total of 18-20 units of academic coursework. Additional requirements for some programs. *Entrance tests:* College Board SAT-Reasoning or ACT with writing component. *For transfer students:* minimum college GPA of 2.5, Some majors require a higher college GPA and/or specific coursework. Advanced placement for postsecondary-level work completed in secondary school. Tutoring available. Noncredit remedial courses offered in summer session and regular academic year.

Degree Requirements: *For all associate degrees:* 60 credit hours; 2 terms in residence. *For all baccalaureate degrees:* 124 credit hours; first 6 or last 2 terms in residence. *For all undergraduate degrees:* 2.0 GPA.

Exemption from some beginning courses possible by passing departmental examinations. *Grading system:* A–F; pass-fail; withdraw (carries time limit).

Distinctive Educational Programs: *For undergraduates:* Dean's Scholar Program; University Honors Program. *For graduate students:* Winterthur Program in Art Conversation; Hagley Program in the History of Industrial America; Longwood Program in Ornamental Horticulture. *Other distinctive programs:* In 1985 the University of Delaware was designated by the National Science Foundation as one of only 12 national research centers in engineering science. The university received the designation for its pioneering work in composites manufacturing science. The University of Delaware has also been named a member of the Association of Research Libraries, a prestigious organization composed of institutions of higher education housing major research library collections. Students also have the opportunity to study abroad in programs located in countries including Switzerland, Spain, Japan, France, Argentina, Australia, Germany, China, Costa Rica, Israel, Italy, Martinique, Mexico, Morocco, New Zealand, South Africa, Tanzania, Sweden.

ROTC: Army and Air Force.

Degrees Conferred: 12 *associate,* 3,255 *baccalaureate*; 817 *master's;* 144 *doctorate.*

Fees and Other Expenses: *Full-time tuition per academic year 2004–05:* resident $6,304; out-of-state $15,990. *Required fees:* $650. *Room per academic year:* $3,668. *Board per academic year:* $2,790.

Financial Aid: Aid from institutionally generated funds is provided on the basis of academic merit, athletic ability, financial need. Institution has a Program Participation Agreement with the U.S. Department of Education for eligible students to receive Pell Grants and other federal aid.

Financial aid to full-time, first-time undergraduate students: need-based scholarships/grants totaling $24,200,000, self-help $25,950,000, parent loans $12,650,000, tuition waivers $565,000, athletic awards $1,300,000; non-need-based scholarships/grants totaling $12,850,000, self-help $9,227,000, parent loans $8,000,000, tuition waivers $2,100,000, athletic awards $3,500,000.

Departments and Teaching Staff: *Total instructional faculty:* 1,379 (full-time 1,121, part-time 258; women 535, men 844; members of minority groups 181). Total faculty with doctorate, first-professional, or other terminal degree: 1,020. Student-to-faculty ratio: 13:1.

Enrollment: Total enrollment 19,058. Undergraduate full-time 6,370 men / 8,739 women, part-time 383m / 531w; graduate fulo-time 1,247m / 1,272w, part-time 400m / 476w.

Characteristics of Student Body: *Ethnic/racial makeup:* number of Black non-Hispanic: 899; American Indian or Alaska Native: 41; Asian or Pacific Islander: 549; Hispanic: 574; White non-Hispanic: 13,596; unknown: 201.

International Students: 163 nonresident aliens enrolled fall 2004. Programs available to aid students whose native language is not English: Social and cultural. English as a Second Language Program. No financial aid specifically designated for international students.

Student Life: On-campus residence halls house approximately 50% of undergraduate student body. 2% of student body reside in Greek housing. *Intercollegiate athletics:* men only: baseball, basketball, cross-country, football, golf, lacrosse, soccer, swimming, tennis, track; women only: basketball, cross-country, field hockey, lacrosse, rowing, soccer, softball, swimming, tennis, track, volleyball. *Special regulations:* Registered cars only permitted on campus. *Special services:* learning resources centers, medical services, bus service to and from off-campus locations; *Student publications, radio: The Review*, a biweekly student newspaper. Radio station WVUD-FM; SLTV, a student-run television station. *Surrounding community:* Newark population 30,000. Located 40 miles from Philadelphia (PA), and 60 miles from Baltimore (MD). Philadelphia International Airport is nearest major terminal; 35 miles from campus. Amtrak train service one mile from campus. Mass transit bus service from Newark and Wilmington to all major cities.

Publications: The University of Delaware Press produces noteworthy scholarly works as they become available.

Library Collections: 2,623,554 volumes including bound books, serial backfiles, electronic documents, and government documents not in separate collections. Online catalog. Current serial subscriptions: 12,476 (paper, microform, and via electronic access). 410 computer work stations. Students have access to the Internet at no charge. Total budget for books, periodicals, audiovisual materials, microforms 2004–05: $7,110,202.

Most important holdings include Unidel History of Chemistry Collection; Unidel History of Horticulture and Landscape Architecture; George Messersmith Diplomatic Papers.

Buildings and Grounds: A total of 453 facilities, including major classroom and laboratory buildings, residence halls and dining halls, athletic, student activity, and farm buildings, constitutes the University's physical plant. Land holdings total 2,047 acres, including 986 acres in Newark, a Marine Studies Complex at Lewes, an Agricultural Substation in Georgetown, and a 34-acre campus in Wilmington. *New buildings:* renovation of DuPont Hall housing the College of Engineering, and the Courtyard by Marriott Hotel on the Newark campus. Cener for the Arts is expected to be completed in 2006; Laaird campus residence hall complex to be completed in 2006.

Chief Executive Officer: Dr. David P. Roselle, President.

Undergraduates address admission inquiries to Louis L. Hirsch, Director of Admissions; graduate/first-professional inquiries to Mary J. Martin, Associate Provost for Graduate Studies.

Alfred Lerner College of Business and Economics

Degree Programs Offered: *Baccalaureate and master's* in accounting, business, finance, management information systems, management, marketing, operations management.

Distinctive Educational Programs: M.B.A.-baccalaureate in engineering with College of Engineering.

College of Agricultural Sciences

Degree Programs Offered: *Baccalaureate* in agricultural business management, agricultural economics, agricultural education, agricultural engineering technology, animal science, entomology, entomology-plant pathology, plant science; *master's* in agricultural economics, animal science, entomology, ornamental horticulture, plant science; *doctorate* in animal science, plant science.

Distinctive Educational Programs: Double-degree program in engineering with College of Engineering. Cooperative master's in public administration with College of Urban Affairs and Public Policy.

College of Arts and Sciences

Degree Programs Offered: *Baccalaureate* in American studies, anthropology, anthropology education, art, art education, art history, biological sciences, biological sciences education, chemistry, chemistry education, classics, communications, comparative literature, computer and information sciences, criminal justice, economics, economics education, English, English education, French, French education, geography, geography education, geology, geophysics, German, German education, history, history education, international relations, Latin, Latin education, liberal studies, mathematical sciences, mathematics education, medical technology, music, philosophy, physical therapy, physics, physics education, political science, political science education, psychology, Russian, Spanish, sociology, sociology education, statistics, technology of artistic and historic objects, theater, visual communication, women's studies; *master's, doctorate* in various fields.

College of Engineering

Degree Programs Offered: *Baccalaureate* in chemical engineering, civil engineering, electrical engineering, mechanical engineering; *master's* in aerospace engineering, chemical engineering, civil engineering, electrical engineering, metallurgy and metals; *doctorate* in applied sciences, chemical engineering.

Distinctive Educational Programs: Accelerated baccalaureate-master's program in mechanical and aerospace engineering. Engineering Experiment Station. *See also* College of Arts and Sciences, and College of Business and Economics.

College of Health and Nursing Sciences

Degree Programs Offered: *Baccalaureate* in applied nutrition, athletic training, dietetics, exercise science, health behavior management, health and physical education, health studies, medical technology, nutritional sciences, nursing. *Master's* in exercise science, health promotion, health services administration, human nutrition, nursing.

College of Human Services, Education, and Public Policy

Degree Programs Offered: *Baccalaureate* in apparel design, educational studies, elementary teacher education, apparel design, early childhood development and education, family and community services, fashion merchandising, hotel/restaurant/institutional management, interdisciplinary studies in human resources, leadership and consumer economics. *Master's* in college counseling, curriculum and instruction, education, environmental and energy policy, educational leadership, educational technology, exceptional children and youth, hospitality information management, human development and family studies, instruction, public administration, reading, school psychology, student affairs practice in higher education, teaching English as a second language, urban affairs and public policy. *Doctorate* in education, educational leadership, environmental and energy policy, human development and faculty studies, urban affairs and public policy.

College of Marine Studies

Degree Programs Offered: *Master's* in marine policy, marine studies, ocean engineering. *Doctorate* in marine studies, oceanography, ocean engineering.

Distinctive Educational Programs: Marine Studies Complex in Lewes includes classroom, Pollution Ecology Laboratory, several research vessels and other research facilities.

Wesley College

120 North State Street
Dover, Delaware 19901-3875

Tel: (302) 736-2300   **E-mail:** jacobsar@.wesley.edu
Fax: (302) 736-2301   **Internet:** www.wesley.edu

Institution Description: Wesley College is a private college affiliated with the United Methodist Church. *Enrollment:* 2,037. *Degrees awarded:* Associate, baccalaureate, master's.

Accreditation: *Regional:* MSA/CHE. *Professional:* nursing

History: Established and chartered as Wilmington Conference Academy 1973; rechartered as Wesley Collegiate Institute and offered first instruction at postsecondary level 1918; first degree (associate) awarded 1924; closed 1932–42; reopened as Wesley Junior College 1942; present name adopted 1958; first baccalaureate awarded 1978.

Institutional Structure: *Governing board:* Board of Trustees; 30 members, all voting, 2 ex officio. *Composition of institution:* Administrators 8 men / 2 woman. Academic affairs headed by vice president for academic affairs. Business finances directed by business manager/treasurer. Full-time instructional faculty 51. Academic governance body, College Senate, meets an average of 8 times per year.

Calendar: Semesters. Academic year Aug. to Aug. Freshmen admitted Aug., Jan., June. Degrees conferred and formal commencement May. Summer session of 2 terms from June to Aug.

Characteristics of Freshmen: 82% (380 students) submitted SAT scores. *25th percentile:* SAT Verbal 460, SAT Math 470. *75th percentile:* SAT Verbal 530, SAT Math 530.

25% of freshmen from Delaware. Freshmen from 13 states and 5 foreign countries.

Admission: Rolling admissions plan. For fall acceptance, apply as early as senior year of secondary school, but not later than opening date of classes. Apply by Nov. for early decision; need not limit application to Wesley. Early acceptance available. *Requirements:* Either 16 secondary school units which must include 4 English, minimum of 2 in a foreign language, 2–3 mathematics, 1 natural science, minimum of 1 social studies; or GED. Lowest acceptable secondary school class standing 5th quintile. *Entrance tests:* College Board SAT or ACT composite recommended. *For transfer students:* 2.0 minimum GPA; 30 hours maximum transfer credit.

College credit and advanced placement for postsecondary-level work completed in secondary school and for extrainstitutional learning on basis of ACE *2006 Guide to the Evaluation of Educational Experiences in the Armed Services.* Tutoring available. Developmental courses offered in summer session and regular academic year; credit given.

Degree Requirements: *For all associate degrees:* 64 credit hours; 24 credit hours in residence. *For all baccalaureate degrees:* 129–132 credit hours; 36 credit hours in residence. *For all undergraduate degrees:* 2.0 GPA; 2 semesters physical education. Fulfillment of some degree requirements and exemption from some beginning courses possible by passing College Board CLEP or departmental tests. *Grading system:* A–F; withdraw (carries time limit); irregular withdrawal, failing.

Distinctive Educational Programs: Work-experience programs. Flexible meeting places and schedules. Off-campus center (at Dover Air Force Base, less than 30 miles away from main institution). Evening classes. Transfer and career curricula. Direct transfer program with over forty 4-year colleges provides automatic transfer for qualified students.

Degrees Conferred: 126 *baccalaureate* (B); 76 *master's* (M): biological/life sciences 11 (B), 2 (M); business/marketing 105 (B), 39 (M); communications/communication technologies 16 (B); education 49 (B), 22 (M); English 4 (B); health professions and related 1 (B), 13 (M); law/legal studies 9 (B); liberal arts/general studies 3 (B); parks and recreation 15 (B); psychology 29 (B); social sciences and history 15 (B).

Fees and Other Expenses: *Full-time tuition per academic year 2005–06:* $14,600 undergraduate; $285 per credit hour for graduate study. *Required fees:* $790. *Room and board per academic year:* $6,900.

Financial Aid: Aid from institutionally generated funds is provided on the basis of academic merit, financial need. Institution has a Program Participation Agreement with the U.S. Department of Education for eligible students to receive Pell Grants and other federal aid.

Financial aid to full-time, first-time undergraduate students: need-based scholarships/grants totaling $2,683,188, self-help $2,368,249; non-need-based scholarships/grants totaling $4,561,659, tuition waivers $285,346.

Departments and Teaching Staff: *Total instructional faculty:* 135 (full-time 61, part-time 74; women 60, men 75; members of minority groups 8). Total faculty with doctorate, first-professional, or other terminal degree: 73. Student-to-faculty ratio: 20:1.

Enrollment: Total enrollment 2,037. Undergraduate full-time 691 men / 863 women, part-time 182m / 105w; graduate full-time 18m / 21w, part-time 30m / 67w.

Characteristics of Student Body: *Ethnic/racial makeup:* number of Black non-Hispanic: 53; American Indian or Alaska Native: 5; Asian or Pacific Islander: 29; Hispanic: 35; White non-Hispanic: 1,107; unknown: 10.

International Students: 15 nonresident aliens enrolled fall 2004. Students from Europe, Asia, Central and South America, Africa, Canada. English as a Second Language Program available. No financial aid specifically designated for international students.

Student Life: On-campus residence halls house 63% of student body. Full-time students under 21 years of age who are single and do not live with parents or relations are required to live in residence halls. *Intercollegiate athletics:* men only: baseball, basketball, football, golf, lacrosse, soccer, tennis. Women only, basketball, field hockey, softball, tennis. *Special regulations:* Cars with decals permitted on campus. Quiet hours from 10pm to 7am Sun.–Thurs. Residence hall visitation from Sun.–Thurs. 1pm to midnight; 1pm to 2am Fri. and Sat. *Special services:* Learning Resources Center, medical services, Career Planning Office. *Student publications: The Wesley Whetstone,* a twice-monthly newspaper; *Eukairia,* a yearbook. *Surrounding community:* Dover population 35,000. Philadelphia, 78 miles from campus, is nearest metropolitan area.

Library Collections: 101,000 volumes including bound books, serial backfiles, electronic documents, and government documents not in separate collections. Online catalog. Current serial subscriptions: 235. 172,600 microform units; 3,572 recordings. 120 computer work stations. Students have access to the Internet at no charge.

Most important special holdings include collections on business, education, religion.

Buildings and Grounds: Campus area 40 acres.

Chief Executive Officer: Dr. Scott D. Miller, President.

Address admission inquiries to Arthur Jacobs, Director of Admissions.

Widener University - Delaware Campus

4601 Concord Pike

Wilmington, Delaware 19803-0474

Tel: (302) 477-2100   **E-mail:** admissions@widener.edu
Fax: (302) 477-2282   **Internet:** www.widener.edu

Institution Description: Widener University - Delaware Campus includes the School of Law. The university is a private institution and is an affiliate of Widener University of Chester, Pennsylvania. *Enrollment:* 1,454. *Degrees offered:* Associate, baccalaureate, doctorate, first-professional (law)

Accreditation: *Regional:* MSA. *Professional:* business, clinical psychology, engineering, health services administration, law, nursing, physical therapy, psychology internship, social work

Calendar: Semesters.

Characteristics of Freshmen: 85 undergraduate applicants (10 men, 75 women). 88.2% of applicants admitted; 43.1% of admitted students enrolled full-time.

Admission: *Requirements:* Graduation from an accredited secondary school; SAT or ACT. Law School: Baccalaureate degree from accredited college or university; LSAT test score.

Degree Requirements: *See* PENNSYLVANIA: Widener University for undergraduate requirements. Law school: 84 credit hours; 2.0 GPA; entire program in residence.

Distinctive Educational Programs: Law School's Clinical Program enables students to earn credit while working for practicing lawyers, state offices.

Degrees Conferred: 12 *associate;* 33 *baccalaureate;* 34 *master's;* 1 *doctorate;* 243 *first-professional:* law. Bachelor's degrees awarded in largest programs: legal professions and studies 14; business, management, marketing, and related support services 8; liberal arts and sciences, general studies and humanities 7; computer and information sciences and support services 4.

Fees and Other Expenses: *Tuition and fees for academic year 2004–05:* $11,520. *Books and supplies:* $750. *Room and board per academic year:* $3,900. Contact the Law School for current tuition and fees.

Financial Aid: Institution has a Program Participation Agreement with the U.S. Department of Education for eligible students to receive Pell Grants and other federal aid.

Departments and Teaching Staff: Faculty are unranked.

Enrollment: Total enrollment 1,454. Undergraduate: 233 (20.2% men, 19.8% women).

Characteristics of Student Body: *Ethnic/racial makeup (undergraduate):* Black non-Hispanic: 9.4%; Asian or Pacific Islander: .4%; White non-Hispanic: 87.1%; unknown: 3.0%.

Chief Executive Officer: Dr. James T. Harris III, President.

Address admission inquiries to Barbara L. Ayers, Director of Admissions.

Wilmington College

320 DuPont Highway
New Castle, Delaware 19720
Tel: (302) 328-9401   **E-mail:** admissions@wilmcoll.edu
Fax: (302) 328-5902   **Internet:** www.wilmcoll.edu

Institution Description: Wilmington College is a private, independent, non-profit college. *Enrollment:* 6,626. *Degrees awarded:* Associate, baccalaureate, master's.

Accreditation: *Regional:* MSA/CHE. *Professional:* counseling, nursing, nursing education

History: Established 1965; chartered 1967; offered first instruction at postsecondary level 1968; awarded first degree (baccalaureate) 1972.

Institutional Structure: *Governing board:* Wilmington College Board of Trustees. Extrainstitutional representation: 18 trustees; institutional representation: president of the college; 1 alumnus. 1 ex officio. 19 voting. *Composition of institution:* Administrators 6 men / 4 women (at dean's level and above; 40% are women). Academic affairs headed by vice president for academic affairs. Management/business/finances directed by business manager. Full-time instructional faculty 67. Academic governance body, Faculty Senate, meets an average of 4 times per year.

Calendar: Semesters. Academic year Sept. to June. Freshmen admitted Sept., Oct., Jan., Mar., May, July. Degrees conferred and formal commencement May.

Characteristics of Freshmen: 100% of applicants accepted. 84% of admitted students enrolled full-time. 40% of entering freshmen expected to graduate within 5 years. 83% of freshmen from Delaware. Freshmen from 5 states.

Admission: Rolling admissions plan. For fall acceptance, apply as early as 18 months prior to enrollment, but not later than beginning of term. Early acceptance available. *Requirements:* Either graduation from accredited secondary school, or GED. *Entrance tests:* College Board SAT or ACT composite recommended. For foreign students TOEFL. *For transfer students:* 2.0 minimum GPA; from accredited institution 75 hours maximum transfer credit; for correspondence/extension students number of credits accepted varies.

College credit for postsecondary-level work completed in secondary school, and for extrainstitutional learning on basis of ACE *2006 Guide to the Evaluation of Educational Experiences in the Armed Services*, portfolio, faculty assessments, and personal interview. Noncredit developmental courses offered during regular academic year.

Degree Requirements: *For all associate degrees:* 60 credit hours. *For all baccalaureate degrees:* 120 hours. *For all undergraduate degrees:* 2.0 GPA; last 30 hours in residence; distribution requirements.

Fulfillment of some degree requirements and exemption from some beginning courses possible by passing departmental examinations, College Board CLEP, or other standardized tests. *Grading system:* A–F; pass; withdraw (deadline after which pass-fail is appended to withdraw); incomplete (deadline after which A–F is assigned).

Distinctive Educational Programs: *For undergraduates:* Internships. Special facilities for using telecommunications in the classroom. Interdepartmental/interdisciplinary programs in aviation management, behavioral science, and criminal justice. Individual majors; doctor of education program. *Available to all students:* Flexible meeting places and schedules, including off-campus centers (at Dover Air Force Base and Silver Lake, 45 miles away from the main campus; Georgetown, 75 miles away) and weekend and evening courses. Accelerated degree programs. Facilities and programs for independent research.

ROTC: Army and Air Force offered in cooperation with University of Delaware.

Degrees Conferred: 728 *baccalaureate* (B), 754 *master's* (M); 23 *doctorate* (D): business/marketing 286 (B); 253 (M); communications/communication technologies 56 (B); computer and information sciences 20 (B); education 96 (B), 435 (M), 23 (D); health professions and related sciences 51 (B), 33 (M); liberal arts/general studies 95 (B); protective services/public administration 33 (M); psychology 13 (B); social sciences and history 111 (B).

Fees and Other Expenses: *Tuition per academic year 2004–05:* undergraduate $7,290; graduate $8,100. *Other fees:* $50.

Financial Aid: Institution has a Program Participation Agreement with the U.S. Department of Education for eligible students to receive Pell Grants and other federal aid.

Financial aid to full-time, first-time undergraduate students: need-based scholarships/grants totaling $2,860,000, self-help $25,799,638, parent loans $241,492; non-need-based scholarships/grants totaling $228,588, self-help $500,000, athletic awards $432,080.

Departments and Teaching Staff: *Total instructional faculty:* 555 (full-time 67, part-time 488; women 265, men 290; members of minority groups 3). Student-to-faculty ratio: 13:1.

Enrollment: Total enrollment 6,626. Undergraduate full-time 762 men / 1,389 women, part-time 725m / 1,533w; graduate full-time 231m / 580w, part-time 547m / 1,259w.

Characteristics of Student Body: *Ethnic/racial makeup:* number of Black non-Hispanic: 626; American Indian or Alaska Native: 12; Asian or Pacific Islander: 39 Hispanic: 98; White non-Hispanic: 2,218; unknown: 1,426.

Student Life: On-campus residence halls house 1% of student body. Residence halls for men only constitute 42% of such space, for women only 58%. *Intercollegiate athletics:* men only: baseball, basketball; women only: basketball, softball, volleyball. *Special regulations:* Cars permitted without restrictions. *Special services:* Learning Resources Center. *Student publications, radio:* The Voyager, a quarterly newspaper; The Odyssey, a yearbook. Radio station WCON broadcasts 20 hours per week. *Surrounding community:* New Castle County, population 400,000, is within Wilmington metropolitan area. Served by mass transit bus system; airport less than 1 mile from campus; passenger rail service 5 miles from campus.

Library Collections: 196,000 volumes. 470 periodical subscriptions. Online catalog. Computer work stations available. Access to online bibliographic retrieval systems. Students have access to the Internet at no charge.

Buildings and Grounds: Campus area 13 acres.

Chief Executive Officer: Dr. Audrey K. Doberstein, President.

Address admission inquiries to Chris Ferguson, Director of Admissions.

District of Columbia

American University

4400 Massachusetts Avenue, N.W.
Washington, District of Columbia 20016
Tel: (202) 885-1000   **E-mail:** afa@american.edu
Fax: (202) 885-6014   **Internet:** www.american.edu

Institution Description: American University is a private institution affiliated with the United Methodist Church. *Enrollment:* 10,978. *Degrees awarded:* Associate, baccalaureate, first-professional (law), master's, doctorate. Certificates also awarded.

Member of Consortium of Universities of the Washington Metropolitan Area.

Accreditation: *Regional:* MSA/CHE. *Professional*: business, clinical psychology, journalism, law, music, public administration, teacher education

History: Established as graduate school, chartered, and incorporated 1893; offered first instruction at postsecondary level 1914; awarded first degrees (master's, doctorate) 1916; added undergraduate level 1925; awarded first baccalaureate 1926.

Institutional Structure: *Governing board:* Board of Trustees. Representation: 47 trustees, including 24 alumni. All voting. *Composition of institution:* Administrators 35 men / 24 women. Academic affairs headed by provost. Management/business/finances directed by vice president for business and fiscal affairs. Vice president for institutional advancement including admissions and financial aid, athletics, development, and university relations. Full-time instructional faculty 441. University Senate meets 9 times per year.

Calendar: Semesters. Academic year Sept. to May. Freshmen admitted Sept., Jan., May. Degrees conferred May, Aug., Dec. Formal commencements May, Jan. Summer session from May to Aug.

Characteristics of Freshmen: 12,198 applicants (4,758 men, 7,440 women). 53.2% of applicants admitted. 18.6% of admitted students enrolled full-time.

95% (1,153 students) submitted SAT scores; 26% (323 students) submitted ACT scores. *25th percentile*: SAT I Verbal 580, SAT I Math 570; ACT Composite 25. *75th percentile*: SAT I Verbal 690, SAT I Math 680; ACT Composite 29.

68% of entering freshmen expected to graduate within 5 years. 3% of freshmen from District of Columbia. Freshmen from 43 states and 57 foreign countries.

Admission: Freshmen may apply for any semester. Deadline for fall semester, Feb. 1; spring Dec. 1; summer April 15. Freshmen early decision Nov. 15. Transfer application deadline Aug. 1. Deadline for applying for financial aid Feb. 1. *Requirements:* either graduation from accredited secondary school with 16 academic units including 4 English and 3 mathematics (including 2 algebra), or GED. Recommend 2 units each in foreign language, natural science, and social science. *Entrance tests:* SAT or ACT composite. *For transfer students:* 2.0 minimum GPA; from 4-year accredited institution 75 semester hours maximum transfer credit from 2-year accredited institution 60 hours.

College credit and advanced placement for postsecondary-level work completed in secondary school. College credit for extrainstitutional learning on basis of ACE *2006 Guide to the Evaluation of Educational Experiences in the Armed Services* and portfolio assessments.

Tutoring available. Developmental courses offered in summer session and regular academic year; credit given.

Degree Requirements: *For all associate degrees:* 60 credit hours. *For all baccalaureate degrees:* 120 credit hours. *For all undergraduate degrees:* 2.0 GPA; 30 hours in residence; general education requirements; exit competency examinations in writing and mathematics.

Fulfillment of some degree requirements and exemption from some beginning courses possible by passing College Board CLEP. *Grading system:* A–F; pass-fail; withdraw.

Distinctive Educational Programs: Work-experience programs. Flexible meeting places and schedules, including off-campus centers (in D.C., Virginia, and Maryland) and evening classes. Special facilities for using telecommunications in the classroom. General interdisciplinary program. Facilities and programs for independent research, including honors programs, individual majors. Study abroad in London, Rome, Copenhagen, Brussels, Buenos Aires, Madrid,

Moscow, Paris, Beijing, Prague, Santiago. Washington Semester Programs provide intercollegiate honors programs for study in D.C. on various aspects of public affairs. *Other distinctive programs:* Continuing education; weekend master's programs in information systems, journalism.

ROTC: Army in cooperation with Georgetown University; Air Force in cooperation with Howard University; Navy in cooperation with George Washington University.

Degrees Conferred: 1,291 *baccalaureate*; 1,349 *master's*; 59 *doctorate*; 346 *first-professional*: law. Bachelor's degrees awarded in top five disciplines: socials sciences 445; business, management, marketing, and related support services 242; communication, journalism, and related programs 161; visual and performing arts 99; security and protective services 91.

Fees and Other Expenses: *Full-time tuition per academic year 2004–05:* undergraduate $25,920. Contact the university for graduate tuition and fees. *Room and board per academic year:* $10,408.

Financial Aid: Institution has a Program Participation Agreement with the U.S. Department of Education for eligible students to receive Pell Grants and other federal aid.

Financial aid to full-time, first-time undergraduate students: 11% received federal grants averaging $3,017; 5% state/local grants averaging $802; 59 institutional grants averaging $13,967; 55% loans averaging $7,740.

Departments and Teaching Staff: American studies *professors* 0, *associate professors* 0, *assistant professors* 0, *part-time faculty* 1; anthropology 3, 3, 2, 1; art 4, 4, 4, 0; biology 1, 4, 4, 0; chemistry 4, 1, 3, 0; computer science 6, 4, 4, 1; economics 6, 10, 5, 0; education 4, 1, 3, 0; health and fitness 0, 1, 3, 0; history 5, 5, 5, 0; languages 5, 6, 4, 5; literature 11, 5, 4, 12; mathematics/statistics 6, 7, 4, 6; performing arts 5, 2, 2, 0; philosophy 3, 2, 2, 0; physics 3, 0, 2, 0; psychology 8, 4, 2, 0; sociology 4, 2, 3, 0.

Total instructional faculty: 475 full-time, part-time 485. *Total tenured faculty:* 246. *Student-to-faculty ratio:* 14:1. 90.9% hold highest degree in their field.

Enrollment: Total enrollment 10,978. Undergraduate 5,763 (28.2% men, 61.8% women).

Characteristics of Student Body: *Ethnic and racial makeup:* Black non-Hispanic: 5.7%; American Indian or Alaska Native: .3%; Asian or Pacific Islander: 4.7%; Hispanic: 4.5%; White non-Hispanic: 61.4%; unknown: 16%.

International Students: 801 nonresident aliens enrolled fall 2003. Students from Europe, Asia, Central and South America, Africa, Canada, Australia, New Zealand, Middle East. Programs available to aid students whose native language is not English: Social, cultural, financial. English as a Second Language Program. International students may apply for scholarships on the same basis as other students.

Student Life: On-campus residence halls house 60% of full-time undergraduate students. Some undergraduate students live in college-operated apartments. 20% of men join fraternities. 15% of women join sororities. *Intercollegiate athletics:* men only: basketball, cross-country, golf, soccer, swimming and diving, tennis, wrestling; women only: basketball, cross-country, field hockey, lacrosse, soccer, swimming and diving, tennis, volleyball. *Special regulations:* Cars permitted for all but freshmen and sophomores. Quiet hours. *Special services:* psychological services, learning services, handicap services, intercultural programs, international student services. Minibus to off-campus locations, including weekend transportation to suburban shopping malls. *Student publications, radio, television:* The Eagle, a weekly newspaper; The Talon, a yearbook. Radio station WAMU-AM and FM broadcasts 24 hours a day. Student operated ATV and WVAU FM and AM. *Surrounding community:* Washington, D.C. population over 550,000. Served by mass transit bus system, airport 10–25 miles from campus, passenger rail service 6 miles from campus.

Publications: *Folio* (Literature Department); *The Law Review* (Washington College of Law); *American University Publications in Philosophy* (Philosophy Department), *Congressional and Presidential Studies* (in conjunction with U.S. Capitol Historical Society, College of Public and International Affairs), *Law Journal of International Law and Policy, Administrative Law Journal*.

Library Collections: 1,150,000 volumes including bound books, serial backfiles, electronic documents, and government documents not in separate collections. Online catalog. Current serial subscriptions: 9,575 paper, 231 electronic.

31,500 recordings; 788 CD-ROMs. 147 computer work stations. Students have access to the Internet at no charge.

Most important holdings include Artemus Martin Collection (rare material on mathematics); Esther Ballou Memorial Collection (on music); Spinks Collection (rare material on Japanese and other Asian cultures).

Buildings and Grounds: Campus area 80 acres.

Chief Executive Officer: Dr. Benjamin Ladner, President.

Address admission inquiries to Cheryl Storie, Assistant Provost, Enrollment.

College of Arts and Sciences

Degree Programs Offered: *Associate* in general studies; *baccalaureate* in American studies, anthropology, art history, arts and cultural management, audio technology, biology, chemistry, computer science, economics, economic theory, education (early childhood and elementary), environmental studies, fine arts, foreign language and communication media, French studies, French-West European area studies, general studies, German studies, German-West European area studies, graphic design, history, information systems, interdisciplinary studies, Jewish studies, literature, literature-cinema studies, mathematics and applied mathematics, music, performing arts (theater), philosophy, physics, psychology, religion, Russian studies, Russian-U.S.S.R. area studies, sociology, Spanish studies, Spanish-Latin American area studies, statistics, studio art, women's and gender studies, health promotion; *master's* and *doctorate* in various fields.

Distinctive Educational Programs: Cooperative programs in engineering with University of Maryland and Washington University (MO). Preprofessional programs in dentistry, medicine, and law.

Kogod School of Business

Degree Programs Offered: *Baccalaureate* in accountancy; finance, international business, management, marketing, real estate and urban development; *master's* in various fields.

Distinctive Educational Programs: *See* Washington College of Law.

School of International Service

Degree Programs Offered: *Baccalaureate* in international studies, language and area studies, interdisciplinary; *master's, doctorate* in various fields.

Admission: Eligibility for freshman consideration normally requires a minimum 3.0 GPA in secondary school computed on academic courses only.

Distinctive Educational Programs: J.D.-M.A. in Law and International Affairs with Washington College of Law.

School of Communication

Degree Programs Offered: *Baccalaureate* in journalism, public communication, visual media, foreign language and communication media, interdisciplinary studies.

School of Public Affairs

Degree Programs Offered: *Baccalaureate* in communication, legal institutions, economics and government, political science, justice, law and society, interdisciplinary; *master's, doctorate* in various fields.

Distinctive Educational Programs: J.D.-M.S. in Law and Justice with Washington College of Law.

Washington College of Law

Degree Programs Offered: *First-professional;* L.L.M. in International Legal Studies.

Admission: Baccalaureate from accredited college or university, LSAT. *For L.L.M.:* law degree from accredited U.S. or international school. Foreign students whose first language is not English must take TOEFL.

Degree Requirements: *J.D.:* 86 credit hours, 2.0 GPA, 3 full academic years in residence; *L.L.M.:* 24 credit hours, 2.0 GPA.

Distinctive Educational Programs: Internships. Joint J.D.-M.B.A. in cooperation with Kogod College of Business Administration; J.D.-M.S. in Law and Justice with School of Public Affairs; J.D.-M.A. in Law and International Affairs with School of International Service.

The Catholic University of America

620 Michigan Avenue, N.E.
Washington, District of Columbia 20064
Tel: (202) 319-5200   **E-mail:** cua-admissions@cua.edu
Fax: (202) 319-4441   **Internet:** www.cua.edu

Institution Description: The Catholic University of America is a private, independent institution affiliated with the Roman Catholic Church. *Enrollment:* 5,740. *Degrees awarded:* Baccalaureate, first-professional (architecture, law, master of divinity, bachelor of sacred theology), master's, doctorate. Licentiates also offered.

Member of Consortium of Universities of the Washington Metropolitan Area.

Accreditation: *Regional:* MSA/CHE. *Professional:* Architecture, chemistry, engineering (civil, electrical, mechanical), law, librarianship, medical technology, music, nursing (baccalaureate, master's), psychology, social work, teacher education (elementary), theology.

History: Established as a graduate institution 1887; offered first instruction at postsecondary level 1889; awarded first degree (master's) 1890; offered first undergraduate instruction 1904.

Institutional Structure: *Governing board:* The Board of Trustees. Extrainstitutional representation: 49 trustees; institutional representation: president of the university. 1 ex officio. All voting. *Composition of institution:* Administrators 23 men / 7 women. Academic affairs headed by Provost. Management/business/finances directed by vice president for finance and treasurer. Full-time instructional faculty 365. Academic governance body, The Senate of the University, meets an average of 10 times per year.

Calendar: Semesters. Academic year late Aug. mid-May. Freshmen admitted Sept., Jan., May, June. Degrees conferred May, Oct., Jan. Formal commencement May. Summer session of 3 sessions from May to Aug.

Characteristics of Freshmen: 2,748 applicants (1,187 men, 561 women). 81.9% of applicants admitted. 28.7% of admitted students enrolled full-time.

93% (627 students) submitted SAT scores; 23% (155 students) submitted ACT scores. *25th percentile:* SAT I Verbal 530, SAT I Math 520; ACT Composite 22. *75th percentile:* SAT I Verbal 640, SAT I Math 630; ACT Composite 28.

70% of entering freshmen expected to graduate within 5 years. 3% of freshmen from the District of Columbia. Freshmen from 42 states and 5 countries.

Admission: Rolling admissions plan. For fall acceptance, apply as early as Sept. of previous year, but not later than Aug. of year of enrollment; for freshmen, no later than Feb. 15 of senior year in high school; for transfer students, by April 1 for following fall semester, Dec. 1 for spring semester. *Requirements:* Graduation from secondary school with 17 academic units which must include 4 English, 2 foreign language, 3 mathematics, 3 science, 4 social studies, 1 fine arts or humanities. *Entrance tests:* College Board SAT and English Achievement or ACT composite. For foreign students TOEFL. *For transfer students:* 2.7 minimum GPA; maximum transfer credit limited only by residence requirement.

College credit and advanced placement for postsecondary-level work completed in secondary school. For extrainstitutional learning, college credit on basis of ACE *2006 Guide to the Evaluation of Educational Experiences in the Armed Services.* Tutoring available.

Degree Requirements: 120 credit hours; 2.0 GPA; 30 hours in residence; distribution requirements; comprehensives in individual fields of study. Fulfillment of some degree requirements and exemption from some beginning courses possible by passing departmental examinations. *Grading system:* A–F; pass-fail (for free electives); withdraw.

Distinctive Educational Programs: Evening classes. Accelerated degree programs. Facilities and programs for independent research, including honors programs, individual majors, tutorials. Study abroad programs in Australia, Belgium, England, France, Germany, Greece, Hungary, Ireland, Italy, Poland, Spain, Venezuela, Zimbabwe. *Other distinctive programs:* Continuing and adult education. Metropolitan College offers General Studies degrees to adult students.

ROTC: Enrollment through cross-registration with Consortium. Army through Georgetown University and Howard University; Air Force through Howard University and University of Maryland, College Park; Navy through George Washington University.

Degrees Conferred: 489 *baccalaureate;* 391 *masters;* 97 *doctorate;* 302 *first-professional.* Bachelor's degrees awarded in top five disciplines: visual and performing arts 58; social sciences 55; architecture and related services 54; communication, journalism, and related programs 38; business, management, marketing, and related support services 37.

Fees and Other Expenses: *Full-time tuition per academic year 2004–05:* $23,000. Contact the university for graduate tuition and fees. *Books and supplies:* $1,000. *Room and board per academic year:* $9,498.

Financial Aid: Aid from institutionally generated funds is provided on the basis of academic merit, financial need. Institution has a Program Participation Agreement with the U.S. Department of Education for eligible students to receive Pell Grants and other federal aid.

Financial aid to full-time, first-time undergraduate students: 9% received federal grants averaging $3,768; 5% state/local grants averaging $1,032; 95% institutional grants averaging $9,884; 62% loans averaging $4,658.

Departments and Teaching Staff: Department of Architecture and Planning *professors* 5, *associate professors* 6, *assistant professors* 2, *instructors* 0, *part-time teachers* 15; Arts and Sciences 57, 76, 27, 1, 79; School of Engineering 9, 3, 15, 0, 10; Columbus School of Law 21, 14, 15, 0, 28; School of Library and Information Science 0, 4, 3, 0, 16; Benjamin t. Rome School of Music 8, 4, 3, 0, 11; School of Nursing 3, 7, 10, 0, 4; School of Philosophy 3, 6, 6, 0, 17; School of Religious Studies 21, 17, 10, 1, 17; National Catholic School of Social Service 4, 9, 3, 0; 18; Metropolitan College 0, 0, 0, 0, 24.

Total instructional faculty: 452. *Total tenured faculty:* 264. *Student-to-faculty ratio:* 10:1. *Degrees held by full-time faculty:* Doctorate 80%, master's 7%, baccalaureate 1%,professional 12%. 96% hold terminal degrees.

Enrollment: Total enrollment 5,740. Undergraduate 2,759 (44.9% men, 55.7% women).

Characteristics of Student Body: *Ethnic and racial makeup:* Black non-Hispanic: 7.1%; Asian or Pacific Islander: 3.4%; Hispanic: 3.7%; White non-Hispanic: 71.7%.

International Students: 120 nonresident aliens enrolled fall 2004. Students from Europe, Asia, Central and South America, Africa, Canada, Australia, New Zealand. Programs available to aid students whose native language is not English: English as a Second Language Program. No financial aid specifically designated for international students.

Student Life: On-campus residence halls house 64% of student body. Freshmen and sophomores are required to live on campus. *Intercollegiate athletics:* men only: baseball, basketball, football, golf, soccer, tennis, track; women only: basketball, field hockey, softball, tennis, track, volleyball. *Special regulations:* Cars with permits allowed; fee charged. Quiet hours. Residence hall visitation from 10am to 2am. *Special services:* Medical services, campus shuttle bus service. *Student publications, radio: Cardinal,* a yearbook; *Tower,* a weekly newspaper. Radio station WCU. *Surrounding community:* Washington, D.C. population over 550,000. Served by mass transit bus and subway systems; airport 6 miles from campus; passenger rail service 2 miles from campus.

Publications: *CUA This Week,* a weekly publication of the Office of Public Affairs; *Inside,* a monthly publication; *CUA Magazine,* quarterly to alumni; *Parents Network,* periodically; *Catholic Historical Review* (quarterly) first published in 1915; *Anthropological Quarterly* first published in 1928; *Law Review,* 1950.

Library Collections: 1,580,000 volumes including bound books, serial backfiles, electronic documents, and government documents not in separate collections. Online catalog. Current serial subscriptions: 5.910. 1,140,000 microform units; 39,200 audiovisual materials. Students have access to the Internet at no charge.

Most important holdings include Oliveira Lima Library; Institute of Christian Oriental Research Collection; Clementine Library.

Buildings and Grounds: Campus area 145 acres.

Chief Executive Officer: Very Rev. David M. O'Connell, C.M., President. Address admission inquiries to Michael Hendricks, Vice President for Enrollment Management.

School of Arts and Sciences

Degree Programs Offered: *Baccalaureate* in accounting, anthropology, art, biochemistry, biology, business management (financial, quantitative, managerial relations), chemical physics, chemistry, computer science, drama, economics, education (early childhood, elementary, music), English, French, German, Greek, history, Latin, mathematics, medical technology, medieval studies, music, oceanography, philosophy, physics, politics, psychology, religion, religious education, social work, sociology, Spanish; *master's, doctorate* in various fields.

Distinctive Educational Programs: Undergraduate honors program. Accelerated baccalaureate-master's program in various fields. 6-year joint baccalaureate-first-professional with School of Law. Joint J.D.-M.A. (in accounting, economics, history, politics, psychology) with School of Law. Joint M.A.-master's in library science program with School of Library Science. Joint M.A.-Ph.D. in psychology and theology with School of Religious Studies. Interdisciplinary master's program in international political economy. Study abroad in England and Spain.

School of Architecture and Planning

Degree Programs Offered: *Baccalaureate* in architecture; *first-professional* in architecture, *master's* in architecture and architectural studies.

Admission: *For first-professional degree:* Baccalaureate in architecture, 2.5 minimum GPA, portfolio.

Degree Requirements: Undergraduate program consists of 137 semester credit hours; minimum GPA of 2.0 after student's first two years of study and C average in design are required for advancement to the Third-Year Design Studio. Minimum 2.0 GPA in all courses is required for graduation. First-professional program consists of 34 semester credit hours and a minimum 3.0 GPA in all courses.

Distinctive Educational Programs: Dual degree program (Bachelor of Science in Architecture and Bachelor of Civil Engineering).

School of Engineering

Degree Programs Offered: *Baccalaureate* in civil, electrical, mechanical engineering, engineering management; *master's, doctorate* in various engineering fields.

Benjamin T. Rome School of Music

Degree Programs Offered: *Baccalaureate* in general choral and combined general choral and instrumental music education, composition, orchestral instruments, organ, piano, voice, musical theater; *master's, doctorate* in music history, music theory, liturgical music, composition, music education, performance (orchestral instruments, organ, piano and piano pedagogy, voice and vocal pedagogy). *Master's* programs are also offered in music librarianship (M.A. and M.S. in L.S.), accompanying and chamber music, instrumental conducting, choral conducting, music education with emphasis on the Kodaly Method.

School of Library and Information Science

Degree Programs Offered: *Master's.* Post-master's certificates also given.

Distinctive Educational Programs: Joint first-professional-master's in library and information science with Schools of Law, Music, and Arts and Sciences. Cooperative graduate program in American civilization and library science with George Washington University. Master's and certificate programs in biomedical information services in affiliation with Georgetown University Medical Center. Information Transfer Lab for use in searching and constructing databases. *See* School of Arts and Sciences.

National Catholic School of Social Service

Degree Programs Offered: *Baccalaureate* in social work; *master's, doctorate* in various fields. Certificate in family therapy also given.

Distinctive Educational Programs: Extended program permits part-time study. Field practicum for all students. 5-year B.A.-M.S.W. program.

School of Nursing

Degree Programs Offered: *Baccalaureate, master's, doctorate.*

School of Philosophy

Degree Programs Offered: *Baccalaureate, master's, doctorate.*

Columbus School of Law

Degree Programs Offered: *First-professional.*

Admission: Baccalaureate from accredited college or university, LSAT.

Degree Requirements: 84 credit hours; 70 GPA (on a scale of 100); 90 weeks in residence (full-time), 120 weeks in residence (part-time), original research paper.

Distinctive Educational Programs: Communications Law Institute; church-state relations; law and public policy, various joint degree programs listed under other schools of the university.

School of Religious Studies

Degree Programs Offered: *First-professional, master's, doctorate* in various fields. Licentiates also given.

Admission: *For first-professional degree:* Baccalaureate from an accredited college or university; 18 semester hours philosophy; GRE or Miller Analogies Test.

Degree Requirements: *For first-professional degree:* 90 semester hours, 2.75 GPA, 24 hours in residence.

Distinctive Educational Programs: Interdisciplinary master's program in liturgical studies.

Corcoran College of Art and Design

500 17th Street, N.W.

Washington, District of Columbia 20006-4804

Tel: (202) 639-1800   **E-mail:** admissions@corcoran.org

Fax: (202) 639-1802   **Internet:** www.corcoran.edu

Institution Description: Corcoran College of Art and Design (formerly named Corcoran School of Art) is a private, independent, nonprofit professional school of art. *Enrollment:* 450. *Degrees awarded:* Baccalaureate, master's. Certificate programs also offered.

Academic offerings subject to approval by District of Columbia licensing body.

Accreditation: *Regional:* MSA/CHE. *Professional:* art

History: Chartered 1867; established and offered first instruction at postsecondary level 1890; awarded first degree (baccalaureate) 1978. *See* Dorothy W. Phillips, *The Corcoran Gallery of Art*, 2 vols. (Washington: The Corcoran Gallery of Art, 1973) for further information.

Institutional Structure: *Governing board:* Trustees of the Corcoran Gallery of Art. Extrainstitutional representation: 30 trustees, including 4 chairmen ermiti and 10 sustaining trustees. Institutional representation: 5 administrators including the dean of the art school. 2 ex officio. Board of Overseers of the School: 28 overseers including 1 ex officio and 1 sustaining overseer. *Composition of institution:* Administrators 3 men / 10 women. Academic affairs headed by associate dean. Management/business/finances: directed by administrative officer. Full-time instructional faculty 44. Academic governance body, the Department Chairs' Council, meets an average of 10 times per year.

Calendar: Semesters. Academic year Sept. to May. Students admitted Sept., Jan. Degrees conferred and formal commencement Jan., May, Aug. Summer session June to July.

Characteristics of Freshmen: 64% of applicants admitted. 485 of admitted students enrolled full-time.

100% (52 students) submitted SAT scores; 12% (6 students) submitted ACT scores. *25th percentile:* SAT Verbal 490, SAT Math 450; ACT Composite 20, ACT English 15, ACT Math 17. *75th percentile:* SAT Verbal 510, SAT Math 560; ACT Composite 22, ACT English 26, ACT Math 25.

58% of entering freshmen expected to graduate within 5 years. 5% of freshmen from the District of Columbia. Freshmen from 16 states and 17 foreign countries.

Admission: Rolling admissions plan. For fall acceptance, apply as early as Sept. of previous year, and on a space available basis through he summer. Early acceptance available. *Requirements:* Either graduation from accredited secondary school with minimum 2.5 GPA or GED. Presentation of portfolio. Recommend college preparatory program with at least 4 units English, 4 art. *Entrance tests:* College Board SAT or ACT Composite; letters of recommendation from teachers or employers. *For transfer students:* 2.0 minimum GPA; maximum transfer credit limited only by residence requirement. Portfolio requirement.

Credit may be awarded for College Board AP examinations and International Baccalaureate higher level examinations.

Degree Requirements: Associate of Fine Arts requires completion of 66 required credits including 36 credits in residence; minimum 2.0 GPA. Bachelor of Fine Arts 126 semester hours; 2.0 GPA; 2 years, including last, in residence; portfolio requirement. Master of Fine Arts in the History of Decorative Arts 48 required credits including a minimum of 39 credits in residence; minimum 3.0 GPA; thesis. Master of Arts in Interior Design 60 required credits including 48 credits in residence; minimum 3.0 GPA; thesis. *Grading system:* A–F; withdraw (deadline after which pass-fail is appended to withdraw); incomplete (carries time limit).

Distinctive Educational Programs: Graphic design and photography internships. Individual majors. Visiting Artists Program. Open Program/Division of Continuing education courses for certificate and nondegree students. Semi-private studios for seniors. The Mobility Program of over 45 colleges and universities allows Corcoran students to pay regular tuition and fees to the Corcoran College of Art and Design and attend a participating host institution on a space-available basis. The college's Department of Continuing Education offers summer study abroad courses.

Degrees Conferred: 82 *baccalaureate:* visual and performing arts. 2 honorary Doctor of Fine Arts awarded 2003-04.

Fees and Other Expenses: *Full-time tuition per academic year 2004–05:* $22,700 undergraduate; Master of Arts in Decorative Arts $23,328; Master of Arts in Interior Design $21,264. *Required fees:* $100 student activities; $1,074 health insurance. *Room and board per academic year:* $10,050.

Financial Aid: Aid from institutionally generated funds is provided on the basis of academic merit, financial need. Institution has a Program Participation Agreement with the U.S. Department of Education for eligible students to receive Pell Grants and other federal aid.

Financial aid to full-time, first-time undergraduate students: need-based scholarships/grants totaling $516,442, self-help $1,174,976, tuition waivers $704,276; non-need-based scholarships/grants totaling $378,655, self-help $586,310, parent loans $1,308,027, tuition waivers $554,725.

Departments and Teaching Staff: *Professors 8, associate professors* 18, *assistant professors* 1, *part-time faculty* 151. *Total instructional faculty:* 178 (full-time 27, part-time 151; women 98, men 80). Total faculty with doctorate, first-professional, or other terminal degree: 67. Student-to-faculty ratio: 10:1. 1 faculty member awarded a sabbatical 2004–05.

Enrollment: Total enrollment 686. Undergraduate full-time 121 men / 213 women, part-time 89m / 218w; graduate full-time 1m / 2w, part-time 3m / 19w. *Transfer students:* in-state 65, out-of-state 151.

Characteristics of Student Body: *Ethnic/racial makeup:* number of Black non-Hispanic: 48; American Indian or Alaska Native: 1; Asian or Pacific Islander: 54; Hispanic: 39; White non-Hispanic: 405; unknown: 119. *Age distribution:* number under 18: 13; 18–19:98; 20–21: 117; 22–24: 101; 25–29: 74; 30–34: 61; 35–39: 40; 40–49: 78; 50–64 55; 65 and over: 6.

International Students: 58 nonresidents enrolled fall 2004. 19 students from Europe, 23 Asia, 14 Central and South America, 1 Canada, 1 Australia. Programs available to aid students whose native language is not English: Social. No financial aid specifically designated for international students.

Student Life: Corcoran-leased housing available. . *Special services:* Medical referrals, counseling services, job-bank, career services office, off-campus housing referrals, internships in related fields. Student gallery with the Corcoran Museum and college facilities. Student Council. *Surrounding community:* District of Columbia 2000 population 610,000. Served by METRO mass transit system; airport 10 miles from campus; passenger rail service 3 miles from campus.

Library Collections: 28,500 volumes. 150 current periodical subscriptions. Online catalog. 5 computer work stations. Students have access to the Internet at no charge. Total budget for books, periodicals, audiovisual materials, microforms 2004–05: $82,000.

Most important holding include 500 rare books dating from 18th century; 250 18th-century journals, other manuscripts; artists' book collection.

Buildings and Grounds: Campus area 1 square block. Additional studio/academic facilities in Georgetown near the intersection of 35th and S Streets.

Chief Executive Officer: Dr. Christina DePaul, Dean.

Address admission inquiries to Elizabeth Smith, Director of Admissions.

Dominican House of Studies

487 Michigan Avenue, N.E.

Washington, District of Columbia 20017

Tel: (202) 529-5300   **E-mail:** admissions@dhs.org

Fax: (202) 529-1700   **Internet:** www.dhs.org

Institution Description: Dominican House of Studies is a private institution affiliated with Dominican Fathers, Roman Catholic Church. *Enrollment:* 67. *Degrees awarded:* First-professional (master of divinity), licentiate.

Member of Washington Theological Consortium.

Accreditation: *Regional:* MSA/CHE. *Nonregional:* ATS. *Professional:* theology

History: Incorporated 1902; established and offered first instruction at postsecondary level 1905; first degree (first-professional) awarded 1906; became pontifical faculty 1941. *See* Reginald Coffey, *The American Dominicans* (New York: St. Martin de Porres Guild, 1970) for further information.

Institutional Structure: *Governing board:* Board of Directors. Extrainstitutional representation: 11 trustees; institutional representation: 2 administrators. 2 ex officio. All voting. *Composition of institution:* Administrators 6 men. Academic affairs headed by president/regent of studies. Management/business/finances directed by treasurer. Full-time instructional faculty 11. Academic governance body, Council of the Faculty, meets an average of 8 times per year.

Calendar: Semesters. Academic year Aug. to May. Entering students admitted Sept. Degrees conferred May. No summer session.

Admission: *Requirements:* For first-professional programs, baccalaureate degree in philosophy or sufficient credits in philosophy to prepare applicant for work in speculative theology. For older students, college credit for extrainstitutional learning (life experience) on basis of faculty assessment, personal interviews.

Degree Requirements: *For first-professional degree:* 110 credit hours; 2.5 GPA; 1 year in residence; chapel attendance 3 times per day; 3 years of prescribed courses in sacred doctrine; basic knowledge of biblical Greek; reading proficiency in scholastic Latin; exit competency examinations-oral comprehensives in individual fields of study. *Grading system:* A–F; withdraw (carries time limit).

Distinctive Educational Programs: Field training programs. Member of Cluster of Independent Theological Schools with De Sales Hall School of Theology (DC) and Oblate College. Evening classes. Tutorials. Study abroad in various countries, including Belgium, France, Germany, Italy, Peru. Master of Theology and Doctor of Ministry programs through the consortium. *Other distinctive programs:* Continuing education for alumni.

Degrees Conferred: 10 *master's:* theology 10; 2 *S.T.L.:* theology 2.

Fees and Other Expenses: *Full-time tuition per academic year:* Contact the institution for current tuition and fees.

Financial Aid: Financial assistance is available in the form of Veterans Administration Benefits, Stafford Loans.

Departments and Teaching Staff: Theology *professors* 3, *associate professors* 5, *assistant professors* 0, *instructors* 1, *part-time teachers* 2. *Total instructional faculty:* 17. Degrees held by full-time faculty: Doctorate 90%, master's 100%, baccalaureate 100%. 90% hold terminal degrees.

Enrollment: Total enrollment 67 (91% men, 9% women).

Characteristics of Student Body: *Ethnic/racial makeup:* Black non-Hispanic: 3%; Asian or Pacific Islander: 3%; Hispanic: 1.5%; White non-Hispanic: 79.1%.

International Students: 9 nonresident aliens enrolled fall 2003. No programs available to aid students whose native language is not English.

Student Life: On-campus residence halls for men only house 97% of student body. *Surrounding community:* Washington, D.C. population 650,000. Served by mass transit bus and subway system; airport 8 miles from campus; passenger rail service 2 miles from campus.

Library Collections: 75,000 volumes. 300 microform titles; 200 audiovisual materials; 320 current periodical subscriptions.

Most important holdings include collection of works by and about St. Thomas Aquinas; collection of Dominican history and works by modern Dominican authors; collection of Dominican works printed before 1800 and incunabula.

Buildings and Grounds: Campus area 8 acres.

Chief Executive Officer: Rev. Reginald Whitt, President.

Address admission inquiries to Veronica Wynnyk, Registrar.

Gallaudet University

800 Florida Avenue, N.E.
Washington, District of Columbia 20002
Tel: (202) 651-5750   **E-mail:** admission@gallaudet.edu
Fax: (202) 651-5744   **Internet:** www.gallaudet.edu

Institution Description: Gallaudet University is a private, independent, nonprofit college for the deaf that receives substantial federal support. *Enrollment:* 1,598. *Degrees awarded:* Associate, baccalaureate, master's, doctorate.

Member of Consortium of Universities of the Washington Metropolitan Area.

Accreditation: *Regional:* MSA/CHE. *Professional:* audiology, business, clinical psychology, counseling, recreation and leisure services, social work, speech-language pathology, teacher education

History: Established as Kendall School 1856; incorporated as Columbia Institution for the Instruction of the Deaf and Dumb and Blind 1857; offered first instruction at postsecondary level and changed name to National Deaf Mute College 1864; changed name to Columbia Institution for the Instruction of the Deaf and Dumb 1865; awarded first degree (baccalaureate) 1869; became Gallaudet College 1954; renamed Gallaudet University 1986.

Institutional Structure: *Governing board:* The Gallaudet University Board of Trustees. Extrainstitutional representation: 12 trustees, President of the U.S., 1 U.S. senator, 2 U.S. representatives; institutional representation: president of the college; 4 alumni. 5 ex officio. All voting. *Composition of institution:* Administrators 12 men / 3 women. Academic affairs headed by provost. Management/business/finances directed by vice president for business affairs. Full-time instructional faculty 267. Academic governance body, The Collegiate Faculty, meets an average of 12 times per year.

Calendar: Semesters. Academic year Sept. to May. Freshmen admitted Aug., Jan. Degrees conferred May, July, Dec. Formal commencement May. Summer session from May to July.

Characteristics of Freshmen: 423 applicants (212 men, 211 women). 75.9% of applicants admitted; 71.6% of admitted students enrolled full-time.

15% (33 students) submitted SAT scores; 85% (192 students) submitted ACT scores. *25th percentile:* ACT Composite 14, ACT English 11, ACT Math 15. *75th percentile:* ACT Composite 18, ACT English 17, ACT Math 18.

Admission: Rolling admissions plan. For fall acceptance, apply no later than Jan. 1. Students are notified of acceptance Apr. Apply by Oct. for early decision; need not limit application to Gallaudet. Early acceptance available. *Requirements:* Recommend college preparatory academic units in English, mathematics (geometry and algebra), physical education, science. Students without these courses may be accepted on completion of a preparatory year at Gallaudet; GED accepted. Require specific health information, including an audiogram. *Entrance tests:* Institutional examination; College Board SAT or ACT composite may be accepted for some students. *For transfer students:* Good standing at previous institution; maximum transfer credit limited by residence requirement.

Tutoring available. Noncredit remedial courses offered in summer session and regular academic year.

Degree Requirements: *For all baccalaureate degrees:* 124 credit hours; 2.0 GPA; 2 semesters in residence; 4 hours of physical education courses; general education requirements. Fulfillment of some baccalaureate degree requirements possible by passing College Board CLEP. *Grading system:* A–F; withdraw (carries time limit).

Distinctive Educational Programs: *For undergraduates:* Special facilities for using telecommunications in the classroom. Interdisciplinary programs in American studies, international studies. Facilities and programs for independent research, including honors programs, tutorials. Study abroad in England, France, Germany, and Spain. Exchange programs with Oberlin College (OH), Western Maryland College. *Available to all students:* Work-experience programs, including cooperative education and internships. Evening classes. Individual majors. Cross-registration through the consortium. *Other distinctive programs:* Associate degree-granting program in interpreting for the deaf for secondary school graduates with one year work experience and well-developed sign-language vocabulary. Associate in Applied Science degree in Office Systems Management offered through School of Preparatory Studies. Kendall Demonstration Elementary School offering 12-month, tuition-free academic, diagnostic, medical and social service program for deaf children, from infancy to 15 years. Model Secondary School for the Deaf prepares students for college, other advanced study, or employment. Division of Public Service offers continuing education, training in physical disabilities to professionals, curriculum development and research, sign language programs. International Center on Deafness. Division of Research specializing in problems of deafness.

Degrees Conferred: 158 *baccalaureate;* 121 *master's;* 9 *doctorate.* Bachelor's degrees awarded in top five disciplines: business, management, marketing, and related support services 20; psychology 17; visual and performing arts 16; family and consumer sciences/human sciences 16; education 14.

Financial Aid: Aid from institutionally generated funds is provided on the basis of academic merit, financial need. Institution has a Program Participation Agreement with the U.S. Department of Education for eligible students to receive Pell Grants and other federal aid.

Financial aid to full-time, first-time undergraduate students: 34% received federal grants averaging $2,510; 62% state/local grants averaging $7,872; 68% institutional grants averaging $4,890; 26% loans averaging $4,657.

Departments and Teaching Staff: *Total instructional faculty:* 267. *Total tenured faculty:* 170. *Student-to-faculty ratio:* 7:1.

Enrollment: Total enrollment 1,598. Undergraduate 1,193 (46.6% men, 53.4% women).

Characteristics of Student Body: *Ethnic/racial makeup:* Black non-Hispanic: 10.8%; American Indian or Alaska Native: 1.8%; Asian or Pacific Islander 5.1%; Hispanic: 7.1%; White non-Hispanic: 61.2%; unknown: 3%.

International Students: 131 nonresident aliens enrolled fall 2004. Programs available to aid students whose native language is not English: English as a Second Language program. No financial aid specifically designated for international students.

Student Life: On-campus residence halls for both men and women house 60% of student body. *Intercollegiate athletics:* men only: baseball, basketball, football, soccer, tennis, track, volleyball; women only, basketball, field hockey, softball, tennis, track, volleyball. *Special regulations:* Registered, insured cars permitted for all but preparatory students. *Special services:* Learning Resources Center, medical services, shuttle bus to city transportation stops. *Student publications: Buff and Blue,* a biweekly newspaper; *Manus,* a biannual literary publication; *The Tower Clock,* a yearbook. *Surrounding community:* Washington, D.C. metropolitan area population over 3 million. Served by mass transit bus, subway, airline, and rail systems.

Library Collections: 215,500 volumes. 375,880 microforms; 4,500 audiovisual materials; 1,415 current periodical subscriptions. Access to online information retrieval systems.

Most important holdings include special collection on deafness covering a period from 1546 to present, including journals, pamphlets, books, photo, manuscripts and other archival material; *Gallaudet Encyclopedia of Deaf People and Deafness.*

Buildings and Grounds: Campus area 99 acres.

Chief Executive Officer: Dr. Irving King Jordan, President.

Address admission inquiries to Charity Reedy-Hines, Director of Admissions.

George Washington University

2121 I Street, N.W.

Washington, District of Columbia 20052

Tel: (202) 994-1000   **E-mail:** gwadm@gwu.edu

Fax: (202) 994-0325   **Internet:** www.gwu.edu

Institution Description: George Washington University is a private, independent, nonprofit institution. *Enrollment:* 23,417. *Degrees awarded:* Associate, baccalaureate, first-professional (law, medicine), master's, doctorate. Certificates also awarded.

Member of the Consortium of Universities of the Washington Metropolitan Area.

Accreditation: *Regional:* MSA/CHE. *Professional:* accounting, athletic training, business, clinical psychology, computer science, counseling, diagnostic medical sonography, engineering, health services administration, interior design, law, medicine, music, physical therapy, physician assisting, psychology internship, public administration, public health, radiation therapy, rehabilitation counseling, speech-language pathology, teacher education

History: Established and chartered as The Columbian College in the District of Columbia and offered first instruction at postsecondary level 1821; awarded first degree (baccalaureate) 1824; changed name to Columbian University 1873; adopted present name 1904; opened Virginia campus in Loudoun County in 1991. *See* Elmer Louis Kayser, *Bricks Without Straw* (New York: Appleton-Century-Crofts, 1970) for further information.

Institutional Structure: *Governing board:* Board of Trustees of The George Washington University. Extrainstitutional representation: 39 trustees; institutional representation: 8 alumni. 1 ex officio. 39 voting. *Composition of institution:* administrators 76 men / 60 women. Full-time instructional faculty 960 men / 468 women.

Calendar: Semesters. Academic year Aug. to May. Freshmen admitted Aug., Jan., May, June, July. Degrees conferred May, Sept., Feb. Formal commencement May. Summer session from May to Aug.

Characteristics of Freshmen: 18,442 applicants (7,753 men, 10,689 women). 38.5% of applicants admitted; 31.8% of admitted students enrolled full-time.

95% (2,148 students) submitted SAT scores; 19% (434 students) submitted ACT scores. *25th percentile:* SAT I Verbal 590, SAT I Math 590; ACT Composite 25. *75th percentile:* SAT I Verbal 690, SAT I Math 680; ACT Composite 29.

68% of entering freshmen expected to graduate within 5 years. 5% of freshmen from District of Columbia. Freshmen from 48 states and 35 foreign countries.

Admission: Priority filing date for fall is Feb. 1. Deadline for early decision Dec. 1. *Requirements:* graduation from an accredited secondary school. *Entrance tests:* College Board SAT and ACT required. SAT recommended. An essay is required. For foreign students, TOEFL is required (minimum score 550). *For transfer students:* from 4- and 2-year accredited institutions maximum transfer credit varies by school.

Degree Requirements: Consult the *Undergraduate Programs Bulletin* for current degree requirements. Fulfillment of some degree requirements and exemption from some beginning courses possible by passing departmental examinations, College Board CLEP, other standardized tests. *Grading system:* A–F; pass-fail; withdraw (carries time limit).

Distinctive Educational Programs: Internships, cooperative education and other work-experience programs for undergraduates and graduate students. Interdisciplinary majors in such areas as political communications, environmental studies and human studies. Doctoral program in policy studies. Formal interschool study: Secondary Fields of Study program allows students in one school to apply for a program in another school. Living-learning residence hall programs. Off-campus programs/courses offered throughout the Washington metropolitan area, including Tri-County Center (MD), and Tidewater (VA). Study abroad includes Academic Year Student Exchange Programs with the Universities of East Anglia, Essex, Lancaster, and Manchester in England, and with the Universidad Catolica del Peru in Peru. Spring Semester Programs with the Institut d'Etudes Francaises and the University of Poitiers in La Rochelle, France. *Other distinctive programs:* Courses in political psychology; Honors Program; Cooperative Education Program; Center for History in the Media; Semester Abroad Programs: Argentina, Australia, Bahamas, Belgium, Brazil, China, Chile, Costa Rica, Czech Republic, England, France, Germany, Hungary, India, Israel, Japan, Korea, Mexico, Morocco, The Netherlands, Spain, Thailand, Taiwan.

ROTC: George Washington University Naval ROTC program is available to students in the Consortium of Washington Area Universities.

Degrees Conferred: 135 *associate;* 1,993 *baccalaureate;* 3,196 *master's;* 252 *doctorate;* 623 *first-professional;* 234 *post-baccalaureate certificates;* 88 *post-master's certificates.* Bachelor's degrees awarded in top five disciplines: social sciences 583; business, management, marketing, and related support services355; psychology 155; English language and literature/letters 143; communication, journalism, and related programs 84.

Fees and Other Expenses: *Full-time tuition per academic year 2004–05:* undergraduate $34,030; contact the university for current graduate tuition and fees. Professional school tuition/fees vary. *Other expenses:* $1,030. *Room and board per academic year:* $10,210.

Financial Aid: Aid from institutionally generated funds is provided on the basis of academic merit, financial need, athletic ability, other criteria. Institution has a Program Participation Agreement with the U.S. Department of Education for eligible students to receive Pell Grants and other federal aid.

Financial aid to full-time, first-time undergraduate students: 11% received federal grants averaging $4,139; 3% state/local grants averaging $713; 60% institutional grants averaging $15,413; 43% loans averaging $6,309.

Departments and Teaching Staff: *Professors* 519, *associate professors* 367, *assistant professors* 358, *instructors* 20, *part-time teachers* 1,396. *Total instructional faculty:* 2,660. Total tenured faculty: 666. Student-to-faculty ratio: 11:1. Degrees held by full-time faculty: Doctorate 56%, master's 8%, baccalaureate 1%, professional 36%. 93% hold terminal degrees.

Enrollment: Total enrollment 23,417. Undergraduate 10,436 (43% men, 57% women).

Characteristics of Student Body: *Ethnic/racial makeup:* Black non-Hispanic: 5.7%; American Indian or Alaska Native: .2%; Asian or Pacific Islander: 9.1%; Hispanic: 4.5%; White non-Hispanic: 63.4%; unknown: 12.5%.

International Students: 480 undergraduate nonresident aliens enrolled fall 2003. Students from Europe, Asia, Central and South America, Africa, Canada, Australia, New Zealand. Programs available to aid students whose native language is not English: Social, cultural. English as a Second Language Program. Some financial aid available for international students.

Student Life: On-campus residence halls available only to full-time undergraduates, 54% of whom live in them. Several residence halls are on-campus institutionally-owned apartments. 18% of undergraduate men join fraternities and 12% of undergraduate women join sororities. *Intercollegiate athletics:* men only: baseball, basketball, crew, cross country golf, soccer, swimming, tennis, water polo; women only: basketball, crew, cross-country, gymnastics, soccer, swimming, tennis, volleyball. *Special regulations:* Cars with decals permitted in designated areas; fee charged. *Special services:* Medical services; Multicultural Student Services; Counseling Center; Career and Cooperative Education Center. *Student publications, radio:* Advocate, a monthly Law School newspaper; *Cherry Tree,* a yearbook; *The George Washington Law Review,* published 5 times per year; *GW Review,* a quarterly literary magazine; *Hatchet,* a biweekly newspaper; *Wooden Teeth,* a biannual literary magazine. Radio Station WRGW broadcasts 88 hours per week. *Surrounding community:* Washington, D.C. metropolitan area population over 3 million. Served by mass transit bus, subway system, airlines, passenger rail service.

Publications: *American Studies International* (quarterly) first published 1975, *GW Forum* 1969, semiannually; *GW Washington Studies* (published intermittently) first published 1974; *Law Review* (1931, published 5 times per year); *ASHE-ERIC Higher Education Reports* (1972, published 8 times per year); *George Washington University Magazine* (1990, quarterly); *By George* (1989, published 8 times per year).

Library Collections: 2,105,000 volumes. 2,771,000 microforms; 207,000 audiovisual materials; 1,100 periodical subscriptions. Online catalog. Access to online information retrieval systems and the Internet.

Most important holdings include papers of former GWU President (when GWU was Columbian College - 1800s); Washingtoniana Research Collections; Greater Washington Board of Trade Records; Freeman Watts Neurosurgery Collection; Edward Kiev Judaica Collection; Charles Suddath Kelly Photographic and Postcards Collection.

Buildings and Grounds: Campus area 40 acres.

Chief Executive Officer: Dr. Stephen J. Trachtenberg, President.

Address undergraduate admission inquiries to Dr. Kathryn M. Napper, Director of Admissions; graduate inquiries to Kristin Williams, Graduate Student Enrollment Management.

Columbian School of Arts and Sciences

Degree Programs Offered: *Baccalaureate* in American civilization, anthropology, applied mathematics, archaeology, art history, biology, chemistry, Chinese language and literature, classical humanities, communication, criminal justice, dance, dramatic literature, economics, East Asian languages and literatures, electronic media, English literature, fine arts, French language and literature, geography, geology, Germanic languages and literature, history, journalism, liberal arts, mathematics, music, philosophy, physics, political science, psychology, radio-television, religion, Russian language and literature, sociology, Spanish-American literature, speech communication, speech and hearing science, statistics, theater. *Master's* in administrative sciences; American civilization, American literature, fine art (ceramics, design, painting, photography, printmaking, sculpture, visual communication), art history, chemical toxicology, clinical microbiology, criminal justice and crime in commerce, English literature, environmental and resource policy, environmental science, immunology, interior design, legislative affairs, museum studies, music, neuroscience, philosophy and social policy, psychology, religion, security management, telecommunications policy, theatre, women's studies, anthropology, economics, history, political science, sociology, applied mathematics, applied statistics, chemistry, forensic sciences, geochemistry, geology, mathematical statistics, mathematics, physics, art therapy, biochemistry, biological sciences, genetics, microbiology, pharmacology, speech-language pathology; *doctorate* in various fields.

Distinctive Educational Programs: Accelerated degree program. Honors program. Joint B.A./M.D., M.D./Ph.D. Interdisciplinary programs available. Cooperative education programs. Secondary concentration with other schools.

Graduate School of Education and Human Development

Degree Programs Offered: *Master's* in counseling (community, employee assistance, rehabilitation, school), curriculum and instruction, education policy studies, education technology leadership, educational leadership and administration, elementary education, human resource development, international education, museum education, secondary education, special education. *Specialist* in educational administration, counseling, curriculum and instruction, higher education administration, human resource development, special education. *Doctorate* in counseling, curriculum and instruction, educational administration and policy studies, higher education administration, human resource development, special education.

School of Engineering and Applied Science

Degree Programs Offered: *Baccalaureate* in civil engineering; computer engineering, computer science, electrical engineering, mechanical engineering, systems engineering; *master's, professional, doctorate* in civil and environmental engineering, computer science, electrical engineering, mechanical and aerospace engineering, systems engineering, telecommunications and computers, engineering management, operations research.

Distinctive Educational Programs: Five-year baccalaureate/master's programs. 3:2 dual-degree programs in engineering with Bowie State College (MD), Gallaudet College (DC), Hood College (MD), St. Joseph's College (CT), St. Thomas Aquinas College, Trinity College of Washington (DC), Wheaton College (MA), and American International University (London, U.K.)

School of Business and Public Management

Degree Programs Offered: *Baccalaureate* in accountancy, business administration; *master's* in accountancy, acquisition management, business administration, public administration, finance, information systems technology, project management, public policy, tourism administration; *doctorate* in accountancy, business administration, health services administration, information and decision systems, management and organization, public administration.

Distinctive Educational Programs: Individualized fields of concentration; secondary fields of study, five year programs; accelerated degree programs; post-MBA certificate program.

Elliott School of International Affairs

Degree Programs Offered: *Baccalaureate* in international affairs, Asian studies, Latin American studies, Middle Eastern studies; *master's* in Asian studies, international affairs; international development studies, international trade and investment policy, Latin American studies; European studies; Russian and East European studies, security policy studies; science, technology, and public policy.

Distinctive Educational Programs: Joint M.A./J.D. program, M.A./M.B.A. program. Graduate certificates in Regional Studies. Institute for European, Russian and Eurasian Studies, Center for International Science and Technology Policy, Gaston Sigur Center for East Asian Studies.

George Washington University Law School

Degree Programs Offered: *First-professional* in law; *master's* in environmental law; government procurement law; international and comparative law;

intellectual property law, litigation and dispute resolution; *doctorate* in various fields.

Admission: *For first-professional degree:* Baccalaureate or equivalent, satisfactory quality of work, acceptable distribution of courses, LSAT.

Degree Requirements: *For first-professional degree:* 84 credit hours, 65 average on 0-100 scale, 56 hours in residence.

Distinctive Educational Programs: Joint first-professional-master's programs in various fields, including business administration, public health, public administration, international affairs.

School of Medicine and Health Sciences

Degree Programs Offered: *Baccalaureate* in clinical laboratory science, emergency medical services, physical therapy, radiologic sciences, sonography; *master's* in physician assistant program; *first-professional* in medicine.

Admission: *For first-professional degree:* 90 semester hours from accredited institution which must include 8 biology, 8 inorganic chemistry, 8 organic chemistry, 8 physics, 6 English composition and literature.

Degree Requirements: *For first-professional degree:* 4 years in residence, 2 year continuum of clerkships (in medicine, surgery, pediatrics, obstetrics-gynecology, psychiatry, and health care science) and elective sequences; 4 week acting internship in medicine, pediatrics, or family medicine; 2 week clerkships in anesthesia, emergency medicine, and a nonclinical (didactic) course. Students choose from options in orthopedics, urology, ophthalmology, pediatric surgery, or otolaryngology. All students must take a clinical course in neurosurgery or neurology.

Distinctive Educational Programs: Joint B.A./M.D.; integrated engineering and M.D. program; joint M.D./Ph.D., joint M.D./M.P.H., joint M.S. in Health Sciences/M.P.H.

School of Public Health and Health Sciences

Degree Programs Offered: *Baccalaureate* in exercise science; *master's* in public health, epidemiology and biostatistics, health services administration, exercise science; *doctorate* in public health, epidemiology and biostatistics.

Distinctive Educational Programs: Joint M.D./M.P.H.; Joint J.D./M.P.H., Master's Internationalist Program in Peace Corps.

Georgetown University

37th and O Street, N.W.
Washington, District of Columbia 20057
Tel: (202) 994-6040   **E-mail:** admissions@georgetown.edu
Fax: (202) 994-0325   **Internet:** www.georgetown.edu

Institution Description: Georgetown University is a private institution affiliated with the Society of Jesus, Roman Catholic Church. Open to students of all faiths. *Enrollment:* 11,730. *Degrees awarded:* Baccalaureate, first-professional (law, medicine), master's, doctorate.

Member of Consortium of Universities of the Washington Metropolitan Area.

Accreditation: *Regional:* MSA/CHE. *Professional:* business, clinical pastoral education, English language education, law, medicine, nurse anesthesia education, nursing-midwifery, nursing, nursing education, ophthalmic medical technology, psychology internship

History: Established as Georgetown College and offered first instruction at postsecondary level 1797; chartered as Georgetown University 1815; awarded first degree 1818; incorporated 1944. *See* John M. Daley, S.J., *Georgetown University: Origin and Early Years* (Washington, DC: Georgetown University Press, 1957); Joseph T. Durkin, S.J., *Georgetown University: The Middle Years 1840–1900* (Washington, DC: Georgetown University Press, 1963) for further information.

Institutional Structure: *Governing board:* The President and Directors of Georgetown College. Extrainstitutional representation: 39 directors; institutional representation: president of the university. 3 ex officio. All voting. *Composition of institution:* Administrators 10 men / 3 women. Academic affairs headed by three vice presidents. Management/business/finances directed by senior vice president. Academic governance body, The Georgetown University Faculty Senate, meets an average of 4 times per year.

Calendar: Semesters. Academic year Sept. to May. Freshmen admitted Sept. Degrees conferred Aug., May, Dec. Formal commencement May. 5 summer sessions of varying lengths offered, May through Aug.

Characteristics of Freshmen: 21.9% of applicants admitted. 47.3% of admitted students enrolled full-time.

83% (1,275 students) submitted SAT scores; 22% (336 students) submitted ACT scores. *25th percentile:* SAT Verbal 640, SAT Math 640; ACT Composite

23, ACT English 28, ACT Math 27. *75th percentile*: SAT Verbal 740, SAT Math 730; ACT Composite 32, ACT English 33, ACT Math 31.

92.5% of entering freshmen expected to graduate within 5 years. 1% of freshmen from District of Columbia. Freshmen from 49 states and 27 foreign countries.

Admission: For fall acceptance, apply as early as Sept. of previous year, but not later than Jan. 10 of year of enrollment. Students are notified of acceptance by May 1. Georgetown does not require that other applications be withdrawn upon early decision acceptance at Georgetown. Early decision candidates have the same acceptance deadline as regular admission candidates. *Requirements:* Graduation from accredited secondary school. Recommend 4 units English, 2 in a foreign language, 2 mathematics, 2 social studies, 1 science. For mathematics and science majors, 4 units mathematics and 3 lab sciences; for nursing students, 3 mathematics, 2-3 science (including biology and chemistry); for business students, 3 mathematics. Additional units in advanced placement and honors courses recommended. *Entrance tests:* College Board SAT or ACT Composite. For foreign students TOEFL.

For transfer students: 3.0 minimum GPA recommended. College credit and advanced placement for postsecondary-level work completed in secondary school. Tutoring available. Noncredit developmental courses offered in summer session.

Degree Requirements: 120–133 credit hours; 2.0 GPA; 4 semesters in residence; general education or core requirements. Additional requirements vary according to program. Fulfillment of some degree requirements and exemption from some beginning courses possible by passing College Board AP. *Grading system:* A–F, pass-fail, withdraw (carries time limit).

Distinctive Educational Programs: Internships. Evening classes. Special facilities for using telecommunications in the classroom. Independent study. Study abroad in various countries, including Argentina, Australia, Austria, Belgium, Brazil, China, Czech Republic, Ecuador, Egypt, England, France, Germany, Ghana, Hungary, Indonesia, Ireland, Israel, Japan, Korea, Morocco, The Netherlands, New Zealand, Niger, Poland, Portugal, Russia, Scotland, Senegal, Spain, Switzerland, Thailand, Turkey, and by individual arrangement. Cross-registration through consortium. *Other distinctive programs:* Continuing education division offers baccalaureate and master's degree programs in liberal studies primarily for older students; courses for credit and enrichment also offered. Research institutes, including th Center for Muslim-Christian Understanding and the Center for Social Justice research, Teaching, and Service.

ROTC: Army. Air Force offered in cooperation with Howard University; Navy offered in cooperation with George Washington University. 25 commissions awarded 2004.

Degrees Conferred: 1,670 *baccalaureate* (B), 1,557 *master's* (M), 71 *doctorate* (D): area and ethnic studies 22 (B), 84 (M); biological/life sciences 59 (B), 173 (M), 12 (D); business/marketing 344 (B), 310 (M); computer and information sciences 11 (B); education 7 (M); English 147 (B); 25 (M); foreign languages and literature 120 (B), 19 (M); 18 (M); health professions and related sciences 110 (B), 53 (M); interdisciplinary studies 36 (B), 69 (M), 7 (D); law/legal studies 368 (M); liberal arts/general studies 22 (B), 61 (M); mathematics 18 (B); philosophy/religion/theology 22 (B), 5 (M), 4 (D); physical sciences 13 (B), 2 (M), 4 (D); protective services/public administration 125 (M); psychology 119 (B), 1 (D); social sciences and history 606 (B), 255 (M); 25 (D); visual and performing arts 21 (B). 863 *first-professional:* law 607, medicine 176. *Honorary degrees awarded 2003–04:* Doctor of Humane Letters 4, Doctor of Laws 1, Doctor of Science 2.

Fees and Other Expenses: *Full-time tuition per academic year 2004–05:* undergraduate $29,805, graduate $27,528. *Required fees:* $355. *Room and board per academic year:* $10,564.

Financial Aid: Aid from institutionally generated funds is provided on the basis of financial need, athletic ability. Institution has a Program Participation Agreement with the U.S. Department of Education for eligible students to receive Pell Grants and other federal aid.

Financial aid to full-time, first-time undergraduate students: need-based scholarships/grants totaling $45,702,000, self-help $17,000,000, tuition waivers $800,000, athletic awards $1,200,000; non-need-based scholarships/grants totaling $2,200,000, self-help $9,900,000, parent loans $15,500,000, tuition waivers $2,500,000, athletic awards $2,500,000. *Graduate aid:* 200 students received federal and state-funded scholarships and grants totaling $1,826,575 (ranging from $430 to $28,650); 1,380 federal and state-funded loans totaling $24,000,000 (ranging from $40 to $24,650); 20 students had work-study jobs yielding $50,000 (ranging from $80 to $13,315).

Departments and Teaching Staff: *Total instructional faculty:* 1,058 (full-time 697, part-time 361; women 398, men 660; members of minority groups 145). Total faculty with doctorate, first-professional, or other terminal degree: 850. Student-to-faculty ratio: 11:1. *Faculty development:* $28,485,520 in grants for research.

Enrollment: Total enrollment 11,730. Undergraduate full-time 2,906 men / 3,408 women, part-time 82m / 126w; graduate full-time 1,555m / 1,539w, part-time 387m / 556w; first-professional full-time 1,338m / 1,224m, part-time 62m / 50w. 2,797 men / 3,288 women. *Transfer students:* 86 m/ 95w.

Characteristics of Student Body: *Ethnic and racial makeup:* number of Black non-Hispanic: 424; American Indian or Alaska Native: 4; Asian or Pacific Islander: 612; Hispanic: 360; White non-Hispanic: 4,375; unknown: 344. *Age distribution:* number under 18: 148; 18–19: 2,903; 20–21: 2,708; 22–24: 402; 25–29: 89; 30–34: 31; 35–39: 14; 40–49: 11; 50–64: 8; 65 and over: 2.

International Students: 1,416 nonresident aliens enrolled fall 2004. 325 students from Europe, 680 Asia, 238 Central and South America, 58 Africa, 67 Canada, 21 Australia, 3 New Zealand, 24 other. Programs available to aid students whose native language is not English: Social. English as a Second Language Program. Financial aid specifically designated for international students: 20 scholarships available annually for undergraduates; 20 totaling $605,814 000 awarded 2004–05; 5 graduate scholarships available annually; 5 totaling $196,554 awarded 2004–05.

Student Life: On-campus residence halls townhouses, and apartments house 78% of undergraduate student body. 3% of student body live off campus in university-owned apartments. *Intercollegiate athletics:* men only: baseball, basketball, crew, cross-country, football, golf, lacrosse, soccer, swimming, tennis, track; women only: basketball, crew, field hockey, lacrosse, swimming, tennis, track, cross-country, volleyball; both sexes: sailing. *Special regulations:* Cars permitted for commuting students. Quiet hours. Residence hall visitation hours determined by residents of each corridor. *Special services:* Disability and Academic Support Services, medical services, university bus transportation to local areas surrounding campus. *Student publications:* Hoya, a twice weekly newspaper; *The Georgetown Journal*, an art and literary magazine published 3 times yearly; *Voice,* a weekly newspaper; *Ye Domesday Booke,* a yearbook; *Independent*bi-weekly news publications. *Surrounding community:* Washington, D.C. population 575,000. Served by mass transit bus, subway system; airport 7 miles from campus; passenger rail service 3 miles from campus.

Publications: *Publisher:* Georgetown University Press.

Library Collections: 2,407,125 volumes. Online catalog. 29,175 current serial subscriptions (paper, microform, electronic); 54,827 recordings, compact discs, audio/videos. 412 400 computer work stations. Students have access to the Internet and online information retrieval services.

Most important holdings include Bowen Collection on Intelligence, Covert Activities, and Espionage; John Gimlary Shea Collection (American History); Graham Greene Papers.

Buildings and Grounds: Campus area 104 acres. *New buildings:* Southwest Quadrangle (residence hall) completed fall 20003; Leo O'Donavan Hall (cafeteria) 2003; Washington Hall (Jesuit Residence) 2003; Performing Arts Center 2005.

Chief Executive Officer: Dr. John J.DeGioria, President.

Address undergraduates address admission inquiries to Charles A. Deacon, Dean of Undergraduate Admissions; Graduate School of Arts and Sciences inquiries to Jennifer Hunt; Law School inquiries to Sophia Sim; School of Medicine inquiries to Eugene T. Ford.

Edmund A. Walsh School of Foreign Service

Degree Programs Offered: *Baccalaureate* in international relations with majors in international economics, international political economy, international history, international politics, regional and comparative studies, culture and politics, science and technology in international affairs. Certificate programs offering regional specializations or a focus on international business diplomacy or justice and peace studies. Five-year BSFS/master's program.

Degree Requirements: Language proficiency examination required for graduation.

Distinctive Educational Programs: Externships. Honors program on Power and Justice in the International System. Institutes and programs for research, publication, and teaching of major international issues, including African Studies Program, Asian Studies Program, Center for Contemporary Arab Studies, Center for Excellence in German and European Studies, Institute for the Study of Diplomacy, Landegger Program in International Business Diplomacy, Latin American Studies Program, Program in German Public and International Affairs, Russian Area Studies Program.

Georgetown College

Degree Programs Offered: *Baccalaureate* in American studies, anthropology, biochemistry, biology, chemistry, Chinese, classics, comparative literature, computer science, economics, English, French, German, government, history, interdisciplinary studies, Italian, Japanese, linguistics, mathematics, medieval studies, philosophy, physics, political economy, Portuguese, psychology, Russian, sociology, Spanish, theology.

Degree Requirements: 120 semester hours and 38 to 40 semester curses; complete general education requirements; field of concentration, GPA 2.0 or better; language and linguistics majors much achieve at least a 2.5 overall in the major; language majors must participate in an overseas study program.

Distinctive Educational Programs: Selective Liberal Arts Seminar (18 credits) fulfills requirements in literature, history, philosophy, and theology. Honors programs in economics, English, government, history. Fourth credit for social action when community service is shown to be complementary to specific course work. Major program in interdisciplinary studies available in junior and senior years if GPA is 3.3.

Graduate School of Arts and Sciences

Degree Programs Offered: *Master's* in Arab studies, bilingual education, biostatistics and epidemiology, business administration, demography, English, foreign service, German and European studies, Latin American studies, liberal studies, national security studies, nursing, public policy, radiation science, Russian area studies, teaching English as a second language; *doctorate* in anatomy and cell biology, biochemistry and molecular biology, economics, government, history, microbiology, pharmacology; *master's* and *doctorate* in Arabic, biochemistry and molecular biology, biology, economics, German, government, history, linguistics, microbiology and immunology, philosophy, physics, physiology and biophysics, Portuguese, Spanish, tumor biology.

McDonough School of Business

Degree Programs Offered: *Baccalaureate* in accounting, finance, international management, management, marketing. Master of Business Administration programs emphasize international/intercultural dimensions of the marketplace, ethical issues, public policy, and business-government relations, communication.

Distinctive Educational Programs: Individual majors.

School of Law

Degree Programs Offered: *First-professional;* also offered in cooperation with Graduate School: JD w/MSFS, J.D. w/MBA, JD w/Philosophy (either MA or PhD) and JD w/MPH offered with Johns Hopkins University. *Master's* in taxation, international and comparative law, labor law, securities regulation, advocacy, common law studies; *doctorate* in judicial science, comparative law.

Admission: *For first-professional degree:* Baccalaureate from accredited university or college. LSAT. Credentials must be assembled by LSDAS.

Degree Requirements: *For first-professional degree:* 83 credit hours, 5.0 GPA on 12.0 scale; 2 upper class writing projects required; 90 weeks in residence.

Distinctive Educational Programs: Joint J.D.-master's degree in foreign service in cooperation with the Graduate School. Legal clinics provide students with practical experience as well as community service.

School of Medicine

Degree Programs Offered: *First-professional.* MA/MD and PhD/MD in bioethics.

Admission: *For first-professional:* 90 semester hours from accredited college or university including 1 year English, 1 year each (including laboratory) biology, inorganic and organic chemistry, mathematics, physics, MCAT. Credentials must be assembled through AMCAS. Baccalaureate recommended.

Degree Requirements: *For first-professional:* Prescribed curriculum in first 2 years, clinical clerkships in 3rd and 4th years, passing grades in all subjects.

Distinctive Educational Programs: Joint M.D.-Ph.D. programs in anatomy, biochemistry, microbiology, pharmacology, physiology.

School of Nursing and Health Studies

Degree Programs Offered: *Baccalaureate* in health studies, nursing; *master's* in health systems administration, nursing.

Distinctive Educational Programs: Study abroad semester in a nursing program in a London hospital setting. A Georgetown faculty member accompanies the students.

Howard University

2400 Sixth Street, N.W.
Washington, District of Columbia 20059
Tel: (202) 806-6100   **E-mail:** admission@howard.edu
Fax: (202) 806-5467   **Internet:** www.howard.edu

Institution Description: Howard University is a private, independent, nonprofit institution. *Enrollment:* 10,658. *Degrees awarded:* Baccalaureate, first-professional (dentistry, law, medicine, theology), master's, doctorate.
Member of Consortium of Universities of the Washington Metropolitan Area.

Accreditation: *Regional:* MSA/CHE. *Professional:* accounting, art, audiology, business, clinical lab scientist, clinical psychology, computer science, dental hygiene, dentistry, dietetics, engineering, health services administration, journalism, law, medicine, music, nursing, occupational therapy, oral and maxillofacial surgery, pediatric dentistry, pharmacy, physical therapy, physician assisting, surgeon assisting, psychology internship, radiation therapy, radiation therapy technology, social work, speech-language pathology, teacher education, theatre

History: Established, chartered, and offered first instruction at postsecondary level 1867; awarded first degree (baccalaureate) 1872. *See* Rayford W. Logan, *Howard University: The First Hundred Years 1867–1967* (Wash., DC: Howard University Press, 1969) for further information.

Institutional Structure: *Governing board:* Howard University Board of Trustees. Extrainstitutional representation: 27 trustees; institutional representation: president of the university, 2 full-time instructional faculty members, 2 students; 2 alumni. 1 ex officio. All voting. *Composition of institution:* Administrators 133 men / 83 women. Academic affairs headed by vice president for academic affairs and vice president for health affairs. Management/business/finances directed by vice president for business and fiscal affairs, treasurer. Full-time instructional faculty 798 men / 371 women. Academic governance body, Council of the Senate, meets an average of 2 times per year.

Calendar: Semesters. Academic year Aug. to May. Freshmen admitted Aug., Jan., June. Degrees conferred and formal commencement May. Summer session from June to July.

Characteristics of Freshmen: 8,860 applicants (2,878 men, 5,982 women). 46.9% of applicants admitted; 34.7% of admitted students enrolled full-time.
56% (1,179 students) submitted SAT scores; 28% (550 students) submitted ACT scores. *25th percentile:* SAT I Verbal 430, SAT I Math 450; ACT Composite 18. *75th percentile:* SAT I Verbal 690, SAT I Math 680; ACT Composite 29.
11% of freshmen from the District of Columbia. Freshmen from 44 states and 52 foreign countries.

Admission: Rolling admissions plan. *Requirements:* Either graduation from accredited secondary school with 16 units, or GED. Additional requirements for some programs. Minimum GPA 2.0. *Entrance tests:* College Board SAT; Achievement tests for some programs. *For transfer students:* 2.0 minimum GPA; from 4-year accredited institution 90 hours maximum transfer credit; from 2-year accredited institution 60 hours. Additional requirements for some programs.
Advanced placement for postsecondary-level work completed in secondary school and for extrainstitutional learning on basis of ACE *2006 Guide to the Evaluation of Educational Experiences in the Armed Services,* portfolio and faculty assessments, personal interviews. Tutoring available. Developmental courses offered in summer session and regular academic year; credit given.

Degree Requirements: Maximum 127 semester hours; 2.0 GPA (2.5 for students in education and social work); last 30 hours in residence; 4 credit hours physical education courses; distribution requirements; comprehensives in all fields of study. Additional requirements for some programs. *Grading system:* A–F; pass-fail; withdraw. Honors-satisfactory-unsatisfactory for medical school only. 100–60 for law school only.

Distinctive Educational Programs: Special facilities for using telecommunications in the classroom. Facilities and programs for independent research, including honors programs; tutorials. Student exchange programs with Davidson College (NC), Denison University (OH), Duke University (NC), Fisk University (TN), Grinnell College (IA), Mills College (CA), Reed College (OR), Smith College (MA), Stanford University (CA), Swarthmore College (PA), University of Missouri, Vassar College (NY), Williams College (MA). Cross-registration through consortium. *Other distinctive programs:* Enrichment and credit programs offered through Continuing Education and Community Service Program Unit. Individualized baccalaureate programs emphasizing independent study offered through the University Without Walls.

ROTC: Army, Air Force.

Degrees Conferred: 1,342 *baccalaureate;* 378 *master's;* 99 *doctorate;* 415 *first-professional.* Bachelor's degrees awarded in top five disciplines: communication, journalism, and related programs 281; business, management, marketing, and related support services 252; health professions and related clinical sciences

172; biological and biomedical sciences 123; computer and information sciences and support services.

Fees and Other Expenses: *Full-time tuition per academic year 2004–05:* $11,645 undergraduate; graduate and professional schools tuition and fees have varying rates; contact the university for current information. *Books and supplies:* $1,020. *Room and board per academic year:* $5,870.

Financial Aid: Aid from institutionally generated funds is provided on the basis of academic merit, financial need, other criteria. Institution has a Program Participation Agreement with the U.S. Department of Education for eligible students to receive Pell Grants and other federal aid.

Financial aid to full-time, first-time undergraduate students: 29% received federal grants averaging $11,304; 3% state/local grants averaging $803; 4% institutional grants averaging $9,604; 48% loans averaging $2,493.

Departments and Teaching Staff: *Professors* 293, *associate professors* 357, *assistant professors* 327, *instructors* 118, *part-time teachers* 726. *Total instructional faculty:* 1,915 (includes lecturers and assistants). 77% of faculty members hold terminal degrees.

Enrollment: Total enrollment 10,658. Undergraduate 7,059 (32.6% men, 67.4% women).

Characteristics of Student Body: *Ethnic/racial makeup:* Black non-Hispanic: 68.7%; American Indian or Alaska Native: .1%; Asian or Pacific Islander: .6%; Hispanic: .5%; White non-Hispanic: .4%; unknown: 20.3%.

International Students: 1,003 nonresident aliens enrolled fall 2003. Programs available to aid students whose native language is not English: cultural; English as a Second Language Program. No financial aid specifically designated for international students.

Student Life: On-campus residences house 30% of student body. Facilities for men only constitute 38% of such space, for women only 61%, for both sexes 1%. *Intercollegiate athletics:* men only: baseball, basketball, football, soccer, swimming, tennis, track; women only: basketball, track, volleyball. *Special regulations:* Cars permitted without restrictions. *Special services:* Learning Resources Center, medical services, campus transportation system. *Student publications, radio, television: The Hilltop,* a weekly student newspaper. Radio station WHUR broadcasts 168 hours per week. TV station WHMM broadcasts 109 hours per week. *Surrounding community:* Served by mass transit bus and subway systems; airport 6 miles from campus; passenger rail service 2 miles from campus.

Library Collections: 2,200,000 volumes. 3,700,000 microforms, 6,600 manuscripts, 3,400,000 audiovisual materials; access to 26300 periodicals. Online catalog. Students have access to online information retrieval services and the Internet.

Most important holdings include Bernard Fall collection on Southeast Asia; Moorland-Springard Collection on black history and culture; Channing Pollock Theater Collection; Paul Robeson Papers, Ralph J. Bunche Oral History Collection.

Buildings and Grounds: Campus area 255 acres.

Chief Executive Officer: Dr. H. Patrick Swygert, President.

Address admission inquiries to Ann M. Waterman, Director of Admissions.

College of Liberal Arts

Degree Programs Offered: *Baccalaureate* in administration of justice, Afro-American studies, anthropology, astronomy, astrophysics, botany, chemistry, classics, economics, English, French, geology, German, history, mathematics, microbiology, philosophy, physical education, physics, political science, psychology, Russian, sociology, Spanish, zoology.

Degree Requirements: 127 credit hours.

Distinctive Educational Programs: Accelerated degree programs in cooperation with Colleges of Dentistry and Medicine leading to baccalaureate and first-professional degrees. Dual-degree program in podiatry with Pennsylvania College of Podiatric Medicine.

College of Allied Health Sciences

Degree Programs Offered: *Baccalaureate* in clinical nutrition, medical dietetics, medical technology, occupational therapy, physical therapy, radiation therapy technology, radiologic technology. Certificates in various fields also given.

Admission: For physician's assistant program, combined SAT score of 750; high school GPA of C or above; ACT composite 16 (English 18, Math 18).

School of Architecture and Planning

Degree Programs Offered: *Baccalaureate, master's* in architecture, city planning.

Admission: SAT 400 verbal; 400 mathematical; GPA 2.5 or above.

School of Business and Public Administration

Degree Programs Offered: *Baccalaureate* in accounting, computer-based information systems, finance, insurance, international business, management, marketing; *master's* in business administration, (general, health services administration), public administration (general, urban).

School of Communications

Degree Programs Offered: *Baccalaureate* in broadcast journalism, broadcast management, communication theory and rhetoric, film directing, journalism, legal communications, news-editorial journalism, radio, speech pathology-audiology, television; *master's* in communication arts, communication sciences, production (radio, television, film), film.

School of Education

Degree Programs Offered: *Baccalaureate* in elementary education, teacher education; *master's* in education, teaching; *doctorate* in education.

School of Engineering

Degree Programs Offered: *Baccalaureate* in chemical engineering, civil engineering, computer systems engineering, electrical engineering, mechanical engineering; *master's* in chemical engineering, civil engineering, computer science, electrical engineering, mechanical engineering, urban systems engineering.

Distinctive Educational Programs: Cooperative education. Joint engineering-M.B.A. program in cooperation with School of Business and Public Administration.

College of Fine Arts

Degree Programs Offered: *Baccalaureate* in applied music, art education, art history, ceramics, composition, design, drama, graphic art, jazz studies, music education, music history and literature, music therapy; *master's* in applied music, art education, art history, composition, music education, music history, musicology, studio art.

Distinctive Educational Programs: Work-experience programs, including apprenticeships, field work, internships. Independent directed study. Center for Ethnic Music specializing in African and African-derived music.

School of Human Ecology

Degree Programs Offered: *Baccalaureate* in consumer education and resource management, human development, human nutrition and food, macroenvironmental and population studies, microenvironmental studies and design.

Distinctive Educational Programs: Interdisciplinary program in international studies in human ecology.

College of Nursing

Degree Programs Offered: *Baccalaureate, master's* in nursing.

Admission: SAT 400 verbal; 400 mathematical or ACT composite of 17 or above; high school ranking in upper 1/3 of class or GED; statement of interest.

Distinctive Educational Programs: Baccalaureate completion program for registered nurses.

College of Pharmacy and Pharmaceutical Sciences

Degree Programs Offered: *Baccalaureate; doctorate* in pharmaceutical science.

School of Social Work

Degree Programs Offered: *Baccalaureate, master's, doctorate.*

Distinctive Educational Programs: Human services evaluation and research division provides practical experience for graduate students. Continuing professional education.

College of Dentistry

Degree Programs Offered: *First-professional.* Certificates in dental hygiene also given.

Admission: *For first-professional degree:* 60 semester hours from accredited college or university which must include 6 in English (composition and literature); 8 each biology, inorganic and organic chemistry, physics; 22 liberal arts electives. DAT. Credentials must be evaluated by American Association of Dental Schools Application Service.

Degree Requirements: *See* general requirements. *For first-professional degree:* 150.5 credit hours; 1 year in residence; prescribed curriculum; exit competency examinations; parts I and II of national dental boards; demonstration of good ethical standards and proficiency in the practice of dentistry. Must be 21 years of age.

Distinctive Educational Programs: Summer internships in Guyana for seniors. Academic reinforcement program provides developmental training for educationally disadvantaged students. *Other distinctive programs:* Continuing professional education. Postdoctoral programs in oral surgery, orthodontics, pedodontics.

School of Law

Degree Programs Offered: *First-professional* in law; *master's* in comparative jurisprudence.

Admission: *For first-professional degree:* Baccalaureate from accredited college or university, LSAT, LSDAS.

Degree Requirements: *For first-professional degree:* 88 credit hours, 70% grade average, final year in residence.

Distinctive Educational Programs: Joint J.D.-M.B.A. program in cooperation with School of Business and Public Administration.

College of Medicine

Degree Programs Offered: *First-professional.*

Admission: 62 semester hours from accredited college or university which must include 6 English; 6 mathematics; 8 each in biology, inorganic and organic chemistry, physics; MCAT; AMCAS. Baccalaureate from accredited college or university recommended.

Degree Requirements: 178-190 credit hours; 2 years in residence, prescribed curriculum, exit competency examination-national medical boards, demonstration of good ethical standards and proficiency in the practice of medicine.

Distinctive Educational Programs: Student exchange programs with various medical schools in the United States and Canada. Joint M.D.-Ph.D. program in cooperation with Graduate School of Arts and Sciences.

Howard University School of Divinity

Degree Programs Offered: *First-professional* in divinity; *master's* in religious studies; *doctorate* in ministry. Certificates in urban ministries also given.

Admission: *For first-professional degree:* Baccalaureate from accredited college or university. Recommend strong liberal arts background, 2.0 GPA.

Degree Requirements: *For first-professional degree:* 84-90 credit hours, 2.0 GPA, 9 months in residence, core curriculum.

Distinctive Educational Programs: Field work. Independent reading. Cross-registration through Washington Theological Consortium. Institute for Urban Religious Studies.

Graduate School of Arts and Sciences

Degree Programs Offered: *Master's* in African studies and research, anatomy, art, biochemistry, botany, chemistry, chemical engineering, civil engineering, communication arts and sciences, computer science, economics, education, electrical engineering, English, genetics and human genetics, German, history, human ecology, mathematics, mechanical engineering, microbiology, pharmacology, philosophy, physical education, physiology and biophysics, political science, psychology, Romance languages, Russian, sociology and anthropology, urban studies, urban systems engineering, zoology. *Doctorate* in various fields.

Joint Military Intelligence College

200 Macdill Boulevard
Washington, District of Columbia 20340-5100
Tel: (202) 231-3319 **E-mail:** jmic@dia.mil
Fax: (202) 231-8652 **Internet:** www.dia.mil

Institution Description: The Joint Military Intelligence College, formerly known as the Defense Intelligence College, is a public (Department of Defense) college offering the Master of Science of Strategic Intelligence degree and other programs and certificate courses. Degree-granting authority legislated by the U.S. Congress. *Degrees awarded:* Baccalaureate, master's. Certificates also awarded.

Accreditation: *Regional:* MSA/CHE.

History: Chartered by the Department of Defense as Defense Intelligence School 1962; awarded first degree (master's) 1981; adopted present name 1993.

Calendar: Quarters. Academic year Sept. to Sept.

Admission: Enrollment limited to military, Department of Defense civilian and other eligible government employees assigned to intelligence functions or pursuing broad careers in intelligence.

Degree Requirements: Completion of prescribed curriculum.

Degrees Conferred: 32 *baccalaureate:* intelligence studies; 154 *master's:* intelligence studies.

Fees and Other Expenses: Contact the college for current information.

Departments and Teaching Staff: School of Intelligence *instructors* 43, *part-time faculty* 86. *Total instructional faculty:* 129.

Enrollment: Total enrollment 532. Undergraduate full-time 32; graduate full-time 150, part-time 350.

Characteristics of Student Body: *Ethnic and racial makeup:* Black non-Hispanic: 18.8%; American Indian or Native: Alaskan 3.1%; Hispanic: 3.1%; White non-Hispanic: 62.5%; unknown: 12.5%.

Library Collections: 80,000 volumes. 2 million microforms; 850 current periodical subscriptions. Access of online information retrieval systems.

Chief Executive Officer: Dr. A. Denis Clift, President.

Address admissions inquiries to Thomas Van Wagner, Director of Enrollment and Student Services.

Potomac College

4000 Chesapeake Street, N.W.
Washington, District of Columbia 20016-1860
Tel: (202) 686-0876 **E-mail:** admissions@potomac.edu
Fax: (202) 686-0818 **Internet:** www.potomac.edu

Institution Description: The curriculum at Potomac College has been designed to be firmly grounded in the realities of the workplace. Traditional classroom lectures are supplemented with participatory learning activities and workplace projects. This process integrates work responsibilities with theory and practical applications. The college has branch in nearby Herndon, Virginia. *Enrollment:* 222. *Degrees awarded:* Baccalaureate.

Accreditation: *Regional:* MSA/CHE. *Nonregional:* ACICS.

Calendar: Potomac College operates on a nontraditional schedule to accommodate working adults. Classes are normally held in the evening and Saturday.

Admission: Rolling admissions plan. *Requirements:* The college admits students who are high school graduate, or the equivalent thereof. Students must have at least four years of post-high school work experience and a minimum of 24 semester credit hours of traditional prior college or nontraditional credits.

Degree Requirements: For the bachelor of science degree, student must complete all required theory course and applied research course requirements satisfactorily. Students must earn a minimum of 39 credits in their major at Potomac College and a total of 123 credits. The 39-credit residency minimum must consist of 10 required courses, a combination of theory and applied research courses and the Capstone Project.

Distinctive Educational Programs: The college offers support courses admission prerequisites for all majors for student who have less than the equivalent of 45 credits and a minimum of 24 credit hours from previous college work, credit for experiential learning, corporate/military training, and/or college equivalency examinations.

The eighteen-month program offers classes on Saturdays or two evenings per week. It is possible to earn six credits every six weeks.

Degrees Conferred: 98 *baccalaureate.* Largest programs for 2003–04: computer and information sciences and support services 50; business, management, marketing, and related support services 48.

Fees and Other Expenses: Contact the college for current tuition/fees.

Financial Aid: Aid from institutionally generated funds is provided on the basis of financial need, other considerations. Institution has a Program Participation Agreement with the U.S. Department of Education for eligible students to receive Pell Grants and other federal aid.

Departments and Teaching Staff: Faculty members are unranked and include part-time instructors.

Enrollment: Total enrollment 222 (22.4% men, 67.6% women)

Characteristics of Student Body: *Ethnic/racial makeup:* Black non-Hispanic: 83.8%; Asian or Pacific Islander: 1.4%; Hispanic: 1.4%; White non-Hispanic: 9.0%; unknown: 4.5%.

Chief Executive Officer: Dr. Florence S. Tate, President.

Address admission inquiries to Hal Levine, Director of Enrollment Services.

Southeastern University

501 I Street, S.W.
Washington, District of Columbia 20024
Tel: (202) 488-8162   **E-mail:** admin@seu.edu
Fax: (202) 484-8337   **Internet:** www.seu.edu

Institution Description: Southeastern University is a private, independent, nonprofit institution operating under a charter from the Congress of the United States. *Enrollment:* 994. *Degrees awarded:* Associate, baccalaureate, master's. Certificates also awarded.

Accreditation: *Regional:* MSA/CHE.

History: Established and offered first instruction at postsecondary level 1879; awarded first degree (baccalaureate) 1917; chartered 1923; formerly Washington School of Accountancy, YMCA College; adopted present name 1930.

Institutional Structure: *Governing board:* Board of Trustees. Representation: 21 trustees, including 8 alumni. All voting. *Composition of institution:* Administrators 15 men / 12 women. Academic affairs headed by dean of academic affairs. Management/business/finances chair, computer science chair, liberal studies chair form academic core. Academic governance bodies, Academic Councils, meet an average of 20 times per year.

Calendar: Quarters. Academic year Sept. to June. Freshmen admitted on a rolling basis. Degrees conferred May, Aug., Dec. Formal commencement June.

Characteristics of Freshmen: 99% of applicants accepted. 48% of accepted applicants enrolled. 12% of freshmen expected to graduate within 5 years.

Admission: Rolling admissions plan. For fall acceptance, apply as late as 1 month prior to beginning of term. Early acceptance available. *Requirements:* Either graduation from accredited secondary school with 4 units English, 3 mathematics; or GED. Minimum GPA 2.0. *Entrance tests:* College Board SAT or institutional placement examination. For foreign students TOEFL. *For transfer students:* 2.0 minimum GPA; from 4-year accredited institution 60 semester hours maximum transfer credit; from 2-year accredited institution 30 hours; correspondence/extension students evaluated individually.

College credit for postsecondary-level work completed in secondary school and for extrainstitutional learning on basis of ACE *2006 Guide to the Evaluation of Educational Experiences in the Armed Services*, portfolio assessment.

Tutoring available. Noncredit developmental courses offered in summer session and regular academic year.

Degree Requirements: *For associate degrees:* 62–72 credit hours; 30 hours in residence. *For all baccalaureate degrees:* 120 hours; 60 hours in residence. *For all undergraduate degrees:* 2.0 GPA; general education requirements.

Fulfillment of some degree requirements and exemption from some beginning courses possible by passing College Board CLEP, AP. *Grading system:* A–F; withdraw (carries time limit).

Distinctive Educational Programs: Internships. Weekend and evening classes. Tutorials.

Degrees Conferred: 39 *associate*; 90 *baccalaureate*; 173 *master's*. Bachelor's degrees awarded in top disciplines: business, management, marketing, and related support services62; liberal arts and sciences, general studies and humanities 12; computer and information sciences and support services 12; health professions and related clinical sciences 4.

Fees and Other Expenses: *Full-time tuition per academic year 2004–05:* $9,705 undergraduate; contact the university for graduate tuition and fees. *Books and supplies:* $1,200. *Room and board per academic year:* $12,078.

Financial Aid: Aid from institutionally generated funds is awarded on the basis of academic merit, financial need. Institution has a Program Participation Agreement with the U.S. Department of Education for eligible students to receive Pell Grants and other federal aid.

Financial aid to full-time, first-time undergraduate students: 43% received federal grants averaging $4,00; 8% received state/local grants; 3% received institutional grants; 43% loans averaging $6,625.

Enrollment: Total enrollment 994. Undergraduate 653 (28.9% men, 71.1% women).

Characteristics of Student Body: *Ethnic/racial makeup:* Black non-Hispanic: 82.1%; American Indian of Alaska Native: .2%; Asian or Pacific Islander: 1.8%; Hispanic: 1.5%; White non-Hispanic: 1.5%; unknown: 5.5%.

International Students: 74 nonresident aliens enrolled fall 2004. Programs available to aid students whose native language is not English: English as a Second Language Program. No financial aid specifically designated for international students.

Student Life: No on-campus housing. *Special regulations:* Learning Resources Center. *Student publications: The Shield*, a yearbook an annual handbook. *Surrounding community:* Washington, D.C. metropolitan area population over 3 million. Served by mass transit bus, rail, and subway system; airport 1.5 miles from campus.

Library Collections: 40,000 volumes including bound books, serial backfiles, electronic documents, and government documents not in separate collections. Online catalog. Current serial subscriptions: 1,200; 20 computer work stations. Students have access to the Internet at no charge.

Most important holdings include collection of annual reports of major United States corporations.

Buildings and Grounds: Campus area 3 acres.

Chief Executive Officer: Dr. Charlene Drew Jarvis, President.

Address admission inquiries to Gwen Kelly, Director of Admissions.

Strayer College

1025 15th Street, N.W.
Washington, District of Columbia 20005
Tel: (202) 408-2400   **E-mail:** admissions@strayer.edu
Fax: (202) 419-1423   **Internet:** www.strayer.edu

Institution Description: Strayer College is an independent, nonsectarian institution that serves business-oriented undergraduate and graduate program. The college serves students from the District of Columbia, Maryland, and Virginia, as well as international students from more than 50 countries. institution. *Enrollment:* 20,138. *Degrees awarded:* Associate, baccalaureate, masters. Diplomas also awarded.

Accreditation: *Regional:* MSA/CHE.

History: Established as Strayer Business College, Inc. in Baltimore (MD) 1898; opened school in Washington, D.C. and offered first instruction at postsecondary level 1904; changed name to Strayer College of Accountancy and awarded first degree (baccalaureate) 1928; incorporated as Strayer Junior College 1959; became 4-year college 1969; awarded first degree (baccalaureate) and adopted present name 1970.

Institutional Structure: Strayer College is a subsidiary of Strayer Education, Inc. *Governing board:* Board of Trustees. Representation: 9 members. All voting. *Composition of institution:* Administrators 8 men / 1 woman. Academics headed by Academic Dean. Management and business affairs directed by the president. Full-time instructional faculty 73.

Calendar: Quarters. Academic year Sept. to June. Freshmen admitted Sept., Jan., Apr., June. Degrees conferred June, Aug., Dec., Mar. Formal commencement June. Summer session of 1 term from late June to early Sept.

Characteristics of Freshmen: 88% of students from District of Columbia. Students from 3 states and 50 foreign countries.

Admission: Rolling admissions plan. Freshman and transfer students applications accepted year-round. *Requirements:* Either graduation from secondary school or GED. *Entrance tests:* Institutional examinations in mathematics, spelling, vocabulary, writing. For foreign students, TOEFL and institutional English proficiency examination also required. *For transfer students:* 2.0 minimum GPA; from 4-year accredited institution 140 hours maximum transfer credit; from 2-year accredited institution 100 hours; for correspondence/extension students, transfer credit varies.

College credit and advanced placement for postsecondary-level work completed in secondary school and for extrainstitutional learning on basis of ACE *2006 Guide to the Evaluation of Educational Experiences in the Armed Services*, portfolio and faculty assessments, personal interviews.

Tutoring available. Developmental/remedial courses offered in summer session and regular academic year; credit given.

Degree Requirements: *For all associate degrees:* 90 credit hours; 27 hours in residence. *For all baccalaureate degrees:* 180 credit hours; 36 hours in residence. *For all degrees:* 2.0 GPA; liberal arts requirements.

Fulfillment of some degree requirements and exemption from some beginning courses possible by passing departmental examinations, College Board CLEP. *Grading system:* A–F; withdraw (deadline after which pass-fail is appended to withdraw).

Distinctive Educational Programs: Work-experience programs including cooperative education, internships. Weekend and evening classes. Accelerated degree programs. Interdisciplinary program in general studies. Individual majors.

Degrees Conferred: 497 *associate*; 1,787 *baccalaureate*; 978 *master's*; 29 *post-baccalaureate certificates*. Bachelor's degrees awarded computer and information sciences and support services 993; business, management, marketing, and related support services 785; social sciences 9.

Fees and Other Expenses: *Full-time tuition per academic year 2004–05:* $9,862. *Books and supplies:* $1,500.

Financial Aid: Aid from institutionally generated funds is awarded on the basis of academic merit, financial need. Institution has a Program Participation Agreement with the U.S. Department of Education for eligible students to receive Pell Grants and other federal aid.

Financial aid to full-time, first-time undergraduate students: 31% received federal grants averaging $1,489; 35% loans averaging $1,511.

Departments and Teaching Staff: *Total instructional faculty: 117. Student-to-faculty ratio: 22:1. Degrees held by full-time faculty:* 55% hold terminal degrees.

Enrollment: Total enrollment 20,138 (including branch campuses). Undergraduate 15,972 (41.1% men, 58.9% women).

Characteristics of Student Body: *Ethnic and racial makeup:* Black non-Hispanic: 43.5%; American Indian or Alaska Native: .5%; Asian or Pacific Islander: 3.9%; Hispanic 3.6%; White non-Hispanic: 32.5%; unknown: 11.8%.

International Students: 671 undergraduate nonresident aliens enrolled fall 2003. Programs to aid students whose native language is not English: English as a Second Language courses.

Student Life: No on-campus housing. *Special services:* Student placement testing, academic advising, career development advising, cooperative education program, financial advising, international student advising, veteran's advising, on-campus CLEP and TOEFL testing, tutoring centers, Learning Resources Centers, student computer labs; student health plans. *Student publications: The Optimist,* a quarterly newspaper. *Surrounding community:* Washington, D.C. metropolitan area population over 3 million. Served by mass transit bus and rail system; subway. Airport 6 miles from campus; passenger rail service 2 miles from campus.

Library Collections: 35,000 volumes. 3,000 audiovisual materials; 550 current periodical subscriptions. Online catalog. Students have access to online information retrieval services and the Internet.

Most important holdings include 32 volumes of official government documents of Watergate investigation proceedings; business management collection.

Buildings and Grounds: Campuses are located in the District of Columbia, suburban northern Virginia, and Spotsylvania County.

Chief Executive Officer: Dr. J. Chris Toe, President.

Address admission inquiries to Office of Admissions.

Trinity College

125 Michigan Avenue, N.E.
Washington, District of Columbia 20017-1094
Tel: (202) 884-9000   **E-mail:** admissions@trinitydc.edu
Fax: (202) 884-9229   **Internet:** www.trinitydc.edu

Institution Description: Trinity College is a private college conducted by the Sisters of Notre Dame de Namur, Roman Catholic Church. *Enrollment:* 1,637. Men admitted as graduate students only. *Degrees awarded:* Baccalaureate, master's. Certificates also awarded.

Member of Consortium of Universities of the Washington Metropolitan Area.

Accreditation: *Regional:* MSA/CHE.

History: Established, chartered, and incorporated 1897; offered first instruction at postsecondary level 1900; awarded first degree (baccalaureate) 1904. *See* Sr. Columba Mullaly, "Trinity College: 75 years," *Trinity College Alumnae Journal* (special issue), June 1972 for further information.

Institutional Structure: *Governing board:* Board of Trustees. Representation: 17 trustees, president of college; 18 voting. *Composition of institution:* Administrators 10 men / 35 women. Academic affairs headed by academic vice president. Management/business/finances directed by vice president for finance and administration. Full-time instructional faculty 52. Academic governance body, the faculty, meets an average of 10 times per year.

Calendar: Semesters. Academic year Sept. to May. Freshmen admitted Sept., Jan. Degrees conferred May (all students), Aug., Dec. (graduate students). Formal commencement May. Summer session of 2 terms from mid-May to early Aug.

Characteristics of Freshmen: 441 applicants. 85.9% of applicants admitted. 38% of admitted students enrolled full-time. Mean SAT scores 500 verbal, 510 mathematical. 80% of entering freshmen expected to graduate within 5 years. 4% of freshmen from Washington, D.C. Freshmen from 20 states and 15 foreign countries.

Admission: Rolling admissions plan. *Requirements:* Graduation from secondary school with 16 units from academic disciplines. *Entrance tests:* College Board SAT or ACT composite. For foreign students TOEFL *For transfer students:* 2.0 GPA; 96 hours maximum transfer credit.

College credit and advanced placement for postsecondary-level work completed in secondary school. College credit for extrainstitutional learning (life experience) on basis of portfolio and faculty assessments, personal interview. Noncredit remedial courses offered.

Degree Requirements: 128 credit hours; 2.0 GPA; 32 hours in residence; comprehensives in individual fields of study; general education requirements.

Fulfillment of some degree requirements and exemption from some beginning courses possible by passing College Board CLEP, AP. *Grading system:* A–F; pass-fail.

Distinctive Educational Programs: *For undergraduates:* Work-experience practica. Accelerated degree programs. Dual-degree program in engineering with University of Maryland at College Park and George Washington University; Weekend college. Cooperative baccalaureate in medical technology with affiliated schools. Interdepartmental majors in American studies; French and history of art; mathematics and economics; medical technology; music education; political sciences and economics; physical sciences. Interdisciplinary programs in international studies, urban studies. Facilities and programs for independent research, including individual majors, tutorials. Institutionally sponsored study abroad through CIEE. Cross-registration through the consortium. *Available for all students:* Evening classes. *Other distinctive programs:* Baccalaureate completion and non-degree-granting continuing education programs.

Degrees Conferred: 132 *baccalaureate;* 221 *master's;* 2 *post-baccalaureate certificates.* Bachelor's degrees awarded in top five disciplines: psychology 53; business, management, marketing, and related support services 31; social sciences 15; communication, journalism, and related programs 13; education 6.

Fees and Other Expenses: *Full-time tuition per academic year 2004–05:* $16,700 undergraduate; contact the university for graduate tuition and fees. *Room and board per academic year:* $7,290. *Books and supplies:* $600.

Financial Aid: Aid from institutionally generated funds is awarded on the basis of academic merit, financial need. Institution has a Program Participation Agreement with the U.S. Department of Education for eligible students to receive Pell Grants and other federal aid.

Financial aid to full-time, first-time undergraduate students: 58% received federal grants averaging $3,467; 41% state/local grants averaging $3,172; 98% institutional grants averaging $6,154; 71% loans averaging $3,840.

Departments and Teaching Staff: *Professors* 11, *associate professors* 17, *assistant professors* 22, *instructors* 2, *part-time teachers* 94. *Total instructional faculty:* 140. *Degrees held by full-time faculty:* Doctorate 90%, master's 100%. 94% hold terminal degrees.

Enrollment: Total enrollment 1,637. Undergraduate 1,011 (2.2% men, 97.8% women).

Characteristics of Student Body: *Ethnic and racial makeup:* Black non-Hispanic: 67.4%; American Indian or Alaska Native: .2%; Asian or Pacific Islander: 2.2%, Hispanic: 8.3%; White non-Hispanic: 8.5%; unknown: 10.8%.

International Students: 27 nonresident aliens enrolled fall 2003. Programs available to aid students whose native language is not English: English as a Second Language Program.

Student Life: On-campus residence halls for women only house 85% of student body. *Intercollegiate athletics:* women only: basketball, crew, field hockey, tennis. *Special regulations:* Registered cars permitted. Residence hall visitation from 8am to 2am. *Special services:* Learning Resources Center, medical services. *Student publications, radio: Record,* a quarterly literary magazine; *Trinity Times,* a biweekly newspaper. Radio Station WRTC. *Surrounding community:* Washington, D.C. metropolitan area population over 3,000,000. Served by mass transit bus and subway system; airport 10 miles from campus; passenger rail service 3 miles from campus.

Library Collections: 215,400 volumes. 6,900 microforms; 13,800 audiovisual materials; 510 current periodical subscriptions. Online catalog. Students have access to online information retrieval services and the Internet.

Most important holdings include art history collection of slides.

Buildings and Grounds: Campus area 26 acres.

Chief Executive Officer: Patricia A. McGuire, President.

Undergraduates address admission inquiries to Lori Kankowski, Director of Admissions.

University of the District of Columbia

4200 Connecticut Avenue, N.W.
Washington, District of Columbia 20008
Tel: (202) 274-6333   **E-mail:** admissions@udc.edu
Fax: (202) 274-5513   **Internet:** www.udc.edu

Institution Description: University of the District of Columbia (Washington Technical Institute, District of Columbia Teachers College and Federal City College until 1977) is a federal institution and land-grant college comprising 3 separately accredited campuses, Georgia/Harvard campus, Mount Vernon Square campus, and Van Ness campus. *Enrollment:* 5,165. *Degrees awarded:* Associate, baccalaureate, and master's.

Member of Consortium of Universities of the Washington Metropolitan Area.

Accreditation: *Regional:* MSA/CHE. *Professional:* business, engineering, engineering technology, law, mortuary science, nursing, planning, radiography, respiratory therapy, social work, speech-language pathology

History: Established as merger of District of Columbia Teachers College (established 1851), Federal City College (established 1966), and Washington Technical College (established 1966) 1975; incorporated 1976; offered first instruction at postsecondary level 1977; awarded first degree (baccalaureate) 1978.

Institutional Structure: *Governing board:* University of the District of Columbia Board of Trustees. Extrainstitutional representation: 14 trustees; institutional representation: 14 trustees; institutional representation: 1 student. All voting. *Composition of institution:* 4 administrators. Academic affairs headed by acting provost and vice president for academic affairs. Management/business directed by acting vice president for university services. Finance directed by chief financial officer for finance. Full-time instructional faculty 226. Academic governance body, Faculty Senate, meets an average of 10 times per year. *Faculty representation:* Faculty served by collective bargaining agent, University of the District of Columbia Faculty Association, affiliated with NEA.

Calendar: Semesters. Academic year Aug. to May. Freshmen admitted Aug., Jan., May. Degrees conferred May, Aug., Dec. Formal commencement May. Summer session of 3 terms from May to July.

Characteristics of Freshmen: 23% of entering freshmen expected to graduate within 5 years. 74% of freshmen from the District of Columbia. Freshmen from 47 states and 57 foreign countries.

Admission: Rolling admissions plan. For fall acceptance, apply as early as senior year of secondary school, but not later than 1 day prior to registration. Early acceptance available. *Requirements:* Open admissions for graduates of approved high schools or those with GED. Recommended 4 units English, 2 in a foreign language, 2 college preparatory mathematics, 2 laboratory science, 2 social studies. *Entrance tests:* For foreign students TOEFL. *For transfer students:* 2.0 minimum GPA, 90 semester hours maximum transfer credit.

College credit for extrainstitutional learning on basis of ACE *2006 Guide to the Evaluation of Educational Experiences in the Armed Services.* Tutoring available. Developmental courses offered in summer session and regular academic year; nondegree credit given.

Degree Requirements: *For all associate degrees:* 60 semester hours. *For all baccalaureate degrees:* 120 hours. *For all degrees:* 2.0 GPA; 30 hours in residence; distribution requirements. Fulfillment of some degree requirements possible by passing departmental examinations. *Grading system:* A–F; withdraw.

Distinctive Educational Programs: Work-experience programs, including cooperative and experiential education. Weekend and evening classes. Interdisciplinary program in environmental science. Honors programs. Cross-registration through consortium. *Other distinctive programs:* Continuing education; degree-granting program at Lorton Correctional Complex; Early Childhood Learning Center; Speech and Hearing Clinic.

ROTC: Army in cooperation with consortium; Air Force in cooperation with Howard University.

Degrees Conferred: 305 *baccalaureate* (B), 67 *master's* (M): architecture 13 (B); biological/life sciences 18 (B); business/marketing 25 (B); 20 (M); communications/communication technologies 26 (B); computer and information sciences 26 (B); education 13 (B), 4 (M); engineering and engineering technologies 19 (B); English 3 (B), 3 (M); foreign languages and literature 3 (B); health professions and related sciences 40 (B); law/legal studies 15 (B); library science 2 (B), 1 (M); military science and technologies 18 (B); philosophy/religion/theology 1 (B); physical sciences 15 (M); protective services/public administration 15 (B), 14 (M); psychology 30 (B); visual and performing 23 (B); other 11 (B), 10 (M). *Honorary degrees awarded 2003–04:* Doctor of Humane Letters 1, Doctor of Science 1, Doctor of Letters 2.

Fees and Other Expenses: *Full-time tuition per academic year 2004–05:* District of Columbia resident $1,800, nonresident $4,440. Contact the university for graduate/professional school tuition and fees.

Financial Aid: Aid from institutionally generated funds is provided on the basis of financial need, athletic ability. Institution has a Program Participation Agreement with the U.S. Department of Education for eligible students to receive Pell Grants and other federal aid.

Financial aid to full-time, first-time undergraduate students: need-based scholarships/grants totaling $5,311,109, self-help $3,571,831, parent loans $13,628; non-need-based scholarships/grants totaling $384,855, self-help $1,675,168.

Departments and Teaching Staff: *Total instructional faculty:* 572 (full-time 223, part-time 289; women 213, men 306; members of minority groups 92). Total faculty with doctorate, first-professional, or other terminal degree: 390. Student-to-faculty ratio: 8:1. 11 faculty members awarded sabbaticals 2004.

Enrollment: Total enrollment 5,165. Undergraduate full-time 809 men / 1,126 women, part-time 977m / 2,054w; graduate full-time 30m / 43w, part-time 47m / 89w.

Characteristics of Student Body: *Ethnic/racial makeup:* number of Black non-Hispanic: 7,068; American Indian or Alaska Native: 4; Asian or Pacific Islander: 120; Hispanic: 283; White non-Hispanic: 271; unknown: 251. *Age distribution:* number under 18: 146; 18–19:489; 20–21: 558; 22–24: 734; 25–29: 951; 30–34: 646; 35–39: 379; 40–49: 683; 50–64: 896; 65 and over: 83.

International Students: 640 nonresident aliens enrolled fall 2004. 6 students from Europe, 4 Asia, 163 Central and South America; 200 Africa, 4 Canada, 2 Australia, 1 New Zealand, 297 other. Programs available to aid students whose native language is not English: Cultural, social. English as a Second Language Program. No financial aid specifically designated for international students.

Student Life: No on-campus housing. *Intercollegiate athletics:* men only: basketball, soccer, tennis, track; women only: basketball, tennis, track. *Special services:* Learning Resources Center, medical services. *Student publications, television:* Newspaper and yearbook. Television station Channel 19. *Surrounding community:* Washington population 650,000. Served by mass transit bus, subway system, airport 15 miles from campus, passenger rail service 10 miles from campus.

Library Collections: 561,627 volumes including bound books, serial backfiles, electronic documents, and government documents not in separate collections. Online catalog. Current serial subscriptions: 661 paper. 607,224 microform units. 19,311 media materials. 152 computer work stations. Students have access to the Internet at no charge.

Most important holdings include Schomburg Clipping Files; engineering and technology collection; Black Biography 1790–1950.

Buildings and Grounds: Campus area 22 acres.

Chief Executive Officer: Dr. William L. Pollard, President.

Address admission inquiries to LaVerne Hill-Flannigan, Director of Admissions.

Washington Theological Union

6896 Laurel Street, N.W.
Washington, District of Columbia 20012-2016
Tel: (800) 334-9922   **E-mail:** admissions@wtu.edu
Fax: (202) 726-1716   **Internet:** www.wtu.edu

Institution Description: Washington Theological Union is a private institution affiliated with the Roman Catholic Church. *Enrollment:* 240. *Degrees awarded:* First-professional (master of divinity, master of arts in pastoral studies), master's.

Member of the Washington Theological Consortium.

Accreditation: *Regional:* MSA/CHE. *Nonregional:* ATS. *Professional:* theology

History: Established as Coalition of Religious Seminaries and offered first instruction at postsecondary level 1968; chartered and changed name to Washington Theological Coalition 1969; awarded first degree 1972; adopted present name 1978.

Institutional Structure: *Governing board:* Board of Trustees. Extrainstitutional representation: 8 trustees; institutional representation: 1 administrator. 1 ex officio. All voting. *Composition of institution:* Administrators 2 men / 2 women. Academic affairs headed by academic dean. Budget/finance directed by business officer. Full-time instructional faculty 22.

Calendar: Semesters (4-1-4 plan). Academic year Sept. to April.

Admission: Rolling admissions plan. *Requirements:* Graduation from accredited college or university with 90 hours in liberal arts, including 18 philosophy. Minimum GPA 2.5.

Degree Requirements: *For master of divinity (first-professional degree):* 102 credit hours; supervised ministries, integrating seminar; for master of arts in pastoral education (first-professional degree): 45 credit hours, supervised ministry, integrating paper; for master of arts in theology (research track): 36 credit hours, thesis or two substantive research papers, proficiency in modern foreign language, general and departmental comprehensive evaluations; for master of arts in theology (general academic track): 42 credit hours, general and departmental comprehensive evaluations; for all degrees: academic residency (two-thirds of coursework), lay ministry program (lay students only) and 3.00 cumulative GPA.

Distinctive Educational Programs: Graduate Certificate Program, Carmelite Chair in Spirituality, Franciscan Center of Theology and Spirituality, Mission and Cross-Cultural Studies Program, Sabbatical Program, Summer Session, Summer Biblical Studies in the Holy Land.

Degrees Conferred: 40 *master of arts:* theology 14; 40 *first-professional:* master of divinity and master of arts in pastoral studies 40.

Fees and Other Expenses: *Full-time tuition per academic year:* $550 per credit. *Room and board per academic year:* $9,900.

Financial Aid: Aid from institutionally generated funds is provided on the basis of financial need, other considerations. 29 fellowships totaling $100,000 awarded (ranging from $1,000 to $20,000).

Departments and Teaching Staff: *Professors* 16, *part-time faculty* 9. *Total instructional faculty:* 25 (full-time 16, part-time 9; women 10, men 15). Total faculty with doctorate, first-professional, or other terminal degree: 25. Student-to-faculty ratio: 9:1.

Enrollment: Total enrollment 240. First-professional full-time 90, part-time 150.

Characteristics of Student Body: *Ethnic/racial makeup:* number of Black non-Hispanic: 20; Asian or Pacific Islander: 25; Hispanic: 20; White non-Hispanic: 131; unknown 34. *Age distribution:* number of: 22–24: 20; 25–29: 20; 30–34: 25; 35–39: 25; 40–49: 60; 50–64: 55, 65 and over: 35.

International Students: 12 nonresident aliens enrolled fall 2004. 6 students from Asia, 3 Central and South America, 3 Africa. Social and cultural programs available to aid students whose native language is not English. No financial aid specifically designated for international students.

Student Life: Enriching variety of cocurricular spiritual, cultural, social, artistic, and intellectual activities are available.

Publications: Washington Theological Union publishes *The New Theology Review.*

Library Collections: 100,000 volumes including bound books, serial backfiles, electronic documents, and government documents not in separate collections. Online catalog. Current serial subscriptions: 402 paper, 2 microform, 30 electronic. 116 recordings. 12 computer work stations. Students have access to the Internet at no charge.

Most important special holdings include the Academy of American Franciscan History Collection; St. Anthony-on-Hudson Collection; Augustine Collection.

Chief Executive Officer: Rev. Daniel McLellan, O.F.M., President.

Address admission inquiries to Peter Barbernitz, Director of Enrollment Services.

Wesley Theological Seminary

4500 Massachusetts Avenue, N.W.
Washington, District of Columbia 20016-5690
Tel: (202) 885-8600   **E-mail:** admissions@wesleysem.org
Fax: (202) 885-8605   **Internet:** wesleysem.org

Institution Description: Wesley Theological Seminary is a private institution affiliated with the United Methodist Church. *Enrollment:* 460. *Degrees awarded:* First-professional (master of divinity), master's, doctorate.

Member of the Washington Theological Consortium.

Accreditation: *Regional:* MSA/CHE. *National:* ATS. *Professional:* theology

History: Established as Westminster Theological Seminary in Westminster (MD) and offered first instruction at postsecondary level 1882; chartered 1884; moved to present location and adopted present name 1958.

Institutional Structure: *Governing board:* Board of Governors of the Wesley Theological Seminary of the United Methodist Church. Extrainstitutional representation: 40 trustees (including 8 alumni), 1 bishop; institutional representation: president of the seminary, 1 full-time instructional faculty member, 1 student. 2 ex officio. 42 voting. *Composition of institution:* Administrators 10 men / 1 woman. Academic affairs headed by dean. Management/business/finances directed by treasurer. Full-time instructional faculty 33. Academic governance body, the faculty, meets an average of 15 times per year.

Calendar: Semesters. Academic year early Sept. to early May. Entering students admitted Sept., Jan., June. Degrees conferred and formal commencement May. Summer sessions from mid-June to mid-July.

Admission: Rolling admissions plan. *Requirements:* Baccalaureate from accredited college or university. *Entrance tests:* Proficiency examination in English. For foreign students TOEFL. *For transfer students:* 2.0 minimum GPA; maximum transfer credit evaluated individually.

Degree Requirements: *For first-professional degree:* 90 credit hours; distribution requirements; completion of teaching and worship-preaching projects; senior project; oral examination on senior project. *For all master's degrees:* 60 credit hours; core curriculum. Additional requirements for some programs. *For all first-professional and master's degrees:* 2.5 GPA; last 30 hours in residence; one course taken through consortium. *Grading system:* A, B, C, F; pass-fail.

Distinctive Educational Programs: Work-experience programs, including field education, internships. Evening classes. Directed study. Institutionally-sponsored study abroad in Greece, Israel, Third World countries. MTS dual degree with American University School of International Service; National Capital Semester. Cross-registration through consortium. Qualified students may enroll at American University. *Other distinctive programs:* Institute for Urban Ministry provides training in inner-city settings.

Degrees Conferred: 24 *doctorate:* theology; 69 *first-professional:* master of divinity.

Fees and Other Expenses: *Tuition per academic year 2004–05:* Contact the seminary for current information.

Financial Aid: Aid from institutionally generated funds is provided on the basis of academic merit, financial need.

Departments and Teaching Staff: *Professors* 12, *associate professors* 2, *assistant professors* 4, *instructors* 10, *part-time faculty* 12.

Total instructional faculty: 45. Degrees held by full-time faculty: Doctorate 88%, master's 100%, professional 75%.

Enrollment: Total enrollment 400 (38.7% men, 61.3% women).

Characteristics of Student Body: *Ethnic/racial makeup:* Black non-Hispanic: 36.5%; Asian or Pacific Islander: 3.5%; Hispanic: 1.1%; White non-Hispanic: 54.8%; unknown: .7%.

International Students: 16 nonresident aliens enrolled fall 2004. No programs available to aid students whose native language is not English. Scholarships awarded annually to qualifying international students.

Student Life: On-campus residence halls and housing available for married students. *Special regulations:* Cars permitted without restrictions. *Special services:* Art Studio. *Student publications, The Firebrand,* a biannual journal; *Wesley Journal,* a weekly newspaper. *Surrounding community:* Washington, D.C. population over 550,000. Served by mass transit bus and subway system, airport 5 miles from campus, passenger rail service 3 miles from campus.

Library Collections: 175,000 volumes. 2,500 microforms; 500 current periodical subscriptions.

Most important holdings include records of the former Methodist Protestant Church; John and Charles Wesley collection; Godsey Collection on Reformed Theology.

Buildings and Grounds: Campus area 1 square block.

Chief Executive Officer: Dr. David McAllister-Wilson, President.

Address admission inquiries to Rev. William D. Aldridge, Director of Admissions.

Florida

Baptist College of Florida

5400 College Drive
Graceville, Florida 32440-1831
Tel: (850) 263-3261   **E-mail:** cbishop@baptistcollege.edu
Fax: (850) 263-7506   **Internet:** www.baptistcollege.edu

Institution Description: The Baptist College of Florida, formerly named Florida Baptist Theological College, is a private institution affiliated with the Florida Baptist Convention. *Enrollment:* 652. *Degrees awarded:* Associate, baccalaureate.

Accreditation: *Regional:* SACS-Comm. on Coll. *National:* ABHE.

History: Established and offered first instruction at postsecondary level 1943; chartered 1957; awarded first degree (baccalaureate) 1977.

Institutional Structure: *Governing board:* Board of Trustees. Extrainstitutional representation: 25 trustees, president and executive director-treasurer of Florida Baptist Convention; institutional representation: president of college. 3 ex officio. 16 voting. *Composition of institution:* Executive administrators 5 men. Academic affairs headed by vice president for academic affairs. Finances directed by senior vice president for business affairs. Full-time instructional faculty 24. Academic governance body, Administrative Council, meets an average of 9 times per year.

Calendar: Semesters. Academic year May to May. Degrees conferred and formal commencement Dec., May. Summer session of 4 terms from late May to late July.

Characteristics of Freshmen: 90% of applicants accepted. 82% of accepted applicants enrolled. 45% of entering freshmen expected to graduate within 5 years. 43% of freshmen from Florida. Freshmen from 20 states and 9 foreign countries.

Admission: Rolling admissions plan. Apply as early as 2 years, but not later than 2 weeks, prior to enrollment. *Requirements:* Either graduation from secondary school or GED. 1 year of approved Christian experience after conversion; good standing in affiliated church. Home schooled students accepted. *For transfer students:* 2.0 minimum GPA; from 2- and 4-year accredited institutions maximum transfer credit limited only by residence requirement; correspondence/extension students 12 hours.

College credit for extrainstitutional learning on basis of ACE *2006 Guide to the Evaluation of Educational Experiences in the Armed Services.* Tutoring available. Noncredit remedial courses offered during regular academic year.

Degree Requirements: 120–130 semester hours; 2.0 GPA; final year in residence; daily chapel attendance; written application for graduation. Fulfillment of some degree requirements possible by passing College Board CLEP. *Grading system:* A–F; pass-fail; withdraw (deadline after which pass-fail is appended to withdraw), DR (course dropped within the drop period).

Distinctive Educational Programs: Bachelor of Arts in Ministry, Bachelor of Arts in Christian Education, Bachelor of Arts in Church Music, Bachelor of Arts in Christian Counseling, Bachelor of Arts in Elementary Education, Bachelor of Arts in Leadership, Bachelor of Music in Church Music, Bachelor of Science in Biblical Studies, Bachelor of Arts in Missions, Bachelor of Music Education, Associate of Divinity, Associate of Christian Education, Associate of Arts in Church Music.

Degrees Conferred: 6 *associate*; 78 *baccalaureate:* education 8, fine and applied arts 3, theology 67.

Fees and Other Expenses: *Full-time tuition per academic year 2004–05:* $6,600. *Room per academic year:* $1,500. *Board per academic year:* $1,872. *Other fees:* $300.

Financial Aid: Aid from institutionally generated funds is provided on the basis of financial need, academic merit. Institution has a Program Participation Agreement with the U.S. Department of Education for eligible students to Receive Pell Grants and other federal aid.

Financial aid to full-time, first-time undergraduate students: Institutional funding: scholarships and grants totaling $444,763; federal and state funding: scholarships and grants totaling $1,284,891; loans totaling $1,258,782; work-study jobs totaling $39,781.

Departments and Teaching Staff: *Total instructional faculty:* 24. *Total tenured faculty:* 10. *Degrees held by full-time faculty:* Doctorate 83%, master's 100%. 83% hold terminal degrees.

Enrollment: Total enrollment 652. Undergraduate full-time 281 men / 170 women, part-time 149m / 52w.

Characteristics of Student Body: *Ethnic/racial makeup:* number of Black non-Hispanic: 25; American Indian or Alaskan Native: 5; Asian or Pacific Islander: 3; Hispanic: 14; White non-Hispanic: 499.

International Students: 3 nonresident aliens enrolled fall 2004. 2 students from Africa, 1 Canada. No programs to aid students whose native language is not English. 3 scholarships totaling $2,500 awarded to international students 2004–05.

Student Life: On-campus residence halls house 36% of student body. 10% of student body housed on campus in apartments, houses, trailers. Housing available for married students. *Special regulations:* Cars with decals permitted. *Student publication: Echoes,* a quarterly newspaper. *Surrounding community:* Graceville population 3,000. Dothan (AL) 20 miles from campus, is nearest major city.

Library Collections: 105,669 volumes including bound books, serial backfiles, electronic documents, and government documents not in separate collections. Online catalog. Current serial subscriptions: 275 paper. 1,700 compact discs; 9,856 videos; 15 DVDs. 2 computer work stations. Students have access to the Internet at no charge. Access to full-text databases through the Florida Electronic Library.

Most important holdings include College Archives; personal library of T.S. Boehm, founding president; complete run of SBC annuals, 1845 to present; Florida Baptist Convention collection received from Stetson University.

Buildings and Grounds: Campus area 220 acres.

Chief Executive Officer: Dr. Thomas A. Kinchen, President.

Address admission inquiries to Christopher M. Bishop, Director of Admissions.

Barry University

11300 N.E. Second Avenue
Miami Shores, Florida 33161-6695
Tel: (305) 839-3000   **E-mail:** admissions@barry.edu
Fax: (305) 899-3054   **Internet:** www.barry.edu

Institution Description: Barry University (Barry College until 1981) is a private, independent, nonprofit institution affiliated with the Roman Catholic Church. *Enrollment:* 9,042. *Degrees awarded:* Baccalaureate, master's, doctorate.

Accreditation: *Regional:* SACS-Comm. on Coll. *Professional:* athletic training, business, counseling, histologic technology, law, nurse anesthesia education, nursing, nursing education, occupational therapy, teacher education, physician assisting, podiatry, social work

History: Established as Barry College, chartered and offered first instruction at postsecondary level 1940; awarded first degree (baccalaureate) 1942; added graduate program 1954; became coeducational 1975; adopted present name 1981.

Institutional Structure: *Governing board:* Barry College Board of Trustees. Extrainstitutional representation: 31 trustees, 2 church officials; institutional representation: president of the college; 1 alumna. 4 ex officio. 31 voting. *Composition of institution:* Administrators 11 men / 10 women. Academic affairs headed by vice president for academic affairs. Management/business/finances directed by vice president for business affairs. Full-time instructional faculty 238. Academic governance body, Academic Affairs Council, meets an average of 15 times per year.

Calendar: Semesters. Academic year Aug. to May. Degrees conferred May, July, Dec. Formal commencement May, Dec. Summer session of 2 terms from mid-May to late July.

Characteristics of Freshmen: 3,186 applicants (1,178 men, 2,010 women). 70.8% of applicants admitted. 22.9% of admitted students enrolled full-time.

85% (440 students) submitted SAT scores; 32% (164 students) submitted ACT scores. *25th percentile*: SAT I Verbal 430, SAT I Math 420; ACT Composite 14, ACT English 16, ACT Math 16. *75th percentile*: SAT I Verbal 530, SAT I Math 520; ACT Composite 23, ACT English 23, ACT Math 21.

56% of freshmen from Florida. Freshmen from 37 states and 56 foreign countries.

Admission: Rolling admissions plan. For fall acceptance, apply as early as May of junior year of secondary school, but not later than Aug. 1 of year of enrollment. Early acceptance available. *Requirements:* Either graduation from accredited secondary school with 16 units which must include English, mathematics, natural science, social studies; or GED. 2 additional units recommended. Additional requirements for some programs. Minimum GPA 3.0. Lowest acceptable secondary school class standing 50th percentile. *Entrance tests:* College Board SAT or ACT composite. For foreign students TOEFL. For nursing majors National League of Nursing examination. *For transfer students:* 2.0 minimum GPA; from 4-year accredited institutions 90 hours maximum transfer credit; from 2-year accredited institutions 64 hours.

College credit and advanced placement for postsecondary-level work completed in secondary school. For extrainstitutional learning, college credit on basis of ACE *2006 Guide to the Evaluation of Educational Experiences in the Armed Services.*

Degree Requirements: 120 credit hours; 2.0 GPA; 30 credits in residence; exit competency examinations-comprehensives in individual fields of study.

Fulfillment of some degree requirements and exemption from some beginning courses possible by passing college Board CLEP or AP (score of 3). *Grading system:* A–F; credit-no credit; withdraw (deadline after which credit-no credit is appended to withdrawal); incomplete (carries time limit).

Distinctive Educational Programs: *For undergraduates:* Accelerated degree program in social work. Facilities and programs for independent research, including tutorials. *Available to all students:* Work-experience programs. Flexible meeting places and schedules, including off-campus center (at Homestead, 46 miles away from main institution) and evening classes. Interdisciplinary programs in international studies; cross-cultural program. Campus exchange program with Aquinas College (MI); Dominican College (CA); St. Mary's Dominican College (LA); St. Thomas Aquinas College (NY). Graduate credit for qualified seniors. Cross-registration through Barry-Biscayne consortium. *Other distinctive programs:* Degree-granting continuing education program. Degree completion program for mature students in cooperation with Embry-Riddle Aeronautical University through Miami Education Consortium.

ROTC: Air Force offered in cooperation with University of Miami.

Degrees Conferred: 1,418 *baccalaureate*; 775 *master's*; 37 *doctorate*; 160 *first-professional*. Bachelor's degrees awarded in top five disciplines: business, management, marketing, and related support services 287; education 257; liberal arts and sciences, general studies and humanities 217; health professions and related clinical sciences 190; computer and information sciences and support sciences 157.

Fees and Other Expenses: *Full-time tuition per academic year 2004–05:* $21,530. *Room and board per academic year:* $7,400. *Books and supplies:* $700.

Financial Aid: Aid from institutionally generated funds is awarded on the basis of academic merit, financial need, other. Institution has a Program Participation Agreement with the U.S. Department of Education for eligible students to receive Pell Grants and other federal aid.

Financial aid to full-time, first-time undergraduate students: 37% received federal grants averaging $3,747; 43% state/local grants averaging $3,493; 96% institutional grants averaging $9,333; 66% loans averaging $3,698.

Departments and Teaching Staff: Academic Computer Center *professors* 0, *associate professors* 0; *assistant professors* 0; *instructors* 0; *part-time teachers* 3; academic and instructional services 0, 0, 0, 0, 7; adult/continuing education 0, 7, 7, 0, 110; arts/sciences 18, 26; 25, 2, 43; business 2, 12, 8, 0, 17; education 4, 13, 13, 3, 45; human performance/leisure science 0, 6, 2, 6, 10; health sciences 3, 6, 11, 0, 43; nursing 3, 5; 22, 0, 16; podiatric medicine 3, 6, 1, 0, 9; social work 11, 8, 5, 0, 10.

Total full-time instructional faculty: 238. *Degrees held by full-time faculty:* Doctorate 70%, master's 100%, professional 3%. 80% of faculty hold terminal degrees.

Characteristics of Student Body: *Ethnic/racial makeup:* Black non-Hispanic: 21.8% American Indian or Alaska Native: .2%; Asian or Pacific Islander: 1.1%; Hispanic: 33.8%; White non-Hispanic: 29.2%; unknown: 9.3%.

International Students: 271 undergraduate nonresident aliens enrolled fall 2003. Programs available to aid students whose native language is not English: noncredit course in English as a Second Language.

Student Life: On-campus residence halls house 27% of undergraduate student body. Dormitories for men only constitute 20% of such space, for women only 80%. *Special regulations:* Cars permitted without restrictions. Quiet hours

from 10pm to 10am Sun.–Thurs., 1am to 10am Fri.–Sat. *Special services:* Nurse run health care on-campus. Van and minibus service available. *Student publications: Hourglass,* a newspaper published 5 times a semester; *Torch and Shield,* a yearbook. *Surrounding community:* Miami population 350,000. Served by mass transit bus system, airport; passenger rail service 8 miles from campus.

Library Collections: 290,600 volumes. 512,000 microforms; 3,600 audiovisual materials; 1,850 current periodical subscriptions. Online catalog. Students have access to online information retrieval systems.

Most important holdings include 2,000 volumes on Catholic Church history and theology; William Lehman Papers.

Buildings and Grounds: Campus area 120 acres.

Chief Executive Officer: Sr. Linda Bevilacqua, O.P., President.

Address admission inquiries Director of Admissions.

Bethune-Cookman College

640 Dr. Mary McLeod Bethune Drive
Daytona Beach, Florida 32114-3099

Tel: (904) 255-1401   **E-mail:** admissions@cookman.edu
Fax: (904) 255-4710   **Internet:** www.cookman.edu

Institution Description: Bethune-Cookman College is a private college related to the United Methodist Church. *Enrollment:* 2,794. *Degrees awarded:* Baccalaureate. Academic offerings in business, education, humanities, science and mathematics, social sciences, nursing.

Accreditation: *Regional:* SACS-Comm. on Coll. *Professional*: business, clinical lab scientist, nursing, teacher education

History: Established and chartered 1923 as Daytona-Cookman Collegiate Institute through a merger of Cookman Institution (established 1872) and Daytona Normal and Industrial Institute for Girls (established 1904); adopted present name 1931; offered first instruction at postsecondary level 1932; added upper division curriculum 1941; awarded first degree (baccalaureate) 1943.

Institutional Structure: *Governing board:* Board of Trustees. Extrainstitutional representation: 40 trustees, including 8 alumni (all voting), 10 trustees emeriti, 4 honorary trustees, 1 institutional administrator (all nonvoting). *Composition of institution:* Administrators 5 men / 4 women. Academic affairs headed by vice president for academic affairs/dean of the faculty. Management/business/finances directed by vice president for fiscal affairs. Full-time instructional faculty 132. Academic governance body, Academic Policies and Curriculum Committee, meets an average of 8 times per year.

Calendar: Semesters. Academic year Aug. to Apr. Freshmen admitted Aug., Jan., June. Degrees conferred and formal commencements Apr., July. Summer session from June to July.

Characteristics of Freshmen: 4,024 applicants (1,500 men, 2,524 women). 66.6% of applicants admitted. 30.8% of admitted students enrolled full-time.

72% (589 students) submitted SAT scores; 28% (234 students) submitted ACT scores. *25th percentile*: SAT I Verbal 360, SAT I Math 350; ACT Composite 14. *75th percentile*: SAT I Verbal 510, SAT I Math 510; ACT Composite 17.

39% of entering freshmen expected to graduate within 5 years. 64% of freshmen from Florida. Freshmen from 32 states and 13 foreign countries.

Admission: Rolling admissions plan. For fall acceptance, apply up to July 30. Apply by Dec. for early decision; need not limit application to Bethune-Cookman. Early acceptance available. *Requirements:* Either graduation from accredited secondary school with 24 units which normally include 4 English, 3 mathematics, 3 natural science, 5 social sciences, 9 electives; or GED. 2 years of a foreign language recommended. Minimum GPA 2.0. *Entrance tests:* College Board SAT or ACT composite. 1 College Board Achievement recommended. *For transfer students:* 2.25minimum GPA; 94 hours maximum transfer credit.

College credit and advanced placement for postsecondary-level work completed in secondary school. Tutoring available. Developmental/remedial courses offered in summer session and regular academic year; nondegree credit given.

Degree Requirements: 124 credit hours; 2.25 GPA (transfer student 2.00 minimum GPA); 1 year in residence; exit competency examinations in writing and mathematics; comprehensives in individual fields of study; weekly chapel attendance; 1 semester physical education; demonstration of sound ethical character. Fulfillment of some degree requirements possible by passing College Board CLEP. *Grading system:* A–F; drop (carries time limit).

Distinctive Educational Programs: Continuing education program provided via Extension Centers in Florida. Dual-degree program in engineering with Tuskegee Institute (AL), University of Florida, University of Central Florida, Florida A&M, Florida Atlantic University. Honors Program. Facilities for independent study including research and tutorials. Study abroad programs in language study in France, Germany, Spain.

ROTC: Army, Air Force offered in cooperation with Embry-Riddle Aeronautical University.

Degrees Conferred: 276 *baccalaureate*. Bachelor's degrees awarded in top five disciplines: business, management, marketing, and related support services 67; psychology 31; education 29; health professions and related clinical sciences 28; security and protective services 27.

Fees and Other Expenses: *Full-time tuition per academic year 2004–05:* $10,610. *Books and supplies:* $790. *Room and board per academic year:* $6,374.

Financial Aid: Aid from institutionally generated funds is provided on the basis of academic merit, financial need, athletic ability, other criteria. Institution has a Program Participation Agreement with the U.S. Department of Education for eligible students to receive Pell Grants and other federal aid.

Financial aid to full-time, first-time undergraduate students: 65% received federal grants averaging $3,610; 59% state/local grants averaging $3,631; 35% institutional grants averaging $9,875; 75% loans averaging $2,605.

Departments and Teaching Staff: Business *professors* 1, *associate professors* 1, *assistant professors* 8, *instructors* 4, *part-time teachers* 3; education 1, 3, 9, 1, 5; humanities 5, 2, 11, 10, 12; nursing 0, 1, 2, 3, 2; science/mathematics 10, 6, 8, 0, 1; social sciences 1, 0, 9; 22, 4. *Total instructional faculty:* 163. Student-to-faculty ratio: 17:1. Degrees held by full-time faculty: doctorate 54%, master's 46%. 54% hold terminal degrees.

Enrollment: Total enrollment 2,794 (41.3% men, 58.7% women).

Characteristics of Student Body: *Ethnic and racial makeup:* Black non-Hispanic: 89.7%; Hispanic: 1%; Asian or Pacific Islander: .3%; White non-Hispanic: 1.8%; unknown: 1.6%.

International Students: 156 nonresident aliens enrolled fall 2003. Students from Europe, Asia, Africa, Canada, Australia. No programs available to aid students whose native language is not English. No financial aid specifically designated for international students.

Student Life: On-campus residence halls house 61% of student body. Dormitories for men only constitute 42% of such space, for women only 58%. *Intercollegiate athletics:* men only: baseball, basketball, cross-country, football, golf, tennis, indoor/outdoor track; women only: basketball, cross-country, golf, softball, tennis, indoor/outdoor track, volleyball. *Special regulations:* Cars permitted for all but freshmen. Curfews begin 11pm weekdays, 2am weekends. Quiet hours from 7pm to 9pm Sun.–Thurs. *Special services:* Learning Resources Center, medical services. *Student publications, radio: B-Cean*, a yearbook; *Pure Pleasure*, a biannual literary magazine; *Voice of the Wildcat*, a monthly newspaper. Radio station WBCC broadcasts 84 hours per week. *Surrounding community:* Daytona Beach population 65,000. Orlando, 60 miles from campus, is nearest metropolitan area. Served by mass transit bus system; airport 3 miles from campus; passenger rail service 30 miles from campus.

Publications: Sources of information about Bethune-Cookman College include Jessie Walters Dees, Jr., *The College Built on Prayer; Mary McLeod Bethune* (Daytona Beach: Bethune-Cookman College, 1963); *B-CC Informer* , a quarterly newspaper for alumni and friends; college catalog.

Library Collections: 170,300 volumes including bound books, serial backfiles, electronic documents, and government documents not in separate collections. Online catalog. 770 current serial subscriptions. 50,000 microforms; 4,500 audiovisual materials. Computer work stations available. Students have access to the Internet at no charge.

Most important holdings include Mary McLeod Bethune papers (founder of B-CC); Black History Collection; Books of Abraham Lincoln.

Buildings and Grounds: Campus area 70 acres.

Chief Executive Officer: Dr. Toudie K. Reed, President.

Address admission inquiries to Les Ferrier, Director of Admissions.

Clearwater Christian College

3400 Gulf-to-Bay Boulevard
Clearwater, Florida 34619-4595
Tel: (727) 726-1153   **E-mail:** admissions@clearwater.edu
Fax: (727) 726-8597   **Internet:** www.clearwater.edu

Institution Description: Clearwater Christian College is a private fundamentalist institution offering programs in business, liberal arts, education, and Bible studies. *Enrollment:* 623. *Degrees awarded:* Associate, baccalaureate.

Accreditation: *Regional:* SACS-Comm. on Coll.

History: Founded 1966.

Calendar: Semesters. Academic year from Aug. to Nay. Freshman admitted in the fall and spring.

Characteristics of Freshmen: 396 applicants (217 men, 179 women). 44.4% of applicants admitted. 100% of admitted students enrolled full-time.

64% (112 students) submitted SAT scores; 58% (102 students) submitted ACT scores. *25th percentile:* SAT I Verbal 480, SAT I Math 450, ACT Composite 19, ACT English 19, ACT Math 17. *75th percentile:* SAT I Verbal 600, SAT I Math 560; ACT Composite 25, ACT English 27, ACT Math 23.

69% of freshmen from Florida.

Admission: Open admissions policy. Notification of acceptance on a rolling basis. *Requirements:* High school graduation or GED; SAT or ACT required.

Degree Requirements: *For baccalaureate degree:* 128 semester hours; 2.0 GPA; completion of required courses.

Distinctive Educational Programs: Nondegree study and work-study programs.

Degrees Conferred: 6 *associate*; 144 *baccalaureate*. Bachelor's degrees awarded in top five disciplines: business, management, marketing, and related support services 31; education 25; theology and ministerial studies 19; liberal arts and sciences, general studies and humanities 12; biological and biomedical sciences 11.

Fees and Other Expenses: *Full-time tuition per academic year 2004–05:* $10,850. *Books and supplies:* $860. *Room and board per academic year:* $4,820.

Financial Aid: Aid from institutionally generated funds is provided on the basis of academic merit, financial need. Institution has a Program Participation Agreement with the U.S. Department of Education for eligible students to receive Pell Grants and other federal aid.

Financial aid to full-time, first-time undergraduate students: 47% received federal grants averaging $2,614; 43 state/local grants averaging $3,658; 56% institutional grants averaging $2,035; 49% loans averaging $2,910.

Departments and Teaching Staff: Bible *professors* 4, *associate professors* 1, *assistant professors* 0; *part-time faculty* 0; business 3, 4, 0, 0; education 6, 2, 1, 0; fine arts 1, 3, 1, 2; humanities 4, 6, 1, 0; science 5, 4, 0, 0.

Total instructional faculty: 48. *Student-to-faculty ratio:* 20:1. *Degrees held by full-time faculty:* Doctorate 67%, master's 100%. 67% hold terminal degrees.

Enrollment: *Total enrollment:* 623 (48.5% men, 51.5% women).

Characteristics of Student Body: *Ethnic/racial makeup:* Black non-Hispanic: 2.9%; Asian or Pacific Islander: .8%; Hispanic: 4%; White non-Hispanic: 91.3%; unknown: 1%.

International Students: 16 nonresident aliens enrolled fall 2003. No programs available to aid students whose native language is not English. No financial aid specifically designated for international students.

Student Life: On-campus housing for 600 students. Cars permitted without restrictions. Intercollegiate and intramural sports. Campus is 10 miles west of Tampa.

Library Collections: 106,820 volumes; 198,000 microform units; 2,100 audiovisual materials. 1,050 current serial subscriptions. Computer work stations available. Students have access to the Internet at no charge.

Most important special collections include Civil War Records and Documentation (contained in bound volumes).

Buildings and Grounds: Campus area 140 acres.

Chief Executive Officer: Dr. Richard A. Stratton, President.

Address admission inquiries to Benjamin J. Puckett, Dean of Enrollment Management.

Eckerd College

4200 54th Avenue South
St. Petersburg, Florida 33711
Tel: (727) 864-8331   **E-mail:** admissions@eckerd.edu
Fax: (727) 866-2304   **Internet:** www.eckerd.edu

Institution Description: Eckerd College is a private, independent, nonprofit college affiliated with the Presbyterian Church (U.S.A.). *Enrollment:* 1,688. *Degrees awarded:* Baccalaureate.

Accreditation: *Regional:* SACS-Comm. on Coll.

History: Established and chartered as Florida Presbyterian College 1958; incorporated 1959; offered first instruction at postsecondary level 1960; awarded first degree (baccalaureate) 1964; adopted present name 1972.

Institutional Structure: *Governing board:* Board of Trustees of Eckerd College. Extrainstitutional representation: 24 trustees (all voting). 11 ex officio (non-voting). *Composition of institution:* Administrators 60 men / 31 women. Academic affairs headed by vice president and dean of faculty. Management/business/finances directed by vice president for finance. Full-time instructional faculty 152. Academic governance body, faculty, meets an average of 9 times per year.

Calendar: Semesters. Academic year Sept. to May. Freshmen admitted Sept., Jan., Feb. Formal commencement May.

Characteristics of Freshmen: 86% (407 students) submitted SAT scores; 40% (191 students) submitted ACT scores. *25th percentile:* SAT Verbal 520,

SAT Math 510; ACT Composite 22, ACT English 21, ACT Math 26. *75th percentile:* SAT Verbal 630, SAT Math 620; ACT Composite 27, ACT English 28, ACT Math 26.

60% of entering freshmen expected to graduate within 5 years. 23% of freshmen from Florida. Freshmen from 37 states and 22 foreign countries.

Admission: Rolling admissions plan. For fall acceptance, apply no later than May 1 of year in which enrollment is sought. Early acceptance available. *Requirements:* Either graduation from secondary school with 4 units in English, 2 in a foreign language, 3 mathematics, 3 science, 3 history and social studies; or GED. Minimum GPA 2.5. Lowest acceptable secondary school class standing 50th percentile. *Entrance tests:* College Board SAT or ACT composite. *For transfer students:* normally 3.0 minimum GPA, maximum transfer credit limited only by residence requirement.

College credit and advanced placement for postsecondary-level work completed in secondary school. For extrainstitutional learning (life experience), college credit and advanced placement on basis of portfolio and faculty assessments, and ACE *2006 Guide to the Evaluation of Educational Experiences in the Armed Services.* Advanced placement for International Baccalaureate Diploma. Tutoring available.

Degree Requirements: 36 courses; 2-year residence requirement; competency requirement in writing; comprehensives in individual fields of study; general education requirements. Fulfillment of some degree requirements and exemption from some beginning courses possible by passing departmental examinations, College Board CLEP or AP. *Grading system:* A–F; withdraw (carries penalty); incomplete (carries time limit).

Distinctive Educational Programs: Marine Science; International Business, Creative Writing, International Relations, Environmental Studies. Autumn Term (for credit) and orientation for freshmen (3 weeks). Academy of Senior Professionals (ASPEC) at Eckerd College (ASPEC) whose members assist with instruction and career guidance. Facilities and programs for independent research and study, including individual majors, tutorials. Study abroad, including Kansai Gaidai (Osaka, Japan), Nanzan University in Nagoya, Japan; University of Foreign Studies (Osaka, Japan); Eckerd London Center; Eckerd Florence, Italy; Aix en Provence and Avignon, France; Madrid, Spain; Freiburg, Germany; affiliation with International Student Exchange Program (ISEP).

ROTC: Army and Air Force in cooperation with University of South Florida.

Degrees Conferred: 329 *baccalaureate:* area and ethnic studies 4, biological and life sciences 67, business 70, communications/communication technologies 14, computer and information science 9, English 15, foreign languages and literature 3, health professions and related clinical sciences 1, mathematics 2, natural resources/environmental science 30, philosophy/religion/theology 8, physical sciences 2, psychology 44, social sciences and history 50, visual and performing arts 10.

Fees and Other Expenses: *Full-time tuition per academic year 2005–06:* $25,804. *Required fees:* $656. *Room and board per academic year:* $7,152.

Financial Aid: Aid from institutionally generated funds is proved on the basis of academic merit, financial need, athletic ability. Institution has a Program Participation Agreement with the U.S. Department of Education for eligible students to receive Pell Grants and other federal aid.

Financial aid to full-time, first-time undergraduate students: need-based scholarships/grants totaling $11,510,379, self-help $5,594,614, parent loans $862,330, tuition waivers $261,488, athletic awards $164; 359; $6,179,695, non-need-based scholarships/grants totaling $6,179,695, self-help $2,634,741, parent loans $1,710,006, tuition waivers $403,290, athletic awards $288,079.

Departments and Teaching Staff: Creative Arts *professors* 8, *associate professors* 3, *assistant professors* 3, *part-time faculty* 13; behavioral sciences 14, 2, 5, 8; comparative cultures 5, 3, 8, 11; letters 8, 4, 7, 5; natural sciences 8, 12, 11, 6; foundations 0, 0, 0, 8. *Total instructional faculty:* 152 (full-time 101, part-time 51; women 53, men 79; members of minority groups 19). Total faculty with doctorate, first-professional, or other terminal degree: 115. Student-to-faculty ratio: 13:1. 16 faculty members awarded sabbaticals 2004–05.

Enrollment: Total enrollment 1.688. Undergraduate full-time 727 men / 929 women, part-time 15m / 17w.

Characteristics of Student Body: *Ethnic/racial makeup:* number of Black non-Hispanic: 54; American Indian or Alaska Native: 4; Asian or Pacific Islander: 30; Hispanic: 30; White non-Hispanic: 1,291; unknown: 130. *Age distribution:* number under 18: 24; 18–19: 765; 20–21: 676; 22–24: 187; 25–29: 29; 30–34: 2; 40–49: 1; 50–64: 1, 65 and over: 1.

International Students: 117 nonresident aliens enrolled fall 2004. 36 students from Europe, 22 Asia, 34 Central and South America, 8 Africa, 5 Canada, 2 Australia, 10 other. Programs available to aid students whose native language is not English: Social, cultural, financial; English as a Second Language. Scholarships available annually for international students.

Student Life: On-campus residence halls house 80% of student body. Residence halls for men only constitute approximately 25% of such space, for women only 25%, coed 50%. Townhouse style residence hall for seniors. *Intercollegiate athletics:* men only: baseball, basketball, golf, soccer, tennis, water skiing, sailing, boardsailing; women only: basketball, softball, tennis, volleyball, water skiing, sailing, boardsailing, soccer; *Special regulations:* Cars permitted without restrictions. *Special services:* Writing Center, career counseling center, medical services. *Student publications, radio: Thimblerig*, a monthly newspaper; *EC Review*, an annual literary magazine; *The Triton*, a student newspaper; a yearbook. Radio station WECX broadcasts 90 hours a week; EC-TV television station. *Surrounding community:* St. Petersburg is within Tampa-St. Petersburg metropolitan area. Served by mass transit bus system; airport 25 miles from campus; passenger rail service 8 miles from campus.

Library Collections: 165,085 volumes including bound books, serial backfiles, electronic documents, and government documents not in separate collections. Online catalog. Current serial subscriptions: 821 paper, 92 microform, 13,375 electronic. 74 recordings; 127 compact discs; 244 CD-ROMs. 22 computer work stations. Students have access to the Internet at no charge. Total budget for books and materials 2004–05: $575,601.

Most important special collections include British history, marine science, and gender studies.

Buildings and Grounds: Waterfront campus area 188 acres situated on bay of the Gulf of Mexico. *New buildings:* Peter H. Armacost Library complete 2004.

Chief Executive Officer: Dr. Donald R. Eastman, President.

Address admission inquiries to Laura E. Schlack, Dean, Admissions and Financial Aid.

Edward Waters College

1658 Kings Road
Jacksonville, Florida 32209

Tel: (904) 470-8000   **E-mail:** tbaldwin@ewc.edu
Fax: (904) 470-8039   **Internet:** www.ewc.edu

Institution Description: Edward Waters College is a private, nonprofit college affiliated with the African Methodist Episcopal Church. *Enrollment:* 1,301. *Degrees awarded:* Baccalaureate.

Accreditation: *Regional:* SACS-Comm. on Coll.

History: Established as Brown Theological Institute 1866; chartered 1872; changed name to Brown University 1874; offered first instruction at postsecondary level and adopted present name 1891; first degree (baccalaureate) awarded 1980. *See* Samuel J. Tucker, *Phoenix from the Ashes* (Jacksonville, FL: Convention Press, 1976) for further information.

Institutional Structure: *Governing board:* Edward Waters College Board of Trustees. Extrainstitutional representation: 34 trustees; institutional representation: president of the college, 1 full-time instructional faculty member, 1 student; 1 alumna. All voting. *Composition of institution:* Administrators 11 men / 7 women. Academic affairs headed by vice president of academic affairs. Management/business/finances directed by executive vice president of business and finance. Full-time instructional faculty 39. Academic governance body, Academic Policy Committee, meets an average of 10 times per year.

Calendar: Semesters. academic year late Aug. to late Apr. Freshmen admitted Aug., Jan., May. Degrees conferred and formal commencement May. Summer session of 2 terms from early May to late July.

Characteristics of Freshmen: 69% of freshmen from Florida. Freshmen from 10 states and 20 foreign countries.

Admission: For fall acceptance, apply by June 30. Spring application deadline Sept. 30. Students are notified of acceptance upon completion of application procedure. *Requirements:* Open admissions; GED accepted. Recommend 4 units English, 2 mathematics, 2 natural science, 2 social science, 5 electives. *Entrance tests:* College Board SAT or ACT composite recommended. *For transfer students:* Automatic transfer for courses in which student has received C or better. From 4-year accredited institution 94 semester hours maximum transfer credit; from 2-year accredited institution 64 hours; correspondence/extension students 31 hours; good standing at institution previously attended.

Tutoring available. Developmental courses offered in summer session and regular academic year; credit given.

Degree Requirements: 120 credit hours; 2.0 GPA; last 30 hours in residence; 2 hours physical education; course, distribution, and general education requirements; exit competency examinations in writing and mathematics. Additional requirements for some degree programs.

Fulfillment of some degree requirements possible by passing College Board CLEP. *Grading system:* A–F; pass-fail; withdraw (no credit, progressing); administrative withdrawal; incomplete.

Distinctive Educational Programs: Cooperative education. Weekend and evening classes. Facilities and programs for independent research, including honors programs (for freshmen and sophomores only), individual majors, independent study. *Other distinctive programs:* Project Upward Bound recruits secondary school seniors who take courses on campus twice a week during academic year and reside on campus for 6 weeks during summer prior to freshman year; credit given. Dual degree program with University of Miami in mathematics and engineering.

Degrees Conferred: 132 *baccalaureate.* Bachelor's degrees awarded in top five disciplines: business, management, marketing, and related support services 78; education 14; security and protective services 11; communication, journalism, and related programs 9; biological and biomedical sciences 4.

Fees and Other Expenses: *Full-time tuition per academic year 2004–05:* $9,176. *Books and supplies:* $60. *Room and board per academic year:* $6,474.

Financial Aid: Aid from institutionally generated funds is awarded on the basis of academic merit, financial need, athletic ability. Institution has a Program Participation Agreement with the U.S. Department of Education for eligible students to receive Pell Grants and other federal aid. 88% received federal grants averaging $2,283; 61% state/local grants averaging $1,232; 38% institutional grants averaging $1,605; 89% loans averaging $3,312.

Departments and Teaching Staff: *Professors 35, part-time teachers 6. Total instructional faculty:* 41. Degrees held by full-time faculty: 40% hold terminal degrees.

Enrollment: Total enrollment 1,301 (52.5% men, 47.5% women).

Characteristics of Student Body: *Ethnic/racial makeup:* Black non-Hispanic: 92.5%; Hispanic: 1.2%; Asian or Pacific Islander: .1%; American Indian or Alaska Native: .2%; White non-Hispanic: .2%; unknown: .4%.

International Students: 2 nonresident aliens enrolled. Students from Europe and Asia. Programs available to aid students whose native language is not English: Social, cultural. No financial aid specifically designated for international students.

Student Life: On-campus residence halls house 18% of student body. Residence halls for men only constitute 46% of such space, for women only 54%. *Intercollegiate athletics:* men only: baseball, basketball, track; women only: basketball, track. *Special regulations:* Cars permitted without restrictions. Quiet hours from 9pm to 8am. Residence hall visitation from 7pm to 9pm Sun.–Thurs., 6pm to 11pm Fri. and Sat. *Special services:* Learning Resources Center, medical services. *Student publications: The Tiger,* a yearbook; *Tiger's Claw,* a monthly newspaper. *Surrounding community:* Jacksonville population 72,000. Served by mass transit bus system; airport 15 miles from campus; passenger rail service 3 miles from campus.

Library Collections: 66.000 volumes; 27,520 microforms; 2,900 audiovisual materials. 1; 350 periodical subscriptions. Online catalog. Computer work stations available. Students have access to the Internet at no charge.

Most important special collections include Obi-Scott Collection of African Art.

Buildings and Grounds: Campus area 50 acres.

Chief Executive Officer: Dr. Jimmy R. Jenkins, President.

Address admission inquiries to Tony Baldwin, Director of Admissions.

Embry-Riddle Aeronautical University

600 South Clyde Morris Boulevard
Daytona Beach, Florida 32114-3900
Tel: (800) 222-3728   **E-mail:** admit@.erau.edu
Fax: (904) 226-7070   **Internet:** www.erau.edu

Institution Description: Embry-Riddle Aeronautical University is a private, independent, nonprofit institution with residential campuses in Daytona Beach and in Prescott, Arizona, and College of Continuing Education operating with residential centers at selected military institutions worldwide. *Enrollment:* 14,676. *Degrees awarded:* Associate, baccalaureate, master's.

Accreditation: *Regional:* SACS—Comm. on Coll. *Professional:* aviation, business, engineering, engineering technology

History: Established as a flying school by Embry-Riddle Corporation 1926; changed name to Embry-Riddle International School of Aviation 1940; changed name to Embry-Riddle Aeronautical Institute and offered first instruction at postsecondary level 1952; awarded first degree (baccalaureate) 1963; adopted present name 1970.

Institutional Structure: *Governing board:* Board of Trustees. Extrainstitutional representation: 22. Institutional representation: 3 faculty, 3 students, 2 alumni. 4 ex officio. 27 voting. *Composition of institution:* Academic affairs headed by provost/vice president academics. University management/business/finances directed by vice president, business and finance. Each campus headed by chancellor. Full-time instructional faculty 190. Academic governance body, Faculty Senate.

Calendar: Semesters. Academic year Sept. to Aug. Freshmen admitted Aug., Jan., May, June. Degrees conferred and formal commencements Apr., Aug., Dec. Summer session of 2 terms from early May to mid-Aug.

Characteristics of Freshmen: Average secondary school rank of freshmen men 32nd percentile, women 24th percentile, class 31st percentile. Mean SAT score men 536 verbal, 569 mathematical; women 535 (v), 556 (m); class 535 (v), 567 (m). Mean ACT Composite class score 24.

78% of applicants accepted. 39% of accepted applicants enrolled. 41% of entering freshmen expected to graduate within 5 years. 22% of freshmen from Florida. Freshmen from 50 states and 36 foreign countries.

Admission: Rolling admissions plan. Early applications encouraged, and early acceptance available. *Requirements:* Graduation from accredited secondary school (or GED) with above minimum SAT or ACT test scores and above minimum high school GPA (depending on academic program). *Entrance tests:* College Board SAT or ACT. For foreign students TOEFL. *For transfer students:* 2.0 or 2.5 minimum GPA; maximum transfer credit limited only by residence requirement.

College credit and advanced placement for postsecondary-level work completed in secondary school. For extrainstitutional learning (life experience), limited college credit and advanced placement on basis of faculty assessment and personal interview, and ACE *2006 Guide to the Evaluation of Educational Experiences in the Armed Services.* Noncredit remedial courses offered in summer session and regular academic terms.

Degree Requirements: *For all associate degrees:* 60–81 credit hours; 15 hours in residence. *For all baccalaureate degrees:* 120–138 credit hours; 30 hours in residence. *For all undergraduate degrees:* 2.0 GPA; core requirements; basic skills courses in communications and mathematics. Fulfillment of some degree requirements and exemption from some beginning courses possible by passing departmental examinations, College Board CLEP, AP. *Grading system:* A–F; pass-fail; withdraw (students are not allowed to withdraw after a specific date in the term).

Distinctive Educational Programs: *For undergraduates:* Cooperative education. *Available to all students:* Evening classes. Independent study. *Other distinctive programs:* The Extended Campus provides instruction through 124 teaching centers in the United States and Europe, through independent study and computerized education.

ROTC: Army, Air Force optional.

Degrees Conferred: 62 *associate;* 932 *baccalaureate; master's.* Bachelor's degrees awarded in top five disciplines: transportation and materials moving 513; engineering 233; engineering technologies/technicians 69; business, management, marketing, and related support services 65; psychology 32.

Fees and Other Expenses: *Full-time tuition per academic year 2004–05:* $22,820. *Required fees:* $680. *Books and supplies:* $920. *Room and board per academic year:* $5,940.

Financial Aid: Aid from institutionally generated funds is provided on the basis of academic merit, financial need. Institution has a Program Participation Agreement with the U.S. Department of Education for eligible students to receive Pell Grants and other federal aid.

Financial aid to full-time, first-time undergraduate students: need-based scholarships/grants totaling $19,891,552; self-help $47,841,196; parent loans $8,706,486, tuition waivers $2,308,875, athletic awards $1,210,966.

Departments and Teaching Staff: *Professors 62, associate professors 67, assistant professors 47, instructors 14, part-time faculty 55.*

Total instructional faculty: 310 (full-time 225, part-time 85; 245; women 72, men 238; members of minority groups 34). Total faculty with doctorate, first-professional, or other terminal degree: 149. Student-to-faculty ratio: 19:1.

Enrollment: Total enrollment 14,676. Undergraduate full-time 1,711 men / 236 women, part-time 8,154m / 1,036w; graduate full-time 1,413m / 261w, part-time 1,568m / 297w.

Characteristics of Student Body: *Ethnic/racial makeup:* number of Black non-Hispanic: 841; American Indian or Alaska Native: 103; Asian or Pacific Islander: 322; Hispanic: 833; White non-Hispanic: 6,310; unknown: 2,633.

International Students: 95 nonresident aliens enrolled fall 2004. Students from Europe, Asia, Central and South, Africa, Canada, New Zealand. Programs available to aid students whose native language is not English: English as a Second Language program. No financial aid specifically designated for foreign students.

Student Life: On-campus residence halls and University-managed off-campus apartments provided. Fraternities and sororities available off-campus. *Special services:* Athletic facilities, student clubs and organizations, campus ministry, health services, counseling office, international student services, career services. *Student publications: Avion,* a weekly newspaper; *Phoenix,* a yearbook. *Surrounding communities:* Daytona Beach area population approximately 150,000 on Florida's east coast near Orlando; Prescott area population approximately 35,000 between the Grand Canyon and Phoenix in the Prescott National Forest.

Library Collections: 144,000 volumes including bound books, serial backfiles, electronic documents, and government documents not in separate collections. Online catalog. 760 current periodical subscriptions; 780 microform items; 7,500 audiovisual materials. Computer work stations available. Students have access to the Internet at no charge.

Most important holdings include computer science, engineering, aviation history; aviation historical collection.

Buildings and Grounds: Campus area 178 acres.

Chief Executive Officer: Dr. George Ebbs, President.

Address admission inquiries to Pam Thomas, Director of Admissions.

Flagger College

74 King Street
P.O. Box 1027
St. Augustine, Florida 32085-1027
Tel: (904) 829-6481   **E-mail:** admiss@flagler.edu
Fax: (904) 824-6017   **Internet:** www.flagler.edu

Institution Description: Flagler College is a private, independent, nonprofit college. *Enrollment:* 787 men / 1,258 women. *Degrees awarded:* Baccalaureate. Member of Northeast Florida Consortium for the Hearing Impaired.

Accreditation: *Regional:* SACS-Comm. on Coll.

History: Chartered 1963; established and offered first instruction at postsecondary level 1968; awarded first degree (baccalaureate) 1972.

Institutional Structure: *Governing board:* Flagler College Board of Trustees. Extrainstitutional representation: 16 trustees. All voting. *Composition of institution:* Administrators 13 men / 12 women. Academic affairs headed by dean. Management/business/finances directed by director of business services. Full-time instructional faculty 66. Academic governance body, College Administrative Council, meets an average of 48 times per year.

Calendar: Semesters. Academic year Sept. to Apr. Freshmen and transfers admitted Sept. and Jan. Degrees conferred and formal commencement Dec. and Apr. One summer session from late Apr. to mid-June.

Characteristics of Freshmen: Middle 50%: SAT Verbal 540–620; SAT Math 520–600; ACT 22–26. 34% of applicants accepted. 70% of accepted applicants enrolled. 50% of entering freshmen expected to graduate within 5 years. 66% of freshmen from Florida. Freshmen from 40 states and 17 foreign countries.

Admission: Early decision plan: deadline Jan. 1; notification Jan. 15. Regular decision plan: notification begins on Mar. 30 and continues on a rolling basis until class fills. *Requirements:* Graduation from recognized secondary school with a minimum of 16 units which should include 4 English, 3 mathematics, 2 science, 4 social studies, 3 electives. Minimum GPA 2.0. Recommendation from secondary school counselor required. *Entrance tests:* College Board SAT or Enhanced ACT. For foreign students minimum TOEFL score 550. *For transfer students:* 2.0 minimum GPA and either SAT or Enhanced ACT scores; 90 semester hours maximum transfer credit; from 2-year institution 64 semester hours maximum transfer credit.

College Level Examination Program (CLEP) credit is generally awarded for scores of 500 or higher on the General Examinations. Advanced Placement (AP) credit is generally given for scores of 3 or higher on the appropriate AP test. Developmental courses offered in English, mathematics, and reading during the regular academic year; credits granted do not count toward degree requirements.

Degree Requirements: 120 semester hours; 2.0 GPA; 45 hours in residence. Fulfillment of some degree requirements and exemption from some beginning courses possible by meeting institutional standards for CLEP or APP. Completion of general education requirements and requirements for a major. Successful completion of all the sub-tests of the College Level Academic Skills Test (CLAST). *Grading system:* A–F; pass-fail; pass; withdraw (deadline after which pass-fail is appended to withdraw).

Distinctive Educational Programs: Deaf degree program. Study abroad in Central America. Preprofessional program in law.

Degrees Conferred: 462 *baccalaureate:* business 115, communications/communication technologies 47, education 57, English 23, foreign languages and literature 10, liberal arts/general studies 18, parks and recreation 22, philosophy/religion/theology 10, psychology 38, social sciences and history 36, visual and performing arts 36.

Fees and Other Expenses: *Full-time tuition per academic year 2004–05:* $8,600. *Room and per academic year:* $5,190.

Financial Aid: Aid from institutionally generated funds is awarded on basis of academic merit, athletic ability, financial need. Institution has a direct lending program. Institution has a Program Participation Agreement with the U.S. Department of Education for eligible students to receive Pell Grants and other federal aid.

Financial aid to full-time, first-time undergraduate students: need-based scholarships/grants totaling $3,713,828, self-help $3,767,247, parent loans $639,129, tuition waivers $19,991, athletic awards $128,744; non-need-based

scholarships/grants totaling $3,256,156, self-help $1,631,864, parent loans $368,209, tuition waivers $76,068, athletic awards $233,516.

Departments and Teaching Staff: Art *professors* 2, *associate professors* 0, *assistant professors* 3, *instructors* 2, *part-time faculty* 8; business 1, 3, 5, 1, 11; communications 0, 0, 4, 3, 7; Education 3, 3, 2, 0, 17; English 2, 0, 5, 1, 9; liberal studies 1, 4, 2, 1, 14; mathematics 0, 1, 3, 4, 7; social/behavioral sciences 1, 2, 2, 1, 11; sport management 1, 0, 1, 0, 2; theatre arts 0, 1, 1, 1, 0, 6.

Total instructional faculty: 158 (full-time 66, part-time 42; women 91, men 87; members of minority groups 14). Total faculty with doctorate, first-professional, or other terminal degree: 75. Student-to-faculty ratio: 21:1.

Enrollment: Total enrollment 2,045. Undergraduate full-time 787 men / 1,258 women, part-time 24m / 37w. *Transfer students:* 92.

Characteristics of Student Body: *Ethnic/racial makeup:* number of Black non-Hispanic: 34; American Indian or Alaska Native: 6; Asian or Pacific Islander: 13; Hispanic: 81; White non-Hispanic: 1,897; unknown: 45. *Age distribution:* number under 18: 8; 18–19: 794; 20–21: 831; 22–24: 368; 25–29: 72; 30–34: 11; 35–39: 9; 40–49: 6; 50–64: 4.

International Students: 27 nonresident aliens enrolled fall 2004. No programs to aid students whose native language is not English. No financial aid specifically designated for international students.

Student Life: *Intercollegiate athletics:* men only: baseball, basketball, cross-country, golf, soccer, tennis; women only: basketball, cross-country, golf, soccer, tennis, volleyball. *Special regulations:* Cars permitted with campus registration. *Special services:* Medical services. *Student publications:* yearbook; *The Flagler Gargoyle,* a biweekly newspaper. *Surrounding community:* St. Augustine population 22,000. Jacksonville, 35 miles from campus, is nearest metropolitan area.

Library Collections: 130,201 volumes including bound books, serial backfiles, electronic documents, and government documents not in separate collections. Online catalog. Current serial subscriptions: 456 paper, 67,500 microform units. 2,400 recordings. 210 computer work stations. Students have access to the Internet at no charge.

Buildings and Grounds: Campus area 72 acres. *New buildings:* Men's dormitory completed 2004.

Chief Executive Officer: Dr. William T. Abare, Jr., President.

Address admission inquiries to Marc G. Williar, Director of Admissions.

Florida Agricultural and Mechanical University

112 Foote-Hilyer Administration Center
South Martin Luther King Boulevard
Tallahassee, Florida 32307-3100
Tel: (850) 599-3000   **E-mail:** admissions@famu.edu
Fax: (850) 589-3952   **Internet:** www.famu.edu

Institution Description: Florida Agricultural and Mechanical University is a state institution. *Enrollment:* 13,067. *Degrees awarded:* Associate, baccalaureate, first-professional (pharmacy), master's, doctorate.

Accreditation: *Regional:* SACS-Comm. on Coll. *Professional:* engineering, engineering technology, health information administration, journalism, nursing, occupational therapy, pharmacy, physical therapy, public health, respiratory therapy, social work, teacher education

History: Established as The State Normal College for Colored Students 1887; became land-grant college 1890; offered first instruction at postsecondary level 1905; changed name to Florida Agricultural and Mechanical College 1909; awarded first baccalaureate 1910; adopted present name 1953.

Institutional Structure: *Governing board:* Board of Regents. Representation: 13 members, including 1 student (appointed by governor of Florida) and commissioner of education. All voting. Total instructional faculty 455. *Composition of institution:* Academic affairs headed by vice president for academic affairs. Management/business/finances directed by chief business officer.

Calendar: Semesters. academic year from May to May.

Characteristics of Freshmen: 70% of applicants accepted. 50% of accepted applicants enrolled. *25th percentile:* SAT Verbal 420, SAT Math 410; ACT Composite 17. *75th percentile:* SAT Verbal 530, SAT I Math 530; ACT Composite 22.

80% entering freshmen expected to graduate within 5 years. 80% of freshmen from Florida. Freshmen from 41 states and 44 foreign countries.

Admission: Rolling admissions plan. *Requirements:* Either graduation from accredited secondary school or GED. Additional requirements for some programs. Minimum GPA 2.0 on academic courses. *Entrance tests:* College Board SAT (combined score of 800) or ACT composite (score of 17). *For transfer students:* 2.0 minimum GPA.

Degree Requirements: *For all associate degrees:* 60 semester hours; 20 of last 30 hours in residence. *For all baccalaureate degrees:* 120 hours; last 2 semesters in residence. *For all undergraduate degrees:* 2.0 GPA; general education requirements. *Grading system:* A–F; satisfactory-unsatisfactory; withdraw.

Distinctive Educational Programs: Work-experience programs. Independent study.

ROTC: Air Force, Army, Navy in cooperation with Florida State University. 4 Air Force, 21 Army, and 12 commissions awarded 2004.

Degrees Conferred: 52 *associate*; 1,605 *baccalaureate* (B); 401 *master's* (M), 24 *doctorate (D)*: agriculture 29 (B), 6 (M); architecture 43 (B), 8 (M); biological/life sciences 55 (B); business/marketing 383 (B), 150 (D); communications/communication technologies 92 (B), 1 (M); computer and information sciences 87 (B), 7 (M); education 144 (B), 83 (M), 16 (D); engineering and engineering technologies 107 (B), 18 (M), 1 (D); English 19 (B); foreign languages and literature 9 (B); health professions and related sciences 180 (B), 46 (M), 6 (D); mathematics 13 (B); natural resources/environmental science 5 (B), 5 (M); philosophy/religion/theology 1 (B); physical sciences 27 (B), 6 (M), 1 (D); protective services/public administration 127 (B), 27 (M); psychology 97 (B), 2 (M); social sciences and history 125 (B), 42 (M); visual and performing arts 47 (B).

Fees and Other Expenses: *Tuition per academic year 2004–05:* undergraduate in-state resident $14,759, out-of-state $29,941; graduate in-state resident $19,859, out-of-state $40,719. *Room and board per academic year:* $5,686 undergraduate; $7,016 graduate.

Financial Aid: Aid from institutionally generated funds is provided on the basis of academic merit, financial need, athletic ability. Institution has a Program Participation Agreement with the U.S. Department of Education for eligible students to receive Pell Grants and other federal aid.

Financial aid to full-time, first-time undergraduate students: need-based scholarships/grants totaling $31,162,392, self-help $31,397,621, tuition waivers $1,439,037; non-need-based scholarships/grants totaling $8,021,658, self-help $19,716,171, athletic awards $2,955,488. *Graduate aid:* 721 students received $2,659,517 in federal and state-funded fellowships/grants; 582 received $8,196,991 in federal and state-funded loans; 368 received $1,823,181 for college-assigned jobs; 87 received other fellowships/grants totaling $171,000; 25 received teaching assistantships totaling $80,467; 144 students were awarded research assistantships totaling $429,625.

Departments and Teaching Staff: *Total instructional faculty:* 621 (full-time women 241, men 380; members of minority groups 484). Total faculty with doctorate, first-professional, or other terminal degree: 160. Student-to-faculty ratio: 21:1.

Enrollment: Total enrollment 13,067. Undergraduate full-time 4,271 men / 5,946 women, part-time 606m / 613w; graduate full-time 252m / 481w, part-time 114w / 211w; first-professional full-time 179m / 335w, part-time 13m / 12w. *Transfer students:* in-state 466, out-of-state 119.

Characteristics of Student Body: *Ethnic/racial makeup:* number of Black non-Hispanic: 10,731; American Indian or Alaska Native: 3; Asian or Pacific Islander: 55; Hispanic: 104; White non-Hispanic: 338; unknown: 7. *Age distribution:* number under 18: 45; 18–19: 672; 20–21: 3,504; 22–24: 2,276; 25–29: 508; 30–34: 104; 35–39: 61; 40–49: 46; 50–64: 13; 65 and over: 2.

International Students: 303 nonresident aliens enrolled fall 2004. Students from Europe, Asia, Central and South America, Africa, Canada. Programs available to aid students whose language is not English: cultural. No financial aid specifically designated for international students.

Student Life: On-campus housing for single and married students. *Student publications:* FAMUAN (campus newspaper); *Cluster News Magazine, FANG* (student handbook). *Surrounding community:* Tallahassee population 200,000.

Library Collections: 879,458 volumes including bound books, serial backfiles, electronic documents, and 455,453 government documents. Online catalog. Current serial subscriptions: 5,636 paper. 5,512 recordings; 197 CD-ROMs. 200 computer work stations. Students have access to the Internet at no charge. Total budget for books, periodicals, audiovisual materials, microforms 2004–05: $1,957,365.

Most important special collections include African American Collection (including the E.A. Copeland Collection); rare book collection; African American Clipping File.

Buildings and Grounds: Campus area 419 acres. *New Buildings:* More than 13 new facilities have been added since 1999. The new University High School is under construction.

Chief Executive Officer: Dr. Castell V. Bryant, President.

Address undergraduate inquiries to Barbara Cox, Director of Admissions; graduate inquiries to Dr. Chanta Haywood, Dean of Graduate Studies.

Florida Christian College

1011 Bill Beck Boulevard
Kissimmee, Florida 34744-4301

Tel: (407) 847-8966	**E-mail:** admissions@fcc.edu
Fax: (407) 847-3925	**Internet:** www.fcc.edu

Institution Description: Florida Christian College is a private institution affiliated with the Christian Churches/Church of Christ. *Enrollment:* 259. *Degrees awarded:* Associate, baccalaureate.

Accreditation: *Regional:* SACS. *National:* ABHE.

History: Established in Orlando 1975; first classes began fall 1976; moved to present campus 1986.

Calendar: Semester. Academic year late Aug. to late Apr.

Characteristics of Freshmen: Average secondary school rank of freshmen men upper 20th percentile, women upper 15th percentile, Freshmen from 8 states and 3 foreign countries.

Admission: High school graduation or GED.

Degree Requirements: Completion of prescribed program.

Degrees Conferred: 8 *associate;* 31 *baccalaureate:* theology and ministerial studies 31.

Fees and Other Expenses: *Full-time tuition per academic year 2004–05:* $8,840. *Books and supplies:* $1,020. *Room and board per academic year:* $4,155.

Financial Aid: Aid from institutionally generated funds is provided on the basis of financial need, other considerations. Institution has a Program Participation Agreement with the U.S. Department of Education for eligible students to receive Pell Grants and other federal aid.

Financial aid to full-time, first-time undergraduate students: 50% received federal grants averaging $2,570; 45% state/local grants averaging $2,199; 71% institutional grants averaging $873; 52% loans averaging $2,001.

Departments and Teaching Staff: *Professors 5, associate professors 1, assistant professors 3, instructors 9, part-time faculty 6. Total instructional faculty:* 25. Degrees held by full-time instructional faculty: Doctorate 40%, master's 100%, baccalaureate 100%. 40% hold terminal degrees.

Enrollment: Total enrollment 259 (51.7% men, 48.3% women).

Characteristics of Student Body: *Ethnic and racial makeup:* Black non-Hispanic: 6.4%; Hispanic: 7.7%; Asian or Pacific Islander: .8%; American Indian or Alaska Native .4%; White non-Hispanic: 84.6%; unknown: .8%.

International Students: 2 nonresident aliens enrolled fall 2003. No programs available to aid students whose native language is not English. No financial aid specifically designated for international students.

Library Collections: 40,000 volumes. Online catalog. 280 current serial subscriptions. 100 CD-ROMs. Computer work stations available. Students have access to the Internet at no charge.

Most important special collections include the Fay Storm Davis Restoration Collections (materials of history of the Restoration Movement); Education Resource Center.

Chief Executive Officer: Dr. Harold E. Armstrong, President.

Address admission inquiries to Phillip Vincent, Director of Admissions.

Florida College

119 North Glen Aven Avenue
Temple Terrace, Florida 33617

Tel: (813) 988-5131	**E-mail:** msmith@floridacollege.edu
Fax: (813) 899-6772	**Internet:** www.floridacollege.edu

Institution Description: Florida College is a private, independent liberal arts college that provides a comprehensive undergraduate experience designed to develop students spiritually, mentally, physically, and socially. It aims to integrate into the students' lives the Bible as the revealed will of God and to prepare students to lives of service to God and humanity. *Enrollment:* 488. *Degrees awarded:* Associate, baccalaureate.

Accreditation: *Regional:* SACS-Comm. on Coll.

History: Established 1944.

Calendar: Semesters. Academic year Aug. to June. Freshmen admitted Aug., Jan., Feb. Degrees conferred June. Formal commencement June. Variable summer session.

Characteristics of Freshmen: 357 applicants (179 men, 178 women). 71.7% of applicants admitted. 99.2% of admitted students enrolled full-time.

57% of applicants submitted SAT scores; 63 submitted ACT scores. *25th percentile*: SAT Verbal 480, SAT Math 480; ACT Composite 20. *75th percentile*: SAT Verbal 600, SAT Math 600; ACT Composite 27.

Freshmen from 40 states and 5 foreign countries.

Admission: Rolling admissions plan.

Degree Requirements: *For degrees:* successful completion of all required credits; 2.0 GPA; satisfied all non-academic requirements for graduation.

Degrees Conferred: 139 *associate*; 14 *baccalaureate*: education 9; theology and ministerial studies 4, liberal arts and sciences, general studies 1.

Fees and Other Expenses: *Full-time tuition per academic year 2004–05:* $10,310. *Books and supplies:* $2,000. *Room and board per academic year:* $5,502.

Financial Aid: Aid from institutionally generated funds is provided on the basis of academic merit, financial need, other criteria. Institution has a Program Participation Agreement with the U.S. Department of Education for eligible students to receive Pell Grants and other federal aid.

Financial aid to full-time, first-time undergraduate students: 17% received federal grants averaging $2,809; 17% state/local grants averaging $2,847; 55% institutional grants averaging $2,943; 53% loans averaging $2,731.

Departments and Teaching Staff: *Total instructional faculty:* 34 (full-time 29, part-time 5; women 7, men 27; members of minority groups 2). Total faculty with doctorate, first-professional, or other terminal degree: 9. Student-to-faculty ratio: 15:1.

Enrollment: *Total enrollment:* 488 (full-time 248 men / 240 women, part-time 9m / 6w).

Characteristics of Student Body: *Ethnic/racial makeup:* number of Black non-Hispanic: 11; Hispanic: 12; White non-Hispanic: 472.

International Students: 8 nonresident aliens enrolled fall 2004.

Student Life: No on-campus housing.

Library Collections: 114m938 volumes including bound books, serial backfiles, electronic documents, and government documents not in separate collections. Online catalog. Current serial subscriptions: 9,224 microform.

Chief Executive Officer: Dr. Charles G. Caldwell, President.

Address admission inquiries to Mari Smith, Assistant Director of Admissions.

Florida Gulf Coast University

10501 FGCU Boulevard, South
Fort Myers, Florida 33965-6565

Tel: (239) 590-1000   **E-mail:** oar@fgcu.edu
Fax: (239) 590-1059   **Internet:** www.fgcu.edu

Institution Description: Florida Gulf Coast University is a public institution of higher education and is the tenth institution in the Florida State University System. It is a comprehensive university offering a full range of baccalaureate programs and graduate education through the master's degree. *Enrollment:* 5,972. *Degrees awarded:* Baccalaureate, master's.

Accreditation: *Regional:* SACS-Comm. on Colleges. *Professional:* business, clinical lab scientist, nurse anesthesia education, occupational therapy, physical therapy, social work

History: The university was founded in 1991 and is located in southwestern Lee County.

Institutional Structure: *Governing board:* Board of Regents. *Composition of institution:* Academic affairs headed by provost and vice president for academic affairs and dean of the college. Administrative services headed by vice president. Foundation headed by vice president. Full-time instructional faculty 170.

Calendar: Semesters. Academic year Aug. to May. Degrees conferred and formal commencement in Dec. and May.

Characteristics of Freshmen: 2,980 applicants (1,191 men, 1,789 women). 73% of applicants admitted. 41.5% of admitted students enrolled full-time.

90% (855 students) submitted SAT scores; 55% (526 students) submitted ACT scores. *25th percentile*: SAT I Verbal 470, SAT I Math 480; ACT Composite 20, ACT English 19, ACT Math 19. *75th percentile*: SAT I Verbal 560, SAT I Math 570; ACT Composite 24, ACT English 24, ACT Math 24.

Admission: Rolling admissions.

Degree Requirements: Earn a minimum of 120 semester hours (certain majors may require more than 120 hours) with a cumulative GPA of 2.0 in all coursework attempted. Colleges and departments may have requirements that exceed these minimums. Earn a minimum of 48 hours of upper division coursework (courses numbered 3000 and above). Complete the General Education and Gordon Rule requirements. Complete 30 of the last 60 hours at Florida Gulf Coast University. Complete the university service learning requirements. Complete the University Colloquium.

Distinctive Educational Programs: Dual degree programs with University of Central Florida; B.S. in Engineering; Doctor of Education. Study abroad through various international programs.

Degrees Conferred: 58 *associate*; 667 *baccalaureate*; 232 *master's*. Bachelor's degrees awarded in top five disciplines: business, management, marketing, and related support services 188; liberal arts and sciences, general studies and humanities 178; health professions and related clinical sciences 100; education 100; security and protective services 56.

Fees and Other Expenses: *Full-time tuition per academic year 2004–05:* undergraduate resident $3,056, out-of-state student $15,152. Contact the university for current graduate tuition/fees. *Room and per academic year:* $6,010.

Financial Aid: Aid from institutionally generated funds is provided on the basis of financial need, other criteria. Institution has a Program Participation Agreement with the U.S. Department of Education for eligible students to receive Pell Grants and other federal aid.

Financial aid to full-time, first-time undergraduate students: 20% received federal grants averaging $2,972; 64% state/local grants averaging $1,911; 38% institutional grants averaging $1,688; 29% loans averaging $3,527.

Departments and Teaching Staff: College of Arts and Sciences *professors* 5, *associate professors* 23, *assistant professors* 19, *instructors* 9, *part-time teachers* 0; College of Business 8, 10, 14, 2, 0; College of Education 9, 13, 4, 5, 1; College of Health 6, 5, 16, 5, 1; College of Public and Social Services 4, 2, 9, 2, 1.

Total instructional faculty: 173. Student-to-faculty ratio: 16:1. Degrees held by full-time faculty: doctorate 77%, master's 23. 77% hold terminal degrees.

Enrollment: Total enrollment 5,972. Undergraduate 4,836 (37.2% men, 62.8% women).

Characteristics of Student Body: *Ethnic/racial makeup:* Black non-Hispanic: 5.1%; American Indian or Alaska Native: .5%; Asian or Pacific Islander: 1.7%; Hispanic: 8.6%; White non-Hispanic: 81.8%; unknown: 1.5%.

International Students: 39 nonresident aliens enrolled fall 2004.

Student Life: On-campus lakefront apartments house 40% of the student body. Campus recreation and leisure services include intramural sports, Wellness Center, outdoor activities, student activities and organizations, multi-access services, counseling, and career planning. *Special services:* Learning Resource Center, health services. *Student publications: The Eagle Newspaper.*

Library Collections: 282,500 volumes including bound books, serial backfiles, electronic documents, and government documents not in separate collections. Online catalog. 1,430 current periodical subscriptions: 528,000 microforms. 2,300 audiovisual materials. Students have access to the Internet at no charge.

Chief Executive Officer: Dr. William C. Merwin, President.

Address admission inquiries to Joseph Shepard, Dean of Enrollment Management.

Florida Institute of Technology

150 West University Boulevard
Melbourne, Florida 32901-6975

Tel: (321) 674-8000   **E-mail:** admissions@fit.edu
Fax: (321) 984-8461   **Internet:** www.fit.edu

Institution Description: Florida Institute of Technology is a private, independent, nonprofit institution. The Colleges of Engineering, and Science and Liberal Arts, and the Schools of Aeronautics, Psychology, and Business are located on the main campus. The School of Extended Graduate Studies is located in thirteen states. *Enrollment:* 4,683. *Degrees awarded:* Associate, baccalaureate, master's, doctorate.

Accreditation: *Regional:* SACS-Comm. on Coll. *Professional:* clinical psychology, computer science, engineering

History: Established as Brevard Engineering College (an evening school), chartered, incorporated, and offered first instruction at postsecondary level 1958; awarded first degree (baccalaureate) 1961; began day program 1962; adopted present name 1966.

Institutional Structure: *Governing board:* Board of Trustees. Representation: 19 trustees, including president of the college. 18 voting. *Composition of institution:* Administrators 15 men / 4 women. Academic affairs headed by provost and chief academic officer. Management/business/finances directed by vice president for financial affairs. Full-time instructional faculty 178. Academic governance body, Faculty Senate, meets an average of 9 times per year.

Calendar: Semesters. Academic year Aug. to May. Freshmen admitted Aug., Jan., Mar., June. Degrees conferred May, Aug., Dec. and formal commencements May, Dec. Summer session from June to Aug.

Characteristics of Freshmen: 82% of applicants accepted. 27% of accepted applicants enrolled full-time.

89% (492 students) submitted SAT scores; 38% (210 students) submitted ACT scores. *25th percentile*: SAT Verbal 500, SAT Math 550; ACT Composite 22, ACT English 20, ACT Math 23. *75th percentile*: SAT Verbal 630, SAT Math 660; ACT Composite 28, ACT English 28, ACT Math 28.

52% of entering freshmen expected to graduate within 5 years. 27% of freshmen from Florida. Freshmen from 40 states and 31 foreign countries.

Admission: Rolling admissions plan. Apply as early as 1 year, but not later than June 1 of enrollment year. Early acceptance available. *Requirements:* either graduation from accredited secondary school or GED. Recommend strong background in mathematics and science. Additional requirements for some programs. Minimum GPA 2.5. Lowest acceptable secondary school class standing 60th percentile. *Entrance tests:* College Board SAT or ACT composite. For foreign students TOEFL. *For transfer students:* 2.0 minimum GPA; maximum transfer credit limited only by residence requirement. College credit and advanced placement for postsecondary-level work completed in secondary school. Tutoring available. Developmental courses offered in summer session and regular academic year; credit given.

Degree Requirements: Completion of all required general education and required courses in the major/minor areas. *For all undergraduate degrees:* 2.0 GPA. Fulfillment of some degree requirements and exemption from some beginning courses possible by passing departmental examinations, College Board CLEP, AP. *Grading system:* A–F; withdraw (carries time limit).

Distinctive Educational Programs: *For undergraduates:* Cooperative education. *For graduate students:* Off-campus centers associated with military bases throughout U.S. Tutorials available. *Other distinctive programs:* Continuing education for graduate students. Senior design projects or Senior Internships and undergraduate research.

ROTC: Army.

Degrees Conferred: 14 *associate;* 467 *baccalaureate* (B), 695 *master's* (M), 47 *doctorate:* biological/life sciences 62 (B), 4 (M), 5 (D); business/marketing 47 (B), 452 (M); communications/communication technologies 7 (B), 1 (M); computer and information sciences 36 (B), 41 (M), 5 (D); education 4 (B), 7 (M), 4 (D); engineering and engineering technologies 178 (B), 112 (M), 9 (D); interdisciplinary studies 6 (B); mathematics 7 (B), 7 (M), 2 (D); natural resources/environmental science 6 (B), 10 (M), 1 (D); physical sciences 33 (B), 12 (M), 1 (D); psychology 19 (B), 42 (M); 20 (D); trade and industry 62 (B), 7 (M).

Fees and Other Expenses: *Full-time tuition per academic year 2004–05:* undergraduate $23,730, graduate $780 per credit. *Room and board per academic year:* $6,220.

Financial Aid: Aid from institutionally generated funds is provided on the basis of academic merit, financial need, athletic ability. Institution has a Program Participation Agreement with the U.S. Department of Education for eligible students to receive Pell Grants and other federal aid.

Financial aid to full-time, first-time undergraduate students: need-based scholarships/grants totaling $17,689,505, self-help $13,498,129, parent loans $2,321,936; tuition waivers $302,708; athletic awards $1,137,458; non-need-based scholarships/grants totaling $4,974,648, self-help $1,490,776, parent loans $300,448, tuition waivers $186,380, athletic awards $741,339. *Graduate aid:* 3 fellowships and grants totaling $4,983; 137 teaching assistantships totaling $2,835,962; 111 research assistantships totaling $968,494.

Departments and Teaching Staff: *Professors* 61, *associate professors* 81, *assistant professors* 57, *instructors* 17, *part-time faculty* 0. *Total instructional faculty:* 390 (full-time 216, part-time 174); women 66, men 329; members of minority groups 44). Total faculty with doctorate, first-professional, or other terminal degree: 312. Student-to-faculty ratio: 12:1. *Faculty development:* $7,710,433 in grants for research. 3 faculty members awarded sabbaticals 2004.

Enrollment: Total enrollment 4,683. Undergraduate full-time 1,510 men / 714 women; part-time 75m / 20w; graduate full-time 365m / 265w, part-time 1,107m / 627w.

Characteristics of Student Body: *Ethnic/racial makeup:* number of Black non-Hispanic: 86; American Indian or Alaska Native: 8; Asian or Pacific Islander: 68; Hispanic: 151; White non-Hispanic: 1,300; unknown: 307. *Age distribution:* number under 18: 67; 18–19 913; 20–21: 824; 22–24: 386; 25–29 67; 30–34: 24; 35–39: 17; 40–49: 14; 65 and over: 7.

International Students: 705 nonresident aliens enrolled fall 2004. 140 students from Europe, 336 Asia, 153 Central and South America, 55 Africa, 14 Canada, 2 Australia, 1 New Zealand, 4 other. Programs available to aid students whose native language is not English: English as a Second Language Program. No financial aid specifically designated for international students.

Student Life: On-campus residence halls house 39% of student body. *Intercollegiate athletics:* men only: baseball, basketball, crew, cross-country, golf, soccer, tennis; women only: basketball, crew, cross-country, golf, soccer, softball, tennis, volleyball. *Special regulations:* Registered cars permitted without restrictions. Quiet hours from 8pm to 8am Mon.–Thurs., 11pm to 9am Fri. and Sat. *Special services:* Learning Resources Center, medical services, shuttle van service to airport. *Student publications, radio: Crimson,* a bimonthly newspaper. Radio station WFIT-FM broadcasts 126 hours per week. *Surrounding commu-*

nity: Melbourne population 100,000. Orlando, 65 miles from campus, is nearest metropolitan area. Served by mass transit bus system; airport 2 miles from campus.

Library Collections: 274,925 volumes including bound books, serial backfiles, electronic documents, and government documents not in separate collections. Online catalog. Current serial subscriptions: 2,073 paper, 984 microform, 10,361 via electronic access. 237 recordings. 2,783 CD-ROMs. 15 computer work stations. Students have access to the Internet at no charge.

Most important holdings include Aerospace Collection (500 volumes, including some autographed editions); John Medaris Collection (personal papers, memorabilia of Major General John B. Medaris, an important figure in space program development); Edwin A. Link Collection; Botanical Collection.

Buildings and Grounds: Campus area 130 acres. *New buildings:* Charles and Ruth Clemente Center; Columbia Residence Hall; Olin Physical Sciences Building.

Chief Executive Officer: Dr. Anthony James Catanese, President.

Address undergraduate admission inquiries to Judith A. Marino, Director, Undergraduate Admissions; graduate admission inquiries to Carolyn P. Farrior, Director of Graduate Admissions.

Florida International University

11200 S.W. 8th Street
University Park
Miami, Florida 33199-0001

Tel: (305) 348-2000   **E-mail:** admiss@fiu.edu
Fax: (305) 348-1908   **Internet:** www.fiu.edu

Institution Description: Florida International University is a state institution with a branch campus in North Miami; 30 miles away from main institution. The institution provides primarily upper division and graduate study. *Enrollment:* 32,228. *Degrees awarded:* Baccalaureate, master's, doctorate. Certificates also awarded.

Member of Southeast Florida Educational Consortium.

Accreditation: *Regional:* SACS-Comm. on Coll. *Professional:* business, computer science, construction education, dietetics, engineering, health information administration, health services administration, journalism, landscape architecture, music, nursing, occupational therapy, physical therapy, public administration, public health, recreation and leisure services, social work, speech-language pathology, teacher education

History: Established and chartered 1965; adopted present name 1969; offered first instruction at postsecondary level 1972; awarded first degree (baccalaureate) 1973; initiated limited lower division program 1981. *See* Rafe Gibbs, *Visibility Unlimited* (Miami: Florida International University Foundations, Inc., 1976) for further information.

Institutional Structure: *Governing board:* Florida Board of Regents. Representation: 13 members, including 1 student (appointed by governor of Florida) and commissioner of education. All voting. *Composition of institution:* Administrators 41 men / 12 women. Academic affairs headed by vice president for academic affairs. Management/business/finances directed by vice president for administrative affairs. Full-time instructional faculty 516. Academic governance body, University Academic Council, meets an average of 12 times per year. *Faculty representation:* Faculty served by collective bargaining agent affiliated with AFT.

Calendar: Semesters. Academic year late Aug. to mid-Apr. Students admitted Aug., Jan., May, June. Degrees conferred Apr., June, Aug., Dec. Formal commencement Apr. Summer session from early May to mid-Aug.

Characteristics of Freshmen: 11,888 applicants (4,948 men, 6,940 women). 31.5% of applicants admitted. 49.4% of admitted students enrolled full-time.

95% (1,927 students) submitted SAT scores; 40% (806 students) submitted ACT scores. *25th percentile:* SAT I Verbal 530, SAT I Math 530; ACT Composite 22, ACT English 21, ACT Math 21. *75th percentile:* SAT I Verbal 600, SAT I Math 610; ACT Composite 26, ACT English 26, ACT Math 26.

60% of entering freshmen expected to graduate within 5 years. 91% of freshmen from Florida. Freshmen from 48 states and 114 countries.

Admission: Rolling admissions plan. *Requirements:* Either associate degree or 60 semester hours from accredited institution with general education course work. Minimum grade average B; minimum scores 1000 SAT or 21 ACT. *Entrance tests:* For foreign students TOEFL. *For transfer students:* 2.0 minimum GPA; from 4-year accredited institution 135 quarter hours maximum transfer credit; from 2-year accredited institution 90 hours.

College credit for extrainstitutional learning on basis ACE *2006 Guide to the Evaluation of Educational Experiences in the Armed Services,* portfolio, and faculty assessments. Tutoring available. Developmental/remedial courses offered.

Degree Requirements: 120 quarter hours; 2.0 GPA; 2 terms in residence. Fulfillment of some degree requirements possible by passing departmental examinations, College Board CLEP. *Grading system:* A–F; credit-noncredit; withdraw.

Distinctive Educational Programs: *For undergraduates:* Cooperative education. Accelerated degree programs. External degree programs through State University System. Interdisciplinary program in environmental studies; interdisciplinary major. *Available to all students:* Weekend and evening classes. *Other distinctive programs:* Division of Centers and Institutes providing cultural programs, training sessions, and conferences on race relations, youth projects, women's research, sexism, labor research. Division of Latin Affairs providing bilingual and consumer education. Nondegree credit courses for professional nurses. Faculty Scholars Program allowing graduates of secondary school to enroll in the upper division program. Joint Center for Environmental and Urban Problems established with Florida Atlantic University. International Institute for Housing and Building. Consumer Affairs Institute sponsored jointly with University of Miami. International Affairs Center providing research, development, and joint programs in international education, research, and training. Continuing education.

ROTC: Army, Air Force in cooperation with University of Miami.

Degrees Conferred: 4,865 *baccalaureate*; 1,883 *master's*; 24 *post-master's certificate*; 78 *doctorate*. Bachelor's degrees awarded in top five disciplines: business, management, marketing, and related support services 1,768; health professions and related clinical sciences 417; psychology 366; education 345; social sciences 328.

Fees and Other Expenses: *Full-time tuition per academic year 2004–05:* $2,914 in-state resident, $15,420 out-of-state. *Room and board per academic year:* $7,341. *Books and supplies:* $1,140.

Financial Aid: Aid from institutionally generated funds is awarded on the basis of academic merit, financial need, athletic ability. Institution has a Program Participation Agreement with the U.S. Department of Education for eligible students to receive Pell Grants and other federal aid.

Financial aid to full-time, first-time undergraduate students: 42% received federal grants averaging $1,539; 34% state/local grants averaging $729; 41% institutional grants averaging $1,023; 11% received loans averaging $630.

Departments and Teaching Staff: *Professors 174, associate professors 267, assistant professors 238, instructors 100, part-time faculty 573. Total instructional faculty: 1; 352.* Degrees held by full-time faculty: Doctorate 75%, master's 21%, baccalaureate 3%, professional 1%. 77% hold terminal degrees.

Enrollment: Total enrollment 33,228. Undergraduate 27,269 (42.8% men, 57.2% women).

Characteristics of Student Body: *Ethnic/racial makeup:* Black non-Hispanic: 13.9%; American Indian or Alaska Native: .2%; Asian or Pacific Islander: 3.8%; Hispanic: 56.4%; White non-Hispanic: 19%; unknown: 1.2%.

International Students: 1,500 undergraduate nonresident aliens enrolled fall 2004. Programs available to aid students whose native language is not English: Social, cultural. English as a Second Language Program. No financial aid specifically designated for international students.

Student Life: No on-campus housing. *Intercollegiate athletics:* men only: baseball, basketball, cross-country, golf, soccer, tennis; women only: basketball, cross-country, golf, softball, tennis, volleyball. *Special services:* Learning Resources Center, medical services, shuttle bus between main and north campuses. *Student publications:* An international magazine, a newspaper, a student handbook, and a yearbook. *Surrounding community:* Miami population 400,000. Served by airport 5 miles from campus; passenger rail service.

Publications: *Caribbean Review* (quarterly) first published 1978.

Library Collections: 1,674,000 volumes. 132,853 government documents; 3,450,000 microforms; 145,000 audiovisual materials; 8,665 periodicals. Online catalog. Students have access to online information retrieval services and the Internet.

Most important holdings include International Collection; Latin American-Caribbean Collection; Narot Collection.

Buildings and Grounds: Campus area 573 acres.

Chief Executive Officer: Modesto A. Maidigue, President.

Address admission inquiries to Carmen Brown, Director of Admissions.

Florida Memorial College

15800 N.W. 42nd Avenue
Miami, Florida 33054-6199
Tel: (305) 626-3600

Institution Description: Florida Memorial College is a private college affiliated with the Baptist Church. *Enrollment:* 2,176. *Degrees awarded:* Baccalaureate.

Accreditation: *Regional:* SACS-Comm. on Coll.

History: Established 1917 as Florida Baptist Academy through merger of Florida Baptist Institute for Negroes (est. 1879) and Florida Normal and Industrial School (est. 1892); offered first instruction at postsecondary level and changed name to Florida Normal and Industrial Institute 1918; chartered 1941; awarded first degree (baccalaureate) 1945; changed name to Florida Normal and Industrial Memorial College 1950; adopted present name 1963.

Institutional Structure: *Governing board:* Florida Memorial College Board of Trustees. Representation: 24 trustees, including 1 alumnus, 6 administrators, 1 student. 1 ex officio. All voting. *Composition of institution:* Administrators 5 men / 1 woman. Academic affairs headed by dean of academic affairs. Management/business/finances directed by business manager. Full-time instructional faculty 57. Academic governance body, Academic Council, meets an average of 12 times per year.

Calendar: Semesters. Freshmen admitted Aug., May, June. Formal commencement Apr.

Characteristics of Freshmen: 5,323 applicants (2,113 men, 3,210 women). 44.4% of applicants admitted. 83.8% of admitted students enrolled full-time. Average secondary school rank men 47th percentile, women 60th percentile, class 53rd percentile.

88% of entering freshmen expected to graduate within 5 years. 80% of freshmen from Florida. Freshmen from 13 states and 10 foreign countries.

Admission: Rolling admissions plan. For fall acceptance, apply as early as junior year of secondary school, but not later than July 15 of year of enrollment. *Requirements:* Either graduation from accredited secondary school or GED. Minimum GPA 2.0. Lowest acceptable secondary school class standing 35th percentile. *Entrance tests:* 2.0 minimum GPA; maximum transfer credit limited only by residence requirement.

Advanced placement for postsecondary-level work completed in secondary school and for extrainstitutional on basis of portfolio and faculty assessments, personal interviews. Tutoring available. Developmental courses offered in summer session and regular academic year; credit given.

Degree Requirements: 124 credit hours; 2.0 GPA; 1 year in residence; weekly chapel attendance; 4 hours physical education; general education requirements; exit competency examination in reading.

Fulfillment of some degree requirements and exemption from some beginning courses possible by passing departmental examinations, standardized test. *Grading system:* A–F; withdraw (carries time limit).

Distinctive Educational Programs: Cooperative education. Weekend and evening classes. Honors programs. Tutorials. Career development program for Haitian adults. Nondegree continuing education for both Protestant clergy and laity.

ROTC: Air Force in cooperation with University of Miami.

Degrees Conferred: 249 *baccalaureate*. Bachelor's degrees awarded in top five disciplines: business, management, marketing, and related support services 70; education 49; security and protective services 36; social sciences 20; psychology 20.

Fees and Other Expenses: *Full-time tuition per academic year 2004–05:* $11,110. *Books and supplies:* $1,200. *Room and board per academic year:* $4,842.

Financial Aid: Aid from institutionally generated funds is awarded on the basis of of financial need, athletic ability, other considerations. Institution has a Program Participation Agreement with the U.S. Department of Education for eligible students to receive Pell Grants and other federal aid.

Financial aid to full-time, first-time undergraduate students: 90% received federal grants averaging $3,563; 42% state/local grants averaging $3,700; 15 % institutional grants averaging $3,700; 59% loans averaging $6,312.

Departments and Teaching Staff: *Total instructional faculty:* 57. Degrees held by full-time faculty: 60% hold terminal degrees.

Enrollment: Total enrollment 2,176 (35.2% men, 64.8% women).

Characteristics of Student Body: *Ethnic/racial makeup:* Black non-Hispanic: 84.1%; Hispanic: 5.3%; White non-Hispanic: .2.4%.

International Students: 178 nonresident aliens enrolled fall 2003.

Student Life: On-campus residence halls house 70% of student body. *Intercollegiate athletics:* men only: basketball, tennis, track, volleyball. *Special regulations:* Cars permitted on campus in designated areas. Curfews. Quiet hours. *Special services:* Medical services. *Student publications: The Lion's Den,* a quarterly newspaper. *Surrounding community:* The campus is located in an urban area of Miami. Served by mass transit bus system; airport.

Library Collections: 88,000 volumes. 7,500 microforms; 350 audiovisual materials; 400 current periodical subscriptions. Students have access to online information retrieval services.

Buildings and Grounds: Campus area 75 acres.

Chief Executive Officer: Dr. Albert E. Smith, President. >p<Address admission inquiries to Roscoe Warren, Director of Enrollment Management.

Florida Metropolitan College

5421 Diplomat Circle
Orlando, Florida 32810
Tel: (407) 628-5870   **E-mail:** info@cci.edu
Fax: (407) 628-2616   **Internet:** www.cci.edu

Institution Description: Florida Metropolitan College - Orlando is a private, independent college. The Orlando campus is one of eight located throughout the state of Florida (Clearwater, Fort Lauderdale, Lakeland, Melbourne, Pompano Beach, Tampa). For specific information regarding the Florida Metropolitan College system, refer to the website for CCI, Inc., corporate owner. *Enrollment:* 1,667. *Degrees awarded:* Associate, baccalaureate, master's.

Accreditation: *Nonregional:* ACICS.

History: Established in Jacksonville 1918; chartered 1947; offered first instruction in Orlando and became Jones College 1953; awarded first degree (associate) 1956; adopted present name 1982; acquired by CCI, Inc. 1998.

Institutional Structure: *Governing board:* Board of Directors. All voting. *Composition of institution:* Administrators 3 men / 5 women. Academic affairs headed by dean of education. Management/business/finances directed by president. Full-time instructional faculty 8. Academic governance body, Academic Committee, meets an average of 6 times per year.

Calendar: Quarters. Academic year Oct. to Oct. Freshmen admitted Oct., Jan., Apr., July. Formal commencement Apr.

Characteristics of Freshmen: 409 applicants (145 men, 264 women). 46.5% of applicants admitted. 50.5% of admitted students enrolled full-time.

Admission: Rolling admissions plan. For fall acceptance, apply no later than first day of classes. Early acceptance available. *Requirements:* Either graduation from accredited secondary school or GED. *For transfer students:* 2.0 minimum GPA; from 4-year accredited institution 135 credit hours maximum transfer credit; from 2-year accredited institution 90 hours. Transfer credit also accepted for correspondence/extension students.

College credit and advanced placement for postsecondary-level work completed in secondary school. For extrainstitutional learning, college credit on basis of ACE *2006 Guide to the Evaluation of Educational Experiences in the Armed Services*; advanced placement on basis of portfolio and faculty assessments. Tutoring available. Developmental courses offered in summer session and regular academic year; credit given.

Degree Requirements: *For associate degrees:* 96 credit hours; 48 hours in residence. *For baccalaureate degrees:* 192 credit hours; 48 hours in residence. *For all undergraduate degrees:* 2.0 GPA. *For master's degree:* 54 credit hours; 3.0 GPA.

Fulfillment of some degree requirements and exemption from some beginning courses possible by passing College Board CLEP. *Grading system:* A–F; withdraw (carries penalty); audit and incomplete.

Distinctive Educational Programs: Work-experience programs. Off-campus centers. Evening classes.

Degrees Conferred: 202 *associate*; 74 *baccalaureate*; 40 *master's*. Bachelor's degrees awarded in disciplines of: business, management, marketing, and related support services 38; security and protective services 17; computer and information sciences and support services 13; health professions and related clinical sciences 6.

Fees and Other Expenses: *Full-time tuition per academic year 2004–05:* $9,180. *Books and supplies:* $700. *Room and board per academic year:* $5,985.

Financial Aid: Aid from institutionally generated funds is provided on the basis of academic merit, other considerations. Institution has a Program Participation Agreement with the U.S. Department of Education for eligible students to receive Pell Grants and other federal aid.

Financial aid to full-time, first-time undergraduate students: 54% of students received federal grants averaging $2,091; 9% state/local grants averaging $516; 1% institutional grants; 60% loans averaging $4,377.

Departments and Teaching Staff: *Instructors* 8, *part-time faculty* 80. *Total instructional faculty:* 88.

Enrollment: Total enrollment 1,667. Undergraduate 1,564 (33.2% men, 68.8% women).

Characteristics of Student Body: *Ethnic/racial makeup:* Black non-Hispanic: 34.4%; American Indian or Alaska Native: .6%; Asian or Pacific Islander: 2%; Hispanic: 17.1%; White non-Hispanic: 28.5%; unknown: 13.6%.

International Students: 59 undergraduate nonresidents enrolled. Students from Asia, Latin America, Africa, Canada. No programs available to aid students whose native language is not English. No financial aid specifically designated for international students.

Student Life: No on-campus housing. *Special regulations:* Cars permitted without restrictions. *Special services:* Learning Resources Center. *Student publications: Newsletter,* a quarterly publication. *Surrounding community:* Orlando metropolitan area population over 1 million. Served by mass transit system; airport 15 miles from campus; passenger rail service 8 miles from campus.

Library Collections: 15,000 volumes. 150 audiovisual materials; 150 current periodical subscriptions.

Most important special holdings include collections on marketing, accounting, and management.

Buildings and Grounds: Campus area 1 acre.

Chief Executive Officer: Ouida B. Kirby, President.

Address admission inquiries to Dave Ritchie, Director of Admissions.

Florida Southern College

111 Lake Hollingsworth Drive
Lakeland, Florida 33801-5698
Tel: (800) 274-4131   **E-mail:** admin@flsouthern.edu
Fax: (863) 680-4120   **Internet:** www.flsouthern.edu

Institution Description: Florida Southern College is a private college affiliated with the Florida Annual Conference of the Methodist Church. *Enrollment:* 1,830. *Degrees awarded:* Baccalaureate, master's.

Accreditation: *Regional:* SACS-Comm. on Coll.

History: Established as Florida Conference College and offered first instruction at postsecondary level 1855; awarded first degree (baccalaureate) 1890; changed name to The Florida Seminary 1902; changed name to Southern College 1906; chartered 1907.

Institutional Structure: *Governing board:* Florida Southern College Board of Trustees. Extrainstitutional representation: 35 trustees; institutional representation: 7 administrators, 1 full-time instructional faculty member, 1 student; 17 alumnus. 1 ex officio. *Composition of institution:* Administrators 3 men / 3 woman. Academic affairs headed by vice president and dean of the college. Management/business/finances directed by vice president for finance. Full-time instructional faculty 109. Academic governance body, the faculty, meets an average of 8 times per year.

Calendar: Semesters. Academic year Sept. to Apr. Freshmen admitted Sept., Jan., July. Degrees conferred and formal commencements May, Dec. Summer session of 2 terms from early June to late July.

Characteristics of Freshmen: 75% of applicants accepted. 31% of accepted students enrolled full-time.

64% (358 students) submitted SAT scores; 35% (199 students) submitted ACT scores. *25th percentile:* SAT Verbal 470, SAT Math 470; ACT Composite 20, ACT English 19, ACT Math 18. *75th percentile:* SAT Verbal 570, SAT Math 570; ACT Composite 25, ACT English 26, ACT Math 25.

52% of entering freshmen expected to graduate within 5 years. 69% of freshmen from Florida. Freshmen from 41 states and 43 foreign countries.

Admission: Rolling admissions plan. For fall acceptance, apply as early as 1 year prior to enrollment, but not later than 6 weeks prior to beginning of term. Early acceptance available. *Requirements:* Graduation from approved secondary school with 4 units English, 3 mathematics, 6 from among foreign languages, natural sciences, social studies. Minimum GPA 2.5 in academic subjects. *Entrance tests:* College Board SAT or ACT composite. *For transfer students:* 2.5 minimum GPA; from 4-year accredited institution 94 semester hours maximum transfer credit; from 2-year accredited institution 64 hours; correspondence/extension students 15 hours.

College credit for extrainstitutional learning on basis of ACE *2006 Guide to the Evaluation of Educational Experiences in the Armed Services.* Tutoring available.

Degree Requirements: 124 credit hours; 2.0 GPA; 2 semesters in residence; monthly Convocation for full-time students; 2 physical education courses; core curriculum; sophomore and senior examinations. Fulfillment of some degree requirements possible by passing College Board CLEP, AP. *Grading system:* A–F; pass-fail; satisfactory-unsatisfactory; withdraw; incomplete.

Distinctive Educational Programs: Flexible meeting places and schedules, including off-campus center (in Orlando) and evening classes. Study abroad in England, Germany, Spain, Switzerland. Study-travel programs. Washington (DC) semester at American University. United Nations semester in cooperation with Drew University (NJ).

ROTC: Air Force, Army. 14 Army commissions awarded 2004.

Degrees Conferred: 524 *baccalaureate:* agriculture 78, biological/life sciences 28, business/marketing 180, communications/communication technologies 41, computer and information sciences 4, education 68, English 9, foreign languages and literature 4, health professions and related sciences 32, liberal arts/general studies 2, mathematics 8, parks and recreation 6, philosophy/religion/theology 10, physical sciences 2, protective services/public administration 24, psychology 24, social sciences and history 28, visual and performing arts 35; 21 *master's* business/marketing.

Fees and Other Expenses: *Full-time tuition per academic year 2004–05:* $17,860 undergraduate; $220 to $350 per credit hour graduate depending on program. *Required fees:* $380. *Room and board per academic year:* $6,410.

Financial Aid: Aid from institutionally generated funds is awarded on the basis of academic merit, financial need, athletic ability. Institution has a Program Participation Agreement with the U.S. Department of Education for eligible students to receive Pell Grants and other federal aid.

Financial aid to full-time, first-time undergraduate students: need-based scholarships/grants totaling $10,229,476, self-help $5,345,678, tuition waivers $484,432, athletic awards $1,315,245; non-need-based scholarships/grants totaling $1,274,436, self-help $318,280, tuition waivers $94,834, athletic awards $108,368. *Graduate aid:* 8 federal and state-funded loans (ranging from $2,500 to $7,500).

Departments and Teaching Staff: *Professors* 40, *associate professors* 31, *assistant professors* 35, *instructors* 3, *part-time faculty* 71. *Total instructional faculty:* 178 (full-time 107, part-time 69; women 67, men 111; members of minority groups 15). Total faculty with doctorate, first-professional, or other terminal degree: 101. Student-to-faculty ratio: 14:1. 2 faculty members awarded sabbaticals 2004.

Enrollment: Total enrollment 1,989. Undergraduate full-time 725 men / 1,105 women, part-time 32m / 72w; graduate part-time 24m / 72w. *Transfer students:* in-state 74; out-of-state 525.

Characteristics of Student Body: *Ethnic/racial makeup:* number of Black non-Hispanic: 121; American Indian or Alaska Native: 6; Asian or Pacific Islander: 19; Hispanic: 77, white non-Hispanic: 1,563; unknown: 8. *Age distribution:* number under 18: 27; 18–19: 818; 20–21: 661; 22–24: 257; 25–29: 28; 30–34: 12; 35–39: 3; 40–49: 10; 50–64: 3.

International Students: 81 nonresident aliens enrolled fall 2004. 22 students from Europe, 13 Asia, 12 Central and South America, 9 Africa, 3 Canada, 1 New Zealand, 19 other. Programs available to aid students whose native language is not English: Social, cultural. English as a Second Language Program. No financial aid specifically designated for international students.

Student Life: Residence halls for men only constitute 34% of such space, for women only 66%. 19% of men join fraternities; 20% of women join sororities. *Intercollegiate athletics:* men only: baseball, basketball, golf, soccer, swimming, tennis, water skiing; women only: basketball, softball, swimming, tennis, volleyball, water skiing. *Special regulations:* Registered cars permitted. Quiet hours. *Special services:* Medical services. *Student publications: The Interlachen Yearbook; The Southern Newspaper,* published weekly. *Surrounding community:* Lakeland population 80,000. Tampa, 30 miles from campus, is nearest metropolitan area. Served by airport 5 miles from campus; passenger rail service 4 miles from campus.

Library Collections: 166,755 volumes including bound books, serial backfiles, electronic documents, and government documents not in separate collections. Online catalog. Current serial subscriptions: 68. 13,598 recordings; 4,025 compact discs. 12 computer work stations. Students have access to the Internet at no charge. Total budget for books, periodicals, audiovisual materials, microforms 2004–05: $360,614.

Most important holdings include Congressman James A. Haley collection; Methodist Archives.

Buildings and Grounds: Campus area 100 acres.

Chief Executive Officer: Dr. Anne B. Kerr, President.

Undergraduates address admission inquiries to William C. Langston, Director of Admissions; graduate inquiries to Larry McLaughlin, Director of Evening Program.

Florida State University

Tallahassee, Florida 32306-2400
Tel: (850) 644-2525   **E-mail:** admissions@admin.fsu.edu
Fax: (850) 644-0197   **Internet:** www.fsu.edu

Institution Description: Florida State University is a state institution. *Enrollment:* 37,269. *Degrees awarded:* Associate, baccalaureate, master's, doctorate, first-professional (law)

Academic offerings subject to approval by statewide coordinating bodies. Budget subject to approval by state governing bodies.

Accreditation: *Regional:* SACS-Comm. on Coll. *Professional:* accounting, art, business, clinical psychology, computer science, counseling, dance, dietetics, engineering, family and consumer science, interior design, law, librarianship, marriage and family therapy, medicine, music, nursing, nursing education, planning, public administration, recreation and leisure services, rehabilitation counseling, social work, speech-language pathology, teacher education

History: Established as Seminary West of the Suwanee 1851; offered first instruction at postsecondary level 1857; awarded first degree (baccalaureate)

1881; became a state college for women 1905; became coeducational and adopted present name 1947.

Institutional Structure: *Governing board:* Florida Board of Education. *Composition of institution:* Administrators 120 men / 78 women. Academic affairs headed by provost and vice president, academic affairs. Management/ business/finances directed by vice president, finance and administration. Full-time instructional faculty 1,104. Academic governance body, Faculty Senate, meets an average of 8 times per year. *Faculty representation:* Faculty served by collective bargaining agent, United Faculty of Florida, affiliated with AFT.

Calendar: Semesters. Academic year Aug. to April. Freshmen admitted Aug., May. Degrees conferred and formal commencements April, Aug., Dec. Summer term of two 6-week sessions from May to Aug.

Characteristics of Freshmen: 65% of applicants admitted. 93% of applicants admitted and enrolled.

63% (3,904 students) submitted SAT scores; 52% (3,247 students) submitted ACT scores. *25th percentile:* SAT Verbal 530, SAT Math 540; ACT Composite 22, ACT English 21, ACT Math 21. *75th percentile:* SAT Verbal 630, SAT Math 630; ACT Composite 27, ACT English 27, ACT Math 26.

61% of entering freshmen expected to graduate within 5 years. 87% of freshmen from Florida. Freshmen from 46 states and 48 foreign countries.

Admission: Rolling admissions. *Requirements:* Graduation from an accredited secondary school with at least 19 academic units with a minimum of 4 units of English; 3 units of mathematics (Algebra I and above); 3 units of natural science (at least 2 with laboratory); 3 units of social science; 2 units of the same foreign language; and 4 elective units preferably from the above academic categories. *Entrance tests:* ACT or SAT. TOEFL required of international applicants. Most Florida students accepted to the University present at least a B+ average in all academic subjects (grades 9–12) and test scores of at least 25 (composite) on the Enhanced ACT or 1100 (verbal plus math) on the SAT. Non-Florida applicants will ordinarily be held to higher standards. *For transfer students:* 3.0 minimum college grade point average unless transferring from a Florida public institution with an A.A. degree and then college grade point average varies according to major. Admission requirements vary from year to year, depending on enrollment limitations and the quantity and quality of applicants. Applicant must have completed two years of foreign language in high school or 8 semester hours in college. Tutoring available.

Degree Requirements: *For all associate degrees:* 60 semester hours; 20 in residence. *For all baccalaureate degrees:* 120 hours; 30 in residence. *For all undergraduate degrees:* 2.0 GPA; liberal studies requirement. Additional requirements for some programs.

Fulfillment of some degree requirements and exemption from some beginning courses possible by passing AP, 1B, or CLEP. *Grading system:* A–F, with use of plus and minus, except no A plus, F plus, or F minus; pass-fail; withdraw (deadline after which pass-fail is appended to withdraw). The College-Level Academic Skills Test (CLAST) is required for admission to upper division status.

Distinctive Educational Programs: Internships. Evening classes. Accelerated degree programs. Interdisciplinary programs in basic studies, Black studies, fashion, international affairs, music, library science, social research, Russian and Eastern European studies, women's studies. Facilities and programs for independent research, including honors programs, individual majors. Exchange programs with Florida Agricultural and Mechanical University, Tallahassee Community College. Study abroad in England, France, Italy, Panama, Russia, Spain, Vietnam. *Other distinctive programs:* Internet-based distance learning, continuing education, and Panama City (FL) Campus.

ROTC: Army, Air Force in cooperation with Florida Agricultural and Mechanical University, Tallahassee Community College. 24 Army and 28 Air Force 23 commissions awarded 2004.

Degrees Conferred: 530 *associate;* 6,578 *baccalaureate* (B), 1,536 *master's* (M), 271 *doctorate* (D): architecture 24 (M), 3 (D); area and ethnic studies 12 (B), 12 (M); biological/life sciences 171 (B), 6 (M), 3 (D); business/marketing 1,477 (B), 139 (M), 11 (D); communications/communication technologies 301 (B), 33 (M), 2 (D); computer and information sciences 271 (B), 44 (M), 6 (D); education 524 (B), 324 (M), 76 (D); engineering and engineering technologies 187 (B), 65 (M), 10 (D); English 310 (B), 33 (M), 10 (D); foreign languages and literature 56 (B), 19 (M), 5 (D); health professions and related sciences 269 (B), 73 (M), 8 (D); home economics and vocational home economics 496 (B), 12 (M), 6 (D); interdisciplinary studies 1 (M), 4 (D); liberal arts/general studies 37 (B), 10 (M), 4 (D); library science 161 (M), 5 (D); parks and recreation 41 (B), 12 (M), 2 (D); philosophy/religion/theology 50 (B), 23 (M), 4 (D); physical sciences 72 (B), 28 (M), 38 (D); protective services/public administration 489 (B), 163 (M), 7 (D); psychology 327 (B), 23 (M), 15 (D); social sciences and history 1,044 (B), 145 (M), 24 (D); visual and performing arts 426 (B), 153 (M), 24 (D). 208 *first-professional:* law. 2 honorary Doctor of Humane Letters awarded 2003–04.

Fees and Other Expenses: *Full-time tuition per academic year 2004–05:* undergraduate in-state resident $2,045, out-of-state nonresident $13,956; graduate in-state resident $4,434, out-of-state nonresident $18,179. *Room and per academic year:* $6,488. *Other fees:* $934 undergraduate, $1,621 graduate.

Financial Aid: Aid from institutionally generated funds is provided on the basis of academic merit, financial need.

Financial aid to full-time, first-time undergraduate students: need-based scholarships/grants totaling $35,362,285, self-help $36,196,844; non-need-based scholarships/grants totaling $33,176,704, self-help $34,889,308, parent loans $10,545,429, tuition waivers $2,925,901, athletic awards $4,199,846. *Graduate aid:* 3,119 federal and state-funded loans totaling $47,189,543 (ranging from $700 to $31,440); 58 work-study jobs totaling $114,000 (ranging from $1,000 to $2,000); 438 fellowships and grants totaling $433,571 (ranging from $330 to $1,700); 7 teaching assistantships totaling $62,000 (ranging from $4,000 to $15,000).

Departments and Teaching Staff: *Professors* 420, *associate professors* 314, *assistant professors* 335, *instructors* 52, *part-time faculty* 1,336. *Total instructional faculty:* 1,255 (women 545, men 941; members of minority groups 187). Student-to-faculty ratio: 22:1. 90% hold terminal degrees. 31 faculty members awarded sabbaticals 2004–05.

Enrollment: Total enrollment 37,269. Undergraduate full-time 11,453 men / 15,087 women, part-time 1,489m / 1,794w; first-professional full-time 488m / 413w, part-time 6m / 10w; graduate full-time 1,899m / 2,199w, part-time 892m / 1,539w. *Transfer students:* in-state 6,395; from out-of-state 967.

Characteristics of Student Body: *Ethnic/racial makeup:* number of Black non-Hispanic: 3,607; American Indian or Alaska Native: 114; Asian or Pacific Islander: 898; Hispanic: 3,147; White non-Hispanic: 21,999; unknown: 435. *Age distribution:* number under 18: 91; 18–19: 10,060; 20–21: 11,490; 22–24: 6,066; 25–29: 1,311; 30–34: 529, 35–39: 306; 40–49: 359; 50–64: 155; 65 and over: 6.

International Students: 1,110 nonresident aliens enrolled fall 2004. 201 students from Europe, 680 Asia, 680 Central and South America and Caribbean, 106 Africa, 22 Canada, 2 Australia, 60 other. Programs available to aid students whose native language is not English: Social, cultural; English as a Second Language. No financial aid specifically designated for international students.

Student Life: On-campus residence halls house 16% of student body. Residence halls for women only 7%; for both sexes 93%. Some students also housed in privately owned and operated residence halls. 13% of men join and 5% live in fraternities. 15% of women join and 4% live in sororities. Housing available for married students. *Intercollegiate athletics:* men only: baseball, football; women only: soccer, softball, volleyball; both sexes: basketball, track, swimming, cross country, golf, tennis. *Special regulations:* Curfews. Dormitory visitation options: non-visitations limited 11am to midnight Sun.–Thurs.; 11am to 2am weekends (Fri. and Sat.); unlimited 24 hours. *Special services:* Learning Resources Center, medical services, on-campus bus service. *Student publications, radio, television:* Annual minority publication; annual student handbook; annual student government handbook; yearbook. Two public radio stations: WFSU-FM and WFSQ-FM, both broadcast 24 hours per day. *Surrounding community:* Tallahassee population 156,703. Jacksonville, 149 miles from campus, is nearest metropolitan area. Served by mass transit bus system; airport 10 miles from campus.

Publications: *FSU Law Review* (quarterly); *Water Resources Atlas of Florida; Resources Atlas of Apalachicola Estuary; Florida Vocational Journal* (bimonthly); *Open Entries* (quarterly); *Research in Review* (quarterly); *Social Theory and Practice* (three times a year); *Proceedings and Reports of Seminars and Research* sponsored by Center for Russian and Eastern European Studies, Research, and Exchanges.

Library Collections: 2,738, 779 volumes including bound books, serial backfiles, electronic documents, and government documents not in separate collections. Online catalog. Current serial subscriptions: 6,797 paper; 196 microform; 31,278 via electronic access. 58,200 recordings; 15,201 compact discs; 8,796 CD-ROMs. 513 computer work stations. Students have access to the Internet at no charge. Total budget for books, periodicals, audiovisual materials, microforms 2004–05: $6,600,669.

Most important holdings include Shaw Childhood in Poetry Collection; Mildred and Claude Pepper Collection; Napoleonic Collection.

Buildings and Grounds: Campus area 1,368 acres.

Chief Executive Officer: Dr. T. K. Wetherll, President.

Address admission inquiries to Janice Finney, Director of Admissions.

College of Arts and Science

Degree Programs Offered: *Baccalaureate* in biochemistry, chemical science, classics and religion, English/business, French/business, German/business, Italian, Italian/business, Latin American and Caribbean studies, Latin American and Caribbean studies/business, medical technology, religion and classics, Russian, Russian/business, secondary science and/or mathematics teaching, Spanish/business; *baccalaureate, master's* in American studies, archaeology, classics, classical archaeology, classical civilizations, Greek and Latin, German, Greek, Latin, religion; *master's* in Slavic languages; *master's,*

doctorate in chemical physics, oceanography, biological oceanography, chemical oceanography, geological oceanography, physical oceanography, cognitive and behavioral science; *baccalaureate, master's, doctorate* in anthropology, biological science, chemistry, analytical chemistry, biochemistry, inorganic chemistry, nuclear chemistry, organic chemistry, physical chemistry, computer science, English, creative writing, literature, French, geology, history, humanities, mathematics, meteorology, philosophy, physics, psychology, clinical psychology, general experimental psychology, Spanish, statistics.

Departments and Teaching Staff: *Professors* 167, *associate professors* 108, *assistant professors* 111, *instructors* 11, *part-time faculty* 24.26 FTE.

Distinctive Educational Programs: Interdepartmental majors in American studies, Asian studies, Asian studies and business, inter-American studies, comparative and world literature, English and librarianship, humanities, medical technology, modern languages and business, modern languages and librarianship.

Enrollment: Total enrollment 7,884.

College of Business

Degree Programs Offered: *Baccalaureate* in business administration/entrepreneurship and small business management, hospitality administration, management/human resource management, management/management information systems, management/purchasing and materials management, multinational business, real estate, risk management and insurance; *master's* in accounting, finance, management, marketing; *baccalaureate, master's, doctorate* in business administration; *doctorate* in business administration/accounting, business administration/finance, business administration/information and management science, business administration/management, business administration/marketing, business administration/risk management and insurance.

Departments and Teaching Staff: *Professors* 43, *associate professors* 20, *assistant professors* 24, *part-time faculty* 12.99 FTE.

Distinctive Educational Programs: Study abroad in Switzerland for 50 selected students in hotel and restaurant management.

Enrollment: Total enrollment 6,280.

College of Communication

Degree Programs Offered: *Baccalaureate* in audiology and speech pathology communication (advertising, communication/art, communication as a liberal art, communication for business, communication/science, communication studies, general communication, interpersonal communication, media communication, media performance, media production, political communication, public relations, sports information management and marketing); *baccalaureate, master's* in audiology and speech pathology communication; *advanced master's* in audiology and speech pathology communication; *baccalaureate, master's, doctorate* in audiology and speech pathology communication (communication theory and research, mass communication, speech communication).

Departments and Teaching Staff: Communication *professors* 3, *associate professors* 8, *assistant professors* 5, *part-time faculty* 4.66 FTE; communication disorders 4, 2, 5, 0, 1.

Distinctive Educational Programs: Special facilities for using telecommunications in the classroom.

Enrollment: Total enrollment 1,856.

School of Criminology

Degree Programs Offered: *Baccalaureate, master's, doctorate.*

Departments and Teaching Staff: *Professors* 5, *associate professors* 4, *assistant professors* 5, *part-time faculty* 4.

Enrollment: Total enrollment 1,526.

College of Education

Degree Programs Offered: *Baccalaureate* in physical education; *baccalaureate, master's* in emotional disturbances/learning disabilities, health education, leisure services and studies, mental retardation, visual disabilities; *master's, specialist* in counseling and human systems; *master's, specialist, doctorate* in adult education, educational administration and supervision, educational policy, planning, and analysis, educational psychology, educational psychology and testing (institutional research, research design and statistics), English education evaluation and measurement (measurement and testing, research and evaluation), foundations of education (history and philosophy of education, international/intercultural development education, social science and education), higher education, instructional systems, physical education (administration and professional preparation), reading education/language arts; *baccalaureate, master's, specialist, doctorate* in early childhood education, elementary education, English education, multilingual/multicultural education, rehabilitation services, science education, social studies education; *specialist, doctorate* in comprehensive vocational education, special education; *doctorate* in counseling psychology and human systems.

Departments and Teaching Staff: *Professors* 20, *associate professors* 35, *assistant professors* 39, *instructors* 1, *part-time faculty* 19.65 FTE.

Enrollment: Total enrollment 2,997.

College of Engineering

Degree Programs Offered: *Baccalaureate, master's, doctorate.*

Departments and Teaching Staff: *Professors* 13, *associate professors* 19, *assistant professors* 15, *part-time faculty* 2.67 FTE.

Enrollment: Total enrollment 1,642.

College of Human Sciences

Degree Programs Offered: *Baccalaureate* in fashion design, textiles, dietetics, food and nutrition science, food services administration, nutrition and fitness; *master's* in food and nutrition; *baccalaureate, master's* in clothing and textiles, fashion merchandising, family/child/consumer sciences, child development, housing, home economics education; *doctorate* in marriage and the family-human sciences; *master's, doctorate* in human economics, exercise physiology, motor behavior.

Departments and Teaching Staff: *Professors* 12, *associate professors* 15, *assistant professors* 6, *part-time faculty* 8.33 FTE.

Enrollment: Total enrollment 2,887.

College of Information

Degree Programs Offered: *Master's, specialist, doctorate.*

Departments and Teaching Staff: *Professors* 4, *associate professors* 5, *assistant professors* 11, *part-time faculty:* 1.67 FTE.

Enrollment: Total enrollment 1,144.

College of Law

Degree Programs Offered: *First-professional.*

Admission: Baccalaureate from accredited college or university; LSAT.

Degree Requirements: 132 hours, 2.0 GPA.

Departments and Teaching Staff: *Professors* 170, *associate professors* 7, *assistant professors* 6, *part-time faculty* 4.

Distinctive Educational Programs: Summer study abroad in England.

Enrollment: Total enrollment 740.

College of Medicine

Degree Programs Offered: *First-professional.*

Admission: Baccalaureate from accredited college or university. GRE.

Departments and Teaching Staff: *Professors* 6, *Associate professors* 3, *assistant professors* 8, *part-time faculty:* 6.33.

Enrollment: Total enrollment 177.

School of Motion Picture, Television, and Recording Arts

Degree Programs Offered: *Baccalaureate, master's.*

Departments and Teaching Staff: *Professors* 1, *associate professors* 6, *assistant professors* 4, *instructors* 3.

Enrollment: Total enrollment 220.

College of Music

Degree Programs Offered: *Baccalaureate, master's, doctorate.* Certificates also given.

Departments and Teaching Staff: *Professors* 33, *associate professors* 23, *assistant professors* 22, *part-time faculty* 4.67 FTE.

Enrollment: Total enrollment 1,151.

School of Nursing

Degree Programs Offered: *Baccalaureate, master's.*

Departments and Teaching Staff: *Professors* 4, *associate professors* 5, *assistant professors* 4, *part-time faculty* 6.33 FTE.

Enrollment: Total enrollment 1,027.

College of Social Sciences

Degree Programs Offered: *Baccalaureate* in Asian studies/business; *master's* in demography, planning; *baccalaureate, master's* in Asian studies, geography, international affairs, Slavic and East European studies, social science;

doctorate in marriage and the family - sociology; *master's, doctorate* in public administration, urban and regional planning; *baccalaureate, master's, doctorate* in economics, political science, sociology.

Departments and Teaching Staff: *Professors* 49, *associate professors* 20, *assistant professors* 31, *instructors* 1, *part-time faculty* 11.65 FTE.

Enrollment: Total enrollment 3,545.

College of Social Work

Degree Programs Offered: *Baccalaureate, master's, doctorate.*

Departments and Teaching Staff: *Professors* 4; *associate professors* 3, *assistant professors* 10, *instructors* 5, *part-time teachers* 8.66 FTE.

Enrollment: Total enrollment 725.

School of Theater

Degree Programs Offered: *Baccalaureate, master's, doctorate.*

Departments and Teaching Staff: *Professors* 9, *associate professors* 4, *assistant professors* 8, *part-time faculty* 1.33 FTE.

Enrollment: Total enrollment 474. part-time 16m / 6w; graduate full-time 42m / 37w, part-time 6m / 5w.

School of Visual Arts and Dance

Degree Programs Offered: *Baccalaureate, master's, specialist, doctorate.*

Departments and Teaching Staff: *Professors* 22, *associate professors* 26, *assistant professors* 15, *part-time faculty* 6.67 FTE.

Enrollment: Total enrollment 1,201.

Hobe Sound Bible College

11298 S.E. Gomez Avenue
P.O. Box 1065
Hobe Sound, Florida 33475-1065

Tel: (772) 546-5534   **E-mail:** info@hsbc.edu
Fax: (772) 545-1422   **Internet:** www.hsbc.edu

Institution Description: Hobe Sound Bible College is a private, interdenominational, nonprofit college. *Enrollment:* 128. *Degrees awarded:* Associate, baccalaureate.

Accreditation: *National:* ABHE.

Institutional Structure: *Governing board:* independent Board of Directors. *Institutional representation:* president of the college. *Composition of institution:* administrators 4 men. Academic affairs headed by academic dean; business/finances directed by Director of finances and development. Full-time instructional faculty 8.

Calendar: Semesters (4-1-4 plan). Academic year Aug. to June. Freshmen admitted Aug., Jan., Feb. Degrees conferred June. Formal commencement June. Variable summer session.

Characteristics of Freshmen: 96 applicants (21 men, 35 women). 73.2% of applicants admitted. 97.6% of admitted students enrolled full-time.

24% (10 students) submitted SAT scores; 34% (14 students) submitted ACT scores. *25th percentile:* SAT Verbal 450, SAT Math 440; ACT Composite 17, ACT English 15, ACT Math 16. *75th percentile:* SAT Verbal 540, SAT Math 600; ACT Composite 24, ACT English 24, ACT Math 24.

Admission: Rolling admissions plan. Apply as early as possible for each term, but not later than first day of classes. *Requirements:* High school diploma or equivalent (GED); SAT or ACT recommended; additional testing required of all new students during orientation.

College credit and/or advanced placement given for CLEP and AP. College transfer credit given for courses with grade of C or above.

Degree Requirements: *For all associate degrees:* 70 credit hours. *For all baccalaureate degrees:* at least 128 credit hours. *For all degrees:* Not less than 30 hours in residence; minimum 2.0 GPA.

Distinctive Educational Programs: All baccalaureate programs provide a double major, one of which is Bible. A variety of opportunities are available for student involvement in Christian outreach ministries. English language institute offered for international students.

Degrees Conferred: 10 *associate;* 15 *baccalaureate:* education 8, theology and ministerial studies 7.

Fees and Other Expenses: *Full-time tuition per academic year 2004–05:* $4,240. *Books and supplies:* $500. *Room and board per academic year:* $3,170.

Financial Aid: Aid from institutionally generated funds is provided on the basis of academic merit, financial need, other criteria. Institution has a Program

Participation Agreement with the U.S. Department of Education for eligible students to receive Pell Grants and other federal aid.

Financial aid to full-time, first-time undergraduate students: 84% received federal grants averaging $2,236; 65% state/local grants averaging $1,780; 77% institutional grants averaging $644; 81% loans averaging $2,561.

Departments and Teaching Staff: *Total instructional faculty:* 19. *Student-to-faculty ratio:* 10:1. *Degrees held by full-time faculty:* Doctorate 25%, master's 100%, baccalaureate 100%.

Enrollment: *Total enrollment:* 128 (45.3% men, 54.7% women).

Characteristics of Student Body: *Ethnic and racial makeup:* Black non-Hispanic: 3.9%; Asian or Pacific Islander: 1.6%; Hispanic: 2.3%; White non-Hispanic: 86.3%.

International Students: 5 nonresident aliens enrolled fall 2004. Students from Europe, Asia, Central and South America, Canada. Programs available to aid students whose native language is not English: English as a Second Language Program.

Student Life: Residence halls on campus for single students; approximately 80 each in men's only and women's dormitories. Other housing on campus available for married students. *Surrounding community:* Hobe Sound is located in southern Florida; 25 miles north of West Palm Beach.

Library Collections: 40,000 volumes including bound books, serial backfiles, electronic documents, and government documents not in separate collections. Online and card catalogs. Current serial subscriptions: 115 paper, 16,745 microform units. 2,515 recordings; 136 compact discs; 5 CD-ROMs. Students have access to the Internet at no charge.

Buildings and Grounds: Eight major buildings occupy the 80-acre campus.

Chief Executive Officer: Dr. Daniel Stetler, President.

Address admission inquiries to Judy Fay, Admission Director.

International Academy of Design and Technology

5225 Memorial Highway
Tampa, Florida 33634-7360
Tel: (813) 881-0007   **E-mail:** admission@academy edu
Fax: (813) 881-0008   **Internet:** www.academy.edu

Institution Description: The International Academy of Design and Technology provides Educational programs that are designed to prepare students for professional opportunities and career success in select design and technology fields. Through the guidance of the faculty, theoretical concepts as well as practical and creative applications are addressed in the curricula and reinforced by interaction with professionals in the various industries. *Enrollment:* 2,405. *Degrees awarded:* Associate, baccalaureate.

Accreditation: *National:* ACICS.

History: Founded in 1977 as a private institution. Tampa campus established 1984. Accreditation as a senior college by ACICS 1990.

Institutional Structure: Florida corporation owned by Career Education Corporation.

Calendar: Quarters. Academic year Aug. to June. Freshmen admitted Aug., Jan., Feb. Degrees conferred June. Formal commencement June. Variable summer session.

Admission: Rolling admissions plan. Early acceptance available. Personal interview required in person or by telephone. Required: graduation from accredited secondary school or GED.

Degree Requirements: *For degrees:* successful completion of all required credits within the maximum credits that may be attempted; current on all financial obligations; 2.0 GPA; satisfied all non-academic requirements for graduation.

Distinctive Educational Programs: Associate and baccalaureate degree programs in select design and technology fields (digital photography, computer animation, digital production, recording arts, fashion design and marketing, graphic design, interior design, interactive media, marketing and design).

Degrees Conferred: 450 *associate;* 154 *baccalaureate:* visual and performing arts 144; communication, journalism, and related programs 8; business, management, marketing, and related support services 2.

Fees and Other Expenses: *Full-time tuition per academic year 2004–05:* $17,250. *Required fees:* $300. *Other fees:* $100 per term.

Financial Aid: Aid from institutionally generated funds is provided on the basis of academic merit, financial need, other criteria. Institution has a Program Participation Agreement with the U.S. Department of Education for eligible students to receive Pell Grants and other federal aid.

Financial aid to full-time, first-time undergraduate students: 34% received federal grants averaging $2,654; 9% institutional grants averaging $898; 66% loans averaging $6,142.

Departments and Teaching Staff: *Total instructional faculty:* 171 (full-time 13, part-time 158; women 89, men 82). Total faculty with doctorate, first-professional, or other terminal degree: 29. Student-to-faculty ratio: 14:1.

Enrollment: *Total enrollment:* 2,405 (full-time 622 men / 1,080 women, part-time 223m / 480w).

International Students: 11 nonresident aliens enrolled fall 2004.

Student Life: No on-campus housing.

Library Collections: Online catalog. 40,000 volumes including bound books, serial backfiles, electronic documents, and government documents not in separate collections. Current serial subscriptions. Students have access to the Internet at no charge.

Buildings and Grounds: Campus area 10 acres.

Chief Executive Officer: Dr. Edmund K. Gross, President.

Address admission inquiries to Harold Saulsby, Vice President of Admission.

International College

2655 Northbrooke Drive
Naples, Florida 34119-7932
Tel: (239) 513-1122   **E-mail:** admit@internationalcollege.edu
Fax: (239) 513-4593   **Internet:** www.internationalcollege.edu

Institution Description: International College is a private, nonprofit, coeducational institution with a main campus in Naples, Florida, and a branch campus in Fort Myers, Florida. *Enrollment:* 1,544. *Degrees awarded:* Associate, baccalaureate, master's.

Accreditation: *Regional:* SACS. *Professional:* health information technician, medical assisting

History: Established in 1990 offering associate in science and bachelor of science degree programs in business-related curricula for adult working students. Curricula expanded to include medical-related programs and paralegal studies; student body expanded to include recent high school graduates as well as adult students.

Institutional Structure: *Governing board:* International College Board of Trustees. 13 trustees; institutional representation: president of the college. All voting. *Composition of institution:* Administrators 9 men / 6 women. Academic affairs headed by Executive Vice President of Academic Affairs. Business/finances directed by Executive Vice President of Finance and Student Services. Full-time instructional faculty: 57.

Calendar: Trimesters. Academic year Sept. to May. Freshmen admitted Sept., Jan., May. Degrees conferred and formal commencement in June.

Admission: Rolling admissions. *Requirements:* Graduation from accredited secondary school or GED. *Entrance tests:* SAT, ACT, CPT or in-house CPAT required. Remedial math and English classes for students not meeting minimum scores. *For transfer students:* 88 hours maximum transfer credit toward bachelor's degree. 40 hours maximum credit toward associate degree.

Advanced placement for postsecondary-level work completed in secondary school and for extrainstitutional learning on basis of ACE *2006 Guide to the Evaluation of Educational Experiences in the Armed Services,* portfolio and faculty assessments, not to exceed 25% of credits required for graduation. Tutoring available. Developmental/remedial courses offered in summer session and regular academic year; credit given.

Degree Requirements: *For all associate degrees:* 60 semester hours; last 20 hours in residence. *For all baccalaureate degrees:* 120 semester hours; last 32 hours in residence; distribution of requirements. *For all undergraduate degrees:* 2.0 GPA. *For master's degrees:* 36–48 hours.

Distinctive Educational Programs: Internships, accelerated management program, and 5th year classes for CPA requirements. Evening classes. Individual majors. Double degree programs.

Degrees Conferred: 93 *associate;* 35 *baccalaureate;* 63 *master's.*

Fees and Other Expenses: *Full-time tuition per academic year 2004–05:* Contact the college for current tuition/fees.

Financial Aid: Aid from institutionally generated funds is provided on the basis of academic merit and other criteria. Institution has a Program Participation Agreement with the U.S. Department of Education for eligible students to receive Pell Grants and other federal aid.

Financial aid to full-time, first-time undergraduate students: need-based scholarships/grants totaling $2,484,207, self-help $6,507,588; non-need-based scholarships/grants totaling $2,209,793, self-help $6,754,460, parent loans $147,049, tuition waivers $125,000. *Graduate aid:* 25 federal and state-funded loans totaling $875,000 (ranging from $500 to $18,500).

Departments and Teaching Staff: *Total instructional faculty:* 109 (full-time 57, part-time 52; women 35, men 74). Total faculty with doctorate, first-professional, or other terminal degree: 48. Student-to-faculty ratio: 16:1.

Enrollment: Total enrollment 1,544. Undergraduate full-time 293 men / 654 women, part-time 134m / 261w; graduate full-time 13m / 24w, part-time 58m / 107w.

Characteristics of Student Body: *Ethnic/racial makeup:* number of Black non-Hispanic: 158; American Indian or Alaska Native: 4; Asian or Pacific Islander: 13; Hispanic: 182; White non-Hispanic: 859; unknown: 20.

International Students: 106 nonresident aliens enrolled fall 2004. No programs available to aid students whose native language is not English. No financial aid specifically designated for international students.

Student Life: Commuter campus at both locations. *Special services:* mentor program, tutor assistance program, class audit and refresher education, alumni association, career development and placement office. *Publications: Panther Press, Compass Times, International Link, The Sextant.* Surrounding community: Naples surrounding population 200,000. Ft. Myers surrounding population 335,000.

Library Collections: 29,711 volumes. Online catalog. 230 current serial subscriptions. Students have access to the Internet at no charge.

Buildings and Grounds: Naples campus located in Gulfgate Plaza; Ft. Myers campus located in Renaissance Building at 8695 College Parkway, Ft. Myers, Florida, 33919.

Chief Executive Officer: Dr. Terry McMahan, President.

Address admission inquiries to Rita Lampus, Director of Admissions.

Jacksonville University

2800 University Boulevard, North
Jacksonville, Florida 32211
Tel: (904) 744-3950   **E-mail:** admissions@jiu.edu
Fax: (904) 745-0101   **Internet:** www.jiu.edu

Institution Description: Jacksonville University is a private, independent, nonprofit institution. *Enrollment:* 3,092. *Degrees awarded:* baccalaureate, master's.

Accreditation: *Regional:* SACS-Comm. on Coll. *Professional:* dance, music, nursing, teacher education

History: Established as William J. Porter University and offered first instruction at postsecondary level 1934; changed name to Jacksonville Junior College 1935; awarded first degree (associate) 1952; changed name to Jacksonville University 1956; added upper division courses 1957; merged with Jacksonville College of Music 1958; added graduate program 1964; added Executive MBA program 1984; added College of Weekend Studies 1986.

Institutional Structure: *Governing board:* Board of Trustees. Representation: 28 trustees, including 3 ex officio. All voting. *Composition of institution:* Administrators 18 men / 11 women. Academic affairs headed by vice president for academic affairs. Business/finances directed by vice president for operations. Development headed by vice president for development. Full-time instructional faculty 144. Academic governance body, Faculty Assembly, meets an average of 8 times per year.

Calendar: Modified trimester plan (two 15-week semesters, optional 12-week summer session or 2 six-week sessions). Academic year begins late Aug. Freshmen admitted Aug., Jan., Apr., June. Degrees conferred and formal commencements Apr. Summer sessions from early May to late July.

Characteristics of Freshmen: 1,974 applicants (1,009 men, 965 women). 71.7% of applicants admitted. 32.6% of admitted students enrolled full-time.

78% (361 students) submitted SAT scores; 46% (212 students) submitted ACT scores. *25th percentile:* SAT I Verbal 450, SAT I Math 480; ACT Composite 19. *75th percentile:* SAT I Verbal 560, SAT I Math 570; ACT Composite 24.

51% of freshmen from Florida. Freshmen from 30 states and 14 foreign countries.

Admission: Rolling admissions plan. For fall acceptance, apply as early as end of junior year of secondary school. Early acceptance available. *Requirements:* Either graduation from accredited secondary school or GED. Recommend 18 secondary school units in academic subjects including 4 English, 3 mathematics, 3 sciences, 2 foreign language, 3 social sciences. Minimum recommended GPA 2.5. Lowest recommended secondary school class standing 50th percentile. *Entrance tests:* College Board SAT or ACT composite. *For transfer students:* 2.0 minimum GPA for consideration; from 4-year accredited institution 96 hours maximum transfer credit; from 2-year accredited institution 64 hours.

College credit and advanced placement for postsecondary-level work completed in secondary school. For extrainstitutional learning, college credit on basis of ACE *2006 Guide to the Evaluation of Educational Experiences in the Armed Services,* portfolio assessment. College credit and advanced placement on basis of faculty assessment. Tutoring available. Developmental courses offered in summer sessions and during regular academic year; nondegree credit given.

Degree Requirements: 128 credit hours; 2.0 GPA; 32 hours, including last 30, in residence; 2 hours physical activity courses; distribution requirements. For baccalaureate in arts, demonstration of foreign language proficiency. Fulfillment of some degree requirements and exemption from some beginning courses possible by passing departmental examinations, College Board Achievement Tests, CLEP, AP. *Grading system:* A–F; pass-fail; withdraw (deadline after which pass-fail is appended to withdraw); incomplete (carries time limit).

Distinctive Educational Programs: *For undergraduates:* Internship programs. College of Weekend Weekend Studies. Dual-degree programs in engineering with Columbia University (NY), Georgia Institute of Technology, University of Florida, University of Miami, Washington University, Mercer University, Stevens Institute of Technology. Facilities and programs for independent research, including honors programs, individual majors. Foreign study by individual arrangement. *For graduate students:* Executive MBA program. *Available to all students:* Evening classes.

ROTC: Navy.

Degrees Conferred: 623 *baccalaureate;* 10 *master's.* Bachelor's degrees awarded in top five disciplines: business, management, marketing, and related support services 157; health professions and related clinical sciences 81; transportation and materials moving 48; liberal arts and sciences, general studies and humanities 39; visual and performing arts 32.

Fees and Other Expenses: *Full-time tuition per academic year 2004–05:* $18,830. *Books and supplies:* $600. *Room and board per academic year:* $6,290.

Financial Aid: Aid from institutionally generated funds is provided on the basis of academic merit, financial need, athletic ability, other criteria. Institution has a Program Participation Agreement with the U.S. Department of Education for eligible students to receive Pell Grants and other federal aid.

Financial aid to full-time, first-time undergraduate students: 30% received federal grants averaging $7,157; 52% state/local grants averaging $3,969; 91% institutional grants averaging $7,521; 52% loans averaging $6,322.

27 freshmen received Navy ROTC scholarships that cover 100% of tuition plus books and living stipend. 49 freshmen were Aviation Management and Flight Operations majors whose flight-related costs average an additional $10,000 per year. Private loans are frequently used to fund the additional expenses.

Departments and Teaching Staff: Education *professors* 2, *associate professors* 2, *assistant professors* 1, *instructors* 0, *part-time teachers* 11; humanities 4, 2, 12, 0, 11; nursing 0, 0, 8, 0, 0; physical education 2, 3, 0, 0, 3; science and mathematics 11, 7, 5, 1, 22; social science 3, 2, 7, 0, 6; art/theatre arts/dance 2, 2, 3, 0; 22; music 4, 5, 0, 0, 18; accounting/economics/finance 0, 4, 5, 0, 12; management/marketing 2, 2, 3, 0, 10; aeronautics 0, 1, 0, 0, 0; other 0, 0, 0, 0, 4. *Total instructional faculty :* 114. Degrees held by full-time faculty: doctorate 63%, master's 36%, baccalaureate 1%. 68% hold terminal degrees.

Enrollment: Total enrollment 3,092. Undergraduate 2,674 (43.1% men, 56.9% women).

Characteristics of Student Body: *Ethnic/racial makeup:* Black non-Hispanic: 13.7%; American Indian or Alaska Native: .7%; Asian or Pacific Islander: 2.5%; Hispanic: 4.5%; White non-Hispanic: 66.7%; unknown: 9.5%.

International Students: 64 undergraduate nonresident aliens enrolled. Students from Europe, Asia, Latin America, Africa, Canada, Australia. Programs available to aid students whose native language is not English: English as a Second Language Program. No financial aid specifically designated for international students.

Student Life: On-campus residence halls house 50% of the student body. *Intercollegiate athletics:* men only: baseball, basketball, crew, cross-country, golf, soccer; women only: crew, cross-country, golf, tennis, indoor and outdoor track and field, volleyball. *Special regulations:* Registered cars permitted without restrictions. *Special services:* academic advising, strong intramural program, placement, medical services, national sororities and fraternities, special services counseling. *Student publications: The Aquarian,* an annual literary magazine; *Navigator,* a biweekly newspaper; *The Riparian,* a yearbook. *Surrounding community:* Jacksonville population 675,000. Airport 21 miles from campus; passenger rail service 20 miles from campus.

Library Collections: 329,000 volumes. 353,000 microforms; 33,400 audiovisual materials; 325 current periodical subscriptions. Online catalog. Students have access to online information retrieval services and the Internet.

Most important holdings include Treasure Collection; Delius Collection; Jacksonville Historical Society.

Buildings and Grounds: Campus area 260 acres.

Chief Executive Officer: Dr. Terry McMahan, President.

Address admission inquiries to Rita Lampus, Director of Admissions.

Jones College

5353 Arlington Expressway
Jacksonville, Florida 32211-5588
Tel: (904) 743-1122   **E-mail:** admissions@jones.edu
Fax: (904) 743-4446   **Internet:** www.jones.edu

Institution Description: Jones College is a private, independent, nonprofit college. *Enrollment:* 777. *Degrees awarded:* Associate, baccalaureate. Certificates also awarded.

Accreditation: *National:* ACICS.

History: Established in Jacksonville 1918.

Institutional Structure: *Governing board:* Board of Trustees. Representation: 5 trustees. *Composition of institution:* Administrators 7 men / 3 women. Academic offices held by dean of college; finances directed by chief executive officer and president. Full-time instructional faculty 8.

Calendar: Semesters. Academic year Sept. to Aug. Freshmen admitted Sept., Jan., May. Degrees conferred Dec., Apr., June, Aug. Annual commencement May.

Characteristics of Freshmen: 90% of applicants accepted. 75% of accepted applicants enrolled. 85% of freshmen from Florida. Freshmen from 12 states and 7 foreign countries.

Admission: Rolling admissions plan. For fall acceptance, apply no later than first day of classes. Early acceptance available. *Requirements:* High school diploma or GED. *For transfer students:* from 4-year accredited institution up to 90 semester hours for baccalaureate degree; from 2-year accredited institution up to 42 semester hours for associate degree.

College credit and advanced placement for postsecondary-level work completed in secondary school. For extrainstitutional learning, college credit on basis of ACE *2006 Guide to the Evaluation of Educational Experiences in the Armed Services.* Advanced placement on basis of portfolio and faculty assessments. Tutoring available. Developmental courses offered in summer session and regular academic year; credit given.

Degree Requirements: *For all associate degrees:* 60 semester hours; 42 hours in residence. *For all baccalaureate degrees:* 120 semester hours; 42 hours in residence. *For all degrees:* 2.0 GPA. Fulfillment of some degree requirements and exemption from some beginning courses possible by passing departmental examinations, College Board CLEP. *Grading system:* A–F; withdraw (carries penalty); audit and incomplete.

Distinctive Educational Programs: Work-experience programs. Off-campus centers. Evening classes.

Degrees Conferred: 48 *associate;* 104 *baccalaureate:* business/marketing 60, computer and information sciences 21, health professions and related sciences 8, interdisciplinary studies 4, law/legal studies 11.

Fees and Other Expenses: *Full-time tuition per academic year 2004–05:* $6,000.

Financial Aid: Aid from institutionally generated funds is provided on the basis of academic merit and financial need.

Financial aid to full-time, first-time undergraduate students: need-based scholarships/grants totaling $2,282,586, self-help $5,591,915, parent loans $15,580.

Departments and Teaching Staff: *Instructors* 4, *part-time faculty* 80. *Total instructional faculty:* 84. *Student-to-faculty ratio:* 13:1. *Degrees held by full-time faculty:* Doctorate 23%, master's 69%, baccalaureate 8%. 10% hold terminal degrees.

Enrollment: Total enrollment 777. Undergraduate full-time 54 men / 172 women, part-time 125m / 426w.

Characteristics of Student Body: *Ethnic/racial makeup:* number of Black non-Hispanic: 300; American Indian or Alaska Native: 3; Asian or Pacific Islander: 10; Hispanic: 136; White non-Hispanic: 234; unknown: 10.

International Students: 4 nonresident aliens enrolled 2004. No programs available to aid students whose native language is not English. No financial aid specifically designated for foreign students.

Student Life: No on-campus housing. *Special regulations:* Cars permitted. *Special services:* local chapters of Phi Theta Pi fraternity, Alpha Iota Sorority, and Data Processing Management Association.

Publications: *Dean's Newsletter.*

Library Collections: 35,000 volumes. 250 microforms; 4,000 audiovisual materials; 150 current periodicals; 5,000 recordings/tapes.

Chief Executive Officer: Dorothy Jones, Chief Executive Officer.

Address admission inquiries to Leanne Osburne, Director of Marketing.

Lynn University

3601 North Military Trail
Boca Raton, Florida 33431-5598
Tel: (561) 237-7000   **E-mail:** admiss@lynn.edu
Fax: (561) 237-7100   **Internet:** www.lynn.edu

Institution Description: Lynn University, formerly known as College of Boca Raton, is a private institution offering a liberal arts and business curriculum. *Enrollment:* 2,276. *Degrees awarded:* Associate, baccalaureate, master's.

Accreditation: *Regional:* SACS-Comm. on Coll.

History: Founded in 1962 as Marymount College, a two-year college for women; became coeducational in 1972; renamed College of Boca Raton in 1974; adopted present name in 1991.

Institutional Structure: *Governing board:* Board of Trustees consisting of 20 members. Board of Overseers. *Composition of institution:* Administrators 30 men / 42 women. Academic affairs headed by a provost/vice president for academic affairs. Management/business/finances directed by an executive vice president. Seven schools headed by deans. Full-time instructional faculty 46. Academic Council, a governance body, meets 8 times per academic year.

Calendar: Semesters. Three summer sessions. Formal commencement in May.

Characteristics of Freshmen: 2,373 applicants (1,080 men, 1,293 women). 79.5% of applicants admitted. 31.8% of admitted students enrolled full-time.

72% (468 students) submitted SAT scores. *25th percentile:* SAT I Verbal 400, SAT I Math 390. *75th percentile:* SAT I Verbal 500, SAT I Math 510.

44% of freshmen from Florida. Students from 36 states and 57 foreign countries.

Admission: Rolling admissions plan. For fall acceptance, apply as early as the end of the junior year, but not later than Aug. 15. *Requirements:* Graduation from accredited secondary school or GED; recommendation of high school teacher or guidance counselor.

Degree Requirements: *For associate degrees:* 63 to 70 credits depending on program pursued. *For baccalaureate degrees:* 120 semester hours; 30 credit hours in residence.

Degrees Conferred: 2 *associate;* 354 *baccalaureate;* 98 *master's;* 13 *doctorate.* Bachelor's degrees awarded in top five disciplines: business, management, marketing, and related support services 173; psychology 34; communication, journalism, and related programs 30; visual and performing arts 26; security and protective services 25.

Fees and Other Expenses: *Full-time tuition per academic year 2004–5:* $23,500. *Books and supplies:* $950. *Room and board per academic year:* $8,600.

Financial Aid: Aid from institutionally generated funds is provided on the basis of academic merit, financial need, athletic ability, other criteria. Institution has a Program Participation Agreement with the U.S. Department of Education for eligible students to receive Pell Grants and other federal aid.

Financial aid to full-time, first-time undergraduate students: 14% received federal grants averaging $4,089; 19% state/local grants averaging $2,926; 50% institutional grants averaging $9,138; 35% loans averaging $6,382.

Departments and Teaching Staff: College of Arts and Sciences *professors* 3, *associate professors* 1, *assistant professors* 2, *instructors* 0, *part-time teachers* 19; Department of Art and Design 1, 1, 0, 0, 2; Department of English and Communications 0, 1, 3, 2, 10; Department of Mathematics and Science 1, 2, 0, 0, 5; School of Business 3, 1, 2, 1, 6; School of Educational 1, 2, 3, 0, 5; School of Hospitality, Tourism, Recreation and Sports 2, 4, 0, 0, 4; School of International Studies 2, 0, 0, 0, 0; School of Professional and Continuing studies 0, 0, 0, 0, 55; Department of Gerontology and Health Services 1, 0, 1, 0, 0; Graduate Studies 11, 0, 0, 0, 7.

Total instructional faculty: 119. *Degrees held by full-time faculty:* Doctorates 63%, master's 32%, professional 5%. 68% hold terminal degrees. Student-to-faculty ratio: 29:1.

Enrollment: Total enrollment 2,276. Undergraduate 1,928 (49.1% men; 50.9% women).

Characteristics of Student Body: *Ethnic/racial makeup:* Black non-Hispanic: 5.5%; American Indian or Alaska Native: .2%; Asian or Pacific Islander: .6%; Hispanic: 5,2%; White non-Hispanic: 28.9%; unknown: 44.7%.

International Students: 289 undergraduate nonresident aliens enrolled fall 2004. No financial aid specifically designated for international students. English study program available.

Student Life: Residence halls available on campus for 680 students. Member of NCAA, Division II. Intercollegiate athletic program: men's and women's basketball, golf, soccer, tennis; men's baseball; women's softball and volleyball. Intramural sports program. Student Government Association. Fraternities, sororities, service organizations. *The Pulse,* student monthly newspaper; *Year-*

book and student literary journal. WLYN student-run radio station. Health services, counseling center, career development center, job fairs, workshops, resume preparation, resume writer software.

Library Collections: 95,000 volumes. 400 periodical subscriptions. 2,000 microforms. 3,500 audiovisual materials. Online catalog. Students have access to online information retrieval services.

Buildings and Grounds: Campus area 123 acres.

Chief Executive Officer: Dr. Donald E. Ross, President.

Address admission inquiries to Dr. Karla Stein, Director, Enrollment Management.

Nova Southeastern University

3301 College Avenue
Fort Lauderdale, Florida 33314
Tel: (954) 262-5392   **E-mail:** info@nova.edu
Fax: (954) 262-3970   **Internet:** www.nova.edu

Institution Description: Nova Southeastern University is a private, independent, nonprofit institution. *Enrollment:* 25,430. *Degrees awarded:* Baccalaureate, master's, doctorate, first-professional (dental medicine, law, optometry, osteopathic medicine, pharmacy).

Member of Southeast Florida Educational Consortium.

Accreditation: *Regional:* SACS-Comm. on Coll. *Professional:* audiology, clinical psychology, dentistry, endodontics, law, marriage and family therapy, optometry, osteopathy, periodontics, pharmacy, physical therapy, physician assisting, psychology internship, public health, speech-language pathology

History: Established and chartered as Nova University of Advanced Technology 1964, and offered first instruction at postsecondary level 1967; awarded first degree (doctorate) 1970; began undergraduate program 1976; adopted present name in 1994 after merger with the Southeastern University of the Health Sciences. *See* Abraham S. Fischler, *The Report of the President on the 15th Anniversary of Nova University* (Fort Lauderdale: Nova University Press 1979) for further information.

Institutional Structure: *Governing board:* Nova Southeastern University Board of Trustees. Extrainstitutional representation: 29 trustees. All voting. *Composition of institution:* Senior administrators 16 men / 3 women. Full-time instructional faculty 542. Academic governance: president's council and council of deans.

Calendar: Trimester. Varies according to program. Academic year Aug. to May. Freshmen admitted on a rolling basis. Undergraduate summer sessions July through August. Degrees conferred as earned.

Characteristics of Freshmen: 1,915 applicants. 61.5% of applicants admitted. 36.4% of admitted students enrolled full-time.

89% (337 students) submitted SAT scores; 43% (165 students) submitted ACT scores. *25th percentile:* SAT Verbal 440, SAT Math 450; ACT Composite 18, ACT English 17, ACT Math 17. *75th percentile:* SAT Verbal 540, SAT Math 560; ACT Composite 23, ACT English 22, ACT Math 24.

63% of freshmen from Florida. Freshmen from 42 foreign countries.

Admission: Rolling admissions. *Undergraduate requirements:* Graduation from accredited secondary school or GED. *For transfer students:* 2.0 minimum GPA; from 4-year accredited institution 90 hours maximum transfer credit; from 2-year accredited institution 66 hours. Advanced placement for postsecondary-level work completed in secondary school, CLEP, other standardized advanced placement tests.

Tutoring available. Developmental courses offered in summer session and regular academic year; credit given.

Degree Requirements: 120–130 credit hours; 2.0–2.5 GPA; 30 credits in residence; general education requirements. Fulfillment of some degree requirements and exemption from some beginning courses possible by passing College Board CLEP, AP, other standardized tests. *Grading system:* A–F; pass.

Distinctive Educational Programs: Combined bachelor's/professional degree programs designed to allow students to complete both degrees in a reduced amount of time. Flexible meeting places and schedules, including off-campus centers throughout the state and in 22 states, weekend, evening, and Internet classes. Work experience programs including cooperative education and internships.

Degrees Conferred: 376 *baccalaureate* (B); 3,585 *master's* (M); 705 *doctorate:* biological/life sciences 79 (B), 5 (M); business/marketing 496 (B), 843 (M), 90 (D); computer and information sciences 36 (B), 77 (M); 45 (D); education 125 (B), 2,019 (M), 381 (D); English 3 (B); health professions and related sciences 23 (B), 244 (M), 29 (D); home economics and vocational home economics 8 (M), 81 (D); interdisciplinary studies 18 (B), 3 (D); law/legal studies 23 (B); liberal arts/general studies 70 (B); parks and recreation 14 (B), 14 (M); protective services/public administration 106 (B), 69 (M); psychology 228 (M), 76

(D); other 1 (B). 835 *first-professional:* dentistry 94, optometry 92, pharmacy 136, law 538, osteopathic medicine 75.

Fees and Other Expenses: *Full-time tuition per academic year 2004–05:* $15,820. *Books and supplies:* $1,200. *Room and board per academic year:* $7,248. Contact the university for current graduate and professional schools tuition/fees.

Financial Aid: Aid from institutionally generated funds is provided on the basis of academic merit, financial need, athletic ability.

Financial aid to full-time, first-time undergraduate students: need-based scholarships/grants totaling $13,861,733, self-help $22,211,111, parent loans $799,259; non-need-based scholarships/grants totaling $6,930,499, self-help $18,792,022, parent loans $76,595, tuition waivers $384,529, athletic awards $1,743,419.

Departments and Teaching Staff: *Total instructional faculty:* 1,539 (full-time 542, part-time 989; women 714, men 817; members of minority groups 292). *Student-to-faculty ratio:* 15:1. 87% of faculty hold terminal degrees.

Enrollment: Total enrollment 25,430. Undergraduate 5,223 (25.2% men, 74.8% women).

Characteristics of Student Body: *Ethnic/racial makeup:* Black non-Hispanic: 27.4%; American Indian or Alaska Native: .4%; Asian or Pacific Islander: 3.2%; Hispanic: 23.9%, 736w; White non-Hispanic: 29.9%; unknown: 6.8%.

International Students: 439 undergraduate nonresident aliens enrolled fall 2003. Programs available for students whose native language is not English: Social. English as a Second Language Program. No financial aid specifically designated for international students.

Student Life: Campus housing available for up to 540 students; married student housing also available. *Special regulations:* Cars permitted without restrictions. *Special services:* Career Resource Center, Academic Support Center. *Surrounding community:* Fort Lauderdale metropolitan area population over 1,000,000. Served by mass transit bus system; airport 8 miles from campus; passenger rail service 10 miles from campus.

Library Collections: 375,000 volumes. 41,000 government document titles; 74,156 microform titles; 1,400 audiovisual materials; 8,073 current periodical subscriptions. Online catalog. Access to online information retrieval systems and the Internet.

Most important holdings include United Nations documents; international law materials; popular culture collection.

Buildings and Grounds: Campus area 300 acres. *New buildings:* Health Professions Division Assembly Building completed 2000; Alvin Sherman Library Research, and Information Technology Center 2001.

Chief Executive Officer: Ray Ferrero, Jr., President.

Address undergraduate admission inquiries to Maria Dillard, Director of Enrollment Management; graduate inquiries to academic center of interest.

Palm Beach Atlantic University

901 South Flagler Avenue
P.O. Box 24708
West Palm Beach, Florida 33416-4708
Tel: (561) 803-2000   **E-mail:** admit@pba.edu
Fax: (561) 803-2186   **Internet:** www.pba.edu

Institution Description: Palm Beach Atlantic University is a nondenominational Christian liberal arts college. *Enrollment:* 3,066. *Degrees awarded:* Associate, baccalaureate, master's, doctorate.

Accreditation: *Regional:* SACS-Comm. on Coll. *Professional:* music, pharmacy

History: Established, chartered, and offered first instruction at postsecondary level 1968; awarded first degree (baccalaureate) 1972.

Institutional Structure: *Governing board:* Palm Beach Atlantic College, Board of Trustees. Representation: 30 trustees, including president of the college, 1 ex officio. All voting. *Composition of institution:* Administrators 14 men / 8 women. Academic affairs headed by academic dean. Management/business/finances directed by Vice President of financial affairs. Full-time instructional faculty 70. Academic governance body, the faculty, meets an average of 9 times per year.

Calendar: Semesters. Academic year Aug. to Aug. Freshmen admitted Aug., Jan., June, July. Degrees conferred May and Dec. Formal commencement May. Extended day summer term from early May to early Aug.

Characteristics of Freshmen: 47% of applicants admitted. 51% of admitted students enrolled full-time.

73% (321 students) submitted SAT scores; 35% (156 students) submitted ACT scores. *25th percentile:* SAT Verbal 490, SAT Math 480; ACT Composite 21, ACT English 20, ACT Math 19. *75th percentile:* SAT Verbal 590, SAT Math 590; ACT Composite 25, ACT English 25, ACT Math 25.

62% of freshmen from Florida. Freshmen from 29 states and 5 foreign countries.

Admission: Rolling admissions plan. Early acceptance available. *Requirements:* Recommend senior status; 4 units in English, a foreign language, mathematics, and natural and/or physical sciences; 2.5 GPA; recommendation by secondary school counselor. GED accepted. *Entrance tests:* College Board SAT minimum score 990 or ACT composite 21 and institutionally designed mathematics placement examination. *For transfer students:* 2.0 minimum GPA; from 4-year accredited institution 96 hours maximum transfer credit; from 2-year accredited institution 67 hours; correspondence/extension students 9 hours. College credit for postsecondary-level work completed in secondary school. Tutoring available. Developmental courses offered in summer session and regular academic year; credit given.

Degree Requirements: 120 credit hours; 2.0 GPA; 32 hours in residence; 4 hours physical education; basic and distribution courses. Fulfillment of some degree requirements and exemption from some beginning courses possible by passing College Board CLEP, APP, or PEP. *Grading system:* A–F; withdraw (carries penalty and time limit).

Distinctive Educational Programs: Evening classes. Special facilities for using telecommunications in the classroom.

Degrees Conferred: 530 *baccalaureate* (B), 103 *master's* (M): biological/life sciences 19 (B); business/marketing 255 (B), 44 (M); communications/communication technologies 64 (B); computer and information sciences 10 (B); education 35 (B), 7 (M); English 3 (B); health professions and related sciences 4 (B); law/legal studies 3 (B); liberal arts/general studies 24 (B); mathematics 2 (B); philosophy/religion/theology 36 (B); psychology 41 (B), 52 (M); social sciences and history 8 (B); visual and performing arts 26 (B). 43 *first-professional:* pharmacy.

Fees and Other Expenses: *Full-time tuition per academic year 2004–05:* $16,160 undergraduate, $11,920 graduate. *Required fees:* $25. *Room and board per academic year:* $6,055.

Financial Aid: Aid from institutionally generated funds is provided on the basis of academic merit, financial need, other criteria.

Financial aid to full-time, first-time undergraduate students: need-based scholarships/grants totaling $5,534,220, self-help $8,082; 355; non-need-based scholarships/grants totaling $10,757,885, self-help $6,570,809, parent loans $3,033,293, tuition waivers $140,702, athletic awards $367,121. *Graduate aid:* 280 federal and state-funded loans totaling $3,065,442; 25 fellowships and grants totaling $17,856.

Departments and Teaching Staff: *Professors* 18, *associate professors* 49, *assistant professors* 65, *instructors* 8, *part-time faculty* 113. *Total instructional faculty:* 253 (full-time 140, part-time 113; women 57, men 83; members of minority groups 8). Total faculty with doctorate, first-professional, or other terminal degree: 103. Student-to-faculty ratio: 12:1.

Enrollment: Total enrollment 3,066. Full-time 830 men / 1,380 women, part-time 81m / 120w; graduate full-time 60m / 153w, part-time 66m / 117w; first-professional full-time 103m / 150w, part-time 2m / 4w.

Characteristics of Student Body: *Ethnic/racial makeup:* number of Black non-Hispanic: 366; American Indian or Alaska Native: 10; Asian or Pacific Islander: 32, Hispanic: 191; White non-Hispanic: 1,661; unknown: 88. *Age distribution:* number under 18: 46; 18–19: 708; 20–21: 730; 22–24: 330; 25–29: 166; 30–34: 104; 35–39: 98; 40–49: 145; 50–64: 50.

International Students: 45 nonresident aliens enrolled fall 2004. No programs available to aid students whose native language is not English. Some financial aid specifically designated for international students.

Student Life: Drama theater group, choral group, student-run newspaper and yearbook. Major annual events: homecoming, Welcome Week, Spring happening. *Intercollegiate athletics:* men only: baseball, basketball, golf, soccer; women only: cross country, soccer, tennis, volleyball. Comprehensive intramural program. *Student publications: The Mast,* a yearbook; *The Compass,* student newspaper. *Surrounding community:* West Palm Beach, population 65,000. Miami, 60 miles from campus, is nearest metropolitan area. Served by mass transit bus system; airport 7 miles from campus; passenger rail service 2 miles from campus.

Library Collections: 106,736 volumes. 230 current periodical subscriptions. 2,534 recordings 278 DVDs; 266 CD-ROMs. 45 computer work stations. Online catalog. Students have access to the Internet at no charge. Total 2004–05 budget for books and materials: $150,000.

Most important holdings include Strouse Theatre Collection.

Buildings and Grounds: Urban campus area 25 acres.

Chief Executive Officer: Dr. David W. Clark, President.

Address undergraduate admission inquiries to Rod Sullivan, Director of Admissions; graduate inquiries to Laura Lein Weber, Director of Graduate and Evening Admission.

Ringling School of Art and Design

2700 North Tamiami Trail
Sarasota, Florida 34234-5895
Tel: (941) 351-5100   **E-mail:** admissions@ringling.edu
Fax: (941) 359-7517   **Internet:** www.ringling.edu

Institution Description: Ringling School of Art and Design is a private, independent, nonprofit institution. *Enrollment:* 540 men / 468 women. *Degrees awarded:* Baccalaureate.

Accreditation: *Regional:* SACS-Comm. on Coll. *National:* NASAD. *Professional:* interior design

History: Established and chartered as School of Fine and Applied Art of the John and Mabel Ringling Art Museum, a branch of Florida Southern College, and offered first instruction at postsecondary level 1931; reincorporated and renamed Ringling School of Art 1933; first degree (baccalaureate) awarded 1935; adopted present name 1979.

Institutional Structure: *Governing board:* Board of Trustees. Representation: 30 trustees, including president of college, 2 ex officio, 2 honorary. *Composition of institution:* President, Vice President for Academic Affairs, Vice President for Business Affairs, Vice President for Institutional Advancement. Full-time instructional faculty 64.

Calendar: Semesters. Academic year Aug. to May. Freshmen admitted Aug. Degrees conferred and formal commencement May. No summer session.

Characteristics of Freshmen: 7% of applicants accepted. 28% of accepted applicants enrolled full-time.

49% (98 students) submitted SAT scores; 10% (21 students) submitted ACT scores. *25th percentile:* SAT Verbal 490, SAT Math 470; ACT Composite 19, ACT English 15, ACT Math 16. *75th percentile:* SAT Verbal 620, SAT Math 590; ACT Composite 26, ACT English 26, ACT Math 25.

69% of freshmen expected to graduate within 5 years. 28% of freshmen from Florida. Freshmen from 30 states and 6 foreign countries.

Admission: Rolling admissions plan. For fall acceptance, apply as early as Dec., but not later than Aug. *Requirements:* Either graduation from secondary school or GED; visual presentation, $30 application fee; letters of recommendation; transcripts. *Entrance tests:* For foreign students TOEFL. *For transfer students:* From 2- and 4-year accredited institution 2.0 GPA

Degree Requirements: 123 credit hours, including a minimum of 75 in art, 12 in art history, and 30 in academics; 2.0 GPA; last 45 credit hours in residency; course and distribution requirements. *Grading system:* A–F; withdraw (carries time limit); incomplete.

Distinctive Educational Programs: Visiting artist program; computer graphics. Extensive incorporation of technology into collegiate art and design education with programs of study that leads to a Bachelor of Fine Arts in six majors: computer animation, fine arts, photography and digital imaging, illustration, interior design, and photography.

Degrees Conferred: 195 *baccalaureate:* visual and performing arts 195.

Fees and Other Expenses: *Full-time tuition per academic year 2004–05:* $19,995. *Room and board per academic year:* $9,242. *Other fees:* $1,290.

Financial Aid: Aid from institutionally generated funds is awarded on the basis of academic merit, financial need. Institution has a Program Participation Agreement with the U.S. Department of Education for eligible students to receive Pell Grants and other federal aid.

Financial aid to full-time, first-time undergraduate students: need-based scholarships/grants totaling $3,099,687, self-help $6,684,987, parent loans $2,158,675; non-need-based scholarships/grants totaling $321,688, self-help $1,456,623, parent loans $1,452,103.

Departments and Teaching Staff: *Total instructional faculty* 121 (full-time 64, part-time 57; women 44, men 77; members of minority groups 3). Total faculty with doctorate, first-professional, or other terminal degree: 77. Student-to-faculty ratio: 12:1. 4 faculty members awarded sabbaticals 2004.

Enrollment: Total enrollment 1,008. Full-time 532 men / 448 women, part-time 8 men / 20 women.

Characteristics of Student Body: *Ethnic/racial makeup:* number of Black non-Hispanic: 20; American Indian or Alaska Native: 10; Asian or Pacific Islander: 40; Hispanic: 93; White non-Hispanic: 794; unknown: 2. *Age distribution:* number under 18: 15; 18–19: 312; 20–21: 578; 22–24: 193; 25–29: 71; 30–34: 25; 35–39: 7; 40–49: 6; 50–64: 6.

International Students: 49 nonresident aliens enrolled fall 2004. 12 students from Europe, 19 Asia, 13 Central and South American. Social and cultural programs to aid students whose native language is not English. No financial aid specifically designated for international students.

Student Life: On-campus residence halls house 48% of student body. Residence halls for men only constitute 58% of such space, for women only 42%. *Special regulations:* No alcohol on campus. *Special services:* Personal counseling; campus ministry; Academic Resource Center. *Surrounding community:* Sarasota population 52,000. Tampa/St. Petersburg; 40 miles from campus, is nearest metropolitan area. Served by airport 2 miles from campus.

Library Collections: 46,802 volumes including bound books, serial backfiles, electronic documents, and government documents not in separate collections. Online catalog. Current serial subscriptions: 340 paper, 4,077 via electronic access. 3,778 recordings; 717 compact discs; 375 CD-ROMs. 34 computer work stations. Students have access to the Internet at no charge. Total budget for books, periodicals, audiovisual materials, microforms 2004–05: $136,000.

Most important holdings include Duff-Stevens Collection (17th-and 18th-century prints), Jackson Collection (Japanese art books and prints), Simmen Collection (portrait prints of 18th-century rulers and statesmen).

Buildings and Grounds: Campus area 35 acres.

Chief Executive Officer: Dr. Larry R. Thompson, Director of Admissions.

Address admission inquiries to James Dean, Director Admissions.

Rollins College

1000 Holt Avenue
Winter Park, Florida 32789-4499

Tel: (407) 646-2000   **E-mail:** admission@rollins.edu
Fax: (407) 646-2600   **Internet:** www.rollins.edu

Institution Description: Rollins College is a private, independent, nonprofit college. *Enrollment:* 2,571. *Degrees awarded:* Baccalaureate, master's.

Accreditation: *Regional:* SACS-Comm. on Coll. *Professional:* business, counseling, music

History: Established and incorporated by 13 Congregational churches and offered first instruction at postsecondary level 1885; awarded first degree (baccalaureate) 1890.

Institutional Structure: *Governing board:* Rollins College Board of Trustees. Extrainstitutional representation: 27 trustees; institutional representation: president of the college. 1 ex officio. All voting. *Composition of institution:* Administrators 25 men / 18 women. Academic affairs headed by vice president for academic affairs and provost. Management/business/finances directed by vice president for business and finance. Full-time instructional faculty 143. Academic governance body, the faculty, meets an average of 6 times per year.

Calendar: Semesters. Academic year from Aug. to May. Degrees conferred May, Aug., Feb. Formal commencement May or June. Summer session from June to Aug.

Characteristics of Freshmen: 59% of applicants accepted. 19% of applicants admitted and enrolled.

15% (461students) submitted SAT scores; 58% (187 students) submitted ACT scores. *25th percentile:* SAT Verbal 540, SAT Math 540. *75th percentile:* SAT Verbal 640, SAT Math 640.

65% of applicants expected to graduate within five years. 44% of freshmen from Florida. Freshmen from 44 states and 43 foreign countries.

Admission: Apply by Feb. 15 for fall term; transfers by Apr. 15; by Dec. 1 for spring; by Nov. 15 for early decision (need not limit application to Rollins). Early admissions available. *Requirements:* Freshmen complete application with $40 processing fee, official high school transcript, counselor's recommendation, SAT or ACT scores, 3 CEEB Achievement tests recommended. Recommend 4 units English, 3 mathematics (including geometry, algebra I and algebra II), 2 history, 2 laboratory science, 2 or more of a foreign language. TOEFL for foreign students. For transfer students, complete application with $40 processing fee, official high school transcript, SAT or ACT scores, official college transcript. Applicant must be in good academic standing and eligible to return to the institution from which transfer is proposed. Each accepted candidate is evaluated for transfer credit on an individual basis. No more than the equivalent of 18 courses and 18 course units of transfer credit will be accepted from a two-year institution.

Degree Requirements: *For undergraduate degrees:* once admitted to full-time degree status, student must complete at least 3/4 of the remaining program of study leading to the B.A. at Rollins or in other programs specifically approved by the dean. 140 credit hours. In the senior year, students must be enrolled on a full-time basis in the College; minimum academic average of 2.0; completion of at least 35 courses of academic work equaling at least 35 course units, including at least 3 winter term courses; 4 terms of physical education for students who enter as freshmen; completion of general education requirements; satisfactory completion of the major requirements with a minimum 2.0 GPA in the major curriculum. Additional requirements for some majors.

Fulfillment of some degree requirements and exemption from some beginning courses possible by passing College Board CLEP, APP. *Grading system:* A–F; withdraw (deadline after which pass-fail is appended to withdraw).

Distinctive Educational Programs: *For undergraduates:* Off-campus center (Brevard Campus) 60 miles away from main institution. Accelerated degree programs: 3-2 BA/MBA Program done in cooperation with Crummer Graduate School of Business. Dual-degree programs in engineering with Auburn University at Montgomery (AL), Columbia University (NY), Georgia Institute of Technology, Washington University (MO); in forestry with Duke University (NC). Interdepartmental programs in area studies, environmental studies, international relations. Facilities for independent research, including honors programs, individual majors. Institutionally sponsored study abroad in Australia and Spain, internship program in London; Verano Espanol, a college-sponsored 6-week summer program in Spain. Affiliated with programs in Germany, Russia, Central Europe, Costa Rica, England, and Spain. With prior approval, students may participate in programs in additional countries. 6-8 January Term off-campus courses. Washington (DC) semester at American University. Rollins College Conference, an integrated seminar for first-year students. Rollins Advantage Program, providing students opportunities for developing the linkages between their undergraduate education and the skills, knowledge, and experiences valued by employers and graduate schools.

Degrees Conferred: 385 *baccalaureate* (B), 321 *master's* (M): area and ethnic studies 1 (B); biological/life sciences 20 (B); business/marketing 40 (B), 233 (M); communications/communication technologies 28 (B); computer and information sciences 10 (B); education 27 (B); 22 (M); English 37 (B); foreign languages and literature 6 (B); interdisciplinary studies 16 (B); liberal arts/general studies 22 (B); mathematics 6 (B); philosophy/religion/theology 6 (B); physical sciences 3 (B); psychology 42 (B), 16 (M); social sciences and history 120 (B); visual and performing arts 51 (B).

Fees and Other Expenses: *Full-time tuition per academic year 2004–05:* $27,700. *Room and board per academic year:* $8,570.

Financial Aid: Aid from institutionally generated funds is provided on the basis of academic merit, financial need, athletic ability, other criteria.

Financial aid to full-time, first-time undergraduate students: need-based scholarships/grants totaling $13,349,473, self-help $3,246,734, parent loans $323,773, athletic awards $300,733; non-need-based scholarships/grants totaling $4,166,385, self-help $1,299,640, parent loans $1,993,744, athletic awards $1,681,105.

Departments and Teaching Staff: *Total instructional faculty:* 229 (full-time 179, part-time 50; women 101, men 128; member of minority groups 27). Total faculty with doctorate, first-professional, or other terminal degree: 180. Student-to-faculty ratio: 11:1.

Enrollment: Total enrollment 2,571. Undergraduate full-time 698 men / 1,061 women; graduate full-time 123m / 112w, part-time 237m / 340w.

Characteristics of Student Body: *Ethnic/racial makeup:* number of Black non-Hispanic: 85; American Indian or Alaska Native: 7; Asian or Pacific Islander: 62; Hispanic: 134; White non-Hispanic: 1,306; unknown: 118.

International Students: 45 nonresident aliens enrolled fall 2004. Students from Europe, Asia, Central and South America, Africa, Canada, Australia. No programs available to aid students whose native language is not English. No financial aid specifically designated for international students.

Student Life: 82% of the student body board in college owned residence halls including fraternity and sorority houses. Halls for men only constitute 11% of residential space and halls for women only constitute 11% of residential space. The remaining 78% of residential space houses both men and women. 27% of all men and women join fraternities and sororities. *Intercollegiate athletics:* men only: baseball, basketball, crew, cross-country, golf, sailing, soccer, tennis, water skiing; women only: basketball, crew, cross country, golf, sailing, soccer, softball, tennis, volleyball, water skiing. *Special regulations:* Cars permitted for all but freshmen. *Special services:* Skills Development Center, Writing Center, Career Development Center, health services, personal counseling. *Student publications, radio:* Brushing, a biannual literary magazine; *R-Times,* an annual handbook; *Sandspur,* a weekly newspaper; *Tomokan,* a yearbook. Radio station WPRK broadcasts 76 hours per week. *Surrounding community:* Orlando metropolitan area population over 1,000,000. Served by mass transit bus system; airport 10 miles from campus; passenger rail service 1 mile from campus.

Publications: *Zygon: Journal of Religion and Science* (quarterly) first published 1980.

Library Collections: 297,021 volumes including bound books, serial backfiles, electronic documents, and government documents not in separate collections. Online catalog. Current serial subscriptions: 1,448 paper, 4,216 electronic. 50 computer work stations. Students have access to the Internet at no charge.

Most important holdings include W. S. Kennedy Collection of Whitmaniana (Whitman Collection); Jessie B. Rittenhouse Poetry Collection; Florida Collection.

Buildings and Grounds: Campus area 67 acres.

Chief Executive Officer: Dr. Lewis Duncan, President.

admission inquiries to David G. Erdmann, Dean of Admissions.

St. John Vianney College Seminary

2900 S.W. 87th Avenue
Miami, Florida 33165-3244
Tel: (305) 223-4561   **E-mail:** admissions@sjvcs.edu
Fax: (305) 223-0650   **Internet:** www.sjvcs.edu

Institution Description: St. John Vianney College Seminary is a four-year undergraduate college providing a preparatory program for men whose objective is to serve the Catholic Church in the priesthood. The Seminary provides an Anglo-Hispanic: bilingual, bicultural program (English/Spanish). *Enrollment:* 58. *Degrees awarded:* Baccalaureate.

Accreditation: *Regional:* SACS-Comm. on Coll.

History: Founded as four-year high school with junior college program and named St. John Vianney Minor Seminary 1959; high school program discontinued 1976; became four-year college and adopted present name 1977.

Calendar: Semesters. Academic year Aug. to May.

Characteristics of Freshmen: 63 applicants (62 men, 1 women). 100 of applicants accepted. 96.8% of admitted students enrolled full-time.

80% of entering students expected to graduate within 5 years. 80% of freshmen from Florida. Freshmen from 2 states and 6 foreign countries.

Admission: Rolling admissions plan. *Requirements:* High school graduation; some exceptions made for GED.

Degree Requirements: 128 semester hours; 2.0 GPA minimum; 35 semester hours in philosophy with a 2.0 GPA minimum.

Distinctive Educational Programs: A two-track system (English/Spanish is offered with intensified courses in Spanish and English as a second language). Enrollment is from English-speaking and Spanish-speaking students; each must take a course in the alternate language each semester with a view to becoming as fluent as possible in the alternate language. *Other distinctive programs:* In addition to its regular four-year program, the Seminary offers a one-year intensive program in pre-theology for men who have already received a bachelor degree from a non-seminary college or university. This program consists of a concentration in philosophy and religion, as well as formation. *Available to all students:* Emphasis on spiritual formation; this growth is fostered in many ways.

Degrees Conferred: 13 *baccalaureate:* philosophy and religious studies 12; theology and ministerial studies 1.

Fees and Other Expenses: *Full-time tuition per academic year 2004–05:* $11,000. *Other expenses:* $3,000. *Books and supplies:* $600. *Room and board per academic year:* $4,000.

Financial Aid: Aid from institutionally generated funds is provided on the basis of financial need. Institution has a Program Participation Agreement with the U.S. Department of Education for eligible students to receive Pell Grants and other federal aid.

Departments and Teaching Staff: Philosophy *professors* 0, *assistant professors* 4, *part-time faculty* 0; theology 1, 2, 0; psychology 1, 0, 0; English 0, 1, 0; humanities 0, 0, 1; science 0, 0, 1; mathematics 0, 0, 1; history 0, 0, 2; sports 0, 0, 1.

Total instructional faculty: 15. Degrees held by full-time faculty: doctorate 33%, master's 60%, baccalaureate 6%. 33% hold terminal degrees.

Enrollment: Total enrollment 58. Undergraduate 55 (94.5% men, 5.5% women).

Characteristics of Student Body: *Ethnic/racial makeup:* Asian or Pacific 1.8%; Hispanic: 36.4%; Black, non-Hispanic: 3.6%; White non-Hispanic: 30.9%.

International Students: 16 nonresident aliens enrolled fall 2004. Programs available to aid students whose native language is not English: Social, cultural. English as a Second Language Program. No financial aid specifically designated for international students.

Student Life: All students are residents. Community living is part of the formation program for the seminarians. *Intramural athletics:* Intramural sports are encouraged, and excellent facilities are available. *Student publications: The Canticle,* a student publication which stresses creative works.

Library Collections: 60,000 volumes including bound books, serial backfiles, electronic documents, and government documents not in separate collections. Online catalog. Current serial subscriptions. Computer work stations available. Students have access to the Internet at no charge.

Most important special holdings include the late Archbishop Coleman F. Carroll collection of personal papers; Antiphonary of Gregorian Chant; collection of Ecclesiastical and Civil law books and Spanish histories.

Buildings and Grounds: Campus area 33 acres in southwestern Dade County.

Chief Executive Officer: Rev. John Noonan, Rector/President.

Address admission inquiries to Bonnie de Angulo, Registrar.

Saint Leo University

33701 State Road 52
P.O. Box 6665
Saint Leo, Florida 33574-6665
Tel: (352) 588-8200   **E-mail:** admission@saintleo.edu
Fax: (352) 588-8917   **Internet:** www.saintleo.edu

Institution Description: Saint Leo University is a Catholic, coeducational liberal arts-based college. *Enrollment:* 1,241. *Degrees awarded:* Associate, baccalaureate, master's.

Accreditation: *Regional:* SACS-Comm. on Coll. *Professional:* business, social work

History: Established and chartered as Saint Leo Military Academy 1889; changed name to Saint Leo Preparatory School 1930; adopted present name and offered first instruction at postsecondary level 1956; opened its doors on the junior college level for both men and women; awarded first degree (baccalaureate) 1967; awarded first master's degree 1996; adopted present name 1999.

Institutional Structure: *Governing board:* Saint Leo University Board of Trustees. Extrainstitutional representation: 30 trustees; institutional representation: 1 faculty member, 1 student, president of the university. 33 voting. *Composition of institution:* Administrators 4 men / 2 woman. Academic affairs headed by vice president, academic affairs. Management/business/finances directed by vice president, business affairs. Full-time instructional faculty 63. Academic governance body, The Academic Council, meets an average of 3 times per year. *Faculty representation:* Faculty served by a faculty agreement.

Calendar: Semesters. Academic year Aug. to May. Freshmen admitted fall and spring terms. Degrees conferred throughout the year; commencement in May.

Characteristics of Freshmen: Mean SAT scores 510 verbal; 508 mathematical. Mean ACT composite score 21.

51% of applicants accepted. 32% of accepted applicants enrolled. 55% of freshmen from Florida. Freshmen from 35 states and 42 foreign countries.

Admission: Rolling admissions plan. Early acceptance available. Common Application is accepted. Online application available on the university website. *Requirements:* Either graduation from accredited secondary school or GED. The admissions committee recommends 16 college preparatory academic units which should include 4 English, 3 mathematics, 2 natural science, 3 social studies and/or history, and 2 foreign language. Recommendation of guidance counselor is required. Minimum high school GPA 2.3 and a minimum combined verbal/mathematical score of 900 or an ACT composite score of 19 also required for admission consideration for a first-time college student. consideration. *Entrance tests:* College Board SAT or ACT scores. *For transfer students:* 2.0 GPA, maximum transfer credit of 66 semester hours from two-year or junior colleges.

College credit and advanced placement for postsecondary-level work completed in secondary school. College credit for extrainstitutional learning (life experience) on basis of USAFI/DANTES. Tutoring available. Developmental courses offered in summer session and regular academic year.

Degree Requirements: *For all associate degrees:* 60 credit hours; 15 of which must be completed at Saint Leo University, 2.0 GPA, comprehensive written examination. *For all baccalaureate degrees:* 120 credit hours, 30 of which must be completed at Saint Leo University and 15 in the major. At least 39 semester hours of coursework must be at the junior/senior (300–400) level, 2.0 GPA. *For all degrees:* 1 physical education course; distribution requirements.

Fulfillment of some degree requirements and exemption from some beginning courses possible by passing departmental examinations, College Board CLEP, AP. *Grading system:* A–F; withdraw (carries time limit).

Distinctive Educational Programs: Evening classes. Cooperative baccalaureate program in medical technology with affiliated hospitals. Tutorials. Honors Program. Ten honor societies with active chapters on campus. Freshman Mentor Program. Study abroad in Australia, Ecuador, England, France, Ireland, Italy, Spain, Switzerland. Liberal Arts in Management (LAMP). Internet-based courses. BA/DO and BA/DDS programs in cooperation with Nova Southeastern University.

ROTC: Army offered on campus. Air Force offered in cooperation with University of South Florida.

Degrees Conferred: 11 *associate;* 173 *baccalaureate:* biological sciences 6, business and management 55, education 25, environmental science 2, letters 23, psychology 11, public affairs and services 35, social sciences and history 18, sport management 9. 1 *honorary degree awarded:* Doctor of Humane Letters.

Fees and Other Expenses: *Full-time tuition per academic year 2005–06:* $14,250. *Room and board per academic year:* $7,460.

Financial Aid: Aid from institutionally generated funds is provided on the basis of academic merit, financial need, athletic ability, other considerations.

$6,205,552 in institutional grants and scholarships. Total federally and state-funded scholarships and grants $3,441,609. Federally-funded loans and Federal Work Study also awarded.

99% of incoming freshmen and all undergraduates received financial aid.Average financial aid package for full-time students $15,130.

Departments and Teaching Staff: *Total instructional faculty:* 122 (full-time 63, part-time 59). Degrees held by full-time faculty: Doctorate 86%, master's 14%. 64% hold terminal degrees. Student-to-faculty ratio: 15:1.

Enrollment: Total enrollment 1,241. Undergraduate full-time 532 men / 655 women, part-time 24m / 30w.

Characteristics of Student Body: *Ethnic/racial makeup:* number of Black non-Hispanic: 90; American Indian or Alaska Native: 8; Asian or Pacific Islander: 14; Hispanic: 89; White non-Hispanic: 835; unknown: 130.

International Students: 75 nonresident aliens enrolled fall 2004. Programs to aid students whose native language is not English: courses in composition and grammar for speakers of other languages. $609,733 in institutional financial aid awarded to 67 nonresident aliens; average award $9,100.

Student Life: On-campus residence halls house 82% of student body. Men only, women only, and coed residence halls, special housing for disabled students, fraternity/sorority housing, and apartments for single student available. *Intercollegiate athletics:* men only: baseball, basketball, cross-country, golf, lacrosse, soccer, swimming, tennis; women only: basketball, cross-country, golf, soccer, softball, swimming, tennis, volleyball. 8 fraternities and 4 sororities on campus. *Special regulations:* Cars with parking stickers permitted. *Special services:* Medical services; Learning Resource Center, Counseling Center, Office of Career Services. Wireless connectivity to the Internet available on campus. Residence hall students are issued a laptop for their use while they attend the university. *Student publications: The Sandhill Review,* a biannual literary magazine; *The Golden Legend,* a yearbook; *The Lion's Pride,* a student newspaper. *Surrounding community:* Saint Leo, population 595, 35 miles north Tampa.

Publications: Biannual alumni magazine.

Library Collections: 141,521 volumes. 28,290 microforms; 6,437 audiovisual materials; 700 current periodical subscriptions. Access to online information retrieval systems.

Most important holdings include a collection of books, some rare, dealing with the history of the Catholic Church and the Benedictine Order in Florida; Catholic periodicals.

Buildings and Grounds: Campus area 186 acres.

Chief Executive Officer: Dr. Arthur F. Kirk, Jr., President.

Address admission inquiries to Gary Bracken, Vice President for Enrollment.

St. Petersburg College

8580 66 Street North
St. Petersburg, Florida 33781
Tel: (727) 341-4772   **E-mail:** admissions@spjc.cc.fl.us
Fax: (727) 341-3318   **Internet:** www.spjc.cc.fl.us

Institution Description: The mission of St. Petersburg College is to provide accessible, learner-centered education for students pursuing selected baccalaureate degrees, technical certificates, applied technology diplomas, and continuing education. *Enrollment:* 23,859./ *Degrees awarded:* Associate, baccalaureate.

Accreditation: *Regional:* SACS-Comm. on Coll.

Calendar: Semesters. Academic year early Sept. to mid-May.

Characteristics of Freshmen: Established 1926.

Admission: Open admission policy.

Degree Requirements: Completion of prescribed curriculum; general education requirements.

Distinctive Educational Programs: The college offers advanced technologies, distance learning, international education opportunities, innovative teaching techniques.

Degrees Conferred: 2,469 *associate;* 123 *baccalaureate.* Bachelor's degrees awarded: education 48; business, management, marketing, and related support 47; health professions and related clinical sciences 28.

Fees and Other Expenses: *Full-time tuition per academic year 2004–05:* lower division in-state $1,833, out-of-state $6,835; upper division in-state $2,201, out-of-state $8,150. *Room and board per academic year:* $5,260.

Financial Aid: Aid from institutionally generated funds is provided on the basis of academic merit, financial need.

Financial aid to full-time, first-time undergraduate students: 34% received federal grants averaging $1,620; 35% state/local grants averaging $664; 11% institutional grants averaging $390; 15% loans averaging $3,313.

Departments and Teaching Staff: Faculty are unranked.

Enrollment: Total enrollment 23,569 (38.3% men, 61.7% women).

Characteristics of Student Body: *Ethnic/racial makeup:* Black non-Hispanic: 10.1%; American Indian or Alaska Native: .7%; Asian or Pacific Islander: 3.2%; Hispanic: 5.4%; White non-Hispanic: 76.3%; unknown: 2.5%.

International Students: 424 nonresident aliens enrolled fall 2003. Programs available to aid students whose native language is not English: English as a Second Language. No financial aid specifically designated for international students.

Student Life: Some residence hall facilities.

Library Collections: Comprehensive library and other information resources available.

Chief Executive Officer: Dr. Karl M. Kuttler, President.

Address admission inquiries to Dr. Martyn Clay, Director of Admissions.

St. Thomas University

16400 N.W. 32nd Avenue
Miami, Florida 33054-6459
Tel: (305) 625-6000   **E-mail:** signup@stu.edu
Fax: (305) 628-6510   **Internet:** www.stu.edu

Institution Description: St. Thomas University is a private liberal arts university sponsored by the Archdiocese of Miami, Roman Catholic Church. *Enrollment:* 2,630. *Degrees awarded:* Baccalaureate, master's, first-professional (law).

Accreditation: *Regional:* SACS-Comm. on Coll. *Professional:* law

Calendar: Semesters. Academic year early Sept. to mid-May.

Characteristics of Freshmen: 74% of freshmen from Florida. Freshmen from 14 states and 21 foreign countries.

Admission: *Requirements:* Graduation from accredited secondary school with C average and 18 units which should include 4 English, 3 mathematics, 2 science, and 3 social science. *Entrance tests:* College Board SAT or ACT.

Degree Requirements: Completion of prescribed curriculum; general education requirements.

Distinctive Educational Programs: Continuing education. Study abroad semester in Spain (near Madrid); Semester Study Abroad for the Earth, Assisi, Italy.

Degrees Conferred: 102 *baccalaureate* (B); 225 *master's degrees* (M): biological/life sciences 4 (B); business/marketing 47 (B), 124 (M); communications/communication technologies 10 (B); computer and information sciences 11 (B), 24 (M); English 1 (B); health professions and related sciences 4 (B), 18 (M); law/legal studies 52 (M); liberal arts/general studies 1 (B); philosophy/religion/theology 7 (M); protective services/public administration 8 (B); psychology 7 (B); social sciences and history 4 (B). 139 *first-professional:* law.

Fees and Other Expenses: *Full-time tuition per academic year:* Contact the university for current tuition/fees for undergraduate, graduate, and first-professional study.

Financial Aid: Aid from institutionally generated funds is provided on the basis of academic merit, financial need.

Financial aid to full-time, first-time undergraduate students: need-based scholarships/grants totaling $6,125,520, self-help $4,210,842, parent loans $640,643, athletic awards $671,569; non-need-based scholarships/grants totaling $1,825,318, self-help $3,538,072.

Departments and Teaching Staff: *Total instructional faculty:* 303 (full-time 92, part-time 211; women 119, men 183; members of minority groups 113). Total faculty with doctorate, first-professional, or other terminal degree: 283. Student-to-faculty ratio: 11:1.

Enrollment: Total enrollment 2,830. Undergraduate full-time 450 men / 640 women, part-time 30m / 49w; graduate full-time 83m / 164w, part-time 181m / 292w; first-professional full-time 397m / 323w, part-time 1m.

Characteristics of Student Body: *Ethnic/racial makeup:* number of Black non-Hispanic: 134; American Indian or Alaska Native: 3; Asian or Pacific Islander: .6; Hispanic: 522; White non-Hispanic: 157; unknown: 18. *Age distribution:* number under 18: 16; 18–19: 306; 20–21: 250; 22–24: 176; 25–29: 121; 30–34: 98, 35–39: 62; 40–49: 96; 50–64: 38, 65 and over: 1.

International Students: 209 nonresident aliens enrolled fall 2004. 17 students from Europe, 17 Asia, 128 Central and South America, 7 Canada. Programs available to aid students whose native language is not English: English as a Second Language. No financial aid specifically designated for international students.

Student Life: Residence hall facilities available on campus.

Library Collections: 228,795 volumes. 357,757 microforms; 1,000 recordings/tape; 900 current periodical subscriptions. 250 computer work stations. Students have access to the Internet at no charge.

Buildings and Grounds: *New buildings:* University Chapel; Science and Technology Building.

Chief Executive Officer: Msgr. Franklyn N. Casale, President.

Address admission inquiries to Lydia Amy, Dean of Enrollment Management.

St. Vincent de Paul Regional Seminary

10701 South Military Trail

Boynton Beach, Florida 33436-4899

Tel: (561) 732-4424

Fax: (561) 737-2205

Institution Description: The St. Vincent de Paul Regional Seminary is a free-standing, graduate professional school of theology to prepare candidates for the Roman Catholic priesthood. The seminary is secondarily committed to providing continuing education for clergy, religious and laity of all denominations. *Enrollment:* 84. *Degrees awarded:* First-professional (theology), master's.

Accreditation: *Regional:* SACS-Comm. on Coll. *National:* ATS. *Professional*: theology

History: Incorporated 1960; established by Vincentian Fathers and offered first instruction at postsecondary level 1963; awarded first degree (baccalaureate) 1964; administration assumed by Archdiocese of Miami 1971; converted to interdiocesan seminary in 1981 under control of dioceses of Miami, St. Petersburg, St. Augustine, Pensacola-Tallahassee, Palm Beach, Venice, and Orlando.

Institutional Structure: *Governing board:* Board of Trustees. Representation: 23 trustees. All voting. *Composition of institution:* Administrators 6. Academic affairs headed by academic dean. Management/business/finances directed by treasurer. Full-time instructional faculty 16. Academic governance body, Faculty Council, meets weekly.

Calendar: Semesters. Academic year Aug. to May. Entering students admitted Aug. Degrees conferred and formal commencement May.

Characteristics of Freshmen: 99% of applicants accepted. 100% of accepted applicants enrolled. 35% of students from Florida. Students from 5 states and 2 foreign countries.

Admission: Rolling admissions plan. *Requirements:* For first-professional degree: baccalaureate from accredited secondary school or its equivalent, with 18 hours in philosophy and 12 in religious studies, personality and psychological tests, medical examination, GRE, language examination in target language (English for Spanish speakers, Spanish for English speakers). For master's degree: baccalaureate from accredited institution or its equivalent, with 12 hours in theology or philosophy, 3.0 GPA, GRE, *Entrance tests:* GRE. For foreign students TOEFL. *For transfer students:* 3.0 minimum GPA. From 4- and 2-year accredited institutions 9 hours maximum transfer credit.

Degree Requirements: *For first-professional degree:* 90 credit hours including 5 credit hours of field education; 6 semesters in residence; daily chapel attendance; exit competency examinations-comprehensives in individual fields of study. *For master's degree:* 39 credit hours; 2 semesters in residence. *For both degrees:* 3.0 GPA; prescribed curriculum. *Grading system:* A–F; pass-fail; withdraw (carries time limit).

Distinctive Educational Programs: Field education. Evening classes. Special facilities for using telecommunications in the classroom. Facilities and programs for independent research, including tutorials, independent study.

Degrees Conferred: 3 *master's:* theology; 11 *first-professional:* master of divinity.

Fees and Other Expenses: *Full-time tuition per academic year 2004–05:* $10,500. *Room and board per academic year:* $7,000.

Financial Aid: Financial aid available through sponsoring diocese.

Departments and Teaching Staff: *Total instructional faculty:* 20 (full-time 15, part-time 5; women 4, men 16; members of minority groups 6.) Total faculty with doctorate, first-professional, or other terminal degree: 18. Student-to-faculty ratio: 4:1.

Enrollment: Total enrollment 65. First-professional full-time 65 men; part-time 15m / 4w.

International Students: 4 nonresident aliens enrolled fall 2004. *Programs available to aid students whose native language is not English:* Cultural; English as a Second Language Program. No financial aid specifically designated for foreign students.

Student Life: On-campus residence halls for seminarians house 92% of student body. *Special regulations:* Cars permitted without restrictions. Appropriate dress for liturgy and classroom. *Special services:* Medical services. *Student publications: Tamar,* a quarterly literary magazine. *Surrounding community:* Boynton Beach population 65,000. Fort Lauderdale; 30 miles from campus, is nearest metropolitan area. Served by airport 20 miles from campus.

Library Collections: 61,000 volumes including bound books, serial backfiles, electronic documents, and government documents not in separate collections. Online catalog. 400 current serial subscriptions. 10 computer work stations.

Most important special collections include theology, Spanish language, philosophy.

Buildings and Grounds: Campus area 70 acres.

Chief Executive Officer: Rev. Msgr. Stephen Bosso, Rector-President.

Address all admission inquiries to Rector-President.

Schiller International University

453 Edgewater Drive

Dunedin, Florida 34698-7532

Tel: (727) 736-5082

Fax: (727) 734-0569

Institution Description: Schiller International University offers a variety of degrees at the undergraduate and graduate levels. In addition to this Florida location, there are campuses in London, Paris, Strasbourg, Heidelberg, Madrid, and Switzerland. Distance learning programs are also available. *Enrollment (Florida campus):* 177. *Degrees awarded:* Associate, baccalaureate, master's.

Accreditation: *Nonregional:* ACICS.

History: Sounded in 1964, Schiller International University is an independent American university with campuses in the United States, United Kingdom, France, Germany, Spain, and Switzerland. The language of instruction is English at all campuses.

Calendar: Semesters. Academic year Aug. to May.

Characteristics of Freshmen: 475 applicants (300 men, 175 women). 44% of applicants accepted. 11.5% of admitted students enrolled full-time.

Admission: Rolling admissions plan. *Requirements:* Graduation from an accredited secondary school or its equivalent.

Degree Requirements: Associate programs are offered in business, hotel and tourism management, resort club management, general studies. Bachelor degree programs include international business, international hotel and tourism management, club resort management, international relations and diplomacy. Master's degree programs (2 years) include international business, hotel and tourism management, management of information technology, international management.

Distinctive Educational Programs: Distance learning programs. Diploma program (1 year, nondegree) in hotel operational management and catering/culinary arts.

Degrees Conferred: 2 *associate*; 45 *baccalaureate*; 52 *master's.* Bachelor's degrees awarded the disciplines of: business, management, marketing, and related support services 33; multidisciplinary studies 8; social sciences 4.

Fees and Other Expenses: *Full-time tuition per academic year 2004–05:* $14,800. *Books and supplies:* $1,305. *Room and board per academic year:* $5,600.

Financial Aid: Institution has a Program Participation Agreement with the U.S. Department of Education for eligible students to receive Pell Grants and other federal aid.

Financial aid to full-time, first-time undergraduate students: 10% of students received federal grants; 5% state/local grants; 5% institutional grants; 5% received loans.

Departments and Teaching Staff: Faculty members are unranked.

Enrollment: Total enrollment 177. Undergraduate 97 (47.4% men, 62.6% women).

Characteristics of Student Body: *Ethnic/racial makeup:* Black, non-Hispanic: 15; Asian or Pacific Islander: 4.1%; Hispanic: 2.1%; White non-Hispanic: 12.4%, nonresident alien: 80.4%.

International Students: 142 undergraduate nonresident aliens enrolled fall 2004.

Chief Executive Officer: Dr. Christoph Lebrecht, President.

Address admission inquiries to Kamala Dontamsetti, Director of Admissions.

Southeastern College of the Assemblies of God

1000 Longfellow Boulevard
Lakeland, Florida 33801-6034

Tel: (941) 667-5000   **E-mail:** admission@secollege.edu
Fax: (941) 667-5200   **Internet:** www.secollege.edu

Institution Description: Southeastern College of the Assemblies of God is a private, independent, nonprofit institution. *Enrollment:* 1,675. *Degrees awarded:* Baccalaureate.

Accreditation: *Regional:* SACS-Comm. on Coll. *National:* ABHE.

History: Established and chartered 1935; offered first program at postsecondary level 1935; awarded first baccalaureate degree 1958; adopted present name 1977.

Calendar: Semesters. Academic year Aug. to Apr. Degrees conferred Dec., Apr. Formal commencement Apr. Summer session of 2 terms from late Apr. to early July.

Characteristics of Freshmen: 630 applicants (250 men, 380 women). 88.6% of applicants accepted. 77.4% of admitted students enrolled full-time.

35% of entering freshmen expected to graduate within 5 years. Freshmen from 27 states and 4 foreign countries.

Admission: Rolling admissions plan. For fall applicants, apply as early as end of junior year of secondary school, but no later than 1 month prior to beginning of term. Early admission available. *Requirements:* Either graduation from secondary school or GED. *Entrance tests:* ACT composite. *For transfer students:* 2.0 minimum GPA for accepted transfer hours; 96 hours maximum transfer credit from 4-year accredited institution; 64 hours maximum transfer credit from 2-year accredited institution.

Degree Requirements: 130 credit hours; 2.0 GPA; 24 semester hours in residence.

Fulfillment of some degree requirements and exemption from some beginning courses possible by passing departmental examinations, College Board CLEP, AP. *Grading system:* A–F; withdraw.

Degrees Conferred: 271 *baccalaureate*. Bachelor's degrees awarded in top five disciplines: theology and ministerial studies 93; business, management, marketing, and related support services 48; education 45; psychology 31; communication, journalism, and related programs 16.

Fees and Other Expenses: *Full-time tuition per academic year 2004–05:* $10,140. *Room and board per academic year:* $5,469. *General fees:* $640. *Books and supplies:* $800.

Financial Aid: Aid from institutionally generated funds is provided on the basis of academic merit, financial need, other criteria. Institution has a Program Participation Agreement with the U.S. Department of Education for eligible students to receive Pell Grants and other federal aid.

Financial aid to full-time, first-time undergraduate students: 35% of students received federal grants averaging $2,998; 48% state/local grants averaging $3,577; 54% institutional grants averaging 54%; 87% loans averaging $2,841.

Departments and Teaching Staff: *Professors* 25, *associate professors* 17, *assistant professors* 11, *instructors* 4, *part-time teachers* 27. *Total instructional faculty:* 66. Degrees held by full-time faculty: Doctorate 49%, master's 51%. 49% hold terminal degrees.

Enrollment: Total enrollment 1,675 (46.7% men, 53.3% women).

Characteristics of Student Body: *Ethnic and racial makeup:* Black non-Hispanic: 6%; American Indian or Alaska Native: .5%; Asian or Pacific Islander: 1.3%; Hispanic 8.7%; White non-Hispanic: 76.9%; unknown: 5.7%.

International Students: 22 nonresident aliens enrolled fall 2004. Students from Europe, Asia, Latin America, Africa, Canada. No programs available to aid students whose native language is not English. No financial aid specifically designated for international students.

Student Life: *Intercollegiate athletics:* basketball, volleyball, baseball, soccer. *Special regulations:* Quiet hours set by dormitory residents. Cars permitted by registration. Religious observance or study required. *Special services:* Personal counseling. *Student publications, radio:* Newspaper, yearbook, weekly news release. *Surrounding community:* Lakeland population 60,000. Located 30 miles from Tampa and less than 50 miles from Disney World in Orlando. Accessible via international airports from Tampa and Orlando. City transit bus system.

Library Collections: 94,000 volumes. 1,660 microform items; 2,875 audiovisual materials; 430 current periodical subscriptions. Online catalog. Students have access to online information retrieval services and the Internet.

Most important special collections include career resources, church buildings, and curriculum laboratory.

Buildings and Grounds: Campus area 60 acres.

Chief Executive Officer: Dr. Mark Rutland, President.
Address admission inquiries to Omar Rashed, Director of Admissions.

Stetson University

421 North Woodland Boulevard
Deland, Florida 32720

Tel: (904) 822-7000   **E-mail:** admission@stetson.edu
Fax: (904) 822-8832   **Internet:** www.stetson.edu

Institution Description: Stetson University is a private institution affiliated with the Florida Baptist Convention of the Southern Baptist Convention. *Enrollment:* 3,439. *Degrees awarded:* Baccalaureate, master's, first-professional.

Accreditation: *Regional:* SACS-Comm. on Coll. *Professional:* accounting, athletic training, business, counseling, law, music, teacher education

History: Established as Deland Academy 1883; offered first instruction at postsecondary level 1884; changed name to Deland Academy and College 1885; chartered and changed name to Deland University 1887; adopted name John B. Stetson University 1889; awarded first degree (baccalaureate) 1893; became Stetson University 1993.

Institutional Structure: *Governing board:* 36 trustees; institutional representation: 1 administrator; 1 alumnus. 2 ex officio. All voting. *Composition of institution:* Administrators 42 men / 25 women. Academic affairs headed by Council of Deans. Management/business/finances directed by vice president for finance. Full-time instructional faculty 100 men/30 women. Academic governance body, Faculty Senate, meets an average of 9 times per year.

Calendar: Semesters. Academic year Aug. to May. Freshmen admitted Aug., Feb., June. Summer session from June to July.

Characteristics of Freshmen: 2,540 applicants (996 men, 1,544 women). 78% of applicants admitted. 30.2% of admitted students enrolled full-time.

92% (553 students) submitted SAT scores; 42% (253 students) submitted ACT scores. *25th percentile:* SAT I Verbal 520, SAT I Math 510; ACT Composite 21, ACT English 21, ACT Math 19. *75th percentile:* SAT I Verbal 620, SAT I Math 610; ACT Composite 27, ACT English 28, ACT Math26.

58% of entering freshmen expected to graduate within 5 years. 73% of freshmen from Florida. Freshmen from 31 states and 18 foreign countries.

Admission: Modified rolling admissions plan. For fall acceptance, apply as early as fall of previous year, but not later than Mar. 15 of year of enrollment. Students are notified of acceptance Dec. 15 through May. Apply by Nov. 1 for early decision. *Requirements:* Either graduation from secondary school with 4 units in English, 3 natural sciences, 3 mathematics, 2 foreign language, 2 social sciences; or GED. *Entrance tests:* College Board SAT or ACT composite. *For transfer students:* 2.0 minimum GPA; from 4-year accredited institution 75 hours maximum transfer credit; from 2-year accredited institution 60 hours; correspondence/extension students 12 hours.

College credit and advanced placement for postsecondary-level work completed in secondary school. Tutoring available. Developmental courses offered in summer session; credit given.

Degree Requirements: 120 credit hours; 2.0 GPA; general education requirements plus specific requirements for College or School and major. Fulfillment of some degree requirements and exemption from some beginning courses possible by passing College Board CLEP. *Grading system:* A–F; pass-fail; pass; withdraw (pass-fail appended to withdrawal).

Distinctive Educational Programs: Stetson University offers study abroad programs in Spain, France, Germany, England, Russia, Hong Kong, and Mexico. Washington semester at American University. Student-designed majors through the Honors Program. 3–2 engineering degrees and a 3–3 law degree with Stetson College of Law. Leadership Development Program, Family Business Center.

Degrees Conferred: 458 *baccalaureate*; 173 *master's*; 270 *first-professional*; 9 *post-master's certificate*. Bachelor's degrees awarded in top five disciplines: business, management, marketing, and related support services 173; social sciences 44; education 38; psychology 32; visual and performing arts 31.

Fees and Other Expenses: *Full-time tuition per academic year 2004–05:* $24,135. Contact the university for graduate/professional school tuition/fees. *Room and board per academic year:* $7,060. *Books and supplies:* $800.

Financial Aid: Aid from institutionally generated funds is provided on the basis of academic merit, financial need, athletic ability, other criteria. Institution has a Program Participation Agreement with the U.S. Department of Education for eligible students to receive Pell Grants and other federal aid.

Financial aid to full-time, first-time undergraduate students: 19% of students received federal grants averaging $3,571; 74% state/local grants averaging $4,974; 94% institutional grants averaging $9,758; 56% loans averaging $5,217.

Departments and Teaching Staff: *Professors* 55, *associate professors* 65, *assistant professors* 41, *instructors* 28.

Total instructional faculty: 182. *Degrees held by full-time faculty:* 88% hold terminal degrees.

Enrollment: Total enrollment 3,439 (includes College of Law). Undergraduate 2,161 (42.6% men, 57.4% women).

Characteristics of Student Body: *Ethnic/racial makeup:* Black non-Hispanic: 5.6%; American Indian or Alaska Native: .4%; Asian or Pacific Islander: 2.1%; Hispanic: 4.8%; White non-Hispanic: 83.3%; unknown: 2.4%.

International Students: 73 undergraduate nonresident aliens enrolled fall 2004. Students from Europe, Asia, Central and South America, Africa, Canada, Australia.

Student Life: On-campus residence halls and apartments house 73% of student body. 27% of student body live off-campus. *Intercollegiate athletics:* men only: baseball, basketball, crew, cross-county, golf, soccer, tennis; women only: basketball, crew, cross-country, golf, soccer, softball, tennis, volleyball. *Special regulations:* Registered cars permitted in designated areas only. *Special services:* Learning Resources Center, medical services, Counseling Center, bookstore. *Student publications, radio: The Stetson Reporter,* a weekly newspaper; *Touchstone,* an annual literary magazine; *Hatter,* a yearbook. Radio station WHAT broadcasts 50 hours per week over the Internet. *Surrounding community:* Deland (population 30,000) is 40 miles for Orlando and 25 miles from Daytona Beach. . Served by airports in both Orlando and Daytona; passenger rail service 5 miles away; bus terminal adjacent to campus.

Library Collections: 390,000 volumes. 414,000 microform units; 18,800 audio/video recordings; 1,145 periodical subscriptions. Approximately 150 computer terminals provided for students use in general access labs. Students are encouraged to have their own computer.

Most important holdings include Florida Baptist Archives; Southern Baptist Archives; government documents (state's first depository for federal documents).

Buildings and Grounds: Campus area 162 acres.

Chief Executive Officer: Dr. H. Douglas Lee, President.

Address admission inquiries to Terry E. Whittum, Director of Admissions.

Stetson University College of Law

1401 61st Street
St. Petersburg, Florida 33707
Tel: (727) 562-7800

Degree Programs Offered: *First-professional.*

Admission: Graduation from accredited college or university; LSAT.

Degree Requirements: 86 credit hours; 6 semesters in residence.

Fees and Other Expenses: Contact the university for current tuition.

Departments and Teaching Staff: *Professors* 23, *associate professors* 4, *assistant professors* 2, *instructors/visiting lecturers* 6.

Total instructional faculty: 35. Degrees held by full-time faculty: Doctorate 100%. 100% hold terminal degrees.

University of Central Florida

4000 Central Florida Boulevard
Orlando, Florida 32816-0002

Tel: (407) 823-2000   **E-mail:** admission@mail.ucf.edu
Fax: (407) 823-3419   **Internet:** www.ucf.edu

Institution Description: University of Central Florida (Florida Technological University until 1978) is a member of the State University System of Florida. *Enrollment:* 42,568. *Degrees awarded:* Associate, baccalaureate, master's, doctorate. Specialist certificate also awarded.

Academic offerings subject to approval by statewide coordinating bodies. Budget subject to approval by state governing boards.

Accreditation: *Regional:* SACS-Comm. on Coll. *Professional:* accounting, athletic training, business, clinical lab scientist, computer science, counseling, engineering, engineering technology, English language education, health information administration, music, nursing, nursing education, physical therapy, public administration, radiography, respiratory therapy, social work, speech-language pathology, teacher education

History: Established and chartered as Florida Technological University 1963; offered first instruction at postsecondary level 1968; awarded first degree (baccalaureate) 1969; adopted present name 1978.

Institutional Structure: *Governing board:* Florida Board of Regents. Representation: 13 members, including 1 student (appointed by governor of Florida). All voting. *Composition of institution:* President, provost, vice president of academic affairs, vice president of student development and enrollment services, vice president of administration and finance, vice president of sponsored research, vice president of university relations. Full-time instructional faculty

877. Academic governance body, Faculty Senate, meets an average of 8 times per year. *Faculty representation:* Faculty served by collective bargaining agent affiliated with AFT.

Calendar: Semesters. Academic year May to May. Freshmen admitted Aug., Jan., May. Degrees conferred May, Aug., Dec. Summer session of 3 terms from May to July.

Characteristics of Freshmen: 55% of applicants admitted. 48% of admitted students enrolled full-time.

75% (4,446 students) submitted SAT scores; 25% (1,452 students) submitted ACT scores. *25th percentile:* SAT Verbal 520, SAT Math 530; ACT Composite 22. *75th percentile:* SAT Verbal 620, SAT Math 630; ACT Composite 27.

50.4% of entering freshmen expected to graduate within 5 years. 93% of freshmen from Florida. Freshmen from 43 states and 67 foreign countries.

Admission: Rolling admissions plan. For fall acceptance, apply no later than March 15 of year of enrollment. Early acceptance available. *Requirements:* Graduates of regionally accredited high schools who meet the admission scale requirements for all academic subjects taken in the 9th through 12th grade may be considered for admission; preference given to those students who have a combined SAT of 970 or above; or 20 and above on the ACT with a high school academic GPA of 2.9 or above; academic units to include English 4, mathematics 3, natural science 3, social science 3, foreign language 2, electives 4 (total minimum of 19). *Entrance tests:* College Board SAT, ACT composite. For foreign students TOEFL. *For transfer students:* From an accredited college or university with 2 years of transferable credit; GPA of 2.0 or above; good standing at last institution attended.

College credit for postsecondary-level work completed in secondary school and for extrainstitutional learning on basis of ACE *2006 Guide to the Evaluation of Educational Experiences in the Armed Services.* Tutoring available. Noncredit developmental courses offered in summer session and regular academic year.

Degree Requirements: *For all associate degrees:* 60 semester hours; 20 hours in residence. *For all baccalaureate degrees:* 120–128 semester hours; 30 hours in residence. *For all undergraduate degrees:* 2.0 GPA; general education requirements. Fulfillment of some degree requirements possible by passing departmental examinations, College Board CLEP, AP, other standardized tests. *Grading system:* A–F; withdraw (carries time limit).

Distinctive Educational Programs: Work-experience programs, including internships, cooperative education. Flexible meeting places and schedules, including off-campus centers (at South Orlando, less than 30 miles away from main institution; Brevard; 40 miles away; at Daytona Beach, 55 miles away) and evening classes. Accelerated degree programs. Special facilities for using telecommunications in the classroom. Facilities and programs for independent research, including individual majors, tutorials, independent study. Study abroad programs in Caribbean, England, Germany, Italy, Mexico, Quebec. Semester and academic year student exchanges with universities in Canada, England, Finland, France, and Germany. *Other distinctive programs:* Continuing education.

ROTC: Army, Air Force. 20 Army and 24 Air Force commissions awarded 2004.

Degrees Conferred: 7,215 *baccalaureate* (B); 1,821 *master's* (M); 37 *doctorate* (D): biological/life sciences 209(B); 20 (M); business/marketing 1,998 (B), 395 (M), 1 (D); communications/communication technologies 392 (B), 32 (M); computer and information sciences 198 (B), 46 (M), 6 (D); education 670 (B), 414 (M), 62 (D); engineering and engineering technologies 487 (B); 259 (M), 44 (D); English 278, (B); 30 (M), 3 (D); foreign languages and literature 25 (B), 5 (M); health professions and related sciences 534 (B), 195 (M); interdisciplinary studies 13 (M); law/legal studies 187 (B); liberal arts/general studies 466 (B), 23 (M); mathematics 26 (B), 38 (M), 5 (D); philosophy/religion/theology 11 (B); physical sciences 16 (B), 19 (M), 3 (D); protective services/public administration 418 (B), 254 (M), 6 (D); psychology 678 (B), 55 (M), 7 (D); social sciences and history 360 (B), 39 (M); visual and performing arts 262 (B), 4 (M).

Fees and Other Expenses: *Full-time tuition per academic year 2004–05:* undergraduate resident $2,982, out-of-state $15,488; graduate resident $5,505, out-of-state $20,876. *Other fees:* $198. *Room and board per academic year:* $7,132.

Financial Aid: Aid from institutionally generated funds is provided on the basis of academic merit, financial need, athletic ability.

Financial aid to full-time, first-time undergraduate students: need-based scholarships/grants totaling $30,765,978, self-help $53,056,175; non-need-based scholarships/grants totaling $48,023,405, self-help $34,576,603, parent loans $4,545,913, athletic awards $1,384,059.

Departments and Teaching Staff: *Professors* 226, *associate professors* 310, *assistant professors* 294, *instructors* 272 *part-time faculty* 468. *Total instructional faculty:* 1,570 (full-time 1,190, part-time 447; women 679, men 958; members of minority groups 312). Total faculty with doctorate, first-professional, or other terminal degree: 1,070. Student-to-faculty ratio: 25:1.

Enrollment: Total enrollment 42,568. Undergraduate full-time 12,092 men / 14,961 women, part-time 3,683m / 4,523w; graduate full-time 1,254m / 1,663w, part-time 4,902m / 2,690w.

Characteristics of Student Body: *Ethnic/racial makeup:* number of Black non-Hispanic: 2,940; American Indian or Alaska Native: 180; Asian or Pacific Islander: 1,742; Hispanic: 4; 353; White non-Hispanic: 24,134; unknown: 1,137. *Age distribution:* number under 18: 97; 18–19: 4,439; 20–21: 10,842, 22–24: 8,491; 25–29 2,091; 30–34: 1,254, 35–39: 612; 40–49: 947; 50–64: 273; 65 and over: 33.

International Students: 1,350 nonresident aliens enrolled fall 2004. Programs available to aid students whose native language is not English: Social. No financial aid specifically designated for international students.

Student Life: On-campus residence halls house 20% of undergraduate student body. *Intercollegiate athletics:* men only: baseball, basketball, cross-country, football, golf, soccer, tennis; women only: basketball, cross-country, golf, tennis, volleyball. *Special regulations:* Cars permitted without restrictions (permit required). *Special services:* Learning Resources Center, medical services, student academic resource center. *Student publications, radio: Future,* a weekly newspaper. Radio station WUCF-FM broadcasts 24 hours a day (168 hours per week). *Surrounding community:* Orlando metropolitan area population 1; 359,000. Served by airport 17 miles from campus; passenger rail service 8 miles from campus.

Library Collections: 1,577,587 volumes. 2,879,241 microforms. 30,889 audiovisual materials. 8,092 serials. Students have access to the Internet at no charge.

Buildings and Grounds: Campus area 1,414 acres.

Chief Executive Officer: Dr. John C. Hitt, President.

Address undergraduate admission inquiries to Gordon Chavis, Jr., Director of Admission; graduate inquiries to Office of Graduate Admissions.

University of Florida

P.O. Box 113150
Gainesville, Florida 32611-3150
Tel: (352) 392-3261   **E-mail:** regadmi@ufl.edu
Fax: (352) 392-8774   **Internet:** www.ufl.edu

Institution Description: University of Florida is a state institution and land-grant college. *Enrollment:* 47,858. *Degrees awarded:* Associate, baccalaureate, first-professional (dentistry, medicine, pharmacy, veterinary medicine, law), master's, doctorate. Specialist degree also awarded.

Academic offerings subject to approval by statewide coordinating bodies. Budget subject to approval by state governing boards.

Accreditation: *Regional:* SACS-Comm. on Coll. *Professional:* accounting, applied science, art, athletic training, audiology, business, clinical psychology, construction education, counseling, dental public health, dentistry, endodontics, engineering, engineering technology, forestry, health services administration, interior design, journalism, landscape architecture, law, medicine, music, nursing-midwifery, nursing, nursing education, occupational therapy, pediatric dentistry, periodontics, pharmacy, physical therapy, physician assisting, planning, psychology internship, recreation and leisure services, rehabilitation counseling, school psychology, speech-language pathology, teacher education, theatre, veterinary medicine

History: Established as East Florida Seminary and offered first instruction at postsecondary level 1853; awarded first degree (baccalaureate) 1882; chartered and adopted present name 1903; became coeducational 1947. *See* Samuel Proctor, *University of Florida: Its Early Years* (Gainesville: University of Florida Press, 1958) for further information.

Institutional Structure: *Governing board:* Florida Board of Regents. Representation: 14 members, including 1 student (appointed by governor of Florida) and commissioner of education. All voting. *Composition of institution:* Administrators 474. Academic affairs headed by vice president for academic affairs who is also University Provost. Management/business/finances directed by vice president for administrative affairs. Full-time instructional faculty 1,531. Academic governance body, University Senate, meets an average of 10 times per year. *Faculty representation:* Faculty served by collective bargaining agent, United Faculty of Florida, affiliated with AFT.

Calendar: Semesters. Academic year Aug. to May. Freshmen admitted Aug., Jan., May, June. Degrees conferred and formal commencements May, Aug., Dec.summer session of 2 terms from May to Aug.

Characteristics of Freshmen: 22,458 applicants (10,040 men, 12,418 women). 53.1% of applicants admitted. 55.8% of admitted students enrolled full-time.

76% (5,145 students) submitted SAT scores. *25th percentile*: SAT I Verbal 570, SAT I Math 590. *75th percentile*: SAT I Verbal 670, SAT I Math 690.

91% of freshmen from Florida. Freshmen from 41 states and 58 foreign countries.

Admission: Early decision/regular decision plan. For fall acceptance, apply as early as Sept. 1 of previous year, but not later than Oct. 15 (for early decision) or Jan. 15 (for regular decision) of year of enrollment. *Requirements:* Graduation from regionally accredited secondary school with 4 years English; 3 years mathematics (algebra I, algebra II, geometry); 3 years science; 3 years social science; 2 years foreign language. *Entrance test:* College Board SAT or ACT composite. For foreign students, SAT or ACT for freshmen or sophomore applicants; TOEFL for junior level applicants. Essay required. 50% of applicants will be admitted on academic credentials, the remainder or the class will be admitted through a holistic review of all the information contained in the application, both academic and personal. *For transfer students:* admission at the transfer freshman or sophomore levels is competitive and limited. Applicants are encouraged to apply at the junior level. Maximum transfer credit from 4-year institutions limited only by residence requirement; from 2-year accredited institutions: 60 semester hours.

College credit and advanced placement for postsecondary-level work completed in secondary school.

Degree Requirements: *For all associate degrees:* 60 semester hours. *For all baccalaureate degrees:* 120–140 semester hours; 30 semester hours in residence. *For all undergraduate degrees:* 2.0 GPA; general education requirements.

Fulfillment of some degree requirements and exemption from some beginning courses possible by passing College Board CLEP IB, AP. *Grading system:* A–F; pass-fail; withdraw (deadline after which pass-fail is appended to withdraw).

Distinctive Educational Programs: Work-experience programs, including cooperative education, internships. Flexible meeting places and schedules, including off-campus centers (at Pensacola; 400 miles away from main institution; at various other locations throughout Florida), evening classes. Accelerated degree programs. Special facilities for using telecommunications in the classroom. Facilities and programs for independent research, including honors programs, tutorials. Institutionally sponsored study abroad in Xian, China; Taipei, Taiwan; Mannheim, Bochum, Leipzig, Germany; Aarhus, Denmark; Kyoto, China, Japan; Paris, Strasbourg, Grenoble, Montpellier, Lille, France; Rio de Janeiro, Brazil; Haifa, Jerusalem, Tel-Aviv, Negev, Israel; Innsbruck, Salzburg, Graz, Austria; London, Cambridge, Lancaster, Manchester, Hull, United Kingdom; Granada, Salamanca, Madrid, Spain; Vicenza, Castelfranco, Rome, Bologna, Milan, Florence, Italy; Coimbre, Portugal; Helsinki, Lahti, Finland; Utrecht, Haarlem, Nijnrode, Leiden, The Netherlands; Moscow, Russia; Merida, Mexico; Sydney, Australia; Kampala, Uganda; Dar es Salaam, Tanzania; Lund, Sweden; Rekjavik, Iceland; Bergen, Oslo, Norway; Thessalonkiki, Greece; Cork, Ireland; Ljubljana, Slovenia; Fez, Morocco; Valletta, Malta; Antwerp, Belgium; Basel, Switzerland.

ROTC: Army, Navy, Air Force.

Degrees Conferred: 415 *associate*; 8,574 *baccalaureate*; 2,961 *master's*; 694 *doctorate*; 964 *first-professional*; 61 *post-master's certificate*. Bachelor's degrees awarded in top five disciplines: business, management, marketing, and related support services 1,715; social sciences 1,106; engineering 828; communication, journalism, and related programs 844; health professions and related clinical sciences 583.

Fees and Other Expenses: *Full-time tuition per academic year 2004–05:* undergraduate in-district/in-state $2,955, out-of-state $15,827. Contact the university for graduate/professional school tuition/fees. *Room and board per academic year:* $6,040.

Financial Aid: Aid from institutionally generated funds is provided on the basis of academic merit, athletic ability, financial need. Institution has a Program Participation Agreement with the U.S. Department of Education for eligible students to receive Pell Grants and other federal aid.

Financial aid to full-time, first-time undergraduate students: 19% of students received federal grants averaging $3,130; 93% state/local grants averaging $2,667; 23% institutional grants averaging $3,311; 22% loans averaging $2,975.

Departments and Teaching Staff: *Professors* 1,348, *associate professors* 820, *assistant professors* 840, *instructors* 24, *part-time faculty* 245, *other* 809. *Total instructional faculty:* 4,126. Student-to-faculty ratio: 17:1. Faculty with doctorate, first-professional, or other terminal degree: 95%.

Enrollment: Total enrollment 47,858. Undergraduate 33,983 (46.6% men, 53.4% women).

Characteristics of Student Body: *Ethnic/racial makeup:* Black non-Hispanic: 8.5%; American Indian or Alaska Native: .5%; Asian or Pacific Islander: 8.9%; Hispanic: 11.9%; White non-Hispanic: 70%; unknown: .9%.

International Students: 574 nonresident aliens enrolled fall 2004. Students from Europe, Asia, Latin America and Caribbean, Africa, Canada, Australia, New Zealand. English as a Second Language Program available. No financial aid specifically designated for international students.

Student Life: On-campus residence halls house 21% of student body. One residence hall for women only. Other residence halls house both men and women, but are separated by floor or section. 68% of residence hall residents are freshmen. 50% of the residents are men and 50% women. Fraternities and sororities house 5% of student body. Family housing is available for 980 families (with or without children, single- or two-parent). *Intercollegiate athletics:* men only: baseball, basketball, football, golf, swimming, tennis, track; women only: fast-pitch softball, basketball, golf, soccer, swimming, tennis, track, volleyball, gymnastics. *Special regulations:* Registered cars permitted in designated areas only. Quiet hours are enforced, but vary from dormitory to dormitory. *Special services:* Learning Resources Center, medical services, shuttle bus system, counseling center, evening escort service (Student Nighttime Auxiliary Patrol). *Student publications, radio, television: Independent Florida Alligator* newspaper published five weekdays during fall and spring semesters, Tuesday and Thursday during summer; *Florida Leader* magazine published every six weeks; *GatorTalk* , sport publication published weekly during the fall. WRUF-AM, WRUF-FM radio stations, WUFT television station (public television affiliate). *Surrounding community:* Alachua County population 185,000 (est.). Jacksonville, 70 miles from campus, is nearest metropolitan area. Served by mass transit bus system; airport 6 miles from campus; passenger rail service 14 miles from campus.

Publications: *Florida Statistical Abstracts* (three times annually) first published 1967; *Florida Estimate of Population* (annually) first published 1972; *Florida Outlook* (quarterly) first published 1978; *Population Studies* (four times a year) first published 1955; *Florida Today* (quarterly) first published 1975; *University of Florida Law Review* (five times a year) first published 1948. University press published 48 titles in 1990.

Library Collections: 5,024,700 volumes including bound books, serial backfiles, electronic documents, and government documents not in separate collections. Online catalog. Current serial subscriptions: 28,100. 6,702,000 microform units; 36,000 audio/visual materials; 16,800 computer files. 650 computer work stations. Students have access to the Internet at no charge.

Most important holdings include the Latin American Collection; the P.K. Yonge Library of Florida History; the Isser and Rae Price Library of Judaica; Baldwin Library of Children's Literature.

Buildings and Grounds: Campus area 2,050 acres.

Chief Executive Officer: Dr. James B. Machen, President.

Address admission inquiries to Patrick C. Herring, Director of Admissions.

College of Liberal Arts and Sciences

Degree Programs Offered: *Baccalaureate, master's, doctorate* in anthropology, astronomy, botany, chemistry, classical studies, computer and information sciences, communications studies, communications science and disorders, criminal justice, East Asian languages and literatures, economics, English, French, geography, geology, German, history, interdisciplinary studies, Jewish studies, linguistics, mathematics, microbiology and cell science, philosophy, physics, political science, Portuguese, psychology, religion, Russian, sociology, Spanish, statistics, zoology.

Distinctive Educational Programs: Interdepartmental and interdisciplinary programs in African studies, Afro-American studies, Asian studies, criminology and law, environmental studies, gerontology, Jewish studies, Soviet and East European studies, women's studies. English Language Institute. Specialization in audiology and speech pathology. *Other distinctive programs:* National High Magnetic Field Laboratory.

College of Agriculture

Degree Programs Offered: *Baccalaureate, master's, doctorate* in agriculture (food and resource), agricultural engineering, agricultural and extension education, agronomy, animal science, botany, dairy science, entomology and nematology, food and resource economics, food science and human nutrition, forest resources and conservation, fruit crops, agricultural operations management, microbiology and cell science, ornamental horticulture, plant pathology, plant sciences, poultry science, soil science, statistics, vegetable crops.

Distinctive Educational Programs: Preprofessional program in veterinary medicine. Pest management and plant protection program. Environmental studies program.

College of Architecture

Degree Programs Offered: *Baccalaureate, master's, doctorate* in architecture; *baccalaureate, master's* in landscape architecture, interior design; master's in urban and regional planning.

College of Business Administration

Degree Programs Offered: *Baccalaureate* in accounting and in business administration with tracks in computer and information science, decision and information sciences, economics, finance, insurance, management, marketing and real estate; *Master of Business Administration, Master of Accounting, master's* in economics and in business administration with tracks in computer and information sciences, decision and information sciences, finance, management, marketing and real estate; *Doctor of Philosophy* in economics and in business administration with tracks in accounting, decision and information sciences, finance, management, marketing and real estate.

Admission: *Undergraduates:* BSBA - 2.50 overall GPA, 2.50 preprofessional; BSAC - 2.8 overall GPA to qualify for applicant pool. *Accounting graduate:* MACC - 1100 GRE combined score or 500 GMAT, Ph.D. - 1200 GRE combined score or 550 GMAT. *Other graduate programs:* requirements vary by degree and department.

Degree Requirements: *Undergraduate:* BSBA - 124 hours, 2.0 overall, major and UF GPAs, and coursework as specified by College; BSAC - 124 hours, 2.0 overall, major and upper division GPA and coursework as specified by School. *Graduate:* Requirements vary by degree and department.

Distinctive Educational Programs: Joint M.B.A.-first-professional degree with School of Law. Master's in health and hospital administration in cooperation with College of Health Related Professions. Bureau of Economic and Business Research.

College of Education

Degree Programs Offered: *Baccalaureate* in elementary education, special education; *advanced degrees* in counselor education, curriculum and instruction, educational administration, elementary education, foundations of education, secondary education, and special education.

Admission: *Undergraduate:* 2.60 GPA; 900 SAT or 20 ACT. *Graduate:* 3.00 GPA; 1,000 GRE.

Degree Requirements: *For baccalaureate degree:* 2.60 GPA. *For graduate degree:* 3.00 GPA.

College of Engineering

Degree Programs Offered: *Baccalaureate* surveying; *baccalaureate, master's, doctorate* in aerospace engineering, agricultural engineering, ceramics engineering, chemical engineering, civil engineering, coastal and oceanographic engineering, computer and information sciences, electrical engineering, engineering graphics, engineering sciences, engineering technology, environmental engineering sciences, general engineering, industrial and systems engineering, land surveying, mechanical engineering, metallurgical engineering, nuclear engineering sciences.

Distinctive Educational Programs: Interdepartmental programs in environmental studies, biomedical engineering. Preprofessional program in biomedical sciences.

College of Fine Arts

Degree Programs Offered: *Baccalaureate* in art, music, theater with emphases in painting, drawing, printmaking, sculpture, ceramics, creative photography, graphic design, art history and art education; music performance, theory, and composition; music history, church music, and music education; acting, music theatre, dance, costume design, scene design, and lighting design; *master's* in music performance, music education, music history and literature, sacred music, theory and composition, conducting, accompanying, and pedagogy; art studio, art history, art education, multi-media, and graphic design, acting and design; *Doctor of Philosophy* in music education.

Admission: Audition or portfolio required, plus 2.5 GPA for art history, art education, and music education. *For graduate degrees:* 3.0 GPA.

Distinctive Educational Programs: University Art Gallery, Center for Latin American and Tropical Arts, Visual Resource Center, Interdisciplinary programs with College of Liberal Arts and Sciences, Latin American Studies, and African Studies; Cooperative Program with College of Architecture in Architectural Preservation; summer repertory theatre program available for theatre majors.

College of Health and Human Performance

Degree Programs Offered: *Baccalaureate, master's* in parks and recreation and management; *baccalaureate, master's, doctorate* in exercise science, physiology, management studies.

College of Health Professions

Degree Programs Offered: *Baccalaureate* in health science; *baccalaureate, master's* in community health liaison; *baccalaureate, master's, doctorate* in physical therapy, public health, vocational rehabilitation counseling; *master's, doctorate* in health services administration; *doctorate* in audiology, rehabilitative services.

College of Journalism and Communications

Degree Programs Offered: *Baccalaureate* in advertising, journalism (print journalism, magazines, editing, photojournalism); public relations; telecommunication (news, production, operations); *interdepartmental programs* in environmental studies, Latin American studies; *master's* and *Doctor of Philosophy* degrees in mass communication.

Admission: 2.5 GPA on 4.0 scale (3.0 for automatic admission).

Distinctive Educational Programs: Interdepartmental programs in environmental studies, Latin American studies, political campaigning (master's only).

College of Nursing

Degree Programs Offered: *Baccalaureate, master's, and doctorate* in nursing.

College of Pharmacy

Degree Programs Offered: *Baccalaureate* in pharmacy, pharmacological sciences; *professional doctorate* in pharmacy.

Admission: *For first-professional:* 8 semester hours in biology, 8 general chemistry, 8 organic chemistry, 8 general physics, 6 English, 3 economics, 9 humanities, 9 social sciences; 2.5 minimum GPA; Pharmacy College Admission Test. *For non-professional:* 8 semester hours in biology, 8 general chemistry, 8 organic chemistry, 8 general physics, 6 English, 3 economics, 9 humanities, 9 social sciences; 3.0 minimum GPA.

Degree Requirements: *See* general requirements. *For baccalaureate:* in pharmacy 96 credit hours, 2.0 GPA, 3 years in residence; in pharmacological sciences 64 credits, 2.0 GPA. *For professional doctorate:* 135 credit hours, 2.0 GPA, 4 years in residence.

College of Dentistry

Degree Programs Offered: *First-professional* in dentistry; *master's* in dental science.

Admission: DAT; 3.0 GPA. Strongly recommend baccalaureate from accredited college or university with 8 semester hours biology with lab, 8 hours general chemistry with lab, 8 hours organic chemistry with lab, and 8 hours physics with lab. Apply through AADSAS 15 months prior to enrollment.

Degree Requirements: 4-year prescribed curriculum; satisfactory completion of all specified clinical and modular objectives.

College of Law

Degree Programs Offered: *First professional* law; *master's, doctorate* in legal specialization.

Admission: Graduation from accredited college or university; LSAT; application processed through LSDAS.

Degree Requirements: 86 credit hours, 2.0 GPA, 58 credit hours in residence.

Distinctive Educational Programs: Joint J.D.-Master's in the following 6 areas: political science/public administration, urban and regional planning, business administration, accounting, sociology, mass communication. Joint J.D.-Ph.D. in history.

College of Medicine

Degree Programs Offered: *First-professional* in medicine; *master's, doctorate* in biochemistry, medical sciences; *master's* in physician assistant.

Admission: *For first-professional:* MCAT; 3.0 GPA. Strongly recommend baccalaureate from accredited college or university, with 8 semester hours biology with lab, 8 general chemistry with lab, 8 organic chemistry with lab, 8 physics, mathematics.

Degree Requirements: *For first-professional:* 4 years prescribed curriculum.

Distinctive Educational Programs: Joint M.D.-Ph.D. program. Honors program.

College of Natural Resources and Environment

Degree Programs Offered: *Baccalaureate* in environmental science; *master's, doctorate* in interdisciplinary ecology.

Distinctive Educational Programs: Minor in environmental science and environmental studies.

College of Veterinary Medicine

Degree Programs Offered: *First-professional* in veterinary medicine; *master's, doctorate* in veterinary medical sciences.

Admission: 80 semester hours from accredited college or university, with 12 biology with lab (including genetics and microbiology), 18 chemistry with lab (including general chemistry, organic chemistry, biochemistry), 8 humanities, 7 animal science, 7 physics with lab, 6 English (including composition), 6 social sciences, 3 calculus; 2.75 GPA in prerequisites; GRE; interview.

Degree Requirements: 151 semester hours, 2.0 GPA, 36 months in residence.

Graduate School

Degree Programs Offered: *Master's, doctorate* in accounting, aerospace engineering, agency correctional and developmental counseling, agricultural engineering, agronomy, anatomical sciences, animal science, anthropology, astronomy, biochemistry and molecular biology, botany, business administration, chemical engineering, chemistry, civil engineering, communication, counseling psychology, counselor education, computer and information science, curriculum and instruction, economics, educational administration, educational psychology, electrical engineering, engineering mechanics, English, entomology and nematology, environmental engineering sciences, finance and insurance, food and resource economics, forest resources and conservation, food science and human nutrition, foundations of education, French, geography, geology, higher education administration, history, horticulture science, immunology and medical microbiology, industrial and systems engineering, international relations, linguistics, management, marketing, mathematics, mechanical engineering, medicinal chemistry, metallurgical and materials engineering, microbiology, neuroscience, nuclear engineering sciences, nursing, pathology, pharmacology, pharmacy, philosophy, physiology, physics, plant pathology, political science, psychology, real estate, research and evaluation methodology, school and counseling and guidance, school psychology, sociology, soil science, Spanish, special education, speech, statistics, student personnel in higher education, veterinary medicine, zoology, architecture, coastal and oceanographic engineering, German, music education, health and human performance, oral biology, geology, decision information science *master's* also in agricultural and extension education, art, building construction, childhood education, dairy science, engineering science, health education, health and hospital administration, insurance, journalism and communication, Latin, Latin American studies, laws in taxation, music, nursing, occupational therapy, physical education, poultry science, rehabilitation counseling, secondary education, theater, veterinary science, vocational technical and adult education, art education, education of emotional disturbed, education of the mentally retarded, elementary education, English education, foreign languages education, history of art, mathematics education, physical therapy, reading education, recreational study, science education, social studies education, specific learning disabilities, and speech pathology; *intermediate* in engineering. Specialist certificate in education, religion, landscape architecture and other graduate certificates also given.

Admission: Upper-division undergraduate GPA of 3.0, GRE general test on verbal, quantitative, and analytical sections — national mean score on each section. *For foreign students:* required TOEFL of 550.

University of Miami

P.O. Box 248025
1540 Comiche Avenue
Coral Gables, Florida 33124
Tel: (305) 284-2211   **E-mail:** admission@miami.edu
Fax: (305) 284-2507   **Internet:** www.miami.edu

Institution Description: University of Miami is a private, independent, nonprofit institution. *Enrollment:* 15,250. *Degrees awarded:* Baccalaureate, master's, doctorate, first-professional (law, medicine).

Member of Southeast Florida Educational Consortium.

Accreditation: *Regional:* SACS-Comm. on Coll. *Professional:* accounting, business, clinical pastoral education, clinical psychology, counseling, engineering, engineering technology, English language education, health services administration, journalism, law, medicine, music, nuclear medicine technology, nursing-midwifery, nursing, oral and maxillofacial surgery, physical therapy, psychology internship, public health, teacher education

History: Established and incorporated 1925; offered first instruction at postsecondary level 1926; awarded first degree (baccalaureate) 1927. *See* Charlton W. Tebeau, *The University of Miami: A Golden Anniversary History* (Coral Gables: University of Miami Press, 1976) for further information.

Institutional Structure: *Governing board:* University of Miami Board of Trustees. Representation: 51 elected, 6 life, 6 ex officio, 17 emeriti. 80 voting. *Composition of institution:* Administrators 576 men / 1,096 women. Academic affairs headed by Executive Vice President and Provost. Business and Finance headed by Senior Vice President. Full-time instructional faculty 752. Academic governance body, Faculty Senate, meets an average of 9 times per year.

Calendar: Semesters. Academic year Aug. to Aug. Freshmen admitted Aug., Jan., May, June. Degrees conferred May, June, Aug., Dec. Formal commencements May, Dec. Summer session of 2 terms.

Characteristics of Freshmen: 77% (1,577 students) submitted SAT scores; 21% (433 students) submitted ACT scores. *25th percentile*: SAT Verbal 570, SAT Math 590; ACT Composite 25, ACT English 25, ACT Math 25. *75th percentile*: SAT Verbal 670, SAT Math 680; ACT Composite 30, ACT English 31, ACT Math 30.

59% of entering freshmen expected to graduate within 5 years. 52% of freshmen from Florida. Freshmen from 43 states and 50 foreign countries.

Admission: Rolling admissions plan. For fall acceptance, apply as early as completion of junior year of secondary school, but not later than July 15 of year of enrollment. Early decision application by Nov. 15; notification date Jan. 15. Regular decision application deadline Mar. 1. Notification date Apr. 15. *Requirements:* Admission is selective and is offered to those applicants whose credentials are academically sound and whose interests, aptitudes, and preparation reflect a well-rounded secondary school experience, inside and outside the classroom. *Entrance tests:* College Board SAT or ACT composite. For 6-year medicine program, Achievement tests. For foreign students TOEFL. *For transfer students:* 2.5 minimum GPA; from 4-year accredited institution and for correspondence/extension students maximum transfer credit limited only by residence requirement; from 2-year accredited institution 64 hours maximum transfer credit.

College credit and advanced placement for postsecondary-level work completed in secondary school and for extrainstitutional learning on basis of ACE *2006 Guide to the Evaluation of Educational Experiences in the Armed Services.* Tutoring available. Developmental courses offered in summer session and regular academic year; credit given.

Degree Requirements: *For all baccalaureate degrees:* 120 semester hours; 2.0 GPA; 2 terms in residence. Architecture degree programs require 171 credits; engineering degree programs require between 129 and 136 credits depending on major field of study. *For all undergraduate degrees:* General education requirements.

Fulfillment of some degree requirements and exemption from some beginning courses possible by passing departmental examinations, College Board CLEP, AP. *Grading system:* A–F; pass-fail; withdraw (carries time limit).

Distinctive Educational Programs: Flexible meeting places and schedules, including weekend classes for graduate students, and evening classes. Accelerated degree programs in medicine, law, marine sciences, business, and engineering. Freshman seminars (with fewer than 25 students per class and taught by distinguished faculty) in fine arts, literature, philosophy, religion, the social sciences and natural sciences. Interdisciplinary programs, including Caribbean, African and Afro-American studies, architectural engineering, international and comparative studies, Latin American studies, Judaic studies, music engineering, women's studies, and a joint degree (M.B.A./M.S.I.E.) program. Facilities and programs for independent research including honors program, individual majors, tutorials. Study abroad in Australia, England, Scotland, Israel, France, Switzerland, Germany, Italy, Spain, Sweden, Czech Republic, The Netherlands, Korea, Argentina, Chile, Colombia, Costa Rica, Ecuador, Japan, Thailand, Canada, Mexico.

ROTC: Army, Air Force in cooperation with Barry University, Florida International University, St. Thomas University, Florida Atlantic University, and Nova Southeastern University.

Degrees Conferred: 2,155 *baccalaureate*; 1,183 *master's*; 159 *doctorate*: 523 *first-professional.* Bachelor's degrees awarded in top five disciplines: business, management, marketing, and related support services 503; visual and performing arts 250; communication, journalism, and related programs 205; biological and biomedical sciences 201; engineering 175.

Fees and Other Expenses: *Full-time tuition per academic year 2004–05:* undergraduate $29,008. Graduate tuition charged per credit hour. Contact the university for current tuition/fees for graduate and first-professional programs. *Required fees:* $483. *Room and board per academic year:* $8,906.

Financial Aid: Aid from institutionally generated funds is provided on the basis of academic merit, financial need, athletic ability, other criteria.

Financial aid to full-time, first-time undergraduate students: need-based scholarships/grants totaling $7,881,581, self-help $37,139,470, parent loans $4,866,079, tuition waivers $4,761,189, athletic awards $2,981,508; non-need-based scholarships/grants totaling $43,203,431, self-help $15,266,249, parent loans $8,366,634, tuition waivers $11,130,097, athletic awards $4,888,066.

Departments and Teaching Staff: *Total instructional faculty:* 1,220 (full-time 877, part-time 343; women 432, men 788; members of minority groups 290). Total faculty with doctorate, first-professional, or other terminal degree: 948. Student-to-faculty ratio: 13:1.

Enrollment: Total enrollment 15,520. Undergraduate full-time 3,936 men / 5.403 women, part-time 260m / 505w; graduate full-time 1; 353m / 1,175w, part-

time 219m / 488w; first-professional full-time 952m / 879w, part-time 33m / 47w.

Characteristics of Student Body: *Ethnic/racial makeup:* number of Black non-Hispanic: 913; American Indian or Alaska Native: 29; Asian or Pacific Islander: 542; Hispanic: 2,324; White non-Hispanic: 5,074; unknown: 279.

International Students: 580 undergraduate nonresident aliens enrolled fall 2004. Students from Europe, Asia, Central and South America, Africa, Canada, Australia, New Zealand. *Programs available to aid students whose native language is not English:* Social, cultural; English as a Second Language. Scholarships for international students awarded annually to qualified applicants.

Student Life: On-campus residence halls house 35% of undergraduate student body. Residential Colleges with faculty Masters have been on the Miami campus since 1984. 14% of undergraduate men join fraternities. 13% of undergraduate women join sororities. *Intercollegiate athletics:* men only: baseball, basketball, crew, cross-country, football, indoor track and field, swimming and diving, tennis, track; women only: basketball, crew, cross-country, golf, indoor track and field, swimming and diving, tennis, track. *Special regulations:* Cars with decals permitted. Freshmen required to live on campus unless living with parents. *Special services:* Multi-cultural student services, health and medical services, counseling services, international student services, career planning and placement services; wellness and recreation, student activities and organizations, women's resource center, leadership programs, volunteer services center, and commuter student services. *Student publications, radio: Hurricane,* a biweekly newspaper; *Ibis,* a yearbook. Radio station WVUM broadcasts 168 hours per week. *Surrounding community:* Coral Gables population 45,000. Miami is nearest metropolitan area. Served by mass transit metrorail and bus systems, airport 7 miles from campus, passenger rail service 10 miles from campus.

Publications: *Aiweek* (monthly) first published in 1987; *Association of Caribbean Studies* (quarterly) first published in 1980; *Bulletin of Marine Science* (quarterly) first published in 1965; *Bulletin: The Louis Calder Memorial Library* (monthly) first published 1979; *Career Strategist* (irregularly) first published 1988; *Caribbean Basin Business Advisor* (irregularly) first published 1986; *Carrell* (irregularly) first published 1960; *Contents of Periodicals on Latin America* (quarterly) first published 1983; *Distaff* (monthly) first published 1955; *Epiphany* (quarterly) first published 1987; *Eye of the Hurricane* (monthly) first published 1989; *Faculty Publications, University of Miami* (annually) first published 1984; *Financial Aid News* (annually) first published 1989; *Florida Jewish Demography* (irregularly) first published 1988; *Hurricane Signals* (monthly) first published 1969; *IIAS News* (quarterly) first published 1983; *International Journal of Hydrogen Energy* (bimonthly); *James Joyce Literary Supplement* (quarterly) first published 1989; *Journal of Interamerican Studies and World Affairs* (quarterly) first published 1959; *Miami Hurricane* (biweekly) first published 1927; *Miami Engineer Magazine* (quarterly) first published 1981; *Miami Faculty* (irregularly) first published 1988; *Miami Tribune* (irregularly) first published 1983; *Miami, The University of Miami Magazine* (quarterly) first published 1989; *Momentum (Coral Gables, FL)* (quarterly) first published 1989; *Quarterly Business Reports* (quarterly) first published 1987; *North South: The Magazine of the Americas* (monthly) first published 1991; *RES IPSA Loquitur* (biweekly) first published 1987; *Research Notes (The University of Miami Research and Sponsored Programs)* (monthly) first published 1963; *Richter RAP* (monthly) first published 1981; *Sea Frontiers (Virginia Key, Miami, FL)* (bimonthly) first published 1988; *Seen and Noted* (quarterly) first published 1983; *Soundings* (quarterly) first published 1967; *Sponsored Program Proposal Action* (monthly) first published 1977; *Tropical Byte* (quarterly) first published 1974; *The University of Miami Bulletin* (annually) first published 1926; *University of Miami Events Calendar* (biweekly) first published 1989; *University of Miami Fact Book* (3 times a year) first published 1973; *University of Miami Inter-American Law Review* first published 1984; *University of Miami Newsletter* (quarterly) first published 1987; *Veritas, for the Faculty, Staff and Friends of the University of Miami* (monthly) first published 1983.

Library Collections: 2,100,000 volumes. 510,000 government documents; 98,000 microforms; Access to 19,600 periodicals. Access to computerized information retrieval systems.

Most important holdings include Floridiana; Cuba, Cuba Exile materials; Jackie Gleason "Entertainment and Unexplained Phenomenon," Pan American World Airways, Inc. Records.

Buildings and Grounds: Campus area over 400 acres.

Chief Executive Officer: Dr. Donna E. Shalala, President.

Undergraduates address admission inquiries to Victor Atherton, Director of Admissions; first-professional students to Law School Director of Admissions; medical students to Office of Admissions, School of Medicine; graduate students to the Graduate School.

College of Arts and Sciences

Degree Programs Offered: *Baccalaureate* in African American studies; American studies, anthropology, art, art history, biochemistry, biology, chemistry, computer science, criminal justice, economics, elementary education, English, French, geography, geology, German, health science, history, international and comparative studies, Judaic studies, Latin American studies, marine affairs, marine science, mathematics, microbiology, music, philosophy, physics, political science, psychobiology, psychology, religion, sociology, Spanish, special education, theatre arts; *graduate degrees* in art, art history, biology, chemistry, computer science, English, French, geography, history, liberal studies, mathematics, philosophy, physics, psychology, sociology, Spanish.

Distinctive Educational Programs: Accelerated degree programs in medicine, interdisciplinary programs in African American studies; American studies, environmental studies, international studies, Judaic studies, Latin American studies, women's studies. Cooperative baccalaureates in marine affairs, marine science with options in biology, chemistry, geology, and physics with Rosenstiel School of Marine and Atmospheric Sciences.

School of Business

Degree Programs Offered: *Baccalaureate* in accounting, business administration, business management and organization, computer information systems, economics, entrepreneurship, finance, human resource management, international finance and marketing, legal studies, marketing, political science, real estate, and sports management; *graduate degrees* in accounting, business administration, business management and organization, computer information systems, economics, health administration, international business, legal implications, management science, marketing, political science, public administration, taxation, telecommunications management.

Distinctive Educational Programs: Entrepreneurship major designed for students who intend to start or manage their own business; sports management major for students intending to seek a career in the management of physical fitness or other sports-related fields.

School of Education

Degree Programs Offered: *Baccalaureate degrees* in education, with the major fields in elementary education and special education. *Graduate degrees:* Master of Science in Education, Specialist in Education, Doctor of Education, and Doctor of Philosophy.

College of Engineering

Degree Programs Offered: *Baccalaureate and graduate* in architectural engineering, biomedical engineering, civil engineering, computer engineering, electrical engineering, engineering, engineering science, industrial engineering, mechanical engineering.

Distinctive Educational Programs: Five-year dual degree programs. Special options in audio and aerospace engineering.

Rosenstiel School of Marine and Atmospheric Sciences

Degree Programs Offered: *Graduate degrees* in applied marine physics, marine and atmospheric chemistry, marine affairs, marine biology and fisheries, marine geology and geophysics, meteorology and physical oceanography.

School of Music

Degree Programs Offered: *Baccalaureate* in instrumental performance, keyboard performance, music, music composition, music education, music engineering technology, music industry, music literature, music theatre, music therapy, studio music-jazz, vocal performance; *graduate degrees* in accompanying, choral conducting, electronic music, instrumental conducting, instrumental performance, jazz pedagogy, jazz performance, keyboard performance, media writing-production, music education, music engineering technology, music industry, musical theatre, music theory-composition, music therapy, musicology, studio jazz writing, vocal performance.

Distinctive Educational Programs: Interdisciplinary and interdepartmental programs for undergraduates in music engineering technology, music therapy, music industry, musical theatre, studio music and jazz (instrumental and vocal).

School of Nursing

Degree Programs Offered: *Baccalaureate, graduate degrees* in nursing.

Distinctive Educational Programs: Transition track offered for R.N. to B.S.N. B.S.N. to Ph.D. program. Continuing education for practicing nurses program.

School of Law

Degree Programs Offered: *First-professional; master's* in estate planning, foreign graduate, international, ocean and coastal, taxation and real property development.

Admission: *First-professional:* Baccalaureate from accredited college or university. Recommend courses in English literature, English language, history, economics, philosophy, political science, psychology, semantics, elements of business operations.

Degree Requirements: *First-professional:* 88 credit hours, 2.0 GPA on a 4.0 scale; 96 weeks in residence.

School of Medicine

Degree Programs Offered: *First-professional; graduate degrees* in molecular cell and developmental biology, biochemistry, cell-molecular biology, epidemiology-public health, microbiology-immunology, neuroscience, molecular and cellular pharmacology, physiology-biophysics, physical therapy, medical informatics, radiology.

Admission: *First-professional:* 90 semester hours of undergraduate study including 2 semesters of English, inorganic chemistry, organic chemistry, physics, biology, 1 semester advanced chemistry, calculus; MCAT.

Degree Requirements: *First-professional:* 4 years in residence.

Distinctive Educational Programs: 2-year M.D. program for students with a doctorate in a biological, physical, or engineering science. Concurrent Ph.D.-M.D. program.

School of Architecture

Degree Programs Offered: *Baccalaureate, graduate degree* in architecture.

Admission: Minimum SAT score of 1,000, 3.0 GPA, and ranking at the top 10% of high school graduating class.

Degree Requirements: Completion of 171 credits.

Distinctive Educational Programs: Study abroad. Visiting Critics Program provides upper-level studios and seminars with internationally distinguished architects and educators.

School of Communication

Degree Programs Offered: *Baccalaureate* in advertising, broadcasting, broadcast journalism, motion pictures, news journalism, organizational communication, photography, public relations, speech communication, video film; *graduate degrees* in communication studies, film production, film scriptwriting, film studies, journalism, public relations.

Admission: A student entering the university as a freshman or as a transfer may enroll in a pre-major status. Before admission to a major, a candidate for the B.S. in communication must achieve sophomore standing, pass typing and grammar tests, and complete at least 9 credits in residence; all grades C or higher, cumulative GPA of 2.5 or higher.

Graduate School of International Studies

Degree Programs Offered: *Undergraduate degree:* International Studies Program is an interdisciplinary program that draws upon the resources of faculty and departments across the university to merge a liberal arts emphasis with the study of international issues and problems. *Graduate degrees* in inter-American studies, international studies.

School of Continuing Studies

Degree Programs Offered: *Baccalaureate* in continuing studies.

Distinctive Educational Programs: Intersession and spring break classes and professional programs; intensive language programs; easy admit adult access program; screenwriting course taught via the Internet; study abroad program; substance abuse education, summer scholars programs for high school juniors and seniors; HIV counseling certificate programs; computer and telecommunication training; human resources management and employee benefits training, off-site master of science programs in total quality management and management of technology; evening courses; institute for retired professionals; continuing education for x-ray technologists; travel professional certification; credit courses for high school students; study skills program for students in grades 5–8; credit certificate programs.

University of North Florida

4567 St. Johns Bluff Road, South
Jacksonville, Florida 32224-2645
Tel: (904) 620-1000   **E-mail:** osprey@unf.edu
Fax: (904) 620-2414   **Internet:** www.unf.edu

Institution Description: University of North Florida is a four-year state university providing full undergraduate and graduate programs of study. *Enrollment:* 14,533. *Degrees awarded:* Baccalaureate, master's, doctorate.

Academic offerings subject to approval by statewide coordinating bodies. Budget subject to approval by state governing boards.

Accreditation: *Regional:* SACS-Comm. on Coll. *Professional:* accounting, athletic training, business, computer science, construction education, counseling, cytotechnology, dietetics, engineering, health services administration, music, nursing, physical therapy, public administration, rehabilitation counseling, teacher education

History: Established 1965; adopted present name 1968; chartered and offered first instruction at postsecondary level 1972; awarded first degree (baccalaureate) 1974.

Institutional Structure: *Governing board:* Board of Trustees reporting to the Florida Board of Governors. Representation: 13 members, including current Student Government and Faculty Association presidents. Remaining members appointed by governor of Florida (5) and Board of Governors (6). All voting. *Composition of institution:* Administrators 41 men / 51 women. Academic affairs headed by vice president of academic affairs. Management/business/ finances directed by vice president of administration and finance. Total instructional faculty 366. Academic governance body, Faculty Association, meets an average of 12 times per year. *Faculty representation:* Faculty served by collective bargaining agent affiliated with AFT.

Calendar: Semesters. Academic year May to Apr. Degrees conferred and formal commencement Apr., Aug., Dec.

Characteristics of Freshmen: 69% of applicants admitted. 40% of admitted students enrolled full-time.

58% (1,332 students) submitted SAT scores; 42% (979 students) submitted ACT scores. *25th percentile:* SAT Verbal 500, SAT Math 500; ACT Composite 20. *75th percentile:* SAT Verbal 600, SAT Math 600; ACT Composite 23.

96% of freshmen from Florida. Freshmen from 34 states and 9 foreign countries.

Admission: Rolling admission plan. Apply as early as 1 year prior to matriculation, but not later than 6 weeks prior to the beginning of the semester. *Requirements:* Lower level - high school GPA of 2.5, SAT of 1050 or ACT of 21; 19 academic units including 4 years of English, 3 years mathematics (Algebra I or higher), 3 years natural sciences, 3 years social sciences, 2 years foreign language, 4 additional electives; college GPA of 2.0, if applicable; upper level - associate of arts degree from a Florida public community college or university or GPA of 2.0; good standing at last institution attended. *Entrance tests:* SAT or ACT if freshman or sophomore; TOEFL for foreign students. *For transfer students:* 2.0 minimum GPA; from 4-year accredited institution 90 semester hours maximum transfer credit; from 2-year accredited institution 60 hours;

College credit for postsecondary-level work completed in secondary school and for credit on the basis of ACE *2006 Guide to the Evaluation of Educational Experiences in the Armed Services.* Tutoring available.

Degree Requirements: 120 semester hours; 2.0 GPA; 30 hours in residence.

Fulfillment of some degree requirements and exemption from beginning courses possible by passing College Board CLEP, AP. *Grading system:* A–F; withdraw (carries time limit).

Distinctive Educational Programs: Work-experience programs. Flexible meeting places and schedules, weekend and evening classes. Accelerated degree programs. Tutorials. Study abroad in Jamaica, Argentina, Uruguay, Spain, Israel, Greece, Peru, Czech Republic, Poland, France. *Other distinctive programs:* Noncredit workshops and seminars for community residents. Seminars for local businesses and industries, governmental agencies, professional associations, and civic organizations. Off-campus degree programs offered at various locations within the adjacent 6-county area.

ROTC: Navy offered in cooperation with Jacksonville University.

Degrees Conferred: 2,226 *baccalaureate* (B), 550 *master's* (M), *doctorate* (D): biological/life sciences 55 (B); business/marketing 512 (B), 189 (M); communications/communication technologies 178 (B); computer and information sciences 132 (B); education 309 (B); 202 (M); 5 (D); engineering and engineering technologies 98 (B); English 85 (B), 23 (M); foreign languages and literature 5 (B); health professions and related sciences 223 (B), 79 (M); interdisciplinary studies 20 (B); mathematics 14 (B); philosophy/religion/theology 13 (B); physical sciences 14 (B); protective services/public administration 95 (B), 24 (M); psychology 195 (B), 17 (M); social sciences and history 174 (B), 3 (M); visual and performing arts 109 (B).

Fees and Other Expenses: *Full-time tuition per academic year 2004–05:* $3,101 undergraduate resident, $14,851 out-of-state nonresident; $3,567 graduate resident, $19,999 out-of-state nonresident. *Room and board per academic year:* $6,278.

Financial Aid: Aid from institutionally generated funds is provided on the basis of academic merit, financial need, athletic ability, other criteria.

Financial aid to full-time, first-time undergraduate students: need-based scholarships/grants totaling $20,753,016, self-help $16,122,147, parent loans $847,621, tuition waivers $400,842, athletic awards $612,202; non-need-based scholarships/grants totaling $2,381,208, self-help $2,455,040, parent loans $849,884, tuition waivers $150,287, athletic awards $133,138. *Graduate aid:* 7 federal fellowships and grants totaling $7,978; 59 federal and state-funded loans totaling $4,976,090; 62 work-study jobs worth $169,787; 37 other fellowships and grants totaling $301,661; 1 teaching assistantship for $10,844; 1 research assistantship for $7,628.

Departments and Teaching Staff: *Professors* 85, *associate professors* 105, *assistant professors* 151, *instructors* 76, *part-time faculty* 234. *Total instructional faculty:* 652 (full-time 421, part-time 231; women 301, men 351; members of minority groups 86). Total faculty with doctorate, first-professional, or other terminal degree: 191. Student-to-faculty ratio: 23:1. 7 faculty members awarded sabbaticals 2004.

Enrollment: Total enrollment 14,533. Undergraduate full-time 3,834 men / 5,225 women, part-time 1,499m / 2,110w; graduate full-time 200m / 437w, part-time 403m / 825w.

Characteristics of Student Body: *Ethnic/racial makeup:* number of Black non-Hispanic: 1,243; American Indian or Alaska Native: 69; Asian or Pacific Islander: 679; Hispanic: 759; White non-Hispanic: 9,976; unknown: 170. *Age distribution:* number under 18: 47; 18–19: 3,412; 20–21: 3,118; 22–24: 2,890; 25–29: 1,498; 30–34: 659; 35–39: 412; 40–49: 483; 50–64: 188; 65 and over: 95.

International Students: 163 nonresident aliens enrolled fall 2004. Programs available to aid students whose native language is not English: Social, cultural. English as a Second Language Program. No financial aid specifically designated for international students.

Student Life: On-campus housing available. *Special services:* Academic Resource Center, Career Services, Counseling Center, Fitness Center, Intramurals, Events Coordinator, bus service between campus and downtown. *Student publications: The Spinnaker,* a biweekly newspaper. *Surrounding community:* Jacksonville population over 1,000,000. Served by airport 23 miles from campus.

Library Collections: 777,860 volumes including bound books, serial backfiles, electronic documents, and government documents not in separate collections. Online catalog. 1,324,219 microforms. Computer work stations available. Students have access to the Internet at no charge.

Most important special collections include personal papers of former Florida Senate President John E. Mathews, Jr.; memorabilia collection of philanthropist Eartha M. M. White; personal papers of Arthur N. Sollee, deceased local transportation official.

Buildings and Grounds: Campus area 1,300 acres. *New buildings:* Fine Arts Building completed 2001; Hayt Golf Learning Center 2001; Science and Engineering Building 2003; Stadium 2003.

Chief Executive Officer: Dr. John A. Delaney, President.

Address admission inquiries to John Yancey, Director of Admissions.

College of Arts and Sciences

Degree Programs Offered: *Baccalaureate* in anthropology, art, biology, chemistry, communications, criminal justice, economics, English, fine arts, history, liberal studies, literature, mathematical sciences, music, political science, psychology, sociology; *master's* in applied sociology, geology, counseling psychology, criminal justice, English, general psychology, history, mathematical sciences, practical philosophy, applied ethics, public administration.

Distinctive Educational Programs: Interdisciplinary program in international studies. Individually designed programs.

College of Business Administration

Degree Programs Offered: *Baccalaureate* in accounting, business management, economics; finance, financial services, international business, marketing, transportation and logistics; *master's* in accounting, general business.

Distinctive Educational Programs: Cooperative education. Skill enrichment courses and seminars for practicing managers offered by Continuing Education Division in cooperation with business and trade associations.

College of Education and Human Services

Degree Programs Offered: *Baccalaureate* in art education, elementary education, English education, mathematics education, middle school education, music education, physical education, science education, social studies education, special education, vocational/technical education; *master's* in counselor education, educational leadership, elementary education, secondary education, special education; *doctorate* in educational leadership.

Admission: The Florida Board of Education requires that applicants for undergraduate teacher education programs submit a copy of their SAT or ACT to support their application for admission. Applicants are required to present a minimum score at or above the 40th percentile. Students who do not meet this requirement may be eligible for special consideration under an exception policy.

Distinctive Educational Programs: Cooperative doctoral degree with University of Florida. Independent study.

College of Health

Degree Programs Offered: *Baccalaureate* in athletic training, health science, nursing; *master's* in community health, health administration, health science, nursing, physical therapy, rehabilitation counseling.

Division of Computer and Information Services

Degree Programs Offered: *Baccalaureate* in computer and information sciences with options in computer science, information science, and information systems; *master's* with options in computer science and information systems.

University of South Florida

4202 East Fowler Avenue
Tampa, Florida 33620-9951
Tel: (813) 974-2011   **E-mail:** askusf@usf.edu
Fax: (813) 974-9689   **Internet:** www.usf.edu

Institution Description: University of South Florida is a state institution with campuses in Lakeland, Sarasota, St. Petersburg, and Tampa. *Enrollment:* 42,566. *Degrees awarded:* Associate, baccalaureate, master's, doctorate, first-professional (medicine). Specialist certificates in education also awarded.

Academic offerings subject to approval by statewide coordinating bodies. Budget subject to approval by state governing boards.

Accreditation: *Regional:* SACS-Comm. on Coll. *Professional:* accounting, applied science, clinical psychology, computer science, engineering, English language education, health services administration, journalism, librarianship, medicine, music, nursing, nursing education, physical therapy, psychology internship, public administration, public health, rehabilitation counseling, school psychology, social work, speech-language pathology, teacher education, theatre

History: Established 1956; chartered and offered first instruction at postsecondary level 1960; awarded first degree (baccalaureate) 1962. *See* Russell M. Cooper and Margaret B. Fisher, *The Vision of a Contemporary University* (Gainesville, Fla.: University Presses of Florida, 1981) for further information.

Institutional Structure: *Governing board:* Florida Board of Regents. Representation: 13 members, including 1 student (appointed by governor of Florida) and commissioner of education. All voting. *Composition of institution:* Administrators 27 men / 6 women. Academic affairs headed by executive vice president and provost. Management/business/finances directed by vice president for administration and finance. Full-time instructional faculty 1,492. *Faculty representation:* Faculty served by collective bargaining agent, United Faculty of Florida, affiliated with AFT.

Calendar: Semesters. Academic year Aug. to Apr. Freshmen admitted Aug., Jan., March, June. Degrees conferred May, Aug., Dec. Formal commencement May. Summer session of 3 terms from May to Aug.

Characteristics of Freshmen: 51% of applicants admitted. 28% of admitted students enrolled full-time.

86% (3,566 students) submitted SAT scores; 33% (2,197 students) submitted ACT scores. *25th percentile:* SAT Verbal 500, SAT Math 510; ACT Composite 21. *75th percentile:* SAT Verbal 600, SAT Math 600; ACT Composite 25.

19% of entering freshmen expected to graduate within 5 years. 91% of freshmen from Florida. Freshmen from 50 states and 133 foreign countries.

Admission: Rolling admissions plan. For fall acceptance, apply as early as one year prior to enrollment, but not later than April 15 of year of enrollment. Early acceptance available. *Requirements:* Either graduation from accredited secondary school or GED. Minimum GPA 2.0. *Entrance tests:* College Board SAT (minimum combined score of 800) or ACT composite. For foreign students TOEFL. *For transfer students:* 2.0 minimum GPA; from 2-year accredited institution 60 hours maximum transfer credit.

Advanced placement for postsecondary-level work completed in secondary school. College credit for extrainstitutional learning on basis of ACE *2006 Guide to the Evaluation of Educational Experiences in the Armed Services.* Tutoring

available. Developmental/remedial courses offered in summer session and regular academic year; credit given.

Degree Requirements: *For all associate degrees:* 60 semester hours; 2.0 GPA; last 30 hours in residence. *For all baccalaureate degrees:* 120 semester hours; 2.0–2.25 GPA; last 30 hours in residence. *For all undergraduate degrees:* Distribution requirements. *Grading system:* A–F; pass-fail; withdraw (carries time limit).

ROTC: Army, Air Force, Navy in cooperation with University of South Florida.

Degrees Conferred: 159 *associate;* 5,376 *baccalaureate* (B), 2,044 *master's* (M), 179 *doctorate* (D): architecture 22 (M); area and ethnic studies 36 (B), 9 (M); biological/life sciences 271 (B), 22 (M), 12 (D); business/marketing 1,444 (B), 327 (M), 5 (D); communications/communication technologies 197 (B), 19 (M); computer and information sciences 91 (B); education 615 (B), 596 (M), 42 (D); engineering and engineering technologies 314 (B); 228 (M); 25 (D); English 382 (B), 23 (M), 17 (D); foreign languages and literature 34 (B), 26 (M); health professions and related sciences 228 (B), 318 (M), 24 (D); interdisciplinary studies 76 (B), 11 (M), 4 (D); liberal arts/general studies 27 (B), 4 (M); library science 149 (M); mathematics 33 (B), 11 (M), 2 (D); natural resources/environmental science 52 (B), 4 (M); philosophy/religion/theology 29 (B), 7 (M), 1 (D); physical sciences 59 (B), 34 (M), 16 (D); protective services/public administration 73 (B), 96 (M); psychology 363 (B); 40 (M), 29 (D); social sciences and history 910 (B), 68 (M), 2 (D); visual and performing arts 142 (B); 30 (M). 89 *first-professional:* medicine 89.

Fees and Other Expenses: *Full-time tuition per academic year 2004–05:* undergraduate resident $3,090, out-of-state student $15,960; graduate resident $5,594, out-of-state student $21,469. *Room and board per academic year:* $6,730.

Financial Aid: Aid from institutionally generated funds is provided on the basis of academic merit, financial need, athletic ability.

Financial aid to full-time, first-time undergraduate students: need-based scholarships/grants totaling $33,577,091, self-help $41,218,898; non-need-based scholarships/grants totaling $48,32,021, self-help $33,3389,285, parent loans $3,763,519, tuition waivers $2,011,530, athletic awards $2,104,914.

Departments and Teaching Staff: *Total instructional faculty:* 1,802 (full-time 1,641, part-time 161). Student-to-faculty ratio: 18:1. Degrees held by full-time faculty: Doctorate 71.7%, master's 6.8%, baccalaureate 1.4%, professional 17%. 96.8% hold terminal degrees.

Enrollment: Total enrollment 42,238. Undergraduate full-time 9,262 men / 13,525, women, part-time 4,322m / 6,157w; graduate full-time 1,360m / 2,004w, part-time 1,791m /3,390w; first-professional full-time 206m / 221w.

Characteristics of Student Body: *Ethnic/racial makeup:* number of Black non-Hispanic: 4,158; American Indian or Alaska Native: 144; Asian or Pacific Islander: 1,842; Hispanic: 3,528; White non-Hispanic: 21,957; unknown: 702. *Age distribution:* number under 18: 124; 18–19: 8,030; 20–21: 8,893; 22–24: 7,994; 25–29: 3,940; 30–34: 1,684; 35–39: 918; 40–49: 1,200; 50–64: 459; 65 and over: 24.

International Students: 1,960 nonresident aliens enrolled fall 2004. 242 students from Europe, 641 Asia, 552 Central and South America, 80 Africa, 64 Canada, 7 Australia, 1 New Zealand. Social and cultural programs to aid students whose native language is not English. English as a Second Language Program. No financial aid specifically designated for international students.

Student Life: On-campus residence halls house 11% of student body. Residence halls for men constitute 39% of such space, for women only 61%. 3% of student body live in university-operated apartments. *Intercollegiate athletics:* men only: baseball, basketball, cross-country, football, golf, soccer, softball, swimming, tennis; women only: basketball, cross-country, golf, softball, swimming, tennis, volleyball. *Special regulations:* Cars permitted on campus; fee charged. *Special services:* Learning Resources Center, medical services. *Student publications, radio, television: Oracle,* a daily newspaper. Radio station WUSF-FM. TV station WUSF. *Surrounding community:* Tampa metropolitan area population over 1.5 million. Served by mass transit bus system; airport 10 miles from campus; passenger rail service 5 miles from campus.

Library Collections: 1.9 million volumes including bound books, serial backfiles, electronic documents, and government documents not in separate collections. Online catalog. Current serial subscriptions: 17,000 paper, 4.2 million microform units. Computer work stations available. Students have access to the Internet at no charge. Total budget for books, periodicals, audiovisual materials, microforms 2004–05: $15 million.

Most important special collections include Centro Asturiano Collection; Dunn Humpton Postcard Collection; Florida and Rare Map Collections.

Buildings and Grounds: Campus area 1,931 acres. *New buildings:* Research Development Park; Natural and Environmental School Building; College of Nursing; Intercollegiate Athletic Training Facility; Joint Military Science Leadership Center; Moffit Cancer Care Research Facility.

Chief Executive Officer: Dr. Judy Genshaft, President.

Address undergraduate inquiries to Julie Hite, Director of Undergraduate Admissions; graduate inquiries to Kelli MacCormack-Brown, Dean of Graduate Studies.

College of Arts and Letters

Degree Programs Offered: *Baccalaureate* in American studies, classics, classics and foreign language, communication, communication-English, communication-theater, English, foreign language, French, German, humanities, Italian, liberal studies, mass communications, philosophy, religious studies, Russian, Spanish; *master's* and *doctorates* in various fields.

College of Business Administration

Degree Programs Offered: *Baccalaureate* in accounting, economics, finance, general business, management, marketing; *master's* in various fields.

College of Education

Degree Programs Offered: *Baccalaureate in* art education, botany education, business and office education, classics education, distributive and marketing education, elementary-early childhood education, elementary education, English education, emotional disturbance education, foreign language education, health education, humanities education, industrial-technical education, mass communications-English education, mathematics education, mental retardation education, music education, physical education, physics education, science education, social science education, specific learning disabilities education, speech communication-English education, zoology education; *master's* in adult education; art education; business and office education; distributive and marketing education; elementary education; emotional disturbance education; English education; foreign language education; gifted education; guidance and counseling education; humanities education; industrial-technical education; library, media, and information studies; mathematics education; mental retardation; music education; physical education; reading education; school psychology; science education; social science education; specific learning disabilities education; speech communication education; *doctorate* in various fields. Specialist certificates also awarded.

College of Engineering

Degree Programs Offered: *Baccalaureate* in chemical engineering; electrical engineering; general engineering; industrial engineering; mechanical engineering; structures, materials, and fluids; *master's* and *doctorate* in various fields.

College of Fine Arts

Degree Programs Offered: *Baccalaureate* in art, dance, music, theater; *master's* in various fields.

Distinctive Educational Programs: The Systems Complex for the Studio and Performing Arts provides instruction and state-of-the-art equipment for research and study by artists, scientists, and students.

College of Natural Sciences

Degree Programs Offered: *Baccalaureate* in biochemistry, biology, botany, chemistry, geology, marine science, mathematics, medical technology, microbiology, physics, zoology; *master's* and *doctorate* in various fields.

Distinctive Educational Programs: Joint Ph.D. program in oceanography with Florida State University.

College of Nursing

Degree Programs Offered: *Baccalaureate, master's.*

College of Social and Behavioral Sciences

Degree Programs Offered: *Baccalaureate* in Afro-American studies, anthropology, criminal justice, economics, geography, history, interdisciplinary social sciences, international studies, political science, psychology, social science education, social work, sociology; *master's* in anthropology, audiology, aural rehabilitation, criminal justice, geography, gerontology, history, political science, psychology, public administration, rehabilitation counseling, sociology, speech pathology.

Distinctive Educational Programs: Interdisciplinary programs in gerontology, urban anthropology, urban community psychology. The Human Resources Institute addresses critical issues in social and behavioral science through research and service; related centers include Center for Applied Anthropology,

Center for Applied Gerontology, Center for Community Development and Analysis, Center for Community Psychology, Center for Evaluation Research. Clinical facilities for speech pathology, audiology, aural rehabilitation, and clinical psychology are open to the public.

College of Medicine

Degree Programs Offered: *First-professional* in medicine; *doctorate* in medical sciences.

Admission: 3 years college or university work required; baccalaureate from accredited college preferred. Credits must include 3 quarters English; 3 each biological science (with laboratory), general chemistry (with laboratory), mathematics, physics (with laboratory); 1 each Mendelian genetics, statistics (mathematics or social science). MCAT.

University of Tampa

401 West Kennedy Boulevard
Tampa, Florida 33606-1490

Tel: (813) 253-3333   **E-mail:** admissions@ut.edu
Fax: (813) 258-7489   **Internet:** www.ut.edu

Institution Description: University of Tampa is a private, independent, nonprofit institution. *Enrollment:* 3,853. *Degrees awarded:* Associate, baccalaureate, master's.

Accreditation: *Regional:* SACS-Comm. on Coll. *Professional:* business, music, nursing, teacher education

History: Chartered as University of Tampa 1930; established and offered first instruction at postsecondary level as Tampa Junior College 1931; added upper division curriculum and readopted present name 1933; awarded first degree (baccalaureate) 1935; began graduate program 1973.

Institutional Structure: *Governing board:* University of Tampa Board of Trustees. Extrainstitutional representation: 48 trustees, past chair of the board, president of the university, chair of the board of overseers, chair of the board of fellows, chair of the board of counselors, president of the National Alumni Association, President of the Chiselers, Inc., President of the Parents' Council, President of the Tampa Chamber of Commerce, Mayor of the City of Tampa. All voting. *Composition of institution:* Administrators 8 men / 4 women. Academic affairs headed by two college deans. Management/business/finances directed by vice president for administration and finance. Full-time instructional faculty 201.

Calendar: Semesters. Academic year Aug. to May. Freshmen admitted Aug., Jan., May, June. Degrees conferred May, Aug., Dec. Formal commencement May and Dec. Summer sessions from May to Aug.

Characteristics of Freshmen: 53% of applicants admitted. 35% of admitted students enrolled full-time.

86% (186 students) submitted SAT scores; 34% (350 students) submitted ACT scores. *25th percentile*: SAT Verbal 480, SAT Math 480; ACT Composite 20, ACT English 20, ACT Math 19. *75th percentile*: SAT Verbal 580, SAT Math 540; ACT Composite 26, ACT English 26, ACT Math 25.

12% of entering freshmen expected to graduate within 5 years. 32% of freshmen from Florida. Freshmen from 30 states and 70 foreign countries.

Admission: Rolling admissions plan. For fall acceptance, apply as early as June of previous year. Early acceptance available. *Requirements:* Either graduation from secondary school with 19 academic units which must include 4 units in English, 3 mathematics, 3 science, 2 foreign language, 3 social studies, 4 academic electives; or GED. Minimum GPA 2.35. *Entrance tests:* College Board SAT or ACT composite. *For transfer students:* 2.2 minimum GPA; minimum number of transfer credits 17 semester credit hours, maximum 64 semester credit hours. Must submit high school transcript if student does not have an associate degree.

College credit and advanced placement for postsecondary-level work completed in secondary school. College credit for USAFI/DANTES, and for extrainstitutional learning on basis of ACE *2006 Guide to the Evaluation of Educational Experiences in the Armed Services.*

Degree Requirements: *For all associate degrees:* 62 credit hours; last 15 semester hours in residence. *For all baccalaureate degrees:* 124 hours; last 31 semester hours in residence. *For all undergraduate degrees:* 2.0 GPA. Fulfillment of some degree requirements and exemption from some beginning courses possible by passing College Board CLEP or APP. *Grading system:* A–F; pass-fail; withdraw; incomplete (carries time limit).

Distinctive Educational Programs: Honors Program. Individual majors. Evening College offers complete degree programs in Bachelor of Science (management, marketing, and computer information systems); Bachelor of Liberal Studies (economics and business, humanities, interdisciplinary studies, and social sciences). Study abroad through affiliation agreement with the American

Institute for Foreign Study; locations in Australia, Mexico, People's Republic of China.

ROTC: Army, Air Force, Navy in cooperation with University of South Florida.

Degrees Conferred: 785 *baccalaureate* (B); 154 *master's* (M): biological/life sciences 53 (B), 28 (M); business/marketing 227 (B); communications/communication technologies 78 (B); computer and information sciences 22 (B); education 83 (B); engineering and engineering technologies 32 (B); English 5 (B); foreign languages and literature 26 (M); health professions and related sciences 26 (M); liberal arts/general studies 15 (B); mathematics 5 (B); natural resources/environmental science 4 (B); physical sciences 1 (B); psychology 61 (B); social sciences and history 133 (B); visual and performing arts 30 (B).

Fees and Other Expenses: *Full-time tuition per academic year 2004–05:* undergraduate $17,250; graduate $6,240. *Room and board per academic year:* $6,670. *Other fees:* $922.

Financial Aid: Aid from institutionally generated funds is provided on the basis of academic merit, financial need, athletic ability.

Financial aid to full-time, first-time undergraduate students: need-based scholarships/grants totaling $22,769,400, self-help $9,247,875, parent loans $5,568,575, athletic awards $586,370; non-need-based scholarships/grants totaling $7,825,595, self-help $6,105,787, parent loans $1,998,407, athletic awards $421,126.

Departments and Teaching Staff: *Total instructional faculty:* 408 (201 full-time; 207 part-time; women 189, men 289; members of minority groups 27). Student-to-faculty ratio: 17:1. Degrees held by full-time faculty: doctorate 85%.

Enrollment: Total enrollment 4,856. Undergraduate full-time 1,462 404 men / 2,391 women, part-time 196m / 296w; graduate full-time 86m / 72w, part-time 175m / 198w.

Characteristics of Student Body: *Ethnic/racial makeup:* number of Black non-Hispanic: 288; American Indian or Alaska Native: 26; Asian or Pacific Islander: 80; Hispanic: 382; White non-Hispanic: 2,705; unknown: 623. *Age distribution:* number under 18: 3; 18–19: 993; 20–21: 1,648; 22–24: 981; 25–29: 143; 30–34: 29, 35–39: 18; 40–49: 21; 50–64: 8.

International Students: 311 nonresident aliens enrolled fall 2004. 60 students from Europe, 31 Asia, 49 Central and South America, 27 Africa, 14 Canada, 107 other. *Programs available to aid students whose native language is not English:* Social and cultural. English as a Second Language Program. Some financial aid designated for international students.

Student Life: On-campus residence halls house 59% of student body. (all coeducational). *Intercollegiate athletics:* men only: baseball, basketball, golf, rifle, soccer; women only: basketball, softball, volleyball; both sexes: crew, swimming, tennis. *Special regulations:* Cars permitted on campus without restrictions. Quiet hours from 9pm to 10am Sun.–Thurs, 1am to 10am Fri.–Sat. *Special services:* Medical services; 115 clubs and student organizations. *Student publications: Minaret,* a weekly newspaper; *Moroccan,* a yearbook; *Quilt,* an annual literary magazine. *Surrounding community:* Tampa, population over 1 million. Served by mass transit bus system; airport 10 miles from campus; passenger rail service 5 miles from campus.

Library Collections: 288,589 volumes including bound books, serial backfiles, electronic documents, and government documents not in separate collections. Online catalog. Current serial subscriptions: paper 5,425; via electronic access 24,006. 2,160 recordings; 31 compact discs; 1,100 CD-ROMs. 43 computer work stations. Students have access to the Internet at no charge.

Most important holdings include Military Affairs - Florida Military Collection; William C. Cramer Collection (the papers of a former U.S. Congressman from Florida); Stanley Kimmel Collection (research and manuscripts for the unpublished works "Mr. Lincoln's Washington," "Mr. Davis' Richmond," and completed work *The Mad Booths of Maryland*).

Buildings and Grounds: Campus area 70 acres.

Chief Executive Officer: Dr. Ronald L. Vaughn, President.

Address admission inquiries to Barbara P. Strickler, Vice President for Enrollment.

University of West Florida

11000 University Parkway
Pensacola, Florida 32514-5750

Tel: (850) 474-2000   **E-mail:** admissions@uwf.edu
Fax: (850) 474-3131   **Internet:** www.uwf.edu

Institution Description: University of West Florida is a state institution offering undergraduate and graduate study. *Enrollment:* 9,452. *Degrees awarded:* Associate, baccalaureate, master's, doctorate.

Academic offerings subject to approval by statewide coordinating bodies. Budget subject to approval by state governing boards.

Accreditation: *Regional:* SACS-Comm. on Coll. *Professional:* business, clinical lab scientist, music, nursing, nursing education, public administration, social work, teacher education

History: Established and incorporated 1963; offered first instruction at post-secondary level 1967; awarded first degree (baccalaureate) 1968; added graduate curriculum 1969; added lower division 1983.

Institutional Structure: *Governing board:* Florida Board of Regents. Representation: 13 members, including 1 student (appointed by governor of Florida), commissioner of education. All voting. *Composition of institution:* Administrators 87 men / 42 women. Academic affairs and administrative affairs headed by vice presidents. Full-time instructional faculty 226.

Calendar: Semesters. Academic year Aug. to Aug. Freshmen admitted Aug., Jan., May, June. Degrees conferred May, Aug., Dec. Formal commencement May, Aug., Dec. Summer session from May to July.

Characteristics of Freshmen: Mean ACT composite score men 23.3, women 22.8, class 23. 83% of applicants accepted. 35% of accepted applicants enrolled. 33% of entering freshmen expected to graduate within 5 years. 84% of freshmen from Florida. Freshmen from 30 states and 23 foreign countries.

Admission: Admission of freshmen and sophomores is on a selective basis. Specific criteria for entering freshmen include: a diploma from a regionally accredited high school, or if foreign, its equivalent, or state approved high school equivalency examinations; scores from SAT or ACT. Students are eligible in one of three ways: (1) a student applying for admissions who has a satisfactory high school record, including at least a B average in the required academic units normally offered in grades 9 through 12 and who submits other evidence that he/she can be expected to carry out successful academic progress in the university; (2) a student applying who has less than a B average in the required academic units must present a combination of high school GPA and entry level test scores equivalent to a 2.5 (on a 4.0 scale) in the required academic units, and a 900 on the combined portions of the SAT or a composite score of 19 on the ACT; (3) a student applying for admissions who does not meet these requirements may bring other important attributes or special talents and may be admitted if, in the judgment of the University Admissions Committee, it is determined from the appropriate evidence that the student can be expected to do successful academic work. Sophomore applicants must meet the freshmen requirements and must have completed a comparable freshman program with a GPA of at least 2.0 (on a 4.0 scale). For admission into the upper division, a transfer student must hold the Associate of Arts degree from a Florida public community college or present a minimum of 60 semester hours of acceptable college level coursework including a minimum of 36 semester hours of specified general education courses. All applicants seeking transfer must have maintained an overall average of at least 2.0 (on a 4.0 scale) on all college work attempted and be in good standing and eligible to return to the last institution attended without academic or disciplinary probation.

Degree Requirements: 120 credit hours; 2.0 GPA (higher for some programs); 30 hours in residence; demonstrated proficiency in English, mathematics. Fulfillment of some degree requirements and exemption from some beginning courses possible by passing departmental examinations, College Board CLEP. *Grading system:* A–F; pass-fail; withdraw (carries time limit).

Distinctive Educational Programs: *For undergraduates:* Interdisciplinary programs in international studies, science. Honors programs. Study abroad in Europe and South America by individual arrangement. *For graduate students:* Cooperative doctorate program in education with Florida State University. *Available to all students:* Cooperative education. Flexible meeting places and schedules, including off-campus centers (at Fort Walton; 50 miles away from main institution) and evening classes. Special facilities for using telecommunications in the classroom. Interdisciplinary programs in humanities, social science. Individual majors.

ROTC: Army in cooperation with Florida State University.

Degrees Conferred: 137 *associate*; 1,481 *baccalaureate*; 359 *master's*; 21 *post-master's certificate*; 21 *doctorate*. Bachelor's degrees awarded in top five disciplines: business, management, marketing, and related support services 290; education 155; communication, journalism, and related programs 151; psychology 124; security and protective services 103.

Fees and Other Expenses: *Full-time tuition per academic year 2004–05:* $2,574 in-state resident, $12,584 out-of-state. Contact the university for current graduate tuition/fees. *Books and supplies:* $800. *Room and board per academic year:* $8,294.

Financial Aid: Aid from institutionally generated funds is provided on the basis of academic merit, financial need, athletic ability. Institution has a Program Participation Agreement with the U.S. Department of Education for eligible students to receive Pell Grants and other federal aid.

Financial aid to full-time, first-time undergraduate students: 21% of students received federal grants averaging $2,772; 65% state/local grants averaging $2,082; 39% institutional grants averaging $1,298; 33% loans averaging $3,456.

Departments and Teaching Staff: *Professors* 57, *associate professors* 64, *assistant professors* 67, *instructors* 24, *part-time teachers* 4. *Total instructional faculty:* 226.3 FTE. Degrees held by full-time faculty: doctorate 78%, master's

Enrollment: Total enrollment 9,452. Undergraduate 7,911 (41.2% men, 58.8% women).

Characteristics of Student Body: *Ethnic/racial makeup:* Black non-Hispanic: 9.7%; American Indian or Alaska Native: 1.1%; Asian or Pacific Islander: 4.5%; Hispanic: 4.3%; White non-Hispanic: 76.2%; unknown: 2.9%.

International Students: 111 undergraduate nonresident aliens enrolled fall 2004. Students from Europe, Asia, Central and South America, Canada. Social and cultural programs available for students whose native language is not English. English as a Second Language Program. No financial aid specifically designated for international students.

Student Life: On-campus residence halls house 15% of student body. *Intercollegiate athletics:* men and women: basketball, cross-country, soccer, tennis; men only: golf and baseball; women only: softball, volleyball. *Special regulations:* Cars with parking decals permitted; fee charged. *Special services:* Learning Resources Center, medical services. *Student publications, radio: The Panhandler,* a biannual poetry publication; *Voyager,* a weekly newspaper. Radio station WUWF broadcasts 126 hours per week. *Surrounding community:* Pensacola population 65,000. New Orleans; 200 miles from campus, is nearest metropolitan area. Served by airport 10 miles from campus.

Publications: Sources of information about University of West Florida include "Inside UWF"and "Nautilus News," TV programs. *Publisher:* Member of State University System Press of Florida.

Library Collections: 609,848 volumes including bound books, serial backfiles, electronic documents, and government documents not in separate collections. Online catalog. 5,035 periodical subscriptions. 1,636,000 microforms. 7,400 audiovisual materials. Computer work stations available. Students have access to the Internet. Fee-based access to online services.

Most important holdings include West Florida Collection (materials on regional history from 16th century to present, including rare books, personal papers of residents, state legislators); estuarine biology collection (30,000 volumes including government documents on regional marine life); Indians of the Southeast collection (3,000 items including illustrations of and books, tapes, and manuscripts on Indian history and culture).

Buildings and Grounds: Campus area 1,600 acres.

Chief Executive Officer: Dr. John C. Cavanaugh, President.

Address admission inquiries to Richard M. Hulett, Director of Admissions.

Warner Southern College

13895 Highway 27
Lake Wales, Florida 33859-8797

Tel: (863) 638-1426   **E-mail:** admissions@warner.edu
Fax: (863) 638-1472   **Internet:** www.warner.edu

Institution Description: Warner Southern College is an independent, nonprofit institution affiliated with the Church of God. *Enrollment:* 989 *Degrees awarded:* Associate, baccalaureate.

Accreditation: *Regional:* SACS-Comm. on Coll.

History: Chartered 1964; established and offered first instruction at postsecondary level 1968; awarded first degree (baccalaureate) 1972.

Institutional Structure: *Governing board:* Board of Trustees. Extrainstitutional representation: 26 trustees, 7 advisory members; institutional representation: 4 administrators, including president of the college, secretary, treasurer. 4 ex officio, 26 voting. *Composition of institution:* Administrators 5 men. Academic affairs headed by vice president of academic affairs. Management/business/finances directed by vice president of business and finance. Full-time instructional faculty 29. Academic governance body, the faculty, meets an average of 10 times per year.

Calendar: Semesters. Academic year Aug. to May. Freshmen admitted Aug. and Jan. Degrees conferred and formal commencement May. Summer session terms from May to July.

Characteristics of Freshmen: 445 applicants (208 men, 237 women). 53.7% of applicants admitted. 56.1% of admitted students enrolled full-time.

6% (87students) submitted SAT scores; 57% (76 students) submitted ACT scores. *25th percentile:* SAT I Verbal 363, SAT I Math 370; ACT Composite 15. *75th percentile:* SAT I Verbal 580, SAT I Math 590; ACT Composite 23.

32% of entering freshmen expected to graduate within 5 years. 68% of freshmen from Florida.

Admission: Rolling admissions plan. For fall acceptance, apply as early as 1 year prior to enrollment, but not later than Sept. 1. Early acceptance available. *Requirements:* Either graduation from secondary school with units which normally include 4 English, 3 social studies, 2 health and physical education, 2 mathematics, 2 science; or GED. Additional units in foreign language recommended. Minimum GPA 2.0. *Entrance tests:* College Board SAT or ACT composite. *For transfer students:* 2.0 minimum GPA; maximum transfer credit limited only by residence requirement.

Advanced placement for postsecondary-level work completed in secondary school. College credit for extrainstitutional learning on basis of ACE *2006 Guide to the Evaluation of Educational Experiences in the Armed Services,* faculty assessment, Noncredit developmental and remedial courses offered during regular academic year.

Degree Requirements: *For all associate degrees:* 64 semester hours. *For all baccalaureate degrees:* 128 hours; competency examinations. *For all undergraduate degrees:* 2.0 GPA; 1 year or 2 semesters in residence; biweekly chapel attendance; fulfillment of church and service requirements. Fulfillment of some degree requirements and exemption from some beginning courses possible by passing College Board CLEP, APP. *Grading system:* A–F; pass-fail; pass; withdraw (carries time limit, deadline after which pass-fail is appended to withdraw).

Distinctive Educational Programs: Evening classes. Adult degree program. H.E.A.R.T. program for relief and development work.

Degrees Conferred: 10 *associate;* 371 *baccalaureate;* 9 *master's.* Bachelor's degrees awarded in top five disciplines: business, management, marketing, and related support services 287; education 28; theology and ministerial studies 21; parks, recreation, leisure and fitness studies 11; biological and biomedical sciences 8.

Fees and Other Expenses: *Full-time tuition per academic year 2004–05:* $11,740. *Room and board per academic year:* $5,160.

Financial Aid: Aid from institutionally generated funds is provided on the basis of academic merit, financial need, athletic ability, other considerations. Institution has a Program Participation Agreement with the U.S. Department of Education for eligible students to receive Pell Grants and other federal aid. 45% received federal grants averaging $3,446; 81% state/local grants averaging $3,148; 93% institutional grants averaging $4; 358; 50% loans averaging $3,955.

Departments and Teaching Staff: Bible *professors* 2, *associate professors* 1, *assistant professors* 1, *instructors* 0, *part-time teachers* 1; business administration 0, 2, 0, 0, 0; communication arts 1, 0, 2, 0, 4; fine arts 1, 0, 1, 0, 0; natural science and mathematics 1, 0, 0, 1, 2; physical education 1, 0, 0, 1, 0, 2; social and behavioral sciences 1, 2, 0, 0, 0; teacher education 1, 1, 2, 0, 0; organizational management 2, 1, 2, 2, 33; Learning Resource Center 0, 1, 0, 1, 0.

Total instructional faculty: 50. Student-to-faculty ratio: 14:1. Degrees held by full-time faculty: doctorate 39%, master's 57%, baccalaureate 4%. 30% hold terminal degrees.

Enrollment: Total enrollment 989. Undergraduate 941 (42.6% men, 57.4% women).

Characteristics of Student Body: *Ethnic/racial makeup:* Black non-Hispanic: 17.5%; American Indian or Alaska Native: .5%; Asian or Pacific Islander: .5%; Hispanic: 7.5%, White non-Hispanic: 67.4%; unknown: 2.9%.

International Students: 34 nonresident aliens enrolled fall 2004. No programs to aid students whose native language is not English.

Student Life: On-campus residence halls house 30% of student body. Dormitories for men only constitute 49% of such space, for women only 51%. *Intercollegiate athletics:* men only: baseball, basketball, cross country; women only: basketball, cross country, volleyball. *Special regulations:* Registered cars permitted without restrictions. Modesty, moderation, cleanliness, and good taste required in dress. Curfews. Quiet hours. *Special services:* Learning Resources Center, medical services. *Student publications: Royal Express,* a bimonthly newspaper. Radio station WSCR. *Surrounding community:* Lake Wales population 10,000. Orlando, 65 miles from campus, is nearest metropolitan area. Served by airport 5 miles from campus; passenger rail service 15 miles from campus.

Library Collections: 74,000 volumes including bound books, serial backfiles, electronic documents, and government documents not in separate collections. Online catalog. 100 current periodical subscriptions; 15,200 audiovisual materials; 7,770 microform units. Computer work stations available. Students have access to the Internet at no charge.

Most important holdings include Church of God historical collection; elementary education curriculum lab.

Buildings and Grounds: Campus area 380 acres.

Chief Executive Officer: Dr. Gregory V. Hall, President.

Address admission inquiries to Jason Roe, Director of Admissions.

Webber International University

1201 Alternate US Highway 27 South
P.O. Box 96
Babson Park, Florida 33827
Tel: (863) 638-1431   **E-mail:** admissions@webber.edu
Fax: (863) 638-2823   **Internet:** www.webber.edu

Institution Description: Webber International University, formerly known as Webber College, is a private 4-year business institution. *Enrollment:* 641. *Degrees awarded:* Associate, baccalaureate, master's.

Accreditation: *Regional:* SACS-Comm. on Coll. *Professional:* business

History: Founded 1927 as a women's college of business; coeducational since 1971.

Calendar: Semesters. Academic year Sept. to Apr.

Characteristics of Freshmen: 79% of applicants admitted. 435 of admitted students enrolled full-time.

68% (95 students) submitted SAT scores; 36% (50 students) submitted ACT scores. *25th percentile:* SAT Verbal 390, SAT Math 420; ACT Composite 16. *75th percentile:* SAT Verbal 470, SAT Math 510; ACT Composite 19.

42.5% of entering freshmen expected to graduate within 5 years. 94% of freshmen from Florida. Freshmen from 10 states and 4 foreign countries.

Admission: Rolling admissions plan; early decision; early admission. *Requirements:* Either graduation from secondary school with minimum 2.0 GPA or GED. *Entrance tests:* 810 SAT or 18 ACT composites required. For foreign students TOEFL score 500 paper or 173 computer-based.

Degree Requirements: Completion of course curriculum and a GPA of at least 2.0.

Degrees Conferred: 14 *associate;* 82 *baccalaureate:* business 82; 22 *master's: business* 22.

Fees and Other Expenses: *Full-time tuition per academic year 2004–05:* $12,300 undergraduate; $380 per credit hour graduate. *Room and board per academic year:* $4,520.

Financial Aid: Aid from institutionally generated funds is provided on the basis of academic merit, financial need, athletic ability, other criteria.

Financial aid to full-time, first-time undergraduate students: need-based scholarships/grants totaling $1,849,556, self-help $1,314,135, parent loans $308,590, tuition waivers $28,051, athletic awards $316,313; non-need-based scholarships/grants totaling $569,938, self-help $265,708, parent loans $63,118, tuition waivers $27,934, athletic awards $598,075.

Departments and Teaching Staff: Business *professors* 19, *part-time faculty* 20. *Total instructional faculty:* 39 (full-time 19, part-time 20; women 13, men 26; members of minority groups 2). Total faculty with doctorate, first-professional, or other terminal degree: 24. Student-to-faculty ratio: 19:1.

Enrollment: Total enrollment 576. Undergraduate full-time 354 men / 180 women, part-time 16m / 35w; graduate full-time 27m / 15w, part-time 7m / 7w. *Transfer students:* 65.

Characteristics of Student Body: *Ethnic/racial makeup:* number of Black non-Hispanic: 129; Asian or Pacific Islander: 2; Hispanic: 36; White non-Hispanic: 336; *Age distribution:* number under 18: 8; 18–19: 180; 20–21: 184; 22–24: 105; 25–29: 47; 30–34: 19, 35–39: 10; 40–49: 22; 50–64: 10.

International Students: 81 nonresident aliens enrolled fall 2004. English as a Second Language Program available. No financial aid specifically designated for international students.

Student Life: Men's and women's residence halls. Men's and women's sports include basketball, baseball, tennis, soccer, golf, football, cross-country, softball track and field, volleyball. *Surrounding community:* The college is located in central Florida near Disney World and Sea World. Served by airport in Orlando; 50 miles from campus.

Library Collections: 25,167 volumes including bound books, serial backfiles, electronic documents, and government documents not in separate collections. Online and card catalogs. Current serial subscriptions: 1,882 paper, 18 microform, 6 electronic. 4 recordings; 4 compact discs; 2 CD-ROMs. 110 computer work stations. Students have access to the Internet at no charge.

Most important special collection is the Fashion History Collection.

Buildings and Grounds: Campus area 40 acres.

Chief Executive Officer: Rex R. Yentes, President.

Address admission inquiries to Julie Razons, Director of Admissions.

Georgia

Agnes Scott College

141 East College Avenue

Decatur, Georgia 30030-3797

Tel: (404) 471-6000　　**E-mail:** admission@agnesscott.edu

Fax: (404) 471-6414　　**Internet:** www.agnesscott.edu

Institution Description: Agnes Scott College is an independent, nonprofit college for women related to the Presbyterian Church U.S.A. *Enrollment:* 923. *Degrees awarded:* Baccalaureate, master's.

Member of the Atlanta Regional Consortium for Higher Education.

Accreditation: *Regional:* SACS-Comm. on Coll.

History: Established as Decatur Female Seminary 1889; changed name to Agnes Scott Institute 1890; offered first instruction at postsecondary level 1902; adopted present name, awarded first degree (baccalaureate) 1906.

Institutional Structure: *Governing board:* Board of Trustees of Agnes Scott College. Extrainstitutional representation: 26 trustees, including 15 alumnae and 1 ex officio alumna. *Composition of institution:* Administrators 2 women. Academic affairs headed by vice president for academic affairs and dean of the college. Management/business/finances directed by vice president for business and finance. Full-time instructional faculty 31 men / 44 women. Academic governance body, the faculty, meets an average of 9 times per year.

Calendar: Semesters. Academic year Aug. to May. Freshmen admitted Aug. and Jan. Degrees conferred and formal commencement May. Limited summer session.

Characteristics of Freshmen: 1,252 applicants (all women). 59.2% of applicants admitted. 34.5% of admitted students enrolled full-time.

89% (230 students) submitted SAT scores; 43% (112 students) submitted ACT scores. *25th percentile:* SAT I Verbal 540, SAT I Math 500-; ACT Composite 22. *75th percentile:* SAT Verbal 680, SAT I Math 620; ACT Composite 28.

70% of entering freshmen expected to graduate within 5 years. 47% of freshmen from Georgia. Freshmen from 30 states.

Admission: Three admission plans for entering freshmen: early decision (deadline Nov. 15); scholarship (deadline Jan. 15); regular decision (deadline Mar. 1). Rolling admissions plan for transfers, priority Mar. 1 and Nov. 1. Early admissions plan for high school juniors. *Requirements:* Recommend 4 secondary school units English, 2 foreign language, 3 mathematics, 2 laboratory science, 2 social studies. GED may be accepted. *Entrance tests:* College Board SAT or ACT. *For transfer students:* 60 semester hours maximum transfer credit.

College credit and advanced placement for postsecondary-level work completed in secondary school.

Degree Requirements: 122 semester hours, including no more than 2 semester hours of physical education; cumulative GPA of 2.0 on a 4.0 scale; 60 semester-hours in residence, not including credit for physical education, with junior and senior years or 3 years including the senior year; specific and distribution requirements.

Fulfillment of some degree requirements possible by College Board AP scores or International Baccalaureate. *Grading system:* A–F; pass-fail, incomplete.

Distinctive Educational Programs: Dual-degree programs in engineering with Georgia Institute of Technology. Interdepartmental/interdisciplinary programs, including English literature/creative writing, mathematics/economics, international relations, sociology/anthropology, astrophysics, mathematics/physics. Business Preparatory Program. Atlanta Semester Program in Women, Leadership, and Social Change. Individual majors, tutorials, independent and special study programs. Global Awareness study programs: Mexico, Japan, Ghana; Global Connections: varies (India '96, England '97). Exchange programs: Kinjo Gakuin, Nagoya, Japan. Summer program in U.S. in marine biology. Internships in Washington, D.C., through American University's Washington Semester program. PLEN Public Policy Semester. Exchange program with Mills College (CA). Return to College Program for women who wish to complete or begin college work. Junior year abroad by individual arrangement in study programs sponsored by American colleges and universities (possibilities all over the world).

Degrees Conferred: 204 *baccalaureate*; 8 *master's*. Bachelor's degrees awarded in top five disciplines: social sciences 59; biological and biomedical sciences 27; psychology 26; English language and literature/letters 21; visual and performing arts 18.

Fees and Other Expenses: *Full-time tuition per academic year 2004–05:* $22,050. *Books and supplies:* $700. *Room and board per academic year:* $7,500.

Financial Aid: Aid from institutionally generated funds is provided on the basis of academic merit, financial need, other considerations. Institution has a Program Participation Agreement with the U.S. Department of Education for eligible students to receive Pell Grants and other federal aid.

Financial aid to full-time, first-time undergraduate students: 25% received federal grants averaging $3,450; 45% state/local grants averaging $3,902; 98% institutional grants averaging $13,131; 53% loans averaging $2,947.

Departments and Teaching Staff: Art *professors* 1, *associate professors* 2, *assistant professors* 2, *instructors* 0, *part-time teachers* 1; biology 3, 1, 2, 0, 1; chemistry 1, 1, 2, 1, 0; classics 0, 2, 0, 0, 0; economics 1, 0, 3, 0, 0; education 0, 1, 2, 0, 3; English 6, 1, 2, 0, 2; history 1, 2, 2, 0, 1; mathematics 2, 1, 1, 0, 1; modern foreign languages 1, 2, 3, 2, 5; music 3, 0, 1, 0, 0; philosophy 2, 0, 0, 0, 1; physics/astronomy 0, 1, 1, 0, 2; political science and sociology/anthropology 2, 3, 2, 0, 2; psychology 1, 2, 2, 0, 0; religious studies 1, 1, 0, 0, 2; theatre/dance 1, 2, 0, 0, 0; women's studies 0, 0, 1, 0, 7; physical education 0, 0, 0, 0, 4.

Total instructional faculty: 88.53 FTE. Student-to-faculty ratio: 10:1. *Degrees held by full-time faculty:* 100% of regular full-time faculty hold terminal degrees.

Enrollment: Total enrollment 923. Undergraduate 898.

Characteristics of Student Body: *Ethnic/racial makeup:* Black non-Hispanic: 19.5%; Asian or Pacific Islander: 4.9%; Hispanic: 3.7%; White non-Hispanic: 56.1%; unknown: 7.7%.

International Students: 73 undergraduate nonresident aliens enrolled fall 2003. Social and cultural programs available to aid students whose native language is not English. Variable number of scholarships available for international students.

Student Life: On-campus residence halls house 90% of traditional-age students. *Intercollegiate athletics:* basketball, cross-country, soccer, softball, swimming, tennis, volleyball. *Special regulations:* Cars permitted without restrictions. *Special services:* Campus Health Center provides medical information, counseling, treatment and referral for health problems. *Student publications:* *Aurora,* a quarterly literary magazine; *Profile,* a biweekly newspaper; *Silhouette,* a yearbook. *Surrounding community:* Decatur population 20,000. Atlanta, 6 miles from campus, is nearest metropolitan area. Served by mass transit rail and bus system; airport 15 miles from campus; passenger rail service 10 miles from campus.

Library Collections: 218,000 volumes including bound books, serial backfiles, electronic documents, and government documents not in separate collections. Online catalog. Current serial subscriptions: 1,460 paper and electronic. 32,700 microform units; 9,800 recordings. Computer work stations available. Students have access to the Internet at no charge.

Most important holdings include Robert Frost collection (manuscripts, personal papers, correspondence, autographed first editions); original manuscripts and papers of deceased alumna author, Catherine Marshall; frontier religion collection (writings by Walter Posey on development of religion on American frontier).

Buildings and Grounds: Campus area 100 acres.

Chief Executive Officer: Dr. Mary B. Bullock, President.

Address admission inquiries to Lee Ann Afton, Director of Admissions.

Albany State University

504 College Drive
Albany, Georgia 31705
Tel: (229) 430-4600
Fax: (229) 430-4830

Institution Description: Albany State University, formerly named Albany State College, is a state institution. *Enrollment: 3,681. Degrees awarded:* Baccalaureate, master's.

Academic offerings subject to approval by statewide coordinating bodies. Budget subject to approval by state governing boards.

Accreditation: *Regional:* SACS-Comm. on Coll. *Professional:* business, nursing, social work, teacher education

History: Established as Albany Bible and Manual Training Institute 1903; changed name to Georgia Normal and Agricultural College and offered first instruction at postsecondary level 1917; awarded first degree (baccalaureate) and became Albany State College 1943; university status awarded 1996.

Institutional Structure: *Governing board:* The Board of Regents of the University System of Georgia. Representation: 15 regents. All voting. *Composition of institution:* 10 administrators. Academic affairs headed by vice president of the university. Management/business/finances directed by vice president for fiscal affairs. Full-time instructional faculty 135. Academic governance body, Faculty Senate, meets an average of 8 times per year.

Calendar: Semesters. Academic year Aug. to July. Freshmen admitted Aug., Jan., May. Degrees conferred and formal commencement May and Dec. Summer session from June to Aug.

Characteristics of Freshmen: 2,106 applicants (747 men, 1,369 women). 83.7% of applicants admitted. 25.9% of admitted students enrolled full-time.

85% (484 students) submitted SAT scores; 27% (152 students) submitted ACT scores. *25th percentile:* SAT I Verbal 430, SAT I Math 420; ACT Composite 16, ACT English 15, ACT Math 16. *75th percentile:* SAT I Verbal 490, SAT I Math 500; ACT Composite 19, ACT English 19, ACT Math 19.

Admission: Rolling admissions plan. Early acceptance available. *Requirements:* Either graduation from accredited secondary school, or GED. Minimum GPA 2.0. *Entrance tests:* College Board SAT or ACT. For foreign students TOEFL. *For transfer students:* 2.0 minimum GPA; 90 semester hours maximum transfer credit.

College credit and advanced placement for postsecondary-level work completed in secondary school. Tutoring available. Noncredit developmental courses offered in summer session and regular academic year.

Degree Requirements: 120 semester hours; 2.0 GPA, some departments higher (for teacher education 2.5); minimum of 30 hours in residence; physical education courses required; general education requirements; exit competency examinations (Regents' Test of Reading and Writing, tests on courses in U.S. and Georgia constitutions and histories, sophomore comprehensives, senior examinations in major fields).

Fulfillment of some degree requirements and exemption from some beginning courses possible by passing College Board CLEP. *Grading system:* A–F; pass-fail; withdraw.

Distinctive Educational Programs: Cooperative education. Some weekend and evening courses. Special facilities for using telecommunications in the classroom. Facilities and programs for independent research, including individual majors, tutorials.

ROTC: Army in cooperation with Fort Valley State College.

Degrees Conferred: 464 *baccalaureate;* 125 *master's;* 65 *post-master's certificate.* Bachelor's degrees awarded in top five disciplines: business, management, marketing, and related support services 155; psychology 69; security and protective services 48; education 47; social sciences 40.

Fees and Other Expenses: *Full-time tuition per academic year 2004–05:* resident undergraduate $2,896, out-of-state $9,864. Contact the university for current graduate tuition/fees. *Books and supplies:* $850. *Room and board per academic year:* $960.

Financial Aid: Institution has a Program Participation Agreement with the U.S. Department of Education for eligible students to receive Pell Grants and other federal aid.

Financial aid to full-time, first-time undergraduate students: 63% received federal grants averaging $3,347; 78% state/local grants averaging $3,188; 11% institutional grants averaging $3,310; 56% loans averaging $2,650.

Departments and Teaching Staff: *Total instructional faculty:* 180.

Enrollment: Total enrollment 3,681. Undergraduate 3,169 (33.5% men, 56.5% women).

Characteristics of Student Body: *Ethnic/racial makeup:* Black non-Hispanic: 93.8%; American Indian or Alaska Native: 1%; Asian or Pacific Islander: .1%; Hispanic: .6%; White non-Hispanic: 5%.

International Students: 13 undergraduate nonresident aliens enrolled fall 2003. No financial aid specifically designated for international students.

Student Life: On-campus housing available. *Intercollegiate athletics:* baseball, basketball, football, tennis, track. *Special services:* Medical services. *Student publications: Albany State Ram,* a yearbook; *Student Voice,* a newspaper. *Surrounding community:* Albany population 44,000. Atlanta, 145 miles from campus, is nearest metropolitan area. Served by mass transit bus system; airport 5 miles from campus.

Buildings and Grounds: Campus area 128 acres.

Chief Executive Officer: Dr. Portia H. Shields, President.

Address admission inquiries to Robin A. McDermott, Director of Admissions.

American Intercontinental University

3330 Peachtree Road, N.E.
Atlanta, Georgia 30326
Tel: (404) 965-5700   **E-mail:** admissions@iuniv.edu
Fax: (404) 965-5701   **Internet:** www.aiuniv.edu

Institution Description: American Intercontinental University (AIU) is a private, coeducational nonsectarian institution. The university has campuses in Fort Lauderdale, Houston, London (England), Los Angeles, Houston, and United Arab Emirates. *Enrollment: 6,368. Degrees awarded:* Associate, baccalaureate. master's.

Accreditation: *Regional:* SACS-Comm. on Colleges. *Professional:* interior design

History: AIU was founded in Europe in 1970. The Atlanta-Buckhead campus was established in 1977.

Institutional Structure: *Governing board:* Oversees president of AIU campuses. *Composition of institution:* Campus president oversees academic dean, student services, admissions, registration, finance, library services. Academic affairs headed by the dean and oversees program chairs for each department.

Calendar: Quarters. Academic year Oct. to May. Two summer terms.

Characteristics of Freshmen: 5,896 applicants (1,982 men, 3,914 women). 44.4% of applicants admitted. 99.4% of admitted students enrolled full-time.

37% of entering freshmen are expected to graduate within 5 years. 48% of freshmen from Georgia (Buckhead Campus).

Admission: Rolling admissions. *Requirements:* Graduation from accredited secondary school or GED; proficiency in the English language; appropriate preparation for collegiate study.

Degree Requirements: *For all associate degrees:* 120 quarter hours; 2.0 GPA. *For all baccalaureate degrees:* 190 quarter hours; 2.0 GPA. Fashion Design and Marketing double major require completion of 200 quarter hours.

Distinctive Educational Programs: English as a Second Language Program; developmental studies program; study tours; exchange program.

Degrees Conferred: 582 *associate;* 2,709 *baccalaureate;* 1,862 *master's.* Bachelor's degrees awarded in top five disciplines: business, management, marketing, and related support services 1,291; computer and information sciences and support services 1,060; visual and performing arts 318; security and protective services 40.

Fees and Other Expenses: *Full-time tuition per academic year 2004–05:* $15,525. *Room per board (off-campus) per academic year:* $6,080. *Books and supplies:* $1,000.

Financial Aid: Institution has a Program Participation Agreement with the U.S. Department of Education for eligible students to receive Pell Grants and other federal aid.

Financial aid to full-time, first-time undergraduate students: 76% received federal grants averaging $1,583; 84% state/local grants averaging $469; 15% institutional grants averaging $434; 78% loans averaging $2,564.

Departments and Teaching Staff: Business *instructors full-time* 2, 18 *part-time;* fashion design 2, 5; fashion design/marketing 2, 5; fashion marketing 1, 6; general education 2, 24; interior design 2, 16; media production 3, 12; visual communication 3, 12. *Total instructional faculty:* 115. Student-to-faculty ratio: 12:1. Degrees held by full-time faculty: doctorate 18%, master's 70%, baccalaureate 12%.

Enrollment: Total enrollment 6,368. Undergraduate 5,277 (44.2% men, 55.8% women).

Characteristics of Student Body: *Ethnic/racial makeup:* Black non-Hispanic: 15.6%; American Indian or Alaska Native: .8%; Asian or Pacific Islander: 1.9%; Hispanic: 5.4%; White non-Hispanic: 31.1%; unknown: 44.9%.

International Students: 141 nonresident aliens enrolled fall 2003. Programs available to aid students whose native language is not English: Social, cultural.

English as a Second Language Program. Scholarships available annually to qualifying international students.

Student Life: Single-student apartments available. Remedial learning services, health insurance, counseling, career services. Various clubs and organizations. *Student publications: The Eagle, Collegian, Source, AIU Review* (student newspaper).

Library Collections: 24,000 volumes. Online catalog. 250 serial subscriptions; 1,200 recordings. Computer work stations available.

Most important special collections include Interior Design and Forecast/Costume Collections.

Buildings and Grounds: Urban campus area 1 acre.

Chief Executive Officer: Dr. Rafael A. Lao, President.

Address admission inquiries to Dave Naylor, Director of Admissions.

Armstrong Atlantic State University

11935 Abercorn Street

Savannah, Georgia 31419-1997

Tel: (912) 927-5211   **E-mail:** admissions@armstrong.edu

Fax: (912) 921-5462   **Internet:** www.armstrong.edu

Institution Description: Armstrong Atlantic State University, formerly Armstrong State College, is a public institution. *Enrollment:* 5,387. *Degrees awarded:* Associate, baccalaureate, master's, doctorate, specialist.

Academic offerings subject to approval by statewide coordinating bodies. Budget subject to approval by state governing boards.

Accreditation: *Regional:* SACS-Comm. on Coll. *Professional:* clinical lab scientist, computer science, dental hygiene, music, nursing, nursing education, physical therapy, public health, radiation therapy, radiography, respiratory therapy, teacher education.

History: Established as Armstrong College of Savannah, chartered, and offered first instruction at postsecondary level 1935; awarded first degree (associate) 1936; incorporated in the University of Georgia system and changed name to Armstrong Junior College 1959; became Armstrong State College 1964; awarded first baccalaureate 1968; adopted present name 1995.

Institutional Structure: *Governing board:* Board of Regents of the University System of Georgia. Representation: 15 regents. *Composition of institution:* Administrators 20 men / 6 women. Academic affairs headed by Vice President. Management/business/finances directed by Vice President for Business and Finance. Full-time instructional faculty 81 men / 63 women. Academic governance body, the faculty, meets an average of 9 times per year.

Calendar: Semesters. Academic year Sept. to June. Freshmen admitted Sept., Jan., Mar., June. Degrees conferred and formal commencement June and Dec. Summer session from June to Aug.

Characteristics of Freshmen: 1,567 applicants (632 men, 935 women). 83.6% of applicants admitted. 26.9% of admitted students enrolled full-time.

79% (672 students) submitted SAT scores; 21% (176 students) submitted ACT scores. *25th percentile:* SAT I Verbal 470, SAT I Math 450; ACT Composite 18, ACT English 17, ACT Math 17. *75th percentile:* SAT I Verbal 570, 5SAT I Math 550; ACT Composite 22, ACT English 24, ACT Math 22.

Admission: Rolling admissions plan. For fall acceptance, apply as early as senior year of secondary school. Early acceptance available. *Requirements:* Either graduation from accredited secondary school with 16 units which must include 4 English, 4 social studies, 2 mathematics, 2 science; or GED. Additional requirements for some programs. Minimum GPA 1.8. *Entrance tests:* College Board SAT. For foreign students TOEFL. *For transfer students:* From 4-year accredited institution maximum transfer credit limited only by residence requirement; from 2-year accredited institution 100 quarter hours; good standing at institution previously attended. Correspondence/extension students 2.0 minimum GPA; 45 quarter hours maximum transfer credit.

College credit for postsecondary-level work completed in secondary school and for extrainstitutional learning (life experience) on basis of ACE *2006 Guide to the Evaluation of Educational Experiences in the Armed Services*; USAFI.

Tutoring available. Noncredit developmental courses offered in summer session and regular academic year.

Degree Requirements: *For all associate degrees:* 60 semester quarter hours; 1 semester hour physical education. *For all baccalaureate degrees:* 120 minimum semester hours; 2 semester hours physical education. *For all undergraduate degrees:* 2.0 GPA; 30 semester hours in residence; general education requirements; exit competency examinations (Regents' Test of Reading and Writing,

tests on or courses in U.S. and Georgia constitutions and histories; comprehensives in major fields of study).

Fulfillment of some degree requirements and exemption from some beginning courses possible by passing departmental examinations, College Board CLEP, AP. *Grading system:* A–F; pass-fail; withdraw.

Distinctive Educational Programs: Evening classes. Dual-degree programs in mathematical sciences and engineering with Georgia Institute of Technology, Auburn University, Clemson University, and Mississippi State University. Dual-degree program in forestry and environmental management with Duke University. Honors programs and independent study. Cross-registration with Savannah State College. *Other distinctive programs:* Continuing education and community service programs.

ROTC: Army in cooperation with University of Georgia; Navy in cooperation with Savannah State College.

Degrees Conferred: 62 *associate*; 632 *baccalaureate*; 247 *master's*. Bachelor's degrees awarded in top five disciplines: health professions and related clinical sciences 227; education 97; liberal arts and sciences, general studies and humanities sciences 85; social sciences 42; security and protective services 30.

Fees and Other Expenses: *Full-time tuition per academic year 2004–05:* $2,602 in-state resident, $9,238 out-of-state. *Room and board per academic year:* $6,192. *Books and supplies:* $800.

Financial Aid: Aid from institutionally generated funds is provided on the basis of academic merit, financial need, athletic ability. Institution has a Program Participation Agreement with the U.S. Department of Education for eligible students to receive Pell Grants and other federal aid.

Financial aid to full-time, first-time undergraduate students: 26% received federal grants averaging $2,897; 76% state/local grants averaging $2,836; 8% institutional grants averaging $922; 26% received loans averaging $2,760.

Departments and Teaching Staff: Biology *professors* 2, *associate professors* 4, *assistant professors* 0, *instructors* 0, *part-time teachers* 0; chemistry 4, 0, 3, 2, 1; fine arts 0, 3, 3, 2, 0; government 4, 2, 3, 0, 0; history 6, 2, 3, 0, 0; languages/literature 5, 2, 9, 0, 0; math/computer science 6, 0, 4, 3, 0; psychology 4, 1, 2, 0, 0; elementary education 3, 3, 1, 0, 0; secondary education 3, 1, 4, 0, 0; asso. nursing 0, 0, 8, 0, 1; bacc. nursing 0, 2, 6, 0, 0; dental hygiene 0, 1, 3, 1, 2; health, phys. ed. 2, 0, 5, 1, 1; respiratory ther. 0, 0, 2, 2, 0; health info mgmt 0, 0, 1, 1, 0; medical technology 0, 0, 2, 0, 0; radiological technology 0, 0, 1, 1, 0; developmental studies 0, 0, 4, 0, 0; military science 0, 0, 2, 0, 0.

Total instructional faculty: 144. Degrees held by full-time faculty: baccalaureate 6%, master's 44%, doctorate 50%. 76% hold terminal degrees.

Enrollment: Total enrollment 6,653. Undergraduate 5,743 (32.2% men, 67.8% women).

Characteristics of Student Body: *Ethnic/racial makeup:* Black non-Hispanic: 21%; American Indian or Native Alaska: 4%; Asian or Pacific Islander: .9%; Hispanic: 2.8%; White non-Hispanic: 71.1%.

International Students: 98 undergraduate nonresident aliens enrolled fall 2004. No programs available to aid students whose native language is not English. No financial aid specifically designated for international students.

Student Life: On-campus housing available. *Intercollegiate athletics:* men only: baseball, basketball, cross-country, golf, soccer, tennis; women only: cross-country, fast-pitch softball, swimming, track, tennis, volleyball. *Special regulations:* Cars with parking decals permitted. *Special services:* Adults Back to College, Academic Computing Center, Counseling and Career Placement, Learning Resources Center, Minority Advisement Program, and a Writing Center. Student organizations include College Union Board, Student Government Association, sororities, religious, special interest, academic honor societies and intramurals. *Student publications: Calliope*, a literary magazine; *Geechee*, the yearbook; *Inkwell*, a bimonthly newspaper. Other publications include *Focus*, a campus/community newspaper published three times yearly; *Maroon & Gold*, a weekly newsletter. *Surrounding community:* Savannah population 175,000. Atlanta, 260 miles from campus, is the nearest metropolitan area. Served by mass transit bus system, airport 21 miles from campus, passenger rail service 15 miles from campus.

Library Collections: 222,100 volumes. 682,000 microforms; 11,200 audiovisual materials; 1,150 current periodicals; 7,150 recordings/tapes. Students have access to online information retrieval services and the Internet.

Most important holdings include works by and about Conrad Aiken (especially first editions); works by other Georgia authors; Library of American Civilization and Library of English Literature.

Buildings and Grounds: Campus area 250 acres.

Chief Executive Officer: Dr. Thomas Z. Jones, President.

Address admission inquiries to Kim West, Director of Admissions.

Art Institute of Atlanta

6600 Peachtree Dunwoody Road

100 Embassy Row

Atlanta, Georgia 30328

Tel: (770) 394-8300   **E-mail:** aiaadm@aii.edu

Fax: (770) 394-0008   **Internet:** www.aia.artinstitutes.edu

Institution Description: The Art Institute of Atlanta is a private college affiliated with the Art Institutes International which is headquartered in Pittsburgh, Pennsylvania. *Enrollment:* 2,651. *Degrees awarded:* Associate, baccalaureate.

Accreditation: *Regional:* SACS. *Professional:* culinary education, interior design

History: Established as Massey College 1949; present name adopted 1974; awarded first associate degree 1963, first baccalaureate 1994.

Institutional Structure: *Governing board:* Board of Trustees: 6 members (3 public, 3 associated with the Art Institutes International). All voting. College president is a nonvoting ex officio member. *Composition of institution:* Administrators 2 men / 5 women. Academic affairs headed by dean of academic affairs. Management/business/finances directed by vice president; Housing, counseling, employment assistance directed by vice president/director of student services. Full-time instructional faculty 91. Adjunct faculty 74.

Calendar: Quarters. Academic year Oct. to Sept. Degrees conferred and formal commencement biannually.

Characteristics of Freshmen: 94% of applicants accepted. 71% of accepted applicants matriculate. 43% of freshmen from Georgia. Freshmen from 28 states.

Admission: Rolling admissions. Early acceptance available for fall. *Requirements:* Graduation from accredited secondary school with high school diploma or GED. *Entrance tests:* None required; SAT or ACT accepted and used for placement purposes. *For transfer students:* 50% of credits must be earned at the college.

Degree Requirements: *For all associate degrees:* 96–128 quarter credit hours. *For all baccalaureate degrees:* 192 quarter credit hours. *For all undergraduate degrees:* 2.0 GPA. *Grading system:* A-F; withdraw (carries time limit).

Distinctive Educational Programs: Internships. Evening and weekend classes. Odyssey Study Abroad.

Degrees Conferred: 264 *associate;* 190 *baccalaureate:* trade and industry 47; visual and performing arts 143.

Fees and Other Expenses: *Full-time tuition per academic year 2004–05:* $17,040. *Room and board per academic year:* $7,311.

Financial Aid: Aid from institutionally generated funds is provided on the basis of academic merit, financial need. Institution has a Program Participation Agreement with the U.S. Department of Education for eligible students to receive Pell Grants and other federal aid.

Departments and Teaching Staff: *Total instructional faculty:* 165 (91 full-time, 74 part-time; women 75, men 90; members of minority groups 34). Total faculty with doctorate, first-professional, or other terminal degree: 79. Student-to-faculty ratio: 21:1. 3 faculty members awarded sabbaticals 2004–05.

Enrollment: Total enrollment 2,651. Full-time 1,237 men / 1,085 women, part-time 186m / 143w.

Characteristics of Student Body: *Ethnic/racial makeup:* number of Black non-Hispanic: 834; American Indian or Alaska Native: 10; Asian or Pacific Islander: 77; Hispanic: 104; White non-Hispanic: 1,295; unknown: 220. *Age distribution:* number under 18: 11; 18–19: 561; 20–21: 545; 22–24: 598; 25–29: 432; 30–34: 169; 35–39: 69; 40–49: 63; 50–64: 6.

International Students: 83 nonresident aliens enrolled fall 2004. Social and cultural programs available to aid students whose native language is not English. No financial aid specifically designated for international students.

Student Life: 23% of student body housed in college-sponsored housing, located off-campus. *Special services:* Career development and services; counseling. *Surrounding community:* Atlanta population 4.9 million.

Library Collections: 40,799 volumes. Online catalog. 27,000 slides; 1,143 video titles; 240 current periodicals. Access to online systems and the Internet.

Buildings and Grounds: The Art Institute of Atlanta moved to a new state-of-the-art industry, built-to-suit facility in 1999.

Chief Executive Officer: Janet S. Day, President.

Address admissions inquiries to Donna C. Scott, Director of Admissions.

Atlanta Christian College

2605 Ben Hill Road

East Point, Georgia 30344

Tel: (404) 761-8861   **E-mail:** admissions@acc.edu

Fax: (404) 669-2024   **Internet:** www.acc.edu

Institution Description: Atlanta Christian College is a private, independent, nonprofit Christian college related to the Christian Churches and Churches of Christ. *Enrollment:* 394. *Degrees awarded:* Associate, baccalaureate.

Accreditation: *Regional:* SACS-Comm. on Coll.

History: Established and chartered 1928; in operation continuously since 1937; awarded first degree (baccalaureate) 1942.

Institutional Structure: *Governing board:* 30 trustees. *Composition of institution:* Administrators 11 men / 2 women. President is chief executive officer. Academic affairs headed by vice president for academic affairs. Fund-raising, publicity, and relations with constituency directed by vice president for development. Full-time instructional faculty 17. Academic governance body, the college faculty, meets on the average of 10 times per year.

Calendar: Semesters. Academic year Aug. to May. Freshmen admitted Aug. and Jan. Degrees conferred May. Formal commencement May.

Characteristics of Freshmen: 515 applicants (238 men, 277 women). 52.6% of applicants admitted. 38.4% of admitted students enrolled full-time.

88% (93 students) submitted SAT scores; 29% (30 students) submitted ACT scores. *25th percentile:* SAT I Verbal 430, SAT I Math 400; ACT Composite 17, ACT English 16, ACT Math 16. *75th percentile:* SAT I Verbal 550, SAT I Math 550; ACT Composite 21, ACT English 21, ACT Math 21.

Admission: For fall acceptance, apply no later than Aug. 1. Apply by Dec. 1 for spring acceptance. *Requirements:* Either graduation from accredited secondary school or GED. Lowest recommended high school GPA 2.0. *Entrance tests:* College Board SAT or ACT. *For transfer students:* 2.0 minimum GPA; from 4-year accredited institution 90 hours maximum transfer credit; from 2-year accredited institution 64 hours.

College credit and advanced placement for postsecondary-level work completed in secondary school.

Degree Requirements: *For all associate degrees:* 64 credit hours. *For all baccalaureate degrees:* 128 credit hours. *For Bachelor of Theology:* 30 hours above first baccalaureate degree. *For all degrees:* 2.0 GPA; 32 hours in residence; internship requirements.

Fulfillment of some degree requirements and exemption from some beginning courses possible by passing College Board CLEP, AP (score of 3). *Grading system:* A–F; withdraw (deadline after which pass-fail is appended to withdraw).

Distinctive Educational Programs: Evening classes. Internship and Christian Service programs.

Degrees Conferred: 3 *associate;* 41 *baccalaureate:* theology and ministerial studies 11; social sciences 10; education 9; business, management, marketing, and related support services 7; visual and performing arts 3.

Fees and Other Expenses: *Full-time tuition per academic year 2004–05:* $11,360. *Books and supplies:* $700. *Room and board per academic year:* $4,400.

Financial Aid: Aid from institutionally generated funds is provided on the basis of academic merit, financial need. Institution has a Program Participation Agreement with the U.S. Department of Education for eligible students to receive Pell Grants and other federal aid.

Financial aid to full-time, first-time undergraduate students: 25% received federal grants averaging $1,500; 88% state/local grants averaging $1,000; 66% institutional grants averaging $1,000; 93% loans averaging $2,625.

Departments and Teaching Staff: *Professors* 14, *associate professors* 1, *assistant professors* 1, *instructors* 1, *part-time teachers* 25. *Total instructional faculty:* 25.3 FTE. Student-to-faculty ratio: 11:1. Degrees held by full-time faculty: Doctorate 60%, master's 100%. 60% hold terminal degrees.

Enrollment: Total enrollment 394 (52.8% men, 47.2% women).

Characteristics of Student Body: *Ethnic/racial makeup:* Black non-Hispanic: 19%; Asian or Pacific Islander: 1%; Americana Indian or Alaska Native: .5%; Hispanic: 1%; White non-Hispanic: 76.5%; unknown: .5%.

International Students: 5 nonresident aliens enrolled fall 2003. No programs available to aid students whose native language is not English. No financial aid specifically designated for international students.

Student Life: On-campus residence halls house 50% of student body. *Intercollegiate athletics:* women only: volleyball; both sexes: basketball, soccer. *Special services:* Campus nurse. *Student publications: Gold and Blue,* quarterly newspaper; *Harvester,* yearbook. *Surrounding community:* Metropolitan Atlanta population 3 million. Served by mass transit bus and rail system; airport 5 miles from campus.

Library Collections: 50,000 volumes including bound books, serial back-files, electronic documents, and government documents not in separate collections. Online catalog. Current serial subscriptions: 257 paper, 1 microform. 374 recordings; 86 compact discs; 3 CD-ROMs. Computer work stations available. Students have access to the Internet at no charge.

Most important special holdings include Alumni Collection; Library of American Civilization - Core Collection; James A. Burns Collection.

Buildings and Grounds: Campus area 52 acres.

Chief Executive Officer: Dr. Edwin Groover, President.

Address admission inquiries to Keith Wagner, Director of Admissions.

Atlanta College of Art

1280 Peachtree Street, N.E.
Atlanta, Georgia 30309
Tel: (404) 733-5100
Fax: (404) 733-5107

Institution Description: The Atlanta College of Art (Atlanta School of Art until 1973) is a private, independent, nonprofit college. *Enrollment:* 322. *Degrees awarded:* Baccalaureate.

Member of the consortia Union of Independent Colleges of Art (UICA) and University Center in Georgia, Inc.

Accreditation: *Regional:* SACS-Comm. on Coll. *Professional*: art

History: Established and incorporated as High Museum School of Art and offered first instruction at postsecondary level 1928; first degree (baccalaureate) awarded 1946; changed name to Atlanta Art Institute 1951; to Atlanta School of Art 1962; adopted present name 1973.

Institutional Structure: *Governing board:* Board of Directors of the Atlanta College of Art. Representation: 49 directors, 8 honorary directors. 4 ex officio. *Composition of institution:* Administrators 2 men / 3 women. Management/business/finances directed by business officer. Full-time instructional faculty 63. Academic governance body, the faculty, meets an average of 10 times per year.

Calendar: Semesters. Academic year early Aug. to May. Freshmen admitted Aug. and Jan. Degrees conferred and formal commencement May. No summer session.

Characteristics of Freshmen: 222 applicants (98 men, 124 women). 69.8% of applicants admitted. 46.5% of admitted students enrolled full-time.

81% (58 students) submitted SAT scores; 31% (22 students) submitted ACT scores. *25th percentile*: SAT I Verbal 450, SAT I Math 440; ACT Composite 17. *75th percentile*: SAT I Verbal 590, SAT I Math 540; ACT Composite 23.

40% of freshmen from Georgia. Freshmen from 26 states and 12 foreign countries.

Admission: Rolling admissions plan. Early acceptance available. *Requirements:* Either graduation from accredited secondary school or GED. Portfolio of minimum 12 pieces of art work. Essay, SAT/ACT scores, high school transcripts. *Entrance tests:* College Board SAT or ACT composite. For foreign students TOEFL.

For transfer students: high school/college transcripts. College credit for postsecondary-level work completed in secondary school. Remedial courses offered during regular academic year; credit awarded.

Degree Requirements: 120 credit hours (39 academic, 81 studio); 2.0 GPA; 4 terms in residence. Fulfillment of some degree requirements and exemption from some beginning courses possible by passing College Board CLEP or APP. *Grading system:* A–F; withdraw (deadline after which pass-fail is appended to withdraw); incomplete.

Distinctive Educational Programs: Daytime and evening classes. Dual-degree program in art with Oglethorpe university. Facilities and programs for independent research, including individual majors and independent study. Cross-registration with 13 colleges and universities in the Atlanta area.

Degrees Conferred: 67 *baccalaureate:* visual and performing arts.

Fees and Other Expenses: *Full-time tuition per academic year 2004–05:* $17,100. *Books and supplies:* $900. *Room and board per academic year:* $6,675.

Financial Aid: Aid from institutionally generated funds is provided on the basis of academic merit, financial need, other criteria. Institution has a Program Participation Agreement with the U.S. Department of Education for eligible students to receive Pell Grants and other federal aid.

Financial aid to full-time, first-time undergraduate students: 37% received federal grants averaging $4,469; 42% state/local grants averaging $2,563; 76% institutional grants averaging $5,037; 69% received loans averaging $3,894.

Departments and Teaching Staff: *Professors* 25; *associate professors* 6, *assistant professors* 8, *instructors* 24, *part-time teachers* 49. *Total instructional faculty:* 79 FTE. Degrees held by full-time faculty: doctorate 25%, master's 75%, baccalaureate 100%. 100% hold terminal degrees.

Enrollment: Total enrollment 322 (49.7% men, 50.3% women).

Characteristics of Student Body: *Ethnic/racial makeup:* Black non-Hispanic: 23%; American Indian or Alaska Native: .3%; Asian or Pacific Islander: 3.1%; Hispanic: 3.4%; White non-Hispanic: 61.2%; unknown: 3.4%.

International Students: 18 nonresident aliens enrolled fall 2003. Students from Europe, Asia, Central and South America, Australia. Social programs available to aid students whose native language is not English. English as a Second Language Program. No financial aid specifically designated for international students.

Student Life: An on-campus residence hall available. *Special regulations:* Cars permitted without restrictions. *Surrounding community:* Atlanta metropolitan area population 3 million. Served by mass transit system (rail station at campus); airport 10 miles from campus.

Publications: *Viewbook;* annual student handbook; quarterly continuing education catalog; newsletter; faculty catalog.

Library Collections: 29,000 volumes. 200 current periodical subscriptions. 100 audiovisual materials. 4 computer work stations. Students have access to the Internet at no charge.

Most important holdings include extensive collection of artists' books; video recordings of visiting artists; statewide artist/artisan registry.

Buildings and Grounds: Campus area 1 square block.

Chief Executive Officer: Ellen L. Meyer, President.

Address admission inquiries to Lucy Leusch, Vice President for Enrollment Management.

Augusta State University

2500 Walton Way
Augusta, Georgia 30904-2200
Tel: (706) 737-1401   **E-mail:** admission@aug.edu
Fax: (706) 667-4353   **Internet:** www.aug.edu

Institution Description: Augusta State University, formerly Augusta College, is a state-supported institution. *Enrollment:* 6,353. *Degrees awarded:* Associate, baccalaureate, master's. Education specialist certificate also awarded.

Academic offerings subject to approval by statewide coordinating bodies. Budget subject to approval by state governing boards. Member of Georgia Consortium.

Accreditation: *Regional:* SACS-Comm. on Coll. *Professional*: business, music, nursing, teacher education

History: With a curriculum beginning as postsecondary courses in the Academy of Richmond County (chartered in 1783), the Junior College of Augusta was formed in 1925; became Augusta College, a unit of the University System of Georgia, in 1958; became 4-year institution 1963; awarded first degree (baccalaureate) 1967; adopted present status and name in 1996. *See* Edward J. Cashin, with Helen Callahan, *A History of Augusta College* (Augusta: Augusta College Press, 1976) for further information.

Institutional Structure: *Governing board:* Board of Regents of the University System of Georgia. Extrainstitutional representation: 15 regents. All voting. *Composition of institution:* Administrators 6 men / 2 women. Academic affairs headed by vice president. Business and student services directed by vice president. Full-time instructional faculty 111 men / 97 women. Academic governance body, the faculty, meets an average of 3 times per year.

Calendar: Semesters. Academic year mid-Aug. to mid-May. Freshmen admitted Aug., Jan., May. Degrees conferred and formal commencement May. Summer session from mid-May to late July.

Characteristics of Freshmen: 100% (602 students) submitted SAT scores. *25th percentile*: SAT Verbal 430, SAT Math 430. *75th percentile*: SAT Verbal 540, SAT Math 540.

95% of freshmen from Georgia. Freshmen from 9 states and 29 foreign countries.

Admission: Rolling admissions plan. For fall acceptance, apply no later than mid-July of year of enrollment. Early acceptance available. *Requirements:* Graduation from accredited secondary school with 4 units English, 3 math, 3 science, 3 social science, 2 foreign language, and 1 other academic credit. GED accepted. Minimum GPA 2.0. *Entrance tests:* College Board SAT. For foreign students TOEFL. *For transfer students:* 2.0 minimum GPA.

Advanced placement for postsecondary-level work completed in secondary school; college credit for extrainstitutional learning on basis of ACE *2006 Guide to the Evaluation of Educational Experiences in the Armed Services.* Tutoring available in most subjects; some at cost to students. Developmental courses offered in summer session and regular academic year; nondegree credit given.

Degree Requirements: *For all associate degrees:* minimum of 60 semester hours; 20 hours in residence. *For all baccalaureate degrees:* minimum of 125 semester hours; 30 hours in residence; comprehensives in individual fields of study. *For all undergraduate degrees:* Regents' Test of reading and writing, tests on or courses in U.S. and Georgia constitutions and histories; 3 semester hours in physical education; core curriculum. *Grading system:* A–F; withdraw (deadline after which pass-fail is appended to withdraw); incomplete.

Distinctive Educational Programs: Work-experience programs. Evening classes. Accelerated degree programs. Special facilities for using telecommunications in the classroom. Interdisciplinary program in third-world cultures. Facilities and programs for independent research, including honors programs, individual majors. Study abroad in France, Spain, Sweden. *Other distinctive programs:* Continuing education. Cooperative education programs and internships.

ROTC: Army in cooperation with Paine College.

Degrees Conferred: 46 *associate;* 518 *baccalaureate (B);* 109 *master's* (M): biological/life sciences 34 (B); business/marketing 126 (B), 48 (M); communications/communication technologies 45 (B); computer and information sciences 25 (B); education 91 (B), 55 (M); English 17 (B); foreign languages and literature 9 (B); mathematics 3 (B); physical sciences 4 (B); protective services/public administration 29 (B), 2 (M); psychology 43 (B), 2 (M); social sciences and history 76 (B); visual and performing arts 16 (B).

Fees and Other Expenses: *Full-time tuition per academic year 2004–05:* $2,702 undergraduate resident, $9,290 out-of-state student. Contact the university for current graduate/professional school tuition and fees. No on-campus housing.

Financial Aid: Aid from institutionally generated funds is provided on the basis of academic merit, athletic ability.

Financial aid to full-time, first-time undergraduate students: need-based scholarships/grants totaling $7,819,411, self-help $7,227,483; non-need-based scholarships/grants totaling $5,906,959, self-help $5,025,282, parent loans $100,076, tuition waivers $3,955,488, athletic awards $465,111.

Departments and Teaching Staff: Biology *professors* 2, *associate professors* 8, *assistant professors* 2, *instructors* 1, *part-time teachers* 5; chemistry/physics 1, 6, 1, 2, 2; fine arts 8, 6, 2, 1, 27; history/philosophy 4, 2, 4, 2, 8; language/literature 9, 12, 11, 7, 11; learning support 0, 1, 7, 6, 8; mathematics/computer science 2, 5, 10, 2, 7; nursing 0, 1, 7, 1, 0; political science 3, 2, 1, 1, 8; psychology 3, 3, 2, 2, 11; sociology 2, 3, 1, 2, 13; business administration 8,7, 4, 2, 2; clinical/professional studies 2, 4, 4, 1, 10; teacher development 0, 4, 4, 1, 2; kinesiology/health 0, 4, 3, 2, 0.

Total instructional faculty: 322. Student-to-faculty ratio: 27:1. Degrees held by full-time faculty: doctorate 70%, master's 29%, baccalaureate 1%. 70% hold terminal degrees.

Enrollment: Total enrollment 6,353. Undergraduate full-time 1,342 men / 2,770 women, part-time 567m / 1,317w; graduate full-time 97m / 213m, part-time 167m / 374.

Characteristics of Student Body: *Ethnic/racial makeup:* number of Black non-Hispanic: 1,512; American Indian or Alaska Native 17; Asian or Pacific Islander: 155; Hispanic: 157; White non-Hispanic: 3,611. *Age distribution:* number under 18: 10; 18–19: 1,229; 20–21: 1,186; 22–24: 1,155; 25–29: 810; 30–34: 406; 35–39: 235; 40–49: 253; 50–64: 69; 65 and over: 3.

International Students: 59 undergraduate nonresident aliens enrolled fall 2004. 3 students from Europe, 10 Asia, 1 Africa, 4 Canada, 2 Australia, 39 other. No programs available to aid students whose native language is not English. No financial aid specifically designated for international students.

Student Life: No on-campus housing. 2% of men join fraternities; 2% of women join sororities. *Intercollegiate athletics:* men only: baseball, basketball, soccer, tennis; women only: basketball, tennis, volleyball, softball; both sexes: cross-country, swimming. *Special regulations:* Cars permitted without restrictions. *Special services:* Learning Resources Center. *Student publications, radio: Bell Ringer,* student newspaper; *Phoenix,* quarterly student magazine; *Sand Hills,* an annual literary magazine. Radio station WAGG broadcasts 86 hours per week. *Surrounding community:* Augusta-Richmond County population 190,000. Atlanta, 145 miles from campus, is nearest metropolitan area. Served by mass transit bus system; airport 13 miles from campus.

Library Collections: 454,590 volumes including bound books, serial backfiles, electronic documents, and government documents not in separate collections. Online catalog. Current serial subscriptions: 33,797 (paper, microform, electronic access). 957,662 microforms. 6,124 audiovisual materials. 50 computer work stations. Students have access to the Internet at no charge. Total budget for books, periodicals, audiovisual materials, microforms 2004–05: $412,018.

Most important holdings include local history and genealogy; Edison Marshall Papers; Augusta Arsenal Records; Richmond Academy Reports. Cumming Family Papers.

Buildings and Grounds: Campus area 80 acres. *New buildings:* University Hall completed 2004; Allgood Hall 2002; Science Building 2002; Student Center 2006.

Chief Executive Officer: William A. Bloodworth, Jr., President.

Address admission inquiries to Katherine Sweeney, Registrar and Director of Admissions.

Berry College

2277 Martha Berry Highway N.W.
Mount Berry, Georgia 30149
Tel: (706) 232-5374   **E-mail:** admissions@berry.edu
Fax: (706) 236-2248   **Internet:** www.berry.edu

Institution Description: Berry College is a private, independent, nonprofit college. *Enrollment:* 2,045. *Degrees awarded:* Baccalaureate, master's, education specialist.

Accreditation: *Regional:* SACS-Comm. on Coll. *Professional:* business, music, teacher education

History: Established 1902; chartered and incorporated as The Boy's Industrial School 1903; changed name to The Berry College 1908; opened The Martha Berry School for Girls 1909; both institutions incorporated as The Berry Schools 1917; opened Berry Junior College and offered first instruction at postsecondary level 1926; awarded first degree (associate) 1928; added upper division curriculum and changed name to The Berry Schools and College 1930; added graduate curriculum 1971; Berry Academy closed and name changed to Berry College 1983. *See* Tracy Byers, *Martha Berry, The Sunday Lady of Possum Trot* (New York, N.Y.; Putnam, 1932); Harnett Kane and Inez Henry, *Miracle in the Mountains* (Garden City, NY: Doubleday and Company, 1956), and Evelyn Hoge Pendley, *A Lady I Loved* (Doraville, GA.: Foote and Davies, 1966) for further information.

Institutional Structure: *Governing board:* The Board of Trustees. Representation: 19 trustees, including 4 alumni. All voting. *Composition of institution:* Administrators 13 men / 5 women. Academic affairs headed by president and provost. Management/business/finances directed by vice president for finance. Full-time instructional faculty 139. Academic governance bodies: Academic Council and Graduate Council, each meet an average of 8 times per year.

Calendar: Semesters. Academic year Aug. to May. Freshmen admitted Aug., Jan., June. Degrees conferred and formal commencements in May, Dec. Summer session of from June to July.

Characteristics of Freshmen: 1,664 applicants (636 men, 1,228 women). 76% of applicants admitted. 36.4% of admitted students enrolled full-time.

79% (408 students) submitted SAT scores; 21% (106 students) submitted ACT scores. *25th percentile:* SAT I Verbal 540, SAT I Math 530; ACT Composite 24, ACT English 24, ACT Math 22. *75th percentile:* SAT I Verbal 640, SAT I Math 620; ACT Composite 28, ACT English 29, ACT Math 27.

47% of entering freshmen expected to graduate within 5 years. 82.5% of freshmen from Georgia. Freshmen from 17 states and 4 foreign countries.

Admission: Rolling admissions plan. Early decision available; need not limit application to Berry. Early acceptance available. *Requirements:* Either graduation from accredited secondary school with 20 units, which must include 4 English, 4 mathematics (algebra I and II, geometry or trigonometry, 4th year of math higher than algebra II), 3 social studies, 3 natural sciences, 2 foreign language; or GED. Admission to the freshman class is based upon probable success as can be determined from high school grades and college entrance test scores combined to derive a predicted GPA for the first year. *Entrance tests:* College Board SAT or ACT. *For transfer students:* 2.5 minimum GPA; no D grades accepted in transfer; a maximum of 67 semester hours of credit including CLEP and other credit by examination is transferable from accredited two-year colleges; correspondence work from other accredited institution to a maximum of 9 semester hours may be allowed in satisfaction of degree requirements.

College credit and advanced placement for postsecondary-level work completed in secondary school, College Board CLEP, credit for International Baccalaureate, and for extrainstitutional learning on basis of ACE *2006 Guide to the Evaluation of Educational Experiences in the Armed Services.* Tutoring available.

Degree Requirements: *For all baccalaureate degrees:* 124 hours; last 30 semester hours in residence; 2.0 GPA; complete general education core requirement in addition to major and/or minor requirements. *For all undergraduate degrees:* 2.0 GPA; exit writing competency examination; exit major field examinations; demonstration of basic competencies in the use of computers and related information technology resources; 3 hours physical education; general education and distribution requirements; English 101 and 102 (or satisfactory completion of writing competency examination for transfer students if 102 taken elsewhere).

Fulfillment of some degree requirements and exemption from some beginning courses possible by passing departmental examinations and College Board CLEP. *Grading system:* A–F; high pass; pass; fail; withdraw (carries time limit, deadline after which pass-fail is appended to withdraw); WS (withdrawal from institution); incomplete.

Distinctive Educational Programs: *For undergraduates:* Cooperative education and internships. Dual-degree programs in engineering with Georgia Institute of Technology and Mercer University, in nursing with Emory University. Interdisciplinary programs may be individually arranged. Summer study abroad programs in Austria, Spain, and other countries. Short courses in Ireland and Italy. Junior semester or year abroad programs in France, Germany, and other western European countries. Summer study in marine science in cooperation with the Gulf Coast Laboratory. *For graduate students:* Flexible meeting places and schedules.

Degrees Conferred: 410 *baccalaureate*; 26 *master's*. Bachelor's degrees awarded in top five disciplines: business, management, marketing, and related support services 67; social sciences 49; communication, journalism, and related programs 42; psychology 33; biological and biomedical sciences 32.

Fees and Other Expenses: *Full-time tuition per academic year 2004–05:* $16,240. Contact the college for graduate tuition/fees. *Books and supplies:* $800. *Room and board per academic year:* $6,450.

Financial Aid: Aid from institutionally generated funds is provided on the basis of academic merit, financial need, athletic ability, other criteria. Institution has a Program Participation Agreement with the U.S. Department of Education for eligible students to receive Pell Grants and other federal aid.

Financial aid to full-time, first-time undergraduate students: 17% received federal grants averaging $3,509; 86% state/local grants averaging $2,895; 82% institutional grants averaging $6,688; 36% loans averaging $2,635.

Departments and Teaching Staff: Campbell School of Business *professors* 3, *associate professors* 5, *assistant professors* 10, *instructors* 1, *part-time teachers* 3; School of Education and Human Sciences 4, 5, 11, 0, 37; Evans School of Humanities and Social Sciences 8, 9, 32, 0, 15; School of Mathematical and Natural Sciences 4, 8, 31, 1, 4.

Total instructional faculty: 156.94 FTE. Student-to-faculty ratio: 12.4:1. Degrees held by full-time faculty: Doctorate 77%, master's 23%. 77% of faculty hold terminal degrees.

Enrollment: Total enrollment 2,045. Undergraduate 1,895 (36.7% men, 63.3% women).

Characteristics of Student Body: *Ethnic/racial makeup:* Black non-Hispanic: 2.6%; American Indian Alaska Native: .1%; Asian or Pacific Islander: .9%; Hispanic: .8%; White non-Hispanic: 91.3%; unknown: 2.3%.

International Students: 38 nonresident aliens enrolled fall 2003. Students from Europe, Asia, Central and South America, Australia. Social and cultural programs available to aid students whose native language is not English: International Club for foreign students. No financial aid specifically designated for international students.

Student Life: On-campus residence halls house 72% of student body. Dormitories for men only constitute 40% of such space, for women only 60%. *Intercollegiate athletics:* men only: basketball, cross-country, golf, soccer, tennis, track; women only: basketball, cross-country, golf, soccer, tennis, track. *Special regulations:* Registered cars permitted to park in designated areas only. *Special services:* Medical services, campus buses. *Student publications: Cabin Log*, a yearbook; *Campus Carrier*, a weekly newspaper; *Ramifications*, a biannual literary magazine. *Surrounding community:* Mount Berry and Rome, Georgia. Atlanta, 65 miles from campus, is nearest metropolitan area.

Library Collections: 707,500 volumes including bound books, serial backfiles, electronic documents, and government documents not in separate collections. Online catalog. Current serial subscriptions: 1,595. 575,000 microform items; 5,000 audiovisual materials. Computer work stations available. Students have access to the Internet at no charge.

Most important holdings include the Martha Berry papers, collection of *Southern Highlander*, published at Berry 1909–66; prints of Andrew Wyeth, limited edition, signed (artist); International Stamp Collection from John Longino.

Buildings and Grounds: Campus area (three locations) 2,800 acres.

Chief Executive Officer: Dr. Scott Colley, President.

Address admission inquiries to Dr. Garreth M. Johnson, Director of Admissions.

Beulah Heights Bible College

892 Berne Street, S.E.
Atlanta, Georgia 30316
Tel: (404) 627-2681   **E-mail:** admissions@beulah.org
Fax: (404) 627-0702   **Internet:** www.beulah.org

Institution Description: Beulah Heights Bible College is owned by the International Pentecostal Church of Christ (IPCC). *Enrollment:* 710. *Degrees awarded:* Associate, baccalaureate.

Accreditation: *National:* ABHE.

History: Beulah Heights Bible College was founded in 1918.

Institutional Structure: *Governing board:* IPCC Executive Committee.

Calendar: Semesters. Academic year Aug. to July.

Characteristics of Freshmen: Average secondary school rank of freshmen men 49th percentile, women 53rd percentile. 100% of applicants accepted. 90% of accepted applicants enrolled.

80% of entering freshmen expected to graduate within 5 years. 90% of freshmen from Georgia. Freshmen from 6 states and 16 foreign countries.

Admission: Graduation from secondary school or GED.

Degree Requirements: Completion of prescribed program.

Degrees Conferred: 41 *associate;* 68 *baccalaureate:* theology and ministerial studies.

Fees and Other Expenses: *Full-time tuition per academic year 2004–05:* $4,540. *Books and supplies:* $500. *Room and board per academic year:* $4,200.

Financial Aid: Aid from institutionally generated funds is provided on the basis of academic merit, financial need, other criteria. Institution has a Program Participation Agreement with the U.S. Department of Education for eligible students to receive Pell Grants and other federal aid.

Financial aid to full-time, first-time undergraduate students: 43% received federal grants averaging $3,086; 47% loans averaging $3,819.

Departments and Teaching Staff: *Professors* 3, *associate professors* 5, *assistant professors* 1, *instructors* 1, *part-time faculty* 24. *Total instructional faculty:* 34. Student-to-faculty ratio: 17:1. Degrees held by full-time faculty: Doctorate 35%, master's 60%, baccalaureate 5%. 35% hold terminal degrees.

Enrollment: Total enrollment 710 (40.6% men, 59.5% women).

Characteristics of Student Body: *Ethnic/racial makeup:* Black non-Hispanic: 59.9%; Asian or Pacific Islander: 1%; Hispanic: 2.1%; White non-Hispanic: 6.9%; American Indian or Alaska Native: .1%.

International Students: 101 nonresident aliens enrolled. Students from Asia, Africa. Social and cultural programs available to aid students whose native language is not English. English as a Second Language Program. Financial aid specifically designated for international students: Scholarships available annually.

Library Collections: Online catalog. 300 Current serial subscriptions. 800 recordings; 4 CD-ROMs. Computer work stations available. Students have access to the Internet at no charge.

Most import special collections include Dr. John Maxwell Resource Center; World Mission Resource Center; Black History.

Chief Executive Officer: Dr. Benson M. Karanja, President.

Address admission inquiries to Jacquelyn B. Armstrong, Director of Admissions

Brenau University

One Centennial Circle
Gainesville, Georgia 30501
Tel: (770) 534-6299   **E-mail:** admissions@brenau.edu
Fax: (770) 534-6114   **Internet:** www.brenau.edu

Institution Description: Brenau University is a private, independent, nonprofit institution. *Enrollment:* 2,067. *Degrees awarded:* Baccalaureate, master's.

Accreditation: *Regional:* SACS-Comm. on Coll. *Professional:* interior design, nursing, occupational therapy, teacher education

History: Established as Georgia Baptist Female Seminary 1878; awarded first degree (baccalaureate) 1879; adopted present name 1900.

Institutional Structure: *Governing board:* Board of Trustees. Representation: 36 trustees (including 9 alumnae). *Composition of institution:* 5 administrators. Academic affairs headed by vice president for academic affairs and provost. Management/business/finances directed by comptroller. Full-time instructional faculty 77.

Calendar: Semesters. Academic year Aug. to May. Freshmen admitted Sept. Formal commencement May. "Maymester" and summer sessions of 2 terms.

Characteristics of Freshmen: 50% of applicants admitted. 15% of admitted students enrolled full-time.

86% (171 students) submitted SAT scores; 32% (64 students) submitted ACT scores. *25th percentile*: SAT Verbal 450, SAT Math 450; ACT Composite 18. *75th percentile*: SAT Verbal 570, SAT Math 540; ACT Composite 22.

44% of entering freshmen expected to graduate within 5 years. 88% of freshmen from Georgia. Freshmen from 13 states and 6 foreign countries.

Admission: Rolling admissions plan. Early acceptance available. *Requirements:* Graduation from accredited secondary school with 16 units, or GED. Recommend 4 units English, 2 college preparatory mathematics, 2 social studies, 1 laboratory science. Additional units recommended for some majors. *Entrance tests:* College Board SAT of ACT composite. For foreign students TOEFL score of 500 or demonstration of proficiency in English through personal interview. *For transfer students:* Statement of honorable withdrawal from previous college or university; maximum transfer credit limited only by residence requirement.

College credit and advanced placement for postsecondary-level work completed in secondary school. College credit for extrainstitutional learning (life experience) on basis of faculty assessment. Developmental courses offered in regular academic year; credit given.

Degree Requirements: 120 semester hours; 2.0 GPA (2.5 in major field). Additional requirements and comprehensives in individual fields of study. Additional requirements for some majors.

Fulfillment of some degree requirements and exemption from some beginning courses possible by passing departmental examinations, College Board CLEP, AP. *Transfer students:* no more than 80 semester hours may be transferred. *Grading system:* A–F; pass-fail; withdraw (carries time limit); incomplete (carries time limit).

Distinctive Educational Programs: Internships. Interdepartmental program in liberal arts studies. Individual majors. Directed independent study. Extensive tutorial services available. Women's College Leadership Development Certificate Programs. Learning disabilities program. Summer program, Brenau in London, is a cooperative program of A.I.F.S. and Richmond College in London. Leadership courses.

Degrees Conferred: 358 *baccalaureate;* 238 *master's;* 44 *education specialist.*

Fees and Other Expenses: *Full-time tuition per academic year 2005–06:* $15,450. Contact the university for graduate and education specialist tuition/fees. *Room and board per academic year:* $8,350.

Financial Aid: Aid from institutionally generated funds is provided on the basis of academic merit, financial need, athletic ability, other criteria. Institution has a Program Participation Agreement with the U.S. Department of Education for eligible students to receive Pell Grants and other federal aid.

Financial aid to full-time, first-time undergraduate students in Women's College: need-based scholarships/grants totaling $6,108,957, self-help $1,219,308, athletic awards $56,900; non-need-based scholarships/grants totaling $1,112,938, self-help $826,183, parent loans $252,898, athletic awards $111,690.

Departments and Teaching Staff: *Total instructional faculty:* 218 (full-time 72, part-time 122; women 122, men 92; members of minority groups 19). Total faculty with doctorate, first-professional, or other terminal degree: 125. Student-to-faculty ratio: 8:1.

Enrollment: Total enrollment 2,067. Undergraduate full-time 87m / 976w, part-time 94m / 345w; graduate full-time 27m / 156w, part-time 88m / 344w.

Characteristics of Student Body: *Ethnic/racial makeup:* number of Black non-Hispanic: 370; American Indian or Alaska Native 8; Asian or Pacific Islander: 20; Hispanic: 33; White non-Hispanic: 929; unknown: 113. *Age distribution:* number under 18: 12; 18–19: 284; 20–21: 219; 22–24: 212; 25–29: 194; 30–34: 189; 35–39: 151; 40–49: 193; 50–64: 45; 65 and over: 1.

International Students: 38 nonresident aliens enrolled fall 2004. No programs available to aid students whose native language is not English. Some financial aid available for qualifying international students.

Student Life: On-campus residence halls, sorority housing, and apartments. *Intercollegiate athletics:* cross-country, softball, soccer, tennis, volleyball. Choral groups, ratio station, television studio, drama/theatre, Student Government. *Student publications: Aurum,* (yearbook); The *Alchemist* (bimonthly student newspaper); *Elixir,* a literary magazine; *Update,* (a weekly newsletter). *Surrounding community:* Gainesville-Hall Country population 145,000; 50 mile northeast of Atlanta.

Library Collections: 73,662 volumes including bound books, serial backfiles, electronic documents, and government documents not in separate collections. Online catalog. Current serial subscriptions: paper, microform, and electronic. 15,772 recordings. 200 computer work stations campus-wide. Students have access to the Internet at no charge.

Most important holdings include Tom Watson Collection of books (mostly historical); archival and rare books collection; Harry Elson Collection of Judaica and

Buildings and Grounds: Campus area 40 acres.

Chief Executive Officer: Dr. Ed Schrader, President.

Address admission inquiries to Christina White, Director of Admissions.

Brewton-Parker College

Highway 280
Mt. Vernon, Georgia 30445-0197
Tel: (912) 583-2241   **E-mail:** admission@bpc.edu
Fax: (912) 583-4498   **Internet:** www.bpc.edu

Institution Description: Brewton-Parker College is a private college offering programs in business, education, liberal arts, and religion. It is affiliated with the Baptist Church. *Enrollment:* 1,136 *Degrees awarded:* Associate, baccalaureate.

Accreditation: *Regional:* SACS-Comm. on Coll.

History: Established as Union Baptist Institute 1904; name changed to Brewton-Parker Institute 1912; offered first instruction at postsecondary level 1923; name changed to Brewton-Parker Junior College 1957; name Brewton-Parker College officially adopted 1978; instituted 4-year program 1984; received full accreditation as 4-year college 1986.

Institutional Structure: *Institutional structure:* Brewton-Parker is owned by the Executive Committee of the Georgia Baptist Convention. The Convention elects a board of trustees that is empowered to operate the college for the Convention. Administrators: president, provost, vice president for enrollment services, vice president for college advancement.

Calendar: Semesters. Academic year Sept. to June. Formal commencement June.

Characteristics of Freshmen: 182 applicants. 117 applicants admitted and enrolled.

86% (177 students) submitted SAT scores; 20% (40 students) submitted ACT scores. *25th percentile*: SAT Verbal 390, SAT Math 400; ACT Composite 17, ACT English 16, ACT Math 16. *75th percentile*: SAT I Verbal 510, SAT I Math 500; ACT Composite 21, ACT English 22, ACT Math 20.

30% of entering freshmen expected to graduate within 5 years. 90% of freshmen from Georgia. Freshmen from 13 states and 8 foreign countries.

Admission: Open admissions policy. Rolling application dates. Early acceptance, transfer, and transient options available. *Requirements:* Graduation from an accredited high school or GED (exam score with a minimum total score 225 and a minimum score of 40 on each section of the exam). High school cumulative GPA of 2.0 indicating credit for a minimum of 13 academic units: English 4 units, mathematics 3 units, natural sciences 3 units, social sciences 3 units. SAT or ACT score.

Degree Requirements: Completion of prescribed curriculum.

Distinctive Educational Programs: Day, evening programs. Classes offered at main campus, and 8 satellite campus locations. Developmental studies and study skills programs. Teacher education and preprofessional programs.

Degrees Conferred: 47 *associate;* 162 *baccalaureate:* biological/life sciences 2, business/marketing 34, education 63, English 1, liberal arts/general studies 10, parks and recreation 6, philosophy/religion/theology 7, psychology 25, social sciences and history 10, visual and performing arts 1.

Fees and Other Expenses: *Full-time tuition per academic year 2004–05:* $11,500. *Required fees:* $1,100. *Room and board per academic year:* $5,200.

Financial Aid: Aid from institutionally generated funds is proved on the basis of academic merit, financial need, athletic ability, other criteria.

Financial aid to full-time, first-time undergraduate students: need-based scholarships/grants totaling $6,107,307, self-help $3,970,137, parent loans $235,054, athletic awards $449,358; non-need-based scholarships/grants totaling $643,361, self-help $447,624, parent loans $281,748, athletic awards $221,551.

Departments and Teaching Staff: *Total instructional faculty:* 115 (full-time 52, part-time 63; women 64, men 51). Total faculty with doctorate, first-professional, or other terminal degree: 38. Student-to-faculty ratio: 9:1.

Enrollment: Total enrollment 1,136. Undergraduate full-time 333 men / 532 women, part-time 79m / 192w.

Characteristics of Student Body: *Ethnic and racial makeup:* number of: Black non-Hispanic: 214; American Indian or Alaska Native: 1; Asian or Pacific Islander: 4; Hispanic: 21; White non-Hispanic: 714; unknown: 140. *Age distribution:* number under 18: 42; 18–19: 296; 20–21: 29: 22–24: 161; 25–29: 134; 30–34: 86; 35–39: 71; 40–49: 80; 50–64: 22; 65 and over: 1.

International Students: 17 nonresident aliens enrolled fall 2004. 2 students from Europe, 2 Asia, 6 Central and South America, 3 Canada, 2 Australia, 4 other. No programs available to aid students whose native language is not English. No financial aid specifically designated for international students.

Student Life: Student support includes orientation program, advising, counseling and guidance, health services, career planning and placement services, student retention and support center, veterans affairs services, social functions, intramural athletics, athletics, and a wide range of service, cultural, religious, musical, athletic, and academic-oriented clubs and organizations. On-campus residence halls house 33% of the student body. Student activities include usage of: track, softball, baseball, and soccer fields; tennis courts; 5-acre lake; swimming pool; general purpose recreation field.

Publications: *The Coronet* (yearbook); *The Lamp* (quarterly magazine).

Library Collections: 77,429 volumes including bound books, serial backfiles, electronic documents, and government documents not in separate collections. Online catalog. Current serial subscriptions: 209 paper, 98 microform. 2,455 recordings; 1,169 compact discs. 8 computer work stations. Students have access to the Internet at no charge. Total budget for books, periodicals, audiovisual materials, microforms 2004–05: $254,900.

Most important special collections include Brewton-Parker College Archives; Baptist Records Collection.

Buildings and Grounds: 280-acre campus with 26 buildings.

Chief Executive Officer: Dr. David R. Smith, President.

Address admission inquiries to Stephanie Whaley, Director of Admissions.

Clark Atlanta University

223 James P. Brawley Drive
Atlanta, Georgia 30314
Tel: (404) 880-8000
Fax: (404) 880-6174

Institution Description: Clark Atlanta University is a private institution affiliated with the United Methodist Church. *Enrollment:* 4,915. *Degrees awarded:* Baccalaureate, master's, doctorate.

Accreditation: *Regional:* SACS-Comm. on Coll. *Professional:* business, health information administration, librarianship, public administration, social work, teacher education

History: Founded in 1988 from the merger of Clark College and Atlanta University. Atlanta University was established 1865; chartered 1867; offered first instruction at postsecondary level 1869; awarded first degree (baccalaureate) 1876. *See* Clarence A. Bacote, *The Story of Atlanta University* (Princeton, N.J.: Princeton University Press, 1969) for further information. Clark University was established 1869; chartered and incorporated 1877; offered first instruction at postsecondary level 1879; awarded first degree (baccalaureate) 1883; became Clark College 1940.

Institutional Structure: *Governing board:* Board of Trustees. Representation: 33 trustees, including president of the university, 1 full-time instructional faculty member, 9 trustees emeriti, 1 alumnus. 3 ex officio. 30 voting. *Composition of institution:* Administrators 9 men / 4 women. Academic affairs headed by vice president of academic affairs. Management/business/finances directed by vice president of resources management. Academic governance bodies, University Senate and Academic Council, each meet an average of 5 times per year.

Calendar: Semesters. Academic year Sept. to May. Degrees conferred and formal commencements May, July. Summer session from early June to late July.

Admission: Rolling admissions plan. For fall acceptance, apply no later than Aug. 1 of year of enrollment. Early acceptance available. *Requirements:* Graduation from accredited secondary school or GED. Recommend 4 units English; 1 foreign language; 1 each in mathematics, natural science, social studies; 5 electives. Minimum GPA 2.0. *Entrance tests:* College Board SAT or ACT composite. *For transfer students:* Credit evaluated on individual basis. *Graduate school requirements:* Graduation from approved college or university with satisfactory evidence of character and other qualifications. Minimum GPA 2.5–3.0. *Entrance tests:* GMAT, GRE, or Miller Analogies.

Tutoring available. Noncredit remedial courses offered in summer session and regular academic year.

Degree Requirements: Completion of prescribed curriculum. *Grading system:* A–F; pass; withdraw (deadline after which pass-fail is appended to withdraw); incomplete.

Distinctive Educational Programs: Work-experience programs. Flexible meeting places and schedules, including weekend and evening classes. Accelerated degree programs. Special facilities for using telecommunications in the classroom. Interinstitutional program in American studies. Doctor of Arts program in humanities. Facilities and programs for independent research, including honors programs, individual majors.

Degrees Conferred: 417 *baccalaureate*; 179 *master's*; 10 *doctorate*. Bachelor's degrees awarded in top five disciplines: business, management, marketing, and related support services 116; communication, journalism, and related programs 83; psychology 34; biological and biomedical sciences 34; security and protective services 24.

Fees and Other Expenses: *Full-time tuition per academic year 2004–05:* $12,936. *Room and board per academic year:* $6,816. *Books and supplies:* $1,000.

Financial Aid: Aid from institutionally generated funds is awarded on the basis of academic merit, financial need. Institution has a Program Participation Agreement with the U.S. Department of Education for eligible students to receive Pell Grants and other federal aid.

Financial aid to full-time, first-time undergraduate students: 63% received federal grants averaging $2,849; 42% state/local grants averaging $1,717; 38% institutional grants averaging $4,825; 70% loans averaging $2,400.

Departments and Teaching Staff: *Total instructional faculty:* 246. Degrees held by full-time faculty: 78% hold terminal degrees.

Enrollment: Total enrollment 4,915. Undergraduate 3,920 (29% men, 71% women).

Characteristics of Student Body: *Ethnic/racial makeup:* Black non-Hispanic: 94.3%; Asian or Pacific Islander: .1%; Hispanic: .2%; White non-Hispanic: .2%; unknown: 5.3%.

International Students: 54 nonresident aliens enrolled. Programs available to aid students whose native language is not English: noncredit course in English as a Second Language.

Student Life: On-campus residence halls house 15% of student body. Dormitories for men only constitute 40% of such space, for women only 60%. *Special regulations:* Cars must be registered. *Special services:* Medical services. *Student publications: Augsba Review,* a School of Business newsletter.

Library Collections: 742,300 volumes. 836,500 microforms; 1,420 periodicals. Online catalog. Students have access to online information retrieval services and the Internet.

Most important holdings include Henry P. Slaughter and Countee Cullen Memorial Collection; Thayer Lincoln Collection.

Buildings and Grounds: Campus area 115 acres.

Chief Executive Officer: Dr. Walter D. Braodnax, President.

Address admission inquiries to Julius Dodds, Director of Admissions.

School of Arts and Sciences

Degree Programs Offered: *Master's* in Afro-American studies, biology, chemistry, criminal justice administration, economics, English, history, mathematical sciences, physics, political science, public administration, Romance languages, social science, sociology and anthropology; *doctorate* in biology, chemistry, political science.

School of Business Administration

Degree Programs Offered: *Master's* in accounting, finance, management and organizational behavior, marketing, operations management, transportation management.

Distinctive Educational Programs: Internships. Career programs available in several concentrations. International Business Institute cosponsored by the Atlanta Chamber of Commerce.

School of Education

Degree Programs Offered: *Master's* in administration and policy studies, curriculum, foundations of education; *doctorate* in administration and policy studies, psychological services. Specialist certificates in education also given.

Distinctive Educational Programs: Dual-degree program in cooperation with the Interdenominational Theological Center leading to master's degrees in education and religious studies. Other cooperative degree programs with the School of Arts and Sciences (Department of Sociology and Anthropology). *Other distinctive programs:* Fifth-year Program enables undergraduates with senior status to work concurrently on master's degree in education while completing the baccalaureate.

School of Library and Information Studies

Degree Programs Offered: *Master's.* Specialist certificates in library service also given.

Distinctive Educational Programs: Internship programs with Lawrence Livermore Laboratory, Georgia Institute of Technology, U.S. Labor Department, Aeromedical Research Laboratory of Fort Rucker, Library of Congress, National Library of Medicine.

Clayton College and State University

5900 North Lee Street
Morrow, Georgia 30260-0285
Tel: (770) 961-3400   **E-mail:** admissions@clayton.edu
Fax: (770) 961-3752   **Internet:** www.clayton.edu

Institution Description: Clayton College and State University, formerly known as Clayton State College, is a public institution. *Enrollment:* 5,954. *Degrees awarded:* Associate, baccalaureate.

Accreditation: *Regional:* SACS. *Professional:* business, dental hygiene, nursing, teacher education

History: Established in 1969 as Clayton Junior College; became a senior college in 1986; awarded first baccalaureate degree 1989; became a university in 1996.

Institutional Structure: Governed by the Board of Regents of the University System of Georgia and headed by president. Academic affairs led by vice president for academic affairs. Management/business/finances head by vice president of operations.

Calendar: Semesters. Academic year late Sept. to mid-June. Degrees conferred May, Aug., Dec. Formal commencement May and Dec. Summer session from mid-May to early Aug.

Characteristics of Freshmen: 58.7% of applicants admitted. 60.7% of admitted students enrolled full-time.

65% (625 students) submitted SAT scores; 18% (172 students) submitted ACT scores. *25th percentile:* SAT Verbal 45, SAT Math 440; ACT Composite 17, ACT English 17, ACT Math 17. *75th percentile:* SAT Verbal 540, SAT Math 540; ACT Composite 21, ACT English 21, ACT Math 21.

11.8% of entering freshmen expected to graduate within 5 years. 90.5% of freshmen from Georgia. Freshmen from 16 states and 33 foreign countries.

Admission: Rolling admissions. Apply as early as one year in advance, but no later than one month prior to start of quarter to be admitted.

Degree Requirements: Completion of prescribed curriculum.

Distinctive Educational Programs: Clayton State College offers a variety of programs. Four-year degrees include biology, communication and media studies, criminal justice, history, integrative studies, middle level education, music, psychology and human services, allied health administration, dental hygiene, health care management, health and fitness management, nursing, administrative management, technology management, business, mathematics, and information technology.

Flexible schedules allow most students to take day or evening classes. Tutoring and developmental studies available. Technical programs include AAS in aviation maintenance technology. Continuing education services and facilities.

ROTC: Army, Air Force, Navy in cooperation with Georgia Institute of Technology.

Degrees Conferred: 309 *associate;* 506 *baccalaureate:* biological/life sciences 12; business/marketing 180; communications/communication technologies 10; computer and information sciences 25; health professions and related sciences 116; liberal arts/general studies 26; psychology 57; visual and performing arts 6.

Fees and Other Expenses: *Full-time tuition per academic year 2004–05:* resident $2,322, out-of-state student $9,290. *Required fees:* $480.

Financial Aid: Aid from institutionally generated funds is provided on the basis of academic merit, financial need, athletic ability.

Financial aid to full-time, first-time undergraduate students: need-based scholarships/grants totaling $2,442,518, self-help $3,842,651; non-need-based scholarships/grants totaling $2,891,789, self-help $3,593,041, parent loans $96,407, tuition waivers $21,270, athletic awards $103,950.

Departments and Teaching Staff: *Professors* 22, *associate professors* 26, *assistant professors* 87, *instructors* 26, *part-time faculty* 138. *Total instructional faculty* 299. Total faculty with doctorate, first-professional, or other terminal degree: 145. Student-to-faculty ratio: 19:1.

Enrollment: Total enrollment 5,954. Undergraduate full-time 963 men / 2,063 women, part-time 815m / 2,113w. *Transfer students:* in-state 2,832; from out-of-state 3,104.

Characteristics of Student Body: *Ethnic and racial makeup:* number of Black non-Hispanic: 2,847; American Indian or Alaska Native: 22; Asian or Pacific Islander: 251; Hispanic: 181; White non-Hispanic: 2,251; unknown: 381. *Age distribution:* number under 18: 27; 18–19: 814; 20–21: 865; 22–24: 1,075; 25–29: 936; 30–34: 813; 35–39: 573; 40–49: 639; 50–64: 52.

International Students: 121 nonresident aliens enrolled fall 2004. 23 students from Europe, 13 Asia, 11 Central and South America, 36 Africa, 7 Canada, 2 Australia, 29 other. Programs available to aid students whose native language is not English: social, cultural. No financial aid specifically designated for international students.

Student Life: Organizations include student government association, cultural and career clubs. Contemporary and classical cultural activities. *Intercollegiate athletics:* basketball for men and women, golf, soccer. Intramural athletics include tennis, softball, volleyball. *Student publications: The Bent Tree,* a monthly newspaper; *Cygnet* a yearly literary magazine.

Library Collections: 110,377 volumes. 750 current periodical subscriptions. Online catalog. Students have access to online information retrieval services and the Internet. Total 2004–05 budget for materials and operations: $227,000.

Extensive collection on Southern history; college archives.

Buildings and Grounds: Campus area 163 acres. *New buildings:* Music Education Building; University Center.

Chief Executive Officer: Dr. Thomas Harden, President.

Address admission inquiries to Jeff Hammer, Director of Admissions.

Columbia Theological Seminary

701 Columbia Drive
Decatur, Georgia 30030
Tel: (404) 378-8821   **E-mail:** admissions@ctheos.edu
Fax: (404) 377-9696   **Internet:** www.ctheos.edu

Institution Description: Columbia Theological Seminary is a graduate seminary of the Presbyterian Church (U.S.A.). *Enrollment:* 290. *Degrees awarded:* Master's, doctorate, first-professional.

Accreditation: *Regional:* SACS-Comm. on Coll. *National:* ATS. *Professional:* theology

Calendar: Semesters (4-1-4 plan). Academic year Sept. to May.

Admission: *Requirements:* Baccalaureate degree from an accredited university or its equivalent; references; church endorsement; autobiographical statement.

Degree Requirements: Completion of prescribed curriculum; requirements vary by program.

Degrees Conferred: 44 *first-professional:* master of divinity; 15 *master's:* theology and ministerial studies; 25 *doctorate:* theology and ministerial studies.

Fees and Other Expenses: *Full-time tuition per academic year 2004–05:* $7,110. Contact the seminary for other information.

Financial Aid: Aid from institutionally generated funds is provided on the basis of academic merit and financial need. Financial assistance is available in the form of Pell Grants, College Work-Study, Veterans Administration Benefits, National Direct Student Loans, Supplemental Education Opportunity Grants (SEOG), Stafford Loans, other federal aid programs.

Departments and Teaching Staff: *Total instructional faculty:* 27.

Enrollment: Total enrollment 290 (51% men, 49% women).

Characteristics of Student Body: *Ethnic/racial makeup:* Black non-Hispanic: 8.3%; Asian or Pacific Islander: 3.1%; Hispanic: 1%; White non-Hispanic: 71.7%; unknown: 8.6%.

International Students: 21 nonresident aliens enrolled fall 2003. Students from Europe, Asia, Central and South America, Africa. Programs available to aid students whose native language is not English: English as a Second Language Program.

Student Life: Residence hall housing available for single men and women; additional on-campus housing for married students.

Library Collections: 175,000 volumes.

Buildings and Grounds: Campus area 60 acres.

Chief Executive Officer: Dr. Laura S. Mendenhall, President.

Address admission inquiries to Rev. Ann Clay Adams, Director of Admissions.

Columbus State University

4225 University Avenue
Columbus, Georgia 31907-5645
Tel: (706) 568-2001   **E-mail:** admissions@colstate.edu
Fax: (706) 568-2123   **Internet:** www.colstate.edu

Institution Description: Columbus State University was formerly known as Columbus College. *Enrollment:* 7,224. *Degrees awarded:* Associate, baccalaureate, master's.

Academic offerings subject to approval by statewide coordinating bodies. Budget subject to approval by state governing boards.

Accreditation: *Regional:* SACS-Comm. on Coll. *Professional:* business, counseling, dental hygiene, music, nursing, occupational therapy, teacher education, theatre

History: Established as a junior college, Columbus College was chartered and offered first instruction at postsecondary level 1958; awarded first degree (associate) 1960 added upper-division program 1966; graduate program 1973; attained university status and adopted present name 1996.

Institutional Structure: *Governing board:* Board of Regents, University System of Georgia. Representation: 15 regents. All voting. *Composition of institution:* Administrators 26 men / 6 women (with faculty rank). Academic affairs headed by vice president for academic affairs. Management/business/finances directed by vice president for business and finance. Full-time instructional faculty 225. Academic governance body, Council of Deans, meets an average of 50 times per year.

Calendar: Semesters. Academic year Aug. to June. Freshmen admitted Aug., Jan., Mar., June. Degrees conferred and formal commencements June, Aug. Summer session June to Aug.

Characteristics of Freshmen: 83% (939 students) submitted SAT scores; 27% (299 students) submitted ACT scores. *25th percentile*: SAT Verbal 440, SAT Math 430; ACT Composite 17; ACT English 17, ACT Math 17. *75th percentile*: SAT Verbal 550, SAT Math 540; ACT Composite 22, ACT English 22, ACT Math 21.

23% of entering freshmen expected to graduate within 5 years.

Admission: Rolling admissions plan. Apply no later than 4 weeks before registration. Early acceptance available. *Requirements:* Either graduation from accredited secondary school or GED. Minimum of 4 units English, 3 mathematics, 3 social studies, 3 science, 1 fine arts elective unit. Additional requirements for some programs. *Entrance tests:* Recentered SAT scores: SAT 430 (v), 400 (M); recentered ACT accepted; TOEFL or satisfactory completion of approved English language program for international applicants whose native language is not English. *For transfer students:* Student must have a 1.8 GPA if transferring less than 30 semester hours or 1.9 GPA if over 30 semester hours.

College credit and advanced placement for postsecondary-level work completed in secondary school. College credit for extrainstitutional learning on basis of ACE *2006 Guide to the Evaluation of Educational Experiences in the Armed Services* and CLEP. Tutoring available. Noncredit developmental courses offered in summer session and regular academic year.

Degree Requirements: *For all associate degrees:* 63 semester hours. *For all baccalaureate degrees:* 123 semester hours; comprehensives in some individual fields of study. *For all undergraduate degrees:* 2.0 GPA and 45 hours in residence for most majors; 3 hours physical education; distribution requirements; Regents Test of Reading and Writing, tests on or courses in U.S. and Georgia constitutions and histories. Additional requirements for some programs.

Fulfillment of some degree requirements and exemption from some beginning courses possible by passing College Board CLEP. *Grading system:* A–F; pass-fail; withdraw (deadline after which pass-fail is appended to withdraw); incomplete (deadline after which A–F is assigned); K (credit by examination).

Distinctive Educational Programs: *For undergraduates:* High school joint enrollment, pre-professional programs. Internships. Off-campus center (at Fort Benning, less than 30 miles away from main institution). Dual-degree program in engineering with Georgia Institute of Technology. Cooperative associate programs in data processing, secretarial science, and electronic technology with Columbus Area Vocational-Technical School. University System of Georgia International Intercultural Studies Program in Spain, France, Germany, and Canada (Quebec). *Available to all students:* Evening classes. Individual majors.

ROTC: Army.

Degrees Conferred: 31 *associate*; 585 *baccalaureate*; 265 *master's*. Bachelor's degrees awarded in top five disciplines: business, management, marketing, and related support services 132; education 79; computer and information sciences and support services 64; English language and literature/letters 53; security and protective services 44.

Fees and Other Expenses: *Full-time tuition per academic year 2004–05:* in-state resident undergraduate $2,808, out-of-state students $9,776; contact the university for current graduate tuition/fees. *Books and supplies:* $800. *Room and board per academic year:* $5,360.

Financial Aid: Aid from institutionally generated funds is provided on the basis of academic merit, financial need. Institution has a Program Participation Agreement with the U.S. Department of Education for eligible students to receive Pell Grants and other federal aid.

Financial aid to full-time, first-time undergraduate students: need-based scholarships/grants totaling $2,896,634, self-help $8,766,206, parent loans $509,215; non-need-based scholarships/grants totaling $3,735,746, self-help $9,721,588, athletic awards $323,350.

Departments and Teaching Staff: *Total instructional faculty:* 390 (full-time 202, part-time 188; women 199, men 191; members of minority groups 56). Total faculty with doctorate, first-professional, or other terminal degree: 191. Student-to-faculty ratio: 19:1.

Enrollment: Total enrollment 7,224. Undergraduate full-time 1,571 men / 2,628 women, part-time 786m / 1,315w; graduate full-time 88m 165w, part-time 307m / 364w.

Characteristics of Student Body: *Ethnic/racial makeup:* number of Black non-Hispanic: 1,901; American Indian or Alaska Native: 23; Asian or Pacific Islander: 122; Hispanic: 223; White non-Hispanic: 3,728; unknown: 219.

International Students: 84 nonresident aliens enrolled fall 2004. No programs available to aid students whose native language is not English. No financial aid specifically designated for international students.

Student Life: On-campus apartment-style housing. *Intercollegiate athletics:* men only: baseball, basketball, cross-country, golf, soccer, tennis; women only: cross-country, softball, tennis. *Special regulations:* Cars must have parking permits. *Special services:* Medical services, accessibility for handicapped (includes on-campus transportation), counseling and placement, Speech Clinic, Academic Support Center, state-of-the-art student computer labs. *Student publications: The Saber*, a weekly newspaper. *Surrounding community:* Columbus population 180,000. Atlanta, 110 miles from campus, is nearest metropolitan area. Served by airport 1 mile from campus.

Library Collections: 265,000 volumes. 224,536 microforms; 1,426 periodicals. Access to online information retrieval systems. Computer work stations available. Students have access to the Internet and online information retrieval services.

Most important holdings include Columbus, Georgia/Chattahoochee Valley Collection; government documents collections; Congressman Jack Brinkley's papers.

Buildings and Grounds: Campus area 135 acres.

Chief Executive Officer: Dr. Frank D. Brown, President.

Address admission inquiries to Susan Lovell, Director of Admissions.

Covenant College

14949 Scenic Highway
Lookout Mountain, Georgia 30750
Tel: (706) 820-1560   **E-mail:** admissions@covenant.edu
Fax: (706) 820-2165   **Internet:** www.covenant.edu

Institution Description: Covenant College is a private college affiliated with the Presbyterian Church in America. *Enrollment:* 1,330. *Degrees awarded:* Associate, baccalaureate, master's.

Member of Christian College Coalition and the Council of Independent Colleges.

Accreditation: *Regional:* SACS-Comm. on Coll.

History: Established, incorporated, and offered first instruction at postsecondary level 1955; first degree (baccalaureate) 1956; master of education program added 1991.

Institutional Structure: *Governing board:* Board of Trustees of Covenant College. Extrainstitutional representation: 28 trustees, all voting. *Composition of institution:* Administrators 8 men. Academic affairs headed by vice president for academic affairs and dean of faculty. Management/business/finances directed by business manager. Full-time instructional faculty 49. Academic governance body, the faculty, meets weekly.

Calendar: Semesters. Academic year Aug. to May. Freshmen admitted Aug., Jan. Degrees conferred and formal commencement May.

Characteristics of Freshmen: 66% of applicants admitted. 37% of admitted students enrolled full-time.

77% (201 students) submitted SAT scores; 47% (123 students) submitted ACT scores. *25th percentile*: SAT Verbal 530, SAT Math 510; ACT Composite 21, ACT English 22, ACT Math 19. *75th percentile*: SAT Verbal 660, SAT Math 620; ACT Composite 29, ACT English 30, ACT Math 26.

66% of entering freshmen expected to graduate within 5 years. 23% of freshmen from Georgia. Freshmen from 39 states.

Admission: Rolling admissions plan. For fall acceptance, apply no later than May 1; for spring acceptance, no later than Nov. 1. *Requirements:* 16 secondary school units, or GED. 4 units in English, 2 foreign language, 2 history, 3 mathematics, 2 natural science, 2 history and social studies, and 3–4 electives. Minimum GPA 2.5. Profession of Christian faith. *Entrance tests:* College Board SAT composite score 1000 or ACT composite score 21. *For transfer students:* 2.0 minimum GPA; from 2-year institution 70 semester hours maximum transfer credit; from 4-year institution 96 hours maximum transfer credit.

College credit given for courses in which a 3, 4, or 5 is scored on Advanced Placement Exams for maximum of 11 credits.

Degree Requirements: *For all undergraduate degrees:* 2.0 GPA; 30 hours in residence; daily chapel attendance; 1 hour first aid. *For all associate degrees:* minimum 62 credit hours; 1 hour health and physical education; 1 year in residence. *For all baccalaureate degrees:* minimum 126 credit units (at least 25 upper division); 1 year in residence; no grade below C- in the major or minor; completion of last 30 units at Covenant. *Grading system:* A–F; pass-fail; withdraw (deadline after which pass-fail is appended to withdraw); incomplete; repeat (erases previous grade).

Distinctive Educational Programs: Work-experience programs. Evening classes. Dual-degree programs in chemistry, engineering, and mathematics with Georgia Institute of Technology. Major in interdisciplinary studies. Preprofessional programs in law, medicine, nursing, and preministerial curriculum. Facilities and programs for independent research. Study abroad in China, Slovak Republic, France, Germany, Kenya, Taiwan. *Other distinctive programs:* Quest Program for working adults (degree in organizational management). Students may receive up to 3 units of credit for work done in connection with a variety of summer service programs sponsored by Mission to the World, the foreign missions agency of the Presbyterian Church in America.

Degrees Conferred: 194 *baccalaureate:* biological/life sciences 9, business/ marketing 12, computer and information sciences 6, education 14, health professions and related sciences 8, interdisciplinary studies 11, mathematics 1, philosophy/religion/theology 19, psychology 19, social sciences and history 49, other 21.

Fees and Other Expenses: *Full-time tuition per academic year 2004–05:* $18,750. *Required fees:* $570. *Room and board per academic year:* $5,600.

Financial Aid: Aid from institutionally generated funds is provided on the basis of academic merit, financial need, athletic ability, other criteria. Institution has a Program Participation Agreement with the U.S. Department of Education for eligible students to receive Pell Grants and other federal aid.

Financial aid to full-time, first-time undergraduate students: need-based scholarships/grants totaling $6,691,812, self-help $2,904,950, parent loans 725,569, athletic awards $402,142; non-need-based scholarships/grants totaling $1,552,002, self-help $201,661, parent loans $257,617, athletic awards $169,900.

Departments and Teaching Staff: *Professors* 25, *associate professors* 23, *assistant professors* 13, *part-time faculty* 17. *Total instructional faculty:* 78 (full-time 61, part-time 17; women 14, men 64; members of minority groups 2). Total faculty with doctorate, first-professional, or other terminal degree: 56. Student-to-faculty ratio: 16:1. 2 faculty members awarded sabbaticals 2004–05.

Enrollment: Total enrollment 1,310. Undergraduate full-time 486 men / 729 women, part-time 25m / 18w; graduate full-time 25m / 43w, part-time 4m / 3w.

Characteristics of Student Body: *Ethnic/racial makeup:* Number of: Black non-Hispanic: 15; American Indian or Alaska Native: 5; Asian or Pacific Islander: 11; Hispanic: 19; White non-Hispanic: 1,100; unknown: 12.

International Students: 9 nonresident aliens enrolled fall 2004. Social and cultural programs available for students whose native language is not English. No financial aid specifically designated for international students.

Student Life: 79% of student body life in on-campus residence halls or student apartments. Dormitories for men constitute 41% of on-campus living accommodations; for women only 53%. 21% of student body live off campus in apartments and houses. *Intercollegiate athletics:* men only: basketball, cross-country; women only: basketball, cross-country, volleyball. Variety of intramural sports for men and women. *Special regulations:* Cars permitted in specified student parking areas. *Special services:* Learning Resources Center, medical services, career planning and placement services; multi-cultural services. *Student publications: Bagpipe,* a weekly newspaper; *Thorn,* a literary magazine; *Tartan,* a yearbook. *Surrounding community:* Dade County population 13,000. Chattanooga (TN), 10 miles from campus, is nearest metropolitan area. Served by airport 30 miles from campus.

Library Collections: 92,000 volumes including bound books, serial backfiles, electronic documents, and government documents not in separate collections. Online catalog. Current serial subscriptions: 410 paper and microform, 144 electronic. 8 computer work stations. Students have access to the Internet at no charge.

Most important special collection is the John Bunyan Collection.

Buildings and Grounds: Campus area 300 acres.

Chief Executive Officer: Dr. Neil B. Nielson, President.

Address admission inquiries to Beth Nedelsky, Admissions Director.

Emmanuel College

181 Springs Street
Franklin Springs, Georgia 30639
Tel: (706) 245-7226   **E-mail:** athompson@emmanuelcollege.edu
Fax: (706) 245-4424   **Internet:** www.emmanuelcollege.edu

Institution Description: Emmanuel College is a private four-year college affiliated with the Pentecostal Holiness Church. *Enrollment:* 754. *Degrees awarded:* Associate, baccalaureate.

Accreditation: *Regional:* SACS-Comm. on Coll.

History: Established as Franklin Springs Institute 1919; adopted present name 1939.

Calendar: Semesters. Academic year Aug. to May.

Characteristics of Freshmen: 90% of applicants submitted SAT scores; 10% submitted ACT scores. *25th percentile*: SAT Verbal 460, SAT Math 450; *75th percentile*: SAT Verbal 550, SAT Math 550.

30% of entering freshmen expected to graduate within 5 years. 75% of freshman from Georgia. Freshmen from 13 states and 3 foreign countries.

Admission: *Requirements:* High school graduation or GED, SAT/ACT scores.

Degree Requirements: *For all associate degrees:* 65 semester hours; *for all baccalaureate degrees:* 120 semester hours; 2.0 GPA; some higher.

Degrees Conferred: 48 *associate;* 107 *baccalaureate:* biological/life sciences 5, business/marketing 20, communications/communication technologies 7, computer and information sciences 7, education 34, English 2, law/legal studies 3, mathematics 1, parks and recreation 8m philosophy/religion/theology 21, psychology 7.

Fees and Other Expenses: *Full-time tuition per academic year 2004–05:* $9,800. *Required fees:* $350. *Room and board per academic year:* $4,700.

Financial Aid: Aid from institutionally generated funds is provided on the basis of academic merit, financial need, athletic ability, other criteria.

Financial aid to full-time, first-time undergraduate students: need-based scholarships/grants totaling $921,361, self-help $1,713,785; non-need-based scholarships/grants totaling $1,873,101, self-help $1,409,351, parent loans $628,693, tuition waivers $54,278, athletic awards $379,135.

Departments and Teaching Staff: *Total instructional faculty:* 72 (full-time 52, part-time 20; women 22, men 50; members of minority groups 1). Total faculty with doctorate, first-professional, or other terminal degree: 30. Student-to-faculty ratio: 128:1.

Enrollment: Total enrollment 744. Undergraduate Full-time 285 men / 359 women, part-time 39m / 71w.

Characteristics of Student Body: *Ethnic/racial makeup:* number of Black non-Hispanic: 122; Asian or Pacific Islander: 2; Hispanic: 7; American Indian or Alaska Native: 2; White non-Hispanic: 609.

International Students: 4 nonresident aliens enrolled fall 2004. Students from Asia, Africa. No programs available to aid students whose native language is not English. No financial aid specifically designated for international students.

Student Life: On-campus residence halls; apartments available for married students.

Library Collections: 80,000 volumes including bound books, serial backfiles, electronic documents, and government documents not in separate collections. Online and card catalogs. 232 current serial subscriptions. 3,124 microform units. Students have access to the Internet at no charge.

Most important special collections include the Pentecostal Holiness Church Archives and the Holiness/Pentecostal Movement History Collection.

Chief Executive Officer: Dr. David R. Hopkins, President.

Address admission inquiries to Kirk M. Connell, Director of Admissions.

Emory University

1380 South Oxford Road
Atlanta, Georgia 30322
Tel: (404) 727-0765   **E-mail:** admiss@emory.edu
Fax: (404) 727-2761   **Internet:** www.emory.edu

Institution Description: Emory University is a private institution affiliated with the United Methodist Church. *Enrollment:* 11,781. *Degrees awarded:* Baccalaureate, first-professional (public health, law, medicine, theology), master's, doctorate. Associate degrees are granted by Oxford College. Diplomas and certificates are also awarded.

Accreditation: *Regional:* SACS-Comm. on Coll. *Professional:* business, clinical pastoral education, clinical psychology, dietetics, law, medicine, music, nursing-midwifery, nursing, nursing education, ophthalmic medical technology, oral and maxillofacial pathology, physical therapy, psychology internship, public health, radiography, teacher education

History: Established in Oxford as Emory College and offered first instruction at postsecondary level 1836; awarded first degree (baccalaureate) 1839; chartered under present name and moved campus to Atlanta 1915. *See* Thomas H. English, *Emory University, 1915-1965: A Semicentennial* (Atlanta: Higgins-McArthur Company, 1966) for further information.

Institutional Structure: *Governing board:* Emory University Board of Trustees. Representation: 29 trustees, 29 trustees emeriti; 9 alumni. 38 voting. *Composition of institution:* president's cabinet: 8 men / 1 woman. Academic affairs headed by provost. Management/business/finances directed by executive vice president for finance and administration. Full-time instructional faculty 2,543. Academic governance body University Senate and Faculty Council.

Calendar: Semesters. Academic year Aug. to May. Freshmen admitted Aug., Jan., Mar., June. Degrees conferred June, Aug., Dec., Mar. Formal commencement June. Summer session from June to Aug.

Characteristics of Freshmen: 38% of applicants admitted. 95% (1,510 students) submitted SAT scores; 30% (477 students) submitted ACT scores. *25th percentile*: SAT Verbal 640, SAT Math 660; ACT Composite 29. *75th percentile*: SAT Verbal 720, SAT I Math 740; ACT Composite 33.

17% of freshmen from Georgia. Freshmen from 48 states and 20 foreign countries.

Admission: Modified rolling admissions plan. For fall acceptance, apply as early as July 15 of previous year, but not later than Feb. 15 of year of enrollment. Students are notified of acceptance Jan.-Apr. Apply by Nov. 1 for early decision; need not limit application to Emory. Early acceptance available. *Requirements:* Graduation from accredited secondary school with 4 units English, 2 in a foreign language, 3–4 college preparatory mathematics (including algebra, geometry), 2 history or social studies, 2 laboratory science, music or art. Minimum GPA 2.0. *Entrance tests:* College Board SAT or ACT composite. *For transfer students:* 2.0 minimum GPA, 90 quarter hours maximum transfer credit.

College credit for postsecondary-level work completed in secondary school.

Degree Requirements: 132 semester hours of which 128 must be academic credits and 4 must be physical education credits; 2.0 GPA; last 4 semesters in residence; general education requirements; exit competency examinations in writing. Fulfillment of some degree requirements and exemption from beginning courses possible by passing departmental examinations. *Grading system:* A–F; satisfactory/unsatisfactory; withdraw (carries penalty and time limit).

Distinctive Educational Programs: Accelerated degree programs. Special facilities for using telecommunications in the classroom. Engineering program in cooperation with Georgia Institute of Technology. Internships at Carter Center of Emory University. Dual-degree programs. Study abroad in many countries.

Degrees Conferred: 240 *associate*; 1,480 *baccalaureate* (B); 993 *master's* (M); 164 *doctorate* (D): area and ethnic studies 26 (B), 3 (M), 2 (D); biological/life sciences 192 (B), 3 (M), 41 (D); business/marketing 224 (B), 337 (M); computer and information sciences 15 (B), 2 (M); education 12 (B), 18 (M), 6 (D); English 90 (B), 2 (M), 8 (D); health professions and related sciences 74 (B), 499 (M), 3 (D); interdisciplinary studies 5 (B), 2 (M), 5 (D); mathematics 23 (B), 9 (M), 6 (D); philosophy/religion/theology 42 (B), 39 (M), 30 (D); physical sciences 39 (B), 9 (M), 14 (D); psychology 148 (B), 7 (M), 12 (D); social sciences and history 506 (B), 23 (M), 28 (D); visual and performing arts 34 (B), 6 (M), 3 (D); other 50 (B), 26 (M), 3 (D). 443 *first-professional:* law 217; medicine 107; theological 163. 4 *honorary degrees awarded 2003–04:* Doctor of Humane Letters 2, Doctor of Laws 1, Doctor of Letters 1.

Fees and Other Expenses: *Full-time tuition per academic year 2004–05:* $28,940. Contact the university for graduate/professional school tuition/fees. *Required fees:* $382. *Room and board per academic year:* $9,650.

Financial Aid: Aid from institutionally generated funds is awarded on the basis of academic merit, financial need.

Financial aid to full-time, first-time undergraduate students: need-based scholarships/grants totaling $40,080,493, self-help $13,138,269, tuition waivers $2,510,472; non-need-based scholarships/grants totaling $12,976,194, self-help $6,830,192, parent loans $11,348,051; tuition waivers $7,491,041. *Graduate aid:* 192 students received federal and state-funded fellowships/grants totaling $1,776,825; 2,792 received federal and state-funded loans totaling $50,013,514; 324 students received work-study jobs worth $786,638; 1,131 received fellowships, grants, teaching assistantships, research assistantships totaling $16,388,810.

Departments and Teaching Staff: Arts and Sciences *professors* 164, *associate professors* 164, *assistant professors* 81, *instructors* 87, *part-time faculty* 1; Business 20, 23, 31, 4, 0; Law 34, 3, 6, 13, 2; Medicine 300, 269, 839, 252, 152; Nursing 9, 8, 6, 10, 28; Oxford College 9, 20, 12, 3, 1; Public Health 41, 29, 29, 41, 4; Theology 20, 10, 6, 0, 3.

Total instructional faculty: 1,445 (without clinical medicine). Full-time 1,244, part-time 201; women 370, men 875; members of minority groups 530. Total faculty with doctorate, first-professional, or other terminal degree: 1,441. 44 faculty members awarded sabbaticals 2004–05.

Enrollment: Total enrollment 11,781. Undergraduate full-time 2,705 men / 3,548 women, part-time 24m / 69w; first-professional full-time 774m / 748w, part-time 27m / 64w; graduate full-time 1,240m / 1,928s, part-time 264m / 390w.

Characteristics of Student Body: *Ethnic/racial makeup:* number of Black non-Hispanic: 320; American Indian or Alaska Native: 14; Asian or Pacific Islander: 984; Hispanic: 181; White non-Hispanic: 3,854; unknown: 465. *Age distribution:* number under 18: 157; 18–19: 2,951; 20–21: 2,718; 22–24: 340; 25–29: 64; 30–34: 45; 35–39: 25; 40–49: 34; 50–64: 12.

International Students: 966 nonresident aliens enrolled fall 2004. 249 students from Europe, 822 Asia, 102 Central and South America, 119 Africa, 74

Canada, 9 Australia, 2 New Zealand, 63 other. Programs available to aid students whose native language is not English: Social, cultural. English as a Second Language Program. Some financial aid designated for international students.

Student Life: On-campus residence halls house 65% of student body. 30% of men join fraternities; 35% of women join sororities. Housing available for married students. *Intercollegiate athletics:* men only: soccer, swimming, tennis, track; women only: tennis, track. *Special regulations:* Cars permitted for all but freshmen. Quiet hours. Dormitory visitation hours. *Special services:* Learning Resources Center, medical services. *Student publications: Archon*, a quarterly literary magazine; *Campus*, a yearbook; *Spoke*, a quarterly humor magazine; *Wheel*, a weekly newspaper; *The Emory Edge*, student-produced nonfiction magazine published once a semester; *Lullwater Review*, Emory's literary journal; *The Fire This Time*, a monthly newsmagazine devoted to promoting African American awareness and discussing related issues; *The Phoenix*, an arts newspaper published on a twice monthly basis throughout the school year; *Spoke*, a quarterly humor magazine; *Campus*, a yearbook. *Surrounding community:* Atlanta. Served by mass transit bus system; airport 15 miles from campus; passenger rail service 4 miles from campus.

Publications: *Emory Law Journal* (quarterly); *Journal of Economic History* (quarterly); *Emory Medicine; Studies in Humanities Series; Law and Religion Series; Momentum; Public Health; Emory Nursing; Goizueta Magazine.*

Library Collections: 2,600,000 volumes including bound books, serial backfiles, electronic documents, and government documents not in separate collections. Online and card catalogs. Current serials: 53,602 (paper, electronic). 37,516 compact discs; 23,919 CD-ROMs. 444 computer work stations. Students have access to the Internet at no charge. Total budget for books, periodicals, audiovisual materials, microforms 2004–05: $12,649,000.

Most important special holdings include Yeats Collection (books, manuscripts, personal papers); Joel Chandler Harris Collections (books, manuscripts, personal papers); Modern Irish Literary Archives; Reformation Studies, including works by and about Martin Luther; American Literary Manuscripts, including Southern regional authors.

Buildings and Grounds: Campus area 784 acres. *New buildings:* Schwartz Center for Performing Arts; Mathematics and Science Center; Winship Cancer Institute; Tarbutton Performing Arts Center at Oxford College; Whitehead Biomedical Research Building; Chandler Library (renovation and expansion); Yerkes Animal Housing and Neurosciences Lab.

Chief Executive Officer: Dr. James W. Wagner, President.

Address admission inquiries to Daniel C. Walls, Dean of Admissions.

Emory College

Degree Programs Offered: *Baccalaureate.*

Distinctive Educational Programs: Internships. Interdisciplinary programs in Afro-American and African studies, international studies, Judaic studies, Latin American studies, liberal studies, Medieval and Renaissance studies. Facilities and programs for independent research, including honors programs, independent study. Study abroad in Austria, England, France, Italy, Spain. Domestic study at Washington (DC) semester program. Early acceptance to School of Medicine for qualified students. *Other distinctive programs:* Summer scholars program for college-bound students; study abroad.

Emory Business School

Degree Programs Offered: *Baccalaureate* and *master's.*
Distinctive Educational Programs: Evening MBA program.

Nell Hodgson Woodruff School of Nursing

Degree Programs Offered: *Baccalaureate* and *master's.*
Distinctive Educational Programs: Cooperative graduate dual-degree program in 12 areas of nursing specialty with the School of Public Health; cooperative degree program in nursing administration and business administration with the Emory Business School.

Emory University School of Law

Degree Programs Offered: *First-professional, master's.*
Admission: Baccalaureate from accredited college or university, LSAT.
Degree Requirements: 88 credit hours, 72 average on 100-point scale, 6 semesters in residence.
Distinctive Educational Programs: Joint J.D.-M.B.A. program with School of Business Administration. Joint J.D.-M.Div. and J.D.-M.T.S. with Candler School of Theology. Interdisciplinary program in law and economics in cooperation with Law and Economics Center; in law and behavioral sciences; additional programs available.

Emory University School of Medicine

Degree Programs Offered: *First-professional.*

Admission: 90 semester hours or 135 quarter hours college work which must include 1 course in English, 18 semester or 27 quarter hours humanities and behavioral science, 1 course in inorganic chemistry, 1 organic chemistry, 1 physics. Recommend baccalaureate.

Degree Requirements: 280 credit hours, 2 years in residence.

Distinctive Educational Programs: Joint first-professional-doctoral program; tuition and stipend awarded. Summer research fellowship. *See also* School of Nursing.

Candler School of Theology

Degree Programs Offered: *First-professional, master's,* and *doctorate.*

Admission: *For first-professional students:* Baccalaureate from accredited college or university, 2.25 GPA.

Degree Requirements: *For first-professional degree:* 84 credit hours, 2.0 GPA, 6 semesters in residence, foundational study requirements.

Distinctive Educational Programs: Cross-registration with Columbia Theological Seminary, Interdenominational Theological Center, Erskine College (SC).

Graduate School of Arts and Sciences

Degree Programs Offered: *Master's* and *doctorate.*

Admission: Baccalaureate from accredited college; GRE.

Distinctive Educational Programs: Interdisciplinary program in general studies.

Oxford College of Emory University

Degree Programs Offered: *Associate.*

Admission: Graduation from secondary school with 16 acceptable units including mathematics through Algebra II, SAT or ACT, brief personal essay.

Degree Requirements: 64 credit hours, 2.0 GPA, 9 months in residence, distribution requirements.

School of Public Health

Degree Programs Offered: *Master's, doctorate.*

Fort Valley State University

1005 State College Drive

Fort Valley, Georgia 31030-4313

Tel: (478) 825-66315   **E-mail:** admissap@fvsu.edu
Fax: (478) 825-6394   **Internet:** www.fvsu.edu

Institution Description: Fort Valley State University, formerly named Fort Valley State College, is a public land-grant college. *Enrollment:* 2,537. *Degrees awarded:* Associate, baccalaureate, master's.

Academic offerings subject to approval by statewide coordinating bodies. Budget subject to approval by state governing boards.

Accreditation: *Regional:* SACS-Comm. on Coll. *Professional:* engineering technology, family and consumer science, rehabilitation counseling, teacher education, veterinary technology

History: Established as Fort Valley High and Industrial School and chartered 1895; changed name to the Fort Valley Normal and Industrial School 1932; merged with State Teachers and Agriculture College at Forsyth, offered first instruction at postsecondary level became Fort Valley State College 1939; awarded first degree (baccalaureate) 1941; adopted present name 1995.

Institutional Structure: *Governing board:* Board of Regents of the University System of Georgia. Representation: 15 regents. All voting. *Composition of institution:* Administrators 14 men / 5 women. Academic affairs headed by dean of academic affairs. Management/business/finances directed by director of business and finance. Full-time instructional faculty 135. Academic governance body, the faculty, meets an average of 9 times per year.

Calendar: Semesters. Academic year Sept. to June. Freshmen admitted Sept., Jan., May, June. Degrees conferred and formal commencements June, Aug. Summer session of 3 terms from mid-June to mid-Aug.

Characteristics of Freshmen: 1,863 applicants (816 men, 1,047 women). 43.7% of applicants admitted. 47.9% of admitted students enrolled full-time.

66% (312 students) submitted SAT scores; 13% (22 students) submitted ACT scores. *25th percentile:* SAT I Verbal 320, SAT I Math 340; ACT Composite 15, ACT English 13, ACT Math 17. *75th percentile:* SAT I Verbal 560, SAT I Math 640; ACT Composite 25, ACT English 25, ACT Math 27. Freshmen from 5 states and 3 foreign countries.

Admission: Rolling admissions plan. Apply no later than 15 days prior to registration. Early acceptance available. *Requirements:* Either graduation from accredited secondary school with 16 units which must include 4 English, 3 social studies, 2 mathematics, 1 biology or natural science, 1 health, 5-7 electives; or GED. Minimum GPA 1.8. *Entrance tests:* College Board SAT. *For transfer students:* 2.0 minimum GPA; from 4-year accredited institution maximum transfer credit limited only by residence requirement; correspondence/extension students 25 quarter hours.

College credit and advanced placement for postsecondary-level work completed in secondary school. For extrainstitutional learning (life experience) college credit on basis of ACE *2006 Guide to the Evaluation of Educational Experiences in the Armed Services.* Advanced placement on basis of faculty assessment. Tutoring available. Developmental courses offered in summer session and regular academic year; credit given.

Degree Requirements: *For all associate degrees:* 60 semester hours. *For all baccalaureate degrees:* 120 minimum semester hours; core curriculum; exit competency examination (Regents Test of reading and writing, tests on or courses in U.S. and Georgia constitutions and histories). *For all undergraduate degrees:* 2.0 GPA; 30 hours in residence; physical education courses.

Fulfillment of some degree requirements and exemption from some beginning courses possible by passing departmental examinations, College Board CLEP, AP. *Grading system:* A–F; pass-fail; withdraw (carries time limit and penalty).

Distinctive Educational Programs: *For undergraduates:* Off-campus centers (at Warner Robins and Macon, each less than 30 miles away from main institution). Interdisciplinary programs. *Available to all students:* Work-experience programs. Flexible schedules, including weekend and evening classes. Facilities and programs for independent research, including individual majors, tutorials. Institutionally arranged study abroad in West Africa; through University of Georgia at various locations, including Europe.

ROTC: Army.

Degrees Conferred: 5 *associate;* 260 *baccalaureate;* 69 *master's.* Bachelor's degrees awarded in top five disciplines: business, management, marketing, and related support services 37; psychology 35; education 29; security and protective services 25; biological and biomedical sciences 24.

Fees and Other Expenses: *Full-time tuition per academic year 2004–05:* in-state resident $2,916, out-of-state $9,884. Contact the university for current graduate tuition/fees. *Books and supplies:* $900. *Room and board per academic year:* $4,386.

Departments and Teaching Staff: *Total instructional faculty:* 135.

Enrollment: Total enrollment 2,537. Undergraduate 2,291 (44.1% men, 55.9% women).

Characteristics of Student Body: *Ethnic/racial makeup:* Black non-Hispanic: 94.7%; Asian or Pacific Islander: .3%, Hispanic: .4%; White non-Hispanic: 3.2%.

International Students: 32 undergraduate nonresident aliens enrolled. Programs available to aid students whose native language is not English: English as a Second Language Program.

Student Life: On-campus residence halls house 54% of student body. *Intercollegiate athletics:* men only: baseball, basketball, cross-country, football, indoor track, tennis, track; women only: basketball, cross-country, indoor track, tennis, track. *Special regulations:* Registered cars with decals permitted in designated areas. *Special services:* Learning Resources Center, medical services. *Student publications: The Flame,* a yearbook; *Peachite,* a monthly newspaper. *Surrounding community:* Fort Valley population 10,000. Atlanta, 100 miles from campus, is nearest metropolitan area. Served by airport 28 miles from campus.

Library Collections: 250,000 volumes. 1170 periodicals; 172,000 microform items; 5,250 audiovisual materials. Online catalog. Students have access to online information retrieval services.

Most important holdings include Ethnic Heritage Collection (books, magazine and newspaper articles, research papers by and about Blacks).

Buildings and Grounds: Campus area 1,375 acres.

Chief Executive Officer: Dr. Kofi Lomotey, President.

Address admission inquiries to Debra McGhee, Director of Admissions.

Georgia College and State University

231 West Hancock Street
Milledgeville, Georgia 31061
Tel: (800) 342-0474   **E-mail:** info@gcsu.edu
Fax: (478) 445-1914   **Internet:** www.gscu.edu

Institution Description: Georgia College and State University is a comprehensive state institution. *Enrollment:* 5,531. *Degrees awarded:* Baccalaureate, master's. Specialist certificate also awarded.

Academic offerings and budget subject to approval by the state governing board.

Accreditation: *Regional:* SACS-Comm. on Coll. *Professional:* business, music, nursing, public administration, teacher education

History: Established and chartered as Georgia Normal and Industrial College 1889; offered first instruction at postsecondary level 1891; awarded first degree (baccalaureate) 1921; changed name to Georgia State College for Women 1922; changed name to The Women's College of Georgia 1961; became coeducational 1967; adopted present name 1996. *See* Hair, Dawson, and Bonner, *History of Georgia College* (Clarksville, Tenn.: Josten's, 1979) for further information.

Institutional Structure: *Governing board:* Board of Regents of the University System of Georgia. Extrainstitutional representation: 18 regents. All voting. *Composition of institution:* Administrators 9 men / 7 women. Academic affairs headed by vice president/dean of faculties. Business affairs directed by vice president for business and finance. Full-time instructional faculty 268. Academic governance body, the faculty, meets at least three times per year and elects a faculty senate to advise administration between meetings.

Calendar: Semesters. Academic year Aug. to May. Freshmen admitted Sept., Jan., June. Degrees conferred and formal commencements May, Dec.

Characteristics of Freshmen: 43.6% of applicants admitted. 70% of admitted students enrolled full-time.

74.6% (683 students) submitted SAT scores; 32.3% (296 students) submitted ACT scores. *25th percentile:* SAT Verbal 520, SAT I Math 520; ACT Composite 21, ACT English 20, ACT Math 19. *75th percentile:* SAT I Verbal 600, SAT I Math 598; ACT Composite 24, ACT English 25, ACT Math 24. 36% of entering freshmen expected to graduate within 5 years. 94% of freshmen from Georgia. Freshmen from 21 states.

Admission: Rolling admission plan. For fall acceptance, apply no later than Apr. 1; for spring Dec. 1; for summer May 1. Early acceptance available. *Requirements:* Either graduation from accredited secondary school with 16 units which must include 4 English, 2 foreign language, 3 mathematics, 3 social studies, 3 science; or GED. Minimum GPA 2.14. *Entrance tests:* College Board SAT or ACT. Students evaluated on entire admissions portfolio. *For transfer students:* From 4-year accredited institution 84 semester hours maximum transfer credit; from 2-year accredited institution 67 semester hours.

Advanced placement for postsecondary-level work completed in secondary school. College credit for extrainstitutional learning on basis of ACE *2006 Guide to the Evaluation of Educational Experiences in the Armed Services;* faculty assessment. Noncredit developmental courses offered in summer session and regular academic year.

Degree Requirements: *For all baccalaureate degrees:* 120 credit hours; 40 hours in residence; exit competency exams (comprehensives in fields of study); 2.0 GPA; exit competency exams (Regent's test of reading and writing, tests on or courses in U.S. and Georgia constitutions and histories). Fulfillment of some degree requirements possible by passing departmental examinations, College Board CLEP, AP. *Grading system:* A–F; withdraw (deadline after which fail is appended to withdraw).

Distinctive Educational Programs: *For undergraduates:* Dual-degree program in engineering with Georgia Institute of Technology. Honors programs. Study abroad in a number of countries. Faculty exchange program in England, China, Mexico, Brazil. Preprofessional college program. *Available to all students:* Work-experience programs, including cooperative education internships. Off-campus residence centers: Georgia College in Macon; Georgia College in Warner Robins operates Logistics Education Center at Robins Air Force Base, Georgia.

ROTC: Army in cooperation with Georgia Military College.

Degrees Conferred: 788 *baccalaureate* (B), 429 *master's* (M): biological/life sciences 18 (B), 19 (M); business/marketing 275 (B), 125 (M); communications/communication technologies 31 (B); computer and information sciences 18 (B); education 19 (B), 223 (M); English 22 (B), 12 (M); foreign languages and literature 14 (B); health professions and related sciences 96 (B), 18 (M); liberal arts/general studies 1 (B); mathematics 2 (B); parks and recreation 10 (B); physical sciences 2 (B); protective services/public administration 38 (B), 38 (M); psychology 61 (B), 4 (M); social sciences and history 45 (B); visual and performing arts 26 (B).

Fees and Other Expenses: *Full-time tuition per academic year 2004–05:* in-state undergraduate $3,152, graduate $3,844; out-of-state undergraduate $12,608, graduate $11,358. *Required fees:* $710. *Room and board per academic year:* $6,452.

Financial Aid: Aid from institutionally generated funds is provided on the basis of academic merit, athletic ability, other considerations. Institution has a Program Participation Agreement with the U.S. Department of Education for eligible students to receive Pell Grants and other federal aid.

Financial aid to full-time, first-time undergraduate students: need-based scholarships/grants totaling $2,610,251, self-help $6,421,252; non-need-based scholarships/grants totaling $10,313,987, self-help $4,332,599, parent loans $905,917, tuition waivers $797,139, athletic awards $511,270.

Departments and Teaching Staff: *Professors* 77, *associate professors* 61, *associate professors* 114, *instructors* 16, *part-time faculty* 139. *Total instructional faculty:* 407 (full-time 268, part-time 139; women 123, men 145; members of minority groups 126). Total faculty with doctorate, first-professional, or other terminal degree: 206. Student-to-faculty ratio: 15:1. *Faculty development:* $1,086,621 in grants for research. 2 faculty members awarded sabbaticals 2004–05.

Enrollment: Total enrollment 5,491. Undergraduate full-time 1,590 men / 2,393 women, part-time 225m / 358w; graduate full-time 100m / 213w, part-time 205m / 447. *Transfer students:* in-state 339; from out-of-state 35.

Characteristics of Student Body: *Ethnic/racial makeup:* number of: Black non-Hispanic: 357; American Indian or Alaska Native: 15; Asian or Pacific Islander: 52; Hispanic: 46; White non-Hispanic: 3,932; unknown: 36. *Age distribution:* under 18: 19; 18–19: 1,480; 20–21: 1,589; 22–24: 976; 22–29: 238; 30–34: 86; 35–39: 77; 40–49: 73; 50–64: 24; 65 and over: 4.

International Students: 118 nonresident aliens enrolled fall 2004. 33 students from Europe, 39 Asia, 16 Central and South America, 18 Africa, 5 Canada, 2 Australia, 4 other. English as a Second Language courses available. Some financial aid available for qualifying international students.

Student Life: On-campus residence halls available. *Intercollegiate athletics:* men only: baseball, basketball, cross country, tennis, golf; women only: basketball, cross country, soccer, softball, tennis. *Special regulations:* Residence halls have various quiet and visitation hours. *Special services:* Learning Resources Center, Student Health Center, Wellness Program. *Student publications, radio:* *Colonnade,* a weekly newspaper. Radio station WGUR. *Surrounding community:* Metropolitan area of Milledgeville has a population of 35,000. Atlanta is approximately 90 miles from campus, Macon 30 miles.

Publications: *The Peacock's Feet-Journal of Creative Arts,* published annually; *The Corinthian, Journal of Student Research,* published annually; *Arts and Letters, Journal of Contemporary Cultures,* published each spring.

Library Collections: 169,735 volumes including bound books, serial backfiles, electronic documents, and government documents not in separate collections. Online and card catalogs. 761 periodical subscriptions with electronic access to 12,402. 180 Computer work stations. Students have access to the Internet at no charge.

Most important holdings include Flannery O'Connor collection of manuscripts, memorabilia; Middle Georgia (Bonner and Sibley) collection of rare materials and manuscripts.

Buildings and Grounds: Campus area 696 acres.

Chief Executive Officer: Dr. Dorothy Leland, President.

Address all admission inquiries to Mike Augustine, Director of Admissions.

Georgia Institute of Technology

225 North Avenue, N.W.
Atlanta, Georgia 30332-0320
Tel: (404) 894-2000   **E-mail:** admissions@gatech.edu
Fax: (404) 894-1277   **Internet:** www.gatech.edu

Institution Description: Georgia Institute of Technology is a state institution. *Enrollment:* 16,841. *Degrees awarded:* Baccalaureate, master's, doctorate.

Academic offerings subject to approval by statewide coordinating bodies. Budget subject to approval by state governing boards. Member of Academic Common Market and Southeastern Consortium for Minorities in Engineering.

Accreditation: *Regional:* SACS-Comm. on Coll. *Professional:* architecture, business, chemistry, computer science, construction education, engineering, planning

History: Established and chartered as Georgia School of Technology 1885; offered first instruction at postsecondary level 1888; awarded first degree (baccalaureate) 1890; adopted present name 1948. See *Engineering the New South, Georgia Tech 1885–1985* (Atlanta: The University of Georgia Press, 1985).

Institutional Structure: *Governing board:* Board of Regents of the University System of Georgia. Extrainstitutional representation: 16 regents. All voting.

Composition of institution: Academic affairs headed by provost and vice president for academic affairs. Management/business/finances directed by senior vice president for administration and finance. Full-time instructional faculty 802. Academic governance body, Academic Senate, meets an average of 10 times per year.

Calendar: Semesters. Academic year Aug. to May. Freshmen admitted Aug., Jan., June. Degrees conferred and formal commencements Aug., Dec., May. Summer session from May to Aug.

Characteristics of Freshmen: 43% of applicants accepted. 43% of accepted students enrolled full-time.

97% (2,492 students) submitted SAT scores; 32% (827 students) submitted ACT scores. *25th percentile*: SAT Verbal 600, SAT Math 650; ACT Composite 25, ACT English 25, ACT Math 27. *75th percentile*: SAT Verbal 690, SAT Math 740; ACT Composite 32, ACT English 30, ACT Math 32. 104 National Merit Scholars.

36% of of freshmen expected to graduate within 5 years. 78% of freshmen from Georgia. Freshmen from 49 states and 31 foreign countries.

Admission: For fall acceptance, apply no later than Jan. 15. Early acceptance available. *Requirements:* Either graduation from accredited secondary school with 4 years English, 4 mathematics (must include 2 algebra, 1 geometry, 1 precalculus including trigonometry); 3 science (1 chemistry; 2 must be laboratory science), 2 foreign language (in one language), 1 social studies, 2 history, 2 academic electives; or GED. *Entrance tests:* College Board SAT. *For transfer students:* completion of 30 semester hours or 45 quarter hours of college coursework with a minimum overall GPA of 2.7 on a 4.0 scale for Georgia residents, 3.0 for nonresidents, and 3.5 for international students.

College credit and advanced placement for postsecondary-level work completed in secondary school. Tutoring available.

Degree Requirements: Undergraduate 2.0 GPA; graduate 2.7 GPA; doctorate 3.0 GPA; general education requirements; exit competency examinations—Regents' Test of Reading and Writing, tests on or courses in U.S. and Georgia constitutions and histories.

Fulfillment of some degree requirements and exemption from some beginning courses possible by passing College Board AP. *Grading system:* A–F; pass-fail; withdraw (carries time limit).

Distinctive Educational Programs: Work-experience programs, including cooperative education, internships. Dual-degree programs in engineering with 29 U.S. colleges and universities. 11 interdisciplinary certificate programs in engineering. Facilities and programs for independent research, including individual majors, tutorials. Senior year abroad in France for study of architecture. *Other distinctive programs:* Continuing education, including videotaped courses offered at private businesses for credit. The Georgia Tech Regional Engineering Program (GTREP) offers undergraduate and graduate engineering degrees in collaboration with Armstrong Atlantic University, Georgia Southern University, and Savannah State University.

ROTC: Army, Navy, Air Force.

Degrees Conferred: 2,594 *baccalaureate* (B); 1,393 *master's* (M); 311 *doctorate* (D): architecture 87 (B), 109 (M), 6 (D); biological/life sciences 71 (B), 27 (M), 3 (D); business/marketing 382 (B), 192 (M), 3 (D); communications/communication technologies 16 (M); computer and information sciences 329 (B), 91 (M), 13 (D); engineering and engineering technologies 1,380 (B), 805 (M), 252 (D); interdisciplinary studies 68 (B); mathematics 22 (B), 24 (M), 8 (D); physical sciences 72 (B), 39 (M), 36 (D); protective services/public administration 17 (B), 21 (M), 2 (D); psychology 26 (B), 13 (M), 7 (D); social sciences and history 91 (B), 30 (M), 1 (D); visual and performing arts 49 (B), 6 (M); other 20 (M).

Fees and Other Expenses: *Full-time tuition per academic year 2004–05:* instate resident undergraduate $3,368, out-of-state student $16,648; resident graduate $4,044, out-of-state $16,940. *Required fees:* $910. *Room and board per academic year:* $6,526.

Financial Aid: Aid from institutionally generated funds is provided on the basis of academic merit, athletic ability, financial need, other criteria. Institution has a Program Participation Agreement with the U.S. Department of Education for eligible students to receive Pell Grants and other federal aid.

Financial aid to full-time, first-time undergraduate students: need-based scholarships/grants totaling $17,655,387, self-help $16,248,466, parent loans $7,076,951, athletic awards $2,825,194; non-need-based scholarships/grants totaling $19,458,113, self-help $7,601,028, parent loans $6,478,520, athletic awards $1,618,437.

Departments and Teaching Staff: *Total instructional faculty:* 813 (full-time 801, part-time 12; women 133, men 680; members of minority groups 182). Total faculty with doctorate, first-professional, or other terminal degree: 782. Student-to-faculty ratio: 14:1. *Faculty development:* $341,885,436 total grants for research (does not include gifts and grants awarded through foundations).

Enrollment: Total enrollment 16,841. Undergraduate full-time 7,749 men / 2,976 women, part-time 581m / 240w; graduate full-time 3,256m / 1,158w, part-time 705m / 176w.

Characteristics of Student Body: *Ethnic and racial makeup:* number of Black non-Hispanic: 882; American Indian or Alaska Native: 29; Asian or Pacific Islander: 1,730; Hispanic: 394; White non-Hispanic: 7,873; unknown: 79. *Age distribution: distribution:* number under 18: 169; 18–19: 4,303; 20–21: 4,183; 22–24: 2,345; 25–29: 359; 30–34: 105; 35–39: 29; 40–49: 28; 50–64: 5.

International Students: 2,872 nonresident aliens enrolled fall 2004. Programs available to aid students whose native language is not English: Social and cultural. English as a Second Language Program. No financial aid specifically designated for international students.

Student Life: On-campus residence halls house 53% of student body. Residence halls for men constitute 14% of such space, for women 2%, for married students 1%, for single students 83%. 21% of men join fraternities; 24% of women join sororities. *Intercollegiate athletics:* men only: baseball, football, swimming; women only: softball, volleyball; both sexes: basketball, cross country, indoor track, tennis, track. *Special regulations:* Registered cars permitted. Quiet hours. Residence hall visitation from 11am to midnight. *Special services:* Medical services, on-campus bus and van service. *Student publications, radio: The Blue Print,* a yearbook; *The Technique,* a weekly newspaper. Radio station WREK broadcasts 168 hours per week. *Surrounding community:* Atlanta metropolitan area population 4,9 million. Served by mass transit bus and subway systems; airport 10 miles from campus; passenger rail service 1 mile from campus.

Library Collections: 4,268,595 cataloged items; 1,406,299 government documents; 2,756,299 technical reports; 196,954 maps; 7,265,347 patents; 5,893 electronic journals. Online catalog. Computer work stations available. Students have access to the Internet at no charge. Total budget for books, periodicals, audiovisual materials, microforms 2004–05: $11,645,893.

Most important special holdings include collections on science/technology; patents; technical reports.

Buildings and Grounds: Campus area 450 acres. *New buildings:* Technology Square; Management Building; Global Learning Center; Georgia Tech Hotel and Conference Center; Economic Development Building; Ford Environmental Science and Technology building; U.A. Whitaker Biomedical Engineering Building; Camus Recreation Center; Business Services Building.

Chief Executive Officer: Dr. G. Wayne Clough, President.

Undergraduates address admission inquiries to Office of Undergraduate Admissions; graduate students should contact the individual school in which they wish to major.

Institute of Paper Science and Technology

500 10th Street, N.W.
Atlanta, Georgia 30318-5794
Tel: (404) 894-5700

Degree Programs Offered: The Institute of Paper Science and Technology (formerly the Institute of Paper Chemistry) is a private, independent institution offering graduate study only. It was established, chartered, and offered first instruction at postsecondary level 1929; awarded first degree (master's) 1931; moved from Wisconsin to Atlanta 1990; became affiliated with Georgia Institute of Technology in 2003. *Degrees awarded:* Master's, doctorate.

Georgia Southern University

Highway 301, South
P.O. Box 8033
Statesboro, Georgia 30460-8033

Tel: (912) 681-5611   **E-mail:** admissions@georgiasouthern.edu
Fax: (912) 486-7240   **Internet:** www.georgiasouthern.edu

Institution Description: Georgia Southern University is a regional state university. *Enrollment:* 16,100. *Degrees awarded:* Baccalaureate, master's, doctorate. Specialist certificate also awarded.

Accreditation: *Regional:* SACS-Comm. on Coll. *Professional*: accounting, business, computer science, construction education, engineering technology, interior design, music, nursing, nursing education, public administration, recreation and leisure services, teacher education

History: Established as First District Agricultural and Mechanical High School and chartered 1906; changed name to Georgia Normal School and offered first instruction at postsecondary level 1924; changed name to South Georgia Teachers College and awarded first degree (baccalaureate) 1929; changed name to Georgia Teachers College 1939; changed name to Georgia Southern College 1959; Georgia Southern's status was changed in 1990 from a Type II (4-year senior college) to a Type 1 (regional university) with a change in name to Georgia Southern University.

Institutional Structure: *Governing board:* University System of Georgia Board of Regents. Extrainstitutional representation: 15 regents. All voting. *Composition of institution:* Administrators 36 men / 11 women. Academic affairs headed by vice president for academic affairs. Management/business/finances directed by vice president for business and finance. Student affairs directed by vice president for student affairs and dean of students. Graduate studies directed by associate vice president for academic affairs and dean of graduate studies. University development directed by vice president for development and university relations. Full-time instructional faculty 630. Academic governance body, Faculty Senate, meets an average of 8 times per year.

Calendar: Semesters. Academic year Sept. to June. Freshmen admitted Sept., Jan., Mar., June. Degrees conferred and formal commencements June, Aug. Summer session June to Aug.

Characteristics of Freshmen: 54% of applicants admitted. 36% of admitted students enrolled full-time.

91% (2,739 students) submitted SAT scores; 21% (635 students) submitted ACT scores. *25th percentile*: SAT Verbal 500, SAT Math 500; ACT Composite 20, ACT English 19, ACT Math 19. *75th percentile*: SAT Verbal 580, SAT Math 580; ACT Composite 23, ACT English 23, ACT Math 24.

34% of entering freshmen expected to graduate within 5 years. 95% of freshmen from Georgia. Freshmen from 28 states and 23 foreign countries.

Admission: Rolling admissions plan. For fall acceptance, apply by May 1. Early acceptance available. *Requirements:* Graduation from accredited secondary school with 16 secondary school units required; 4 English, 4 mathematics, 3 social studies, 3 sciences, 2 foreign language, 4 electives. Minimum GPA 2.0; SAT 980 or ACT 20. *Entrance test:* SAT Reasoning Test or ACT. *For transfer students:* 2.0 minimum GPA; from 2-year accredited institution 68 hours maximum transfer credit. No limit on transfer credits from accredited 4-year institutions, but the last 30 hours must be completed at Georgia Southern. Additional for School of Business, School of Education, and School of Nursing.

College credit and advanced placement for postsecondary-level work completed in secondary school. College credit for College Board CLEP, AP, and for extrainstitutional learning on basis of ACE *2006 Guide to the Evaluation of Educational Experiences in the Armed Services*. Tutoring available. Developmental courses offered in summer session and regular academic year; institutional credit given.

Degree Requirements: *For all baccalaureate degrees:* 125 minimum credit hours. *For all undergraduate degrees:* 2.0 GPA; 38 credit hours in residence; exit competency examinations (Regents' Tests of Reading and Writing, tests on or courses in U.S. and Georgia constitutions and histories); distribution requirements. *For education majors:* Comprehensive examinations. *Grading system:* A–F; withdraw (deadline after which pass-fail is appended to withdraw); satisfactory-unsatisfactory; incomplete.

Distinctive Educational Programs: *For undergraduates:* Cooperative education programs in School of Technology, Study Abroad Program. Preprofessional programs in dentistry, forestry, medicine, pharmacy, law, optometry, veterinary medicine. Engineering programs in conjunction with the Georgia Institute of Technology. Baccalaureate degree offerings in education at Brunswick Center. External degree programs; Honors Programs; independent study; Weekend College for business students. *For graduate students:* Off-campus centers (at Brunswick, 100 miles away from main institution). *Available to all students:* Evening classes.

ROTC: Army. 10 commissions awarded 2004.

Degrees Conferred: 2,033 *baccalaureate*; 488 *master's*; 70 *post-master's certificates*; 23 *doctorate*. Bachelor's degrees awarded in top five disciplines: business, management, marketing, and related support services 622; education 209; parks, recreation, leisure, and fitness studies 161; family and consumer sciences/human sciences 129; health professions and related clinical sciences 127.

Fees and Other Expenses: *Full-time tuition per academic year: 2004–05:* undergraduate resident $2,322, out-of-state student $9,290; graduate resident $2,106, out-of-state student $8,370. *Required fees:* $830. *Room and board per academic year:* $6,000.

Financial Aid: Aid from institutionally generated funds is provided on the basis of academic merit, financial need, athletic ability, other criteria. Institution has a Program Participation Agreement with the U.S. Department of Education for eligible students to receive Pell Grants and other federal aid.

Financial aid to full-time, first-time undergraduate students: need-based scholarships/grants totaling $22,052,902; self-help $23,316,496, parent loans $2,238,011, tuition waivers $378,502, athletic awards 793,905; non-need-based scholarships/grants totaling $10,735,181, self-help $11,113,699, parent loans $1,943,607, tuition waivers $1,217,607, athletic awards $863,521. *Graduate aid:* 119 students received federal and state-funded fellowships and grants totaling $178,275 (ranging from $150 to $3,750); 694 received federal and state-funded loans totaling $6,598,351 (ranging from $180 to $18,000); 8 received work-study jobs worth $46,656; 100 college-assigned jobs totaling $150,694; 6 fellowships worth $3,800; 22 teaching assistantships totaling $110,000; 287 research assistantships totaling $1,353,239 (ranging from $407 to $10,281).

Departments and Teaching Staff: *Total instructional faculty:* 708 (full-time 630, part-time 78; women 320, men 388; members of minority groups 81). Total faculty with doctorate, first-professional, or other terminal degree: 506. Student-to-faculty ratio: 20:1. *Faculty development:* $135,774 in grants for research. 7 faculty members awarded sabbaticals 2004–05.

Enrollment: Total enrollment 16,100. Undergraduate full-time 6,441 men / 6,217 women, part-time 703m / 731w; graduate full-time 233m / 441w, part-time 370m / 994w. *Transfer students:* 760 in-state; 68 from from out-of-state.

Characteristics of Student Body: *Ethnic/racial makeup:* number of Black non-Hispanic: 3,274; American Indian or Alaska Native: 26; Asian or Pacific Islander: 174; Hispanic: 194; White non-Hispanic: 10,045; unknown: 246. *Age distribution:* number under 18: 140; 18–19: 5,018; 20–21: 4,563; 22–24: 3,131; 25–29: 30–34: 239; 35–39: 137; 40–49: 157; 50–64: 48; 65 and over: 2.

International Students: 192 nonresident aliens enrolled fall 2004. 24 students from Europe, 74 Asia, 23 Central and South America, 34 Africa, 5 Canada, 1 Australia, 31 other. Programs available to aid students whose native language is not English: cultural, social. English as a Second Language Program. Tuition waivers for some international students.

Student Life: On-campus residence halls house 68% of freshmen and 23% of all undergraduate students. *Intercollegiate athletics:* men only: baseball, basketball, cross-country, football, golf, soccer, swimming, tennis; women only: basketball, softball, swimming, tennis, cross-country, volleyball. *Special regulations:* Cars permitted for all students; parking in designated areas. *Special services:* Learning Resources Center, medical services. *Student publications, radio: George-Anne*, a daily newspaper; *Miscellany*, a biannual literary magazine; *Southern Reflector* student magazine is produced 4 times per semester. a yearbook. Radio station WVGS 91.9 has continuous air play. *Surrounding community:* Statesboro population 16,000. Savannah, 55 miles from campus, is nearest metropolitan area.

Library Collections: 568,551 volumes. 585,340 government documents. Current serial subscriptions: 2,697 paper; 884,997 microform; 17,775 via electronic access. 28,913 recordings. 310 computer work stations. Online catalog. Students have access to online information retrieval services and the Internet. Total 2004–05 budget for materials and operations: $1,186,769.

Most important holdings include collections of Congressmen Ronald "BO' Ginn's papers; Zachert Collection of private press books; Commander William Rigdon papers (naval aide to President Roosevelt); local history manuscript collection.

Buildings and Grounds: Campus area 600 acres. *New buildings:* College of Information Technology; Nursing/Chemistry; Ceramic/Sculpture Studio; Wild Life Center Pavilion; Southern Courtyard Residence Complex; Southern Pines Residence Complex; McAnderson Pavilion; Eagle Village Residence Complex.

Chief Executive Officer: Dr. Bruce Grube, President.

Address admission inquiries to Susan Davies, Director of Admissions.

Georgia Southwestern State University

800 Wheatley Street
Americus, Georgia 31709-4693

Tel: (229) 928-1279   **E-mail:** gswapps@gsw.edu
Fax: (229) 931-2059   **Internet:** www.gsw.edu

Institution Description: Georgia Southwestern State University, formerly named Georgia Southwestern College, is a member institution of the University of Georgia System. *Enrollment:* 2,569. *Degrees awarded:* Associate, baccalaureate, master's. Specialist certificate also awarded.

Academic offerings subject to approval by statewide coordinating bodies.Budget subject to approval by state governing boards.

Accreditation: *Regional:* SACS-Comm. on Coll. *Professional*: business, nursing, teacher education

History: Established as Third District Agricultural and Mechanical School 1906; changed name to Third District Agricultural and Normal College, chartered and offered first instruction at postsecondary level 1926; awarded first degree (associate) 1928; became Georgia Southwestern College 1932; added baccalaureate program 1964; awarded first baccalaureate 1968; adopted present name 1996.

Institutional Structure: *Governing board:* Board of Regents of the University System of Georgia. Extrainstitutional representation: 15 regents. All voting. *Composition of institution:* Administrators 6. Academic affairs headed by vice president for academic affairs and dean of the faculty. Management/business/ finances directed by vice president for business and finance. Academic governance body, Faculty Senate, meets an average of 4 times per year.

Calendar: Semesters. Academic year Aug. to May. Freshmen admitted Aug., Jan., Mar., June. Degrees conferred and formal commencements June, Dec. Summer session from June to Aug.

Characteristics of Freshmen: 69% (269 students) submitted SAT scores; 13% (51 students) submitted ACT scores. *25th percentile*: SAT Verbal 440, SAT Math 440; ACT Composite 17. *75th percentile*: SAT Verbal 530, SAT Math 520; ACT Composite 20.

24% of entering freshmen expected to graduate within 5 years. 94% of freshmen from Georgia. Freshmen from 18 states and 35 foreign countries.

Admission: Rolling admissions plan. For fall acceptance, apply as early as 1 year prior to enrollment, but not later than 20 days prior to enrollment. Early acceptance and early decision available. *Requirements:* Graduation from accredited secondary school. Recommend 4 English, 4 mathematics, 3 social science, 3 natural science, 2 foreign language, 2 academic electives, 3 physical education units. GED accepted for students out of school 5 years or longer. *Entrance tests:* College Board SAT (minimum combined score of 830). *For transfer students:* 2.0 GPA; from 4-year accredited institution 90 hours maximum transfer credit; from 2-year accredited institution 65 hours; correspondence/extension students 45 hours.

College credit and advanced placement for postsecondary-level work completed in secondary school. College credit for extrainstitutional learning on basis of ACE *2006 Guide to the Evaluation of Educational Experiences in the Armed Services* and departmental examinations. Remedial courses offered in summer session and regular academic year; credit given.

Degree Requirements: *For all baccalaureate degrees:* 120 credit hours; 6 physical education courses; exit competency examinations—Regents' Test of reading and writing, comprehensives in individual fields of study. *For all undergraduate degrees:* 2.0 GPA; 2 semesters in residence; distribution requirements; exit competency examinations—tests on or courses in U.S. and Georgia constitutions and histories.

Fulfillment of some degree requirements and exemption from some beginning courses possible by passing departmental examinations, College Board CLEP, AP. *Grading system:* A–F; withdraw (deadline after which pass-fail is appended to withdraw); incomplete (deadline after which A–F is assigned).

Distinctive Educational Programs: *For undergraduates:* Cooperative education. Dual-degree baccalaureate program in engineering with Georgia Institute of Technology. Honors programs. Study abroad in varying locations through University System of Georgia Study Abroad program. Internships in most fields. *Available to all students:* Evening classes.

Degrees Conferred: 320 *baccalaureate* (B), 136 *master's* (M): biological sciences 13 (B); business/marketing 105 (B), 29 (M); computer and information sciences 6 (M); education 77 (B), 101 (M); English 7 (B); 119, health professions and related sciences 21 (B); mathematics 4 (B); parks and recreation 1 (B); physical sciences 4 (B); psychology 46 (B); social sciences and history 35 (B); visual and performing arts 7 (B).

Fees and Other Expenses: *Full-time tuition per academic year 2004–05:* resident undergraduate $2,522, out-of-state student $9,295; graduate in-state resident $2,786, out-of-state $11,146. *Room per academic year:* $2,580. *Board per academic year* $2,064.

Financial Aid: Aid from institutionally generated funds is provided on the basis of academic merit, athletic ability. Institution has a Program Participation Agreement with the U.S. Department of Education for eligible students to receive Pell Grants and other federal aid.

Financial aid to full-time, first-time undergraduate students: need-based scholarships/grants totaling $2,356,544, self-help $2,753,807; non-need-based scholarships/grants totaling $2,450,806, self-help $1,882,535, parent loans $57,992, athletic awards $275,617.

Departments and Teaching Staff: *Professors* 21, *associate professors* 25, *assistant professors* 36, *instructors* 7, *part-time faculty* 43. *Total instructional faculty:* 132 (full-time 89, part-time 27; women 57, men 59; members of minority groups 10). Degrees held by full-time faculty: doctorate 65%, master's 100%. 68% hold terminal degrees. Student-to-faculty ration 16:1.

Enrollment: Total enrollment 2,313. Undergraduate full-time 587 men / 998 women, part-time 151m / 366w; graduate full-time 14m / 20w, part-time 52m / 125w.

Characteristics of Student Body: *Ethnic and racial makeup:* number of Black non-Hispanic: 679; American Indian or Alaska Native: 10; Asian or Pacific Islander: 21; Hispanic: 19; White non-Hispanic: 1,311. *Age distribution:* number under 18: 35; 18–19: 503; 20–21: 486; 22–24: 442; 25–29: 253; 30–34: 154; 35–39: 98; 40–49: 104; 50–64: 26; 65 and over: 2.

International Students: 67 nonresident aliens enrolled fall 2004. 8 students from Europe, 36 Asia, 9 Central and South America, 4 Africa, 2 Canada, other 8. English as a Second Language program. No financial aid specifically designated for international students.

Student Life: On-campus residence halls house 26% of student body. Residence halls for men only constitute 35% of such space, for women only 65%. 11% of men join and 3% of members live in fraternities. *Intercollegiate athletics:* men only: baseball, basketball, cross country, golf, tennis; women only: basketball, cross country, softball, tennis, volleyball. *Special regulations:* Registered cars permitted; parking fee charged. Quiet hours, and limited dormitory

visitation in some residence halls. *Special services:* Learning Resources Center, medical services. *Student publications: Gate,* a yearbook; *Clay and Pine,* an annual literary magazine; *Sou'Wester,* a weekly newspaper. *Surrounding community:* Americus population 18,000. Atlanta, 140 miles from campus, is nearest metropolitan area. Served by airport 42 miles from campus; passenger rail service 142 miles from campus.

Library Collections: 344,361 volumes. 144,809 government documents; 652,749 microforms; 1,849 audiovisual materials; current periodical subscriptions paper 345, microform 224, via electronic access 7. 3,314 recordings; 31 compact discs; 3,816 CD-ROMs. 50 computer work stations. Students have access to the Internet.

Most important special holdings include rare book collection.

Buildings and Grounds: Campus area 325 acres. *New buildings:* Newman Alumni Center, Crawford Wheatley Hall, and Jackson Hall have been completely renovated.

Chief Executive Officer: Dr. Michael Hanes, President.

Address admission inquiries to Gaye Hayes, Director of Admissions.

Georgia State University

University Plaza
33 Gilmer Street S.E.
Atlanta, Georgia 30303-3083

Tel: (404) 651-2000   **E-mail:** admissions@gsu.edu
Fax: (404) 451-3567   **Internet:** www.gsu.edu

Institution Description: Georgia State University is a state institution. *Enrollment:* 27,261. *Degrees awarded:* Associate, baccalaureate, master's, doctorate. Specialists certificates in education also awarded.

Academic offerings subject to approval by statewide coordinating bodies. Budget subject to approval by state governing boards.

Accreditation: *Regional:* SACS-Comm. on Coll. *Professional:* business, clinical psychology, counseling, counseling psychology, dietetics, health services administration, law, music, nursing, physical therapy, public administration, rehabilitation counseling, respiratory therapy, respiratory therapy technology, school psychology, social work, speech-language pathology, teacher education

History: Established as Georgia Institute of Technology, Evening School of Commerce, and offered first instruction at postsecondary level 1913; awarded first degree (baccalaureate) 1916; changed name to University System Center 1932, to Atlanta Division, University of Georgia 1947, to Georgia State College of Business Administration 1955, to Georgia State College 1962; adopted present name 1969. *See* Bertram Holland Flanders, *A New Frontier in Education* (Atlanta: University of Georgia, 1955) for further information.

Institutional Structure: *Governing board:* Board of Regents of the University System of Georgia. Representation: 15 regents. All voting. *Composition of institution:* Administrators 31 men / 16 women. Academic affairs headed by provost and vice president for academic affairs. Management/business/finances directed by vice president for financial affairs. Full-time instructional faculty 513 men / 246 women. Academic governance body, University Senate, meets an average of 3 times per year.

Calendar: Semesters. Academic year Sept. to June. Freshmen admitted Aug., Nov., Feb., May. Degrees conferred and formal commencements Mar., June, Aug., Dec.

Admission: Rolling admissions plan. For fall acceptance, apply by July 1. Early acceptance available. *Requirements:* Either graduation from accredited secondary school with 15 units which must include 4 English, 3 mathematics (algebra I and II, geometry), 3 natural sciences (2 units in laboratory science), 3 social studies (American history, world history, economics, government), 2 foreign language. *Entrance tests:* College Board SAT or ACT. For foreign students TOEFL. *For transfer students:* 2.1 minimum GPA; from 4-year accredited institution 140 quarter hours maximum transfer credit; from 2-year accredited institution 95 hours; correspondence/extension students 45 hours.

College credit for postsecondary-level work completed in secondary school. Tutoring available. Noncredit developmental courses offered in summer session and regular academic year.

Degree Requirements: *For all associate degrees:* 60 credit hours. *For all baccalaureate degrees:* 120 credit hours. *For all undergraduate degrees:* 2.0 GPA; 2 terms in residence; core curriculum; exit competency examinations in writing, comprehensives in individual fields of study, Regents' Test of reading and writing, tests on or courses in U.S. and Georgia constitutions and histories.

Fulfillment of some degree requirements and exemption from some beginning courses possible by passing College Board CLEP, AP. *Grading system:* A–F; withdraw (deadline after which pass-fail is appended to withdraw).

Distinctive Educational Programs: Flexible meeting places and schedules, including off-campus courses (at DeKalb and Gwinnett Counties, 20 miles away and Valdosta, 250 miles away) and evening classes. Interdisciplinary programs in communications, community development, human resources, urban government and administration, urban studies. Honors programs. Study abroad in Belgium, France, Great Britain, Greece, Italy, Japan, Mexico, Spain, West Germany. *Other distinctive programs:* Learning Support Services for students who wish to pursue a college education but have not demonstrated college-level competence in the necessary academic skills.

ROTC: Army.

Degrees Conferred: 3,061 *baccalaureate*; 18 *post-baccalaureate certificates*; 2,073 *master's*; 81 *post-master's certificate*; 113 *doctorate*; 208 *first-professional.* Bachelor's degrees awarded in top five disciplines: business, management, marketing, and related support services 947; social sciences 236; psychology 263; computer and information sciences and support services 227; visual and performing arts 206.

Fees and Other Expenses: *Full-time tuition per academic year 2004–05:* in-state resident $4,154, out-of-state student $14,260. Contact the university for current graduate tuition/fees. *Books and supplies:* $1,000. *Room and board per academic year:* $6,730.

Financial Aid: Aid from institutionally generated funds is provided on the basis of academic merit, financial need, athletic ability. Institution has a Program Participation Agreement with the U.S. Department of Education for eligible students to receive Pell Grants and other federal aid.

Financial aid to full-time, first-time undergraduate students: 30% received federal grants averaging $3,108; 91% state/local grants averaging $4,497; 2% institutional grants averaging $4,104; 33% received loans averaging $2,724.

Departments and Teaching Staff: Arts and Sciences *professors* 94, *associate professors* 124, *assistant professors* 84, *instructors* 18, *part-time teachers* 141; Business Administration 81, 37, 46, 0, 79; Education 49, 45, 28, 6, 29; Health Sciences 8, 26, 25, 2, 13; Law 12, 12, 3, 3, 4; Public and Urban Affairs 5, 15, 14, 4, 20; Developmental Studies 1, 1, 12, 4, 25.

Total instructional faculty: 862.4 FTE. *Degrees held by full-time faculty:* Doctorate 83%, master's 11%, baccalaureate 1%, professional 5%. 90% hold terminal degrees.

Enrollment: Total enrollment 27,261. Undergraduate 19,889 (39.1% men, 60.9% women).

Characteristics of Student Body: *Ethnic and racial makeup:* Black non-Hispanic: 34.0%; American Indian or Native Alaskan: .2%; Asian or Pacific Islander: 10.6%; Hispanic: 3.4%; White non-Hispanic: 48.9%.

International Students: 576 undergraduate nonresident aliens enrolled fall 2003. Students from Europe, Africa, Australia. Programs available to aid students whose native language is not English: Social, cultural, financial. English as a Second Language Program.

Student Life: No on-campus housing. Housing available on Georgia Tech's campus a the Georgia State Olympic Village. *Intercollegiate athletics:* men only: basketball, cross-country, soccer, tennis; women only: basketball, cross-country, softball, tennis, volleyball; both sexes: golf, swimming. *Special services:* Counseling Center, Learning Resources Center, medical services. *Student publications, radio:* Rampway, a yearbook; *Review*, a literary magazine; *The Signal*, a weekly newspaper. Radio station WRAS broadcasts 168 hours per week. *Surrounding community:* Atlanta 18-county metropolitan area population over 3 million. Served by mass transit bus and trains (AMTRAK); airport 10 miles from campus; passenger rail service 3 miles from campus.

Publications: *Criminal Justice Review* (twice a year) first published in 1976; *Directory of Foreign Manufacturers in the U.S.* (every other year) first published in 1975; *Emphasis GSU* (5 times a year) first published in 1971; *Georgia State Literary Studies Series* (annually) first published in 1986; *Georgia State University FACT Book* (annually) first published in 1970; *Georgia State University Law Review* (irregularly) first published in 1985; *International Criminal Justice Review* (annually) first published in 1990; *Marketing Information - A Professional Reference Guide* (irregularly) first published in 1982; *Profile* (four times a year) first published in 1982; *Research Monograph Series* (irregularly) first published in 1973; *Studies in the Literary Imagination* (twice a year) first published in 1968; *Working Paper Series* (irregularly) first published in 1978.

Library Collections: 1,522,000 volumes. 761,585 government documents; 264,000 microforms; 23,000 audiovisual materials; 7535 periodical subscriptions. Online catalog. Students have access to online information retrieval services and the Internet.

Most important special holdings include Southern Labor Archives; Popular Music Collection (includes Johnny Mercer Collection); Jane and O'Neal Photographic Collections.

Buildings and Grounds: Campus area 257 acres (44 acres in main campus and 232 acres in suburban/research properties and president's home).

Chief Executive Officer: Dr. Carl V. Patton, President.

Address admission inquiries to Diane M. Weber, Director of Admissions; College of Law inquiries to Director of Admissions.

College of Arts and Sciences

Degree Programs Offered: *Baccalaureate* in anthropology, art history, art education, art studio concentrations, biological sciences, chemistry, computer science, economics, English, film and video, French, geography, geology, German, history, interdisciplinary studies, journalism, mathematics, music (applied) concentrations, music education, music industry (music management or sound recording technology), philosophy, physics, political science, psychology, sociology, Spanish, speech, theatre; *master's* in various fields; *doctorate* in astronomy, biological sciences, chemistry, English, history, physics, political science, psychology, sociology.

Distinctive Educational Programs: African American studies program; applied program in philosophy; bachelor of interdisciplinary studies; cartography production laboratory; center for biotechnology and drug design; center for brain sciences and health; center for high angular resolution astronomy with a program in speckle interferometry; center for Latin American and Hispanic studies; center for technology and the humanities, center for applied research in anthropology; commercial language program; creative writing program; gerontology center and certification program; ground water/hydrogeology program; heritage preservation degree and certificate program; laboratory for microbial and biochemical sciences; language research center with programs in non-human primate language acquisition and language assistance for handicapped children; premedical and prelaw programs; sacred music program; translation/interpretation program; tutorial assistance and workshops in English composition and mathematics; women's studies institute.

College of Business Administration

Degree Programs Offered: *Baccalaureate* in accounting, actuarial science, economics, finance, computer information systems, decision sciences, hospitality administration, management, marketing, real estate, risk management and insurance; *master's* in various fields; *doctorate* in accountancy, computer information systems, decision sciences, finance, management, marketing, operations management, personnel and employment relations, real estate, risk management and insurance.

Distinctive Educational Programs: Joint program with College of Law (MBA/JD); academic common market programs in actuarial science, health administration, real estate, and taxation.

College of Education

Degree Programs Offered: *Baccalaureate* in early childhood education, exercise science, health and related physical education, middle childhood education, recreation. *master's* in various education and education-related fields. *specialist degree* (6th year degree) in various fields; *doctorate* in counselor education, counseling psychology, early childhood education, education of students with exceptionalities, educational administration and supervision, educational psychology, higher education, instructional technology, language and literacy education, library media technology, mathematics education, research-measurement-statistics, school psychology, science education, social foundations of education, social studies education, sports science, vocational leadership.

Distinctive Educational Programs: Gifted education certification program. Master's-level initial certification programs in early childhood, English, mathematics, science, and social studies education. Collaborative master's-level program in early childhood education. Cooperative initial certification programs with Georgia Institute of Technology.

College of Health Sciences

Degree Programs Offered: *Baccalaureate* in criminal justice, medical technology, nursing, nutrition and dietetics, physical therapy, respiratory therapy, social work; *master's* in allied health professions, criminal justice and nursing; *doctorate* in nursing. *Master's* programs in physical therapy and social work are projected to begin fall 1998. health and human

Distinctive Educational Programs: Master's programs in the allied health professions include concentrations in medical technology, nutrition and dietetics, physical therapy and respiratory therapy. Master's programs in nursing include clinical nurse specialist programs in adult health, child and adolescent psychiatric/mental health, adult psychiatric/mental health and gerontology. A family nurse practitioner program is available as well as nurse practitioner programs in perinatal/women's health and child health. The focus area of the doctoral program in nursing is in Health Promotion, Protection, and Restoration with a special emphasis on vulnerable populations.

School of Policy Studies

Degree Programs Offered: *Baccalaureate* in urban studies with specializations in aviation management, gerontology, human resources, planning and economic development, urban governance; *master's* in public administration, urban studies; *doctorate* in economics.

Distinctive Educational Programs: Graduate students may participate in several nationally prominent research centers, including the Policy Research Center which conducts research on both domestic issues and the international economy, and in the GSU Economic Forecasting Center which publishes national and regional forecasts. Interdisciplinary programs in community development, human resources, urban government administration, urban studies, and public administration.

Interdenominational Theological Center

700 Martin L. King, Jr. Drive S.W.

Atlanta, Georgia 30314-4143

Tel: (404) 527-7700   **E-mail:** admissions@itc.edu
Fax: (404) 527-0901   **Internet:** www.itc.edu

Institution Description: The Interdenominational Theological Center is an ecumenical professional graduate school of theology. The constituent seminaries of the Center are Gammon Theological Seminary, Charles H. Mason Theological Seminary, Morehouse School of Religion, Phillips School of Theology, Johnson C. Smith Theological Seminary, and Turner Theological Seminary. *Enrollment:* 406. *Degrees awarded:* First-professional, master's, doctorate.

Accreditation: *Regional:* SACS-Comm. on Coll. *National:* ATS. *Professional*: theology

Institutional Structure: *Governing board:* Board of Trustees. 40 members. Extrainstitutional representation: 28 trustees from the six participating schools; 12 members-at-large. Full-time instructional faculty 21. Academic governance body, meets on the average of times per year.

Calendar: Semesters. Academic year Aug. to May. Summer session.

Admission: *Requirements:* Bachelor of Arts degree or its equivalent from an accredited college or university; certificate from a major official of the applicant's denomination indicating that the applicant is an acceptable candidate for service in the denomination and that admission to the Center is approved.

Degree Requirements: Completion of prescribed curriculum; requirements vary by program.

Distinctive Educational Programs: Continuing education program.

Degrees Conferred: 11 *master's*; 7 *doctorate:* Doctor of Ministry; 80 *first-professional:* Master of Divinity.

Fees and Other Expenses: *Full-time tuition per academic year 2004–05:* $8,858.

Financial Aid: Financial assistance is available in the form of College Work-Study, Veterans Administration Benefits, National Direct Student Loans, Stafford Loans.

Departments and Teaching Staff: Biblical studies *professors* 3, *associate professors* 2, *assistant professors* 0; philosophy/theology/ethics/church history 2, 2, 1; persons/society/culture 1, 3, 1; church and its mission 3, 2, 1.

Total instructional faculty: 21. Total tenured faculty: 12. Degrees held by full-time instructional faculty: professional 100%, doctorate 50%, masters 100%. 50% of faculty hold terminal degrees.

Enrollment: Total enrollment 406 (52.2% men, 47.8% women).

Characteristics of Student Body: *Ethnic/racial makeup:* Black non-Hispanic: 89.7%; Asian or Pacific Islander: .2%; White non-Hispanic: 3%; unknown: .5%.

International Students: 27 nonresident aliens enrolled fall 2003. No programs available to aid students whose native language is not English. No financial aid specifically designated for international students.

Student Life: Residence hall accommodations as well as efficiency housing and trailers are available. *Student publications: ITC Journal*, student yearbook, campus newsletter.

Library Collections: ITC holdings are included in Robert C. Woodruff Library of Atlanta University Center, Inc.

Most important theological collections are the C. Eric Lincoln Collection; Harry V. Richardson Collection; Gammon Theological Seminary Archival Collection.

Chief Executive Officer: Dr. Michael A. Battle, President.

Address admission inquiries to Quintin L. Robertson, Director of Admissions.

Kennesaw State University

1000 Chastain Road

Marietta, Georgia 30144-5591

Tel: (770) 423-6300   **E-mail:** ksuadmit@kennesaw.edu
Fax: (770) 423-6541   **Internet:** www.kennesaw.edu

Institution Description: Kennesaw State University is a 4-year institution of the University System of Georgia. *Enrollment:* 17,355. *Degrees awarded:* Baccalaureate, master's.

Accreditation: *Regional:* SACS-Comm. on Coll. *Professional*: business, engineering, nursing, teacher education

History: Established 1963; incorporated 1965 as Kennesaw Junior College; offered first instruction at postsecondary level 1966; awarded first degree (associate) 1967; awarded first baccalaureate degree 1980; offered first graduate programs in MBA and Medicine 1985; became Kennesaw State College in 1988 and Kennesaw State University 1996

Institutional Structure: *Governing board:* Board of Regents of the University System of Georgia. Extrainstitutional representation: 18 regents. All voting. *Composition of institution:* Administrators 13 men / 7 women. Academic affairs headed by vice president of academic affairs. Management/business/finances directed by vice president of business and finance. Full-time instructional faculty 537. Academic governance body, the faculty (including the administration), meets an average of 10 times per year.

Calendar: Semesters. Academic year Aug. to May. Freshmen admitted fall, winter, spring, summer. Degrees conferred and formal commencement Mar., June, Dec.

Characteristics of Freshmen: 61% of applicants admitted. 52% of admitted students enrolled full-time.

84% (1,627 students) submitted SAT scores; 7% (137 students) submitted ACT scores. *25th percentile*: SAT Verbal 490, SAT Math 490; ACT Composite 20, ACT English 20, ACT Math 19. *75th percentile*: SAT Verbal 580, SAT Math 570; ACT Composite 24, ACT English 24, ACT Math 23.

13% of entering freshmen expected to graduate within 5 years. 91% of freshmen from Georgia. Freshmen from 17 states and 47 foreign countries.

Admission: Rolling admissions plan. Apply by May 27 for fall admissions. Early admission available. *Requirements:* Either graduation from accredited secondary school with satisfactory SAT/ACT scores. Full standing admission requires a 950 combine minimum on the SAT and 2.5 GPA. Adults out of high school for five years or more with no previous college are reviewed as nontraditional students with only high school graduation nor GED required. Students who are less than 23 years of age should attend a two-year private college and qualify as a transfer. *For transfer students:* Students qualify as transfers if they have earned 30 transferable semester hours of 45 quarter transferable hours. GPA is calculated on all academic work attempted from all institutions attended.; minimum 2.0 GPA required to be considered.

College credit and advanced placement for extrainstitutional learning (life experience) on basis of College Board CLEP or departmental examinations. Tutoring available. Developmental courses offered in summer session and regular academic year; institutional credit given.

Degree Requirements: *For all baccalaureate degrees:* 120 semester hours with a minimum 2.0 GPA. At least 30 semester hours in residence and satisfactory completion of the University System of Georgia Regents' Testing Program. *Grading system:* A–F.

Distinctive Educational Programs: Cooperative (work-study) program; cross-registration; distance learning; double major; ESL; Honors program; internships; study abroad. Teacher certification program. Weekend College.

ROTC: Army, Air Force.

Degrees Conferred: 1,801 *baccalaureate* (B), 705 *master's* (M): biological/life sciences 61 (B); business/marketing 517 (B), 309 (M); communications/communication technologies 118 (B); computer and information sciences 149 (B), 65 (M); education 344 (B), 225 (M); English 37 (B), 25 (M); foreign languages and literature 19 (B); health professions and related sciences 133 (B), 44 (M); interdisciplinary studies 11 (B); mathematics 13 (B); parks and recreation 58 (B); physical sciences 10 (B); protective services/public administration 63 (B), 26 (M); psychology 106 (B); social sciences and history 125 (B); visual and performing arts 46 (B).

Fees and Other Expenses: *Full-time tuition per academic year 2004–05:* in-state undergraduate $2,322, out-of-state $9,290; in-state graduate $2,786, out-of-state $11m146, *Required fees:* $576. *Other fees:* $1,000. Contact the university for housing costs.

Financial Aid: Aid from institutionally generated funds is provided on the basis of academic merit, financial need, athletic ability. Institution has a Program Participation Agreement with the U.S. Department of Education for eligible students to receive Pell Grants and other federal aid.

Financial aid to full-time, first-time undergraduate students: need-based scholarships/grants totaling $10,063,938, self-help $19,141,426; non-need-based scholarships/grants totaling $18,443,084, self-help $14,908,106, parent loans $732,888, tuition waivers $723,761, athletic awards $1,384,652. *Graduate aid:* 473 federal and state-funded loans totaling $3,764,307 (ranging from $244 to $8,130); 1 work-study job worth $952.

Departments and Teaching Staff: Full-time *professors* 130, *associate professors* 133, *assistant professors* 163, *instructors* 91, *part-time faculty* 537. *Total instructional faculty:* 858 (full-time 537, part-time 321; women 377, men 461; members of minority groups 138). Total faculty with doctorate, first-professional, or other terminal degree: 480. Student-to-faculty ratio: 19:1. *Faculty development:* $364,045 in grants for research. 5 faculty members awarded sabbaticals 2004–05.

Enrollment: Total enrollment 17,355. Undergraduate full-time 4,234 men / 6,413 women, part-time 1,938m / 3,488w; graduate full-time 240m / 270w, part-time 575m / 847w.

Characteristics of Student Body: *Ethnic/racial makeup:* number of Black non-Hispanic: 1,627; American Indian or Alaska Native: 47; Asian or Pacific Islander: 523; Hispanic: 542; White non-Hispanic: 13,075; unknown: 265. *Age distribution:* number under 18: 181; 18–19: 3,239' 20–21: 3,467; 22–24: 3,542; 25–29: 2,396; 30–34: 1,206; 35–39: 301; 40–49: 970; 50–64: 254; 65 and over: 23.

International Students: 1,524 nonresident aliens enrolled fall 2004. 239 students from Europe, 363 Asia, 385 Central and South America, 402 Africa, 73 Canada, 5 Australia, 4 New Zealand, 53 other. Programs available to aid students whose native language is not English: English as a Second Language Program. No financial programs specifically designate for international students.

Student Life: On-campus housing available for single students. *Student publications: The Sentinel,* newspaper; *Talon,* student feature magazine. Sororities and fraternities. Intramural and intercollegiate athletics. *Surrounding community:* Cobb County population 607,00. Atlanta, 26 miles from campus, is nearest metropolitan area.

Publications: *Secolas Annuals,* first published in 1968; *Journal of Georgia Historians* (annually), first published 1981; and *Faculty Research Journal* (annually) first published 1981. *College Bound,* adult learners publication; *The Kennesaw Magazine,* alumni news.

Library Collections: 276,315 volumes. 295,749 government documents; 1,078,483 microforms; 3,507 current periodical subscriptions. Online catalog. Students have access to the Internet at no charge.

Most important special collections include Bentley Rare Books; DiFazio Children's Collection.

Buildings and Grounds: Campus area 183 acres. *New buildings:* Athletic Complex; Clendenin Building; English Building; Convocation/Classroom Building.

Chief Executive Officer: Dr. Betty L. Siegel, President. Address admission inquiries to Joe F. Head, Dean of Enrollment Service; graduate inquiries to Steven P. KIng, Director of Graduate Admissions.

LaGrange College

601 Broad Street
LaGrange, Georgia 30240
Tel: (706) 880-8000   **E-mail:** admission@lgc.edu
Fax: (706) 880-8358   **Internet:** www.lgc.edu

Institution Description: LaGrange College is a private, independent, non-profit college affiliated with North Georgia Annual Conference of the United Methodist Church. *Enrollment:* 1,044. *Degrees awarded:* Associate, baccalaureate, master's.

Accreditation: *Regional:* SACS-Comm. on Coll. *Professional:* business, nursing

History: Established as LaGrange Female Academy 1831; changed name to LaGrange Female Institute and offered first instruction at postsecondary level 1847; changed name to LaGrange Female College and awarded first degree (baccalaureate) 1851; adopted present name 1934; became coeducational 1953.

Institutional Structure: *Governing board:* LaGrange College Board of Trustees. Extrainstitutional representation: 35 trustees, including 3 alumni; institutional representation: president of the college, 1 student. 6 ex officio. All voting. *Composition of institution:* Administrators 7 men / 4 women (at dean's level and above, 33% are women). Academic affairs headed by academic dean. Management/business/finances directed by executive vice president. Academic governance body, Board of Trustees (advised by academic dean and the faculty), meets an average of 2 times per year.

Calendar: Semesters. Academic year Sept. to June. Freshmen admitted Sept., Jan., Mar., June, July. Degrees conferred and formal commencement June.

Characteristics of Freshmen: 38% of applicants admitted. 18% of admitted students enrolled full-time.

86% (189 students) submitted SAT scores; 31% (69 students) submitted ACT scores. *25th percentile:* SAT Verbal 460, SAT Math 460; ACT Composite 17, ACT English 17, ACT Math 17. *75th percentile:* SAT Verbal 570, SAT Math 570; ACT Composite 21, ACT English 21, ACT Math 21.

46% of entering freshmen expected to graduate within 5 years. 88% of freshmen from Georgia. Freshmen from 10 states and 5 foreign countries.

Admission: Rolling admissions plan. For fall acceptance, apply as early as Sept. of previous year but not later than 1 month prior to enrollment. Early acceptance available. *Requirements:* Either graduation from accredited secondary school with 11 units which must include 4 English, 3 social studies, 4 mathematics, 3 science; or GED. Recommend 2 units foreign language, 1 additional mathematics, 1 additional science. Minimum GPA 2.0. *Entrance tests:* College Board SAT or ACT composite. *For transfer students:* Maximum transfer credit limited only by residence requirement; from 2-year accredited institution 54 semester hours.

College credit and advanced placement for postsecondary-level work completed in secondary school. Tutoring available.

Degree Requirements: *For all associate degrees:* 60 semester hours. *For all baccalaureate degrees:* 120 semester hours; last 60 semester hours in residence. *For all degrees:* 2.0 GPA; 2 semester hours physical education; distribution requirements.

Fulfillment of some degree requirements and exemption from some beginning courses possible by passing departmental examinations, College Board CLEP, AP. *Grading system:* A–F; pass-fail; withdraw (deadline after which pass-fail is appended to withdrawal); incomplete (deadline after which A–F is assigned); incomplete (deadline after which A–F is assigned).

Distinctive Educational Programs: *For undergraduates:* Dual-degree program in engineering with Auburn University (AL) and Georgia Institute of Technology. Foreign study opportunities include summer religion seminar in Israel and Europe and January term travel courses to Europe, England, Costa Rica. Spanish language study in Mexico in cooperation with InterAmerican Workshop in Mexico. *Available to all students:* Work-experience programs. Leadership programs. Evening classes.

Degrees Conferred: 2 *associate;* 96 *baccalaureate:* biological/life sciences 3, business/marketing 31, computer and information sciences 3, education 13, engineering and engineering technologies 1, English 3, foreign languages and literature 1, health professions and related sciences 2, liberal arts/general studies 1, mathematics 1, philosophy/religion/theology 3, physical sciences 6, protective services/public administration 1, psychology 8, social sciences and history 11, visual and performing arts 12.

Fees and Other Expenses: *Full-time tuition per academic year 2004–05:* $15,206. *Room and board per academic year:* $6,318.

Financial Aid: Aid from institutionally generated funds is provided on the basis of academic merit, financial need. Institution has a Program Participation Agreement with the U.S. Department of Education for eligible students to receive Pell Grants and other federal aid.

Financial aid to full-time, first-time undergraduate students: need-based scholarships/grants totaling $5,620,222, self-help $3,386,128, parent loans $557,909, tuition waivers $109,584; non-need-based scholarships/grants totaling $1,338,233, self-help $348,565, parent loans $302,980, tuition waivers $165,508.

Departments and Teaching Staff: *Professors* 22, *associate professors* 18, *assistant professors* 26, *instructors* 1, *part-time faculty* 45. *Total instructional faculty:* 103 (full-time 66, part-time 37; women 45, men 58; members of minority groups 5). Total faculty with doctorate, first-professional, or other terminal degree: 69. Student-to-faculty ratio: 13:1. Degrees held by full-time faculty: doctorate 59%, master's 100%, professional 9%. 86% hold terminal degrees.

Enrollment: Total enrollment 1,044. Undergraduate full-time 314 men / 562 women, part-time 42m / 75w; graduate full-time 10m / 41w. *Transfer students:* in-state 172; from out-of-state 113.

Characteristics of Student Body: *Ethnic/racial makeup:* number of Black non-Hispanic: 188; American Indian or Alaska Native: 5; Asian or Pacific Islander: 13; Hispanic: 11; White non-Hispanic: 753; unknown: 23. *Age distribution:* number under 18: 34; 18–19: 344; 20–21: 304; 25–29: 62; 30–34: 47; 35–39: 55; 40–49: 58; 50–64: 13.

International Students: 18 nonresident aliens enrolled fall 2004. 2 students from Europe, 98 Asia, 3 Central and South America, 5 Africa. Programs available to aid students whose native language is not English: social, cultural. No financial aid specifically designated for international students.

Student Life: On-campus residence halls house 80% of student body. 37% of men join fraternities. 28% of freshmen women join sororities. *Intercollegiate athletics:* men only: basketball, baseball, football, soccer, tennis; women only: soccer, volleyball, softball, tennis. *Special regulations:* Cars permitted without restrictions. *Student publications: Hilltop News,* a campus newspaper published twice a quarter; *The Quadrangle,* a college yearbook; *The Scroll,* an annual art and literary magazine. *Surrounding community:* LaGrange population 27,000. Atlanta, 65 miles from campus, is nearest metropolitan area.

Library Collections: 114,366 volumes including bound books, serial backfiles, electronic documents, and government documents not in separate collections. Online catalog. Current serial subscriptions: 512 via electronic access. Phono discs 860; compact discs 391. 39 computer work stations. Students have access to the Internet at no charge.

Most important holdings include Lafayette Collection (manuscripts, papers, pamphlets on the life of the Marquis de Lafayette); Grogan Papers (original manuscripts).

Buildings and Grounds: Campus area 35 acres. *New buildings:* Two apartment style residence halls completed in 2003.

Chief Executive Officer: Dr. Stuart Gulley, President.

Address all admission inquiries to Phil Dodson, Director of Admission.

Life University

1269 Barclay Circle
Marietta, Georgia 30060
Tel: (770) 426-2600   **E-mail:** admissions@lifenet.life.edu
Fax: (770) 429-4819   **Internet:** www.life.edu

Institution Description: Life University (formerly known as Life College and Life Chiropractic College) a private, independent, nonprofit institution. *Enrollment:* 1,210. *Degrees awarded:* Baccalaureate, master's, first-professional.

Accreditation: *Regional:* SACS. *Professional:* chiropractic education

History: Founded and chartered as Life Chiropractic College 1974; first degree (chiropractic) awarded 1978; adopted present name 1996.

Institutional Structure: Board of Trustees. *Institutional representation:* President of the University. *Composition of institution:* Provost, vice president of operations and finance, deans of the College of Chiropractic and College of Arts and Sciences. Full-time instructional faculty 91. Academic representative body, Faculty Senate, meets 6 or more times per year.

Calendar: Quarters. Freshmen admitted each quarter. Degrees conferred June, Sept., Dec., March. Formal commencements June, Dec.

Characteristics of Freshmen: 59% of applicants admitted. 36% of admitted students enrolled full-time.

57% (16 students) submitted SAT scores; 43% (12 students) submitted ACT scores. *25th percentile:* SAT Verbal 418, SAT Math 438; ACT Composite 17, ACT English 16, ACT Math 16. *75th percentile:* SAT Verbal 530, SAT Math 503; ACT Composite 21, ACT English 20, ACT Math 20.

16% of entering students expected to graduate within 5 years. 40% of freshmen from Georgia.

Admission: Undergraduate: GPA 2.0 or higher (4.0 scale); SAT 840, ACT 18; graduate: GPA 3.0; GRE 800; MAT 40; first-professional: preprofessional background of not less that 90 semester hours or 135 quarter hours

Degree Requirements: Completion of prescribed program.

Degrees Conferred: 70 *baccalaureate:* biological/life sciences 24, business/marketing 19, health professions and related sciences 27; 16 *master's* health professions and related sciences; 340 *first-professional:* chiropractic.

Fees and Other Expenses: *Full-time tuition per academic year 2004–05:* Contact the university for current undergraduate, graduate, and first-professional tuition and fees.

Financial Aid: Aid from institutionally generated funds is provided on the basis of academic merit, financial need. Institution has a Program Participation Agreement with the U.S. Department of Education for eligible students to receive Pell Grants and other federal aid.

Financial aid to full-time, first-time undergraduate students: need-based scholarships/grants totaling $688,200, self-help $230,500; non-need-based scholarships/grants totaling $234,600, self-help $950,000, parent loans $124,000. *Graduate aid:* 800 federal and state-funded loans totaling $22,000,000; 250 work-study jobs worth $200,000.

Departments and Teaching Staff: *Professors* 12, *associate professors* 23, *assistant professors* 18, *instructors* 33, *part-time faculty* 24.

Total instructional faculty: 115 (full-time 91, part-time 24). Total faculty with doctorate, first-professional, or other terminal degree: 97. Student-to-faculty ratio: 12:1.

Enrollment: Total enrollment 1,233. Undergraduate full-time 159 men / 145 women, part-time 70m / 93w; graduate full-time 7m / 6w, part-time 15m / 5w; first-professional 416m / 242w, part-time 54m / 22w.

Characteristics of Student Body: *Ethnic and racial makeup:* number of Black non-Hispanic: 51; Asian or Pacific Islander: 8; Hispanic: 8; White non-Hispanic: 57; unknown: 266. *Age distribution:* number of 18–19: 25; 20–21: 45; 22–24: 114; 25–29: 105; 30–34: 52; 35–39: 21; 40–49: 24; 50–64: 6.

International Students: 147 nonresident aliens enrolled fall 2004. Programs available to aid students whose native language is not English: English as a Second Language. Scholarships available for international students.

Student Life: Student clubs and organizations including Student Council and intramural sports; Student Success Center offers personal/academic/career counseling, academic assistance, disability services; Wellness Center fitness center available to students.

Library Collections: 56,715 volumes. 124 periodical subscriptions; access to 2,000 journals via electronic access. 8,514 recordings; 134 compact discs; 173 CD-ROMs. 30 computer work stations. Students have access to the Internet at no charge. Total budget for books and materials 2004–05: $172,400.

Most important special holdings include chiropractic and health sciences; sports sciences; English/history/mathematics.

Buildings and Grounds: Campus area 90 acres. *New buildings:* Administration Building; Student Services and Learning Resource Building; College of Arts and Sciences Center; College of Chiropractic Center; Human Performance Facility; Student Activities Center.

Chief Executive Officer: Dr. Guy F. Riekeman, President.

Address admission inquiries to Dr. Deborah Heairlston, Director of New Students Development.

Macon State College

100 College Station Drive
Macon, Georgia 31296-5144
Tel: (478) 471-2700   **E-mail:** admissions@lmaconstate.edu
Fax: (478) 471-2846   **Internet:** www.maconstate.edu

Institution Description: The purpose of Macon State College is to advance the intellectual, cultural, social, economic, recreational, and physical development of those within commuting distance. Flexible and accommodating, the college has since its beginning served district constituencies including military personnel, early enrollment students, tradition and nontraditional, day and evening students. *Degrees awarded:* Associate, baccalaureate.

Accreditation: *Regional:* SACS. *Professional:* dental hygiene, health information technician, nursing, respiratory therapy

Institutional Structure: Board of Trustees. *Institutional representation:* President of the University. *Composition of institution:* Provost, vice president of operations and finance.

Calendar: Semesters.

Characteristics of Freshmen: 3,556 applicants (1,147 men, 2,409 women). 60% of applicants admitted. 35.8% of admitted students enrolled full-time.

67% (643 students) submitted SAT scores; 12% (114 students) submitted ACT scores. *25th percentile:* SAT I Verbal 400, SAT I Math 390; ACT Composite 15, ACT English 14, ACT Math 15. *75th percentile:* SAT I Verbal 530, SAT I Math 510; ACT Composite 19, ACT English 19, ACT Math 18.

Admission: Graduation from an accredited secondary school with 16 curse units: 4 English, 4 mathematics, 3 science, 3 social science, 2 foreign language. Apply by July 22 for fall semester; December 2 for spring semester.

Degree Requirements: Completion of prescribed program.

Degrees Conferred: 364 *associate;* 208 *baccalaureate.* Bachelor's degrees awarded in top five disciplines: computer and information sciences and support services 94; business, management, marketing, and related support services 61; health professions and related clinical sciences 30; public administration and social service professions 18; communication, journalism, and related programs.

Fees and Other Expenses: *Full-time tuition per academic year 2004–05:* in-state resident $1,626, out-of-state $6,030. *Books and supplies:* $866. *Room and board per academic year:* $2,922.

Financial Aid: Aid from institutionally generated funds is provided on the basis of academic merit, financial need. Institution has a Program Participation Agreement with the U.S. Department of Education for eligible students to receive Pell Grants and other federal aid.

Financial aid to full-time, first-time undergraduate students: 46% received federal grants averaging $3,157; 67% state/local grants averaging $1,868; 27% loans averaging $3,398.

Departments and Teaching Staff: Faculty are unranked.

Enrollment: Total enrollment 5,733 (33.3% men, 66.7% women).

Characteristics of Student Body: *Ethnic and racial makeup:* Black non-Hispanic: 36.4%; American Indian or Alaska Native: .2%; Asian or Pacific Islander: 2.1%; Hispanic: 1.6%; White non-Hispanic: 59%.

International Students: 34 nonresident aliens enrolled fall 2004. Programs available to aid students whose native language is not English: English as a Second Language.

Student Life: Student clubs and organizations.

Library Collections: 83,000 volumes. 327 periodical subscriptions; access to journals via electronic access. Library has access to GALILEO, the Georgia statewide information network. Computer work stations available.

Buildings and Grounds: Macon metropolitan area population 75,000; located 75 miles southeast of Atlanta.

Chief Executive Officer: Dr. David A. Bell, President.

Address admission inquiries to Terrell M. Mitchell, Director of Admissions.

Medical College of Georgia

1120 15th Street
Augusta, Georgia 30912
Tel: (706) 721-0211   **E-mail:** cnobles@mail.mcg.edu
Fax: (706) 721-0186   **Internet:** www.mcg.edu

Institution Description: Medical College of Georgia is a state institution. *Enrollment:* 769 men / 1,312 women. *Degrees awarded:* Associate, baccalaureate, master's, doctorate, first-professional (dentistry, medicine). Certificates also warded.

Accreditation: *Regional:* SACS-Comm. on Coll. *Professional*; clinical lab scientist, combined prosthodontics, dental hygiene, dentistry, diagnostic medical sonography, endodontics, health information administration, medical illustration, medicine, nuclear medicine technology, nurse anesthesia education, nursing, occupational therapy, oral and maxillofacial surgery, pediatric dentistry, periodontics, physical therapy, physician assisting, prosthodontics, psychology internship, radiation therapy, radiography, respiratory therapy

History: Established 1828; offered first instruction at postsecondary level 1829; awarded first degree (first-professional) 1833; became part of university system and adopted present name 1950.

Institutional Structure: *Governing board:* Board of Regents of the University System of Georgia. Extrainstitutional representation: 16 regents. All voting. *Composition of institution:* President, Vice Presidents for Academic Affairs, Clinical Activities, and Fiscal Affairs and Planning.

Calendar: Semesters. Academic year Aug. to May. Entering students admitted Aug. and Jan. Degrees conferred and formal commencement May.

Admission: *Entrance tests:* For School of Dentistry DAT; for School of Medicine MCAT; undergraduate programs SAT or ACT graduate programs GRE.

Degree Requirements: *For first-professional degree:* Requirements vary by program. *Grading system:* A–F; withdraw.

Degrees Conferred: Health professions and related sciences: 39 *associate;* 343 *baccalaureate;* 73 *master's;* 8 *doctorate.* 220 *first-professional:* dentistry 47, medicine 173.

Fees and Other Expenses: *Full-time tuition per academic year 2004–05:* Undergraduate in-state resident $3,368, out-of-state $13,474; graduate in-state resident $4,044, out-of-state $16,170. *Required fees:* $586. *Graduate housing/apartments:* $3,824 per semester.

Financial Aid: Aid from institutionally generated funds is provided on the basis of academic merit, financial need.

Financial aid to full-time, first-time undergraduate students: need-based scholarships/grants totaling $1,268,309, self-help $3,081,554, parent loans $22,133; non-need-based scholarships/grants totaling $522,820, self-help $861,321, parent loans $33,769. *Graduate aid:* 14 students received federal and state-funded fellowships and grants totaling $493,446 (ranging from $24,018 to $55,754); 189 federal and state-funded loans totaling $2,399,777 (ranging from $200 to $8,500); 50 work-study jobs worth $742,706 (ranging from $500 to $6,192); 16 other fellowships and grants totaling $308,988; 4 teaching assistantships totaling $76,000; 82 research assistantships totaling $1,584,500.

Departments and Teaching Staff: *Professors* 143, *associate professors* 176, *assistant professors* 252, *instructors* 39, *part-time faculty:* 118, *other ranks* 36. *Total instructional faculty:* 764 (full-time 646, part-time 118; women 137, men 519; members of minority groups 134). Total faculty with doctorate, first-professional, or other terminal degree: 671.

Enrollment: Total enrollment 2,081. Undergraduate full-time 90 men / 540 women, part-time 9m / 77w; first-professional full-time 535m / 400w, part-time 7m / 3w; graduate full-time 108m / 248w, part-time 17m / 47w.

Characteristics of Student Body: *Ethnic/racial makeup:* number of Black non-Hispanic: 109; American Indian or Alaska Native: 3; Asian or Pacific Islander: 23; Hispanic: 4; White non-Hispanic: 560; unknown: 12. *Age distribution:* number of 18–19: 2; 20–21: 232; 22–24: 220; 25–29: 111; 30–34: 64; 35–39: 33; 40–49: 42; 50–64: 12.

International Students: 202 nonresident aliens enrolled fall 2004. No programs to aid students whose native language is not English. No financial aid specifically designated for international students.

Student Life: On-campus housing for single and married students available. *Special regulations:* Cars permitted without restrictions. *Special student ser-*

vices: campus employment opportunities, campus safety program, career counseling, child day-care facilities, free psychological counseling, international student services, low-cost health insurance, multicultural affairs office. *Surrounding community:* Augusta area population 200,000. Atlanta, 135 miles from campus, is nearest major city.

Library Collections: 180,000 volumes. 7,114 microforms; 12,831 audiovisual materials; 430 current periodical subscriptions; access to journals via electronic access 1,733. 43 computer work stations. Students have Internet access no charge.

Most important holdings include landmark collection of medical textbooks; 19th Century Medical Library of the Medical College of Georgia; personal papers of Robert B. Greenblatt, M.D.

Buildings and Grounds: Campus area 100 acres. *New buildings:* Cancer Research Facility (home of Augusta Cancer Center of Excellence) completed 2005.

Chief Executive Officer: Daniel W. Rahn, M.D., President. Undergraduates address admission inquiries to Carol Nobles, Director of Student Recruitment and Admissions; graduate inquiries to Patricia Cameron, Assistant Dean for Recruitment and Admissions-Graduate Studies.

Mercer University

1400 Coleman Avenue
Macon, Georgia 31207
Tel: (478) 301-2700   **E-mail:** admissions@mercer.edu
Fax: (478) 301-2655   **Internet:** www.mercer.edu

Institution Description: Mercer University is composed of schools located in Macon and Atlanta and offers programs at the baccalaureate, master's, doctorate, and first-professional levels. The university is a private institution affiliated with the Georgia Baptist Convention. It is the second largest Baptist-affiliated institution in the world, and the only independent university of its size in the United States that combines programs in liberal arts, business, engineering, education, medicine, pharmacy, law, and theology. *Enrollment:* 7,180.

Accreditation: *Regional:* SACS-Comm. on Coll. *Professional*: applied science, business, computer science, engineering, law, marriage and family therapy, medicine, music, nursing, nursing education, pharmacy, teacher education

History: Chartered 1830; established as Mercer Institute 1833; offered first instruction at postsecondary level and adopted present name 1838; awarded first degree (baccalaureate) 1841. *See* Spright Dowell, *A History of Mercer University 1833–1953* (Atlanta, Ga.: Foote and Davis, Inc., 1958) for further information.

Institutional Structure: *Governing board:* Board of Trustees. *Composition of institution:* President, executive vice president and provost; senior vice president for university advancement; senior vice president for finance; senior vice president for administration; senior vice president-Atlanta. Full-time instructional faculty 343.

Calendar: Semesters. Academic year Aug. to May. Entering students admitted Aug., Jan., June, July. Degrees conferred and formal commencement May.

Characteristics of Freshmen: 85% of applicants admitted; 21% of admitted students enrolled full-time.

93% (537 students) submitted SAT scores; 41% (237 students) submitted ACT scores. *25th percentile*: SAT Verbal 530, SAT Math 540; ACT Composite 22, ACT English 22, ACT Math 22. *75th percentile*: SAT Verbal 640, SAT Math 640; ACT Composite 27, ACT English 27, ACT Math 27.

43% of entering freshmen expected to graduate within 5 years. 75% of freshmen from Georgia. Freshmen from 29 states and 8 foreign countries.

Admission: Rolling admissions plan. Early action deadline Nov. 1; regular action deadline Apr. 1. *Requirements:* Either graduation from secondary school with 16 units, including 4 English, 4 mathematics, 3 science (of these, 2 units must be lab), 2 foreign language, 3 social studies. *Entrance tests:* College Board SAT or ACT. *For transfer students:* 2.5 minimum GPA.

College credit and advanced placement for postsecondary-level work completed in secondary school. Tutoring available at no charge. Developmental courses offered in summer session and regular academic years; credit given.

Degree Requirements: 120–130 semester hours; 2.0 GPA; last 2 semesters in residence; general education requirements; exit competency examinations (comprehensives in individual fields of study). Fulfillment of some degree requirements and exemption from some beginning courses possible by passing College Board CLEP, AP. *Grading system:* A–F; satisfactory-unsatisfactory; withdraw (carries time limit).

Distinctive Educational Programs: Work-experience programs. Flexible meeting places and schedules, including weekend and evening classes. Special facilities for using telecommunications in the classroom. Facilities and programs for independent research, including individual majors, tutorials. First-Year Seminar, Great Books, Senior Capstone. Pre-professional work is offered for students expected to enter theology, education, law, medicine, pharmacy, dentistry, medical technology, veterinary medicine. Teacher certification program available.

ROTC: Army. 10 commissions awarded 2004.

Degrees Conferred: 941 *baccalaureate* (B); 386 *master's* (M); 8 *doctorate* (D): biological/life sciences 27 (B); business/marketing 202 (B), 213 (M); communications/communication technologies 44 (B), computer and information sciences 37 (B), 5 (M); education 157 (B), 92 (M); engineering and engineering technologies 62 (B), 26 (M); English 16 (B); foreign languages and literature 10 (B); health professions and related sciences 82 (B), 36 (M), 3 (D); interdisciplinary studies 69 (B); liberal arts/general studies 6 (B); mathematics (3); natural resources/environmental science 5 (B); philosophy/religion/theology 16 (B); physical sciences 10 (B); protective services/public administration 113 (B); psychology 29 (B), 10 (M); social sciences and history 39 (B), 2 (M); visual and performing arts 14 (B). 351 *first-professional:* pharmacy 149, law 129, medicine 42, theological 31.

Fees and Other Expenses: *Full-time tuition per academic year 2004–05:* undergraduate $22,050; graduate varies by program. *Room per academic year:* $7,060.

Financial Aid: Aid from institutionally generated funds is awarded on the basis of academic merit, financial need, athletic ability, other criteria. Institution has a Program Participation Agreement with the U.S. Department of Education for eligible students to receive Pell Grants and other federal aid.

Financial aid to full-time, first-time undergraduate students: need-based scholarships/grants totaling $19,703,391, self-help $6,946,665, parent loans $833,399, tuition waivers $423,853, athletic awards $687,853; non-need-based scholarships/grants totaling $11,738,069, self-help $3,406,960, parent loans $2,275,424, tuition waivers $795,109, athletic awards $1,891,360. *Graduate aid:* 184 students received federal and state-funded fellowships and grants totaling $1,324,973; 1,759 received federal and state-funded loans totaling $31,260,198; 44 work-study jobs worth $135,253; 859 other fellowships and grants totaling $5,694,503.

Departments and Teaching Staff: *Total instructional faculty:* 577 (full-time 343, part-time 234; women 242, men 335; members of minority groups 82). Total faculty with doctorate, first-professional, or other terminal degree: 381. Student-to-faculty ratio: 14:1. 15 faculty members awarded sabbaticals 2004–05.

Enrollment: Total enrollment: 7,180. Undergraduate full-time 1,285 men / 2,605 women, part-time 195m / 543w; first-professional full-time 551m / 780w, part-time 32m / 58w; graduate full-time 145m / 506w, part-time 245m / 535w.

Characteristics of Student Body: *Ethnic/racial makeup:* number of Black non-Hispanic: 1,323; American Indian or Alaska Native: 7; Asian or Pacific Islander: 147; Hispanic: 78; White non-Hispanic: 2,817; unknown: 138. *Age distribution:* number under 18: 18; 18–19: 1,042; 20–2: 1,064; 22–24: 646; 25–29: 451; 30–34: 465; 35–39: 365; 40–49: 460; 50–64: 115; 65 and over: 2.

International Students: 118 nonresident aliens enrolled fall 2004. English as a Second Language Program. Limited scholarships are available for qualifying international students.

Student Life: On-campus residence halls and additional on-campus apartments available for upperclass students. *Intercollegiate athletics:* men's baseball, basketball, golf, soccer, tennis, cross country, rifle; women's basketball, tennis, soccer, volleyball, cross country, golf. Member of the National Collegiate Athletic Association and the Trans American Athletic Conference. *Special regulations:* Registered cars permitted. Residence hall visitation hours from 11am to 11:30pm weekdays and 11am to 2am weekends. *Special services:* Learning Center, Counseling Center, International Student Services, Disabled Student Services, Career Services. *Student activities:* Over 100 registered student organizations. 17 social fraternities; 10 with chapter houses. 16 social fraternities and sororities, with chapter houses. Student leadership programs include the Freshmen Leadership Experience. Campus recreation offers formal competition, outdoor recreation program, fitness assessments, swimming pool, fitness center, aerobics, co-recreational sports. *Student publications: Cluster,* a student weekly newspaper; *The Caldron,* annual; *Mercer Law Review,* a quarterly publication. *Surrounding community:* Macon metropolitan area population 300,000. Atlanta is 70 miles from campus. Served by mass transit bus system; airport 12 miles from campus.

Publications: Mercer University Press published 40 scholarly and literary works each year, primarily in the areas of religion, philosophy, and Southern studies and literature.

Library Collections: 692,225 volumes. Current serial titles: 3,055,812 microforms; 57,166 video and audio titles. Students have access to the Internet at no charge.

Most important special holdings include collection of Georgia Baptist history; James H. Kilpatrick papers; Robert Burns collection.

Buildings and Grounds: Campus area 315 acres (Atlanta and Macon campuses). *New buildings:* McCorkle Music Building; University Center.

Chief Executive Officer: R. Kirby Godsey, President.

Address admission inquiries to Vice President, Admissions.

Walter F. George School of Law

Degree Programs Offered: *First-professional.*

Admission: Baccalaureate degree from college or university, LSAT.

Degree Requirements: 90 semester hours, 76 grade average on 100 scale, 90 weeks in residence.

Departments and Teaching Staff: *Total instructional faculty:* 26.

Southern School of Pharmacy

Degree Programs Offered: *First-professional; doctorate.*

Admission: Rolling admissions. New classes begin in Aug. Early application encouraged. PCAT scores, recommendations, pharmacy experience considered.

Departments and Teaching Staff: *Total full-time instructional faculty:* 39.

School of Medicine

Degree Programs Offered: *Master's, doctorate.*

Admission: Before beginning study, all accepted applicants must have successfully completed 3 years of course work leading to the baccalaureate degree, and 1-year laboratory courses in biology, inorganic or general chemistry, biochemistry, and physics. New MCAT; applications must be initiated through the American Medical College Application Service.

Departments and Teaching Staff: *Total full-time instructional faculty:* 74.

School of Theology

Degree Programs Offered: *Master of Divinity, Doctor of Ministry.*

Admission: Minimum requirements for admission include a baccalaureate degree from an accredited college or university in the United States, or proof of an equivalent degree from a foreign university.

Morehouse College

830 Westview Drive, S.W.
Atlanta, Georgia 30314
Tel: (404) 681-2800   **E-mail:** admissions@morehouse.edu
Fax: (404) 659-6536   **Internet:** www.morehouse.edu

Institution Description: Morehouse College is a private, independent, nonprofit college for men. *Enrollment:* 2,891. *Degrees awarded:* Baccalaureate.

Member of Atlanta University Center.

Accreditation: *Regional:* SACS-Comm. on Coll. *Professional:* business

History: Established as the Augusta Institute 1867; chartered and changed name to Atlanta Baptist Seminary and to Atlanta Baptist College 1879; offered first instruction at postsecondary level 1894; awarded first degree (baccalaureate) 1897. *See* Edward A. Jones, *A Candle in the Dark* (Valley Forge, PA.: Judson Press, 1967) for further information.

Institutional Structure: *Governing board:* Board of Trustees of Morehouse College. Extrainstitutional representation: 31 trustees; institutional representation: president of the college, 3 full-time instructional faculty members, 3 students. 3 ex officio. 35 voting. *Composition of institution:* Administrators 19 men / 5 women. Academic affairs headed by academic dean. Management/business/finances directed by business manager. Full-time instructional faculty 150. Academic governance body, The Faculty of Morehouse College meets an average of 8 times per year.

Calendar: Semesters. Academic year Aug. to May. Freshmen admitted Aug., Jan. Degrees conferred and formal commencement May. No summer session.

Characteristics of Freshmen: 2,277 applicants (2,227 men). 67.5% of applicants admitted. 46.3% of admitted students enrolled full-time.

79% (568 students) submitted SAT scores; 29% (210 students) submitted ACT scores. *25th percentile*: SAT I Verbal 470, SAT I Math 470; ACT Composite 19, ACT English 17, ACT Math 18. *75th percentile*: SAT I Verbal 580, SAT I Math 590; ACT Composite 24, ACT English 24, ACT Math 25.

Freshmen from 40 states and 10 foreign countries.

Admission: Rolling admissions plan. For fall acceptance, apply as early as Sept. 15 of previous year, but not later than Feb. 15 of year of enrollment. *Requirements:* Either graduation from accredited secondary school with 11 units which normally include 4 English, 3 college preparatory mathematics, 2 science (1 laboratory), 2 social studies; or GED. Minimum GPA 2.0. *Entrance tests:* College Board SAT. For foreign students TOEFL. *For transfer students:* 2.5 minimum GPA; 60 semester hours maximum transfer credit.

Tutoring available. Remedial courses offered during regular academic year; institutional credit given.

Degree Requirements: 124 credit hours; 2.0 GPA; 2 terms in residence; 2 physical education courses; distribution requirements, 6 nonacademic hours in freshmen orientation and college assembly. *Grading system:* A–F; pass-fail; withdraw; incomplete (carries time limit).

Distinctive Educational Programs: Dual-degree program in engineering with Georgia Institute of Technology. Preprofessional programs in law and medicine. Interdisciplinary programs in international studies, urban studies. Honors programs. Study abroad may be individually arranged. Cross-registration and cooperative academic programs through consortium.

ROTC: Army, Navy, Air Force offered in cooperation with Georgia Institute of Technology.

Degrees Conferred: 452 *baccalaureate.* Bachelor's degrees awarded in top five disciplines: business, management, marketing, and related support services 165; social sciences 70; psychology 34; computer and information sciences and support services 33; biological and biomedical sciences 27.

Fees and Other Expenses: *Full-time tuition per academic year:* $15,740. *Books and supplies:* $850. *Room and board per academic year:* $8,748.

Financial Aid: Aid from institutionally generated funds is awarded on the basis of academic merit, financial need, athletic ability. Institution has a Program Participation Agreement with the U.S. Department of Education for eligible students to receive Pell Grants and other federal aid.

Financial aid to full-time, first-time undergraduate students: 42% received federal grants averaging $3,813; 25% state/local grants averaging $1,165; 47% institutional grants averaging $12,013; 68% loans averaging $5,945.

Departments and Teaching Staff: *Total instructional faculty:* 150. Degrees held by full-time faculty: 74% hold terminal degrees.

Enrollment: Total enrollment 2.891 (100% men).

Characteristics of Student Body: *Ethnic/racial makeup:* Black non-Hispanic: 94.5%; Hispanic: 2.2%; American Indian or Alaska Native: .1%; White non-Hispanic: .1%; unknown: 1.9%.

International Students: 84 nonresident aliens enrolled fall 2003. Students from Europe, Asia, Africa, and other countries. Programs available to aid students whose native language is not English: social and cultural.

Student Life: On-campus residence halls house 50% of student body. *Intercollegiate athletics:* Baseball, basketball, cross-country, football, tennis, track. *Special regulations:* Registered cars permitted without restrictions. *Special services:* Learning Resources Center, medical services, counseling center; career placement. *Student publications: The Maroon Tiger,* a monthly newspaper; *Torch,* a yearbook. *Surrounding community:* Atlanta metropolitan area population over 3 million. Served by mass transit subway system; airport 9 miles from campus; passenger rail service 5 miles from campus.

Library Collections: 550,000 volumes. 15,000 microforms; 8,000 audiovisual materials; 110 periodical subscriptions.

Most important holdings include Japanese collection; Afro-American collection.

Buildings and Grounds: Campus area 60 acres.

Chief Executive Officer: Dr. William E. Massey, President.

Address admission inquiries to Sterling H. Hudson, Dean of Admissions.

Morehouse School of Medicine

720 Westview Drive, S.W.
Atlanta, Georgia 30310-1495

Tel: (404) 752-1650   **E-mail:** karen@msm.edu
Fax: (404) 752-1012   **Internet:** www.msm.edu

Institution Description: The Morehouse School of Medicine is a private professional school. *Enrollment:* 253. *Degrees awarded:* Master's, doctorate, first-professional.

Member of Georgia State University System.

Accreditation: *Regional:* SACS-Comm. on Coll. *Professional:* medicine, public health

Calendar: Semesters.

Admission: Contact the school for current entrance requirements.

Degree Requirements: Completion of prescribed curriculum.

Degrees Conferred: 16 *master's:* health professions and related sciences; 3 *doctorate:* health professions and related sciences; 39 *first-professional:* medicine.

Fees and Other Expenses: *Tuition and fees per academic year:* $17,402. Contact the school housing and other costs.

Financial Aid: Aid from institutionally generated funds is provided on the basis of financial need. Institution has a Program Participation Agreement with the U.S. Department of Education for eligible students to receive Pell Grants and other federal aid.

Institutional funding for graduate students: fellowships and grants are available to qualifying students.

Departments and Teaching Staff: Anatomy *professors* 3, *associate professors* 4, *assistant professors* 5, *instructors* 2, *part-time teachers* 0; biochemistry 0, 3, 4, 1, 0; microbiology/immunology 1, 2, 4, 3, 0; pathology 1, 1, 1, 0, 0; pharmacology/toxicology 2, 3, 2, 0, 0; physiology 3, 0, 4, 0, 0; medical education 2, 1, 1, 0, 0; community health and preventive medicine 3, 4, 14, 4, 0; family medicine 0, 4, 11, 7, 1; medicine 4, 5, 21, 2, 7; obstetrics and gynecology 0, 3, 3, 4, 5; pediatrics 2, 5, 4, 2, 2; psychiatry 2, 6, 2, 4, 3; surgery 3, 2, 7, 1, 4.

Total instructional faculty: 204. *Degrees held by full-time faculty:* Doctorate 33%, master's 8%, baccalaureate 1%, professional 77%. 86% hold terminal degrees.

Enrollment: Total enrollment 253 (32.4% men, 67.6% women).

International Students: No programs to aid students whose native language is not English.

Chief Executive Officer: Dr. James R. Gavin III, President.

Address admission inquiries to Dean of Admissions.

North Georgia College and State University

College Avenue
Dahlonega, Georgia 30597

Tel: (706) 864-1400   **E-mail:** admission@ngcsu.edu
Fax: (706) 864-1478   **Internet:** www.ngcsu.edu

Institution Description: North Georgia College and State University is a state institution. *Enrollment:* 4,552. *Degrees awarded:* Associate, baccalaureate, master's, education specialist. Academic offerings subject to approval by statewide coordinating bodies. Budget subject to approval by state governing boards.

Accreditation: *Regional:* SACS-Comm. on Coll. *Professional:* business, nursing, physical therapy, teacher education

History: Established and chartered 1872; offered first instruction at postsecondary level 1873; awarded first degree (baccalaureate) 1878; changed from 4-year to 2-year college 1931; became 4-year college again 1946; adopted present name 1996.

Institutional Structure: *Governing board:* Board of Regents of the University System of Georgia. *Composition of institution:* 16 regents. All voting. *Faculty representation:* Administrators 12 men / 4 women. Academic affairs headed by vice president for academic affairs. Management/business/finances directed by vice president for business and finance. Full-time instructional faculty 163. Academic governance body, Faculty Senate, meets approximately 8 times per year.

Calendar: Semesters. Academic year Aug. to Aug. Freshmen admitted Aug., Jan., Mar., May. Degrees conferred and formal commencement Aug., Dec., May.

Characteristics of Freshmen: 59.8% of applicants admitted. 15.9% of admitted students enrolled full-time.

90% (665 students) submitted SAT scores; 25% (185 students) submitted ACT scores. *25th percentile:* SAT Verbal 500, SAT Math 490; ACT Composite 19, ACT English 19, ACT Math 19. *75th percentile:* SAT Verbal 580, SAT Math 580; ACT Composite 23, ACT English 24, ACT Math 24.

18% of entering freshmen expected to graduate within 5 years. 88% of freshmen from Georgia. Freshmen from 29 states and 21 foreign countries.

Admission: Rolling admissions plan. Apply no later than 20 days prior to registration. Early acceptance available. *Requirements:* Either graduation from accredited secondary school with 18 academic units which must include 4 English, 4 math (2 algebra, 1 geometry, 1 higher math), 3 social science, 3 laboratory science, 4 foreign language, 2 additional credits from any of the above areas; or GED. Minimum GPA 2.0. *Entrance tests:* College Board SAT (minimum scores 480 verbal, 440 mathematical). *For transfer students:* 2.0 minimum GPA; from 4-year accredited institution 140 quarter hours maximum transfer credit; from 2-year accredited institution 95 hours. International and transfer students apply no later than 30 days prior to start of quarter.

College credit and advanced placement for postsecondary-level work completed in secondary school. College credit for extrainstitutional learning (life experience) on basis of ACE *2006 Guide to the Evaluation of Educational Experiences in the Armed Services;* faculty assessment. Tutoring available. Noncredit developmental courses offered in summer session and regular academic year.

Degree Requirements: *For all associate degrees:* 60 semester hours. *For all baccalaureate degrees:* 120 semester hours; foreign language requirement; comprehensives in individual fields of study.

Fulfillment of some degree requirements possible by passing College Board CLEP. *Grading system:* A–F.

Distinctive Educational Programs: Internships. Evening classes. Dual-degree programs in chemistry, computer science, engineering, industrial management, mathematics, and physics with Georgia Institute of Technology and Clemson University. Preprofessional programs in medicine. Master's program in physical therapy, education, and public administration. Special facilities for using telecommunications in the classroom. Interdisciplinary programs in social science. Independent study. Study abroad in various locations through university system. *Other distinctive programs:* Continuing education program. Foreign language programs in Canada and France; business program in London, England.

ROTC: All resident male students must be a member of the Corps of Cadets. Out-of-state tuition waived for members of the Corps. Georgia residents receive $1,500 per year from the state for participating in the Corps.

Degrees Conferred: 47 *associate;* 690 *baccalaureate* (B), 170 *master's* (M): biological/life sciences 53 (B), 7 (M); business/marketing 185; computer and information sciences 19 (B); education 152 (B), 83 (M); English 30 (B), 34 (M); foreign languages and literature 8 (B); health professions and related sciences 30 (B), 34 (M); mathematics 9 (B), 7 (M); physical sciences 18 (B); protective services/public administration 56 (B), 6 (M); psychology 69 (B), 17 (M); social sciences and history 41 (B), 6 (M); other 26 (B).

Fees and Other Expenses: *Full-time tuition per academic year 2004–05:* undergraduate in-state resident $2,322, out-of-state student $9,290; graduate resident $2,786, out-of-state student $11,146. *Required fees:* $606. *Room and board per academic year:* $4,424.

Financial Aid: Aid from institutionally generated funds is provided on the basis of academic merit, financial need, athletic ability, other criteria.

Financial aid to full-time, first-time undergraduate students: need-based scholarships/grants totaling $1,797,267, self-help $2,104,821. non-need-based scholarships/grants totaling $6,587,470, self-help $3,679,027, parent loans $126,775, athletic awards $302,147.

Departments and Teaching Staff: *Professors* 50, *associate professors* 49, *assistant professors* 90, *instructors* 39, *part-time faculty* 132. *Total instructional faculty:* 330 (full-time 200, part-time 130; women 169, men 161; members of minority groups 10). Total faculty with doctorate, first-professional, or other terminal degree: 187. Student-to-faculty ratio: 14:1.

Enrollment: Total enrollment 4,552. Undergraduate full-time 1,357 men / 1,870 women, part-time 257m / 530w; graduate full-time 39m / 112w, part-time 100m / 287w. *Transfer students:* in-state 4,229; from out-of-state 271.

Characteristics of Student Body: *Ethnic/racial makeup:* number of Black non-Hispanic: 119; American Indian or Alaska Native: 15; Asian or Pacific Islander: 68; Hispanic: 79; White non-Hispanic: 3,682; unknown: 51. *Age distribution:* number under 18: 9; 18–19: 795; 20–21: 1,270; 22–24: 1,002; 25–29: 313; 30–34: 149; 35–39: 119; 40–49: 157; 50–64: 50; 65 and over: 7.

International Students: 44 nonresident aliens enrolled fall 2004. 15 students from Europe, 12 Asia, 3 Central and South America, 7 Africa, 3 Canada, 3 unknown. Social programs available to aid students whose native language is not English. English as a Second Language Program. No financial aid specifically designated for international students.

Student Life: On-campus residence halls house 40% of student body. *Intercollegiate athletics:* men: baseball, basketball; women: softball; both sexes: basketball, soccer, tennis, rifle. *Special regulations:* Registered cars permitted without restrictions. *Special services:* Medical services. *Surrounding community:* Dahlonega population 31,500. Atlanta, 65 miles from campus, is nearest metropolitan area.

Library Collections: 175,330 volumes. 25,751 government documents; 540,662 microforms; 3,210 audiovisual materials; 550 current periodical subscriptions. 15 computer work stations. Students have access to the Internet at no charge.

Most important holdings include collections on military history; children's literature; the New York Times on microfilm (all issues); ERIC microfiche collection; business reference materials; literary reference materials; The Owen Papers.

Buildings and Grounds: Campus area 206 acres. *New buildings:* Military Leadership Center occupied 2005.

Chief Executive Officer: Dr. David Potter, President.

Address undergraduate admission inquiries to Linda Smith, Admission Specialist; graduate inquiries to Dr. Donna Gressel, Director of Graduate Studies.

Oglethorpe University

4484 Peachtree Road, N.E.
Atlanta, Georgia 30319-2797
Tel: (404) 261-1441 **E-mail:** admission@oglethorpe.edu
Fax: (404) 364-8500 **Internet:** www.oglethorpe.edu

Institution Description: Oglethorpe University is a private, independent, nonprofit institution. *Enrollment:* 1,053. *Degrees awarded:* Baccalaureate, master's.

Member of the consortium University Center in Georgia.

Accreditation: *Regional:* SACS-Comm. on Coll.

History: Established as Oglethorpe University 1835; offered first instruction at postsecondary level 1838; awarded first degree (baccalaureate) 1839; changed name to Oglethorpe College 1964; readopted present name 1971.

Institutional Structure: *Governing board:* Oglethorpe University Board of Trustees. Extrainstitutional representation: 35 trustees; institutional representation: president of the university. 1 ex officio. All voting. *Composition of institution:* Administrators 36 men / 25 women. Academic affairs headed by provost. Management/business/finances directed by executive vice president. Full-time instructional faculty 57. Academic governance body, Faculty Council, meets an average of 6 times per year.

Calendar: Semesters. Academic year Aug. to May. Freshmen admitted on rolling admissions basis when file is complete. Degrees conferred and formal commencements May, Aug. Summer session of 2 terms from May to Aug.

Characteristics of Freshmen: 1,239 applicants (424 men, 815 women). 65.5% of applicants admitted. 28% of admitted students enrolled full-time.

85% (190 students) submitted SAT scores; 39% (88 students) submitted ACT scores. *25th percentile:* SAT I Verbal 550, SAT I Math 490; ACT Composite 20. *75th percentile:* SAT I Verbal 660, SAT I Math 620; ACT Composite 27.

85% of freshmen expected to graduate within 5 years. 50% of freshmen from Georgia. Freshmen from 25 states and 8 foreign countries.

Admission: For fall acceptance, candidates for regular decision may submit their applications at any time, although the University will accept applicants after Mar. 1 only on a space-available basis. To be considered, freshmen applicants should submit a completed application form, high school transcripts, standardized test scores, and recommendations. Decisions will be mailed on February 1 to all candidates whose applications are complete by Jan. 24. After Jan. 24, decisions will be mailed on a rolling basis. *Requirements:* Either graduation from accredited secondary school with 16 units which must include 4 English, 4 social studies, 2 mathematics, 2 science, 4 academic electives; or GED. Average GPA 3.28. *Entrance tests:* College Board SAT or ACT composite. *For transfer students:* 2.3 minimum GPA; 90 semester hours maximum transfer credit; good standing at institution previously attended. Home school students individually evaluated.

College credit and advanced placement for postsecondary-level work completed in secondary school. College credit for USAFI.

Degree Requirements: 132 credit hours; 2.0 GPA; 30 of last 60 hours in residence; distribution requirements; core curriculum.

Fulfillment of some degree requirements and exemption from some beginning courses possible by passing College Board AP. Fulfillment of some degree requirements also possible by passing College Board CLEP. *Grading system:* A–F with plus and minus.

Distinctive Educational Programs: *For undergraduates:* Weekend classes. Dual-degree programs in engineering with Georgia Institute of Technology, Auburn University (AL), University of Southern California, and University of Florida; in art with Atlanta College of Art. Urban Leadership Program. Interdepartmental/interdisciplinary program in international studies, American studies, business/behavioral science, business/computer science, mathematics/computer science. Study abroad in Argentina, France, Germany, Japan, The Netherlands, Monaco. Cross-registration with 19 Atlanta area colleges and universities. Atlanta College of Art. Joint enrollment program for eligible secondary school students. Writing program. *Available to all students:* Evening classes. Individual majors.

ROTC: Available through arrangement with Georgia State University and Georgia Institute of Technology.

Degrees Conferred: 210 *baccalaureate;* 47 *master's.* Bachelor's degrees awarded in top five disciplines: business, management, marketing, and related support services 70; English language and literature/letters 37; psychology 27; social sciences 17; history 11.

Fees and Other Expenses: *Full-time tuition per academic year 2004–05:* $21,000. *Books and supplies:* $600. *Room and board per academic year:* $7,100.

Financial Aid: Aid from institutionally generated funds is provided on the basis of academic merit, financial need. Institution has a Program Participation

Agreement with the U.S. Department of Education for eligible students to receive Pell Grants and other federal aid.

Financial aid to full-time, first-time undergraduate students: 23% received federal grants averaging $3,967; 62% state/local grants averaging $3,629; 97% institutional grants averaging $11,580; 60% loans.

Departments and Teaching Staff: *Professors* 18, *associate professors* 9, *assistant professors* 20, *instructors* 10, *part-time teachers* 56.

Total instructional faculty: 113. Degrees held by full-time faculty: doctorate 94%, master's 4%, professional 2%. 96% hold terminal degrees.

Enrollment: Total enrollment 1,053. Undergraduate 972 (34.2% men, 65.8% women).

Characteristics of Student Body: *Ethnic/racial makeup:* Black non-Hispanic: 20.7%; Asian or Pacific Islander: 2.6%; Hispanic: 3.1%; White non-Hispanic: 58.4%; unknown: 10.5%.

International Students: 46 undergraduate nonresident aliens enrolled fall 2003. Programs available to aid students whose native language is not English: social, cultural. No financial aid specifically designated for international students.

Student Life: On-campus residence halls house 60% of full-time students. Residence halls for men only constitute 50% of such space, for women only 50%. 33% of men join and 4% live in fraternities; 25% of women join and 2% live in sororities. *Intercollegiate athletics:* men only: basketball, baseball, soccer, tennis, track, cross-country; women only: basketball, volleyball, soccer, tennis, track, cross-country. *Special regulations:* Cars permitted without restrictions. Quiet hours from 10pm to 8am. Residence hall visitation from 9am to 12 midnight Sun.-Thurs., 9am to 2am Fri. and Sat. *Special services:* Medical services, counseling. *Student publications: The Stormy Petrel,* a biweekly newspaper; *The Tower,* a biannual literary magazine; *Yamacraw,* a yearbook. *Surrounding community:* Atlanta population 3 million. Served by mass transit bus and train systems; airport 15 miles from campus; passenger rail service 7 miles from campus.

Library Collections: 130,000 volumes. 4,500 audiovisual materials; 775 current periodical subscriptions. Access to online information retrieval systems. Students have access to the Internet at no charge.

Most important special holdings include collections on Japan; Walt Whitman Collection; University Archives.

Buildings and Grounds: Campus area 120 acres.

Chief Executive Officer: Dr. Larry D. Large, President.

Address admission inquiries to Joseph Tinsley, Director of Admissions.

Paine College

1235 15th Street
Augusta, Georgia 30901-3182
Tel: (706) 821-8200   **E-mail:** tinsley@mail.paine.edu
Fax: (706) 821-8293   **Internet:** www.paine.edu

Institution Description: Paine College is a private college affiliated with the Christian Methodist Episcopal Church and the United Methodist Church. *Enrollment:* 882. *Degrees awarded:* Baccalaureate.

Accreditation: *Regional:* SACS-Comm. on Coll. *Professional:* business

History: Established as Paine Institute 1882; chartered 1883; offered first instruction at postsecondary level 1891; awarded first degree (baccalaureate) 1895; adopted present name 1903.

Institutional Structure: *Governing board:* Paine College Board of Trustees. Extrainstitutional representation: 30 trustees. Ex-officio: president of the College, 1 full-time instructional faculty member and 1 student. 33 voting. *Composition of institution:* Administrators: 13 men / 18 women. Academic affairs headed by academic dean. Management/business/finances directed by business manager. Instructional faculty 102. Academic governance body, the faculty, meets an average of 9 times per year.

Calendar: Semesters. Academic year Aug. to May. Freshmen admitted year round. Degrees conferred and formal commencement May. Summer session June to July.

Characteristics of Freshmen: 26% of applicants admitted. 26% of admitted students enrolled full-time.

81.4% (157 students) submitted SAT scores; 34.2% (66 students) submitted ACT scores. *25th percentile*: SAT Verbal 350, SAT Math 350; ACT Composite 15. *75th percentile*: SAT Verbal 450, SAT Math 450; ACT Composite 19.

24% of entering freshmen expected to graduate within 5 years. 77% of freshmen from Georgia. Freshmen from 13 states.

Admission: Rolling admissions plan. For fall acceptance, apply no later than Aug. 1 of year of enrollment. Students are notified of acceptance beginning Mar. Apply by Jan. for early decision; need not limit application to Paine College.

Early acceptance available. *Requirements:* Either graduation from accredited secondary school with 4 units in English, 3 mathematics, 3 natural sciences, 3 social studies (1 history), 3 electives; or GED. Minimum GPA 2.0. *Entrance tests:* College Board SAT or ACT composite. *For transfer students:* 2.0 minimum GPA.

Advanced placement for postsecondary-level work in secondary school. College credit for extrainstitutional learning on basis of faculty assessment. Tutoring available. Noncredit developmental courses offered during regular academic year and during the summer session.

Degree Requirements: 124 credit hours; 2.0 GPA; weekly chapel attendance; 2 hours physical education; general education requirements. Fulfillment of some degree requirements and exemption from some beginning courses possible by passing departmental examinations. College Board CLEP, other standardized tests. *Grading system:* A–F; withdraw (carries time limit).

Distinctive Educational Programs: Work-experience programs, including internships, cooperative education. Flexible meeting places and schedules, including off-campus center (at Fort Gordon) and evening classes. Cross-registration with Augusta State University. Dual-degree programs in engineering with Georgia Institute of Technology and Tuskegee University; in engineering with Florida A&M University. Cooperative baccalaureate in mass communications with Clark College (Atlanta, GA) and Augusta State University. Transfer agreement for premedical students with the Medical College of Georgia (Augusta, GA) and Tuskegee University (AL); transfer program for nursing with Medical College of South Carolina School of Nursing. Honors Program, tutorials. Study abroad.

ROTC: Army in cooperation with Augusta State University. 1 commission awarded 2004.

Degrees Conferred: 109 *baccalaureate:* biological/life sciences 9; business/marketing 27; communications/communication technologies 2; education 15; English 9; interdisciplinary studies 21 mathematics 1; philosophy/religion/theology 11; psychology 16; social sciences and history 27.

Fees and Other Expenses: *Full-time tuition per academic year 2004–05:* $14,086. *Required fees:* $674. *Other fees:* $765. *Room and board per academic year:* $4,178.

Financial Aid: Aid from institutionally generated funds is provided on the basis of academic merit, financial need, athletic ability, other criteria. Institution has a Program Participation Agreement with the U.S. Department of Education for eligible students to receive Pell Grants and other federal aid.

Departments and Teaching Staff: Business administration *professors* 1, *associate professors* 1, *assistant professors* 5,5, *instructors* 0, *part-time faculty* 4.5; education 0, 2, 4, 1, 1.5; humanities 5, 1, 17, 4, 8.5; natural sciences and mathematics .5, 4, 10, 4, 8.5; social sciences 3.5, 7, 1.5, 0, 6.5; general education support services 0, 1, 0, 6, 0.

Total instructional faculty: 102 (full-time 79, part-time 23; women 43, men 59; members of minority groups 42). Total faculty with doctorate, first-professional, or other terminal degree: 42. Student-to-faculty ratio: 10:1.

Enrollment: Total enrollment 882. Full-time 235 men / 571 women, part-time 22m / 54w. Transfer students: 52.

Characteristics of Student Body: *Ethnic/racial makeup:* number of Black non-Hispanic: 864; Asian or Pacific Islander: 2; Hispanic: 3; White non-Hispanic: 6. *Age distribution:* number under 18: 3; 18–19: 248; 20–21: 286; 22–24: 200; 25–29: 40; 30–34: 21; 35–39: 17; 40–49: 28; 50–64: 14; 65 and over: 1; unknown: 24. 36% of student body attend summer sessions.

International Students: 5 nonresident aliens enrolled 2004. 3 students from Africa, 2 other. No programs available to aid students whose native language is not English. No financial aid specifically designated for international students.

Student Life: On-campus residence halls house 57% of student body. Residence halls for men only constitute 31% of such space, for women only 69%. *Intercollegiate athletics:* men and women: baseball, basketball, cross-country, softball, track, volleyball. *Special regulations:* Cars permitted without restrictions. Quiet hours. Residence hall visitation in lounges from noon to midnight. *Special services:* Learning Resources Center, medical services, Tutorial and Enrichment Center; Mathematics Support and Fitness Center. *Student publications: Lion,* a yearbook; *Paineite,* a student newspaper. *Surrounding community:* Augusta population 60,000. Atlanta, 150 miles from campus, is nearest metropolitan area. Served by mass transit system, airport 8 miles from campus.

Library Collections: 90,000 volumes. Online catalog. 10,200 microforms; 305 periodicals. 62 computer work stations. Students have access to online information retrieval services.

Most important holdings include the Frank Yerby Collection (autographed editions); Howard Thurman Meditation Collection; Martin Luther King, Jr. Collection (books by and about Blacks); Charles G. Gomillion Collection (mostly sociology books).

Buildings and Grounds: Campus area 58 acres.

Chief Executive Officer: Shirley A.R. Lewis, President.

Address admission inquiries to Joseph Tinsley, Director of Admissions.

Piedmont College

165 Central Avenue
P.O. Box 10
Demorest, Georgia 30535-0010
Tel: (706) 778-3000   **E-mail:** admission@piedmont.edu
Fax: (706) 776-2811   **Internet:** www.piedmont.edu

Institution Description: Piedmont College is a private, independent college historically related to the Congregational Christian Churches of America. *Enrollment:* 2,222. *Degrees awarded:* Baccalaureate, master's.

Accreditation: *Regional:* SACS-Comm. on Coll.

History: Established as J.S. Green Collegiate Institute, chartered, and offered first instruction at postsecondary level 1897; changed name to J.S. Green College 1899; adopted present name 1903; awarded first degree (baccalaureate) 1910.

Institutional Structure: *Governing board:* Piedmont College Board of Trustees. Extrainstitutional representation: 23 trustees; institutional representation: president of the college, ex officio, non-voting; 2 alumni including president of alumni association, ex officio. *Composition of institution:* Administrators 7 men / 3 women. Academic affairs headed by vice president for academic affairs. Management/business/finances directed by vice president for administration and finance. Full-time instructional faculty 100. Academic governance body, the faculty, meets an average of 9 times per year.

Calendar: Semesters. Academic year Aug. to May. Freshmen admitted Aug., Jan., May. Degrees conferred May, Aug., Dec. Formal commencement May. Summer session of 2 terms from June through Aug.

Characteristics of Freshmen: 62% of applicants admitted. 21% of admitted students enrolled full-time.

82% (147 students) submitted SAT scores; 24% (44 students) submitted ACT scores. *25th percentile*: SAT Verbal 450, SAT Math 459; ACT Composite 18. *75th percentile*: SAT Verbal 540, SAT Math 560; ACT Composite 23.

42% of entering freshmen expected to graduate within 5 years. 99% of freshmen from Georgia. Freshmen from 1 foreign country.

Admission: Rolling admissions. For fall acceptance, apply by Aug. 1. Early acceptance available. *Requirements:* Either graduation from secondary school or GED. Recommend 4 units English, 3 mathematics, 2 natural sciences, 2 social studies, 7 additional academic units, additional units in algebra and geometry. *Entrance tests:* College Board SAT. *For transfer students:* 2.0 minimum GPA; from 4-year accredited institution 90 hours maximum transfer credit; from 2-year accredited institution 60 hours; correspondence/extension students 30 hours.

Advanced placement for postsecondary-level work completed in secondary school. Advanced placement and college credit on basis of College Board CLEP. Tutoring available. A comprehensive 6-week college preparatory program (remedial) is offered in the summer. Noncredit remedial courses are offered during the regular academic year.

Degree Requirements: 124 semester hours; 2.0 GPA; last 30 hours in residence; demonstrated proficiency in English. Fulfillment of some degree requirements and exemption from some beginning courses possible by passing departmental examinations, College Board CLEP. *Grading system:* A–F; withdraw (deadline after which pass-fail is appended to withdraw); incomplete (carries time limit).

Distinctive Educational Programs: Evening classes. Preprofessional programs in dentistry, chiropractic, forestry and wildlife management, medical technology, medicine, nursing, optometry, osteopathy, pharmacy, veterinary medicine. Facilities and programs for independent research including individual majors, tutorials. Honors College based on the Oxford model; Program for Academic Success (an intensive summer program for students needing additional preparatory work for college). Each year the college offers study/travel options for academic credit (Russian archaeology/history and English literature/theatre are examples).

Degrees Conferred: 251 *baccalaureate* (B); 595 *master's* (M); biological/life sciences 4 (B); business/marketing 62 (B), 23 (M); communications/communication technologies 9 (B); Education 64 (B), 572 (M); English 5 (B); foreign languages and literature 2 (B); health professions and related sciences 15 (B); interdisciplinary studies 2 (B); mathematics 4 (B); philosophy/religion/theology 4 (B); physical sciences 11 (B); psychology 15; social sciences and history 37 (M); visual and performing arts 17 (B).

Fees and Other Expenses: *Full-time tuition per academic year 2004–05:* $15,500 undergraduate; $310 per credit hour graduate. *Room and board per academic year:* $5,300.

Financial Aid: Aid from institutionally generated funds is provided on the basis of academic merit, athletic ability, financial need, other criteria. Institution

has a Program Participation Agreement with the U.S. Department of Education for eligible students to receive Pell Grants and other federal aid.

Financial aid to full-time, first-time undergraduate students: need-based scholarships/grants totaling $1,706,884, self-help $155,479; non-need-based scholarships/grants totaling $4,306,512, self-help $1,638,765, parent loans $1,224,475, tuition waivers $127,430.

Departments and Teaching Staff: *Professors 20, associate professors 35, assistant professors 36, instructors 5; part-time faculty: 80. Total instructional faculty:* 176 (full-time 96, part-time 80; women 94, men 78; members of minority groups 13). Total faculty with doctorate, first-professional, or other terminal degree: 110. Student-to-faculty ratio: 141.

Enrollment: Total enrollment 2,222. Undergraduate full-time 332 men / 602 women, part-time 58m / 104w; graduate full-time 122m / 326w, part-time 105m / 373w.

Characteristics of Student Body: *Ethnic/racial makeup:* number of Black non-Hispanic: 55; American Indian or Alaska Native: 1; Asian or Pacific Islander: 10; Hispanic: 22; White non-Hispanic: 981; unknown: 23. *Age distribution:* number under 18: 90; 18–19: 242; 20–21: 248; 22–24: 176; 25–29: 135; 30–34: 70; 35–39: 55; 40–49: 51; 50–64: 22.

International Students: 31 nonresident aliens enrolled fall 2004. 11 students from Europe, 5 Asia, 8 Central and South America, 7 other. No programs available to aid students whose native language is not English. No financial aid specifically designated for international students.

Student Life: On-campus residence halls house 30% of student body. Dormitories for men only constitute 50% of such space, for women only 50%. 33% of married students request institutional housing and are so housed. *Intercollegiate athletics:* men only: baseball, basketball, soccer; women only: basketball, soccer, volleyball. *Student publications: The Lions Roar,* a student newspaper; *Yonahian,* a yearbook. *Surrounding community:* Demorest population 2,000. Atlanta, 85 miles from campus, is nearest metropolitan area.

Library Collections: 118,750 volumes. 48,462 microforms; 366 current periodical subscriptions. Computer work stations available. Students have access to the Internet at no charge.

Buildings and Grounds: Campus area 50 acres.

Chief Executive Officer: W. Ray Cleere, Chief Executive Officer.

Address undergraduate admission inquiries Cynthia Peterson, Director of Undergraduate Admissions; graduate inquires to Carol Kokesh, Director of Graduate Admissions.

Reinhardt College

7300 Reinhardt College Circle
Waleska, Georgia 30183-2981
Tel: (770) 720-5600   **E-mail:** admissions@reinhardt.edu
Fax: (770) 720-5602   **Internet:** www.reinhardt.edu

Institution Description: Reinhardt College is a private college affiliated with the United Methodist Church. *Enrollment:* 1,079. *Degrees awarded:* Associate, baccalaureate.

Accreditation: *Regional:* SACS.

Calendar: Semesters. Academic year Aug. to May.

Characteristics of Freshmen: 773 applicants (356 men, 417 women). 68.2% of applicants admitted. 41.4% of admitted students enrolled full-time.

88% (221 students) submitted SAT scores; 10% (25 students) submitted ACT scores. *25th percentile*: SAT I Verbal 450, SAT I Math 430; ACT Composite 17. *75th percentile*: SAT I Verbal 550, SAT I Math 530; ACT Composite 22.

97% of freshmen from Georgia. Freshmen from 5 states and 14 foreign countries.

Admission: *Requirements:* High school graduation or GED; SAT. College credit and advanced placement for postsecondary-level work completed in secondary school and for extrainstitutional learning on basis of ACE *2006 Guide to the Evaluation of Educational Experiences in the Armed Services.*

Developmental/remedial courses offered in summer session and regular academic year; credit given.

Degree Requirements: Completion of courses prescribed for the degree program.

Degrees Conferred: 16 *associate*; 182 *baccalaureate.* Bachelor's degrees awarded in top five disciplines: business, management, marketing, and related support services 73; education 30; communication, journalism, and related programs 18; biological and biomedical sciences 17; visual and performing arts 11.

Fees and Other Expenses: *Full-time tuition per academic year 2004–05:* $12,000. *Books and supplies:* $850. *Room and board per academic year:* $6,400.

Financial Aid: Aid from institutionally generated funds is provided on the basis of academic merit, financial need, athletic ability. Institution has a Program

Participation Agreement with the U.S. Department of Education for eligible students to receive Pell Grants and other federal aid.

Financial aid to full-time, first-time undergraduate students: 27% received federal grants averaging $2,510; 82% state/local grants averaging $1,225; 71% institutional grants averaging $1,425; 46% loans averaging $1,849.

Departments and Teaching Staff: Mathematics/science *professors* 2, *associate professors* 3, *assistant professors* 1, *instructors* 1, *part-time teachers* 4; business 2, 2, 0, 0, 7; education 1, 1, 1, 0, 1; fine arts 2, 1, 1, 0, 0; social science 1, 1, 4, 3, 9; humanities 1, 3, 5, 1, 0; physical education 0, 1, 2, 4, 0.

Total instructional faculty: 73. Student-to-faculty ratio: 10:1. Degrees held by full-time faculty: doctorate 65%, master's 35%. 71% hold terminal degrees.

Enrollment: Total enrollment 1,079 (42.5% men, 57.5% women).

Characteristics of Student Body: *Ethnic/racial makeup:* Black non-Hispanic: 6.1%; American Indian or Alaska Native: .5%; Asian or Pacific Islander: .7%; Hispanic: 2.2%; White non-Hispanic: 64.5%.

International Students: 11 nonresident aliens enrolled fall 2003. Students from Europe, Asia, Central and South America, Africa, Canada, Australia, New Zealand. English as a Second Language Program available. No financial aid specifically designated for international students.

Library Collections: 48,000 volumes. 2,000 microforms; 3,600 audiovisual materials; 315 current periodical subscriptions. 1,306 recordings; 410 compact disks; 169 CD-ROMs. 40 computer work stations. Students have access to the Internet at no charge.

Buildings and Grounds: Campus area 600 acres.

Chief Executive Officer: Dr. J. Thomas Isherwood, President.

Address admissions inquiries to Julie T. Cook, Dean of Enrollment Services.

Savannah College of Art and Design

342 Bull Street
P.O. Box 3146
Savannah, Georgia 31402-3146
Tel: (912) 525-5000   **E-mail:** admission@scad.edu
Fax: (912) 525-5986   **Internet:** www.scad.edu

Institution Description: Savannah College of Art and Design is a private institution offering programs in architecture, art, and design. *Enrollment:* 6,776. *Degrees awarded:* Baccalaureate, master's.

Accreditation: *Regional:* SACS-Comm. on Coll.

History: Established 1978.

Calendar: Quarters. Academic year Sept. to May.

Characteristics of Freshmen: 73% of applicants admitted. 43% of admitted students enrolled full-time.

74% (963 students) submitted SAT scores; 24% (317 students) submitted ACT scores. *25th percentile:* SAT Verbal 440, SAT Math 480; ACT Composite 20. *75th percentile:* SAT Verbal 610, S SAT Math 590; ACT Composite 26.

59% of entering students are expected to graduate in 5 years. 15% of freshmen from Georgia. Freshmen from 50 states and 60 foreign countries.

Admission: Graduation from an accredited high school in upper 50% of class; minimum 2.0 GPA; SAT or ACT.

Degree Requirements: 180 quarter hour credits for Bachelor of Fine Arts; 225 quarter hours for Bachelor of Architecture; required distribution courses; 2.0 GPA overall, 3.0 GPA in major.

Distinctive Educational Programs: Architectural history, sequential art, computer art, fibers, graphic design, historic preservation, video/film. Study abroad programs in France all year. Summer off-campus program in Italy.

Degrees Conferred: 997 *baccalaureate* (B); 321 *master's* (M): architecture 10 (B), 81 (M); communications/communication technologies 18 (B), 8 (M); computer and information sciences 217 (B), 59 (M); interdisciplinary studies 21 (B), 15 (M); visual and performing arts 711 (B), 158 (M).

Fees and Other Expenses: *Full-time tuition per academic year 2004–05:* $21,600 undergraduate; $22,050 graduate. *Matriculation fee:* $500. *Room and board per academic year:* $8,700.

Financial Aid: Financial aid from institutionally generated funds is provided on the basis of academic merit, financial need, other criteria.

Financial aid to full-time, first-time undergraduate students: need-based scholarships/grants totaling $3,002,267, self-help $10,400,426; non-need-based scholarships/grants totaling $15,712,706, self-help $4,597,822, parent loans $30,768,362, tuition waivers $462,158, athletic awards $978,813.

Departments and Teaching Staff: *Professors* 523, *adjunct faculty* 48. *Total instructional faculty:* 371 (full-time 324, part-time 47; women 153, men 218; members of minority groups 28). Total faculty with doctorate, first-professional, or other terminal degree: 287. Student-to-faculty ratio: 18:1.

Enrollment: Total enrollment 6,776. Full-time undergraduate 2,587 men / 2,657 women, part-time 275m / 222w; graduate full-time 423m / 433w, part-time 82m / 97w.

Characteristics of Student Body: *Ethnic and racial makeup:* number of Black non-Hispanic: 290; American Indian or Alaska Native: 14; Asian or Pacific Islander: 118; Hispanic: 172; White non-Hispanic: 2,561; unknown: 2,336. *Age distribution:* number under 18: 1,104; 18–19: 2.020; 20–21: 22–24: 427; 25–29: 144; 30–34: 41; 35–39: 9; 40–49: 9; 50–64: 3.

International Students: 448 nonresident aliens enrolled fall 2004. 36 students from Europe, 305 Asia, 122 Central and South America, 20 Africa, 12 Canada, 2 Australia, 2 New Zealand. Programs available to aid students whose native language is not English: English as a Second Language. No financial aid specifically designated for international students.

Student Life: Campus housing available for 2,300 students. Over 44 student organizations. Intercollegiate and intramural sports. Cars permitted without restrictions. *Student publications: The District,* student newspaper.

Library Collections: 126,680 volumes. Online catalog. 926 current periodical subscriptions. 6,080 microforms units. Students have access to the Internet at no charge.

Buildings and Grounds: *New buildings:* American Hall; Arnold Hall; numerous new facility buildings for various departments.

Chief Executive Officer: Paula S. Wallace, President.

Address admission inquiries to Ginger Kent, Director of Recruitment; graduate inquiries to Darrell Thornton, Director of Graduate Enrollment.

Savannah State University

State College Branch
P.O. Box 20449
Savannah, Georgia 31404
Tel: (912) 356-2186
Fax: (912) 356-2998

Institution Description: Savannah State University is a senior university of the University System of Georgia. *Enrollment:* 2,800.. *Degrees awarded:* Baccalaureate, master's.

Accreditation: *Regional:* SACS-Comm. on Coll. *Professional:* business, engineering technology, social work, teacher education

History: Established and chartered as Georgia State Industrial College for Colored Youth 1890; offered first instruction at postsecondary level 1926; awarded first degree (baccalaureate) 1930; changed name to Georgia State College 1931; changed name to Savannah State College 1950; adopted present name 1996.

Institutional Structure: *Governing board:* Board of Regents of the University System of Georgia. Extrainstitutional representation: 15 regents. All voting. *Composition of institution:* Administrators 11 men / 1 woman. Academic affairs headed by vice-president for academic affairs. Business operations headed by a vice president for business and finance. Student Affairs headed by a vice president for student affairs. Full-time instructional faculty 142. Academic governance body, Faculty Senate, meets once each month in academic year.

Calendar: Semesters. Academic year Sept. to June. Freshmen admitted Sept., Jan., Mar., June. Degrees conferred and formal commencement June.

Characteristics of Freshmen: 2,652 applicants (965 men, 1,687 women). 48.9% of applicants admitted. 40.4% of admitted students enrolled full-time.

84% (562 students) submitted SAT scores; 29% (196 students) submitted ACT scores. *25th percentile:* SAT I Verbal 410, SAT I Math 400; ACT Composite 16, ACT English 15, ACT Math 16. *75th percentile:* SAT I Verbal 480, SAT I Math 470; ACT Composite 19, ACT English 19, ACT Math 18.

55% of entering freshmen expected to graduate within 5 years. 85% of freshmen from Georgia. Freshmen from 23 states and 15 foreign countries.

Admission: Rolling admissions plan. For fall acceptance, apply as early as fall of previous year, but not later than 20 days prior to registration. *Requirements:* Either graduation from accredited secondary school or GED. Minimum recentered SAT score 880 with at least 430 verbal. Students with less than the total composite recentered SAT score of 879 or less may be admitted to Learning Support Program. *For transfer students:* 2.0 GPA from accredited 2 or 4 year institutions; SAT score; 135 quarter hours maximum transfer credit; credit for extension, correspondence, CLEP or military experience 45 quarter hours maximum. For foreign students minimum TOEFL score 500.

Credit granted for CLEP, military experience according to ACE *2006 Guide to the Evaluation of Educational Experiences in the Armed Services*; AP examinations of the College Board. Noncredit developmental courses are available each quarter.

Degree Requirements: *For all associate degrees:* 60 semester hours. *For all baccalaureate degrees:* 120–124 semester hours. *For all undergraduate degrees:*

2.0 GPA; 1 year in residence; 6 hours physical education; Regent's Test of reading and writing; courses on U.S. and Georgia constitutions and histories. Master's degree requires a minimum of 30 semester hours. *Grading system:* A–F; withdraw (carries time limit).

Distinctive Educational Programs: Excellent academic computing facilities available to all major programs at the College. Computing is fully integrated into the instructional program of the School of Business. Cooperative education. Dual-degree program with Georgia Institute of Technology. Georgia Legislative Internship Program. Opportunities for student participation in research projects in the natural sciences. Distinctive major programs include business, information systems, marine biology, engineering technology and social work. A minor program in forensic science is available.

ROTC: Army, Navy in cooperation with Armstrong State College.

Degrees Conferred: 3 *associate;* 264 *baccalaureate;* 60 *master's.* Bachelor's degrees awarded in top five disciplines: business, management, marketing, and related support services 66; computer and information sciences and support services 32; engineering technologies/technicians 29; communication, journalism, and related programs 27; security and protective services 25.

Fees and Other Expenses: *Full-time tuition per academic year 2004–05:* $2,940 in-state resident, $9,904 out-of-state student. *Books and supplies:* $1,000. *Room and board per academic year:* $4,616.

Financial Aid: Aid from institutionally generated funds is provided on the basis of academic merit, financial need, athletic ability. Institution has a Program Participation Agreement with the U.S. Department of Education for eligible students to receive Pell Grants and other federal aid.

Financial aid to full-time, first-time undergraduate students: 64% received federal grants averaging $3,340; 87% state/local grants averaging $3,905; 5% institutional grants averaging $1,941; 12% received loans averaging $3,067.

Departments and Teaching Staff: Business administration *professors* 10, *associate professors* 4, *assistant professors* 13, *instructors* 1, *part-time teachers* 1; humanities 3, 9, 6, 2, 7; fine arts 3, 4, 1, 0, 2; social and biological sciences 6, 7, 4, 0, 11; social work 0, 4, 1, 0, 0; recreation and athletics 0, 3, 1, 1, 1; public administration 2, 1, 1, 0, 0; chemistry 3, 2, 0, 0, 0; biology 7, 3, 0, 0, 3; mathematics and physics 5, 7, 1, 0, 3; engineering technology 3, 7, 0, 0, 0; learning support 1, 6, 8, 2, 6.

Total instructional faculty: 176. Degrees held by instructional faculty: doctorate 68%, master's 32%. 68% hold terminal degrees.

Enrollment: Total enrollment 2,800. Undergraduate 2,665 (43.2% men, 56.8% women).

Characteristics of Student Body: *Ethnic/racial makeup:* Black non-Hispanic: 94.8%; Asian or Pacific Islander: .4%; Hispanic: .5%; White non-Hispanic: 2.8%.

International Students: 40 nonresident aliens enrolled fall 2003. Students from Europe, Asia, Central and South America, Africa, Canada. Programs available to aid students whose native language is not English: social, cultural, financial.

Student Life: On-campus residence halls house 50% of student body. Housing is also available for married students. *Intercollegiate athletics:* men only: baseball, basketball, football, track; women only: basketball. *Special services:* Health services, entertainment and cultural activities, Career Office Service and Co-Op. *Student publications, radio: The Tiger,* a yearbook; *Tiger's Roar,* a newspaper; campus radio station WHJC. *Surrounding community:* Savannah, a historic coastal community, population 275,000. Savannah is served by bus, rail and airline service.

Library Collections: 200,000 volumes. 558,000 microforms; 4,175 audiovisual materials; 832 current periodical subscriptions. Online catalog. Students have access to online information retrieval services and the Internet.

Most important special collections include an extensive collection of Afro-American material.

Buildings and Grounds: Campus area 164 acres.

Chief Executive Officer: Dr. Carleton E. Brown, President.

Undergraduates address admission inquiries to Judith Edwin, Dean of Enrollment Management.

Shorter College

315 Shorter Avenue
Rome, Georgia 30165-4298

Tel: (706) 291-2121   **E-mail:** admissions@shorter.edu
Fax: (706) 236-1515   **Internet:** www.shorter.edu

Institution Description: Shorter College is a private college affiliated with the Georgia Baptist Convention. *Enrollment:* 895. *Degrees awarded:* Baccalaureate, master's.

Accreditation: *Regional:* SACS-Comm. on Coll. *Professional:* music

History: Established, chartered as Cherokee Baptist Female College, and offered first instruction at postsecondary level 1873; changed name to Shorter Female College 1877; awarded first degree (baccalaureate) 1892; adopted present name 1923. *See* Robert G. Gardner, *On the Hill* (Rome, Ga.: Shorter College, 1973) for further information.

Institutional Structure: *Governing board:* Shorter College Board of Trustees. Extrainstitutional representation: 30 trustees. All voting. *Composition of institution:* Administrators 4 men / 1 woman. Academic affairs headed by provost. Management/business/finances headed by Senior Vice President. Full-time instructional faculty 43 men / 22 women. Academic governance body, Board of Trustees (advised by Curriculum Committee of the Faculty), meets an average of 2 times per year.

Calendar: Semesters. Academic year Aug. to May. Freshmen admitted Aug., Jan., June. Degrees conferred and formal commencement May, Dec. Summer session of 1 term from June to July.

Characteristics of Freshmen: 87% of applicants admitted. 35% of admitted students enrolled full-time.

88% (198 students) submitted SAT scores; 39% (89 students) submitted ACT scores. *25th percentile:* SAT Verbal 490, SAT Math 470; ACT Composite 19, ACT English 19, ACT Math 18. *75th percentile:* SAT Verbal 610, SAT Math 590; ACT Composite 25, 85% of entering freshmen expected to graduate within 5 years. 95% of freshmen from Georgia.

Admission: Rolling admission plan. For fall acceptance, apply as early as 1 year prior to year of enrollment, but not later than first day of classes. Early admission and joint enrollment available. *Requirements:* Either graduation from secondary school with 16 academic units including 4 English, 3 mathematics, 3 history, 3 science; or GED. 2 additional units in a foreign language recommended. CLEP credit accepted. *Entrance tests:* College Board SAT or ACT composite. *For transfer students:* From 4-year accredited institution maximum transfer credit limited only by residence requirement; from 2-year accredited institution 66 hours maximum transfer credit; for correspondence/extension students maximum transfer credit varies.

Advanced placement for postsecondary-level work completed in secondary school. College credit for extrainstitutional learning on basis of ACE *2006 Guide to the Evaluation of Educational Experiences in the Armed Services.* Tutoring available. Noncredit developmental courses offered during regular academic year.

Degree Requirements: 126–133 semester hours depending on major; 150 hours for 5-year accounting CPA track degree; 2.0 GPA; last 2 semesters in residence; core curriculum; competency exam in writing, cultural events attendance. *Grading system:* A–F; incomplete (deadline after which A–F is assigned); pass-fail; pass; satisfactory-unsatisfactory; withdraw (deadline after which pass-fail is appended to withdraw).

Distinctive Educational Programs: Interdisciplinary programs in fine arts, natural science, and social science; individually designed majors available. School of Professional Programs offers continuous enrollment, lockstep programs to working adults evenings and weekends. Study abroad in Austria, England, China, Hong Kong.

Degrees Conferred: 195 *baccalaureate:* biological/life sciences 14; business/marketing 36; communications/communication technologies 17; computer and information sciences 3; education 46; English 5; foreign languages and literature 6; law/legal studies 5; mathematics 1; natural resources/environmental science 1; parks and recreation 6; philosophy/religion/theology 9; psychology 14; social sciences and history 15; visual and performing arts 16.

Fees and Other Expenses: *Full-time tuition per academic year 2004–05:* $12,500. *Required fees:* $270. *Room and board per academic year:* $5,900.

Financial Aid: Aid from institutionally generated funds is provided on the basis of academic merit, financial need, athletic ability, other criteria.

Financial aid to full-time, first-time undergraduate students: need-based scholarships/grants totaling $3,952,720, self-help $1,995,166, parent loans $873,866, athletic awards $406,576; non-need-based scholarships/grants totaling $2,603,328, self-help $642,157, parent loans $455,366, athletic awards $558,381.

Departments and Teaching Staff: *Total instructional faculty:* 106 (full-time 62, part-time 44; women 51, men 55; members of minority groups 4). Total faculty with doctorate, first-professional, or other terminal degree: 55. Student-to-faculty ratio: 11:1.

Enrollment: Total enrollment 895. Undergraduate full-time 374 men / 475 women, part-time 15m / 32w. *Transfer students:* in-state 51; from out-of-state 26.

Characteristics of Student Body: *Ethnic/racial makeup:* number of Black non-Hispanic: 55; Asian or Pacific Islander: 101 Hispanic: 121 White non-Hispanic: 749; unknown: 19. *Age distribution:* number under 18: 8; 18–19: 360; 20–21: 319; 22–24: 140; 25–29: 22; 30–34: 14; 35–39: 19; 40–49: 12; 50–64: 5; 65 and over: 2. 27% of total student body attend summer sessions.

International Students: 51 nonresident aliens enrolled fall 2004. 12 students from Europe, 2 Asia, 20 Central and South America, 12 Africa, 5 Canada. *Pro-*

grams available to aid students whose native language is not English: Social. Some financial aid available to international students.

Student Life: On-campus residence halls house 65% of traditional semester student body. Dormitories for men only constitute 38% of such space, for women only 62%. *Intercollegiate athletics:* men only: basketball, cross-country, golf, soccer, softball, tennis, track; women only: basketball, cross-country, golf, soccer, softball, tennis, volleyball. *Special regulations:* Cars permitted without restrictions. Dormitory visitation from 12 noon to 10pm Sun.–Thurs., 12 noon to 1am. Fri.–Sat., 12 noon to 10pm day before classes. *Special services:* Medical services, Career Development Office. *Student publications: Argo,* a yearbook; *The Chimes,* an annual literary magazine; *The Periscope,* a monthly newspaper. Student radio station WSOS. *Surrounding community:* Rome population 30,000. Atlanta, 70 miles from campus, is nearest metropolitan area. Served by airport 6 miles from campus.

Library Collections: 150,000 volumes. 11,004 audiovisual materials; 599 current periodical subscriptions. Access to online bibliographic information retrieval systems. Computer work stations available. Students have access to the Internet at no charge.

Most important special holdings include local Baptist history; music library.

Buildings and Grounds: Campus area 150 acres.

Chief Executive Officer: Dr. Harold E. Newman, President.

Address undergraduate admission inquiries to Dr. John Head, Vice President for Enrollment Management.

South University

709 Mall Boulevard
Savannah, Georgia 31406
Tel: (912) 201-8000   **E-mail:** admission@southuniversity.edu
Fax: (912) 201-8070   **Internet:** www.southuniversity.edu

Institution Description: South University, formerly named South College, is a private institution offering a select group of course offerings geared to community needs. The university operates branch campuses in West Palm Beach, Florida and Columbia, South Carolina, and Montgomery, Alabama. *Enrollment:* 784. *Degrees awarded:* Associate, baccalaureate, master's, first-professional.

Accreditation: *Regional:* SACS.

History: Established in 1899 as Draughons Practical Business College, South University is a four-year institution offering a variety of degrees in health care, business, and paralegal studies.

Calendar: Quarters. Academic year Oct. to June.

Characteristics of Freshmen: 93% of applicants accepted. 74% of accepted applicants enrolled. 92% of freshmen from Georgia.

Admission: *Requirements:* High school graduation or GED; bachelor's degree or higher for master's programs.

Degree Requirements: *For all degrees:* Completion of all courses prescribed for the degree program.

Distinctive Educational Programs: Physician assistant; anesthesiologist assistant, doctor of pharmacy.

Degrees Conferred: 87 *associate* : data processing, health services and paramedical technologies; 38 *baccalaureate:* business/marketing 16; computer and information sciences 1; health professions and related sciences 17; law and legal studies 4; 28 *master's:* health professions and related studies.

Fees and Other Expenses: *Full-time tuition per academic year 2004–05:* $14,780 undergraduate; $23,580 graduate (average).

Financial Aid: Aid from institutionally generated funds is provided on the basis of financial need.

Financial aid to full-time, first-time undergraduate students: need-based scholarships/grants totaling $1,325,677, self-help $2,076,989, parent loans $179,373; non-need-based scholarships/grants totaling $540,712, self-help $2,840,937, parent loans $32,560. *Graduate aid:* 21 students received federal and state-funded fellowships and grants totaling $64,000; 180 received federal and state-funded loans totaling $4,080,000.

Departments and Teaching Staff: *Total instructional faculty:* 109 (full-time 39, part-time 70). Degrees held by full-time faculty: baccalaureate 18%, master's 51%, doctorate 31%. 28% hold terminal degrees.

Enrollment: Total enrollment 784. Undergraduate full-time 109 men / 242 women, part-time 60m / 151w; graduate full-time 66m / 151w, part-time 2m / 3w.

Characteristics of Student Body: *Ethnic/racial makeup:* number of Black non-Hispanic: 195; American Indian or Alaska Native: 6; Asian or Pacific Islander: 9; Hispanic: 11; White non-Hispanic: 285; unknown: 46. *Age distribution:* number under 18: 1; 18–19: 40; 20–21: 70; 22–24: 128; 25–29: 135; 30–34: 72; 35–39: 45; 40–49: 56; 50–64: 17.

International Students: 10 nonresident aliens enrolled fall 2004. 2 students from Europe, 6 Asia, 1 Africa. No programs to aid students whose native language is not English. No financial aid specifically designated for international students.

Student Life: Students may participate in the Student Affairs Advisory Committee and several professional clubs. The college publishes an annual catalog, student handbook, and a variety of newsletters for students, employees, and the community.

Library Collections: 22,240 volumes. 80 current periodical subscriptions. 29 computer work stations. Students have access to the Internet at no charge.

Buildings and Grounds: Campus area 6.5 acres. *New buildings:* School of Pharmacy Building completed 2004.

Chief Executive Officer: John T. South, III, Chancellor.

Address admissions inquiries to Michael Thompson, Vice President/Director of Admissions.

Southern Polytechnic State University

1100 South Marietta Parkway
Marietta, Georgia 30060-2896
Tel: (678) 915-7778   **E-mail:** admissions@spsu.edu
Fax: (678) 915-7292   **Internet:** www.spsu.edu

Institution Description: Southern Polytechnic State University (formerly Southern College of Technology) is a senior college in the University System of Georgia. *Enrollment:* 3,803. *Degrees awarded:* Associate, baccalaureate, master's.

Accreditation: *Regional:* SACS-Comm. on Coll. *Professional:* business, construction education, engineering technology

History: Established as a division of Georgia Institute of Technology in 1948; awarded first associate degree in 1949; initiated baccalaureate program in 1970; became an independent institution in 1980; became Southern College of Technology in 1986; adopted present name 1996.

Institutional Structure: *Governing board:* Board of Regents of the University System of Georgia. Extrainstitutional representation: 18 regents. All voting. *Composition of institution:* Administrators 27 men / 23 women. Academic Affairs headed by the Vice President for Academic Affairs. Business operations directed by the Vice President for Business and Finance. Full-time instructional faculty 106 men / 23 women. Academic governance body, the Faculty Senate, meets an average of 8 times per year.

Calendar: Semesters. Academic year Aug. to June. Freshmen admitted Sept., Jan., Mar., June. Degrees conferred Dec., May. Formal commencement May and Dec. Summer term from June to Sept.

Characteristics of Freshmen: 1,069 applicants (898 men, 171 women). 62.5% applicants admitted. 62.3% of admitted students enrolled full-time.

92% (400 students) submitted SAT scores; 10% (43 students) submitted ACT scores. *25th percentile:* SAT I Verbal 500; SAT I Math 530; ACT Composite 19, ACT English 19, ACT Math 19. *75th percentile:* SAT I Verbal 610, SAT I Math 630; ACT Composite 25, ACT English 24, ACT Math 25.

40% of entering freshmen expected to graduate within 5 years. 95% of freshmen from Georgia. Freshmen from 30 states and 80 foreign countries.

Admission: Rolling admissions plan. Early acceptance available. *Requirements:* Either graduation from high school or GED. *Entrance tests:* College Board SAT. For foreign students TOEFL. *For transfer students:* 2.0 minimum GPA; from 4-year accredited institution 3 years maximum transfer credit; from 2-year accredited institution 2 years; correspondence/extension students evaluated individually. College credit for extrainstitutional learning (life experience) on basis of portfolio assessment.

Degree Requirements: *For all associate degrees:* 60 hours; 20 credit hours in residence. *For all baccalaureate degrees:* 120–152 hours; 30 credit hours in residence. *For all degrees:* 2.0 GPA; exit competency examinations—Regents' Test of Reading and Writing, tests on or courses in U.S. and Georgia constitutions and histories.

Fulfillment of some degree requirements possible by passing College Board CLEP. *Grading system:* A–F; withdraw (carries time limit).

Distinctive Educational Programs: Cooperative education programs. Evening classes. Cooperative educational programs with other institutions. *Other distinctive programs:* Continuing education.

ROTC: Army, Navy, Air Force in cooperation with Georgia Institute of Technology.

Degrees Conferred: 50 *associate;* 421 *baccalaureate;* 192 *master's.* Bachelor's degrees awarded in top five disciplines: engineering technologies/technicians 197; consumer and information sciences and support services 96; business, management, marketing, and related support services 77; architecture and related services 29; mathematics and statistics 10.

Fees and Other Expenses: *Full-time tuition per academic year 2004–05:* $2,892 in-state resident undergraduate, $10,174 out-of-state. Contact the university for current graduate tuition/fees. *Books and supplies:* $1,000. *Room and board per academic year:* $6,418.

Financial Aid: Aid from institutionally generated funds is provided on the basis of academic merit, financial need, athletic ability, other criteria. Institution has a Program Participation Agreement with the U.S. Department of Education for eligible students to receive

Financial aid to full-time, first-time undergraduate students: 20% received federal grants averaging $2,958; 77% state/local grants averaging $3,223; 27% loans averaging $2,489.

Departments and Teaching Staff: *Total instructional faculty:* 139. Student-to-faculty ratio: 13:1. Degrees held by full-time faculty: Doctorate 54%, master's 45%, baccalaureate 1%. 57% hold terminal degrees.

Enrollment: Total enrollment 3,801. Undergraduate 3,255 (83.2% men, 16.8% women).

Characteristics of Student Body: *Ethnic/racial makeup:* Black non-Hispanic: 21%; American Indian or Alaska Native: .2%; Asian or Pacific Islander: 6.5%; Hispanic: 2.7%; White non-Hispanic: 64.3%. *Age distribution:* number under 18: 9; 18–19: 628; 20–21: 688; 22–24: 795; 25–29: 548; 30–34: 269; 35–39: 145; 40–49: 144; 50–64: 38; 65 and over: 2. 35% of student body attend summer sessions.

International Students: 177 undergraduate nonresident aliens enrolled fall 2004. Programs available to aid students whose native language is not English: social and cultural. No financial aid specifically designated for international students.

Student Life: On-campus residence halls house 19% of student body. *Intercollegiate athletics:* men only: baseball, basketball, tennis. *Special regulations:* Cars permitted without restrictions. *Special services:* Learning Resources Center, medical services, Student Recreation Center. *Student radio:* Radio station WGHR broadcasts 105 hours per week. *Surrounding community:* Marietta, population 35,000, is located in Atlanta metropolitan area. Served by airport 35 miles from campus; passenger rail service 20 miles from campus.

Library Collections: 119,780 volumes. 1,256 serial subscriptions; 9 electronic serial subscriptions. Online and card catalogs. 12 computer work stations. Students have access to the Internet at no charge.

Buildings and Grounds: Campus area 250 acres.

Chief Executive Officer: Dr. Lisa A. Rossbacher, President.

Address admission inquiries to Virginia Head, Director of Admissions.

Spelman College

350 Spelman Lane, S.W.
Atlanta, Georgia 30314-4399

Tel: (404) 681-3643   **E-mail:** admiss@spelman.edu
Fax: (404) 270-5118   **Internet:** www.spelman.edu

Institution Description: Spelman College is a private, independent, nonprofit college for women. *Enrollment:* 2,186. *Degrees awarded:* Baccalaureate.

Accreditation: *Regional:* SACS-Comm. on Coll. *Professional:* music, teacher education

History: Established as Atlanta Baptist Female Seminary 1881; changed name to Spelman Seminary 1884; chartered 1888; offered first instruction at postsecondary level 1897; awarded first degree (baccalaureate) 1901; adopted present name 1924. *See* Florence Matilda Read, *The Story of Spelman College* (Princeton: Princeton University Press, 1961) for further information.

Institutional Structure: *Governing board:* Spelman College Board of Trustees. Extrainstitutional representation: 18 trustees, president of the consortium; institutional representation: president of the college, 1 full-time instructional faculty member, 1 student; 2 alumnae. 2 ex officio. All voting. *Composition of institution:* Administrators 5 men / 14 women. Academic affairs headed by president. Management/business/finances directed by business manager. Full-time instructional faculty 138. Academic governance body, the faculty, meets an average of 9 times per year.

Calendar: Semesters. Academic year Aug. to May. Freshmen admitted Aug., Jan. Degrees conferred and formal commencement May. No summer session.

Characteristics of Freshmen: 4,341 applicants (women). 38.9% of applicants admitted. 29.2% of admitted students enrolled full-time.

84% (415 students) submitted SAT scores; 15% (75 students) submitted ACT scores. *25th percentile*: SAT I Verbal 500, SAT I Math 490; ACT Composite 20. *75th percentile*: SAT I Verbal 580, SAT I Math 580; ACT Composite 24.

17% of freshmen from Georgia. Freshmen from 46 states and 18 foreign countries.

Admission: Rolling admissions plan. For fall acceptance, apply as early as junior year of secondary school, but not later than Mar. 1 of year of enrollment. Apply by Nov. 1 for early action; must limit application to Spelman. Early acceptance available. *Requirements:* Either graduation from accredited secondary school with 15 units which must include 4 English, 2 history, 2 mathematics, 2 science, 2 from among foreign language, literature, social studies, science; or GED. Minimum GPA 2.0. *Entrance tests:* College Board SAT or ACT composite. For foreign students TOEFL. *For transfer students:* 2.0 minimum GPA; from 4-year accredited institution maximum transfer credit 90 hours; from 2-year accredited institution 60 hours.

College credit and advanced placement for postsecondary-level work completed in secondary school. For extrainstitutional learning, college credit and advanced placement on basis of ACE *2006 Guide to the Evaluation of Educational Experiences in the Armed Services*, portfolio assessment. College credit on basis of faculty assessment.Tutoring available. Credit and noncredit developmental/remedial courses offered during regular academic year.

Degree Requirements: 120 credit hours; 2.0 GPA; 30 hours in residence; 2–3 hours physical education including hours in activity sports; freshmen orientation classes; core curriculum.

Fulfillment of some degree requirements and exemption from some beginning courses possible by passing ACT College Board CLEP, AP (score of 3). *Grading system:* A–F; pass-fail; withdraw (deadline after which pass-fail is appended to withdraw).

Distinctive Educational Programs: Cooperative education. Dual-degree program in engineering with Georgia Institute of Technology, Boston University, Auburn University, and Rochester Institute of Technology. Cross-registration and cooperative academic programs through the consortium.

ROTC: Army, Navy, Air Force in cooperation with Georgia Institute of Technology.

Degrees Conferred: 533 *baccalaureate*. Bachelor degrees awarded in top five disciplines: social sciences 163; psychology 88; English language and literature/letters 58; biological and biomedical sciences 54; computer and information sciences and support services 30.

Fees and Other Expenses: *Full-time tuition per academic year 2004–05:* $15,190. *Books and supplies:* $1,658. *Room and board per academic year:* $8,010.

Financial Aid: Aid from institutionally generated funds is provided on the basis of academic merit, financial need. Institution has a Program Participation Agreement with the U.S. Department of Education for eligible students to receive Pell Grants and other federal aid.

Financial aid to full-time, first-time undergraduate students: 51% received federal grants averaging $2,500; 25% state/local grants averaging $2,000; 6% institutional grants averaging $2,000; 86% loans averaging $2,000.

Departments and Teaching Staff: Art *professors* 1, *associate professors* 4, *assistant professors* 12, *instructors* 0; biology 2, 2, 4, 3; chemistry 2, 3, 3, 3; computer and information science 0, 1, 2, 2; drama and dance 1, 2, 1, 1; economics 0, 5, 0, 1; education 2, 2, 1, 2; English 3, 3, 6, 5; foreign language 1, 5, 3, 4; health and physical education 0, 1, 0, 3; history 0, 3, 2, 1; mathematics 4, 3, 3, 1; music 2, 1, 2, 1; philosophy and religion 1, 2, 2, 1; physics 1, 2, 2, 1; political science 1, 2, 3, 0; psychology 2, 3, 1, 1; sociology 3, 3, 1, 0.

Total instructional faculty: 138. 84% hold terminal degrees.

Enrollment: Total enrollment 2,186 (.1% men, 99.9% women).

Characteristics of Student Body: *Ethnic/racial makeup:* Black non-Hispanic: 94.1%; Hispanic: .1%; American Indian or Alaska Native: 1%; unknown: .8%.

International Students: 35 nonresident aliens enrolled. No programs available to aid students whose native language is not English. No financial aid specifically designated for international students.

Student Life: On-campus residence halls house 62% of student body. 2% of student body live off campus in the consortium's Interdenominational Theological Center. *Special regulations:* Registered cars permitted for juniors and seniors; fee required. Curfews. Quiet hours. Residence hall visitation from 3:30pm to 11:50pm Sun., 6pm to 11:50pm Mon.–Sat. *Special services:* Medical services. *Student publications: Focus*, an irregularly published literary magazine; *Reflections*, a yearbook; *Spotlight*, a monthly newspaper. *Surrounding community:* Atlanta metropolitan area population 3 million. Served by mass transit bus and train system; airport 7 miles from campus; passenger rail service 7 miles from campus.

Library Collections: 500,000 titles. 386,000 microforms; 10,000 audiovisual materials; 1,440 current periodicals. Online catalog. Students have access to online retrieval services and the Internet.

Most important holdings include John Henrick Clarke Africana Collection; Countee Cullens Memorial Collection; Henry Slaughter Collection; Margaret Nabrit Curry Collection (on women, 1,309 volumes); drama collection (275 items).

Buildings and Grounds: Campus area 32 acres.

Chief Executive Officer: Dr. Beverly D. Tatum, President.

Address admission inquiries to Mitchell Fagler, Director of Admissions. Services.

Thomas University

1501 Millpond Road

Thomasville, Georgia 31792

Tel: (229) 226-1621 **E-mail:** admission@thomasu.edu

Fax: (229) 226-1653 **Internet:** www.thomasu.edu

Institution Description: Thomas University, formerly Thomas College, is a private institution. *Degrees offered:* Associate, baccalaureate.

Accreditation: *Regional:* SACS. *Professional:* nursing, social work

Institutional Structure: President, executive vice president, vice president of academic affairs, director of student affairs, business office manager. Board of Trustees. Full-time instructional faculty 41.

Calendar: Semesters. Academic year Aug. to May.

Characteristics of Freshmen: Average secondary school rank of freshmen men top 19th percentile, women top 35th percentile. 100% of applicants accepted. 67% of accepted applicants enrolled.

73% of entering freshmen expected to graduate within 5 years. 90% of freshmen from Georgia. Freshmen from 5 states and 4 foreign countries.

Admission: Graduation from an accredited high school or GED. College credit and advanced placement for postsecondary-level work completed in secondary school and for extrainstitutional learning on basis of ACE *2006 Guide to the Evaluation of Educational Experiences in the Armed Services*. Developmental/remedial courses offered in summer session and regular academic year; credit given.

Degree Requirements: Completion of all prescribed courses and residence requirement.

Degrees Conferred: 9 *associate*; 131 *baccalaureate*; 12 *master's*. Bachelor's degrees awarded in top five disciplines: education 40; health professions and related clinical sciences 27; security and protective services 25; business, management, marketing, and related support services 14; public administration and social service professions: 10.

Fees and Other Expenses: *Full-time tuition per academic year 2004–05:* $9,800. *Books and supplies:* $1,100. *Room and board per academic year:* $4,800.

Financial Aid: Aid from institutionally generated funds is provided on the basis of academic merit, financial need, athletic ability, other considerations. Institution has a Program Participation Agreement with the U.S. Department of Education for eligible students to receive Pell Grants and other federal aid.

Financial aid to full-time, first-time undergraduate students: 63% received federal grants averaging $3,441; 74% state/local grants averaging $1,440; 40% institutional grants averaging $5,239; 60% loans averaging $5,146.

Departments and Teaching Staff: Business *professors* 1, *associate professors* 4, *assistant professors* 0, *instructors* 0, *part-time teachers* 5; education 3, 0, 1, 0, 5; human services 2, 6, 2, 1, 4; liberal arts 1, 2, 3, 2, 8; mathematics/natural science 2, 2, 3, 2, 8; allied health 2, 3, 1, 1, 0; developmental 0, 0, 4, 0, 0.

Total instructional faculty: 78. Student-to-faculty ratio: 13:1. Degrees held by full-time faculty: doctorate 50%, master's 46%, baccalaureate 4%.

Enrollment: Total enrollment 679. Undergraduate full-time 747 (37.6% men, 62.4% women).

Characteristics of Student Body: *Ethnic/racial makeup:* Black non-Hispanic: 33.9%; American Indian or Alaska Native: .5%; Asian or Pacific Islander: .8%; Hispanic: 1.2%; White non-Hispanic: 55.3%.

International Students: 47 nonresident aliens enrolled fall 2003. Students fro Asia, Central and South America. No programs available to aid students whose native language is not English.

Library Collections: 54,200 volumes. 418 current periodical subscriptions. 825 audiovisual units; 83 compact discs. 40 computer work stations. Students have access to the Internet at no charge.

Buildings and Grounds: Campus area 25 acres.

Chief Executive Officer: Dr. John M. Hutchinson, President.

Address admissions inquiries to Director of Student Affairs.

Toccoa Falls College

P.O. Box 800899

Toccoa Falls, Georgia 30598

Tel: (706) 886-6831 **E-mail:** admission@toccoafalls.edu

Fax: (706) 282-6012 **Internet:** www.toccoafalls.edu

Institution Description: Toccoa Falls College is a private, independent, nonprofit institution affiliated with the Christian and Missionary Alliance. *Enrollment:* 829. *Degrees awarded:* Associate, baccalaureate.

Accreditation: *Regional:* SACS-Comm. on Coll. *National:* ABHE. *Professional:* business, music, teacher education

History: Established as Golden Valley Institute at Golden, North Carolina 1907; moved to present location and changed name to Toccoa Falls Institute 1911; authorized to grant baccalaureate 1939; adopted present name 1975.

Institutional Structure: *Governing board:* Board of Trustees. Representation: 27 trustees. All voting. *Composition of institution:* Academic affairs headed by dean of the college. Management/business/finances directed by director of finance. Full-time instructional faculty 43.

Calendar: Semesters. Academic year Aug. to May. Formal commencement Dec., May. Summer session from June to July.

Characteristics of Freshmen: 64% of applicants admitted. 31% of admitted students enrolled full-time.

80% (128 students) submitted SAT scores; 40% (65 students) submitted ACT scores. *25th percentile:* SAT Verbal 460, SAT Math 460; ACT Composite 18. *75th percentile:* SAT Verbal 600, SAT Math 580; ACT Composite 24.

42% of entering freshmen expected to graduate within 5 years. 54% of freshmen from Georgia. Freshmen from 22 states.

Admission: Rolling admissions plan. Early acceptance available. *Requirements:* Either graduation from secondary school or GED. *Entrance tests:* College Board SAT or ACT composite. For foreign students TOEFL. *For transfer students:* Minimum 2.0 GPA.

Degree Requirements: *For all associate degrees:* 60 credit hours. *For all baccalaureate degrees:* 126 hours; exit competency examination in Bible content; Christian service requirement. *For all degrees:* 2.0 GPA; 30 hours in residence; weekly chapel attendance; core curriculum.

Fulfillment of some degree requirements and exemption from some beginning courses possible by passing College Board CLEP. *Grading system:* A–F; withdraw (deadline after which pass-fail is appended to withdraw).

Degrees Conferred: 11 *associate;* 160 *baccalaureate:* business/marketing 8; communications/communication technologies 10; education 31; philosophy/religion/theology 75; psychology 28; visual and performing arts 5.

Fees and Other Expenses: *Full-time tuition per academic year 2004–05:* $12,050. *Required fees:* $475 matriculation fee. *Room and board per academic year:* $4,600.

Financial Aid: Aid from institutionally generated funds is provided on the basis of academic merit and financial need.

Financial aid to full-time, first-time undergraduate students: need-based scholarships/grants totaling $1,917,284, self-help $2,264,506; non-need-based scholarships/grants totaling $2,645,720, self-help $1,470,571, parent loans $843,626, tuition waivers $133,557.

Departments and Teaching Staff: *Total instructional faculty:* 68 (full-time 43, part-time 25; women 18, men 50; members of minority groups 4). Total faculty with doctorate, first-professional, or other terminal degree: 30. Student-to-faculty ratio: 15:1.

Enrollment: Total enrollment 829. Full-time 346 men / 427 women, part-time 17m / 39w.

Characteristics of Student Body: *Ethnic/racial makeup:* number of Black non-Hispanic: 23; Asian or Pacific Islander: 41; Hispanic: 16; White non-Hispanic: 731; unknown: 1. *Age distribution:* number under 18: 10; 18–19: 254; 20–21: 287; 22–24: 178; 25–29: 40; 30–34: 21; 35–39: 15; 40–49: 12; 50–64: 10; 65 and over: 2.

International Students: 16 nonresident aliens enrolled fall 2004. 4 students from Europe, 1 Asia, 4 Central and South America, 3 Africa, 4 Canada. Social and financial aid available to aid international students.

Student Life: On-campus housing available. Housing available for married students. Toccoa Falls College provides many opportunities for Christian fellowship. *Intercollegiate athletics:* Member of NCCAA. men's and women's soccer, men's baseball; men's and women's basketball, women's volleyball. The International Student Association provides opportunities for support to students in new surroundings. The Married Student Association provides socials, projects, and other activities for the married population. Student Missions Fellowship provides reports of missionaries (representatives of many missionary organizations actively engage in the program). Campus Wives Association, Outdoor Club, Teacher Education Club, Communications Club, African American Student

Association, Philosophy Club. *Special regulations:* Registered cars with decals permitted; fee charged. *Special services:* Learning Resources Center. *Student publications: Forrester,* a yearbook; *Talon,* a biweekly newspaper; *Student Directory,* an annual publication. *Surrounding community:* Toccoa population 9,000. Atlanta, 90 miles from campus, is nearest metropolitan area.

Library Collections: 159,082 volumes. 4,418 audiovisual materials. Access to 41,595 serials via electronic access. 60 computer work stations campus-wide. Students have access to the Internet at no charge.

Most important holdings include collections on Bible, theology, and Christian education; personal library of Richard A. Forrest, founder of institution; collections on world missions..

Buildings and Grounds: *New buildings:* Scholl of Counseling expanded with new classrooms and offices.

Chief Executive Officer: W. Wayne Gardner, President.

Address admission inquiries to Christy Meadows, Director of Admissions.

University of Georgia

436 East Broad Street
Athens, Georgia 30602
Tel: (706) 542-3000   **E-mail:** admissions@uga.edu
Internet: www.uga.edu

Institution Description: The University of Georgia is a state institution and land-grant college. *Enrollment:* 33,405. *Degrees awarded:* Baccalaureate, first-professional (law, pharmacy, veterinary medicine), master's, doctorate. Specialist certificate in education also awarded.

Budget subject to approval by state governing boards.

Accreditation: *Regional:* SACS-Comm. on Coll. *Professional:* accounting, art, audiology, business, clinical psychology, counseling, counseling psychology, engineering, environmental health, family and consumer science, forestry, interior design, journalism, landscape architecture, law, marriage and family therapy, music, pharmacy, psychology internship, public administration, recreation and leisure services, rehabilitation counseling, school psychology, social work, speech-language pathology, teacher education, theatre, veterinary medicine

History: Established and chartered 1785; offered first instruction at postsecondary level 1801; awarded first degree (baccalaureate) 1804. *See* Robert Preston Brooks, *The University of Georgia Under Sixteen Administrations 1785–1955* (Athens: The University of Georgia Press, 1956) and Thomas G. Dyer, *The University of Georgia: A Bicentennial History, 1785–1985* (Athens: The University of Georgia Press, 1985) for further information.

Institutional Structure: *Governing board:* Board of Regents of the University System of Georgia. Representation: 18 regents. All voting. *Composition of institution:* Administrators 21 men / 8 women. Academic affairs headed by senior vice president for academic affairs and provost. Management/business/finances directed by senior vice president for finance and administration. Full-time instructional faculty 1,661. Academic governance body, The University Council, meets an average of 6 times per year.

Calendar: Semesters. Academic year Aug. to May. Freshmen admitted Aug., Jan., June. Degrees conferred May, Aug., Dec. Formal commencement May and Dec.

Characteristics of Freshmen: 62% of applicants admitted. 34% of admitted students enrolled full-time.

96% (4,339 students) submitted SAT scores; 33% (1,502 students) submitted ACT scores. *25th percentile:* SAT Verbal 560, SAT Math 570; ACT Composite 24, ACT English 23, ACT Math 24. *75th percentile:* SAT Verbal 660, SAT Math 660; ACT Composite 28, ACT 29, English ACT Math 28. 44 National Merit Scholars.

83% of entering freshmen expected to graduate within 5 years. 83% of freshmen from Georgia. Freshmen from 41 states and 33 foreign countries.

Admission: Early enrollment (with acceptable credentials, students can enroll at the end of the senior year) and joint enrollment (with acceptable credentials can enroll during the senior year). For fall acceptance, apply as early as beginning of senior year of secondary school, but not later than 20 days prior to beginning of term. *Requirements:* Either graduation from accredited secondary school with 16 units which must include 4 English, 4 mathematics, 3 science (2 laboratory and 1 physical science), 3 social science (world history, U.S. history, economics/government); or GED. *Entrance tests:* College Board SAT or ACT. *For transfer students:* 2.5 minimum GPA for applicants with 60 or more hours of transfer credit; 3.2 minimum GPA for applicants with 30 to 59 hours of transfer credit; maximum transfer credit 60 semester hours from a junior college or 100 semester hours from a senior college; minimum of 45 semester hours in residence.

College credit and advanced placement for postsecondary-level work completed in secondary school. College credit for extrainstitutional learning on basis of ACE *2006 Guide to the Evaluation of Educational Experiences in the Armed Services.* Tutoring available. Noncredit developmental and remedial courses offered in summer session and regular academic year.

Degree Requirements: 120 semester hours; 2.2 GPA; 45 semester hours in residence; 1 semester hour in basic physical education; exit competency examinations (Regents' Test of Reading and Writing, tests on or courses in U.S. and Georgia constitutions and histories); environmental literacy and cultural diversity requirements.

Fulfillment of some degree requirements and exemption from some beginning courses possible by passing departmental examinations, College Board CLEP, AP, other standardized tests. *Grading system:* A–F; pass-fail; withdraw (deadline after which pass-fail is appended to withdraw).

Distinctive Educational Programs: Cooperative education. Accelerated degree programs. Combination bachelor's/master's degree program sponsored by the Honors Program in conjunction with the Graduate School. Interdepartmental and interdisciplinary programs in area studies, engineering, women's studies, interdisciplinary Field Program offers 8 weeks of geology, anthropology, and ecology courses in the field rather than in the classroom. Center for Undergraduate Research Opportunities offers research apprentice program and summer research fellows program. Institutionally sponsored study abroad and exchange programs in 36 foreign countries; residential study abroad sites in Oxford, England; Cortina, Italy; and Costa Rica. Participant in National Student Exchange.

ROTC: Army, Air Force. 11 Army and 23 Air Force commissions awarded 2004.

Degrees Conferred: 5,779 *baccalaureate* (B), 1,612 *master's* (M), 404 *doctorate* (D): agriculture 182 (B), 54 (M), 27 (D); architecture 66 (B), 10 (M); biological/life sciences 370 (B), 30 (M), 51 (D); business/marketing 1,578 (B), 399 (M), 16 (D); communications/communication technologies 484 (B), 59 (M), 3 (D); computer and information sciences 51 (B), 51 (M), 2 (D); education 613 (B), 492 (M), 123 (D); engineering and engineering technologies 29 (B), 2 (M); English 264 (B), 18 (M), 15 (D); foreign languages and literature 142 (B), 27 (M), 11 (D); health professions and related sciences 105 (B), 48 (M), 28 (D); home economics and vocational home economics 264 (B), 20 (M), 10 (D); interdisciplinary studies 49 (B), 19 (M); law/legal studies 20 (M); liberal arts/general studies 36 (B); mathematics 33 (B), 36 (M), 9 (D); natural resources/environmental science 57 (B), 39 (M), 11 (D); parks and recreation 36 (B); philosophy/religion/theology 54 (B), 6 (M), 1 (D); physical sciences 33 (B), 9 (M), 15 (D); protective services/public administration 112 (B), 164 (M), 12 (D); psychology 301 (B), 39 (M), 36 (D); social sciences and history 667 (B), 31 (M), 21 (D); visual and performing arts 248 (B), 39 (M), 13 (D). 428 *first-professional:* pharmacy 114; veterinary medicine 87; law 227.

Fees and Other Expenses: *Full-time tuition per academic year 2004–05:* in-state resident undergraduate $3,368, out-of-state $14,684; in-state graduate $4,044, out-of-state $17,378. *Room and board per academic year:* $6,006.

Financial Aid: Aid from institutionally generated funds is provided on the basis of academic merit, financial need, athletic ability, other criteria.

Financial aid to full-time, first-time undergraduate students: need-based scholarships/grants totaling $26,728,690, self-help $18,823,531, parent loans $1,819,943, tuition waivers $851,022, athletic awards $1,196,570; non-need-based scholarships/grants totaling $59,005,534, self-help $17,562,137, parent loans $7,047,192, tuition waivers $6,790,155, athletic awards $3,623,336.

Departments and Teaching Staff: *Professors* 686, *associate professors* 494, *assistant professors* 364, *instructors* 45, *part-time faculty* 340. *Total instructional faculty:* 2,080 (full-time 1,661, part-time 419; women 995, men 1,385; members of minority groups 274). Total faculty with doctorate, first-professional, or other terminal degree: 1,805. Student-to-faculty ratio: 17.7:1. *Faculty development:* $159,909,578 in grants for research.

Enrollment: Total enrollment 33,405. Undergraduate full-time 9,702 men / 12,914 women, part-time 1,060m / 1,343w; first-professional full-time 568m / 972w, part-time 14m / 40w; graduate full-time 1,912m / 2,433w, part-time 872m / 1,575w. *Transfer students:* in-state 719; out-of-state 51.

Characteristics of Student Body: *Ethnic/racial makeup:* number of Black non-Hispanic: 1,153; American Indian or Alaska Native: 39; Asian or Pacific Island: 1,134; Hispanic: 439; White non-Hispanic: 22,009. *Age distribution:* number under 18: 124; 18–19: 8,504; 20–21: 9,917; 22–24: 4,923; 25–29: 881; 30–34: 276; 35–39: 126; 40–49: 299; 50–64: 62; 65 and over: 5.

International Students: 1,322 nonresident aliens enrolled fall 2004. 301 students from Europe, 1,180 Asia, 146 Central and South America, 180 Africa, 132 Canada, 8 Australia, 8 New Zealand, 79 other. Programs available to aid students whose native language is not English: social, cultural. English as a Second Language Program.

Student Life: On-campus residence halls house 20% of student body. Residence halls for women 20%, for both sexes 80%. 19% of men join and 5% live in fraternities; 24% of undergraduate women join and 6% live in sororities. *Inter-*

collegiate athletics: men only: baseball, basketball, cross-country, football, golf, swimming and diving, tennis, track; women only: basketball, cross-country, equestrian, golf, gymnastics, soccer, softball, swimming and diving, track, volleyball. *Special regulations:* Registered cars with permits allowed. *Special services:* Learning Resources Center, medical services, campus bus service. *Student publications, radio, television: The Georgia Agriculturist,* a quarterly news magazine; *The Georgia Law Review,* a quarterly publication; *Georgia Pharmacist Magazine,* an annual news publication; *Pandora,* a yearbook; *Red and Black,* a newspaper published 5 times per week. Radio station WUOG broadcasts 147 hours per week; WUGA-FM radio is part of the Georgia public radio network. *Surrounding community:* Athens-Clarke County population 108,000. Atlanta, 70 miles from campus, is nearest metropolitan area. Served by mass transit bus system; airport 5 miles from campus.

Library Collections: 4,028,611 volumes. 6,487,755 microforms; 253,388 recordings; electronic access to 40,899 serials. 652 computer work stations. Students have access to the Internet at no charge.

Most important special holdings include Confederate Imprints; Margaret Mitchell Papers; Richard B. Russell Memorial Library; Peabody Award Archive; Hagrett Rare Book and Manuscript Library..

Buildings and Grounds: Main campus area 614 acres. *New buildings:* Student Learning Center; Women's Athletic Comples; East Campus Village Housing and Dining Commons; Paul D. Coverdell Center for Biomedical and Health Sciences.

Chief Executive Officer: Dr. Michael F. Adams, President.

Undergraduates address admission inquiries to Nancy McDuff, Vice President for Admissions and Enrollment Management; graduate inquiries to Janet A. Sandor, Director, Graduate Admissions.

University of West Georgia

1600 Maple Street
Carrollton, Georgia 30118

Tel: (678) 839-5000   **E-mail:** admis@westga.edu
Fax: (678) 839-4766   **Internet:** www.westga.edu

Institution Description: The University of West Georgia, formerly named State University of West Georgia, is a coeducational, liberal arts, residential institution. *Enrollment:* 10,216. *Degrees awarded:* Baccalaureate, master's, doctorate. Educational specialist certificate also awarded.

Accreditation: *Regional:* SACS-Comm. on Coll. *Professional:* accounting, art, business, counseling, music, nursing, nursing education, public administration, teacher education, theatre

History: Established as 4th District Agricultural and Mechanical School 1906; chartered, offered first instruction at postsecondary level, and adopted present name 1933; became 4-year institution 1957; awarded first degree (baccalaureate) 1958; in 1967, initiated a graduate program at the master's level; became a state university in 1996; appointed in 1999 to offer the institution's first doctoral program in education; current name adopted in 2005.

Institutional Structure: *Governing board:* Board of Regents of University System of Georgia. Extrainstitutional representation: 18 regents. All voting. *Composition of institution:* Administrators 8 men / 5 women. Academic affairs headed by vice president and dean of faculties. Management/business/finances directed by vice president for business and finance. Full-time instructional faculty 384. Academic governance body, Faculty Senate, meets an average of 10 times per year. Student services headed by vice president for student services.

Calendar: Semesters. Academic year Sept. to June. Freshmen admitted Jan., June, Aug. Degrees conferred May, July, Dec. Formal commencement May, July, Dec. Summer session of 2 terms from June to Aug.

Characteristics of Freshmen: 61% of applicants admitted. 66% of admitted students enrolled full-time.

86% (1,417 students) submitted SAT scores; 26.5% (437 students) submitted ACT scores. *25th percentile:* SAT Verbal 460, SAT Math 450; ACT Composite 18, ACT English 18, ACT Math 18. *75th percentile:* SAT Verbal 540, SAT Math 540; ACT Composite 22, ACT English 22, ACT Math 22.

14% of entering freshmen expected to graduate within 5 years. 98% of freshmen from Georgia. Freshmen from 16 states and 23 foreign countries.

Admission: Rolling admissions plan. Early acceptance available. *Requirements:* either graduation from accredited secondary school with 4 units English, 4 mathematics, 3 science, 1 social studies, 2 foreign language; or GED. *Entrance tests:* College Board SAT. *For transfer students:* 2.0 minimum GPA; from 4-year accredited institution 60 semester hours maximum transfer credit; from 2-year accredited institution 30 hours.

College credit and advanced placement for postsecondary-level work completed in secondary school. Tutoring available. Noncredit developmental courses offered in summer session and regular academic year.

Degree Requirements: *For all baccalaureate degrees:* minimum 120 semester hours of academic college work in an approved program and completion of the physical education requirement of the college from which one takes a degree. The approved program must include 60 semester hours in the Core Curriculum. Minimum of 39 semester hours of work in courses numbered 3000 or above. Twenty-one of these hours must be in the major field and 12 of these hours must be taken at West Georgia. Thirty-three semester hours must be complete din residence. Twenty of these hours must be in the senior year. Attain a minimum overall GPA of 2.0 and a minimum GPA of 2.0 in the courses used to satisfy the major. Students must pass the Regents' Test of the University System of Georgia.

Fulfillment of some degree requirements and exemption from some beginning courses possible by passing College Board CLEP, AP. *Grading system:* A–F; withdraw (deadline after which pass-fail is appended to withdraw).

Distinctive Educational Programs: *For undergraduates:* Work-experience programs including cooperative education and internships. Dual-degree program in engineering with Georgia Institute of Technology, Auburn University (AL), and Mercer University. Various preprofessional programs available. Honors program. Study abroad includes a variety of programs in France, Canada, Ivory Coast, England, Spain, Mexico, Germany, Italy and Israel, available through the University System of Georgia. *Available to all students:* Evening classes. Special facilities for using telecommunications in the classroom. *Other distinctive programs:* Continuing education. Georgia Water and Wastewater Institute offers in-service training program through cooperative efforts of college and Georgia Department of Natural Resources. Joint doctoral program in education with University of Georgia. Advanced Academy of Georgia.

ROTC: Army.

Degrees Conferred: 29 *associate;* 1,070 *baccalaureate;* (B); 419 *master's* (M); 1 *doctorate:* biological/life sciences 56 (B), 9 (M); business/marketing 303 (B), 48 (M); communications/communication technologies 37 (B); computer and information sciences 8 (B), 1 (M); education 220 (B), 261 (M); English 19 (B), 5 (M); foreign languages and literature 3 (B); health professions and related sciences 63 (B), 27 (M); interdisciplinary studies 3 (M); mathematics 9 (B); natural resources/environmental science 3 (B); parks and recreation 34 (B); philosophy/religion/theology 1 (B); physical sciences 22 (B); protective services/public administration 38 (B), 12 (M); psychology 78 (B), 30 (M); social sciences and history 136 (B), 14 (M); visual and performing arts 40 (B). 139 *education specialists certificates.*

Fees and Other Expenses: *Full-time tuition per academic year 2004–05:* undergraduate resident $2,322; out-of-state $9,290; graduate resident $2,106, out-of-state $8,370. *Required fees:* $584 (undergraduate); $489 (graduate). *Room and board per academic year:* $4,550.

Financial Aid: Aid from institutionally generated funds is provided on the basis of academic merit, financial need, athletic ability.

Financial aid to full-time, first-time undergraduate students: need-based scholarships/grants totaling $13,116,804, self-help $10,129,176, athletic awards $310,718; non-need-based scholarships/grants totaling $7,252,965, self-help $4,480,911, parent loans $1,126,617, athletic awards $332,733. *Graduate aid:* 129 federal and state-funded fellowships and grants totaling $163,287; 488 federal and state-funded loans totaling $4,319,633; 1 work-study job worth $2,364; 49 other fellowships and grants totaling $92,270.

Departments and Teaching Staff: *Total instructional faculty:* 511 (full-time 384, part-time 127; women 258, men 253; members of minority groups 71). Total faculty with doctorate, first-professional, or other terminal degree: 347. Student-to-faculty ratio: 19:1.

Enrollment: Total enrollment 10,216. Undergraduate full-time 2,817 men / 4,082 women, part-time 515m / 865w; graduate full-time 116m / 265w, part-time 332m / 1,234w. *Transfer students:* in-state 4,127; from out-of-state 302.

Characteristics of Student Body: *Ethnic/racial makeup:* number of Black non-Hispanic; 1,900; American Indian or Alaska Native: 20; Asian or Pacific Islander: 109; Hispanic: 118; White non-Hispanic: 5,908; unknown: 135. *Age distribution:* number under 18: 184; 18–19: 2,999; 20–21: 2,291; 22–24: 1,555; 25–29: 468; 30–34: 275; 35–39: 220; 40–49: 229; 50–64: 53; 65 and over: 5. 49% of student body attend summer sessions.

International Students: 121 nonresident aliens enrolled fall 2004. 56 students from Europe, 73 Asia, 59 Central and South America, 75 Africa, 15 Canada, 1 Australia. No programs available to aid students whose native language is not English. No financial aid specifically designated for international students.

Student Life: On-campus residence halls house 25% of student body. 11 fraternities and 9 sororities. *Intercollegiate athletics:* men only: baseball, basketball, cross-country, football, golf; women only: basketball, softball, cross-country, soccer, volleyball. *Special regulations:* Cars permitted without restrictions. Quiet hours from 7pm to 7am. Residence hall visitation from 10am to midnight Sun.–Thurs., 10am to 2am Fri. and Sat. *Special services:* EXCEL Center, medical services, daytime intracampus bus service. *Student publications, radio: Eclectic,* an annual literary magazine; *The West Georgian,* a weekly newspaper. Radio station WWGC broadcasts 112 hours per week. *Surrounding community:*

Carrollton population over 19,000. Atlanta, 50 miles from campus, is nearest metropolitan area. Served by airport 12 miles from campus.

Library Collections: 391,330 volumes. 1,132,936 microforms. 26,000 audiovisual units; 1,155 current periodical subscriptions. Online catalog. 745 computer work stations. Students have access to online information retrieval services and the Internet.

Most important holdings include College Archives; Newt Gingrich Papers; Robert D. Tisinger (REA Files).

Buildings and Grounds: Campus area 394 acres. *New buildings:* Adamson Hall completed 2003.

Chief Executive Officer: Dr. Beheruz N. Sethna, President.

Undergraduates address admission inquiries to Dr. Bobby Johnson, Director of Undergraduate of Admissions; graduate inquires to Dr. Jack O. Jenkins, Dean, Graduate School.

Valdosta State University

1500 North Patterson Street
Valdosta, Georgia 31698
Tel: (800) 618-1878
Fax: (229) 333-5482

Institution Description: Valdosta State University is a state institution. *Enrollment:* 10,400. *Degrees awarded:* Associate, baccalaureate, master's, doctorate. Specialist certificates in education also awarded.

Budget subject to approval by state governing boards.

Accreditation: *Regional:* SACS-Comm. on Coll. *Professional:* business, dental hygiene, music, nursing, nursing education, public administration, social work, speech-language pathology, teacher education, theatre

History: Established by the state legislature 1906; incorporated 1911; became South Georgia Normal College and offered first instruction at postsecondary level as a 2-year institution for women 1913; changed name to Georgia State Woman's College and became 4-year institution 1922; adopted present name and became coeducational 1950; became a regional university of the University System of Georgia in 1993.

Institutional Structure: *Governing board:* Board of Regents of the University System of Georgia. Extrainstitutional representation: 18 regents. All voting. *Composition of institution:* Administrators 43 men / 14 women. Academic affairs headed by vice president and assistant vice president. Management/business/finances directed by vice president for business and finance. Full-time instructional faculty 420. Academic governance body, General Faculty, meets an average of 4 times per year.

Calendar: Semesters. Academic year Aug. to May. Freshmen admitted Aug., Jan., May, June. Degrees conferred and formal commencements May, Aug., and Dec. Summer session of one 8-week session and two 4-week sessions.

Characteristics of Freshmen: 66% of applicants admitted. 49% of admitted students enrolled full-time.

84% (1,430 students) submitted SAT scores; 12% (206 students) submitted ACT scores. *25th percentile:* SAT Verbal 480, SAT Math 470; ACT Composite 20, ACT English 20, ACT Math 19. *75th percentile:* SAT Verbal 560, SAT Math 560; ACT Composite 24, ACT English 25, ACT Math 24.

32% of entering freshmen are expected to graduate within 5 years. 95% of freshmen from Georgia. Freshmen from 28 states.

Admission: Rolling admissions plan. Apply as early as 1 year before beginning of quarter, but not later than 20 days before registration. Early acceptance available. *Requirements:* Either graduation from accredited secondary school with 16 units, earned between grades 9-12, which must include 4 English, 4 mathematics, 3 science, 3 social studies, 2 foreign language; must have 3 of 5 areas in college preparatory curriculum complete. Minimum GPA 2.0. *Entrance tests:* College Board SAT or ACT. *For transfer students:* 2.0 minimum GPA; from 4-year accredited institution 90 hours maximum transfer credit; from 2-year accredited institution 60 hours; correspondence/extension students 30 hours.

College credit and advanced placement for postsecondary-level work completed in secondary school. College credit for extrainstitutional learning on basis of ACE *2006 Guide to the Evaluation of Educational Experiences in the Armed Services,* faculty assessment. Tutoring available.

Degree Requirements: *For all associate degrees:* 60 semester hours; 20 hours in residence. *For all baccalaureate degrees:* 120 semester hours; 30 hours in residence; junior core curriculum. *For all undergraduate degrees:* 2.0 GPA; courses in English, mathematics, humanities, science, and social sciences as well as Regents' Test of Reading and Writing.

Fulfillment of some degree requirements and exemption from some beginning courses possible by passing institutional examinations, College Board CLEP, AP. *Grading system:* A–F.

Distinctive Educational Programs: Flexible meeting places and schedules, including off-campus centers (at various locations 30 to 90 miles away from main institution) and evening classes. Dual-degree program in engineering with Georgia Institute of Technology. Special facilities for using telecommunications in the classroom. Facilities and programs for independent research, including honors programs, individual majors, tutorials. *Other distinctive programs:* Office of Public Services offers on- and off-campus credit and noncredit programs.

ROTC: Air Force. 11 commissions awarded 2004.

Degrees Conferred: 46 *associate*; 1,274 *baccalaureate* (B); 340 *master's* (M), 18 *doctorate(D):* biological/life sciences 48 (B); business/marketing 34 (B), 20 (M); communications/communication technologies 44 (B); computer and information sciences 35 (B); education 252 (B), 184 (M), 18 (D); engineering and engineering technologies 15 (B); English 88 (B), 7 (M); foreign languages and literature 6 (B); health professions and related sciences 89 (B), 52 (M); law/legal studies 7 (B); liberal arts/general studies 13 (B); library science 1 (M); mathematics 3 (B); natural resources/environmental science 4 (B); parks and recreation 20 (B); philosophy/religion/theology 4 (B); physical sciences 11 (B); protective services/public administration 55 (B), 54 (M); psychology 66 (B), 10 (M); social sciences and history 110 (B), 12 (M); visual and performing arts 80 (B).

Fees and Other Expenses: *Full-time tuition per academic year 2004–05:* undergraduate in-state resident $2,322, out-of-state $9,290; graduate resident $2,786, out-of-state $11,146. *Room and board per academic year:* $5,208.

Financial Aid: Aid from institutionally generated funds is awarded on the basis of academic merit, financial need, athletic ability.

Financial aid to full-time, first-time undergraduate students: need-based scholarships/grants totaling $13,712,784, self-help $15,436,633, parent loans $5,503,080, athletic awards $241,403; non-need-based scholarships/grants totaling $8,498,428, self-help $17,752,348, parent loans $12,221,104, athletic awards $641,500. *Graduate aid:* 797 federal and state-funded loans totaling $6,698,574 (ranging from $200 to $18,500); 15 work-study jobs worth $35,900 (ranging from $1,000 to $4,000); 133 other college-assigned job (nonteaching, nonresearch) totaling $242,526.

Departments and Teaching Staff: *Professors* 115, *associate professors* 89, *assistant professors* 128, *instructors* 58, *part-time faculty* 71. *Total instructional faculty:* 491 (includes faculty on 11/12 month contracts). Full-time 420, part-time 71; women 239, men 232. Student-to-faculty ratio: 21:1. *Faculty development:* $247,303 in grants for research. 2 faculty members awarded sabbaticals 2004–05.

Enrollment: Total enrollment 10,400. Full-time undergraduate 3,063 men / 4,340 women, part-time 608m / 942w; full-time graduate 106m / 364w, part-time 220m / 697w.

Characteristics of Student Body: *Ethnic/racial makeup:* number of White non-Hispanic: 6,713; Black non-Hispanic: 1,908; American Indian or Alaska Native: 25; Asian or Pacific Islander: 107; Hispanic: 145. *Age distribution:* number under 18: 31; 18–19: 2,615; 20–21: 2,788; 22–24: 1,952; 25–29: 809; 30–34: 303; 35–39: 209; 40–49: 248; 50–64: 55; 65 and over: 3.

International Students: 144 nonresident aliens enrolled 2004. 63 students from Europe, 52 Asia, 28 Central and South America, 31 Africa, 13 Canada, 4 Australia, 20 other. Social, cultural, and financial programs available to aid students whose native language is not English.

Student Life: On-campus residence halls house 17% of student body. 10% of men join fraternities. 2% of student body live in university-owned apartments. *Intercollegiate athletics:* men only: baseball, basketball, football, cross country, golf, tennis; women only: basketball, cross country, softball, tennis, volleyball. *Special regulations:* Cars with parking decals permitted. Quiet hours. Residence hall visitation from 7pm to midnight Mon.-Thurs., noon to 1am Fri., 9am to 1am Sat., 9am to midnight Sun. *Special services:* Learning Resources Center, medical services, campus bus service. *Student publications, radio, television:* Oradeck, literary magazine; *Spectator,* a weekly newspaper. Radio and television stations WVVS broadcast 133 hours and 9½ hours per week, respectively. *Surrounding community:* Valdosta population 121,400. Jacksonville, Florida, 130 miles from campus, is nearest metropolitan area. Served by airport 4 miles from campus.]

Library Collections: 467,500 volumes including bound books, serial backfiles, electronic documents, and government documents not in separate collections. Online catalog. Current serial subscriptions: 2,815 paper, 78 microform, 600 electronic. 15,183 recordings; 2,553 compact discs. 300 computer work stations. Students have access to the Internet at no charge. Total 2004–05 budget for books and materials: $1,005,740.

Most important special holdings include the Archives of South Georgia History; Emily Hendree Park Collection—United Daughters of the Confederacy; Joyce Ann Joyce Collection; Janice Dougherty Collection. Valdosta State University Archives.

Buildings and Grounds: Campus area 168 acres. *New buildings:* Biology/Chemistry Building; Odum Library Addition; Centennial Hall East.

Chief Executive Officer: Dr. Ronald Zaccari, President.

Undergraduates address admission inquiries to Walter Peacock, Director of Admissions; graduate inquiries to Dr. Brian Adler, Dean of Graduate Studies.

Wesleyan College

4760 Forsyth Road
Macon, Georgia 31210-4462

Tel: (478) 477-1110   **E-mail:** admissions@wesleyan-college.edu
Fax: (478) 757-4030   **Internet:** www.wesleyan-college.edu

Institution Description: Wesleyan College is a private, nonprofit college affiliated with the United Methodist Church. *Enrollment:* 654 women. Wesleyan awards degrees to women only. *Degrees awarded:* Baccalaureate, master's.

Teacher education program subject to approval by statewide coordinating bodies.

Accreditation: *Regional:* SACS-Comm. on Coll. *Professional:* music, teacher education

History: Established as Georgia Female College, chartered, and offered first instruction at postsecondary level 1836; first degree (baccalaureate) awarded 1840; changed name to Wesleyan Female College 1843; adopted present name 1919; moved to present campus 1928. *See* Samuel Luttrell Akers, *The First One Hundred Years of Wesleyan College: 1836–1936* (Savannah, Ga.: Beehive Press, 1976) for further information.

Institutional Structure: *Governing board:* Board of Trustees: 31 regular, 4 ex officio, 3 alumnae; meets 3 times per year. *Composition of institution:* Administrators 3 men / 2 women. Full-time instructional faculty 21 men / 22 women. Faculty meets formally 10 times per year. *Faculty representation:* Faculty-student committees in all areas except personnel (faculty only).

Calendar: Semesters. Academic year Aug. to May. Degrees conferred May, Aug. Formal commencement May.

Characteristics of Freshmen: 400 applicants. 54.8% of applicants admitted. 34.2% of admitted students enrolled full-time.

92% (69 students) submitted SAT scores; 36% (27 students) submitted ACT scores. *25th percentile*: SAT I Verbal 490, SAT I Math 470; ACT Composite 20, ACT English 19, ACT Math 18. *75th percentile*: SAT I Verbal 610, SAT I Math 590; ACT Composite 25, ACT English 23, ACT Math 23.

48% of entering freshmen expected to graduate within 5 years. 62% of freshmen from Georgia. Freshmen from 14 states and 1 foreign country.

Admission: Rolling admissions plan. Freshman early decision: application deadline Nov. 1; decision notification, Dec. 1; candidate's reply date, Jan. 1. Freshman regular decision: application deadline Mar. 1 (Jan. 15 for academic scholarship competition); decision notification, rolling but no later than Apr. 1; candidate's reply date, May 1. Freshman late decision: application deadline (after admission), rolling; candidate's reply date, May 1. Transfer admission: rolling; candidate's reply date two weeks after notification. *Requirements:* 4 units in English, 3 mathematics, 2 natural sciences, 4 units electives. *Entrance tests:* College Board SAT or ACT composite. *For transfer students:* 2.0 minimum GPA from accredited institution; 60 semesters hours maximum transferable from a junior college; 90 semester hours maximum from a senior college.

Advanced placement for extrainstitutional learning (life experience) on basis of portfolio and faculty assessments. College credit and advanced placement for postsecondary-level work completed in secondary school.

Degree Requirements: 120 semester hours; 2.0 GPA; general education requirements. Fulfillment of some degree requirements and exemption from some beginning courses possible by passing College Board CLEP and APP.

Grading system: A–F; withdraw (carries time limit and deadline after which pass-fail is appended to withdraw); credit-no credit; satisfactory (for noncredit work).

Distinctive Educational Programs: Internships in summer session and regular academic year. Honors program. Weekend and evening classes. Dual-degree programs in engineering with Auburn University (AL), Georgia Institute of Technology, and Mercer University (GA). Videotape and playback facilities. Self-designed interdisciplinary programs. Computer Focus program. Preprofessional programs in law and medicine. Facilities and programs for independent research and tutorials. Exchange program with International Christian University in Japan and Sofia University in Bulgaria. Interdisciplinary freshmen seminar courses.

Degrees Conferred: 126 *baccalaureate*; 27 *master's*. Bachelor's degrees awarded in top five disciplines: business, management, marketing, and related support services 32; psychology 16; communication, journalism, and related programs 15; visual and performing arts 13; biological and biomedical sciences 12.

Fees and Other Expenses: *Full-time tuition per academic year 2004–05:* $10,900. *Books and supplies:* $800. *Room and board per academic year:* $7,450.

Financial Aid: Aid from institutionally generated funds is provided on the basis of academic merit, financial need, other criteria. Institution has a Program Participation Agreement with the U.S. Department of Education for eligible students to receive Pell Grants and other federal aid.

Financial aid to full-time, first-time undergraduate students: 49% received federal grants averaging $2,615; 74% state/local grants averaging $3,000; 92% institutional grants averaging $6,437; 76% loans averaging $4,585.

Departments and Teaching Staff: *Professors* 8, *associate professors* 9, *assistant professors* 19, *instructors* 7, *part-time teachers* 12. *Total instructional faculty:* 55. Degrees held by full-time faculty: doctorate 70%, master's 84%, baccalaureate 100%. 80% of faculty hold terminal degrees.

Enrollment: Total enrollment 654. Undergraduate 582.

Characteristics of Student Body: *Ethnic/racial makeup:* Black non-Hispanic: 30.9%; Asian or Pacific Islander: 2.2%; Hispanic: 2.2%; White non-Hispanic: 42.8%; unknown: 4%.

International Students: No programs available to aid students whose native language is not English. No financial aid specifically designated for international students.

Student Life: On-campus residence halls for women house 75% of student body. *Intercollegiate athletics:* NCAA Div. III basketball, softball, soccer, tennis, volleyball; equestrian team, member of Intercollegiate Horse Show Association. *Special regulations:* Cars must be parked in specified lots. *Special services:* Health Center; tutorial services; a 4-year career exploration, preparation, and placement program; community service program. *Student publications: The Pioneer*, a newspaper published 7 times per year; *Veterropt*, a yearbook; *Wesleyan Magazine of Creative Arts*, published biannually. *Surrounding community:* Macon population 150,000. Atlanta, 80 miles from campus, is nearest metropolitan area. Served by the Atlanta international airport as well as the Macon airport 15 miles from campus.

Library Collections: 143,000 volumes. 33,000 microforms; 6,500 audiovisual materials; 630 current periodical subscriptions. Online catalog. Students have access to online information retrieval services and the Internet.

Most important special collections include Park Collection of Georgiana; McGregor Collection of Americana; Eugenia Rawls papers.

Buildings and Grounds: Campus area 206 acres.

Chief Executive Officer: Dr. Ruth A. Knox, President.

Address admission inquiries to Patricia R. Hardeman, Registrar.

Hawaii

Brigham Young University - Hawaii Campus

55-220 Kulanui Street

Laie, Oahu, Hawaii 96762-1266

Tel: (808) 293-3211   **E-mail:** admissions@byuh.edu

Fax: (808) 293-3329   **Internet:** www.byuh.edu

Institution Description: Brigham Young University-Hawaii Campus (Church College of Hawaii until 1974) is a private institution affiliated with The Church of Jesus Christ of Latter-day Saints. *Enrollment:* 2,486. *Degrees awarded:* Associate, baccalaureate. Certificates also awarded.

Accreditation: *Regional:* WASC-Sr. *Professional:* business, social work

History: Established as the Church College of Hawaii, chartered and offered first instruction at postsecondary level 1955; awarded first degree (associate) 1956; adopted present name 1974.

Institutional Structure: *Governing board:* Board of Trustees. Representation: 12 trustees. All voting. *Composition of institution:* Administrators 45 men / 24 women. Academic affairs headed by vice president for academics. Management/business/finances directed by secretary-treasurer and business manager. Full-time instructional faculty 115. Academic governance body, Academic Planning Council, meets an average of 40 times per year.

Calendar: Semesters. Academic year Aug. to Apr. Freshmen admitted Sept., Jan., Apr. Degrees conferred June, Dec. Formal commencement June, Dec. Summer session from June to Aug.

Characteristics of Freshmen: 12% of applicants admitted. 83% of accepted applicants enrolled full-time.

14% (28 students) submitted SAT scores; 34% (70 students) submitted ACT scores. *25th percentile:* SAT Verbal 422, SAT Math 442; ACT Composite 20, ACT English 19, ACT Math 19. *75th percentile:* SAT Verbal 527, SAT Math 557; ACT Composite 26, ACT English 25, ACT Math 26.

32% of entering freshmen expected to graduate within 5 years. 22% of freshmen from Hawaii. Freshmen from 15 states and 29 foreign countries.

Admission: Rolling admissions plan. Apply no later than Feb. 15. Early acceptance available. *Requirements:* Graduation from secondary school or GED. For Philippine students 1 year of college recommended. Minimum GPA 3.0. *Entrance tests:* College Board ACT composite. For foreign students TOEFL or demonstrated proficiency in English. *For transfer students:* 3.0 minimum GPA; from 4-year accredited institution 102 hours maximum transfer credit; from 2-year accredited institution 66 hours; correspondence/extension students 36 hours.

College credit for postsecondary-level work completed in secondary school and for extrainstitutional learning on basis of ACE *2006 Guide to the Evaluation of Educational Experiences in the Armed Services.* Tutoring available. Developmental courses offered in summer session and regular academic year; credit given.

Degree Requirements: *For all associate degrees:* 60 credit hours; 20 hours in residence; 1 hours physical education. *For all baccalaureate degrees:* 120 credit hours; 30 hours in residence; 2 hours physical education courses; demonstrated proficiency in English; GPA 2.5. *For all undergraduate degrees:* 2.0 GPA; religion courses; general education requirements. Fulfillment of some] degree requirements possible by passing departmental examinations, College Board CLEP, AP. *Grading system:* A–F; pass; withdraw (deadline after which pass-fail is appended to withdraw); incomplete.

Distinctive Educational Programs: Work-experience programs. Weekend classes. Interdisciplinary programs in history-government, Hawaiian studies, marine studies, mathematics-physical science, Polynesian studies. Facilities and programs for independent research, including honors programs, individual majors, tutorials. Study abroad through Brigham Young University (UT). Hawaiian oral history program. Cooperative program with Polynesian Cultural Center. Summer session study of Polynesian and Asian peoples. *Other distinctive programs:* Credit and noncredit continuing education, including extension programs in Asia and Pacific communities. Annual Know Your Religion lecture series.

ROTC: Army an Air Force in cooperation with University of Hawaii - Manoa.

Degrees Conferred: 22 *associate;* 545 *baccalaureate:* area and ethnic studies 9; biological/sciences 19; business/marketing 141; computer and information sciences 59; education 14; English 10; interdisciplinary studies 76; mathematics 7; parks and recreation 24; protective services and public administration 25; psychology 46; social sciences and history 40; visual and performing arts 15.

Fees and Other Expenses: *Full-time tuition per academic year 2004–05:* $2,660. *Room and board per academic year:* $4,800.

Financial Aid: Aid from institutionally generated funds is provided on the basis of academic merit, financial need, athletic ability. Institution has a Program Participation Agreement with the U.S. Department of Education for eligible students to receive Pell Grants and other federal aid.

Financial aid to full-time, first-time undergraduate students: need-based scholarships/grants totaling $2,916,000, self-help $6,129,217; non-need-based scholarships/grants totaling $1,700,000, self-help $4,982,283, parent loans $96,440, tuition waivers $195,773, athletic awards $406,000.

Departments and Teaching Staff: *Professors* 39, *associate professors* 36, *assistant professors* 27, *instructors* 13, *part-tie faculty* 109. *Total instructional faculty:* 224 (full-time 111, part-time 113; women 82, men 142; members of minority groups 70). Total faculty with doctorate, first-professional, or other terminal degree: 100. Student-to-faculty ratio: 15:1. *Faculty development:* $82,095 in grants for research.

Enrollment: Total enrollment 2,486. Full-time 961 men / 1,229 women, part-time 104m / 192w. *Transfer students:* in-state 20; from out-of-state 217.

Characteristics of Student Body: *Ethnic/racial makeup:* number of Black non-Hispanic: 10; American Indian or Alaska Native: 13; Asian or Pacific Islander: 677; Hispanic: 38; White non-Hispanic: 687; unknown: 44. *Age distribution:* number under 18: 12; 18–19: 341; 20–21: 489; 22–24: 816; 25–29: 520; 30–34: 147; 35–39: 50; 40–49: 64; 50–64: 26; 65 and over: 1. 54% of student body attend summer sessions.

International Students: 1,117 nonresident aliens enrolled fall 2004. 36 students from Europe, 588 Asia, 36 Central and South America, 10 Africa, 24 Canada, 13 Australia, 58 New Zealand, 352 other. Programs available to aid students whose native language is not English: social, cultural. English as a Second Language Program. No financial aid specifically designated for international students.

Student Life: On-campus residence halls house 60% of student body. Residence halls for men only constitute 42% of such space, for women only 58%. 95% of married students request institutional housing; 90% are so housed. 80% of students live on campus. *Intercollegiate athletics:* men only: basketball, cross-country, golf, tennis, water polo; women only: cross-country, softball, tennis, volleyball. *Special regulations:* Cars must be registered. Dress code requires adherence to standards of modesty, humility, decency and propriety. Curfews and quiet hours. *Special services:* Learning Resources Center, medical services. *Student publications:* weekly newspaper. *Surrounding community:* Laie, Oahu population 5,000. Honolulu, 40 miles from campus, is nearest metropolitan area. Served by mass transit bus system; airport 40 miles from campus.

Library Collections: 321,400 volumes including bound books, serial backfiles, electronic documents, and government documents not in separate collections. Online catalog. Access to current serial subscriptions via electronic access: 11,825. 465 computer work stations campus-wide. Students have access to the Internet at no charge.

Most important special holdings include Pacific Island Collection; University Archives; Moronism Collection.

Buildings and Grounds: Campus area 200 acres. *New buildings:* Stake Center completed 2002.

Chief Executive Officer: Dr. Eric B. Shumway, President.

Address admission inquiries to Jeffrey Bunker, Dean of Admissions and Records.

Chaminade University of Honolulu

3140 Waialae Avenue
Honolulu, Hawaii 96816-1578
Tel: (808) 735-4711   **E-mail:** admissions@lava.net
Fax: (808) 739-4647   **Internet:** www.chaminade.edu

Institution Description: Chaminade University of Honolulu is a private institution affiliated with the Society of Mary, Roman Catholic Church. *Enrollment:* 1,783. *Degrees awarded:* Associate, baccalaureate, master's.

Accreditation: *Regional:* WASC-Sr.

History: Established, chartered as St. Louis Junior College, and offered first instruction at postsecondary level 1955; became 4-year institution and changed name to Chaminade College of Honolulu 1957; awarded first degree (baccalaureate) 1959; incorporated with St. Louis High School and became St. Louis-Chaminade Education Center 1968; adopted present name 1977.

Institutional Structure: *Governing board:* St. Louis Chaminade Education Center Board of Directors (policy-making body for St. Louis High School and Chaminade University). Extrainstitutional representation: 8 directors. All voting. Board of Regents (for Chaminade University). Extrainstitutional representation: 34 regents, all voting; 1 honorary; institutional representation: 4 administrators, 1 full-time instructional faculty member. 2 ex officio. *Composition of institution:* Administrators 15 men / 11 women. Academic affairs headed by vice president/academic affairs. Management/business/finances directed by vice president for finance and operations. Full-time instructional faculty 49. Academic governance body, Dean's Council, meets weekly.

Calendar: Semesters. Academic year July to June. Freshmen admitted Aug., Jan., May, June, July. Degrees conferred and formal commencements May, Dec. Summer session of 2 terms from May to Aug.

Characteristics of Freshmen: 97% of applicants admitted. 23% of admitted students enrolled full-time.

82% (203 students) submitted SAT scores; 18% (44 students) submitted ACT scores. *25th percentile:* SAT Verbal 430, SAT Math 430; ACT Composite 17, ACT English 16, ACT Math 17. *75th percentile:* SAT Verbal 510, SAT Math 530; ACT Composite 23, ACT English 23, ACT Math 24.

34% of entering freshmen expected to graduate within 5 years. 46% of freshmen from Hawaii. Freshmen from 28 states and 5 foreign countries.

Admission: Rolling admissions plan. For fall acceptance, apply no later than Aug. 1 of year of enrollment. Early acceptance available. *Requirements:* Either graduation from accredited secondary school or GED. Recommend college preparatory program, including 3 units English, 2 mathematics, 2 social studies, 1 science, 2 academic electives. Minimum GPA 2.0. *Entrance tests:* College Board SAT or ACT composite. For foreign students TOEFL. *For transfer students:* 2.0 minimum GPA; from 4-year accredited institution 94 hours maximum transfer credit; from 2-year accredited institution 45 hours.

College credit and advanced placement for postsecondary-level work completed in secondary school; college credit for extrainstitutional learning on basis of ACE *2006 Guide to the Evaluation of Educational Experiences in the Armed Services.* Tutoring available. Developmental/remedial courses offered during regular academic year; nondegree credit given.

Degree Requirements: *For all associate degrees:* 60 semester hours; 1 semester in residence. *For all baccalaureate degrees:* 124 hours; 1 year in residence. *For all undergraduate degrees:* 2.0 GPA; general education requirements. *Grading system:* A–F; credit-no credit; withdraw; incomplete (carries time limit).

Distinctive Educational Programs: Flexible meeting places and schedules, including various locations in Honolulu and at several military bases within 30 miles of main institution; evening and weekend classes. Accelerated degree programs. Early Childhood Education with Montessori emphasis; English as a Foreign Language program. Interdepartmental/interdisciplinary programs in humanities, with emphasis in American Studies, Asian Studies, European Studies, Pacific Island Studies, Hawaiian Studies, Ethnic Studies, International Studies, and in Behavioral Sciences with emphasis in anthropology, sociology, or social services. Graduate degrees in Japanese business studies, criminal justice, counseling psychology. Facilities and programs for independent research, including individual majors, tutorials. Study abroad in Japan. Students may register for courses at University of Hawaii at Manoa, Brigham Young University Hawaii Campus, Hawaii Loa College, Hawaii Pacific University. *Other distinctive programs:* Qualified secondary school students may enroll in courses for credit. Servicemembers Opportunity College.

ROTC: Army, Air Force in cooperation with University of Hawaii - Manoa.

Degrees Conferred: 190 *associate;* 310 *baccalaureate* (B); 251 *master's* (M): biological/life sciences 7 (B); business/marketing 47 (B), 53 (M); communications/communication technologies 1 (B); computer and information sciences 13 (B); education 33 (B); English 13 (B), 72 (M); interdisciplinary studies 5 (B); liberal arts/general studies 1 (B); philosophy/religion/theology 7 (B), 6

(M); protective services/public administration 61 (B), 20 (M); psychology 48 (B), 100 (M); social sciences and history 55; visual and performing arts 9 (B).

Fees and Other Expenses: *Full-time tuition per academic year 2004–05:* undergraduate $14,330; graduate $10,560. *Required fees:* $120. *Room and board per academic year:* $8,870.

Financial Aid: Institution has a Program Participation Agreement with the U.S. Department of Education for eligible students to receive Pell Grants and other federal aid.

Financial aid to full-time, first-time undergraduate students: need-based scholarships/grants totaling $6,425,625, self-help $4,507,805, parent loans $765,968, athletic awards $370,088; non-need-based scholarships/grants totaling $1,007,942, self-help $1,445,977, parent loans $1,445,977, athletic awards $114,119. *Graduate aid:* 490 federal and state-funded loans totaling $5,503,642; 6 college-assigned jobs (nonresearch, nonteaching) totaling $28,635.

Departments and Teaching Staff: *Total instructional faculty:* 136 (full-time 77, part-time 59; women 56, men 80; members of minority groups 60). Total faculty with doctorate, first-professional, or other terminal degree: 55. Student-to-faculty ratio: 11:1. 2 faculty members awarded sabbaticals 2004–05.

Enrollment: Total enrollment 1,783. Undergraduate full-time 333 men / 716 women, part-time 4m / 16w; graduate full-time 143m / 343w, part-time 75m / 143w.

Characteristics of Student Body: *Ethnic/racial makeup:* number of Black non-Hispanic: 60; American Indian or Alaska Native: 12; Asian or Pacific Islander: 1,145; Hispanic: 101; White non-Hispanic: 432,

International Students: 33 nonresident aliens enrolled fall 2004. 6 students from Europe, 20 Asia, 3 Canada, 4 other. No programs available to aid students whose native language is not English. No financial aid specifically designated for international students.

Student Life: On-campus residence halls house 20% of student body. Off-campus dormitory houses another 6% of student body. *Intercollegiate athletics:* men only: basketball; women only: volleyball; men and women: cross-country, golf, tennis, water polo. *Special regulations:* Cars permitted with valid registration, insurance and payment of parking fees. *Special services:* Learning Resources Center, medical services. *Student publications: Ahinahina*, a yearbook; *Aulama*, a biannual literary magazine; *Silversword*, a monthly newspaper. *Surrounding community:* Honolulu population 837,000. Served by mass transit bus system; airport 10 miles from campus.

Library Collections: 76,773 volumes including bound books, serial backfiles, electronic documents, and government documents not in separate collections. Online catalog. Current serial subscriptions: 300 paper, 12 microform, 4,677 via electronic access. 165 recordings; 43 compact discs; 122 CD-ROMs. 19 computer work stations. Students have access to the Internet at no charge.

Most important special holdings include Hawaiiana; Julius J. Nodel Judaica Library Collection; Oceania Collection; David L. Carlson Japan Collection; Catholic Authors Collection.

Buildings and Grounds: Campus area 22 acres. *New buildings:* Behavioral Sciences Center; Education Building; Castle Science Building.

Chief Executive Officer: Dr. Sue Wesselkamper, President.

Address admission inquiries to Director of Admissions.

Hawaii Pacific University

1166 Fort Street Mall
Honolulu, Hawaii 96813
Tel: (808) 544-0200   **E-mail:** admissions@hpu.edu
Fax: (808) 544-1136   **Internet:** www.hpu.edu

Institution Description: Hawaii Pacific University is a private, independent, nonprofit institution. *Enrollment:* 7,800. *Degrees awarded:* Associate, baccalaureate, master's. Certificates also awarded.

Accreditation: *Regional:* WASC-Sr. *Professional:* nursing, social work

History: Established and offered first instruction at postsecondary level 1965; awarded first degree (baccalaureate) 1972; merged with Honolulu Christian College (established 1953) 1966; launched graduate school 1986; university status 1990; merged with Hawaii Loa College in 1992; affiliated with Oceanic Institute in 2003.

Institutional Structure: *Governing board:* Board of Trustees. Representation: 24 trustees. *Composition of institution:* Full-time instructional faculty 132 men / 102 women.

Calendar: Semesters (4-1-4 plan). Academic year Sept. to May. Formal commencements Jan., May, Aug. Summer session of 4 terms.

Characteristics of Freshmen: 79% of applicants admitted. 28% of admitted students enrolled full-time.

70% (574 students) submitted SAT scores; 32% (237 students) submitted ACT scores. *25th percentile:* SAT Verbal 430, SAT Math 440; ACT Composite

18, ACT English 17, ACT Math 17. *75th percentile*: SAT Verbal 560, SAT Math 570; ACT Composite 24, ACT English 25, ACT Math 25. 42% of entering freshmen expected to graduate within 5 years. 38% of freshmen from Hawaii. Freshmen from 50 states and 10o foreign countries.

Admission: Applications processed on a rolling basis. *Requirements:* graduation from accredited secondary school with a 2.5 GPA, or GED. *For transfer students:* Maximum transfer credit limited only by residence requirement of 30 semester credits (for baccalaureate). College credit for extrainstitutional learning on basis of ACE *2006 Guide to the Evaluation of Educational Experiences in the Armed Services.*

Degree Requirements: *For all associate degrees:* 60 credit hours; 15 hours in residence. *For all baccalaureate degrees:* 124 credit hours; 30 hours in residence. *For master's degrees:* 36–45 credit hours; 24–27 hours in residence.

Fulfillment of some degree requirements and exemption from some beginning courses possible by passing departmental examinations, College Board CLEP. *Grading system:* A–F; credit-no credit; withdraw pass-withdraw fail; incomplete (carries time limit).

Distinctive Educational Programs: Cooperative education and internships throughout six-year program. Off-campus programs on military installations. Tutoring laboratories and developmental education programs in math, English, and computer literacy. Degree programs in accounting, business, communications, computer information, computer science, economics, English, environmental science, human resource management, humanities, management, marine science, nursing, oceanography, political science, psychology, public administration, teaching education, TESL, travel industry management, and in 22 other areas. Individualized majors and pre-law certificate programs. *Other distinctive programs:* Honors curriculum and certificate program. Small Business Institute. Early admissions program for well-prepared high school juniors. English language foundations program. Academic counseling for adults. Study abroad programs in Japan (Hokkaido, Osaka, Nagasaki).

ROTC: Army, Air Force in cooperation with University of Hawaii. 6 Air Force and 12 Army commissions awarded 2004.

Degrees Conferred: 249 *associate;* 1,139 *baccalaureate* (B); 334 *master's* (M): biological/life sciences 31 (B); business/marketing 518 (B), 203 (M); communications/communication technologies 83 (B), 28 (M); computer and information sciences 24 (B), 75 (M); education 9 (B), 11 (M); English 6 (B); health professions and related sciences 167 (B), 6 (M); interdisciplinary studies 19 (B), 5 (M); liberal arts/general studies 2 (B); mathematics 2 (B); natural resources/environmental science 19 (B); physical sciences 3 (B); protective services/public administration 99 (B); psychology 52 (B); social sciences and history 55 (B), 6 (M).

Fees and Other Expenses: *Full-time tuition per academic year 2005–06:* $11,550 undergraduate; $11,760 graduate. *Required fees:* $80. *Room and board per academic year:* $9,450.

Financial Aid: Aid from institutionally generated funds is provided on the basis of academic merit, financial need, athletic ability, other criteria.

Financial aid to full-time, first-time undergraduate students: need-based scholarships/grants totaling $2,646,117, self-help $14,074,541, parent loans $6,507,702; non-need-based scholarships/grants totaling $7,782,734, tuition waivers $235,863, athletic awards $1,103,984. *Graduate aid:* 429 federal and state-funded loans totaling $7,436,500; 6 work-study jobs worth $8,674; other college-assigned jobs (nonresearch, nonteaching) totaling $57,784; 133 other fellowships and grants totaling $502,322.

Departments and Teaching Staff: *Professors* 23, *associate professors* 69, *assistant professors* 87, *instructors* 55, *part-time faculty* 353. *Total instructional faculty:* 587 (full-time 284, part-time 353; women 253, men 334; members of minority groups 193). Total faculty with doctorate, first-professional, or other terminal degree: 276. Student-to-faculty ratio: 18:1. *Faculty development:* $7,717,528 in grants for research.

Enrollment: Total enrollment 7,800. Undergraduate full-time 1,503, 2,530 women, part-time 1,249m / 1,323w; graduate full-time 288m / 343w, part-time 272m / 282w.

Characteristics of Student Body: *Ethnic/racial makeup:* number of Black non-Hispanic: 498; American Indian or Alaska Native: 71; Asian or Pacific Islander: 2,075; Hispanic: 443; White non-Hispanic: 2,534; unknown: 37. *Age distribution:* number under 18: 82; 18–19: 1,066; 20–21: 1,181; 22–24:1,560; 25–29: 1,301; 30–34: 591; 35–39: 385; 40–49: 373; 50–64: 76.

International Students: 1,429 nonresident aliens enrolled fall 2004. 489 students from Europe, 814 Asia, 44 Central and South America, 36 Africa, 25 Canada, 3 Australia, 8 other. Programs available to aid students whose native language is not English: social and cultural. English as a Second Language Program. No financial aid specifically designated for international students.

Student Life: Institutional housing available. *Intercollegiate athletics:* men's baseball, basketball, soccer, cross country, tennis; women's soccer, softball, cross country, tennis, volleyball. *Special services:* Tutoring Center (free service); computer center. *Student publications: Kalamalama,* a student newspaper; *Hawaii Pacific Review,* a literary magazine. 80 student organizations. *Sur-*

rounding community: Honolulu and the island of Oahu population 800,000. Served by mass transit bus system; airport.

Library Collections: 162,000 volumes including bound books, serial backfiles, electronic documents, and government documents not in separate collections. Online catalog. Current serial subscriptions: 12,000 paper and microform. Computer work stations available. Students have access to the Internet at no charge.

Most important special holdings include Hawaiian-Pacific Collection; Corporate Information Center Collection; Cooperative Education Collection; Hawaii State Certified Public Accountancy Collection.

Buildings and Grounds: School has two distinctive campuses operating as one: downtown campus in 8 modern buildings in Honolulu and a residential 135-acre campus in a suburb of Honolulu.

Chief Executive Officer: Dr. Chatt G. Wright, President.

Address undergraduate admissions inquiries to Cherie Andrade, Director of Admissions: graduate inquiries to Harry Byerly, Director of Graduate and Adult Services Center.

University of Hawaii at Hilo

200 West Kawili Street
Hilo, Hawaii 96720-4091

Tel: (808) 974-7311   **E-mail:** admissions@uhh.hawaii.edu
Fax: (808) 974-7622   **Internet:** www.uhh.hawaii.edu

Institution Description: *Enrollment:* 3,288. *Degrees awarded:* Baccalaureate, master's.

Accreditation: *Regional:* WASC-Sr.

History: Established as Extension Division of University of Hawaii and offered first instruction at postsecondary level 1947; added junior level 1969; became 4-year institution and changed name to Hilo College 1970; awarded first degree (baccalaureate) 1971; added College of Agriculture 1975; adopted present name 1979; separated from Hawaii Community College 1991.

Institutional Structure: *Composition of institution:* Administrators 8. Full-time instructional faculty 134.

Calendar: Semesters. Academic year late Aug. to mid-May. Summer session.

Characteristics of Freshmen: 1,548 applicants (547 men, 999 women). 64.1% of applicants admitted. 43.4% of admitted students enrolled full-time.

70% (300 students) submitted SAT scores; 20% (89 students) submitted ACT scores. *25th percentile*: SAT I Verbal 430, SAT I Math 440; ACT Composite 18, ACT English 17, ACT Math 17. *75th percentile*: SAT I Verbal 540, SAT I Math 560; ACT Composite 24, ACT English 23, ACT Math 24.

16% of entering freshmen expected to graduate within 5 years. 82% freshmen from Hawaii. Freshmen from 19 states and 5 foreign countries.

Admission: For fall acceptance, apply no later than July 1; for spring acceptance no later than Dec. 15. *Requirements:* 17 units from secondary school including 4 English, 3 mathematics beyond pre-algebra, 3 natural sciences, 7 electives, not including physical education or ROTC. Additional requirements for some programs. Minimum GPA 2.5. *Entrance tests:* College Board SAT or ACT composite. For international students TOEFL.

College credit and advanced placement for extrainstitutional learning on basis of ACE *2006 Guide to the Evaluation of Educational Experiences in the Armed Services.*

Degree Requirements: *For baccalaureate degrees:* 120–123 credit hours; 30 hours, including final term, in residence. *For all undergraduate degrees:* 2.0 GPA; area requirements. Additional requirements for some programs. Fulfillment of some degree requirements and exemption from some beginning courses possible by passing departmental examinations, College Board AP. Fulfillment of some degree requirements possible by passing College Board CLEP. *Grading system:* A–F; credit-no credit; withdraw.

Distinctive Educational Programs: Interdisciplinary program in liberal studies. Student exchange through National Student Exchange Program. *Other distinctive programs:* Center for continuing education and community services. Selected secondary school junior and seniors may enroll in college courses.

Degrees Conferred: 13 *associate;* 518 *baccalaureate.* Bachelor's degrees awarded in top five disciplines: social sciences 86; psychology 83; biological and biomedical sciences 66; business, management, marketing, and related support services 49; communication, journalism, and related programs 40.

Fees and Other Expenses: *Full-time tuition per academic year 2004–05:* in-state resident $2,543; out-of-state student $8,111. *Books and supplies:* $1,107. *Room and board per academic year* $4,916.

Financial Aid: Aid from institutionally generated funds is provided on the basis of academic merit, financial need, athletic ability, other criteria. Institution has a Program Participation Agreement with the U.S. Department of Education for eligible students to receive Pell Grants and other federal aid.

Financial aid to full-time, first-time undergraduate students: 30% received federal grants averaging $3,158; 17% institutional grants averaging $1,999; 37% loans averaging $3,220.

Departments and Teaching Staff: College of Agriculture *professors* 4, *associate professors* 6, *assistant professors* 2, *instructors* 4, *part-time teachers* 0; College of Arts and Sciences 39, 39, 30, 0, 73.

Total instructional faculty: 197. Degrees held by full-time instructional faculty: doctorate 83%, master's 17%. 83% hold terminal degrees.

Enrollment: Total enrollment 3,288. Undergraduate 3,182 (40.6% men, 59.4% women).

Characteristics of Student Body: *Ethnic/racial makeup:* Black non-Hispanic: 1.4%; American Indian or Alaska Native: .7%; Asian or Pacific Islander: 46.3%; Hispanic: 2.7%; White non-Hispanic: 42.4%; unknown: .1%.

International Students: 204 nonresident aliens enrolled fall 2004. *Programs available to aid students whose native language is not English:* Social, cultural. English as a Second Language program. No financial aid specifically designated for international students.

Student Life: On-campus residence halls and apartments. Privately owned off-campus apartments for single and married students. *Special services:* Learning Resources Center, medical services. *Student publications: Vulcan News,* a weekly newspaper; *Kanilehua,* quarterly art and literary magazine. *Student government:* elected officers and senators serve as student voice on issues and concerns of total student body. *Student activities:* Student Activities Council provides dances, films, special events, cultural activities for the campus community. *Surrounding community:* Hilo population 46,000.

Library Collections: 240,000 volumes. 350,000 government documents; 11,000 microforms; 12,000 audiovisual materials; 1,700 periodicals. Students have access to online information retrieval services.

Most important holdings include Hawaiian Collection.

Buildings and Grounds: Campus area 115 acres.

Chief Executive Officer: Dr. Rose Y. Tseng, Chancellor.

Address admission inquiries to James Cromwell, Director of Admissions.

University of Hawaii at Manoa

2444 Dole Street
Honolulu, Hawaii 96822

Tel: (808) 956-8111   **E-mail:** info@manoa.hawaii.edu
Fax: (808) 956-4148   **Internet:** www.manoa.hawaii.edu

Institution Description: *Enrollment:* 20,549. *Degrees awarded:* Associate, baccalaureate, master's, doctorate, first-professional (medicine, law). Professional diploma in education and other certificates also awarded.

Budget subject to approval by Board of Regents and legislature. Member of the consortium National Student Exchange.

Accreditation: *Regional:* WASC-Sr. *Professional:* audiology, business, clinical lab scientist, clinical psychology, counseling, dental hygiene, engineering, law, librarianship, medicine, music, nursing, nursing education, planning, psychology internship, public health, rehabilitation counseling, social work, speech-language pathology, teacher education

History: Established and chartered as College of Hawaii 1907; offered first instruction at postsecondary level 1908; awarded first degree (baccalaureate) 1912; incorporated and changed name to University of Hawaii 1920; adopted present name 1972.

Institutional Structure: *Composition of institution:* Chancellor. The following are of equal stature and report to the Chancellor. Vice chancellors for Academic Affairs; Research and Graduate Education; Students; Administration; Finance and Operations. Deans of: John A. Burns School of Medicine; Richardson School of Law. Athletic Director of Intercollegiate Athletics. Administrators 70 men / 33 women. Full-time instructional faculty 1,126. Academic governance body, Faculty Senate, meets once a month.

Calendar: Semesters. Academic year Aug. to May. Freshmen admitted Aug., Jan., May. Degrees conferred and formal commencements May, Aug., Dec. Two summer sessions beginning May and July.

Characteristics of Freshmen: 87.4% (1,758 students) submitted SAT scores; 14.5% (291 students) submitted ACT scores. *25th percentile:* SAT Verbal 490, SAT Math 520; ACT Composite 21, ACT English 20, ACT Math 21. *75th percentile:* SAT Verbal 580, SAT Math 620; ACT Composite 25, ACT English 26, ACT Math 26.

Freshmen from 44 states.

Admission: Modified rolling admissions plan. For fall acceptance, apply as early as Dec. 1 of previous year, but not later than June 15. Students are notified of acceptance beginning Jan. 15. . *Requirements:* Either graduation from accredited secondary school with 22 units (17 from college preparatory curriculum), including 4 English, 3 mathematics, 3 science, 4 social studies, 4 other from

among English, mathematics, foreign language, physical and biological sciences, social sciences; or GED. Additional mathematics, science units required for engineering, mathematics, and science students. Minimum GPA 2.8. Lowest acceptable secondary school class standing 40th percentile. *Entrance tests:* College Board SAT or ACT composite. For foreign students TOEFL also. *For transfer students:* In-state residents 2.0 minimum GPA, out-of-state students 2.5 GPA; from 4-year accredited institution maximum transfer credit limited only by residence requirement; from 2-year accredited institution 60 hours.

College credit and advanced placement for postsecondary-level work completed in secondary school. College credit for extrainstitutional learning on basis of ACE *2006 Guide to the Evaluation of Educational Experiences in the Armed Services.*

Tutoring available. Noncredit developmental courses offered in summer sessions and regular academic year.

Degree Requirements: *For all associate degrees:* 67 credit hours. *For all baccalaureate degrees:* 124–154 credit hours; general education requirements. Additional requirements for some programs. *For all undergraduate degrees:* 2.0 GPA; 30 credits in residence. Some colleges and degree programs have higher requirements.

Fulfillment of some degree requirements and exemption from some beginning courses possible by passing departmental examinations, College Board CLEP, AP (score of 3). *Grading system:* A–F; credit-no credit; I (incomplete); L (audit).

Distinctive Educational Programs: Extensive course offerings in East Asian and Indo-Pacific languages. Interdisciplinary study in the ocean and earth sciences and in marine studies. Travel industry management program with an international focus. Problem-based medical program. Special facilities for using telecommunications in the classroom. Study abroad in East Asia, Europe, Japan, Pacific Islands, Southeast Asia, and Tahiti. *Other distinctive programs:* Community service programs including Center for Labor Education, and Research and Small Business Management Program. English Language Institute and intensive course in English. Certificate program in interpretation and translation.

ROTC: Army, Air Force.

Degrees Conferred: 2,584 *baccalaureate;* 94 *post-bachelor certificates;* 1,040 *master's;* 112 *doctorate;* 147 *first-professional.* Bachelor's degrees awarded in top five disciplines: business, management, marketing, and related support services 564; education 253; social sciences 233; psychology 147; English language and literature/letters 141.

Fees and Other Expenses: *Full-time tuition per academic year 2004–05:* undergraduate in-state resident $3,580; out-of-state $19m960. Contact the university for current graduate/professional schools tuition/fees. *Books and supplies:* $1,017. *Room and board per academic year:* $8,043.

Financial Aid: Aid from institutionally generated funds is provided on the basis of academic merit, financial need, athletic ability, other criteria. Institution has a Program Participation Agreement with the U.S. Department of Education for eligible students to receive Pell Grants and other federal aid.

Financial aid to full-time, first-time undergraduate students: need-based scholarships/grants totaling $9,770,899, self-help $10,677,079, tuition waivers $2,012,107, athletic awards $21,447; non-need-based scholarships/grants totaling $3,262,819, self-help $6,940,110, parent loans $5,420,078, tuition waivers $1,748,003, athletic awards $3,401,940.

Departments and Teaching Staff: *Total instructional faculty:* 1,495 (full-time 1,243, part-time 252; women 562, men 933; members of minority groups 578). Total faculty with doctorate, first-professional, or other terminal degree: 1,254. Student-to-faculty ratio: 12:1. *Faculty development:* $199,944,709 in grants for research. 65 faculty members awarded sabbaticals 2004–05.

Enrollment: Total enrollment 20,549. Undergraduate full-time 5,138 men / 6,631 women, part-time 1,095m / 1,367w; first-professional 254m / 334w, part-time 7m / 4w; graduate full-time 1,036 / 1,554w, part-time 1,251m / 1,838w.

Characteristics of Student Body: *Ethnic/racial makeup:* number of undergraduate Black non-Hispanic: 142; American Indian or Alaska Native: 52; Asian or Pacific Islander: 8,881; Hispanic: 302; White non-Hispanic: 3,706; unknown: 495. *Age distribution:* number under 18: 276; 18–19: 1,669; 20–21: 24; 22–24: 10; 25–29: 16; 30–34: 15; 35–39: 3; 40–49: 3; 50–64: 2; 65 and over: 1.

International Students: 673 undergraduate nonresident aliens enrolled fall 2004. Programs available to aid students whose native language is not English: English as a Second Language Program. Scholarships available annually to qualifying international students.

Student Life: On campus residence halls house 15% of student body. Residence halls for men only constitute about 1% of such space, for women only 2%, for both sexes 97%. *Intercollegiate athletics:* men only: baseball, football; women only: cross-country, softball; both sexes: basketball, golf, swimming/ diving, tennis, volleyball. *Special regulations:* Cars permitted in designated areas only. *Special services:* Learning Resources Center, Student Health Service, Student Employment Office, Cooperative Education Program, Center for Student Development, child care. *Student publications, radio: Hawaii Review,* a biannual literary magazine; *Ka Leo O Hawaii,* a newspaper published 5 times per week; *Manoa Student-Faculty Directory, Student Handbook.* Radio station

KTUH broadcasts 168 hours per week. *Surrounding community:* Honolulu metropolitan area population 840,000. Served by mass transit bus system; airport 12 miles from campus.

Publications: *Asian Perspectives* (biannually) first published 1957; *Asian Studies of Hawaii* (triennially) first published 1965; *Biography* (quarterly) first published 1978; *Biography Monographs* (biannually) first published 1980; *Culture Learning Institute Monographs* (triennially) first published 1976; *Korean Studies* (annually) first published 1977; *Mon-Khmer Studies* (annually) first published 1977; *Monographs of the Center for Southeast Asian Studies* (biannually) first published 1975; *Monographs for the Society for Asian and Comparative Philosophy* (biannually) first published 1974; *Oceanic Linguistics* (biannually) first published 1962; *Oceanic Linguistics Special Publications* (biannually) first published 1966; *Pacific Science* (quarterly) first published 1947; *Philosophy East and West* (quarterly) first published 1951; *Proceedings of the Hawaii Topical Conference in Particle Physics* (biannually) first published 1968; *Asian Theatre Journal* (biannually) first published 1984; *The Contemporary Pacific* (biannually) first published 1989; *Buddhist-Christian Studies* (annually) first published 1981; *Manoa: A Pacific Journal of International Writing* (biannually) first published 1989; *Journal of World History* (biannually) first published 1990.

Library Collections: 3,100,401 volumes including bound books, serial backfiles, electronic documents, and government documents not in separate collections. Online catalog. 26,838 microform units; 75 electronic subscriptions providing access to over 2,000 databases. 3,878 recordings; 6,984 compact discs; 65 CD-ROMs. 85 computer work stations. Students have access to the Internet at no charge. Total budget for books, periodicals, audiovisual materials 2004–05: $5 million.

Most important holdings include Jean Charlot Collection, Hawaiian and Pacific Collections; Asia Collections (includes material on East, Southeast, and South Asia).

Buildings and Grounds: Campus area 305 acres. *New buildings:* restoration of Hawai'i Hall; Krauss Hall.

Chief Executive Officer: Dr. Peter Englert, Chancellor.

Address admission inquiries to Jan Heu, Director of Admissions and Records; graduate inquiries to Graduate Division Admissions Office.

College of Arts and Sciences

Degree Programs Offered: *Baccalaureate:* American studies, anthropology, art, Asian studies, biology, botany, chemistry, Chinese, classics, communication, computer science, dance ethnology, dance theater, drama and theater, economics, English, ethnic studies, French, geography, geology, geology and geophysics, German, Greek, Hawaiian language, Hawaiian studies, history, Japanese, journalism, Latin, liberal studies, mathematics, meteorology, microbiology, music, Philippine studies, philosophy, physics, political science, psychology, religion, Russian, sociology, Spanish, speech, women's studies, zoology; *master's, doctorate* in various fields. Certificates also given.

Departments and Teaching Staff: Arts and Humanities *professors* 68, *associate professors* 43, *assistant professors* 21, *instructors* 0, *part-time teachers* 0; languages, linguistics, & literature 61, 64, 22, 34, 36; natural sciences 79, 25, 14, 5, 29; social sciences 79, 25, 14, 5, 29; academic affairs 2, 0, 2, 0, 0.

Distinctive Educational Programs: Interdisciplinary programs in environmental studies, Pacific Island studies, population studies, Russian area studies, women's studies. Preprofessional programs in allied health fields, medicine.

Enrollment: Total enrollment 9,946.

School of Architecture

Degree Programs Offered: *Baccalaureate* in architecture; *master's* in high technology architecture, transitional cultures architecture, urban design; *doctorate* in architecture.

Admission: Separate School of Architecture application must be submitted in addition to the university common application.

Degree Requirements: 212 approved credits; 2.5 cumulative GPA; comprehensive portfolio review.

Departments and Teaching Staff: Total instructional faculty 50.

Enrollment: Total enrollment 275.

College of Business Administration

Degree Programs Offered: *Baccalaureate* in accounting, finance, international business, management, management information systems, marketing, human resources management; *master's* in accounting, business administration, human resources management, executive MBA, Japan-focused MBA, China-focused MBA, Vietnam MBA.

Departments and Teaching Staff: Total instructional faculty 62. 90% hold terminal degrees.

Distinctive Educational Programs: Executive MBA programs for working professionals offers degree study primarily through weekend courses. Japan and China focused MBA programs offer one-year MBA with internships. Fellowships for study abroad.

Enrollment: Total enrollment 1,283.

College of Education

Degree Programs Offered: *Baccalaureate* in elementary education, secondary education, health, exercise science, and lifestyle management; *master's* in counseling and guidance, curriculum studies, early childhood education administration, educational communications and technology, educational foundations, educational psychology, kinesiology, leisure science, special education teaching; *doctorate in* education, educational psychology.

Departments and Teaching Staff: Total instructional faculty: 90. 92% 1old terminal degrees.

Distinctive Educational Programs: Field-based undergraduate and graduate teacher educational programs in partnership with K-12 grade schools in the state. Specializations within doctorate of education in curriculum and instruction, educational administration, educational foundations, and exceptionalities.

Enrollment: Total enrollment 1,337 (undergraduate 399, graduate 938).

College of Engineering

Degree Programs Offered: *Baccalaureate, master's, doctorate* in civil, electrical and mechanical engineering.

Departments and Teaching Staff: Total instructional faculty 49. 98% hold terminal degrees.

Enrollment: Total enrollment 726.

School of Nursing and Dental Hygiene

Degree Programs Offered: *Baccalaureate* in nursing, dental hygiene; *master's* in nursing (concentration in advanced practice nursing and clinical systems management); *doctorate* in nursing.

Departments and Teaching Staff: Total instructional faculty 62. 43% hold terminal degrees.

Distinctive Educational Programs: Ph.D. with focus on development of nurse scientist sensitive to cultural preferences and education needs of disadvantaged students, primary health care in rural sites; B.S. completion programs; generic M.S. for students with B.S. degrees in related areas.

Enrollment: Total enrollment 365. Full-time undergraduate 230, part-time 20; graduate full-time 38, part-time 63; first-professional full-time 1, part-time 13.

School of Social Work

Degree Programs Offered: Provides upper-division and graduate study only. *Baccalaureate* in social work; *master's* in social work; *doctorate* in social welfare.

Departments and Teaching Staff: Total instructional faculty 16. 100% hold terminal degrees.

Distinctive Educational Programs: Advanced Standing awarded to eligible BSW graduates. Advanced curriculum concentrations in Child and Family, Health, Mental Health, and Gerontology. Practicum experiences in community agencies required at the baccalaureate and master's levels.

Enrollment: Total enrollment 356. Full-time 28 men / 155 women; part-time 28m / 147w.

College of Tropical Agriculture and Human Resources

Degree Programs Offered: *Baccalaureate, master's, doctorate* in various fields.

Departments and Teaching Staff: Total instructional faculty 38.47 FTE. 90% hold terminal degrees.

Distinctive Educational Programs: Tropical food production, bioengineering, dietetics, tropical biotechnology, integrated research, instruction, extension programs.

Enrollment: Total enrollment 763.

William S. Richardson School of Law

Degree Programs Offered: *First-professional.*

Admission: Baccalaureate from accredited college or university; LSAT; LSDAS.

Degree Requirements: 89 credit hours, 2.0 GPA, 6 semesters in residence.

Departments and Teaching Staff: Total instructional faculty 18. 100% hold terminal degrees.

Distinctive Educational Programs: Strong clinical emphasis; Pacific-Asian Legal Studies (China, Japan, Pacific Islands), native Hawaiian rights; environmental law. Year-long pre-admission program for students who are socially and/or economically disadvantaged. Dual degree program with other graduate programs on campus such as MBA, Asian Studies, Social Work, and Urban Planning.

Enrollment: Total enrollment 245.

John A. Burns School of Medicine

Degree Programs Offered: Provides upper-division, first-professional and graduate study only. *Baccalaureate* in medical technology, speech pathology and audiology; *first-professional* in medicine; *master's* in speech pathology and audiology; *master's, doctorate* in biochemistry, biophysics, genetics, pharmacology, physiology, reproductive biology, tropical medicine; *doctorate* in biostatistics and epidemiology.

Admission: *For first-professional degree:* 90 semester hours from accredited college or university which must include 4 semester hours chemistry (organic, inorganic), 8 biology, 4 molecular and cell biology, 3 biochemistry, 8 physics; MCAT; must be processed by AMCAS. Recommend additional units in calculus, embryology, general genetics, physical chemistry, quantitative analysis, statistics.

Degree Requirements: *For first-professional:* 4 semesters in residence, demonstration of high ethical standards and proficiency in the practice of medicine.

Departments and Teaching Staff: Total instructional faculty 225 FTE.

Distinctive Educational Programs: Problem-based learning curriculum. Academic and other support services provided in prematriculation and in decelerated degree programs for educationally and economically disadvantaged students primarily from the Pacific Basin.

School of Hawaiian, Asian, and Pacific Studies

Degree Programs Offered: *Baccalaureate* in Asian Studies, Hawaiian Studies; *master's* in Asian Studies, Pacific Island Studies; *graduate certificate* in Asian Studies.

Departments and Teaching Staff: Total instructional faculty 24. 100% hold terminal degrees.

Enrollment: Total enrollment 316.

School of Ocean and Earth Science and Technology

Degree Programs Offered: *Baccalaureate, master's, doctorate.*

Departments and Teaching Staff: Total instructional faculty 65. 100% hold terminal degrees.

Enrollment: Total enrollment 225.

School of Travel Industry Management

Degree Programs Offered: *Baccalaureate, master's.*

Departments and Teaching Staff: Total instructional faculty 14.

Enrollment: Total enrollment 273.

University of Hawaii at West Oahu

96-043 Ala Ike
Pearl City, Hawaii 96782-3699

Tel: (808) 454-4700   **E-mail:** admissions@uhwo.edu
Fax: (808) 453-6076   **Internet:** www.uhwo.edu

Institution Description: University of Hawaii at West Oahu (formerly West Oahu College) is located on campus of Leeward Community College. It provides

upper division baccalaureate study only. *Enrollment:* 834. *Degrees awarded:* Baccalaureate.

Accreditation: *Regional:* WASC-Sr.

History: Established and chartered 1974; offered first instruction at postsecondary level 1976; awarded first degree (baccalaureate) 1977; present name adopted 1989.

Institutional Structure: *Composition of institution:* Administrators 3 men / 1 woman. Academic affairs headed by chancellor. Management/business/finances directed by director of administrative services. Full-time instructional faculty 12 men / 4 women. Academic governance body, Faculty Senate, meets an average of 8 times per year.

Calendar: Semesters. Academic year Aug. to May. New students admitted Aug., Jan., June. Degrees conferred and formal commencement May.

Admission: Rolling admissions plan. Apply no later than last day of registration. *Requirements:* 55 credit hours at accredited university or college which must include 18 humanities, 15 social science, 12 natural science. Minimum GPA 2.0. *Entrance tests:* For foreign students TOEFL. *For transfer students:* 2.0 minimum GPA, maximum transfer credit limited only by residence requirement.

College credit for extrainstitutional learning on basis of ACE *2006 Guide to the Evaluation of Educational Experiences in the Armed Services.*

Degree Requirements: 120 credit hours; 2.0 GPA; 30 credit hours in residence; core courses; senior research project or practicum.

Fulfillment of some degree requirements and exemption from some beginning courses possible by passing departmental examinations, College Board CLEP. *Grading system:* A–F; withdraw (carries time limit).

Distinctive Educational Programs: Internships. Weekend and evening classes. Interdisciplinary thematic studies, including American studies, Asian studies, European studies, international studies, justice administration, Pacific studies. Individual majors. *Other distinctive programs:* Hawaii residents over 60 years of age may attend courses for credit tuition-free.

ROTC: Army in cooperation with University of Hawaii at Manoa.

Degrees Conferred: 212 *baccalaureate.* Bachelor's degrees awarded in top five disciplines: business, management, marketing, and related support services 79; psychology 44; social sciences 40; security and protective services 19; history 14. letters 7, psychology 26, public affairs and services 34, social sciences 21.

Fees and Other Expenses: *Full-time tuition per academic year:* $2,184 in-state resident.

Financial Aid: Aid from institutionally generated funds is provided on the basis of academic merit, financial need. Institution has a Program Participation Agreement with the U.S. Department of Education for eligible students to receive Pell Grants and other federal aid.

Departments and Teaching Staff: Humanities *professors* 2, *associate professors* 2, *part-time teachers* 1; social sciences 1, 2, 5; professional studies 1, 2, 4. *Total instructional faculty:* 20. Degrees held by full-time faculty: doctorate 100%. 100% hold terminal degrees.

Enrollment: Total enrollment 834 (29.7% men, 70.3% women).

Characteristics of Student Body: *Ethnic/racial makeup:* Black non-Hispanic: 1.8%; American Indian or Alaska Native: .1%; Asian or Pacific Islander: 67%; Hispanic: 3.1%; White non-Hispanic: 27.1%; unknown: .1%.

International Students: 4 nonresident aliens enrolled fall 2004.

Student Life: No on-campus housing. *Special regulations:* Cars permitted without restrictions. *Student publications:* An irregularly published newsletter. *Surrounding community:* Pearl City is located in the Honolulu metropolitan area. Served by mass transit bus system, airport 7 miles from campus.

Publications: Monthly newsletter.

Library Collections: 30,000 volumes. 550 microform titles; 445 audiovisual materials; 135 current periodical subscriptions. Students have access to online information services and the Internet.

Chief Executive Officer: Dr. Linda J. Johnsrud, Chancellor.

Address admission inquiries to Terri Ota, Registrar.

Idaho

Albertson College of Idaho

2112 Cleveland Boulevard
Caldwell, Idaho 83605
Tel: (208) 459-5011   **E-mail:** admission@albertson.edu
Fax: (208) 454-2077   **Internet:** www.albertson.edu

Institution Description: Albertson College of Idaho is a private, independent, nonprofit college. *Enrollment:* 807. *Degrees awarded:* Baccalaureate, master's.

Accreditation: *Regional:* NWCCU.

History: Established 1891; offered first instruction at postsecondary level 1906; awarded first degree (baccalaureate) 1911.

Institutional Structure: *Governing board:* Board of Trustees. Representation: 42 trustees, including the president of the college, 12 alumni. *Composition of institution:* Administrators 6 men / 3 women (at dean's level and above, 20% are women). Academic affairs headed by vice president for academic affairs. Management/business/finances directed by chief financial officer. Full-time instructional faculty 58. Academic governance body, Faculty Assembly, meets an average of 9 times per year.

Calendar: 13-week fall and spring terms, 6 week winter term. Academic year Sept. to June. Formal commencement May. Summer session of 1 term early June to late July.

Characteristics of Freshmen: 647 applicants (262 men, 365 women). 81.5% of applicants admitted. 36.7% of admitted students enrolled full-time.

65% (129 students) submitted SAT scores; 79% (156 students) submitted ACT scores. *25th percentile:* SAT I Verbal 520, SAT I Math 500; ACT Composite 21, ACT English 20, ACT Math 20. *75th percentile:* SAT I Verbal 640, SAT I Math 620; ACT Composite 26, ACT English 27, ACT Math 26.

50% of entering freshmen expected to graduate within 5 years. 73% of freshmen from Idaho. Freshmen from 24 states and 7 foreign countries.

Admission: Rolling admissions plan. Early acceptance available. *Requirements:* Either graduation from accredited secondary school or GED. Recommend 4 units English, 3 history and social studies, 3 mathematics, 2 laboratory science. Interview required. *Entrance tests:* College Board SAT or ACT composite. For foreign students minimum TOEFL combined score 500 (with no score less than 45). *For transfer students:* From 4-year accredited institution 94 hours maximum transfer credit, from 2-year accredited institution 62 credit hours.

Study skills course, remedial classes and tutoring available.

Degree Requirements: 124 credit hours; 1 year in residence; general graduation requirements in English, fine arts, literature, natural sciences, mathematics, philosophy, religion, social sciences, physical education, Western civilization.

Fulfillment of some degree requirements and exemption from some beginning courses possible through College Board CEEB, CLEP. *Grading system:* A–F; pass-fail; pass; withdraw; withdraw/pass or fail.

Distinctive Educational Programs: *For undergraduates:* Gipson Scholars (those with GPAs of at least 3.75 and ACT or SAT scores of 90th percentile or above may design their own courses of study and present senior projects); honors projects; 5th year internship program in education; preprofessional programs in medicine, veterinary science, dentistry, law, engineering; dual-degree engineering programs with Columbia University (NY), Stanford University (CA), University of Idaho, Washington University (MO); MBA with Gonzaga University and Boise State University; Master of Management with Willamette; Master of Natural Resources with University of Idaho.

Degrees Conferred: 183 *baccalaureate;* 7 *master's.* Bachelor degrees awarded in top five disciplines: biological and biomedical sciences 28; psychology 23; visual and performing arts 21; social sciences 21; business, management, marketing, and related support services 18.

Fees and Other Expenses: *Full-time tuition per academic year 2004–05:* $15,550. *Other expenses:* $1,250. *Books and supplies:* $800. *Room and board per academic year:* $5,150.

Financial Aid: Aid from institutionally generated funds is provided on the basis of academic merit, financial need, athletic ability, other criteria. Institution has a Program Participation Agreement with the U.S. Department of Education for eligible students to receive Pell Grants and other federal aid.

Financial aid to full-time, first-time undergraduate students: 35% received federal grants averaging $3,403; 59% state/local grants averaging $612; 97% institutional grants averaging $6,007; 71% loans averaging $4,727.

Departments and Teaching Staff: *Total instructional faculty:* 58. Total tenured faculty: 44. Student-to-faculty ratio: 12:1. Degrees held by full-time faculty: 94% hold terminal degrees.

Enrollment: Total enrollment 807. Undergraduate 789 (45.1% men, 54.9% women).

Characteristics of Student Body: *Ethnic/racial makeup:* Black non-Hispanic: .8%; American Indian or Alaska Native: .5%; Asian or Pacific Islander: 2.9%; Hispanic: 3.8%; White non-Hispanic: 74.3%; unknown: 15.5%.

International Students: 18 undergraduate nonresident aliens enrolled fall 2004. No programs to aid students whose native language is not English.

Student Life: On-campus residence halls house 55% of student body; most residence halls have wings for men and for women, but there is one for women only. *Intercollegiate athletics:* men only: basketball, baseball, golf, skiing, soccer; women only: soccer, skiing, tennis, volleyball. *Special regulations:* Registered cars permitted. Quiet hours observed. *Special services:* Medical, counseling and career planning and placement services; campus chaplain; outdoor program which rents out sports equipment, sponsors excursions. *Student publications:* Coyote, a bimonthly newspaper; The Trail, a yearbook. *Surrounding community:* Caldwell population 25,000. Boise, 25 miles from campus, population 250,000. Served by airport 25 miles from campus.

Library Collections: 184,000 volumes. 75,000 government documents; 17,000 microforms; 1,700 audiovisual materials. 700 current periodical subscriptions. Computer work stations available. Students have access to the Internet at no charge.

Most important holdings include Idaho Governor Robert Smylie Papers; Vardis Fisher Collection; Boone Collection of Journals (1891–1936); papers of former U.S. Senator Steve Symms.

Buildings and Grounds: Campus area 48 acres.

Chief Executive Officer: Dr. Robert Hoover, President.

Address admission inquiries to Dean of Admissions.

Boise Bible College

8695 West Marigold Street
Boise, Idaho 83714-1220
Tel: (208) 376-7731   **E-mail:** admissions@boisebible.edu
Fax: (208) 376-7743   **Internet:** www.boisebible.edu

Institution Description: Boise Bible College is a private institution affiliated with the Christian Churches/Churches of Christ. *Enrollment:* 122. *Degrees awarded:* Associate, baccalaureate.

Accreditation: *National:* ABHE.

Calendar: Semesters. Academic year Aug. to May.

Characteristics of Freshmen: 44 applicants (24 men, 20 women). 100% of applicants admitted. 61.4% of admitted students enrolled full-time.

33% (9 students) submitted SAT scores; 59% (16 students) submitted ACT scores. *25th percentile:* SAT I Verbal 510, SAT I Math 460; ACT Composite 20, ACT English 18, ACT Math 18. *75th percentile:* SAT I Verbal 550, SAT I Math 540; ACT Composite 25, ACT English 25, ACT Math 21.

Admission: *Requirements:* Graduation from an accredited secondary school or GED, appropriate recommendations.

Degree Requirements: Completion of prescribed curriculum.

Degrees Conferred: 5 *associate;* 11 *baccalaureate:* theology and ministerial studies 9; philosophy and religious studies 2.

Fees and Other Expenses: *Full-time tuition per academic year 2004–05:* $6,300. *Other expenses:* $2,000. *Books and supplies:* $700. *Room and board per academic year* $4,200.

Financial Aid: Aid from institutionally generated funds is provided on the basis of academic merit, other criteria. Institution has a Program Participation Agreement with the U.S. Department of Education for eligible students to receive Pell Grants and other federal aid.

Financial aid to full-time, first-time undergraduate students: 52% received federal grants; 52% institutional grants; 57% received loans.

Departments and Teaching Staff: Christian ministries *professors* 1, *associate professors* 0, *part-time teachers* 1; Christian education 1, 0, 1; missions 1, 0, 0; music 0, 1, 0; Greek and New Testament 1, 0, 0; theology and New Testament 1, 0, 0; library and information management 0, 1, 0; theology and Old Testament 0, 0, 1; social sciences 0, 0, 1; history 0, 0, 1; applied music 0, 0, 1.

Total instructional faculty: 12. Degrees held by full-time faculty: doctorate 18%, master's 66%, baccalaureate 16%. 18% hold terminal degrees.

Enrollment: Total enrollment 122 (53.3% men, 46.7% women).

Characteristics of Student Body: *Ethnic and racial makeup:* Black non-Hispanic: 2.5%; Asian or Pacific Islander: 2.5%; Hispanic: .8%; White non-Hispanic: 92.6%.

International Students: 2 nonresident aliens enrolled fall 2004. Some financial aid available to international students.

Library Collections: 34,000 volumes. 950 microform titles; 1,000 audiovisual materials; 102 current periodical subscriptions.

Most important special collection is the Rare Bible Collection.

Chief Executive Officer: Dr. Charles A. Crane, President.

Address admission inquiries to Ross Knudsen, Director of Enrollment Services.

Boise State University

1910 University Drive
Boise, Idaho 83725
Tel: (208) 426-1820   **E-mail:** bsuinfo@boisestate.edu
Fax: (208) 426-3765   **Internet:** www.boisestate.edu

Institution Description: Boise State University (Boise State College until 1974) is a state institution. *Enrollment:* 18,335. *Degrees awarded:* Associate, baccalaureate, master's, doctorate.

Academic offerings subject to approval by statewide coordinating bodies. Budget subject to approval by state governing boards. Member of Western Interstate Commission for Higher Education.

Accreditation: *Regional:* NWCCU. *Professional:* accounting, athletic training, business, computer science, construction education, counseling, culinary education, dental assisting, engineering, environmental health, health information technician, music, nursing, public administration, radiography, respiratory therapy, social work, surgical technology, teacher education, theatre

History: Established as Boise Junior College and offered first instruction at postsecondary level 1932; incorporated 1934; became public institution 1939; became 4-year institution and changed name to Boise College 1965; awarded first degree (baccalaureate) 1967; became part of state system of higher education and changed name to Boise State College 1969; adopted present name 1974. *See* Eugene Chaffee, *An Idea Grows* (Boise: Syms-York Co., 1970) for further information.

Institutional Structure: *Governing board:* State Board of Education and Board of Regents of the University of Idaho. Representation: 7 members (appointed by governor of Idaho), state superintendent of public instruction. 1 ex officio. All voting. *Composition of institution:* Administrators 47 men / 15 women. Academic affairs headed by provost. Management/business/finances directed by vice president for financial affairs. Full-time instructional faculty 561. Academic governance body, Boise State University Faculty, meets an average of 15 times per year.

Calendar: Semesters. Academic year Aug. to May. Freshmen admitted Aug., Jan., June. Degrees conferred May, Aug., Dec. Formal commencement May. Summer session from June to Aug.

Characteristics of Freshmen: 90% of applicants admitted. 67% of admitted students enrolled full-time.

34% (863 students) submitted SAT scores; 68% (1,726 students) submitted ACT scores. *25th percentile:* SAT Verbal 460, SAT Math 450; ACT Composite 17, ACT English 16, ACT Math 17. *75th percentile:* SAT Verbal 590, SAT Math 575; ACT Composite 26, ACT English 26, ACT Math 27.

20% of entering freshmen expected to graduate within 5 years. 87% of freshmen from Idaho. Freshmen from 35 states and 28 foreign countries.

Admission: Rolling admissions plan. Deadline for submission of all application materials is July 29 for fall semester, Nov. 25 for spring semester. *Requirements:* Graduation from accredited secondary school with at least 2.0 GPA in the following subjects: 4 years English; 3 years mathematics (algebra and higher); 3 years science; 2½ years social sciences; 1 year foreign language or humanities;

1½ years other college preparation. Students with GEDs also considered. *Entrance tests:* ACT or SAT for students under 21 years of age. TOEFL required for foreign students. *For transfer students:* 2.0 minimum GPA.

College credit and advanced placement for postsecondary-level work completed in secondary school. College credit for extrainstitutional learning may be granted on basis of ACE *2006 Guide to the Evaluation of Educational Experiences in the Armed Services* or through Prior Learning Program. Tutoring available. Noncredit developmental courses offered in summer session and regular academic year.

Degree Requirements: *For all associate degrees:* 64 credit hours. *For all baccalaureate degrees:* 128–145 credit hours; last 30 hours in residence; general education and distribution requirements; exit competency examinations in writing. *For all undergraduate degrees:* 2.0 GPA.

Fulfillment of some degree requirements and exemption from some beginning courses possible by passing departmental examinations, College Board CLEP, AP. *Grading system:* A–F; pass-fail; withdraw (deadline after which pass-fail is appended to withdraw).

Distinctive Educational Programs: Work-experience programs, including cooperative education, internships. Flexible meeting places and schedules, including off-campus centers (at Mt. Home Air Force Base, 60 miles away, and in Twin Falls, Canyon County, Gowen Field), weekend and evening classes. Cooperative baccalaureate program in medical technology with approved hospitals. Interdisciplinary multi-ethnic studies program. Preprofessional programs in architecture; allied health sciences, including chiropractic, dental hygiene, dentistry, medicine, occupational therapy, optometry, pharmacy, physical therapy, and veterinary medicine; engineering; forestry and wildlife. Honors programs. Study abroad through consortium in England, France, Germany, Spain. Major in bilingual-multicultural elementary education.

ROTC: Army, Air Force.

Degrees Conferred: 289 *associate;* 1,320 *baccalaureate* (B), 234 *master's* (M), 4 *doctorate* (D): biological/life sciences 35 (B), 7 (M); business/marketing 302 (B), 34 (M); communications/communication technologies 45 (B), 3 (M); computer and information sciences 76 (B), 1 (M); education 140 (B), 115 (M), 4 (D); engineering and engineering technologies 77 (B), 7 (M); English 46 (B), 9 (M); foreign languages and literature 31 (B); health professions and related sciences 109 (B), 5 (M); interdisciplinary studies 40 (B), 3 (M); mathematics 4 (B); parks and recreation 19 (B), 5 (M); philosophy/religion/theology 6 (B); physical sciences 10 (B), 4 (M); protective services/public administration 91 (B), 38 (M); psychology 55 (B); social sciences and history 147 (B), 2 (M); trade and industry 19 (B); visual and performing arts 69 (B); other 1 (M).

Fees and Other Expenses: *Full-time tuition per academic year 2004–05:* undergraduate resident $3,520, out-of-state student $10,576; graduate resident $4,232, out-of-state student $11,288. *Room and board per academic year:* $5,384.

Financial Aid: Boise State University offers a direct lending program. Aid from institutionally generated funds is provided on the basis of academic merit, financial need, athletic ability. Institution has a Program Participation Agreement with the U.S. Department of Education for eligible students to receive Pell Grants and other federal aid.

Financial aid to full-time, first-time undergraduate students: need-based scholarships/grants totaling $16,330,000, self-help $28,875,000, tuition waivers $900,000, athletic awards $450,000; non-need-based scholarships/grants totaling $2,362,000, self-help $9,050,000, tuition waivers $1,500,000, athletic awards $2,500,000. *Graduate aid:* 103 teaching assistantships totaling $1,150,000 (ranging from $7,000 to $12,000).

Departments and Teaching Staff: *Professors* 137, *associate professors* 143, *assistant professors* 126, *instructors* 123, *part-time faculty* 509. *Total instructional faculty:* 1,038 (full-time 529, part-time 509; women 490, men 648; members of minority groups 77). Total faculty with doctorate, first-professional, or other terminal degree: 690. Student-to-faculty ratio: 18:1. *Faculty development:* $20 million in grants for research. 17 faculty members awarded sabbaticals 2004.

Enrollment: Total enrollment 18,355. Undergraduate full-time 5,021 men / 5,557 women, part-time 2,747m / 3,394w; graduate full-time 204m / 240w, part-time 490m / 679w.

Characteristics of Student Body: *Ethnic/racial makeup:* number of Black non-Hispanic: 167; American Indian or Alaska Native: 150; Asian or Pacific Islander: 314; Hispanic: 734; White non-Hispanic: 12,175; unknown: 961. *Age distribution:* number under 18: 675; 18–19: 2,792; 20–21: 3,066; 22–24:3,688; 25–29: 3,006; 30–34: 1,559; 35–39: 864; 40–49: 1,219; 50–64: 351; 65 and over: 50.

International Students: 437 nonresident aliens enrolled fall 2004. 80 students from Europe, 230 Asia, 90 Central and South America, 13 Africa, 28 Canada, 5 Australia, 1 New Zealand. Programs available to aid students whose native language is not English: English as a Second Language Program. No financial aid specifically designated for international students.

Student Life: On-campus residence halls house 8% of student body. Residence halls for men constitute 40% of such space, for women only 50%, for both sexes 10%. 2% of men join and 1% live in fraternities; 2% of women join and 1% live in sororities. Housing available for married students. 25% of married students request institutional housing; 10% are so housed. *Intercollegiate athletics:* men only: baseball, football, track. Women only, track, volleyball. *Special regulations:* Registered cars permitted on campus in designated areas only. Quiet hours. *Special services:* Learning Resources Center, medical services. *Student publications, radio, television: Cold Drill,* an annual literary magazine; *University News,* a weekly newspaper. Radio station KBSU-FM broadcasts 168 hours per week. TV station KAID 112 hours per week. *Surrounding community:* Boise population 105,000. Portland (OR), 450 miles from campus, is nearest metropolitan area. Served by mass transit bus system; airport 3 miles from campus; passenger rail service 3 miles from campus.

Publications: *Western Writers Series* (5 times per year) first published in 1972.

Library Collections: 675,000 volumes. 1,223,235 microforms; 59,694 audiovisual materials; 5,000 periodicals. Access to online information retrieval systems. 200 computer work stations. Students have access to the Internet at no charge. Total 2004–05 budget for books and materials: $5,200,000.

Most important special holdings include Len B. Jordan Senatorial Papers; Frank Church Papers; Robert Limbert Papers; Cecil Andras Papers.

Buildings and Grounds: 115 acres. *New buildings:* Taylor Hall, Kaiser Hall completed 2004; West Campus Center 2005.

Chief Executive Officer: Dr. Robert Kastra, President.

Address undergraduate admission inquiries to Mark Wheeler, Director of Enrollment Services.

Idaho State University

921 South 8th Avenue
Pocatello, Idaho 83209
Tel: (208) 282-3620   **E-mail:** info@isu.edu
Fax: (208) 282-4122   **Internet:** www.isu.edu

Institution Description: *Enrollment:* 13,802. *Degrees awarded:* Associate, baccalaureate, master's, doctorate. Specialist certificate in education and other certificates also awarded.

Academic offerings subject to approval by statewide coordinating bodies. Budget subject to approval by state governing boards.

Accreditation: *Regional:* NWCCU. *Professional:* accounting, audiology, business, clinical lab scientist, counseling, culinary education, dental hygiene, dentistry, dietetics, engineering, health information technician, medical assisting, music, nursing, nursing education, occupational therapy, pharmacy, physical therapy, physician assisting, surgeon assisting, public health, social work, speech-language pathology, teacher education

History: Incorporated as The Academy of Idaho, a secondary school, 1901; changed name to The Idaho Technical Institute 1915; became Southern Branch of University of Idaho and offered first instruction at postsecondary level 1927; awarded first degree (baccalaureate) 1930; became independent institution, Idaho State College, 1947; adopted present name 1963. *See* Merrill D. Beal, *History of Idaho State College* (Pocatello: Idaho State University, 1952) for further information.

Institutional Structure: *Governing board:* The State Board of Education and Board of Regents of the University of Idaho. Representation: 7 members (appointed by governor of Idaho), superintendent of public instruction. All voting. *Composition of institution:* Administrators 59 men / 41 women. Institution governed by a president. Academic affairs headed by academic vice president. Management/business/finances directed by vice president for finance. Full-time instructional faculty 548. Academic governance body, Faculty Affairs Council, meets an average of 12 times per year.

Calendar: Semesters. Academic year June to May. Freshmen admitted Aug., Jan., June. Degrees conferred May, Aug., Dec. Formal commencements May, Aug. Summer session from May to Aug.

Characteristics of Freshmen: 71% of applicants admitted. 41% of admitted students enrolled full-time.

6% (140 students) submitted SAT scores; 59% (1,325 students) submitted ACT scores. *25th percentile*: SAT Verbal 460, SAT Math 460; ACT Composite 18, ACT English 16, ACT Math 17. *75th percentile*: SAT Verbal 590, SAT Math 610; ACT Composite 23, ACT English 23, ACT Math 23.

11% of entering freshmen expected to graduate within 5 years. 95% of freshmen from Idaho. Freshmen from 19 states and 10 foreign countries.

Admission: Rolling admissions plan. *Requirements:* Graduation from accredited secondary school or completion of GED with average score 450 or better. ACT of SAT scores for students younger than 21, those older than 21 are

exempt. The credit requirements are as follows: 8 English (1989 onward), 4 mathematics for students graduating in 1989 or 1990, 6 credits math for students graduating in 1991, and 6 math for students graduating 1992 onward, with additional credits strongly recommended; 4 natural science for students graduating 1989 and 1990, 6 credits natural science for students graduating from 1991 onward, 5 social science, 4 fine arts/foreign languages/humanities, 2 humanities/ foreign language, 1 speech, 3 extra college preparation credits. Students not meeting core may be considered for provisional admission based on predicted Idaho State University GPA of 2.00, calculated by combining high school core GPA and ACT/SAT scores. Students below 2.00 predicted Idaho State University GPA may petition admissions committee to be considered. *For transfer students:* 2.00 GPA from other institutions attended; 64 credit hours maximum transfer from two-year institutions; from four-year institutions maximum transfer limited only by residence requirement. *For foreign students:* TOEFL 500 minimum; 2.00 equivalent grades from secondary or postsecondary schools; financial statement from sponsor verifying ability to cover educational costs.

Degree Requirements: *For all associate degrees:* 64 semester hours. *For all baccalaureate degrees:* 128 hours. *For all undergraduate degrees:* 2.0 GPA; 32 of last 40 credits in residence; general education requirements.

Fulfillment of some degree requirements and exemption from some beginning courses possible by passing departmental examination, College Board CLEP, AP. *Grading system:* + and - A–F; pass-fail; withdraw.

Distinctive Educational Programs: Flexible meeting places and schedules, including off-campus centers (at Idaho Falls, 50 miles away from main institution; Twin Falls, 100 miles away; Boise, 250 miles away); evening classes. Interdepartmental program in American studies. Individual majors. *Other distinctive programs:* Idaho Dental Education Program, a cooperative first-professional program with the Creighton University Boyne School of Dental Science (for Idaho residents only).

ROTC: Army.

Degrees Conferred: 25 *associate;* 1,188 *baccalaureate* (B), 301 *master's* (M), 31 *doctorate* (D): area and ethnic studies 9 (B); biological/life sciences 141 (B), 21 (M), 1 (D); business/marketing 194 (B), 54 (M); communications/communication technologies 50 (B), 2 (M); computer and information sciences 30 (B); education 213 (B), 93 (M), 12 (D); engineering and engineering technologies 49 (B), 9 (M), 3 (D); English 20 (B), 7 (M), 5 (D); foreign languages and literature 19 (B); health professions and related sciences 215 (B), 69 (M), 4 (D); home economics and vocational home economics 3 (B); interdisciplinary studies 16 (B), 3 (M); liberal arts/general studies 18 (B); mathematics 6 (B), 2 (M), 1 (D); philosophy/religion/theology 3 (B); physical sciences 17 (B), 14 (M); protective services/public administration 62 (B), 8 (M); psychology 28 (B), 4 (M), 3 (D); social sciences and history 82 (B), 14 (M), 2 (D); visual and performing arts 19 (B), 1 (M). 62 *first-professional:* pharmacy.

Fees and Other Expenses: *Full-time tuition per academic year 2004–05:* Idaho resident undergraduate required fees: $4,380; out-of-state student $7,080 plus required fees $4,380; graduate resident $4,380 required fees, out-of-state student $7,090 plus $4,380 required fees. *Room and board per academic year:* undergraduate $4,850, graduate $7,290.

Financial Aid: Idaho State University has a direct lending program. Aid from institutionally generated funds is provided on the basis of academic merit, financial need, other criteria. Institution has a Program Participation Agreement with the U.S. Department of Education for eligible students to receive Pell Grants and other federal aid.

Financial aid to full-time, first-time undergraduate students: need-based scholarships/grants totaling $17,479,879, self-help $23,728,513, tuition waivers $191,400, athletic awards $25,902; non-need-based scholarships/grants totaling $8,069,670, self-help $16,688,967, parent loans $448,967, tuition waivers $13,647,663, athletic awards $2,185,429. *Graduate aid:* federal and state-funded fellowships and grants totaling $242,429; federal and state-funded loans $6,724,682; work-study jobs $68,478; other fellowships and grants $663,392; 233 teaching assistantships totaling $2,821,603; 95 research assistantships totaling $1,303,264.

Departments and Teaching Staff: *Total instructional faculty:* 763 (full-time 548, part-time 205; women 250, men 503; members of minority groups 41). Total faculty with doctorate, first-professional, or other terminal degree: 335. Total tenured faculty 231. Student-to-faculty ratio: 15:1. *Faculty development:* $28 million in grants for research. 17 faculty members awarded sabbaticals 2004–05.

Enrollment: Total enrollment 13,802. Undergraduate full-time 3,587 men / 4,289 women, part-time 1,525m / 2,262w; graduate full-time 345m / 465w, part-time 405m / 662w; first-professional full-time 137m / 85w, part-time 17m / 23w. *Transfer students:* in-state 375; from out-of state 459.

Characteristics of Student Body: *Ethnic and racial makeup:* number of Black non-Hispanic: 93; American Indian or Alaska Native: 230; Asian or Pacific Islander: 193; Hispanic: 498; White non-Hispanic: 11,530; unknown: 910. *Age distribution:* number under 18: 1,920; 18–19: 992; 20–21: 1,845; 22–

24: 3,279; 25–29: 2,500; 30–34: 1,199; 35–39: 762; 40–49: 1,213; 50–64: 681; 65 and over: 1.

International Students: 325 nonresident aliens enrolled fall 2004. 39 students from Europe, 164 Asia, 12 Central and South America, 87 Africa, 19 Canada, 3 Australia. English as a Second Language Program. Some scholarships available for qualifying international students.

Student Life: On campus residence halls house 18% of student body. Some men and women live in fraternities and sororities. Housing available for married students. *Intercollegiate athletics:* men only: baseball, football, golf, skiing, tennis, track; women only: basketball, soccer, skiing, tennis, track, volleyball. *Special regulations:* Cars permitted on campus in designated areas only. *Special services:* Learning Resources Center, medical services, career center, ADA and Disabilities Resource Center, Child Care Services, Gender Resource Center, student organizations and Greek life, campus transportation system. *Student publications, radio, television:* The Bengal, a weekly newspaper. TV station KISU. Radio station KISU FM 91.1. *Surrounding community:* Pocatello population 60,000. Salt Lake City (UT), 175 miles from campus, is nearest metropolitan area. Served by airport 15 miles from campus.

Library Collections: 712,041 volumes including bound books, serial backfiles, electronic documents, and government documents not in separate collections. Online and card catalogs. Current serial subscriptions: 6,672 paper, 1,961,706 microform. 923 recordings. 62 computer work stations. Students have access to the Internet at no charge. Total budget for books and materials 2004–05: $1.1 million.

Most important special holdings include Intermountain West Collection; papers of Minnie Howard, early Pocatello physician; Fred T. DuBois Collection; local history collections.

Buildings and Grounds: Campus area 274 acres. *New buildings:* Physical Science Complex; Performing Arts Center; Davis Field House.

Chief Executive Officer: Dr. Richard L. Bowen, President.

Address admission inquiries to Julie Mead, Director of Admissions; graduate inquiries to Dr. Paul Tate, Dean, Graduate School.

College of Arts and Sciences

Degree Programs Offered: *Associate* in art, biological sciences, chemistry, criminal justice, English French, German, history, Latin, mathematics, political science, Russian, Shoshoni, Spanish, speech communication; *baccalaureate* in American studies, anthropology, art, biochemistry, biology, botany, chemistry, drama, ecology, economics, English, fine arts, French, general studies, geology, German, history, international studies, mathematics, mass communication, medical technology, microbiology, music, philosophy, physics, political science, psychology, social work, sociology, Spanish, speech, zoology; *master's* and *doctorate* awarded through Graduate School.

Departments and Teaching Staff: Total instructional faculty 267.

Distinctive Educational Programs: Cooperative baccalaureate in medical technology with approved hospitals. Preprofessional programs in dentistry, medicine, optometry, osteopathic medicine, podiatric medicine, veterinary medicine.

Enrollment: Total enrollment 5,065.

College of Business

Degree Programs Offered: *Associate* in general business; *baccalaureate* in accounting, business administration, business education, computer science and information systems, finance, general business, management and organization, marketing; *master's* awarded through Graduate School.

Departments and Teaching Staff: Total instructional faculty: 39.

Enrollment: Total enrollment: 1,418.

College of Education

Degree Programs Offered: *Baccalaureate* in early childhood education, elementary education, family and consumer sciences, human exceptionality, music education, physical education, secondary education; *master's, doctorate,* and specialist certificate in education awarded through Graduate School. Vocational-technical teacher education program also available.

Departments and Teaching Staff: Total instructional faculty 39.

Enrollment: Total enrollment 1,703.

College of Engineering

Degree Programs Offered: *Baccalaureate* in computer science, engineering, engineering management; *master's* in nuclear engineering, measurement and control engineering; waste management and environmental science; engineering structures and mechanics, environmental engineering; *doctorate* in engineering and applied science, nuclear science and engineering.

Departments and Teaching Staff: Total instructional faculty 20.

Distinctive Educational Programs: Preprofessional program in architecture.

Enrollment: Total enrollment 570.

College of Health Professions

Degree Programs Offered: *Associate* in radiography, sign language studies; *baccalaureate* in dental hygiene, dietetics, educational interpreting, health care administration, health education, nursing, physician assistant studies, radiography, speech pathology and audiology; *master's* in audiology, counseling, health education, nursing, occupational therapy, physical therapy, public health, speech pathology and audiology, education of hearing impaired.

Departments and Teaching Staff: Total instructional faculty 105.

Enrollment: Total enrollment 2,511.

College of Pharmacy

Degree Programs Offered: *First-professional; master's* in pharmacy (pharmaceutical chemistry), pharmaceutics, pharmacognosy, pharmacology or pharmacy administration; *doctorate* in pharmacology, pharmacokinetics, biopharmaceutics, biopharmaceutical analysis, pharmacy administration.

Admission: *For first-professional degree:* Completion of 6 credits of composition, 8–10 general chemistry, 8 organic chemistry, 4 calculus and analytical geometry, 6 physics, and 18–24 social sciences and humanities; overall 2.5 GPA. Applications due Feb. 15 for fall enrollment including: 3 letters of recommendation, application, transcripts, personal interview. Competitive process with limited admissions.

Degree Requirements: *For first-professional degree:* 224 semester credits; 2.0 GPA; meet degree requirements in proper sequence.

Departments and Teaching Staff: Total instructional faculty 18.

Enrollment: Total enrollment 513.

School of Applied Technology

Degree Programs Offered: *Associate in* applied science (aircraft maintenance mechanics), automotive collision repair and refinishing, civil engineering technology, computer programming/systems technology, dental laboratory technology, diesel/diesel electric technology, drafting/design technology, electromechanical drafting technology, electromechanical technology, electronic systems technology, electronic RF/telcom technology graphics arts/printing technology; instrumentation technology, laser/electro-optics technology, machining technology, marketing and management, office occupations; *associate* in technology (civil engineering, computer programming/systems, communication electronics, drafting/design, electromechanical drafting, electromechanical, electronic systems, instrumentation, laser/electro-optics, telecommunications); *baccalaureate* in applied technology (civil engineering, computer programming/systems, communication electronics, drafting/design, electromechanical drafting, electromechanical, electronic RF/telcom, electronic systems, instrumentation, laser/electro-optics, telecommunications); *master's* in human resource training and development.

Degree Requirements: Associate of applied science requires a minimum of 72 credits in the applied technology major.

Departments and Teaching Staff: Total instructional faculty 96.

Enrollment: Total enrollment 1,698.

Interdisciplinary Programs

Degree Programs Offered: *Baccalaureate* in applied technology, university studies; *master's* in general interdisciplinary studies, waste management and environmental science.

Departments and Teaching Staff: Faculty members are drawn from other colleges.

Enrollment: Total enrollment 186.

Lewis-Clark State College

500 8th Avenue
Lewiston, Idaho 83501
Tel: (208) 792-2210   **E-mail:** admissions@lcsc.edu
Fax: (209) 792-2876   **Internet:** www.lcsc.edu

Institution Description: Lewis-Clark State College is a state institution. *Enrollment:* 3,325. *Degrees awarded:* Associate, baccalaureate.

Academic offerings subject to approval by statewide coordinating bodies. Budget subject to approval by state governing boards.

Accreditation: *Regional:* NWCCU. *Professional:* nursing, nursing education, social work, teacher education

History: Established as Lewis-Clark Normal School and offered first instruction at postsecondary level 1893; awarded first degree (associate) 1895; adopted present name 1971.

Institutional Structure: *Governing board:* The State Board of Education and Board of Regents of the University of Idaho. Representation: 7 members (appointed by governor of Idaho), superintendent of public instruction. *Composition of institution:* Administrators 7 men / 3 women. Academic affairs headed by academic vice president. Management/business/finances directed by financial vice president and bursar. Full-time instructional faculty 120. Academic governance body, Faculty Association, meets an average of 4 times per year.

Calendar: Semesters. Academic year Aug. to May. Freshmen admitted Aug., Jan., June. Degrees conferred and formal commencement May. 1997 summer session of 2 terms from early June to late July.

Characteristics of Freshmen: 71% of applicants admitted. 39% of admitted students enrolled full-time.

20% (91 students) submitted SAT scores; 61% (284 students) submitted ACT scores. *25th percentile:* SAT Verbal 400, SAT Math 410; ACT Composite 17, ACT English 15, ACT Math 16. *75th percentile:* SAT Verbal 520, SAT Math 540; ACT Composite 22, ACT English 22, ACT Math 21.

24% of entering freshmen expected to graduate in 5 years. 67% of freshmen from Idaho. Freshmen from 27 states and 33 foreign countries.

Admission: Rolling admissions plan. For fall acceptance, apply no later than 10 days after registration. Early acceptance available. *Requirements:* Either graduation from accredited secondary school or GED. *For transfer students:* 2.0 GPA; from 4-year accredited institution 96 semester hours maximum transfer credit; from 2-year accredited institution 64 hours; transfer credit also available for correspondence/extension students.

College credit and advanced placement for postsecondary-level work completed in secondary school. College credit for extrainstitutional learning on basis of ACE *2006 Guide to the Evaluation of Educational Experiences in the Armed Services*, portfolio assessment.

Tutoring available. Developmental courses offered in summer session and regular academic year.

Degree Requirements: *For all associate degrees:* 64 credit hours; general education requirements for academic majors; 16 hours in residence. *For all baccalaureate degrees:* 128 credit hours; 32 hours in residence; general education requirements.

Fulfillment of some degree requirements and exemption from some beginning courses possible by passing departmental examinations, College Board CLEP, AP. *Grading system:* A–F; pass-fail; withdraw (carries time limit; IP for individualized instruction classes not completed by end of semester).

Distinctive Educational Programs: Cooperative education. Off-campus centers in various northern Idaho communities. Weekend and evening classes. Interdepartmental programs in general studies. Honors programs. Individual majors.

ROTC: Air Force offered in cooperation with Washington State University; Army and Navy offered in cooperation with University of Idaho. 1 Army commission awarded 2004.

Degrees Conferred: 113 *associate;* 319 *baccalaureate:* biological/life sciences 15; business/marketing 581 communications/communication technologies 10; computer and information sciences 5; education 34; English 8; health professions and related sciences 44; interdisciplinary studies 26; law/legal studies 3; liberal arts/general studies 12; mathematics 5; natural resources/environmental science 71 physical sciences 17; psychology 20; social sciences and history 55.

Fees and Other Expenses: *Full-time tuition per academic year 2005–06:* resident $3,712, out-of-state student $10,266. *Room and board per academic year:* $3,855.

Financial Aid: Aid from institutionally generated funds is provided on the basis of academic merit, financial need, athletic ability. Institution has a Program Participation Agreement with the U.S. Department of Education for eligible students to receive Pell Grants and other federal aid.

Financial aid to full-time, first-time undergraduate students: need-based scholarships/grants totaling $4,551,408, self-help $6,344,990; non-need-based scholarships/grants totaling $1,221,815, self-help $2,389,202, tuition waivers $621,294, athletic awards $578,851.

Departments and Teaching Staff: Business *professors* 2, *associate professors* 1, *assistant professors* 4, *instructors* 1, *part-time faculty* 0; education 10, 4, 3, 3, 0; humanities 10, 5, 2, 4 0; natural science and mathematics 5, 5, 5, 4, 0; nursing and health sciences 6, 5, 6, 0, 1; social science 8, 2, 5, 3, 1; business technology 6, 4, 3, 0, 4; technical and industrial 9, 4, 5, 0, 0.

Total instructional faculty: 140 (full-time 134, part-time 6; women 64, men 96; members of minority groups 9). Total faculty with doctorate, first-professional, or other terminal degree: 93. Student-to-faculty ratio: 17:1. 1 faculty member awarded sabbatical 2004–05.

Enrollment: Total enrollment 3,325. Full-time 990 men / 1,339 women, part-time 291m / 705w.

Characteristics of Student Body: *Ethnic/racial makeup:* number of Black non-Hispanic: 14; American Indian or Alaska Native: 163; Asian or Pacific Islander: 27; Hispanic: 149; White non-Hispanic: 2,675; unknown: 198. *Age distribution:* number under 18: 242; 18–19: 674; 20–21: 535; 22–24: 512; 25–29: 426; 30–34: 263; 35–39: 180; 40–49: 343; 50–64: 135; 65 and over: 12.

International Students: 99 nonresident aliens enrolled fall 2004. 12 students from Europe, 61 Asia, 5 Central And South America, 10 Africa, 7 Canada, 2 Australia. Programs available to aid students whose native language is not English: social, cultural. English as a Second Language Program. No financial aid specifically designated for international students.

Student Life: On-campus residence halls house 6% of student body. Dormitories for men only constitute 47% of such space, for women only 53%. *Intercollegiate athletics:* men only: baseball, basketball; women only: basketball, volleyball. *Special regulations:* Cars permitted in designated areas. Limited residence hall visitation. *Special services:* Learning Resources Center, medical services. *Student publications, radio, television:* Lewiston population 28,000. Seattle, 470 miles from campus, is nearest metropolitan area. Served by airport 5 miles from campus.

Library Collections: 256,927 volumes. Online catalog. 18,167 government documents; 39,725 microforms; 6,800 audiovisual materials. Current serial subscriptions: paper 816; microform 29; via electronic access 11,951. 7,000 recordings. 17 computer work stations. Students have access to the Internet at no charge.

Most important holdings include Pacific Northwest Collection; Children's Literature Collection; Library of American Civilization.

Buildings and Grounds: Campus area 40 acres.

Chief Executive Officer: Dr. Dene Kay Thomas, President.

Address admission inquiries to Director of Enrollment Management.

New St. Andrews College

205 East Fifth Street
Moscow, Idaho 83843
Tel: (208) 882-1566   **E-mail:** admissions@nsa.edu
Fax: (208) 882-4293   **Internet:** www.nsu.edu

Institution Description: *Enrollment:* 135. *Degrees awarded:* Associate, baccalaureate.

Accreditation: *National:* Transnational Association of Christian Colleges and Schools (TRACS).

History: The college was established in 1994 as a Christian postsecondary institution. The college is committed to the pursuit of knowledge and wisdom in the light of the Holy Scriptures. Its mission is to provide the highest quality undergraduate education in the liberal arts and culture from a biblical worldview.

Institutional Structure: The college's primary objective for its administration is to provide academic leadership for the faculty, students, and the college as a whole.

Calendar: Quarters.

Characteristics of Freshmen: 68 applicants (35 men, 33 women). 82.4% of applicants admitted. 73.2% of admitted students enrolled full-time.

73% (35 students) submitted SAT scores; 31% (15 students) submitted ACT scores. *25th percentile:* SAT I Verbal 570, SAT I Math 520; ACT Composite 24, ACT English 26, ACT Math 23. *75th percentile:* SAT I Verbal 710, SAT I Math 640; ACT Composite 29, ACT English 33 ACT Math 26.

Admission: *Requirements:* Graduation from accredited secondary school with a B or better average. Previous Latin and classical languages no required but helpful. Applicant should have an ACT score of 20 or above or SAT composite score of 1000. Statement of Christian faith is required.

Degree Requirements: *For all associate and baccalaureate degrees:* completion of the prescribed program.

Distinctive Educational Programs: Programs require four years of language study in Latin and the classical languages.

Degrees Conferred: 6 *associate;* 18 *baccalaureate:* liberal arts and sciences, general studies, and humanities: 18.

Fees and Other Expenses: *Full-time tuition per academic year 2004–05:* $6,800. *Books and supplies:* $1,500. *Off-campus room and board per academic year:* $4,500.

Financial Aid: Institution does not have a Program Participation Agreement with the U.S. Department of Education.

Departments and Teaching Staff: Faculty are unranked.

Enrollment: Total enrollment 135.

Student Life: No on-campus housing.

Chief Executive Officer: Dr. Roy Alden Atwood, President.

Address admission inquiries to John Lewis, Director Admissions.

Northwest Nazarene University

623 Holly Street
Nampa, Idaho 83686-5897
Tel: (208) 467-8011   **E-mail:** admissions@nnu.edu
Fax: (208) 467-8099   **Internet:** www.nnu.edu

Institution Description: Northwest Nazarene University is a private college affiliated with the Church of the Nazarene. *Enrollment:* 1,587. *Degrees awarded:* Associate, baccalaureate, master's.

Accreditation: *Regional:* NWCCU. *Professional:* business, counseling, music, nursing education, social work, teacher education

History: Established and incorporated as an elementary school 1913; offered first instruction at postsecondary level 1915; first degree (baccalaureate) became Northwest Nazarene College 1917; attained university status in 1999 and adopted the present name.

Calendar: Semesters. Academic year Sept. to June. Freshmen admitted Sept., Jan., Mar., June. Degrees conferred June, Aug., Dec., Mar. Formal commencement June.

Characteristics of Freshmen: Average secondary school rank of freshmen 66th percentile. Mean ACT composite score 22. 98% of applicants accepted. 37.3% of entering freshmen expected to graduate within 5 years.

Admission: Rolling admissions plan. For fall acceptance, apply as early as end of junior year, but not later than Sept. of year of enrollment. *Requirements:* High school diploma (2.5 GPA for regular admission) or GED (Standard Score Average of 45 for regular admission). *Entrance tests:* ACT. For foreign students TOEFL. *For transfer students:* A minimum of 36 credits is required to be admitted as a transfer student; students with less than 36 credits must provide high school and transcript information. From 4-year accredited institution 152 quarter credits maximum transfer credit; from 2-year accredited institution 94 credits; correspondence/extension students 47 credits. Regular admission is routinely granted to students in good "academic status" (defined as a 2.0 GPA) and who would be eligible for continued enrollment at their current institutions.

College credit and advanced placement for postsecondary-level work completed in secondary school and for extrainstitutional learning (life experience) on basis of ACE *2006 Guide to the Evaluation of Educational Experiences in the Armed Services.* Developmental courses offered during regular academic year; credit given.

Degree Requirements: *For all associate degrees:* 60 semester credits. *For all baccalaureate degrees:* 124 semester credits; demonstrated competence in mathematics. *For all undergraduate degrees:* 2.0 GPA; 1 year of quarters in residence; chapel attendance required; demonstrated competence in writing; general education requirements.

Fulfillment of some degree requirements and exemption from some beginning courses possible by passing departmental examinations, College Board CLEP, APP. *Grading system:* A–F; pass-fail; withdraw (carries time limit); incomplete (carries time limit).

Distinctive Educational Programs: *For undergraduates:* Field experience programs. Dual-degree program in engineering with University of Idaho. Interdisciplinary majors in engineering physics, food service management, general studies, mathematics and natural science, psychology and sociology, and by individual arrangement. Preprofessional program in medical technology. Facilities and programs for independent research, including individual majors, tutorials. *Available to all students:* Internships. Evening classes. *Other distinctive programs:* The Riley Intellectual Life Lecture Series, sponsored annually for Christian scholars.

Degrees Conferred: 258 *baccalaureate*; 99 *master's.* Bachelor's degrees awarded in top five disciplines: business, management, marketing, and related support services biological and life sciences 61; education 38; public administration ad social service professions: 29; liberal arts and sciences, general studies, and humanities 16; visual and performing arts 15.

Fees and Other Expenses: *Full-time tuition per academic year 2004–05:* $16,570. *Books and supplies:* $760. *room and board per academic year:* $4,630.

Financial Aid: Aid from institutionally generated funds is provided on the basis of academic merit, financial need, athletic ability. Institution has a Program Participation Agreement with the U.S. Department of Education for eligible students to receive Pell Grants and other federal aid.

Financial aid to full-time, first-time undergraduate students: 45% received federal grants averaging $1,951, 36% state/local grants averaging $557, 29% institutional grants averaging $2,657; 57% loans averaging $4,934.

Departments and Teaching Staff: Study skills *professors* 6, *part-time faculty* 3; business/economics 6, 4; education 9, 3; philosophy and religion 9, 3; social work 2, 2; art and music 10, 16; communication studies 2, 1; English 6, 1; history and political science 4, 0; modern language 2, 2; psychology and sociology 4, 1; biology 5, 0; chemistry 4, 1; kinesiology 7, 3; mathematics/computer science 5, 2; nursing 2, 0; physics 3, 0; military science 0, 2.

Total instructional faculty: 98. Student-to-faculty ratio: 14.3:1. Degrees held by full-time faculty: doctorate 69%, master's 27%.

Enrollment: Total enrollment 1,587. Undergraduate 1,172 (41.2% men, 58.8% women).

Characteristics of Student Body: *Ethnic/racial makeup:* Black non-Hispanic: .6%; American Indian or Alaska Native: .5%; Asian or Pacific Islander: 1.4%; Hispanic: 1.4%; White non-Hispanic: 67.1%; unknown: 28.6%.

International Students: 6 nonresident aliens enrolled fall 2004. No programs to aid students whose native language is not English. No financial aid specifically designated for international students.

Student Life: On-campus residence halls and apartments house 70% of student body. Housing for men only constitutes 45% of such space, for women only 55%. 2% of student body live off campus in college-owned houses. *Intercollegiate athletics:* men only: baseball, basketball, cross-country, golf, soccer, tennis, track and filed; women only: basketball, cross-country, soccer, tennis, track and field, volleyball. *Special regulations:* Cars permitted without restrictions. *Special services:* Learning Resources Center, medical services. *Student publications: Crusader,* a weekly newspaper; *Oasis,* a yearbook. *Surrounding community:* Nampa population 40,000. Boise is nearest metropolitan area. Served by airport 20 miles from campus; passenger rail service 2 miles from campus.

Publications: *The Messenger,* a quarterly publication from University Advancement.

Library Collections: 120,000 volumes. 35,803 government documents. 20,000 microform units; 3,500 audiovisual materials. 820 periodical subscriptions. Computer work stations available. Students have access to the Internet.

Most important holdings include Library of American Civilization (microfiche); Annie Laurie Bird Collection (on Nampa, Idaho); Wesley Collection (life, work, theology of John Wesley).

Buildings and Grounds: Campus area 85 acres.

Chief Executive Officer: Dr. Richard A. Hagood, President.

Address undergraduate admission inquiries to Dr. Eric Forseth, Director of Enrollment Services.

University of Idaho

Moscow, Idaho 83844
Tel: (208) 885-6111   **E-mail:** admissions@uidaho.edu
Fax: (208) 885-9119   **Internet:** www.uidaho.edu

Institution Description: University of Idaho is a state institution and land-grant college. *Enrollment:* 12,824. *Degrees awarded:* Baccalaureate, master's, doctorate, first-professional (law). Specialist certificates also awarded.

Academic offerings subject to approval by statewide coordinating bodies. Budget subject to approval by state governing boards. Member of the consortium Associated Western Universities.

Accreditation: *Regional:* NWCCU. *Professional:* architecture, athletic training, counseling, dietetics, forestry, landscape architecture, law, music, recreation and leisure services, rehabilitation counseling, teacher education

History: Chartered 1890; established and offered first instruction at postsecondary level 1892; awarded first degree (baccalaureate) 1896; added master's program 1913; doctorate program 1959. *See* Rafe Gibbs, *Beacon for Mountain and Plain* (Caldwell, Idaho: The Caxton Printers, 1962) for further information.

Institutional Structure: *Governing board:* The State Board of Education and Board of Regents of the University of Idaho. Representation: 8 members (appointed by governor of Idaho), state superintendent of public instruction. All voting. *Composition of institution:* Administrators 35 men / 10 women. Academic affairs headed by academic vice president. Management/business/finances directed by financial vice president. Full-time instructional faculty 532. Academic governance body, Faculty Council, meets an average of 25 times per year.

Calendar: Semesters. Academic year Aug. to May. Freshmen admitted on a rolling basis. Degrees conferred May, Aug., Dec. Formal commencement May. Summer session from May to Aug.

Characteristics of Freshmen: *25th percentile*: SAT Verbal 460, SAT Math 490; ACT Composite 20, ACT English 18, ACT Math 19. *75th percentile*: SAT Verbal 610, SAT Math 610; ACT Composite 26, ACT English 26, ACT Math 26.

Admission: Rolling admissions plan. For fall acceptance, apply no later than Aug. 1. For priority consideration for financial aid and scholarships by Feb. 1. Early acceptance available. $40 nonrefundable application fee for new applications in an undergraduate degree program; $55 for graduate programs. *Requirements:* Graduation from a regionally accredited high school. Completion of the following high school core subjects with a 2.0 GPA: English 8 units, math 6 units, natural sciences 6 units, humanities 2 units, social science 5 units, and additional college prep courses 3 units. *Entrance tests:* College Board SAT or ACT Composite. *For transfer students:* 2.0 minimum GPA (except for engineering 2.8 GPA and landscape architecture 2.5 GPA). From 4-year accredited institutions courses are evaluated on a course-by-course basis; 2-year accredited institutions 70 semester hours maximum transfer credit; correspondence/extension students 48 hours.

College credit and advanced placement for postsecondary-level work completed in secondary school. For extrainstitutional learning, college credit on basis of ACE *2006 Guide to the Evaluation of Educational Experiences in the Armed Services*; advanced placement on basis of portfolio and faculty assessments,personal interviews.

Tutoring available. Remedial courses in English and chemistry offered during the regular academic year; no credit given.

Degree Requirements: *For all undergraduate degrees:* minimum of 128 credit hours; 2.0 GPA; 32 credit hours in residence; 33 credits in four core categories.

Fulfillment of some degree requirements and exemption from some beginning courses possible by passing departmental examinations, College Board CLEP. *Grading system:* A–F; pass-fail; withdraw.

Distinctive Educational Programs: Evening classes. Interdisciplinary program in general studies. Honors programs. Individual majors. Tutorials. Cooperative programs in medicine, veterinary medicine, and cross-registration with Washington State University and Lewis-Clark State College. Cooperative program in veterinary medicine with Washington State University. Cooperative master's program in public administration with Idaho State University and Boise State University. *Other distinctive programs:* Continuing education. Research and service facilities, including the Center for Native American Development, Institute of Human Behavior, Bureau of Public Affairs Research, Cooperative Extension Service, Idaho Water and Energy Resources Institute. International student exchange program.

ROTC: Army; Navy in cooperation with Washington State University.

Degrees Conferred: 1,554 *baccalaureate*; 458 *master's*: 33 *post-master's*; 70 *doctorate*. Bachelor's degrees awarded in top five disciplines: business, management, marketing, and related support services 189; engineering 168; education 162; communication, journalism, and related programs 118; natural resources and conservation 116. *First-professional* law 103.

Fees and Other Expenses: *Full-time tuition per academic year 2004–05:* in-state undergraduate $3,532; out-of-state $11,652. *Books and supplies:* $1,266. *Room and board per academic year:* $5,034. Contact the university for graduate/first-professional tuition/fees.

Financial Aid: Aid from institutionally generated funds is provided on the basis of academic merit, financial need, athletic ability, other criteria. Institution has a Program Participation Agreement with the U.S. Department of Education for eligible students to receive Pell Grants and other federal aid.

Financial aid to full-time, first-time undergraduate students: need-based scholarships/grants totaling $11,765,392, self-help $21,293,113; non-need-based scholarships/grants totaling $7,890,220, self-help $13,618,740, parent loans $1,875,430, tuition waivers $3,661,683, athletic awards $2,892,206.

Departments and Teaching Staff: *Total instructional faculty:* 557 (full-time 532, part-time 25; women 146, men 411; members of minority groups 46). Total faculty with doctorate, first-professional, or other terminal degree: 462.

Enrollment: Total enrollment 12,824. Undergraduate full-time 4,630 men / 3,772 women, part-time 614m / 634w; graduate full-time 665m / 536w, part-time 898m / 855w; first-professional full-time 179m / 132w, part-time 6m / 3w.

Characteristics of Student Body: *Ethnic/racial makeup:* number of Black non-Hispanic: 83; American Indian or Alaska Native: 115; Asian or Pacific Islander: 224; Hispanic: 363; White non-Hispanic: 7,986; unknown: 551.

International Students: 238 undergraduate nonresident aliens enrolled fall 2003. *Programs available to aid students whose native language is not English:* Social. English as a Second Language program. Some financial aid available annually for undergraduate international students.

Student Life: On-campus residence halls, including married student housing, house 19% of student body. 21% of undergraduate men join fraternities and 16% live in fraternity houses; 18% of women join sororities and 15% live in sorority houses. College-leased cooperatives also offer residence space. *Intercollegiate athletics:* men only: basketball, cross-country, football, golf, tennis, track and field; women only: basketball, cross-country, golf, soccer, swimming, tennis, track and field, volleyball. *Special regulations:* Registered cars permitted. *Special services:* Academic Assistance Programs; medical services. *Student publications, radio, television:* Biweekly newspaper: *the Argonaut.* Annual magazine: *The Blot.* Radio station KUOI. TV station KUID. *Surrounding community:* Moscow population 21,207. Spokane (WA), 90 miles from campus, is nearest metropolitan area. Served by airport 6 miles from campus.

Publications: *Fugue* (biannual) literary magazine first published in 1990.

Library Collections: 2,648,274 volumes. Online catalog. Current serial subscriptions: 1,700 paper; 3,845 via electronic access. 1,881 recordings; 1,794

compact discs; 3,860 CD-ROMs. 75 computer work stations. Students have access to the Internet at no charge. Total 2004–05 operating budget: $2,612,439.

Most important holdings include Sir Walter Scott Collection; State of Idaho Historical Collection; Barnard-Stockbridge Collection (mining pictures); regional manuscripts and archives.

Buildings and Grounds: Campus area 1,400 acres. *New buildings:* Gauss-Johnson Engineering Complex (renovation); Idaho Commons; Vandal Enrollment Services Center; Agricultural Biotechnology Laboratory; Vandal Athletic Center; Student Recreation Center; Living Learning Center; Teaching and Learning Center.

Chief Executive Officer: Dr. Timothy P. White, President.

Undergraduates address admission inquiries to Director of Admissions; graduate inquiries to Graduate Admissions Office.

College of Agricultural and Life Sciences

Degree Programs Offered: *Baccalaureate* in agribusiness, agricultural economics, agricultural education, agricultural mechanization, animal science, bacteriology, crop management, crop science, entomology, general agriculture, horticultural science, landscape horticulture, natural resources and rural development, plant protection, poultry science, range-livestock management, soil science, veterinary science; home economics (child development and family relations); clothing, textiles, and home design; food and nutrition; home economics education; *master's* in agricultural economics, agricultural education, animal science, entomology, family and consumer sciences, food science, microbiology, molecular biology and biochemistry, plant science, soil and land resources, veterinary science; *doctorate* in animal physiology, entomology, food science, microbiology, molecular biology and biochemistry, plant science, soil and land resources.

Distinctive Educational Programs: Agricultural experiment station.

College of Business and Economics

Degree Programs Offered: *Baccalaureate* in accounting, economics, finance, management, marketing; *master's* in business administration, economics.

Distinctive Educational Programs: Center for Business Development and Research.

College of Education

Degree Programs Offered: *Baccalaureate* in athletic training, early childhood development and education, dance, elementary education, office administration, physical education, recreation, technology; *master's, doctorate* in various fields. Specialist certificates also awarded.

College of Engineering

Degree Programs Offered: *Baccalaureate* in biological and agricultural engineering, chemical engineering, civil engineering, computer engineering, computer science, electrical engineering, materials science and engineering, mechanical engineering, metallurgical engineering; *master's* in biological and agricultural engineering, chemical engineering, civil engineering, computer engineering, computer science, electrical engineering, environmental engineering, geological engineering, materials science and engineering, mechanical engineering, metallurgical engineering; metallurgy, nuclear engineering, systems engineering; *doctorate* in biological and agricultural engineering, chemical engineering, civil engineering, computer science, electrical engineering, materials science and engineering, mechanical engineering, nuclear engineering.

Distinctive Educational Programs: Master's programs in nuclear engineering through the facilities at Idaho National Engineering Laboratory at Idaho Falls. Engineering Experiment Station.

College of Graduate Studies

Degree Programs Offered: *Master's* and *doctorate* in bioinformatics and biology; neuroscience.

College of Law

Degree Programs Offered: *First-professional.*

Admission: Baccalaureate from accredited college or university. Lowest acceptable class standing 50th percentile. LSAT score above national median. LSDAS registration.

Degree Requirements: 84 credit hours, 2.0 GPA, 6 semesters in residence.

College of Letters, Arts, and Social Sciences.

Degree Programs Offered: *Baccalaureate* in advertising; American studies; anthropology; architecture; art; bacteriology; biology; botany; chemistry; child development; classical studies; clothing, textiles, and design; communication; economics; English; foreign languages; French; geography; German; history; home economics; home economics education; interdisciplinary studies; interior design; journalism; landscape architecture; Latin; medical technology; museology; music; music education; naval science; philosophy; physics; political science; psychology; radio-television; religious studies; sociology; Spanish; speech; theater arts; zoology; *master's* and *doctorate* in environmental science, history, political science.

College of Natural Resources

Degree Programs Offered: *Baccalaureate* in ecology and conservation biology; fishery resources; forest products; forest resources; rangeland ecology and management; range livestock management; resource recreation and tourism; wildlife resources; *master's* fishery resources; forest products; forest resources; natural resources; rangeland ecology and management; resource recreation and tourism; wildlife resources; *doctorate* in natural resources.

Distinctive Educational Programs: Forest, Wildlife, and Range Experiment Station.

Illinois

Adler School of Professional Psychology

65 East Wacker Place
Suite 2100
Chicago, Illinois 60601-7298
Tel: (312) 201-5900   **E-mail:** information@adler.edu
Fax: (312) 201-5917   **Internet:** www.adler.edu

Institution Description: Adler School of Professional Psychology, formerly known as the Alfred Adler Institute of Chicago, is a private, independent, non-profit college. *Enrollment:* 480. *Degrees awarded:* Master's, doctorate.

Accreditation: *Regional:* NCA.

History: Offered first instruction at postsecondary level as a division of the Individual Psychological Association 1952; established as Alfred Adler Institute of Chicago 1952; chartered and incorporated 1963; awarded first degree (master's) 1978; adopted present name 1993.

Institutional Structure: *Governing board:* Board of Directors of the Alfred Adler Institute of Chicago. Extrainstitutional representation: 2 directors; institutional representation: 4 administrators, 3 faculty members, 4 ex officio. All voting. *Composition of institution:* Administrators 3 men / 3 women. Academic affairs headed by dean of faculty. Management/business/finances directed by president. Academic governance body, the faculty, meets an average of 4 times per year.

Calendar: Quarters. Academic year June to June. Degrees conferred and formal commencement Oct. Summer session of 1 term from June to Sept.

Admission: Rolling admissions plan. *Requirements:* Baccalaureate from accredited college or university with 18 credit hours in psychology, including at least one course each in abnormal psychology, developmental psychology, personality theories, and psychological tests and measurements.

Degree Requirements: *For master's degrees:* 22 courses; 3.0 GPA; 3 courses in residence; core requirements; term paper; field experience observing and practicing counseling techniques, therapeutic experience with psychologist or other approved therapist; final oral and written examinations. *Grading system:* A–F; pass-fail.

Distinctive Educational Programs: Weekend and evening classes. Accelerated degree programs. *Other distinctive programs:* Family Learning Service provides professionals and laypersons with training in the principles and techniques of Adlerian psychology. Courses available for educators. Human Dynamics Consultants outreach program.

Degrees Conferred: 78 *master's:* psychology; 5 *post-master's certificate;* 23 *doctorate:* psychology.

Fees and Other Expenses: *Full-time tuition per academic year:* Contact the school for current tuition and fees.

Financial Aid: Scholarships available on basis of academic merit, financial need. Institution has a Program Participation Agreement with the U.S. Department of Education for eligible students to receive Pell Grants and other federal aid.

Departments and Teaching Staff: Psychology *professors* 18, *part-time faculty:* 33. *Total instructional faculty:* 51. Degrees held by full-time faculty: doctorate 80%, master's 100%. 100% hold terminal degrees.

Enrollment: Total enrollment 480 (22.7% men, 77.3% women).

Characteristics of Student Body: *Ethnic/racial makeup:* Black non-Hispanic: 9.4%; Asian or Pacific Islander: 5%; Hispanic: 4%; White non-Hispanic: 74.4%; unknown: 7.3%.

International Students: No programs available to aid students whose native language is not English. No financial aid specifically designated for international students.

Student Life: No on-campus housing. *Special services:* Learning Resources Center. *Student publications: Alfred Adler Institute Student Association Newsletter,* a quarterly. *Surrounding community:* Chicago population over 3,000,000. Served by mass transit bus and commuter rail system, airport, and passenger rail service.

Library Collections: 20,000 volumes. 60 current periodical subscriptions.

Chief Executive Officer: Dr. Raymond E.Crissman, President.
Address admission inquiries to Susan Greenwald, Director of Admissions.

Augustana College

639 Thirty-eighth Street
Rock Island, Illinois 61201
Tel: (309) 794-7000   **E-mail:** admissions@augustana.edu
Fax: (309) 794-7422   **Internet:** www.augustana.edu

Institution Description: Augustana College is a private, undergraduate college affiliated with the Evangelical Lutheran Church in America. *Enrollment:* 2,292. *Degrees awarded:* Baccalaureate.

Member of the consortium Quad-Cities Graduate Study Center.

Accreditation: *Regional:* NCA. *Professional:* music, teacher education

History: Established as Augustana Seminary and offered first instruction at postsecondary level 1860; incorporated 1863; changed name to Augustana College and Theological Seminary 1865; awarded first degree (baccalaureate) 1877; adopted present name 1948. *See* Conrad Bergendoff, *Augustana, a Profession of Faith* (Davenport, Iowa: Wagners Printers, 1969) for further information.

Institutional Structure: *Governing board:* Board of Trustees, 27 outside members plus college president. Extrainstitutional representation: 27 trustees; institutional representation: president of the college. 2 ex officio. All voting. *Composition of institution:* Administrators 21 men / 17 women. (2.5% are members of minority groups). Academic affairs headed by president. Management/business/finances directed by vice president for financial affairs. Full-time instructional faculty 144. Academic governance body, Faculty Senate, meets an average of 10 times per year.

Calendar: Quarters. Academic year Sept. to May. Freshmen admitted Sept., Nov., Mar., June. Degrees conferred May, Aug., Nov., Mar. Formal commencement May. Summer session from June to Aug.

Characteristics of Freshmen: 77% of applicants admitted. 27% of students admitted enrolled full-time.

10% (58 students) submitted SAT scores; 99% (596 students) submitted ACT scores. *25th percentile:* ACT Composite 23.6. *75th percentile:* ACT Composite 28.6.

75% entering freshmen expected to graduate within 5 years. 90% of freshmen from Illinois. Freshmen from 14 states and 23 foreign countries.

Admission: Rolling admissions plan. For fall acceptance, apply as early as Sept. 1 of previous year, with applications preferred by Feb. 1, but not later than Aug. 15 of year of enrollment. *Requirements:* Either graduation from accredited secondary school or GED. Strongly recommends 4 units English, 1 foreign language, 3 mathematics, 2 natural science, 2 social studies (including history). For engineering, mathematics, and science programs, recommend 1½ units algebra, 1 geometry, ½ trigonometry. Minimum GPA 2.5. Lowest acceptable secondary school class standing 50th percentile. *Entrance tests:* College Board SAT or ACT composite. *For transfer students:* 2.0 minimum GPA; from 4-year accredited institution maximum transfer credit limited only by residence requirement.

College credit and advanced placement for postsecondary-level work completed in secondary school. Tutoring available.

Degree Requirements: 123 semester credits; 2.0 GPA; last 60 hours in residence; core and distribution requirements.

Fulfillment of some degree requirements and exemption from some beginning courses possible by passing College Board AP. Exemption from foreign language courses also possible by passing departmental examinations. *Grading system:* A–F; pass-fail; withdraw (carries time limit).

Distinctive Educational Programs: Internships and cooperative education program. Coordinated degree programs with different universities in engineering, forestry, environmental management, landscape architecture, dentistry, and occupational therapy. Interdisciplinary honors programs. Institutionally sponsored study abroad in Argentina, Brazil, China, Colombia, Ecuador, England, France, Hong Kong, Japan, Mexico, Peru, Spain, Sweden. Weekly community convocations featuring speakers and performers. Centers of distinction include the Center for Vocational Reflection, Center for the Study of Ethics, Freistat Center for Studies in World Peace, and the Institute for Leadership and Advice.

Degrees Conferred: 730 *baccalaureate:* area and ethnic studies 7; biological/life sciences 95; business/marketing 134; communications/communication technologies 32; computer and information science 26; education 55; engineering/engineering technologies 7; English 59; foreign languages and literature 34; health professions and related sciences 48; mathematics 19; philosophy/religion/theology 17; physical sciences 25; psychology 41; social sciences and history 124; visual and performing arts 19.

Fees and Other Expenses: *Full-time tuition per academic year 2004–05:* $21,672. *Room and board per academic year:* $6,042.

Financial Aid: Aid from institutionally generated funds is provided on the basis of academic merit, financial need. Institution has a Program Participation Agreement with the U.S. Department of Education for eligible students to receive Pell Grants and other federal aid.

Financial aid to full-time, first-time undergraduate students: need-based scholarships/grants totaling $17,396,058, self-help $11,088,086, parent loans $3,081,802, tuition waivers $883,381; non-need-based scholarships/grants totaling $2,855,932.

Departments and Teaching Staff: *Professors* 47, *associate professors* 47, *assistant professors* 46, *instructors* 4, *part-time faculty* 83. *Total instructional faculty:* 132 (full-time 144, part-time 87; women 103, men 28; members of minority groups 20). Total faculty with doctorate, first-professional, or other terminal degree: 157. Student-to-faculty ratio: 12:1. *Faculty development:* 15 faculty members awarded sabbaticals 2004–05.

Enrollment: Total enrollment 2,292. Undergraduate full-time 971 men / 1,295 women, part-time 14m / 12w. *Transfer students:* in-state 61; from out-of-state 16.

Characteristics of Student Body: *Ethnic/racial makeup:* number of Black non-Hispanic: 51; American Indian or Alaska Native: 7; Asian or Pacific Islander: 51; Hispanic: 60; White non-Hispanic: 2,113. *Age distribution:* number under 18: 12; 18–19: 1,114; 20–21: 995; 22–24: 133; 25–29: 18; 30–34: 9; 35–39: 3; 40–49: 8.

International Students: 17 nonresident aliens enrolled fall 2004. 9 students from Europe, 11 Asia, 2 Central and South America, 5 Africa, 1 Canada. Programs to aid students whose native language is not English: Social and cultural. English as a Second Language Program. Some scholarships specifically designated for international students.

Student Life: On-campus residence halls house 67% of student body. Residence halls are 62% coed, 23% for women, 15% for men. 3% of student body live in college-owned housing off-campus. *Intercollegiate athletics:* men only: baseball, basketball, cross-country, football, golf, soccer, swimming, tennis, track, wrestling; women only: basketball, cross-country, golf, soccer, softball, swimming, tennis, track, volleyball. *Special services:* career planning and placement, counseling services, campus ministry. *Student publications, radio:* *Observer*, a weekly newspaper; *Saga*, an annual literary magazine. Radio station WAUG broadcasts 75 hours per week; National Public Radio station WVIK broadcasts 24 hours per day. *Surrounding community:* Quad Cities metropolitan area population 350,000. Served by mass transit bus system; airport 3 miles from campus; passenger rail service 40 miles from campus.

Library Collections: 248,000 volumes. Online catalog. 127,000 microforms; 2,030 audiovisual materials; 1,330 current periodical subscriptions. Access to online information retrieval systems. Computer work stations available. Students have access to the Internet at no charge.

Most important holdings include Swenson Swedish Immigration Research Center (books, manuscripts, microfilms, and periodicals dealing with the development of Swedish Culture in the U.S. beginning in the 1860s, with some historical material about the Augustana Lutheran Synod); Hauberg Upper Mississippi Valley History Collection (local and Indian history from the middle 1800s to the middle 1900s); Charles XV Collection (materials on 18th-century French radicalism, including original source materials and books dating from 1789–1848).

Buildings and Grounds: Campus area 115 acres.

Chief Executive Officer: Dr. Steven Bahls, President.

Address admission inquiries to Martin Sauer, Dean of Admissions.

Aurora University

347 South Gladstone Avenue
Aurora, Illinois 60506-4892
Tel: (630) 892-6431   **E-mail:** admissions@admin.aurora.edu
Fax: (630) 844-5463   **Internet:** www.aurora.edu

Institution Description: Aurora University is a private, independent, non-profit liberal arts college founded by the Advent Christian Church in 1893. *Enrollment:* 3,326. *Degrees awarded:* Baccalaureate, master's, doctorate.
Member of the consortium Council of West Suburban Colleges.

Accreditation: *Regional:* NCA. *Professional:* business, nursing, nursing education, recreation and leisure services, social work

History: Established as Mendota College and offered first instruction at postsecondary level 1893; awarded first degree (baccalaureate) 1894; chartered 1899; adopted name Aurora College and moved to present location 1912. Changed name to Aurora University in January, 1985.

Institutional Structure: *Governing board:* Aurora University Board of Directors. Extrainstitutional representation: 34 directors; institutional representation: president of the university, 1 full-time faculty member, president of student association, and president of alumni association. *Composition of institution:* president and four vice presidents (academic affairs, finance, development), Academic affairs headed by provost and six deans.

Calendar: Semesters. Academic year early Sept. to late May. Freshmen admitted Sept., Nov., Jan., Mar., May, June. Degrees conferred May, Aug. Formal commencement May. Summer session from late May to mid-Aug.

Characteristics of Freshmen: 1,650 applicants (661 men, 989 women). 83% of applicants admitted. 33.5% of admitted students enrolled full-time.
6% (15 students) submitted SAT scores; 94% (279 students) submitted ACT scores. *25th percentile:* SAT I Verbal 470, SAT I Math 460; ACT Composite 19, ACT English 18, ACT Math 18. *75th percentile:* SAT I Verbal 540, SAT I Math 580; ACT Composite 23, ACT English 23, ACT Math 23.
46% of entering freshmen expected to graduate within 5 years. 85% of freshmen from Illinois. Freshmen from 5 states.

Admission: Rolling admissions plan. For fall acceptance, apply as early as end of junior year in secondary school, but not later than Aug. 31 of year of enrollment. *Requirements:* Either graduation from an accredited secondary school or GED. Minimum GPA 2.0. Lowest acceptable secondary school class standing 50th percentile. Consideration may be given students with lower GPA and class standing. *Entrance tests:* College Board SAT or ACT composite. *For transfer students:* 2.0 GPA; from 4-year accredited institution 86 semester hours maximum transfer credit; from 2-year accredited institution and for correspondence/extension students 60 hours.
College credit and advanced placement for postsecondary-level work completed in secondary school. College credit for extrainstitutional learning on the basis of ACE *2006 Guide to the Evaluation of Educational Experiences in the Armed Services* and portfolio assessment. Tutoring available. Noncredit developmental courses offered during regular academic year.

Degree Requirements: 120 semester hours; 2.0 GPA in the 40 courses counted toward graduation; 3 terms in residence; communications requirement; distribution requirements.
Fulfillment of some degree requirements and exemption from some beginning courses possible by passing College Board CLEP, APP, or other standardized tests. LEAP program provides up to 30 semester hours credit for prior learning. *Grading system:* A–F; pass-fail; withdraw (deadline after which pass-fail is appended to withdraw).

Distinctive Educational Programs: *For undergraduates:* Accelerated degree programs. Cooperative programs in medical technology, nursing with area hospitals. Baccalaureate completion program for registered nurses. Interdepartmental/interdisciplinary programs in computer science and business, environmental science, humanities. Facilities and programs for independent research, including honors programs, individual majors. Study abroad through programs offered by other institutions. *Available to all students:* Work-experience programs. Evening classes. Interdepartmental/interdisciplinary program in criminal justice management.

Degrees Conferred: 323 *baccalaureate*; 911 *master's*; 11 *doctorate*. Bachelor's degrees awarded in to five disciplines: business, management, marketing, and related support services 89; education 55; health professions and related clinical sciences 44; psychology 23; public administration and social service professions 22.

Fees and Other Expenses: *Full-time tuition per academic year 2004–05:* $14,750 undergraduate; contact the university for current graduate tuition. *Books and supplies:* $900. *Room and board per academic year:* $6,541.
Institution has a Program Participation Agreement with the U.S. Department of Education for eligible students to receive Pell Grants and other federal aid.

Financial aid to full-time, first-time undergraduate students: 34% received federal grants averaging $2,629; 48% state/local grants averaging $4,109; 98% institutional grants averaging $7,083; 71% loans averaging $3,609.

Departments and Teaching Staff: Accounting *professors* 0, *associate professors* 1, *assistant professors* 0, *instructors* 1, *part-time teachers* 2; criminal justice 1, 0, 0, 0, 4; communications 3, 1, 1, 0, 2; computer science 0, 0, 2, 2, 1; economics and business 1, 0, 2, 4, 4; education 0, 1, 4, 1, 10; English 3, 0, 1, 0, 0; history 1, 0, 0, 0, 1; mathematics 0, 2, 0, 1, 0; natural science 4, 2, 0, 0, 2; nursing 1, 2, 2, 7, 6; philosophy 1, 0, 0, 0, 0; physical education 0, 4, 0, 2, 1; political science 1, 0, 0, 0, 2; psychology 1, 1, 2, 0, 3; recreation administration 0, 1, 1, 1, 2; religion 1, 0, 0, 0, 0; sociology 0, 0, 1, 0, 1; Spanish 0, 0, 0, 1, 0; social work 3, 2, 5, 6, 4.

Total instructional faculty: 130. Degrees held by full-time faculty: master's 46%, doctorate 54%.

Enrollment: Total enrollment 3,326. Undergraduate 1,719 (34.3% men, 65.7% women).

Characteristics of Student Body: *Ethnic/racial makeup:* Black non-Hispanic: 13.7%; American Indian or Alaska Native: .2%; Asian or Pacific Islander: 2.3%; Hispanic: 12.4%; White non-Hispanic: 70.8%; unknown .5%.

International Students: 17 undergraduate nonresident aliens enrolled 2004. Students from Asia, Latin America, Canada. No programs available for students whose native language is not English. No financial aid specifically designated for international students.

Student Life: On-campus residence halls house 28% of student body. Dormitories for men only constitute 50% of such space, for women only 50%. Fraternities and sororities available. *Intercollegiate athletics:* men only: baseball, basketball, cross-country running, football, golf, soccer, tennis; women only: basketball, softball, tennis, volleyball. *Special regulations:* Cars permitted without restrictions. Quiet hours from 7pm to 10pm weekdays. Residence hall visitation from noon to midnight Sun.–Thurs., noon to 2am Fri. and Sat. *Special services:* Learning Resources Center, medical services. *Student publications: Borealis*, a biweekly newspaper; *Pharos*, a yearbook; *Wings in the Dawn*, an annual literary magazine. *Surrounding community:* Aurora population 117,000. Chicago, 40 miles from campus, is nearest metropolitan area. Served by mass transit bus system; passenger rail service 2 miles from campus.

Library Collections: 105,000 volumes. 46,000 microforms; 11,000 audiovisual materials; 718 current periodical subscriptions. Online catalog. Students have access to online information retrieval services and the Internet.

Most important holdings include Jenks Collection of Adventual Materials; Prouty Shakespeare Collection; University Archives.

Buildings and Grounds: Campus area 26 acres.

Chief Executive Officer: Dr. Rebecca L. Sherrick, President.

Address admission inquiries Dr. Carol Dunn, Vice President for Enrollment.

Barat College of DePaul University

700 East Westleigh Road

Lake Forest, Illinois 60045-3263

Tel: (847) 234-3000   **E-mail:** admissions@barat.edu

Fax: (847) 234-6300   **Internet:** www.barat.edu

Institution Description: Barat College of DePaul University is a private college in the Catholic tradition. *Enrollment:* 636. *Degrees awarded:* Baccalaureate, master's.

Accreditation: *Regional:* NCA.

History: Established as Barat College of the Sacred Heart, chartered, and offered first instruction at postsecondary level 1858; moved from Chicago to Lake Forest 1904; offered baccalaureate starting 1918; first degree (baccalaureate) awarded 1920; present name adopted 1969. *See* Helen Condon, *75th Anniversary Report* (Lake Forest: Barat College, 1979) for further information.

Institutional Structure: *Governing board:* Board of Trustees. Extrainstitutional representation: 31 trustees; institutional representation: 1 administrator, 1 full-time faculty member, 5 representatives of the Religious of the Sacred Heart; 8 alumnae, 41 voting. *Composition of institution:* Administrators 2 men / 3 women. Academic affairs headed by assistant vice president for academic affairs. Management/business/finances directed by treasurer. Full-time instructional faculty 35. Academic governance body, Faculty Assembly, meets an average of 10 times per year.

Calendar: Semesters. Academic year Sept. to May. Freshmen admitted June, Sept., Jan. Degrees conferred Dec., May, Aug. Formal commencement May. Two summer sessions from mid-May to mid-Aug.

Characteristics of Freshmen: 70% of applicants accepted. 30% of accepted applicants enrolled.

Average secondary school rank of freshmen men 56th percentile, women 45th percentile, class 48th percentile. Mean ACT composite class score 21. 30 National Merit Scholars.

70% of entering freshmen expected to graduate within 5 years. 76% of freshmen from Illinois. Freshmen from 14 states and 3 foreign countries.

Admission: Rolling admissions plan. For fall acceptance, apply as early as Sept. of previous year. Early acceptance available. *Requirements:* Official transcripts from accredited secondary school or GED. Minimum GPA 2.5. *Entrance tests:* College Board SAT or ACT composite. *For transfer students:* 2.5 minimum GPA; from 2-year institution 60 hours maximum transfer credit, from 4-year institution 75 hours.

College credit for postsecondary-level work completed in secondary school, for College Board CLEP, and for extrainstitutional learning on basis of ACE *2006 Guide to the Evaluation of Educational Experiences in the Armed Services*, portfolio, and faculty assessments.

Tutoring available. Developmental courses offered in summer session and regular academic year; credit given.

Degree Requirements: 120 credit hours; 2.0 GPA; first 90 or final 45 hours in residence; core requirements; 75 credits maximum accepted in transfer. culminating exercise prescribed by major department. Fulfillment of some degree requirements possible by passing College Board CLEP, AP. *Grading system:* A–F; pass-fail; withdraw (carries time limit).

Distinctive Educational Programs: Work-experience program. Flexible meeting places and schedules, including weekend and evening classes. Interdepartmental/interdisciplinary programs in art therapy, interdisciplinary science, international studies, communication arts, management and business/psychology, human resources emphasis and human behavior. Facilities and programs for independent research, including individual majors and tutorials. Individually designed interdisciplinary majors. Double majors. Study abroad in England, France, Italy. Cross-registration with Lake Forest College. Learning Opportunities Center offers special program to limited number of students with diagnosed learning disabilities.

Degrees Conferred: 203 *baccalaureate:* biological and life 39, business 211, communications 3, computer and information sciences 4, education 16, fine and applied arts 12, health professions 14, letters 9, mathematics 4, physical sciences 2, psychology 12, social sciences 16.

Fees and Other Expenses: *Full-time tuition per academic year:* Contact the college for current tuition, fees, and other expenses.

Financial Aid: Barat College offers a direct lending program. Aid from institutionally generated funds is provided on the basis of academic merit, financial need. Institution has a Program Participation Agreement with the U.S. Department of Education for eligible students to receive Pell Grants and other federal aid.

Departments and Teaching Staff: *Total full-time instructional faculty:* 35. Degrees held by full-time faculty: doctorate 63%, master's 17%, professional 2%. 63% hold terminal degrees. *Faculty development:* $18,500 grants for research. 1 faculty member awarded a sabbatical 1998–99.

Enrollment: Total enrollment 636.

Student Life: On-campus residence halls house 32% of student body. *Student activities:* basketball and volleyball teams; Student Government; various clubs and activities. *Special regulations:* Cars permitted without restrictions. *Special services:* Counseling and medical services, career planning and placement. *Student publications: Journaux*, school newspaper; *Ecrivez*, an annual literary magazine; yearbook. *Surrounding community:* Lake Forest population 15,250. Chicago, 30 miles from campus, is nearest metropolitan area. Served by mass transit systems; airport 24 miles from campus; passenger rail service 5 miles from campus.

Publications: *Communique*, a magazine for the alumni and friends of Barat College.

Library Collections: 120,000 volumes. 10,000 microforms; 1,500 audiovisual materials; 264 current periodical subscriptions. 567 recordings. Access to online information retrieval systems. Students have access to the Internet at no charge.

Most important holdings include Middle English Literature Collection; 19th-century women's rights periodicals; Roman Catholic Theology and Philosophy of Religion collection.

Buildings and Grounds: Campus area 31 acres.

Chief Executive Officer: Dr. Lucy Morros, President.

Address admission inquiries to Director of Admissions.

Benedictine University

5700 College Road
Lisle, Illinois 60532
Tel: (630) 829-6090   **E-mail:** admissions@ben.edu
Fax: (630) 960-1126   **Internet:** www.ben.edu

Institution Description: Benedictine University, formerly named Illinois Benedictine College, is a private college affiliated with the Roman Catholic Church. *Enrollment:* 3,232. *Degrees awarded:* Baccalaureate, master's.

Member of Council of West Suburban Colleges and West Suburban Regional Academic Consortium.

Accreditation: *Regional:* NCA. *Professional:* dietetics, nursing

History: Established by the Benedictine monks of Saint Procopius Abbey as Saint Procopius College 1887; chartered and offered first instruction at postsecondary level 1890; awarded first degree (baccalaureate) 1915; became Illinois Benedictine College 1971; adopted present name 1996.

Institutional Structure: *Governing board:* Board of Trustees. Extrainstitutional representation: 34 trustees; institutional representation: president of the college, 1 full-time instructional faculty member, chair of alumni association. 5 ex officio. All voting. *Composition of institution:* Administrators 7 men / 2 women. Full-time instructional faculty 88. Professional administrative staff 56 men / 43 women.

Calendar: Semesters. Academic year Aug. to May. Formal commencement May. Summer session of 2 terms.

Characteristics of Freshmen: 952 applicants (454 men, 498 women). 732.8% of applicants admitted. 43.1% of admitted students enrolled full-time.

10% (30 students) submitted SAT scores; 99% (30 students) submitted ACT scores. *25th percentile:* ACT Composite 20, ACT English 20, ACT Math 20. *75th percentile:* ACT Composite 26, ACT English 27, ACT Math 27.

55% of freshmen class expected to graduate within 5 years. 96% of freshmen from Illinois. Freshmen from 6 states.

Admission: Rolling admissions plan. For fall acceptance, apply as early as beginning of senior year. *Requirements:* Either graduation from secondary school with 16 units which must include 4 English, 2 foreign language, 1 algebra, 1 geometry, 1 history, 1 laboratory science; or GED. Lowest acceptable secondary school class standing 50th percentile. *Entrance tests:* College Board SAT or ACT composite (minimum score 21). *For transfer students:* Minimum grade average of C; from 4-year accredited institution, maximum transfer credit limited only by residence requirement; from 2-year accredited institution 60 hours. Persons not meeting these standards for admission may be considered by the Admissions Committee.

Degree Requirements: 120 credit hours; 2.0 GPA; last 45 hours in residence; liberal education core curriculum. Fulfillment of some degree requirements and exemption from some beginning courses possible by passing College Board CLEP. *Grading system:* A–F; withdraw.

Distinctive Educational Programs: *For undergraduate students:* Interdisciplinary programs in business and the arts and humanities. Certificate program for managers. *For graduate students:* Interdisciplinary master's program in management, computer sciences, and exercise physiology. Study abroad: students can earn 12–15 semester hours during a semester abroad. Coursework can be combined with an internship or and entire semester can be internship only. Students have studied in England, Austria, Germany, France, Greece, Spain, Japan, Mexico, Costa Rica, and China. There are study abroad opportunities in almost every country.

Degrees Conferred: 32 *associate;* 428 *baccalaureate;* 232 *master's;* 2 *doctorate.* Bachelor's degrees awarded in top five disciplines: business, management, marketing, and related support services 155; biological and biomedical sciences 41; health professions and related clinical sciences 39; education 37; psychology 30.

Fees and Other Expenses: *Full-time tuition per academic year 2004–05:* $17,800 undergraduate; graduate tuition charged per credit hour. *Books and supplies:* $840. *Room and board per academic year:* $6,390.

Financial Aid: Aid from institutionally generated funds is provided on the basis of academic merit, financial need. Institution has a Program Participation Agreement with the U.S. Department of Education for eligible students to receive Pell Grants and other federal aid.

Financial aid to full-time, first-time undergraduate students: 22% received federal grants averaging $4,622; 39% state/local grants averaging $3,961; 96% institutional grants averaging $7,216; 49% loans averaging $8,120.

Departments and Teaching Staff: *Professors* 43, *associate professors* 22, *assistant professors* 20, *instructors* 3, *part-time faculty* 128. *Total instructional faculty:* 130. Student-to-faculty ratio: 14:1. Degrees held by full-time faculty: doctorate 80%, baccalaureate 100%.

Enrollment: Total enrollment 3,232. Undergraduate 2,148 (37.7% men, 62.3% women).

Characteristics of Student Body: *Ethnic/racial makeup:* Black non-Hispanic: 9.2%; American Indian or Alaska Native: .2%; Asian or Pacific Islander: 2.8%; Hispanic: 7.2%; White non-Hispanic: 48.6%; unknown: 21%.

International Students: 21 nonresident aliens enrolled fall 2004. Programs available to aid students whose native language is not English: Social, cultural. English as a Second Language Program. No financial aid specifically designated international students.

Student Life: On-campus residence halls house 33% of undergraduate student body. *Intercollegiate athletics:* men only: baseball, basketball, cross-country, football, golf, soccer, swimming, track; women only: basketball, cross-country, golf, soccer, softball, swimming, tennis, track, volleyball. *Student publications, television: Candor,* a weekly student newspaper; *Black on White,* a literary journal. Broadcast club video productions for cable. *Surrounding community:* Suburban adjoining Lisle, population 19,000, and Naperville, population 95,000, in the business corridor 25 miles west of Chicago.

Library Collections: 176,450 volumes. 34,500 government documents; 331,148 microforms; 5,700 audiovisual materials; 7,720 periodical subscriptions. Online catalog. Access to online information retrieval systems and the Internet.

Most important holdings include Lincoln Collection; international marketing materials; federal and Illinois documents depository collections.

Buildings and Grounds: Campus area 108 acres.

Chief Executive Officer: Dr. Rev. Dismas B. Calcic, O.S.B, President.

Address admission inquiries to Karl Gibbons, Director of Admissions.

Blackburn College

700 College Avenue
Carlinville, Illinois 62626-1498
Tel: (217) 854-3231   **E-mail:** admit@blackburn.edu
Fax: (217) 854-3713   **Internet:** www.blackburn.edu

Institution Description: Blackburn College is a private, independent, nonprofit institution. *Enrollment:* 594. *Degrees awarded:* Baccalaureate, master's.

Member of the consortium The Metro East St. Louis Regional Council on Inter-Institutional Cooperation.

Accreditation: *Regional:* NCA.

History: Established 1837; chartered as Blackburn Theological Seminary 1857; offered first instruction at postsecondary level 1864; awarded first degree (baccalaureate) 1868; adopted present name 1869; added associate degree-granting program 1916; abandoned baccalaureate 1918; reinstituted 4 year-curriculum 1947.

Institutional Structure: *Governing board:* Board of Trustees. Representation: 24 trustees (including 10 alumni). 1 ex officio. 24 voting. *Composition of institution:* Administrators 6 men. Academic affairs headed by provost and dean of the college. Management/business/finances directed by business manager-treasurer. Full-time instructional faculty 35. Academic governance body, the All College Assembly, meets an average of 9 times per year.

Calendar: Semesters. Academic year early Sept. to late May. Freshmen admitted Sept., Jan. Degrees conferred May, Oct. Formal commencement May. No summer session.

Characteristics of Freshmen: 916 applicants (521 men, 395 women). 56.1% of applicants admitted. 34.8% of admitted students enrolled full-time.

1% (3 students) submitted SAT scores; 97% (175 students) submitted ACT scores. *25th percentile:* SAT I Verbal 475, SAT I Math 475; ACT Composite 18, ACT English 18, ACT Math 18. *75th percentile:* SAT I Verbal 560, SAT I Math 560; ACT Composite 24, ACT English 24, ACT Math 24. 50% entering freshmen expected to graduate within 5 years. 78% of freshmen from Illinois. Freshmen from 10 states and 3 foreign countries.

Admission: Rolling admissions plan. For fall acceptance, apply as early as end of junior year (when grades available), but not later than July 15 of year of enrollment. Early acceptance available. *Requirements:* Either evidence of ability to do college work or GED. 3–4 secondary school units English, 3–4 social sciences, 2–3 mathematics, 2–3 natural sciences recommended. *Entrance tests:* College Board SAT or ACT composite. *For transfer students:* 2.0 minimum GPA; maximum transfer credit limited only by residence requirement.

College credit and advanced placement for postsecondary-level work completed in secondary school. Tutoring available. Developmental courses offered during regular academic year; credit given.

Degree Requirements: 122 credit hours; 2.0 GPA; last 2 semesters in residence; distribution requirements.

Fulfillment of some degree requirements and exemption from some beginning courses possible by passing College Board CLEP, APP, or departmental examinations. *Grading system:* A–F; pass-fail; withdraw (carries time limit; deadline after which pass-fail is appended to withdraw).

Distinctive Educational Programs: Blackburn College Work Program (each resident college student works 15 hours per week for the college. By performing all jobs on campus related to the operation of the physical plant, students partially offset the cost of room and board by receiving a Work Grant). Facilities and programs for independent research, including individual majors, tutorials. Study abroad in Mexico. Government internships in Washington (DC) through American University and the Washington Center for Learning Alternatives.

Degrees Conferred: 124 *baccalaureate:* degrees awarded in top five disciplines: education 43; business, management, marketing, and related support services 31; biological and biomedical sciences 10; computer and information sciences and support services 8; parks, recreation, leisure, and fitness studies 7.

Fees and Other Expenses: *Full-time tuition per academic year 2004–05:* $14,600. *Room and board per academic year:* $3,580. *Books and supplies:* $700.

Financial Aid: Aid from institutionally generated funds is provided on the basis of academic merit, financial need. Institution has a Program Participation Agreement with the U.S. Department of Education for eligible students to receive Pell Grants and other federal aid.

Financial aid to full-time, first-time undergraduate students: 43% received federal grants averaging $3,078; 56% state/local grants averaging $4,178; 95% institutional grants averaging $4,755; 72% received loans averaging $2,956.

Departments and Teaching Staff: Art *professors* 2, *part-time faculty* 1; biology 3, 0; business administration 2, 0; chemistry/physics 2, 0; economics 2, 0; education 2, 2; English 3, 3; history 2, 0; mathematics/computer science 5, 1; modern language 2, 1; music 2, 3; philosophy and religion 1, 1; physical education 2, 3; political science 2, 0; psychology 2, 1; speech/communications 1, 1.

Total instructional faculty: 52. Degrees held by full-time faculty: doctorate 75%, master's 23%, baccalaureate 3%. 80% hold terminal degrees.

Enrollment: Total enrollment 594 (44.4% men, 55.6% women).

Characteristics of Student Body: *Ethnic/racial makeup:* Black non-Hispanic: 8.2%; American Indian or Alaska Native: .5%; Asian or Pacific Islander: .5%; Hispanic: 1.2%; White non-Hispanic: 82.8%; unknown: 4%.

International Students: 16 nonresident aliens enrolled fall 2004. No programs available to aid students whose native language is not English. Financial aid specifically designated for international students: Variable number of scholarships available annually.

Student Life: On-campus residence halls house 95% of student body. Residence halls for men constitute 12% of such space, for women 35%, for both sexes 53%. *Intercollegiate athletics:* men only: basketball, baseball, cross-country, golf, soccer, swimming, track and field; women only: badminton, basketball, cross-country, track and field, tennis, volleyball. *Special regulations:* Cars must be registered. Quiet hours and visitation policies set by each residence hall. *Student publications: Beaver Tales,* a yearbook; *The Burnian,* a newspaper. *Surrounding community:* Carlinville population 5,500. Springfield, 45 miles from campus, is nearest metropolitan area. Served by passenger rail service 1.5 miles from campus.

Library Collections: 83,000 volumes. 35,000 microforms; 390 periodical subscriptions; 4,500 recordings/tapes. Students have access to online information retrieval services.

Most important holdings include collections on botany; 18th-century literature; religion; Blackburn College Archives.

Buildings and Grounds: Campus area 80 acres.

Chief Executive Officer: Dr. Miriam R. Pride, President.

Address admission inquiries to John Malin, Director of Enrollment Management.

Bradley University

1501 West Bradley Avenue
Peoria, Illinois 61625

Tel: (309) 676-7611   **E-mail:** admissions@bradley.edu
Fax: not available   **Internet:** www.bradley.edu

Institution Description: Bradley University is a private, independent, non-profit institution. *Enrollment:* 5,861. *Degrees awarded:* Baccalaureate, master's, doctorate.

Accreditation: *Regional:* NCA. *Professional:* accounting, art, business, construction education, counseling, engineering, music, nurse anesthesia education, nursing, physical therapy, social work, teacher education, theatre

History: Established and incorporated as Bradley Polytechnic Institute, and offered first instruction at postsecondary level 1897; awarded first degree (baccalaureate) 1920; adopted present name 1946. *See* Louis A. R. Yates, *A Proud*

Heritage: Bradley's History 1897–1972 (Peoria: Observer Press, 1974) for further information.

Institutional Structure: *Governing board:* Board of Trustees. Extrainstitutional representation: 31 trustees; institutional representation: 4 administrators, 1 faculty member, 1 student. 2 ex officio. 31 voting. *Composition of institution:* administrators 22 men / 5 women. Academic affairs headed by provost and vice president for academic affairs. Management/business/finances directed by vice president for business affairs. Total instructional faculty 341. Academic governance body, Bradley University Senate, meets an average of 8 times per year.

Calendar: Semesters. Academic year Aug. to May. Freshmen admitted Aug., Jan., June, July. Degrees conferred and formal commencements May, Dec. Summer session of 3 terms from May to Aug.

Characteristics of Freshmen: 64% of applicants admitted. 27.5% of admitted students enrolled full-time.

15% (152 students) submitted SAT scores; 95% (968 students) submitted ACT scores. *25th percentile:* SAT Verbal 540, SAT Math 550; ACT Composite 32, ACT English 22, ACT Math 22. *75th percentile:* SAT Verbal 640, SAT Math 570; ACT Composite 28, ACT English 28, ACT Math 28.

69% of entering freshmen expected to graduate within 5 years. 85% of freshmen from Illinois. Freshmen from 31 states and 7 foreign countries.

Admission: Rolling admissions plan. For fall acceptance, apply as early as Aug. 1 of year prior to enrollment. *Requirements:* Either graduation from secondary school with 3 units in English, 2 college preparatory mathematics, 2 social studies, 1 laboratory science; or GED. Additional requirements vary according to program. Undergraduate admission is based on a review of a student's academic and extracurricular records. *Entrance tests:* College Board SAT or ACT composite. For foreign students TOEFL. *For transfer students:* 2.0 minimum GPA, maximum transfer credit limited only by residence requirement; from 2-year accredited institution 66 hours.

College credit and advanced placement for postsecondary-level work completed in secondary school.

Degree Requirements: 124 credit hours; 2.0 GPA; 30 semester hours in residence; general education requirements. *For B.A.:* 2 years college-level foreign language or equivalent. *For B.S.* 6 hours of courses selected from natural and physical science, mathematics, computer science, statistics or quantitative methods in addition to University basic skills general education requirements.

Fulfillment of some degree requirements and exemption from some beginning courses possible by passing departmental examinations, College Board CLEP, AP. *Grading system:* A–F; pass-fail; withdraw.

Distinctive Educational Programs: Internships. Evening classes. Cooperative program in administration of criminal justice with Illinois Central College. Cooperative education. Special facilities for using telecommunications in the classroom. Interdisciplinary programs in environmental science, international business, social services. Facilities and programs for independent research, including individual majors, tutorials. Study abroad in Africa, Austria, Czechoslovakia, Denmark, England, France, Germany, Hong Kong, Hungary, Italy, Japan, Jerusalem, Malta, Mexico, Russia, Scotland, Spain, Sweden, Wales. *Other distinctive programs:* Continuing education, honors program, international business, Residence Hall of the Future (computerized dormitory facilities). Special degree completion program for place-bound students. Center for Student Leadership. Academic Exploration Program.

ROTC: Army in cooperation with Illinois State University.

Degrees Conferred: 1,117 *baccalaureate* (B), 276 *master's* (M): biological/life sciences 23 (B); business/marketing 283 (B), 100 (M); communications/communication technologies 173 (B); computer and information sciences 26 (B), 32 (M); education 109 (B), 68 (M); engineering and engineering technologies 132 (B), 57 (M); English 23 (B), 5 (M); foreign languages and literature 7 (B); health professions and related sciences 80 (B), 26 (M); home economics and vocational home economics 15 (B); liberal arts/general studies 2 (B), 4 (M); mathematics 10 (B); natural resources/environmental science 3 (B); philosophy/religion/theology 3 (M); physical sciences 12 (B); protective services/public administration 29 (B); psychology 68 (B); social sciences and history 56 (B); visual and performing arts 63 (B), 4 (M).

Fees and Other Expenses: *Full-time tuition per academic year 2004–05:* undergraduate $17,600, graduate $10,170. *Required fees:* $130. *Room and board per academic year:* $6,150.

Financial Aid: Bradley University has a direct lending program. Aid from institutionally generated funds is provided on the basis of academic merit, financial need, athletic ability, other criteria. Institution has a Program Participation Agreement with the U.S. Department of Education for eligible students to receive Pell Grants and other federal aid.

Financial aid to full-time, first-time undergraduate students: need-based scholarships/grants totaling $30,121,371, self-help $14,069,974, parent loans $1,555,239, tuition waivers $1,000,302, athletic awards $782,874; non-need-based scholarships/grants totaling $6,635,097, self-help $5,780,437, parent loans $4,452,437, tuition waivers $985,000, athletic awards $1,024,375.

Departments and Teaching Staff: *Professors* 93, *associate professors* 115, *assistant professors* 83, *instructors* 46, *part-time faculty* 195. *Total instructional faculty:* 532 (full-time 337, part-time 195; women 212, men 320; members of minority groups 52). Total faculty with doctorate, first-professional, or other terminal degree: 278. Student-to-faculty ratio: 14:1. 19 faculty members awarded sabbaticals 2004–05.

Enrollment: Total enrollment 5,861. Undergraduate full-time 2,252 men / 2,586 women, part-time 104m / 145w; graduate full-time 108m / 107w, part-time 279m / 260w.

Characteristics of Student Body: *Ethnic and racial makeup:* number of Black non-Hispanic: 292; American Indian or Alaska Native: 10; Asian or Pacific Islander: 148; Hispanic: 107; White non-Hispanic: 4,464; unknown: 335. *Age distribution:* under 18: 28; 18–19: 2,033; 20–21: 2,143; 22–24: 671; 25–29: 145; 30–34: 55; 35–39: 23; 40–49: 35.

International Students: 273 nonresident aliens enrolled fall 2004. 20 students from Europe, 213 Asia, 8 Central and South America, 20 Africa, 5 Canada, 3 Australia, 2 other. No programs available to aid students whose native language is not English. No financial aid specifically designated for international

Student Life: On-campus residence halls house 42% of undergraduate student body. *Intercollegiate athletics:* men only: baseball, basketball, golf, tennis, track, cross-country, soccer; women only: basketball, softball, tennis, track, cross-country, golf, volleyball. *Special regulations:* Registered cars permitted without restrictions; fee charged. Quiet hours. *Special services:* Academic support services, medical and counseling services. *Student publications, radio, television: Scout,* a weekly newspaper; two literary magazines. Radio station WCBU-FM broadcasts 24 hours per day, every day. T.V. station WTVP broadcasts over 100 hours per week. *Surrounding community:* Peoria population 115,000. Chicago (IL) and St. Louis (MO) 150 miles from campus, are nearest metropolitan areas. Served by mass transit bus system, airport 5 miles from campus, bus service to Chicago and St. Louis from campus.

Library Collections: 537,995 volumes including bound books, serial backfiles, electronic documents, and government documents not in separate collections. Online catalog. Current serial subscriptions: 1m488 paper, 236 microform, 1,000 via electronic access. 7,637 CD-ROMs. 141 computer work stations. Students have access to the Internet at no charge. Total budget for books, periodicals, audiovisual materials, microforms 2004–05: $1,047,882.

Most important holdings include Charles H. Bennett Collection (industrial arts history); Chase Collection (Bishop Philander Chase and Jubilee College); Peoria Historical Society Library (Central Illinois Historical Society).

Chief Executive Officer: Dr. David Brosky, President.

Address admission inquiries to Angela Roberson, Associate Provost for Enrollment Management; graduate inquiries to Dr. Robert Bolla, Dean of the Graduate School.

Chicago School of Professional Psychology

325 North Wells Street
Chicago, Illinois 60610
Tel: (312) 786-9443   **E-mail:** admission@csopp.edu
Fax: (312) 322-3273   **Internet:** www.csopp.edu

Institution Description: The Chicago School of Professional Psychology is a private institution offering graduate study only. *Enrollment:* 845. *Degrees awarded:* Doctorate.

Accreditation: *Regional:* NCA. *Professional:* clinical psychology

Calendar: Semesters. Academic year Aug. to July.

Admission: *Requirements:* baccalaureate degree from an accredited institution; 18 hours of psychology coursework including abnormal psychology, statistics, theories of personality; 3 letters of recommendation; official transcripts; official copies of GRE scores.

Degree Requirements: Residency requirement which may be satisfied by completion of two consecutive regular semester of full-time study (12 credits or more) or completion of 30 credit hours within one 12-month period including summer session.

Degrees Conferred: 28 *doctorate:* psychology.

Fees and Other Expenses: *Full-time tuition per academic year 2004–05:* $21,900.

Financial Aid: Aid from institutionally generated funds is provided on the basis of academic merit, financial need. Institution has a Program Participation Agreement with the U.S. Department of Education for eligible students to receive Pell Grants and other federal aid.

Departments and Teaching Staff: *Professors* 1, *associate professors* 13, *assistant professors* 3, *part-time faculty* 36. *Total instructional faculty:* 53. Student-to-faculty ratio: 12:1. Degrees held by full-time faculty: doctorate 100%.

Enrollment: Total enrollment 845 (19.2% men, 80.8% women).

Characteristics of Student Body: *Ethnic/racial makeup:* Black non-Hispanic: 10.2%; Asian or Pacific Islander: 5.3%; American Indian or Alaska Native .1%; Hispanic: 6.5%; White non-Hispanic: 70.2%.

International Students: No programs available to aid students whose native language is not English. No financial aid specifically designated for international students.

Library Collections: 15,000 volumes including bound books, serial backfiles, electronic documents, and government documents not in separate collections. Card catalog. Current serial subscriptions: 149 paper, 123 microform, fulltext titles available through OCLC and PREQUEST. 390 recordings; 5 CD-ROMs. Computer work stations available. Students have access to the Internet at no charge.

Most important special holdings in clinical psychology, psychotherapy, and cross-cultural studies and counseling; collective works of C.G. Jung.

Chief Executive Officer: Dr. Michael Horowitz, President.

Address admission inquiries to Magdelen Kellogg, Director of Admissions.

Chicago State University

9501 South King Drive
Chicago, Illinois 60629-1598
Tel: (773) 995-2000   **E-mail:** ug-admissions@csu.edu
Fax: (773) 995-3584   **Internet:** www.csu.edu

Institution Description: Chicago State University is an urban, nonresidential state institution. *Enrollment:* 6,835. *Degrees awarded:* Baccalaureate, master's.

Academic offerings subject to approval by statewide coordinating bodies. Budget subject to approval by state governing board. Member of Chicago Consortium of Colleges and Universities.

Accreditation: *Regional:* NCA. *Professional:* business, counseling, health information administration, music, nursing, occupational therapy, social work, teacher education

History: Established as Cook County Normal School 1867; changed name to Chicago Normal School 1896, to Chicago Teachers College 1910, to Chicago Normal School 1913; changed name to Chicago Teachers College 1938; awarded first degree (baccalaureate) 1939; changed name to Illinois Teachers College Chicago-South 1965, to Chicago State College 1967; adopted present name 1971. *See* Edmund Kearney and E. Maynard Moore, *A History: Chicago State University 1867–1979* (Chicago: Chicago State University, 1979) for further information.

Institutional Structure: *Governing board:* Illinois Board of Governors of State Colleges and Universities. Extrainstitutional representation: 14 members, including 5 students (1 from each university under board jurisdiction). 9 voting. *Composition of institution:* Administrators 103 men / 80 women. University headed by president and vice presidents for academic affairs (provost), administrative affairs, institutional advancement. Full-time instructional faculty 299. Academic governance body, Faculty Senate, meets an average of 10 times per year. *Faculty representation:* Faculty served by collective bargaining agent affiliated with AFT.

Calendar: Semesters. Academic year Aug. to May. Freshmen admitted Aug., Jan., May, July. Degrees conferred May, June, Aug., Dec. Formal commencement July, Jan. Summer session from late May to late July.

Characteristics of Freshmen: 94% of applicants admitted. 14% of admitted students enrolled full-time.

Student scores in *25th percentile:* ACT Composite 17, ACT English 15, ACT Math 15. *75th percentile:* ACT Composite 19, ACT English 20, ACT Math 18.

89% of entering freshmen expected to graduate within five years. 94% of freshmen from Illinois. Freshmen from 16 states and 3 foreign countries.

Admission: Rolling admissions plan. For fall acceptance, apply as early as Oct. of previous year, but not later than July of year of enrollment. Early acceptance available. *Requirements:* Freshmen must score a minimum ACT Composite of 18 and a GPA of 2.5 on a 4 point scale in high school or GED score of 225. Students over 25 years of age are not required to submit ACT scores. *For transfer students:* Students transferring 24 or more semester hours should have a minimum GPA of 2.0. Those transferring with less than 30 hours must meet both freshman and transfer requirements. From two-year accredited institutions, 66 semester hours maximum transfer credit. Foreign students are required to submit TOEFL scores. Additional requirements for some programs.

College credit and advanced placement for postsecondary-level work completed in secondary school. College credit for extrainstitutional learning on basis of ACE *2006 Guide to the Evaluation of Educational Experiences in the Armed Services;* portfolio assessment. Tutoring available. Developmental and remedial courses offered throughout the school year.

Degree Requirements: 120 credit hours; 2.0 GPA; last 30 hours in residence. All students must pass proficiency examinations in reading and English and tests on or courses in U.S. and Illinois constitutions. Depending on their major, most students must pass proficiency examinations in mathematics. Students must successfully complete two semesters instruction in a foreign language.

Fulfillment of some degree requirements and exemption from some beginning courses possible by passing departmental examinations, College Board CLEP, APP, other standardized test. *Grading system:* A–F; pass-fail; withdraw.

Distinctive Educational Programs: *For undergraduates:* Work-experience programs. Interdisciplinary program in cultural studies. Facilities and programs for independent research, including honors programs, individual majors, tutorials. Institutionally sponsored study abroad in Germany and The Netherlands. *For graduate students:* Ed.D. in educational leadership, GIS graduate certificate program, M.F.A. in creative writing, master's in education, criminal justice, and computer science. *Available to all students:* Weekend and evening classes. Special facilities for using telecommunications in the classroom. *Other distinctive programs:* University Without Walls, an individualized degree-granting program for nontraditional students;. extension services offering continuing education programs.

ROTC: Army; Air Force offered in cooperation with Illinois Institute of Technology.

Degrees Conferred: 798 *baccalaureate;* 396 *master's.*

Fees and Other Expenses: *Full-time tuition per academic year 2004–05:* $5,633 undergraduate resident, $9,822 out-of-state; graduate resident $3,174; out-of-state $5,910. *Required fees:* $656. *Room and board per academic year:* $56,030.

Financial Aid: Aid from institutionally generated funds is awarded on the basis of academic merit, financial need. Institution has a Program Participation Agreement with the U.S. Department of Education for eligible students to receive Pell Grants and other federal aid.

Financial aid to full-time, first-time undergraduate students: need-based scholarships/grants totaling $17,225,904, self-help $9,253,501, non-need-based scholarships/grants totaling $2,678,273, self-help $5,482,049, parent loans $145,345, tuition waivers $958,357, athletic awards $739,241. *Graduate aid:* 7 students received federal and state-funded scholarships and grants totaling $9,886; 402 federal and state-funded loans totaling $3,418,460; 2 work-study jobs worth $4,000; 318 other fellowships and grants totaling $339,630; 1 research assistantship at $1,722.

Departments and Teaching Staff: *Professors* 75, *associate professors* 84, *assistant professors* 77, *instructors* 63, *part-time faculty* 77. *Total instructional faculty:* 876 (full-time 299, part-time 77; women 213, men 216; members of minority groups 259). Total faculty with doctorate, first-professional, or other terminal degree: 276. Student-to-faculty ratio: 18:1. *Faculty development:* $1,931,651 in grants for research. 8 faculty members awarded sabbaticals 2004–05.

Enrollment: Total enrollment 6,835. Undergraduate full-time 935 men / 2,301 women, part-time 380m / 1,251w; graduate full-time 110m / 244w, part-time 464m / 1,150w. *Transfer students:* in-state 385; from out-of-state 172.

Characteristics of Student Body: *Ethnic/racial makeup:* number of Black non-Hispanic: 4,215; American Indian or Alaska Native: 8; Asian or Pacific Islander: 21; Hispanic: 10; White non-Hispanic: 155; unknown: 130. *Age distribution:* under 31; 18: 18–19: 698; 20–21: 650; 22–24: 868; 25–29: 807; 30–34: 613; 35–39: 347; 40–49: 572; 50–64: 259; 65 and over: 22. 35% of student body attend summer sessions.

International Students: 31 nonresident aliens enrolled fall 2004. 7 students from Europe, 5 Asia, 2 Central and South America, 9 Africa, 3 Canada, 5 other. No programs available to aid students whose native language is not English. No financial aid specifically designated for international students.

Student Life: 360-bed residence hall. *Intercollegiate athletics:* NCAA Division I men's and women's basketball, cross-country, golf, tennis, track; women only: volleyball; men only: baseball. *Special services:* Learning Resources Center, child-care center, wellness center. *Student publications: Tempo,* a weekly newspaper; *Amandala,* a monthly library journal. *Surrounding community:* Chicago population over 3,000,000. Served by mass transit bus, rail systems; airport 15 miles from campus; passenger rail service 1 mile from campus.

Publications: *Illinois Schools Journal* (quarterly).

Library Collections: 420,676 volumes. Online catalog. Current serial subscriptions: paper 1,008; microform 618,816; via electronic access 14,000. 46 computer work stations. Students have access to the Internet at no charge.

Most important holdings include Schomburg Collection; Slavery Collection; Madhubuti Collections. Total 2004–05 budget for books and materials: $502,215.

Buildings and Grounds: Campus area 161 acres. *New buildings:* Library; Convocation/Performance Center; Conference Center; Outreach Center.

Chief Executive Officer: Dr. Elnora D. Daniel, President.

Address undergraduates inquiries to Ms. Addie Epps, Director of Admissions; graduate inquiries to to Dr. Anitra Ward, Director of Graduate Studies.

Chicago Theological Seminary

5757 South University Avenue
Chicago, Illinois 60637
Tel: (773) 752-5757 **E-mail:** admissions@ctschicago.edu
Fax: (773) 752-0905 **Internet:** www.ctschicago.edu

Institution Description: Chicago Theological Seminary is a seminary of the United Church of Christ which is committed to an ecumenical academic environment, and currently enrolls students from 22 Protestant as well as Roman Catholic, Jewish, Eastern Orthodox, and other traditions. *Enrollment:* 119. *Degrees awarded:* Master's, doctorate, first-professional.

Accreditation: *Regional:* NCA. *National:* ATS. *Professional:* theology

History: The seminary is was founded in 1855 and is the oldest institution of higher learning in Chicago. Students are prepared for ministry within the context of religious and social issues that affect the daily lives of all human beings.

Calendar: Semesters. Academic year Sept. to May.

Admission: *Requirements:* Bachelor of Arts degree or its equivalent.

Degree Requirements: Requirements vary by program; completion of prescribed curriculum.

Distinctive Educational Programs: Emphases in liberation theologies, Jungian psychology and spirituality, and Jewish-Christian studies. Dual degree programs in social work and counseling psychology. Cooperative programs in preaching and religious education.

Degrees Conferred: 6 *master's:* theology; 16 *doctorate:* theology; 21 *first-professional:* master of divinity.

Fees and Other Expenses: *Full-time tuition per academic year 2004–05:* $8,960. *Required fees:* $140. *Room and board per academic year:* $7,980.

Financial Aid: Aid from institutionally generated funds is provided on the basis of academic merit, financial need. *Graduate aid:* 58 students received federal and state-funded loans totaling $750,000 (ranging from $1,000 to $18,500); 19 received college-assigned jobs (nonteaching, nonresearch) totaling $63,000; 8 teaching assistantships at $4,500.

Departments and Teaching Staff: *Total instructional faculty:* 12 (full-time 12; women 3, men 9; member of minority groups 6). Total faculty with doctorate, first-professional, or other terminal degree: 12. Student-to-faculty ratio: 17:1. 4 faculty members awarded sabbaticals 2004–05.

Enrollment: Total enrollment 119. First-professional full-time 10 men / 12 women, part-time 27m / 41w; graduate full-time 26m / 23w, part-time 37m / 33w.

Characteristics of Student Body: *Ethnic/racial makeup:* Black non-Hispanic: 21.5%; Asian or Pacific Islander: 1.5%; White non-Hispanic: 61%. *Age distribution:* 22–24: 1.5%; 25–29: 5.4%; 30–34: 13.4%; 35–39: 16.3%; 40–49: 40.1%; 50–59: 20%; 60–and over: 3.3%.

International Students: 28 nonresident aliens enrolled fall 2004. No programs available to aid students whose native language is not English. No financial aid specifically designated for international students.

Student Life: Residence halls and apartments available. 6 student organizations focus on issues of racism, homophobia, sexism, and other peace and justice issues. Regular worship and social opportunities.

Publications: *Tower News; The Chicago Theological Seminary Register.*

Library Collections: 110,000 volumes. Card catalog. 2,500 microforms; 865 audiovisual materials; 129 current periodical subscriptions. 5 computer work stations. Students have access to the Internet at no charge.

Most important special collections include Congregational and Puritan history; religion and the human sciences, including sexuality; Jewish-Christian and Afro-American Studies.

Chief Executive Officer: Rev. Dr. Susan Brooks Thistlethwaite, President.
Address admission inquiries to Director of Admissions.

Columbia College Chicago

600 South Michigan Avenue
Chicago, Illinois 60605
Tel: (312) 663-1600 **E-mail:** admissions@colum.edu
Fax: (312) 344-8069 **Internet:** www.colum.edu

Institution Description: Columbia College is a private, independent, non-profit college. *Enrollment:* 10,294. *Degrees awarded:* Baccalaureate.

Accreditation: *Regional:* NCA.

History: Established, chartered, and incorporated as Columbia College of Oratory 1980; changed name to Columbia College of Expression and offered first instruction at postsecondary level 1907; first degree (baccalaureate) awarded 1911; adopted present name 1944.

Institutional Structure: *Governing board:* Board of Trustees of Columbia College. Extrainstitutional representation: 44 positions on board. All voting. *Composition of institution:* Administrators 8 men / 7 women. Academic affairs headed by Provost. Finances directed by Vice President of Finance. Management/business directed by Executive Vice President. Full-time instructional faculty 252.

Calendar: Semesters. Academic year Sept. to May. Freshmen admitted Sept., Feb., June. Degrees conferred and formal commencement June.

Characteristics of Freshmen: 90% of applicants admitted. 65% of admitted students enrolled full-time.

72% submitted ACT scores. *25th percentile*: ACT Composite 17, ACT English 17, ACT Math 16. *75th percentile*: ACT Composite 24, ACT English 25, ACT Math 23.

35% of entering freshmen expected to graduate within 5 years. 90% of freshmen from Illinois. Freshmen from 30 states and 73 foreign countries.

Admission: Rolling admissions plan. Apply at any time. Early decision available; need not limit application to Columbia. Early acceptance available. Last day for submission of application July 1. *Requirements:* Either graduation from accredited secondary school or GED. *Entrance tests:* College Board SAT or ACT composite recommended. *For transfer students:* from 4-year accredited institution 88 hours maximum transfer credit; from 2-year accredited institution 62 hours; correspondence/extension students 16 hours.

College credit and advanced placement for postsecondary-level work completed in secondary school. For extrainstitutional learning (life experience), college credit and advanced placement on basis of ACE *2006 Guide to the Evaluation of Educational Experiences in the Armed Services*; faculty assessment, portfolio assessment, and personal interview. Tutoring available.

Degree Requirements: 124 credit hours; 2.0 GPA; 1 term in residence; distribution requirements; 2 writing courses.

Fulfillment of some degree requirements and exemption from some beginning courses possible by passing College Board CLEP and AP. *Grading system:* A–F; pass-fail; withdraw (carries time limit); incomplete.

Distinctive Educational Programs: Cooperative baccalaureate programs in Chicago with the Adler Planetarium and Astro-Science Center, Zenith Flash, Paragon Studios, and Media International. Weekend and evening classes. Accelerated degree programs. Interdisciplinary programs in broadcast communications, contemporary studies, photojournalism, and advertising art. Facilities and programs for independent research, including individual majors, tutorials, and co-op/internship programs. Off-campus programs with the Associated Colleges of the Midwest in urban education practicum. Individualized study abroad. *For graduate students:* Programs in photography, film/video, creative writing and the teaching of writing, public affairs journalism, dance therapy, interdisciplinary arts education, and in arts, entertainment, and media management, all of which confer the Master of Arts degree. Educational studies program leading to M.A.T.; Film/Video and Photography Department now offers the M.F.A.

Degrees Conferred: 1,415 *baccalaureate* (B), 127 *master's* (M): area and ethnic studies 1 (M); business/marketing 137 (B); communications/communication technologies 279 (B), 6 (M); computer and information sciences 8 (M); interdisciplinary studies 16 (B), 17 (M); liberal arts/general studies 217; visual and performing arts 704 (B), 39 (M).

Fees and Other Expenses: *Full-time tuition per academic year 2005–06:* $15,588. *Required fees:* $410. *Room and board per academic year:* $7,600.

Financial Aid: Aid from institutionally generated funds is provided on the basis of academic merit, financial need, talent. Institution has a Program Participation Agreement with the U.S. Department of Education for eligible students to receive Pell Grants and other federal aid.

Financial aid to full-time, first-time undergraduate students: need-based scholarships/grants totaling $20,966,697, self-help $40,876,997, tuition waivers $953,911; non-need-based scholarships/grants $53,132.

Departments and Teaching Staff: *Total instructional faculty:* 1,616 (full-time 299, part-time 1,317; women 743, men 883; member of minority groups 227).

Enrollment: Total enrollment 10,294. Undergraduate full-time 4,060 men / 4,266 women, part-time 676m / 706w; graduate full-time 99m / 247w, part-time 88m / 212w.

Characteristics of Student Body: *Ethnic/racial makeup:* number of Black non-Hispanic: 1,516; American Indian or Alaska Native: 88; Asian or Pacific Islander: 333; Hispanic: 961; White non-Hispanic: 6,098; unknown: 531. *Age distribution:* number under 18: 61; 18–19: 2,599; 20–21: 2,996; 22–24: 2,375; 25–29: 1,037; 30–34: 321; 35–39: 121; 40–49: 138; 50–64: 49; 65 and over: 2.

International Students: 212 nonresident aliens enrolled fall 2004. Programs available to aid students whose native language is not English: Social, cultural. English as a Second Language Program. No financial aid specifically designated for international students.

Student Life: On-campus housing available. *Student publications, radio:* Columbia Chronicle, a weekly newspaper; *Hair Trigger*, a biannual literary publication. Radio station WCRX broadcasts 40 hours per week. *Surrounding community:* Chicago population over 3 million. Served by mass transit system; airport 10 miles from campus; passenger rail service 1 mile from campus.

Library Collections: 234,698 volumes. Online catalog. Current serial subscriptions: 1,226. 26,902 microforms; 115,912 audiovisual materials. Students have access to the Internet at no charge.

Most important holdings include George Lurie Fine Art Collection (books and prints); Black American Literature Collection (includes first editions of contemporary black authors); Center for the Study of Black Music.

Buildings and Grounds: Campus includes 15 buildings.

Chief Executive Officer: Dr. Warrick L. Carter, President.

Undergraduates address admission inquiries to Murphy Monroe, Director of Admissions.

Concordia University River Forest

7400 Augusta Street
River Forest, Illinois 60305
Tel: (708) 771-8300   **E-mail:** crfadmis@curf.edu
Fax: (708) 209-3176   **Internet:** www.curf.edu

Institution Description: Concordia University (Concordia College until 1988) is a private institution affiliated with the Lutheran Church-Missouri Synod. *Enrollment:* 2,056. *Degrees awarded:* Baccalaureate, master's, doctorate.

Accreditation: *Regional:* NCA. *Professional:* counseling, music, teacher education

History: Established in Addison as Concordia Teachers College, a secondary school and 1-year college, and offered first instruction at postsecondary level 1864; chartered 1865; added second year 1908; moved to present location 1913; incorporated 1915; added third year 1933; fourth year 1939; awarded first degree (baccalaureate) 1940; added graduate curriculum 1957; became Concordia College 1978; attained university status 1988; added doctoral programs 2000. *See* A. Freitag, *College with a Cause* (St. Louis, MO.: Concordia Publishing House, 1964) for further information.

Institutional Structure: *Governing board:* Board of Control. Representation: 10 directors, including 2 alumni, president of the college. 1 ex officio. 9 voting. *Composition of institution:* Administrators 8 men / 3 women. Academic affairs headed by academic dean. Management/business/finances directed by vice president of administrative services. Full-time instructional faculty 75. Academic governance body, the Senate, meets an average of 8 times per year.

Calendar: Semesters. Academic year late-Aug. to early-May. Freshmen admitted Aug., Jan., June. Degrees conferred Dec., May, Aug. Formal commencements Dec., May, Aug.

Characteristics of Freshmen: 1,529 applicants (661 men, 868 women). 51.5% of applicants admitted. 23.5% of admitted students enrolled full-time.

22% (42 students) submitted SAT scores; 91% (168 students) submitted ACT scores. *25th percentile*: SAT I Verbal 450, SAT I Math 460; ACT Composite 19, ACT English 18, ACT Math 18. *75th percentile*: SAT I Verbal 590, SAT I Math 590; ACT Composite 25, ACT English 25, ACT Math 25.

60% of entering freshmen expected to graduate within 5 years. 51% of freshmen from Illinois. Freshmen from 25 states and 2 foreign countries.

Admission: Rolling admissions plan. For fall acceptance, apply as early as 1 year, but not later than 1 week, prior to enrollment. *Requirements:* Either graduation from accredited secondary school with 15 units (11 in academic subjects) which must include 3 English, 1 algebra, 1 science, 1 social studies; or GED. Minimum GPA 2.0. *Entrance tests:* ACT minimum composite score 20. *For transfer students:* 2.0 minimum GPA. 67 semester hours maximum lower-level transfer credit; no upper-level limit.

College credit and advanced placement for postsecondary-level work completed in secondary school. College credit for extrainstitutional learning on basis of Ace *2006 Guide to the Evaluation of Educational Experiences in the Armed Services.*

Degree Requirements: 128–149 semester hours; 2.0 GPA; 32 semester hours in residence; 2–3 semester hours physical education. Fulfillment of some degree requirements and exemption from some beginning courses possible by passing departmental examinations. *Grading system:* A–F; pass-fail; withdraw (carries time limit); incomplete (carries time limit).

Distinctive Educational Programs: *For undergraduates:* Interdisciplinary programs in communications, humanities and the performing arts, natural science and mathematics, social and behavioral science. Independent study. Cross-registration with Dominican University and Triton College. Baccalaureate nursing programs with West Suburban College of Nursing. *For graduate students:* Weekend classes. *Available to all students:* Evening classes.

Degrees Conferred: 228 *baccalaureate*; 189 *master's*; 1 *doctorate.* Bachelor's degrees awarded in top five disciplines: education 105; business, management, marketing, and related support services 54; psychology 14; theology and ministerial studies 8; visual and performing arts 7.

Fees and Other Expenses: *Full-time tuition per academic year 2004–05:* $18,700. *Books and supplies:* $600. *Room and board per academic year:* $5,900.

Financial Aid: Aid from institutionally generated funds is provided on the basis of academic merit, financial need, other criteria. Institution has a Program Participation Agreement with the U.S. Department of Education for eligible students to receive Pell Grants and other federal aid.

Financial aid to full-time, first-time undergraduate students: 26% received federal grants averaging $3,282; 28% state/local grants averaging $3,956; 88% institutional grants averaging $6,937; 67% loans averaging $3,258.

Departments and Teaching Staff: *Professors* 22, *associate professors* 27, *assistant professors* 25, *instructors* 1, *part-time faculty* 133. *Total full-time instructional faculty:* 75. Student-to-faculty ratio: 15:1. Degrees held by full-time faculty: doctorate 68%, master's 100%. 65% hold terminal degrees.

Enrollment: Total enrollment 2,056. Undergraduate 1,134 (34.8% men, 65.2% women).

Characteristics of Student Body: *Ethnic/racial makeup:* Black non-Hispanic: 6.3%; American Indian or Alaska Native .3%; Asian or Pacific Islander: 1.4%; Hispanic: 5.7%; White non-Hispanic: 66.7%.

International Students: 5 nonresident aliens enrolled fall 2004. No programs available to aid students whose native language is not English. No financial aid specifically designated for international students.

Student Life: On-campus residence halls house 65% of the undergraduate student body. Dormitories for men only constitute 37% of such space, for women only 63%. *Intercollegiate athletics:* men only: baseball, basketball, football, tennis, track, wrestling; women only: basketball, softball, tennis, track, volleyball. *Special regulations:* Cars permitted without restrictions. Residence hall visitation from 5pm to 10:30pm Mon.–Thurs., 3pm to midnight Fri., noon to midnight Sat., and noon to 10:30pm Sun. *Student publications: The Spectator,* a newspaper printed weekly during the academic year. *Surrounding community:* River Forest population 15,000. Chicago, 1 mile from campus, is nearest metropolitan area. Served by mass transit bus and rail systems; airport 10 miles from campus; passenger rail service 1 mile from campus.

Library Collections: 165,000 volumes including bound books, serial backfiles, electronic documents, and government documents not in separate collections. Online catalog. 470 current serial subscriptions: 630,000 microform units; 4,039 recordings; 3,895 audiovisual materials. Computer work stations available. Students have access to the Internet at no charge.

Most important holdings include Education Resources Information Center (ERIC) microfiche collection; theology; hymnal collection.

Buildings and Grounds: Campus area 40 acres.

Chief Executive Officer: Dr. Manfred B. Boos, President.

Address admission inquiries to Evelyn P. Burdick, Vice President for Enrollment.

DePaul University

25 East Jackson Boulevard
Chicago, Illinois 60604-2287

Tel: (312) 362-8000   **E-mail:** admitdpu@depaul.edu
Fax: (312) 362-3222   **Internet:** www.depaul.edu

Institution Description: DePaul University is a private institution affiliated with Congregation of the Mission, Roman Catholic Church. *Enrollment:* 23,570. *Degrees awarded:* Baccalaureate, master's, doctorate, first-professional (juris doctor). Certificates also awarded.

Accreditation: *Regional:* NCA. *Professional:* accounting, business, clinical psychology, law, music, nurse anesthesia education, nursing, nursing education, teacher education

History: Established as Vincent's College, chartered, and offered first instruction at postsecondary level 1898; first degree (baccalaureate) awarded 1899; present name adopted 1907. See Reverend Patrick J. Mullins, "A History of the University," *DePaul University Magazine,* 27 (Winter, Spring, Summer 1976, pp. 7–13; 7–11; 7–14) for further information.

Institutional Structure: *Governing board:* Board of Trustees. Extrainstitutional representation: 43 trustees; institutional representation: 1 administrator. All voting. *Composition of institution:* 5 officers of the university; 8 academic officers, 13 administrative officers. Academic governance body, Faculty Council

meets an average of 10 times per year. Additional governing councils: Staff Council and Student Government Association.

Calendar: Quarters. Academic year Sept. to June. Freshmen admitted Sept. through July. Degrees conferred and formal commencement June. Summer session of 2 terms from mid-June to late Aug.

Characteristics of Freshmen: 69% of applicants admitted. 23% of admitted students enrolled full-time.

26.9% (823 students) submitted SAT scores; 83.99% (1,946 students) submitted ACT scores. *25th percentile:* SAT Verbal 520, SAT Math 500; ACT Composite 21, ACT English 21, ACT Math 20. *75th percentile:* SAT Verbal 620, SAT Math 610; ACT Composite 26, ACT English 27, ACT Math 26.

56% of entering freshmen expected to graduate within 5 years. 75% of freshmen from Illinois. Freshmen from 43 states.

Admission: Rolling admissions plan. For fall acceptance, apply no later than one month before term begins. *Requirements:* Either graduation from accredited secondary school or GED. Recommend 4 units English, 3 mathematics, 2 social science, 7 electives (recommended: 2 laboratory sciences). Auditions required for both Music and Theatre School. *Entrance tests:* College board SAT or ACT composite. For foreign students TOEFL. *For transfer students:* 2.0 minimum GPA except for Commerce program which is 2.5; from 4-year accredited institution 132 quarter hours maximum transfer credit; from 2-year accredited institution 99 hours.

College credit and advanced placement for postsecondary-level work completed in secondary school. Tutoring available. Developmental courses offered during regular academic year; credit given.

Degree Requirements: 188 quarter hours; 2.0 GPA; 3 quarters in residence; general education requirement. Fulfillment of some degree requirements and exemption from some beginning courses possible by passing departmental examination, College Board CLEP, APP. *Grading system:* A–F; pass-fail; withdraw; (carries time limit, deadline after which pass-fail is appended to withdraw).

Distinctive Educational Programs: Weekend and evening classes. Dual-degree programs in engineering with University of Illinois (Urbana and Chicago), University of Notre Dame (IN), University of Detroit, Marquette University. Interdisciplinary programs, including American studies, environmental studies, Jewish studies, Latin American studies, women's studies. Honors program. Preprofessional program in engineering. Quarter programs: Florence, Italy; Sheffield, England; Beijing, China; Merida, Mexico; Athens, Greece; Budapest, Hungary; Paris, France; Bonn, Germany; Mito, Japan. Excursion programs: Puerto Rico; Zimbabwe; Israel. *Other distinctive programs:* Baccalaureate completion program for registered nurses. College credit available for secondary school students; credit given.

ROTC: Air Force (on-campus, freshmen and sophomore); in cooperation with University of Illinois at Chicago and Chicago State University (juniors and seniors).

Degrees Conferred: 2,615 *baccalaureate* (B); 1,351 *master's* (M); 18 *doctorate* (D): area and ethnic studies 16 (B); biological/life sciences 50 (B), 6 (M); business/marketing 873 (B), 84 (M); communications/communication technologies 178 (B), 19 (M); computer and information sciences 212 (B), 261 (M), 2 (D); education 212 (B), 470 (M), 5 (D); English 64 (B), 77 (M); health professions and related sciences 3 (B), 56 (M); interdisciplinary studies 3 (B), 58 (M); liberal arts/general studies 354 (B), 20 (M); mathematics 13 (B), 21 (M); natural resources/environmental science 6 (B); philosophy/religion/theology 21 (B), 5 (M), 3 (D); physical sciences 16 (B), 13 (M); protective services/public administration 10 (B), 61 (M); psychology 162 (B), 21 (M), 8 (D); social sciences and history 251 (B), 34 (M); visual and performing arts 162 (B), 45 (M). 299 *first-professional:* law.

Fees and Other Expenses: *Full-time tuition per academic year 2004–05:* undergraduate $19,700; graduate $410 to $650 per quarter hour depending on program. *Required fees:* $65. *Room and board per academic year :* $9,307.

Financial Aid: Institution has a direct lending program. Aid from institutionally generated funds is provided on the basis of academic merit, financial need, other criteria. Institution has a Program Participation Agreement with the U.S. Department of Education for eligible students to receive Pell Grants and other federal aid.

Financial aid to full-time, first-time undergraduate students: need-based scholarships/grants totaling $60,180,000, self-help $56,420,000; non-need-based scholarships/grants totaling $18,850,000, self-help $25,980,000, parent loans $94,000,000, tuition waivers $4,200,000, athletic awards $3,000,000. *Graduate aid:* 20 students received federal and state-funded fellowships and grants totaling g$99,174; 3,3210 federal and state-funded loans totaling $48,785,591; 38 students held work-study jobs worth $192,000; 848 other fellowships and grants totaling $9,459,785; 433 research assistantships totaling $2,087,288.

Departments and Teaching Staff: *Professors* 174, *associate professors* 261, *assistant professors* 324, *instructors* 80, *part-time faculty* 707. *Total instructional faculty:* 1,546 (full-time 839, part-time 707; women 678, men 868; members of minority groups 254). Total faculty with doctorate, first-professional, or other terminal degree: 680. Student-to-faculty ratio: 17:1. *Faculty development:* $4,085,417 total grants for research. 46 faculty members awarded sabbaticals 2004–05.

Enrollment: Total enrollment 23,570. Undergraduate full-time 4,729 men / 6,419 women, part-time 1,432m / 2,117w; graduate full-time 1,986m / 2,006w, part-time 1,798m / 1,861w; first-professional full-time 434m / 487w, part-time 141m / 140w. *Transfer students:* in-state 1,163; from out-of-state 124.

Characteristics of Student Body: *Ethnic/racial makeup:* number of Black non-Hispanic: 1,450; American Indian or Alaska Native: 49; Asian or Pacific Islander: 1,323; Hispanic: 1,916; White non-Hispanic: 8,9875; unknown: 894. *Age distribution:* number under 18: 141; 18–19: 4,026; 20–21: 1,153; 22–24: 2,459; 25–29: 1,218; 30–34: 763; 35–39: 570 40–49: 753; 50–64: 212; 65 and over: 6.

International Students: 814 nonresident aliens enrolled fall 2004. Programs available to aid students whose native language is not English: Social, cultural. English as a Second Language Program. No financial aid specifically designated for international students.

Student Life: On-campus residence halls house 18% of student body. *Intercollegiate athletics:* basketball, cross-country, golf, rifle, softball, tennis, track. *Special regulations:* Cars with parking stickers permitted (fee charged). *Special services:* Medical services; academic tutoring, counseling services; academic and career advising; multicultural student affairs; university ministry. *Student activities:* student government, programming board, Greek organizations, over 100 student organizations, on-campus entertainment. *Student media: The Depaulian,* student newspaper. *Surrounding community:* Chicago population 3,005,000. Served by mass transit bus and train system; airport 12 miles from campus; passenger rail service 1 mile from campus.

Library Collections: 896,864 volumes. 1,350,000 microforms; 14,000 audiovisual materials; 11,220 current serial subscriptions. 6,754 recordings; 8,707 compact discs; 240 CD-ROMS. 126 computer work stations. Online catalog. Students have access to the Internet at no charge.

Most important holdings include collections on Napoleon, Charles Dickens, Irish; Book Arts; Verrona Williams Derr African/American Collection; antiquarian treasury of St. Thomas More's work.

Buildings and Grounds: Campus area 35 acres. *New buildings:* Belden-Racine Residence Hall; Clifton-Fullerton Residence Hall; Athletic Training Center; Student Center (Lincoln Park Campus).

Chief Executive Officer: Rev. Dennis H. Holtschneider, C.M,. President.

Undergraduates address admission inquiries to Carlene Klaas, Director of Undergraduate Admissions; graduate inquiries to Andre Lewis, Director of Graduate and Adult Admissions.

DeVry University

One Tower Lane

Oakbrook Terrace, Illinois 60181-4663

Tel: (630) 571-7700   **E-mail:** info@devry.edu

Fax: (630) 571-o317   **Internet:** www.devry.edu

Institution Description: DeVry University provides applications-oriented undergraduate and graduate programs in business, technology, and management to more than 49,000 students at 70 locations in the United States and online. *Degrees awarded:* Baccalaureate, master's.

Information about any program and location can be found in the undergraduate 2005–06 catalog online (www.devry.edu) in PDF format. The graduate catalog for the Keller Graduate School of Management of DeVry University is also available in PDF format. *Note:* Adobe Acrobat Reader is necessary to view a PDF file.

Accreditation: *Regional:* NCA. *Professional:* business, engineering technology

Degree Requirements: Contact DeVry University for current admission requirements, degree completion requirements, tuition/fees, and financial aid.

Chief Executive Officer: Ronald L. Taylor, President and Chief Executive Officer.

Dr. William M. Scholl College of Podiatric Medicine

3333 Green Bay Road

North Chicago, Illinois 60064-3095

Tel: (800) 843-3059   **E-mail:** admissions@rfums.edu

Fax: (847) 578-3401   **Internet:** www.rfums.edu/scpm

Institution Description: Dr. William M. Scholl College of Podiatric Medicine is a nonprofit private institution and is a unit of the Roslind Franklin University of Medicine and Science (RFUMS). *Enrollment:* 270. *Degrees awarded:* First-professional (doctor of podiatric medicine), baccalaureate.

Accreditation: *Regional:* NCA. *Professional:* podiatry

History: Established 1912; incorporated 1959; Foot Clinics of Chicago established 1928; awarded first baccalaureate degree 1976; adopted present name 1981. The college's patient care facilities were established in 1928 and currently are known as the Scholl Chicago Foot Health Centers. Scholl College became a member of the Rosalind Franklin University of Medicine and Science in 2001.

Institutional Structure: *Governing board:* Extrainstitutional representation: 19 trustees; institutional representation: 1 administrator, 1 faculty, 1 student, 1 alumnus. *Composition of institution:* Administrators 16 men / 8 women. Academic affairs headed by dean of academic and clinical affairs. Business/finances directed by chief financial officer. Full-time instructional faculty 26. Academic governance body, the faculty, meets an average of 4 times per year.

Calendar: Semesters. Academic year mid-Aug. to early May. Degrees conferred and formal commencement May.

Admission: Rolling admissions plan. Deadline for application to fall entering class is Apr. 1. Early admission decision: applications must be complete by July 1 of 2nd or 3rd year of undergraduate study (3.25 overall GPA and MCAT scores equivalent to the national average). *Requirements:* minimum of 90 semester hours (120 quarter hours) of coursework at an accredited college or university including the following preprofessional requirements: 12 semester hours of biological sciences; 8 semester hours each of general chemistry, organic chemistry, and physics; 6 semester hours of English. *Entrance tests:* Medical College Admission Test (MCAT); scores on the spring MCAT are acceptable for fall admission.

Degree Requirements: 162-172 semester hours; 2.00 GPA; successful completion of four-year academic and clinical curriculum. *Grading system:* A–F; pass/fail; withdraw.

Distinctive Educational Programs: Swanson Foundation Independent Scholar Program, an alternative educational track for academically gifted students interested in research.

Degrees Conferred: 88 *baccalaureate:* biological sciences (issued concurrently with the first-professional degree); 102 *first-professional:* podiatric medicine.

Fees and Other Expenses: *Full-time tuition per academic year 2004–05:* $23,507. *Books and supplies:* $1,050. *Living expenses:* $13,395.

Financial Aid: Aid from institutionally generated funds is provided on the basis of academic merit, financial need, and other criteria. Institution has a Program Participation Agreement with the U.S. Department of Education for eligible students to receive Pell Grants and other federal aid.

127 students shared $700,000 in scholarships 2004–05.

Departments and Teaching Staff: *Total instructional faculty:* 26. Degrees held by full-time faculty: doctorate 21%, baccalaureate 100%, professional 54%.

Enrollment: Total enrollment 270.

Characteristics of Student Body: *Ethnic/racial makeup:* Black non-Hispanic: 2.6%, American Indian or Alaska Native: .9%; Asian or Pacific Islander: 12.4%; Hispanic: 2%; White non-Hispanic: 79.3%.

International Students: No programs available to aid students whose native language is not English. No financial aid specifically designated for international students.

Student Life: Students live in the surrounding community in private apartments. No on-campus residence halls. The Office of Student Services provides assistance in locating apartments and roommates. *Intercollegiate athletics:* men only: basketball. Intramural activities include basketball, flag football, water volleyball, and indoor soccer. Indoor swimming pool located on campus. *Special services:* Student health services available Mon.–Fri.; student counseling. *Student publications: The First Ray,* publishes journal articles 3 times per year. *Surrounding community:* Campus is located on Chicago's Near North Side, also called the Gold Coast. It is an urban residential area, close to shopping, entertainment. Close access to mass transportation, bus and subway; passenger rail service 2 miles from campus; airport 10 miles from campus.

Library Collections: Students have access to the resources of the Boxer Library and online information retrieval services.

Most important Scholl College special holdings include collections on podiatric medicine, orthopedics, and dermatology.

Chief Executive Officer: Dr. Terence B. Albright, Dean.

Address admission inquiries to Office of Admissions.

Dominican University

7900 West Division Street
River Forest, Illinois 60305

Tel: (708) 366-2490   **E-mail:** domadmis@dom.edu
Fax: (708) 524-6990   **Internet:** www.dom.edu

Institution Description: Dominican University, formerly known as Rosary College, is a private, independent, nonprofit college owned and conducted by the Sisters of St. Dominic of Sinsinawa, Roman Catholic Church. *Enrollment:* 841 men / 2,347 women. *Degrees awarded:* Baccalaureate, master's.

Accreditation: *Regional:* NCA. *Professional:* business, librarianship, social work

History: Chartered as St. Clara Academy, a women's secondary school, in Wisconsin 1848; founded as St. Clara College and offered first instruction at postsecondary level 1901; moved to Illinois, incorporated, and adopted present name 1918; awarded first degree (baccalaureate) 1923; became coeducational 1970; adopted present name 1997. *See* Sister Aurelia Altenhofen, O.P., *Rosary College: Transition and Progress, 1901–1974* (n.p., 1977) for further information.

Institutional Structure: *Governing board:* Dominican University Board of Trustees. Extrainstitutional representation: 31 trustees, including 10 alumnae; institutional representation: 1 full-time instructional faculty member, 1 student. 1 ex officio. 29 voting. *Composition of institution:* Administrators 3 men / 7 women (at dean's level and above, 82% are women). Academic affairs headed by provost. Management/business/finances directed by vice president for business affairs. Full-time instructional faculty 44 men / 56 women. Academic governance body, Academic Council, meets an average of 8 times per year.

Calendar: Semesters. Academic year Aug. to May. Freshmen admitted Aug., Jan., May, July. Degrees conferred and formal commencement May, Jan. Summer session from May to Aug.

Characteristics of Freshmen: 83% of applicants admitted. 33% of admitted students enrolled full-time.

13% (36 students) submitted SAT scores; 98% (265 students) submitted ACT scores. *25th percentile:* SAT Verbal 500, SAT Math 500; ACT Composite 20, ACT English 19, ACT Math 18. *75th percentile:* SAT Verbal 610, SAT Math 600; ACT Composite 25, ACT English 25, ACT Math 24. 61% of entering freshmen expected to graduate within 5 years. 91% of freshmen from Illinois. Freshmen from 9 states and 2 foreign countries.

Admission: Rolling admissions plan. For fall acceptance, apply as early as Sept. of previous year, but not later than Aug. of year of enrollment. Early acceptance available. *Requirements:* Either graduation from accredited secondary school with 16 units which should include 14 units in English, foreign language, laboratory science, mathematics, and social studies and 2 electives; or GED. Lowest acceptable secondary school standing 50th percentile. *Entrance tests:* College Board SAT or ACT composite. *For transfer students:* 2.3 minimum GPA; from 4-year accredited institution 90 hours maximum transfer credit; from 2-year accredited institution 68 hours.

College credit and advanced placement for postsecondary-level work completed in secondary school. College credit for College Board CLEP and for extrainstitutional learning on basis of faculty assessment. Tutoring available. Developmental courses offered during regular academic year; credit given.

Degree Requirements: 124 semester hours; 2.0 GPA; 2 terms in residence; distribution requirements. Humanities seminar required. Fulfillment of some degree requirements and exemption from some beginning courses possible by passing College Board CLEP. *Grading system:* A–F; pass-fail; withdraw (carries time limit); withdraw failing (no penalty, carries time limit); incomplete; no credit.

Distinctive Educational Programs: *For undergraduates:* Internships. Interdepartmental/interdisciplinary programs in American studies, international business. Facilities for independent research, including honors programs, tutorials. Study abroad through programs offered by other institutions in England, France, Italy, Salamanca. Cross-registration through Concordia-Dominican Exchange. Research facilities of Argonne National Laboratories available. *For graduate students:* Dual-degree program in business and in law with John Marshall Law School. *Available to all students:* Weekend and evening classes. Special facilities for using telecommunications in the classroom. Individual majors.

Degrees Conferred: 269 *baccalaureate* (B), 525 *master's* (M): area and ethnic studies 3 (B); biological/life sciences 8 (B); business/marketing 72 (B), 101 (M); communications/communication technologies 18 (B); computer and information sciences 19 (B), 13 (M); education 111 (B); English 8 (B); foreign languages and literature 6 (B); health professions and related sciences 5 (B); home economics and vocational home economics 3 (B); liberal arts/general studies 6 (B); library science 249 (M); mathematics 3 (B); philosophy/religion/theology 5 (B); protective services/public administration 51 (M); psychology 22 (B); social sciences and history 54 (B); visual and performing arts 77 (B).

Fees and Other Expenses: *Full-time tuition per academic year 2004–05:* $18,900 undergraduate; $600 per credit hour graduate (varies). *Required fees:* $100. *Room and board per academic year:* $6,800.

Financial Aid: Aid from institutionally generated funds is provided on the basis of academic merit, financial need. Institution has a Program Participation Agreement with the U.S. Department of Education for eligible students to receive Pell Grants and other federal aid.

Financial aid to full-time, first-time undergraduate students: need-based scholarships/grants totaling $5,279,898, self-help $2,698,496; non-need-based scholarships/grants totaling $3,139,012, self-help $1,411,591, parent loans $517,886, tuition waivers $596,921. *Graduate aid:* 12 students received federal and state-funded fellowships/grants totaling g$39,850; 594 federal and state-funded loans totaling $6,144,388; 14 college-assigned jobs worth $20,160; 319 other fellowships/grants totaling $544,884; 2 teaching assistantships at $3,420 each.

Departments and Teaching Staff: *Professors* 19, *associate professors* 35, *assistant professors* 38, *instructors* 8, *part-time faculty* 209. *Total instructional faculty:* 309. Student-to-faculty ratio: 11:1. Degrees held by full-time faculty: doctorate 79%, master's 16%, professional 2%. 81% hold terminal degrees. 3 faculty members awarded sabbaticals 2004–05.

Enrollment: Total enrollment 3,388. Undergraduate full-time 328 men / 756 women, part-time 52m / 140w; graduate full-time 139m / 227w, part-time 322m / 1,224w. *Transfer students:* in-state 84; from out-of-state 15.

Characteristics of Student Body: *Ethnic and racial makeup:* number of Black non-Hispanic: 88; American Indian or Alaska Native: 1; Asian or Pacific Islander: 27; Hispanic: 199; White non-Hispanic: 880; unknown: 58. *Age distribution:* under 18: 1; 18–19: 911; 20–21: 421; 22–24: 234; 25–29: 80; 30–34: 29; 35–39: 24; 40–49: 44; 50–64: 26; 65 and over: 2.

International Students: 149 nonresident aliens enrolled fall 2004. Students from Europe, Asia, Central and South America, Africa. No programs available to aid students whose native language is not English. No financial aid specifically designated for international students.

Student Life: On-campus residence halls house 30% of undergraduate student body. Minimal graduate housing and group apartment sharing is available. Residence halls for men only constitute 25% of such space, for women only 55%. Language Institute for English (LIFE) houses about 20%. Performing Arts Residencies: Chicago Sinfonietta. *Intercollegiate athletics:* men only: basketball, soccer, volleyball, baseball, tennis; women only: basketball, tennis, volleyball, soccer, softball. *Special regulations:* Quiet hours from 11pm daily; guest registration noon to 3am. *Special services:* Learning Resources Center, Language Lab, Child Care Center, Computer Labs, Counseling Center, Career Advising, Writing Lab. *Student publications, radio:* Eagle, an annual literary magazine; *Eagle,* an annual literary magazine; *The Rosary Reporter,* a bimonthly newspaper. *Surrounding community:* River Forest population 13,000. Chicago, 15 miles from campus, is nearest metropolitan area. Served by mass transit bus system; airport 5 miles from campus; passenger rail service 1 mile from campus.

Library Collections: 308,714 volumes. 104,805 government documents; 37,000 microforms; 4,745 audiovisual materials; 814 current periodical subscriptions. Online catalog. Access to online information retrieval services. Students have access to the Internet at no charge. Total budget for books, periodicals, audiovisual materials, microforms 2004–05: $278,000.

Most important special holdings include collections on library science, American and English literature, juvenile literature, sheet music.

Buildings and Grounds: Campus area 30 acres.

Chief Executive Officer: Dr. Donna M. Carroll, President.

Address admission inquiries to Pamela Johnson, Vice President of Enrollment Management.

Graduate School of Business

Degree Programs Offered: *Master's* in business administration with concentrations in accounting, finance, health care administration, management information systems, marketing, human resource management, entrepreneurship. international business administration, and general management. *Additional degree programs:* Master of Science in accounting, master of science in management information systems, master of science in organizational management.

Admission: Baccalaureate from accredited institution with an appropriate general education component. No prior business courses are required. Satisfactory scores on the Graduate Management Admission Test and three references from professors an/or supervisors. International students must have a demonstrated proficiency in English by scoring 550 or higher on the TOEFL and evidence of adequate financial support.

Degree Requirements: Completion of a minimum of thirty semester hours of graduate credit including completion of core and foundation MBA courses; 3.0 GPA and proficiency in standard microcomputer software.

Graduate School of Education

Degree Programs Offered: Master of Science in Education (Early Childhood), Master of Arts in Teaching, Master of Science in Special Education, and Master of Arts in Educational Administration.

Admission: Baccalaureate from accredited institution with an appropriate general education component; 3.0 GPA; three letters of recommendation with at least one from school principal or supervisor and assessment of written communication skills. For the Educational Administration program, candidates must have completed two full years of successful full-time teaching and/or student personnel work in an elementary or secondary school. For international students, demonstrated proficiency in English by scoring 550 or higher on the TOEFL.

Degree Requirements: Satisfactory completion of 32 to 40 semester hours of graduate credit; 3.0 GPA; successful completion of 100 clinical hours in accordance with the policies and procedures for each specific program.

Graduate School of Library and Information Science

Degree Programs Offered: *Master's* in librarianship with concentrations in technical services, public services, and focus areas in special libraries, academic libraries, public libraries, school libraries, information resources management, health sciences librarianship, law libraries, theological libraries, music librarianship, and rare books and special collections.

Admission: *For Master of Library Science:* Baccalaureate from accredited institution with 60 semester hours in the liberal arts or sciences; 3.0 GPA; indication of professional promise based on recommendations and personal interview; GRE Aptitude Test in certain cases. For foreign students demonstrated proficiency in English or University of Michigan Language Examination.

Degree Requirements: *See* general requirements. *For Master of Library Science:* 36 credit hours; 3.0 GPA; 12 months in residence; distribution requirements; completion of degree within 5 years or 6 summers.

Graduate School of Social Work

Degree Programs Offered: *Master's* in social work.

Admission: 3.0 GPA required for advanced standing students and 2.75 GPA for regular students; personal statement; 3 letters of recommendation with 1 completed by an academic reference while the other 2 by work or volunteer-related reference.

Degree Requirements: 64 credit hours including 16 credit hours in the first year followed by 20 credits hour in the second year of supervised fieldwork. Degree expected to be completed in 5 contiguous semesters for full-time and 4 calendar years for part-time. Applicants with a bachelor's degree in social work from a CSWE accredited program may be eligible for advanced standing. The advanced standing program currently consists of 32 credit hours of coursework, including 20 hours of fieldwork (per week) and related integrated seminars. This program requires 1 calendar year of study for full-time students and 2 years for part-time students.

East-West University

816 South Michigan Avenue
Chicago, Illinois 60605
Tel: (312) 939-0111   **E-mail:** admissions@eastwest.edu
Fax: (312) 939-0083   **Internet:** www.eastwest.edu

Institution Description: East-West University is a private institution offering programs of study for commuter students. *Enrollment:* 1,031. *Degrees offered:* Associate, baccalaureate.

Accreditation: *Regional:* NCA.

History: Established 1978.

Calendar: Quarters.

Characteristics of Freshmen: 100% of applicants accepted.

Admission: Graduation from an accredited secondary school or GED; ACT recommended; English and mathematics placement examinations.

Degree Requirements: 180 quarter hours (60 in the major field); 2.0 GPA.

Degrees Conferred: 50 *associate*; 34 *baccalaureate*: business, management, marketing, and related support services 16; computer and information sciences

and support services 8; liberal arts and sciences, general studies, and humanities 5; engineering technologies/technicians 5.

Fees and Other Expenses: *Full-time tuition per academic year 2004–05:* $10,815. *Books and supplies:* $1,700. No on-campus housing. *Off-campus room and board:* $7,800.

Financial Aid: Institution has a Program Participation Agreement with the U.S. Department of Education for eligible students to receive Pell Grants and other federal aid.

Financial aid to full-time, first-time undergraduate students: 90% received federal grants averaging $2,454; 72% state/local grants averaging $3,327; 26% institutional grants averaging $1.449; 41% loans averaging $2,284.

Departments and Teaching Staff: *Total instructional faculty:* 11. Student-to-faculty ratio: 8:1. 9% hold terminal degrees.

Enrollment: Total enrollment 1,031 (34.6% men, 65.4% women).

Characteristics of Student Body: *Ethnic/racial makeup:* Black non-Hispanic: 72.6%; Asian or Pacific Islander: .7%; Hispanic: 12.1%; White non-Hispanic: 2.4%; unknown: 1%.

International Students: 152 nonresident aliens enrolled fall 2004.

Student Life: All students commute to the campus.

Library Collections: 32,000 volumes. 10,000 microforms; 95 current periodical subscriptions. Students have access to online information retrieval services.

Buildings and Grounds: The university occupies a building in the Loop area of downtown Chicago.

Chief Executive Officer: Dr. M. Wasuillah Kahn, Chancellor.

Address admission inquiries to William Link, Director of Admissions.

Eastern Illinois University

600 Lincoln Avenue
Charleston, Illinois 61920-3099
Tel: (217) 581-5000   **E-mail:** admissns@eiu.edu
Fax: (217) 581-7060   **Internet:** www.eiu.edu

Institution Description: Eastern Illinois University is a comprehensive state institution. *Enrollment:* 11,651. *Degrees awarded:* Baccalaureate, master's. Specialist certificates also awarded.

Academic offerings subject to approval by statewide coordinating bodies. Budget subject to approval by state governing boards.

Accreditation: *Regional:* NCA. *Professional:* accounting, art, athletic training, business, counseling, dietetics, family and consumer science, industrial technology, journalism, music, recreation and leisure services, speech-language pathology, teacher education

History: Established as Eastern Illinois State Normal School 1895; offered first instruction at postsecondary level 1899; changed name to Eastern Illinois State Teachers College 1921; awarded first degree (baccalaureate) 1922; changed name to Eastern Illinois State College 1947; adopted present name 1957.

Institutional Structure: *Governing board:* Board of Trustees of Eastern Illinois University. Representation: 8 members including 1 student. 7 voting. *Composition of institution:* Administrators 13 men / 4 women. Academic affairs headed by provost and vice president for academic affairs. Management/business/finances directed by vice president for business affairs. Full-time instructional faculty 633. Academic governance body, Council on Academic Affairs, meets an average of 25 times per year. *Faculty representation:* Faculty served by collective bargaining agent, University Professionals of Illinois, affiliated with AFT.

Calendar: Semesters. Academic year Aug. to May. Freshmen admitted Aug., Jan., June. Degrees conferred and formal commencements May, Aug., Dec.

Characteristics of Freshmen: 76% of applicants admitted. 20% of admitted students enrolled full-time.

3% of students submitted SAT scores; 97% ACT scores. *25th percentile*: ACT Composite 19, ACT English 18, ACT Math 18. *75th percentile*: ACT Composite 23, ACT English 24, ACT Math 23.

56% of entering freshmen expected to graduate in five years. 99% of freshmen from Illinois. Freshmen from 6 states and 5 foreign countries.

Admission: Rolling admissions plan. For fall acceptance, apply as early as 1 year prior to enrollment, but no later than 10 days prior to beginning of term. $30 application fee.Early acceptance available. *Requirements:* Either graduation from accredited secondary school or GED. Recommend 4 units in English, 4 mathematics, 3 laboratory science, 3 social studies. Lowest acceptable secondary school class standing 25th percentile with ACT of at least 18; 50th percentile with ACT of at least 19, 75th percentile with ACT of at least 22. *Entrance tests:* ACT composite or SAT. *For transfer students:* 2.0 minimum GPA (C average); transfer credit limited by residence requirement (42 hours).

College credit and advanced placement for postsecondary-level work completed in secondary school. College credit for extrainstitutional learning on basis of ACE *2006 Guide to the Evaluation of Educational Experiences in the Armed Services;* portfolio assessment.

Degree Requirements: 120 semester hours; 2.0 GPA; 42 hours in residence; general education requirements; tests on or courses in U.S. and Illinois constitutions.

Fulfillment of some degree requirements and exemption from some beginning courses possible by passing departmental examinations, College Board CLEP, APP. *Grading system:* A–F; pass-fail; withdraw (deadline after which pass-fail is appended to withdraw).

Distinctive Educational Programs: *For undergraduates:* Pre-Engineering program in cooperation with University of Illinois at Urbana-Champaign. Interdisciplinary programs in African American studies, social science education. Honors programs. *For graduate students:* Off-campus centers (at Champaign, 50 miles away from main institution; Danville, 65 miles away; Decatur, 55 miles; Centralia, 40 miles; Mt. Vernon, 100 miles; Olney, 60 miles; Rantoul, 55 miles; Robinson, 70 miles; Salem, 100 miles). Interdisciplinary programs in gerontology; M.A. option in historical administration. *Available to all students:* internships. Evening classes. Interdisciplinary program in environmental biology. Summer 1997 study abroad: Art in Paris; Spanish in Mexico and Spain. *Other distinctive programs:* B.A. degree in an individualized, nontraditional program designed for working adults. B.S. degree in Career Occupations for individuals with significant employment experience and technical expertise.

ROTC: Army. 12 commissions awarded 2004.

Degrees Conferred: 2,022 *baccalaureate;* 609 *master's;* 56 *specialist;* 22 *post-baccalaureate certificates.*

Fees and Other Expenses: *Full-time tuition per academic year 2004–05:* in-state undergraduate resident $146 per semester hour, out-of-state $421 per semester hour; graduate resident $142 per semester hour, out-of-state $411 per semester hour. *Required fees:* $705 per semester. *Room and board per academic year:* $5,750.

Financial Aid: Aid from institutionally generated funds is provided on the basis of academic merit, athletic ability, other considerations. Institution has a Program Participation Agreement with the U.S. Department of Education for eligible students to receive Pell Grants and other federal aid.

Financial aid to full-time, first-time undergraduate students: need-based scholarships/grants totaling $14,531,050, self-help $20,183,000, parent loans $2,409,198, tuition waivers $1,206,546, athletic awards $579,994l non-need-based scholarships/grants totaling $2,967,304, self-help $5,734,579, parent loans $1,266,370, tuition waivers $1,668,232, athletic awards $1,596,742. *Graduate aid:* 73 students received $171,603 in federal and state-funded fellowships/grants; 870 received $4,400,194 in federal and state-funded loans; 18 received $61,444 for college-assigned jobs; 877 received other fellowships/grants totaling $3,279,235; 144 teaching assistantships awarded totaling $627,245; 30 research assistantships were awarded totaling $124,186.

Departments and Teaching Staff: *Professors* 206, *associate professors* 119, *assistant professors* 117, *instructors* 183, *part-time faculty* 97. *Total instructional faculty:* 730 (full-time 633, part-time 97; 322 women, 408 men; members of minority groups 57). Student-to-faculty ratio: 15;1.

Enrollment: Total enrollment 11,651. Undergraduate full-time 3,864 men / 5,094 women, part-time 316m / 654w; graduate full-time 266m / 381w, part-time 383m / 693w.

Characteristics of Student Body: *Ethnic/racial makeup:* number of Black non-Hispanic: 724; American Indian or Alaska Native: 23; Asian or Pacific Islander: 114; Hispanic: 241; White non-Hispanic: 724; unknown: 243. *Age distribution:* number under 18: 43; 18–19: 3,543; 20–21: 3,733; 22–24: 1,607; 25–29: 352; 30–34: 174; 35–39: 141; 40–49: 248; 50–64: 87.

International Students: 143 nonresident aliens enrolled fall 2004. Cultural and financial programs available to aid students whose native language is not English. English as a Second Language Program. Scholarships available annually for undergraduate and graduate international students.

Student Life: On-campus housing available for over 50% of student population: men-only, women-only, and co-ed residence halls (capacity: 4,400) with varying visitation policies and quiet floors; student and married student apartments (capacity: 700); Greek Court complex (capacity: 340). 18% of men join fraternities; 15% of women join sororities. *Intercollegiate athletics:* men only: baseball, basketball, cross-country, football, golf, soccer, swimming, tennis, track, wrestling; women only: basketball, cross-country, golf, soccer, softball, swimming, tennis, track, volleyball. *Special regulations:* Cars with parking tags permitted in designated areas; fee charged. *Special services:* Reading, Writing, Math Diagnostic Centers, legal services, medical services. *Student publications, radio, television: The Daily Eastern News,* a newspaper; *Minority Today,* a monthly newspaper; *The Vehicle,* a literary magazine; *Heartland,* a general interest magazine; *The Warbler,* yearbook. Radio station WEIU-FM/Television station WEIU-TV, Channel 51. *Surrounding community:* Charleston, population 26,000, is 1 hour south of University of Illinois at Urbana-Champaign; approxi-

mately midway between St. Louis (MO) and Indianapolis (IN). Served by airport 5 miles from campus; passenger rail service 12 miles from campus.

Publications: *Educational Journal* (annually) first published in 1967; *Karamu* (literary journal) published semiannually.

Library Collections: 1,013,336 volumes including bound books, serial backfiles, electronic documents, and government documents not in separate collections. Online catalog. Current serial subscriptions: 2,021 paper, 60 microform, 16,820 via electronic access. 9,139 recordings; 4,287 compact discs; 2,378 CD-ROMs. 20,321 audiovisual materials. 250 computer work stations. Students have access to the Internet at no charge.

Most important special collection: Remo Belli Percussion Music Collection.

Buildings and Grounds: Campus area 320 acres.

Chief Executive Officer: Dr. Luis V. Hencken, President.

Address undergraduate admission inquiries to Brenda Ross, Director of Admissions; graduate inquiries to Dr. Robert Augustine, Dean, Graduate School.

Elmhurst College

190 Prospect
Elmhurst, Illinois 60126
Tel: (630) 617-3500   **E-mail:** admit@elmhurst.edu
Fax: (630) 617-5501   **Internet:** www.elmhurst.edu

Institution Description: Elmhurst College is a private, independent, nonprofit college affiliated with the United Church of Christ. *Enrollment:* 2,681. *Degrees awarded:* Baccalaureate, master's.

Accreditation: *Regional:* NCA. *Professional:* nursing, nursing education, teacher education

History: Established as Elmhurst Pro-Seminary and Academy 1871; reorganized into Elmhurst Academy and Junior College and offered first instruction at postsecondary level 1919; adopted present name 1924; awarded first degree (baccalaureate) 1925; became coeducational in 1930; chartered 1942. *See* Robert C. Stanger, *The Elmhurst Years* (Elmhurst: Elmhurst College, 1971) for further information.

Institutional Structure: *Governing board:* Board of Trustees. Representation: 36 members, including 8 alumni, 1 ex officio (president of the college), 8 honorary trustees; 29 voting. *Composition of institution:* Administrators 34 men / 27 women. Academic affairs headed by dean of the college. Management/business/finances directed by vice president of finance. Full-time instructional faculty 107. Academic governance body, the faculty, meets an average of 8 times per year.

Calendar: Semesters. 4-1-4 plan. Academic year Aug. to May. Freshmen admitted Aug., Jan., June. Degrees conferred May, Jan. Formal commencements May and February. 4 summer sessions.

Characteristics of Freshmen: 1,124 applicants admitted. 386 students admitted and enrolled full-time.

12% submitted SAT scores; 87% submitted ACT scores. *25th percentile:* ACT Composite 19. *75th percentile:* ACT Composite 26.

73% of freshmen expected to graduate within 5 years. 89% of freshmen from Illinois. Freshmen from 13 states and 21 foreign countries.

Admission: Rolling admissions plan. For fall acceptance, apply as early as end of junior year of secondary school, but not later than Aug. 15 of year of enrollment. Early acceptance available. *Requirements:* Either graduation from accredited secondary school with 16 units or GED. Recommend 4 units English, 2 in a foreign language, 2 mathematics, 2 laboratory science, 2 social studies, 6 academic electives. Minimum GPA 2.75 on 4.00 scale. *Entrance tests:* SAT or ACT. For foreign students TOEFL. *For transfer students:* 2.7 minimum GPA; from 4-year accredited institution 96 hours maximum transfer credit; from 2-year accredited institution 64 hours.

College credit and advanced placement for postsecondary-level work completed in secondary school. College credit for extrainstitutional learning on basis of ACE *2006 Guide to the Evaluation of Educational Experiences in the Armed Services,* portfolio, and faculty assessments. Tutoring available. Learning Center with study skills, time management, and other workshops available throughout the academic year; audiovisual aids available.

Degree Requirements: 128 credit hours; 2.0 GPA; last 2 terms in residence; distribution requirements; residency requirement is the last 32 semester hours of credit. Fulfillment of some degree requirements and exemption from some beginning courses possible by passing College Board CLEP, APP (score of 3). *Grading system:* A–F; pass-fail; withdraw (carries time limit); incomplete (carries time limit).

Distinctive Educational Programs: Work-experience and field-experience programs. Flexible meeting places and schedules, including off-campus centers, weekend and evening classes. Dual-degree programs in engineering with Illinois

Institute of Technology. Northwestern University, University of Illinois at Urbana-Champaign, Washington University (MO). Preprofessional program in actuarial science, allied health, dentistry, engineering, law, library science, medicine, pharmacy, physical therapy, seminary, veterinary medicine. Facilities and programs for independent research, including interdisciplinary honors program, student-designed interdepartmental majors, tutorials. Institutionally sponsored foreign study tours during January interim. Study abroad through Institute for American Universities in Aix-en-Provence, France; through University of Illinois in Austria, France, Spain; through Wayne State University in Germany. Central college programs in Spain, France, England, and Austria. Off-campus study in U.S. through Washington (DC) semester at American University.

ROTC: Air Force offered in cooperation with Illinois Institute of Technology; Army offered in cooperation with Wheaton College.

Degrees Conferred: 614 *baccalaureate* (B), 74 *master's* (M): biological/life sciences 23 (B); business/marketing 210 (B), 38 (M); communications/communication technologies 35 (B); computer and information sciences 30 (B), 16 (M); education 105 (B), 6 (M); English 37 (B), 6 (M); foreign languages and literature 8 (B); health professions and related sciences 42 (B); interdisciplinary studies 1 (B); liberal arts/general studies 3 (B); mathematics 12 (B); natural resources/environmental science 4 (B); philosophy/religion/theology 5 (B); physical sciences 10 (B); psychology 26 (B), 8 (M); social sciences and history 30 (B); visual and performing arts 38 (B).

Fees and Other Expenses: *Full-time tuition per academic year 2004–05:* $20,090 undergraduate; $637 per semester hour graduate. *Required fees:* $80. *Other fees:* $100. *Room and board per academic year:* $6,304.

Financial Aid: Elmhurst College offers a direct lending program. Aid from institutionally generated funds is provided on the basis of academic merit, financial need, other considerations. Institution has a Program Participation Agreement with the U.S. Department of Education for eligible students to receive Pell Grants and other federal aid.

Financial aid to full-time, first-time undergraduate students: need-based scholarships/grants totaling $16,177,696, self-help $5,202,922; non-need-based scholarships/grants totaling $3,095,020, self-help $5,110,162, parent loans $2,940,425. *Graduate aid:* 36 fellowships and grants totaling $34,421.

Departments and Teaching Staff: *Professors 37, associate professors 35, assistant professors 36, instructors 6, part-time faculty 160. Total instructional faculty:* 276 (full-time 116, part-time 160; women 138, men 138). Total faculty with doctorate, first-professional, or other terminal degree: 145. Student-to-faculty ratio: 13:1. 9 faculty members awarded sabbaticals 2004–05.

Enrollment: Total enrollment 2,681. Undergraduate full-time 781 men / 1,348 women, part-time 124m / 231w; graduate part-time 105m 92w. *Transfer students:* in-state 1,234; from out-of-state 35.

Characteristics of Student Body: *Ethnic/racial makeup:* number of Black non-Hispanic: 131; American Indian or Alaska Native: 9; Asian or Pacific Islander: 72; Hispanic: 125; White non-Hispanic: 1,938; unknown: 180. *Age distribution:* under 18: 6; 18–19: 708; 20–21: 802; 22–24: 430; 25–29: 256; 30–34: 148; 35–39: 98; 40–49: 176; 50–64: 50; 65 and over: 25. 23% of student body attend summer sessions.

International Students: 28 nonresident aliens enrolled fall 2004. 14 students from Europe, 4 Asia, 3 Africa, 1 other. Programs available to aid students whose native language is not English: Social, cultural. No financial aid specifically designated for international students.

Student Life: On-campus residence halls house 32% of student body. *Intercollegiate athletics:* men only: baseball, basketball, cross-country, football, golf, tennis, track, wrestling; women only: basketball, cross-country, golf, soccer, softball, tennis, track, volleyball. *Special regulations:* Registered cars permitted without restrictions. *Special services:* Learning Resources Center, medical services, counseling center, chaplain. *Student publications, radio: The Elmhurst College Leader,* a weekly newspaper. Radio station WRSE broadcasts 56 hours per week. *Surrounding community:* Elmhurst population 40,000. Chicago, 16 miles from campus, is nearest metropolitan area. Served by mass transit bus system; airport 7 miles from campus; passenger rail service 1 mile from campus.

Library Collections: 218,107 volumes including bound books, serial backfiles, electronic documents, and government documents not in separate collections. Online catalog. Current serial subscriptions: 743 paper, microform 53, via electronic access 432. 2,839 recordings. 212 compact discs; 35 CD-ROMs. 60 computer work stations. Students have access to the Internet at no charge.

Most important holdings include German hymnals and hymnology books dating from the late 18th century; annual reports of corporations and associations; nursing collection; English literature collection. Total 2004–05 budge for books and materials: $333,913.

Buildings and Grounds: Campus area 38 acres. *New buildings:* Circle Hall completed 2004; library entrance renovation 2004.

Chief Executive Officer: Dr. Bryant L. Cureton, President.

Address admission inquiries to Gary Rold, Dean of Admissions; graduate inquiries to Dr. Patricia Lynott, Dean for the School of Advanced Learning.

Erikson Institute

420 North Wabash Avenue
Chicago, Illinois 60611-5627

Tel: (312) 755-2250   **E-mail:** info@erikson.edu
Fax: (312) 755-0928   **Internet:** www.erikson.edu

Institution Description: The Erikson Institute is an independent, private graduate school. *Enrollment:* 253. *Degrees awarded:* Master's.

Accreditation: *Regional:* NCA.

History: Founded in 1966.

Institutional Structure: Governing board: Board of Trustees. 36 trustees; 4 life trustees.

Calendar: Semesters. Academic year Sept. to May. Fall admission only. Formal commencement May. Degrees awarded My, Sept. Summer session late May to early Aug.

Admission: Rolling admissions. *Requirements:* baccalaureate degree from an accredited institution; minimum 2.75 GPA.

Degree Requirements: 3.0 GPA; 38–48 credit hours depending on program; comprehensive examination.

Degrees Conferred: 2 *master's:* : education 1; home economics and vocational home economics 2.

Fees and Other Expenses: *Full-time tuition per academic year 2004–05:* $565 per credit hour. *Required fees:* $160.

Financial Aid: Aid from institutionally generated funds is provided on the basis of academic merit, financial need. Institution has a Program Participation Agreement with the U.S. Department of Education for eligible students to receive Pell Grants and other federal aid. *Graduate aid:* 4 students received $!3,673 in federal and state-funded fellowships/grants; 122 received federal and state-funded loans totaling $1,390,336 (ranging from $2,000 to $18,500); 203 other fellowships and grants totaling $993,930 (ranging from $424 to $13,320); 2 research assistantships worth $30,000.

Departments and Teaching Staff: Child development/early childhood education *professors 4, associate professors 2, assistant professors 4, instructors 1. part-time faculty 14. Total instructional faculty:* 25.

Enrollment: Total enrollment 253. Graduate full-time 2 men / 58 women, part-time 7m / 186w.

International Students: 3 nonresident aliens from Asia enrolled fall 2004. No programs available to aid students whose native language is not English. No financial aid specifically designated for international students.

Library Collections: 12,600 volumes including bound books, serial backfiles, electronic documents, and government documents not in separate collections. Online catalog. 85 current serial subscriptions. 30 computer work stations. Students have access to the Internet at no charge.

Chief Executive Officer: Dr. Samuel J. Meisels, President.

Address admission inquiries to Office of Admissions.

Eureka College

300 East College Avenue
Eureka, Illinois 61530-1500

Tel: (309) 467-3721   **E-mail:** admissions@eureka.edu
Fax: (309) 467-6386   **Internet:** www.eureka.edu

Institution Description: Eureka College is a private college affiliated with the Christian Church (Disciples of Christ). *Enrollment:* 520. *Degrees awarded:* Baccalaureate.

Accreditation: *Regional:* NCA.

History: Established as Walnut Grove Academy 1848; chartered, adopted present name, and offered first instruction at postsecondary level 1855; awarded first degree (baccalaureate) 1860. *See* Elmira Dickinson, *A History of Eureka College* (St. Louis, MO: Christian Publishing Co., 1894) and Harold Adams, *The History of Eureka College* (Henry, IL: M & D Printing Co., 1982) for further information.

Institutional Structure: *Governing board:* The Trustees of Eureka College. Extrainstitutional representation: 24 trustees; institutional representation: president of the college. 1 ex officio. All voting. *Composition of institution:* Administrators 8 men / 2 women. Academic affairs headed by dean of the college. Management/business/finances directed by director of finance and planning. Full-time instructional faculty 61. Academic governance body, the faculty, meets an average of 9 times per year.

Calendar: Semesters. Academic year Aug. to May. Freshmen admitted Aug., Oct., Jan., Mar. Degrees conferred and formal commencement May. No summer session.

Characteristics of Freshmen: 588 applicants (283 men, 305 women). 32.7% of applicants admitted. 96.9% of admitted students enrolled full-time.

100% (192 students) submitted ACT scores. *25th percentile:* ACT Composite 18, ACT English 17, ACT Math 21. *75th percentile:* ACT Composite 25, ACT English 25, ACT Math 24.

51% of entering freshmen expected to graduate within 5 years. 88% of freshmen from Illinois. Freshmen from 11 states and 1 foreign country.

Admission: Rolling admissions plan. For fall acceptance, apply as early as end of junior year of secondary school. *Requirements:* Either graduation from secondary school with 16 units which must include 12 college preparatory; or GED. *Entrance tests:* ACT composite. *For transfer students:* 2.0 minimum GPA, 68 hours maximum transfer credit.

Credit and advanced placement for postsecondary-level work completed in secondary school and for College Board CLEP.

Degree Requirements: 124 semester hours; 2.0 GPA; last 30 semester hours in residence; 2 hours physical education; exit competency examination in writing; distribution requirements.

Fulfillment of some degree requirements and exemption from some beginning courses possible by passing departmental examinations, College Board CLEP, other standardized tests. *Grading system:* A–F; pass-fail; withdraw (carries time limit); incomplete (carries time limit).

Distinctive Educational Programs: Summer exchange program with Sofia University in Tokyo. Extensive internship program. Mentorship program with college alumni. Writing Excellence Program.

Degrees Conferred: 99 *baccalaureate:* bachelor's degrees awarded in top five disciplines: business, management, marketing, and related support services 33; education 20; communication, journalism, and related programs 12; visual and performing arts 6; social sciences 5.

Fees and Other Expenses: *Full-time tuition per academic year 2004–05:* $19,100. *Room per academic year:* $5,880.

Financial Aid: Aid from institutionally generated funds is provided on the basis of academic merit, financial need. Institution has a Program Participation Agreement with the U.S. Department of Education for eligible students to receive Pell Grants and other federal aid.

Financial aid to full-time, first-time undergraduate students: 44% received federal grants averaging $3,536; 57% state/local grants averaging $4,272; 100% institutional grants averaging $8,063; 87% loans averaging $3,647.

Departments and Teaching Staff: *Total instructional faculty:* 44. Student-to-faculty ratio: 18:1. Degrees held by full-time faculty: doctorate 85%.

Enrollment: Total enrollment 520 (48.1% men, 51.9% women).

Characteristics of Student Body: *Ethnic/racial makeup:* Black non-Hispanic: 8.5%; Asian or Pacific Islander: 1.2%; American Indian or Alaska Native: .4%; Hispanic: 1.2%; White non-Hispanic: 87.9%.

International Students: 5 nonresident aliens enrolled fall 2004. No programs available to aid students whose native language is not English. No financial aid specifically designated for international students.

Student Life: On-campus residence halls house 85% of student body. Dormitories for men only constitute 50% of such space, for women only 50%. 12% of men join and 9% live in fraternities. 85% of the student body live on campus. *Intercollegiate athletics:* men only: basketball, football, golf, swimming, tennis, track. Women only, basketball, softball, tennis, track, volleyball; both sexes: swimming. *Special regulations:* Registered cars permitted. Residence hall visitation from noon to midnight. *Special services:* Medical services. *Student publications: Impressions,* an annual literary magazine; *The Pegasus,* a monthly newspaper; *The Prism,* a yearbook. *Surrounding community:* Eureka population 6,000. Chicago, 150 miles from campus, is nearest metropolitan area.

Library Collections: 85,000 volumes including bound books, serial backfiles, electronic documents, and government documents not in separate collections. Online catalog. Current serial subscriptions: 345 paper, 4,989 microform, 800 electronic databases. 15 CD-ROMs. Computer work stations available. Students have access to the Internet at no charge.

Most important special holdings include 19th-century English literature; history of Disciples of Christ (Christian Church); early publications of Alexander Campbell; college publications 1928–32, the years Ronald Reagan attended; history of Eureka College.

Buildings and Grounds: Campus area 112 acres.

Chief Executive Officer: Dr. Paul R. Lister, President.

Address admission inquiries to Brian Sajko, Dean of Admissions.

Garrett-Evangelical Theological Seminary

2121 Sheridan Road
Evanston, Illinois 60201
Tel: (847) 866-3900   **E-mail:** admissions@garrett.edu
Fax: (847) 866-3957   **Internet:** www.garrett.edu

Institution Description: Garrett-Evangelical Theological Seminary (Garrett Theological and Evangelical Theological Seminaries until 1974) is a private institution affiliated with The United Methodist Church. *Enrollment:* 329. *Degrees awarded:* First-professional (master of divinity), master's, doctorate.

Accreditation: *Regional:* NCA. *National:* ATS. *Professional:* theology

History: Established as Garrett Theological Seminary 1853; chartered and offered first instruction at postsecondary level 1855; awarded first degree (first-professional) 1858; merged with Evangelical Theological Seminary (established 1873) and adopted present name 1974. *See* Frederick A. Norwood, *From Dawn to Midday at Garrett* (Evanston: Garrett-Evangelical Theological Seminary, 1978) for further information.

Institutional Structure: *Governing board:* Board of Trustees of Garrett-Evangelical Theological Seminary. Extrainstitutional representation: 32 trustees, 5 life trustees, resident bishop; institutional representation: president of the seminary, 2 full-time instructional faculty members, 4 students; 2 alumni. 42 voting. *Composition of institution:* Administrators 7 women / 5 men. Academic affairs headed by vice president for academic affairs and dean. Management/business/finances directed by vice president for administration. Full-time instructional faculty 25. Academic governance body, the faculty, meets an average of 7 times per year.

Calendar: Semesters. Academic year Sept. to June. Entering students admitted Sept., Jan. Degrees conferred and formal commencement May. Summer session from June to July.

Characteristics of Freshmen: 64% of applicants accepted. 51% of accepted applicants enrolled. 45% of students from Illinois. Students from 20 states and 5 foreign countries.

Admission: Rolling admissions plan. Apply as early as end of junior year of college, but not later than 2 months prior to registration. *Requirements:* Graduation from accredited 4-year college with acceptable academic performance and recommendations giving evidence of professional competency, potential for leadership in the ministry, and ability to do graduate work. Provisional admission possible. *Entrance tests:* For foreign students TOEFL. *For transfer students:* 2.5 minimum GPA; from accredited graduate theological school transfer credit for up to one third of academic program.

Degree Requirements: *For first-professional degree:* 31 units; core courses; ministry project; field education; senior colloquy and consultation; evaluation conference. *For M.A. in Christian Education degree:* 20 units; core courses; ministry project; field education; retreats; professional evaluation conference. *For Master of Theological Studies degree:* 21 units; evaluation conference. *For M.A. in Music Ministry degree:* 20 units. *Doctor of Ministry & Ph.D. dual degree:* with Northwestern University Medill School of Journalism in Religion and News Media. *For all degrees:* Grade average of C+. *Grading system:* A–F; pass-fail; withdraw (deadline after which pass-fail is appended to withdraw); descriptive reports.

Distinctive Educational Programs: Evening classes. Cooperative master's and doctorate programs with Northwestern University. Special facilities for using telecommunications in the classroom. Facilities and programs for independent research, including tutorials, independent study. Institutionally sponsored study abroad in varying locations. Cross-registration through consortium. The Institute for Black Religious Research, The Peace Institute. *Other distinctive programs:* General and special lecture programs. Degree and nondegree continuing education.

Degrees Conferred: 7 *post-baccalaureate certificates;* 17 *master's;* 38 *first-professional;* 7 *doctorate.*

Fees and Other Expenses: *Full-time tuition per academic year 2004–05:* $12,015. *Room per academic year:* $4,590. *Board per academic year:* $2,715.

Financial Aid: Aid from institutionally generated funds is provided on the basis of academic merit, leadership ability. Institution has a Program Participation Agreement with the U.S. Department of Education for eligible students to receive Pell Grants and other federal aid.

Departments and Teaching Staff: Bible *professors* 0, *associate professors* 2, *assistant professors* 2, *instructors* 0; church history 1, 1, 2, 0; theology 4, 1, 1, 0; ethics and society 1, 0, 0, 0; Christian education 2, 0, 1, 0; pastoral psychology/counseling 1, 2, 0, 1; preaching and worship 1, 1, 0, 0; church administration/evangelism and spiritual formation 0, 2, 1, 0.

Total instructional faculty: 25. Degrees held by full-time faculty: doctorate 95%, master of divinity 5%. 95% hold terminal degrees.

Enrollment: Total enrollment 329 (41.9% men, 58.1% women).

Characteristics of Student Body: *Ethnic/racial makeup:* Black non-Hispanic: 17.3%; American Indian or Alaska Native: .3%; Asian or Pacific Islander: 4.6%; Hispanic: .9%; White non-Hispanic: 66.9%; unknown 1.2%.

International Students: 29 nonresident aliens enrolled fall 2004. Students from Asia, Central and South America, Africa. Programs available to aid students whose native language is not English: Social, cultural, financial. English as a Second Language Program.

Student Life: On-campus residence halls house 11% of student body. Residence halls for men only constitute 53% of such space, for women only 47%. Some students, including married students, live off campus in seminary-owned apartments. *Special regulations:* Cars with registration stickers permitted. *Special services:* Learning Resources Center, medical services. *Student publications: Rough Edges*, a literary magazine published irregularly by female students. *Surrounding community:* Evanston, 2000 population 75,000, is located in the Chicago metropolitan area. Served by mass transit bus and subway systems; airport and passenger rail service each 12–15 miles from campus.

Publications: Sources of information about Garrett-Evangelical Theological Seminary include United Methodist publications; *Aware*, a quarterly.

Library Collections: 300,000 volumes. 8,745 microforms; 1,400 periodicals. Access to online information retrieval systems.

Most important holdings include Methodistica (monographs, manuscripts, biographies, and official documents on the Methodist Church in England and the United States, including information on major church leaders and figures associated with Garrett-Evangelical Theological Seminary); Patristic Collection (monographs about the Church Fathers and translations of their works); Paul Edwin Keene Bible Collection (examples of the English Bible, including a Matthews Bible from 1537 and a King James Bible from 1611).

Buildings and Grounds: Campus area 5.2 acres.

Chief Executive Officer: Dr. Ted A. Campbell, President.

Address admission inquiries to Rev. David A. Newhouse, Director of Admissions.

Governors State University

1 University Parkway
University Park, Illinois 60466-0975
Tel: (708) 534-5000   **E-mail:** info@govst.edu
Fax: (708) 534-1640   **Internet:** www.govst.edu

Institution Description: Governors State University is a state institution providing upper division and graduate study only. *Enrollment:* 5,652. *Degrees awarded:* Baccalaureate, master's.

Academic offerings subject to approval by statewide coordinating bodies. Budget subject to approval by state governing boards. Member of Chicago Consortium of Colleges and Universities.

Accreditation: *Regional:* NCA. *Professional:* business, counseling, health services administration, nursing, occupational therapy, physical therapy, public administration, social work, speech-language pathology

History: Established and chartered 1969; offered first instruction at postsecondary level 1971; awarded first degrees (baccalaureate, master's) 1972.

Institutional Structure: *Governing board:* Board of Trustees of 7 members. *Composition of institution:* Administrators 57 men / 49 women (17% are members of minority groups). Academic affairs headed by provost and vice president for academic affairs. Management/business/finances directed by vice president for administration. Full-time instructional faculty 148. Academic governance body, Faculty Senate, meets an average of 10 times per year. *Faculty representation:* Faculty served by collective bargaining agent, UPI.

Calendar: Trimesters. Academic year Sept. to Aug. Degrees conferred Apr., Aug., Dec. Formal commencement June.

Admission: Rolling admissions plan. *Requirements:* For undergraduates, an associate degree or 60 semester hours (90 quarter hours) from accredited institution. Minimum GPA 2.0. For graduate students, a bachelor's degree from a regionally accredited college or university. Satisfy collegial and/or major criteria, if applicable, for graduate study in a specified major. *Entrance tests:* For foreign students TOEFL; certain graduate programs GRE, GMAT. *For transfer students:* 2.0 minimum GPA.

College credit for extrainstitutional learning on basis of ACE *2006 Guide to the Evaluation of Educational Experiences in the Armed Services*, portfolio, and faculty assessments. Tutoring available.

Degree Requirements: 120 credit hours; 2.0 GPA; 24 hours in residence. Individual degree programs may impose additional requirements. *Grading system:* A–F; pass-no credit; withdraw (carries time limit).

Distinctive Educational Programs: *For undergraduates:* Individualized program recognizing experiential learning in cooperation with Chicago State, Eastern Illinois, Northeastern Illinois, and Western Illinois. *For graduate stu-

dents: Cooperative master's program in Educational Administration and Supervision with Chicago State and Northeastern Illinois. *Available to all students:* Flexible schedules including day, evening, and weekend courses. Facilities and opportunities for independent research and tutorials. Work experience programs. *Other distinctive programs:* Individualized, degree-granting continuing education program in cooperation with Eastern Illinois, Northeastern Illinois, Western Illinois and Chicago State Universities. Study abroad at Oldenburg, Germany (exchange program with Carl-von-Ossietzky Universitat).

ROTC: Air Force offered in cooperation with Illinois Institute of Technology. Army offered in cooperation with University of Illinois at Chicago.

Degrees Conferred: 780 *baccalaureate;* 745 *master's.* Bachelor's degrees awarded in top five disciplines include liberal arts and sciences, general studies, and humanities 267; business, management, marketing, and related support services 120; education 110; health professions and related clinical sciences 71, security and protective services 51.

Fees and Other Expenses: *Full-time tuition per academic year 2004–05:* undergraduate resident $3,716. Contact the university for current nonresident undergraduate and graduate tuition/fees.

Financial Aid: Aid from institutionally generated funds is provided on the basis of academic merit, financial need. Institution has a Program Participation Agreement with the U.S. Department of Education for eligible students to receive Pell Grants and other federal aid.

Departments and Teaching Staff: *Professors* 138; *lecturers* 17, *part-time teachers* 180. *Total instructional faculty:* 335. Degrees held by full-time faculty: doctorate 78%, master's 22%. 81% hold terminal degrees.

Enrollment: Total enrollment 5,652. Undergraduate 2,752 (29.5% men, 70.5% women).

Characteristics of Student Body: *Ethnic/racial makeup:* Black non-Hispanic: 36.2%, American Indian or Alaska Native: .1%; Asian or Pacific Islander: 1.2%; Hispanic: 5.4%; White non-Hispanic: 49.8%; unknown 6.7%.

International Students: 14 undergraduate nonresident aliens enrolled fall 2004. Students from Europe, Asia, Latin America. Programs available to aid students whose native language is not English: Social, cultural. No financial aid specifically designated for international students.

Student Life: No on-campus housing. *Special regulations:* Cars permitted with paid parking. *Special services:* University Library, and Center for Learning Assistance. *Student publication: The Innovator*, a biweekly newspaper. *Surrounding community:* University Park, population 10,000, is located in Chicago metropolitan area. Served by mass transit train and bus systems.

Library Collections: 285,000 volumes. 265,000 government documents; 25,500 audiovisual materials; 480,000 microforms; 2,300 current periodicals. Students have access to online information retrieval services.

Most important holdings include Kuper Collection (plays of the 20th century); African American Literature.

Buildings and Grounds: Campus area 753 acres.

Chief Executive Officer: Dr. Stuart I. Fagan, President.

Address admission inquiries to Director of Admissions.

Greenville College

315 East College Avenue
Greenville, Illinois 62246
Tel: (618) 664-2800   **E-mail:** admission@greenville.edu
Fax: (618) 664-9841   **Internet:** www.greenville.edu

Institution Description: Greenville College is a private, nonprofit college affiliated with the Free Methodist Church of North America. *Enrollment:* 1,315. *Degrees awarded:* Baccalaureate, master's.

Member of Council for Christian Colleges and Universities; Christian College Consortium and Coalition, Council of Independent Colleges; Federation of Independent Illinois Colleges and Universities.

Accreditation: *Regional:* NCA. *Professional:* teacher education

History: Established, chartered, and offered first instruction at postsecondary level 1892; first degree (baccalaureate) awarded 1898.

Institutional Structure: *Governing board:* Board of Trustees. Representation: 28 trustees. 1 ex officio. All voting. *Composition of institution:* Administrators 27 men / 30 women. Academic affairs headed by vice president for academic affairs. Management/business/finances directed by vice president for finance. Full-time instructional faculty 56. Academic governance body, Faculty Assembly, meets an average of 16 times per year.

Calendar: Semesters (4-1-4 plan). Academic year Sept. to May. Freshmen admitted for all terms. Degrees conferred May, Aug., Dec. Formal commencement May. Summer session of 3 terms from May to July.

Characteristics of Freshmen: 69% of applicants admitted. 41% of admitted students enrolled full-time.

13% (32 students) submitted SAT scores; 87% (207 students) submitted ACT scores. *25th percentile*: SAT Verbal 455, SAT Math 478; ACT Composite 19, ACT English 19, ACT Math 18. *75th percentile*: SAT Verbal 573, SAT Math 573; ACT Composite 26, ACT English 26, ACT Math 25.

2 National Merit Scholars. 43% of entering freshmen expected to graduate within 5 years. 58% of freshmen from Illinois. Freshmen from 29 states and 2 foreign countries.

Admission: Rolling admissions plan. For fall acceptance, apply as early as June 1 after junior year, but not later than Aug. 1 of year of enrollment. Early acceptance available. *Requirements:* Either graduation from accredited secondary school or GED. 16 secondary school units, including 4 English, 2 foreign languages, 1 American history, 1 algebra, 1 geometry, 1 laboratory science recommended. Minimum GPA 2.0. Lowest acceptable secondary school class standing 50th percentile. *Entrance tests:* College Board SAT or ACT composite. *For transfer students:* 2.0 GPA; from 4-year institution 86 credit hours maximum transfer credit; from 2-year institution 60 hours; correspondence/extension students 30 hours.

College credit and advanced placement for postsecondary-level work completed in secondary school. Tutoring available. Developmental courses offered during regular academic year; credit given.

Degree Requirements: 126 credit hours; 2.0 GPA; three-quarters of college career or 40 of final 60 credits in residence; half of major and minor credits must be earned at Greenville College. Chapel attendance 3 times per week, unless excused; specific and distributed general education requirements.

Fulfillment of some degree requirements and exemption from some beginning courses possible by passing College Board CLEP. *Grading system:* A–F; withdraw (carries time limit and deadline after which pass/fail is appended to withdraw).

Distinctive Educational Programs: Work-experience programs. Evening classes. Dual-degree program in engineering with University of Illinois at Urbana-Champaign. Facilities and programs for independent research, including honors programs, individual majors. Study programs include: American Studies in Washington, D.C.; Australian Studies Center; China Studies Program; Contemporary Music Program in Martha's Vineyard; Latin American Studies Program in Costa Rica; Los Angeles Film studies Center; Middle East Studies Program in Egypt; Oxford Program; Russian Studies Program; Uganda Studies Program; Au Sable Institute of Environmental Studies in Mancelona, Michigan; Christian Center for Urban Studies in Chicago, Illinois; Daystar University in Kenya; Institute for Family Studies-Focus on the Family in Colorado Springs, Colorado.

Degrees Conferred: 338 *baccalaureate:* biological/life sciences 21; business/marketing 162; communications/communication technologies 17; computer and information sciences 5; education 60; English 10, foreign languages and literature 3; interdisciplinary studies 4; liberal arts/general studies 6; mathematics 1; parks and recreation 4; philosophy/religion/theology 11; physical sciences 7; protective services/public administration 6; psychology 4; social sciences and history 14; visual and performing arts 19. *Master's:* philosophy/religion/theology 6.

Fees and Other Expenses: *Full-time tuition per academic year 2004–05:* $17,142 undergraduate, $320 per credit graduate. *Required fees:* $100. *Room and board per academic year:* $5,904.

Financial Aid: Greenville College offers a direct lending program. Aid from institutionally generated funds is awarded on the basis of academic merit, financial need, other considerations. Institution has a Program Participation Agreement with the U.S. Department of Education for eligible students to receive Pell Grants and other federal aid.

Financial aid to full-time, first-time undergraduate students: need-based scholarships/grants totaling $7,353,359, self-help $3,823,091; parent loans $668,174; non-need-based scholarships/grants totaling $735,864; self-help $691,250, parent loans $1,077,962.

Departments and Teaching Staff: *Professors* 14, *associate professors* 10, *assistant professors* 25, *instructors* 7, *part-time faculty* 75. *Total instructional faculty:* 131 (full-time 56, part-time 75; women 45, men 86; members of minority groups 6). Total faculty with doctorate, first-professional, or other terminal degree: 56. Student-to-faculty ratio: 14:1. 3 faculty members awarded sabbaticals 2004.

Enrollment: Total enrollment 1,168. Undergraduate full-time 535 men / 583 women, part-time 27m / 25w; graduate full-time 13m / 37w, part-time 33m / 62w. *Transfer students:* in-state 115; from out-of-state 28.

Characteristics of Student Body: *Ethnic/racial makeup:* number Black non-Hispanic: 76; American Indian or Alaska Native: 6; Asian or Pacific Islander: 10; Hispanic: 26; White non-Hispanic: 184; unknown: 48. *Age distribution:* number under 18: 7; 18–19: 361; 20–21: 350; 22–24:152; 25–29: 64; 30–34: 71; 35–39: 30; 40–49: 85; 50–64: 47; 65 and over: 3.

International Students: 19 nonresident aliens enrolled fall 2004. 1 student from Europe, 3 Asia, 4 Central and South America, 7 Africa, 4 Canada. No programs available to aid students whose native language is not English. No financial aid specifically designated for international students.

Student Life: On-campus residence halls house 69% of student body. Residence halls for men only constitute 57% of such space, for women only 43%. *Intercollegiate athletics:* men only: baseball, basketball, cross-country, football, soccer, tennis, track; women only: basketball, cross-county, soccer, softball, tennis, track, volleyball. *Special regulations:* Cars must be parked in designated areas. Quiet hours from 11:00pm to 7:00am. Residence hall visitation on special occasions only. *Special services:* Learning Resources Center. *Student publications, radio: The Papyrus,* a newspaper; *The Vista,* a yearbook. Radio station WGRN broadcasts 108 hours per week. *Surrounding community:* Greenville population 5,500. St. Louis (Mo.), 50 miles from campus, is nearest metropolitan area. Served by airport 55 miles from campus; passenger rail service 45 miles from campus.

Library Collections: 131,425 volumes including bound books, serial backfiles, electronic documents, and government documents not in separate collections. Online catalog. Current serial subscriptions: 490 paper, 13,909 microform units, 1,500 electronic. 4,600 recordings. 45 computer work stations. Students have access to the Internet at no charge. Total budget for books, periodicals, audiovisual materials, microforms 2004–05: $75,000.

Most important special collections include the Richard W. Bock Sculpture Collection of over 1,000 objects including sculpture, photographs, and drawings.

Buildings and Grounds: Campus area 40 acres. *New buildings:* College Avenue Apartments completed 2001; Dietzman Center 2001; Maves Art Center 2003; Music Center 2005.

Chief Executive Officer: Dr. V. James Mannoia, Jr., President.

Address admission inquiries to Michael Ritter, Director of Admissions.

Harrington College of Design

200 West Madison
Chicago, Illinois 60606-3433
Tel: (312) 939-4976 **E-mail:** info@interiordesign.edu
Fax: (312) 939-8005 **Internet:** www.interiordesign.edu

Institution Description: The Harrington College of Design is a private college offering full- and part-time programs devoted solely to interior design. *Enrollment:* 1,588. *Degrees awarded:* Associate, baccalaureate.

Accreditation: *National:* NASAD. *Professional:* interior design

History: Established in 1931, the college remains the Midwest's only college devoted exclusively to professional interior design.

Calendar: Semesters. Academic year Sept. to June.

Admission: Contact the Admissions Office for catalog and application.

Degree Requirements: Completion of prescribed curriculum.

Distinctive Educational Programs: Study abroad program with Interior Architecture Department of Rotterdam College of Art, The Netherlands.

Degrees Conferred: 120 *associate:* interior design; 73 *baccalaureate:* visual arts.

Fees and Other Expenses: *Full-time tuition per academic year 2004–05:* $16,205. *Room and board per academic year:* $7,100. *Books and supplies:* $1,300. *Other expenses:* $2,788.

Financial Aid: Aid from institutionally generated funds is provided on the basis of financial need, other criteria. Institution has a Program Participation Agreement with the U.S. Department of Education for eligible students to receive Pell Grants and other federal aid.

Financial aid to full-time, first-time undergraduate students: 20% received federal grants averaging $2,858; 81% loans averaging $8,554.

Departments and Teaching Staff: *Total instructional faculty:* 40.

Enrollment: Total enrollment 1,558 (16.5% men, 99.5% women).

Characteristics of Student Body: *Ethnic/racial makeup:* Black non-Hispanic: 8.7%; American Indian or Alaska Native: .6%; Asian or Pacific Islander: 4.3%; Hispanic: 9.3%; White non-Hispanic: 71.5%; unknown: 5.6%.

International Students: 12 nonresident aliens enrolled fall 2004. No programs available to aid students whose native language is not English. No financial aid specifically designated for international students.

Library Collections: 25,000 volumes. 90 current periodical subscriptions. 26,000 audiovisual materials.

Most important special holdings: major collection of current catalogs from manufacturers of furniture, lighting, etc.

Buildings and Grounds: The Institute is housed in the historic Landmark Fine Arts Building.

Chief Executive Officer: Patricia Comstock, President.

Address admission inquiries to Wendi Franczyk, Director of Admissions.

Illinois College

1101 West College Avenue
Jacksonville, Illinois 62650
Tel: (217) 245-3000   **E-mail:** admissions@hilltop.ic.edu
Fax: (217) 245-3093   **Internet:** www.ic.edu

Institution Description: Illinois College is a private college affiliated with the United Presbyterian Church in the U.S.A. and the United Church of Christ. *Enrollment:* 1,037. *Degrees awarded:* Baccalaureate.

Member of Sangamon Valley Academic Library Consortium.

Accreditation: *Regional:* NCA.

History: Established and chartered 1829; offered first instruction at postsecondary level 1830; awarded first degree (baccalaureate) 1835; merged with Jacksonville Female Academy and became coeducational 1903. *See* Charles E. Frank, *Pioneer's Progress: Illinois College 1829–1879* (Carbondale, Ill.: Southern Illinois University Press, 1979) for further information.

Institutional Structure: *Governing board:* The board of Trustees of Illinois College. Extrainstitutional representation: 22 trustees; institutional representation: President of the college; 5 alumni. 1 ex officio. All voting. *Composition of institution:* Administrators 5 men / 2 women (at dean's level and above, 29% are women). Academic affairs headed by vice president for academic affairs. Management/business/finances directed by business manager. Full-time instructional faculty 61. Academic governance body, The Faculty of Illinois College, meets an average of 9 times per year.

Calendar: Semesters. Academic year Aug. to May. Freshmen admitted Aug., Jan. Degrees conferred and formal commencement May.

Characteristics of Freshmen: 1,145 applicants (579 men, 566 women). 55.2% of applicants admitted. 34.6% of admitted students enrolled full-time.

7% (19 students) submitted SAT scores; 98% (252 students) submitted ACT scores. *25th percentile:* SAT I Verbal 500, SAT I Math 480; ACT Composite 21, ACT English 21, ACT Math 20. *75th percentile:* SAT I Verbal 600, SAT I Math 660; ACT Composite 26, ACT English 26, ACT Math 26.

53% of entering freshmen expected to graduate within 5 years. 97% of freshmen from Illinois. Freshmen from 5 states and 2 foreign countries.

Admission: Rolling admissions plan. For fall acceptance, apply as early as end of junior year of secondary school, but not later than Aug. 15 of year of enrollment. *Requirements:* Either graduation from an accredited secondary school with 15 units which must include 3 English and 7 foreign language, history, laboratory science, mathematics, social studies; or GED. 4 English, 2 algebra, 1 geometry recommended. Minimum GPA 2.0. *Entrance tests:* College Board SAT or ACT composite. *For transfer students:* 2.0 minimum GPA, 90 hours maximum transfer credit; from 2-year accredited institution 66 hours.

College credit and advanced placement for postsecondary-level work completed in secondary school.

Degree Requirements: 120 credit hours; 2.0 GPA; last two terms in residence; attendance at 60 convocations (programs of general cultural interest); distribution requirements. Fulfillment of some degree requirements and exemption from some beginning courses possible by passing departmental examinations, College Board CLEP, APP. *Grading system:* A–F; credit-fail, withdraw (deadline after which pass-fail is appended to withdraw).

Distinctive Educational Programs: Work-experience programs. Dual-degree programs in engineering with University of Illinois, cytochemistry with Mayo School of Health-Related Sciences (MN); occupational therapy with Washington University (MO) and medical technology with St. John's Hospital in Springfield (IL). External degree program in nursing with Mennonite College of Nursing. Study abroad in England, France, Germany, and Spain. Intercultural exchange program with Ritsumeikan University in Kyoto, Japan.

Degrees Conferred: 186 *baccalaureate.* Bachelor's degrees awarded in top five disciplines: education 39; business, management, marketing, and related support services 34; biological and biomedical sciences 28; social sciences 22; English language and literature/letters 18.

Fees and Other Expenses: *Full-time tuition and fees per academic year 2004–05:* $14,000. *Books and supplies:* $800. *Room and board per academic year:* $8,200.

Financial Aid: Aid from institutionally generated funds is provided on the basis of academic merit, financial need. Institution has a Program Participation Agreement with the U.S. Department of Education for eligible students to receive Pell Grants and other federal aid.

Financial aid to full-time, first-time undergraduate students: 31% received federal grants averaging $2,858; 53% state/local grants averaging $4,059; 99% institutional grants averaging $5,368; 76% loans averaging $3,235.

Departments and Teaching Staff: *Professors* 13, *associate professors* 23, *assistant professors* 18, *instructors* 7, *part-time faculty* 39. *Total instructional*

faculty: 100. Student-to-faculty ratio: 14:1. Degrees held by full-time faculty: doctorate 76%, master's 24%.

Enrollment: Total enrollment 1,037 (45.8% men, 54.2% women).

Characteristics of Student Body: *Ethnic/racial makeup:* Black non-Hispanic: 2.6%; American Indian or Alaskan Native: .4%; Asian or Pacific Islander: .6%; Hispanic: 1.5%; White non-Hispanic: 92%. *Age distribution:* 17–21: 89.7%; 22–24: 7%; 25–29: 1.3%; 30–34: .4%; 35–39: .8%; 40–49: 3%; 50–59: .1%.

International Students: 12 nonresident aliens enrolled fall 2004. Students from Europe, Asia, Africa. No programs available to aid students whose native language is not English. No financial aid specifically designated for international students.

Student Life: On-campus residence halls house 47% of student body. Residence halls for men constitute 47% of such space, for women 40%, for both sexes 13%. *Intercollegiate athletics:* men only: baseball, basketball, cross-country, football, golf, soccer, tennis, track, wrestling; women only: basketball, cross-country, soccer, softball, tennis, track, volleyball. *Special regulations:* Cars permitted without restrictions. Quiet hours and residence hall visitation hours are established by residence hall committees. *Special services:* Medical services. *Student publications, radio: Forte,* a biannual literary magazine; *Rambler,* the college newspaper; *Rig Veda,* the yearbook. *Surrounding community:* Jacksonville population 20,000. Springfield (IL), 35 miles from campus, is nearest metropolitan area. Served by mass transit bus system, airport, and passenger rail service.

Publications: *Par Rapport* (biannually) first published in 1977.

Library Collections: 160,000 volumes including bound books, serial backfiles, electronic documents, and government documents not in separate collections. Online catalog. Current serial subscriptions: 620 paper, 100 microform, 3,000 electronic. 7,000 microform units; 3,000 recordings; 3,000 compact discs; 100 CD-ROMs. Computer work stations available. Students have access to the Internet at no charge.

Most important holdings include the Packard Lincoln Collection; Ben J. Thomas Civil War Collection; Illinois College History Collection.

Buildings and Grounds: Campus area 62 acres.

Chief Executive Officer: Dr. Axel D.Steuer, President.

Address admission inquiries to Richard Bystry, Director of Admissions.

Illinois College of Optometry

3241 South Michigan Avenue
Chicago, Illinois 60616
Tel: (312) 225-1700   **E-mail:** admission@ico.edu
Fax: (312) 225-1724

Institution Description: Illinois College of Optometry is a private, independent, nonprofit college, primarily for graduate study. *Enrollment:* 593. *Degrees awarded:* First-professional (optometry). Baccalaureate also available.

Accreditation: *Regional:* NCA. *Professional:* optometry

History: Established as Northern Illinois College of Ophthalmology and Otology 1872; changed name to Chicago College of Ophthalmology and Otology 1891; merged with Needles Institute of Optometry (established 1907) and changed name to Northern Illinois College of Optometry 1926; awarded first degree (first-professional) 1927; merged with Chicago College of Optometry (established 1937) and adopted present name 1955.

Institutional Structure: *Governing board:* Board of Trustees. Representation: 10 trustees, 2 faculty, 1 student. All voting. *Composition of institution:* Academic affairs headed by vice president for academic affairs/dean. Management/business/finances directed by chief financial officer. Full-time instructional faculty 50.

Calendar: Quarters. Academic year Aug. to May. Entering students admitted Aug. Degrees conferred and formal commencement May. Summer session of 2 terms from May to Aug.

Characteristics of Freshmen: 42% of applicants accepted. 55% of accepted applicants enrolled. 22% of entering students from Illinois. Entering students from 30 states and 2 foreign countries.

Admission: Rolling admissions plan. For fall acceptance, apply as early as Sept. of previous year, but not later than Apr. 1 of year of enrollment. Early acceptance available. *Requirements:* 90 semester hours or 135 quarter hours of prescribed college courses, including preprofessional curriculum in optometry from accredited junior college, college, or university. *Entrance tests:* Optometry College Admissions Test (OAT).

Degree Requirements: *For first-professional degrees:* 264 quarter hours; 2.0 GPA; 4 years in residence; completion of prescribed curriculum. *Grading system:* A–F; satisfactory-unsatisfactory; withdraw (deadline after which pass-fail is appended to withdraw).

Distinctive Educational Programs: *Available to all students:* Externships and residency programs. *Other distinctive programs:* Nondegree continuing education program for license renewal.

Degrees Conferred: 8 *baccalaureate*: health professions and related sciences; 165 *first-professional:* optometry.

Fees and Other Expenses: *Full-time tuition per academic year 2004–05:* $24,978.

Financial Aid: Aid from institutionally generated funds is provided on the basis of academic merit, financial need. Institution has a Program Participation Agreement with the U.S. Department of Education for eligible students to receive Pell Grants and other federal aid.

Departments and Teaching Staff: Basic health sciences *professors* 3, *associate professors* 1, *assistant professors* 2, *instructors* 0; clinical education 2, 1, 2, 0; dean's office education 6, 14, 15, 3. *Total instructional faculty:* 50. Degrees held by full-time faculty: professional 94%, master's 26%, doctorate .1%, baccalaureate 100%. 94% hold terminal degrees.

Enrollment: Total enrollment 593 (32.7% men, 67.3% women).

Characteristics of Student Body: *Ethnic/racial makeup:* Black non-Hispanic: 2.7%; Asian or Pacific Islander: 23,3%; Hispanic: 1.3%; White non-Hispanic: 57.7%; unknown: .8%.

International Students: 84 nonresident aliens enrolled fall 2004. No programs available to aid students whose native language is not English. No financial aid specifically designated for international students.

Student Life: On-campus residence halls house 26% of student body. Residence halls for both sexes constitute 100% of such space. *Special regulations:* Cars permitted in designated areas. *Special services:* Learning Resources Center. *Surrounding community:* Chicago metropolitan population 7,921,514. Served by airport 20 miles from campus; passenger rail service 8 miles from campus.

Library Collections: 30,000 volumes. 242 serial subscriptions. 3,053 microforms; 3,622 audiovisual materials. 46 CD-ROMS. 21 computer work stations. Online catalog. Students have access to the Internet at no charge.

Most important special holdings include collections on optometry, ophthalmology, and vision science.

Chief Executive Officer: Dr. Arol R. Augsburger, President.

Address admission inquiries to Ms. Asha Davis, Director of Admissions.

Illinois Institute of Technology

3300 South Federal Street
Chicago, Illinois 60616-3793
Tel: (312) 567-3000 **E-mail:** admission@iit.edu
Fax: (312) 567-3004 **Internet:** www.iit.edu

Institution Description: Illinois Institute of Technology is a private, independent, nonprofit institution. *Enrollment:* 6,378. *Degrees awarded:* Baccalaureate, master's, first-professional (law), doctorate. Certificates also awarded.

Accreditation: *Regional:* NCA. *Professional:* business, clinical psychology, engineering, law, rehabilitation counseling

History: Established by merger of Armour Institute of Technology (established 1890) and Lewis Institute (established 1895), merged with Institute of Design (established 1937), and adopted present name 1940; merged with Chicago-Kent College of Law 1969; founded Stuart Graduate School of Business 1969. *See* Irene Macauley, *The Heritage of Illinois Institute of Technology* (Chicago: Privately printed, 1978) for further information.

Institutional Structure: *Governing board:* Board of Trustees-Illinois Institute of Technology. Extrainstitutional representation: 65 trustees, including 21 alumni; institutional representation: president of the institute, 1 administrator. 2 ex officio. All voting. *Composition of institution:* Administrators 15 men / 5 women. Academic affairs headed by chief academic officer. Management/business/finances directed by vice president for business and finance. Full-time instructional faculty 288 men / 52 women. Academic governance body, Faculty Senate, meets an average of 3 times per year.

Calendar: Semesters (quarters for School of Business, Center for Law and Financial Markets). Academic year Aug. to May. Freshmen admitted Aug., Jan. Degrees conferred and formal commencements May, Dec. Summer session May to Aug.

Characteristics of Freshmen: 2,609 applicants (1,909 men, 700 women). 61.4% of applicants admitted. 28.9% of admitted students enrolled full-time.

53% (248 students) submitted SAT scores; 75% (350 students) submitted ACT scores. *25th percentile:* SAT I Verbal 570, SAT I Math 630; ACT Composite 26, ACT English 25, ACT Math 26. *75th percentile:* SAT I Verbal 670, SAT I Math 710; ACT Composite 30, ACT English 30, ACT Math 32.

43% of entering freshmen expected to graduate within 5 years. 39% of freshmen from Illinois. Freshmen from 35 states and 17 foreign countries.

Admission: Rolling admissions plan for freshmen and transfer students. For fall acceptance, apply as early as Sept. 1 of senior year of secondary school. *Requirements:* Diploma from accredited secondary school with 12.5 units of high school (4 English, 3.5 mathematics, 3 science (2 of which are lab)) 2 social science. *Entrance tests:* College Board SAT or ACT required of all freshmen. TOEFL required of all international students. *For transfer students:* minimum of 15 semester hours of transferable courses at an accredited community college, four-year college/university; cumulative GPA and individual grades in all classes that apply toward major are considered.

College credit and advanced placement for postsecondary-level work completed in secondary school. College credit for extrainstitutional learning on basis of ACE *2006 Guide to the Evaluation of Educational Experiences in the Armed Services;* portfolio assessment. Tutoring available.

Degree Requirements: 120–167 credit hours; 1.85 GPA (2.0 in major field); last 45 hours in residence; distribution requirements. Fulfillment of some degree requirements and exemption from some beginning courses possible by passing departmental examination, College Board CLEP, AP. *Grading system:* A–F; pass-fail; withdraw (carries time limit).

Distinctive Educational Programs: Career Development, with on-campus interviewing, summer internships, job books, development assistance, career counseling and testing, resume writing/interviewing techniques, employer library and videotape collection workshops, resume critiques and mock employment interviews; cooperative education. Evening classes. Special facilities for using telecommunications in the classroom. Interdisciplinary education. Honor programs. Tutorials. Study abroad programs available. Over 30 extension centers in the greater Chicago area that receive video educational broadcasts from Illinois Institute of Technology.

ROTC: Army Navy, Air Force.

Degrees Conferred: 403 *baccalaureate;* 992 *master's;* 64 *doctorate;* 280 *first-professional.* Bachelor's degrees awarded in top five disciplines: engineering 212; computer and information sciences and support services 83; architecture and related services 35; biological and biomedical sciences 25; social sciences 14.

Fees and Other Expenses: *Full-time tuition per academic year 2004–05:* $21,528 undergraduate; graduation tuition charged per credit hour. *Books and supplies:* $1,000. *Room and board per academic year:* $6,946.

Financial Aid: Aid from institutionally generated funds is awarded on the basis of academic merit, financial need, athletic ability, other criteria. Institution has a Program Participation Agreement with the U.S. Department of Education for eligible students to receive Pell Grants and other federal aid.

Financial aid to full-time, first-time undergraduate students: 25% received federal grants averaging $5,971; 29% state/local grants averaging $3,607; 98% institutional grants averaging $12,224; 59% loans averaging $8,333.

Departments and Teaching Staff: *Professors* 106, *associate professors* 72, *assistant professors* 77, *instructors* 25, *part-time teachers* 226.

Total instructional faculty: 506. Student-to-faculty ratio: 12:1. Degrees held by full-time faculty: doctorate 65%, master's 14%, baccalaureate 1%, professional 20%. 97% hold terminal degrees.

Enrollment: Total enrollment 6,378. Undergraduate 2,090 (75.4% men, 24.6% women).

Characteristics of Student Body: *Ethnic/racial makeup:* Black non-Hispanic: 5.8%; American Indian or Alaska Native: .3%; Asian or Pacific Islander: 13.7%; Hispanic: 7.4%; White non-Hispanic: 48.3%; unknown: 9%.

International Students: 326 undergraduate nonresident aliens enrolled fall 2004. Students from Europe, Asia, Central and South America, Africa, Canada, Australia. Programs available to aid students whose native language is not English: Social, cultural, financial. English as a Second Language Program.

Student Life: On-campus residence halls house 53% of full-time undergraduates. 15% of men join and 13% live in fraternities. Off-campus housing and housing available for married students. 65% of full-time undergraduates live on campus. *Intercollegiate athletics:* men only: baseball, basketball, cross-country, swimming; women only: basketball, cross-country, swimming, volleyball. *Special regulations:* Cars permitted without restrictions. *Special services:* Learning Resources Center, medical and psychological services, bus service between main campus and downtown campuses. *Student publications, radio:* Technology News, a weekly newspaper. Radio station WOUI broadcasts 84 hours per week. *Surrounding community:* Chicago population over 3,000,000. Served by mass transit bus, subway, train systems; airport 10 miles from campus; passenger rail service 2 miles from campus.

Library Collections: 594,500 volumes. 184,500 microforms; 54,300 audiovisual materials. 700 current periodical subscriptions. Students have access to the Internet at no charge.

Most important special collections include rare books (science and engineering) 1400–1900; Marvin Cameras Papers; NASA and NACA Technical Reports.

Buildings and Grounds: Campus area 120 acres.

Chief Executive Officer: Lewis M. Collens, President.
Address admission inquiries to Dean for Admissions.

College of Architecture

Degree Programs Offered: *Baccalaureate, master's* in architecture, city and regional development, design.

Armour College

Degree Programs Offered: *Baccalaureate* in chemical engineering, civil engineering, electrical engineering, environmental engineering, fire protection and safety engineering, gas engineering, mechanics, mechanical and aerospace engineering, metallurgical engineering; *master's* in chemical engineering, civil engineering, electrical engineering, environmental engineering, gas engineering, gas technology, mechanical and aerospace engineering, mechanical engineering, metallurgical and aerospace engineering; *doctorate* in chemical engineering, civil engineering, electrical engineering, environmental engineering, gas engineering, mechanics, mechanical and aerospace engineering, metallurgical and materials engineering.

Stuart School of Business

Degree Programs Offered: *Master's* in business administration, environmental management, financial markets and trading, operations and technology management; *doctorate* in management.

Chicago-Kent College of Law

Degree Programs Offered: *First-professional* in law; *master's* in law.

Admission: For *first-professional:* Baccalaureate, or, for exceptional students, completion of 65 per cent of undergraduate work. LSAT; registration with LSDAS. For *master's:* J.D., personal interview.

Distinctive Educational Programs: Legal Services Center administers prepaid legal services to senior citizens and other private cases.

Institute of Design

Degree Programs Offered: *Master's* in design, public works; *doctorate* in design.

Institute of Psychology

Degree Programs Offered: *Baccalaureate* in psychology; *master's* in personnel and human resources development, psychology, rehabilitation counseling; *doctorate* in psychology.

Illinois State University

North and School Streets
Normal, Illinois 61790
Tel: (309) 438-2111   **E-mail:** admissions@ilstu.edu
Fax: (309) 438-3932   **Internet:** www.ilstu.edu

Institution Description: Illinois State University is a state institution. *Enrollment:* 20,757. *Degrees awarded:* Baccalaureate, master's, doctorate.

Academic offerings subject to approval by statewide coordinating bodies. Budget subject to approval by state governing boards. Member of Illinois Education Consortium.

Accreditation: *Regional:* NCA. *Professional:* accounting, art, audiology, business, dietetics, environmental health, family and consumer science, health information administration, industrial technology, interior design, music, nursing, nursing education, psychology internship, recreation and leisure services, school psychology, social work, speech-language pathology, teacher education, theatre

History: Documents establishing institution were drawn by Abraham Lincoln; established as Illinois State Normal University and offered first instruction at postsecondary level 1857; awarded first degree (baccalaureate) 1907; incorporated and adopted present name 1964. *See* Helen Marshall, *The Grandest of Enterprises* (Normal: Illinois State Normal University, 1957) for further information.

Institutional Structure: *Governing board:* Illinois State University Board of Trustees appointed by Illinois governor. *Composition of institution:* Administrators 6 men / 7 women. Academic affairs headed by vice president and provost. Management/business/finances directed by vice president for finance and planning. Vice presidents for student affairs and university advancement. Full-time

instructional faculty 831. Academic governance body, Academic Senate, meets an average of 20 times per year.

Calendar: Semesters. Academic year Aug. to May. Freshmen admitted Aug., Jan., June. Degrees conferred May, Aug., Dec. Formal commencements May, Dec. Summer session from May to Aug.

Characteristics of Freshmen: 75% of applicants accepted. 37% of accepted students enrolled full-time.

99% (2,800 students) submitted ACT scores. *25th percentile:* ACT Composite 22, ACT English 21, ACT Math 21. *75th percentile:* ACT Composite 26, ACT English 26, ACT Math 26.

50% of entering freshmen expected to graduate within 5 years. 99% of freshmen from Illinois.

Admission: Rolling admissions plan. For fall acceptance, apply as early as Aug. 1 of previous year. Early acceptance available. *Requirements:* Either graduation from secondary school or GED. Additional requirements for some programs. *Entrance tests:* College Board SAT or ACT composite. *For transfer students:* 2.0 minimum GPA, maximum transfer credit limited only by residence requirement.

College credit for postsecondary-level work completed in secondary school and for extrainstitutional learning on basis of ACE *2006 Guide to the Evaluation of Educational Experiences in the Armed Services*; portfolio and faculty assessment. Tutoring available. Noncredit developmental remedial courses offered in summer session and regular academic year.

Degree Requirements: 120 semester hours; 2 semesters in residence; distribution requirements; examinations on the U.S. and Illinois constitutions and on the proper use of the national flag. Additional requirements for some programs.

Fulfillment of some degree requirements and exemption from some beginning courses possible by passing departmental examinations, College Board CLEP, APP. *Grading system:* A–F; pass-fail; withdraw (carries penalty and time limit).

Distinctive Educational Programs: Work-experience programs. Extended University, Distance Education, Extension courses at Bolingbrook, Brimfield, Champaign, Chicago Newberry Library, East Peoria, Kishwaukee, Pekin, Peoria, Quad Cities, Rochester, Woodstock, Wilmington. Accelerated degree programs. Dual-degree program in engineering with University of Illinois at Urbana-Champaign. Special facilities for using telecommunications in the classroom. Interdisciplinary courses in British studies, humanities, interracial dynamics, women's studies. Facilities and programs for independent research, including honors programs, individual majors, tutorials. Study abroad in Australia, Austria, England, France, Germany, Italy, Japan, Russia, Scotland, Spain, Sweden, Wales.

ROTC: Army. .

Degrees Conferred: 4,148 *baccalaureate;* 678 *master's;* 43 *doctorate.* Bachelor's degrees awarded in top five disciplines: education 890; business, management, marketing, and related support services 810; communication, journalism, and related programs 276; social sciences 269; health professions and related clinical sciences 220.

Fees and Other Expenses: *Full-time tuition per academic year 2004–05:* resident undergraduate $4,800, out-of-state $10,020. Contact the university for current graduate tuition/fees. *Required fees:* $1,528. *Room and board per academic year:* $5,676.

Financial Aid: Aid from institutionally generated funds is provided on the basis of academic merit, financial need, athletic ability. Institution has a Program Participation Agreement with the U.S. Department of Education for eligible students to receive Pell Grants and other federal aid.

Financial aid to full-time, first-time undergraduate students: need-based scholarships/grants totaling $31,756,919, self-help $33,049,167, parent loans $2,550,999, tuition waivers $384,982, athletic awards $565,248; non-need-based scholarships/grants totaling $6,592,422, self-help $19,365,341, parent loans $8,771,014, tuition waivers $1,007,766, athletic awards $1,970,024.

Departments and Teaching Staff: *Professors* 265, *associate professors* 198, *assistant professors* 267, *instructors* 128, *part-time faculty* 230. *Total instructional faculty:* 1,088 (full-time 831, part-time 257; women 509, men 579; members of minority groups 103). Total faculty with doctorate, first-professional, or other terminal degree: 784. Student-to-faculty ratio: 19:1.

Enrollment: Total enrollment 20,757. Undergraduate full-time 7,062 men / 9,551 women, part-time 589m / 676w; graduate full-time 454m / 691w, part-time 561m / 1,173w.

Characteristics of Student Body: *Ethnic and racial makeup:* number of Black non-Hispanic: 1,105; American Indian or Alaska Native: 51; Asian or Pacific Islander: 292; Hispanic: 536; White non-Hispanic: 15,360; unknown: 321.

International Students: 141 nonresident aliens enrolled fall 2004. Students from Europe, Asia, Central and South America, Africa, Canada, Australia, New Zealand. Programs available to aid students whose native language is not English: Social, cultural. English as a Second Language Program. No financial aid specifically designated for international students.

Student Life: Family/student apartments available. 22 fraternities and 17 sororities. *Intercollegiate athletics:* men only: baseball, basketball, cross-country, football, golf, tennis, track; women only: basketball, cross-country, golf, gymnastics, tennis, soccer, softball, swimming, volleyball. *Special regulations:* Cars with decals permitted in designated areas. Quiet hours on specified residence hall floors. *Special services:* Learning Resources Center, medical services. *Student publications, radio: Amistad*, a bimonthly newsletter; *The Daily Vidette*, a newspaper; *Orbit*, a quarterly literary magazine. Radio station WGLT broadcasts 133 hours per week. *Surrounding community:* Normal population 45,000; Bloomington (twin city to Normal) population 60,000. Chicago, 125 miles from campus, is nearest metropolitan area. Served by mass transit bus system; airport 5 miles from campus; passenger rail service 2 blocks from campus.

Publications: Sources of information include *Educational Studies* (quarterly) first published in 1970, *Illinois Quarterly* first published 1939, *Illinois School Law Quarterly* first published 1980, *Planning and Changing* (quarterly) first published 1970, *Proceedings of the Philosophy of Education Society* (annually) first published 1952.

Library Collections: 1,566,500 volumes including bound books, serial backfiles, electronic documents, and government documents not in separate collections. Online catalog. 12,255 current serial subscriptions. 24,720 audiovisual materials. 1,885,500 microform units. Students have access to the Internet at no charge.

Most important holdings include collection on the history of the circus and allied arts; collection on 20th century English and American authors; collection of books from private presses.

Buildings and Grounds: Campus area 950 acres.

Chief Executive Officer: Dr. C. Alvin Bowman, Jr. President.

Address admission inquiries to Molly K. Arnold, Director of Admissions.

Mennonite College of Nursing

804 North East Street
Bloomington, Illinois 61701-3078
Tel: (309) 829-0715

Degree Programs Offered: Generic program: 60 credit hours; specified prerequisites; 2.0 GPA. For RNs: same as for generic program plus proof of RN license.

Degree Requirements: Completion of prescribed program.

Illinois Wesleyan University

1312 North Park Street
Bloomington, Illinois 61702

Tel: (309) 556-1000   **E-mail:** iwuadmit@iwu.edu
Fax: (309) 556-3970   **Internet:** www.iwu.edu

Institution Description: Illinois Wesleyan University is a private, independent, residential liberal arts university. *Enrollment:* 2,118. *Degrees awarded:* Baccalaureate.

Accreditation: *Regional:* NCA. *Professional:* music, nursing, teacher education

History: Established 1850; offered first instruction at postsecondary level 1851; chartered and awarded first degree (baccalaureate) 1853. *See* Minor Myers, Jr. and Carl Teichman, *Illinois Wesleyan University: Continuity and Change, 1850-2000* (Bloomington, privately printed, 2001) for further information.

Institutional Structure: *Governing board:* Board of Trustees. Extrainstitutional representation: 39 elected, voting members, at least 12 of whom must be alumni; 4 ex officio members, including the president of the university. *Composition of institution:* Cabinet officers (10 men, 3 women). Academic affairs headed by provost/dean of the university. Management/business/finances directed by vice president for business and finance. Full-time instructional faculty 159. General faculty meets once a month; 4 major elected faculty committees meet weekly and biweekly; other elected and appointed committees meet as needed.

Calendar: Semesters and optional 3-week May term (4-4-1). Academic year late Aug. to May. First-year students admitted Aug., Jan. Degrees conferred Dec., May (formal commencement), Aug.

Characteristics of Freshmen: 49% of applicants admitted. 38% of admitted students enrolled full-time.

35% (192 students) submitted SAT scores; 93% (513 students) submitted ACT scores. *25th percentile:* SAT Verbal 580, SAT Math 600; ACT Composite 27, ACT English 26, ACT Math 26. *75th percentile:* SAT Verbal 690, SAT Math 690; ACT Composite 31, ACT English 32, ACT Math 30.

13 National Merit Scholars. 64% of entering freshmen expected to graduate within 5 years. 90% of freshmen from Illinois. Freshmen from 12 states and 5 foreign countries.

Admission: Rolling admissions plan with notification starting Dec. 15; priority application date Nov. 1. *Requirements:* Either graduation from accredited secondary or GED; minimum of 15 academic units recommended (4 English, 3 math, 3 science with 2 labs, 3 foreign language 2 history). *Entrance tests:* College Board SAT or ACT composite; writing component accepted but not required. For foreign students TOEFL. *For transfer students:* 2.0 minimum GPA; from 4-year accredited institution maximum transfer credit 64 semester hours.

College credit and advanced placement for postsecondary-level work completed in secondary school. Tutoring available.

Degree Requirements: 32 course units (128 semester hours); 2.0 GPA; 2 years in residence; general education requirements.

Fulfillment of some degree requirements and exemption from some beginning courses up to 32 semester hours (8 course units) of AP credit awarded for scores of 4 or 5. *Grading system:* A–F; pass-fail; withdraw (carries time limit).

Distinctive Educational Programs: Internships. Evening classes. Dual-degree programs in engineering with Case Western Reserve University (OH), Northwestern University, Washington University (MO); in forestry with Duke University (NC). Cooperative baccalaureate in medical technology with approved hospitals. Special facilities for using telecommunications in the classroom. Interdepartmental programs in American Studies, arts management, humanities, music theater, natural science. Facilities and programs for independent research, including honors programs, individual majors. Study abroad in Europe; domestic off-campus study in Washington (DC).

Degrees Conferred: 468 *baccalaureate:* Degrees awarded in top five disciplines: biological/life sciences 48, business management 102; psychology 41, social sciences and history 71, visual and performing arts 55.

Fees and Other Expenses: *Full-time tuition per academic year 2005–06:* $27,474. *Room and board per academic year:* $6,426. *Required fees:* $150.

Financial Aid: Aid from institutionally generated funds is awarded on the basis of academic merit, financial need. Institution has a Program Participation Agreement with the U.S. Department of Education for eligible students to receive Pell Grants and other federal aid.

Financial aid to full-time, first-time undergraduate students: need-based scholarships/grants totaling $15,154,340, self-help $6,145,048; non-need-based scholarships/grants totaling $6,548,449, self-help $1,783,448, parent loans $2,556,954, tuition waivers $97,425.

Departments and Teaching Staff: *Professors* 47, *associate professors* 63, *assistant professors* 45, *instructors* 5, *part-time faculty* 63. *Total instructional faculty:* 223 (full-time 160, part-time 63; women 109, men 114; members of minority groups 32). Total faculty with doctorate, first-professional, or other terminal degree: 162.

Enrollment: Total enrollment 2,118. Full-time 924 men / 1,188 women, part-time 6m / 3w.

Characteristics of Student Body: *Ethnic/racial makeup:* number of Black non-Hispanic: 67; American Indian or Alaska Native: 5; Asian or Pacific Islander: 46; Hispanic: 57; White non-Hispanic: 1,811; unknown: 99. *Age distribution:* under 18: 25; 18–19: 1,059; 20–21: 965; 22–24: 64; 25–29: 2; 30–34: 2; 40–49: 1.

International Students: 31 nonresident aliens enrolled fall 2004. 10 students from Europe, 14 Asia, 1 Central and South America, 6 Africa, 2 other. No programs available to aid students whose native language is not English. No financial aid specifically designated for international students.

Student Life: On-campus residence halls house 81% of student body. Residence halls for men constitute 27% of such space, for women 46%, for both sexes 27%. 30% of men join and 25% live in fraternities; 30% of women join and 23% live in sororities. *Intercollegiate athletics:* men only: baseball, basketball, football, golf, tennis, track, wrestling; women only: basketball, softball, tennis, track, volleyball. *Special regulations:* Cars permitted without restrictions. Quiet hours. Residence hall visitation from noon to 11:30pm Sun.–Thurs., noon to 12:30am Fri. and Sat. *Special services:* Learning Resources Center, medical services. *Student publications, radio: The Argus*, a weekly newspaper; *Unicorn*, an annual literary magazine; *Wesleyana*, a yearbook. Radio station WESN broadcasts 147 hours per week. *Surrounding community:* Bloomington population 45,000. Chicago, 130 miles from campus, is nearest metropolitan area. Served by mass transit bus system; airport 3 miles from campus; passenger rail service 2 miles from campus.

Library Collections: 357,239 volumes. Current serial subscriptions: 1,058 paper; 10 microform; 8,953 via electronic access. 6,650 recordings; 3,800 compact discs; 178 CD-ROMs. 100 computer work stations. Students have access to online information retrieval services and the Internet.

Most important special holdings include works by and about John Wesley Powell and exploration of the West; works by and about John Gay and the 18th-

19th century British stage. Total budget for books and materials 2004–05: $693,217.

Buildings and Grounds: Campus area 79 acres with 51 buildings. *New buildings:* Ames Library opened 2002; Hansen Student Center 2002.

Chief Executive Officer: Dr. Richard F. Wilson, President.

Address admission inquiries to Jerry Pope, Dean of Admissions.

John Marshall Law School

315 South Plymouth Court

Chicago, Illinois 60604

Tel: (312) 427-2737   **E-mail:** admission@jmls.edu
Fax: (312) 427-5136   **Internet:** www.jmls.edu

Institution Description: John Marshall Law School is a private professional school. *Enrollment:* 1,571. *Degrees awarded:* First-professional, master's.

Accreditation: *Regional:* NCA. *Professional:* law

History: Established 1899.

Institutional Structure: Governing board: board of trustees. Administration: Dean, five associate deans, law library director, 2 assistant deans.

Calendar: Semesters. Academic year Aug. to May.

Admission: Entering classes begin in Aug. and Jan. for full-time study. Students must take the Law School Admission Test, and apply by Apr. 1 for fall admissions or Oct. 1 for spring admission.

Degree Requirements: 90 semester hours; overall GPA of at least 2.0 over three years full-time and four years part-time.

Distinctive Educational Programs: Legal writing and intellectual property. Center for Real Estate; Center for Taxation and Employee Benefits; Center for International and Comparative Law; Center for Information Technology and Privacy Law; Fair Housing Legal Support Center; Center for Advocacy and Dispute Resolution. Advanced degrees in intellectual property, taxation and employee benefits, real estate, international law (for international students), information technology law, and international business transactions.

Degrees Conferred: 96 *master's:* law/legal studies; 375 *first-professional:* law.

Fees and Other Expenses: *Full-time tuition per academic year 2004–05:* $28,660.

Financial Aid: Aid from institutionally generated funds is provided on the basis of academic merit and financial need. Institution has a Program Participation Agreement with the U.S. Department of Education for eligible students to receive Pell Grants and other federal aid.

Departments and Teaching Staff: *Professors* 37, *associate professors* 13, *assistant professors* 5, *part-time faculty* 78. *Total instructional faculty:* 133. Student-to-faculty ratio: 9:1. Degrees held by full-time faculty: doctorate 7%, master's 45%, baccalaureate 100%, professional 100%.

Enrollment: Total enrollment 1,571 (57.3% men, 42.7% women).

Characteristics of Student Body: *Ethnic/racial makeup:* Black non-Hispanic: 5%; American Indian or Alaska Native: .4%; Asian or Pacific Islander: 5.7%; Hispanic: 4.2%; White non-Hispanic: 78.9%; unknown: 3.1%.

International Students: 31 nonresident aliens enrolled fall 2004. No programs available to students whose native language is not English. No financial aid specifically designated for international students.

Student Life: John Marshall Law School has over 30 student organizations providing opportunities for students to plan social activities and community service initiatives. *Student publications: John Marshall Law Review* and *Journal of Computer and Information Law. John Marshall Magazine* is published 3 times per year.

Library Collections: 235,000 volumes. 128,845 microforms; 1,340 audiovisual materials; 800 current periodical subscriptions. 150 computer workstations. Access to online information retrieval systems and the Internet.

Chief Executive Officer: Patricia Mell, Dean.

Address admission inquiries to William B. Powers, Associate Dean for Admission and Student Affairs.

Judson College

1151 North State Street

Elgin, Illinois 60123

Tel: (847) 695-2500
Fax: (847) 628-2046

Institution Description: Judson College is an independent college, affiliated with the American Baptist Churches, USA. *Enrollment:* 1,220. *Degrees awarded:* Baccalaureate, master's.

Member of Christian College Coalition.

Accreditation: *Regional:* NCA.

History: Established, chartered, incorporated, and offered first instruction at postsecondary level 1963; awarded first degree 1964.

Institutional Structure: *Governing board:* Board of Trustees. Representation: 36 trustees, including 2 alumni, 1 administrator, 1 part-time instructional faculty member. 1 ex officio. All voting. *Composition of institution:* President's cabinet comprised of: provost and vice president for academic affairs, vice presidents for: advancement, business affairs, enrollment and technology services, student development; senior dean for graduate, adult, and continuing education. Full-time instructional faculty 53. Academic governance body is the Faculty Business Meeting that meets once per month.

Calendar: Semesters. Academic year Aug. to May. Freshmen admitted Aug., Jan. Degrees conferred and formal commencement May, Dec. No summer session.

Characteristics of Freshmen: 68% of applicants accepted. 50% of accepted applicants enrolled.

Average secondary school rank of freshmen class 61st percentile. Mean SAT class scores 533 verbal, 504 mathematical. Mean ACT composite class score 22.

57% of freshmen expected to graduate within 5 years. 66% of freshmen from Illinois. Freshmen from 24 states.

Admission: Rolling admissions plan. For fall acceptance, apply by Aug. 15. Early decision available; need not limit application to Judson. Early acceptance available. *Requirements:* Either graduation from accredited secondary school or GED. 15 units, the majority in college preparatory subjects recommended. Minimum 2.0 GPA. ACT composite 18. *Entrance tests:* ACT composite. *For transfer students:* 2.0 minimum GPA, 66 hours maximum transfer credit.

Advanced placement for postsecondary-level work completed in secondary school. Advanced placement credit given. Tutoring available. Remedial courses offered during regular academic year.

Degree Requirements: 126 credit hours; 2.0 GPA; 30 hours in residence; general education core of 47 hours required including biblical studies, English proficiency requirement. Fulfillment of some degree requirements possible by participation in college activities, passing College Board CLEP. *Grading system:* A–F; pass; withdraw; incomplete (carries time limit).

Distinctive Educational Programs: Architecture, Worship Arts, and accelerated degree completion programs including a general education liberal arts cohort program. There are more than 60 academic majors, minors, and concentrations, including 10 pre-professional programs. Study abroad available in various foreign locations as well s off-campus programs in Washington,D.C. Hollywood, Martha's Vineyard, and other locations in the United States.

Degrees Conferred: 384 *baccalaureate:* architecture 28 (17 *master's* also awarded); biological/life sciences 3; business/marketing 136; communications/communication technologies 8; education 26; English 4; interdisciplinary studies 7; mathematics 3; philosophy/religion/theology 27; physical sciences 2; protective services/public administration 13; psychology 13; social sciences and history 50; visual and performing arts 26.

Fees and Other Expenses: *Full-time tuition per academic year 2004–05:* undergraduate $15,900l; graduate $595 per credit hour. *Required fees:* $260. *Room and board per academic year:* $6,200.

Financial Aid: Judson College offers a direct lending program. Aid from institutionally generated funds is provided on the basis of academic merit, financial need, athletic ability, other criteria. Institution has a Program Participation Agreement with the U.S. Department of Education for eligible students to receive Pell Grants and other federal aid.

Departments and Teaching Staff: *Professors* 13, *associate professors* 21, *assistant professors* 18, *instructors* 1, *part-time faculty* 56. *Total instructional faculty:* 111 (full-time 53, part-time 58; women 42, men 69; members of minority groups 10). Total faculty with doctorate, first-professional, or other terminal degree: 53. Student-to-faculty ratio: 15:1. *Faculty development:* $86,857 total grants for research. 2 faculty members awarded sabbaticals 2004–05.

Enrollment: Total enrollment 1,220. Undergraduate full-time 390 men / 477 women, part-time 96m / 184w; graduate full-time 12m / 4w, part-time 26m / 31w.

Characteristics of Student Body: *Ethnic/racial makeup:* number of Black non-Hispanic: 49; American Indian or Alaska Native: 2; Asian or Pacific Islander: 14; Hispanic: 63; White non-Hispanic: 854; unknown: 203. *Age distribution:* number under 18: 11; 18–19: 243; 20–21: 280 22–24: 188; 25–29: 104; 30–34: 74; 35–39: 76; 40–49: 118; 50–64: 36; unknown: 17.

International Students: 35 nonresident aliens enrolled fall 2004. 11 students from Europe, 7 Asia, 8 Central and South America, 7 2 Africa, 2 Canada. Programs available to aid students whose native language is not English: English as a second language program. Financial aid in the form of scholarships available annually on a contingent basis.

Student Life: On-campus residence halls house 70% of student body. *Intercollegiate athletics:* men only: baseball; women only: softball, both sexes: basketball, soccer. *Special regulations:* Cars permitted with campus registration. Curfews, residence hall visitation, and quiet hours vary according to residence hall. *Special services:* computer lab, medical services. *Surrounding community:* Elgin population 90,000. Chicago, 40 miles from campus, is nearest metropolitan area. Served by mass transit bus system; airport 30 miles from campus; passenger rail service and bus service two miles from campus.

Publications: Sources of information about Judson include *Judson Today Magazine.*

Library Collections: 103,433 volumes. Online catalog. Current serial subscriptions: 422 paper, 1 microform; 18,697 via electronic access. 11,000 recordings. 25 computer work stations. Students have access to the Internet at no charge.

Most important holdings include collection of Jeffersonian Americana; microbook Library of American civilization; Schofield Music collection; Baptist History and Missions.

Buildings and Grounds: Campus area 85 acres. *New buildings:* Clarkside-South Architecture Building completed 2000.

Chief Executive Officer: Dr. Jerry B. Cain, President.

Address admission inquiries to Philip Guth, Director of Enrollment Services.

Keller Graduate School of Management of DeVry University

1 Tower Lane
Chicago, Illinois 60181

Tel: (630) 571-7700   **E-mail:** admissions@keller.edu
Fax: (630) 571-0317   **Internet:** www.keller.edu

Institution Description: Keller Graduate School of Management of DeVry University (CBA Institute until 1975) is a private, proprietary institution. *Enrollment:* 1,856. *Degrees awarded:* Master's.

Accreditation: *Regional:* NCA. *Professional:* business

History: Established and incorporated as CBA Institute and offered first instruction at postsecondary level 1973; offered master's program and adopted present name 1975; first degree (master's) awarded 1976; became a unit of DeVry University in 2004.

Institutional Structure: *Governing board:* Board of Directors. Extrainstitutional representation: 6 directors; institutional representation: 2 administrators. All voting. *Composition of institution:* Administrators 8 men / 6 women. Academic affairs headed by dean. Management/business/finances directed by president. Academic governance body, the administration, meets an average of 12 times per year.

Calendar: Quarters. Academic year Sept. to June. Entering students admitted Sept., Nov., Feb., Apr., June. Degrees conferred and formal commencements June, Jan. Summer session from late June to early Sept.

Admission: Rolling admissions plan. *Requirements:* Baccalaureate from accredited college or university. Interview. *Entrance tests:* GMAT. *For transfer students:* 3.0 minimum GPA; 12 hours maximum transfer credit.

Degree Requirements: 60 quarter hours; 2.5 minimum GPA; 8 core and 7 advanced courses, including business planning seminar.

Fulfillment of some degree requirements and exemption from some beginning courses possible by passing departmental examinations. *Grading system:* A–F; withdraw (excessive number carries penalty).

Distinctive Educational Programs: Internships. Flexible meeting places and schedules including off-campus centers, weekend and evening classes. Special facilities for using telecommunications in the classroom.

Degrees Conferred: 346 *master's:* business and management.

Fees and Other Expenses: *Full-time tuition per academic year 2004–05:* Contact the school for current tuition and fees.

Financial Aid: Fellowships, grants, and nonteaching/nonresearch college-assigned jobs available.

Departments and Teaching Staff: *Total instructional faculty:* 73.

Enrollment: Total enrollment 1,856.

Student Life: No on-campus housing. *Special regulations:* Cars permitted without restrictions. *Special services:* Learning Resources Center. *Surrounding community:* Chicago population over 3,000,000. Served by mass transit bus and train system; airport 20 miles from campus.

Kendall College

900 North Branch Street
Chicago, Illinois 60822

Tel: (312) 752-2000   **E-mail:** tfitzgibbon@kendall.edu
Fax: (312) 752-2057   **Internet:** www.kendall.edu

Institution Description: Kendall College is a private college affiliated with the United Methodist Church. *Enrollment:* 715. *Degrees awarded:* Associate, baccalaureate.

Academic offerings subject to approval by statewide coordinating bodies.

Accreditation: *Regional:* NCA. *National:* American Culinary Federation. *Professional:* culinary education

History: Established as Evanston Collegiate Institute and offered first instruction at postsecondary level 1934; first degree (associate) awarded 1936; incorporated 1941; present name adopted 1950; offered first baccalaureate degree instruction 1979; moved to Chicago campus 2004.

Institutional Structure: *Governing board:* Kendall College Corporation. Representation: 24 trustees, including 7 directors and president of the college; 5 administrators; 5 honorary trustees. 2 ex officio. 24 voting. *Composition of institution:* Administrators 5 men / 5 women. Management/business/finances directed by president. Full-time instructional faculty 28. Academic governance body, Faculty Senate, meets an average of 9 times per year.

Calendar: Quarters. Academic year Sept. to June. Students admitted Sept., Jan., Apr., July. Degrees conferred and formal commencement June. Summer session full quarter term.

Characteristics of Freshmen: 49% of applicants admitted. 24% of admitted students enrolled full-time.

14% (26 students) submitted SAT scores; 78% (50 students) submitted ACT scores. *25th percentile:* SAT Verbal 470, SAT Math 440; ACT Composite 18, ACT English 18, ACT Math 17. *75th percentile:* SAT Verbal 530, SAT Math 560; ACT Composite 21, ACT English 22, ACT Math 23.

38% of entering freshmen expected to graduate within 5 years. 81% of freshmen from Illinois. Freshmen from 11 states and 1 foreign country.

Admission: Rolling admissions plan. For fall acceptance, apply as early as Oct. 1 of previous year, but not later than Sept. 1 of year of enrollment. Early acceptance available. *Requirements:* Either 10-11 secondary school units which must include 4 English, 2 mathematics, 2 science, 2-3 history/social studies; or GED. 2 units in a foreign language and additional courses in mathematics, speech, science recommended. *Entrance tests:* College Board SAT or ACT composite. *For transfer students:* 2.0 minimum GPA; from 4-year institution 90 hours maximum transfer credit; for 2-year institution 60 hours. Advanced placement for 3–5. Tutoring available. Developmental courses offered during regular academic year; credit given.

Degree Requirements: *For all associate degrees:* 96 quarter hours; 1 year in residence. *For all baccalaureate degrees:* 184 quarter hours; 1 year in residence. *For all degrees:* 2.0 GPA. *Grading system:* A–F; satisfactory/unsatisfactory; withdraw (carries time limit; deadline after which satisfactory/unsatisfactory appended to withdraw).

Distinctive Educational Programs: Work-experience programs. Evening classes. All programs provide students with internship/work opportunities. State-of-the-art information technology, leadership and advocacy, early childhood education, culinary arts, and hospitality management programs.

Degrees Conferred: 59 *associate;* 49 *baccalaureate:* business/marketing 31; education 11; interdisciplinary studies 2; protective services/public administration 5.

Fees and Other Expenses: *Full-time tuition per academic year 2004–05:* $18,360. *Required fees:* $300. *Room and board per academic year:* $9,000.

Financial Aid: Aid from institutionally generated funds is provided on the basis of academic merit, financial need. Institution has a Program Participation Agreement with the U.S. Department of Education for eligible students to receive Pell Grants and other federal aid.

Financial aid to full-time, first-time undergraduate students: need-based scholarships/grants totaling $2,449,550, self-help $1,023,333, athletic awards $362,327; non-need-based self-help $846,245, parent loans $916,080.

Departments and Teaching Staff: *Professors* 2, *associate professors* 6, *assistant professors* 3, *instructors* 24, *part-time faculty* 35. *Total instructional faculty:* 70. *Student-to-faculty ratio:* 9:1.

Enrollment: Total enrollment 715. Full-time 216 men / 222 women, part-time 55m / 122w. *Transfer students:* in-state 101; from out-of-state 24.

Characteristics of Student Body: *Ethnic/racial makeup:* number of Black non-Hispanic: 64; American Indian or Alaska Native: 2; Asian or Pacific Islander: 47; Hispanic: 50; White non-Hispanic: 401; unknown: 20. *Age distribution:* number 18–19: 101; 20–21: 128; 22–24: 127; 25–29: 86; 30–34: 64; 35–39: 35; 40–49: 50; 50–64: 23; 65 and over: 1.

International Students: 31 nonresident aliens enrolled fall 2004. Social and cultural programs available to aid students whose native language is not English. Financial aid specifically designated for international students.

Student Life: *Special services:* Computer labs; student lounge; pre-admission counseling and testing; class-related tutorial and academic advisement; career services. Access to state-of-the-art fitness center; student cafeteria food prepared by culinary arts students. *Student publications:* Weekly newspaper. *Surrounding community:* Chicago, a major metropolitan area. Served by mass transit bus and rail systems.

Library Collections: 31,210 volumes. Online catalog. 150 serial subscriptions. 10 computer work stations. Access to online information retrieval systems. Students have access to the Internet at no charge.

Most important holdings include culinary arts collection; Native American culture collection; early childhood education; human services collection.

Chief Executive Officer: Dr. Howard A. Tullman, President.

Address admission inquiries to Director of Admissions.

Knox College

2 East South Street
Galesburg, Illinois 61401

Tel: (309) 341-7000   **E-mail:** admission@knox.edu
Fax: (309) 341-7090   **Internet:** www.knox.edu

Institution Description: Knox College is a private, independent, nonprofit college. *Enrollment:* 1,205 *Degrees awarded:* Baccalaureate.
Member of Associated Colleges of the Midwest.

Accreditation: *Regional:* NCA.

History: Established and chartered as Knox Manual Labor College 1837; offered first instruction at postsecondary level 1841; awarded first degree (baccalaureate) 1846; adopted present name 1857. *See* Earnest Elmo Calkins, *They Broke the Prairie* (New York: Charles Scribner's Sons, 1937) for further information.

Institutional Structure: *Governing board:* Knox College Board of Trustees. Extrainstitutional representation: 36 trustees; institutional representation: 1 administrator. 36 voting. *Composition of institution:* Administrators 6 men / 2 women. Academic affairs headed by dean of the college and vice president for academic affairs. Management/business/finances directed by vice president for finance, treasurer. Full-time instructional faculty 62 men / 37 women. Academic governance body, the faculty, meets an average of 9 times per year.

Calendar: Three 10-week terms. Academic year Sept. to June. Freshmen admitted Sept., Mar., Jan. Degrees conferred June, Oct., Jan., Apr. Formal commencement June.

Characteristics of Freshmen: 72% of applicants admitted. 19% of admitted students enrolled full-time.

48% (174 students) submitted SAT scores; 73% (265 students) submitted ACT scores. *25th percentile:* SAT Verbal 570, SAT Math 560; ACT Composite 25, ACT English 25, ACT Math 23. *75th percentile:* SAT Verbal 700, SAT Math 670; ACT Composite 30, ACT English 31, ACT Math 28.

75% of entering freshmen expected to graduate within 5 years. 54% of freshmen from Illinois. Freshmen from 36 states and 20 foreign countries.

Admission: Rolling admissions plan. For fall acceptance, apply as early as Sept. 15 of previous year, but not later than Aug. 15 of year of enrollment. Early action application date Dec. 1. *Requirements:* Either graduation from accredited secondary school with 15 units in English, foreign language, mathematics, natural science, and social studies; or GED. 3 additional units recommended. *Entrance tests:* College Board SAT or ACT composite. *For transfer students:* 22.5 course credits maximum accepted toward degree; from 2-year accredited institution 18.0 course credits maximum accepted. Good standing at institution previously attended.

College credit for postsecondary-level work completed in secondary school. Tutoring available. Developmental/remedial courses offered during regular academic year; credit given.

Degree Requirements: 36 course credits; 2.0 GPA; key competencies in language, mathematics, writing, speaking, diversity information literacy; foundation area requirements in arts, humanities, science, social science; experiential learning requirements. Fulfillment of some degree requirements and exemption

from some beginning courses possible by passing College Board A-level or 1B. *Grading system:* A–F; pass-fail; withdraw (carries time limit).

Distinctive Educational Programs: Honors Program for Seniors. Rush Medical School-Knox College Early Identification Program for freshmen planning on medical school. Three study abroad programs run by Knox College but open to other students: Barcelona, in conjunction with the university there; and Buenos Aires in conjunction with a university there. Besancon in conjunction with the university there. Consortial programs (Knox is a member of the Associated Colleges of the Midwest and the Institute of European Studies): China, Costa Rica, England, India, Italy, Japan, Russia, Germany, Yugoslavia; One-semester research program in the natural sciences and social sciences at Oak Ridge National Laboratory (TN), Urban Teaching Term for education students, summer program at Wilderness Field Station (MN). Washington, D.C. semester in cooperation with The American University. Dual degree programs in architecture with Washington University (MO); engineering with Columbia University (NY), University of Illinois, Washington University (MO), and Rensselaer Polytechnic Institute (NY); forestry and environmental management with Duke University (NC); law with Columbia University and University of Chicago; nursing with Rush University; Green Oaks Interdisciplinary Environmental Term; Clinical Psychology Term; Repertory Theatre Term.

Degrees Conferred: 265 *baccalaureate:* area and ethnic studies 4; biological/life sciences 30; computer and information sciences 6; education 20; English 33; foreign languages and literature 15; liberal arts/general studies 4; mathematics 9; natural resources/environmental science 7; philosophy/religion/theology 10; physical sciences 13; psychology 27; social sciences and history 67; visual and performing arts 20.

Fees and Other Expenses: *Full-time tuition per academic year 2004–05:* $24,960. *Required fees:* $276. *Room and board per academic year:* $6,102.

Financial Aid: Aid from institutionally generated funds is provided on the basis of academic merit, financial need. Institution has a Program Participation Agreement with the U.S Department of Education for eligible students to receive Pell Grants and other federal aid.

Financial aid to full-time, first-time undergraduate students: need-based scholarships/grants totaling $12,960,170, self-help $4,263,903; non-need-based scholarships/grants totaling $3,045,107, self-help $1,530,487, parent loans $1,776,106.

Departments and Teaching Staff: *Professors* 25, *associate professors* 30, *assistant professors* 28, *instructors* 5, *part-time faculty* 28. *Total instructional faculty:* 116 (full-time 88, part-time 28; women 49, men 67; members of minority groups 11). Total faculty with doctorate, first-professional, or other terminal degree: 101. Student-to-faculty ratio: 12:1. 17 faculty members awarded sabbaticals 2004–05.

Enrollment: Total enrollment 1,205. Full-time 330 men / 648 women, part-time 10m / 17w. *Transfer students:* in-state 52; from out-of-state 54.

Characteristics of Student Body: *Ethnic/racial makeup:* number of Black non-Hispanic: 56; American Indian or Alaska Native: 4; Asian or Pacific Islander: 58; Hispanic: 55; White non-Hispanic: 869; unknown: 73. *Age distribution:* number under 18: 22; 18–19: 576; 20–21: 480; 22–24: 81; 25–29: 14; 30–34: 0l 35–39: 1; 40–49: 2; 50–64: 1.

International Students: 90 nonresident aliens enrolled fall 2004. 15 students from Europe, 52 Asia, 1 Central and South America, 15 Africa, 2 Canada, 5 other. No programs available to aid students whose native language is not English. No financial aid specifically designated for international students.

Student Life: On-campus residence halls house 95% of student body. Residence halls for men only constitute 8% of such space, for women only 19%, for both sexes 58%. 5% of student body is housed in college-controlled student houses. 10% live in fraternity/sorority houses. *Intercollegiate athletics:* men only: baseball, basketball, cross-country, football, golf, soccer, swimming, tennis, track, wrestling; women only: basketball, cross-country, soccer, softball, swimming, tennis, track, volleyball. *Special regulations:* Cars permitted without restrictions. Quiet hours vary according to living unit. *Special services:* Learning Resources Center, medical services. *Student publications, radio: Catch,* a literary magazine (published 2–3 times annually); *The Gale,* a yearbook; *Knox Student,* a weekly newspaper. Radio station WVKC-FM broadcasts 138 hours per week. *Surrounding community:* Galesburg population 35,000. Chicago, 180 miles from campus, is nearest metropolitan area. Served by airport 4 miles from campus; passenger rail service less than 1 mile from campus.

Library Collections: 308,614 volumes. Online and card catalogs. Current serial subscriptions: paper 927; microform 98,696; 1,094 audiovisual materials; 7,159 recordings. Access to online information retrieval systems. Total 2004–05 budget for books and materials: $1,062,507.

Most important holdings include Finley Collection on the Old Northwest; Strong Collection of 18th- and 19th-century maps and photographs; Hughes Collection of manuscripts and first editions of Hemingway and the "Lost Generation" of American expatriate writers; Smith Collection on the Civil War.

Buildings and Grounds: Campus area 60 acres.

Chief Executive Officer: Dr. Roger L. Taylor, President.
Address admission inquiries to Paul Steenis, Dean of Admissions.

Lake Forest College

555 North Sheridan Road
Lake Forest, Illinois 60045-2399
Tel: (847) 234-3100   **E-mail:** admissions@lakeforest.edu
Fax: (847) 735-6291   **Internet:** www.lakeforest.edu

Institution Description: Lake Forest College is a private, nonprofit college affiliated with the Presbyterian Church. *Enrollment:* 1,408. *Degrees awarded:* Baccalaureate, master's.

Accreditation: *Regional:* NCA.

History: Established and chartered as Lind University 1857; changed name to Lake Forest University 1865; offered first instruction at postsecondary level 1876; first degree (baccalaureate) awarded 1879; present name adopted 1965; added master's program in liberal studies 1977.

Institutional Structure: *Governing board:* Board of Trustees. Representation: 45 trustees, including president of the college and 21 alumni; 1 full-time instructional faculty member; 2 students. 3 ex officio. 25 voting. *Composition of institution:* Administrators 32 men / 59 women. Academic affairs headed by dean of faculty. Management/business/finances directed by vice president-business, treasurer. Academic governance body, the faculty, meets an average of 8 times per year.

Calendar: Semesters. Academic year Aug. to May. Freshmen admitted Aug., Jan. Degrees conferred May, Oct., Mar. Formal commencement May.

Characteristics of Freshmen: 63% of applicants admitted. 28% of admitted students enrolled full-time.

50% (201 students) submitted SAT scores; 70% (285 students) submitted ACT scores. *25th percentile:* SAT Verbal 530, SAT Math 530; ACT Composite 23, ACT English 24, ACT Math 23. *75th percentile:* SAT Verbal 650, SAT Math 640; ACT Composite 28, ACT English 29, ACT Math 28.

59% of entering freshmen expected to graduate within 5 years. 42% of freshmen from Illinois. Freshmen from 37 states and 13 foreign countries.

Admission: For fall acceptance, apply as early as Sept. 1 of previous year, but not later than Feb. 1. Students are notified of acceptance Mar. Apply by Jan. 15 for early decision; need not limit application to Lake Forest. Early acceptance available. *Requirements:* Either graduation from accredited secondary school or GED. 4 years English, 3 in a foreign language, 4 mathematics, 1–2 history, and 1–2 natural sciences recommended. *Entrance tests:* College Board SAT or ACT composite. *For transfer students:* 2.0 minimum GPA; from 4-year accredited institution 60 hours maximum transfer credit; from 2-year accredited institution 60 hours.

College credit and advanced placement for postsecondary-level work completed in secondary school. Tutoring available.

Degree Requirements: At the college, credit is earned, recorded, and tallied by courses rather than by semester hours. For conversion purposes, a course is valued at 4 semester hours. Students are expected to pass 32 courses, fulfill the general education requirements, attain a 2.00 overall GPA, and complete the requirements of a major.

Fulfillment of some degree requirements and exemption from some beginning courses possible by passing achievement tests. *Grading system:* A–F; credit-D-fail; withdraw (may carry penalty); X (conditional grade); incomplete (may carry penalty); MW (medical withdraw).

Distinctive Educational Programs: *For undergraduates:* Internships. Consortial colleges. Dual-degree programs in engineering with Washington University (MO), social service with University of Chicago. Programs for independent research, including honors programs and individual majors. International internship programs in Paris and Madrid. Ancient Mediterranean Civilization program in Turkey and Greece. Marine biology on San Salvador Island. *Available to all students:* Evening classes. Special facilities for using telecommunications in the classroom. Interdisciplinary programs. Tutorials. Computer labs, including labs in 6 dorms, a 24-hour access lab in science complex as well as labs in academic buildings and library.

Degrees Conferred: 286 *baccalaureate*; 3 *master's*. 4 honorary degrees awarded: Doctor of Laws 2, Doctor of Letters 1; Doctor of Arts 1.

Fees and Other Expenses: *Full-time tuition per academic year 2004–05:* $27,000. *Required fees:* $334. *Room and board per academic year:* $6,526.

Financial Aid: Aid from institutionally generated funds is provided on the basis of academic merit, financial need, other criteria. Institution has a Program Participation Agreement with the U.S. Department of Education for eligible students to receive Pell Grants and other federal aid.

Financial aid to full-time, first-time undergraduate students: need-based scholarships/grants totaling $16,905,000, self-help $3,868,932, parent loans $1,431,909, tuition waivers $284,327; non-need-based scholarships/grants totaling $2,909,530, self-help $202,750, parent loans $281,326, tuition waivers $923,849.

Departments and Teaching Staff: *Professors* 31, *associate professors* 29, *assistant professors* 29, *part-time faculty* 81. *Total instructional faculty:* 170 (89 full-time, 81 part-time; women 80, men 90; members of minority groups 18). Total faculty with doctorate, first-professional, or other terminal degree: 134. Student-to-faculty ratio: 12:1. *Faculty development:* 8 faculty members awarded sabbaticals 2004–05.

Enrollment: Total enrollment 1,408. Undergraduate full-time 564 men / 802 women, part-time 10m / 15w; graduate part-time 1m, part-time 3m / 13w.

Characteristics of Student Body: *Ethnic and racial makeup:* number of Black non-Hispanic: 57; American Indian or Alaska Native: 4; Asian or Pacific Islander: 50; Hispanic: 74; White non-Hispanic: 1,083. *Age distribution:* number under 18: 17; 18–19: 610; 20–21: 585; 22–24:135; 25–29: 14; 30–34: 1; 35–39: 2; 40–49: 3.

International Students: 124 nonresident aliens enrolled fall 2004. 24 students from Europe, 32 Asia, 8 Central and South America; 2 Africa, 45 Canada, 12 other. Social and cultural programs available to students whose native language is not English. Variable number of scholarships available annually for international students.

Student Life: On-campus residence halls house 88% of student body. Residence halls for for women 8%, for both sexes 88%. *Intercollegiate athletics:* men: basketball, diving, football, handball, ice hockey, lacrosse, soccer, swimming, tennis; women: basketball, diving, handball, soccer, softball, swimming, tennis, volleyball. Wide variety of active club sports. Twelve-sport intramural athletic program. *Special regulations:* quiet hours from 10pm to 10am; courtesy hours from 10am to 10pm. No on-campus cars allowed for freshmen. *Special services:* Student Health Center and Counseling Center. *Student publications:* *The Stentor,* a weekly newspaper; *The Forester,* a yearbook; *Tusitala,* a fine arts magazine; *Collages,* a foreign language literary magazine; *Lake Forest Papers,* a publication of award-winning student papers. *Surrounding community:* Lake Forest population 18,000. Chicago, 30 miles from campus, is nearest metropolitan area. Served by O'Hare airport 30 miles from campus; Northwestern passenger train 1 mile from campus.

Library Collections: 259,977 volumes. 101,709 microforms; 11,047 audiovisual materials; current periodical subscriptions: 665 paper, 15 microform, 633 via electronic access. Students have access to the Internet at no charge.

Most important holdings include the Joseph Medill Patterson Papers and Library (founder of the New York Daily News); Railroad History Collection (Elliott Donnelley, James Sloss, Munson Paddock); O'Kieffe Collection of Americana and Rare Books.

Buildings and Grounds: Campus area 107 acres. *Renovations and expansions:* Donnelley and Lee Library; Farwell Field; Nollen Hall and Deerpath Hall; Halas Hall; Lily Reid Hold Memorial Chapel.

Chief Executive Officer: Dr. Stephen D. Schutt, President.

Undergraduates address admission inquiries to William G. Motzer, Jr., Director of Admissions; graduate inquiries to Daniel L. LeMahieu, Director, Master of Liberal Studies Program.

Lake Forest Graduate School of Management

280 North Sheridan Road
Lake Forest, Illinois 60045
Tel: (847) 234-5005   **E-mail:** admiss@lfgsm.edu
Fax: (847) 234-3656   **Internet:** www.lfgsm.edu

Institution Description: Lake Forest Graduate School of Management (Lake Forest School of Management until 1985, Industrial Management Institute until 1972, Advanced Management Institute until 1979) is a private, independent, nonprofit institution. *Enrollment:* 791. *Degrees awarded:* Master's.

Accreditation: *Regional:* NCA.

History: Established and chartered as Industrial Management Institute, an independent institution, on the campus of Lake Forest College 1946; offered first instruction at postsecondary level 1968; awarded first degree (master's) and changed name to Advanced Management Institute 1972; changed name to Lake Forest School of Management 1979. Changed name in 1985 to Lake Forest Graduate School of Management; moved headquarters and camp to new state-of-the art campus in Conway Park.

Institutional Structure: *Governing board:* Board of Directors. Extrainstitutional representation: directors; institutional representation: 1 administrator; 2 alumni. 1 ex officio. All voting. *Composition of institution:* Administrators 4 men / 3 women. Academic affairs headed by executive vice president and chief administrative officer. Management/business/finances directed by vice president. Academic governance bodies, ad hoc curriculum review committees, meet on an irregular basis.

Calendar: Quarters. Academic year Aug. to June. New students admitted Aug., Nov., Feb., and April. Degrees conferred and formal commencement June.

Admission: Rolling admissions plan. *Requirements:* Minimum 4 years business experience; undergraduate degree required. Interview required. *Entrance tests:* GRE can be substituted for GMAT. *For transfer students:* Maximum of 3 courses from comparable program with minimum grade of B.

Degree Requirements: *For master's degrees:* For MBA, 16 courses with GPA of 2.7 or better. *Grading system:* A–F; withdraw (carries time limit).

Distinctive Educational Programs: Weekend and evening classes. Accelerated degree programs.

Degrees Conferred: 210 *master's:* business/marketing.

Fees and Other Expenses: *Full-time tuition per academic year 2004–05:* $2,275 per course.

Financial Aid: *Federal and state funding:* 232 loans totaling $2,685,289 (ranging from $500 to $18,500).

Departments and Teaching Staff: *Total instructional faculty:* 153 (153 part-time; 33 women, 120 men; members of minority groups 9). Total faculty with doctorate, first-professional, or other terminal degree: 25.

Enrollment: Total enrollment 791. Graduate part-time 475 men / 316 women.

Student Life: No on-campus housing. *Special regulations:* Cars permitted without restrictions. *Surrounding community:* Lake Forest population 20,000. Chicago, 35 miles from campus, is nearest metropolitan area. Served by mass transit commuter train system, airport 25 miles from campus, passenger rail service 1 mile from campus.

Library Collections: Computer work stations. Students have access to the Internet at no charge.

Buildings and Grounds: Campus area 2 acres.

Chief Executive Officer: John N. Popoli, President.

Address admission inquiries to Nell McKitrick, Associate Dean, Admissions.

Lincoln Christian College

100 Campus View Drive
Lincoln, Illinois 62656
Tel: (217) 732-3168
Fax: (217) 732-5718

Institution Description: Lincoln Christian College is an private institution affiliated with the Christian Churches/Churches of Christ. *Enrollment:* 1,025. *Degrees awarded:* Associate, baccalaureate, master's, first-professional (master of divinity).

Accreditation: *Regional:* NCA. *National:* AHBE.

History: The college was founded in 1944.

Calendar: Semesters.

Characteristics of Freshmen: 211 applicants (75 men, 136 women). 73.5% of applicants admitted. 75.5% of admitted students enrolled full-time.

6% (7 students) submitted SAT scores; 93% (113 students) submitted ACT scores. *25th percentile:* ACT Composite 19, ACT English 19, ACT Math 17. *75th percentile:* ACT Composite 26, ACT English 26, ACT Math 24.

Admission: *Requirements:* High school transcript; 3 recommendations; ACT. TOEFL for international students.

Degree Requirements: *For all associate degrees:* 66 semester hours for associate.. *For all undergraduate degrees:* 130 semester hours. *Grading system:* A–F.

Degrees Conferred: 19 *associate;* 129 *baccalaureate;* 27 *master's;* 19 *first-professional.* Bachelor's degrees awarded: theology and ministerial studies 100; business, management, marketing, and related support services 29.

Fees and Other Expenses: *Full-time tuition per academic year:* undergraduate $4,776. *Room and board per academic year:* $3,936.

Financial Aid: Aid from institutionally generated funds is provided on the basis of academic merit, financial need.Institution has a Program Participation Agreement with the U.S. Department of Education for eligible students to receive Pell Grants and other federal aid.

Financial aid to full-time, first-time undergraduate students: 42% received federal grants averaging $1,963; 34% state/local grants averaging $3,429; 52% institutional grants averaging $2,532; 64% loans averaging $3,408.

Departments and Teaching Staff: *Total instructional faculty:* 41.

Enrollment: Total enrollment 1,025. Undergraduate 714 (49% men, 51% women).

Characteristics of Student Body: *Ethnic/racial makeup:* Black non-Hispanic: 3.6%; American Indian or Alaska Native: .1%; Asian or Pacific Islander: .3%; Hispanic: .6%; White non-Hispanic: 94.5%.

International Students: 3 undergraduate nonresident aliens enrolled fall 2004.

Student Life: *Intercollegiate athletics:* men only: baseball, basketball soccer, tennis, volleyball; women only: basketball, volleyball.

Library Collections: 92,000 volumes. 5,500 microforms; 450 current periodical subscriptions; 25,000 recordings/tapes. Access to online information retrieval systems.

Buildings and Grounds: Campus area 227 acres.

Chief Executive Officer: Dr. Keith H. Ray, President.

Address admissions inquiries to Dr. Greg Taylor, Director of Admissions.

Lewis University

One University Parkway
Romeoville, Illinois 60446-2298
Tel: (815) 838-0500   **E-mail:** info@lewisu.edu
Fax: (815) 838-9456   **Internet:** www.lewisu.edu

Institution Description: Lewis University is a private institution conducted by the Brothers of the Christian Schools, a Roman Catholic teaching order. *Enrollment:* 4,848 *Degrees awarded:* Associate, baccalaureate, master's. Certificates also awarded.

Accreditation: *Regional:* NCA. *Professional:* nursing, nursing education, teacher education

History: Established as Holy Name Technical School 1932; incorporated and changed name to Lewis Holy Name Technical School 1934; changed name to Lewis School of Aeronautics 1940; offered first instruction at postsecondary level and changed name to Lewis College of Science and Technology 1944; changed name to Lewis College 1960; adopted present name 1973.

Institutional Structure: *Governing board:* Lewis University Board of Trustees. Representation: 30 trustees, including president of the university. 20 voting. *Composition of institution:* Administrators 22. Academic affairs headed by vice president for academic affairs. Management/business/finances directed by vice president for business and finance; vice president for institutional advancement. Full-time instructional faculty 113. Academic governance body, Academic Affairs Committee, meets an average of 24 times per year.

Calendar: Semesters. Academic year late Aug. to mid-May. Freshmen admitted Aug., Jan., June. Degrees conferred May, Aug., Jan. Formal commencement May. Summer session of 3 concurrent terms beginning after Memorial Day.

Characteristics of Freshmen: 1,878 applicants (834 men, 1,044 women). 67.6% of applicants admitted. 40.1% of admitted students enrolled full-time.

2% (13 students) submitted SAT scores; 97% (494 students) submitted ACT scores. *25th percentile:* SAT I Verbal 460, SAT I Math 430; ACT Composite 19, ACT English 19, ACT Math 17. *75th percentile:* SAT I Verbal 550, SAT I Math 580; ACT Composite 24, ACT English 24, ACT Math 24.

50% of entering freshmen expected to graduate within 5 years. 96% of freshmen from Illinois. Freshmen from 6 states and 7 foreign countries.

Admission: Rolling admissions plan. For fall acceptance, apply by Sept. 1. Early acceptance available. *Requirements:* Either graduation from accredited secondary school with 15 units which must include 3 in English and 12 in college preparatory subjects; or GED. Minimum grade average C. Lowest recommended secondary school class standing upper half of class. *Entrance tests:* ACT composite preferred; College Board SAT accepted. For foreign students TOEFL or demonstrated proficiency in English. *For transfer students:* 2.0 minimum GPA; from 4-year accredited institution and for correspondence/extension students 96 semester hours maximum transfer credit; from 2-year accredited institution 72 hours. >

College credit and advanced placement for postsecondary-level work completed in secondary school and for extrainstitutional learning on basis of ACE *2006 Guide to the Evaluation of Educational Experiences in the Armed Services,* portfolio and faculty assessments, personal interview. Developmental courses offered during regular academic year; credit given.

Degree Requirements: *For all associate degrees:* 76 semester hours. *For all baccalaureate degrees:* 128 hours. *For all undergraduate degrees:* 2.0 GPA (some majors have higher major GPA requirement); 32 hours in residence; 50 hour liberal arts core plus writing and library skills competency exams; course in religious dimension of man; distribution requirements. *Grading system:* A–F; pass-fail; withdraw (carries time limit).

Distinctive Educational Programs: Internships. Weekend and evening classes. Special facilities for using telecommunications in the classroom. Interdisciplinary programs in ethnic studies and women's studies. Facilities for independent research, including honors programs, individual majors, independent study. *Other distinctive programs:* Lewis University Airport provides technical training for students and repair services for small aircraft owners in the community.

ROTC: Army, Navy, and Air Force offered through cooperating institutions.

Degrees Conferred: 2 *associate;* 741 *baccalaureate;* 354 *master's;* 12 *postmaster's certificates.* Bachelor's degrees awarded in top five disciplines business, management, marketing, and related support services 196; health professions and related clinical sciences 150; security and protective services 85; transportation and materials moving 59; education 43.

Fees and Other Expenses: *Full-time tuition per academic year 2004–05:* undergraduate $16,906. Contact the university for graduate tuition/fees. *Room and board per academic year:* $7,200. *Books and supplies:*$500.

Financial Aid: Aid from institutionally generated funds is provided on the basis of academic merit, financial need, athletic ability, other criteria. Institution has a Program Participation Agreement with the U.S. Department of Education for eligible students to receive Pell Grants and other federal aid.

Financial aid to full-time, first-time undergraduate students: 23% received federal grants averaging $3,687; 44% state/local grants averaging $4,109; 69% institutional grants averaging $7,142; 71% loans averaging $3,364.

Departments and Teaching Staff: Arts and sciences *professors* 23, *associate professors* 20, *assistant professors* 16, *instructors* 3, *part-time teachers* 44; business 4, 4, 2, 5, 36; nursing 2, 3, 5, 5, 12. *Total instructional faculty:* 169 FTE. Degrees held by full-time faculty: doctorate 58%, master's 40%, baccalaureate 2%. 58% hold terminal degrees.

Enrollment: Total enrollment 4,848. Undergraduate 3,459 (39.3% men, 60.7% women).

Characteristics of Student Body: *Ethnic/racial makeup:* Black non-Hispanic: 13.8%; American Indian or Alaska Native: .1%; Asian or Pacific Islander: 2.7%; Hispanic: 7.3%; White non-Hispanic: 68.9%; unknown: 3.6%.

International Students: 128 undergraduate nonresident aliens enrolled fall 2004. Students from Europe, Asia, Central and South America, Africa, Canada. Programs available to aid students whose native language is not English: English as a Second Language. Financial aid specifically designated for international students: Scholarships available annually.

Student Life: Seven residence halls house 395 males and 357 females. An additional 60 men reside in a private residence hall on campus. *Intercollegiate athletics:* men only: baseball, basketball, cross country, soccer, tennis, track and field, volleyball; women only: basketball, cross country, golf, soccer, tennis, volleyball, softball, track and field. *Special regulations:* Cars permitted without restrictions. Quiet hours. Residence hall visitation from 11am to midnight Sun.–Thurs., 11am to 2am Fri.–Sat. *Special services:* Learning Resources Center, medical services. *Student publications: The Flyer,* a weekly newspaper; *Windows,* a literary magazine. *Surrounding community:* Romeoville population 15,500. Chicago, 35 miles from campus, is nearest metropolitan area. Served by mass transit bus system; airport 30 miles from campus; passenger rail service 1 mile from campus.

Library Collections: 180,000 volumes. 5,000 government documents; 13,100 microforms; 2,300 audiovisual materials; 800 current periodical subscriptions. Online catalog. Students have access to online information retrieval services and the Internet.

Most important special holdings include I & M Canal Archives; federal documents depository; Martin S. Ackerman Art and Print Collection.

Buildings and Grounds: Campus area 336 acres.

Chief Executive Officer: Brother James Gaffney, F.S.C., President.

Address admission inquiries to Raymond Kennelly, Director of Enrollment Management.

College of Arts and Sciences

Degree Programs Offered: *Associate* in aviation; *baccalaureate* in art, applied science, athletics, aviation maintenance and avionics, aviation maintenance and non-destructive evaluation, biology, chemistry, computer science, education, elected studies, English, fire science management, history, human resource management, journalism, liberal arts, mathematics, medical technology, music, music merchandising, philosophy, physics, political science, psychology, public administration, radio-tv broadcasting, religious studies, criminal/social justice, social work, sociology, speech-drama, theatre; *master's* in education, social justice.

Admission: *See* general requirements. *For master's degree:* GRE; MAT; baccalaureate; GPA.

College of Business

Degree Programs Offered: *Baccalaureate* in accounting, business administration, economics, finance, management information systems, management science, marketing; *master's* in business administration.

Admission: *See* general requirements. *For master's degree:* Baccalaureate from accredited college or university; GMAT; GPA.

Degree Requirements: *For master's degree:* 36 credit hours, 3.0 GPA, 24 hours in residence.

College of Nursing

Degree Programs Offered: *Baccalaureate, master's.*

Admission: *See* general requirements; GRE; BSN; GPA.

Degree Requirements: In addition to general requirements, approval of dean and nursing faculty.

Lutheran School of Theology at Chicago

1100 East 55th Street
Chicago, Illinois 60615
Tel: (773) 256-0700   **E-mail:** admissions@lstc.edu
Fax: (773) 256-0782   **Internet:** www.lstc.edu

Institution Description: The Lutheran School of Theology at Chicago is a private institution affiliated with the Evangelical Lutheran Church in America. *Enrollment:* 349. *Degrees offered:* Master's, first-professional, doctorate.

Accreditation: *Regional:* NCA. *National:* ATS. *Professional:* theology

History: Formed in 1962 as the result of the merging of four Lutheran seminaries: Augustana Theological Seminary, Grand View Seminary, Chicago Lutheran Theological Seminary, Suomi Theological Seminary. Christ-Seminex of Chicago came into the School shortly thereafter.

Calendar: Quarters. Academic year Sept. to June.

Admission: Baccalaureate degree or the equivalent from an accredited college or university.

Degree Requirements: Completion of prescribed program (Master of Divinity, Master of Arts, Master of Theology, Doctor of Theology).

Degrees Conferred: 39 *master's;* 24 *doctorate.*

Fees and Other Expenses: *Full-time tuition per academic year:* $8,279.

Financial Aid: Financial assistance, usually in the form of a grant-in-aid, is awarded on the basis of need. Merit grants based on academic performance also available.

Departments and Teaching Staff: Bible *professors* 5, *associate professors* 0, *assistant professors* 1; *part-time teachers* 3; theology/history 3, 3, 1, 3; ministry 2, 2, 1, 3.

Total instructional faculty: 21. Degrees held by full-time faculty: doctorate 90%, master's 100%. 90% hold terminal degrees. *Faculty development:* $14,000 total grants for research. 5 faculty members awarded sabbaticals 995–96.

Enrollment: Total enrollment 349. Full-time 142, part-time 157.

Characteristics of Student Body: *Ethnic/racial makeup:* number of Black non-Hispanic: 25; American Indian or Alaska Native: 1; Asian or Pacific Islander: 7; Hispanic: 17; Whitevnon-Hispanic: 245. *Age distribution:* 22–24: 15%; 25–29: 23%; 30–34: 10%; 35–39: 13%; 40–49: 23%; 50–59: 16%.

International Students: 62 nonresident aliens enrolled fall 2004. 18 students from Europe, 25 Asia, 4 Central and South America, 8 Africa, 7 Middle East. Programs available to aid students whose native language is not English: Social, cultural. English as a Second Language. Scholarships available annually for international students.

Student Life: Worship services are held each school day and the Eucharist is celebrated each week.

Library Collections: 400,000 volumes.

Buildings and Grounds: The school occupies a 3-square block area in the Hyde Park section of Chicago.

Chief Executive Officer: James K. Echols, President.

Address admission inquiries to Marilyn Olson, Director of Admissions.

Loyola University of Chicago

820 North Michigan Avenue
Chicago, Illinois 60611
Tel: (312) 915-6500   **E-mail:** admission@luc.edu
Fax: (312) 915-7003   **Internet:** www.luc.edu

Institution Description: Loyola University of Chicago is a private, independent, nonprofit Jesuit institution affiliated with the Roman Catholic Church, with Lake Shore, Medical Center, and Water Tower campuses in Chicago and a campus in Rome, Italy. *Enrollment:* 13,909. *Degrees awarded:* Baccalaureate, first-professional (dentistry, law, medicine, master of divinity), master's, doctorate.

Member of the Chicago Consortium of Colleges and Universities.

Accreditation: *Regional:* NCA. *Professional:* accounting, business, clinical pastoral education, clinical psychology, counseling psychology, dentistry, dietetics, law, medicine, nursing, nursing education, oral and maxillofacial surgery, social work, theatre

History: Established as St. Ignatius College and offered first instruction at postsecondary level 1870; awarded first degree (baccalaureate) 1874; moved to Lake Shore Campus 1906; incorporated and adopted present name 1909; opened downtown Water Tower Campus 1945; began Rome Center Campus 1962; opened Loyola University Medical Center and Foster G. McGaw Hospital 1969.

Institutional Structure: *Governing board:* Board of Trustees. Representation: 30 trustees. All voting. *Composition of institution:* Administrators 165 men / 38 women. Academic affairs headed by academic senior vice president; of medical center, by provost. Management/business/finances directed by senior vice president of management services and vice president for finance. Full-time instructional faculty 804. Academic governance body, Faculty Council, meets an average of 10 times per year.

Calendar: Semesters. Academic year Aug. to Apr. Freshmen admitted Aug., Jan., May. Degrees conferred and formal commencements May, Jan. Summer session from May to Aug.

Characteristics of Freshmen: 13,056 applicants (4,196 men, 8,860 women). 71.9% of applicants admitted. 19% of admitted students enrolled full-time.

40% (716 students) submitted SAT scores; 96% (1,541 students) submitted ACT scores. *25th percentile:* SAT I Verbal 530, SAT I Math 520; ACT Composite 22, ACT English 22, ACT Math 21. *75th percentile:* SAT I Verbal 640, SAT I Math 630; ACT Composite 28, ACT English 29, ACT Math 27.

60% of entering freshmen expected to graduate within 5 years. 71% of freshmen from Illinois. Freshmen from 37 states.

Admission: Rolling admissions plan. For fall acceptance, apply as early as Oct. 1 of previous year, but not later than the beginning of Aug. of year of enrollment. Early acceptance available. *Requirements:* Either graduation from accredited secondary school with 15 units which must include English, 2 mathematics, 1 science, 1 social studies, 5 from among above areas; or GED. For business, mathematics, science students recommend additional units in mathematics, science. Minimum GPA 2.0. *Entrance tests:* College Board SAT or ACT composite. For foreign students TOEFL. *For transfer students:* 2.0 minimum GPA; from 4-year accredited institution maximum transfer credit limited only by residence requirements; from 2-year accredited institution 64 hours; correspondence/extension students 30 hours (15 hours of extension work). For dental hygiene, nursing, business administration students 2.5 minimum GPA.

College credit and advanced placement for postsecondary-level work completed in secondary school; college credit for extrainstitutional learning on basis of ACE *2006 Guide to the Evaluation of Educational Experiences in the Armed Services.* Tutoring available. Developmental and remedial courses offered during regular academic year; limited credit given.

Degree Requirements: 128 credit hours; 2.0 GPA; last 45 hours in residence; core curriculum. Fulfillment of some degree requirements possible by passing College Board CLEP, AP, other standardized tests. *Grading system:* A–F; pass-fail; withdraw.

Distinctive Educational Programs: Weekend and evening classes. Facilities and programs for independent research, including honors programs, individual majors, tutorials. Study abroad at Loyola University Rome Center, Italy and Mexico. Students considering Roman Catholic priesthood are eligible for admission to St. Joseph Seminary for junior and senior years. Unique master's degree program in Health Care Law at Law School. Strong commitment to core curriculum.

ROTC: Air Force, Army, Navy at neighboring institutions.

Degrees Conferred: 1,196 *baccalaureate*; 1,160 *master's*; 142 *doctorate*; 389 *first-professional*. Bachelor's degrees awarded in top five disciplines: business, management, marketing, and related support services 264; health professions and related clinical sciences 140; biological and biomedical sciences 137; social sciences 135; psychology 120.

Fees and Other Expenses: *Full-time tuition per academic year 2004–05:* $21,750 undergraduate; contact the university for graduate and first-professional tuition/fees. *Room and board per academic year:* $8,924. *Books and supplies:* $844.

Financial Aid: Aid from institutionally generated funds is provided on the basis of academic merit, financial need, athletic ability, other criteria. Institution has a Program Participation Agreement with the U.S. Department of Education for eligible students to receive Pell Grants and other federal aid.

Financial aid to full-time, first-time undergraduate students: 27% received federal grants averaging $3,439; 32% state/local grants averaging $4,192; 90% institutional grants averaging $8,973; 73% loans averaging $5,354.

Departments and Teaching Staff: *Professors* 226, *associate professors* 268, *assistant professors* 270, *instructors* 40, *part-time teachers* 509. *Total instructional faculty:* 804. Degrees held by full-time faculty: 97% hold terminal degrees.

Enrollment: Total enrollment 13,909. Undergraduate 8,319 (34% men, 66% women).

Characteristics of Student Body: *Ethnic/racial makeup:* Black non-Hispanic: 7%; American Indian or Alaska Native: .2%; Asian or Pacific Islander: 10.3%; Hispanic: 9.8%; White non-Hispanic: 58.1%; unknown: 12.8%.

International Students: 141 undergraduate nonresident aliens enrolled fall 2004. Programs available to aid students whose native language is not English: Social and cultural. No financial aid specifically designated for international students.

Student Life: On-campus residence halls house 29% of undergraduate student body. Residence halls for men only constitute 19% of such space, for women only 11%, for both sexes 70%. 1% of student body housed in cooperative facilities. *Intercollegiate athletics:* men only: basketball, cross-country, golf, soccer, swimming, tennis, track, water polo; women only: basketball, cross-country, golf, track, volleyball. *Special regulations:* Cars permitted; parking space distributed by lottery. Residence hall visitation from noon to midnight Sun.–Thurs., from noon to 2am Fri.–Sat. *Special services:* Learning Resources Center, Career and Placement Center, medical services. *Student publications, radio: Cadence,* a biannual literary magazine; *Phoenix,* a weekly newspaper. Radio station WLUW broadcasts 100 hours per week. *Surrounding community:* Chicago population over 3,000,000. Served by mass transit bus and train system; airport 8 miles from campus; passenger rail service 1 mile from campus.

Publications: History department publishes *Mid-America: An Historical Review;* English department publishes *Restoration and 18th-Century Theatre Research; Keats-Shelley Journal, Essays in Medieval Studies.*

Library Collections: 1.5 million volumes. 1.6 million microforms; 33,100 audiovisual materials; access to 110,500 periodicals (paper, microform, electronic retrieval). Online catalog. Students have access to online information retrieval services and the Internet.

Most important holdings include Paul Claudell collection; Jesuitica; Samuel Insull Papers.

Buildings and Grounds: Campus area 100 acres.

Chief Executive Officer: Rev. Michael J. Garanzini, S.J., President.

Undergraduates address admission inquiries to April Hansen, Director of Admissions; graduate inquiries to Dean of Graduate School.

College of Arts and Sciences

Degree Programs Offered: *Baccalaureate* in anthropology, applied psychology, biology, chemistry, classical civilization, communication, computer science, criminal justice, dental hygiene, English, fine arts, Greek, history, Latin, mathematics, modern languages, philosophy, physics, political science, psychology, social work, sociology, theater, theology.

Distinctive Educational Programs: Interdisciplinary programs in Afro-American studies, Latin American studies, linguistic studies, women's studies. Honors program. Exchange program with Mundelein College. Study abroad program at Rome Center of Liberal Arts.

School of Business Administration

Degree Programs Offered: *Baccalaureate* in accounting, economics, finance, information systems, managerial accounting, marketing, personnel management, production management, public accounting; *master's* in various fields.

School of Education

Degree Programs Offered: *Baccalaureate* in elementary education, secondary education, special education; *master's* and *doctorate* in counseling and educational psychology, curriculum and human resource development, educational leadership and policy studies.

Distinctive Educational Programs: School of Education associated with Erikson Institute of Early Childhood Education. Initiation of master's in non-public school administration; master's, doctorate in higher education.

Marcella Niehoff School of Nursing

Degree Programs Offered: *Baccalaureate, master's.*

Distinctive Educational Programs: Continuing education, workshops.

School of Social Work

Degree Programs Offered: *Master's, doctorate.*

Distinctive Educational Programs: Joint master's-first-professional program with School of Law; Type 73 School of Social Work certificate.

School of Dentistry

Degree Programs Offered: *First-professional* in dentistry; *master's* in oral biology. Certificates also awarded.

Admission: *For first-professional:* 90 semester hours from college or university with 6 semester hours organic chemistry, 8 semester hours physics, 16 semester hours biology/zoology; DAT and AADAS.

Degree Requirements: *For first-professional:* 172 credit hours; 2.0 GPA; 4 years in residence.

School of Law

Degree Programs Offered: *First-professional* in law; *master's* in health law, child law; *doctorate* in health law, child law.

Admission: For first-professional: 86 credit hours (43 in required courses); 2.0 GPA.

Stritch School of Medicine

Degree Programs Offered: *First-professional.*

Admission: *For first-professional:* Bachelor's degree required with 1 year in biology, 1 inorganic chemistry, 1 physics, 1 organic chemistry or biochemistry; MCAT; AAMCAS.

Graduate School

Degree Programs Offered: *Master's* and *doctorate* in a wide range of research and applied areas in Arts and Sciences, Education, Pastoral Studies, Workplace Studies, Nursing and Basic Health Sciences.

Departments and Teaching Staff: 390 graduate faculty and 115 associate graduate faculty drawn from the College of Arts and Sciences and the Schools of Nursing, Dentistry, Medicine, and Education.

Distinctive Educational Programs: Institutes in Pastoral Studies, Industrial Relations, Community and Organizational Development, Parmly Hearing Research Institute, Doyle Center for Children and Families and Day School.

Mundelein College (formerly University College)

Degree Programs Offered: *Baccalaureate* in anthropology, biology, chemistry, classical civilization, communication, computer science, criminal justice, economics, elementary education, English, fine arts, finance, French, German, Greek, history, information systems, Italian, Latin, managerial accounting, marketing, mathematics, personnel management, philosophy, physics, political science, production and operations management, psychology, public accounting, social work, sociology, Spanish, special education, theatre, theology.

Admission: Admission to degree candidacy is granted only after a minimum of 20 semester hours with a 2.0 GPA; student must be 21 years of age or 3 years out of high school.

Degree Requirements: 128 semester hours with 2.0 GPA; final 45 semester hours in residence or a total of 64 semester hours earned at parent institution.

Departments and Teaching Staff: Mundelein College has no academic departments proper to itself, but rather culls its teaching staff from the other undergraduate colleges of the University, thus permitting its students to benefit from the resources and expertise of the established faculty in Arts and Sciences, Business Administration, Education, and Nursing. Because of this arrangement, the constituency of the faculty of University College changes from semester to semester, varying in rank and status.

McCormick Theological Seminary

5460 South University Avenue
Chicago, Illinois 60615

Tel: (773) 284-4687   **E-mail:** choward@mccormick.edu
Fax: (773) 284-2612   **Internet:** www.mccormick.edu

Institution Description: McCormick Theological Seminary is an autonomous institution with an ecumenical student body and related to the Presbyterian Church (U.S.A.) through its general assembly. *Enrollment:* 275. *Degrees awarded:* Master's, doctorate, first-professional. Certificate in Theological Studies also awarded.
Member of: Association of Chicago Theological Schools.

Accreditation: *Regional:* NCA. *National:* ATS. *Professional:* theology

History: Lane Theological Seminary (founded 1829) of Cincinnati, Ohio suspended operations and became affiliated with McCormick Theological Seminary 1932; moved into new facility 2003.

Institutional Structure: *Governing board:* Board of Directors (52 members); 4 officers; 2 honorary members.

Calendar: Semesters. Academic year Sept. to May. Summer session for all levels of degrees.

Admission: *Requirements:* Bachelor of Arts or its academic equivalent; readiness and aptitude for study at graduate level. Doctor of Ministry requires 3 years in ministry post Master of Divinity degree.

Degree Requirements: Completion of prescribed curriculum; requirements vary by program.

Distinctive Educational Programs: Hispanic Ministries Program. Certificate in Theological Studies program.

Degrees Conferred: 10 *master's:* theology; 50 *doctorate:* theology; 32 *first-professional:* master of divinity.

Fees and Other Expenses: *Full-time tuition per academic year 2004–05:* $7,930.

Financial Aid: Aid from institutionally generated funds is provided on the basis of financial need, other criteria. *Graduate aid:* 32 federal and state-funded loans totaling $302,593; 14 work-study jobs worth $30,000; 65 college—assigned jobs (nonteaching, nonresearch) totaling $110,000; 56 other fellowships and grants totaling $353,376.

Departments and Teaching Staff: *Professors* 11, *associate professors* 8, *assistant professors* 2, *instructors* 1, *part-time faculty* 9. *Total instructional faculty:* 43 (full-time 22, part-time 21; women 19, men 24; members of minority groups 17). Total faculty with doctorate, first-professional, or other terminal degree: 20. 4 faculty members awarded sabbaticals 2004–05.

Enrollment: Total enrollment 275. First-professional full-time 32 men / 37 women, part-time 25m / 44w; graduate full-time 80m / 40w, part-time 12m / 5w.

Characteristics of Student Body: 26 nonresident aliens enrolled fall 2004.

International Students: Programs available to aid students whose native language is not English: Social, cultural. English as a Second Language Program. Financial aid available to qualifying international students.

Student Life: The Seminary owns two apartment houses and rents space from nearby Lutheran School of Theology.

Library Collections: 377,431 volumes. Online and card catalogs. Current serial subscriptions: 930 paper, 35 microform, 88 via electronic access. 672 recordings; 865 CD-ROMs. 30 computer work stations. Total 2004–05 budget for books and materials: $158,740.

Buildings and Grounds: *New buildings:* New facility complete March 2003; houses all faculty offices and administrative offices on the campus of the Lutheran School of Theology of Chicago.

Chief Executive Officer: Dr. Cynthia M. Campbell, President.

Address admission inquiries to Craig Howard, Director of Recruitment and Admissions.

McKendree College

701 College Road
Lebanon, Illinois 62254-1299

Tel: (618) 537-4481   **E-mail:** inquiry@mckendree.edu
Fax: (618) 537-6496   **Internet:** www.mckendree.edu

Institution Description: McKendree College is a private, independent, liberal arts college affiliated with the United Methodist Church. *Enrollment:* 2,257. *Degrees awarded:* Baccalaureate.

Accreditation: *Regional:* NCA.

History: Established as Lebanon Seminary 1828; adopted present name 1830; chartered 1835; awarded first degree (baccalaureate) 1840.

Institutional Structure: *Governing board:* Board of Trustees. Extrainstitutional representation: 40 trustees, 13 trustees emeriti, 4 honorary members; institutional representation: president of the college. 1 ex officio. 40 voting. *Composition of institution:* Academic affairs headed by provost and dean of the college. Management/business/finances directed by vice president for administration and finance. Full-time instructional faculty 70. Academic governance body, the faculty, meets an average of 10 times per year.

Calendar: Semesters. Academic year Aug. to May. Degrees conferred May, Aug., Dec. Formal commencement May. Summer session of 2 terms from June to Aug.

Characteristics of Freshmen: 71% of applicants admitted. 29% of admitted students enrolled full-time.

7% (24 students) submitted SAT scores; 92% (313 students) submitted ACT scores. *25th percentile:* SAT Verbal 420, SAT Math 430; ACT Composite 20, ACT English 19, ACT Math 19. *75th percentile*: SAT Verbal 530, SAT Math 630; ACT Composite 26, ACT English 26, ACT Math 26.

57% of entering freshmen expected to graduate within 5 years. 83% of freshmen from Illinois. Freshmen from 10 states and 6 foreign countries.

Admission: Rolling admissions plan. For fall acceptance, apply as early as end of junior year of secondary school. Early acceptance available. *Requirements:* Either graduation from accredited secondary school with 16 academic units or GED; minimum GPA 2.50 on 4.00 scale; 20 ACT composite; top 50% class rank. *Entrance tests:* ACT composite preferred; College Board SAT accepted. *For transfer students:* 2.0 minimum GPA; from 4-year accredited institution 96 semester hours maximum transfer credit; from 2-year accredited institution 70 hours.

College credit and advanced placement for postsecondary-level work completed in secondary school. College credit for USAFI-DANTES and for extrainstitutional learning (life experience) on basis of ACE *2006 Guide to the Evaluation of Educational Experiences in the Armed Services.*

Degree Requirements: 128 semester hours; 2.0 GPA; 64 hours in residence; 32 of last 40 hours in residence; 2 physical activity courses; general education requirements. Fulfillment of some degree requirements and exemption from some beginning courses possible by passing departmental examinations, College Board CLEP. *Grading system:* A–F; pass-fail; withdraw (carries penalty).

Distinctive Educational Programs: Internships. Flexible meeting places and schedules, including off-campus centers (at Louisville and Radcliff, Kentucky, both 240 miles away from main institution) and evening classes. McKendree at Scott Air Force Base offers coursework in an accelerated on-month format. Service learning requirements are built into many courses. Capstone nursing program offered at several sites in southern Illinois. Facilities for independent research, including honors programs, individual majors. Study abroad programs.

ROTC: Army and Air force offered in cooperation with Southern Illinois University-Edwardsville.

Degrees Conferred: 545 *baccalaureate:* biological/life sciences 15; business/marketing 179; communications/communication technologies 23; computer and information sciences 60; education 74; English 12; health professions and related sciences 95; liberal arts/general studies 3; library science 4; philosophy/religion/theology 1; psychology 31; social sciences and history 45; visual and performing arts 3.

Fees and Other Expenses: *Tuition per academic year 2004–05:* $16,400 undergraduate; $4,435 graduate. *Required fees:* $200. *Room and board per academic year:* $6,480.

Financial Aid: Aid from institutionally generated funds is provided on the basis of academic merit, financial need, athletic ability, musical talent, community service, Methodist scholarships. Institution has a Program Participation Agreement with the U.S. Department of Education for eligible students to receive Pell Grants and other federal aid.

Financial aid to full-time, first-time undergraduate students: need-based scholarships/grants totaling $9,756,533, self-help $4,104,566. parent loans $407,844, athletic awards $1,108,951; non-need-based scholarships/grants totaling $2,213,564, self-help $1,636,209, parent loans $1,249,945, athletic awards $955,321. *Graduate aid:* 65 federal and state-funded loans totaling $542,518.

Departments and Teaching Staff: *Professors 17, associate professors 16, assistant professors 24, instructors 13, part-time faculty 156. Total instructional faculty:* 226 (full-time 68, part-time 156; women 122, men 104; members of minority groups 15). Total faculty with doctorate, first-professional, or other terminal degree: 84. Student-to-faculty ratio: 15:1. 2 faculty members awarded sabbaticals 2004–05.

Enrollment: Total enrollment 2,257. Undergraduate full-time 741 men / 874 women, part-time 196m / 345w; graduate full-time 6m / 18w, part-time 15m / 62w. *Transfer students:* in-state 140; from out-of-state 173.

Characteristics of Student Body: *Ethnic/racial makeup:* number of Black non-Hispanic: 265; American Indian or Alaska Native: 2; Asian or Pacific Islander: 19; Hispanic: 36; White non-Hispanic: 1,749; unknown: 47. *Age distribution:* number under 18: 6; 18–19: 535; 20–21: 564; 22–24: 277; 25–29: 200; 30–34: 161; 35–39: 139; 40–49: 223; 50–64: 50; 65 and over: 1.

International Students: 38 nonresident aliens enrolled fall 2004. 9 students from Europe, 8 Asia, 16 Central and South America, 3 Africa, 1 Australia. Programs available to aid students whose native language is not English: Social and cultural. English as a Second Language Program. Some financial aid specifically designated for qualifying international students.

Student Life: On-campus residence halls house 56% of student body. Residence halls for men constitute 45% of such space, for women 55%. *Intercollegiate athletics:* men only: baseball, basketball, bowling, cross-country, football, golf, soccer, swimming, tennis, track and field; women only: basketball, cross-country, golf, soccer, softball, tennis, track and field, volleyball. *Special regulations:* Cars permitted without restrictions. Quiet hours set by residents in individual halls. Dormitory visitation from 10am to midnight Sun. through Thurs., 10am to 2am Fri. and Sat. *Special services:* Learning Resources Center, medical services, career development, writing lab, multicultural programs, freshman transition program. *Student publications: The McKendrean,* a yearbook; *Montage,* annual literary magazine; *Bearchat,* weekly newsletter; *The Review,* a biweekly newspaper. *Surrounding community:* Lebanon population 3,700. St.

Louis (MO), 23 miles from campus, is nearest metropolitan area. Served by mass transit bus system.

Library Collections: 96,265 volumes including bound books, serial backfiles, electronic documents, and government documents not in separate collections: Online catalog. Current serial subscriptions 501 paper. 3,576 recordings; 1,355 compact discs; 674 CD-ROMs. 13 computer work stations. Students have access to the Internet at no charge. Total budget for books, periodicals, audiovisual materials, microforms 2004–05: $154,350.

Most important special holdings include archives of Southern Illinois Conference of the United Methodist Church; U.S. depository for U.S. government documents; Sherlock Holmes Baker Street Journals.

Buildings and Grounds: Campus area 110 acres. *New buildings:* Marion K. Piper Academic Center; Intramural Gymnasium; Russel E. and Fern M. Hettenhausen Center for the Arts.

Chief Executive Officer: Dr. James M. Dennis, President.

Address admission inquiries to Mark e. Campbell, Vice President of Admissions and Financial Aid.

MacMurray College

447 East College Avenue
Jacksonville, Illinois 62650-2590

Tel: (217) 479-7000   **E-mail:** admiss@mac.edu
Fax: (217) 245-0405   **Internet:** www.mac.edu

Institution Description: MacMurray College is a private college affiliated with the United Methodist Church. *Enrollment:* 667. *Degrees awarded:* Associate, baccalaureate.

Accreditation: *Regional:* NCA. *Professional:* nursing, nursing education, social work, teacher education

History: Established as Illinois Conference Female Academy 1846; chartered 1847; offered first instruction at postsecondary level and changed name to Illinois Conference Female College 1851; changed name to Illinois Female College 1863, to Illinois Woman's College 1899; awarded first degree (baccalaureate) 1900; changed name to MacMurray College for Women 1930; adopted present name 1953; merged with coordinate MacMurray College for men (established 1955) 1969; celebrated the college's sesquicentennial in 1996. *See* Walter B. Hendrickson, *Forward in the Second Century of MacMurray College: a History of 125 Years* (Jacksonville: MacMurray College, 1972) for further information.

Institutional Structure: *Governing board:* MacMurray College Board of Trustees. Extrainstitutional representation: 40 trustees, including 6 representatives of the United Methodist Church; 6 alumni trustees; remaining elected by the Board. Institutional representation: president (voting); 6 administrators (non-voting); 2 full-time instructional staff members (non-voting), 2 students (non-voting). 41 voting. *Composition of institution:* Administrators 7 men / 6 women. Academic affairs headed by dean of the college. Management/business/finances directed by business manager. Full-time instructional faculty 45. Academic governance body, the faculty, meets an average of 8 times per year.

Calendar: Semesters (4-1-4 plan). Academic year Aug. to June. Freshmen admitted Aug., Jan., May, June. Degrees conferred May, June, July, Dec. Formal commencement early May. Summer session of 6 weeks from June to July.

Characteristics of Freshmen: 50% of applicants admitted. 27% of admitted students enrolled full-time.

7% (11 students) submitted SAT scores; 87% (141 students) submitted ACT scores. *25th percentile:* SAT Verbal 430, SAT Math 410; ACT Composite 17, ACT English 17, ACT Math 16. *75th percentile:* SAT Verbal 550, SAT Math 550; ACT Composite 23, ACT English 23, ACT Math 21.

50% of freshmen expected to graduate within 5 years. 82% of freshmen from Illinois. Freshmen from 11 states.

Admission: Rolling admissions plan. Apply as early as 1 year prior to, but not later than Aug. 1. Early acceptance available. *Requirements:* Either graduation from accredited secondary school or GED. Recommend 4 units in English, 2 foreign language, 2 laboratory science, 2 mathematics, 2 social studies. *Entrance tests:* College board SAT or ACT composite recommended. For foreign students TOEFL. *For transfer students:* From 4-year accredited institution 90 credit hours maximum transfer credit; from 2-year accredited institution 60 hours maximum; correspondence/extension students 16 hours.

College credit and advanced placement for postsecondary-level work completed in secondary school.

Degree Requirements: *For all associate degrees:* 60 credit hours; freshman rhetoric sequence; one core course and three breadth requirements; quantitative reasoning; writing proficiency. *For all baccalaureate degrees:* 120 credit hours in addition to the above three core courses and one breadth component. *For all degrees:* 2.0 GPA; last 30 hours in residence.

Fulfillment of some degree requirements and exemption from some beginning courses possible by passing departmental examinations, College Board CLEP, AP. *Grading system:* A–F; pass-fail; withdraw.

Distinctive Educational Programs: Cooperative education. Evening classes. Dual-degree programs in engineering with Columbia University (NY), Washington University (MO); dual-degree programs in medical sciences may be individually arranged. Facilities and programs for independent research, including honors programs, individual majors, directed study. Off-campus study in the U.S. includes Washington (DC) Semester at American University. Study abroad programs available through association with Central College (Iowa).

Degrees Conferred: 146 *baccalaureate:* biological/life sciences 5; business/marketing 22; communications/communication technologies 1; education 36; English 4; foreign languages and literature 3; health professions and related sciences 12; mathematics 1; parks and recreation 10; philosophy/religion/theology 4; physical sciences 3; protective services/public administration 20; psychology 15; social sciences and history 5; visual and performing arts 5.

Fees and Other Expenses: *Full-time tuition per academic year 2004–05:* $15,000. *Required fees:* $250. *Room and board per academic year:* $5,600.

Financial Aid: Aid from institutionally generated funds is provided on the basis of academic merit, financial need. Institution has a Program Participation Agreement with the U.S. Department of Education for eligible students to receive Pell Grants and other federal aid.

Financial aid to full-time, first-time undergraduate students: need-based scholarships/grants totaling $5,250,173, self-help $2,611,736, parent loans $239,713; non-need-based scholarships/grants totaling $536,633, self-help $975,699, parent loans $237,657.

Departments and Teaching Staff: *Total instructional faculty:* 75 (full-time 43, part-time 32; women 46, men 29; members of minority groups 2). Total faculty with doctorate, first-professional, or other terminal degree: 30. Student-to-faculty ratio: 13:1.

Enrollment: Total enrollment 667. Undergraduate full-time 257 men / 356 women, part-time 14m / 40w. *Transfer students:* in-state 60; from out-of-state 16.

Characteristics of Student Body: *Ethnic/racial makeup:* number of Black non-Hispanic: 88; American Indian of Alaska Native: 3; Asian or Pacific Islander: 3; Hispanic: 19; White non-Hispanic: 529; unknown: 18. *Age distribution:* number under 18: 4; 18–19: 205; 20–21: 212; 22–24: 138; 25–29: 41; 30–34: 23; 35–39: 12; 40–49: 29; 50–64: 3.

International Students: 8 nonresident aliens enrolled fall 2004. Programs available to aid students whose native language is not English: Social, cultural, financial. No financial aid specifically designated for international students.

Student Life: On-campus residence halls house 75% of student body. Residence halls for men only constitute 15% of such space, for women only 43%, for both sexes 42%. *Intercollegiate athletics:* men only: baseball, basketball, football, soccer, tennis, wrestling; women only: basketball, soccer, softball, tennis, volleyball; both sexes: golf. *Special regulations:* Cars permitted without restrictions. *Special services:* Medical services. *Student publications: The Bagpipe,* a newspaper; *Montage,* an annual literary magazine; *Tartan,* a yearbook. *Surrounding community:* Jacksonville population 20,000. St. Louis (MO), 80 miles from campus, is nearest metropolitan area. Served by airport 35 miles from campus; passenger rail service 35 miles from campus.

Library Collections: 160,000 volumes. 230,000 government documents; 590 microforms; 1,020 audiovisual materials; 200 current periodical subscriptions. Online catalog. 40 computer work stations. Students have access to online information retrieval systems and the Internet.

Most important holdings include Birdseye Pepys Collection (books by and about 17th-century British diarist, Samuel Pepys); Austin-Ball Collection (early 20th-century materials about singing and voice instruction); selective federal government document depository.

Buildings and Grounds: Campus area 80 acres. *New buildings:* Putnam Center for the Arts completed 2002; William H. Springer Center for Music 2002.

Chief Executive Officer: Dr. Lawrence D. Bryan, President.

Address admission inquiries to Rhonda Cors, Vice President for Enrollment Management.

Mennonite College of Nursing

804 North East Street
Bloomington, Illinois 61701-3078
Tel: (309) 829-0715   **E-mail:** admissions@ilstu.edu
Fax: (309) 829-0765   **Internet:** www.ilstu.edu

Institution Description: The Mennonite College of Nursing offers professional training for nurses. It became affiliated with Illinois State University in 2003. *SEE* Illinois State University.

Midstate College

411 West North Moor Road
Peoria, Illinois 61614
Tel: (309) 692-4092   **E-mail:** midstate@midstate.edu
Fax: (309) 692-4873   **Internet:** www.midstate.edu

Institution Description: Midstate College is a private institution. *Enrollment:* 550. *Degrees awarded:* Associate, baccalaureate. Diplomas are also awarded.

Academic offering are subject to approval by Illinois Board of Higher Education.

Accreditation: *Regional:* NCA. *Professional:* medical assisting

History: Established in 1888, Midstate College is a private college with a strong background of providing students with essential business skills. The first of several baccalaureate degrees was accredited in 1999.

Institutional Structure: Governing board: Midstate College Board of Directors.

Calendar: Quarters. Academic year Aug. to Aug. Diplomas and degrees conferred quarterly. Formal commencement May and November.

Admission: Rolling admissions. *Requirements:* High school diploma or GED. Students must have an acceptable Midstate College entrance examination score.

Degree Requirements: 2.0 GPA; complete minimum requirements (required quarter hours, upper-level courses, and competencies) as stated in their program. *Transfer students:* must earn one-third of their quarter hours at Midstate College and complete their last quarter in residence.

Degrees Conferred: 17 *baccalaureate:* business, management, marketing, and related support services.

Fees and Other Expenses: *Full-time tuition per academic year 2004–05:* $9,300. *Required fees:* $100.

Financial Aid: Aid from institutionally generated funds is provided on the basis of academic merit, financial need. Institution has a Program Participation Agreement with the U.S. Department of Education for eligible students to receive Pell Grants and other federal aid.

Departments and Teaching Staff: *Total instructional faculty:* 62 (full-time 18, part-time 44; women 23, men 21; members of minority groups 6). Total faculty with doctorate, first-professional, or other terminal degree: 4.

Enrollment: Total enrollment 727. Full-time 29 men / 158 women, part-time 52m / 288w.

Characteristics of Student Body: *Ethnic/racial makeup:* number of Black non-Hispanic: 105; Asian or Pacific Islander: 1; Hispanic: 5; White non-Hispanic: 405; unknown: 11. *Age distribution:* number 18–19: 10; 20–21: 36; 22–24: 136; 25–29: 156; 30–34: 97; 35–39: 54; 40–49: 78; 50–64: 10.

International Students: No programs available to aid students whose native language is not English. No financial aid specifically designated for international students.

Student Life: Students come from the surrounding metropolitan area, all of Illinois, and many other states. Students are responsible for housing and routine health care. *Clubs and organizations:* Alpha Iota Sorority; Paralegal Association; American Association of Medical Assistants; Midstate Medics; Judicial Reporting Club; Student Senate.

Publications: *Midstate Voice* and *Midstate Reporter.*

Library Collections: 5,400 volumes including bound books, serial backfiles, electronic documents, and government documents not in separate collections. Online catalog. 23 periodical subscriptions. 17 computer work stations. Students have access to the Internet at no charge.

Buildings and Grounds: 3.2 acres with 2 buildings.

Chief Executive Officer: Dr. R. Dale Bunch, Chairman of the Board and President;

Address admission inquiries to Jessica Aver, Director of Admissions.

Midwestern University

555 31st Street
Downers Grove, Illinois 60515
Tel: (630) 969-4400   **E-mail:** admissil@midwestern.edu
Fax: (630) 515-7319   **Internet:** www.midwestern.edu

Institution Description: Formerly known as the Chicago College of Osteopathic Medicine, Midwestern University is a private professional school. The university has a branch campus (Arizona College of Osteopathic Medicine) in

Glendale, Arizona. *Enrollment:* 1,499. *Degrees awarded:* Baccalaureate, master's, first-professional.

Accreditation: *Regional:* NCA. *Professional:* computer science, occupational therapy, osteopathy, pharmacy, physical therapy, physician assisting, surgeon assisting

Calendar: Quarters. Academic year Aug. to May.

Characteristics of Freshmen: 12% of applicants accepted. 8% of accepted applicants enrolled.

Degrees Conferred: *Master's:* biological/life sciences 12; health professions and related sciences 85; 283 *first-professional:* osteopathic medicine 160; pharmacy 123.

Fees and Other Expenses: *Full-time tuition per academic year 2004–05:* $18,624. Contact the university for undergraduate health professions and graduate medical school fees. *Room and board per academic year:* Contact the university for current rates.

Financial Aid: Aid from institutionally generated funds is provided on the basis of academic merit, financial need, other considerations. Institution has a Program Participation Agreement with the U.S. Department of Education for eligible students to receive Pell Grants and other federal aid.

Departments and Teaching Staff: *Professors* 47, *associate professors* 53, *assistant professors* 70, *instructors* 27, *part-time teachers* 127, *volunteers* 246. *Total instructional faculty:* 570. Degrees held by full-time faculty: doctorate 23%, master's 10%, professional 57%. 90% hold terminal degrees.

Enrollment: Total enrollment 1,791. Undergraduate 49 (49% men, 51% women).

Characteristics of Student Body: *Ethnic/racial makeup:* Black non-Hispanic: 4.1%; Asian or Pacific Islander: 10.2%; Hispanic: 10.2%; White non-Hispanic: 73.5%; unknown: 2%.

Library Collections: 80,000 volumes. 8 microform titles; 15,860 audiovisual materials; 1,089 current periodical subscriptions. Access to 6 online information retrieval systems; CD-ROM databases.

Most important special holdings include osteopathic medicine; basic sciences; clinical medicine.

Chief Executive Officer: Dr. Kathleen H. Goeppinger, President.

Address admission inquiries Mark T. Clancy, Director of Admissions

Arizona College of Osteopathic Medicine

19555 North 59th Avenue
Glendale, Arizona 85308
Tel: (623) 572-3300

Degree Programs Offered: First-professional degree in osteopathic medicine.

Distinctive Educational Programs: Contact the college for entrance requirements and other information necessary for enrollment, tuition, fees. and living accommodations.

Enrollment: 549

Millikin University

1184 West Main Street
Decatur, Illinois 62522-2084

Tel: (217) 424-6211   **E-mail:** admis@millikin.edu
Fax: (217) 425-3993   **Internet:** www.millikin.edu

Institution Description: Millikin University is a private, independent, nonprofit institution affiliated with The Presbyterian Church in the United States of America. *Enrollment:* 2,676. *Degrees awarded:* Baccalaureate, master's.

Accreditation: *Regional:* NCA. *Professional:* music, nursing, nursing education, teacher education

History: Established and chartered 1901; offered first instruction at postsecondary level 1903; awarded first degree (baccalaureate) 1907; adopted present name 1953.

Institutional Structure: *Governing board:* Extrainstitutional representation: 34 trustees, all voting; institutional representation: 1 administrator. 1 ex officio. *Composition of institution:* Administrators 13 men / 27 women. Academic affairs headed by provost-vice president for academic affairs. Management/business/finances directed by vice president for business affairs. Full-time instructional faculty 129. Academic governance body, the university faculty, meets an average of 9 times per year.

Calendar: Semesters. Academic year late Aug. to mid-May. Degrees conferred and formal commencement May. Summer session of 1 term from mid-June to late July.

Characteristics of Freshmen: 2,762 applicants (1,165 men, 1,597 women). 73.8% of applicants admitted. 25.9% of admitted students enrolled full-time.

13% (68 students) submitted SAT scores; 95% (501 students) submitted ACT scores. *25th percentile:* SAT I Verbal 460, SAT I Math 450; ACT Composite 20, ACT English 19, ACT Math 18. *75th percentile:* SAT I Verbal 600, SAT I Math 570; ACT Composite 26, ACT English 26, ACT Math 25.

64% of entering freshmen expected to graduate within 5 years. Freshmen from 14 states and 3 foreign countries.

Admission: Rolling admissions plan. For fall acceptance, apply as early as end of junior year of secondary school, but not later than 1 month prior to beginning of term. Apply by Dec. 1 for early decision; must limit application to Millikin. Early acceptance available. *Requirements:* Either graduation from accredited secondary school with 15 units which normally include 4 English, 2 mathematics, 2 science, 2 social studies; or GED. Lowest recommended secondary school class standing 50th percentile. *Entrance tests:* College Board SAT or ACT composite. *For transfer students:* 2.0 minimum GPA; from 4-year accredited institution 91 hours maximum transfer credit; from 2-year accredited institution 66 hours.

College credit and advanced placement for postsecondary-level work completed in secondary school. Advanced placement for extrainstitutional learning on basis of faculty assessment. Tutoring available.

Degree Requirements: 124-138 credit hours; 2.0 GPA; 2 (of last 3) semesters in residence; general education requirements. Fulfillment of some degree requirements and exemption from some beginning courses possible by passing departmental examinations, College Board CLEP, AP (score of 3). *Grading system:* A–F; pass-fail; withdraw (deadline after which pass-fail is appended to withdraw).

Distinctive Educational Programs: Evening classes. Interdepartmental programs. Facilities and programs for independent research, including honors programs, individual majors; also includes James Millikin scholars program, a 4-year program for qualified students, involving self-designed curriculum, honors seminars and project, financial aid. College of Fine Arts offers programs in commercial music, art therapy, musical theatre, computer graphics. Study abroad in Austria, England, France, Japan, Mexico, Singapore, Spain, West Germany through the Institute of European Studies. Off-campus study in U.S. includes United Nations Semester (for juniors) through Drew University (NJ) and Washington Semester (for juniors and seniors) through American University (DC). *Other distinctive programs:* Degree and nondegree continuing education.

Degrees Conferred: 505 *baccalaureate.* Bachelor's degrees awarded in top five disciplines: business, management, marketing, and related support services 109; visual and performing arts 109; education 76; health professions and related clinical sciences 25; communication, journalism, and related programs 25; 32 *master's* business, management, marketing, and related support services.

Fees and Other Expenses: *Full-time tuition per academic year 2004–05:* $19,900. *Room and board per academic year:* $6,512. *Books and supplies:* $800.

Financial Aid: Aid from institutionally generated funds is provided on the basis of academic merit, financial need, other criteria. Institution has a Program Participation Agreement with the U.S. Department of Education for eligible students to receive Pell Grants and other federal aid.

Financial aid to full-time, first-time undergraduate students: 31% received federal grants averaging $3,265; 51% state/local grants averaging $4,208; 99% institutional grants averaging $8,861; 94% loans averaging $4,245.

Departments and Teaching Staff: *Professors* 33, *associate professors* 37, *assistant professors* 45, *instructors* 14, *part-time faculty* 71. *Total instructional faculty:* 200. Degrees held by full-time faculty: doctorate 60.9%, master's 92%, baccalaureate 100%. 89% hold terminal degrees.

Enrollment: Total enrollment 2,576. Undergraduate 2,649 (43% men, 57% women).

Characteristics of Student Body: *Ethnic/racial makeup:* Black non-Hispanic: 8.8%; American Indian or Alaska Native: .1%; Asian or Pacific Islander: 1%; Hispanic: 2.4%; White non-Hispanic: 82.6%; unknown: 4.3%.

International Students: 19 nonresident aliens enrolled fall 2004. Students from Europe, Asia, Central and South America, Africa. Programs available to aid students whose native language is not English: Social, cultural. No Financial aid specifically designated for international students.

Student Life: On-campus residence halls house 60% of student body. Residence halls for men only constitute 20% of such space, for women only 30%, for both sexes 50%. 30% of men join and 15% live in fraternities; 31% of women join and 21% live in sororities. *Intercollegiate athletics:* men only: baseball, basketball, cross-country, football, golf, tennis, track, wrestling; women only: basketball, tennis, track, volleyball; both sexes: cross country, soccer, swimming. *Special regulations:* Registered cars permitted for upperclass students. Freshmen and sophomores may petition for permission. Quiet hours set by dormitory residents. Dormitory visitation from noon to 1am. *Special services:* Medical services. *Student publications, radio: Collage,* a biannual literary magazine; *Decaturian,* a weekly newspaper; *Millidek,* a yearbook; *Echo,* a biweekly student newspaper. Radio station WJMU broadcasts 120 hours per week. *Surrounding community:* Decatur population 95,000. St. Louis (MO), 120 miles from campus, is nearest metropolitan area. Served by mass transit bus system; airport 11 miles from campus; passenger rail service 40 miles from campus.

Library Collections: 212,200 volumes. 21,500 microforms; 2,300 audiovisual materials; 500 periodical subscriptions; Online catalog. Students have access to online information retrieval services and the Internet.

Most important holdings include Carlyle Baer Bookplate collection (over 5,000 items); Alice in Wonderland collection; Lincolniana and Civil War Memorial Collection; Stephen Decatur Collection; Music Collection.

Buildings and Grounds: Campus area 70 acres.

Chief Executive Officer: Douglas E. Zemke, President.

Address admission inquiries to Lin F. Stoner, Dean Admissions.

College of Arts and Sciences

Degree Programs Offered: *Baccalaureate* in biology, chemistry, communications, computer science, elementary education, English, French, German, history, human services, literature, mathematics, music, philosophy, physical education, physics, political science, psychology, religion, school nursing, sociology, social sciences, Spanish, writing.

Admission: *See* general requirements.

Degree Requirements: *See* general requirements. *For baccalaureate of arts:* 3 credit hours literature; foreign language competency requirement. *For baccalaureate of science:* 10 hours in science and mathematics; 3 literature.

Distinctive Educational Programs: Cooperative baccalaureate programs in medical technology and physical therapy with approved schools and hospitals. Interdisciplinary programs in American studies, art management, art therapy, continental European studies, environmental studies, music-theater, psychology-sociology, urban studies. Individual research for students in biology, chemistry, and physics.

Tabor School of Business

Degree Programs Offered: *Baccalaureate* in accounting, business administration, economics, finance, international business, human resource management, management information systems, marketing, production/operations management.

Admission: GPA of 2.25 and Foundation courses required for admission as a major to upper-division.

Degree Requirements: *See* general requirements.

College of Fine Arts

Degree Programs Offered: *Baccalaureate* in art, art education, art therapy, commercial art, applied music (performance), church music, commercial music, music/business, music education, theatre (acting, directing, and design), music/theatre, dance (minor).

Admission: *See* general requirements. In addition to general requirements, audition.

Degree Requirements: *See* general requirements.

School of Nursing

Degree Programs Offered: *Baccalaureate* in nursing.

Admission: *See* general requirements. In addition to general requirements, ACT composite (score of 24) secondary school class standing top quarter.

Degree Requirements: *See* general requirements. BSN completion program offered for registered nurses. *For baccalaureate in nursing:* 2.5 GPA, 4 semesters in residence.

Distinctive Educational Programs: Generic purist program with teaching by clinical associates as well as regular faculty members. Practicums; simulation laboratory; computer facilities.

Monmouth College

700 East Broadway
Monmouth, Illinois 61462
Tel: (309) 457-2131　　**E-mail:** admit@monm.edu
Fax: (309) 457-2141　　**Internet:** www.monm.edu

Institution Description: Monmouth College is a private college affiliated with the United Presbyterian Church in the United States of America. *Enrollment:* 1,252. *Degrees awarded:* Baccalaureate.

Member of Associated Colleges of the Midwest (ACM).

Accreditation: *Regional:* NCA.

History: Established as Monmouth Academy 1853; offered first instruction at postsecondary level 1856; adopted present name and chartered 1857; awarded first degree (baccalaureate) 1858. *See* Francis Garvin Davenport, *Monmouth College: The First One Hundred Years, 1853–1953* (Cedar Rapids, Iowa: Privately printed, 1953); William L. Urban, *A History of Monmouth College* (Monmouth: Monmouth College, 1979) for further information.

Institutional Structure: *Governing board:* The Monmouth College Senate. Extrainstitutional representation: 9 charter trustees (includes 1 emeritus); 33 trustees; institutional representation: president of the college. 37 voting members; 9 non-voting members. *Composition of institution:* Administrators 35 men / 26 women. Academic affairs headed by vice president for academic affairs. Management/business/finances directed by vice president for finance and business. Full-time instructional faculty 70. Academic governance body, the faculty, meets an average of 9 times per year.

Calendar: Semesters. Academic year Aug. to May. Freshmen admitted on a rolling basis. Degrees conferred and formal commencement May. No summer session.

Characteristics of Freshmen: 72% of applicants admitted. 33% of admitted students enrolled full-time.

25th percentile: SAT Verbal 550, SAT Math 560; ACT Composite 20, ACT English 21, ACT Math 20. *75th percentile:* SAT Verbal 580, SAT Math 580; ACT Composite 26, ACT English 26, ACT Math 26.

61% of entering freshmen expected to graduate within 5 years.

Admission: For fall acceptance, apply as early as 1 year prior to enrollment, but not later than Mar. 1 of year of enrollment. *Requirements:* Either graduation from an accredited secondary school or GED. Recommend 15 units. Minimum recommended GPA 2.0. Lowest recommended secondary school class standing 50th percentile. *Entrance tests:* College Board SAT or ACT composite. For foreign students minimum TOEFL score 550. *For transfer students:* 2.3 minimum GPA; from 4-year accredited institution maximum of 62 semester hours accepted.

College credit and advanced placement for postsecondary-level work completed in secondary school. Tutoring available.

Degree Requirements: *For all baccalaureate degrees:* 124 semester hours. *For all degrees:* 2.0 GPA; general education requirements. Fulfillment of some degree requirements and exemption from some beginning courses possible by passing departmental examinations, College Board AP, and/or satisfactory score(s) on International Baccalaureate examinations. *Grading system:* A–F.

Distinctive Educational Programs: Business, communications, and public internship programs. Dual-degree programs in engineering with Case Western Reserve University (OH), Washington University (MO), and University of Southern California; in nursing and medical technology with Rush University in Chicago; in architecture with Washington University; individual majors. Institutionally sponsored study abroad in Costa Rica, England, France, Japan, Greece, Sweden, Ireland, and others through Associated Colleges of the Midwest and the Great Lakes Colleges Association.l Institutionally sponsored off-campus programs in the U.S. including urban education, urban studies, and women in management, all in Chicago; semester in Washington (DC). Other opportunities for domestic off-campus study include ACM's Wilderness Field Station (MN) program and through ACM/GLCA programs at Oak Ridge (TN) National Laboratory and at Chicago's Newberry Library. Semester in Washington also available through American University. *Other distinctive programs:* Honors program.

ROTC: Army offered in cooperation with Western Illinois University.

Degrees Conferred: 230 *baccalaureate:* biological/life sciences 18; business/marketing 15; communications/communication technologies 26; computer and information sciences 1; education 49; English 10; foreign languages and literature 7; interdisciplinary studies 5; mathematics 11; natural resources/environmental science 2; philosophy/religion/theology 4; physical sciences 6; psychology 13; social sciences and history 20; visual and performing arts 7.

Fees and Other Expenses: *Full-time tuition board per academic year 2005–06:* $20,200. *Room and board per academic year:* $5,750.

Financial Aid: Aid from institutionally generated funds is provided on the basis of academic merit, financial need. Institution has a Program Participation Agreement with the U.S. Department of Education for eligible students to receive Pell Grants and other federal aid.

Financial aid to full-time, first-time undergraduate students: need-based scholarships/grants totaling $9,837,626, self-help $2,913,606; non-need-based scholarships/grants totaling $3,203,803, self-help $2,353,176, waivers athletic $447,706.

Departments and Teaching Staff: *Professors* 22, *associate professors* 17, *assistant professors* 24, *instructors* 7, *part-time faculty* 35. *Total instructional faculty:* 105 (full-time 70, part-time 35; women 50, men 56; members of minority groups 8). Total faculty with doctorate, first-professional, or other terminal degree: 64. Student-to-faculty ratio: 14:1. 5 faculty members awarded sabbaticals 2004–05.

Enrollment: Total enrollment 1,252. Undergraduate full-time 584 men / 663 women, part-time 1m / 4w.

Characteristics of Student Body: *Ethnic/racial makeup:* number of Black non-Hispanic: 42; American Indian or Alaska Native 1; Asian or Pacific

Islander: 10; Hispanic: 8; White non-Hispanic: 1,140; unknown: 3. *Age distribution:* number under 18: 4; 18–19: 655; 20–21: 471; 22–24: 95; 25–29: 7; 30–34: 35–39: 8; 40–49: 3; 50–64: 2.

International Students: 18 nonresident aliens enrolled fall 2004. 5 students from Europe, 7 Asia, 2 Africa, 4 Canada. Programs available to aid students whose native language is not English: Social, Cultural. English as a Second Language Program. No financial aid specifically designated for international students.

Student Life: On-campus residence halls house 90% of student body. Residence halls for men constitute 45% of such space, for women 55%. 35% of men join and live in fraternities. 30% of women join sororities but all live in the residence halls. *Intercollegiate athletics:* men only: baseball, basketball, football, golf, soccer, track; women only: basketball, golf, softball, volleyball. *Special regulations:* Cars permitted without restrictions. Quiet hours and dormitory visitation hours vary according to residence hall. *Special services:* Teaching Learning Center, Counseling Services. *Student publications, radio: Oracle,* a weekly newspaper; *Ravelings,* a yearbook; *Carillon,* an annual literary magazine; *The Coil,* a creative arts magazine. Radio station WMCR broadcasts 100 hours per week. *Surrounding community:* Monmouth population 12,000. Chicago, 200 miles from campus, is nearest metropolitan area. Served by airport 14 miles from campus; passenger rail service 14 miles from campus.

Library Collections: 320,522 volumes. 463 current serial subscriptions; access to 861 via electronic access. 10,138 recordings. 79 computer work stations. Students have access to the Internet at no charge. Total budget for books, periodicals, audiovisual materials, microforms 2004–05: $210,389.

Most important special holdings include Monmouthiana; Presbyterian and local history; U.S. Government Documents Depository since 1860; James Christy Shields Collection of Arts and Antiquities.

Buildings and Grounds: Campus area 15 square blocks. *New buildings:* Bowers Residence Hall completed 2001; Huff Athletic Center 2003; Founders Village 2004.

Chief Executive Officer: Dr. Richard F. Giese, President.

Address admission inquiries to Christine Johnson, Director of New Student Enrollment.

Moody Bible Institute

820 North LaSalle Boulevard
Chicago, Illinois 60610-3284
Tel: (312) 329-4400   **E-mail:** admissions@moody.edu
Fax: (312) 329-8987   **Internet:** www.moody.edu

Institution Description: Moody Bible Institute is a private interdenominational professional institution. *Enrollment:* 1,732. *Degrees awarded:* Associate, baccalaureate, master's.

Accreditation: *Regional:* NCA. *National:* ABHE. *Professional:* music

History: Founded by D. L. Moody in 1886.

Calendar: Semesters. Academic year Aug. to May.

Characteristics of Freshmen: ACT composite class score 25. 60% of applicants accepted. 65% of freshmen expected to graduate within 5 years. 205 of freshmen from Illinois. Freshmen from 36 states and 16 foreign countries.

Admission: *Requirements:* Graduation from accredited secondary school or equivalent; good Christian character; membership in an evangelical Protestant church and acceptance of the Institute's doctrinal statement. *Entrance tests:* ACT.

Degree Requirements: *For baccalaureate degree:* 130 semester hours; completion of prescribed curriculum. *For graduate degree:* 36 semester hours.

Distinctive Educational Programs: Extensive correspondence program offered. Study abroad at Belfast Bible College (Ireland), Glasgow Bible College (Scotland), and European Bible Institute (France).

Degrees Conferred: 322 *baccalaureate:* degrees awarded in top five disciplines: communications/communications technologies 30; theology and religious vocations 266; mechanics/repairers; 19; 68 *master's:* theology.

Fees and Other Expenses: *Full-time tuition per academic year:* paid for by donors; student fees $1,415. *Room and board per academic year:* $5,670.

Financial Aid: Aid from institutionally generated funds is provided on the basis of academic merit, financial need.

Departments and Teaching Staff: Bible *professors* 8, *associate professors* 1, *assistant professors* 0, *instructors* 1; theology 3, 2, 2, 0; educational ministries 3, 1, 3, 0; pastoral studies 1, 0, 2, 0; international ministry 4, 3, 1, 0; communications 1, 4, 2, 0; general education 2, 0, 1, 1; music 10, 4, 0, 0; physical education 1, 4, 0, 0.

Total instructional faculty: 80 FTE. Degrees held by full-time instructional faculty: doctorate 51.4%, master's 93.1%. 51.4% hold terminal degrees.

Enrollment: Total enrollment 1,403; undergraduate 1,388.

Characteristics of Student Body: *Ethnic/racial makeup:* Black non-Hispanic: 1.9%; American Indian or Alaska Native: .5%; Asian or Pacific Islander: 2.5%; Hispanic: 3%; White non-Hispanic: 85.8%.

International Students: 81 nonresident aliens enrolled. No programs available to aid students whose native language is not English. No financial aid specifically designated for international students.

Student Life: Residence halls available on campus.

Library Collections: 140,000 volumes. 4,500 item music library; 950 current periodical subscriptions.

Buildings and Grounds: Campus area 15 city blocks.

Chief Executive Officer: Dr. Joseph M. Stowell, III, President.

Address admission inquiries to Annette Moi, Dean of Admissions.

Meadville/Lombard Theological School

5701 South Woodlawn Avenue
Chicago, Illinois 60637
Tel: (773) 256-3000   **E-mail:** admissions@meadville.edu
Fax: (773) 753-1323   **Internet:** www.meadville.edu

Institution Description: Meadville/Lombard Theological School is a graduate professional school offering programs of study for preparation for professional religious leadership. It is affiliated with the University of Chicago. *Enrollment:* 123. *Degrees awarded:* Master's, doctorate, first-professional.

Accreditation: *National:* ATS. *Professional:* theology

History: Founded in Meadville, Pennsylvania as a seminary for Unitarians and members of the Christian Connection 1844; moved to University of Chicago 1926; acquired the charter of Lombard College (Galesburg, IL) and became Meadville Theological School of Lombard College 1964.

Institutional Structure: *Governing board:* Board of Trustees. Extrainstitutional representation: 21 trustees. *Composition of institution:* Administrative head is the dean and chief executive. Instructional faculty 13. Academic governance body is the School Council.

Calendar: Quarters. No summer session.

Admission: *Requirements:* Academic records of graduation from accredited college; GRE examination; personal statement; letters of recommendation.

Degree Requirements: *For master of divinity degree:* 3 years of academic study and internship of 6 months. *For doctor of ministry:* thesis; related courses.

Degrees Conferred: 12 *first-professional:* master of divinity; 1 *master's;* 1 *doctorate.*

Fees and Other Expenses: *Full-time tuition per academic year:* $15,600. Contact the school for current fees/expenses.

Financial Aid: Aid from institutionally generated funds is provided on the basis of academic merit, financial need, other criteria. Institution has a Program Participation Agreement with the U.S. Department of Education for eligible students to receive Pell Grants and other federal aid.

Departments and Teaching Staff: *Total instructional faculty:* 13.

Enrollment: Total enrollment 123 (35% men, 65% women).

Characteristics of Student Body: *Ethnic/racial makeup:* Black non-Hispanic: 4.9%; Hispanic: 3.3%; White non-Hispanic: 89.4%. *Age distribution:* 22–24: 6%; 25–29: 20%; 30–34: 16%; 35–39: 23%; 40–49: 26%; 50–59: 3%; 60-and over: 3%.

International Students: No programs available to aid students whose native language is not English. Some financial aid specifically designated for international students.

Student Life: Some housing for single students is available at Meadville/ Lombard. Married student housing is available at the University of Chicago. Housing for both single and married students is available at neighboring theological schools.

Publications: The *M/L News* is issued 3 times a year. The *Announcements* is published every other year.

Library Collections: 130,000 volumes. 125 current periodical subscriptions. Students have access to the Regenstein Library of the University (1 block away) and also to several libraries of the Association of Chicago Theological Schools.

Most important special holdings include collections of papers of important Unitarian and Universalist ministers, including William Ellery Channing, Jenkin Lloyd Jones, A. Powell Davies, Vincent B. Silliman, Charles Lyttle, Clinton Lee Scott, and Jack Mendelsohn.

Buildings and Grounds: School activities are mainly concentrated in a main building on the University of Chicago campus. Three additional buildings are used for offices and housing.

Chief Executive Officer: Dr. Lee Barker, President.

Address admission inquiries to Dr. John W. Tolley, Director of Enrollment Management.

NAES College

2838 West Peterson
Chicago, Illinois 60659
Tel: (312) 761-5000   **E-mail:** admissions@naes.edu
Fax: (312) 761-3608   **Internet:** www.naes.edu

Institution Description: NAES College, formerly Native American Educational Services, is a private, independent, nonprofit institution with centers in Chicago, Fort Peck and Northern Cheyenne (MT), and Santo Domingo Pueblo (NM). The Chicago center houses the central administration. *Enrollment:* 80. *Degrees awarded:* Baccalaureate.

Accreditation: *Regional:* NCA.

History: Established and incorporated 1974; offered first instruction at post-secondary level 1975; awarded first degree (baccalaureate) 1977.

Institutional Structure: *Governing board:* NAES Board of Directors. Extrainstitutional representation: 8 directors; institutional representation: 1 student; 1 alumna. All voting. *Composition of institution:* Administrators 2 men / 3 women. Academic affairs headed by president. Management/business/finances directed by fiscal officer. Full-time instructional faculty 2. Academic governance body, Resident Faculty, meets an average of 4 times per year.

Calendar: Semesters. Academic year Sept. to July. Freshmen admitted Sept., Jan., Apr., Aug. Degrees conferred July, Dec., Apr. Formal commencement July. Summer session from early to late Aug.

Admission: Rolling admissions plan. Apply anytime during semester prior to intended enrollment. *Requirements:* Applicant must be employed, or a volunteer, in an Indian organization or agency serving Indian people in the community where the center is located. Must have secondary school diploma or GED, be 24 years of age, and have completed at least 60 semester hours of transferable credit from another college. *For transfer students:* 2.0 minimum GPA from accredited institution; maximum transfer credit limited only by residence requirement.

College credit for extrainstitutional learning on basis of ACE *2006 Guide to the Evaluation of Educational Experiences in the Armed Services*, portfolio, faculty assessments, personal interviews. Tutoring available.

Degree Requirements: 120 credit hours; 3 terms in residence; core seminars; educational planning and professional development courses; oral examinations before degree committee. *Grading system:* Pass-fail.

Distinctive Educational Programs: Work-experience programs. Evening classes. Accelerated degree programs. External degree-program in cooperation with local community colleges and Governors State University (IL). All programs are interdisciplinary and include the areas of community and human services, community development, and community education. Students integrate coursework with community needs, working full-time and attending classes full-time. Tutorials. Part-time study permitted only through summer institute, special NAES projects, and courses designated by faculty members as open to part-time students. *Other distinctive programs:* Board Training Project for development of professional operational systems among Indian community boards and staff members. Contemporary Issues in Indian Communities, a summer institute, open to students and nonstudents.

Degrees Conferred: 14 *baccalaureate*.

Fees and Other Expenses: *Full-time tuition per academic year:* $6,090. Contact NAES in Chicago for current information.

Financial Aid: Financial assistance is available in the form of Pell Grants, College Work-Study, Veterans Administration Benefits, Supplemental Education Opportunity Grants (SEOG), Stafford Loans, other federal aid programs.

Departments and Teaching Staff: *Instructional faculty:* 3. Student-to-faculty ratio: 22:1.

Enrollment: Total enrollment 80.

Characteristics of Student Body: *Ethnic/racial makeup:* Black non-Hispanic: 1.4%; American Indian or Alaska Native: 90%; White non-Hispanic: 7.1%; unknown: 1.4%.

International Students: No programs to aid students whose native language is not English. No financial aid specifically designated for international students.

Student Life: No on-campus housing. *Special services:* Learning Resources Center. *Surrounding community:* Chicago population over 3,000,000. Served by mass transit bus system; airport 12 miles from campus; passenger rail service 6 miles from campus.

Buildings and Grounds: Campus area 1 building.

Chief Executive Officer: Faith Smith, President.

Address admission inquiries to Registrar.

National University of Health Sciences

200 East Roosevelt Road
Lombard, Illinois 60148
Tel: (630) 629-2000   **E-mail:** admissions@nuhs.edu
Fax: (630) 889-6554   **Internet:** www.nuhs.edu

Institution Description: The National University of Health Sciences, formerly known as the College of Chiropractic, is a private, independent, nonprofit college providing upper division undergraduate and professional study only. *Enrollment:* 524. *Degrees awarded:* Baccalaureate, first-professional (chiropractic).

Accreditation: *Regional:* NCA. *National:* AMTA. *Professional:* chiropractic education

History: Established as National School of Chiropractic, offered first instruction at postsecondary level, and awarded first degree (first-professional) 1906; chartered 1908; adopted present name 1920; incorporated 1942; awarded first baccalaureate degree 1966; adopted present name 2002.

Institutional Structure: *Governing board:* National University of Health Sciences Board of Trustees. Representation: 12 trustees. All voting. *Composition of institution:* Administrators 10 men. Academic affairs headed by chancellor. Management/business/finances directed by vice president for administration. Full-time instructional faculty 54 men / 14 women. Academic governance body, Curriculum Committee, meets an average of 4 times per year.

Calendar: Trimesters. Academic year early Sept. to Apr. New classes admitted Sept., Jan., Apr. Degrees conferred and formal commencements Apr., Aug., Dec. Summer session from late Apr. to mid-Aug.

Admission: Modified rolling admissions plan. *Requirements:* Either graduation from accredited secondary school or GED, and the equivalent of 60 semester hours from an accredited college or university to include 6 hours biology, 6 hours inorganic chemistry, 6 hours organic chemistry, 6–12 hours English, 18–24 hours humanities and social sciences (general psychology required), 6 hours physics.

Degree Requirements: *For all baccalaureate degrees:* 68 hours at National College; 4 trimesters in residence. *For first-professional degrees:* 198 hours; 10 trimesters in residence; prescribed curriculum clinical internship. *For all degrees:* 2.0 GPA.

Fulfillment of some degree requirements possible by passing departmental examinations. *Grading system:* A–F; pass-fail; withdraw (deadline after which pass-fail is appended to withdraw).

Distinctive Educational Programs: *For graduate students:* Weekend classes. *Other distinctive programs:* National-Lincoln School of Postgraduate Education provides programs to assist practitioners in maintaining their expertise and in developing clinical specialties.

Degrees Conferred: 65 *baccalaureate:* biological and biomedical sciences; 135 *first-professional:* chiropractic.

Fees and Other Expenses: *Full-time tuition per academic year:* Contact the university for current tuition, fees, and expenses.

Financial Aid: Institutional, federal, and state funding for first-professional students available; awarded on basis of academic merit, financial need. Institution has a Program Participation Agreement with the U.S. Department of Education for eligible students to receive Pell Grants and other federal aid.

Departments and Teaching Staff: *Professors* 18, *associate professors* 19, *assistant professors* 16, *instructors* 21, *part-time teachers* 20. *Total instructional faculty:* 84. Degrees held by full-time faculty: doctorate 24.3%, master's 6.8%, baccalaureate 2.7%, professional 66.2%. 94.6% hold terminal degrees.

Enrollment: Total enrollment 524 (21.7% men, 78.3% women).

Characteristics of Student Body: *Ethnic/racial makeup:* Black non-Hispanic: 6.6%; Asian or Pacific Islander: 5.3%; Hispanic: 5.9%; White non-Hispanic: 79.6%. *Age distribution:* 17–21: 4.8%; 22–24: 35.9%; 25–29: 40.1%; 30–34: 8.8%; 35–39: 5.1%; 40–49: 4.1%; 50–59: .2%.

International Students: No programs available to aid students whose native language is not English. Some financial aid available to international students.

Student Life: On-campus housing accommodates 33% of student population. *Special regulations:* Registered cars permitted in designated areas. *Special services:* Learning Resources Center, medical services. *Student publication: The Synapse,* a bimonthly newspaper. *Surrounding community:* Lombard population 39,000; located in Chicago metropolitan area. Served by airport 15 miles from campus; passenger rail service 2 miles from campus.

Publications: *Journal of Manipulative and Physiological Therapeutics* (9 times per year) first published in 1978; *Journal of Chiropractic Humanities* (annual) first published in 1991; *Chiropractic Technique* (quarterly) first published in 1988.

Library Collections: 30,000 volumes. 2,000 audiovisual materials; 2,649 reels of microfilm; 473 current periodical subscriptions. Students have access to online information retrieval services.

Most important special collections include Joseph Janse Papers; alternative and natural medicine; chiropractic material.

Buildings and Grounds: Campus area 16 acres.

Chief Executive Officer: Dr. James F. Winterstein, President.

Address admission inquiries Ron Mensching, Director of Admissions.

National-Louis University

122 South Michigan Avenue
Chicago, Illinois 60603-6191
Tel: (888) 8632   **E-mail:** nluinfo@nl.edu
                        Internet: www.nl.edu

Institution Description: National-Louis University, formerly the National College of Education, is a private college with branch campuses in Chicago, Wheeling (IL), Wheaton (IL), and centers in St. Louis, Atlanta, Milwaukee, Elgin (IL), Tampa/Orlando, northern Virginia/Washington, D.C., and Heidelberg, Germany. *Enrollment:* 7,433. *Degrees awarded:* Baccalaureate, master's, doctorate. Certificates and diplomas also awarded.

Accreditation: *Regional:* NCA. *Professional:* clinical lab scientist, radiation therapy, respiratory therapy, teacher education

History: Established as Chicago Training School and offered first instruction at postsecondary level 1886; became National Kindergarten College 1912; became 4-year institution and renamed National College of Education 1930; awarded first degree (baccalaureate) 1932; adopted present name 1989.

Institutional Structure: *Governing board:* Board of Trustees. Extrainstitutional representation: 31 members, 7 officers. *Composition of institution:* three colleges: Arts and Sciences, Education, Management/Business. Full-time instructional faculty 253.

Calendar: Quarters. Academic year Sept. to June. Freshmen admitted Sept., Jan., Mar. Summer session begins June.

Characteristics of Freshmen: 165 applicants (39 men, 126 women). 94.5% of applicants admitted. 41% of admitted students enrolled full-time.

91% (64 students) submitted ACT scores. *25th percentile*: ACT Composite 14, ACT English 13, ACT Math 14. *75th percentile*: ACT Composite 19, ACT English 20, ACT Math 19.

95% of freshmen from Illinois. Freshmen from 3 states.

Admission: Rolling admissions plan. *Requirements:* Recommend either graduation from secondary school with 4 units English, 2 or more laboratory science, mathematics, 1 U.S. history or government; or GED. Lowest recommended secondary school class standing 50th percentile. *Entrance tests:* College Board SAT or ACT composite. *For transfer students:* 2.0 minimum GPA. Exceptions possible. *For graduate students:* GRE, MAT, Watson-Glaser or other test usually required.

Degree Requirements: Minimum 180 quarter hours; exit competency examination in English for most programs; 2.0 GPA. For liberal arts studies program, last 45 hours in residence. For liberal arts in teacher education program, last 90 hours in residence; minimum 2.5 GPA.

Fulfillment of some degree requirements possible by passing College Board CLEP, AP, departmental examinations. *Grading system:* A–C, no credit; pass-no credit; withdraw.

Distinctive Educational Programs: Field experience. Special scheduling for adult students, especially in management and business programs. Demonstration school offers students opportunity for extensive classroom observation and participation. Cooperative programs in medical technology, radiation therapy, and respiratory therapy with affiliated area hospitals.

Degrees Conferred: 1,134 *baccalaureate*; 1,974 *master's*; 147 *post-master's certificates*; 18 *doctorate*. Bachelor's degrees awarded in top five disciplines: business, management, marketing, and related support services 609; multidisciplinary studies 256; education 111; health professions and related clinical sciences 84; social sciences 20.

Fees and Other Expenses: *Full-time tuition per academic year 2004–05:* undergraduate $16,200; graduate tuition per semester hour. *Books and supplies:* $992. *Room and board per academic year:* $6,213.

Financial Aid: Aid from institutionally generated funds is provided on the basis of academic merit, financial need. Institution has a Program Participation Agreement with the U.S. Department of Education for eligible students to receive Pell Grants and other federal aid.

Financial aid to full-time, first-time undergraduate students: 84% received federal grants averaging $3,354; 63% state/local grants averaging $4,100; 87% institutional grants averaging $2,946; 32% loans averaging $5,946.

Departments and Teaching Staff: *Total instructional faculty:* 156. Degrees held by full-time faculty: doctorate 65%, master's 35%. 65% hold terminal degrees.

Enrollment: Total enrollment 7,433. Undergraduate 2,113 (26.1% men, 73.9% women).

Characteristics of Student Body: *Ethnic/racial makeup:* Black non-Hispanic: 22.5%, American Indian or Alaska Native: .3%; Asian or Pacific Islander: 1.6%; Hispanic: 6.6%; White non-Hispanic: 16.8%; unknown: 52.1%. *Age distribution:* 17–21: 7.6%; 22–24: 11.6%; 25–29: 20.2%; 30–34: 13.5%; 35–39: 13.4%; 40–49: 26.8%; 50–59: 6.7%; 60–and over: .7%.

International Students: Programs available to aid student whose native language is not English: Social and cultural. English as a Second Language Program. No financial aid specifically designated for international students.

Student Life: On-campus housing available in Evanston. Many university-sponsored clubs. Student governance. Limited health services on Evanston and Chicago campuses. *Special regulations:* Limited parking for upperclass students, with preference given to commuters; fee charged. Quiet hours. *Student publications: Celebration*, an annual art and literature publication; *Futura*, a yearbook; a newspaper. *Surrounding community:* Evanston population 85,000, is located in Chicago metropolitan area. Served by mass transit bus and rail system.

Library Collections: 153,000 volumes. 926,000 microforms; 3,490 current periodicals; 5,100 audiovisual materials. Online catalog. Students have access to online information retrieval services and the Internet.

Most important special collections include Elizabeth Harrison's Papers and Personal Collection; central series collection of journals; William Gray Reading Collection.

Chief Executive Officer: Dr. Curtis L. McCray, President.

Address admission inquiries to Kathleen Thompson, Director of Enrollment Management.

North Central College

30 North Brainard Street
Naperville, Illinois 60566-7063
Tel: (630) 637-5100   **E-mail:** admissions@noctrl.edu
Fax: (630) 637-5121   **Internet:** www.noctrl.edu

Institution Description: North Central College is an independent liberal arts college, related to the United Methodist Church. *Enrollment:* 2,377. *Degrees awarded:* Baccalaureate, master's.

Member of the consortia Council of West Suburban Colleges and West Suburban Regional Academic Consortium.

Accreditation: *Regional:* NCA.

History: Established as The Plainfield College of the Evangelical Association of North America 1861 and offered first instruction at postsecondary level 1863; changed name to North Western College 1864; incorporated 1865; first degree (baccalaureate) awarded 1866; adopted present name 1926. *See* Clarence R. Roberts, *A Century of Liberal Education 1861–1961* (Naperville, Ill.: North Central College, 1960) for further information.

Institutional Structure: *Governing board:* The Board of Trustees of North Central College. Extrainstitutional representation: 34 active trustees (also 22 life and 5 honorary trustees); 19 alumni among active trustees. *Composition of institution:* Administrators 16 men / 12 women. Academic affairs headed by vice president for academic affairs/dean of faculty; dean of graduate and continuing education. Management/business/finances directed by vice president of institutional advancement and vice president of business affairs. Full-time instructional faculty 125. Academic governance body, The College Faculty, meets an average of 9 times per year.

Calendar: Trimesters. Academic year Sept. to June. Freshmen admitted Sept., Dec., Apr., June. Formal commencement June. Summer session June to Aug. Weekend College, a degree-completion program for adults in which classes meet on alternate weekends, is offered each term during the academic year.

Characteristics of Freshmen: 69% of applicants admitted. 21% of admitted students enrolled full-time.

11% (43 students) submitted SAT scores; 95% (362 students) submitted ACT scores. *25th percentile*: SAT Verbal 510, SAT Math 540; ACT Composite 21, ACT English 21, ACT Math 21. *75th percentile*: SAT Verbal 610, SAT Math 670; ACT Composite 27, ACT English 27, ACT Math 27.

61% of entering freshmen expected to graduate within 5 years. 89% of freshmen from Illinois. Freshmen from 15 states and 10 foreign countries.

Admission: Rolling admissions plan. For fall acceptance, apply as early as Sept. of previous year, but not later than early August of year of enrollment. Early decision available; need not limit application to North Central. *Requirements:* Either graduation from an accredited secondary school with 15 units from college preparatory curriculum; or GED. Lowest acceptable secondary school class standing 50th percentile. *Entrance tests:* College Board and/or ACT composite. *For transfer students:* 2.3 minimum GPA. From 4-year institution 3 years maximum transfer credit; from 2-year institution 2 years; from any state-system accredited correspondence program all courses that meet degree requirements completed with grade of D or better; from other programs credits accepted after individual review.

College credit for extrainstitutional learning on the basis of ACE *2006 Guide to the Evaluation of Educational Experiences in the Armed Services* and assessment by faculty and dean of faculty. Tutoring available. Noncredit developmental/remedial courses offered during regular academic year.

Degree Requirements: 120 semester hours; 2.0 GPA; last 30 hours in residence; general education requirements; completion of major. Fulfillment of some degree requirements possible by passing College Board CLEP exams. *Grading system:* A–F; withdraw (carries time limit).

Distinctive Educational Programs: Weekend and evening classes. Master of Arts degree in Liberal Studies. Master of Science degrees in computer science, management information systems. Master's degree in business administration. Leadership, ethics, and values interdisciplinary program. Dual-degree programs in engineering and computer science with Washington University (MO), University of Illinois, Urbana-Campaign, Purdue University (IN), Marquette University (WI), and University of Minnesota. Cooperative master's program in business administration with Stuart School of Management at Illinois Institute of Technology. Cooperative baccalaureate programs in engineering with the Illinois Institute of Technology; in nursing and medical technology with Rush University (IL); banking and bank management with the American Institute of Banking. Combined preprofessional programs in medicine, dentistry, nursing with 1 year at professional school. Facilities and programs for independent research, including honors programs, individual majors, tutorials, on- and off-campus independent study, Richter Fellowship for Independent Study to support special projects. Study abroad through the Institute of International Education or by individual arrangement. Off-campus study in Washington (DC) semester through American University, at the United Nations through Drew University (NJ), and elsewhere. Off-campus study in marine sciences through the Gulf Coast Research Laboratory (MS). Cross-registration with members of the consortium. Continuing education program offered by Illinois Institute of Technology on the North Central College campus.

ROTC: Air Force in cooperation with Illinois Institute of Technology; Army in cooperation with Wheaton College.

Degrees Conferred: 504 *baccalaureate* (B); 135 *master's* (M): biological/life sciences 16 (B); business/marketing 143 (B), 30 (M); communications/communication technologies 57 (B); computer and information sciences 23 (B), 4 (M); education 75 (B), 65 (M); English 22 (B); foreign languages and literature 10 (B); health professions and related sciences 5 (B); interdisciplinary studies 5 (B); liberal arts/general studies 1 (B), 16 (M); mathematics 7 (B); philosophy/religion/theology 7 (B); physical sciences 9 (B); psychology 29 (B); social sciences and history 66 (B); visual and performing arts 18 (B). 1 honorary degree awarded 2004: Doctor of Laws.

Fees and Other Expenses: *Full-time tuition per academic year 2004–05:* undergraduate $20,160; graduate $545 per credit hour. *Other fees:* $180. *Room and board per academic year:* $6,757.

Financial Aid: Aid from institutionally generated funds is provided on the basis of academic merit, financial need. Institution has a Program Participation Agreement with the U.S. Department of Education for eligible students to receive Pell Grants and other federal aid.

Financial aid to full-time, first-time undergraduate students: need-based scholarships/grants totaling $13,582,985, self-help $5,460,833, parent loans $1,407,935, tuition waivers $167,813; non-need-based scholarships/grants totaling $3,475,236, self-help $2,739,906, tuition waivers $530,636.

Departments and Teaching Staff: *Total instructional faculty:* 209 (full-time 125, part-time 89; women 106, men 103; members of minority groups 13). Total faculty with doctorate, first-professional, or other terminal degree: 127. Student-to-faculty ratio: 13:1.

Enrollment: Total enrollment 2,377. Undergraduate full-time 712 men / 1,076 women, part-time 127m / 121w; graduate full-time 26m / 23w, part-time 131m / 161w. *Transfer students:* 236.

Characteristics of Student Body: *Ethnic and racial makeup:* number of Black non-Hispanic: 69; American Indian or Alaska Native: 2; Asian or Pacific Islander: 60; Hispanic: 96; White non-Hispanic: 1,670; unknown: 103. *Age distribution:* number under 18: 51; 18–19: 689; 20–21: 748; 22–24: 298; 25–29: 99; 30–34: 49; 35–39: 29; 40–49: 60; 50–64: 12.

International Students: 36 nonresident aliens enrolled fall 2004. 24 students from Europe, 10 Asia, 1 Central and South America, 1 Africa, 1 Canada. Programs available to aid students whose native language is not English: Social and cultural. English as a Second Language Program. No financial aid specifically designated for international students.

Student Life: On-campus residence halls house 42% of student body. *Intercollegiate athletics:* men only: baseball, basketball, cross-country, football, golf, soccer, swimming, tennis, track, wrestling; women only: basketball, cross-country, softball, swimming, tennis, track, volleyball. *Special regulations:* Cars with decals permitted on campus in designated areas only. Residence hall visitation from 10am to 12:30am weekdays, 10am to 2am weekends. *Special services:* Academic advising center, medical services, counseling services. *Student publications, radio:* The Cardinal, annual literary magazine; The Chronicle, a biweekly newspaper. A 3,900-watt, stereo radio station WONC-FM (89.1) broadcasts 18 hours daily to a potential audience of more than one million listeners. *Surrounding community:* Naperville population 85,000. Chicago, 29 miles from campus, is nearest metropolitan area. Served by mass transit bus and train system; airport 21 miles from campus; passenger rail service 2 blocks from campus.

Library Collections: 150,777 volumes. 603 current periodical subscriptions. 2,508 recordings. 44 computer work stations. Total 2004–05 budget for books and materials: $281,844.

Most important holdings include the Leffler Lincoln Collection; Sang Jazz Collection; Sang Limited Edition Collection; North Central College archival papers and photographs; Harris N. Fanell Congressional Papers.

Buildings and Grounds: Campus area 56 acres.

Chief Executive Officer: Dr. Harold R. Wilde, President.

Undergraduates address admission inquiries to Director of Admissions; graduate inquiries to Director of Graduate and Continuing Education Admissions.

North Park University

3225 West Foster Avenue
Chicago, Illinois 60625

Tel: (773) 244-6200 **E-mail:** admission@northpark.edu
Fax: (773) 244-4953 **Internet:** www.northpark.edu

Institution Description: North Park University, formerly known as North Park College and Theological Seminary, is a private institution affiliated with the Evangelical Covenant Church of America. *Enrollment:* 2,563. *Degrees awarded:* Baccalaureate, first-professional (theology), master's, doctorate.

Accreditation: *Regional:* NCA. *Professional:* music, nursing, nursing education, theology

History: Established as a two-year institution 1891; named Swedish Evangelical Mission Covenant College and Seminary 1892; became North Park College and Seminary 1894; incorporated 1902; became 4-year college 1958; adopted present name 1997. *See* Leland H. Carlson, *A History of North Park College* (Chicago: North Park College and Theological Seminary, 1941) for further information.

Institutional Structure: *Governing board:* Board of Directors. Extrainstitutional representation: 36 trustees, president of the university, 3 full-time instructional faculty members, 3 students, liaison member of denomination's executive board. 36 voting. *Composition of institution:* Administrators 20 men / 4 women. Academic affairs headed by provost of the university and vice president and dean of the seminary. Management/business/finances directed by vice president for administration and finance. Full-time instructional faculty 100. Academic governance body, the faculty, meets an average of 15 times per year.

Calendar: Semesters. Academic year Sept. to May. Entering students admitted Sept., Nov., Mar., June. Degrees conferred and formal commencement May. Summer session from early June to late July.

Characteristics of Freshmen: 1,111 applicants (381 men, 730 women). 32.1% of applicants admitted. 69.1% of admitted students enrolled full-time.

23% (77 students) submitted SAT scores; 79% (262 students) submitted ACT scores. *25th percentile:* SAT I Verbal 490, SAT I Math 480; ACT Composite 18, ACT English 18, ACT Math 17. *75th percentile:* SAT I Verbal 640, SAT I Math 590; ACT Composite 25, ACT English 25, ACT Math 24.

60% entering freshmen expected to graduate within 5 years. 63% of freshmen from Illinois. Freshmen from 27 states and 5 foreign countries.

Admission: Rolling admissions plan. First priority deadline Jan. 15; second priority deadline Mar. 15. Early acceptance available. *Requirements:* Either graduation from accredited secondary school or GED. Recommend secondary school units in English, foreign language, mathematics, science, social studies. Minimum GPA 2.0. Lowest acceptable secondary school class standing 50th percentile. *Entrance tests:* College Board SAT or ACT composite. *For transfer students:* 2.0 minimum GPA; from 4-year accredited institution 90 semester hours maximum transfer credit; from 2-year accredited institution 60 hours.

Advanced placement for postsecondary-level work completed in secondary school. Tutoring available. Noncredit developmental/remedial courses offered during regular academic year.

Degree Requirements: 120–124 semester hours; 2.0 GPA; 3 terms in residence; physical education courses; general education requirements; exit competency examination in writing; comprehensives in individual fields of study.

Fulfillment of some degree requirements and exemption from some beginning courses possible by passing departmental examinations, College Board CLEP. *Grading system:* A–F; pass-fail.

Distinctive Educational Programs: Over 200 Internships in the Chicago areas. Evening classes. Cooperative baccalaureate in medical technology with affiliated hospitals. Interdisciplinary programs in international affairs, music-business, urban studies. Facilities and programs for independent research, including individual majors, tutorials. International study programs in Sweden, Mexico, Finland, Ecuador, Israel, England, and South America. Innovative and dynamic honors program.

Degrees Conferred: 371 *baccalaureate*; 135 *master's*. Bachelor's degrees awarded in top five disciplines: business, management, marketing, and related support services 120; biological and biomedical sciences 37; communication, journalism, and related programs 33; health professions and related clinical sciences 30; psychology 25.

Fees and Other Expenses: *Full-time tuition per academic year 2004–05:* $20,350. *Books and supplies:* $800. *Room nd board per academic year:* $6,980.

Financial Aid: Aid from institutionally generated funds is awarded on the basis of academic merit, financial need. Institution has a Program Participation Agreement with the U.S. Department of Education for eligible students to receive Pell Grants and other federal aid.

Financial aid to full-time, first-time undergraduate students: 52% received federal grants averaging $3,121; 52% state/local grants averaging $3,980; 98% institutional grants averaging $9,918; 83% loans averaging $3,326.

Departments and Teaching Staff: *Professors 35, associate professors 25, assistant professors 15, instructors 3. Total instructional faculty:* 78. Student-to-faculty ratio: 15:1. Degrees held by full-time faculty: doctorate 74.6%, master's 100%. 78% hold terminal degrees.

Enrollment: Total enrollment 2,563. Undergraduate 1,716 (35.5% men, 64.5% women).

Characteristics of Student Body: *Ethnic/racial makeup:* Black non-Hispanic: 11.6%; American Indian or Alaska Native: .3%; Asian or Pacific Islander: 8.2%; Hispanic: 9.4%; White non-Hispanic: 58.9%; unknown: 8.8%.

International Students: 48 undergraduate nonresident aliens enrolled fall 2004. Students from Europe, Asia, Central and South America, Africa, Canada. Programs available to aid students whose native language is not English: Social, cultural. English as a Second Language Program. Scholarships available for international students annually.

Student Life: On-campus residence halls house 67% of student body. *Intercollegiate athletics:* men only: baseball, basketball, cross-country, football, golf, soccer, tennis track; women only: basketball, cross-country, golf, soccer, softball, tennis, track, volleyball. *Special regulations:* Cars of upperclass students (no first-year students) permitted in designated areas. Residence hall visitation from 12pm to 12am on week nights, 12pm to 2am on weekends. *Special services:* Learning Resources Center, medical services. *Student publications: North Park Press,* a weekly newspaper; *Cupola,* a yearbook; *North Branch,* an annual literary magazine. *Surrounding community:* Chicago population over 3,000,000. Served by mass transit bus and rail systems; airport and passenger rail service, each 10 miles from campus.

Library Collections: 255,000 volumes including bound books, serial backfiles, electronic documents, and government documents not in separate collections. Online catalog. 1,197 serial subscriptions; 6,500 audiovisual materials; 93,000 microform units; Computer work stations available. Students have access to the Internet at no charge.

Most important holdings include Scandinavian collection (including Jenny Lind collection); rare books collection; Abraham Lincoln collection.

Buildings and Grounds: Campus area 25 acres.

Chief Executive Officer: Dr. David G. Horner, President.

Address admission inquiries to Rev. Mark Olson, Dean of Enrollment.

Northeastern Illinois University

5500 North St. Louis Avenue
Chicago, Illinois 60625

Tel: (773) 583-4050   **E-mail:** admrec@neiu.edu
Fax: (773) 442-4900   **Internet:** www.neiu.edu

Institution Description: Northeastern Illinois University is a state institution. *Enrollment:* 12,164. *Degrees awarded:* Baccalaureate, master's.

Academic offerings subject to approval by statewide coordinating bodies. Member of Illinois Education Consortium and Union for Experimenting Colleges and Universities.

Accreditation: *Regional:* NCA. *Professional:* business, counseling, social work, teacher education

History: Predecessor established in Elmwood as Cook County Normal School 1867; changed name to Chicago Normal School 1896, Chicago Teacher College 1910, Chicago Normal College 1913, Chicago Teachers College 1938; reestablished as Chicago Teachers College North 1957; offered first instruction at postsecondary level, and awarded first degree (baccalaureate) 1961; incorporated and changed name to Illinois Teachers College-Chicago North 1965, to Northeastern Illinois State College 1967; adopted present name 1971. *See* Melvin George, "Northeastern Illinois University: The History of a Comprehensive University" (Diss., University of Chicago, 1979) for further information.

Institutional Structure: *Governing board:* Board of Governors of State Colleges and Universities of Illinois. Representation: 14 members including 5 students (1 from each university under board jurisdiction). 9 voting. *Composition of institution:* 4 vice presidential areas: academic affairs, student affairs, development and public affairs, administrative affairs. 185 administrative staff members. Full-time instructional faculty 375 plus 496 civil service staff. Academic governance performed by University Senate. *Faculty representation:* Faculty served by collective bargaining agent, University Professionals of Illinois, affiliated with AFT.

Calendar: Semesters. Academic year Aug. to May. Freshmen admitted Aug., Jan., May, July. Degrees conferred May, Aug., Dec. Summer term of 3 sessions from May to Aug.

Characteristics of Freshmen: 2,652 applicants (1,109 men, 1,743 women). 75.4% of applicants admitted. 45.2% of admitted students enrolled full-time.

60% (957 students) submitted ACT scores. *25th percentile*: ACT Composite 16, ACT English 14, ACT Math 15. *75th percentile*: ACT Composite 21, ACT English 21, ACT Math 21.

98% of freshmen from Illinois. Freshmen from 6 states and 14 foreign countries.

Admission: Rolling admissions plan. For fall acceptance, apply as early as Sept. 1 of senior year of secondary school, but not later than Aug. 1 of year of enrollment. *Requirements:* Either graduation from accredited secondary school or GED. Require college preparatory curriculum. Lowest acceptable secondary school class standing 50th percentile or minimum enhanced ACT composite score 19. *Entrance tests:* ACT composite. For foreign students TOEFL. *For transfer students:* 2.0 minimum GPA on a 4.0 scale; from 2-year accredited institution 60 hours.

College credit and advanced placement for postsecondary-level work completed in secondary school. Tutoring available. Developmental courses offered in summer session and regular academic year; credit given but does not count toward graduation.

Degree Requirements: 120 credit hours; 2.0 GPA on 4.0 scale; last 30 hours in residence; general education requirements; exit competency examination in writing, and reading, and examination or courses in U.S. and Illinois constitutions. Additional requirements for some programs.

Fulfillment of some degree requirements and exemption from some beginning courses possible by passing College Board CLEP, AP. *Grading system:* A–F; pass-fail; incomplete (carries time limit).

Distinctive Educational Programs: *For undergraduates:* Accelerated degree programs. Interdisciplinary programs in educational studies, environmental studies, leisure studies, natural science, social science, women's studies. Honors programs. Study abroad in Japan and Mexico. *For graduate students:* Cooperative master's program in educational administration and supervision. Interdisciplinary program in urban land use. *Available to all students:* Work-experience programs. Weekend and evening classes. Facilities and programs for independent research and individualized majors. Tutorial and peer helper programs. *Other distinctive programs:* Outreach program for the Hispanic-American community. Community service programs. Center for Inner City Studies. University Without Walls, a self-paced, interdisciplinary undergraduate program for mature students. Board of Governors Bachelors Degree Program offering individualized nontraditional study in cooperation with Chicago State University, Eastern Illinois University, Governors State University, and Western Illinois University. Continuing education. Study abroad in Mexico (Spanish study) and Costa Rica (Spanish study and internships); Spain (Spanish study).

ROTC: Air Force in cooperation with Illinois Institute of Technology; Army in cooperation with Loyola University.

Degrees Conferred: 1,162 *baccalaureate*; 507 *master's*. Bachelor's degrees awarded in top five disciplines: education 229; liberal arts and sciences, general studies and humanities 203; business, management, marketing, and related support services 106; computer and information sciences and support services 124; social sciences 81.

Fees and Other Expenses: *Full-time tuition per academic year 2004–05:* undergraduate resident $3,956, out-of-state students $6,572. Contact the university for current graduate tuition/fees. *Books and supplies:* $1,200. *Off-campus room and board per academic year:* $7,272.

Financial Aid: Aid from institutionally generated funds is provided on the basis of academic merit, financial need, athletic ability, other criteria. Institution has a Program Participation Agreement with the U.S. Department of Education for eligible students to receive Pell Grants and other federal aid.

Financial aid to full-time, first-time undergraduate students: 47% received federal grants averaging $2,998; 48% state/local grants averaging $2,448; 6% institutional grants averaging $1,269; 9% loans averaging $2,783.

Departments and Teaching Staff: Anthropology *professors* 2, *associate professors* 1, *assistant professors* 2, *instructors* 2, *part-time teachers* 4; art 5, 2, 4, 0, 8; biology 11, 2, 0, 0, 2; chemistry 3, 2, 2, 0, 2; computer science 5, 1, 6, 4, 2; criminal justice 1, 2, 4, 0, 1; earth science 4, 0, 1, 1, 1; economics 3, 4, 2, 0, 0; English Language Program 4, 1, 0, 2, 0; English 14, 2, 1, 0, 6; foreign language 2, 2, 9, 0, 6; geography and environment 4, 1, 3, 0, 2; history 9, 3, 0, 2, 0; linguistics 3, 3, 3, 1, 5; mathematics 5, 5, 2, 1, 3; mathematics lab 0, 1, 1, 1, 3; philosophy 2, 1, 2, 0, 1; physics 5, 1, 0, 0, 1; political science 9, 1, 1, 0, 1; psychology 8, 1, 4, 1, 8; social work 1, 2, 2, 1, 3; sociology 6, 0, 1, 1, 5; speech and performing arts 7, 1, 3, 0, 3; accounting/business law/finance 0, 8, 9, 2, 12; management and marketing 2, 5, 4, 2, 13; counselor education 6, 2, 2, 0, 2; curriculum and instruction 12, 4, 7, 2, 5; educational foundations 5, 7, 3, 2, 20; exercise physics and cardiac rehabilitation 1, 1, 1, 1, 0; health/physical education/recreation and athletics 3, 2, 6, 0, 1; inner city studies education 4, 4, 0, 0, 1; reading 4, 0, 3, 0, 4; special education 6, 6, 4, 0, 5.

Total instructional faculty: 508. 78% hold terminal degrees.

Enrollment: Total enrollment 12,164. Undergraduate 9,305 (37.3% men, 62.7% women).

Characteristics of Student Body: *Ethnic and racial makeup:* Black non-Hispanic: 12.1%; American Indian or Alaska Native: .3%; Asian or Pacific Islander: 10.8%; Hispanic: 29.1%; White non-Hispanic: 44%. *Age distribution:* 17–21: 55%; 22–24: 16%; 25–29: 12%; 30–34: 8%; 35–39: 5%; 40–49: 4%.

International Students: 344 undergraduate nonresident aliens enrolled fall 2004. No programs available to aid students whose native language is not English. No financial aid specifically designated for international students.

Student Life: No on-campus housing. *Intercollegiate athletics:* men only: baseball, football, golf; women only: softball, volleyball; both sexes: basketball, cross-country, tennis. Intramural athletics available in a variety of sports. *Special services:* Medical services. *Student publications, radio: Apocalypse*, a quarterly literary magazine; *The Beehive*, a yearbook; *The Northeastern Illinois Print*, a weekly newspaper; *Que Ondee Sola*, a monthly Latino newspaper; *Aperture*, a filmmaking and recording publication. Radio station WZRD broadcasts 94 hours per week. *Surrounding community:* Chicago population over 3 million. Served by mass transit bus system; airport 10 miles from campus; passenger rail service 7 miles from campus.

Library Collections: 650,000 volumes. 191,023 government documents; 786,486 microforms; 3,010 audiovisual materials; 3,816 current periodicals. Access to online information retrieval systems. Students have access to the Internet at no charge.

Most important special holdings include Chicago and Cook County Archives; William Gray Reading Collection; Afro-American studies collection; curriculum guides/elementary and secondary school textbooks.

Buildings and Grounds: Campus area 64 acres.

Chief Executive Officer: Dr. Salme H. Steinberg, President.

Undergraduates address admission inquiries to Miriam Rivera, Director of Admissions and Records; graduate inquiries to Dean Mohan Sood, Graduate School.

Northern Seminary

660 East Butterfield Road
Lombard, Illinois 60148
Tel: (630) 620-2100   **E-mail:** admissions@seminary.edu
Fax: (630) 620-2194   **Internet:** www.seminary.edu

Institution Description: Northern Seminary, formerly Northern Baptist Theological Seminary, is a private institution affiliated with the American Baptist Churches, U.S.A. *Enrollment:* 225. *Degrees awarded:* First-professional (theology), master's, doctorate.

Member of the Consortium Association of Chicago Theological Schools.

Accreditation: *Regional:* NCA. *National:* ATS. *Professional:* theology

History: Established, chartered, incorporated, and offered first instruction at postsecondary level 1913; awarded first degree 1916; added 4-year college 1920; absorbed Norwegian Baptist Seminary (founded 1871) 1956; moved to present campus and college separated from Seminary to become Judson College 1963; present name adopted 2004..

Institutional Structure: *Governing board:* Board of Trustees. Representation: 61 trustees, including president of the alumni association, president of the

seminary, dean of the seminary, 1 full-time instructional faculty member, 2 students. 7 ex officio. 2 Regional Executive Ministers Advisory Council representatives. 7 honorary members. 52 voting. *Composition of institution:* Administrators 8 men / 6 women. Academic affairs headed by dean of the seminary. Management/business/finances directed by assistant to the president for business affairs. Full-time instructional faculty 13. Academic governance body, the faculty, meets an average of 20 times per year.

Calendar: Quarters. Academic year Sept. to June. Entering students admitted Sept., Jan., Mar. Degrees conferred and formal commencement June. Summer session June to Aug.

Characteristics of Freshmen: 88% of applicants accepted. 100% of accepted applicants enrolled. 80% of freshmen from Illinois. Freshmen from 4 states.

Admission: Rolling admissions plan. *Requirements:* Baccalaureate from accredited college or university. Minimum GPA 2.50. *Entrance tests:* For foreign students TOEFL.

Degree Requirements: *For first-professional degrees:* 102 quarter hours plus field education; 40 hours in residence. *For master's degrees:* 60 quarter hours; 38 hours in residence. *For both degrees:* 2.25 GPA; distribution requirements. *Grading system:* 4-point numerical scale; credit-no credit; withdraw (carries deadline).

Distinctive Educational Programs: Work-experience programs. Association of Chicago Theological Schools. Evening classes. Special facilities for using telecommunications in the classroom. Interdisciplinary program in urban ministries. Off-campus study in Chicago sponsored by the Seminary Consortium for Urban Pastoral Education. Cross-registration with Wheaton College.

Degrees Conferred: 9 *master's:* theology and ministerial studies; 26 *first-professional:* master of divinity; 8 *doctorate:* pastoral counseling/counseling.

Fees and Other Expenses: *Tuition per academic year 2004–05:* $11,550.

Financial Aid: Aid from institutionally generated funds is provided on the basis of academic merit, financial need. Institution has a Program Participation Agreement with the U.S. Department of Education for eligible students to receive Pell Grants and other federal aid.

Departments and Teaching Staff: Theology *professors* 10, *associate professors* 1, *assistant professors* 2, *part-time faculty* 18. *Total instructional faculty:* 31. Degrees held by full-time faculty: 100% hold terminal degrees.

Enrollment: Total enrollment 225.

International Students: Students from Europe, Asia, Central and South America, Africa, Canada. Programs available to aid students whose native language is not English: Cultural. Limited scholarship aid available for international students.

Student Life: On-campus apartments house 50% of student body. Housing available for married students. *Special regulations:* Cars registered with housing office permitted without restrictions. *Surrounding community:* Lombard, population 40,000, is located within Chicago metropolitan area. Served by mass transit bus and train system; airport 18 miles from campus, passenger rail service 3 miles from campus.

Publications: Sources of information about Northern Seminary include *The American Baptist Magazine*.

Library Collections: 46,000 volumes. 2,500 audiovisual materials; 635 current periodical subscriptions. 16 computer work stations. Students have access to the Internet at no charge.

Most important special holdings include Abraham H. Cassel Collection of 16th–19th century theological books and pamphlets; Ora Huston Collection of English Bibles; Baptist historical records.

Buildings and Grounds: Campus area 28 acres.

Chief Executive Officer: Dr. Charles W. Moore, President.

Address admission inquiries to Charles Dresser, Director of Enrollment.

Northern Illinois University

DeKalb, Illinois 60115-2854
Tel: (815) 753-1000   **E-mail:** admissions@niu.edu
Fax: (815) 753-0198   **Internet:** www.niu.edu

Institution Description: Northern Illinois University is a state institution. *Enrollment:* 24,820. *Degrees awarded:* Baccalaureate, first-professional (law), master's, doctorate. Certificates also awarded.

Academic offerings subject to approval by statewide coordinating bodies. Budget subject to approval by state governing boards.

Accreditation: *Regional:* NCA. *Professional:* accounting, art, athletic training, audiology, business, counseling, dietetics, engineering, industrial technology, law, marriage and family therapy, music, nursing, nursing education, physical therapy, psychology internship, public administration, public health, rehabilitation counseling, speech-language pathology, teacher education

History: Established as Northern Illinois State Normal School 1895; offered first instruction at postsecondary level 1899; changed name to Northern Illinois State Teachers College, became 4-year institution, awarded first degree (baccalaureate) 1921; changed name to Northern Illinois State College 1955; adopted present name 1957; added College of Law 1979. *See* Earl W. Hayter, *Education in Transition* (DeKalb: Northern Illinois University Press, 1974) for further information.

Institutional Structure: *Governing board:* Illinois Board of Regents. Representation: 9 regents (appointed by governor of Illinois), 3 students. 9 voting. *Composition of institution:* Administrators 191 men / 67 women. Academic affairs headed by vice president and provost. Management/business/finances directed by vice president of business affairs. Full-time instructional faculty 1,015. Academic governance body, Council on Institution, meets an average of 18 times per year.

Calendar: Semesters. Academic year Aug. to May. Freshmen admitted Aug., Jan., June. Degrees conferred and formal commencements May, Aug., Dec. Summer session from late May to mid-Aug.

Characteristics of Freshmen: 15,861 applicants (7,072 men, 8,789 women). 63.6% of applicants admitted. 29.1% of admitted students enrolled full-time.

3% (112 students) submitted SAT scores; 98% (3,190 students) submitted ACT scores. *25th percentile:* SAT I Verbal 465, SAT I Math 485; ACT Composite 19, ACT English 18, ACT Math 18. *75th percentile:* SAT I Verbal 590, SAT I Math 620; ACT Composite 24, ACT English 24, ACT Math 25.

97% of freshmen from Illinois. Freshmen from 21 states and 16 foreign countries.

Admission: Rolling admissions plan. For fall acceptance, apply as early as Oct. 1 of previous year, but not later than Aug. 7 of year of enrollment. Early acceptance available. *Requirements:* Either graduation from accredited secondary school, or GED with ACT composite score of 22. Lowest acceptable secondary school class standing 50th percentile with ACT composite score of 17 or 33rd percentile with ACT composite score of 22. *Entrance tests:* ACT composite. For foreign students TOEFL. *For transfer students:* 2.0 minimum GPA; maximum transfer credit limited only by residence requirement; correspondence students 30 semester hours.

College credit and advanced placement for postsecondary-level work completed in secondary school. Advanced placement for extrainstitutional learning on basis of ACE *2006 Guide to the Evaluation of Educational Experiences in the Armed Services.* Tutoring available. Developmental-remedial courses offered in summer session and regular academic year; credit given in some cases.

Degree Requirements: 124 semester hours; 2.0 GPA; 30 hours in residence; general education requirements; exit competency examination on U.S. and Illinois Constitutions.

Fulfillment of some degree requirements and exemption from some beginning courses possible by passing departmental examinations, College Board CLEP, APP. *Grading system:* A–F; pass-fail; withdraw (carries time limit).

Distinctive Educational Programs: Internships. Flexible meeting places and schedules, including off-campus centers (at Oregon, Ill., 35 miles away from main institution, and at various locations throughout northern Illinois) and evening classes. Special facilities for using telecommunications in the classroom. Interdisciplinary programs in applied communication, black studies, comparative literature, environmental studies. Latino studies, linguistics, medieval studies, Southeast Asian studies, urban studies. Facilities and programs for independent research, including honors programs, individual majors, independent study. Institutionally sponsored study abroad in Austria, Denmark, Ecuador, England, France, Spain.

ROTC: Army.

Degrees Conferred: 3,658 *baccalaureate;* 1,519 *master's;* 25 *post-master's certificates;* 90 *doctorate;* 96 *first-professional:.* Bachelor's degrees awarded in top five disciplines: business, management, marketing, and related support services 915; education 518; social sciences 269; communication, journalism, and related programs 269; health professions and related clinical sciences 251.

Fees and Other Expenses: *Full-time tuition per academic year 2004–05:* undergraduate resident $6,617; out-of-state student $11,228. Contact the university for current tuition/fees for graduate/first-professional programs. *Room and board per academic year:* $5,340. *Books and supplies:* $1,000.

Financial Aid: Aid from institutionally generated funds is provided on the basis of academic merit, athletic ability. Institution has a Program Participation Agreement with the U. S. Department of Education for eligible students to receive Pell Grants and other federal aid.

Financial aid to full-time, first-time undergraduate students: 30% received federal grants averaging $3,242; 43% state/local grants averaging $3,675; 9% institutional grants averaging $3,155; 54 % loans averaging $3,898.

Departments and Teaching Staff: *Professors* 302, *associate professors* 287, *assistant professors* 255, *instructors* 120, *part-time faculty* 149. *Total instructional faculty:* 1,014 FTE. Degrees held by full-time faculty: doctorate 73%, master's 24%, baccalaureate 3%. 82% hold terminal degrees.

Enrollment: Total enrollment 24,820. Undergraduate 18,031 (47.1% men, 52.9% women).

Characteristics of Student Body: *Ethnic and racial makeup:* Black non-Hispanic: 12.4%; American Indian or Alaska Native: .2%; Asian or Pacific Islander: 5.7%; Hispanic: 6.5%; White non-Hispanic: 71.2%.

International Students: 162 undergraduate nonresident aliens enrolled fall 2004.

Student Life: On-campus residence halls house 28% of student body. Residence halls for men constitute 34% of such space, for women 47%, for both sexes 19%. 6% of men join and 4% live in fraternities; 6% of women join and 4% live in sororities. Housing available for married students. *Intercollegiate athletics:* men only: baseball, basketball, football, gymnastics, hockey, soccer, swimming, tennis, track, wrestling; women only: basketball, gymnastics, swimming, tennis, track, volleyball. *Special regulations:* Cars with decals permitted in designated areas; fee charged. *Special services:* Learning Resources Center, medical services, student fee-supported bus system providing transportation throughout city. *Student publications, radio: Northern Star,* a daily newspaper; *Towers,* an annual literary magazine. Radio stations WNIU and WKDI broadcast 145 hours and 168 hours per week. *Surrounding community:* DeKalb population 35,000. Chicago, 60 miles from campus, is nearest metropolitan area.

Library Collections: 3,157,000 volumes. 1,241,460 government documents; 3,010,000 microforms; 18,290 periodical subscriptions. Online catalog. Students have access to online information retrieval services and the Internet.

Most important holdings include Donn V. Hart Southeast Asia collection; Earl W. Hayter Regional History Center; Jeremy Taylor Collection; James Hanley Collection.

Buildings and Grounds: Campus area 550 acres.

Chief Executive Officer: Dr. John G. Peters, President.

Address admission inquiries to Robert H. Burk, Director of Admissions.

College of Law

Degree Programs Offered: *First-professional.*

Admission: Baccalaureate from accredited college or university; LSAT, LSDAS.

Degree Requirements: 90 credit hours, 2.0 GPA.

Northwestern University

633 Clark Street
Evanston, Illinois 60208-3854

Tel: (847) 491-3741   **E-mail:** admissions@northwestern.edu
Fax: (847) 491-7364   **Internet:** www.northwestern.edu

Institution Description: Northwestern University is a private, independent nonprofit institution with campuses in Evanston and Chicago. *Enrollment:* 17,747. *Degrees awarded:* Baccalaureate, first-professional (business, law, medicine), master's, doctorate. Certificates also awarded.

Accreditation: *Regional:* NCA. *Professional:* business, clinical psychology, dentistry, endodontics, engineering, health services administration, journalism, law, marriage and family therapy, medicine, music, oral and maxillofacial surgery, pediatric dentistry, periodontics, physical therapy, psychology internship, public health, speech-language pathology, theatre

History: Established 1850; chartered as North Western University 1851; offered first instruction at postsecondary level 1855; awarded first degree (baccalaureate) 1859; adopted present name 1867. *See* Harold F. Williamson and Payson S. Wild, *Northwestern University: A History 1850–1975* (Evanston: Northwestern University, 1976) and Jay Pridmore, *Northwestern University: Celebrating 150 Years* (Evanston: Northwestern University, 2000) for further information.

Institutional Structure: *Governing board:* Northwestern Board of Trustees. Representation: 117 trustees- 34 charter trustees, 27 national trustees, 4 life trustees, 10 alumni. 34 voting. *Composition of institution:* Academic affairs headed by provost. Management/business/finances directed by senior vice president for business and finance. Full-time instructional faculty 2,538. Academic governance body, University Senate, meets an average of 3 times per year.

Calendar: Quarters (semesters for Law School and School of Continuing Studies). Academic year late Sept. to early June. Freshmen admitted Sept., Jan., Mar., June. Degrees conferred June. Formal commencement June. Summer session from mid-June to mid-Aug.

Characteristics of Freshmen: 14,137 applicants (6,504 men, 7,633 women). 33.3% of applicants admitted. 41.3% of admitted students enrolled full-time.

86% (1,677 students) submitted SAT scores; 49% (956 students) submitted ACT scores. *25th percentile:* SAT I Verbal 650, SAT I Math 660; ACT Composite 29, ACT English 29, ACT Math 28. *75th percentile*: SAT I Verbal 730, SAT I Math 750; ACT Composite 33, ACT English 34, ACT Math 33.

91% of entering freshmen expected to graduate within 5 years. 25% of freshmen from Illinois. Freshmen from 50 states and 25 foreign countries.

Admission: Freshman candidates should submit Part I of application no later than Jan. 1 of the year of enrollment. Students are notified of acceptance Apr. 15. Early decision candidates apply by Nov. 1; notification by Dec. 15. *Requirements:* Either graduation from accredited secondary school with 4 units in English, 2 foreign language, 3 mathematics, 2 history/social studies, 2 laboratory science; or GED. Audition for music majors. 3 additional academic electives recommended. *Entrance tests:* College Board SAT 1 or ACT. 3 achievements for some programs (recommended for all candidates). *For transfer students:* 3.0 minimum GPA; 2 years maximum transfer credit. Undergraduates apply to 1 of 6 schools. Applications may be submitted via the Internet. Advanced placement credit for scores of 4 and 5 on AP examinations; credit for higher level of International Baccalaureate. Tutoring available.

Degree Requirements: 45–48 quarter courses; last 23 must be taken while student enrolled as an undergraduate in Northwestern University. The last 3 quarters must be completed while the student is enrolled in the school or college of the university that is to grant the degree. Minimum 2.0 GPA. For the Weinberg College of Arts and Sciences, students must demonstrate proficiency in writing, foreign language. *Grading system:* A–F; pass with credit (P); no grade, no credit (N).

Distinctive Educational Programs: Work-experience programs, including field studies, internships. Evening classes. Independent study (seniors only). Academic options include combined bachelor and master's degree programs, combined bachelor and professional degree programs, combined college and dental program, combined college and management program, combined college and medical program. Special certificate program for African studies, Asian studies, Jewish studies, science in human culture, women's studies. Freshmen seminars, Chicago field studies internship. Teaching certification in art, biological sciences, chemistry, English, French, German, history, Latin, mathematics, physical science, Russian, social sciences, Spanish. Four units of P-pass or N-no credit option each term. Study abroad programs in Canada, China, Egypt, England, France, Germany, Japan, Israel, Italy, Mexico, Russia, Spain. *Other distinctive programs:* Teaching Magazine and Teaching TV programs added to School of Journalism; Integrated Science Program; Mathematical Methods in Social Sciences Program; certificate program in musical theater; certificate program in leadership; 5-year degree program in journalism/engineering; Cognitive Science major in College of Arts and Sciences. Junior Tutorial Program.

ROTC: Navy; Air Force in cooperation with Illinois Institute of Technology; Army in cooperation with University of Illinois-Chicago.

Degrees Conferred: 1,999 *baccalaureate*; 2,616 *master's*; 367 *doctorate*; 394 *first-professional*. Bachelor's degrees awarded in top five disciplines: communication, journalism, and related programs 380; social sciences 339; engineering 329; visual and performing arts 207; psychology 196.

Fees and Other Expenses: *Full-time tuition per academic year 2004–05:* $30,085. *Books and supplies:* $1,353. *Room and board per academic year:* $9,393.

Financial Aid: Aid from institutionally generated funds is provided on the basis of academic merit, financial need, athletic ability, Institution has a Program Participation Agreement with the U.S. Department of Education for eligible students to receive Pell Grants and other federal aid.

Financial aid to full-time, first-time undergraduate students: 8% received federal grants averaging $5,824; 15% state/local grants averaging $2,435; 45% institutional grants averaging $18434; 34% loans averaging $3,486.

Departments and Teaching Staff: *Professors* 606, *associate professors* 323, *assistant professors* 477, *instructors* 218, *part-time teachers* 690. *Total instructional faculty:* 2,538. Student-to-faculty ratio: 7:1. Degrees held by full-time faculty: 100% hold terminal degrees.

Enrollment: Total enrollment 17,747. Undergraduate 9,115 (46.2% men, 53.8% women).

Characteristics of Student Body: *Ethnic/racial makeup:* Black non-Hispanic: 5.5%; American Indian or Alaska Native: .3%; Asian or Pacific Islander: 15.6%; Hispanic: 5.3%; White non-Hispanic: 59.9%.

International Students: 456 undergraduate nonresident aliens enrolled fall 2004. Students from Europe, Asia, Central and South America, Africa, Canada, Australia, New Zealand, other. No programs available to aid students whose native language is not English. No financial aid specifically designated for international students.

Student Life: On-campus residence halls, fraternity and sorority houses, and residential colleges at Evanston campus house 71% of undergraduates. *Intercollegiate athletics:* men only: baseball, football, wrestling; women only: cross-country, fencing, field hockey, softball, volleyball; both men and women: basketball, diving, golf, soccer, swimming, tennis. *Special regulations:* Cars with decals permitted in designated areas for all but resident freshmen; fee charged.

Special services: Medical services, campus bus system. *Student publications, radio:* Byline Magazine, a journalism publication; *Daily Northwestern*, a newspaper; *Helicon*, an annual magazine; *Northwestern Engineer*, a quarterly magazine; *Northwestern Review*, a biweekly newspaper; *Rubber Teeth*, a quarterly magazine; *Syllabus*, a yearbook. Radio station WNUR-FM broadcasts 168 hours per week. *Surrounding community:* Evanston, population 75,000, is located in Chicago metropolitan area. Served by mass transit bus and rail systems; airport 17 miles from campus.

Publications: *Tri Quarterly*, published by The College of Arts and Sciences.

Library Collections: 4,320,000 volumes, including government documents; 4,226,000 microforms; 75,360 audiovisual materials. 40,000 periodicals. Computerwork stations available. Students have access to the Internet at no charge. Access to online information retrieval systems.

Most important holdings include Herskovits Library of African Studies; Transportation Collection; 20th Century Music Collection.

Buildings and Grounds: Campus area 250 acres.

Chief Executive Officer: Dr. Henry S. Bienen, President.

Undergraduates address admission inquiries Dr. Carol Lunkenheimer, Director of Undergraduate Admissions; graduate/first-professional students to respective admissions office of Law, Medical, and Graduate Schools.

Weinberg College of Arts and Sciences

Degree Programs Offered: *Baccalaureate.* Certificates also awarded.

Distinctive Educational Programs: Individual majors. Interdisciplinary programs in computer studies, humanities, urban studies, women's studies. Honors programs. Writing program. Combined bachelor's and master's degree programs. Combined college and dental program, management program, medical program, music program. 4-year baccalaureate-master's programs.

School of Education and Social Policy

Degree Programs Offered: *Baccalaureate* in human development and social policy, teacher education; *master's*.

Distinctive Educational Programs: Tutorials.

Medill School of Journalism

Degree Programs Offered: *Baccalaureate* in journalism; *master's* in advertising, journalism.

Distinctive Educational Programs: Internships. Washington Program allows students to cover federal government for Medill News Service. Student placement on newspaper staff. Broadcasting program. National High School Institute summer program. Gannett Urban Journalism Center offers seminars and study programs for urban editors and publishers.

School of Music

Degree Programs Offered: *Baccalaureate, master's, doctorate.*

Distinctive Educational Programs: Internships. Opera workshop. National High School Institute summer program. *See also* Wienberg College of Arts and Sciences.

School of Speech

Degree Programs Offered: *Baccalaureate* in communication studies, communication sciences and disorders, performance studies, radio/television/film, speech education, theatre; *master's* in communication.

Distinctive Educational Programs: Interdepartmental studies. Clinical program in speech pathology. Intercollegiate debating. Joint baccalaureate-master's program in communication studies. National High School Institute summer program.

McCormick School of Engineering and Applied Science

Degree Programs Offered: *Baccalaureate* and *master's* in applied mathematics, biomedical engineering, chemical engineering, civil engineering, computer sciences, electrical engineering, environmental engineering, industrial engineering and management sciences, materials science and engineering, mechanical engineering, nuclear engineering, science engineering, urban and regional planning; *master's* in transportation engineering, theoretical and applied mechanics.

Distinctive Educational Programs: Cooperative engineering program provides industrial engineering experience. Combined baccalaureate in industrial engineering and master's program in management with Kellogg Graduate School of Management. Joint baccalaureate/first-professional program with dental and medical schools. *See also* College of Arts and Sciences.

Medical School

Degree Programs Offered: *Baccalaureate* in medicine, physical therapy; *BS-MD, MD-PhD, Doctor of Medicine.*

Admission: *For first-professional:* 3 years study from accredited college or university with 1 year general biology, 1 year general physics, 2 years inorganic and organic chemistry, 1 year English; MCAT. Baccalaureate recommended.

Distinctive Educational Programs: Honors program in medical education requires two years on Evanston campus in College of Arts and Sciences with courses in chemistry, biology, physics. The combined M.D.-Ph.D. program offered by the medical school and the graduate school, designed for careers in biomedical research or academic medicine coupled with the clinical practice of medicine. The Master of Public Health Program, M.D./M.P.H. with comprehensive instruction in epidemiology and key aspects of contemporary public health care services. Cooperative program in medical education with McGaw Medical Center. Cancer Center coordinates research with member hospitals.

School of Law

Degree Programs Offered: *First-professional, master's, doctorate.*

Admission: *For first-professional:* Baccalaureate from accredited college or university; LSAT.

Distinctive Educational Programs: Small classes and seminars; the case method, the problem method; clinical training; legal writing skills; senior research program; legal clinic program; extended study program. Joint first-professional master's program in management with graduate school of management. Joint first-professional/doctoral program in law and social services with graduate school.

Graduate School

Degree Programs Offered: *Master's* in art theory and practice; *master's* and *doctorate* in anthropology; art history; audiology and hearing impairment; biochemistry; classics; clinical medicine; communication sciences and disorders; comparative literature and theory; economics; education and social policy (administration and policy studies, counseling psychology, human development and social policy, teaching-learning processes); English; French and Italian; geological sciences; German language and literature; Hispanic studies; history; history and literature of religions; learning disabilities; linguistics; management; medical and dental sciences; molecular biology and cell biology; music (education, history and literature, theory); neurobiology and physiology; performance studies; philosophy; physics and astronomy; political science; radio, television, film; Slavic languages and literatures; sociology; speech (education, interdepartmental studies, speech and language pathology, theatre, theatre and drama); technological institute (applied mathematics, biomedical engineering, chemical engineering, civil engineering, electrical engineering and computer science, industrial engineering and management science and engineering, materials science and engineering, mechanical engineering, theoretical and applied mechanics); transportation; *doctorate* in ecology and evolutionary biology; geography; mathematics; psychology; tumor cell biology.

Departments and Teaching Staff: Faculty drawn from other colleges within the university.

Distinctive Educational Programs: Interdepartmental programs. Cooperative doctorate in religion with Garrett-Evangelical Theological Seminary. African studies program awards certificates and coordinates seminars and conferences. Traveling scholar program through Committee on Institutional Cooperation allows doctoral students the use of cooperating institutions. Interdisciplinary program in molecular, cellular, and integrative biomedical sciences. Transportation Center. Urban Systems and Policy Planning. Probability and Statistics. Computer Studies in Music.

Kellogg Graduate School of Management

Degree Programs Offered: *Master's.*

Distinctive Educational Programs: The evening master of management program. Program on business management. Joint major in international business. Program in hospital and health services management. Program in public and nonprofit management. Program in transportation management. Executive master's program. Accounting and informational systems department.

Olivet Nazarene University

One University Avenue
Bourbonnais, Illinois 60914
Tel: (815) 939-5011   **E-mail:** admissions@olivet.edu
Fax: (815) 935-4898   **Internet:** www.olivet.edu

Institution Description: Olivet Nazarene University is a private, independent, nonprofit college affiliated with the Church of the Nazarene. *Enrollment:* 4,364. *Degrees awarded:* Associate, baccalaureate, master's. Certificates also awarded.

Accreditation: *Regional:* NCA. *Professional:* engineering, music, nursing, nursing education, social work, teacher education

History: Established as elementary school 1907; chartered as Illinois Holiness University and offered first instruction at postsecondary level 1909; awarded first degree (baccalaureate) 1914; changed name to Olivet University 1915, Olivet College 1921; became Olivet Nazarene College 1940; achieved university status and adopted present name 2000.

Institutional Structure: *Governing board:* Board of Trustees of Olivet Nazarene University. Representation: 47 trustees (including 3 alumni), president of the college. 1 ex officio. All voting. *Composition of institution:* Administrators 15 men. Academic affairs headed by vice president and dean of the college. Management/business/finances directed by chief financial officer. Full-time instructional faculty 85. Academic governance body, the faculty, meets an average of 7 times per year.

Calendar: Semesters. Academic year Sept. to May. Freshmen admitted Sept., Jan., Feb., June, July, Aug. Degrees conferred and formal commencement May. Summer session of 3 terms from early June to late Aug.

Characteristics of Freshmen: 2,270 applicants (652 men, 1,424 women). 78.9% of applicants admitted. 38.9% of admitted students enrolled full-time.

95% (669 students) submitted ACT scores. *25th percentile:* ACT Composite 20, ACT English 20, ACT Math 20. *75th percentile:* ACT Composite 26, ACT English 26, ACT Math 26.

40% of entering freshmen expected to graduate within 5 years. 37% of freshmen from Illinois. Freshmen from 28 states and 17 foreign countries.

Admission: Rolling admission plan. Apply as early as 2 years prior to enrollment, but not later than Aug. 1 of year of enrollment. Early acceptance available. *Requirements:* Either graduation from accredited secondary school or GED. Minimum GPA 2.0. *Entrance tests:* ACT composite. For foreign students TOEFL. *For transfer students:* 2.0 GPA; from 4-year accredited institution maximum transfer credit limited only by residence requirement; from 2-year accredited institution 68 hours.

College credit and advanced placement for postsecondary-level work completed in secondary school. Tutoring available. Developmental courses offered during regular academic year; credit awarded.

Degree Requirements: *For all associate degrees:* 64 credit hours. *For all baccalaureate degrees:* 128 credit hours. *For all undergraduate degrees:* 2.0 GPA; last 30 hours in residence, or 45 hours in residence including 15 of last 30; chapel attendance 3 days per week; 2 hours physical education; distribution requirements.

Fulfillment of some degree requirements and exemption from some beginning courses possible by passing departmental examination, College Board CLEP, AP, other standardized test. *Grading system:* A–F; pass-fail; withdraw (carries time limit).

Distinctive Educational Programs: *For undergraduates:* Dual-degree program in engineering with University of Illinois. Cooperative baccalaureate in medical technology and in nursing with affiliated hospitals. Interdisciplinary programs in general studies, physical science. Facilities and programs for independent research including honors programs, independent study. Baccalaureate completion program for registered nurses. *Other distinctive programs:* Continuing education program, including Institute for Church Management.

Degrees Conferred: 406 *baccalaureate:* degrees awarded in top five disciplines: business, management, marketing, and related support services 78; education 60; health professions and related clinical sciences 41; psychology 33; English language and literature/letters 25.

Fees and Other Expenses: *Full-time tuition per academic year 2004–05:* $15,470. *Books and supplies:* $800. *Room and board per academic year:* $6,800.

Financial Aid: Aid from institutionally generated funds is awarded on the basis of academic merit, financial need, athletic ability, other considerations. Institution has a Program Participation Agreement with the U.S. Department of Education for eligible students to receive Pell Grants and other federal aid.

Financial aid to full-time, first-time undergraduate students: 27% received federal grants averaging $3,045; 35% state/local grants averaging $3,148; 94% institutional grants averaging $6,466; 71% received loans averaging $4,779.

Departments and Teaching Staff: *Total instructional faculty:* 113. *Degrees held by full-time faculty:* 34% hold terminal degrees.

Enrollment: Total enrollment 4,364. Undergraduate 2,633 (39.7% men, 60.3% women).

Characteristics of Student Body: *Ethnic/racial makeup:* Black non-Hispanic: 8.5%; American Indian or Alaska Native: .25; Asian or Pacific Islander: 1.4%; Hispanic: 2.8%; White non-Hispanic: 86%.

International Students: 29 undergraduate nonresident aliens enrolled fall 2004.

Student Life: On-campus residence halls house 75% of student body. Residence halls for men constitute 40% of such space, for women 60%. Housing available for married students. *Intercollegiate athletics:* men only: baseball, basketball, football, soccer, track, wrestling; women only: basketball, volleyball. *Special regulations:* Cars must be registered and insured. Curfews begin midnight Sun.–Thurs., 1am Fri. and Sat. *Special services:* Learning Resources Center, medical services. *Student publications, radio: Aurora,* a yearbook; *Glimmerglass,* a biweekly newspaper. Radio station WKOC broadcasts 60 hours per week. *Surrounding community:* Bourbonnais is 60 miles south of Chicago.

Library Collections: 175,000 volumes. 42,000 microforms; 4,800 audiovisual materials; 1,000 current periodical subscriptions; 6,000 recordings/tapes. Online catalog. Students have access to online information retrieval services and the Internet.

Most important holdings include John Wesley Collection (original manuscripts and pamphlets of the English founder of Methodism); James Arminius' theological writings.

Buildings and Grounds: Campus area 190 acres.

Chief Executive Officer: De John C. Bowling, President.

Address admission inquiries to Brian Parker, Director of Admissions.

Principia College

1 Maybeck Place
Elsah, Illinois 62028
Tel: (618) 374-2131   **E-mail:** admissions@prin.edu
Fax: (618) 374-4000   **Internet:** www.prin.edu

Institution Description: Principia College is a private college affiliated with Christian Scientists. The College is a unit of the Principia, which also includes lower, middle, and upper schools, all located in St. Louis, MO. *Enrollment:* 537. *Degrees awarded:* Baccalaureate.

Accreditation: *Regional:* NCA.

History: Established in St. Louis, MO, as 2-year institution and offered first instruction at postsecondary level 1910; incorporated 1912; became 4-year institution 1932; awarded first degree (baccalaureate) 1934; moved to present location 1935.

Institutional Structure: *Governing board:* Board of Trustees. Representation: 15 trustees. All voting. *Composition of institution:* Full-time instructional 79.

Calendar: Quarters. Academic year Sept. to June.

Characteristics of Freshmen: 87% of applicants admitted. 53% of admitted students enrolled full-time.

85% (91 students) submitted SAT scores; 42% (45 students) submitted ACT scores. *25th percentile:* SAT Verbal 510, SAT Math 500; ACT Composite 21, ACT English 20, ACT Math 21. *75th percentile:* SAT Verbal 650, SAT Math 620; ACT Composite 30, ACT English 30, ACT Math 29.

74% of entering freshmen expected to graduate within 5 years. 3% of freshmen from Illinois. Freshmen from 27 states and 10 foreign countries.

Admission: Rolling admissions plan. For fall acceptance, apply no later than May 1 of year of enrollment. Apply by Dec. 1 for winter acceptance. *Requirements:* Graduation from accredited secondary school. Recommend 4 units English, 3 foreign language, 3 college preparatory mathematics, 2-3 natural science, 2-3 social studies. Minimum GPA 2.0. *Entrance tests:* College Board SAT or ACT composite. For foreign students TOEFL.

Tutoring available. Noncredit developmental-remedial courses offered during regular academic year.

Degree Requirements: 180 quarter hours; 2.0 GPA; 4 quarters, including 45 quarter hours under direct Principia faculty supervision during 15 months just prior to graduation; distribution requirements; demonstrated proficiency in writing. *Grading system:* A–F; withdraw.

Distinctive Educational Programs: Internships. Interdisciplinary programs in Asian studies, coaching fundamentals, environmental studies, German studies, international relations, Russian studies, sports management, women's studies, and world perspectives. Facilities and programs for independent research, including individual majors, independent projects. Study abroad in China, England, Scotland, Italy, New Zealand, Spain, France, Germany, Vietnam.

Degrees Conferred: 116 *baccalaureate:* area and ethnic studies 2; biological/life sciences 5; business/marketing 14; communications/communication technologies 5; computer and information sciences 8; education 5; English 4; foreign languages and literature 4; interdisciplinary studies 5; mathematics 3; philosophy/religion/theology 4; physical sciences 6; social sciences and history 24; visual and performing arts 24.

Fees and Other Expenses: *Full-time tuition per academic year 2005–06:* $20,145. *Required fees:* $220. *Room and board per academic year:* $7,350.

Financial Aid: Aid from institutionally generated funds is provided on the basis of academic merit, financial need. Institution has a Program Participation Agreement with the U.S. Department of Education for eligible students to receive Pell Grants and other federal aid.

Financial aid to full-time, first-time undergraduate students: need-based scholarships/grants totaling $4,019,021, self-help $1,436,607; non-need-based scholarships/grants totaling $2,403,890.

Departments and Teaching Staff: *Total instructional faculty:* 71 (full-time 50, part-time 21; women 31, men 40; members of minority groups 1). Total faculty with doctorate, first-professional, or other terminal degree: 35. Student-to-faculty ratio: 9:1. 8 faculty members awarded sabbaticals 2004–05.

Enrollment: Total enrollment 537 (full-time 250 men / 281 women, part-time 1m / 6w).

Characteristics of Student Body: *Ethnic/racial makeup:* number of Black non-Hispanic: 5; Asian or Pacific Islander: 5; Hispanic: 7; White non-Hispanic: 438; unknown: 12.

International Students: 74 nonresident aliens enrolled fall 2004. 11 Students from Europe, 9 Asia, 5 Central and South America, 46 Africa, 5 Canada, 2 Australia. Programs available to aid students whose native language is not English: Social, cultural. No financial aid specifically designated for international students.

Student Life: On-campus residence halls house 99% of student body. *Intercollegiate athletics:* men only: baseball, basketball, cross-country, football, golf, soccer, swimming-diving, tennis, track; women only: basketball, cross-country, soccer, softball, swimming-diving, tennis, track, volleyball. *Special services:* Academic Advising Center; Career Development Center. *Student publications, radio: Pilot,* weekly newspaper. Radio station WTPC. *Surrounding community:* Elsah population 1,000. St. Louis (MO), 40 miles from campus, is nearest metropolitan area. Served by airport 35 miles from campus.

Library Collections: 211,460 volumes. 63,000 government documents; 200,000 microforms; 7,792 audiovisual materials (records, tapes, films); 900 current periodical subscriptions. Online and card catalogs. Students have access to online information retrieval services and the Internet. Total 2004–05 budget for books and materials: $155,832.

Most important holdings include The Treasure Room (rare book collection); Christian Science materials; English and American literature collections; history collection; religious and Bible-related materials; Ernest Vogel Third Reich Collection; David Anderson Collection on the Russian Revolution.

Buildings and Grounds: Campus area 3,000 acres.

Chief Executive Officer: Dr. George D. Moffett, III, President.

Address admission inquiries to Martha Green Quirk, Dean of Admissions.

Quincy University

1800 College Avenue
Quincy, Illinois 62301-2699
Tel: (800) 688-4295   **E-mail:** admissions@quincy.edu
Fax: (217) 228-5376   **Internet:** www.quincy.edu

Institution Description: Quincy University is a private Catholic, coeducational, liberal arts university founded in 1860 by Franciscan Friars. *Enrollment:* 1,294. *Degrees awarded:* Associate, baccalaureate, master's.

Accreditation: *Regional:* NCA. *Professional:* music

History: Established as St. Francis Solanus College 1860; awarded first degree (baccalaureate) 1864; incorporated 1873; changed name to Quincy College 1917; became coeducational 1923; changed name to Quincy University 1993.

Institutional Structure: *Governing board:* Board of Trustees. Extrainstitutional representation: 25 trustees; institutional representation: president of the college. All voting. *Composition of institution:* Administrators 19 men / 15 women. Academic affairs headed by vice president for academic affairs. Finances directed by vice president for financial affairs. Full-time instructional faculty 34 men / 12 women. Academic governance body, Faculty Assembly, meets an average of 6 times per year.

Calendar: Semesters. Academic year Aug. to May. Freshmen admitted Aug., Jan., June. Degrees conferred and formal commencement May.

Characteristics of Freshmen: 74% of applicants admitted. 23% of admitted students enrolled full-time.

9% (21 students) submitted SAT scores; 91% (207 students) submitted ACT scores. *25th percentile*: SAT Verbal 440, SAT Math 470; ACT Composite 24, ACT English 18, ACT Math 18. *75th percentile*: SAT Verbal 520, SAT Math 550; ACT Composite 24, ACT English 24, ACT Math 24.

49% of entering freshmen expected to graduate within 5 years. 66% of freshmen from Illinois. Freshmen from 16 states and 1 foreign country.

Admission: Rolling admissions plan. For fall acceptance, apply as early as end of junior year of secondary school, but not later than Aug. 15 of year of enrollment. Early acceptance available. *Requirements:* Either graduation from accredited secondary school with 16 units or GED. Recommend 4 units English, 2 in a foreign language, 3 mathematics, 2 social studies, 2 science, 3 electives. Minimum GPA 2.0. *Entrance tests:* ACT composite preferred; College Board SAT accepted; letter of recommendation; personal statement. *For transfer students:* 2.0 minimum GPA; students with fewer than 24 semester hours of credit must also submit an official copy of their high school transcript; 60 hours maximum transfer credit.

College credit and advanced placement for postsecondary-level work completed in secondary school, for USAFI, and for extrainstitutional learning (life experience) on basis of portfolio and faculty assessments. Tutoring available.

Degree Requirements: *For all baccalaureate degrees:* 124 credit hours; 30 hours in residency, including 18 hours in the major area of concentration. *For all degrees:* 2.0 GPA; general education requirements. Fulfillment of some degree requirements and exemption from some beginning courses possible by passing departmental examinations, College Board CLEP, APP. *Grading system:* A–F; pass-fail; withdraw (carries time limit).

Distinctive Educational Programs: Early exploratory internship program; Freshman Mentor Program; First Year Seminar; Contract Majors; Honors program; credit for academically related experience. Interdisciplinary studies in humanities, music, business. Preprofessional programs in medicine, dentistry, veterinary medicine, law, engineering, physical therapy. Baccalaureate program in clinical laboratory sciences. Teacher certification programs (elementary, special education, and secondary). Reading Center laboratory for education majors. Facilities and programs for independent research including student designed majors and independent studies. Writing across-the-curriculum program supported through the Ameritech Center; collaborative learning opportunities; internships and practica available in all majors. Academic honor societies. On-campus television studio and national public radio station. Summer study abroad program in Assisi, Italy. International study opportunities in over 25 countries through College Consortium for International Studies.

Degrees Conferred: 231 *baccalaureate* (B); 47 *master's* (M): biological/life sciences 8 (B); business/marketing 43 (B), 21 (M); communications/communication technologies 6 (B); computer and information sciences 11 (B); education 48 (B), 26 (M); English 3 (B); health professions and related sciences 17 (B); interdisciplinary studies 1 (B); mathematics 5 (B); parks and recreation 7 (B); philosophy/religion/theology 6 (B); physical sciences 4 (B); protective services/public administration 27 (B); psychology 12 (B); social sciences and history 11 (B); visual and performing arts 7 (B); other 15 (B). 1 honorary degree awarded 2004: Doctor of Laws.

Fees and Other Expenses: *Full-time tuition per academic year 2004–05:* $17,800. *Required fees:* $530. *Room and board per academic year:* $6,590.

Financial Aid: Aid from institutionally generated funds is provided on the basis of academic merit, financial ability, athletic ability, other criteria. Institution has a Program Participation Agreement with the U.S. Department of Education for eligible students to receive Pell Grants and other federal aid.

Financial aid to full-time, first-time undergraduate students: need-based scholarships/grants totaling $6,013,535, self-help $2,723,792, parent loans $145,454, tuition waivers $84,844, athletic awards $315,860; non-need-based scholarships/grants totaling $1,673,264, self-help $16,060, parent loans $1,020,418, tuition waivers $242,224, athletic awards $1,440,875.

Departments and Teaching Staff: *Professors* 15, *associate professors* 17, *assistant professors* 13, *instructors* 1, *part-time faculty* 74. *Total instructional faculty:* 120 (full-time 46, part-time 74; women 58, men 62; members of minority groups 3). Total faculty with doctorate, first-professional, or other terminal degree: 60. Student-to-faculty ratio: 14:1. 1 faculty member awarded a sabbatical 2004–05.

Enrollment: Total enrollment 1,294. Undergraduate full-time 905 men / 535 women, part-time 65m / 81w; graduate full-time 3m / 17w, part-time 65m / 123w. *Transfer students:* in-state 72; from out-of-state 16.

Characteristics of Student Body: *Ethnic and racial makeup:* number of Black non-Hispanic: 65; American Indian or Alaska Native: 1; Asian or Pacific Islander: 8; Hispanic: 30; White non-Hispanic: 844; unknown: 131. *Age distribution:* number under 18: 1; 18–19: 343; 20–21: 341; 22–24: 173; 25–29: 61; 30–34: 33; 35–39: 20; 40–49: 33; 50–64: 5.

International Students: 9 nonresident aliens enrolled fall 2004. 3 students from Europe, 1 Asia, 1 Central and South America. No programs available to aid students whose native language is not English. No financial aid specifically designated for international students.

Student Life: On-campus residence halls house 70% of student body. Campus housing options are varied with single-sex and coed residence halls, apartments, and houses. Housing available for married students. *Intercollegiate athletics:* men: basketball, cross-country, football, soccer, tennis, volleyball; women: basketball, cross-country, soccer, softball, tennis, volleyball. *Special services:* Shuttle bus service between Main and North campuses; freshmen mentor program. *Student publications, radio, television: Falcon*, a weekly newspaper; *Gyrfalcon*, a yearbook, *Riverrun*, a literary magazine. Radio station WQUB-FM; television studio. *Surrounding community:* Quincy has a population of 50,000. St. Louis (MO), 120 miles from campus, is nearest metropolitan area. Served by mass transit bus system; airport 10 miles from campus; passenger rail service 2 miles from campus.

Library Collections: 239,482 volumes. Online and card catalogs. Current serial subscriptions: 464 paper, 41 microform, 19 via electronic access. 161,612 microforms; 3,150 audiovisual materials. 3,857 recordings; 90 compact discs. 10 computer work stations. Students have access to online information retrieval services and the Internet. Total 2004–05 budget for materials and operations: $382,088.

Most important special collections include Rare Book Collection; Bonaventure Collection; Fraborese Collection.

Buildings and Grounds: Campus area 73 acres.

Chief Executive Officer: Sr. Margaret Feldner, O.S.F., President.

Address admission inquiries to Mark Clynes, Director of Admissions.

Robert Morris College

401 South State Street
Chicago, Illinois 60605

Tel: (312) 935-6800   **E-mail:** enroll@rmcil.edu
Fax: (312) 935-6660   **Internet:** www.rmcil.edu

Institution Description: Robert Morris is the fifth largest private, independent, not-for-profit institution of higher education in Illinois. *Enrollment:* 5,520. *Degrees awarded:* Associate, baccalaureate. Professional diplomas also awarded.

Accreditation: *Regional:* NCA. *Professional:* business

History: Founded 1913 as the Moser School in Chicago; acquired by Robert Morris College in 1975; awarded first baccalaureate degree 1992.

Institutional Structure: *Governing board:* Robert Morris College Board of Trustees. *Institutional representation:* president of the college. Administrators 2 men / 11 women. Academic affairs headed by senior vice president for academics. Management/business/finances directed by vice president for business affairs.

Calendar: Quarters. Five 10-week sessions per year that begin July 1 and end June 30. Degrees conferred throughout the year with formal commencement in May and Sept.

Characteristics of Freshmen: 82% of applicants admitted. 48% of admitted applicants enrolled. 83% of entering freshmen expected to graduate within 5 years. 96% of freshmen from Illinois. Freshmen from 21 states and 17 foreign countries.

Admission: *Requirements:* Applications accepted throughout the year. Graduation from accredited high school or GED; official transcript from high school or college demonstrating the ability to successfully complete college-level coursework. Minimum 2.0 GPA on a 4.0 scale. *For transfer students:* Minimum GPA of 2.0 on 4.0 scale; minimum 64 quarter hours or 43 semester hour of accepted credit from a regionally accredited institution of higher education.

Degree Requirements: *For all associate degrees:* completion of 92 quarter hours including a minimum of 52 major elective credits; 36 general education credits; 4 electives. *For baccalaureate degrees:* completion of 188 quarter hours including a minimum of 104 major elective credits; 68-76 general education credits; balance in free electives. *For all professional diplomas:* completion of a minimum of 60 quarter hours that include 40 major credits, 16 general education credits, and 4 electives.

Distinctive Educational Programs: Cooperative education; internships and externships; evening and weekend classes; summer advantage program; study abroad in Austria and England.

ROTC: Army in cooperation with University of Illinois-Chicago.

Degrees Conferred: 1,345 *associate*; 1,050 *baccalaureate:* business/marketing 759; computer and finformation sciences 195; visual and performing arts 96.

Fees and Other Expenses: *Full-time tuition per academic year 2005–06:* $15,575. *Room and board per academic year:* $6,600.

Financial Aid: Aid from institutionally generated funds is provided on the basis of academic merit, financial need, athletic ability. Institution has a Program

Participation Agreement with the U.S. Department of Education for eligible students to receive Pell Grants and other federal aid.

Financial aid to full-time, first-time undergraduate students: need-based scholarships/grants totaling $36,196,867, self-help $24,526,790, parent loans $1,901,021, tuition waivers $121,284, athletic awards $1,399,712; non-need-based scholarships/grants totaling $556,112, self-help $1,738,354, parent loans $1,738,354, tuition waivers $14,609, athletic awards $410,284.

Departments and Teaching Staff: *Instructors* 139, *part-time faculty* 250. *Total instructional faculty:* 1389 (full-time 139, part-time 250; women 175, men 214; members of minority groups 79). Total faculty with doctorate, first-professional, or other terminal degree: 79. Student-to-faculty ratio: 21:1.

Enrollment: Total enrollment 5,520. Full-time 1,705 men / 3,340 women; part-time 144m / 331w. *Transfer students:* in-state 1,079; from out-of-state 34.

Characteristics of Student Body: *Ethnic/racial makeup:* number of Black non-Hispanic: 2,323; American Indian or Alaska Native: 23; Asian or Pacific Islander: 120; Hispanic: 1,305; White non-Hispanic: 1,611; unknown: 111. *Age distribution:* number under 18: 239; 18–19: 1,276; 20–21: 1,142; 22–24: 907; 25–29: 812; 30–34: 510; 35–39: 164; 40–49: 303; 50–64: 66; 65 and over: 1.

International Students: 27 nonresident aliens enrolled fall 2004. 4 students from Europe, 3 Asia, 4 Central and South America, 9 Africa, 2 Canada, 5 other. No programs available to aid students whose native language is not English. No financial aid specifically designated for international students.

Student Life: The college is a commuter institution. *Intercollegiate athletics:* men: basketball, cross-country, baseball, soccer; women: basketball, cross-country, soccer, volleyball. *Student publication: The Eagle,* newspaper. Numerous clubs and organizations for student participation. *Surrounding community:* Chicago population over 3 million.

Library Collections: 121,737 volumes. Online catalog. 2,362 audiovisual materials; 193 current periodical subscriptions. 3,523 compact discs; 1,174 CD-ROMs. 123 computer work stations. Students have access to the Internet at no charge. Total 2004–05 budget for books, periodicals, audiovisual materials, microforms: $400,000.

Most important special collections include business; African American material; health studies.

Buildings and Grounds: In addition to the Chicago campus, the college maintains locations in Oaklawn, Bensenville, Naperville, Lyons Township, and Springfield.

Chief Executive Officer: Michael P. Viollt, President.

Address admissions inquiries to Ana Mendez, Dean of Admissions.

Rockford College

5050 East State Street
Rockford, Illinois 61108-2393

Tel: (815) 236-4000   **E-mail:** admission@rockford.edu
Fax: (815) 226-4119   **Internet:** www.rockford.edu

Institution Description: Rockford College is a private, independent, non-profit college. *Enrollment:* 1,458. *Degrees awarded:* Baccalaureate, master's. Member of the consortium Rockford Regional Academic Center.

Accreditation: *Regional:* NCA.

History: Established 1846; chartered and incorporated as Rockford Female Seminary 1847; offered first instruction at postsecondary level 1851; awarded first degree (baccalaureate) 1882; adopted present name 1892; became coeducational 1958. *See* C. Hal Nelson, ed., *Rockford College: A Retrospective Look* (Rockford: Rockford College, 1980) for further information.

Institutional Structure: *Governing board:* Rockford College Board of Trustees. Representation: 40 trustees (including 15 alumni), 18 honorary trustees, president of the college. 41 voting. *Composition of institution:* Administrators 17 men / 14 women. Academic affairs headed by vice president and dean. Management/business/finances directed by business manager. Full-time instructional faculty 80. Academic governance body, the faculty, meets an average of 9 times per year.

Calendar: Semesters. Academic year Aug. to May. Freshmen admitted Aug., Sept. Degrees conferred and formal commencement May. Summer session from June to Aug.

Characteristics of Freshmen: 1,308 applicants (549 men, 759 women). 54.1% of applicants admitted. 39.1% of admitted students enrolled full-time.

100% (277 students) submitted ACT scores. *25th percentile:* ACT Composite 22, ACT English 18, ACT Math 16. *75th percentile:* ACT Composite 28, ACT English 24, ACT Math 22.

73% of freshmen from Illinois. Freshmen from 13 states and 6 foreign countries.

Admission: Rolling admissions plan. For fall acceptance, apply as early as Sept. of previous year, but not later than day of registration. Early acceptance

available. *Requirements:* Either graduation from secondary school with 4 units English, 2 foreign language, 1 algebra, 1 geometry, 7 electives; or GED. *Entrance tests:* College Board SAT and ACT composite. *For transfer students:* 2.0 minimum GPA; from 4-year accredited institution 80 hours maximum transfer credit; from 2-year accredited institution 70 hours; correspondence students 6 hours; extension students 30 hours.

College credit and advanced placement for postsecondary-level work completed in secondary school and for extrainstitutional learning on basis of ACE *2006 Guide to the Evaluation of Educational Experiences in the Armed Services,* faculty assessment. Tutoring available. Developmental courses offered in summer and interim sessions, and regular academic year; credit given.

Degree Requirements: *For all baccalaureate degrees:* 124 hours; 30 hours in residence; 2 hours physical education; attendance at college forum series, distribution requirements. *For most undergraduate degrees:* minimum 2.0 GPA; selected programs require a minimum 2.5 GPA.

Fulfillment of some degree requirements and exemption from some beginning courses possible by passing departmental examinations, College Board CLEP, APP. *Grading system:* A–F; pass-fail; withdraw (deadline after which pass-fail is appended to withdraw); incomplete (carries time limit).

Distinctive Educational Programs: *For undergraduates:* Internships. Interdisciplinary programs in environmental studies, humanities, public policy, science, social science, urban studies. Study abroad at Regent's College, London founded by Rockford College in 1983; in Madrid, Spain; Paris, France; and Munich, Germany. United Nations semester with Drew University (NJ); Washington semester at American University (DC). *For graduate students:* Interdisciplinary program in women's studies. *Available to all students:* Flexible meeting places and schedules, including weekend and evening classes. Special facilities for using telecommunications in the classroom. Facilities and programs for independent research, including honors programs, individual majors, tutorials. *Other distinctive programs:* Degree-granting continuing education.

Degrees Conferred: 239 *baccalaureate*; 172 *master's.* Bachelor's degrees awarded in top five disciplines: education 69; business, management, marketing, and related support services 34; social sciences 26; psychology 21; health professions and related clinical sciences 20.

Fees and Other Expenses: *Full-time tuition per academic year 2004–05:* $21,200. *Books and supplies:* $960. *Room and board per academic year:* $6,780.

Financial Aid: Aid from institutionally generated funds is provided on the basis of academic merit, financial need, other criteria. Institution has a Program Participation Agreement with the U.S. Department of Education for eligible students to receive Pell Grants and other federal aid.

Financial aid to full-time, first-time undergraduate students: 85% received federal grants averaging $2,192; 64% state/local grants averaging $3,732; 97% institutional grants averaging $4,172; 69% loans averaging $1,891.

Departments and Teaching Staff: *Professors* 26, *associate professors* 28, *assistant professors* 24, *instructors* 2, *part-time faculty* 62. *Total instructional faculty:* 101. Degrees held by full-time faculty: doctorate 57%, master's 43%. 70% hold terminal degrees.

Enrollment: Total enrollment 1,458. Undergraduate 887 (39.9% men, 60.1% women).

Characteristics of Student Body: *Ethnic and racial makeup:* Black non-Hispanic: 8.1%; American Indian or Alaska Native: .3%; Asian or Pacific Islander: 1.9%; White non-Hispanic: 77%; unknown: 6.8%. *Age distribution:* 17–21: 36%; 22–24: 17%; 25–29: 15%; 30–34: 9%; 35–39: 8%; 40–49L 12%; 50–59: 3%.

International Students: 8 nonresident aliens enrolled fall 2004. Students from Europe, Asia, Central and South America, Canada. Programs available to aid students whose native language is not English: English as a Second Language Program. No financial aid specifically designated for international students.

Student Life: On-campus residence halls house 33% of student body. *Intercollegiate athletics:* men only: baseball, football, golf; women only: softball, volleyball; coed: soccer, basketball, swimming, tennis. *Special regulations:* Registered cars permitted in designated areas. Women only and men only dorms have visitation policies; coed dorms have 24-hour visitation. *Special services:* Learning Resources Center, medical services van shuttle service. *Student publications, radio:* Regent Tribune, student newspaper; WRCR broadcasts 98 hours per week. *Surrounding community:* Rockford population 140,000. Chicago, 70 miles from campus, is nearest metropolitan area. Served by mass transit bus system; airport 6 miles from campus; passenger rail service 3 miles from campus.

Library Collections: 168,000 volumes including bound books, serial backfiles, electronic documents, and government documents not in separate collections. Online catalog. Current serial subscriptions: 815 paper. 7,590 microform units; 9,900 audiovisual materials. 10,000 recordings. Computer work stations available. Students have access to the Internet at no charge.

Most important holdings include the papers of Jane Addams; ABC Book Collection (1,000 volumes); Julia Lathrop Papers; Holbrook ABC Children's Collection.

Buildings and Grounds: Campus area 130 acres.

Chief Executive Officer: Dr. Paul C. Pribbenow, President.

Undergraduates address admission inquiries to Gary Lubbert, Director of Admissions; graduate inquiries to Winston McKean, Dean of Continuing and Graduate Education.

Roosevelt University

430 South Michigan Avenue
Chicago, Illinois 60605

Tel: (312) 341-3530   **E-mail:** applyru@roosevelt.edu
Fax: (312) 341-3660   **Internet:** www.roosevelt.edu

Institution Description: Roosevelt University is a private, independent, non-profit institution. *Enrollment:* 7,385. *Degrees awarded:* Baccalaureate, master's, doctorate. Certificates also awarded.

Member of Chicago Consortium of Colleges and Universities and Chicago Metropolitan Higher Education Council.

Accreditation: *Regional:* NCA. *Professional:* counseling, music, teacher education

History: Established as Roosevelt College of Chicago, chartered, and offered first instruction at postsecondary level 1945; awarded first degree (baccalaureate) 1946; adopted present name 1954.

Institutional Structure: *Governing board:* Board of Trustees. Extrainstitutional representation: 57 trustees; institutional representation: president of the university, 5 full-time instructional faculty members; 1 alumnus, 2 students, 1 ex officio. All voting. *Composition of institution:* Administrators 71 men / 107 women. Academic affairs headed by provost. Management/business/finances directed by vice president for business and finance. Full-time instructional faculty 212. Academic governance body, University Faculty Senate, meets an average of 7 times per year.

Calendar: Semesters. Academic year Aug. to May. Freshmen admitted Aug., Sept., Jan., May, June, July. Degrees conferred May, Sept., Jan. Formal commencement May, Jan. Summer sessions from early May to late Aug.

Characteristics of Freshmen: 78% of applicants accepted. 48% of accepted applicants enrolled.

20.4% (56 students) submitted SAT scores; 72% (198 students) submitted ACT scores. *25th percentile:* SAT I Verbal 522.5, SAT I Math 620; ACT Composite 19, ACT English 18, ACT Math 17. *75th percentile:* SAT I Verbal 480, SAT I Math 587.5; ACT Composite 24, ACT English 24, ACT Math 23.

40% of entering freshmen expected to graduate within 5 years. 90% of freshmen from Illinois. Freshmen from 11 states and 10 foreign countries.

Admission: Rolling admissions plan. Early acceptance available. *Requirements:* Either graduation from secondary school with 15 academic units in subjects which normally include English, foreign language, history, mathematics, science; or GED. Additional requirements for some majors. Minimum grade average C. Lowest acceptable secondary school class standing 25th percentile. *Entrance tests:* College Board SAT or ACT composite. *For transfer students:* 2.0 minimum GPA; from 4-year accredited institution 90 semester hours maximum transfer credit; from 2-year accredited institution 66 hours; correspondence/ extension students 30 hours.

College credit for postsecondary-level work completed in secondary school and for extrainstitutional learning on basis of ACE *2006 Guide to the Evaluation of Educational Experiences in the Armed Services,* portfolio and faculty assessments, personal interviews. Tutoring available. Developmental/remedial courses offered in summer session and regular academic year; credit given.

Degree Requirements: 120–136 semester hours; 2.0 GPA; 30 hours in residence; general education requirements; distribution requirements; demonstrated proficiency in writing. Additional requirements for some majors. Fulfillment of some degree requirements possible by passing College Board CLEP. *Grading system:* A–F; pass-fail; withdraw (carries time limit).

Degrees Conferred: 925 *baccalaureate;* 952 *master's;* 13 *doctorate.* Bachelor's degrees awarded in to five disciplines: business, management, marketing, and related support services 310; computer and information sciences and support services 104; education 84; psychology 77; communication, journalism, and related programs 66.

Fees and Other Expenses: *Full-time tuition per academic year 2004–05:* $18,000 undergraduate; contact the university for graduate tuition. *Books and supplies:* $900. Contact the university for on-campus housing accommodations.

Financial Aid: Aid from institutionally generated funds is awarded on the basis of academic merit, financial need, other criteria. Institution has a Program

Participation Agreement with the U.S. Department of Education for eligible students to receive Pell Grants and other federal aid.

Departments and Teaching Staff: *Professors* 43, *associate professors* 75, *assistant professors* 81, *instructors* 13, *part-time faculty* 437. *Total instructional faculty:* 649 (full-time 212, part-time 437; women 269, men 380; members of minority groups 20). Degrees held by full-time faculty: 80% hold terminal degrees.

Enrollment: Total enrollment 7,385. Undergraduate 4,103; graduate 3,282. *Transfer students:* in-state 436; from out-of-state 118.

Characteristics of Student Body: *Ethnic/racial makeup:* number of Black non-Hispanic: 1,063; American Indian or Alaska Native: 20; Asian or Pacific Islander: 193; Hispanic: 454; White non-Hispanic: 1,929; unknown: 349. *Age distribution:* number under 18: 2; 354; 18–19: 528; 20–21: 761; 22–24: 761; 25–29: 749; 30–34: 446; 35–39: 329; 40–49: 517; 50–64: 170; 65 and over: 5.

International Students: 324 nonresident aliens enrolled fall 2004. 63 students from Europe, 201 Asia, 15 Central and South America, 33 Africa, 4 Canada, 2 Australia, 2 New Zealand. Programs available to aid students whose native language is not English: English for International Students Program. No financial aid specifically designated for international students.

Student Life: On-campus residence halls house 12% of student body. *Intercollegiate athletics:* men only: basketball, cross-country, golf, soccer, tennis, track; both sexes: bowling. *Special regulations:* Cars permitted without restrictions. *Special services:* Learning Resources Center, medical services. *Student publications, radio:* Oyez Review, a quarterly art and literary magazine; Torch, a weekly newspaper. WRBC broadcasts 65 hours per week. *Surrounding community:* Chicago population over 3,000,000. Served by mass transit bus; train system; airport 25 miles from campus; passenger rail service less than 1 mile from campus.

Publications: *Business and Society* (biannually) first published 1960.

Library Collections: 186,096 volumes. Online catalog. 52,900 microforms; 22,300 audiovisual materials; 1,129 current periodicals. 90 computer work stations. Students have access to online information retrieval services and the Internet. Total 2004–05 budget for materials and operations: $800,252.

Most important holdings include collection of music books, recordings, and scores; Microbook Library of American Civilization.

Buildings and Grounds: Campus area one-half square block.

Chief Executive Officer: Dr. Charles R. MIddleton, President.

Address admission inquiries to Admissions Director.

College of Arts and Sciences

Degree Programs Offered: *Baccalaureate* and *master's* in fine and applied arts, foreign languages, letters, physical sciences, public affairs and services, social sciences; *doctorate* in psychology. Certificates also given.

Degree Requirements: *See* general requirements. *For bachelor of science degree:* 60 credit hours in natural science or psychology. Additional requirements for some majors. Graduate requirements vary by program.

Distinctive Educational Programs: *For undergraduates:* Cooperative baccalaureate program in medical nuclear medicine, and radiological technologies with local hospitals; in podiatric science with accredited schools of podiatric medicine. Cooperative degree program with the Art Institute of Chicago, The Harrington Institute of Interior Design, and Spertus College of Judaica. Interdisciplinary programs in actuarial science; African, Afro-American, Black studies; American studies; computer studies; culture studies; cytotechnology; journalism; labor relations; public administration, speech communication; theater. Preprofessional programs in dentistry, medicine, and pharmacology. Dual-degree program in Jewish studies with Spertus College of Judaica. Facilities for independent research, including honors programs, tutorials. *For graduate students:* Accelerated degree programs. Interdisciplinary programs in women's studies, integrated marketing communications, and gerontology. *Available to all students:* Flexible meeting places and schedules, including off-campus centers (3 satellites within metropolitan area), weekend and evening classes. Special facilities for using telecommunications in the classroom. Interdisciplinary program in comparative literature. Individual majors. Study abroad by individual arrangement.

Chicago Musical College

Degree Programs Offered: *Baccalaureate* in composition, jazz studies, music business, music education, music history, music theory, performance, piano pedagogy; *master's* in piano pedagogy, vocal pedagogy, composition, keyboard, music education, musicology, theory, string, voice, wind or percussion instruments.

Admission: Examinations in music theory and keyboard facility; placement test in performance; for performance majors, examination in major instrument. For composition/theory/musicology: evidence of creative work or original writing.

Degree Requirements: *See* General requirements. *For baccalaureate:* Senior performance or paper. Additional requirements for some majors. Graduate degree requirements vary. Comprehensive exam for all majors.

College of Education

Degree Programs Offered: *Baccalaureate* in early childhood education, elementary teacher education, secondary teacher education, special education; *master's* in early childhood education, educational administration and supervision, guidance and counseling, reading, special education, teacher education; bilingual-bicultural studies.

Admission: *See* general requirements. Basic skills test. For early childhood education, apply during first semester; for elementary and secondary education, apply before registering for introductory education classes.

Degree Requirements: *See* general requirements. *For baccalaureate:* 2.5 GPA, field experience and student teaching. Graduate degree requirements vary.

Walter E. Heller College of Business Administration

Degree Programs Offered: *Baccalaureate* in accounting, advertising, business administration, business law, business teacher education, finance, management, marketing, personnel administration; *master's* in accounting, business administration, information systems, international business, marketing communications. Certificates also given.

Degree Requirements: *See* general requirements. Core business curriculum; quantitative methods courses. Additional requirements vary by major. Graduate degree requirements vary.

Distinctive Educational Programs: Small business management seminars. Individual and interdepartmental majors in business teacher education, management, and marketing.

Evelyn T. Stone University College

Degree Programs Offered: *Baccalaureate* and *master's* in general studies, computer science, hospitality management, telecommunications, professional studies. Certificates also given.

Degree Requirements: 80 credit hours. *Degrees held by full-time faculty:* 90% hold terminal degrees.

Distinctive Educational Programs: Bachelor of general studies degree program, especially designed for adults over 25, is accelerated through the use of College Board CLEP and supplemented by seminars in humanities, natural, and social sciences. Program to give qualified students without baccalaureate degrees access to graduate schools. External degree program through independent study. Noncredit skill enrichment workshops, courses, seminars.

Rosalind Franklin University of Medicine and Science

3333 Green Bay Road
North Chicago, Illinois 60064
Tel: (847) 578-3000   **E-mail:** info@rfums.edu
Fax: (847) 578-3401   **Internet:** www.rfums.edu

Institution Description: Rosalind Franklin University of Medicine and Science is a four-year university specializing the health sciences. *Enrollment:* 1,687. *Degrees awarded:* Baccalaureate, master's, doctorate, first-professional.

Accreditation: *Regional:* NCA. *Professional:* medicine

History: The university has been built around the Chicago Medical School that was founded in 1912. The university is comprised of the Chicago Medical School, College of Health Professions, School of Graduate and Postdoctoral Studies, and Dr. William M. Scholl College of Podiatric Medicine. The current name was adopted in 2004.

Calendar: Quarter system.

Admission: *Requirements:* Each professional graduate program has specific admissions requirements. Contact the university for current information.

Degrees Conferred: *baccalaureate* 1; *master's* 180; *doctorate* 34; *first-professional* 210.

Fees and Other Expenses: *Full-time tuition 2005–06:* Contact the university for current tuition/fees. Apartment-style housing is available on-campus.

Financial Aid: Aid from institutionally generated funds is provided on the basis of academic merit, athletic ability, financial need, other criteria. Institution has a Program Participation Agreement with the U.S. Department of Education for eligible students to receive Pell Grants and other federal aid.

Departments and Teaching Staff: *Total instructional faculty:* 731.

Enrollment: Total enrollment 1,687.

Library Collections: The Boxer Library is housed in the Basic Sciences Building and includes bound books, serial backfiles, electronic documents, and government documents. Access to online information retrieval systems including Medline, PsychInfo, and other scientific resources.

Buildings and Grounds: Major hospital affiliates include North Chicago Veterans Affairs Medical Center, John H. Stroger, Jr. Hospital of Cook County, Mount Sinai Hospital and Medical Center, and Advocate Lutheran General Hospital.

Chief Executive Officer: Dr. K. Michael Welch, President and Chief Executive Officer.

Address admission inquires to Office of Admissions.

Rush University

600 South Paulina Street
Chicago, Illinois 60612
Tel: (312) 942-7100   **E-mail:** admissions@rushu.rush.edu
Fax: (312) 942-2219   **Internet:** www.rush.edu

Institution Description: Rush University is a private, independent, nonprofit institution providing upper division, professional, and graduate degree study only. *Enrollment:* 1,362. *Degrees awarded:* Baccalaureate, first-professional (medicine), master's, doctorate.

Accreditation: *Regional:* NCA. *Professional:* audiology, clinical lab scientist, health services administration, medicine, nurse anesthesia education, nursing, nursing education, occupational therapy, perfusion, speech-language pathology

History: Established as Rush-Presbyterian-St. Luke's Medical Center 1969 with merger of Rush Medical College (established 1837) and Presbyterian-St. Luke's Hospital and Health Center (formed 1956 by merger of Central Free Dispensary, St. Luke's Hospital and Presbyterian Hospital); admitted first medical students 1971; academic component established as Rush University 1972; awarded first degree (first-professional) and added College of Nursing 1973; added College of Health Sciences 1975, added The Graduate College 1981.

Institutional Structure: *Governing board:* Board of trustees. Extrainstitutional representation: 80 trustees; director of medical college alumni association. All voting. *Composition of institution:* Administrators 15 men / 9 women. Academic affairs headed by dean of academic support services. Business/finances directed by vice president for finance. Academic governance body, University Council, meets an average of 1 time per year.

Calendar: Quarters. Academic year Sept. to June. Entering students admitted Sept. Degrees conferred and formal commencement June. Summer session from late June to late Aug.

Admission: *For first-professional degree:* For fall acceptance, apply to AMCAS as early as June 15, but not later than Nov. 15 of year prior to enrollment. Students are notified of acceptance beginning Nov. Apply by Aug. 1 for early decision; must limit application to Rush Medical College. *Requirements: See* individual colleges below.

Degree Requirements: *See* individual colleges below.

Distinctive Educational Programs: Tutorials. Dual-degree programs and transfer agreements with various U.S. colleges and universities. Joint M.D.-Ph.D. program. Affiliation with 16 area hospitals for clinical work. *Other distinctive programs:* Continuing education for practicing physicians, nurses, and other health professionals.

Degrees Conferred: 82 *baccalaureate:* health professions and related sciences; 130 *master's;* 35 *doctorate;* 108 *first-professional.*

Fees and Other Expenses: *Full-time tuition per academic year 2004–05:* Tuition and fees vary by program. Contact the university for current information.

Financial Aid: Aid from institutionally generated funds is provided on the basis of academic merit, financial need. Institution has a Program Participation Agreement with the U.S. Department of Education for eligible students to receive Pell Grants and other federal aid.

Financial aid to full-time, first-time undergraduate students: need-based scholarships/grants totaling $1,013,043, self-help $2,068,527, parent loans $47,417, tuition waivers $18071; non-need-based scholarships/grants totaling $160,632, self-help $295,294, parent loans $227,712, tuition waivers $18,071. *Graduate aid:* 71 students received $806,412 in federal and state-funded fellowships/grants; 650 received $20,242,739 in federal and state-funded loans; 75 received $246,145 for work-study jobs; 334 other fellowships/grants totaling $3,673,071; 6 research assistantships were awarded totaling $15,500.

Departments and Teaching Staff: Biochemistry *professors* 4, *associate professors* 2, *assistant professors* 6, *instructors* 7; immunology/micro 1, 3, 9, 6; psychology and social sciences 1, 1, 5, 1; dermatology .5, .5, 2, .5; diagnostic radiology and nuclear medicine 5, 4, 4, 6; internal medicine 7, 11, 29, 49; neurological science 1, 1, 4, 1; pediatrics 2, 3, 16, 21; preventive medicine .5, 1,

3, 0; psychiatry 1, 1, 14, 7; family practice 2, 2, 14, 16; anesthesiology 1, 1, 4, 6; cardiovascular thoracic surgery 1, 1, 2, 2; general surgery 1, 3, 9, 11; neurological surgery .5, .5, 1, 1; obstetrics and gynecology 1, 2, 13, 16; orthopedic surgery 1, 2, 4, 7; otolaryngology and bronchoscopy 1, 1, 3, 3; pathology 2, 2, 2, 2; therapeutic radiology 1, 1, 3, .5; urology .5, 1, 2, 2; pharmacology 1, 1, 3, 2; ophthalmology .5, .5, 4, 4; physical medicine and rehabilitation .5, 0, 2, .5; community health nursing 0, 1, 2, 2; psychiatric nursing .5, .5, 2, 4; psychiatric nursing 0, 0, 1, 5; medical nursing 0, 1, 4, 9; gerontological nursing .5, .5, 1, 4; surgical nursing 0, .5, 4, 8; obstetrics and gynecological nursing .5, 0, 1.5, 4; religion and health 0, 1, 1, .5; health systems management .5, 2, 5, 12; physiology 2, 1, 1, 2; clinical nutrition 0, 0, 1, 2; medical technology 0, 1, 1, 10; anatomy 1.5, 1, 2.5, .5; plastic and reconstruction surgery .5, .5, 1, 1; occupational therapy 0, .5, .5, 2; medical physics 0, .5, 0, 0.

Total instructional faculty: 524. Degrees held by full-time faculty: doctorate 15%, master's 14%, baccalaureate 2%, professional 70%. 85% hold terminal degrees.

Enrollment: Total enrollment 1,362. Undergraduate 212 (13.7% men, 86.3% women).

Characteristics of Student Body: *Ethnic/racial makeup:* Black non-Hispanic: 7.1%; Asian or Pacific Islander: 10.8%; Hispanic: 7.1%; White non-Hispanic: 2.2%.

International Students: 7 undergraduate nonresident aliens enrolled fall 2004. No programs available to aid students whose native language is not English. No financial aid specifically designated for international students.

Student Life: On-campus residence halls house 25% of student body. Apartments for both men and women constitute 100% of such space. *Special regulations:* Cars permitted without restrictions. *Special services:* Learning Resources Center, Academic Skills Center, personal counseling, medical services. *Surrounding community:* Chicago population over 3,000,000. Served by mass transit bus, subway, and train systems; airport 20 miles from campus; passenger rail service 2 miles from campus.

Library Collections: 130,000 volumes. 5,000 audiovisual materials; 2,000 periodicals. Online catalog. Students have access to information retrieval services and the Internet.

Most important holdings include books by and about Dr. Benjamin Rush; books and pamphlets on cholera and cholera epidemics of the 19th century; books on 16th- and 17th-century medicine.

Buildings and Grounds: Campus area 6 square blocks.

Chief Executive Officer: Dr. Lucy J. Goodman, President.

Address admission inquiries to Director of Admissions.

College of Health Sciences

Degree Programs Offered: *Baccalaureate* in medical technology; *master's* in audiology, clinical nutrition, health systems management, medical physics, occupational therapy (entry level and advanced), speech-language pathology.

Admission: *For baccalaureate:* 60 semester hours of lower division in prehealth curriculum to include 12 hours of behavioral sciences, 8 of human anatomy and physiology, 8 inorganic chemistry, 4 microbiology, 4 organic chemistry, 4 quantitative analysis, 3 statistics, 17 academic electives. Requirements for admission to master's programs vary by program. Contact College Admission Services for information.

Degree Requirements: Degree requirements, including hours, thesis, curriculum and length of study, vary by program.

College of Nursing

Degree Programs Offered: *Baccalaureate, master's* with practitioner programs in anesthesia, community health, gerontology, neonatal and pediatric; *clinical specialist* programs in gerontology, home health care, medical/surgical, oncology, parent/child health and psychiatry/mental health; *doctorate* in nursing science.

Admission: *For baccalaureate:* two years of prehealth and liberal studies with a minimum of 60 semester hours as prerequisite, including courses in inorganic and organic chemistry, human anatomy and physiology, microbiology, statistics, growth and development and behavioral sciences. *For graduate programs:* criteria include evidence of good academic ability (3.0 on 4.0 scale; 3.5 on 4.0 scale for master's level); GRE results; licensure as a professional nurse in Illinois; three recommendations; acceptable interview; passing grade in statistics.

Degree Requirements: *For baccalaureate:* 90 quarter hours at Rush with a 2.0 or better grade point average in specified curriculum. *For master's degree:* 55 quarter hours minimum (nurse practitioner programs require additional hours); 3.0 grade point average (4.0 scale). *For doctorate:* 125 quarter hours post-baccalaureate minimum; 3.0 grade point average (4.0 scale); dissertation; equivalent of three quarters of full-time graduate study.

Distinctive Educational Programs: RN completion program; summer doctoral program.

Graduate College

Degree Programs Offered: *Master's* in anatomical sciences, medical physics, and pharmacology; *doctorate* in anatomical sciences, biochemistry, immunology, medical physics, pharmacology, physiology, psychology.

Admission: Requirements vary by particular program. Contact Graduate College Admissions Office.

Degree Requirements: Length of program and credit hour requirements vary by program. All require 8 quarters of full-time residence, dissertation (master's thesis).

Distinctive Educational Programs: Concurrent Doctor of Medicine/Doctor of Philosophy.

Rush Medical College

Degree Programs Offered: *Doctor of Medicine.* (Concurrent Doctor of Medicine/Doctor of Philosophy with the Graduate College).

Admission: Minimum of 90 semester (135 quarter hours) of undergraduate study to include two semesters of physics, two semesters of biology (emphasis in zoology), two semesters of inorganic and organic chemistry each (in lieu of two semesters of organic chemistry, students may take one semester of organic chemistry and one of biochemistry), Medical College Admission Test, interview.

Degree Requirements: Minimum of 35 months of enrollment; passing of all courses in preclinical curriculum and all required clerkships and Part I of the National Board of Medical Examiners.

Distinctive Educational Programs: Rush Medical College offers the Alternative Curriculum, a problem-based approach to preclinical curriculum.

Saint Anthony College of Nursing

5658 East State Street
Rockford, Illinois 61108-2468

Tel: (815) 395-5091   **E-mail:** admissions@sacn.edu
Fax: (815) 395-2275   **Internet:** www.sacn.edu

Institution Description: Saint Anthony College of Nursing is a private Catholic college offering a bachelor of science in nursing. Successful graduates are prepared for entry into registered professional nursing and graduate-level education. *Enrollment:* 123. *Degrees awarded:* Baccalaureate.

Accreditation: *Regional:* NCA. *Professional:* nursing

History: The college was established in 1915 as Saint Anthony Medical Center School of Nursing; changed to a baccalaureate degree-granting institution in 1990.

Institutional Structure: *Governing board:* Board of Trustees.

Calendar: Semesters. Academic year Aug. to May.

Admission: Rolling admission plan. Transfers admitted to upper division twice per year. *Requirements:* Minimum 2.5 GPA and 64 prerequisite credits from regionally accredited college.

Degree Requirements: *For all baccalaureate degrees:* 64 upper division credits with a minimum 2.0 GPA and other educational activities required.

Distinctive Educational Programs: *For undergraduates:* Traditional program leading to licensure as RN and BSN and an accelerated program for licensed RNs seeking BSN.

Degrees Conferred: 38 *baccalaureate:* nursing.

Fees and Other Expenses: *Full-time tuition per academic year 2005–06:* $15,400. *Other fees:* $112.

Financial Aid: Aid from institutionally generated funds is provided on the basis of academic merit, financial need. Institution has a Program Participation Agreement with the U.S. Department of Education for eligible students to receive Pell Grants and other federal aid.

Financial aid to full-time, first-time undergraduate students: need-based scholarships/grants totaling $279,830, self-help $389,796; non-need-based scholarships/grants totaling $47,058, self-help $207,410, parent loans $81,941.

Departments and Teaching Staff: *Total instructional faculty:* 11 (full-time 10, part-time 1; women 10, men 1; members of minority groups 2). Student-to-faculty ratio: 10:1.

Enrollment: Total enrollment 111. Full-time 8 men / 85 women, part-time 3w / 16m.

Characteristics of Student Body: *Ethnic/racial makeup:* number of Black non-Hispanic: 5; Asian or Pacific Islander: 3; Hispanic: 4; White non-Hispanic:

95; unknown: 4. *Age distribution:* number of 20–21: 13, 22–24: 35; 25–29: 20; 30–34: 13; 35–39: 9; 40–49: 12; 50–64: 5.

International Students: 1 nonresident alien enrolled fall 2004. No programs available to aid students whose native language is not English. No financial aid specifically designated for international students.

Library Collections: 3,000 volumes including bound books, serial backfiles, electronic documents, and government documents not in separate collections. Card catalog. Current serial subscriptions: paper and microform. 23 CD-ROMs. 8 computer work stations. Students have access to the Internet at no charge.

Buildings and Grounds: New library, updated computer lab, and nursing skill lab completed 1999.

Chief Executive Officer: Dr. Terese A. Burch, Dean.

Address admission inquiries to Nancy A. Sanders, Dean of Admissions and Student Affairs.

Saint Francis Medical Center College of Nursing

511 N.E. Greenleaf Street
Peoria, Illinois 61603-3783
Tel: (309) 655-2201   **E-mail:** admissions@sfmc.con.edu
Fax: (309) 624-8973   **Internet:** www.sfmc.con.edu

Institution Description: The college is a private, Roman Catholic, upper division institution offering the bachelor of science degree in nursing. It is located on the campus of OSF Saint Francis Medical Center. *Enrollment:* 272. *Degrees awarded:* Baccalaureate, master's.

Accreditation: *Regional:* NCA. *Professional:* nursing

History: Saint Francis Hospital School of Nursing was organized in 1905 for Sisters only and opened to lay students in 1918. The school became the College of Nursing in 1985.

Institutional Structure: *Governing board:* The Sisters of the Third Order of Saint Francis. *Composition of institution:* Board of Directors with 19 members.

Calendar: Semesters. Academic year Aug. to May.

Admission: *Requirements:* All students must complete 62 semester hours of prenursing requirements at another accredited institution. A minimum GPA of 2.50 is required for enrollment in the upper division baccalaureate nursing program. For master's degree: BSN from accredited program; minimum 2.8 GPA; proof of licensure as a registered professional nurs; one year of professional nursing experience preferred.

Degree Requirements: *For all baccalaureate degrees:* Completion of prescribed curriculum of 62 semester hours in nursing courses. *For master's degree:* 45 hours.

Distinctive Educational Programs: RN (previous baccalaureate degree not in nursing to MSN program).

Degrees Conferred: 69 *baccalaureate:* nursing; 8 *master's:* nursing.

Fees and Other Expenses: *Full-time tuition per academic year 2005–06:* $10,200. *Other fees:* $210. *Room per academic year:* $1,880.

Financial Aid: Aid from institutionally generated funds is provided on the basis of academic merit, other considerations. Institution has a Program Participation Agreement with the U.S. Department of Education for eligible students to receive Pell Grants and other federal aid.

Financial aid to full-time, first-time undergraduate students: need-based scholarships/grants totaling $1,028,343, self-help $598,752, parent loans $5,876, tuition waivers $44,750; non-need-based scholarships/grants totaling $317,984, self-help $130,864, parent loans $10,557, tuition waivers $28,368. *Graduate aid:* 10 federal and state-funded loans totaling $94,958 (ranging from $970 to $18,196).

Departments and Teaching Staff: Nursing *professors* 3, *associate professors* 5, *assistant professors* 7, *instructors* 3, *part-time faculty* 7. *Total instructional faculty:* 25 (full-time 18, part-time 7; women 25). Total faculty with doctorate, first-professional, or other terminal degree: 7. Student-to-faculty ratio: 10:1. 1 faculty member awarded a sabbatical 2004–05.

Enrollment: Total enrollment 272. Undergraduate full-time 25m / 157 women, part-time 2m / 16w; graduate full-time 3w, part-time 3m / 46w.

Characteristics of Student Body: *Ethnic/racial makeup:* number of Black non-Hispanic: 4; Hispanic: 3; White non-Hispanic: 213. *Age distribution:* number of 20–21: 43; 22–24: 65; 25–29: 41; 30–34: 36; 35–39: 18; 40–49: 16; 50–64: 1.

International Students: 4 nonresident aliens from enrolled fall 2004. 2 students from Europe, 1 Asia, 1 Africa. No programs available to aid students whose native language is not English. No financial aid specifically designated for international students.

Student Life: On-campus housing is available in the College of Nursing residence that provides three floors of private rooms for male/female students. Peoria population 365,000.

Library Collections: 6,300 volumes. 125 journal titles. Over 300 videocassettes. 21 computer work stations. Online catalog. Students have access to the Internet at no charge. Total 2004–05 budget for books and materials: $30,000.

Most import special collections include nursing books and periodicals; material supporting nursing.

Chief Executive Officer: Dr. Lois Hamilton, Dean.

Address admission inquiries to Janice Farquharson, Director of Admissions/Registrar.

St. John's College

421 North Ninth Street
Springfield, Illinois 62702-5380
Tel: (217) 544-6464   **E-mail:** admissions@st-johns.org
Fax: (217) 527-5533   **Internet:** www.st-johns.org

Institution Description: St. John's College is a Catholic-sponsored, private single purpose college for upper division nursing education. *Enrollment:* 82. *Degrees awarded:* Baccalaureate.

Accreditation: *Regional:* NCA. *Professional:* clinical lab scientist, nursing

Calendar: Semesters. Academic year mid-Aug. to mid-May.

Admission: *Requirements:* Students admitted into junior year and must have completed 60 semester hours of lower division credit prior to admission.

Degree Requirements: *For baccalaureate degree:* 125 semester hours of specified coursework; minimum 24 semester hours completed at St. John's College.

Degrees Conferred: 26 *baccalaureate:* nursing.

Fees and Other Expenses: *Full-time tuition per academic year 2004–05:* $4,752. *Required fees:* $366.

Financial Aid: Aid from institutionally generated funds is provided on the basis of academic merit, financial need. Institution has a Program Participation Agreement with the U.S. Department of Education for eligible students to receive Pell Grants and other federal aid. Institutional funding for scholarships available to qualifying students.

Departments and Teaching Staff: *Total instructional faculty:* 14 (full-time 13, part-time ; women 14). Total faculty with doctorate, first-professional, or other terminal degree: 2. Student-to-faculty ratio: 5:1.

Enrollment: Total enrollment 82.

Characteristics of Student Body: *Ethnic/racial makeup:* number of Black non-Hispanic: 1; American Indian or Alaska Native: 1; White non-Hispanic: 79. *Age distribution:* number 18–19: 1, 20–21: 36; 22–24: 27; 25–29: 8; 30–34: 6; 35–39: 2; 40–49: 2.

International Students: 1 nonresident alien from Asia enrolled fall 2004. No programs available to aid students whose native language is not English. No financial aid designated for international students.

Library Collections: 9,000 volumes. Online catalog. 700 audiovisual materials; 380 current periodical subscriptions.

Most important special collections comprised of medical information.

Chief Executive Officer: Dr. Jane Schachtsiek, RN, Chancellor.

Address admissions inquiries to Linda Quigley, Admissions Officer.

Saint Xavier University

3700 West 103rd Street
Chicago, Illinois 60655
Tel: (773) 298-3000   **E-mail:** admissions@sxu.edu
Fax: (773) 779-9061   **Internet:** www.sxu.edu

Institution Description: Saint Xavier University is a private college affiliated with the Sisters of Mercy—Chicago Province, Roman Catholic Church. *Enrollment:* 5,722. *Degrees awarded:* Baccalaureate, master's.

Accreditation: *Regional:* NCA. *Professional:* business, music, nursing, nursing education, speech-language pathology, teacher education

History: Chartered as Saint Francis Xavier Academy for Females 1847; offered first instruction at postsecondary level 1908; awarded first degree (baccalaureate) 1912; became Saint Xavier College 1956; became coeducational 1969; adopted present name 1989.

Institutional Structure: *Governing board:* Board of Trustees. Extrainstitutional representation: 25 trustees; institutional representation: 1 administrator. 1 ex officio. *Composition of institution:* Administrators 5 men / 8 women. Academic affairs headed by dean of faculty. Management/business/finances directed by vice president for business and finance. Full-time instructional faculty 162.

Calendar: Semesters. Academic year early Sept. to late May. Degrees conferred May, Aug., Jan. Formal commencement May. Summer session of 2 terms from late May to early Aug.

Characteristics of Freshmen: 1,812 applicants (594 men, 1,218 women). 69.8% of applicants admitted. 32.3% of admitted students enrolled full-time.

3% (13 students) submitted SAT scores; 95% (396 students) submitted ACT scores. *25th percentile:* SAT I Verbal 470, SAT I Math 480; ACT Composite 20, ACT English 20, ACT Math 19. *75th percentile:* SAT I Verbal 500, SAT I Math 500; ACT Composite 24, ACT English 25, ACT Math 24.

97% of freshmen from Illinois. Freshmen from 6 states.

Admission: Rolling admissions plan. For fall acceptance, apply as early as fall of year prior to enrollment. Early acceptance available. *Requirements:* Graduation from accredited secondary school with 16 units. Recommend 4 units English, 2 in a foreign language, 4 natural science and social studies. For nursing students 1 additional unit in chemistry. *Entrance tests:* College Board SAT or ACT composite. For foreign students TOEFL. *For transfer students:* 20 minimum GPA; from 4-year accredited institution maximum transfer credit limited only by residence requirement; from 2-year accredited institution 70 hours.

College credit and advanced placement for postsecondary-level work completed in secondary school.

Degree Requirements: 120 credit hours; 2.0 GPA; last 30 hours in residence; core requirements. Fulfillment of some degree requirements and exemption from some beginning courses possible by passing departmental examinations, College Board CLEP, AP, other standardized tests. *Grading system:* A–F; pass-fail; incomplete.

Distinctive Educational Programs: Individual majors. *Other distinctive programs:* Continuing education. Noncredit adult education. Special program for senior citizens.

ROTC: Air Force in cooperation with Illinois Institute of Technology.

Degrees Conferred: 683 *baccalaureate*; 4 *post-baccalaureate certificates*; 1,034 *master's*. Bachelor's degrees awarded in top five disciplines: business, management, marketing, and related support services 141; health professions and related clinical sciences 140; education 121; liberal arts and sciences, general studies and humanities 48; biological and biomedical sciences 40.

Fees and Other Expenses: *Full-time tuition per academic year 2004–05:* undergraduate $17,320, graduate tuition varies by program. *Books and supplies:* $900. *Room and board per academic year:* $6,724.

Financial Aid: Aid from institutionally generated funds is provided on the basis of academic merit, financial need, athletic ability. Institution has a Program Participation Agreement with the U.S. Department of Education for eligible students to receive Pell Grants and other federal aid.

Financial aid to full-time, first-time undergraduate students: 37% received federal grants averaging $3m793; 51% state/local grants averaging $4,432; 97% institutional grants averaging $6,091; 71% loans averaging $4,289.

Departments and Teaching Staff: *Professors* 23, *associate professors* 98, *assistant professors* 26, *instructors* 15, *part-time faculty* 141. *Total full-time instructional faculty:* 162. Degrees held by full-time faculty: doctorate 76%.

Enrollment: Total enrollment 5,722. Undergraduate 3,075 (28.7% men, 71.3% women).

Characteristics of Student Body: *Ethnic/racial makeup:* Black non-Hispanic: 18.1%; American Indian or Alaska Native: .3%; Asian or Pacific Islander: 1.8%; Hispanic: 11.7%; White non-Hispanic: 61.8%; unknown: 6%.

International Students: 9 undergraduate nonresident aliens enrolled fall 2004. No programs to aid students whose native language is not English. No financial aid specifically designated for international students.

Student Life: On-campus housing available. *Intercollegiate athletics:* men only: baseball, basketball, cross-country; women only: basketball, softball, volleyball. *Special services:* Learning Resources Center, medical services. *Surrounding community:* Chicago population over 3 million. Served by mass transit bus system, airport and passenger rail service.

Library Collections: 172,200 volumes. 10,620 microforms; 2,300 current serial subscriptions. Online catalog. Students have access to online information retrieval services and the Internet.

Buildings and Grounds: Campus area 70 acres.

Chief Executive Officer: Dr. Judith A. Dwyer, President.

Address admission inquiries to Beth Gerach, Managing Director of Admissions.

Seabury-Western Theological Seminary

2122 Sheridan Road
Evanston, Illinois 6020-29381
Tel: (847) 228-9300   **E-mail:** swts@nwu.edu
Fax: (847) 228-9624   **Internet:** www.swts.nwu.edu

Institution Description: Seabury-Western Theological Seminary is an accredited seminary of the Episcopal Church. *Enrollment:* 158. *Degrees awarded:* Master's, first-professional, licentiate. Certificates of study also awarded.

Accreditation: *Regional:* NCA. *National:* ATS. *Professional* theology

History: Formed by merger of Seabury Divinity School (founded 1857 in Faribault, Minnesota) and Western Theological Seminary (founded in Chicago 1885) in Evanston 1933.

Institutional Structure: *Governing board:* Board of Trustees. 36 members. *Composition of institution:* Dean and president. Academic affairs headed by Associate dean for academic affairs. Management/business/finance directed by comptroller.

Calendar: Quarters. Academic year Sept. to May. No summer sessions.

Admission: Bachelor's degree; aptitude portion of the GRE; on-campus interview; approval of Bishop or other ecclesiastical authority.

Degree Requirements: Completion of prescribed curriculum.

Distinctive Educational Programs: Students not holding a baccalaureate degree or its equivalent and who fulfill all requirements for the master of divinity degree will be awarded the diploma of licentiate in theology.

Degrees Conferred: 193 *first-professional:* master of divinity; 6 *master's:* theology/theological studies; 15 *doctorate:* ministerial studies.

Fees and Other Expenses: *Full-time tuition per academic year 2004–05:* $13,700.

Financial Aid: Aid from institutionally generated funds awarded on the basis of academic merit, financial need. Institution has a Program Participation Agreement with the U.S. Department of Education for eligible students to receive Pell Grants and other federal aid.

Departments and Teaching Staff: Theology *professors* 4, *part-time professors* 7, *adjunct professors* 18. *Total instructional faculty:* 29. Degrees held by full-time faculty: doctorate 100%.

Enrollment: Total enrollment 158 (53.8% men, 46.2% women).

Characteristics of Student Body: *Ethnic/racial makeup:* Black non-Hispanic: 2.5%; Asian or Pacific Islander: 3.8%; Hispanic: 2.5%; White non-Hispanic: 87.3%.

International Students: 6 nonresident aliens enrolled fall 2004. No programs available to aid students whose native language is not English. No financial aid specifically designated for international students.

Library Collections: 320,000 volumes. 7,500 microforms; 500 audiovisual materials; 1,800 current periodical subscriptions. Computer work stations available. Access to online information retrieval systems. Students have access to the Internet at no charge.

Most important holdings include Hale Rare Book Collection; Hibbard Egyptian Collection.

Buildings and Grounds: Dr. James B. Lemler, Dean and President.

Address admission inquiries to Elizabeth Donohue, Coordinator of Admissions.

School of the Art Institute of Chicago

37 South Wabash
Chicago, Illinois 60603
Tel: (312) 899-5100   **E-mail:** info@artic.edu/saic
Fax: (312) 263-0141   **Internet:** www.artic.edu/saic

Institution Description: The School of the Art Institute of Chicago is a private, independent, nonprofit school. *Enrollment:* 2,660. *Degrees awarded:* Baccalaureate, master's. Preprofessional certificates also awarded.

Accreditation: *Regional:* NCA. *Professional:* art

History: Established as Chicago Academy of Design and offered first instruction at postsecondary level 1866; incorporated and changed name to Chicago Academy of Fine Arts 1879; adopted present name 1882; awarded first degree (baccalaureate) 1925. *See* Roger Gilmore, ed., *Over a Century* (Chicago: The School of the Art Institute of Chicago, 1981) for further information.

Institutional Structure: *Governing board:* Board of Governors of the School of the Art Institute of Chicago. Representation: 35 governors. 3 ex officio. *Composition of institution:* Academic affairs headed by vice president of academic affairs and dean of faculty. . Management/business/finances directed by vice president for finance. Full-time instructional faculty 103. Academic governance body, Faculty Senate, meets an average of 32 times per year.

Calendar: Semesters. Academic year Sept. to May. Freshmen admitted June. Degrees conferred and formal commencement May. Summer session of 3 terms from May to Aug.

Characteristics of Freshmen: 1,194 applicants (337 men, 857 women). 83.7% of applicants admitted. 33.4% of admitted students enrolled full-time.

52% (174 students) submitted SAT scores; 34% (112 students) submitted ACT scores.

17% of freshmen from Illinois. Freshmen from 43 states.

Admission: Rolling admissions plan. For fall acceptance, apply as early as Oct. of previous year, and no later than March 1 of year of enrollment for priority consideration. *Requirements:* Either graduation from accredited secondary school or GED; portfolio; minimum 500 SAT 1 verbal score (minimum 20 ACT English); statement of purpose. Academic credentials and recommendations are considered. Interview recommended. *For transfer students:* From 4-year accredited institution 96 semester hours maximum transfer credit; from 2-year accredited institution 60 hours.

Tutoring available. Developmental course offered during regular academic year; credit given.

Degree Requirements: 132 semester hours; 36 hours in residence; general education and studio art requirements; entrance competency examination in writing.

Fulfillment of some degree requirements and exemption from some beginning courses possible by passing College Board CLEP. *Grading system:* Credit; no credit; withdraw.

Distinctive Educational Programs: Cooperative education. Flexible meeting places and schedules, including weekend and evening classes. Facilities and programs for independent research, including individual majors, tutorials. Study abroad: Australia, Canada, Columbia, France, Germany, Iceland, Israel, Italy, Jamaica, Japan, The Netherlands, Portugal, Spain, United Kingdom, Northern Ireland. Individual off-campus study program. Cross-registration with Roosevelt University.

Degrees Conferred: 461 *baccalaureate*; 29 *post-baccalaureate certificates*; 241 *master's*. Bachelor's degrees awarded: visual and performing arts 433; education 16; architecture and related services 12.

Fees and Other Expenses: *Full-time tuition per academic year 2004–05:* $25,660. *Books and supplies:* $2,300. *Room and board per academic year:* $10,620.

Financial Aid: Aid from institutionally generated funds is provided on the basis of academic merit, financial need. Institution has a Program Participation Agreement with the U.S. Department of Education for eligible students to receive Pell Grants and other federal aid.

Financial aid to full-time, first-time undergraduate students: 22% received federal grants averaging $3,859; 11% state/local grants averaging $3,639; 67% institutional grants averaging $9,048; 54% loans averaging $7,453.

Departments and Teaching Staff: *Professors* 46, *associate professors* 34, *assistant professors* 20, *instructors* 3, *part-time teachers* 363. *Total instructional faculty:* 466. Student-to-faculty ratio: 13:1. Degrees held by full-time faculty: doctorate 17%, master's 69%, baccalaureate 13%. 86% hold terminal degrees.

Enrollment: Total enrollment 2,660. Undergraduate 2,093 (32.8% men, 67.2% women).

Characteristics of Student Body: *Ethnic/racial makeup:* Black non-Hispanic: 3.1%; American Indian or Alaska Native: .7%; Asian or Pacific Islander: 9.6%; Hispanic: 7.1%; White non-Hispanic: 60.8%; unknown: 4.1%.

International Students: 306 nonresident aliens enrolled fall 2004. Programs available to aid students whose native language is not English: Social, cultural. English as a Second Language Program. No financial aid specifically designated for international students.

Student Life: Two residence hall facilities available. *Special services:* Learning Resources Center, on-site registered nurse. *Student publications:* A student newspaper. *Surrounding community:* Chicago population over 3 million. Served by mass transit systems; airport 15 miles from campus; passenger rail service 1 mile from campus.

Library Collections: 65, 00 volumes including bound books, serial backfiles, electronic documents, and government documents not in separate collections. Online catalog. Current serial subscriptions: 360 paper. 7 recordings; 720 compact discs; 67 CD-ROMs. Computer work stations available. Students have access to the Internet at no charge.

Most important special holdings include artists books; film center collection; alumni slide registry.

Chief Executive Officer: Anthony Jones, President.

Address admission inquiries to Kathy Amato, Director of Enrollment Management.

Southern Illinois University Carbondale

Carbondale, Illinois 62901-4304

Tel: (618) 536-4405   **E-mail:** admrec@siuc.edu
Fax: (618) 453-4609   **Internet:** www.siuc.edu

Institution Description: Southern Illinois University Carbondale is a comprehensive, public university. *Enrollment:* 21,589. *Degrees awarded:* Associate, baccalaureate, first-professional (law, medicine), master's, doctorate. Specialist certificates in education also awarded.

Academic offerings subject to approval by statewide coordinating body. Budget subject to approval by state governing board.

Accreditation: *Regional:* NCA. *Professional:* accounting, art, athletic training, business, counseling psychology, dental hygiene, dental laboratory technology, dietetics, engineering, forestry, funeral service education, industrial technology, interior design, journalism, law, medicine, music, physical therapy, psychology internship, public administration, radiography, recreation and leisure services, rehabilitation counseling, respiratory therapy, social work, speech-language pathology, teacher education, theatre

History: Established as Southern Illinois Normal University and chartered 1869; offered first instruction at postsecondary level 1874; awarded first degree (baccalaureate) 1908; adopted present name 1947. *See* E. G. Lentz, *75 Years in Retrospect* (Carbondale: Southern Illinois University Press, 1956) for further information.

Institutional Structure: *Composition of institution:* Administrators 233 men / 203 women. Academic affairs headed by vice chancellor for academic affairs. Management/business/finances directed by vice chancellor for financial affairs. Full-time instructional faculty 869. Academic governance bodies, Graduate Council and Faculty Senate, each meet an average of 11 times per year.

Calendar: Semesters. Academic year Aug. to May. Freshmen admitted Aug., Jan., June. Degrees conferred and formal commencements May, Aug. Summer session from June to Aug.

Characteristics of Freshmen: 6% (161 students) submitted SAT scores; 98% (2,472 students) submitted ACT scores. *25th percentile:* SAT Verbal 450, SAT Math 480; ACT Composite 19, ACT English 18, ACT Math 18. *75th percentile:* SAT Verbal 570, SAT Math 590; ACT Composite 24, ACT English 24, ACT Math 24.5.

33% of entering freshmen are expected to graduate within 5 years. 91% of freshmen from Illinois.

Admission: Rolling admissions plan. For fall acceptance, apply as early as end of junior year in secondary school, but not later than July 15 of year of enrollment. Early acceptance available. *Requirements:* Either graduation from accredited secondary school or GED. Lowest acceptable secondary school class standing 50th percentile. *Entrance tests:* ACT composite. For foreign students TOEFL. *For transfer students:* 2.0 minimum GPA; transfer credit varies.

College credit and advanced placement for postsecondary-level work completed in secondary school and for extrainstitutional learning on basis of ACE *2006 Guide to the Evaluation of Educational Experiences in the Armed Services*, portfolio, and faculty assessments. Tutoring available. Developmental-remedial courses offered during regular academic year; credit given.

Degree Requirements: *For all associate degrees:* 60 credit hours, last year (30 semester hours) in residence. *For all baccalaureate degrees:* 120 credit hours, last year (30 semester hours) or 3 years credit (90 semester hours) in residence. *For all undergraduate degrees:* 2.0 GPA; 4 credit hours human health and well being courses; general education requirements.

Fulfillment of some degree requirements and exemption from some beginning courses possible by passing departmental examinations, College Board CLEP, AP. *Grading system:* A–F; pass-fail.

Distinctive Educational Programs: Work-experience programs, including internships, cooperative education. Flexible meeting places and schedules, including off-campus centers (at military bases in various locations in the United States) and evening classes. Facilities and programs for independent research, including honors programs, individual majors, tutorials. Study abroad programs in Africa, Asia, Australia, Austria, Brazil, China, Costa Rica, Dominican Republic, Ecuador, Canada, France, Germany, Hungary, India, Indonesia, Jamaica, Japan, Liberia, Mexico, Poland, Russia, United Kingdom.

ROTC: Army, Air Force.

Degrees Conferred: 4,219 *baccalaureate* (B), 1,085 *master's* (M), 256 *doctorate* (D): agriculture 114 (b), 18 (M); architecture 17 (B); biological/life sciences 125 (B), 30 (M), 17 (D); business/marketing 365 (B), 365 (M), 145 (D); communications/communication technologies 198 (B), 21 (M), 5 (D); computer and information sciences 124 (B), 13 (M); education 920 (B), 221 (M), 28 (D); engineering and engineering technologies 550 (B), 107 (M), 7 (D); English 153 (B), 82 (M), 11 (D); foreign languages and literature 21 (B), 6 (M); health professions and related sciences 212 (B), 105 (M), 7 (D); home economics and vocational home economics 71 (B), 6 (M); interdisciplinary studies 28 (B); law/

legal studies 21 (B); liberal arts/general studies 83 (B); mathematics 19 (B), 18 (M), 5 (D); natural resources/environmental science 47 (B), 9 (D); parks and recreation 39 (B), 6 (M); personal and miscellaneous services 13 (B); philosophy/religion/theology 14 (B), 3 (M), 6 (D); physical sciences 23 (B), 24 (M); protective services/public administration 291 (B), 22 (M); psychology 143 (B), 14 (M), 10 (D); social sciences and history 119 (B), 15 (M), 14 (D); trade and industry 192 (B), 9 (M), 1 (D); visual and performing arts 207 (B), 41 (M); other 30 (B). 174 *first-professional:* law 104, medicine 70.

Fees and Other Expenses: *Full-time tuition per academic year 2004–05:* resident undergraduate $5,310, out-of-state $13,275; contact the university for graduate tuition/fees and on-campus housing. *Books and supplies:* $840. *Other fees:* $2,397.

Financial Aid: Aid from institutionally generated funds is provided on the basis of academic merit, athletic ability. Institution has a Program Participation Agreement with the U.S. Department of Education for eligible students to receive Pell Grants and other federal aid.

Financial aid to full-time, first-time undergraduate students: need-based scholarships/grants totaling $29,695,635, self-help $30,976,215, parent loans $609,248, tuition waivers $546,495, athletic awards $701,351; non-need-based scholarships/grants totaling $13,222,679, self-help $20,867,775, parent loans $4,365,594, tuition waivers $4,365,594, athletic awards $1,732,911.

Departments and Teaching Staff: *Total instructional faculty:* 1,061 (full-time 869, part-time 192; women 362, men 699; members of minority groups 129). Total faculty with doctorate, first-professional, or other terminal degree: 829. Student-to-faculty ratio: 18.1.

Enrollment: Total enrollment 21,589. Undergraduate full-time 8,564 men / 6,468 women, part-time 1,096m / 744w; graduate full-time 794m / 875w, part-time 1,131m / 1,236w; first-professional full-time 385m / 296w.

Characteristics of Student Body: *Ethnic and racial makeup:* number of Black non-Hispanic: 2,555; American Indian or Alaska Native: 62; Asian or Pacific Islander:320; Hispanic: 560; White non-Hispanic: 11,723. *Age distribution:* number under 18: 9l 18–19: 3,738; 20–21: 4,593; 22–24: 3,677; 25–29: 1,503; 30–34: 571; 35–39: 394l 40–49: 465; 50–64: 82.

International Students: 1,318 undergraduate nonresident aliens enrolled fall 2004. International students from 109 countries. No programs available to aid students whose native language is not English. No financial aid specifically designated for international students.

Student Life: On-campus residence halls house 22% of student body. Residence halls for men constitute 60% of such space, for women 40%. Sororities, fraternities, and off-campus residence halls also offer residence space. Housing available for married students. 22% of students live on campus. *Intercollegiate athletics:* men only: baseball, basketball, football, golf, gymnastics, swimming and diving, tennis, track and cross-country; women only: basketball, field hockey, golf, softball, swimming and diving, tennis, track and cross-country, volleyball. *Special regulations:* Cars permitted for graduate, handicapped, and continuing students and for those students requiring a car for work. *Special services:* Learning Resources Center, medical services, evening transportation from campus for women. *Student radio, television:* Radio station WSIU-FM broadcasts 168 hours per week. TV station WSIU broadcasts 63 hours per week. *Surrounding community:* Carbondale population 27,000. St. Louis (MO), 120 miles from campus, is nearest metropolitan area. Served by airport 5 miles from campus; passenger rail service 1 mile from campus.

Library Collections: 7,715,918 volumes including government documents, serials, and microforms. 36,000 audiovisual materials. Access to online information retrieval systems. Students have access to the Internet at no charge.

Most important holdings include John Dewey papers (modern American philosophy); James Joyce (Irish Literary Renaissance) Collection; collection on American and British expatriate writers.

Buildings and Grounds: Campus area 1,139 acres.

Chief Executive Officer: Dr. Walter Wendler, Chancellor.

Address admission inquiries to Anne DeLuca, Director of Admissions

College of Agriculture

Degree Programs Offered: *Baccalaureate* in agribusiness economics, agricultural education, agriculture education and mechanization, food and nutrition, forestry and plant and soil science, general agriculture; *master's* available through Graduate School.

Admission: *See* general requirements.

Degree Requirements: *For agribusiness economics major:* higher level math required.

College of Business and Administration

Degree Programs Offered: *Baccalaureate* in accounting, business and administration, business economics, finance, management, marketing; *master's* and *doctorate* available through Graduate School.

Distinctive Educational Programs: *See* School of Law.

College of Mass Communication and Media Arts

Degree Programs Offered: *Baccalaureate* in art, cinema and photography, communication disorders and sciences, journalism, music, radio-television, speech communication, theater; *master's* and *doctorate* available through Graduate School.

College of Education

Degree Programs Offered: *Baccalaureate* in agricultural education, art, biological sciences, botany, business education, chemistry, classics, early childhood education, economics, elementary education, English, French, geography, German, health education, history, home economics education, language arts and social studies, mathematics, music, occupational education, physical education, physics, political science, recreation, Russian, social studies, Spanish, special education, speech communication, speech pathology and audiology, zoology; *master's* and *doctorate* available through Graduate School.

Distinctive Educational Programs: Off-campus baccalaureate program in occupational education, postsecondary education specialization, is offered at various military bases.

College of Engineering

Degree Programs Offered: *Baccalaureate* in civil engineering, electrical engineering, mechanical engineering, mining engineering, engineering technology, industrial technology; *master's, doctorate* available through Graduate School.

Admission: Minimum ACT score of 23 and in upper half of class, or ACT score of 18–22 and in upper quarter of class. Transfer students need average GPA of 2.4 for engineering if transferring more than 26 hours.

College of Liberal Arts

Degree Programs Offered: *Baccalaureate* in administration of justice, African studies, aging studies, anthropology, Asian studies, Black American studies, classics, community development, earth science, economics, English, foreign languages and literatures, foreign language and international trade, French, German, geography, history, linguistics, mathematics, museum studies (minor), paralegal studies for legal assistant, philosophy, political science, psychology, religious studies, Russian, sociology, Spanish, speech communication, university studies; *master's* and *doctorate* available through Graduate School.

Distinctive Educational Programs: Interdepartmental-interdisciplinary programs in Asian studies, East European studies, Inter-American studies, religious studies, Russian studies.

College of Sciences

Degree Programs Offered: *Baccalaureate* in biological sciences, chemistry, computer science, geology, mathematics, microbiology, physics, physiology, plant biology, zoology.

Distinctive Educational Programs: *For undergraduates:* Interdepartmental programs in biological sciences. *For graduate students:* Interdisciplinary programs in molecular science. Research facilities include an electron microscopy center, experimental ponds, greenhouse, outdoor laboratory accommodations, vivarium, wildlife enclosure. Research shops available for electronics, fine instruments, glass-blowing, large equipment.

Graduate School

Degree Programs Offered: *Master's* in accountancy, administration of justice, agribusiness economics, agricultural education and mechanization, animal industries, anthropology, applied linguistics, art, behavior analysis and therapy, biological sciences, botany, business administration, business education, chemistry, cinema and photography, communication disorders and sciences, community development, computer science, curriculum and instruction, economics, educational administration, educational psychology, engineering, English, English as a foreign language, foreign languages and literatures, forestry, geography, geology, health education, higher education, history, journalism, mathematics, microbiology, mining engineering, music, occupational education, philosophy, physical education, physics, physiology, plant and soil science, political science, psychology, public affairs, recreation, rehabilitation administration and services, rehabilitation counseling, social work, sociology, special education, speech communication, statistics, telecommunications, theater, zoology; *doctorate* in anthropology, botany, business administration, chemistry, communications disorders and sciences, economics, education (curriculum and instruction, educational administration, educational psychology, health education, higher education, occupational education, physical education, special education), engineering science, English, geography, historical studies, journalism, mathematics, microbiology, molecular science, philosophy, physiology, political science, psychology, sociology, speech communication, zoology. Specialist degrees in curriculum and instruction, educational administration, educational psychology. Doctorate of Rehabilitation also awarded.

Departments and Teaching Staff: Faculty members drawn from other colleges within the university.

School of Law

Degree Programs Offered: *First-professional.*

Admission: Baccalaureate from accredited institution; LSAT; LSDAS.

Degree Requirements: 90 credit hours, 2.0 GPA on 4.0 scale, 6 semesters in residence.

Distinctive Educational Programs: Joint J.D.-master's in accountancy, J.D.-M.B.A., J.D.-master's in public affairs with Graduate School. Computer-based legal research program. Prison Legal Aid service. Legal Aid to the Elderly.

Southern Illinois University Edwardsville

SIUE Campus Box 1151
Edwardsville, Illinois 62026-1151

Tel: (618) 692-3705   **E-mail:** admissions@siue.edu
Fax: (618) 650-5013   **Internet:** www.siue.edu

Institution Description: Southern Illinois University Edwardsville is a state institution. *Enrollment:* 13,794. *Degrees awarded:* Baccalaureate, first-professional (dentistry), master's. Specialist certificates also awarded.

Academic offerings subject to approval by statewide coordinating bodies. Member of the Consortia Higher Education Center of St. Louis, Illinois Education Consortium, Metro East St. Louis Regional Council on Interinstitutional Cooperation.

Accreditation: *Regional:* NCA. *Professional:* accounting, business, construction education, dental hygiene, dental laboratory technology, dentistry, music, nurse anesthesia education, nursing, nursing education, public administration, social work, speech-language pathology, teacher education

History: Established as a branch campus of Carbondale 1957; awarded first degree (baccalaureate) 1960. *See* David L. Butler, *Retrospect at a Tenth Anniversary* (Carbondale and Edwardsville: Southern Illinois University Press, 1976) for further information.

Institutional Structure: *Governing board:* Board of Trustees of Southern Illinois University. Extrainstitutional representation: 7 trustees; institutional representation: 2 students. 8 voting. One of the student trustees is selected by the governor to be a voting member. *Composition of institution:* Academic affairs headed by vice chancellor and provost. Management/business/finances directed by vice chancellor for administration. Full-time instructional faculty 528. Academic governance body, Faculty Senate, meets an average of 12 times per year.

Calendar: Semesters. Academic year Aug. to May. Freshmen admitted Aug., Jan., May. Degrees conferred May, Aug., Dec. Formal commencement May, Aug., Dec. Summer session of 1 term.

Characteristics of Freshmen: Average secondary school rank of freshmen is 68th percentile. Mean ACT Composite score is 22.3. 78% of applicants admitted. 47% of accepted applicants enrolled.

37% of entering freshmen expected to graduate within 5 years. 92% of freshmen from Illinois.

Admission: Rolling admissions plan. For fall acceptance, apply at the end of the 6th semester o high school, but no later than May 1 prior to the start of the fall semester. *Requirements:* Either graduation from accredited secondary school or GED; high school course requirements; grade point average, and class rank also considered. *Entrance tests:* ACT/SAT Composite. For international students TOEFL. *For transfer students:* 2.0 GPA and 30 semester hours of transferable credit.

Tutoring available. Developmental courses offered in summer session and regular academic year; credit given.

Degree Requirements: 124 credit hours; 2.0 GPA on a 4.0 scale; 30 semester hours in residence; 60 senior college hours; general education requirements.

Distinctive Educational Programs: Work-experience programs. Flexible meeting places and schedules, including off-campus centers; weekend and evening classes. Accelerated degree program. Special facilities for using telecommunications in the classroom. Interdisciplinary programs. Interdisciplinary course sequence in gerontology for graduate students pursuing traditional disciplines. Study abroad programs in England, France, Germany, The Netherlands.

ROTC: Air Force, Army. 4 Air Force and 9 Army commissions awarded 2004.

Degrees Conferred: 1,860 *baccalaureate* (B), 121 *master's* (M): biological/life sciences 92 (B), 12 (M); business/marketing 469 (B), 123 (M); communications/communication technologies 75 (B), 6 (M); computer and information sciences 42 (B), 27 (M); education 192 (B), 164 (M); engineering and engineering technologies 133 (B), 73 (M); English 82 (B), 21 (M); foreign languages and literature 9 (B); health professions and related sciences 140 (B), 84 (M); liberal arts/general studies 88 (B), 8 (M); mathematics 9 (B), 8 (M); parks and recreation 44 (B), 32 (M); philosophy/religion/theology 9 (B); physical sciences 16 (B), 11 (M); protective services/public administration 67 (B), 62 (M); psychology 127 (B), 28 (M); social sciences and history 161 (B), 44 (M); visual and performing arts 105 (B), 14 (M). 43 *first-professional:* dentistry.

Fees and Other Expenses: *Full-time tuition per academic year 2005–06:* undergraduate resident $4,320, out-of-state $10,800. Contact the university for current graduate/first-professional tuitions/fees. *Required fees:* $859. *Room and board per academic year:* $5,819.

Financial Aid: The university offers a direct lending program. Aid from institutionally generated funds is provided on the basis of academic merit, financial need, athletic ability, other criteria. Institution has a Program participation Agreement with the U.S. Department of Education for eligible students to receive Pell Grants and other federal aid.

Financial aid to full-time, first-time undergraduate students: need-based scholarships/grants totaling $18,656,447, self-help $19,009,901; parent loans $916,408, tuition waivers $643,151, athletic awards $90,926; non-need-based scholarships/grants totaling $2,140,900, self-help $14,223,100, parent loans $4,148,096; tuition waivers $1,448,905, athletic awards $148,986. *Graduate aid:* 238 students received federal and state-funded fellowships and grants totaling $509,794; 970 federal and state-funded loans totaling $11,712,027; 28 work-study jobs worth $39,922; 262 other college-assigned jobs totaling $550,815; 121 other fellowships/grants totaling $119,443; 147 teaching assistantships totaling $5556,582; 91 research assistantships totaling g$209,118.

Departments and Teaching Staff: *Professors* 109, *associate professors* 114, *assistant professors* 174, *instructors* 75, *lecturers* 25, *part-time faculty* 230.

Total instructional faculty: 758 (full-time 528, part-time 230; women 332, men 426; members of minority groups 104). Total faculty with doctorate, first-professional, or other terminal degree: 430. Student-to-faculty ratio: 18:1. *Faculty development:* $18.8 million total grants for research. 15 faculty members awarded sabbaticals 2004–05.

Enrollment: Total enrollment 13,493. Undergraduate full-time 4,023 men / 5,026 women, part-time 805m / 957w; first-professional full-time 110m / 88w; graduate full-time 288m / 423w, part-time 616m / 1,157w.

Characteristics of Student Body: *Ethnic and racial makeup:* number of Black non-Hispanic: 1,157; American Indian or Alaska Native: 27; Asian or Pacific Islander: 216; Hispanic: 173; White non-Hispanic: 9,104. *Age distribution:* number under 18: 311; 18–19: 3,611; 20–21: 3,438; 22–24: 2,334; 25–29: 967; 30–34: 400; 35–39: 232; 40–49: 264; 50–64: 84.

International Students: 452 nonresident aliens enrolled fall 2004. 28 students from Europe, 325 Asia, 13 Central and South America, 74 Africa, 4 Canada, 1 Australia, 7 other. Social and cultural programs available to aid students whose native language is not English. English as a Second Language Program. No financial aid specifically designated for international students.

Student Life: 57% of new freshmen live on campus. 22% of student body live in college-operated apartments and residence halls. *Intercollegiate athletics:* men only: baseball, basketball, cross-country, golf, soccer, tennis, track and field, wrestling; women only: basketball, softball, tennis, track and field, volleyball, cross-country. *Special regulations:* Cars permitted without restrictions. *Special services:* Textbook Rental Program, Learning Resources Center, medical services, bus service between student housing, campus core, and surrounding communities. *Student publications, radio: Alestle,* a biweekly newspaper; *J-Student,* a quarterly paper; *Sou'wester,* an irregularly published literary magazine; *River Bluff Review.* Radio station WSIE-FM. *Surrounding community:* Edwardsville population 16,000. St. Louis, 20 miles from campus, is nearest metropolitan area. Served by mass transit bus system; airport 35 miles from campus; passenger rail service 15 miles from campus.

Publications: *Papers on Language and Literature* (quarterly) first published in 1965; *Drumvoices Revue.*

Library Collections: 827,403 volumes including bound books, serial backfiles, electronic documents, and government documents not in separate collections. Online and card catalogs. Current serial subscriptions: 5,792 paper and microform, 9,680 electronic. 22,150 recordings; 5,400 compact discs. Computer work stations available. Students have access to the Internet and other online services. Total budget for books, periodicals, audiovisual materials, microforms 2004–05: $1,594,363.

Most important holdings include collections on music (especially jazz); Louis Sullivan buildings ornaments; materials relating to Illinois region.

Buildings and Grounds: Campus area 2,660 acres. *New buildings:* Bluff Residence Hall; Nursing Complex (Sprngfield, IL); East St. Louis Higher Education Center.

Chief Executive Officer: Dr. Vaughn Vendegrift, Chancellor.

Address admission inquiries to Judy Bartel, Assistant Director of Admissions.

Spertus Institute of Jewish Studies

618 South Michigan Avenue
Chicago, Illinois 60605

Tel: (312) 322-1769   **E-mail:** college@spertus.edu
Fax: (312) 922-6406   **Internet:** www.spertus.edu

Institution Description: Spertus Institute of Jewish Studies, formerly known as Spertus College, is a private, nonsectarian, nonprofit institution offering graduate study only. *Enrollment:* 291. *Degrees awarded:* Master's, doctorate.

Accreditation: *Regional:* NCA.

History: Established and incorporated as College of Jewish Studies 1925; offered first instruction at postsecondary level 1926; awarded first degree (baccalaureate) 1932; became Spertus College of Judaica 1970; became College in 1992; adopted present name 2002.

Institutional Structure: *Governing board:* Spertus College Board of Trustees. Extrainstitutional representation: 45 trustees; institutional representation: president of the college, 45 voting. *Composition of institution:* Administrators 5 men / 3 women. Academic affairs headed by dean. Management/business/finances directed by director of administration. Full-time instructional faculty 3. Academic governance body, the faculty, meets an average of 4 times per year.

Calendar: Quarters. Academic year Sept. to June. Students admitted Sept., Jan., Mar., June. Degrees conferred and formal commencement June. 1997 summer session from mid-June to late July.

Admission: Rolling admissions plan. *Requirements:* Baccalaureate degree. Five graduate programs available in Judaica and nonprofit management, each with varying requirements.

Degree Requirements: Completion of prescribed curriculum. *Grading system:* A–F; pass-fail; withdraw (carries time limit); incomplete (carries time limit).

Distinctive Educational Programs: Maurice Spertus Museum of Judaica, a research and cultural resource center. Distance learning program.

Degrees Conferred: 71 *master's:* philosophy/religion/theology 8; nonprofit management 63.

Fees and Other Expenses: *Tuition 2004–05:* $250 per quarter hour.

Financial Aid: Aid from institutionally generated funds is provided on the basis of academic merit, financial need. Institution has a Program Participation Agreement with the U.S. Department of Education for eligible students to receive Pell Grants and other federal aid. *Graduate financial aid:* 102 federal and state-funded loans totaling $1,153,297; 88 fellowships and grants totaling $63,265.

Departments and Teaching Staff: *Total instructional faculty:* 35 (full-time 3, part-time 12; 12 women, 23 men; members of minority groups 2). Total faculty with doctorate, first-professional, or other terminal degree: 2. Student-to-faculty ratio: 8:1.

Enrollment: Total enrollment 291 (part-time 114 men / 177 women).

Student Life: No on-campus housing. *Surrounding community:* Chicago population over 3,000,000. Served by mass transit bus and rail system; airport 30 miles from campus; 2 passenger rail stations within 5 miles of campus.

Publications: *Publisher:* Spertus College of Judaica Press.

Library Collections: 110,000 volumes. 1,500 microforms; 300 audiovisual materials; 550 current periodical subscriptions.

Most important holdings include Chicago Jewish Archives (250 feet of manuscripts, archives, photographs about Chicago Jewish community dating back to mid-18000's); Katzin Rare Book Room (500 volumes dealing with Jewish studies); Levin Microform Collection (1,500 microforms of dissertations, periodicals, newspapers on Jewish Studies).

Buildings and Grounds: Campus area 100,000 square feet (1 building).

Chief Executive Officer: Dr. Howard A. Sulkin, President.

Address admission inquiries to Student Records Coordinator.

Telshe Yeshiva-Chicago

3535 West Foster Avenue
Chicago, Illinois 60625

Tel: (773) 463-7738   **E-mail:** info@telzchicago.edu
Fax: (773) 463-2849   **Internet:** www.telzchicago.edu

Institution Description: Telshe Yeshiva-Chicago is a private, professional institution. *Enrollment:* 76. *Degrees offered:* First-professional (first and second rabbinic).

Accreditation: *Professional:* rabbinical and Talmudic education.

Calendar: Semesters. Academic year Aug. to July.

Characteristics of Freshmen: 12 applicants (12 men). 100% of applicants admitted. 100% of admitted students enrolled full-time.

Degree Requirements: Completion of prescribed program.

Degrees Conferred: 4 *baccalaureate:* theology/ministerial studies.

Fees and Other Expenses: *Tuition per academic year:* $10,000. *Room and board per academic year (off-campus):* $10,613.

Financial Aid:
Financial aid to full-time, first-time undergraduate students: 75% received federal grants; 33% state/local grants; 75% institutional grants.

Enrollment: Total enrollment 76. Full-time 71, part-time 5.

Chief Executive Officer: Rabbi Abraham C. Levin, President.
Address admission inquiries to Rabbi A. Levin.

Trinity Christian College

6601 West College Drive
Palos Heights, Illinois 60463

Tel: (708) 597-3000   **E-mail:** admissions@trnty.edu
Fax: (708) 239-3986   **Internet:** www.trnty.edu

Institution Description: Trinity Christian College is a private, independent, nonprofit institution. *Enrollment:* 1,234. *Degrees awarded:* Baccalaureate. Member of the Council of Christian College Coalition.

Accreditation: *Regional:* NCA.

History: Established, chartered, and offered first instruction at postsecondary level 1959; awarded first degree (associate) 1961.

Institutional Structure: *Governing board:* Board of Trustees. Representation: 29 trustees, including president of the college. 1 ex officio. All voting. *Composition of institution:* Administrators 4 men / 2 women. Management/business finances directed by comptroller. Full-time instructional faculty 65. Academic governance body, Academic Affairs Committee, meets an average of 12 times per year.

Calendar: Semesters. Academic year Sept. to May. Freshmen admitted Sept., Jan. Degrees conferred May, Dec. Formal commencement Dec., May.

Characteristics of Freshmen: 94% of applicants admitted. 79% of admitted students enrolled full-time.

89% (191 students) submitted ACT scores. *25th percentile*: ACT Composite 19, ACT English 18, ACT Math 17. *75th percentile*: ACT Composite 26, ACT English 26, ACT Math 25.

59% of entering freshmen expected to graduate within 5 years. 46% of freshmen from Illinois. Freshmen from 27 states and 3 foreign countries.

Admission: Rolling admissions plan. For fall acceptance, apply as early as Sept. of previous year, but not later Sept. of year of enrollment. Early acceptance available. *Requirements:* Either graduation from accredited secondary school with 16 units or GED. Recommend 4 units English, 3 or more units in 2 subjects, 2 units in 2 subjects (1 of which is a foreign language). Minimum GPA 2.1. *Entrance tests:* ACT composite preferred; College Board SAT accepted. For foreign students TOEFL score of 500 or higher. *For transfer students:* 2.0 minimum GPA.

College credit and advanced placement for postsecondary-level work completed in secondary school. Developmental courses offered during regular academic year.

Degree Requirements: 125 semester hours; 2.0 GPA; 2 terms in residence; 2 physical education courses; core and distribution requirements; participation in 2 interim sessions. Fulfillment of some degree requirements and exemption from some beginning courses possible by passing College Board CLEP, AP. *Grading system:* A–F; pass-fail; withdraw (carries time limit); incomplete (carries time limit).

Distinctive Educational Programs: Work-experience programs. Evening classes. Interdisciplinary program in metropolitan studies. Independent study. Institutionally sponsored study abroad in Spain.

Degrees Conferred: 269 *baccalaureate:* biological/life sciences 3; business/marketing 57; communications/communication technologies 4; computer and information sciences 8; education 109; English 1; health professions and related sciences 20; mathematics 6; parks and recreation 9; philosophy/religion/theology 6; physical sciences 3; protective services/public administration 12; psychology 17; social sciences and history 9; visual and performing arts 5.

Fees and Other Expenses: *Full-time tuition per academic year 2005–06:* $16,985. *Room and board per academic year:* $6,600.

Financial Aid: Aid from institutionally generated funds is provided on the basis of academic merit, financial need, athletic ability, other criteria. Institution has a Program Participation Agreement with the U.S. Department of Education for eligible students to receive Pell Grants and other federal aid.

Financial aid to full-time, first-time undergraduate students: need-based scholarships/grants totaling $3,234,702, self-help $4,142,667; non-need-based scholarships/grants totaling $2,307,649, self-help $1,696,609, athletic awards $385,153.

Departments and Teaching Staff: *Professors* 19, *associate professors* 14, *assistant professors* 32, *part-time faculty* 62. *Total instructional faculty:* 127 (full-time 65, part-time 62; women 54, men 73; members of minority groups 17). Total faculty with doctorate, first-professional, or other terminal degree: 52. Student-to-faculty ratio: 13:1. 4 faculty members awarded sabbaticals 2004–05.

Enrollment: Total enrollment 1,234. Undergraduate full-time 385 men / 665 women, part-time 60m / 24w.

Characteristics of Student Body: *Ethnic/racial makeup:* number of Black non-Hispanic: 84; American Indian or Alaska Native: 3; Asian or Pacific Islander: 27; Hispanic: 53; White non-Hispanic: 996; unknown: 49. *Age distribution:* number under 18: 10; 18–19: 403; 20–21: 437; 22–24: 172; 25–29: 55; 30–34: 44; 35–39: 41; 40–49: 57; 50–64: 15.

International Students: 22 undergraduate nonresident aliens enrolled fall 2004. No programs available to aid students whose native language is not English. No financial aid specifically designated for international students.

Student Life: On-campus residence halls house 60% of student body. *Intercollegiate athletics:* men only: baseball, basketball, soccer; women only: basketball, soccer, softball, volleyball. *Special regulations:* Cars permitted in designated areas. Residence hall visitation from 5pm to midnight Tues.–Fri., noon to midnight Sat. and Sun. *Special services:* Learning Resources Center. *Student publications: Bulletin,* college magazine (published 3 times per year); *Allelu,* a yearbook; *Courier,* a monthly newspaper. *Surrounding community:* Palos Heights population 12,000. Chicago, 15 miles from campus, is nearest metropolitan area. Served by mass transit bus system; airport 20 miles from campus; passenger rail service 2 miles from campus.

Library Collections: 77,000 volumes including bound books, serial backfiles, electronic documents, and government documents not in separate collections. Online and card catalogs. Current serial subscriptions: 461 paper, 2 microform, 9,255 via electronic access. 850 recordings; 198 compact discs. 11 computer work stations. Students have access to the Internet at no charge. Total budget for books, periodicals, audiovisual materials, microforms 2004–05: $166,000.

Most important holdings include Dutch Heritage Center Collection; Elton Williams Collection; Vander Weele Curriculum Center.

Buildings and Grounds: Campus area 50 acres. *New buildings:* Chapel/Performing Arts Center; Science Center.

Chief Executive Officer: Dr. Steven Timmermans, President.

Address admission inquiries to Josh Lenarz, Director of Admissions.

Trinity International University

2065 Half Day Road
Deerfield, Illinois 60015

Tel: (847) 948-8800 **E-mail:** admissions@tiu.edu
Fax: (847) 317-8090 **Internet:** www.tiu.edu

Institution Description: Trinity International University, formerly named Trinity College, is a private, independent, nonprofit college affiliated with the Evangelical Free Church of America. *Enrollment:* 2,815. *Degrees awarded:* Baccalaureate.

Member of the Christian College Consortium.

Accreditation: *Regional:* NCA.

History: Established 1897; merged with Trinity Seminary and Bible Institute of Minneapolis 1946; offered first instruction at postsecondary level 1952; awarded first degree (baccalaureate) 1954; separated administratively from Trinity Evangelical Divinity School 1974; the divinity school became a graduate school of the university in 1995.

Institutional Structure: *Governing board:* Trinity International University Board of Trustees. Extrainstitutional representation: 21 trustees, president of the

university. 1 ex officio. 21 voting. *Composition of institution:* Administrators 10 men / 3 women. Academic affairs headed by vice president for academic affairs and dean of the college. Management/business/finances directed by business manager. Full-time instructional faculty 24 men / 7 women. Academic governance body, Trinity College Faculty, meets an average of 15 times per year.

Calendar: Semesters. Academic year early Sept. to early May. Freshmen admitted Sept., Jan., May. Summer session of 4-weeks from mid-May.

Characteristics of Freshmen: 78% of applicants admitted. 36% of admitted students enrolled full-time.

19% of applicants submitted SAT scores; 81% submitted ACT scores. *25th percentile:* SAT Verbal 520, SAT I Math 490; ACT Composite 20. *75th percentile:* SAT Verbal 650, SAT Math 660; ACT Composite 26.

53% of freshmen from Illinois. Freshmen from 24 states and 4 foreign countries.

Admission: Rolling admissions plan. For fall acceptance, apply as early as completion of junior year of secondary school, but not later than the week of registration. Early acceptance available. *Requirements:* Either graduation from accredited secondary school with 15 units which must include 12 academic; or GED. Minimum 2.0 GPA. Lowest acceptable secondary school class standing 50th percentile. *Entrance tests:* ACT composite preferred. College Board SAT accepted. *For transfer students:* 2.0 minimum GPA; maximum transfer credit limited only by residence requirement; from 2-year institution 60 semester hours maximum.

College credit for postsecondary-level work completed in secondary school. Tutoring available. Remedial courses offered during regular academic year; credit given.

Degree Requirements: 126 credit hours; 2.0 GPA; 30 of final 45 hours in residence; twice-weekly chapel attendance; 2 credit hours in physical education; 3 units of off-campus Christian service; distribution requirements, successful completion of 46 hours of general education plus an English Usage Examination.

Fulfillment of some degree requirements and exemption from some beginning courses possible by passing departmental examinations, College Board CLEP, APP. *Grading system:* A–C, no credit; withdraw (carries time limit); incomplete (carries time limit).

Distinctive Educational Programs: Work-experience programs. Internships. Evening classes. Interdepartmental program in liberal arts; divisional majors. Facilities for independent research, including honors programs, individual majors, tutorials. Institutionally sponsored off-campus study includes the Oregon Extension Program in environmental studies. Consortium-sponsored off-campus programs include American Studies in Washington (DC) and Latin American Studies in Costa Rica.

Degrees Conferred: 243 *baccalaureate*; 182 *master's*; 26 *doctorate.*

Fees and Other Expenses: *Full-time tuition per academic year 2005–06:* $19,050 undergraduate; $12,126 graduate. $12,126. *Room and board per academic year:* $6,320.

Financial Aid: Aid from institutionally generated funds is provided on the basis of academic merit, financial need. Institution has a Program Participation Agreement with the U.S. Department of Education for eligible students to receive Pell Grants and other federal aid.

Financial aid to full-time, first-time undergraduate students: need-based scholarships/grants totaling $4,896,427, self-help $3,552,837, parent loans $1,865,560, athletic awards $2,157,893; non-need-based scholarships/grants totaling $1,342,583, self-help $2,127,585.

Departments and Teaching Staff: *Total instructional faculty:* 241 (full-time 84, part-time 157; women 68, men 173; members of minority groups 13). Total faculty with doctorate, first-professional, or other terminal degree: 131. Degrees held by full-time faculty: doctorate 46%, master's 48%, baccalaureate 6%. 74% hold terminal degrees.

Enrollment: Total enrollment 2,815. Undergraduate 1,816; graduate 969.

Characteristics of Student Body: *Ethnic/racial makeup:* number of Black non-Hispanic: 211; American Indian or Alaska Native: 8; Asian or Pacific Islander: 48; Hispanic: 53; White non-Hispanic: 1,582; unknown: 648.

International Students: 165 nonresident aliens enrolled fall 2004. Programs available to aid students whose native language is not English: Social, cultural. English as a Second Language Program. No financial aid specifically designated for international students.

Student Life: On-campus residence halls house 16% of student body. Residence halls for men constitute 82% of such space, for women 18%. 7% of student body housed in institutionally controlled apartments. 50% of married students request institutional housing; 14% are so housed. 23% of students live on campus. *Intercollegiate athletics:* women only: softball. *Special regulations:* Registered cars permitted (fee charged). *Special services:* Medical services. *Surrounding community:* Deerfield population 20,000. Chicago, 30 miles from campus, is nearest metropolitan area. Served by airport 20 miles from campus; passenger rail service 3 miles from campus.

Publications: Sources of information about Trinity include a magazine, *Voices. Trinity Journal* (biannually) first published 1971.

Library Collections: 215,000 volumes. 138,000 microforms; 4,500 recordings/tapes; 1,600 periodicals. Students have access to online information retrieval services and the Internet.

Chief Executive Officer: Dr. Gregory L. Waybright, President.

Address undergraduate admission inquiries Matt Yoder, Director of Undergraduate Admissions; graduate inquiries to Ken Bottom, Director of Graduate Admissions.

Trinity Evangelical Divinity School

2065 Half Day Road
Deerfield, Illinois 60015
Tel: (708) 945-8800

Degree Programs Offered: *Master's, doctorate.*

Admission: *Requirements:* Baccalaureate degree from approved college or university, or its equivalent. Recommend 60 credits in liberal arts; Greek for some degrees. Minimum GPA 2.0 for first-professional and master of religious education programs; 2.5 for other master's programs. *Entrance tests:* GRE or Miller Analogies Test. For foreign students TOEFL. *For transfer students:* Maximum transfer credit limited by residence requirements.

Degree Requirements: *For first-professional degrees:* 136 quarter hours; 2.0 GPA; credit hours. *For master's degree:* 48–84 hours; 2.0-2.5 GPA; comprehensives in individual fields of study. *For first-professional and master's degrees:* Last 3 terms, including last 36 hours, in residence; comprehensive bible content examination; field education.

Fees and Other Expenses: Contact the seminary for current information; tuition and fees vary by program.

Departments and Teaching Staff: *Total instructional faculty:* 97.

Enrollment: Total enrollment 676 full-time, 830 part-time.

University of Chicago

5801 South Ellis Avenue
Chicago, Illinois 60637

Tel: (773) 702-1234   **E-mail:** college-admissions@uchicago.edu
Fax: (773) 702-4119   **Internet:** www.uchicago.edu

Institution Description: The University of Chicago is a private, independent, nonprofit institution. *Enrollment:* 13,870. *Degrees awarded:* Baccalaureate, first-professional (law, medicine, theology), master's, doctorate. Graduate certificates also awarded.

Member of the consortium Committee on Institutional Cooperation.

Accreditation: *Regional:* NCA. *Professional:* accounting, applied science, art, blood bank technology, business, clinical lab scientist, clinical psychology, computer science, dentistry, dietetics, endodontics, engineering, English language education, health information administration, medical illustration, medicine, nursing-midwifery, nursing, nursing education, occupational therapy, oral and maxillofacial surgery, pediatric dentistry, periodontics, pharmacy, physical therapy, planning, psychology internship, public administration, public health, social work

History: Established and offered first instruction at postsecondary level 1857; discontinued instruction 1886; reopened and chartered 1890; first instruction offered by reopened institution 1892; awarded first degree (baccalaureate) 1893.

Institutional Structure: *Governing board:* Board of Trustees. Representation: 40 trustees. *Composition of institution:* Administrators 20. Academic affairs headed by president. Management/business/finances directed by vice president for business and finance. Full-time instructional faculty 2,113. Academic governance body, Council of the University Senate, meets an average of 9 times per year.

Calendar: Quarters. Freshmen admitted Oct., Jan., Mar., June. Degrees conferred and formal commencement June, Aug., Dec., Mar. Summer session from mid-June to late Aug.

Characteristics of Freshmen: 40% of applicants admitted. 34% of admitted applicants enrolled.

45 % of students submitted SAT scores; 40% submitted ACT scores. *25th percentile:* SAT Verbal 670, SAT I Math 660; ACT Composite 28. *75th percentile:* SAT Verbal 770, SAT Math 760; ACT Composite 33.

86% of entering students expected to graduate within five years. 19% of freshmen from Illinois. Freshmen from 49 states and 20 foreign countries.

Admission: For fall acceptance, apply as early as Oct. 1 of previous year, but not later than Jan. 1 of year of enrollment. Students are notified of acceptance Apr. Apply by Dec. 1 for early decision; need not limit application to University of Chicago. Early acceptance available. *Requirements:* Graduation from accredited secondary school. *Entrance tests:* College Board SAT or ACT composite. *For transfer students:* 3.0 minimum GPA; 2 years maximum transfer credit.

College credit and advanced placement for postsecondary-level work completed in secondary school. Tutoring available.

Degree Requirements: *For undergraduate degrees:* 42 courses; 1.75 GPA; 6 quarters in residence; 1 year physical education; core requirements. Fulfillment of some degree requirements and exemption from some beginning courses possible by passing institutional examinations, College Board CLEP, AP. *Grading system:* A–F; pass-fail; withdraw; incomplete (carries time limit, penalty until course completed).

Distinctive Educational Programs: Evening and weekend classes. Accelerated degree programs. Interdisciplinary programs within the New Collegiate Division (fundamentals, law, letters and society, ideas and methods, gender studies, film and media studies). Facilities for independent research, including honors programs, individual majors, tutorials. Study abroad programs in Paris, France; Bologna, Italy; Mexico City; Kyoto, Japan; Mussourie, India; Seville, Spain; University College in London, England; Trinity College at Cambridge, England through ACM; Florence, Italy; Krasnodar, Commonwealth of Independent States; Zagreb, Yugoslavia; Puna, India; Hong Kong; Tokyo, Japan; Costa Rica; Zimbabwe.

Degrees Conferred: 1,014 *baccalaureate* (B); 2,397 *master's* (M); 331 *doctorate* (D): area and ethnic studies 13 (B), 25 (M); biological/life sciences 115 (B), 9 (M), 54 (D); business/marketing 1,273 (B), 10 (M); computer and information sciences 10 (B), 74 (M), 2 (D); education 1 (D); English 51 (B), 7 (M), 11 (D); foreign languages and literature 72 (B), 28 (M); 26 (D); health professions and related sciences 4 (M); interdisciplinary studies 2 (B), 1 (D); law/legal studies 48 (B), 3 (D); liberal arts/general studies 28 (B), 128 (M); mathematics 48 (B), 68 (M), 26 (D); natural resources/environmental science 8 (B); philosophy/religion/theology 46 (B), 39 (M), 30 (D); physical sciences 56 (B), 65 (M),36 (D); protective services/public administration 22 (B), 293 (M), 5 (D); psychology 78 (B), 4 (M), 12 (D); social sciences and history 430 (B), 307 (M), 98 (D); visual and performing arts 35 (B), 35 (M), 16 (D). 201 *first-professional:* law 191; medicine 102; master of divinity 8.

Fees and Other Expenses: *Full-time tuition per academic year 2004–05:* undergraduate $30,123, graduate $31,650. Contact the university for first-professional tuition and fees. *Other fees:* $606. *Room and board per academic year:* $9,623.

Financial Aid: Aid from institutionally generated funds is provided on the basis of academic merit, financial need, other criteria. Institution has a Program Participation Agreement with the U.S. Department of Education for eligible students to receive Pell Grants and other federal aid.

Financial aid to full-time, first-time undergraduate students: 150 students received federal aid averaging $5,493; 724 students received institutional aid averaging $17,563; 82 students received scholarships from external sources averaging $4,532.

Departments and Teaching Staff: *Professors* 466, *associate professors* 1,861, *assistant professors* 236, *instructors* 34, *part-time faculty* 368. *Total instructional faculty:* 1,404 (full-time 1,036, part-time 368; women 449, men 935; members of minority groups 205). Total faculty with doctorate, first-professional, or other terminal degree: 1,194. Student-to-faculty ratio: 10:1.

Enrollment: Total enrollment 13,870. Undergraduate full-time 2,250 men / 2,263 women, part-time 14m / 18w; graduate full-time 3,231m / 2,598w, part-time 1,716m / 127w; first-professional full-time 598m / 502w, part-time 3w

Characteristics of Student Body: *Ethnic/racial makeup:* number of Black non-Hispanic: 584; American Indian or Alaska Native: 38; Asian or Pacific Islander: 1,634; Hispanic: 715; White non-Hispanic: 7,137; unknown: 1,401. *Age distribution:* number under 18: 42; 18–19: 1,933; 20–21: 2,046; 22–24: 440; 25–29: 29; 30–34: 12; 35–39: 1; 40–49: 1.

International Students: 2,363 nonresident aliens enrolled fall 2004. Students from Europe, Asia, Central and South America, Africa, Canada, Australia, New Zealand. Programs available to aid students whose native language is not English: English as a Second Language Program. No financial aid specifically designated for international students.

Student Life: On-campus residence halls house 43% of student body. Residence halls for men constitute 15% of such space, for women 6%, for both sexes 79%. 5% of men join and 4% live in fraternities. 46% of married students request institutional housing and are so housed. 51% of student body lives on campus. *Intercollegiate athletics:* men only: baseball, basketball, football, soccer, swimming, tennis, track, wrestling; women only: basketball, field hockey, softball, swimming, tennis, track, volleyball; both sexes: fencing. *Special regulations:* Cars permitted without restrictions. *Special services:* Learning Resources Center, medical services, campus bus system. *Student publications, radio:* Publications include *Cap and Gown,* a yearbook; *Chicago Review,* a quarterly magazine; *Chicago Maroon,* a biweekly newspaper; *Counterpoint,* a bimonthly magazine; *Primavera,* a quarterly magazine. Radio station WHPK broadcasts 168 hours per week. *Surrounding community:* Chicago population over

3,000,000. Served by mass transit system; airport and passenger rail service 8 miles from campus.

Library Collections: 7,145,087 printed volumes. Online catalog. 2,308,586 microforms; 18,900 audiovisual materials; 47,790 periodicals. 200 public computer work stations. Students have access to online information retrieval services and the Internet. Total 2003–04 budget for materials and operations: $13,462,639.

The Department of Special Collections houses the library's collection of rare books, archives, and manuscripts, including Crerar Library's rare book collection. The rare book collections contain more than 250,000 volumes covering all fields of knowledge. Particular strengths are in the history of science and medicine; English, American, and Continental drama; children's literature; theology and religion; Judaica.

Buildings and Grounds: Campus area 171 acres. *New buildings:* Max Palevsky Residential Commons; Ratner Gymnasium; Graduate School of Business (Hyde Park Center); Interdisciplinary Research Building; University Press Building.

Chief Executive Officer: Dr. Donald Randel, President.

Address admission inquiries to Theodore A. O'Neill, Dean, College Admissions.

College

Degree Programs Offered: *Baccalaureate.*

Departments and Teaching Staff: Faculty drawn from other divisions and schools of the university.

Distinctive Educational Programs: Joint baccalaureate-master's program in social sciences and economics in cooperation with Division of the Social Sciences. Program in Arts and Sciences Basic to Human Biology and Medicine in cooperation with Division of the Biological Sciences and Pritzker School of Medicine, leading to a master's degree in human biology. Joint baccalaureate-master's program in biochemistry in cooperation with Division of the Biological Sciences. New Collegiate Division offers interdisciplinary experimental programs, including politics, economics, rhetoric, and law; ideas and methods; tutorial studies.

Divinity School

Degree Programs Offered: *First-professional, master's, doctorate.*

Admission: *For first-professional:* Baccalaureate or equivalent with good academic record from accredited college or university; GRE aptitude section.

Degree Requirements: *For first-professional:* 27 courses; Biblical Hebrew or New Testament Greek; 1 year field education; dissertation.

Distinctive Educational Programs: Cross-registration with members of Chicago Cluster of Theological Schools.

Division of Biological Sciences

Degree Programs Offered: *Master's, doctorate.*

Departments and Teaching Staff: Faculty is shared with the Pritzker School of Medicine.

Distinctive Educational Programs: *See* The College and Pritzker School of Medicine.

Division of Humanities

Degree Programs Offered: *Master's, doctorate.*

Division of Physical Sciences

Degree Programs Offered: *Master's, doctorate.*

Division of Social Sciences

Degree Programs Offered: *Master's, doctorate.*

Distinctive Educational Programs: Master's program in the social sciences with concentrations in areas and language studies, cross-cultural studies, economics and policy concerns, history and philosophy of the social sciences, social change, social policy and survey research, urban studies. Master's programs also available in international relations, Latin American studies, Middle Eastern studies.

Graduate School of Business

Degree Programs Offered: *Doctorate.*

Law School

Degree Programs Offered: *First-professional, master's, doctorate.*

Admission: *For first-professional:* Recommend general college education, including study of a foreign language, history, social sciences; LSAT required; applications through LSDAS.

Degree Requirements: *For first-professional:* 140 credit hours; 68 grade average; 27 months in residence.

Distinctive Educational Programs: Joint first-professional-master's program with Graduate School of Business. Clinical program, criminal justice studies, law and economics, legal history, and comparative law programs.

Pritzker School of Medicine

Degree Programs Offered: *First-professional.*

Admission: 90 semester hours or 135 quarter hours of college work with 16 semester hours of chemistry (including general, aliphatic, and aromatic organic), 12 biology (including 8 hours with laboratory), 8 physics (with laboratory), and work in English composition, humanities, mathematics, social sciences; MCAT.

Degree Requirements: 43.5 course credits; 8 quarters in residence.

Distinctive Educational Programs: Joint M.D.-Ph.D. programs in cooperation with Division of Biological Sciences, including federally funded Medical Scientist Training Program. Research conducted at Ben May Laboratory for Cancer Research, La Rabida Research Center - University of Chicago Institute, and the Walter G. Zoller Memorial Dental Clinic. *See also* The College.

School of Social Service Administration

Degree Programs Offered: *Master's, doctorate.*

University of Illinois at Chicago

601 South Morgan Street
Chicago, Illinois 60607-7128
Tel: (312) 996-7000 **E-mail:** cgadmit@uic.edu
Fax: (312) 413-3393 **Internet:** www.uic.edu

Institution Description: The University of Illinois at Chicago is a state institution. *Enrollment:* 24,865. *Degrees awarded:* Baccalaureate, master's, doctorate, first-professional (dentistry, medicine, pharmacy).

Accreditation: *Regional:* NCA. *Professional:* accounting, applied science, art, blood bank technology, business, clinical lab scientist, clinical psychology, computer science, dentistry, dietetics, endodontics, engineering, English language education, health information administration, medical illustration, medicine, nursing-midwifery, nursing, nursing education, occupational therapy, oral and maxillofacial surgery, pediatric dentistry, periodontics, pharmacy, physical therapy, planning, psychology internship, public administration, public health, social work

History: Adopted present name 1982 after consolidation of the two Chicago campuses formerly known as the University of Illinois at the Medical Center and the University of Illinois at Chicago Circle. Medical instruction dates back to 1896 when the Chicago College of Pharmacy became the School of Pharmacy; College of Physicians and Surgeons, now College of Medicine, became affiliated 1897; Columbian Dental College became affiliated 1901; all 3 officially became part of the University 1913. Two-year Chicago Undergraduate Division established at navy Pier 1946; renamed the University of Illinois at Chicago Circle and opened as four-year university 1965. College of Nursing established 1953, School of Associated Health Professions 1963.

Institutional Structure: *Composition of institution:* Administrators 21 men / 3 women. Academic affairs/business and finance headed by Executive Vice Chancellor/Vice Chancellor for Academic Affairs. Management services and physical plant directed by Vice Chancellor for Administration. Student support services and activities by Vice Chancellor for Student Affairs. Clinical health services and hospital by Vice Chancellor for Health Services. Academic governance body, Senate, meets an average of 9 times per year.

Calendar: Semesters. Academic year Aug. to May. Freshmen admitted Aug., Jan.. Degrees conferred May, Aug., Dec. Formal commencement May. Summer session from early June to mid-July.

Characteristics of Freshmen: 12,362 applicants (6,318 men, 7,044 women). 61.7% of applicants admitted. 35% of admitted students enrolled full-time.

97% (2,647 students) submitted ACT scores. *25th percentile*: ACT Composite 20, ACT English 20, ACT Math 19. *75th percentile*: ACT Composite 25, ACT English 26, ACT Math 26.

26% of entering freshmen expected to graduate within 5 years. 97.6% of freshmen from Illinois. Freshmen from 24 states and 6 foreign countries.

Admission: Rolling admissions plan. For fall acceptance, apply as early as Sept. 1 of previous year, but not later than May 30 of year of enrollment. Early acceptance available. *Requirements:* Either graduation from accredited secondary school with 16 academic units which must meet (follow) required high school subject patterns; or GED. *Entrance tests:* College Board SAT or ACT composite. For foreign students TOEFL. *For transfer students:* 3.0 minimum GPA on 5.0 scale; from 4-year accredited institution hours maximum transfer credit limited only by residence requirement; from 2-year accredited institution 90 quarter hours.

College credit for extrainstitutional learning on basis of *2006 Guide to the Evaluation of Educational Experiences in the Armed Services.* Tutoring available. Remedial courses offered in summer and regular academic year; nondegree credit given.

Degree Requirements: 120 semester hours for most programs; 3.0 GPA on 5.0 scale; first 90 or last 30 semester hours in residence; general education requirements. Fulfillment of some degree requirements and exemption from some beginning courses possible by passing departmental examinations, CLEP, AP. *Grading system:* A–E; pass-fail; withdraw.

Distinctive Educational Programs: Evening classes. Special facilities for using telecommunications in the classroom. Facilities and programs for independent research, including Honors College, individual majors, tutorials. Study abroad programs include architecture in Versailles; liberal arts in Paris, Barcelona, Baden, Austria. Independent study abroad also available.

ROTC: Army; Navy, Air Force in cooperation with Illinois Institute of Technology.

Degrees Conferred: 3,262 *baccalaureate;* 1,879 *master's;* 233 *doctorate;* 515 *first-professional.* Bachelor's degrees awarded in top five disciplines: business, management, marketing, and related support services 577; engineering 324; biological and biomedical sciences 322; psychology 298; social sciences 248.

Fees and Other Expenses: *Full-time tuition per academic year 2004–05:* $7,824 resident, $19,072 out-of-state student. Contact the university for graduate and first-professional tuition/fees. *Books and supplies:* $850. *Room and board per academic year:* $7,534.

Financial Aid: Aid from institutionally generated funds is provided on the basis of academic merit, financial need, athletic ability. Institution has a Program Participation Agreement with the U.S. Department of Education for eligible students to receive Pell Grants and other federal aid.

Financial aid to full-time, first-time undergraduate students: 33% received federal grants averaging $2,958; 47% state/local grants averaging $3,832; 40% institutional grants averaging $2,459; 33% loans averaging $4,036.

Departments and Teaching Staff: *Total instructional faculty:* 2,613. 74% hold terminal degrees. Student-to-faculty ratio: 15:1.

Enrollment: Total enrollment 24,865. Undergraduate 15,462 (45.8% men, 54.2% women).

Characteristics of Student Body: *Ethnic/racial makeup:* Black non-Hispanic: 8.9%; American Indian or Alaska Native: .2%; Asian or Pacific Islander: 24.9%; Hispanic: 16.3%; White non-Hispanic: 43%; unknown: 5.5%. *Age distribution:* 17–21: 38.9%; 22–24: 22.9%; 25–29: 19.8%; 30–34: 8.2%; 35–39: 4.3%; 40–49: 4.8%; 50–59: .9%; 65–and over: 0.1%.

International Students: 170 undergraduate nonresident aliens enrolled fall 2004. Students from Europe, Asia, Central and South America, Africa, Canada, Australia, New Zealand. Programs available to aid students whose native language is not English: English as a Second Language Program. No financial aid specifically designated for international students.

Student Life: On-campus residence halls house approximately 2,500 students. *Intercollegiate athletics:* men only: baseball, basketball, cross-country, gymnastics, soccer, swimming, tennis; *women only:* basketball, cross-country, gymnastics, softball, swimming, tennis, volleyball. *Student organizations:* Over 200 student organizations covering such areas as athletics and sports, ethnic, fraternities, sororities, honoraries, literary/publication, military, performing arts, professional, political/social, religious, special interests. *Special services:* Academic Center for Excellence, African American Academic Network, Latin American Recruitment and Educational Services Program, Native American Support Program, Health Services, Career Services, Children's Center. *Student publications: Chicago Flame,* a weekly newspaper. *Surrounding community:* Chicago population over 3,000,000. Served by mass transit bus, train, subway systems, 2 major airports 10 and 25 miles from campus, passenger rail service 1 mile from campus.

Publications: *Advances in Thermodynamics Book Series; AIDS Book Review Journal: An E-Journal; AIDS Information Source Book; Journal of Algebraic Geometry; Journal of Allied Health; American Journal of Orthodontics and Dentofacial Orthopedics; The Eighteenth Century: A Current Bibliography; Journal of Electromagnetic Waves and Applications; European Transactions on Telecommunications; Forum Linguisticum; Heat Transfer-Japanese Research; Heat Transfer-Soviet Research; IEEE Transactions on Antennas and Propagation; IEEE-CS Press; International Communications in Heat and Mass Trans-*
fer; International Journal of Heat and Mass Transfer; Libri; Literature and Medicine; Medical Decision Making; Numerical Heat Transfer; Other Voices Literary Magazine; Physical Therapy; Political Communication; Probus; International Journal of Latin and Romance Linguistics; Research in Governmental and Nonprofit Accounting; Still in Spin; 3 Sources, The Region 3 Newsletter, NN/LM; Visual Anthropology.

Library Collections: 2,165,000 volumes. 3,800,000 microforms; 29,000 audiovisual materials; 15,500 serial subscriptions. Online catalog. Students have access to online information retrieval services and the Internet.

Most important special holdings include Robert Hunter Middleton Design Printing Collection; Corporate Archives of the Chicago Board of Trade; Jane Addams Memorial Collection; Midwest Women's Historical Collection.

Buildings and Grounds: Campus area 240 acres.

Chief Executive Officer: Dr. Sylvia Manning, Chancellor.

Address admission inquiries to Thomas Glenn, Director of Admissions.

College of Liberal Arts and Sciences

Degree Programs Offered: *Baccalaureate* in African American studies, anthropology, Black studies, chemistry, classical civilization, classical languages and literature, communication, criminal justice, economics, English (literature and writing), French, geography, German, history, Italian, Latin American studies, music, philosophy, physics, Polish, political science, psychology (general and applied), Russian, sociology, Spanish, biological sciences, geological sciences, mathematics; *specialized curricula* includes baccalaureates in biochemistry, chemistry, geography, mathematics and computer science, physics, statistics and operations research, French business studies; *teacher education curriculum for secondary schools* in biological sciences, chemistry, geography, mathematics, physics, English, French, German, history, Russian,Spanish; *master's* in anthropology, communication, criminal justice, English (specializations in literature, creative writing, and the teaching of English), French, environmental and urban geography, German, Hispanic studies, history, linguistics, mathematics, philosophy, political science, psychology, Slavic studies, sociology, biological sciences, chemistry, geological sciences, mathematics, physics, teaching of history, teaching of mathematics; *doctorate* anthropology, biological sciences, chemistry, mathematics, English, geotechnical engineering and geosciences, German (in cooperation with Urbana-Champaign), history, philosophy, physics, political science (Public Policy Analysis Program), psychology, Slavic languages and literatures, sociology.

Distinctive Educational Programs: Interdisciplinary program in ethnic studies. Preprofessional programs in dentistry, medical dietetics, medical laboratory sciences, medical record administration, medicine, nursing, occupational therapy, pharmacy, physical therapy, veterinary medicine. Study abroad in Austria, France, Poland, Spain; study also available by individual arrangement.

College of Architecture and the Arts

Degree Programs Offered: *Baccalaureate* in architecture, art education, graphic design, industrial design, photography/film/electronic media, studio arts, art history, music, theatre; *master's* in architecture, art therapy, art history, graphic design, industrial design, photography, film/animation/video, electronic visualization, studio arts.

Distinctive Educational Programs: Study abroad in Europe.

College of Business Administration

Degree Programs Offered: *Baccalaureate* in accounting, economics, finance, information and decision sciences, management, marketing; *master's* in accounting, business administration (MBA), management information systems, urban and quantitative economics; *doctorate* in business economics, finance, human resource management, management information systems, marketing.

College of Education

Degree Programs Offered: *Baccalaureate* in elementary education; *master's* in instructional leadership, leadership and administration, special education; *doctorate* in curriculum and instruction, educational policy and administration, special education.

Distinctive Educational Programs: Research and laboratory opportunities in urban education. Child study facility. Bilingual education program. Catholic teacher education program.

College of Engineering

Degree Programs Offered: *Baccalaureate* in bioengineering, chemical engineering, civil engineering, computer engineering, computer science, electrical engineering, industrial engineering, mechanical engineering, engineering physics, engineering management; *master's* in bioengineering, chemical engineering, civil engineering, electrical engineering and computer science, industrial engineering, materials science and engineering, mechanical engineering; *doctorate* in bioengineering, chemical engineering, civil engineering, electrical engineering and computer science, geotechnical engineering and geosciences, industrial engineering and operations research, materials science and engineering, mechanical engineering.

Distinctive Educational Programs: Work-experience programs.

College of Associated Health Professions

Degree Programs Offered: *Baccalaureate* in health information management, human nutrition and dietetics, kinesiology, medical laboratory sciences, occupational therapy, physical therapy; *master's* in biomedical visualization, human nutrition and dietetics, kinesiology, medical laboratory sciences, occupational therapy, physical therapy; *doctorate* in human nutrition and dietetics.

Distinctive Educational Programs: Corrective therapy program. Community recreation program.

Jane Addams College of Social Work

Degree Programs Offered: *Baccalaureate, master's, doctorate.*

Distinctive Educational Programs: Social planning-policy administration or social work-treatment, theories, and research.

College of Dentistry

Degree Programs Offered: *Baccalaureate* in dentistry; *master's* in oral sciences; *doctorate* dental surgery.

Admission: 90 quarter hours from accredited college or university, including 9 English, 21 chemistry, 9 biological science, 9 physics, additional electives.

Degree Requirements: *For first-professional degree:* 218 hours, 3.0 GPA on a 5.0 scale, 36 months in residence.

Distinctive Educational Programs: Concurrent registration in the School of Public Health possible for qualified students.

College of Medicine

Degree Programs Offered: *Master's* in anatomy and cell biology, biochemistry, health professions education, microbiology and immunology, pathology, pharmacology, physiology and biophysics, surgery; *doctor of medicine; doctor of philosophy* in anatomy and cell biology, biochemistry, mammalian genetics, microbiology and immunology, pathology, pharmacology, physiology and biophysics.

Admission: Baccalaureate from accredited college or university, MCAT.

Degree Requirements: 156 weeks credit, 36 months in residence.

Distinctive Educational Programs: Combined M.D.-Ph.D. program through Medical Scholars Program for students in the School of Basic Medical Sciences, Urbana-Champaign, in cooperation with other divisions of the university at Urbana-Champaign.

School of Public Health

Degree Programs Offered: *Master's* in public health, public health sciences; *doctorate* in public health, public health sciences.

Distinctive Educational Programs: Cooperative master's and doctoral programs in community health education with Department of Health and Safety Education, Urbana-Champaign campus; in bioengineering with College of Engineering, Chicago Circle campus. Joint D.D.S.-M.P.H. and M.D.-M.P.H. degree programs with colleges of Dentistry and Medicine, Medical Center Campus.

College of Nursing

Degree Programs Offered: *Baccalaureate, master's, doctorate.*

Admission: *For baccalaureate:* 45 quarter hours college coursework, including 8 rhetoric and composition, 8 humanities, 8 zoology or general biology with laboratory, 4 general or inorganic chemistry with laboratory, 4 organic chemistry with laboratory, 4 psychology, 4 sociology, additional electives.

Degree Requirements: *For baccalaureate degree:* 188 quarter hours, 3.0 GPA on a 5.0 scale, 3 quarters in residence.

College of Pharmacy

Degree Programs Offered: *Master's* in forensic science, medicinal chemistry, pharmacognosy, pharmacy; *doctorate* in pharmacy; *doctor of philosophy* in medicinal chemistry, pharmacognosy, pharmacy.

Admission: *For baccalaureate:* 45 quarter hours from accredited college or university, including 4 semesters English, 8 general or inorganic chemistry with laboratory, 8 biology with laboratory, 3 algebra, 2 trigonometry, additional electives; 3.25 GPA on a 5.0 scale; ACT or SAT; PCAT.

Degree Requirements: *For baccalaureate degree:* 234 quarter hours, 3.0 GPA on a 5.0 scale, 27 months in residence.

School of Urban Planning and Public Affairs

Departments and Teaching Staff: *Total instructional faculty:* 23. *Degrees held by full-time faculty:* doctorate 80%, master's 18%, professional 2%. 82% hold terminal degrees.

University of Illinois at Springfield

One University Plaza
Springfield, Illinois 62707-5407
Tel: (217) 206-6600   **E-mail:** admissions@uis.edu
Fax: (217) 206-6511   **Internet:** www.uis.edu

Institution Description: University of Illinois at Springfield, formerly known as Sangamon State University. is a public institution providing upper division and graduate study only. *Enrollment:* 4,396. *Degrees awarded:* Baccalaureate, master's.

Academic offerings subject to approval by statewide coordinating bodies. Budget subject to approval by state governing boards. Member of Center Illinois Arts Consortium and Illinois Educational Consortium.

Accreditation: *Regional:* NCA. *Professional:* clinical lab scientist, counseling, nursing, public administration, social work

History: Established and chartered 1969; offered first instruction at postsecondary level 1970; awarded first degrees (baccalaureate, master's) 1971; adopted present name 1995.

Institutional Structure: *Governing board:* Illinois Board of Regents. Representation: 9 regents (appointed by governor of Illinois), 3 students. 9 voting. *Composition of institution:* Administrators 27 men / 5 women (6% are members of minority groups; at dean's level and above, 25% are women). Academic affairs headed by vice president for academic affairs and dean of the faculty. Management/business/finances directed by vice president for business and administrative services. Full-time instructional faculty 170. Academic governance body, Faculty Senate, meets an average of 20 times per year.

Calendar: Semesters. Academic year Aug. to May. Entering students admitted Aug., Jan., June. Degrees conferred May, Aug., Dec. Formal commencement May. Summer session from early June to early Aug.

Characteristics of Freshmen: 432 applicants (180 men, 252 women). 43.3% of applicants admitted. 48.1% of admitted students enrolled full-time.

100% (90 students) submitted ACT scores. *25th percentile:* ACT Composite 23, ACT English 22, ACT Math 23. *75th percentile:* ACT Composite 28, ACT English 28, ACT Math 27.

97% of entering students from Illinois.

Admission: Rolling admissions plan. For fall acceptance, apply no later than registration period. *Requirements:* Admission to the junior year is granted to applicants who have completed 60 semester (90 quarter) hours of credit with an average of C or better from a regionally accredited college or university. These hours must include a minimum of 3 semester hours of transferable English composition. An additional 22 hours of general education requirements must be met prior to graduation. Students are urged to complete the general education requirements prior to admission. Admission also open to students demonstrating adequate preparation through proficiency examinations or evaluation of extrainstitutional learning (life experience). Maximum transfer credit limited only by residence requirement.

Degree Requirements: 60 upper division semester hours; 30 hours in residence; 6 hours Public Affairs Colloquia; demonstrated proficiency in communication skills; exit examinations on U.S. and Illinois Constitutions at least once at the collegiate level. *Grading system:* A, B, C, D, U; credit-no credit; withdraw; incomplete; and R (deferred).

Distinctive Educational Programs: *Available to all students:* Internships. Flexible meeting places and schedules, including off-campus centers (at downtown Springfield, 7 miles from the main campus; Peoria, 90 miles away), weekend and evening classes. Interdisciplinary programs in environmental studies, women's studies. Facilities and programs for independent research, including individual majors, tutorials. *Other distinctive programs:* Continuing education. Center for Legal Studies. Community Arts Management. Credit for Prior Learning. Gerontology. Facilities and programs for study of public affairs at state and local levels, including Center for Policy Studies and Program Evaluation, Center for the Study of Middle-Size Cities, Illinois Legislative Studies Center.

Degrees Conferred: 625 *baccalaureate*; 453 *master's*; 1 *doctorate*. Bachelor's degrees awarded in top five disciplines: business, management, marketing, and related support services 181; psychology 64; liberal arts and sciences, general studies and humanities 62; security and protective services 56; communication, journalism, and related programs 45.

Fees and Other Expenses: *Full-time tuition per academic year 2004–05:* undergraduate resident $5,539, out-of-state student $13,549. *Books and supplies:* $1,200. *Room and board per academic year:* $6,816.

Financial Aid: Aid from institutionally generated funds is provided on the basis of academic merit, financial need, athletic ability, other criteria. Institution has a Program Participation Agreement with the U.S. Department of Education for eligible students to receive Pell Grants and other federal aid.

Financial aid to full-time, first-time undergraduate students: 20% received federal grants averaging $2,293; 40% state/local grants averaging $2,684; 100% institutional grants averaging $3,248; 63% loans averaging $2,532.

Departments and Teaching Staff: *Professors* 56, *associate professors* 65, *assistant professors* 42, *instructors* 7, *part-time teachers* 62. *Total instructional faculty:* 191. Student-to-faculty ratio: 16:1. Degrees held by full-time faculty: doctorate 71.6%, master's 24.3%, baccalaureate .6%, professional 3.6%.

Enrollment: Total enrollment 4,396. Undergraduate 2,507 (39.7% men, 60.3% women).

Characteristics of Student Body: *Ethnic/racial makeup:* Black non-Hispanic: 8.4%; American Indian or Alaska Native: .3%; Asian or Pacific Islander: 2.3%; Hispanic: 1.8%; White non-Hispanic: 81.6%; unknown: 4.9%.

International Students: 13 undergraduate nonresident aliens enrolled 2004. Students from Europe, Asia, Central and South America, Africa. Programs available to aid students whose native language is not English: Social, cultural, financial. English as a Second Language Program.

Student Life: 6% of student body live on campus in institutionally owned apartments. Housing available for married students. *Intercollegiate athletics:* men only: soccer, tennis; women only: tennis. *Special regulations:* Cars permitted without restrictions. *Special services:* Learning Resources Center, medical services. *Student publications, radio: Alchemist Review,* an annual literary magazine; *SSU News,* a biweekly newspaper. Radio station WSSR broadcasts 147 hours per week. *Surrounding community:* Springfield population 100,000. St. Louis (MO), 95 miles from campus, is nearest metropolitan area. Served by mass transit bus system; airport 8 miles from campus; passenger rail service 5 miles from campus.

Publications: *The Psychohistory Review,* published 3 times per year; *Illinois Issues,* published monthly, first published in 1975.

Library Collections: 505,000 volumes. 10,000 microforms titles; 9,300 recordings/tapes; 4,400 audiovisual materials; 2,950 periodicals. Online catalog. Students have access to online information retrieval services and the Internet.

Most important special holdings include Illinois Regional Documents Depository; Richard Phillips Illinois Photography Collection; Handy Writers' Colony Collection.

Buildings and Grounds: Campus area 746 acres.

Chief Executive Officer: Dr. Richard D. Ringeisen, President.

Address admission inquiries Darren Bush, Director of Admissions and Records.

University of Illinois at Urbana-Champaign

601 East John Street
Urbana, Illinois 61820
Tel: (217) 333-1000   **E-mail:** admission@uiuc.edu
Fax: (217) 333-9758   **Internet:** www.uiuc.edu

Institution Description: *Enrollment:* 40,687. *Degrees awarded:* Baccalaureate, first-professional (law, veterinary medicine), master's, doctorate. Certificates also awarded.

Member of Committee on Institutional Cooperation, National Association of State Universities and Land Grant Colleges; American Council on Education, Association of American Universities, North Central Association, Midwest Universities Consortium for International Activities.

Accreditation: *Regional:* NCA. *Professional:* accounting, art, athletic training, audiology, business, clinical psychology, counseling psychology, dance, dietetics, engineering, forestry, journalism, landscape architecture, law, music, planning, psychology internship, recreation and leisure services, rehabilitation counseling, social work, speech-language pathology, theatre, veterinary medicine

History: The university was chartered in 1867 as the Illinois Industrial University; opened 1868; first certificates awarded 1871; first baccalaureate degree conferred June 1878. For further information, see Winton Solberg's *University*

of Illinois 1867–1894, published 1968 and Burt Powell's *The Semi-Centennial History of the University of Illinois,* published in 1918.

Institutional Structure: Administrators 17 men / 11 women. Financial and academic affairs headed by provost and vice chancellor for academic affairs. Student affairs headed by vice chancellor for student affairs. Full-time instructional faculty 1,598 men / 540 women. Academic governance body, Senate, meets an 7 or 8 times per year.

Calendar: Semesters. Academic year Sept. to May. Freshmen admitted Aug., Jan., June. Degrees conferred May, Aug., Oct., Jan. Formal commencement May. Summer session from May to Aug.

Characteristics of Freshmen: 68% of applicants admitted. 48.47% of admitted applicants enrolled.

29.4% (2,134 students) submitted SAT scores; 99.9% (7,240 students) submitted ACT scores. *25th percentile:* SAT Verbal 560, SAT Math 620; ACT Composite 25, ACT English 25, ACT Math 26. *75th percentile:* SAT Verbal 670, SAT Math 730; ACT Composite 31, ACT English 31, ACT Math 31.

74% of entering freshmen expected to graduate within 5 years. 92% of freshmen from Illinois. Freshmen from 44 states and 29 foreign countries.

Admission: For fall acceptance, apply as early as Oct. 1; by Nov. 1 for early decision if "very well qualified" (need not limit application to University of Illinois at Urbana-Champaign); by Nov. 15 for consideration advantage; space-available acceptance basis after Dec. 15. Students notified of acceptance as early as Oct., most in Jan. For College of Veterinary Medicine, apply by Oct. 15. *Requirements:* Either graduation from accredited secondary school with 15 academic units which must include 3 English, 1 each algebra and plane geometry, other college preparatory subjects; or GED. Additional requirements for some programs. Secondary school rank and SAT or ACT scores must indicate a predictive GPA of 2.00 on a 3.00 scale. *Entrance tests:* College Board SAT or ACT composite. For foreign students TOEFL. *For transfer students:* 2.25 minimum GPA on a 4.0 scale (3.5 for teacher education program), maximum transfer credit limited only by residence requirement.

Tutoring available. Remedial courses offered in summer session and regular academic year; credit may be given.

Degree Requirements: *For undergraduates:* 120–134 semester hours; 2.0 GPA on a 4.0 scale; first 3 years or final year in residence; general education requirements. Additional requirements for some programs. Fulfillment of some degree requirements and exemption from some beginning courses possible by passing College Board AP. *Grading system:* A–E.

Distinctive Educational Programs: Work experience programs. Weekend and evening classes. Accelerated degree programs. Special facilities for using telecommunications in the classroom. Facilities and programs for independent research, including honors programs, individual majors, tutorials. Institute of Aviation offers flight training to students in other divisions of the university, and research opportunities through general aviation training simulators. Study abroad programs in over 40 countries. Programs are offered through International Association for the Exchange of Students for Technical Experience; Engineering Alliance for Global Education; Exchange scholarships at Munich and Darmstadt, Germany; Individual programs with many universities and countries. Freshman Discovery Program; Women in Math, Science and Engineering Program. The university offers several living and learning communities that connects curricular and cocurricular activities and programs and by bringing academics into the residence halls.

ROTC: Army, Navy, Air Force. Commissions awarded 2004: Army 14, Navy 27, Air Force 22.

Degrees Conferred: 6,994 *baccalaureate* (B), 2,746 *master's* (M), 574 *doctorate* (D): agriculture 328 (B), 87 (M), 32 (D); architecture 181 (B), 150 (M), 6 (D); area and ethnic studies 28 (B), 17 (M); biological/life sciences 495 (B), 56 (M), 52 (D); business/marketing 1,211 (B), 663 (M), 12 (D); communications/communication technologies 236 (B), 38 (M), 5 (D); computer and information sciences 204 (B), 128 (M), 25 (D); education 241 (B), 238 (M), 53 (D); engineering and engineering technologies 178 (B), 450 (M), 129 (D); English 534 (B), 37 (M), 20 (D); foreign languages and literature 133 (B), 33 (M), 24 (D); health professions and related sciences 252 (B), 53 (M), 10 (D); home economics and vocational home economics 62 (B), 2 (D); interdisciplinary studies 37 (B), 5 (M), 5 (D); law/legal studies 29 (M); liberal arts/general studies 19 (B); library science 235 (M), 1 (D); mathematics 102 (B), 48 (B), 17 (D); natural resources/environmental science 52 (B), 30 (M), 4 (D); parks and recreation 179 (B), 37 (M), 10 (D); personal and miscellaneous services 1 (B); philosophy/religion/theology 42 (B), 8 (M), 5 (D); physical sciences 121 (B), 67 (M), 58 (D); protective services/public administration 31 (M), 6 (D); psychology 512 (B), 62 (M), 25 (D); social sciences and history 178 (B), 74 (M), 39 (D); visual and performing arts 65 (B), 70 (M), 34 (D). 308 *first-professional:* law 213, veterinary science 95.

Fees and Other Expenses: *Full-time tuition per academic year 2005–06:* undergraduate resident $7,042, out-of-state $21,128; graduate resident $7,160, out-of-state $20,000. *Required fees:* $1,626. *Room and board per academic year:* $7,176.

Financial Aid: The university offers a direct lending program. Aid from institutionally generated funds is provided on the basis of academic merit, athletic ability, financial need, other considerations. Institution has a Program Participation Agreement with the U.S. Department of Education for eligible students to receive Pell Grants and other federal aid.

Financial aid to full-time, first-time undergraduate students: need-based scholarships/grants totaling $57,273,422, self-help $49,757,266, parent loans $14,802,261, tuition waivers $5,808,199, athletic awards $1,357,713; non-need-based scholarships/grants totaling $9,556,701, self-help $16,668,397, parent loans $12,654,828, tuition waivers $6,412,764, athletic awards $3,963,111.

Departments and Teaching Staff: *Total instructional faculty:* 2,549 (full-time 2,158, part-time 391; women 847, men 1,702; members of minority groups 224). Total faculty with doctorate, first-professional, or other terminal degree: 2,080. Student-to-faculty ratio: 14:1. *Faculty development:* $318,339,000 in grants for research. 129 faculty members awarded sabbaticals 2004–05.

Enrollment: Total enrollment 40,687. Undergraduate full-time 15,066 men / 13,620 women, part-time 535m / 411w; first-professional full-time 471m / 573w, part-time 9m / 17w; graduate full-time 4,476m / 3,347w, part-time 493m / 1,169w. *Transfer students:* in-state 823, from out-of-state 129.

Characteristics of Student Body: *Ethnic and racial makeup:* number of Black non-Hispanic: 1,993; American Indian or Alaska Native: 73; Asian or Pacific Islander: 3,773; Hispanic: 1,862; White non-Hispanic: 19,876; unknown: 768. *Age distribution:* number under 18: 451; 18–19: 13,104; 20–21: 12,483; 22–24: 2,906; 25–29: 441; 30–34: 116; 35–39: 54; 40–49: 52; 50–64: 22; 65 and over: 7.

International Students: 4,748 nonresident aliens enrolled fall 2004. 500 students from Europe, 3,611 Asia, 260 Central and South Latin America, 103 Africa, 100 Canada, 19 Australia, 13, New Zealand, 147 other. Programs available to aid students whose native language is not English: Social, cultural. English as a Second Language Program. No financial aid specifically designated for international students.

Student Life: On-campus residence halls house 27% of student body. 22 undergraduate residence halls; 5 privately-owned certified residence halls and 19 certified houses. Graduate student housing includes 2 residence halls. Housing available for married students. 18.6% of male students belong to fraternities and 22.6% of females belong to sororities. *Intercollegiate athletics:* men only: baseball, football, wrestling; women only: basketball, golf, gymnastics, soccer, track, tennis. *Special services:* Medical services, child care, group and individual psychological counseling, bus service for all students (including students with disabilities) and Institute of Aviation students. *Student publications, radio: Daily Illini,* a daily newspaper; *Illio,* a yearbook. Radio station WPGU broadcasts 24 hours a day. *Surrounding communities:* Twin cities population, Urbana 36,000, Champaign 59,000. Chicago, 135 miles from campus, is nearest metropolitan area. Served by mass transit bus system; airport 7 miles from campus; passenger rail and bus services 1 mile from campus.

Publications: *American Journal of Psychology* (quarterly) first published 1887, *Comparative Literature Studies* (quarterly) first published 1963, *Educational Theory* (quarterly) first published 1951, *Illinois Journal of Mathematics* (quarterly) first published 1957, *Illinois Teacher* (5 times per year) first published 1957, *International Journal of Accounting* (biannually) first published 1965, *International Regional Science Review* (biannually) first published 1965, *Journal of Aesthetic Education* (quarterly) first published 1966, *Journal of Business Communication* (quarterly) first published 1963, *Journal of Consumer Research* (quarterly) first published 1971, *Journal of English and Germanic Philology* (quarterly) first published 1897, *Journal of Vocational Behavior* (6 times per year) first published 1971, *Law Forum* (quarterly) first published 1949, *Library Trends* (quarterly) first published 1952, *Quarterly Review of Economics and Business* first published 1961, *Review of Research in Visual Arts Education* (biannually) first published 1973; *The Ninth Letter* (biannually) first published 2004.

Library Collections: 10,189,657 volumes (includes government documents). 9,201,301 microforms; 6,741 computer titles; 30,292 manuscripts and archives; 868,358 audiovisual materials. Online and card catalogs. Students have access to the Internet at no charge. Access to online bibliographic information retrieval systems. Total 2004–05 budget for books and materials: $14,245,664.

Most important holdings include T.W. Baldwin Elizabethan Library (5,779 volumes of authors' texts and commentaries on their works and prayer books, rhetoric, histories, and school books of the period); Mark Twain Collection (2,100 volumes of manuscripts and other materials by or about the author); Milton Collection (including all first editions and collections of variant texts, later editions, and critical works); Carl Sandberg Collection; H.G. Wells Collection.

Buildings and Grounds: Campus area 1,470 acres with 200 major buildings in Champaign, Urbana, and surrounding areas. *New buildings:* Admissions and Records Building; Indoor Football Stadium/Indoor Tennis Center; Siebel Computer Science Building; Spurlock Museum; Campbell Hall Communications Center.

Chief Executive Officer: Dr. Richard Herman, Chancellor.

Address admission inquiries to Keith Marshall, Office of Admissions and Records.

College of Liberal Arts and Sciences

Degree Programs Offered: *Baccalaureate* in actuarial science; anthropology; art history; astronomy; Asian studies; biochemistry; bioengineering; biology; biophysics; chemical engineering; chemistry; classics; comparative literature; English; entomology; French; geography; geology; Germanic languages and literatures; history; humanities; Italian; Latin American studies; linguistics; mathematics and computer science; microbiology; music; philosophy; physics; physiology; plant biology; political science; Portuguese; psychology; religious studies; rhetoric; Russian; Russian and East European studies; sociology; Spanish; statistics; *master's* and *doctorate* in various fields.

Admission: 4 units English, 3–3½ math, 2 science, 2 social studies, 2 foreign language.

Degree Requirements: 120 total semester credits, include 21 advanced credits.

Departments and Teaching Staff: *Professors* 315, *associate professors* 152; *assistant professors* 125, *instructors* 29. *Total instructional faculty:* 650.

Distinctive Educational Programs: Cooperative program in teacher education with College of Education. Interdepartmental programs in Afro-American studies, American civilization, cinema studies, medieval civilization, Renaissance studies, West European studies, women's studies. Preprofessional programs in dentistry, medical dietetics, medical laboratory sciences, medical record administration, medicine, nursing, occupational therapy, pharmacy, veterinary medicine. Study abroad in Austria, France, Italy, Japan, Mexico, Spain, Soviet Union.

Enrollment: Total enrollment 16,605.

College of Agriculture, Consumer and Environmental Sciences

Degree Programs Offered: *Baccalaureate, master's, doctorate.*

Departments and Teaching Staff: *Professors* 101, *associate professors* 63, *assistant professors* 37, *instructors* 5, *part-time faculty* 21. *Total instructional faculty:* 216. Degrees held by full-time faculty: Doctorate 88%, master's 100%. 88% hold terminal degrees.

Distinctive Educational Programs: Double-degree program in agricultural science and agricultural engineering. Cooperative programs in agricultural education and home economics with College of Education. Interdepartmental graduate-level programs in nutrition, plant physiology. Research and instructional opportunities through college-operated farms, forest plantation, orchards, greenhouses, laboratories.

Enrollment: Total enrollment: 2,783.

College of Applied Life Studies

Degree Programs Offered: *Baccalaureate* in community health, kinesiology, leisure studies, speech and hearing science; *master's, doctorate* in various fields.

Departments and Teaching Staff: *Professors* 16,5, *associate professors* 19.4, *assistant professors* 12, *part-time teachers* 10.2. *Total instructional faculty:* 58.1 FTE. *Degrees held by full-time faculty:* Doctorate 98%, professional 2%. 100 hold terminal degrees.

Distinctive Educational Programs: Cooperative master's program with School of Public Health at the Medical Center in Chicago. Biomechanics Laboratory. Exercise Therapy Clinic. Motor Behavior Laboratory. Physical Fitness Research Laboratory. Health Education Research Laboratory. Safety and Traffic Safety Education Research Laboratory. *Other distinctive programs:* Recreation and Tourism Development. Experimental summer sports fitness day school for children. Division of Rehabilitation-Education Services offering medical services, physical therapy and functional training, prosthetics, counseling, services for visually and hearing impaired, occupational therapy, recreation and athletics, and transportation services.

Enrollment: Total enrollment 1,684.

College of Commerce and Business Administration

Degree Programs Offered: *Baccalaureate, master's,* and *doctorate* in accountancy, business administration, economics, finance.

Departments and Teaching Staff: Accountancy *professors* 8, *associate professors* 8, *assistant professors* 11, *instructors* 5, *part-time faculty* 9; business administration 18, 6, 18, 0, 6; economics 21, 12, 7, 0, 6; finance 8, 6, 3, 0, 12. *Total instructional faculty:* 146 FTE. Degrees held by full-time faculty: doctorate 96.4%, master's 3.6%.

Enrollment: Total enrollment 3,704. Full-time undergraduate 2,846, unclassified 35, graduate 777.

College of Communications

Degree Programs Offered: *Baccalaureate* in advertising, communication, journalism; media studies; *master's, doctorate* in various fields.

Departments and Teaching Staff: *Professors* 11, *associate professors* 11, *assistant professors* 9, *instructors* 2, *part-time teachers* 8. *Total instructional faculty:* 41. Degrees held by full-time faculty: Doctorate 70%, master's 95%. 100% hold terminal degrees.

Enrollment: Total enrollment 649.

College of Education

Degree Programs Offered: *Baccalaureate, master's, doctorate.*

Departments and Teaching Staff: *Professors* 47, *associate professors* 36, *assistant professors* 49. *Total instructional faculty:* 112. Degrees held by full-time faculty: doctorate 100%.

Distinctive Educational Programs: Joint degree programs with College of Law and MBA program with College of Commerce and Business Administration.

Enrollment: Total enrollment 1,552.

College of Engineering

Degree Programs Offered: *Baccalaureate, master's, doctorate.*

Departments and Teaching Staff: *Total instructional faculty:* 371. Degrees held by full-time faculty: doctorate 100%.

Distinctive Educational Programs: 5-year cooperative education program. Study abroad; on-the-job training available in foreign countries. Coordinated Science Laboratory provides interdisciplinary research in physical electronics and information sciences. Materials Research Laboratory. Materials Engineering Research Laboratory. Highway Traffic Safety Center.

Enrollment: Total enrollment 7,764. Undergraduate full-time 5,123, unclassified full-time 67, graduate full-time 2,473.

College of Fine and Applied Arts

Degree Programs Offered: *Baccalaureate, master's, doctorate.*

Admission: Art and Design has a professional interest statement requirement for entering freshmen.

Departments and Teaching Staff: *Total instructional faculty:* 16. Degrees held by full-time faculty: doctorate 39%, master's 31%, baccalaureate 3%. 27% hold terminal degrees.

Distinctive Educational Programs: Band internship program. Cooperative degree programs with Parkland College. Interdepartmental programs in architecture, engineering, ecology, urban design. Study abroad in France. Visual Research Laboratory. Urban design studio. *Other distinctive programs:* Summer Art School for secondary school students. Summer Youth Music. Conferences and institutes for professionals, including architecture workshop, conference on campus planning, urban planning. Bureau of Urban and Regional Planning Research. Small Homes Council-Building Research Council, Krannert Center for the Performing Arts, Krannert Art Museum.

Enrollment: Total enrollment 2,692. Undergraduate full-time 1,870, graduate full-time 793.

School of Social Work

Degree Programs Offered: *Baccalaureate, master's, doctorate.*

Departments and Teaching Staff: *Total instructional faculty:* 25 FTE. Degrees held by full-time faculty: professional 85%, doctorate 85%, master's 100%, baccalaureate 100%. 100% hold terminal degrees.

Enrollment: Total enrollment 297. Graduate full-time 284, part-time 13.

College of Law

Degree Programs Offered: *First-professional, master's, doctorate.*

Admission: *For first-professional students:* Baccalaureate from accredited college or university; LSAT.

Degree Requirements: *For first-professional degree:* 90 credit hours, 2.0 GPA on a 4.0 scale, 90 weeks in residence.

Departments and Teaching Staff: *Professors:* 24, *associate professors* 4, *assistant professors* 8, *instructors* 8, *part-time teachers* 45. *Total instructional faculty:* 59 FTE. *Degrees held by full-time faculty:* Professional 98%, doctorate 2%, master's 18%, baccalaureate 100%. 100% hold terminal degrees.

Distinctive Educational Programs: Joint-degree program with Institute of Labor and Industrial Relations.

Enrollment: Total enrollment 711.

College of Veterinary Medicine

Degree Programs Offered: *First-professional, master's, doctorate .*

Admission: *For first-professional students:* 60 semester hours prescribed college courses, 2.75 GPA on a 4.0 scale.

Degree Requirements: *For first-professional degree:* 156 credit hours, 2.25 cumulative GPA.

Departments and Teaching Staff: *Professors* 39, *associate professors* 34, *assistant professors* 30; *part-time faculty* 1. *Total instructional faculty:* 104. Degrees held by full-time faculty: professional 73%, doctorate 67%, master's 63%.

Enrollment: Total enrollment 473.

Graduate College

Degree Programs Offered: *Master's, doctorate.*

Departments and Teaching Staff: Faculty members are drawn from other colleges and schools of the university.

Distinctive Educational Programs: The Graduate College/Office of the Vice Chancellor for Research houses a number of interdisciplinary units, including the National Center for Supercomputing Applications, the Biotechnology Center, and the Program in Ancient Technologies and Archaeological Materials. Interdisciplinary graduate programs include biophysics, computational science and engineering, neuroscience, and nutritional sciences. There are numerous joint degree programs between departments. All graduate programs are under the jurisdiction of the Graduate College.

Enrollment: Total enrollment 8,692. First-professional full-time 439 men / 505 women, part-time 6m / 6w; graduate full-time 3,789m / 2,577w, part-time 664m / 706w.

Institute of Labor and Industrial Relations

Degree Programs Offered: *Master's, doctorate.*

Departments and Teaching Staff: Institute of Labor and Industrial Relations *professors* 8, *associate professors* 2, *assistant professors* 4, *instructors* 1, *part-time teachers* 1. *Total instructional faculty:* 16. *Degrees held by full-time faculty:* Doctorate 100%. 100% hold terminal degrees.

Distinctive Educational Programs: *See* College of Law.

Enrollment: Total enrollment 149.

Graduate School of Library and Information Science

Degree Programs Offered: *Master's, doctorate.* Certificates also given.

Departments and Teaching Staff: Library and information science *professors* 5, *associate professors* 3, *assistant professors* 11, *part-time teachers* 2. *Total instructional faculty:* 19. *Degrees held by full-time faculty:* Doctorate 93%, master's 100%, baccalaureate 100%.

Enrollment: Total enrollment 267.

University of St. Francis

500 North Wilcox Street
Joliet, Illinois 60435

Tel: (800) 735-7500   **E-mail:** information@stfrancis.edu
Fax: (815) 740-5032   **Internet:** www.stfrancis.edu

Institution Description: The University of St. Francis, formerly the College of St. Francis, is a Catholic, Franciscan private institution. *Enrollment:* 2,110. *Degrees awarded:* Baccalaureate, master's.

Accreditation: *Regional:* NCA. *Professional:* physical therapy, physician assisting, surgeon assisting, recreation and leisure services, social work

History: Established in 1920 as the New College which became Assisi Junior College for women and offered first instruction 1925; added senior college and adopted present name 1930; awarded first degree (baccalaureate) 1933; incorporated 1962; became coeducational 1971.

Institutional Structure: *Governing board:* Board of Trustees. Extrainstitutional representation: 29 trustees; institutional representation: 4 alumni, president of college (ex officio). Academic affairs headed by vice president of academic affairs, deans of the colleges of arts and sciences, business education, nursing, allied health and professional studies. Business/finances directed by vice president for business affairs. Full-time instructional faculty 72.

Calendar: Semesters. Academic year Aug. to May.

Characteristics of Freshmen: 46% of applicants admitted. 17% of admitted students enrolled full-time.

100% (157 students) submitted ACT scores. *25th percentile*: ACT Composite 20, ACT English 19, ACT Math 19. *75th percentile*: ACT Composite 25, ACT English 25, ACT Math 26.

52% of entering freshmen expected to graduate within 5 years. 98% of freshmen from Illinois. Freshmen from 3 states.

Admission: Although each freshman applicant is considered individually, it is expected that each student demonstrate preparation for rigorous, selective college courses by successful academic performance. All candidates are evaluated on the strength of their transcripts, ACT or SAT scores, references, interviews, personal statement, extracurricular activities, and talent/ability. Rolling admissions plan. *Requirements:* Either graduation from accredited secondary school, or GED. For most students, lowest acceptable secondary school class standing 50th percentile, minimum ACT composite score of 20. *Entrance tests:* College Board SAT or ACT composite. *For transfer students:* 2.0 minimum GPA; from 4-year accredited institution maximum transfer credit limited only by resident requirement; from 2-year accredited institution 70 hours maximum transfer credit.

Degree Requirements: 128 credit hours; 2.0 GPA; 32 hours in residence; general education requirements. *Grading system:* A–F; withdraw (carries time limit).

Distinctive Educational Programs: Living-learning program for science students; internships in most majors; part-time evening baccalaureate programs; on- and off-campus programs: degree completion program in health arts (in 12 states), master's in health services administration (in 13 states), several baccalaureate and master's programs available entirely online. Study abroad with the American Institute for Foreign Study.

Degrees Conferred: 277 *baccalaureate* (B), 234 *master's* (M): biological/life sciences 12 (B); business/marketing 44 (B), 67 (M); communications/communication technologies 25 (B); computer and information sciences 23 (B); education 71 (B), 166 (M); English 4 (B); health professions and related sciences 40 (B), 1 (M); mathematics 5 (B); parks and recreation 14 (B); protective services/public administration 3 (B); psychology 10 (B); social sciences and history 14 (B); visual and performing arts 17 (B).

Fees and Other Expenses: *Full-time tuition per academic year 2004–05:* $18,310. *Required fees:* $360. *Room and board per academic year:* $6,180.

Financial Aid: Aid from institutionally generated funds is provided on the basis of academic merit, financial need, athletic ability. Institution has a Program Participation Agreement with the U.S. Department of Education for eligible students to receive Pell Grants and other federal aid.

Financial aid to full-time, first-time undergraduate students: need-based scholarships/grants totaling $5,376,884, self-help $2,646,710, parent loans $585,057, athletic awards $1,071,891; non-need-based scholarships/grants totaling $1,554,738, self-help 3,005,303, parent loans $1,053,149, athletic awards $995,350.

Departments and Teaching Staff: *Professors* 14, *associate professors* 14, *assistant professors* 40, *instructors* 4, *part-time faculty* 136. *Total instructional faculty:* 206 (full-time 72, part-time 136; women 115, men 93; members of minority groups 18). Total faculty with doctorate, first-professional, or other terminal degree: 76. Student-to-faculty ratio: 13:1. 2 faculty members awarded sabbaticals 2004–05.

Enrollment: Total enrollment 2,110. Full-time undergraduates 355 men / 721 women, part-time 41m / 132w; full-time graduates 49m / 111w, part-time 157m / 544w. *Transfer students:* in-state 172; from out-of-state 7.

Characteristics of Student Body: *Ethnic/racial makeup:* number of Black non-Hispanic: 100; American Indian or Alaska Native: 4; Asian or Pacific Islander: 32; Hispanic: 84; White non-Hispanic: 976; unknown: 37. *Age distribution:* under 18: 2; 18–19: 291; 20–21: 415' 22–24: 258; 25–29: 105; 30–34: 61; 35–39: 45; 40–49: 57; 50–64: 13; 65 and over: 1; unknown: 1.

International Students: 17 nonresident aliens enrolled fall 2004. No programs available to aid students whose native language is not English. No financial aid specifically designated for international students.

Student Life: On-campus housing available. *Surrounding community:* Joliet, population 85,000, is 40 miles from Chicago.

Library Collections: 106,346 volumes. Online and card catalogs. 776 current periodical subscriptions (1,308 microform). Access to online information retrieval systems. Students have access to the Internet at no charge.

Most important special collection in Franciscan (books on St. Francis of Assisi and the Franciscan Order); Mariology (books about the Blessed Virgin Mary); John L. Raymond Collection (books on many subjects—some rare, fine bindings, etc.).

Chief Executive Officer: Dr. Michael Vinciguerra, President.

Address undergraduate admission inquiries to Meghan Connolly, Director of Undergraduate Admissions; graduate inquiries to Mary Spreitzer, Director of Graduate Admissions.

University of St. Mary of the Lake - Mundelein Seminary

1000 East Maple Avenue
Mundelein, Illinois 60060

Tel: (847) 566-6401   **E-mail:** admsn@usml.edu
Fax: (847) 566-7330   **Internet:** www.usml.edu

Institution Description: The University of St. Mary of the Lake - Mundelein Seminary offers professional training and is operated by the Roman Catholic Church. *Enrollment:* 217. *Degrees offered:* First-professional, master's, doctorate.

Accreditation: *National:* ATS. *Professional:* theology

Calendar: Quarters. Academic year Sept. to May.

Degree Requirements: Completion of prescribed curriculum.

Degrees Conferred: 6 *master's:* theology; 1 *doctorate:* theology; 38 *first-professional:* master of divinity.

Fees and Other Expenses: *Full-time tuition per academic year 2004–05:* $14,765. *Room and board per academic year:* $6,310.

Financial Aid: Aid from institutionally generated funds is provided on the basis of financial need.

Departments and Teaching Staff: Biblical exegesis and proclamation *professors* 1, *associate professors* 0, *assistant professors* 2, *instructors* 1, *part-time teachers* 3; systematic theology 1, 1, 2, 0, 3; Christian life 1, 1, 1, 0, 3; Church history 0, 2, 0, 0, 3; worship 0, 0, 0, 1, 3; pastoral life 0, 0, 0, 0, 9. *Total instructional faculty:* 22. Degrees held by full-time instructional faculty: doctorate 80%, master's 95%, professional 100%.

Enrollment: Total enrollment 217.

International Students: 78 nonresident aliens enrolled fall 2004. 27 students from Europe, 8 Asia, 26 Central and South America, 16 Africa, 1 Canada. No programs available to aid students whose native language is not English, No financial aid specifically designated for international students.

Library Collections: 198,000 volumes. 2,000 microforms; 4,000 audiovisual materials; 420 current periodicals. 5 computer work stations.Students have access to online information retrieval services and the Internet.

Most important special holdings include Mundelein Collection; Carey Collection; Americana.

Chief Executive Officer: Rev. John F. Canary, Rector/President.

Address admission inquiries to Director of Admissions.

VanderCook College of Music

3140 South Federal Street
Chicago, Illinois 60616

Tel: (312) 225-6288   **E-mail:** admissions@vandercook.edu
Fax: (312) 225-5211   **Internet:** www.vandercook.edu

Institution Description: VanderCook College of Music is a private institution. *Enrollment:* 188. *Degrees awarded:* Baccalaureate, master's.

Accreditation: *Regional:* NCA. *Professional:* music

History: Established as the VanderCook Cornet School 1909; incorporated as the VanderCook School of Music 1928; adopted present name 1950.

Calendar: Semesters. Academic year late Aug. to late July. Summer graduate session of 1 term from early June to late July.

Characteristics of Freshmen: 89% of applicants admitted. 61% of admitted students enrolled full-time.

18% (5 students) submitted SAT scores; 82% (23 students) submitted ACT scores. *25th percentile:* SAT Verbal 440, SAT Math 490; ACT Composite 16, ACT English 15, ACT Math 15. *75th percentile:* SAT Verbal 540, SAT Math 540; ACT Composite 22, ACT English 25, ACT Math 20.

63% of freshmen from Illinois. Freshmen from 6 states.

Admission: *Requirements:* Either graduation from accredited secondary school or GED. Recommend 3 years English, 3 social studies, 2 science, 2 foreign language, 2 mathematics. Minimum recommended GPA 3.0. Audition, theory examination. *Entrance tests:* College Board SAT or ACT composite.

Degree Requirements: 140.5 semester hours; 2.0 GPA; senior comprehensives; general education requirements.

Fulfillment of some degree requirements in performance possible by passing institutional examinations. *Grading system:* A–F; withdraw (pass-fail appended); incomplete (carries time limit).

Distinctive Educational Programs: Teacher certification program.

Degrees Conferred: 15 *baccalaureate:* education; 75 *master's:* education.

Fees and Other Expenses: *Full-time tuition per academic year 2005–06:* $15,890 undergraduate; contact the college for current graduate tuition/fees. *Required fees:* $720. *Room and board per academic year:* $7,200.

Financial Aid: Aid from institutionally generated funds is provided on the basis of academic merit, financial need, talent. Institution has a Program Participation Agreement with the U.S. Department of Education for eligible students to receive Pell Grants and other federal aid.

Financial aid to full-time, first-time undergraduate students: need-based scholarships/grants totaling $365,489, self-help $435,154; non-need-based scholarships/grants totaling $225,926, self-help $156,539, parent loans $256,972.

Departments and Teaching Staff: *Total instructional faculty:* 36 (full-time 9, part-time 27; women 15, men 21; members of minority groups 2). Total faculty with doctorate, first-professional, or other terminal degree: 7. Student-to-faculty ratio: 6:1.

Enrollment: Total enrollment 188. Undergraduate full-time 46 men / 45 women, part-time 18m / 14w; graduate full-time 3m / 5w, part-time 25m / 32w. *Transfer students:* in-state 3; from out-of-state 4.

Characteristics of Student Body: *Ethnic/racial makeup:* number of Black non-Hispanic: 14; Asian or Pacific Islander: 2; Hispanic: 8; White non-Hispanic: 66; unknown: 31.

International Students: 2 nonresident aliens enrolled fall 2004. No programs available to aid students whose native language is not English. No financial aid specifically designated for international students.

Student Life: Cooperative housing facilities with Illinois Institute of Technology available. *Special services:* Medical services available in cooperation with Illinois Institute of Technology. *Surrounding community:* Chicago population over 3 million. Served by mass transit system, airport, and passenger rail service.

Library Collections: 13,885 volumes. 91 current periodical subscriptions; 3,016 recordings and tapes. 1,940 compact discs; 24 CD-ROMs. Students have access to online information retrieval services.

Most important holdings include Performance Library (15,000 selections for band, chorus, orchestra); H.A. VanderCook personal papers.

Buildings and Grounds: The college occupies a building on the 120-acre campus of the Illinois Institute of Technology.

Chief Executive Officer: Charles T. Menghini, President.

Address admission inquiries to Admissions Coordinator.

Western Illinois University

One University Circle
Macomb, Illinois 61455-1390
Tel: (309) 298-1414   **E-mail:** wiuadm@wiu.edu
Fax: (309) 298-3111   **Internet:** www.wiu.edu

Institution Description: Western Illinois University is a state institution. *Enrollment:* 13,558. *Degrees awarded:* Baccalaureate, master's, doctorate. Specialist certificates in education and school psychology also awarded.

Academic offerings subject to approval by statewide coordinating bodies. Budget subject to approval by state governing boards. Member of the consortium Quad Cities Graduate Study Center.

Accreditation: *Regional:* NCA. *Professional:* accounting, athletic training, audiology, business, counseling, English language education, music, recreation and leisure services, social work, speech-language pathology, teacher education

History: Established as Western Illinois State Normal School 1899; offered first instruction at postsecondary level 1902; awarded first degree (baccalaureate) 1918; changed name to Western Illinois State Teachers College 1921; changed name to Western Illinois State College 1947; adopted present name 1957; Rock Island Regional Undergraduate Center opened on the campus of Black Hawk College in Moline, Illinois 1988; IBM building in Moline purchased and WIU-Regional Center established 1995. *See* Victor Hicken, *The Purple and the Gold* (Macomb: Western Illinois University Foundation, 1970) for further information.

Institutional Structure: *Governing board:* Western Illinois Board of Trustees. Extrainstitutional representation: 8 members including 1 student. 9 voting. *Composition of institution:* Administrators 127 men / 130 women. Academic affairs headed by provost and academic vice president. Management/business/finances directed by vice president for administrative services. Full-time instructional faculty 615, Academic governance body, Faculty Senate, meets an average of 9 times per year. *Faculty representation:* Faculty served by collective bargaining agent University Professionals of Illinois, affiliated with AFT.

Calendar: Semesters. Academic year Aug. to May. Freshmen admitted Aug., Jan., June. Degrees conferred May, Aug., Dec. Formal commencements May, Dec. Summer session early June to late July.

Characteristics of Freshmen: 705 of applicants admitted. 38% of admitted4 applicants enrolled.

97% (2,025 students) submitted ACT scores. *25th percentile:* ACT Composite 19. *75th percentile:* ACT Composite 24.

52% of entering freshmen expected to graduate within 5 years. 96% of freshmen from Illinois. Freshmen from 14 states and 6 foreign countries.

Admission: Rolling admissions plan. For fall acceptance, apply as early as Sept. 1 of previous year, but not later than May 15. Early acceptance available. *Requirements:* Either graduation from a state recognized high school, or GED. Recommend 4 years English, 3 years social studies (emphasizing history and government), 3 years mathematics (with at least 1 course from advanced algebra, geometry, trigonometry, pre-calculus or calculus)m 3 years laboratory science, 2 years to be selected from art, film, foreign language, music, speech, theatre, journalism, religion, philosophy, and vocational education. *Entrance tests:* ACT score of 20, SAT 920 or with an ACT score of at least 18 (SAT 850) if they rank in the upper 50% of high school graduating class and have a 2.2 GPA. *For transfer students:* 2.0 minimum GPA; from 2-year and 4-year accredited institutions; maximum transfer credit limited only by residence requirement; correspondence/extension students 90 hours maximum transfer credit.

College credit and advanced placement for postsecondary-level work completed in secondary school, USAFI/DANTES, and for extrainstitutional learning on basis of ACE *2006 Guide to the Evaluation of Educational Experiences in the Armed Services*; portfolio assessment. Tutoring available. Developmental courses offered in summer session and regular academic year; nondegree credit given.

Degree Requirements: 120 semester hours; 2.0 GPA; 2 terms in residence; core curriculum. Fulfillment of some degree requirements and exemption from some beginning courses possible by passing College Board CLEP, AP, other standardized tests. *Grading system:* A–F; pass-fail; withdraw (carries time limit).

Distinctive Educational Programs: Flexible meeting places and schedules, including off-campus centers (at Rock Island, 76 miles away from main institution; Moline, 80 miles away; Springfield, 84 miles away), and evening classes. The Western Illinois University Regional Center located at Black Hawk College—Quad City campus, offers separate undergraduate degrees. External degrees through the Board of Governors program with Chicago State University, Northeastern Illinois University, Governors State University, and Eastern Illinois University. Special facilities for using telecommunications in the classroom. Interdisciplinary programs in Afro-American studies, Latin American studies, Middle Eastern studies, Russian and East European studies, urban and community studies. Facilities and programs for independent research, including honors programs, individual majors, tutorials. Study abroad in England. *Other distinctive programs:* Alice B. Kibbe Life Science Station on Mississippi River; Kaskaskia-interdisciplinary undergraduate program; regional telecommunications consortium system broadcasting educational programming. Office of Aquatic Studies at the Shedd Aquarium in Chicago that will enable faculty and students to expand their research activities into new areas; delivery of classes to K-12 students and in-service programming for teachers using satellite-delivered interactive programs.

ROTC: Army.

Degrees Conferred: 2,370 *baccalaureate* (B), 692 *master's* (M): agriculture 7 (B); area and ethnic studies 6 (B); biological/life sciences 62 (B), 15 (M); business/marketing 308 (B), 95 (M); communications/communication technologies 218 (B), 8 (M); computer and information sciences 50 (B), 27 (M); education 306 (B), 347 (M); engineering and engineering technologies 62 (B), 13 (M); English 60 (B), 18 (M); foreign languages and literature 14 (B); health professions and related sciences 36 (B), 19 (M); home economics and vocational home economics 46 (B); interdisciplinary studies 3 (B); liberal arts/general studies 306 (B); mathematics 13 (B), 8 (M); parks and recreation 107 (B), 14 (M); philosophy/religion/theology 5 (B); physical sciences 17 (B), 12 (M); protective services/public administration 351 (B), 27 (M); psychology 101 (B), 21 (M); social sciences and history 147 (B), 54 (M); visual and performing arts 76 (B), 11 (M).

Fees and Other Expenses: *Full-time tuition per academic year 2005–06:* undergraduate resident $4,968, out-of-state $7,452; graduate resident $4,382, out-of-state $8,765. *Required fees:* $1,443. *Room and board per academic year:* $6,113.

Financial Aid: Aid from institutionally generated funds is provided on the basis of academic merit, financial need, athletic ability, other criteria. Institution has a Program Participation Agreement with the U.S. Department of Education for eligible students to receive Pell Grants and other federal aid.

Financial aid to full-time, first-time undergraduate students: need-based scholarships/grants totaling $22,568,718, self-help $20,171,190, parent loans $3,120,765, tuition waivers $20,797, athletic awards $627,995; non-need-based scholarships/grants totaling $3,085,714, self-help $11,221,342, parent loans $1,569,410, tuition waivers $50,192, athletic awards $976,420.

Departments and Teaching Staff: *Professors* 189, *associate professors* 153, *assistant professors* 170, *instructors* 96, *part-time faculty* 89. *Total instructional*

faculty: 704 (full-time 615, part-time 89; women 277, men 427; members of minority groups 71). Total faculty with doctorate, first-professional, or other terminal degree: 451. Student-to-faculty ratio: 17:1. 25 faculty members awarded sabbaticals 2004–o5.

Enrollment: Total enrollment 13,558. Undergraduate full-time 5,251 men / 4,879 women, part-time 557m / 628w; graduate full-time 404m / 398w, part-time 462m / 984w. *Transfer students:* in-state 1,032; from out-of-state 293.

Characteristics of Student Body: *Ethnic and racial makeup:* number of Black non-Hispanic: 699; American Indian or Alaska Native: 21; Asian or Pacific Islander: 139; Hispanic: 361; White non-Hispanic: 8,533; unknown: 445. *Age distribution:* number under 18: 80; 18–19: 3,681; 20–21: 399; 22–24: 1,992; 25–29: 628; 30–34: 277; 35–39: 198; 40–49: 348; 50–64: 23; 65 and over: 4.

International Students: 292 nonresident aliens enrolled fall 2004. 31 students from Europe, 209 Asia, 18 Central and South America, 10 Africa, 7 Canada. Programs available to aid students whose native language is not English: English as a Second Language Program. Some financial aid specifically designated for international students.

Student Life: On-campus residence halls, fraternities, and sororities house 48% of student body. Accommodations for men only constitute 28% of such space, for women only 25%, for both sexes 53%. 18% of men join and 7% live in fraternities; 13% of women join and 3% live in sororities. 3% of student body live in married and graduate student apartments. 52% of students live on campus. *Intercollegiate athletics:* men only: baseball, basketball, football, golf, diving, soccer, swimming, tennis, track; women only: basketball, cross-country, diving, golf, softball, swimming, tennis, track, volleyball. *Special regulations:* Cars permitted without restrictions. *Special services:* Learning Resources Center, medical services; services for the disabled, Gwendolyn Brooks Cultural Center, Casa Latina, Supportive Services Program Student Advocate. *Student publications, radio, television:* *Courier*, a newspaper published 3 times per week. Radio stations WIUM-FM and WIUS broadcast 168 and 112 hours per week, respectively. Television station WMAC broadcasts ½ to 1 hour per week. *Surrounding community:* Macomb population 20,000. St. Louis (MO), 150 miles from campus, is nearest metropolitan area. Served by passenger rail and bus service 1 mile from campus.

Publications: *Mississippi Valley Review; Newsletter of the Center for Icarian Studies; Journal of Behavioral Economics; The Journal of Developing Areas; State of Illinois Industrial Education Association Journal; Journal of Business Leadership; Journal of Contemporary Business Issues; WIU Journal of Business; The Journal of Socio-Economics.*

Library Collections: 718,241 volumes including bound books, serial backfiles, electronic documents, and government documents not in separate collections. Online and card catalogs. Current serial subscriptions: 3,445 paper. 200 computer work stations. Students have access to the Internet at no charge. Total budget for books, periodicals, audiovisual materials, microforms 2004–05: $1,571,200.

Most important special holdings include Icarian Studies Collection; Center for Regional Authors; Burl Ives Collection; Nauvoo and Mormon Collection.

Buildings and Grounds: Campus area 1,050 acres. *New buildings:* Residence hall completed 2004.

Chief Executive Officer: Dr. Al Goldfarb, President.

Address admission inquiries to David Garcia, Director of Admissions.

Wheaton College

501 College Avenue
Wheaton, Illinois 60187
Tel: (630) 752-5005   **E-mail:** admissions@wheaton.edu
Fax: (630) 752-5285   **Internet:** www.wheaton.edu

Institution Description: Wheaton College is a private, nondenominational college committed to Christian liberal arts education. *Enrollment:* 2,892. *Degrees awarded:* Baccalaureate, master's, doctorate.

Member of Christian College Consortium; Council for Christian Colleges and Universities.

Accreditation: *Regional:* NCA. *Professional:* clinical psychology, music, teacher education

History: Established, offered first instruction at postsecondary level, and awarded first degree (baccalaureate) 1860; chartered and incorporated 1861.

Institutional Structure: *Governing board:* The Trustees of Wheaton College. Representation: 20 trustees. All voting. *Composition of institution:* Administrators 33 men / 19 women. Chief academic officer is Provost. Management/business/finances directed by vice president for finance. Full-time instructional faculty 188. Academic governance body, Faculty of Wheaton College.

Calendar: Semesters. Academic year Aug. to May. Summer sessions begin May and June.

Characteristics of Freshmen: 54% of applicants accepted. 55% of accepted applicants enrolled.

73% (434 students) submitted SAT scores; 58% (348 students) submitted ACT scores. *25th percentile:* SAT Verbal 620, SAT Math 610; ACT Composite 26. *75th percentile:* SAT Verbal 720, SAT Math 700; ACT Composite 31.

82% of entering freshmen expected to graduate within 5 years. 19% of freshmen from Illinois. Freshmen from 45 states and 9 foreign countries.

Admission: For fall admission, apply as early as spring of previous year, but not later than Jan. 15 of year of enrollment. Students are notified of acceptance April 1. Early decision available. *Requirements:* Graduation from approved secondary school with 18 units, including 16 in English, foreign language, mathematics, science, social studies. Additional requirements for music majors. Lowest acceptable secondary school class standing 50th percentile. The GED and International Baccalaureate also acceptable for admission. *Entrance tests:* College Board SAT or ACT composite. *For transfer students:* 3.0 GPA.

College credit and advanced placement for postsecondary-level work completed in secondary school.

Degree Requirements: *For all undergraduate degrees:* 124 semester hours; 2.0 GPA; 48 semester hours must be completed at Wheaton, including 12 of last 20 hours; chapel attendance 3 days per week; 3 semester hours physical education; distribution requirements; demonstrated competency in foreign language, mathematics, speech, writing; comprehensives in individual fields of study.

Fulfillment of some degree requirements and exemption from some beginning courses possible by passing departmental examinations, College Board SAT subject examinations, APP. *Grading system:* A–F; pass-fail; withdraw; incomplete.

Distinctive Educational Programs: *For undergraduates:* Institutionally sponsored study abroad in Asia, England, France, Germany, Mexico, Russia. Study abroad also by individual arrangement. Human Needs and Global Resources program, including internships. Moscow State University student exchange program. Internships available in all departments. Cooperative programs in social science at American University (DC). Programs through the consortium, including American Studies Program (DC) and Latin American studies. Summer programs in botany, geology, and zoology at Wheaton College Science Station (SD) and in leadership training at Honey Rock Camp (WI). *Other distinctive programs:* Wilderness and stress education through High Road Program in northern Wisconsin.

ROTC: Army offered as a supplement to the college curriculum and is integrated with the goals of the college.

Degrees Conferred: 604 *baccalaureate*; 201 *master's*; 17 *doctorate*. Bachelor's degrees awarded in top five disciplines: social sciences 96; business, management, marketing, and related support services 58; visual and performing arts 56; English language and literature/letters 51; communication, journalism, and related programs 46.

Fees and Other Expenses: *Full-time tuition per academic year 2004–05:* $21,100. *Room and board per academic year:* $6,660. *Books and supplies:* $714.

Financial Aid: Aid from institutionally generated funds is provided on the basis of academic merit, financial need. Institution has a Program Participation Agreement with the U.S. Department of Education for eligible students to receive Pell Grants and other federal aid.

Financial aid to full-time, first-time undergraduate students: need-based scholarships/grants totaling $14,048,315, self-help $6,893,624, parent loans $1,762,224; non-need-based scholarships/grants totaling $1,351,656, self-help $882,391, parent loans $1,360,322.

Departments and Teaching Staff: *Total instructional faculty:* 272 (full-time 188, part-time 84; women 91, men 181; members of minority groups 23). Total faculty with doctorate, first-professional, or other terminal degree: 204. Student-to-faculty ratio: 13:1.

Enrollment: Total enrollment 2,892. Undergraduate full-time 1,259 men / 12,429; part-time 84m / 76w; graduate full-time 123m / 147w, part-time 106m / 82w.

Characteristics of Student Body: *Ethnic and racial makeup:* number of Black non-Hispanic: 53; American Indian or Alaska Native: 9; Asian or Pacific Islander: 181; Hispanic: 68; White non-Hispanic: 2,066; unknown: 28. *Age distribution:* 17–21: 80%; 22–24: 7%; 25–29: 5%; 30–34: 2%; 35–339: 2%; 40–49: 2%.

International Students: 34 undergraduate nonresident aliens enrolled fall 2004. Students from Europe, Asia, Central and South America, Africa, Canada. Programs available to aid students whose native language is not English: Social, cultural. No financial aid specifically designated for international graduate students.

Student Life: 90% of students live on-campus. *Intercollegiate athletics:* men only: baseball, basketball, cross-country, football, golf, soccer, swimming, tennis, track, wrestling; women only: basketball, cross-country, soccer, softball, swimming, tennis, track, volleyball. *Special regulations:* Cars permitted for all but freshmen. Freshmen curfews begin midnight Sun.–Thurs., 2am Fri. and Sat.

Special services: Learning Resources Center, medical services. *Student publications, radio: Kodon*, a quarterly literary magazine; *Record*, a weekly newspaper; *Tower*, a yearbook. Radio station WETN-FM and TV Cable Channel WETN. *Surrounding community:* Wheaton, population 52,000, is located in Chicago metropolitan area. Served by airport 25 miles from campus; passenger rail service 1 mile from campus.

Library Collections: 490,306 volumes. 24,697 government documents; 215,280 microforms; 26,475 audiovisual materials; 3,216 current periodicals. 62 computer work stations. Students have access to the Internet at no charge.

Most important holdings include Wade Collection, consisting of first and rare editions of books by C.S. Lewis, J.R.R. Tolkien, Dorothy L. Sayers, Charles Williams and others; Akin Collection, more than 4,000 rare and unusual books on English literature and colonial history; books, manuscripts, personal papers, art work of novelist and children's writer Madeleine l'Engle.

Buildings and Grounds: Campus area 80 acres.

Chief Executive Officer: Dr. Duane Litfin, President.

Undergraduates address admission inquiries to Shawn P. Leftwich, Director of Admissions; graduate inquiries to Julie A. Huebner, Director of Graduate Admissions.

Indiana

Anderson University

1100 East Fifth Street
Anderson, Indiana 46012-3495
Tel: (765) 649-9071   **E-mail:** info@anderson.edu
Fax: (765) 641-3851   **Internet:** www.anderson.edu

Institution Description: Anderson University is a private institution affiliated with the Church of God. *Enrollment:* 2,677. *Degrees awarded:* Associate, baccalaureate, first-professional (master of divinity, master of religious education), master's, doctorate.

Accreditation: *Regional:* NCA. *Professional:* athletic training, business, music, nursing, social work, teacher education

History: Established as Anderson Bible Training School 1917; chartered as Anderson Bible School and Seminary 1925; offered first instruction at postsecondary level and changed name to Anderson College and Theological Seminary 1929; awarded first degree (baccalaureate) 1932; became Anderson College 1964; became Anderson University 1987.

Institutional Structure: *Governing board:* Board of Trustees. Representation: 32 trustees, including president of the university and 1 trustee-emeritus. *Composition of institution:* Academic affairs headed by vice president of academic affairs and dean. Academic affairs headed by Dean of the School of Theology. Management/business/finances directed by vice president for finance and treasurer. Vice president for student life and human resources. Vice president for business and administrative services. Vice president of enrollment management and information systems. Academic programs based in 18 academic departments, which in turn are grouped into three colleges: College of the Arts, College of Professional Studies, College of Science and Humanities. Each school has its own dean, who is its chief operational officer in regard to all programs and personnel of that school.

Calendar: Semesters. Academic year Sept. to May. Summer session from May to Aug.

Characteristics of Freshmen: 2,060 applicants (610 men, 1,250 women). 70.9% of applicants admitted. 35.3% of admitted students enrolled full-time.

73% (422 students) submitted SAT scores; 52% (300 students) submitted ACT scores. *25th percentile:* SAT I Verbal 470, SAT I Math 470; ACT Composite 21, ACT English 20, ACT Math 19. *75th percentile:* SAT I Verbal 590, SAT I Math 580; ACT Composite 26, ACT English 27, ACT Math 25.

45% of entering freshmen expected to graduate within 5 years. 61% of freshmen from Indiana. Freshmen from 29 states and 6 foreign countries.

Admission: Rolling admissions plan. *Requirements:* Either graduation from accredited secondary school or GED. *Entrance tests:* College Board SAT or ACT composite. For foreign students SAT or ACT composite and TOEFL or other demonstration of English proficiency. *For transfer students:* From 4- and 2-year accredited institutions maximum transfer credit limited only by residence requirement; correspondence students 12 semester hours.

College credit and advanced placement for postsecondary-level work completed in secondary school.

Degree Requirements: *For all associate degrees:* 62–64 credit hours. *For all baccalaureate degrees:* 124 credit hours. *For all undergraduate degrees:* 2.0 GPA; last 24 hours in residence; biweekly chapel attendance; liberal arts requirements.

Fulfillment of some degree requirements and exemption from some beginning courses possible by passing departmental examinations, College Board CLEP, AP. *Grading system:* A–F; satisfactory-unsatisfactory; credit-noncredit; withdraw (carries time limit); incomplete (carries time limit).

Distinctive Educational Programs: Interdepartmental programs in family science, graphic design, mass communication, mathematics/economics, and social work. Professional programs in dentistry, health science, law, medicine, seminary; in engineering leading to baccalaureate awarded by Purdue University, Ohio State University, University of Dayton, University of Evansville, Tri-State University, University of Michigan, University of Illinois, University of Missouri-Rolla. Professional programs in criminal justice, early childhood education, secretarial studies, nursing (4-year), and teacher education. Facilities and programs for independent research, including honors programs, individual majors, tutorials, independent study. Individually arranged study abroad. Center for Public Service provides students with practical research experience. Cooperative associate programs in computer programming technology, computer manufacturing technology, and electrical engineering technology with Purdue University.

Degrees Conferred: 2 *associate;* 394 *baccalaureate;* 102 *master's;* 1 *doctorate;* 9 *first-professional.* Bachelor's degrees awarded in top five disciplines: business, management, marketing, and related support services sciences 74; education 72; health professions and related clinical sciences 42; protective services/public administration 36; theology and ministerial studies 24.

Fees and Other Expenses: *Full-time tuition per academic year 2004–05:* undergraduate $17,990, graduate tuition varies by program. *Books and supplies:* $750. *Room and board per academic year:* $5,820.

Financial Aid: Aid from institutionally generated funds is provided on the basis of academic merit, financial need. Institution has a Program Participation Agreement with the U.S. Department of Education for eligible students to receive Pell Grants and other federal aid.

Financial aid to full-time, first-time undergraduate students: 30% received federal grants averaging $3,157; 35% state/local grants averaging $4,480; 96% institutional grants averaging $7,304; 88% loans averaging $4,613.

Departments and Teaching Staff: Art and design *professors* 4, *associate professors* 1, *assistant professors* 0, *instructors* 1, *part-time teachers* 10; business/economics 6, 7, 2, 0, 3; biology 4, 0, 0, 0, 1; chemistry & physics 3, 0, 1, 0, 1; communication 2, 2, 1, 0, 8; computer science 3, 0, 1, 0, 1; education 5, 4, 1, 0, 5; English 3, 1, 0, 6, 2; foreign language 0, 3, 1, 4, 0; history/political science 1, 1, 1, 1, 4; mathematics 3, 1, 0, 0, 0; music 4, 4, 3, 2, 14; nursing 2, 0, 5, 1, 1; physical education 3, 3, 3, 1, 7; psychology 4, 0, 0, 0, 1; religious studies 6, 2, 1, 0, 5; sociology/social work 2, 3, 2, 0, 7; theology 5, 3, 0, 0, 3; general education/adult education 0, 0, 0, 0, 10.

Total instructional faculty: 214. Student-to-faculty ratio: 14:1. Degrees held by full-time faculty: doctorate 61%, master's 39%.

Enrollment: Total enrollment 2,677. Undergraduate full-time 2,270 (41.5% men, 58.5% women).

Characteristics of Student Body: *Ethnic and racial makeup:* Black non-Hispanic: 7%; American Indian or Alaska Native: .2%; Asian or Pacific Islander: 1.9%; Hispanic: 1.1%; White non-Hispanic: 88.1%; unknown: 1.6%. *Age distribution:* 17–21: 68%; 22–24: 11%; 25–29: 6%; 30–34: 5%; 35–39: 3%; 40–49: 5%; 50–59: 2%.

International Students: 25 undergraduate nonresident aliens enrolled fall 2004. Students from Europe, Asia, Central and South America, Africa, Canada. No programs available to aid students whose native language is not English. No financial aid specifically designated for international students.

Student Life: On-campus residence halls and apartments available for single and married students. *Special regulations:* Registered cars permitted without restrictions. *Special services:* Learning Resources Center, medical services. *Student publications, radio:* Newspaper, yearbook. Radio station WQME. *Surrounding community:* Anderson population 65,000. Indianapolis is nearest metropolitan area. Served by mass transit bus system; airport 25 miles from campus.

Publications: *Signatures,* international alumni magazine published quarterly.

Library Collections: 265,000 volumes including bound books, serial backfiles, electronic documents, and government documents not in separate collections. Online catalog. Current serial subscriptions: 950 paper. 90,000 microforms. 2,765 recordings; 250 compact discs; 12,000 audiovisual materials. Computer work stations available. Students have access to the Internet at no charge.

Most important holdings include Charles E. Wilson (former Secretary of Defense) personal papers; Gaither Hymnal Collection; Warner Collection of Church of God authors and related topics.

Buildings and Grounds: Campus area 100 acres.

Chief Executive Officer: Dr. James L. Edwards, President.

Address admission inquiries Dr. Michael E. Collette, Director of Enrollment Management.

Associated Mennonite Biblical Seminary

3003 Benham Avenue
Elkart, Indiana 46517
Tel: (219) 295-3726   **E-mail:** admissions@ambs.edu
Fax: (219) 295-0092   **Internet:** www.ambs.edu

Institution Description: Associated Mennonite Biblical Seminary was created by merger of Goshen Biblical Seminary and Mennonite Biblical Seminary. The seminary is a graduate ministerial and church leadership training school of the Mennonite Church. *Enrollment:* 168. *Degrees awarded:* First-professional, master's.

Accreditation: *Regional:* NCA. *Professional:* theology

History: Established as Bible School of Elkhart Institute 1895; moved campus to Goshen, reorganized as Bible School of Goshen College, and offered first instruction at postsecondary level 1903; adopted present name 1946; entered into cooperative relationship with Mennonite Biblical Seminary 1958; moved campus back to Elkhart 1969; incorporated under its current name in 1993.

Institutional Structure: *Governing Board:* AMBS Board of Overseers.

Calendar: Semesters. January interterm. Academic year Sept. to May.

Admission: *Requirements:* Graduation from a liberal arts course of an accredited college; a statement in regard to the candidate's Christian faith convictions.

Degree Requirements: Master of Divinity 90 semester hours; Master of Arts 60 semester hours.

Distinctive Educational Programs: Master of Arts in Peace Studies; Conference-based Theological Education Program; Black and Hispanic Leadership Training; Mission Training Center.

Degrees Conferred: 12 *master's:* theology; 23 *first-professional:* master of divinity.

Fees and Other Expenses: *Full-time tuition per academic year 2004–05:* $9,980. *Other fees:* $28.

Financial Aid: Aid from institutionally generated funds is provided on the basis of financial need. Institution has a Program Participation Agreement with the U.S. Department of Education for eligible students to receive Pell Grants and other federal aid.

Departments and Teaching Staff: *Total instructional faculty:* 16.

Enrollment: Total enrollment 168.

Characteristics of Student Body: *Ethnic/racial makeup:* Black non-Hispanic: .6%; Asian or Pacific Islander: 1.2%; American Indian or Alaska Native: .6%; White non-Hispanic: 74.4%.

International Students: 39 nonresident aliens enrolled fall 2004. Students from Europe, Asia, Central and South America, Africa, Canada. No programs available to assist students whose native language is not English. No financial aid specifically designated for international students.

Student Life: Both on- and off-campus housing is available for single and married students. *Surrounding community:* Elkart is located 5 miles south of the Michigan-Indiana border, 20 miles from the city of South Bend and the University of Notre Dame.

Library Collections: 110,000 volumes. 1,500 microforms; 1,500 audiovisual materials; 530 current periodical subscriptions. Computer work stations available. Access to online information retrieval systems. Students have access to the Internet at no charge.

Most important special collections include the Studer Bible Collection; Anabaptist-Mennonite Studies; Biblical Studies.

Buildings and Grounds: Campus area 32 acres.

Chief Executive Officer: Dr. J. Nelson Kraybill, President.

Address admission inquiries to Randall C. Miller, Director of Admissions.

Ball State University

2000 University Avenue
Muncie, Indiana 47306
Tel: (765) 289-1241   **E-mail:** askus@wp.bsu.edu
Fax: (765) 285-1632   **Internet:** www.bsu.edu

Institution Description: Ball State University is a state institution. *Enrollment:* 9,324 men / 11,220 women. *Degrees awarded:* Associate, baccalaureate, master's, doctorate.

Academic offerings subject to approval by statewide coordinating bodies. Budget subject to approval by state governing boards.

Accreditation: *Regional:* NCA. *Professional:* accounting, architecture, art, athletic training, audiology, business, counseling, counseling psychology, chemistry, dietetics, engineering technology, journalism, landscape architecture,

music, nuclear medicine technology, nursing, planning, psychology internship, radiation therapy, radiography, respiratory therapy, school psychology, social work, speech-language pathology, teacher education, theatre

History: Established as Indiana State Normal School, Eastern Division, chartered, and offered first instruction at postsecondary level 1918; awarded first degree (baccalaureate) 1919; became known as Ball State Teachers College 1929; adopted present name 1965.

Institutional Structure: *Governing board:* Ball State University Board of Trustees. Extrainstitutional representation: 9 trustees; institutional representation: 1 student. All voting. *Composition of institution:* Administrators 20. Academic affairs headed by provost. Management/business/finances directed by vice president for business affairs. Full-time instructional faculty 903.

Calendar: Semesters academic terms. Academic year Aug. to May. Summer terms available. Formal commencements May, Dec. July.

Characteristics of Freshmen: 76% of applicants admitted. 35% of applicants admitted and enrolled.

83% (2,801 students) submitted SAT scores; 16% (545 students) submitted ACT scores. *25th percentile:* SAT Verbal 470, SAT Math 470; ACT Composite 19, ACT English 19, ACT Math 19. *75th percentile:* SAT Verbal 570, SAT I Math 580; ACT Composite 24, ACT English 24, ACT Math 25.

44% of entering freshmen expected to graduate within 5 years. 91% of freshmen from Indiana. Freshmen from 34 states and 88 foreign countries.

Admission: Submit completed application before Mar. 1 for fall semester, Apr. 1 for summer semester, and before Dec. 1 for spring semester for priority consideration. *Requirements:* Graduation from accredited secondary school or its equivalent. Recommend college preparatory curriculum. *Entrance tests:* College Board SAT or ACT composite. For foreign students TOEFL.

College credit and advanced placement for postsecondary-level work completed in secondary school and for extrainstitutional learning on basis of ACE *2006 Guide to the Evaluation of Educational Experiences in the Armed Services,* portfolio and faculty assessments, personal interviews. Tutoring available. Developmental courses offered in summer session and regular academic year; credit given.

Degree Requirements: *For all associate degrees:* 63 semester hours. *For all baccalaureate degrees:* 126 semester hours. *For all undergraduate degrees:* 2.0 GPA; 3 terms in residence; core curriculum. Fulfillment of some degree requirements possible by passing departmental examinations, College Board CLEP, AP. *Grading system:* A–F with +/- grading; pass/fail; withdraw (carries time limit).

Distinctive Educational Programs: *For undergraduates:* Interdepartmental programs, including Afro-American studies, American studies, ancient studies, Asian studies, energy, gerontology, humanities, Latin-American studies, legal administration, mathematical economics, medieval and renaissance studies, Native American studies, Peace Studies and Conflict Resolution, Sports Studies, women and gender studies. Academic opportunity and honors programs. Preprofessional programs in dentistry, medicine, pharmacy, engineering, law. Institutionally-sponsored study abroad in England, Australia, and other locations. *For graduate students:* Interdepartmental programs arranged on individual basis. *Available to all students:* Work-experience programs, including field experience, internships. Special facilities for using telecommunications in the classroom. Facilities and programs for independent research. *Other distinctive programs:* Credit-granting continuing education.

ROTC: Army. 17 commissions awarded 2004.

Degrees Conferred: 300 *associate;* 3,172 *baccalaureate* (B), 941 *master's* (M), 67 *doctorate* (D): architecture 167 (B), 29 (M); biological/life sciences 134 (B), 22 (M); business/marketing 429 (B), 119 (M); communications/communication technologies 360 (B), 94 (M); computer and information sciences 23 (B), 32 (M); education 349 (B), 295 (M), 42 (D); engineering and engineering technologies 71 (B), 11 (M); English 81 (B), 18 (M), 5 (D); foreign languages and literature 54 (B); health professions and related sciences 237 (B), 145 (M), 6 (D); home economics and vocational home economics 109 (B), 18 (M); studies 51 (B), 21 (M); mathematics 22 (B), 15 (M); natural resources/environmental science 11 (B), 8 (M); philosophy/religion/theology 14 (B); physical sciences 38 (B), 11 (M); protective services/public administration 189 (B); psychology 68 (B), 65 (M), 7 (D); social sciences and history 151 (B), 19 (M); visual and performing arts 173 (B), 25 (M), 6 (D); other 581 (B), 4 (M), 6 (D).

Fees and Other Expenses: *Full-time tuition per academic year 2004–05:* undergraduate resident $5,752, out-of-state $14,928; graduate varies by credit hour. *Room and board per academic year:* $6,328.

Financial Aid: Institution has a direct lending program. Aid from institutionally generated funds is provided on the basis of academic merit, financial need, athletic ability, other criteria. Institution has a Program Participation Agreement with the U.S. Department of Education for eligible students to receive Pell Grants and other federal aid.

Financial aid to full-time, first-time undergraduate students: need-based scholarships/grants totaling $28,344,060, self-help $30,850,252; non-need-based scholarships/grants totaling $18,025,067, self-help $32,668,552, parent loans $74,345,117, tuition waivers $7,892,887, athletic awards $3,873,291.

Graduate aid: 83 federal and state-funded fellowships and grants totaling $225,731; 1,124 federal and state-funded loans totaling $12,429,951; 293 other fellowships and grants totaling $761,232; teaching and research assistantships totaling $6,275,518.

Departments and Teaching Staff: *Total instructional faculty:* 1,169 (903 full-time, 266 part-time; 503 women, 666 men; 93 members of minority groups). Total faculty with doctorate, first-professional, or other terminal degree: 748. Student-to-faculty ratio: 16:1. *Faculty development:* $9,996,608 in grants for research. 37 faculty members awarded sabbaticals 2004–05.

Enrollment: Total enrollment 20,544. Undergraduate full-time 7,642 men / 8,554 women, part-time 535m / 804w; graduate full-time 451m / 626w, part-time 696m / 1,236w. *Transfer students:* in-state 574; from out-of-state 89.

Characteristics of Student Body: *Ethnic and racial makeup:* Black non-Hispanic: 1,209; American Indian or Alaska Native: 51; Asian or Pacific Islander: 121; Hispanic: 237; White non-Hispanic: 15,323; unknown: 391. *Age distribution:* under 18: 65; 18–22: 13,984; 23–25: 1,175; 25 and over: 907.

International Students: Programs available to aid students whose native language is not English: English as Second Language Program. Scholarships available annually for both qualifying undergraduate and graduate international students.

Student Life: On-campus residence halls house 34% of student body. 34% of students live on campus. *Intercollegiate athletics:* men only: baseball, cross-country, football, golf, swimming, tennis, track and field, volleyball; women only: basketball, cross-country, field hockey, gymnastics, softball, swimming and diving, tennis, track and field (indoor and outdoor), volleyball. *Special regulations:* Cars permitted for all students. *Special services:* Career services, counseling and psychological services, disabled student development, early outreach programs, health services, multicultural affairs, bus service, learning center, campus child care center. *Student publications, radio, television:* The Ball State News, a daily newspaper; *Orient,* a yearbook. Radio station WBST; TV station WIPB. *Surrounding community:* Muncie population 80,000. Indianapolis, 60 miles from campus, is nearest metropolitan area. Served by mass transit bus system; airport and passenger rail service, both 3 miles from campus.

Library Collections: 1.5 million volumes including bound books, serial backfiles, electronic documents, and government documents not in separate collections. Online catalog. Current serial subscriptions: 3,661 paper, 604 electronic. 2,335 recordings; 9,954 compact discs; 1,530 CD-ROMs. 125 computer work stations. Students have access to the Internet at no charge.

Most important holdings include The John Steinbeck Collection in honor of Elizabeth Otis (more than 800 cataloged works by and about Steinbeck and honoring his friend and literary agent, including first editions, autographed copies, original manuscripts and letters, galley proofs, posters of various movie adaptations of his works); Sir Norman Angell Collection (2,300 books, periodicals, and personal papers); collections on American poetry and Middletown Studies; Middletown Studies Collection.

Buildings and Grounds: Campus area 31 acres. *New buildings:* Art and Journalism Building; Music Instruction Building.

Chief Executive Officer: Dr. JoAnn M. Gora, President.

Address admission inquiries to Dr. Larry Waters, Dean of Admissions and Enrollment Services.

Bethany Theological Seminary

615 National Road West
Richmond, Indiana 47374-4019
Tel: (765) 983-1500   **E-mail:** admissions@brethren.org/bethany
Fax: (765) 983-1840   **Internet:** www.brethren.org/bethany

Institution Description: Bethany Theological Seminary is a private institution offering graduate study only. *Enrollment:* 61. *Degrees offered:* Master's, first-professional.

Accreditation: *Regional:* NCA. *Professional:* Theology.

Calendar: Semesters. Academic year Sept. to May.

Admission: *Requirements:* Baccalaureate degree from an accredited institution; 2.75 GPA.

Degree Requirements: *For all degrees:* Completion of prescribed curriculum.

Degrees Conferred: 8 *master's:* master of divinity; 11 *first-professional:* theology.

Fees and Other Expenses: *Full-time tuition per academic year:* Contact the seminary for current tuition/fees.

Financial Aid: Aid from institutionally generated funds is provided on the basis of academic merit, financial need, other criteria. Institution has a Program Participation Agreement with the U.S. Department of Education for eligible students to receive Pell Grants and other federal aid.

Departments and Teaching Staff: *Total instructional faculty:* 18. Degrees held by full-time faculty: doctorate 85%, master's 100%. 85% hold terminal degrees. *Faculty development:* 1 faculty member awarded a sabbatical each year.

Enrollment: Total enrollment 61. First-professional full-time 10 men / 14 women, part-time 12m / 7w; graduate full-time 4m / 2w, part-time 2m / 1w.

Characteristics of Student Body: *Ethnic/racial makeup:* White non-Hispanic: 61. *Age distribution:* 22–24: 16%; 25–29: 20%; 30–34: 11%; 35–39: 13%; 40–49: 20%; 50–59: 16%; 60 and over: 3%.

International Students: 2 nonresident aliens from Africa enrolled fall 2004. Programs available to aid students whose native language is not English: Social, cultural, financial.

Library Collections: 37,000 volumes. 152,000 microforms. Online and card catalogs. Students have access to the Internet at no charge.

Chief Executive Officer: Eugene F. Roop, President.

Address admission inquiries Director of Admissions.

Bethel College

1001 West McKinley Avenue
Mishawaka, Indiana 46545
Tel: (574) 259-8511
Fax: (574) 257-3326

Institution Description: Bethel College is a private college affiliated with the Missionary Church. *Enrollment:* 1,988. *Degrees awarded:* Associate, baccalaureate, master's.

Member of Northern Indiana Consortium for Education.

Accreditation: *Regional:* NCA. *Professional:* nursing, teacher education

History: Established and offered first instruction at postsecondary level 1947; awarded first degree (baccalaureate) 1948.

Institutional Structure: *Governing board:* Board of Directors. Representation: 22 directors, including president of the college, 6 alumni. 2 ex officio. 22 voting. *Composition of institution:* Administrators 6 men. Academic affairs headed by dean of faculty. Management/business/finances directed by director of business services. Full-time instructional faculty 79. Academic governance body, the faculty, meets an average of 18 times per year.

Calendar: Semesters. Academic year Aug. to May. Freshmen admitted Aug., Jan. Degrees conferred May, Aug., Dec. Formal commencement May. Summer session of 1 term from mid-May to mid-Aug.

Characteristics of Freshmen: 1,215 applicants (456 men, 759 women). 55.9% of applicants admitted. 68.3% of admitted students enrolled full-time.

47% (261 students) submitted SAT scores; 30% (167 students) submitted ACT scores. *25th percentile:* SAT I Verbal 470, SAT I Math 460; ACT Composite 19, ACT English 18, ACT Math 18. *75th percentile:* SAT I Verbal 580, SAT I Math 590; ACT Composite 26, ACT English 26, ACT Math 26. 50% of entering freshmen expected to graduate within 5 years. 75% of freshmen from Indiana. Freshmen from 16 states and 6 foreign countries.

Admission: Rolling admissions plan. For fall acceptance, apply as early as end of junior year of high school, but not later than registration period. Early acceptance available. *Requirements:* Either graduation from accredited secondary school or GED. Recommend 4 units English, 2 foreign language, 2 laboratory science, 2 mathematics, 2 social studies. Typing also recommended. Minimum 1.90 GPA. Lowest acceptable secondary school class standing 30th percentile. *Entrance tests:* College Board SAT or ACT composite. *For transfer students:* 2.0 minimum GPA; 90 semester hours maximum transfer credit; from 2-year accredited institution 60 hours; correspondence/extension students 6 hours.

College credit and advanced placement for postsecondary-level work completed in secondary school. Tutoring available. Remedial courses offered during regular academic year; credit given.

Degree Requirements: *For all associate degrees:* 62 credit hours; 1 hour physical education. *For all baccalaureate degrees:* 124 credit hours; 2 hours physical education. *For all undergraduate degrees:* 2.0 GPA; 30 semester hours in residence; chapel attendance 3 times per week; core curriculum; distribution requirements.

Fulfillment of some degree requirements and exemption from some beginning courses possible by passing College Board CLEP, AP (score of 3). *Grading system:* A–F; pass-fail; withdraw (carries time limit).

Distinctive Educational Programs: Work-experience programs. Evening and Saturday classes. Dual-degree program in engineering with University of Notre Dame. Special facilities for using telecommunications in the classroom. Institution-sponsored study abroad in Ecuador, China, and Russia. Semester in Jerusalem in cooperation with the American Institute of Holy Land Studies. Some courses available in 8-week blocks.

ROTC: Navy offered in cooperation with University of Notre Dame.

Degrees Conferred: 53 *associate*; 305 *baccalaureate*; 23 *master's*. Bachelor's degrees awarded in top five disciplines: business, management, marketing, and related support services 100; liberal arts and sciences, general studies and humanities 37; education 37; health professions and related clinical sciences 28; visual and performing arts 16.

Fees and Other Expenses: *Full-time tuition per academic year 2004–05:* $15,200 undergraduate; contact the college for graduate tuition/fees. *Books and supplies:* $100. *Room and board per academic year:* $4,930.

Financial Aid: Aid from institutionally generated funds is provided on the basis of academic merit, financial need, athletic ability. Institution has a Program Participation Agreement with the U.S. Department of Education for eligible students to receive Pell Grants and other federal aid.

Financial aid to full-time, first-time undergraduate students: 43% received federal grants averaging $1,461; 42% state/local grants averaging $2,218; 93% institutional grants averaging $2,381; 96% loans averaging $3,000.

Departments and Teaching Staff: *Total instructional faculty:* 79. Student-to-faculty ratio: 18:1. Degrees held by full-time faculty: doctorate 61%, master's 39%.

Enrollment: Total enrollment 1,988 (38.5% men, 63.5% women).

Characteristics of Student Body: *Ethnic/racial makeup:* Black non-Hispanic: 10.4%; American Indian or Alaska Native .5%; Asian or Pacific Islander: 1.4%; Hispanic: 2.7%; White non-Hispanic: 83%. *Age distribution:* 17–21: 52%; 22–24: 10%; 25–29: 7%; 30–34: 7%; 35–39: 7%; 40–49: 12%; 50–59: 4%; 60–and over: 1%.

International Students: 35 Undergraduate nonresident aliens enrolled fall 2004. No programs available to aid students whose native language is not English. No financial aid specifically designated for international students.

Student Life: On-campus residence halls house 57% of student body. Residence halls for men only constitute 45% of such space, for women only 55%. *Intercollegiate athletics:* men only: baseball, basketball, cross-country, golf, soccer, tennis, track; women only: basketball, cross-country, softball, track, volleyball. *Special regulations:* Cars with decals permitted. Curfews begin 11:30pm weekdays, 12:30am Fri. and Sat., midnight Sun. Quiet hours begin 10:30pm. *Special services:* Medical services. *Student publications: Beacon,* a monthly newspaper; *Helm,* a yearbook. *Surrounding community:* Mishawaka-Southbend combined population 150,000. Chicago, 90 miles from campus, is nearest metropolitan area. Served by mass transit bus system.

Library Collections: 104,100 volumes. 4,380 microforms; 450 current periodical subscriptions. 4,000 audiovisual materials. Students have access to the Internet.

Buildings and Grounds: Campus area 70 acres.

Chief Executive Officer: Dr. Steven R. Kramer, President.

Address admission inquiries to Randy Beachy, Vice President for Enrollment Management.

Butler University

4600 Sunset Avenue
Indianapolis, Indiana 46208

Tel: (317) 940-8000   **E-mail:** admission@butler.edu
Fax: (317) 940-9930   **Internet:** www.butler.edu

Institution Description: Butler University is a private, independent, nonprofit institution. *Enrollment:* 4,415. *Degrees awarded:* Associate, baccalaureate, first-professional (pharmacy), master's. Specialist certificates in education also awarded.

Accreditation: *Regional:* NCA. *Professional:* business, counseling, dance, music, pharmacy, physician assisting, surgeon assisting, psychology internship, teacher education, theatre

History: Chartered as North Western Christian University 1850; established and offered first instruction at postsecondary level 1855; awarded first degree (baccalaureate) 1849; adopted present name 1877.

Institutional Structure: *Governing board:* Board of Trustees. Extrainstitutional representation: 24 trustees, including 13 alumni; institutional representation: president of the university. 1 ex officio. 31 voting. *Composition of institution:* Administrators 38 men / 19 women. Academic affairs headed by dean of academic affairs. Management/business/finances directed by vice president for finance and administration. Full-time instructional faculty 247. Academic governance body, Faculty Assembly, meets an average of 10 times per year.

Calendar: Semesters. Academic year Aug. to May. Freshmen admitted Aug., Jan., June, Aug. Degrees conferred May, Aug., Dec. Formal commencement May. Summer session of 2 terms from early June to mid-Aug.

Characteristics of Freshmen: 72% of applicants admitted. 27% of applicants admitted and enrolled.

58% (536 students) submitted SAT scores; 42% (390 students) submitted ACT scores. *25th percentile:* SAT Verbal 530, SAT Math 540; ACT Composite 25, ACT English 24, ACT Math 24. *75th percentile:* SAT Verbal 630, SAT Math 650; ACT Composite 29, ACT English 29, ACT Math 29.

94% of entering freshmen expected to graduate within 5 years. 54% of freshmen from Indiana. Freshmen from 31 states and 20 foreign countries.

Admission: Rolling admissions plan. For fall acceptance, apply as early as Sept. of previous year, but not later than Aug. of year of enrollment. Early acceptance available. *Requirements:* Either graduation from accredited secondary school or GED. Recommend 4 units in English, 2 foreign languages, 3 units of lab science, 2 mathematics (algebra, geometry), 2 science, 2 social studies, 3 electives. Additional requirements for some programs. *Entrance tests:* College Board SAT or ACT composite. *For transfer students:* 2.0 minimum GPA; from 4-year accredited institution maximum transfer credit limited only by residence requirement; from 2-year accredited institution 63 hours; correspondence/extension students 6 hours.

College credit and advanced placement for postsecondary-level work completed in secondary school and for extrainstitutional learning on basis of ACE *2006 Guide to the Evaluation of Educational Experiences in the Armed Services;* faculty assessment. Tutoring available. Noncredit developmental/remedial courses offered in summer session and regular academic year.

Degree Requirements: *For all baccalaureate degrees:* 126–136 hours; 45 hours in residence. *For all undergraduate degrees:* 2.0 GPA; 2 hours physical education courses; core curriculum requirements. Fulfillment of some degree requirements and exemption from some beginning courses possible by passing departmental examinations, College Board CLEP, APP. *Grading system:* A–F; pass-fail; withdraw (deadline after which pass-fail is appended to withdraw).

Distinctive Educational Programs: Evening classes. Cross-registration with Heron School of Art of Indiana University-Purdue University at Indianapolis.Interdisciplinary programs in public and corporate communication and in modern languages and business. Honors programs.Institute for Study Abroad programs in Argentina, Australia, Chile, Costa Rica, England, Ireland, Scotland, New Zealand.

ROTC: Air Force with Indiana University-Bloomington; Navy on-campus.

Degrees Conferred: 668 *baccalaureate* (B), 170 *master's* (M): biological/life sciences 32 (B); business/marketing 161 (B), 87 (M); communications/communication technologies 68 (B); computer and information sciences 13 (B); education 94 (B), 60 (M); English 35 (B), 2 (M); interdisciplinary studies 2 (B); mathematics 9 (B); philosophy/religion/theology 6 (B); physical sciences 28 (B); protective services/public administration 2 (B); psychology 17 (B); social sciences and history 4 (B), 6 (M); visual and performing arts 70 (B), 11 (M). 80 *first-professional:* pharmacy 80.

Fees and Other Expenses: *Tuition per academic year 2004–05:* $22,250 undergraduate, per credit hour for graduate study. *Room and board per academic year:* $5,850. *Other fees:* $180.

Financial Aid: Aid from institutionally generated funds is provided on the basis of academic merit, financial need, athletic ability, other criteria. Institution has a Program Participation Agreement with the U.S. Department of Education for eligible students to receive Pell Grants and other federal aid.

Departments and Teaching Staff: College of Liberal Arts and Sciences *professors* 42, *associate professors* 29, *assistant professors* 31, *instructors* 22, *part-time faculty* 62; College of Education 7, 10, 5, 4, 22; College of Business 11, 16, 4, 3, 14; College of Pharmacy and Health Sciences 9, 8, 23, 3, 2; College of Fine Arts 14, 20, 10, 4, 55.

Total instructional faculty: 435 (full-time 280, part-time 155; women 88, men 247; members of minority groups 38). Total faculty with doctorate, first-professional, or other terminal degree: 271. Student-to-faculty ratio: 12:1. *Faculty development:* $1.5 million in grants for research. 17 faculty members awarded sabbaticals 2004–05.

Enrollment: Total enrollment 4,415. Undergraduate full-time 1,359 men / 12,292 women, part-time 27m / 44w; graduate 34m / 28w, part-time 216m / 230w; first-professional full-time 54m / 124w, part-time 3m / 4w. *Transfer students:* in-state 68; from out-of-state 27.

Characteristics of Student Body: *Ethnic/racial makeup:* number of Black non-Hispanic: 141; American Indian or Alaska Native: 6; Asian or Pacific Islander: 78; Hispanic: 78; White non-Hispanic: 3,337; unknown: 201. *Age distribution:* number under 18: 7; 18–19: 1,413; 20–21: 1,692; 22–24: 644; 25–29: 76; 30–34: 29; 35–39: 11; 40–49: 25; 50–64: 8.

International Students: 102 nonresident aliens enrolled fall 2004. 26 students from Europe, 30 Asia, 14 Central and South America 14, 10 Africa, 10 Canada, 1 Australia, 11 other. No programs to aid students whose native language is not English, No financial aid specifically designated for international students.

Student Life: Residence hall space: 1/3 women only, 2/3 coed. 57% of student body live on-campus. *Intercollegiate athletics:* men only: baseball, basketball, cross-country, football, golf, soccer, swimming, tennis, track; women only: cross-country, basketball, golf, softball, tennis, track, volleyball. *Special regula-*

tions: Cars permitted in designated areas. Quiet hours. Open visitation in residence halls. *Special services:* Learning Resources Center, health services. *Student publications: The Collegian,* a weekly newspaper; *Drift,* yearbook; *MSS,* a quarterly literary magazine. *Surrounding community:* Indianapolis population 701,000. Served by mass transit bus and train systems, airport 7 miles from campus, rail and bus service 5 miles from campus.

Library Collections: 311,429 volumes. Online catalog. Current serial subscriptions: 1,124 paper; 72 microform; 8,672 via electronic access. 16,500 audiovisual materials. 40 computer work stations. Students have access to the Internet at no charge. Total 2004–05 budget for books and materials: $900,000.

Most important special holdings include University Archives; Jean Sibelius Collection (music); Charters Collection (South Pacific); National Track and Field Hall of Fame Library; Abraham Lincoln and the Civil War Collection.

Buildings and Grounds: Campus area 290 acres. *New buildings:* Fine Arts Building completed 2003; Edison-Duckwall Recital Hall 2005.

Chief Executive Officer: Dr. Robert Fong, President.

Address admission inquiries to William Preble, Dean of Admission.

Calumet College of Saint Joseph

2400 New York Avenue
Whiting, Indiana 46394-2195
Tel: (219) 473-7770   **E-mail:** admissions@ccsj.edu
Fax: (219) 473-4259   **Internet:** www.ccsj.edu

Institution Description: Calumet College of St. Joseph is a private, independent, nonprofit college conducted by the Precious Blood Missionaries, Roman Catholic Church. *Enrollment:* 1,339. *Degrees awarded:* Associate, baccalaureate. Certificates also awarded.

Accreditation: *Regional:* NCA.

History: Established as Saint Joseph's College Calumet Center, a 2-year extension of Saint Joseph's College (established 1889) and offered first instruction at postsecondary level 1951; became 4-year college and changed name to Saint Joseph's College Calumet Campus 1960; awarded first degree (baccalaureate) 1961; changed name to Saint Joseph's Calumet College 1971; separated from Saint Joseph's College, incorporated, and changed name to Calumet College 1973; adopted present name 1980.

Institutional Structure: *Governing board:* Calumet College of Saint Joseph Board of Trustees. Extrainstitutional representation: 40 trustees, 6 religious, 2 faculty members, 2 students. All voting. *Composition of institution:* Management/business/finances directed by vice president for finance. Academic affairs directed by Dean of Academic and Student Affairs. Enrollment management directed by vice president of enrollment/management. Full-time instructional faculty 21. Academic governance body, Faculty Assembly, meets an average of 15 times per year.

Calendar: Semesters. Academic year Aug. to May. Freshmen admitted Aug., Jan., Apr. Degrees conferred Dec., May, Aug. Formal commencement May. Summer session of 2 terms from late Apr. to early Aug.

Characteristics of Freshmen: 75% of applicants accepted. 53% of accepted applicants enrolled. 79% of freshmen from Indiana. Freshmen from 3 states.

Admission: Rolling admissions plan. For fall acceptance, apply as early as June of previous year, but not later than Sept. of year of enrollment. Early acceptance available. *Requirements:* Either graduation from accredited secondary school with 15 academic units which must include 10 from among English, foreign language, mathematics, natural sciences, social studies; or GED. Minimum 2.0 GPA. Different requirements for admission to associate degree and certificate programs. *Entrance tests:* Reading, Writing, and Math Tests with additional writing sample. *For transfer students:* 2.0 minimum GPA; from 4-year accredited institution 94 hours maximum transfer credit; from 2-year accredited institution 66 hours; correspondence students 12 hours; extension student 60 hours.

College credit and advanced placement for postsecondary-level work completed in secondary school and for extrainstitutional learning on basis of ACE *2006 Guide to the Evaluation of Educational Experiences in the Armed Services;* portfolio assessment. Tutoring available. Developmental courses offered in summer session and regular academic year; credit given, but not applied toward degree.

Degree Requirements: *For all associate degrees:* 60 semester hours; 15 hours in residence. *For all baccalaureate degrees:* 124 semester hours; 30 hours in residence; 2.0 GPA in major field. *For all degrees:* 2.0 GPA; distribution requirements.

Fulfillment of some degree requirements and exemption from some beginning courses possible by passing departmental examinations, College Board CLEP, other standardized test. *Grading system:* A–F; pass-fail; withdraw (carries time limit); incomplete (carries time limit).

Distinctive Educational Programs: Program of granting credit for prior learning experience. Special degree completion program for students with 54 hours and work experience. Cooperative education. Flexible meeting places and schedules, including off-campus centers and evening classes. Interdisciplinary programs, including media and fine arts, general education, general studies, liberal arts. Facilities and programs for independent research, including honors programs, individual majors, tutorials, independent study. Study abroad may be individually arranged. *Other distinctive programs:* Certification classes.

Degrees Conferred: 22 *associate;* 249 *baccalaureate;* 61 *master's.* Bachelor's degrees awarded in top five disciplines: security and protective services 103; business, management, marketing, and related support services 76; education 17; health professions and related clinical sciences 15; computer and information sciences and support services: 10.

Fees and Other Expenses: *Full-time tuition per academic year 2004–05:* $7,560. *Books and supplies:* $1,050. *Room and board per academic year:* $4,500.

Financial Aid: Aid from institutionally generated funds is provided on the basis of academic merit, financial need. Institution has a Program Participation Agreement with the U.S. Department of Education for eligible students to receive Pell Grants and other federal aid.

Financial aid to full-time, first-time undergraduate students: 40% received federal grants averaging $3,847; 23% state/local grants averaging $4,738; 65% institutional grants averaging $3,038; 44% loans averaging $3,701.

Departments and Teaching Staff: *Professors* 8, *associate professors* 3, *assistant professors* 6, *instructors* 4, *part-time teachers* 142. *Total instructional faculty:* 68 FTE. Total tenured faculty: 10. Student-to-faculty ratio: 15:1. Degrees held by full-time faculty: doctorate 52%, master's 38%, professional 10%. 81% of faculty hold terminal degrees.

Enrollment: Total enrollment 1,339. Undergraduate 1,260 (41% men, 59% women).

Characteristics of Student Body: *Ethnic/racial makeup:* Black non-Hispanic: 27.9%; American Indian or Alaska Native: .2%; Asian or Pacific Islander: .5%; Hispanic: 19.8%; White non-Hispanic: 51.4%; unknown: .1%. *Age distribution:* 17–21: 13%; 22–29: 11%; 25–29: 13%; 30–34: 13%; 35–39: 13%; 40–49: 26%; 50–59: 10%; 60 and over: 1%.

International Students: 2 undergraduate nonresident aliens enrolled fall 2004. Programs available to aid students whose native language is not English: English as a Second Language Program. No financial aid specifically designated for international students.

Student Life: No on-campus housing. *Special services:* Tutoring and Testing Center. Intramural sports program, theatre group, student clubs. *Student publications: Shavings,* a weekly newspaper. *Surrounding community:* Hammond population 85,000. Chicago (IL), 20 miles from campus, is nearest metropolitan area. Served by mass transit bus system; airport 30 miles from campus; passenger rail service 4 miles from campus.

Library Collections: 105,000 volumes. 3,500 microforms; 6,500 audiovisual materials; 355 current periodical subscriptions. Computer work stations available. Students have access to the Internet at no charge.

Most important special holdings include 10,000 items dealing with contemporary theology; 8,000 items on education; 3,000 volumes on the North American Indian (including some 19th-century and many out-of-print editions); Missionaries of the Precious Blood Collection.

Buildings and Grounds: CCSJ has a main campus in Whiting and two smaller campuses in Merrillville, Indiana and Chicago, Illinois. In addition, classes are offered at sites in Crown Point, Gary, and Munster, Indiana and Homewood, Illinois.

Chief Executive Officer: Dr. Dennis C. Rittenmeyer, President.

Address admission inquiries to Chuck Walz, Director Admissions.

Christian Theological Seminary

1000 West 42nd Street
Indianapolis, Indiana 46208-3301
Tel: (317) 924-1331   **E-mail:** admissions@cts.edu
Fax: (317) 924-1961   **Internet:** www.cts.edu

Institution Description: Christian Theological Seminary is an ecumenical graduate school of the Christian Church (Disciples of Christ). Emphasis is on preparing for the pastoral ministry through the study of Bible, Church History, Theology and Culture and Personality. *Enrollment:* 295. *Degrees awarded:* First-professional (theology), master's, doctorate.

Accreditation: *Regional:* NCA. *National:* ATS. *Professional:* theology

History: Established as Bible Department of Butler University 1889; became Butler Bible College 1898; changed name to College of Religion 1924; became separate corporation and adopted present name 1958.

Institutional Structure: *Governing board:* Board of Trustees. Extrainstitutional representation: 23 trustees; institutional representation: president of the institution. 1 ex officio. *Composition of institution:* Academic affairs headed by vice president and dean of the seminary. Management/business/finances directed by treasurer and business manager. Full-time instructional faculty 23.

Calendar: Semesters. Academic year early Sept. to mid-May.

Admission: Rolling admissions plan. *Requirements:* Baccalaureate from accredited college or university. Recommend concentrated studies in literature, history, classical philosophy, religion. Minimum GPA 2.5.

Degree Requirements: *For first-professional:* 90 credit hours; field education. *For master's:* 60 credit hours; thesis. *For both degrees:* 2.0 GPA; 1 year in residence. *Grading system:* A–D.

Distinctive Educational Programs: Extensive field education program, Pastoral Care and Counseling training center. Approved polity courses by several denominations.

Degrees Conferred: 14 *master's:* philosophy/religion/theology 8, psychology 6; 3 *doctorate* psychology 3; 26 *first-professional:* master of divinity. Honorary degrees awarded 2004: Doctor of Humane Letters 2. Doctor of Public Service 2.

Fees and Other Expenses: *Full-time tuition per academic year:* Contact the seminary for current information.

Financial Aid: Aid from institutionally generated funds is provided on the basis of academic merit, financial need. Financial assistance is available in the form of Pell Grants, College Work-Study, Veterans Administration Benefits, National Direct Student Loans, Supplemental Education Opportunity Grants (SEOG), Stafford Loans, other federal aid programs.

Departments and Teaching Staff: Bible *professors* 2, *associate professors* 2, *assistant professors* 0, *part-time teachers* 1; church history 1, 1, 3, 1; systematic and philosophical theology 2, 0, 0, 1; Christianity and culture 2, 1, 1, 3; pastoral theology and psychology 1, 1, 2, 4; Christian ministries 2, 0, 2, 6.

Total instructional faculty: 39. Total tenured faculty: 13. Degrees held by full-time faculty: Doctorate 100%. 70% hold terminal degrees.

Enrollment: Total enrollment 295 (123 men, 172 women). Graduate full-time 54, part-time 110; first-professional full-time 106, part-time 25.

Characteristics of Student Body: *Ethnic/racial makeup:* Black non-Hispanic: 19/9%; Asian or Pacific Islander: .6%; Hispanic: .9%; White non-Hispanic: 75.8%; unknown: 1.2%. *Age distribution:* 22–24: 14; 25–29: 39; 30–34: 29; 35–39: 27; 40–49: 88; 50–64: 82; 65 and over: 16.

International Students: 6 nonresident aliens enrolled fall 2004. 2 students from Asia, 2 Africa, 2 other. No programs available to aid students whose native language is not English. Some financial aid available for qualifying international students.

Student Life: 36 units student apartments on campus. Many students live in parsonages where they serve as student ministers. *Student publications: Koinonia,* a newspaper. *Surrounding community:* Located adjacent to Butler University, Indianapolis Art Museum.

Publications: *Encounter,* a scholarly journal; *CTS Bulletin* and *Link,* both newsletters.

Library Collections: 220,000 volumes. 1,400 microforms; 500 audiovisual titles; 1,400 current periodical subscriptions. 900 recordings. 500 compact discs. 80 CD-ROMs. Online catalog. Students have access to online information retrieval services and the Internet.

Most important holdings include Significant Disciples and Rare Bibles Collection; regional religious history; Stone-Campbell/Christian Church Collection.

Buildings and Grounds: Architecturally modern complex on 40 acres; chapel, repertory theatre, library wing, dining hall, large academic wing, apartment complex.

Chief Executive Officer: Dr. Edward L. Wheeler, President.

Address admission inquiries to Director of Admissions.

Concordia Theological Seminary

6600 North Clinton Street
Fort Wayne, Indiana 46825-4996

Tel: (219) 452-2100   **E-mail:** cfwadmis@crf.cuis.edu
Fax: (219) 452-2121   **Internet:** www.ctsfw.edu

Institution Description: Concordia Theological Seminary is a private institution affiliated with the Lutheran Church-Missouri Synod. *Enrollment:* 389. *Degrees awarded:* First-professional (theology), master's, doctorate.

Accreditation: *Regional:* NCA. *Professional:* theology

History: Established in Fort Wayne and offered first instruction at postsecondary level 1846; passed into control of Missouri Synod 1847; moved to St. Louis (MO) and merged with another seminary 1861; moved to Springfield (IL). 1875; awarded first degree (baccalaureate) 1964; returned to Fort Wayne 1976.

Institutional Structure: *Governing board:* The Board of Control. Extrainstitutional representation: 9 members, including 3 alumni; institutional representation: president of the college, 1 administrator. 2 ex officio. All voting. *Composition of institution:* Administrators 9 men. Academic affairs headed by academic dean. Management/business/finances directed by dean of administration. Full-time instructional faculty 31. Academic governance body, Administrative Council, meets an average of 36 times per year.

Calendar: Quarters. Academic year mid-Sept. to mid-May. Entering students admitted Sept., Dec., Mar., June. Degrees conferred May., Aug., Nov., Mar. Formal commencement May. Summer sessions from mid-May to mid-July.

Characteristics of Freshmen: 91% of applicants accepted. 82% of accepted applicants enrolled.

Admission: Rolling admissions plan. Apply as early as 12 months, but not later than 6 weeks, prior to enrollment. *Requirements:* Baccalaureate degree from regionally accredited institution. Students without a baccalaureate degree but with a minimum of 96 hours in specified courses will be considered. Minimum GPA 2.25. *Entrance tests:* GRE, Ohio State University Psychological Test. *For transfer students:* 2.25 minimum GPA; maximum transfer credits 79 quarter hours.

Degree Requirements: *For all first-professional degrees:* 137 quarter hours; 2.0 GPA; 4 quarters in residence; distribution requirements; participation in supervised pastoral education programs; theological exit interview. Master of Sacred Theology requires a Master of Divinity degree, a 3.00 GPA; 42 credit hours for the program (6 of them thesis credit). Master of Arts requires 72 quarter hours plus a 30-40 page essay. Daily chapel attendance. Doctor of Missiology degree requires a Master of Divinity degree; minimum of 3 years of full-time experience in cross-cultural ministry or evangelism; 72 quarter hour program plus dissertation. *For Doctor of Ministry degree:* requires Master of Divinity degree, minimum 3 years in the ministry; 51 credit hours for the program (9 of them for project/dissertation). *Grading system:* A–F; pass-fail; withdraw (carries time limit); incomplete (carries time limit).

Distinctive Educational Programs: *For first-professional students:* Work-experience programs. Study abroad in Oberursal, Germany, through institutionally sponsored seminary exchange program. *Available to all students:* Evening classes. Independent study.

Degrees Conferred: 14 *master's:* theology and ministerial studies; 5 *doctorate:* theology and religious vocations; 72 *first-professional:* master of divinity.

Fees and Other Expenses: *Full-time tuition per academic year:* Contact the seminary for current information; tuition varies by program.

Financial Aid: Aid from institutionally generated funds is provided on the basis of academic merit, financial need, other criteria. Institution has a Program Participation Agreement with the U.S. Department of Education for eligible students to receive Pell Grants and other federal aid.

Departments and Teaching Staff: Exegetical theology *professors* 3, *associate professors* 4, *assistant professors* 2, *instructors* 0, *part-time faculty* 0; historical theology 2, 1, 1, 0, 0; systematic theology 1, 2, 0, 0, 3; pastoral ministry/missions 3, 3, 3, 1, 27; *Total instructional faculty:* 36. Degrees held by full-time faculty: first-professional 16%, doctorate 80%, master's 100%. 80% hold terminal degrees.

Enrollment: Total enrollment 389 (93.3% men, 6.7% women).

Characteristics of Student Body: *Ethnic/racial makeup:* Black non-Hispanic: 1.5%; Asian or Pacific Islander: .5%; Hispanic: .8%; White non-Hispanic: 85.1%; unknown: 8.5%.

International Students: 14 nonresident aliens enrolled fall 2004. No programs available to aid students whose native language is not English. Scholarships available to qualifying international students.

Student Life: On-campus residence halls house 25% of student body. Residence halls for men constitute 100% of such space. *Intercollegiate athletics:* men only: basketball, soccer. *Special regulations:* Insured cars permitted; parking permit required. *Surrounding community:* Fort Wayne population 166,000. Indianapolis, 100 miles from campus, is nearest metropolitan area. Served by airport 12 miles from campus; passenger rail service 6 miles from campus.

Publications: Sources of information about Concordia include *Called to Serve Newsletter. Concordia Theological Quarterly* first published in 1936.

Library Collections: 155,000 volumes. 3,500 microforms; 7,600 audiovisual materials; 820 current periodical subscriptions.

Most important holdings include the Sasse Collection (Australian Lutheranism); 4,000 volumes of primary source material of the 16th- and 17th-century Lutheranism.

Chief Executive Officer: Dr. Dean O. Wenthe, President.

Address admission inquires to Rev. Scott C. Klemsz, Director of Admissions.

DePauw University

313 South Locust Street

Greencastle, Indiana 46135-1772

Tel: (765) 658-4800   **E-mail:** admissions@depauw.edu

Fax: (765) 658-4177   **Internet:** www.depauw.edu

Institution Description: DePauw University is a private, nonprofit institution affiliated with the United Methodist Church. *Enrollment:* 2,391. *Degrees awarded:* Baccalaureate.

Member of the consortium Great Lakes Colleges Association.

Accreditation: *Regional:* NCA. *Professional:* athletic training, music, music, teacher education

History: Established and chartered as Indiana Asbury University and offered first instruction at postsecondary level 1837; awarded first degree (baccalaureate) 1840; admitted women 1867; School of Music founded 1884; adopted present name 1884. *See* George B. Manhart, *DePauw Through the Years*, (Chicago, IL, and Crawfordsville, IN: The Lakeside Press, 1962) for further information.

Institutional Structure: *Governing board:* Board of Trustees. Extrainstitutional representation: maximum of 40 voting members of which not less than 50% are graduates of DePauw and not less than 25% are members of the United Methodist Church. 3 voting trustees are student reps elected to serve after graduation. Ex officio trustees: 11 life, 11 advisory. *Composition of institution:* Administrators 20 men / 14 women (at dean's level and above, 44% are women). Academic affairs headed by provost. Management/business/finances directed by vice president for finance. Full-time instructional faculty 188. Academic governance body, the faculty, meets an average of 7 times per year.

Calendar: Semesters. Academic year Aug. to May. Freshmen admitted Aug., Jan., Feb. Degrees conferred and formal commencement May.

Characteristics of Freshmen: 3,423 applicants (1,546 men, 1,877 women). 69.8% of applicants admitted. 27.7% of admitted students enrolled full-time.

81% of students submitted SAT scores; 84% submitted ACT scores. *25th percentile*: SAT I Verbal 550, SAT I Math 570; ACT Composite 24, ACT English 24, ACT Math 24. *75th percentile*: SAT I Verbal 660, SAT I Math 680; ACT Composite 29, ACT English 30, ACT Math 28.

78% of entering freshmen expected to graduate within 5 years. 56% of freshmen from Indiana. Freshmen from 33 states and 7 foreign countries.

Admission: Deadline for regular admission is Feb. 1. Students notified of decision by Apr. 1. Early notification deadline is Dec. 1. Decisions are mailed the final week in Jan.; need not limit application to DePauw. *Requirements:* Either graduation from accredited secondary school or GED. Recommend 4 units English, 4 in a foreign language, 4 college preparatory mathematics, 4 physical sciences, 4 social studies. *Entrance tests:* College Board SAT or ACT composite. *For transfer students:* From 4-year accredited institution 96 semester hours maximum transfer credit; from 2-year accredited institution 60 hours; correspondence/extension students 4 hours.

College credit and advanced placement for postsecondary-level work completed in secondary school. Tutoring available. Developmental and remedial courses offered during regular academic year; credit given for some courses.

Degree Requirements: *For all undergraduate degrees:* 31 courses (124 semester hours) except Bachelor of Music Education which requires 32 courses (128 semester hours); 2.0 GPA; 6 of last 8 courses in residence; distribution requirements; competency requirements in writing, oral communication, and quantitative reasoning.

Fulfillment of some degree requirements and exemption from some beginning courses possible by passing departmental examinations, College Board AP, other standardized tests. *Grading system:* A–F; pass-fail withdraw (carries time limit); incomplete (carries time limit).

Distinctive Educational Programs: *For undergraduates:* Dual-degree programs in engineering with Case Western Reserve University (OH), Columbia University (NY), Georgia Institute of Technology, Washington University (MO); in dentistry, medical technology or medicine by individual arrangement. Center for Contemporary Media offering state of the art broadcasting and communication facilities. Interdisciplinary majors available in Asian Studies, Russian Studies, and Women's Studies as well as self-designed majors. Interdisciplinary programs in conflict studies, business administration, business and public service, institutional management, international business, philosophy, public administration, religion, and by individual arrangement. Opportunities for collaborative research with faculty members, limited number of research grants available, and individualized majors. Honor Scholar Program; Management Fellows, Media Fellows, and Science Research Fellows Programs. Fifth Year Scholar Program. Fifth Year Teacher Classification Program. Study abroad through opportunities through institutionally-arranged programs in Vienna, Budapest, Freiburg, and Athens; options available through GLCA, CIEE, and ACM; direct entry into select universities in the United Kingdom and Germany; programs in cooperation with Brethren Colleges Abroad in France, Germany, and Spain; exchange programs in Japan with Nanzan University of Nagoya. Off-campus study in the U.S. includes arts program in New York, Newberry Library Program in the Humanities (IL), Oak Ridge (TN) science semester, and urban semester in Philadelphia (PA) through the GLCA consortium and ACM; Drew University (NJ) semester on the United Nations; Washington (DC) semester at American University.

ROTC: Air Force offered in cooperation with Indiana University-Bloomington. Army offered in cooperation with Rose-Hulman Institute of Technology in Terre Haute (IN).

Degrees Conferred: 522 *baccalaureate*. Bachelor's degrees awarded in top five disciplines: social sciences 97; communication, journalism, and related programs 91; English language and literature/letters 81; biological and biomedical sciences 43; visual and performing arts 41.

Fees and Other Expenses: *Full-time tuition per academic year 2004–05:* $25,000. *Books and supplies:* $600. *Room and board per academic year:* $7,000. *Other expenses:* 1,000.

Financial Aid: Aid from institutionally generated funds is provided on the basis of academic merit, financial need, special talent. Institution has a Program Participation Agreement with the U.S. Department of Education for eligible students to receive Pell Grants and other federal aid.

Financial aid to full-time, first-time undergraduate students: 13% received federal grants averaging $3,458; 14% state/local grants averaging $4,236; 58% institutional grants averaging $12,272; 32% loans averaging $3,720.

Departments and Teaching Staff: Art *professors* 3, *associate professors* 0, *assistant professors* 2, *instructors* 1, *part-time teachers* 3; biology 4, 3, 5, 0, 0; chemistry 1, 3, 3, 0, 0; classical studies 1, 0, 3, 0, 0; computer science 2, 2, 1, 0, 0; communication 2, 3, 5, 1, 3; economics 4, 2, 3, 0, 2; education 2, 2, 3, 1, 1; English 8, 5, 5, 3, 3; geography & geology 1, 1, 1, 0, 1; history 5, 2, 4, 0, 0; health and physical education 4, 2, 1, 0, 0; mathematics 4, 3, 1, 0, 0; modern languages 5, 2, 9, 2, 2; music 6, 5, 6, 0, 25; philosophy 4, 1, 0, 1, 0; physics 2, 1, 1, 0, 0; political science 5, 1, 1, 0, 0; psychology 2, 3, 3, 0, 0; religious studies 4, 1, 0, 0, 1; sociology & anthropology 4, 2, 2, 1, 0; university studies 0, 0, 1, 0, 1.

Total instructional faculty: 202 FTE. Student-to-faculty ratio: 11:1. Degrees held by full-time faculty: doctorate 82%, master's 17%, professional 1%. 93% hold terminal degrees.

Enrollment: Total enrollment 2,391 (45% men, 55% women).

Characteristics of Student Body: *Ethnic and racial makeup:* Black non-Hispanic: 5.4%; American Indian or Alaska Native: .4%; Asian or Pacific Islander: 2.2%; Hispanic: 3.1%; White non-Hispanic: 85.7%; unknown: 1.2%. *Age distribution:* 17–21: 72%; 22–24: 27%; 25–up: 1%.

International Students: 50 nonresident aliens enrolled fall 2004. English as a Second Language Program. Variable number of scholarships available for qualifying international students.

Student Life: On-campus residence halls house 48% of student body. 78% of men join and 49% live in on-campus fraternities; 72% of women join and 44% live in on-campus sororities. 94% of all students live on campus. *Intercollegiate athletics:* men only: baseball, basketball, cross-country, football, golf, soccer, swimming, tennis, track; women only: basketball, cross-country, field hockey, golf, softball, soccer, swimming, tennis, track, volleyball. *Special regulations:* Cars with decals permitted on campus in designated areas only; fee charged. Quiet hours and residence hall visitation hours vary according to residence hall. *Special services:* Medical services. Transportation to and from airport during vacation periods. *Student publications, radio:* The DePauw, a semiweekly newspaper; The Mirage, a yearbook; Midwestern Review, a quarterly magazine of arts and issues. Radio station WGRE broadcasts 24 hours per day, 7 days a week while students are on campus. *Surrounding community:* Greencastle population 10,000. Indianapolis, 45 miles from campus, is nearest metropolitan area. Served by airport 43 miles from campus.

Library Collections: 284,000 volumes. 250,000 government documents; 372,000 microforms; 15,700 audiovisual materials; 4,020 current periodical subscriptions. 300 recordings. 200 computer work stations. Access to online information retrieval systems. Students have access to the Internet at no charge.

Most important holdings include Bret Harte Collection (first editions); Charles and Mary Ritter Beard Papers; Indiana Methodist Episcopal Circuit Preacher's Journals; Governor James Whitcomb's Library; Thomas Bond Wood Papers.

Buildings and Grounds: Campus area 175 acres.

Chief Executive Officer: Dr. Robert G. Bottoms, President.

Address admission inquiries to Madeleine R. Eagon, Vice President for Admissions and Financial Aid.

Earlham College

701 National Road West

Richmond, Indiana 47374-4095

Tel: (765) 983-1200   **E-mail:** admission@earlham.edu

Fax: (765) 983-1560   **Internet:** www.earlham.edu

Institution Description: Earlham College is an independent, nonprofit college affiliated with the Society of Friends. *Enrollment:* 1,190. *Degrees awarded:* Baccalaureate. Earlham School of Religion offers first-professional and master's degrees.

Member of consortium Great Lakes Colleges Association.

Accreditation: *Regional:* NCA. *National:* ATS. *Professional:* teacher education, theology

History: Established as Friends Boarding School 1847; first instruction at postsecondary level and present name adopted 1859; awarded first degree (baccalaureate) 1862; incorporated 1881. *See* Opal Thornburg, *Earlham: The Story of the College 1847–1962*, (Richmond: Earlham College Press, 1963) for further information.

Institutional Structure: *Governing board:* The Board of Trustees. Extrainstitutional representation: 6 trustees, 6 members appointed by Indiana Yearly Meeting of Friends, 6 appointed by Western Yearly Meeting of Friends, 6 honorary trustees; institutional representation: president of college; 4 alumni. 1 ex officio. 23 voting. *Composition of institution:* Administrators 91 men / 63 women. Academic affairs headed by president. Management/business/finances directed by vice president for financial affairs. Full-time instructional faculty 95. Academic governance body, the faculty, meets an average of 12 times per year.

Calendar: Semesters. Academic year Aug. to May. First-year students admitted Aug. and Jan. Degrees conferred May. May term. No summer session.

Characteristics of Freshmen: 72% of applicants admitted. 31% of admitted applicants enrolled.

31% (271 students) submitted SAT scores; 34% (115 students) submitted ACT scores. *25th percentile*: SAT Verbal 580, SAT Math 530; ACT Composite 24. *75th percentile*: SAT Verbal 690, SAT Math 650; ACT Composite 29.

69% of entering freshmen expected to graduate within 5 years. 25% of freshmen from Indiana. Freshmen from 49 states and 53 foreign countries.

Admission: Feb. 15 is deadline for regular decision. Apply by Dec. 1 for early decision; need not limit application to Earlham. Early acceptance available. *Requirements:* Either at least 15 secondary school units in academic subjects, which normally include 4 English, at least 2 in a foreign language, 3 mathematics, at least 2 each in history/social studies, science; or GED. Students who do not meet usual class rank and College Board SAT scores criteria but who can offer other evidence of their intellectual ability are invited to write dean of admissions to explain their situation. Minimum GPA 3.0. *Entrance tests:* SAT or ACT composite (SAT preferred). *For transfer students:* 3.0 minimum GPA, 60 semester hours maximum transfer credit.

College credit and advanced placement for postsecondary-level work completed in secondary school. College credit by individual consideration for extrainstitutional learning on basis of ACE *2006 Guide to the Evaluation of Educational Experiences in the Armed Services*; faculty assessment. Tutoring available.

Degree Requirements: 122 credit hours; 2.0 GPA; 4 semesters in residence; 4 physical education courses; requirements specific to major fields; general education requirements; faculty approval; comprehensives in individual fields of study. Some degree requirements can be fulfilled by taking achievement tests. Exemption from beginning courses possible by passing CLEP, offered before classes start in the fall. *Grading system:* A–D for courses successfully completed; no passes not recorded.

Distinctive Educational Programs: *For undergraduates:* Interdepartmental and interdisciplinary majors including African/African-American studies, Japanese studies, Latin American studies, human development and social relations, peace and conflict studies, women's studies. Individually designed majors. Preprofessional programs in business and engineering, environmental education, law, medicine, ministry, nursing. Five-year engineering degree program in cooperation with Case-Western Reserve University (OH), Washington University (MO), University of Rochester (NY), Rensselaer Polytechnic Institute (NY), or University of Michigan at Ann Arbor. 5-year nursing degree program in cooperation with Case-Western Reserve. Study abroad in England, France, Germany, Kenya, Japan, Mexico, elsewhere. Interterm and domestic programs, including tropical biology, marine biology, Southwest field studies, Wilderness program in August. Living/learning programs. Other programs available through consortium and Associated Colleges of the Midwest.

Degrees Conferred: 266*baccalaureate:* area and ethnic studies 18; biological/life sciences 41; business/marketing 20; communications/communication technologies 2; computer and information sciences 10; education 1; English 13; foreign languages and literature 16; interdisciplinary studies 27; mathematics 4; philosophy/religion/theology 11; physical sciences 11; psychology 23; social sciences and history 55; visual and performing arts 14; 6 *master's*: education 6.

Fees and Other Expenses: *Full-time tuition per academic year 2004–05:* $25,364 undergraduate, $7,506 Earlham School of Religion. *Required fees:* $678. *Room and board per academic year:* $5,740.

Financial Aid: Aid from institutionally generated funds is provided on the basis of academic merit, financial need. Institution has a Program Participation Agreement with the U.S. Department of Education for eligible students to receive Pell Grants and other federal aid.

Financial aid to full-time, first-time undergraduate students: need-based scholarships/grants totaling $11,442,329, self-help $3,275,823, parent loans $217,751; non-need-based scholarships/grants totaling $2,765,101, self-help $1,413,864, parent loans $1,088,616. *Graduate aid:* 38 federal and state-funded loans totaling $584,551 (ranging from $1,537 to $27,750); 42 scholarships totaling $170,319 (ranging from $636 to $13,420).

Departments and Teaching Staff: *Professors* 42, *associate professors* 17, *assistant professors* 34, *instructors* 2, *part-time faculty* 95.

Total instructional faculty: 114 (full-time 91, part-time 23; women 48, men 66; members of minority groups 21). Total faculty with doctorate, first-professional, or other terminal degree: 98. Student-to-faculty ratio: 12:1. *Faculty development:* $53,891 in grants for research. 13 faculty members awarded sabbaticals 2004–05.

Enrollment: Total enrollment 1,274. Full-time undergraduate 492 men / 678 women, part-time 7m / 13w; full-time first-professional 10m / 24w, part-time 8m / 6w; full-time graduate 14 / 7w, part-time 5m / 10w. *Transfer students:* in-state 5; from out-of-state 10.

Characteristics of Student Body: *Ethnic/racial makeup:* number of Black non-Hispanic: 82; American Indian or Alaska Native: 3; Asian or Pacific Islander:22; Hispanic: 32; White non-Hispanic: 898; unknown 71. *Age distribution:* under 18: 4; 18–19: 454; 20–21: 519; 22–24: 191; 25–29: 10; 30–34: 1; 35–39: 1; 50–64: unknown: 9.

International Students: 85 nonresident aliens enrolled fall 2004. 21 students from Europe, 28 Asia, 7 Central and South America, 11 Africa, 2 Canada, 1 Australia, 11 other. No programs to aid students whose native language is not English. Some financial aid designated specifically for qualifying international students.

Student Life: On-campus residence halls house for both men and women house 67% of the student body; 15% of the student body live off-campus in 25 houses owned by the college (including language houses: French, German, Japanese, Spanish). Housing is available for married students. *Intercollegiate athletics:* men only: baseball, basketball, football, tennis, track, cross-country, soccer; women only: basketball, field hockey, tennis, track, cross-country, volleyball, lacrosse, soccer. *Special regulations:* Established quiet hours in 1 hall; elsewhere according to consensus of residents. *Special services:* Learning Center, medical services. *Student publications, radio:* The Earlham Word, a weekly newspaper; *Crucible*, published annually. *Sargasso*, a college yearbook. Radio station WECI broadcasts 24 hours per day all week. . *Surrounding community:* Richmond population 42,000. Dayton (OH), 40 miles from campus, is nearest metropolitan area. Served by mass transit bus system; airport 40 miles from campus.

Publications: Sources of information about Earlham include *The Earlhamite*, the quarterly college alumni magazine; the annual *President's Report; Ideas That Make a Difference*; the college admissions prospectus; and the college curriculum guide.

Library Collections: 403,639 volumes. Online catalog. Current serial subscriptions: 1,027 paper; access to 19,000 via electronic access. 91,000 government documents; 196,000 microforms; 50,000 audiovisual materials. 96 computer work stations. Access to online information retrieval systems. Total budget for books and materials 2004–05: $515,000.

Most important holdings include collections on the Society of Friends; Uyesugi Japanese-American Collection; peace studies.

Buildings and Grounds: Campus area 800 acres. *New buildings:* Landrum Bolling Center for Interdisciplinary Studies and Social Sciences opened 2002; Susanne Hoerner Jackson Equestrian Center (indoor riding arena) 2003.

Chief Executive Officer: Dr. Douglas C. Bennett, President.

Address admission inquiries to Jeff Rickey, Director of Admissions and Financial Aid; inquires for Earlham School of Religion to Susan Axtell, Director of Recruitment/Admissions.

Franklin College of Indiana

101 Branigin Boulevard
Franklin, Indiana 46131-2623
Tel: (317) 738-8000   **E-mail:** admissions@franklincollege.edu
Fax: (317) 736-6030   **Internet:** franklincollege.edu

Institution Description: Franklin College of Indiana is a private college affiliated with Indiana Baptist Convention of the American Baptist Churches in the U.S.A. *Enrollment: 994. Degrees awarded:* Baccalaureate.

Accreditation: *Regional:* NCA.

History: Established as Indiana Baptist Manual Labor Institute 1834; chartered 1836; offered first instruction at postsecondary level and adopted present name 1844; awarded first degree (baccalaureate) 1848.

Institutional Structure: *Governing board:* Board of Trustees. Extrainstitutional representation: 33 trustees, including Executive Minister of Indiana Baptist Convention; institutional representation: president of the college; 1 alumnus. 2 ex officio. 33 voting. *Composition of institution:* 6 administrators. Academic affairs headed by vice president and dean of the college. Management/business/finances directed by vice president for finance. Full-time instructional faculty 38 men / 16 women. Academic governance body, the faculty, meets an average of 12 times per year.

Calendar: Semesters. Academic year early Sept. to mid-May. Freshmen admitted Sept., Jan., Feb., June. Degrees conferred and formal commencement May. Summer session of 1 term from early June to late July.

Characteristics of Freshmen: 1,078 applicants (610 men, 408 women). 76.3% of applicants admitted. 34% of admitted students enrolled full-time.

92% (255 students) submitted SAT scores; 38% (105 students) submitted ACT scores. *25th percentile:* SAT Verbal 470, SAT Math 480; ACT Composite 20, ACT English 19, ACT Math 19. *75th percentile:* SAT Verbal 580, SAT Math 590; ACT Composite 26, ACT English 26, ACT Math 26.

46% of freshmen from Indiana. Freshmen from 13 states and 5 foreign countries.

Admission: Rolling admissions plan. For fall acceptance, apply as early as June 1 of previous year, but not later than Aug. 15 of year of enrollment. Early acceptance available. *Requirements:* Either graduation from accredited secondary school with 3 units English, 3 social studies, 2 mathematics, 1 science; or GED. 5 additional units recommended. *Entrance tests:* College Board SAT or ACT composite. *For transfer students:* 2.0 minimum GPA, 108 hours maximum transfer credit; correspondence/extension students 30 hours.

College credit and advanced placement for postsecondary-level work completed in secondary school and for extrainstitutional learning on basis of ACE *2006 Guide to the Evaluation of Educational Experiences in the Armed Services.* Tutoring available.

Degree Requirements: 138 credit hours; 2.0 GPA; 2 terms in residence; general education requirements; exit competency examinations (comprehensives in individual fields of study). Fulfillment of some degree requirements and exemption from some beginning courses possible by passing College Board CLEP, AP. *Grading system:* A–F; pass-fail; withdraw (carries time limit).

Distinctive Educational Programs: Work-experience programs. Extensive internship program. Cooperative baccalaureate program in engineering with Washington University (MO); in forestry with Duke University (NC); in medical technology with Methodist Hospital; in nursing with DePauw University. Interdisciplinary program in business-journalism. Facilities and programs for independent research, including honors programs, tutorials. Study abroad in England and Switzerland. Study also available by individual arrangement. Washington (DC) semester at American University. United Nations (NY) semester in cooperation with Drew University (NJ). Students may pursue a minor in theater at Indiana Central University.

ROTC: Army in cooperation with Indiana University-Purdue University at Indianapolis.

Degrees Conferred: 216 *baccalaureate.* Bachelors; degrees awarded in top five disciplines: education 51; communication, journalism, and related programs 35; social sciences 22; biological and biomedical sciences 17; business, management, marketing, and related support services 15.

Fees and Other Expenses: *Full-time tuition per academic year 2004–05:* $18,275. *Room and board per academic year:* $5,730. *Books and supplies:*$1,000.

Financial Aid: Aid from institutionally generated funds is provided on the basis of academic merit, financial need. Institution has a Program Participation Agreement with the U.S. Department of Education for eligible students to receive Pell Grants and other federal aid.

Financial aid to full-time, first-time undergraduate students: 31% received federal grants averaging $2,709; 48% state/local grants averaging $4,577; 100% institutional grants averaging $6,370; 94% loans averaging $6,209.

Departments and Teaching Staff: Art *professors* 0, *associate professors* 1, *assistant professors* 0, *instructors* 0, *part-time teachers* 1; biology 1, 2, 1, 0, 0; chemistry 1, 1, 0, 0, 0; economics/business/accounting 1, 1, 1, 0, 4; education 1, 1, 1, 0, 2; English 4, 0, 2, 0, 1; history 0, 1, 1, 1, 0; journalism 0, 1, 3, 0, 1; modern languages 2, 0, 0, 0, 0; mathematics 3, 0, 1, 0, 2; music 1, 0, 0, 0, 2; philosophy and religion 2, 1, 2, 0, 0; physical education 3, 1, 1, 1, 0; physics 0, 0, 1, 0, 0; political science 1, 1, 0, 0, 0; psychology 0, 1, 1, 0, 0; sociology 0, 1, 0, 1, 0; speech 0, 0, 0, 0, 2.

Total instructional faculty: 66. Total tenured faculty: 33. Degrees held by full-time faculty: doctorate 50%, master's 50%. 52% hold terminal degrees.

Enrollment: Total enrollment 994 (48.5% men, 51.5% women).

Characteristics of Student Body: *Ethnic/racial makeup:* Black non-Hispanic: 4.4%; American Indian or Alaska Native: .3%; Asian or Pacific Islander: .6%; Hispanic: 1.5%; White non-Hispanic: 86.3%; unknown: .1%.

International Students: 7 nonresident aliens enrolled fall 2004. Programs available to students whose native language is not English: Social and cultural. No financial aid specifically designated for international students.

Student Life: On-campus residence halls house 89% of student body. Residence halls for men constitute 55% of such space, for women 45%. 33% of men join and 15% live in fraternities. *Intercollegiate athletics:* men only: baseball, basketball, cross-country, football, golf, tennis, track, wrestling; women only: basketball, field hockey, tennis, track, volleyball. *Special regulations:* Cars permitted for all but first-semester freshmen. Quiet hours. Residence hall visitation from 11am to midnight Sun.–Thurs., 11am to 2am Fri. and Sat. *Special services:* Learning Resources Center, medical services. *Student publications, radio: The Almanack,* a yearbook; *The Apoqee,* an annual literary magazine; *The Franklin,* a weekly newspaper. Radio station WFCI broadcasts 72 hours per week. *Surrounding community:* Franklin population 12,000. Indianapolis, 20 miles from campus, is nearest metropolitan area. Served by airport 27 miles from campus.

Publications: *Mennonite Quarterly Review* first published 1927. Pinchpenny Press published 5 titles in 1990.

Library Collections: 125,000 volumes. 215,500 microforms; 7,450 audiovisual materials; 810 periodical subscriptions; Access to online information retrieval services and the Internet.

Most important holdings include David Demaree Banta collection of Indiana history; Indiana Baptist Collection; Roger D. Branigin Papers.

Buildings and Grounds: Campus area 75 acres.

Chief Executive Officer: Dr. James G. Moseley, President. >p<Address admission inquiries to Kathryn Coffman, Director of Admissions.

Goshen College

1700 South Main Street
Goshen, Indiana 46526
Tel: (574) 535-7000   **E-mail:** admissions@goshen.edu
Fax: (574) 535-7660   **Internet:** www.goshen.edu

Institution Description: Goshen College is a private college affiliated with the Mennonite Church. *Enrollment: 908. Degrees awarded:* Baccalaureate.

Member of Northern Indiana Consortium for Education.

Accreditation: *Regional:* NCA. *Professional:* nursing, nursing education, social work, teacher education

History: Established, chartered, and incorporated as Elkhart Institute 1894; offered first instruction at postsecondary level 1903; awarded first degree (baccalaureate) 1910. *See* John S. Umble, *Goshen College: 1894–1954* (Scottdale, PA: Mennonite Publishing House, 1954) and Susan Fisher Miller, *Culture for Service: A History of Goshen College 1894–1994* (Nappanee, IN: Evangel Press, 1994) for further information.

Institutional Structure: *Governing board:* Goshen College Board of Overseers. Representation: 12 trustees, including 10 alumni. All voting. *Composition of institution:* Administrators 33 men / 22 women. Academic affairs headed by academic dean. Management/business/finances directed by business manager. Full-time instructional faculty 58. Academic governance body, the faculty, meets an average of 16 times per year.

Calendar: Semesters. Academic year Aug. to May. Freshmen admitted Aug., Jan., Apr. Degrees conferred May, Aug., Dec. Formal commencement May.

Characteristics of Freshmen: 775 of applicants admitted. 41% of applicant admitted and enrolled.

75% (121 students) submitted SAT scores; 33% (53 students) submitted ACT scores. *25th percentile:* SAT Verbal 490, SAT Math 490; ACT Composite 20, ACT English 21, ACT Math 21. *75th percentile:* SAT Verbal 670, SAT Math 630; ACT Composite 28, ACT English 30, ACT Math 28.

66% of entering freshmen expected to graduate within 5 years. 47% of freshmen from Indiana. Freshmen from 22 states and 4 foreign countries.

Admission: Rolling admissions plan. For fall acceptance, apply as early as 1 year prior to enrollment, but not later than Aug. 15. Early acceptance available. *Requirements:* Graduation from accredited secondary school with 16 academic units. GED accepted from applicants 19 years of age or older. 4 units English, 2-4 foreign language, 2-4 mathematics, 2 science, 2 social studies recommended. Minimum GPA 2.0. Lowest acceptable secondary school class standing 50th percentile. Combined SAT scores of 920 or ACT composite score of 21. *Entrance tests:* College Board SAT or ACT composite. *For transfer students:* 2.0 minimum GPA; from 4-year accredited institution 90 hours maximum transfer credit; correspondence/extension students 15 hours.

College credit and advanced placement for postsecondary-level work completed in secondary school, for departmental examinations, and for extrainstitutional learning on basis of ACE *2006 Guide to the Evaluation of Educational Experiences in the Armed Services*; faculty assessment. Tutoring available.

Degree Requirements: 120 credit hours; 3 terms in residence; international education (at Goshen or abroad). Fulfillment of some degree requirements possible by passing College Board CLEP, APP, departmental examinations. *Grading system:* A–F; pass-fail; withdraw (carries time limit); descriptive reports may be appended to A–F or pass-fail.

Distinctive Educational Programs: International education is part of general education for all students. Normally done through Study-Service Trimester in Costa Rica, Dominican Republic, Indonesia, Germany, People's Republic of China. Other study abroad in Europe, Asia and Latin America through programs sponsored by Brethren Colleges Abroad. Council on International Education Exchanges, Council of Mennonite Colleges. TESOL (Teaching English to Speakers of Other Languages) minor. Work-study programs. Evening classes. Dual-degree program in engineering with Case Western Reserve University and Washington University. Domestic off-campus study with Urban Life Center in Chicago (IL). Tropical Agriculture Study at University of Florida and Washington (DC), Study and Service Year sponsored by Eastern Mennonite University.

Degrees Conferred: 244 *baccalaureate:* biological/life sciences 8; business/marketing 40; communications/communication technologies 12; computer and information science 14; education 17; English 9; foreign languages literature 12; health professions and related sciences 17; mathematics 4; natural resources/environmental science 4; parks and recreation 2; philosophy/religion/theology 7; physical sciences 5; protective services/public administration 12; psychology 11; social sciences and history 16; visual and performing arts 28.

Fees and Other Expenses: *Full-time tuition per academic year 2004–05:* $18,200. *Room and board per academic year:* $6,200.

Financial Aid: Goshen College offers a direct lending program. Aid from institutionally generated funds is provided on the basis of academic merit, financial need, athletic ability, other criteria. Institution has a Program Participation Agreement with the U.S. Department of Education for eligible students to receive Pell Grants and other federal aid.

Financial aid to full-time, first-time undergraduate students: need-based scholarships/grants totaling $6,310,255, self-help $2,574,618, tuition waivers $323,197, athletic awards $582,725; non-need-based scholarships/grants totaling $1,298,632, self-help $1,015,027, parent loans $719,914, tuition waivers $190,695, athletic awards $68,800.

Departments and Teaching Staff: *Professors* 25, *associate professors* 19, *assistant professors* 14, *part-time teachers* 74. *Total instructional faculty:* 110 (full-time 64, part-time 46; women 50, men 60; members of minority groups 6). Total faculty with doctorate, first-professional, or other terminal degree: 48. Student-to-faculty ratio: 10:1. Degrees held by full-time faculty: doctorate 62%, master's 34%. 62% hold terminal degrees. *Faculty development:* $73,800 in grants for research. 1 faculty member awarded a sabbatical 2004–05.

Enrollment: Total enrollment 908. Undergraduate full-time 344 men / 462 women, part-time 30m / 72w. *Transfer students:* 57.

Characteristics of Student Body: *Ethnic and racial makeup:* number of Black non-Hispanic: 30; American Indian or Alaska Native: 2; Asian or Pacific Islander: 9; Hispanic: 37; White non-Hispanic: 755; unknown: 2. *Age distribution:* number under 18: 5; 18–19: 301; 20–21: 286; 22–24: 126; 25–29: 62; 30–34: 32; 35–39: 32; 40–49: 45; 50–64: 10; unknown: 9.

International Students: 73 nonresident aliens enrolled fall 2004. 5 students from Europe, 30 Asia, 14 Africa, 14 Canada, 3 other. Programs available to aid students whose native language is not English: Social, cultural, financial. English as a Second Language Program. Variable number of scholarships available annually for qualifying international students.

Student Life: On-campus residence halls house 67% of student body. Residence halls for women only constitute 13% of such space, for both sexes 87%. 10% live in small-group housing of 5-15 students per unit. 46% of married students request institutional housing; 41% are so housed. *Intercollegiate athletics:* men only: baseball, cross-country, golf, soccer, tennis, track; women only: basketball, baseball, cross-country, soccer, tennis, volleyball. *Special regulations:* Standard of Life Together: Even though people of diverse backgrounds make up the college community, each member is expected to affirm and show serious intent to live according to a set of minimal standards: (1) non-use of alcohol,

tobacco, illegal drugs; (2) opposition to sexual discrimination, sexual coercion, sexual exploitation and sexual abuse; (3) prohibition of the possession and use of firearms or fireworks. Quiet hours from 11pm to 7am Sun.–Thurs. Residence hall visitation hours vary. *Special services:* Learning Resources Center, medical services. *Student publications, radio: Maple Leaf*, a yearbook; *Record*, a weekly newspaper. Radio station WGCS broadcasts 96 hours per week. *Surrounding community:* Goshen population 23,000. Chicago (IL), 120 miles from campus, is nearest metropolitan area. Served by airports 16 and 35 miles from campus. Passenger rail service 13 miles from campus.

Publications: *Mennonite Quarterly Review* first published 1927.

Library Collections: 180,577 volumes. Online catalog. 564 periodical subscriptions. 159,300 microforms. 48 computer work stations. Access to online information retrieval systems. Students have access to the Internet at no charge. Total 2004–05 budget for books and materials: $161,300.

Most important special collections include the Mennonite Historical Library (45,000 books and periodicals on Mennonite and Anabaptist history); Hartzler Music Collection of 3,300 volumes of early American hymnody; Peace and War Collection.

Buildings and Grounds: Campus area 135 acres. *New buildings:* Music Building/Performing Arts Center completed 2002.

Chief Executive Officer: Dr. John Yordy, President.

Address admission inquiries to Karen L. Raftus, Director of Admissions.

Grace College and Theological Seminary

200 Seminary Drive
Winona Lake, Indiana 46590

Tel: (574) 372-5110   **E-mail:** admissions@grace.edu
Fax: (574) 372-5114   **Internet:** www.grace.edu

Institution Description: Grace College is a private, independent, nonprofit college affiliated with Fellowship of Grace Brethren Churches. *Enrollment:* 1,258. *Degrees awarded:* Associate, baccalaureate. Certificates also awarded.

Accreditation: *Regional:* NCA. *Professional:* music, social work, teacher education

History: Grace Theological Seminary chartered 1937; Collegiate Division of Grace Theological Seminary established and offered first instruction at postsecondary level 1948; adopted present name and awarded first degree (associate) 1950; became 4-year institution 1954.

Institutional Structure: *Governing board:* Board of Trustees. Extrainstitutional representation: 27 trustees; institutional representation: 1 administrator, president of the college. 2 ex officio. All voting. *Composition of institution:* Administrators 5 men. Academic affairs headed by academic dean. Management/business/finances directed by director of business affairs. Full-time instructional faculty 39. Academic governance body, the faculty, meets an average of 15 times per year.

Calendar: Semesters. Academic year Aug. to May. Freshmen admitted Aug., May, June, July. Degrees conferred May, Aug., Dec. Formal commencement May.

Characteristics of Freshmen: 72% of applicants admitted. 31% of applicants admitted and enrolled.

25th percentile: SAT Verbal 480, SAT Math 470; ACT Composite 19, ACT English 18, ACT Math 19. *75th percentile:* SAT Verbal 600, SAT Math 580; ACT Composite 26, ACT English 26, ACT Math26.

28% of entering freshmen expected to graduate within 5 years. 52% of freshmen from Indiana. Freshmen from 19 states.

Admission: Rolling admissions plan. *Requirements:* Either graduation from accredited secondary school or GED. Recommend 4 units English, 2 in a foreign language, 2–3 mathematics, 2–3 science, 3 social studies. Lowest acceptable secondary school class standing 50th percentile. *Entrance tests:* ACT or SAT. *For transfer students:* No limit on transfer hours from an accredited institution.

College credit and advanced placement for postsecondary-level work completed in secondary school. Tutoring available.

Degree Requirements: *For all associate degrees:* 78 semester hours; 1 physical education course. *For all baccalaureate degrees:* 124 semester hours; 2 physical education courses. *For all degrees:* 2.0 GPA; 30 hours in residence; daily chapel attendance; distribution requirements. Fulfillment of some degree requirements and exemption from some beginning courses possible by passing departmental examinations, College Board CLEP, AP. *Grading system:* A–F; pass-fail.

Distinctive Educational Programs: Internships. Evening classes. Cooperative baccalaureate programs in home economics, industrial technology, and nursing with Ball State University. Facilities and programs for independent research including individual majors, independent study. Associate's program offered in state prison. Study abroad in France through University of Grenoble, in Spain through University of Valencia.

Degrees Conferred: 228 *baccalaureate* (B); 25 *master's* (M): biological/life sciences 8 (B); business/marketing 49 (B); communications/communication technologies 16 (B); computer and information sciences 3 (B); education 35 (B); English 4 (B); foreign languages and literature 6 (B); interdisciplinary studies 1 (B); mathematics 1 (B); parks and recreation 3 (B); philosophy/religion/theology 57 (B), 20 (M); physical sciences 1 (B); protective services/public administration 10 (B); psychology 33 (B), 5 (M); social sciences and history 1 (B); visual and performing arts 11 (B). 8 *first-professional:* master of divinity 8.

Fees and Other Expenses: *Full-time tuition per academic year 2004–05:* $14,630 undergraduate; graduate programs $417 per credit hour. *Required fees:* $40. *Room and board per academic year:* $6,150.

Financial Aid: Aid from institutionally generated funds is provided on the basis of academic merit, financial need, athletic ability. Institution has a Program Participation Agreement with the U.S. Department of Education for eligible students to receive Pell Grants and other federal aid.

Financial aid to full-time, first-time undergraduate students: need-based scholarships/grants totaling $4,372,043, self-help $4,003,790, parent loans $577,995, tuition waivers $271,348, athletic awards $395,028; non-need-based scholarships/grants totaling $860,185, self-help $1,201,842, parent loans $1,688,400, tuition waivers $280,584, athletic awards $190,482.

Departments and Teaching Staff: *Total instructional faculty:* 107 (full-time 46, part-time 61; women 25, men 82; members of minority groups 4). Total faculty with doctorate, first-professional, or other terminal degree: 36. Student-to-faculty ratio: 18:1.

Enrollment: Total enrollment 1,258. Undergraduate full-time 495 men / 467 women, part-time 88m / 63w; part-time 88m / 63w; first-professional full-time 12m, part-time 13m; graduate full-time 26m / 12w, part-time 60m / 22w.

Characteristics of Student Body: *Ethnic and racial makeup:* number of Black non-Hispanic: 96; American Indian or Alaska Native: 6; Asian or Pacific Islander: 4; Hispanic: 4; White non-Hispanic: 480. *Age distribution:* number under 18: 42; 18–19: 315; 20–21: 355; 22–24: 122; 25–29: 71; 30–34: 56; 35–39: 51; 40–49: 75; 50–64: 25; 65 and over: 1.

International Students: 9 nonresident aliens enrolled fall 2004. 2 students from Europe, 2 Asia, 2 Central and South America, 1 Africa, 2 Canada. No programs available to aid students whose native language is not English. No financial aid specifically designated for international students.

Student Life: On-campus residence halls house 80% of student body. Residence halls for men only constitute 40% of such space, for women only 60%. *Intercollegiate athletics:* men only: baseball, basketball, cross-country, golf, soccer, track; women only: basketball, soccer, softball, volleyball. *Special regulations:* Cars permitted without restrictions. Dress should adhere to traditional Christian standards. Quiet hours from 11pm to 6am Sun.–Thurs. *Special services:* Learning Resources Center, medical services. *Student publications: The Heritage*, a yearbook; *The Sounding Board*, a weekly newspaper. *Surrounding community:* Winona Lake population 3,000. Indianapolis, 120 miles from campus, is nearest metropolitan area. Served by 2 airports 50 miles from campus.

Library Collections: 140,000 volumes including bound books, serial backfiles, electronic documents, and government documents not in separate collections. Online catalog. Current serial subscriptions: 369 paper, 23,000 microform, 20,000 via electronic access. 1,900 recordings; 610 compact discs. 17 computer work stations. Students have access to the Internet at no charge. Total budget for books, periodicals, audiovisual materials, microforms 2004–05: $96,000.

Most important holdings include Billy Sunday Collection, Grace Brethren Church Collection, Near East Archeology Collection; Winona Lake local history.

Buildings and Grounds: Campus area 400 acres.

Chief Executive Officer: Dr. Ronald E. Manahan, President.

Address admission inquiries to Anecia R. Miller, Director of Admissions.

Huntington College

2303 College Avenue
Huntington, Indiana 46750
Tel: (219) 356-6000   **E-mail:** admissions@huntington.edu
Fax: (219) 356-4086   **Internet:** www.huntington.edu

Institution Description: Huntington College is a private, Christian liberal arts college affiliated with Church of the United Brethren in Christ. *Enrollment:* 959. *Degrees awarded:* Baccalaureate.

Accreditation: *Regional:* NCA.

History: Established and chartered as Central College at Huntington and offered first instruction at postsecondary level 1897; awarded first degree (baccalaureate) 1899; adopted present name 1917.

Institutional Structure: *Governing board:* Board of Trustees. Extrainstitutional representation: 29 trustees, 8 church-elected members; institutional representation: 1 trustee, 1 student. *Composition of institution:* Administrators 14 men / 2 women. Academic affairs headed by academic dean. Business/finances directed by business manager. Full-time instructional faculty 41. Academic governance body, the College Faculty, meets biweekly.

Calendar: Semesters (4-1-4 plan). Academic year Sept. to May. Freshmen admitted Sept., Jan., Feb., June, July. Degrees conferred May, July, Jan. Formal commencement May. Summer session of 2 terms from late May to mid-July.

Characteristics of Freshmen: 659 applicants (230 men, 429 women). 90.4% of applicants admitted. 34.2% of admitted students enrolled full-time.

77% (157 students) submitted SAT scores; 56% (115 students) submitted ACT scores. *25th percentile:* SAT I Verbal 460, SAT I Math 450; ACT Composite 20, ACT English 21, ACT Math 19. *75th percentile:* SAT I Verbal 630, SAT I Math 620; ACT Composite 28, ACT English 28, ACT Math 27.

47.3% of entering freshmen expected to graduate within 5 years. 57% of freshmen from Indiana. Freshmen from 18 states and 2 foreign countries.

Admission: Rolling admissions plan. For fall acceptance, apply as early as May of previous year, but not later than Aug. 15 of year of enrollment. Early acceptance available. *Requirements:* 2.3 high school GPA/850 SAT, ACT18. Recommend 4 units English, 3 social studies, 3 mathematics, 3 science. *Entrance tests:* College Board SAT or ACT, English and mathematics placement tests. *For transfer students:* 2.0 minimum GPA.

Credit awarded for acceptable scores on CLEP, AP and GCE Advanced Level examinations. Tutoring and remedial courses offered during regular academic year; credit given for most remedial courses. English as a Second Language instruction for international students.

Degree Requirements: *For all baccalaureate degrees:* 128 credit hours; either last final 30 or minimum 90 hours in residence. *For all undergraduate degrees:* 2.0 GPA; liberal arts core requirements. Fulfillment of some degree requirements and exemption from some beginning courses possible with acceptable scores on CLEP, AP. *Grading system:* A–F; withdraw (carries time limit); incomplete (deadline after which A–F assigned).

Distinctive Educational Programs: *For undergraduates:* Study semester in Jamaica. Latin American Studies in Costa Rica, Hollywood Film Studies, and American Studies program in Washington, DC available. Short term overseas and U.S. study-travel courses available at northern Michigan environmental studies facility. Study opportunities in Israel offered in cooperation with American Institute of Holy Land Studies. Graphic arts curriculum includes instruction in computer-assisted design. Independent study and internship experiences encouraged for upper division students. Institute for Family Studies in Colorado Springs, Colorado.

Degrees Conferred: 19 *associate*; 177 *baccalaureate*; 1 *master's*. Bachelor's degrees awarded in top five disciplines: education 56; business, management, marketing, and related support services 34; theology and ministerial studies 19; communication, journalism, and related programs 14; psychology 12.

Fees and Other Expenses: *Full-time tuition per academic year 2004–05:* $18,490. *Books and supplies:* $750. *Room and board per academic year:* $5,500.

Financial Aid: Aid from institutionally generated funds is provided on the basis of academic merit, financial need, athletic ability, other criteria. Institution has a Program Participation Agreement with the U.S. Department of Education for eligible students to receive Pell Grants and other federal aid.

Financial aid to full-time, first-time undergraduate students: 24% received federal grants averaging $3,170; 33% state/local grants averaging $4,812; 90% institutional grants averaging $5,561; 83% loans averaging $3,198.

Departments and Teaching Staff: *Professors* 14, *associate professors* 12, *assistant professors* 13; *instructors* 2, *part-time faculty* 19. *Total instructional faculty:* 60. Highest degrees held by full-time faculty: doctorate 81%, master's 19%. 81% hold terminal degrees.

Enrollment: Total enrollment 959 (43.1% men, 66.9% women).

Characteristics of Student Body: *Ethnic/racial makeup:* Black non-Hispanic: .8%; Asian or Pacific Islander: .9%; American Indian or Alaska Native .1%; Hispanic: .7%; White non-Hispanic: 95.3%.*Age distribution:* 17–21: 68%; 22–24: 25%; 25–29: 3%; 30–34: 2%; 35–39: 1%; 40–49: 6%; 50–59: 2%; 60–up: .2%.

International Students: 21 nonresident aliens enrolled fall 2004. Students from Europe, Asia, Latin America, Canada. Programs available to aid students whose native language is not English: English as a Second Language Program. Financial aid specifically designated for international students: undergraduate scholarships available annually.

Student Life: On-campus residence halls house 88% of undergraduate student body. Residence halls for men only constitute 50 % of capacity; for women 50%. *Intercollegiate athletics:* men only: baseball, basketball, cross-country, golf, soccer, tennis, track; women only: basketball, cross-country, soccer, softball, tennis, track, volleyball. *Special regulations:* Cars permitted without restrictions. *Special services:* Learning Center, Writing Center, microcomputer lab, tutoring, extended orientation course, medical services. *Student publications: Huntingtonian*, a biweekly newspaper. *Surrounding community:* Huntington population 16,500. Indianapolis, 100 miles from campus, is nearest metropolitan area. Served by airport 25 miles from campus.

Publications: *Alumni News and Views* published quarterly for alumni.

Library Collections: 130,000 volumes. 17,500 microforms; 5,400 audiovisual materials; 522 current periodical subscriptions.

Most important holdings include collections on Eastern European Studies; United Brethren in Christ Church Archives; curriculum materials collection.

Buildings and Grounds: Campus area 170 acres.

Chief Executive Officer: Dr. G. Blair Dowden, President.

Address admission inquiries to Jeffrey c. Breggren, Vice President for Enrollment Management.

Hanover College

One College Avenue
P.O. Box 108
Hanover, Indiana 47243
Tel: (812) 866-7000
Fax: (812) 866-6879

Institution Description: Hanover College is a private, independent college related to the Synod of Lincoln Trails, Presbyterian Church (U.S.A.). *Enrollment:* 1,062. *Degrees awarded:* Baccalaureate.

Accreditation: *Regional:* NCA. *Professional*: teacher education

History: Established as Hanover College, a school for men, and offered first instruction at postsecondary level 1827; chartered 1828; awarded first degree (baccalaureate) 1830; established Henry C. Long College for Women 1947; merged with Henry C. Long College 1978.

Institutional Structure: *Governing board:* Board of Trustees of Hanover College. Representation: 32 trustees, 19 of which are alumni. All voting. *Composition of institution:* Administrators 105. Academic affairs headed by vice president for academic affairs. Management/business/finances directed by vice president for business affairs. Total instructional faculty 99. Academic governance body, the faculty, meets an average of 9 times per year.

Calendar: Semesters. Academic year Sept. through May. Freshmen admitted Sept., Jan. Degrees conferred May, Aug., Dec. Formal commencement May. No summer session.

Characteristics of Freshmen: 74% of applicants admitted. 31% of applicants admitted and enrolled.

65% (247 students) submitted SAT scores; 34% (130 students) submitted ACT scores. *25th percentile*: SAT Verbal 530, SAT Math 540; ACT Composite 22. *75th percentile*: SAT Verbal 640, SAT Math 640; ACT Composite 28.

69% of entering freshmen expected to graduate within 5 years. 65% of freshmen from Indiana. Freshmen from 21 states and 5 foreign countries.

Admission: Rolling admissions plan. For fall acceptance, apply as early as Sept. 1 of previous year, but not later than Mar. 1 of year of enrollment. Early acceptance available. Apply by Dec. 1 for early notification I; Jan. 15 for early notification II; Mar. 1 is the priority date. *Requirements:* Either graduation from an accredited secondary school with 16 units, including 4 English, 2–3 in a foreign language, 2–3 history and social studies, 2–3 laboratory science, 2–3 college preparatory mathematics. Lowest acceptable secondary school class standing 50th percentile. *Entrance tests:* College Board SAT or ACT composite. For transfer students: 2.5 minimum GPA; from 4-year accredited institution 70 hours maximum transfer credit;

College credit and advanced placement for postsecondary-level work completed in secondary school. Tutoring available. Noncredit remedial courses offered during regular academic year.

Degree Requirements: 36 courses; 2.0 GPA; final year in residence; 4 semester hours physical education; demonstrated competence in the liberal arts and natural sciences; exit competency examinations-comprehensives in individual fields of study. Fulfillment of some degree requirements and exemption from some beginning courses possible by passing departmental examinations, College Board Achievement Tests, APP. *Grading system:* A–F; pass-fail; withdraw (carries time limit); incomplete (deadline after which A–F is given).

Distinctive Educational Programs: Work-experience programs, including internships, field experience. Interdepartmental/interdisciplinary programs in environmental studies; non-Western studies. Facilities and programs for independent research, including tutorials, independent study courses. Study abroad programs in Australia, Belgium, France, Germany, Mexico, Spain, Turkey. Off-campus study in the U.S. through Washington (DC) semester at American University; Philadelphia Urban Semester; Rivers Institute at Hanover College; Career Connections Program; Center for Business Preparation; Center for Free Inquiry. Cross-registration through Spring Term Consortium.

Degrees Conferred: 226 *baccalaureate:* biological/life sciences 17; business/marketing 26; communications/communication technologies 18; computer and information sciences 4; education 3; foreign languages and literature 10; interdisciplinary studies 4; mathematics 5; philosophy/religion/theology 21; physical sciences 12; psychology 24; social sciences and history 59; visual and performing arts 11.

Fees and Other Expenses: *Full-time tuition per academic year 2005–06:* $21,150. *Required fees:* $500. *Room and board per academic year:* $6,500.

Financial Aid: Aid from institutionally generated funds is provided on the basis of academic merit, financial need, other considerations. Institution has a Program Participation Agreement with the U.S. Department of Education for eligible students to receive Pell Grants and other federal aid.

Financial aid to full-time, first-time undergraduate students: need-based scholarships/grants totaling $1,653,860, self-help $1,653,360, parent loans $241,734, tuition waivers $156,764; non-need-based scholarships/grants totaling $1,883,449, self-help $1,053,436, parent loans $1,177,647, tuition waivers $134,017.

Departments and Teaching Staff: *Professors* 29, *associate professors* 25, *assistant professors* 29, *instructors* 3, *part-time faculty* 11. *Total instructional faculty:* 97 (full-time 86, part-time 11; women 34, men 63; members of minority groups 12). Total faculty with doctorate, first-professional, or other terminal degree: 88. Student-to-faculty ratio: 10.7:1. *Faculty development:* $90,772 in grants for research. 7 faculty members awarded sabbaticals 2004–05.

Enrollment: Total enrollment 1,062. Undergraduate full-time 480 men / 572 women, part-time 4m / 6w.

Characteristics of Student Body: *Ethnic/racial makeup:* number of Black non-Hispanic: 21; American Indian or Alaska Native: 2; Asian or Pacific Islander: 32; Hispanic: 13; White non-Hispanic: 901; unknown: 50. *Age distribution:* under 18: 13; 18–19: 573; 20–21: 411; 22–24: 52; 25–29: 6; 30–34: 1; 35–39: 3; 40–49: 2; 50–64: 1.

International Students: 43 nonresident aliens enrolled fall 2004. Programs available to aid students whose native language is not English: Social, cultural. Some financial aid available for qualifying international students.

Student Life: On-campus residence halls house 70% of student body. 45% of men join and live in fraternities; 53% of women join and 40% live in sororities. 98% of students live on campus. *Intercollegiate athletics:* men only: baseball, basketball, cross-country, football, track; women only: basketball, field hockey, tennis, volleyball, softball. *Special regulations:* Freshmen who live within a 50-mile radius of campus must have special permission to have a vehicle on campus. Quiet hours set by individual residence halls. Most residence hall visitation is 24/7. *Special services:* Medical and counseling services. *Student publications: Kennings*, an annual literary magazine; *The Revonah*, a yearbook; *The Triangle*, a biweekly newspaper; *The Hanover Historical Review*, a student scholarly journal. *Surrounding community:* Hanover population 4,500. Louisville (KY), 45 miles from campus, is nearest metropolitan area.

Library Collections: 233,416 volumes including bound books, serial backfiles, electronic documents, and government documents not in separate collections. Online catalog. Current serial subscriptions: 1,007 paper, 755 via electronic access. 7,804 recordings; 596 compact discs. 9 computer work stations. Students have access to the Internet at no charge. Total budget for books, periodicals, audiovisual materials, microforms 2004–05: $433,150.

Most important holdings include archives of the Presbyterian Church of Indiana; Papers of Senator William E. Jenna; Charles J. Lynn Rare Book Collection; Gene Stratton Porter First Edition Collection.

Buildings and Grounds: Campus area 650 acres. *New buildings:* Science Center completed 2000; Ogle Center 2000; Greenwood Suites 2002; Beta Theta Pi House 2002; Shoe Box (student gathering place) 2004.

Chief Executive Officer: Dr. Russell L. Nichols, President.

Address admission inquiries to Kenneth Moyer, Director of Admission.

Indiana Institute of Technology

1600 East Washington Boulevard
Fort Wayne, Indiana 46803
Tel: (219) 422-5561   **E-mail:** admissions@indtech.edu
Fax: (219) 422-7696   **Internet:** www.indtech.edu

Institution Description: Indiana Institute of Technology is a private, independent, nonprofit institution. *Enrollment:* 3,200. *Degrees awarded:* Associate, baccalaureate, master's.

Accreditation: *Regional:* NCA. *Professional:* engineering

History: Established as Indiana Technical College and incorporated 1930; offered first instruction at postsecondary level 1931; awarded first degree (baccalaureate) 1933; adopted present name 1963.

Institutional Structure: *Governing board:* The Board of Trustees. Extrainstitutional representation: 14 trustees; institutional representation: 2 administrators, 1 full-time instructional faculty member. 1 student. 18 voting. *Composition of institution:* Administrators 16 men / 6 women. Management/business/finances directed by controller. Full-time instructional faculty 19 men / 4 women. Academic governance body, Faculty Assembly, meets an average of 4 times per year.

Calendar: Semesters. Academic year Aug. to May. Freshmen admitted Aug., Jan., June, July. Degrees conferred and formal commencement May. Summer session of 3 terms from June to Aug.

Characteristics of Freshmen: Average secondary school rank of freshmen 77th percentile. Mean SAT class score 453 verbal, 484 mathematical. Mean ACT composite score 22. 98% of applicants accepted. 20% of accepted applicants enrolled.

42% of entering freshmen expected to graduate within 5 years. 48% of freshmen from Indiana. Freshmen from 30 states and 8 foreign countries.

Admission: Rolling admissions plan. For fall acceptance, apply as early as spring of junior year of secondary school, but not later than last day of registration. *Requirements:* Either graduation from accredited secondary school with 4 units in English, 2 mathematics and science, 7 academic electives; or GED. Additional requirements for engineering majors. Minimum GPA 2.0. *Entrance tests:* College Board SAT or ACT composite required. For foreign students minimum TOEFL score 500. *For transfer students:* 2.0 minimum GPA; from 4-year accredited institution maximum transfer credit limited only by residence requirement; from 2-year accredited institution 48 hours.

College credit and advanced placement for postsecondary-level work completed in secondary school. For extrainstitutional learning (life experience), college credit on basis of ACE *2006 Guide to the Evaluation of Educational Experiences in the Armed Services*, portfolio assessment, faculty assessment. Tutoring available. Developmental courses offered in summer session and regular academic year; credit given.

Degree Requirements: *For all associate degrees:* 60 semester hours; 15 semester hours in residence. *For all baccalaureate degrees:* 120 semester hours for business; 124 computer science; 130 engineering; 30 semester hours in residence. *For all degrees:* 2.00 GPA and 2.00 major point average. Competency assessment required in all associate and baccalaureate degrees.

Fulfillment of some degree requirements and exemption from some courses possible by passing departmental exams, transfer credit, College Board CLEP, AP, or experiential credit. *Grading system:* A–F; withdraw (deadline after which grade of W is assigned).

Distinctive Educational Programs: Cooperative education. Evening classes. Extended Studies Program for off-campus correspondence degree completion for associate and bachelor's degrees. Early admission for qualified high school juniors/seniors. competency-based education requires Communication Skills and Major Area Assessment for associate degree; Communication Skills, Humanities/Social Science, Support Knowledge, and Major Area Assessment for baccalaureate degree. All students required to have personal computer. College leases Apple PCs, but student may bring previously-owned PC in lieu of leasing college machine.

Degrees Conferred: 590 *baccalaureate*; 116 *master's*: business/marketing 546 (B), 116 (M); computer and information sciences 4 (B); engineering/engineering technologies 33 (B); parks and recreation 7 (B).

Fees and Other Expenses: *Full-time tuition per academic year 2005–06:* $17,600 undergraduate; $333 per credit hour for graduate programs. *Room and board per academic year:* $6,750.

Financial Aid: Aid from institutionally generated funds is provided on the basis of academic merit, financial need, athletic ability, other criteria. Institution has a Program Participation Agreement with the U.S. Department of Education for eligible students to receive Pell Grants and other federal aid.

Financial aid to full-time, first-time undergraduate students: need-based scholarships/grants totaling $4,325,459, self-help $6,358,773, parent loans $56,823, tuition waivers $4,612,802, athletic awards $4,612,802; non-need-based scholarships/grants totaling $3,534,183, self-help $2,556,442, parent loans $655,581, tuition waivers $339,528, athletic awards $125,670.

Departments and Teaching Staff: Engineering and science *professors* 3, *associate professors* 8, *assistant professors* 3, *part-time faculty* 5; business 4, 5, 14, 224; computer studies 0, 1, 2, 12. *Total instructional faculty:* 281 (full-time 42, part-time 239; women 96, men 184; members of minority groups 31). Total faculty with doctorate, first-professional, or other terminal degree: 24. Student-to-faculty ratio: 19:1.

Enrollment: Total enrollment 3,425. Undergraduate full-time 969 men / 831 women, part-time 555m / 842w; graduate full-time 116m / 113w, part-time 118m / 80w. *Transfer students:* in-state 272; from out-of-state 32.

Characteristics of Student Body: *Ethnic/racial makeup:* number of Black non-Hispanic: 402; American Indian or Alaska Native: 24; Asian or Pacific Islander: 34; Hispanic: 71; White non-Hispanic: 2,157; unknown: 299. *Age dis-*

tribution: under 18: 2; 18–19: 107; 20–21: 296; 22–24: 289; 25–29: 424; 30–34: 347; 35–39: 413; 40–49: 600; 50–64: 117; 65 and over: 1.

International Students: 30 nonresident aliens enrolled fall 2004. Students from Europe, Asia, Africa, Canada. Programs available to aid students whose native language is not English: English as a Second Language Program.

Student Life: On-campus residence halls house 50% of student body. One residence hall for flat-style residence; male/female residents. One residence hall with limited access wing for female residents only; remainder of residence hall for male residents. Some men live in fraternity housing. *Intercollegiate athletics:* men only: basketball, baseball, soccer; women only: basketball, softball, volleyball. *Special regulations:* Registered cars permitted without restrictions. Quiet hours from 7:00pm to 12:00 noon. Residence hall visitation from 2:00pm until 11:00pm Sun.–Thurs. Visitation Fri. and Sat. from 2:00pm until 1:00am. *Special services:* Learning Resources Center, Computer Center, Microcomputer Center, Computer-Aided Design (CAD) Center. *Student publications, radio: Tech Times* published biweekly during academic year. Radio station for on-campus transmission. *Surrounding community:* Fort Wayne population 165,000. Indianapolis, 120 miles south of campus, is nearest metropolitan area. Served by mass transit bus system; airport 8 miles from campus; passenger rail service 4 miles from campus.

Library Collections: 50,000 volumes. 500 microform titles; 125 current periodical subscriptions. 12 computer work stations. Access to online information retrieval systems. Students have access to the Internet at no charge.

Most important holdings include NASA special publications and reports (microfiche).

Buildings and Grounds: Campus area 25 acres. *New buildings:* Andorfer Commons; Yergens-Rogers Residence Hall.

Chief Executive Officer: Dr. Arthur Snyder, President.

Address admission inquiries to Allison Carnahan, Vice President of Enrollment Management.

Indiana State University

210 North 7th Street
Terre Haute, Indiana 47809

Tel: (812) 237-6311   **E-mail:** admissions@isu.indstate.edu
Fax: (812) 237-2291   **Internet:** www.isu.indstate.edu

Institution Description: Indiana State University is a comprehensive, residential, state-assisted institution of higher education serving the community, state and nation through undergraduate and graduate instruction, research and public service. *Enrollment:* 11,200. *Degrees awarded:* Associate, baccalaureate, master's, doctorate. Educational specialist certificate also awarded.

Accreditation: *Regional:* NCA. *Professional:* art, athletic training, business, clinical psychology, construction education, counseling psychology, dietetics, electronic technology, English language education, environmental health, family and consumer science, industrial technology, manufacturing technology, marriage and family therapy, mechanical technology, music, nursing, recreation and leisure services, school psychology, social work, speech-language pathology, teacher education

History: Established as Indiana State Normal School 1865; offered first instruction at postsecondary level 1900; awarded first degree (baccalaureate) 1908; changed name to Indiana State Teachers College 1929, to Indiana State College 1961; adopted present name 1965.

Institutional Structure: *Governing board:* Indiana State University Board of Trustees. Representation: 9 trustees, including 1 student and 2 alumni (all appointed by the governor of Indiana). All voting. *Composition of institution:* Administrators 24 men / 7 women. Academic affairs headed by vice president for academic affairs. Management/business/finances directed by vice president for business affairs. Academic governance body, Faculty Senate, meets an average of 12 times per year.

Calendar: Semesters. Academic year Aug. to May. Degrees conferred May, Dec. Formal commencement May. Two summer terms.

Characteristics of Freshmen: 5,399 applicants (2,580 men, 2,819 women). 83.3% of applicants admitted. 40.3% of admitted students enrolled full-time.

80% (1,479 students) submitted SAT scores; 23% (431 students) submitted ACT scores. *25th percentile:* SAT I Verbal 420, SAT I Math 420; ACT Composite 17, ACT English 16, ACT Math 17. *75th percentile:* SAT I Verbal 520, SAT I Math 530; ACT Composite 22, ACT English 22, ACT Math 23.

94% of freshmen from Indiana. Freshmen from 47 states and 64 foreign countries.

Admission: Rolling admissions plan. For fall acceptance, apply as early as 1 year prior to enrollment, but not later than Aug. 15 of year of enrollment. Early acceptance available. Freshman applicants are normally expected to be ranked in the upper 50% of their high school class. Students whose academic achievement is below this level are reviewed on an individual basis. Additional consideration will be given to standardized test scores, the rigor of the students' high school curriculum, grades earned in academic subjects, and other evidence that the applicants have the potential for success in university course work. A limited number of students may be admitted conditionally if they agree to participate in a program offered through the Student Academic Services Center. *Entrance tests:* College Board SAT; ACT composite. For foreign students TOEFL or equivalent English proficiency test scores. *For transfer students:* 2.0 minimum GPA; from 4-year accredited institution 94 semester hours maximum transfer credit; from 2-year accredited institution 64 hours; correspondence/extension students 31 hours.

College credit and advanced placement for postsecondary-level work completed in secondary school and for extrainstitutional learning on basis of ACE *2006 Guide to the Evaluation of Educational Experiences in the Armed Services,* portfolio and faculty assessments. Tutoring available. Noncredit developmental and remedial courses offered.

Degree Requirements: *For undergraduates:* 124 semester hours; 2.0 GPA; 30 hours in residence; 2 credit hours of physical education; general education requirements. Fulfillment of some degree requirements and exemption from some beginning courses possible by passing departmental examinations, College Board CLEP, AP, Achievement Tests, ACT. *Grading system:* A–F.

Distinctive Educational Programs: Work-experience programs. Flexible meeting places and schedules, including off-campus centers (at Washington, Vincennes, Putnamville, Sellersburg, Booneville, Hammond, Indianapolis, 80 miles away; Jasper, 110 miles away; Evansville, 112 miles away; Merrillville, 165 miles away), weekend and evening classes. Special facilities for using telecommunications in the classroom. Interdisciplinary programs in African studies, Honors Program, General Studies, International Studies, International Business, Latin American Studies, Women's Studies. Study abroad offered in cooperation with other universities. Interactive programs through Indiana Higher Education Telecommunication Services. *Other distinctive programs:* Academic Enrichment and Learning Skills Center.; First-Year Experience Program; Supplemental Instruction Program; Center for Teaching and Learning, Student Outcomes Assessment Program; University 101 Program; Student Academic Services Center. Study abroad in Austria, Costa Rica, France, Germany, Russia, Spain.

ROTC: Army in cooperation with Rose-Hulman Institute of Technology; Air Force in cooperation with Indiana State University.

Degrees Conferred: 155 *associate*; 1,413 *baccalaureate*; 431 *master's*; 33 *doctorate.* Bachelor's degrees awarded in top five disciplines: business, management, marketing, and related support services 259; education 249; social sciences 159; engineering technologies/technicians 133; visual and performing arts 74.

Fees and Other Expenses: *Full-time tuition per academic year 2004–05:* $5,640 resident, $12,368 out-of-state student. Contact the university for graduate tuition/fees. *Room and board per academic year:* $5,428. *Books and supplies:* $1,020.

Financial Aid: Aid from institutionally generated funds is provided on the basis of academic merit, financial need, athletic ability. Institution has a Program Participation Agreement with the U.S. Department of Education for eligible students to receive Pell Grants and other federal aid.

Financial aid to full-time, first-time undergraduate students: 28% received federal grants averaging $2,864; 30% state/local grants averaging $3.366; 35% institutional grants averaging $2,542; 50% loans averaging $3,813.

Departments and Teaching Staff: College of Arts and Sciences *professors* 125, *associate professors* 87, *assistant professors* 77, *instructors* 2, *part-time faculty* 92; School of Business 18, 15, 10, 0, 14; School of Education 34, 23, 18, 1, 13; School of Health and Human Performance 13, 9, 13, 0, 16; School of Nursing 2, 8, 16, 0, 19; School of Technology 15, 11, 14, 2, 6.

Total instructional faculty: 663. Degrees held by full-time faculty: doctorate 77.4%, master's 22.6%. 85% hold terminal degrees.

Enrollment: Total enrollment 11,200. Undergraduate 9,321 (49% men, 51% women).

Characteristics of Student Body: *Ethnic and racial makeup:* Black non-Hispanic: 12%; American Indian or Alaska Native: .4%; Asian or Pacific Islander: .7%; Hispanic: 1.2%; White non-Hispanic: 81.4%; unknown: 2.6%.

International Students: 149 undergraduate nonresident aliens enrolled fall 2004. Programs available to aid students whose native language is not English: Social, cultural. English as a Second Language Program. Some financial aid designated for international students.

Student Life: On-campus residence halls house 33% of student body and 71% of freshman class. Housing available: coed dorms, women's dorms, apartments for married and single students, fraternities, and sororities. 9% of men join fraternities and 6% of women join sororities. *Intercollegiate athletics:* men: basketball, baseball, football, cross-country, tennis, track and field; women: basketball, tennis, track and field, volleyball, softball, cross-country. *Special regulations:* Registered cars permitted in designated areas. Visitor parking available. Residence hall visitation choice of residents. *Special services:* African-Ameri-

can Cultural Center, Career Center, Center for Teaching and Learning, Child Care Center, Learning Resource Center, Student Counseling Center, Student Health Center, and numerous other student service organizations. *Student publications, radio:* Indiana Statesman, a newspaper published Mon., Wed., Fri. during regular academic year and weekly during summer; *Sycamore,* a yearbook; *Indiana State Quarterly,* published 4 times a year. Radio station WISU-FM broadcasts 75 hours per week. *Surrounding community:* Terre Haute population 60,000. Indianapolis, 75 miles east of campus, is nearest metropolitan area. Served by mass transit bus system; 2 airports five and six miles from campus.

Publications: *Contemporary Education* (quarterly); *Black American Literature Forum* (quarterly); *Classical and Modern Literature* (quarterly); *Midwestern Journal of Language and Folklore* (twice each year); *The Hoosier Science Teacher* (quarterly); *Indiana English* (three times a year); *Global Business and Finance Review* (twice per year), and *Journal of Education for MIS* (yearly).

Library Collections: 1,355,000 volumes. 100,000 microforms; 38,000 audiovisual materials; 2,500 current periodical subscriptions. Students have access to online information retrieval services and the Internet.

Most important special holdings include Cordell Collection of Early English Dictionaries; Eugene V. Debs Collection; early textbook collection.

Buildings and Grounds: The 92-acre main campus adjoins Terre Haute's downtown business district. Married student apartment complexes are located nearby on the 15-acre south campus. Two miles to the east, located on 51 acres, are ISU's 20,500-seat Memorial Stadium and a nine-hole golf course. The ISU baseball field is located on the 95-acre river campus along the Wabash River.

Chief Executive Officer: Dr. Lloyd W. Benjamin, III, President.

Address admission inquiries to Richard J. Toomey, Director of Admissions.

College of Arts and Sciences

Degree Programs Offered: *Baccalaureate* in Afro-American studies, anthropology, computer science, social work, theater, and urban regional studies; *baccalaureate* and *master's* in art, chemistry, communication, criminology, economics, English, foreign languages, geography and geology, history, home economics, humanities, library science, life sciences, mathematics, music, philosophy, physics, political science, public administration, psychology, science teaching, social studies, sociology; *doctorate* in geography, life sciences and psychology.

Admission: In addition to general requirements, additional requirements for fine arts program. Graduate requirements vary according to program and level.

Degree Requirements: *See* general requirements. 2.2 GPA required in courses from major department. Requirements vary according to program and level.

Distinctive Educational Programs: Cooperative baccalaureate program in clinical laboratory science with approved hospitals. medical technology with approved hospitals. Preprofessional programs in dental hygiene, dentistry, engineering, medicine, law, optometry, pharmacy, theology, veterinary medicine. *See* School of Business.

School of Business

Degree Programs Offered: *Associate* and *baccalaureate* in accounting, marketing, management, management information systems, business administration, business education, insurance, marketing education, administrative systems; *master's* and *doctorate* in business administration, business education.

Admission: International students: required score of 550 on TOEFL.

Distinctive Educational Programs: Interdisciplinary programs offered in cooperation with departments of music, speech, home economics, and nursing. Mentoring and internship opportunities with business executives.

School of Education

Degree Programs Offered: Child Development and Early Childhood Education; Teaching Curricula.

Admission: Predicted first semester ISU GPA of 2.4 based on SAT and high school rank, or 2.5 ISU GPA.

Degree Requirements: *See* general requirements. *For baccalaureate degree:* 2.5 GPA. Graduate requirements vary.

Distinctive Educational Programs: License-granting, post-master's, nondegree program, school administrators.

School of Health and Human Performance

Degree Programs Offered: *Baccalaureate, master's* in community health, environmental health, health education, physical education, recreation, safety management.

Degree Requirements: Student in Physical Education must have a 2.5 GPA in their major courses and in overall GPA to graduate.

Distinctive Educational Programs: Baccalaureate and master's in athletic training and adult fitness. Master's in safety management through televised educational network safety and management (1 of 5 accredited in the country).

School of Nursing

Degree Programs Offered: *Associate, baccalaureate* and *master's.*

Admission: In addition to general requirements, 2 units mathematics (including 1 algebra), 1 chemistry. Lowest acceptable secondary school class standing 75th percentile. *Entrance tests:* College Board SAT (combined score of 900, score of 400 on verbal and mathematics each), ACT Composite (score of 23). *For master's:* Baccalaureate degree from NLN accredited program; academic research course, preferably nursing. Health assessment competence, RN licensure. IND, CPR certification, and GRE required.

Degree Requirements: *For associate degree:* 63 credit hours, 2.0 GPA, 15 hours in residence. *For baccalaureate degree:* 124 credit hours.

Distinctive Educational Programs: Continuing education for graduates of the programs and other nurses. Coordinated master's/MBA in nursing and business administration to prepare nurses for administrative positions.

School of Technology

Degree Programs Offered: *Baccalaureate* in aerospace administration, professional pilot, computer hardware technology, electronics technology, industrial automotive technology, mechanical technology, general industrial technology, packaging technology, computer integrated manufacturing, manufacturing technology, technology education, secondary education, vocational trade/industrial technical; construction technology, general industrial supervision, graphic arts management; *master's* in technology education, industrial professional technology, electronics and computer technology, vocational-technical education.

Admission: Enrollment in General Industrial Technology restricted to persons who have completed approximately one-half of their academic work toward a degree in another institution of higher education or in another school within the university.

Distinctive Educational Programs: Cooperative professional practice program in industry; credit granted. Interdisciplinary program Ph.D. program in technical education with curriculum and instruction. Uniquely designed integrated programs in packaging, human resource development, and computer integrated manufacturing.

Indiana University

System Administration

Bloomington, Indiana 47405

Tel: (812) 322-0211   **E-mail:** www.indiana.edu

Institution Description: Indiana University is one of the oldest state universities in the midwestern United States. It was founded in 1820, only four years after Indiana achieved statehood, and has grown to eight campuses. The residential campus at Bloomington and the urban campus at Indianapolis are the largest. Other campuses are located in Gary, Kokomo, New Albany, Richmond, and South Bend, and courses are offered in Columbus, Elkhart, and many other sites. With an enrollment of nearly 93,000 students on eight campuses, Indiana University ranks as one of the largest institutions of higher education in the United States.

History: System formally established 1968. *See* Thomas D. Clark, *Indiana University; Midwestern Pioneer* (Bloomington: Indiana University Press, 1970) for further information.

Institutional Structure: *Governing board:* The Trustees of Indiana University. There are 9 voting trustees: 3 elected by alumni, 5 appointed by governor of Indiana, and 1 student trustee appointed by governor. Academic governance body, University Faculty Council, is composed of representatives from each campus and meets 10 times per year.

Calendar: Semesters. Freshmen admitted Aug., Jan., May, June. Degrees conferred May, June, Aug., Dec. (graduate degrees conferred as earned). Formal commencement May. Summer sessions vary according to campus.

Admission: Rolling admissions plan. For fall acceptance, apply as early as end of junior year of secondary school, but not later than Feb. 15. *Minimum requirements:* 8 semesters of English, 6 semesters of mathematics, 2 semesters of laboratory science, 2 semesters of social science. Students must submit either SAT or ACT results. There are additional requirements for some programs. Students must submit either SAT or ACT results. *For transfer students:* In-state residents 2.0 minimum GPA, out-of-state students 2.5 minimum GPA; from 4-year accredited institution 96 hours maximum transfer credit; from 2-year accredited institution 60 hours. Transfer credit also accepted for correspondence/extension students.

Distinctive Educational Programs: Undergraduate and graduate study at off-campus centers throughout the state. Undergraduate and graduate external degree programs through School of Continuing Education. Indiana Higher Education Telecommunications System provides televised classroom instruction. Overseas programs are available in Bologna, Italy; Canterbury, United Kingdom; Costa Rica; Dijon, France; Florence, Italy; Graz, Austria; Hamburg, Germany; Leiden, Maastricht, and Rotterdam, The Netherlands; St. Petersburg, Russia; Ljubljana, Yugoslavia; Madrid, Spain; Mexico City, Mexico; Salamanca, Spain; Singapore; Strasbourg, France; Zomba, Malawi; and 35 others through cooperative programs.

Publications: Indiana University publishes a number of scholarly periodicals, including *International Folklore Review, Research in African Literatures, Journal of Women's History, Discourse: Journal for Theoretical Studies in Media and Culture, Middle East Journal,* and *Religion and American Culture: A Journal of Interpretation.* The Indiana University Press published 175 tiles in fiscal year 1990. Indian University also houses the editorial offices of several scholarly journals, including *American Historical Review, Anthropological Linguistics, Business Horizons, Journal of Folklore Research, Indiana Business Review, Indiana Magazine of History, Indiana Magazine of History, Indiana University Mathematics Journal,* and *Journal of American History.*

Buildings and Grounds: Dr. Adam W. Herbert, Jr., President.

Address admission inquiries to individual campuses.

Indiana University Bloomington

300 North Jordan Avenue

Bloomington, Indiana 47405-1106

Tel: (812) 855-4848   **E-mail:** iuadmit@indiana.edu

Fax: (812) 855-5102   **Internet:** www.indiana.edu

Institution Description: *Enrollment:* 37,821. *Degrees awarded:* Associate, baccalaureate, first-professional (optometry, law), master's, doctorate, specialist.

Academic offerings subject to approval by statewide coordinating bodies. Budget subject to approval by state governing boards. Member of Committee on Institutional Cooperation and Midwest University Consortium for International Activities.

Accreditation: *Regional:* NCA. *Professional:* accounting, art, athletic training, audiology, business, clinical psychology, counseling, counseling psychology, interior design, journalism, law, librarianship, music, optometry, psychology internship, public administration, public health, recreation and leisure services, school psychology, social work, speech-language pathology, teacher education, theatre

History: Established as Indiana State Seminary and chartered 1820; offered first instruction at postsecondary level 1830; adopted present name 1838. *See* Thomas D. Clark, *Indiana University: Midwestern Pioneer* (Bloomington: Indiana University Press, 1970) for further information.

Institutional Structure: *Composition of institution:* Academic affairs headed by Dean of the Faculties. Management/business/finances directed by Dean, Budgetary Administration and Planning. Full-time instructional faculty 1,319. Academic governance body, Bloomington Faculty Council, meets an average of 12 times per year.

Calendar: Semesters. Academic year early Sept. to early May. Freshmen admitted Aug., Jan., May, June. Degrees conferred May, Aug., Jan. (graduate degrees conferred as earned). Formal commencement May. Summer sessions vary according to campus.

Characteristics of Freshmen: 80.8% of applicants accepted. 39.1% of accepted applicants enrolled.

84.4% (5,361 students) submitted SAT scores; 37.8% (2,404 students) submitted ACT scores. *25th percentile:* SAT Verbal 490, SAT Math 500; ACT Composite 22, ACT English 21, ACT Math 21. *75th percentile:* SAT Verbal 600, SAT Math 620; ACT Composite 27, ACT English 28, ACT Math 27.

63.6% of entering freshmen expected to graduate within 5 years. 70.5% of freshmen from Indiana. Freshmen from 47 states and 65 foreign countries.

Admission: Rolling admissions plan. For fall acceptance, apply as early as end of junior year of secondary school, but not later than Feb. 15. *Minimum requirements:* 8 semesters of English, 6 semesters of mathematics, 2 semesters of laboratory science, 2 semesters of social science. Students must submit either SAT or ACT results. *For transfer students:* In-state residents 2.0 minimum GPA, out-of-state students 2.5 minimum GPA; from 4-year accredited institution 96 hours maximum transfer credit; from 2-year accredited institution 60 hours. Transfer credit also accepted for correspondence/extension students.

College credit for postsecondary-level work completed in secondary school. Tutoring available. Developmental courses offered during regular academic year; credit given.

Degree Requirements: *For all associate degrees:* 60–68 credit hours. *For all baccalaureate degrees:* minimum 120 credit hours. *For all undergraduate degrees:* 2.0 GPA, residency requirement (varies with program).

Distinctive Educational Programs: Flexible meeting places and schedules, including weekend and evening classes. Accelerated degree programs. Interdisciplinary programs: American studies, African studies, arts administration, Afro-American studies, film studies, Latin American and Caribbean Studies, medieval studies, Renaissance studies, Russian and East European studies, Victorian studies, women's studies, West European studies, Jewish studies. Special facilities available for using telecommunications in the classroom. Facilities and programs for independent research, including honors programs, individual majors. Overseas study and domestic exchange programs available.

ROTC: Army, Air Force.

Degrees Conferred: 78 *associate*; 6,172 *baccalaureate*; 1,680 *master's*; 375 *doctorate*; 272 *first-professional*. Bachelor's degrees awarded in top five disciplines: business, management, marketing, and related support services 1,221; education 1,006; communication, journalism, and related programs 661; public administration and social service professions 421; biological and biomedical sciences 348.

Fees and Other Expenses: *Full-time tuition per academic year 2004–05:* undergraduate resident $4,946, out-of-state $16,739; contact the university for current graduate/first-professional programs tuition/fees. Contact individual professional schools for current information. *Books and supplies:* $740. *Room and board per academic year:* $6,006.

Financial Aid: Aid from institutionally generated funds is provided on the basis of academic merit, financial need, athletic ability, other criteria. Institution has a Program Participation Agreement with the U.S. Department of Education for eligible students to receive Pell Grants and other federal aid.

Financial aid to full-time, first-time undergraduate students: need-based scholarships/grants totaling $29,867,006, self-help $38,974,012; non-need-based scholarships/grants totaling $29,183,862, self-help $19,142,699, parent loans $29,680,627, tuition waivers $1,723,818, athletic awards $3,258,178.

Departments and Teaching Staff: *Professors* 588, *associate professors* 342, *assistant professors* 318, *instructors* 71, *part-time teachers* 252.

Total instructional faculty: 1,562. Student-to-faculty ratio: 18:1. Degrees held by full-time faculty: doctorate 81.7%, master's 13.6%, baccalaureate 2.8%, professional .2%. 91.6% hold terminal degrees.

Enrollment: Total enrollment 37,821. Undergraduate full-time 13,390 men / 14,303 women, part-time 869m / 937w; first-professional full-time 442m / 383w, part-time 51m / 61w; graduate full-time 2,285m / 2,252w, part-time 1,257m / 1,541w. *Transfer students:* in-state 196 men / 181 women, from out-of-state 125m / 109w.

Characteristics of Student Body: *Ethnic and racial makeup:* number of Black non-Hispanic: 1,216; American Indian or Alaska Native: 67; Asian or Pacific Islander: 949; Hispanic: 647; White non-Hispanic: 24,961; unknown: 393. *Age distribution:* 17–21: 61%; 22–24: 18%; 25–29: 11%; 30–34: 5%; 35–39: 2%; 40–49: 2%; 50–64: 1%.

International Students: 1,316 nonresident aliens enrolled fall 2004. Students from Europe, Asia, Central and South America, Africa, Canada, Australia, New Zealand,. Programs available to aid students whose native language is not English: Social, cultural, financial. English as a Second Language Program.

Student Life: On-campus residence halls house 39% of student body. Some students live on campus in cooperative facilities and in university-owned apartments and houses. 7% of undergraduate men join fraternities; 9% of undergraduate women join sororities; a combined 14% live in them. Married student housing available. *Intercollegiate athletics:* men only: baseball, basketball, cross-country, football, golf, soccer, swimming and diving, tennis, track and field, wrestling; women only: basketball, cross-country, golf, soccer, swimming and diving, tennis, track and field, volleyball. *Special regulations:* Cars allowed for juniors and seniors without restrictions; freshmen and sophomores must obtain special permission. *Special services:* Learning Skills Center, International Student Center, various minority cultural centers, medical services, disabled student services, campus bus service. *Student publications, radio, television: Indiana Daily Student,* a daily newspaper. Radio station WFIU broadcasts 168 hours per week. TV station WTIU broadcasts 124 hours per week. *Surrounding community:* Bloomington population 65,000. Indianapolis, 50 miles from campus, is nearest metropolitan area. Served by mass transit bus system, airport 5 miles from campus.

Library Collections: 6,647,355 volumes. 59,439 serial subscriptions; 4,902,515 microforms; 252,970 audiovisual materials. Computer work stations throughout the campus. Students have access to the Internet (charges included in mandatory student fees).

Most important special holdings include Lilly Library rare book collection of over 336,000 volumes and 6,000,000 manuscripts; Archives of Traditional Music; Kinsey Institute.

Buildings and Grounds: Campus area 1,878 acres.

Chief Executive Officer: Dr. Kenneth Gros-Louis, Chancellor.

Address admission inquiries to Mary Ellen Anderson, Director of Admissions; graduate inquiries to Kimberly Bunch, Director of Graduate Admissions.

College of Arts and Sciences

Degree Programs Offered: *Baccalaureate* in Afro-American studies, anthropology, apparel merchandising, astronomy and astrophysics, biochemistry, biology, chemistry, classical studies, comparative literature, computer science, criminal justice, East Asian languages and literatures, East Asian studies, economics, English, folklore, French, geography, geology, Germanic studies, history, history of art, individualized major program, interior design, Italian, linguistics, mathematics, microbiology, music, Near Eastern languages and cultures, philosophy, physics, political science, Portuguese, psychology, religious studies, Slavic languages and literature, sociology, Spanish, speech communication, speech and hearing sciences, studio art, telecommunications, and theatre and drama.

Distinctive Educational Programs: Interdisciplinary programs in various fields including African studies, film studies, Jewish studies, medieval studies, women's studies. Joint baccalaureate-first-professional with School of Optometry and School of Dentistry (IUPUI).

Kelley School of Business

Degree Programs Offered: *Baccalaureate* with concentrations in accounting, business economics and public policy, computer information systems, finance, finance/insurance, finance/real estate, management, marketing, marketing/advertising, marketing/distribution management, operations management, human resource management, international studies; *master's* and *doctorate* in business administration. *Certificate* also given.

Distinctive Educational Programs: Internships.

School of Continuing Studies

Degree Programs Offered: *Associate, baccalaureate* in general studies.

Departments and Teaching Staff: Faculty in this school function only as administrators. The school's degrees are designed primarily for adults and part-time learners who earn credits toward degrees through attending courses throughout the university. *Professors* 2, *associate professors* 1.

School of Education

Degree Programs Offered: *Baccalaureate, master's, doctorate* in various teacher education areas. Specialist also given.

Admission: GPA of 2.5 required for admission to teacher education program.

Degree Requirements: Cumulative GPA of 2.5 required for graduation.

Distinctive Educational Programs: Cooperative student teaching arrangements with schools from a variety of cultural and economic backgrounds, including opportunities with the American Indian, Latin, and rural education projects. *Other distinctive programs:* Teacher as Decision Maker program for post baccalaureate certification students. Distance education programs. Programs under development to enhance collaboration in schools. Enhanced efforts in technology applications in developmental stage.

Graduate School

Degree Programs Offered: *Master's, doctorate.*

Departments and Teaching Staff: Faculty members are drawn from the departments of the College of Arts and Sciences and from other schools within the university.

School of Health, Physical Education, and Recreation

Degree Programs Offered: *Baccalaureate, master's, doctorate, director* in various fields within health and safety education, kinesiology/physical education, recreation and park administration. *Certificate, associate* in hazard control technology, *master's* in public health also given. *Doctorate* in human performance awarded through Graduate School.

Distinctive Educational Programs: School operates Bradford Woods, a 2,300-acre outdoor education center for instruction and camping programs.

School of Law

Degree Programs Offered: *Master's, first-professional.*

Admission: Baccalaureate from accredited college or university with 90 semester hours coursework that would be acceptable toward a baccalaureate in the College of Arts and Sciences or the School of Business; LSAT.

Degree Requirements: *For first-professional:* 86 credit hours, all in residence; cumulative 2.3 GPA; writing and research requirement.

Distinctive Educational Programs: Clinical internships. Joint first-professional-master's degrees in cooperation with the Schools of Business, Public and Environmental Affairs, and Library and Information Sciences.

School of Journalism

Degree Programs Offered: *Baccalaureate* in journalism.

School of Library and Information Science

Degree Programs Offered: *Master's, specialist. Doctorate* awarded through Graduate School.

Distinctive Educational Programs: Dual master's degree programs in cooperation with the Graduate School, School of Music, School of Public and Environmental Affairs, and School of Law.

School of Music

Degree Programs Offered: *Baccalaureate* offered in various fields, including audio recording, ballet, composition, early instrument, guitar, jazz studies, music education, music history and literature, music theory, opera scenic technique, orchestral instrument, organ, piano, piano accompanying, voice, woodwind instruments; *master's, doctorate* in various fields. *Associate* in various technologies also given. *Artist Diploma* and *Performer Diploma* offered.

School of Optometry

Degree Programs Offered: *Associate* in optometric technology, optician; *baccalaureate, first-professional, master's* and *doctorate* in visual sciences and physiological optics awarded through Graduate School.

Admission: *For first-professional:* Minimum of 90 credit hours preprofessional study with required courses in English composition, a foreign language, arts and humanities, animal biology, calculus, general physics, inorganic and organic chemistry, psychology, statistics, social and behavioral science, advanced science.

Degree Requirements: *For first-professional:* 136 credit hours, all hours in residence, 2.0 GPA.

School of Public and Environmental Affairs

Degree Programs Offered: *Associate* in public affairs; *baccalaureate* in public affairs; *master's* in public affairs, environmental science; *doctorate* in environmental science, public policy.

Indiana University East

2325 Chester Boulevard
Richmond, Indiana 47374-1289
Tel: (765) 973-8208   **E-mail:** eaadmit@indiana.edu
Fax: (765) 973-8288   **Internet:** www.indiana.edu

Institution Description: *Enrollment:* 2,516. *Degrees awarded:* Associate, baccalaureate. Certificate also awarded.

Accreditation: *Regional:* NCA. *Professional:* business, nursing, social work, teacher education

History: In 1946 Earlham College and Indiana University established the Eastern Indiana Center, which was originally administered as a cooperative program to give adults in the community an opportunity to pursue college-level study as part-time students. In October 1970, Indiana University assumed complete administrative control and began working toward the development of the new campus. In January 1975, a new Indiana University East campus was opened and occupied on a 194-acre site on the north edge of Richmond, Indiana. The primary mission of Indiana University East is to provide opportunities for formal learning through instructional programs that lead to the completion of baccalaureate or associate degrees. Also, the campus provides educational opportunities for the development of personal and professional interests of people in the region.

Institutional Structure: *Composition of institution:* 5 administrators. Academic affairs, student affairs, and management/business/finances each headed by vice chancellor. Full-time instructional faculty 61. Academic governance body, Indiana University East Senate, meets an average of 8 times per year.

Calendar: Semesters. Academic year late Aug. to early May.

Characteristics of Freshmen: 93% of applicants admitted. 92% of applicants admitted and enrolled.

15.74% (202 students) submitted SAT scores; 27.41% (116 students) submitted ACT scores. Mean SAT Verbal 450, SAT Math 435; mean ACT Composite 18.25.

47% of entering freshmen expected to graduate within 5 years. 77% of freshmen from Indiana. Freshmen from 4 states.

Admission: Rolling admissions plan. For fall acceptance, apply as early as end of junior year of secondary school, but not later than Feb. 15. *Minimum requirements:* 8 semesters of English, 6 semesters of mathematics, 2 semesters of laboratory science, 2 semesters of social science. Students must submit either SAT or ACT results. *For transfer students:* In-state residents 2.0 minimum GPA, out-of-state students 2.5 minimum GPA; from 4-year accredited institution 96 hours maximum transfer credit; from 2-year accredited institution 60 hours. Transfer credit also accepted for correspondence/extension students.

Distinctive Educational Programs: School offers college credit for postsecondary-level work completed in secondary school. Courses offered in some undergraduate and master's programs for credit at other Indiana University campuses. Transfer agreements with other Indiana University campuses. Cooperative degree programs in technology fields with Purdue University.

Degrees Conferred: 70 *associate;* 172 *baccalaureate:* biological/life sciences 9; business/marketing 28; communications/communication technologies 2; computer and information sciences 6; education 39; health professions and related sciences 24; liberal arts/general studies 24; mathematics 2; personal and miscellaneous services 13; protective services/public administration 13; psychology 10; social sciences and history 4.

Fees and Other Expenses: *Full-time tuition per academic year 2004–05:* undergraduate resident $3,762, out-of-state student $10,143. *Required fees:* $318. Contact the university for graduate tuition/fees.

Financial Aid: Aid from institutionally generated funds is provided on the basis of academic merit, financial need, other criteria. Institution has a Program Participation Agreement with the U.S. Department of Education for eligible students to receive Pell Grants and other federal aid.

Financial aid to full-time, first-time undergraduate students: need-based scholarships/grants totaling $3,660,593, self-help $2,488,065; non-need-based scholarships/grants totaling $552,655, self-help $2,120,943, parent loans $90,232, tuition waivers $21,740.

Departments and Teaching Staff: *Professors* 9, *associate professors* 22, *assistant professors* 16m *instructors* 34, *part-time faculty* 112. *Total instructional faculty:* 193 (full-time 84, part-time 112; women 93, men 100; members of minority groups 14). Total faculty with doctorate, first-professional, or other terminal degree: 67. Student-to-faculty ratio: 13:1. *Faculty development:* 5 faculty members awarded sabbaticals 2004–05.

Enrollment: Total enrollment 2,516. Undergraduate full-time 358 men / 906 women, part-time 373m / 849w.

Characteristics of Student Body: *Ethnic and racial makeup:* number of Black non-Hispanic: 110; American Indian or Alaska Native: 11; Asian or Pacific Islander: 15; Hispanic: 17; White non-Hispanic: 2,293; unknown: 70. *Age distribution:* number 18–19: 381; 20–24: 532; 25–29: 274; 30–34: 184; 35–39: 135; 40–49: 192; 50–64: 57.

International Students: No programs available to aid students whose native language is not English. No financial aid specifically designated for international students.

Student Life: No on-campus housing. *Special services:* Student Government Association; Student Development Center. *Student publications: New Voice*, a biweekly paper; *Pioneer Press*, a biweekly paper. *Surrounding community:* Richmond population 40,000. Dayton, 41 miles from campus, is nearest metropolitan area. Indianapolis is 68 miles from campus.

Library Collections: 65,336 volumes. Online catalog. 45,000 microforms; 9,434 audiovisual materials; 87 current periodical subscriptions. 47 computer work stations. Access to online information retrieval systems. Students have access to the Internet (charges included in mandatory fees).

Buildings and Grounds: Campus area 194 acres.

Chief Executive Officer: Dr. David J. Fulton, Chancellor.

Address admission inquiries to James Bland, Director of Admissions.

Indiana University Kokomo

2300 South Washington Street
P.O. Box 9003
Kokomo, Indiana 46904-9003
Tel: (765) 455-2000   **E-mail:** iuadmis@iuk.edu
Fax: (765) 455-9587   **Internet:** www.iuk.edu

Institution Description: *Enrollment:* 2,903. *Degrees awarded:* Associate, baccalaureate, master's. Certificates also awarded.

Accreditation: *Regional:* NCA. *Professional:* business, nursing, nursing education, teacher education

History: Established as Kokomo Center of Indiana University and offered first instruction at postsecondary level 1945; adopted present name 1968; awarded first degree (baccalaureate) 1970.

Institutional Structure: *Composition of institution:* Administrators 6. Academic affairs, student affairs, and management/business/finances each headed by vice chancellor. Full-time instructional faculty 99. Academic governance body, Indiana University at Kokomo Faculty Senate, meets an average of 8 times per year.

Calendar: Semesters. Academic year late Aug. to early May.

Characteristics of Freshmen: 84.5% of applicants accepted. 74.2% of accepted applicants enrolled.

67.8% (316 students) submitted SAT scores; 24.9% (116 students) submitted ACT scores. *25th percentile:* SAT I Verbal 430, SAT I Math 430; ACT Composite 17, ACT English 16, ACT Math 16. *75th percentile:* SAT I Verbal 540, SAT I Math 530; ACT Composite 21, ACT English 21, ACT Math 21.

14.7% of entering freshmen expected to graduate within 5 years. 99.5% of entering freshmen from Indiana.

Admission: Rolling admissions plan. For fall acceptance, apply as early as end of junior year of secondary school, but not later than Feb. 15. *Minimum requirements:* 8 semesters of English, 6 semesters of mathematics, 2 semesters of laboratory science, 2 semesters of social science. Students must submit either SAT or ACT results. *For transfer students:* In-state residents 2.0 minimum GPA, out-of-state students 2.5 minimum GPA; from 4-year accredited institution 96 hours maximum transfer credit; from 2-year accredited institution 60 hours. Transfer credit also accepted for correspondence/extension students.

College credit for extrainstitutional learning on basis of ACE *2006 Guide to the Evaluation of Educational Experiences in the Armed Services*; portfolio and faculty assessment. Tutoring available. Developmental courses offered in summer session and regular academic year; credit given.

Degree Requirements: *For all associate degrees:* 60–63 semester hours. *For all baccalaureate degrees:* 120–124 hours. *For all degrees:* 2.0 GPA; residence requirement; demonstrated proficiency in writing. Additional requirements for some programs. Fulfillment of some degree requirements and exemption from some beginning courses possible by passing departmental examinations, College Board CLEP, Achievement Tests. *Grading system:* A–F; pass-fail; withdraw (deadline after which pass-fail is appended to withdraw).

Distinctive Educational Programs: Flexible meeting places and schedules, including weekend and evening classes. Cooperative baccalaureate program in medical technology with affiliated hospitals. Cooperative degree programs in technology fields with Purdue University. Interdisciplinary program in labor studies. *Other distinctive programs:* Masters program in elementary education and M.B.A. in business.

Degrees Conferred: 174 *associate:* 243 *baccalaureate;* 23 *master's.* Bachelor's degrees awarded in top five disciplines: education 50; health professions and related clinical sciences 48; business, management, marketing, and related support services 44; liberal arts and sciences, general studies and humanities 42; computer and information sciences and support services 10.

Fees and Other Expenses: *Full-time tuition per academic year 2004–05:* undergraduate resident $3,762, out-of-state student $10,143. Contact the university for current graduate tuition/fees. *Required fees:* $349. *Books and supplies:* $840.

Financial Aid: Aid from institutionally generated funds is provided on the basis of academic merit, financial need, other considerations. Institution has a Program Participation Agreement with the U.S. Department of Education for eligible students to receive Pell Grants and other federal aid.

Financial aid to full-time, first-time undergraduate students: need-based scholarships/grants totaling $2,629,360, self-help $1,892,903; non-need-based scholarships/grants totaling $852,105, self-help $1,531,801, parent loans $104,508, tuition waivers $14,832.

Departments and Teaching Staff: *Total instructional faculty:* 164 (full-time 99, part-time 85; women 105, men 79; members of minority groups 18). Total faculty with doctorate, first-professional, or other terminal degree: 72. Student-to-faculty ratio: 15.8:1.

Enrollment: Total enrollment 2,903. Undergraduate full-time 415 men / 1,011 women, part-time 337m / 969w; graduate full-time 6m / 9w, part-time 64m / 92w. *Transfer students:* in-state 132, from out-of-state 4.

Characteristics of Student Body: *Ethnic and racial makeup:* number of Black non-Hispanic: 86; American Indian or Alaska Native: 12; Asian or Pacific Islander: 23; Hispanic: 29; White non-Hispanic: 2,490; unknown: 84. *Age distribution:* 17–21: 39%; 22–24: 14%; 25–29: 15%; 30–34: 11%; 35–39: 8%; 40–49: 10%; 50–64: 3%.

International Students: 8 nonresident aliens enrolled fall 2004. Student from Europe, Asia, Africa, Canada. No programs available to aid students whose native language is not English.

Student Life: No on-campus housing. Limited athletic program. *Special services:* Learning Enhancement Center; day-care center. *Student publications: The Correspondent*, a newspaper. *Surrounding community:* Kokomo population 45,000. Indianapolis, 50 miles from campus, is nearest metropolitan area. Served by regional airport 6 miles from campus.

Library Collections: 133,433 volumes. 50,000 government documents; 1,445 audiovisual materials; 466,893 microforms; 1,448 serial subscriptions. Students have access to the Internet (charges included in mandatory fees).

Buildings and Grounds: Campus area 51 acres.

Chief Executive Officer: Dr. Ruth J. Person, Chancellor.

Address admission inquiries to Jackie Kenney-Fletcher, Darren Bush, Director of Admissions.

Indiana University Northwest

3400 Broadway
Gary, Indiana 46408
Tel: (219) 980-6500   **E-mail:** admit@iun.edu
Fax: (219) 981-4219   **Internet:** www.iun.edu

Institution Description: *Enrollment:* 5,138. *Degrees awarded:* Associate, baccalaureate, master's.

Accreditation: *Regional:* NCA. *Professional:* clinical lab technology, dental hygiene, health information technician, nursing, nursing education, phlebotomy, public administration, radiation therapy, radiography, respiratory therapy, social work, teacher education

History: Established and offered first instruction at postsecondary level 1922; discontinued operation 1933; assumed control of Gary College (established 1933) and made it an extension center 1948; joined with Calumet Center to form Indiana University Northwest 1963; awarded first baccalaureate 1967.

Institutional Structure: *Composition of institution:* 22 administrators. Academic affairs, student affairs, management/business/finances each headed by vice chancellor; vice chancellor for technology; vice-chancellor for external relations. Full-time instructional faculty 190. Academic governance body, Indiana University Northwest Faculty Organization, meets an average of 8 times per year.

Calendar: Semesters. Academic year mid-Aug. to early May.

Characteristics of Freshmen: 79.3% of applicants accepted. 73.1% of accepted applicants enrolled.

72% (549 students) submitted SAT scores; 10.5% (80 students) submitted ACT scores. *25th percentile:* SAT I Verbal 400, SAT I Math 390; ACT Composite 15, ACT English 14, ACT Math 15. *75th percentile:* SAT I Verbal 500, SAT I Math 500; ACT Composite 21, ACT English 21, ACT Math 19.

17.6% of entering freshmen expected to graduate within 5 years. 98.7% of freshmen from Indiana. Freshmen from 5 states and 11 foreign countries.

Admission: Rolling admissions plan. For fall acceptance, apply as early as end of junior year of secondary school, but not later than Feb. 15. *Minimum requirements:* 8 semesters of English, 6 semesters of mathematics, 2 semesters of laboratory science, 2 semesters of social science. Students must submit either SAT or ACT results. *For transfer students:* In-state residents 2.0 minimum GPA, out-of-state students 2.5 minimum GPA; from 4-year accredited institution 96 hours maximum transfer credit; from 2-year accredited institution 60 hours. Transfer credit also accepted for correspondence/extension students.

Degree Requirements: *For all associate degrees:* 60 credit hours. *For all baccalaureate degrees:* 120-124 credit hours; 26 hours of final year in residence, including 10 hours in major. *For all undergraduate degrees:* 2.0 GPA. *Grading system:* A–F; pass-fail; withdraw (deadline after which pass-fail is appended to withdraw).

Distinctive Educational Programs: High involvement of full-time faculty in all aspects of undergraduate education including preprofessional programs. Nationally recognized graduate program in Urban Teacher Education and nationally accredited M.P.A., M.S.W, and M.B.A. programs.

ROTC: Army.

Degrees Conferred: 231 *associate;* 365 *baccalaureate;* 93 *master's.* Bachelor's degrees awarded in top five disciplines: business, management, marketing, and related support services 71; liberal arts and sciences, general studies and humanities 54; security and protective services 46; health professions and related clinical sciences 45; education 40.

Fees and Other Expenses: *Full-time tuition per academic year 2004–05:* undergraduate resident $3,762, out-of-state student $10,143. Contact the university for graduate tuition/fees. *Required fees:* $424.

Financial Aid: Aid from institutionally generated funds is provided on the basis of academic merit, financial need, other considerations. Institution has a Program Participation Agreement with the U.S. Department of Education for eligible students to receive Pell Grants and other federal aid.

Financial aid to full-time, first-time undergraduate students: need-based scholarships/grants totaling $3,892,202, self-help $3,583,656; non-need-based scholarships/grants totaling $924,460, self-help $2,166,946, parent loans $177,108, tuition waivers $32,912, athletic awards $1,800.

Departments and Teaching Staff: *Total instructional faculty:* 293 (full-time 190, part-time 203; women 208, men 185; members of minority groups 81). Total faculty with doctorate, first-professional, or other terminal degree: 159. Student-to-faculty ratio: 14:1.

Enrollment: Total enrollment 5,138. Undergraduate full-time 811 men / 1,774 women, part-time 565m / 1,366w; graduate full-time 20m / 64w, part-time 142m / 376w.

Characteristics of Student Body: *Ethnic and racial makeup:* number of Black non-Hispanic: 983; American Indian or Alaska Native: 18; Asian or Pacific Islander: 59; Hispanic: 519; White non-Hispanic: 2,821; unknown: 126. *Age distribution:* 17–21: 34%; 22–24: 16%; 25–29: 16%; 30–34: 9%; 35–39: 7%; 40–49: 13%; 50–64: 5%.

International Students: 10 nonresident aliens enrolled fall 2004. Students from Europe, Asia, Latin America, Africa, Canada. No programs available to aid students whose native language is not English. No financial aid specifically designated for international students.

Student Life: No on-campus housing. *Intercollegiate athletics:* NAIA Division II. Men only: baseball, basketball, golf; women only: basketball, volleyball. *Special regulations:* Cars permitted without restrictions. *Special services:* Learning Resources Center, on-campus day-care facility. *Student publications: Spirits,* a student literary magazine published once a semester. *Surrounding community:* Campus is located in the middle of Gary-Hammond-East Chicago urbanized area with a population of 240,000. Served by Gary regional airport 6 miles from campus.

Library Collections: 252,500 volumes. 223,500 government documents; 330 audiovisual materials; 344,000 microforms; 1,530 periodicals subscriptions. Students have access to the Internet (charges included in mandatory fees).

Buildings and Grounds: Campus area 38 acres.

Chief Executive Officer: Dr. Bruce Bergland, Chancellor.

Address admission inquiries to Dr. Linda B. Templeton, Director of Admissions.

Indiana University - Purdue University Fort Wayne

2101 Coliseum Boulevard East
Fort Wayne, Indiana 46805-1499
Tel: (260) 481-6100   **E-mail:** ipfwadms@ipfw.edu
Fax: (260) 481-6880   **Internet:** www.ipfw.edu

Institution Description: *Enrollment:* 11,810. *Degrees awarded:* Associate, baccalaureate, master's.

Member of National Student Exchange.

Accreditation: *Regional:* NCA. *Professional:* business, clinical psychology, computer science, dental hygiene, dental laboratory technology, engineering, engineering technology, health information technician, music, nursing, public administration, teacher education

History: Established as Fort Wayne Center of Indiana University and offered first instruction at postsecondary level 1917; Purdue University establish a campus in Fort Wayne 1941; initiated cooperative arrangement with Purdue University 1964; awarded first baccalaureate 1967; changed name to Indiana University-Purdue University Fort Wayne 1968;

Institutional Structure: *Composition of institution:* Academic affairs headed by vice chancellor for academic affairs. Management/business/finances directed by vice chancellor for financial affairs. Full-time instructional faculty 352. Academic governance body, Faculty Senate, meets an average of 9 times per year.

Calendar: Semesters. Academic year Aug. to May.

Characteristics of Freshmen: 96% of applicants admitted. 66% of applicants admitted and enrolled.

93% (1,517 students) submitted SAT scores; 20% (333 students) submitted ACT scores. *25th percentile:* SAT Verbal 430, SAT Math 430; ACT Composite 17, ACT English 16, ACT Math 17. *75th percentile:* SAT Verbal 530, SAT Math 550; ACT Composite 23, ACT English 23, ACT Math 23.

10% of freshmen expected to graduate within 5 years. 93% of freshmen from Indiana.

Admission: Graduation for accredited secondary school or equivalent. College credit for post-secondary-level work completed in secondary school and for extrainstitutional learning on basis of ACE *2006 Guide to the Evaluation of Educational Experiences in the Armed Services*; portfolio assessment; advanced placement on basis of faculty assessment and personal interview. Tutoring avail-

able. Developmental courses offered in summer session and regular academic year; nondegree credit given.

Degree Requirements: *For all associate degrees:* 60–66 credit hours. *For all baccalaureate degrees:* 122–128 credit hours. *For all undergraduate degrees:* 2.0 GPA; 32 hours in residence.

Fulfillment of some degree requirements and exemption from some beginning courses possible by passing departmental examinations. *Grading system:* A–F; pass-fail; withdraw (carries time limit).

Distinctive Educational Programs: Weekend and evening classes. Wide variety of cooperative undergraduate and graduate programs. Interdisciplinary programs in ethnic studies, women's studies, urban studies. Facilities for independent research, including honors programs, individual majors, tutorials.

Degrees Conferred: 444 *associate;* 869 *baccalaureate* (B), 201 *master's* (M): area and ethnic studies 1; biological/life sciences 24 (B), 6 (M); business/marketing 166 (B), 47 (M); communications/communication technologies 24 (B), 10 (M); computer and information sciences 29 (B), 12 (M); education 187 (B), 106 (M); engineering and engineering technologies 89 (B); English 14 (B), 4 (M); foreign languages and literature 10 (B); health professions and related sciences 23 (B), 1 (M); liberal arts/general studies 106 (B), 8 (M); mathematics 14 (B), 4 (M); philosophy/religion/theology 7 (B); physical sciences 8 (B); protective services/public administration 42 (B), 3 (M); psychology 37 (B); social sciences and history 48 (B); visual and performing arts 40 (B). Honorary degrees awarded 2004: Doctor of Literature 2; Doctor of Engineering 1.

Fees and Other Expenses: *Full-time tuition per academic year 2004–05:* undergraduate resident $4,740, out-of-state $11,678; graduate resident $4,793, out-of-state $10,940. *Required fees:* $572 undergraduate, $457 graduate. *room and board per academic year:* $4,480.

Financial Aid: Aid from institutionally generated funds is provided on the basis of academic merit, financial need, athletic ability, other criteria. Institution has a Program Participation Agreement with the U.S. Department of Education for eligible students to receive Pell Grants and other federal aid.

Financial aid to full-time, first-time undergraduate students: need-based scholarships/grants totaling $11,587,945, self-help $14,843,511; non-need-based scholarships/grants totaling $2,129,022, self-help $12,223,059, parent loans $617,005, tuition waivers $191,448, athletic awards $935,201.

Departments and Teaching Staff: *Professors* 66, *associate professors* 113, *assistant professors* 121. *instructors* 52, *part-time faculty* 384. *Total instructional faculty:* 736 (full-time 352, part-time 384; women 330, men 406; members of minority groups 74). Total faculty with doctorate, first-professional, or other terminal degree: 360. Student-to-faculty ratio: 17:1. *Faculty development:* $5,003,282 in grants for research. 29 faculty members awarded sabbaticals 2004–05.

Enrollment: Total enrollment 11,810. Undergraduate full-time 2,926 men / 3,722 women, part-time 1,750m / 2,691w; graduate full-time 37m / 53w, part-time 257m / 374w. *Transfer students:* 708.

Characteristics of Student Body: *Ethnic and racial makeup:* number of Black non-Hispanic: 573; American Indian or Alaska Native: 40; Asian or Pacific Islander: 228; Hispanic: 275; White non-Hispanic: 9,592; unknown: 250. *Age distribution:* number under 18: 117; 18–19: 2,317; 20–21: 2,268; 22–24: 2,373; 25–29: 1,663; 30–34: 562; 35–39: 562; 40–49: 733; 50–64: 215; 65 and over: 9. 31% of student body attend summer sessions.

International Students: 158 nonresident aliens enrolled fall 2004. Students from Europe, Asia, Central and South America, Africa, Canada. Programs available to aid students whose native language is not English: Social, cultural. English as a Second Language Program. No financial aid specifically designated for international students.

Student Life: No on-campus housing. *Intercollegiate athletics:* men only: baseball, basketball, soccer, tennis, track and field, volleyball; women only: basketball, soccer, softball, tennis, track, volleyball. *Special regulations:* All students pay parking fees per credit hour enrolled. *Special services:* Learning Resources Center; Women's Center; Writing Center. *Student publications: Communicator,* a student newspaper. *Surrounding community:* Fort Wayne population 200,000. Indianapolis, 120 miles from campus, is nearest metropolitan area. Served by mass transit bus system; airport 13 miles from campus; passenger rail service 5 miles from campus.

Publications: *CLIO* (3 times per year) first published 1977.

Library Collections: 1,017,043 volumes including bound books, serial backfiles, electronic documents, and government documents not in separate collections. Online catalog. Current serial subscriptions: paper 1,500, via electronic access 22,000. 285 computer work stations. Students have access to the Internet at no charge. Total budget for books, periodicals, audiovisual materials, microforms 2004–05: $611,131.

Buildings and Grounds: Campus area 566 acres. *New buildings:* Waterfield Campus Student Housing completed 2003.

Chief Executive Officer: Dr. Michael A. Wartell, Chancellor.

Address admission inquiries to Carol B. Isaacs, Director of Admissions.

Indiana University - Purdue University Indianapolis

425 University Boulevard
Indianapolis, Indiana 46202-5143
Tel: (317) 274-5555   **E-mail:** apply@iupui.edu
Fax: (317) 278-1862   **Internet:** www.indiana.edu

Institution Description: *Enrollment:* 29,953. *Degrees awarded:* Associate, baccalaureate, first-professional (dentistry, medicine, law), master's, doctorate.

Accreditation: *Regional:* NCA. *Professional:* art, clinical lab scientist, dental hygiene, dentistry, dietetics, engineering, engineering technology, health information technician, health services administration, histologic technology, law, medicine, nuclear medicine technology, nursing, nursing education, occupational therapy, pediatric dentistry, periodontics, physical therapy, public administration, public health, radiation therapy, radiography, respiratory therapy, social work

History: Established as a branch of Indiana University and offered first instruction at postsecondary level 1914; merged with Purdue University regional campus at Indianapolis, adopted present name, and incorporated 1969; awarded first degree (baccalaureate) 1970.

Institutional Structure: Institution is governed jointly by the Trustees of Indiana University and the Board of Trustees of Purdue University. *Composition of institution:* Administrators 140. Academic affairs headed by Executive Vice Chancellor and Dean of the Faculties. Management/business/finances directed by Vice Chancellor for Budgeting and Fiscal Affairs. Full-time instructional faculty 2,163. Academic governance body, IUPUI Faculty Council, meets an average of 8 times per year.

Calendar: Semesters. Academic year mid-Aug. to early May.

Characteristics of Freshmen: 86% of applicants accepted. 65.6% of accepted applicants enrolled.

73.1% (1,988 students) submitted SAT scores; 25.4% (692 students) submitted ACT scores. *25th percentile:* SAT I Verbal 440, SAT I Math 440; ACT Composite 18, ACT English 17, ACT Math 17. *75th percentile:* SAT I Verbal 550, SAT I Math 550; ACT Composite 23, ACT English 23, ACT Math 24.

15.6% of entering freshmen expected to graduate within 5 years. 99.4% of freshmen from Indiana. Freshmen from 38 states and 59 foreign countries.

Admission: *See* Indiana University, System Administration (above).

Degree Requirements: *For all associate degrees:* 60 credit hours; residence requirements vary by program. *For all baccalaureate degrees:* 120–124 credit hours; minimum 26 hours of final year in residence, including 10 hours in major. *For all undergraduate degrees:* 2.0 GPA. *Grading system:* A–F; pass-fail; withdraw (deadline after which pass-fail is appended to withdraw).

Distinctive Educational Programs: Interdisciplinary studies offered in women's studies, biomechanical engineering, American studies. Weekend College; Community Learning network; Continuing Studies; Honors programs. School offers college credit for postsecondary-level work completed in secondary school and for extrainstitutional learning (life experience) on basis of ACE *Military Guide.* Tutoring available.

ROTC: Army, Air Force.

Degrees Conferred: 647 *associate;* 2,527 *baccalaureate;* 615 *master's;* 35 *doctorate;* 605 *first-professional.* Bachelor's degrees awarded in top five disciplines: business, management, marketing, and related support services 424; health professions and related clinical sciences 392; liberal arts and sciences, general studies and humanities 386; education 265; computer and information sciences and support services 126.

Fees and Other Expenses: *Full-time tuition per academic year 2004–05:* undergraduate resident $4,526, out-of-state student $14,346. (Graduate and professional schools vary; contact the school of choice for current information). *Required fees:* $573. *Books and supplies:* $840.

Financial Aid: Aid from institutionally generated funds is provided on the basis of academic merit, financial need, other considerations. Institution has a Program Participation Agreement with the U.S. Department of Education for eligible students to receive Pell Grants and other federal aid.

Financial aid to full-time, first-time undergraduate students: need-based scholarships/grants totaling $24,682,704, self-help $25,487,625; non-need-based scholarships/grants totaling $7,385,189, self-help $19,192,967, parent loans $1,249,656, tuition waivers $723,570, athletic awards $635,204.

Departments and Teaching Staff: *Total instructional faculty:* 3,107 (full-time 2,163, part-time 944; women 1,262, men 1,845; members of minority groups 502). Total faculty with doctorate, first-professional, or other terminal degree: 1,977. Student-to-faculty ratio: 17:1.

Enrollment: Total enrollment 29,953. Undergraduate full-time 5,564 men / 8,073 women, part-time 3,174m / 4,361w; graduate full-time 501m / 910w, part-time 2,093m / 2,806w; first-professional full-time 1,192m / 986w, part-time 157m / 136w.

Characteristics of Student Body: *Ethnic and racial makeup:* number of Black non-Hispanic: 2,291; American Indian or Alaska Native: 71; Asian or Pacific Islander: 525; Hispanic: 419; White non-Hispanic: 16,929; unknown: 668. *Age distribution:* 17–21: 30%; 22–24: 21%; 25–29: 21%; 30–34: 10%; 35–39: 6%; 40–49: 9%; 50–64: 2%; 65–and over: 1%.

International Students: 369 undergraduate nonresident aliens enrolled fall 2004. Students from Europe, Asia, Central and South America, Africa, Canada, Australia, New Zealand. Programs available to aid students whose native language is not English: Social, cultural, financial. English as a Second Language Program. No financial aid specifically designated for international students.

Student Life: Limited on-campus housing available for single and married students. 2% of students live on campus. *Intercollegiate athletics:* men only: baseball, basketball, soccer, tennis; women only: basketball, softball, tennis, volleyball. *Special services:* Integrated technologies, medical services, counseling and psychological services. *Student publications: Genesis,* a biannual literary magazine; *Sagamore,* a weekly newspaper. *Surrounding community:* Indianapolis population 800,000. Greater Indianapolis metropolitan area population 1,500,000. Served by mass transit bus system; airport 8 miles from campus.

Library Collections: 1,592,200 volumes. 80,500 government documents; 10,160 serial subscriptions; 159,000 audiovisual materials; 2,461,500 microforms. Students have access to the Internet (charges included in mandatory fees).

Most important special holdings: School of Medicine Library.

Buildings and Grounds: Campus area 515 acres.

Chief Executive Officer: Dr. Charles R. Bantz, Chancellor.

Address admission inquiries to Dr. Rebecca Porter, Director of Enrollment Management.

School of Liberal Arts

Degree Programs Offered: *Associate* in various fields; *baccalaureate* in anthropology, communication and theater, economics, English, French, geography, German, history, philosophy, political science, religious studies, sociology, Spanish; *master's* in history, economics.

Herron School of Art

Degree Programs Offered: *Baccalaureate* in art education, art history, ceramics, fine arts, painting, photography, printmaking, sculpture, visual communication, woodworking; *master's* in art education.

Admission: Portfolio review.

School of Engineering and Technology

Degree Programs Offered: *Associate* in architectural technology, biomedical electronics technology, civil engineering technology, computer technology, electrical engineering technology, food service and lodging supervision, mechanical drafting-design technology, mechanical engineering technology, supervision; *baccalaureate* in computer integrated manufacturing technology, computer technology, construction technology, electrical engineering, electrical engineering technology, interdisciplinary engineering, mechanical engineering, mechanical engineering technology, supervision; *master's* in electrical engineering, interdisciplinary engineering, mechanical engineering. *Certificate* in technical drafting also given.

Distinctive Educational Programs: Interdisciplinary majors. Minority Engineering Advancement Program. Alternative science careers program.

School of Nursing

Degree Programs Offered: *Associate, baccalaureate. Master's* in nursing administration and teacher education, community health nursing, nursing of adults, parent/child nursing, psychiatric/mental health nursing, primary health care nursing. *Doctorate* in nursing administration, nursing of adults, psychiatric/mental health nursing, health policies, health of the community.

School of Physical Education

Degree Programs Offered: *Baccalaureate.*

School of Science

Degree Programs Offered: *Baccalaureate* and *master's* in biology, chemistry, computer science, geology (IU programs), mathematics, physics, psychology; *doctorate* in rehabilitation psychology.

Distinctive Educational Programs: Undergraduate research opportunities; peer tutoring.

School of Social Work

Degree Programs Offered: *Baccalaureate, master's* in social work.

School of Dentistry

Degree Programs Offered: *Associate* in dental hygiene; *baccalaureate* in public health dental hygiene; *first-professional; master's* in dental diagnostic sciences, dental materials, endodontics, operative dentistry, oral and maxillofacial surgery, oral pathology, orthodontics, pediatric dentistry, periodontics, preventive dentistry, prosthodontics; *master's* and *doctorate* awarded through Graduate School. *Certificate* in dental assisting also given.

Admission: *For first-professional:* 90 semester hours (135 quarter hours) of approved predental credit which must include 2 semesters biology or zoology, 2 general chemistry, 1 organic chemistry, 2 general physics (all with laboratory), 1 psychology, 1 business; 2.5 overall and science GPA.

Degree Requirements: *For first-professional:* 3-year core curriculum, 4th year in clinical practice.

School of Law

Degree Programs Offered: *First-professional.*

Admission: Baccalaureate from accredited college or university with 90 semester hours considered acceptable toward an arts and sciences or business degree; LSAT.

Degree Requirements: 85 credit hours, 2.0 GPA.

Distinctive Educational Programs: Accelerated program. Joint degree programs in cooperation with the Schools of Business and Public and Environmental Affairs.

Enrollment: *Total enrollment:* 884. Full-time first-professional 314 men / 269 women, part-time 168m / 129w.

School of Medicine

Degree Programs Offered: *Associate* in paramedic science, radiography; *baccalaureate* in cytotechnology, medical imaging technology, health information administration, medical technology, nuclear medicine technology, occupational therapy, physical therapy, radiation therapy; *respiratory therapy; first-professional, master's,* and *doctorate* in medical science; *master's* and *doctorate* in health sciences awarded through Graduate School.

Admission: *For first-professional:* 90 semester hours from accredited college or university which must include 1 year biological sciences, 1 general chemistry, 1 organic chemistry, 1 physics (all with laboratory); MCAT. Baccalaureate from accredited college or university strongly recommended.

Degree Requirements: *For first-professional:* 8 full semesters within 4 years, last 2 years in residence.

Distinctive Educational Programs: Accelerated baccalaureate-first-professional program.

School of Business

Degree Programs Offered: *Baccalaureate* with concentrations in accounting, business economics and public policy, finance, finance/insurance, finance/real estate, management, marketing, marketing/distribution management, human resources management; *master's* in business administration. *Certificate* also given.

Distinctive Educational Programs: Internships. *See also* School of Law.

School of Continuing Studies

Degree Programs Offered: *Associate, baccalaureate* in general studies, labor studies. Certificate in labor studies also given.

Fees and Other Expenses: Faculty members are drawn from other schools within the university.

School of Education

Degree Programs Offered: *Baccalaureate, master's, doctorate* in various teacher education areas. Specialist also given.

Distinctive Educational Programs: Cooperative student teaching arrangements with schools from a variety of cultural and economic backgrounds, including opportunities with the American Indian, Latino, and rural education projects. *Other distinctive programs:* Teacher as Decision Maker program for post baccalaureate certification students. Distance education programs. Programs under development to enhance collaboration in schools. Enhanced efforts in technology applications in developmental stage.

School of Public and Environmental Affairs

Degree Programs Offered: *Associate* in criminal justice, public affairs; *baccalaureate* in criminal justice, health services management, public affairs, public health; *master's* in health administration, planning, public affairs.

Distinctive Educational Programs: Combined degree programs in cooperation with the Schools of Law and Nursing.

School of Journalism

Degree Programs Offered: *Baccalaureate* in journalism.

Graduate School

Degree Programs Offered: *Master's, doctorate.*

Departments and Teaching Staff: Faculty drawn from various schools within the university.

Indiana University South Bend

1700 Mishawaka Avenue
P.O. Box 7111
South Bend, Indiana 46634-7111
Tel: (574) 520-IUSB   **E-mail:** admissions@iusb.edu
Fax: (219) 520-4834   **Internet:** www.iusb.edu

Institution Description: Indiana University at South Bend is a state institution. *Enrollment:* 7,501. *Degrees awarded:* Associate, baccalaureate, master's. Certificates also award.

Member of Northern Indiana Consortium for Education (NICE).

Accreditation: *Regional:* NCA. *Professional:* business, dental hygiene, nursing, nursing education, public administration, radiation therapy, radiography, social work, teacher education

History: Established and offered first instruction at postsecondary level 1940; awarded first degree (baccalaureate) 1967; adopted present name 1968.

Institutional Structure: *Composition of institution:* Administrators 41. Academic affairs, student affairs, management/business/finances each headed by a vice chancellor. Full-time instructional faculty 179. Academic governance body, Academic Senate, meets an average of 9 times per year.

Calendar: Semesters. Academic year late Aug. to early May.

Characteristics of Freshmen: 81.9% of applicants accepted. 19.1% of accepted applicants enrolled.

73% (653 students) submitted SAT scores; 9.2% (82 students) submitted ACT scores. *25th percentile:* SAT I Verbal 430, SAT I Math 430; ACT Composite 17, ACT English 16, ACT Math 17. *75th percentile:* SAT I Verbal 540, SAT I Math 530; ACT Composite 23, ACT English 22, ACT Math 23.

19% of entering freshmen are expected to graduate within 5 years. 96.2% of freshmen from Indiana. Freshmen from 10 states and 32 foreign countries.

Admission: Rolling admissions plan. For fall acceptance, apply as early as end of junior year of secondary school, but not later than Feb. 15. *Minimum requirements:* 8 semesters of English, 6 semesters of mathematics, 2 semesters of laboratory science, 2 semesters of social science. Students must submit either SAT or ACT results. *For transfer students:* in-state residents 2.0 minimum GPA, out-of-state students 2.5 minimum GPA; from 4-year accredited institution 96 hours maximum transfer credit; from 2-year accredited institution 60 hours. Transfer credit also accepted for correspondence/extension students.

College credit for extrainstitutional learning on basis of ACE *2006 Guide to the Evaluation of Educational Experiences in the Armed Services*, portfolio and faculty assessments. Tutoring available; developmental/remedial courses offered during regular academic year.

Degree Requirements: *For all associate degrees:* 60 credit hours. *For all baccalaureate degrees:* 120–24 credit hours; 30 hours in residence; exit competency examinations in some disciplines. *For all undergraduate degrees:* 2.0 GPA; core curriculum.

Fulfillment of some degree requirements and exemption from some beginning courses possible by passing departmental examinations, College Board CLEP, Achievement Tests, APP. *Grading system:* A–F; pass-fail; withdraw (carries time limit, deadline after which pass-fail is appended to withdraw).

Distinctive Educational Programs: Work-experience programs. Flexible meeting places and schedules, including off-campus centers (at Elkhart, Warsaw, and other locations), weekend and evening classes. Interdepartmental programs in the arts, international relations, public affairs. Full range of nursing degrees. Preprofessional programs in dentistry, engineering, medicine, optometry, pharmacy, law. Facilities and support for independent research, including honors programs, tutorials. Cross-registration through consortium. Transfer agreements with other Indiana University campuses. Study abroad in Ireland, England, Peru,

Japan. System-wide overseas study programs in many European cities, Mexico, China, and Israel. *Other distinctive programs:* Degree, certificate, professional training, and general interest programs through School of Continuing Studies. Cooperative degree program with Purdue University to offer engineering technology degrees. Servicemembers Opportunity College.

ROTC: Army, Navy, Air Force in cooperation with University of Notre Dame.

Degrees Conferred: 161 *associate*; 538 *baccalaureate*; 251 *master's*. Bachelor's degrees awarded in top five disciplines: education 103; business, management, marketing, and related support services 90; liberal arts and sciences, general studies and humanities 77; health professions and related clinical sciences 54; psychology 36.

Fees and Other Expenses: *Full-time tuition per academic year 2004–05:* resident $3,828. out-of-state students $10,890. Contact the university for current graduate tuition/fees. *Required fees:* $406. *Books and supplies:* $976.

Financial Aid: Aid from institutionally generated funds is provided on the basis of academic merit, financial need, other criteria. Institution has a Program Participation Agreement with the U.S. Department of Education for eligible students to receive Pell Grants and other federal aid.

Financial aid to full-time, first-time undergraduate students: need-based scholarships/grants totaling $5,023,396, self-help $5,429,492; non-need-based scholarships/grants totaling $1,200,529, self-help $3,059,110, parent loans $313,630, tuition waivers $35,706, athletic awards $41,000.

Departments and Teaching Staff: *Total instructional faculty:* 551 (full-time 291, part-time 260; women 288, men 263; members of minority groups 62). Total faculty with doctorate, first-professional, or other terminal degree: 232. Student-to-faculty ratio: 13.6:1.

Enrollment: Total enrollment 7,501. Undergraduate full-time 1,325 men / 2,219 women, part-time 991m / 1,787w; graduate full-time 78m / 118w, part-time 320m / 663w.

Characteristics of Student Body: *Ethnic and racial makeup:* number of Black non-Hispanic: 400; American Indian or Alaska Native: 32; Asian or Pacific Islander: 80; Hispanic: 178; White non-Hispanic: 5,299; unknown: 204. *Age distribution:* 17–21: 34%; 22–24: 17%; 25–29: 17%; 30–34: 10%; 35–39: 7%; 40–49: 11%; 50–64: 3%.

International Students: 129 nonresident aliens enrolled fall 2004. Students from Europe, Asia, Central and South America, Africa, Canada, New Zealand. Programs available to aid students whose language is not English: Social, cultural. English as a Second Language program. No financial aid specifically designated for international students.

Student Life: No on-campus housing. *Special regulations:* Cars permitted without restrictions. *Special services:* Learning Resources Center. *Student publications, radio:* Analecta, an annual literary magazine; *Preface,* a newspaper published 32 times per year. *Surrounding community:* South Bend population 106,000. Served by mass transit bus system; airport 4 miles from campus; passenger rail service 9 miles from campus.

Library Collections: 303,203 volumes. 451,621 microforms; 7,824 audiovisual materials; 1,713 serial subscriptions. Students have access to the Internet (charges included in mandatory fees).

Most important holdings include James Lewis Cassaday Theater Collection; Christianson Lincoln Collection.

Buildings and Grounds: Campus area 80 acres.

Chief Executive Officer: Dr. Una Mae Reck, Chancellor.

Address admission inquiries to Jeff M. Johnson, Director of Admissions.

Indiana University Southeast

4201 Grand Line Road
New Albany, Indiana 47150
Tel: (812) 941-2212   **E-mail:** admissions@ius.edu
Fax: (812) 941-2595   **Internet:** www.ius.edu

Institution Description: *Enrollment:* 6,238. *Degrees awarded:* Associate, baccalaureate, master's.

Member of the consortium Kentuckiana Metroversity.

Accreditation: *Regional:* NCA. *Professional:* business, engineering technology, nursing, nursing education, teacher education

History: Established as Falls City Center and offered first instruction at postsecondary level 1941; adopted present name and awarded first degree (associate) 1968. *See* Gerald O. Haffner, *Indiana University Southeast: A Brief, Informal History,* (Bloomington: Indian University Publications, 1973) for further information.

Institutional Structure: *Composition of institution:* 7 administrators. Academic affairs, student affairs, management/business/finances each headed by vice chancellor. Full-time instructional faculty 199. Academic governance body,

Indiana University Southeast Faculty Senate, meets an average of 8 times per year.

Calendar: Semesters. Academic year late Aug. to late Apr.

Characteristics of Freshmen: 93.6% of applicants accepted. 73.8% of accepted applicants enrolled.

50.8% (414 students) submitted SAT scores; 16.7% (136 students) submitted ACT scores. *25th percentile:* SAT I Verbal 420, SAT I Math 410; ACT Composite 17, ACT English 22, ACT Math 21. *75th percentile:* SAT I Verbal 520, SAT I Math 530; ACT Composite 22, ACT English 22, ACT Math 21.

91.6% of freshmen from Indiana. Freshmen from 6 states and 9 foreign countries.

Admission: Rolling admissions plan. For fall acceptance, apply as early as end of junior year of secondary school, but not later than Feb. 15. *Minimum requirements:* 8 semesters of English, 6 semesters of mathematics, 2 semesters of laboratory science, 2 semesters of social science. Students must submit either SAT or ACT results. *For transfer students:* In-state residents 2.0 minimum GPA, out-of-state students 2.5 minimum GPA; from 4-year accredited institution 96 hours maximum transfer credit; from 2-year accredited institution 60 hours. Transfer credit also accepted for correspondence/extension students.

College credit for extrainstitutional learning on basis of ACE *2006 Guide to the Evaluation of Educational Experiences in the Armed Services,* portfolio and faculty assessments. Tutoring available; developmental/remedial courses offered during regular academic year.

Degree Requirements: *For all associate degrees:* 60 credit hours; 15 hours in residence. *For all baccalaureate degrees:* 120–124 credit hours; 26 hours of final year in residence, including 10 in major. *For all undergraduate degrees:* 2.0 GPA.

Fulfillment of some degree requirements and exemption from some beginning courses possible by passing standardized tests. *Grading system:* A–F; pass-fail; withdraw (deadline after which pass-fail is appended to withdraw).

Distinctive Educational Programs: School offers college credit for postsecondary-level work completed in secondary school and for extrainstitutional learning on basis of ACE *2006 Guide to the Evaluation of Educational Experiences in the Armed Services* and faculty assessment. Tutoring available. Developmental courses offered in summer session and regular academic year; nondegree credit given. Work-experience programs. Cross-registration through consortium. Flexible meeting places and schedules, weekend and evening classes. Accelerated degree programs. Cooperative program in engineering with Purdue University. Interdisciplinary program in women's studies.

ROTC: Army in cooperation with Indiana University Bloomington; Air Force through consortium.

Degrees Conferred: 145 *associate*; 610 *baccalaureate*; 264 *master's*. Bachelor's degrees awarded in top five disciplines: education 142; business, management, marketing, and related support services 140; liberal arts and sciences, general studies and humanities 121, psychology 37; health professions and related clinical sciences 30.

Fees and Other Expenses: *Full-time tuition per academic year 2004–05:* undergraduate resident $3,762, out-of-state $10,673. Contact the university for current graduate tuition/fees. *Required fees:* $390.

Financial Aid: Aid from institutionally generated funds is provided on the basis of academic merit, financial need, other considerations. Institution has a Program Participation Agreement with the U.S. Department of Education for eligible students to receive Pell Grants and other federal aid.

Financial aid to full-time, first-time undergraduate students: need-based scholarships/grants totaling $5,384,190, self-help $4,289,525; non-need-based scholarships/grants totaling $1,424,207, self-help $2,816,158, parent loans $205,024, tuition waivers $50,990, athletic awards $49,300.

Departments and Teaching Staff: *Total instructional faculty:* 425 (full-time 199, part-time 226; women 213, men 212; members of minority groups 44). Total faculty with doctorate, first-professional, or other terminal degree: 167. Student-to-faculty ratio: 16:1.

Enrollment: Total enrollment 6,238. Undergraduate full-time 1,222 men / 2,050 women, part-time 833m / 1,314w; graduate full-time 16m / 14w, part-time 282m / 507w.

Characteristics of Student Body: *Ethnic and racial makeup:* number of Black non-Hispanic: 187; American Indian or Alaska Native: 16; Asian or Pacific Islander: 48; Hispanic: 54; White non-Hispanic: 4,924; unknown: 174.

International Students: 16 nonresident aliens enrolled fall 2004. No programs available to aid students whose native language is not English. No financial aid specifically designated for international students.

Student Life: No on-campus housing. *Intercollegiate athletics:* men only: baseball, basketball; women only: basketball, volleyball. *Special regulations:* Cars permitted without restrictions. *Special services:* Student Development Center; Adult Student Center; day-car facility. *Student publications:* The Horizon, a weekly newspaper; *The Literary Magazine,* published once each semester. *Surrounding community:* New Albany population 36,500. Louisville, 10 miles from campus, is nearest metropolitan area. Served by airport 20 miles from campus.

Library Collections: 233,181 volumes. 112,200 government documents; 366,077 microforms; 9,497 audiovisual materials; 851 current periodicals. Students have access to the Internet (charges included in mandatory fees).

Buildings and Grounds: Campus area 177 acres.

Chief Executive Officer: Dr. Sandra R. Patterson-Randles, Chancellor.

Address admission inquiries to Annie Skuce, Director of Admissions.

Indiana Wesleyan University

4201 South Washington Street
Marion, Indiana 46953
Tel: (715) 677-2138   **E-mail:** admissions@indwes.edu
Fax: (715) 677-2333   **Internet:** www.indwes.edu

Institution Description: Indiana Wesleyan University, formerly Marion College, is a private, independent, nonprofit college affiliated with The Wesleyan Church. *Enrollment:* 11,412. *Degrees awarded:* Associate, baccalaureate, master's, doctorate.

Member of the Small College Consortium.

Accreditation: *Regional:* NCA. *Professional:* clinical lab scientist, music, nursing, nursing education, social work, teacher education

History: Established 1919; chartered and offered first instruction at postsecondary level 1920; awarded first degree (baccalaureate) 1921; added master's program 1979; adopted present name 1987. *See* Willard G. Smith, "History of Church-Controlled Colleges of the Wesleyan Methodist Church" (Diss., New York University, 1951) for further information.

Institutional Structure: *Governing board:* Board of Trustees of Indiana Wesleyan University. Extrainstitutional representation: 30 trustees, including 11 alumni and 4 women; institutional representation: 9 administrators plus 6 representatives from the university, faculty, staff, alumni, and 2 from the sponsoring denomination. 17 ex officio (non-voting). *Composition of institution:* Administrators 9 men (at dean's level and above). Academic affairs headed by vice president of academic affairs. Management/business/finances directed by vice president for financial affairs. Academic governance body, the Senate, meets an average of 8 times per year.

Calendar: Semesters. Academic year Sept. to May. Freshmen admitted Sept., Jan., June, July. Degrees conferred Apr., Aug., Dec. (formal commencements).

Characteristics of Freshmen: 73% of applicants admitted. 33.4% of applicants admitted and enrolled.

50% of students submitted SAT scores; 50% submitted ACT scores. *25th percentile*: SAT Verbal 500, SAT Math 475; ACT Composite 24, ACT English 24, ACT Math 24. *75th percentile*: SAT Verbal 625, SAT Math 625; ACT Composite 24, ACT English 24, ACT Math 24.

55% of entering freshmen expected to graduate within 5 years. 52% of freshmen from Indiana. Freshmen from 32 states.

Admission: For fall acceptance, apply as early as completion of junior year of secondary school. Students are encouraged to apply in the academic year prior to the term of their intended enrollment. Students must complete the application process at least 10 business days prior to the start of the semester of their intended enrollment. Consideration will be given as space allows. *Requirements:* Either graduation from secondary school with 10 college preparatory units; or GED. *Entrance tests:* College Board SAT or ACT Composite. *For transfer students:* Correspondence/extension students 6 hours maximum transfer credit.

Advanced placement for postsecondary-level work completed in secondary school. College credit for extrainstitutional learning (life experience) on basis of *ACE 2006 Guide to the Evaluation of Educational Experiences in the Armed Services.* Tutoring available. Developmental courses offered in summer session and regular academic year; credit given.

Degree Requirements: *For all associate degrees:* 62 semester hours. *For all baccalaureate degrees:* 124 semester hours; 2.5 GPA overall; GPA in major(s) vary. *For all undergraduate degrees:* 2.0 GPA; 2 semesters in residence; chapel attendance 3 times weekly; general education requirements.

Fulfillment of some degree requirements and exemption from some beginning courses possible by passing College Board CLEP, AP, other standardized tests. *Grading system:* A–F; credit-noncredit; withdraw (fail appended if failing at time of withdrawal).

Distinctive Educational Programs: Weekend and evening classes. Cooperative baccalaureate in medical technology with approved hospitals. Interdisciplinary programs in general science, social sciences. Facilities and programs for independent research, including honors programs, individual majors. Travel opportunities available. Adult Education Program sites in Indiana, Kentucky, and Ohio. Education sites in Indiana: Indianapolis, Fort Wayne, Columbus, Kokomo, Shelbyville.

Degrees Conferred: 1,515 *baccalaureate* (B); 1,386 *master's* (M): area and ethnic studies 12 (B); biological/life sciences 10 (B); business/marketing 977 (B), 792 (M); communications/communication technologies 19 (B); computer and information sciences 11 (B); education 45 (B), 561 (M); English 14 (B); health professions and related sciences 233 (B), 27 (M); liberal arts/general studies 10 (B); parks and recreation 24 (B); philosophy/religion/theology 53 (B), 7 (M); physical sciences 2 (B); protective services/public administration 29 (B); psychology 31 (B); social sciences and history 10 (B); visual and performing arts 30 (B).

Fees and Other Expenses: *Full-time tuition per academic year 2005*06:* $16,184. *Room and board per academic year:* $5,840.

Financial Aid: Aid from institutionally generated funds is provided on the basis of academic merit, financial need, athletic ability, other criteria. Institution has a Program Participation Agreement with the U.S. Department of Education for eligible students to receive Pell Grants and other federal aid.

Departments and Teaching Staff: *Professors* 26, *associate professors* 37, *assistant professors* 47, *instructors* 5. *Total instructional faculty:* 121 (full-time 121; women 43, men 78; members of minority groups 8). Total faculty with doctorate, first-professional, or other terminal degree: 70. Student-to-faculty ratio: 18:1.

Enrollment: Total enrollment 11,412. Undergraduate full-time 6,909, part-time 830; graduate full-time 3,442, part-time 231.

Characteristics of Student Body: *Ethnic/racial makeup:* number of Black non-Hispanic: 817; American Indian or Alaska Native: 23; Asian or Pacific Islander: 55; Hispanic: 93; White non-Hispanic: 5,334; unknown: 194. *Age distribution:* number under 18: 12; 18–19: 1.128; 20–21: 1,012; 22–24: 280; 25–29: 37; 30–34: 20; 35–39: 4; 40–49: 20; 50–64: 8.

International Students: 17 nonresident aliens enrolled. 1 student from Europe, 2 Asia, 1 Africa, 3 Canada, 10 other. Programs available for students whose native language is not English: Social, cultural. No financial aid specifically designated for international students.

Student Life: On-campus residence halls house 77% of student body. Residence halls for men constitute 37% of such space, for women 63%. *Intercollegiate athletics:* men only: baseball, basketball, cross-country, soccer, softball, tennis, track, volleyball; women only: basketball, cross-country, soccer, softball, tennis, track, volleyball. *Special regulations:* Cars permitted without restrictions. Campus dress should reflect the Christian standards of modesty, appropriateness, and simplicity. *Special services:* Clinical counseling, tutoring, testing, disability services, medical services. *Student publications, radio: Journal,* a bimonthly newspaper; *Legacy,* a yearbook. WTWU-TV station. *Surrounding community:* Marion population 31,000. Indianapolis, 65 miles from campus, is nearest metropolitan area. Served by mass transit bus system; airport 50 miles from campus.

Library Collections: 133,196 volumes. 189,358 microform titles; 10,657 audiovisuals (including recordings and tapes); 659 periodicals. Students have access to online information retrieval services and the Internet.

Most important holdings include Wesleyana Collection; Nursing Collection.

Buildings and Grounds: Campus area 132 acres.

Chief Executive Officer: James Dr. Barnes, President.

Address admission inquiries to Director of Admissions.

ITT Technical Institute

9511 Angola Court
Indianapolis, Indiana 46268-1119
Tel: (317) 875-8640   **E-mail:** admissions@itt-tech.edu
Fax: (317) 875-8641   **Internet:** www.itt-tech.edu

Institution Description: ITT Technical Institute is owned and operated by ITT Educational Services, Inc. of Indianapolis, Indiana. *Degrees awarded:* Associate, baccalaureate. Campuses are located throughout the United States. Contact the institute for localities (www.itt-tech.edu).

Accreditation: *National:* ACICS.

Calendar: Quarters. Classes held year round beginning in De., Mar., June, and Sept.

Characteristics of Freshmen: 1,462 applicants (832 men, 630 women). 25.7% of applicants admitted. 71.5% of admitted students enrolled full-time.

Admission: The student must provide documented proof of his or her high school diploma or recognized equivalency certificate.

Degree Requirements: Student must attain an overall 2.0 cumulative grade point average for the entire program pursued; must successfully complete all courses specified in the catalog for the program.

Degrees Conferred: 211 *associate*; 67 *baccalaureate.* Bachelor's degrees awarded in top disciplines: engineering technologies/technicians 55; computer and information sciences and support services 12.

Fees and Other Expenses: *Full-time tuition per academic year 2004–05:* $13,548. *Room and board per academic year:* $5,958.

Financial Aid: Financial assistance is available in the form of Pell Grants, College Work-Study, Veterans Administration Benefits, National Direct Student Loans, Supplemental Education Opportunity Grants (SEOG), Stafford Loans, other federal aid programs.

Financial aid to full-time, first-time undergraduate students: 50% received federal grants averaging $2,433; 5% institutional grants averaging $1,149; 95% loans averaging $4,515.

Departments and Teaching Staff: *Instructors* 32. *Degrees held by full-time faculty:* baccalaureate 82%, master's 15%, doctorate 3%.

Enrollment: *Total enrollment* 1,787. Undergraduate 1,695 (76.7% men, 23.3% women).

Characteristics of Student Body: *Ethnic/racial makeup:* Black non-Hispanic: 16.3%; American Indian or Alaska Native .5%; Asian or Pacific Islander: 2.2%; Hispanic: 3.7%; White non-Hispanic: 59.8%; unknown: 17.6%.

International Students: No programs to aid students whose native language is not English. No financial aid specifically designated for international students.

Student Life: The school helps organize wholesome recreational activities by providing equipment, faculty sponsorship, and financial support.

Buildings and Grounds: The school occupies 59,000 square feet with available parking on site in northwest Indianapolis.

Chief Executive Officer: Steven E. Brooks, Director.

Address admissions inquiries to Director of Recruitment.

Manchester College

604 East College Avenue
North Manchester, Indiana 46962
Tel: (260) 982-5000   **E-mail:** admitinfo@manchester.edu
Fax: (260) 982-5043   **Internet:** www.manchester.edu

Institution Description: Manchester College is a private college affiliated with the Church of the Brethren. *Enrollment:* 1,075. *Degrees awarded:* Associate, baccalaureate, master's.

Accreditation: *Regional:* NCA. *Professional:* athletic training, social work, teacher education

History: Established and chartered as Manchester College and Bible School, and offered first instruction at postsecondary level 1889; awarded first degree (baccalaureate) 1900; adopted present name 1902. See Ira H. Frantz, ed., *Manchester College* (Elgin, IL: The Brethren Press, 1964) for further information.

Institutional Structure: *Governing board:* Board of Trustees. Extrainstitutional representation: 6 representatives of church districts, 5 representatives of alumni association, president of the college ex officio; 25 at-large members approved by church districts. All voting. *Composition of institution:* Administrators 4 men / 3 women. Academic affairs headed by vice president of academic affairs. Management/business/finances directed by president and treasurer. Full-time instructional faculty 66. Academic governance body, the faculty, meets an average of 16 times per year.

Calendar: Semesters. Academic year Sept. to May. Freshmen admitted Sept., Jan., Feb., June, July. Degrees conferred and formal commencement May. Summer term of 3 sessions.

Characteristics of Freshmen: 76% of applicants accepted. 34.5% accepted applicants enrolled.

90% (250 students) submitted SAT scores; 30% (83 students) submitted ACT scores. *25th percentile:* SAT Verbal 450, SAT Math 460; ACT Composite 20. *75th percentile:* SAT Verbal 560, SAT Math 570; ACT Composite 25.

50% entering freshmen expected to graduate within 5 years. 88% of freshmen from Indiana. Freshmen from 11 states and 10 foreign countries.

Admission: Rolling admissions plan. Apply as early as June following junior year in secondary school. Early acceptance available. *Requirements:* Either graduation from accredited secondary school or GED. *Entrance tests:* College Board SAT preferred; ACT composite accepted. *For transfer students:* 2.0 minimum GPA.

Degree Requirements: *For all associate degrees:* 64 credit hours; 1 hour Values, Ideas, and the Arts. *For all baccalaureate degrees:* 128 hours; comprehensives in individual fields of study; 2 hours physical education; 2 hours Values, Ideas, and the Arts. *For all undergraduate degrees:* 2.0 GPA; 32 hours in residence; distribution requirements.

Fulfillment of some degree requirements and exemption from some beginning courses possible by passing departmental examinations, College Board CLEP or APP. *Grading system:* A–F; pass-fail; withdraw.

Distinctive Educational Programs: *For undergraduates:* Interdisciplinary programs in environmental studies, gerontology, and peace studies. Foreign study through Brethren Colleges Abroad in Ecuador, England, France, Germany, Greece, India, Mexico, Spain and other locations by special arrangement. Republic of China, Spain; also available in cooperation with Council of Mennonite Colleges by special arrangement. *Available to all students:* Facilities and programs for independent research, including individual majors, tutorials.

Degrees Conferred: 12 *associate;* 208 *baccalaureate:* biological/life sciences 16; business/marketing 53; communications/communication technologies 18; computer and information sciences 5; education 40; English 2; foreign languages and literature 11; health professions and related sciences 12; interdisciplinary studies 6; mathematics 4; natural resources/environmental science 3; parks and recreation 3; philosophy/religion/theology 8; physical sciences 2; protective services/public administration 13; psychology 12; social sciences and history 18; visual and performing arts 5; 16 *master's:* business/marketing.16.

Fees and Other Expenses: *Full-time tuition per academic year 2005–06:* $18,750. *Required fees:* $610. *Room and board per academic year:* $6,500.

Financial Aid: Aid from institutionally generated funds is provided on the basis of academic merit, financial need, other criteria. Institution has a Program Participation Agreement with the U.S. Department of Education for eligible students to receive Pell Grants and other federal aid.

Financial aid to full-time, first-time undergraduate students: need-based scholarships/grants totaling $10,652,587, self-help $3,709,473, parent loans $1,140,022, tuition waivers $111,800; non-need-based scholarships/grants totaling $1,903,843, self-help $433,855, parent loans $138,886, tuition waivers $70,686.

Departments and Teaching Staff: *Total instructional faculty:* 83 (full-time 66, part-time 17; women 30, men 42; members of minority groups 1). Total faculty with doctorate, first-professional, or other terminal degree: 65. Student-to-faculty ratio: 14:1. *Faculty development:* 5 faculty members awarded sabbaticals 2004–05.

Enrollment: Total enrollment 1,078. Undergraduate full-time 456 men / 554 women, part-time 22m / 31w; graduate full-time 5m / 7w. *Transfer students:* 38.

Characteristics of Student Body: *Ethnic and racial makeup:* number of Black non-Hispanic: 31; American Indian or Alaska Native: 7; Asian or Pacific Islander: 8; Hispanic: 22; White non-Hispanic: 930; unknown: 8. *Age distribution:* number under 18: 12; 18–19: 456; 20–21: 421; 22–24: 148; 25–29: 12; 30–34: 5; 35–39: 6; 40–49: 10; 50–64: 2.

International Students: 69 nonresident aliens enrolled fall 2004. 8 students from Europe, 49 Asia, 3 Central and South America, 5 Africa, 4 Canada. Programs available to aid students whose native language is not English: Social, cultural. No financial aid specifically designated for international students.

Student Life: On-campus residence halls house 79% of student body. Dormitories for men only constitute 35% of such space, for women only 40%, for both sexes 25%. Housing available for married students. 10% of married students request institutional housing; 90% are so housed. *Intercollegiate athletics:* men only: baseball, basketball, cross-country, football, golf, soccer, tennis, track, wrestling; women only: basketball, cross-country, golf, soccer, softball, tennis, track, volleyball. *Special regulations:* Cars permitted with campus registration. *Special services:* Learning Resources Center, medical services. *Student publications, radio:* The Aurora, a yearbook; Oak Leaves, a weekly newspaper. Radio station WBKE broadcasts 24 hours daily. *Surrounding community:* North Manchester population 6,500. Served by mass transit bus and passenger rail service 20 miles away; airport 40 miles. Fort Wayne (IN) is 35 miles from campus.

Library Collections: 179,000 volumes. 21,943 microforms; 4,913 audiovisual materials; 617 current periodical subscriptions. Online catalog. Access to online information retrieval systems. 41 computer work stations. Students have access to the Internet (charges included in mandatory fees).

Most important special holdings include Church of the Brethren Collection; Peace Studies Library (3 separate collections: Peace, Nonviolence, Pacifism); Africana.

Buildings and Grounds: Campus area 120 acres. *New buildings:* Science Center completed 2005.

Chief Executive Officer: Dr. Jo Young Switzer, President.

Address admission inquiries to Jolane Rohr, Director of Admissions.

Marian College

3200 Cold Spring Road
Indianapolis, Indiana 46222-1997
Tel: (317) 955-6000   **E-mail:** www.marian.edu
Fax: admissions@marian.edu

Institution Description: Marian College is a coeducational, comprehensive liberal arts college developed by the Sisters of Saint Francis, Oldenburg, Indiana,

Roman Catholic Church. *Enrollment:* 1,685. *Degrees awarded:* Associate, baccalaureate.

Member of Consortium for Urban Education.

Accreditation: *Regional:* NCA. *Professional:* dietetics, nursing, teacher education

History: Established at Oldenburg (IN) as Saint Francis Normal School for Women, and offered first instruction at postsecondary level 1851; merged with Immaculate Conception Junior College (founded 1924) and adopted present name 1936, chartered and moved to present site 1937; awarded first degree (baccalaureate) 1938; became coeducational 1954.

Institutional Structure: *Governing board:* Board of Trustees of Marian College. Extrainstitutional representation: 34 trustees, including 3 alumni; institutional representation: 1 administrator. All voting. *Composition of institution:* Administrators 6 men / 2 women. Academic affairs headed by dean for academic affairs. Management/business/finances directed by chief financial officer. Full-time instructional faculty 80. Academic governance body, College Council, meets an average of 9 times per year.

Calendar: Semesters. Academic year late Aug. to mid-May. Freshmen admitted Aug., Jan., June. Degrees conferred May, Aug. Formal commencement May. Summer sessions of 2 terms from mid-May to early Aug.

Characteristics of Freshmen: 915 applicants (268 men, 647 women). 72.7% of applicants admitted. 35.9% of admitted students enrolled full-time.

71% (168 students) submitted SAT scores; 45% (107 students) submitted ACT scores. *25th percentile*: SAT I 450, Verbal SAT I Math 440; ACT Composite 19, ACT English 18, ACT Math 17. *75th percentile*: SAT I Verbal 560, SAT I Math 560; ACT Composite 24, ACT English 24, ACT Math 24. 55% of entering freshmen expected to graduate within 5 years. 96% of freshmen from Indiana. Freshmen from 9 states and 16 foreign countries.

Admission: Rolling admissions plan. For fall acceptance, apply no later than Aug. 25. Early acceptance available. *Requirements:* Either graduation from accredited secondary school with 16 units which must include 3 English, 2 in a foreign language, 2 mathematics, 1 laboratory science, 1 social studies; or GED. Additional units in algebra, geometry, and speech recommended. Minimum 2.0 GPA. Lowest acceptable secondary school class standing 50th percentile. *Entrance tests:* College Board SAT or ACT composite. *For transfer students:* 2.0 minimum GPA; from 4-year accredited institution 96 hours maximum transfer credit; from 2-year accredited institution 64 hours; correspondence/extension students 10 hours. College credit and advanced placement for postsecondary-level work completed in secondary school. College credit for extrainstitutional learning (life experience) on basis of faculty assessment, and testing (for nurses training) and advanced placement on basis of ACE *2006 Guide to the Evaluation of Educational Experiences in the Armed Services.*

Degree Requirements: *For all associate degrees:* 64 semester hours; 15 hours in residence. *For all baccalaureate degrees:* 128 hours; 30 hours in residence; College Board Undergraduate Assessment Program Area of Field Tests. *For all degrees:* 2.0 GPA; comprehensives in individual fields of study; general education requirements.

Fulfillment of some degree requirements possible by passing departmental examinations and College Board CLEP. *Grading system:* A–F; pass-fail; withdraw.

Distinctive Educational Programs: Cooperative education. Evening classes. Non-West Studies. Study abroad. Pre-engineering program articulated with University of Detroit Mercy. Other pre-professional programs.

ROTC: Army offered in cooperation with Indiana University-Purdue at Indianapolis.

Degrees Conferred: 48 *associate*; 19 *baccalaureate*; 15 *master's.* Bachelor's degrees awarded in top five disciplines: business, management, marketing, and related support services 60; education 31; health professions and related clinical sciences 27; psychology 11; visual and performing arts 10.

Fees and Other Expenses: *Full-time tuition per academic year 2004–05:* $18,240. *Room and board per academic year:* $6,000. *Books and supplies:* $700.

Financial Aid: Aid from institutionally generated funds is provided on the basis of academic merit, financial need, athletic ability, other criteria. Institution has a Program Participation Agreement with the U.S. Department of Education for eligible students to receive Pell Grants and other federal aid.

Financial aid to full-time, first-time undergraduate students: 30% received federal grants averaging $3,596; 38% state/local grants averaging $5,519; 90% institutional grants averaging $8,684; 83% loans averaging $3,276.

Departments and Teaching Staff: *Professors* 15, *associate professors* 20, *assistant professors* 33, *instructors* 12, *part-time faculty* 52. *Total instructional faculty:* 132. Degrees held by full-time instructional faculty: doctorate 25%, master's 100%.

Enrollment: Total enrollment 1,685. Undergraduate 1,666 (26.3% men, 73.7% women).

Characteristics of Student Body: *Ethnic/racial makeup:* Black non-Hispanic: 18.8%; American Indian or Alaska Native: .4%; Asian or Pacific Islander: .6%; Hispanic: 1.6%; White non-Hispanic: 66.7%; unknown: 10.8%. *Age distribution:* 17–21: 51%; 22–24: 11%; 25–29: 9%; 30–34: 8%; 35–39: 8%; 40–49: 10%; 50–59: 2%; 60–and over: 1%.

International Students: 18 undergraduate nonresident aliens enrolled fall 2004. Students from Europe, Asia, Central and South America, Africa, Canada. No programs available to aid students whose native language is not English. No financial aid specifically designated for international students.

Student Life: On-campus residence halls house 40% of student body. Residence halls for both sexes constitute 54% of such space, for women only 46%. *Intercollegiate athletics:* men only: baseball, basketball, golf; women only: basketball, volleyball, softball; both sexes: tennis, track, cross-country. *Special regulations:* Cars permitted without restrictions. Quiet hours from 7pm to 7am Mon.–Thurs. Residence hall visitation from noon to 11pm Sun., 5pm to 11pm Mon.–Thurs., 5pm to 1:30am Fri., noon to 1:30am Sat. *Special services:* Medical services. *Student publications: Carbon,* a weekly newspaper; *Fioretti,* a quarterly literary magazine; *The Marian,* a school yearbook. *Surrounding community:* Indianapolis population 750,000. Served by mass transit bus system; airport 4 miles from campus; passenger rail service 5 miles from campus.

Library Collections: 144,000 volumes. 2,500 recordings/tapes; 590 current periodical subscriptions. Online catalog. Students have access to online information retrieval services and the Internet.

Most important holdings include Archbishop Paul. C. Schulte Historical Collection (history of the midwest, particularly Illinois and Missouri); Deutsche National-Litteratur (collection of German literature from middle ages to 19th century); Collective History of North American Indian Tribes; Catholic Identity Collection.

Buildings and Grounds: Campus area 114 acres.

Chief Executive Officer: Daniel J. Elsener, President.

Address admission inquiries to Dean of Enrollment Management.

Martin University

2171 Avondale Place
Indianapolis, Indiana 46218
Tel: (317) 543-3235 **E-mail:** info@martin.edu
Fax: (317) 543-3675 **Internet:** www.martin.edu

Institution Description: Martin University, formerly known as Martin Center College, is a private, independent, nonprofit college primarily for adults. *Enrollment:* 829. *Degrees awarded:* Baccalaureate.

Accreditation: *Regional:* NCA.

History: Established and offered first instruction at postsecondary level 1977; incorporated 1979; awarded first degree (baccalaureate) 1981; adopted present name 1994.

Institutional Structure: *Governing board:* Martin University Board of Trustees. Extrainstitutional representation: 19 trustees; institutional representation: president of the college. 2 ex officio. 17 voting. *Composition of institution:* Administrators 7 men / 2 women. Academic affairs headed by academic dean. Management/business/finances directed by business manager. Full-time instructional faculty 37. Academic governance body, Administrative Council, meets an average of 12 times per year.

Calendar: Semesters. Academic year Aug. to Apr. Freshmen admitted any month. Degrees conferred and formal commencement Oct. Summer session from early July to late Sept.

Characteristics of Freshmen: Average secondary school rank 50th percentile. Freshmen from 1 state and 1 foreign country.

Admission: Rolling admissions plan. *Requirements:* Either graduation from accredited secondary school or GED. Open admissions policy. *For transfer students:* 95 hours maximum transfer credit. College credit for extrainstitutional learning (life experience) on basis of ACE *2006 Guide to the Evaluation of Educational Experiences in the Armed Services*; portfolio reviewed by faculty committee. Developmental courses offered in summer session and regular academic year; credit given.

Degree Requirements: 126 semester hours; 2.0 GPA; 3 terms in residence; general education requirements; senior thesis or project. Fulfillment of some degree requirements possible by passing College Board CLEP. *Grading system:* A–F; withdraw.

Distinctive Educational Programs: Each student helps to design own degree plan consisting of a series of learning contracts. Students may fulfill contracts through courses, internships, apprenticeships, tutorials, or other learning methods. Weekend and evening classes. Accelerated degree programs. Interdisciplinary programs in public administration, social problems management. *Other distinctive programs:* Institute of Afro-American Studies, publishing *The Afro-*

American Journal and presenting public lectures, exhibits and weekly radio program. Sickle Cell Center.

Degrees Conferred: 52 *baccalaureate*; 17 *master's*. Bachelor's degrees awarded in top five disciplines: business, management, marketing, and related support services 17; psychology 9; philosophy and religious studies 5; biological and biomedical sciences 5; education 5.

Fees and Other Expenses: *Full-time tuition per academic year 2004–05:* $10,970. *Books and supplies:* $820. *Room and board per academic year:* $5,530.

Financial Aid: Aid from institutionally generated funds is provided on the basis of academic merit, financial need, availability. Institution has a Program Participation Agreement with the U.S. Department of Education for eligible students to receive Pell Grants and other federal aid.

Financial aid to full-time, first-time undergraduate students: 57% received federal grants averaging $3,262; 30% state/local grants; 10% institutional grants; 60% loans averaging $4,338.

Departments and Teaching Staff: *Total instructional faculty:* 37. 50% of faculty hold terminal degrees.

Enrollment: Total enrollment 629. Undergraduate 532 (27.3% men, 72.7% women).

Characteristics of Student Body: *Ethnic/racial makeup:* Black non-Hispanic: 93.65; Hispanic: .2%; White non-Hispanic: 5.1%; unknown: .4%. *Age distribution:* 17–21: 9%; 22–24: 6%; 25–29: 13%; 30–34: 13%; 35–39: 10%; 40–449: 30%; 50–59: 14%; 60–and over: 5%.

International Students: 4 undergraduate nonresident aliens enrolled fall 2004. No programs available to aid students whose native language is not English. No financial aid specifically designated for international students.

Student Life: No on-campus housing. *Special regulations:* Cars permitted without restrictions. *Surrounding community:* Indianapolis population over 1 million. Served by airport 12 miles from campus; passenger rail service 5 miles from campus.

Library Collections: Students use interlibrary loan and reference services of 65 area libraries.

Most important holdings include Afro-American studies collection (940 volumes and 2,237 audiovisual materials housed at college that pertain to Afro-American history, culture, literature, and sociological topics).

Buildings and Grounds: Campus area 1 square block.

Chief Executive Officer: Rev. Fr. Boniface Hardin, President.

Address admission inquiries to Brenda Shaheed, Director of Admissions.

Oakland City University

143 North Lucretia Street
Oakland City, Indiana 47660-1099

Tel: (812) 749-4781   **E-mail:** ocuadmit@oak.edu
Fax: (812) 749-1233   **Internet:** www.oak.edu

Institution Description: Oakland City University, formerly named Oakland City College, is a private college affiliated with the General Association of General Baptists. *Enrollment:* 1,985 *Degrees awarded:* Associate, baccalaureate, master's. Certificates and diplomas also awarded.

Accreditation: *Regional:* NCA. *Professional:* teacher education

History: Established and chartered 1885; offered first instruction at postsecondary level 1877; awarded first degree (baccalaureate) 1895; present name adopted 1995.

Institutional Structure: *Governing board:* Board of Trustees. Extrainstitutional representation: 24 trustees, 1 denominational representative; institutional representation: 2 administrators, 1 full-time faculty member, 1 student, 1 alumni representative. 3 ex officio. 24 voting. *Composition of institution:* Administrators 6 cabinet, 17 staff; 31% are women. Academic affairs headed by vice president for academic affairs. Management/business/finances directed by business manager. Full-time instructional faculty 37. Academic governance body, Faculty Assembly, meets monthly during academic year.

Calendar: Semesters. Academic year Aug. to May. Freshmen admitted Sept., Jan., May, June, July. Degrees conferred and formal commencement May. Summer sessions May to Aug.

Characteristics of Freshmen: 504 applicants (195 men, 309 women). 47.2% of applicants admitted.

2.1% of admitted students enrolled full-time. 49% (197 students) submitted SAT scores; 26% (109 students) submitted ACT scores. *25th percentile:* SAT I Verbal 450, SAT I Math 440; ACT Composite 17, ACT English 15, ACT Math 18. *75th percentile:* SAT I Verbal 580, SAT I Math 600; ACT Composite 23, ACT English 21, ACT Math 23.

57% of entering freshmen expected to graduate within 5 years. 68% of freshmen from Indiana. Freshmen from 17 states and 8 foreign countries.

Admission: Rolling admissions plan. Apply no later than first day of class. Early acceptance available. *Requirements:* Either graduation from approved, accredited, or commissioned secondary school or GED. Minimum recommended GPA 2.0. *Entrance tests:* College Board SAT preferred; ACT composite accepted. College proficiency tests in mathematics and English. *For transfer students:* 2.0 minimum GPA; last year must be in residence; from 2-year accredited institution 64 semester hours maximum transfer credit; correspondence/extension students 18 hours. *For foreign students:* TOEFL.

College credit and advanced placement for postsecondary-level work completed in secondary school and for extrainstitutional learning on basis of ACE *2006 Guide to the Evaluation of Educational Experiences in the Armed Services*, portfolio, and faculty assessments. Tutoring available. Developmental courses offered; credit given.

Degree Requirements: *For all associate degrees:* 64 semester hours. *For all baccalaureate degrees:* 128 semester hours; 2.3 GPA in major field except for education majors which require 2.5 GPA in major area; distribution requirements; general education. *For Master of Divinity degree:* baccalaureate degree plus 90 graduate semester hours. Special requirements for teacher education degrees. Accelerated Master of Science in Management (36 semester hours/18 months).

Fulfillment of some degree requirements and exemption from some beginning courses possible by passing College Board CLEP, ETS DANTES, divisional examinations, Advanced Placement Programs, proficiency examinations, work or service experience, military services credit. *Grading system:* A–F; pass/no fail; withdraw (deadline after which fail is appended to withdraw); incomplete (carries time limit).

Distinctive Educational Programs: Work-experience programs. Flexible meeting places and schedules, including off-campus center (at Bedford, 90 miles away from main institution), evening classes. Interdisciplinary course in contemporary and world problems. Facilities and programs for independent research and study. School of Adult Degrees and Professional Studies offers accelerated associates, baccalaureate, and master's degrees. Associate degrees are the accelerated associate degree in business and in criminal justice. The baccalaureate degrees are the Management of Human Resources and the Organizational Management degrees. The master's degree is the Master of Science in Management. All programs are offered in a nontraditional format (evening classes, Saturday classes) at different locations in southern and mid-state Indiana.

Degrees Conferred: 122 *associate*; 271 *baccalaureate*; 171 *master's*; 2 *first-professional*. Bachelor's degrees awarded in top five disciplines: business, management, marketing, and related support services 172; education 49; liberal arts and sciences, general studies and humanities 12; biological and biomedical sciences 10; philosophy and religious studies 9.

Fees and Other Expenses: *Full-time tuition per academic year 2004–05:* $12,000 undergraduate; contact the university for graduate tuition/fees. *Books and supplies:* $1,000. *Room and board per academic year:* $4,800.

Financial Aid: Aid from institutionally generated funds is provided on the basis of academic merit, financial need, athletic ability, other criteria. Institution has a Program Participation Agreement with the U.S. Department of Education for eligible students to receive Pell Grants and other federal aid.

Financial aid to full-time, first-time undergraduate students: 46% received federal grants averaging $2,496; 62% state/local grants averaging $4,751; 86% institutional grants averaging $3,824; 61% loans averaging $2,438.

Departments and Teaching Staff: *Professors* 8, *associate professors* 12, *assistant professors* 14, *instructors* 3, *part-time faculty* 29. *Total instructional faculty:* 37. Student-to-faculty ratio: 17:1. Degrees held by full-time faculty: doctorates 64.8%, master's 16.2%, baccalaureates 8.1%, professional 2.7%. 70.3% hold terminal degrees.

Enrollment: Total enrollment 1,985. Undergraduate 1,616 (47.8% men, 52.2% women).

Characteristics of Student Body: *Ethnic and racial makeup:* Black non-Hispanic: 9.9%; American Indian or Alaska Native: .4%; Asian or Pacific Islander: .4%; Hispanic: 1.4%; White non-Hispanic: 83.8%; unknown: 1.4%. *Age distribution:* 17–21: 21%; 22–24: 18%; 25–29: 10%; 30–34: 12%; 35–39: 12%; 40–49: 10%; 50–59: 105; 60–and over: 7%.

International Students: 39 nonresident aliens enrolled fall 2004. Social and cultural programs and English as a Second Language program available to aid students whose native language is not English. Scholarships available for undergraduate qualifying international students.

Student Life: On-campus residence halls house 28% of student body. Residence halls for men constitute 65% of such space, for women 35%. *Intercollegiate athletics:* (NCAA II, NCCAA) men: baseball, basketball, softball, cross-country, golf. *Special regulations:* Cars permitted without restrictions. Curfews begin midnight Sun.–Thurs., 2am Fri. and Sat. Quiet hours from 11pm to 8am daily. *Special services:* Student support services which offers tutoring, personal counseling, career counseling, and freshman studies. *Student publications: The Mirror*, a yearbook; *The O.C. Collegian*, a student monthly newspaper. *Sur-*

rounding community: Oakland City population 3,000. Evansville, 30 miles from campus, is nearest metropolitan area. Served by Evansville airport; bus transportation 12 miles from campus.

Library Collections: 85,000 volumes. 1000,400 microforms; 2,600 audiovisual materials; 460 current periodical subscriptions. 1,840 recordings; 544 compact discs; 60 CD-ROMs. Access to online information retrieval systems. Students have access to the Internet at no charge.

Special collections include General Association minutes (1891–present) and the minutes of the Liberty Association of General Baptists (1824–present).

Buildings and Grounds: Campus area 20 acres.

Chief Executive Officer: Dr. James W. Murray, President.

Address admission inquiries to Buddy Harris, Director of Admissions

Purdue University

West Lafayette, Indiana 47907

Tel: (765) 494-4600   **E-mail:** admissions@purdue.edu
Fax: (765) 494-0544   **Internet:** www.purdue.edu

Institution Description: Purdue University is a state university and land-grant college. Regional campuses are at Hammond (Calumet Campus), Fort Wayne, and Westville (North Central Campus). Purdue academic programs are also offered at Indiana University-Purdue University at Indianapolis (IUPUI). The Fort Wayne campus is called Indiana University-Purdue University at Fort Wayne. Purdue academic programs are offered through its Statewide Technology program at several locations around the state. *Enrollment:* 38,653. *Degrees awarded:* Associate, baccalaureate, first-professional (pharmacy, veterinary medicine), master's, doctorate.

Accreditation: *Regional:* NCA. *Professional:* applied science, athletic training, audiology, business, chemistry, clinical psychology, construction education, counseling, dietetics, engineering, engineering technology, forestry, industrial technology, interior design, landscape architecture, marriage and family therapy, nursing, nursing education, pharmacy, psychology internship, speech-language pathology, teacher education, theatre, veterinary medicine

History: In 1869, the Indiana General Assembly decided to establish the state's land-grant college near Lafayette. They accepted $150,000 from John Purdue, $50,000 from Tippecanoe County and 100 acres from local residents. The legislators named the new institution Purdue University. Classes began in 1874 with six instructors and 39 students. The first degree was awarded in 1875.

Institutional Structure: *Governing board:* Board of Trustees. Extrainstitutional representation: 10 trustees; institutional representation: 1 student. *Composition of institution:* Administrators 11 men / 1 woman (vice presidents); 5 men (chancellors); 8 men / 2 woman (deans). Academic affairs headed by executive vice president for academic affairs. Management/business/finances directed by executive vice president and treasurer. Full-time instructional faculty 1,911.

Calendar: Semesters. Academic year Aug. to May. Freshmen admitted Aug., Jan., June. Degrees conferred and formal commencement Aug, Dec., May. Summer session.

Characteristics of Freshmen: 80.2% of applicants admitted. 35.2% of applicants admitted and enrolled.

84.8% (5,604 students) submitted SAT scores; 41% (2,709 students) submitted ACT scores. *25th percentile:* SAT Verbal 500, SAT Math 530; ACT Composite 22, ACT English 21, ACT Math 23. *75th percentile:* SAT Verbal 610, SAT Math 650; ACT Composite 28, ACT English 27, ACT Math 29.

60.6% of entering freshmen expected to graduate within 5 years. 50% of freshmen from Indiana. Freshmen from 50 states, 3 territories, and 47 foreign countries.

Admission: Rolling admissions plan. For fall acceptance, apply as early as end of junior year of secondary school, but not later than 30 days prior to registration. Early acceptance available. Two programs have application deadlines of Nov. 15: Flight Technology and Veterinary Technology. *Requirements:* Graduation from accredited secondary school. Specific requirements vary by program. *Entrance tests:* College Board SAT or ACT. For foreign students, TOEFL. *For transfer students:* C-plus minimum grade average; evaluation on individual basis.

College credit for postsecondary-level work completed in secondary school. Tutoring available. Developmental/remedial courses offered.

Degree Requirements: *For all associate degrees:* 2.0 GPA on 4.0 scale. *For all baccalaureate degrees:* 2.0 GPA on 4.0 scale, proficiency in English composition. *For all undergraduate degrees:* 2 semesters in residence; general education requirements. Credit hours vary by program.

Fulfillment of some degree requirements and exemption from some beginning courses possible by passing College Board CLEP, AP. *Grading system:* A–F; pass-not pass; satisfactory/unsatisfactory; withdraw; incomplete.

Distinctive Educational Programs: Cooperative education. Special facilities for using telecommunications in the classroom. Interdisciplinary programs in many areas. The Programs for Study Abroad currently offers 289 programs in various countries: Argentina, Australia, Austria, Belgium, Brazil, Canada, Chile, Costa Rica, Czech Republic, Denmark, Dominican Republic, England, France, Germany, Ghana, Honduras, Hungary, Italy, Japan, Mexico, Netherlands, New Zealand, Norway, Poland, Russia, Scotland, Singapore, Spain, Sweden, Switzerland, Turkey, Ukraine, Vietnam, Wales. *Other distinctive programs:* Continuing education, Extension Service, and agricultural experiment station. Distance learning; Honors Program; teacher certification program; Weekend College.

ROTC: Air Ford, Army., Navy, Marine. 25 Air Force commissions awarded 2004; 14 Army; 15 Navy; 8 Marine.

Degrees Conferred: 6,154 *baccalaureate* (B), 1,583 *master's* (M), 446 *doctorate* (D): agriculture 334 (B), 78 (M), 27 (D); architecture 25 (B); area and ethnic studies 3 (B); biological/life sciences 145 (B), 29 (M), 28 (D); business/marketing 898 (B), 423 (M), 16 (D); communications/communication technologies 270 (B), 22 (M), 12 (D); computer and information sciences 312 (B), 64 (M), 4 (D); education 487 (B), 163 (M), 40 (D); engineering and engineering technologies 1,657 (B), 517 (M), 136 (D); English 146 (B), 19 (M), 6 (D); foreign languages and literature 35 (B), 19 (M), 6 (D); health professions and related sciences 317 (B), 47 (M), 26 (D); home economics and vocational home economics 379 (B), 11 (M), 19 (D); interdisciplinary studies 7 (B); liberal arts/general studies 8 (B); mathematics 86 (B), 46 (M), 12 (D); natural resources/environmental science 73 (B), 9 (M), 4 (D); philosophy/religion/theology 20 (B), 3 (M), 8 (D); physical sciences 83 (B), 29 (M), 55 (D); psychology 210 (B), 9 (M), 11 (D); social sciences and history 375 (B), 51 (M), 19 (D); trade and industry 144 (B); visual and performing arts 140 (B), 34 (M). 216 *first-professional:* pharmacy 152, veterinary medicine 64.

Fees and Other Expenses: *Full-time tuition per academic year 2004–05:* resident $6,092, out-of-state student $18,700. Some programs have higher fees. *Books and supplies:* $940. *Room and board per academic year:* $7,020.

Financial Aid: Aid from institutionally generated funds is provided on the basis of academic merit, financial need. Institution has a Program Participation Agreement with the U.S. Department of Education for eligible students to receive Pell Grants and other federal aid.

Financial aid to full-time, first-time undergraduate students: need-based scholarships/grants totaling $58,722,789, self-help $54,011,646, parent loans $22,093,322, tuition waivers $12,561,962; non-need-based scholarships/grants totaling $8,964,444, self-help $40,622,144, parent loans $108,283,060, athletic awards $5,283,146.

Departments and Teaching Staff: Total faculty for Agriculture 304, Consumer and Family Science 71, Education 102, Engineering 324, Liberal Arts 478, Management 131, Pharmacy/Nursing/Health Sciences 121, Science 356, Technology 169, Veterinary Medicine 91, other 77.

Total instructional faculty: 2,224 (full-time 1,911, part-time 313; women 651, men 1,573; members of minority groups 308). Total faculty with doctorate, first-professional, or other terminal degree: 2,151. Student-to-faculty ratio: 14.7:1.

Enrollment: Total enrollment 38,653. Undergraduate full-time 17,232 men / 11,722 women, part-time 899m / 894w; first-professional full-time 278m / 632w, part-time 2m / 12; graduate full-time 3,095m / 1,786w, part-time 1,277m / 824w. *Transfer students:* in-state 671 (undergraduate), from out-of-state 448.

Characteristics of Student Body: *Ethnic and racial makeup:* number of Black non-Hispanic 1,058; American Indian or Alaska Native: 137; Asian or Pacific Islander: 1,547; Hispanic: 746; White non-Hispanic: 746. *Age distribution:* number under 18: 233; 18–19: 11,500; 20–21: 11,871; 22–24: 5,472; 25–29: 868; 30–35: 391; 36–40: 150; 41–45: 106; 46–50: 84; 51–60: 62; 61–and over: 10.

International Students: 4,921 nonresident aliens enrolled fall 2004. 582 students from Europe, 3,612 Asia, 453 Central and South America, 136 Africa, 102 Canada, 21 Australia, 2 New Zealand, 13 other. Programs available to aid students whose native language is not English: Social, cultural. No financial aid specifically designated for international students.

Student Life: On-campus residence halls accommodate 30% of all students. 5% reside in fraternities or sororities. Cooperative houses are available as are apartments for married students. *Intercollegiate athletics:* men only: baseball, basketball, cross-country, football, golf, swimming, wrestling, track and field, tennis, women only: basketball, cross-country, golf, soccer, softball, swimming, track and field, tennis, volleyball. *Special regulations:* Registered cars permitted. *Special services:* Medical services. Students ride free on all local bus routes. *Student publications: Debris,* a yearbook; *Exponent,* a daily newspaper; many specialized newspapers, magazines, and newsletters. *Surrounding community:* The population of Lafayette and West Lafayette is 75,000. It is served by a scheduled airline, bus lines, and an interstate highway. Lafayette is located 65 miles northwest of Indianapolis.

Publications: There are many publications dedicated and distributed to special interests for various colleges/schools, student organizations, faculty and staff, and alumni for Purdue University. A few examples are Wellness, Benefits, |Student Organizations, Business Services, IFC/Panhellenic Alumni, Physical Plant.

Library Collections: 2,459,943 volumes. Online catalog. Current serial subscriptions: 16,651 paper; 4,178 via electronic access. 945 recordings; 5,915 CD-ROMs. 194 computer work stations. Access to online information retrieval systems.

Most important special holdings: Krannert Collection on the History of Economics and Economic Thought; Goss Library of Engineering History; Gilbreth Library of Industrial Management.

Buildings and Grounds: Campus area 1,565 acres. *New buildings:* Aquatics Center completed 2000; Bindley Bioscience Center 2003; Birck Nanotechnology Center 2003; Computer Science Building 2004; Martell Forest Research and Education Center 2002; Distance Learning Facility 2001; Dick and Sandy Dauch Alumni Center 2002.

Chief Executive Officer: Dr. Martin C. Jischke, President.

Address admission inquiries to Dr. Douglas L. Christiansen, Director of Admissions.

Graduate School

Degree Programs Offered: *Master's, educational specialist, doctorate* in departments of aeronautics and astronautics, agricultural economics, agricultural engineering, agronomy, American studies, animal sciences, audiology and speech sciences, biochemistry, biological sciences, botany and plant pathology, chemical engineering, chemistry, child development and family studies, civil engineering, communication, comparative literature, computer sciences, consumer sciences and retailing, earth and atmospheric sciences, economics; education: curriculum and instruction, educational studies; electrical engineering, English, entomology, food science, foods and nutrition, foreign languages and literatures, forestry and natural resources, health, kinesiology and leisure studies, health sciences, history, horticulture, industrial engineering, industrial and physical pharmacy, industrial technology, management, materials engineering, mathematics, mechanical engineering, medicinal chemistry and pharmacognosy, nuclear engineering, organizational behavior and human resource management, pharmacology and toxicology, pharmacy practice, philosophy, physics, plant physiology, political science, psychological sciences, restaurant/hotel/institutional management, sociology and anthropology, statistics, veterinary anatomy, veterinary clinical sciences, veterinary pathobiology, veterinary physiology and pharmacology, visual and performing arts.

Admission: For degree-seeking graduates, students must: (1) hold a baccalaureate degree from a college or university of recognized standing; (2) submit two complete official transcripts of all previous college and university studies; (3) demonstrate a minimum grade point index of 5.0 (B) or equivalent. Individual departments may set higher grade point requirements and may require the submission of additional evidence of academic performance. Foreign students are required to have a minimum score of 550 on TOEFL.

Degree Requirements: Students must earn grades of A, B, or C which are acceptable in fulfilling Graduate School requirements in any plan of study; demonstrate acceptable proficiency in English composition; some departments require a reading knowledge of French, German, Russian, or Spanish for conferring the master's degree; for the doctorate, individual departments determine a foreign language requirement; at least one-half of the total credit hours used to satisfy degree requirements must be earned in residence on the Purdue campus.

Departments and Teaching Staff: *See* Departments and Teaching Staff above.

School of Pharmacy

Degree Programs Offered: *First-professional.*

Admission: To the straight-through program students must have: (1) completed one year of prepharmacy and at least two years of the B.S. in Pharmacy curriculum; (2) a record of high-level academic performance during the first three years of college, with no grade lower than C in all core pharmacy courses; (3) demonstrated motivation and interest in a career in the health-care professions; and (4) possess good oral and written communication skills and the ability to work well with people.

Degree Requirements: For professional, 74 credit hours; entire program in residence; 30 hours clerkship.

School of Veterinary Medicine

Degree Programs Offered: *Associate* in applied science, *first-professional.*

Admission: *For first-professional:* Complete a two- to three-year preprofessional or preveterinary curriculum at accredited college or university.

Degree Requirements: *For first-professional:* 159 credits, entire program in residence. Internship.

Distinctive Educational Programs: School manages 360-acre veterinary research farm.

School of Agriculture

Degree Programs Offered: *Associate* in agriculture; *baccalaureate* in forestry, landscape architecture, agricultural engineering.

School of Consumer and Family Sciences

Degree Programs Offered: *Associate* in applied science; *baccalaureate.*

School of Education

Degree Programs Offered: *Baccalaureate.*

Schools of Engineering

Degree Programs Offered: *Baccalaureate* in aeronautical and astronautical engineering, chemical engineering, civil engineering, computer and electrical engineering, construction engineering, electrical engineering, engineering, industrial engineering, interdisciplinary engineering, land surveying, materials engineering, mechanical engineering, nuclear engineering.

School of Health Sciences

Degree Programs Offered: *Baccalaureate* in environmental health.

School of Liberal Arts

Degree Programs Offered: *Baccalaureate.*

School of Management

Degree Programs Offered: *Baccalaureate* in industrial management.

School of Nursing

Degree Programs Offered: *Baccalaureate.*

Admission: Preferential application deadline Apr. 10. Achievement tests may be required for nonaccredited high schools of home-schooled students.

School of Science

Degree Programs Offered: *Associate* in science; *baccalaureate.*

School of Technology

Degree Programs Offered: *Associate* in applied science; *baccalaureate.*

Purdue University Calumet

2200 169th Street
Hammond, Indiana 46323-2094
Tel: (219) 989-2993   **E-mail:** admis@calumet.purdue
Fax: (219) 989-2581   **Internet:** www.calumet.Purdue

Institution Description: *Enrollment:* 9,222. *Degrees awarded:* Associate, baccalaureate, master's.

Academic offerings subject to approval by statewide coordinating bodies.

Accreditation: *Regional:* NCA. *Professional:* engineering, marriage and family therapy, nursing, teacher education

History: Established as Purdue University Center, Hammond, and offered first instruction at postsecondary level 1946; changed name to Purdue University, Calumet Center 1959, to Purdue University-Calumet Campus 1962; awarded first degree (baccalaureate) 1967; adopted present name 1978.

Institutional Structure: *Composition of institution:* Administrators 34 men / 28 women. Academic affairs headed by vice chancellor for academic affairs. Management/business/finances directed by directed by vice chancellor. Full-time instructional faculty 141 men / 92 women. Academic governance body, Council of Faculty Delegates, meets an average of 9 times per year.

Calendar: Semesters. Academic year mid-Aug. to mid-May. Freshmen admitted Aug., Jan., June. Degrees conferred May, Aug., Dec. Formal commencement May. Summer session of 3 terms from early June to early Aug.

Characteristics of Freshmen: 2,178 applicants (2,178 men, 991 women). 81.5% of applicants admitted. 41.5% of admitted students enrolled full-time.

65% (794 students) submitted SAT scores; 15% (187 students) submitted ACT scores. *25th percentile*: SAT I Verbal 390, SAT I Math 390; ACT English 15, ACT Math 16. *75th percentile*: SAT I Verbal 510, SAT I Math 510; ACT English 22, ACT Math 22.

30% of entering freshmen expected to graduate within 5 years. 92% of freshmen from Indiana.

Admission: Rolling admissions plan. For fall acceptance, apply as early as end of junior year of secondary school, but not later than May 1 of year of enrollment. Early acceptance available. *Requirements:* Either graduation from accredited secondary school with 15 units, or GED. Recommend 3–4 in English, 1–3 mathematics, 1–2 laboratory science, 1 history or science, 2 foreign language for some humanities programs. Lowest acceptable secondary school class standing upper half to upper third. *Entrance tests:* College Board SAT. Out-of-state students may substitute ACT composite. *For transfer students:* Minimum grade average C; maximum transfer credit limited only by residence requirement.

College credit and advanced placement for postsecondary-level work completed in secondary school. College credit for extrainstitutional learning (life experience) on basis of ACE *Military Guide,* faculty assessment. Tutoring available. Remedial courses offered in summer session and regular academic year; credit given.

Degree Requirements: *For all associate degrees:* 63–76 semester hours. *For all baccalaureate degrees:* 120–130 semester hours. *For all undergraduate degrees:* 4.0 on 2.0–6.0 scale; 32 hours in residence; general education requirements; exit competency examinations in writing.

Fulfillment of some degree requirements and exemption from some beginning courses possible by passing departmental examinations, College Board CLEP, AP. *Grading system:* A–F; pass-fail; withdraw; incomplete.

Distinctive Educational Programs: Cooperative education. Flexible meeting places and schedules, including weekend and evening classes. Special facilities for using telecommunications in the classroom. Interdisciplinary programs in communication and creative arts, chemistry-physics. Preprofessional programs in dentistry, medicine, pharmacy. Associate degree programs in dietetic technology and business. Study abroad. *Other distinctive programs:* 'Open access' policy for students to utilize extensive computing capabilities (mainframes, microcomputers, and PCs). Continuing education.

Degrees Conferred: 329 *associate*; 765 *baccalaureate*; 186 *master's.* Bachelor's degrees awarded in top five disciplines: business, management, marketing, and related support services 227; engineering technologies/technicians 68; communication, journalism, and related programs 64; social sciences 63; computer and information sciences and support services 63.

Fees and Other Expenses: *Full-time tuition per academic year 2004–05:* undergraduate resident $4,838, out-of-state student $10,396. *Books and supplies:* $950. *Room and board per academic year:* $6,716.

Financial Aid: Aid from institutionally generated funds is provided on the basis of academic merit, financial need, athletic ability. Institution has a Program Participation Agreement with the U.S. Department of Education for eligible students to receive Pell Grants and other federal aid.

Financial aid to full-time, first-time undergraduate students: 23% received federal grants averaging $2,387; 23% state/local grants averaging $2,184; 3% institutional grants averaging $1,991; 31% loans averaging $2,440.

Departments and Teaching Staff: School of Liberal Arts and Sciences: behavioral sciences *professors* 3, *associate professors* 7, *assistant professors* 9, *instructors* 0; biology 5, 4, 0, 0; chemistry/physics 3, 6, 5, 0; communication/creative arts 0, 7, 5, 0; English/philosophy 6, 7, 8, 0; foreign languages and literature 1, 4, 1, 0; history/political science 3, 4, 0, 0; mathematics 9, 5, 5, 0; School of Professional Studies: construction technologies 1, 4, 2, 0; education 4, 5, 4, 0; electrical engineering technology 2, 4, 5, 0; engineering 3, 8, 4, 0; information systems and computer programing 2, 4, 6, 0; manufacturing engineering technology 1, 6, 2, 0; management 2, 6, 6, 3; Nursing: 4, 12, 15, 0.

Total instructional faculty: 233 plus part-time teachers with FTE of 70.22. Total tenured faculty: 78%.

Enrollment: Total enrollment 9,222. Undergraduate 8,283 (43.5% men, 56.5% women).

Characteristics of Student Body: *Ethnic/racial makeup:* Black non-Hispanic: 15.1%, American Indian or Alaska Native: .3%; Asian or Pacific Islander: 1.4%; Hispanic: 14.9%; White non-Hispanic: 67.4%. *Age distribution:* 17–21: 34.7%; 22–24: 26.2%; 25–29: 9.1%; 30–34: 22.2%; 35–39: 3%; 40–49: 3.2%; 50–59: 1.4%; 60*+*and over: 2%.

International Students: 66 undergraduate nonresident aliens enrolled fall 2004. No programs available to aid students whose native language is not English. No financial aid specifically designated for international students.

Student Life: No on-campus housing. *Intercollegiate athletics:* men only: basketball, soccer; women only: basketball, volleyball. *Special regulations:* Registered cars with permits allowed. *Special services:* Fitness Center, medical services. *Student publications: Skylark,* an annual literary magazine; *The Purdue Chronicle,* a biweekly newspaper. *Surrounding community:* Hammond population 95,000. Chicago (IL), 25 miles from campus, is nearest metropolitan area. Served by airport 10 miles from campus; passenger rail service 3 miles from campus.

Library Collections: 216,000 volumes. 40,000 microforms; 1,650 periodicals. Students have access to online information retrieval services.

Most important special holdings include Black History and Literature; Northwest Indiana materials; Purdue University Calumet materials.

Buildings and Grounds: Campus area 165 acres.

Chief Executive Officer: Dr. Howard Cohen, Chancellor.

Address admission inquiries to Director of Admissions.

Purdue University North Central

1401 South U.S. 421
Westville, Indiana 46391-9528

Tel: (219) 785-5200   **E-mail:** admissions@purduenc.edu
Fax: (219) 785-5538   **Internet:** www.purduenc.edu

Institution Description: Purdue University North Central is a regional campus. *Enrollment:* 3,442. *Degrees awarded:* Associate, baccalaureate, master's.

Accreditation: *Regional:* NCA. *Professional:* business, engineering technology, nursing

Calendar: Semesters. Academic year Aug. to May.

Characteristics of Freshmen: 86% of applicants admitted. 71% of applicants admitted and enrolled.

60% (389 students) submitted SAT scores; 17% (110 students) submitted ACT scores. *25th percentile*: SAT Verbal 430, SAT Math 430; ACT Composite 17, ACT English 17, ACT Math 17. *75th percentile*: SAT Verbal 530, SAT Math 530; ACT Composite 22, ACT English 22, ACT Math 22.

24% of freshmen are expected to graduate within 5 years. 99% of freshmen from Indiana. Freshmen from 4 states and 1 foreign country.

Admission: *Requirements:* See Purdue University, West Lafayette.

Degree Requirements: Completion of prescribed curriculum.

Degrees Conferred: 224 *associate;* 254 *baccalaureate*: biological/life sciences 10; business/marketing 47; computer and information sciences 10; education 45; engineering and engineering technologies 11; English 8; liberal arts/general studies 77; social sciences and history 10, trade and industry 32, other 4.

Fees and Other Expenses: *Full-time tuition per academic year 2004–05:* resident undergraduate $4,900, out-of-state student $11,500; graduate resident $4,850, out-of-state student $10,600.

Financial Aid: Aid from institutionally generated funds is provided on the basis of academic merit, financial need, other criteria. Institution has a Program Participation Agreement with the U.S. Department of Education for eligible students to receive Pell Grants and other federal aid.

Departments and Teaching Staff: *Total instructional faculty:* 239 (full-time 104, part-time 135; women 103, men 136; members of minority groups 23). Total faculty with doctorate, first-professional, or other terminal degree: 123.

Enrollment: Total enrollment 3,442. Undergraduate full-time 942 men / 1,105 women, part-time 501m / 872w; graduate part-time 3m / 19w.

Characteristics of Student Body: *Ethnic/racial makeup:* number of Black non-Hispanic: 125; American Indian or Alaska Native: 31; Asian or Pacific Islander: 35; Hispanic: 138; White non-Hispanic: 2,988; unknown: 103. *Age distribution:* number under 18: 40; 18–19: 836; 20–21: 614; 22–24: 569; 25–29: 449; 30–34: 331; 35–39: 189; 40–49: 311; 50–64: 97; 65 and over: 5.

International Students: 11 nonresidents aliens enrolled 2003. 1 student from Europe, 6 Asia, 1 Central and South America, 1 Africa, 1 Australia, 1 Canada. No programs available to aid students whose native language is not English. No financial aid specifically designated for international students.

Library Collections: 90,000 volumes. Online and card catalogs. Current serial subscriptions: 397 paper, 1 microform, 1,2424 via electronic access. 23 computer work stations. Students have access to online information retrieval services and the Internet.

Buildings and Grounds: Campus area 265 acres.

Chief Executive Officer: Dr. James Dworkin, Chancellor.

Address admission inquiries to Cathy Buckman, Director of Admissions.

Rose-Hulman Institute of Technology

5500 Wabash Avenue
Terre Haute, Indiana 47803
Tel: (812) 877-1511   **E-mail:** admis.ofc@rose-hulman.edu
Fax: (812) 877-9925   **Internet:** www.rose-hulman.edu

Institution Description: Rose-Hulman Institute of Technology (Rose Polytechnic Institute until 1971) is a private, independent, nonprofit institution. *Enrollment:* 1,904. *Degrees awarded:* Baccalaureate, master's. Certificates in Technical Translation also awarded.

Accreditation: *Regional:* NCA. *Professional*: engineering

History: Established and incorporated as Rose Polytechnic Institute 1874; offered first instruction at postsecondary level 1883; awarded first degree (baccalaureate) 1885; adopted present name 1971. *See* John L. Bloxsome, *Rose: The First Hundred Years* (Terre Haute: Rose-Hulman, 1973) for further information.

Institutional Structure: *Governing board:* Board of Trustees. Extrainstitutional representation: 36 directors; institutional representation: 1 administrator; 2 alumni. All voting. *Composition of institution:* Administrators 24 men / 6 women. Academic affairs headed by vice president for academic affairs. Management/business/finances directed by vice president for administration and finance. Full-time instructional faculty 119. Academic governance body, the faculty, meets an average of 9 times per year.

Calendar: Quarters. Academic year Sept. to May. Freshmen admitted Sept. Degrees conferred May and Mar. Formal commencement May. No summer session.

Characteristics of Freshmen: 3,088 applicants (2,401 men, 687 women). 69.6% of applicants admitted. 22% of admitted students enrolled full-time.

85% (404 students) submitted SAT scores; 56% (267 students) submitted ACT scores. *25th percentile:* SAT I Verbal 570, SAT I Math 630; ACT Composite 27, ACT English 25, ACT Math 28. *75th percentile*: SAT I Verbal 680, SAT I Math 720; ACT Composite 32, ACT English 31, ACT Math 34.

69% of entering freshmen expected to graduate within 5 years. 48% of freshmen from Indiana. Freshmen from 45 states and 12 foreign countries.

Admission: Rolling admissions plan. For fall acceptance, apply as early as Aug. 1 of previous year, but not later than Feb. 1 of year of enrollment. Students are notified of acceptance Oct. 1 to Mar. 1. *Requirements:* 4 years in English, 4 mathematics, 2 social studies, 1 chemistry, 1 physics. Recommend 4 years academic electives from among biology, foreign language, history, mathematics, mechanical drawing, speech; personal interview. *Entrance tests:* College Board SAT or ACT composite. *For transfer students:* Transfer credit limited only by residence requirement.

College credit and advanced placement for postsecondary-level work completed in secondary school. Tutoring available.

Degree Requirements: *For all undergraduate degrees:* 195–197 credit hours; senior year in residence; 1 year military training.

Fulfillment of some degree requirements and exemption from some beginning courses possible by passing College Board AP. *Grading system:* A–F.

Distinctive Educational Programs: Center for Technology Assessment and Policy Studies. Institutionally arranged study abroad in England, Germany. *Other distinctive programs:* Technical Translation Program at University of Stuttgart.

ROTC: Air Force and Army.

Degrees Conferred: 346 *baccalaureate*; 43 *master's*. Bachelors' degrees awarded in top five disciplines: engineering 269; computer and information sciences and support services 55; physical sciences 17; biological and biomedical sciences 3; mathematics and statistics 2.

Fees and Other Expenses: *Full-time tuition per academic year 2004–05:* $26,136. *Room and board per academic year:* $7,065. *Books and supplies:* $1,200.

Financial Aid: The institute offers students a direct lending program. Aid from institutionally generated funds is provided on the basis of academic merit and financial need. Institution has a Program Participation Agreement with the U.S. Department of Education for eligible students to receive Pell Grants and other federal aid.

Financial aid to full-time, first-time undergraduate students: 17% received federal grants averaging $3,264; 19% state/local grants averaging $4,617; 84% institutional grants averaging $6,571; 71% loans averaging $5,293.

Departments and Teaching Staff: Chemical engineering *professors* 4, *associate professors* 2, *assistant professors* 2, *part-time teachers* 2; chemistry 3, 5, 2, 0; civil engineering 3, 2, 1, 0; computer science 4, 1, 3, 0; electrical engineering 7, 6, 4 0; humanities 7, 6, 5, 11; mathematics 7, 7, 3, 0; mechanical engineering 9, 5, 3, 1; management engineering 0, 0, 1, 0; physics 6, 2, 6, 0; biomedical engineering 0, 1, 4, 0.

Total instructional faculty: 133. Total tenured faculty: 118. Student-to-faculty ratio: 14:1. Degrees held by full-time faculty: doctorates 99%, master's 1%. 98% hold terminal degrees.

Enrollment: Total enrollment 1,904. Undergraduate 1,765 (80.6% men, 19.4% women).

Characteristics of Student Body: *Ethnic/racial makeup:* Black non-Hispanic: 2.5%; American Indian or Alaska Native: .1%; Asian or Pacific Islander: 3.5%; Hispanic: 1.6%; White non-Hispanic: 91%; unknown: .1%. *Age distribution:* 17–21: 90%; 22–24: 9%; 25–29: 8%; 30–34: 2%.

International Students: 19 undergraduate nonresident aliens enrolled fall 2004. Students from Europe, Asia, Africa. No programs available to aid students whose native language is not English. No financial aid specifically designated for international students.

Student Life: On-campus residence halls. *Intercollegiate athletics:* Baseball, basketball, cross-country, football, golf, rifle, soccer, tennis, track and field, wrestling. *Special regulations:* Cars permitted without restrictions. *Special services:* Medical services. *Student publications: The Modulus*, a yearbook; *The Thorn*, a weekly newspaper. *Surrounding community:* Terre Haute metropolitan area population 180,000.

Library Collections: 73,000 volumes. 795 current periodical subscriptions. 535 microform units.650 audiovisual materials. Computer work stations available.

Most important special collections include the Rose-Hulman History Archives and the engineering collection.

Buildings and Grounds: Campus area 200 acres.

Chief Executive Officer: Dr. John J. Midgley, President.

Address admission inquiries to Charles G. Howard, Vice President for Admissions

Saint Joseph's College

U.S. Highway 231
Rensselaer, Indiana 47978
Tel: (800) 447-8781   **E-mail:** admissions@saintjoe.edu
Fax: (219) 866-6122   **Internet:** www.saintjoe.edu

Institution Description: Saint Joseph's College is a private, independent, nonprofit college sponsored by the Missionaries of the Precious Blood, Roman Catholic Church. *Enrollment:* 1,010. *Degrees awarded:* Associate, baccalaureate, master's. Member of the Indiana Consortium for International Programs.

Accreditation: *Regional:* NCA. *Professional*: teacher education

History: Established as secondary school and junior college and incorporated 1889; offered first instruction at postsecondary level 1891; awarded first degree (associate) 1896; became minor seminary 1925; reestablished as accredited junior college 1931; became 4-year college 1936; became coeducational 1968.

Institutional Structure: *Governing board:* Board of Trustees, Saint Joseph's College. Extrainstitutional representation: 41 trustees, including 10 religious, president of alumni association; president of parents' association; institutional representation: president of the college, 1 full-time instructional faculty member, 1 student. 4 ex officio. All voting. *Composition of institution:* Administrators 9 men / 12 women (at dean's level and above, 22% are women). Academic affairs headed by provosts/vice president for academic affairs. Management/business/finances directed by vice president for business affairs. Full-time faculty 57. Academic governance body, Faculty Assembly, meets an average of 8 times per year.

Calendar: Semesters. Academic year Aug. to May. Freshmen admitted Aug., Jan., May. Degrees conferred and formal commencements May, July.

Characteristics of Freshmen: 79% of applicants admitted. 25% of applicants admitted and enrolled.

57% (117 students) submitted SAT scores; 43% (89 students) submitted ACT scores. *25th percentile:* SAT Verbal 430, SAT Math 430; ACT Composite 19, ACT English 18, ACT Math 17. *75th percentile*: SAT Verbal 540, SAT Math 550; ACT Composite 24, ACT English 24, ACT Math 24.

50% od entering freshmen expected to graduate within 5 years. 64% of freshmen from Indiana. Freshmen from 11 states and 2 foreign countries.

Admission: Rolling admissions plan. For fall acceptance, apply as early as Sept. 1 of previous year, but not later than Aug. 1 of year of enrollment. Early acceptance available. *Requirements:* Either graduation from accredited secondary school with 15 units, including 10 from among English, foreign languages, mathematics, natural sciences, social studies; or GED. Minimum GPA 2.0. *Entrance tests:* College Board SAT or ACT composite. *For transfer students:* 2.0 minimum GPA; from 4-year accredited institution 90 semester hours maximum transfer credit; from 2-year accredited institution 60 hours; correspondence/extension students 12 hours.

College credit and advanced placement for postsecondary-level work completed in secondary school and for extrainstitutional learning on basis of ACE *2006 Guide to the Evaluation of Educational Experiences in the Armed Services.* Tutoring available. One-credit study skills course offered during regular academic year.

Degree Requirements: *For all associate degrees:* 60 credit hours. *For all baccalaureate degrees:* 120 credit hours. *For all undergraduate degrees:* 2.0 GPA; last 30 hours in residence; core curriculum.

Fulfillment of some degree requirements and exemption from some beginning courses possible by passing departmental examinations, College Board CLEP. *Grading system:* A–F plus/minus (no A+ or D–); pass-no pass; withdraw (non-punative with time limit); incomplete (with time limit); audit.

Distinctive Educational Programs: *For undergraduates:* Work-experience programs, including internships. Cooperative baccalaureate in medical technology with affiliated hospitals. Interdisciplinary programs in athletic training, biology-chemistry, criminal justice, environmental science, humanities, international studies, music-business administration. Preprofessional programs in dentistry, law, medicine, physical therapy. Independent study program. Unique and innovative Liberal Arts curriculum called "Core." Study abroad by individual arrangement; 6 locations in Europe, 1 in Latin America. *Available to all students:* Special facilities for using telecommunications in the classroom.

Degrees Conferred: 6 *associate;* 176 *baccalaureate:* biological/life sciences 7; business/marketing 38; communications/communication technologies 16; computer and information sciences 9; education 32; English 10; health professions and related sciences 6; mathematics 8; natural resources/environmental science 4; philosophy/religion/theology 2; physical sciences 2; protective services/public administration 3; psychology 12; social sciences and history 13; visual and performing arts 4. 5 *master's:* philosophy/religion/theology 5.

Fees and Other Expenses: *Full-time tuition per academic year 2005–06:* $19,960. *Required fees:* $160. *Room per academic year:* $2,960. *Board per academic year:* $3,520.

Financial Aid: Aid from institutionally generated funds is provided on the basis of academic merit, athletic ability, other criteria.Institution has a Program Participation Agreement with the U.S. Department of Education for eligible students to receive Pell Grants and other federal aid.

Financial aid to full-time, first-time undergraduate students: need-based scholarships/grants totaling $5,696,532, self-help $2,173,918, parent loans $492,820, tuition waivers $176,139, athletic awards $1,194,942; non-need-based scholarships/grants totaling $958,644, self-help $1,575,006, parent loans $1,149,913, tuition waivers $75,488, athletic awards $797,761. *Graduate aid:* 6 federal and state-funded loans totaling $21,411 (ranging from $2,160 to $4,135); 2 fellowship totaling $1,500 ($500 and $1,000).

Departments and Teaching Staff: Commerce *professors* 0, *associate professors* 4, *assistant professors* 3, *part-time faculty* 4; humanities 2, 7, 8, 15; mathematics/science 1, 2, 3, 3; natural science 3, 4, 3, 6; social science 3, 4, 10, 7.

Total instructional faculty: 92 (full-time 57, part-time 25; women 39, men 53; members of minority groups 4). Total faculty with doctorate, first-professional, or other terminal degree: 47. Student-to-faculty ratio: 14:1.

Enrollment: Total enrollment 1,010. Undergraduate full-time 361m / 438w; part-time 26m / 85w. *Transfer students:* in-state 19; from out-of-state 11.

Characteristics of Student Body: *Ethnic and racial makeup:* number of Black non-Hispanic: 46; American Indian or Alaska Native 2; Asian or Pacific Islander: 4; Hispanic: 41; White non-Hispanic: 893; unknown: 14. *Age distribution:* under 18: 96; 18–19: 432; 20–21: 276; 22–24: 66; 25–29: 42; 30–34: 37; 35–39: 32; 40–49: 21; 50–64: 8.

International Students: 10 nonresident aliens enrolled fall 2004. 3 students from Europe, 2 Asia, 5 Canada. No programs available to aid students whose native language is not English. No financial aid specifically designated for international students.

Student Life: On-campus residence halls house 66% of student body. Single gender, coed, and apartment housing available. All residence halls are computer ready. *Intercollegiate athletics:* men only: baseball, basketball, cross-country, football, golf, soccer, tennis, track; women only: basketball, cross-country, golf, soccer, softball, tennis, track, volleyball. *Special regulations:* Registered cars permitted without restrictions. Quiet hours and visitation hours established in each residence hall. *Special services:* Freshman Seminar Course, Learning Resources Center, medical services, Freshman Academic Support Program. *Student publications, radio: Measure,* a semester literary magazine; *Observer,* a bimonthly newspaper. Radio station WPUM broadcasts 125 hours per week. WPUM-TV broadcasts 24 hours each day over a closed circuit cable TV system which is provided in each residence hall. *Student activities:* Student government sponsors 36 clubs and organizations. *Surrounding community:* Rensselaer population 5,500. Chicago (IL), 83 miles from campus, is nearest metropolitan area. Served by airport 40 miles from campus; passenger rail service 2 miles from campus.

Library Collections: 157,021 volumes. Online and card catalogs. Current serial subscriptions; 109 paper, 69,136 microform. 22,885 recordings. 290 CD-ROMs. Students have access to the Internet at no charge. Total 2004–05 budget for books and materials: $112,256.

Most important holdings include collections regarding the Roman Catholic Church, American history, music.

Buildings and Grounds: Campus area 130 acres.

Chief Executive Officer: Dr. Ernest R. Mills, III, J.D., President.

Address admission inquiries to Admissions Office.

Saint Mary-of-the-Woods College

Saint Mary's Road
Saint Mary-of-the-Woods, Indiana 47876
Tel: (812) 535-5151   **E-mail:** admission@smwc.edu
Fax: (812) 535-5010   **Internet:** www.smwc.edu

Institution Description: Saint Mary-of-the-Woods College is a private women's college affiliated with the Roman Catholic Church. Men are accepted as graduate students only. *Enrollment:* 1,705. *Degrees awarded:* Associate, baccalaureate, master's.

Member of College Consortium of Western Indiana.

Accreditation: *Regional:* NCA. *Professional:* music, teacher education

History: Established as Saint Mary's Female Institute 1841; offered first instruction at postsecondary level 1845; chartered 1846; offered first first degree (baccalaureate) 1899; adopted present name 1909.

Institutional Structure: *Governing board:* Board of Trustees. Extrainstitutional representation: 20 trustees; institutional representation: 1 administrator; 5 alumnae. 3 ex officio. 25 voting. *Composition of institution:* Administrators 3 men / 31 women. Academic affairs headed by vice president for academic affairs. Management/business/finances directed by chief business officer. Full-time instructional faculty 12 men / 46 women. Academic governance body, Faculty Assembly, meets an average of 14 times per year.

Calendar: Semesters. Academic year Aug. to May. Freshmen and transfers admitted Aug., Jan; nontraditional students in the external degree program can begin semesters in Aug., Oct., Dec., Jan., Mar., Apr., and June. Formal commencement May. No summer session.

Characteristics of Freshmen: 54% of applicants accepted. 42% of accepted applicants enrolled.

Average secondary school rank of freshmen: 72nd percentile. Mean SAT scores 498 verbal, 464 mathematical. Mean ACT class score 23.5.

57% of entering freshmen expected to graduate in 5 years. 75% of freshmen from Indiana. Freshmen from 10 states and 2 foreign countries.

Admission: Rolling admissions plan. For fall acceptance, apply as early as junior year of secondary school, but not later than Aug. 15 of year of enrollment. Early acceptance available. *Requirements:* 16 secondary school units which should include 3 English, 2 foreign language, 2 mathematics, 1 history, 1 science, and 5 additional units from these areas. GED accepted. 2 additional units recommended. *Entrance tests:* College Board SAT, or ACT composite. For foreign students TOEFL. *For transfer students:* 2.0 minimum GPA; 90 hours maximum transfer credit.

College credit and advanced placement for postsecondary-level work completed in secondary school and for extrainstitutional learning on basis of ACE *2006 Guide to the Evaluation of Educational Experiences in the Armed Services;* portfolio and faculty assessments. Tutoring available.

Degree Requirements: *For all associate degrees:* 61 credits hours; 1 semester physical education. *For all baccalaureate degrees:* 125 credit hours; 2 semesters physical education. *For all degrees:* 2.0 GPA; 2 semesters in residence for traditional students; distribution requirements.

Fulfillment of some degree requirements and exemption from some beginning courses possible by passing College Board CLEP, Achievement Tests, or AP. *Grading system:* A–F; pass-fail option for elective courses; withdraw (deadline after which pass-fail is appended to withdraw).

Distinctive Educational Programs: Internships in major field; credit and noncredit supplemental learning experience programs. Women's External Degree (WED) contract learning program for persons unable to complete baccalaureate through regular college programs. Interdisciplinary programs in fine arts and humanities. Facilities and programs for independent research, including individual majors and tutorials. Study abroad through programs offered by other institutions or by individual arrangement. Cross-registration with other consortium members.

Degrees Conferred: 4 *associate;* 151 *baccalaureate:* biological and life sciences 3; business 26; communications/communication technologies 5; computer and information science 3; education 45; English 7; home economics 1; interdisciplinary studies 30; liberal arts/general studies 8; mathematics 3; philosophy/religion 3; psychology 15, visual and performing arts 3. 14 *master's:* health professions and related sciences 2; interdisciplinary studies 2; theology 10.

Fees and Other Expenses: *Full-time tuition per academic year 2004–05:* $17,360 undergraduate, $379 per credit hour graduate. *Required fees:* $500. *Room and board per academic year:* $6,560.

Financial Aid: Aid from institutionally generated funds is provided on the basis of academic merit, financial need, athletic ability, other criteria. Institution has a Program Participation Agreement with the U.S. Department of Education for eligible students to receive Pell Grants and other federal aid.

Departments and Teaching Staff: *Total instructional faculty:* 61 (full-time 61; women 39, men 22; members of minority groups 1). Total tenured faculty: 34. Student-to-faculty ratio: 12:1. Degrees held by full-time faculty: Doctorate 54%, master's 24%, baccalaureate 2%, professional 17%. 65% of faculty hold terminal degrees.

Enrollment: Total enrollment 1,705. Undergraduate full-time 354 women, part-time 25m / 1,207w; graduate part-time 16m / 110w.

Characteristics of Student Body: *Ethnic/racial makeup:* number of Black non-Hispanic: 54; American Indian Alaska Native: 11; Asian or Pacific Islander: 4; Hispanic: 22; White non-Hispanic: 1,245.

International Students: 5 nonresident aliens enrolled fall 2004. Programs available to aid students whose native language is not English: Social, cultural. No financial aid specifically designated for international students.

Student Life: On-campus residence halls house 89% of student body. *Intercollegiate athletics:* Basketball, softball, tennis, volleyball, cross-country. *Special regulations:* Cars with stickers permitted. *Special services:* Learning Resources Center, medical services. *Student publications: Aurora,* a biannual literary magazine; *The Woods,* a biweekly news magazine. *Surrounding community:* Terre Haute population 62,000. Indianapolis, 70 miles from campus, is nearest metropolitan area. Served by airport 12 miles from campus.

Library Collections: 155,000 volumes. 447 current periodical subscriptions. Computer work stations available. Students have access to the Internet at no charge.

Most important special holdings include Gladys McKenney Molony Collection of fore-edge paintings; Samuel Taylor Coleridge Collection (works and criticism); original library of the Sisters of Providence dating from 1840.

Buildings and Grounds: Campus area 67 acres.

Chief Executive Officer: Dr. Joan Jescinski, C.S.J., President.

Address admission inquiries to James Malley, Admission Director.

Saint Mary's College

Notre Dame, Indiana 46556

Tel: (574) 284-4000   **E-mail:** admissions@saintmarys.edu
Fax: (574) 284-4716   **Internet:** www.saintmarys.edu

Institution Description: Saint Mary's College is a private women's college affiliated with the Congregation of the Sisters of the Holy Cross, Roman Catholic Church. Men are admitted as special students. *Enrollment:* 1,418. *Degrees awarded:* Baccalaureate.

Member of Northern Indiana Consortium for Education.

Accreditation: *Regional:* NCA. *Professional:* art, music, social work, teacher education

History: Established in Bertrand (MI) as Saint Mary's Academy 1844; chartered by state of Michigan 1851; moved to present location and chartered by state of Indiana 1855; offered first instruction at postsecondary level 1870; awarded first degree (baccalaureate) 1892; adopted present name 1903. *See* Sister Mary Immaculate Greek, *A Panorama: 1844–1977 Saint Mary's College* (Notre Dame, IN: Saint Mary's College, 1977) for further information.

Institutional Structure: *Governing board:* The Corporation of Saint Mary's College, Notre Dame. Extrainstitutional representation: 26 trustees, 8 or more of whom are Sisters of the Holy Cross or members of other Roman Catholic Religious congregations; institutional representation: 1 administrator, 1 full-time instructional faculty member, 1 student; 1 alumna; all voting. *Composition of institution:* Administrators 18 men / 64 women. Academic affairs headed by vice president and dean of faculty. Management/business/finances directed by vice president for fiscal affairs. Mission affairs guided by vice president for missions. Development activities directed by vice president for college relations. Student life activities directed by vice president for student affairs. Full-time instructional faculty 136. Academic governance body, Faculty Assembly, meets an average of 8 times per year.

Calendar: Semesters. Academic year Aug. to May. Freshmen admitted Aug., Jan. Degrees conferred and formal commencement May. No summer session.

Characteristics of Freshmen: 76% of applicants admitted. 36% of applicants admitted and enrolled.

75% (264 students) submitted SAT scores; 68% (239 students) submitted ACT scores. *25th percentile:* SAT Verbal 525, SAT Math 510; ACT Composite

22, ACT English 22, ACT Math 22. *75th percentile:* SAT Verbal 610, SAT Math 610; ACT Composite 27, ACT English 29, ACT Math 26.

86% of entering freshmen expected to graduate within 5 years. 26% of freshmen from Indiana. Freshmen from 32 states and 2 foreign countries.

Admission: Rolling admissions plan. For fall acceptance, apply as early as Aug. 1 of previous year, but not later than Mar. 1 of year of enrollment. Also an Early Decision Program. Application for this program must be in by Nov. 15. Admission notifications for the EDP are mailed by Dec. 15. Applications may be submitted on regular program at any time but after March 15 are admitted on a space available basis. *Requirements:* Either graduation from accredited secondary school with 4 units English, 2 in a foreign language, 2 college preparatory mathematics, 2 social studies, 1 laboratory science, 5 academic electives; or GED. Minimum GPA 2.5. Lowest acceptable secondary school class standing 66th percentile. *Entrance tests:* College Board SAT or ACT composite. For foreign students TOEFL. *For transfer students:* 2.5 minimum GPA; 68 semester hours maximum transfer credit; 60 semester hours in residence.

College credit and advanced placement for postsecondary-level work completed in secondary school. Tutoring available. Developmental/remedial courses offered during regular academic year; credit given.

Degree Requirements: 128 semester hours; 2.0 GPA; 60 hours, and half of major courses in residence; distribution requirements; grade of C in all major courses; demonstrated proficiency in writing and in a foreign language; comprehensives in individual fields of study.

Fulfillment of some degree requirements and exemption from some beginning courses possible by passing College Board CLEP, Achievement Tests, AP. *Grading system:* A–F; pass/fail; honors-satisfactory-unsatisfactory; withdraw (carries time limit); incomplete (carries time limit).

Distinctive Educational Programs: Work-experience programs, including field experience, internships. Evening classes. Dual-degree program in engineering with University of Notre Dame. Special facilities for using telecommunications in the classroom. Interdepartmental/interdisciplinary programs in American studies, humanistic studies, urban studies, Latin American studies. Independent study and research projects. Institutionally sponsored study abroad in Ireland and India; at off-campus center in Rome; summer programs in England, France, Italy. Study abroad also through University of Notre Dame, in Australia, Austria, France, Japan, Jerusalem, Mexico, Spain; elsewhere by individual arrangement. Off-campus study through Washington (DC) semester at American University. Library facilities and some courses, student activities shared with University of Notre Dame. Cross-registration through consortium. *Other distinctive programs:* Center for Spirituality program of lectures and seminars on spirituality and women in the church; accelerated program in nursing; student-designed major.

ROTC: Army, Navy, Air Force offered in cooperation with University of Notre Dame.

Degrees Conferred: 371 *baccalaureate:* biological/life sciences 21; business/marketing 68; communications/communication technologies 47; computer and information sciences 2; education 51; English 38; foreign languages and literature 24; mathematics 9; philosophy/religion/theology 6; physical sciences 11; protective services/public administration 23; psychology 25; social sciences and history 37; visual and performing arts 14; student designed major 1.

Fees and Other Expenses: *Full-time tuition per academic year 2004–05:* $22,922. *Required fees:* $362. *Room and board per academic year:* $7,663.

Financial Aid: Aid from institutionally generated funds is provided on the basis of academic merit, financial need. Institution has a Program Participation Agreement with the U.S. Department of Education for eligible students to receive Pell Grants and other federal aid.

Financial aid to full-time, first-time undergraduate students: need-based scholarships/grants totaling $8,708,075, self-help $3,985,320, parent loans $564,140, tuition waivers $988,345; non-need-based scholarships/grants totaling $5,140,646, self-help $3,509,125, parent loans $2,971,725, tuition waivers $531,787.

Departments and Teaching Staff: *Total instructional faculty:* 201 (full-time 136, part-time 65; women 124, men 77; members of minority groups 10). Student-to-faculty ratio: 11:1. Degrees held by full-time faculty: doctorate 76%, master's 4%, professional 20%. 96% hold terminal degrees.

Enrollment: Total enrollment 1,418. Undergraduate full-time 1 man / 1,382 women, part-time 1m / 35w. *Transfer students:* in-state 1; from out-of-state 39.

Characteristics of Student Body: *Ethnic and racial makeup:* number of Black non-Hispanic: 17; American Indian or Alaska Native: 9; Asian or Pacific Islander:33; Hispanic: 71; White non-Hispanic: 1,279. *Age distribution:* number under 18: 17; 18–19: 627; 20–21: 664; 22–24: 81; 25–29: 8; 30–34: 5; 35–39: 5; 40–49: 10; 50–64: 2; 65 and over: 1.

International Students: 11 nonresident aliens enrolled 2004. 4 students from Europe, 4 Asia, 1 Central and South America, 2 Africa. No programs available to aid students whose native language is not English. No financial aid specifically designated for international students.

Student Life: On-campus residence hall house 86% of student body. Residence hall for women constitute 100% of such space. *Intercollegiate athletics:* women only: basketball, crew, fencing, golf, gymnastics, skiing, soccer, softball, swimming, tennis, track, volleyball. *Special regulations:* Quiet hours set by dormitory residents. Dormitory visitation from 10am to midnight Sun.–Thurs., 10am to 2am Fri.–Sat. *Special services:* Medical services, shuttle bus to and from off-campus locations. *Student publications: The Blue Mantle*, a yearbook; *Chimes*, a biannual literary magazine. *The Observer*, a daily newspaper is published jointly with University of Notre Dame. *Surrounding community:* South Bend population 110,000. Chicago, 100 miles from campus, is nearest metropolitan area. Served by mass transit bus system, airport 3 miles from campus, passenger rail service 4 miles from campus.

Library Collections: 215,616 volumes. 7,100 microforms; 3,300 audiovisual materials; 760 current periodical subscriptions. Online catalog. Students have access to online information retrieval services and the Internet.

Most important holdings include Dante Collection.

Buildings and Grounds: Campus area 275 acres. *New buildings:* Welcome Center complete 2000; Qpus Hall Apartments 2004; Student Center/Dining Hall 2005.

Chief Executive Officer: Dr. Carol Ann Mooney, President.

Address admission inquiries to Mona Bowe, Director of Admissions.

Saint Meinrad School of Theology

One Hill Drive
Saint Meinrad, Indiana 47577
Tel: (812) 357-6611   **E-mail:** apply@saintmeinrad.edu
Fax: (812) 357-6964   **Internet:** www.saintmeinrad.edu

Institution Description: Saint Meinrad School of Theology is a private Roman Catholic Seminary conducted by the Order of St. Benedict. Lay men and women are admitted to the Master of Theological Studies and Master of Arts in Catholic thought. *Enrollment:* 156. *Degrees awarded:* First-professional (master of divinity), master's.

Member of the consortium Theological Education Association of Mid-America.

Accreditation: *Regional:* NCA. *National:* ATS. *Professional*: theology

History: Established as Saint Meinrad Seminary 1857; offered first instruction at postsecondary level 1861; incorporated as Saint Meinrad's Abbey 1890; awarded first degree (first-professional), incorporated as theological school and adopted present name 1969. *See* Albert Kleber, O.S.B., *History of Saint Meinrad Archabbey* (Saint Meinrad, IN: Grail Publications, 1954) for further information.

Institutional Structure: *Governing board:* Saint Meinrad School of Theology Board of Trustees. Extrainstitutional representation: 7 trustees, including the archabbot; institutional representation: president-rector, business manager, 5 other administrators, 2 full-time instructional faculty members, 2 alumni. 3 ex officio. All voting. *Composition of institution:* Administrators 4 men / 2 women. Academic affairs headed by academic dean. Management/business/finances directed by treasurer and business manager. Total instructional faculty 30. Academic governance body, School of Theology Faculty, meets twice monthly.

Calendar: Semesters. 4-1-4 plan. Academic year Aug. to May. Summer session mid-June to late July. Entering students admitted June, Aug. Degrees conferred and formal commencement May.

Admission: Rolling admissions plan. For fall acceptance, apply as early as Sept. of previous year, but not later than Aug. of year of enrollment. *Requirements:* Baccalaureate degree from accredited college or university. For first-professional students 18 semester hours in philosophy which must include logic, metaphysics, history of philosophy; 12 semester hours in theology. International students must have English competency examination. *For transfer students:* 2.0 minimum GPA; for first-professional students 56 hours maximum transfer credit; master's students 15 hours.

Degree Requirements: *For first-professional degree:* 116 credit hours, 4 interterms and 15 practicum units required, plus distribution requirements. *For master's degree:* 48 credit hours. *For all degrees:* 2.0 GPA; distribution requirements. *Grading system:* A–F; pass-fail; withdraw (carries time limit); incomplete (carries time limit).

Distinctive Educational Programs: *For first-professional degree:* Work-experience programs. Facilities and programs for independent research, including tutorials. Study abroad during interterm in Rome. Off-campus study in the U.S., in Hispanic-American ministry programs. *Available to all students:* Special facilities for using telecommunications in the classroom. *Other distinctive programs:* Continuing education.

Degrees Conferred: 27 *master's:* theology; 10 *first-professional:* master of divinity.

Fees and Other Expenses: *Full-time tuition per academic year 2005–06:* $14,618. *Other fees:* $275 retreat fee. *Room and board per academic year:* $8,179.

Financial Aid: Aid from institutionally generated funds is provided on the basis of financial need. Institution has a Program Participation Agreement with the U.S. Department of Education for eligible students to receive Pell Grants and other federal aid. *Graduate aid:* 20 students received federal and state-funded loans totaling $39,600; 40 work-study jobs totaling $44,000; 95 other fellowships totaling $554,869 (ranging $150 to $2,712).

Departments and Teaching Staff: Philosophy/systematics *professors* 1, *associate professors* 0, *assistant professors* 3, *instructors* 0, *part-time faculty* 12; pastoral studies 1, 3, 2, 2, 0; Biblical/historical 2, 1, 1, 0, 2.

Total instructional faculty: 24 (full-time 21, part-time 3; women 3, men 21; member of minority group 1). Total faculty with doctorate, first-professional, or other terminal degree: 19. Student-to-faculty ratio: 5:1. *Faculty development:* 3 faculty members awarded sabbaticals 2004–05.

Enrollment: Total enrollment 156.First-professional full-time 78 men; graduate full-time 2m / 4w, part-time 33m / 39w.

Characteristics of Student Body: *Ethnic and racial makeup:* Black non-Hispanic: 1; Asian or Pacific Islander: 1; Hispanic: 31; White non-Hispanic: 96.

International Students: 10 nonresident aliens enrolled full-time fall 2004. No programs available to aid students whose native language is not English. No financial aid specifically designated for international students.

Student Life: On-campus residence halls for men house 75% of the student body. *Special regulations:* Cars permitted without restrictions. *Special services:* Learning Resources Center, medical services. *Surrounding community:* Saint Meinrad population 500. Louisville (KY), 80 miles from campus, is nearest metropolitan area.

Publications: Sources of information about Saint Meinrad School of Theology include the *Saint Meinrad Newsletter*.

Library Collections: 170,542 volumes. Online catalog. Current serial subscriptions: paper 369; microform 10,464; via electronic access 5. 3,724 recordings; 433 compact discs; 38 CD-ROMs. Students have access to the Internet at no charge. Total budget for books and materials 2004–05: $70,000.

Buildings and Grounds: Campus area 350 acres.

Chief Executive Officer: Rev. Mark O'Keefe, O.S.B., President-Rector.

Address admission inquiries to Rev. John Thomas, Director of Enrollment Management.

Taylor University

500 West Reade Avenue
Upland, Indiana 46989-1001
Tel: (765) 998-5134   **E-mail:** admissions@taylor.edu
Fax: (765) 998-4925   **Internet:** www.taylor.edu

Institution Description: Taylor University is a private, independent, nonprofit, evangelical Christian college. *Enrollment:* 1,887. *Degrees awarded:* Associate, baccalaureate.

Member of Christian College Consortium.

Accreditation: *Regional:* NCA. *Professional:* music, social work, teacher education

History: Established by Methodist Episcopal Church as Fort Wayne Female College and offered first instruction at postsecondary level 1846; awarded first degree (baccalaureate) 1850; changed name to Fort Wayne College 1855; adopted present name 1890. *See* William Ringenberg, *Taylor University: The First 125 Years* (Grand Rapids, Mich.: Eerdmans Publishing Co., 1973) for further information.

Institutional Structure: *Governing board:* Taylor University Board of Trustees. Extrainstitutional representation: 20 trustees; institutional representation: president of the university; 5 alumni. 1 ex officio. All voting. *Composition of institution:* Administrators 7 men / 4 women. Academic affairs headed by vice president for academic affairs. Management/business/finances directed by executive vice president. Full-time instructional faculty 140. Academic governance body, Taylor University Faculty, meets an average of 12 times per year.

Calendar: Semesters (4-1-4 plan). Academic year Sept. to May. Freshmen admitted Sept., Jan., Feb., June. Degrees conferred and formal commencement May. Summer session of 2 terms from late May to late July.

Characteristics of Freshmen: 61% of applicants accepted. 49% of accepted applicants enrolled.

48% (228 students) submitted SAT scores; 52% (249 students) submitted ACT scores. *25th percentile:* SAT I Verbal 530, SAT I Math 530; ACT Composite 23, ACT English 24, ACT Math 23. *75th percentile:* SAT I Verbal 660, SAT I Math 660; ACT Composite 29, ACT English 31, ACT Math 29.

Admission: Rolling admissions plan. For fall acceptance, apply as early as 1 year prior to enrollment, but not later than July 1 of year of enrollment. Early acceptance available. *Requirements:* Either graduation from accredited secondary school with 4 units English, 2 mathematics, 2 social studies, 1 laboratory science; or GED. 2 units in foreign language recommended. *Entrance tests:* College Board SAT or ACT composite. *For transfer students:* 2.0 minimum GPA; from 4-year accredited institution maximum transfer limited only by residence requirement; from 2-year accredited institution 66 hours; correspondence/extension students 6 hours.

College credit and advanced placement for postsecondary-level work completed in secondary school and for extrainstitutional learning basis of ACE *2006 Guide to the Evaluation of Educational Experiences in the Armed Services.* Tutoring available. Developmental courses offered in summer session and regular academic year; credit given.

Degree Requirements: *For all associate degrees:* 68 credit hours; 2 terms in residence. *For all baccalaureate degrees:* 128 credit hours; one-half of major credits earned at Taylor and final 30 hours in residence; general education requirements. *For all degrees:* 2.0 GPA (higher GPA in some majors); chapel attendance; 3 physical education courses; entrance competency examination in writing and mathematics; computer literacy.

Fulfillment of some degree requirements and exemption from some beginning courses possible by passing College Board CLEP and standardized testing for credit. *Grading system:* A–F; withdraw (deadline after which pass-fail is appended to withdraw); incomplete (carries time limit).

Distinctive Educational Programs: Work-experience programs. Physics engineering program with Washington University. Cooperative baccalaureate program in nursing with Ball State University; in medical technology with approved hospitals. Special facilities for using telecommunications in the classroom. Interdepartmental majors possible in combination with environmental studies or systems analysis; inter-area studies in education-physical education, humanities, natural science, and social sciences. Preprofessional program in medicine. Facilities for independent research, including honors programs, individual majors, tutorials. Institutionally sponsored programs in Dominican Republic, Israel, Mexico; history and economics programs in Europe in cooperation with Wheaton College (IL); study elsewhere by individual arrangement. Interterm study tours to Israel, England, and Europe. Latin American summer programs. American studies program in Washington (DC). *Other distinctive programs:* Credits-in-Escrow summer program for secondary school students.

Degrees Conferred: 2 *associate*; 406 *baccalaureate*; 1 *master's*. Bachelor's degrees awarded in top five disciplines: education 88; business, management, marketing, and related support services 78; computer and information sciences and support services 43; psychology 29; theology and ministerial studies 29.

Fees and Other Expenses: *Full-time tuition per academic year 2004–05:* $20,520. *Required fees:* $226. *Books and supplies:* $700. *Room and board per academic year:* $5,630.

Financial Aid: Aid from institutionally generated funds is provided on the basis of academic merit, financial need, athletic ability. Institution has a Program Participation Agreement with the U.S. Department of Education for eligible students to receive Pell Grants and other federal aid.

Financial aid to full-time, first-time undergraduate students: need-based scholarships/grants totaling $8,643,252, self-help $4,780,852, parent loans $3,182,484, tuition waivers $819,332, athletic awards $533,079; non-need-based scholarships/grants totaling $2,254,847, self-help $2,088,993, parent loans $9,223,368, tuition waivers $443,807, athletic awards $343,642.

Departments and Teaching Staff: *Total instructional faculty:* 187 (full-time 140, part-time 47; women 63, men 124; members of minority groups 8). Total faculty with doctorate, first-professional, or other terminal degree: 99. Student-to-faculty ratio: 13:1.

Enrollment: Total enrollment 1,887. Undergraduate 1,868, graduate 19.

Characteristics of Student Body: *Ethnic/racial makeup:* number of Black non-Hispanic: 26; American Indian or Alaska Native: 5; Asian or Pacific Islander: 25; Hispanic: 17; White non-Hispanic: 1,738; unknown: 20.

International Students: 20 nonresident aliens enrolled fall 2004. Students from Europe, Asia, Central and South America, Africa, Canada. No programs available to aid students whose native language is not English. No financial aid specifically designated for international students.

Student Life: On-campus residence halls house 74% of student body. Residence halls for men constitute 46% of such space, for women 54%. 7% of student body, including some married students, live off campus in university owned and operated apartments. Approximately 19% of the student body are commuters or live in non-university owned facilities. *Intercollegiate athletics:* men only: baseball, basketball, cross-country, football, golf, tennis, track, wrestling; women only: basketball, field hockey, soccer, softball, tennis, track, volleyball. *Special regulations:* Registered cars permitted; freshmen may have cars after Thanksgiving. Residence hall visitation during open houses arranged by hall residents. *Special services:* Learning Resources Center, medical services, Leadership Development Program includes 300+ opportunities for leadership experi-

ence. Nationally recognized. Annual sponsor of the National Student Leadership Conference for Christian Colleges and the Christian Leadership Conference for High School Students. *Student publications: The Echo*, student newspaper; *Taylor Magazine; Profile. Surrounding community:* Upland. Indianapolis, 65 miles from campus, is nearest metropolitan area.

Library Collections: 186,200 volumes. 10,900 microforms; 7,900 audiovisual materials; 690 current periodical subscriptions. Online catalog. Students have access to online information services and the Internet.

Most important special holdings include James DeWeerd Rare Documents and Bibles; Wengate African Artifacts Collection; Alfred Backus Collection of Wesley and Backus Sermons and Journals.

Buildings and Grounds: Campus area 250 acres.

Chief Executive Officer: Dr. Daniel J. Gyertson, President.

Address admission inquiries to Stephen Mortland, Vice President, Enrollment Services.

Tri-State University

1 University Avenue
Angola, Indiana 46703

Tel: (260) 665-4100   **E-mail:** admit@tristate.edu
Fax: (260) 665-4292   **Internet:** www.tristate.edu

Institution Description: Tri-State University is a private, independent, nonprofit institution. *Enrollment:* 1,233. Branch campuses are located at Fort Wayne and South Bend. *Degrees awarded:* Associate, baccalaureate.

Accreditation: *Regional:* NCA. *Professional:* engineering, teacher education

History: Chartered and incorporated 1883; offered first instruction at postsecondary level 1884; awarded first degree (baccalaureate) 1886; adopted present name 1976. *See* Alice Parrott, *History of Tri-State College* (Angola: Tri-State College, 1959) and Elizabeth Brown Orlosky, *From Carriage to Computer* (Angola: Tri-State University, 1984) for further information.

Institutional Structure: *Governing board:* Board of Trustees. Representation: 22 trustees, 3 alumni. All voting. *Composition of institution:* Administrators 12 men / 14women. Academic affairs headed by vice president for academic affairs. Finances/fiscal headed by vice president fiscal and financial affairs. Vice presidents for institutional advancement, campus and student operations, enrollment management, administration. Full-time instructional faculty 73. Academic governance bodies: Academic Council meets weekly; faculty meets 6 times per year.

Calendar: Semesters. Academic year Aug. to May. Freshmen and transfer students admitted Aug., Dec., Mar., June, July. Degrees conferred May, July, Aug., Nov., Feb. Formal commencement in May.

Characteristics of Freshmen: 76% of applicants admitted. 25% of applicants admitted and enrolled.

54% (173 students) submitted SAT scores; 46% (147 students) submitted ACT scores. *25th percentile:* SAT Verbal 460, SAT Math 490; ACT Composite 19, ACT English 18, ACT Math 19. *75th percentile:* SAT Verbal 550, SAT Math 600; ACT Composite 25, ACT English 24, ACT Math 26.

50% of freshmen expected to graduate within 5 years. 62% from Indiana. Freshmen from 11 states and 1 foreign country.

Admission: Rolling admissions plan. Mar. 1 priority application deadline. Early acceptance available. *Requirements:* Graduation from accredited secondary school with 4 units English, 2 social studies. Mathematics and science requirements vary according to program. Minimum 2.0 GPA. Lowest acceptable secondary school class standing 50th percentile. *Entrance tests:* College Board SAT or ACT composite. *For transfer students:* Maximum transfer credit limited only by residence requirement and program area requirements.

College credit and advanced placement for postsecondary-level work completed in secondary school and for extrainstitutional learning on basis of ACE *2006 Guide to the Evaluation of Educational Experiences in the Armed Services;* departmental evaluations. Remedial courses offered in summer session and during regular academic year.

Degree Requirements: *For all associate degrees:* 65–70 semester hours; 3 hours physical education courses. *For all baccalaureate degrees:* 128–132 semester hours; 3 hours physical education courses. *For all degrees:* 2.0 GPA; 3 terms in residence; general education requirements.

Fulfillment of some degree requirements and exemption from some beginning courses possible by passing departmental examinations, College Board CLEP, ETS Advanced Placement, other standardized tests. *Grading system:* A–F; pass-fail; withdraw (carries time limit, deadline after which pass-fail is appended to withdraw).

Distinctive Educational Programs: Cooperative education programs. Internships. Work-experience programs. Interdepartmental programs in computer science, criminal justice and psychology, business, entrepreneurship, environmental science and engineering, golf management, sport management, social science, communications, business and engineering.

Degrees Conferred: 14 *associate;* 231 *baccalaureate:* biological and life sciences 5; business/marketing 73; computer and information science 1; education 27; engineering/engineering technologies 76; mathematics 2; natural resources/environmental science 1; parks and recreation 12; physical sciences 2; protective services/public administration 17; psychology 6; social sciences and history 1.

Fees and Other Expenses: *Full-time tuition per academic year 2004–05:* $19,260. *Room and board per academic year:* $5,700.

Financial Aid: Aid from institutionally generated funds is provided on the basis of academic merit, financial need, athletic ability. Institution has a Program Participation Agreement with the U.S. Department of Education for eligible students to receive Pell Grants and other federal aid.

Departments and Teaching Staff: *Professors* 21, *associate professors* 26, *assistant professors* 26, *part-time faculty* 22. *Total instructional faculty:* 95 (full-time 73, part-time 22; women 26, men 69; members of minority groups 3). Total faculty with doctorate, first-professional, or other terminal degree: 52. Student-to-faculty ratio: 14:1.

Enrollment: Total enrollment 1,233. Undergraduate full-time 693 men / 328 women, part-time 72m / 132w; graduate full-time 1m / 2w, part-time 5m.

Characteristics of Student Body: *Ethnic/racial makeup:* number of Black non-Hispanic: 32; American Indian or Alaska Native: 3; Asian or Pacific Islander: 13; Hispanic: 5; White non-Hispanic: 1,024; unknown: 121. *Age distribution:* under 18: 30; 18–19: 426; 20–21: 395; 22–24: 195; 25–29: 62; 30–34: 41; 35–39: 23; 40–49: 48.

International Students: 18 nonresident aliens enrolled fall 2004. 2 students from Europe, 8 Asia, 4 Central and South America, 4 Africa. Programs available to aid students whose native language is not English: English as a Second Language Program. No financial aid specifically designated for international students.

Student Life: On-campus residence halls house 45% of student body. Some men and women join and live in fraternities and sororities. *Intercollegiate athletics:* men only: baseball, basketball, cross-country, golf, soccer, swimming, tennis, track, volleyball; women only: basketball, cross-country, fencing, golf, soccer, softball, swimming, track, volleyball. *Special regulations:* Cars permitted in designated areas. Curfews, quiet hours. *Student radio:* WEAX broadcasts 102 hours per week. *Surrounding community:* Angola population 7,000. Fort Wayne, 40 miles from campus, is nearest metropolitan area. Angola is 3 to 4 hours drive from Detroit, Chicago, Cleveland, and Indianapolis. Served by airport 50 miles from campus; passenger rail service 35 miles from campus.

Library Collections: 142,500 volumes. Online and card catalogs. 165 serial subscriptions. 15,440 microforms; 6,100 audiovisual materials. 5,948 recordings. Computer work stations available. Students have access to the Internet at no charge. Total 2004–05 budget for books and materials: $117,833.

Most important special holdings include NASA, AGARD, and NATO reports; elementary education, textbooks and curriculum materials; Fortune 500 companies annual reports.

Buildings and Grounds: Campus area 400 acres.

Chief Executive Officer: Dr. Earl D. Brooks, II, President.

Address admission inquiries to Scott Goplin, Vice President, Enrollment Management and Dean of Admissions.

University of Evansville

1800 Lincoln Avenue
Evansville, Indiana 47722
Tel: (812) 479-2468   **E-mail:** admissions@evansville.edu
Fax: (812) 474-4076   **Internet:** www.evansville.edu

Institution Description: University of Evansville is a private institution affiliated with The United Methodist Church. *Enrollment:* 2,687. *Degrees awarded:* Associate, baccalaureate, master's.

Member of Association of Urban Universities, Indiana Consortium for International Programs, American Council on Education, Indiana Conference of Higher Education.

Accreditation: *Regional:* NCA. *Professional:* engineering, music, nursing, physical therapy, teacher education

History: Established, chartered, and incorporated as Moore's Hill Male and Female Collegiate Institute 1854; offered first instruction at postsecondary level 1856; awarded first degree (baccalaureate) 1858; changed name to Moore's Hill College 1887, to Evansville College 1919; adopted present name 1967. *See* Ralph E. Olmstead, *From Institute to University* (Evansville: University of Evansville Press, 1973) or George Klinger, *We Face the Future Unafraid: A Narrative History of the University of Evansville* (Evansville: University of Evansville Press, 2003) for further information.

Institutional Structure: *Governing board:* Board of Trustees of the University of Evansville. Extrainstitutional representation: 41 trustees—2 ex officio and 39 elected members (representatives of South Indiana Conference, United Methodist Church); North Indiana Conference; bishop of the Indiana area; president of the university; alumni-elected members, and student-elected members form the graduating class. All voting. *Composition of institution:* Major administrators 9 men / 4 woman. Academic affairs headed by vice president for academic affairs. Management/business/finances directed by vice president for fiscal affairs and administration. Full-time instructional faculty 169. Academic governance body, Faculty Senate, meets an average of 9 times per year.

Calendar: Semesters. Academic year Aug. to May. Freshmen admitted Aug., Jan. Degrees conferred at formal commencement in Dec. and May. Summer session of 2 terms mid-May to mid-July.

Characteristics of Freshmen: 88.1% of applicants admitted. 28.4% of applicants admitted and enrolled.

70% (443 students) submitted SAT scores; 56% (355 students) submitted ACT scores. *25th percentile:* SAT Verbal 510, SAT Math 500; ACT Composite 23, ACT English 22, ACT Math 21. *75th percentile:* SAT Verbal 630, SAT Math 630; ACT Composite 28, ACT English 29, ACT Math 28.

59% of entering freshmen expected to graduate within 5 years. 52% of freshmen from Indiana. Freshmen from 29 states and 18 foreign countries.

Admission: Rolling admissions plan. For fall acceptance, apply as early as completion of junior of secondary school, but not later than Aug. of year of enrollment. Early acceptance available. *Requirements:* Either graduation from accredited secondary school with 4 units in English, 3 mathematics, 2 science, 1, history, or GED. Additional units in mathematics, science, and foreign language; minimum GPA 2.5 recommended. Lowest acceptable secondary school class standing 40th percentile. *Entrance tests:* College Board SAT or ACT Composite. For foreign students TOEFL. *For transfer students:* 2.0 minimum GPA.

College credit and advanced placement for postsecondary-level work completed in secondary school. College credit for extrainstitutional learning on basis of ACE *2006 Guide to the Evaluation of Educational Experiences in the Armed Services;* portfolio assessment. Tutoring available.

Degree Requirements: *For all associate degrees:* 62 semester hours. *For all baccalaureate degrees:* Minimum of 124 hours. *For all undergraduate degrees:* 2.0 GPA; 30 hours in residence; general education requirements.

Fulfillment of some degree requirements and exemption from some beginning courses possible by passing departmental or advanced placement examinations, or College Board CLEP. *Grading system:* A–F; pass-fail; withdraw (carries time limit).

Distinctive Educational Programs: Interdisciplinary programs in continuing studies, environmental administration, environmental science, humanities, psychobiology, and urban affairs. Facilities and programs for cooperative education, independent research, individualized majors, and honors. Study abroad available through the Institute of European Studies in Austria, France, Germany, Mexico, and Spain. Harlaxton College provides British campus near Grantham, and for majors in archaeology and British studies as well as undergraduates in general.

Degrees Conferred: 16 *associate;* 444 *baccalaureate* (B), 48 *master's* (M): biological/life sciences 10 (B); business/marketing 59 (B); communications/communication technologies 18 (B); computer and information sciences 19 (B); education 58 (B); engineering and engineering technologies 35 (B); English 13 (B); foreign languages and literature 3 (B); health professions and related sciences 45 (B), 28 (D); law/legal studies 3 (B); liberal arts/general studies 39 (B); mathematics 4 (B); natural resources/environmental science 3 (B); parks and recreation 17 (B); philosophy/religion/theology 5 (B); protective services/public administration 48 (M); psychology 22 (B); social sciences and history 44 (B); visual and performing arts 44 (B).

Fees and Other Expenses: *Full-time tuition per academic year 2005–06:* $21,120 undergraduate; $560 per credit hour for graduate courses. *Required fees:* $540. *Room and board per academic year:* $6,840.

Financial Aid: Aid from institutionally generated funds is provided on the basis of academic merit, financial need, athletic ability, other criteria. Institution has a Program Participation Agreement with the U.S. Department of Education for eligible students to receive Pell Grants and other federal aid.

Financial aid to full-time, first-time undergraduate students: need-based scholarships/grants totaling $20,931,983, self-help $7,162,022, parent loans $3,443,028, tuition waivers $1,146,368, athletic awards $1,115,969; non-need-based scholarships/grants totaling $5,335,690, self-help $639,204, parent loans $677,204, tuition waivers $359,330, athletic awards $1,639,061. *Graduate aid:* 22 federal and state-funded loans totaling $234,406 (ranging from $522 to $8,780).

Departments and Teaching Staff: *Professors* 52, *associate professors* 59, *assistant professors* 68, *instructors* 10, *part-time faculty* 60. *Total instructional faculty:* 229 (full-time 169, part-time 60; women 88, men 141). Total faculty with doctorate, first-professional, or other terminal degree: 140. Student-to-faculty ratio: 13:1. *Faculty development:* $85,000 in grants for research. 5 faculty members awarded sabbaticals 2004–05.

Enrollment: Total enrollment 2,687. Undergraduate full-time 888 men / 1,405 women, part-time 131m / 208w; graduate full-time 14m / 31w, part-time 2m / 8w.

Characteristics of Student Body: *Ethnic and racial makeup:* number of Black non-Hispanic: 55; American Indian or Alaska Native: 6; Asian or Pacific Islander: 28; Hispanic: 27; White non-Hispanic: 1,820; unknown: 268. *Age distribution:* under 18: 168; 18–19: 1,118; 20–21: 889; 22–24: 232; 25–29: 65; 30–34: 39; 35–39: 21; 40–49: 72; 50–64: 36; 65 and over: 1.

International Students: 128 nonresident aliens enrolled fall 2004. 18 students from Europe, 62 Asia, 6 Central and South America, 18 Africa, 6 Canada, 4 Caribbean, 14 Middle East. Programs available to aid students whose native language is not English: Social, cultural. English as a Second Language Program. Financial aid specifically designated for international students: Variable number scholarships available annually; 47 totaling $507,627 awarded 2004–05.

Student Life: On-campus residence halls house 67% of student body. Residence halls for men only constitute 35% of such space, for women only 63%. 28% of men fraternities; 21% of women join sororities. *Intercollegiate athletics:* men only: baseball, basketball, cross-country, diving, golf, soccer, swimming; women only: basketball, cross-country, diving, golf, soccer, softball, swimming, tennis, volleyball. *Special regulations:* Parking permitted in designated areas only. Residence hall visitation from 10am to midnight Sun.-Thur.; 10am to 2am Fri. and Sat. Some 24-hour visitation floors available in each residence hall. *Special services:* health services; writing center. *Student publications, radio: The Crescent,* a biweekly newspaper; *LINC,* a yearbook; a student handbook. Radio station WUEV broadcasts 24 hours per day. *Surrounding community:* Evansville metropolitan area population 122,000. Indianapolis, 180 miles from campus, is nearest metropolitan area. Served by airport 7 miles from campus.

Library Collections: 282,820 volumes. Current serial subscriptions: paper 1,000; microform 465,000; via electronic access 13,065. 11,230 recordings. Online catalog. Access to online information retrieval systems. Students have access to the Internet at no charge. Total 2004–05 budget books and materials: $600,000.

Most important holdings include James L. Clifford Collection of 18th-century British Literature and Johnsoniana; editorial cartoons of K.K. Knecht; Library of American Civilization and Library of English Literature.

Buildings and Grounds: Campus area 72 acres.

Chief Executive Officer: Dr. Stephen Jennings, President.

Address admission inquiries to Dr. Tom Bear, Dean of Admission.

College of Arts and Sciences

Degree Programs Offered: *Baccalaureate* in archaeology, art history, art, biology, chemistry, biochemistry, classical studies, composition, criminal justice, economics, environmental administration, environmental science, French, German, health and physical education, history, international studies, interpersonal communication, journalism, literature, mathematics, medical technology, philosophy, physics, political science, pre-theology, psychobiology, psychology, public administration, public relations, religion, sociology, Spanish, telecommunications.

School of Business Administration

Degree Programs Offered: *Baccalaureate* in accounting, business administration with an emphasis in economics, finance, global studies, management, marketing, or a self-designed cognate.

College of Education and Health Sciences

Degree Programs Offered: *Associate* in physical therapist assistant; *baccalaureate* in physical education, special education, elementary education, English education, foreign language education, mathematics education, science education, social studies, education, music education, theatre education, art education, athletic training, exercise science, movement science, sport studies, nursing, health services administration; *master's* in health services administration, physical therapy.

College of Engineering and Computing Science

Degree Programs Offered: *Baccalaureate* in computer science, computer engineering, electrical engineering, engineering management, Internet technology, civil engineering, mechanical engineering; *master's* in computer science, electrical engineering.

College of Fine Arts

Degree Programs Offered: *Baccalaureate* in art, art education, art history, art studio, art therapy, commercial art; music, music performance, music education, music management, music therapy; theatre, theatre performance, theatre design and technology, theatre management.

Admission: Admission to music and theatre programs is by audition and/or portfolio presentation in addition to university requirements. Art scholarships require portfolio presentation.

Degree Requirements: Specific degree requirements vary with each program.

Center for Continuing Education

Degree Programs Offered: *Baccalaureate* in external studies, liberal studies; *master's* in public service administration.

Departments and Teaching Staff: Full-time faculty members are drawn from other colleges within the university. Part-time instructors with appropriate terminal degrees are occasionally utilized.

University of Indianapolis

1400 East Hanna Avenue
Indianapolis, Indiana 46227-3697

Tel: (800) 232-8634   **E-mail:** admissions@uindy.edu
Fax: (317) 788-3300   **Internet:** www.uindy.edu

Institution Description: University of Indianapolis is a private, independent, nonprofit institution affiliated with the United Methodist Church. *Enrollment:* 4,188. *Degrees awarded:* Associate, baccalaureate, master's, doctorate.

Accreditation: *Regional:* NCA. *Professional:* business, music, nursing, nursing education, occupational therapy, physical therapy, social work, teacher education

History: Established and incorporated as Indiana Central University, 1902; offered first instruction at postsecondary level 1905; awarded first degree (baccalaureate) 1908. For further information *see* Russell E. Vance, Jr., *Fifty Years of Christian Education: A Short History of Indiana Central College, 1905–1955* (Indianapolis: 1955); and Marvin L Henricks, *From Parochialism to Community* (Indianapolis: 1977).

Institutional Structure: *Governing board:* University of Indianapolis Board of Trustees. Extrainstitutional representation: 32 trustees, United Methodist Bishop of Indiana area; institutional representation: president of the university; president of Alumni Association, 8 alumni. 3 ex officio. All voting. *Composition of institution:* College of Arts and Sciences, School of Business, School of Education, School of Nursing, Krannert School of Physical Therapy, Graduate Business Programs, Occupational Therapy Programs, Center for Continuing Education and Management Development. Administrators 14 men / 8 women. Academic affairs headed by academic dean. Management/business/finances directed by treasurer and business manager. Full-time instructional faculty 76 men / 78 women. Academic governance body, the faculty, meets an average of 9 times per year.

Calendar: Semesters. 4-4-1 plan. Academic year Aug. to Apr. Freshmen admitted Aug., Jan., Apr., June. Degrees conferred Dec., Apr./May, Aug. Formal commencement Apr. or May. Summer session of 2 terms from May to Aug.

Characteristics of Freshmen: 76% of applicants admitted. 32% of applicants admitted and enrolled.

84% (568 students) submitted SAT scores; 45% (271 students) submitted ACT scores. *25th percentile:* SAT Verbal 450, SAT Math 460; ACT Composite 18, ACT English 18, ACT Math 18. *75th percentile:* SAT Verbal 560, SAT Math 570; ACT Composite 25, ACT English 25, ACT Math 24.

55% of entering freshmen expected to graduate within 5 years. 87% of freshmen from Indiana. Freshmen from 21 states and 13 foreign countries.

Admission: Rolling admissions plan. Early acceptance available. *Requirements:* Either graduation from accredited secondary school with 16 units which must include 12 from among English and literature, foreign language, history, laboratory science, mathematics, social studies; or GED. Lowest recommended secondary school class standing 50th percentile. *Entrance tests:* College Board SAT or ACT composite. For foreign students TOEFL.

College credit and advanced placement for postsecondary-level work completed in secondary school. Developmental courses offered in summer session and regular academic year; credit given.

Degree Requirements: *For all associate degrees:* 62 credit hours; 30 hours in residence. *For all baccalaureate degrees:* 124 credit hours; 30 hours in residence. *For all undergraduate degrees:* 2.0 GPA on 4.0 scale; general education requirements; at least one academic major.

Fulfillment of some degree requirements and exemption from some beginning courses possible by passing departmental examinations, College Board CLEP, AP, other standardized tests. *Grading system:* A–F; pass-fail; withdraw (carries time limit).

Distinctive Educational Programs: Dual degree programs in engineering and physics offered with Purdue University/ Indianapolis. Study abroad offered in 27 countries through the College Consortium for International Studies and in Cyprus, Greece, and Taiwan. BUILD Program for learning-disabled students. Cooperative education program. Evening and weekend classes; accelerated degree programs. Special facilities for using telecommunications in the classroom. Independent study. Cross-registration through metropolitan consortium. Television courses through cable TV. Noncredit continuing education classes.

ROTC: Army in cooperation with Indiana University-Purdue University at Indiana.

Degrees Conferred: 128 *associate;* 467 *baccalaureate* (B); 255 *master's* (M); 13 *doctorate* (D): biological/life sciences 27 (B), 3 (M); business/marketing 137 (B), 35 (D); communications/communication technologies 33 (B); computer and information sciences 3 (B); education 65 (B), 44 (M); English 5 (M); foreign languages and literature 6 (B); health professions and related sciences 35 (B), 152 (M); 4 (D); interdisciplinary studies 1 (M); liberal arts/general studies 37 (B); mathematics 2 (B); natural resources/environmental science 4 (B); parks and recreation 11 (B); philosophy/religion/theology 8 (B); physical sciences 11 (B); protective services/public administration 17 (B); psychology 39 (B), 8 (M); social sciences and history 24 (B), 6 (M); visual and performing arts 18 (B), 1 (M).

Fees and Other Expenses: *Full-time tuition per academic year 2005–06:* $17,980 undergraduate; $18,765 graduate. *Required fees:* $100. *Room and board per academic year:* $6,550.

Financial Aid: Aid from institutionally generated funds is provided on the basis of academic merit, financial need, athletic ability, other criteria. Institution has a Program Participation Agreement with the U.S. Department of Education for eligible students to receive Pell Grants and other federal aid.

Financial aid to full-time, first-time undergraduate students: need-based scholarships/grants totaling $7,961,516, self-help $10,016,225, tuition waivers $1,379,068; non-need-based scholarships/grants totaling $9,724,672, self-help $9,218,271, tuition waivers $2,184,559. *Graduate aid:* 400 students received federal and state-funded loans totaling $6,210,675 (ranging from $100 to $25,000); 110 other fellowships/grants totaling $400,115 (ranging from $900 to $23,000).

Departments and Teaching Staff: Arts and sciences *professors* 14, *associate professors* 31, *assistant professors* 28, *instructors* 11, *part-time faculty* 163; business 2, 7, 4, 1, 39; psychology 1, 1, 8, 0, 9; physical therapy 1, 3, 6, 1, 1; nursing 0, 7, 5, 5, 22; occupational therapy 0, 3, 5, 0, 5; education 0, 3, 12, 0, 17.

Total instructional faculty: 417 (full-time 161, part-time 117; women 197, men 220; members of minority groups 32). Total faculty with doctorate, first-professional, or other terminal degree: 208. Student-to-faculty ratio: 14:1. *Faculty development:* 13 faculty members awarded sabbaticals 2004–05.

Enrollment: Total enrollment 4,188. Undergraduate full-time 798 men / 1,412 women, part-time 220m / 715w; graduate full-time 127m / 285w, part-time 184m / 447w.

Characteristics of Student Body: *Ethnic and racial makeup:* number of Black non-Hispanic: 316; American Indian or Alaska Native: 10; Asian or Pacific Islander: 38; Hispanic: 49; White non-Hispanic: 2,497; unknown: 130. *Age distribution:* 17–21: 36%; 22–24: 15%; 25–29: 18%; 30–34: 12%; 35–39: 8%; 40–49: 10%; 50–59: 1%.

International Students: 145 nonresident aliens enrolled fall 2004. 23 students from Europe, 89 Asia, 4 Central and South America, 16 Africa, 5 Canada, 1 Australia, 7 other. Programs available to aid students whose native language is not English: social, cultural, financial. English as a Second Language Program. Financial aid specifically designated for international students: unlimited number of scholarships are available annually for undergraduate students; 33 totaling $186,740 awarded 2004–05.

Student Life: On-campus residence halls house 70% of undergraduates in 5 residence halls; apartments comprise 18% of college housing. *Intercollegiate athletics:* men: baseball, basketball, cross-country, football, golf, soccer, swimming and diving, tennis, track and field, wrestling; women: basketball, cross-country, golf, soccer, softball, swimming and diving, tennis, track and field, volleyball. *Special regulations:* Cars with parking stickers permitted in designated areas. Residence hall visitation from 12 noon to 11pm Sun. through Thurs; 12 noon to 2am Friday and Saturday. *Special services:* Health services, personal and spiritual counseling, tutoring, math laboratory, writing laboratory. *Student publications, radio: Oracle,* a yearbook; *Reflector,* a weekly newspaper. Radio station WICR-FM broadcasts 24 hours per day. *Surrounding community:* Indianapolis population over 1 million. Served by mass transit bus system, airport 10 miles from campus, passenger rail service 5 miles from campus.

Library Collections: 190,441 volumes. Online catalog. Current serial subscriptions: paper 1,004; microform 20,406. 500 recordings; 645 compact discs.

15 computer work stations. Access to online information retrieval systems and the Internet.

Most important holdings include Krannert Collection of rare books and fine bindings; University Archives (documents and artifacts); EUB and United Brethren Church books.

Buildings and Grounds: Campus area 65 acres.

Chief Executive Officer: Dr. Beverly J. Pitts, President.

Address admission inquiries to Ron Wilks, Director of Admissions.

University of Notre Dame

210 Main Building
Notre Dame, Indiana 46556
Tel: (574) 631-5000   **E-mail:** admissions@nd.edu
Fax: (574) 631-5872   **Internet:** www.nd.edu

Institution Description: The University of Notre Dame is a private, independent, nonprofit institution affiliated with the Congregation of Holy Cross, Indiana Province of Priests, Roman Catholic Church. *Enrollment:* 11,479. *Degrees awarded:* Baccalaureate, first-professional (law, master of divinity), master's, doctorate.

Accreditation: *Regional:* NCA. *Professional:* accounting, architecture, business, counseling psychology, engineering, law, psychology internship, theology

History: Established under present official name, University of Notre Dame du Lac, as secondary school and college, and offered first instruction at postsecondary level 1842; chartered 1844; awarded first degree (baccalaureate) 1849; discontinued secondary school 1927. *See* Thomas J. Schlereth, *The University of Notre Dame—A Portrait of Its History and Campus* (Notre Dame: University of Notre Dame Press, 1991) for further information.

Institutional Structure: *Governing board:* Fellows of the University of Notre Dame du Lac and the Board of Trustees. Extrainstitutional representation: 89 trustees, 12 fellows (6 laymen, 6 Holy Cross priests), 57 trustees active (all voting), 32 life trustees (nonvoting); institutional representation: president of the university, provost, executive vice-president, Religious Superior of Holy Cross Community at Notre Dame, Provincial Superior of Congregation of Holy Cross (Indiana Province). *Composition of institution:* Administrators to academic administrators 36 men / 8 women. Academic affairs headed by provost. Management/business/finances directed by executive vice president. Total instructional faculty 190. Academic governance body, Academic Council, meets an average of 4 times per year.

Calendar: Semesters. Academic year late Aug. to early May. Freshmen admitted Aug. Degrees conferred and formal commencement May.

Characteristics of Freshmen: 30% of applicants admitted. 57% of applicants admitted and enrolled.

67% (1,349 students) submitted SAT scores; 33% (635 students) submitted ACT scores. *25th percentile:* SAT Verbal 630, SAT Math 650; ACT Composite 30. *75th percentile:* SAT Verbal 730, SAT Math 740; ACT Composite 33.

8% of freshmen from Indiana. Freshmen from 49 states and 34 foreign countries.

Admission: Early action is the option for those who apply by Nov. 1. Decision letters are mailed in mid-Dec. Regular action is the option for those who apply by Dec. 31. Decision letters are mailed in early Apr. *Requirements:* Graduation from accredited secondary school with 4 units in English, 2 in a foreign language, 3–4 mathematics, 2 laboratory science, 1 history, 3–4 electives in above disciplines. Recommend additional units in history, language, science. *Entrance tests:* College Board SAT. *For transfer students:* 3.0 minimum GPA; from 4- and 2-year accredited institutions, 60 hours maximum transfer credit.

Advanced placement for postsecondary-level work completed in secondary school. College credit and advanced placement on basis of faculty assessment. Tutoring available.

Degree Requirements: *For all undergraduate degrees:* 120–162 credit hours; 2.0 GPA; 60 credit hours, including final year, in residence; 14 courses of university requirements; additional requirements for some programs. Exemption from some beginning courses possible by passing departmental examinations, International Baccalaureate, College Board AP. *Grading system:* A–F; pass-fail; withdraw (requires permission of dean); satisfactory-unsatisfactory.

Distinctive Educational Programs: Work-experience programs. Student involvement in faculty research. First year small seminary experience. Special facilities for using telecommunications in the classroom. Facilities and programs for independent research; including honors programs, tutorials. Study abroad in Innsbruck, Austria; Angers, France; Mexico City, Mexico; Rome, Italy; Jerusalem, Israel; London, England; Nagoya and Tokyo, Japan; Toledo, Spain; Dublin, Ireland; Freemantle, Australia; Cairo, Egypt; Santiago, Chile; Tianjin, China; and the Caribbean Program.

ROTC: Air Force, Army, Navy. 34 Air Force commissions awarded 2004; 12 Army commissions; 34 Navy commissions.

Degrees Conferred: 2,052 *baccalaureate* (B), 940 *master's* (M), 149 *doctorate* (D): architecture 43 (B), 7 (M); area and ethnic studies 44 (B); biological/life sciences 90 (B), 6 (M), 13 (D); business/marketing 580 (B), 484 (M); computer and information sciences 41 (B); education 1 (B), 156 (M); engineering and engineering technologies 194 (B), 74 (M), 33 (D); English 95 (B), 29 (M), 9 (D); foreign languages and literature 37 (B), 8 (M); health professions and related sciences 113 (B); interdisciplinary studies 25 (M), 8 (D); law/legal studies 23 (B), 1 (D); liberal arts/general studies 55 (B); mathematics 40 (B), 6 (M), 9 (D); natural resources/environmental science 16 (B); philosophy/religion/theology 58 (B), 28 (M), 26 (D); physical sciences 18 (B), 14 (M), 14 (D); protective services/public administration 15 (M); psychology 130 (B), 12 (M), 12 (D); social sciences and history 416 (B), 35 (M), 24 (D); visual and performing arts 81 (B), 18 (M). 176 *first-professional:* law 166, master of divinity 10.

Fees and Other Expenses: *Full-time tuition per academic year 2005–06:* undergraduate $31,100; graduate $31,000. *Required fees:* $442. *Room and board per academic year:* $8,010.

Financial Aid: Aid from institutionally generated funds is provided on the basis of academic merit, financial need, athletic ability, other criteria. Institution has a Program Participation Agreement with the U.S. Department of Education for eligible students to receive Pell Grants and other federal aid.

Financial aid to full-time, first-time undergraduate students: need-based scholarships/grants totaling $67,230,824, self-help $21,336,479, parent loans $34,136, tuition waivers $2,048,302, athletic awards $1,861,857; non-need-based scholarships/grants totaling $11,991,490, self-help $23,587,902, parent loans $7,318,333, tuition waivers $4,882,402, athletic awards $8,529,973.

Departments and Teaching Staff: *Professors* 359, *associate professors* 232, *assistant professors* 181, *instructors:* 8, *part-time faculty* 410.

Total instructional faculty: 1,190 (full-time 780, part-time 410; women 305, men 885; members of minority groups 126). Student-to-faculty ratio: 12.65:1.

Enrollment: Total enrollment 11,479. Undergraduate full-time 4,413 men / 3,896 women, part-time 16m / 7w; first-professional full-time 327m / 259w, part-time 1w; graduate full-time 1,493m / 809w, part-time 145m / 113w.

Characteristics of Student Body: *Ethnic/racial makeup:* number of Black non-Hispanic: 308; American Indian or Alaska Native: 57; Asian or Pacific Islander: 448; Hispanic: 682; White non-Hispanic: 6,515. *Age distribution:* under 18: 26; 18–19: 3,250; 20–21: 4,133; 22–24: 904; 25–29: 13; 30–34: 4; 35–39: 1; 40–49: 1.

International Students: 322 undergraduate non-resident aliens enrolled. Students from Europe, Asia, Central and South America, Africa, Canada, Australia, New Zealand. No programs available to aid students whose native language is not English. Financial aid for international students available on a limited basis.

Student Life: On-campus residence halls house 77% of student body. Residence halls for men constitute 53% of such space, for women 47%. Housing available for married and single graduate students. *Intercollegiate athletics:* men: baseball, basketball, cross-country, fencing, football, golf, hockey, lacrosse, soccer, swimming, tennis, track, wrestling; women: basketball, cross-country, fencing, golf, lacrosse, softball, swimming, tennis, track, volleyball. *Special regulations:* Parking in lots adjacent to campus. Quiet hours set by hall residents. Residence hall visitation until midnight Mon.-Thurs., until 2am Fri. and Sat. *Special services:* Office of Campus Ministry, Center for Social Concerns, Learning Resources Center, medical services, counseling services, shuttle bus to and from St. Mary's College and other off-campus locations. *Student publications, radio: The Dome,* a yearbook; *Juggler,* a biannual journal of arts; *The Observer,* a daily newspaper; *Scholastic,* a weekly magazine. Periodically published: *Notre Dame Student Business Review, Science Quarterly, Technical Review, Hunamitas.* Radio station WSND-FM and AM, each broadcasting 133 hours per week (AM does not broadcast during official school vacations). *Surrounding community:* South Bend population 108,000. Chicago, 90 miles from campus, is nearest metropolitan area. Served by airport and bus 5 miles from campus; passenger rail service 3 miles from campus.

Publications: *American Journal of Jurisprudence* (annually) first published in 1956, *American Midland Naturalist* (quarterly) first published 1908, *Journal of College and University Law,* (quarterly), first published in 1984; *Journal of Legislation* (biannually) first published 1974, *Notre Dame English Journal* (biannually) first published 1957, *Notre Dame Journal of Formal Logic* (quarterly) first published 1959, *Notre Dame Journal of Law, Ethics, and Public Policy,* (biannually), first published 1986; *Notre Dame Law Review* (published 5 times a year) first published 1925, *Review of Politics* (quarterly) first published 1939.

Library Collections: 2,797,065 volumes including bound periodicals and government documents not in separate collections. Current serial subscriptions: 9,885 paper; 5,750 via electronic access. 6,132 recordings. 6,669 compact discs. 47 CD-ROMS. 145 computer work stations. Online catalog. Students have access to online information retrieval services. Access to the Internet is at no charge.

Most important holdings include collections on Medieval Studies, including Ambrosiano Library Mss. (Milan, Italy); Catholic Americana; Dante Collection.

Buildings and Grounds: Campus area 1,250 acres. *New buildings:* Coleman-Morse Center completed 2000; Visiting Faculty Housing 2002; Hammes Mosbry Hall 2004; Performing Arts Center 2004.

Chief Executive Officer: Rev. Rev. John I. Jenkins, C.S.C., President.

Undergraduates address admission inquiries to Director of Admissions; graduate student inquiries to Graduate Recruitment and Admissions.

Notre Dame Law School

Degree Programs Offered: *First-professional.*

Admission: Graduation from approved college or university; LSAT, LSDAS.

Degree Requirements: 90 credit hours; 6 semester in residence.

Distinctive Educational Programs: Joint J.D.-M.B.A.; joint J.D.-M.Div. with Graduate School; LL.M. offered both in South Bend, Indiana and London England. Notre Dame is the only American law school offering a full year of study abroad for the J.D. student.

Graduate School

Degree Programs Offered: *Master's, doctorate* in various fields; *first-professional* (master of divinity).

Admission: *For first-professional:* Baccalaureate from university or college, including 18 hours philosophy; GRE.

Degree Requirements: *For first-professional:* 72 credit hours; 3.0 GPA; 12 months in residence.

Departments and Teaching Staff: Faculty drawn from the university.

Distinctive Educational Programs: Interdisciplinary programs in African studies, Asian studies, biochemistry, biophysics, chemical physics, Latin American studies, Soviet and East European studies, West European studies. Research facilities include Center for Philosophy of Religion, Center for the Study of Man in Contemporary Society, Computing Center, Cushwa Center for the Study of American Catholicism, Kellogg Institute for International Studies, Institute for Urban Studies, Laboratory of Biology (LOBUND), Radiation Laboratory, Social Science Training Research Laboratory, Vector Biology Laboratory, Center for Applied Mathematics, Center for Bioengineering and Pollution Control, Center for Catalysis and Reaction Engineering.

University of Saint Francis

2701 Spring Street
Fort Wayne, Indiana 46808-3994

Tel: (260) 434-3279   **E-mail:** admis@sf.edu
Fax: (260) 434-7590   **Internet:** www.sf.edu

Institution Description: University of Saint Francis is a private, independent, nonprofit institution affiliated with the Sisters of St. Francis of Perpetual Adoration, Roman Catholic Church. *Enrollment:* 1,883. *Degrees awarded:* Associate, baccalaureate, master's.

Accreditation: *Regional:* NCA. *Professional:* art, nursing, nursing education, occupational therapy, physician assisting, surgeon assisting, social work, teacher education

History: Established in Layfayette, Indiana and offered first instruction at postsecondary level 1890; accredited as a two-year normal school 1928; awarded first degree (baccalaureate) 1940; relocated to Fort Wayne 1944; . absorbed Lutheran College of Health Professions and achieved university status 1998.

Institutional Structure: *Governing board:* University of Saint Francis Board of Trustees. Extrainstitutional representation: 13 trustees, Provincial of the Order, Vice-Provincial and Provincial Treasurer, Chairman of Citizens' (Advisory) Board; institutional representation: 3 administrators. 7 ex officio. All voting. *Composition of institution:* Administrators 4 men / 8 women. Academic affairs headed by vice president for academic affairs. Management/business/finances directed by vice president for finance. Full-time instructional faculty 95. Academic governance body, Faculty Forum, meets 6 times per year.

Calendar: Semesters. Academic year Aug. to May. Freshmen admitted Aug., Jan., June. Degrees conferred and formal commencement May. Summer session from early June to early Aug.

Characteristics of Freshmen: 81% of applicants accepted. 39% of accepted applicants enrolled.

74% (259 students) submitted SAT scores; 34% (120 students) submitted ACT scores. *25th percentile:* SAT Verbal 430, SAT Math 430; ACT Composite

18, ACT English 16, ACT Math 16. *75th percentile*: SAT Verbal 530, SAT Math 540; ACT Composite 22, ACT English 22, ACT Math 23.

81% of freshmen from Indiana. Freshmen from 3 states.

Admission: Rolling admissions plan. For fall acceptance, apply as early as the end of junior year of secondary school, but not later than the first day of classes. Early acceptance available. *Requirements:* Either graduation from accredited secondary school or GED. Recommend 4 units English, 2 in a foreign language, 2 mathematics, 2 science, 2 social studies. *Entrance tests:* College Board SAT or ACT composite. For foreign students TOEFL. *For transfer students:* 2.0 minimum GPA; from 4-year accredited institution 92 semester hours maximum transfer credit.

Advanced placement for postsecondary-level work completed in secondary school. Tutoring available. Remedial courses offered; credit awarded.

Degree Requirements: *For all associate degrees:* 64 credit hours; 16 hours in residence. *For all baccalaureate degrees:* 128 credit hours; 32 hours in residence; exit competency examination (Academic Profile; English Proficiency). *For all undergraduate degrees:* 2.0 GPA; general education requirements. Fulfillment of some degree requirements and exemption from some beginning courses possible by passing departmental examination, College Board CLEP. *Grading system:* A–F; satisfactory-unsatisfactory; withdraw (deadline after which satisfactory-unsatisfactory appended to withdraw); incomplete (carries time limit).

Distinctive Educational Programs: *For undergraduates:* Work-experience programs, including internships and practica. Cooperative baccalaureate program in medical technology with affiliated hospitals. Cooperative associate degree in radiology technology with area hospital. Interdepartmental programs in American studies, biology-chemistry, communications, English, environmental studies, health and safety, international studies, social studies, and social work. Study abroad by individual arrangement. Honors Program. Preprofessional programs in dentistry, medicine. *Available to all students:* Evening classes. Tutorials. *Other distinctive programs:* Bachelor of Liberal Studies for adult learners. Weekend College available for working adults over the age of 25.

Degrees Conferred: 142 *associate;* 176 *baccalaureate* (B); 61 *master's* (M): biological/life sciences 4 (B); business/marketing 43 (B), 17 (M); education 23 (B), 21 (M); English 2 (B); health professions and related sciences 41 (B), 12 (M); liberal arts/general studies 10 (B); natural resources/environmental science 1 (B); philosophy/religion/theology 3 (B); physical sciences 6 (B); protective services/public administration 3 (B); psychology 7 (B), 8 (M); visual and performing arts 26 (B), 3 (M).

Fees and Other Expenses: *Tuition per academic year 2004–05:* $14,900. Graduate study charged per credit hour. *Required fees:* $588. *Room and board per academic year:* $5,450.

Financial Aid: Aid from institutionally generated funds is provided on the basis of academic merit, financial need, athletic ability, other criteria. Institution has a Program Participation Agreement with the U.S. Department of Education for eligible students to receive Pell Grants and other federal aid.

Financial aid to full-time, first-time undergraduate students: need-based scholarships/grants totaling $8,094,734, self-help $6,698,369, parent loans $516,183, tuition waivers $167,659, athletic awards $1,616,878; non-need-based scholarships/grants totaling $712,862, self-help $2,256,510, parent loans $928,268, tuition waivers $172,457, athletic awards $442,566. *Graduate aid:* 157 federal and state-funded loans totaling $1,996,389 (ranging from $130 to $18,500).

Departments and Teaching Staff: *Total instructional faculty:* 192 (full-time 95, part-time 97; women 120, men 72; members of minority groups 13). Total faculty with doctorate, first-professional, or other terminal degree: 53. Student-to-faculty ratio: 11:1.

Enrollment: Total enrollment 1,834. Undergraduate full-time 414 men / 815 women, part-time 58m / 321w; graduate full-time 19m / 58w, part-time 39m / 110w. *Transfer students:* in-state 765; from out-of-state 46.

Characteristics of Student Body: *Ethnic/racial makeup:* number of Black non-Hispanic: 70; American Indian or Alaska Native: 5; Asian or Pacific Islander: 18' Hispanic: 28; White non-Hispanic: 1,151; unknown: 374. *Age distribution:* under 18: 1; 18–19: 326; 20–21: 446; 22–24: 344; 25–29: 185; 30–34: 101; 35–39: 88; 40–49: 113; 50–64: 44; 65 and over: 2.

International Students: 7 nonresident aliens enrolled fall 2004. Programs available to aid students whose native language is not English: English as a Second Language Program. No financial aid specifically designated for international students.

Student Life: On-campus residence halls house 32% of the full-time undergraduate student body. Residence halls for women constitute 58% of available space; for men 42% of such space. *Intercollegiate athletics:* men only: baseball, basketball, cross-country, football, golf, soccer, track and field; women only: basketball, cross-country, golf, soccer, softball, tennis, track and field, volleyball. *Special regulations:* Cars must have parking decals. *Special services:* Learning Resources Center, medical services. *Student publications, Broadsheet,* a triannual literary publication. *Surrounding community:* Fort Wayne population

175,000. Indianapolis, 120 miles from campus, is nearest metropolitan area. Served by mass transit bus system; airport and passenger rail service 3 miles from campus.

Library Collections: 85,600 volumes. 618,500 microforms; 1,500 audiovisual materials; 510 current periodical subscriptions. Online catalog. Students have access to online information retrieval services and the Internet.

Most important special holdings include ERIC and Psychlit.

Buildings and Grounds: Campus area 75 acres.

Chief Executive Officer: Sr. M. Elise Kriss, O.S.F., President.

Address admission inquiries Jamie McGrath, Enrollment Services Data Manager.

University of Southern Indiana

8600 University Boulevard
Evansville, Indiana 47712
Tel: (812) 465-8600   **E-mail:** enroll@usi.edu
Fax: (812) 464-1956   **Internet:** www.usi.edu

Institution Description: *Enrollment:* 10,050. *Degrees awarded:* Associate, baccalaureate, masters.

Accreditation: *Regional:* NCA. *Professional:* accounting, business, chemistry, dental assisting, dental hygiene, engineering, nursing, nursing education, occupational therapy, radiography, respiratory therapy, social work, teacher education

History: Established as the Evansville regional campus of Indiana State University (Terre Haute) and offered first instruction at postsecondary level 1965; awarded first degrees 1971; made separate state university by Indiana General Assembly and adopted present name 1985.

Institutional Structure: *Governing board:* 9 members appointed by the Governor of Indiana (one must be a resident of Vanderburgh County; one must be a graduate of the institution; one must be a student). *Composition of institution:* Administrators 118 men / 166 women. Academic affairs headed by provost/vice president for academic affairs. Business and finance headed by vice president for business affairs. Student Services headed by vice president for student affairs. Public Relations and Development headed by vice president for advancement. Academic governance body, Faculty Senate, meets an average of 15 times per year.

Calendar: Semesters. Academic year Aug. to May. Freshmen admitted Aug., Jan., June, July. Degrees conferred and formal commencement May.

Characteristics of Freshmen: 92.1% of applicants admitted. 50.2% of applicants admitted and enrolled.

79% (1,667 students) submitted SAT scores; 32% (733 students) submitted ACT scores. *25th percentile:* SAT Verbal 420, SAT Math 420; ACT Composite 17, ACT English 16, ACT Math 16. *75th percentile:* SAT Verbal 530, SAT Math 530; ACT Composite 22, ACT English 22, ACT Math 22.

18.4% of entering freshmen expected to graduate within 5 years. 95.1% of freshmen from Indiana. Freshmen from 18 states and 4 foreign countries.

Admission: Rolling admissions plan. For fall acceptance, apply as early as completion of junior year of secondary school, but not later than Aug. 15 of year of enrollment. Early acceptance available. *Requirements* and *entrance tests:* See main entry. *For transfer students:* 2.0 minimum GPA; from 4-year accredited institution 94 semester hours maximum transfer credit; from 2-year accredited institution 64 hours.

College credit and advanced placement for postsecondary-level work completed in secondary school. College credit for extrainstitutional learning on basis of ACE *2006 Guide to the Evaluation of Educational Experiences in the Armed Services.* Tutoring available. Noncredit remedial courses offered during regular academic year.

Degree Requirements: *For all associate degrees:* 64 semester hours; 18 hours in residence. *For all baccalaureate degrees:* 124 semester hours; 2.0 GPA; 30 hours in residence; 2 credit hours of physical education; general education requirements. *Grading system:* A–F; pass-fail; withdraw (carries penalty and time limit).

Distinctive Educational Programs: Weekend and evening classes. Accelerated degree programs. Study abroad in over 50 countries. Internet baccalaureate completion in nursing.

ROTC: 7 Army commissions awarded 2004.

Degrees Conferred: 174 *associate;* 1,091 *baccalaureate* (B); 164 *master's* (M): biological/life sciences 27 (B); business/marketing 250 (B), 42 (M); communications/communication technologies 139 (B); computer and information sciences 37 (B); education 161 (B), 36 (M); engineering and engineering technologies 6 (B); English 33 (B); foreign languages and literature 12 (B); health professions and related sciences 167 (B), 42 (M); interdisciplinary studies 3 (B); liberal arts/general studies 9 (B), 1 (M); mathematics 5 (B); parks and recreation

12 (B); philosophy/religion/theology 3 (B); physical sciences 12 (B); protective services/public administration 37 (B), 43 (M); psychology 48 (B); social sciences and history 92 (B); visual and performing arts 38 (B). *Honorary degrees awarded 2004:* Doctor of Civil Law 1, Doctor of Law 2.

Fees and Other Expenses: *Full-time tuition per academic year 2004–05:* undergraduate in-state resident $4,017, out-of-state student $9,582; graduate resident $3,510, out-of-state student $6,430. *Required fees:* $122 freshmen, $60 other. *Room and board per academic year:* $5,480.

Financial Aid: Aid from institutionally generated funds is provided on the basis of academic merit, financial need, athletic ability, other criteria. Institution has a Program Participation Agreement with the U.S. Department of Education for eligible students to receive Pell Grants and other federal aid.

Financial aid to full-time, first-time undergraduate students: need-based scholarships/grants totaling $13,068,758, self-help $13,974,299, parent loans $2,619,384, tuition waivers $258,268, athletic awards $304,317; non-need-based scholarships/grants totaling $2,081,507, self-help $4,740,741, parent loans $1,692,797, tuition waivers $392,671, athletic awards $391,252. *Graduate aid:* 93 students received federal and state-funded fellowships and grants totaling $56,136 (ranging from $2,100 to $5,000); 142 federal and state-funded loans totaling $1,431,580 (ranging from $596 to $18,500).

Departments and Teaching Staff: *Professors* 40, *associate professors* 72, *assistant professors* 90, *instructors* 85, *part-time faculty* 281. *Total instructional faculty:* 576 (full-time 295, part-time 281; women 296, men 280; members of minority groups 35). Total faculty with doctorate, first-professional, or other terminal degree: 237. Student-to-faculty ratio: 18.8:1. *Faculty development:* $156,792 in grants for research. 7 faculty members awarded sabbaticals 2004–05.

Enrollment: Total enrollment 10,050. Undergraduate full-time 3,049 men / 4,377 women, part-time 659m / 1,132w; graduate full-time 33m / 83w, part-time 189m / 528w.

Characteristics of Student Body: *Ethnic and racial makeup:* number of Black non-Hispanic: 417; American Indian or Alaska Native: 20; Asian or Pacific Islander: 53; Hispanic: 63; White non-Hispanic: 8,596. *Age distribution:* under 18: 7; 18–19: 2,722; 20–21: 2,752; 22–24: 1,973; 25–29: 769; 30–34: 368; 35–39: 221; 40–49: 296; 50–64: 104; 65 and over: 5.

International Students: 73 nonresident aliens enrolled fall 2004. 16 students from Europe, 53 Asia, 7 Central and South America, 7 Africa, 3 Canada, 2 other. Programs available to aid students whose native language is not English: English as a Second Language Program. No financial aid specifically designated for international students.

Student Life: Privately owned and operated student housing for 3,000 students adjacent to campus. *Intercollegiate athletics:* men only: baseball, basketball, golf, soccer, tennis, cross-country; women only: basketball, cross-country, soccer, softball, tennis, volleyball. *Special services:* Health services, intramurals, Greek Life, orientation. *Student publications: The Shield,* a weekly student newspaper. *Surrounding community:* Evansville population 180,500. Louisville (KY), St. Louis (MO), Nashville (TN), Indianapolis (IN) are all within 2-4 hours travel time. Served by mass transit system. Airport 12 miles from campus.

Library Collections: 247,329 volumes. Online catalog. Current serial subscriptions: 661 paper, 577,668 microform, 11,763 via electronic access. 586 compact discs; 294 CD-ROMs. 94 computer work stations. Students have access to the Internet at no charge. Total 2004–05 budget for books and materials: $582,531.

Most important holdings include Mead Johnson Company Archives; Petroleum Information Geological Data Library; Don Blair Collection of photos.

Buildings and Grounds: *New buildings:* Recreation and Fitness Center completed 2001; Science and Education Center 2003.

Chief Executive Officer: Dr. H. Ray Hoops, President.

Address undergraduate admission inquiries to Eric Otto, Director of Admissions; graduate inquiries to Dr. Peggy Harrel, Director of Graduate Studies.

Valparaiso University

U.S. HIghway 30
Valparaiso, Indiana 46383
Tel: (219) 464-5000   **E-mail:** admissions@valpo.edu
Fax: (219) 464-5381   **Internet:** www.valpo.edu

Institution Description: Valparaiso University is a private institution affiliated with the Lutheran Church-Missouri Synod. *Enrollment:* 3,969. *Degrees awarded:* Associate, baccalaureate, first-professional (law), master's. Education specialist certificate also awarded.

Accreditation: *Regional:* NCA. *Professional:* business, chemistry, engineering, law, music, nursing, nursing education, social work, teacher education

History: Established and chartered as Valparaiso Male and Female Academy, and offered first instruction at postsecondary level 1859; awarded first degree (baccalaureate) 1863; closed 1869; reopened as Northern Indiana Normal School and Business Institute 19873; changed name to Valparaiso College 1900; adopted present name 1907. Purchased by the Lutheran University Association in 1925, and independent organization promoting higher education in the Lutheran-Christian tradition. *See* John H. Strietelmeier, *Valparaiso's First Century* (Valparaiso: Valparaiso University, 1959) for further information.

Institutional Structure: *Governing board:* Lutheran University Association. Representation: 33 directors including president of the university, president of the University Guild, president of the Alumni Association, ex officio. All voting. *Composition of institution:* Administrators 35 men / 23 women. Academic affairs headed by provost and vice president for academic affairs. Management/business/finances directed by vice president for administration and finance. Full-time instructional faculty 237. Academic governance body, University Council, meets at least once a month during the regular academic year.

Calendar: Semesters. Academic year Aug. to May. Freshmen admitted Aug., Jan., May, June. Degrees conferred May, Aug., Dec. Formal commencement May. Summer session mid-June to early Aug.

Characteristics of Freshmen: 81% of applicants admitted. 21% of applicants admitted and enrolled.

55% (415 students) submitted SAT scores; 71% (536 students) submitted ACT scores. *25th percentile*: SAT Verbal 530, SAT Math 530; ACT Composite 23, ACT English 23, ACT Math 23. *75th percentile*: SAT Verbal 630, SAT Math 640; ACT Composite 29, ACT English 29, ACT Math 29.

73% of entering freshmen expected to graduate within 5 years. 32% of freshmen from Indiana. Freshmen from 39 states and 6 foreign countries.

Admission: Rolling admissions plan. Early action available. *Requirements:* Either graduation from accredited secondary school or GED. Recommend 4 units English, 3 college preparatory mathematics, 2 laboratory science, 2 history, 3 additional science, history, social sciences, language, English, and mathematics courses. Additional requirements: College of Arts and Sciences - 2 foreign language; College of Business Administration - 2 units of algebra and 1 unit of geometry; College of Engineering - a 4th unit of mathematics with at least precalculus, 3 laboratory science including chemistry and physics; College of Nursing - 3 laboratory science including biology and chemistry. *Entrance tests:* College Board SAT and ACT accepted. *For transfer students:* 2.0 minimum GPA, 3.0 GPA for Nursing. 94 semester hours maximum transfer credit. For engineering program, 106 hours.

College credit and advanced placement for postsecondary-level work completed in secondary school. College credit for extrainstitutional learning on basis of ACE *2006 Guide to the Evaluation of Educational Experiences in the Armed Services.* Tutoring available. Noncredit developmental courses offered.

Degree Requirements: *For all associate degrees:* 60-61 semester hours. *For all baccalaureate degrees:* 124–150 hours; 1 credit physical education. *For all undergraduate degrees:* 2.0 GPA; 2 semesters in residence; general education requirements.

Fulfillment of some degree requirements and exemption from some beginning courses possible by passing institutional examinations, College Board CLEP, AP. *Grading system:* A–F; pass-fail; withdraw (carries time limit).

Distinctive Educational Programs: Evening classes. Combined liberal arts-engineering program. Special facilities for using telecommunications in the classroom. Minors in applied statistics, business administration, Chinese and Japanese studies, criminology, ethnic studies, film studies, gender studies, human aging, American studies, environmental science, international business, global studies, bioethics, electronics, liberal arts, business, manufacturing management, and political communication. Facilities and programs for independent research, including honors program, individual majors, tutorials. Programs of studies in deaconess ministry. Independent group studies program. Washington (DC) semester at American University. United Nations (NY) semester with Drew University (NJ). Christ College, an honors college emphasizing liberal studies, draws members from the 4 undergraduate schools within the university. Study abroad in China, England, France, Germany, Greece, Japan, Mexico, Namibia.

ROTC: Air Force in cooperation with University of Notre Dame. 5 commissions awarded 2004.

Degrees Conferred: 669 *baccalaureate* (B), 86 77 *master's* (M): area and ethnic studies 1 (B); biological/life sciences 33 (B); business/marketing 97 (B), 9 (M); communications/communication technologies 44 (B); computer and information sciences 9 (B); education 35 (B), 23 (M); engineering and engineering technologies 75 (B); English 34 (B), 3 (M); foreign languages and literature 14 (B); health professions and related sciences 31 (B), 3 (M); interdisciplinary studies 25 (B), 12 (M); law/legal studies 4 (M); mathematics 10 (B); natural resources/environmental science 2 (B); parks and recreation 20 (B), 1 (M); philosophy/religion/theology 14 (B), 1 (M); physical sciences 29 (B); protective services/public administration 11 (B); psychology 32 (B), 17 (M); social sciences and history 95 (B), 11 (M); visual and performing arts 58 (B). *First-professional:* law 145.

Fees and Other Expenses: *Full-time tuition per academic year 2005–06:* $22,000 undergraduate; $375 per credit hour for graduate/first-professional programs. *Required fees:* $750. *Room and board per academic year:* $6,220.

Financial Aid: Valparaiso University has a direct lending program. Aid from institutionally generated funds is provided on the basis of academic merit, financial need, athletic ability, other criteria. Institution has a Program Participation Agreement with the U.S. Department of Education for eligible students to receive Pell Grants and other federal aid.

Financial aid to full-time, first-time undergraduate students: need-based scholarships/grants totaling $24,420,000, self-help $9,050,000, tuition waivers $900,000, athletic awards $1,030,000; non-need-based scholarships/grants totaling $5,500,000, self-help $7,210,000, parent loans $3,000,000, tuition $600,000, waivers athletic awards $1,070,000. *Graduate aid:* 5 students received federal and state-funded fellowships and grants totaling $13,878; 121 federal and state-funded loans totaling $1,567,732 (ranging from $700 to $18,500); 1 work-study job worth $989; 24 other college-assigned jobs totaling $119,042.

Departments and Teaching Staff: *Professors 65, associate professors 76, assistant professors 71, instructors 25, part-time faculty 125. Total instructional faculty:* 362 (full-time 237, part-time 125; women 141, men 221; members of minority groups 29). Total faculty with doctorate, first-professional, or other terminal degree: 275. Student-to-faculty ratio: 13:1. *Faculty development:* $184,000 in grants for research. 10 faculty members awarded sabbaticals 2004–05.

Enrollment: Total enrollment 3,969. Undergraduate full-time 1,401 men / 1,496 women, part-time 50m / 120w; first-professional full-time 247m / 266w, part-time 27m / 21w; graduate full-time 58m / 104w, part-time 61m / 118w. *Transfer students:* in-state 103; from out-of-state 180.

Characteristics of Student Body: *Ethnic/racial makeup:* number of Black non-Hispanic: 114; American Indian or Alaska Native: 8; Asian or Pacific Islander: 50; Hispanic: 92; White non-Hispanic: 2,618; unknown: 123. *Age distribution:* number under 18: 26; 18–19: 1,845; 20–21: 1,273; 22–24: 256; 25–29: 45; 30–34: 25; 35–39: 26; 40–49: 51; 50–64: 19; 65 and over: 2.

International Students: 88 nonresident aliens enrolled fall 2004. 20 students from Europe, 28 Asia, 10 Central and South America, 6 Africa, 2 Canada, 22 Middle East. Programs available to aid students whose native language is not English: English as a Second Language Program. Variable number of scholarships available annually for international students; $85,000 awarded 2004–05.

Student Life: On-campus residence halls house 65% of student body. Approximately 21% of students join fraternities and sororities. *Intercollegiate athletics:* men only: baseball, basketball, cross-country, football, soccer, swimming, tennis, track; women only: basketball, cross country, soccer, softball, swimming, tennis, track, volleyball. *Special regulations:* Cars permitted for all but freshmen. Quiet hours. *Special services:* Writing Center, Health Center. . *Student publications, radio:* The Beacon, a yearbook; The Lighter, a biannual literary magazine; The Torch, a weekly newspaper. Radio station WVUR broadcasts 143 hours per week. *Surrounding community:* Valparaiso population 26,000 is 50 miles from South Bend and 60 miles from Chicago. Major airports serve Chicago and South Bend.

Publications: *The Cresset* (5 times per year) first published 1937.

Library Collections: 1,148,473 volumes including bound books, serial backfiles, electronic documents, and government documents not in separate collections. Online catalog. 21,360 total serial subscriptions. 1,453 recordings. 1,140 compact discs. 1,821 CD-ROMs. 758 computer work stations on campus. Students have access to the Internet at no charge. Total 2004–05 budget for books and materials: $1,333,623.

Most important special holdings include Lutheran File; Restoration era theology materials; Indiana legal materials.

Buildings and Grounds: Campus area 310 acres. *New buildings:* Christopher Center for Library and Information Resources completed 2004.

Chief Executive Officer: Dr. Alan F. Harre, President.

Undergraduates address admission inquiries to Janice Lantz, Director of Admissions; graduate study inquiries to Dr. David Rowland, Dean of Graduate Studies; School of Law inquiries to Tony Credit, Executive Director of Admissions.

College of Arts and Sciences

Degree Programs Offered: *Associate* in general science; *baccalaureate* in American studies, applied music, art, biology, broadcast meteorology, chemistry, Chinese and Japanese studies, communications, economics, economics and computer analysis, elementary education, secondary education, English, environmental science, French, German, classics, Spanish, geography, meteorology, geology, history, individualized, international economics and cultural affairs, international service, mathematics, computer science, modern European stud-

ies, music, church music, music composition, music performance, music equation, music enterprises, music/theatre, philosophy, pre-seminary studies, physical education, athletic training, sports management, exercise science, physics, political science, psychology, social work, sociology, criminology, theatre and television arts, theology; *master's* in counseling, school psychology, English, history, human behavior and society, individualized, teaching and learning, special education, music, music performance, church music, music education.

Distinctive Educational Programs: Cooperative program in geological and geographical sciences with Indiana University Northwest through Valparaiso-Indiana Geography and Geology Association. Combined liberal arts-medical arts program. Interdisciplinary program in applied statistics, business administration, ethnic studies, film studies, gender studies, human aging, manufacturing management, political communication, liberal arts business minor.

Enrollment: Total enrollment: 2,291. Undergraduate full-time 1,931, part-time 120; graduate full-=time 133, part-time 107.

College of Business Administration

Degree Programs Offered: *Baccalaureate* in accounting, decision science, finance, management, marketing, international business.

Distinctive Educational Programs: Cooperative education, internships, and double major in the College of Business Administration.

Enrollment: Total enrollment: 492. Undergraduate full-time 420, part-time 12; graduate full-time 16, part-time 34.

College of Engineering

Degree Programs Offered: *Baccalaureate* in civil, computer, electrical, and mechanical engineering.

Distinctive Educational Programs: Cooperative education, internships, Valparaiso International engineering Program. Minors in digital systems design and manufacturing management. Double-degree program in engineering and arts and sciences and business administration.

Enrollment: Total enrollment: 350. Undergraduate full-time 343, part-time 7.

College of Nursing

Degree Programs Offered: *Baccalaureate, master's, post-master's* nursing, family nurse practitioner.

Distinctive Educational Programs: Register nurses, accelerated, and transfer students may complete the requirements for the baccalaureate degree in less than 4 years. Registered nurses in the RN-MSN program may complete the BSN and MSN degree in less than 3 years. Parish nurse program and advanced nurse education program for graduate students.

Enrollment: Total enrollment: 270. Undergraduate full-time 193 part-time 32; graduate full-time 11, part-time 34.

School of Law

Degree Programs Offered: *J.D., L.L.M., JD/MBA, JD/MA, JD/MALS, JD/MS.*

Admission: Baccalaureate degree; LSAT.

Degree Requirements: 90 credit hours; average GPA 2.00 and pro bono internship requirement. Passing grade in all courses on a scale of A-F; S/U (Satisfactory/Unsatisfactory).

Enrollment: Total enrollment: 567. First-professional full-time 513, part-time 48.

Wabash College

301 West Wabash Avenue
P.O. Box 352
Crawfordsville, Indiana 47933-0352

Tel: (765) 361-6100   **E-mail:** admissions@wabash.edu
Fax: (765) 361-6437   **Internet:** www.wabash.edu

Institution Description: Wabash College is a private, independent, college. *Enrollment:* 857. *Degrees awarded:* Baccalaureate.

Member of the consortium Great Lakes Colleges Association (GLCA).

Accreditation: *Regional:* NCA.

History: Established as Wabash Manual Labor College and Teachers Seminary 1832; chartered 1834; awarded first degree (baccalaureate) 1838; adopted present name 1851. *See* James Insley Osborne and Theodore Gregory Gronert, *Wabash College The First Hundred Years* (Crawfordsville, IN: R.E. Banta, 1932) for further information.

Institutional Structure: *Governing board:* The Board of Trustees. Representation: 31 trustees (including 6 elected by alumni), 12 emeritus trustees; institutional representation: president of the college. 1 ex officio. 31 voting. *Composition of institution:* Administrators 5 men, 1 woman. Academic affairs headed by dean of the college. Management/business/finances directed by financial officer. Total instructional faculty 90. Academic governance body, the faculty, meets an average of 15 times per year.

Calendar: Semesters. Academic year Aug. to May. Freshmen admitted Aug., Jan. Degrees conferred and formal commencement May. No summer session.

Characteristics of Freshmen: 49% of applicants admitted. 37% of applicants admitted and enrolled.

90% (224 students) submitted SAT scores; 45% (111 students) submitted ACT scores. *25th percentile:* SAT Verbal 530, SAT Math 550; ACT Composite 23, ACT English 21, ACT Math 23. *75th percentile:* SAT Verbal 650, SAT Math 660; ACT Composite 28, ACT English 28, ACT Math 28.

69% of entering freshmen expected to graduate within 5 years. 72% of freshmen from Indiana. Freshmen from 18 states and 10 foreign countries.

Admission: Rolling admissions plan. Early decision closing date is Dec. 1 with notification by Dec. 15. Non-binding early action: apply by Dec. 1, notification by Dec. 15. For fall acceptance, apply as early as Oct. 1 of previous year, but not later than July 1 of year of enrollment. *Requirements:* Graduation from accredited secondary school with 13 units which normally include 4 English, 2 foreign language, 3 mathematics, 2 laboratory science, 2 social studies; GED accepted in exceptional cases. Preferred minimum GPA 3.0. Preferred secondary school class standing top one third. *Entrance tests:* College Board SAT or ACT composite. *For transfer students:* 2.0 minimum GPA, 17 liberal arts courses maximum transfer credit, 3 terms in residence.

College credit and advanced placement for postsecondary-level work completed in secondary school.

Degree Requirements: 34 course credits; 2.0 GPA; 4 terms in residence; distribution and course requirements; oral and written examination in individual fields of study. Fulfillment of some degree requirements and exemption from some beginning courses possible by passing departmental examinations, College Board CLEP, APP. *Grading system:* A–F; withdraw (deadline after which pass-fail is appended to withdraw); incomplete (must finish by semester's end); condition (a failing grade which may be improved to D by semester's end); credit only.

Distinctive Educational Programs: Work-experience programs. Dual degree programs in engineering with Columbia University (NY), Washington University (MO). Interdepartmental/interdisciplinary programs in cultures and traditions, environmental problems, Far Eastern area studies, international studies, physical sciences. Facilities for independent research, including individual majors, tutorials. Institutionally sponsored study abroad in Greece, Italy. Study abroad through the Institute of European Studies in Austria, England, France, Germany, and Spain. Study abroad through Associated Colleges of the Midwest (ACM) and GLCA at the Chinese University in Hong Kong, in India, at the Waseda University in Tokyo (cosponsored by Waseda). Study abroad through GLCA in Colombia; in Africa in Ghana, Kenya, Liberia, Nigeria, Sierra Leone; and at the University of Dakar in Senegal. Also through GLCA, Comparative Urban Studies in Europe at the University of Aberdeen in Scotland. Individually arranged study abroad. Informal program with Queen Elizabeth College of the University of London. Off-campus study in the U.S. through ACM and GLCA includes Newberry Library Program (Chicago, IL), Oak Ridge Science Semester (TN); through GLCA, New York Arts Program, Philadelphia Urban Semester (PA). Washington (DC) Semester in cooperation with American University.

Degrees Conferred: 181 *baccalaureate:* biological/life science 9; English 29; foreign languages and literature 17; mathematics 14; philosophy/religion/theology 24; physical sciences 10; psychology 22; social science and history 73; visual and performing arts 5.

Fees and Other Expenses: *Full-time tuition per academic year 2004–05:* $22,964. *Required fees:* $424. *Room and board per academic year:* $6,728.

Financial Aid: Wabash College has a direct lending program. Aid from institutionally generated funds is provided on the basis of academic merit, financial need, other criteria. Institution has a Program Participation Agreement with the U.S. Department of Education for eligible students to receive Pell Grants and other federal aid.

Financial aid to full-time, first-time undergraduate students: need-based scholarships/grants totaling $8,258,569, self-help $2,531,683, tuition waivers $186,792; non-need-based scholarships/grants totaling $3,559,747, self-help $2,420,243, tuition waivers $21,870.

Departments and Teaching Staff: *Total instructional faculty:* 90 (full-time 87, part-time 2; women 19, men 71; members of minority groups 5). Total faculty with doctorate, first-professional, or other terminal degree: 82. Student-to-faculty ratio: 10:1. *Faculty development:* $2,763,893 in grants for research.

Enrollment: Total enrollment 853. Undergraduate full-time 845 men, part-time 8.

Characteristics of Student Body: *Ethnic/racial makeup:* number of Black non-Hispanic: 59; American Indian or Alaska Native 1; Asian or Pacific Islander; 27; Hispanic: 35; White non-Hispanic: 680; unknown: 17. *Age distribution:* 99% of students under 23.

International Students: 34 nonresident aliens enrolled fall 2004. 5 students from Europe, 18 Asia, 2 Central and South America, 6 Africa, 3 Canada. Programs available to aid students whose native language is not English: Financial. Variable number of scholarships awarded annually.

Student Life: On-campus residence halls house 16% of student body. 75% of men join and 68% live in fraternities. *Intercollegiate athletics:* men only: baseball, basketball, cross-country, football, golf, soccer, swimming, tennis, track, wrestling. *Special regulations:* Cars permitted without restrictions. *Special services:* Medical services. *Student publications, radio:* The Bachelor, a weekly newspaper; *The Wabash Review,* a biannual literary magazine; *The Wabash Yearbook.* Radio station WNDY broadcasts 126 hours per week. *Surrounding community:* Crawfordsville population 15,000. Indianapolis, 45 miles from campus, is nearest metropolitan area. Served by airport 45 miles from campus; passenger rail service 1 mile from campus.

Library Collections: 434,460 volumes. Online and card catalogs. Current serial subscriptions: 5,530 paper; 11,359 microform. 11,151 recordings. Access to online information retrieval systems. 75 computer work stations. Total 2004–05 for books and materials: $1,190,276. >p<Most important holdings include collections of classics, early British and American history, Wabash College archives.

Buildings and Grounds: Campus area 50 acres. *New buildings:* Trippet Hall completed 2003; Hays Hall 2004; Goodrich Hall 2004.

Chief Executive Officer: Dr. Andrew T. Ford, President.

Address admission inquiries to Steven J. Klein, Director of Admissions.

Iowa

Allen College

1815 Logan Avenue
Waterloo, Iowa 50703-1999
Tel: (319) 226-2000   **E-mail:** admissions@allencollege.edu
Fax: (319) 226-2051   **Internet:** www.allencollege.edu

Institution Description: Allen College is a private nonprofit college and a subsidiary of Allen Health Systems, Inc. It is affiliated with Iowa Health System. *Enrollment:* 364. *Degrees awarded:* Associate, baccalaureate, master's.

Accreditation: *Regional:* NCA. *Professional:* nursing

History: Allen Memorial Hospital's involvement in nursing education began in 1925 and terminated in 1997 when Allen College was incorporated as a subsidiary of Allen Health Systems, Inc. to establish a degree-granting institution offering nursing ans allied health programs.

Institutional Structure: *Governing board:* Board of Trustees. Representation: 9 trustees. *Composition of institution:* Academic affairs headed by dean of academic affairs. Management and finance headed by chancellor. Full-time instructional faculty 18. The faculty organization meets monthly.

Calendar: Semesters. Academic year begins June 1 to mid-May and operates using three semesters. Degrees conferred Dec., May. Formal commencement May.

Characteristics of Freshmen: 74% of applicants admitted. 54% of applicants admitted and enrolled.

100% (33 students) submitted ACT scores. *25th percentile:* ACT Composite 19, ACT English 18, ACT Math 18. *75th percentile:* ACT Composite 22, ACT English 21, ACT Math 23.

53% of entering freshmen expected to graduate within 5 years. 100% of freshmen from Iowa. Freshmen from 7 states.

Admission: Rolling admissions plan. Undergraduate students must also apply for admission to either the University of Northern Iowa or Wartburg College. Students are accepted for entrance in fall, spring, and summer semesters. Radiology students enter in the summer semester only. *Requirements:* Graduation from accredited high school with rank in the upper 50% of graduating class. All programs require a high school GPA of 3.0 on a 4.0 scale.

Entrance tests: ACT with a composite score of 20 or above. TOEFL with minimum score of 550 for international students whose first language is not English. *Transfer students:* Grade of C or above is required for nay courses transferred from other institutions. In addition, a minimum of 3.0 GPA is required for students transferring. Applicants with less than 24 semester hours must also meet the admission requirements as those students entering directly from high school.

Degree Requirements: *For associate degree:* completion of a course of study with a minimum of 73 semester hours and a cumulative GPA of 2.0 or higher. *For baccalaureate degree:* completion of a course of study with a minimum of 124 semester hours with a grade of C or above in each course taken; cumulative GPA of 2.0 or higher. *For master's degree:* Completion of at least 34 semester hours with a GPA of 3.0 or higher.

Degrees Conferred: 41 *baccalaureate:* health professions and related sciences 41; 11 *master's:* health professions and related sciences.

Fees and Other Expenses: *Tuition per academic year 2005–06:* undergraduate $11,171; graduate $10,700. *Room and board per academic year:* $5,519.

Financial Aid: Aid from institutionally generated funds is provided on the basis of academic merit, financial need. Institution has a Program Participation Agreement with the U.S. Department of Education for eligible students to receive Pell Grants and other federal aid.

Financial aid to full-time, first-time undergraduate students: need-based scholarships/grants totaling $779,372, self-help $1,018,339, parent loans $121,670; non-need-based scholarships/grants totaling $17,877, self-help $766,184, parent loans $324,165. *Graduate aid:* 16 students received federal and state-funded fellowships and grants totaling $15,664 (ranging from $500 to $1,500).

Departments and Teaching Staff: *Total instructional faculty:* 27 (full-time 18, part-time 9; women 27;). Total faculty with doctorate, first-professional, or other terminal degree: 3. Student-to-faculty ratio: 13:1.

Enrollment: Total enrollment 364. Undergraduate full-time 13 men / 262 women, part-time 4m / 54w; graduate full-time 1m / 9w, part-time 21w. *Transfer students:* in-state 94.

Characteristics of Student Body: *Ethnic/racial makeup:* number of Asian or Pacific Islander: 2; Hispanic: 4; White non-Hispanic: 322. *Age distribution:* under 18–19: 11; 20–21: 71; 22–24: 70; 25–29: 29; 30–34: 12; 35–39: 9; 40–49: 14; 50–64: 4.

Student Life: Limited on-campus housing. Residence housing is available to all Allen College students either at the University of Northern Iowa or Wartburg College. Married student housing is available. *Special Services:* Child Care Center, Counseling Center, Health Services, Pastoral Care, Wellness/Fitness Center. Services are free to students with the exception of Health Services. *Student publications: The Pulse,* a biweekly student newsletter. *Surrounding community:* Waterloo and Cedar Falls population 101,000. Airport 5 miles from campus. Bus system runs from Allen College to University of Northern Iowa.

Library Collections: 1,100 volumes including bound books, serial backfiles, electronic documents, and govern documents not in separate collections. Current serial subscriptions: 106 paper. 13 CD-ROMs. 18 computer work stations. Students have access to the Internet (fee included in activity fee).

Most import special collections include nursing (historical works); radiography (historical works); Allen Hospital Historical Interview Tapes (audiocassettes).

Chief Executive Officer: Dr. Jane Hasek, Chancellor.

Address admission inquiries to Joanna Ramsden-Meier, Enrollment Management Director.

Ashford University

400 North Bluff Boulevard
P.O. Box 2967
Clinton, Iowa 52733-2967
Tel: (563) 242-4023   **E-mail:** admissns@tfu.edu
Fax: (563) 242-8684   **Internet:** www.tfu.edu

Institution Description: Ashford University College, formerly Mount Saint Clare College and most recently The Franciscan University, is a private institution affiliated with Sisters of St. Francis, Roman Catholic Church. *Enrollment:* 459. *Degrees awarded:* Associate, baccalaureate.

Accreditation: *Regional:* NCA.

History: Established as Mount Saint Clare College and Academy 1895; chartered separately and adopted present name 1918; became 4-year institution 1979; awarded first degree (baccalaureate) 1981; The Franciscan University 2000; became Ashford University in 2002.

Institutional Structure: *Governing board:* Board of Trustees. Representation: trustees. All voting. Academic affairs headed by academic dean. Management/business/finances headed by Director of Administrative Services. Full-time instructional faculty 27.

Calendar: Semesters. Academic year Aug. to May. Freshmen admitted Aug., Jan., June. Degrees conferred May, July, Dec. Formal commencement May. Summer sessions from May to July.

Characteristics of Freshmen: 295 applicants (161 men, 134 women). 71.5% of applicants admitted. 24.6% of admitted students enrolled full-time.

96% (50 students) submitted ACT scores. *25th percentile:* ACT Composite 18, ACT English 16, ACT Math 16. *75th percentile:* ACT Composite 22, ACT English 21, ACT Math 21.

40% of entering freshmen expected to graduate within 5 years. 56% of freshmen from Iowa. Freshmen from 5 states and 3 foreign countries.

Admission: Rolling admissions plan. *Requirements:* Either graduation from accredited secondary school or GED. Minimum GPA 2.0. Lowest acceptable secondary school class standing top 66th percentile. *Entrance tests:* College Board SAT, ACT composite. *For transfer students:* 2.0 minimum GPA, maximum transfer credit 64 credit hours from a 2-year institution; 90 credit hours from a 4-year institution.

College credit and advanced placement for postsecondary-level work completed in secondary school. Tutoring available. Noncredit developmental courses offered during regular academic year.

Degree Requirements: *For all associate degrees:* 62 semester hours; last 15 hours in residence. *For all baccalaureate degrees:* 122 hours; last 30 hours in residence. *For all degrees:* 2.0 GPA; general education requirements. Fulfillment of some degree requirements possible by passing departmental examinations, College Board CLEP. *Grading system:* A–F; withdraw (carries time limit).

Distinctive Educational Programs: Work-experience programs. Evening classes. Opportunities for independent studies, including honors programs, tutorials. Study abroad in Italy. Bridge Program designed to help under prepared students gain the academic skills needed to succeed in college.

Degrees Conferred: 4 *associate*; 109 *baccalaureate*; 27 *master's*. Bachelor's degrees awarded in top five disciplines: business, management, marketing, and related support services 26; education 26; social sciences 20; liberal arts and sciences, general studies and humanities 15; visual and performing arts 9.

Fees and Other Expenses: *Full-time tuition per academic year 2004–05:* $14,690. *Books and supplies:* $700. *Room and board per academic year* $5,250. *Other expenses:* $1,000.

Financial Aid: Aid from institutionally generated funds is provided on the basis of academic merit, financial need, athletic ability, other criteria. Institution has a Program Participation Agreement with the U.S. Department of Education for eligible students to receive Pell Grants and other federal aid.

Financial aid to full-time, first-time undergraduate students: 41% received federal grants averaging $2,908; 30% state/local grants averaging $3,331; 98% institutional grants averaging $5,526; 76% loans averaging $3,120.

Departments and Teaching Staff: Business *professors* 1, *associate professors* 2, *assistant professors* 2, *unranked instructors* 1, *part-time teachers* 1, *adjunct* 3; education 0, 1, 2, 2, 1, 3; fine arts 0, 1, 2, 0, 1, 5; humanities 2, 1, 1, 1, 2, 4; science 1, 2, 0, 2, 0, 3; social sciences 2, 0, 1, 0, 1, 3.

Total instructional faculty: 60. Student-to-faculty ratio: 12.8:1. Degrees held by full-time faculty: Doctorate 28%, master's 64%, baccalaureate 8%. 30% hold terminal degrees.

Enrollment: Total enrollment 459. Undergraduate 391 (men 42.7%, women 57.3%).

Characteristics of Student Body: *Ethnic/racial makeup:* Black non-Hispanic: 6.9%; Asian or Pacific Islander: 1.5%; American Indian or Alaska Native: .5%; Hispanic: 1.5%; White non-Hispanic: 87.2%; unknown: .5%. *Age distribution:* 17–21: 51%; 22–24: 10%; 25–29: 8%; 30–34: 6%; 35–39: 8%; 40–49: 14%; 50–59: 2%; 60–and over: 1%.

International Students: 7 undergraduate nonresident aliens enrolled fall 2004. Programs available to aid students whose native language is not English: English as a Second Language Program. No financial aid specifically designated for foreign students.

Student Life: On-campus residence halls house 35% of student body. *Intercollegiate athletics:* men only: baseball, basketball, cross-country, golf, track, wrestling; women only: basketball, cheerleading, cross-country, softball, track, volleyball. *Student publications:* Weekly newsletter. *Surrounding community:* Clinton population 28,000. Quad-cities 40 miles from campus; Des Moines, 199 miles. Served by mass transit bus system; airport 35 miles from campus.

Library Collections: 81,000 volumes. 74,500 microforms; 2,500 audiovisual materials; 645 current periodical subscriptions. Online catalog. Computer work stations available. Students have fee-based access to online services.

Most important special holdings include the DaMour Collection of Literature and Fine Arts; the Durham Collection of Theology and History; Clare Collection (St. Francis/St. Clare/Medieval Women); Children's Literature Collection.

Buildings and Grounds: Campus area 25 acres.

Chief Executive Officer: Dr. Michael E. Kaelke, President.

Address admission inquiries to Waunita Sullivan, Director of Enrollment.

Briar Cliff University

3303 Rebecca Street
Sioux City, Iowa 51104
Tel: (712) 279-5321   **E-mail:** admissions@briar-cliff.edu
Fax: (712) 279-5410   **Internet:** www.briar-cliff.edu

Institution Description: Briar Cliff University is a private, independent, nonprofit institution affiliated with the Catholic Church and Franciscan order. *Enrollment:* 1,116. *Degrees awarded:* Associate, baccalaureate, master's

Accreditation: *Regional:* NCA. *Professional:* social work, nursing

History: Established as a junior college for women, chartered, and offered first instruction at the postsecondary level 1930; awarded first degree (associate) 1931; became 4-year college 1936; incorporated 1963; became coeducational

1966. *See* Sister Mary Eunice Mousel, *They Have Taken Root* (N.Y.: Bookman Associates, 1954) for further information.

Institutional Structure: *Governing board:* Briar Cliff University College Board of Trustees. Extrainstitutional representation: 27 trustees, including 2 alumni; institutional representation: president of college. All voting. *Composition of institution:* Administrators 27 men / 28 women (at dean's level and above, 40% are women). Academic affairs headed by vice president of academic development. Management/business/finances directed by vice president of financial development. Academic governance body, Academic Affairs Committee, meets an average of 10 times per year.

Calendar: Modified 3-3 plan. Academic year Sept. to May. Freshmen admitted Sept., Dec., Mar., June. Degrees conferred May, Aug., Nov. Formal commencement May.

Characteristics of Freshmen: 73% of applicants admitted. 19% of applicants admitted and enrolled.

3% (8 students) submitted SAT scores; 97% (242 students) submitted ACT scores. *25th percentile:* SAT Verbal 470, SAT Math 370; ACT Composite 19, ACT English 17, ACT Math 17. *75th percentile:* SAT Verbal 560, SAT Math 510; ACT Composite 24, ACT English 23, ACT Math 24. 50% of entering freshmen expected to graduate within 5 years. 56% of freshmen from Iowa. Freshmen from 16 states and 1 foreign country.

Admission: Rolling admissions plan. For fall acceptance, apply as early as 1 year prior to enrollment, but not later than Sept. of year of enrollment. Early acceptance available. *Requirements:* Either graduation from accredited secondary school with 16 units or GED. Minimum GPA 2.0. Lowest acceptable secondary school class standing 20th percentile. *Entrance tests:* ACT composite 18 minimum score. For foreign students TOEFL. *For transfer students:* 2.0 minimum GPA; from 4-year accredited institution 90 semester hours; from 2-year accredited institution 60 hours; correspondence/extension students evaluated individually. Advanced placement for postsecondary-level work completed in secondary school.

College credit for extrainstitutional learning on basis of ACE *2006 Guide to the Evaluation of Educational Experiences in the Armed Services*; portfolio and faculty assessments. Tutoring available. Developmental/remedial courses offered in summer session and regular academic year; credit given.

Degree Requirements: *For all associate degrees:* 60 credit hours; last 15 hours in residence. *For all baccalaureate degrees:* 120 credit hours; last 30 hours in residence. *For all degrees:* 2.0 minimum GPA; distribution requirements.

Fulfillment of some degree requirements and exemption from some beginning courses possible by passing College Board CLEP or other standardized test. *Grading system:* A–F; pass-fail (limited); withdraw (carries time limit); incomplete (deadline after which A–F is assigned).

Distinctive Educational Programs: Internships. Weekend and evening classes. Dual-degree program in engineering with Iowa State University. Cooperative baccalaureate in medical technology with approved hospitals, in radiologic technology with Marian Health Center. Interdepartmental/interdisciplinary programs in medical technology, natural science, philosophy/theology, psychology/sociology, radiologic technology, religious education, pre-engineering; individually arranged interdepartmental programs. Facilities and programs for independent research, including individual majors and tutorials.

Degrees Conferred: 188 *baccalaureate:* biological/life sciences 10; business/marketing 60; communications/communication technologies 4; computer and information sciences 5; education 28; English 4; health professions and related sciences 22; parks and recreation 14; philosophy/religion/theology 1; protective services/public administration 13; psychology 10; social sciences and history 3; visual and performing arts 188; 13 *master's:* education 13.

Fees and Other Expenses: *Full-time tuition per academic year 2004–05:* $16,560 undergraduate; $229 to $395 per credit hour for graduate study. *Required fees:* $465. *Room and board per academic year:* $5,433.

Financial Aid: Aid from institutionally generated funds is provided on the basis of academic merit, financial need, athletic ability. Institution has a Program Participation Agreement with the U.S. Department of Education for eligible students to receive Pell Grants and other federal aid.

Financial aid to full-time, first-time undergraduate students: need-based scholarships/grants totaling $3,095,387, self-help $5,059,298, parent loans $212,635, tuition waivers $246,919, athletic awards $1,090,247.

Departments and Teaching Staff: *Professors* 17, *associate professors* 11, *assistant professors* 20, *instructors* 4, *part-time faculty* 6.

Total instructional faculty: 97 (full-time 53, part-time 44; women 51, men 34; members of minority groups 1). Total faculty with doctorate, first-professional, or other terminal degree: 42. Student-to-faculty ratio: 12:1.

Enrollment: Total enrollment 1,116. Undergraduate full-time 399 men / 533 women, part-time 49m / 103w; graduate full-time 2m / 8w, part-time 2m / 20w. *Transfer students:* in-state 93, from out-of-state 36.

Characteristics of Student Body: *Ethnic/racial makeup:* number of Black non-Hispanic: 24; American Indian or Alaska Native: 12; Asian or Pacific Islander: 13; Hispanic: 36; White non-Hispanic: 497. *Age distribution:* under 18:

2; 8–19: 384; 20–21: 313; 22–24: 145; 25–29: 67; 30–34: 49; 35–39: 33; 40–49: 100; 50–64: 23.

International Students: 2 nonresident aliens from Asia enrolled fall 2004. No programs to aid students whose native language is not English. No financial aid specifically designated for international students.

Student Life: On- and off-campus residence halls house 66% of full-time students. *Intercollegiate athletics:* men only: baseball, basketball, cross-country, golf, soccer, track, wrestling; women only: basketball, cross-country, golf, soccer, softball, track. tennis, volleyball. *Special regulations:* Cars with decals permitted on campus in designated areas only; fee charged. Quiet hours from 10am to 10pm Sun.–Thurs., noon to midnight Fri. and Sat. Residence hall visitation noon to midnight Sun.–Thurs. and noon–2am Fri. and Sat. *Special services:* Learning Resources Center, medical services. *Student publications: Cliff News,* a weekly newspaper; *Briar Cliff Review,* an annual literary magazine. *Surrounding community:* Sioux City population 85,000. Omaha, 100 miles from campus, is nearest metropolitan area. Served by mass transit bus system; airport 10 miles from campus; passenger rail service 100 miles from campus.

Library Collections: 83,856 volumes including bound books, serial backfiles, electronic documents, and government documents not in separate collections. Online catalog. Current serial subscriptions: 10,706 (combined paper, microform, and via electronic access). 130 computer work stations. Students have access to the Internet at no charge.

Buildings and Grounds: Campus area 70 acres. *New buildings:* Stark Student Center.

Chief Executive Officer: Dr. Beverly Wharton, President.

Address admission inquiries to Sharisue Wilcoxon, Vice President for Enrollment Management.

Buena Vista University

610 West Fourth
Storm Lake, Iowa 50588
Tel: (712) 749-2400   **E-mail:** admissions@bvu.edu
Fax: (712) 749-2037   **Internet:** www.bvu.edu

Institution Description: Buena Vista University is a private, independent, nonprofit institution affiliated with the United Presbyterian Church U.S.A. *Enrollment:* 1,316. *Degrees awarded:* Baccalaureate, master's.

Accreditation: *Regional:* NCA. *Professional:* Social work, teacher education

History: Established, incorporated, and offered first instruction at postsecondary level 1891; first degree (baccalaureate) awarded 1893; adopted present name 1995. *See* William B. Cumberland, *History of Buena Vista College* (Ames: Iowa State University Press, 1966) for further information.

Institutional Structure: *Governing board:* Buena Vista College Board of Trustees. Extrainstitutional representation: 30 trustees, including 1 alumnus, 1 church official; institutional representation: president of college, all voting. *Composition of institution:* Administrators 19 men / 18 women. Academic affairs headed by executive vice president and dean of faculty. Management/business/finances directed by vice president for business services. Full-time instructional faculty 81. Academic governance body, Board of Trustees Academic Affairs Committee (advised by Faculty Senate and Faculty Academic Affairs Committee), meets an average of 12 times per year.

Calendar: Semesters (4-1-4 plan). Academic year Aug. to May. Freshmen admitted Aug., Jan., Feb., summer sessions. Degrees conferred May, Aug., Dec. Formal commencement May. Summer sessions of 3 terms from late May to late July.

Characteristics of Freshmen: 81% of applicants admitted. 26% of applicants admitted and enrolled.

2% (7 students) submitted SAT scores; 100% (331 students) submitted ACT scores. *25th percentile:* ACT Composite 20. *75th percentile:* ACT Composite 25. 59% of entering freshmen expected to graduate within 5 years. 75% of freshmen from Iowa. Freshmen from 10 states.

Admission: Rolling admissions plan. For fall acceptance, apply as early as September of previous year. Apply by Dec. 1 of previous year for early decision. Early acceptance available. *Requirements:* Graduation from accredited secondary school. 4 units in English, 3 history, 3 mathematics, 3 science recommended. Minimum GPA 2.5. Lowest acceptable secondary school class standing 50th percentile. *Entrance tests:* ACT of SAT. *For transfer students:* 2.5 GPA; from 4-year accredited institution maximum transfer credit limited only by residence requirement; from 2-year accredited institution 68 hours maximum; must be in good standing at institution previously attended.

College credit and advanced placement for postsecondary-level work completed in secondary school. College credit for extrainstitutional learning (life experience) on basis of assessment by academic dean. Tutoring available.

Degree Requirements: 128 credit hours; 2.0 cumulative GPA (higher in many major/minor areas). Education students must maintain 2.5 cumulative GPA in major and minor areas; last 30 hours in residence; skills proficiency in mathematics and written communication. Academic and Cultural Events Series (ACES) requirement. The ACES program consists of lecture series and concert/major events series. The program is designed to enrich the curriculum and enhance the college's commitment to the liberal arts.

Fulfillment of some degree requirements possible by passing departmental examination and College Board APP, CLEP, AP. *Grading system:* A–F; honors pass no credit (HPNC), withdrawal, incomplete.

Distinctive Educational Programs: Required internships. Honors program. Florida business interim. Republic of China Language Fellowship. Washington Semester with American University. Presidential Fellows, Career Development Program, dual-degree program in engineering with Washington University (MO), dentistry with the University of Iowa. Individualized majors. Study abroad programs in China, England, Japan, Spain, Taiwan, Mexico, Korea, Hong Kong, Poland.

Degrees Conferred: 711 *baccalaureate* (B); 24 *master's* (M): biological/life sciences 18 (B); business/marketing 232 (B); communications/communication technologies 23 (B); computer and information sciences 5 (B); education 194 (B), 24 (M); English 11 (B); foreign languages and literature 2 (B); health professions and related sciences 9 (B); interdisciplinary studies 65 (B); parks and recreation 12 (B); philosophy/religion/theology 2 (B); physical sciences 3 (B); protective services/public administration 44 (B); psychology 57 (B); social sciences and history 28 (B); visual and performing arts 10 (B).

Fees and Other Expenses: *Full-time tuition per academic year 2005–06:* $21,688 undergraduate, $266 per credit hour graduate. *Room and board per academic year:* $6,054.

Financial Aid: Aid from institutionally generated funds is provided on the basis of academic merit, financial need. Institution has a Program Participation Agreement with the U.S. Department of Education for eligible students to receive Pell Grants and other federal aid.

Financial aid to full-time, first-time undergraduate students: need-based scholarships/grants totaling $14,898,791, self-help $5,456,534; non-need-based scholarships/grants totaling $2,062,282, self-help $982,626, tuition waivers $525,302.

Departments and Teaching Staff: Communication and arts *professors* 2, *associate professors* 7, *assistant professors* 12; *instructors* 3, *part-time faculty* 14; business 5, 1, 4, 1, 2; social sciences/philosophy and religion 3, 5, 7, 0, 5; education 4, 1, 7, 4, 14; science 7, 3, 5, 1, 5.

Total instructional faculty: 121 (full-time 81, part-time 40; women 55, men 66; members of minority groups 4). Total faculty with doctorate, first-professional, or other terminal degree: 57. Student-to-faculty ratio: 15:1. *Faculty development:* 2 faculty members awarded sabbaticals 2004–05.

Enrollment: Total enrollment 1,316. Undergraduate full-time 583 men / 659 women, part-time 14m / 20w; graduate full-time 11m / 29w.

Characteristics of Student Body: *Ethnic/racial makeup:* number of Black non-Hispanic: 26; American Indian or Alaska Native: 3; Asian or Pacific Islander: 25; Hispanic: 23; White non-Hispanic: 1,132; unknown: 56. *Age distribution:* number under 18: 28; 18–19: 565; 20–21: 518; 22–24: 115; 25–29: 13; 30–34: 12; 35–39: 6; 40–49: 13; 50–64: 6.

International Students: 11 nonresident aliens enrolled fall 2004. 11 students from Asia. Programs available to aid students whose language is not English: Social, cultural, financial. English as a Second Language Program. Variable number of scholarships available to qualifying international students. 21 totaling $405,489 were awarded 2004–05.

Student Life: On-campus residence halls house 84% of student body. Residence halls for men only constitute 44% of such space, for women only 66%. *Intercollegiate athletics:* men only: baseball, basketball, cross-country, football, golf, swimming, tennis, track, wrestling; women only, basketball, cross-country, softball, tennis, track, volleyball. *Special regulations:* Cars permitted on campus. Quiet hours from 11pm to 10am Sun.–Thurs. Residence hall visitation from noon to midnight Sun.–Thurs. *Special services:* Learning Resources Center, medical services. *Student publications, radio: The Tack,* a weekly newspaper. Radio station KBVC broadcasts approximately 30 hours of live coverage each week on the local cable channel. *Surrounding community:* Storm Lake population 10,000. Des Moines and Omaha, 150 miles from campus, are nearest metropolitan areas. Sioux City is 65 miles from the campus.

Library Collections: 136,000 volumes. Online catalog. Current periodical subscriptions. 640 paper; 14,929 via electronic access. 2,348 audiovisual materials. 24 computer work stations. Students have access to the Internet at no charge. Total 2004–05 budget for books and materials: $263,095.

Most important special collections on Buena Vista History; U.S. Civil War History; Iowa History.

Buildings and Grounds: Campus area 54 acres. *New buildings:* Lamberti Recreation Center completed 2001; Liberty Hall (residence hall) 2002; Estelle Strebens Science Center 2004.

Chief Executive Officer: Dr. Frederick V. Moore, President.

Address admission inquiries to Ronda Bacon, Director of Admissions; Graduate inquiries to Jean Bral, Graduate Recruiter.

Central College

812 University
Pella, Iowa 50219-1902
Tel: (817) 462-3687   **E-mail:** admission@central.edu
Fax: (641) 628-5316   **Internet:** www.central.edu

Institution Description: Central College, formerly known as Central University of Iowa, is a private institution affiliated with the Reformed Church in America. *Enrollment:* 1,750. *Degrees awarded:* Baccalaureate.

Accreditation: *Regional:* NCA. *Professional*: music, teacher education

History: Established by Iowa Baptist Convention and incorporated 1853; offered first instruction at postsecondary level 1858; awarded first degree (baccalaureate) 1861. *See* Josephine E. Thostenson, *Central College Bulletin: One Hundred Years of Service* (Pella, Iowa: Central College, 1953) for further information.

Institutional Structure: *Governing board:* Central College Board of Trustees. Extrainstitutional representation: 24 trustees including 3 alumni; institutional representation: president of the university, 2 full-time instructional faculty members, 2 students; 3 ministers. 4 ex officio. All voting. *Composition of institution:* Administrators 4 men / 3 women (at dean's level and above, 49% are women). Academic affairs headed by vice president for academic affairs. Management/business/finances directed by vice president for business and treasurer. Full-time instructional faculty 50. Academic governance body, the faculty (advised by the Curriculum Committee) meets monthly.

Calendar: Semesters. Academic year Aug. to May. Freshmen admitted Sept., Nov., Mar. Degrees conferred May, Aug., Nov., Feb. Formal commencement May. Summer session of 2 five-week sessions and a ten-week session (overlaps the five-week sessions).

Characteristics of Freshmen: 83% of applicants admitted. 26% of applicants admitted and enrolled.

5% (22 students) submitted SAT scores; 49% (440 students) submitted ACT scores. *25th percentile*: SAT Verbal 500, SAT Math 520; ACT Composite 21. *75th percentile*: SAT Verbal 600, SAT Math 630; ACT Composite 26.

68% of entering freshmen expected to graduate within 5 years. 80% of freshmen from Iowa. Freshmen from 17 states and 3 foreign countries.

Admission: Rolling admissions plan. For fall acceptance, apply as early as Sept. 1 of previous year, but not later than July 1. Early acceptance available. *Requirements:* Graduation from accredited secondary school or GED. Recommend 16 academic units including 4 English, 2 in a foreign language, 3 social studies, 2 mathematics, 2 science. Lowest acceptable secondary school class standing 50th percentile. *Entrance tests:* College Board ACT composite. *For transfer students:* 2.0 minimum GPA; from accredited 4-year institution 135 quarter hours maximum transfer credit; from 2-year accredited institution 100 quarter hours.

Advanced placement for postsecondary-level work completed in secondary school. Tutoring available. Developmental courses offered during regular academic year; credit given for some courses.

Degree Requirements: 120 semester hours (15 semester hours must be taken in residence); 2.0 GPA; distribution requirements; demonstrated proficiency in communications.

Grading system: A–F; pass; withdraw (deadline after which pass-fail is appended to withdraw); incomplete (deadline after which A–F is assigned).

Distinctive Educational Programs: Internships. Interdepartmental/interdisciplinary programs in linguistics, pre-law, pre-ministry, international studies, systems management. Facilities for independent research, including honors programs, individual majors, tutorials. Study abroad in Austria, China, England, France, Kenya, Mexico, The Netherlands, Spain, Wales. Off-campus study in urban studies at Chicago Metropolitan Center and Washington DC Center.

Degrees Conferred: 318 *baccalaureate:* area and ethnic studies 12; biological/life sciences 16; business/marketing 56; communications/communication technologies 21; computer and information sciences 13; education 48; English 8; foreign languages and literature 10; health professions and related sciences 33; liberal arts/general studies 27; mathematics 6; natural resources/environmental science 4; philosophy/religion/theology 9; physical sciences 9; psychology 15; social sciences and history 29; visual and performing arts 12.

Fees and Other Expenses: *Full-time tuition per academic year 2004–05:* $18,648. *Required fees:* $244. *Room and board per academic year:* $6,486.

Financial Aid: Central College offers a direct lending program. Aid from institutionally generated funds is provided on the basis of academic merit, financial need. Institution has a Program Participation Agreement with the U.S.

Department of Education for eligible students to receive Pell Grants and other federal aid.

Departments and Teaching Staff: *Total instructional faculty:* 153 (full-time 99, part-time 54; women 53, men 92; members of minority groups 8). Total faculty with doctorate, first-professional, or other terminal degree: 100. Student-to-faculty ratio: 14:1. *Faculty development:* $17,000 in grants for research. 7 faculty members awarded sabbaticals 2004–05.

Enrollment: Total enrollment 1,750. Undergraduate full-time 749 men / 957 women, part-time 25m / 19w.

Characteristics of Student Body: *Ethnic/racial makeup:* number of Black non-Hispanic: 14; American Indian or Alaska Native: 3; Asian or Pacific Islander: 20; Hispanic: 22; White non-Hispanic: 1,553; unknown: 116.

International Students: 22 nonresident aliens enrolled fall 2004. 7 students form Europe, 7 Asia, 4 Central and South America, 3 Africa. Programs available to aid students whose native language is not English: Social, cultural. Scholarships are available for qualifying international students.

Student Life: On-campus residence halls house 90% of student body. Residence halls for men constitute 41% of such space, for women 31%, for both sexes 28%. Housing available for married students. 52% of married students request institutional housing; 24% are so housed. 86% of students live on campus. *Intercollegiate athletics:* men only: baseball, basketball, cross-country, football, golf, tennis, track, wrestling; women only: basketball, cross-country, golf, softball, tennis, track, volleyball. *Special regulations:* Cars permitted without restrictions. Quiet hours set by individual residence halls. Residence hall visitation from noon to midnight Sun.–Thurs., noon to 1am Fri. and Sat. *Special services:* Learning Resources Center, medical services. *Student publications, radio: The Knickerbocker*, an annual literary magazine; *The Ray*, a weekly newspaper; *Writing Anthology*, an Annual Collection of Student Writings. Radio station KCUI broadcasts 94 hours per week. *Surrounding community:* Pella, population 10,000. Des Moines, 40 miles from campus, is nearest metropolitan area. Served by airport and passenger rail service, each 40 miles from campus.

Library Collections: 195,000 volumes. Online catalog. 54,000 microforms; 8,800 audiovisual materials; 3,500 recordings. 925 current periodical subscriptions. Computer work stations available. Access to online information retrieval systems and the Internet.

Most important holdings include manuscripts, diaries, etc. relating to the Dutch in America; Paper of Hendrik P. Scholte, founder of Pella; Helen Van Dyke Miniature Book Collection.

Buildings and Grounds: Campus area 130 acres. *New buildings:* Vermeer Science Center.

Chief Executive Officer: Dr. David H. Roe, President.

Address admission inquiries to Carol Williamson, Dean of Admissions.

Clarke College

1550 Clarke Drive
Dubuque, Iowa 52001-3198
Tel: (563) 588-6300   **E-mail:** admissions@clarke.edu
Fax: (563) 588-6789   **Internet:** www.clarke.edu

Institution Description: Clarke College is a private college affiliated with the Sister of Charity of the Blessed Virgin Mary, Roman Catholic Church. *Enrollment:* 980. *Degrees awarded:* Associate, baccalaureate, master's.

Member of the consortium Tri-College Cooperative Effort.

Accreditation: *Regional:* NCA. *Professional*: music, nursing, nursing education, physical therapy, social work, teacher education

History: Established as St. Mary's Academy 1843; changed name to St. Joseph's Academy 1846; adopted name Mount St. Joseph College 1879; offered first instruction at postsecondary level 1901; awarded first degree (baccalaureate) 1904; chartered 1912; adopted present name 1928. Graduate studies added 1961. College became coeducational 1979.

Institutional Structure: *Governing board:* 37 trustees, including 7 alumni, president of the college, 3 ex officio. *Composition of institution:* Administrators 25 men / 33 women. At dean's level and above: 2 men, 5 women. President's executive council includes: executive vice president, vice presidents for academic affairs, business affairs, enrollment management and institutional marketing, institutional advancement, student life. Full-time instructional faculty 92. Academic governance body, the Educational Policy Committee, meets an average of 9 times a year.

Calendar: Semesters. Academic year Aug. to May. Freshmen admitted Aug., Jan., June. Degrees conferred and formal commencement May. Summer session June to July.

Characteristics of Freshmen: 78% of applicants accepted. 35% of accepted applicants enrolled.

7% (14 students) submitted SAT scores; 76% (195 students) submitted ACT scores. *25th percentile*: SAT Verbal 460, SAT Math 460; ACT Composite 20. *75th percentile*: SAT Verbal 542, SAT Math 542; ACT Composite 24.

65% entering freshmen expected to graduate within 5 years. 40% of freshmen from Iowa. Freshmen from 17 states and 11 foreign countries.

Admission: Rolling admissions plan. For fall acceptance, apply no later than Aug. 21. Early acceptance available. *Requirements:* Recommend 16 secondary school units which normally include 4 English, 2 in a foreign language, 3 history/social studies, 3 mathematics, 3 science, 5 electives. GED accepted. Minimum GPA 2.0. Lowest acceptable secondary school class standing 50th percentile. *Entrance tests:* College Board SAT or ACT composite. *For transfer students:* 2.25 minimum GPA; from 4-year accredited institution 90 semester hours maximum transfer credit; from 2-year accredited institution 64 hours; correspondence/extension students 30 hours.

College credit for postsecondary-level work completed in secondary school and for extrainstitutional learning on basis of ACE *2006 Guide to the Evaluation of Educational Experiences in the Armed Services*, portfolio and faculty assessments, personal interviews. Credit given for developmental courses does not count toward graduation.

Degree Requirements: *For all associate degrees:* 62 semester hours. *For all baccalaureate degrees:* 124 hours; distribution requirements; exit competency examinations (comprehensives in individual fields of study, senior performance or project). *For all undergraduate degrees:* 2.0 GPA; 30 hours in residence; exit competency examination in English composition.

Fulfillment of some degree requirements and exemption from some beginning courses possible by passing College Board CLEP, AP. *Grading system:* A–F; Satisfactory/Unsatisfactory; withdraw (carries time limit); incomplete (carries time limit).

Distinctive Educational Programs: Internships, cooperative education opportunities, and service learning opportunities offered. Accelerated evening degree program for adults. Contract majors and independent study opportunities. Individual study abroad experiences are tailored to students' interests. Ground trips frequently sponsored by academic departments.

Degrees Conferred: 211 *baccalaureate* (B), 48 *master's* (M): biological/life sciences 7 (B); business/marketing 42 (B); communications/communication technologies 17 (B), 6 (M); computer and information sciences 25 (B); education 28 (B), 13 (M); English 9 (B); foreign languages and literature 2 (B); health professions and related sciences 19 (B), 24 (M); mathematics 3 (B); philosophy/religion/theology 8 (B); protective services/public administration 7 (B); psychology 20 (B); social sciences and history 14 (B); visual and performing arts 14 (B).

Fees and Other Expenses: *Full-time tuition per academic year 2005–06:* $18,360 undergraduate, $4,365 graduate. *Required fees:*$585. *Room and board per academic year:* $6,445.

Financial Aid: Aid from institutionally generated funds is provided on the basis of academic merit, financial need, other considerations. Institution has a Program Participation Agreement with the U.S. Department of Education for eligible students to receive Pell Grants and other federal aid.

Financial aid to full-time, first-time undergraduate students: need-based scholarships/grants totaling $7,695,934, self-help $3,115,385, parent loans $429,789, tuition waivers $365,350; non-need-based scholarships/grants totaling $692,331, self-help $2,583,070, parent loans $115,878, tuition waivers $113,477.

Departments and Teaching Staff: *Total instructional faculty:* 142 (full-time 81, part-time 61; women 64, men 34; members of minority groups 2). Total faculty with doctorate, first-professional, or other terminal degree: 78. Student-to-faculty ratio: 10:1. *Faculty development:* 2 faculty members awarded sabbaticals 2004–05.

Enrollment: Total enrollment 1,190. Undergraduate full-time 226 men / 641 women, part-time 49m / 137w; graduate full-time 15m / 49w, part-time 14m / 49w.

Characteristics of Student Body: *Ethnic/racial makeup:* number of Black non-Hispanic: 25; American Indian or Alaska Native: 3; Asian or Pacific Islander: 4; Hispanic: 24; White non-Hispanic: 1,120, unknown: 4. *Age distribution:* 17–21: 49%; 22–24: 11.3%; 25–29: 7,2%; 30–34: 6.5%; 35–39: 5,8%; 40–49: 9.8%; 50–59: 4.4%; 60–and over: .01%, unknown 4.9%.

International Students: 10 nonresident aliens enrolled fall 2004. Students from Europe, Asia, Central and South America, Canada. Programs available to aid students whose native language is not English: social, cultural. English as a Second Language Program. Unlimited number of scholarships available for qualifying international students.

Student Life: On-campus residence halls house 42% of student body. One coed residence hall, 1 males-only and 1 females-only residence hall, one apartment building for males and females. *Athletics:* men only: alpine skiing, baseball, basketball, cross-country, golf, tennis, soccer; women only: basketball, volleyball. *Special regulations:* Quiet hours from 11pm to noon; residence hall visitation hours from noon to 11pm Sun.–Thurs., noon to 2am Fri. and Sat. Cars

permitted in designated areas only. *Special services:* Health service, counseling, bookstore and post office on campus, physical activities center. Active campus ministry. Tri-college intercampus bus Mon.–Fri. *Student publications, television: Catalyst,* a quarterly magazine; *Courier,* a weekly newspaper. TV station KLRK, broadcasts 2–5 hours per week. *Surrounding community:* Dubuque population 59,000. Chicago, 180 miles from campus, is nearest metropolitan area. Served by municipal transit bus system; airport 10 miles from campus.

Publications: *On Campus,* a quarterly publication; *The Collegian,* a triannual newsletter.

Library Collections: 135,000 volumes including bound books, serial backfiles, electronic documents, and government documents not in separate collections. Online catalog. Current serial subscriptions: 500 paper, 350 microform. 551 recordings; 12 CD-ROMS. Computer work stations available. Students have access to the Internet at no charge.

Most important special collections include the BVM Heritage Collection; Mayan Art Books; East Asian Collection.

Buildings and Grounds: Campus area 55 acres.

Chief Executive Officer: Sr. Catherine Dunn, BVM, President.

Address admission inquiries to Director of Admissions.

Coe College

1220 First Avenue N.E.
Cedar Rapids, Iowa 52402-5092

Tel: (319) 399-8000	**E-mail:** admissions@coe.edu
Fax: (319) 399-8830	**Internet:** www.coe.edu

Institution Description: Coe College is a private institution affiliated with the United Presbyterian Church in the United States of America. *Enrollment:* 1,355. *Degrees awarded:* Baccalaureate, master's.

Member of the consortia Associated Colleges of the Midwest (ACM).

Accreditation: *Regional:* NCA. *Professional:* music, nursing, nursing education, teacher education

History: Established as Cedar Rapids Collegiate Institute and offered first instruction at postsecondary level 1851; changed name to Parsons Seminary 1866, to Coe Collegiate Institute 1875; incorporated and adopted present name 1881; awarded first degree (baccalaureate) 1884; absorbed Leander Clark College (which had absorbed Western College) 1919; Phi Kappa Phi established 1925; Phi Beta Kappa established 1949. *See* Grace Hartzell Douma and Catherine Covert Stepanek, *Coe College "Courier," The Centennial Edition* (Cedar Rapids, Iowa: Coe College, 1951) for further information.

Institutional Structure: *Governing board:* Coe College Board of Trustees. Extrainstitutional representation: 40 trustees, 29 alumni, college president (ex officio). *Composition of institution:* Administrators 6 men / 1 woman. Academic affairs headed by vice president for academic affairs and dean of the faculty. Management/business/finances directed by vice president for administrative services. Full-time instructional faculty 80. Academic governance body, the faculty, meets an average of 10 times per year.

Calendar: Semesters (4-1-4 plan). Academic year Aug. to May. Freshmen admitted Aug., Jan., Feb., June. Summer session from May to July.

Characteristics of Freshmen: 1,177 applicants (621 men, 556 women). 71.8% of applicants admitted. 37.4% of admitted students enrolled full-time.

13% (41 students) submitted SAT scores; 94% (296 students) submitted ACT scores. *25th percentile*: SAT I Verbal 550, SAT I Math 540; ACT Composite 22, ACT English 21, ACT Math 21. *75th percentile:* SAT I Verbal 650, SAT I Math 650; ACT Composite 27, ACT English 27, ACT Math 27.

59% of entering freshmen expected to graduate within 5 years. 59% of freshmen from Iowa. Freshmen from 22 states and 6 foreign countries.

Admission: Early action Dec. 1 deadline, notification by Dec. 15; regular decision deadline Mar. 1, notification by Mar. 15. *Requirements:* The high school program should be of a college preparatory nature; 4 years of English, 3 mathematics, 3 each of science and history, and 2 foreign language are recommended for admission. GED accepted. *Entrance tests:* College Board SAT or ACT composite required. SAT average is 1100; ACT composite average is 24. *For transfer students:* 2.0 minimum GPA, 27 courses maximum transfer credit.

College credit for postsecondary-level work completed in secondary school and for extrainstitutional learning on basis of ACE *2006 Guide to the Evaluation of Educational Experiences in the Armed Services*; personal interview. Tutoring available.

Degree Requirements: 36 courses; 2.0 GPA; last 9 courses in residence; completion of 10 courses distributed across the areas of social science, natural science, humanities, and non-western studies (a foreign language may substitute for the latter); comprehensive examinations in some departments.

Fulfillment of some degree requirements and exemption from some beginning courses possible by passing College Board CLEP or AP, or departmental examinations. *Grading system:* A–F; pass-fail; withdraw (carries penalty after deadline).

Distinctive Educational Programs: Internship programs for juniors and seniors. Evening classes. Accelerated degree programs. Engineering and architecture therapy with Washington University (MO); social service administration with University of Chicago (IL). Special facilities for using telecommunications in the classroom. Interdepartmental/interdisciplinary majors in African American studies, American studies, Asian studies, biochemistry, environmental science, gender studies, general science, literature, molecular biology, and public relations. Study abroad through ACM includes programs in Costa Rica, London, and Florence; at Palacky University, Czech Republic, Tanzania; University of Poona, India; Waseda University, Japan; University of Zimbabwe. Study abroad also available by individual arrangement. Other programs through ACM include science semester at Oak Ridge (TN); humanities program at Newberry Library in Chicago; urban education and urban studies programs in Chicago; and summer program at Wilderness Field Station for biology study. Through Coe College programs, Washington (DC) and New York City terms. Other off-campus study through Coe/University of Iowa exchange program and cross-registration with Mount Mercy College.

ROTC: Army and Air Force offered in cooperation with University of Iowa.

Degrees Conferred: 253 *baccalaureate*; 9 *master's*. Bachelor's degrees awarded in top five disciplines: business, management, marketing, and related support services area and ethnic studies 44; social sciences 36; psychology 27; visual and performing arts 24; biological and biomedical sciences 20.

Fees and Other Expenses: *Full-time tuition per academic year 2004–05:* $22,650. *Books and supplies:* $700. *Room and board per academic year:* $5,950.

Financial Aid: Coe College offers a direct lending program. Aid from institutionally generated funds is provided on the basis of academic merit, financial need, other criteria. Institution has a Program Participation Agreement with the U.S. Department of Education for eligible students to receive Pell Grants and other federal aid.

Financial aid to full-time, first-time undergraduate students: 31% received federal grants averaging $3,391; 48% state/local grants averaging $3,213; 99% institutional grants averaging $10,920; 77% loans averaging $5,774.

Departments and Teaching Staff: Art studies *professors* 1, *associate professors* 2, *assistant professors* 1, *part-time teachers* 4; biology 2, 2, 2, 0; business administration/economics 4, 1, 3, 4; chemistry 1, 1, 2, 0; English 4, 1, 1, 3; foreign language 2, 2, 1, 4; history 2, 0, 1, 0; mathematical sciences 2, 1, 2, 1; music 3, 1, 1, 22; nursing 0, 0, 4, 6; philosophy/religion 2, 2, 1, 3; physical education 0, 0, 4, 5; physics 1, 1, 1, 0; political science 1, 1, 1, 0; psychology 2, 2, 1, 0; rhetoric 0, 1, 0, 7; sociology 2, 0, 1, 1; teacher education 1, 0, 2, 7; theater 0, 2, 1, 0.

Total instructional faculty: 148. Student-to-faculty ratio: 12:1. Degrees held by full-time faculty: doctorate 77%, master's 100%, first-professional 15%, baccalaureate 100%. 92% hold terminal degrees.

Enrollment: Total enrollment 1,355. Undergraduate 1,337 (men 44.6%, women 55.4%).

Characteristics of Student Body: *Ethnic/racial makeup:* Black non-Hispanic: 1.7%; American Indian or Alaska Native: .3%; Asian or Pacific Islander: .7%; Hispanic: 1.4%; White non-Hispanic: 90.1%; unknown: 1.2%.

International Students: 62 undergraduate nonresident aliens enrolled fall 2004. Students from Europe, Asia, Africa, Canada. Programs available to aid students whose native language is not English: English as a Second Language Program. Some financial aid designated for qualifying international students.

Student Life: On campus residence halls house 72% of student body. Residence halls for men only constitute 22% of such space, for women only 21%, for both sexes 48%. 9% of student body rent apartments owned by college. *Intercollegiate athletics:* men: baseball, basketball, cross-country, football, golf, soccer, swimming, tennis, track, wrestling; women: basketball, cross-country, golf, soccer, softball, swimming, tennis, track, volleyball. *Special regulations:* Cars permitted subject to payment of registration fee. *Special services:* Writing Center, counseling services, medical services. *Student publications: Cosmos,* a weekly newspaper; *Coe Review* and *Pearl,* annual literary magazines; *Acorn,* a yearbook. *Surrounding community:* Cedar Rapids area population 150,000. Chicago, 225 miles from campus, is nearest metropolitan area. Served by mass transit bus system; airport 5 miles from campus.

Publications: Sources of information about Coe College include *Coe Courier,* an alumni publication.

Library Collections: 217,000 volumes including bound books, serial backfiles, electronic documents, and government documents not in separate collections. Online catalog. Current serial subscriptions: 1,380. 5,900 microforms; 9,100 audiovisual materials. Computer work stations available. Students have access to the Internet at no charge.

Most important holdings include William L. Shirer manuscripts, first editions and personal papers; Charles Abraham Lincoln monograph collection of Charles J. Lynch; published works of Paul Engle.

Buildings and Grounds: Campus area 52 acres.

Chief Executive Officer: Dr. James R. Phifer, President.

Address admission inquiries to John P. Grundig, Director of Admissions.

Cornell College

600 First Street West
Mount Vernon, Iowa 52314-1098
Tel: (319) 895-4000   **E-mail:** admissions@cornellcollege.edu
Fax: (319) 895-4451   **Internet:** www.cornellcollege.edu

Institution Description: Cornell College is a private, nonprofit college affiliated with The United Methodist Church. *Enrollment:* 1,155. *Degrees awarded:* Baccalaureate.

Member of Associated Colleges of the Midwest.

Accreditation: *Regional:* NCA. *Professional:* music, teacher education

History: Established as Iowa Conference Seminary 1853; incorporated as Mount Vernon College and offered first instruction at postsecondary level 1855; adopted present name 1857, awarded first degree (baccalaureate) 1858.

Institutional Structure: *Governing board:* Cornell College Board of Trustees. Representation: 32 trustees, including 24 alumni, college president. 1 ex officio. All voting. *Composition of institution:* Administrators 8 men / 4 women. Academic affairs headed by dean of the college. Management/business/finances directed by vice president and treasurer. Full-time instructional faculty 45 men / 24 women. Academic governance body, Corporate Faculty of the College, meets an average of 17 times per year.

Calendar: One-Course-At-A-Time. The calendar year (Aug. to May) has nine 3-1/2 week terms with four days off between terms. Freshmen admitted at beginning of each term. Degrees conferred and formal commencement May.

Characteristics of Freshmen: 64% of applicants admitted. 27% of applicants admitted and enrolled.

30% (87 students) submitted SAT scores; 83% (242 students) submitted ACT scores. *25th percentile:* SAT Verbal 560, SAT Math 470; ACT Composite 23, ACT English 22, ACT Math 22. *75th percentile:* SAT Verbal 660, SAT Math 670; ACT Composite 29, ACT English 50, ACT Math 28. 66% of entering freshmen expected to graduate within 5 years. 35% of freshmen from Iowa. Freshmen from 28 states and 6 foreign countries.

Admission: Dated admission plan. Early decision application deadline Nov. 15 with notification by Dec. 15. Early action application deadline is Dec. 15 with notification by Jan. 15. Regular decision application deadline Mar. 1 with notification by Apr. 1. *Requirements:* Good secondary school preparation and ability to complete degree program at Cornell.

Entrance tests: College board SAT or ACT composite. *For transfer students:* 2.80 minimum GPA; may transfer in any number of credits but will need to complete one full-year at Cornell to earn a Cornell degree.

Degree Requirements: 32 courses; 2.0 GPA; 1 year in residence; distribution requirements for B.A. Fulfillment of some degree requirements and exemption from beginning courses possible by passing departmental examinations, College Board CLEP, AP, International Baccalaureate, and other standardized examinations. *Grading system:* A–F (plus/minus); pass-fail; withdraw (carries time limit); incomplete (carries time limit).

Distinctive Educational Programs: Work-experience programs. Flexible meeting places and schedules. Accelerated degree program. Dual-degree programs in engineering in cooperation with Washington University (MO), in environmental design and forestry with Duke University (NC), in social service administration with University of Chicago (IL), may also be individually arranged. Cooperative baccalaureate degree programs in nursing and allied health sciences with Rush University (IL). Interdepartmental/interdisciplinary programs in environmental studies, German studies, Medieval and Renaissance studies, origins of behaviors, Russian studies. Facilities for independent research, including honors programs, individual majors, tutorials. Study abroad through the consortium in England, Hong Kong, India, Italy, Japan, and Latin America. Foreign study and travel also available through Experiment in International Living. Off-campus study programs in territorial U.S. include Washington (DC) semester in cooperation with American University and one-semester exchange programs with Fisk University (TN), Rust College (MS), University of Puerto Rico. Through the consortium, Geology in the Rocky Mountains, Newberry Library (IL) Program in the Humanities, Oak Ridge (TN) Science Semester, Urban Studies and Urban Education Programs in Chicago, study at Wilderness Field Station (MN).

Degrees Conferred: 303 *baccalaureate:* area and ethnic studies 9; biological/ life sciences 12; business/marketing 6; computer and information sciences 9; education 34; English 25; foreign languages and literature 15; interdisciplinary studies 21; liberal arts/general studies 3; mathematics 12; natural resources/environmental science 3; parks and recreation 9; philosophy/religion/theology 15;

physical sciences 9; psychology 36; social sciences and history 64; visual and performing arts 8; other 3.

Fees and Other Expenses: *Full-time tuition per academic year 2005–06:* $23,500. *Required fees:* $180. *Room and board per academic year:* $6,4300.

Financial Aid: Aid from institutionally generated funds is provided on the basis of academic merit, financial need. Institution has a Program Participation Agreement with the U.S. Department of Education for eligible students to receive Pell Grants and other federal aid.

Financial aid to full-time, first-time undergraduate students: need-based scholarships/grants totaling $13,147,317, self-help $3,472,694, tuition waivers $468,957; non-need-based scholarships/grants totaling $3,671,170, self-help $140,134, parent loans $804,891, tuition waivers $171,293.

Departments and Teaching Staff: *Total instructional faculty:* 102 (full-time 85, part-time 17; women 48, men 54; members of minority groups 8). Total faculty with doctorate, first-professional, or other terminal degree: 84. Student-to-faculty ratio: 11:1. *Faculty development:* 8 faculty members awarded sabbaticals2004–05.

Enrollment: Total enrollment: 1,155. Undergraduate full-time 489 men / 656 women, part-time 4m / 6w. *Transfer students:* in-state 53; from out-of-state 52.

Characteristics of Student Body: *Ethnic/racial makeup:* number of Black non-Hispanic: 31; American Indian or Alaska Native: 3; Asian or Pacific Islander: 13; Hispanic: 38; White non-Hispanic: 989; unknown: 50. *Age distribution:* number under 18: 11; 18–19: 539; 20–21: 508; 22–24:82; 25–29: 12; 30–34: 235–39: 50–64: 1.

International Students: 31 nonresident aliens enrolled fall 2004. 5 students from Europe, 17 Asia, 1 Central and South America, 7 Africa, 1 Canada. Programs available to aid students whose native language is not English: Social, cultural. English as a Second Language Program. Financial aid specifically designated for international students: scholarships are available annually; 23 were awarded 2004–05.

Student Life: On-campus residence halls house 95% of student body. 64% of students live in coed housing; 25% live in women only housing; 6% live in men only housing. *Intercollegiate athletics:* men: baseball, basketball, cross-country, football, golf, soccer, tennis, track, wrestling; women: basketball, cross-country, golf, soccer, softball, tennis, track, volleyball. *Special regulations:* Cars permitted without restrictions. *Special services:* Medical services. *Student publications, radio: The Cornelian,* a newspaper published 3 times per month; *Open Field,* an annual literary magazine; *Royal Purple,* a yearbook. Radio station KRNL broadcasts 99 hours per week. *Surrounding community:* Mt. Vernon population 4,000. Cedar Rapids, 14 miles from campus, is nearest metropolitan area. Served by airport 18 miles from campus.

Publications: Sources of information about Cornell College include *Cornell Report,* the alumni magazine.

Library Collections: 182,740 volumes. Online catalog. 7,500 audiovisual materials; 495 current periodical subscriptions. 6,727 recordings. Computer work stations available. Students have access to online information retrieval systems and the Internet.

Most important holdings include works on Middle East; ornithology collection.

Buildings and Grounds: Campus area 112 acres.

Chief Executive Officer: Dr. Leslie H. Garner, Jr., President.

Address admission inquiries Jonathan Stroud, Vice President for Enrollment.

Des Monies University - Osteopathic Medical Center

3200 Grand Avenue
Des Moines, Iowa 50312
Tel: (515) 271-1400   **E-mail:** admissions@dmu.edu
Fax: (515) 271-1532   **Internet:** www.dmu.edu

Institution Description: Des Moines University- Osteopathic Medical Center, formerly named University of Osteopathic Medicine and Health Sciences, is a private, independently organized, nonprofit institution. *Enrollment:* 1,306. *Degrees awarded:* Master's, first-professional (osteopathic medicine, physical therapy, podiatric medicine).

Accreditation: *Regional:* NCA. *Professional:* osteopathy, physical therapy, physician assisting, podiatry, public health, surgeon assisting

History: Founded as Dr. S.S. Still College of Osteopathy 1898; name changed to College of Osteopathic Medicine and Surgery 1958; achieved university status and named University of Osteopathic Medicine and Health Sciences in 1980; adopted present name 2002.

Institutional Structure: *Composition of institution:* Colleges of Osteopathic Medicine and Surgery, Podiatric Medicine and Surgery, and Health Sciences.

Board of Trustees appoints president. Full-time instructional faculty 83. Academic governance body, University Faculty, meets monthly.

Calendar: Trimester and yearly calendars (varies for each program).

Admission: Admission requirements vary for different programs. Contact the university for details.

Degree Requirements: Successful completion of all academic and clinical requirements.

Distinctive Educational Programs: Osteopathic medicine and surgery; podiatric medicine and surgery, physician's assistant; health care administration; physical therapy.

Degrees Conferred: 47 *master's:* physician assistant 36; public health 5; health care 6; 210 *first-professional:* osteopathic medicine 187; podiatric medicine 23.

Fees and Other Expenses: *Full-time tuition per academic year:* varies by program; osteopathic medicine $29,050; podiatric medicine $22,175; physician assistant $20,175; physical therapy $17,650; public health $380 per credit hour; health management $380 per credit hour. No on-campus housing.

Financial Aid: Some scholarships available to qualifying students.

Departments and Teaching Staff: *Total instructional faculty:* 85 (full-time 58, part-time 27; women 17, men 68; members of minority groups 2). Total faculty with doctorate, first-professional, or other terminal degree: 85.

Enrollment: Total enrollment 1,306. First-professional full-time 562 men / 475 women, part-time 27m / 62w; graduate full-time 19m / 56w, part-time 28m / 57w.

Characteristics of Student Body: *Ethnic/racial makeup:* number of Black non-Hispanic: 16; American Indian or Alaska Native: 7; Asian or Pacific Islander: 45; Hispanic: 29; White non-Hispanic: 1,161.

International Students: 15 nonresident aliens enrolled fall 2004. No programs available to aid students whose native language is not English. No financial aid specifically designated for international students.

Library Collections: 54,121 volumes. Online and card catalogs. 5,074 recordings, compact discs, CD-ROMs. 570 current periodical subscriptions. 75 computer work stations. Students have access to online information retrieval services and the Internet. Total 2004–05 budget for books and materials: $702,000.

Most important special holdings include historic medical and osteopathic publications.

Buildings and Grounds: Campus area 16 acres. *New buildings:* Student Education Building completed 2000; Student Education Center 2005.

Chief Executive Officer: Terry E. Branstad, President/Chief Executive Officer. Address admission inquiries to Margie Gehringer, Director of Admissions.

Divine Word College

102 Jacoby Drive, S.W.
Epworth, Iowa 52045
Tel: (563) 876-3353   **E-mail:** admissions@dwci.edu
Fax: (563) 876-3407   **Internet:** www.dwci.edu

Institution Description: Divine Word College, a private college affiliated with Divine Word Missionaries, Roman Catholic Church, trains men for the priesthood and brotherhood. *Enrollment:* 78. *Degrees awarded:* Associate, baccalaureate.

Accreditation: *Regional:* NCA.

History: Established as St. Paul's Mission House 1931; chartered and offered first instruction at postsecondary level 1932; adopted present name and became 4-year college 1964; awarded first degree (baccalaureate) 1966.

Institutional Structure: *Governing board:* Divine Word College Board of Trustees. Extrainstitutional representation: 21 trustees; institutional representation: 1 full-time instructional faculty member, president of the college. 1 ex officio. All voting. *Composition of institution:* Administrators 11 men. Academic affairs headed by academic dean. Management/business/finances directed by business manager. Full-time instructional faculty 13. Academic governance body, Committee on Academic Affairs, meets an average of 18 times per year.

Calendar: Semesters. Academic year Aug. to May. Freshmen admitted Aug., Jan. Degrees conferred and formal commencement May. No summer session.

Characteristics of Freshmen: 25 male applicants. 84% of applicants admitted. 100% of admitted students enrolled full-time.

50% (2 students) submitted SAT scores; 50% (2 students) submitted ACT scores. *25th percentile:* SAT Verbal 380, SAT I Math 500; ACT Composite 20, ACT English 20, ACT Math 21. *75th percentile:* SAT Verbal 480, SAT Math 580; ACT Composite 24, ACT English 21, ACT Math 27.

Freshmen from 18 states and 2 foreign countries.

Admission: Rolling admissions plan. For fall acceptance, apply as early as 1 year prior to enrollment, but not later than Aug. 1 of year of enrollment. Early acceptance available. *Requirements:* Either graduation from accredited secondary school or GED. Recommend 4 units English, 2 mathematics, 1 natural science, 1 social studies, 8 academic electives. *Entrance tests:* College Board SAT or ACT composite. *For transfer students:* 2.0 minimum GPA, maximum transfer credit limited only by residence requirements.

College credit and advanced placement for postsecondary-level work completed in secondary school.

Degree Requirements: *For all associate degrees:* 60 credit hours; last two semesters in residence. *For all baccalaureate degrees:* 128 credit hours; last 30 hours in residence; comprehensives in individual fields of study. *For all degrees:* 2.0 GPA; daily chapel attendance; distribution requirements.

Fulfillment of some degree requirements and exemption from some beginning courses possible by passing departmental examinations, College Board CLEP, Achievement Tests, AP, other standardized tests. *Grading system:* A–F; pass; withdraw (deadline after which pass-fail is appended to withdraw); incomplete (carries time limit).

Distinctive Educational Programs: Institutionally sponsored study abroad in Japan, Philippines.

Degrees Conferred: 2 *associate*; 7 *baccalaureate:* philosophy and religious studies 7.

Fees and Other Expenses: *Full-time tuition per academic year:* $9,300. *Room and board per academic year:* $2,200. *Books and supplies:* $500. *Other expenses:* $1,740.

Financial Aid: Institution has a Program Participation Agreement with the U.S. Department of Education for eligible students to receive Pell Grants and other federal aid.

Departments and Teaching Staff: *Total instructional faculty:* 13.

Enrollment: Total enrollment 68. Full-time 78 (men 78).

Characteristics of Student Body: *Ethnic/racial makeup:* Black non-Hispanic: 15.4%; Asian or Pacific Islander: 65.4%; White non-Hispanic: 3.8%;.

International Students: 12 nonresident aliens enrolled fall 2004. Programs available for students whose native language is not English: English as a Second Language Program.

Student Life: On-campus residence halls house 100% of student body. *Special regulations:* Cars permitted without restrictions. Quiet hours from 10pm to 8am. *Special services:* Medical services; college-owned cars available for student use. *Student publications: The Penship,* an annual literary magazine. *Surrounding community:* Epworth population 1,500. Chicago, 200 miles from campus, is nearest metropolitan area. Served by mass transit bus system; airport and passenger rail service, each 15 miles from campus.

Library Collections: 110,000 volumes. 2,000 microform titles; 4,500 audiovisual materials; 400 current periodical subscriptions; 10,000 recordings/tapes. Students have access to online information retrieval services.

Buildings and Grounds: Campus area 40 acres.

Chief Executive Officer: Dr. Michael W. Hutchins, President.

Address admission inquiries to Leo Uhal, Director of Admissions.

Dordt College

498 4th Avenue N.E.
Sioux Center, Iowa 52150-1697
Tel: (712) 722-6000   **E-mail:** admissions@dordt.edu
Fax: (712) 722-1185   **Internet:** www.dordt.edu

Institution Description: As an institution of higher education committed to the Reformed Christian perspective, the mission of Dordt College is to equip students, alumni, and the broader community to work effectively toward Christ-centered renewal in all aspects of contemporary life. *Enrollment:* 1,290. *Degrees awarded:* Associate, baccalaureate, master's. Certificates are also awarded.

Accreditation: *Regional:* NCA. *Professional:* engineering, social work, teacher education

History: Dordt College was established in 1955.

Institutional Structure: *Governing board:* Board of Trustees. Academic affairs headed by dean of education; management/business/finance directed by executive vice president and business administrator. Academic governance body, the faculty, meets biannually.

Calendar: Semesters. Freshmen and transfer students admitted Aug. and Jan. Degrees conferred in May with formal commencement.

Characteristics of Freshmen: 814 applicants (352 men, 42 women). 93.6% of applicants admitted. 45.3% of admitted students enrolled full-time.

19% (66 students) submitted SAT scores; 89% (307 students) submitted ACT scores. *25th percentile:* SAT I Verbal 470, SAT I Math 480; ACT Composite 21,

ACT English 20, ACT Math 21. *75th percentile:* SAT I Verbal 600, SAT I Math 580; ACT Composite 27, ACT English 27, ACT Math 27.

Admission: Rolling admission. For fall acceptance, apply as early as Sept. of senior year in secondary school, but not later than Aug. 1 of year of enrollment. Priority given to applicants who apply before June 1. *Requirements:* Graduation from accredited secondary school or GED. *Entrance tests recommended:* ACT or SAT. Transfer students must have a 2.0 minimum GPA.

Degree Requirements: *For all baccalaureate degrees:* 132 to 136 credit hours depending upon program of study. All programs include general and physical education credits. Fulfillment of some degree requirements possible by passing College Board CLEP and AP. GPA requirements: 2.0 or 2.5 on a 4.0 scale depending upon program.

Degrees Conferred: 29 *associate*; 257 *baccalaureate*; 3 *master's.* Bachelor's degrees awarded in top five disciplines: education 58; business, management, marketing, and related support services 49; visual and performing arts 18; engineering 17; psychology 14.

Fees and Other Expenses: *Full-time tuition per academic year 2004–05:* $16,450. *Books and supplies:* $780. *Room and board per academic year:* $4,850.

Financial Aid: Aid from institutionally generated funds is provided on the basis of academic merit, financial need, other criteria. Institution has a Program Participation Agreement with the U.S. Department of Education for eligible students to receive Pell Grants and other federal aid.

Financial aid to full-time, first-time undergraduate students: 34% received federal grants averaging $3,168; 30% state/local grants averaging $3,585; 100% received institutional grants averaging $4,784; 92% loans averaging $5,671.

Departments and Teaching Staff: *Total instructional faculty:* 75. Degrees held by full-time faculty: 85% hold doctorates. Student-to-faculty ratio: 16:1.

Enrollment: Total enrollment 1,290 (45.8% men, 54.2% women).

Characteristics of Student Body: *Ethnic/racial makeup:* Black non-Hispanic: .2%; Asian or Pacific Islander: .9%; Hispanic: .2%; White non-Hispanic: 89.2%; unknown: .5%.

International Students: 115 nonresident aliens enrolled fall 2004. No programs available to aid students whose native language is not English. No financial aid specifically designated for international students.

Student Life: College housing can accommodate 1,250 students. *Intercollegiate athletics:* 7 sports for men; 7 sports for women; 10 intramural sports each for men and women. *Special services:* counseling and information services; reading service for the visually handicapped. *Special regulations:* Cars permitted. *Surrounding area:* Sioux Center is located 42 miles south of Sioux City.

Library Collections: 185,000 volumes including bound books, serial backfiles, electronic documents, and government documents not in separate collections. Online catalog. 15,000 microform items; 5,000 audiovisual materials; 700 current serial subscriptions. Computer work stations available. Students have access to the Internet at no charge.

Buildings and Grounds: Campus area 110 acres.

Chief Executive Officer: Dr. Carl E. Zylstra, President.

Address admission inquiries to Quentin Van Essen, Executive Director of Admissions.

Drake University

2507 University Avenue
Des Moines, Iowa 50311
Tel: (515) 271-3181   **E-mail:** admitinfo@drake.edu
Fax: (515) 271-3016   **Internet:** www.drake.edu

Institution Description: Drake University is a private, independent, nonprofit institution. *Enrollment:* 5,221. *Degrees awarded:* Baccalaureate, first-professional (law, pharmacy), master's, doctorate.

Accreditation: *Regional:* NCA. *Professional:* accounting, art, business, journalism, law, music, nursing, pharmacy, rehabilitation counseling, teacher education

History: Founded by Disciples of Christ through transfer of faculty of Oskaloosa College, chartered, incorporated, and offered first instruction at postsecondary level 1881; awarded first degree (baccalaureate) 1885. *See* Charles J. Ritchey, *Drake University: Through 75 Years* (Des Moines: Drake University, 1956) for further information.

Institutional Structure: *Governing board:* Board of Governors has authority on matters pertaining to University; Board of Trustees acts in advisory capacity. Extrainstitutional representation: Board of Governors 32 members, Board of Trustees 43 members. Institutional representation: president of the university; 33 alumni, 3 emeriti, 3 ex officio. All voting. *Composition of institution:* Administrators 123 men / 102 women. Academic affairs headed by provost. Management/business/finances directed by vice president, business and finance. Full-time instructional faculty 153 men / 96 women. Academic governance body, University Senate, meets an average of 9 times per year.

Calendar: Semesters. Academic year Aug. to May. Freshmen admitted June, Aug., Jan. Degrees conferred and formal commencement May. Summer session of two 5-week terms and two 4-week terms, offered concurrently, plus a 3-week interim term.

Characteristics of Freshmen: 84% of applicants admitted. 27% of applicants admitted and enrolled.

26% (206 students) submitted SAT scores; 94% (738 students) submitted ACT scores. *25th percentile:* SAT Verbal 530, SAT Math 560; ACT Composite 24, ACT English 24, ACT Math 23. *75th percentile*: SAT Verbal 650, SAT Math 670; ACT Composite 29, ACT English 29, ACT Math 29.

86% of entering freshmen expected to graduate within 5 years. 31% of freshmen from Iowa. Freshmen from 28 states and 10 foreign countries.

Admission: Rolling admissions for all majors except pharmacy. Early acceptance available. *Requirements:* Either graduation from accredited secondary school or GED. Additional requirements for some programs, including mathematics for business and pharmacy students, auditions for some music majors. Minimum GPA 2.5. *Entrance tests:* College Board SAT or ACT composite. For foreign students TOEFL. *For transfer students:* 2.0 GPA (pharmacy 3.5 GPA, journalism 2.25 GPA, education 2.5 GPA at 60 hours, actuarial science 2.5 TPA, accounting 2.5 GPA at 42 hours); from 4-year accredited institution 94 hours maximum transfer credit (with the exception of students in the College of Pharmacy and Health Sciences where 129 hours of transfer credit may be applied); from 2-year accredited institution 66 hours.

College credit for postsecondary-level work completed in secondary school and for extrainstitutional learning on basis of ACE *2006 Guide to the Evaluation of Educational Experiences in the Armed Services*, portfolio assessment. Tutoring available. Developmental courses offered in summer session and regular academic year; credit given.

Degree Requirements: 124 credit hours (158 for pharmacy degree); 2.0 minimum GPA; last 30 hours in residence; general education requirements.

Fulfillment of some degree requirements and exemption from some beginning courses possible by passing departmental examinations, College Board AP exams, CLEP, other standardized tests. *Grading system:* A–F; credit/noncredit; withdraw (carries time limit).

Distinctive Educational Programs: The University Honors Program is designed for the highly qualified, motivated, and committed student who is searching for additional challenges, enrichment, and enlightenment in a college education. The program consists of a core of honors courses, upper-level seminars, and a senior honors thesis or project. Drake's Computer Intensive University Program provides a learning environment in which Drake undergraduates experience computer applications across the curriculum. From the residence halls, students access an electronic network with direct connections to other students, faculty, library, university information source, central research and instructional computing facilities, and two international computer networks.

Through the University's International Programs Abroad, which maintains affiliations with several institutions and consortia, students can arrange to study overseas for a semester or a year. Programs are available in Australia, Austria, Belgium, Brazil, Canada, China, Columbia, Costa Rica, Czechoslovakia, Cyprus, Dominican Republic, Fiji, Finland, France, Germany, Honduras, Hong Kong, Hungary, India, Indonesia, Israel, Italy, Japan, Kenya, Korea, Malta, Mexico, The Netherlands, Nigeria, Philippines, Poland, Russia, Singapore, Spain, Sweden, Switzerland, Taiwan, Tanzania, Thailand, Togo, United Kingdom, Uruguay, Vietnam, Wales, Zimbabwe.

ROTC: Army. 2 commissions awarded 2004–05.

Degrees Conferred: 588 *baccalaureate* (B); 354 *master's* (M); 8 *doctorate* (D): biological/life sciences 58 (B); business/marketing 180 (B), 112 (M); communications/communication technologies 109 (B), 3 (M); computer and information sciences 5 (B); education 51 (B), 179 (M), 8 (D); English 15 (B); health professions and related sciences 5 (B); law/legal studies 6 (B); liberal arts/general studies 1 (B); mathematics 1 (B); natural resources/environmental science 8 (B); philosophy/religion/theology 2 (B); physical sciences 6 (B); protective services/public administration 60 (M); psychology 32 (B); social sciences and history 35 (B); visual and performing arts 44 (B). 234 *first-professional:* pharmacy 101; law 133.

Fees and Other Expenses: *Full-time tuition per academic year 2004–05:* $20,200. *Required fees:* $350. *Room and board per academic year:* $5,920.

Financial Aid: Aid from institutionally generated funds is provided on the basis of academic merit, financial need, athletic ability, other criteria. Institution has a Program Participation Agreement with the U.S. Department of Education for eligible students to receive Pell Grants and other federal aid.

Financial aid to full-time, first-time undergraduate students: need-based scholarships/grants totaling $20,420,460, self-help $15,095,645, parent loans $2,272,658, athletic awards $672,697; non-need-based scholarships/grants

totaling $10,721,083, self-help $13,251,867, parent loans $18,571,627, athletic awards $1,879,280. *Graduate aid:* 892 students received federal and state-funded loans totaling $13,124,346 (ranging from $100 to $18,500); 350 received fellowships and grants totaling $275,415 (ranging from $500 to $22,600).

Departments and Teaching Staff: *Total instructional faculty:* 374 (full-time 249, part-time 125; women 161, men 213; members of minority groups 28). Total faculty with doctorate, first-professional, or other terminal degree: 234. Student-to-faculty ratio: 14.7:1. *Faculty development:* 15 faculty members awarded sabbaticals 2004–05.

Enrollment: Total enrollment 5,221. Undergraduate full-time 1,214 men / 1,699 women, part-time 112m / 139w; first-professional full-time 357m/ 269w, part-time 9m / 12w; graduate full-time 14m / 28w, part-time 415m / 655w. *Transfer students:* in-state 93; from out-of-state 32.

Characteristics of Student Body: *Ethnic and racial makeup:* number of Black non-Hispanic: 107; American Indian or Alaska Native: 7; Asian or Pacific Islander: 108; Hispanic: 43; White non-Hispanic: 2,522; unknown: 231. *Age distribution:* under 18: 36; 18–19: 1,462; 20–21: 1,147; 22–24: 296; 25–29: 88; 30–34: 42; 35–39: 30; 40–49: 38; 50–64: 21; 65 and over: 4.

International Students: 204 nonresident aliens enrolled fall 2004. Students from Europe, Asia, Central and South America, Africa, Canada, Australia. Programs available to aid students whose native language is not English: social, cultural. English as a Second Language Program. Financial aid specifically designated for international students: variable number of scholarships available for qualifying undergraduate students. 102 scholarships totaling $1,200,000 awarded 2004–05.

Student Life: On-campus residence halls house 52% of student body. 29% of men join and 15% live in fraternities; 28% of women join and 14% live in sororities. *Intercollegiate athletics:* men only: basketball, football, golf, soccer, tennis, track; women only: basketball, softball, tennis, track, volleyball. *Special regulations:* Cars permitted without restrictions. Quiet hours. Residence hall visitation 24 hours, 7 days a week. *Special services:* Medical, counseling, Disability Resource Center. *Student publications: Drake Magazine,* a literary publication; *Periphery,* a student magazine; *Times Delphic,* a biweekly newspaper. *Surrounding community:* Des Moines population over 300,000. Served by mass transit bus system, airport 8 miles from campus.

Library Collections: 683,948 volumes. Online and card catalogs. Current serial subscriptions: paper 1,865, microform 894,663, via electronic access 15,000. Students have access to online information retrieval services.

Most important holdings include Philip Duffield Strong papers; Gardner Cowles papers; John Cowles papers.

Buildings and Grounds: Campus area 120 acres.

Chief Executive Officer: Dr. David Maxwell, President.

Address admission inquiries to Thomas F. Delahunt, Director of Admissions.

College of Arts and Sciences

Degree Programs Offered: *Baccalaureate* in astronomy; biology; chemistry; computer science; earth science; economics; economics-business administration; English; foreign languages; geography; history; humanities; international relations; Latin American area studies; marine science; mathematics; philosophy; physics; political science; psychology; religion; sociology; speech communication; art; graphic design; music; music education; theatre arts; *master's* in various fields, including music, music education.

Distinctive Educational Programs: Dual-degree program in physics and engineering with Cornell University (NY) and Washington University (MO). Interdisciplinary programs in Asian studies, human aging, humanities, international relations, Latin American studies. Preprofessional programs in church vocations, dentistry, marine science, medical technology, medicine, social welfare.

School of Education

Degree Programs Offered: *Baccalaureate* in elementary education; secondary education; art education; music education. *Master of Arts* in teaching (American history; art; biology; business education; chemistry; earth science; English; foreign language; general science; geography; journalism; mathematics; physics; physical science; sociology; speech communication/theatre; world history); *Master of Science* in elementary education; counselor education; education (adult education/training and development); elementary school counseling; secondary school counseling; educational administration (elementary and secondary); higher education; teacher education and curriculum studies; *Specialist* in education (adult education; curriculum and teaching; educational administration; higher education); *doctorate* in education (adult education; counselor education; curriculum studies; educational administration; higher education).

School of Journalism and Mass Communication

Degree Programs Offered: *Baccalaureate* in advertising, account management, creative advertising, broadcast news, journalism teaching, magazines, news-editorial, public relations, radio-television management, radio-television production.

College of Pharmacy and Health Sciences

Degree Programs Offered: *Baccalaureate* and *master's* in nursing; *first-professional* and *doctorate* in pharmacy.

Law School

Degree Programs Offered: *First-professional.*

Admission: Baccalaureate from accredited institution, LSAT.

Degree Requirements: 90 credit hours, 6 residence credits, 2.0 minimum GPA.

Distinctive Educational Programs: Doctor of Jurisprudence joint degree programs offered.

Emmaus Bible College

2570 Asbury Road
Dubuque, Iowa 52001-3096
Tel: (563) 588-8000 **E-mail:** info@emmaus.edu
Fax: (563) 588-1216 **Internet:** www.emmaus.edu

Institution Description: Emmaus Bible college is a private, nonprofit, independent college. *Enrollment:* 257. *Degrees awarded:* Baccalaureate.

Accreditation: *National:* ABHE. *Professional*: teacher education

History: Established as Emmaus Bible School in 1941 in Toronto, Canada. A second campus was opened in Chicago in 1947. In 1953 the two campuses were merged at the new location in Oak Fork, IL. In 1984 the campus moved to its present location in Dubuque, IA and changed its name to Emmaus Bible College.

Institutional Structure: *Governing board:* Board of Trustees. Representation: 20 trustees. *Composition of institution:* Academic affairs headed by dean of education; management/business/finance directed by executive vice president and business administrator. Academic governance body, the faculty, meets biannually.

Calendar: Semesters. Two-week WinterTerm. Academic year Aug. to May. Freshmen and transfer students admitted Aug. and Jan. Degrees conferred in Dec. and May with formal commencement in May.

Characteristics of Freshmen: 83 applicants (83 men, 51 women). 85.5% of applicants admitted. 80.3% of admitted students enrolled full-time.

29% (17 students) submitted SAT scores; 51% (30 students) submitted ACT scores. *25th percentile*: SAT Verbal 510, SAT Math 450; ACT Composite 18, ACT English 17, ACT Math 17. *75th percentile*: SAT Verbal 650, SAT Math 660; ACT Composite 24, ACT English 24, ACT Math 22.

Admission: Rolling admission. For fall acceptance, apply as early as Sept. of senior year in secondary school, but not later than Aug. 1 of year of enrollment. Priority given to applicants who apply before June 1. *Requirements:* Graduation from accredited secondary school or GED. *Entrance tests recommended:* ACT or SAT. Transfer students must have a 2.0 minimum GPA.

Degree Requirements: *For all baccalaureate degrees:* 132 to 136 credit hours depending upon program of study. All programs include a Bible major with Bible credits ranging from 52 to 94, and a core list of required courses. All programs include general and physical education credits.

Fulfillment of some degree requirements possible by passing College Board CLEP and AP. GPA requirements: 2.0 or 2.5 on a 4.0 scale depending upon program.

Distinctive Educational Programs: *For undergraduates:* One-year Bible Certificate and Continuing Education Certificate available for college graduates.

Degrees Conferred: 37 *baccalaureate*: computer and information sciences and support services 2; education 11; theology and ministerial studies 24.

Fees and Other Expenses: *Full-time tuition per academic year 2004–05:* $7,330. *Books and supplies:* $600. *Room and board per academic year:* $3,580.

Financial Aid: Aid from institutionally generated funds is provided on the basis of academic merit, financial need, other criteria. Institution has a Program Participation Agreement with the U.S. Department of Education for eligible students to receive Pell Grants and other federal aid.

Financial aid to full-time, first-time undergraduate students: 21% received federal grants averaging $2,513; 34% institutional grants averaging $2,052; 41% loans averaging $4,920.

Departments and Teaching Staff: Bible and theology *professors* 6, *part-time teachers* 4; elementary education 3, 1; music 1, 1; Christian education 1, 1; missions 2, 0; general education studies 2, 4.

Total instructional faculty: 26. Student-to-faculty ratio: 15:1. Degrees held by full-time faculty: doctorate 33%, master's 40%, baccalaureate 27%. 33% hold terminal degrees.

Enrollment: Total enrollment 257 (43.6% men, 56.4% women).

Characteristics of Student Body: *Ethnic/racial makeup:* Black non-Hispanic: 1.6%; American Indian or Alaska Native: .4%; Asian or Pacific Islander: 3.1%; Hispanic: 2.7%; White non-Hispanic: 90.3%; unknown: 1.2%. *Age distribution:* 17–21: 72%; 22–24: 15%; 25–29: 5%; 30–34: 3%; 35–39: 2%; 40–49: 1%; unknown: 2%.

International Students: 25 nonresident aliens enrolled fall 2004. No programs available to aid students whose native language is not English. No financial aid specifically designated for international students.

Student Life: All single students required to live on campus (unless living with family in immediate area). *Intercollegiate athletics:* Member of NCAA. Basketball for men and women. Intramural sports include basketball, volleyball, field hockey, flag football, softball, badminton, table tennis. Club level sports: outdoor and indoor soccer. *Special regulations:* Cars permitted (restricted to one per student). *Student radio:* On-campus radio stations. *Surrounding area:* Dubuque population 60,000. Served by bus system. Airport with 3 major airlines.

Publications: *The Emmaus Journal,* theological journal.

Library Collections: 85,200 volumes including bound books, serial backfiles, electronic documents, and government documents not in separate collections. Online catalog. 300 current serial subscriptions. Computer work stations available. Students have access to the Internet at no charge.

Buildings and Grounds: Campus area 23 acres.

Chief Executive Officer: Dr. Kenneth A. Daughters, President.

Address admission inquiries to Kathryn L. Van Dine, Registrar.

Faith Baptist Bible College and Theological Seminary

1900 N.W. Fourth Street
Ankeny, Iowa 50021-2152
Tel: (515) 964-0601 **E-mail:** admissions@faith.edu
Fax: (515) 964-1638 **Internet:** www.faith.edu

Institution Description: Faith Baptist Bible College and Theological Seminary is a private, nonprofit institution affiliated with the General Association of Regular Baptist Churches. *Enrollment:* 506. *Degrees awarded:* Associate, baccalaureate, master's. Certificates also awarded.

Accreditation: *Regional:* NCA. *National:* ABHE.

History: Founded as Omaha Bible Institute 1921; name changed to Omaha Baptist Bible College 1960; moved to Ankeny and changed name to Faith Baptist Bible College 1967; Seminary established 1986.

Institutional Structure: *Governing board:* Board of Directors (32 members). *Composition of institution:* Administrative Council: president, executive vice president, vice presidents for academic services, student enrichment and services, business and finance, enrollment and constituent services, institutional advancement.

Calendar: Semesters. Academic year Aug. to May. Summer session of 2 terms from May to June. Formal commencement May.

Characteristics of Freshmen: 77% of applicants admitted. 55% of applicants admitted and enrolled.

10% (11 students) submitted SAT scores; 87% (99 students) submitted ACT scores. *25th percentile*: SAT Verbal 490, SAT Math 430; ACT Composite 19, ACT English 19, ACT Math 17. *75th percentile*: SAT Verbal 520, SAT Math 560; ACT Composite 26, ACT English 26, ACT Math 24.

41% of entering freshmen expected to graduate within 5 years. 49% of freshmen from Iowa. Freshmen from 22 states and 5 foreign countries.

Admission: All application forms, including references and transcripts, should be in the hands of the Admissions Committee one month prior to registration. *Requirements:* Definite knowledge of Christ as Savior; graduation from high school or GED. *For transfer students:* Full credit for equivalent and parallel courses from accredited institutions. Must have C grade or above. Other credits accepted on provisionary basis.

Degree Requirements: 130–142 credit hours; at least one full year (24 hours) of resident study; 2.0 GPA on 4.0 scale; acceptance of doctrinal statement of Faith Baptist Bible College and Seminary; completion of program requirements.

Distinctive Educational Programs: Secondary Education Program with English and Bible major.

Degrees Conferred: 13 *associate;* 76 *baccalaureate:* education 29; philosophy/religion/theology 45; visual and performing arts 2; 14 *master's:* theology 14; 11 *first-professional:* master of divinity.

Fees and Other Expenses: *Full-time tuition per academic year 2005–06:* $10,804 undergraduate, $9,322 graduate. *Required fees:* $400. *Room and board per academic year:* $4,316.

Financial Aid: Aid from institutionally generated funds is provided on the basis of academic merit, financial need, other considerations. Institution has a Program Participation Agreement with the U.S. Department of Education for eligible students to receive Pell Grants and other federal aid.

Financial aid to full-time, first-time undergraduate students: need-based scholarships/grants totaling $1,019,247, self-help $1,191,523, parent loans $108,901; non-need-based scholarships/grants totaling $342,197, self-help $339,324, parent loans $12,200. *Graduate aid:* 24 federal and state-funded loans totaling $158,700 (ranging from $758 to $11,500).

Departments and Teaching Staff: *Professors* 7, *associate professors* 10, *assistant professors* 4, part-time faculty 13.

Total instructional faculty: 34 (full-time 21, part-time 13; women 10, men 24; members of minority groups 4). Total faculty with doctorate, first-professional, or other terminal degree: 17. Student-to-faculty ratio: 17:1.

Enrollment: Total enrollment 506. Undergraduate full-time 159 men / 159 women, part-time 19m / 21w; first-professional full-time 25m / 1w, part-time 14m; graduate full-time 12m / 1w, part-time 56m / 39w.

Characteristics of Student Body: *Ethnic/racial makeup:* number of Black non-Hispanic: 1; American Indian or Alaska Native: 1; Asian or Pacific Islander: 3; Hispanic: 7; White non-Hispanic: 346. *Age distribution:* number under 18: 7; 18–19: 153; 20–21: 123; 22–24: 58; 25–29: 11; 30–34: 2; 35–39: 2; 40–49: 2.

International Students: 5 nonresident aliens enrolled fall 2004. 4 students from Asia, 1 Africa. No programs available to aid students whose native language is not English. No financial aid specifically designated for international students.

Student Life: On-campus housing for single students available. Limited number of apartments available for married students. *Special regulations:* Dress code and standards of conduct established. Use of alcoholic beverages, tobacco and nonprescribed drugs prohibited.

Publications: *Faith Witness,* a general quarterly publication; *Alumni Update,* biannual publication to alumni; *Faith Pulpit,* monthly seminary publication.

Library Collections: 67,040 volumes. Online catalog. 3,005 microforms; 7,940 audiovisual materials; 435 current periodical subscriptions. 2,758 recordings. 30 computer work stations. Students have access to the Internet at no charge.

Most important special holdings include collections on Bible commentaries, theology, and Christian living.

Buildings and Grounds: Campus area 52 acres.

Chief Executive Officer: Dr. Richard W. Houg, President.

Address admission inquiries to Tim Nilius, Vice President of Enrollment.

Graceland University

700 College Avenue
Lamoni, Iowa 50140

Tel: (641) 784-5000   **E-mail:** admissions@graceland.edu
Fax: (641) 784-5480   **Internet:** www.graceland.edu

Institution Description: Graceland University, formerly Graceland College is a private college affiliated with Reorganized Church of Jesus Christ of Latter-day Saints. *Enrollment:* 2,351. *Degrees awarded:* Baccalaureate, master's. Certificates also awarded.

Accreditation: *Regional:* NCA. *Professional:* nursing, nursing education, teacher education

History: Established, incorporated, offered first instruction at postsecondary level 1895; awarded first degree (baccalaureate) 1898; reorganized as junior college 1920; reestablished senior level 1960; became Graceland University in 2000. *See* Paul M. Edwards, *The Hilltop Where* (Independence, MO: Herald House, 1972) and Barbara J. Higdon, Editor, *An Illustrated History of Graceland* (Independence, MO: Herald House, 1989) for further information.

Institutional Structure: *Governing board:* Graceland University Board of Trustees. Extrainstitutional representation: 24 trustees. All voting. *Composition of institution:* Administrators 31 men / 31 women. Six vice presidents: Independence Education Center/Outreach and dean of nursing; academic affairs and dean of faculty, student life and dean of students, business affairs and treasurer, enrollment management and dean of admissions, institutional advancement. Full-time instructional faculty 79. Academic governance body, the faculty, meets an average of 10 times per year.

Calendar: Semesters (4-1-4 plan). Academic year Aug. to May. Freshmen admitted Aug., Jan., Feb., June. Degrees conferred May, Aug., Dec., Jan. Formal commencement May. Summer session of multiple terms from June to July.

Characteristics of Freshmen: 1,170 applicants (672 men, 498 women). 55.4% of applicants enrolled. 47.5% of admitted students enrolled full-time.

21% (65 students) submitted SAT scores; 66% (204 students) submitted ACT scores. *25th percentile:* SAT Verbal 410, SAT Math 410; ACT Composite 17, ACT English 16, ACT Math 16. *75th percentile:* SAT Verbal 540, SAT Math 540; ACT Composite 24, ACT English 24, ACT Math 24.

40% of entering freshmen expected to graduate within 5 years. 33% of freshmen from Iowa. Freshmen from 27 states and 9 foreign countries.

Admission: Rolling admissions plan. For fall acceptance, apply as early as 1 year prior to enrollment, but not later than Aug. 15 of year of enrollment. Early acceptance available. *Requirements:* Either graduation from accredited secondary school or GED. Must meet 2 of the following 3 requirements: 2.0 GPA, secondary school class standing 50th percentile, ACT composite 21 or SAT combined score 960. Additional requirements for some programs. *Entrance tests:* College Board SAT or ACT composite. *For transfer students:* 2.0 minimum GPA; from 4-year accredited institution maximum transfer credit limited only by residence requirement; from 2-year institution 75 semester hours maximum transfer credit; correspondence/extension students, 12 hours.

College credit and advanced placement for postsecondary-level work completed in secondary school. Tutoring available. Developmental courses offered in summer session and regular academic year; credit given.

Degree Requirements: 128 semester hours; 2.0 GPA; 32 hours in residence; distribution requirements. Fulfillment of some degree requirements and exemption from some beginning courses possible by passing departmental examinations, College Board CLEP, APP. *Grading system:* A–F; pass-fail; withdraw (carries time limit); incomplete (carries time limit).

Distinctive Educational Programs: Flexible meeting places and schedules, including off-campus center (at Independence, MO, 120 miles away from main institution) and evening classes. Accelerated degree program. Facilities for independent research, including honors programs, individual majors. Outreach Nursing Program (home study); CHANCE program for students with learning dysfunction; honors program available in all majors.

Degrees Conferred: 434 *baccalaureate;* 85 *master's.* Bachelor's degrees awarded in top five disciplines: education 121; health professions and related clinical sciences 101; business, management, marketing, and related support services 96; liberal arts and sciences, general studies and humanities 23; psychology 19.

Fees and Other Expenses: *Full-time tuition per academic year 2004–05:* $15,000. *Books and supplies:* $1,000. *Room and board per academic year:* $5,150.

Financial Aid: Graceland University offers a direct lending program. Aid from institutionally generated funds is provided on the basis of academic merit, financial need, athletic ability, other criteria. Institution has a Program Participation Agreement with the U.S. Department of Education for eligible students to receive Pell Grants and other federal aid.

Financial aid to full-time, first-time undergraduate students: 27% received federal grants averaging $3,182; 13% state/local grants averaging $3,538; 100% institutional grants averaging $8,703; 69% loans averaging $4,648.

Departments and Teaching Staff: Fine arts *professors* 3, *associate professors* 3, *assistant professors* 3, *instructors* 0, *part-time faculty* 2; health and education 5, 2, 8, 1, 2; humanities 5, 2, 3, 0, 4; nursing 3, 2, 11, 0, 0; science/mathematics 6, 3, 3, 1, 0; social science 3, 4, 6, 2, 4.

Total instructional faculty: 91. Student-to-faculty ratio: 16.6:1. Degrees held by full-time instructional faculty: doctorate 56%, master's 34%, baccalaureate 1%. 65% hold terminal degrees.

Enrollment: Total enrollment 2,351. Undergraduate 1,845 (38.3% men, 61.7% women).

Characteristics of Student Body: *Ethnic/racial makeup:* Black non-Hispanic: 6.3%; American Indian or Alaska Native: .5%; Asian or Pacific Islander: 1.7%; Hispanic: 2.8%; White non-Hispanic: 62.2%. *Age distribution:* 17–21: 24%; 22–24: 9%; 25–29: 4%; 30–34: 6%; 35–39: 11%; 40–49: 29%; 50–59: 12%; 60–and over: 2%.

International Students: 154 undergraduate nonresident aliens enrolled fall 2004. Programs available to aid students whose native language is not English: Social, cultural, financial. English as a Second Language Program. Financial aid specifically designated for international students: scholarships available annually to qualifying students.

Student Life: On-campus residence halls house 70% of student body. Residence halls for men constitute 49% of such space, for women 51%. Limited housing available for married students. *Intercollegiate athletics:* men only: baseball, basketball, football, golf, soccer tennis, track, volleyball; women only: basketball, golf, soccer, softball, tennis, track, volleyball. *Special regulations:* Cars permitted without restrictions. Quiet hours from 12am to 7am. Residence hall visitation from noon to midnight Sun.–Thurs.; noon to 2am Fri. and Sat. *Special* *services:* Academic Skills Center, medical services. *Student publications: Acacia,* a yearbook; *Graceland Tower,* a weekly newspaper. *Surrounding community:* Lamoni population 3,000. Des Moines, 80 miles from campus, is nearest metropolitan area.

Library Collections: 199,500 volumes including bound books, serial backfiles, electronic documents, and government documents not in separate collections. Online catalog. 625 current serial subscriptions. 3,700 audiovisual materials. 925 microforms. Computer work stations available. Students have access to the Internet at no charge.

Most important holdings include Restoration History Manuscript Collection (including manuscripts from the early days of the Mormon Church); contemporary literature; education; sociology.

Buildings and Grounds: Campus area 165 acres.

Chief Executive Officer: Dr. John K. Menzies, President.

Address admission inquiries to Brian Shantz, Director of Admissions.

Grand View College

1200 Grandview Avenue
Des Moines, Iowa 50316
Tel: (515) 263-2810   **E-mail:** admiss@gvc.edu
Fax: (515) 263-2974   **Internet:** www.gvc.edu

Institution Description: Grand View College is a private college affiliated with the Evangelical Lutheran Church in America. *Enrollment:* 1,759. *Degrees awarded:* Associate, baccalaureate.

Accreditation: *Regional:* NCA. *Professional:* nursing, nursing education

History: Established and chartered 1896; offered first instruction at postsecondary level 1924; added 3-year program 1968, baccalaureate 1975.

Institutional Structure: *Governing board:* Board of Directors. Extrainstitutional representation: 32 directors, 4 honorary directors, 1 church official. 2 ex officio. 9 honorary. 34 voting. *Composition of institution:* Administrators 12 men / 2 women. Academic affairs headed by academic dean. Management/business/finances directed by vice president for finance. Full-time instructional faculty 81. Academic governance body, the faculty, meets an average of 8 times per year.

Calendar: Semesters. Academic year Aug. to late Apr. Freshmen admitted Aug., Jan., May, June, July. Degrees conferred and formal commencement Apr. Summer session of 2 terms from May to early Aug.

Characteristics of Freshmen: 80% of applicants accepted. 28% of accepted applicants enrolled.

3.7% (8 students) submitted SAT scores; 95.9% (209 students) submitted ACT scores. *25th percentile:* SAT Verbal 420, SAT Math 470; ACT Composite 18; *75th percentile:* SAT Verbal 550, SAT Math 560; ACT Composite 23.

90% of freshmen from Iowa. Freshmen from 11 states and 5 foreign countries.

Admission: Rolling admissions plan. For fall acceptance, apply as early as junior year of secondary school, but not later than Aug. 15 of year of enrollment. Early acceptance available. *Requirements:* Either graduation from accredited secondary school or GED. *Entrance tests:* ACT or SAT. *For transfer students:* 2.0 minimum GPA, maximum transfer credit limited only by residence requirement.

College credit and advanced placement for postsecondary-level work completed in secondary school. College credit for extrainstitutional learning on basis of ACE *2006 Guide to the Evaluation of Educational Experiences in the Armed Services.* Tutoring available. Remedial courses offered during regular academic year; credit given.

Degree Requirements: *For all associate degrees:* 62 credit hours; 30 credit hours (or last 12 hours) in residence. *For all baccalaureate degrees:* 124 hours; last 30 hours in residence; demonstrated proficiency in English and mathematics. *For all degrees:* 2.0 GPA; 2.2 GPA in major field; exit competency examinations in writing; distribution requirements.

Fulfillment of some degree requirements and exemption from some beginning courses possible by passing departmental examinations, College Board CLEP, AP. *Grading system:* A–F.

Distinctive Educational Programs: Work-experience programs, including internships, cooperative education. Evening classes. Interdisciplinary programs by individual arrangement. Facilities for independent research, including honors programs, individual majors. Study abroad in Austria, England, France, Mexico, Spain, and Wales in cooperation with Central College. Cross-registration with Des Moines Area Community College and Drake University. Students may enroll in classes at Des Moines Art Center and receive credit from Grand View. *Other distinctive programs:* Degree-granting continuing education.

ROTC: Army and Air Force offered in cooperation with Drake University.

Degrees Conferred: 2 *associate;* 334 *baccalaureate.* Bachelor's degrees awarded in top five disciplines: health professions and related clinical sciences

72; business, management, marketing, and related support services 63; education 41; liberal arts and sciences, general studies and humanities 31; security and protective services 19.

Fees and Other Expenses: *Full-time tuition per academic year 2004–05:* $15,342. *Books and supplies:* $800. *Room and board per academic year:* $5,436.

Financial Aid: Aid from institutionally generated funds is provided on the basis of academic merit, financial need, athletic ability, other criteria. Institution has a Program Participation Agreement with the U.S. Department of Education for eligible students to receive Pell Grants and other federal aid.

Financial aid to full-time, first-time undergraduate students: 39% received federal grants averaging $2,806, 65% state/local grants averaging $3,446, 98% institutional grants averaging $5,363, 64% loans averaging $5,770.

Departments and Teaching Staff: *Professors* 23, *associate professors* 20, *assistant professors* 17, *instructors* 3, *part-time teachers* 78.

Total instructional faculty: 141. Student-to-faculty ratio: 12:1. Degrees held by full-time faculty: 52% hold terminal degrees.

Enrollment: Total enrollment 1,759 (30.1% men, 69.9% women).

Characteristics of Student Body: *Ethnic/racial makeup:* Black non-Hispanic: 3.1%; American Indian or Alaska Native: .4%; Asian or Pacific Islander: 1.7%; Hispanic: 1.3%; White non-Hispanic: 63.1%; unknown: 29%. *Age distribution:* 17–21: 53%; 22–24: 17%; 25–29: 8%; 35–39: 7%; 40–49: 5%; 50–59: 9%; 60–and over: 1%.

International Students: 25 nonresident aliens enrolled fall 2004. Students from Europe, Asia, Canada. No programs available to aid students whose native language is not English. No financial aid specifically designated for international students.

Student Life: On-campus residence halls house 20% of student body. *Intercollegiate athletics:* men only: baseball, basketball, golf, soccer; women only: basketball, soccer, softball, volleyball. *Special regulations:* Cars permitted without restrictions. *Special services:* Learning Resources Center, medical services, Adult Learning Center. *Student publications, radio: Grand View,* a weekly newspaper. Radio station KDPS; campus television station. *Surrounding community:* Des Moines metropolitan area population 350,000. Served by mass transit bus system; airport 10 miles from campus.

Library Collections: 105,000 volumes. 186,000 microforms; 6,500 audiovisual materials; 355 current periodical subscriptions. Access to online information retrieval systems and the Internet.

Most important holdings include N.F.S. Grundtuig Collection; collection of books, diaries, manuscripts by and about Danish immigrants, dating from the late 19th- and early 20th-centuries.

Buildings and Grounds: Campus area 25 acres.

Chief Executive Officer: Dr. Kent L. Henning, President.

Address admission inquiries to Debbie M. Barger, Vice President for Enrollment Management.

Grinnell College

1121 Park Avenue
Grinnell, Iowa 50112
Tel: (641) 269-3600   **E-mail:** askgrin@grin.edu
Fax: (641) 269-4800   **Internet:** www.grin.edu

Institution Description: Grinnell College is a private, independent, nonprofit college. *Enrollment:* 1,556. *Degrees awarded:* Baccalaureate.

Member of the consortium Associated Colleges of the Midwest.

Accreditation: *Regional:* NCA.

History: Established as the Trustees of Iowa College 1846; chartered 1847; offered first instruction at postsecondary level 1848; first degree (baccalaureate) awarded 1854, adopted present name 1909. *See* John S. Nollen, *Grinnell College* (Iowa City: State Historical Society of Iowa, 1953) for further information.

Institutional Structure: *Governing board:* The Board of Trustees. Extrainstitutional representation: 30 trustees, 10 life trustees and 1 ex officio. institutional representation: 1 administrator; 1 ex officio. 49 voting. *Composition of institution:* Administrators 6 men / 2 women. Academic affairs headed by dean of the faculty. Management/business/finances directed by treasurer of the college. Full-time instructional faculty 150. Academic governance body, The Executive Council, meets an average of 28 times per year.

Calendar: Semesters. Academic year Aug. to May. First-year students admitted for fall only. Degrees conferred and formal commencement May. No summer session.

Characteristics of Freshmen: 51% of applicants admitted. 29% of applicants admitted and enrolled.

60% (261 students) submitted SAT scores; 39% (169 students) submitted ACT scores. *25th percentile:* SAT Verbal 640, SAT Math 650; ACT Composite

28, ACT English 27, ACT Math 27. *75th percentile*: SAT Verbal 760, SAT Math 730; ACT Composite 32, ACT English 34, ACT Math 32.

85% of entering freshmen expected to graduate within 5 years. 11% of freshmen from Iowa. Freshmen from 50 states and 45 foreign countries.

Admission: For fall acceptance, apply as early as Aug. of previous year. Students are notified of acceptance Dec. 15 and Apr. 1. Apply by Nov. 30 for early decision, first choice. Early admission available. *Requirements:* Graduation from accredited secondary school with 4 units in English, 3 mathematics, 9 academic electives. *Entrance tests:* College Board SAT or ACT composite. *For transfer students:* 3.0 minimum GPA; maximum transfer credit from accredited institutions limited only by residence requirement.

Advanced placement for postsecondary-level work completed in secondary school. Tutoring available. Developmental courses offered during regular academic year; credit given.

Degree Requirements: 124 credit hours; 4 semesters in residence; freshman tutorial; major requirements. Fulfillment of some degree requirements and exemption from some beginning courses possible by passing College Board APP. *Grading system:* A–F; Pass/Fail.

Distinctive Educational Programs: First semester tutorial with writing focus, taught by student's academic advisor. New Science Project pre-orientation for students from under-represented groups. Extensive opportunities for student-faculty research in most disciplines. Plus-2 option to pursue an extra-credit independent project connected to a regular course. Internships for academic credit with faculty supervision Center for Prairie Studies. Interdisciplinary concentrations such as global Development Studies, Linguistics, and Technology Studies. Cooperative professional programs in architecture, engineering, and law. Ninth semester student teaching program leading to certification. Urban teaching program in Chicago. Off-campus study opportunities at various locations throughout the world and at universities in the United States.

Degrees Conferred: 428 *baccalaureate:* biological/life sciences 48; computer and information sciences 25; English 47; foreign languages and literature 43; mathematics 15; philosophy/religion/theology 20; physical sciences 19; psychology 19; social sciences and history 146; visual and performing arts 38; other 8. *Honorary degrees awarded 2004:* Doctor of Science 2; Doctor of Humane Letters 2.

Fees and Other Expenses: *Full-time tuition per academic year 2004–05:* $25,200. *Required fees:* $620. *Room and board per academic year:* $6,870.

Financial Aid: Aid from institutionally generated funds is provided on the basis of academic merit, financial need. Institution has a Program Participation Agreement with the U.S. Department of Education for eligible students to receive Pell Grants and other federal aid.

Financial aid to full-time, first-time undergraduate students: need-based scholarships/grants totaling $14,203,938, self-help $4,171,382, tuition waivers $304,942; non-need-based scholarships/grants totaling $5,627,388, self-help $211,168, tuition waivers $843,564.

Departments and Teaching Staff: *Total instructional faculty:* 190 (full-time 150, part-time 40; women 80, men 110; member of minority groups 190). Total faculty with doctorate, first-professional, or other terminal degree: 171. Student-to-faculty ratio: 9:1. *Faculty development:* 29 faculty members awarded sabbaticals 2004–05.

Enrollment: Total enrollment 1,556. Undergraduate full-time 694 men / 835 women, part-time 15m / 12w.

Characteristics of Student Body: *Ethnic/racial makeup:* number of Black non-Hispanic: 61; American Indian or Alaska Native: 11; Asian or Pacific Islander: 76; Hispanic: 55; White non-Hispanic: 1,060; unknown: 128. *Age distribution:* number under 18: 28; 18–19: 756; 20–21: 655; 22–24: 90.

International Students: 187 nonresident aliens enrolled fall 2004. Programs available to aid students whose native language is not English: social, cultural, financial. 157 international students received financial aid in 2004–05 totaling $3,536,882.

Student Life: On-campus residence halls house 85% of student body. *Intercollegiate athletics:* men only: baseball, basketball, cross-country, football, golf, soccer, swimming, tennis, track; women only: basketball, cross-country, golf, soccer, softball, swimming, tennis, track, volleyball. *Special regulations:* Cars permitted without restrictions. *Special services:* Reading, writing, science, and math labs, medical services. *Student publications, radio: Cyclone,* a yearbook; *Scarlet and Black,* a weekly newspaper. Radio station KDIC broadcasts 154 hours per week. *Surrounding community:* Grinnell population 9,000. Des Moines, 55 miles from campus, is nearest metropolitan area.

Library Collections: 521,465 volumes. 541,925 government documents; 392,573 microform items; 29,452 audiovisual items; 5,147 periodicals subscribed to (including electronic serials). Students have access to the Internet at no charge.

Most important holdings include James Norman Hall Collection (manuscripts and books); Pinne Collection; East Asian Collection.

Buildings and Grounds: Campus area 90 acres. *New buildings:* John Crystal Center completed 2002; 4 residence halls completed 2003.

Chief Executive Officer: Dr. Russell K. Osgood, President.

Address admission inquiries to James Sumner, Dean of Admission and Financial Aid.

Hamilton College

3165 Edgewood Parkway S.W.
Cedar Rapids, Iowa 52404

Tel: (319) 363-0481   **E-mail:** admissions@hamiltonia.edu
Fax: (319) 363-3812   **Internet:** www.hamiltonia.edu

Institution Description: Hamilton College is an institution of higher education offering programs that integrate general education, professional skills, and career-focused education. The college employs instructional methods based on adult learning theory and is committed to the development of each student's intellectual, analytical, and critical thinking abilities. In addition to the main campus in Cedar Rapids, there are branch campuses in Cedar Falls, Des Moines, and Mason City. *Enrollment:* 689. *Degrees awarded:* Associate, baccalaureate.

Accreditation: *Regional:* NCA. *National:* ACICS.

History: The college was established in 1900.

Institutional Structure: *Governing board:* Board of Trustees. Academic affairs headed by dean of education; management/business/finance directed by executive vice president and business administrator.

Calendar: Quarters.

Admission: Rolling admission. For fall acceptance, apply as early as Sept. of senior year in secondary school, but not later than Aug. 1 of year of enrollment. Priority given to applicants who apply before June 1. *Requirements:* Graduation from accredited secondary school or GED. *Entrance tests recommended:* ACT or SAT. Transfer students must have a 2.0 minimum GPA.

Degree Requirements: Completion of prescribed curriculum for program in which the student is enrolled.

Degrees Conferred: 95 *associate;* 40 *baccalaureate.* Bachelor's degrees awarded in largest programs: business, management, marketing, and related support services 22; computer and information sciences and support services 18.

Fees and Other Expenses: *Full-time tuition per academic year 2004–05:* $11,520. *Room and board per academic year:* $7,722. *Other expenses:* $4,248.

Financial Aid: Aid from institutionally generated funds is provided on the basis of academic merit, financial need, other criteria. Institution has a Program Participation Agreement with the U.S. Department of Education for eligible students to receive Pell Grants and other federal aid.

Financial aid to full-time, first-time undergraduate students: 60% received federal grants averaging $1,138; 14% state/local grants; 5% received institutional grants; 83% loans averaging $2,173.

Departments and Teaching Staff: *Total instructional faculty:* Faculty members are unranked.

Enrollment: Total enrollment 669 (32.7% men, 67.3% women).

Characteristics of Student Body: *Ethnic/racial makeup:* Black non-Hispanic: 7.8%; American Indian or Alaska Native: .1%; Asian or Pacific Islander: 1.6%; Hispanic: 1.5%; White non-Hispanic: 45.9%; unknown: 43%.

International Students: No programs available to aid students whose native language is not English. No financial aid specifically designated for international students.

Student Life: Intercollegiate and intramural sports available. *Special services:* counseling and information services; tutoring services. *Surrounding community:* Cedar Rapids is 230 miles west of Chicago.

Library Collections: Students have access to the Internet and other online retrieval systems.

Buildings and Grounds: Campus is located in central Cedar Rapids.

Chief Executive Officer: Dr. Ken Sigmon, President.

Address admission inquiries to Director of Admissions.

Iowa State University of Science and Technology

Ames, Iowa 50011
Tel: (515) 294-4111   **E-mail:** admissions@iastate.edu
Fax: (515) 294-2592   **Internet:** www.iastate.edu

Institution Description: Iowa State University of Science and Technology is a state institution. *Enrollment:* 26,380. *Degrees awarded:* Baccalaureate, first-professional (veterinary medicine), master's, doctorate. Certificates and specialist degrees are also awarded.

Academic offerings subject to approval by statewide coordinating bodies. Budget subject to approval by state governing boards.

Accreditation: *Regional:* NCA. *Professional:* accounting, business, computer science, counseling psychology, dietetics, engineering, family and consumer science, forestry, industrial technology, interior design, journalism, landscape architecture, marriage and family therapy, music, planning, psychology internship, veterinary medicine

History: Established and incorporated as Iowa Agricultural College 1858; offered first instruction at postsecondary level 1868; awarded first degree (baccalaureate) 1872; changed name to Iowa State College of Agriculture and Mechanic Arts 1898; adopted present name 1959. *See* Earle Dudley Ross, *The History of Iowa State College* (Ames: Iowa State Press, 1942), for further information.

Institutional Structure: *Governing board:* Iowa Board of Regents, State of Iowa. Representation: 9 regents (appointed by governor of Iowa). All voting. *Composition of institution:* Administrators 71 men / 14 women. Academic affairs headed by provost. Management/business/finances directed by vice president for business and finance. Full-time instructional faculty 1,084 men / 351 women. Academic governance body, Faculty Senate, meets monthly.

Calendar: Semesters. Academic year Aug. to May. Freshmen admitted Aug., Jan., June. Degrees conferred and formal commencements May, Aug., Dec. Summer session of 1 term from June to July.

Characteristics of Freshmen: 9,172 applicants (5,002 men, 4,170 women). 90.2% of applicants admitted. 44.1% of admitted students enrolled full-time.

15% (551 students) submitted SAT scores; 96% (3,572 students) submitted ACT scores. *25th percentile:* SAT Verbal 530, SAT Math 550; ACT Composite 22, ACT English 21, ACT Math 22. *75th percentile:* SAT Verbal 650, SAT Math 690; ACT Composite 27, ACT English 27, ACT Math 28.

54% of entering freshmen expected to graduate within 5 years. 74.4% of freshmen from Iowa.

Admission: Rolling admissions plan. For fall acceptance, apply 6 to 9 months in advance. *Requirements:* Graduation from accredited secondary school or GED; 4 units English, 3 mathematics, 3 science, 2 social science; class standing 50th %ile minimum. *Entrance tests:* SAT I or ACT. For foreign students TOEFL. *For transfer students:* 2.0 GPA and 24 transferable credits from accredited institution; maximum transfer credit from 2-year accredited institution 65 semester hours.

Degree Requirements: 120–169.5 semester hours; 2.0 GPA; 32 hours in residence; general education requirements; demonstrated proficiency in English composition.

Fulfillment of some degree requirements possible by passing College Board CLEP. *Grading system:* A–F; satisfactory-fail, pass-not pass, withdraw.

Distinctive Educational Programs: Evening classes. External degree programs in liberal studies with University of Iowa, University of Northern Iowa. Interdisciplinary programs in environmental studies, international studies. Honors programs. Institutionally sponsored study abroad programs in more than 30 countries including Australia, Costa Rica, Ecuador, England, Germany, Greece, Italy, Korea, Mexico, Scotland, Spain, Switzerland, Wales. International Student Exchange Program. *Other distinctive programs:* Continuing education. Intensive English and Orientation Program, a full-time course of instruction which prepares students to enter American colleges and universities.

ROTC: Air Force, Army, Navy.

Degrees Conferred: 4,523 *baccalaureate*; 818 *master's*; 228 *doctorate*. Bachelor's degrees awarded in top five disciplines: business, management, marketing, and related support services 920; engineering 806; agriculture, agriculture operations and related sciences 423; education 363; visual and performing arts 279.

Fees and Other Expenses: *Full-time tuition per academic year 2004–05:* resident undergraduate $5,426, out-of-state student $15,128. Contact the university for graduate tuition/fees. *Books and supplies:* $850. *Room and board per academic year:* $5,958.

Financial Aid: Iowa State University offers a direct lending program. Aid from institutionally generated funds is provided on the basis of academic merit, financial need, athletic ability, other criteria. Institution has a Program Participation Agreement with the U.S. Department of Education for eligible students to receive Pell Grants and other federal aid.

Financial aid to full-time, first-time undergraduate students: 24% received federal grants averaging $2,865; 12% state/local grants averaging $1,092; 67% institutional grants averaging $3,665; 60% loans averaging $7,864.

Departments and Teaching Staff: *Professors* 603, *associate professors* 442, *assistant professors* 335 instructors 55, *part-time* 232. *Total instructional faculty:* 1,667. Student-to-faculty ratio: 14:1. Degrees held by full-time faculty: doctorate 86.6%, master's 8.5%, baccalaureate .7%, professional 4.1%. 94.4% hold terminal degrees.

Enrollment: Total enrollment 26,380. Undergraduate 21,354 (56.1% men, 43.9% women).

Characteristics of Student Body: *Ethnic and racial makeup:* Black non-Hispanic: 2.8%; American Indian or Alaska Native: .3%; Asian or Pacific Islander: 3.2%; Hispanic: 2.1%; White non-Hispanic: 83.1%; unknown: 5%. *Age distribution:* 15–21: 58%; 22–24: 20%; 25–29: 10%; 30–34: 4%; 35–39: 2%; 40–49: 3%; 50–59: 1%; 60–and over: less than 1%.

International Students: 747 undergraduate nonresident aliens enrolled fall 2003. Students from Europe, Asia, Central and South America, Africa, Canada, Australia, New Zealand. Programs available to aid students whose native language is not English: Social, cultural, financial. English as a Second Language Program. Some financial aid specifically designated for qualifying international students.

Student Life: On-campus residence halls house 29.6% of student body. 8% of men fraternity houses; 6% of women live in sorority houses. 3.8% of students live in university owned student apartments. 33% of students live in institutional housing. *Intercollegiate athletics:* men only: baseball, basketball, cross country, football, golf, indoor track, outdoor track, swimming, wrestling; women only: basketball, cross country, golf, gymnastics, indoor/outdoor track, softball, swimming, tennis, volleyball. *Special services:* Medical services. *Student publications, radio: Iowa State Daily,* a daily newspaper; *Ethos,* a quarterly literary magazine. Radio station KURE. *Surrounding community:* Ames population 50,000. Des Moines, 30 miles from campus, is nearest metropolitan area. Served by mass transit bus system, airport 38 miles from campus.

Library Collections: 2,387,000 volumes including bound books, serial backfiles, electronic documents, and government documents not in separate collections. Online catalog. Current serial subscriptions: 28,500 (paper, microform, electronic). 3,413,000 microforms; 65,000 audiovisual materials. 175 computer work stations. Students have access to the Internet at no charge.

Most important holdings include books and serials on natural, mathematical, and physical sciences; manuscripts and papers on agriculture; history of Iowa.

Buildings and Grounds: Campus area 1,790 acres.

Chief Executive Officer: Dr. Gregory L. Geoffroy, President.

Address admission inquiries to Marc Harding, Director of Admissions.

College of Agriculture

Degree Programs Offered: *Baccalaureate* in agricultural biochemistry, agricultural business, agricultural education, agricultural extension education, agricultural journalism, agricultural mechanization, agricultural microbiology, agricultural studies-farm operation, agronomy, animal ecology, animal science, biometry, dairy science, entomology, fisheries and wildlife biology, food technology and science, forestry, genetics, horticulture, international agriculture, international studies, pest management, plant pathology, professional agriculture, public service and administration in agriculture, seed science. *Master's* and *doctorate* in various fields. Certificates also awarded.

Degree Requirements: 120–128 credits.

College of Business Administration

Degree Programs Offered: *Baccalaureate* in accounting, finance, general business, management, marketing, transportation and logistics; *master's* in business administrative sciences.

Degree Requirements: 124.5 credits.

College of Design

Degree Programs Offered: *Baccalaureate* and *master's* in art and design, architecture, community and regional planning, landscape architecture.

Degree Requirements: 120.5–169.5 credits.

College of Education

Degree Programs Offered: *Baccalaureate* in community health education, elementary education, environmental studies, industrial education and technology, leisure studies, occupational safety, physical education. *Master's* and *doctorate* in various fields.

Degree Requirements: 121.5–135.5 credits.

College of Engineering

Degree Programs Offered: *Baccalaureate* in aerospace engineering, agricultural engineering, chemical engineering (including construction engineering, surveying engineering), civil engineering, electrical engineering (including computer engineering), engineering science, industrial engineering (including engineering journalism, engineering operations), ceramic engineering, metallurgical engineering, mechanical engineering, nuclear engineering. *Master's* and *doctorate* in various fields.

Degree Requirements: 122.5–134.5 credits.

Distinctive Educational Programs: Cooperative work-experience program.

College of Family and Consumer Sciences

Degree Programs Offered: *Baccalaureate* in adult home economics education; apparel design; child, parent, and community services; community nutrition; consumer food science; dietetics; educational services in family and consumer sciences; family environment; family resource management and consumer services; family services; fashion merchandising; food science; food service management; general studies in home economics; growth and development of children; home economics education; family and consumer sciences journalism; hotel and restaurant management; housing and the near environment; international studies in family and consumer sciences; nutritional science; teaching prekindergarten-kindergarten children; textiles and clothing related science. *Master's* and *doctorate* in various fields.

Degree Requirements: 120–128.5 credits.

College of Liberal Arts and Sciences

Degree Programs Offered: *Baccalaureate* in anthropology, biochemistry, biology, biological/pre-medical illustration, biophysics, botany, chemistry, computer science, distributed studies, earth science (geology, meteorology), economics, English, environmental studies, foreign languages and literatures (French, German, Russian, Spanish), history, individual major, international studies, journalism and mass communication, liberal studies, linguistics, mathematics, metallurgy, microbiology, music, naval science, philosophy, physics, political science, psychology, religious studies, social work, sociology, speech communication, statistics, telecommunicative arts, zoology. *Master's* and *doctorate* in various fields.

Degree Requirements: 124–130.5 credits.

College of Veterinary Medicine

Degree Programs Offered: *First-professional* in veterinary medicine. *Master's* and *doctorate* in various fields.

Admission: *For first-professional degree:* 60 semester hours from regionally accredited college or university, 2.5 minimum GPA for preprofessional credits. Preference given to in-state residents and residents of states having contracts with Iowa State for educating veterinary medical students.

Degree Requirements: *For first-professional degree:* 151 credit hours, 2.0 GPA, 32 hours in residence, comprehensive examinations, 2.0 GPA.

Iowa Wesleyan College

601 North Main Street

Mount Pleasant, Iowa 52641

Tel: (319) 385-8021   **E-mail:** admitrwl@iwc.edu
Fax: (319) 385-6296   **Internet:** www.iwc.edu

Institution Description: Iowa Wesleyan College is a private college affiliated with the United Methodist Church. *Enrollment:* 776. *Degrees awarded:* Baccalaureate.

Accreditation: *Regional:* NCA. *Professional:* nursing

History: Established and chartered as Mount Pleasant Collegiate Institute and incorporated 1842; changed name to Iowa Wesleyan University 1855; awarded first degree (baccalaureate) 1856; adopted present name 1912. *See* Louis A. Haselmayer, *A 125th Anniversary History* (Mount Pleasant: Iowa Wesleyan College, 1967) for further information.

Institutional Structure: *Governing board:* Iowa Wesleyan College Board of Trustees. Extrainstitutional representation: 35 trustees, including 8 alumni; institutional representation: president of the college, chairman of the faculty, president of the student body. 6 ex officio. All voting. *Composition of institution:* Administrators 4 men / 6 women. Academic affairs headed by vice president for academic affairs. Management/business/finances directed by vice president for financial affairs. Full-time instructional faculty 40. Academic governance body, the faculty, meets an average of 9 times per year.

Calendar: Semesters. Academic year Aug. to May. Degrees conferred May, Aug., Dec., Feb. Formal commencement May. Summer session of 1 term from early June to mid-Aug.

Characteristics of Freshmen: 587 applicants (326 men, 261 women). 64.4% of applicants admitted. 25.4% of admitted students enrolled full-time.

4% (4 students) submitted SAT scores; 84% (81 students) submitted ACT scores. *25th percentile:* SAT Verbal 330, SAT Math 300; ACT Composite 18, ACT English 17, ACT Math 17. *75th percentile:* SAT Verbal 520, SAT Math 520; ACT Composite 23, ACT English 22, ACT Math 23.

46% of entering freshmen expected to graduate within 5 years. 50% of freshmen from Iowa. Freshmen from 14 states and 3 foreign countries.

Admission: Rolling admissions plan. Apply no later than Aug. 15 of year of enrollment. Apply by middle of junior year of secondary school for early decision; need not limit application to Iowa Wesleyan. Early acceptance available. *Requirements:* Graduation from accredited secondary school or GED. Recommend 15 units including 4 English, 1 foreign language, 3 mathematics, 2 fine arts, 2 history. Minimum GPA 2.0. *Entrance tests:* College Board SAT or ACT composite. *For transfer students:* 2.0 minimum GPA.

College credit and advanced placement for postsecondary-level work completed in secondary school. Tutoring available. Developmental courses offered during regular academic year; credit given.

Degree Requirements: *For all baccalaureate degrees:* 124 credit hours; distribution requirements; career experiences; responsible social involvement project. *For all undergraduate degrees:* 2.0 GPA; last 30 hours in residence. Fulfillment of some degree requirements possible by passing College Board CLEP, AP; exemption from some beginning courses possible by passing College Board AP. *Grading system:* A–F; satisfactory-unsatisfactory; withdraw.

Distinctive Educational Programs: Life skills, service learning, career experience. Cooperative baccalaureate in medical technology with approved schools. Interdisciplinary programs in life sciences, environmental health. Individual majors. Study abroad during interim period.

Degrees Conferred: 151 *baccalaureate.* Bachelor's degrees awarded in top five disciplines: education 52; business, management, marketing, and related support services31; health professions and related clinical sciences 9; psychology 9; biological and biomedical sciences 8.

Fees and Other Expenses: *Full-time tuition per academic year 2004–05:* $16,070. *Books and supplies:* $800. *Room and board per academic year:* $5,920.

Financial Aid: Aid from institutionally generated funds is provided on the basis of academic merit, financial need, athletic ability, other criteria. Institution has a Program Participation Agreement with the U.S. Department of Education for eligible students to receive Pell Grants and other federal aid.

Financial aid to full-time, first-time undergraduate students: 66% received federal grants averaging $3,040; 28% state/local grants averaging $3,124; 99% institutional grants averaging $3,731; 98% loans averaging $5,551.

Departments and Teaching Staff: Business *professors* 0, *associate professors* 1, *assistant professors* 3, *instructors* 0, *part-time faculty* 0; education 0, 2, 2, 2, 3; fine arts 3, 2, 1, 0, 2; human studies 3, 0, 1, 1, 1; languages/literature 1, 4, 2, 0, 4; nursing 1, 2, 2, 3, 1; science 1, 2, 2, 0, 1.

Total instructional faculty: 56. Degrees held by full-time faculty: doctorate 33%, master's 100%. 39% hold terminal degrees.

Enrollment: Total enrollment 776 (38.8% men, 61.2% women).

Characteristics of Student Body: *Ethnic/racial makeup:* Black non-Hispanic: 9.9%; Asian or Pacific Islander: .8%; American Indian or Alaska Native: .3%; Hispanic: 7.35; White non-Hispanic: 73.5%; unknown: 1.7%. *Age distribution:* 17–21: 35%; 22–24: 15%; 25–29: 8%; 30–34: 11%; 35–39: 11%; 40–49: 13%; 50–59: 2%.

International Students: 51 nonresident aliens enrolled fall 2004. Programs available to aid students whose native language is not English: English as a Second Language Program. Scholarships awarded annually to qualifying international students.

Student Life: On-campus residence halls house 65% of student body. *Intercollegiate athletics:* men only: baseball, basketball, football, track; women only; basketball, field hockey, softball, track, volleyball; both sexes: cross-country, golf, soccer, swimming, tennis, track. *Special regulations:* Cars permitted without restrictions. Quiet hours from 10pm to 10am. *Special services:* Learning Resources Center, medical services. *Student publications, television: The Croaker*, a yearbook; *Iowa Wesleyan Courier*, a bimonthly newspaper; Sigma Tau Delta annual literary publication. *Surrounding community:* Mount Pleasant population 7,400. Chicago (IL), 250 miles from campus, is nearest metropolitan area. Served by airport 25 miles from campus; passenger rail service less than 1 mile from campus.

Library Collections: 110,000 volumes. 21,000 microforms; 3,500 audiovisual materials. 400 current periodical subscriptions. Access to online information retrieval systems.

Most important holdings include Iowa Conference of the United Methodist Conference Archives, German Americanism Collection, contemporary graphic artists' prints and books.

Chief Executive Officer: Dr. William N. Johnston, President.

Address admission inquiries to Gary Owens, Director of Admissions.

Loras College

1450 Alta Vista Street
Dubuque, Iowa 52004-0178
Tel: (563) 588-7100   **E-mail:** adms@loras.edu
Fax: (563) 588-7119   **Internet:** www.loras.edu

Institution Description: Loras College is a private college affiliated with the Archdiocese of Dubuque, Roman Catholic Church. *Enrollment:* 1,743. *Degrees awarded:* Associate, baccalaureate, master's.

Accreditation: *Regional:* NCA. *Professional:* social work, teacher education

History: Established as Saint Raphael's Seminary for men 1839; changed name to Mount St. Bernard 1850, St. Joseph's College 1873; incorporated, chartered, and offered first instruction at postsecondary level 1894; awarded first degree (baccalaureate) 1895; changed name to Dubuque College 1914; Columbia College 1920; adopted present name 1939; admitted women 1971. *See* M. M. Hoffmann, *The Story of Loras College* (Dubuque, Iowa: Loras College Press, 1939) and F.P. Friedl, *The Loras College Story* (Dubuque, Iowa: Loras College Press, 1989) for further information.

Institutional Structure: *Governing board:* Loras College Board of Regents. Extrainstitutional representation: 24 regents, archbishop of Dubuque; institutional representation: president of the college. 2 ex officio. All voting. *Composition of institution:* Administrators 4 men / 4 women. Academic affairs headed by vice president for academic affairs. Business/finances directed by vice president for finance and administrative service. Full-time instructional faculty 113. Academic governance body, Academic Council, meets an average of 18 times per year.

Calendar: Semesters. Academic year Aug. to May. Freshmen admitted Aug., Jan., June. Degrees conferred May, Aug., Dec. Formal commencement May.

Characteristics of Freshmen: 81% of applicants admitted. 34% of applicants admitted and enrolled.

90% (387 students) submitted ACT scores. *25th percentile:* ACT Composite 20, ACT English 18, ACT Math 18. *75th percentile:* ACT Composite 25, ACT English 25, ACT Math 25.

68% of entering freshmen expected to graduate within 5 years. 48% of freshmen from Iowa. Freshmen from 23 states and 8 foreign countries.

Admission: Rolling admissions plan. For fall acceptance, apply as early as junior year of secondary school, but not later than Aug. of year of enrollment. Early acceptance available. *Requirements:* Either graduation from accredited secondary school in upper half or GED. Recommend 4 units English, 3 or more of mathematics, 3 or more of natural science, 2 or more of foreign language. Minimum GPA 2.0. *Entrance tests:* College Board SAT or ACT composite (score of 20). *For transfer students:* 2.0 GPA, from 2-year accredited institution 60 hours maximum transfer credit. Consideration will be given to students with GPA below 2.0.

Advanced placement for postsecondary-level work completed in secondary school. College credit for extrainstitutional learning on basis of ACE *2006 Guide to the Evaluation of Educational Experiences in the Armed Services;* portfolio assessment. Tutoring available. Noncredit developmental courses offered in summer session and regular academic year.

Degree Requirements: *For all associate degrees:* 60 credit hours; 15 hours in residence. *For all baccalaureate degrees:* 120 credit hours; 30 hours in residence; exit-competency examinations—comprehensives, including theses, projects, and oral reports, in some departments. *For all undergraduates:* 2.0 GPA; distribution requirements; competency in speech, logic, composition.

Fulfillment of some degree requirements and exemption from some beginning courses possible by passing College Board CLEP and AP. *Grading system:* A–F; pass-fail; withdraw (deadline after which pass-fail is appended to withdraw); incomplete.

Distinctive Educational Programs: *For undergraduates:* Dual-degree programs in medical technology and engineering with various schools, including University of Iowa. Interdisciplinary program in humanities and sophomore honors interdisciplinary program. Other honors programs. Individualized study abroad in Western Europe, including programs in Austria, England (social work), Spain, France, and Germany. Marine biology study in Central America. Cross-registration through consortium. Consortium also offers adult degree program for students over 24. *Available to all students:* Cooperative education. Evening classes. Special facilities for using telecommunications in the classroom. Facilities and programs for independent research, including individual majors, independent study.

Degrees Conferred: 4 *associate;* 439 *baccalaureate* (B); 37 *master's* (M): architecture 4 (B); biological/life sciences 16 (B); business/marketing 125 (B); communications/communication technologies 34 (B); education 84 (B), 17 (M); engineering and engineering technologies 25 (B); English 8 (B), 5 (M); mathematics 7 (B); parks and recreation 9 (B); philosophy/religion/theology 8 (B), 4 (M); physical sciences 11 (B), 7 (M); protective services/public administration

219 (B); psychology 16 (B), 4 (M); social sciences and history 58 (B); visual and performing arts 3 (B).

Fees and Other Expenses: *Full-time tuition per academic year 2004–05:* $18,670. Contact the college for current graduate tuition/fees. *Required fees:* $69.50. *Other fees:* $800. *Room and board per academic year:* $5,845.

Financial Aid: Aid from institutionally generated funds is provided on the basis of academic merit, financial need, other considerations. Institution has a Program Participation Agreement with the U.S. Department of Education for eligible students to receive Pell Grants and other federal aid.

Financial aid to full-time, first-time undergraduate students: need-based scholarships/grants totaling $11,177,319, self-help $5,335,701; non-need-based scholarships/grants totaling $4,303,242, self-help $4,029,550, parent loans $751,096, tuition waivers $1,095,619.

Departments and Teaching Staff: *Professors* 43 *associate professors* 35, *assistant professors* 30, *instructors* 3, *part-time faculty:* 30. *Total instructional faculty:* 141 (full-time 111, 30 part-time; women 49, men 93; members of minority groups 5). Total faculty with doctorate, first-professional, or other terminal degree: 120. Student-to-faculty ratio: 13:1. *Faculty development:* 2 faculty members awarded sabbaticals 2004–05.

Enrollment: Total enrollment 1,743. Undergraduate full-time 777 men / 774 women, part-time 24m / 43w; graduate full-time 3m / 9w, part-time 49m / 64w. *Transfer students:* in-state 200; from out-of-state 83.

Characteristics of Student Body: *Ethnic/racial makeup:* number of Black non-Hispanic: 18; American Indian or Alaska Native: 1; Asian or Pacific Islander: 14; Hispanic: 17; White non-Hispanic: 478; unknown: 63. *Age distribution:* number under 18: 6; 18–19: 730; 20–21: 633; 22–24: 150; 25–29: 50; 30–34: 16; 35–39: 16; 40–49: 14; 50–64: 3.

International Students: 28 nonresident aliens enrolled fall 2004. Students from Europe, Asia, Central and South America, Africa, Canada. Programs available to aid students whose native language is not English: social and cultural; English as a Second Language Program. Financial aid specifically designated for international students: 24 scholarships totaling $246,288 were awarded 2004–05.

Student Life: On-campus residence halls house 60% of student body. Residence halls for men only constitute 114% of such space, for women only 13%, for both sexes 75%. *Intercollegiate athletics:* men: baseball, basketball, cross-country, football, golf, indoor/outdoor track, soccer, swimming/diving, tennis, wrestling; women: basketball, cross-country, soccer, softball, swimming, volleyball, swimming, tennis, track. *Special regulations:* Cars with registration stickers permitted. Quiet hours from 7pm to 10pm and 11pm to 8am Sun.–Thurs., midnight to 8am Fri. and Sat. Residence hall visitation from 9am to 2am daily. *Special services:* Instructional Resources Lab, Writing Center, Accounting Lab, Finance Lab, Statistics Lab, Mathematics Lab, Computer Center, Learning Disabilities Program, medical services, peer counselors, consortium intercampus bus. *Student publications, radio: The Lorian,* a bimonthly newspaper; *Loras Faculty Review,* published triannually; *The Purgold,* a yearbook. Radio station KLCR broadcasts 98 hours per week. *Surrounding community:* Dubuque population 90,000. Chicago, 180 miles from campus, is nearest metropolitan area. Served by mass transit bus system; airport 7 miles from campus; passenger rail service 3 miles from campus.

Library Collections: 290,517 volumes including bound books, serial backfiles, electronic documents, and government documents not in separate collections. Online catalog. Current serial subscriptions: 750 paper, 12 microform, 8,719 electronic. 20 computer work stations. Students have access to the Internet at no charge.

Most important holdings include Furness Collection (writings of Horace, including primary source translations and editions from 15th century to the present); detailed history of the region and city of Dubuque; largest known collection of Torch Press Imprints, fine printing and limited editions of the private press from the early 1900s to the middle 1960s.

Buildings and Grounds: Campus area 60 acres. *New buildings:* Academic Resource Center completed 2002; Apartment Complex 2002.

Chief Executive Officer: Dr. Joachim W. Froehlich, President.

Address admission inquiries to Tim Hauber, Director of Admissions.

Luther College

700 College Drive
Decorah, Iowa 52101-1045
Tel: (563) 387-1287   **E-mail:** admissions@luther.edu
Fax: (563) 387-2158   **Internet:** www.luther.edu

Institution Description: Luther College is a private institution affiliated with The Evangelical Lutheran Church in America. *Enrollment:* 2,573. *Degrees awarded:* Baccalaureate.

Member of the consortium Upper Midwest Association for International Education.

Accreditation: *Regional:* NCA. *Professional:* music, nursing, nursing education, social work, teacher education

History: Established as a college for men, chartered and offered first instruction at postsecondary level 1861; awarded first degree (baccalaureate) 1866; became coeducational 1936. *See* David T. Nelson, *Luther College 1861–1961* (Decorah: Luther College Press, 1961), for further information.

Institutional Structure: *Governing board:* Luther College Board of Regents. Extrainstitutional representation: 25 regents; institutional representation: 5 administrators, 4 full-time instructional faculty members, 4 students. 2 ex officio. 25 voting. *Composition of institution:* Administrators 48 men / 56 women (3% are members of minority groups). Academic affairs headed by vice president for academic affairs. Management/business/finances directed by vice president for finance and administration. Full-time instructional faculty 167. Academic governance body, College Council, meets an average of 8 times per year.

Calendar: Semesters (4-1-4 plan). Academic year Sept. to May. Freshmen admitted Sept., Jan., Feb., June, July. Degrees conferred May, June, July, Aug., Dec., Jan. Formal commencement May. Summer session of 2 terms from early June to late July.

Characteristics of Freshmen: 2,233 applicants (998 men, 1,235 women). 71.3% of applicants admitted. 41.5% of admitted students enrolled full-time.

16% (103 students) submitted SAT scores; 96% (633 students) submitted ACT scores. *25th percentile:* SAT Verbal 545, SAT Math 560; ACT Composite 22, ACT English 21, ACT Math 21. *75th percentile:* SAT Verbal 655, SAT Math 670; ACT Composite 28, ACT English 29, ACT Math 28.

77% of entering freshmen expected to graduate within 5 years. 37% of freshmen from Iowa. Freshmen from 25 states and 18 foreign countries.

Admission: Rolling admissions plan. For fall acceptance, apply as early as Sept. of previous year, but not later than March 1 of year of enrollment. Early acceptance available. *Requirements:* Either graduation from accredited secondary school with units which must include 4 English, 3 mathematics, 3 social science, and 2 natural science; or GED. An additional 2 units of modern language recommended. Lowest acceptable secondary school class standing 50th percentile. *Entrance tests:* College Board SAT or ACT composite. *For transfer students:* 2.5 minimum GPA, 96 hours maximum transfer credit; from 2-year institution 64 hours.

College credit for postsecondary-level work completed in secondary school. College credit and advanced placement for College Board CLEP. For extrainstitutional learning (life experience) college credit and advanced placement on basis of faculty assessment; college credit on basis of portfolio assessment.

Tutoring available. Noncredit remedial courses offered during regular academic year.

Degree Requirements: 128 credit hours; 2 terms in residence; 2 physical education courses; senior research paper in major field; distribution requirements. Fulfillment of some degree requirements and exemption from some beginning courses possible by passing departmental examinations, College Board CLEP, AP. *Grading system:* A–F; pass-fail; withdraw (carries time limit), incomplete (carries time limit).

Distinctive Educational Programs: Internships. Dual-degree programs in engineering with Washington University (MO) and with University of Minnesota-Minneapolis. Cooperative baccalaureate programs in medical technology, cytotechnology, and nuclear medicine technology with approved area hospitals. Interdepartmental programs in international management studies, Latin American area studies, museum studies, arts management programs, and sports management program. Preprofessional programs in dentistry, hospital and health administration, medicine, optometry, physical therapy. Individual majors. Study abroad through institutionally sponsored and consortium January term programs. Off-campus study in the U.S. includes nursing year in Rochester (MN) and Washington (DC) semester at American University or through Lutheran College Consortium.

Degrees Conferred: 555 *baccalaureate.* Bachelor's degrees awarded in top five disciplines: business, management, marketing, and related support services 93; education 70; visual and performing arts 68; biological and biomedical sciences 67; social sciences 43.

Fees and Other Expenses: *Full-time tuition per academic year 2004–05:* $23,070. *Room and board per academic year:* $4,170. *Books and supplies:* $775.

Financial Aid: Luther College offers a direct lending program. Aid from institutionally generated funds is provided on the basis of academic merit, financial need, other considerations. Institution has a Program Participation Agreement with the U.S. Department of Education for eligible students to receive Pell Grants and other federal aid.

Financial aid to full-time, first-time undergraduate students: 21% received federal grants averaging $3,250; 58% state/local grants averaging $2,401; 96% institutional grants averaging $8,618; 76% loans averaging $3,762.

Departments and Teaching Staff: Africana studies *professors* 1, *associate professors* 0, *assistant professors* 1, *instructors* 0, *part-time teachers* 1; art 1,1, 3, 0, 1; biology 5, 2, 2, 0, 2; chemistry 3, 2, 1, 0, 1; classics 0, 0, 2, 0, 0; communications/linguistics 1, 2, 1, 1, 1; computer science 1, 1, 1, 0, 0; economics/business 4, 6, 1, 1, 1; education 3, 1, 4, 2, 5; English 6, 3, 1, 0, 4; history 2, 2, 1, 0, 2; health and physical education 2, 3, 3, 0, 1; mathematics 3, 2, 1, 0, 4; modern language and literatures 3, 2, 3, 3, 4; music 7, 6, 7, 5, 17; nursing 1, 3, 1, 0, 0; physics 2, 1, 1, 0, 0; political science 3, 1, 0, 0, 0; psychology 3, 1, 2, 1, 0; religion and philosophy 6, 2, 5, 1, 1; sociology/anthropology/social work 2, 3, 5, 0, 0; theatre/dance 1, 2, 1, 0, 1.

Total instructional faculty: 183.52 FTE. Student-to-faculty ratio: 13:1. Degrees held by full-time faculty: doctorate 75%, master's 16%, baccalaureate 1%. 83% hold terminal degrees.

Enrollment: Total enrollment 2,573 (40.1% men, 59.9% women).

Characteristics of Student Body: *Ethnic/racial makeup:* Black non-Hispanic: .7%; American Indian or Alaska Native: .3%; Asian or Pacific Islander: 1.4%; Hispanic: 1.1%; White non-Hispanic: 89.8%; unknown: 3.6%. *Age distribution:* 17–21: 90%; 22–24: 6.5%; 25–29: 1.3%; 30–34: .6%; 35–39: .4%; 40–49: .7%; 50–59: .4%; 60–and over: .1%.

International Students: 80 nonresident aliens enrolled fall 2004. Students from Europe, Asia, Central and South America, Africa. Programs available to aid students whose native language is not English: Social, cultural, and financial. Financial aid specifically designated for international students: Variable number of scholarships available annually for undergraduate international students.

Student Life: Students choose from traditional coed residence halls (by floor), college apartments, townhouses, and language houses. Floor options include quiet, wellness, and chemical free. First-year students are housed together. *Intercollegiate athletics:* men only: baseball, basketball, cross-country, football, golf, soccer, swimming, tennis, track, wrestling; women only: basketball, cross-country, golf, soccer, softball, swimming, tennis, track, volleyball. *Special regulations:* Cars permitted without restriction. Quiet hours set by individual residence halls. Intervisitation in first-year halls 10am to 2am; upper class halls have extended visitation (24 hours) on Fri. and Sat. *Special services:* Learning Resources Center, medical services. *Student publications, radio: College Chips,* a weekly newspaper; *Pioneer,* a yearbook; *The New Oneota Review,* an annual literary magazine. Radio station KWLC broadcasts 42 hours per week. *Surrounding community:* Decorah population 8,000. Minneapolis (MN), 170 miles from campus, is nearest metropolitan area.

Publications: Sources of information about Luther College include Luther College news releases distributed throughout the surrounding community. *Publisher:* Luther College Press.

Library Collections: 337,600 volumes including bound books, serial backfiles, electronic documents, and government documents not in separate collections. Online catalog. Current serial subscriptions: 1,610 paper, 100 electronic. 6,095 recordings; 2,258 compact discs; 76 CD-ROMs. Computer work stations available. Students have access to the Internet at

Most important holdings include Norwegian-American newspapers on microfilm from 19th century to present; papers and historical materials about Norwegian-American Lutheranism in the 19th century; papers of 19th- and 20th-century Norwegian-American church leaders; Bible collection; art collection.

Buildings and Grounds: Campus area 800 acres.

Chief Executive Officer: Dr. Richard L. Torgerson, President.

Address admission inquiries to Jon Lund, Vice President for Enrollment and Marketing.

Maharishi University of Management

1000 North Fourth Street
Fairfield, Iowa 52557-1113
Tel: (641) 472-7000   **E-mail:** admissions@mum.edu
Fax: (641) 472-1179   **Internet:** www.mum.edu

Institution Description: Maharishi University of Management has pioneered a system of higher education based on developing students' full alertness and creative intelligence. The system integrates the content of traditional discipline-based education with knowledge and technologies for developing students' mental potential. *Enrollment:* 695. *Degrees awarded:* Baccalaureate, master's, doctorate.

Accreditation: *Regional:* NCA.

History: The university was founded in 1971 by His Holiness Maharisi Mahesh Yogi.

Institutional Structure: *Governing board:* Board of Trustees. Academic affairs headed by dean of education; management/business/finance directed by executive vice president and business administrator. Academic governance body, the faculty, meets biannually.

Calendar: Semesters. Academic year Aug. to June.

Characteristics of Freshmen: 67% of applicants admitted. 71% of applicants admitted and enrolled.

42% (4 students) submitted SAT scores; 21% (5 students) submitted ACT scores. *25th percentile*: SAT Verbal 510, SAT Math 470; ACT Composite 19, ACT Math 18. *75th percentile*: SAT Verbal 640, SAT Math 620; ACT Composite 25, ACT Math 25.

Admission: Rolling admission. For fall acceptance, apply as early as Sept. of senior year in secondary school, but not later than Aug. 1 of year of enrollment. Priority given to applicants who apply before June 1. *Requirements:* Graduation from accredited secondary school or GED. *Entrance tests recommended:* ACT or SAT. Transfer students must have a 2.0 minimum GPA.

Degree Requirements: *For all baccalaureate degrees:* 166 credit units with a minimum of 60 credits in the major and completion of the core curriculum of 18 units as well as 20 units in a distribution of academic fields. All students must maintain a 2.0 GPA.

Degrees Conferred: 55 *baccalaureate* (B); 96 *master's* (M); 6 *doctorate* (D): biological/life sciences 5 (B); business/marketing 3 (B), 25 (M); computer and information sciences 51 (M); education 2 (B); engineering and engineering technologies 2 (B); health professions and related sciences 12 (B), 9 (M), 1 (D); liberal arts and sciences, general studies and humanities 19 (B), 2 (M); mathematics 5 (B); physical sciences 1 (B), 1 (M); psychology 1 (B); other 5 (B), 8 (M), 5 (D).

Fees and Other Expenses: *Full-time tuition per academic year 2005–06:* $24,000. *Required fees:* $430. *Room and board per academic year:* $6,000.

Financial Aid: Aid from institutionally generated funds is provided on the basis of academic merit, financial need, other criteria. Institution has a Program Participation Agreement with the U.S. Department of Education for eligible students to receive Pell Grants and other federal aid.

Financial aid to full-time, first-time undergraduate students: need-based scholarships/grants totaling $2,577,673, self-help $2,282,652; non-need-based scholarships/grants totaling $98,235, self-help $192,466, parent loans $6,800. *Graduate aid:* 55 students received federal and state-funded loans totaling $709,428; 31 students had work-study jobs totaling $87,196; 27 students held other college-assigned jobs (nonteaching, nonresearch) totaling $166,842; 101 students had other fellowships and grants totaling $758,174; 6 students held research assistantships totaling $24,856.

Departments and Teaching Staff: *Total instructional faculty:* 56 (full-time 44, part-time 12; women 16, men 40). Total faculty with doctorate, first-professional, or other terminal degree: 36. Student-to-faculty ratio: 14:1.

Enrollment: Total enrollment 695. Undergraduate full-time 122 men / 93 women, part-time 7m / 5w; graduate full-time 305m / 90w, part-time 58m / 15w.

Characteristics of Student Body: *Ethnic/racial makeup:* number of Black non-Hispanic: 7; American Indian or Alaska Native: 1; Asian or Pacific Islander: 12; Hispanic: 3; White non-Hispanic: 161; unknown: 6. *Age distribution:* number of 18–19: 52; 20–21: 87; 22–24: 162; 25–29: 174; 30–34: 94; 35–39: 37; 40–49: 33; 50–64: 41; 65 and over: 4.

International Students: 505 nonresident aliens enrolled fall 2004. 25 students from Europe, 362 Asia, 8 Central and South America, 73 Africa, 19 Canada, 8 Australia, 2 New Zealand, 2 other. No programs available to aid students whose native language is not English. Financial aid specifically designated for qualifying international students.

Student Life: 73% of students live on campus. Intercollegiate and intramural sports available. *Special services:* counseling and information services; tutoring services. *Surrounding community:* Fairfield is located 115 miles southeast of Des Moines.

Library Collections: 153,832 volumes including bound books, serial backfiles, electronic documents, and government documents not in separate collections. Online catalog. Current serial subscriptions: paper 293; 10,853 via electronic access. 10,400 recordings; 300 compact discs; 200 CD-ROMs. 26 computer work stations available. Students have access to the Internet at no charge.

Most important special collection is the Vedic Research Collection.

Buildings and Grounds: Campus area 275 acres.

Chief Executive Officer: Dr. Beyan Morris, President.

Address admission inquiries to Ron Barnett, Dean of Admissions.

Mercy College of Health Sciences

928 Sixth Avenue
Des Moines, Iowa 50309-1239
Tel: (515) 643-3180   **E-mail:** admissions@mchs.edu
Fax: (515) 643-6698   **Internet:** www.mchs..edu

Institution Description: Mercy College of Health Sciences is a health-system-affiliated Catholic institution of higher education. Guided by the core values of the Spirit of Mercy - reverence, integrity, compassion, excellence - the primary purpose of the college is to prepare students for service and leadership roles in health care. By providing coherent general and professional educational experiences, the college offers programs leading to academic degrees, certificates, and continuing professional development in selected health care disciplines. *Degrees awarded:* Associate, baccalaureate.

Accreditation: *Regional:* NCA. *Professional:* clinical lab scientist, cytotechnology, diagnostic medical sonography, EMT-paramedic, nursing education, radiography, surgical technology

History: the college was established in 1995.

Institutional Structure: *Governing board:* Board of Regents. Extrainstitutional representation: 28 trustees; institutional representation: president of the college. *Composition of institution:* Academic affairs directed by vice president for academic affairs. Student services directed by vice president for student life. Management/business/finances directed by vice president for administration and finance. Development/college relations/alumni directed by vice president for institutional advancement.

Calendar: Semesters (4-4-1 plan). Academic year from Sept. to May.

Characteristics of Freshmen: 461 applicants (34 men, 427 women). 93.3% of applicants admitted. 12.8% of admitted students enrolled full-time.

80% (37 students) submitted ACT scores. *25th percentile*: ACT Composite 20, ACT English 18, ACT Math 17. *75th percentile*: ACT Composite 23, ACT English 23, ACT Math 22.

Admission: Rolling admissions plan. Early acceptance available. *Requirements:* Graduation from accredited secondary school or GED. Recommend 4 units in English, 2 in a foreign language, 3 mathematics, 3 science, 2 social studies, introduction to computers. *Entrance tests:* College Board SAT, ACT composite, or other standardized test. For foreign students TOEFL.

Degree Requirements: Completion of required courses and specified program. demonstrated proficiency in writing and math. Fulfillment of some degree requirements possible by passing departmental examinations, College Board CLEP, AP. Exemption from some beginning courses possible by passing College Board AP. *Grading system:* A to F, pass/D/no

Degrees Conferred: 121 *associate*; 14 *baccalaureate*. Bachelor's degrees awarded in the largest program: health professions and related clinical sciences 14.

Fees and Other Expenses: *Full-time tuition per academic year 2004–05:* $11,300. *Books and supplies:* $1,200. *Room and board per academic year:* $6,000.

Financial Aid: Aid from institutionally generated funds is provided on the basis of academic merit, financial need. Institution has a Program Participation Agreement with the U.S. Department of Education for eligible students to receive Pell Grants and other federal aid.

Financial aid to full-time, first-time undergraduate students: 33% received federal grants averaging $2,592; 51% state/local grants averaging $3,531; 62% institutional grants averaging $2,833; 91% loans averaging $11,338.

Departments and Teaching Staff: *Total instructional faculty:* Faculty members are unranked.

Enrollment: Total enrollment 659 (8.6% men, 91.41% women).

Characteristics of Student Body: *Ethnic/racial makeup:* of Black non-Hispanic: 1.2%; Asian American Indian or Pacific Islander: .2%; Hispanic: 1.7%; White non-Hispanic: 92.1%; unknown: 2.7%.

International Students: No programs to aid students whose native language is not English. No financial aid specifically designated for international students.

Student Life: On-campus housing available.

Library Collections: 6,000 volumes. 1,100 audiovisual materials. 46 periodical subscriptions. Students have access to online information retrieval services and the Internet. Computer work stations available.

Buildings and Grounds: Campus area 4 acres.

Chief Executive Officer: Dr. Deanne M. Remer, President.

Address admission inquiries to Dr. John Nies, Director of Enrollment/Student Services.

Morningside College

1501 Morningside Avenue
Sioux City, Iowa 51106
Tel: (712) 274-5000   **E-mail:** mscadm@.morningside.edu
Fax: (712) 274-5101   **Internet:** www.morningside.edu

Institution Description: Morningside College is a private college affiliated with The United Methodist Church. *Enrollment:* 1,204. *Degrees awarded:* Associate, baccalaureate, master's.

Accreditation: *Regional:* NCA. *Professional:* music, nursing, teacher education

History: Established as University of the Northwest 1889; came under the auspices of the Northwest Town Conference of the Methodist Episcopal Church, chartered, adopted present name, and offered first instruction at postsecondary level 1894; awarded first degree (baccalaureate) 1895; absorbed Charles City College 1914.

Institutional Structure: *Governing board:* Board of Directors. Extrainstitutional representation: 39 directors, including 19 alumni; institutional representation: president of the college, 1 full-time instructional faculty member, 1 student. 8 ex officio. All voting. *Composition of institution:* Administrators 3 men / 2 women. Academic affairs headed by vice president for academic affairs. Management/business/finances directed by vice president for business affairs. *Total instructional faculty* 91. Academic governance body, Faculty Senate, meets an average of 10 times per year.

Calendar: Semesters. Academic year late Aug. to early May. Freshmen admitted Aug., June, July. Degrees conferred and formal commencements May, Aug. May interim. Summer session of 2 terms from early June to early Aug.

Characteristics of Freshmen: 78% of applicants admitted. 35% of applicants admitted and enrolled.

7% (21 students) submitted SAT scores; 96% (299 students) submitted ACT scores. *25th percentile:* ACT Composite 19, ACT English 17, ACT Math 17. *75th percentile:* ACT Composite 24, ACT English 24, ACT Math 24.

21% entering freshmen expected to graduate within 5 years. 61% of freshmen from Iowa. Freshmen from 13 states and 11 foreign countries.

Admission: Rolling admissions plan. For fall acceptance, apply as early as June of previous year, but not later than Aug. 15 of year of enrollment. Early acceptance available. *Requirements:* Either graduation from accredited secondary school or GED, 2 years of mathematics. Recommend 3 years English, 3 social science, 2 science. Lowest acceptable secondary school class standing 50th percentile. *Entrance tests:* College Board SAT or ACT composite. *For transfer students:* 2.0 minimum GPA with 24 transferable hours; from 4-year accredited institution maximum transfer credit limited only by residence requirement; from 2-year accredited institution 62 hours; correspondence/extension students 10 hours. Some students with GPA below 2.0 accepted on probationary status.

College credit and advanced placement for postsecondary-level work completed in secondary school. College credit for extrainstitutional learning on basis of ACE *2006 Guide to the Evaluation of Educational Experiences in the Armed Services.* Tutoring available. Remedial courses offered during regular academic year; credit given.

Degree Requirements: *For all associate degrees:* 62 credit hours. *For all baccalaureate degrees:* 124 credits; core curriculum; minor requirement. *For all undergraduate degrees:* 2.0 GPA; 30 hours in residence; writing endorsement within major. Fulfillment of some degree requirements and exemption from some beginning requirements possible by passing College Board CLEP, AP (score of 3). *Grading system:* A–F (minus and plus implemented); pass-fail; withdraw; incomplete (carries time limit).

Distinctive Educational Programs: Interdisciplinary programs including corporate communications, advertising, and human resource management. Professional program in engineering leading to baccalaureate awarded by University of Iowa, South Dakota State University, Washington University (MO). Independent study. Institutionally sponsored study abroad in England, France, Japan, and Mexico.

Degrees Conferred: 155 *baccalaureate:* biological/life sciences 8; business/marketing 31; communications/communication technologies 9; computer and information sciences 8; education 51; engineering and engineering technologies 1; English 2; health professions and related sciences 6; interdisciplinary studies 3; mathematics 2; parks and recreation 1; philosophy/religion/theology 3; protective services/public administration 2; psychology 9; social sciences and history 5; visual and performing arts 14. 86 *master's:* education 86. 2 honorary degrees awarded 2004: Doctor of Science, Doctor of Music.

Fees and Other Expenses: *Full-time tuition per academic year 2004–05:* $16,260. *Required fees:* $910. *Room and board per academic year:* $5,400.

Financial Aid: Aid from institutionally generated funds is provided on the basis of academic merit, financial need, athletic ability, other criteria. Institution has a Program Participation Agreement with the U.S. Department of Education for eligible students to receive Pell Grants and other federal aid.

Financial aid to full-time, first-time undergraduate students: need-based scholarships/grants totaling $4,204,329, self-help $3,736,243; non-need-based scholarships/grants totaling $5,294,163, self-help $4,299,475, parent loans $328,109, tuition waivers $372,235, athletic awards $1,181,354. *Graduate aid:* 5 federal and state-funded loans totaling $22,103 (ranging from $1,700 to $8,820).

Departments and Teaching Staff: *Total instructional faculty:* 109 (full-time 65, part-time 44; women 55, men 54; members of minority groups 2). Total faculty with doctorate, first-professional, or other terminal degree: 44. Student-to-

faculty ratio: 15:1. *Faculty development:* 3 faculty members awarded sabbaticals 2004–05.

Enrollment: Total enrollment 1,205. Undergraduate full-time 442 men / 538 women, part-time 21m / 36w; graduate part-time 29m / 138w.

Characteristics of Student Body: *Ethnic/racial makeup:* number of Black non-Hispanic: 26; American Indian or Alaska Native: 2; Asian or Pacific Islander: 13; Hispanic: 39; White non-Hispanic: 826; unknown: 108. *Age distribution:* number under 18: 4; 18–19: 395; 20–21: 365; 22–24: 172; 25–29: 42; 20; 30–34: 20; 35–39: 7; 40–49: 17; 50–64: 4; 65 and over: 2.

International Students: 23 nonresident aliens enrolled fall 2004. 8 students from Europe, 13 Asia, 2 Africa. Programs available to aid students whose native language is not English: Social and cultural. English as a Second Language Program. Financial aid specifically designated for international students: scholarships available annually; 20 awarded 2004–05.

Student Life: On-campus residence halls for undergraduates house 62% of student body. Dormitories for men only constitute 50% of such space, for women only 50%. Some men join and live in fraternities; some women join and live in sororities. Housing available for married students. *Intercollegiate athletics:* men only: baseball, basketball, cross-country, football, track; women only: basketball, cross-country, soccer, softball, track, volleyball. *Special regulations:* Cars permitted in designated areas only. *Special services:* Learning Resources Center, student health services. *Student publications, radio: Collegian Reporter,* a weekly newspaper; *KIOSK,* an annual literary magazine; *The Sioux,* a yearbook. Radio station KMSC broadcasts 100 hours per week. *Surrounding community:* Sioux City population 85,000. Omaha (NE), 100 miles from campus, is nearest metropolitan area. Served by mass transit bus system; airport 6 miles from campus.

Library Collections: 113,169 volumes including bound books, serial backfiles, electronic documents, and government documents not in separate collections. Online catalog. Current serial subscriptions: 176 paper, 52 microform, 15,000 electronic (web-based). 5,601 recordings. 19 computer work stations. Students have access to the Internet at no charge.

Most important holdings include Indian Studies Collection; Morningside College Archives.

Buildings and Grounds: Campus area 27 acres. *New buildings:* Science Center renovation completed 2001; Student Apartment Complexes (2) 2003.

Chief Executive Officer: Dr. John C. Reynders, President.

Address admission inquiries to Joel Wayand, Director of Admissions.

Mount Mercy College

1330 Elmhurst Drive, N.E.
Cedar Rapids, Iowa 52402-4797
Tel: (319) 363-8213   **E-mail:** admission@mtmercy.edu
Fax: (319) 363-5270   **Internet:** www.mtmercy.edu

Institution Description: Mount Mercy College is a private college affiliated with the Sisters of Mercy, Roman Catholic Church. *Enrollment:* 1,486. *Degrees awarded:* Baccalaureate.

Accreditation: *Regional:* NCA. *Professional:* nursing, social work, teacher education

History: Established and chartered as Mount Mercy Junior College, a school for women, 1928; offered first instruction at postsecondary level and awarded first degree (associate) 1930; adopted present name 1956; became 4-year college 1957; incorporated 1962; became coeducational 1969. *See* Sister Mary Augustine Roth, *Courage and Change* (Cedar Rapids, Iowa: Stamats Communications, Inc., 1980) for further information.

Institutional Structure: *Governing board:* Mount Mercy College Board of Trustees. Extrainstitutional representation: 35 trustees, including 6 honorary members, 7 alumni; institutional representation: president of the college, 1 ex officio. All voting. *Composition of institution:* Administrators 15 men / 26 women. Academic affairs headed by academic dean. Management/business/finances directed by vice president for finance and planning. Full-time instructional faculty 63. Academic governance body, the faculty, meets an average of 9 times per year.

Calendar: Semesters (4-1-4 plan). Academic year late Aug. to mid-May. Freshmen admitted Aug., Jan., Feb., June, July. Degrees conferred and formal commencement May. Summer session of 2 terms from early June to mid-Aug.

Characteristics of Freshmen: 541 applicants (139 men, 402 women). 86.3% of applicants admitted. 45.8% of admitted students enrolled full-time.

1% (3 students) submitted SAT scores; 99% (211 students) submitted ACT scores. *25th percentile:* ACT Composite 20, ACT English 18, ACT Math 19. *75th percentile:* ACT Composite 25, ACT English 24, ACT Math 24.

59% of entering freshmen expected to graduate within 5 years. 90% of freshmen from Iowa. Freshmen from 7 states.

Admission: Rolling admissions plan. For fall acceptance, apply as early as June 15 of previous year, but not later than Aug. 15 of year of enrollment. Early acceptance available. *Requirements:* Either graduation from accredited secondary school with 16 academic units or GED. Recommend 4 units English, 2 history and social studies, 2 mathematics, 1 laboratory science. Additional requirements for some programs. Lowest acceptable secondary school class standing 40th percentile. *Entrance tests:* College Board SAT or ACT composite. *For transfer students:* 2.5 minimum GPA, 63 semester hours maximum transfer credit.

College credit and advanced placement for postsecondary-level work completed in secondary school and for extrainstitutional learning on basis of portfolio and faculty assessments. Tutoring available. Developmental courses offered during regular academic year; credit given.

Degree Requirements: 123 credit hours; 2.0 GPA; 30 hours in residence; distribution requirements; minimum of 9 credit hours in the major must be completed at Mt. Mercy College. Fulfillment of some degree requirements and exemption from some beginning courses possible by passing departmental] examinations. College Board CLEP, AP. *Grading system:* A–F; pass-fail; withdraw; incomplete (carries time limit).

Distinctive Educational Programs: Internships. Evening classes. Cooperative baccalaureate program in medical technology with area hospitals. Independent study; individual majors. Cross-registration with Coe College. Honors Program and curriculum. Exchange programs.

Degrees Conferred: 391 *baccalaureate:* Bachelor's degrees awarded in top five disciplines: business, management, marketing, and related support services 138; education 78; health professions and related clinical sciences 45; security and protective services 26; public administration and social service professions 19.

Fees and Other Expenses: *Full-time tuition per academic year 2004–05:* $16.880. *Room and board per academic year:* $6,400. *Books and supplies:* $800.

Financial Aid: Aid from institutionally generated funds is provided on the basis of academic merit, financial need, other criteria. Institution has a Program Participation Agreement with the U.S. Department of Education for eligible students to receive Pell Grants and other federal aid.

Financial aid to full-time, first-time undergraduate students: 34% received federal grants averaging $2,823; 54% state/local grants averaging $3,506; 100% institutional grants averaging $7,076; 86% loans averaging $5,829.

Departments and Teaching Staff: Art *professors* 2, *associate professors* 2, *assistant professors* 1, *part-time teachers* 2; business 0, 1, 7, 1; science 2, 2, 1, 3; computer science/mathematics 0, 2, 2, 0; criminal justice 0, 0, 2, 1; economics 1, 0, 0, 0; humanities 2, 6, 4, 5; education 1, 1, 3, 6; nursing 1, 2, 9, 3; social science 3, 3, 1, 1; public relations/communications 0, 0, 2, 3; social work 1, 1, 1, 1.

Total instructional faculty: 92. Degrees held by full-time faculty: doctorate 54%, master's 46%. 62% hold terminal degrees.

Enrollment: Total enrollment 1,486 (men 30.3%, women 69.7%).

Characteristics of Student Body: *Ethnic/racial makeup:* Black non-Hispanic: 1.7%; American Indian or Alaska Native: .3%; Asian or Pacific Islander: .7%; Hispanic: 1.3%; White non-Hispanic: 86.6%; unknown: 9.4%. *Age distribution:* 17–21: 40%; 22–24: 14%; 25–29: 13%; 30–34: 7.8%; 35–39: 11%; 40–49: 9%; 50*59: 1%.

International Students: 12 nonresident aliens enrolled. Students from Europe, Asia. No programs available to aid students whose native language is not English. No financial aid specifically designated for foreign students.

Student Life: On-campus residence halls and apartments house 36% of student body. *Intercollegiate athletics:* men only: baseball, basketball, golf, soccer, track, cross-country; women only: basketball, softball, golf, volleyball, track, cross-country. *Special regulations:* Cars permitted for all students; some parking restrictions. Minimal established quiet hours from midnight to 8am Sun. to Thurs., 2am to 8am. Fri. and Sat. Residence hall visitation from 8am to 2am daily. *Special services:* Medical services. *Student publications: Reflections,* a biennial literary magazine; *Minstril,* student newspaper; *Echos from the Mount,* a quarterly publication highlighting student achievements. *Surrounding community:* Cedar Rapids population 111,000. Chicago (IL), 250 miles from campus, is nearest metropolitan area. Served by mass transit bus system; airport 10 miles from campus.

Library Collections: 125,000 volumes. 2,250 microform titles; 4,100 audiovisual materials; 715 current periodical subscriptions. Online catalog. Students have access to online information retrieval services and the Internet.

Most important holdings include nursing and Catholicism collections.

Buildings and Grounds: Campus area 40 acres.

Chief Executive Officer: Dr. Robert W. Pearce, President.

Address admission inquiries to Margaret Jackson, Dean of Admissions.

Northwestern College

101 Seventh Street, S.W.
Orange City, Iowa 51041

Tel: (712) 737-7000   **E-mail:** admissions@nwciowa.edu
Fax: (712) 737-7164   **Internet:** www.nwciowa.edu

Institution Description: Northwestern College is a private Christian liberal arts college affiliated with the Reformed Church in America. *Enrollment:* 1,284. *Degrees awarded:* Associate, baccalaureate.

Member of Colleges of Mid-America and Coalition for Christian Colleges and Universities.

Accreditation: *Regional:* NCA. *Professional:* social work, teacher education

History: Established as Northwestern Classical Academy 1882; chartered, changed name to Northwestern Classical Academy and Junior College, and offered first instruction at postsecondary level 1927; awarded first degree (associate) 1929; became 4-year college and adopted present name 1957.

Institutional Structure: *Governing board:* Board of Trustees of Northwestern College. Extrainstitutional representation: 32 trustees; institutional representation: president of the college. 1 ex officio. All voting. *Composition of institution:* Administrators 15 men / 10 women. Academic affairs headed by vice president for academic affairs. Management/business/finances directed by vice president of financial affairs. Full-time instructional faculty 52 men / 14 women. Academic governance body, Academic Policies Committee meets an average of 12 times per year.

Calendar: Semesters. Academic year Aug. to May. Degrees conferred and formal commencement May. Summer session May to June.

Characteristics of Freshmen: 85% of applicants admitted. 33% of applicants admitted and enrolled.

Applicants submitted ACT scores. *25th percentile:* ACT Composite 21. *75th percentile:* ACT Composite 27.

60% of entering freshmen expected to graduate within 5 years. 53% of freshmen from Iowa. Freshmen from 20 states and 4 foreign countries.

Admission: Rolling admissions plan. For fall acceptance, apply as early as Sept. 1 of previous year, but not later than Aug. 15 of year of enrollment. Early acceptance available. *Requirements:* Either graduation from accredited secondary school or GED. Recommend 4 units English, 3 mathematics, 3 social studies, 2 natural science. Minimum recommended GPA 2.0. Lowest recommended secondary school class standing 50th percentile. *Entrance tests:* College Board SAT or ACT composite. For foreign students TOEFL. *For transfer students:* 2.0 minimum GPA; from 4-year accredited institution 96 semester hours maximum transfer credit; from 2-year accredited institution 64 hours; correspondence/extension students 30 hours.

College credit and advanced placement for postsecondary-level work completed in secondary school. Tutoring available. Developmental courses offered during regular academic year; credit given.

Degree Requirements: 124 credit hours; 2.0 GPA (2.50 for teacher education students); 48 credit general education program, 30 credits in residence; chapel attendance 3 times weekly. Fulfillment of some degree requirements and exemption from some beginning courses possible by passing College Board CLEP, AP. *Grading system:* A–F; pass-fail; withdraw (carries time limit); incomplete (carries time limit).

Distinctive Educational Programs: Departmental internships, Summer Institute for International Students, Off-Campus Study Programs in the Chicago Metropolitan Center; AuSable Trails Institute of Environmental Studies in Mancelona, MI. American Studies Program in Washington, D.C.; Los Angeles Film Studies Program in Los Angeles, CA; Latin American Studies Program in San Jose, Costa Rica; Middle East Studies Program in Cairo, Egypt and Russian Studies Program in Nizhni Novgorod. In addition to the majors in liberal arts, athletic training, and actuarial science, the college offers 11 career concentrations and 19 preprofessional programs.

Degrees Conferred: 2 *associate;* 238 *baccalaureate:* biological/life sciences 12; business/marketing 47; communications/communication technologies 10; computer and information sciences 6; education 61; English 11; foreign languages and literature 2; liberal arts/general studies 10; mathematics 2; natural resources/environmental science 2; parks and recreation 9; philosophy/religion/theology 10l physical sciences 3; protective services/public administration 11; psychology 14; social sciences and history 25; visual and performing arts 4; other 19.

Fees and Other Expenses: *Full-time tuition per academic year 2004–05:* $16,360. *Room per academic year:* $4,656.

Financial Aid: Aid from institutionally generated funds is provided on the basis of academic merit, financial need, athletic ability, other criteria. Institution has a Program Participation Agreement with the U.S. Department of Education for eligible students to receive Pell Grants and other federal aid.

Financial aid to full-time, first-time undergraduate students: need-based scholarships/grants totaling $4,243,548, self-help $6,432,666; non-need-based scholarships/grants totaling $4,606,234, self-help $1,088,337, parent loans $827,473, athletic awards $717,075.

Departments and Teaching Staff: *Total instructional faculty:* 130 (full-time 72, part-time 33; women 51, men 79; members of minority groups 2). Total faculty with doctorate, first-professional, or other terminal degree: 70. Student-to-faculty ratio: 15:1.

Enrollment: Total enrollment 1,284. Undergraduate full-time 465 men / 760 women, part-time 27m / 32w.

Characteristics of Student Body: *Ethnic/racial makeup:* number of Black non-Hispanic: 5; American Indian or Alaska Native: 1; Asian or Pacific Islander: 1; Hispanic: 1; White non-Hispanic: 965. *Age distribution:* number under 18: 9; 18–19: 555; 20–21: 538; 22–24: 112; 25–29: 4; 30–34: 5; 40–49: 1; 50–64: 1.

International Students: 36 nonresident aliens enrolled fall 2004. 3 students from Europe, 23 Asia, 3 Central and South America, 7 Africa, 1 Canada. Programs available to aid students whose native language is not English: social, cultural. English as a Second Language Program. Some financial aid available for qualifying international students.

Student Life: On-campus residence halls house 85% of student body. Dormitories for men only constitute 47% of such space, for women only 53%. 5% of student body housed on campus in apartments, cottages, mobile homes. 80% of married students request institutional housing; 50% are so housed. *Intercollegiate athletics:* men: baseball, basketball, cross-country, football, golf, soccer, tennis, track, wrestling; women: basketball, cross-country, golf, soccer, softball, tennis, track, volleyball. *Special regulations:* Cars permitted without restrictions. *Special services:* Learning Resources Center, extensive computer center, computer search library catalog system, student center and fitness facility, medical services. *Student publications: Beacon,* a weekly newspaper; *The Cornerstone,* a yearbook; *Spectrum,* an annual literary magazine. *Surrounding community:* Orange City population 5,000. Nearby major cities include Sioux City (IA), 45 miles away; Sioux Falls (SD), 70 miles away; Omaha (NE) 140 miles away.

Library Collections: 110,000 volumes. Online catalog. Current serial subscriptions: paper 125,000; microform 110,000. 9,600 audiovisual materials; 5,000 recordings. Students have access to the Internet at no charge.

Most important holdings include modern literature collection; mainstream Protestantism; Dutch Heritage Collection.

Buildings and Grounds: Campus area 40 acres. *New buildings:* Korver Visual Arts Center completed 2003; DeWitt Theatre Arts Center 2004.

Chief Executive Officer: Doug Beukelmon, Vice President.

admission inquiries to Mark Bloemendaal, Director of Admissions.

Palmer College of Chiropractic

1000 Brady Street
Davenport, Iowa 52803-5287
Tel: (563) 884-5000   **E-mail:** pcadmit@palmer.edu
Fax: (563) 884-5409   **Internet:** www.palmer.edu

Institution Description: Palmer College of Chiropractic is a private, independent, nonprofit college. *Enrollment:* 2,028. *Degrees awarded:* Associate, baccalaureate, master's, first-professional (doctor of chiropractic).

Accreditation: *Regional:* NCA. *Professional:* chiropractic education

History: Established as Palmer School of Chiropractic 1895; offered first instruction at postsecondary level and awarded first degree (first-professional) 1896; chartered 1907; adopted present name 1966.

Institutional Structure: *Governing board:* Palmer College of Chiropractic Board of Trustees. Extrainstitutional representation: 12 trustees, including 7 alumni. All voting. *Composition of institution:* Administrators 5 men. Academic affairs headed by vice president for academic affairs. Management/business/finances directed by vice president for business affairs. Full-time instructional faculty 87 men / 29 women. Academic governance body, Faculty Senate, meets an average of 23 times per year.

Calendar: Quarters. Academic year Oct. to Oct. Freshmen admitted Oct., Jan., Mar., July. Degrees conferred and formal commencements June, Oct., Dec., Mar.

Characteristics of Freshmen: 17 applicants (3 men, 14 women). 100% of applicants admitted. 88.2% of admitted students enrolled full-time.

93% of entering freshmen expected to graduate within 5 years. Freshmen from 50 states and 17 foreign countries.

Admission: Rolling admissions plan. Apply as early as 1 year prior to enrollment, but not later than 1 week after classes commence. *Requirements:* Either graduation from accredited secondary school or GED; and the equivalent of 60 semester hours in college, with overall GPA of 2.25; including 6 hours biology, 6 hours organic chemistry, 6 hours inorganic chemistry, 6 hours physics; and

additional units including 6 hours English, 3 hours psychology, and 3 hours social science or humanities.

Developmental courses offered during regular academic year; nondegree credit given.

Degree Requirements: 251 credit hours; 2.0 GPA; 12 quarters in residence; National Board of Chiropractic Examiners test; satisfactory completion of required curriculum, including 20 hours clinical work for the D.C. degree. 90 semester hours in undergraduate studies and 30 semester hours in Basic Sciences, which is included in the chiropractic curriculum, to obtain the B.S. degree.

Fulfillment of some degree requirements possible by passing departmental examinations. *Grading system:* A–F; pass-fail; withdraw (carries time limit); incomplete (deadline after which A–F is assigned).

Distinctive Educational Programs: Internships. 3-year preprofessional program in cooperation with St. Ambrose College. 2-year preprofessional and baccalaureate completion programs in cooperation with St. Ambrose, Loras College, and California State College (PA). Baccalaureate completion program also available in cooperation with Upper Iowa University. Facilities and programs for independent research, including honors programs, tutorials. Nondegree continuing education courses and seminars on campus and at varying locations in U.S.

Degrees Conferred: 14 *associate;* 72 *baccalaureate;* 1 *master's;* 456 *first-professional:* chiropractic. Bachelor's degrees awarded in multidisciplinary studies.

Fees and Other Expenses: *Full-time tuition per academic year 2004–05:* $5,640. Contact the college for first-professional tuition/fees. *Books and supplies:* $951. *Room and board per academic year:* $16,539.

Financial Aid: Aid from institutionally generated funds is provided on the basis of academic merit, financial need. Institution has a Program Participation Agreement with the U.S. Department of Education for eligible students to receive Pell Grants and other federal aid.

Financial aid to full-time, first-time undergraduate students: 60% received federal grants; 81% loans.

Departments and Teaching Staff: *Total instructional faculty:* 128. Degrees held by full-time faculty: doctorate 14%, master's 32%, baccalaureate 68%, professional 73%. 83% hold terminal degrees.

Enrollment: Total enrollment 2,028. Undergraduate 97 (37.15 men, 62.9% women).

Characteristics of Student Body: *Ethnic/racial makeup:* Black non-Hispanic: 3.1%; Asian or Pacific Islander: 2.1%; Hispanic: 2.1%; White non-Hispanic: 90.7%; unknown: 2.1%.

International Students: 2 undergraduate nonresident aliens enrolled fall 2004. No programs available to aid students whose native language is not English. No financial aid specifically designated for international students.

Student Life: No on-campus housing. 10% of men join and 2% live in fraternities. *Intercollegiate athletics:* men only: rugby, soccer. *Special regulations:* Cars permitted without restrictions. *Special services:* Learning Resources Center. *Student publications: The Beacon,* a monthly newspaper; *PCC,* a yearbook. *Surrounding community:* Davenport population 105,000. Chicago (IL), 180 miles from campus, is nearest metropolitan area. Served by mass transit bus system, airport 6 miles from campus.

Library Collections: 55,000 volumes. 17,000 microforms; 24,000 audiovisual items; 705 current periodical subscriptions. Online catalog. Students have access to online information retrieval services and the Internet.

Most important holdings include chiropractic and alternative health care books.

Buildings and Grounds: Campus area 6 square blocks.

Chief Executive Officer: Dr. Donald P. Kern, President.

Address admission inquiries to Karen Eden, Director of Admissions.

St. Ambrose University

518 West Locust Street
Davenport, Iowa 52803-2898
Tel: (563) 333-6000   **E-mail:** admit@sau.edu
Fax: (563) 333-6243   **Internet:** www.sau.edu

Institution Description: St. Ambrose University, formerly St. Ambrose College, is a private, nonprofit institution affiliated with the Roman Catholic Church. *Enrollment:* 3,500. *Degrees awarded:* Baccalaureate, master's, doctorate.

Accreditation: *Regional:* NCA. *Professional:* business, engineering, nursing education, occupational therapy, physical therapy, social work

History: Established as St. Ambrose Seminary and offered first instruction at postsecondary level 1882; incorporated 1885; awarded first degree (baccalaureate) 1905; adopted St. Ambrose College name 1928; name officially changed to St. Ambrose University 1987.

Institutional Structure: *Governing board:* Board of Directors. Representation: 29 directors. 5 ex officio. All voting. *Composition of institution:* Administrators 6 men / 3 women. Academic affairs headed by vice president for academic affairs. Management/business/finances directed by vice president for finance. Full-time instructional faculty 116. Academic governance body, Faculty Assembly, meets an average of 6 times per year.

Calendar: Semesters. Academic year late Aug. to mid-May. Freshmen admitted Jan., May, June, July, Aug. Degrees conferred and formal commencement May and December. Summer session of 2 terms from mid-May to mid-July.

Characteristics of Freshmen: 84% of applicants accepted. 52% of accepted applicants enrolled. Average secondary school class rank 41st percentile. Mean ACT composite score 21.9. 53% of entering freshmen expected to graduate within 5 years. 52% of freshmen from Iowa. Freshmen from 11 states and 2 foreign countries.

Admission: Rolling admissions plan. For fall acceptance, apply as early as 1 year prior to enrollment, but not later than Aug. 1. Early acceptance available. *Requirements:* Either graduation from accredited secondary school or GED. Minimum GPA 2.5 and either a high school rank in the upper 50% of the graduation class or an ACT of 20 or above. *Entrance tests:* College Board SAT or ACT composite required for students. *For transfer students:* 2.0 minimum GPA; from 4-year accredited institutions 90 credit hours maximum transfer credit; from 2-year accredited institutions 60 hours; correspondence/extension students 60 hours.

College credit for postsecondary-level work completed in secondary school and for extrainstitutional learning on basis of ACE *2006 Guide to the Evaluation of Educational Experiences in the Armed Services*, portfolio and faculty assessments. Tutoring available. Developmental/remedial courses offered.

Degree Requirements: 120 semester hours; 2.0 GPA; last 30 or 45 of last 60 hours in residence; 2 credits physical education. Fulfillment of some degree requirements and exemption from some beginning courses possible by passing College Board CLEP, AP, other standardized tests.

Grading system: A–F; withdraw (deadline after which pass-fail is appended to withdraw).

Distinctive Educational Programs: Work-experience programs. Weekend and evening classes. Accelerated degree programs: Bachelor of Applied Management Technology, Bachelor of Elected Studies. Interdepartmental program in women's studies, peace and justice. Facilities and programs for independent research, including individual majors and tutorials. Study abroad for semester or year in many countries. Specific exchange programs with institutions in Ecuador and England.

Degrees Conferred: 533 *baccalaureate*; 376 *master's*; 1 *doctorate*. Bachelor's degrees awarded in top five disciplines: business, management, marketing, and related support services: 152; education 81; communication, journalism, and related programs 50; psychology 47; computer and information sciences 37.

Fees and Other Expenses: *Full-time tuition per academic year 2004–05:* $17,565. *Room and board per academic year:* $6,150. *Books and supplies:* $710.

Financial Aid: Aid from institutionally generated funds is provided on the basis of academic merit, financial need, athletic ability, other criteria. Institution has a Program Participation Agreement with the U.S. Department of Education for eligible students to receive Pell Grants and other federal aid.

Financial aid to full-time, first-time undergraduate students: 22% received federal grants averaging $1,414; 28% state/local grants averaging $2,959; 99% institutional grants averaging $4,096; 75% loans averaging $3,599.

Departments and Teaching Staff: Accounting *professors* 3, *associate professors* 1, *assistant professors* 1, *instructors* 0, *part-time faculty* 2l; art 2, 1, 1, 0, 2; biology 2, 2, 2, 0, 0; chemistry 1, 0, 2, 0, 0; communications 6, 1, 0, 0, 1; criminal justice 0, 0, 0, 0, 7; business and economics 6, 7, 8, 0, 12; education 1, 3, 0, 0, 5; English 1, 2, 1, 0, 2; foreign language 1, 0, 1, 0, 3; industrial engineering 2, 0, 2, 0, 0; mathematics/computer science 5, 2, 0, 0 0; social work 0, 1, 0, 0, 2; music 2, 0, 1, 0, 10; occupational therapy 4, 0, 0, 1, 2; philosophy 2, 0, 3, 0, 0; physical education 1, 1, 3, 0, 9; physical therapy 5, 1, 1, 1, 0; physics 1, 0, 3, 0, 0; political science 1, 1, 0, 0, 0; psychology 3, 2, 1, 0, 1; sociology 0, 0, 2, 0, 2; special education 2, 0, 1, 0, 4; theology 2, 1, 1, 0, 5.

Total instructional faculty: 138. Degrees held by full-time faculty: doctorate 64%, master's 33%, baccalaureate 2%, professional 2%. 68% hold terminal degrees. Student-to-faculty ratio: 13:1.

Enrollment: Total enrollment 3,500. Full-time 847 men / 1,136 women, part-time 175m / 325w.

Characteristics of Student Body: *Ethnic/racial makeup:* Black non-Hispanic: 3.1%; American Indian or Alaska Native: .3%, Asian or Pacific Islander: .9%; Hispanic: 2.5%; White non-Hispanic: 92.3%. *Age distribution:* 17–21: 38%; 22–24: 15%; 25–29: 15%; 30–34: 9%; 35–39: 8%; 40–49: 12%; 50–59: 2%; 60–and over: 1%.

International Students: 23 nonresident aliens enrolled fall 2004. Students from Europe, Asia, Central and South America, Africa, Canada. Programs available to aid students whose native language is not English: social and cultural. No financial aid specifically designated for international students.

Student Life: On-campus residence halls available, some configured as suites or townhouses. *Special regulations:* Cars permitted without restrictions. *Special services:* Academic Support Center; Multicultural Affairs Office; Office for Students with Physical or Academic Disabilities; Career Development Office; Transition Center for individuals leaving the work force to become students; Counseling Center, Health Services, Student Activities Board, Safety and Security Services, Residence Life Services, Remedial Education Programs, Intramural Sports Office. *Student radio, television:* Radio station KALA–FM broadcasts to the Quad Cities all but 5 hours weekly. TV station TV-11 broadcasts 24 hours per day. *Surrounding community:* Davenport population 95,500. Chicago, 160 miles from campus, is nearest metropolitan area. Served by mass transit system; airport 10 miles from campus.

Library Collections: 180,400 volumes. 32,000 microform units; 4,200 audiovisual materials; 615 current periodical subscriptions. Online catalog. Students have access to online information retrieval services.

Most important holdings include business and management, economics, and religious studies materials.

Buildings and Grounds: Campus area 48 acres.

Chief Executive Officer: Dr. Edward J. Rogalski, President.

Address admission inquiries to Meg Halligan, Director of Admissions.

Simpson College

701 North C Street
Indianola, Iowa 50125
Tel: (800) 362-2454
Fax: (515) 961-1498

Institution Description: Simpson College is a private college affiliated with The United Methodist Church. *Enrollment:* 1,966. *Degrees awarded:* Baccalaureate.

Accreditation: *Regional:* NCA. *Professional:* music, teacher education

History: Established and incorporated as Indianola Male and Female Seminary 1860; changed name to Des Moines Conference Seminary 1866; offered first instruction at postsecondary level and changed name to Simpson Centenary College 1867; first degree (baccalaureate) awarded 1870; present name adopted 1885.

Institutional Structure: *Governing board:* Simpson College Board of Trustees. Representation: 42 voting members, 5 ex officio, 16 lifetime honorary members. *Composition of institution:* Administrators 36 men / 37 women. Academic affairs headed by vice president of the college and dean of academic affairs. Management/business/finances directed by vice president for business affairs. Full-time instructional faculty 55 men / 25 women. Academic governance body, Simpson College Faculty, meets an average of 10 times per year.

Calendar: Semesters. Academic year Aug. to May. Freshmen admitted Sept., Jan., May, June, July. Degrees conferred and formal commencement May. Summer session of 2 terms.

Characteristics of Freshmen: 86% of applicants admitted. 365 of applicants admitted and enrolled.

5% (18 students) submitted SAT scores; 98% (386 students) submitted ACT scores. *25th percentile*: ACT Composite 21, ACT English 21, ACT Math 21. *75th percentile*: ACT Composite 26, ACT English 26, ACT Math 26.

69% of entering freshmen expected to graduate within 5 years. 86% of freshmen from Iowa. Freshmen from 14 states and 3 foreign countries.

Admission: Rolling admissions plan. Apply as early as end of junior year in secondary school, but not later than one week after classes begin. Early acceptance available. *Requirements:* Either graduation from secondary school with recommendation of principal or guidance counselor or GED. *Entrance tests:* College Board SAT or ACT composite. *For transfer students:* 2.0 minimum GPA, 96 semester hours maximum transfer credit; from 2-year accredited institution 64 hours; correspondence/extension students minimum GPA determined individually, 6 hours maximum transfer credit. Simpson accepts the International Baccalaureate (IB).

College credit and advanced placement for postsecondary-level work completed in secondary school and for extrainstitutional learning on basis of portfolio assessment. College credit on basis of ACE *2006 Guide to the Evaluation of Educational Experiences in the Armed Services.* Tutoring available. Developmental/remedial courses offered in summer session and regular academic year; credit given.

Degree Requirements: 128 hours and 2.0 GPA for Bachelor of Arts degree; 132 hours and 2.0 GPA for Bachelor of Music degree. 1 year (including internship) in residence; 40–41 hours Cornerstone Studies (distributive education); foreign language competency; writing competency requirement; mathematics proficiency requirement. Fulfillment of some degree requirements possible by passing departmental examinations, College Board CLEP or AP. *Grading system:* A–F; honors/pass/non-pass; withdraw (carries time limit), incomplete, credit.

Distinctive Educational Programs: Cooperative education. Summer, evening, and weekend classes in Indianola and Des Moines. FASTrack Program (ten-week modules). Dual-degree program in engineering with Washington University (MO) and Iowa State University. Cooperative baccalaureate degree in medical technology with Methodist Hospital.Interdisciplinary programs in environmental studies. Master of Arts in Teaching program. Study abroad at Institute of Italian Studies, Florence and Rome, Italy; Simpson Semester in Caen, France; England Semester in London, German Semester in Schorndorf, Germany; Spanish Semester in Merida, Mexico; Interims in Greece, Japan, Russia. Washington (DC) semester at American University. United Nations semester at Drew University (NJ). Certificates in management, accounting, or computer science. Domestic studies: Washington Center Internship and Symposia, Washington (DC); Appalachian Semester at Union College (KY); Washington, DC semester at American University; United Nations semester at Drew University (NJ).

Degrees Conferred: 398 *baccalaureate:* biological/life sciences 27; business/marketing 112; communications/communication technologies 26; computer and information sciences 23; education 56;engineering and engineering technologies 1; English 9; foreign languages and literature 12; mathematics 13; natural resources/environmental science 2; parks and recreation 2; personal and miscellaneous services 21; philosophy/religion/theology 6; physical sciences 2; protective services/public administration 23; psychology 20; social sciences and history 18; visual and performing arts 25.

Fees and Other Expenses: *Full-time tuition per academic year 2005–06:* $20,693. *Required fees:* $218. *Room and board per academic year:* $5,922.

Financial Aid: Aid from institutionally generated funds is provided on the basis of academic merit, financial need, other considerations. Institution has a Program Participation Agreement with the U.S. Department of Education for eligible students to receive Pell Grants and other federal aid.

Financial aid to full-time, first-time undergraduate students: need-based scholarships/grants totaling $16,300,815; self-help $6,916,845, parent loans $318,347, tuition waivers $373,395; non-need-based scholarships/grants totaling $1,773,834, self-help $3,550,417, parent loans $985,727, tuition waivers $220,517. *Graduate aid:* 11 students received federal and state-funded loans totaling $55,387 (ranging from $1,500 to $17,776).

Departments and Teaching Staff: Education *professors* 1, *associate professors* 3, *assistant professors* 2, *instructors* 1, *part-time faculty* 2; physical education 0, 0, 4, 2, 2; social science 1,1, 3, 0, 1; English 3, 0, 3, 0, 5; foreign languages 1, 2, 0, 0, 3; history 2, 1, 1, 0, 4; philosophy/religion 1, 1, 2, 1, 0; biology 1, 1, 4, 0, 1; chemistry/physics 3, 1, 0, 0, 0; computer science 0, 2, 0, 2, 2; mathematics 3, 1, 0, 0, 0; communications 1, 0, 2, 0, 1; business administration 4, 1, 3, 0, 4; political science 1, 1, 0, 1, 1; art 0, 1, 1, 0, 4; music 3, 2, 0, 5, 5; psychology 1, 2, 0, 0, 3; theatre 1, 2, 0, 0, 1.

Total instructional faculty: 127 (full-time 87, part-time 40; women 50, men 77; members of minority groups 8). Total faculty with doctorate, first-professional, or other terminal degree: 83. Student-to-faculty ratio: 13:1. *Faculty development:* $10,000 in grants for research. 6 faculty members awarded sabbaticals 2004–05.

Enrollment: Total enrollment 1,966. Undergraduate full-time 598 men / 854 women, part-time 164m / 339w; graduate part-time 4m / 7w.

Characteristics of Student Body: *Ethnic/racial makeup:* number of Black non-Hispanic: 34; American Indian or Alaska Native: 2; Asian or Pacific Islander: 23; Hispanic: 25; White non-Hispanic: 1,793; unknown: 58. *Age distribution:* number under 18: 4; 18–19: 586; 20–21: 637; 22–24: 270; 25–29: 128; 30–34: 103; 35–39: 72; 40–49: 109; 50–64: 30; 65 and over: 3.

International Students: 31 nonresident aliens enrolled fall 2004. 7 students from Europe, 13 Asia, 4 Central and South Latin America, 4 Africa, 2 Canada, 1 other. Programs available to aid students whose native language is not English: social, cultural. Financial aid specifically designated for international students: 30 scholarships available annually. Awards in 2004 totaled $504,892.

Student Life: Institutionally controlled residence halls, including fraternities and sororities, house 82% of full-time student body. Dormitories for men constitute 32% of such space, for women 35%, for both sexes 33%. 32% of full-time men join and 34% live in fraternities; 30% of full-time women join and 25% live in sororities. *Intercollegiate athletics:* men only: baseball, basketball, football, golf, tennis, track and field, wrestling, cross-country; women only: basketball, golf, soccer, softball, tennis, track and field, volleyball, cross-country. *Special regulations:* Cars permitted without restrictions. Quiet hours from 7pm to 10am. *Special services:* Hawley Resource Center; Career Planning Center. *Student publications: Sequel,* an annual literary magazine; *Simpsonian,* a weekly newspaper; *Zenith,* a yearbook. Radio station KSTM 88.9 FM student-run with all varieties of music. *Surrounding community:* Indianola population 12,000. Des

Moines, 12 miles from campus, is nearest metropolitan area. Served by airport 16 miles from campus.

Library Collections: 197,713 volumes including bound books, serial backfiles, electronic documents, and government documents not in separate collections. Online catalog. Current serial subscriptions: 528 paper, 28 microform, 4 via electronic access. 2,012 recordings; 936 compact discs; 104 CD-ROMs. 24 computer work stations. Students have access to the Internet at no charge.

Most important holdings include Avery O. Craven Collection on the Antebellum South; Sears Lehmann Collection of Ancient Pottery (25 pieces).

Buildings and Grounds: Campus area 63 acres. *New buildings:* Barker Hall (residence hall for undergraduate men) addition completed 2005.

Chief Executive Officer: Dr. John W. Byrd, President.

Address admission inquiries to Deborah Tierney, Vice President for Admissions.

University of Dubuque

2000 University Avenue
Dubuque, Iowa 52001-5050
Tel: (563) 589-3200   **E-mail:** admissions@dbq.edu
Fax: (563) 589-3690   **Internet:** www.dbq.edu

Institution Description: University of Dubuque is a private institution affiliated with the Presbyterian Church (U.S.A.). The university consists of a College of Liberal Arts and a Theological Seminary. *Enrollment:* 1,361. *Degrees awarded:* Associate, baccalaureate, first-professional, master's.

Accreditation: *Regional:* NCA. *National:* ATS. *Professional:* theology

History: Established as German Theological School of the Northwest 1852; offered first instruction at postsecondary level and awarded first degree (baccalaureate) 1905.

Institutional Structure: *Governing board:* Board of Trustees. Representation: 45 trustees. *Composition of institution:* Administrators 31 men / 27 women. Management/business/finances directed by vice president of finance. Full-time instructional faculty 57.

Calendar: Semesters. Academic year Aug. to May.

Characteristics of Freshmen: 80% of applicants admitted. 50% of applicants admitted and enrolled.

14% (56 students) submitted SAT scores; 88% (268 students) submitted ACT scores. *25th percentile:* SAT Verbal 400, SAT Math 410; ACT Composite 17, ACT English 16, ACT Math 17. *75th percentile:* SAT Verbal 500, SAT Math 550; ACT Composite 22, ACT English 21, ACT Math 23.

32% of freshmen expected to graduate within 5 years. 35% of freshmen from Iowa. Freshmen from 23 states and 3 foreign countries.

Admission: *Requirements:* Graduation from secondary school with 15 units, including 10 from academic fields. *Entrance tests:* College Board SAT or ACT composite. *For transfer students:* 2.0 minimum GPA; from 2-year accredited institution 60 hours maximum transfer credit; from 4-year accredited institution maximum transfer credit limited only by residence requirement; correspondence/extension students 24 hours. TOEFL required for foreign students.

College credit for postsecondary-level work completed in secondary school and for extrainstitutional learning on basis of ACE *2006 Guide to the Evaluation of Educational Experiences in the Armed Services.* Credit for experiential learning through portfolio development.

Degree Requirements: *For all associate degrees:* 64 credit hours. *For all baccalaureate degrees:* 120 credit hours. *For all undergraduate degrees:* 2.0 GPA; 30 of last 36 hours in residence; general education and general skills requirements. For teacher education students 2.75 GPA; minor required for B.A. and B.S. degrees.

Fulfillment of some degree requirements and exemption from some beginning courses possible by passing departmental examinations, College Board CLEP, other standardized tests. *Grading system:* A–F; pass/fail, withdraw.

Distinctive Educational Programs: Work-experience programs. Joint baccalaureate-M.Div./M.A.R. in theology with Theological Seminary. Interdisciplinary program in environmental science. Education and Social Work Departments combined with Clarke College and Loras College; with Wartburg Theological Seminary joint M.B.A.-M.Div/M.A.R. programs. International M.B.A. program in Singapore and Malaysia. Ed.S. offered in cooperation with National-Louis University. Study abroad through special arrangement. *Other distinctive programs:* Credit and non-credit continuing education. HECUA off-campus and overseas study semester. Environmental Studies Semester at Northwoods Audubon Center (MN).

ROTC: Army. 3 commissions awarded 2004.

Degrees Conferred: 158 *baccalaureate* (B), 70 *master's* (M); 18 *doctorate* (D): business/marketing 29 (B), 62 (M); communications/communication technologies 3 (M); computer and information sciences 22 (B); education 17 (B);

English 6 (B); liberal arts/general studies 1 (B); mathematics 1 (B); natural resources/environmental science 2 (B); parks and recreation 7 (b); philosophy/religion/theology 8 (B), 5 (M), 18 (D); protective services/public administration 8 (B); psychology 11 (B); social sciences and history 2 (B); trade and industry 34 (B). 29 *first-professional:* master of divinity 29.

Fees and Other Expenses: *Full-time tuition per academic year 2004–05:* $16,660. *Required fees:* $200. Graduate study changed per credit hour. *Room per academic year:* $5,700.

Financial Aid: Aid from institutionally generated funds is provided on the basis of academic merit, financial need. Institution has a Program Participation Agreement with the U.S. Department of Education for eligible students to receive Pell Grants and other federal aid.

Financial aid to full-time, first-time undergraduate students: need-based scholarships/grants totaling $8,747,159, self-help $10,958,942, parent loans $182,717; non-need-based scholarships/grants totaling $710,628, self-help $1,132,004, parent loans $172,328. *Graduate aid:* 15 students received federal and state-funded loans totaling $127,156.

Departments and Teaching Staff: *Total instructional faculty:* 136 (full-time 57, part-time 79; women 57, men 79; members of minority groups 5). Total faculty with doctorate, first-professional, or other terminal degree: 33. Student-to-faculty ratio: 23:1. 230 Total enrollment 1,361. Undergraduate full-time 677 men / 369 women, part-time 24m / 31w; first-professional full-time 85m / 50w, part-time 16m / 8w; graduate full-time 24m / 17w, part-time 34m / 26w. *Transfer students:* in-state 106; from out-of-state 8.

Characteristics of Student Body: *Ethnic/racial makeup:* number of Black non-Hispanic: 114; American Indian or Alaska Native: 29; Asian or Pacific Islander: 14; Hispanic: 43; White non-Hispanic 864; unknown: 32. *Age distribution:* number under 18: 9; 18–19: 467; 20–21: 371; 22–24: 128; 25–29: 51; 30–34: 21; 35–39: 11; 40–49: 23; 50–64: 6,

International Students: 44 nonresident aliens enrolled fall 2004. 2 students from Europe, 33 Asia, 1 Central and south America, 1 Africa, 6 Canada, 1 Australia. Programs available to aid students whose native language is not English: social and cultural. English as a Second Language Program. No financial aid specifically designated for international students.

Student Life: On-campus housing available. Housing available for married seminary students. *Intercollegiate athletics:* men only: basketball, baseball, football, wrestling; women only: basketball, softball, volleyball; both sexes: tennis, golf, indoor and outdoor track, soccer. . *Special services:* Counseling and medical services. *Student publications: Under the Bell Tower,* a newspaper; *The Key,* a yearbook. *Surrounding community:* Dubuque population 58,000. Nearby metropolitan areas: Madison, 95 miles away; Quad Cities, 65 miles away.

Library Collections: 168,500 volumes including bound books, serial backfiles, electronic documents, and government documents not in separate collections. Online catalog. Current serial subscriptions: 484 paper, 20,000 microform, 7,115 via electronic access. 78 CD-ROMs. 80 compact discs. 63 computer work stations. Students have access to the Internet at no charge. Total budget for books, periodicals, audiovisual materials, microforms 2004–05: $211,500.

Most important special collections include William C. Brown Collection; William J. Petersen Collection; Joseph L. Minelic Collection; University Archives.

Buildings and Grounds: Campus area 70 acres. *New buildings:* Seminary Village completed 2000; Charles C. Myers Library 2001; University Park Village 2004.

Chief Executive Officer: Dr. Jeffrey F. Bullock, President.

Address admission inquiries to Jesse James, Director of Admissions. Admission inquiries for Theological Seminary to Donna Warhover, Director of Seminary Admission.

Theological Seminary

Degree Programs Offered: *First-professional, master's.*

Admission: *For first-professional:* Baccalaureate or equivalent from accredited college or university. Recommend major in the humanities, social sciences, history, or philosophy. 2.0 minimum GPA.

Degree Requirements: *For first-professional:* 96 credit hours, 2.0 GPA, 1 year in residence.

University of Iowa

Iowa City, Iowa 52242

Tel: (319) 335-3847   **E-mail:** admissions@uiowa.edu
Fax: (319) 335-1535   **Internet:** www.uiowa.edu

Institution Description: The University of Iowa is a state institution. *Enrollment:* 28,442. *Degrees awarded:* Baccalaureate, first-professional (dentistry, law, medicine), master's, doctorate. Certificates also awarded.

Accreditation: *Regional:* NCA. *Professional:* accounting, applied science, athletic training, audiology, business, clinical lab scientist, pastoral counseling, clinical psychology, counseling, counseling psychology, dentistry, diagnostic medical sonography, dietetics, endodontics, engineering, English language education, health services administration, journalism, law, librarianship, medicine, music, nuclear medicine technology, nurse anesthesia education, nursing, nursing education, oral and maxillofacial pathology, pediatric dentistry, periodontics, pharmacy, physical therapy, physician assisting, surgeon assisting, planning, public health, radiation therapy, recreation and leisure services, rehabilitation counseling, social work, speech-language pathology, theatre

History: Chartered under present official name, State University of Iowa, 1847; offered first instruction at postsecondary level 1855; awarded first degree (baccalaureate) 1858.

Institutional Structure: *Governing board:* Iowa State Board of Regents. Representation: 9 regents appointed by governor. *Composition of institution:* Administrators 47% men / 53% women. Academic affairs headed by provost. Management/business/finances directed by vice president for finance and university services. *Total instructional faculty* 1,702.

Calendar: Semesters. Academic year late Aug. to early May. Degrees conferred and formal commencements Dec., May, July. Summer session of 3 terms from late May to the end of July.

Characteristics of Freshmen: 83% of applicants accepted. 41% of accepted applicants enrolled.

12% (494 students) submitted SAT scores; 96% (3,870 students) submitted ACT scores. *25th percentile:* SAT Verbal 530, SAT Math 540; ACT Composite 22, ACT English 21, ACT Math 21. *75th percentile:* SAT Verbal 660, SAT Math 670; ACT Composite 27, ACT English 27, ACT Math 27.

64% of freshmen from Iowa. Freshmen from 44 states and 15 foreign countries.

Admission: *Requirements:* Iowa residents must have class rank in top 50% or have acceptable admission index score. Nonresidents must rank top 30% or acceptable admission index. Index score is a combination of class rank and ACT or SAT. Engineering admission requirements are higher. Applicants must also have completed a prescribed set of high school courses. *Entrance tests:* College Board SAT or ACT composite. For foreign students TOEFL. *For transfer students:* 2.25 minimum GPA and 24 hours acceptable graded credit or if fewer than 24 hours completed the admission decision is based on a combination of high school and college records and ACT or SAT.

College credit and advanced placement for postsecondary-level work completed in secondary school.

Degree Requirements: 120 credit hours; 2.0 GPA; last 30 consecutive hours, 45 of last 60 hours, or 90 total hours, in residence; general education requirements. Fulfillment of some degree requirements and exemption from some beginning courses possible by passing College Board CLEP, AP, other standardized test. *Grading system:* A–F; pass-fail; pass; withdraw; satisfactory-unsatisfactory; honors; no grade; audit.

Distinctive Educational Programs: Work-experience programs. Joint degree programs between School of Social Work and College of Law, School of Social Work and Department of Urban and Regional Planning, College of Law and Department of Sociology, Colleges of Business Administration and Law and the School of Library Science, Department of Economics and College of Law. Interdepartmental programs in Afro-American studies; global studies; Latin American studies; literature, science, and the arts; women's studies. Honors programs. Study abroad in over 55 countries.

ROTC: Army and Air Force offered.

Degrees Conferred: 4,013 *baccalaureate* (B), 1,358 *master's* (M), 300 *doctorate* (D): architecture 20 (M); area and ethnic studies 43 (B), 13 (M), 3 (D); biological/life sciences 117 (B), 33 (M), 6 (D); business/marketing 768 (B), 330 (M), 6 (D); communications/communication technologies 438 (B), 19 (M), 13 (D); computer and information sciences 71 (B), 32 (M), 1 (D); education 201 (B), 150 (M), 13 (D); engineering and engineering technologies 248 (B), 76 (M), 36 (D); English 240 (B), 75 (M), 7 (D); foreign languages and literature 86 (B), 28 (M), 6 (D); health professions and related sciences 262 (B), 188 (M), 21 (D); interdisciplinary studies 42 (B), 3 (M), 1 (D); law/legal studies 16 (M); liberal arts/general studies 29 (M); library science 31 (M); mathematics 29 (B), 47 (M), 16 (D); natural resources/environmental science 16 (B); parks and recreation 177 (B), 24 (M), 3 (D); philosophy/religion/theology 39 (B), 12 (M), 3 (D); physical sciences 39 (B), 20 (M), 17 (D); protective services/public administration 44 (B), 94 (M), 1 (D); psychology 284 (B), 7 (M), 10 (D); social sciences and history 568 (B), 32 (M), 26 (D); visual and performing arts 272 (B), 108 (M), 28 (D). 547 *first-professional:* dentistry 78; law 233; medicine 131; pharmacy 105.

Fees and Other Expenses: *Full-time tuition per academic year 2004–05:* undergraduate resident $4,980, out-of-state student $16,276. Contact the university for current graduate/professional school tuition/fees. *Books and supplies:* $840. *Room and board per academic year:* $6,560.

Financial Aid: Aid from institutionally generated funds is provided on the basis of academic merit, financial need. Institution has a Program Participation Agreement with the U.S. Department of Education for eligible students to receive Pell Grants and other federal aid.

Financial aid to full-time, first-time undergraduate students: need-based scholarships/grants totaling $23,074,374, self-help $29,592,808; non-need-based scholarships/grants totaling $11,504,954, self-help $33,082,074, parent loans $27,414,360, athletic awards $5,741,759.

Departments and Teaching Staff: *Total instructional faculty:* 1,713 (full-time 1,622, part-time 91; women 458, men 1,245; members of minority groups 237). Total faculty with doctorate, first-professional, or other terminal degree: 1,656. Student-to-faculty ratio: 14:1.

Enrollment: Total enrollment 28,442. Undergraduate full-time 8,201 men / 9,678 women, part-time 1,035m / 1,221w; first-professional full-time 1,561m / 1214w, part-time 79m / 55w; graduate full-time 1,310m / 1,585w, part-time 1,573m / 1,714w. *Transfer students:* in-state 1,624; from out-of-state 1,174.

Characteristics of Student Body: *Ethnic and racial makeup:* number of Black non-Hispanic: 449; American Indian or Alaska Native: 87; Asian or Pacific Islander: 733; Hispanic: 459; White non-Hispanic: 17,422; unknown: 634. *Age distribution:* under 18: 148; 18–19: 7,347; 20–21: 1,659; 22–24:3,269; 25–29: 837; 30–34: 319; 35–39: 238; 40–49: 220; 50–64: 98.

International Students: 351 undergraduate nonresident aliens enrolled fall 2004. Students from Europe, Asia, Central and South America, Africa, Canada, Australia, New Zealand. Programs available to aid students whose native language is not English: social, cultural. English as a Second Language Program. No financial aid specifically designated for international students.

Student Life: On-campus housing available for single and married students. Men and women may join and live in fraternities and sororities. *Intercollegiate athletics:* men only: baseball, basketball, cross-country, football, golf, gymnastics, rowing, soccer, swimming, tennis, track, wrestling; women only: basketball, cross-country, field hockey, golf, gymnastics, softball, swimming, tennis, track, volleyball. *Special services:* Medical services. *Student operated radio station:* KRUI. *University operated radio stations:* WSUI, KSUI. *Surrounding community:* Iowa City population 60,000.

Publications: *Publisher:* The University of Iowa Press.

Library Collections: 4,382,000 volumes including bound books, serial backfiles, electronic documents, and government documents not in separate collections. Online catalog. Access to 50,000 serials via electronic access; 7,885,000 microforms; 276,000 audiovisual materials. Computer work stations available. Students have access to the Internet at no charge.

Most important holdings include Leigh Hunt Collection (over 2,500 manuscripts and letters and over 700 books); Henry A. Wallace papers (200 linear feet); Iowa Authors Collection (10,000 books and manuscripts); John Martin History of Medicine (3,000 titles); Iowa Women's Archives.

Chief Executive Officer: Dr. David Skorton, President.

Address admission inquiries to Michael Barron, Director of Admissions.

University of Northern Iowa

1227 West 27th Street
Cedar Falls, Iowa 50614
Tel: (319) 273-2281   **E-mail:** admissions@uni.edu
Fax: (319) 273-2885   **Internet:** www.uni.edu

Institution Description: University of Northern Iowa is a state institution. *Enrollment:* 12,727. *Degrees awarded:* Baccalaureate, master's, doctorate. Specialist certificate in education also awarded.

Accreditation: *Regional:* NCA. *Professional:* art, audiology, business, construction technology, counseling, industrial technology, manufacturing technology, music, recreation and leisure services, social work, speech-language pathology

History: Established and chartered as Iowa State Normal School 1876; offered first instruction at postsecondary level 1900; awarded first degree (baccalaureate) 1905; changed name to Iowa State Teachers College 1909, State College of Iowa 1961; adopted present name 1967.

Institutional Structure: *Governing board:* Iowa State Board of Regents. Representation: 9 regents. All voting. *Composition of institution:* Administrators 442 men / 26 women. Academic affairs headed by vice president and provost. Management/business/finances directed by vice president for administrative services. Academic governance body, Faculty Senate, meets an average of 15 times per year. *Faculty representation:* Faculty served by collective bargaining agent affiliated with AAUP.

Calendar: Semesters. Academic year Aug. to May. Freshmen admitted Aug., Jan., June. Degrees conferred May, June, Dec., Formal commencements May, July, Dec. Summer session of 6 terms from May to July.

Characteristics of Freshmen: 79.7% of applicants admitted. 40.3% of applicants admitted and enrolled.

4.3% (73 students) submitted SAT scores; 95.7% (1,643 students) submitted ACT scores. *25th percentile*: SAT Verbal 430, SAT Math 480; ACT Composite 20, ACT English 19, ACT Math 19. *75th percentile*: SAT Verbal 600, SAT Math 610; ACT Composite 25, ACT English 25,ACT Math 25.

54.6% of entering freshmen expected to graduate within 5 years. 91.5% of freshmen from Iowa. Freshmen from 19 states and 16 foreign countries.

Admission: Rolling admissions plan. For fall acceptance, apply as early as 1 year prior to enrollment, but not later than 2 weeks before first day of class. *Requirements:* Graduation from accredited secondary school. Require 4 years in English, (must include 1 year of composition); 3 mathematics (must include equivalents of algebra, geometry, and advanced algebra); 3 science (1 with lab); 3 social studies; and 2 years electives from above areas, and/or language and/or fine arts. Lowest acceptable secondary school class standing 50th percentile. *Entrance tests:* ACT composite. *For transfer students:* Requires GPA based on number of credits accepted for transfer (60 or more 2.00, 42–59 2.25, 24–41 2.50). Students with fewer than 24 semester hours will be considered for admission on the basis of their high school records. For those from 4-year accredited institution maximum transfer credit limited only by residence requirement; from 2-year institution maximum 65 hours; correspondence/extension students maximum 32 hours.

College credit for extrainstitutional learning on basis of ACE *2006 Guide to the Evaluation of Educational Experiences in the Armed Services.* Tutoring available. Noncredit developmental courses offered in summer session and regular academic year.

Degree Requirements: 129–139 credit hours; 2.0–2.5 GPA; 2 terms in residence; 3 semester hours in personal fellness which includes 2 activity courses in physical education; general education requirements.

Fulfillment of some degree requirements possible by passing College Board CLEP. *Grading system:* A–F; withdraw (carries time limit).

Distinctive Educational Programs: Work-experience programs. Weekend and evening classes. External degree program. Special facilities for using telecommunications in the classroom. Interdisciplinary programs in American studies, Asian studies, general studies, inter-American studies, individual studies, Russia and East European studies, chemistry-marketing, humanities. Facilities and programs for independent research, including individual majors, tutorials. Institutionally-sponsored study abroad in Australia, Austria, Chile, China, Costa Rica, Denmark, England, France, Germany, Ghana, Japan, Poland, Portugal, Russia, Slovakia, Spain, Wales. Student exchange with Iowa State University, University of Iowa; with various other institutions through National Student Exchange program.

ROTC: Army. 20 commissions awarded 2004.

Degrees Conferred: 2,384 *baccalaureate* (B), 434 *master's* (M), 10 *doctorate* (D): area and ethnic studies 5 (B), 1 (M); biological/life sciences 101 (B), 3 (M); business/marketing 575 (B), 44 (M); communications/communication technologies 184 (B), 15 (M); computer and information sciences 32 (B), 8 (M); education 541 (B), 192 (M), 8 (D); engineering and engineering technologies 63 (B), 13 (M), 2 (D); English 60 (B), 4 (M); foreign languages and literature 26 (B), 23 (M); health professions and related sciences 72 (B), 17 (M); home economics and vocational home economics 72 (B); interdisciplinary studies 4 (B), 2 (M); liberal arts/general studies 131 (B); library science 7 (M); mathematics 13 (B), 5 (M); natural resources/environmental science 2 (B), 3 (M); parks and recreation 77 (B); philosophy/religion/theology 16 (M); physical sciences 29 (B), 1 (M); protective services/public administration 72 (B), 41 (M); psychology 91 (B), 33 (M); social sciences and history 283 (B), 13 (M); visual and performing arts 135 (B), 9 (M).

Fees and Other Expenses: *Full-time tuition per academic year 2004–2006* undergraduate resident $4,702; out-of-state student $12,020; graduate resident $5,488, out-of-state student $13,012. *Required fees:* $685. *Room per academic year:* $2,431. *Board per academic year:* $2,830.

Financial Aid: University of Northern Iowa offers a direct lending program. Aid from institutionally generated funds is provided on the basis of academic merit, financial need, athletic ability, other criteria. Institution has a Program Participation Agreement with the U.S. Department of Education for eligible students to receive Pell Grants and other federal aid.

Financial aid to full-time, first-time undergraduate students: need-based scholarships/grants totaling $11,871,109, self-help $28,110,607; non-need-based scholarships/grants totaling $24,800,049, self-help 5,843,721, parent loans $10,166,553, athletic awards $2,648,450. *Graduate aid:* 107 students received federal and state-funded fellowships and grants totaling $286,805; 660 received federal and state-funded loans totaling $7,328,029; 20 students had work-study jobs worth $30,656; 523 students received other fellowships and grants totaling $2,030,936; 416 students received assistantships totaling $2,255,046.

Departments and Teaching Staff: *Total instructional faculty:* 784 (full-time 649, part-time 135; women 335, men 449; members of minority groups 80).

Total faculty with doctorate, first-professional, or other terminal degree: 578. Student-to-faculty ratio: 16:1. *Faculty development:* $2,567,447 in grants for research. 20 faculty members awarded sabbaticals 2004–05.

Enrollment: Total enrollment 12,2927. Undergraduate full-time 4,264 men / 5,725 women, part-time 592m / 685w; graduate full-time 225m / 417w, part-time 331m / 688w.

Characteristics of Student Body: *Ethnic/racial makeup:* number of Black non-Hispanic: 325; American Indian or Alaska Native: 30; Asian or Pacific Islander: 114; Hispanic: 197; White non-Hispanic: 10,401. *Age distribution:* number under 18: 107;18–19: 3,176; 20–21: 4,340; 22–24: 2,654; 25–29: 512; 30–34: 184; 35–39: 98; 40–49: 140; 50–64: 54; 65 and over: 1.

International Students: 375 nonresident aliens enrolled fall 2004. 95 students from Europe, 156 Asia, 42 Central and South America, 33 Africa, 11 Canada, 2 Australia, 36 other. Programs available to aid students whose native language is not English: cultural. English as a Second Language Program. No financial aid loans specifically designated for international students.

Student Life: On-campus residence halls house 33% of student body. Residence halls for are designated as substance-free and upper classmen areas. Residence halls for men constitute 17% of such space, for women only 31%, for both sexes 52%. 2% of men join fraternities and 2% of women join sororities. Housing available for married students. *Intercollegiate athletics:* men only: baseball, basketball, football, golf, track and cross-country, wrestling; women only: basketball, golf, softball, swimming, tennis, track and cross-country, volleyball. *Special regulations:* Cars permitted without restrictions. *Special services:* Center for Academic Achievement, medical services. *Student publications, radio: Northern Iowan*, a biweekly newspaper; *Old Gold*, a yearbook. Radio station KUNI-FM broadcasts 168 hours per week; KHKE-FM 126 hours; KCRS 84 hours. *Surrounding community:* Cedar Falls population 37,000. Des Moines (IA) 120 miles from campus, is nearest metropolitan area. Served by mass transit bus system; airport 8 miles from campus.

Publications: *North American Review* (quarterly) first published in 1815.

Library Collections: 2,353,037 volumes. Online catalog. Current serial subscriptions: 2,775 paper; 1,035 via electronic access. 15,132 recordings; 3,409 CD-ROMs. 101 computer work stations. Students have access to the Internet and online services.

Most important holdings include collections on American fiction of 1960s–70s; children's literature; education; papers of Senator Charles Grassley.

Buildings and Grounds: Campus area 910 acres.

Chief Executive Officer: Dr. Robert D. Koob, President.

Address admission inquiries to Roland Carillo, Director of Enrollment Management.

Upper Iowa University

605 Washington Street
P.O. Box 1857
Fayette, Iowa 52142
Tel: (563) 425-5281   **E-mail:** admission@uiu.edu
Fax: (563) 425-5277   **Internet:** www.uiu.edu

Institution Description: Upper Iowa University is a private, independent, nonprofit institution. *Enrollment:* 4,989. *Degrees awarded:* Baccalaureate, master's.

Academic offerings subject to approval by statewide coordinating bodies.

Accreditation: *Regional:* NCA.

History: Chartered as The Fayette Seminary of Upper Iowa Conference 1850; incorporated 1856; established, changed name to Collegiate Institute, and offered first instruction at postsecondary level 1857; adopted present name 1858; awarded first degree (baccalaureate) 1862; *See* M.H. Alderson "Upper Iowa University" *Palimpsest* 46, no. 3 (1965) for further information.

Institutional Structure: *Governing board:* Board of Trustees of Upper Iowa University. Extrainstitutional representation: 13 trustees, including 5 alumni; institutional representation: president of the college; 1 full-time instructional faculty member. 1 ex officio. 14 voting. *Composition of institution:* Administrators 10 men / 16 women. Academic affairs headed by provost. Management/business/finances directed by business manager. Full-time instructional faculty 17 men / 3 women. Academic governance body, Academic Council, meets an average of 9 times per year.

Calendar: Semesters with two 8-week terms per semester. Academic year Aug. to May. Freshmen admitted Aug., Oct., Jan., Mar, June, July. Degrees conferred Feb., May, June, Aug., Oct, Dec. Formal commencement May. Summer session from early June to late July.

Characteristics of Freshmen: 674 applicants (438 men, 236 women). 68.5% of applicants admitted. 32.5% of admitted students enrolled full-time.

10% (16 students) submitted SAT scores; 90% (134 students) submitted ACT scores. *25th percentile*: SAT Verbal 370, SAT Math 380; ACT Composite 19, ACT English 14, ACT Math 16. *75th percentile*: SAT Verbal 510, SAT Math 490; ACT Composite 20, ACT English 19, ACT Math 21.

55% of entering freshmen expected to graduate within 5 years. 70% of freshmen from Iowa. Freshmen from 10 states and 4 foreign countries.

Admission: Rolling admissions plan; applications accepted throughout the year. Early acceptance available. *Requirements:* Either graduation from accredited secondary school or GED. Minimum GPA 2.0. Lowest acceptable secondary school class standing 60th percentile. *Entrance tests:* College Board SAT or ACT composite. *For transfer students:* 2.0 GPA; from 4-year accredited institution maximum transfer credit limited only by residence requirement; from 2-year accredited institution 60 semester hours.

College credit for postsecondary-level work completed in secondary school and for extrainstitutional learning on basis of ACE *2006 Guide to the Evaluation of Educational Experiences in the Armed Services* (45 semester hours maximum). Tutoring available. Noncredit developmental courses offered during regular academic year.

Degree Requirements: 120 semester hours; 2.00 GPA; 1 term in residence; distribution requirements. Fulfillment of some degree requirements and exemption from some beginning courses possible by passing departmental examinations, College Board CLEP, other standardized test. *Grading system:* A–F; pass-fail; pass; withdraw (deadline after which A–F is appended to withdraw); incomplete (carries time limit).

Distinctive Educational Programs: Internships and cooperative education. Flexible meeting places and schedules, including off-campus centers (at Waterloo, 50 miles away from main institution; Des Moines, 175 miles away, and Madison, WI, 150 miles away). Interdepartmental/interdisciplinary programs in conservation/recreation management, recreation. *Other distinctive programs:* External Degree Program offers courses leading to baccalaureates in accounting, marketing, management, and public administration.

ROTC: Army.

Degrees Conferred: 29 *associate;* 854 *baccalaureate*; 52 *master's.* Bachelor's degrees awarded in top five disciplines: business, management, marketing, and related support services 407; public administration and social service professions 176; education 91; psychology 71; social sciences 66.

Fees and Other Expenses: *Full-time tuition per academic year 2004–05:* $16,556 undergraduate; graduate study charged per credit hour. *Books and supplies:* $1,150. *Room and board per academic year:* $5,272.

Financial Aid: Aid from institutionally generated funds is provided on the basis of academic merit, financial need. Institution has a Program Participation Agreement with the U.S. Department of Education for eligible students to receive Pell Grants and other federal aid.

Financial aid to full-time, first-time undergraduate students: 49% received federal grants averaging $1,332; 36% state/local grants averaging $3,366; 85% institutional grants averaging $6,834; 80% loans averaging $3,444.

Departments and Teaching Staff: Art *professors* 0, *associate professors* 1, *assistant professors* 0, *instructors* 0; biology 1, 0, 1, 0; business administration 0, 0, 0, 3; chemistry 0, 1, 1, 0; education 0, 0, 1, 1; English 1, 0, 1, 0; foreign language 0, 1, 0, 0; health, physical education and recreation 0, 1, 1, 3; mathematics, physics 2, 1, 0, 0; music 1, 0, 0, 0; history 0, 1, 0, 0; political science 0, 1, 0, 0; psychology and sociology 0, 0, 1, 0; speech and theatre 0, 1, 0, 0.

Total instructional faculty: 28. Student-to-faculty ratio: 16:1. Degrees held by full-time faculty: 11 doctorate, 15 master's. 55% hold terminal degrees.

Enrollment: Total enrollment 4,989. Undergraduate 4,855 (40.8% men, 59.2% women).

Characteristics of Student Body: *Ethnic/racial makeup:* Black non-Hispanic: 14.7%; American Indian or Alaska Native: .4%; Asian or Pacific Islander: 2%; Hispanic: 3.3%; White non-Hispanic: 76.7%; unknown: 2.9%.

International Students: 28 nonresident aliens enrolled fall 2004. No programs available to aid students whose native language is not English. No financial aid specifically designated for international students.

Student Life: On-campus residence halls house 67% of student body. Housing available for married students. 2% of married students request institutional housing and are so housed. *Intercollegiate athletics:* men only: baseball, basketball, cross-country, football, golf, soccer, tennis, track, wrestling; women only: basketball, soccer, tennis, volleyball, softball, cross-country, golf, track. *Special regulations:* Registered cars permitted in designated areas only. Quiet hours from 10pm to 10am Sun.–Sat. Residence hall visitation from 10am to 1am Sun.–Thurs. (to 3am Fri. and Sat.). *Special services:* Snack bar, bowling alley (free bowling), automatic teller banking, trips to nearby shopping centers, free golfing, cable TV, recreation room, sauna, medical and dental services readily available. *Student publications: The Collegian*, a weekly newspaper. *Surrounding community:* Fayette population 1,500. Chicago (IL), 250 miles from campus, is nearest large metropolitan area.

Library Collections: 152,000 volumes. 32,000 government documents; 9,000 microforms; 2,100 audiovisual materials; 290 current periodical subscriptions. Online catalog. Students have access to the Internet at no charge.

Most important holdings include pictures, tapes, and slides of NASA projects.

Buildings and Grounds: Campus area 100 acres.

Chief Executive Officer: Dr. Adam G. Walker, President.

Address admission inquiries to Linda Hoopes, Director of Admissions

Vennard College

2300 Eighth Avenue, East
University Park, Iowa 52595
Tel: (641) 673-8391   **E-mail:** admissions@vennard.edu
Fax: (641) 673-8365   **Internet:** vennard.edu

Institution Description: Vennard College is a private, interdenominational Bible college. *Enrollment:* 72. *Degrees awarded:* Associate, baccalaureate.

Accreditation: *National:* ABHE.

Calendar: Semesters.

Characteristics of Freshmen: 37 applicants (16 men, 21 women). 29.7% of applicants admitted. 100% of admitted students enrolled full-time.

16% (2 students) submitted SAT scores; 82% (9 students) submitted ACT scores. *25th percentile:* ACT Composite 17, ACT English 16, ACT Math 16. *75th percentile:* ACT Composite 20, ACT English 21, ACT Math 21.

Admission: *Requirements:* Graduation from secondary school.

Degree Requirements: Completion of prescribed curriculum.

Distinctive Educational Programs: Bachelor of Theology (5-year program in pastoral theology).

Degrees Conferred: 3 *associate*; 4 *baccalaureate:* theology and ministerial studies.

Fees and Other Expenses: *Full-time tuition per academic year:* $9,020. *Books and supplies:* $775. *Room and board per academic year:* $4,600.

Financial Aid: Aid from institutionally generated funds is provided on the basis of academic merit, financial need, other criteria. Institution has a Program Participation Agreement with the U.S. Department of Education for eligible students to receive Pell Grants and other federal aid.

Financial aid to full-time, first-time undergraduate students: 75% received federal grants; 100% institutional grants; 75% received loans.

Departments and Teaching Staff: Bible/theology *professors* 3, *associate professors* 1, *assistant professors* 0, *part-time teachers* 1; education/Christian education 0, 1, 0, 2; general education 1, 0, 2, 5; missiology 0, 0, 1, 0; music 0, 0, 1, 1.

Total instructional faculty: 13. Degrees held by full-time faculty: master's 50%, baccalaureate 20%.

Enrollment: Total enrollment 72 (52.8% men, 47.2% women).

Characteristics of Student Body: *Ethnic/racial makeup:* Asian or Pacific Islander: 1.4%; Hispanic: 1.4%; White non-Hispanic: 97.2%.

International Students: 2 nonresident aliens enrolled. Programs available to aid students whose native language is not English: Social, cultural. English as a Second Language Program. No financial aid specifically designated for international students.

Library Collections: 30,000 volumes. 140 current periodical subscriptions.

Most important special holdings include collections on holiness, preaching, and the Bible.

Chief Executive Officer: Dr. Bruce E. Moyer, President.

Address admission inquiries to Robyn E. Chrisman, Director of Admissions.

Waldorf College

106 South Sixth Street
Forest City, Iowa 50436
Tel: (841) 585-2450   **E-mail:** admissions@waldorf.edu
Fax: (841) 585-8194   **Internet:** www.waldorf.edu

Institution Description: The mission of Waldorf College is to education the whole person in the spirit of Jesus Christ, enabling the individual to experience fulfillment through a life of service. It is affiliated with the Evangelical Lutheran Church in America. *Enrollment:* 629. *Degrees awarded:* Baccalaureate.

Accreditation: *Regional:* NCA.

History: Waldorf College was established in 1903.

Institutional Structure: *Governing board:* Board of Regents. Extrainstitutional representation: 28 trustees; institutional representation: president of the college. *Composition of institution:* Academic affairs directed by vice president

for academic affairs. Student services directed by vice president for student life. Management/business/finances directed by vice president for administration and finance. Development/college relations/alumni directed by vice president for institutional advancement.

Calendar: Semesters (4-4-1 plan). Academic year from Sept. to May.

Characteristics of Freshmen: 761 applicants (437 men, 324 women). 62.5% of applicants admitted. 43.1% of admitted students enrolled full-time.

91% (192 students) submitted ACT scores. *25th percentile:* ACT Composite 16, ACT English 16, ACT Math 17. *75th percentile:* ACT Composite 23, ACT English 23, ACT Math 23.

Admission: Rolling admissions plan. Early acceptance available. *Requirements:* Graduation from accredited secondary school or GED. Recommend 4 units in English, 2 in a foreign language, 3 mathematics, 3 science, 2 social studies, introduction to computers. *Entrance tests:* College Board SAT, ACT composite, or other standardized test. For foreign students TOEFL.

Degree Requirements: Completion of required courses and specified program. demonstrated proficiency in writing and math. Fulfillment of some degree requirements possible by passing departmental examinations, College Board CLEP, AP. Exemption from some beginning courses possible by passing College Board AP. *Grading system:* A to F, pass/D/no

Degrees Conferred: 37 *associate*; 112 *baccalaureate.* Bachelor's degrees awarded into five disciplines: business, management, marketing, and related support services 38; communication, journalism, and related programs; education 17; computer and information sciences and support services; history 9.

Fees and Other Expenses: *Full-time tuition per academic year 2004–05:* $14,500. *Books and supplies:* $790. *Room and board per academic year:* $4,400. *Other expenses:* $2,460.

Financial Aid: Aid from institutionally generated funds is provided on the basis of academic merit, financial need. Institution has a Program Participation Agreement with the U.S. Department of Education for eligible students to receive Pell Grants and other federal aid.

Financial aid to full-time, first-time undergraduate students: 65% received federal grants averaging $1,259; 46% state/local grants averaging $3,241; 95% institutional grants averaging $3,089; 95% loans averaging $3,251.

Departments and Teaching Staff: *Total instructional faculty:* Faculty members are unranked.

Enrollment: Total enrollment 629 (45.9% men, 54.1% women).

Characteristics of Student Body: *Ethnic/racial makeup:* Black non-Hispanic: 3.5%; Asian or Pacific Islander: .5%; Hispanic: .5%; White non-Hispanic: 90.5%.

International Students: 32 nonresident aliens enrolled fall 2004. Students from Europe, Asia, Central and South America, Africa. Programs to aid students whose native language is not English: social, cultural, financial. English as a Second Language Program. Some financial aid to qualifying international students.

Student Life: On-campus housing available. *Sports activities:* intercollegiate and intramural athletics. *Special services:* testing services, counseling services.

Library Collections: Students have access to online information retrieval services and the Internet. Computer work stations available.

Buildings and Grounds: Campus is located in the downtown urban area of Forest City.

Chief Executive Officer: Rev. Thomas L. Jolivette, President.

Address admission inquiries to Steven Lovik, Vice President for Admissions.

Wartburg College

222 Ninth Street, N.W.
Waverly, Iowa 50677-1003
Tel: (319) 352-8264   **E-mail:** admissions@wartburg.edu
Fax: (319) 352-8579   **Internet:** www.wartburg.edu

Institution Description: Wartburg College is a private institution affiliated with The Evangelical Lutheran Church in America. *Enrollment:* 1,804. *Degrees awarded:* Baccalaureate.

Accreditation: *Regional:* NCA. *Professional:* music, social work, teacher education

History: Chartered as Wartburg Normal School 1852; offered first instruction at postsecondary level 1885; awarded first degree (baccalaureate) 1898; changed name to Wartburg Normal College 1920; merged with 4 other Lutheran colleges and adopted present name 1935.

Institutional Structure: *Governing board:* Board of Regents. Extrainstitutional representation: 28 trustees; institutional representation: president of the college. *Composition of institution:* Academic affairs directed by vice president for academic affairs. Student services directed by vice president for student life.

Management/business/finances directed by vice president for administration and finance. Development/college relations/alumni directed by vice president for institutional advancement. Enrollment management (admissions, financial aid, Pathways Center) directed by vice president for enrollment management. Full-time instructional faculty 57 men / 46 women.

Calendar: Semesters (4-1-4 plan). Academic year from Sept. to May.

Characteristics of Freshmen: 87% of applicants accepted. 34% of accepted applicants enrolled.

8% (37 students) submitted SAT scores; 92% (459 students) submitted ACT scores. *25th percentile*: SAT Verbal 480, SAT Math 490; ACT Composite 21, ACT English 20, ACT Math 20. *75th percentile*: SAT Verbal 630, SAT Math 650; ACT Composite 26, ACT English 27, ACT Math 26.

73% of entering freshmen expected to graduate within 5 years. 73% of freshmen from Iowa. Freshmen from 16 states and 10 foreign countries.

Admission: Rolling admissions plan. Early acceptance available. *Requirements:* Graduation from accredited secondary school or GED. Recommend 4 units in English, 2 in a foreign language, 3 mathematics, 3 science, 2 social studies, introduction to computers. *Entrance tests:* College Board SAT, ACT composite, or other standardized test. For foreign students TOEFL.

Degree Requirements: 36 courses; 2.0 GPA; 7 of last 9 courses in residence; complete courses in a major; liberal arts requirements; demonstrated proficiency in writing and math. Fulfillment of some degree requirements possible by passing departmental examinations, College Board CLEP, AP. Exemption from some beginning courses possible by passing College Board AP. *Grading system:* A to F, pass/D/no credit.

Distinctive Educational Programs: Special academic programs at Wartburg include those in leadership education and global and multicultural studies. Internships are available in all majors and there are internship programs in Denver, Washington, D.C., and abroad. Study abroad in 18 countries. On-campus work-study, numerous baccalaureate degrees, dual majors in any combination, and individualized majors are possible. A 3-2 engineering degree is offered with Iowa State University, the Universities of Iowa and Illinois, and Washington University in St. Louis, Other 3-2 degrees are possible in medical technology, occupational therapy, and public health education. An array of experiential learning opportunities are offered.

Degrees Conferred: 414 *baccalaureate:* biological/life sciences 33; business/marketing 83; communications/communication technologies 34; computer and information sciences 15; education 68; English 21; foreign languages and literature 3; health professions and related sciences 5; mathematics 13; parks and recreation 19; philosophy/religion/theology 26; physical sciences 13; protective services/public administration 16; psychology 19; social sciences and history 27; visual and performing arts 19.

Fees and Other Expenses: *Full-time tuition per academic year 2005–06:* $20,500. *Room and board per academic year:* $5,765. *Other fees:* $630.

Financial Aid: Aid from institutionally generated funds is provided on the basis of academic merit, financial need, talent (music, art). Institution has a Program Participation Agreement with the U.S. Department of Education for eligible students to receive Pell Grants and other federal aid.

Financial aid to full-time, first-time undergraduate students: need-based scholarships/grants totaling $16,203,852, self-help $9,076,670, parent loans $445,413, tuition waivers $583,094; non-need-based scholarships/grants totaling $4,160,494, self-help $13,751,545, parent loans $440,772, tuition waivers $429,788.

Departments and Teaching Staff: *Total instructional faculty:* 165 (full-time 105, part-time 60; women 74, men 91; members of minority groups 9). Student-to-faculty ratio: 13:1.

Enrollment: Total enrollment 1,804. Undergraduate full-time 780 men / 945 women, part-time 36m / 43w. *Transfer students:* 37.

Characteristics of Student Body: *Ethnic/racial makeup:* number of Black non-Hispanic: 61; American Indian or Alaska Native: 1; Asian or Pacific Islander: 27; Hispanic: 20; White non-Hispanic: 1,480; unknown: 39.

International Students: 94 nonresident aliens enrolled fall 2004. Students from Europe, Asia, Central and South America, Africa, West Indies. Programs to aid students whose native language is not English: social, cultural, financial. English as a Second Language Program. Financial aid specifically designated for international students: variable scholarships available annually.

Student Life: On-campus housing available. *Intercollegiate athletics:* men only: baseball, basketball, cross-country, football, golf, soccer, tennis, track, wrestling; women only: basketball, cross-country, golf, soccer, softball, tennis, track, volleyball. *Special services:* testing services, Career Development and Placement Center, Writing/Reading Laboratory, counseling services, Pathways Center, International Student Services, Diversity Student Services, substance abuse education, Student Health and Wellness Center. *Student publications, radio: Castle*, a literary magazine; *Fortress*, a yearbook; *The Page*, a daily information bulletin; *Wartburg Trumpet*, a weekly newspaper. Radio Station KWAR; TV station.

Library Collections: 186,089 volumes including bound books, serial backfiles, electronic documents, and government documents not in separate collections. Online catalog. Current serial subscriptions: 704 paper, 28 microform, 12,473 via electronic access. 7,774 microforms; 4,717 audiovisual materials. Computer work stations available. Students have access to the Internet at no charge.

Most important holdings include Wartburg College Archives; Koob Collection of Hostage Memorabilia; Lutheranism; Namibia Collection; Archives of Iowa Broadcasting.

Buildings and Grounds: Campus area 118 acres plus 75 acres of farmland. *New buildings:* Campus entrance completed 2005; renovation and addition to Science Center, 2005; renovation and addition to Saemann Student Center 2005; Lohe Hall 2005.

Chief Executive Officer: Dr. Jack R. Ohle, President. Address admission inquiries to Doug Bowman, Director of Admissions.

Wartburg Theological Seminary

333 Wartburg Place
Dubuque, Iowa 52004
Tel: (563) 589-0200   **E-mail:** info@wartburgseminary.edu
Fax: (563) 589-0333   **Internet:** www.wartburgseminary.edu

Institution Description: Wartburg Theological Seminary is a private institution affiliated with The Evangelical Lutheran Church in America. *Enrollment:* 189. *Degrees awarded:* First-professional (master of divinity).

Accreditation: *Regional:* NCA. *National:* ATS. *Professional:* theology

Institutional Structure: *Governing board:* Division for Ministry of the Evangelical Lutheran Church in America. Board of Directors for Wartburg Seminary. Representation: 25 board members (1 from each of the 18 synods to which Wartburg relates); 5 at-large members appointed by the Division for Ministry; 2 Bishops from the 18 supporting synods. *Composition of institution:* Academic affairs headed by dean of the faculty. Management/business/finances directed by director of business and finance. Full-time instructional faculty 13.

Calendar: Semesters. Academic year early Sept. to mid-May. Degrees conferred May, Dec. Formal commencement May. Summer language session of 5 or 6 weeks from mid-July to late Aug.

Admission: Rolling admissions plan. *Requirements:* Baccalaureate from accredited college or university, which should include 12 semester hours each English, Greek, a modern foreign language; 6 hours each history, natural science, philosophy, social science.

Degree Requirements: *For first-professional degree:* 123 semester hours. *For M.A. degree:* 54 semester hours. *For S.T.M.:* 36 semester hours. *Grading system:* A–F; credit-no credit; incomplete (carries time limit).

Distinctive Educational Programs: Independent study. Off-campus study in the U.S. at Lutheran Seminary Program in the Southwest at Austin, Texas. Cross-registration through consortium. Study abroad program. *Other distinctive programs:* Continuing professional education.

Degrees Conferred: 11 *master's:* theology; 36 *first-professional:* master of divinity.

Fees and Other Expenses: *Full-time tuition per academic year 2004–05:* Contact the seminary for current information.

Financial Aid: Aid from institutionally generated funds is provided on the basis of academic merit, financial need. Institution has a Program Participation Agreement with the U.S. Department of Education for eligible students to receive Pell Grants and other federal aid.

Departments and Teaching Staff: *Professors* 7, *associate professors* 4, *assistant professors* 4, *part-time faculty* 10. *Total instructional faculty:* 25. Degrees held by full-time faculty: doctorate 86%, master's 100%. 86% hold terminal degrees.

Enrollment: Total enrollment 189 (50.3% men, 49.7% women).

Characteristics of Student Body: *Ethnic and racial makeup:* Black non-Hispanic: 1.1%; American Indian or Alaska Native: 1.1%; White non-Hispanic: 86.8%; unknown: 6.3%.

International Students: 9 nonresident aliens enrolled fall 2004. Students form Europe, Asia, Central and South America, Africa. No programs available to aid students whose native language is not English. Some financial aid available for graduate international students.

Student Life: On-campus residence halls. Houses and apartments available for married students. *Surrounding community:* Dubuque population 65,000. Chicago, 140 miles from campus, is nearest metropolitan area. Served by airport.

Library Collections: Resources shared with consortium. 12,000 volumes. 260 current periodical subscriptions; 194 audiovisual materials. Students have access to online information retrieval services and the Internet.

Most important special collections include the Rare Book Collection (7,000 volumes; includes 1,035 books from the 16th century); Latin American Liberation Theology Collection; Papua New Guinea Collection; J. Michael Reu Collection of the writings of Wartburg Seminary professor (1899–1937).

Buildings and Grounds: Campus area 30 acres.

Chief Executive Officer: Dr. Duane H. Larson, President.

Address admission inquiries to Rev. Wayne Teig, Director of Admissions.

William Penn University

201 Trueblood Avenue
Oskaloosa, Iowa 52577
Tel: (515) 673-1001   **E-mail:** admissions@wmpenn.edu
Fax: (515) 673-1396   **Internet:** www.wmpenn.edu

Institution Description: William Penn University, formerly William Penn College, is a private college affiliated with the Society of Friends (Quaker). *Enrollment:* 1,682. *Degrees awarded:* Baccalaureate.

Accreditation: Regional: NCA. *Professional:* nursing, teacher education

History: Established and chartered as Penn College and offered first instruction at postsecondary level 1873; awarded first degree (baccalaureate) 1875; became William Penn College 1933; achieved university status 2001. *See* S. Arthur Watson, *William Penn College—A Product and A Producer* (Oskaloosa: William Penn College, 1971) for further information.

Institutional Structure: *Governing board:* Board of Trustees. Representation: 45 trustees, including 15 appointed by Iowa Yearly Meeting, 18 nominated and elected by Board, 9 nominated by alumni and elected by Board, 2 nominated by faculty and elected by Board, 1 nominated by students and elected by Board. All voting. *Composition of institution:* Administrators 12 men / 10 women. Academic affairs headed by academic dean. Management/business/finances directed by business manager. Full-time instructional faculty 59. Academic governance body, Academic Committee, meets an average of 9 times per year.

Calendar: Semesters. Academic year Aug. to May. Freshmen admitted Aug., Jan., June, July. Degrees conferred May, Aug., and Jan. Formal commencement May. Summer session of 2 terms and 1 pre-summer session from mid-May to early Aug.

Characteristics of Freshmen: 63% of applicants admitted. 32% of applicants admitted and enrolled.

24.3% (44 students) submitted SAT scores; 72.4% (131 students) submitted ACT scores. *25th percentile:* SAT Verbal 400, SAT Math 420; ACT Composite 16, ACT English 15, ACT Math 16. *75th percentile:* SAT Verbal 510, SAT Math 530; ACT Composite 22, ACT English 21, ACT Math 22.

43% of entering freshmen expected to graduate within 5 years. 46% of freshmen from Iowa. Freshmen from 28 states and 4 foreign countries.

Admission: Rolling admissions plan. For fall acceptance, apply as early as Sept. 1 of previous year, but not later than Aug. 15 of year of enrollment. Early acceptance available. *Requirements:* Either graduation from accredited secondary school with 15 units, or GED. Recommend 3–4 English, 2 in a modern foreign language, 2 mathematics, 2 natural science, 2 social studies, 3–4 electives. Minimum GPA 2.0. *Entrance tests:* College Board SAT (minimum combined score of 8600) or ACT composite (minimum score minimum 18). *For transfer students:* 2.0 minimum GPA; from 4-year accredited institution 94 hours maximum transfer credit; from 2-year accredited institution 64 hours; correspondence/extension students 15 hours.

College credit for extrainstitutional learning on basis of ACE *2006 Guide to the Evaluation of Educational Experiences in the Armed Services.* Tutoring available. Developmental courses offered during regular academic year; credit given.

Degree Requirements: 124 credit hours; 2.0 GPA; 30 hours in residence; Undergraduate Assessment Program examination; 2 physical education courses; distribution requirements.

Fulfillment of some degree requirements and exemption from some beginning courses possible by passing College Board CLEP General and Subject examinations. *Grading system:* A–F; pass-no credit; incomplete (carries time limit).

Distinctive Educational Programs: Evening classes. Cooperative baccalaureate program with Indian Hills Community College leading to vocational certification in computer programming, criminal justice, culinary arts, early childhood, electronics, telecommunication technology, lasers electro-optics technology, robotics and automation technology, health information technology, nursing, physical therapy, radiologic technology. College for Working Adults: enrollment of 800 at sites in Oskaloosa, West Des Moines, Ames.

Degrees Conferred: 88 *baccalaureate.* Bachelor's degrees awarded in top five disciplines include biological and life sciences 7, business and management 12, education 29, parks and recreation 8, social sciences and history 7.

Fees and Other Expenses: *Full-time tuition per academic year 2004–05:* $14,334. *Required fees:* $370. *Room and board per academic year:* $4,746.

Financial Aid: Aid from institutionally generated funds is provided on the basis of academic merit, financial need, activities. Institution has a Program Participation Agreement with the U.S. Department of Education for eligible students to receive Pell Grants and other federal aid.

Financial aid to full-time, first-time undergraduate students: need-based scholarships/grants totaling $157,829, self-help $2,915,4446, parent loans $60,218, tuition waivers $102,154, athletic awards $2,746,030; non-need-based scholarships/grants totaling $196,870, self-help $1,894,265, parent loans $1,445,230, tuition waivers $198,298, athletic awards $484,594.

Departments and Teaching Staff: *Total instructional faculty:* 36 (full-time 33, part-time 3; women 13, men 23; members of minority groups 1). Total faculty with doctorate, first-professional, or other terminal degree: 19. Student-to-faculty ratio: 14:1.

Enrollment: Total enrollment 1,682. Undergraduate full-time 136 men / 141 women, part-time 45m / 160w. *Transfer students:* in-state 333; from out-of-state 405.

Characteristics of Student Body: *Ethnic/racial makeup:* number of Black non-Hispanic: 28; American Indian or Alaska Native: 13; Asian or Pacific Islander: 15; Hispanic: 48; White non-Hispanic: 1,398; unknown: 69. *Age distribution:* number of 18–19: 214; 20–21: 290; 22–24: 364; 25–29: 203; 30–34: 148; 35–39: 115; 40–49: 124; 50–64: 19.

International Students: 21 nonresident aliens enrolled 2004. 1 student from Europe, 14 Asia, 1 Central and South America, 2 Africa, 3 Canada. Programs available to aid students whose native language is not English: English as a Second Language Program. Financial aid specifically designated for international students. 25 scholarships available annually; $132,000 awarded 2004–05.

Student Life: On-campus residence halls house 51% of student body. Residence halls for men only constitute 61% of such space, for women only 39%. *Intercollegiate athletics:* men only: baseball, basketball, cross-country, football, soccer, track; women only: basketball, cross-country, soccer, softball, track, volleyball. *Special regulations:* Cars permitted without restrictions. Quiet hours and residence hall visitation hours set by residents. *Student publications, radio: Penn n' Ink,* an annual literary magazine; *Penn Chronicle,* a bimonthly newspaper; *Quaker,* a yearbook. Radio station KIGG broadcasts 48 hours per week. *Surrounding community:* Oskaloosa population 11,000. Des Moines, 50 miles from campus, is nearest metropolitan area.

Library Collections: 76,327 volumes. Current periodical subscriptions: 205 paper, 4,012 microform, 11,521 via electronic access. Online catalog. Students have access to online information retrieval services and the Internet. Total budget for books and materials 2004–05: $61,628.

Most important holdings include collections of works on Quaker history; Peace Collection.

Buildings and Grounds: Campus area 40 acres.

Chief Executive Officer: Dr. Richard E. Sours, President.

Address admission inquiries to John Ottoson, Vice President for Enrollment Management.

Kansas

Baker University

618 Eighth Street
Baldwin City, Kansas 66006-0065
Tel: (785) 594-6451　　**E-mail:** adm@baker.edu
Fax: (785) 594-8372　　**Internet:** www.baker.edu

Institution Description: Baker University is a private, independent, non-profit institution affiliated with the United Methodist Church. *Enrollment:* 856. *Degrees awarded:* Baccalaureate, master's.

Member of the consortium Kansas City Regional Council for Higher Education.

Accreditation: *Regional:* NCA.

History: Established, chartered, and offered first instruction at post secondary level 1858. First degree (baccalaureate) offered 1866. Master's program in liberal arts added 1976. *See* H. K. Ebright, *The History of Baker University* (Baldwin, Kansas: Baker University, 1951), for further information.

Institutional Structure: *Governing board:* Board of Trustees. Extrainstitutional representation: 32 trustees; institutional representation: 5 administrators, 1 full-time instructional faculty member. 4 ex officio. 32 voting. *Composition of institution:* Administrators 10 men. Academic affairs headed by provost and dean of the university. Management/business/finances directed by treasurer. Full-time instructional faculty 50. Academic governance body, the faculty, meets an average of 8 times per year.

Calendar: Semesters (4-1-4 plan). Academic year Sept. to May. Freshmen admitted Jan., May, Aug. Degrees conferred May, Dec., Jan. Formal commencement May. Summer session of 2 terms from early June to mid-Aug.

Characteristics of Freshmen: 823 applicants (324 men, 499 women). 81.2% of applicants admitted. 30.45 of admitted students enrolled full-time.

9% (19 students) submitted SAT scores; 96% (194 students) submitted ACT scores. *25th percentile*: SAT I Verbal 430, SAT I Math 430; ACT Composite 21, ACT English 20, ACT Math 19. *75th percentile*: SAT I Verbal 660, SAT I Math 600; ACT Composite 26, ACT English 26, ACT Math 26.

45% of entering freshmen expected to graduate within 5 years. 66% of freshmen from Kansas. Freshmen from 19 states and 2 foreign countries.

Admission: Rolling admissions plan. For fall acceptance, apply as early as second semester of junior year of secondary school, but not later than Sept. 1. Early acceptance available. *Requirements:* Either graduation from accredited secondary school or GED. College preparatory courses in English, a foreign language, mathematics, natural science, and social studies strongly recommended. Minimum GPA 2.0. Lowest acceptable secondary school class standing 50th percentile. *Entrance tests:* College Board SAT or ACT composite. *For transfer students:* 2.0 minimum GPA; from 4-year accredited institution 92 hours maximum transfer credit; from 2-year accredited institution 62 hours; correspondence/extension students 6 hours.

College credit for postsecondary-level work completed in secondary school and for College Board CLEP. Advanced placement for extrainstitutional learning on basis of ACE *2006 Guide to the Evaluation of Educational Experiences in the Armed Services.* Tutoring available. Developmental courses offered in summer session and regular academic year; credit given.

Degree Requirements: 124 credit hours; 2.0 GPA; 2 terms in residence; exit competency examination in writing; comprehensives in individual fields of study; 4 hours physical education. Fulfillment of some degree requirements possible by passing College Board CLEP. *Grading system:* A–F; pass-fail; withdraw (carries time limit).

Distinctive Educational Programs: *For undergraduates:* Dual-degree programs in forestry with Duke University (NC); in engineering with Kansas State University, University of Kansas, and Washington University (MO). Interdisciplinary programs. Study abroad in Spain. *For graduate students:* Evening master's program in liberal arts for Kansas City residents is offered at off-campus center (Leawood, 40 miles away from main institution) in cooperation with Southern Methodist University. Weekend classes. *Available to all students:* Evening classes.

Degrees Conferred: 165 *baccalaureate*. Bachelor's degrees awarded in top five disciplines: business, management, marketing, and related support services 42; social sciences 15; parks, recreation, leisure, and fitness studies 15; history 14; education 14.

Fees and Other Expenses: *Full-time tuition per academic year 2004–05:* $15,575. *Room and board per academic year:* $5,450. *Books and supplies:*$1,000.

Financial Aid: Aid from institutionally generated funds is provided on the basis of academic merit, athletic ability, financial need, other criteria. Institution has a Program Participation Agreement with the U.S. Department of Education for eligible students to receive Pell Grants and other federal aid.

Financial aid to full-time, first-time undergraduate students: 29% received federal grants averaging $2,965; 38% state/local grants averaging $2,676; 95% institutional grants averaging $5,850; 73% loans averaging $4,618.

Departments and Teaching Staff: *Total instructional faculty:* 50.

Enrollment: Total enrollment 856 (47.4% men, 52.6% women).

Characteristics of Student Body: *Ethnic/racial makeup:* Black non-Hispanic: 5.6%; American Indian or Alaska Native: .8%; Asian or Pacific Islander: .9%; Hispanic: 2.9%; White non-Hispanic: 85.6%; unknown: 3.7%.

International Students: 3 nonresident aliens enrolled fall 2004. No programs available to aid students whose native language is not English. No financial aid specifically designated for international students.

Student Life: On-campus residence halls house 42% of student body. Dormitories for men only constitute 55% of such space, for women only 45%. 31% of men join and 20% live in fraternities; 55% of women join and 32% live in sororities. *Intercollegiate athletics:* men only: baseball, basketball, bowling, football, golf, tennis, track; women only: basketball, bowling, softball, tennis, track, volleyball. *Special regulations:* Cars permitted without restrictions. Residence hall visitation from 10am to 11pm. Mon.–Thurs., 10am to 1am Fri. and Sat., 10am to midnight Sun. *Special services:* Learning Resources Center, medical services. *Student publications, radio: Orange,* a weekly newspaper. Radio station KNBU broadcasts 89 hours per week. *Surrounding community:* Baldwin City population 3,000. Kansas City, 40 miles from campus, is nearest metropolitan area.

Library Collections: 97.000 volumes. 7,500 microforms; 345 current periodical subscriptions. Online catalog. 3,400 audiovisual materials. Students have access to online information retrieval services and the Internet.

Most important holdings include the Quayle Bible Collection, Kansas Methodist Archives, and Baker Archives.

Buildings and Grounds: Campus area 26 acres.

Chief Executive Officer: Dr. Daniel M. Lambert, President.

Address admission inquiries to Louise Cummings-Simmons, Director of Enrollment Management.

Barclay College

607 North Kingman
Haviland, Kansas 67059
Tel: (620) 862-5252　　**E-mail:** admissions@barclaycollege.edu
Fax: (620) 862-5242　　**Internet:** www.barclaycollege.edu

Institution Description: Barclay College, formerly Friends Bible College, is a private, independent, nonprofit institution affiliated with the Friends Church (Quaker) of the Evangelical Friends Alliance, Friends United Meeting and with formal ties to several other Evangelical Church bodies such as the Evangelical Methodist Church. *Enrollment:* 183. *Degrees awarded:* Associate, baccalaureate.

Accreditation: *Regional:* NCA. *National:* ABHE.

History: Founded 1917 as a Bible Institute with an existing Quaker Academy founded 1892; became two-year college 1925; became four-year college 1968; accredited 1975.

Institutional Structure: *Governing board:* Board of Trustees appointed by Barclay College Association, Inc. *Composition of institution:* Administrators 5.

Total full-time faculty 3 men / 3 women; adjunct faculty 3 men / 1 woman. Full-time faculty meets weekly.

Calendar: Semesters. Academic year Aug. to May.

Characteristics of Freshmen: 10% (3 students) submitted SAT scores; 82% (23 students) submitted ACT scores. *25th percentile*: SAT Verbal 510, SAT Math 480; ACT Composite 18, ACT English 15, ACT Math 16. *75th percentile*: SAT Verbal 590, SAT Math 570; ACT Composite 26, ACT English 25, ACT Math 21,

40% of entering freshmen class expected to graduate within 5 years. 36% of freshmen from Kansas. Freshmen from 7 states and 1 foreign country.

Admission: *Requirements:* Graduation from secondary school or equivalency diploma. Rolling admission and advanced placement plans available. *Entrance tests:* SAT or ACT composite.

Degree Requirements: 64–128 credit hours; 2.0 GPA with 2.5 GPA in major field; at least 30 semester hours in residence and 30–40 hours completed in Bible/theology; 8 units of Christian service required.

Distinctive Educational Programs: Youth Ministry Program with relationship with Youth for Christ International.

Degrees Conferred: 41 *baccalaureate:* business/marketing 2; education 5; philosophy/religion/theology 12; psychology 22.

Fees and Other Expenses: *Full-time tuition per academic year 2004–05:* $9,250. *Room and board per academic year:* $4,700.

Financial Aid: Aid from institutionally generated funds is provided on the basis of academic merit, financial need. Institution has a Program Participation Agreement with the U.S. Department of Education for eligible students to receive Pell Grants and other federal aid.

Financial aid to full-time, first-time undergraduate students: need-based scholarships/grants totaling $427,904, self-help $384,422; non-need-based scholarships/grants totaling $236,610, self-help $135,011, parent loans $18,650, tuition waivers $19,738.

Departments and Teaching Staff: *Total instructional faculty:* 8 (2 women, 6 men; 1 member of a minority group). Total faculty with doctorate, first-professional, or other terminal degree: 5. Student-to-faculty ratio: 6:1.

Enrollment: Total enrollment 183. Undergraduate full-time 86 men / 76 women, part-time 9m / 12w. *Transfer students:* in-state 28; from out-of-state 60.

Characteristics of Student Body: *Ethnic/racial makeup:* number of Black non-Hispanic: 10; American Indian or Alaska Native: 3; Asian or Pacific Islander: 3; Hispanic: 4; White non-Hispanic: 60; unknown: 2. *Age distribution:* number under 18: 1; 18–19: 44; 20–21: 37; 22–24: 23; 25–29: 17; 30–34: 13; 35–39: 15; 40–49: 21; 50–64: 72.

International Students: 1 nonresident alien enrolled fall 2004. No programs available to aid students whose native language is not English. No financial aid specifically designated for international students.

Student Life: Men and women residence halls house 85% of student body. *Student publications: Crimsayvista,* a yearbook. *Surrounding community:* Small rural community.

Library Collections: 63,759 volumes. Online catalog. Access to 21,988 serials (paper, microform, electronic access). 17 computer work stations. Access to online information retrieval systems and the Internet. Total 2004–05 budget for books and materials: $44,957.

Most important special collection contains books by and about Quakers.

Buildings and Grounds: Campus area 17 acres including 7 major buildings.

Chief Executive Officer: Dr. David Hietala, President.

Address admission inquiries to Ryan Kendall, Director of Admissions.

Benedictine College

1020 North 2nd Street
Atchison, Kansas 66002

Tel: (913) 367-5340   **E-mail:** bcadmiss@benedictine.edu
Fax: (913) 367-3673   **Internet:** www.benedictine.edu

Institution Description: Benedictine College is a private, nonprofit college affiliated with the Roman Catholic Church. *Enrollment:* 1,441. *Degrees awarded:* Associate, baccalaureate, master's.

Member of the consortium Kansas City Regional Council for Higher Education.

Accreditation: *Regional:* NCA. *Professional:* music, teacher education

History: Saint Benedict's College established to train men for the priesthood 1859; incorporated 1868; offered first instruction at postsecondary level 1915; first degree (baccalaureate) awarded 1920. Saint Scholastica's Academy for women established 1863; name changed to Mount Saint Scholastica Junior College 1924; first degree (baccalaureate) awarded 1932. Saint Benedict's College merged with Mount Saint Scholastica College to form Benedictine College 1971.

Institutional Structure: *Governing board:* Board of Directors. Extrainstitutional representation: 27 directors; institutional representation: 1 administrator, 22 alumni. 1 ex officio. 26 voting. *Composition of institution:* Administrators 7 men / 6 women. Academic affairs headed by dean of the college. Management/business/finances directed by business manager. Full-time instructional faculty 51. Academic governance body, the faculty, meets an average of 9 times per year.

Calendar: Semesters. Academic year Aug. to May. Freshmen admitted Aug., Jan., June. Degrees conferred May, Aug., Dec. Formal commencement May. Summer session from June to July.

Characteristics of Freshmen: 99% of applicants admitted. 51% of applicants admitted and enrolled.

8% (26 students) submitted SAT scores; 89% (278 students) submitted ACT scores. *25th percentile*: SAT Verbal 440, SAT Math 450; ACT Composite 19, ACT English 19, ACT Math 19. *75th percentile*: SAT Verbal 575, SAT Math 575; ACT Composite 25, ACT English 26, ACT Math 26.

32% of entering freshmen expected to graduate within 5 years. 40% of freshmen from Kansas. Freshmen from 25 states and 1 foreign country.

Admission: Rolling admissions plan. For fall acceptance, apply as early as summer after junior year, but not later than Aug. 1 of year of enrollment. Early acceptance available. *Requirements:* Either 16 units from an accredited secondary school which should include 4 units English, 2–3 foreign language, 2–3 mathematics, 2 social studies, 1–2 science; or GED. Minimum GPA 2.0. Lowest acceptable secondary school class standing 40th percentile. *Entrance tests:* College Board SAT or ACT composite. For foreign students minimum TOEFL score 535. *For transfer students:* 2.0 minimum GPA; from 2-year institutions 64 hours maximum transfer credit, from 4-year institutions 92 hours.

College credit and advanced placement for postsecondary-level work completed in secondary school and for College Board CLEP. College credit for extrainstitutional learning on basis of ACE *2006 Guide to the Evaluation of Educational Experiences in the Armed Services.* Tutoring available. Developmental courses offered during regular academic year; credit given.

Degree Requirements: *For all baccalaureate degrees:* 128 credit hours; final 30 hours in residence; comprehensives in individual fields of study; general education requirements. *For all undergraduates:* 2.0 GPA; 2 hours physical education. *For all associate degrees:* 65 credit hours. Fulfillment of some degree requirements and exemption from some beginning courses possible by passing College Board APP, CLEP, departmental exams. *Grading system:* A–F; pass-no pass; withdraw (carries time limit); incomplete.

Distinctive Educational Programs: Work-experience programs. Flexible meeting places. Dual-degree programs in engineering with other schools by arrangement. Interdisciplinary programs. Facilities and programs for independent research, including minor in international studies and individual majors. Cross registration and exchange programs with other colleges in consortium. International studies program in China, Ireland, The Netherlands, Spain, France, Germany, Mexico, England, Wales. Discovery College learning opportunities.

ROTC: Army in cooperation with Missouri Western State College. 2 commissions awarded 2004.

Degrees Conferred: 215 *baccalaureate* (B), 53 *master's* (M): biological/life sciences 19 (B); business/marketing 38 (B), 41 (M); communications/communication technologies 16 (B); computer and information sciences 2 (B); education 34 (B), 12 (M); English 6 (B); foreign languages and literature 8 (B); health professions and related sciences 1 (B); liberal arts/general studies 5 (B); mathematics 6 (B); philosophy/religion/theology 32 (B); physical sciences 3 (B); psychology 8 (B); social sciences and history 34 (B); visual and performing arts 3 (B).

Fees and Other Expenses: *Full-time tuition per academic year 2004–05:* undergraduate $14,576; graduate $16,000. *Required fees:* $550. *Room and board per academic year:* $6,128.

Financial Aid: Aid from institutionally generated funds is provided on the basis of academic merit, financial need, athletic ability. Institution has a Program Participation Agreement with the U.S. Department of Education for eligible students to receive Pell Grants and other federal aid.

Financial aid to full-time, first-time undergraduate students: need-based scholarships/grants totaling $6,327,396, self-help $4,180,066, tuition waivers $179,354, athletic awards $1,331,249; non-need-based scholarships/grants totaling $356,160, self-help $264,125, parent loans $1,341,631, tuition waivers $14,576, athletic awards $58,600.

Departments and Teaching Staff: *Total instructional faculty:* 99 (full-time 59, part-time 40; women 33, men 66; members of minority groups 7). Total faculty with doctorate, first-professional, or other terminal degree: 54. Student-to-faculty ratio: 16:1. *Faculty development:* 2 faculty members awarded sabbaticals 2004–05.

Enrollment: Total enrollment 1,441. Full-time undergraduate 550 men / 536 women, part-time 118m / 190; graduate full-time 34m / 12w, part-time 1m. *Transfer students:* 90.

Characteristics of Student Body: *Ethnic/racial makeup:* number of Black non-Hispanic: 47; American Indian or Alaska Native: 5; Asian or Pacific

Islander: 26; Hispanic: 93; White non-Hispanic: 1,123; unknown: 52. *Age distribution:* number under 18: 207; 18–19: 505; 20–21: 464; 22–24: 131; 25–29: 31; 30–34: 9; 35–39: 73; 40–49: 20; 50–64: 13; 65 and over: 1.

International Students: 48 nonresident aliens enrolled fall 2004. 7 students from Europe, 29 Asia, 6 Central and South America, 1 Africa, 3 other. Programs available to aid students whose native language is not English: social, cultural. English as a Second Language Program. Financial aid available for international students: 27 scholarships totaling $131,865 were awarded 2004–05.

Student Life: On-campus residence halls house 81% of student body. Residence halls for men only constitute 52% of such space, for women only 48%. *Intercollegiate athletics:* men only: baseball, basketball, golf, soccer, tennis, track; women only: basketball, golf, soccer, softball, tennis, volleyball. *Student publications: The Circuit,* a biweekly newspaper; *Loomings,* an annual magazine of the arts; *The Raven,* a yearbook. *Surrounding community:* Atchison population 11,000. Kansas City, 50 miles from campus, is nearest metropolitan area. Served by airport 33 miles from campus.

Library Collections: 368,558 volumes. Online catalog. 504 serial subscriptions. 857 recordings, compact discs, CD-ROMs. 83 computer work stations. Access to online information retrieval systems and the Internet.

Most important special collections include Monastic History (especially Benedictines); Medieval History; Jean Mabillon Collection on History and Historiography.

Buildings and Grounds: Campus area 150 acres. *New buildings:* Woman's Dormitory completed 2005.

Chief Executive Officer: Dr. Stephen D. Minnis, President.

Address admission inquiries to Ms. Kelly Vowels, Dean of Enrollment Management.

Bethany College

421 North First Street
Lindsborg, Kansas 67456

Tel: (785) 227-3311   **E-mail:** admissions@bethany.edu
Fax: (785) 227-2860   **Internet:** www.bethany.edu

Institution Description: Bethany College is a private college affiliated with the Central State Synod of the Evangelical Lutheran Church in America. *Enrollment:* 586. *Degrees awarded:* Baccalaureate.

Accreditation: *Regional:* NCA. *Professional:* music, social work, teacher education

History: Established as Bethany Academy 1881; chartered 1882; amended charter and adopted present name 1886; offered first instruction at postsecondary level 1887; awarded first degree (baccalaureate) 1891. *See* Emory Lindquist, *Bethany in Kansas* (Lindsborg: Bethany College Publications, 1975) for further information.

Institutional Structure: *Governing board:* Board of Directors of Bethany College. Extrainstitutional representation: 34 directors, including 3 bishops; institutional representation: 2 administrators, including president of the college; 4 alumni. 5 ex officio. All voting. *Composition of institution:* Administrators 21 men / 14 women. Academic affairs headed by academic dean. Management/business/finances directed by director of business and finance. Full-time instructional faculty 47. Academic governance body, the faculty, meets an average of 9 times per year.

Calendar: Semesters (4-1-4 plan). Academic year early Sept. to mid-May. Freshmen admitted on a rolling basis. June. Degrees conferred May, Aug., Dec., Jan. Formal commencement May. Summer session from early to late June.

Characteristics of Freshmen: 778 applicants (459 men / 319 women). 67.7% of applicants admitted. 29% of admitted students enrolled full-time.

11% (17 students) submitted SAT scores; 86% (133 students) submitted ACT scores. *25th percentile:* SAT I Verbal 420, SAT I Math 430; ACT Composite 18, ACT English 16, ACT Math 17. *75th percentile:* SAT I Verbal 570, SAT I Math 500; ACT Composite 24, ACT English 25, ACT Math 24.

36% of entering freshmen expected to graduate within 5 years. 48% of freshmen from Kansas. Freshmen from 9 states and 4 foreign countries.

Admission: The Admissions Committee interprets grade point average and class rank in relation to the quality of the curriculum which the applicant has pursued in high school. It is recommended that students have the following coursework: 4 years of English, 3 years of mathematics, 3 years of social studies, 1 year of foreign language, and 1 year of physical education. Rolling admissions and early acceptance plans available. *Requirements:* Graduation from accredited secondary school or GED; minimum high school GPA 2.5 on a 4.0 scale. *Entrance tests:* Minimum ACT composite of 19 or combined SAT verbal and

math scores of 750. *Transfer students:* minimum transfer cumulative GPA of 2.3 on a 4.0 scale. *International students:* TOEFL score of 525 or higher.

College credit for postsecondary-level work completed in secondary school and for extrainstitutional learning (life experience) on basis of ACE *2006 Guide to the Evaluation of Educational Experiences in the Armed Services.* Tutoring available. Developmental courses offered during regular academic year and Jan. interterm; credit given.

Degree Requirements: 128 semester hours; 2.0 GPA; 32 of the last 40 hours in residence; general education requirements. Fulfillment of some degree requirements and exemption from some beginning courses possible through CLEP, ACT scores, Advanced Placement and International Baccalaureate examination results. *Grading system:* A–F; pass-fail; withdraw, incomplete.

Distinctive Educational Programs: Internship program (Experience-based Education) with special programs with the Washington Center and the Chicago Urban Life Center. Three plus two master's degree program in aerospace, electrical, mechanical, and industrial engineering with Wichita State University. Contract major available. Study travel abroad during January Interterm. Affiliated with Associated Colleges of Central Kansas, cross registration, joint courses in computer science, education, and special education.

Degrees Conferred: 115 *baccalaureate.* Bachelor's degrees awarded in top five disciplines: education 38; biological and biomedical sciences 16; business, management, marketing, and related support services 11; public administration and social service professions 7; security and protective services 7.

Fees and Other Expenses: *Full-time tuition per academic year 2004–05:* $15,010. *Room and board per academic year:* $5,150. *Books and supplies:* $900.

Financial Aid: Aid from institutionally generated funds is provided on the basis of academic merit, financial need, athletic ability, other criteria. Institution has a Program Participation Agreement with the U.S. Department of Education for eligible students to receive Pell Grants and other federal aid.

Financial aid to full-time, first-time undergraduate students: 42% received federal grants averaging $2,405; 31% state/local grants averaging $2,758; 95% institutional grants averaging $6,296; 79% loans averaging $4,376.

Departments and Teaching Staff: Art *professors* 0, *associate professors* 0, *assistant professors* 2, *instructors* 0; *part-time teachers* 2; English/theatre/communications 1, 1, 2, 0, 1; foreign languages 0, 0, 0, 0, 3; music 1, 0, 3, 1, 13; religion/philosophy 0, 2, 0, 0, 2; biology 0, 1, 1, 0, 0; mathematics/physical sciences 4, 0, 1, 0, 1; economics/business 4, 0, 2, 0, 0; education 0, 0, 4, 0, 3; health/physical education/recreation 0, 1, 3, 1, 1; history/political science 1, 1, 1, 0, 0; psychology 2, 1, 0, 0, 1; sociology/social work 1, 3, 0, 0, 3.

Total instructional faculty 75. Degrees held by full-time faculty: doctorate 55.5%, master's 40, baccalaureate 2.2%, professional 2.2%.

Enrollment: Total enrollment 586 (50.2% men, 49.8% women).

Characteristics of Student Body: *Ethnic/racial makeup:* Black non-Hispanic: 8.4%; American Indian or Alaska Native: 1.2%; Asian or Pacific Islander: 1%; Hispanic: 4.3%; White non-Hispanic: 81.7%; unknown: 3.2%. *Age distribution:* 17–21: 78%; 22–24: 12%; 25–29: 2%; 30–34: 2%; 35–39: 2%; 40–49: 2%; 50–59: 1%; unknown: 1%.

International Students: 2 nonresident aliens enrolled 2004. No programs available to aid students whose native language is not English. Some financial aid available for qualifying international students.

Student Life: On-campus residence halls house 77% of student body. *Intercollegiate athletics:* men: baseball, basketball, cross-country, football, golf, soccer, indoor track, outdoor track; women: basketball, cross-country, golf, soccer, indoor track, outdoor track, softball, volleyball. *Special regulations:* Vehicles permitted (registration fee). Visitation in residence halls from 9am to 1am Sun.–Thurs., 9am to 2am Fri.–Sat. No alcohol. 35 campus organizations including 4 fraternities and 3 sororities. *Special services:* Academic Support Center, career services, counseling service, Health Center. *Student publications: The Bethanian,* a yearbook; *The Bethany Messenger,* a weekly newspaper. *Surrounding community:* Lindsborg population 3,500. Salina is 20 miles from campus; Wichita 70 miles. Served by airports in Salina and Wichita; passenger rail service 50 miles from campus.

Library Collections: 122,000 volumes. 38,670 microforms; 2,563 audiovisual materials; 610 current periodical subscriptions. Students have access to online information retrieval services.

Most important holdings include papers and letters (in Swedish) of Carl Swensson, founder and second president of the college; books and materials on 18th- and 19th-century Swedish immigrants, including Swedish periodicals and Bibles; letters and poems by Carl Sandburg, including original and unpublished material.

Buildings and Grounds: Campus area 80 acres.

Chief Executive Officer: Dr. Paul K. Formo, President.

Address admission inquiries to T. B. Maceo, Director of Enrollment Management.

Bethel College

300 East 27th Street
North Newton, Kansas 67117
Tel: (316) 283-2500   **E-mail:** admissions@bethelks.edu
Fax: (316) 284-5845   **Internet:** www.bethelks.edu

Institution Description: Bethel College is a private college affiliated with the General Conference Mennonite Church. *Enrollment:* 509. *Degrees awarded:* Baccalaureate.

Accreditation: *Regional:* NCA. *Professional:* nursing, nursing education, social work, teacher education

History: Established as the Bethel College of the Mennonite Church of North America, chartered, and incorporated 1887; offered first instruction at postsecondary level 1893; awarded first degree (baccalaureate) 1912; adopted present name 1961. *See* Peter J. Wedel, E. G. Kaufman, eds., *The Story of Bethel College* (North Newton: Bethel College, 1954) for further information.

Institutional Structure: *Governing board:* Bethel College Board of Directors. Extrainstitutional representation: 29 directors, including 35 alumni. 29 voting. *Composition of institution:* Administrative Cabinet 7 persons. Academic affairs headed by vice president. Management/business/finances directed by controller. Full-time instructional faculty 44.43 (includes FTE). Academic governance bodies, Advisory Committee to the Academic Dean and Educational Policies Committee, meet an average of 4 times per month.

Calendar: Semesters (4-1-4 plan): fall semester, interterm, spring semester, summer session. Academic year Aug. to May. Degrees conferred May, Dec., Jan., summer. Formal commencement May.

Characteristics of Freshmen: 79.5% of applicants admitted. 35.8% of applicants admitted and enrolled.

13% (15 students) submitted SAT scores; 87% (104 students) submitted ACT scores. *25th percentile:* SAT Verbal 460, SAT Math 530; ACT Composite 20, ACT English 20, ACT Math 19. *75th percentile:* SAT Verbal 670, SAT Math 700; ACT Composite 27, ACT English 28, ACT Math 27.

45% of entering freshmen expected to graduate within 5 years. 87% of freshmen from Kansas. Freshmen from 9 states and 2 foreign countries.

Admission: Rolling admissions plan. Early acceptance available. *Requirements:* Either graduation from accredited secondary school or GED. Minimum GPA 2.0. Lowest acceptable secondary school class standing 66th percentile. Exceptions are considered by committee. *Entrance tests:* College Board SAT or ACT composite. *For transfer students:* 2.0 minimum GPA; from 4-year accredited institution unlimited transfer hours but student must have 30 residence hours; from 2-year accredited unlimited transfers hours but student must earn 60 baccalaureate hours.

College credit and advanced placement for postsecondary-level work completed in secondary school. Advanced placement for extrainstitutional learning on basis of ACE *2006 Guide to the Evaluation of Educational Experiences in the Armed Services.* Tutoring available. Developmental courses offered in summer session and regular academic year; credit given.

Degree Requirements: *For all baccalaureate degrees:* 124 credit hours; demonstrated proficiency in writing, speech, mathematics, and computer literacy; *For all degrees:* 2.0 GPA; 30 hours in residence; general education requirements. Fulfillment of some degree requirements and exemption from some beginning courses possible by passing departmental examinations, College Board CLEP, IB, AP. *Grading system:* A–F; credit-no credit; withdraw (deadline after which pass-fail appended to withdraw).

Distinctive Educational Programs: Work-experience programs. Evening classes. Dual-degree programs in engineering with Kansas State University and Washington University (St. Louis, MO). Facilities and programs for independent research, including honors programs, tutorials. Domestic off-campus study in Chicago and Washington, D.C. Study abroad in China, Costa Rica, England, Ecuador, Egypt, France, Germany, Greece, Japan, Mexico, Spain, Russia, and other one-month travel experiences during January term. *Other distinctive programs:* Continuing education for social work professionals. Life Enrichment Program for senior citizens.

Degrees Conferred: 97 *baccalaureate:* biological/life sciences 2; business/marketing 15; communications/communication technologies 4; computer and information sciences 4; education 10; English 4; foreign languages and literature 4; health professions and related sciences 11; interdisciplinary studies 2; mathematics 4; parks and recreation 4; philosophy/religion/theology 4; physical sciences 4; protective services/public administration 9; psychology 2; social sciences and history 7; visual and performing arts 10.

Fees and Other Expenses: *Full-time tuition per academic year 2005–06:* $15,500. *Room and board per academic year:* $6,100.

Financial Aid: Aid from institutionally generated funds is provided on the basis of academic merit, financial need, athletic ability, other criteria. Institution

has a Program Participation Agreement with the U.S. Department of Education for eligible students to receive Pell Grants and other federal aid.

Financial aid to full-time, first-time undergraduate students: need-based scholarships/grants totaling $1,142,436, self-help $2,238,772; non-need-based scholarships/grants totaling $1,825,282, self-help $620,409, parent loans $448,475, tuition waivers $366,826, athletic awards $331,087.

Departments and Teaching Staff: *Total instructional faculty:* 60 (full-time 45, part-time 15; women 21, men 39). Total faculty with doctorate, first-professional, or other terminal degree: 33. Student-to-faculty ratio: 10:1. *Faculty development:* $20,000 in grants for research. 3 faculty members awarded sabbaticals 2004–05.

Enrollment: *Total enrollment:* 509. Undergraduate full-time 228 men / 249 women, part-time 13m / 19w.

Characteristics of Student Body: *Ethnic/racial makeup:* number Black non-Hispanic: 28; American Indian or Alaska Native: 3; Asian or Pacific Islander: 12; Hispanic: 24; White non-Hispanic: 423. *Age distribution:* 9% of students are over age 25.

International Students: 19 nonresident aliens enrolled fall 2004. 3 students from Europe, 2 Asia, 4 Central and South Latin America, 9 Africa, 1 Canada. No programs available to aid students whose native language is not English. Financial aid specifically designated for undergraduate international students: unlimited number of scholarships available annually; 6 totaling $74,664 were awarded 2004–05.

Student Life: On-campus residence halls house 68% of student body. *Intercollegiate athletics:* men only: basketball, cross-country, football, golf, soccer, tennis, track; women only: basketball, cross-country, golf, soccer, tennis, track, volleyball. *Special regulations:* Cars permitted in designated parking areas. *Special services:* Center for Academic Development; career development and placement; Personal Assistance System (PAS Counseling); international student advisor. *Student publications:* Collegian, a biweekly newspaper; Thresher, a yearbook. *Surrounding community:* Newton population 18,000. Wichita, 25 miles from campus, is nearest metropolitan area. Served by airport 30 miles from campus; passenger rail service 2 miles from campus, Interstate I-35, ½ mile from campus.

Publications: *Mennonite Life* (quarterly) first published in 1946; now online at www.bethelks.edu/mennonitelife/

Library Collections: 140,408 volumes. 14,001 microforms. Current periodical subscriptions: paper 537, via electronic access 19,177. 3,506 recordings, 971 compact discs, 13 CD-ROMS. Online catalog. 10 computer work stations. Access to online information retrieval systems and the Internet. Total 2004–05 budget for books and materials: $56,645.

Most important holdings include materials related to peace and conflict resolution; H.R. Voth papers (anthropologist and missionary to Hopi Indians); The Mennonite Library and Archives (25,000 items, including works of Mennonite history and theology, personal papers, letters, as well as rare books from Europe dating back to the 15th century).

Buildings and Grounds: Campus area 90 acres.

Chief Executive Officer: Dr. E. Laverne Epp, President.

Address admission inquiries to Allan Bartel, Director of Admissions and Enrollment.

Central Baptist Theological Seminary

741 North 31st Street
Kansas City, Kansas 66102-3964
Tel: (913) 371-5313   **E-mail:** enrollment@cbts.edu
Fax: (913) 371-8110   **Internet:** www.cbts.edu

Institution Description: Central Baptist Theological Seminary is a private institution affiliated with the American Baptist Churches. *Enrollment:* 94. *Degrees awarded:* First-professional (master of divinity), master's. Diplomas also awarded.

Accreditation: *Regional:* NCA. *National:* ATS. *Professional:* theology

History: Established 1901.

Institutional Structure: *Governing board:* Board of Directors. Extrainstitutional representation: 39 directors; institutional representation: president of the seminary; 2 student representative. 1 ex officio. Full-time instructional faculty 11.

Calendar: Semesters (15 weeks each semester). Academic year Aug. to May.

Admission: Apply no later than July 15. *Requirements:* Baccalaureate from accredited college or university.

Degree Requirements: *For M. Div. degree:* 75 credit hours. *For M.A.R.S. degree:* 48 credit hours. *For all graduate degrees:* 2.3 GPA on 4.0 scale; 2 terms in residence. *Grading system:* A–F; satisfactory-unsatisfactory; incomplete.

Distinctive Educational Programs: Work-experience programs, including clinical pastoral education, field education, Native American Program. Annual mission day. *Other distinctive programs:* Continuing education, long distance learning.

Degrees Conferred: 7 *master's:* religious studies; 14 *first-professional:* master of divinity. *Honorary degrees awarded 2004:* Doctor of Divinity 2.

Fees and Other Expenses: *Tuition 2004–05:* $273 per credit hour. *Required fees:* $270. *Room per academic year:* $2,295.

Financial Aid: Aid from institutionally generated funds is provided on the basis of academic merit, financial need. Institution has a Program Participation Agreement with the U.S. Department of Education for eligible students to receive Pell Grants and other federal aid.

Departments and Teaching Staff: Biblical studies *professors* 1, *associate professors* 0, assistant professors 0, *part-time faculty* 2; church history 0, 1, 0, 1; evangelism 0, 1, 0, 0; church/community 0, 1, 0, 0; homiletics/worship 1, 0, 0, 0; religious education 1, 0, 0, 1; learning resources 0, 1, 0, 0; pastoral theology 1, 1, 1, 0; theology/spirit formation 1, 0, 0, 2.

Total instructional faculty: 17 (full-time 11, part-time 6; women 6, men 11; member of minority group 1). Total faculty with doctorate, first-professional, or other terminal degree: 17.

Enrollment: Total enrollment 94. Undergraduate full-time 1 man; part-time 1m / 3w; first-professional full-time 21m / 20w, part-time 20m / 14w; graduate full-time 1m / 1w, part-time 6m / 6w.

Characteristics of Student Body: *Ethnic/racial makeup:* number of Black non-Hispanic: 24, American Indian or Alaska Native: 3; Asian or Pacific Islander: 3; White non-Hispanic: 61.

International Students: 3 nonresident aliens enrolled fall 2004. 2 students from Central and South America, 1 Africa. No programs available to aid students whose native language is not English. No financial aid specifically designated for international students.

Student Life: On-campus residence halls and apartments. Housing available for married students. *Special regulations:* Cars permitted without restrictions. *Surrounding community:* Kansas City population 161,000.

Publications: *Voice,* published quarterly; *Fact,* published weekly.

Library Collections: 85,000 volumes. Online catalog. 12,000 microforms; 7,500 audiovisual materials; 330 current periodical subscriptions. 13 computer work stations. Most important holdings include collections on Baptist church history and the Fred E. Young Qumran Collection.

Chief Executive Officer: Thomas Dr. Molly T. Marshall, President.

Address admission inquiries to Mary Beth Robertson, Director of Enrollment Services.

Central Christian College

1200 South Main Street
P.O. Box 1402
McPherson, Kansas 67460
Tel: (620) 241-0723   **E-mail:** admissions@centralchristian.edu
Fax: (620) 241-6032   **Internet:** www.centralchristian.edu

Institution Description: Central Christian College, formerly a junior college, is an independent college affiliated with the Free Methodist Church. *Enrollment:* 320. *Degrees awarded:* Associate, baccalaureate.

Accreditation: *Regional:* NCA.

History: Central Christian College was founded in 1884.

Calendar: Semesters (4-1-4 plan). Academic year Sept. to May.

Characteristics of Freshmen: 46% of applicants admitted. 15% of applicants admitted and enrolled.

18% (16 students) submitted SAT scores; 82% (73 students) submitted ACT scores. *25th percentile*: SAT Verbal 370, SAT Math 370; ACT Composite 17, ACT English 15, ACT Math 17. *75th percentile*: SAT Verbal 530, SAT Math 560; ACT Composite 22, ACT English 23, ACT Math 23.

25% of entering freshmen expected to graduate within 5 years. 30% of freshmen from Kansas. Freshmen from 23 states and 1 foreign country.

Admission: *Requirements:* Graduation from accredited secondary school or GED.

Degree Requirements: *For all associate degrees:* Completion of 64 semester hours. *For all baccalaureate degrees:* Completion of 128 semester hours.

Distinctive Educational Programs: New bachelor of science majors added: communication, natural science, music, social science, exercise science, sport management, psychology.

Degrees Conferred: 50 *associate;* 51 *baccalaureate:* business/marketing 21; liberal arts and sciences, general studies and humanities 19; philosophy/religion/theology 11.

Fees and Other Expenses: *Full-time tuition per academic year 2005–06:* $13,600. *Required fees:* $500. *Room and board per academic year:* $4,500.

Financial Aid: Aid from institutionally generated funds is provided on the basis of academic merit, athletic ability, financial need, other criteria. Institution has a Program Participation Agreement with the U.S. Department of Education for eligible students to receive Pell Grants and other federal aid.

Financial aid to full-time, first-time undergraduate students: need-based scholarships/grants totaling $627,730, self-help $1,671,883; non-need-based scholarships/grants totaling $1,318,500, self-help $757,643, parent loans $240,000, tuition waivers $77,000, athletic awards $160,000.

Departments and Teaching Staff: *Total instructional faculty:* 33 (full-time 16, part-time 17; women 7, men 27). Total faculty with doctorate, first-professional, or other terminal degree: 6. Student-to-faculty ratio: 16:1.

Enrollment: Total enrollment 320. Full-time 141 men / 159 women, part-time 12m / 8w. *Transfer students:* in-state 6; from out-of-state 10.

Characteristics of Student Body: *Ethnic/racial makeup:* number of Black non-Hispanic: 33; American Indian or Alaska Native: 5, Hispanic: 18; White non-Hispanic 258. *Age distribution:* number under 18: 14; 18–19: 139; 20–21: 103; 22–24: 37; 25–29: 7; 30–34: 4; 35–39: 4; 40–49: 9; 0–64: 3.

International Students: 6 nonresident aliens enrolled fall 2004. 5 students from Asia, 1 Australia. No programs available to students whose native language is not English. No financial aid specifically designated for international students.

Student Life: On-campus housing available.

Library Collections: 36,432 volumes including bound books, serial backfiles, electronic documents, and government documents not in separate collections. Online catalog. Current serial subscriptions: paper, microform, electronic. 892 recordings; 282 compact discs; 12 CD-ROMs. 8 computer work stations. Students have access to the Internet at no charge.

Most important special holdings include Free Methodist Collection; Japanese Book Collection.

Buildings and Grounds: Campus area 210 acres.

Chief Executive Officer: Dr. Donald Mason, President.

Address admission inquiries to David Ferrell, Dean of Admissions.

Emporia State University

1200 Commercial Street
Emporia, Kansas 66801-5087
Tel: (620) 341-1200   **E-mail:** go2esu@emporia.edu
Fax: (620) 341-5073   **Internet:** emporia.edu

Institution Description: Emporia State University (formerly Emporia Kansas State College) is a public institution. *Enrollment:* 6,194. *Degrees awarded:* Baccalaureate, master's, doctorate. Specialist degree also awarded.

Academic offerings subject to approval by statewide coordinating bodies. Budget subject to approval by state governing boards.

Accreditation: *Regional:* NCA. *Professional*: athletic training, business, counseling, librarianship, music, nursing, rehabilitation counseling, teacher education

History: Established as Kansas State Normal School and chartered 1863; offered first instruction at postsecondary level 1865; awarded first degree (baccalaureate) 1867; changed name to Kansas State Teachers College 1923, to Emporia Kansas State College 1974; adopted present name 1977. *See* P.J. Wyatt, *A History of the First 100 Years of the Kansas State Teachers College 1863–1963* (Emporia: Emporia State University Press, 1963) for further information.

Institutional Structure: *Governing board:* Board of Regents, State of Kansas. Extrainstitutional representation: 9 regents, 1 president, 1 ex officio. 9 voting. *Composition of institution:* Administrators 30 men / 30 women (3% are members of minority groups). Academic affairs headed by vice president of academic affairs. Management/business/finances directed by vice president of administration and fiscal affairs. Full-time instructional faculty 251. Academic governance body, Faculty Senate, meets an average of 30 times per year.

Calendar: Semesters. Academic year Aug. to May. Freshmen admitted Aug., Jan., June. Degrees conferred May, Aug., Dec. Formal commencements May, Dec. Summer session of 3 terms from June to Aug.

Characteristics of Freshmen: 72% of applicants admitted. 57% of applicants admitted and enrolled.

1.8% (13 students) submitted SAT scores; 90.5% (660 students) submitted ACT scores. *25th percentile*: ACT Composite 18.9, ACT English 17.9, ACT Math 17.7. *75th percentile*: ACT Composite 24.7, ACT English 24.6, ACT Math 24.2.

37% of entering freshmen expected to graduate within 5 years. 91% of freshmen from Kansas. Freshmen from 10 states and 8 foreign countries.

Admission: Rolling admissions plan. For fall acceptance, apply as early as junior year of secondary school, but not later than one week prior to enrollment.

Early acceptance available. *Requirements:* Graduation from an accredited secondary school or GED; ACT 21 ore above or top 1/3 of class or 2.0 GPA on Kansas Core Curriculum. *For transfer students:* 64 hours maximum transfer credit; 2.0 minimum GPA.

College credit and advanced placement for postsecondary-level work completed in secondary school. For extrainstitutional learning on basis of ACE *2006 Guide to the Evaluation of Educational Experiences in the Armed Services*; college credit and advanced placement on basis of faculty assessment. Tutoring available. Noncredit remedial courses offered in summer session and regular academic year.

Degree Requirements: *For all baccalaureate degrees:* 124 credit hours; 30 of last 45 hours in residence; exit competency examinations in writing, reading, and mathematics. *For all undergraduate degrees:* 2.0 minimum GPA; 2 courses in physical education. Fulfillment of some degree requirements and exemption from some beginning courses possible by passing departmental examinations, College Board CLEP, APP. *Grading system:* A–F; pass; withdraw; incomplete (carries time limit).

Distinctive Educational Programs: *For undergraduates:* Dual-degree programs in engineering with University of Kansas and Kansas State University. Interdisciplinary programs. 2+2 program for business majors taught at Johnson County and Butler County Community College. *For graduates:* Accredited master and doctorate in library science, student personnel. Online master's degree in business education, curriculum and instruction, educational administration, physical education, instructional technology, and master teacher. *Available to all students:* Flexible meeting places and schedules, weekend and evening classes. Special facilities for using telecommunications in the classroom. Facilities and programs for independent research, including honors programs, individual majors, tutorials.

Degrees Conferred: 854 *baccalaureate* (B), 440 *master's* (M), 3 *doctorate* (D): biological/life sciences 33 (B), 11 (M); business/marketing 147 (B), 19 (M); communications/communication technologies 39 (B); computer and information sciences 46 (B); education 288 (B), 227 (M); English 18 (B), 8 (M); foreign languages and literature 10 (B); health professions and related sciences 67 (B), 12 (M); interdisciplinary studies 2 (B); liberal arts/general studies 28 (B); library science 133 (M), 3 (D); parks and recreation 22 (B); physical sciences 13 (B), 2 (M); psychology 35 (B), 16 (M); social sciences and history 79 (B), 5 (M); education specialist 4 (M).

Fees and Other Expenses: *Full-time tuition per academic year 2004–05:* resident undergraduate $2,410, out-of-state student $9,130; ; graduate resident $2,890, out-of-state student $9,258. *Required fees:* $626. *Room and board per academic year:* $4,474.

Financial Aid: Aid from institutionally generated funds is provided on the basis of academic merit, financial need, athletic ability, other criteria. Institution has a Program Participation Agreement with the U.S. Department of Education for eligible students to receive Pell Grants and other federal aid.

Financial aid to full-time, first-time undergraduate students: need-based scholarships/grants totaling $6,294,793, self-help $8,897,730, parent loans $80,533, tuition waivers $2,763, athletic awards $375,153; non-need-based scholarships/grants totaling $1,229,955, self-help $4,158,369, parent loans $433,283, tuition waivers $1,596, athletic awards $419,798. *Graduate aid:* 617 students received federal and state-funded loans totaling $4,797,125 (ranging from $100 to $16,070); 154 teaching assistantships worth $831,570; 49 research assistantships worth $230,581.

Departments and Teaching Staff: *Total instructional faculty:* 273 (full-time 251, part-time 22; women 115, men 158; members of minority groups 23). Total faculty with doctorate, first-professional, or other terminal degree: 210. Student-to-faculty ratio: 18:1. *Faculty development:* $330,118. 8 faculty members awarded sabbaticals 2004–05.

Enrollment: Total enrollment 6,194. Undergraduate full-time 1,457 men / 2,339 women, part-time 197m / 377w; graduate full-time 987m / 147w, part-time 422m / 1,157w. *Transfer students:* in-state 440; from out-of-state 74.

Characteristics of Student Body: *Ethnic/racial makeup:* number of Black non-Hispanic: 169; American Indian or Alaska Native: 31; Asian or Pacific Islander: 22; Hispanic: 190; White non-Hispanic: 3,723; unknown: 136. *Age distribution:* number under 18: 37; 18–19: 1,230; 20–21: 1,372; 22–24: 966; 25–29: 358; 30–34: 124; 35–39: 76; 40–49: 132; 50–64: 44; 65 and over: 31.

International Students: 166 nonresident aliens enrolled fall 2004. 33 students from Europe, 70 Asia, 22 Central and South America, 16 Africa, 2 Canada, 23 other. Programs available to aid students whose native language is not English: English as a Second Language. Some financial aid specifically designated for international students: 10 scholarships awarded annually.

Student Life: All first-year students reside on-campus. Residence halls house 24% of student population. 9% of undergraduate students are involved in the Greek system. *Intercollegiate athletics:* men only: baseball, basketball, cross-country, football, tennis, track; women only: basketball, cross-country softball, swimming, tennis, track, volleyball. *Special regulations:* Registered cars permit-

ted without restrictions. *Special services:* Learning Resources Center, medical services. *Student publications: Bulletin,* a weekly newspaper; *Spotlight,* a quarterly alumni magazine; *Sunflower,* a yearbook. *Surrounding community:* Emporia population 27,000. Kansas City, 110 miles from campus, is nearest metropolitan area. Served by Interstate 35. Passenger rail service 2 miles from campus.

Publications: Emporia State University publishes *The Best of Emporia State, Heritage of the Great Plains,the Kansas School Naturalist, Kansas Science Teacher, Quivira, Teaching History Journal Methods, Emporia State Research Studies.*

Library Collections: 2,364,320 volumes including bound books, serial backfiles, electronic documents, and government documents. Online catalog. 1,256 recordings; 503 compact discs; 143 CD-ROMs. 62 public computer work stations. Access to online information retrieval systems and the Internet. Total 2004–05 budget for books and materials: $393,828.

Most important holdings include William Allen White Collection (diary, letters, manuscripts, travelogues of Pulitzer Prize winner); Mary Massee Collection (original art, resources for children's books, manuscripts); Normaliana; Lois Lenski Collection.

Buildings and Grounds: Campus area 211 acres. *New buildings:* Student Recreation Center completed 2001.

Chief Executive Officer: Dr. Kay Schallenkamp, President.

Address admission inquiries to Laura Eddy, Director of Admissions; graduate inquiries to Dr. Robert Grover, Dean of Graduate Studies and Research.

Fort Hays State University

600 Park Street
Hays, Kansas 67601-4099
Tel: (785) 628-4222   **E-mail:** admissions@fhsu.edu
Fax: (785) 628-4085   **Internet:** www.fhsu.edu

Institution Description: Fort Hays State University (Fort Hays Kansas State College until 1977) is a state institution and land-grant college. *Enrollment:* 8,500. *Degrees awarded:* Associate, baccalaureate, master's. Specialist certificate also awarded.

Accreditation: *Regional:* NCA. *Professional:* music, nursing, nursing education, radiography, social work, speech-language pathology, teacher education

History: Established as Western Branch of Kansas Normal School of Emporia, chartered, and offered first instruction at postsecondary level 1902; awarded first degree (baccalaureate) 1910; changed name to Fort Hays Kansas State Normal School 1914, Kansas State Teachers College of Hays 1923, Fort Hays Kansas State College 1931; adopted present name 1977. *See* James Forsythe, *The First 75 Years* (Topeka, Kans.: Fort Hays State University, 1977) for further information.

Institutional Structure: *Governing board:* Board of Regents, State of Kansas. Extrainstitutional representation: 9 members (appointed by governor of Kansas). All voting. *Composition of institution:* Administrators 14 men / 2 women. Academic affairs headed by provost. Management/business/finances directed by vice president for administration and finance. Academic governance body, Faculty Senate, meets an average of 26 times per year.

Calendar: Semesters. Academic year Aug. to May. Freshmen admitted Aug., Jan., June. Degrees conferred May, July, and Dec. Formal commencement May.

Characteristics of Freshmen: 95% of freshmen from Kansas. Freshmen from 34 states.

Admission: Early acceptance available. *Requirements:* Either graduation from accredited secondary school or GED. Score of 21 or higher on the ACT or rank in the top third of high school graduating class or in-state students a GPA of 2.0 in prescribed core courses; out-of-state students minimum GPA 2.5 in prescribed core courses. *Entrance tests:* ACT composite preferred; College Board SAT accepted. For foreign students TOEFL. *For transfer students:* 2.0 minimum GPA in at least 24 hours; from 4-year accredited institution all hours transferable, however, student must complete a minimum of 30 hours and fulfill the requirements as specified for the degree; from 2-year accredited institution all hours are transferable, however, student must complete the last 60 credit hours in residence and fulfill the requirements as specified for the degree.

College credit and advanced placement for postsecondary-level work completed in secondary school and for extrainstitutional learning on basis of ACE *2006 Guide to the Evaluation of Educational Experiences in the Armed Services.* Developmental courses offered in summer session and regular academic year; credit given.

Degree Requirements: *For all associate degrees:* a minimum of 60 credit hours; 2 physical education courses. *For all baccalaureate degrees:* a minimum of 124 credit hours. *For all undergraduate degrees:* 2.0 GPA; 30 hours in residence; general education requirements.

Fulfillment of some degree requirements and exemption from some beginning courses possible by passing departmental examination, College Board CLEP and AP. *Grading system:* A–U; pass-fail; pass; withdraw (carries time limit).

Distinctive Educational Programs: *For undergraduates:* Social work with Kansas State University. Pre-professional programs in dentistry, engineering, forestry, law, medicine, medical diagnostic imaging, medical technology, optometry, osteopathy, pharmacy, public administration and management, radiologic technology, theology, veterinary medicine. *For graduate students:* Collaborative doctoral (Ed.D.) program with Kansas State University. *Available to all students:* Work-experience programs, including internships, field experience, practicum. Weekend and evening classes. Special facilities for using telecommunications in the classroom.

Degrees Conferred: 51 *associate*; 949 *baccalaureate*; 245 *master's*. Bachelor's degrees awarded in top five disciplines: liberal arts and sciences, general studies and humanities 192; education 158; business, management, marketing, and related support services 152; visual and performing arts 55; health professions and related clinical sciences 49.

Fees and Other Expenses: *Full-time tuition per academic year 2004–05:* $2,901 resident undergraduate, $9,026 out-of-state student. *Books and supplies:* $850. *Room and board per academic year:* $4,949.

Financial Aid: Aid from institutionally generated funds is provided on the basis of academic merit, financial need. Institution has a Program Participation Agreement with the U.S. Department of Education for eligible students to receive Pell Grants and other federal aid.

Financial aid to full-time, first-time undergraduate students: 26% received federal grants averaging $2,400; 5% state/local grants averaging $625; 30% institutional grants averaging $1,100; 42% loans averaging $2,750.

Departments and Teaching Staff: *Total instructional faculty:* 296. *Degrees held by full-time faculty:* doctorate 67.97%, master's 30.47%, baccalaureate 1.17%, professional .40%. 80.86% hold terminal degrees.

Enrollment: Total enrollment 8,500. Undergraduate 7,173 (45.3% men, 54.7% women).

Characteristics of Student Body: *Ethnic/racial makeup:* Black non-Hispanic: 1.5%; American Indian or Alaska Native: .6%; Asian or Pacific Islander: 25.7%l Hispanic: 2.1%; White non-Hispanic: 66.3%; unknown: 3.8%. *Age distribution:* 17–21: 43%; 22–24: 21%; 25–29: 11%; 30–39: 12%; 40–49: 10%; 50–up: 3%.

International Students: Social and cultural programs available to aid students whose native language is not English. English as a Second Language Program.

Student Life: On-campus residence halls house 24% of student body. Dormitories for men only constitute 40% of such space, for women only 48%, for both sexes 12%. 2% of men join and live in fraternities; 2% of women join and live in sororities. Housing available for married students. *Intercollegiate athletics:* men only: baseball, basketball, cross-country, football, golf, tennis, track, wrestling; women only: basketball, cross-country, softball, tennis, volleyball. *Special regulations:* Cars with permits allowed. Quiet hours and dormitory visitation hours vary according to residence hall. *Special services:* Medical services. *Student publications, radio, television: Big Creek Review,* a biannual literary magazine; *The Reveille,* a yearbook; *University Leader,* a biweekly newspaper. Radio station KFHS broadcasts 35 hours per week. TV station KFHS broadcasts 18 hours per week. *Surrounding community:* Hays population 16,500. Kansas City, 270 miles from campus, is nearest metropolitan area. Served by airport 3 miles from campus.

Library Collections: 300,000 volumes. 700,000 government documents; 275,000 microforms; 400 audiovisual materials; 2,500 current periodicals. Access to online information retrieval systems.

Most important holdings include German Heritage Collection; Curry Collection of Military History; Kansas Collection.

Buildings and Grounds: Campus area 4,300 acres.

Chief Executive Officer: Dr. Edward H. Hammond, President.

Address admission inquiries to Joseph G. Linn, Director of Admissions.

Friends University

2100 University Street
Wichita, Kansas 67213-3397

Tel: (316) 295-5000   **E-mail:** admissions@friends.edu
Fax: (316) 262-5027   **Internet:** www.friends.edu

Institution Description: Friends University is a private, independent, nonprofit institution. Enrollment 2,749. *Degrees awarded:* Associate, baccalaureate, master's.

Accreditation: *Regional:* NCA. *Professional:* marriage and family therapy, music, teacher education

History: Established and offered first instruction at postsecondary level 1898; awarded first degree (baccalaureate) 1901; incorporated 1920. *See* Floyd and Norma Souders, *Friends University* (North Newton, Kansas: Mennonite Press, 1974) for further information.

Institutional Structure: *Governing board:* Friends University Board of Trustees. Extrainstitutional representation: 21 trustees, including 1 alumnus; institutional representation: president of the university. 1 ex officio. All voting. *Composition of institution:* Administrators 7 men / 1 woman. Academic affairs headed by vice president for academic affairs. Management/business/finances directed by vice president for administration and finance. Full-time instructional faculty 38 men / 17 women. Academic governance body, Academic Affairs Committee, meets an average of 9 times per year.

Calendar: Semesters. Academic year late Aug. to early May. Freshmen admitted Aug., Jan. Degrees conferred May, Dec. Formal commencement May. Summer session from late May to early July.

Characteristics of Freshmen: 642 applicants (273 men, 369 women). 72.6% of applicants admitted. 65% of admitted students enrolled full-time.

4% (12 students) submitted SAT scores; 78% (235 students) submitted ACT scores. *25th percentile:* SAT I Verbal 440, SAT I Math 420; ACT Composite 18, ACT English 17, ACT Math 17. *75th percentile*: SAT I Verbal 600, SAT I Math 610; ACT Composite 24, ACT English 24, ACT Math 24.

Admission: Rolling admissions plan. For fall acceptance, apply as early as 18 months prior to registration, but not later than 2 weeks after beginning of term. Early acceptance available. *Requirements:* Either graduation from accredited secondary school with 16 units which must include 3 English, 2 laboratory science, 2 mathematics, 2 social studies; or GED. Minimum GPA 2.0. *Entrance tests:* College Board SAT or ACT composite. For foreign students TOEFL. *For transfer students:* 2.0 GPA; from 4-year accredited institution maximum transfer credit limited only by residence requirements; from 2-year accredited institution 64 hours maximum transfer credit.

College credit for postsecondary-level work completed in secondary school and for extrainstitutional learning (life experience) on basis of committee assessment. Tutoring available. Developmental courses offered during regular academic year; credit given.

Degree Requirements: *For all associate degrees:* 62 credit hours; 15 hours in residence. *For all baccalaureate degrees:* 124 credit hours; 30 hours in residence; exit competency examinations. *For all undergraduate degrees:* 2.0 GPA; distribution requirements.

Fulfillment of some degree requirements and exemption from some beginning courses possible by passing departmental examinations, College Board CLEP, other standardized tests. *Grading system:* A–F; pass-fail; withdraw (carries penalty); incomplete (deadline after which A–F is assigned).

Distinctive Educational Programs: Internship. Degree completion program with major in Human Resources Management for persons with 62 hours previous work. Interdepartmental/interdisciplinary programs in human services and international business. Tutorials. Cross-registration with Kansas Newman College.

Degrees Conferred: 56 *associate*; 662 *baccalaureate*; 269 *master's*. Bachelor's degrees awarded in top five disciplines: business, management, marketing, and related support services 381; computer and information sciences and support services 117; education 48; psychology 31; biological and biomedical sciences 24.

Fees and Other Expenses: *Full-time tuition per academic year 2004–05:* $14,520. *Room and board per academic year:* $4,700. *Books and supplies:* $900.

Financial Aid: Aid from institutionally generated funds is provided on the basis of academic merit, financial need, and performance. Institution has a Program Participation Agreement with the U.S. Department of Education for eligible students to receive Pell Grants and other federal aid.

Financial aid to full-time, first-time undergraduate students: 41% received federal grants averaging $3,661; 25% state/local grants averaging $2,309; 71% institutional grants averaging $5,433; 71% loans averaging $4,920.

Departments and Teaching Staff: Business *professors* 3, *associate professors* 3, *assistant professors* 4, *instructors* 1, *part-time teachers* 0; education/behavioral sciences 4, 6, 3, 1, 2; fine arts 2, 4, 3, 0, 6; natural sciences 4, 1, 3, 0, 1; religion/humanities 3, 3, 2, 2, 2.

Total instructional faculty: 50. Degrees held by full-time faculty: doctorate 58%, master's 39%, professional 3%. 59% hold terminal degrees.

Enrollment: Total enrollment 2,749. Undergraduate 2,271 (41.5% men, 58.5% women).

Characteristics of Student Body: *Ethnic/racial makeup:* Black non-Hispanic: 11.4%, American Indian or Alaska Native: 1.8%; Asian or Pacific Islander: 1.5%; Hispanic: 5.3%; White non-Hispanic: 78.7%.

International Students: 30 undergraduate nonresident aliens enrolled fall 2004. No programs available to aid students whose native language is not English. No financial aid specifically designated for international students.

Library Collections: 120,000 volumes. 2,225 microforms; 4,500 audiovisual materials; 860 current periodical subscriptions; 8,000 recordings/tapes. Students have access to online information retrieval services and the Internet.

Most important holdings include Quaker collection (books by and about Quakers, from 17th century to present).

Buildings and Grounds: Campus area 54 acres.

Chief Executive Officer: Dr. Biff Green, President.

Address admission inquiries to Director of Admissions.

Kansas State University

119 Anderson Hall
Manhattan, Kansas 66506-0113
Tel: (785) 532-6250   **E-mail:** kstate@ksu.edu
Fax: (785) 532-6393   **Internet:** www.ksu.edu

Institution Description: Kansas State University is a state land-grant institution. *Enrollment:* 23,151. *Degrees awarded:* Associate, baccalaureate, first-professional (veterinary medicine), master's, doctorate.

Academic offerings subject to approval by statewide coordinating bodies. Budget subject to approval by state governing boards.

Accreditation: *Regional:* NCA. *Professional:* accounting, art, athletic training, business, computer science, construction education, counseling, dietetics, engineering, interior design, journalism, landscape architecture, marriage and family therapy, music, planning, psychology internship, public administration, recreation and leisure services, social work, speech-language pathology, teacher education, theatre, veterinary medicine

History: Chartered as Kansas State Agricultural College 1858; established and offered first instruction at postsecondary level 1863; awarded first degree (baccalaureate) 1867; changed name to Kansas State College of Agriculture and Applied Science 1931; adopted present name 1959. *See* James C. Carey, *Kansas State University, The Quest for Identity* (Lawrence, KS: Regents Press of Kansas, 1977) for further information.

Institutional Structure: *Governing board:* Board of Regents, State of Kansas. Extrainstitutional representation: 9 members (appointed by governor of Kansas). All voting. *Composition of institution:* Administrators 388 (233 men / 155 women). Academic affairs headed by provost. Management/business/finances directed by vice president for administration and finance. Full-time instructional faculty 893. Academic governance body, Kansas State University Faculty Senate, meets an average of 10 times per year.

Calendar: Semesters. Academic year Aug. to May. Freshmen admitted Aug., Jan., June. Degrees conferred May, Dec.

Characteristics of Freshmen: 65% of applicants accepted. 52of accepted applicants enrolled.

92% (3,197 students) submitted ACT scores. *25th percentile:* ACT Composite 20.6, ACT English 19.7, ACT Math 19.7. *75th percentile:* ACT Composite 26.2, ACT English 26.3, ACT Math 26.8.

79% of entering freshmen expected to graduate within 5 years. 85% of freshmen from Kansas. Freshmen from 39 states and 17 foreign countries.

Admission: Rolling admissions plan. Apply no later than a few days after registration. Early acceptance available. *Requirements:* Academic rank in top one third of high school class and score 21 or higher on the ACT; complete the Kansas Pre-College Curriculum with a 2.0 GPA. Recommend 3 units English, 1 college preparatory mathematics, 1 college preparatory science. *Entrance tests:* ACT composite or SAT. For foreign students TOEFL or demonstrated proficiency in English. *For transfer students:* 2.0 minimum GPA; maximum transfer credit of up to one half of degree requirements.

College credit and advanced placement for postsecondary-level work completed in secondary school and for extrainstitutional learning on basis of ACE *2006 Guide to the Evaluation of Educational Experiences in the Armed Services.* Advanced placement for USAFI/DANTES. Tutoring available. Developmental courses offered in summer session and regular academic year; nondegree credit given.

Degree Requirements: *For all associate degrees:* 60–61 semester hours. *For all baccalaureate degrees:* 120–160 hours. *For all undergraduate degrees:* 2.0 GPA; 30 hours, including 20 of last 30 hours, in residence; 1 physical education course; prescribed curriculum; 6 credits English composition; 2 oral composition.

Fulfillment of some degree requirements and exemption from some beginning courses possible by passing departmental examinations, College Board CLEP, APP. *Grading system:* A–F; A–pass-fail; withdraw (deadline after which pass-fail is appended to withdraw).

Distinctive Educational Programs: *For undergraduates:* Work-experience programs. Dual-degree program in social work with College of Arts and Sciences. Interdisciplinary programs in gerontology, laser science, life sciences, linguistics, physical science, social science, women's studies; interdisciplinary major in humanities. Major in nutrition and exercise sciences. Facilities and programs for independent research, including honors programs, tutorials. Institutionally sponsored study abroad in Australia, Czech Republic, England, France, Germany, Mexico, Switzerland. Personalized study leading to bachelor of general studies through Non-Traditional Study Program. *For graduate students:* Interdisciplinary programs in animal sciences, biochemistry, crop protection, engineering, food science, genetics, home economics, parasitology, veterinary pathology. Domestic study with member schools of the Mid-America State Universities Association. *Available to all students:* Flexible meeting places and schedules, including off-campus centers (at Fort Riley, an associate degree-granting center; agricultural experiment station; other varying locations, all within 30 miles of main institution) and evening classes. Special facilities for using telecommunications in the classroom. *Other distinctive programs:* Credit-noncredit continuing education programs offered in communities throughout the state. Summer school classes open to nonmatriculated students. Outreach degree-granting programs available in computer science, education, history, industrial engineering. Courses made available in 33 centers throughout state via telephone line and audiovisual equipment. Intersession classes open to public without prior enrollment. Conferences, short courses, workshops, special interest programs, noncredit programs available to individuals and organizations through University Conference Office. Servicemembers' Opportunity College. Community Activities Program for adults and children on topics relating to recreational and leisure time activities.

ROTC: Army, Air Force.

Degrees Conferred: 104 *associate;* 3,371 *baccalaureate* (B), 713 *master's* (M), 146 *doctorate* (D): agriculture 379 (B), 72 (M), 28 (D); architecture 99 (B), 21 (M); biological/life sciences 160 (B), 22 (M), 21 (D); business/marketing 600 (B), 55 (M); communications/communication technologies 165 (B), 21 (M); computer and information sciences 110 (B), 58 (M), 3 (D); education 355 (B), 217 (M), 32 (D); engineering and engineering technologies 398 (B), 73 (M), 17 (D); English 42 (B), 26 (M); foreign languages and literature 19 (B), 5 (M); health professions and related sciences 92 (B), 6 (M), 3 (D); home economics and vocational home economics 222 (B), 42 (M), 12 (D); liberal arts/general studies 3 (B); mathematics 17 (B), 9 (M), 6 (D); natural resources/environmental science 1 (m); parks and recreation 102 (b), 11 (M); philosophy/religion/theology 4 (B); physical sciences 27 (B), 10 (M), 12 (D); protective services/public administration 28 (B), 6 (M); psychology 75 (B), 17 (M), 4 (D); social sciences and history 304 (B), 28 (M), 9 (D); trade and industry 48 (B); visual and performing arts 123 (B), 13 (M). 107 *first-professional:* veterinary medicine.

Fees and Other Expenses: *Full-time tuition per academic year 2004–05:* in-state resident $4,110, out-of-state $12,870; contact the university for current graduate tuition/fees. *Room and board per academic year:* $5,738. *Required fees:* $555. *Books and supplies:* $1,030.

Financial Aid: Aid from institutionally generated funds is provided on the basis of academic merit, financial need. Institution has a Program Participation Agreement with the U.S. Department of Education for eligible students to receive Pell Grants and other federal aid.

Financial aid to full-time, first-time undergraduate students: need-based scholarships/grants totaling $26,604,689, self-help $56,934,779, tuition waivers $3,267,158, athletic awards $3,376,183; non-need-based scholarships/grants totaling $3,010,899, self-help $27,537,119, athletic awards $254,406.

Departments and Teaching Staff: *Total instructional faculty:* 1,048 (full-time 893, part-time 155; women 368, men 680; members of minority groups 118). Student-to-faculty ratio: 21:1. Degrees held by full-time faculty: doctorate 76.2%, master's 21.5%, baccalaureate 2.6%. 84.7% hold terminal degrees.

Enrollment: Total enrollment 23,151. Undergraduate full-time 8,607 men / 1,551 women, part-time 1,161m / 1,257w; first-professional 141m / 287w, part-time 1m / 5w; graduate full-time 709m / 599w, part-time 940m / 1,371w.

Characteristics of Student Body: *Ethnic/racial makeup:* number of Black non-Hispanic: 551; American Indian or Alaska Native: 95; Asian or Pacific Islander: 252; Hispanic: 461; White non-Hispanic: 16,856; unknown: 653. *Age distribution:* 17–21: 58.1%; 22–24: 21.3%; 25–29: 9%; 30–39: 3.8%; 40–49: 3.9%; 50–up: 1.4%.

International Students: 230 undergraduate nonresident aliens enrolled fall 2004. Programs available to aid students whose native language is not English: social, cultural; English as a Second Language. No financial aid specifically designated for international students.

Student Life: On-campus residence halls house 22% of student body. Dormitories for men only constitute 30% of such space, for women only 32%, for both sexes 38%. 1% of student body housed on campus in cooperative facilities; 3% in institutionally controlled living space; 62% in privately owned and operated apartments. 15% of men join and 9% live in fraternities; 15% of women join and 6% live in sororities. Housing available for married students. *Intercollegiate athletics:* men only: baseball, basketball, cross-country, football, golf, track; women only: basketball, cross-country, equestrian, golf, rowing/crew, tennis, track, volleyball. *Special services:* Learning Resources Center, medical services.

Student radio: Radio station KSDB-FM broadcasts 40 hours per week. *Surrounding community:* Manhattan population 35,000. Kansas City, 110 miles from campus, is nearest metropolitan area. Served by airport 5 miles from campus.

Publications: Participant with other universities under State Board of Regents in sponsoring Regents Press of Kansas.

Library Collections: 3,478,500 volumes. Online catalog. Access to 19,445 serials (paper, microform, electronic). Students have access to online information retrieval systems and the Internet.

Most important holdings include Carolus Linnaeus Collection; Robert Graves Collection; pre-1900 cookery collection.

Buildings and Grounds: Campus area 668 acres.

Chief Executive Officer: Dr. Jon Wefald, President.

Undergraduates address admission inquiries to Larry Moeder, Director of Admissions; graduate inquiries to Paul Isaac; veterinary medicine students to Jody Johnson.

College of Arts and Sciences

Degree Programs Offered: *Associate* in art; *baccalaureate, master's* in biochemistry, biology, communications, fine and applied arts, foreign languages, health professions, letters, physical sciences, public affairs and services, social sciences, interdisciplinary studies; *doctorate* in biochemistry, biology, chemistry, computer science, economics, English, history, mathematics, physics, psychology, sociology, statistics.

Admission: In addition to general requirements, 1 unit algebra (geometry may be substituted for some programs); additional requirements for some programs.

Distinctive Educational Programs: *For undergraduates:* Cooperative baccalaureate in physical therapy with School of Therapy of Mayo Foundation. Cooperative program for teacher certification with College of Education. Joint baccalaureate and master's degree in economics. Preprofessional programs in medical technology (in cooperation with affiliated institutions) and veterinary medicine. Summer reading program for credit. *Other distinctive programs:* Vascular plant and mycological herbarium and several research facilities in physical science area.

College of Agriculture

Degree Programs Offered: *Baccalaureate, master's, doctorate.*

Admission: In addition to general requirements, 1–4 units algebra, 1 geometry.

Degree Requirements: Prescribed curriculum.

Distinctive Educational Programs: *For undergraduates:* Senior internship in horticultural therapy with psychiatric hospitals, rehabilitation centers, Veterans Administration hospitals, correctional agencies, geriatric and retirement centers, and community-based agencies. Dual-degree program in business administration with College of Business Administration. Joint program for baccalaureate in agriculture and master's in business administration with College of Business Administration. Preprofessional programs in forestry and veterinary medicine. Honors program. 2-year technical program in retail floriculture. *Other distinctive programs:* Experimental work available on 4,000 acres near campus. Feed and flour mills, bakery, greenhouses, and hotbeds on campus.

College of Business Administration

Degree Programs Offered: *Associate* in accounting; *baccalaureate* in accounting, business administration and management, finance, marketing; *master's* in accounting, business (general).

Admission: In addition to general requirements, 1–4 units algebra, 1 geometry. For graduate programs GMAT.

Degree Requirements: Core requirements.

Distinctive Educational Programs: *For undergraduates:* Internships. Dual-degree program in business administration and any nonbusiness field. Cooperative program with the division of continuing education leading to associate degree for military personnel.

College of Education

Degree Programs Offered: *Baccalaureate* in elementary education; secondary education in agriculture and natural resources, biological sciences, communications, engineering, fine and applied arts, foreign languages, health professions, home economics, letters, mathematics, physical sciences, social sciences; *master's* in administration, agriculture and natural resources, continuing education, elementary education, home economics, occupational education, second-

ary education, special education; *doctorate* in administration and foundations, adult and occupational education, curriculum and instructive education.

Admission: Students enter as juniors after completing liberal arts curriculum including 2 semesters of English composition and oral communication (2.0 GPA), and other courses varying with teaching field. 2.2 GPA in all courses taken in residence, 2.5 in all teaching-field work completed in residence.

Distinctive Educational Programs: Center for Extended Services addressing problems common to schools in Kansas. Instructional media center developing teaching aids. Center for Rural Education and Small Schools. Center for Economic Education, Center for Community Education.

College of Engineering

Degree Programs Offered: *Baccalaureate* in agricultural, architectural, chemical, civil engineering; construction science; electrical engineering; engineering technology; industrial, mechanical, nuclear engineering; *master's* in agricultural, chemical, civil, electrical, industrial, mechanical, nuclear engineering; *doctorate* in agricultural, bioenvironmental, chemical, civil, electrical engineering; energy processes; industrial, mechanical engineering; information processing; materials science; nuclear engineering; systems engineering.

Admission: In addition to general requirements, 2 units algebra, 1 geometry, 1–4 trigonometry.

Distinctive Educational Programs: *For undergraduates:* Dual-degree program in chemical engineering with Pittsburg State University. Joint programs in engineering with colleges of Business Administration, Arts and Sciences, Architecture. Combined baccalaureate and master's degrees in engineering. 5-year cooperative education program. *Other distinctive programs:* Institute for Environmental Research. Institute for Systems Design and Optimization. Center for Energy Studies. Center for Transportation Research and Training. Institute for Computational Research in Engineering. Nuclear Engineering Shielding Facility. Nuclear Reactor Facility.

College of Human Ecology

Degree Programs Offered: *Baccalaureate, master's, doctorate* in clothing, textiles, and interior design; dietetics, restaurant and institutional management; family and child development, family economics, food and nutrition, human ecology.

Admission: In addition to general requirements, 2 units algebra or 1 algebra and 1 geometry.

Distinctive Educational Programs: *For undergraduates:* Dual-degree program in consumer affairs and social work; in family and child development and social work, both with College of Arts and Sciences. Dual-degree program in liberal arts with Kansas Independent Colleges.

College of Architecture and Design

Degree Programs Offered: *Baccalaureate* in architecture, interior architecture, landscape architecture; *master's* in architecture; city/urban, community and regional planning; landscape architecture.

Admission: In addition to general requirements, 2 units algebra, 1 geometry, 4 trigonometry; completion of 2-year pre-design professions program offered through the college, and including courses in art history, concepts of structure, mathematics, oral communication, physics, theory of environmental design, Western civilizations.

Distinctive Educational Programs: Research at Center for Regional and Community Planning.

College of Veterinary Medicine

Degree Programs Offered: *Master's* in pathology (human and animal), physiology (human and animal), vet clinical sciences; *doctorate* in pathology (human and animal), physiology (human and animal); *first-professional* in veterinary medicine.

Admission: In addition to general requirements, 71 semester hours college credit in prescribed preveterinary curriculum; proof of secondary school units required for preveterinary program, including 1–4 units algebra, 1 geometry. Nonresidents from states having colleges of veterinary medicine will not be considered.

Distinctive Educational Programs: Students entering without baccalaureates may be awarded baccalaureate degree upon completion of first 2 years of the curriculum in veterinary medicine. Clinical sciences facility for animal treatment and student instruction. Library consisting of 17,000 volumes on veterinary medicine and allied fields.

Kansas State University—Salina, College of Technology and Aviation

2409 Scanlan Avenue
Salina, Kansas 67401
Tel: (913) 536-2560

Degree Programs Offered: *Associate in Applied Science; Associate of Technology; Bachelor of Science in Engineering Technology.*

Degree Requirements: Associate degree by specific programming, 66–69 credit hours. Bachelor of Science degree by specific programming, 126–128 credit hours.

Kansas Wesleyan University

100 East Claflin
Salina, Kansas 67401-6146
Tel: (785) 827-5541 **E-mail:** admissions@kwu.edu
Fax: (785) 827-0927 **Internet:** www.kwu.edu

Institution Description: Kansas Wesleyan University is a private institution affiliated with the United Methodist Church. *Enrollment:* 825. *Degrees awarded:* Associate, baccalaureate.

Member of the consortium Associated Colleges of Central Kansas.

Accreditation: *Regional:* NCA.

History: Chartered as Kansas Wesleyan University 1885; offered first instruction at postsecondary level 1886; awarded first degree (baccalaureate) 1887; adopted present name 1969.

Institutional Structure: *Governing board:* Board of Trustees. Representation: 30 trustees, 3 trustees emeriti, 1 honorary trustee. 30 voting. *Composition of institution:* Academic affairs headed by vice president and dean of faculty. Management/business/finances directed by business manager. Full-time instructional faculty 32.

Calendar: Semesters (4-1-4 plan). Academic year late Aug. to late May. Freshmen admitted Sept., June. Degrees conferred and formal commencement May. Summer session of 4 terms from early June to late July.

Characteristics of Freshmen: 9% (12 students) submitted SAT scores; 91% (118 students) submitted ACT scores. *25th percentile:* SAT Verbal 400, SAT Math 480; ACT Composite 19, ACT English 18, ACT Math 19. *75th percentile:* SAT Verbal 500, SAT Math 510; ACT Composite 23, ACT English 24, ACT Math 24.

Admission: Rolling admissions plan. *Requirements:* Either graduation from accredited secondary school or GED. Minimum GPA 2.5; ACT 18 and over. *For transfer students:* From 4- and 2-year accredited institutions maximum transfer credit limited only by residence requirement; correspondence/extension students 30 semester hours.

College credit and advanced placement for postsecondary-level work completed in secondary school. College credit for extrainstitutional learning (life experience) on basis of portfolio and faculty assessments. Tutoring available.

Degree Requirements: *For all associate degrees:* 62 semester hours; 48 hours in residence. *For all baccalaureate degrees:* 123 hours; for bachelor of arts, 24 of last 33 hours in residence, for bachelor of science, 48 of last 62 hours in residence. *For all degrees:* 2.0 GPA; 3 credit hours physical education courses; core curriculum; exit competency examinations in writing and mathematics.

Fulfillment of some degree requirements and exemption from some beginning courses possible by passing departmental examinations, College Board CLEP, AP.

Distinctive Educational Programs: Evening classes. Dual-degree programs in engineering with University of Kansas, Kansas State University, Columbia University (NY); in agricultural economics and agricultural education with Kansas State University. Cooperative baccalaureate program in cytotechnology, medical technology, nursing with affiliated hospitals. Interdisciplinary program in environmental studies in cooperation with Land Institute of Salina. Facilities and programs for independent research, including individual majors, independent study. Study abroad available through consortium. Cross-registration through consortium.

Degrees Conferred: 27 *associate;* 122 *baccalaureate.* Bachelor's degrees awarded in top five disciplines: business, management, marketing, and related support services 35; protective services/public administration 23; education 17; parks and recreation 10; biological/biomedical sciences 9. 20 *master's:* business, management, marketing, and related support services 20.

Fees and Other Expenses: *Full-time tuition per academic year 2005–06:* $15,800. *Room and board per academic year:* $5,600. *Books and supplies:* $650.

Financial Aid: Aid from institutionally generated funds is provided on the basis of academic merit, financial need, other criteria. Institution has a Program Participation Agreement with the U.S. Department of Education for eligible students to receive Pell Grants and other federal aid.

Financial aid to full-time, first-time undergraduate students: need-based scholarships/grants totaling $3,305,000, self-help $2,326,000; non-need-based scholarships/grants totaling $2,517,000, self-help $2,193,000. *Graduate aid:* 29 students received federal and state-funded loans totaling $178.000.

Departments and Teaching Staff: *Total instructional faculty:* 32. Student-to-faculty ratio: 15:1.

Enrollment: Total enrollment 825. Undergraduate full-time 235 men / 352 women, part-time 47m / 127w; graduate full-time 8m / 4w, part-time 24m / 28w.

Characteristics of Student Body: *Ethnic/racial makeup:* number of Black non-Hispanic: 39; American Indian or Alaska Native: 6; Asian or Pacific Islander: 8; Hispanic: 28; White non-Hispanic: 674. *Age distribution:* number under 18: 16; 18–19: 217; 20–21: 207; 22–24: 115; 25–29: 56; 30–34: 44; 35–39: 31; 40–49: 61; 50–64: 12; 65 and over: 2.

International Students: 34 nonresident aliens enrolled fall 2004. Programs available to aid students whose native language is not English: English as a Second Language. Unlimited scholarships available annually to qualifying international students.

Student Life: On-campus residence halls and apartments house 50% of student body. Housing available for married students. *Intercollegiate athletics:* men only: baseball, basketball, cross-country, football, golf, soccer, softball, track; women only: basketball, cross-country, golf, soccer, tennis, track, volleyball. *Special regulations:* Cars permitted without restrictions. *Special services:* Learning Resources Center. *Student publications:* Newspaper, yearbook. *Surrounding community:* Salina population 45,000. Wichita, 89 miles from campus, is nearest metropolitan area. Served by airport 6 miles from campus.

Library Collections: 100,000 volumes. 38,000 government documents; 1,000 microforms; 420 current periodical subscriptions. Online catalog. Students have access to online information retrieval services and the Internet.

Most important special collection is the Methodist Church Collection.

Buildings and Grounds: Campus area 28 acres.

Chief Executive Officer: Dr. Philip P. Kerstetter, President.

Address admission inquiries to James Allen, Director of Admissions.

Manhattan Christian College

1415 Anderson Avenue
Manhattan, Kansas 66502-4081
Tel: (785) 539-3571 **E-mail:** admit@mccks.edu
Fax: (785) 539-0832 **Internet:** www.mccks.edu

Institution Description: Manhattan Christian College is a private Bible college. *Enrollment:* 331. *Degrees awarded:* Associate, baccalaureate.

Accreditation: *Regional:* NCA. *National:* ABHE.

Calendar: Semesters. Academic year Aug. to May.

Characteristics of Freshmen: 79% of applicants admitted. 51% of applicants admitted and enrolled.

Average secondary school rank of freshmen men 72nd percentile, women 74th percentile, class 73rd percentile. Mean ACT Composite score 21.4.

37.5% of entering freshmen expected to graduate within 5 years. 65% of freshmen from Kansas. Freshmen from 12 states.

Admission: *Requirements:* Graduation from accredited secondary school or equivalent. *Entrance tests:* ACT.

Degree Requirements: Completion of prescribed courses; Bible curriculum.

Degrees Conferred: 71 *baccalaureate:* business/marketing 25; education 6; philosophy/religion/theology 40.

Fees and Other Expenses: *Full-time tuition per academic year 2004–05:* $8,826. *Room and board per academic year:* $4,482.

Financial Aid: Aid from institutionally generated funds is provided on the basis of academic merit, financial need, other criteria. Institution has a Program Participation Agreement with the U.S. Department of Education for eligible students to receive Pell Grants and other federal aid.

Financial aid to full-time, first-time undergraduate students: need-based scholarships/grants totaling $882,466, self-help $803,229; non-need-based scholarships/grants totaling $470,210, self-help $325,271, parent loans $111,776, tuition waivers $30,068.

Departments and Teaching Staff: *Professors* 1, *associate professors* 5, *assistant professors* 4, *part-time faculty* 20. *Total instructional faculty:* 30 (full-time 10, part-time 20; women 9, men 21; members of minority groups 2). Total faculty with doctorate, first-professional, or other terminal degree: 7. Student-to-faculty ratio: 15:1.

Enrollment: Total enrollment 331. Full-time 133 men / 129 women; part-time 26m / 43w. *Transfer students:* in-state 15; from out-of-state 7.

Characteristics of Student Body: *Ethnic/racial makeup:* number of Black non-Hispanic: 12; Asian or Pacific Islander: 1; Hispanic: 5; White non-Hispanic: 306; unknown: 6. *Age distribution:* under 18: 1; 18–19: 112; 20–21: 114; 22–24: 51; 25–29: 13; 30–34: 10; 35–39: 8; 40–49: 17; 50–64: 5.

International Students: 1 nonresident alien enrolled fall 2004. No programs to aid students whose native language is not English. No scholarships specifically designated for international students.

Student Life: Residence hall facilities available for single men and women; housing available for married students.

Library Collections: 43,250 volumes. 1,805 microform titles; 195 audiovisual materials; 202 current periodical subscriptions. Online and card catalogs. 1,886 recordings; 30 CD-ROMs. 2 computer work stations. Access to online information retrieval systems and the Internet. Total 2004–05 budget for books and materials: $17,000.

Most important special collections include Commentaries; Christian Education; Video Collection.

Chief Executive Officer: Dr. Randall L. Ingmire, President.

Address admission inquiries to Paul Schmidt, Director of Admissions.

McPherson College

1600 East Euclid Street
McPherson, Kansas 67460-1402
Tel: (620) 241-0731   **E-mail:** admiss@mcpherson.edu
Fax: (620) 241-8443   **Internet:** www.mcpherson.edu

Institution Description: McPherson College is a private college affiliated with the Church of the Brethren. *Enrollment:* 480. *Degrees awarded:* Associate, baccalaureate.

Member of Associated Colleges of Central Kansas and Small College Consortium.

Accreditation: *Regional:* NCA.

History: Established as McPherson College and Industrial Institute 1887; offered first instruction at postsecondary level 1890; awarded first degree (baccalaureate) 1894; adopted present name and chartered 1898. *See* Elmer LeRoy Craik, *History of the Church of the Brethren in Kansas* (McPherson: Privately printed, 1922) for further information.

Institutional Structure: *Governing board:* McPherson College Board of Trustees. Representation: 35 trustees, including president of the college. 1 ex officio. All voting. *Composition of institution:* Administrators: President, 3 Vice Presidents. Academic affairs headed by vice president for academic services. Management/business/finances directed by Vice President for Financial Services. Full-time instructional faculty 39. Academic governance body, the faculty, meets an average of 8 times per year.

Calendar: Semesters. Academic year early Sept. to late May. Freshman admitted Sept., Jan., Feb., June. Degrees conferred and formal commencement May.

Characteristics of Freshmen: 855 applicants (362 men, 193 women). 76% of applicants admitted. 28.1% of admitted applicants enrolled full-time.

16% (21 students) submitted SAT scores; 86% (101 students) submitted ACT scores. *25th percentile:* SAT I Verbal 440, SAT I Math 440; ACT Composite 19, ACT English 16, ACT Math 17. *75th percentile:* SAT I Verbal 540, SAT I Math 530; ACT Composite 23, ACT English 22, ACT Math 24.

53% of entering freshmen expected to graduate within 5 years. 46% of freshmen from Kansas. Freshmen from 17 states and 2 foreign countries.

Admission: Rolling admissions plan. For fall acceptance, apply as early as June of previous year, but not later than Aug. of year of enrollment. *Requirements:* Either graduation from secondary school or GED. Minimum GPA 2.0. Lowest acceptable secondary school class standing 50th percentile. *Entrance tests:* ACT composite. For foreign students TOEFL. *For transfer students:* 2.0 minimum GPA; from 4-year accredited institution 94 hours maximum transfer credit; from 2-year accredited institution 62 hours.

College credit and advanced placement for postsecondary-level work completed in secondary school and for extrainstitutional learning (life experience) on basis of ACE *2006 Guide to the Evaluation of Educational Experiences in the Armed Services.* Tutoring available. Remedial courses offered during regular academic year; credit given.

Degree Requirements: *For all associate degrees:* 62 credit hours. *For all baccalaureate degrees:* 124 credit hours. *For all degrees:* 2.0 GPA; 32 hours in residence; distribution requirements; attendance at convocations; demonstrated proficiency in English.

Fulfillment of some degree requirements and exemption from some beginning courses possible by passing departmental examinations, College Board CLEP,

APP. *Grading system:* A–F; pass-fail; withdraw (carries time limit); incomplete (carries time limit).

Distinctive Educational Programs: Work-experience programs, including cooperative education, internships, field experiences. Flexible meeting places and schedules, including off-campus center (at Hutchison, less than 30 miles away from main institution) and evening classes. Dual-degree programs in agriculture, home economics with Kansas State University. Associate of Technology degree in antique automobile restoration. Campus-wide computer networking with 1 computer for every 10 students. Junior year student teaching. Special facilities for using telecommunications in the classroom. Interdisciplinary programs in agricultural economics-agribusiness, anthropology, audiovisual communications, environmental science, interior design, Latin American studies. Preprofessional program in nursing. Facilities and programs for independent research, including individual majors, independent study, research, and reading courses. Study abroad at Dalion Institute in China; in Cheltenham, England; Strasbourg, France; Marburg, West Germany through Brethren Colleges Abroad; in Colombia, Ethiopia, Kenya through Council of Mennonite Colleges; elsewhere through ACCK. Off-campus study at various locations in the U.S. through ACCK; inner-city internships for teaching students. *Other distinctive programs:* Degree-granting evening division; credit and noncredit continuing education programs.

Degrees Conferred: 18 *associate;* 48 *baccalaureate.* Bachelor's degrees awarded in top five disciplines: business, management, marketing, and related support services 10; education 8; visual and performing arts 4; social sciences 4; psychology 4.

Fees and Other Expenses: *Full-time tuition per academic year 2004–05:* $14,645. *Books and supplies:* $750. *Room and board per academic year:* $5,620.

Financial Aid: Aid from institutionally generated funds is provided on the basis of academic merit, financial need. Institution has a Program Participation Agreement with the U.S. Department of Education for eligible students to receive Pell Grants and other federal aid.

Financial aid to full-time, first-time undergraduate students: 44% received federal grants averaging $3,308; 28% state/local grants averaging $3,014; 98% institutional grants averaging $7,017; 84% loans averaging $4,416.

Departments and Teaching Staff: Art *professors* 0, *associate professors* 0, *assistant professors* 2, *instructors* 0; *part-time teachers* 0; business/accounting 1, 0, 2, 0, 1; music 2, 0, 2, 0, 3; psychology 0, 2, 0, 0, 0; sociology 0, 0, 2, 0, 0; mathematics/computer science 0, 3, 0, 0, 1; foreign languages 1, 0, 1, 0, 0; English 0, 1, 1, 0, 2; technology 1, 0, 2, 1, 0; agriculture 0, 1, 0, 0, 0; biology 0, 0, 2, 0, 0; physical education 0, 3, 2, 0, 0; chemistry and physical science 1, 1, 0, 0, 0; education 0, 1, 1, 0, 0; history 1, 0, 0, 0, 0; philosophy/religion 1, 0, 0, 0, 0; speech 0, 1, 0, 0, 0.

Total instructional faculty: 46. Degrees held by full-time faculty: doctorate 68%, master's 100%. 68% hold terminal degrees.

Enrollment: Total enrollment 480 (men 59.6%, women 40.4%).

Characteristics of Student Body: *Ethnic/racial makeup:* Black non-Hispanic: 8.6%; American Indian or Alaska Native: .2%; Asian or Pacific Islander: .2%; Hispanic: 5.2%; White non-Hispanic: 83.3%; unknown: .6%. *Age distribution:* 17–21: 55%; 22–24: 12%; 25–29: 4%; 30–34: 9%; 35–39: 7%; 40–49: 9%; 50–59: 3%; 60–up: 1%.

International Students: 7 nonresident aliens enrolled 2004. Students from Europe, Asia, Africa. No programs available to aid students whose native language is not English. No financial aid specifically designated for international students.

Student Life: On-campus residence halls house 70% of student body. Residence halls for men constitute 44% of such space, for women 41%, for both sexes 15%. 10% of student body live off-campus in married student housing. *Intercollegiate athletics:* men only: basketball, football, tennis, track; women only: basketball, tennis, track, volleyball; both sexes: cross-country, golf. *Special regulations:* Registered cars permitted without restrictions. Quiet hours from 7pm to 7am Sun.–Thurs. Residence hall visitation hours vary according to residence halls. *Special services:* Learning Resources Center, medical services. *Student publications: Spectator,* a newspaper. *Surrounding community:* McPherson population 12,000. Wichita, 50 miles from campus, is nearest metropolitan area. Served by airport 3 miles from campus.

Library Collections: 90,000 volumes. 70,200 microforms; 20,000 audiovisual materials; 455 current periodical subscriptions. Online catalog. Students have access to online information retrieval services.

Most important holdings include Church of the Brethren materials and historical materials; Kansas Collection (several thousand official records of the city and county of McPherson).

Buildings and Grounds: Campus area 22 acres.

Chief Executive Officer: Ronald D. Hovis, President.

Address admission inquiries to Carol Williams, Director of Admissions.

MidAmerica Nazarene College

2030 East College Way
Olathe, Kansas 66062-1899
Tel: (913) 782-3750   **E-mail:** admissions@mnu.edu
Fax: (913) 791-3290   **Internet:** www.mnu.edu

Institution Description: MidAmerica Nazarene College is a private college affiliated with the International Church of the Nazarene. *Enrollment:* 1,985. *Degrees awarded:* Associate, baccalaureate, master's.

Member of Eight College Consortium, Small College Consortium.

Accreditation: *Regional:* NCA.

History: Established and chartered 1966; offered first instruction at postsecondary level 1968; first degree (baccalaureate) awarded 1972.

Institutional Structure: *Governing board:* Board of Trustees. Extrainstitutional representation: 33 trustees; institutional representation: 1 administrator. 34 voting. *Composition of institution:* Administrators 17 men / 4 women (at dean's level and above, 19% are women). Academic affairs headed by academic dean. Management/business/finances directed by business manager. Academic governance body, the faculty, meets an average of 9 times per year.

Calendar: Semesters. Academic year Aug. to May. Freshmen admitted Sept., Jan., Feb., May. Degrees conferred and formal commencement May.

Characteristics of Freshmen: 100% of applicants accepted. 63% of accepted applicants enrolled.

9% of students submitted SAT scores; 92% submitted ACT scores. *25th percentile:* SAT Verbal 455, SAT Math 440; ACT Composite 19, ACT English 18, ACT Math 17. *75th percentile:* SAT Verbal 610, SAT Math 610; ACT Composite 26, ACT English 28, ACT Math 26.

48% of freshmen from Kansas. Freshmen from 21 states.

Admission: Rolling admissions plan. For fall acceptance, apply as early as Sept. of previous year, but not later than Sept. of year of enrollment. Apply at any time for early decision; need not limit application to Mid-America Nazarene. Early acceptance available. *Requirements:* Either graduation from accredited secondary school with 15 units, or GED. 4 English, 3 mathematics, 3 science, 3 social studies, 1 foreign language (recommended). Open enrollment for nondegree students. *Entrance tests:* ACT composite score of 12 required. *For transfer students:* From 2-year accredited institution 1 to 23 hours with minimum GPA 1.50; with 24 to 55 hours, minimum GPA 2.0.

College credit for postsecondary-level work completed in secondary school and for extrainstitutional learning on basis of ACE *2006 Guide to the Evaluation of Educational Experiences in the Armed Services* and faculty assessment. Tutoring available. Developmental courses offered during regular academic year; credit given.

Degree Requirements: *For all associate degrees:* 63 semester hours. *For all baccalaureate degrees:* 126 semester hours; exit competency examinations in writing and comprehensives in individual fields of study; 1 physical activity course. *For all undergraduate degrees:* 2.0 GPA; 2 terms in residence; weekly chapel attendance.

Fulfillment of some degree requirements possible by passing College Board CLEP. *Grading system:* A–F; pass-no credit; withdraw (does not affect GPA).

Distinctive Educational Programs: Evening classes. Accelerated degree programs. Joint baccalaureate degree program in religion with European Bible College, Switzerland. Other individually and institutionally arranged study-abroad programs. Travel- and experience-based credit. Directed and independent study available.

ROTC: Air Force, Army.

Degrees Conferred: 1 *associate*; 388 *baccalaureate* (B); 217 *master's* (M): agriculture 3 (B); biological/life sciences 9 (B); business/marketing 209 (B), 59 (M); communications/communication technologies 8 (B); computer and information sciences 10 (B); education 36 (B), 144 (M); English 5 (B); foreign languages and literature 2 (B); health professions and related sciences 14 (B); mathematics 3 (B); parks and recreation 10 (B); philosophy/religion/theology 20 (B); physical sciences 2 (B); psychology 34 (B), 14 (M); social sciences and history 19 (B); visual and performing arts 4 (B).

Fees and Other Expenses: *Full-time tuition per academic year 2005–06:* $13,830 undergraduate; graduate charges vary by program. *Required fees:* $1,000. *Room and board per academic year:* $5,828.

Financial Aid: Aid from institutionally generated funds is provided on the basis of academic merit, financial need, athletic ability, other criteria. Institution has a Program Participation Agreement with the U.S. Department of Education for eligible students to receive Pell Grants and other federal aid.

Financial aid to full-time, first-time undergraduate students: need-based scholarships/grants totaling $4,147,713, self-help $4,503,994, parent loans $710,209, tuition waivers $393,469, athletic awards $1,063,640; non-need-based scholarships/grants totaling $744,182, self-help $4,017,565, parent loans

$125,172, tuition waivers $98,816, athletic awards $322,232. *Graduate aid:* 257 students received federal and state-funded loans totaling $2,708,145 (ranging $100 to $18,500).

Departments and Teaching Staff: *Professors 26 associate professors 21, assistant professors 21, instructors 66, part-time faculty 113. Total instructional faculty:* 172 (full-time 76, part-time 96; women 72, men 100). Total faculty with doctorate, first-professional, or other terminal degree: 94. Student-to-faculty ratio: 19:1. *Faculty development:* 3 faculty members awarded sabbaticals 2004–05.

Enrollment: Total enrollment 1,985. Undergraduate full-time 630 men / 690 women, part-time 72m / 74w; graduate full-time 76m / 99w, part-time 68m / 276w.

Characteristics of Student Body: *Ethnic/racial makeup:* number of Black non-Hispanic: 105; American Indian or Alaska Native: 16; Asian or Pacific Islander: 15; Hispanic: 45; White non-Hispanic: 1,238; unknown: 22. *Age distribution:* number under 18: 7; 18–19: 417; 20–21: 448; 22–24: 214; 25–29: 130; 30–34: 69; 35–39: 63; 40–49: 100; 50–64: 18.

International Students: 34 nonresident aliens enrolled fall 2004. No programs available to aid students whose native language is not English. No financial aid specifically designated for international students.

Student Life: On-campus residence halls house 71% of student body. Dormitories for men only constitute 49% of such space, for women only 51%. *Intercollegiate athletics:* men only: baseball, basketball, cross-country, football, golf, tennis, track; women only: basketball, cross-country, tennis, track, volleyball. *Special regulations:* Cars permitted in designated areas only. Curfews from 11pm to 6am. Quiet hours from 7pm to 10pm. *Special services:* Learning Resources Center, medical services. *Student publications: Conestoga,* a yearbook; *Trailblazer,* a biweekly newspaper. *Surrounding community:* Olathe population 38,000. Kansas City (MO), 19 miles from campus, is nearest metropolitan area.

Publications: Sources of information about MidAmerica include *Accent Magazine,* distributed to alumni and friends of the college.

Library Collections: 120,134 volumes including bound books, serial backfiles, electronic documents, and government documents not in separate collections. Online catalog. Current serial subscriptions: 225 paper, 800 electronic. 1,200 recordings; 227 compact discs; 495 CD-ROMs. Students have access to the Internet at no charge. Total budget for books, periodicals, audiovisual materials, microforms 2004–05: $111,000.

Most important special collections include Lantz Books on Holiness; Heritage Collection; Americana Collection.

Buildings and Grounds: Campus area 105 acres.

Chief Executive Officer: Dr. Richard L. Spindle, President.

Address admission inquiries to Dennis Troyer, Director of Admissions.

Newman University

3100 McCormick Avenue
Wichita, Kansas 67213-2097
Tel: (316) 942-4291   **E-mail:** admissions@newman.edu
Fax: (316) 942-4483   **Internet:** www.newman.edu

Institution Description: Newman University, formerly Newman College, is a private regional and international Catholic university. *Enrollment:* 2,179. *Degrees awarded:* Associate, baccalaureate, master's.

Accreditation: *Regional:* NCA.

History: Established as Sacred Heart Junior College, a college for women, and offered first instruction at postsecondary level 1933; awarded first degree (associate) 1935; added upper division curricula and changed name to Sacred Heart College 1952; incorporated 1958; became coeducational 1965; became Kansas Newman College in 1973 and Newman College in 1998; achieved university status and adopted present name 2002.

Institutional Structure: *Governing board:* Newman College Board of Directors. Extrainstitutional representation: 22 trustees; institutional representation: 1 administrator. All voting. *Composition of institution:* Administrators 17 men / 12 women. Academic affairs headed by vice president for academic affairs. Management/business/finances directed by vice president for finance and administration. Full-time instructional faculty 74. Academic governance body, the faculty, meets an average of 8 times per year.

Calendar: Semesters. Academic year Aug. to May. Freshmen admitted Aug., Jan., June. Degrees conferred and formal commencement Dec. and May. Summer session of 4-week, 5-week, 8-week terms from mid-May to mid-Aug.

Characteristics of Freshmen: 99% of applicants admitted. 47% of applicants admitted and enrolled.

12% (27 students) submitted SAT scores; 68% (150 students) submitted ACT scores. *25th percentile:* SAT Verbal 440, SAT Math 400; ACT Composite 19,

ACT English 18, ACT Math 18. *75th percentile*: SAT Verbal 560, SAT Math 590; ACT Composite 25, ACT English 26, ACT Math 25.

47% of entering freshmen expected to graduate within 5 years. 54% of freshmen from Kansas. Freshmen from 12 states and 7 foreign countries.

Admission: Rolling admissions plan. For fall acceptance, apply no later than Aug. 15. Early decision and early acceptance available. *Requirements:* Either graduation from accredited secondary school or GED. Minimum GPA 2.0. *Entrance tests:* ACT Composite. *For transfer students:* 2.0 minimum GPA. 90 hours maximum transfer credit; from 2-year accredited institution 62 hours.

College credit for postsecondary-level work completed in secondary school and for extrainstitutional learning on basis of ACE *2006 Guide to the Evaluation of Educational Experiences in the Armed Services* and faculty assessment. Tutoring available. Developmental courses offered during regular academic year; credit given.

Degree Requirements: *For all associate degrees:* 62 credit hours. *For all baccalaureate degrees:* 124 credit hours. *For all undergraduate degrees:* 2.0 GPA; 30 semester in residence. *For all master's degrees:* 3.0 GPA. Fulfillment of some degree requirements possible by passing departmental examinations or College Board CLEP. *Grading system:* A–F; pass/fail; withdraw (carries time limit).

Distinctive Educational Programs: Work-experience programs. Flexible meeting places and schedules, including off-campus centers and evening classes. Cross-registration with Friends University.

Degrees Conferred: 45 *associate;* 260 *baccalaureate* (B), 140 *master's* (M): biological/life sciences 14 (B); business/marketing 70 (B), 72 (M); communications/communication technologies 4 (B); computer and information sciences 5 (B); education 77 (B), 31 (M); health professions and related sciences 55 (B), 15 (M); liberal arts/general studies 1 (B); mathematics 1 (B); philosophy/religion/theology 12 (B); physical sciences 3 (B); protective services/public administration 22 (M); psychology 11 (B); social sciences and history 5 (B); visual and performing arts 1 (B).

Fees and Other Expenses: *Full-time tuition per academic year 2004–05:* $14,650 undergraduate; contact the university for graduate tuition/fees. *Required fees:* $6 per credit hour. *Room and board per academic year:* $5,060.

Financial Aid: Aid from institutionally generated funds is provided on the basis of academic merit, financial need, athletic ability, other criteria. Institution has a Program Participation Agreement with the U.S. Department of Education for eligible students to receive Pell Grants and other federal aid.

Financial aid to full-time, first-time undergraduate students: need-based scholarships/grants totaling $2,205,000, self-help $4,496,169; non-need-based scholarships/grants totaling $3,304,835, self-help $5,193,949, parent loans $499,019, tuition waivers $337,397, athletic awards $928,291. *Graduate aid:* 188 students received federal and state-funded loans totaling $2,158,368 ($135 to $18,500).

Departments and Teaching Staff: *Total instructional faculty:* 80 (full-time 74, part-time 6; women 39, men 41; members of minority groups 2). Total faculty with doctorate, first-professional, or other terminal degree: 46. Student-to-faculty ratio: 17:1.

Enrollment: Total enrollment 2,179. Undergraduate full-time 440 men / 163 women, part-time 255m / 385w; graduate full-time 20m / 48w, part-time 71m / 187w. *Transfer students:* in-state 279; from out-of-state 43.

Characteristics of Student Body: *Ethnic/racial makeup:* number of Black non-Hispanic: 117; American Indian or Alaska Native: 34; Asian or Pacific Islander: 58; Hispanic: 153; White non-Hispanic: 1,673; unknown: 13. *Age distribution:* number 18–19: 343; 20–21: 301; 22–24: 256; 25–29: 169; 30–34: 137; 35–39: 66; 40–49: 139; 50–64: 80; 65 and over: 9.

International Students: 131 nonresident aliens enrolled fall 2004. 16 students from Europe, 70 Asia, 3 Central and South America, 37 Africa, 1 Canada, 1 New Zealand, 3 other. No programs to aid students whose native language is not English. Financial aid specifically designated for international students: 107 undergraduate scholarships were awarded in 2004–05 totaling $205,800.

Student Life: On-campus residence halls house 11% of student body. *Intercollegiate athletics:* men only: baseball, basketball, bowling, cross-country, golf, soccer; tennis, wrestling, volleyball; women only: basketball, bowling, cross-country, golf, soccer, softball, tennis, volleyball. *Special regulations:* Cars permitted without restriction. *Special services:* Learning Resources Center. *Student publications: Vantage,* a weekly newspaper. *Surrounding community:* Wichita population 300,000. Served by mass transit bus system; airport 5 miles from campus.

Publications: Sources of information about Newman University include the university catalog and *Viewbook.*

Library Collections: 108,765 volumes including bound books, serial backfiles, electronic documents, and government documents not in separate collections. Online catalog. Current serial subscriptions: 166 paper, 43 microform, 7,000 electronic. 1,688 recordings; 33 compact discs; 23 CD-ROMs. 11 computer work stations. Students have access to the Internet at no charge.

Most important special collections include the John Henry Cardinal Newman Collection; Wichita Blues Society Collection.

Buildings and Grounds: Campus area 61 acres. *New buildings:* De Mattias Fine Arts completed 2000; Mabee Dining Center 2000; Beata Residence Hall 2000.

Chief Executive Officer: Dr. Aidan Donleavy, President.

Address admission inquiries to Director of Admissions.

Ottawa University

1001 South Cedar Street
Ottawa, Kansas 66067-3399

Tel: (785) 242-5200   **E-mail:** admiss@ottawa.edu
Fax: (785) 229-1007   **Internet:** www.ottawa.edu

Institution Description: Ottawa University is a private institution affiliated with the American Baptist Church. *Enrollment:* 447. *Degrees awarded:* Baccalaureate.

Accreditation: *Regional:* NCA.

History: Established and chartered 1865; offered first instruction at postsecondary level 1872; awarded first degree (baccalaureate) 1886. *See* Haworth B. Smith, *Ottawa University: Its History and Its Spirit* (Ottawa: Ottawa University, 1957) for further information.

Institutional Structure: *Governing board:* Ottawa University Board of Trustees. Extrainstitutional representation: 36 trustees; institutional representation: president of the college. 1 ex officio. All voting. *Composition of institution:* Administrators 5 men / 1 woman. Academic affairs headed by vice president for academic affairs. Management/business/finances directed by business manager. Full-time instructional faculty 46. Academic governance body, Academic Council, meets an average of 18 times per year.

Calendar: Semesters. Academic year Aug. to May. Freshmen admitted Aug., Jan., June, July. Degrees conferred and formal commencement May.

Characteristics of Freshmen: 81% of applicants admitted. 37% of applicants admitted and enrolled.

25th percentile: SAT Verbal 400, SAT Math 420; ACT Composite 18, ACT English 16, ACT Math 16. *75th percentile*: SAT Verbal 510, SAT Math 550; ACT Composite 22, ACT English 21, ACT 24.

26% of entering freshmen expected to graduate within 5 years. 70% of freshmen from Kansas. Freshmen from 9 states and 1 foreign country.

Admission: Rolling admissions plan. Early acceptance available. *Requirements:* Either graduation from accredited secondary school with 10 units which must include 4 in communications or related areas and 6 from among arts, humanities, and behavioral, natural, and social sciences; or GED. Minimum GPA 2.4. *Entrance tests:* College Board SAT or ACT composite. *For transfer students:* 2.0 minimum GPA, 94 semester hours maximum transfer credit.

College credit for postsecondary-level work completed in secondary school and for extrainstitutional learning on basis of ACE *2006 Guide to the Evaluation of Educational Experiences in the Armed Services*; portfolio and faculty assessments. Tutoring available. Developmental courses offered during regular academic year; credit given.

Degree Requirements: 124 credit hours; 2.0 GPA; 2 terms in residence; 2 physical education courses; distribution requirements. Fulfillment of some requirements and exemption from some beginning courses possible by passing College Board CLEP, AP. *Grading system:* A–F; withdraw (carries time limit); incomplete (carries time limit).

Distinctive Educational Programs: Three majors identified as distinctive majors university-wide: business, education, human services. Degree completion sites offer individualized degree plans for all majors. Online programs in health care management and human resources. Partnership with Rio Salada Community College (Phoenix, AZ) offers online police science program. *Other distinctive programs:* Degree completion programs at centers in Overland Park, Kansas; Milwaukee, Wisconsin; Phoenix, Arizona; and 3 locations on the Pacific Rim. Master's degree programs at Overland Park and Phoenix.

Degrees Conferred: 78 *baccalaureate:* biological/life sciences 7; business/marketing 28; communications/communication technologies 6; computer and information sciences 1; education 8; liberal arts/general studies 8; mathematics 4; parks and recreation 6; psychology 2; social sciences and history 9.

Fees and Other Expenses: *Full-time tuition per academic year 2004–05:* $13,850. *Room and board per academic year:* $5,420.

Financial Aid: Aid from institutionally generated funds is provided on the basis of academic merit, financial need, athletic ability, other criteria. Institution has a Program Participation Agreement with the U.S. Department of Education for eligible students to receive Pell Grants and other federal aid.

Financial aid to full-time, first-time undergraduate students: need-based scholarships/grants totaling $3,449,223, self-help $1,691,725, athletic awards

$698,475; non-need-based scholarships/grants totaling $110,162, self-help $881,314.

Departments and Teaching Staff: *Professors* 2, *associate professors* 6, *assistant professors* 5, *instructors* 7, *part-time faculty* 2. *Total instructional faculty:* 22. Student-to-faculty ratio: 16:1.

Enrollment: Total enrollment 447. Undergraduate full-time 231 men / 194 women, part-time 8m / 14w. *Transfer students:* in-state 23; from out-of-state 15.

Characteristics of Student Body: *Ethnic/racial makeup:* number of Black non-Hispanic: 42; American Indian or Alaska Native: 11; Asian or Pacific Islander: 6; Hispanic: 14; White non-Hispanic: 339; unknown: 13. *Age distribution:* number under 4; 18–19: 144; 20–21: 158; 22–24: 97; 25–29: 19; 30–34: 9; 35–39: 8l 40–49: 6; 50–64: 2.

International Students: 19 nonresident aliens enrolled fall 2004. 3 students from Europe, 8 Asia, 6 Africa, 1 Canada, 1 other. Programs available to aid students whose native language is not English: English as a Second Language. No financial aid specifically designated for international students.

Student Life: Residence halls include a men's hall, a women's hall, and a coeducational hall. *Intercollegiate athletics:* men only: baseball, basketball, cross-country, football, soccer, track; women only: basketball, cross-country, soccer, softball, track, volleyball. *Special regulations:* Registered cars permitted without restrictions. *Special services:* Learning Resources Center, medical services. *Student publications, radio: The Campus*, a bimonthly newspaper; *The Ottawan*, a yearbook. Radio station KTJO broadcasts 35 hours per week. *Surrounding community:* Ottawa population 12,000. Kansas City (MO), 45 miles from campus, is nearest metropolitan area.

Library Collections: 79,985 volumes. Online catalog. Current serial subscriptions: paper 169, microform 18,326, via electronic access 204. 428 recordings; 12 compact discs, 35 CD-ROMs. 7 computer work stations. Students have access to the Internet at no charge. Total 2004–05 budget for books, periodicals, audiovisual materials, microforms: $32,000.

Most important holdings include 2,000 rare and scholarly books on Chinese art and ceramics, Native Americans, Baptist history.

Buildings and Grounds: Campus area 69 acres.

Chief Executive Officer: Dr. John E. Neal, President.

Address admission inquiries to Fola Akande, Director of Admissions.

Pittsburg State University

1701 South Broadway
Pittsburg, Kansas 66762
Tel: (620) 235-7000   **E-mail:** psuadmit@pittstate.edu
Fax: (620) 235-4080   **Internet:** www.pittstate.edu

Institution Description: Pittsburg State University (Kansas State College of Pittsburg until 1977) is a state institution. *Enrollment:* 6,537. *Degrees awarded:* Associate, baccalaureate, master's. Certificates also awarded.

Academic offerings subject to approval by campus coordinating body and state board. Budget subject to approval by state governing boards.

Accreditation: *Regional:* NCA. *Professional:* business, counseling, engineering, music, nursing, social work, teacher education

History: Established and chartered as Kansas State Manual Training Normal School, and offered first instruction at postsecondary level 1903; awarded first degree (baccalaureate) 1904; changed name to Kansas State Teachers College of Pittsburg 1925, Kansas State College of Pittsburg 1959; adopted present name 1978.

Institutional Structure: *Governing board:* Board of Regents, State of Kansas. Representation: 9 members (appointed by governor of Kansas). All voting. *Composition of institution:* Administrators 24 men / 11 women. Academic affairs headed by academic vice president. Management/business/finances directed by vice president for business. Full-time instructional faculty 286. Academic governance body, Faculty Senate, meets monthly. *Faculty representation:* Faculty served by collective bargaining agent affiliated with NEA.

Calendar: Semesters. Academic year Aug. to May. Freshmen admitted Aug., Jan., June. Degrees conferred May, Aug., Dec. Formal commencement May, Dec.

Characteristics of Freshmen: 95% of applicants admitted. 95% (825 students) submitted ACT scores. *25th percentile*: ACT Composite 19, ACT English 17, ACT Math 18. *75th percentile*: ACT Composite 24, ACT English 24, ACT Math 24.

41% of entering g freshmen expected to graduate within 5 years. 72% of freshmen from Kansas. Freshmen from 13 states and 8 foreign countries.

Admission: Rolling admissions plan. For fall acceptance, apply as early as 1 year prior to enrollment, but not later than Aug. 1 of year of enrollment. Early acceptance available. *Requirements:* Graduation from accredited secondary school or GED. For out-of-state students lowest acceptable secondary school

class standing 50th percentile. *Entrance tests:* ACT composite. *For transfer students:* 2.0 minimum GPA; from 4-year accredited institution 94 hours maximum transfer credit; from 2-year accredited institution 64 hours; correspondence/extension students 30 hours.

College credit and advanced placement for postsecondary-level work completed in secondary school and for extrainstitutional learning (life experience) on basis of ACE *2006 Guide to the Evaluation of Educational Experiences in the Armed Services.* Tutoring available. Developmental and remedial courses offered during regular academic year; credit given.

Degree Requirements: *For all associate degrees:* 64 credit hours; 15 semester hours in residence. *For all baccalaureate degrees:* 124 to 127 credit hours; 30 semester hours in residence. For bachelor of arts students 10 hours in a foreign language. *For all undergraduate degrees:* 2.0 GPA; general education requirements. *For master's degrees:* Requirements vary by program.

Fulfillment of some degree requirements and exemption from some beginning courses possible by passing departmental examinations. College Board CLEP, AP (score of 3). *Grading system:* A–F; pass-fail; withdraw; incomplete (carries time limit).

Distinctive Educational Programs: Work-experience programs, including cooperative education, internships. Weekend and evening classes. Special facilities for using telecommunications in the classroom. Facilities and programs for independent research, including honors programs, individual majors, tutorials. Institutionally sponsored study abroad in China, Costa Rica, France, Korea, Mexico, Paraguay, Ukraine. *Other distinctive programs:* Credit and enrichment continuing education.

ROTC: Army. 17 commissions awarded 2004.

Degrees Conferred: 37 *associate;* 1,026 *baccalaureate*: biological/life sciences 57; business/marketing 163; communications/communication technologies 46; computer and information sciences 23; education 144; engineering and engineering technologies 253; English 16; foreign languages and literature 1; health professions and related sciences 50; home economics and vocational home economics 32; liberal arts/general studies 46; mathematics 11; parks and recreation 18; physical sciences 11; psychology 75; social sciences and history 65; visual and performing arts 15. 413 *master's* in various disciplines.

Fees and Other Expenses: *Full-time tuition per academic year 2004–05:* resident undergraduate $2,632, out-of-state student $8,990; resident graduate $3,066, out-of-state $8,494. *Required fees:* $662. *Room and board per academic year:* $4,334.

Financial Aid: Aid from institutionally generated funds is provided on the basis of academic merit, financial need, athletic ability. Institution has a Program Participation Agreement with the U.S. Department of Education for eligible students to receive Pell Grants and other federal aid.

Financial aid to full-time, first-time undergraduate students: need-based scholarships/grants totaling $8,180,563, self-help $10,078,559, parent loans $51,183, athletic awards $405,473; non-need-based scholarships/grants totaling $1,197,266, self-help $4,520,288, parent loans $917,401, athletic awards $415,380. *Graduate aid:* 262 students received federal and state-funded loans totaling $1,805,537; 57 students held work-study jobs worth $138,676.

Departments and Teaching Staff: *Professors* 110, *associate professors* 70; *assistant professors:* 57; *instructors* 49, *part-time faculty* 90. *Total instructional faculty:* 376 (full-time 286, part-time 90; women 149, men 227; members of minority groups 21). Total faculty with doctorate, first-professional, or other terminal degree: 255. Student-to-faculty ratio: 18:1. *Faculty development:* 11 faculty members awarded sabbaticals 2004–05.

Enrollment: Total enrollment 6,537. Undergraduate full-time 2,548 men / 2,486 women, part-time 246m / 313w; graduate full-time 192m / 204w, part-time 209m / 439w. *Transfer students:* 530.

Characteristics of Student Body: *Ethnic/racial makeup:* number of Black non-Hispanic: 128; American Indian or Alaska Native: 110; Asian or Pacific Islander: 27; Hispanic: 90; White non-Hispanic: 4,724; unknown 152. *Age distribution:* number under 18: 53; 18–19: 1,442; 20–21: 1,843; 22–24: 1,309; 25–29: 410; 30–34: 154; 35–39: 96; 40–49: 135; 50–64: 47; 65 and over: 4.

International Students: 262 nonresident aliens enrolled fall 2004. Programs available to aid students whose native language is not English: social and cultural. No scholarships specifically designated for international students.

Student Life: On-campus residence halls house 15% of student body. All residence halls are considered co-ed. Housing available for married students. *Intercollegiate athletics:* men only: basketball, cross-country, football, track; women only: basketball, cross-country, softball, track volleyball. *Special regulations:* Registered cars permitted in designated areas only. *Special services:* Learning Resources Center, Student Health Center, Counseling Center, Writing Center, Career Services. Multiple computer labs across campus with extended evening and weekend hours. *Student publications:* weekly newspaper; yearbook. *Surrounding community:* Pittsburg population 20,000. Kansas City, 100 miles from campus, is nearest metropolitan area. Served by airport 30 miles from campus.

Library Collections: 639,136 volumes. Online and card catalogs. Current serial subscriptions: paper 7,038, microform 842,616. 3,800 audiovisual materials. Access to online information retrieval systems. 104 computer work stations. Total 2004–05 budget for books and materials: $657,400.

Most important special collections include the Haldemann Julius Collection (socialism, literature); Kansas Collection; Eva Jessye Collection (Black music, history).

Buildings and Grounds: Campus area 233 acres. *New buildings:* Family and Consumer Science Building completed 2003.

Chief Executive Officer: Dr. Thomas Bryant, President.

Address admission inquiries to Angela D. Peterson, Director of Admission and Enrollment Services; graduate inquiries to Dr. Peggy Snyder, Dean of Continuing and Graduate Studies.

College of Arts and Sciences

Degree Programs Offered: *Baccalaureate* in art, biology, biology education, chemistry, communication, English, family and consumer sciences, foreign language, general studies, history, mathematics, music, nursing, physics, social science; *master's* in art, biology, chemistry, communication, English, history, mathematics, music, nursing, physics, social science.

Distinctive Educational Programs: Social work, international studies, music performance. Minors in women's studies, multicultural studies, environmental management, earth and space science.

College of Business

Degree Programs Offered: *Baccalaureate* in accounting, computer science, information systems, economics, finance, international business, management, marketing; *master's* in accounting and general administration.

Distinctive Educational Programs: International business major; internal auditing minor.

College of Education

Degree Programs Offered: *Baccalaureate* in early childhood/late childhood K-6, physical education, psychology; *master's* in teaching, reading, physical education, psychology, counseling psychology, educational leadership, educational technology, special education teaching; *specialist degrees* in counseling, school psychology, community college and higher education, general school administration.

College of Technology

Degree Programs Offered: *Associate* in automotive service technician, air conditioning, heating and refrigeration, electrical technology, wood technology; *baccalaureate* in engineering technology, commercial graphics, printing management, vocational-technical education, technology management and sales, automotive technology, technology education and wood technology; *master's* in engineering technology, human resource development, technical teaching education, technology, printing management and technology education; *specialist* in education industrial education.

Distinctive Educational Programs: Plastics engineering technology, automotive technology, wood technology majors - multimedia, industrial safety, industrial management minors.

Southwestern College

100 College Street
Winfield, Kansas 67156-2499

Tel: (620) 229-6000   **E-mail:** scadmit@sckans.edu
Fax: (620) 229-6224   **Internet:** www.sckans.edu

Institution Description: Southwestern College is a private college affiliated with the Kansas West Conference of the United Methodist Church. *Enrollment:* 1,417. *Degrees awarded:* Baccalaureate, master's.

Accreditation: *Regional:* NCA. *Professional:* music, nursing, nursing education

History: Established as The Southwest Kansas Conference College and chartered 1885; offered first instruction at postsecondary level 1886; awarded first degree (baccalaureate) 1889; adopted present name 1908; merged with Winfield College of Music 1926.

Institutional Structure: *Governing board:* Board of Trustees. Extrainstitutional representation: 41 trustees. All voting. *Composition of institution:* Administrators 10. Academic affairs directed by dean of faculty. Management/business/finances directed by vice president for business affairs. Full-time instructional faculty 48. Academic governance body, the faculty, meets an average of 10 times per year.

Calendar: Semesters. Academic year Aug. to May. Freshmen admitted Aug., Jan., summer. Degrees conferred and formal commencement May. Summer session offers courses from May to July.

Characteristics of Freshmen: 23% (32 students) submitted SAT scores; 87% (122 students) submitted ACT scores. *25th percentile:* SAT Verbal 430, SAT Math 420; ACT Composite 19, ACT English 18, ACT Math 18. *75th percentile:* SAT Verbal 550, SAT Math 590; ACT Composite 24, ACT English 25, ACT Math 24.

29% of entering freshmen expected to graduate within 5 years. 53% of freshmen from Kansas. Freshmen from 11 states and 1 foreign country.

Admission: Rolling admissions plan. For fall acceptance, apply as early as Sept. of previous year, but not later than Aug. 1. Early acceptance available. *Requirements:* Either graduation from accredited secondary school or GED. Minimum GPA 2.0 in academic courses. *For transfer students:* 2.0 minimum GPA; from 4-year accredited institution 94 semester hours maximum transfer credit; from 2-year accredited institution 64 hours.

College credit and advanced placement for postsecondary-level work completed in secondary school. College credit for extrainstitutional learning (life experience) and faculty assessment. Tutoring available. Developmental courses offered during regular academic year; credit given.

Degree Requirements: 124 credit hours including specific requirements for major field of study and the integrative studies program with an overall grade point average of 2.0. At lest 30 credit hours must be from Southwestern College with 15 of the last 30 taken at the college.

Fulfillment of some degree requirements and exemption from some beginning courses possible by passing departmental examinations, College Board CLEP, APP, other standardized tests. *Grading system:* A–F; satisfactory-unsatisfactory; withdraw (carries time limit); incomplete (carries time limit).

Distinctive Educational Programs: Unusual general education component, identified as the integrative study program, emphasizes synthesis of knowledge, and stresses writing, speaking, and research across academic disciplines. Individually arranged study abroad.

Degrees Conferred: 449 *baccalaureate:* biological/life sciences 22; business/marketing 224; computer and information sciences 10; education 23; engineering and engineering technologies 1; English 1; health professions and related sciences 40; liberal arts/general studies 3; mathematics 2; parks and recreation 13; philosophy/religion/theology 7; physical sciences 3; protective services/public administration 18; psychology 7; social sciences and history 5; visual and performing arts 10. 66 *master's:* business/marketing 46; education 20.

Fees and Other Expenses: *Full-time tuition per academic year 2005–06:* $16,118. *Room and board per academic year:* $5,228.

Financial Aid: Aid from institutionally generated funds is provided on the basis of academic merit, financial need, athletic ability, other criteria. Institution has a Program Participation Agreement with the U.S. Department of Education for eligible students to receive Pell Grants and other federal aid.

Financial aid to full-time, first-time undergraduate students: need-based scholarships/grants totaling $2,977,954, self-help $3,922,313, parent loans $455,468, tuition waivers $97,186, athletic awards $477,150; non-need-based scholarships/grants totaling $447,113, self-help $680,219, parent loans $188,500, tuition waivers $88,533, athletic awards $109,600. *Graduate aid:* 68 students received federal and state-funded loans totaling $624,093 (ranging from $500 to $18,500); 3 students held teaching assistantships totaling $17,000 (ranging from $4,400 to $6,500).

Departments and Teaching Staff: *Total instructional faculty:* 154 (full-time 48, part-time 106; women 68, men 85; members of minority groups 3). Total faculty with doctorate, first-professional, or other terminal degree: 25. Student-to-faculty ratio: 10:1.

Enrollment: Total enrollment 1,417. Undergraduate full-time 316 men / 351 women, part-time 344m / 238w; graduate part-time 71m / 97w.

Characteristics of Student Body: *Ethnic/racial makeup:* number of Black non-Hispanic: 98; American Indian or Alaska Native: 21; Asian or Pacific Islander: 9; Hispanic: 45; White non-Hispanic: 51; unknown: 175. *Age distribution:* 18–24: 56%; 25–34: 16%; 35–49: 23%; 50–up: 4%.

International Students: 23 nonresident aliens enrolled fall 2004. 2 students from Europe, 6 Asia, 2 Central and South America, 11 Africa, 2 other. No programs available to aid students whose native language is not English. Some financial aid specifically designated for international students.

Student Life: On-campus residence halls house 60% of full-time students. Residential living options include 2 all-female halls, 1 all-male hall, and 3 apartment complexes. *Intercollegiate athletics:* men only: basketball, football, cross country, golf, soccer, tennis, track; women only: basketball, cross country, soccer, tennis, track, volleyball. *Special regulations:* Full-time students required to live on campus until 20 years of age or junior classification; other exceptions apply. Alcohol prohibited on campus; no smoking permitted in buildings.] Registered cars permitted; no parking fees. *Special services:* Cooperative Learning Center, computer access in every residence hall room and apartment; mail center; computer centers; career planning office; counseling services; campus nurse.

Student publications, radio: The Collegian, a bimonthly newspaper; *The Moundbuilder,* a yearbook. Radio station KSWC-FM broadcasts 75 hours per week. *Surrounding community:* Winfield population 12,000. Served by airport 45 miles from campus.

Library Collections: 78,657 volumes. Online catalog. Current serial subscriptions: paper 135, microform 1, via electronic access 17,000. 11 computer work stations. Access to online information retrieval systems. Students have access to the Internet at no charge.

Most important holdings include William Joyce Griffith Collection (600 volumes on history, economy, politics of Central and South America; some written in Spanish); Ludgood Walker Collection (400 volumes on Afro-American history); Watumull India Collection (450 volumes on literature and history of India and Southeast Asia).

Buildings and Grounds: Campus area 85 acres.

Chief Executive Officer: Dr. W. Richard Merriman, Jr., President.

Address admission inquiries Todd Moore, Director of Admissions.

Sterling College

125 West Cooper Street
P.O. Box 98
Sterling, Kansas 67579
Tel: (620) 278-2173   **E-mail:** admissions@sterling.edu
Fax: (620) 278-3887   **Internet:** www.sterling.edu

Institution Description: Sterling College is a private, nonprofit college affiliated with The United Presbyterian Church in the United States of America. *Enrollment:* 480. *Degrees awarded:* Baccalaureate.

Member of Associated Colleges of Central Kansas.

Accreditation: *Regional:* NCA. *Professional:* teacher education

History: Chartered as Cooper Memorial College 1886; established and offered first instruction at postsecondary level 1887; awarded first degree (baccalaureate) 1892; changed name to Cooper College 1909; adopted present name 1920.

Institutional Structure: *Governing board:* Board of Trustees. Extrainstitutional representation: 26 voting trustees; 5 ex-officio members. Institutional representation: 5 non-voting administrator; *National Advisory Board:* 39 members. *Composition of institution:* president and 5 vice presidents who oversee the areas of academics, student life, finance advancement, and enrollment services. Full-time instructional faculty 31. Academic governance body, the Faculty of Sterling College, meets an average of 9 times per year.

Calendar: Semesters (4-1-4 plan). Academic year Aug. to May. Freshmen admitted Sept., Jan., Feb. Degrees conferred May, Aug., Dec., Jan. Formal commencement May. No summer session.

Characteristics of Freshmen: 55% of applicants admitted. 25% of applicants admitted and enrolled.

17% (23 students) submitted SAT scores; 83% (111 students) submitted ACT scores. *25th percentile:* SAT Verbal 390, SAT Math 430; ACT Composite 19, ACT English 17, ACT Math 18. *75th percentile:* SAT Verbal 540, SAT Math 580; ACT Composite 25, ACT English 25, ACT Math 25.

38% of entering freshmen expected to graduate within 5 years. 50% of freshmen from Kansas. Freshmen from 13 states and 1 foreign country.

Admission: Rolling admissions plan. For fall acceptance, apply up to Aug. 15. Early decision and early acceptance available. *Requirements:* Either graduation from accredited secondary school with 3 units in English, 2 mathematics, 2 social studies, 1 health and physical education, 1 laboratory science, 8 electives; or GED. 1 additional unit in English recommended. Minimum GPA 2.0. *Entrance tests:* ACT Composite. *For transfer students:* 2.2 minimum GPA, maximum transfer credit limited only by residence requirement.

College credit for postsecondary-level work completed in secondary school and for extrainstitutional learning (life experience) on basis of ACE *2006 Guide to the Evaluation of Educational Experiences in the Armed Services.* Tutoring available. Developmental courses offered during regular academic year; credit given.

Degree Requirements: 124 credit hours; 2.0 GPA; 24 of last 30 hours in residence; comprehensive test of general education; writing proficiency requirement; 2 units physical education classroom study, 1 unit physical education activity; general education requirements; chapel attendance required.

Fulfillment of some degree requirements and exemption from some beginning courses possible by passing College Board CLEP or APP. *Grading system:* A–F; pass-no credit; withdraw (carries time limit, deadline after which pass-fail is appended to withdraw).

Distinctive Educational Programs: Work-experience programs. 2- to 3-year honors program requiring study in foreign language and civilization, great books course, honors project outside major field, honors project in major field. Prepro-

fessional programs in engineering, medical technology, medicine, nursing. Special Interterm study and travel programs sponsored by Sterling or a consortium of central Kansas colleges. Dual degree program in medical technology with Wichita State University. Special semester and summer programs, including semesters abroad, available through Council of Christian Colleges and Universities: China, Russia, Middle East, United Kingdom, Los Angeles Film Studies, and American Studies (Washington DC).

Degrees Conferred: 86 *baccalaureate:* biological/life sciences 5; business/marketing 8; communications/communication technologies 7; computer and information sciences 1; education 16; English 3; health professions and related sciences 2; interdisciplinary studies 4; mathematics 1; parks and recreation 3; philosophy/religion/theology 12; psychology 5; social sciences and history 8; visual and performing arts 11.

Fees and Other Expenses: *Full-time tuition per academic year 2004–05:* $13,807. *Required fees:* $100. *Room per academic year:* $2,279. *Board per academic year:* $3,510.

Financial Aid: Aid from institutionally generated funds is provided on the basis of academic merit, athletic ability, financial need, other criteria. Institution has a Program Participation Agreement with the U.S. Department of Education for eligible students to receive Pell Grants and other federal aid.

Financial aid to full-time, first-time undergraduate students: need-based scholarships/grants totaling $1,710,360, self-help $636,261, athletic awards $346,170; non-need-based scholarships/grants totaling $417,148, self-help $201,693, parent loans $94,622, tuition waivers $53,782, athletic awards $109,561.

Departments and Teaching Staff: *Professors* 4, *associate professors* 12, *assistant professors* 17, *instructors* 5, *part-time faculty* 22. *Total instructional faculty:* 60 (full-time 38, part-time 22; women 19, men 41; members of minority groups 3). Total faculty with doctorate, first-professional, or other terminal degree: 26. Student-to-faculty ratio: 10:1.

Enrollment: Total enrollment 487. Full-time 226 men / 212 women, part-time 22m / 27w.

Characteristics of Student Body: *Ethnic/racial makeup:* number of Black non-Hispanic: 29; American Indian or Alaska Native: 10; Asian or Pacific Islander: 2; Hispanic: 23; White non-Hispanic: 410; unknown: 2. *Age distribution:* under 18: 25; 18–19: 195; 20–21: 154; 22–24: 63; 25–29: 11; 30–39: 1; 40–49: 2; 50–64: 2; 65 and over: 1.

International Students: 11 nonresident aliens enrolled fall 2004. 1 student from Europe, 4 Asia, 2 Central and South America, 3 Africa, 1 Canada. No programs available to aid students whose native language is not English. No financial aid specifically designated for international students.

Student Life: On-campus residence halls house 90% of student body. Separate residence halls for men and women. *Intercollegiate athletics:* men: baseball, basketball, cross-country, football, soccer, track; women: basketball, cross-country, soccer, softball, track, volleyball. *Special regulations:* Cars permitted (registration required). *Special services:* Career Center, Coffee House. *Student publications: Roundup,* a yearbook; *The Stir,* a biweekly newspaper; *The Skirl,* weekly campus newsletter. *Surrounding community:* Sterling population 2,500. Wichita, 70 miles from campus, is nearest metropolitan area with major airport. Passenger rail service 25 miles from campus.

Library Collections: 100,000 volumes including bound books, serial backfiles, electronic documents, and government documents not in separate collections. Online catalog. Current serial subscriptions: 269 paper. 38,064 microform. 115 computer work stations. Students have access to the Internet at no charge. Fee-based access to online services.

Special collections include the Heritage Collection (books written or edited by alumni).

Buildings and Grounds: Campus area 43 acres.

Chief Executive Officer: Dr. Al Anderson, Interim President.

Address admission inquiries to Dennis Dutton, Director of Admissions.

Tabor College

400 South Jefferson Street
Hillsboro, Kansas 67063
Tel: (620) 947-3121   **E-mail:** admissions@tabor.edu
Fax: (316) 947-2607   **Internet:** www.tabor.edu

Institution Description: Tabor College is a private college affiliated with the conference of the Mennonite Brethren Church of North America. *Enrollment:* 536. *Degrees awarded:* Associate, baccalaureate, master's.

Member of Associated Colleges of Central Kansas.

Accreditation: *Regional:* NCA. *Professional:* athletic training, music, nursing education

History: Established and offered first instruction at postsecondary level 1908; awarded first degree (baccalaureate) 1913; incorporated 1952.

Institutional Structure: *Governing board:* Tabor College Board of Directors. Extrainstitutional representation: 27 directors; institutional representation: 1 full-time instructional faculty member, 1 student. All voting. *Composition of institution:* Administrators 13 men / 8 women. Academic affairs headed by vice president of academic affairs. Management/business/finances directed by vice president for business and fiance. Full-time instructional faculty 36. Academic governance body, Tabor College Faculty, meets an average of 12 times per year.

Calendar: Semesters. Academic year Sept. to May. Freshmen admitted Sept., Jan., Feb. Degrees conferred and formal commencement May. No summer session.

Characteristics of Freshmen: 9% (13 students) submitted SAT scores; 91% (126 students) submitted ACT scores. *25th percentile*: ACT Composite 19, ACT English 19, ACT Math 19. *75th percentile*: ACT Composite 25, ACT English 25, ACT Math 25.

45% of entering freshmen expected to graduate within 5 years. 66% of freshmen from Kansas. Freshmen from 11 states and 1 foreign country.

Admission: Rolling admissions plan. For fall acceptance, apply as early as completion of first semester senior year in secondary school, but not later than Aug. 15. Early acceptance available. *Requirements:* Either graduation from secondary school or GED. High school GPA is multiplied by ACT composite score; must equal a 45 and ACT minimum of 18 (SAT-I 860) or better to be admitted. *Entrance tests:* ACT composite. *For transfer students:* 64 credit cap on transfer credit.

College credit and advanced placement for postsecondary-level work completed in secondary school. College credit for extrainstitutional learning on basis of ACE *2006 Guide to the Evaluation of Educational Experiences in the Armed Services*, portfolio assessment. Tutoring available.

Degree Requirements: *For all associate degrees:* 64 credit hours; 2 hours physical education. *For all baccalaureate degrees:* 124 hours; 3 hours physical education. *For all undergraduate degrees:* 2.0 GPA; 1 year in residence; general education requirements.

Fulfillment of some degree requirements and exemption from some beginning courses possible by passing College Board CLEP or APP. *Grading system:* A–F; pass-no credit; withdraw (carries time limit).

Distinctive Educational Programs: Evening classes. Facilities and programs for independent research, including individual majors, tutorials, and directed study contracts during summer session. During interterm, off-campus study at other institutions in consortium, and traveling seminars. Program in environmental studies through AuSable Institute; cooperative programs of study in agriculture and piano pedagogy. Field study programs in Washington (DC); in San Jose, Costa Rica, through Christian College Coalition. Programs in mathematics, language (German and Spanish), and special education through consortium. Accelerated degree completion programs in business administration, Christian ministry, RN to RSN program. Master's programs in education and accounting.

Degrees Conferred: 2 *associate;* 148 *baccalaureate:* agriculture 1; biological/life sciences 6; business/marketing 33; communications/communication technologies 8; computer and information sciences 6; education 30; health professions and related sciences 9; liberal arts/general studies 1; mathematics 2; parks and recreation 6; philosophy/religion/theology 28; physical sciences 1; psychology 5; social sciences and history 7; visual and performing arts 5. 7 *master's*: business/marketing 4; education 3.

Fees and Other Expenses: *Full-time tuition per academic year 2005–06:* $15,575 undergraduate; $290 per credit hour for graduate courses. *Required fees:* $370. Room and board per academic year: $5,670.

Financial Aid: Aid from institutionally generated funds is provided on the basis of academic merit, financial need, athletic ability, other criteria. Institution has a Program Participation Agreement with the U.S. Department of Education for eligible students to receive Pell Grants and other federal aid.

Financial aid to full-time, first-time undergraduate students: need-based scholarships/grants totaling $1,034,122, self-help $2,909,322, parent loans $319,089; non-need-based scholarships/grants totaling $2,360,960, tuition waivers $206,869, athletic awards $677,206. *Graduate aid:* 10 students received federal and state-funded loans totaling $76,408.

Departments and Teaching Staff: *Professors* 10, *associate professors* 11, *assistant professors* 10, *instructors* 5, *part-time faculty* 19. *Total instructional faculty:* 55 (full-time 36, part-time 19; women 20, men 35; members of minority groups 1). Total faculty with doctorate, first-professional, or other terminal degree: 23. Student-to-faculty ratio: 11:1. *Faculty development:* 3 faculty members awarded sabbaticals 2004–05.

Enrollment: Total enrollment 536. Undergraduate full-time 250 men / 213 women, part-time 39m / 84w; graduate full-time 5m / 3w, part-time 5m / 7w. *Transfer students:* in-state 56; from out-of-state 38.

Characteristics of Student Body: *Ethnic/racial makeup:* number of Black non-Hispanic: 33; American Indian or Alaska Native: 7; Asian or Pacific Islander: 5; Hispanic: 16; White non-Hispanic: 537; unknown: 2. *Age distribution:* number of 18–19: 165; 20–21: 178; 22–24: 108; 25–29: 24; 30–34: 29; 35–39: 22; 40–49: 39; 50–64: 18.

International Students: 5 nonresident aliens enrolled fall 2004. 2 students from Asia, 2 Central and south America, 1 Canada. No programs available to aid students whose native language is not English. No financial aid specifically designated for international students.

Student Life: On-campus residence halls house 79% of student body. Residence halls for men constitute 53% of such space, for women 47%. *Intercollegiate athletics:* men: baseball, basketball, cross country, football, golf, soccer, tennis, track; women: basketball, cross country, golf, soccer, softball, tennis, track, volleyball. *Special regulations:* Cars permitted without restrictions. Quiet hours 11pm to 8am. *Special services:* Writing Center; Disability Services; Center for Academic Development; Career Services Center. *Student publications:* The View, a biweekly newspaper; The Bluejay, a yearbook. *Surrounding community:* Hillsboro, population 3,000. Wichita (KS), 55 miles from campus, is nearest metropolitan area.

Library Collections: 81,384 volumes including bound books, serial backfiles, electronic documents, and government documents not in separate collections. Online and card catalogs. Current serial subscriptions: paper 146, via electronic access 18,500. 1,934 recordings; 673 compact discs; 11 CD-ROMS. 11 computer work stations. Students have access to the Internet at no charge. Total budget for books, periodicals, audiovisual materials, microforms 2004–05: $47,141.

important holdings include works of C.S. Lewis, Solzhenitsyn, and J. Michener; Mennonite Brethren history and information.

Buildings and Grounds: Campus area 26 acres.

Chief Executive Officer: Dr. Larry Nikkel, President.

Address admission inquiries to Rusty Allen, Dean of Enrollment Management.

United States Army Command and General Staff College

1 Reynolds Avenue
Fort Leavenworth, Kansas 66027

Tel: (913) 684-2903   **E-mail:** info@leavenworth.army.mil
Fax: (913) 684-2906   **Internet:** www.cgsc.army.mil

Institution Description: The United States Army Command and General Staff College is a federal institution. *Enrollment:* 1,000. *Degrees awarded:* Master's. Diplomas also awarded.

Accreditation: *Regional:* NCA.

History: Established as a school for the cavalry and infantry and offered first instruction at postsecondary level 1881; adopted name U.S. Infantry and Cavalry School 1886; changed name to Command and Staff College 1946; adopted present name 1952; awarded first degree (master's) 1976. *See* Roger Spiller, *CGSC 1881–1981* (Fort Leavenworth: Command and General Staff College, 1981) for further information.

Institutional Structure: *Governing board:* Department of the Army Training and Doctrine Command. Advisory committee of 9 members. All voting. *Composition of institution:* Administrators 101 men / 1 woman. Academic affairs headed by commandant. Management/business/finances directed by comptroller. Full-time instructional faculty 159 men / 3 women. Academic governance body, Faculty Board, meets an average of 40 times per year.

Calendar: Trimesters. Academic year Aug. to June. Students admitted Aug. Degrees conferred and formal commencement June. No summer session.

Admission: Students are notified of selection by June 1. *Requirements:* Officer in U.S. Army with rank of major or captain, promotable, with exemplary military record, and degree from accredited college or university.

Tutoring available. Noncredit remedial courses offered during regular academic year.

Degree Requirements: 30 semester hours, 2.0 GPA; 9–15 hours in residence; exit competency examinations in military art and science; 1 hour per day physical training; core curriculum. *Grading system:* A–F.

Distinctive Educational Programs: Master's program in military art and science. Cooperative master's programs in operations research with Kansas State University; in history, political science, and journalism with University of Kansas; in public administration with University of Missouri-Kansas City; in contract management, logistics management, and transportation management with Florida Institute of Technology.

Degrees Conferred: 182 *master's:* military science and technology.

Fees and Other Expenses: *Full-time tuition per academic year:* Tuition, fees, room, and board provided by U.S. Army.

Enrollment: Total enrollment 1,000 (917 men / 83 women). Number enrolled varies depending on Army operational requirements.

Characteristics of Student Body: Correspondence courses offered for credit.

Student Life: *Special regulations:* Cars permitted without restrictions. Military attire required for classes and other specified times. *Special services:* Learning Resources Center, medical services. *Surrounding community:* Leavenworth population 35,000. Kansas City (MO), 40 miles from campus, is nearest metropolitan area. Served by airport 25 miles from campus.

Library Collections: 270,000 volumes. 250,000 reports and studies. 1,000 current periodical subscriptions; access to 19,000 via electronic access. Access to online information retrieval systems. Students have access to the Internet at no charge. *Most important special holdings:* 1.5 million microforms on military history.

Buildings and Grounds: Campus area 2 city blocks.

Chief Executive Officer: Lt. Gen. William S. Wallace, Commandant.

Admission restricted to selected military personnel.

University of Kansas

Lawrence, Kansas 66045

Tel: (785) 864-2700   **E-mail:** adm@ukans.edu
Fax: (785) 864-5017   **Internet:** www.ukans.edu

Institution Description: The University of Kansas is a multi-campus state institution with the main campus at Lawrence and the Medical Center in Kansas City. *Enrollment:* 28,905. *Degrees awarded:* Baccalaureate, first-professional (law, medicine, pharmacy), master's, doctorate. Specialists and other certificates also awarded.

Academic offerings subject to approval by state governing board. Budget subject to approval by state governing board.

Accreditation: *Regional:* NCA. *Professional:* accounting, art, audiology, business, clinical psychology, computer science, counseling psychology, engineering, English language education, health services administration, journalism, law, music, pharmacy, planning, psychology internship, public administration, social work, speech-language pathology, teacher education

History: Established and chartered 1864; offered first instruction at postsecondary level 1866; awarded first degree (baccalaureate) 1873. *See:* Clifford S. Griffin, *University of Kansas - A History* (Lawrence: Regents Press of Kansas, 1974) for further information.

Institutional Structure: *Governing board:* Board of Regents, State of Kansas. Representation: 9 members (appointed by governor of Kansas). All voting. *Composition of institution:* The University of Kansas is a single institution with academic programs and facilities at two primary campuses: Lawrence and Kansas City. Undergraduate, graduate, and professional education are the principal missions of the Lawrence campus with medicine and related health professional education the focus of the Kansas City campus.

Calendar: Semesters. Academic year Aug. to May. Freshman admitted Aug., Jan., June. Degrees conferred May, Aug., Dec. Formal commencement May. Summer session of 1 term from June to July.

Characteristics of Freshmen: 69% of applicants admitted. 67% of applicants admitted and enrolled.

99% (4,215 students) submitted ACT scores. *25th percentile:* ACT Composite 21. *75th percentile:* ACT Composite 27.

51% of entering freshmen expected to graduate within 5 years. 68% of freshmen from Kansas. Freshmen from 42 states and 29 foreign countries.

Admission: Rolling admissions plan. For fall acceptance apply as early as Sept. of previous year, but not later than Feb. of year of enrollment. *Requirements:* Complete the Kansas Board of Regents' Qualified Admission curriculum with at least a 2.0 GPA on a 4.0 scale; achieve an ACT score of 21 or above or an SAT score of 980 or above or rank in the top one-third of high school graduating class. Out-of-state applicants must complete the Kansas Board of Regents' Qualified Admission curriculum with at least a 2.5 GPA on a 4.0 scale or achieve an ACT score of 24 or above or an SAT score of 1090 or rank in the top one-third of high school graduating class. Additional requirements for some programs. *Entrance tests:* ACT or SAT accepted. *For transfer students:* 2.0 minimum GPA; from 4-year accredited institution 94 semester hours maximum transfer credit; from 2-year accredited institution 64 hours.

College credit and advanced placement for postsecondary-level work completed in secondary school. Tutoring available. Remedial math courses offered during regular academic year; nondegree credit given.

Degree Requirements: 124–132 semester hours; 2.0 GPA; 2 terms in residence; exit requirements vary according to college or school. Fulfillment of some degree requirements possible by passing College Board CLEP, AP. *Grading system:* A–F; withdraw (carries time limit).

Distinctive Educational Programs: Thematic Learning Communities, Global Awareness Program. 100 study abroad programs in over 50 countries. Languages Across the Curriculum, service learning experience, undergraduate research experience, Writing Center, Freshman Summer Institute; University Honors Program; Mount Oread Scholars Program; Haskell Mentor Program; Center for Teaching Excellence, Continuing Education, evening classes, and off-campus instruction sites.

ROTC: Army, Navy, Air Force. 14 Army, 9 Navy, 11 Air Force commissions awarded 2004.

Degrees Conferred: 3,889 *baccalaureate* (B), 1,506 *master's* (M), 256 *doctorate* (D): architecture 77 (B), 36 (M); area and ethnic studies 43 (B), 25 (M), 4 (D); biological/life sciences 273 (B), 18 (M), 28 (D); business/marketing 461 (B), 199 (M), 28 (D); communications/communication technologies 359 (B), 33 (M); computer and information science 53 (B), 39 (M); education 161 (B), 339 (M), 56 (D); engineering/engineering technologies 237 (B), 139 (M), 13 (D); English 442 (B), 37 (M), 12 (D); foreign languages and literature 152 (B), 21 (M), 11 (D); health professions and related sciences 278 (B), 231 (M), 25 (D); interdisciplinary studies 78 (B), 33 (M), 8 (D); liberal arts/general studies 24 (B); mathematics 37 (B), 12 (M), 8 (D); natural resources/environmental science 29 (B); parks and recreation 104 (B); philosophy/religion/theology 24 (B), 8 (M), 4 (D); physical sciences 41 (B), 19 (M), 16 (D); protective services/public administration 39 (B), 197 (M), 3 (D); psychology 277 (B), 44 (M), 27 (D); social sciences and history 376 (B), 47 (M), 19 (D); visual and performing arts 324 (B), 39 (M), 20 (D). 478 *first-professional:* law 197; medicine 160; pharmacy 121.

Fees and Other Expenses: *Full-time tuition per academic year 2004–05:* undergraduate resident $4,163, out-of-state student $12,117; graduate resident $4,291, out-of-state student $11,018. *Required fees:* $574. *Room and board per academic year:* $5,216.

Financial Aid: Aid from institutionally generated funds is provided on the basis of academic merit, financial need, athletic ability, other criteria. Institution has a Program Participation Agreement with the U.S. Department of Education for eligible students to receive Pell Grants and other federal aid.

Financial aid to full-time, first-time undergraduate students: need-based scholarships/grants totaling $17,574,676, self-help $22,093,495, tuition waivers $2,983,585, athletic awards $1,584,531; non-need-based scholarships/grants totaling $6,903,663, self-help $18,659,130, parent loans $17,746,377, tuition waivers $1,119,785, athletic awards $2,878,852.

Departments and Teaching Staff: College of Liberal Arts and Sciences *professors* 226, *associate professors* 177, *assistant professors* 169, *instructors/lecturers* 19, *part-time faculty* 163; Journalism/Mass Communications 6, 11, 5, 2, 15; School of Architecture 9, 12, 9, 0, 17; School of Business 25, 13, 6, 2, 12; School of Education 24, 36, 14, 1, 29; School of Engineering 43, 30, 17, 1, 20; School of Fine Arts 35, 34, 29, 2, 23; School of Law 32, 2, 0, 0, 13; School of Pharmacy 32, 15, 17, 0, 1; School of Social Welfare 8, 8, 6, 1, 43.

Total instructional faculty: 1,312 (full-time 1,185, part-time 127; women 451, men 864; members of minority groups 179). Total faculty with doctorate, first-professional, or other terminal degree: 1,249. Student-to-faculty ratio: 20:1. *Faculty development:* $274 million in grants for research. 55 faculty members awarded sabbaticals 2004–05.

Enrollment: Total enrollment 28,905. Undergraduate full-time 9,133 men / 9,534 women, part-time 1,347m / 1,309w; first-professional full-time 777m / 699w, part-time 20m / 30w; graduate full-time 1,031m / 1,655w, part-time 1,497m / 1,853w. *Transfer students (undergraduate):* in-state 781; from out-of-state 718.

Characteristics of Student Body: *Ethnic/racial makeup (undergraduate):* number of Black non-Hispanic: 746; American Indian or Alaska Native: 260; Asian or Pacific Islander: 851; Hispanic: 692; White non-Hispanic: 17,595; unknown: 553. *Age distribution:* number under 18: 102; 18–19: 7,424; 20–21: 7,884; 22–24: 4,376; 25–29: 1,026; 30–34: 314; 35–39: 173; 40–49: 193; 50–64: 95; 65 and over: 9. 39% of student body attend summer sessions.

International Students: 1,683 nonresident aliens enrolled fall 2004. 218 students from Europe, 1,205 Asia, 198 Central and South America, 85 Africa, 43 Canada, 4 Australia. Programs available to aid students whose native language is not English: social, cultural. English as a Second Language Program. No financial aid specifically designated for international students.

Student Life: On-campus residence halls house about 13% of student body. 4% housed on campus in single apartments, 1% in married housing. On-campus scholarship halls house 2% of student body. 14% of undergraduate men join fraternities, 17% of undergraduate women join sororities. *Intercollegiate athletics:* men only: baseball, basketball, cross-country, football, golf, swimming, tennis, indoor/outdoor track; women only: basketball, cross-country, golf, rowing, soccer, softball, swimming, tennis, indoor/outdoor track, volleyball. *Special regulations:* Cars permitted in designated zoned areas; fee charged according to zone. Quiet hours in residence halls; visitation varies according to hall. *Special services:* Legal Aid, Student Development Center, Student Fitness Center, Academic Resource Center, Advising Center, Orientation Program, Child Care Center, Placement Services, Medical Services, campus bus system, 2 student union facilities, Services for Students with Disabilities arranges handicapped assistance; extensive intramural sports program and recreational facilities, Applied English Center; reduced rates to all sporting events, theatrical productions, speakers; Women's Resource Center, Writing Center, wide range of student clubs (musical, scientific, language, sports, religious, professional, foreign student groups); Counseling Center, Financial Aid Office. *Student publications, radio: Jayhawker,* a yearbook; *University Daily Kansan,* a daily campus-wide newspaper. Radio stations KJHK and KANU each broadcast 168 hours per week. *Surrounding community:* Lawrence population 80,000. Kansas City, 40 miles east of campus, is nearest metropolitan area. Served by airport 50 miles from campus; passenger rail service 1 mile from campus.

Publications: *Accolades; American Studies; Architectural Management; Auslegung; Biota; Books and Libraries; Bulletin; Catalyst; Channels; Child Development Abstracts and Bibliography; Children's Services: Social Policy, Research and Practices; Chimeres; Coal City Review; Connections; Cottonwood Review; Current Research in Earth Sciences; Directions; East Asian Series; Families and Disability Newsletter; The Geological Record; the Government of Kansas, HBC News (Higuchi Biosciences Center); Horizons; Horizons Unlimited; Human Biology: The International Journal of Population Biology and Genetics; Humanistic Studies Series; Innovations in Education; Institution of Haitian Studies (occasional papers); Journal of Applied Behavioral Analysis; Journal of Dramatic Theory and Criticism; Journal of Social and Clinical Psychology; Kansas Academy of Science Transactions; Kansas Alumni Magazine; Kansas Business Review; Kansas Engineer; Kansas Geological Survey Bulletins, Educational Series, Technical Series; Kansas Journal of Law and Public Policy; Kansas Law Review; The Kansas Legislature: Parliamentary Procedures; The Kansas Legislature: Structure and Process; Kansas Statistical Abstract; Kansas Trans Reporter; Kansas Working Papers in Linguistics, KATESOL; KU Anthropologist; KU Laws; KUCLIMAT Newsletter; Latin American Theatre Review; Library Series; Lindley Lecture Series; M.E. Vibrations; Momentum; Monograph Series (KU Public Management Center); Murphy Lectures in Art; The Nabokovian; Natural Resources Research; News and Notes: Women's Studies; Oread Engineer; Paleontological Contributions; Panorama; pc-trans; Phamakan; Preview; Proceedings of the Research Symposium on the Psychology and Acoustics of Music; Register of the Spencer Museum of Art; Research Opportunities in Renaissance Drama; Russkii Tekst; Scientific Papers (Natural History Museum); Slovene Linguistic Studies; Social Thought and Research; Strategram; Teaching Matters; Treatise of Invertebrate Paleontology; Update; Yearbook of German-American Studies.*

Library Collections: 4,768,862 volumes. Maps, graphics, audio, film, video: 3,391,510 units. 41,380 current serial subscriptions (paper, microform, electronic). 4,108,857 microforms; 55,284 audiovisual materials. 11,278 computer files. Total library expenditures 2004–05: $19,076,850.

Most important holdings include Natural History; History of Economics; 18th Century British History and Literature; Ellis Collection on Ornithology; Wilcox Collection on Contemporary Political Movements; Clendening History of Medicine Collection; Central American and Caribbean Collection; Irish Cultural History Collection.

Buildings and Grounds: Campus area over 1,000 acres. *New buildings:* Robert J. Dole Institute of Politics complete 2003; Eaton Hall 2003; Student Recreation and Fitness Center 2003; Hall Center for the Humanities 2004; Multidisciplinary Research Building 2005; Scholarship Hall 2005.

Chief Executive Officer: Robert E. Hemenway, Chancellor.

Undergraduates address admission inquiries to Lisa Pinamonti Kiess, Director of Admissions; graduate study inquiries to individual departments; professional school inquires should be directed to the school of interest.

College of Liberal Arts and Sciences

Degree Programs Offered: *Baccalaureate* in African and African-American studies, American studies, anthropology, astronomy, atmospheric science and meteorology, biochemistry, biology, chemistry, classical antiquity, classical languages, communication studies, East Asian languages and cultures, economics, English, environmental studies, European studies, French, geography, geology, Germanic languages and literatures, history, history of art, human biology, human development and family life, humanities, international studies, Latin American area studies, special major, linguistics, mathematics, microbiology, philosophy, physics, political science, psychology, religious studies, Slavic languages and literatures, sociology, Soviet and East European studies, Spanish, speech-language-hearing sciences and disorders, theatre and film, women's studies. *Master's* and *doctorate* offered through the Graduate School.

Distinctive Educational Programs: Interdisciplinary programs in African studies, American studies, Eastern civilizations, environmental studies, history and philosophy of science, human biology, humanities, Latin American area studies, Soviet and East European studies, Western civilization, women's studies. Undergraduate research facilities are available in most departments. Joint doctorate in computer science with Kansas State University. Cooperative doctorate in educational administration and higher education with Emporia State

University. Resident fee rate agreement between Missouri and Kansas in selected programs. *See* School of Architecture.

School of Architecture and Urban Design

Degree Programs Offered: *Baccalaureate* in architecture, architectural studies, architectural engineering; *master's* offered through the Graduate School.

Degree Requirements: 5 years, 165 hours.

Distinctive Educational Programs: 5-year bachelor or architecture with 9-month internship. Joint master's degrees in urban planning and law, public administration, or American studies. Exchange program with University of Missouri.

School of Business

Degree Programs Offered: *Baccalaureate* in accounting, business administration, or business and another field; *master's* accounting; *doctorate* offered through the Graduate School.

Fees and Other Expenses: Additional master-level fee $61.80 per credit hour.

Distinctive Educational Programs: Bachelor of science in business with concentration in any of 55 fields throughout the University. Combined M.B.A./J.D. (law) program. *See also* School of Law.

School of Education

Degree Programs Offered: *Baccalaureate* in elementary education, exercise science, secondary education, health education, physical education, music education, music therapy, visual arts education. *Master's* and *doctorate* offered through the Graduate School.

Distinctive Educational Programs: Cooperative Transfer Programs in educational administration and higher education with Emporia, Pittsburg, and Wichita State Universities. Special laboratory facilities including media, microcomputer, curricula, statistics, exercise physiology, music education, microteaching, kinesiology-biomechanics. Perceptual motor clinic. Music therapy clinic and wellness center.

School of Engineering

Degree Programs Offered: *Baccalaureate* in aerospace engineering, architectural engineering, chemical engineering, civil engineering, computer engineering, computer science, electrical engineering, engineering physics, mechanical engineering and petroleum engineering. *Master's* and *doctorate* offered through the Graduate School.

Degree Requirements: Semester hours required for engineering degrees range from 128–137 hours.

Fees and Other Expenses: Additional $30 per credit hour for engineering courses.

Distinctive Educational Programs: Interdisciplinary master's-doctorate in engineering with the School of Business. Environmental health laboratories. Tertiary Oil Recovery Project. Wind tunnel for aerospace students. Flight research laboratory. Center for engineering and related interdisciplinary research. *See* School of Business.

School of Fine Arts

Degree Programs Offered: *Baccalaureate* in art, design, ceramics, industrial design, interior design, metalsmithing/jewelry, textile design, visual communication (graphic design, illustration), history of art, painting, printmaking, sculpture, theatre design, dance, music, music composition, music education, music history, music performance/instrumental music performance (voice, music theory, theatre and voice), music therapy, visual arts education.

Distinctive Educational Programs: Practical experience producing advertising art for the performing arts programs. Interdisciplinary programs in theater-voice, theater-design. Program of visiting artists, piano artist-in-residence. Electronic music studio.

William Allen White School of Journalism and Mass Communication

Degree Programs Offered: *Baccalaureate* in advertising, business communications, broadcast news, broadcast management (promotion and sales), community journalism, magazine journalism, news and editorial, photojournalism. *Master's* offered through the Graduate School.

Admission: To be candidates for admission to the school, students must have completed all first- and second-year requirements and a total of 60 hours of coursework.

Distinctive Educational Programs: Interdisciplinary programs in journalism and business, in science writing. Internships in Kansas and the U.S. Laboratory facilities in advertising, broadcasting, magazine, newspaper, photography.

School of Social Welfare

Degree Programs Offered: *Baccalaureate, master's, doctorate* in social work.

Distinctive Educational Programs: BSW and MSW programs in Lawrence and metro Kansas City. One year master's program for selected BSW applicants; opportunities in research and training projects in child welfare, case management, and work with the chronically mentally ill; post-graduate courses for practitioners. Joint degree program in social work and law (MSW/JD).

School of Law

Degree Programs Offered: *First-professional.*

Admission: Baccalaureate from accredited institution; LSAT.

Degree Requirements: 90 credit hours, 2.0 GPA, 6 semesters of full-time residence or equivalent.

Fees and Other Expenses: Additional $112.30 per credit hour for Law School courses.

Distinctive Educational Programs: Joint degree programs include JD with MBA; MA economics; Master of health services administration; MA philosophy; MA public administration; MA social work; MA urban planning. Certificate programs in tribal law and in media, law, and policy. Moot Court program, clinical programs in criminal justice, law and entrepreneurship, legal aid, legislative, judicial clerkship, media law, public policy, Paul E. Wilson Defender Project; Tribal Law and Government Center, international semester in London through the London Law Consortium, specially equipped courtroom, law library.

School of Pharmacy

Degree Programs Offered: *First-professional.*

Degree Requirements: *For baccalaureate:* 200 credit hours (6 years of study) required for graduation.

Fees and Other Expenses: Additional $95.45 per credit hour for pharmacy courses.

Distinctive Educational Programs: Intersearch doctoral program, a pharmaceutical graduate research program conducted at the international level by the U.S.A. and Australia.

Graduate School

Degree Programs Offered: *Master's, doctorate* in various fields. Specialist and other certificates also given.

Departments and Teaching Staff: Faculty are drawn from other colleges within the university.

University of Saint Mary

4100 South Fourth Street
Leavenworth, Kansas 66048

Tel: (913) 682-5151   **E-mail:** admiss@stmary.edu
Fax: (913) 758-6140   **Internet:** www.stmary.edu

Institution Description: University of Saint Mary, formerly named Saint Mary College, is a private, liberal arts, coeducational college founded and sponsored by the Sisters of Charity of Leavenworth, Roman Catholic. *Enrollment:* 824. *Degrees awarded:* Associate, baccalaureate, master's.

Member of Kansas City Regional Council for Higher Education.

Accreditation: *Regional:* NCA. *Professional:* teacher education

History: Chartered as St. Mary's Academy 1860; changed name to St. Mary's Junior College and offered first instruction at postsecondary level 1923; first degree (associate) awarded 1925; adopted present name and added upper division curricula 1930; offered master's program in education in 1950. adopted present name 2003.

Institutional Structure: *Governing board:* Board of Trustees of University of Saint Mary. Extrainstitutional representation: 19 trustees. *Composition of institution:* Administrators 3 men / 3 women. Academic affairs headed by academic vice president and dean of the college. Management/business/finances directed by vice president for administrative services. Full-time instructional faculty 43. All faculty and professional staff meet 8 times per year regarding college concerns.

Calendar: Semesters. Academic year Aug. to May. Freshmen admitted Aug., Jan., June. Degrees conferred May, Dec. Formal commencement May. Summer session of 1 term from June to July.

Characteristics of Freshmen: 75% of applicants admitted. 19% of applicants admitted and enrolled.

9% of students submitted SAT scores; 92% of students submitted ACT scores. *25th percentile*: SAT Verbal 450, SAT Math 440; ACT Composite 18. *75th percentile*: SAT Verbal 580, SAT Math 610; ACT Composite 23.

41% of entering freshmen expected to graduate within 5 years. 48% of freshmen from Kansas. Freshmen from 14 states and 2 foreign countries.

Admission: Rolling admissions plan. For fall acceptance, apply as early as the end of junior year of secondary school. *Requirements:* Graduation from accredited secondary school with 16 units which must include 4 units in English, 2 in a foreign language, 2 mathematics, 2 social science, 1 laboratory science; or GED. *Entrance tests:* ACT composite or SAT. *For transfer students:* 2.0 minimum GPA; from 2-year accredited institutions 64 hours maximum transfer credit; from 4-year, 90 hours.

College credit and advanced placement for postsecondary-level work completed in secondary school. Advanced placement for extrainstitutional learning (life experience) on basis of institutional examinations. Tutoring available.

Degree Requirements: *For all associate degrees:* 64 credit hours; 15 hours in residence. *For all baccalaureate degrees:* minimum 128 hours; 30 hours in residence. *For all undergraduate degrees:* 2.0 GPA. *For graduate degrees:* Contact program department for requirements.

Fulfillment of some degree requirements and exemption from some beginning courses possible by passing departmental examinations or College Board CLEP. *Grading system:* A–F; pass-fail; withdraw (carries time limit).

Distinctive Educational Programs: Work-experience programs. Flexible meeting places and schedules, including off-campus centers, weekend and evening classes. Facilities for independent research, including honors programs, individual majors, and independent studies. Exchange program with Sophia University in Tokyo, Japan. Study may be arranged through a cooperative program with Central College (IA) and with other colleges. Semester at University of Kansas through cooperative program. Cross-registration with consortium colleges. 2+2 programs leading to baccalaureate degrees in various programs in education, business, and social sciences. Master's degree offered in education, business, and psychology.

ROTC: Air Force and Army offered in cooperation with University of Kansas.

Degrees Conferred: 1 *associate;* 140 *baccalaureate:* biological/life sciences 5; business/marketing 29; communications/communication technologies 1; computer and information sciences 17; education 17; English 5; home economics and vocational home economics 1; liberal arts/general studies 2; mathematics 2; parks and recreation 11; philosophy/religion/theology 9; psychology 19; social sciences and history 16; visual and performing arts 6. 200 *master's:* business/marketing 36; education 157; psychology 7.

Fees and Other Expenses: *Full-time tuition per academic year 2004–05:* $14,400 undergraduate; $5,850 graduate. *Required fees:* $190. *Room and board per academic year:* $5,540.

Financial Aid: Aid from institutionally generated funds is provided on the basis of academic merit, financial need, athletic ability. Institution has a Program Participation Agreement with the U.S. Department of Education for eligible students to receive Pell Grants and other federal aid.

Financial aid to full-time, first-time undergraduate students: need-based scholarships/grants totaling $670,887, self-help $1,380,414; non-need-based scholarships/grants totaling $1,590,051, self-help $901,825, parent loans $430,099, athletic awards $432,346.

Departments and Teaching Staff: *Total instructional faculty:* 97 (full-time 43, part-time 54; women 54, men 43). Student-to-faculty ratio: 12:1. *Degrees held by full-time faculty:* doctorate 44.7%, master's 38.5%, professional 15.8%. 45% hold terminal degrees.

Enrollment: Total enrollment 824. Undergraduate full-time 195 men / 202 women, part-time 40m / 100w; graduate full-time 5m / 34w, part-time 66m / 192w. *Transfer students:* in-state 38; from out-of-state 37.

Characteristics of Student Body: *Ethnic/racial makeup:* number of Black non-Hispanic: 63; American Indian or Alaska Native: 2; Asian or Pacific Islander: 14; Hispanic: 36; White non-Hispanic: 345; unknown: 68. *Age distribution:* under 18: 63; 18–19: 150; 20–21: 136; 22–24: 76; 25–29: 30; 30–34: 20; 35–39: 16; 40–49: 32; 50–64: 13; 65 and over: 1.

International Students: 14 nonresident aliens enrolled fall 2004. 2 students from Europe, 3 Asia, 5 Central and South America, 2 Canada, 2 Australia. No programs available to aid students whose native language is not English. No financial aid specifically designated for international students.

Student Life: On-campus residence halls house 45% of students in main-campus programs. *Intercollegiate athletics:* women: baseball, soccer, softball, volleyball, basketball; men: baseball, basketball, football, soccer. *Special regulations:* Cars permitted without restrictions. *Special services:* Health services.

Student publications: The Taper, a bimonthly newspaper. *Surrounding community:* Leavenworth population 36,000. Kansas City (MO), 26 miles from campus, is nearest metropolitan area. Served by airport 23 miles from campus.

Library Collections: 118,195 volumes including bound books, serial backfiles, electronic documents, and government documents not in separate collections. Online and card catalogs. Current serial subscriptions: paper 205, microform 18, via electronic access 7,000. 600 recordings, 65 compact discs, 65 CD-ROMs. 8 computer work stations. Students have access to the Internet at no charge.

Most important holdings include Americana, Lincoln Collection, and Bible Collection.

Buildings and Grounds: Campus area 240 acres.

Chief Executive Officer: Sister Diane Steele, President.

Address admission inquiries to Jessica Goffinet, Director of Admissions and Recruitment.

Washburn University

1700 S.W. College Avenue
Topeka, Kansas 66621

Tel: (785) 231-1010   **E-mail:** admissions@washburn.edu
Fax: (785) 231-1089   **Internet:** www.washburn.edu

Institution Description: Washburn University of Topeka is a public urban institution. *Enrollment:* 7,251. *Degrees awarded:* Associate, baccalaureate, first-professional (law), master's.

Accreditation: *Regional:* NCA. *Professional:* law, music, nursing, radiography, social work, teacher education

History: Established by Congregational Church and chartered as Lincoln College 1865; offered first instruction at postsecondary level 1866; changed name to Washburn College and awarded first degree (baccalaureate) 1868; became Washburn Municipal University of Topeka 1941; adopted present name 1952.

Institutional Structure: *Governing board:* Washburn University of Topeka Board of Regents. Representation: 9 regents, including mayor of Topeka. 1 ex officio. 9 voting. *Composition of institution:* Administrators 55 men / 32 women. Academic affairs headed by vice president for academic affairs. Management/business/finances directed by vice president for administration and treasurer. Full-time instructional faculty 211. Academic governance body, University Council, meets an average of 9 times per year.

Calendar: Semesters. Academic year late Aug. to mid-May. Freshmen admitted Aug., Jan., June. Degrees conferred May, Aug., Dec. Formal commencement May. Summer session of 2 terms from early June to late July.

Characteristics of Freshmen: 100% of applicants admitted. 64% of applicants admitted and enrolled. 86% (801 students) submitted ACT scores. *25th percentile:* ACT Composite 19, ACT English 18, ACT Math 17. *75th percentile:* ACT Composite 25, ACT English 25, ACT Math 25.

56% of entering freshmen expected to graduate within 5 years. 95% of freshmen from Kansas. Freshmen from 13 states and 2 foreign countries.

Admission: Rolling admissions plan. For fall acceptance, apply no later than 15 days before enrollment. Early acceptance available. *Requirements:* Either graduation from accredited secondary school or GED. ACT required for all students applying with less than 24 hours of credit. *Entrance tests:* ACT composite recommended. For foreign students TOEFL. *For transfer students:* 2.0 minimum GPA; from 4-year accredited institution maximum transfer credit limited only by residence requirement; from 2-year accredited institution 64 hours.

College credit for postsecondary-level work completed in secondary school and for extrainstitutional learning on basis of ACE *2006 Guide to the Evaluation of Educational Experiences in the Armed Services,* faculty assessment. Tutoring available. Noncredit developmental courses offered during regular academic year.

Degree Requirements: *For all associate degrees:* 62 credit hours; 24 hours in residence. *For all baccalaureate degrees:* 124 hours; 30 hours in residence. *For all undergraduate degrees:* 2.0 GPA; 2 hours physical education courses; general education requirements.

Fulfillment of some degree requirements possible by passing departmental examinations, College Board CLEP. *Grading system:* A–F; pass-fail; withdraw (carries time limit).

Distinctive Educational Programs: Work-experience programs, including internships, cooperative education. Weekend and evening classes. Cooperative baccalaureate in clinical laboratory sciences and engineering. Special facilities for using telecommunications in the classroom. Interdepartmental program in general studies. Preprofessional programs in dentistry, medicine, law, nursing, pharmacy, theology, and veterinary medicine. Facilities and programs for inde-

pendent research, including honors programs, individual majors, tutorials. Institutionally sponsored study abroad in Europe, Asia, Africa, and Central America.

ROTC: Air Force, Army, Navy in cooperation with University of Kansas.

Degrees Conferred: 136 *associate;* 729 *baccalaureate* (B); 150 *master's* (M): biological/life sciences 14 (B); business/marketing 188 (B), 35 (M); communications/communication technologies 47 (B); computer and information sciences 24 (B); education 58 (B), 24 (M); engineering and engineering technologies 14 (B); English 18 (B); foreign languages and literature 18 (B); health professions and related sciences 99 (B); interdisciplinary studies 16 (B); liberal arts/general studies 3 (M); mathematics 8 (B); parks and recreation 16 (B); philosophy/religion/theology 2 (B); physical sciences 11 (B); protective services/public administration 122 (B), 83 (M); psychology 24 (B), 5 (M); social sciences and history 16 (B); visual and performing arts 15 (B). 142 *first-professional:* law 142.

Fees and Other Expenses: *Full-time tuition per academic year 2004–05:* undergraduate resident $4,500, out-of-state student $10,170; graduate resident $3,708, out-of-state $7,242. *Room and board per academic year:* $4,588. *Required fees:* $62. First-professional tuition and fees vary; contact the university for current information.

Financial Aid: Aid from institutionally generated funds is provided on the basis of academic merit, financial need, athletic ability, other criteria. Institution has a Program Participation Agreement with the U.S. Department of Education for eligible students to receive Pell Grants and other federal aid.

Financial aid to full-time, first-time undergraduate students: need-based scholarships/grants totaling $10,402,196, self-help $19,631,444, parent loans $4,184,832, athletic awards $733,930; non-need-based scholarships/grants totaling $1,303,187, self-help $4,503,363, parent loans $1,429,893, athletic awards $141,836.

Departments and Teaching Staff: *Professors* 73, *associate professors* 66, *assistant professors* 68, *instructors* 50, *part-time faculty* 259. *Total instructional faculty:* 516 (full-time 257, part-time 259; women 255, men 261; members of minority groups 41). Total faculty with doctorate, first-professional, or other terminal degree: 325. Student-to-faculty ratio: 17:1. *Faculty development:* 7 faculty members awarded sabbaticals 2004–05.

Enrollment: Total enrollment 7,251. Undergraduate full-time 1,637 men / 2,572 women, part-time 718m / 1,471w; first-professional full-time 251m / 201w, part-time 8m / 6w; graduate full-time 35m / 102w, part-time 90m / 1560w.

Characteristics of Student Body: *Ethnic/racial makeup:* number of Black non-Hispanic: 289; American Indian or Alaska Native: 84; Asian or Pacific Islander: 54; Hispanic: 179; White non-Hispanic: 3,457; unknown: 2,241. . *Age distribution:* number under 18: 66; 18–19: 1,221; 20–21: 1,442; 22–24: 1,371; 25–29: 835; 30–34: 476; 35–39: 314; 40–49: 431; 50–64: 193; 65 and over: 12; unknown: 37.

International Students: 101 nonresident aliens enrolled fall 2004. Students from Europe, Asia, Latin America, Africa, Canada, New Zealand. Programs available to aid students whose native language is not English: social, cultural. No financial aid specifically designated for international students.

Student Life: On-campus residence halls house 14% of student body. Residence halls for men constitute 39% of such space, for women 42%, for both sexes 19%. 3% of men join fraternities; 5% of women join sororities. *Intercollegiate athletics:* male: baseball, basketball, football, golf, tennis; female: basketball, softball, tennis, volleyball. *Special regulations:* Cars permitted in designated parking areas. *Special services:* Learning Resources Center, medical services. *Student publications, radio, television:* Weekly newspaper, yearbook. TV station KTWU broadcasts 87 hours per week. *Surrounding community:* Topeka population 120,000. Kansas City, Missouri, 70 miles from campus, is nearest metropolitan area. Served by mass transit bus system; airport 7 miles from campus.

Library Collections: 338,842 volumes. Online and card catalogs. Current serial subscriptions: paper 1,733, microform 17, via electronic access 1,770. 67 recordings; 876 compact discs; 11 CD-ROMs. 13 computer work stations. Students have access to the Internet at no charge. Total 2004–05 budget for books and materials: $587,605.

Most important holdings include archives of the University and of the Kansas Nebraska Conference of the Congregational Church; Bradbury Thompson Collection; Brown vs. Board of Education Archives; Patent and Trademark Collection (law emphasis); Wolf Creek (NRC) Collection; Robert F.W. Whitcomb Rare Book Collection; William I. Koch Art History Collection.

Buildings and Grounds: Campus area 160 acres. *New buildings:* Living Learning Center; Washburn Village; Student Recreation and Wellness Center.

Chief Executive Officer: Dr. Jerry B. Farley, President.

Address admission inquiries to Kirk Haskins, Director of Admissions; School of Law inquiries to Karla Beam, Director of Admissions, Washburn University School of Law.

School of Law

Degree Programs Offered: *First-professional.*
Admission: Baccalaureate degree; LSAT; LSDAS.
Degree Requirements: 90 credit hours; 18 months in residence; 2.0 GPA.

Wichita State University

1845 Fairmount Street
Wichita, Kansas 67260-0001

Tel: (316) 973-3085   **E-mail:** admissions@wichita.edu
Fax: (316) 978-3174   **Internet:** www.wichita.edu

Institution Description: *Enrollment:* 14,297. *Degrees awarded:* Associate, baccalaureate, master's, doctorate. Certificates also awarded.

Academic offerings subject to approval by statewide coordinating bodies. Budget subject to approval by state governing boards.

Accreditation: *Regional:* NCA. *Professional:* accounting, audiology, business, clinical lab scientist, dance, dental hygiene, engineering, music, nursing, nursing education, physical therapy, public administration, public health, social work, speech-language pathology, teacher education

History: Incorporated as Fairmount College 1887; established by Congregational Church as Fairmount Institute 1892; chartered as Fairmount College and offered first instruction 1895; awarded first degree (baccalaureate) 1899; became municipal institution and changed name to Municipal University of Wichita 1926; changed name to University of Wichita 1956; became part of state system and became Wichita State University in 1964. *See* Craig Miner, *Uncloistered Halls: The Centennial History of Wichita State University* (Wichita, Kansas: Wichita State Endowment Association, 1995) and John Rydjord, *A History of Fairmount College* (Lawrence, Kansas: The Regents Press of Kansas, 1977) for further information.

Institutional Structure: *Governing board:* Kansas Board of Regents and the Wichita State University Board of Trustees. *Composition of institution:* Academic affairs and computing/telecommunication services headed by vice president, academic affairs. Management/business/finances directed by vice president, administration and finance. Development, alumni and university relations directed by vice president, university advancement. Full-time instructional faculty 469. Academic governance body, Faculty Senate, meets an average of 18 times per year.

Calendar: Semesters. Academic year Aug. to May. Freshmen admitted Aug., Jan., June. Degrees conferred May, Aug., Dec. Formal commencement Dec., May. Summer session of 4 terms from May to Aug.

Characteristics of Freshmen: 82% of applicants admitted. 51% of applicants admitted and enrolled.

7% (86 students) submitted SAT scores; 85% (981 students) submitted ACT scores. *25th percentile:* SAT Verbal 470, SAT Math 492; ACT Composite 20, ACT English 19, ACT Math 19. *75th percentile:* SAT Verbal 590, SAT Math 630; ACT Composite 26, ACT English 25, ACT Math 26.

30% of entering freshmen expected to graduate within 5 years. 90% of Freshmen from Kansas. Freshmen from 28 states and 18 foreign countries.

Admission: Rolling admissions plan. For fall acceptance, apply as early as end of junior year of secondary school, but not later than Aug. 1 of year of enrollment. Early acceptance available. *Requirements:* Either graduation from secondary school or GED for Kansas state residents. Recommend pre-college curriculum with 4 units English, 2 in a foreign language, 3 mathematics, 3 science, 2 history and social studies, 1 computer literacy. Minimum GPA 2.0 for nonresidents. *Entrance tests:* ACT composite. For foreign students TOEFL. *For transfer students:* 2.0 minimum GPA (foreign students 2.25); from 2- and 4-year accredited institutions maximum transfer credit limited only by residence requirement; correspondence/extension students 30 hours.

Tutoring available. Developmental and remedial courses offered in summer session and regular academic year; credit given for developmental courses.

Degree Requirements: *For all associate degrees:* 60–64 credit hours; 1 term in residence. *For all baccalaureate degrees:* 124–143 credit hours; 2 terms in residence. *For all undergraduate degrees:* 2.0–2.50 GPA (depending on college); completion of general education program.

Fulfillment of some degree requirements possible by passing departmental examinations, College Board CLEP, ACT. *Grading system:* A–F; withdraw.

Distinctive Educational Programs: Bachelor's degree programs in entrepreneurship, international business, and aerospace engineering; master's degree program in sports administration. Interdisciplinary programs in general liberal arts and sciences, gerontology, minority studies, urban affairs, women's studies. Facilities and programs for independent research, including honors programs. Special exchange program with the University of Orleans (France); Spanish program in Puebla (Mexico). Summer program in Strasbourg (France).

Degrees Conferred: 168 *associate;* 1,817 *baccalaureate* (B), f914 *master's* (M), 28 *doctorate* (D): area and ethnic studies 23 (B); biological/life sciences 40 (B), 2 (M); business/marketing 427 (B), 108 (M); communications/communication technologies 100 (B), 15 (M); computer and information sciences 47 (B), 36 (M); education 207 (B), 220 (M), 5 (D); engineering and engineering technologies 148 (B), 220 (M), 8 (D); English 27 (B), 8 (M); foreign languages and literature 29 (B), 5 (M); health professions and related sciences 191 (B), 109 (M); interdisciplinary studies 3 (B), 6 (M); liberal arts/general studies 4 (B), 5 (M); mathematics 19 (B), 2 (M), 1 (D); natural resources/environmental science 2 (M); parks and recreation 25 (B), 28 (M); philosophy/religion/theology 4 (B); physical sciences 36 (B), 16 (M), 1 (D); protective services/public administration 161 (B), 60 (M); psychology 108 (B), 8 (M), 13 (D); social sciences and history 135 (B), 37 (M); visual and performing arts 83 (B), 27 (M).

Fees and Other Expenses: *Full-time tuition per academic year 2004–05:* undergraduate resident $3,150, out-of-state student $10,603; graduate resident $2,700, out-of-state student $8,100. *Required fees:* $758. *Room and board per academic year:* $4,900.

Financial Aid: Aid from institutionally generated funds is provided on the basis of academic merit, financial need, athletic ability, other criteria. Institution has a Program Participation Agreement with the U.S. Department of Education for eligible students to receive Pell Grants and other federal aid.

Financial aid to full-time, first-time undergraduate students: need-based scholarships/grants totaling $13,527,504, self-help $44,927,998; non-need-based scholarships/grants totaling $4,938,529, parent loans $1,057,404, athletic awards $1,783,009.

Departments and Teaching Staff: *Total instructional faculty:* 522 (full-time 469, part-time 53; women 208, men 314; members of minority groups 56). Total faculty with doctorate, first-professional, or other terminal degree: 397. Student-to-faculty ratio: 18:1. *Faculty development:* $35,925,319 in grants for research. 14 faculty members awarded sabbaticals 2004–05.

Enrollment: Total enrollment 14,297. Undergraduate full-time 3,159 men / 4,058 women, part-time 1,668m / 2,314w; graduate full-time 504m / 539w, part-time 879m / 1,176w.

Characteristics of Student Body: *Ethnic/racial makeup:* number of Black non-Hispanic: 726; American Indian or Alaska Native: 145; Asian or Pacific Islander: 787; Hispanic: 542; White non-Hispanic: 7,899; unknown: 551. *Age distribution:* number under 18: 393; 18–19: 1,891; 20–21: 2,630; 22–24: 2,508; 25–29: 1,587; 30–34: 726; 35–39: 417; 40–49: 643; 50–64: 284; 65 and over: 20.

International Students: 549 undergraduate nonresident aliens enrolled fall 2004. Programs available to aid students whose native language is not English: social and cultural. English as a Second Language Program. Some financial aid designated for international students.

Student Life: On-campus residence halls house 8% of student body. 7% of men join fraternities; 5% of women join sororities. *Intercollegiate athletics:* men only: baseball, basketball, cross-country, golf, tennis, track; women only: basketball, cross-country, golf, softball, tennis, track, volleyball. *Special regulations:* Cars permitted without restrictions. *Special services:* Learning Resources Center, medical services, shuttle bus service during evening hours. *Student publications, radio, television:* Sunflower, triweekly newspaper. Radio station KMUW broadcasts 131 hours per week; WSU cable channel 13 broadcasts 125 hours per week. *Surrounding community:* Wichita metropolitan area population 500,000. Served by mass transit bus system; airport 10 miles from campus.

Publications: *Business and Economic Report* (quarterly) alternates with the monthly *Kansas Economic Indicators* as a publication of the Center for Economic Development and Business Research, a service of the W. Frank Barton School of Business, Wichita State University. *Publisher:* University Press of Kansas is operated jointly by the University of Kansas, Kansas State University, The Wichita State University, Emporia State University, Ft. Hays State University and Pittsburg State University.

Library Collections: 1,552,180 volumes. 503,000 government documents; 1,100,000 microforms; 15,000 audiovisual materials; 2,055 current periodicals. Access to online information retrieval systems and the Internet.

Most important holdings include W.H. Auden Collection; William Lloyd Garrison Collection; collection on hypnotism, mesmerism, and animal magnetism; Baughman Collection (early Kansas maps); Aviation History of World War II Collection.

Buildings and Grounds: Campus area 380 acres.

Chief Executive Officer: Dr. Donald L. Beggs, President.

Address admission inquiries to Gina Crabtree, Director of Admissions.

Fairmount College of Liberal Arts and Sciences

Degree Programs Offered: *Associate* in arts, electrical engineering technology; *baccalaureate* in anthropology, biological sciences, chemistry, communication, computer science, criminal justice, economics, English, French, general studies/liberal arts, geology, gerontology, history, mathematics, minority studies, philosophy, physics, political science, psychology, social work, sociology,

Spanish, women's studies (field majors: biochemistry, chemistry/business, classical studies, international studies, and all LAS majors); *master's* in general studies/liberal studies, geology, gerontology, history, mathematics, physics, political science, public administration, social work, sociology, Spanish, and women's studies; *doctorate* in mathematics, psychology.

W. Frank Barton School of Business

Degree Programs Offered: *Associate* in legal assisting; *baccalaureate* in accounting, business administration, economics, entrepreneurship, finance, human resource management, international business, management, management information systems, and marketing; *master's* in accounting, business, business administration, and economics.

College of Education

Degree Programs Offered: *Baccalaureate* in communicative disorders and sciences, elementary education, secondary education, sports administration; *master's* in communicative disorders and sciences, counseling, curriculum and instruction, educational administration and supervision, educational psychology, physical education, special education, sports administration; *doctorate* in communicative disorders and sciences, educational administration and supervision.

College of Engineering

Degree Programs Offered: *Baccalaureate* in aerospace engineering, computer engineering, electrical engineering, industrial engineering, manufacturing engineering, mechanical engineering; *master's* in aerospace engineering, electrical engineering, engineering management, industrial engineering, mechanical engineering; *doctorate* in aerospace engineering, electrical engineering, mechanical engineering.

Distinctive Educational Programs: Interdisciplinary baccalaureate program in engineering, including emphases in biomedical engineering, engineering management, engineering analysis, other fields.

College of Fine Arts

Degree Programs Offered: *Baccalaureate* in art education, art history, art-studio art (emphases in ceramics, drawing and painting, printmaking, sculpture), graphic design, music (emphases in history-literature, performance, piano pedagogy, theory-composition), music education, musical theatre, performing arts-dance, and theatre; *master's* in music, music education.

College of Health Professions

Degree Programs Offered: *Associate* in dental hygiene, physical therapist assisting; *baccalaureate* in health services organization and policy, medical technology, nursing, physician assisting; *master's* in nursing, physical therapy.

Kentucky

Alice Lloyd College

100 Purpose Road
Pippa Passes, Kentucky 41844-9701
Tel: (606) 368-2101   **E-mail:** admissions@alc.edu
Fax: (606) 368-2125   **Internet:** www.alc.edu

Institution Description: Alice Lloyd College is a private liberal arts college. *Enrollment:* 611. *Degrees awarded:* Associate, baccalaureate.

Accreditation: *Regional:* SACS-Comm. on Coll.

History: Established 1923.

Calendar: Semesters. Academic year late Aug. to early May.

Characteristics of Freshmen: 881 applicants (363 men, 528 women). 58.6% of applicants admitted. 33.9% of admitted students enrolled full-time.

9 students submitted SAT scores; 165 students submitted ACT scores. *25th percentile:* ACT Composite 17, ACT English 16, ACT Math 17. *75th percentile:* ACT Composite 24, ACT English 24, ACT Math 24.

45% of entering freshmen expected to graduate within 5 years. 65% of freshmen from Kentucky. Freshmen from 5 states and 3 foreign countries.

Admission: Rolling admissions plan. *Requirements:* Graduation from accredited secondary school.

Degree Requirements: Completion of prescribed curriculum; general education requirements.

Degrees Conferred: 99 *baccalaureate.* Bachelor's degrees awarded in top five disciplines: education 34; business, management, marketing, and related support services life sciences 23; biological and biomedical sciences 14; history 8; English language and literature/letters 8.

Fees and Other Expenses: *Full-time tuition per academic year 2004–05:* $7,450. *Books and supplies:* $850. *Room and board per academic year:* $3,800.

Financial Aid: Aid from institutionally generated funds is provided on the basis of academic merit, financial need, athletic ability. Institution has a Program Participation Agreement with the U.S. Department of Education for eligible students to receive Pell Grants and other federal aid.

Financial aid to full-time, first-time undergraduate students: 48% received federal grants averaging $3,210; 68% state/local grants averaging $3,364; 81% institutional grants averaging $3,380; 9% received loans averaging $1,189.

Departments and Teaching Staff: Social science/education *professors* 5, *associate professors* 2, *assistant professors* 3, *instructors* 3, *part-time faculty* 1; humanities 0, 2, 3, 3, 3; natural science/mathematics 2, 2, 3, 1, 1. *Total instructional faculty:* 44. Degrees held by full-time faculty: doctorate 55%, master's 100%. 55% hold terminal degrees.

Enrollment: Total enrollment 611 (48.8% men, 53.2% women).

Characteristics of Student Body: *Ethnic/racial makeup:* Black non-Hispanic: 1%; American Indian or Alaska Native: .2%; Asian or Pacific Islander: .3%; Hispanic: .5%; White non-Hispanic: 97.9%.

International Students: 2 nonresident aliens enrolled fall 2004. Students from Asia, Central and South America, Africa. No programs available to aid students whose native language is not English. No financial aid specifically designated for international students.

Library Collections: 80,000 volumes. 4,600 microform units (92 titles); 2,440 audiovisual materials; 400 current periodical subscriptions. Online catalog. Students have access to online information retrieval services and the Internet.

Most important holdings include the Appalachian Studies Monographs; oral history taped interviews from Eastern Kentucky; original photographic work of Astor Dobson.

Buildings and Grounds: Campus area 225 acres.

Chief Executive Officer: Dr. Joe A. Stepp, President.

Address admission inquiries to Sean Damron, Director of Admissions.

Asbury College

1 Macklem Drive
Wilmore, Kentucky 40390-1198
Tel: (859) 858-3511   **E-mail:** admissions@asbury.edu
Fax: (859) 858-3912   **Internet:** www.asbury.edu

Institution Description: Asbury College is a private, independent, nonprofit college. *Enrollment:* 1,278. *Degrees awarded:* Baccalaureate, master's.

Member of Christian College Consortium and Coalition for Christian Colleges and Universities.

Accreditation: *Regional:* SACS-Comm. on Coll. *Professional:* music, social work

History: Established and offered first instruction at postsecondary level 1890; awarded first degree (baccalaureate) 1893; incorporated 1904; awarded first master's degree 2001.

Institutional Structure: *Governing board:* Asbury College Board of Trustees. Extrainstitutional representation: 26 trustees. *Composition of institution:* Administrators 20 men / 7 women. Academic affairs headed by provost. Management/business/finances directed by vice president for business affairs and treasurer. Full-time instructional faculty 65 men / 23 women. Academic governance body, The Faculty Assembly of Asbury College, meets an average of 8 times per year.

Calendar: Semesters. Academic year Aug. to May. Freshmen admitted Aug., Jan., May. Degrees conferred May, Aug., Dec. Formal commencement May. Summer session of 2 terms May to July.

Characteristics of Freshmen: 74% of applicants admitted. 50% of applicants admitted and enrolled.

60% (182 students) submitted SAT scores; 70% (210 students) submitted ACT scores. *25th percentile:* SAT Verbal 530, SAT Math 500; ACT Composite 21, ACT English 21, ACT Math 19. *75th percentile:* SAT Verbal 640, SAT Math 620; ACT Composite 27, ACT English 29, ACT Math 26. 4 National Merit Scholars.

62% of entering freshmen expected to graduate within 5 years. 30% of freshmen from Kentucky. Freshmen from 37 states and 5 foreign countries.

Admission: Rolling admissions plan. For fall acceptance, apply as early as junior year of secondary school, but not later than Aug. 1 of year of enrollment. Early acceptance available. *Requirements:* Either graduation from secondary school or GED. Recommend 4 units English (1 year composition), 2 social studies (1 year history), 2-3 laboratory science, 3-4 mathematics, 2 foreign language. Minimum GPA 2.5. *Entrance tests:* SAT 1020, ACT 22 Composite. *For transfer students:* 2.5 minimum GPA, 75 semester hours from accredited institutions and 60 semester hours from unaccredited institutions maximum transfer credit.

College credit and advanced placement possible through College Board CLEP, APP, and institutional foreign language examinations. Tutoring available. Remedial math and English courses.

Degree Requirements: 124 semester hours; 2.5 GPA (B.A.), 2.75 (B.S.); 3 semesters in residence; chapel attendance 3 times weekly; general education requirements. For M.A.: 3.0 GPA; 32 to 53 semester hours.

Grading system: A–F; credit/no credit; withdraw; incomplete (carries time limit).

Distinctive Educational Programs: Through the Coalition for Christian Colleges and Universities: study abroad programs in Australia, China, Egypt, France, Kenya, Russia, England, Costa Rica, Israel, Uganda, Spain, and off-campus programs in Washington, D.C., Massachusetts, Michigan, Illinois, Colorado, California. Dual-degree programs with the University of Kentucky in engineering. Pre-law, pre-dental, pre-medical, pre-veterinary education. ROTC program.

ROTC: Air Force and Army in cooperation with the University of Kentucky.

Degrees Conferred: 267 *baccalaureate:* biological/life sciences 11; business/marketing 18; communications/communication technologies 35; education 20; English 34; foreign languages and literature 23; health professions and related sciences 1; mathematics 4; parks and recreation 10; philosophy/religion/

theology 41; physical sciences 7; psychology 23; social sciences and history 23; visual and performing arts 9. 12 *master's:* education 12.

Fees and Other Expenses: *Full-time tuition per academic year 2005–06:* $18,808. *Required fees:* $148. *Room and board per academic year:* $4,806.

Financial Aid: Aid from institutionally generated funds is provided on the basis of academic merit, financial need, other criteria. Institution has a Program Participation Agreement with the U.S. Department of Education for eligible students to receive Pell Grants and other federal aid.

Financial aid to full-time, first-time undergraduate students: need-based scholarships/grants totaling $7,844,775, self-help $5,032,035, parent loans $946,662, tuition waivers $300,299, athletic awards $56,148; non-need-based scholarships/grants totaling $1,340,511, self-help $408,635, parent loans $167,879, tuition waivers $572,709, athletic awards $10,107. *Graduate aid:* 44 students received federal and state-funded loans totaling $461,033 (ranging from $136 to $18,500).

Departments and Teaching Staff: *Professors* 47, *associate professors* 23, *assistant professors* 18, *part-time faculty* 66. *Total instructional faculty:* 154 (full-time 88, part-time 66; women 57, men 97; members of minority groups 2). Total faculty with doctorate, first-professional, or other terminal degree: 85. Student-to-faculty ratio: 10:1. *Faculty development:* 6 faculty members awarded sabbaticals 2004–05.

Enrollment: Total enrollment 1,278. Undergraduate full-time 473 men / 678 women, part-time 25m / 42w; graduate full-time 3w, part-time 19m / 38w. *Transfer students:* in-state 13; from out-of-state 39.

Characteristics of Student Body: *Ethnic/racial makeup:* number of: Black non-Hispanic: 11; American Indian or Alaska Native: 4; Asian or Pacific Islander: 15; Hispanic: 16; White non-Hispanic: 1,164. *Age distribution:* number under 18: 26; 18–19: 447; 20–21: 522; 22–24: 171; 25–29: 23; 30–34: 6; 35–39: 8; 40–49: 14; 50–64: 1.

International Students: 18 nonresident aliens enrolled fall 2004. 2 students from Europe, 7 Asia, 7 Africa, 2 Canada. Programs available to aid students whose native language is not English: social. No financial aid specifically designated for international students.

Student Life: On-campus residence halls house 84% of student body. Married student housing: 50–55% of married students request institutional housing; 95–98% are so housed. *Intercollegiate athletics:* men: basketball, cross-country, soccer, swimming, tennis; women: basketball, cross-country, swimming, tennis, volleyball. *Special regulations:* Cars permitted; registration required. Curfews from 11pm to 6am Sun.–Thurs. Quiet hours from 7pm to 7am daily. *Special services:* Tutoring Service, counseling services, leadership and career development, health services. *Student publications: Collegian,* a weekly student newspaper; *The Asburian,* a yearbook. *Surrounding community:* Wilmore population 5,905. Lexington (KY), 14 miles from campus, is nearest metropolitan area.

Publications: Sources of information about Asbury include the *Ambassador* (the alumni, constituent magazine) and the annual college catalog.

Library Collections: 145,424 volumes including bound books, serial backfiles, electronic documents, and government documents not in separate collections. Online catalog. Current serial subscriptions: 517 paper, 22,120 microform. 9,197 audiovisual materials. 12 computer work stations. Students have access to the Internet at no charge.

Most important holdings include Ford Philpot Collection; Alexander Reid Collection; Bishop J. Waskom Pickett Collection.

Buildings and Grounds: Campus area 65 acres. *New buildings:* Aldergate Commons completed 2001; Dennis F. and Elsie B. Kinlaw Library 2001.

Chief Executive Officer: Dr. Paul A. Rader, President.

Address admission inquiries to Dr. Jack P. Powell, Vice President of Enrollment Management.

Asbury Theological Seminary

204 North Lexington Avenue
Wilmore, Kentucky 40390-1199
Tel: (859) 858-3581   **E-mail:** admissions@asburyseminary.edu
Internet: www.asburyseminary.edu

Institution Description: Asbury Theological Seminary is a multidenominational graduate level institution that prepares men and women for ministry. *Enrollment:* 1,741. *Degrees awarded:* Master's, first-professional, doctorate (cooperative program with University of Kentucky).

Accreditation: *Regional:* SACS-Comm. on Coll. *National:* ATS. *Professional:* theology

History: Established as integral part of Asbury College 1923; incorporated as a separate institution 1931.

Institutional Structure: *Governing board:* Board of Trustees. Representation: 34 trustees. *Composition of institution:* Administered by president, vice

president/provost, vice president for finance, vice president for Seminary Advancement, dean of students. Full-time instructional faculty 59.

Calendar: Semesters (4-1-4 plan). Academic year late June to May. Degrees conferred Jan., May, Aug., Dec. Formal commencement May. Summer sessions June to Aug.

Admission: Rolling admissions plan. Application must be on file 2 months prior to beginning of term. *Requirements:* For M.Div, M.A., student must have baccalaureate degree with GPA 2.25 on 4.00 scale from an accredited college or university; for Th.M. and D.Min., student must have M.Div. degree with GPA of 3.00 on 4.00 scale; for D.Miss. program, student must have Master of Theology. *Entrance tests:* For M.Div. and M.A., students below 2.25 GPA need to supply GRE or MAT scores; all Th.M. applicants need to supply GRE or MAT scores. *For transfer students:* transfer credit given for work done at accredited institutions; last 30 hours must be completed at Asbury.

Degree Requirements: *For Master of Arts:* 60 semester hours; 2.0 GPA; 30 semester hours in residence; 7 year limit. *For Master of Divinity:* 90 semester hours; 2.00 GPA; 60 semester hours in residence; 10 year limit; knowledge of Greek prerequisite. *For Master of Theology:* 30 semester hours; 3.0 GPA. *For Doctor of Ministry:* 27 semester hours; thesis required; 3.0 GPA; major concentration required. *For Doctor of Missiology:* 60 semester hours; major area studies required; dissertation required.

Distinctive Educational Programs: Inner City Ministries Program; Appalachian Studies Program; Five Seminary Consortium; Internship Studies; Scholarship Programs; nondegree continuing education. January Course: The Church Abroad.

Degrees Conferred: 83 *master of arts;* 138 *master of divinity;* 20 *doctorate:* theology.

Fees and Other Expenses: *Tuition per academic year:* varies by program. Contact the seminary for current tuition and fees.

Financial Aid: Aid from institutionally generated funds is provided on the basis of academic merit, financial need, other considerations. Financial assistance is available in the form of Pell Grants, College Work-Study, Veterans Administration Benefits, National Direct Student Loans, Supplemental Education Opportunity Grants (SEOG), Stafford Loans, other federal aid programs.

Departments and Teaching Staff: *Total instructional faculty:* 53.4 FTE. *Total tenured faculty:* 33. Degrees held by full-time faculty: doctorate 83%, master's 11%, professional 6%. 89% hold terminal degrees.

Enrollment: Total enrollment 1,741.

Characteristics of Student Body: *Ethnic/racial makeup:* Black non-Hispanic: 3%; American Indian or Alaska Native: 1%; Asian or Pacific Islander: 2%; Hispanic: 15; White non-Hispanic: 64%; unknown: 5.6%. *Age distribution:* 22–24: 18%; 25–29: 28%; 30–34: 15%; 35–39: 8%; 40–49: 9%; 50–59: 2%.

International Students: 131 nonresident aliens enrolled fall 2004. Students from Europe, Asia, Central and South America, Africa, Canada, Australia.

Student Life: Campus housing for singles includes 200 beds (150 men, 50 women), 156 units of seminary-owned apartments. Many apartments and housing opportunities available in the surrounding community. *Special services:* Day care center, campus activities center including gym, lounge, racquetball court, exercise room, and student offices.

Publications: Quarterly ministry magazine, *The Asbury Herald,* contains helpful/inspirational articles and institutional alumni news; semiannual faculty publication, *The Asbury Journal,* contains scholarly/research articles.

Library Collections: 275,000 volumes. 5,000 microforms; 15,500 audiovisual materials; 750 current periodical subscriptions.

Most important special holdings include OMS International Papers; Hanna Whithall Smith Papers; Christian Holiness Association Papers; W.W. White Papers.

Chief Executive Officer: Dr. Jeffrey E. Greenway, President.

Address admission inquiries to Janette Vernon, Director of Admissions.

Bellarmine College

2001 Newburg Road
Louisville, Kentucky 40205-0671
Tel: (502) 452-8000   **E-mail:** admissions@bellarmine.edu
Fax: (502) 452-8002   **Internet:** www.bellarmine.educ

Institution Description: Bellarmine College is a private college affiliated with the Roman Catholic Church. *Enrollment:* 2,888. *Degrees awarded:* Associate, baccalaureate, master's. Certificates also awarded.

Accreditation: *Regional:* SACS-Comm. on Coll. *Professional:* clinical lab scientist, nursing, nursing education, teacher education

History: Established as Bellarmine College, a men's college and offered first instruction at postsecondary level 1950; awarded first degree (baccalaureate)

1954; merged with Ursuline College, a women's college, and changed name to Bellarmine-Ursuline College 1968; re-adopted present name 1971.

Institutional Structure: *Governing board:* Board of Trustees; extrainstitutional representation: 30 trustees, archbishop of Louisville; institutional representation: president of the college, 2 full-time instructional faculty members, president of the student body. 3 ex officio. All voting. *Composition of institution:* Administrators 10 men / 18 women (at dean's level 1 is a woman). Academic affairs headed by vice president and dean, academic affairs. Management/business/finances directed by vice president for financial affairs. Full-time instructional faculty 101. Academic governance body, Educational Affairs Committee, meets an average of 20 times per year.

Calendar: Semesters. Academic year Aug. to May. Freshmen admitted Aug., Jan., June. Degrees conferred May, Dec. Formal commencement May. Summer session of 4 terms from May to Aug.

Characteristics of Freshmen: 1,504 applicants (406 men, 1,038 women). 78.5% of applicants admitted. 34.7% of admitted students enrolled full-time.

33% (137 students) submitted SAT scores; 67% (272 students) submitted ACT scores. *25th percentile:* SAT I Verbal 500, SAT I Math 490; ACT Composite 21, ACT English 21, ACT Math 20. *75th percentile:* SAT I Verbal 610, SAT I Math 610; ACT Composite 26, ACT English 27, ACT Math 26.

57% of entering freshmen expected to graduate within 5 years. 80% of freshmen from Kentucky. Freshmen from 12 states and 4 foreign countries.

Admission: Rolling admissions plan. For fall acceptance, apply as early as Sept. of previous year, but not later than Aug. of year of enrollment. Early acceptance available. *Requirements:* Either graduation from accredited secondary school with 16 academic units which must include 4 English, 2 mathematics, 2 natural science, 2 social studies; or GED. Minimum grade average of C. Lowest acceptable secondary school class standing 40th percentile. *Entrance tests:* College Board SAT or ACT composite. For foreign students TOEFL. *For transfer students:* 2.0 GPA, 90 semester hours maximum transfer credit; from 2-year accredited institution 70 hours; correspondence/extension students 12 hours.

College credit and advanced placement for postsecondary-level work completed in secondary school and for extrainstitutional learning (life experience) on basis of ACE *2006 Guide to the Evaluation of Educational Experiences in the Armed Services.* Tutoring available. Developmental courses offered during regular academic year; credit given.

Degree Requirements: *For all associate degrees:* 63 credit hours. *For all baccalaureate degrees:* 126 credit hours; exit competency examination—GRE or other standardized tests. *For all undergraduate degrees:* 2.0 GPA; 1 year in residence; distribution requirements; exit competency examination in writing.

Fulfillment of some degree requirements and exemption from some beginning courses possible by passing departmental examinations, College Board CLEP, APP. *Grading system:* A–F, pass-fail, withdraw (deadline after which pass-fail is appended to withdraw); incomplete (carries time limit).

Distinctive Educational Programs: *For undergraduates:* Internships. Interdisciplinary program in liberal studies; senior comprehensive seminars. Facilities for independent research including honors programs, tutorials. Institutionally sponsored summer study abroad in varying locations; International Student Exchange Program: over 40 countries and 100 universities. Off-campus study in U.S. may be individually arranged. Degree-completion program in liberal studies for former students of Bellarmine. *Available to all students:* Weekend and evening classes. Independent study. Cross-registration through consortium. *Other distinctive programs:* Thomas Merton Studies Center sponsors national symposium, courses, seminars, lectures, retreats, and cultural events. Credit and non-credit education program.

ROTC: Air Force and Army offered in cooperation with University of Louisville.

Degrees Conferred: 351 *baccalaureate*; 227 *master's.* Bachelor's degrees awarded in top five disciplines: health professions and related clinical sciences 90; business, management, marketing, and related support services 70; psychology 26; biological and biomedical sciences 22; communication, journalism, and related programs 22.

Fees and Other Expenses: *Full-time tuition per academic year 2004–05:* $19,950. *Books and supplies:* $620. *Room and board per academic year:* $6,080.

Financial Aid: Aid from institutionally generated funds is provided on the basis of academic merit, financial need, athletic ability, other considerations. Institution has a Program Participation Agreement with the U.S. Department of Education for eligible students to receive Pell Grants and other federal aid.

Financial aid to full-time, first-time undergraduate students: 25% received federal grants averaging $2,959; 67% state/local grants averaging $3,435; 84% institutional grants averaging $9,146; 59% received loans averaging $3,087.

Departments and Teaching Staff: Biology *professors* 2, *associate professors* 2, *assistant professors* 2, *part-time faculty* 5; chemistry 0, 3, 0, 3; communications 2, 0, 0, 1; computer science 1, 1, 0, 6; education 3, 2, 1, 8; English 2, 3, 2, 4; fine and performing arts 1, 2, 2, 15; foreign languages 0, 0, 1, 5; history/political science 2, 1, 1, 3; mathematics 3, 1, 1, 2; philosophy 2, 1, 1, 1; psychol-

ogy/sociology 0, 2, 2, 8; theology 2, 0, 1, 1; accounting 0, 2, 3, 1; business 4, 3, 1, 2; economics 3, 2, 0, 0; nursing 1, 3, 9, 18.

Total instructional faculty: 135 FTE. Student-to-faculty ratio: 14:1. Degrees held by full-time faculty: doctorate 75%, master's 20%, professional 5. 80% hold terminal degrees.

Enrollment: Total enrollment 2,888. Undergraduate 2,327 (men 34.5%, women 65.5%).

Characteristics of Student Body: *Ethnic/racial makeup:* Black non-Hispanic: 4.1%; American Indian or Alaska Native: .1%; Asian or Pacific Islander: 1.5%; Hispanic: 1.1%; White non-Hispanic: 82.6%; unknown: .1%. *Age distribution:* 17–21: 61%; 22–24: 9%; 25–29: 9%; 30–34: 6%; 35–39: 5%; 40–49: 7%; 50–59: 2%; 60–and over: 1%.

International Students: 26 nonresident aliens enrolled fall 2004. Programs available to aid students whose native language is not English: cultural. English as a Second Language Program. No financial aid specifically designated for international students.

Student Life: On-campus residence halls house 38% of student body. Residence halls for men constitute 48% of such space, for women 52%. *Intercollegiate athletics:* men only: baseball, basketball, cross-country, golf, soccer, tennis, track; women only, basketball, cross-country, field hockey, golf, soccer, softball, tennis, track, volleyball. *Special regulations:* Cars permitted without restrictions. Quiet hours from 9pm to 7am. Residence hall visitation from 11am to 2am daily. *Special services:* Medical services. *Student publications: The Concord,* a bimonthly newspaper; *The Lance,* a yearbook. *Surrounding community:* Louisville population 1,000,000. Served by mass transit bus system, airport 5 miles from campus.

Publications: *Merton Seasonal* (quarterly) first published 1976; *Kentucky Poetry Review,* 1983.

Library Collections: 115,000 volumes. 694,000 microforms; 4,900 audiovisual materials; 550 current periodical subscriptions. 4,784 recordings. 60 computer work stations. Access to online information retrieval systems and the Internet.

Most important holdings include Thomas Merton Collection (30,000 items including manuscripts, first editions, correspondence, journals, memorabilia); John Lyons Kentucky Catholic History; Data Courier Collection; Henry T. Miles Collection of Civil War literature.

Buildings and Grounds: Campus area 124 acres.

Chief Executive Officer: Dr. Joseph J. McGowan, President.

Address admission inquiries to Timothy A. Sturgeon, Dean of Admission.

Berea College

Berea, Kentucky 40404

Tel: (859) 985-3000   **E-mail:** admissions@berea.edu
Fax: (859) 985-3917   **Internet:** www.berea.edu

Institution Description: Berea College is a private, independent, nonprofit, nondenominational Christian college. *Enrollment:* 1,556. *Degrees awarded:* Baccalaureate.

Accreditation: *Regional:* SACS-Comm. on Coll. *Professional:* nursing, nursing education, teacher education

History: Established 1855; incorporated 1859; offered first instruction at postsecondary level 1869; awarded first degree (baccalaureate) 1873. *See* Elizabeth Peck, *Berea's First Century, 1855–1955* (Lexington: University of Kentucky Press, 1955) for further information.

Institutional Structure: *Governing board:* Berea College Board of Trustees. Representation: 30 trustees, including 12 alumni; president of the college. All voting. *Composition of institution:* Central administrative officer include the president, academic vice president and provost, dean of the faulty, vice president for alumni relations and development, vice president for business and administration, vice president for finance, vice president for labor and student life. Full-time instructional faculty 131. Academic governance body, the faculty, meets an average of 8 times per year.

Calendar: Semesters (4-1-4 plan). Academic year Sept. to May. Freshmen admitted Sept., Feb., June. Degrees conferred May, Sept., Feb. Formal commencement May. Summer session of 1 term from June to July.

Characteristics of Freshmen: 34% of applicants accepted. 71% of accepted applicants enrolled.

23% (91 students) submitted SAT scores; 74% (297 students) submitted ACT scores. *25th percentile:* SAT Verbal 490, SAT Math 510; ACT Composite 21, ACT English 21, ACT Math 19. *75th percentile:* SAT Verbal 615, SAT Math 615; ACT Composite 26, ACT English 28, ACT Math 25.

89% of entering freshmen expected to graduate within 5 years. 40% of freshmen from Kentucky. Freshmen from 25 states and 22 foreign countries.

Admission: Rolling admissions plan. Apply as early as 15 months, but not later than 90 days, prior to enrollment. Early acceptance available. *Requirements:* Graduation from an accredited secondary school, completion of homeschool curriculum, or GED. Recommend 4 units English, 3 mathematics, 2 science, 2 social studies, 2 years of foreign language. Lowest acceptable secondary school class standing 40th percentile. *Entrance tests:* College Board SAT or ACT. For foreign students TOEFL. *For transfer students:* 2.4 minimum GPA; from 4-year accredited institution 90 semester hours maximum transfer credit; from 2-year accredited institution 67 hours.

College credit and advanced placement for postsecondary-level work completed in secondary school. Tutoring available. Developmental courses offered in summer session and regular academic year; nondegree credit given.

Degree Requirements: 33 courses (35 for nursing); minimum 2.0 overall GPA; convocation attendance 10 times per term. All student participate in labor program by working at least 10 hours per week maintaining the college.

Fulfillment of some degree requirements and exemption from some beginning courses possible by passing departmental examinations, College Board CLEP, AP. *Grading system:* A–F; incomplete (carries time limit).

Distinctive Educational Programs: Work-experience programs. Individually arranged interdisciplinary programs. Institutionally sponsored study abroad in many countries. Exchange program with many colleges.

Degrees Conferred: 337 *baccalaureate.* Bachelor's degrees awarded in top five disciplines: business, management, marketing, and related support services 48; education 34; social sciences 26; biological and biomedical sciences 24; engineering technologies/technicians 24.

Fees and Other Expenses: *Full-time tuition per academic year 2005–06:* $21,600. *Required fees:* 516. *Room and board per academic year:* $4,980.

Financial Aid: Aid from institutionally generated funds is provided on the basis of financial need. Institution has a Program Participation Agreement with the U.S. Department of Education for eligible students to receive Pell Grants and other federal aid.

Financial aid to full-time, first-time undergraduate students: need-based scholarships/grants totaling $40,405,407, self-help $3,150,277, parent loans $1,400; non-need-based scholarships/grants totaling $656,483.

Departments and Teaching Staff: *Professors* 45, *associate professors* 43, *assistant professors* 37, *instructors* 6, *part-time faculty* 29. *Total instructional faculty:* 160 (full-time 131, part-time 29; women 64, men 96). Total faculty with doctorate, first-professional, or other terminal degree: 119. Student-to-faculty ratio: 10:1. *Faculty development:* 13 faculty members awarded sabbaticals 2003-04.

Enrollment: Total enrollment 1,556. Undergraduate full-time 628 men / 888 women, part-time 21m / 19w.

Characteristics of Student Body: *Ethnic/racial makeup:* number of: Black non-Hispanic: 285; American Indian or Alaska Native: 8; Asian or Pacific Islander: 22; Hispanic: 26; White non-Hispanic: 1,070; unknown: 31. *Age distribution:* 17–21: 81%; 22–24: 13%; 25–29: 3%; 30–34: 1%; 35–39: less than 1%; 40–49: 1%; 50–and over: 1%.

International Students: 114 nonresident aliens enrolled fall 2004. Students from Europe, Asia, Central and South Latin America, Africa. Programs available to aid students whose native language is not English: social, cultural, financial.

Student Life: On-campus residence halls house 82% of student body. Residence halls for men constitute 42% of such space, for women 58%. Limited housing available for married or single parent students. *Intercollegiate athletics:* men: baseball, basketball, cross-country, golf, soccer, swimming, tennis, track and field; women: basketball, cross-country, soccer, softball, swimming, tennis, track and field, volleyball. *Special services:* Medical services. *Student publications, radio: The Chimes,* a yearbook; *The Pinnacle,* a monthly newspaper. *Surrounding community:* Berea population 10,000. Lexington, 40 miles from campus, is nearest metropolitan area.

Library Collections: 358,556 volumes including bound books, serial backfiles, electronic documents, and government documents not in separate collections. Online and card catalogs. Current serial subscriptions: 1,268 paper, 188 microform, 11 electronic. 306 compact discs; 54 CD-ROMs. Computer work stations available. Students have access to the Internet at no charge. Total budget for books, periodicals, audiovisual materials, microforms 2004–05: $412,446.

Most important holdings include the Weatherford-Hammond Collection (9,000 items pertaining to the history and culture of the Southern Appalachian region, including books, pamphlets, other printed materials, and 350 feet of archival and manuscript materials); the rare book collection (items dating back to the 16th century and including a 1st edition of the King James Bible, other Bibles, ballads, hymnals, early editions of works of English and American literature, works on Black history); Berea College Archives.

Buildings and Grounds: Campus area 140 acres.

Chief Executive Officer: Larry D. Shinn, President.

Address admission inquiries to James Ealy, Director of Admissions.

Brescia University

717 Frederica Street
Owensboro, Kentucky 42301-3023

Tel: (270) 685-3131   **E-mail:** admissions@brescia.edu
Fax: (270) 686-8422   **Internet:** www.brescia.edu

Institution Description: Brescia University, formerly Brescia College, is a private institution affiliated with the Roman Catholic Church. *Enrollment:* 674. *Degrees awarded:* Associate, baccalaureate, master's. Post-baccalaureate certificates also awarded.

Accreditation: *Regional:* SACS-Comm. on Coll.

History: Established as Mount Saint Joseph Junior College and offered first instruction at postsecondary level 1925; became 4-year college and became Brescia College 1950; awarded first degree (baccalaureate) 1953; became Brescia University 1998.

Institutional Structure: *Governing board:* Board of Trustees of Brescia University, Inc. with 41 members. *Composition of institution:* President's cabinet 3 men / 3 women. Academic affairs headed by vice president for academic affairs. Management/business/finances directed by director of business affairs. Full-time instructional faculty 40. Academic governance body, Faculty Assembly, meets an average of once per month.

Calendar: Semesters. Academic year Aug. to May. Freshmen admitted Aug., Jan., May, July. Degrees conferred and formal commencement May. Summer session from early June to early July.

Characteristics of Freshmen: 933 applicants (371 men, 562 women). 73.4% of applicants admitted. 23.6% of admitted students enrolled full-time.

44% of entering freshmen expected to graduate within 5 years. 82% of freshmen from Kentucky. Freshmen from 3 states and 4 foreign countries.

Admission: Rolling admissions plan. Apply as early as 1 year prior to registration, but not later than last day of late registration. Early acceptance available. $25 nonrefundable application fee for full-time and transfer applicants. *Requirements:* Either graduation from accredited secondary school or GED. Recommend 4 units English, 3 mathematics, 2 science, 2 social studies. Other strongly recommended include 2 units of foreign language, 2 units of fine arts, 2 units of computer science. Minimum GPA 2.0. *Entrance tests:* College Board SAT or ACT composite. *For transfer students:* 2.0 minimum GPA; maximum transfer credit limited only by residence requirement.

College credit and advanced placement for postsecondary-level work completed in secondary school. For extrainstitutional learning (life experience), college credit or advanced placement on basis of faculty assessment, ACE *2006 Guide to the Evaluation of Educational Experiences in the Armed Services.* Tutoring available. Developmental courses offered in summer session and regular academic year; credit given.

Degree Requirements: *For all associate degrees:* 63 credit hours (minimum). *For all baccalaureate degrees:* 128 credit hours. *For all undergraduate degrees:* 2.0 GPA; 42 hours in residence; distribution requirements.

Fulfillment of some degree requirements and exemption from some beginning courses possible by passing departmental examinations, College Board CLEP, AP. *Grading system:* A–F; pass-fail; withdraw (carries time limit); incomplete (carries time limit).

Distinctive Educational Programs: Optional minors offered in accounting, biology, business, chemistry, computer studies, economics, English, history, math, philosophy, physics, political science, professional writing (English); psychology, religious studies, sociology, Spanish, women's studies. Self-designed majors. Independent study. Internships. Preprofessional programs in art therapy, dentistry, engineering, law, medicine, optometry, pharmacy, veterinary science; 2-2 engineering program with University of Kentucky; speech and communication disorders. Weekend program for adult students.

Degrees Conferred: 19 *associate*; 107 *baccalaureate*; 9 *master's.* Bachelor's degrees awarded in top five disciplines: public administration and social science professions 24; business, management, marketing, and related support services 22; education 14; psychology 10; liberal arts and sciences, general studies and humanities 10.

Fees and Other Expenses: *Full-time tuition per academic year 2004–05:* $11,300 undergraduate; graduate study charged per credit hour. *Books and supplies:* 1,000. *Room and board per academic year:* $5,000.

Financial Aid: Aid from institutionally generated funds is provided on the basis of academic merit, financial need, athletic ability, other criteria. Institution has a Program Participation Agreement with the U.S. Department of Education for eligible students to receive Pell Grants and other federal aid.

Financial aid to full-time, first-time undergraduate students: 32% received federal grants averaging $2,726; 72% state/local grants averaging $2,972; 87% institutional grants averaging $6,283; 60% received loans averaging $2,893.

Departments and Teaching Staff: Business *professors* 1, *associate professors* 1, *assistant professors* 3 *instructors* 1, *part-time faculty* 6; education/social and behavioral sciences 0, 2, 6, 1, 9; fine arts 0, 2, 4, 0, 3; humanities 2, 3, 4, 0, 7; mathematics/natural sciences 1, 3, 3, 3, 5.

Total instructional faculty: 80. Student-to-faculty ratio: 14:1. Degrees held by full-time faculty: doctorate 50%, master's 30. 70% hold terminal degrees.

Enrollment: Total enrollment 674. Undergraduate 634 (44% men, 56% women).

Characteristics of Student Body: *Ethnic/racial makeup:* Black non-Hispanic: 4.3%; American Indian or Alaska Native: .3%; Asian or Pacific Islander: .9%; Hispanic: 1.7%; White non-Hispanic: 81.5%; unknown: .6%. *Age distribution:* 17–21: 42%; 22–24: 14%; 25–39: 12%; 31–40: 14; 41–50: 12%; 51–and over: .6%.

International Students: 67 undergraduate nonresident aliens enrolled fall 2004. Students from Europe, Central and South America, Africa. Programs available to aid students whose native language is not English: English as a Second Language Program. Some financial aid available for qualifying international students.

Student Life: On-campus residence halls house 23% of student body. *Special regulations:* Cars permitted without restrictions. *Special services:* Student Support Services; Learning Resources Center, medical services. *Student publications: Brescia Yearbook,* an annual; *The Broadcast,* weekly newspaper. *Surrounding community:* Owensboro population 55,000. Louisville, 145 miles from campus, is nearest metropolitan area. Served by mass transit bus system; airport 3 miles from campus.

Publications: Sources of information about Brescia include "Brescia Now," published 3 times per year for alumni.

Library Collections: 184,000 volumes including bound books, serial backfiles, electronic documents, and government documents not in separate collections. Online catalog. Current serial subscriptions: 5,340 electronic full-text titles. 5,119 recordings; 156 compact discs. Computer work stations available. Students have access to the Internet.

Most important holdings include books and other published materials by and about Kentucky authors and Kentucky history and culture from the 18th and 19th centuries; Catholic Lay Ministry Collection; collections in women's studies and business.

Buildings and Grounds: Campus area 6 acres.

Chief Executive Officer: Sister Vivian Marie Bowles, O.S.U., Ed.D., President.

Address admission inquiries to Dr. William Kuba, Director of Enrollment Management.

Campbellsville University

1 University Drive
Campbellsville, Kentucky 42718

Tel: (270) 789-5000   **E-mail:** admissions@campbellsvil.edu
Fax: (270) 789-5050   **Internet:** www.campbellsvil.edu

Institution Description: Campbellsville College is a private college affiliated with Kentucky Baptist Convention (Southern Baptist). *Enrollment:* 2,187. *Degrees awarded:* Associate, baccalaureate, master's. Certificates also awarded.

Accreditation: *Regional:* SACS-Comm. on Coll.

History: Established as Russell Creek Academy and incorporated 1906; offered first instruction at postsecondary level and became Campbellsville College 1924; awarded first degree (associate) 1926; became Campbellsville University 1996.

Institutional Structure: *Governing board:* Board of Trustees of Campbellsville University. Representation: 44 trustees, including 15 alumni. All voting. *Composition of institution:* Administrators 5 men. Academic affairs headed by academic vice president. Management/business/finances directed by business vice president and treasurer. Full-time instructional faculty 82. Academic governance body, the faculty, meets an average of 20 times per year.

Calendar: Semesters. Academic year Aug. to May. Freshmen admitted Aug., Jan., June, July. Degrees conferred and formal commencement May. Summer session from early June to late July.

Characteristics of Freshmen: 73% of applicants admitted. 40% of applicants admitted and enrolled. 13% of students submitted SAT scores; 82% submitted ACT scores. *25th percentile:* SAT Verbal 420, SAT Math 430; ACT Composite 18. *75th percentile:* SAT Verbal 560, SAT Math 570; ACT Composite 24. 34% of entering freshmen expected to graduate within 5 years. 81% of freshmen from Kentucky. Freshmen from 17 states and 2 foreign countries.

Admission: Rolling admissions plan. For fall acceptance, apply as early as completion of junior year of secondary school, but not later than beginning of Sept. of year of enrollment. Early acceptance available. *Requirements:* Either graduation from accredited secondary school or GED. Minimum GPA 2.0. Teacher education programs require a 2.5 GPA (on a 4.0 scale). *Entrance tests:* College Board SAT or ACT composite. *For transfer students:* 2.0 minimum GPA, 73 semester hours maximum transfer credit.

College credit and advanced placement for postsecondary-level work completed in secondary school and for extrainstitutional learning on the basis of ACE *2006 Guide to the Evaluation of Educational Experiences in the Armed Services;* faculty assessment. Developmental courses offered in summer session and regular academic year; credit given.

Degree Requirements: *For all associate degrees:* 64 credit hours; 2.1 GPA in major; 1 physical activity course; 3 semesters convocation. *For all baccalaureate degrees:* 128 credit hours; 2.25 in major; 3 hours physical education, including 1 activity course; 6 semesters convocation; GRE. *For all undergraduate degrees:* 2.0 GPA; 30 semester hours in residence; weekly chapel attendance; distribution requirements. Fulfillment of some degree requirements and exemption from some beginning courses possible by passing departmental examinations, College Board CLEP, APP. *Grading system:* A–F; pass; withdraw (deadline after which pass-fail is appended to withdraw); satisfactory-unsatisfactory; incomplete (carries time limit).

Distinctive Educational Programs: Evening classes. Accelerated degree program. Dual-degree program in engineering with Georgia Institute of Technology. Cooperative baccalaureate in medical technology with approved hospitals. Independent study. Institutionally sponsored study abroad in Israel and Europe.

Degrees Conferred: 37 *associate;* 197 *baccalaureate;* 58 *master's.*

Fees and Other Expenses: *Full-time tuition per academic year:* $15,140 undergraduate, graduate tuition per credit hour. *Room and board per academic year:* $5,868. *Other fees:* $320.

Financial Aid: Aid from institutionally generated funds is provided on the basis of academic merit, financial need, athletic ability, other criteria. Institution has a Program Participation Agreement with the U.S. Department of Education for eligible students to receive Pell Grants and other federal aid.

Financial aid to full-time, first-time undergraduate students: need-based scholarships/grants totaling $8,831,449, self-help $3,989,198, parent loans $303,176, tuition waivers $434,595, athletic awards $807,889; non-need-based scholarships/grants totaling $880,197, self-help $742,154, parent loans $240,644, tuition waivers $48,401, athletic awards $321,819.

Departments and Teaching Staff: *Total instructional faculty:* 210 (82 full-time, 128 part-time; women 106, men 104; members of minority groups 10). Total faculty with doctorate, first-professional, or other terminal degree: 55. Student-to-faculty ratio: 13:1.

Enrollment: Total enrollment 2,187. Undergraduate full-time 558 men / 617 women, part-time 191m / 335w; graduate full-time 7m / 9w, part-time 134m / 223w. *Transfer students:* in-state 113; from out-of-state 14.

Characteristics of Student Body: *Ethnic/racial makeup:* number of Black non-Hispanic: 80; American Indian or Alaska Native: 3; Asian or Pacific Islander: 5; Hispanic: 11; White non-Hispanic: 1,550; unknown: 52. *Age distribution:* number under 18: 290; 18–19: 619; 20–21: 370; 22–24: 241; 25–29: 103; 30–34: 61; 35–39: 42; 40–49: 64; 50–64: 61; 65 and over: 7.

International Students: 132 nonresident aliens enrolled fall 2004. Programs available to aid students whose native language is not English: social, cultural. English as a Second Language Program. Financial aid available for qualifying international students.

Student Life: On-campus residence halls house 40% of student body. Residence halls for men constitute 40% of such space, for women 57%. Housing available for married students. 45% of married students request institutional housing; 5% of student body are so housed. *Intercollegiate athletics:* men only: baseball, basketball, golf, soccer, tennis, wrestling; women only: basketball, soccer, softball, swimming, tennis, volleyball. *Special regulations:* Cars with decals permitted. Quiet hours from 8pm to 8am. Residence hall visitation from 11am to midnight. *Special services:* Medical services. *Student publications: The Campus Tymes,* a monthly newspaper; *Maple Trail,* a yearbook. *Surrounding community:* Campbellsville population 9,000. Louisville, 80 miles from campus, is nearest metropolitan area.

Library Collections: 90,687 volumes including bound books, serial backfiles, electronic documents, and government documents not in separate collections. Online and card catalogs. Current serial subscriptions: 518 paper. 97,000 microforms. 5,313 recordings. Students have access to the Internet at no charge.

Buildings and Grounds: Campus area 75 acres.

Chief Executive Officer: Dr. Michael V. Carter, President.

Address admission inquiries to Coordinator of Recruiting.

Centre College

600 West Walnut Street
Danville, Kentucky 40422-1394
Tel: (859) 238-5200   **E-mail:** admission@centre.edu
Fax: (859) 238-9610   **Internet:** www.centre.edu

Institution Description: Centre College (formerly Centre College of Kentucky) is a private, independent, nonprofit college. *Enrollment:* 1,069. *Degrees awarded:* Baccalaureate.

Member of the consortium Associated Colleges of the South.

Accreditation: *Regional:* SACS-Comm. on Coll.

History: Established and chartered 1819; offered first instruction at postsecondary level 1820; awarded first degree (baccalaureate) 1824; merged with Central University at Richmond 1901; merged with Kentucky College for Women 1926; adopted Centre College as official name 1982.

Institutional Structure: *Governing board:* Board of Trustees. Extrainstitutional representation: 30 trustees. All voting. *Composition of institution:* Administrators 12. Academic affairs headed by vice president and dean of the college. Business/finances headed by vice president for business and finance. External affairs headed by vice president for planning and resources. Full-time instructional faculty 92. Academic governance body, The College Council (includes all full-time faculty, some staff members, and students) meets an average of 3 times per year.

Calendar: Semesters (4-2-4 plan). Academic year Sept. to May. Freshmen admitted Sept., Jan. Degrees conferred May, July. Formal commencement May. Independent study available during summer.

Characteristics of Freshmen: 60% of applicants accepted. 27% of accepted applicants enrolled.

Average secondary school rank top 40th percentile. Mean SAT mid-range class scores 570–690 verbal, 580–680 mathematical. Median range of ACT composite score 25–30. 9 National Merit Scholars.

79% of entering freshmen expected to graduate within 5 years. 74% of freshmen from Kentucky.

Admission: Rolling admissions plan. For fall acceptance, apply as early as Sept. of previous year, but not later than Mar. 1 of year of enrollment. Early decision available. Early action deadline Nov. 15. *Requirements:* Graduation from accredited secondary school with 4 units English, 4 mathematics, 2 science, 2 social studies; 2 units foreign language. GED acceptable. *Entrance tests:* College Board SAT or ACT. *For transfer students:* 2.5 minimum GPA, 69 hours maximum transfer credit. Advanced placement; CLEP scores reviewed for credit.

Degree Requirements: 111 credit hours; 42 credit hours required in residence; 2.0 GPA; demonstrated proficiency in expository writing, foreign language, and mathematics; physical education requirement; convocation requirement (attendance at 12 programs per year). *Grading system:* A–U; pass-unsatisfactory; withdraw passing or withdraw failing (with time limits).

Distinctive Educational Programs: Dual-degree (3-2) programs in engineering in cooperation with Columbia University (NY), Georgia Institute of Technology, University of Kentucky, Texas A & M University, Vanderbilt University (TN), Washington University (MO). Special facilities for using telecommunications in the classroom. Interdepartmental/interdisciplinary programs, including self-designed majors. Study off-campus during short term in varying locations in the U.S. and abroad. International programs run by Centre College in London and Strasbourg for fall or spring semesters or entire year. Internships for academic credit. Special career advising program. John C. Young Scholars Program.

ROTC: Army and Air Force offered in cooperation with University of Kentucky. Centre College provides room and board for ROTC (Army, Air Force) scholarship recipients.

Degrees Conferred: 258 *baccalaureate:* biological/life sciences 20; computer and information science 6; English 28; interdisciplinary studies 14; liberal arts/general studies 1; mathematics 10; philosophy and religion 15; physical sciences 6; psychology 29; social sciences 96; visual and performing arts 19. *Honorary degrees awarded 2004–05:* Doctor of Humane Letters 1, Doctor of Laws 1, Doctor of Divinity 1.

Fees and Other Expenses: *Full-time tuition per academic year 2004–05:* $21,800. *Room per academic year:* $3,700. *Board per academic year:* $3,600.

Financial Aid: Aid from institutionally generated funds is provided on the basis of academic merit, financial need. Institution has a Program Participation Agreement with the U.S. Department of Education for eligible students to receive Pell Grants and other federal aid.

Financial aid to full-time, first-time undergraduate students: need-based scholarships/grants totaling $10,018,031, self-help $2,294,895; non-need-based scholarships/grants totaling $3,336,385, self-help $756,383.

Departments and Teaching Staff: Anthropology/sociology *professors* 1, *associate professors* 2, *assistant professors* 2, *instructors* 0, *part-time faculty* 1; art 3, 0, 2, 0, 0; biochemistry and molecular biology 0, 3, 0, 0, 0; biology 3, 3, 2, 0, 0; chemical physics 1, 4, 0, 0, 0; chemistry 1, 4, 2, 0, 0; classical studies 1, 1, 0, 0, 0; computer science 1, 2, 2, 0, 0; dramatic arts 2, 1, 2, 1, 0; economics 3, 1, 3, 0, 1; education 1, 2, 0, 2, 0; English 4, 3, 3, 1, 1; environmental studies 1, 4, 0, 0, 0; French 2, 0, 1, 0, 1; German studies 2, 0, 0, 1, 0; government 3, 1, 1, 1, 0; history 3, 4, 1, 0, 0; international studies 2, 2, 2, 0, 0; mathematics 3, 1, 3, 0, 0; music 2, 0, 2, 12, 0; philosophy 2, 1, 1, 0, 0; physics 2, 2, 1, 0, 0; political economy 3, 1, 1, 0, 0; psychobiology 5, 0, 1, 0, 0; psychology 4, 0, 2, 0, 0; religion 3, 1, 2, 0, 0; Spanish 1, 1, 4, 1, 0.

Total instructional faculty: 108. Student-to-faculty ratio: 10:1. Degrees held by full-time faculty: doctorate or other terminal degree 98%.

Enrollment: Total enrollment 1,069. Undergraduate full-time 506 men / 552 women, part-time 1m / 1w; unclassified full-time 1m / 5w, part-time 1m / 4w.

Characteristics of Student Body: *Ethnic/racial makeup:* number of Black non-Hispanic: 25; American Indian or Alaska Native: 2; Asian or Pacific Islander: 28; White non-Hispanic: 987. *Age distribution:* 17–21: 91%; 22–24: 8%; 25–up: less than 1%.

International Students: 19 nonresident aliens enrolled fall 2004. No programs available to aid students whose native language is not English. International students are eligible for financial aid.

Student Life: On-campus residence halls house 94% of student body. Dormitories and college-owned fraternity houses for men only constitute 40% of such space, for women only 10%, for both sexes 50%. 38% of men join fraternities; 39% of women join sororities. Each fraternity has a residence that accommodates 10 students. Sororities have chapter rooms in dormitories but members do not live together in one dormitory. *Intercollegiate athletics:* men only: baseball, basketball, cross-country, field hockey, golf, soccer, swimming, tennis, track; women only: basketball, cross-country, field hockey, swimming, soccer, tennis, track, volleyball. Women have "club sports" in soccer and volleyball. 90% of students participate in one or more of 21 intramural sports. *Special regulations:* Cars permitted, with campus registration, except for first 6 weeks for freshmen. Residence hall visitation from 10am to 10:30pm Sun.–Thurs., 10am to 2am Fri. and Sat., except for freshmen during fall term. *Special services:* Medical and counseling services. *Special advising:* Both faculty and staff academic advisors and peer counselors are used in special freshman advising program. *Student judicial system:* Academic and social infractions adjudicated by student-elected Student Judiciary. *Student publications: The Cento*, a students newspaper; *Olde Centre*, a yearbook. *Surrounding community:* Danville population 18,000. Lexington, 35 miles from campus, is nearest metropolitan area. Served by Lexington airport.

Publications: Catalog published annually online; annual donor report. *Centrepiece* alumni magazine published quarterly.

Library Collections: 218,343 volumes. 52,659 microforms; 1,162 current periodical subscriptions. Students have access to online information retrieval systems and the Internet.

Most important holdings include Dante collection of 19th century editions, criticism, and commentary; Le Compte Davis Collection, including 19th- and 20th-century popular fictions and history of the American West; Kentucky history collection, including religious and church history; Centre College Archives; Ed McLanahan manuscripts. Library is partial depository for U.S. government documents.

Buildings and Grounds: Campus area 115 acres.

Chief Executive Officer: Dr. John A. Roush, President.

Address admission inquiries to J. Carey Thompson, Dean of Admissions.

Clear Creek Baptist Bible College

300 Clear Creek Road
Pineville, Kentucky 40977-9754
Tel: (606) 337-3196   **E-mail:** admissions@ccbbc.edu
Fax: (606) 337-2372   **Internet:** www.ccbbc.edu

Institution Description: Clear Creek Baptist Bible College prepares adults for Christian service. *Enrollment:* 207. *Degrees awarded:* Baccalaureate.

Accreditation: *Regional:* SACS. *National:* ABHE.

History: College began in 1926 with summer campus and a 2-week class period for mountain preachers training; changed in 1946 to year round school for preachers, ministers, and missionaries; accredited 1986 as a college for the training of ministers.

Institutional Structure: *Governing board:* Kentucky Baptist Convention.

Calendar: Semesters. Academic year from Aug. to May. Summer session of 2 terms of 3 weeks each.

Characteristics of Freshmen: 88% of applicants admitted. 86% of accepted applicants enrolled. 57% of entering freshmen expected to graduate within 5 years. 39% of of freshmen from Kentucky. Freshmen from 10 states.

Admission: *Requirements:* Open admissions.

Degree Requirements: *For baccalaureate degree:* 100 hours of core requirements; 28 hours of ministry; chapel attendance and several Christian service activities required.

Distinctive Educational Programs: Biblical theological education programs.

Degrees Conferred: 29 *baccalaureate:* theology.

Fees and Other Expenses: *Full-time tuition per academic year 2004–05:* $4,110. *Required fees:* $360. *Room and board per academic year:* $3,310.

Financial Aid: Aid from institutionally generated funds is provided on the basis of financial need. Institution has a Program Participation Agreement with the U.S. Department of Education for eligible students to receive Pell Grants and other federal aid.

Financial aid to full-time, first-time undergraduate students: need-based scholarships/grants totaling $739,704; self-help $38,083; non-need-based scholarships/grants totaling $174,660.

Departments and Teaching Staff: *Professors* 2, *associate professors* 4, *assistant professors* 1, *part-time faculty* 15. *Total instructional faculty:* 22 (full-time 7, part-time 15; women 1, men 21). Total faculty with doctorate, first-professional, or other terminal degree: 11. Student-to-faculty ratio: 12.69:1.

Enrollment: Total enrollment 207. Undergraduate full-time 125 men / 24 women, part-time 39m / 9w.

Characteristics of Student Body: *Ethnic/racial makeup:* number of Black non-Hispanic: 1; White non-Hispanic: 206. *Age distribution:* number 18–19: 11; 20–21: 24; 22–24: 27; 25–29: 30; 30–34: 35; 35–39: 31; 40–49: 36; 50–64: 2.

International Students: 2 nonresident aliens enrolled fall 2004. . No programs available to aid students whose native language is not English. Some financial aid designated for international students; 1 scholarship for $650 awarded 2004–05.

Student Life: Family life center on campus. Students offer ministry to local people and churches. *Student publications: Weekly Campus News Bulletin; Mountain Voice,* quarterly bulletin to students, alumni, and friends.

Library Collections: 47,309 volumes including bound books, serial backfiles, electronic documents, and government documents not in separate collections. Online and card catalogs. Current serial subscriptions: 266 paper, 178 microform, 9,585 via electronic access. 2,726 recordings; 159 CD-ROMs. 16 computer work stations. Students have access to the Internet at no charge. Total budget for books, periodicals, audiovisual materials,microforms 2004–05: $17,927.

Most important special holdings include theological and biblical material.

Buildings and Grounds: *New buildings:* Kelly Hall renovated (male dormitory and dining hall) completed 2003.

Chief Executive Officer: Dr. Bill D. Whitaker, President.

Address admissions inquiries to Billy Howell, Director of Admissions.

Cumberland College

6191 College Station Drive
Williamsburg, Kentucky 40769

Tel: (606) 549-2000   **E-mail:** admiss@cumber.edu
Fax: (609) 539-4490   **Internet:** www.cumber.edu

Institution Description: Cumberland College is a private institution affiliated with the Southern Baptist Church. *Enrollment:* 1,744. *Degrees awarded:* Baccalaureate, master's.

Accreditation: *Regional:* SACS-Comm. on Coll. *Professional:* music

History: Established as Williamsburg Institute 1889; offered first instruction at postsecondary level and adopted present name 1913; awarded first degree (baccalaureate) 1961.

Institutional Structure: *Governing board:* Board of Trustees. Representation: 28 trustees. *Composition of institution:* 22 administrators. Academic affairs headed by academic dean. Management/business/finances directed by director of business affairs-treasurer. Full-time instructional faculty 100.

Calendar: Semesters. Academic year Aug. to May. Freshmen admitted Aug., Jan. Formal commencement May. Summer session from early June to mid-Aug.

Characteristics of Freshmen: 1,115 applicants (635 men, 480 women). 74% of applicants admitted. 50.7% of admitted students enrolled full-time.

23% (96 students) submitted SAT scores; 89% (379 students) submitted ACT scores. *25th percentile:* SAT I Verbal 420, SAT I Math 430; ACT Composite 19, ACT English 18, ACT Math 17. *75th percentile:* SAT I Verbal 540, SAT I Math 530; ACT Composite 24, ACT English 24, ACT Math 23.

55% of freshmen from Kentucky. Freshmen from 36 states and 15 foreign countries.

Admission: For fall acceptance, apply as early as beginning of senior year of secondary school, but not later than Aug. 1. *Requirements:* Either graduation from secondary school or GED. *Entrance tests:* ACT composite or SAT. For foreign students TOEFL or other evidence of English language proficiency.

Degree Requirements: *For all baccalaureate degrees:* 128 credit hours (minimum). *For all undergraduate degrees:* 2.0 GPA, weekly convocation attendance, general education requirements. *Grading system:* A–F; withdraw (deadline after which pass-fail is appended to withdraw); incomplete.

Distinctive Educational Programs: Cooperative degree programs in medical technology with approved hospitals. Preprofessional programs in dentistry, engineering, medicine, optometry, pharmacy, physical therapy. Honors program. Ministerial Training Program. *Other distinctive programs:* Qualified high school students may take courses on campus.

ROTC: Army.

Degrees Conferred: 202 *baccalaureate;* 45 *master's.* Bachelor's degrees awarded in top five disciplines: education 31; business, management, marketing, and related support services 30; psychology 19; biological and biomedical sciences 18; health professions and related clinical sciences 15.

Fees and Other Expenses: *Full-time tuition per academic year 2004–05:* $11,858 undergraduate; graduate study charged per credit hour. *Books and supplies:* $800. *Room and board per academic year:* $5,126.

Financial Aid: Aid from institutionally generated funds is provided on the basis of academic merit, financial need, athletic ability, other criteria. Institution has a Program Participation Agreement with the U.S. Department of Education for eligible students to receive Pell Grants and other federal aid.

Financial aid to full-time, first-time undergraduate students: 55% received federal grants averaging $2,806; 49% state/local grants averaging $3,297; 97% institutional grants averaging $5,382; 59% received loans averaging $2,595.

Departments and Teaching Staff: 15 departments with 100 faculty members. *Total instructional faculty:* 100. Student-to-faculty ratio: 16:1. Degrees held by full-time faculty: doctorate 65%, master's 35%. 65% hold terminal degrees.

Enrollment: Total enrollment 1,744. Undergraduate 1,603 (46.1% men, 51.9% women).

Characteristics of Student Body: *Ethnic/racial makeup:* Black non-Hispanic: 6.1%; American Indian or Alaska Native: .3%; Asian or Pacific Islander: .5%; Hispanic: 1.5%; White non-Hispanic: 89.1%; unknown: .25.

International Students: 35 nonresident aliens enrolled fall 2004. Students form Europe, Asia, Central and South America, Africa. No programs available to aid students whose native language is not English. No financial aid specifically designated for international students.

Student Life: On-campus housing available. *Special services:* Learning Resources Center, medical services. *Surrounding community:* Williamsburg population 6,000. Cincinnati (OH), 200 miles from campus, is nearest metropolitan area. Served by mass transit bus system.

Library Collections: 190,500 volumes including bound books, serial backfiles, electronic documents, and government documents not in separate collections. Online catalog. 771,000 microforms. 660 current serial subscriptions. 3,800 audiovisual materials. Students have access to the Internet at no charge.

Most important special collections include the Kentucky Collection.

Buildings and Grounds: Campus area 50 acres.

Chief Executive Officer: Dr. James H. Taylor, President.

Address admission inquiries to Erica Harris, Director of Admissions.

Eastern Kentucky University

521 Lancaster Avenue
Richmond, Kentucky 40475-3102

Tel: (859) 622-1000   **E-mail:** admissions@eku.edu
Fax: (859) 622-1020   **Internet:** www.eku.edu

Institution Description: Eastern Kentucky University is a state institution. *Enrollment:* 15,683. *Degrees awarded:* Associate, baccalaureate, master's. Specialist certificates also given.

Academic offerings subject to approval by statewide coordinating bodies.

Accreditation: *Regional:* SACS-Comm. on Coll. *Professional:* athletic training, business, clinical lab scientist, clinical lab technology, computer science, construction education, dietetics, EMT-paramedic, electronic technology, environmental health, health information administration, industrial technology, medical assisting, music, nursing, nursing education, occupational therapy, public administration, recreation and leisure services, social work, speech-language pathology, teacher education

History: Established as Eastern Kentucky State Normal School, chartered, and offered first instruction at postsecondary level 1906; became 4year institution and changed name to Eastern Kentucky State Normal School and Teachers College 1922; awarded first degree (baccalaureate) 1925; changed name to Eastern Kentucky State Teachers College 1930; added master's program 1935; changed name to Eastern Kentucky State College 1948; adopted present name 1966. See J. T. Dorris, *Five Decades of Progress* (Richmond: Eastern Kentucky University, 1956) for further information.

Institutional Structure: *Governing board:* Board of Regents. Extrainstitutional representation: 11 regents; institutional representation: 1 full-time instructional faculty member, 1 staff member, 1 student. All voting. *Composition of institution:* Administrators 82 men 54 women. Academic affairs headed by vice president for academic affairs and provost. Management/business/finances directed by vice president for administration and finance and by vice president for governmental relations and budget. Full-time instructional faculty 595. Academic governance body, Faculty Senate, meets an average of 9 times per year.

Calendar: Semesters. Academic year Aug. to May. Freshmen admitted Aug., Jan., June. Degrees conferred and formal commencements May, Aug., Dec. Summer session from mid-June to early Aug. Intersession from mid-May to mid-June.

Characteristics of Freshmen: 94% of applicants admitted. 11% (269 students) submitted SAT scores; 98% (2,501 students) submitted ACT scores. *25th percentile:* SAT Verbal 450, SAT Math 440; ACT Composite 18, ACT English 17, ACT Math 17. *75th percentile:* SAT Verbal 560, SAT Math 580; ACT Composite 23, ACT English 23, ACT Math 22.

20% of entering freshmen expected to graduate within 5 years. 92% of freshmen from Kentucky. Freshmen from 33 states and 23 foreign countries.

Admission: Rolling admissions plan. Early acceptance available. *Requirements:* Graduation from accredited secondary school; ACT score of 18 or higher. GED (minimum score of 45) accepted for students older than 17 years of age, whose secondary school class has graduated. Lowest acceptable secondary school class standing 50th percentile for out-of-state students. *Entrance tests:* ACT. *For transfer students:* 2.0 minimum GPA; maximum transfer credit limited only by residence requirement.

College credit and advanced placement for postsecondary-level work completed in secondary school. College credit for extrainstitutional learning on basis of ACE *2006 Guide to the Evaluation of Educational Experiences in the Armed Services.*

Tutoring available. Noncredit developmental/remedial courses offered in summer session and regular academic year.

Degree Requirements: *For all associate degrees:* 68 semester hours; 15 of last 18 hours in residence. *For all baccalaureate degrees:* 136 hours; 30 of last 36 hours in residence. *For all undergraduate degrees:* 2.0 GPA; 2 credit hours of physical education courses; distribution requirements.

Fulfillment of some degree requirements and exemption from some beginning courses possible by passing departmental examinations, College Board CLEP. *Grading system:* A–F; pass-fail; withdraw (deadline after which pass-fail is appended to withdraw).

Distinctive Educational Programs: Asset Protection; Aviation; Fire Safety Engineering Technology; Forensic Science; Interpreting for Deaf Individuals; Insurance; Occupational Therapy; Women's Studies; Police and Corrections; Gerontology. *Available to all students:* Work-experience programs. Flexible meeting places and schedules, including off-campus centers (at varying locations), weekend and evening classes. Special facilities for using telecommunications in the classroom. Interdisciplinary program in planning and development. Facilities and programs for independent research, including individual majors, tutorials.

ROTC: Army.

Degrees Conferred: 237 *associate;* 1,078 *baccalaureate* (B), 612 *master's* (M): agriculture 33 (B); biological/life sciences 39 (B), 17 (M); business/marketing 119 (B), 36 (M); communications/communication technologies 61 (B); computer and information sciences 15 (B), 6 (M); education 265 (B), 396 (M); engineering and engineering technologies 72 (B); English 46 (B), 11 (M); foreign languages and literature 13 (B); health professions and related sciences 270 (B), 39 (M); home economics and vocational home economics 51 (B); law/legal studies 10 (B); liberal arts/general studies 4 (B); mathematics 5 (B), 1 (M); parks and recreation 36 (B), 6 (M); philosophy/religion/theology 7 (B); physical sciences 18 (B), 6 (M); protective services/public administration 290 (B), 34 (M); psychology 85 (B), 14 (M); social sciences and history 142 (B), 6 (M); trade and industry 17 (B); visual and performing arts 33 (B), 10 (M).

Fees and Other Expenses: *Full-time tuition per academic year 2004–05:* undergraduate resident $3,332, out-of-state student $10,004. *Required fees:* $460. *Room and board per academic year:* $4,658.

Financial Aid: Aid from institutionally generated funds is provided on the basis of academic merit, financial need, athletic ability. Institution has a Program Participation Agreement with the U.S. Department of Education for eligible students to receive Pell Grants and other federal aid.

Financial aid to full-time, first-time undergraduate students: need-based scholarships/grants totaling $24,254,636, self-help $37,495,126, parent loans $6,811,591, tuition waivers $552,990, athletic awards $588,575; non-need-based scholarships/grants totaling $6,192,240, self-help $9,084,331, parent loans $4,034,261, tuition waivers $1,109,887, athletic awards $1,000,300.

Departments and Teaching Staff: *Total instructional faculty:* 456 (full-time 553, part-time 403; women 482, men 474; members of minority groups 93). Student-to-faculty ratio: 17:1. 67% of faculty hold terminal degrees.

Enrollment: Total enrollment 15,683. Undergraduate full-time 4,312 men / 6,521 women, part-time 1,019m / 1,985w; graduate full-time 121m / 332w, part-time 500m / 1,333w.

Characteristics of Student Body: *Ethnic/racial makeup (undergraduate):* number of Black non-Hispanic: 640; American Indian or Alaska Native: 58; Asian or Pacific Islander: 146; Hispanic: 93; White non-Hispanic: 12,645; unknown: 175. *Age distribution:* 17–21: 32%; 22–24: 33%; 25–29: 15%; 30–39: 12%; 40–49: 6%; 50–and over: 2%.

International Students: 80 nonresident aliens enrolled fall 2004. Students from Europe, Asia, Central and South America, Africa, Canada. Programs available to aid students whose native language is not English: social, cultural. English as a Second Language Program. No financial aid specifically designated for international students.

Student Life: On-campus residence halls house 57% of student body. Residence halls for men constitute 41% of such space, for women 59%. 4% of men join fraternities; 3% of women join sororities. College-owned off-campus housing available for married students. 27% of married students request institutional housing and are so housed. *Intercollegiate athletics:* men only: baseball, basketball, cross-country, football, golf, gymnastics, swimming, tennis, track; women only: basketball, cross-country, field hockey, gymnastics, swimming, tennis, track, volleyball. *Special regulations:* Registered cars permitted; fee charged. Residence hall visitation hours set by residents within designated limits. *Special services:* Learning Resources Center, medical services, shuttle bus between main campus and law enforcement complex. *Student publications, radio:* *Aurora,* an annual literary magazine; *The Eastern Progress,* a student-run newspaper; *Milestone,* a CD yearbook. WXII-FM, a student-run radio station. *Surrounding community:* Richmond population 28,000. Cincinnati (OH), 100 miles from campus, is nearest metropolitan area. Served by Lexington & Bluegrass Airport 30 miles from campus.

Library Collections: 838,000 volumes including bound books, serial backfiles, electronic documents, and government documents not in separate collections. Online catalog. Current serial subscriptions: 3,670. 4,300 audiovisual materials. 1,410,000 microforms. 140 computer work stations adjacent to library. Students have access to the Internet at no charge.

Most important holdings include Townsend Room Collection of Kentuckiana (includes books about Kentucky, by and about Kentuckians; manuscripts; letters; maps; genealogy collection); Congressman Carl Perkins Papers; EKU institutional records.

Buildings and Grounds: Campus area 630 acres.

Chief Executive Officer: Dr. Joanne K. Glasser, President.

Address admission inquiries to Stephen Byrn, Director of Admissions.

Georgetown College

400 East College Street
Georgetown, Kentucky 40324

Tel: (502) 863-8000   **E-mail:** admissions@georgetowncollege.edu
Fax: (502) 868-7733   **Internet:** www.georgetowncollege.edu

Institution Description: Georgetown College is a private college affiliated with the Kentucky Baptist Convention. *Enrollment:* 1,835. *Degrees awarded:* Baccalaureate, master's.

Accreditation: *Regional:* SACS-Comm. on Coll.

History: Established and chartered as a men's institution 1829; offered first instruction at postsecondary level 1830; awarded first degree (baccalaureate) 1844; merged with Georgetown Female Seminary and became coeducational 1892. See Robert Snyder, *A History of Georgetown College* (Georgetown: Georgetown College, 1979) for further information.

Institutional Structure: *Governing board:* Georgetown College Board of Trustees. Extrainstitutional representation: 36 trustees. 36 voting. *Composition of institution:* Administrators 23 men / 11 women. Academic affairs headed by vice president for academic affairs and provost. Management/business/finances directed by vice president and chief financial officer. Full-time instructional faculty 93. Academic governance body, the faculty, meets an average of 8 times per year.

Calendar: Semesters. Academic year Aug. to May. Freshmen admitted Aug., Jan., June, July. Degrees conferred and formal commencement May. Summer session of 2 terms from June to Aug.

Characteristics of Freshmen: 94% of applicants admitted. 41% of applicants admitted and enrolled.

21% (75 students) submitted SAT scores; 97% (343 students) submitted ACT scores. *25th percentile*: ACT Composite 20, ACT English 19, ACT Math 19. *75th percentile*: ACT Composite 26, ACT English 27, ACT Math 26.

58% of entering freshmen expected to graduate within 5 years. 83% of freshmen from Kentucky. Freshmen from 21 states and 11 foreign countries.

Admission: Rolling admissions plan. For fall acceptance, apply as early as Sept. 8 of previous year, but not later than Aug. 1 of year of enrollment. *Requirements:* Either graduation from accredited secondary school with 16 units or GED. Recommend 4 units English, 2 in a foreign language, 2 mathematics, 2 science, 2 social studies. Minimum GPA 2.0. *Entrance tests:* ACT composite. *For transfer students:* 2.0 minimum GPA; from 4-year accredited institution 98 hours maximum transfer credit; from 2-year accredited institution 66 hours; correspondence/extension students 9 hours.

College credit and advanced placement for postsecondary-level work completed in secondary school. Noncredit developmental courses offered during regular academic year.

Degree Requirements: 120 semester hours; 2.0 GPA; 2 terms in residence; 2 hours physical education; general education requirements; comprehensives in individual fields of study. Fulfillment of some degree requirements and exemption from some beginning courses possible by passing departmental examinations, College Board CLEP, AP. *Grading system:* A–F; pass-fail; withdraw (deadline after which pass-fail is appended to withdraw); incomplete (carries time limit).

Distinctive Educational Programs: *For undergraduates:* Dual-degree programs in engineering with University of Kentucky. Cooperative baccalaureate program in medical technology with approved schools of medical technology. Interdisciplinary programs in American studies, child development, environmental studies, European studies, social studies, youth ministries. Facilities for independent research, including honors programs, individual majors. Independent study. Study abroad in England, France, Spain, Austria; other countries through consortium. Georgetown College-Regent's Park College in the University of Oxford provides up to one year of study in Oxford (England). *For graduate students:* Weekend and evening classes.

ROTC: Army, Air Force offered in cooperation with University of Kentucky.

Degrees Conferred: 233 *baccalaureate*; 106 *master's*. Bachelor's degrees awarded in top five disciplines business, management, marketing, and related support services 41; visual and performing arts 40; biological and biomedical sciences 31; psychology 22; education 19.

Fees and Other Expenses: *Full-time tuition per academic year 2004–05:* $19,170. *Room and board per academic year:* $5,780.

Financial Aid: Aid from institutionally generated funds is provided on the basis of academic merit, financial need, athletic ability, other criteria. Institution has a Program Participation Agreement with the U.S. Department of Education for eligible students to receive Pell Grants and other federal aid.

Financial aid to full-time, first-time undergraduate students: need-based scholarships/grants totaling $9,086,892, self-help $2,168,231, tuition waivers $110,109, athletic awards $664,159; non-need-based scholarships/grants totaling $4,345,410, self-help $1,208,130, parent loans $669,101, tuition waivers $104,515, athletic awards $303,222.

Departments and Teaching Staff: *Total instructional faculty:* 160 (full-time 101, part-time 59; women 30, men 29). Total faculty with doctorate, first-professional, or other terminal degree: 88. Student-to-faculty ratio: 11:1.

Enrollment: Total enrollment 1,835. Undergraduate full-time 569 men / 690 women, part-time 39m / 36w; graduate full-time 11m / 33w, part-time 71m / 386w.

Characteristics of Student Body: *Ethnic/racial makeup:* number of Black non-Hispanic: 49; American Indian or Alaska Native: 3; Asian or Pacific Islander: 10; Hispanic: 9; White non-Hispanic: 1,249. *Age distribution:* 17–21: 90%; 22–24: 9%; 25–29: 1%.

International Students: 14 nonresident aliens enrolled fall 2004. Students from Europe, Asia, Central and South America. No programs available to aid students whose native language is not English. No financial aid specifically designated for international students.

Student Life: On-campus residence halls, fraternities, and sororities house 89% of student body. Housing for men only constitutes 45% of such space, for women only 55%. 31% of men join and 95% live in fraternities; 32% of women join and 60% live in sororities. President's House Association also offers residence space for men. Limited housing available for married students. Less than 1% of student body is so housed. *Intercollegiate athletics:* men: baseball, basketball, cross country, football, golf, soccer, tennis; women: basketball, cross country, golf, soccer. softball, tennis, volleyball. *Special regulations:* Co-ed visitation hours 3pm to midnight Monday-Thursday; Friday 3pm to 1am; Saturday

noon to 1am; Sunday noon to midnight. Visitors must sign in at a registration area. *Special services:* Medical services. *Student publications, radio: The Georgetonian*, a weekly newspaper; *Inscape*, an annual literary journal; *The Belle of the Blue*, a yearbook. *Surrounding community:* Georgetown population 13,000. Lexington, 12 miles from campus, is nearest metropolitan area. Served by airport 15 miles from campus.

Publications: *Georgetown College Faculty Lectures* (annually) first published 1973. Member of University Press of Kentucky.

Library Collections: 160,862 volumes including bound books, serial backfiles, electronic documents, and government documents not in separate collections. Online catalog. Current serial subscriptions: 541 paper. 1,356 compact discs. 120 computer work stations. Students have access to the Internet at no charge.

Most important special holdings include Smith Law Library; Spears Collection (Kentucky authors); Thompson Collection of Biblical Literature.

Buildings and Grounds: Campus area 104 acres. *New buildings:* Fitness Center completed 2002.

Chief Executive Officer: William H. Crouch, Jr., President.

Address undergraduate admission inquiries to Johnnie Johnson, Director of Admissions.

Kentucky Christian College

100 Academic Parkway
Grayson, Kentucky 41143-1199
Tel: (606) 474-3000   **E-mail:** admissions@kcc.edu
Fax: (606) 474-3155   **Internet:** www.kcc.edu

Institution Description: Kentucky Christian College is a privately supported college offering programs designed to prepare students for Christian leadership and service in the church and in professions throughout the world. *Enrollment:* 601. *Degrees awarded:* Associate, baccalaureate.

Accreditation: *Regional:* SACS-Comm. on Coll. *National:* ABHE.

History: The college was founded in 1919 with an emphasis in training public school teachers. The college has maintained an affiliation with the Churches of Christ and Christian Churches.

Calendar: Semesters. Academic year late Aug. to early May

Characteristics of Freshmen: 336 applicants (131 men, 205 women). 71.7% of applicants admitted. 60.6% of admitted students enrolled full-time.

21% (31 students) submitted SAT scores; 82% (119 students) submitted ACT scores. *25th percentile:* SAT I Verbal 440, SAT I Math 430; ACT Composite 18, ACT English 17, ACT Math 17. *75th percentile:* SAT I 560, Verbal SAT I Math 580; ACT Composite 24,ACT English 25, ACT Math 24.

47% of entering freshmen expected to graduate within five years. 35% of freshmen from Kentucky. Freshmen from 18 states and 3 foreign countries.

Admission: High school graduation with completion of 16 units including 4 English, 2 mathematics, 2 social science. *Entrance tests:* ACT. Early admission, early decision.

Degree Requirements: Completion of prescribed curriculum.

Distinctive Educational Programs: Baccalaureate programs in pre-law/history, Bible, ministries, music, teacher education, psychology, social work, business administration.

Degrees Conferred: 91 *baccalaureate*; 4 *master's*. Bachelor's degrees awarded in top five disciplines: theology and ministerial studies 41; education 21; business, management, marketing, and related support services business and management 11; psychology 6; public administration and social service professors 4.

Fees and Other Expenses: *Full-time tuition per academic year 2004–05:* $10,640. *Room and board per academic year:* $850. *Books and supplies:* $850.

Financial Aid: Aid from institutionally generated funds is provided on the basis of academic merit, financial need, other criteria. Institution has a Program Participation Agreement with the U.S. Department of Education for eligible students to receive Pell Grants and other federal aid.

Financial aid to full-time, first-time undergraduate students: 35% received federal grants averaging $2,318; 25% state/local grants averaging $3,759; 98% institutional grants averaging $2,841; 77% received loans averaging $3,486.

Departments and Teaching Staff: Behavioral sciences *professors* 1, *associate professors* 0, *assistant professors* 2, *part-time teachers* 2; Bible and ministries 6, 0, 2, 3; business administration 0, 0, 2, 2; general studies 3, 1, 2, 5; music 1, 1, 1, 2; teacher education 3, 0, 1, 0.

Total instructional faculty: 40. Degrees held by full-time faculty: doctorate 58%, master's 100%.

Enrollment: Total enrollment 601. Undergraduate 585 (258 men, 327 women).

Characteristics of Student Body: *Ethnic/racial makeup:* Black non-Hispanic: .35; American Indian or Alaska Native: .35; Hispanic: .2%; White non-Hispanic: 94.9%; unknown: 2.9%.

International Students: 8 nonresident aliens enrolled fall 2004. Students from Europe, Central and South America, Africa, Canada. No programs available to aid students whose native language is not English. Some financial aid available for qualifying international students.

Student Life: Residence hall and student apartment accommodations available. Intercollegiate and intramural men's and women's sports teams. College-sponsored traveling music groups/ensembles. College-sponsored drama and theater opportunities. Spiritual growth/service groups.

Library Collections: 102,000 volumes. 740 microform titles; 3,600 audiovisual materials; 440 current periodical subscriptions. Students have access to online information retrieval services and the Internet.

Most important holdings include Religion/Restoration Research Collection.

Buildings and Grounds: Campus area 121 acres.

Chief Executive Officer: Dr. Keith P. Keeran, President.

Address admission inquiries to Sandra Deakins, Vice President for Enrollment Management.

Kentucky Mountain Bible College

855 Kentucky Highway 541
Vancleve, Kentucky 41385-0010
Tel: (606) 666-5000   **E-mail:** admissions@kmbc.edu
Fax: (606) 666-7744   **Internet:** www.kmbc.edu

Institution Description: Kentucky Mountain Bible College, formerly known as Kentucky Mountain Bible Institute, is a private institution affiliated with the Kentucky Mountain Holiness Association. *Enrollment:* 92. *Degrees awarded:* Associate, baccalaureate.

Accreditation: *National:* ABHE.

History: Founded 1931 as Kentucky Mountain Bible Institute; adopted present name in 1991.

Calendar: Semesters. Academic year late Aug. to late May.

Characteristics of Freshmen: 19 applicants (45 men, 34 women). 22.6% of applicants admitted. 94.4% of admitted students enrolled full-time.

7% (2 students) submitted SAT scores; 78% (17 students) submitted ACT scores. *25th percentile:* ACT Composite 15, ACT English 16, ACT Math 17. *75th percentile:* ACT Composite 23, ACT English 27, ACT Math 24.

Admission: *Requirements:* High school graduation or GED. Christian students must meet standards of character, conduct, and health; acceptable SAT or ACT.

Degree Requirements: *For all undergraduate degrees:* 130 credits in Bible theology and professional studies; GPA of 2.0. *For associate degree:* 65 credit hours; completion of prescribed program. *Grading system:* A–F.

Distinctive Educational Programs: Programs in ministerial training, Christian education, sacred music, missions, and communications.

Degrees Conferred: 3 *associate;* 4 *baccalaureate:* education 2; theology and ministerial studies 1; communication, journalism, and related programs 1.

Fees and Other Expenses: *Full-time tuition per academic year 2004–05:* $4,930. *Room and board per academic year:* $3,000. *Books and supplies:* $400.

Financial Aid: Aid from institutionally generated funds is provided on the basis of academic merit, financial need, musical talent. Institution has a Program Participation Agreement with the U.S. Department of Education for eligible students to receive Pell Grants and other federal aid.

Financial aid to full-time, first-time undergraduate students: 60% received federal grants; 67% institutional grants; 33% received loans.

Departments and Teaching Staff: *Part-time faculty:* 14. *Total instructional faculty:* 14. Degrees held by part-time faculty: doctorate 10%, master's 70%, baccalaureate 20%.

Enrollment: Total enrollment 92 (43 men, 49 women).

Characteristics of Student Body: *Ethnic/racial makeup:* White non-Hispanic: 88%; other 12%.

International Students: 11 nonresident aliens enrolled fall 2004. Students from Asia, Africa. No programs available to aid students whose native language is not English. No financial aid specifically designated for international students.

Student Life: Student life centers around college functions, student activities center, outdoor outings, and religious life. *Student publications: Silver Trumpet* (four times yearly); *KMBCian Yearbook.*

Library Collections: 25,000 volumes. 90 microform titles; 350 audiovisual materials; 200 current periodical subscriptions. Online catalog.

Most important special holdings include Holiness Collection; Missions Collection.

Chief Executive Officer: Dr. Philip Speas, President.

Address admission inquiries to Rev. Dana Beland, Admissions Counselor.

Kentucky State University

400 East Main Street
Frankfort, Kentucky 40601
Tel: (502) 597-6000   **E-mail:** jburrell@.kysu.edu
Fax: (502) 597-5814   **Internet:** www.kysu.edu

Institution Description: Kentucky State University is a state-assisted, public, liberal studies-oriented institution. *Enrollment:* 2,335. *Degrees awarded:* Associate, baccalaureate, master's.

Academic offerings subject to approval by statewide coordinating bodies. Budget subject to approval by state governing boards.

Accreditation: *Regional:* SACS-Comm. on Coll. *Professional:* music, nursing social work, teacher education

History: Established as Kentucky Normal Institute 1886; offered first instruction at postsecondary level 1887; changed name to Kentucky Normal and Industrial Institute for Colored Persons 1902; to Kentucky Industrial College for Colored Persons 1926; awarded first degree (baccalaureate) 1929; changed name to Kentucky State College for Negroes 1938; to Kentucky State College 1952; adopted present name 1972; liberal studies academic emphasis adopted 1982. *See* John A. Hardin, *Onward and Upward, A Centennial History of Kentucky State University, 1886–1986* (Frankfort: Kentucky State University, 1987) for further information.

Institutional Structure: *Governing board:* Board of Regents. Extrainstitutional representation: 8 regents; institutional representation: 1 full-time instructional faculty member, 1 Kentucky resident full-time student. All voting. *Composition of institution:* Administrators 24 men / 8 women. Academic affairs, business affairs, student affairs, policy and management, and university relations units each headed by a vice president. Six schools and colleges, plus international Graduate Center headed by deans. Full-time instructional faculty 150. Academic governance body, Faculty Senate, meets an average of 16 times per year.

Calendar: Semesters with intersession. Academic year Aug. to July. Freshmen admitted any of four academic terms which begin Aug., Jan., May, June. Degrees conferred and formal commencement May. Summer sessions June to July.

Characteristics of Freshmen: 59% of applicants accepted. 44% of accepted applicants enrolled.

18% (138 students) submitted SAT scores; 82% (634 students) submitted ACT scores. *25th percentile:* SAT Verbal 390, SAT Math 380; ACT Composite 15, ACT English 14, ACT Math 15. *75th percentile:* SAT Verbal 500, SAT Math 500; ACT Composite 19, ACT English 19, ACT Math 19.

32% of entering freshmen expected to graduate within 5 years. 55% of freshmen from Kentucky. Freshmen from 23 states and 10 foreign countries.

Admission: Rolling admissions plan. Early acceptance available. *Requirements:* General requirements include graduation from accredited secondary school, complete pre-college curriculum, ACT, and prior to enrollment must take placement tests in English, reading, mathematics, and foreign languages. *Pre-college curriculum requirement:* Completion of 20 high school units, or presentation of requisite competence in English (4 units), mathematics (3 units, including algebra and geometry), science (2 units, including biology or chemistry or physics), and social studies (2 units including world civilization and U.S. history). Kentucky residents in addition must meet one of the following requirements: rank in upper half of high school class, or score a composite of 16 or higher on the ACT, or cumulative GPA 2.75 or higher. Non-Kentucky residents in addition to general requirements must meet at least one of the following requirements: rank in upper half of high school class, or score at the national average or above on the ACT, or demonstrate through other acceptable means ability to pursue university academic program without substantial remedial aid. Foreign student requirement of 3.0 GPA. *Entrance tests:* ACT composite. For foreign students TOEFL, minimum score of 525. *For transfer students:* Must be eligible for readmittance to institution previously attended; those with fewer than 30 transferable credits must also satisfy applicable freshman admission requirements; a maximum of 64 credit hours acceptable from a junior college; final 32 credit hours must be earned at KSU. *Graduate admissions requirements:* For unconditional admission, earned baccalaureate from accredited college or university with minimum 3.0 GPA; GRE Part I, aptitude minimum score of 1400 or GMAT minimum score of 425; three letters of recommendation from former professors; typed statement of goals and career objectives; admission interview may be required. For conditional admissions, earned baccalaureate degree from accredited college or university; 3 letters of recommendation from former professors or employers; typed statement of goals and career objectives; applications must be received by July 15 for fall semester, Dec. 15 for spring semester,

May 1 for summer session. Up to one-half the number of credit hours required for completion of a baccalaureate or an associate degree may be earned through credit by examination/certification; departmental challenge exams, advanced placement program, credit for life experience, CLEP, PEP, and Armed Services Certification for Credit.

Tutoring available; reading, writing, and math clinics. Developmental courses offered during academic year. Credits for latter not applicable to degree requirements.

Degree Requirements: *For all associate degrees:* 64–73 credit hours, including general education requirements. *For all baccalaureate degrees:* 128–144 credit hours, including 53 credit hours of the Liberal Studies requirements; student must successfully complete a senior exam which includes an assessment of written communication skills. At least one-half of a student's major field academic credit hours must be earned at KSU. For all graduates a minimum of 2.0 GPA is required. *Grading system:* A–F (4 points); limited pass-fail; withdraw (carries time limit). *For graduate (public affairs) degree:* curriculum follows National Association of Schools of Public Affairs and Administration standards for professional degree programs; 36 credit hours of graduate coursework required, including 8 core courses of 24 credit hours. Five specialty options each require minimum of 6 credit hours in specialty courses. Last 6 credit hours from 3 different options: thesis (6 hours), professional project (6 hours), or additional coursework (6 hours); a student is placed on probation when GPA falls below 3.0. Probationary student who does not earn a 3.0 is dismissed from program.

Distinctive Educational Programs: Baccalaureate degree curricula fully integrated with a model liberal studies core curriculum, which includes a 12-credit hour integrative studies sequence. "Great Books" program, leading to major or minor in liberal studies, taught by seminar/tutorial method, offered by Whitney M. Young, Jr. College of Leadership Studies. Work-experience programs, include cooperative education and internships, among the latter a program in the Kentucky Attorney General's office for junior and senior prelaw students. Weekend and evening classes. Study abroad through Cooperative Center for Study in Britain (summer term, junior year abroad) and December-January interim programs at Kings College of the University of London.

ROTC: Army offered in cooperation with University of Kentucky.

Degrees Conferred: 73 *associate;* 280 *baccalaureate:* biological/life sciences 23; business/marketing 39; computer and information sciences 26; education 21; engineering and engineering technologies 27; English 23; health professions and related sciences 30; home economics and vocational home economics 24; law/legal studies 16; liberal arts/general studies 28; mathematics 2; personal and miscellaneous services 15; psychology 11; social sciences and history 17; visual and performing arts 11; 42 *master;s:* biological/life sciences 3; protective services/public administration 39.

Fees and Other Expenses: *Full-time tuition per academic year 2004–05:* undergraduate resident $1,617, out-of-state student $4,552; graduate resident $1,771, out-of-state student $5,014. *Required fees:* $459. *Room and board per academic year:*$2,811.

Financial Aid: Aid from institutionally generated funds is provided on the basis of academic merit, financial need, athletic ability, other considerations. Institution has a Program Participation Agreement with the U.S. Department of Education for eligible students to receive Pell Grants and other federal aid.

Financial aid to full-time, first-time undergraduate students: need-based scholarships/grants totaling self-help parent $9,520,399, self-help $8,447,174, parent loans $1,268,404.

Departments and Teaching Staff: *Professors* 30, *associate professors* 51, *assistant professors* 57, *instructors* 11, *part-time faculty* 5. *Total instructional faculty:* 153 (full-time 148, part-time 5; women 57, men 84; members of minority groups 61). Total faculty with doctorate, first-professional, or other terminal degree: 76. Student-to-faculty ratio: 15:1.

Enrollment: Total enrollment 2,325. Undergraduate full-time 723 men / 894 women; part-time 176m / 411w; graduate full-time 21m / 33w, part-time 38m / 39w. *Transfer students:* in-state 98; from out-of-state 41.

Characteristics of Student Body: *Ethnic/racial makeup:* number of Black non-Hispanic: 1,342; American Indian or Alaska Native: 5; Asian or Pacific Islander: 33; Hispanic: 15; White non-Hispanic: 790; unknown: 163. *Age distribution:* number under 18: 14; 18–19: 488; 20–21: 517; 22–24: 481; 25–29: 334; 30–34: 178; 35–39: 117; 40–49: 146; 50–64: 42; 65 and over: 18. 43% of student body attend summer sessions.

International Students: 92 nonresident aliens enrolled fall 2004. 10 students from Europe, 7 Asia, 23 Central and South America, 39 Africa, 5 Canada, 8 other. No programs available to aid students whose native language is not English. No financial aid specifically designated for international students.

Student Life: On-campus residence halls house 57% of full-time student body. Single rooms available. Some residence halls reserved for freshmen, others for upperclass students, and for men and women students. In-room telephones available. *Intercollegiate athletics:* men only: baseball, basketball, football, golf, tennis, track, cross-country; women only: basketball, softball, tennis,

track, cross-country, volleyball. *Special regulations:* Cars permitted without restrictions. Residence hall quiet hours 9pm to 6am daily. Open visitation 6pm to 11pm. Sun.–Thurs, noon to 2am Fri., Sat. *Special services:* Medical, dental, and mental health care. *Student publications: The Thorobred News,* a student/campus newspaper; *The Thorobred,* a yearbook; *Kentucky River,* an annual literary publication. *Surrounding community:* Frankfort population 28,000. Lexington, 25 miles from campus, and Louisville, 50 miles from campus, are nearest metropolitan areas. Served by mass transit bus system; airport 20 miles from campus; passenger rail services 75 miles from campus.

Publications: *Notes from Alumni Affairs, KSU Magazine, KSU Experts on Call, Faculty Information Bulletin.*

Library Collections: 325,586 volumes. Online catalog. 122,000 government documents; 127,000 microforms; 885 periodicals. 1,925 recordings. Access to online information retrieval systems and the Internet.

Most important special holdings include Rufus B. Atwood Papers (KSU president, 1929–1962); Whitney M. Young, Sr. Memorabilia; African/African American Book Collection.

Buildings and Grounds: Main campus area 310 acres; university farm 166 acres. *New buildings:* The university has participated in several renovation project that include the Carl M. Hill Student Center, Hathaway Hall, Business Annex, Carver Hall, Young Hall.

Chief Executive Officer: Dr. Mary Evans Slas, President.

Address admission inquiries to James Burrell, Director of Admissions; graduate inquiries to Dr. Mark Garrison, Director of Graduate Studies.

Kentucky Wesleyan College

3000 Frederica Street
P.O. Box 1039
Owensboro, Kentucky 42302-1039

Tel: (270) 926-3111   **E-mail:** admitme@kwc.edu
Fax: (270) 926-3196   **Internet:** www.kwc.edu

Institution Description: Kentucky Wesleyan College is a private college affiliated with the United Methodist Church. *Enrollment:* 679. *Degrees awarded:* Baccalaureate.

Accreditation: *Regional:* SACS-Comm. on Coll.

History: Established as Millersburg Male and Female Collegiate Institute and chartered 1858; incorporated 1860; offered first instruction at postsecondary level 1864; awarded first degree (baccalaureate) and changed name to Kentucky Wesleyan University 1866; moved to Winchester, Kentucky 1890; moved to Owensboro, Kentucky 1951.

Institutional Structure: *Governing board:* Board of Trustees of Kentucky Wesleyan College (40 permitted); 12 must be UMC clergy or lay members of the Kentucky Annual conference, 2 church officials, 1 full-time institutional faculty member, 1 student, 1 alumnus, 5 ex officio. *Composition of institution:* Administrators 5 men / 2 women. Academic affairs headed by academic dean. Management/business/finances directed by business manager and treasurer. Full-time instructional faculty 38. Academic governance body, the faculty, meets an average of 9 times per year.

Calendar: Semesters. Academic year Aug. to May. Freshmen admitted Aug., Jan., June. Degrees conferred May, Aug., Dec. Formal commencement May. Summer session June to July.

Characteristics of Freshmen: 72.8% of applicants admitted. 19.75% of applicants admitted and enrolled.

23% (49 students) submitted SAT scores; 94 (199 students) submitted ACT scores. *25th percentile:* SAT Verbal 460, SAT I Math 480; ACT Composite 20, ACT English 19, ACT Math 18. *75th percentile:* SAT I Verbal 610, SAT I Math 580; ACT Composite 25; ACT English 25; ACT Math 26.

46.5% of entering freshmen expected to graduate within 5 years. 83.6% of freshmen from Kentucky. Freshmen from 13 states and 3 foreign countries.

Admission: Rolling admissions plan. For fall acceptance, apply as early as Sept. of previous year, but not later than last day of registration. Early acceptance available. *Requirements:* Either graduation from accredited secondary school or GED. Some exceptions. Additional requirements for some programs. Minimum GPA 2.25. *Entrance tests:* ACT Composite with minimum score 19. *For transfer students:* 2.00 minimum GPA in core courses; from 4-year accredited institution 98 hours maximum transfer; from 2-year accredited institution 67 hours; correspondence/extension students 16 hours.

College credit and advanced placement for postsecondary-level work completed in secondary school and for extrainstitutional learning on basis of ACE *2006 Guide to the Evaluation of Educational Experiences in the Armed Services;* faculty assessment. Tutoring available. Noncredit developmental courses offered during regular academic year.

Degree Requirements: *For all baccalaureate degrees:* 128 credit hours. *For all undergraduate degrees:* 2.0 GPA; 1 term in residence; 2 hours physical education; distribution requirements.

Fulfillment of some requirements and exemption from some beginning courses possible by passing departmental examinations, College Board CLEP, AP. *Grading system:* A–F; pass-fail; withdraw (deadline after which pass-fail is appended to withdraw); incomplete (carries time limit).

Distinctive Educational Programs: Internships. Evening classes. Dual-degree program in engineering with Auburn University (AL) and University of Kentucky. Cooperative baccalaureate program in medical technology with approved hospitals and accredited schools of medical technology. Cooperative associate program in radiologic technology with Owensboro-Davies County Hospital. Special facilities for using telecommunications in the classroom. Individually designed interdisciplinary programs. Preprofessional programs in dentistry, medicine, optometry, pharmacy, physical therapy. Facilities for independent research, including honors programs, tutorials. Study abroad program (England Semester) may be individually arranged.

Degrees Conferred: 114 *baccalaureate:* biological/life sciences ; business/marketing 16; communications/communication technologies 13; computer and information sciences 8; education 3; English 4; foreign languages and literature 1; health professions and related sciences 1; interdisciplinary studies 2; mathematics 3; parks and recreation 4; philosophy/religion/theology 1; physical sciences 3; protective services/public administration 10; psychology 13; social sciences and history 12; visual and performing arts 3.

Fees and Other Expenses: *Full-time tuition per academic year 2004–05:* $12,160. *Required fees:* $400. *Room and board per academic year:* $5,450. *Other fees:* $175.

Financial Aid: Aid from institutionally generated funds is provided on the basis of academic merit, financial need, athletic ability, other criteria. Institution has a Program Participation Agreement with the U.S. Department of Education for eligible students to receive Pell Grants and other federal aid.

Financial aid to full-time, first-time undergraduate students: need-based scholarships/grants totaling $2,831,804, self-help $1,989,506, parent loans $423,016, athletic awards $721,413.

Departments and Teaching Staff: *Professors* 14, *associate professors* 7, *assistant professors* 14, *instructors* 3, *part-time faculty* 35. *Total instructional faculty:* 69 (full-time 35, part-time 34; women 30, men 39; members of minority groups 3). Total faculty with doctorate, first-professional, or other terminal degree: 33. Student-to-faculty ratio: 14:1.

Enrollment: Total enrollment 679. Undergraduate full-time 330 men / 311 women, part-time 19m / 19w.

Characteristics of Student Body: *Ethnic/racial makeup:* number of Black non-Hispanic: 53; American Indian or Alaska Native 1; Asian or Pacific Islander: 4; Hispanic: 14; White non-Hispanic: 551; unknown: 45. *Age distribution:* number 18–19: 315; 20–21: 213; 22–24: 90; 25–29: 26; 30–34: 12; 35–39: 4; 40–49: 11; 50–and over: 1.

International Students: 11 nonresident aliens enrolled fall 2004. 5 students from Europe, 1 Asia, 2 Central and South America, 3 Canada. No programs available to aid students whose native language is not English. No financial aid specifically designated for international students.

Student Life: On-campus residence halls house 47% of student body. *Intercollegiate athletics:* men: baseball, basketball, football, golf, soccer. Women: basketball, golf, soccer, softball, tennis, volleyball. *Special regulations:* Cars permitted without restrictions. Quiet hours from 10pm to 10am. Residence hall visitation from 11am to midnight Sun.-Thurs.; 11am to 2am Fri. and Sat. *Special services:* Learning Resources Center, medical services. *Student publications, radio, television:* Panagram, a bimonthly newspaper; Porpyrian, a yearbook. Radio station broadcasts only on campus 70 hours per week. Closed-circuit TV broadcasts 10 hours per week. *Surrounding community:* Owensboro population 54,000. St. Louis, 163 miles from campus, is nearest metropolitan area. Served by mass transit bus system; airport 3 miles from campus.

Library Collections: 108,407 volumes including bound books, serial backfiles, electronic documents, and government documents not in separate collections. Online catalog. Current serial subscriptions: 312 paper. 146,285 microforms. 3,268 recordings. 46 computer work stations. Students have access to the Internet at no charge.

Most important holdings include the Kentucky United Methodist Heritage Collection; Dr. and Mrs. M. David Orrahood Collection (English literature of the 19th and 20th centuries).

Buildings and Grounds: Campus area 63 acres.

Chief Executive Officer: Dr. Anne Cairns, Federlein, President.

Address admission inquiries to Ken R. Kasp, Dean of Admissions and Financial Aid.

Lexington Theological Seminary

631 South Limestone Street
Lexington, Kentucky 40508
Tel: (859) 252-0361   **E-mail:** admissions@lextheo.edu
Fax: (859) 281-6042   **Internet:** www.lextheo.edu

Institution Description: Lexington Theological Seminary is affiliated with the Christian Church (Disciples of Christ). *Enrollment:* 163. *Degrees awarded:* Master's, doctorate (divinity).

Accreditation: *Regional:* SACS-Comm. on Coll. *National:* ATS. *Professional:* theology

History: Founded 1865; adopted present name 1965.

Institutional Structure: *Governing board:* Board of Trustees. 48 members. *Composition of institution:* Administrators 6 men / 3 women. Administrative officers include the president, dean, vice president for development, business manager, comptroller. Full-time instructional faculty 12.

Calendar: Semesters (4-1-4 plan). Academic year Aug. to May.

Admission: *Requirements:* Bachelor's degree.

Degree Requirements: *For Master of Divinity:* 90 semester hours. *For Master of Arts:* 48 semester hours. *For Doctor of Ministry:* 33 semester hours.

Degrees Conferred: 22 *first-professional:* master of divinity 13; 7 *master's:* pastoral studies; 2 *doctorate:* theology.

Fees and Other Expenses: *Tuition academic year 2004–05:* $4,230. *Room and board per academic year:* $3,194.

Financial Aid: Aid from institutionally generated funds is provided on the basis of academic merit, financial need. Institution has a Program Participation Agreement with the U.S. Department of Education for eligible students to receive Pell Grants and other federal aid. *Graduate aid:* 16 students received federal and state-funded loans totaling $108,661 (ranging from $4,250 to $8,500).

Departments and Teaching Staff: Church history *professors* 1, *associate professors* 0, *part-time teachers* 4; theology 1, 1, 0; practice of ministry 2, 1, 0; church music 0, 0, 3; Old Testament 1, 0, 0; ethics and society 1, 0, 0; New Testament 1, 0, 1; religious education 0, 1, 0; pastoral care 1, 0, 0; homiletics 1, 0, 0. *Total instructional faculty:* 20. Degrees held by full-time faculty: doctorate 88%, professional 12%. 88% hold terminal degrees.

Enrollment: Total enrollment 163.

Characteristics of Student Body: *Ethnic/racial makeup:* Black non-Hispanic: 20; White non-Hispanic: 143. *Age distribution:* 22–24: 15%; 25–29: 20%; 30–34: 20%; 35–39: 15%; 40–49: 15%; 50–59: 10%; 60–up 5%.

International Students: 2 nonresident aliens from Asia enrolled fall 2004. No programs to aid students whose native language is not English. No financial aid specifically designated for international students.

Publications: *Lexington Theological Quarterly.*

Library Collections: 155,000 volumes. Online and card catalogs. 15,000 microforms; 1,000 current periodical subscriptions. Access to online information retrieval systems and the Internet.

Most important special collections include the John Mason Neale Papers; materials from the history of the Christian Church.

Buildings and Grounds: Campus area consists of Administration Building, library, chapel, and 4 student apartment buildings, 16 townhouse units.

Chief Executive Officer: Dr. Robert Cueni, President.

Address admission inquiries to Director of Admissions.

Lindsey Wilson College

210 Lindsey Wilson Street
Columbia, Kentucky 42728-1223
Tel: (270) 384-2126   **E-mail:** admissions@lindsey.edu
Fax: (270) 384-8200   **Internet:** www.lindsey.edu

Institution Description: Lindsey Wilson College is a private, independent, nonprofit college affiliated with the United Methodist Church. *Enrollment:* 1,846. *Degrees awarded:* Associate, baccalaureate.

Accreditation: *Regional:* SACS-Comm. on Coll.

History: Established as Lindsey Wilson Training School 1903 and offered a college preparatory curriculum and a course of study preparatory to county and state certification; lower division college curriculum added and became Lindsey Wilson College 1923; awarded first baccalaureate degree 1988.

Institutional Structure: *Institutional structure:* Governing Board: Lindsey Wilson College Board of Trustees. *Extrainstitutional representation:* 46 trustees; *institutional representation:* president of the college. 3 ex officio. 1 student. All voting. *Composition of institution:* Administrators 21 men / 19 women. Academic affairs headed by provost and dean of the faculty. Management/business/finances directed by executive vice president for administration and director of financial affairs. Full-time instructional faculty 44.

Calendar: Semesters. Academic year late Aug. to mid-May 12. Freshmen admitted Aug., Jan. Degrees conferred May, Aug., Dec. Formal commencement May.

Characteristics of Freshmen: 85% of applicants accepted. 40% of accepted applicants enrolled. Average ACT composite score 19. 93% of freshmen from Kentucky. Freshmen from 6 states and 11 foreign countries.

Admission: Rolling admissions plan. For fall acceptance, apply as early as Aug. of previous year. *Requirements:* Either graduation from accredited secondary school or GED. *Entrance tests:* ACT composite. *For transfer students:* Lindsey Wilson College accepts students from 2-year and 4-year colleges accredited by a regional accrediting commission for colleges and schools. Students with a GPA below 2.0 on a 4.0 scale will be accepted on academic probation.

Tutoring available. Developmental and remedial courses offered during the regular academic year.

Degree Requirements: *For all associate degrees:* 64 semester hours; 28 hours in residence. *For all baccalaureate degrees:* 128 semester hours; 30 of the last 36 in residence. *For all undergraduate degrees:* 2.0 GPA (education majors cumulative GPA must be 2.5); distribution requirements.

Fulfillment of some degree requirements and exemption from some beginning courses possible by passing CLEP or APP standardized tests. *Grading system:* A–F; pass-fail; credit; withdraw; incomplete (carries time limit).

Distinctive Educational Programs: Evening, weekend, satellite, and correctional program classes. Accelerated degree programs. Higher Education Opportunity Program in cooperation with state education department offers financial and academic support to disadvantaged students.

Degrees Conferred: 71 *associate;* 229 *baccalaureate*; 20 *master's.* Bachelor's degrees awarded in top five disciplines: multidisciplinary studies 115; education 26; business, management, marketing, and related support services 21; communication, journalism, and related programs 15; biological and biomedical sciences 11.

Fees and Other Expenses: *Full-time tuition per academic year 2004–05:* $12,984. *Books and supplies:* $400. *Room and board per academic year:* $5,698.

Financial Aid: Aid from institutionally generated funds is provided on the basis of academic merit, financial need, athletic ability, other criteria. Institution has a Program Participation Agreement with the U.S. Department of Education for eligible students to receive Pell Grants and other federal aid.

Financial aid to full-time, first-time undergraduate students: 71% received federal grants averaging $2,012; 85% state/local grants averaging $1,453; 97% institutional grants averaging $2,920; 75% received loans averaging $2,685.

Departments and Teaching Staff: Business *professors* 0, *associate professors* 1, *assistant professors* 1, *instructors* 5, *part-time teachers* 34; developmental studies 0, 0, 0, 2, 6; education/physical education 0, 1, 3, 1, 5; English 0, 0, 1, 6, 25; fine arts 0, 1, 2, 1, 3; humanities 0, 1, 0, 4, 4; human services 0, 1, 0, 3, 22; mathematics 0, 0, 1, 4, 2; science 0, 1, 2, 2, 7. *Total instructional faculty:* 152. Degrees held by full-time faculty: doctorate 18%, master's 80%, baccalaureate 2%. 20% hold terminal degrees.

Enrollment: Total enrollment 1,846. Undergraduate 1,565 (men 34.2%, women 63.8%).

Characteristics of Student Body: *Ethnic/racial makeup:* Black non-Hispanic: 7.5%; American Indian or Alaska Native: .3%; Asian or Pacific Islander: .8%; Hispanic: 1.5%; White non-Hispanic: 83%.

International Students: 59 undergraduate nonresident aliens enrolled fall 2004. Students from Europe, Asia, Africa. Programs available to aid students whose native language is not English: social, cultural, financial.

Student Life: On-campus residence halls. *Intercollegiate athletics:* (men and women) baseball, basketball, cross-country, golf, soccer. *Special regulations:* Cars permitted without restrictions. *Special services:* Learning Resources Center with tutorial services. *Surrounding community:* Columbia population 4,000. Lexington, Louisville, and Nashville, all major metropolitan cities, are each a two-hour drive from Columbia.

Library Collections: 85,000 volumes. 60,000 microforms; 40,000 government documents; 1,350 periodicals; 6,000 recordings/tapes. Students have access to online information retrieval services and the Internet.

Most important special collections include Churchmanship Collection; United Methodist History Collection; Lindsey Wilson College Archives.

Buildings and Grounds: Campus area 40 acres.

Chief Executive Officer: Dr. William T. Luckey, Jr., President.

Address admission inquiries David W. Alls, Director of Admissions.

Louisville Presbyterian Theological Seminary

1044 Alta Vista Road
Louisville, Kentucky 40205-1798
Tel: (502) 895-3411   **E-mail:** admissions@lpts.edu
Fax: (502) 895-1096   **Internet:** www.lpts.edu

Institution Description: Louisville Presbyterian Theological Seminary is a private institution affiliated with the Presbyterian Church in the U.S.A. *Enrollment:* 184. *Degrees awarded:* First-professional (master of divinity), master's, doctorate.

Member of the consortia Kentuckiana Metroversity and Theological Education Association of Mid-America, Appalachian Ministries Educational Resource Center, Seminary Consortium for Urban Pastoral Education.

Accreditation: *Regional:* SACS-Comm. on Coll. *National:* ATS. *Professional*: theology

History: Established as Danville Theological Seminary and offered first instruction at postsecondary level 1853; awarded first degree (first-professional) 1856; chartered 1893; merged with Louisville Theological Seminary (established 1893) and changed name to Presbyterian Theological Seminary 1901; added master's and doctoral programs, adopted present name 1927. *See* Robert Stuart Sanders, *History of Louisville Presbyterian Theological Seminary, 1853–1953* (Louisville: Louisville Presbyterian Theological Seminary, 1953) for further information.

Institutional Structure: *Governing board:* Board of Trustees, Louisville Presbyterian Theological Seminary. Extrainstitutional representation: 37 trustees; institutional representation: president of the seminary. 37 voting. *Composition of institution:* Administrators 28. Academic affairs headed by vice president for academic affairs and dean. Management/business/finances directed by vice president for finance and treasurer. Development affairs directed by vice president for seminary relations. Full-time instructional faculty 17. Academic governance body, Academic Council, meets an average of 9 times per year.

Calendar: Semesters (4-1-4 plan). Academic year Aug. to May. Entering students admitted Sept., Jan., Feb. Degrees conferred and formal commencement May. Summer sessions.

Admission: Rolling admissions plan. Apply as early as 1 year, but not later than 1 month, prior to registration. *Requirements:* Baccalaureate from accredited college or university. Liberal arts background recommended. Provisional admission possible for graduates from nonaccredited institution. Recommend minimum GPA 2.5 for master's; 3.0 GPA for D.Min. 45 hours maximum transfer credit.

Tutoring available. Remedial courses offered during regular academic year.

Degree Requirements: *For first-professional degrees:* 90 credit hours; 45 credits in residence; distribution requirements; field education; oral examination on statement of faith and ministry. *For master's degrees:* 55 to 68 credit hours; thesis and oral examination; 2.5 GPA. *For first-professional degrees:* 3.0 GPA. *Grading system:* A–F; withdraw (carries time limit); incomplete (carries time limit).

Distinctive Educational Programs: Work-experience programs. Evening classes. Accelerated degree programs. Dual-degree programs in theology and law and in theology and social work with University of Louisville. Cooperative program in education with University of Louisville. Facilities and programs for independent research, including individual majors, tutorials. Study abroad by individual arrangement. Off-campus study in the U.S. at Overseas Ministries Study Center, Ventnor (NJ). *Other distinctive programs:* Continuing education for lay education. Certificate of Homelitic Studies Program.

Degrees Conferred: 20 *master's:* theology 2; marriage and family therapy 10; master of theology 10; *first-professional:* 26 master of divinity; 6 *doctorate:* ministry.

Fees and Other Expenses: *Full-time tuition per academic year 2004–05:* $8,250. *Required fees:* $71. *Room and per academic year:* $2,320. *Board per academic year:* 1,130.

Financial Aid: Aid from institutionally generated funds is provided on the basis of academic merit, financial need. Institution has a Program Participation Agreement with the U.S. Department of Education for eligible students to receive Pell Grants and other federal aid. *Graduate aid:* 47 students received federal and state-funded loans totaling $304,055 (ranging from $1,500 to $13,341); 21 students held work-study jobs worth $30,434 (ranging from $48 to $1,350).

Departments and Teaching Staff: *Professors* 13, *associate professors* 6, *part-time faculty* 30. *Total instructional faculty:* 49 (full-time 19, part-time 30; women 20, men 29; members of minority groups 3). Degrees held by full-time faculty: doctorate 100%. 100% hold terminal degrees. Student-to-faculty ratio: 10:1. *Faculty development:* 4 faculty members awarded sabbaticals 2004–05.

Enrollment: Total enrollment 184. First-professional full-time 35m / 52w, part-time 6m / 6w; graduate full-time 7m / 15w, part-time 35m / 28w.

Characteristics of Student Body: *Age distribution:* 17–21: 1%; 22–24: 5%; 25–29: 13%; 30–34: 8%; 35–39: 16%; 40–49: 39%; 50–59: 17%; 60–up: 1%.

International Students: 2 nonresident aliens enrolled fall 2004. 1 student from Europe, 1 Asia. Programs available to aid students whose native language is not English: English as a Second Language Program. No Financial programs specifically designated for international students.

Student Life: Elected students have high profile in the seminary's governance structure. Existence of cohesive campus community. 63% of student enrollment is housed in on-campus housing including residence halls, efficiencies, 1,2, and 3 bedroom apartments. Residence halls are co-ed. Married and family housing available. Pets are allowed. One car per apartment, with extra cars in a guest lot. *Special services:* Learning and Resource Center. Intra-community computer network as well as Internet hook-up for students and staff. *Surrounding community:* Louisville metropolitan population 1 million. Served by mass transit bus system; airport 7 miles from campus.

Publications: Sources of information about Louisville Presbyterian Theological Seminary include *Mosaic.*

Library Collections: 163,716 volumes including bound books, serial backfiles, electronic documents, and government documents not in separate collections. Online catalog. Current serial subscriptions: 597 paper, 145 via electronic access. Online catalog. 4,591 recordings; 89 compact discs; 92 CD-ROMs. 17 computer work stations. Students have access to the Internet at no charge. Total budget for books, periodicals, audiovisual materials, microforms 2004–05: $229,323.

Most important holdings include 100 manuscripts and printed records of the Presbyterian Church Courts of Kentucky dating from the 18th century; 500 printed Bibles dating from the 16th century.

Buildings and Grounds: Campus area 55 acres.

Chief Executive Officer: Dr. Dean K. Thompson, President.

Address admission inquiries to Kerry Rice, Director of Admissions.

Mid-Continent College

99 Powell Road East
Mayfield, Kentucky 42066-9007
Tel: (270) 247-9521   **E-mail:** admissions@mid-continent.edu
Fax: (270) 247-3115   **Internet:** www.mid-continent.edu

Institution Description: Mid-Continent College, formerly names Mid-Continent Baptist Bible College, is an independent, four-year college affiliated with the Baptist Church. *Enrollment:* 814. *Degrees awarded:* Baccalaureate.

Accreditation: *Regional:* SACS. *National:* ABHE.

History: The college was founded in 1949.

Calendar: Semesters.

Characteristics of Freshmen: 204 applicants (109 men, 95 women). 66.7% of applicants admitted. 69.9% of admitted students enrolled full-time.

9% (4 students) submitted SAT scores; 57% (25 students) submitted ACT scores. *25th percentile:* SAT I Verbal 450, SAT I Math 510; ACT Composite 17, ACT English 15, ACT Math 16. *75th percentile:* SAT I Verbal 490, SAT I Math 590; ACT Composite 21, ACT English 21, ACT Math 20.

Admission: Open admissions. *Requirements:* Secondary school transcript; recommendations; interview; SAT I or ACT. TOEFL for international students. College credit and advanced placement for postsecondary-level work completed in secondary school and for extrainstitutional learning on basis of ACE *2006 Guide to the Evaluation of Educational Experiences in the Armed Services.* Developmental/remedial courses offered in summer session and regular academic year; credit given.

Degree Requirements: *For all undergraduate degrees:* 128 semester hours; 10 semester hours of mathematics/science; computer literacy. *Grading system:* A–F.

Degrees Conferred: 133 *baccalaureate.* Bachelor's degrees awarded in top five disciplines: business, management, marketing, and related support services 111; theology and ministerial studies 7; social sciences 5; multidisciplinary studies 6; psychology 3.

Fees and Other Expenses: *Full-time tuition per academic year 2004–05:* $9,390. *Room and board per academic year:* $5,485. *Books and supplies:* $800.

Financial Aid: Aid from institutionally generated funds is provided on the basis of academic merit, financial need, other criteria. Institution has a Program Participation Agreement with the U.S. Department of Education for eligible students to receive Pell Grants and other federal aid.

Financial aid to full-time, first-time undergraduate students: 47% received federal grants averaging $1,40-6; 48% state/local grants averaging $1,719; 58% institutional grants averaging $2,191; 58% loans averaging $2,013.

Departments and Teaching Staff: *Total instructional faculty:* 21.

Enrollment: Total enrollment 814 (46.7% men, 54.3% women).

Characteristics of Student Body: *Ethnic/racial makeup:* Black non-Hispanic: 12.5%; Asian or Pacific Islander: .4%; Hispanic: .7%; White non-Hispanic: 81.9%; unknown: .5%.

International Students: 6 nonresident aliens enrolled fall 2004. No programs available to aid students whose native language is not English.

Student Life: College housing available. Off-campus living permitted. Baptist Student Union; Student Government Association.

Library Collections: 35,000 volumes. 2,000 recordings/tapes; 185 current periodical subscriptions. Students have access to online information retrieval services and the Internet.

Buildings and Grounds: Campus area 60 acres.

Chief Executive Officer: Dr. Robert J. Imoff, President.

Address admissions inquiries to Darla Zakowicz, Director of Admissions.

Midway College

512 East Stephens Street
Midway, Kentucky 40347-1120
Tel: (606) 846-5346   **E-mail:** admissions@midway.edu
Fax: (606) 846-5823   **Internet:** www.midway.edu

Institution Description: Midway College is an independent college affiliated with the Christian Church (Disciples of Christ). *Enrollment:* 1,271. *Degrees awarded:* Associate, baccalaureate.

Accreditation: *Regional:* SACS. *Professional:* nursing, physical therapy, teacher education

History: Established and chartered as Kentucky Female Orphans School, a school for orphan girls, in 1847. Offered first post-secondary degrees 1945. Operated as Midway Junior College 1945 to 1973; present name adopted 1974; first men admitted in separate evening division 1988; first baccalaureate degrees offered 1989.

Institutional Structure: *Governing board:* Representation: Midway College Board of Trustees. 32 members. All voting. Administrators 2 men / 3 women. Academic affairs headed by vice-president for academic affairs. Full-time instructional faculty 48. Academic governance body, Midway College Faculty Assembly, meets an average of 8 times per year.

Calendar: Semesters. Academic year Aug. to May. Freshmen admitted Aug., Jan., May, June. Degrees conferred and formal commencement May. Summer session of 2 terms from May to Aug.

Characteristics of Freshmen: 97% of applicants accepted. 40% of accepted applicants enrolled.

Average secondary school rank of freshmen top 25th percentile. Mean SAT class score 497 verbal, 471 mathematical. Mean ACT composite score 20.

57% of entering freshmen expected to graduate within 5 years. 83% of freshmen from Kentucky. Freshmen from 15 states and 1 foreign country.

Admission: Rolling admissions plan. Students applying for fall acceptance may apply for admission as early as the end of junior year in high school. Priority is given to those that apply prior to Mar. 1. *Requirements:* Students must submit official transcripts from high school, official college transcripts (where applicable), ACT/SAT test scores. In some cases, an interview with the Admissions Committee, essay, and letters of recommendation may be required. Graduation from and accredited secondary school. College preparatory coursework is encouraged. *Entrance tests:* College Board SAT or ACT are required.

Degree Requirements: *For all associate degrees:* 68 to 72 semester hours. *For all baccalaureate degrees:* 130 semester hours; distribution requirements. *For all degrees:* 2.00 GPA minimum and C or higher in English, math, and speech courses.

Fulfillment of some degree requirements and exemptions from some beginning courses possible by passing College Board CLEP or AP. *Grading system:* A-F; pass-fail; withdraw (carries time limit).

Distinctive Educational Programs: Equine Studies; Equine Management. Study abroad at Bishop Burton College in Beverly, North Humberside, United Kingdom.

Degrees Conferred: 64 *associate;* 200 *baccalaureate.* Bachelor's degrees awarded in top five disciplines: business, management, marketing, and related support services 102; education 56; agriculture, agriculture operations and related sciences 29; biological and biomedical science 5; health professions and related clinical sciences 4.

Fees and Other Expenses: *Full-time tuition per academic year 2004–05:* $12,600. *Books and supplies:* $1,800. *Room and board per academic year:* $5,800.

Financial Aid: Aid from institutionally generated funds is provided on the basis of academic merit, financial need, athletic ability, other criteria. Institution has a Program Participation Agreement with the U.S. Department of Education for eligible students to receive Pell Grants and other federal aid.

Financial aid to full-time, first-time undergraduate students: 44% received federal grants averaging $3,461; 54% state/local grants averaging $3,678; 51% institutional grants averaging $4,112; 47% loans averaging $3,796.

Departments and Teaching Staff: *Professors* 4, *associate professors* 4, *assistant professors* 29, *instructors* 11, *part-time teachers* 7. *Total instructional faculty:* 55. Student-to-faculty ratio: 12.4:1. Degrees held by full-time faculty: doctorate 42%, master's 56%, baccalaureate 2%. 42% hold terminal degrees.

Enrollment: Total enrollment 1,271 (11.3% men, 88.7% women).

Characteristics of Student Body: *Ethnic/racial makeup:* Black non-Hispanic: 5.2%; American Indian or Alaska Native .5%; Asian or Pacific Islander: .25; Hispanic: .2%; White non-Hispanic: 91%; unknown: 2.4%. *Age distribution:* 17–21: 33%; 22–24: 13%; 25–29: 17%; 30–34: 8%; 35–39: 14%; 40–49: 3%; 50–59: less than 1%.

International Students: 3 nonresident aliens enrolled fall 2004. 1 student from Europe, 1 Asia, 1 Canada. No programs available to aid students whose native language is not English. No financial aid specifically designated for international students.

Student Life: On campus residence halls house 40% of day college enrollment. *Intercollegiate athletics:* women: basketball, tennis, volleyball, soccer, equestrian events, cross country. *Surrounding community:* Midway population 9,000. Lexington is 15 miles from campus.

Library Collections: 52,000 volumes including bound books, serial backfiles, electronic documents, and government documents not in separate collections. Online and card catalogs. Current serial subscriptions: 450 paper. 52,000 microform units. 8,900 recordings. 25 computer work stations. Students have access to the Internet at no charge.

Most important special holdings include Equine Studies, Women's Studies, Nursing, Paralegal Library.

Buildings and Grounds: Campus area 105 acres.

Chief Executive Officer: Dr. William b. Drake, Jr., President.

Address admissions inquiries to Dr. James Wombles, Dean of Admissions.

Morehead State University

University Boulevard
Morehead, Kentucky 40351-1689
Tel: (606) 783-2221   **E-mail:** admissions@moreheadstate.edu
Fax: (606) 783-5038   **Internet:** www.moreheadstate.edu

Institution Description: Morehead State University is a state institution. *Enrollment:* 9,393. *Degrees awarded:* Associate, baccalaureate, master's. Specialist in education; co-doctoral programs in higher education, guidance and counseling. Certificates also awarded.

Academic offerings subject to approval by statewide coordinating bodies. Budget subject to approval by state governing boards.

Accreditation: *Regional:* SACS-Comm. on Coll. *Professional:* business, industrial technology, music, nursing, radiography, social work, teacher education, veterinary technology

History: Chartered as Morehead State Normal School 1922; offered first instruction at postsecondary level 1923; changed name to Morehead State Normal School and Teachers College 1926; awarded first degree (baccalaureate) 1927; changed name to Morehead State Teachers College 1930, to Morehead State College 1948; adopted present name 1966.

Institutional Structure: *Governing board:* Board of Regents. Extrainstitutional representation: 8 regents; institutional representation: 1 faculty member, 1 staff member, 1 student. All voting. *Composition of institution:* Administrators 34 men / 11 women. Academic affairs headed by provost. Full-time instructional faculty 213 men / 145 women. Academic governance by President, Cabinet, Faculty Senate, and Board of Regents.

Calendar: Semesters. Academic year mid-Aug. to mid-May. Freshmen admitted Aug., Jan., May, July. Degrees conferred Dec., May, July, Aug. Formal commencements May and Aug. Summer session from mid-June to late July.

Characteristics of Freshmen: 66% of applicants admitted. 88% of applicants admitted and enrolled.

3% (41 students) submitted SAT scores; 97% (1,243 students) submitted ACT scores. *25th percentile*: ACT Composite 17, ACT English 15, ACT Math 16. *75th percentile*: ACT Composite 22, ACT English 21, ACT Math 21.

18% of entering freshmen expected to graduate within 5 years. 79% of freshmen from Kentucky. Freshmen from 24 states and 4 foreign countries.

Admission: Rolling admissions plan. Early acceptance available. *Requirements:* Graduation from accredited secondary school or GED. Exceptions possible for in-state residents. Additional requirements for some programs. Lowest acceptable secondary school class standing for out-of-state students 50th percentile. *Entrance tests:* ACT composite. For foreign students TOEFL. *For transfer students:* 2.0 minimum GPA.

College credit for postsecondary-level work completed in secondary school and for extrainstitutional learning on basis of ACE *2006 Guide to the Evaluation of Educational Experiences in the Armed Services;* faculty assessment. Tutoring available. Developmental courses offered in summer session and regular academic year; credit given.

Degree Requirements: *For all associate degrees:* 64 credit hours. *For all baccalaureate degrees:* 128 hours; 2 hours physical education; general education requirements. *For all undergraduate degrees:* 2.0 GPA, 2 semesters (including last) in residence.

Fulfillment of some degrees requirements possible by passing departmental examinations, College Board CLEP, other standardized tests. *Grading system:* A–E; pass-fail; withdraw (carries time limit); incomplete (carries time limit).

Distinctive Educational Programs: *For undergraduates:* Work-experience programs. Accelerated degree programs. Facilities for independent research, including honors programs and tutorials. *For graduate students:* Joint doctoral program in education in cooperation with the University of Kentucky. Interdepartmental/interdisciplinary program in vocational education. *Available to all students:* Flexible meeting places and schedules, including off-campus centers (at Marshland, Prestonsburg, Jackson, Mt. Sterling, West Liberty) and evening classes. Special facilities for using telecommunications in the classroom. Individual majors. Study abroad in cooperation with other institutions in Kentucky International Association. Servicemembers Opportunity College.

ROTC: Army.

Degrees Conferred: 146 *associate*, 991 *baccalaureate* (B), 359 *master's* (M): agriculture 29 (B); biological/life sciences 43 (B); business/marketing 189 (B), 68 (M); communications/communication technologies 69 (B), 11 (M); computer and information sciences 6 (B); education 184 (B), 281 (M); engineering and engineering technologies 28 (B), 6 (M); English 22 (B), 6 (M); foreign languages and literature 5 (B); health professions and related sciences 32 (B); home economics and vocational home economics 6 (B); interdisciplinary studies 1 (B); law/legal studies 12 (B); liberal arts/general studies 107 (B); mathematics 9 (B); parks and recreation 23 (B); philosophy/religion/theology 4 (B); physical sciences 16 (B); protective services/public administration 40 (B); psychology 32 (B), 12 (M); social sciences and history 94 (B), 5 (M); visual and performing arts 41 (B), 10 (M).

Fees and Other Expenses: *Full-time tuition per academic year 2004–05:* $3,840 resident undergraduate, $10,200 nonresident; graduate resident $4,160, nonresident $11,140. *Room and board per academic year:* $4,410.

Financial Aid: Aid from institutionally generated funds is provided on the basis of academic merit, financial need, athletic ability. Institution has a Program Participation Agreement with the U.S. Department of Education for eligible students to receive Pell Grants and other federal aid.

Financial aid to full-time, first-time undergraduate students: need-based scholarships/grants totaling $14,483,465, self-help $10,230,202; non-need-based scholarships/grants totaling $7,231,139, self-help $8,424,583, parent loans $1,429,929, tuition waivers $1,984,303.

Departments and Teaching Staff: Full-time faculty 488 (full-time 358, part-time 130; women 225, men 263; members of minority groups 42). Total faculty with doctorate, first-professional, or other terminal degree: 260. Student-to-faculty ratio: 19:1. *Faculty development:* 3 faculty members awarded sabbaticals 2004–05.

Enrollment: Total enrollment 9,393. Undergraduate full-time 2,748 men / 3,028 women, part-time 386m / 1,095w; graduate full-time 120m / 183w, part-time 379m / 354w. *Transfer students:* 457.

Characteristics of Student Body: *Ethnic/racial makeup:* number of Black non-Hispanic: 270; American Indian or Alaska Native: 19; Asian or Pacific Islander: 21; Hispanic: 56; White non-Hispanic: 1,345. *Age distribution:* number under 18: 124; 18–19: 1,936; 20–21: 2,073; 22–24: 1,696; 25–29: 763; 30–34: 585; 35–39: 279; 40–49: 359; 50–64: 186; 65 and over: 6. 45% of student body attend summer sessions.

International Students: 87 nonresident aliens enrolled fall 2004. 14 students from Europe, 99 Asia, 15 Central and South America, 3 Africa, 8 Canada, 8 Australia, 1 other. Programs available for students whose native language is not English: social and cultural. English as a Second Language Program. No financial aid specifically designated for international students.

Student Life: On-campus residence halls house 65% of student body. Residence halls for men, women, and coed. Housing available for married students. *Intercollegiate athletics:* men only: baseball, basketball, football, golf, tennis, track; women only: basketball, softball, tennis, track, volleyball. *Special regulations:* Registered cars allowed in designated areas only. Visitation in lobbies 9am to 12 midnight Sun.–Thurs., 9am to 2am Fri. and Sat. Opposite sex allowed to visit in rooms from 12 noon to 12 midnight Sun. through Thurs. and from 12 noon to 2am Fri. and Sat. *Special services:* Learning Resources Center, medical services. *Student publications, radio:* Inscape, a literary magazine, published irregularly during year; *Raconteur*, a yearbook; *Trail Blazer*, a weekly newspaper. Radio station WMKY broadcasts 126 hours per week. *Surrounding commu-*

nity: Morehead population 9,000. Cincinnati (OH), 140 miles from campus, is nearest metropolitan area.

Library Collections: 569,769 volumes. Current serial subscriptions: 1,824 paper, 200 microform, 1,002 via electronic access. 6,440 recordings; 4,016 compact discs; 2,762 DC-ROMs. 140 computer work stations. Online catalog. Students have access to online information retrieval services and the Internet. Total 2004–05 budget for materials and operations: $981,682.

Most important holdings include Appalachian Collection; James Still Collection; Jesse Stuart Collection.

Buildings and Grounds: Campus area 809 acres.

Chief Executive Officer: Dr. Wayne D. Andrews, President.

Undergraduates address admission inquiries to Joel Pace, Director of Admissions; graduate inquiries to Susan Maxey, Graduate Advisor.

Murray State University

15th and Main
Murray, Kentucky 42071
Tel: (270) 762-3011   **E-mail:** admissions@murraystate.edu
Fax: (250) 762-3413   **Internet:** www.murraystate.edu

Institution Description: Murray State University is a public institution. *Enrollment:* 10,120. *Degrees awarded:* Associate, baccalaureate, master's, doctorate. Specialist certificates in education also awarded.

Academic offerings subject to approval by statewide coordinating bodies. Budget subject to approval by state governing boards.

Accreditation: *Regional:* SACS-Comm. on Coll. *Professional:* applied science, art, business, counseling, engineering, engineering technology, journalism, music, nurse anesthesia education, nursing, social work, speech-language pathology, teacher education, veterinary technology

History: Established and chartered as Murray Normal School 1922; offered first instruction at postsecondary level 1923; changed name to Murray Normal School and Teachers College and awarded first degree (baccalaureate) 1926; changed name to Murray State Teachers College 1930, to Murray State College 1948; adopted present name 1966.

Institutional Structure: *Governing board:* Murray State University Board of Regents. Extrainstitutional representation: 10 regents. *Composition of institution:* president; 4 vice presidents (academic, student affairs, institutional advancement, administrative services). Academic governance body, Academic Council, meets every 2 weeks.

Calendar: Semesters. Academic year Aug. to May. Freshmen admitted Aug., Jan., June. Degrees conferred May, Aug., Dec. Formal commencements May, Dec.

Characteristics of Freshmen: 2,972 applicants (1,186 men, 1,766 women). 87.4% of applicants admitted. 53.9% of admitted students enrolled full-time.

97% (1,412 students) submitted ACT scores. *25th percentile*: ACT Composite 20, ACT English 19, ACT Math 18. *75th percentile*: ACT Composite 26, ACT English 26, ACT Math 24.

Admission: Rolling admissions plan. Early acceptance available. *Requirements:* For freshmen, accredited secondary school and, for unconditional in-state, minimum ACT score of 18; for unconditional out-of-state, minimum ACT score of 20; all others considered using a combination of GED scores, ACT scores, class rank, precollege curriculum, and SAT scores. *For transfer students:* 2.0/4.0 GPA for unconditional admission for all applicants. All degree credit from accredited colleges is accepted for transfer; a maximum of 96 transfer hours from 4-year institutions will apply toward a degree; a maximum of 67 transfer hours from a 2-year institution will apply toward a degree.

College credit and advanced placement for postsecondary-level work completed in secondary school; college credit for extrainstitutional learning on basis of ACE *2006 Guide to the Evaluation of Educational Experiences in the Armed Services;* faculty assessment. Tutoring available. Developmental courses offered in summer session and regular academic year; credit given.

Degree Requirements: *For all associate degrees:* 64–67 semester hours; 24 hours in residence. *For all baccalaureate degrees:* 128 hours (137–149 in College of Creative Expression); 32 hours in residence. *For all undergraduate degrees:* 2.0 GPA; general education requirements.

Fulfillment of some degree requirements possible by passing College Board CLEP. *Grading system:* A–E; pass; withdraw.

Distinctive Educational Programs: Honors Program; Bachelor of Independent Studies degree; Mid-America Remote Sensing Center (MARC), which is a satellite remote sensing facility; work-experience programs; national and international student exchange programs. Study abroad through Kentucky Institute for European Studies (KIES) offers academic programs in Austria, Spain, France, and Italy; Cooperative Center for Study in Britain (CCSB) provides sev-

eral options for study in Britain; faculty and student exchange agreements with Kenyatta University in Nairobi, Kenya, Belize College of Arts, Science and Technology (BELCAST) and the Technological Institute, Costa Rica, in South America, Darling Downs Institute, Toowoomba, Queensland, Australia, Jordanhill College of Education, Glasgow, Scotland, and the University of Sarajevo, Yugoslavia; semester at sea offers study aboard ship traveling to various parts of the world. Management and Information Systems degree program.

Degrees Conferred: 32 *associate;* 1,440 *baccalaureate;* 570 *master's.* Bachelor's degrees awarded in top five disciplines: education 250; business, management, marketing, and related support services 214; communication, journalism, and related programs 151; health professions and related clinical sciences 142; engineering technologies/technicians 92.

Fees and Other Expenses: *Full-time tuition per academic year 2004–05:* undergraduate and graduate resident $3,984; out-of-state $10,836. *Room and board per academic year:* $4,662. *Books and supplies;* $700.

Financial Aid: Aid from institutionally generated funds is provided on the basis of academic merit, financial need, athletic ability. Institution has a Program Participation Agreement with the U.S. Department of Education for eligible students to receive Pell Grants and other federal aid.

Financial aid to full-time, first-time undergraduate students: 19% received federal grants averaging $2,999; 39% state/local grants averaging $2,075; 35% institutional grants averaging $3,535; 32% loans averaging $4,367.

Departments and Teaching Staff: *Total instructional faculty:* 187. Student-to-faculty ratio: 16:1. Degrees held by full-time faculty: doctorate 90%, master's 100%. 100% hold terminal degrees.

Enrollment: Total enrollment 10,120. Undergraduate 8,363 (42.3% men, 57.7% women).

Characteristics of Student Body: *Ethnic/racial makeup:* Black non-Hispanic: 5.6%; American Indian or Alaska Native: .6%; Asian or Pacific Islander: .8%; Hispanic: .8%; White non-Hispanic: 89.1%; unknown: .9%.

International Students: 184 undergraduate nonresident aliens enrolled fall 2004. Programs available to aid students whose native language is not English: social, cultural. English as a Second Language Program. Some financial aid for international students.

Student Life: On-campus residence halls house over 50% of full-time students. Residence halls for men constitute 39% of such space, for women 49%, coed housing 12%. Housing available for married students. *Intercollegiate athletics:* men only: baseball, basketball, cross-country, football, golf, tennis, track; women only: basketball, cross-country, tennis, track, volleyball. *Special regulations:* Registered cars with decals permitted in designated areas. Quiet hours. Residence hall visitation during daytime and evening hours; hours set by residents in individual residence halls. *Special services:* Learning Resources Center, medical services. *Student publications, radio, television: Murray State News,* a weekly newspaper; *The Shield,* a yearbook. Radio station WKMS-FM broadcasts 140 hours per week. TV station MSU-TV broadcasts educational and cultural programming 7 hours per week. WPAD is carrier current on campus radio station. *Surrounding community:* Murray population 14,500. Nashville (TN), 120 miles from campus, is nearest metropolitan area. Served by airport in Paducah (KY).

Publications: *Business and Public Affairs* (quarterly) first published 1979; *Shagbark Review* (biannually) first published 1973; *The Minority Connection* for the Office of Minority Affairs; *International Update* for the Center for International Programs; *The Graduate Bulletin* and *The Undergraduate Bulletin* catalogs (biennial); *The Times* (bimonthly alumni newspaper); *The Alumnus* magazine.

Library Collections: 390,000 volumes. 212,000 government documents; 201,000 microform units; 10,500 audiovisual materials; 2,385 current periodicals. Access to online information retrieval systems and the Internet.

Most important holdings include Jesse Stuart Collection; genealogy and local history collection; Tennessee Valley Authority collection; Forrest Pogue War and Diplomacy Collection; Irvin Cobb Collection.

Buildings and Grounds: Campus area 250 acres.

Chief Executive Officer: Dr. F. King Alexander, President.

Address admission inquiries to James T. Vaughan, Vice President for Enrollment Management.

College of Education

Degree Programs Offered: *Associate* in child care, food service management; *baccalaureate* in child studies, communication disorders, elementary education, health, library science, mental retardation, physical education, recreation, rehabilitation, secondary education, special education, speech and hearing; *master's* in various fields.

Distinctive Educational Programs: Integrated science/mathematics/education program.

College of Business and Public Affairs

Degree Programs Offered: *Associate* in computer data processing, general business administration, real estate, secretarial training; *baccalaureate* in accounting, business administration, business education, computer science, criminal justice, economics, management, marketing, political science, real estate; *master's* in business administration, economics, public administration.

College of Creative Expression

Degree Programs Offered: *Baccalaureate, master's* in art, journalism, music, radio, speech and theater, television.

Distinctive Educational Programs: Interdepartmental course in the arts; interdepartmental programs through journalism and radio-television, and speech and theater departments.

College of Science

Degree Programs Offered: *Associate* in chemical technology, horticulture; *baccalaureate* in aquatic biology, astronomy, biological sciences, chemistry, earth science, engineering physics, fisheries biology, geography, geology, mathematics, medical technology, nursing, physical science, physics, urban and regional planning, wildlife biology; *master's* various fields.

Distinctive Educational Programs: Integrated science-mathematics-education program.

College of Humanistic Studies

Degree Programs Offered: *Baccalaureate* in English, foreign language, history, philosophy, sociology; *master's* in English, history.

College of Industry and Technology

Degree Programs Offered: *Associate* in civil engineering technology, computer engineering technology drafting and design technology, electrical engineering technology, environmental engineering technology, mechanical engineering technology, occupational safety and health, graphic arts technology, vocational technical education; *baccalaureate* in agriculture, civil engineering technology, construction technology, electrical engineering technology, engineering technology, graphic arts technology, home economics, industrial arts education, manufacturing technology, military science, occupational safety and health technology, printing management, vocational technical education; *master's* in various fields.

Distinctive Educational Programs: Emergency medical training program. Vocational handicapped operators program.

Northern Kentucky University

Nunn Drive
Highland Heights, Kentucky 40199
Tel: (859) 572-5100   **E-mail:** admitnku@nku.edu
Fax: (859) 572-5566   **Internet:** www.nku.edu

Institution Description: Northern Kentucky University is a state institution. *Enrollment:* 13,903. *Degrees awarded:* Associate, baccalaureate, master's, first-professional (law).

Academic offerings subject to approval by Northern Kentucky University Board of Regents and the Kentucky Council on Higher Education. Member of Greater Cincinnati Consortium of Colleges and Universities.

Accreditation: *Regional:* SACS-Comm. on Coll.*Professional:* business, chemistry, construction technology, engineering technology, law, music, nursing, radiography, respiratory therapy, social work, teacher education

History: Established as Northern Kentucky State College 1968; offered first instruction at postsecondary level 1970; first degree (associate) awarded 1971; Salmon P. Chase College of Law, an independent law school in Cincinnati, Ohio, merged with the college in 1972; university status was achieved in 1976. First master's program (business administration) offered in 1980.

Institutional Structure: *Governing board:* Board of Regents. Extrainstitutional representation: 8 regents; institutional representation: 1 full-time instructional faculty member, 1 full-time classified staff, 1 student. 1 ex officio. All revolving. *Composition of institution:* Administrators 39 men / 34 women. Academic affairs headed by vice provost. Management/business/finances directed by vice president/treasurer. Full-time instructional faculty 549. Faculty Senate meets at least once a month during both semesters and during the summer.

Calendar: Semesters. Academic year Aug. to May. Freshmen admitted fall, spring, summer. Degrees conferred and formal commencement Dec., May. Summer session of 10 terms from May to Aug.

Characteristics of Freshmen: 81% of applicants admitted.47% of applicants admitted and enrolled.

14% (286 students) submitted SAT scores; 79% (1,628 students) submitted ACT scores. *25th percentile:* SAT Verbal 420, SAT Math 410; ACT Composite 18, ACT English 16, ACT Math 16. *75th percentile:* SAT Verbal 550, SAT Math 550; ACT Composite 23, ACT English 22, ACT Math 23.

18% of entering freshmen expected to graduate within 5 years. 70% of freshmen from Kentucky. Freshmen from 16 states and 10 foreign countries.

Admission: Rolling admissions plan. For fall acceptance, apply as early as August 1 of senior year in secondary school, but not later than August 1 of year of enrollment. Early acceptance available. *Requirements:* No specific requirements; graduates of state-accredited secondary schools accepted. GED accepted if applicant is 19 or older. *Entrance tests:* ACT Composite. *See* Salmon P. Chase College of Law for additional requirements. *For transfer students:* From 4- and 2-year institutions no set GPA requirements. Must be in good academic standing from the sending school or meet with an associate dean to be admitted. No maximum transfer hours.

Tutoring available. Developmental courses offered in summer session and regular academic year; credit given.

Degree Requirements: *For all associate degrees:* 64 credit hours, at least 2.0 GPA and the last 20 hours in residence. *For all baccalaureate degrees:* 128 credit hours, at least a 2.0 GPA;last 30 hours in residence. *See* College of Law for other requirements. Fulfillment of some degree requirements and exemption from some beginning courses possible by passing College Board CLEP, AP, or departmental examinations. *Grading system:* A–F; pass-fail; withdraw (carries time limit).

Distinctive Educational Programs: *For undergraduates:* Honors program. Cooperative education program, evening classes, web-based classes and degree programs. Interdepartmental/interdisciplinary majors in international studies and urban studies; minors in environmental, Latin American, and women's studies, health care, international studies, Japanese studies, medieval studies, legal and social justice studies. Dual-degree programs in engineering (agricultural, chemical, civil, electrical, mechanical, metallurgical, mining) with University of Kentucky. Study abroad through Cooperative Center for study in England; Kentucky Institute for European studies; direct exchanges with universities in India, Japan, Scotland, Spain, and other countries.

ROTC: Air Force in cooperation with University of Cincinnati; Army in cooperation with Xavier University.

Degrees Conferred: 223 *associate;* 1,421 *baccalaureate* (B); 252 *master's* (M): biological/life 38 (B); business/marketing 377 (B), 82 (M); communications/communication technologies 63 (B); computer and information sciences 28 (B), 9 (M); education 188 (B), 202 (M); engineering and engineering technologies 65 (B), 8 (M); English 143 (B); foreign languages and literature 6 (B); health professions and related sciences 74 (B), 15 (M); mathematics 14 (B); natural resources/environmental science 10 (B); philosophy/religion/theology 6 (B); physical sciences 22 (B); protective services/public administration 87 (B), 36 (M); psychology 77 (B); social sciences and history 150 (B); visual and performing arts 93 (B). 102 *first-professional:* law.

Fees and Other Expenses: *Full-time tuition per academic year 2005–06:* undergraduate resident $4,968, nonresident $9,696; graduate resident $4,806, nonresident $9,846. *Room and board per academic year:* $5,358.

Financial Aid: Aid from institutionally generated funds is provided on the basis of academic merit, financial need, athletic ability, other criteria. Institution has a Program Participation Agreement with the U.S. Department of Education for eligible students to receive Pell Grants and other federal aid.

Financial aid to full-time, first-time undergraduate students: need-based scholarships/grants totaling $9,531,169, self-help $25,884,028; non-need-based scholarships/grants totaling $10,360,674, self-help $2,951,743, parent loans $2,789,351, tuition waivers $2,645,248, athletic awards $617,269.

Departments and Teaching Staff: *Professors* 110, *associate professors* 91, *assistant professors* 149, *instructors* 3; *lecturers* 185, *part-time faculty* 433, *unranked* 11. *Total instructional faculty:* 788 (full-time 487, part-time 301; women 386, men 402; members of minority groups 69). Total faculty with doctorate, first-professional, or other terminal degree: 331. Student-to-faculty ratio: 18:1. *Faculty development:* 11 faculty members awarded sabbaticals 2004–05.

Enrollment: Total enrollment 13,903. Undergraduate full-time 3,723 men / 5,266 women, part-time 1,248m / 1,815w; first-professional full-time 179m / 139w, part-time 146m / 115w; graduate full-time 72m / 94w, part-time 370m / 736w. *Transfer students:* 680.

Characteristics of Student Body: *Ethnic and racial makeup:* number of Black non-Hispanic: 567; American Indian or Alaska Native: 26; Asian or Pacific Islander: 106; Hispanic: 113; White non-Hispanic: 10,647. *Age distribution:* under 18: 18; 18–19: 2,862; 20–21: 2,852; 22–24: 2,790; 25–29: 1,467; 30–34: 638; 35–39: 401; 40–49: 498; 50–64: 126; 65 and over: 9. 39% of student body attend summer sessions.

International Students: 218 nonresident aliens enrolled fall 2004. Programs available to aid students whose native language is not English: social, cultural.

English as a Second Language Program. No financial aid specifically designated for international students.

Student Life: On-campus housing for 1,400 students in traditional single/double dormitory rooms and apartment suites. *Intercollegiate athletics:* men only: baseball, basketball, cross-country, golf, soccer, tennis; women only: basketball, cross-country, golf, softball, tennis, volleyball. *Special regulations:* Cars permitted without restrictions. *Special services:* Learning Resources Center, campus nurse. *Student publications, radio: The Collage,* an annual literary magazine; *The Northerner,* a weekly newspaper; WRFN, an on-campus student radio station. *Surrounding community:* Cincinnati metropolitan area population 2 million. Served by mass transit bus system; airport 10 miles from campus; passenger rail service 8 miles from campus.

Publications: *Journal of Kentucky Studies* (annually) first published in 1984; *The Northern Kentucky Law Review* (annually) first published 1975.

Library Collections: 307,000 volumes. 900,000 government documents; 735,000 microforms; 1,886 current periodicals. Online catalog. Access 1,881 recordings. 70 computer work stations. Students have access to online information retrieval systems and the Internet.

Most important special holdings include Kentuckiana Collection; Confederate Imprints (microform); early English books (microform);Harry M. Candill Appalachian Collection; Carl Bogardus Inland River Collection.

Buildings and Grounds: Campus area 397 acres. *New buildings:* University Suites completed 2003; Dorothy Westerman Hermann Science Center 2002.

Chief Executive Officer: Dr.James C. Votruba, President.

Address admission inquiries to Melissa Gorbandt, Director of Admissions; graduate school inquiries to Peg Griffin, Director of Graduate Programs; law school inquiries to Gerald St. Amand, Dean, Salmon F. Chase College of Law.

Salmon P. Chase College of Law

Degree Programs Offered: *J.D., J.D./M.B.A.*

Admission: Baccalaureate from accredited college or university; LSAT; LSDAS registration.

Degree Requirements: 88 semester hours, 2.0 GPA, 90 weeks in residence for full-time students, 120 weeks for part-time students.

Departments and Teaching Staff: Law teaching staff 13 men / 6 women. *Total instructional faculty:* 19.

Pikeville College

214 Sycamore Street
Pikeville, Kentucky 41501
Tel: (606) 218-5250
Fax: (606) 218-5255

Institution Description: Pikeville College is a private, independent, nonprofit college affiliated with the United Presbyterian Church (U.S.A.). *Enrollment:* 1,100. *Degrees awarded:* Associate, baccalaureate, doctor of osteopathic medicine. Certificates also awarded/

Accreditation: *Regional:* SACS-Comm. on Coll. *Professional:* clinical lab scientist, osteopathy

History: Established and incorporated as Pikeville Collegiate Institute 1889; adopted present name 1909; offered first instruction at postsecondary level 1918; became 4-year institution 1955; awarded first degree (baccalaureate) 1957; School of Osteopathic Medicine (doctoral level) added 1997.

Institutional Structure: *Governing board:* The Board of Trustees. 34 trustees; president of the college; president of the alumni association. 1 ex officio. 31 voting. *Composition of institution:* Administrators 6 vice presidents (4 men / 2 women). Full-time instructional faculty 55. Academic governance body, the faculty, meets an average of 9 times per year.

Calendar: Semesters. Academic year June to Aug. Freshmen admitted Aug., Jan., May. Degrees conferred May, Aug., Dec. Formal commencement May. Summer session of from May to Aug.

Characteristics of Freshmen: 100% of applicants admitted. 28% of applicants admitted and enrolled.

100% (177 students) submitted ACT scores. *25th percentile*: ACT Composite 17, ACT English 16, ACT Math 16. *75th percentile*: ACT Composite 21, ACT English 22, ACT Math 21.

35% of entering freshmen expected to graduate within 5 years. 86% of freshmen from Kentucky. Freshmen from 10 states and 2 foreign countries.

Admission: Rolling admissions plan. Early acceptance available. *Requirements:* Either graduation from accredited secondary school with program which emphasized English, foreign language, mathematics, natural sciences, social studies; or GED. *Entrance tests:* ACT Composite preferred; College Board SAT

accepted. For foreign students TOEFL. *For transfer students:* submittal of college transcripts and must take a writing proficiency exam.

College credit and advanced placement for postsecondary-level work completed in secondary school and for extrainstitutional learning (life experience) on basis of ACE *2006 Guide to the Evaluation of Educational Experiences in the Armed Services;* portfolio and faculty assessments. Tutoring available. Developmental/remedial courses offered in summer session and regular academic year; credit given.

Degree Requirements: *For all associate degrees:* 64 credit hours; 2 credit hours physical education; core requirements, including 12hours in humanities, 3 mathematics, and 6 social science; at least 50% of credit hours required in the major, and a total of 25% must be earned in residence. *For all degrees:* 2.0 GPA (2.0 in major field); last 30 hours in residence; grades of C or higher in all major courses; completion of college assessment requirements.

Fulfillment of some degree requirements and exemption from some beginning courses possible by passing departmental examinations, College Board CLEP, AP. *Grading system:* A–F; pass-fail; withdraw (carries time limit).

Distinctive Educational Programs: Work-experience programs including internships, field experience, in-service training, practicums. Evening classes. Interdisciplinary courses in humanities. Independent study. Community education program. The Elizabeth Akers Elliott Nursing Program. The Pikeville College School of Osteopathic Medicine.

Degrees Conferred: 23 *associate;* 166 *baccalaureate:* biological/life sciences 8; business/marketing 43; computer and information sciences 4; education 24; English 2; mathematics 4; philosophy/religion/theology 2; physical sciences 2; protective services/public administration 10; psychology 39; social sciences and history 17; visual and performing arts 2. 59 *first-professional:* osteopathic medicine.

Fees and Other Expenses: *Full-time tuition per academic year 2004–05:* $10,500. Graduate (osteopathic program) $27,000. *Room and board per academic year:* $5,000.

Financial Aid: Aid from institutionally generated funds is generated on the basis of academic merit, athletic ability, financial need, other considerations. Institution has a Program Participation Agreement with the U.S. Department of Education for eligible students to receive Pell Grants and other federal aid.

Financial aid to full-time, first-time undergraduate students: need-based scholarships/grants totaling $3,858,575, self-help $2,227,132, parent loans $19,126; non-need-based scholarships/grants totaling $2,551,781, self-help $71,560, tuition waivers $144,646, athletic awards $1,055,890. *Graduate aid (first-professional):* 232 students received federal and state-funded loans totaling $8,372,421; 129 students received fellowships and grants totaling $1,573,881.

Departments and Teaching Staff: *Professors* 15, *associate professors* 19, *assistant professors* 18, *instructors* 3, *part-time faculty* 15. *Total instructional faculty:* 70 (full-time 55, part-time 15; women 36, men 34). Total faculty with doctorate, first-professional, or other terminal degree: 27. Student-to-faculty ratio: 13:1.

Enrollment: Total enrollment 1,066. Undergraduate full-time 325 men / 427 women, part-time 10m / 39w; first-professional full-time 150m / 115w, part-time 10m / 39w. Transfer students: in-state 46; from out-of-state 18.

Characteristics of Student Body: *Ethnic/racial makeup:* number of Black non-Hispanic: 51; American Indian or Alaska Native: 3; Asian or Pacific Islander: 2; Hispanic: 6; White non-Hispanic: 737; unknown: 6. *Age distribution:* number 18–19: 232; 20–21: 251; 22–24: 171; 25–29: 67; 30–34: 29; 35–39: 24; 40–49: 23; 50–64: 4.

International Students: 13 nonresident aliens enrolled fall 2004. 2 students from Europe, 3 Central and South America, Africa 4,Canada 3, New Zealand 1. No programs available to aid students whose native language is not English. No financial aid specifically designated for international students.

Student Life: On-campus residence halls house 41% of student body. *Special regulations:* Registered cars permitted without restrictions. *Special services:* Medical services. *Student publications: The Bear Facts,* a weekly student newspaper; *The Highlander,* a yearbook. *Surrounding community:* Pikeville population 6,500. Lexington-Fayette, 140 miles from campus, is nearest metropolitan area.

Library Collections: 72,673 volumes. Online and card catalogs. Current serial subscriptions: paper 219; 1,811 via electronic access. 36 computer work stations. Access to online information retrieval systems and the Internet. Total 2004–05 budget for books and materials: $311,766.

Most important special collection is the Hatfield-McCoy Feud Collection; Gov. Patten's Historical Papers.

Chief Executive Officer: Dr. Harold Smith, President.

Address admission inquiries to Melinda Lynch, Dean of Admissions; firs-professional program inquiries to Stephen Payson, Associate Dean, Student Services.

Southern Baptist Theological Seminary

2825 Lexington Road
Louisville, Kentucky 40280-0001
Tel: (502) 897-4011   **E-mail:** admissions@sbts.edu
Fax: (502) 887-4880   **Internet:** www.sbts.edu

Institution Description: The Southern Baptist Theological Seminary is a private institution affiliated with the Southern Baptist Convention. A baccalaureate-degree granting branch campus, Nigerian Theological Seminary, is located in Ogbomosho, Nigeria. *Enrollment:* 2,983. *Degrees awarded:* First-professional (master of divinity), master's, doctorate.

Member of the consortia Kentuckiana Metroversity, Theological Education Association of Mid-America.

Accreditation: *Regional:* SACS-Comm. on Coll. *National:* ATS. *Professional:* music, theology

History: Chartered 1858; established and offered first instruction at postsecondary level 1859; awarded first degree 1861. *See* William A. Mueller, *A History of Southern Baptist Theological Seminary* (Nashville: Broadman Press, 1959) for further information.

Institutional Structure: *Governing board:* Board of Trustees. Representation: 62 trustees, including 30 alumni. All voting. *Composition of institution:* Administrators 28 men / 12 women. Academic affairs headed by provost. Management/business/finances directed by vice president for business affairs. Full-time instructional faculty 68. Academic governance body, the faculty, meets an average of 5 times per year.

Calendar: Semesters. Academic year Aug. to May. Entering students admitted Aug., Jan., Feb., June, July. Degrees conferred and formal commencements June, Dec. Summer session of 2 terms from late May to mid-July.

Characteristics of Freshmen: 95 applicants (45 men, 50 women).88.4% of applicants admitted. 77.4% of admitted students enrolled full-time.

Admission: Rolling admissions plan. Apply as early as 1 year, but not later than 1 month, prior to entry. *Requirements:* Baccalaureate from accredited college. For master's of divinity and master's of religious education, 60 semester hours of liberal arts courses. Minimum GPA 2.0. *Entrance tests:* GRE, Miller Analogy Test for some programs. For foreign students TOEFL.

Remedial course in written communication offered in regular academic year; nondegree credit given.

Degree Requirements: *For first-professional degree:* 85 credit hours. *For master's degree:* 32–35 credit hours. *For both degrees:* 4.0 GPA on 12.0 scale (8.0 for master's of theology); 1 year in residence; demonstrated proficiency in English. *Grading system:* A–F; pass-fail; withdraw (deadline after which pass-fail is appended to withdraw).

Distinctive Educational Programs: Field education. Evening classes. Special facilities for using telecommunications in the classroom. Interdisciplinary formation in Christian ministry course. Study tour of Israel. *Other distinctive programs:* Continuing education in theology. Seminary Extension Department in cooperation with other seminaries of the Southern Baptist Convention. Flexible diploma programs to prepare adults for Baptist ministries, through Boyce Bible College.

Degrees Conferred: Theology and ministerial studies: 71 *baccalaureate*; 59 *master's*; 79 *doctorates*; 164 *first-professional*: master of divinity.

Fees and Other Expenses: *Full-time tuition per academic year 2004–05:* $4,290. *Room and board per academic year:* $6,372. *Books and supplies:* $1,400.

Financial Aid: Aid from institutionally generated funds is provided on the basis of academic merit, financial need, other criteria. Institution has a Program Participation Agreement with the U.S. Department of Education for eligible students to receive Pell Grants and other federal aid.

Financial aid to full-time, first-time undergraduate students: 33% received institutional grants averaging $159; 8% received loans averaging $1,587.

Departments and Teaching Staff: *Total instructional faculty:* 68.

Enrollment: Total enrollment 2,983. Undergraduate 753 (80.4% men, 39.6% women).

Characteristics of Student Body: *Ethnic/racial makeup:* Black non-Hispanic: 5.2%; American Indian or Alaska Native: .7%; Asian or Pacific Islander: 3.1%; Hispanic: 1.3%; White non-Hispanic: 85.9%. unknown: 3.9%.

International Students: 30 undergraduate nonresident aliens enrolled fall 2004. Some financial aid available for qualifying international students.

Student Life: On-campus residence halls house 33% of student body. Housing available for men only, for women only, and for married students. 35% of married students request institutional housing; 33% are so housed. *Special regulations:* Registered cars with decals permitted in designated areas. *Special services:* Learning Resources Center, medical services. *Student publications: The Towers,* a weekly newspaper. *Surrounding community:* Louisville metropolitan area population over 1 million. Served by mass transit bus system; airport 12 miles from campus.

Publications: *Review and Expositor* (quarterly) first published 1904.

Library Collections: 280,000 volumes. 25,000 microforms; 40,000 audiovisual materials; 1,275 periodicals. Students have access to online information retrieval services.

Most important holdings include Baptist historical collection, church music collection.

Buildings and Grounds: Campus area 106 acres.

Chief Executive Officer: Dr. R. Albert Mohler, Jr., President.

Address admission inquiries to Scott M. Davis, Director of Admissions.

Spalding University

851 South Fourth Street
Louisville, Kentucky 40203-2188
Tel: (502) 585-9911   **E-mail:** admissions@spalding.edu
Fax: (502) 585-7158   **Internet:** www.spalding.edu

Institution Description: Spalding University is a private, independent, non-profit institution affiliated with the Sisters of Charity of Nazareth, Roman Catholic Church. *Enrollment:* 1,698. *Degrees awarded:* Baccalaureate, master's, doctorate. Specialist certificates also awarded. Member of the consortium Kentuckiana Metroversity.

Accreditation: *Regional:* SACS-Comm. on Coll. *Professional:* clinical psychology, dietetics, nursing, nursing education, occupational therapy, social work, teacher education

History: Established in Louisville 1920 as Nazareth College, a branch campus of Nazareth Academy in Nazareth (established 1814, chartered 1829, offered first instruction at postsecondary level 1890); awarded first degree (baccalaureate) 1924; changed name to Catherine Spalding College 1963; merged with Nazareth Academy, became coeducational, and changed name to Spalding College 1969; became Spalding University 1984.

Institutional Structure: *Governing board:* Spalding University Board of Trustees. Extrainstitutional representation: 23 trustees; institutional representation: president of the university, 1 full-time instructional faculty member, 1 student; 1 alumna/alumnus. 1 ex officio. All voting. *Composition of institution:* Administrators 68. Academic affairs headed by provost. Management/business/finances directed by vice president for finance; administration and external affairs headed by vice president for administration. Full-time instructional faculty 17 men / 44 women. Academic governance body, the faculty, meets monthly.

Calendar: Semesters. Academic year late Aug. to mid-May. Freshmen admitted Aug., Jan., May. Degrees conferred and formal commencement May. Summer session of 3 terms from mid-May to mid-Aug.

Characteristics of Freshmen: 330 applicants (42 men, 288 women). 52.7% of applicants admitted. 32.7% of admitted students enrolled full-time.

10% (5 students) submitted SAT scores; 90% (51 students) submitted ACT scores. *25th percentile:* SAT I Verbal 410, SAT I Math 440; ACT Composite 16, ACT English 15, ACT Math 16. *75th percentile:* SAT I Verbal 530, SAT I Math 580; ACT Composite 21, ACT English 21, ACT Math 20.

Freshmen from 7 states and 9 foreign countries.

Admission: Rolling admissions plan. For fall acceptance, apply as early as 1 year prior to enrollment, but not later than week of registration. Early acceptance available. *Requirements:* Either graduation from accredited secondary school or GED. Recommend 12 academic units which normally include 4 English, 2 in a foreign language, 2 mathematics, 2 natural science, 2 social studies. Additional requirements for some programs. Lowest recommended acceptable secondary school class standing 50th percentile. *Entrance tests:* College Board SAT or ACT composite. For foreign students TOEFL. *For transfer students:* 2.0 minimum GPA; from 4-year accredited institution 96 semester hours maximum transfer credit; from 2-year accredited institution 64 hours; correspondence/extension students 12 hours.

College credit for postsecondary-level work completed in secondary school and for extrainstitutional learning on basis of ACE *2006 Guide to the Evaluation of Educational Experiences in the Armed Services;* portfolio assessment. Tutoring available.

Degree Requirements: 128 credit hours; 2.0 GPA; 2 terms in residence; distribution requirements. Fulfillment of some degree requirements and exemption from some beginning courses possible by passing College Board CLEP, AP. *Grading system:* A–F; pass-fail; withdraw (carries time limit); incomplete (carries time limit).

Distinctive Educational Programs: *For undergraduates:* Internships. Preprofessional programs in dentistry, medicine, optometry, pharmacy. Independent study. Study abroad through consortium. *Available to all students:* Evening classes. Special facilities for using telecommunications in the classroom. Individual majors. *Other distinctive programs:* Continuing education. Weekend College (baccalaureate degree available by attending classes on weekends only). Theatre program promotes working relationship with local artists and arts-producing organizations such as Actors Theatre and the Kentucky Center for the Arts. Study abroad programs in Belize, Ecuador, and Ireland.

Degrees Conferred: 5 *associate;* 221 *baccalaureate;* 220 *master's;* 36 *doctorate.* Bachelor's degrees awarded in top five disciplines: health professions and related clinical sciences 68; business, management, marketing, and related support services 49; education 20; psychology 15; communication, journalism, and related programs 15.

Fees and Other Expenses: *Full-time tuition per academic year 2004–05:* undergraduate $14,250; contact the university for current graduate tuition/fees. *Room and board per academic year:* $4,572. *Books and supplies:* $500.

Financial Aid: Aid from institutionally generated funds is provided on the basis of academic merit, financial need, other criteria. Institution has a Program Participation Agreement with the U.S. Department of Education for eligible students to receive Pell Grants and other federal aid.

Financial aid to full-time, first-time undergraduate students: 39% received federal grants averaging $3,081; 75% state/local grants averaging $3,368; 73% institutional grants averaging $5,643; 85% loans averaging $4,235.

Departments and Teaching Staff: Social work *professors* 1, *associate professors* 0, *assistant professors* 3, *instructors* 0, *part-time faculty* 2; sociology 1, 0, 1, 0, 2; art 0, 1, 1, 0, 3; business 0, 1, 2, 0, 4; communications 0, 2, 1, 0, 3; dietetics 0, 0, 1, 1, 0; education 3, 3, 3, 0, 8; English 1, 1, 2, 0, 1; history 2, 0, 0, 0, 0; mathematics 0, 1, 2, 0, 4; natural science 1, 1, 3, 0, 6; nursing 0, 6, 12, 4, 6; occupational therapy 1, 0, 2, 0, 0; philosophy 0, 1, 1, 0, 0; psychology 3, 5, 3, 0, 12; religion 1, 0, 2, 0, 8; French 0, 0, 0, 0, 1; Spanish 0, 0, 0, 0, 1; music 0, 0, 0, 0, 2; computer science 0, 0, 0, 0, 1.

Total instructional faculty: 76. Degrees held by full-time faculty: 62% hold terminal degrees.

Enrollment: Total enrollment 1,698. Undergraduate 989 (20% men, 80% women).

Characteristics of Student Body: *Ethnic and racial makeup:* Black non-Hispanic: 16.5%; American Indian or Alaska Native: .4%; Asian or Pacific Islander: 1.5%; Hispanic: .6%; White non-Hispanic: 46.4%; unknown: 30.3%. *Age distribution:*17–21: 23%; 22–24: 14%; 25–29: 18%; 30–34: 11%; 35–39: 10%; 40–49: 17%; 50–59: 5%; 60–and over: 2%.

International Students: 42 undergraduate nonresident aliens enrolled fall 2004. Students from Europe, Asia, Central and South America, Africa, Canada, Australia. No programs available to aid students whose native language is not English. Some financial aid available for qualifying international students.

Student Life: On-campus residence halls house 7% of student body. Residence halls for men constitute 33% of such space, for women 67% (1 floor for men; 2 floors for women). *Special regulations:* Cars permitted without restrictions. *Special services:* Center for Academic Development, counseling services. *Student publications: Spectrum,* a monthly newspaper. *Surrounding community:* Louisville metropolitan area population 970,000 Served by mass transit bus system; airport 3 miles from campus.

Library Collections: 220,300 volumes. 16,300 microforms; 8,700 audiovisual materials; 600 current periodical subscriptions. Online catalog. Students have access to online information retrieval services and the Internet.

Most important special holdings include the Flaget (an early Catholic Kentucky Bishop) Collection of religious and other books; nursing archival books collection; Edith Stein papers; Archdiocese Ecumenical Collection.

Buildings and Grounds: Campus area 5.2 acres.

Chief Executive Officer: Dr. Dr. JoAnn Rooney, President.

Address admission inquiries to Christ Houk, Director of Enrollment Management.

Sullivan University

3101 Bardstown Road
Louisville, Kentucky 40205-3013
Tel: (502) 456-6504   **E-mail:** stfd@corp.sullivan.edu
Fax: (502) 456-0040   **Internet:** www.sullivan.edu

Institution Description: Sullivan University is a private 4-year coeducational institution. *Enrollment:* 2,968. *Degrees awarded:* Associate, baccalaureate, master's.

Accreditation: *Regional:* SACS. *National:* American Culinary Federation, Inc. *Professional:* culinary education

History: The college was founded in 1864.

Calendar: Quarters.

Characteristics of Freshmen: 95% of applicants accepted. 60% of freshmen return for sophomore year. 83% of freshmen from Kentucky.

Admission: *Requirements:* Graduation from an accredited secondary school or GED. College credit and advanced placement for postsecondary-level work completed in secondary school and for extrainstitutional learning on basis of ACE *2006 Guide to the Evaluation of Educational Experiences in the Armed Services.* Developmental/remedial courses offered in summer session and regular academic year; credit given.

Degree Requirements: *For all associate degrees:* 95 quarter hours. *For all baccalaureate degrees:* 180 quarter hours. *For all degrees:* Computer literacy; internship for some majors. *Grading system:* .A–F.

Degrees Conferred: 379 *associate;* 315 *baccalaureate;* 96 *master's.* Bachelor's degrees awarded in top disciplines: business, management, marketing, and related support services; legal professions and studies 16.

Fees and Other Expenses: *Full-time tuition per academic year 2004+=05:* $12,750. *Room and board per academic year:* $5,340. *Books and supplies:* $1,500.

Financial Aid: Aid from institutionally generated funds is provided on the basis of academic merit, financial need, other criteria. Institution has a Program Participation Agreement with the U.S. Department of Education for eligible students to receive Pell Grants and other federal aid.

Financial aid to full-time, first-time undergraduate students: 17% received federal grants averaging $2,804; 8% state/local grants averaging $2,106; 8% institutional grants averaging $1,344; 19% received loans averaging $4,587.

Departments and Teaching Staff: *Total instructional faculty:* 85.

Enrollment: Total enrollment 4,860. Undergraduate 4,559 (41.5% men, 58.5% women).

Characteristics of Student Body: *Ethnic/racial makeup:* Black non-Hispanic: 21.4%; American Indian or Alaska Native: .8%; Hispanic: .6%; White non-Hispanic: 74.2%; unknown: .4%.

International Students: 41 nonresident aliens enrolled fall 2004. Programs available to aid students whose native language is not English: social, cultural, financial.

Student Life: *Intercollegiate athletics:* men and women's basketball.

Library Collections: 25,000 volumes. 7,000 microform titles; 225 current periodical subscriptions. Students have access to online information retrieval services.

Buildings and Grounds: Campus area 10 acres.

Chief Executive Officer: A. R. Sullivan, President.

Address admissions inquiries to Greg Cawthon, Director of Admissions.

Thomas More College

333 Thomas More Parkway
Crestview Hills, Kentucky 41017-3495
Tel: (859) 341-5800   **E-mail:** admissions@thomasmore.edu
Fax: (859) 344-3345   **Internet:** www.thomasmore.edu

Institution Description: Thomas More College is a Catholic, coeducational, liberal arts college affiliated with the Diocese of Covington, Kentucky. Its purpose is to educate men and women in a Roman Catholic tradition so that they make real in their own lives the scholarship, service, and integrity of Saint Thomas More. *Enrollment:* 1,465. *Degrees awarded:* Associate, baccalaureate, master's. Certificates also awarded.

Academic offerings subject to approval by faculty and Board of Trustees and licensing by Kentucky Council on Higher Education. Budget subject to approval by Board of Trustees. Member of the Greater Cincinnati Consortium of Colleges and Universities.

Accreditation: *Regional:* SACS-Comm. on Coll. *Professional:* nursing, teacher education

History: Established as Villa Madonna College and offered first instruction at postsecondary level 1921; chartered 1923; awarded first degree (baccalaureate) 1929; adopted present name 1968. *See* Sr. M. Irmina Saelinger, *Retrospect and Vista: The First Fifty Years of Thomas More College* (Covington: Thomas More College, 1971) for further information.

Institutional Structure: *Governing board:* The Board of Trustees of Thomas More College. Extrainstitutional representation: 27 trustees, including bishop of diocese, provincials of Benedictine Sisters, Congregation of Divine Providence, and Sisters of Notre Dame; institutional representation: president of the college, 2 full-time instructional faculty members, 1 student. *Composition of institution:* Administrators 9 men / 14 women. Academic affairs headed by vice president for academic affairs. Business/finances handled by vice president for finance. Full-time instructional faculty 72. Academic governance body, Faculty General Assembly, meets an average of 9 times per year.

Calendar: Semesters. Academic year mid-Aug. to mid-May. Freshmen admitted Aug., Jan., May, July. Degrees conferred and formal commencement May. Summer session from mid-May to mid-Aug.

Characteristics of Freshmen: 63% of applicants admitted. 17% of applicants admitted and enrolled.

34% (60 students) submitted SAT scores; 88% (154 students) submitted ACT scores. *25th percentile:* SAT Verbal 430, SAT Math 450; ACT Composite 19, ACT English 18, ACT Math 18. *75th percentile:* SAT Verbal 580, SAT Math 560; ACT Composite 23, ACT English 23, ACT Math 23.

54% of entering freshmen expected to graduate within 5 years. 53% of freshmen from Kentucky. Freshmen from 10 states and 10 foreign countries.

Admission: Rolling admissions plan. For fall acceptance, apply as early as Sept. 1 of previous year, but not later than Aug. 15 of year of enrollment. Early acceptance available. *Requirements:* Either graduation from accredited secondary school with 16 units which normally include 4 units English, 2 in a foreign language, 2 mathematics, 2 science, 2 social studies; or GED. Minimum 80 average in college preparatory courses. Lowest acceptable secondary school class standing 50th percentile. *Entrance tests:* ACT composite preferred; College Board SAT accepted. Minimum ACT English and composite scores 20; minimum SAT verbal score 530, combined score 1010. For foreign students TOEFL. *For transfer students:* 2.0 minimum GPA; 90 semester hours maximum transfer credit.

College credit and advanced placement for postsecondary-level work completed in secondary school and for extrainstitutional learning on basis of ACE *2006 Guide to the Evaluation of Educational Experiences in the Armed Services*; portfolio assessment. Tutoring available. Note taking, extended time testing also available. Developmental courses offered during regular academic year; credit given.

Degree Requirements: *For all associate degrees:* 64 credit hours; last 15 hours in residence. *For all baccalaureate degrees:* 128 credit hours; last 30 hours in residence. *For master's degree:* 45 credit hours; all in residence; 3.0 GPA. *For all degrees:* 2.0 GPA; distribution requirements; demonstrated proficiency in writing and oral communication, and computer literacy.

Fulfillment of some degree requirements and exemption of some beginning courses possible by passing College Board CLEP, AP, other standardized tests. *Grading system:* A–F; pass-fail; withdraw (deadline after which pass-fail is appended to withdraw); incomplete (carries time limit).

Distinctive Educational Programs: Work-experience programs, including cooperative education, field experience, internships, practicums. Flexible meeting places and schedules, including weekend and evening classes, plus accelerated degree program format for completion of baccalaureate and master's degree in administration. Dual-degree program in physics and engineering with engineering school of the student's choice. Special facilities for using telecommunications in the classroom. Individually arranged interdisciplinary programs. Accelerated degree program format for completion of associate degree. Facilities for independent research, including honors programs, individual majors, independent study. Study abroad by individual arrangement. Cross-registration through consortium. *Other distinctive programs:* Degree-granting continuing education programs.

ROTC: Air Force in cooperation with University of Cincinnati (OH), Army in cooperation with Xavier University (OH).

Degrees Conferred: 65 *associate;* 235 *baccalaureate:* biological/life sciences 16; business/marketing 118; communications/communication technologies 7; computer and information sciences 5; education 11; English 10; health professions and related sciences 8; liberal arts/general studies 20; mathematics 2; philosophy/religion/theology 4; physical sciences 2; protective services/public administration 3; psychology 10; social sciences and history 15; visual and performing arts 4. 78 *master's:* business/marketing 78.

Fees and Other Expenses: *Full-time tuition per academic year 2005–06:* $17,660. *Required fees:* $320. *Room and board per academic year:* $6,150.

Financial Aid: Aid from institutionally generated funds is provided on the basis of academic merit, financial need, other considerations. Institution has a Program Participation Agreement with the U.S. Department of Education for eligible students to receive Pell Grants and other federal aid.

Financial aid to full-time, first-time undergraduate students: need-based scholarships/grants totaling $1,721,686, self-help $2,956,170; non-need-based scholarships/grants totaling $5,316,779, self-help $2,328,186, parent loans $1,095,610, tuition waivers $661,700. *Graduate aid:* 45 students received federal and state-funded loans totaling $451,433 (ranging from $2,575 to $14,535).

Departments and Teaching Staff: *Professors* 15, *associate professors* 34, *assistant professors* 20, *instructors* 3, *part-time faculty* 57. *Total instructional faculty:* 129 (full-time 72, part-time 57; women 53, men 76). Total faculty with doctorate, first-professional, or other terminal degree: 47. Student-to-faculty ratio: 15:1.

Enrollment: Total enrollment 1,465. Undergraduate full-time 548 men / 324 women, part-time 116m / 151w; graduate full-time 68m / 58w.

Characteristics of Student Body: *Ethnic/racial makeup:* number of Black non-Hispanic: 65; American Indian or Alaska Native: 3; Asia or Pacific Islander: 7; Hispanic: 8; White non-Hispanic: 192; unknown: 255. *Age distribution:* number under 18: 438; 18–19: 279; 20–21: 113; 22–24: 117; 25–29: 117 30–34: 88; 35–39: 101; 40–49: 43; 50–64: 29; 65 and over: 3.

International Students: 11 nonresident aliens enrolled. 5 students from Europe, 2 Asia, 3 Central and South America, 1 Africa. Programs available to aid students whose native language is not English: social, cultural. 2 scholarships available annually (sister school exchange) for full tuition.

Student Life: On-campus residence halls house 15% of student body. Residence halls for men only constitute 33% of such space, for women only 33%, coed 34%. *Intercollegiate athletics:* men only: baseball, basketball, football, golf, soccer, tennis; women only: basketball, golf, soccer, softball, tennis, volleyball. *Special regulations:* Cars permitted without restrictions. Quiet hours from 10pm to 8am weekdays and midnight to 8am weekends. Residence hall visitation from noon to midnight weekdays and noon to 2am weekends. *Special services:* Learning Resources Center, Writing Center, Math Center, medical services. *Student publications: More News,* a monthly newspaper; *Utopian,* a bimonthly newspaper; *Words,* an annual literary magazine. *Surrounding community:* Crestview Hills population 3,500. Cincinnati, 8 miles from campus, is nearest metropolitan area. Served by mass transit bus system; airport 5 miles from campus; passenger rail service 10 miles from campus.

Library Collections: 113,056 volumes. Online and card catalogs. 601 current periodical subscriptions. 19,058 microforms, 2,242 recordings. Students have access to online information retrieval services and the Internet.

Most important holdings include a collection of several hundred volumes by and about Thomas More; Kentuckiana.

Buildings and Grounds: Campus area 60 acres.

Chief Executive Officer: Sr. Margaret A. Stallmeyer, C.O.P., President.

Address admission inquiries to Carl Goodmonson, Director of Admissions.

Transylvania University

300 North Broadway
Lexington, Kentucky 40508-1797
Tel: (859) 233-8300   **E-mail:** admissions@transy.edu
Fax: (859) 233-8797   **Internet:** www.transy.edu

Institution Description: Transylvania University is a private, independent, nonprofit institution affiliated with the Christian Church (Disciples of Christ). *Enrollment:* 1,114. *Degrees awarded:* Baccalaureate.

Accreditation: *Regional:* SACS-Comm. on Coll.

History: Established and chartered as Transylvania Seminary 1780; offered first instruction at postsecondary level 1785; changed name to Transylvania University 1799; first degree (baccalaureate) awarded 1802; changed name to Kentucky University 1865; readopted name Transylvania 1908; changed name to Transylvania College 1915; present name readopted 1969. See John D. Wright, Jr., *Transylvania: Tutor to the West* (Lexington, Kentucky: University Press of the West, 1980) for further information.

Institutional Structure: *Governing board:* The Board of Trustees. Representation: 67 trustees (including 20 alumni), 2 honorary trustees, 9 life trustees, 1 administrator. 1 ex officio. 58 voting. *Composition of institution:* Administrators 6 men / 1 woman. Academic affairs headed by vice president and dean of the college. Management/business/finances directed by vice president for finance. Full-time instructional faculty 65. Academic governance body, Faculty Meeting, meets an average of 7 times per year.

Calendar: Semesters (4-4-1). Academic early Sept. to late May. Freshmen admitted Sept., Jan., June, July. Degrees conferred and formal commencement May. Summer session of 2 terms from early June to late July.

Characteristics of Freshmen: 1,134 applicants (407 men, 727 women). 28.3% of applicants admitted. 100% of admitted students enrolled full-time.

22% (65 students) submitted SAT scores; 90% (270 students) submitted ACT scores. *25th percentile:* SAT I Verbal 490, SAT I Math 463; ACT Composite 23, ACT English 23, ACT Math 22. *75th percentile:* SAT I Verbal 690, SAT I Math 663; ACT Composite 28, ACT English 28, ACT Math 27.

77% of freshmen from Kentucky. Freshmen from 21 states and 4 foreign countries.

Admission: Selective admissions. For fall acceptance, apply as early as Sept. of senior year, but not later than Mar. of year of enrollment. Early opinion available. *Requirements:* Either 12 college preparatory secondary school units in English, mathematics, natural sciences, and social sciences; or GED. *Entrance tests:* College Board SAT or ACT composite. For foreign students minimum TOEFL score 550. *For transfer students:* 2.75 minimum GPA; from 2-year institution 19 course units maximum transfer credit; from 4-year institution 19 units.

College credit for postsecondary-level work completed in secondary school and for extrainstitutional learning on basis of ACE *2006 Guide to the Evaluation of Educational Experiences in the Armed Services* and College Board CLEP. Tutoring available. Noncredit developmental courses offered during regular academic year.

Degree Requirements: 36 course units; 2.0 GPA; final 2 terms in residence; general education requirements, writing requirement. Fulfillment of some degree requirements possible by passing College Board AP or International Baccalaureate. *Grading system:* A–F; pass-fail (for specified courses only); withdraw through midterm.

Distinctive Educational Programs: Internships in business administration, hotel and restaurant management, public administration, sociology, and political science (in Kentucky and national governments). Evening classes. Accelerated degree programs. Dual-degree programs in engineering with Washington University (MO), Vanderbilt University (TN) and University of Kentucky. Transylvania is affiliated with the Kentucky Institute for International Studies and the Washington Center. Videotape recording and playback facilities available. Pre-professional programs in engineering, medicine. Facilities and programs for independent research. Individual majors. Tutorials. Study in England and France through the Institute of American Universities; competitive scholarship for summer study in England (for graduating seniors); the European experience (a summer study-travel course); study in Mexico at the University of the Americas; May term study-travel course in Hispano-Mexican civilization; Washington (DC) semester at American University.

ROTC: Army, Air Force.

Degrees Conferred: 253 *baccalaureate*. Bachelor's degrees awarded in five top disciplines: business, management, marketing, and related support services 54; social sciences 31; psychology 31; biological and biomedical sciences 31; history 15.

Fees and Other Expenses: *Full-time tuition per academic year 2004–05:* $18,690. *Room and board per academic year:* $6,340. *Books and supplies:* $750.

Financial Aid: Aid from institutionally generated funds is provided on the basis of academic merit, financial need, athletic ability, other criteria. Institution has a Program Participation Agreement with the U.S. Department of Education for eligible students to receive Pell Grants and other federal aid.

Financial aid to full-time, first-time undergraduate students: 22% received federal grants averaging $2,934; 77% state/local grants averaging $3,408; 100% institutional grants averaging $7,152; 65% received loans averaging $3,215.

Departments and Teaching Staff: Business administration and economics *professors* 2, *associate professors* 4, *assistant professors* 0, *part-time teachers* 3; education and physical education 0, 5, 2, 0; fine arts 3, 4, 2, 3; humanities 3, 3, 7, 8; natural sciences and mathematics 5, 4, 6, 4; social sciences 4, 1, 6, 5.

Total instructional faculty: 88. Degrees held by full-time faculty: doctorate 85%, master's 82%, baccalaureate 100%. 95% hold terminal degrees.

Enrollment: Total enrollment 1,114 (41.3% men, 58.7% women).

Characteristics of Student Body: *Ethnic/racial makeup:* Black non-Hispanic: 2.2%; American Indian or Alaska Native: .4%; Asian or Pacific Islander: 1.4%; Hispanic: 1.3%; White non-Hispanic: 86.9%; unknown: 7.6%.

International Students: 5 nonresident aliens enrolled fall 2004. Students from Europe, Asia, Central and South America, Africa. No programs available to aid students whose native language is not English. No financial aid specifically designated for international students.

Student Life: On-campus residence halls house 80% of student body. Residence halls for men constitute 45% of such space, for women 55%. 60% of men join fraternities; 60% of women join sororities. *Intercollegiate athletics:* men only: baseball; women only: field hockey, softball; both sexes: swimming, tennis, cross country, basketball, soccer. *Special regulations:* Cars must be parked in designated areas. *Student services:* Learning Resources Center, Fitness Center, limited medical services. *Student publications, radio: Crimson,* a yearbook; *Rambler,* a weekly newspaper; *Transylvanian,* a biannual literary magazine. Radio station WTLX broadcasts 10 hours per week. *Surrounding community:* Lexington-Fayette population 240,000. Louisville, 90 miles from campus, is nearest metropolitan area. Served by mass transit bus system; airport 4 miles from campus.

Library Collections: 120,000 volumes. 3,000 microform units; 1,635 audiovisual materials; 540 current periodical subscriptions. Online catalog. Students have access to online information retrieval services and the Internet.

Most important holdings include Transylvania University Archives; Transylvania Medical Library (pre-1850); J. Winston Coleman Kentuckiana Collection (Kentucky history); Clara S. Peck Natural History Collection; Henry Clay Papers.

Buildings and Grounds: Campus area 45 acres.

Chief Executive Officer: Dr. Charles L. Shearer, President.

Address admission inquiries to Sarah E. Coen, Director of Admissions.

Union College

310 College Street
Barbourville, Kentucky 40906-1499
Tel: (606) 546-4151   **E-mail:** enroll@unionky.edu
Fax: (606) 546-1217   **Internet:** www.unionky.edu

Institution Description: Union College is a private college affiliated with the United Methodist Church. *Enrollment:* 1,011. *Degrees awarded:* Associate, baccalaureate, master's. Specialist certificates also awarded.

Member of the consortia Council of Independent Kentucky Colleges and Universities.

Accreditation: *Regional:* SACS-Comm. on Coll.

History: Established, chartered, and incorporated 1879; offered first instruction at postsecondary level 1880; awarded first degree (baccalaureate) 1893. *See* W. G. Marigold, *Union College 1879–1979* (Barbourville: Union College, 1979) for further information.

Institutional Structure: *Governing board:* Union College Board of Trustees consisting of 53 trustees, 37 of whom are voting trustees (includes 1 faculty trustee); the president of the college, plus 2 additional ex officio trustees (includes 1 administrator); 2 student associate trustees; and 11 emeriti trustees. *Composition of institution:* Executive Leadership Team consists of the president of the college, plus 6 vice president (3 men and 3 women). Academic affairs headed by vice president for academic affairs. Management/business/finances directed by vice president for business affairs. The faculty meets an average of 9 times per year.

Calendar: Semesters. Academic year Aug. to May. Freshmen admitted Aug., May. Degrees conferred and formal commencement May. Summer session from June to Aug.

Characteristics of Freshmen: 692 applicants (484 men, 208 women). 72.4% of applicants admitted. 25.3% of admitted students enrolled full-time.

13% (17 students) submitted SAT scores; 86% (109 students) submitted ACT scores. *25th percentile:* SAT I Verbal 410, SAT I Math 420; ACT Composite 16, ACT English 15, ACT Math 20. *75th percentile:* SAT I Verbal 450, SAT I Math 490; ACT Composite 21, ACT English 20, ACT Math 20.

30% of entering freshmen expected to graduate within 5 years. 68% of freshmen from Kentucky. Freshmen from 10 states and 4 foreign countries.

Admission: Rolling admissions plan. Early acceptance available. *Requirements:* Either graduation from accredited secondary school with 11 units which normally include 4 English, 3 mathematics, 2 social studies, 2 laboratory science; or GED. Foreign language units recommended. Minimum GPA 2.0. *Entrance tests:* College Board SAT or ACT composite. *For transfer students:* 2.0 minimum GPA; from 4-year accredited institution 98 hours maximum transfer credit; from 2-year accredited institution 67 hours; correspondence/extension students 32 hours.

College credit and advanced placement for postsecondary-level work completed in secondary school. College credit for extrainstitutional learning on basis of ACE *2006 Guide to the Evaluation of Educational Experiences in the Armed Services;* portfolio assessment. Tutoring available.

Degree Requirements: *For all associate degrees:* 66 semester hours; 15 hours in residence. *For all baccalaureate degrees:* 128 hours; 32 hours in residence. *For all undergraduate degrees:* 2.0 GPA; distribution requirements.

Fulfillment of some degree requirements and exemption from some beginning courses possible by passing College Board CLEP, AP. *Grading system:* A–F; pass-fail; withdraw (carries time limit); incomplete (carries time limit).

Distinctive Educational Programs: *For undergraduates:* Dual-degree programs in engineering with Auburn University (AL), University of Kentucky; in physical therapy with Jefferson Community College. Interdisciplinary program in Appalachian Regional Studies. Facilities for independent research, including honors programs, tutorials. Washington (DC) semester at American University. *For graduate students:* Flexible meeting places and schedules, including off-campus centers (at Manchester, less than 30 miles away from main institution); Middlesboro, 32 miles away; Williamsburg, 33 miles away; Harlan, 50 miles away; Whitley City, 58 miles away; Monticello, 75 miles away; weekend classes. *Available to all students:* Internships. Evening classes. Facilities and programs for independent research. Study abroad through Kentucky Institute for European Studies (Austria, France, Germany, Italy, Spain). *Other distinctive programs:* Qualified high school students may enroll in certain summer session courses for half tuition.

Degrees Conferred: 132 *baccalaureate;* 122 *master's.* Bachelor's degrees awarded in top five disciplines: education 45; business, management, marketing, and related support services 35; psychology 19; security and protective services 6; social sciences 5.

Fees and Other Expenses: *Full-time tuition per academic year 2004–05:* $13,750. *Books and supplies:* $900. *Room and board per academic year:* $4,400.

Financial Aid: Aid from institutionally generated funds is provided on the basis of academic merit, athletic ability. Institution has a Program Participation Agreement with the U.S. Department of Education for eligible students to receive Pell Grants and other federal aid.

Financial aid to full-time, first-time undergraduate students: 55% received federal grants averaging $3,333; 61% state/local grants averaging $3,507; 79% institutional grants averaging $3,785; 79% received loans averaging $3,590.

Departments and Teaching Staff: Business *professors* 0, *associate professors* 1, *assistant professors* 3, *instructors* 1; education 4, 5, 1, 0; English/journalism 2, 1, 1, 2; health/physical education 1, 1, 1, 1; history/religion 2, 0, 2, 0; library 0, 2, 2, 0; music 4, 0, 0, 0; natural science 2, 4, 1, 0; social science 4, 1, 3, 0.

Total instructional faculty 52. Student-to-faculty ratio: 12:1. Degrees held by full-time faculty: doctorate 34%, master's 17%. 58.8% hold terminal degrees.

Enrollment: Total enrollment 1,011. Undergraduate 535 (52.9% men, 47.1% women).

Characteristics of Student Body: *Ethnic/racial makeup:* Black non-Hispanic: 9.9%; American Indian or Alaska Native: 1.7%; Asian or Pacific Islander: .7%; Hispanic: 1.3%; White non-Hispanic: 84.7%; unknown: .6%.

International Students: 5 undergraduate nonresident aliens enrolled fall 2004. No programs available to aid students whose native language is not English. Some financial aid designated for international students.

Student Life: On-campus residence halls house 35% of student body. Residence halls for men only constitute 50% of such space, for women only 50%. *Intercollegiate athletics:* men only: baseball, basketball, golf, football, soccer; women only: basketball, soccer, softball, volleyball; both sexes: swimming, tennis. *Special regulations:* Registered cars with decals permitted in designated areas only. Curfews, quiet hours and hours for residence hall visitation set according to residence hall. *Special services:* Learning Resources Center. *Surrounding community:* Barbourville population 3,500. Knoxville (TN), 100 miles from campus, is nearest metropolitan area. Served by airport 25 miles from campus; passenger rail service 13 miles from campus.

Library Collections: 108,000 volumes including bound books, serial backfiles, electronic documents, and government documents not in separate collections. Online catalog. 2,450 current serial subscriptions. 419,000 microforms. 5,700 audiovisual materials. Computer work stations available. Students have access to the Internet at no charge.

Most important holdings include the Lincoln Civil War Collection (rare books, memorabilia, medals); curriculum library; music scores and recordings.

Buildings and Grounds: Campus area 100 acres.

Chief Executive Officer: Dr. Edward C. Derosset, President.

Address admission inquiries to Andre Washington, Director of Admissions.

University of Kentucky

206 Administration Building
Lexington, Kentucky 40506
Tel: (859) 257-9000   **E-mail:** admissio@uky.edu
Fax: (859) 257-3823   **Internet:** www.uky.edu

Institution Description: University of Kentucky is a state institution and land-grant college. *Enrollment:* 25,686. *Degrees awarded:* Baccalaureate, first-professional (dentistry, law, pharmacy, medicine), master's, doctorate. Special certificates in education also awarded. Academic offerings subject to approval by statewide coordinating bodies. Budget subject to approval by state and governing board.

Accreditation: *Regional:* SACS-Comm. on Coll. *Professional:* accounting, business, clinical lab scientist, clinical pastoral education, counseling psychology, dentistry, dietetics, engineering, family and consumer science, forestry, health services administration, interior design, journalism, landscape architecture, law, librarianship, marriage and family therapy, medicine, music, nursing, nursing education, pediatric dentistry, periodontics, pharmacy, physical therapy, public administration, radiation therapy, rehabilitation counseling, school psychology, speech-language pathology, teacher education

History: Established as Agricultural and Mechanical College of Kentucky University and chartered 1865; offered first instruction at postsecondary level 1869; changed name to Agricultural and Mechanical College of Kentucky 1878, to State University of Kentucky 1908; adopted present name 1916. *See* James F. Hopkins, *The University of Kentucky: Origins and Early Years* (Lexington: University of Kentucky Press, 1951) and Charles G. Talbot, *The University of Kentucky: The Maturing Years* (Lexington: University of Kentucky Press, 1965) for further information.

Institutional Structure: *Governing board:* Board of Trustees consisting of 20 members. 16 appointed by the governor of which 3 represent agricultural interests and 3 are alumni of the university, 3 faculty, 1 student. *Composition of*

institution: The president is the chief executive officer of the university. Management/business/finances directed by vice president for administration. Full-time instructional faculty 1,238. Academic governance body, University Senate, meets an average of 8 times per year.

Calendar: Semesters. Academic year late Aug. to early May. Freshmen admitted Aug., Jan., May, June. Degrees conferred May, Aug., Dec. Formal commencement May. Summer session of 2 terms from mid-May to early Aug.

Characteristics of Freshmen: 78% of applicants accepted. 45% of accepted applicants enrolled.

30% (1,196 students) submitted SAT scores; 91% (3,609 students) submitted ACT scores. *25th percentile:* SAT Verbal 510, SAT Math 510; ACT Composite 21, ACT English 21, ACT Math 21. *75th percentile:* SAT Verbal 620; SAT Math 640; ACT Composite 27, ACT English 27, ACT Math 27.

40% of freshmen expected to graduate within 5 years. 77% of freshmen from Kentucky. Freshmen from 40 states and 30 foreign countries.

Admission: Rolling admissions plan. For fall acceptance, apply no later than June 1. Early acceptance available. *Requirements:* Either graduation from accredited secondary school or GED and meet pre-college curriculum requirements. Minimum GPA 2.0. *Entrance tests:* Enhanced ACT composite with minimum score greater than 18. For foreign students TOEFL with minimum score 525. *For transfer students:* 2.0 minimum GPA; from 4-year accredited institution maximum transfer credit limited only by requirement that 30 of last 36 hours must be completed in residence; from 2-year accredited institution 67 hours maximum transfer credit; correspondence/extension students 30 hours and one-third of major requirements.

College credit for extrainstitutional learning. Tutoring available. Note: All applicants should be aware that some programs have selective admissions, application procedures, and deadlines which differ from those from general university admission.

Degree Requirements: 120–176 credit hours; 2.0 GPA; 30 of last 36 hours in residence; general education requirements.

Fulfillment of some degree requirements and exemption from some beginning courses possible by passing departmental examinations, College Board CLEP, AP. *Grading system:* A–F; pass-fail; audit; incomplete, repeat option, and withdraw (carries time limit).

Distinctive Educational Programs: Honors program; Academic Common Market with 14 southern states in selected academic programs; accelerated programs and credit-by-examination programs; University Scholars program which integrates undergraduate and graduate or professional courses of study into a single, continuous program culminating in both a baccalaureate degree and a master's degree; Donovan Scholars Program for students over age 60. Internships. Interdisciplinary programs; joint degrees with a number of public and private institutions. Flexible meeting places and schedules, including off-campus centers and evening classes. Special facilities for using telecommunications in the classroom. Interdepartmental program in general studies. Multidisciplinary Centers, Research Institutes and Programs, Research Support Units, and Inter-University Affiliations. Facilities and programs for independent research. Study abroad programs include Traveling Scholars Program, Heidelberg Scholarships, Deauville Exchange, Fulbright Graduate Scholarships, Rhodes Scholarships, Marshall Scholarships, and English-speaking Union Scholarships.

ROTC: Army, Air Force.

Degrees Conferred: 3,373 *baccalaureate*; 1,242 *master's*; 233 *doctorate*; 372 *first-professional*. Bachelors degrees awarded in top five disciplines: business, management, marketing, and related support services 732; communication, journalism, and related programs 335; education 281; social sciences 251; engineering 249.

Fees and Other Expenses: *Full-time tuition per academic year 2004–05:* undergraduate resident $5,163, nonresident $12,148. Contact the university for current graduate and professional schools tuition/fees. *Books and supplies:* $700. *Room per academic year:* $3,363. *Board per academic year:* $1,766.

Financial Aid: Aid from institutionally generated funds is provided on the basis of academic merit, financial need, athletic ability, other criteria. Institution has a Program Participation Agreement with the U.S. Department of Education for eligible students to receive Pell Grants and other federal aid.

Financial aid to full-time, first-time undergraduate students: need-based scholarships/grants totaling $51,962,087, self-help $3,603,545, parent loans $9,923,640, tuition waivers $493,637, athletic awards $5,582,600.

Departments and Teaching Staff: *Total instructional faculty:* 1,695 (full-time 1,198, part-time 497; women 604, men 1,091). Total faculty with doctorate, first-professional, or other terminal degree: 1,000. Student-to-faculty ratio: 16.5:1. 94% of faculty hold terminal degrees.

Enrollment: Total enrollment 25,686. Undergraduate full-time 7,988 men / 8,607 women, part-time 887m / 952w; first-professional full-time 707m / 701w, part-time 11m / 8w; graduate full-time 1,416m / 1682w, part-time 1,034m / 1693w.

Characteristics of Student Body: *Ethnic/racial makeup:* number of undergraduate Black non-Hispanic: 1,041; American Indian or Alaska Native: 27;

Asian or Pacific Islander: 322; Hispanic: 182; White non-Hispanic: 16,293; unknown: 386.

International Students: 183 undergraduate nonresident aliens enrolled fall 2004. Programs available to aid students whose native language is not English: social, cultural. English as a Second Language Program. No financial aid specifically designated for international students.

Student Life: On-campus residence halls (including dorms and undergraduate and graduate apartments) house 25% of student body. Dormitories for men only, women only, and undergraduate co-ed. There are 149 apartments for upperclass men and women. Single graduate and advanced student apartments are available as well as apartments for married students and families. Some men and women join and live in fraternity and sorority houses. *Intercollegiate athletics:* men only: basketball, football, baseball, tennis, golf, track, swimming/diving, ice hockey, soccer, rugby, riflery; women only: basketball, volleyball, golf, gymnastics, swimming/diving, tennis, track, riflery, cross-country. *Special regulations:* Cars permitted on campus in designated areas. Dependent upon availability of parking spaces, commuter and residence hall parking permits are issued by student classification on a first-come basis. Handicapped parking is available. Free shuttle and bus service on campus, Mon.–Fri. 7:30am to 4:50pm; Mon.–Thur. 6:30pm to 11:30 pm. *Special services:* Health services (including medical, surgical, and mental), health insurance, University Counseling and Testing Center, Health Education Office, Learning Services Center, Handicapped Student Services, Campus Recreation, Student Center, Student Commuter Office, Student Organizations, Leadership Program, American Ombudsman, Office of International Affairs, Office of Minority Affairs, University Career Center, Health Careers Opportunity Program; Professional Education Preparation Program. Many cultural opportunities and facilities. *Student publications: Kentucky Kernel*, a daily student newspaper (published once weekly during summer sessions). Radio station WUKY and WRFL (run by students). *Surrounding community:* Lexington population 205,000. Cincinnati (OH), 80 miles from campus, is nearest metropolitan area. Served by airport; passenger rail service 5 miles from campus.

Publications: *Kentucky Review*, a book published by the Library 3 times per year; *Proceedings*, a book of papers presented each year at Eastern Oil Shale Symposium; *Crossroads*, a booklet published annually for the Dean of Students' Office; *Kentucky Law Journal*, a book published quarterly; *Hospital Marketing*, a referring physicians annual. The University Press has published *Romance* quarterly and *Southern Folklore* 3 times per year.

Library Collections: 2,793,000 volumes including bound periodicals and government documents not in separate collections. 5,873,000 microforms; 73,500 audiovisual materials; 26,500 535 periodicals (paper, microform, electronic). Online catalog. Students have access to online information retrieval services and the Internet.

Most important holdings include W. Hugh Peal collection of British and American Victorian/Romantic Period literature; Wilson Kentuckiana Collection; Combs Appalachian Collection (including Appalachian Regional Commission Archives); Modern Political Papers (30 Kentucky politicians from the 20th century).

Buildings and Grounds: Campus area 765 acres.

Chief Executive Officer: Dr. Lee. T. Todd, Jr., President.

Address undergraduate admission inquiries to Don Witt, Director of Admissions; graduate inquiries to: Graduate School; College of Dentistry, College of Law, College of Medicine; College of Pharmacy.

College of Arts and Sciences

Degree Programs Offered: *Baccalaureate.*

College of Agriculture

Degree Programs Offered: *Baccalaureate.*

College of Allied Health Professions

Degree Programs Offered: *Baccalaureate* in allied health education, clinical nutrition, community health, medical technology, physical therapy.

College of Architecture

Degree Programs Offered: *Baccalaureate, master's.*

College of Business and Economics

Degree Programs Offered: *Baccalaureate* in accounting, business administration, economics.

College of Communications and Information Studies

Degree Programs Offered: *Baccalaureate* in communication, journalism, speech, telecommunications; *master's* in library science.

College of Education

Degree Programs Offered: *Baccalaureate.*

College of Engineering

Degree Programs Offered: *Baccalaureate* in agricultural engineering, chemical engineering, civil engineering, electrical engineering, mechanical engineering, metallurgical engineering, mining engineering.

College of Fine Arts

Degree Programs Offered: *Baccalaureate* in applied music, art education, art history, art studio, individual studies, music, music education, theater arts.

College of Home Economics

Degree Programs Offered: *Baccalaureate* in consumer studies; early childhood education; home economics education; housing and interior design; individual and family development; nutritional and food science; textiles, clothing, and merchandising.

College of Nursing

Degree Programs Offered: *Baccalaureate.*

College of Social Work

Degree Programs Offered: *Baccalaureate.*

College of Dentistry

Degree Programs Offered: *First-professional.*
Admission: College background in biological sciences and chemistry; DAT.
Degree Requirements: Completion of prescribed curriculum.

College of Law

Degree Programs Offered: *First-professional.*
Admission: Baccalaureate from accredited institution; LSAT.
Degree Requirements: 18 months in residence.

College of Medicine

Degree Programs Offered: *First-professional.*
Admission: 90 semester hours from accredited institution with strong background in biological sciences and chemistry; MCAT.
Degree Requirements: Completion of prescribed curriculum.

College of Pharmacy

Degree Programs Offered: *Baccalaureate, first-professional.*
Admission: *For first-professional:* Strong college background in chemistry; PCAT.
Degree Requirements: *For first-professional:* Completion of prescribed curriculum.

Graduate School

Degree Programs Offered: *Master's* in accounting; art history; business education; classics; clinical and college teaching; clinical nutrition; diplomacy and international commerce; elementary education; family economics and management; forestry; horticulture; housing and interior design; individual development within the family; library science; medical radiation dosimetry; mining engineering; nuclear engineering; nursing; nutrition and food science; operations research; orthodontics; periodontics; public administration; radiologic health; rehabilitation counseling; secondary education; social work; speech and hearing; studio art; textiles, clothing, and merchandising; theater arts; *master's, doctorate* in agricultural engineering; anatomy; animal science; anthropology; biochemistry; biological sciences; business administration; chemical engineering; chemistry; civil engineering; clinical psychology; communication; crop science; curriculum and instruction; economics; educational administration and supervision; educational psychology and counseling; electrical engineering; engineering mechanics; English; entomology; experimental psychology;

French; geography; geology; German; health, physical education, and recreation; higher educational administration; history; mathematics; mechanical engineering; metallurgical engineering; microbiology; applied music; music history and appreciation; pharmaceutical sciences; philosophy; physics; physiology and biophysics; plant pathology; political science; social and philosophical studies; social psychology; sociology; soil science; Spanish; special education; statistics; toxicology; veterinary science; vocational education; *doctorate* in administration and supervision, curriculum and instruction, educational psychology and testing, higher education administration, social and philosophical studies, special education, vocational education.

Departments and Teaching Staff: Faculty drawn from other colleges of the university.

University of Louisville

2301 South Third Street
Louisville, Kentucky 40292-0001
Tel: (502) 852-6169   **E-mail:** admitme@louisville.edu
Fax: (502) 852-2344   **Internet:** www.louisville.edu

Institution Description: University of Louisville is a state institution with three campuses: Belknap, Shelby, and Health Sciences (located in downtown Louisville). *Enrollment:* 20,731. *Degrees awarded:* Associate, baccalaureate, first-professional (dentistry, law, medicine), master's, doctorate. Certificates also awarded.

Accreditation: *Regional:* SACS-Comm. on Coll. *Professional:* accounting, audiology, business, clinical lab scientist, clinical pastoral education, clinical psychology, computer science, counseling psychology, cytotechnology, dental hygiene, dentistry, endodontics, engineering, interior design, law, marriage and family therapy, medicine, music, nursing, nursing education, periodontics, physical therapy, psychology internship, public administration, radiation therapy, radiography, respiratory therapy, social work, speech-language pathology, teacher education

History: Established as Jefferson Seminary 1798; chartered as Louisville Collegiate Institute 1837; offered first instruction at postsecondary level 1813; awarded first degree 1814; adopted present name 1846. *See* Kentucky Writers Project, *A Centennial History of the University of Louisville* (Louisville: University of Louisville, 1939) for further information.

Institutional Structure: *Governing board:* Board of Trustees. Extrainstitutional representation: 20 trustees; institutional representation: 1 full-time faculty, 1 full-time staff, 1 student, 2 alumni. All voting. *Composition of institution:* Academic affairs headed by university provost. Management/business/finances directed by vice president for finance and administration. Full-time instructional faculty 1,195. Academic governance body, Faculty Senate, meets an average of 10 times per year.

Calendar: Semesters. Academic year June to May. Freshmen admitted Aug., Jan., May, June, July. degrees conferred May, Aug., Dec. Formal commencement May. Summer session of 7 terms from mid-May to mid-Aug.

Characteristics of Freshmen: 66% of applicants accepted. 42% of accepted applicants enrolled.

31% (727 students) submitted SAT scores; 90% (2,122 students) submitted ACT scores. *25th percentile:* SAT Verbal 490, SAT Math 490; ACT Composite 21, ACT English 20, ACT Math 19. *75th percentile:* SAT Verbal 620, SAT I Math 610; ACT Composite 26, ACT English 23, ACT Math 26.

20% of entering freshmen expected to graduate within 5 years. 93% of freshmen from Kentucky. Freshmen from 26 states and 80 foreign countries.

Admission: Rolling admissions plan. Apply by July 1 of previous year for early decision; need not limit application to University of Louisville. Early acceptance available. *Requirements:* Either graduation from accredited secondary school with 4 units in English, 2 foreign language, 2 social studies, units courses in algebra I and II, and geometry; or GED. Additional requirements for some programs. Minimum GPA 2.0–3.0. For out-of-state students lowest acceptable secondary school class standing 50th percentile. *Entrance tests:* ACT composite. *For transfer students:* From 4-year accredited institution 2.0–2.5 minimum GPA, maximum transfer credit limited only by residence requirement; from 2-year accredited institution 2.0 minimum GPA, 62 hours.

College credit for postsecondary-level work completed in secondary school.

Tutoring available. Noncredit developmental/remedial courses offered in summer session and regular academic year.

Degree Requirements: *For all associate degrees:* 60 credit hours, with last 15 in residence. *For all baccalaureate degrees:* 120 credit hours, with last 30 in residence; 2 semesters physical education. *For all undergraduate degrees:* 2.0 GPA; distribution and general education requirements. Additional requirements for some programs.

Fulfillment of some degree requirements and exemption from some beginning courses possible by passing College Board CLEP, AP. *Grading system:* A–F; pass-fail; withdraw.

Distinctive Educational Programs: Off-campus center (at Fort Knox, 40 miles away from main institution). Evening classes. Special facilities for using telecommunications in the classroom. Honors programs. Individual majors. *Other distinctive programs:* Continuing education.

ROTC: Air Force; Army.

Degrees Conferred: 45 *associate:* 1,890 *baccalaureate:* 1,322 *master's;* 106 *doctorate;* 330 *first-professional.* Bachelor's degrees awarded in top five disciplines: business, management, marketing, and related support services 454; social sciences 176; engineering 169; psychology 158; communication, journalism, and related programs 140.

Fees and Other Expenses: *Full-time tuition per academic year 2004–05:* undergraduate resident $4,450, nonresident $12,166. Contact the university for current graduate/first-professional tuition and fees. *Room and board per academic year:* $6,036. *Books and supplies:* $800.

Financial Aid: Aid from institutionally generated funds is proved on the basis of academic merit, financial need, athletic ability, other criteria. Institution has a Program Participation Agreement with the U.S. Department of Education for eligible students to receive Pell Grants and other federal aid.

Financial aid to full-time, first-time undergraduate students: need-based scholarships/grants totaling $29,136,114, self-help $23,894,237, parent loans $882,144, tuition waivers $1,022,600, athletic awards $1,804,383; non-need-based scholarships/grants totaling $15,185,374, self-help $2,855,049, parent loans $1,035,067, tuition waivers $927,680, athletic awards $3,145,050.

Departments and Teaching Staff: *Total instructional faculty:* 1,271 (full-time 796, part-time 477; women 526, men 745). Total faculty with doctorate, first-professional, or other terminal degree: 755. Student-to-faculty ratio: 18:1. Degrees held by full-time faculty: doctorate 56.2%, master's 9.7%, baccalaureate 1%, professional 32.8%. 99% hold terminal degrees.

Enrollment: Total enrollment 20,731. Undergraduate full-time 5,166 men / 5,919 women, part-time 1,765m / 2,002w; first-professional full-time 646m / 578w, part-time 38m / 39w; graduate full-time 950m /1,232w, part-time 980m / 1,396w.

Characteristics of Student Body: *Ethnic/racial makeup:* number of undergraduate Black non-Hispanic: 1,988; American Indian or Alaska Native: 37; Asian or Pacific Islander: 430; Hispanic: 197; White non-Hispanic: 11,870; unknown: 120.

International Students: 230 undergraduate nonresident aliens enrolled fall 2004. Students from Europe, Asia, Central and South America, Africa, Canada, Australia, New Zealand. Programs available to aid students whose native language is not English: social, cultural. English as a Second Language Program. No financial aid specifically designated for international students.

Student Life: On-campus residence halls for both sexes house 7% of student body. Housing available for married students. Separate housing available for students joining fraternities and sororities. *Intercollegiate athletics:* men: baseball, basketball, football, golf, soccer, tennis, track, cross-country; women: basketball, field hockey, gymnastics, softball, tennis, track and cross-country, volleyball. *Special regulations:* Cars must display parking permits. Residence hall visitation from noon to midnight; some residence halls have 24-hour visitation; quiet hours. *Special services:* Learning Resources Center, Multicultural Center, Disability Resource Center, medical services. *Student publications, radio: Cardinal,* a weekly newspaper; *Louisville Review,* a triennial literary digest; *Minerva,* a yearbook; *Thinker,* a quarterly magazine. Radio station WLCV broadcasts 105 hours per week. *Surrounding community:* Louisville population 270,000. Served by mass transit bus system, airport 2 miles from campus.

Library Collections: 1,983,162 volumes. 24,910 serial subscriptions (paper, microform, electronic). 2,180,187 microforms; 34,429 audiovisual materials. Online catalog. Students have access to online information retrieval services and the Internet.

Most important holdings include the Bullitt Collection (mathematics and astronomy); Cain Collection of Irish Literary Renaissance; McWhorter's Edgar Rice Burroughs Collection.

Buildings and Grounds: Campus area 660 acres. *New buildings:* Belknap Research Building completed 2005; William F. Ekstrom Library Expansion 2005; Ralph Wright Natatorium 2005; Jim Patterson Stadium.

Chief Executive Officer: Dr. James R. Ramsey, President.

Address admission inquiries to Jenny L. Sawyer, Director of Admissions.

College of Arts and Sciences

Degree Programs Offered: *Associate* in police administration; *baccalaureate* in American studies, anthropology, art, art history, biology, chemistry, economics, English, French, general studies, geography, geology, German, Greek, history, home economics, humanities, Latin, linguistics, mathematics, music history, philosophy, physics, political science, political science-international studies, psychology, Russian, sociology, Soviet area studies, Spanish, theater arts, urban studies, botany, chemistry, foods and nutrition, Pan-American studies, political science-policy analysis, recreation education, science-dental hygiene, sociology with social work option, zoology.

Distinctive Educational Programs: Interdisciplinary programs in American studies, linguistics, religious studies, Soviet studies, urban studies, women's studies. Interdisciplinary freshman symposium. Cooperative baccalaureate program in sociology and social work with Spalding College. Chemistry major with business option. Urban studies center at Gardencourt in Cherokee Park. Study abroad in Ecuador, France, Germany, Spain.

Division of Allied Health

Degree Programs Offered: *Associate* in dental hygiene, radiologic technology; *baccalaureate* in cytotechnology, medical technology, nuclear medicine.

School of Business

Degree Programs Offered: *Associate, baccalaureate.*

School of Education

Degree Programs Offered: *Baccalaureate* in counseling and guidance, elementary education, health education, health occupations education, vocational teacher education.

Distinctive Educational Programs: Education multimedia center.

School of Music

Degree Programs Offered: *Baccalaureate* in applied music, piano, and vocal pedagogy; music history, public school music, theory-composition.

Distinctive Educational Programs: 5-year double-degree program leading to Bachelor of Music and Bachelor of Music Education degrees. Apprenticeships for qualified students with Louisville Orchestra.

College of Urban and Public Affairs

Degree Programs Offered: *Associate, baccalaureate, master's.*

School of Nursing

Degree Programs Offered: *Baccalaureate.*

Speed Scientific School - Engineering

Degree Programs Offered: *Associate, baccalaureate, master's.*

School of Dentistry

Degree Programs Offered: *First-professional.* Specialist certificates also given.

Admission: 90 semester hours from accredited liberal arts college with 1 year in English; 1 year each in general biology, general inorganic chemistry, general physics, organic chemistry, all with laboratory; competence in reading and communication skills; DAT. Recommend courses in algebra, trigonometry, analytical geometry, or calculus.

Degree Requirements: 195½ credit hours, 2.0 GPA, final year in residence.

Distinctive Educational Programs: Combined baccalaureate—first-professional and master's—first-professional programs. Extensive research program. Off-campus clinical externship programs. Dual-degree programs. Accelerated degree program. Honors program. Summer clinical program. Family practice clinical program. Affiliation with local hospitals, children's home, county health department.

School of Law

Degree Programs Offered: *First-professional.*

Admission: Baccalaureate from approved college or university, LSAT, LSDAS, competence in communication skills. Recommend 3 hours in college accounting and ability to type.

Degree Requirements: 2.0 GPA, 90 semester hours in residence, writing requirement, prescribed curriculum, satisfactory completion of moot court program.

Distinctive Educational Programs: Double-degree program in law and theology in cooperation with Louisville Presbyterian Theological Seminary.

School of Medicine

Degree Programs Offered: *First-professional.*

Admission: 3 years from accredited liberal arts college with 2 semesters in English; 2 each in general biology, general chemistry, organic chemistry, physics, all with laboratory; 1 calculus (or 2 other college mathematics); MCAT. For out-of-state applicants, 3.6 GPA and scores equal to national average or higher in each section of MCAT.

Degree Requirements: Satisfactory completion of prescribed course of study in medicine.

Graduate School

Degree Programs Offered: *Master's, doctorate.* Specialist certificates in education also given.

Departments and Teaching Staff: Faculty drawn from other schools and colleges of the university.

Distinctive Educational Programs: Interdisciplinary master's program. Joint doctorate in musicology with University of Kentucky.

Western Kentucky University

1 Big Red Way
Bowling Green, Kentucky 42101-3576
Tel: (270) 745-0111   **E-mail:** admissions@wku.edu
Fax: (270) 745-5387   **Internet:** www.wku.edu

Institution Description: Western Kentucky University is a state institution. *Enrollment:* 18,485. *Degrees awarded:* Associate, baccalaureate, master's. Certificates also awarded.

Accreditation: *Regional:* SACS-Comm. on Coll. *Professional:* applied science, art, business, computer science, dental hygiene, engineering technology, health information technician, industrial technology, journalism, music, nursing, nursing education, public health, recreation and leisure services, social work, speech-language pathology, teacher education

History: Established as Western Kentucky State Normal School 1906; changed name to Western Kentucky State Normal School and Teachers College 1922; awarded first degree (baccalaureate) 1924; changed name to Western Kentucky State Teachers College 1930, to Western Kentucky State College 1948; adopted present name 1966.

Institutional Structure: *Governing board:* Board of Regents. Representation: 11 regents. *Composition of institution:* Academic affairs headed by provost/vice president for academic affairs. Finances directed by chief financial officer. Development and alumni affairs directed by vice president for development and alumni relations. Student affairs headed by vice president for student affairs. Full-time instructional faculty 562.

Calendar: Semesters. Academic year Aug. to May.

Characteristics of Freshmen: 6,002 applicants (8,082 men, 2,726 women). 93.3% of applicants admitted. 54.4% of admitted students enrolled full-time.

4% (132 students) submitted SAT scores; 90% (2,720 students) submitted ACT scores. *25th percentile:* SAT I Verbal 455, SAT I Math 440; ACT Composite 18, ACT English 17, ACT Math 17. *75th percentile:* SAT I Verbal 550, SAT I Math 560; ACT Composite 23, ACT English 24, ACT Math 23.

18.3% of entering freshmen expected to graduate within 5 years. 81.8% of freshmen from Kentucky. Freshmen from 27 states and 10 foreign countries.

Admission: Rolling admissions plan. For fall acceptance, apply as early as one year prior to admission, but not later than June 1 (out-of-state students) or Aug. 1 (Kentucky residents) of year of enrollment. Early acceptance available. *Requirements:* Either graduation from accredited secondary school, or GED; minimum high school GPA 2.5. Pre-college curriculum required for students not in Community College: 4 years English, 3 years mathematics, 2 years social studies, 2 years science. *Entrance tests:* ACT composite score of 20 or SAT total of 930 for out-of-state graduates. For foreign students TOEFL score of 500 required. *For transfer students:* 2.0 minimum GPA; maximum transfer credit limited only by residence requirement.

College credit for postsecondary-level work completed in secondary school. Developmental courses offered.

Degree Requirements: *For all associate degrees:* 60 credit hours; 16 hours in residence. *For all baccalaureate degrees:* 128 hours; 32 hours in residence. *For all undergraduate degrees:* 2.0 GPA; general education requirements. Fulfillment of some degree requirements and exemption from some beginning courses possible by passing departmental examinations, College Board CLEP, AP. *Grading system:* A–F; withdraw (deadline after which pass-fail is appended to withdrawal).

Distinctive Educational Programs: Work-experience programs. Interdisciplinary study programs. Preprofessional programs in engineering, forestry, medicine, optometry, pharmacy, physical therapy, theology, veterinary medicine. Facilities and programs for independent research, including honors programs, tutorials. Study abroad in Austria, Belize, Canada, China, Japan, Mexico, Australia, Ecuador, England, France, Germany, Ireland, Italy, Scotland, South Africa, Spain. Semester at Sea Program. Continuing education programs. Servicemembers Opportunity College. *Other distinctive programs:* Extended Campus Centers in Elizabethtown, Glasgow, Owensboro, and Russellville, KY. Community College provides academic enrichment and associate degrees.

ROTC: Army.

Degrees Conferred: 315 *associate*; 2,116; *baccalaureate*; 761 *master's*. Bachelor's degrees awarded in top five disciplines: education 374; business, management, marketing, and related support services 362; communication, journalism, and related programs 217; social sciences 190; liberal arts and sciences, general studies and humanities 186.

Fees and Other Expenses: *Full-time tuition per academic year 2004–05:* undergraduate resident $4,698, nonresident $11,286. Contact the university for current graduate tuition/fees. *Room and board per academic year:* $3,990.

Financial Aid: Aid from institutionally generated funds is provided on the basis of academic merit, athletic ability, other criteria. Institution has a Program Participation Agreement with the U.S. Department of Education for eligible students to receive Pell Grants and other federal aid.

Financial aid to full-time, first-time undergraduate students: 33% received federal grants averaging $2,720; 73% state/local grants averaging $2,078; 22% institutional grants averaging $2,993; 40% received loans averaging $2,664.

Departments and Teaching Staff: Accounting and finance *professors* 6, *associate professors* 4, *assistant professors* 5, *instructors* 1, *part-time* 6; agriculture 3, 4, 4, 2, 0; allied health and human services 0, 4, 2, 0, 3; art 5, 3, 1, 1, 8; biology 4, 4, 9, 2, 10; chemistry 10, 2, 3, 1, 11; communication 4, 4, 3, 3, 23; community college 2, 2, 6, 15, 61; computer science 4, 2, 1, 6, 0; consumer and family sciences 3, 1, 3, 3, 13; economics and marketing 12, 7, 2, 1, 1; educational leadership 7, 7, 8, 0, 20; engineering technology 2, 4, 4, 0, 3; English 12, 11, 8, 3, 42; geography and geology 5, 5, 6, 2, 5; government 1, 3, 3, 1, 6; history 11 2, 6, 0, 11; industrial technology 3, 1, 2, 1, 3; integrative studies in teacher education 13, 10, 13, 4, 14; management and information systems 5, 7, 5, 3, 9; mathematics 10, 4, 4, 11, 14; modern languages and intercultural studies 4, 6, 5, 1, 11; music 7, 4, 4, 1, 17; nursing 1, 8, 11, 4, 5; physical education and recreation 5, 2, 2, 5, 2; philosophy and religion 8, 3, 1, 0, 6; physics and astronomy 8, 1, 5, 1, 1; psychology 14, 12, 5, 1, 16; public health 5, 2, 4, 3, 10; school of journalism and broadcasting 4, 10, 2, 2, 9; sociology 6, 1, 5, 1, 6; theatre and dance 4, 1, 2, 1, 0.

Total instructional faculty: 562. Student-to-faculty ratio: 18:1. Degrees held by full-time faculty: doctorate 71%, master's 26%, baccalaureate 2%, professional 1%. 84% hold terminal degrees.

Enrollment: Total enrollment 18,485. Undergraduate 15,818 (51.4% men, 58.6% women).

Characteristics of Student Body: *Ethnic/racial makeup:* Black non-Hispanic: 8.8%; American Indian or Alaska Native: .3%; Asian or Pacific Islander: 1%; Hispanic: .9%; White non-Hispanic: 86.5%; unknown: 1.1%.

International Students: 221 undergraduate nonresident aliens enrolled fall 2004. Students from Europe, Asia, Central and South America, Africa, Canada, Australia. Programs available to aid students whose native language is not English: social, cultural. English as a Second Language Program. No financial aid specifically designated for international students.

Student Life: On-campus residence halls. Co-ed residence halls available. *Intercollegiate athletics:* baseball, basketball, football, cross-country, golf, soccer, swimming, tennis, track, volleyball. *Special services:* Learning Resources Center, medical services. *Student publications: Herald,* a newspaper; WKRX-AM, a student radio station; WKYU-TV, a public television station. *Surrounding community:* Bowling Green population 50,000. Nashville, 65 miles from campus, is nearest metropolitan area.

Library Collections: 592,000 volumes. 2,652,000 microforms; 94,000 audiovisual materials; 4,565 periodicals. Online catalog. Access to online information retrieval systems and the Internet.

Most important special collections include Kentuckiana (books, periodicals, manuscripts, personal papers); Mammouth Cave materials; Kentucky Shakers, South Union, and Kentucky materials.

Buildings and Grounds: Campus area 200 acres.

Chief Executive Officer: Dr. Gary A. Ransdell, President.

Address admission inquiries to Dr. Luther Hughes, Director of Enrollment Management.

Louisiana

Centenary College of Louisiana

2911 Centenary Boulevard
Shreveport, Louisiana 71134-1188
Tel: (318) 869-5011   **E-mail:** admissions@centenary.edu
Fax: (318) 869-5026   **Internet:** www.centenary.edu

Institution Description: Centenary College of Louisiana is a private college affiliated with the United Methodist Church. *Enrollment:* 1,032. *Degrees awarded:* Baccalaureate, master's.

Member of the consortium Associated Colleges of the South.

Accreditation: *Regional:* SACS-Comm. on Coll. *Professional:* chemistry, music

History: Established and chartered in Jackson as College of Louisiana and offered first instruction at postsecondary level 1825; awarded first degree (baccalaureate) 1827; merged with Centenary College (established 1839) and adopted present name 1845; moved to present location 1908. *See* Walter McGehee Lowrey, *Centenary College of Louisiana: Sesquicentennial 1825–1975* (Shreveport: Centenary College Alumni Association, 1975) for further information.

Institutional Structure: *Governing board:* Board of Trustees. Extrainstitutional representation: 67 trustees, including 16 life members; institutional representation: 2 full-time instructional faculty members, 1 student; 1 alumnus. 6 ex officio. 56 voting. *Composition of institution:* Administrators 7 men / 5 women. Academic affairs headed by dean of the college. Management/business/finances directed by business manager and comptroller. Full-time instructional faculty 44. Academic governance body, the faculty, meets an average of 10 times per year.

Calendar: Semesters. Academic year from June to May. Freshmen admitted Aug., Feb., June, July. Degrees conferred and formal commencement May. Summer session of 1 term.

Characteristics of Freshmen: 70% of applicants admitted. 35% of applicants admitted and enrolled.

48% (134 students) submitted SAT scores; 87% (244 students) submitted ACT scores. *25th percentile:* SAT Verbal 510, SAT Math 520; ACT Composite 22, ACT English 22, ACT Math 20. *75th percentile:* SAT Verbal 640, SAT Math 630; ACT Composite 26, ACT English 29, ACT Math 27.

54% of entering freshmen expected to graduate within 5 years. 60% of freshmen from Louisiana. Freshmen from 31 states and 14 foreign countries.

Admission: Rolling admissions plan. For fall acceptance, apply as early as spring of junior year of secondary school, but not later than registration period. Early acceptance available. *Requirements:* Either graduation from accredited secondary school with 15 units which must include 3 units in English, 2 mathematics, 2 natural science, 2 social studies; or GED. 1 additional unit in English and 2 in a foreign language recommended. *Entrance tests:* College Board SAT or ACT composite. For foreign students TOEFL. *For transfer students:* 2.0 minimum GPA; from 2-year accredited institution 64 hours maximum transfer credit.

College credit for postsecondary-level work completed in through a college prior to earning high school diploma. College credit for life experience based on *2006 Guide to the Evaluation of Educational Experiences in the Armed Services.* Tutoring available.

Degree Requirements: *For all baccalaureate degrees:* 124 credit hours. *For all undergraduate degrees:* 2.0 GPA; 45 hours in residence; complete requirements for Intercultural Experiences, Service Learning, Career Exploration; distribution requirements and exemption from some beginning courses possible by passing College Board AP. Two semesters of First Year Experience (FYE) for every student except those who transfer English 100 (who then require one semester of FYE). *Grading system:* A–F; pass-fail; withdraw (carries time limit).

Distinctive Educational Programs: *For undergraduates:* Accelerated degree programs. Dual-degree programs in engineering with Case Western Reserve University (OH), Louisiana Tech University, Texas Agricultural and Mechanical University, Tulane University (LA), University of Southern California; Washington University in St. Louis, MO. Interdisciplinary program in busi-

ness and Spanish. Preprofessional program in law. Honors programs. Study abroad in Belgium, Canada, Denmark, England, France, Italy, Senegal. Through consortium, semester at Oak Ridge National Laboratory (TN), Washington (DC) semester in cooperation with American University. *Available to all students:* Independent study. *Other distinctive programs:* Continuing education for community service workers (free for senior citizens).

Degrees Conferred: 176 *baccalaureate:* biological/life sciences 30; communications/communication technologies 36; computer and information sciences 13; education 6; English 7; foreign languages and literature 4; interdisciplinary studies 4; mathematics 7; parks and recreation 11; philosophy/religion/theology 5; physical sciences 6; psychology 13; social sciences and history 21; visual and performing arts 13. 46 *master's:* business/marketing 10; education 36. *Honorary degrees awarded 1004–05:* Doctor of Science 1, Doctor of Letters 1, Doctor of Laws 1.

Fees and Other Expenses: *Full-time tuition per academic year 2004–05:* $16,750. *Required fees:* $610. *Room and board per academic year:* $6,070. *Other fees:* $110.

Financial Aid: Aid from institutionally generated funds is provided on the basis of academic merit, financial need, athletic ability, other criteria. Institution has a Program Participation Agreement with the U.S. Department of Education for eligible students to receive Pell Grants and other federal aid.

Financial aid to full-time, first-time undergraduate students: need-based scholarships/grants totaling $6,008,116, self-help $1,332,540, tuition waivers $132,928, athletic award $846,390; non-need-based scholarships/grants totaling $3,771,987, self-help $983,573, tuition waivers $102,493, athletic awards $1,293,058.

Departments and Teaching Staff: *Professors* 31, *associate professors* 16, *assistant professors* 17, *instructors* 6, *part-time faculty* 43. *Total instructional faculty:* 113 (full-time 70, part-time 43; women 47, men 66; members of minority groups 5). Total faculty with doctorate, first-professional, or other terminal degree: 82. Student-to-faculty ratio: 12:1.

Enrollment: Total enrollment 1,092. Undergraduate full-time 317 men / 563 women, part-time 15m / 10w; graduate full-time 2w / 7w, part-time 29m / 97w.

Characteristics of Student Body: *Ethnic/racial makeup:* number of Black non-Hispanic: 67; American Indian or Alaska Native: 5; Asian or Pacific Islander: 25; Hispanic: 21; White non-Hispanic: 755; unknown: 3. *Age distribution:* number under 18: 19; 18–19: 437; 20–21: 353; 22–24: 79; 25–29: 6; 30–34: 4; 35–39: 2; 40–49: 5.

International Students: 29 nonresident aliens enrolled fall 2004. 19 students from Europe, 3 Asia, 1 Central and South America, 6 Canada. No programs available to aid students whose native language is not English. No financial aid specifically designated for international students.

Student Life: On-campus residence halls house 68% of student body. 26% of men join and 28% of women join Greek organizations. *Intercollegiate athletics:* male sports include baseball, basketball, golf, soccer, tennis, cross country, swimming; female sports include basketball, cross-country, golf, gymnastics, swimming, softball, tennis, volleyball. *Special regulations:* Registered vehicles permitted in designated parking areas. Defined quiet hours. Residence hall visitation from 11am to 3am daily. *Student publications, radio: The Conglomerate,* a weekly newspaper; *Pandora,* an annual literary magazine; *Yoncopin,* a yearbook. Radio station KSCL. *Surrounding community:* Shreveport/Bossier City population 500,000. Served by airport 7 miles from campus.

Publications: *Centenary Today,* a quarterly tabloid.

Library Collections: 180,000 volumes. 311,000 microforms; 425 audiovisual materials; 996 current periodical subscriptions. Access to online information retrieval systems.

Most important holdings include archives of Louisiana Conference of the United Methodist Church; religion collection; geology collection; business/economics collection; Pierce Cline Rare Book Room; Jack London Collection; John William Carrinton Papers.

Buildings and Grounds: Campus area 65 acres. *New buildings:* Anderson Choral Building completed 2002; Feazel Instrumental Hall 2002; Centenary Fitness Center and Natatorium 2000.

Chief Executive Officer: Dr. Kenneth L. Schwab, President.

Address admission inquiries to Tim Crowley, Director of Admissions.

Dillard University

2601 Gentilly Boulevard
New Orleans, Louisiana 70122
Tel: (504) 816-4670   **E-mail:** admissions@dillard.edu
Fax: (504) 816-4895   **Internet:** www.dillard.edu

Institution Description: Dillard University is a private institution affiliated with the United Methodist Church and the United Church of Christ. *Enrollment:* 2,155. *Degrees awarded:* Baccalaureate.

Accreditation: *Regional:* SACS-Comm. on Coll. *Professional:* music, nursing

History: Established and incorporated 1930 through merger of New Orleans University and Straight College (both established 1869); offered first instruction at postsecondary level 1935; awarded first degree (baccalaureate) 1937.

Institutional Structure: *Governing board:* Board of Trustees. Representation: 22 trustees, including president of the university, 2 alumni. All voting. *Composition of institution:* Administrators 14 men / 11 women. Academic affairs headed by vice president for academic affairs. Management/business/finances directed by vice president for fiscal affairs. Full-time instructional faculty 64 men / 57 women. Academic governance body, the faculty, meets an average of 8 times per year.

Calendar: Semesters. Academic year mid-Aug. to mid- May. Freshmen admitted Aug., Jan., June. Degrees conferred May, Dec., Aug. Formal commencement May. Summer session of 2 terms.

Characteristics of Freshmen: 46% of applicants admitted. 34% of applicants admitted and enrolled.

34% (485 students) submitted SAT scores; 61% (884 students) submitted ACT scores. *25th percentile:* SAT Verbal 450, SAT Math 440; ACT Composite 19, ACT English 19, ACT Math 17. *75th percentile:* SAT Verbal 530, SAT Math 520; ACT Composite 22, ACT English 24, ACT Math 21.

9.5% of entering freshmen expected to graduate within 5 years. 50% of freshmen from Louisiana. Freshmen from 36 states and 9 foreign countries.

Admission: For fall acceptance, apply as early as Sept. of previous year, but not later than Apr. of year of enrollment. Students are notified of acceptance May. Apply by July 15 of previous year for early decision; need not limit application to Dillard. Early acceptance available. *Requirements:* Either graduation from accredited secondary school with 3-4 units English, 4 mathematics and science, 2 social studies, 5 other academic subjects, 2 electives; or GED. Additional requirements for nursing program. *Entrance tests:* College Board SAT or ACT composite. For foreign students TOEFL. *For transfer students:* 2.0 minimum GPA, 60 hours maximum transfer credit.

Advanced placement for postsecondary-level work completed in secondary school. Tutoring available. Noncredit developmental courses offered in summer session and regular academic year.

Degree Requirements: 124 credit hours; 2.0 GPA; last 30 hours in residence; 4 hours physical education; core curriculum. Additional requirements for nursing degree.

Fulfillment of some degree requirements and exemption from some beginning courses possible by passing departmental examinations. Fulfillment of some degree requirements also possible by passing College Board AP, other standardized tests. Exemption from some courses also possible for exceptional ACT or College Board SAT scores. *Grading system:* A–F; withdraw (deadline after which pass-fail is appended to withdraw).

Distinctive Educational Programs: Work-experience programs. Dual-degree program in engineering with Columbia University (NY) and Georgia Institute of Technology. Interdisciplinary programs in criminal justice, urban studies. Facilities for independent research, including honors programs, tutorials. Institutionally sponsored study abroad in France; Council of the Development of French in Louisiana; Goethe Institute (exchange program for students of German).

ROTC: Army offered in cooperation with Tulane University.

Degrees Conferred: 343 *baccalaureate:* biological/life sciences 40; business/marketing 65; communications/communication technologies 35; computer and information sciences 17; education 17; English 17; foreign languages and literature 1; health professions and related sciences 37; mathematics 1; physical sciences 9; protective services/public administration 25; psychology 59; trade and industry 17; visual and performing arts 3.

Fees and Other Expenses: *Full-time tuition per academic year 2004–05:* $11,200. *Required fees:* $380. *Room and board per academic year:* $6,840.

Financial Aid: The university offers a direct lending program. Aid from institutionally generated funds is provided on the basis of financial need. Institution has a Program Participation Agreement with the U.S. Department of Education for eligible students to receive Pell Grants and other federal aid.

Financial aid to full-time, first-time undergraduate students: need-based scholarships/grants totaling $11,348,584; self-help $6,497,990; non-need-based scholarships/grants totaling $5,145,654, self-help $5,571,269, parent loans $2,622,487, tuition waivers $299,506, athletic awards $461,438.

Departments and Teaching Staff: *Professors 17, associate professors 33, assistant professors 65, instructors 29, part-time faculty 56. Total instructional faculty:* 144 (full-time 145, part-time 56; women 113, men 88; members of minority groups 175). Total faculty with doctorate, first-professional, or other terminal degree: 175. Student-to-faculty ratio: 12:1. *Faculty development:* $1,554,145 total grants for research.

Enrollment: Total enrollment 2,155. Full-time 428 men / 1,492 women, part-time 42m / 193w.

Characteristics of Student Body: *Ethnic/racial makeup:* number of Black non-Hispanic: 2,139; Asian or Pacific Islander: 1; Hispanic: 2; White non-Hispanic: 6; unknown: 1. *Age distribution:* number under 18: 30; 18–19: 834; 20–21: 739; 22–24: 261; 25–29: 89; 30–34: 33; 35–39: 30; 40–49: 68; 50–64: 45.

International Students: 14 nonresident aliens enrolled fall 2004. 4 students from Europe, 1 Canada, 9 other. No programs available to aid students whose native language is not English. No financial aid specifically designated for international students.

Student Life: On-campus residence halls house 46% of student body. Residence halls for men only constitute 29% of such space, for women only 71%. *Intercollegiate athletics:* For men and for women, basketball. *Special regulations:* Cars permitted without restrictions. *Special services:* Learning Resources Center, medical services. *Student publications: Courtbouillon,* a monthly newspaper; *Le Diable Bleu,* a yearbook. *Surrounding community:* New Orleans population 560,000. Served by mass transit bus system; airport 7 miles from campus; passenger rail service 3 miles from campus.

Library Collections: 106,119 volumes. Online catalog. Current serial subscriptions: 422 paper. 430 recordings. Computer work stations available. Students have access to online information retrieval services and the Internet.

Most important special collection: Harold Patton Collection.

Buildings and Grounds: Campus area 62 acres. *New buildings:* International Center for Economic Freedom Building.

Chief Executive Officer: Dr. Marvalene Hughes, President.

Address admission inquiries to Linda G. Nash, Director of Admissions.

Grambling State University

100 Main Street
P.O. Drawer 607
Grambling, Louisiana 71245
Tel: (318) 274-6142   **E-mail:** admissions@gram.edu
Fax: (318) 274-3240   **Internet:** www.gram.edu

Institution Description: Grambling State University (Grambling College until 1974) is a state institution. *Enrollment:* 5,040. *Degrees awarded:* Associate, baccalaureate, master's, doctorate.

Academic offerings subject to approval by statewide coordinating bodies. Budget subject to approval by state governing boards.

Accreditation: *Regional:* SACS-Comm. on Coll. *Professional*; business, computer science, journalism, music, nursing, public administration, recreation and leisure services, social work, teacher education

History: Established as Colored Industrial and Agricultural School 1901; changed name to North Louisiana Agricultural and Industrial Institute 1905; changed name to Lincoln Parish Training School 1918; changed name to Louisiana Normal and Industrial Institute, became a state junior college 1928; became four-year college 1940; awarded first degree (baccalaureate) 1944; changed name to Grambling College 1947; adopted present name 1974.

Institutional Structure: *Governing board:* State of Louisiana Board of Trustees for State Colleges and Universities. Representation: 18 trustees, including 1 student (all appointed by the governor of Louisiana). All voting. State of Louisiana Board of Regents for State Colleges and Universities Representation: 16 regents including 1 student (all appointed by the governor of Louisiana). All voting. *Composition of institution:* Administrators 18 men / 6 women. Academic affairs headed by vice president for academic affairs. Management/business/finances directed by vice president for administration. Full-time instructional faculty 241. Academic governance body, Faculty Senate, meets an average of 9 times per year.

Calendar: Semesters. Academic year Aug. to May. Freshmen admitted Aug., Jan., June. Degrees conferred and formal commencements May, July, and Dec. Summer session from June to July.

Characteristics of Freshmen: 58% of applicants admitted. 51% of applicants admitted and enrolled.

17% (195 students) submitted SAT scores; 83% (986 students) submitted ACT scores. *25th percentile*: SAT Verbal 380, SAT Math 370; ACT Composite 15, ACT English 13, ACT Math 15. *75th percentile*: SAT Verbal 460, SAT Math 470; ACT Composite 18, ACT English 18, ACT Math 17.

27% of entering freshmen expected to graduate within 5 years. 55% of freshmen from Louisiana. Freshmen from 34 states and 16 foreign countries.

Admission: Modified rolling admissions plan. For fall acceptance, apply as early as Jan. 1, but not later than Aug. 15. Students are notified of acceptance beginning Mar. 1. Apply by Jan. 1 for early decision; need not limit application to Grambling State. Early acceptance available. *Requirements:* Either graduation from accredited secondary school with 3 units in English, 2½ social studies, 2 mathematics, 2 science, 7 electives; or GED. 1 additional unit in English recommended. Minimum recommended GPA 2.0. *Entrance tests:* Minimum ACT 17 or SAT 810. For foreign students minimum TOEFL score 450. *For transfer students:* 2.0 minimum GPA; maximum transfer credit limited only by residence requirement. Good standing at institution previously attended.

College credit and advanced placement for postsecondary-level work completed in secondary school. College credit for extrainstitutional learning on basis of ACE *2006 Guide to the Evaluation of Educational Experiences in the Armed Services.* Tutoring available. Developmental courses offered in summer session and regular academic year; credit given.

Degree Requirements: *For all associate degrees:* 61–76 credit hours. *For all baccalaureate degrees:* 128 credit hours; attendance at all lyceum and college-sponsored cultural events during freshman and sophomore years; comprehensive examinations in basic skills and in individual fields of study. *For all undergraduate degrees:* 2.0 GPA; complete senior year in residence; physical education requirement.

Fulfillment of some degree requirements and exemption from some beginning courses possible by passing departmental examinations, College Board AP. *Grading system:* A–F; withdraw.

Distinctive Educational Programs: *For undergraduates:* Dual-degree program in engineering with Louisiana Tech University. interdisciplinary programs, including, Afro-American studies, Asian studies, Latin American studies, urban studies. Preprofessional programs in dentistry, law, medicine, nursing. Facilities for independent research, including honors programs, individual majors, tutorials. *For graduate students:* Off-campus centers (at Homer, approximately 60 miles away from main institution; Natchitoches, 75 miles away). *Available to all students:* Work-experience programs including cooperative education, internships. Weekend and evening classes. Special facilities for using telecommunications in the classroom. Exchange programs for study abroad with Brazil, China, India, Malaysia, Mexico. Cross-registration with Louisiana Tech University. *Other distinctive programs:* Continuing education offering undergraduate and graduate program. Summer enrichment program for superior secondary school seniors.

ROTC: Army offered in cooperation with Louisiana Tech University and University of Louisiana at Monroe; Air Force. 13 Army and 3 Air Force commissions awarded 2004.

Degrees Conferred: 25 *associate;* 563 *baccalaureate* (B); 109 *master's* (M); 2 *doctorate* (D): biological/life sciences 43 (B); business/marketing 89 (B); communications/communication technologies 37 (B), 9 (M); computer and information sciences 89 (B); education 22 (B), 18 (M), 2 (D); engineering and engineering technologies 18 (B); English 9 (B); foreign languages and literature 1 (B); health professions and related sciences 34 (B), 16 (M); law/legal studies 16 (B); liberal arts/general studies 1 (M); mathematics 2 (B); parks and recreation 30 (B), 16 (M); personal and miscellaneous services 2 (B); physical sciences 4 (B); protective services/public administration 95 (B), 71 (M); psychology 38 (B); social sciences and history 26 (B); visual and performing arts 8 (B).

Fees and Other Expenses: *Full-time tuition per academic year 2004–05:* undergraduate resident $2,136, nonresident $7,486. Contact the university for current graduate tuition/fees. *Required fees:* $1,274. *Room per academic year:* $1,938. *Board per academic year:* $1,674.

Financial Aid: Aid from institutionally generated funds is provided on the basis of academic merit, athletic ability, other criteria. Institution has a Program Participation Agreement with the U.S. Department of Education for eligible students to receive Pell Grants and other federal aid.

Financial aid to full-time, first-time undergraduate students: need-based scholarships/grants totaling $11,058,283, self-help (loans $11,631,475, federal work study $786,814); non-need-based scholarships/grants totaling $1,943,307, self-help $873,743, athletic awards $1,096,745. *Graduate aid:* 549 students received federal and state-funded loans totaling $2,925,000 (ranging from $4,000 to $18,500); 17 received work-study jobs totaling $27,391, 29 received fellowships and grants totaling $101,280 (ranging from $300 to $3,000).

Departments and Teaching Staff: *Total instructional faculty:* 247 (full-time 244, part-time 3; women 115, men 132; member of minority groups 186). Total faculty with doctorate, first-professional, or other terminal degree: 141. Student-to-faculty ratio: 20:1. *Faculty development:* $830,289 total grants for research. 1 faculty member awarded a sabbatical 2004–05.

Enrollment: Total enrollment 5,040. Undergraduate full-time 1,673 men / 2,417 women, part-time 156m / 195w; graduate full-time 105m / 278w, part-time 52m / 164w. *Transfer students:* in-state 125; from out-of-state 81.

Characteristics of Student Body: *Ethnic/racial makeup:* number of Black non-Hispanic: 4,179; American Indian or Alaska Native: 9; Asian or Pacific Islander: 6; Hispanic: 13; White non-Hispanic: 23; unknown: 38.

International Students: 80 nonresident aliens enrolled fall 2004. Programs available to aid students whose native language is not English: social, cultural. Financial aid available annually for qualifying international students.

Student Life: On-campus residence halls house 67% of student body. Residence halls for men constitute 50% of such space, for women 50%. *Intercollegiate athletics:* men only: baseball, basketball, football, golf, tennis, track; women only, basketball, tennis, track. *Special regulations:* Cars must be registered with campus police. Curfews during first and last 2 weeks of each semester from midnight to 6am. Quiet hours vary according to residence hall. Visitation from 7pm to 11pm. *Special services:* Learning Resources Center, medical services. *Student publications, radio:* The Gramblinite, a weekly newspaper; The Tiger, a yearbook. Radio station KGRM broadcasts 56 hours per week. The Television Center cablecast public service programs for 8 hours a day. *Surrounding community:* Grambling population 4,500. Shreveport, 65 miles from campus, is nearest metropolitan area. Served by airport 40 miles from campus.

Publications: *The Grambling Papers in Political Science* (annually) first published in 1976, *The International Review of Cross-Cultural Studies* (semiannually) first published in 1979, *The Journal of Social and Behavioral Science* (quarterly) first published in 1979, *The Liberal Arts Bulletin* (annually) first published in 1967, *The Proceedings of the Third World Symposium* (semiannually) first published in 1979.

Library Collections: 307,000 volumes including bound books, serial backfiles, electronic documents, and government documents not in separate collections. Online catalog. Current serial subscriptions: 985 paper, 2 microform, 5,607 electronic. 122,000 microform items; 6,285 audiovisual materials. Computer work stations available. Students have access to the Internet at no charge.

Most important holdings include Afro-American Center Collection (rare and contemporary books, manuscripts, personal papers, and microfilm on the history of black Americans); papers and letters of Arthur Schumburg (Black book collector, 1874–1938); papers of John Quincy Adams (on microfilm).

Buildings and Grounds: Campus area 340 acres.

Chief Executive Officer: Dr. Horace A. Judson, President.

Address all admission inquiries Nora b. Taylor, Director of Admissions.

Louisiana College

1140 College Drive
Pineville, Louisiana 71359

Tel: (318) 487-7011   **E-mail:** admissions@lacollege.edu
Fax: (318) 487-7550   **Internet:** www.lacollege.edu

Institution Description: Louisiana College is a private college affiliated with the Louisiana Baptist Convention (Southern Baptist). *Enrollment:* 1,085. *Degrees awarded:* Baccalaureate.

Accreditation: *Regional:* SACS-Comm. on Coll. *Professional*: business, nursing, social work, teacher education

History: Established, chartered, and offered first instruction at postsecondary level 1906; awarded first degree (baccalaureate) 1907. *See* Oscar Hoffmeyer, Jr., *Louisiana College 75 Years/A Pictorial History* (Charlotte, NC: Delmar, 1981) for further information.

Institutional Structure: *Governing board:* Louisiana College Board of Trustees. Representation: 34 trustees. 1 ex officio. 33 voting. *Composition of institution:* Administrators 10 men / 2 women. Academic affairs headed by vice president for academic affairs. Management/business/finances directed by vice president for business affairs. Full-time instructional faculty 64. Academic governance body, the faculty, meets an average of 10 times per year.

Calendar: Semesters. Academic year late Aug. to mid-May. Freshmen admitted Aug., Jan., June, July. Degrees conferred and formal commencement May. Summer session of 2 terms from early June to mid-Aug.

Characteristics of Freshmen: 76% of applicants accepted. 47% of accepted applicants enrolled.

3% (9 students) submitted SAT scores. 96% (227 students) submitted ACT scores. Average secondary school rank of freshmen men 70th percentile, women 74th percentile, class 72nd percentile. Mean ACT composite class score 23.5.

43% of entering freshmen expected to graduate within 5 years. 89% of freshmen from Louisiana. Freshmen from 7 states.

Admission: Rolling admissions plan. For fall acceptance, apply as early as summer following junior year of secondary school, but not later than Aug. 31 of year of enrollment. Apply by end of junior year for early decision; must limit application to Louisiana. Early acceptance available. *Requirements:* Either graduation from accredited secondary school with 17 units, including 4 English, 3 social studies, 3 mathematics, 3 science; or GED (score of 50 or above). Minimum GPA 2.0. Lowest acceptable secondary school class standing 50th percentile. *Entrance tests:* College Board SAT (minimum combined score 930), or ACT composite (minimum score 20). For foreign students minimum TOEFL score 550. *For transfer students:* 2.0 minimum GPA; from 4-year accredited institution 97 hours maximum transfer credit; from 2-year accredited institution 66 hours.

College credit and advanced placement for postsecondary-level work completed in secondary school. Tutoring available. Developmental courses offered in summer session and regular academic year; credit given.

Degree Requirements: *For all baccalaureate degrees:* 127 credit hours; 4 hours physical education. *For all degrees:* 2.0 GPA; last 30 hours in residence; weekly chapel attendance; core curriculum.

Fulfillment of some degree requirements and exemption from some beginning courses possible by passing departmental examinations, College Board CLEP, AP. *Grading system:* A–F; pass-fail; withdraw (deadline after which pass-fail is appended to withdraw).

Distinctive Educational Programs: Flexible meeting places and schedules. Cooperative baccalaureate programs in dental hygiene, occupational therapy, respiratory therapy. Preprofessional programs in architecture, dentistry, engineering, law, medicine, pharmacy, physicians assistant, veterinary medicine. Facilities and classes for independent research, including honors programs, individual majors, independent study. Study abroad through programs offered by other institutions and by individual arrangement; Mary D. Bowman Louisiana College Overseas Study Program in London, England.

ROTC: Army in cooperation with Northwestern State University. 1 commission awarded 2004.

Degrees Conferred: 198 *baccalaureate:* biological/life sciences 18; business/marketing 30; communications/communication technologies 13; education 27; English 11; foreign languages and literature 1; health professions and related sciences 15; law/legal studies 2; liberal arts/general studies 8; mathematics 5; parks and recreation 18; philosophy/religion/theology 13; physical sciences 1; protective services/public administration 10; psychology 4; social sciences and history 17; visual and performing arts 5.

Fees and Other Expenses: *Full-time tuition per academic year 2004–05:* $9,500. *Required fees:* $425. *Room per academic year:* $3,330.

Financial Aid: Aid from institutionally generated funds is provided on the basis of academic merit, financial need, athletic ability, other criteria. Institution has a Program Participation Agreement with the U.S. Department of Education for eligible students to receive Pell Grants and other federal aid.

Financial aid to full-time, first-time undergraduate students: need-based scholarships/grants totaling $1,729,966, self-help $1,729,966; non-need-based scholarships/grants totaling $125,400, self-help $1,374,704.

Departments and Teaching Staff: *Professors* 25, *associate professors* 15, *assistant professors* 21, *instructors* 3, *part-time faculty* 28. *Total instructional faculty:* 92 (full-time 64, part-time 28; women 44, men 48; members of minority groups 2). Total faculty with doctorate, first-professional, or other terminal degree: 44. Student-to-faculty ratio: 17:1. *Faculty development:* 2 faculty members awarded sabbaticals 2004–05.

Enrollment: Total enrollment 1,085. Undergraduate full-time 402 men / 518 women, part-time 56m / 109w. *Transfer students:* in-state 61.

Characteristics of Student Body: *Ethnic/racial makeup:* number of Black non-Hispanic: 98; American Indian or Alaska Native: 3; Asian or Pacific Islander: 15; Hispanic: 16; White non-Hispanic: 942; unknown: 2. *Age distribution:* number under 18: 46; 18–19: 398; 20–21: 332; 22–24: 152; 25–29: 63; 30–34: 27; 35–39: 26; 40–49: 26; 50–64: 13; 65 and over: 2.

International Students: 8 nonresident aliens enrolled fall 2004. 4 students from Asia, 3 Central and South America, 1 Africa. No programs available to aid students whose native language is not English. No financial aid specifically designated for international students.

Student Life: On-campus residence halls house 49% of student body. Residence halls for men only constitute 44% of such space, for women only 55%. College-owned, off-campus housing available for married students; 1% of married students are so housed. *Recreational athletics:* men only: baseball, basketball, football, golf, soccer; women only: basketball, cross-country, soccer, softball, soccer. tennis. *Special regulations:* Registered cars permitted in designated areas only. *Special services:* Learning Resources Center, medical services. *Surrounding community:* Pineville population 18,000. New Orleans, 200 miles from campus, is nearest metropolitan area. Served by mass transit bus system; airport 5 miles from campus.

Library Collections: 335,300 volumes. Online catalog. Current serial subscriptions: 191 paper; 189 microform; 13,269 via electronic access. 2,900 recordings; 298 CD-ROMs. 15 computer work stations. Students have access to online information retrieval services and the Internet. Total 2004–05 budget for materials and operations: $84,650.

Most important holdings include the Central Louisiana Collection; Louisiana Baptist Collection; Mt. Lebanon Records.

Buildings and Grounds: Campus area 81 acres. *New buildings:* Baker Health and Wellness Center completed 2001.

Chief Executive Officer: Dr. Joe Aguillard, President.

Address admission inquiries to Byron McGee, Director of Admissions.

Louisiana State University and Agricultural and Mechanical College

156 Thomas Boyd Hall
Baton Rouge, Louisiana 70803
Tel: (225) 388-6977   **E-mail:** admissions@lsu.edu
Fax: (225) 388-5982   **Internet:** www.lsu.edu

Institution Description: *Enrollment:* 31,561. *Degrees awarded:* Baccalaureate, first-professional (law, veterinary medicine), master's, doctorate. Certificate of educator specialist and advanced certificate in library and information science are also awarded.

Accreditation: *Regional:* SACS-Comm. on Coll.*Professional*: art, audiology, business, clinical psychology, counseling, dietetics, engineering, family and consumer science, forestry, interior design, journalism, landscape architecture, law, librarianship, music, school psychology, social work, speech-language pathology, teacher education, veterinary medicine

History: Established as Louisiana State Seminary of Learning and Military Academy 1853; offered first instruction at postsecondary level 1860; awarded first degree (baccalaureate) 1869; changed name to Louisiana State University 1870; adopted present name 1877.

Institutional Structure: *Composition of institution:* Administrators 41 men / 9 women. Chief administrative officer is the chancellor. Academic affairs headed by executive vice chancellor and provost. Management/business/finances directed by vice chancellor for business affairs. Full-time instructional faculty 1,297. Academic governance body, Faculty Senate, meets an throughout the year.

Calendar: Semesters. Academic year Aug. to Aug. Freshmen admitted Aug., Jan., June. Degrees conferred and formal commencements May, Dec. Two summer sessions (8-week and 5-week) in June/July.

Characteristics of Freshmen: 78% of applicants accepted. 66% of applicants accepted and enrolled.

13.4% (763 students) submitted SAT scores; 86.4% (4,924 students) submitted ACT scores. *25th percentile*: SAT Verbal 520, SAT Math 530; ACT Composite 22, ACT English 22, ACT Math 20. *75th percentile*: SAT Verbal 630, SAT Math 640; ACT Composite 27, ACT English 28, ACT Math 26.

49% of entering freshmen expected to graduate within 5 years. 81% of freshmen from Louisiana. Freshmen from 45 states and 33 foreign countries.

Admission: Rolling admissions plan. For fall acceptance, apply as early as Sept. 1 of previous year, but not later than April 1. Early acceptance available. *Requirements:* Applicants for freshmen admission, and all applicants who have earned fewer that 24 semester hours of college-level work must graduate from an approved high school and have an overall GPA of 3.0 on 4.0 scale on 18 specific high school units. *Entrance tests:* ACT/SAT for freshmen, TOEFL for foreign students. *For transfer students:* A transfer student who has earned fewer that 30 semester hours of college-level work must meet the unit requirements for freshmen. All transfer applicants must have at least a 2.5 average on all college work attempted. In general, credit earned in colleges and universities accredited by regional accrediting associations is given full value. Graduate requirements vary; see current university graduate catalog.

College credit for postsecondary-level work completed in secondary school and for extrainstitutional learning on basis of ACE *2006 Guide to the Evaluation of Educational Experiences in the Armed Services.* Tutoring available. Developmental courses offered during regular academic year; nondegree credit given.

Degree Requirements: 120–160 hours; 2.0 GPA; 39 credit hour general education requirement; 2 semesters in residence; at least 25% of total numbers of hours at the university. Graduate requirements vary; see current university graduate catalog. Fulfillment of some degree requirements and exemption from some beginning courses possible by passing departmental examinations, College Board CLEP, AP, other standardized tests. *Grading system:* A–F; pass-fail; withdraw.

Distinctive Educational Programs: Evening classes. Preprofessional program in nursing. Facilities and programs for independent research, including honors programs, individual majors, tutorials. Study abroad in England, France, Germany, Honduras, Italy, Japan, Spain, and other countries worldwide. LSU is a member of both national and international student exchange programs (NSE, ISEP). Cross-registration with Southern University and Agricultural and Mechanical College. *Other distinctive programs:* continuing education. Audubon Sugar Institute provides training, research, and service for the sugar cane industry. Center for Computation and Technology; Center for Community engagement, Learning, and Leadership; Honors College; service learning components in many classes. Prospective secondary education teachers earn degrees in content areas with certifications in education, certification.

ROTC: Army; Navy in cooperation with Southern University. 16 Air Force, 15 Army, and 2 Navy commissions awarded 2004.

Degrees Conferred: 4,312 *baccalaureate* (B), 1,073 *master's* (M), 240 *doctorate* (D): agriculture 86 (B), 21 (M), 6 (D); architecture 114 (B), 19 (M); area and ethnic studies 4 (B); biological/life sciences 364 (B), 8 (M), 20 (D); business/marketing 987 (B), 195 (M); 13 (D); communications/communication technologies 214 (B), 12 (M), 2 (D); computer and information sciences 45 (B), 12 (M), 6 (D); education 505 (B), 184 (M), 33 (D); engineering and engineering technologies 370 (B), 118 (M), 22 (D); English 168 (B), 9 (M), 15 (D); foreign languages and literature 29 (B), 14 (M), 6 (D); health professions and related sciences 86 (B), 38 (M), 8 (D); home economics and vocational home economics 43 (B), 10 (M), 3 (D); interdisciplinary studies 20 (B), 15 (M); law/legal studies 11 (M); liberal arts/general studies 389 (B), 28 (M); library science 69 (M); mathematics 20 (B), 29 (M), 4 (D); natural resources/environmental science 47 (B), 25 (M), 6 (D); philosophy/religion/theology 20 (B), 3 (M); physical sciences 41 (B), 14 (M), 27 (D); protective services/public administration 127 (M), 4 (D); psychology 219 (B), 13 (M), 16 (D); social sciences and history 401 (B), 38 (M), 20 (D); visual and performing arts 140 (B), 35 (M), 19 (D). 299 *first-professional:* law 222; veterinary medicine 27. *Honorary degrees awarded 2004–05:* Doctor of Science 2.

Fees and Other Expenses: *Full-time tuition per academic year 2004–05:* undergraduate resident $4,325, nonresident $11,125; graduate resident $5,310, nonresident $11,110. *Room per academic year:* $3,140 to $4,000. *Board per academic year:* $956 to $2,542.

Financial Aid: Aid from institutionally generated funds is provided on the basis of academic merit, financial need, athletic ability, other criteria. Institution has a Program Participation Agreement with the U.S. Department of Education for eligible students to receive Pell Grants and other federal aid.

Financial aid to full-time, first-time undergraduate students: need-based scholarships/grants totaling $38,690,444, self-help $34,123,457, parent loans $2,324,434, tuition waivers $3,222,603, athletic awards $1,565,756;non-need-based scholarships/grants totaling $33,308,368, self-help $20,642,552, parent loans $7,101,370, tuition waivers $1,406,370, athletic awards $2,550,953. *Graduate aid:* 270 students received federal and state-funded fellowships/grants totaling $2,301,500; 2,287 received federal and state-funded loans totaling $33,423,000, 1,142 students held other college-assigned jobs (nonteaching, non-reserach) totaling $2,478,425; 1,054 received other fellowships and grants totaling $2,879,400; 1,729 received teaching/research assistantships totaling $17,795,23

Departments and Teaching Staff: *Total instructional faculty:* 1,475 (full-time 1,293, part-time 182; women 502, men 473; members of minority groups 155). Total faculty with doctorate, first-professional, or other terminal degree: 1,186. Student-to-faculty ratio: 22:1. *Faculty development:* $54,449,584 in grants for research. 61 faculty members awarded sabbaticals 2004–05.

Enrollment: Total enrollment: 31,561. Undergraduate full-time 24,363, part-time 2,034; graduate full-time 3,617, part-time 1,547. *Transfer students:* in-state 1,026; from out-of-state 162.

Characteristics of Student Body: *Ethnic/racial makeup:* number of Black non-Hispanic: 2,406; American Indian or Alaska Native: 104; Asian or Pacific Islander: 953; Hispanic: 654; White non-Hispanic: 21,217; unknown: 712. *Age distribution:* number under 18: 503; 18–19: 10,298; 20–21: 8,930; 22–24: 4,680; 25–29: 1,103; 30–34: 364; 35–39: 167; 40–49: 230; 50–64: 102; 65 and over: 20.

International Students: 1,830 nonresident aliens enrolled fall 2004. 349 students from Europe, 1,034 Asia, 322 Central and South America, 168 Africa, 37 Canada, 5 Australia. Programs available to aid students whose native language is not English: social, cultural, financial. English as a Second Language Program. Some financial aid in the form of institutional scholarships available to international students; 135 awarded in 2003–04 totaling $753,255.

Student Life: On-campus residence halls house 19% of student body. Residence halls for men constitute 43% of such space, for women only 57%. 12% of undergraduate men join and 32% live in fraternities; 14% of undergraduate women join and 35% live in sorority housing. On-campus apartments also available; 3% of student body so housed. 22% of students live on campus. *Intercollegiate athletics:* men: baseball, football, cross country, track and field, basketball, golf, swimming, tennis; women: basketball, golf, gymnastics, swimming, tennis, track and field, cross country, soccer, volleyball. *Special regulations:* Registered cars permitted in designated areas only. *Special services:* Student Health Center, Office of Multicultural Affairs, Career Services, International Services, Office of Disability Services. Child Care Center; Center for Student Leadership and Involvement; Center for Academic Success. Residential Colleges provide living-learning community experience with focus on technology, economic and community development, honors college, or transition and peer

monitoring. Herbarium houses plant species collection, offers research opportunities. Anglo-American Art Museum. Museum of Geoscience. Museum of Natural Science. Rural Life Museum on Burden Research Plantation. *Student publications, radio: The Daily Reveille*, a newspaper; *The Gumbo*, a yearbook, *Legacy* (magazine). FM radio station KLSU broadcasts 24 hours a day, 7 days a week; Tiger TV, campus television station. *Surrounding community:* East Baton Rouge Paris population over 500,000. New Orleans, 89 miles from campus, is nearest metropolitan area. Served by mass transit bus system; airport 15 miles from campus.

Publications: *The Southern Review* (quarterly). LSU Press published 70 titles in 2003–04.

Library Collections: 3,300,000 volumes including bound books, serial backfiles, electronic documents, and government documents not in separate collections. Online catalog. 300 computer work stations. Students have access to the Internet at no charge.

Most important holdings include McIlhenny Natural History Collection; Louisiana and Lower Mississippi Valley Collection; Political Papers Collection.

Buildings and Grounds: Campus area 1,944 acres. *New buildings:* Life Sciences Annex; Energy, Coast, and Environment Building; West Campus Apartments; LSU Child Care Center.

Chief Executive Officer: Dr. Sean O'Keefe, Chancellor.

Address undergraduate admission inquiries to Clive Brooks, Director of Undergraduate Admissions; graduate inquiries to Renee Renegar, Director of Graduate Admissions; law school inquiries to Eric Eden Director of Law School Admissions.

College of Agriculture

Degree Programs Offered: *Baccalaureate* in agricultural business, family and consumer sciences, textile, apparel and merchandising, natural resource ecology and management, nutritional sciences, food science and technology, plant and soil systems, environmental management systems, sciences, vocational education; *master's, doctorate* in wildlife and fisheries, vocational education; *baccalaureate, master's* in agriculture, animal science, dairy science, poultry science; *master's* in applied statistics; *master's, doctorate* in agricultural economics, agronomy, entomology, horticulture, human ecology, human resources education, food science, plant health; *doctorate* in animal and dairy sciences.

Departments and Teaching Staff: *Professors 23, associate professors 16, assistant professors 9, instructors 115, part-time faculty 3. Total instructional faculty:* 66.

Distinctive Educational Programs: Cooperative program with LSU Agricultural Center.

College of Art and Design

Degree Programs Offered: *Baccalaureate* in interior design; *baccalaureate, master's* in architecture, studio art, landscape architecture; *master's* in art history.

Departments and Teaching Staff: *Professors 23, associate professors 16, assistant professors 9, instructors 15, part-time faculty 3. Total instructional faculty:* 66.

Distinctive Educational Programs: Computer-aided design; Geographic Information System Research Laboratory.

College of Arts and Sciences

Degree Programs Offered: *Baccalaureate* in economics, general studies, international studies, Russian area studies, Spanish, German, Latin, women's and gender studies; *baccalaureate, master's* in anthropology, liberal arts, philosophy; *baccalaureate, master's, doctorate* in communication disorders, English, French, geography, history, mathematics, political science, psychology, sociology, communication studies; liberal arts. *master's, doctorate* in comparative literature, linguistics.

Departments and Teaching Staff: *Professors 133, associate professors 68, assistant professors 66, instructors 160, part-time faculty 41. Total instructional faculty:* 468.

Distinctive Educational Programs: Honors and interdisciplinary studies; Center for French and Francophone Studies; Louisiana Population Data Center; Southern Regional Climate Center; U.S. Civil War Center; Voegelin Institute for American Renaissance Studies.

College of Basic Sciences

Degree Programs Offered: *Baccalaureate, master's, doctorate* in biological sciences; *baccalaureate, doctorate* in computer science; *masters* in medical physics and health physics.

Departments and Teaching Staff: *Professors 76, associate professors 35, assistant professors 37, instructors 32, part-time faculty 10. Total instructional faculty:* 190.

Distinctive Educational Programs: Preprofessional programs in medicine and dentistry; Biodynamics Institute.

E. J. Ourso College of Business

Degree Programs Offered: *Baccalaureate* in international trade and finance, management; *baccalaureate, master's* in finance, information systems and decision sciences, marketing; *master's* in public administration; *baccalaureate, master's, doctorate* in accounting, economics; *doctorate* in business administration.

Departments and Teaching Staff: *Professors 36, associate professors 11, assistant professors 28, instructors 29, part-time faculty 12. Total instructional faculty:* 116.

Distinctive Educational Programs: Executive MBA Program; Internal Audit Program; Louisiana Business and Technology Center; Louisiana Real Estate Research Institute; Public Management Program; Technology Transfer.

College of Education

Degree Programs Offered: *Baccalaureate* in elementary grades education, secondary education; *baccalaureate, master's, doctorate* in kinesiology, *master's* in education, guidance administration; *doctorate* in curriculum and instruction, educational leadership and research; *certificate of education specialist* in education.

Departments and Teaching Staff: *Professors 15, associate professors 22, assistant professors 21, instructors 22, part-time faculty 9. Total instructional faculty:* 89.

Distinctive Educational Programs: Louisiana Educational Policy Research Center; Center for Scientific and Mathematical Literacy; Holmes Consortium.

College of Engineering

Degree Programs Offered: *Baccalaureate* in biological engineering, computer engineering, construction management, early childhood education, environmental engineering; PK-3 teacher certification; *baccalaureate, master's* in industrial engineering; *master's, doctorate* in engineering science; *baccalaureate, master's, doctorate* in chemical engineering, civil engineering, electrical engineering, mechanical engineering, petroleum engineering; *master's* in biological and agricultural engineering.

Departments and Teaching Staff: *Professors 46, associate professors 34, assistant professors 27, instructors 13, part-time faculty 28. Total instructional faculty:* 138.

Distinctive Educational Programs: Remote Sensing and Image Processing laboratory; Hazardous Waste Research Center; Hazardous Substance Research Center; Louisiana Transportation Research Center; Louisiana Water Resources Research Institute; Institute for Recyclable Materials.

College of Music and Dramatic Arts

Degree Programs Offered: *Baccalaureate* in music education; *Baccalaureate, master's, doctorate* in music, theatre; *doctorate* in music.

Departments and Teaching Staff: *Professors 24, associate professors 17, assistant professors 19, instructors 2, part-time faculty 5. Total instructional faculty:* 67.

School of the Coast and Environment

Degree Programs Offered: *Master's* in environmental science; *master's, doctorate* in oceanography, coastal sciences.

Departments and Teaching Staff: *Professors 1, associate professors 0, assistant professors 0, part-time faculty 1. Total instructional faculty:* 2.

Distinctive Educational Programs: Coastal Ecology Institute; Coastal Fisheries Institute; Coastal Studies Institute; Institute for Environmental Studies; Oceanography and Coastal Sciences; Wetland Biogeochemistry Institute.

School of Library and Information Science

Degree Programs Offered: *Master's; certificate of advanced study* in library science.

Departments and Teaching Staff: *Professors 0, associate professors 3, assistant professors 7, instructors 0, part-time faculty 1. Total instructional faculty:* 11.

Manship School of Mass Communication

Degree Programs Offered: *Baccalaureate, master's* in mass communication; *doctorate* in mass communication and public affairs.

Departments and Teaching Staff: *Professors 8, associate professors 5, assistant professors 10, instructors 2, part-time faculty 6. Total instructional faculty* 31.

Distinctive Educational Programs: Ph.D. program is the only such program in the United States devoted exclusively to media and politics.

School of Social Work

Degree Programs Offered: *Master's, doctorate* in social work.

Departments and Teaching Staff: *Professors 2, associate professors 2, assistant professors 6, instructors 2, part-time faculty 13. Total instructional faculty:* 25.

Distinctive Educational Programs: Students can specialize in gerontological or medical social work or corrections for M.S.W. and in forensic social work or corrections for Ph.D.

School of Veterinary Medicine

Degree Programs Offered: *First-professional, master's, doctorate.*

Admission: 66 semester hours preprofessional curriculum; objective evaluation based on GPA and MCAT scores; subjective evaluation.

Degree Requirements: 174 credit hours; 2.0 GPA.

Departments and Teaching Staff: *Professors 37, associate professors 22, assistant professors 18, instructors 10, part-time faculty 4. Total instructional faculty:* 91.

Distinctive Educational Programs: Programs in epidemiology and community health; veterinary anatomy and cell biology; veterinary clinical sciences, veterinary microbiology and parasitology; veterinary pathology; pharmacology; toxicology; captor rehabilitation research, equine research.

Louisiana State University Health Center

433 Bolivar Street
New Orleans, Louisiana 70112-2223
Tel: (504) 568-4800   **E-mail:** admissions@lsumc.edu
Fax: (504) 568-5177   **Internet:** www.lsumc.edu

Institution Description: One of the institution's two public academic health science centers located in Louisiana. *Enrollment:* 2,238. *Degrees awarded:* Associate, baccalaureate, first-professional (dentistry, medicine), master's, doctorate.

Accreditation: *Regional:* SACS-Comm. on Coll. *Professional:* audiology, cardiovascular technology, clinical lab scientist, dental hygiene, dental laboratory technology, dentistry, endodontics, maxillofacial prosthodontics, medicine, nursing, nursing education, occupational therapy, ophthalmic medical technology, pediatric dentistry, periodontics, physical therapy, prosthodontics, psychology internship, public health, rehabilitation counseling, respiratory therapy, speech-language pathology

History: Established, chartered and offered first instruction at postsecondary level 1931; awarded first degree (first-professional) 1933.

Institutional Structure: *Governing board:* Board of Supervisors, Louisiana State University System. 15 members including 1 student. *Composition of institution:* Administrators 14 men / 2 women. Vice chancellors for: academic affairs, administration and finance, clinical affairs, institutional services, administrative/community/security affairs, health care services division. Full-time instructional faculty 960 full-time, 316 part-time. Academic governance body, Council of Deans, meets 12 times per year.

Calendar: Semesters. Academic year from Aug. to Aug. Degrees conferred May, Aug., Dec. Formal commencements May.

Degrees Conferred: 145 *baccalaureate:* health professions and related sciences; 127 *master's:* biological sciences 13; health professions and related sciences 114; 21 *doctorate:* biological/life sciences 14, health professions and related sciences 7. 127 *first-professional:* dentistry 52; medicine 175.

Fees and Other Expenses: *Full-time tuition per academic year 2004–05:* undergraduate in-state $2,506; out-of-state $4,206; graduate in-state $4,066, out-of-state $6,566. Professional tuition/fees vary by school and academic program. Contact the Health Center for current tuition, fees, and expenses.

Financial Aid: Aid from institutionally generated funds is provided on the basis of academic merit, financial need, other considerations. Institution has a Program Participation Agreement with the U.S. Department of Education for eligible students to receive Pell Grants and other federal aid.

Financial aid to full-time, first-time undergraduate students:

Financial aid to full-time, first-time undergraduate students: need-based scholarships/grants totaling $283,562, self-help $2,444,971, parent loans $42,497, tuition waivers $18,002; non-need-based scholarships/grants totaling $265,383, self-help $588,811, parent loans $109,562, tuition waivers $32,622. *Graduate aid:* 28 students received federal and state-funded fellowships and grants totaling $401,754; 1,115 received federal and state-funded loans totaling $27,460,786; 37 teaching assistantships were awarded totaling $121,419; 111 research assistantships awarded totaling $364,244.

Departments and Teaching Staff: *Total instructional faculty:* 1,276 (full-time 960, part-time 316; women 507, men 769; members of minority groups 272). *Faculty development:* $54,244,402 in grants for research.

Enrollment: Total enrollment 2,238. Full-time undergraduate 74 men / 511 women, part-time 12m / 45w; first-professional full-time 494m / 436; graduate full-time 150m / 231w, part-time 27m / 158w.

Characteristics of Student Body: *Ethnic/racial makeup:* number of Black non-Hispanic: 74; American Indian or Alaska Native: 3; Asian or Pacific Islander: 49; Hispanic: 24; White non-Hispanic: 487; unknown: 1. *Age distribution:* number 18–19: 1; 20–21: 140; 22–24: 305; 25–29: 113; 30–34: 41; 35–39: 16; 40–49: 21; 50–64: 5.

International Students: 3 nonresident aliens enrolled fall 2004. No programs available to aid students whose native language is not English. No financial aid specifically designated for international students.

Student Life: On-campus residence halls house 15% of student body. Residence hall rooms are open to all students with quotas based on enrollment in each school. *Special regulations:* Cars permitted without restrictions. *Student publications:* The student body publishes the institution's yearbook, the *Murmur. Special services:* student health service; on-campus shuttle; computer labs. *Surrounding community:* New Orleans population approximately 500,000. Served by mass transit system; airport and passenger rail service.

Library Collections: 232,617 volumes. 4,800 microform titles; 7,200 audiovisual materials; 2,950 current periodicals. Access to online information retrieval systems and the Internet. 52 computer work stations. Total 2004–05 budget for books and materials: $1,316,921.

Most important holdings include collections on yellow fever, Louisiana medical history.

Buildings and Grounds: Campus area (3 campuses) 6 square blocks.

Chief Executive Officer: Dr. John A. Rock, Chancellor.

Address admission inquiries to Office of Admissions.

School of Allied Health Professions

Degree Programs Offered: *Baccalaureate* degrees offered on the New Orleans campus in cardiopulmonary science, medical technology, ophthalmic medical technology, rehabilitation services; *master's* degree in occupational therapy, physical therapy, rehabilitation counseling, speech-language pathology; *doctorate* in audiology.

Admission: *Baccalaureate* in cardiopulmonary science and ophthalmic medical technology; 60 semester hours in preprofessional curriculum from accredited college or university required; 73 preprofessional credit hours required in medical technology and 85 preprofessional credit hours required in rehabilitation services.

Degree Requirements: *Baccalaureate* programs required credit hours range from 43 to 73 depending on the program; students are in residence from 12 to 26 months depending on the program; a 2.0 GPA is required in all programs.

Departments and Teaching Staff: *Total instructional faculty:* 158. Degrees held by full-time faculty: 35 doctorate, 82 master's, 19 baccalaureate. 89% hold terminal degrees.

Distinctive Educational Programs: Fourth-year medical technology program in cooperation with affiliated hospitals. *Other distinctive programs:* Assessment Center provides vocational services in cooperation with the City of New Orleans and sponsors research and student internships. Children's Center provides educational and related services to handicapped children. Developmental Disability Center for Children. Therapeutic Nursery School serves emotionally disturbed children.

Enrollment: Total enrollment 300.

School of Nursing

Degree Programs Offered: *Baccalaureate, master's, doctorate.*

Admission: Prenursing curriculum from accredited college or university, 2.5 GPA for associate degree; 2.8 GPA for baccalaureate degree.

Degree Requirements: *For baccalaureate degree:* 130 credit hours, 2.0 GPA, 9 months in residence.

Enrollment: Total enrollment 751.

School of Dentistry

Degree Programs Offered: *Associate, baccalaureate* in dental laboratory technology; *baccalaureate* in dental hygiene; *first-professional* in dentistry. Specialist certificates also awarded.

Admission: *For first-professional:* 90 semester hours from approved college of arts and science with 9 hours English, 8 each in general physics, general zoology, organic chemistry (all with laboratory), DAT.

Degree Requirements: *For first-professional:* 4,670 clock hours; 2.0 GPA, 2 years in residence.

Distinctive Educational Programs: Joint first-professional and doctorate program with School of Graduate Studies. *Other distinctive programs:* Continuing education for practicing dentists.

Enrollment: Total enrollment 414.

School of Medicine in New Orleans

Degree Programs Offered: *First-professional.*

Admission: Three full-time academic years in approved college with a minimum of 90 hours of acceptable credits which must include 9 English, 8 general chemistry, 8 biology, 8 organic chemistry, and 8 physics; MCAT; applications through AMCAS.

Degree Requirements: 4,564 clock hours, minimum grade of pass, final 2 years in residence.

Distinctive Educational Programs: Joint first-professional and doctorate program with School of Graduate Studies. *Other distinctive programs:* Continuing education for state physicians, which includes distribution of videotape cassettes.

Enrollment: Total enrollment 703.

School of Graduate Studies

Degree Programs Offered: *Master's* and *doctorate* in anatomy, biochemistry, biostatistics, human genetics, microbiology, neuroscience, pathology, pharmacology, physiology.

Admission: Baccalaureate from accredited college or university, GPA of at least 3.0 for undergraduate work and 3.0 for graduate work, GRE (minimum of 1000 on combined verbal and quantitative), TOEFL (minimum of 550).

Degree Requirements: *For master's:* 30 semester hours, at least one academic year in residence, thesis. *For doctorate:* at least 3 years in residence, dissertation.

Distinctive Educational Programs: *See* School of Dentistry and Medical School.

Enrollment: Total enrollment 119.

School of Public Health

Degree Programs Offered: *Master* of public health with concentrations in behavioral and community health sciences; biostatistics; environmental and occupational health sciences; epidemiology; health policy and systems management.

Admission: Baccalaureate from accredited college or university, GPA of at least 3.0 for undergraduate work and 3.0 for graduate work, GRE (minimum of 1000 on combined verbal and quantitative), When appropriate, the Medical College Admissions Test or Dental Admissions Test may be substituted, and satisfactory standing at the most recent educational institution attended. All international students must present a minimum score of 585 on the paper-based or 215 on the computer-based Test of English as a Foreign Language (TOEFL).

Degree Requirements: Two-year course of study involving practice experience and capstone project; a 3.0 GPA is required in all programs.

Departments and Teaching Staff: Behavioral and community health sciences *professors* 5, *associate professors* 1, *assistant professors* 2, *instructors* 2; biostatistics 3, 2, 2, 1; environmental health sciences 1, 2, 0, 0; epidemiology 2, 2, 9, 0; health policy and systems management 3, 0, 2, 0; research and service 0, 1, 7, 6.

Enrollment: Total enrollment 19.

Louisiana State University in Shreveport

One University Place
Shreveport, Louisiana 71115-2399

Tel: (318) 797-5000   **E-mail:** admission@lsus.edu
Fax: (318) 797-5286   **Internet:** www.lsus.edu

Institution Description: *Enrollment:* 4,401. *Degrees awarded:* Baccalaureate, master's. Specialist certificate also awarded.

Accreditation: *Regional:* SACS-Comm. on Coll. *Professional:* business, chemistry, teacher education

History: Established and chartered 1965; offered first instruction at postsecondary level 1967; awarded first degree (associate) 1973; added senior level 1974; added graduate level 1978.

Institutional Structure: *Composition of institution:* Administrators 16 men / 29 women. Academic affairs headed by vice chancellor for academic affairs. Management/business/finances directed by vice chancellor for administration. Student affairs headed by vice chancellor for student affairs. Full-time instructional faculty 132.

Calendar: Semesters. Academic year Aug. to May. Freshmen admitted Aug., Jan., June. Degrees conferred and formal commencements May, Aug., Dec. Summer session of 3 terms from early June to early Aug.

Characteristics of Freshmen: 100% of applicants admitted. 63% of applicants admitted and enrolled.

95% (305 students) submitted ACT scores. Mean ACT Composite class score 20.5.

18% of entering freshmen expected to graduate within 5 years. 99% of freshmen from Louisiana. Freshmen from 10 states.

Admission: Rolling admissions plan. For fall acceptance, apply as early as Jan. 1, but not later than registration. Early acceptance available. *Requirements:* Open admissions for graduates of Louisiana secondary schools; out-of-state students must be graduated from accredited secondary school. Recommended college preparatory courses of 15 units to include 4 English, 3 mathematics, 3 sciences, 3 social studies. *Entrance tests:* ACT composite recommended. *For transfer students:* 2.0 minimum GPA; from 4-year accredited institution 98 semester hours maximum transfer credit; from 2-year accredited institution 60 hours; correspondence/extension students 62 hours.

College credit for extrainstitutional learning on basis of *2006 Guide to the Evaluation of Educational Experiences in the Armed Services.* Remedial courses offered; nondegree credit given.

Degree Requirements: *For all baccalaureate degrees:* 128 semester hours minimum; 30 of last 40 hours in residence; distribution requirements. Fulfillment of some degree requirements possible by passing departmental examinations, College Board CLEP, AP. *Grading system:* A–F; pass-fail; withdraw (carries penalty).

Distinctive Educational Programs: Flexible meeting places and schedules, including off-campus centers and evening classes. Accelerated degree programs. Combined program in science and medicine or dentistry allows students to substitute first year in a professional school for final year at Shreveport. Cooperative baccalaureate in medical technology with Louisiana State University School of Medicine. Preprofessional programs in animal science, forestry and wildlife, general agriculture, pharmacy, physical therapy, physicians assistant, speech pathology, veterinary medicine. Interdisciplinary program in social sciences. Facilities and programs for independent research, including honors programs, individual majors, tutorials. Credit and noncredit continuing education. American Studies Washington Semester offered in summer.

ROTC: Army in cooperation with Northwestern State University of Louisiana.

Degrees Conferred: 604 *baccalaureate:* biological/life sciences 11; business/marketing 188; communications/communication technologies 21; computer and information sciences 16; education 71; engineering and English 6; foreign languages and literature 2; health professions and related sciences 6; liberal arts/general studies 46; mathematics 6; physical sciences 3; protective services/public administration 16; psychology 32; social sciences and history 11; visual and performing arts 9. 89 *master's:* business/marketing 29; computer and information sciences 10; education 16; liberal arts/general studies 4; protective services/public administration 18; psychology 12.

Fees and Other Expenses: *Full-time tuition per academic year 2004–05:* undergraduate resident $4,325, nonresident $11,125; graduate resident $5,310, nonresident $11,110. *Room per academic year:* $3,140 to $4,000. *Board per academic year:* $956 to $2,542.

Financial Aid: Aid from institutionally generated funds is provided on the basis of academic merit, financial need, athletic ability. Institution has a Program Participation Agreement with the U.S. Department of Education for eligible students to receive Pell Grants and other federal aid.

Departments and Teaching Staff: *Professors* 48, *associate professors* 32, *assistant professors* 37, *instructors* 28, *part-time faculty* 100. *Total instructional faculty:* 245 (full-time 146, part-time 99; women 104, men 141; members of minority groups 23). Total faculty with doctorate, first-professional, or other terminal degree: 129. Student-to-faculty ratio: 18:1. *Faculty development:* 5 faculty members awarded sabbaticals 2004–05.

Enrollment: Total enrollment 4,401. Undergraduate full-time 967 men / 1,681 women, part-time 402m / 703w; graduate full-time 46m / 112w, part-time 136m / 354w.

Characteristics of Student Body: *Ethnic/racial makeup:* number of Black non-Hispanic: 857; American Indian or Alaska Native: 38; Hispanic: 125; White non-Hispanic: 2,376; unknown 298. *Age distribution:* number under 18: 12; 18–19: 803; 20–21: 793; 22–24: 982; 25–29: 749; 30–34: 409; 35–39: 197; 40–49: 280; 50–64: 120; 65 and over: 13. 40% of student body attend summer sessions.

International Students: 69 nonresident aliens enrolled fall 2004. Students from Europe, Asia, Central and South America, Canada. No programs available to aid students whose native language is not English. No financial aid specifically designated for international students.

Student Life: On-campus apartment style housing available. *Special regulations:* $20 parking fee. *Special services:* Learning Resource Center. Math and English labs. Full component of student activities. *Surrounding community:* Shreveport population 206,000. Dallas (TX), 200 miles from campus, is nearest metropolitan area. Served by mass transit bus system; airport 10 miles from campus.

Library Collections: 279,821 volumes. 70,000 government documents; 335,000 microforms; 1,500 audiovisual materials; 1,190 current periodical subscriptions. Online and card catalogs. 25 computer work stations. Access to online information retrieval systems and the Internet. Total 2004–05 budget for books and materials: $650,000.

Most important holdings include Northwest Louisiana book collection; Northwest Louisiana archives; Noel Collection.

Buildings and Grounds: Campus area 200 acres.

Chief Executive Officer: Dr. Vincent Marsala, Chancellor.

Address admission inquiries to Jennifer Carter, Director of Admissions.

Louisiana Tech University

305 Wisteria
Ruston, Louisiana 71272
Tel: (318) 257-0211   **E-mail:** admissions@latech.edu
Fax: (318) 257-2928   **Internet:** www.latech.edu

Institution Description: Louisiana Tech University is a state institution. *Enrollment:* 11,691. *Degrees awarded:* Associate, baccalaureate, master's, doctorate.

Academic offerings subject to approval by statewide coordinating bodies. Budget subject to approval by state governing boards.

Accreditation: *Regional:* SACS-Comm. on Coll. *Professional:* accounting, art, audiology, business, computer science, dietetics, engineering, engineering technology, family and consumer science, forestry, health information administration, health information technician, interior design, music, nursing, speech-language pathology, teacher education

History: Established as Industrial Institute and College of Louisiana 1894; chartered and offered first instruction at postsecondary level 1895; awarded first degree (baccalaureate) 1897; changed name to Louisiana Polytechnic Institute 1920; adopted present name 1970. *See* Ruby B. Pearce, Sally Robinson, Helen Graham, *Alma Mater: 1895–1945* (Ruston: Louisiana Tech Alumni Association, 1945) for further information.

Institutional Structure: *Governing board:* Board of Trustees for State Colleges and Universities. Representation: 18 trustees, including 1 student (all appointed by governor of Louisiana). All voting. *Composition of institution:* President; administrators 36; vice president for academic affairs; vice president for administrative affairs; vice president for student affairs, vice president for development and external affairs. Full-time instructional faculty 371. Academic governance body, Council of Academic Deans, meets an average of 12 times per year.

Calendar: Semesters. Academic year late Aug. to mid-May. Freshmen admitted Sept., Dec., Mar., June. Degrees conferred and formal commencements May, Aug., Nov., Feb. Summer session from June to Aug.

Characteristics of Freshmen: 3,897 applicants (2,143 men, 1,754 women). 86.4% of applicants admitted. 48.9% of admitted students enrolled full-time.

93% (1,789 students) submitted ACT scores. *25th percentile:* ACT Composite 20, ACT English 20, ACT Math 19. *75th percentile:* ACT Composite 25, ACT English 25, ACT Math 24.

33% of entering freshmen expected to graduate within 5 years. 84% of freshmen from Louisiana. Students from 15 states and 1 foreign country.

Admission: Selective admission. Apply as early as 2 years, but not later than 2 weeks, prior to enrollment. Early acceptance available. *Requirements:* Graduation from accredited secondary school with 2.0 GPA in core curriculum (4 units English, 3 mathematics, 3 social studies, 3 science, 4½ electives) or rank in upper 50% of high school class or score of 22 on ACT composite. *Entrance tests:* ACT composite. *For transfer students:* 2.0 minimum GPA; from 4-year accredited institution maximum transfer credit limited only by residence requirement;

from 2-year accredited institution 68 semester hours; correspondence/extension students 6 hours.

College credit and advanced placement for postsecondary-level work completed in secondary school. College credit for extrainstitutional learning (life experience) on basis of ACE *2006 Guide to the Evaluation of Educational Experiences in the Armed Services*. Tutoring available.

Degree Requirements: *For all associate degrees:* 60–68 semester hours. *For all baccalaureate degrees:* 130–140 semester hours; senior year in residence. Fulfillment of some degree requirements possible by passing College Board CLEP. *Grading system:* A–F; pass-fail; withdraw (carries time limit).

Distinctive Educational Programs: Cooperative education. Flexible meeting places and schedules, including off-campus center (at Barksdale Air Force Base, 65 miles away from main institution) and evening classes. Facilities and programs for independent research, including honors programs. Study abroad in Italy, Mexico. Cross-registration and faculty exchange with Grambling State University. Research opportunities through Center for Rehabilitation Science and Biomedical Engineering, Institute for Manufacturing, Water Resources Center. *Other distinctive programs:* Continuing education. Speech and Hearing Clinic offers diagnostic and remedial services.

Degrees Conferred: 94 *associate*; 1,390 *baccalaureate*; 366 *master's*; 33 *doctorate*. Bachelor's degrees awarded in top five disciplines: business, management, marketing, and related support services 305; engineering 169; liberal arts and sciences, general studies, and humanities 118; education 99; social sciences 71.

Fees and Other Expenses: *Full-time tuition per academic year 2004–05:* undergraduate resident $3,914, nonresident $8,939. *Books and supplies:* $900. *Room and board per academic year:* $4,035. Contact the university for current information regarding tuition and fees for graduate study.

Financial Aid: Aid from institutionally generated funds is provided on the basis of academic merit, financial need, athletic ability, other criteria. Institution has a Program Participation Agreement with the U.S. Department of Education for eligible students to receive Pell Grants and other federal aid.

Financial aid to full-time, first-time undergraduate students: 24% received federal grants averaging $2,719; 35% state/local grants averaging $2,608; 23% institutional grants averaging $1,747; 21% received loans averaging $4,244.

Departments and Teaching Staff: *Professors* 130, *associate professors* 94, *assistant professors* 111, *instructors* 36. *Total instructional faculty:* 371. Degrees held by full-time faculty: doctorate 67%, master's 31%, baccalaureate 2%. 79% hold terminal degrees.

Enrollment: Total enrollment 11,691. Undergraduate 9,318 (51.6% men, 48.4% women).

Characteristics of Student Body: *Ethnic/racial makeup:* Black non-Hispanic: 15.9%; American Indian or Alaska Native: .6%; Asian or Pacific Islander: .7%; Hispanic: 1.8%; White non-Hispanic: 72%; unknown: 7%. *Age distribution:* 17–21: 39%; 22–24: 30%; 25–29: 12%; 30–34: 5%; 35–39: 4%; 40–49: 5%; 50–59: 1%; 60–up 4%.

International Students: 177 nonresident aliens enrolled fall 2004. Programs available to aid students whose native language is not English: social, cultural. English as a Second Language Program. No financial aid specifically designated for international students.

Student Life: On-campus residence halls house 46% of student body. Residence halls for men constitute 55% of such space, for women 45%. 12 fraternities for men, 6 sororities for women. Housing available for married students. *Intercollegiate athletics:* men only: baseball, basketball, cross-country, football, golf, tennis, track; women only: basketball, softball, track, volleyball. *Special regulations:* Registered cars permitted without restrictions. Residence hall visitation hours vary according to individual residence halls. *Special services:* Learning Resources Center, medical services. *Student publications, radio:* The *Tech Talk*, a weekly newspaper. Radio station KLPI. *Surrounding community:* Ruston population 20,000. Shreveport, 60 miles from campus, is nearest metropolitan area. Served by Monroe airport 3o miles east of campus and Shreveport 65 miles west.

Library Collections: 1,131,600 volumes. 2,140,600 microforms; 520 audiovisual materials; 2,930 current periodical subscriptions. Online catalog. Students have access to online information retrieval services and the Internet.

Most important special collections include Joe. D. Waggoner Congressional Papers; American Foreign Policy Collection; Hartner Forestry Collection.

Buildings and Grounds: Campus area 235 acres.

Chief Executive Officer: Dr. Daniel D. Reneau, President.

Address admission inquiries to Jan B. Albritton, Director of Admissions.

College of Arts and Sciences

Degree Programs Offered: *Baccalaureate* in architecture, art, chemistry, English, foreign languages, history, journalism, mathematics, music, physics, professional aviation, social sciences, speech; *master's* in art, chemistry, English, history, mathematics, Romance languages, speech.

Distinctive Educational Programs: Cooperative baccalaureate program in medical technology with affiliated hospitals. Preprofessional programs in law, optometry, pharmacy, social welfare, speech pathology. General studies degree program.

College of Administration and Business

Degree Programs Offered: *Associate, baccalaureate, master's* in business administration, professional accountancy; *doctorate* in business administration.

College of Education

Degree Programs Offered: *Baccalaureate* in business education, counseling and guidance, early childhood education, elementary education, health and physical education, human relations and supervision, mathematical education, psychology, science education, special education; *master's* in various fields.

College of Engineering

Degree Programs Offered: *Baccalaureate* in biomedical engineering, chemical engineering, civil engineering, computer engineering, construction engineering technology, electrical engineering, electrical engineering technology, geology industrial engineering, mechanical engineering, petroleum engineering; *master's* in biomedical, chemical, civil, computer science, electrical, industrial, mechanical, and petroleum engineering; manufacturing systems engineering; *doctorate* in biomedical engineering.

College of Home Economics

Degree Programs Offered: *Associate, baccalaureate* in apparel and textile merchandising, child life and family studies, consumer affairs, consumer services, early childhood education, fashion merchandising, food science, general home economics, home economics (secondary education)g, nutrition and dietetics; *master's* in general home economics education, human ecology, human ecology education, institution management, nutrition and dietetics.

Distinctive Educational Programs: Cooperative undergraduate program in general dietetics with area hospitals.

College of Life Sciences

Degree Programs Offered: *Associate* in medical record technology, nursing; *baccalaureate* in agricultural business, agricultural education, animal science, agronomy, botany, forestry, horticulture, medical record administration, medical technology, microbiology, wildlife conservation, zoology.

Distinctive Educational Programs: Field experience through forestry camp program. Preprofessional program in nursing, veterinary medicine.

Loyola University New Orleans

6363 St. Charles Avenue
New Orleans, Louisiana 70118-6195

Tel: (504) 865-3240   **E-mail:** admit@loyno.edu
Fax: (504) 865-3383   **Internet:** www.loyno.edu

Institution Description: Loyola University New Orleans is a private institution affiliated with the Society of Jesus, Roman Catholic Church. *Enrollment:* 5,423. *Degrees awarded:* Baccalaureate, first-professional (law), master's.

Accreditation: *Regional:* SACS-Comm. on Coll. *Professional:* accounting, business, counseling, law, music, nursing

History: Established as Preparatory College of Immaculate Conception 1847; offered first instruction at postsecondary level 1849; awarded first degree (baccalaureate) 1856; changed name to Loyola College 1904; chartered under present name 1912.

Institutional Structure: *Governing board:* Board of Trustees. All voting. Academic affairs headed by provost/vice president for academic affairs. Management/business/finances directed by vice president for business and finance. Full-time instructional faculty 246. Academic governance body, Faculty Senate, meets an average of 10 times per year.

Calendar: Semesters. Academic year Aug. to May. Freshmen admitted Aug., Jan., June. Degrees conferred and formal commencement May. Summer session of 2 terms from early June to mid-Aug.

Characteristics of Freshmen: 86% of applicants accepted. 45% of applicants accepted and enrolled.

70% (576 students) submitted SAT scores; 61% (497 students) submitted ACT scores. *25th percentile:* SAT Verbal 570, SAT Math 560; ACT Composite

24, ACT English 26, ACT Math 23. *75th percentile*: SAT Verbal 680, SAT Math 660; ACT Composite 29, ACT English 32, ACT Math 28.

54% of entering freshmen expected to graduate within 5 years. 47% of freshmen from Louisiana. Freshmen from 48 states and 11 foreign countries.

Admission: Rolling admissions plan. Early acceptance available. *Requirements:* Either graduation from accredited secondary school or GED. *Entrance tests:* College Board SAT or ACT composite. For foreign students TOEFL. *For transfer students:* 2.25 minimum GPA; maximum transfer credit limited only by residence and core requirements.

College credit and advanced placement for postsecondary-level work completed in secondary school. Tutoring available. Developmental courses offered during regular academic year; credit given.

Degree Requirements: 120–140 credit hours (varies by program); 2.0 GPA; core requirements. Fulfillment of some degree requirements and exemption from some beginning courses possible by passing departmental examinations, College Board CLEP, AP. *Grading system:* A–F; withdraw (carries time limit).

Distinctive Educational Programs: Honors program. Combined juris doctor/master of business administration program. External degree program (New Orleans Consortium). International study in Belgium, England, China, Czech Republic, Italy, Mexico, Spain. Internships and cooperative education. Weekend and evening classes. Special facilities for using telecommunications in the classroom. Interdisciplinary studies available. Facilities for independent research, including honors programs, individual majors, independent study.

ROTC: Offered in conjunction with Tulane University.

Degrees Conferred: 784 *baccalaureate* (B), 220 *master's* (M): biological/life sciences 42 (B); business/marketing 144 (B), 56 (M); communications/communication technologies 102 (B), 2 (M); computer and information science 16 (B); education 17 (B), 19 (M); engineering/engineering technologies 1 (B); English 42 (B); fine and applied arts 11 (B); foreign languages and literature 9 (B); health professions and related sciences 75 (B); liberal arts/general studies 3 (B); mathematics 5 (B), 3 (M); physical sciences 14 (B); philosophy/religion 15 (B), 131 (M); protective services/public administration 25 (B); psychology 46 (B); social sciences and history 83 (B); visual and performing arts 39 (B), 3 (M). 276 *first-professional:* law.

Fees and Other Expenses: *Full-time tuition per academic year 2005–06:* undergraduate $24,410; graduate varies by program. *Required fees:* $836. *Room per academic year:* $5,166. *Board per academic year:* $3,146.

Financial Aid: Aid from institutionally generated funds is provided on the basis of academic merit, financial need. Institution has a Program Participation Agreement with the U.S. Department of Education for eligible students to receive Pell Grants and other federal aid.

Financial aid to full-time, first-time undergraduate students: need-based scholarships/grants totaling $20,907,608, self-help $8,341,646, parent loans $1,004,478, tuition waivers $659,550; non-need-based scholarships/grants totaling $14,064,121, self-help $3,343,591, tuition waivers $904,280.

Departments and Teaching Staff: *Total instructional faculty:* 483 (full-time 306, part-time 177; women 189, men 294; members of minority groups 55). Total faculty with doctorate, first-professional, or other terminal degree: 210. Student-to-faculty ratio: 11.43:1.

Enrollment: Total enrollment 5,423. Undergraduate full-time 1,283 men / 1,937 women, part-time 155m / 313w; graduate full-time 56m / 66w, part-time 243m / 566w; first-professional full-time 289m / 342w, part-time 94m / 79w.

Characteristics of Student Body: *Ethnic/racial makeup:* number of Black non-Hispanic: 369; American Indian or Alaska Native: 19; Asian or Pacific Islander: 151; Hispanic: 400; White non-Hispanic: 2,356; unknown: 253.

International Students: 140 undergraduate nonresident aliens enrolled fall 2004. Students from Europe, Asia, Central and South America, Africa, Canada, Australia. Programs available to aid students whose native language is not English: English as a Second Language Program. No financial aid specifically designated for international students.

Student Life: On-campus residence halls house 22% of student body. Residence halls for men constitute 36% of such space, for women 64%. 17% of men join fraternities and 17% of women are members of sororities. *Intercollegiate athletics* for men: basketball, baseball, cross-country, swimming, track and field. For women: basketball, cross-county, soccer, track and field, volleyball. *Special regulations:* Freshmen residents are not be allowed to purchase permits to park on campus. Upperclassmen residents and commuters may park on campus after purchasing a permit. There are no curfews for residents. Residents may turn to LSCN to get university-sponsored videos, announcements, and movies. *Special services:* Learning Resources Center, counseling, career, and medical services. *Student publications, radio, television: The Maroon,* a weekly newspaper; *The Wolf* a yearbook. *Surrounding community:* New Orleans population over 500,000. Served by mass transit bus and streetcar system; airport 10 miles from campus, passenger rail service 2 miles from campus.

Publications: *New Orleans Review,* a national literary magazine.

Library Collections: 447,380 volumes including bound books, serial backfiles, electronic documents, and government documents not in separate collections. Online catalog. Current serial subscriptions: 1,339. 671,775 microforms; 14,872 audiovisual materials; 14,330 E-books. /computer work stations available. Students have access to the Internet at no charge.

Most important special holdings include Moon Landrieu Collection; Louis J. Twomey Papers, Archives of the New Orleans Province of the Society of Jesus; J. Edgar Monroe Collection; Walker Percy and His Circle Collection.

Buildings and Grounds: Campus area 19 acres at main campus (St. Charles Avenue); 4 acres at the Broadway Campus.

Chief Executive Officer: Rev. Kevin William Wildes, S.J. President.

Address undergraduate admission inquiries to Deborah C. Stieffel, Dean of Admissions and Enrollment Management.

McNeese State University

4100 Ryan Street
Lake Charles, Louisiana 70609-2215
Tel: (337) 475-5000   **E-mail:** admissions@mcneese.edu
Fax: (337) 475-5012   **Internet:** www.mcneese.edu

Institution Description: McNeese State University is a state institution. *Enrollment:* 8,785. *Degrees awarded:* Associate, baccalaureate, master's. Specialist certificate in education also awarded.

Academic offerings subject to approval by statewide coordinating bodies. Budget subject to approval by state governing boards. Member of the consortium Southwest Louisiana Regional Council for Cooperation.

Accreditation: *Regional:* SACS-Comm. on Coll. *Professional:* business, clinical lab scientist, computer science, dietetics, engineering, family and consumer science, journalism, music, nursing, radiography, teacher education

History: Established as Lake Charles Junior College, a division of Louisiana State University and offered first instruction at postsecondary level 1939; changed name to John McNeese Junior College 1940; awarded first degree (associate) 1941; became 4-year institution, separated from Louisiana State, and changed name to McNeese State College 1950; adopted present name 1970.

Institutional Structure: *Governing board:* State of Louisiana Board of Supervisors for State Colleges and Universities. Representation: 18 trustees, including 1 student (all appointed by governor of Louisiana). All voting. *Composition of institution:* Administrators 29 men / 3 women. Academic affairs headed by vice president for academic affairs. Management/business/finances directed by chief fiscal officer. Full-time instructional faculty 264. Academic governance body, University Council, meets an average of 40 times per year.

Calendar: Semesters. Academic year late Aug. to mid-May. Freshmen admitted Aug., Jan., June. Degrees conferred and formal commencements May, July, Dec. Summer session from early June to late July.

Characteristics of Freshmen: 2,313 applicants (991 men, 1,322 women). 88.5% of applicants admitted. 78.5% of admitted students enrolled full-time.

5% (77 students) submitted SAT scores; 87% (1,360 students) submitted ACT scores. *25th percentile*: ACT Composite 17, ACT English 17, ACT Math 16. *75th percentile*: ACT Composite 22, ACT English 23, ACT Math 21.

50% of entering freshmen expected to graduate within 5 years. 95% of freshmen from Louisiana. Freshmen from 35 states and 26 foreign countries.

Admission: Rolling admissions plan. For fall acceptance, apply as early as Oct. of senior year of secondary school, but not later than 1 month prior to registration. Apply by Apr. 1 for early decision; need not limit application to McNeese State. Early acceptance available. *Requirements:* Graduation from accredited secondary school. Admission possible for nongraduates 18 years of age and older who satisfactorily complete institutional entrance examination. *Entrance tests:* ACT composite for placement. For foreign students minimum TOEFL score 500. *For transfer students:* Maximum transfer credit limited only by residence requirement; correspondence/extension students 45 semester hours. Good standing at institution previously attended.

College credit and advanced placement for postsecondary-level work completed in secondary school. For extrainstitutional learning (life experience), advanced placement for faculty assessment, personal interviews. Tutoring available. Developmental courses offered in summer session and regular academic year; credit given.

Degree Requirements: *For all associate degrees:* 64–81 semester hours. *For all baccalaureate degrees:* 124–135 hours. *For all undergraduate degrees:* 2.0 GPA; 2 terms in residence; general education and core requirements.

Fulfillment of some degree requirements and exemption from some beginning courses possible by passing departmental examinations, College Board CLEP, AP. *Grading system:* A–F; pass-fail; withdraw (carries penalty and time limit).

Distinctive Educational Programs: Cooperative education. Flexible meeting places and schedules, including off-campus centers (at DeQuincy, less than

30 miles away from main institution; Kinder, 34 miles away; Jennings, 36 miles; Lake Arthur, 42 miles; Oberlin, 44 miles; DeRidder, 47 miles) and evening classes. Cooperative baccalaureate program in medical technology with approved schools of medical technology. Interdisciplinary degree program in liberal studies. Preprofessional programs include architecture, dentistry, medicine, veterinary medicine. Facilities and programs for independent research, including honors programs, tutorials. *Other distinctive programs:* Reading conferences. Environmental science workshops. Science institutes.

Degrees Conferred: 179 *associate;* 900 *baccalaureate;* 243 *master's.* Bachelor's degrees awarded in top five disciplines: business, management, marketing, and related support services 210; education 119; liberal arts and sciences, general studies, and humanities 114; health professions and related clinical sciences 79; engineering 56.

Fees and Other Expenses: *Full-time tuition per academic year 2004–05:* resident $3,098, nonresident $9,164. *Books and supplies:* $1,000. *Room and board per academic year:* $3,996.

Financial Aid: Aid from institutionally generated funds is provided on the basis of academic merit, athletic ability. Institution has a Program Participation Agreement with the U.S. Department of Education for eligible students to receive Pell Grants and other federal aid.

Financial aid to full-time, first-time undergraduate students: 39% received federal grants averaging $3,110; 46% state/local grants averaging $2,110; 40% institutional grants averaging $2,800; 40% received loans averaging $2,890.

Departments and Teaching Staff: *Total full-time faculty:* 264. 66% of faculty hold terminal degrees.

Enrollment: Total enrollment 8,785. Undergraduate 7,726 (40.4% men, 59.6% women).

Characteristics of Student Body: *Ethnic/racial makeup:* Black non-Hispanic: 20.1%; American Indian or Alaska Native: .8%; Asian or Pacific Islander: .8%; Hispanic: .5%; White non-Hispanic: 74.8%; unknown: .5%. *Age distribution:* 17–21: 50.8%; 22–24: 17.5%; 25–29: 11.2%; 30–34: 6.6%; 35–39: 4.8%; 40–49: 6.9%; 50–59: 1.9%.

International Students: 124 undergraduate nonresident aliens enrolled 2004. No programs available to aid students whose native language is not English. No financial aid specifically designated for international students.

Student Life: On-campus residence halls house 20% of student body. Dormitories for men only constitute 50% of such space, for women only 50%. 6% of men join and live in fraternities. 19% of married students request institutional housing; 13% are so housed. 24% of students live on campus. *Intercollegiate athletics:* men only: baseball, basketball, cross-country, football, golf, tennis, track; women only: basketball, softball, tennis. *Special regulations:* Registered cars permitted in designated areas (fee charged). Curfews. Residence hall visitation from 6pm to 10pm. *Special services:* Learning Resources Center, medical services. *Student publications: Arena,* a literary magazine; *The Contraband,* a weekly newspaper; *The Log,* a yearbook. *Surrounding community:* Lake Charles population 75,000. Houston (TX), 161 miles from campus, is nearest metropolitan area. Served by mass transit bus system; airport 5 miles from campus; passenger rail service 7 miles from campus.

Publications: *McNeese Review* (annually) first published in 1948.

Library Collections: 546,200 volumes including bound books, serial backfiles, electronic documents, and government documents not in separate collections. Online catalog. 1,810 current serial subscriptions. 1,437,500 microfilm units; 1,385 audiovisual materials. Computer work stations available. Students have access to the Internet at no charge.

Most important holdings include Southwest Louisiana collection; Southern Writers First Edition collection; fore-edge paintings collection; Rosa Hart/Little Theatre Collection.

Buildings and Grounds: Campus area 500 acres.

Chief Executive Officer: Dr. Robert D. Herbert, President.

Address admission inquiries to Tammie E. Pettis, Director of Admissions.

New Orleans Baptist Theological Seminary

3939 Gentilly Boulevard
New Orleans, Louisiana 70126-4858
Tel: (504) 282-4455   **E-mail:** admissions@nobts.edu
Fax: (505) 283-3621   **Internet:** www.nobts.edu

Institution Description: New Orleans Baptist Theological Seminary is a private institution affiliated with the Southern Baptist Convention. *Enrollment:* 2,846. *Degrees awarded:* Associate, first-professional (master of divinity), master's, doctorate.

Accreditation: *Regional:* SACS-Comm. on Coll. *National:* ATS. *Professional:* music, theology

History: Chartered as Baptist Bible Institute 1917; offered first instruction at postsecondary level 1918; awarded first baccalaureate 1921; adopted present name 1946.

Institutional Structure: *Governing board:* Board of Trustees. Representation: 37 trustees. *Composition of institution:* Academic affairs headed by vice president for academic affairs. Management/business/finances directed by vice president for business affairs. Full-time instructional faculty 49.

Calendar: Academic year Aug. to July. 4 eight-week terms and 2 summer terms.

Characteristics of Freshmen: 151 applicants admitted (103 men, 48 women). 88.7% of admitted students enrolled full-time.

Admission: Rolling admissions plan. *Requirements:* For first-professional, baccalaureate or equivalent from accredited college or university.

Degree Requirements: *For first-professional degree:* 88 semester hours; 1.0 GPA on 3.0 scale. *For master of religious education degree:* 66 hours; 1.0 GPA on 3.0 scale. *For master of church music degree:* 56 hours; 2.0 GPA on 3.0 scale. *For all degrees:* Field education. *Grading system:* A–F; withdraw.

Degrees Conferred: 15 *associate;* 72 *baccalaureate:* theology and ministerial studies; 59 *master's:* theology and ministerial studies; 126 *first-professional:* master of divinity.

Fees and Other Expenses: *Full-time tuition per academic year 2004–05:* $3,700. *Books and supplies:* $900. *Room and board per academic year:* $2,400. Contact the seminary for current graduate and first-professional tuition and fees.

Financial Aid: Aid from institutionally generated funds is provided on the basis of financial need.Institution has a Program Participation Agreement with the U.S. Department of Education for eligible students to receive Pell Grants and other federal aid. Contact the seminary for information regarding financial aid.

Departments and Teaching Staff: *Total instructional faculty:* 89.

Enrollment: Total enrollment 2,846. Undergraduate 1,083 (74.2% men, 25.8% women).

Characteristics of Student Body: *Ethnic/racial makeup:* Black non-Hispanic: 14.1%; American Indian or Alaska Native: .6%; Asian or Pacific Islander: 1.6%; Hispanic: 16.6%; White non-Hispanic: 66.4%.

International Students: 8 undergraduate nonresident aliens enrolled fall 2004. Programs available to aid students whose native language is not English: social, cultural.

Student Life: On-campus housing for single and married students. *Surrounding community:* New Orleans population over 500,000.

Library Collections: 235,000 volumes.

The library is a depository for Baptist materials, and contains specialized book collections, manuscripts, and memorabilia from outstanding church leaders; specialized collection of music materials includes 9,000 books, 9,500 scores, 1,500 hymnals and psalters; 3,000 recordings; and several thousand anthems and larger classical works (The Edmond D. Keith collection of 5,000 books, hymnals, and scores is a special feature of this collection).

Buildings and Grounds: Campus area 81 acres.

Chief Executive Officer: Charles S. Kelley, Jr., President.

Address admission inquiries to Dr. Paul E. Gregoire, Director of Admissions.

Nicholls State University

Louisiana Highway 1
Thibodaux, Louisiana 70310
Tel: (877) 642-4555   **E-mail:** admissions@nich.edu
Fax: (985) 448-4929   **Internet:** www.nich.edu

Institution Description: Nicholls State University (Francis T. Nicholls State College until 1970) is a state institution. *Enrollment:* 7,473. *Degrees awarded:* Associate, baccalaureate, master's. Specialist certificates in education also awarded.

Academic offerings subject to approval by statewide coordinating bodies. Budget subject to approval by state governing boards. Member of LUM-CON.

Accreditation: *Regional:* SACS-Comm. on Coll. *Professional:* accounting, art, business, chemistry, computer science, cytotechnology, EMT-paramedic, family and consumer science, journalism, music, nursing, nursing education, respiratory therapy, teacher education

History: Established as Francis T. Nicholls Junior College of Louisiana State University and offered first instruction at postsecondary level 1948; became independent institution, added upper division, and changed name to Francis T. Nicholls State College 1956; awarded first degree (baccalaureate) 1958; adopted present name 1970.

Institutional Structure: *Governing board:* State of Louisiana Board of Supervisors for State College and Universities. Representation: 15 supervisors, including 1 student. All voting. *Composition of institution:* Administrators 20

men / 1 woman. Academic affairs headed by vice president of academic affairs. Management/business/finances directed by vice president of business affairs. *Total instructional faculty* 264. Academic governance body, Faculty Senate, meets an average of 12 times per year.

Calendar: Semesters. Academic year June to May. Freshmen admitted Aug., Jan., June. Degrees conferred and formal commencements May, Dec. Summer session of 1 term from early June to early Aug.

Characteristics of Freshmen: 99% of applicants admitted. 57% of applicants admitted and enrolled.

3% (41 students) submitted SAT scores; 96% (1,568 students) submitted ACT scores. *25th percentile:* ACT Composite 17, ACT English 17, ACT Math 16. *75th percentile:* ACT Composite 22, ACT English 23, ACT Math 22.

13% of entering freshmen expected to graduate within 5 years. 97% of freshmen from Louisiana. Freshmen from 16 states and 7 foreign countries.

Admission: Rolling admissions plan. For fall acceptance, apply by Aug. 15 of year of enrollment. Early acceptance available. *Requirements:* Either graduation from secondary school or GED. *Entrance tests:* ACT composite. For foreign students TOEFL. *For transfer students:* 1.0 GPA; 65 hours maximum transfer credit; good standing at institution previously attended. College credit and advanced placement for postsecondary-level work completed in secondary school. College credit for extrainstitutional learning on basis of ACE *2006 Guide to the Evaluation of Educational Experiences in the Armed Services.* Tutoring available. Developmental/remedial courses offered in summer session and regular academic year; nondegree credit given.

Degree Requirements: *For all associate degrees:* 60 semester hours; 12 hours in residence. *For all baccalaureate degrees:* 120 hours; 30 hours in residence; 2 semesters physical education. *For all undergraduate degrees:* 2.0 GPA; general education and core curriculum requirements. Additional requirements for some programs. Fulfillment of some degree requirements and exemption from some beginning courses possible by passing departmental examinations, College Board CLEP, AP, other standardized tests. *Grading system:* A–F; pass-fail; withdraw (carries penalty, carries time limit).

Distinctive Educational Programs: Internships. Evening classes. Preprofessional programs in dentistry, engineering, medicine, optometry, pharmacy, physical therapy, veterinary medicine. Facilities for independent research, including honors programs, individual majors. Study abroad in France through institutionally sponsored program, and in Rome, in cooperation with Louisiana Tech University. *Other distinctive programs:* High Ability Program for outstanding secondary school students. Upward Bound Program for secondary school juniors. Credit and noncredit continuing education programs and baccalaureate in general studies.

Degrees Conferred: 149 *associate;* 777 *baccalaureate* (B); 141 *master's* (M): agriculture 11 (B); biological/life sciences 25 (B), 2 (M); business/marketing 222 (B), 40 (M); communications/communication technologies 34 (B); computer and information sciences 6 (B); education 87 (B), 77 (M); engineering and engineering technologies 14 (B); English 10 (B); health professions and related sciences 138 (B); home economics and vocational home economics 21 (B); liberal arts/general studies 95 (B); mathematics 3 (B), 7 (M); personal and miscellaneous services 27 (B); physical sciences 7 (B); psychology 11 (B), 15 (M); social sciences and history 42 (B); visual and performing arts 24 (B).

Fees and Other Expenses: *Full-time tuition per academic year 2004–05:* resident $2,135, nonresident $7,583. *Required fees:* $1,105. *Room per academic year:* $1,800. *Board per academic year:* $1,734.

Financial Aid: Aid from institutionally generated funds is provided on the basis of academic merit, financial need, athletic ability. Institution has a Program Participation Agreement with the U.S. Department of Education for eligible students to receive Pell Grants and other federal aid.

Financial aid to full-time, first-time undergraduate students: need-based scholarships/grants totaling $6,880,636, self-help $4,317,595, parent loans $11,449, tuition waivers $217,556, athletic awards $216,474; non-need-based scholarships/grants totaling $3,733,238, self-help $7,305,234, parent loans $289,119, tuition waivers $406,458, athletic awards $700,729.

Departments and Teaching Staff: *Total instructional faculty:* 285 (women 142, men 143; members of minority groups 30). Total faculty with doctorate, first-professional, or other terminal degree: 161. Student-to-faculty ratio: 21:1.

Enrollment: Total enrollment 7,473. Undergraduate full-time 2,170 men / 3,432 women, part-time 364m / 818w; graduate full-time 47m / 104w, part-time 113m / 425w.

Characteristics of Student Body: *Ethnic/racial makeup:* number of Black non-Hispanic: 1,238; American Indian or Alaska Native: 134; Asian or Pacific Islander: 61; Hispanic: 104; White non-Hispanic: 5,025, unknown: 176. *Age distribution:* number under 18: 170; 18–19: 2,319; 20–21: 1,606; 22–24: 1,195; 25–29: 592; 30–34: 366; 35–39: 200; 40–49: 267; 50–64: 66; 65 and over: 3.

International Students: 69 nonresident aliens enrolled fall 2004. 12 students from Europe, 18 Asia, 16 Central and South America, 2 Africa, 14 Canada, 2 Australia. English as a Second Language Program available to aid students whose native language is not English. No financial aid specifically designated for international students.

Student Life: On-campus residence halls house 18% of student body. Residence halls for men constitute 40% of such space, for women 60%. Housing available for married students. *Intercollegiate athletics:* men only: baseball, basketball, cross-country, football, golf, tennis, track; women only: basketball, cross-country, indoor and outdoor track, soccer, softball, tennis, volleyball. *Special regulations:* Registered cars permitted without restrictions. *Special services:* Learning Resources Center; medical services; disability services; women's resource and services office; family resource center; Center for Study of Dyslexia. *Student publications, radio: La Pirogue,* a yearbook; *The Mosaic,* an annual literary magazine; *The Nicholls Worth,* a weekly newspaper. Radio station KVFG broadcasts 60 hours per week. *Surrounding community:* Thibodaux population 16,000. New Orleans, 68 miles from campus, is nearest metropolitan area. Served by mass transit system; airport 5 miles from campus; passenger rail service 3 miles from campus.

Library Collections: 540,948 volumes including bound books, serial backfiles, electronic documents, and government documents not in separate collections. Online catalog. Current serial subscriptions: 1,341. Computer work stations available. Students have access to the Internet at no charge.

Most important holdings include archives of former U.S. Senator Allen J. Ellender; J. Wilson Lepine Laurel Valley Plantation Collection; Thibodaux and Lafourche Parish collections of photographs and documents.

Buildings and Grounds: Campus area 210 acres.

Chief Executive Officer: Dr. Stephen T. Hulbert, President.

Address admission inquiries to Becky LeBlanc-Durocher, Director of Admissions.

Northwestern State University of Louisiana

College Avenue
Natchitoches, Louisiana 71497
Tel: (318) 357-5964   **E-mail:** admissions@nsula.edu
Fax: (318) 357-4223   **Internet:** www.nsula.edu

Institution Description: Northwestern State University of Louisiana is a state institution and land-grant college. *Enrollment:* 10,546. *Degrees awarded:* Associate, baccalaureate, master's.

Academic offerings subject to approval by statewide coordinating bodies. Budget subject to approval by state governing boards.

Accreditation: *Regional:* SACS-Comm. on Coll. *Professional:* business, chemistry, counseling, family and consumer science, industrial technology, journalism, music, nursing, nursing education, radiography, social work, teacher education, theatre, veterinary technology

History: Established as Louisiana Normal School 1884; offered first instruction at postsecondary level 1885; became 4-year institution and changed name to Louisiana State Normal College 1918; awarded first degree (baccalaureate) 1919; changed name to Northwestern State College of Louisiana 1944; chartered 1957; adopted present name 1970.

Institutional Structure: *Governing board:* State of Louisiana Board of Trustees for State Colleges and Universities. Representation: 15 trustees, including 1 student (all appointed by governor of Louisiana). All voting. *Composition of institution:* Administrators 50. Academic affairs headed by provost and vice president of academic affairs. Business/finances directed by vice president for business affairs and controller. Full-time instructional faculty 303. Academic governance body, Curriculum Review Council, meets an average of 10 times per year.

Calendar: Semesters. Academic year Aug. to May. Freshmen admitted Aug., Jan., June. Degrees conferred and formal commencements May, Dec. Summer session from May to Aug.

Characteristics of Freshmen: 90.7% of applicants admitted. 54.7% of applicants admitted and enrolled.

7% (138 students) submitted SAT scores; 89% (1,663 students) submitted ACT scores. *25th percentile:* SAT Verbal 430, SAT Math 430; ACT Composite 16, ACT English 15, ACT Math 16. *75th percentile:* SAT Verbal 580, SAT Math 580; ACT Composite 21, ACT English 22, ACT Math 20.

28% of entering freshmen expected to graduate within five years. 92% of freshmen from Louisiana. Freshmen from 23 states and 5 foreign countries.

Admission: Rolling admissions plan. Apply as early as 1 year before registration. *Requirements:* In-state freshmen must complete the Louisiana core curriculum, need no more than one developmental class and meet one of the following: minimum of 20 on ACT Composite score or minimum of 940 of combined math/verbal, or have a high school GPA of 2.0, or rank in top 50% of high school graduating class. Out-of-state freshmen must meet the same requirements as in-state students or score a minimum of 20 on ACT (or 940 on SAT) and need no more than one developmental course and have a high school GPA of 20 or above or rank in top 50% of high school class or score a minimum o 23 on ACT (1060 on SAT). *For transfer students:* Transfer credit varies. Students with fewer than 12 earned hours must meet freshmen requirements.

Advanced placement for postsecondary-level work completed in secondary school. College credit for extrainstitutional learning on basis of ACE *2006 Guide to the Evaluation of Educational Experiences in the Armed Services.*

Degree Requirements: *For all associate degrees:* 60 credit hours excluding physical activity; minimum of 2.0 GPA on required courses; minimum of 25% of earned degree hours from NSU. *For all baccalaureate degrees:* 120 credit hours; last 30 hours in residence. *For all undergraduate degrees:* 2.0 GPA; general education requirements.

Fulfillment of some degree requirements possible by passing departmental examinations, College Board CLEP. *Grading system:* A–F; pass-fail; withdraw; incomplete.

Distinctive Educational Programs: Flexible meeting places; Online degree programs in various fields. Facilities and programs for independent research, including honors programs, individual majors. *Other distinctive programs:* Continuing education for nontraditional students. Louisiana Scholars College, a selective admissions college for exceptional college students is located on the NSU campus.

ROTC: Army. 14 commissions awarded 2004.

Degrees Conferred: 193 *associate*; 1,019 *baccalaureate* (B); 232 *master's*(M): biological/life sciences 47 (B); business/marketing 184 (B); communications/communication technologies 25 (B); computer and information sciences 39 (B); education 89 (B), engineering and engineering technologies 27 (B); English 13 (B), 9 (M); health professions and related sciences 118 (B), 22 (M); home economics and vocational home economics 19 (B); liberal arts/general studies 192 (B); mathematics 8 (B); physical sciences 6 (B); protective services/public administration 83 (B); psychology 78 (B), 8 (M); social sciences and history 49 (B), 1 (M); visual and performing arts 42 (B), 9 (M).

Fees and Other Expenses: *Full-time tuition per academic year 2004–05:* undergraduate resident $2,144, nonresident $8,222. Contact the university for current graduate tuition/fees. *Required fees:* $1,097. *Room per academic year:* $1,850. *Board per academic year:* $1,576.

Financial Aid: Aid from institutionally generated funds is provided on the basis of academic merit, athletic ability, other criteria. Institution has a Program Participation Agreement with the U.S. Department of Education for eligible students to receive Pell Grants and other federal aid.

Financial aid to full-time, first-time undergraduate students: need-based scholarships/grants totaling $12,810,262, self-help $13,078,368; non-need-based scholarships/grants totaling $8,190,727, self-help $11,992,376, parent loans $224,936, tuition waivers $2,153,816, athletic awards $1,575,047. *Graduate aid:* 10 students received federal and state-funded fellowships/grants totaling $10,760; 338 received federal and state-funded loans totaling $98,815, 19 students held held college-assigned jobs totaling $15,654; 339 received fellowships and grants totaling $42,029.

Departments and Teaching Staff: *Professors* 42, *associate professors* 69, *assistant professors* 131, *instructors* 61, *part-time faculty* 313. *Total instructional faculty:* 616 (full-time 303, part-time 313; women 324, men 292; members of minority groups 70). Total faculty with doctorate, first-professional, or other terminal degree: 70. Student-to-faculty ratio: 21:1.

Enrollment: Total enrollment 10,546. Undergraduate full-time 2,636 men / 4,314 women, part-time 562m / 1,902w; graduate full-time 95m / 178w, part-time 167m / 692w. *Transfer students:* in-state 567; from out-of-state 68.

Characteristics of Student Body: *Ethnic/racial makeup:* number of Black non-Hispanic: 2,951; American Indian or Alaska Native: 182; Asian or Pacific Islander: 82; Hispanic: 168; White non-Hispanic: 5,530; unknown: 439. *Age distribution:* number under 18: 245; 18–19: 2,735; 20–21: 2,334; 22–24: 1,552; 25–29: 942; 30–34: 371; 35–39: 390; 40–49: 50–64: 482; 65 and over: 22.

International Students: 48 nonresident aliens enrolled fall 2004. 15 students from Europe, 4 Asia, 11 Central and South America, 6 Africa, 8 Canada, 2 Australia, 1 other. No programs available to aid students whose native language is not English. No financial aid specifically designated for international students.

Student Life: On-campus residence halls house 23% of student body. Some men join and live in fraternities. Housing available for married students. *Intercollegiate athletics:* men only: baseball, basketball, football, track; women only, basketball, softball, tennis, volleyball, track. *Special regulations:* Cars permitted without restrictions. *Special services:* Medical services. *Student publications, radio:* ARGUS, a biannual magazine; *Current Sauce,* a weekly newspaper; *Potpourri,* a yearbook. Radio station KNWD broadcasts 42 hours per week. *Surrounding community:* Natchitoches population 18,000. New Orleans, 300 miles from campus, is nearest metropolitan area.

Publications: *Southern Studies: An Interdisciplinary Journal of the South* (quarterly). Northwestern State University Press, established in 1979, is one of two university presses in the state of Louisiana dedicated to the publication and distribution of scholarly materials.

Library Collections: 323,931 volumes. 30,000 government documents; Current serial subscriptions: 1,898 paper; 11,423 microform. 145 compact discs. 530 CD-ROMs. Online catalog. Access to online information retrieval systems and the Internet.

Most important holdings include Melrose Plantation Collection; Caroline Dorman Collection; C.F. Gauss Collection.

Buildings and Grounds: Campus area 840 acres. *New buildings:* Wellness and Recreation Center completed 2005; Modified Residential Housing 2005.

Chief Executive Officer: Dr. Randall J. Webb, President.

Address inquiries to Jana Lucky, Director of Admissions.

Notre Dame Seminary Graduate School of Theology

2901 South Carrollton Avenue
New Orleans, Louisiana 70118-4391

Tel: (504) 866-7426   **E-mail:** admissions@nds.edu
Fax: (504) 866-1301   **Internet:** www.nds.edu

Institution Description: Notre Dame Seminary Graduate School of Theology is a private institution affiliated with the Archdiocese of New Orleans, Roman Catholic Church. *Enrollment:* 151. *Degrees awarded:* First-professional (master of divinity), master's.

Member of New Orleans Consortium.

Accreditation: *Regional:* SACS-Comm. on Coll. *National:* ATS. *Professional:* theology

History: Established as Notre Dame Seminary and offered first instruction at postsecondary level 1923; chartered 1948; incorporated and awarded first degree (baccalaureate) 1950; discontinued baccalaureate program and adopted present name 1968.

Institutional Structure: *Governing board:* Notre Dame Seminary Board of Trustees. Representation: 17 trustees, including president-rector of the institution, 1 student; 7 alumni. 23 voting. *Composition of institution:* Administrators 9 men / 2 women. Academic affairs headed by president-rector. Management/business/finances directed by Business Manager. Full-time instructional faculty 14.

Calendar: Semesters. Academic year late Aug. to mid-May. Freshmen admitted Aug., Jan. Degrees conferred and formal commencement May.

Characteristics of Freshmen: 99% of applicants accepted. 99% of accepted applicants enrolled. 80% of entering students expected to graduate within 5 years. 95% of entering students from Louisiana. Entering students from 6 states, 1 foreign country.

Admission: Rolling admissions plan. For fall acceptance, apply no later than July. *For first-professional degree:* minimum GPA 2.0. *For master's degree:* proficiency examination in foreign language. Minimum GPA 2.7. *For both degrees:* baccalaureate degree from accredited college or the equivalent with 18 semester hours philosophy. *Entrance tests:* GRE.

Degree Requirements: *For first-professional degree:* 125 credit hours (master's); 2.0 GPA; 2 terms in residence; exit competency examinations (oral and written comprehensives in individual field of study). *For master's degree:* 37 credit hours; 3.0 GPA; exit competency examinations (written comprehensives in individual field of study; thesis). *For both degrees:* Distribution requirements. *Grading system:* A–F; pass-fail; withdraw (carries time limit).

Distinctive Educational Programs: Internships. Cross-registration through consortium. *Other distinctive programs:* First-professional degree program available through continuing education.

Degrees Conferred: 2 *master's:* theology/theological studies; 19 *first-professional:* master of divinity.

Fees and Other Expenses: *Full-time tuition per academic year 2004–05:* Contact the seminary for current information.

Financial Aid: Aid from institutionally generated funds is provided on the basis of financial need. Institution has a Program Participation Agreement with the U.S. Department of Education for eligible students to receive Pell Grants and other federal aid.

Departments and Teaching Staff: Theology *professors* 14, *part-time teachers* 18. *Total instructional faculty:* 32. Degrees held by full-time faculty: doctorate 71%, master's 29%.

Enrollment: Total enrollment 151 (84.8% men, 15.2% women).

Characteristics of Student Body: *Ethnic/racial makeup:* Black non-Hispanic: 1.3%; Asian or Pacific Islander: 4.6%; Hispanic: 2%; White non-Hispanic: 72.8%.

International Students: 14 undergraduate nonresident aliens enrolled fall 2004. No programs available to aid students whose native language is not English. No financial aid specifically designated for international students.

Student Life: On-campus residence halls house 72% of student body. Residence halls for men constitute 100% of such space. *Special regulations:* Cars permitted without restrictions. *Student radio/TV:* Archdiocesan Educational Television Station WLAE-TV broadcasts instructional television for school children, adult learning courses, and daily presentations of the Rosary and weekly vigil mass. *Surrounding community:* New Orleans population over 500,000. Served by mass transit bus and rail system; airport 30 miles from campus, passenger rail service 7 miles from campus.

Library Collections: 97,000 volumes including bound periodicals.

Most important holdings include *Complutensian Polyglot* (a 6-volume Bible dating from early 16th century).

Chief Executive Officer: V. Rev. Patrick J. Williams, President-Rector.

Address admission inquiries to Academic Dean.

Our Lady of Holy Cross College

4123 Woodland Drive
New Orleans, Louisiana 70131-7399
Tel: (504) 394-7744   **E-mail:** admissions@olhcc.edu
Fax: (504) 391-2421   **Internet:** www.olhcc.edu

Institution Description: Our Lady of Holy Cross College is a private institution affiliated with the Roman Catholic Church. *Enrollment:* 1,997. *Degrees awarded:* Associate, baccalaureate, master's.

Accreditation: *Regional:* SACS-Comm. on Coll. *Professional:* nursing

History: Established 1916.

Institutional Structure: *Governing board:* Board of Regents. Extrainstitutional representation: 25 trustees; institutional representation: president of college. 2 ex officio. All voting. *Composition of institution:* Administrators 10. Academic affairs headed by academic dean. vice president. Management/business/finances directed by controller. Full-time instructional faculty 31.

Calendar: Semesters. Academic year July to May. Summer session of 2 terms from June to Aug.

Characteristics of Freshmen: 90% of applicants accepted. 89% of accepted applicants enrolled.

Mean ACT composite score 20. 75% of entering freshmen expected to graduate within 5 years. 99% of freshmen from Louisiana.

Admission: Rolling admissions plan. Early acceptance available. *Requirements:* Either graduation from accredited secondary school or GED. *Entrance tests:* College Board SAT or ACT composite. For international students TOEFL. *For transfer students:* Correspondence/extension students 60 credit hours maximum transfer credit.

Degree Requirements: 130 credit hours; minimum grade of C in all courses of academic specialization; last 30 hours in residence; core curriculum. Exemption from some beginning courses possible by passing departmental examinations. *Grading system:* A–F; pass; withdraw (deadline after which pass-fail is appended to withdraw); incomplete.

Distinctive Educational Programs: Independent study. Experiential learning.

ROTC: Air Force in cooperation with University of New Orleans and Tulane University.

Degrees Conferred: 3 *associate;* 147 *baccalaureate:* biological/life sciences 5; business/marketing 27; computer and information sciences 2; education 4; English31 home economics and vocational home economics 53; liberal arts/general studies 19; philosophy/religion/theology 1; social sciences and history 25.

Fees and Other Expenses: *Full-time tuition per academic year 2004–05:* undergraduate $7,350; graduate $5,720.

Financial Aid: Aid from institutionally generated funds is provided on the basis of academic merit, financial need.Institution has a Program Participation Agreement with the U.S. Department of Education for eligible students to receive Pell Grants and other federal aid.

Departments and Teaching Staff: Applied, Natural, and Social Sciences *professors* 0, *associate professors* 3, *assistant professors* 2, *instructors* 2, *part-time teachers* 41; Humanities, Education, and Counseling 3, 5, 4, 3, 28; Nursing 0, 3, 5, 1, 5.

Total instructional faculty: 125 (full-time 43, part-time 82). Student-to-faculty ratio: 21:1. Degrees held by full-time faculty: doctorate 61%, master's 39%.

Enrollment: Total enrollment 1,997. Undergraduate full-time 295 men / 998 women, part-time 100m / 377w; graduate full-time 16m / 13w, part-time 22m / 77w. *Transfer students:* in-state 205.

Characteristics of Student Body: *Ethnic/racial makeup:* number of Black non-Hispanic: 139; American Indian or Alaska Native: 23; Asian or Pacific Islander: 42; Hispanic: 75; White non-Hispanic: 964. *Age distribution:* 17–21: 28%; 22–27: 39%; 28–33 14%; 34–39: 8%; 40–49: 7%; 50–59: 3%; 60–up: .3%. 43% of total student body attend summer sessions.

International Students: 5 nonresident aliens enrolled fall 2004. 1 student from Asia, 4 Africa. No programs available to aid students whose native language is not English. No financial aid specifically designated for international students.

Student Life: *Special regulations:* Cars permitted in designated areas. *Special services:* Medical services. *Student activities:* Social, professional, honor clubs and organizations; intramural sports; access to fitness center. *Student publications:* Calliope, a literary magazine; *The Hurricane Watch*, a newspaper. *Surrounding community:* New Orleans population over 500,000.

Publications: *Crossnotes*, a newsletter; *The Holy Cross Report*, and *Parlons*.

Library Collections: 85,500 volumes including bound books, serial backfiles, electronic documents, and government documents not in separate collections. Online catalog. Current serial subscriptions: 970 paper, microform, and electronic. 18 CD-ROMs. 8 computer work stations. Students have access to the Internet at no charge.

Most important holdings include Richard Dixon Collection; Tom Fox Collection; Sidney Villere Genealogy Collection.

Buildings and Grounds: Campus area 40 acres.

Chief Executive Officer: Dr. Paul T. Ceasar, O.S.C, President.

Address admissions inquiries to Kristine Kopecky, Vice President for Enrollment Services.

St. Joseph Seminary College

75376 River Road
St. Benedict, Louisiana 70457
Tel: (504) 867-2232   **E-mail:** acdean@sjasc.edu
Fax: (504) 867-2270   **Internet:** www.sjasc.edu

Institution Description: St. Joseph Seminary College is a private men's college affiliated with the Order of St. Benedict, Roman Catholic Church. *Enrollment:* 171. Women are admitted as unclassified students. *Degrees awarded:* Baccalaureate.

Accreditation: *Regional:* SACS-Comm. on Coll.

History: Established as St. Joseph Preparatory Seminary 1891; offered first instruction at postsecondary level 1892; awarded first degree (associate) 1894; changed name to St. Joseph's College 1898; chartered 1903; changed name to St. Joseph Seminary 1911; adopted present name 1969.

Institutional Structure: *Governing board:* Board of Trustees of St. Joseph Seminary College. Extrainstitutional representation: 21 trustees, including archbishop of New Orleans; institutional representation: president of the college. 2 ex officio. 21 voting. *Composition of institution:* Administrators 11 men / 2 women. Academic affairs headed by academic dean. Management/business/finances directed by business officer. Academic governance body, Academic Affairs Committee, meets an average of 6 times per year.

Calendar: Semesters. Academic year Aug. to May. Freshmen admitted Aug., Jan. Degrees conferred and formal commencement May.

Characteristics of Freshmen: 27 applicants (27 men). 100% of applicants admitted. 100% of admitted students enrolled. Mean ACT Composite score 21.

70% of entering freshmen expected to graduate within 5 years. 92% of freshmen from Louisiana. Freshmen from 2 states.

Admission: Rolling admissions plan. For fall acceptance, apply as early as Jan. of year of enrollment, but not later than day of registration. *Requirements:* Either graduation from accredited secondary school with 17 academic units which normally include 3 English, 2 foreign language, 2 mathematics, 2 science, 1 U.S. history, additional units from among English, a secondary foreign language, mathematics, and social studies; or GED. Minimum GPA 2.0. *Entrance tests:* ACT composite. *For transfer students:* 2.0 GPA; 100 semester hours maximum transfer credit; correspondence/extension students 6 hours.

Advanced placement for postsecondary-level work completed in secondary school. Tutoring available. Developmental courses offered during regular academic year; credit given.

Degree Requirements: 124 semester hours; 2.0 GPA; 2 semesters in residence; daily chapel attendance; distribution requirements. Fulfillment of some degree requirements and exemption from some beginning courses possible by passing departmental examinations, College Board CLEP. *Grading system:* A–F; pass-fail; withdraw (deadline after which pass-fail is appended to withdraw).

Distinctive Educational Programs: Special facilities for using telecommunications in the classroom. Interdisciplinary courses in religion and history, philosophy, and psychology. Tutorials.

Degrees Conferred: 20 *baccalaureate:* liberal arts and sciences, general studies, and humanities.

Fees and Other Expenses: *Full-time tuition per academic year 2004–05:* $10,085. *Books and supplies:* $1,000. *Room and board per academic year:* $5,915.

Financial Aid: Aid from institutionally generated funds is provided on the basis of financial need. Institution has a Program Participation Agreement with the U.S. Department of Education for eligible students to receive Pell Grants and other federal aid.

Financial aid to full-time, first-time undergraduate students: 25% received federal grants; 25% state/local grants.

Departments and Teaching Staff: *Total instructional faculty:* 26. Student-to-faculty ratio: 12.5:1. Degrees held by faculty: doctorate 13%, master's 13%. 50% hold terminal degrees.

Enrollment: Total enrollment 171 (66.1% men, 33.9% women).

Characteristics of Student Body: *Ethnic/racial makeup:* Black non-Hispanic: 2.3%; Asian or Pacific Islander: 2.9%; Hispanic: 13.5%; White non-Hispanic: 80.1%; unknown: 2.9%.

International Students: Programs to aid students whose native language is not English: English as a Second Language. No financial aid specifically designated for international students.

Student Life: On-campus residence halls house 84% of student body. Residence halls for men only constitute 100% of such space. *Special regulations:* Cars must be registered ($5 fee). Quiet hours 24 hours per day. Residence hall visitation from 6am to 11:15pm. *Special services:* Medical services. *Surrounding community:* St. Benedict is located in St. Tammany Parish. New Orleans, 45 miles from campus, is nearest metropolitan area.

Library Collections: 65,000 volumes including bound books, serial backfiles, electronic documents, and government documents not in separate collections. Online and card catalogs. Current serial subscriptions: 157 paper. 150 recordings; 50 compact discs; 32 CD-ROMs. Computer work stations available. Students have access to the Internet at no charge.

Most important holdings include the philosophy collection (3,800 volumes on Plato, Aristotle, Thomas Aquinas, Kant, and the existentialists); the Natchez Collection (2,800 volumes published between 1610 and 1940, and mid-19th century Catholic newspapers and Bible commentaries, all part of the library of the office of the bishop of Natchez, Miss., between 1837 and 1940). Library serves as depository for St. Tammany Parish Historical Society (some original material dates back to 1870; copies of older material included).

Buildings and Grounds: Campus area 31 acres.

Chief Executive Officer: Rev. Gregory M. Boquet, OSB, President-Rector.

Address admission inquiries to Dr. Edward Dupuy, Academic Dean.

Southeastern Louisiana University

SLU 107784
University Station
Hammond, Louisiana 704020001

Tel: (985) 549-2000   **E-mail:** admissions@selu.edu
Fax: (985) 549-5632   **Internet:** www.selu.edu

Institution Description: Southeastern Louisiana University is a state institution. *Enrollment:* 15,462. *Degrees awarded:* Associate, baccalaureate, master's.

Accreditation: *Regional:* SACS-Comm. on Coll. *Professional:* accounting, business, chemistry, computer science, counseling, family and consumer science, industrial technology, music, nursing, social work, speech-language pathology, teacher education

History: Established and chartered as Hammond Junior College, and offered first instruction at postsecondary level 1925; became 4-year institution and changed name to Southeastern Louisiana College 1928; awarded first degree (baccalaureate) 1939; adopted present name 1970. *See* LeRoy Ancelet, *A History of Southeastern Louisiana College* (Baton Rouge: Louisiana State University, 1971) for further information.

Institutional Structure: *Governing board:* Supervisors for the University of Louisiana System. Representation: 2 members from each congressional district and 1 member from the state at large, appointed by the governor with consent of the Senate. *Composition of institution:* Administrators 105 men / 99 women. Academic affairs headed by vice president for academic affairs. Management/business/finances directed by vice president for administration and finance. Full-time instructional faculty 497. Academic governance body, Faculty Senate, meets an average of 10 times per year.

Calendar: Semesters. Academic year early June to late May. Freshmen admitted Aug., Jan., June. Degrees conferred and formal commencements May, Dec. Summer session from early June to late July.

Characteristics of Freshmen: 94% of applicants admitted. 77% of applicants admitted and enrolled.

100% 2,538 (students) submitted ACT scores. *25th percentile:* ACT Composite 18, ACT English 18, ACT Math 17. *75th percentile:* ACT Composite 22, ACT English 23, ACT Math 22.

19% of entering freshmen expected to graduate within 5 years. 97% of freshmen from Louisiana. Freshmen from 28 states and 19 foreign countries.

Admission: Rolling admissions plan. Apply no later than 1 month before registration. Early acceptance available. *Requirements:* Graduation from accredited secondary school in the upper 50% of graduating class or ACT composite of 20 or higher or high school GPA of 2.0 on the core set of courses listed below. English 4 units; mathematics 3 units, science 3 units, social studies 3 units, electives 4.5 units for a total of 17.5 units. *Entrance tests:* ACT. For foreign students TOEFL. *For transfer students:* Student transferring with less than 12 hours of college credit must meet the admissions criteria of entering freshmen mentioned above; student with 12 hours or more of college credit must have a cumulative GPA of 2.0.

College credit and advanced placement for postsecondary-level work completed in secondary school. College credit for extrainstitutional learning on basis of ACE *2006 Guide to the Evaluation of Educational Experiences in the Armed Services.* Tutoring available. Noncredit developmental courses offered in summer session and regular academic year.

Degree Requirements: *For all associate degrees:* 60–69 credit hours; completion of the last final 15 hours in residence. *For all baccalaureate degrees:* 119–132 credit hours; final 30 hours in residence. *For all undergraduate degrees:* 2.0 GPA; general education requirements. Additional requirements for some programs.

Fulfillment of some degree requirements and exemption from some beginning courses possible by passing departmental examinations, College Board CLEP, AP, other standardized tests. *Grading system:* A–F; pass-fail; pass; withdraw (carries time limit).

Distinctive Educational Programs: Work-experience programs, including cooperative education, internships. Flexible meeting places and schedules, including off-campus centers (at Mandeville, 30 miles away from main campus; New Orleans, 40 miles away); Internet courses, compressed video courses, live TV courses, evening classes. Honors Programs. Institutionally sponsored study abroad in Austria, Brazil, Canada, Costa Rica, Honduras, Italy, France, United Kingdom. *Other distinctive programs:* Continuing education; MBA Program; Integrated Science and Technology Program; Master of Arts in Teaching Program.

ROTC: Army in cooperation with Louisiana State University.

Degrees Conferred: 69 *associate;* 1,586 *baccalaureate* (B); 323 *master's* (M): agriculture 3 (B); biological/life sciences 59 (B), 8 (M); business/marketing 584 (B), 99 (M); communications/communication technologies 60 (B), 11 (M); computer and information sciences 25 (B); education 231 (B), 133 (M); engineering and engineering technologies 44 (B); English 25 (B), 6 (M); health professions and related sciences 115 (B), 41 (M); home economics and vocational home economics 35 (B); interdisciplinary studies 4 (M); liberal arts/general studies 160 (B); mathematics 10 (B); physical sciences 3 (B); protective services/public administration 91 (B); psychology 47 (B), 8 (M); social sciences and history 54 (B), 5 (M); visual and performing arts 35 (B), 8 (M).

Fees and Other Expenses: *Full-time tuition per academic year 2004–05:* undergraduate resident $3,191, nonresident $8,519; graduate resident $2,986, nonresident $6,982. *Room and board per academic year:* $4,290.

Financial Aid: Aid from institutionally generated funds is provided on the basis of academic merit, financial need, athletic ability, other criteria. Institution has a Program Participation Agreement with the U.S. Department of Education for eligible students to receive Pell Grants and other federal aid.

Financial aid to full-time, first-time undergraduate students: need-based scholarships/grants totaling $16,109,695, self-help $19,077,552; non-need-based scholarships/grants totaling $7,695,893, self-help $15,597,108, parent loans $719,137, tuition waivers $528,175, athletic awards $642,959. *Graduate aid:* 26 students received $53,325 in federal and state-funded fellowships/grants; 730 received $5,609,883 in federal and state-funded loans; 10 received $14,839 for work-study jobs; 167 received $421,759 for college-assigned jobs; 12 received other fellowships/grants totaling $25,000; 17 teaching assistantships awarded totaling $55,610; 66 research assistantships awarded totaling $235,382.

Departments and Teaching Staff: *Professors 66, associate professors 84, assistant professors 146, instructors 183. Total instructional faculty:* 730 (full-time 497, part-time 233; women 408, men 322; members of minority groups 65). Total faculty with doctorate, first-professional, or other terminal degree: 342. Student-to-faculty ratio: 27:1. *Faculty development:* $4,071,125 in grants for research.

Enrollment: Total enrollment 15,462. Undergraduate full-time 4,459 men / 6,698 women, part-time 787m / 1,720w; graduate full-time 158m / 321w, part-time 250m / 1,079w. *Transfer students:* in-state 3,330; from out-of-state 751.

Characteristics of Student Body: *Ethnic/racial makeup:* number of Black non-Hispanic: 2,203; American Indian or Alaska Native: 51; Asian or Pacific Islander: 80; Hispanic: 192; White non-Hispanic: 10,766; unknown: 272. *Age distribution:* number under 18: 257; 18–19: 4,147; 20–21: 3,444; 22–24: 2,903; 25–29: 1,392; 30–34: 604; 35–39: 325; 40–49: 426; 50–64: 168; 65 and over: 18. 36% of student body attend summer sessions.

International Students: 153 nonresident aliens enrolled fall 2004. 63 students from Europe, 36 Asia, 25 Central and South America, 13 Africa, 15 Canada, 1 Australia, 1 New Zealand, 9 other. Programs available to aid students whose native language is not English: social, cultural. English as a Second Language. Financial aid available for qualifying undergraduate international students. 3 scholarships awarded in 2004–05 totaling $7,281.

Student Life: On-campus residence halls house 10% of student body. *Intercollegiate athletics:* men: baseball, basketball, cheerleading, cross-country, football, golf, tennis, track and field; women: basketball, cheerleading, cross-country, soccer, softball, tennis, track and field, volleyball. *Special regulations:* Registered cars permitted in designated areas only. *Special services:* Learning Resources Center, counseling and medical services. *Student publications, radio:* Lion's Roar, a weekly newspaper. Radio station KSLU. Southern Channel TV station. *Surrounding community:* Hammond population 18,000. New Orleans, 55 miles from campus, is nearest metropolitan area. Served by passenger rail service 1 mile from campus.

Publications: *Economic Reporter* is published quarterly and contains articles and statistic data of the economy of the region; *Louisiana Literature* is a literary magazine published twice yearly; *The Gambit* is a biannual journal of creative writing. *The Pick* is an annual journal of exceptional writing from across the curriculum.

Library Collections: 603,303 volumes including bound books, serial backfiles, electronic documents, and government documents not in separate collections. Online catalog. Current serial subscriptions: 1,542 paper, 15,498 microform; 301 via electronic access. 280 computer work stations. Students have access to the Internet at no charge. Total budget for books, periodicals, audiovisual materials, microforms 2004–05: $972,760.

Special collections are housed in the Center for Regional Studies. Most important holdings include Congressman James Morrison Papers; Kennedy Assassination Papers; local genealogy collection.

Buildings and Grounds: Campus area 365 acres. *New buildings:* Student Activity Center completed 2001; Fayard Hall 2001; Southeastern Oaks 2001; major addition to Teacher Education Center 2003; President Residence 2005.

Chief Executive Officer: Dr. Randy Moffett, President.

Address admission inquiries to Sam Dominano, Director of New Student Enrollment and Student Aid; graduate inquiries to Sandra Meyers, Graduate Admissions.

College of Arts, Humanities, and Social Sciences

Degree Programs Offered: *Associate* in criminal justice, industrial technology, general studies; *baccalaureate* in art, biology, chemistry, communication, criminal justice, cultural resource management, English, French, general studies, history, horticulture, industrial technology, liberal arts studies, mathematics, music, physics, political science, psychology, sociology, social work, Spanish; *master's* in biology, English, history, music, psychology.

College of Business

Degree Programs Offered: *Associate* in office administration; *baccalaureate* in accounting, management, marketing, general business; *master's* in business administration.

College of Education and Human Development

Degree Programs Offered: *Baccalaureate* in communication education, business education, elementary education, English education, music education, special education, speech/language and hearing, communication education, family and consumer science, French education, kinesiology, science education, social studies teaching, Spanish education; *master's* in special education, communication sciences and disorders, health and kinesiology, curriculum and instruction.

College of General Studies

Degree Programs Offered: *Associate, baccalaureate* in general studies.

College of Nursing and Health Sciences

Degree Programs Offered: *Baccalaureate* in speech, language, and hearing; kinesiology, athletic training, health education and promotion; nursing; *master's* in nursing, communication sciences and disorders, health, kinesiology.

College of Science and Technology

Degree Programs Offered: *Associate* in industrial technology; *baccalaureate* in biological sciences, horticulture, chemistry, physics, computer science, mathematics, industrial technology, occupational health.

Southern University and A&M College

Southern University Branch Post Office
Baton Rouge, Louisiana 70813
Tel: (225) 771-2430   **E-mail:** admissions@subr.edu
Fax: (225) 771-2500   **Internet:** www.subr.edu

Institution Description: *Enrollment:* 9,400. *Degrees awarded:* Associate, baccalaureate, first-professional (law), master's, doctorate Special education certificates also awarded.

Accreditation: *Regional:* SACS-Comm. on Coll. *Professional:* architecture, business, computer science, dietetics, engineering, family and consumer science, journalism, law, music, nursing, nursing education, public administration, rehabilitation counseling, social work, speech-language pathology, teacher education

History: Established as Southern University in New Orleans and chartered 1880; offered first instruction on postsecondary level 1881; adopted present name 1890; recognized as land-grant college 1892; awarded first degree (baccalaureate) 1912. Law Center established 1947; Graduate School established 1957.

Institutional Structure: *Composition of institution:* Campus administration is headed by chancellor; vice chancellors for academic affairs, finance and administration, research and strategic initiatives, university college. Senior leadership includes directors of planning, assessment and institutional research, athletics, Office of Technology and Network services, executive assistant to the chancellor, associate vice chancellor fore academic affairs, assistant to the chancellor for public relations, corporate scholarship coordinator. Full-time instructional 420. Faculty governance body, Faculty Senate, meets regularly.

Calendar: Semesters. Academic year Aug. to May. Freshmen admitted Aug., Jan., June. Degrees conferred and formal commencements May, Aug., Dec. Maymester 3 weeks prior to summer session. 3 summer sessions from early June to early Aug.

Characteristics of Freshmen: 54.4% of applicants admitted. 61.3% of applicants admitted and enrolled.

15% (224 students) submitted SAT scores; 99% (1,494 students) submitted ACT scores. *25th percentile:* SAT Verbal 380, SAT Math 370; ACT Composite 16, ACT English 15, ACT Math 15. *75th percentile:* SAT Verbal 470, SAT Math 480; ACT Composite 20, ACT English 20, ACT Math 18.

18.4% of entering freshmen expected to graduate within 5 years. 77% of freshmen from Louisiana. Freshmen from 33 states and 9 foreign countries.

Admission: Open admissions plan. Apply as early as 1 year prior to enrollment. Early acceptance available. *Requirements:* Graduation from secondary school or GED. First-time freshmen must submit an ACT score of 17 or 830 SAT or a 2.2GPA on a 4.0 scale; 4 units of English, 3 math, 3 natural science, 3 social science. Admission standards will change effective January 2006. Contact the university catalog for the new requirements. *Entrance tests:* ACT Composite or SAT. For foreign students TOEFL. *For transfer students:* 2.0 minimum GPA; 93 hours maximum transfer credit; good standing at institution previously attended.

College credit and advanced placement for postsecondary-level work completed in secondary school.

Degree Requirements: Degree requirements are measured in terms of quantitative and qualitative standards. Requirements for individual colleges and school may differ. The total number of credit hours and the quality points required may vary according to curricula. Baccalaureate degrees require a minimum of 124 semester hours; master's degrees 30 semester hours; doctoral degrees 60 semester hours beyond the bachelors degree. Refer to the college catalog for specific requirements.

Distinctive Educational Programs: Study Abroad Program is coordinated by the Division of Continuing Education. Evening and Weekend Program. Distance Education provides select courses for bachelor's, master, degree, or certification programs through a variety of delivery options. Programs for persons over 55; persons who register for one or more courses and are residents of Louisiana, are exempt from the payment of tuition and registration fees.

ROTC: Army, Navy, Air Force. 1 Air Force, 4 Navy, and 5 Army commissions awarded 2004.

Degrees Conferred: 18 *associate;* 941 *baccalaureate* (B), 263 *master's:* (M), 11 *doctorate* (D): agriculture 12 (B); architecture 3 (B); biological/life sciences 27 (B), 5 (M); business/marketing 144 (B); communications/communication technologies 44 (B), 9 (M); computer and information sciences 54 (B), 18 (M); education 47 (B), 123 (M); 6 (D); engineering and engineering technologies 84 (B), 6 (M); English 8 (B); foreign languages and literature 1 (B); health professions and related sciences 179 (B), 45 (B), 4 (D); home economics and vocational home economics 47 (B); mathematics 10 (B), 5 (M); natural resources/environmental science 6 (B), 6 (M); physical sciences 17 (B), 6 (M); protective services/public administration 97 (B), 33 (M), 1 (D); psychology 75 (B); social sciences and history 75 (B), 7 (M); visual and performing arts 11. *Honorary degrees awarded 2004–05:* Doctorate of Business 2, Doctorate of Public Policy 2, Doctorate of Humane Letters 1.

Fees and Other Expenses: *Full-time tuition per academic year 2004–05:* resident undergraduate $3,488, nonresident $9,280; resident graduate $3,506, nonresident $8,672. *Room per academic year:* $2,756. *Board per academic year:* $1,780.

Financial Aid: Aid from institutionally generated funds is provided on the basis of academic merit, financial need, athletic ability. Institution has a Program Participation Agreement with the U.S. Department of Education for eligible students to receive Pell Grants and other federal aid.

Financial aid to full-time, first-time undergraduate students: need-based scholarships/grants totaling $75,228,000, self-help $46,911; non-need-based scholarships/grants totaling $57,500,000, self-help $750,000. *Graduate aid:* 267 students received $497,310 in federal and state-funded fellowships/grants; 1,421 received $10,422,243 in federal and state-funded loans; 6 received $11,967 for college-assigned jobs; 1 student received a fellowship for $4,832; 180 research assistantships were awarded totaling $808,564.

Departments and Teaching Staff: *Professors* 112, *associate professors* 98, *assistant professors* 140, *instructors* 70, *part-time faculty* 141. *Total instructional faculty:* 561 (full-time 420, part-time 141; women 286, men 275; members of minority groups 412). Total faculty with doctorate, first-professional, or other terminal degree: 339. Student-to-faculty ratio: 18:1. *Faculty development:* $25,861,632 total grants for research. 1 faculty member awarded a sabbatical 2004–5.

Enrollment: Total enrollment 9,400. Undergraduate full-time 2,850 men / 4,458 women, part-time 244m / 471w; graduate full-time 184m / 436w; part-time 190m / 567w. *Transfer students:* in-state 183; from out-of-state 70.

Characteristics of Student Body: *Ethnic/racial makeup:* number of Black non-Hispanic: 8,924; American Indian or Alaska Native: 5; Asian or Pacific Islander: 106; Hispanic: 8; White non-Hispanic: 233. *Age distribution:* number under 18: 25; 18–19: 2,366; 20–21: 2,195; 22–24: 2,043; 25–29: 770; 30–34: 290; 35–39: 129; 40–49: 173; 50–64: 39; 65 and over: 3. 33.4% of student body attend summer sessions.

International Students: 124 nonresident aliens enrolled fall 2004. Programs available to aid students whose native language is not English: social, cultural. English as a Second Language Program. No financial aid specifically designated for international students.

Student Life: On-campus residence halls. All unmarried full-time undergraduate first-time freshmen students regardless of age are required to live in on-campus residence halls and are required to purchase a meal plan. *Intercollegiate athletics:* men only: baseball, basketball, cross-country, football, indoor track and field, tennis, track; women only: basketball, cross-country, indoor track and field, track, volleyball. *Special regulations:* Parking restrictions. Curfews. Quiet hours. Residence hall visitation policy must be followed. Freshmen are not permitted to participate in visitation until they have satisfactorily completed 15 credit hours. *Special services:* Career Services, Student Health Services, Counseling Center, Student Disability Services, Student Media Services, Student Union. *Student publications: Digest,* a weekly newspaper; *The Jaguar,* a yearbook. Served by airport 3 miles from campus; passenger rail service 50 miles from campus.

Publications: *Southern University Law Review,* published biannually.

Library Collections: John B. Cade Library houses 831,983 volumes. Serial subscriptions: 1,675 paper, 3 microform, 181 via electronic access. 1,756 recordings; 2,856 compact discs; 1,568 CD-ROMs. 141 computer work stations. Online catalog. Students have access to the Internet at no charge. Total 2004–05 budget for books and materials: $323,926.

Most important holdings include Black Heritage Collection; J.S. Clark Papers; John Brother Cade Manuscript Collection; Camille S. Shade African American Collection; Slave Archives.

Buildings and Grounds: Campus area 964 acres including extension agricultural site. *New buildings:* Engineering Building complete 2000; Honors College 2000; C. Shade Dormitory 2000; Infirmary and Health Center 2001; Baseball Stadium 2002.

Chief Executive Officer: Dr. Edward R. Jackson, Chancellor.

Address admission inquiries to Nathaniel Harrison, Executive Director, Office of Admissions and Recruitment; graduate inquiries to Eura Adams, Director, Graduate Admissions and Recruitment.

Southern University at New Orleans

6400 Press Drive
New Orleans, Louisiana 70126

Tel: (504) 286-5000   **E-mail:** admissions@suno.edu
Fax: (504) 286-5131   **Internet:** www.suno.edu

Institution Description: *Enrollment:* 3,647. *Degrees awarded:* Associate, baccalaureate, master's.

Accreditation: *Regional:* SACS-Comm. on Coll. *Professional:* social work

History: Established and offered first instruction at postsecondary level 1959; awarded first degree (baccalaureate) 1963.

Institutional Structure: *Composition of institution:* Administrators 8 men / 3 women. Academic affairs headed by dean of academic affairs. Management/business/finances directed by comptroller and business manager. Full-time instructional faculty 125. Academic governance body, University Senate, meets an average of 10 times per year.

Calendar: Semesters. Academic year Aug. to May. Freshmen admitted Aug., Jan., May. Degrees conferred and formal commencements May, Dec. Summer session of 1 term from late May to late July.

Characteristics of Freshmen: 95% of applicants accepted. 39% of accepted applicants enrolled. 98% of freshmen from Louisiana.

Admission: Graduation from an accredited secondary school or GED; ACT Composite required.

Distinctive Educational Programs: Tutoring available. Developmental courses offered in summer session and regular academic year; credit given. Work-experience programs, including cooperative education, internships. Weekend and evening class. Individual majors. Institutionally sponsored study abroad in France. Special facilities for research; business-economics statistical laboratory through Division of Business.

ROTC: Army in cooperation with Loyola University, University of New Orleans.

Degrees Conferred: 198 *associate;* 484 *baccalaureate;* 141 *master's.* Degrees awarded in top five disciplines: business, management, marketing, and related support services 100; liberal arts and sciences, general studies, and humanities 75; computer and information sciences and support services 80; public administration and social service professions 53; psychology 50.

Fees and Other Expenses: *Full-time tuition per academic year 2004–05:* resident $2,904; nonresident $6,642. *Books and supplies:* $1,000. *Room and board per academic year:* $7,173.

Financial Aid: Aid from institutionally generated funds is provided on the basis of academic merit, financial need, other criteria. Institution has a Program Participation Agreement with the U.S. Department of Education for eligible students to receive Pell Grants and other federal aid.

Financial aid to full-time, first-time undergraduate students: 84% received federal grants averaging $1,884; 39% received loans averaging $1,715.

Departments and Teaching Staff: *Total instructional faculty:* 235 (125 full-time).

Enrollment: Total enrollment 3,647. Undergraduate 2,824 (30.7% men, 69.3% women).

Characteristics of Student Body: *Ethnic/racial makeup:* Black non-Hispanic: 94.2%; Asian or Pacific Islander: .6%; Hispanic: .3%; White non-Hispanic: 1.7%; unknown: 3.2%.

International Students: 90 nonresident aliens enrolled fall 2004. Programs available to aid students whose native language is not English: social, cultural. No financial aid specifically designated for international students.

Student Life: *Intercollegiate athletics:* men only: basketball, track; women only: basketball, track. *Special regulations:* Cars permitted in designated areas; fee charged. *Special services:* Learning Resources Center, medical services. *Student publications:* Bimonthly newspaper; yearbook. *Surrounding community:* New Orleans population over 500,000. Served by mass transit system; airport 25 miles from campus; passenger rail service 8 miles from campus.

Library Collections: 3000,000 volumes. Online catalog. Students have access to online information retrieval databases and the Internet.

Most important holdings include Afro-French collection; collection on Blacks; Kellogg business collection.

Buildings and Grounds: Campus area 22 acres.

Chief Executive Officer: Dr. Paul L. Robinson, Sr., Chancellor.

Address admission inquiries Timotea Bailey, Director of Admissions.

Tulane University

6823 St. Charles Avenue
New Orleans, Louisiana 70118
Tel: (504) 802-8000   **E-mail:** admission@tulane.edu
Fax: (504) 862-8715   **Internet:** www.tulane.edu

Institution Description: Tulane University is a private, independent, non-profit institution that includes Tulane College for Men and Newcomb College for Women. The graduate, architecture, engineering, and professional schools are coeducational. *Enrollment:* 12,691. *Degrees awarded:* Baccalaureate, first-professional (law, medicine), master's, doctorate.

Member of the consortium Association of American Universities.

Accreditation: *Regional:* SACS: Comm. on Coll. *Professional:* applied science, business, computer science, dietetics, engineering, health services administration, law, medicine, psychology internship, public health, school psychology, social work

History: Established as Medical College of Louisiana 1834; incorporated and offered first instruction at postsecondary level 1835; awarded first degree (first-professional) 1936; became part of University of Louisiana 1847; reverted to private control and adopted present official name, Tulane University of Louisiana, 1884; admitted women 1887. *See* John P. Dyer, *Tulane, The Biography of a University* (New York: Harper & Row, 1966) for further information.

Institutional Structure: *Governing board:* Board of Administrators. Extrainstitutional representation: 25 trustees, 17 emeritus members; institutional representation: 3 full-time instructional faculty members, 3 students; 2 alumni. 3 ex officio. 25 voting. *Composition of institution:* Administrators 23 men / 5 women. Academic affairs headed by academic vice president and provost. Management/business/finances directed by executive vice president. Full-time instructional faculty 915. Academic governance body, University Senate, meets an average of 9 times per year.

Calendar: Semesters. Academic year early Aug. to May. Freshmen admitted Aug., Jan., May, June, July. Degrees conferred May, Aug., Dec., Jan. (Law School). Formal commencements May, June (Medical School). Summer sessions of 4, 6, and 8 weeks offered.

Characteristics of Freshmen: 45% of applicants admitted. 20% of applicants admitted and enrolled.

75% (1,210 students) submitted SAT scores; 25% (403 students) submitted ACT scores. *25th percentile*: SAT Verbal 628, SAT Math 503; ACT Composite 28. *75th percentile*: SAT Verbal 725, SAT Math 700; ACT Composite 32. 71% of entering freshmen expected to graduate within 5 years. 30% of freshmen from Louisiana. Freshmen from 30 states.

Admission: Rolling admissions plan. For fall acceptance, freshmen apply as early as Sept. 1 of previous year, but not later than Feb. 1 of year of enrollment. Apply by Nov. 1 for early decision and early notification plans; need not limit application to Tulane. *Requirements:* Either graduation from accredited secondary school or GED. Recommend 4 units English, 3 preferably in mathematics, (students who plan to enter scientific fields should have 4 years), at least 2 and preferably 3 or 4 years of a classical or modern language; at least 2 years of laboratory science (students who plan to enter scientific fields should take at least 3 years); at least 2 social studies with an emphasis on history; architecture students should also take full of advantage of fine arts coursework available. *Entrance tests:* College Board SAT or ACT, 3 Achievement tests recommended. SAT II required for home-schooled students. *For transfer students:* 3.0 minimum GPA.

Entering Tulane students who score well on the Advanced Placement Examination of the College Board usually receive both advanced placement and credit for the appropriate subjects.

Degree Requirements: 128 credit hours; 2.0 GPA; 2 terms in residence; 2 physical education courses; distribution requirements; demonstrated proficiency in English, mathematics, and in a foreign language. Individual schools may have requirements that vary. *Grading system:* A–F; pass-fail; withdraw (carries time limit).

Distinctive Educational Programs: Internships. Off-campus centers (at F. Edward Herbert Riverside Research Center and Delta Primate Research Center). Evening classes. State-of-the art computer facilities and special facilities for using telecommunications in the classroom. Innovative programs include accelerated program, Tulane Honors Program, dual-degrees, advanced placement, independent studies, colloquia, self-designed majors, women's studies, Mellon Professorship, international relations, cognitive studies, communication, Jewish studies, Latin American studies, political economy, Urban Village. Junior year abroad programs in various countries.

ROTC: Army, Navy. Air Force in cooperation with University of New Orleans.

Degrees Conferred: 1,452 *baccalaureate;* 1,135 *master's;* 127 *doctorate.* Bachelor's degrees awarded in top five disciplines: business, management, mar-keting, and related support services 330; social sciences 260; engineering 126; psychology 93; computer and information sciences and support services 81. 495 *first-professional:* law, medicine.

Fees and Other Expenses: *Full-time tuition per academic year 2004–05:* $29,800. Tuition for professional schools vary; contact the school of interest for current information. *Required fees:* 2,310. *Room and board per academic year:* $8,172.

Financial Aid: Aid from institutionally generated funds is provided on the basis of academic merit, financial need, athletic ability. Institution has a Program Participation Agreement with the U.S. Department of Education for eligible students to receive Pell Grants and other federal aid.

Financial aid to full-time, first-time undergraduate students: need-based scholarships/grants totaling $40,928,511, self-help $14,995,897, parent loans $1,235,670, tuition waivers $2,470,197, athletic awards $2,727,352; non-need-based scholarships/grants totaling $30,910,618, self-help $4,607,024, parent loans $10,105,738,tuition waivers $3,350,238, athletic awards $5,115,795.

Departments and Teaching Staff: *Professors* 340, *associate professors* 285, *assistant professors* 260, *instructors* 64, *part-time faculty* 272. *Total instructional faculty:* 1,371 (full-time 1,099, part-time 272; women 451, men 920; members of minority groups 298). Total faculty with doctorate, first-professional, or other terminal degree: 1,207. Student-to-faculty ratio: 13:1.

Enrollment: Total enrollment 12,691. Undergraduate full-time 3,025 men / 3,126 women, part-time 738m / 1,097w; first-professional full-time 851m / 160w, part-time 3m / 3w; graduate full-time 1,091m / 1,339w. part-time 372m / 296w.

Characteristics of Student Body: *Ethnic/racial makeup:* number of Black non-Hispanic: 738; American Indian or Alaska Native: 41; Asian or Pacific Islander: 340; Hispanic: 272; White non-Hispanic: 5,763, unknown: 634.

International Students: 188 nonresident aliens enrolled fall 2004. Students from Europe, Asia, Central and South America, Africa, Canada, Australia, New Zealand. Programs available to aid students whose native language is not English: social and cultural. English as a Second Language Program. No financial aid specifically designated for international students.

Student Life: On-campus housing is available for 50% of the undergraduate students. Apartment facilities are also available for married and single students. *Intercollegiate athletics:* men only: baseball, cross-country, football, golf, swimming, tennis; women only: basketball, cross-country, indoor and outdoor track, swimming, tennis, volleyball. *Special regulations:* Freshmen may not park on campus. Parking permits required 24 hours per day. *Special services:* Learning Resources Center, medical services, disabled student services, legal aid. *Student publications, radio: Jambalaya,* a yearbook; *The Maritime Lawyer,* a biannual journal; *Tulane Hullabaloo,* a weekly newspaper; *Tulane Law Review,* a quarterly publication; *Tulane Literary Magazine,* a annual publication; *Voxhumana,* a monthly publication; an annual student directory. Radio station WTUL-FM broadcasts 24 hours per day. *Surrounding community:* New Orleans metropolitan area population over 1 million. Served by mass transit bus and street car systems; airport 10 miles from campus; passenger rail service 2 miles from campus.

Publications: *The Human Mosaic,* anthropology (2 volumes published annually) first published in 1966; *The Tulane Architectural Review* (annually) first published 1975; *Tulane Studies in Geology and Paleontology* (quarterly) first published 1962; *Tulane Studies in Philosophy* (annually) first published 1952; *Tulane Studies in Political Science* (annually) first published 1954; *Tulane Studies in Social Welfare* (irregularly) first published 1957; *Tulane Studies in Zoology and Botany* (semiannually); *Tulanian* (quarterly) university/alumni magazine first published 1929; *Inside Tulane* (monthly) university faculty staff tabloid first published 1981.

Library Collections: 2,100,000 volumes. 2,500,000 microforms; approximately 55,000 audiovisual materials; 16,500 periodicals. Access to online information retrieval systems.

Most important holdings include Latin American Library; Louisiana Collection; jazz archive.

Buildings and Grounds: Main campus area 110 acres.

Chief Executive Officer: Dr. Scott Cowen, President.

Address admission inquiries to Richard Whiteside, Vice President for Enrollment Management; graduate and professional school inquiries to various entities concerned.

Tulane College for Men

Degree Programs Offered: *Baccalaureate* in American studies, anthropology, art (history or studio), biological chemistry, biology, chemistry, communication, earth sciences, economics, English, French, geology, German, Greek, history, Italian, Latin, Latin American studies, mathematical economics, mathematics (pure, applied, computer science, or statistics), medieval studies, music, philosophy, physics, political economy, political science, political science-international relations, psychology, Russian, sociology, Spanish, theater.

Distinctive Educational Programs: Interdepartmental majors in American studies, art and biology, Asian studies, biological chemistry, cognitive studies, environmental studies, Jewish studies, Latin American studies, linguistics, mathematical economics, medieval studies, political economy, religious studies, Russian and Soviet studies. Cross-registration with Loyola University in designated courses. Junior Year Abroad Program. Washington Semester Program. Dual degree programs with architecture, business, law, medicine, and social work.

Newcomb College for Women

Degree Programs Offered: *Baccalaureate* in anthropology, art (art history or studio), biology, chemistry, classics, communication, earth sciences, economics, English, French, geology, German, Greek history, Italian, Latin, mathematics, music, philosophy, physics, political science, psychology, Russian, sociology, Spanish, theatre.

Degree Requirements: General University requirements except 4 physical education courses are required instead of 2. Grading system utilizes satisfactory-unsatisfactory instead of pass-fail.

Distinctive Educational Programs: Interdepartmental majors in American studies, art and biology, Asian studies, biological chemistry, cognitive studies, environmental studies, international relations, Jewish studies, Latin American studies, linguistics, mathematical economics, medieval studies, political economy, religious studies, Russian and Soviet studies. Washington (D.C.) semester with American University. Cross-registration with Loyola University in designated courses in communications, drama and speech, journalism.

School of Architecture

Degree Programs Offered: *Baccalaureate, master's.*

Degree Requirements: For bachelor of architecture: 186 credit hours; for bachelor of architecture with accredited undergraduate degree: 130 credit hours.

Distinctive Educational Programs: Joint program with Graduate School of Business Administration allows architecture students to complete first year of M.B.A. program before graduation.

A. B. Freeman School of Business

Degree Programs Offered: *Baccalaureate* and *master's* in accounting; economic analysis; finance; general management; international business; law, regulation, and taxation; management science; marketing; organizational behavior.

Distinctive Educational Programs: Joint master's in business administration and public health with School of Public Health and Tropical Medicine. Joint first-professional-master's in business administration with School of Law. Dual-degree program for minority students with Xavier University of Louisiana.

School of Engineering

Degree Programs Offered: *Baccalaureate* in biomedical engineering, chemical engineering, computer science, electrical engineering, mechanical engineering. *Master's* and *doctorate* in various fields.

Distinctive Educational Programs: Tulane Chemical Engineering Practice School Program provides experience in solving actual plant problems at local chemical plants or oil refineries. Individually arranged interdisciplinary programs in engineering.

Tulane School of Law

Degree Programs Offered: *First-professional; master's* in energy and environment, Latin American studies; *master's* and *doctorate* in admiralty law, comparative law, corporate law, general practice law, international law, public interest law, resource development law, various other fields.

Admission: Bachelor's degree from an accredited university is required to enter Law School. Exceptional students only may be admitted with 96 semester hours from an accredited university.

Distinctive Educational Programs: Tulane Law School offers a J.D. in both civil and common law. Third year students may participate in an extensive clinical program (juvenile law, civil law, criminal law) or serve as clerks to federal district judges. The Admiralty program which offers an LL.M. in Admiralty is the most extensive in the United States and one of the two most comprehensive in the world. The Institute of Comparative Law emphasizes comparison of the jural method with techniques used in Latin American, European legal systems. Tulane Law School offers joint degrees with the School of Business Administration, School of Public Health and Tropical Medicine, and the School of Social Work. It also offers a specialized program leading to an M.C.L.-M.A. in Latin American Studies.

Tulane University School of Medicine

Degree Programs Offered: *First-professional.*

Admission: Apply by Dec. 15. 90 semester hours prescribed college curriculum from approved institution; MCAT.

Degree Requirements: 4-year prescribed program.

Distinctive Educational Programs: Joint first-professional-master's in public health with School of Public Health and Tropical Medicine. Other first-professional-master's, first-professional-doctorate programs also available. Interdisciplinary courses in clinical pathology, neuroscience.

The Graduate School

Degree Programs Offered: *Master's* and *doctorate* in various fields.

Departments and Teaching Staff: Graduate faculty have primary appointments in other divisions of the university. There is no singular faculty for the Graduate School.

Distinctive Educational Programs: Middle American Research Institute, Center for Latin American Studies, Murphy Institute for political Economy and Policy Analysis, Delta Regional Primate Research Center, International Collaboration in Infectious Diseases Research Program in Cali, Colombia, Center for Archaeology. Student exchange programs with the University of Strasbourg (France) and the Free University of Berlin (Germany).

School of Public Health and Tropical Medicine

Degree Programs Offered: *Master's* and *doctorate* in biostatistics, community health nursing, environmental health sciences, epidemiology, health systems management, international health, maternal and child health, nutrition, tropical medicine; joint MHA/MBA, MHA/JD, MPH and TM/MD.

Distinctive Educational Programs: Interdepartmental International Health Program. Joint master's programs in social work and public health, and in business and public health. *See* Schools of Law and Medicine.

School of Social Work

Degree Programs Offered: *Master's.* General and Clinical *Doctor of Social Work.*

Admission: Admission to the Clinical Doctor of Social Work requires a Master of Social Work.

Degree Requirements: Clinical Doctor of Social Work requires a 12 month clinical internship.

Distinctive Educational Programs: Interdisciplinary doctoral sequence. Continuing education. *See* Schools of Law and Public Health.

University College

Degree Programs Offered: *Baccalaureate* in computer information systems, criminal justice, paralegal studies, physical education, social studies. Certificates also given.

University of Louisiana at Lafayette

104 University Circle
Lafayette, Louisiana 70503

Tel: (337) 482-1000   **E-mail:** admissions@louisiana.edu
Fax: (337) 482-6195   **Internet:** www.louisiana.edu

Institution Description: University of Louisiana at Lafayette, formerly named University of Southwestern Louisiana, is a state institution. *Enrollment:* 16,561. *Degrees awarded:* Associate, baccalaureate, master's, doctorate.

Academic offerings subject to approval by statewide coordinating bodies. Budget subject to approval by state governing boards.

Accreditation: *Regional:* SACS-Comm. on Coll. *Professional:* art, business, computer science, dietetics, EMT-paramedic, engineering, family and consumer science, health information administration, industrial technology, interior design, journalism, music, nursing, speech-language pathology, teacher education

History: Established as Southwestern Louisiana Industrial Institute 1898; became junior college and offered first instruction at postsecondary level 1916; became 4-year institution, awarded first degree (baccalaureate), and changed name to Louisiana Institute of Liberal and Technical Learning 1921; name changed to University of Southwestern Louisiana 1960; became University of Louisiana at Lafayette 1999. *See* Lea L. Seale, *A Brief History of Southwestern Louisiana Institute 1901–1958* (Lafayette: University of Southwestern Louisiana, 1959) for further information.

Institutional Structure: *Governing board:* University of Louisiana System Board of Supervisors. Representation: 18 trustees, including 1 student (all appointed by governor of Louisiana). All voting. *Composition of institution:* Administrators 74 men / 30 women. Academic affairs headed by vice president for academic affairs. Management/business/finances directed by vice president for business affairs. Full-time instructional faculty 555. Academic governance body, University Council, meets an average of 45 times per year.

Calendar: Semesters. Academic year mid-Aug. to mid-May. Freshmen admitted Aug., Jan. May. Degrees conferred May, Dec. Formal commencements May, Dec. Summer session from early June to early Aug.

Characteristics of Freshmen: 5,165 applicants (2,197 men, 2,968 women). 85% of applicants admitted. 59.9% of admitted students enrolled full-time.

7% of applicants submitted SAT scores; 93% (2,742 students) submitted ACT scores. *25th percentile:* ACT Composite 18, ACT English 18, ACT Math 17. *75th percentile:* ACT Composite 24, ACT English 25, ACT Math 24.

Admission: Rolling admissions plan. Apply as early as 1 year, but not later than 1 month, prior to enrollment. Early acceptance available. *Requirements:* Graduation from accredited secondary school or GED. State applicants and out-of-state applicants must meet certain criteria. 17.5 units of high school courses including 4 English, 3 mathematics, 3 science, 3 social studies, 4.5 electives. *Entrance tests:* ACT or SAT. For foreign students TOEFL. *For transfer students:* 2.0 minimum GPA; from 4-year accredited institution maximum transfer credit limited only by residence requirement; from 2-year accredited institution 62 hours.

College credit and advanced placement for postsecondary-level work completed in secondary school. College credit for extrainstitutional learning on basis of ACE *2006 Guide to the Evaluation of Educational Experiences in the Armed Services*; portfolio assessment. Tutoring available. Limited noncredit remedial courses offered during regular academic year.

Degree Requirements: *For all associate degrees:* 60 credit hours; 21 semester hours in residence. *For all baccalaureate degrees:* 124 credit hours; 30 semester hours in residence; 2 physical education courses. *For all undergraduate degrees:* 2.0 GPA; general education requirements.

Fulfillment of some degree requirements and exemption from some beginning courses possible by passing departmental examinations, College Board CLEP, other standardized tests. *Grading system:* A–F; credit-no credit.

Distinctive Educational Programs: Evening classes. Facilities and programs for independent research, including honors programs, individual majors, tutorials. Institutionally sponsored study abroad in France. Summer program in France at Toulon. *Other distinctive programs:* Continuing education. Computer Aided Design used in engineering, architecture, and computer science majors; Integrated Computer Assisted Design and Computer Assisted Manufacturing "Factory of the Future" in use for undergraduate mechanical engineering education.

ROTC: Army.

Degrees Conferred: 160 *associate*; 2,021 *baccalaureate*; 364 *master's*; 29 *doctorate*. Bachelor's degrees awarded in top five disciplines: business, management, marketing, and related support services 437; education 264; liberal arts and sciences, general studies, and humanities 260; health professions and related clinical sciences 211; engineering 127.

Fees and Other Expenses: *Full-time tuition per semester 2004–05:* resident undergraduate $3,228, nonresident $9,408. Contact the university for current graduate tuition/fees. *Books and supplies:* $1,000. *Room and board per academic year:* $3,386.

Financial Aid: Aid from institutionally generated funds is provided on the basis of academic merit, financial need, athletic ability. Institution has a Program Participation Agreement with the U.S. Department of Education for eligible students to receive Pell Grants and other federal aid.

Financial aid to full-time, first-time undergraduate students: 33% received federal grants averaging $2,930; 56% state/local grants averaging $2,227; 28% institutional grants averaging $1,724; 32% received loans averaging $2,784.

Departments and Teaching Staff: *Professors* 150, *associate professors* 133, *assistant professors* 136, *instructors* 112, *part-time teachers* 162. *Total instructional faculty:* 693. Student-to-faculty ratio 24:1. Degrees held by full-time faculty: doctorate 71.6%, master's 26.9%, baccalaureate 1.1%. 78.6% hold terminal degrees.

Enrollment: Total enrollment: 16,561. Undergraduate 15,043 (41.6% men, 58.4% women).

Characteristics of Student Body: *Ethnic/racial makeup:* Black non-Hispanic: 18.6%; American Indian or Alaska Native: .5%; Asian or Pacific Islander: 1.4%; Hispanic:1.7%; White non-Hispanic: 74.5%; unknown: 1.6%. *Age distribution:* 17–21: 49.9%; 22–24: 21.9%; 25–29: 13%; 30–34: 4.9%; 35–39: 3.1%; 40–49: 4%; 50–59: 1%; 60–up: 2%.

International Students: 256 undergraduate nonresident aliens enrolled fall 2004. Students from Europe, Asia, Central and South America, Africa, Canada, Australia. Programs available to aid students whose native language is not English: social and cultural. English as a Second Language Program. No financial aid specifically designated for international students.

Student Life: On-campus residence halls house 12% of student body. Residence halls for men constitute 46% of such space, for women 54%. 4% of married students request institutional housing; 1% are so housed. *Intercollegiate athletics:* men only: baseball, basketball, cross-country, football, tennis, track; women only: basketball, cross-country, soccer, softball, tennis, track. volleyball. *Special regulations:* Nonresident student cars permitted in designated areas only. Curfews and quiet hours. Residence hall visitation varies according to residence halls. *Special services:* Learning Resources Center, medical services, bus service between parking lot and main campus. *Student publications, radio:* Vermillon, a weekly newspaper. Radio station KRVS broadcasts 168 hours per week. *Surrounding community:* Lafayette population 82,000. New Orleans, 140 miles from campus, is nearest metropolitan area. Served by mass transit bus system; airport 3 miles from campus; passenger rail service 1 mile from campus.

Publications: The Center for Louisiana Studies publishes the historical journals *Louisiana History* and the *Attakapas Gazette*, as well as an extensive series of books on Louisiana history, architecture, and culture. The English department publishes the journals *Explorations in Renaissance Culture; Explorations: The Age of Enlightenment; The Griot* (official publication of the Southern Conference on Afro-American Studies); *The Roundtable* (official publication of the South Central College English Association); and *The Southwestern Review*.

Library Collections: 873,200 volumes. 1,768,370 microforms; 255,992 audiovisual materials; 4,965 current periodical subscriptions. Online catalog. Access to online information retrieval systems and the Internet.

Most important holdings include horticulture and ornamental herbarium collection; southwestern Louisiana archives and manuscripts collection.

Buildings and Grounds: Campus area 1,375 acres.

Chief Executive Officer: Dr. Ray P. Authement, President.

Undergraduates address admission inquiries to Leroy Broussard, Director of Admissions; graduate inquiries to Dr. Lewis Pyenson, Dean of Graduate School.

College of Liberal Arts

Degree Programs Offered: *Associate* in criminal justice; *baccalaureate* in modern languages, history, philosophy, psychology, anthropology, sociology, political science, pre-law, criminal justice, speech pathology and audiology, interpersonal public communication, mass communication, public relations; *master's* in English, French, history, rehabilitation counseling, psychology, communication/speech pathology/audiology; *doctorate* in English, Francophone studies.

Degree Requirements: Core curriculum including 6 hours of each of the following: English, history, mathematics, arts and humanities electives, behavioral science, and (for B.S. degree) foreign language; 8 hours science; 4 hours physical education; 3 hours communication elective; and 12 hours foreign language.

College of Applied Life Sciences

Degree Programs Offered: *Two year transfer programs* in pre-agricultural engineering, pre-forestry, and pre-veterinary; *baccalaureate* in environmental/sustainable resources, sustainable agriculture, apparel design and merchandising, child and family studies, dietetics, hospitality management; *master's* in human resources.

Distinctive Educational Programs: Center for Crawfish Research. Center for Greenhouse Research.

College of Sciences

Degree Programs Offered: *Two year transfer programs* in pre-physical therapy, pre-medical technology, pre-pharmacy; *baccalaureate* in biology, resource biology, biodiversity, microbiology, chemistry, computer science, geology, mathematics, health information management, physics; *master's* in biology, computer science, geology, mathematics, physics; *doctorate in* environmental and evolutionary biology, computer science, mathematics, cognitive science.

College of Business Administration

Degree Programs Offered: *Baccalaureate* in accounting, business systems, analysis and technology, economics, finance, insurance and risk management, management, professional land and resource management and marketing; *master's of business administration* in business administration, health care administration; *post-master's certificate* in health care administration.

College of Education

Degree Programs Offered: *Baccalaureate* in elementary education, vocational education, special education, music education, secondary education, health and physical education; *master's* in education of the gifted, curriculum and instruction, guidance and counseling, administration and supervision.

College of Engineering

Degree Programs Offered: *Associate* in industrial technology; *baccalaureate* in chemical engineering, civil engineering, electrical engineering, computer engineering, telecommunications engineering, industrial technology, mechanical engineering, petroleum engineering; *master's* in chemical engineering, civil engineering, computer engineering, telecommunications, engineering management, mechanical engineering; *doctorate* in computer engineering.

Distinctive Educational Programs: Interdisciplinary master's programs in engineering management, engineering systems.

College of Nursing

Degree Programs Offered: *Associate* in emergency health science; *baccalaureate* and *master's* in nursing.

College of the Arts

Degree Programs Offered: *Baccalaureate* in architecture, interior design, industrial design, performing arts, visual arts, music; *master's* in music.

College of General Studies

Degree Programs Offered: *Associate* and *baccalaureate* in general studies.

Admission: Students must be eligible to exit junior division, i.e. have completed at least 30 hours of non-remedial courses, have a cumulative GPA of 2.0 and have declared a major in General Studies.

Degree Requirements: *For associate degree:* 64 hours, 21 in residence. *For baccalaureate degree:* 124 hours, 30 in residence with a minimum of 30 hours at the junior/senior level and 15 hours at the senior level.

Departments and Teaching Staff: Faculty is drawn from the entire university faculty.

University of Louisiana at Monroe

700 University Avenue
Monroe, Louisiana 71209
Tel: (318) 342-5252   **E-mail:** admissions@ulm.edu
Fax: (318) 342-1409   **Internet:** www.ulm.edu

Institution Description: University of Louisiana at Monore, formerly named Northeast Louisiana University, is a state institution. *Enrollment:* 8,831. *Degrees awarded:* Associate, baccalaureate, master's, doctorate. Specialist and other certificates also awarded.

Academic offerings subject to approval by statewide coordinating bodies. Budget subject to approval by state governing boards.

Accreditation: *Regional:* SACS-Comm. on Coll. *Professional:* accounting, business, computer science, construction education, counseling, dental hygiene, family and consumer science, journalism, marriage and family therapy, music, nursing, nursing education, occupational therapy, pharmacy, radiography, social work, speech-language pathology, teacher education

History: Established as Ouachita Parish Junior College, chartered, and offered first instruction at postsecondary level 1931; changed name to Northeast Center of Louisiana State University 1934, to Northeast Junior College of Louisiana State University 1939; added senior level and changed name to Northeast Louisiana State College 1950; achieved university status in 1970; adopted present name 2001.

Institutional Structure: *Governing board:* Board of Trustees for State Colleges and Universities. Representation: 18 trustees, including 1 student (all appointed by governor of Louisiana). All voting. *Composition of institution:* Academic affairs headed by vice president. Management/business/finances directed by vice president. Full-time instructional faculty 369. Academic governance body, Faculty Senate, meets an average of 12 times per year.

Calendar: Semesters. Academic year late Aug. to mid-May. Freshmen admitted Aug., Jan., June. Degrees conferred and formal commencements May, Aug., Dec. Summer session from early June to mid-Aug.

Characteristics of Freshmen: 2,423 applicants (908 men, 1,515 women). 90.3% of applicants admitted. 67.9% of admitted students enrolled full-time.

5% (80 students) submitted SAT scores; 92% (1,441 students) submitted ACT scores. *25th percentile:* SAT I Verbal 458, SAT I Math 448; ACT Composite 18, ACT English 18, ACT Math 17. *75th percentile:* SAT I Verbal 560, SAT I Math 570; ACT Composite 23, ACT English 25, ACT Math 23.

22% of entering freshmen expected to graduate within 5 years. 94% of freshmen from Louisiana. Freshmen from 44 states and 42 foreign countries.

Admission: Rolling admissions plan. For fall acceptance, apply no later than July. Early acceptance available. *Requirements:* Either graduation from accredited secondary school or GED. *For transfer students:* From 4-year accredited institution 98 hours maximum transfer credit; from 2-year accredited institution 60 hours. Good standing at institution previously attended.

College credit and advanced placement for postsecondary-level work completed in secondary school. College credit for extrainstitutional learning on basis of ACE *2006 Guide to the Evaluation of Educational Experiences in the Armed Services.* Tutoring available. Noncredit developmental courses offered in summer session and regular academic year.

Degree Requirements: *For all associate degrees:* 60–70 credit hours; 1 semester in residence; 2 hours physical education. *For all baccalaureate degrees:* 128–138 credit hours; 2 semesters in residence; 2–4 hours physical education. *For all undergraduate degrees:* 2.0 GPA; general education requirements.

Fulfillment of some degree requirements and exemption from some beginning courses possible by passing College Board CLEP, other standardized tests. *Grading system:* A–F; withdraw.

Distinctive Educational Programs: Evening classes. Special facilities for using telecommunications in the classroom.

ROTC: Army.

Degrees Conferred: 34 *associate;* 937 *baccalaureate;* 278 *master's;* 11 *doctorate;* 78 *first-professional.* Bachelor's degrees awarded in top five disciplines:health professions and related clinical sciences 226; business, management, marketing, and related support services 202; liberal arts and sciences, general studies, and humanities 80; education 80; psychology 48.

Fees and Other Expenses: *Full-time tuition per academic year 2004–05:* undergraduate resident $3,196, nonresident $9,148. Contact the university for current tuition for graduate study. *Books and supplies:* $1,000. *Room and board per academic year:* $4,000.

Financial Aid: Aid from institutionally generated funds is provided on the basis of academic merit, financial need, other criteria. Institution has a Program Participation Agreement with the U.S. Department of Education for eligible students to receive Pell Grants and other federal aid.

Financial aid to full-time, first-time undergraduate students: 56% received federal grants averaging $7,094; 41% state/local grants averaging $2,292; 70% institutional grants averaging $1,619; 68% received loans averaging $2,624.

Departments and Teaching Staff: Accounting *professors* 3, *associate professors* 0, *assistant professors* 6, *instructors* 3, *part-time faculty* 0; agriculture 1, 1, 1, 1, 1; allied health sciences 0, 4, 5, 10, 3; art 0, 3, 4, 0, 3; aviation 0, 1, 2, 2, 1; chemistry 4, 9, 3, 2, 1; criminal justice, social work, sociology 3, 8, 6, 0, 6; office information systems 2, 3, 3, 2, 0; communication 1, 8, 10, 5, 5; construction 0, 2, 4, 1, 0; computer science 2, 2, 2, 3, 2; curriculum and instruction 6, 2, 4, 11, 2; economics and finance 4, 2, 8, 2, 0; educational leadership and counseling 3, 3, 9, 1, 4; English 3, 3, 13, 16, 1; foreign languages 2, 1, 3, 4, 1; geosciences 6, 5, 1, 0, 0; health and human performance 1, 3, 6, 7, 3; history 4, 5, 5, 0, 4; home economics 0, 3, 2, 2, 0; mathematics 0, 6, 4, 10, 2; management and marketing 10, 1, 6, 3, 0; music 3, 7, 8, 4, 3; nursing 1, 8, 13, 1, 8; pharmacy 8, 8, 18, 0, 2; physics 2, 2, 2, 2, 0; psychology 5, 1, 6, 3, 7.

Total instructional faculty: 494.

Enrollment: Total enrollment 8,631. Undergraduate 7,475 (36.7% men, 64.3% women).

Characteristics of Student Body: *Ethnic/racial makeup:* Black non-Hispanic: 28.35; American Indian or Alaska Native: .4%; Asian or Pacific Islander: 2.2%; Hispanic: .7%; White non-Hispanic: 67.5%. *Age distribution:* 17–21: 51%; 22–24: 21%; 25–29: 12%; 30–34: 6%; 35–39: 4%; 40–49: 5%; 50–59: 1%.

International Students: 75 nonresident aliens enrolled fall 2004. Programs available to aid students whose native language is not English: English as a Second Language Program. No financial aid specifically designated for international students.

Student Life: On-campus residence halls house 29% of student body. *Intercollegiate athletics:* men only: baseball, basketball, football, rifle, soccer, swimming, tennis, track, volleyball; women only: basketball, softball, swimming, tennis, track, volleyball. *Special regulations:* Freshmen must park away from academic areas. *Special services:* Learning Resources Center, medical services. *Student publications, radio: Chacohoula,* a yearbook; *The Helicon,* an annual literary magazine; *Pow Wow,* a weekly newspaper. Radio station KNLU. Monroe population 55,000. Orleans, 300 miles from campus, is nearest metropolitan area. Served by airport 3 miles from campus.

Library Collections: 605,000 volumes. 168,000 government documents; 551,000 microforms; 2,910 current periodical subscriptions. 330 audiovisual units. Online catalog. Students have access to online information retrieval services and the Internet.

Most important holdings include Otto Passman Congressional Papers; Historic Cartographic Collection for U.S. Corps of Engineers; Durwood Griffin Photographic Collection.

Buildings and Grounds: Campus area 240 acres.

Chief Executive Officer: Dr. James E. Cofer, Sr., President.

Address undergraduate admission inquiries to Lisa Miller, Director of Admissions; graduate inquiries to Dean of Graduate Studies and Research.

University of New Orleans

Lake Front

New Orleans, Louisiana 70148

Tel: (800) 256-5866   **E-mail:** admissions@uno.edu
Fax: (504) 280-5522   **Internet:** www.uno.edu

Institution Description: *Enrollment:* 17,350. *Degrees awarded:* Associate, baccalaureate, master's, doctorate.

Accreditation: *Regional:* SACS-Comm. on Coll. *Professional:* accounting, business, computer science, counseling, engineering, music, planning, teacher education, theatre

History: Established as Louisiana State University in New Orleans 1956; offered first instruction at postsecondary level 1958; awarded first degree (baccalaureate) 1962; chartered 1965; adopted present name 1974.

Institutional Structure: *Composition of institution:* Administrators 19 men / 3 women. Academic affairs headed by provost/vice chancellor for academic affairs. Management/business/finances directed by vice chancellor for business affairs. Full-time instructional faculty 433. Academic governance body, University Senate, meets an average of 9 times per year.

Calendar: Semesters. Academic year Aug. to May. Freshmen admitted Aug., Jan., May. Degrees conferred and formal commencement May, Aug., Dec. Summer sessions from June to July.

Characteristics of Freshmen: 635 of applicants admitted4. 29% of applicants admitted and enrolled.

12% (245 students) submitted SAT scores; 90% (1,845 students) submitted ACT scores. *25th percentile:* SAT Verbal 450, SAT Math 450; ACT Composite 18, ACT English 18, ACT Math 17. *75th percentile:* SAT Verbal 590, SAT Math 580; ACT Composite 23, ACT English 25, ACT Math 23.

13% of entering freshmen expected to graduate within 5 years. 91% of freshmen from Louisiana. Freshmen from 39 states and 19 foreign countries.

Admission: Rolling admissions plan. For fall acceptance, apply as early as senior year of secondary school, but not later than July 1 of year of enrollment. Early acceptance available. *Requirements:* Entering freshmen are required to have a minimum of 17½ core units and a minimum ACT score of 20. *For transfer students:* 2.0 minimum GPA; from 4-year accredited institution maximum transfer credit limited only by residence requirement; from 2-year accredited institution maximum transfer credit limited to one half of degree requirement; correspondence/extension student 30 hours.

College credit and advanced placement for postsecondary-level work completed in secondary school. College credit for extrainstitutional learning on basis of ACE *2006 Guide to the Evaluation of Educational Experiences in the Armed Services.* Tutoring available. Developmental/remedial courses offered in summer session and regular academic year; credit given.

Degree Requirements: *For all associate degrees:* 70 hours. *For all baccalaureate degrees:* 128 hours; 30 hours in residence; additional requirements for some programs. Fulfillment of some degree requirements and exemption from some beginning courses possible by passing College Board CLEP, AP. *Grading system:* A–F; pass-fail; withdraw (deadline after which A–F is appended to withdraw).

Distinctive Educational Programs: Cooperative education. Flexible meeting places and schedules, including off-campus centers, evening classes. Interdisciplinary graduate programs in urban studies. Preprofessional programs in occupational therapy, rehabilitation counseling, respiratory therapy. Honors programs. Summer study abroad in Austria. Special Education Center provides educational, diagnostic, and consultative services to exceptional children. Center for bio-organic studies sponsors research on environmental and health science. International Marketing Institute assists development of international business in Louisiana. Division of Business and Economic Research sponsors faculty research and provides information to community and government agencies. Noncredit continuing education. *Other distinctive programs:* "European Experience" (for gifted high school students) in England, Belgium, France, Germany,

Austria, and Italy; "Glories of France": (for gifted high school students) in France; summer school at Innsbruck, Austria; geology field camp in Mexico.

ROTC: Army, Air Force in cooperation with Tulane University.

Degrees Conferred: 1,727 *baccalaureate* (B), 867 *master's* (M), 79 *doctorate* (D): architecture 11 (M); biological/life sciences 59 (B), 7 (M); business/marketing 647 (B), 337 (M), 4 (D); communications/communication technologies 133 (B), 5 (M); computer and information sciences 33 (B), 19 (M); education 136 (B), 239 (M), 43 (D); engineering and engineering technologies 116 (B), 58 (M), 11 (D); English 57 (B), 13 (M); foreign languages and literature 10 (B), 5 (M); health professions and related sciences 43 (M); liberal arts/general studies 191 (B); mathematics 10 (B), 12 (M); natural resources/environmental science 1 (B); philosophy/religion/theology 16 (B); physical sciences 15 (B), 18 (M), 13 (D); protective services/public administration 7 (M); psychology 101 (B), 7 (M), 4 (D); social sciences and history 136 (B), 37 (M), 4 (D); visual and performing arts 66 (B), 49 (M).

Fees and Other Expenses: *Full-time tuition per academic year 2004–05:* undergraduate $3,184, graduate $10,228. *Required fees:* $518. *Room and board per academic year:* $4,590.

Financial Aid: Aid from institutionally generated funds is provided on the basis of academic merit, financial need, athletic ability, other criteria. Institution has a Program Participation Agreement with the U.S. Department of Education for eligible students to receive Pell Grants and other federal aid.

Financial aid to full-time, first-time undergraduate students: need-based scholarships/grants totaling $13,695,884, self-help $24,286,436; non-need-based scholarships/grants totaling $6,642,105, self-help $22,512,738, parent loans $875,237, tuition waivers $3,308,459, athletic awards $1,013,087.

Departments and Teaching Staff: *Professors* 199, *associate professors* 109, *assistant professors* 123, *instructors* 105, *part-time faculty* 229. *Total instructional faculty:* 785 (full-time 556, part-time 229; women 310, men 475; members of minority groups 101). Total faculty with doctorate, first-professional, or other terminal degree: 101. Student-to-faculty ratio: 21:1.

Enrollment: Total enrollment 17,350. Undergraduate full-time 4,315 men / 5,236 women, part-time 1,512m / 2,162w; graduate full-time 736m / 937w, part-time 866m / 1,506w. *Transfer students:* 1,156.

Characteristics of Student Body: *Ethnic/racial makeup:* number of Black non-Hispanic: 3,250; American Indian or Alaska Native: 57; Asian or Pacific Islander: 737; Hispanic: 873; White non-Hispanic: 7,230; unknown: 118. *Age distribution:* number under 18: 359; 18–19: 3,341; 20–21: 3,035; 22–24: 2,888; 25–29: 1,737; 30–34: 795; 35–39: 417; 40–49: 467; 50–64: 134; 65 and over: 52.

International Students: 867 nonresident aliens enrolled fall 2004. Students from Europe, Asia, Central and South America, Africa, Canada. Programs available to aid students whose native language is not English: English as a Second Language Program. No financial aid specifically designated for international students.

Student Life: On-campus residence halls house 5% of student body. Dormitories for men only constitute 50% of such space, for women only 50%. *Intercollegiate athletics:* men only: baseball, basketball, golf, tennis; women only, basketball, tennis, volleyball. *Special regulations:* Cars permitted for $20 fee. *Special services:* Learning Resources Center, medical services. *Student publications:* Driftwood, a weekly newspaper; *Ellipsis*, a monthly literary magazine. *Surrounding community:* New Orleans metropolitan area population 1.5 million. Served by mass transit bus system; airport 17 miles from campus; passenger rail service 5 miles from campus.

Publications: *Louisiana Business Survey* (quarterly) first published 1970, *Plantation Society* (triennially) first published 1981, *Review of Business and Economic Research* (triennially) first published 1965.

Library Collections: 850,000 volumes including bound books, serial backfiles, electronic documents, and government documents not in separate collections. Online and card catalogs. Current serial subscriptions: 4,916 paper, 56 microform, 401 electronic. 22,003 recordings; 2,587 compact discs. 24 computer work stations. Students have access to the online services and the Internet. Total budget for books and materials 2004–05: $1,675,348.

Most important holdings include collection on Marcus Christian (black poet and historian); archives of Supreme Court of Louisiana; William Faulkner Collection; Crabites Collection of Egyptology; Orleans Paris School Board Records.

Buildings and Grounds: Campus area 195 acres. *New buildings:* Kirschman Hall -College of Business Administration completed 2005; Recreation/Fitness Center 2003.

Chief Executive Officer: Dr. Timothy P. Ryan, Chancellor.

Address admission inquiries to Roslyn Sheley, Director of Admissions.

Xavier University of Louisiana

7325 Palmetto Street
New Orleans, Louisiana 70125
Tel: (504) 486-7411   **E-mail:** apply@xula.edu
Fax: (504) 520-7388   **Internet:** www.xula.edu

Institution Description: Xavier University of Louisiana is a private institution affiliated with the Sisters of the Blessed Sacrament, Roman Catholic Church. *Enrollment:* 4,121. *Degrees awarded:* Baccalaureate, first-professional (pharmacy), master's.

Accreditation: *Regional:* SACS-Comm. on Coll. *Professional:* chemistry, music, pharmacy

History: Established as Xavier University, a secondary school, 1915; became 2-year normal school and offered first instruction at postsecondary level 1917; chartered 1918; became 4-year college 1925; awarded first degree (baccalaureate) 1928; added master's program 1933.

Institutional Structure: *Governing board:* Xavier University of Louisiana Board of Trustees. Extrainstitutional representation: 19 trustees, institutional representation: president of the college. 1 ex officio. 19 voting. *Composition of institution:* Administrators 21 men / 11 women. Academic affairs headed by vice president for academic affairs. Management/business/finances directed by vice president for fiscal affairs. Full-time instructional faculty 262. Academic governance body, University Academic Assembly, meets an average of 6 times per year.

Calendar: Semesters. Academic year late Aug. to early May. Freshmen admitted Aug., Jan., June. Degrees conferred and formal commencement May. Summer session of 2 terms from mid-May to late July.

Characteristics of Freshmen: 88% of applicants accepted. 32% of applicants accepted and enrolled.

52% (519 students) submitted SAT scores; 76% (765 students) submitted ACT scores. *25th percentile:* SAT Verbal 440, SAT Math 430; ACT Composite 18, ACT English 18, ACT Math 17. *75th percentile:* SAT Verbal 470, SAT Math 540; ACT Composite 24, ACT English 25, ACT Math 23.

57% of entering freshmen expected to graduate within 5 years. 46% of freshmen from Louisiana. Freshmen from 36 states and 1 foreign country.

Admission: Rolling admissions plan. For fall acceptance, apply by Mar. 1. Early acceptance available. *Requirements:* Either graduation from accredited secondary school with 16 units which should include 4 English, 1 algebra, 1 geometry, 1 natural science, 1 social studies, 8 academic electives; or GED. Additional units recommended for some programs. Minimum GPA 2.0. Lowest acceptable secondary school class standing 50th percentile. *Entrance tests:* College Board SAT or ACT composite. For foreign students TOEFL. *For transfer students:* 2.0 minimum GPA; from 4-year accredited institution 90 semester hours maximum transfer credit; from 2-year accredited institution 60 hours.

College credit and advanced placement for postsecondary-level work completed in secondary school. Tutoring available. Developmental-remedial courses offered in summer session and regular academic year; nondegree credit given.

Degree Requirements: 128–166 semester hours; 2.0 GPA; 2 semesters in residence; core curriculum; minor requirements; exit competency examinations-GRE or other standardized tests. Additional requirements for some majors. Fulfillment of some degree requirements and exemption from some beginning courses possible by passing College Board CLEP Subject Examinations, APP (score of 3). *Grading system:* A–F; pass-fail; withdraw (deadline after which pass-fail appended to withdraw).

Distinctive Educational Programs: Cooperative education. Accelerated degree programs. Dual-degree programs in business with Tulane University; in engineering with Tulane University, University of Detroit (MI). Interdisciplinary program in urban studies. Preprofessional program in medicine. Facilities for independent research, including honors programs, tutorials. Cooperative major programs and cross-registration through consortium. *Other distinctive programs:* Credit and enrichment continuing education program. Center for Intercultural Studies (students attend various Central American, African, and European countries).

ROTC: Army, Navy, Air Force.

Degrees Conferred: 441 *baccalaureate.* Bachelor's degrees awarded in top five disciplines: biological/life sciences 169; business/marketing 43; communications/communication technologies 24; physical sciences; 57, psychology 51; 80 *master's:* various disciplines; 96 *first-professional:* pharmacy.

Fees and Other Expenses: *Full-time tuition per academic year 2004–05:* $11,300. *Required fees:* $900. *Room and board per academic year:* $7,100. *Books and supplies:* $1,000. Contact the university for current information regarding tuition and fees for graduate and first-professional study.

Financial Aid: Aid from institutionally generated funds is provided on the basis of academic merit, athletic ability, other criteria. Institution has a Program Participation Agreement with the U.S. Department of Education for eligible students to receive Pell Grants and other federal aid.

Financial aid to full-time, first-time undergraduate students: need-based scholarships/grants totaling $7,675,345, self-help $13,345,998; non-need-based scholarships/grants totaling $8,652,493, self-help $10,161,110, parent loans $9,854,659, tuition waivers $533,595, athletic awards $943,438.

Departments and Teaching Staff: *Professors* 49, *associate professors* 64, *assistant professors* 104, *instructors* 24 *part-time faculty* 48. *Total instructional faculty:* 289 (full-time 241, part-time 48; women 124, men 165; members of minority groups 134). Total faculty with doctorate, first-professional, or other terminal degree: 230. Student-to-faculty ratio: 15.6:1.

Enrollment: Total enrollment 4,121. Undergraduate full-time 772 men / 2,371 women, part-time 38m / 109w; first-professional full-time 136m / 445w, part-time 2m / 6w; graduate full-time 32m / 128w, part-time 16m / 66w.

Characteristics of Student Body: *Ethnic/racial makeup:* number of Black non-Hispanic: 2,750; American Indian or Alaska Native: 2; Asian or Pacific Islander: 161; Hispanic: 14; White non-Hispanic: 52; unknown: 243.

International Students: 68 nonresident aliens enrolled fall 2004. Students from Europe, Asia, Central and South America, Africa, Canada. Programs available to aid students whose native language is not English: social, cultural. No financial aid specifically designated for international students.

Student Life: On-campus residence halls house 25% of student body. Residence halls for men only constitute 37% of such space, for women only 63%. *Intercollegiate athletics:* men only: basketball; women only: basketball. *Special regulations:* Cars permitted without restrictions. Curfews. Residence hall visitation restrictions. *Special services:* Learning Resources Center, medical services. *Student publications:* A semimonthly newspaper. *Surrounding community:* New Orleans population over 500,000. Served by mass transit system; airport 8 miles from campus; passenger rail service 2 miles from campus.

Publications: *Xavier Review* (biannually) first published 1981.

Library Collections: 125,000 volumes. Online catalog. 1,865 current periodical subscriptions. 4,800 audiovisual units. Students have access to online information retrieval services and the Internet. Total 2004–05 budget for books and materials: $650,000.

Most important holdings include Charles F. Hartman Collection of manuscripts dealing with Civil War reconstruction period; New Orleans Crusader Collection; African American Collection, including materials by and about black persons; Treasury Department War Bond Literary Collection.

Buildings and Grounds: Campus area 27 acres.

Chief Executive Officer: Dr. Norman C. Francis, President.

Address admission inquiries to Warren D. Brown, Director of Admissions.

Maine

Bangor Theological Seminary

300 Union Street
Bangor, Maine 04401

Tel: (207) 942-6781   **E-mail:** admissions@bts.edu
Fax: (207) 990-1267   **Internet:** www.bts.edu

Institution Description: Bangor Theological Seminary is a private, independent, nonprofit seminary affiliated with the United Church of Christ. In addition to its professional program, the school offers a 2-year liberal studies program to prepare students without baccalaureate degrees for entrance to the theological studies program. *Enrollment:* 132. *Degrees awarded:* First-professional (master of divinity), master of theological studies, doctor of ministry.

Accreditation: *Regional:* NEASC. *National:* ATS. *Professional:* theology

History: Established in Hampden 1811; incorporated 1812; chartered 1814; offered first instruction at postsecondary level 1816; moved to present location 1819; adopted present name 1820; awarded first degree (first-professional) 1905. *See* Walter L. Cook, *Bangor Theological Seminary: A Sesquicentennial History* (Bangor: University of Maine Press, 1971) for further information.

Institutional Structure: *Governing board:* Board of Trustees of Bangor Theological Seminary. Extrainstitutional representation: 17 trustees; institutional representation: 5 alumni/ae, all voting. *Composition of institution:* Administrators 1 man / 3 women. Academic affairs headed by dean of the seminary. Management/business/finances directed by business treasurer. Full-time instructional faculty 5 men / 4 women. Academic governance body, the faculty, meets an average of 15 times per year.

Calendar: Semesters. Academic year early Sept. to mid-May. Entering students admitted Sept., Jan. Degrees conferred and formal commencement May.

Admission: Rolling admissions plan. For fall acceptance, apply as early as Sept. 1 of previous year, but not later than Aug. 1 of year of enrollment. *Requirements:* Either graduation from accredited secondary school or GED. For applicants under 21 years of age, 1 year college-level work; for applicants under 20, 2 years college-level work. Baccalaureate degree recommended. *For transfer students:* From accredited theological school maximum transfer credit limited only by residence requirement.

Degree Requirements: 90 credits for M.Div.; 50 credits for M.T.S.; 2.5 GPA; distribution requirements; baccalaureate degree from accredited college or university; demonstrated proficiency in writing. *Grading system:* A–F; pass-fail; withdraw (carries time limit).

Distinctive Educational Programs: *For first-professional students:* Facilities and programs for independent research, including individual majors, tutorials, independent study during summer and January session. *Available to all students:* Field education. Special facilities for using telecommunications in the classroom.

Degrees Conferred: 4 *master's:* theology; 16 *first-professional:* master of divinity; 3 *doctorate:* theology.

Fees and Other Expenses: *Full-time tuition per academic year 2004–05:* undergraduate $9,840. *Books and supplies:* $800. *Room and board per academic year:* $11,145. Contact the seminary for current graduate/professional program tuition/fees.

Financial Aid: Aid from institutionally generated funds is provided on the basis of academic merit. Institution has a Program Participation Agreement with the U.S. Department of Education for eligible students to receive Pell Grants and other federal aid.

Departments and Teaching Staff: *Professors 7, associate professors 3, part-time faculty 26. Total instructional faculty:* 36. Degrees held by full-time faculty: doctorate 80%, master's 20%. 80% hold terminal degrees.

Enrollment: Total enrollment 132. Undergraduate 29 (37.9% men, 82.1% women).

Characteristics of Student Body: *Ethnic/racial makeup (undergraduate):* Black non-Hispanic: 3.4%; White non-Hispanic: 93.1%.

International Students: No programs available to aid students whose native language is not English. No financial aid specifically designated for international students.

Student Life: 20 on-campus student apartments. *Special regulations:* On-campus parking is provided for all students. *Surrounding community:* Bangor population 35,000. Boston, 250 miles from campus, is nearest metropolitan area. Served by mass transit bus system; airport 2 miles from campus.

Publications: Sources of information about Bangor Theological Seminary include *The Open Door*, a quarterly publication.

Library Collections: 130,000 volumes. 775 microform titles; 770 audiovisual materials; 425 current periodical subscriptions.

Most important special holdings include 19th Century Sermon Collection, resources in Bible, theology, missions, and church history.

Buildings and Grounds: Campus area 12 acres.

Chief Executive Officer: Dr. William C. Imes, President.

Address admission inquiries to Michael Ruddy, Director of Admissions.

Bates College

2 Andrews Road
Lewiston, Maine 04240

Tel: (207) 786-6000   **E-mail:** admissions@bates.edu
Fax: (207) 786-6025   **Internet:** www.bates.edu

Institution Description: Bates College is a private, independent, nonprofit liberal arts college. *Enrollment:* 1,743. *Degrees awarded:* Baccalaureate.

Accreditation: *Regional:* NEASC. *Professional:*

History: Established as Maine State Seminary by Freewill Baptists and incorporated 1855; offered first instruction at postsecondary level 1863; adopted present name 1864; awarded first degree (baccalaureate) 1867. *See* Alfred Williams Anthony *Bates College and Its Background* (Philadelphia: Judson Press, 1936) for further information.

Institutional Structure: *Governing board:* President and Trustees of Bates College. Extrainstitutional representation: 40 trustees; institutional representation: 1 administrator; 1 ex officio. 40 voting. *Composition of institution:* Administrators 4 men / 4 women. Academic affairs headed by dean of the faculty. Management/business/finances directed by vice president for finance and administration and treasurer. Full-time instructional faculty 177. Academic governance body, the faculty, meets an average of 9 times per year.

Calendar: Semesters (4-4-1 plan). Academic year early Sept. to late May. First-year admitted Sept., Jan. Degrees conferred in May at formal commencement. Summer session devoted to special programs.

Characteristics of Freshmen: 64.7% of entering freshmen ranked in top 10% of high school class. 29.6% of applicants accepted. 38% of accepted applicants enrolled. 88% of entering first-years expected to graduate within 5 years. 10% of freshmen from Maine. Freshmen from 38 states and 33 foreign countries.

Admission: For fall acceptance, apply no later than Jan. 1 of year of enrollment. Students are notified of acceptance Apr. 1. Apply by Nov. 15 or Jan. 1 for early decision; need not limit application to Bates, but must withdraw other applications if accepted. Early acceptance and deferred admission available. On campus or alumni interview recommended. *Requirements:* Recommended secondary courses: 4 years of English, at least 3 mathematics, 3 foreign language, at least 1 laboratory science, 3 social science and/or history. GED accepted in exceptional cases. *Entrance tests:* By faculty vote, all standardized tests are optional. Nontraditional applicants welcome. *For transfer students:* 3.0 minimum GPA, 16 courses maximum transfer credit.

College credit and advanced placement for postsecondary-level work completed in secondary school. Tutoring, writing, and math workshops available.

Degree Requirements: 32 courses and 2 short-term units; 2.0 GPA; 2 years in residence; thesis or comprehensives in major field of study, 2 semesters physical education; general education requirements. Accelerated three-year degree program available. Fulfillment of some degree requirements and exemption from some beginning courses with College Board AP exam scores of 4 and 5. *Grading system:* A–F.

Distinctive Educational Programs: First-year seminars in many fields for entering students; thesis required for most majors with senior honors program available. 4-4-1 (semester-semester-short term) calendar. Innovative teaching approaches emphasized in the short term when students focus on one topic, including field study in U.S. and abroad. 32 majors offered, including African-American, American cultural, classical, medieval, Asian, environmental, and women's studies, as well as biological chemistry and neuroscience. Student designed interdisciplinary majors available. Liberal arts-engineering degree plan with Case Western, Columbia, Washington Universities, Dartmouth College, and RPI. Extensive student involvement in faculty research, including summer research internships. Bates sponsors a nationally recognized service-learning program providing over 40,000 hours of service to more than 100 community groups each year. Active Junior Year and Junior Semester Abroad program with over one-half of junior class participating in locations worldwide. Special fall semester abroad programs available to entering students. Washington semester program at American University. Williams College-Mystic Seaport Program in maritime studies. Exchange programs with Washington and Lee University, Morehouse and Spelman Colleges, and McGill University. Research program at Jackson Laboratory in Bar Harbor, Maine and Memorial Sloan-Kettering Career Center in New York.

Degrees Conferred: 450 *baccalaureate:* area and ethnic studies 18; biological/life 56; English 45; foreign languages and literature 26; interdisciplinary studies 12; mathematics 11; natural resources/environmental science 26; philosophy/religion/theology 26; physical sciences 20; psychology 50; social sciences and history 160; visual and performing arts 33.

Fees and Other Expenses: *Comprehensive fee per academic year 2004–05:* $39,900.

Financial Aid: Aid from institutionally generated funds is provided on the basis of financial need. Institution has a Program Participation Agreement with the U.S. Department of Education for eligible students to receive Pell Grants and other federal aid.

Financial aid to full-time, first-time undergraduate students: need-based scholarships/grants totaling $15,216,609, self-help $2,868,714; non-need-based scholarships/grants totaling $53,364, self-help $1,177,195, parent loans $1,696,782.

Departments and Teaching Staff: *Professors* 52, *associate professors* 53, *assistant professors* 40, *instructors* 4, *lecturers* 22, *part-time faculty* 26.

Total instructional faculty: 189 (full-time 163, part-time 26; women 66, men 103; members of minority groups 22). Student-to-faculty ratio: 10:1. Degrees held by full-time faculty: 99.2% hold terminal degrees.

Enrollment: Total enrollment 1,743. Undergraduate full-time 857 men / 886 women.

Characteristics of Student Body: *Ethnic/racial makeup:* number of Black non-Hispanic: 39; American Indian or Alaska Native: 3; Asian or Pacific Islander: 63; Hispanic: 49; White non-Hispanic: 1,440; unknown: 51. *Age distribution:* number under 18: 19; 18–19: 836; 20–21: 764; 22–24: 120; 25–29: 2; 30–34: 2.

International Students: 98 nonresident aliens enrolled fall 2004. Students from Europe, Asia, Central and South America, Africa, Canada. Programs available to aid students whose native language is not English: social, cultural. Financial aid specifically designated for international students: variable number of scholarships available annually,

Student Life: Guaranteed housing with on-campus residence halls and houses accommodating 90% of student body. Single sex residences available; most students choose co-ed residences. First-year students reside in "centers" with 8–15 other first-years and a junior advisor. Quiet houses, chemical-free houses, and theme houses available. No fraternities or sororities. 90 recognized student organizations, including volunteer, political, social, and multicultural groups. Intramural, club, and varsity sports. *Intercollegiate athletics:* men: soccer, football, cross-country, basketball, skiing, squash, swimming and diving, indoor track, rowing, tennis, baseball, lacrosse, outdoor track, golf; women: field hockey, volleyball, cross-country, golf, basketball, soccer, skiing, squash, swimming and diving, indoor track, tennis, rowing, softball, lacrosse, outdoor track. *Special services:* Health Center, Office of Career Services, Writing Workshop, community internship programs. *Student publications, radio: The Bates Student,* a weekly newspaper; *Garnet,* a literary magazine (published irregularly); *Mirror,* a yearbook. Radio station WRBC broadcasts 24 hours a day, 7 days per week. *Surrounding community:* Lewiston and nearby Auburn have populations of 40,000 and 24,000 respectively. Portland is 35 miles from campus; Boston (MA), 140 miles from campus. Served by interstate and local bus system.

Library Collections: 499,777 volumes including bound books, serial backfiles, electronic documents, and government documents not in separate collections. Online catalog. Current serial subscriptions: 726 paper, 175 microform, 61 electronic. 24,994 recordings; 8,131 compact discs; 1,597 CD-ROMs. 46 computer work stations. Students have access to the Internet at no charge.

Most important holdings include early Freewill Baptist collection; Maine Small Press Collection; Rice Collection (historical and economic material in French and German); Stanton Natural History Collection; Dorothy Freeman Collection; Edmund S. Muskie Archives.

Buildings and Grounds: Campus area 109 acres.

Chief Executive Officer: Dr. Elaine T. Hansen, President.

Address admission inquiries to Wylie L. Mitchell, Dean of Admissions.

Bowdoin College

Brunswick, Maine 04011

Tel: (207) 725-3100   **E-mail:** admissions@bowdoin.edu
Fax: (207) 725-3101   **Internet:** www.bowdoin.edu

Institution Description: Bowdoin College is a private, independent, liberal arts college. *Enrollment:* 1,677. *Degrees awarded:* Baccalaureate.

Accreditation: *Regional:* NEASC.

History: Established and chartered 1794; offered first instruction at postsecondary level 1802; awarded first degree (baccalaureate) 1806; became coeducational 1971; celebrated bicentennial June 1994. *See* Charles C. Calhoun, *A Small College in Maine: Two Hundred Years of Bowdoin* (Penmor Lithographers, Lewiston, Maine: 1993). Patricia McGraw Anderson, *The Architecture of Bowdoin College* (Brunswick, Maine: Bowdoin College Museum of Art, 1988).

Institutional Structure: *Governing board:* Unicameral, Board of Trustees. Extrainstitutional representation: 50 trustees; institutional representation: the president of the college. *Composition of institution:* Administrators 135 men / 203 women. Academic affairs headed by dean for academic affairs. Management/business/finances directed by vice president for finance and administration. Student affairs headed by dean of student affairs. Full-time instructional faculty 152. Academic governance body, the faculty, meets an average of 9 times per year.

Calendar: Semesters. Academic year late Aug. to mid-May. Freshmen admitted Sept. Degrees conferred and formal commencement May. No summer session.

Characteristics of Freshmen: 24% of applicants admitted. 40% of applicants admitted and enrolled. 64% (346 students) submitted SAT scores. *25th percentile:* SAT Verbal 640, SAT Math 650. *75th percentile:* SAT Verbal 740, SAT 720.

89% of entering freshmen expected to graduate within 5 years. 11% of freshmen from Maine. Freshmen from 39 states and 13 foreign countries.

Admission: For fall acceptance, apply no later than Jan. 1 for Early Decision II and regular admission. Students notified of decision by mid-Apr. For Early Decision I, apply no later than Nov. 15; must limit to Bowdoin. Notification by late December. *Requirements:* Graduation from secondary school or general college preparatory program recommended. Recommend 4 units English, foreign language, mathematics (including trigonometry), and social science, and 3-4 years of laboratory science. Interview strongly recommended. Recommendations from school guidance counselor, two teacher recommendations, essay and school transcript considered very important as well as other factors such as extracurricular participation, special talents, and cultural or regional backgrounds that will contribute to the diversity of the college. Student's interests and personality matched with aims and objectives of the college. *Entrance tests:* SAT or ACT optional. *For transfer students:* March 1 deadline for fall admission; 3.0 minimum GPA; 16 courses maximum transfer credit.

College credit and advanced placement for postsecondary-level work completed in secondary school in conjunction with the CEEB Advanced Placement Program.

Degree Requirements: Successfully pass the equivalent of 32 full-credit courses; complete a departmental major or majors, an interdisciplinary major, or a student-designed major (a minor may be declared with any of the above); 4 semesters in residence (completing at least 16 courses), at least 2 during the junior and senior years; complete at least 2 semester courses in each of the 3 areas of the curriculum: natural science and mathematics, social and behavioral sciences, humanities and fine arts; and two semester courses in non-Eurocentric studies.

Some degree requirements and exemption from some beginning courses possible with College Board AP credit. *Grading system:* A, B, C, D, F (plus and minus grading system); credit/fail option available for a limited number of courses.

Distinctive Educational Programs: Interdisciplinary majors in Africana studies, art history and archaeology, art history and visual arts, Asian studies, biochemistry, chemical physics, computer science and mathematics, English and theater, environmental studies, Eurasian and East European studies, geology and chemistry, geology and physics, Latin American studies, mathematics and economics, neuroscience, gender and women's studies. Departmental and interdepartmental majors offered in Africana studies, anthropology, art history, Asian studies, biochemistry, biology, chemistry, classics, computer science, economics, English, environmental studies, French, geology, German, government history, mathematics, music, neuroscience, philosophy, physics, psychology, religion, Romance languages, Russian, sociology, Spanish, visual arts. Minor programs offered by most departments including dance, Greek, Latin, theater, education, Latin American Studies. Opportunities for double and student-designed majors. Facilities for independent research and study, including honors program. State-accredited teacher certification program. Off-campus marine biology and ornithology research facilities at Kent Island, New Brunswick (Canada) and at two coastal facilities near the campus. Foreign study encouraged. College sponsors the South India Term Abroad (SITA) program and the Intercollegiate Sri Lanka Education (ISLE) program; Swedish Program in Organizations Studies and Public Policy (Stockholm) and the Intercollegiate Center for Classical Studies (Rome); member of the American College Consortium for East-West Cultural and Academic Exchange (with republics formerly in the Soviet Union). Programs for East Asian studies in Nepal, Japan, and People's Republic of China. Programs for studies in Africa, South and Central America, Australia, Caribbean, New Zealand, Israel, Turkey, Bowdoin participates in the Twelve-College Exchange Program. Off-campus domestic study programs include the Williams College-Mystic Seaport Program, the National Theater Institute, the Washington Semester at American University, and the SEA Semester at Woods Hole Oceanographic Institution (Cape Cod, MA). Dual-degree programs in engineering with California Institute of Technology, Columbia University (NY); and in legal studies with Columbia University (NY). *Other distinctive programs:* College-owned art museum sponsors symposium and special lectures. Its collection includes over 140 Old Master drawings, ancient art (including sculpture, pottery, bronzes), American colonial and federal portraits, Winslow Homer memorabilia, 19th- and 20th-century works of American artists.

Degrees Conferred: 415 *baccalaureate:* area and ethnic studies 13; biological/life sciences 36; computer and information sciences 3; English 31; foreign languages and literature 50; interdisciplinary studies 10; mathematics 9; natural resources/environmental science 15; philosophy/religion/theology 18; physical sciences 18; psychology 18; social sciences and history 160; visual and performing arts 34. *Honorary degrees awarded 2004–05:* Doctor of Humane Letters 1, Doctor of Science 1, Doctor of Laws 1, Doctor of Letters 1, Doctor of Music 1.

Fees and Other Expenses: *Full-time tuition per academic 2004–05:* $30,944. *Required fees:* $682. *Room and board per academic year:* $8,054.

Financial Aid: Aid from institutionally generated funds is provided on the basis of financial need, other considerations. Institution has a Program Participation Agreement with the U.S. Department of Education for eligible students to receive Pell Grants and other federal aid.

Financial aid to full-time, first-time undergraduate students: need-based scholarships/grants totaling $17,067,790, self-help $3,139,535; non-need-based scholarships/grants totaling $577,172, self-help $880,228, parent loans $3,412,858.

Departments and Teaching Staff: *Total instructional faculty:* 183 (full-time 152, part-time 31; women 84, men 99; members of minority groups 19). Total faculty with doctorate, first-professional, or other terminal degree: 170. Student-to-faculty ratio: 10:1. *Faculty development:* $2,643,233 in grants for research. 26 faculty members awarded sabbaticals 2004–05.

Enrollment: Total enrollment 1,677. Undergraduate full-time 851 men / 817 women, part-time 3m / 6w. *Transfer students:* in-sate 7; from out-of-state 14.

Characteristics of Student Body: *Ethnic/racial makeup:* number of Black non-Hispanic: 90; American Indian or Alaska Native: 13; Asian or Pacific Islander: 185; Hispanic: 96; White non-Hispanic: 1,201; unknown: 36. *Age distribution:* number under 18: 33; 18–19: 830; 20–21: 693; 22–24: 115; 25–29: 5; 30–34: 40–49: 1.

International Students: 56 nonresident aliens enrolled fall 2004. 9 students from Europe, 12 Asia, 1 Africa, 21 Canada, 3 Middle East, 10 other. No programs available to aid students whose native language is not English. No financial aid specifically designated for international students.

Student Life: On-campus residence halls house 85% of student body. All residences are coeducational and vary from traditional residence halls: the Coles Tower, small "family-style" houses, and college-owned apartments. *Intercollegiate athletics:* men: baseball, basketball, cross country, football, ice hockey, lacrosse, soccer, squash, swimming, tennis, track/field (indoor and outdoor), skiing; women: basketball, cross country, field hockey, ice hockey, lacrosse, skiing, soccer, softball, squash, swimming, tennis, track/field (indoor and outdoor), volleyball; coeducational: golf, sailing. 80% of the student body participates in either intramural or intercollegiate sports. *Special regulations:* All students are permitted to have cars on campus. *Special services:* Career services, medical and counseling services, evening shuttle-bus service. *Student publications, radio: The Bowdoin Orient,* a weekly newspaper; *Bugle,* a yearbook; *Quill,* a biannual literary magazine; *WBOR,* a student-run radio station. Bowdoin Cable Network, a student-run cable broadcasting system. *Surrounding community:* Brunswick (ME), population 21,500, is situated on the Maine coast, 25 miles from Portland and 120 miles from Boston.

Library Collections: 981,704 volumes including bound books, serial backfiles, electronic documents, and government documents not in separate collections. Online catalog. Current serial subscriptions: 1,819 paper and microform; 3,846 via electronic access. 8,099 recordings; 4,521 compact discs; 1,099 CD-ROMs. 116 computer work stations. Students have access to the Internet at no charge. Total budget for books, periodicals, audiovisual materials, microforms 2004–05: $1,873,850.

Most important holdings include special collections of books on the Civil War, Abolition, Anti-Slavery and Reconstruction, including the Joshua Lawrence Chamberlain Collection and the Oliver Otis Howard Papers; Literary Life in the Late 18th- and 19th Centuries, including the Abbot Memorial Collection, the Nathaniel Hawthorne Collection, and the Henry Wadsworth Longfellow Collection; collections on the history of Bowdoin and the State of Maine; Senator George J. Mitchell Papers.

Buildings and Grounds: Campus area 200 acres. *New buildings:* Kanbar Hall completed 2004; Thane Dining Hall 2000; Wish Theater 2000.

Chief Executive Officer: Dr. Barry Mills, President.

Address admission inquiries to James S. Miller, Dean of Admissions and Financial Aid.

Colby College

Mayflower Hill Drive
Waterville, Maine 04901
Tel: (207) 872-3168 **E-mail:** admission@colby.edu
Fax: (207) 872-3474 **Internet:** www.colby.edu

Institution Description: Colby College is a private, independent, nonsectarian, nonprofit liberal arts college. *Enrollment:* 1,821. *Degrees awarded:* Baccalaureate.

Accreditation: *Regional:* NEASC.

History: Established and chartered as Maine Literary and Theological Institution 1813; offered first instruction at postsecondary level 1818; changed name to Waterville College 1821; awarded first degree (baccalaureate) 1822; changed name to Colby University 1867; first admitted women 1871; adopted present name 1899. *See* Ernest C. Marriner, *A History of Colby* (Waterville: Colby College Press, 1963) for further information.

Institutional Structure: *Governing board:* Board of Trustees of Colby College. Extrainstitutional representation: 30 voting members of the board including 9 alumni trustees; 51 overseers; institutional representation: 2 faculty members, 2 students. 4 ex officio. *Composition of institution:* Administrators 55 men / 46 women. Academic affairs headed by vice president for academic affairs and dean of the faculty. Management/business/finances directed by administrative vice president. Full-time instructional faculty 156. Academic governance board, the faculty, meets an average of 10 times per year.

Calendar: Semesters (4-1-4 plan). Academic year early Sept. to late May. Freshmen admitted Sept., Feb. Degrees conferred May, Oct. Formal commencement May. No summer session.

Characteristics of Freshmen: 37% of applicants admitted. 36% of applicants admitted and enrolled.

82% (414 students) submitted SAT scores; 25% (125 students) submitted ACT scores. *25th percentile*: SAT Verbal 640, SAT I Math 640; ACT Composite 27, ACT English 28, ACT Math 26. *75th percentile*: SAT I Verbal 720, SAT I Math 710; ACT Composite 31, ACT English 32, ACT Math 30.

87% of entering freshmen expected to graduate within 5 years. 11% of freshmen from Maine. Freshmen from 34 states and 27 foreign countries.

Admission: For fall acceptance, apply no later than Jan. 15 of year of enrollment. Students are notified of acceptance Apr. Apply by Nov. 15 or Jan. 1 for early decision; must limit application to Colby College. Early acceptance available. *Recommended:* Graduation from accredited secondary school with 16 units which must include 4 English, 2 foreign language, 3 mathematics, 1 history or social studies, 1 laboratory science. *Entrance tests:* College Board SAT or ACT composite. For foreign students TOEFL. *For transfer students:* 3.0 minimum GPA, 64 credit hours must be earned in resident as of the class of 2005.

College credit and advanced placement for postsecondary-level work completed in secondary school. Tutoring available.

Degree Requirements: 120 semester hours (128 semester hours as of class of 2005); 2.0 GPA; 4 semesters in residence; wellness requirement; distribution requirements. Fulfillment of some degree requirements and exemption from some beginning courses possible by passing departmental examinations, College Board CLEP, AP. *Grading system:* A–F; pass-fail; withdraw (carries penalty).

Distinctive Educational Programs: January Program of Independent Study; Colby Outdoor Orientation Trips for freshmen; Senior Scholars. Exchange programs with Fisk University (TN), Howard University (DC), and Pitzer and

Pomona Colleges (CA). Interdisciplinary programs in American studies, East Asian studies, French studies, Latin American studies, Jewish studies, human development, and performing arts. Concentrations in cell and molecular biology/biochemistry, education, environmental science, financial markets, earth science, public policy, studio art, art history, quantitative analysis. The Associated Kyoto Program; China Cooperative Language Program; Intercollegiate Sri Lanka Education Consortium. London Program in theater and drama. Colby in Washington (DC); Colby in Cuernavaca (Mexico); Colby in Dijon (France); Colby in Costa Rica; Colby in Frieburg (Germany); Colby in St. Petersburg (Russia); Colby in Salamanca (Spain); Colby in Cork (Ireland). Five-year engineering degree program with the Dartmouth College. Preprofessional programs in law, theology, government service, medicine, and dentistry; extensive computer resources and instruction in computer sciences.

Degrees Conferred: 486 *baccalaureate:* area and ethnic studies 59; biological/life sciences 41; business/marketing 2; computer and information sciences 14; English 52; foreign languages and literature 34; interdisciplinary studies 12; mathematics 20; natural resources/environmental science 15; philosophy/religion/theology 22; physical sciences 23; psychology 23; social sciences and history 135; visual and performing arts 35.

Fees and Other Expenses: *Full-time tuition per academic year 2005–06:* comprehensive fee $41,770 (includes tuition, room and board, mandatory fees).

Financial Aid: Aid from institutionally generated funds is provided on the basis of financial need.

Financial aid to full-time, first-time undergraduate students: need-based scholarships/grants totaling $16,269,365, self-help $2,299,763; non-need-based self-help $1,982,344, parent loans $2,534,013.

Departments and Teaching Staff: *Professors* 70, *associate professors* 38, *assistant professors* 50, *instructors* 2, *part-time faculty* 64. *Total instructional faculty:* 224 (full-time 160, part-time 64; women 105, men 119; members of minority groups 21). Total faculty with doctorate, first-professional, or other terminal degree: 189. Student-to-faculty ratio: 10:1. *Faculty development:* 22 faculty members awarded sabbaticals 2004–05.

Enrollment: Total enrollment 1,821. Full-time 849 men / 972 women. *Transfer students:* from out-of-state 10.

Characteristics of Student Body: *Ethnic/racial makeup:* number of Black non-Hispanic: 26; American Indian or Alaska Native: 11; Asian or Pacific Islander: 97; Hispanic: 48; White non-Hispanic: 1,502. *Age distribution:* number under 18: 20; 18–19: 879; 20–21: 806; 22–24: 115; 25–29: 1.

International Students: 157 nonresident aliens enrolled fall 2004. 59 students from Europe, 57 Asia, 13 Central and South America, 18 Africa, 31 Canada, 3 Australia, 6 other. No programs available to aid students whose native language is not English. No financial aid designated for international students.

Student Life: *Intercollegiate athletics:* men only: baseball, basketball, cross-country, football, golf, ice hockey, lacrosse, skiing, soccer, squash, swimming, tennis, indoor and outdoor track; women only: basketball, cross-country, field hockey, ice hockey, lacrosse, skiing, soccer, softball, squash, swimming, tennis, indoor and outdoor track; both sexes: rugby, crew, and sailing. Colby is a charter member of the New England Small College Athletic Conference and does not grant athletic scholarships of any kind. *Special regulations:* Cars permitted without restrictions. *Special services:* Learning Resources Center, medical services, van transportation to nearby community; Farnham Writer's Center. *Student publications, radio:* The Colby Echo, a weekly newspaper; *Colby Reader,* quarterly political paper, *The Oracle,* a yearbook; *The Pequod,* for art, literature, and photography; *New Moon Rising,* feminist journal. Radio station WMHB-FM broadcasts 126 hours per week. *Surrounding community:* Waterville population 18,000. Boston, 180 miles from campus, is nearest metropolitan area. Served by airport 3 miles from campus.

Publications: *Colby Library Quarterly* first published 1943; *Colby,* quarterly magazine for alumni, parents, and friends of the college.

Library Collections: 944,000 volumes including bound books, serial backfiles, electronic documents, and government documents not in separate collections. Online catalog. Current serial subscriptions: 1,145 paper, 6,455 via electronic access. 8,400 recordings. 63 computer work stations. Students have access to the Internet at no charge.

Most important holdings include Edwin Arlington Robinson Collection of the Maine Poets' books, manuscripts, letters, memorabilia; Thomas Hardy Collection; James Augustine Healy Collection of Modern Irish Literature comprising 6,000 primary and critical sources representing the Irish Literary Renaissance, 1880–1940.

Buildings and Grounds: Campus area 714 acres. *New buildings:* Harold and Bibby Alford Residence Complex.

Chief Executive Officer: Dr. William D. Adams, President.

Address admission inquiries to Steven Thomas, Dean of Admissions.

College of the Atlantic

105 Eden Street
Bar Harbor, Maine 04609

Tel: (207) 288-5015   **E-mail:** inquiry@coa.edu
Fax: (207) 288-4126   **Internet:** www.coa.edu

Institution Description: College of the Atlantic is a private, independent, nonprofit college. *Enrollment:* 283. *Degrees awarded:* Baccalaureate, master's.

Accreditation: *Regional:* NEASC.

History: Incorporated 1969; offered first instruction at postsecondary level 1971; awarded first degree (baccalaureate) 1974.

Institutional Structure: *Governing board:* Board of Trustees. Representation: 27 trustees, including 2 alumni, the president of the college. 1 ex officio. 27 voting. *Composition of institution:* Administrators 23. Academic affairs headed by academic dean. Management/business/finances directed by director of finance and administration. Full-time instructional faculty 19. Self-governance system directed by All College Meeting; meets an average of 16 times per year.

Calendar: Trimesters. Academic year mid-Sept. to early June. New students admitted Sept., Dec., Mar. Degrees conferred and formal commencement May. Limited summer courses offered.

Characteristics of Freshmen: 73% of applicants accepted. 43% of accepted applicants enrolled. 62% of applicants submitted SAT scores; 12% submitted ACT scores. *25th percentile:* SAT Verbal 550, SAT Math 510; ACT Composite 23. *75th percentile:* SAT Verbal 680, SAT Math 620; ACT Composite 31.

63% of entering freshmen expected to graduate within 5 years. 20% of freshmen from Maine. Freshmen from 33 states and 9 foreign countries.

Admission: Rolling admissions plan. For fall acceptance, apply no later than Jan. 10. For Early Decision I, Dec. 1; Early Decision II, Jan 1. *Requirements:* Either graduation from secondary school or GED; personal interview recommended; written statement expressing commitment to the study of human ecology; personal interview recommended. *Entrance tests:* College Board SAT optional.

College credit for postsecondary-level work completed in secondary school and for extrainstitutional learning on basis of ACE *2006 Guide to the Evaluation of Educational Experiences in the Armed Services;* committee assessment; personal interview. Tutoring available. Remedial courses offered during regular academic year; credit given.

Degree Requirements: 36 COA credits; 2 years in residence; core course in human ecology; 2 courses in each of 3 resource areas; 1-term internship; human ecology essay demonstrating competence in writing; quantitative reasoning requirement; 1-term final project. Fulfillment of some degree requirements possible by passing College Board CLEP, AP. *Grading system:* A–F; pass-fail; withdraw (deadline after which pass-fail is appended to withdraw); descriptive reports.

Distinctive Educational Programs: Non-departmental interdisciplinary program in human ecology, stressing the dynamic interactions between humans and the environment; two-day academic and social orientation; seminary-style classes. Independent study, tutorials; residency. Cross-registration with the University of Maine. Five-day orientation consisting of wilderness expedition in the fall for entering and returning students.

Degrees Conferred: 49 *baccalaureate:* military policy studies; 2 *master's:* interdisciplinary studies.

Fees and Other Expenses: *Full-time tuition per academic year 2004–05:* $26,238. *Required fees:* $375. *Room and board per academic year:* $7,089.

Financial Aid: Aid from institutionally generated funds is provided on the basis of academic merit, financial need. Institution has a Program Participation Agreement with the U.S. Department of Education for eligible students to receive Pell Grants and other federal aid.

Financial aid to full-time, first-time undergraduate students: need-based scholarships/grants totaling $4,238,524, self-help $1,032,122, tuition waivers $24,404; non-need-based scholarships/grants totaling $22,500, self-help $278,777, parent loans $268,386.

Departments and Teaching Staff: *Total instructional faculty:* 35 (full-time 27, part-time 8; women 12, men 22). Total faculty with doctorate, first-professional, or other terminal degree: 26. Student-to-faculty ratio: 9:1.

Enrollment: Total enrollment 283. Undergraduate full-time 98 men / 162 women, part-time 2m / 10w; graduate full-time 1m / 8w, part-time 2m.

Characteristics of Student Body: *Age distribution:* 17–21: 84%; 22–24: 13%; 25–29: 1%; 30–34: 1%; 40–49: 1%.

International Students: 50 nonresident aliens enrolled fall 2004. Programs available to aid students whose native language is not English: social, cultural, financial.

Student Life: On-campus coeducational cooperative residences house 43% of student body. *Special regulations:* Pets are not allowed on campus. Cars permitted without restrictions. *Special services:* Learning Resources Center. *Student publications: Off the Wall,* a weekly news sheet; *Voices,* a biannual literary magazine. *Surrounding community:* Bar Harbor population 5,000. Boston (MA), 250 miles from campus, is nearest metropolitan area. Served by Bar Harbor Airport 9 miles from campus.

Library Collections: 38,500 volumes. Current serial subscriptions: 400 paper; 275 microform. 1,950 audiovisual materials. Access to online information retrieval systems and the Internet.

Most important holdings include R. Amory Thorndike Humanities Collection (books); Philip Darlington Evolution Collection (books); Dorcas Crary Natural History and Horticulture Collection (books); John Nason Collection.

Buildings and Grounds: Campus area 26 shorefront acres.

Chief Executive Officer: Dr. Steven K. Katona, President.

Address admission inquiries to Sarah Baker, Director of Admissions.

Husson College

One College Circle
Bangor, Maine 04401-2999
Tel: (207) 941-7100   **E-mail:** admit@husson.edu
Fax: (207) 941-7988   **Internet:** www.husson.edu

Institution Description: Husson College is a private, independent, nonprofit college of business and professional studies. *Enrollment:* 2,039. *Degrees awarded:* Associate, baccalaureate, master's.

Accreditation: *Regional:* NEASC. *Professional:* nursing, nursing education, occupational therapy, physical therapy

History: Established and incorporated as Shaw Business College 1898; offered first instruction at postsecondary level 1910; changed name to Maine School of Commerce-Bangor Branch 1926, to Bangor Maine School of Commerce 1933; adopted present name 1947; awarded first degree (baccalaureate) 1954; initiated graduate programs 1978; initiated baccalaureate nursing program 1982.

Institutional Structure: *Governing board:* Husson College Board of Trustees. Representation: 33 trustees, including 2 alumni, president of the college, 1 student. 2 ex officio. All voting. *Composition of institution:* Administrators 7 men. Academic affairs headed by vice-president and dean for academic affairs. Management/business/finances directed by vice-president for financial affairs and treasurer. Full-time instructional faculty 53. Academic governance body, Academic Committee, meets an average of 10 times per year.

Calendar: Semesters. Academic year Sept. to May. Students admitted Sept., Jan., June. Degrees conferred and formal commencement May. Summer session of 2 terms from June to Aug.

Characteristics of Freshmen: 98% of applicants admitted. 525 of applicants admitted and enrolled.

99% (262 students) submitted SAT scores; 4% (10 students) submitted ACT scores. *25th percentile:* SAT Verbal 410, SAT Math 410; ACT Composite 17; ACT English 14, ACT Math 16. *75th percentile:* SAT Verbal 490, SAT Math 510; ACT Composite 27, ACT English 28, ACT Math 27.

56% of entering freshmen expected to graduate within 5 years. 88% of freshmen from Maine. Freshmen from 15 states and 13 foreign countries.

Admission: Rolling admissions plan. For fall acceptance, apply no later than 2 weeks before beginning of semester. *Requirements:* Either graduation from secondary school or GED. Recommendation from secondary school counselor or principal. Interview may be required. *Entrance tests:* College Board SAT or ACT Composite recommended. *For transfer students:* 2.0 minimum GPA, 90 hours maximum transfer credit; from 2-year accredited institution 45 hours.

College credit for postsecondary-level work completed in secondary school and extrainstitutional learning on basis of ACE *2006 Guide to the Evaluation of Educational Experiences in the Armed Services.* Tutoring available. Noncredit developmental/remedial courses offered during regular academic year.

Degree Requirements: *For all associate degrees:* 60–90 credit hours. *For all baccalaureate degrees:* 120–135 credit hours. *For all undergraduate degrees:* 2.0 GPA; last 2 terms in residence; distribution requirements. *For M.S. in physical therapy:* 177 credit hours.

Fulfillment of some degree requirements and exemption from some beginning courses possible by passing departmental examinations, College Board CLEP, AP. *Grading system:* A–F; withdraw (deadline after which pass-fail is appended to withdraw); incomplete (deadline after which A–F is assigned).

Distinctive Educational Programs: *For undergraduates:* Cooperative education programs. Flexible meeting places and schedules, including off-campus centers at South Portland, and Caribou; evening and weekend classes. *For graduate students:* Internships. *Available to all students:* Individual majors. *Other distinctive programs:* Continuing Education and Extension Division offers associate and baccalaureate degree programs. Language studies center on campus

offers intensive English training to foreign students who plan to study at U.S. colleges and universities.

ROTC: Army and Navy offered in cooperation with University of Maine at Orono.

Degrees Conferred: 21 *associate;* 259 *baccalaureate* (B); 107 *master's* (M): biological/life sciences 4 (B); business/marketing 144 (B), 76 (M); computer and information sciences 24 (B); education 16 (B); health professions and related sciences 43 (B), 34 (M); law/legal studies 6; protective services/public administration 12 (B); psychology 10 (B).

Fees and Other Expenses: *Full-time tuition per academic year 2005–06:* $11,130. *Required fees:* $250. *Room and board per academic year:* $6,030.

Financial Aid: Aid from institutionally generated funds is provided on the basis of academic merit, financial need. Institution has a Program Participation Agreement with the U.S. Department of Education for eligible students to receive Pell Grants and other federal aid.

Financial aid to full-time, first-time undergraduate students: need-based scholarships/grants totaling $7,057,899, self-help $6,320,944, parent loans $520,120; non-need-based scholarships/grants totaling $762,295, self-help $2,887,682, parent loans $714,841.

Departments and Teaching Staff: *Professors* 11, *associate professors* 14, *assistant professors* 12, *instructors* 3, *part-time teachers* 11.

Total instructional faculty: 51 (full-time 46, part-time 5; women 23, men 28). Total faculty with doctorate, first-professional, or other terminal degree: 42. Student-to-faculty ratio: 18:1.

Enrollment: Total enrollment 2,039. Undergraduate full-time 332 men / 702 women, part-time 162m / 382w; graduate full-time 20m / 37w, part-time 64m / 140w.

Characteristics of Student Body: *Ethnic/racial makeup:* number of Black non-Hispanic: 30; American Indian or Alaska Native: 3; Asian or Pacific Islander: 24; Hispanic: 6; White non-Hispanic: 1,681.

International Students: 44 nonresident aliens enrolled fall 2004. Programs available to aid students whose native language is not English: English as a Second Language Program. No financial aid specifically designated for international students.

Student Life: On-campus residence halls house 59% of student body. Residence halls for both sexes constitute 100% of such space. 3% of men join and live in fraternities; 3% of women join and live in sororities. Fraternities and sororities are located in residence halls. *Intercollegiate athletics:* men: baseball, basketball, cross-country, football, golf, soccer; women : basketball, cross-county, field hockey, soccer, softball, swimming, volleyball. *Special regulations:* Cars permitted for $25 fee. Quiet hours from 10pm to 7am Mon.–Thurs., 1am to 7am Fri.–Sun. *Special services:* Learning Resources Center, medical services, Academic Development specialists. *Student publications, radio: The Chieftain,* a yearbook; *The Spectator,* a weekly newspaper. Radio station WHSN broadcasts 84 hours per week. *Surrounding community:* Bangor population 35,000. Boston (MA), 250 miles from campus, is nearest metropolitan area. Served by airport 2 miles from campus.

Publications: *Crosscuts,* student and faculty literary publication; *Ledger,* alumni publication; *Business Law Review,* faculty publication.

Library Collections: 37,871 volumes. 15,147 microforms; 500 current periodical subscriptions. 6 computer work stations. Access to online information retrieval systems and the Internet. Total 2004–05 budget for books and materials: $125,000.

Buildings and Grounds: Campus area 170 acres. *New buildings:* Center for Family Business; Swan Fitness Center; The Commons.

Chief Executive Officer: Dr. William Beardsley, President.

Address admission inquiries to Jane M. Goodwin, Director of Admissions.

Maine College of Art

97 Spring Street
Portland, Maine 04101-3913
Tel: (207) 775-3052   **E-mail:** admsns@meca.edu
Fax: (207) 772-5069   **Internet:** www.meca.edu

Institution Description: Maine College of Art, formerly named Portland School of Art, is a private, nonprofit college. *Enrollment:* 465. *Degrees awarded:* Baccalaureate.

Accreditation: *Regional:* NEASC. *Professional:* art

History: Established as Portland School of Fine and Applied Arts 1882; incorporated and offered first instruction at postsecondary level 1911; awarded first degree (baccalaureate) 1975; adopted present name 1994.

Institutional Structure: *Governing board:* Portland Society of Art Board of Trustees. Extrainstitutional representation: 36 trustees. 2 ex officio. All voting. *Composition of institution:* Administrators 4 men / 6 women. Academic affairs headed by assistant director. Management/business/finances directed by business manager. Full-time instructional faculty 15. Academic governance body, the faculty, meets an average of 18 times per year.

Calendar: Semesters. Academic year Sept. to May. Freshmen admitted Sept. Degrees conferred and formal commencement May. Summer session from mid-June to late July.

Characteristics of Freshmen: 445 applicants (164 men, 291 women). 64.5% of applicants admitted. 33.8% of admitted students enrolled full-time.

60% (90 students) submitted SAT scores; 6% (10 students) submitted ACT scores. *25th percentile*: SAT I Verbal 490, SAT I Math 460; ACT Composite 15. *75th percentile*: SAT I Verbal 590, SAT I Math 560; ACT Composite 20.

40% of freshmen from Maine. Freshmen from 18 states and 3 foreign countries.

Admission: Rolling admissions plan. For fall acceptance, recommended deadline Mar. 1. *Requirements:* Graduation from secondary school, or GED. Portfolio of 10 to 20 pieces, including 5 drawings from direct observation. *For transfer students:* 2.0 GPA, 36 semester hours maximum transfer credit for academic subjects. Maximum transfer credit for studio subjects based on performance and portfolio evaluation.

Degree Requirements: 134 credit hours; 2.0 GPA; 4 semesters in residence; 18 credits art history. *Grading system:* A–F; withdraw (carries time limit).

Distinctive Educational Programs: Study abroad by individual arrangement. Evening programs for adults; Saturday studio workshops for secondary school students.

Degrees Conferred: 89 *baccalaureate:* visual and performing arts; 13 *master's:* visual and performing arts.

Fees and Other Expenses: *Full-time tuition per academic year 2004–05:* $22,343. *Books and supplies:* $1,800. *Room and board per academic year:* $6,000.

Financial Aid: Aid from institutionally generated funds is provided on the basis of academic merit, financial need, artistic ability.Institution has a Program Participation Agreement with the U.S. Department of Education for eligible students to receive Pell Grants and other federal aid.

Financial aid to full-time, first-time undergraduate students: 31% received federal grants averaging $4,246; 18% state/local grants averaging $898; 100% institutional grants averaging $6,261; 66% received loans averaging $4,282.

Departments and Teaching Staff: *Total instructional faculty:* 40.

Enrollment: Total enrollment 465. Undergraduate 431 (40.8% men, 59.2% women).

Characteristics of Student Body: *Ethnic/racial makeup:* Black non-Hispanic: .2%; American Indian or Alaska Native: .7%; Asian or Pacific Islander: .2%; Hispanic: 2.6%; White non-Hispanic: 80.5%; unknown: 13.2%.

International Students: 11 nonresident aliens enrolled fall 2004. No programs to aid student whose native language is not English. Limited financial aid for international students.

Student Life: On-campus housing available. *Special regulations:* Cars permitted without restrictions. *Special services:* Medical services. *Surrounding community:* Portland population 65,000. Boston (MA), 90 miles from campus, is nearest metropolitan area. Served by airport 3 miles from campus.

Library Collections: 19,000 volumes. 100 videos; 45,000 slides.

Most important special collections include pre-1900 imprints; artists' books.

Chief Executive Officer: Dr. Christine J. Vincent, President.

Address admission inquiries to Joshua Bergey, Director of Admissions.

Maine Maritime Academy

Castine, Maine 04420

Tel: (207) 326-2206   **E-mail:** admissions@mma.edu
Fax: (207) 326-2515   **Internet:** www.mma.edu

Institution Description: Maine Maritime Academy is a state institution offering degree programs in marine engineering, marine transportation operations, marine science, marine biology, small vessel operations, international business and logistics. *Enrollment:* 819. *Degrees awarded:* Associate, baccalaureate, master's.

Accreditation: *Regional:* NEASC. *Professional:* business, engineering, engineering technology

History: Established as Maine Nautical Training School, chartered, and offered first instruction at postsecondary level 1941; adopted present name 1942; awarded first degree (bachelor of marine science) 1943. *See* James Aldrich, *A Fair Winds, Stormy Seas: 50 Years of Main Maritime Academy* (Penobscot Books, 1991) for further information.

Institutional Structure: *Governing board:* Board of Trustees, Maine Maritime Academy. Representation: 12 trustees meet 4 times per year. All voting. *Composition of institution:* Academic affairs headed by academic dean. Student

affairs head by dean of students. Management/business/finances directed by vice president for administration and finance. Full-time instructional faculty 52. Academic governance body, the Faculty, meets an average of 7 times per year.

Calendar: Semesters. Academic year Aug. to Apr. Freshmen admitted Sept.

Characteristics of Freshmen: 64% of applicants admitted. 95% of applicants admitted and enrolled.

Mean SAT scores 525 verbal, 513 mathematical.

68% of entering freshmen expected to graduate within 5 years. 65% of freshmen from Maine. Freshmen from 35 states and 6 foreign countries.

Admission: Rolling admissions plan. For fall acceptance, apply no later than July 1. *Requirements:* Either graduation from secondary school with 4 units in English, 3 units science, 4 units mathematics, or GED. Must be in good mental and physical health. *Entrance tests:* College Board SAT or ACT composite. Test for color blindness. *For transfer students:* 2.0 minimum GPA; maximum transfer credit limited only by residence requirement.

College credit and advanced placement for postsecondary-level work completed in secondary school.

Degree Requirements: *Bachelor of Science (four-year):* 128–142 credit hours depending on major; *Five-Year Systems Engineering major:* 181 credit hours. *Associate of Science:* 67 credit hours depending on major; *Master of Science (Global Supply Chain Management, Maritime Management, International Business, Defense Logistics):* 33 credit hours. 3.0 GPA for all programs. Additional requirements for all 4–5 year U.S. Coast Guard License programs: ship laboratory and watchstanding requirements, 3 sea training cruises.

Fulfillment of some degree requirements and exemption from some beginning courses possible by life experience credits, military schooling, and through College Board AP credits. *Grading system:* A–F; pass-fail for selected courses.

Distinctive Educational Programs: Co-op participation and credits in power engineering, systems engineering, small vessel operations, and marine transportation majors. Cadet shipping program on operating merchant ships and two 2-month training cruises on Maine Maritime Academy Training Vessel for fulfillment of sea time requirement. Since 1988, required successful completion of U.S. Coast Guard approved Fire Training Program. New regulations for Nautical Science and Marine Transportation students are 360 days or equivalent of sea time for license.

ROTC: Navy. 18 commissions awarded 2004.

Degrees Conferred: 13 *associate;* 119 *baccalaureate:* biological/life 9; business/marketing 9; engineering and engineering technologies 57; interdisciplinary studies 2; trade and industry 33; 3 *master's:* business/marketing.

Fees and Other Expenses: *Full-time tuition per academic year 2004–05:* undergraduate in-district resident $5,960, in-state (out-of-district) $8,940, out-of-state $11,500; graduate in-district $7,560, out-of-state $13,500. *Room and board per academic year:* $6,400 to $10,100.

Financial Aid: Aid from institutionally generated funds is provided on the basis of academic merit, financial need. Institution has a Program Participation Agreement with the U.S. Department of Education for eligible students to receive Pell Grants and other federal aid.

Financial aid to full-time, first-time undergraduate students: need-based scholarships/grants totaling $1,890,598, self-help $2,802,126, parent loans $223,218; non-need-based scholarships/grants totaling $205,186, self-help $1,211,422, parent loans $422,773, tuition waivers $124,060. *Graduate aid:* 2 students received federal and state-funded loan at $14,750 each; 2 teaching assistantships were awarded totaling $10,500.

Departments and Teaching Staff: Arts and sciences *professors* 2, *associate professors* 9, *assistant professors* 3, *instructors* 0, *part-time faculty* 1; engineering 4, 7, 6, 2, 0; international business and logistics 1, 3, 0, 0, 0; marine science 3, 0, 3, 0, 0; marine transportation 3, 2, 2, 2, 0.

Total instructional faculty: 52 (full-time 51, part-time 1; women 13, men 39; members of minority groups 2). Total faculty with doctorate, first-professional, or other terminal degree: 29. Student-to-faculty ratio: 16.2: 1. *Faculty development:* $237,050 in grants for research. 2 faculty members awarded sabbaticals 2004–05.

Enrollment: Total enrollment 819. Undergraduate full-time 675 men / 121 women, part-time 7m / 2w; graduate full-time 11m / 3w.

Characteristics of Student Body: *Ethnic/racial makeup:* number of Black non-Hispanic: 3; American Indian or Alaska Native: 2; Asian or Pacific Islander: 5; Hispanic: 8; White non-Hispanic: 181; unknown: 8. *Age distribution:* number of 18–19: 309; 20–21: 192; 22–24: 244; 25–29: 50; 30–34: 12; 35–39: 4; 40–49: 7; 65 and over: q.

International Students: 24 nonresident aliens enrolled fall 2004. No programs available to aid students whose native language is not English. No financial aid specifically designated for international students.

Student Life: Except for married students, veterans, those over 23 years of age, or those with 6 semesters completed: on-campus residence is mandatory. *Student activities:* varsity basketball, cross-country, football, lacrosse, sailing, soccer. Other activities include band, drill team, cheerleading, club rugby, ice hockey, rifle/pistol, golf, bicycling, indoor soccer, outing, drama, photography; intramural activities in 13 areas. Social council, professional student organizations. No social Greek system. *Special regulations:* Cars are permitted for all students. Students in Coast Guard License Program are required to be in uniformed regiment of midshipmen (currently 70% of students) and subject to drug testing. *Special services:* Learning resources center, writing lab, tutoring program, peer educators, peer counselors, on-campus medical services. *Student publications, radio:* Yearbook, newspaper. *Surrounding community:* Castine population 1,500. Bangor, a town of over 80,000, is 40 miles away.

Library Collections: 208,290 volumes. Online catalog. Current serial subscriptions: paper 382; via electronic access 38. 1,310 recordings; 210 compact discs; 184 CD-ROMs. 14 computer work stations. Access to online information retrieval systems and the Internet.

Most important special collections include Maritime History Collection; Leslie L. Kanuk Federal Maritime Commission Collection; Schieffelin Collection on U.S. Civil War and other military history.

Buildings and Grounds: Campus area 37 acres.

Chief Executive Officer: Dr. Leonard Tyler, President.

Address undergraduate admission inquiries to Jeffrey C. Wright, Director of Admissions.

Saint Joseph's College

278 Whites Bridge Road
Standish, Maine 04084-5263

Tel: (800) 338-7057   **E-mail:** admissions@sjcme.edu
Fax: (207) 893-7862   **Internet:** www.sjcme.edu

Institution Description: Saint Joseph's College is a private college conducted by the Sisters of Mercy, Roman Catholic Church. *Enrollment:* 986. *Degrees awarded:* Baccalaureate.

Accreditation: *Regional:* NEASC. *Professional:* nursing

History: Established as St. Joseph's College for women and offered first instruction at postsecondary level 1912; chartered 1915; offered first degree (baccalaureate) 1938; changed name to The College of Our Lady of Mercy 1949; readopted original name 1956; became coeducational 1970.

Institutional Structure: *Governing board:* Board of Trustees. Extrainstitutional representation: 5 trustees. All voting. Board of Overseers. Extrainstitutional representation: 31 governors; institutional representation: 1 student, president of the college. 2 ex officio. All voting. *Composition of institution:* Administrators 6 men / 12 women. Academic affairs headed by dean of the college. Finances directed by vice president for finance and administration. Full-time instructional 67. Academic governance body, Faculty Senate, meets an average of 8 times per year.

Calendar: Semesters. Academic year Sept. to May. Freshmen admitted Sept., Jan. Degrees conferred and formal commencement May. Summer session of 2 terms from June to July.

Characteristics of Freshmen: 73% of applicants admitted. 35% of applicants admitted and enrolled.

93% (274 students) submitted SAT scores; 6% (18 students) submitted ACT scores. *25th percentile:* SAT Verbal 460, SAT Math 460; ACT Composite 17. *75th percentile:* SAT Verbal 560, SAT Math 550; ACT Composite 20.

65% of entering freshmen expected to graduate within 5 years. 55% of freshmen from Maine. Freshmen from 10 states and 1 foreign country.

Admission: Early admission and regular admissions plans. For fall acceptance, apply as early as Oct. 1, but not later than Aug. 1 of year of enrollment. *Requirements:* Either graduation from secondary school with 16 units which must include 4 English, 3-4 mathematics, 1 or 2 science, 2 social science, 6-8 academic electives (of which 2 are preferably a foreign language); or GED. Additional requirements for some programs. *Entrance tests:* College Board SAT. *For transfer students:* 2.0 minimum GPA, maximum transfer credit limited only by residence requirement.

Advanced placement for postsecondary-level work completed in secondary school. Noncredit remedial courses offered during regular academic year.

Degree Requirements: 128 credit hours; 2.0 GPA; last 2 terms in residence; distribution requirements, senior seminar, research paper. Fulfillment of some degree requirements possible by passing College Board CLEP. Exemption from some beginning courses possible by passing APP (score of 3). *Grading system:* A–F; withdraw (deadline after which fail is appended to withdraw); incomplete (carries time limit).

Distinctive Educational Programs: Campus-based programs include clinical learning experience for nursing students in cooperating health care agencies; degree completion program in radiologic technology; RN to BSN completion program. Preprofessional field experience and student teaching for education students; internships for communications and business majors; fieldwork for

sociology majors. FM radio and television stations for communications majors. Facilities for independent study and research. Study abroad by individual arrangement. *Other distinctive programs:* Through the External Degree and Continuing Education Department, adults participate in directed independent distance learning. Associate degree in management; bachelor degrees in professional arts, health care administration, business administration; master's degree in health services administration. A cooperative venture with the Diocese of Portland offers religious studies and pastoral ministry programs at the certificate and bachelor levels.

Degrees Conferred: 173 *baccalaureate:* biological/life sciences 16; business/marketing 26; communications/communication technologies 21; education 43; English 12; health professions and related sciences 21; liberal arts/general studies 1; mathematics 2; natural resources/environmental science 4; philosophy/religion/theology 3; psychology 10; social sciences and history 14.

Fees and Other Expenses: *Full-time tuition per academic year 2004–05:* $19,890. *Room and board per academic year:* $8,580. *Other fees:* $715.

Financial Aid: Aid from institutionally generated funds is provided on the basis of academic merit, financial need, other criteria. Institution has a Program Participation Agreement with the U.S. Department of Education for eligible students to receive Pell Grants and other federal aid.

Financial aid to full-time, first-time undergraduate students: need-based scholarships/grants totaling $7,522,537, self-help $4,888,155, parent loans $658,178, tuition waivers $308,706; non-need-based scholarships/grants totaling $985,249; self-help $2,070,532, parent loans $992,885, tuition waivers $87,134.

Departments and Teaching Staff: *Total instructional faculty:* 118 (full-time 57, part-time 51; women 59, men 59; member of minority group 1). Total faculty with doctorate, first-professional, or other terminal degree: 70. Student-to-faculty ratio: 13:1. *Faculty development:* $214,389 in grants for research. 3 faculty members awarded sabbaticals 2004–05.

Enrollment: Total enrollment 986. Full-time 351 men / 609 women, part-time 8m / 18w. *Transfer students:* in-state 31.

Characteristics of Student Body: *Ethnic/racial makeup:* number of Black non-Hispanic: 11; Asian or Pacific Islander: 5; Hispanic: 6; White non-Hispanic: 829; unknown: 134. *Age distribution:* number under 18: 11; 18–19: 414; 20–21: 86; 22–24: 327; 25–29: 6; 30–34: 8; 35–39: 40–49: 4; 50–64: 2.

International Students: 4 nonresident aliens enrolled fall 2004. No programs available to aid students whose native language is not English. Financial aid on merit basis only for qualifying international students.

Student Life: Primarily a residential institution with more than 83% of students living on campus. *Intercollegiate athletics:* men only: baseball, basketball, cross-country, golf, soccer; women only: basketball, cross-country, field hockey, soccer, softball, volleyball. *Special services:* Van service provided to the greater Portland area on a scheduled basis. *Student publications, radio: E.G.,* an annual literary magazine; *The Shield,* a yearbook; *Spectrum,* a biweekly newspaper. Radio station WSJB broadcasts 140 hours per week. *Surrounding community:* Portland (ME), 20 miles from campus, is nearest metropolitan area. Served by airport 20 miles from campus.

Publications: *Saint Joseph's College News,* college and alumni newsletter.

Library Collections: 98,626 volumes. Online catalog. Current serial subscriptions: paper 368; microform 29,010; via electronic access 11,461. Access to online information retrieval systems and the Internet.

Most important special holdings include Maine Collection; Irish Collection; Bishops' Collection (books, papers, periodicals).

Buildings and Grounds: Campus area 350 acres. *New buildings:* Reeney Hall and Carrier Hall (dormitories); Harold Alford Hall completed 2004.

Chief Executive Officer: Dr. David House, President.

Address admission inquiries to Dr. Alexander Popovics, Vice President for Enrollment Management; Distance Education inquiries, Lynne Robinson, Director of Admissions, Graduate and Professional Studies.

Thomas College

180 West River Road
Waterville, Maine 04901-5097

Tel: (207) 859-1111   **E-mail:** admissions@thomas.edu
Fax: (207) 859-1114   **Internet:** www.thomas.edu

Institution Description: Thomas College is a private, independent, nonprofit college. *Enrollment:* 870. *Degrees awarded:* Associate, baccalaureate, master's.

Accreditation: *Regional:* NEASC.

History: Established as Keist Business College 1894; changed name to Morgan Business College 1903; adopted name Thomas Business College 1912; incorporated, changed name to Thomas Junior College, and offered first instruction at postsecondary level 1956; awarded first degree (associate) 1959; offered first baccalaureate and adopted present name 1963; offered first master's 1976.

Institutional Structure: *Governing board:* Thomas College Board of Trustees. Representation: 24 trustees including president of the college. All voting. *Composition of institution:* Administrators 6 men / 6 women. Academic affairs headed by vice president for academic affairs. Management/business/finances directed by vice president for financial affairs. Full-time instructional faculty 23.

Calendar: Semesters. Academic year early late Aug. to early May. Freshmen admitted Sept., Jan. Degrees conferred Jan., May, Aug.; formal commencement May.

Characteristics of Freshmen: 72% of applicants admitted. 36% of applicants admitted and enrolled.

96% (173 students) submitted SAT scores; 2% (4 students) submitted ACT scores. *25th percentile:* SAT Verbal 400, SAT Math 410. *75th percentile:* SAT Verbal 510, SAT Math 520.

56% of freshmen expected to graduate within 5 years. 78% of freshmen from Maine. Freshmen from 9 states.

Admission: Rolling admissions plan. For fall acceptance, apply as early as Aug. of previous year, but not later than May 1 of year of enrollment. Early acceptance available. *Requirements:* Either graduation from accredited secondary school with 16 units which must include 4 English, 2 mathematics, 2 science, 3 social science, 6 academic electives (preferably business); or GED. 1 additional unit mathematics and interview recommended. Minimum GPA 2.0. Lowest acceptable secondary school class standing 50th percentile. *Entrance tests:* College Board SAT or ACT composite. For foreign students TOEFL. *For transfer students:* 2.0 minimum GPA; from 4-year accredited institution 90 hours maximum transfer credit; from 2-year accredited institution 60 hours.

College credit and advanced placement for postsecondary-level work completed in secondary school. College credit for extrainstitutional learning on the basis of *2006 Guide to the Evaluation of Educational Experiences in the Armed Services.* Tutoring available.

Degree Requirements: *For all associate degrees:* 60 credit hours; 1 term in residence. *For all baccalaureate degrees:* 120 credit hours; 2 terms in residence. *For all undergraduate degrees:* 2.0 GPA; distribution requirements.

Fulfillment of some degree requirements and exemption from some beginning courses possible by passing College Board CLEP, APP (score of 3). *Grading system:* A–F; pass-fail; withdraw (carries time limit; deadline after which pass-fail is appended to withdraw).

Distinctive Educational Programs: *For undergraduates:* Work-experience programs. Individual majors. Cross-registration with Colby College. *For graduate students:* Off-campus center (at Portland, 80 miles away). *Available to all students:* Evening classes. Tutorials.

Degrees Conferred: 33 *associate;* 87 *baccalaureate:* business/marketing 68; computer and information sciences 16; education 2, psychology 1. 37 *master's:* business/marketing 30; computer and information sciences 1. 2 *honorary degrees awarded 2004–05:* Doctor of Humane Letters 1, Doctor of Business Administration 1.

Fees and Other Expenses: *Full-time tuition per academic year 2004–05:* $15,520. *Required fees:* $370. *Room and board per academic year:* $6,760.

Financial Aid: The college offers a direct lending program. Aid from institutionally generated funds is provided on the basis of academic merit, financial need. Institution has a Program Participation Agreement with the U.S. Department of Education for eligible students to receive Pell Grants and other federal aid.

Financial aid to full-time, first-time undergraduate students: need-based scholarships/grants totaling $3,259,215, self-help $1,885,296; non-need-based scholarships/grants totaling $916,014, self-help $1,719,843, parent loans $345,378, athletic awards $78,650. *Graduate aid:* 25 students received federal and state-funded loans totaling $64,199 (ranging from $866 to $2,124).

Departments and Teaching Staff: *Professors* 5, *associate professors* 7, *assistant professors* 11, *part-time faculty* 85.

Total instructional faculty: 85 (full-time 23, part-time 63; women 23, men 65). Total faculty with doctorate, first-professional, or other terminal degree: 18. Student-to-faculty ratio: 15:1.

Enrollment: Total enrollment 870. Undergraduate full-time 331 men / 269 women, part-time 37m / 100w; graduate full-time 2m / 1w, part-time 57m / 73w. *Transfer students:* in-state 46.

Characteristics of Student Body: *Ethnic/racial makeup:* number of Black non-Hispanic: 6; American Indian or Alaska Native: 4; Asian or Pacific Islander: 2; Hispanic: 7; White non-Hispanic: 652; unknown: 66. *Age distribution:* number 18–19: 239; 20–21: 240; 22–24: 82; 25–29: 21; 30–34: 6; 35–39: 7; 40–49: 5.

International Students: No programs available to aid students whose native language is not English. No financial aid specifically designated for international students.

Student Life: On-campus residence halls house 60% of student body. Residence halls for both sexes constitute 100% of such space. *Intercollegiate athletics:* men only: baseball, basketball, golf, lacrosse, tennis, soccer; women only: basketball, field hockey, lacrosse, soccer, softball. *Special regulations:* Cars permitted without restrictions. *Special services:* Medical services. *Student publications: The Voice,* a weekly student newspaper; *The Thomasonian,* a yearbook. *Surrounding community:* Waterville population 16,000. Portland, 75 miles from campus, is nearest metropolitan area.

Library Collections: 28,000 volumes. 230 current periodical subscriptions. Online catalog. 14 computer work stations. Students have access to online information retrieval services and the Internet. Total 2004–05 budget for books and materials: $35,000.

Most important special holdings include materials relating to the fields of business and computer science.

Buildings and Grounds: Campus area 70 acres.

Chief Executive Officer: Dr. George R. Spann, President.

Address admission inquiries to Robert Callahan, Dean of Admissions.

Unity College

Quaker Hill Road
HC78
Unity, Maine 04988-9502
Tel: (207) 948-3131   **E-mail:** admissions@unity.edu
Fax: (207) 948-6277   **Internet:** www.unity.edu

Institution Description: Unity College is a private, independent, nonprofit college. *Enrollment:* 519. *Degrees awarded:* Associate, baccalaureate.

Accreditation: *Regional:* NEASC.

History: Established as Unity Institute of Liberal Arts and Sciences 1965; offered first instruction at postsecondary level 1966; chartered and adopted present name 1967; awarded first degree (baccalaureate) 1969.

Institutional Structure: *Governing board:* The Board of Trustees. Extrainstitutional representation: 23 trustees, including 4 trustees emeriti; institutional representation: 1 faculty member, 1 student; 1 alumnus. All voting. *Composition of institution:* Administrators 4 men / 3 woman. Academic affairs headed by provost. Management/business/finances directed by business manager. Full-time instructional faculty 33. Academic governance body, Faculty Academic Council, meets an average of 35 times per year.

Calendar: Semesters. Academic year Aug. to May. Freshmen admitted Aug., Jan. Degrees conferred May, Dec. Formal commencement May. No summer session.

Characteristics of Freshmen: 91% of applicants accepted. 39% of accepted applicants enrolled. 48% of entering freshmen expected to graduate within 5 years. 38% of freshmen from Maine. Freshmen from 21 states.

Admission: Rolling admissions plan. For fall acceptance, apply as early as middle of junior year in secondary school, but not later than registration. Early acceptance available. *Requirements:* High school graduation or GED. Admission is selective. Recommend: 3 years mathematics, 2 years laboratory science. SAT or ACT recommended but are not required. May require on-campus interview, on-campus testing, successful completion of the Summer Institute, or submission of additional supporting materials from candidates for admission whose overall academic profile may raise questions as to the ability to do college-level work.

College credit and advanced placement for postsecondary-level work completed in secondary school and for extrainstitutional learning (life experience) on basis of faculty assessment. Tutoring available. Developmental/remedial courses offered during regular academic year; credit given.

Degree Requirements: *For all associate degrees:* 60–credit hours; 30 hours in residence. *For all baccalaureate degrees:* 120 credit hours; 60 hours in residence. *For all degrees:* 2.0 GPA; required courses in English composition, oral communication; distribution requirements.

Fulfillment of some degree requirements and exemption from some beginning courses possible by passing departmental examinations, College Board CLEP, AP. *Grading system:* A–no credit; incomplete (carries time limit).

Distinctive Educational Programs: Work-experience programs. Weekend and evening classes. Interdepartmental/interdisciplinary programs in conservation law enforcement, natural resources administration, wildlife and fisheries technology. Facilities and programs for independent research, including tutorials, independent study, directed study.

ROTC: Army in cooperation with University of Maine, Orono.

Degrees Conferred: 12 *associate;* 124 *baccalaureate:* biological and life sciences 29, liberal arts/general studies 6, natural resources and environmental science 65, parks and recreation 24.

Fees and Other Expenses: *Full-time tuition per academic year 2004–05:* $15,790. *Required fees:* $735. *Room and board per academic year:* $6,250.

Financial Aid: Aid from institutionally generated funds is provided on the basis of academic merit, financial need, other criteria. Institution has a Program Participation Agreement with the U.S. Department of Education for eligible students to receive Pell Grants and other federal aid.

Institutional funding for undergraduates: 334 scholarships and grants totaling $991,542 (ranging from $500 to $7,000); 6 college-assigned jobs totaling $5,800. *Federal and state funding for undergraduates:* 112 scholarships and grants totaling $621,082 (ranging from $300 to $5,375); 367 loans totaling $1,872,627 (ranging from $1,000 to $10,500); 292 work-study jobs totaling $499,701 (ranging from $800 to $2,200).

Departments and Teaching Staff: *Total instructional faculty:* 50 (full-time 30, part-time 20; women 19, men 31, members of minority groups 2). Total faculty with doctorate, first-professional, or other terminal degree: 32. Student-to-faculty ratio: 13.2:1.

Enrollment: Total enrollment 521. Undergraduate full-time 352 men / 183 women, part-time 5m / 1w.

Characteristics of Student Body: *Ethnic/racial makeup:* number of Black non-Hispanic: 2; Hispanic: 2; White non-Hispanic: 514. *Age distribution:* number 18–19: 167, 20–21: 192, 22–24: 180, 25–29: 28, 30–34: 5, 35–39: 3.

International Students: 3 nonresident aliens enrolled fall 2004. 2 students from Asia, 1 Canada. No programs available to aid students whose native language is not English. No financial aid specifically designated for foreign students.

Student Life: On-campus residence halls house 61% of student body. *Intercollegiate athletics:* men only: basketball, cross-country, soccer; women only: basketball, cross-country, volleyball. *Special regulations:* Cars permitted without restrictions. *Special services:* Learning Resources Center, medical services. *Surrounding community:* Unity population 1,500. Boston (MA) 200 miles from campus, is nearest metropolitan area.

Publications: *Northwinds Magazine* (2 times annually); *Northeaster Magazine* (2 times annually).

Library Collections: 52,236 volumes. Online and card catalogs. Access to 65 serials via electronic access. 606 audiovisual materials; 12 computer work stations. Students have access to online information retrieval services and the Internet. Total 2004–05 budget for books, periodicals, audiovisual materials, microforms: $68,000.

Most important holdings include American Indians Collection (basket collection); Environmental Studies Collection.

Buildings and Grounds: Campus consists of 200 acres of fields and woodlands overlooking Lake Winecook and a total of over 500 acres of land.

Chief Executive Officer: Dr. David Glenn-Lewin, President.

Address admission inquiries to Kay Fiedler, Director of Admissions.

University of Maine

5713 Chadbourne Hall
Orono, Maine 04469-0001

Tel: (207) 581-1110   **E-mail:** um-admit@maine.edu
Fax: (207) 581-1517   **Internet:** www.umaine.edu

Institution Description: University of Maine, Orono, offers undergraduate and graduate programs through five colleges: Applied Sciences and Agriculture, Arts and Humanities, Business Administration, Education, Engineering, Forest Resources, Sciences, Social and Behavioral Science, and University College. *Enrollment:* 11,358. *Degrees awarded:* Baccalaureate, master's, doctorate. Certificates also awarded.

Accreditation: *Regional:* NEASC. *Professional:* business, clinical psychology, computer science, dental assisting, dental hygiene, dietetics, engineering, engineering technology, forestry, health information technician, nursing, nursing education, psychology internship, public administration, social work, speech-language pathology, teacher education

History: Established and incorporated as State College of Agriculture and Mechanic Arts 1865; offered first instruction at postsecondary level 1868; awarded first degree (baccalaureate) 1872; changed name to University of Maine 1897. *See* David C. Smith, *The First Century: A History of the University of Maine 1865–1965* (Orono: The University of Maine Press, 1979) for further information.

Institutional Structure: *Composition of institution:* Administrators 58 men / 25 women. President, vice president and provost for academic affairs, vice president for administration, dean of research, vice president for research. Full-time instructional faculty 503. Academic governance body, Faculty Senate, meets an average of 12 times per year.

Calendar: Semesters. Academic year Sept. to May. Freshmen admitted Jan., Sept. Degrees conferred May, Aug., Dec. Formal commencement May, Dec. Summer session from mid-May to mid-Aug.

Characteristics of Freshmen: 79% of applicants admitted. 38% of applicants admitted and enrolled.

94.5% (1,609 students) submitted SAT scores; 7.4% (126 students) submitted ACT scores. *25th percentile:* SAT Verbal 480, SAT Math 480; ACT Composite 20. *75th percentile:* SAT Verbal 590, SAT Math 600; ACT Composite 26.

51% of entering freshmen expected to graduate within 5 years. 83% of freshmen from Maine. Freshmen from 30 states and 21 foreign countries.

Admission: Rolling admissions plan. For full consideration for student financial aid, apply no later than Mar 1. Early acceptance available. *Requirements:* Either graduation from secondary school with 4 units in English, 1 laboratory science, 3 mathematics, 1 history/social science; or GED. Additional units for some programs. Minimum GPA 3.0 preferred. Lowest acceptable secondary school class standing 30th percentile. *Entrance tests:* College Board SAT or ACT, For foreign students TOEFL. *For transfer students:* 2.5 minimum GPA; from 2- and 4-year accredited institutions, maximum transfer credit limited only by residence requirements and pending review by individual colleges within the university.

College credit and advanced placement for postsecondary-level work completed in secondary school. College credit for language study through military defense schools upon approval by program. Tutoring available.

Degree Requirements: *For all baccalaureate degrees:* 120–139 credit hours; 30 hours in residence. *For all undergraduate degrees:* 2.0 GPA; distribution requirements. Fulfillment of some degree requirements and exemption from some beginning courses possible by passing departmental examinations, College Board CLEP, AP. *Grading system:* A–F; pass-fail.

Distinctive Educational Programs: Canadian Studies. Interdisciplinary programs in natural resources, sustainable agriculture, and numerous other areas. Work-experience programs. Evening classes. University-wide honors program. Study abroad programs in Austria, Bulgaria, Canada, German, France, Ireland, Japan, New Zealand, Spain, republics of the former Soviet Union, and the United Kingdom. Student exchange programs with opportunities in 35 countries.

ROTC: Army, 11 commissions awarded 2004; Navy offered in cooperation with Maine Maritime Academy.

Degrees Conferred: 3 *associate;* 1,492 *baccalaureate* (B), 479 *master's* (M), 41 *doctorate* (D): agriculture 77 (B), 18 (M), 1 (D); area and ethnic studies 5 (B); biological/life sciences 69 (B), 15 (M), 1 (D); business/marketing 185 (B), 44 (M); communications/communication technologies 86 (B); computer and information sciences 21 (B), 7 (M); education 199 (B), 213 (M), 3 (D); engineering and engineering technologies 266 (B), 33 (M), 4 (D); English 98 (B), 21 (M); foreign languages and literature 11 (B), 5 (M); health professions and related sciences 106 (B), 22 (M); home economics and vocational home economics 35 (B), 3 (M); interdisciplinary studies 4, (B), 8 (D); liberal arts/general studies 15 (B), 4 (M); mathematics 16 (B), 4 (M); natural resources/environmental science 60 (B), 23 (M), 7 (D); parks and recreation 18 (B); philosophy/religion/theology 8 (B); physical sciences 12 (B), 6 (M), 8 (D); protective services/public administration 42 (B), 38 (M); psychology 81 (B), 12 (M), 7 (D); social sciences and history 121 (B), 4 (M), 2 (D); visual and performing arts 27 (B), 7 (M).

Fees and Other Expenses: *Full-time tuition per academic year 2005–06:* undergraduate resident $5,520, nonresident $15,660; 11,250; graduate resident $4,932, nonresident $14,076. *Other fees:* $1,390. *Room and board per academic year:* $6,732.

Financial Aid: Aid from institutionally generated funds is provided on the basis of academic merit, financial need, athletic ability, other criteria. Institution has a Program Participation Agreement with the U.S. Department of Education for eligible students to receive Pell Grants and other federal aid.

Financial aid to full-time, first-time undergraduate students: need-based scholarships/grants totaling $19,245,637, self-help $23,083,612, tuition waivers $1,746,394, athletic awards $1,333,951; non-need-based scholarships/grants totaling $3,770,787, self-help $8,616,796, tuition waivers $2,316,250. *Graduate aid:* 513 students received federal and state-funded loans totaling $5,371,764 (ranging from $100 to $18,500); 118 received work-study jobs totaling $683,123 (ranging from $600 to $9,000).

Departments and Teaching Staff: *Total instructional faculty:* 740 (full-time 503, part-time 237; women 290, men 450; members of minority groups 28). Total faculty with doctorate, first-professional, or other terminal degree: 504. Student-to-faculty ratio: 15:1. *Faculty development:* $57,568,688 in grants for research.

Enrollment: Total enrollment 11,358. Undergraduate full-time 3,810 men / 3,657 women, part-time 573m / 1,046w; graduate full-time 434m / 709w, part-time 315m / 815w. *Transfer students:* in-state 429; from out-of-state 56.

Characteristics of Student Body: *Ethnic/racial makeup:* number of Black non-Hispanic: 81; American Indian or Alaska Native: 167; Asian or Pacific Islander: 111; Hispanic: 71; White non-Hispanic: 8,437; unknown: 59. *Age distribution:* number under 18: 89; 18–19: 2,895; 20–21: 2,932; 22–24: 1,630; 25–29: 534; 30–34: 310; 35–39: 196; 40–49: 370; 50–64: 136; 65 and over: 3.

International Students: 336 nonresident aliens enrolled fall 2004. 64 students from Europe, 183 Asia, 22 Central and South America 22, Africa 29, 76

Canada, 2 Australia, 20 other. Programs available to aid students whose native language is not English: social, cultural, financial. English as a Second Language Program. Financial aid specifically designated for international students: 23 scholarships available annually.

Student Life: On-campus residence halls house 30% of student body. Residence halls are co-ed and include engineering and science wings, non-smoking areas, Honors College dorms, "Outdoor Adventure: floors, and married student housing. Over 230 club and organizations; 15 fraternities and 6 sororities. *Intercollegiate athletics:* men only: baseball, basketball, cross-country, football, golf, hockey, soccer, swimming, track; women only: basketball, cross country, field hockey, soccer, softball, swimming, tennis, track. *Special regulations:* Registered cars with decals permitted on campus except during school breaks. Quiet hours vary according to residence hall. *Special services:* Medical services, bus service between University College and main campus. *Student publications, radio: The Maine Campus,* a daily newspaper; *The Maine Review,* a student literary magazine; *The Prism,* a yearbook. Radio station WMEB-FM broadcasts 126 hours per week. *Surrounding community:* Orono population 10,000. Boston (MA), 250 miles from campus, is nearest metropolitan area. Served by mass transit bus system; airport 10 miles from campus.

Publications: *American Potato Journal* (monthly) first published in 1974, *Paideuma* (triennially) first published 1972, *Thoreau Quarterly Journal* first published 1969.

Library Collections: 1,034,248 volumes. Online catalog. Current serial subscriptions: paper 3,889, microform 1,600,000. 10,320 audiovisual materials. 300 computer work stations.

Most important special holdings include State of Maine Collection; Hamlin Family Papers; Stephen King Papers; Cole Collection (maritime history); William S. Cohen Papers; Canadiana.

Buildings and Grounds: Campus area 3,150 acres.

Chief Executive Officer: Dr. Robert Kennedy, President.

Address undergraduate admission inquiries to Sharon Oliver, Director of Admissions; graduate inquiries to Scott Delcourt, Director of Graduate School.

College of Natural Sciences, Forestry, and Agriculture

Degree Programs Offered: *Baccalaureate* in agribusiness administration; animal, veterinary, and aquatic sciences; biochemistry; bioresource engineering; bioresource engineering technology; botany; clinical laboratory sciences; food science and human nutrition; forest engineering; forestry; geological sciences; landscape horticulture; microbiology, molecular, and cellular biology; parks, recreation, and tourism; resource management and environmental policy; sustainable agriculture; wildlife ecology; ecology and environmental sciences; wood science and technology; zoology; *master's* in agricultural and resource economics, agricultural engineering, animal and veterinary science, biochemistry, biology, botany, community development, entomology, food and nutrition, food science, plant and soil science, resource utilization; *doctorate* in biochemistry, biological sciences, ecology and environmental sciences, forest resources, geological sciences, marine bioresources, microbiology, nutritional science, oceanography, plant science, zoology.

College of Business, Public Policy, and Health

Degree Programs Offered: *Baccalaureate* in business administration (concentrations in accounting, finance, management, marketing), public administration, nursing, social work; *master's* in business administration, nursing, public administration, social work.

College of Education and Human Development

Degree Programs Offered: *Baccalaureate* in child development/family relations, elementary education; secondary education, kinesiology and physical education; *master's* in elementary and secondary education, literacy education, science education, social studies education, counselor education, educational leadership, special education, physical education, human development and family studies; *doctorate* in language arts, educational leadership, literacy, educational administration.

College of Liberal Arts and Sciences

Degree Programs Offered: *Baccalaureate* in anthropology, art, chemistry, communication, communication disorders, computer science, economics, English, French, German, history, international affairs, journalism and mass communication, Latin, mathematics and statistics, modern languages, music, Spanish, philosophy, physics, political science, psychology, Romance languages, sociology theatre/dance; *master's* in computer science, quaternary studies, chemistry, communication, communication disorders, economics, English, history, mathematics, French, teaching, music, physics, psychology, theatre; *doctorate* in chemistry, history, physics, psychology, clinical psychology.

College of Engineering

Degree Programs Offered: *Baccalaureate* in bioresource engineering, chemical engineering, civil engineering, electrical and computer engineering, electrical engineering technology, construction management technology, engineering physics, forest engineering, mechanical engineering, mechanical engineering technology, pulp and paper technology, spatial engineering technology; *master's* in chemical engineering, environmental and water resources engineering, computer engineering, thermal science, engineering mechanics, spatial information science and engineering; *doctorate* in chemical engineering, environmental and water resources engineering, geotechnical engineering, structural and mechanical engineering; spatial information science and engineering.

University of Maine at Augusta

46 University Drive
Augusta, Maine 04330-9410

Tel: (207) 621-3000   **E-mail:** umaar@uma.maine.edu
Fax: (207) 621-3116   **Internet:** www.uma.maine.edu

Institution Description: *Enrollment:* 5,528. *Degrees awarded:* Associate, baccalaureate.

Accreditation: *Regional:* NEASC. *Professional:* clinical lab technology, nursing

History: Established 1965.

Calendar: Semesters. Academic year from early Sept. to mid-May.

Admission: *Requirements:* Graduation from accredited secondary school or equivalent; completion of 16 units.

Degree Requirements: 120 credit hours minimum; GPA 2.0; 72 hours in major.

Degrees Conferred: 392 *associate;* 259 *baccalaureate.* Bachelor's degrees awarded in top five disciplines: business and management 38, English language and literature 7, mathematics 2, public administration and services 4, social sciences and history 29.

Fees and Other Expenses: *Full-time tuition per academic year 2004–05:* $3,690 resident, $8,950. *Books and supplies:* $720. *Room and board per academic year:* $4,926.

Financial Aid: Aid from institutionally generated funds is provided on the basis of financial need. Financial assistance is available in the form of Pell Grants, College Work-Study, Veterans Administration Benefits, National Direct Student Loans, Supplemental Education Opportunity Grants (SEOG), Stafford Loans, other federal aid programs.

Percentage of student body receiving various forms of financial aid: federal scholarships and grants 69% (average $2,351); state/local scholarships and grants 555 (average $909); institutional fellowships 20% (average $1,270); loans 81% (average $3,199).

Departments and Teaching Staff: *Professors* 30, *associate professors* 41, *assistant professors* 18, *instructors* 12, *part-time teachers* 95.

Total instructional faculty: 196. Degrees held by full-time faculty: doctorate 26%, master's 64%, baccalaureate 7%.

Enrollment: Total enrollment 5,528.

Characteristics of Student Body: *Ethnic/racial makeup:* Black non-Hispanic: .4%; American Indian or Native Alaskan: 3%; Asian or Pacific Islander: .3%; Hispanic: .5%; White non-Hispanic: 96.7%. *Age distribution:* 22 or less: 27%, 22–30: 25%; 31–40: 22%; 41–50: 175; over 51: 7%.

International Students: 6 nonresident aliens enrolled. No programs to aid students whose native language is not English.

Student Life: Commuter campus.

Library Collections: 45,000 volumes. 1,370 microform titles; 480 current periodical subscriptions. Students have access to online information retrieval services and the Internet.

Most important special collections include the Kennebec Valley Historical Society Collection.

Chief Executive Officer: Dr. Richard Randall, President.

Address admission inquiries to Director of Admissions.

University of Maine at Farmington

111 South Street
Farmington, Maine 04938-1911
Tel: (207) 778-7000   **E-mail:** umfadmit@maine.edu
Fax: (207) 778-8182   **Internet:** www.umf.main.edu

Institution Description: *Enrollment:* 2,349. *Degrees awarded:* Baccalaureate. Certificates also awarded.

Accreditation: *Regional:* NEASC. *Professional:* teacher education

History: Established as Western Maine Normal School 1863; offered first instruction at postsecondary level 1864; changed name to Farmington State Normal School 1868; awarded first degree (baccalaureate) 1924; changed name to Farmington State Teachers College 1945, to Farmington State College 1965, to Farmington State College of the University of Maine 1968; adopted present name 1970; now operating as the liberal arts college of the University of Maine System.

Institutional Structure: *Composition of institution:* Administrators 19. Academic affairs headed by provost. Management/business/finances directed by executive director for finance and administration. Full-time instructional faculty 119.

Calendar: Semesters. Academic year early Sept. to mid-May. Formal commencement in May.

Characteristics of Freshmen: 70% of applicants admitted. 32% of applicants admitted and enrolled.

87% (454 students) submitted SAT scores. *25th percentile*: SAT Verbal 460, SAT Math 450. *75th percentile*: SAT Verbal 560, SAT Math 550.

52% of entering freshmen expected to graduate within 5 years. 87% of freshmen from Maine. Freshmen from 19 states and 4 foreign countries.

Admission: Rolling admissions plan. For fall acceptance, apply as early as Sept. 1 of previous year, but not later than Mar. 15 of year of enrollment. Early acceptance available. *Requirements:* Either graduation from approved secondary school, or GED. Recommend 16 college preparatory units, including 4 English, 2 foreign language, 3 mathematics, 2 laboratory science, 2 social studies. Additional requirements for some programs. Lowest recommended secondary school class standing 50th percentile. *Entrance tests:* College Board SAT not required but considered if submitted.

Degree Requirements: *For all baccalaureate degrees:* 120–122 credit hours; 2.0 GPA for B.A. and B.F.A. degrees; 2.50 GPA for B.S. degrees. Additional requirements for some programs. *For all degrees:* Freshmen writing requirement; distribution requirements. Fulfillment of some degree requirements and exemption from some beginning courses possible by passing departmental examinations, College Board CLEP, AP. *Grading system:* A–F; withdraw; incomplete (carries time limit); H grade (must be completed prior to graduation).

Distinctive Educational Programs: Interdisciplinary program in general studies. Individual majors. Early childhood education; rehabilitation services. Interdisciplinary programs in liberal arts and general studies; individual majors. *Other distinctive programs:* Ski Industry Certificate Program. Study abroad in Canada, United Kingdom, France.

Degrees Conferred: 354 *baccalaureate:* biological/life sciences 5; business/marketing 24; computer and information sciences 4; education 156; English 18; health professions and related sciences 19; interdisciplinary studies 33; liberal arts/general studies 7; mathematics 3; natural resources/environmental science 2; psychology 38; social sciences and history 16; visual and performing arts 2. other 27.

Fees and Other Expenses: *Tuition per academic year 2004–05:* $4,650 resident, $11,340 nonresident. *Required fees:* $500. *Room and board per academic year:* $5,700.

Financial Aid: Aid from institutionally generated funds is provided on the basis of academic merit, financial need. Institution has a Program Participation Agreement with the U.S. Department of Education for eligible students to receive Pell Grants and other federal aid.

Financial aid to full-time, first-time undergraduate students: need-based scholarships/grants totaling $4,585,260, self-help $5,707,229; non-need-based scholarships/grants totaling $1,433,528, self-help $3,823,385, parent loans $650,866, tuition waivers $152,381.

Departments and Teaching Staff: *Total instructional faculty:* 159 (full-time 119, part-time 40; women 82, men 77; members of minority groups 9). Total faculty with doctorate, first-professional, or other terminal degree: 113. Student-to-faculty ratio: 17:1.

Enrollment: Total enrollment 2,349. Full-time 724 men / 1,337 women, part-time 73m / 215w.

Characteristics of Student Body: *Ethnic/racial makeup:* number of Black non-Hispanic: 4; American Indian or Alaska Native: 19; Asian or Pacific Islander: 17; Hispanic: 16; White non-Hispanic: 2,176.

International Students: 12 nonresident aliens enrolled fall 2004. 4 students from Europe, 3, Asia, 2 Central and South America 2, Canada 1, other 2. No programs to aid students whose native language is not English. Some financial aid available to qualifying international students.

Student Life: On-campus residence halls house nearly all first-year students and about 50% of the student body. WUMF, a student run radio station; 80 other student activities. *Surrounding community:* Farmington population 7,450.

Publications: *The Maine Stream*, a monthly newspaper; *The Sandy River Review*, a literary magazine featuring the poetry, artwork, and prose of students and faculty is published twice a year; *Dirigo*, a yearbook.

Library Collections: 100,464 volumes. Online and card catalogs. 610 periodical subscriptions. 8,370 audiovisual materials. 180 computer work stations. Students have access to online information retrieval services. Most important special holdings: Children's Literature Collection.

Buildings and Grounds: Campus areas 55 acres.

Chief Executive Officer: Dr.Theodora J. Kalikow, President.

Address admission inquiries to William Geller, Director of Admissions.

University of Maine at Fort Kent

25 University Drive
Fort Kent, Maine 04743
Tel: (207) 834-7500   **E-mail:** umfkadm@maine.edu
Fax: (207) 834-7503   **Internet:** www.umfk.maine.edu

Institution Description: *Enrollment:* 1,076. *Degrees awarded:* Associate, baccalaureate. Member of Northern Maine Consortium.

Accreditation: *Regional:* NEASC.

History: Established and chartered as Madawaska Training School 1878; offered first instruction at postsecondary level 1934; changed name to Fort Kent State Normal School 1955, to Fort Kent State Teachers College 1961; awarded first degree (baccalaureate) 1963; changed name to Fort Kent State College 1965, to Fort Kent College of the University of Maine 1968; adopted present name 1970. *See* Roger L. Grindle, *Century of Progress* (Madawaska, Maine: St. John Valley Publishing Co., 1978) for further information.

Institutional Structure: *Composition of institution:* Administrators 9 men / 14 women. Academic affairs headed by president. Management/business/finances directed by business manager. Full-time instructional faculty 36. Academic governance body, Faculty Senate, meets monthly.

Calendar: Semesters. Academic year Sept. to May. Freshmen admitted Sept., Jan., June. Degrees conferred May, Aug., Dec. Formal commencement May. Summer session from May to Aug.

Characteristics of Freshmen: 81% of applicants admitted. 56% of applicants admitted and enrolled.

70% (124 students) submitted SAT scores; 2% (4 students) submitted ACT scores. Mean SAT scores for class 455 verbal, 487 math.

38% of entering freshmen expected to graduate within 5 years. 83% of freshmen from Maine. Freshmen from 10 states and 7 foreign countries.

Admission: Rolling admissions plan. For fall acceptance, apply as early as Sept. 2 of previous year, but not later than Aug. 15 of year of enrollment. Early acceptance available. *Requirements:* Graduation from secondary school. Recommend 4 units in English, units in a foreign language, 2 mathematics, 2 science, 2 social science. GED accepted for associate of arts or baccalaureate of university studies programs. *Entrance tests:* College Board SAT. *For transfer students:* 1.0 minimum GPA; 90 hours maximum transfer credit.

College credit and advanced placement for postsecondary-level work completed in secondary school and for extrainstitutional learning on basis of ACE *2006 Guide to the Evaluation of Educational Experiences in the Armed Services*; portfolio assessment; assessment by Academic Affairs Committee. Tutoring available. Developmental courses offered during regular academic year; credit given.

Degree Requirements: *For all associate degrees:* 60 credit hours. *For all baccalaureate degrees:* 120–128 credit hours. *For all degrees:* 2.0 GPA; 2 full-time terms in residence; general education requirements (except for baccalaureate of university studies).

Fulfillment of some degree requirements and exemption from some beginning courses possible by passing institutional examination, College Board CLEP, APP. *Grading system:* A–F; pass-fail; withdraw.

Distinctive Educational Programs: Five baccalaureate programs and an associate program provide both traditional and innovative degree options. Environmental studies; interdisciplinary studies; Franco-American bilingual-bicultural studies; nursing; liberal arts; teacher preparation; business management; computer applications; rural public safety; E-commerce; honors. Cooperative education internships, and clinical practica provide options for applications of classroom theories. Summer and evening programs provide access to area residents including in-service for professionals and options for nontraditional adults. Students may take classes for credit at nearby College Universitaire St. Louis Maillet in Edmundston, New Brunswick (Canada). Students may make individual arrangements for study abroad or may enroll in a program directed by an accredited college/university.

Degrees Conferred: 34 *associate;* 192 *baccalaureate:* biological/life sciences 4; business/marketing 20; computer and information sciences 5; education 119; health professions and related sciences 13; natural resources/environmental science 3; protective services/public administration 6; social sciences and history 24.

Fees and Other Expenses: *Full-time tuition per academic year 2004–05:* undergraduate resident $3,960, nonresident $9,607. *Other fees:* $554. *Room and board per academic year:* $6,003.

Financial Aid: Aid from institutionally generated funds is provided on the basis of academic merit, financial need. Institution has a Program Participation Agreement with the U.S. Department of Education for eligible students to receive Pell Grants and other federal aid.

Financial aid to full-time, first-time undergraduate students: need-based scholarships/grants totaling $1,394,848, self-help $1,229,811, tuition waivers $101,098; non-need-based scholarships/grants totaling $192,213, self-help $44,937, parent loans $148,567, tuition waivers $275,583.

Departments and Teaching Staff: Arts and humanities *professors* 3, *associate professors* 2, *assistant professors* 2, *instructors* 1, *part-time faculty* 5; natural and behavioral sciences 6, 4, 7, 1, 18; education 2, 2, 0, 3, 12; nursing 0, 1, 1, 2, 4.

Total instructional faculty: 76 (full-time 37, part-time 39; women 20, men 19). Total faculty with doctorate, first-professional, or other terminal degree: 21.

Enrollment: Total enrollment 1,076. Full-time 319 men / 467 women, part-time 65m / 225w. *Transfer students:* in-state 43; from out-of-state 161

Characteristics of Student Body: *Ethnic/racial makeup:* number of Black non-Hispanic: 13; American Indian or Alaska Native: 16; Asian or Pacific Islander: 1; Hispanic: 5; White non-Hispanic: 749. *Age distribution:* number under 18: 5; 18–19: 241; 20–21: 189; 22–24: 231; 25–29: 190; 30–34: 58; 35–39: 48; 40–49: 68; 50–64: 22; 65 and over: 4.

International Students: 293 nonresident aliens enrolled fall 2004. 5 students from Europe, 2 Asia, 5 Central and South America, 9 Africa, 268 Canada, 3 other. No programs available to aid students whose native language is not English. Financial aid specifically designated for international students: 20 scholarships for undergraduates are available annually. 19 totaling $158,555 awarded 2004–05.

Student Life: On-campus residence halls house 20% of student body. Residence halls for men constitute 43% of such space, for women 57%. *Intercollegiate athletics:* men and women: alpine skiing, basketball, soccer. *Special regulations:* Cars permitted without restrictions. Quiet hours. Residence halls and hall activities open to commuted students. *Special services:* Learning Resources Center, health services, transportation service to and from airport at beginning and end of school recess. *Campus publications: Valley Vision,* monthly newsletter; *Currents,* weekly news bulletin. *Surrounding community:* Fort Kent population 5,000. Bangor, 200 miles from campus, is nearest metropolitan area. Served by airport 65 miles from campus.

Library Collections: 67,507 volumes. Online catalog. Current serial subscriptions: paper 335, microform 223, via electronic access 143. 3,963 recordings, 223 compact discs; 143 CD-ROMs. 19 computer work stations. Students have access to online information retrieval systems and the Internet.

Most important special holdings include Maine history; Acadian Archives (circulating and non-circulating); Curriculum Collection.

Buildings and Grounds: Campus area 52 acres. Nadeau Hall completed 2000; The Lodge (residence hall) 2004; Acadian Archives Building 2004.

Chief Executive Officer: Dr. Richard W. Cost, President.

Address admission inquiries to Cathy Saucier, Admissions Director.

University of Maine at Machias

9 O'Brien Avenue
Machias, Maine 04654-1397
Tel: (207) 255-1200   **E-mail:** admissions@umm.maine.edu
Fax: (207) 255-4864   **Internet:** www.umm.maine.edu

Institution Description: The University of Maine at Machias is one of the seven University of Maine System campuses. *Enrollment:* 1,191. *Degrees awarded:* Baccalaureate.

Accreditation: *Regional:* NEASC. *Professional:* recreation and leisure services

History: Established as Washington State Normal School and offered first instruction at postsecondary level 1909; changed name to Washington State Teachers College 1952; awarded first degree (baccalaureate) 1953; changed

name to Washington State College of the University of Maine 1968; adopted present name 1970.

Institutional Structure: *Composition of institution:* Administrators 2 men / 2 women. Academic affairs headed by vice president for academic affairs. Management/business/finances directed by chief financial officer. Student affairs headed director of student life. Full-time instructional faculty 30. Academic governance body, the faculty, meets 7 to 8 times per year.

Calendar: Semesters. Academic year Aug. to May. Freshmen admitted Sept., Jan., June. Degrees conferred and formal commencement May. Summer session from mid-May to mid-Aug.

Characteristics of Freshmen: 84.5% of applicants admitted. 30% of applicants admitted and enrolled.

84.4% (76 students) submitted SAT scores; 11% (10 students) submitted ACT scores. *25th percentile:* SAT Verbal 410, SAT Math 400; ACT Composite 19, ACT English 17, ACT Math 17. *75th percentile:* SAT Verbal 540, SAT Math 540; ACT Composite 21, ACT English 23, ACT Math 25.

43% of entering freshmen expected to graduate within 5 years. 71% of freshmen from Maine. Freshmen from 14 states and 3 foreign countries.

Admission: To qualify as a UMM applicant, students must be high school graduates or have successfully complete the GED exam. All applicants entering directly from high school must submit SAT or ACT scores. It is recommended that applicants entering directly from high school follow a college preparatory program, achieve a B average, and rank in the top half of their graduating class. Consideration will be given to work and life experience for applicants who have been out of school for some time. Transfer students must be in good academic standing at their previous college/university and have a minimum grade point average of 2.0.

Degree Requirements: *For all baccalaureate degrees:* 120 hours minimum; 2.0 GPA; core requirements. *Residency requirement:* 30 hours in residence, including 12 hours in the major, at least 9 of which must be at 300-level or better.

Credit awarded for appropriate scores on CLEP and AP exams. Credit awarded for prior learning and military/training experience with appropriate documentation. *Grading system:* A–F; pass-fail; withdraw.

Distinctive Educational Programs: Cooperative education and internships in many programs. Weekend and evening classes. Bachelor of College Studies program.International exchange programs with University of Wales and Bath Spa University College in the United Kingdom.

Degrees Conferred: 88 *baccalaureate:* biological/life sciences 4; business/marketing 15; education 8; English 2; interdisciplinary studies 18; liberal arts/general studies 11; natural resources/environmental science 9; parks and recreation 14; social sciences and history 5; visual and performing arts 2.

Fees and Other Expenses: *Full-time tuition per academic year 2005–06:* $4,290 resident, $11,640 nonresident. *Required fees:* $555. *Room and board per academic year:* $5,678.

Financial Aid: Aid from institutionally generated funds is provided on the basis of academic merit, financial need. Institution has a Program Participation Agreement with the U.S. Department of Education for eligible students to receive Pell Grants and other federal aid.

Financial aid to full-time, first-time undergraduate students: need-based scholarships/grants totaling $2,039,566, self-help $1,611,953, tuition waivers $99,344; non-need-based scholarships/grants totaling $471,346, self-help $680,597, parent loans $279,456, tuition waivers $11,061.

Departments and Teaching Staff: Arts and Letters *professors* 1, *associate professors* 5, *assistant professors* 4, *part-time faculty:* 30; Environmental and Biological Sciences 2, 4, 4, 8; Professional Studies 2, 4, 4, 24.

Total instructional faculty: 92 (full-time 30, part-time 62; women 40, men 52; members of minority groups 2). Total faculty with doctorate, first-professional, or other terminal degree: 40. Student-to-faculty ratio: 14.5:1.

Enrollment: Total enrollment 1,191. Full-time 178 men / 330 women, part-time 148m / 535w. *Transfer students:* in-state 29; from out-of-state 6.

Characteristics of Student Body: *Ethnic/racial makeup:* number of Black non-Hispanic: 9; American Indian or Alaska Native: 45; Asian or Pacific Islander: 3; Hispanic: 14; White non-Hispanic: 1,065. *Age distribution:* number under 18: 37; 18–19: 179; 20–21: 208; 22–24: 186; 25–29: 140; 30–34: 124; 35–39: 83; 40–49: 138; 50–64: 85; 65 and over: 11.

International Students: 55 nonresident aliens enrolled fall 2004. 14 students from Europe, 8 Asia, 3 Central and South America, 3 Africa, 26 Canada, 1 Australia. Programs available to aid students whose native language is not English: social. No financial aid specifically designated for international students.

Student Life: On-campus residence halls house 43% of degree-seeking students. *Intercollegiate athletics:* men only: basketball, cross-country, soccer; women only: basketball, cross-country, soccer, volleyball. *Special regulations:* Registered cars permitted in designated areas. Quiet hours. *Special services:* Health and counseling services. *Student publications: Binnacle,* an annual literary magazine. The Center for Lifelong Learning provides the campus and local communities with programs in aquatics, fitness, and wellness. *Surrounding com-*

munity: Machias population 2,500. Portland (ME) 210 miles from campus, is nearest metropolitan area. Served by airport 2 miles from campus.

Library Collections: 91,000 volumes including bound books, serial back-files, electronic documents, and government documents not in separate collections. Online catalog. Current serial subscriptions: 353 paper, 75 microform, 12,000 via electronic access. 645 recordings; 1,568 compact discs; 49 CD-ROMs. 24 computer work stations. Students have access to the Internet at no charge. Total 2004–05 budget for books and materials: $84,058.

Most important holdings include Maine Collection (state history); Juvenile Collection (curriculum materials for teachers).

Buildings and Grounds: Campus area 46 acres. *New buildings:* Elizabeth Clarke Flaherty Early Care and Education Center completed 2001; addition to Dorward Hall (residence hall) 2003.

Chief Executive Officer: Dr. Cynthia E. Huggins, President.

Address admission inquiries to Stewart Bennett, Director of Admissions.

University of Maine at Presque Isle

181 Main Street
Presque Isle, Maine 04769-2888
Tel: (207) 768-8400   **E-mail:** info@umpi.maine.edu
Fax: (207) 768-9534   **Internet:** www.umpi.maine.edu

Institution Description: *Enrollment:* 1,652. *Degrees awarded:* Associate, baccalaureate. In addition to certificates, the university also offers articulated transfer arrangements with campuses of the University of Maine System and continuing education for practicing professionals.

Accreditation: *Regional:* NEASC. *Professional:* clinical lab technology, recreation and leisure services, social work

History: Established as Aroostook State Normal School, chartered and offered first instruction at postsecondary level 1903; changed name to Aroostook State Teachers College 1952; awarded first degree (baccalaureate) 1953; changed name to Aroostook State College 1965, to Aroostook State College of the University of Maine 1968; present name adopted 1970.

Institutional Structure: *Composition of institution:* Administrators 17 men / 11 women. Academic affairs headed by vice president for academic affairs. Management/business/finances directed by vice president for business and financial affairs. Academic governance body, University Senate, meets monthly during the academic year.

Calendar: Semesters. Academic year early Sept. to mid-May. Freshmen admitted Sept., Jan. Degrees conferred May, Dec. Formal commencement May. Summer session of 2 terms from mid-May to end of Aug.

Characteristics of Freshmen: 820 applicants (220 men, 300 women). 87.3% of applicants admitted. 42.5% of admitted students enrolled full-time.

Average secondary school rank men 47th percentile, women 61st percentile, class 55th percentile.

94% of freshmen from Maine. Freshmen from 6 states and 3 foreign countries.

Admission: Rolling admissions plan. For fall acceptance, apply as early as Sept. 1 of previous year, but not later than Sept. 1 of year of enrollment. Apply by Nov. 15 for early decision. Early acceptance available. *Requirements:* Either graduation from accredited secondary school or GED. Recommend 4 units English, 2 in a foreign language, 3 mathematics, 2 laboratory science, 2 social studies, 3 electives. *Entrance tests:* College Board SAT. *For transfer students:* 2.0 minimum GPA; from 4-year accredited institution 90 hours maximum transfer credit; from 2-year accredited institution 60 hours.

College credit and advanced placement for postsecondary-level work completed in secondary school. College credit for extrainstitutional learning on basis of ACE *2006 Guide to the Evaluation of Educational Experiences in the Armed Services.* Tutoring available. Noncredit developmental courses offered during regular academic year.

Degree Requirements: *For all associate degrees:* 60–70 credit hours; 1 term in residence. *For all baccalaureate degrees:* 120–128+ hours; 1 year in residence; general education core curriculum. *For all degrees:* 2.0 GPA.

Fulfillment of some degree requirements possible by passing College Board CLEP, AP. *Grading system:* A–F; pass-fail; withdraw (carries penalty and time limit).

Distinctive Educational Programs: Work-experience programs. Flexible meeting places and schedules, including off-campus centers, evening classes. Environmental studies program offers student exchange possibilities with other campuses in system. Transfer arrangements in engineering and applied science and agriculture with University of Maine. Nursing transfer program with University of Southern Maine, University of Maine at Orono, and University of Maine at Fort Kent. Certificate program in Russian and East European studies. Atlantic Community studies. Special facilities for using telecommunications in the classroom. Tutorials. Servicemembers Opportunity College.

Degrees Conferred: 25 *associate;* 233 *baccalaureate.* Bachelor's degrees awarded in top five disciplines: liberal arts and sciences, general studies, and humanities 75; education 80; business, management, marketing, and related support services 19; public administration and social service professions 15; multidisciplinary studies 15.

Fees and Other Expenses: *Full-time tuition per academic year 2004–05:* resident $4,460, nonresident $10,400. *Books and supplies:* $700. *Room and board per academic year:* $5,114.

Financial Aid: Aid from institutionally generated funds is provided on the basis of academic merit, financial need. Institution has a Program Participation Agreement with the U.S. Department of Education for eligible students to receive Pell Grants and other federal aid.

Financial aid to full-time, first-time undergraduate students: 73% received federal grants averaging $3,259; 48% state/local grants averaging $922; 57% institutional grants averaging $1,313; 58% received loans averaging $2,504.

Departments and Teaching Staff: International studies *professors* 3, *associate professors* 1, *assistant professors* 2, *instructors* 0, *part-time teachers* 1; communication and literature 7, 0, 2, 1, 0; science 1, 7, 0, 3, 0; fine arts 3, 0, 1, 0, 0; mathematics and physics 1, 3, 1, 0, 0; recreation/leisure 0, 1, 2, 0, 0; human and social services 3, 0, 4, 0, 0; education 2, 1, 1, 0, 2; business 2, 2, 2, 0, 0; physical education and health education 1, 3, 2, 2, 0.

Total instructional faculty: 80. Degrees held by full-time faculty: doctorate 67%, master's 30%. 80% hold terminal degrees.

Enrollment: Total enrollment 1,652.

Characteristics of Student Body: *Ethnic/racial makeup:* Black non-Hispanic: .5%; American Indian or Alaska Native: 3.6%; Asian or Pacific Islander: .6%; Hispanic: .7%; White non-Hispanic: 88.1%. *Age distribution:* 17–21: 44.6%; 22–24: 18.6%; 25–29: 12.6%; 30–34: 6.7%; 35–39: 6.9%; 40–49: 9%; 50–59: 1.2%; 60–and over: .3%.

International Students: 103 undergraduate nonresident aliens enrolled fall 2004. Students from Europe, Asia, Central and South America, Africa, Canada, Australia. Programs available for students whose native language is not English: social, cultural, financial.

Student Life: On-campus residence halls house 30% of student body. All residence halls are coeducational, with freshmen men and women on separate floors. *Intercollegiate athletics:* men only: baseball, basketball, soccer; women only: basketball, field hockey, soccer, volleyball. *Special regulations:* Cars permitted without restrictions. *Special services:* Learning Resources Center, medical services. *Student publications, radio: The University Times,* a biweekly newspaper. WUPI broadcasts up to 24 hours per day. *Surrounding community:* Presque Isle population 10,500. Portland, 300 miles from campus, is nearest metropolitan area. Served by airport 2.5 miles from campus.

Publications: *Image,* a biweekly newsletter; *Blue and Gold,* an alumni association newsletter issued 3 times per year.

Library Collections: 85,000 volumes. 68,000 government documents. 750,000 microforms. 2,275 audiovisual materials; 470 current periodical subscriptions. Online catalog. Students have access to online information retrieval services and the Internet.

Most important holdings include collection of documents, books, newspapers, and periodicals related to history of Aroostook County; collection of geological specimens (including minerals, fossils, and taxidermy) and publications; Maine Authors Collection.

Buildings and Grounds: Campus area 150 acres.

Chief Executive Officer: Dr. William Shields, President.

Address admission inquiries to Brain M. Manter, Director of Admissions.

University of New England

11 Hills Beach Road
Biddeford, Maine 04005-9988
Tel: (207) 283-0171   **E-mail:** admissions@une.edu
Fax: (207) 283-3678   **Internet:** www.une.edu

Institution Description: University of New England (Saint Francis College until 1978) is a private, independent, nonprofit institution with two campuses in southern Maine. Three colleges include the College of Arts and Sciences, College of Health Professions, and College of Osteopathic Medicine. *Enrollment:* 3,327. *Degrees awarded:* Associate, baccalaureate, master's, first-professional, doctorate.

Accreditation: *Regional:* NEASC. *Professional:* dental hygiene, nurse anesthesia education, nursing, occupational therapy, osteopathy, physical therapy, occupational therapy, osteopathy, physical therapy, social work

History: Established as Saint Francis High School 1939; changed name to Saint Francis College and offered first instruction at postsecondary level 1943; chartered and awarded first degree (baccalaureate) 1953; initiated first-professional program 1978; merged with Westbrook College (founded 1831) 1996; the Westbrook College Campus is a designated national historic site in the city of Portland.

Institutional Structure: *Governing board:* Board of Trustees. Representation: 45 trustees, 13 trustees emeriti. *Composition of institution:* Senior administrators 7 men / 3 women. Academic affairs headed by 3 academic deans. Management/business/finances directed by vice president. Full-time instructional faculty 134. Academic governance body, University Council, meets an average of 10 times per year.

Calendar: Semesters (4-1-4 plan). Academic year mid-May to mid-May. Freshmen admitted Sept., Jan., Feb. Degrees conferred and formal commencement May. No summer session.

Characteristics of Freshmen: 91% of applicants admitted. 31% of applicants admitted and enrolled. 97% (477 students) submitted SAT scores. *25th percentile:* SAT Verbal 460, SAT Math 460. *75th percentile:* SAT Verbal 560, SAT Math 570.

38% of entering freshmen expected to graduate within 5 years. 33% of freshmen from Maine. Freshmen from 38 states and 2 foreign countries.

Admission: Rolling admissions plan. For fall acceptance, apply as early as Sept. of previous year, but not later than Aug. of year of enrollment; through Dec. 15 for spring term. *Requirements:* Either graduation from accredited secondary school with 4 units English, 3 mathematics, 2 laboratory science, 2 social studies; or GED. Recommend majors in health or life sciences have additional units in mathematics and science. Some degree programs offer conditional acceptance to applicants with incomplete or deficient credentials. *Entrance tests:* College Board SAT or ACT composite. For foreign students TOEFL; 2 letters of recommendation. *For transfer students:* 2.5 minimum GPA; from 4-year accredited institution 90 semester hours maximum transfer credit; from 2-year accredited institution 60 hours.

College credit and advanced placement for postsecondary-level work completed in secondary school. Tutoring available through the Learning Assistance Center. Noncredit developmental courses offered during regular academic year.

Degree Requirements: *For baccalaureate degrees:* 120 credits. *For all associate degrees:* 68 credits. One year in residence for all degrees; 2.0 GPA. Distribution requirements.

Fulfillment of some degree requirements and exemption from some beginning courses possible by passing College Board CLEP, AP. *Grading system:* A–F; pass-fail; withdraw.

Distinctive Educational Programs: *For undergraduates:* Internships. Evening classes. Facilities and programs for independent research, including honors programs, individual majors, tutorials, independent study. Cooperative education programs, field placements, and practicums. Study abroad by individual arrangement.

Degrees Conferred: 63 *associate;* 223 *baccalaureate* (B); 448 *master's* (M): biological/life sciences 46 (B); business/marketing 13 (B); education 10 (B), 245 (M); English 4 (B), health professions and related clinical sciences 97 (B), 132 (M); natural resources/environmental science 10 (B); parks and recreation 15 (B); protective services/public administration 71 (M); psychology 22 (B); social sciences and history 6 (M). 104 *first-professional:* osteopathic medicine.

Fees and Other Expenses: *Full-time tuition per academic year 2005–06:* $21,540 undergraduate. Contact the university for tuition/fees for graduate and first-professional programs. *Required fees:* $735. *Room and board per academic year:* $8,730.

Financial Aid: Aid from institutionally generated funds is provided on the basis of academic merit, financial need, other criteria. Institution has a Program Participation Agreement with the U.S. Department of Education for eligible students to receive Pell Grants and other federal aid.

Financial aid to full-time, first-time undergraduate students: need-based scholarships/grants totaling $11,271,213, self-help $9,799,704, parent loans $443,821, tuition waivers $92,275; non-need-based scholarships/grants totaling $1,704,754, self-help $6,640,693, parent loans $1,756,473, tuition waivers $86,204.

Departments and Teaching Staff: *Total instructional faculty:* 271 (full-time 134, part-time 137; women 138, men 133; members of minority groups 5). Total faculty with doctorate, first-professional, or other terminal degree: 117. Student-to-faculty ratio: 12:1.

Enrollment: Total enrollment 3,327. Undergraduate full-time 325 men / 1,089 women, part-time 73m / 20w; graduate full-time 115m / 329w, part-time 178m / 519w; first-professional full-time 229m / 262w.

Characteristics of Student Body: *Ethnic/racial makeup:* number of Black non-Hispanic: 11; American Indian or Alaska Native: 3; Asian or Pacific Islander: 13; Hispanic: 12; White non-Hispanic: 1,571; unknown: 82.

International Students: 13 nonresident aliens enrolled fall 2004.

Student Life: On-campus residence halls house 85% of student body. Total of 5 residence halls: 1 female, 4 co-ed (by floor). *Intercollegiate athletics:* men only: basketball, lacrosse, soccer; women only: basketball, softball, volleyball.

Special regulations: Cars permitted with regulations. Freshmen residency requirement. *Special services:* Learning Assistance Center, medical services. *Surrounding community:* Located on the southern coast of Maine in Biddeford which has a population of 22,000. Portland, 18 miles from campus, is nearest metropolitan area. Boston is 90 miles to the south. Served by bus system; airport 18 miles from campus.

Library Collections: 142,181 volumes. 6,281 microforms; 9,879 audiovisual materials; 2,443 current periodical titles. Online catalog. Students have access to online information retrieval services and the Internet.

Most important holdings include History of Osteopathic Medicine Collection; Main Women Writers Collection; Dental History Collection; personal papers of Booth Tarkington (American novelist and playwright, 1869–1946).

Buildings and Grounds: Biddeford campus area 540; Westbrook campus (Portland) 41 acres. *New buildings:* Marine Science Education and Research Center; East and West Residence Halls.

Chief Executive Officer: Dr. Sandra G. Featherman, President.

Address admission inquiries to Dean of Admissions and Enrollment Management.

University of Southern Maine

96 Falmouth Street
Portland, Maine 04103
Tel: (207) 780-4141   **E-mail:** usmadm@maine.maine.edu
Fax: (207) 780-4933   **Internet:** www.usm.maine.edu

Institution Description: *Enrollment:* 11,089. *Degrees awarded:* Associate, baccalaureate, first-professional (law), master's.

Accreditation: *Regional:* NEASC. *Professional:* art, business, computer science, counseling, engineering, industrial technology, law, music, nursing, public administration, rehabilitation counseling, social work, teacher education

History: Established as Western Maine Normal School and chartered 1878; offered first instruction at postsecondary level 1879; awarded first degree (baccalaureate) 1938; changed name to Gorham State Teachers College 1945, Gorham State College 1965, to Gorham State College of the University of Maine 1968; merged with the University of Maine in Portland and changed name to University of Maine at Portland-Gorham 1970; adopted present name 1978.

Institutional Structure: Member of University of Main System. *Composition of institution:* Administrators 15. Academic affairs headed by provost/vice president for academic affairs. Management/business/finances directed by executive director for financial resources. Full-time instructional faculty 320, part-time 226. Academic governance body, The Faculty Senate, meets an average of 18 times per year.

Calendar: Semesters. Academic year Sept. to May. Degrees conferred May, Aug., Dec. Formal commencement May. Summer session from mid-May to mid-Aug.

Characteristics of Freshmen: 3,742 applicants (1,832 men / 2,110 women). 82.8% of applicants admitted. 28.4% of admitted students enrolled full-time.

93% (881 students) submitted SAT scores; 4% (34 students) submitted ACT scores. *25th percentile:* SAT I Verbal 450, SAT I Math 450; ACT Composite 18; ACT English 18, ACT Math 17. *75th percentile:* SAT I Verbal 560, SAT I Math 550; ACT Composite 24, ACT English 24, ACT Math 24.

93% of freshmen from Maine. Freshmen from 28 states.

Admission: Rolling admissions plan. For fall acceptance, application deadline July 15. Early acceptance available. *Requirements:* Either graduation from accredited secondary school with 4 units in English, 2 history or social studies, 2 laboratory science, 2 Algebra I and II, 1 geometry; or GED. Recommend 2 additional units in foreign language for Arts and Sciences. Applicants to vocation-occupation education and vocation education programs must have 3 years occupational experiences. Music majors must audition. Most associate and baccalaureate degree programs, excluding nursing, offer conditional acceptance to applicants with incomplete or deficient credentials. *Entrance tests:* College Board SAT or ACT composite. For foreign students TOEFL. *For transfer students:* 2.0 minimum GPA; from 4-year accredited institution 90 semester hours maximum transfer credit; from 2-year accredited institution 60 hours.

College credit and advanced placement for postsecondary-level work completed in secondary school. Tutoring available. Noncredit developmental/remedial courses offered in summer session and regular academic year.

Degree Requirements: *For all associate degrees:* 60 semester hours; 1 term in residence. *For all baccalaureate degrees:* 120 semester hours; 2 terms in residence; general education requirements. *For all degrees:* 2.0 GPA. Fulfillment of some degree requirements and exemption from some beginning courses possible by passing College Board CLEP, AP. *Grading system:* A–F; pass-fail; withdraw (carries time limit).

Distinctive Educational Programs: Work-experience programs. Flexible meeting places and schedules, including off-campus center, evening classes. Facilities and programs for independent research, including individual majors. Center for Research and advanced Study. Study abroad through British exchange program. *Other distinctive programs:* The Department of Conferences and Special Programs offers seminars, institutes, workshops, conferences, and short courses for information sharing purposes, skills development, and professional advancement. Honors Program. University-wide core curriculum; interactive instructional television system between campuses.

ROTC: Army.

Degrees Conferred: 41 *associate;* 972 *baccalaureate*; 389 *master's*: Bachelor's degrees awarded in top five disciplines: social sciences 185; health professions and related clinical sciences 136; business, management, marketing, and related support services 130; communication, journalism, and related programs 104; visual and performing arts 67. 82 *first-professional*: law.

Fees and Other Expenses: *Full-time tuition per academic year:* undergraduate resident $5,510, nonresident $13,670. Contact the university for current graduate tuition/fees. *Other fees:* $380. *Room and baord per academic year:* $6,502.

Financial Aid: Aid from institutionally generated funds is provided on the basis of financial need. Institution has a Program Participation Agreement with the U.S. Department of Education for eligible students to receive Pell Grants and other federal aid.

Financial aid to full-time, first-time undergraduate students: 47% received federal grants averaging $2,557; 31% state/local grants averaging $937; 16% institutional grants averaging $3,078; 62% received loans averaging $3,252.

Departments and Teaching Staff: Business *professors* 1, *associate professors* 10, *assistant professors* 3, *instructors* 0, *part-time faculty* 15; accounting 2, 3, 2, 0, 0; applied medical sciences 2, 0, 1, 0, 1; American New England studies 1, 1, 1, 0, 0; art 2, 7, 3, 0, 11; biology 3, 4, 3, 0, 2; communication 1, 3, 2, 0, 1; criminology 2, 1, 2, 0, 1; computer science 2, 2, 2, 0, 0; academic support 0, 3, 0, 0, 18; extended academic programs 0, 0, 0, 0, 7; economics 1, 4, 1, 0, 2; education 11, 19, 6, 1, 38; electrical engineering 1, 2, 2, 0, 0; English 5, 7, 5, 0, 19; environmental science and policy 0, 1, 3, 0, 2; foreign languages and classics 0, 7, 2, 0, 8; geography/anthropology 1, 5, 2, 0, 1; geosciences 2, 1, 2, 0, 2; history 7, 6, 0, 0, 4; Lewiston-Auburn College 0, 4, 7, 1, 21; linguistics 0, 2, 0, 0, 3; mathematics 5, 7, 2, 0, 13; music 4, 6, 1, 0, 17; Professional Development Center 0, 0, 0, 0, 4; nursing 1, 13, 4, 1, 12; philosophy 4, 4, 1, 0, 3; physics 0, 4, 0, 0, 2; political science 2, 4, 0, 0, 6; public policy and management 1, 2, 1, 0, 3; psychology 1, 5, 3, 0, 0; sociology 1, 3, 3, 0, 0; social work 1, 5, 2, 0, 3; industrial technology 0, 5, 2, 0, 6; theatre 3, 3, 2, 0, 2; therapeutic recreation 0, 2, 2, 1, 3.

Total instructional faculty: 376. Degrees held by full-time faculty: doctorate 61%, master's 42%, professional 8%. 61% hold terminal degrees.

Enrollment: Total enrollment 11,089. Undergraduate 8,736 (39.5% men, 60.5% women).

Characteristics of Student Body: *Ethnic/racial makeup:* Black non-Hispanic: 1.2%; American Indian or Alaska Native: 1.2%; Asian or Pacific Islander: 1.4%; Hispanic: .8%; White non-Hispanic: 95.5%.

International Students: 9 nonresident aliens enrolled fall 2004. Programs available to aid students whose native language is not English: English as a Second Language Program. Financial aid available for qualifying international students.

Student Life: On-campus residence halls house 11.5% of undergraduate student body. All residence halls are co-ed. *Intercollegiate athletics:* men only: baseball, basketball, cross country, golf, hockey, soccer, tennis; women only, basketball, field hockey, soccer, softball, tennis, volleyball. *Special regulations:* Registered cars permitted for all. Quiet hours and visitation vary according to residence hall. All visitors must sign in at security desks of residence halls. *Special services:* Learning Resources Center, medical services, bus service between campuses. *Student publications, radio: Free Press,* a weekly newspaper; *Portland Review of the Arts,* a biannual literary magazine; *Reflection,* a yearbook. Radio station WMPG broadcasts 168 hours a week. *Surrounding community:* Portland population 67,000. Boston, 100 miles from campus, is nearest metropolitan area. Served by mass transit bus system; airport 2 miles from campus.

Publications: *Maine Law Review,* a triennial publication.

Library Collections: 570,000 volumes. 100,000 government document titles; 1,025,000 microform units: 2,700 audiovisual materials; 3,000 periodicals. Online catalog. Students have access to online information retrieval systems and the Internet.

Most important holdings include Anthoenson Collection of Fine Printing; Other and Smith Collection of rare maps, globes, and atlases dating from 1400s; University Archives dating back to 1878; nursing collection; education collection.

Buildings and Grounds: Campus area 144 acres.

Chief Executive Officer: Dr. Richard L. Pattenaude, President.

Address admission inquiries to Dee Gardner, Director of Admissions.

College of Arts and Sciences

Degree Programs Offered: *Baccalaureate* in art, biology, chemistry, communication, criminology, economics, English, French, geography/anthropology, geology, history, liberal studies, mathematics, music philosophy, political science, psychology, self-designed, social science, sociology, social work, theatre. In addition, bachelor of fine arts (B.F.A.) is offered by the Art Department; bachelor of science (B.S.) is offered by the Departments of Chemistry, Art, Mathematics, and Music; and bachelor of music in performance (B.M.) is offered by the Music Department. The College of Arts and Sciences offers a 2-year degree program leading to the associate of arts (A.A.) degree in liberal arts.

Degree Requirements: *For associate of arts degree:* minimum proficiency requirements; core curriculum requirements; electives from the College of Arts and Sciences. *For baccalaureate degree:* minimum proficiency requirements; core curriculum requirements; departmental or program requirements; minimum of 120 credits of accepted courses; minimum of 2.0 cumulative grade point average.

Distinctive Educational Programs: Interdepartmental programs. Independent study. Cooperative baccalaureate in engineering and engineering physics, cooperative master's in history, both with University of Maine in Orono.

School of Business

Degree Programs Offered: The School of Business offers a number of different programs to meet student needs. The School offers a 2-year program in business administration leading to an associate of science in business administration degree. 4-year undergraduate programs leading to the degree of bachelor of science in business administration are available in 2 areas of study: accounting and business administration. The School also provides a graduate program leading to the degree of master of business administration.

Admission: Any high school student may seek admission to the 2-year associate degree program. A college preparatory background, while desirable, is not necessary. Applicants should complete the University of Maine application and specify the associate in business administration program. Candidates also must complete the Scholastic Aptitude Test. To be admitted to a baccalaureate major within the School of Business, a student must have completed at least 53 semester hours with a minimum cumulative grade point average of 2.00 and have completed the required set of courses for the designated major, also with a minimum cumulative GPA of 2.00.

Degree Requirements: *For Associate of Science in Business Administration:* A minimum of 60 credits. *For baccalaureate degree:* All students must complete at least 120 credit hours of coursework. To be eligible for the B.S. degree, a student must have attained an cumulative GPA of 2.00 or higher in all courses taken in baccalaureate programs at the University and in all baccalaureate courses in accounting, business, and economics. Accounting majors must also attain a 2.00 or higher cumulative GPA in all accounting designated courses. Transfer students majoring in accounting normally will need to complete at least 12 credits of 300-level or 400-level accounting designated courses at USM to obtain a B.S. degree.

School of Nursing

Degree Programs Offered: *Associate* in therapeutic recreation; *baccalaureate, master's* in nursing, health sciences, sports medicine, therapeutic recreation.

Admission: In addition to general university requirements, applicants to the School of Nursing must have 2 units of science (with lab) and 2 units of history/social science. Early admission is offered to candidates with 950 combined SAT scores and in the top third of their high school graduating class.

Degree Requirements: *For Associate in Therapeutic Recreation:* 60 credit hours. *For baccalaureate degree:* in nursing, a minimum of 121–126 credits including nursing, core competencies, general education, liberal arts and sciences, and other supporting courses; in therapeutic recreation, 122.5 credit hours.

Distinctive Educational Programs: Bureau of Continuing Education for Nursing provides programs to update skills and knowledge in specialized areas of nursing care.

University of Maine School of Law

Degree Programs Offered: *First-professional.*

Admission: LSAT; registration with LSDAS.

Degree Requirements: 89 credit hours. 2.0 GPA.

Departments and Teaching Staff: Law *professors* 12, *associate professors* 5, *part-time teachers* 12.

College of Education

Degree Programs Offered: The College of Education is organized into two departments. The Professional Educational Department-Graduate Division offers degrees in reading, instructional leadership, and educational administration. The Department of Human Resource Development offers graduate degrees in counselor education, adult education, and community agency/rehabilitation counseling. Additionally, undergraduate degree programs are offered with the College of Arts and Sciences in art education, music education, and secondary mathematics; undergraduate degrees are offered with the School of Applied Science in technology education and applied technology education.

Admission: Admission to an undergraduate program in the College of Education is initiated through the Admissions Office. Candidates for admission must be graduates of approved secondary schools or hold the high school equivalency diploma.

Degree Requirements: General university requirements.

Distinctive Educational Programs: Practica, internships, student teaching. The Educational Placement Office provides professional assistance in preparing students for employment opportunities.

School of Applied Science

Degree Programs Offered: The School is organized into 4 departments: the Department of Computer Science, the Department of Technology, the Department of Engineering, and the Department of Applied Immunology. Through these departments, the School offers bachelor's and master's degrees, including the B.S. in computer science, industrial technology, and vocational technology. The School provides industrial arts and vocational/occupational courses in support of B.S. degrees in industrial arts education and vocational/occupational education offered by the College of Education. The School offers the M.S. degree in computer science, and through a cooperative arrangement, the M.S. degree in engineering is extended from the University of Maine in Orono. In September 1987, the M.S. degree in applied immunology was offered in collaboration with the Maine Medical Center and with the Foundation for Blood Research. The Department of Engineering also offers introductory undergraduate courses in engineering to prepare students for transfer to the University of Maine in Orono's engineering programs.

Admission: Admission to an undergraduate program in the School of Applied Science is initiated through the University Admissions Office. Candidates for admission must be graduates of an approved secondary school and meet such other admissions requirements as are set out for all undergraduate applicants of the University.

Degree Requirements: *For Bachelor of Science in Computer Science:* minimum of 47 credits (in addition to core curriculum). Total minimum credits required for graduation is 120. Minimum cumulative GPA of 2.0 in major courses. *For Bachelor of Science in Industrial Technology:* 127 credits. *For Bachelor of Science in Electrical Engineering:* 134 credits. *For Bachelor of Science Applied Technical Leadership:* 121 credits. *For Bachelor of Science in Technical Education:* 127 credits. *For Bachelor of Science in Safety and Health:* 131.5 credits.

Maryland

Baltimore Hebrew University

5800 Park Heights Avenue
Baltimore, Maryland 21215
Tel: (410) 578-6900   **E-mail:** admissions@bhu.edu
Fax: (410) 578-6940   **Internet:** www.bhu.edu

Institution Description: Baltimore Hebrew University is a private, independent, nonprofit institution. *Enrollment:* 105. *Degrees awarded:* Baccalaureate, master's, doctorate.

Accreditation: *Regional:* MSA.

History: Established 1919.

Institutional Structure: *Governing board:* Board of Trustees. Extrainstitutional representation: 1 administrator. 1 ex officio. *Composition of institution:* Administrators 7. Academic affairs headed by dean of the school of undergraduate studies. Management/business/finances directed by controller.

Calendar: Semesters. Academic year Sept. to May. Formal commencement May. Summer session from June to July.

Admission: *Requirements:* Graduation from accredited secondary school. *Entrance tests:* College Board SAT. *For transfer students:* Transfer credit varies.

Degree Requirements: *For all undergraduate degrees:* 120 credit hours; 2.75 GPA on 4.25 scale; 2 years in residence; general education requirements, including proficiency in Hebrew. *Grading system:* A–F; withdraw; incomplete.

Distinctive Educational Programs: Work-experience programs. Dual degree in Jewish Communal Service with University of Maryland; in Jewish education with Towson State University. Cooperative programs with Goucher College, The Johns Hopkins University. Individual majors. Study abroad in Israel. Upland Program enables students to study Hebrew as a living spoken language. *Other distinctive programs:* Center for the Study of Soviet Jewish Resettlement in American Society provided research for Soviet Jewish emigres in Jewish and general communities. The Jewish Historical Society of Maryland.

Degrees Conferred: 4 *baccalaureate:* Jewish studies; 24 *master's:* Jewish studies.

Fees and Other Expenses: *Full-time tuition per academic year 2005–06:* $10,400 undergraduate, $9,450 graduate. No on-campus housing.

Financial Aid: Financial aid to full-time, first-time undergraduate students: need-based scholarships/grants totaling $20,275; non-need based $2,550. *Graduate aid:* 10 students received federal and state-funded loans totaling $117,296 (ranging from $5,983 to $18,500); 4 students held work-study jobs totaling $5,090 (ranging from $205 to $1,310); 48 fellowships and grants totaling $265,625 (ranging from $675 to $20,000).

Departments and Teaching Staff: *Total instructional faculty:* 10. 100% hold terminal degrees.

Enrollment: Total enrollment 105.

International Students: 4 nonresident aliens enrolled fall 2004. 2 students from Asia, 2 Central and South America.

Student Life: *Special services:* Learning Resources Center. *Surrounding community:* Baltimore population 790,000. Served by mass transit bus system, airport, passenger rail service.

Library Collections: 85,000 volumes. 7,500 microforms; 350 current periodical subscriptions; 12,000 recordings/tapes. Access to online information retrieval systems and the Internet.

Most important holdings include collection of rare books from 16th to 18th centuries.

Buildings and Grounds: Campus area 2 acres.

Chief Executive Officer: Dr. Rela Geffen, President.

Address admission inquiries to Laurie Shoemaker, Director of Admissions.

Baltimore International College

17 Commerce Street
Baltimore, Maryland 21202-3230
Tel: (410) 752-4710   **E-mail:** admissions@bic.edu
Fax: (410) 752-3730   **Internet:** www.bic.edu

Institution Description: *Enrollment:* 556. *Degrees awarded:* Baccalaureate.
Accreditation: *Regional:* MSA.

History: Baltimore International College was formerly known as Baltimore International Culinary College.

Calendar: Trimesters. Academic year begins in Sept.

Characteristics of Freshmen: 252 applicants (127 men, 125 women). 52% of applicants admitted. 99.2% of admitted students enrolled full-time.

60% of freshmen from Maryland. Freshmen from 23 states and 5 foreign countries.

Admission: *Requirements:* Graduation from an accredited secondary school or GED.

Degree Requirements: *For all baccalaureate degrees:* Completion of the prescribed curriculum.

Distinctive Educational Programs: *For undergraduates:* Business and management programs; culinary arts.

Degrees Conferred: 152 *associate;* 16 *baccalaureate:* business/marketing.

Fees and Other Expenses: *Full-time tuition per academic year 2004–05:* $19,990. *Books and supplies:* $1,500. *Room and board per academic year:* $6,294.

Financial Aid: Aid from institutionally generated funds is provided on the basis of academic merit, athletic ability. Institution has a Program Participation Agreement with the U.S. Department of Education for eligible students to receive Pell Grants and other federal aid.

Financial aid to full-time, first-time undergraduate students: 55% received federal grants averaging $2,159; 25% state/local grants averaging $1,411; 93% institutional grants averaging $2,325; 88% received loans averaging $5,472.

Departments and Teaching Staff: School of Business and Management *instructors 7, part-time teachers 7;* School of Culinary Arts 9, 6. *Total instructional faculty:* 29. Student-to-faculty ratio: 16:1. Degrees held by full-time faculty: doctorate 13%, master's 31%, baccalaureate 6%. 38% hold terminal degrees.

Enrollment: Total enrollment 556 (44.8% men, 55.2% women).

Characteristics of Student Body: *Ethnic/racial makeup:* Black non-Hispanic: 38.7%; American Indian or Alaska Native: .4%; Asian or Pacific Islander: 4.5%; Hispanic: 2.3%; White non-Hispanic: 38.7%; unknown: 2.7%. *Age distribution:* 17–21: 46%; 22–24: 15%; 25–29: 14%; 30–34: 9%; 35–39: 5%; 40–49: 7%; 50–59: 2%; 60–and over: 1%. 85% of total student body attend summer trimester.

International Students: 8 nonresident aliens enrolled fall 2004. Students from Europe, Africa. No programs available to aid students whose native language is not English. No financial programs specifically designated for international students.

Library Collections: 16,000 volumes including bound books, serial backfiles, electronic documents, and government documents not in separate collections. Current serial subscriptions: paper, microform, electronic. 34 computer work stations. Students have access to the Internet at no charge.

Most important special collections include culinary arts, hospitality management, and specialized periodicals and indexes.

Buildings and Grounds: Dr. Roger Chylinski, President.

Address admissions inquiries to Brian Booher, Director of Admissions.

Bowie State University

14000 Jericho Park Road
Bowie, Maryland 20715
Tel: (301) 464-3000   **E-mail:** admissions@bowiestate.edu
Fax: (301) 464-3510   **Internet:** www.bowiestate.edu

Institution Description: Bowie State University is a state institution. *Enrollment:* 5,415. *Degrees awarded:* Baccalaureate, master's, doctorate. Certificates also awarded.

Academic offerings subject to approval by statewide coordinating bodies. Budget subject to approval by state governing boards.

Accreditation: *Regional:* MSA. *Professional:* business, computer science, nursing, social work, teacher education

History: Established as Industrial School for Colored Youth 1865; offered first instruction at postsecondary level 1893; chartered as Normal School No. 3 1908; awarded first degree (baccalaureate) 1912; changed name to Bowie Normal and Industrial School for the Training of Colored Youth 1925, to Maryland State Teachers College 1935; became Bowie State College 1963; adopted present name and joined the University System of Maryland in 1988.

Institutional Structure: *Governing board:* Board of Regents for the University System of Maryland. Representation: 11 board members, including 1 student (replaced annually to represent 6 state institutions on a rotating basis). All voting. *Composition of institution:* Administrators 121, Academic affairs headed by vice president of academic affairs and dean of the college office. Management/business/finances directed by vice president for business and financial affairs. Full-time instructional faculty 159. Academic governance body, Faculty Senate, meets an average of 9 times per year.

Calendar: Semesters. Academic year Sept. to May. Freshmen admitted Aug., Jan., May. Degrees conferred and formal commencement May.

Characteristics of Freshmen: 5,443 applicants (1,835 men, 3,608 women). 44.3% of applicants admitted. 26% of admitted students enrolled full-time.

91% (589 students) submitted SAT scores; 7% (43 students) submitted ACT scores. *25th percentile:* SAT I Verbal 400, SAT I Math 400; ACT Composite 16. *75th percentile:* SAT I Verbal 490, SAT I Math 440; ACT Composite 19.

29% of entering freshmen expected to graduate within 5 years. 92% of freshmen from Maryland. Freshmen from 27 states.

Admission: Rolling admissions plan. For fall acceptance, apply as early as Sept. of previous year, but not later than Aug. of year of enrollment. Early acceptance available. *Requirements:* Either graduation from secondary school or GED; GPA of 2.2 (or a minimum ACT score of 19). Out-of-state residents should have a minimum cumulative GPA of 2.6 and a minimum recentered SAT I score of 950 (or a minimum ACT score of 20). Required high school courses: English 4 credits; social science/history 3 credits; mathematics 3 credits; laboratory science 2 credits; foreign language 2 credits; electives 6 credits. *Entrance tests:* College Board SAT. For foreign students TOEFL. *For transfer students:* minimum 2.0 GPA for a minimum of 24 transferable credits, or SAT 1 scores will be required.

College credit for postsecondary-level work completed in secondary school and for extrainstitutional learning on basis of ACE *2006 Guide to the Evaluation of Educational Experiences in the Armed Services.* Tutoring available. Developmental-remedial courses offered; credit given.

Degree Requirements: 120 credit hours; 2.0 GPA; 6 months in residence, developmental studies course requirements; national standardized exit tests; exit competency examination in English. Additional requirements for some programs. Fulfillment of some degree requirements possible by passing College Board CLEP. *Grading system:* A–F.

Distinctive Educational Programs: Cooperative education. Flexible meeting places and schedules, including off-campus centers (at Andrews Air Force Base, Belair Junior High School, Computer Sciences Technicolor Associates, Fort George G. Meade, Goddard Space Flight Center, Prince George's and Anne Arundel counties departments of social services), weekend and evening classes. Dual-degree program in engineering with University of Maryland. Facilities and programs for independent research, including honors programs, individual majors, tutorials. Cooperative enrollment with other Maryland state colleges and universities. Certificate programs in child development, family counseling, psychotherapy through Adler-Dreikurs Institute of Human Relations. Study abroad opportunities. *Other distinctive programs:* Continuing education. Graduate programs in administrative management and management information systems.

ROTC: Army in cooperation with Howard University (DC); Air Force in cooperation with University of Maryland at College Park.

Degrees Conferred: 596 *baccalaureate;* 367 *master's.* Bachelor's degrees awarded in top five disciplines: business, management, marketing, and related support services 146; social sciences 93; computer and information sciences and support services 82; communication, journalism, and related programs 55; psychology 54. x\200 *Full-time tuition per academic year 2004–05:* $5,218 under-

graduate resident, $13,583 out-of-state student: $13,583. Contact the university for current graduate tuition/fees/other costs. *Room and board per academic year:* $6,321.

Financial Aid: Aid from institutionally generated funds is provided on the basis of academic merit, financial need, athletic ability, other criteria. Institution has a Program Participation Agreement with the U.S. Department of Education for eligible students to receive Pell Grants and other federal aid.

Financial aid to full-time, first-time undergraduate students: 12% received federal grants averaging $2,954; 20% state/local grants averaging $2,056;14% institutional grants averaging $3,965; 22% received loans averaging $2,785.

Departments and Teaching Staff: *Total instructional faculty:* 251 (full-time 139, part-time 112). Student-to-faculty ratio: 18:1. Degrees held by full-time faculty: doctorate 43%, master's 50%, baccalaureate 4%. 75% hold terminal degrees.

Enrollment: Total enrollment 5,415. Undergraduate 4,027 (36.3% men, 63.&% women).

Characteristics of Student Body: *Ethnic/racial makeup:* Black non-Hispanic: 89.1%; American Indian or Alaska Native: .3%; Asian or Pacific Islander: 1.5%; Hispanic: 1.4%; White non-Hispanic: 5.6%; unknown: 1.3%.

International Students: 40 undergraduate nonresident aliens enrolled fall 2004. No programs available to aid students whose native language is not English. Financial aid available for qualifying international students.

Student Life: On-campus residence halls house 25% of undergraduate student body. *Intercollegiate athletics:* men only: baseball, basketball, football, tennis; women only: basketball, softball, tennis, volleyball. *Special regulations:* Registered cars permitted. *Special services:* Career Services and Cooperative Education, Counseling and Student Development, Financial Aid, Health Services, Special Services Project, International and Disabled Student Services, and Student Activities. *Student publications: The Spectrum,* a monthly newspaper; the *Bulldog,* a yearbook; the *Torch,* a literary magazine. *Surrounding community:* Bowie population 37,000. Washington (DC), 15 miles from campus, is nearest metropolitan area. Served by mass transit bus system; airport 20 miles from campus; passenger rail service 1 mile from campus.

Library Collections: 295,000 volumes. 640,000 microforms; 1,300 audiovisual materials; 1,396 current periodical subscriptions. 200 computer work stations campus-wide. Online catalog. Students have access to online information retrieval systems and the Internet.

Most important holdings include North Star Collection (formerly Negro Collection); Maryland Room; archives.

Buildings and Grounds: Campus area 238 acres.

Chief Executive Officer: Dr. Calvin W. Lowe, President.

Address admission inquiries to Director of Admissions.

Capitol College

11301 Springfield Road
Laurel, Maryland 20708
Tel: (301) 953-200   **E-mail:** admissions@capitol-college.edu
Fax: (301) 953-1442   **Internet:** www.capitol-college.edu

Institution Description: Capitol College (formerly Capitol Institute of Technology) is a private, independent institution. *Enrollment:* 739. *Degrees awarded:* Associate, baccalaureate, master's.

Accreditation: *Regional:* MSA. *Professional:* engineering

History: Established as a correspondence school and offered first instruction at postsecondary level 1927; became Capitol Radio Engineering Institution 1932; awarded first degree (associate) 1954; chartered as Capitol Institute of Technology 1964; licensed to confer baccalaureate degrees in 1965; name changed to present 1987; master's program instituted in 1989.

Institutional Structure: *Governing board:* Board of Trustees. Representation: 16 trustees, 2 trustees emeriti, 16 voting. *Composition of institution:* Administrators 5. Academic affairs headed by vice president for academic affairs. Management/business/finances directed by vice president for administration and finance. Full-time instructional faculty 14.

Calendar: Semesters. Academic year late Aug. to early Aug. New students admitted Aug., Jan., May. Degrees conferred once each year at formal commencement in May. Summer session late May through mid-Aug.

Characteristics of Freshmen: 60% of applicants admitted. 255 of applicants admitted and enrolled.

100% (264 students) submitted SAT scores. Mean SAT scores 450 verbal, 480 mathematical.

90% of freshmen from Maryland. Freshmen from 12 states and 3 foreign countries.

Admission: Rolling admissions plan. *Requirements:* Graduation from accredited secondary school or GED and 3 years of college preparatory mathematics. *For foreign students:* score of 500 on TOEFL, 3 years college preparatory mathematics and proof of English proficiency.

College credit and advanced placement for extrainstitutional learning on basis of ACE *2006 Guide to the Evaluation of Educational Experiences in the Armed Services;* faculty assessment. Tutoring available.

Degree Requirements: *For all associate degrees:* 66–68 semester hours; 30 hours must be taken at Capitol College. *For all baccalaureate degrees:* 123–136 semester hours; 40 hours must be taken at Capitol College.

Fulfillment of some degree requirements and exemption from some beginning courses possible by passing departmental examinations. Exemption from courses also possible by passing College Board CLEP. *Grading system:* A–F; withdraw (carries time limit).

Distinctive Educational Programs: Offer BS, MS, and MBA degrees in engineering, computer sciences, information technologies and business. Online master's degrees in government and corporate training are available.

Degrees Conferred: 12 *associate;* 72 *baccalaureate* (B); 162 *master's* (M): business/marketing 11 (B), 28 (M); computer and information sciences 22 (B), 134 (M); engineering and engineering technologies 39 (B).

Fees and Other Expenses: *Full-time tuition per academic year 2004–05:* $17,244 undergraduate; graduate study $410 per credit hour. *Room and board per academic year:* $5,746. *Required fees:* $310 (undergraduate).

Financial Aid: Aid from institutionally generated funds is provided on the basis of academic merit, financial need. Institution has a Program Participation Agreement with the U.S. Department of Education for eligible students to receive Pell Grants and other federal aid.

Financial aid to full-time, first-time undergraduate students: need-based scholarships/grants totaling $1,009,156, self-help $1,537,196, parent loans $470,722, tuition waivers $68,290; non-need-based scholarships/grants totaling $275,184, self-help $296,613, parent loans $268,012.

Departments and Teaching Staff: Electrical, electronics, telecommunications engineering technology *professors* 5, *associate professors* 0, *assistant professors* 0, *part-time faculty* 7; computer technology/mathematics and science 1, 3, 1, 11; management 1, 0, 3, 8.

Total instructional faculty: 40 (full-time 14, part-time 26; women 8, men 32; members of minority groups 10). Total faculty with doctorate, first-professional, or other terminal degree: 15. Student-to-faculty ratio: 18:1. Degrees held by full-time faculty: doctorate 29%, master's 100%.

Enrollment: Total enrollment 679. Undergraduate full-time 144 men / 47 women, part-time 113m / 20w; graduate full-time 61m / 21w, part-time 265m / 68w.

Characteristics of Student Body: *Ethnic/racial makeup:* number of Black non-Hispanic: 138; Asian or Pacific Islander: 23; Hispanic: 12; White non-Hispanic: 137; unknown: 3.

International Students: 11 nonresident aliens enrolled fall 2004. Programs available to aid students whose native language is not English: social, cultural. English as a Second Language Program. No financial aid specifically designated for international students.

Student Life: Apartment-style living on campus. Intramural sports available. Honor societies, student government association, minority student associations, professional associations. School newspaper. *Surrounding community:* Laurel (MD) population 5,000. Washington (DC), 19 miles from campus, and Baltimore (MD), 22 miles from campus, are nearest metropolitan areas.

Library Collections: 10,000 volumes. 200 microform collections; 125 audiovisual materials; 87 current periodical subscriptions. Online catalog. 32 computer work stations. Students have access to online information retrieval services and the Internet. Total 2004–05 budget for materials and operations: $10,000.

Buildings and Grounds: Campus area 52 acres. *New buildings:* William G. McGowan Academic Center completed 2005.

Chief Executive Officer: Dr. Michael Wood, President.

Address admission inquiries Darnell Edwards, Director of Admissions; graduate inquiries to Ken Crockett, Director of Graduate Admissions.

College of Notre Dame of Maryland

4701 North Charles Street
Baltimore, Maryland 21210-2476
Tel: (410) 435-0100
Fax: (410) 532-5791

Institution Description: College of Notre Dame of Maryland is a private college primarily for women affiliated with the Roman Catholic Church. *Enrollment:* 3,307. *Degrees awarded:* Baccalaureate, master's.

Accreditation: *Regional:* MSA. *Professional:* nursing, teacher education

History: Established as Notre Dame of Maryland Collegiate Institute for Young Ladies and offered first instruction at postsecondary level 1873; chartered as 4-year college and adopted present name 1896; first degree (baccalaureate) awarded 1899; incorporated 1957. *See* Sister Mary David, *The College of Notre Dame of Maryland: 1895–1945* (New York: Declan X. McMullen Co., Inc., 1947) for further information.

Institutional Structure: *Governing board:* Board of Trustees. Extrainstitutional representation: 24 trustees; institutional representation: president of the college, 1 full-time instructional faculty member; 1 alumna, 1 student representative. 3 ex officio - emeriti. 1 special advisor to president. 24 voting. *Composition of institution:* Administrators 5 men / 47 women (at dean's level and above 67% are women). Academic affairs headed by vice president. Management/business/finances directed by chief financial officer. Full-time instructional faculty 26 men / 55 women. Academic governance body, Curriculum Committee, meets an average of 8 times per year.

Calendar: Semesters (4-1-4 plan). Academic year Sept. to May. Freshmen admitted Sept., Feb. Degrees conferred May, Aug., Dec. Formal commencement May. Winter term in January.

Characteristics of Freshmen: 450 applicants (450 women). 72.4% of applicants admitted. 45.7% of admitted students enrolled full-time.

96% (143 students) submitted SAT scores. *25th percentile:* SAT I Verbal 490, SAT I M450. *75th percentile:* SAT I Verbal 580, SAT I Math 580.

65% of entering freshmen expected to graduate within 5 years. 78% of freshmen from Maryland. Freshmen from 15 states and 3 foreign countries.

Admission: Rolling admissions plan. For fall acceptance, apply as early as Oct. 1 of previous year, but not later than Aug. 15. Apply by Dec. 3 for early action; priority deadline for maximum consideration for admissions scholarships and financial aid is Feb. 15; need not limit application to College of Notre Dame of Maryland. Early acceptance available. *Requirements:* Graduation from accredited secondary school with 18 units which include 4 English, 3 foreign language, 3 college preparatory mathematics, 2 history, 2 science, 4 electives. Exceptions may be made. Lowest acceptable secondary school class standing 40th percentile. *Entrance tests:* College Board SAT. For foreign students TOEFL. *For transfer students:* 2.5 minimum GPA; 60 hours maximum transfer credit.

College credit and advanced placement for postsecondary-level work completed in secondary school. Tutoring available. Noncredit developmental English course offered during regular academic year.

Degree Requirements: 120 credit hours; 2.0 GPA; 2 years in residence; general education distribution requirements. Fulfillment of some degree requirements and exemption from some beginning courses possible by passing College Board CLEP, AP. *Grading system:* A–F; pass-fail; withdraw (carries time limit), incomplete.

Distinctive Educational Programs: Internships; work-study program for chemistry, engineering, pre-dental and pre-medical students. Weekend classes. Accelerated degree programs. Dual-degree program in engineering and cooperative program in nursing with University of Maryland. Interdisciplinary program in liberal arts. Facilities and programs for independent research, including individual majors, tutorials. Study abroad by individual arrangement. Cooperative academic program with Loyola College (MD). Coppin State, Goucher, and Morgan State Colleges, Johns Hopkins and Towson Universities (MD). Degree programs through Continuing Education and Weekend College, and Weekend Graduate program.

Degrees Conferred: 322 *baccalaureate;* 349 *master's.* Bachelor's degrees awarded in top five disciplines: business, management, marketing, and related support services 83; liberal arts and sciences, general studies, and humanities 34; health professions and related clinical sciences 31; communication, journalism, and related programs 24, public administration and social service professions 20.

Fees and Other Expenses: *Full-time tuition per academic year 2004–05:* $19,900. *Room and board per academic year:* $7,800.

Financial Aid: Aid from institutionally generated funds is provided on the basis of academic merit, financial need, leadership/talent/achievement/service. Institution has a Program Participation Agreement with the U.S. Department of Education for eligible students to receive Pell Grants and other federal aid.

Financial aid to full-time, first-time undergraduate students: 51% received federal grants averaging $3,638; 45% state/local grants averaging $4,307; 93% institutional grants averaging $9,104; 75% received loans averaging $4,625.

Departments and Teaching Staff: *Professors* 24, *associate professors* 34, *assistant professors* 22, *instructors* 1, *part-time teachers* 10.

Total instructional faculty: 91 plus 148 associate faculty who teach in part-time weekend college and graduate schools. Student-to-faculty ratio: 15:1. Degrees held by full-time faculty: doctorate 68%, master's 32%. 68% hold terminal degrees.

Enrollment: Total enrollment 3,907. Undergraduate 1,686 (6.1% men, 93.9% women).

Characteristics of Student Body: *Ethnic/racial makeup:* Black non-Hispanic: 26.4%; American Indian or Alaska Native: .5%; Asian or Pacific Islander: 2.8%; Hispanic: 2.6%; White non-Hispanic: 65.5%; unknown: .7%.

International Students: 27 undergraduate nonresident aliens enrolled fall 2004. Programs available to aid students whose native language is not English: social, cultural. English as a Second Language Program. No financial aid specifically designated for undergraduate international students but they are eligible for academic and achievement awards.

Student Life: On-campus residence halls house 65% of student body. Residence halls women only constitute 100% of such space. *Intercollegiate athletics:* women only: basketball, swimming, volleyball, lacrosse, field hockey, soccer (club). *Special regulations:* Cars permitted without restrictions. Dormitory visitation in upperclass residence hall Sun.–Thurs. noon to midnight, Fri.–Sat. noon to 2am; freshman-sophomore residence hall Mon.–Thurs. 4pm to midnight, Fri.–Sat. noon to 2am Sun. noon to midnight.

Library Collections: 380,000 books and bound periodicals; 26,000 audiovisual items; 2,100 periodical subscriptions. Online catalog. Students have access to the Internet at no charge.

Most important special holdings include Gerard Manley Hopkins collection; Knott collection of fore-edge paintings; Henry James first editions.

Buildings and Grounds: Campus area 58 acres.

Chief Executive Officer: Dr. Mary Pat Seurkamp, President.

Address admission inquiries to Dr. Jennifer Blair, Director of Admissions.

Columbia Union College

7600 Flower Avenue
Takoma Park, Maryland 20912
Tel: (301) 891-4000   **E-mail:** enroll@cuc.edu
Fax: (301) 891-4230   **Internet:** www.cuc.edu

Institution Description: Columbia Union College is a private institution affiliated with the Seventh-Day Adventists. *Enrollment:* 1,116. *Degrees awarded:* Associate, baccalaureate, master's. Certificates also awarded.

Accreditation: *Regional:* MSA. *Professional:* nursing, respiratory therapy, teacher education

History: Established as Washington Training College and offered first instruction at postsecondary level 1904; changed name to Washington Foreign Mission Seminary 1907, to Washington Missionary College 1913; awarded first degree (baccalaureate) 1915; adopted present name 1961.

Institutional Structure: *Governing board:* Board of Trustees. Representation: 34 trustees. *Composition of institution:* Administrators 5. Academic affairs headed by vice president for academic affairs. Financial affairs directed by vice president for financial administration. Full-time instructional faculty 50.

Calendar: Semesters. Academic year Sept. to Apr. Formal commencement May, July. Summer session from mid-May to late July.

Characteristics of Freshmen: 82% of applicants admitted. 35% of applicants admitted and enrolled.

71% (148 students) submitted SAT scores; 22% (53 students) submitted ACT scores. *25th percentile:* SAT Verbal 400, SAT Math 360; ACT Composite 16, ACT English 15, ACT Math 15. *75th percentile:* SAT Verbal 530, SAT Math 490; ACT Composite 23, ACT English 25, ACT Math 22.

28% of entering freshmen expected to graduate within 5 years. 41% of freshmen from Maryland. Freshmen from 32 states.

Admission: Rolling admissions plan. *Requirements:* Either graduation from approved secondary school with units which normally include 4 English, 2 mathematics, 2 science, history 2, 4 academic electives; or GED. Minimum 2.0 GPA. *Entrance tests:* College Board SAT I, SAT II, or ACT. For foreign students TOEFL score 550. *For transfer students:* 2.0 minimum GPA; from 4-year accredited institution maximum transfer credit 90 hours; from 2-year accredited institution 70 hours.

College credit and advanced placement for postsecondary-level work completed in secondary school. College credit for extrainstitutional learning (life experience) on basis of portfolio assessment. Developmental/remedial courses offered during regular academic year.

Degree Requirements: *For all associate degrees:* 64 semester hours; last 24 hours in residence; 1 hour physical education. *For all traditional baccalaureate degrees:* 128 hours; last 30 hours in residence; 1 hour physical education. *For all degrees:* 2.0 GPA; 2.25 GPA in major field; general education requirements, including 6–12 hours religious studies.

Fulfillment of some degree requirements and exemption from some beginning courses possible by passing departmental examinations, College Board CLEP, APP, other standardized tests. *Grading system:* A–F; pass-fail; satisfactory-unsatisfactory; withdraw; incomplete (carries time limit).

Distinctive Educational Programs: Adult continuing education (noncredit); cooperative education; remedial/development program; preprofessional programs. Foreign study; independent study; national honor societies; external degree; student missionary program; Honors Program.

Degrees Conferred: 16 *associate;* 286 *baccalaureate:* biological/life sciences 1; business/marketing 74; communications/communication technologies 8; computer and information sciences 38; education 9; English 1; health professions and related sciences 60; liberal arts/general studies 24; philosophy/religion/theology 7; psychology 58; social sciences and history 1; visual and performing arts 5. 5 *master's:* business/marketing.

Fees and Other Expenses: *Full-time tuition per academic year 2005–06:* Contact the college for current information.

Financial Aid: Aid from institutionally generated funds is provided on the basis of academic merit, financial need, other criteria. Institution has a Program Participation Agreement with the U.S. Department of Education for eligible students to receive Pell Grants and other federal aid.

Departments and Teaching Staff: *Total instructional faculty:* 57 (full-time 51, part-time 6; women 26, men 31; members of minority groups 23). Total faculty with doctorate, first-professional, or other terminal degree: 25. Student-to-faculty ratio: 13.7:1.

Enrollment: Total enrollment 1,115. Full-time 299 men / 486 women, part-time 101m / 200w; graduate full-time 1m, part-time 8m / 20w.

Characteristics of Student Body: *Ethnic/racial makeup:* number of Black non-Hispanic: 584; American Indian or Alaska Native: 2; Asian or Pacific Islander: 58; Hispanic: 90; White non-Hispanic: 198; unknown: 119.

International Students: 35 nonresident aliens enrolled fall 2004. Programs available to aid students whose native language is not English: English as a Second Language Program. No financial aid specifically designated for international students.

Student Life: On-campus housing for single and married students available. *Intercollegiate athletics:* men only: baseball, basketball, soccer, track and field; women only: basketball, soccer, softball, track and field. Men's and women's intramurals. *Special regulations:* Students must dress in accordance with standards of Christian modesty. *Special services:* Medical services. *Student publications, radio:* The Columbia Journal, a student newspaper; Golden Memories, a yearbook; Line Up, a student directory. *Surrounding community:* Suburban and residential, 7 miles north of Washington, DC; served by mass transit bus and subway system; 10 miles from National Airport.

Library Collections: 141,152 volumes. Online and card catalogs. Current serial subscriptions: 382 paper; 9,000 via electronic access. 6 computer work stations. Students have access to the Internet at no charge. Most important special holdings include Heritage Room with materials associated with Seventh-day Adventists; curriculum library to support teacher education program.

Buildings and Grounds: Campus area 19 acres.

Chief Executive Officer: Dr. Randel Wisbey, President.

Address admission inquiries to Emile John, Director of Admissions.

Coppin State College

2500 West North Avenue
Baltimore, Maryland 21216-3698
Tel: (410) 951-5400   **E-mail:** admissions@coppin.edu
Fax: (410) 523-7238   **Internet:** www.coppin.edu

Institution Description: Coppin State College is a state institution and a member of the University of Maryland System. *Enrollment:* 3,875. *Degrees awarded:* Baccalaureate, master's.

Academic offerings subject to approval by statewide coordinating bodies. Budget subject to approval by state governing boards.

Accreditation: *Regional:* MSA. *Professional:* nursing, rehabilitation counseling, social work, teacher education

History: Established as teacher training program housed in Douglas High School and offered first instruction at postsecondary level 1900; became Fannie Jackson Coppin Normal School 1926; became 4-year college and changed name to Coppin Teachers College 1930; awarded first degree (baccalaureate) ca. 1942; became part of State of Maryland system and changed name to Coppin State Teachers College 1950; adopted present name 1967.

Institutional Structure: *Governing board:* The Board of Regents of the University of Maryland System. 19 board members. *Composition of institution:* Administrators 15 men / 16 women. Academic affairs headed by vice president for academic affairs. Management/business/finances directed by vice president for business and finance. Full-time instructional faculty 109. Academic governance body, Curriculum Committee, meets an average of 12 times per year.

Calendar: Semesters. Academic year Sept. to May. Freshmen admitted Aug., Jan. Degrees conferred and formal commencement May. Summer sessions.

Characteristics of Freshmen: 2,845 applicants (761 men, 2,084 women). 56.5% of applicants admitted. 36.1% of admitted students enrolled full-time.

76% (472 students) submitted SAT scores; 9% (44 students) submitted ACT scores. *25th percentile*: SAT I Verbal 400, SAT I Math 350; ACT Composite 14. *75th percentile*: SAT I Verbal 500, SAT I Math 500; ACT Composite 18.

Admission: Rolling admissions plan. For fall acceptance, apply following first semester of senior year of secondary school, but not later than July 27. Apply by end of junior year for early decision; need not limit application to Coppin State. Early acceptance available. *Requirements:* Either graduation from accredited secondary school with 4 units English, 3 social studies, 3 mathematics, 2 science, 7 electives; or GED. Additional requirements for nursing program. Minimum GPA 2.0. *Entrance tests:* College Board SAT. For foreign students TOEFL. *For transfer students:* 2.0 minimum GPA; from 4-year accredited institution 70 hours maximum transfer credit.Good standing at institution previously attended.

Tutoring available. Developmental-remedial courses offered in summer session and regular courses offered in summer session and regular academic year; credit given.

Degree Requirements: *For undergraduate degrees:* 128 credit hours; 2.0 GPA; last 30 hours in residence; 2 physical education courses; general education requirements; exit competency examination in English; GRE, professional, or other standardized proficiency examination. Additional requirements for nursing degree. Up to 60 credits accepted from a two-year college.

Fulfillment of some degree requirements and exemption from some beginning courses possible by passing departmental examinations, College Board APP. *Grading system:* A–F; withdraw (carries time limit).

Distinctive Educational Programs: *For undergraduates:* Work-experience programs. Dual-degree programs in engineering with University of Maryland, College Park in social work, and in dentistry and pharmacy with University of Maryland, Baltimore County. Interdepartmental programs in general science, international studies, social science. Honors programs. Tutorials. Cross-registration with other Maryland state colleges and with private colleges in the Baltimore area. Coppin Industrial Cluster, a program through which local industries help students prepare for employment in business, industry, education, and government by advising school on faculty, curriculum development and by providing internships, part-time and summer employment, scholarship aid, or other assistance. *For graduate students:* Off-campus centers. Evening classes. *Available to all students:* Facilities and programs for independent research. *Other distinctive programs:* Degree-granting Evening School.

Degrees Conferred: 304 *baccalaureate*; 149 *master's*. Bachelor's degrees awarded in top five disciplines: business, management, marketing, and related support services 50; health professions and related clinical sciences 43; security and protective services 42; psychology 38; liberal arts and sciences, general studies, and humanities 34.

Fees and Other Expenses: *Full-time tuition per academic year 2004–05:* $4,599 resident, $10,771 nonresident. *Books and supplies:* $600. *Room and board per academic year:* $6,236.

Financial Aid: Aid from institutionally generated funds is provided on the basis of academic merit, athletic ability. Institution has a Program Participation Agreement with the U.S. Department of Education for eligible students to receive Pell Grants and other federal aid.

Financial aid to full-time, first-time undergraduate students: 62% received federal grants averaging $3,408; 21% state/local grants averaging $1,070; 44% institutional grants averaging $1,506; 60% received loans averaging $2,684.

Departments and Teaching Staff: *Professors* 25, *associate professors* 31, *assistant professors* 38, *instructors* 4, *lecturers* 8, *part-time teachers* 85.

Total instructional faculty: 191. Student-to-faculty ratio: 17:1.

Enrollment: Total enrollment 3,875. Undergraduate 3,290 (23.8% men, 76.2% women).

Characteristics of Student Body: *Ethnic/racial makeup:* Black non-Hispanic: 94.4%; American Indian or Alaska Native: .1%; Asian or Pacific Islander: .2%; Hispanic: .2%; White non-Hispanic: 1.8%; unknown: .3%. *Age distribution:* 17–21: 35%; 22–24: 14%; 25–29: 16%; 30–34: 9%; 35–39: 8%; 40–49: 14.1%; 50–59: 3.5%; 60–and over: .4%.

International Students: 99 undergraduate nonresident aliens enrolled fall 2004. No programs available to aid students whose native language is not English. No financial aid specifically designated for international students.

Student Life: On campus housing: Dedmon Hall is a 300-bed residence hall. *Intercollegiate athletics:* men only: baseball, basketball, soccer, tennis, track, volleyball; women only: volleyball; both sexes: cross-country. *Special regulations:* Cars with decals permitted on campus in designated areas. *Special services:* Learning Resources Center, medical services. Shuttle service for nursing students to and from Provident Hospital. *Student publications: The Coppin Courier*, a monthly newspaper; *The Coppin Eagle*, a yearbook. *Surrounding community:* Baltimore population 790,000. Served by mass transit bus system, airport, and passenger rail service.

Library Collections: 200,000 volumes. 233,000 microforms; 620 audiovisual materials; 715 current periodical subscriptions. Online catalog. Students have access to online information retrieval services and the Internet.

Buildings and Grounds: Campus area 45 acres.

Chief Executive Officer: Dr. Stanley F. Battle, President.

Address admission inquiries to Michelle Gross, Director of Admissions.

Frostburg State University

101 Braddock Road
Frostburg, Maryland 21532-1099
Tel: (301) 687-4000   **E-mail:** fsuadmissions@frostburg.edu
Fax: (301) 687-4737   **Internet:** www.frostburg.edu

Institution Description: Frostburg State University is a state institution. *Enrollment:* 5,327. *Degrees awarded:* Baccalaureate, master's.

Academic offerings subject to approval by statewide coordinating bodies. Budget subject to approval by state governing boards.

Accreditation: *Regional:* MSA. *Professional:* teacher education

History: Established as State Normal School at Frostburg, a 2-year institution, 1898; offered first instruction at postsecondary level 1902; became 4-year institution and awarded first degree (baccalaureate) 1934; changed name to State Teachers College at Frostburg 1935; changed name to Frostburg State College 1963; adopted present name 1987.

Institutional Structure: *Governing board:* Board of Regents of the University of Maryland System. Representation: 17 board members, including 1 student regent. All voting. *Composition of institution:* Administrators 37 men / 20 women. Four major administrative divisions: Academic Affairs, Administrative Services, Student Services, University Advancement (all headed by vice presidents). Full-time instructional faculty 228. Academic governing body, University Faculty Senate, meets monthly.

Calendar: Semesters. Academic year late Aug. to early May. Freshmen admitted all terms. Degrees conferred May, Aug., Dec. Formal commencement May, Dec. Summer session of two 6-week and three 4-week terms.

Characteristics of Freshmen: 80% of applicants accepted. 41% of accepted applicants enrolled.

97% (927 students) submitted SAT scores; 3% (24 students) submitted ACT scores. *25th percentile*: SAT Verbal 450, SAT Math 460; ACT Composite 17. *75th percentile*: SAT Verbal 550, SAT Math 560; ACT Composite 22. 48% of entering freshmen expected to graduate within 5 years. 84% of freshmen from Maryland. Freshmen from 16 states and 4 foreign countries.

Admission: For fall acceptance, apply as early as mid-Sept. of previous year. Early acceptance available. *Requirements:* Either graduation from accredited secondary school or GED. Lowest acceptable secondary school class standing 50th percentile. Consideration will be given to students with class standing below 50th percentile. *Entrance tests:* College Board SAT. *For transfer students:* 2.0 minimum GPA; from 2-year accredited institution 70 hours maximum transfer credit.

Tutoring available. Credit for remedial math courses offered during regular academic year.

Degree Requirements: 120 semester hours; 2.0 GPA overall and in major; last 30 hours and half of major credits in residence; completion of general education program including 17 credits in basic requirements (grade of C or better in freshman composition, advanced composition, speech, computer science, mathematics, and health fitness) and 32 credits minimum in liberal arts component; completion of a minimum of 15 elective credits outside the general education program and the major department; completion of minimum of 40 credits at upper division level.

Fulfillment of some degree requirements and exemption from some beginning courses possible by passing departmental examinations, College Board CLEP, AP. *Grading system:* A–F; pass/fail; withdraw (carries penalty, carries time limit); PT (pass by examination); NC (no credit); CS (continuous study required).

Distinctive Educational Programs: *For undergraduates:* Internships. Dual-degree programs in engineering with University of Maryland College Park; 6-year BA/BS-JD program with University of Baltimore. Preprofessional transfer programs in dental hygiene, medical technology, nursing, occupational therapy, pharmacy, and physical therapy. Undergraduate majors in wildlife and fisheries. Interdisciplinary programs in environmental analysis and planning, general science, international studies, justice studies, recreation, and social sciences. BFA in visual arts. Honors program. Study abroad in various countries through International Student Exchange Program and official university exchange agreements. Teacher certification in most fields. Evening-only program in business administration for part-time working adults. *For graduate students:* Master's program in human performance. Master's programs offered in applied ecology and conservation biology, fisheries management, and wildlife management. *Available to all students:* Off-campus center at Hagerstown offers undergraduate programs in accounting, business administration, justice studies, and sociology; master's programs in education and business scheduled to meet needs of adult part-time students.

Degrees Conferred: 797 *baccalaureate* (B); 253 *master's* (M): architecture 2 (B); biological/life sciences 11 (B); business/marketing 135 (B), 96 (M); communications/communication technologies 49 (B); computer and information sciences 30 (B), 4 (M); education 102 (B), 135 (M); English 22 (B); foreign languages and literature 3 (M); liberal arts/general studies 50 (B), 4 (M); mathematics 7 (B); natural resources/environmental science 13 (B), 7 (M); parks and recreation 36 (B), 4 (M); philosophy/religion/theology 3 (B); physical sciences 22 (B); protective services/public administration 36 (B); psychology 64 (B), 3 (M); social sciences and history 118 (B); visual and performing arts 74 (B).

Fees and Other Expenses: *Full-time tuition per academic year 2004–05:* $5,000 undergraduate resident, out-of-state student $13,250; graduate resident $5,040, out-of-state $5,778. *Required fees:* $1,230. *Other fees:* $59 per credit hour. *Room and board per academic year:* $6,148.

Financial Aid: Aid from institutionally generated funds is provided on the basis of academic merit, financial need. Institution has a Program Participation Agreement with the U.S. Department of Education for eligible students to receive Pell Grants and other federal aid.

Financial aid to full-time, first-time undergraduate students: need-based scholarships/grants totaling $6,978,284, self-help $6,002,342; non-need-based scholarships/grants totaling $6,524,644, self-help $6,524,644, parent loans $4,104,852, tuition waivers $734,752.

Departments and Teaching Staff: *Professors* 85, *associate professors* 59, *assistant professors* , *part-time faculty* 118.

Total instructional faculty: 346 (full-time 228, part-time 118; women 147, men 199; members of minority groups 27). Total faculty with doctorate, first-professional, or other terminal degree: 226. Student-to-faculty ratio: 18:1.

Enrollment: Total enrollment 5,357. Undergraduate full-time 2,164 men / 2,063 women, 136m / 159w; graduate full-time 96m / 146w, part-time 211m / 362w. *Transfer students:* in-state 284; from out-of-state 65.

Characteristics of Student Body: *Ethnic/racial makeup:* number of Black non-Hispanic: 572; American Indian or Alaska Native: 22; Asian or Pacific Islander: 69; Hispanic: 86; White non-Hispanic: 3,634; unknown: 105.*Age distribution:* number under 18: 219; 18–19: 1,714; 20–21: 1,525; 22–24: 745; 25–29: 141; 30–34: 71; 35–39: 37; 40–49: 22; 50–64: 18.

International Students: 52 nonresident aliens enrolled fall 2004. 14 students from Europe, 14 Asia, 4 Central and South America 4, 18 Africa, 3 Canada. No programs available to aid students whose native language is not English. No financial aid specifically designated for international students.

Student Life: On-campus residence halls house. Private residence facilities also offer residence space. *Intercollegiate athletics:* men only: baseball, basketball, football, soccer, swimming, tennis, track; women only: basketball, field hockey, lacrosse, swimming, tennis, track; co-ed golf. *Special regulations:* Registered cars permitted for all students. *Special services:* Learning Resources Center, medical services, programs of academic support services; student special services, counseling services. *Student publications, radio: Arts and Letters,* an annual literary magazine; *Bittersweet,* an annual literary magazine; *Nemacolin,* a yearbook; *Bottom Line,* a weekly newspaper. Radio station WFWM broadcasts 98 hours per week. *Surrounding community:* Frostburg has a population of 8,000. Pittsburgh (PA), 120 miles from campus, is nearest metropolitan area. Served by mass transit bus system, airport 15 miles from campus, passenger rail service 15 miles from campus.

Publications: Sources of information about Frostburg State include *Academic Programs in Maryland's Colleges and Universities,* published by Maryland Higher Education Commission.

Library Collections: 260,000 volumes. 158,000 microforms; 7,100 audiovisual items; 182,000 government documents; 1,965 periodical subscriptions. Online catalog. Students have access to online information retrieval services and the Internet.

Most important special holdings include U.S. Senator J. Glenn Beall's papers (60 drawers); U.S.G.S. and Defense Mapping Agency (35,000); Davis Collection (WWII, 4,000 items); Meyer's Collection on Communist Party U.S.A. (3,000 items).

Buildings and Grounds: Campus area 243 acres.

Chief Executive Officer: Dr. Catherine Gira, President.

Address admission inquiries to Patricia Gregory, Director of Admissions; graduate inquires to Patricia Spiker, Director of Graduate Services.

Goucher College

1021 Dulaney Valley Road
Baltimore, Maryland 21204-2794

Tel: (410) 337-6000   **E-mail:** admissions@goucher.edu
Fax: (410) 337-6354   **Internet:** www.goucher.edu

Institution Description: Goucher College is a private, independent, nonprofit college. *Enrollment:* 2,349. *Degrees awarded:* Baccalaureate, master's.

Accreditation: *Regional:* MSA.

History: Established as Woman's College of Baltimore City 1885; offered first instruction at postsecondary level 1888; changed name to Woman's College of Baltimore 1890; awarded first degree (baccalaureate) 1892; adopted present name 1910; became coeducational 1986. *See* Anna H. Knipp and Thaddeus P. Thomas, *The History of Goucher* (Baltimore: Goucher College, 1938) and Frederic O. Musser, *The History of Goucher College, 1930–1985* (Baltimore: The Johns Hopkins University Press, 1990) for further information.

Institutional Structure: *Governing board:* Board of Trustees. Extrainstitutional representation: 41 trustees (including 25 alumni); 15 trustees emeriti; institutional representation: president of the college. 2 ex officio. 44 voting. *Composition of institution:* Administrators 34 women / 21 men. Academic affairs headed by dean/vice president. Management/business/finances directed by vice president for finance. Full-time instructional faculty 38 men / 66 women.

Calendar: Semesters. Academic year Aug to May. Freshmen admitted Sept., Jan. Degrees conferred and formal commencement May. No summer session.

Characteristics of Freshmen: 68% of applicants admitted. 21% of applicants admitted and enrolled.

97% (385 students) submitted SAT scores; 21% (87 students) submitted ACT scores. *25th percentile:* SAT Verbal 560, SAT Math 530; ACT Composite 23, ACT 22, English ACT Math 21. *75th percentile*: SAT Verbal 660, SAT Math 630; ACT Composite 27, ACT English 29, ACT Math 26.

68% of entering freshmen expected to graduate within 5 years. 33% of freshmen from Maryland. Freshmen from 47 states.

Admission: Deadlines: early action Dec. 15 (notification Feb. 1); transfer May 1. *Requirements:* Either graduation from accredited secondary school with 16 units that must include 4 English, 3 or 4 in a foreign language, 3 mathematics, 2 or 3 social studies, 1 or 2 laboratory sciences; or GED. *Entrance tests:* College Board SAT-I or ACT, both with writing. For foreign students TOEFL. *For transfer students:* 2.8 minimum GPA; 60 hours maximum transfer credit.

Degree Requirements: 120 credit hours; 2.0 GPA; last 2 years in residence; 3 semesters physical education; distribution requirements. Fulfillment of some degree requirements and exemption from some beginning courses possible by passing departmental examinations, College Board CLEP, APP. *Grading system:* A–F; pass-fail; withdraw (carries time limit); incomplete.

Distinctive Educational Programs: Internships and other off-campus study. Study abroad programs with institutions in England, France, Germany, Spain, Israel, Mexico. Majors in 18 departments and five interdisciplinary areas. Option for individualized majors. Cooperative academic programs with Baltimore Hebrew University, Johns Hopkins University, Loyola College, Morgan State University, College of Notre Dame, Towson State, Essex Community College, Maryland Institute, College of Art. *Other distinctive programs:* Dance, international studies, equestrian, M.Ed., M.A. Historic Preservation, M.A. Creative Nonfiction, Post-baccalaureate program, Goucher II program for returning adult students.

ROTC: Army in cooperation with Loyola College of Maryland.

Degrees Conferred: 272 *baccalaureate* (B); 148 *master's* (M): area and ethnic studies 1 (B); biological/life sciences 14 (B); business/marketing 17 (B);communications/communication technologies 22 (B); computer and information sciences 4 (B); education 14 (B), 103 (M); English 25 (B), 18 (M); foreign languages and literature 6 (B); interdisciplinary studies 2 (B), 14 (M); mathematics 3 (B); philosophy/religion/theology 60 (B); physical sciences 9 (B); social sciences and history 53 (B); visual and performing arts 13 (B).

Fees and Other Expenses: *Full-time tuition per academic year 2004–05:* $27,100. *Other fees:* $425. *Room and beard per academic year:* $8,875.

Financial Aid: Aid from institutionally generated funds is provided on the basis of financial need. Institution has a Program Participation Agreement with the U.S. Department of Education for eligible students to receive Pell Grants and other federal aid.

Financial aid to full-time, first-time undergraduate students: need-based scholarships/grants totaling $12,721,644, self-help $3,311,416, parent loans $1,833,724, tuition waivers $630,199; non-need-based scholarships/grants totaling $1,747,602, self-help $947,841, parent loans $1,714,702, tuition waivers $60,641.

Departments and Teaching Staff: *Total instructional faculty:* 182 (full-time 104, part-time 78; women 118, men 63). Total faculty with doctorate, first-professional, or other terminal degree: 95. Student-to-faculty ratio: 10:1.

Enrollment: Total enrollment 2,349. Undergraduate full-time 431 men / 891 women, part-time 11m / 33w; graduate full-time 37m / 101w, part-time 185m / 660w.

Characteristics of Student Body: *Ethnic/racial makeup:* number of Black non-Hispanic: 64; American Indian or Alaska Native: 4; Asian or Pacific Islander: 46; Hispanic: 42; White non-Hispanic: 881; unknown: 321.

International Students: 10 nonresident aliens enrolled fall 2004. No programs available to aid students whose native language is not English. No financial aid specifically designated for international students.

Student Life: On-campus residence halls house 75% of student body. *Intercollegiate athletics:* men only: cross-country, soccer, swimming, basketball, lacrosse, tennis; women only: cross-country, tennis, field hockey, volleyball, basketball, swimming, lacrosse, soccer; men and women: equestrian sports. Sixty student clubs and organizations on campus. *Special regulations:* Cars permitted without restrictions. All residence halls have public areas and residence wings. Access to residence wings limited to only students and authorized employees. Public areas of the residence halls open 7am to 6:30pm. *Special services:* Medical services. *Student publications, radio: Donnybrook Fair,* a yearbook; *The Goucher Quindecim,* a newspaper; *Preface,* an annual arts magazine. *Surrounding community:* Baltimore metropolitan area population 2,300,000. Served by airport 30 miles from campus, passenger rail service 8 miles from campus.

Library Collections: 309,792 volumes including bound books, serial backfiles, electronic documents, and government documents not in separate collections. Online catalog. Current serial subscriptions: 1,615 paper, 1 microform, 985 via electronic access. 8,572 audiovisual materials. 24 computer work stations. Students have access to the Internet at no charge. Total budget for books, periodicals, audiovisual materials, microforms 2004–05: $426,920.

Most important special holdings include Jane Austen Collection (first editions, memorabilia, and collateral material); Mark Twain Collection (American and English first editions, biographies); H.L. Mencken Collection (books, pamphlets, periodicals, manuscripts, photographs).

Buildings and Grounds: Campus area 287 acres.

Chief Executive Officer: Dr. Sanford J. Ungar, President.

Undergraduates address admission inquiries to Carlton Surbeck, III, Director of Admissions; graduate inquires to Frederick Mauk, Dean for Graduate and Professional Studies.

Hood College

401 Rosemont Avenue
Frederick, Maryland 21701
Tel: (301) 663-3131 **E-mail:** admissions@hood.edu
Fax: (301) 694-7653 **Internet:** www.hood.edu

Institution Description: Hood College is a private, independent, nonprofit college, primarily for women, historically affiliated with the United Church of Christ. *Enrollment:* 1,948. Men accepted as commuter students. *Degrees awarded:* Baccalaureate, master's.

Accreditation: Regional: MSA. *Professional:* social work, teacher education

History: Established as Women's College of Frederick, Maryland and offered first instruction at postsecondary level 1893; awarded first degree (baccalaureate) 1895; incorporated 1897; adopted present name 1913.

Institutional Structure: *Governing board:* Board of Trustees. Extrainstitutional representation: 43 trustees including 19 alumnae; institutional representation: president of the college. 29 voting. *Composition of institution:* Administrators 13 men / 40 women. Academic affairs headed by provost and dean of academic affairs. Management/business/finances directed by vice president for administration. Full-time instructional faculty 30 men / 43 women.

Calendar: Semesters. Academic year Aug. to May. Freshmen admitted Aug., Jan., June. Degrees conferred May, Sept., Jan. Formal commencement May. Summer session of 2 six-week terms from June to Aug.

Characteristics of Freshmen: 1,426 applicants (550 men, 1,076 women). 57.% of applicants admitted. 29.7% of admitted students enrolled full-time. 98% (239 students) submitted SAT scores; 18% (43 students) submitted ACT scores. *25th percentile:* SAT Verbal 490, SAT I Math 490; ACT Composite 20. *75th percentile:* SAT I Verbal 620, SAT I Math 600; ACT Composite 25.

65% of entering freshmen expected to graduate within 5 years. 57% of freshmen from Maryland. Freshmen from 18 states and 15 foreign countries.

Admission: Rolling admissions plan. Early action plan deadline Nov. 15, regular admission plan priority deadline Mar.1 (notification Mar. 31); admission seminar option; early admissions for qualified applicants who have completed high school. *Requirements:* 16 accredited secondary school units or GED. English, foreign language, mathematics, natural science, social studies. Open Campus Day (prospective students have interviews with admissions and financial aid staffs; attend presentations by faculty and students; tour campus). "Hood Start" program allows qualified secondary school students to take Hood course. *Entrance tests:* College Board SAT or ACT composite. For foreign students TOEFL. *For transfer students:* 2.0 minimum GPA; from 2-year accredited institution 70 hours maximum transfer credit.

Tutoring available. Developmental courses offered during regular academic year. Blazer Days (prospective students meet with faculty and students, tour campus, learn about scholarships and financial aid, and meet with admissions staff; some students stay overnight and attend class the next day).

Degree Requirements: 124 credit hours; completion of major core curriculum and senior year requirements; cumulative 2.0 GPA; final 30 hours in residence; 1 year physical education (none required for students 25 or older). Fulfillment of some degree requirements and exemption from some beginning courses possible by passing departmental examinations, College Board CLEP, Achievement Tests, or APP. *Grading system:* A–F; withdraw (carries time limit); limited S/U; incomplete.

Distinctive Educational Programs: *For undergraduates:* Dual-degree program in engineering with George Washington University (DC). Interdisciplinary majors in biochemistry, communication arts, environmental studies, Latin American studies, law and society, psychobiology, religion and philosophy. Double majors. Honors programs. Study abroad through institutionally sponsored program in France (University of Strasbourg); through Council on International Education Exchange programs in Spain (University of Seville); and by individual arrangement in Germany. French, German, and Spanish language residence halls. Off-campus study through Washington (DC) semester in cooperation with American University. *Available to all students:* Internships. Evening classes. Facilities and programs for independent research including individual majors, tutorials. Cross-registration with Frederick Community College, Hagerstown Junior College.

ROTC: Army in cooperation with Western Maryland College and Mount St. Mary's College.

Degrees Conferred: 177 *baccalaureate;* 162 *master's.* Bachelor's degrees awarded in top five disciplines: biological and biomedical sciences 25; psychology 24; education 23; business, management, marketing, and related support services 20; social sciences 14.

Fees and Other Expenses: *Full-time tuition per academic year 2004–05:* $21,275 undergraduate; graduate study charged per credit hour. *Books and supplies:* $800. *Room and board per academic year:* $7,200.

Financial Aid: Aid from institutionally generated funds is provided on the basis of academic merit, financial need, other considerations. Institution has a Program Participation Agreement with the U.S. Department of Education for eligible students to receive Pell Grants and other federal aid.

Financial aid to full-time, first-time undergraduate students: 29% received federal grants averaging $4,083; 43% state/local grants averaging $4,409; 99% institutional grants averaging $10,566; 67% received loans averaging $5,287.

Departments and Teaching Staff: Art *professors* 1, *associate professors* 1, *assistant professors* 1, *instructors* 0, *part-time teachers* 4; biology 2, 5, 4, 0, 4; chemistry/physics 2, 1, 1, 0, 0; communications 0, 2, 0, 0, 1; economics 1, 1, 2, 0, 0; education 2, 5, 1, 0, 5; English 3, 1, 1, 0, 0; foreign languages 1, 0, 4, 0, 1; history 3, 0, 0, 0, 0; management 0, 1, 2, 1, 0; mathematics/computer science 2, 3, 3, 0, 3; music 1, 0, 0, 0, 0; philosophy/religion 1, 0, 0, 0, 1; political science 0, 1, 2, 0, 1; psychology 2, 1, 2, 0, 1; social work 0, 0, 2, 0, 1; sociology 1, 2, 0, 0, 1; physical education 1, 0, 0, 0, 0.

Total instructional faculty: 91. *Total tenured faculty:* 46. Student-to-faculty ratio: 10:1. Degrees held by full-time faculty: 96% hold terminal degrees.

Enrollment: Total enrollment 1,948. Undergraduate 1,027 (19% men, 81% women).

Characteristics of Student Body: *Ethnic/racial makeup:* Black non-Hispanic: 11%; American Indian or Alaska Native: 3%; Asian or Pacific Islander: 2%; Hispanic: 2.3%; White non-Hispanic: 69.2%; unknown: 10.3%.

International Students: 49 undergraduate nonresident aliens enrolled fall 2004. Students from Europe, Asia, Central and South America, Africa, Canada. Programs available to aid students whose native language is not English: social and cultural. Financial aid specifically designated for international students: 15 scholarships available annually for undergraduates.

Student Life: On-campus residence halls house 51% of student body. Residence halls for women only constitute 100% of such space. *Intercollegiate athletics:* women only: basketball, field hockey, lacrosse, soccer, swimming, tennis, volleyball. *Special regulations:* Cars permitted without restrictions. Quiet hours determined by dormitory residents. Academic and social honor codes. *Special services:* Learning Resources Center, medical services, weekend bus to Washington, D.C. Leadership and wellness programs. *Student publications: Blue and Grey,* a weekly newspaper; *The Herald,* a biannual literary magazine; *Touch-*

stone, a yearbook. *Surrounding community:* Frederick population 49,000. Washington (DC), 42 miles from campus, is nearest metropolitan area.

Publications: *Hood Today,* bimonthly newspaper.

Library Collections: 207,000 volumes including bound books, serial backfiles, electronic documents, and government documents not in separate collections. Online catalog. Current serial subscriptions: 910 paper, 2,502 via electronic access. 566,000 microform units. 2,550 recordings; 1,000 compact discs; 200 CD-ROMs. Computer work stations available. Students have access to the Internet and other online information retrieval services.

Most important special holdings include Irving M. Landauer Civil War Collection; Samuel Cole Hogarth Print Collection of Engravings; Sylvia Meagher Archive (Kennedy assassination); Harold Weisberg Collection (relating to Kennedy and King assassinations).

Buildings and Grounds: Campus area 50 acres.

Chief Executive Officer: Dr. Ronald J. Volpe, President.

Address admission inquiries to Susan Hallenbeck, Director of Admissions; graduate inquiries Graduate Enrollment Manager.

Johns Hopkins University

3400 North Charles Street
Baltimore, Maryland 21218-2688

Tel: (410) 516-8000   **E-mail:** gotojhu@jhu.edu
Fax: (410) 516-6025   **Internet:** www.jhu.edu

Institution Description: Johns Hopkins University is a private, independent, nonprofit institution. *Enrollment:* 18,626. *Degrees awarded:* Baccalaureate, first-professional (medicine), master's, doctorate. Associate offered through School of Continuing Studies.

Accreditation: *Regional:* MSA. *Professional:* blood bank technology, clinical pastoral education, cytotechnology, diagnostic medical sonography, engineering, health services administration, medical illustration, medicine, nuclear medicine technology, nursing, nursing education, perfusion, public health

History: Incorporated 1867; offered first instruction at postsecondary level 1876; awarded first degree (doctorate) 1876. *See* John C. French, *A History of the University Founded by Johns Hopkins* (Baltimore: Johns Hopkins University Press, 1946) for further information.

Institutional Structure: *Governing board:* The Johns Hopkins University Board of Trustees. Representation: 58 trustees, including president of the university, 35 alumni, 20 trustees emeriti, 1 ex officio. 58 voting. *Composition of institution:* Administrators 264 men / 237 women. Academic affairs headed by provost. Management/business/finances directed by vice president for finance and treasurer. Full-time instructional faculty 2,423. Academic governance body, Academic Council, meets an average of 20 times per year.

Calendar: Semesters. Academic year early Sept. to early May. Intersession month of Jan. Freshmen admitted Sept., June. Degrees conferred May, Nov., Mar. Formal commencement May. Summer session of 2 terms from mid-June to late Aug.

Characteristics of Freshmen: 11,763 applicants (6,256 men, 5,507 women). 30.7% of applicants admitted. 31.2% of admitted students enrolled full-time.

96% (1,082 students) submitted SAT scores; 17% (190 students) submitted ACT scores. *25th percentile:* SAT I Verbal 630, SAT I Math 660; ACT Composite 27, ACT English 27, ACT Math 26. *75th percentile:* SAT I Verbal 730, SAT I Math 780; ACT Composite 32, ACT English 32, ACT Math 33.

88% of entering freshmen expected to graduate within 5 years. 13% of from Maryland. Freshmen from 46 states and 38 foreign countries.

Admission: For fall acceptance, apply as early as Sept. of previous year, but not later than Jan. 1 of year of enrollment. Students are notified of acceptance Apr. 15. Apply by Nov. 15 for early decision; must commit to acceptance to Johns Hopkins. *Requirements:* Either graduation from accredited secondary school or GED. Recommend 4 units English, 3–4 foreign language, 4 mathematics, 2–3 laboratory science, 2–3 social studies. *Entrance tests:* SAT I and 3 SAT II tests including writing or ACT. For foreign students TOEFL. *For transfer students:* 3.0 minimum GPA; 60 hours maximum transfer credit.

Tutoring available. Developmental courses offered in summer session and regular academic year; credit given.

Degree Requirements: 120–130 credit hours; 2.0 GPA in major field; 4 semesters in residence; distribution requirements; additional requirements for some programs; writing requirement: must take four 'writing emphasis' courses to fulfill degree requirements; for students matriculating from high school, maximum of 12 transfer credits allowed toward degree.

Fulfillment of some degree requirements and exemption from some beginning courses possible by passing College Board AP. *Grading system:* A–F; pass-fail; withdraw (carries time limit).

Distinctive Educational Programs: Facilities and programs for independent research, including individual majors, tutorials, independent study. Five-year BA/BM program with Peabody Institute; BA/MA with School of Advanced International Studies; BS/MS in Engineering; BA/MAT with School of Continuing Studies. Study abroad: Bologna Center in Bologna, Italy; the Hopkins-Nanjing Center for Chinese and American Studies in Nanjing, China. Exchange programs also exist with universities in Kenya, Jordan, Argentina, Japan, Brazil, Mexico, and France. Exchange programs in Berlin and Slovenia. Study abroad opportunities through Center of International Education Exchange. Affiliated research centers and institutes include Space Telescope Science Institute, Applied Physics Laboratory, Carnegie Institute of Washington, Center for Metropolitan Planning and Research, Institute for the Academic Advancement of Youth.

ROTC: Army.

Degrees Conferred: 1,288 *baccalaureate*; 3,565 *master's*; 382 *doctorate*; 115 *first-professional*. Bachelor;'s degrees offered in top five disciplines: health professions and related clinical sciences 241; social sciences 230; engineering computer and information sciences and support services 84; biological and biomedical sciences 83.

Fees and Other Expenses: *Full-time tuition per academic year 2004–05:* $30,140. undergraduate; contact the university for current information regarding tuition and fees for graduate and first-professional study. *Room and board per academic year:* $9,516. 7,870. *Books and supplies:* $850.

Financial Aid: Aid from institutionally generated funds is provided on the basis of academic merit, financial need. Institution has a Program Participation Agreement with the U.S. Department of Education for eligible students to receive Pell Grants and other federal aid.

Financial aid to full-time, first-time undergraduate students: 15% received federal grants averaging $5,213; 7% state/local grants averaging $2,661; 44% institutional grants averaging $16,996; 35% received loans averaging $5,782.

Departments and Teaching Staff: Arts and sciences *professors* 199, *associate professors* 20, *assistant professors* 37, *instructors* 45, *part-time faculty* 172; engineering 52, 19, 27, 8, 338; Peabody (music) 111, 0, 0, 52, 0; medicine 225, 325, 409, 354, 100; public health 86, 57, 57, 158, 65; nursing 4, 6, 13, 28, 45; international studies 18, 7, 3, 20, 146; continuing studies 3, 1, 24, 9, 1,481.

Total instructional faculty: 3,160 FTE. Student-to-faculty ratio: 10:1 (undergraduate). Degrees held by full-time faculty: doctorate 98%. 99% hold terminal degrees.

Enrollment: Total enrollment 18,626. Undergraduate 5,710 (2,878 men, 2,832 women).

Characteristics of Student Body: *Ethnic/racial makeup:* Black non-Hispanic: 8.3%; American Indian or Alaska Native: .4%; Asian or Pacific Islander: 17.8%; Hispanic: 4.6%; White non-Hispanic: 63.9%.

International Students: 286 undergraduate nonresident aliens enrolled fall 2004. No programs available to aid students whose native language is not English. No financial aid specifically designated for foreign students.

Student Life: Residence halls for men and women constitute 100% of on-campus residence hall space. Fraternities and sororities available. University-owned apartments also offer residence space. Housing available for married students. *Intercollegiate athletics:* men only: lacrosse, football, soccer, cross-country, basketball, wrestling, swimming, fencing, baseball, track, water polo, tennis; women only: tennis, fencing, soccer, swimming, basketball, field hockey, squash, cross-country, track, lacrosse. *Special regulations:* Cars permitted for students who live more than 1 mile from campus. *Special services:* Learning Resources Center, medical services, shuttle bus to and from School of Medicine and Peabody Institute. *Student publications: The Newsletter,* a weekly newspaper; *Hullabaloo,* class annual, *Zeniada,* a literary magazine *Surrounding community:* Baltimore. Served by mass transit bus system; airport 14 miles from campus; passenger rail service 2 miles from campus.

Publications: The Johns Hopkins University Press, founded in 1878, is the oldest university press in continuous operation.

Library Collections: 6.8 million titles. 1,600,000 microforms; 56,950 audiovisual materials; 23,050 periodical subscriptions. Online catalog. Students have access to online information retrieval services and the Internet.

Most important special holdings include the Abram G. Hutzler Collection of Economic Classics; Fowler Collection of Early Architectural History; Tudor and Stuart Club Collection of English Literature.

Buildings and Grounds: Campus area 140 acres.

Chief Executive Officer: Dr. William R. Brody, President.

Address admission inquiries to John Letting, Director of Admissions.

School of Arts and Sciences

Degree Programs Offered: *Baccalaureate, masters, doctorate* in chemistry, classics, cognitive science, earth and planetary sciences, environmental studies, English, German, history, history of art, history of science, humanities, Latin American studies, mathematics, music, Near Eastern studies, political economics, psychology, sociology; *baccalaureate, master's* in writing; *baccalaureate, doctorate* in anthropology, biology, biophysics, cognitive science, philosophy, French, Hispanic and Italian studies, physics and astronomy, political science.

Distinctive Educational Programs: Internships. Independent Study and Independent Research. Accelerated degree programs leading to baccalaureate and master's in German, history, humanities, mathematics, political economy, psychology, writing, in international studies in cooperation with School of Advanced International Studies; in music in cooperation with Peabody Conservatory; Flex-Med Program; interdisciplinary programs in Atlantic history, culture and society; behavioral biology; humanistic studies; natural sciences; public health; social and behavioral sciences. Honors programs. Double degree (BA/BM) with Peabody; minor in women's studies. Undergraduate study abroad program at Bologna Center in Italy as well as opportunities to study abroad in other parts of the world; graduate study programs in France, Germany, Italy, Spain.

G.W.C. Whiting School of Engineering

Degree Programs Offered: *Baccalaureate, master's, doctorate* in biomedical engineering, chemical engineering, civil engineering, computer science, electrical and computer engineering, geography and environmental engineering, materials science and engineering, mathematical sciences, mechanical engineering. Part-Time Programs offer separate degree programs under the Whiting School of Engineering (separate from the School of Continuing Studies).

Peabody Institute of Johns Hopkins University, Conservatory of Music

Degree Programs Offered: *Baccalaureate, master's, doctorate, graduate performance diploma, artist diploma, performer's certificate,* in conducting, composition, fretted instruments, keyboard instruments, orchestral instruments, voice, recording arts and sciences, music history and music criticism.

Distinctive Educational Programs: Internships. Interdisciplinary baccalaureate program in music performance and recording arts and sciences in cooperation with the G.W.C. Whiting School of Engineering. Master of Music program in Music Criticism in cooperation with the School of Arts and Sciences.

Paul H. Nitze School of Advanced International Studies

Degree Programs Offered: *Master's, doctorate.*

Admission: Language and economics requirement for applicants. GRE required. TOEFL required of non-native English speakers. Deadline February 1st.

Degree Requirements: 2 out of 3 core examinations required for M.A. Language proficiency required. Oral examination for M.A. in area of specialization and international economics. 16 one-semester non-language courses.

Distinctive Educational Programs: *Other distinctive programs:* One-year master's program in international public policy for U.S. and foreign government officers and international business executives. Annual Christian A. Herter Lecture Series on international topics.

School of Continuing Studies (formerly Evening College)

Degree Programs Offered: Credit programs are centered in three degree-granting divisions: Business and Management, Liberal Arts, and Education and Human Services. *Undergraduate:* Associate of Science, Bachelor of Science, Bachelor of Liberal Arts; *Graduate:* Master of Science in Business, Master of Science in Real Estate, Master of Science in Behavioral Science, Master of Science in Special Education, Master of Arts in Teaching, Master of Liberal Arts, Master of Drama Studies. *Certificate programs:* Economic Education Leadership, Leadership Development, Hopkins Fellows in Change Management, Advanced Study in Liberal Arts, Advanced Study in Education with concentrations in Special Education and Counseling.

Admission: For information on admission and degree requirements, contact School of Continuing studies, Office of Admissions and Advising, 204 Shaffer Hall, 3400 North Charles Street, Baltimore, MD 21218.

Distinctive Educational Programs: Flexible formats, six locations, and convenient meeting times for adult, working professionals. Leadership Development Program for Minority Managers. Master of Drama Studies. Large noncredit program in a wide variety of disciplines, including liberal arts, computer technology, business and management available at most campuses.

School of Hygiene and Public Health

Degree Programs Offered: *Master of Health Science, Master of Public Health, Master of Science, Doctor of Public Health, Doctor of Science, Doctor of Philosophy.*

School of Medicine

Degree Programs Offered: *First-professional* in medicine; *master's* in medical and biological illustration; *doctorate* in cell biology and anatomy, biophysics, history of medicine, immunology, molecular genetics, pharmacology and molecular science, neuroscience, physiology, biochemistry, cellular and molecular biology, biomedical engineering, human genetics.

Admission: ACT, SAT, GRE, or MCAT required.

Degree Requirements: Completion of prescribed curriculum.

Distinctive Educational Programs: Joint M.D.-Ph.D. programs in any of the degree programs offered. For graduate and first-professional students, interdepartmental programs in biochemistry, cellular and molecular biology.

School of Nursing

Degree Programs Offered: *Bachelor of science* degree with a major in nursing; *master of science* in nursing with a double major in clinical nursing science and management; *master of science* with majors in acute care nursing, chronic care nursing, or nursing care delivery and management.

Admission: For information on admission and degree requirements, contact the School of Nursing Office of Admissions at the above address.

Loyola College in Maryland

4501 North Charles Street
Baltimore, Maryland 21210-2699
Tel: (410) 617-2000   **E-mail:** admissions@loyola.edu
Fax: (410) 617-2176   **Internet:** www.loyola.edu

Institution Description: Loyola College in Maryland is a private, nonprofit college affiliated with the Society of Jesus, Roman Catholic Church. *Enrollment:* 6,156. *Degrees awarded:* Baccalaureate, master's, doctorate.

Accreditation: *Regional:* MSA. *Professional:* accounting, business, computer science, engineering, speech-language pathology

History: Established as a men's college, offered first instruction at postsecondary level and awarded first degree (baccalaureate) 1852; incorporated 1853; merged with Mount Saint Agnes College for Women 1971; School of Business and Management established 1980. *See* Nicholas Varga, *Baltimore's Loyola, Loyola's Baltimore 1851–1986* (Maryland Historical Society, 1990).

Institutional Structure: *Governing board:* Loyola College in Maryland Board of Trustees. Extrainstitutional representation: 30 trustees; institutional representation: president of the college. All voting. *Composition of institution:* Three operating divisions: Academic, Administration and Finance, Development and College Relations. Full-time instructional faculty 149 men / 64 women.

Calendar: Semesters. Academic year Sept. to Aug. Degrees conferred May, Aug., Dec. Formal commencement May. Summer terms June to mid-July and mid-July to Aug.

Characteristics of Freshmen: 99.5% (948 students) submitted SAT scores; 10% (98 students) submitted ACT scores. *25th percentile:* SAT Verbal 560, SAT Math 570; ACT Composite 24, ACT English 22, ACT Math 24. *75th percentile:* SAT Verbal 650, SAT I Math 650; ACT Composite 29, ACT English 29, ACT Math 28.

71% of entering freshmen expected to graduate within 5 years. 23% of freshmen from Maryland. Freshmen from 29 states, Puerto Rico, and the Virgin Islands.

Admission: Admission deadline Jan. 15, but students should apply as early in the senior year of high school as possible. Some well-qualified applicants accepted early. Preparation in secondary school should normally total 16 units including classical or modern foreign language 3–4 units; 4 English, 2–3 units history, 3–4 units mathematics, and 3–4 science. *Entrance tests:* College Board SAT. International students from non-English speaking countries must achieve a minimum score of 550 on TOEFL exam.

Degree Requirements: 40 courses, 120 credits; 2.0 GPA; last 2 years in residence; core and distribution requirements. Fulfillment of some degree requirements and exemption from some beginning courses possible by passing departmental examinations, College Board CLEP, AP. *Grading system:* A–F.

Distinctive Educational Programs: Honors Program. Freshmen Year Experience (course designed to ease the transition from high school to college). Internship courses that provide practical experience in a particular discipline. Study abroad programs in Leuven, Belgium; Bangkok, Thailand; Newcastle, England. Humanities Center student research fellowships.

ROTC: Army; Air Force through cooperative arrangement with University of Maryland.

Degrees Conferred: 802 *baccalaureate*; 795 *master's*; 13 *doctorate*. Bachelor's degrees awarded in top five disciplines: business, management, marketing, and related support services 273; communication, journalism, and related programs 97; social sciences 88; psychology 58; education 47.

Fees and Other Expenses: *Full-time tuition per academic year 2004–05:* $28,470. *Books and supplies:* $780. *Room and board per academic year:* $8,100. Contact the college for current tuition/fees for graduate study.

Financial Aid: Aid from institutionally generated funds is provided on the basis of academic merit, financial need, athletic ability. Institution has a Program Participation Agreement with the U.S. Department of Education for eligible students to receive Pell Grants and other federal aid.

Financial aid to full-time, first-time undergraduate students: need-based scholarships/grants totaling $19,326,992, self-help $7,609,108, tuition waivers $590,819, athletic awards $416,491; non-need-based scholarships/grants totaling $5,551,163, self-help $4,966,200, parent loans $12,497,692, tuition waivers $1,320,974, athletic awards $3,100,875.

Departments and Teaching Staff: *Total instructional faculty:* 541 (full-time 295, part-time 246; women 244, men 297; members of minority groups 43). Student-to-faculty ratio: 13:1. Degrees held by full-time faculty: doctorate 86%, master's 11%, professional 3%. 91% hold terminal degrees.

Enrollment: Total enrollment 6,156. Undergraduate full-time 1,399 men / 1,999 women; part-time 23m / 20w; graduate full-time 248m / 439w, part-time 788m / 1,240w.

Characteristics of Student Body: *Ethnic/racial makeup (undergraduate):* number of Black non-Hispanic: 171; American Indian or Alaska Native: 1; Asian or Pacific Islander: 63; Hispanic: 71; White non-Hispanic: 2,993; unknown: 115.

International Students: 27 undergraduate nonresident aliens enrolled fall 2004. No programs available to aid students whose native language is not English. No financial aid specifically designated for international students.

Student Life: On-campus residence halls and apartments house 75% of student body. *Intercollegiate athletics:* Teams compete in Division I of the National Collegiate Athletic Association and the Metro Atlantic Athletic Conference. 14 intercollegiate sports including basketball, cross-country, golf, soccer, lacrosse, tennis, swimming/diving, volleyball. *Special services:* IBM and Apple computer labs; health and career planning and placement services. *Student publications, radio: The Greyhound,* a weekly newspaper; *The Forum* and *The Garland,* literary magazines; yearbook. Radio station WLCR. *Surrounding community:* Baltimore population 760,000, served by mass transit bus system, airport 20 miles from campus, passenger rail service 3 miles from campus.

Library Collections: 438,000 volumes. 425,000 microforms; 39,500 audiovisual materials; 14,900 periodical subscriptions. Access to online information retrieval services and the Internet.

Most important special holdings include Gerard Manley Hopkins Collection (books, articles, reviews); Henry and Marion Knott Fore-Edge Painting Collection; Henry James first editions (approximately 50).

Buildings and Grounds: Campus area 89 acres.

Chief Executive Officer: Rev. Harold E. Ridley, S.J., President.

Undergraduates address admission inquiries to William J. Brossemeyer III, Director of Undergraduate Admissions; graduate inquiries to Scott Greatorex, Director of Graduate Admissions.

McDaniel College

2 College Hill
Westminster, Maryland 21157
Tel: (410) 848-7000   **E-mail:** admissions@mcdaniel.edu
Fax: (410) 857-2729   **Internet:** www.mcdaniel.edu

Institution Description: McDaniel College, formerly Western Maryland College, is a private, four-year college of liberal arts and sciences. *Enrollment:* 3,304. *Degrees awarded:* Baccalaureate, master's.

Accreditation: *Regional:* MSA. *Professional:* social work

History: Established and offered first instruction at postsecondary level 1867; chartered 1868; named for Western Maryland Railroad; awarded first degree (baccalaureate) 1871; adopted present name 2002.

Institutional Structure: *Governing board:* Board of Trustees. Extrainstitutional representation: 36 trustees, 20 trustees emeriti, honorary trustees; institutional representation: 4 administrators, 3 faculty visitors, 3 student visitors, 6 alumni visitors. 7 ex officio. 43 voting. *Composition of institution:* President, academic affairs headed by provost; management/business/finances directed by vice president for administration and finance; student affairs directed by vice president, dean of student affairs; institutional advancement directed by vice president for institutional advancement. Full-time instructional faculty 84. Academic governance body, the faculty, meets an average of 8 times per year.

Calendar: Semesters (4-1-4 plan). Academic year Aug. to May. Freshmen matriculate Aug., Jan., Feb. Degrees conferred May, Aug., Dec. Formal commencement May. Summer session from June to Aug.

Characteristics of Freshmen: 2,041 applicants (1,037 men, 1,004 women). 76.3% of applicants admitted. 22.9% of admitted students enrolled full-time.

94% (347 students) submitted SAT scores. *25th percentile:* SAT I Verbal 510, SAT I Math 510. *75th percentile:* SAT I Verbal 610, SAT I Math 610.

62% of entering freshmen expected to graduate within 5 years. 70% of freshmen from Maryland. Freshmen from 20 states and 5 foreign countries.

Admission: For fall acceptance, apply as early as end of junior year of secondary school for the Mar. 15 application deadline. Early action applications due on or before Dec. 1. *Requirements:* Either graduation from accredited secondary school with 16 units which must include 4 English, 2 foreign language, 3 mathematics, 2 laboratory sciences, 3 social studies; or GED. 1 additional unit foreign language recommended. *Entrance tests:* College Board SAT. For foreign students TOEFL. *For transfer students:* 2.0 minimum GPA; from 4-year accredited institution 90 hours maximum transfer credit; from 2-year accredited institution 64 hours; correspondence/extension students 30 hours.

College credit and advanced placement for postsecondary-level work completed in secondary school. For extrainstitutional learning college credit on basis of ACE *2006 Guide to the Evaluation of Educational Experiences in the Armed Services,* portfolio assessment, personal interviews. Tutoring available.

Degree Requirements: 128 credit hours; 2.0 GPA; 2 terms in residence; major requirements; competence requirements in English composition and mathematics; liberal arts requirements; foreign language, heritage sequence, cross cultural distribution requirements in arts, humanities, social science, natural science, quantitative analysis; physical education.

Fulfillment of some degree requirements and exemption from some beginning courses possible by passing College Board CLEP, AP. *Grading system:* A–F; pass-fail; withdraw (carries time limit).

Distinctive Educational Programs: Internships, collaborative research, double majors. Dual degree programs in engineering with Washington University (MO), University of Maryland College park; in forestry with Duke University (NC). Cooperative baccalaureate in nursing with Emory University (GA). Study abroad through Central College (Iowa) Consortium and the University of Maryland Study in London, and Harlaxton College. Other study abroad opportunities in Europe and Asia. Washington (DC) semester at American University; United Nations semester at Drew University (NJ). Appalachian semester at Union College (KY). Branch campus in Budapest, Hungary.

ROTC: Army.

Degrees Conferred: 415 *baccalaureate*; 433 *master's.* Bachelor's degrees in top five disciplines: business, management, marketing, and related support services 67; social sciences 63; biological and biomedical sciences 37; visual and performing arts 36; communication, journalism, and related programs 36.

Fees and Other Expenses: *Full-time tuition per academic year 2004–05:* undergraduate $24,800. Contact the college for current tuition/fees for graduate programs. *Room and board per academic year:* $5,600.

Financial Aid: Aid from institutionally generated funds is provided on the basis of academic merit, financial need, other considerations. Institution has a Program Participation Agreement with the U.S.. Department of Education for eligible students to receive Pell Grants and other federal aid.

Financial aid to full-time, first-time undergraduate students: 18% received federal grants averaging $3,478; 27% state/local grants averaging $2,897; 93% institutional grants averaging $11,195; 61% received loans averaging $3,795.

Departments and Teaching Staff: *Professors* 33, *associate professors* 26, *assistant professors* 22, *instructors* 3, *part-time faculty* 65. *Total instructional faculty:* 105.67 FTE. Student-to-faculty ratio: 12.23:1. Degrees held by full-time faculty: doctorate 90%, master's 10%. 96.4% hold terminal degrees.

Enrollment: Total enrollment 3,304. Undergraduate 1,621 (41.9% men, 58.1% women).

Characteristics of Student Body: *Ethnic/racial makeup (undergraduate):* Black non-Hispanic: 8.2%; American Indian or Alaska Native: .9%; Asian or Pacific Islander: 1.5%; Hispanic: 1.4%; White non-Hispanic: 80.5%; unknown: 6.2%. *Age distribution:* 17–21: 43%; 22–24: 11%; 25–29: 19%; 30–34: 8%; 35–39: 5%; 40–49: 9%; 50–59: 3%; 60–and up: 1.5.%

International Students: 21 undergraduate nonresident aliens enrolled fall 2004. Students from Europe, Asia, Central and South America, Africa, Canada. Programs available to aid students whose native language is not English: English as a Second Language Program. Financial aid specifically designated for international students: scholarships available.

Student Life: On-campus coed residence halls, garden apartments, and college-owned houses house 90% of student body. Freshmen and sophomores are required to live on campus. Affinity housing available for students with similar interests who want to live together, i.e., Honors Housing. *Intercollegiate athletics:* men only: baseball, basketball, cross-country, football, golf, lacrosse, soccer, swimming, tennis, track, wrestling; women only: basketball, cross-country, field hockey, lacrosse, softball, swimming, tennis, track, volleyball. The golf team is coed. *Special regulations:* Registered cars with decals permitted in designated areas. No freshmen cars allowed. *Special services:* Medical services, professional counseling. *Student publications: Contrast,* an annual literary magazine; *Phoenix,* a biweekly newspaper; a yearbook. *Surrounding community:* Westminster population 10,000. Baltimore, 30 miles from campus, is nearest metropolitan area. Served by airport two miles from campus.

Library Collections: 197,500 volumes. 230,000 government documents; 1,445,000 microfiche. 162,500 audiovisual materials. 4,340 periodicals. Computer work stations available. Access to online information retrieval services and the Internet.

Most important special holdings include the Lincoln Collection; 20th-Century First Editions Collection.

Buildings and Grounds: Campus area 160 acres.

Chief Executive Officer: Dr. Joan Develin Coley, President.

Address admission inquiries to Martha O'Connell, Dean of Admissions.

Maryland Institute College of Art

1300 Mount Royal Avenue
Baltimore, Maryland 21217
Tel: (410) 669-9200   **E-mail:** admissions@mica.edu
Fax: (410) 669-9206   **Internet:** www.mica.edu

Institution Description: Maryland Institute College of Art is a private, independent, nonprofit institution. *Enrollment:* 1,608. *Degrees awarded:* Baccalaureate, master's.

Accreditation: *Regional:* MSA. *National:* NASAD. *Professional:* art

History: Chartered 1826; offered first instruction at postsecondary level 1907; awarded first degree (baccalaureate) 1935.

Institutional Structure: *Governing board:* Board of Trustees. Representation: 38 trustees. All voting. *Composition of institution:* Administrators 33 men / 48 women. Academic affairs headed by vice president for academic affairs. Management/business/finances directed by vice president for finance and chief financial officer. Full-time instructional faculty 115.

Calendar: Semesters. Academic year Aug. to May. Freshmen admitted Sept., Jan. Degrees conferred and formal commencement May.

Characteristics of Freshmen: 44% of applicants admitted. 37% of applicants admitted and enrolled. 98% (399 students) submitted SAT scores;. *25th percentile:* SAT Verbal 540, SAT I Math 510. *75th percentile:* SAT Verbal 660, SAT Math 620.

68% of freshmen expected to graduate within 5 years. 17% of freshmen from Maryland. Freshmen from 41 states and 14 foreign countries.

Admission: Fall application closing date Feb. 15. Early acceptance available. *Requirements:* Either graduation from accredited secondary school or GED; portfolio. *Entrance tests:* College Board SAT. For foreign students TOEFL.

College credit and advanced placement for postsecondary-level work completed in secondary school.

Degree Requirements: 126–132 credit hours; 2.0 GPA; general education requirements. Fulfillment of some degree requirements and exemption from some beginning courses possible by passing College Board AP. *Grading system:* A–D, F; withdraw; incomplete.

Distinctive Educational Programs: Internships. Independent study. Institutionally arranged study abroad: studio art in Ireland, Italy, France, Israel, Japan, Korea, The Netherlands, Scotland; photography in England, Scotland.

ROTC: Army offered in cooperation with Johns Hopkins University.

Degrees Conferred: 260 *baccalaureate:* visual and performing arts 260; 87 *master's:* education 35, visual and performing arts 32. *Honorary degrees awarded 2004–05:* Doctor of Humane Letters 3.

Fees and Other Expenses: *Full-time tuition per academic year 2004–05:* $24,474. *Room and board per academic year:* $7,080. *Required fees:* $730.

Financial Aid: Aid from institutionally generated funds is provided on the basis of academic merit, financial need. Institution has a Program Participation Agreement with the U.S. Department of Education for eligible students to receive Pell Grants and other federal aid.

Departments and Teaching Staff: *Total instructional faculty:* 241 (full-time 115, part-time 126; women 113, men 128). Total faculty with doctorate, first-professional, or other terminal degree: 207. Student-to-faculty ratio: 10:1. Degrees held by full-time faculty: doctorate 17%, master's 75%, baccalaureate 6%. 77% hold terminal degrees.

Enrollment: *Total enrollment* 1,608. Undergraduate full-time 520 men / 862 women, part-time 9m / 11w; graduate full-time 72m / 125w, part-time 9w. *Transfer students:* in-state 21; from out-of-state 32.

Characteristics of Student Body: *Ethnic/racial makeup:* number of Black non-Hispanic: 51; American Indian or Alaska Native: 9; Asian or Pacific Islander: 111; Hispanic: 64; White non-Hispanic: 956; unknown: 132. *Age distribution:* number under 18: 26; 18–19: 647; 20–21: 551; 22–24: 128; 25–29: 34; 30–34: 9; 35–39: 3; 40–49: 2; 50–64: 1.

International Students: 88 nonresident aliens enrolled fall 2004. 8 students from Europe, 38 Asia, 5 Central and South America, 1 Africa, 2 Canada. Programs available to aid students whose native language is not English: English as a Second Language. No financial programs specifically designated for international students.

Student Life: *Surrounding community:* Baltimore population 785,000. Served by mass transit bus system, airport, and passenger rail service.

Library Collections: 55,000 volumes. 366 periodical subscriptions. Online catalog. 4,200 recordings. 305 computer work stations campus-wide. Students have access to the Internet at no charge.

Most important special holdings: over 120,000 slides of contemporary and historical art.

Buildings and Grounds: *New buildings:* Meyerhoff House purchase and renovation 2002; Brown Center 2004; Station Building renovation 2005.

Chief Executive Officer: Fred Lazarus IV, President.

Address undergraduate admission inquiries to Theresa Lynch Bedoya, Vice President and Dean of Admissions; graduate inquiries to Scott Kelly, Director of Graduate Admissions.

Morgan State University

1700 East Cold Spring Lane
Baltimore, Maryland 21251
Tel: (443) 885-3333   **E-mail:** admissions@morgan.edu
Fax: (443) 885-3698   **Internet:** www.morgan.edu

Institution Description: Morgan State University (Morgan State College until 1975) is a state institution. *Enrollment:* 6,891. *Degrees awarded:* Baccalaureate, master's, doctorate.

Accreditation: *Regional:* MSA. *Professional:* accounting, business, clinical lab scientist, engineering, landscape architecture, music, planning, social work, teacher education

History: Chartered as Centenary Bible Institute and offered first instruction at postsecondary level 1867; changed name to Morgan College 1890; awarded first degree (baccalaureate) 1895; became state institution and changed name to Morgan State College 1939; adopted present name 1975.

Institutional Structure: *Governing board:* Board of Regents of Morgan State University. Representation: 13 regents, including 1 student. *Composition of institution:* Administrators 22. Academic affairs headed by vice president of academic affairs. Management/business/finances directed by vice president of finance and management. Full-time instructional faculty 243.

Calendar: Semesters. Academic year early Sept. to mid-May. Freshmen admitted Sept., Jan. Formal commencement May. Summer session from late June to early Aug.

Characteristics of Freshmen: 11,393 applicants (4,069 men, 7,324 women). 34.7% of applicants admitted. 30.9% of admitted students enrolled full-time.

90% (1,170 students) submitted SAT scores. *25th percentile:* SAT I Verbal 423, SAT I Math 407. *75th percentile:* SAT I Verbal 500, SAT I Math 480.

Admission: Rolling admissions plan. For fall acceptance, out-of-state students apply by Apr. 15. *Requirements:* Normally, graduation from secondary school or GED. *Entrance tests:* College Board SAT or ACT. *For transfer students:* Good standing at institution previously attended.

Degree Requirements: 120 semester hours; 2.0 GPA; last 30 hours in residence; 2 credits physical education; general education requirements; exit competency examinations in writing and speech; comprehensives in major fields of study. *Grading system:* A–F (A, B, C, U for freshmen); pass-fail; withdraw (carries time limit).

Distinctive Educational Programs: Work-experience programs. Flexible meeting places and schedules, including off-campus centers, weekend and evening classes. Dual-degree programs in engineering with University of Pennsylvania, University of Rochester (NY); in physical therapy with University of Maryland at Baltimore. Cooperative baccalaureate program in medical technology with area hospitals. Interdepartmental and interdisciplinary programs in international studies, mental health, religious studies, urban studies. Honors programs. Study abroad. Cross-registration with Bowie State College, College of Notre Dame of Maryland, Coppin State College, Frostburg State College, Goucher College, Johns Hopkins University, Salisbury State College, Towson State University, University of Baltimore, University of Maryland at Baltimore.

ROTC: Army.

Degrees Conferred: 868 *baccalaureate;* 94 *master's;* 26 *doctorate.* Bachelor's degrees awarded in top five disciplines: business, management, marketing, and related support services 197; engineering 91; communication, journalism, and related programs 84; education 79; computer and information sciences and support services 75.

Fees and Other Expenses: *Full-time tuition per academic year 2004–05:* resident $5,718, out-of-state student $12,958; graduate resident and out-of-state student charged per credit hour (contact the university for current rates). *Room and board per academic year:* $6,780. *Books and supplies:* $2,000.

Financial Aid: Aid from institutionally generated funds is provided on the basis of academic merit, financial need, athletic ability, other criteria. Institution has a Program Participation Agreement with the U.S. Department of Education for eligible students to receive Pell Grants and other federal aid.

Financial aid to full-time, first-time undergraduate students: 47% received federal grants averaging $2,817; 2% state/local grants averaging $3,086; 32% received loans averaging $2,847.

Departments and Teaching Staff: *Professors* 47, *associate professors* 65, *assistant professors* 75, *instructors* 18; *part-time faculty* 77.

Total instructional faculty: 230.67 FTE. Student-to-faculty ratio: 18:1. Degrees held by full-time faculty: doctorate 80%.

Enrollment: Total enrollment 6,891. Undergraduate 6,243 (2,697 men, 3,546 women).

Characteristics of Student Body: *Ethnic/racial makeup:* Black non-Hispanic: 92.5%; American Indian or Alaska Native: .2%; Asian or Pacific Islander: .6%; Hispanic: .5%; White non-Hispanic: 1%; unknown: 2.9%.

International Students: 137 undergraduate nonresident aliens enrolled fall 2004. No programs available to aid students whose native language is not English. No financial aid specifically designated for international students.

Student Life: On-campus housing available. *Special regulations:* Cars with decals permitted; fee charged. *Student publications: Spokesman,* a weekly newspaper. *Surrounding community:* Baltimore metropolitan population over 3 million.

Library Collections: 389,500 volumes. Online catalog. 738,000 microfilm items. 46,000 audiovisual materials. Current serial subscriptions: 3,010. Students have access to online information retrieval services and the Internet.

Most important special holdings include Beulah Davis Room which contains one of the nation's largest Afro-American collections.

Buildings and Grounds: Campus area 140 acres.

Chief Executive Officer: Dr. Earl S. Richardson, President.

Address admission inquiries to Edwin T. Johnson, Director of Admissions.

Mount Saint Mary's University

16300 Old Emmitsburg Road
Emmitsburg, Maryland 21727-7797
Tel: (301) 447-6122   **E-mail:** admissions@msmary.edu
Fax: (301) 447-5860   **Internet:** www.msmary.edu

Institution Description: Mount Saint Mary's University, formerly named Mount Saint Mary's College and Seminary is a private, independent, nonprofit institution affiliated with the Roman Catholic Church. *Enrollment:* 2,125. *Degrees awarded:* Baccalaureate, master's, first-professional.

Accreditation: *Regional:* MSA.

History: Established and offered first instruction at postsecondary level 1808; awarded first degree (baccalaureate) 1810; chartered 1830; incorporated 1831. *See* Mary M. Meline and Rev. Edward F.X. McSweeney, *The Story of the Mountain* (Emmitsburg: The Weekly Chronicle, 1911) for further information; adopted present name 2004.

Institutional Structure: *Governing board:* Board of Trustees of Mount Saint Mary's University. Representation: 32 trustees, including 19 alumni, 1 ex officio. All voting. *Composition of institution:* Administrators 50 men / 41 women. Academic affairs headed by vice president. Finances directed by vice president/treasurer. Full-time instructional faculty 68 men / 35 women. Academic governance body, Academic Affairs Committee, meets an average of 6 times per year.

Calendar: Semesters. Academic year Aug. to May. Freshmen admitted Aug., Jan. Degrees conferred and formal commencement May. Summer session of 2 terms from May to Aug.

Characteristics of Freshmen: 85% of applicants admitted. 21% of applicants admitted and enrolled.

98% (385 students) submitted SAT scores. *25th percentile:* SAT Verbal 480, SAT Math 470. *75th percentile:* SAT Verbal 590, SAT Math 580.

67% of entering freshmen expected to graduate within 5 years. 62% of freshmen from Maryland. Freshmen from 15 states and 4 foreign countries.

Admission: April 1 admissions notification plan. Admission decision notification on a rolling basis beginning De. 1. *Requirements:* Either graduation from accredited secondary school with 16 units which must include 4 English, 2 foreign language, 3 mathematics, 3 history, 3 science; or GED. Acceptable secondary school class standing depending on strength of secondary school and stu-

dent's curriculum. *Entrance tests:* College Board SAT. *For transfer students:* 2.0 minimum GPA; 60 credit hours will be accepted for transfer except from 2-year institution; 90 credits from 4-year institution.

College credit and advanced placement for postsecondary-level work completed in secondary school and for extrainstitutional learning on basis of ACE *2006 Guide to the Evaluation of Educational Experiences in the Armed Services;* advanced placement on basis of faculty assessment. Tutoring available. Developmental courses offered during regular academic year; credit given. Disabilities services available.

Degree Requirements: 120 credit hours; 2.0 GPA; 2.0 GPA in major; senior year in residence; general education requirements. Fulfillment of some degree requirements and exemption from some beginning courses possible by passing College Board CLEP, AP. *Grading system:* A–F; pass-fail; withdraw (carries time limit); FA (failure because of absence).

Distinctive Educational Programs: Work-experience programs, including internships. Evening classes. Special facilities for using multimedia in the classroom. Interdepartmental programs in American culture, classical studies, international studies, biopsychology. 3-3 and 4-2 programs with Sacred Heart; 3-2 programs in nursing with Johns Hopkins University. Student designed majors. Study abroad programs in Costa Rica, England, Ireland, Italy. Affiliation with other institutions abroad. Facilities and programs for independent research; tutorials.

ROTC: Army in cooperation with McDaniel College. 2 commissions awarded 2004.

Degrees Conferred: 357 *baccalaureate* (B); 106 *master's* (M): biological/life sciences 16 (B); business/marketing 156 (B), 75 (M); communications/communication technologies 19 (B); computer and information sciences 6 (B); education 46 (B), 23 (M); English 16 (B); foreign languages and literature 5 (B); interdisciplinary studies 2 (B); mathematics 5 (B); philosophy/religion/theology 6 (B), 8 (M); physical sciences 1 (B); protective services/public administration 1 (B); psychology 1 (B); social sciences and history 69 (B); visual and performing arts 4 (B). 21 *first-professional:* master of divinity.

Fees and Other Expenses: *Full-time tuition per academic year 2005–06:* $22,500 undergraduate; graduate tuition varies by program (contact the university for current information). *Required fees:* $400. *Room and board per academic year:* $8,030.

Financial Aid: Aid from institutionally generated funds is provided on the basis of academic merit, financial need, athletic ability. Institution has a Program Participation Agreement with the U.S. Department of Education for eligible students to receive Pell Grants and other federal aid.

Financial aid to full-time, first-time undergraduate students: need-based scholarships/grants totaling $9,483,046, self-help $3,959,229, parent loans 593,018, tuition waivers $250,000, athletic awards $521,634; non-need-based scholarships/grants totaling $4,565,635, self-help $2,492,173, parent loans $1,845,971, tuition waivers $330,000, athletic awards $1,224,816. *Graduate aid:* 104 students received federal and state-funded loans totaling $769,906 (ranging from $177 to $11,000); 162 received fellowships and grants totaling $2,519,894 (ranging from $1,000 to $17,220).

Departments and Teaching Staff: *Professors* 24, *associate professors* 26, *assistant professors* 31, *instructors* 12, *part-time faculty* 80.

Total instructional faculty: 183 (full-time 103, part-time 80; women 74, men 109; members of minority groups 7). Total faculty with doctorate, first-professional, or other terminal degree: 109. Student-to-faculty ratio: 13:1. *Faculty development:* 5 faculty members awarded sabbaticals 2004–05.

Enrollment: Total enrollment 2,125. Undergraduate full-time 608 men / 811 women, part-time 64m / 129w; graduate full-time 75m / 47w, part-time 146m / 146w; first-professional full-time 99m. *Transfer students:* in-state 264; from out-of-state 64.

Characteristics of Student Body: *Ethnic/racial makeup (undergraduate):* number of Black non-Hispanic: 91; American Indian or Alaska Native: 3; Asian or Pacific Islander: 38; Hispanic: 52; White non-Hispanic: 1,395; unknown: 18. *Age distribution:* number under 18: 3; 18–19: 655; 20–21: 592; 22–24: 122; 25–29: 38; 30–34: 41; 35–39: 46; 40–49: 86; 50–64: 26; 65 and over: 1.

International Students: 42 nonresident aliens enrolled fall 2004. 11 students from Europe, 9 Asia, 17 Central and South America, 3 Africa, 1 Canada, 1 Australia. No programs available to aid students whose native language is not English, No financial aid specifically designated for international students.

Student Life: On-campus residence halls house 80% of student body. *Intercollegiate athletics:* men only: baseball, basketball, cross-country, golf, lacrosse, soccer, tennis, track, club rugby; women only: basketball, cross country, golf, soccer, softball, swimming, tennis, track, lacrosse. *Special regulations:* Cars permitted in designated areas for all students. Quiet hours. Residence hall visitation from 8am to midnight Sun.–Thurs., from 8am to 2am. Fri. and Sat; senior apartments and annex 24-hour visitation. *Special services:* Writing Center, medical services. Learning Resources Center, disabilities services. *Student publications, radio: Mountain Echo,* a weekly newspaper; *Lighted Corners,* a biannual literary magazine. Radio station WMTB-FM broadcasts 24 hours a day. *Surrounding* *community:* Emmitsburg population 2,000. Baltimore, 50 miles from campus, is nearest metropolitan area; Washington, D.C. is 65 miles from campus.

Library Collections: 210,359 volumes including bound books, serial backfiles, electronic documents, and government documents not in separate collections. Online catalog. 926 current serial subscriptions. 18,615 microform units. Computer work stations available. Students have access to the Internet at no charge. Total budget for books, periodicals, audiovisual materials, microforms 2004–05: $295,000.

Most important special holdings include 19th-century Catholic Americana; Marylandia; theology collection.

Buildings and Grounds: Campus area 1,400 acres. *New construction:* Renovation of McGowan Campus Center and Borders Learning Center.

Chief Executive Officer: Dr. Thomas H. Powell, President.

Undergraduates address admission inquiries to Steven Neitz, Executive Director of Admissions and Financial Aid; graduate inquiries to specific programs.

St. John's College

60 College Avenue
Annapolis, Maryland 21404
Tel: (410) 626-2522   **E-mail:** admissions@sjca.edu
Fax: (410) 269-7216   **Internet:** www.sjca.edu

Institution Description: St. John's College is a nonsectarian, private, independent, nonprofit college with a summer Graduate Institute in Liberal Education and a sister campus in Santa Fe, New Mexico. *Enrollment:* 564. *Degrees awarded:* Baccalaureate, master's.

Accreditation: *Regional:* MSA.

History: Established as King William's School 1696; chartered as St. John's College 1784; offered first instruction at postsecondary level 1789; awarded first degree (baccalaureate) 1793; opened Santa Fe campus 1964.

Institutional Structure: *Governing board:* Board of Visitors and Governors. Representation: 56 trustees, including governors of Maryland and New Mexico, 27 alumni, 5 emeritus members. 7 ex officio. 49 voting. *Composition of institution:* Administrators 8 men / 10 women. Academic affairs headed by dean. Operations/business/finances directed by treasurer. Full-time instructional faculty 55 men / 18 women. Academic governance body, The Faculty of St. John's College in Annapolis, meets an average of 9 times per year.

Calendar: Semesters. Academic year Aug. to May. Freshmen admitted Aug., Jan. Undergraduate degrees conferred May; graduate degrees Aug. Formal commencements May, Sept. Graduate Institute summer session of 1 term from June to Aug.

Characteristics of Freshmen: 67% of applicants admitted. 38% of applicants admitted and enrolled.

87% (118 students) submitted SAT scores. *25th percentile*: SAT Verbal 660, SAT Math 600. *75th percentile*: SAT Verbal 760, SAT Math 690.

75% of entering freshmen expected to graduate within 5 years. 13% of Freshmen from Maryland. Freshmen from 33 foreign countries.

Admission: Rolling admissions plan. For fall acceptance, suggested Mar. 1 deadline; late applications considered. Early acceptance available. *Requirements:* Either graduation from accredited secondary school with 3 years mathematics, 2 foreign language, 2–3 natural science; or GED. Strong college preparatory background and additional units in foreign language and science recommended.

Degree Requirements: 132 credit hours; 4 years in residence; senior essay and oral examination. *Grading system:* A–F.

Distinctive Educational Programs: St. John's does not have formal departments or majors. All students follow the same curriculum, the reading and seminar discussion of books that stand among the sources of Western intellectual tradition, exercises in translation, mathematical demonstration, music analysis, and laboratory science. Intercampus transfer to Santa Fe campus available. Evening classes.

Degrees Conferred: 102 *baccalaureate:* liberal arts/general studies; 51 *master's:* liberal arts/general studies.

Fees and Other Expenses: *Full-time tuition per academic year 2005–06:* Contact the college for current information.

Financial Aid: Aid from institutionally generated funds is provided on the basis of financial need. Institution has a Program Participation Agreement with the U.S. Department of Education for eligible students to receive Pell Grants and other federal aid.

Financial aid to full-time, first-time undergraduate students: need-based scholarships/grants totaling $4,709,243, self-help $1,903,368. *Graduate aid:* 75 students received federal and state-funded fellowships and grants totaling

$299,605 (ranging from $500 to $4,700); 80 students received federal and state-funded loans totaling $834,953 (ranging from $500 to $18,500).

Departments and Teaching Staff: *Total instructional faculty:* 81 (full-time 73, part-time 8; women 20, men 61; members of minority groups 5). Total faculty with doctorate, first-professional, or other terminal degree: 57. Student-to-faculty ratio: 8:1. *Faculty development:* 7 faculty members awarded sabbaticals 2004–05.

Enrollment: Total enrollment 564. Undergraduate full-time 261 men / 210 women, part-time 1m / 1w; graduate full-time 48m / 30w, part-time 6m / 7w.

Characteristics of Student Body: *Ethnic/racial makeup:* number of Black non-Hispanic: 4; American Indian or Alaska Native: 4; Asian or Pacific Islander: 8; Hispanic: 13; White non-Hispanic: 422; unknown: 18. *Age distribution:* number under 18: 4; 18–19: 185; 20–21: 192; 22–24: 83; 25–29: 7; 30–34: 2.

International Students: 4 nonresident aliens enrolled fall 2004. 1 student from Europe, 1 Asia, 1 Africa, 1 Canada. No programs available to aid students whose native language is not English. No financial aid specifically designated for international students.

Student Life: On-campus residence halls house 75% of student body. Residence halls are co-ed with floors allocated to men or women. *Special regulations:* Cars permitted for all but freshmen (exceptions possible). *Special services:* Medical services. *Student publications: The Gadfly,* a weekly newspaper; *The Collegian,* short essays, photography, and poetry; *Energeria,* long essays and poetry. *Surrounding community:* Annapolis population 35,000. Baltimore and Washington, D.C., each 25 miles from campus, are nearest metropolitan areas. Served by airport 20 miles from campus.

Publications: *The St. John's Review* (first published as *The College,* 1969), biannually. *Publisher:* The St. John's College Press.

Library Collections: 108,000 volumes. Online catalog. 1,400 microforms; 4,000 audiovisual materials; 122 current periodical subscriptions. 17 computer work stations. Students have access to the Internet at no charge.

Most important special holdings include Henry L. Bowen Collection of Myths and Place Symbolism in Architecture; Rev. Thomas Bray Collection of 1696 (first public library in America); Zenith J. Brown (Leslie Ford/David Frome) Mystery Collection.

Buildings and Grounds: Campus area 30 acres.

Chief Executive Officer: Dr. Christopher Nelson, President.

Undergraduates address admission inquiries to John Christensen, Director of Admissions; graduate inquiries to Joan Silver, Director of Graduate Institute.

St. Mary's College of Maryland

St. Mary's City, Maryland 20686-3001
Tel: (240) 892-2000   **E-mail:** admissions@smcm.edu
Fax: (240) 895-5001   **Internet:** www.smcm.edu

Institution Description: St. Mary's College of Maryland is a state institution with the special mission of providing an undergraduate liberal arts curriculum and experience similar to a private college. *Enrollment:* 1,935. *Degrees awarded:* Baccalaureate.

Accreditation: *Regional:* MSA.

History: Established as St. Mary's Female Seminary 1840; became the first junior college in Maryland 1926; initiated baccalaureate curriculum 1967; designated a public honors college 1992.

Institutional Structure: *Governing board:* Board of Trustees. Extrainstitutional representation: 24 trustees. All voting. *Composition of institution:* Administrators 26 men / 17 women. Academic affairs headed by provost. Management/business/finances directed vice president of business and finance. Full-time instructional faculty 122. Academic governance body, Faculty Senate, meets an average of 18 times per year.

Calendar: Semesters. Academic year early Sept. to mid-May. Degrees conferred and formal commencement May. Summer session from May to July.

Characteristics of Freshmen: 57.3% of applicants admitted. 32.4% of applicants admitted and enrolled.

97% (418 students) submitted SAT scores; 3% (13 students) submitted ACT scores. *25th percentile:* SAT Verbal 580, SAT Math 570. *75th percentile:* SAT Verbal 690, SAT Math 660.

79% of entering freshmen expected to graduate within 5 years. 78% of freshmen from Maryland. Freshmen from 23 states and 10 foreign countries.

Admission: For fall acceptance, apply as early as 1 year prior to enrollment. For early decision plan, submit all materials by Dec. 15; for regular admission by Jan. 15. For spring semester apply by Oct. 15. Selection of early decision plan requires the student to withdraw applications to other colleges if accepted by St. Mary's. *Requirements:* Either graduation from accredited secondary school with 4 units English, 3 mathematics, 1 social studies, 3 science, 7 academic electives; or GED. Interview recommended. *Entrance tests:* College Board SAT. For foreign students TOEFL. *For transfer students:* 2.5 minimum GPA; from 4-year accredited institution 90 semester hours maximum transfer credit; from 2-year accredited institution 70 hours. Tutoring available.

Degree Requirements: 128 credit hours; 2.0 GPA; 30 of last 36 hours of degree course in residence; distribution requirements. Fulfillment of some degree requirements and exemption from some beginning courses possible by passing departmental examinations, College Board CLEP, AP. *Grading system:* A–F; credit-no credit; withdraw (carries time limit; deadline after which fail is appended to withdraw); incomplete (carries time limit).

Distinctive Educational Programs: *Available to all students:* Internships. Evening classes. Dual-degree program in engineering with University of Maryland College Park. Interdepartmental/interdisciplinary programs in human development, natural science, social studies. Facilities and programs for independent research, including honors program, individual majors, independent study, and study abroad. *Other distinctive programs:* St. Mary's City Field School in Archaeology; tuition waivers available for senior citizens; concurrent enrollment possible for outstanding high school seniors. Teacher Education Program offers summer credit workshops for education students and classroom teachers. Curriculum Materials Center for in-service and pre-service teachers. Study abroad in England, France, Germany, China, Costa Rica, Hong Kong, Thailand, and other countries by arrangement. . National Student Exchange Program. Cross-disciplinary studies are offered in five areas: African and African Diaspora Studies; East Asian Studies; Environmental Studies; the Neurosciences; Women, Gender, and Sexuality Studies.

Degrees Conferred: 465 *baccalaureate:* biological sciences 58; computer and information sciences 11; letters 53; natural sciences 1; mathematics 6; human studies 13; physical sciences 11; psychology 97; public policy studies 4; social sciences 165; student designed major 15; visual and performing arts 31.

Fees and Other Expenses: *Full-time tuition per academic year 2005–06:* $9,063 undergraduate, $17,940 graduate. *Required fees:* $1,833. *Room and board per academic year:* $7,980.

Financial Aid: Aid from institutionally generated funds is provided on the basis of academic merit, financial need. Institution has a Program Participation Agreement with the U.S. Department of Education for eligible students to receive Pell Grants and other federal aid.

Financial aid to full-time, first-time undergraduate students: need-based scholarships/grants totaling $3,223,766, self-help $2,164,004; non-need-based scholarships/grants totaling $3,554,152, self-help $2,367,449, parent loans $5,069,241, tuition waivers $502,299.

Departments and Teaching Staff: *Professors* 33, *associate professors* 34, *assistant professors* 47, *instructors* 8, *part-time faculty* 80.

Total instructional faculty: 202 (full-time 122, part-time 80; women 98, men 104). Total faculty with doctorate, first-professional, or other terminal degree: 149. Student-to-faculty ratio: 13.5:1. *Faculty development:* $306,722 in grants for research. 9 faculty members awarded sabbaticals 2004–05.

Enrollment: Total enrollment 1,935. Undergraduate full-time 758 men / 1,072 women, part-time 51m / 54w. *Transfer students:* in-state 67; from out-of-state 2.

Characteristics of Student Body: *Ethnic/racial makeup:* number of Black non-Hispanic: 121; American Indian or Alaska Native: 4; Asian or Pacific Islander: 70; Hispanic: 48; White non-Hispanic: 1,478; unknown: 125. *Age distribution:* number under 18: 68; 18–19: 608; 20–21: 865; 22–24: 246; 25–29: 33; 30–34: 11; 35–39: 9; 40–49: 13; 50–64: 5.

International Students: 12 nonresident aliens enrolled fall 2004. 2 students from Europe, 1 Central and South America, 5 Africa, 2 Canada, 2 Bahamas. No programs available to aid students whose native language is not English. No financial aid specifically designated for international students.

Student Life: On-campus residences house 83% of full-time student body. Residences for men constitute 11% of such space, for women 10%, both sexes 27%, apartments for single students 27%; housing for disabled students 1%, additional 24% other housing options. *Intercollegiate athletics:* men only: baseball, basketball, lacrosse, sailing, soccer, swimming, tennis; women only: basketball, lacrosse, sailing, soccer, swimming, tennis, volleyball. *Special regulations:* Cars permitted; yearly parking fee charged. *Special services:* Writing Center, Health Center, Career Services. *Student publications, radio: Avatar,* an annual literary magazine; *The Dove,* a yearbook; *The Point News,* a biweekly newspaper. WSMC, the radio station; TV6, campus cable television station. *Surrounding community:* St. Mary's County population 86,211. Washington, D.C. and Annapolis each 70 miles from campus, are nearest metropolitan areas.

Publications: Sources of information about St. Mary's College of Maryland catalogue; *Mulberry Tree Papers,* published 3 times per year.

Library Collections: 155,077 volumes. 155 microform items; 8,343 current periodical subscriptions; 6,472 recordings/tapes. Online catalog. Students have access to online information retrieval services and the Internet.

Most important special holdings include the Maryland Collection and College Archives.

Buildings and Grounds: Campus area 319 acres. *New buildings:* Campus Center completed 2000; Edward T. Lewis Quadrangle 2001; Waring Commons 2003; Somerset Athletics and Recreation Center renovation 2005.

Chief Executive Officer: Dr. Jane M. O'Brien, President.

Address admission inquiries to Director of Admissions.

St. Mary's Seminary and University

5400 Roland Avenue
Baltimore, Maryland 21210-1994

Tel: (410) 864-4000   **E-mail:** admissions@stmarys.edu
Fax: (410) 864-4278   **Internet:** www.stmarys.edu

Institution Description: Saint Mary's Seminary and University is a private institution affiliated with the Society of St. Sulpice, Roman Catholic Church. *Enrollment:* 261. *Degrees awarded:* Baccalaureate, first-professional (divinity), master's, licentiate, doctorate.

Accreditation: *Regional:* MSA. *National:* ATS. *Professional:* theology

History: Established as St. Mary's Seminary and offered first instruction at postsecondary level 1791; chartered 1805; awarded first degree (baccalaureate) 1808; consolidated undergraduate instruction on campus of St. Charles College (established 1858) and changed name to St. Mary's Seminary College 1969; adopted present name 1977.

Institutional Structure: *Governing board:* Board of Trustees. Extrainstitutional representation: 25 trustees; institutional representation: president of the college, 1 full-time instructional staff member. 3 ex officio. All voting. *Composition of institution:* Administrators 6 men / 6 women. Academic affairs headed by academic dean. Management/business/finances directed by vice president for administration and finance. Full-time instructional faculty 27. Academic governance body, Academic Senate, meets an average of 12 times per year.

Calendar: Semesters. Academic year Sept. to May. Freshmen admitted Sept. Degrees conferred and formal commencement May. Summer session of 1 term from early June to early July.

Admission: Rolling admissions plan. For fall acceptance, apply no later than 1 week after beginning of classes. *Requirements:* Baccalaureate from accredited institution with 18 semester hours in philosophy, 12 in theology or religious studies. Additional requirements for seminary candidates. *Entrance tests:* GRE. *For transfer students:* 48 hours maximum transfer credit. Seminarians contact the Director of Admissions; non-seminarians contact Dean, School of Theology.

Tutoring available. Noncredit developmental/remedial courses offered during regular academic year.

Degree Requirements: *For first-professional degree:* 103 semester hours; 2.0 GPA; 52 hours in residence; comprehensives in individual fields of study; fulfillment of prescribed curriculum. For seminarians chapel attendance. *Grading system:* A–F; pass-fail; withdraw (deadline after which pass-fail is appended to withdraw).

Distinctive Educational Programs: Externships. Evening classes. Tutorials. Specialized ministry programs offered at various locations in U.S. and abroad. *Other distinctive programs:* Continuing education.

Degrees Conferred: 2 *baccalaureate:* liberal arts/general studies; 27 *master's:* theology/ministerial studies; 10 *first-professional:* master of divinity; 1 *doctorate:* theology/ministerial studies.

Fees and Other Expenses: *Full-time tuition per academic tuition 2004–05:* Contact the institution for current tuition/fees, housing, and other costs.

Departments and Teaching Staff: Theology *professors* 15, *associate professors* 8, *assistant professors* 2, *instructors* 2, *part-time teachers* 15.

Total instructional faculty: 42. Student-to-faculty ratio: 6:1. Degrees held by full-time faculty: doctorate 67%, master's 100%, professional 16%. 83% hold terminal degrees.

Enrollment: Total enrollment 261. Undergraduate 4 men.

Characteristics of Student Body: *Ethnic/racial makeup:* White non-Hispanic: 100%.

Student Life: On-campus residence halls house 95% of student body. Residence halls for men only constitute 100% of such space. *Special regulations:* Cars permitted without restrictions. Conservative dress required. *Surrounding community:* Baltimore population 785,000. Served by mass transit bus system; airport 25 miles from campus; passenger rail service 6 miles from campus.

Chief Executive Officer: Rev. Robert F. Leavitt, S.S., President.

Address admission inquiries to Director of Admissions.

Salisbury University

1101 Camden Avenue

Salisbury, Maryland 21801-6837

Tel: (410) 543-6000   **E-mail:** admissions@salisbury.edu

Fax: (410) 546-6016   **Internet:** www.salisbury.edu

Institution Description: Salisbury University, formerly named Salisbury State University, is a member institution of the University of Maryland System. *Enrollment:* 6,942. *Degrees awarded:* Baccalaureate, master's.

Academic offerings subject to approval by statewide coordinating bodies. Budget subject to approval by state governing boards.

Accreditation: *Regional:* MSA. *Professional:* athletic training, business, clinical lab scientist, environmental health, nursing, nursing education, respiratory therapy, social work, teacher education

History: Established as Maryland State Normal School at Salisbury, a 2-year institution, 1925; became 3-year institution 1931, 4-year 1934; changed name to State Teacher's College at Salisbury 1935; awarded first degree (baccalaureate) 1936; added master's program 1962; became Salisbury State College 1963 and Salisbury State University 1988; adopted present name 1999. *See* Henrietta Spencer Purnell, *School and College Days at Salisbury, Maryland: A Chronological History in Three Parts, 1925–1967* (available at Salisbury State University library) for further information.

Institutional Structure: *Governing board:* The Board of Regents of the University of Maryland System. Representation: 16 board members, including 1 student (replaced annually to represent 6 state institutions on a rotating basis). All voting. *Composition of institution:* Administrators 27 men / 26 women. Academic affairs headed by vice president for academic affairs. Management/business/finances directed by director of business and finance. Full-time instructional faculty 178 men / 136 women. Academic governance body, SSU Forum, meets an average of 9 times per year.

Calendar: Semesters (4-1-4). Academic year early Sept. to mid-May. Freshmen admitted Sept., Feb. Degrees conferred May, Dec. Formal commencement May. Three summer sessions from early June to mid-Aug.

Characteristics of Freshmen: 61% of applicants admitted. 32% of applicants admitted and enrolled.

99% (977 students) submitted SAT scores. *25th percentile*: SAT Verbal 510, SAT Math 530. *75th percentile*: SAT Verbal 590, SAT Math 610.

65% of entering freshmen expected to graduate within 5 years. 83% of freshmen are from Maryland.

Admission: Rolling admissions plan. For fall acceptance, apply as early as Sept. 15 of previous year. Students are notified of acceptance beginning Nov. 1. Early acceptance available. *Requirements:* Either graduation from accredited secondary school or GED. *Entrance tests:* College Board SAT I or ACT. For foreign students TOEFL. *For transfer students:* 2.0 minimum GPA; from 4-year accredited institution 90 hours maximum transfer credit; from 2-year accredited institution 70 hours; correspondence/extension students maximum transfer credit determined on individual basis.

College credit and advanced placement for postsecondary-level work completed in secondary school; for departmental examinations, College Board CLEP, and APP; for extrainstitutional learning (life experience) on basis of *ACE 2006 Guide to the Evaluation of Educational Experiences in the Armed Services.* Peer tutoring available. Developmental courses offered during regular academic year; credit given for some courses.

Degree Requirements: 120 credit hours; 2.0 GPA; last 30 hours in residence (up to 6 hours waived in unusual circumstances); 3 physical education credits; general education requirements; competence in writing.

Fulfillment of some degree requirements and exemption from some beginning courses possible by passing departmental examinations, College Board CLEP, Achievement Tests, APP. *Grading system:* A–F; pass-no credit; incomplete (carries time limit); CS (satisfactory work in progress).

Distinctive Educational Programs: *For undergraduates:* Dual-degree program in engineering with University of Maryland at College Park, Old Dominion University (VA), Widener University (PA). Dual-degree programs in biology/environmental science and social work/sociology with University of Maryland Eastern Shore and University of Maryland (College Park). Master of Arts in Teaching, collaborative with University of Maryland Eastern Shore. Preprofessional programs. Honors programs. Interdisciplinary minors in American studies, anthropology, comparative literature, environmental studies, interdisciplinary science, international studies, planning, religious studies, social studies, women's studies/gender studies. Dual-minors with University of Maryland Eastern Shore available in agribusiness, animal and poultry science, clothing and tex-

tiles, construction management, fashion merchandising, food and beverage management, hotel administration, plant/soil science, technology education. Individually arranged study abroad in England, France, Spain. Teacher certification in most fields. *Available to all students:* Work-experience programs. Student clubs and organizations. Facilities and programs for independent research, including individual majors, tutorials. *Other distinctive programs:* Noncredit continuing education program. Service member's Opportunity College program.

ROTC: Army in cooperation with University of Delaware.

Degrees Conferred: 1,301 *baccalaureate* (B); 208 *master's* (M): biological/life sciences 71 (B); business/marketing 217 (B), 51 (M); communications/communication technologies 135 (B); computer and information sciences 51 (B); education 205 (B), 87 (M); English 46 (B), 22 (M); foreign languages and literature 9 (B); health professions and related sciences 8 (B), 15 (M); liberal arts/general studies 98 (B); mathematics 63 (B); natural resources/environmental science 24 (B); physical sciences 8 (B); protective services/public administration 65 (B), 29 (M); psychology 84 (B), 1 (M); social sciences and history 131 (B), 3 (M); visual and performing arts 59 (B); other 27 (B).

Fees and Other Expenses: *Full-time tuition per academic year 2004–05:* undergraduate resident $4,546, out-of-state student $12,124; graduate resident $236 per credit, out-of-state student $506 per credit. *Required fees:* $1,430. *Room and board per academic year:* $7,050.

Financial Aid: Aid from institutionally generated funds is provided on the basis of federal methodology. Institution has a Program Participation Agreement with the U.S. Department of Education for eligible students to receive Pell Grants and other federal aid.

Financial aid to full-time, first-time undergraduate students: need-based scholarships/grants totaling $5,023,288, self-help $7,298,453; non-need-based scholarships/grants totaling $4,270,436, self-help $7,391,092, parent loans $10,836,809, tuition waivers $939,361.

Departments and Teaching Staff: *Professors* 70, *associate professors* 98, *assistant professors* 87, *instructors* 19, *lecturers* 49, *part-time faculty* 180.

Total instructional faculty: 494 (full-time 314, part-time 180; women 252, men 236; members of minority groups 32). Total faculty with doctorate, first-professional, or other terminal degree: 271. Student-to-faculty ratio: 16:1. *Faculty development:* $4,730,622 in grants for research. 12 faculty members awarded sabbaticals 2004–05.

Enrollment: Total enrollment 6,942. Undergraduate full-time 2,466 men / 3,182 women, part-time 316m / 402w; graduate full-time 50m / 117w, part-time 93m / 316w. *Transfer students:* in-state 631; from out-of-state 94.

Characteristics of Student Body: *Ethnic/racial makeup (undergraduate):* number of Black non-Hispanic: 621; American Indian or Alaska Native: 20; Asian or Pacific Islander: 167; Hispanic: 146; White non-Hispanic: 5,019;

International Students: 43 nonresident aliens enrolled fall 2004. Students from Europe, Asia, Africa, Canada. Programs available to aid students whose native language is not English: social, cultural. No financial aid specifically designated for international students.

Student Life: On-campus residence halls house 50% of full-time undergraduate student body. Residence halls for men constitute 11% of such space, for women 14%, for both sexes 75%. *Intercollegiate athletics:* men: baseball, basketball, cross-country, football, lacrosse, soccer, swimming, tennis, track and field; women: basketball, cross-country, field hockey, lacrosse, soccer, softball, swimming, tennis, track and field, volleyball. *Special regulations:* Registered cars permitted for all students except for freshmen residents. *Special services:* Health center, counseling services, career services, student employment, recreation and intramurals, student clubs and organizations, honors programs. *Student publications, radio: Evergreen,* a yearbook; *The Flyer,* a newspaper published 13 times per semester; *Scarab,* an annual literary magazine. Radio station WSUR broadcasts 24 hours a day. *Surrounding community:* Salisbury population 21,000. Washington, D.C./Baltimore, 100 miles from campus, are the nearest metropolitan areas. Served by airport 5 miles from campus.

Library Collections: 254,151 volumes. Online catalog. Current serial subscriptions: paper 1,271, microform 747,871; via electronic access Ex Libris Alpha System. 54 computer work stations. Access to online information retrieval services and the Internet. Total 2004–05 budget for books and other materials: $2,105,525.

Most important special holdings include Maryland Collection; John E. Jacob Collection (maps, ephemera); LesCallette Civil War Collection; Benjamin Lankford Collection.

Buildings and Grounds: Campus area 130 acres. *New buildings:* Scarborough Leadership Center completed 2001; Henson Science Hall 2002.

Chief Executive Officer: Dr. Janet Dudley-Eschbach, President.

Address admission inquiries to Laura Thorpe, Jane Dane, Dean of Admissions.

Sojourner-Douglass College

500 North Caroline Street
Baltimore, Maryland 21205-1898
Tel: (410) 276-0306   **E-mail:** admissions@sdc.edu
Fax: (410) 575-1810   **Internet:** www.sdc.edu

Institution Description: Sojourner-Douglass College is a private, independent, nonprofit institution. *Enrollment:* 1,082. *Degrees awarded:* Baccalaureate.

Accreditation: *Regional:* MSA.

History: Established as Homestead-Montebello Center, an off-campus center of Antioch University (OH), 1972; became independent, awarded first degree (baccalaureate), and adopted present name 1980.

Institutional Structure: *Governing board:* Board of Directors. Academic affairs headed by dean. Management/business/finances directed by business manager. Full-time instructional faculty 5 men / 2 women.

Calendar: Semesters.

Admission: Rolling admissions plan. Apply no later than 6 weeks prior to beginning of term. Early acceptance available. *Requirements:* Recommend graduation from accredited secondary school or GED; institutional placement examinations.

College credit and advanced placement for postsecondary-level work completed in secondary school. College credit for extrainstitutional learning (life experience) on basis of portfolio and faculty assessments, personal interviews.

Degree Requirements: *For undergraduate degrees:* 132 credit hours; 1 year in residence; internship. *Grading system:* A–F; withdraw (carries time limit).

Distinctive Educational Programs: Flexible meeting places and schedules, including off-campus center in eastern Maryland, weekend and evening classes. Interdisciplinary programs in administration, human growth and development, human and social resources. *Other distinctive programs:* Televised courses. Nontraditional work-experience programs for adults.

Degrees Conferred: 176 *baccalaureate:* public administration and social science professions 125; psychology 51. 24 *master's:* psychology 24.

Fees and Other Expenses: *Full-time tuition per academic year 2004–05:* $6,000. The institution is a commuter school.

Departments and Teaching Staff: *Total instructional faculty:* 50 (33 full-time).

Enrollment: Total enrollment 1,082 (162 men, 840 women).

Characteristics of Student Body: *Ethnic/racial makeup:* Black non-Hispanic: 97.1%; American Indian or Alaska Native: .1%; Asian or Pacific Islander: .1%; Hispanic: .2%; White non-Hispanic: 1.4%; unknown: 1.1%.

Student Life: No on-campus housing. *Surrounding community:* Baltimore metropolitan population over 3 million.

Buildings and Grounds: Campus area 15 acres.

Chief Executive Officer: Dr. Charles W. Simmons, President.

Address admission inquiries to Diana Samuels, Coordinator of Admissions.

Towson University

8000 York Road
Towson, Maryland 21252-0001
Tel: (410) 830-2000   **E-mail:** admissions@towson.edu
Fax: (410) 830-3488   **Internet:** www.towson.edu

Institution Description: Towson University is an institutional member of the University of Maryland System. *Enrollment:* 17,667. *Degrees awarded:* Baccalaureate, master's, doctorate. Certificates also awarded.

Academic offerings subject to approval by statewide coordinating bodies. Budget subject to approval by state governing boards.

Accreditation: *Regional:* MSA. *Professional:* accounting, athletic training, audiology, business, computer science, dance, music, nursing, nursing education, occupational therapy, psychology internship, speech-language pathology, teacher education

History: Established and chartered as Maryland State Normal School and offered first instruction at postsecondary level 1866; changed name to State Teachers College at Towson 1935; awarded first degree (baccalaureate) 1938; changed name to Towson State College and became a liberal arts institution 1963; adopted present name 1976.

Institutional Structure: *Governing board:* The University of Maryland Board of Regents. *Extrainstitutional representation:* 17 board members, including 1 student. All voting. *Composition of institution:* Administrators: 38 men / 23 women. Four major administrative divisions: academic affairs, administration and finance, student life, institutional advancement; each headed by a vice pres-

ident reporting to the president. Full-time instructional faculty 311 men / 210 women. Academic governance body: The University Senate meets once a month during the academic year. *Faculty representation:* The Faculty Association, affiliated with AAUP.

Calendar: Semesters (4-1-4 plan). Academic year Sept. to May. Freshmen admitted Sept., Jan. Degrees conferred May, Aug., Jan. Formal commencements Dec. and May. Summer session of 2 day terms and 1 evening term.

Characteristics of Freshmen: 10,683 applicants (6,727 men, 3,936 women). 67.2 of applicants admitted. 29.1% of admitted students enrolled full-time.

97% (2,024 students) submitted SAT scores. *25th percentile:* SAT I Verbal 490, SAT I Math 500. *75th percentile:* SAT I Verbal 580, SAT I Math 590.

51% of entering freshmen expected to graduate within 5 years. 73% of freshmen from Maryland. Freshmen from 49 states and 37 foreign countries.

Admission: Priority admission given to freshman applicants whose secondary school records indicate B-level work (3.00 or above on a 4.00 scale) from grades 9–11. These applicants must also possess a minimum 1100 combined SAT I. Applicants with a lower profile will be considered after mid-year senior grades are available. *For transfer students:* With 56 or more credits, a 2.0 minimum cumulative GPA; 30–55 credits with a 2.25 minimum cumulative GPA; less than 30, a 2.50 minimum GPA and high school requirements.

No minimum GPA for those who have been out of school for at least 3 years as long as they attain minimum score on university administered math, reading, and writing tests. College credit and advanced placement for postsecondary-level work completed in secondary school. College credit for extrainstitutional learning (life experience) on basis of portfolio and faculty assessments.

Degree Requirements: 120 minimum credit hours; 2.0 GPA; normally last 30 hours in residence; distribution requirements including 1 credit in physical education and 2 courses in writing as well as 15 other courses from the following academic groupings: fine and performing arts, humanities, natural and mathematical sciences, social and behavioral sciences; exit competency examinations in writing, mathematics. For baccalaureate of arts, foreign language requirements. Additional requirements for some programs.

Fulfillment of some degree requirements and exemption from some beginning courses possible by passing College Board CLEP, AP. *Grading system:* A–F; pass-D-fail; withdraw (deadline after which fail is appended to withdraw).

Distinctive Educational Programs: Work-experience programs, including cooperative education. Weekend and evening classes. Accelerated degree programs. Dual-degree programs in engineering with University of Maryland at College Park; Cooperative baccalaureate in special education with Coppin State College. Special facilities for using telecommunications in the classroom. Interdisciplinary programs in African-American studies, American studies, environmental studies, ethnic studies, health services, international studies, Latin American studies, law enforcement, management, medieval and renaissance studies, natural science, sports studies, women's studies. Travel-study courses in England, France, Italy, The Netherlands, Germany, and elsewhere. Study abroad in varying locations by individual arrangement. Semester or year exchange at other U.S. colleges and universities through National Student Exchange. Cross-registration with other institutions within the University of Maryland System; College of Notre Dame of Maryland; Goucher and Loyola Colleges; Johns Hopkins University; Morgan State University. *Other distinctive programs:* Evening college; off-campus center in Columbia; College in Escrow (for high school seniors); Directed Independent Study (for those unable to attend regular classes); Second Bachelors Program; television courses; all through the College of Continuing Studies.

ROTC: Army in cooperation with Loyola College; Air Force with University of Maryland at College Park.

Degrees Conferred: 2,740 *baccalaureate*; 777 *master's*, 2 *doctorate*. Bachelor's degrees awarded in top five disciplines: business, management, marketing, and related support services 474; education 378; social sciences 283; psychology 269; communication, journalism, and related programs 253.

Fees and Other Expenses: *Full-time tuition per academic year 2004–05:* undergraduate resident $6,672, nonresident $15,352; graduate student tuition charged per credit hour (contact the university for current rates). *Room and board per academic year:* $6,828.

Financial Aid: Aid from institutionally generated funds is provided on the basis of academic merit, financial need, athletic ability. Institution has a Program Participation Agreement with the U.S. Department of Education for eligible students to receive Pell Grants and other federal aid.

Financial aid to full-time, first-time undergraduate students: 13% received federal grants averaging $2,878; 23% state/local grants averaging $2,688; 29% institutional grants averaging $4,418; 41% received loans averaging $3,096.

Departments and Teaching Staff: *Professors* 170, *associate professors* 121, *assistant professors* 158, *instructors* 72, *part-time teachers* 615.

Total instructional faculty: 1,136. Student-to-faculty ratio: 16.1: 1. Degrees held by full-time faculty: doctorate 46%, master's 44%, baccalaureate 6%, professional 2%.

Enrollment: Total enrollment 17,667. Undergraduate 14,311 (5,553 men, 8,758 women).

Characteristics of Student Body: *Ethnic/racial makeup:* Black non-Hispanic: 10.1%; American Indian or Alaska Native: .2%; Asian or Pacific Islander: 3.5%; Hispanic: 2.1%; White non-Hispanic: 73.3%; unknown: 8.3%. *Age distribution:* 18–21; 50%; 22–24: 21%; 25–29: 13%; 30–34: 5%; 35–39: 4%; 40–49: 5%; 50–and over: 2%.

International Students: 358 undergraduate nonresident aliens enrolled fall 2004. Programs available to aid students whose native language is not English: social, cultural. English as a Second Language Program. No financial aid specifically designated for international students.

Student Life: On-campus residence halls house 30% full-time undergraduate enrollment. *Intercollegiate athletics:* men: baseball, basketball, cross-country, football, lacrosse, soccer, swimming, tennis, track; women: basketball, cross-country, field hockey, gymnastics, lacrosse, softball, swimming, tennis, track, volleyball. *Special regulations:* Registered cars permitted for all but freshmen and sophomores living on campus. *Special services:* Women's Center, services for students with disabilities, tutoring, personal and career counseling, student health services, Office of Multicultural Student Life, student government association, fraternities and sororities; students serve on university policy-making committees; shuttle buses between campus and all university parking areas. *Student publications, radio:* Grub Street Wit, an annual literary magazine; *Tower Echoes*, a yearbook; *Towerlight*, a weekly newspaper. Radio station WTMD-FM broadcasts 162 hours per week. *Surrounding community:* Baltimore metropolitan area population over 2 million. Served by mass transit bus system; airport 30 miles from campus; passenger rail service 10 miles from campus.

Publications: *TSU Undergraduate and Graduate catalogs; TSU Compass; Student Handbook; Transitions: A Guidebook for Adult Students at TSU.*

Library Collections: 365,000 volumes. Online catalog. Current serial subscriptions: 2,165. 830,200 microform units. 14,200 audiovisual materials. 120 computer work stations. Students have access to the Internet at no charge.

Most important special holdings include women's studies; music collection; education collection.

Buildings and Grounds: Campus area 328 acres.

Chief Executive Officer: Dr. Robert L. Caret, President.

Undergraduate admission inquiries to Susanna Craine, Director of Undergraduate Admissions; graduate inquiries Graduate Admissions and Outreach.

Uniformed Services University of the Health Sciences

4301 Jones Bridge Road
Bethesda, Maryland 20814-4799

Tel: (301) 295-3101   **E-mail:** admissions@usuhs.mil
Fax: (301) 295-3545   **Internet:** www.usuhs.mil

Institution Description: Uniformed Services University of the Health Sciences is a federal institution. *Enrollment:* 843. *Degrees awarded:* First-professional (medicine), master's, doctorate.

Accreditation: *Regional:* MSA. *Professional:* medicine, public health

History: Chartered by an act of Congress 1972; established and offered first instruction at postsecondary level 1976; awarded first degree (first-professional) 1980.

Institutional Structure: *Governing board:* Uniformed Services University of the Health Sciences Board of Regents. Extrainstitutional representation: 9 regents appointed by the President of the United States and confirmed by the Senate. Ex officio: Secretary of Defense or his representative, the Surgeons General of the uniformed services of the Army, Navy, Air Force, and the U.S. Public Health Service; all voting; institutional representation: president of the university; non-voting. Full-time instructional faculty 275. Academic governance body, Faculty Assembly, meets an average of 4 times per year.

Calendar: Academic year Aug. to June.

Characteristics of Freshmen: 11% of applicants accepted. 8% of accepted applicants enrolled.

Admission: First-professional students apply as early as June 1 of previous year] for fall acceptance, but not later than Nov. 1. Students are notified of acceptance on a rolling basis, beginning in Nov. For graduate programs, apply 6 months prior to registration for fall acceptance, but not later than Mar. 1. *Requirements:* For first-professional degree, baccalaureate from accredited academic institution in the United States, Canada, or Puerto Rico by June 15 of the year of desired matriculation. Academic prerequisites include 1 academic year each of the following with laboratory: general or inorganic chemistry, physics, organic chemistry, and biology. In addition, 1 semester of calculus and college English are required. Applicants must be U.S. citizens 18 years or older at time

of matriculation, but no older than 30 years of age as of June 30 in the year of admission; however, the age of any student who has served on active duty as a commissioned officer in the uniformed services may exceed the age limit by a period equal to the time served on active duty, provided the student is no older than 35 as of June 30 in the year of admission; must meet requirements for holding a regular] commission in the uniformed services. Military personnel and ROTC students must have approval from their military departments or sponsoring components. Registration with AMCAS. For graduate degrees, baccalaureate or equivalent from accredited academic institutions. *Entrance tests:* MCAT for medical students; GRE for graduate students. *For transfer students:* All students are accepted as first-year students.

Degree Requirements: *For first-professional degree:* 2.0 GPA; courses in military studies and medical history, and in military medical field studies (must be taken during first 2 years); core curriculum; parts I and II of examination given by the National Board of Medical Examiners. *For master's degrees:* 3.0 GPA; qualifying examinations. *For all degrees:* Entire program in residence. *Grading system:* A–F; pass-fail.

Degrees Conferred: 44 *master's;* 13 *doctorate;* 166 *first-professional.*

Fees and Other Expenses: No tuition. Students are required to pay for housing, food, and other expenses from their annual salary.

Financial Aid: *Federal and state funding:* All first-professional students receive salaries as officers at the 0–1 level (Second Lieutenant in the Army and Air Force, Ensign in the Navy). *For graduates:* 49 stipends totaling $1,078,000 (ranging from $22,000 to $23,000).

Departments and Teaching Staff: *Professors* 275, *part-time teachers* 2,370. *Total instructional faculty:* 280 basic sciences; 2,465 clinical program. *Faculty development:* $23,253,055 total grants for research.

Enrollment: Total enrollment 843.

Characteristics of Student Body: *Ethnic/racial makeup:* number of Black non-Hispanic: 19; American Indian or Native Alaskan: 5; Asian or Pacific Islander: 200; Hispanic: 17; White non-Hispanic: 563. *Age distribution:* 17–21: 12%; 22–24: 35%; 25–29: 20%; 30–34: 2%; 35–39: 1%.

International Students: No programs available to aid students whose native language is not English. No financial aid specifically designated for international students.

Student Life: No on-campus housing. *Special regulations:* Cars permitted without restrictions. M.D. students must wear military uniforms. *Special services:* Learning Resources Center, student health service. *Student publications:* Vector, a quarterly newspaper; *CADUSUHS*, the student yearbook. *Surrounding community:* Bethesda (MD) population 81,000. Washington (DC), 2 miles from campus, is nearest metropolitan area. Served by mass transit subway (15 minute walk to campus from Medical Center stop) and bus systems; airport 25 miles from campus, passenger rail service 20 miles from campus (both airport and rail service accessible by subway).

Library Collections: 550,000 volumes. Online and card catalogs. 1,000 current periodical subscriptions. 100 computer work stations. Students have access to online information retrieval services and the Internet.

Most important special holdings include collection on military medicine.

Buildings and Grounds: Campus area 20 acres.

Chief Executive Officer: Dr. Larry W. Laughlin, President.

Address admission inquiries to Joan C. Stearman, Director, Office of Admissions; first-professional inquiries to Eleanor Metcalf, Dean for Graduate Education.

United States Naval Academy

121 Blake Road
Annapolis, Maryland 21402-5000

Tel: (410) 293-1000   **E-mail:** webmail@usna.edu
Fax: (410) 293-4348   **Internet:** www.usna.edu

Institution Description: United States Naval Academy is a federal institution. *Enrollment:* 4,150. *Degrees awarded:* Baccalaureate.

Accreditation: *Regional:* MSA. *Professional:* computer science, engineering,

History: Established as the Naval School and offered first instruction at postsecondary level 1845; reorganized as the U.S. Naval Academy 1850–51; offered first degree (baccalaureate) 1932 (authorized by act of Congress, retroactive to 1931); admitted women 1976. *See* Jack Sweetman, *The United States Naval Academy: An Illustrated History* (Annapolis: Naval Institute Press, 1979) for further information.

Calendar: Semesters. Academic year Aug. to May. Entering students admitted July. Degrees conferred and formal commencement May. Summer session of 3 terms from late May to mid-Aug.

Characteristics of Freshmen: 14% of applicants admitted. 95 of applicants admitted and enrolled.

92% (1,145 students) submitted SAT scores; 59% (739 students) submitted ACT scores. *25th percentile:* SAT Verbal 580, SAT Math 610; ACT English 25, ACT Math 26. *75th percentile:* SAT Verbal 680, SAT Math 710; ACT English 30, ACT Math 31.

86% of entering students expected to graduate within 5 years. 4% of freshmen cadets from Maryland. Freshmen from 50 states and 21 foreign countries.

Admission: Rolling admissions plan. For fall acceptance, apply as early as Apr. of previous year, but not later than Jan. 31 of year of enrollment. *Requirements:* Strongly recommend 4 secondary school units English, 3 modern language, 4 mathematics (including trigonometry), 1 chemistry, 1 European or world history, 1 physics. Nomination to Naval Academy by specified official source. Candidates must be of good moral character; unmarried; 17–23 years of age on July 1 of year of admissions; U.S. citizens, except for limited quota of foreign students authorized by Congress. *Entrance tests:* College Board SAT or ACT English and Mathematics; medical and physical aptitude examinations.

College credit and advanced placement for postsecondary-level work completed in secondary school. Tutoring available. Remedial courses offered during regular academic year; credit given.

Degree Requirements: 140 credit hours; 2.0 GPA; 4 years in residence; 4 years military training; physical education requirements in boxing, cardiovascular fitness, gymnastics, strength fitness, swimming, wrestling; achievement of standards of performance in at-sea training, conduct, honor, military performance; acceptance of a commission in U.S. Navy or U.S. Marine Corps if proffered; comprehensives in individual fields of study.

Fulfillment of some degree requirements and exemption from some beginning courses possible by passing departmental examinations, College Board AP. *Grading system:* A–F.

Distinctive Educational Programs: Special facilities for using telecommunications in the classroom. Facilities and programs for independent research, including honors programs (for humanities and social science majors), individual majors, tutorials. Trident Scholar program for independent research and study during senior year. Extensive computer facilities include over 300 remote computer terminals throughout the academy that are accessible 16 hours a day, 7 days a week. Each freshman will purchase a personal computer.

ROTC: Commissions awarded 2004: Air Force 3; Army 2; Navy 784; Marine Corps 195.

Degrees Conferred: 1,009 *baccalaureate:* computer and information sciences 56; engineering and engineering technologies 341; English 63; mathematics 23; physical sciences 155; social sciences and history 571.

Fees and Other Expenses: *Full-time tuition per academic year:* None. Entrance deposit $2,200.

Departments and Teaching Staff: *Total instructional faculty:* 579 (full-time 549, part-time 30; women 126, men 403; members of minority groups 47). Total faculty with doctorate, first-professional, or other terminal degree: 335. Student-to-faculty ratio: 7:1. Degrees held by full-time faculty: doctorate 54%, master's 34%, baccalaureate 12%. 54% hold terminal degrees.

Enrollment: Total enrollment 4,349. Full-time 3,626 men / 723 women.

Characteristics of Student Body: *Ethnic/racial makeup:* number of Black non-Hispanic: 284; American Indian or Alaska Native: 83; Asian or Pacific Islander: 215; Hispanic: 386; White non-Hispanic: 3,340. *Age distribution:* number under 18: 45; 18–19: 1,675; 20–21: 1,986; 22–24: 616; 25–29: 27.

International Students: 40 nonresident aliens enrolled fall 2004. 9 students from Europe, 8 Asia, 11 Central and South America, 4 Africa, 8 other. Programs available to aid students whose native language is not English: social, cultural. No financial aid specifically designated for international students.

Student Life: On-campus residence halls for both men and women house 100% of student body. *Intercollegiate athletics:* men only: baseball, basketball, football, soccer, swimming, tennis, track; women only: basketball, swimming, track, volleyball. *Special regulations:* Cars permitted for senior midshipmen and for junior midshipmen by special permission. Prescribed naval uniforms are worn daily. Quiet hours from 8pm to 11pm. *Special services:* Medical services. *Student publications, radio: The Log,* a monthly magazine. Radio station WRNV. *Surrounding community:* Annapolis population 35,000. Washington (DC), 30 miles from campus, is nearest metropolitan area. Served by airport 30 miles from campus.

Library Collections: 662,575 volumes including bound periodicals. 1,685 current serial subscriptions. Current serial subscriptions: paper 2,709; microform 130,816. Students have access to the Internet and online information retrieval services.

Most important special holdings include William J. Sebald Collection of personal papers; Admiral William Adger Moffett Collection (9 feet of papers of first head of Bureau of Naval Aeronautics dating from 1920–1933); A.A. Michelson Collection (16 feet of papers, books, photographs, and instruments belonging to first American to win Nobel Prize in physics); Captain Joel Abbot Collection

(official and personal letterbooks dating from 1815–1855; includes 25 reels microfilm); Dr. Thomas Paine Collection (submarine books); Edward Steichen Photographs Collection.

Buildings and Grounds: Campus area 329 acres. The academy grounds are a Registered National Historic Landmark. *New buildings:* Glenn Warner Soccer Facility completed 2004; Uriah P. Levy Center and Jewish Chapel 2005.

Chief Executive Officer: J. R. Ryan, Vice Admiral, USN, Superintendent.

Address admission inquiries to Director of Admissions.

University of Baltimore

1420 North Charles Street
Baltimore, Maryland 21201

Tel: (410) 837-4200   **E-mail:** admissions@ubalt.edu
Fax: (410) 837-4793   **Internet:** www.ubalt.edu

Institution Description: University of Baltimore is a state institution providing upper division, first-professional, and graduate study. *Enrollment:* 5,045. *Degrees awarded:* Baccalaureate, first-professional (law), master's, doctorate. Certificates also awarded.

Academic offerings subject to approval by statewide coordinating bodies. Budget subject to approval by state governing boards.

Accreditation: *Regional:* MSA. business, law, public administration

History: Established, chartered; and offered first instruction at postsecondary level 1925; awarded first degrees (baccalaureate, first-professional) 1927; merged with Easter College and Mount Vernon School of Law 1970; became public, upper-division, and professional institution 1975; became part of the University of Maryland System 1988.

Institutional Structure: *Governing board:* The Board of Regents of the University of Maryland System. Representation: 16 board members, including 1 student. All voting. *Composition of institution:* Administrators 39 men / 17 women. Academic affairs headed by provost for academic and administrative affairs. Management/business/finances directed by vice president for business and financial affairs. Full-time instructional faculty 150. Academic governance body, University Faculty Senate, meets an average of 4 times per year.

Calendar: Semesters. Academic year Sept. to May. Entering students admitted Sept., Aug., Jan., June. Degrees conferred May, Aug., Dec. Formal commencement May. Summer session from June to Aug.

Admission: Rolling admissions plan. *Requirements:* Associate of arts degree or 56 credit hours from accredited college or university. Minimum 2.0 GPA. *Entrance tests:* For foreign students, minimum TOEFL score 550. *For transfer students:* 2.0 minimum GPA; from 4-year accredited institution 90 hours maximum transfer credit; from 2-year accredited institution 70 hours.

College credit for extrainstitutional learning (life experience) on basis of ACE *2006 Guide to the Evaluation of Educational Experiences in the Armed Services.* Tutoring available. Noncredit developmental courses offered during regular academic year.

Degree Requirements: *For undergraduate degrees:* 120 credit hours 2.0 GPA; last 30 hours in residence; for liberal art students, English-communication courses. Fulfillment of some degree requirements and exemption from some beginning courses possible by passing College Board CLEP. *Grading system:* A–F; pass-fail; pass; withdraw (carries time limit, deadline after which pass-fail is appended to withdraw); incomplete (carries time limit).

Distinctive Educational Programs: Work-experience programs. Flexible meeting places and schedules, weekend and evening classes. Accelerated degree programs. Honors programs. Web-based baccalaureate and master's programs.

Degrees Conferred: 468 *baccalaureate* (B), 470 *master's* (M); 3 *doctorate* (D): business/marketing 212 (B), 21 (M); communications/communication technologies 23 (B), 64 (M), 2 (D); computer and information sciences 37 (B); English 13 (B); health professions and related sciences 20 (B), 38 (M); interdisciplinary studies 42 (B); law/legal studies 20 (B), 61 (M); protective services/public administration 55 (B), 13 (M); psychology 22 (B), 18 (M); social sciences and history 24 (B), 44 (M), 1 (D). *First-professional:* law 261.

Fees and Other Expenses: *Full-time tuition per academic year 2004–05:* undergraduate resident $6,448; out-of-state student $17,790; graduate resident $8,259, out-of-state student $12,205.

Financial Aid: Aid from institutionally generated funds is provided on the basis of academic merit, financial need. Institution has a Program Participation Agreement with the U.S. Department of Education for eligible students to receive Pell Grants and other federal aid.

Departments and Teaching Staff: *Total instructional faculty:* 328 (full-time 156, part-time 172; women 108, men 220; members of minority groups 42). Total faculty with doctorate, first-professional, or other terminal degree: 236. Student-to-faculty ratio: 16:1.

Enrollment: Total enrollment 5,045. Undergraduate full-time 455 men / 596 women, part-time 384m / 682w; first-professional full-time 475m / 504w, part-time 42m / 56w; graduate full-time 165m / 277w, part-time 549m / 863.

Characteristics of Student Body: *Ethnic/racial makeup (undergraduate):* number of Black non-Hispanic: 694; American Indian or Alaska Native: 16; Asian or Pacific Islander: 60; Hispanic: 25; White non-Hispanic: 991; unknown: 156. *Age distribution:* number 18–19: 7; 20–21: 225; 22–24: 445; 25–29: 490; 30–34: 294; 35–39: 209; 40–49: 367; 50–64: 81; 65 and over: 2.

International Students: 327 nonresident aliens enrolled fall 2004. Students from Europe, Asia, Central and South America, Africa. No programs available to aid students whose native language is not English. No financial aid specifically designated for international students.

Student Life: No on-campus housing. *Special regulations:* Cars permitted without restrictions. *Special services:* Learning Resources Center, medical services. *Student publications: Law Forum,* a law student newspaper; *Ubique,* the campus newspaper. *Surrounding community:* Baltimore regional population over 2 million. Served by mass transit bus and train systems; light rail to campus. Airport 9 miles from campus.

Publications: *Small Business Economics: An International Journal; International Property Law Journal; Environmental Law Journal; Journal of Information Technology Management; Production and Operations Management Journal.*

Library Collections: 240,000 volumes. 167,000 government documents; 345,000 microforms; 900 audiovisual materials; 985 current periodical subscriptions. Access to online information retrieval services and the Internet.

Most important special holdings include Steamship Heritage Collection; Herwood Collection of Accountancy; Decker Collection of American History; WMAR Television News films.

Buildings and Grounds: Campus area 45 acres.

Chief Executive Officer: Dr. Robert L. Bogomolny, President.

Address admission inquiries to Director of Admissions.

Yale Gordon College of Liberal Arts

Degree Programs Offered: *Baccalaureate* in applied statistics, computer science, corporate communications, criminal justice, English, history, jurisprudence; political science, psychology, sociology; *master's* in applied psychology, criminal justice, legal and ethical studies, public administration, publications design, sociology, urban recreation.

Distinctive Educational Programs: Cooperative master's programs in publications design with Maryland Institute, College of Art; in sociology with Morgan State University. Interdisciplinary programs in advertising; aging; English and advertising, oral and written communication, theater arts; general studies; jurisprudence; legal studies; regional development, urban arts; interdisciplinary honors courses. Cross-registration with Coppin, Morgan, and Towson State universities; Peabody Conservatory of Music; University of Maryland, Baltimore County. Computer satellite center. Graphics and media laboratories.

Robert G. Merrick School of Business

Degree Programs Offered: *Baccalaureate, master's* in business; *master's* in business administration. Undergraduate certificates in accounting and computer information systems.

Distinctive Educational Programs: Joint degree programs in cooperation with School of Law. Cooperative programs with area community colleges in administration for nursing, fire protection technology, hotel-motel administration, restaurant administration. *Other distinctive programs:* Business management counseling by students through Small Business Institute. Certificates through Women's Program in Management. Bureau of Business Research.

School of Law

Degree Programs Offered: *First-professional; master's* in taxation. Joint and combined programs: BA/JD; MA/JD, JD/MBA, JD/MPA, JD/MS.

Admission: Baccalaureate degree from an accredited college or university; LSAT.

Degree Requirements: 84 credit hours, 2.0 GPA, 2 years in residence.

Distinctive Educational Programs: Internships. *Other distinctive programs:* Criminal Practices, Juvenile Law, and Legal Services to the Elderly clinics. *See also* School of Business.

University of Maryland Baltimore

520 West Lombard Street
Baltimore, Maryland 21201-1627
Tel: (410) 706-3100   **E-mail:** admit@umd.edu
Fax: (410) 706-0234   **Internet:** www.umaryland.edu

Institution Description: University of Maryland Baltimore is a major operating unit of the state-owned University of Maryland System. *Enrollment:* 5,602. *Degrees awarded:* Baccalaureate, first-professional, master's, doctorate.

Accreditation: *Regional:* MSA. *Professional:* clinical lab scientist, prosthodontics, dental hygiene, dentistry, dietetics, EMT-paramedic, endodontics, engineering, law, medicine, nursing-midwifery, nursing, pediatric dentistry, periodontics, pharmacy, physical therapy, prosthodontics, social work

History: Established as College of Medicine of Maryland 1807; chartered as University of Maryland 1812; Baltimore College of Dental Surgery chartered 1840; Maryland College of Pharmacy established 1841; Maryland College of Pharmacy merged with University of Maryland to form School of Pharmacy 1904; present name adopted 1920; School of Social Work and Community Planning established 1961.

Institutional Structure: *Governing Board:* The Board of Regents of the University of Maryland System. *Composition of institution:* Administrators 53 men / 26 women. Chancellor is chief executive officer. Academic affairs headed by special assistant to the chancellor for academic affairs. Management/business/finances directed by director of business services. Full-time instructional faculty 322.

Calendar: Semesters. 4-1-4 plan. Academic year early Sept. to mid-May. Formal commencement May. Summer sessions.

Admission: Students are admitted to the various schools on the campus according to set procedures for each school. Students are generally categorized as undergraduate, graduate, or professional according to the degree sought. Each of the programs has an application for admission and an admissions committee.

Degree Requirements: Depends on specific program of study.

Distinctive Educational Programs: Practicum experiences and interdisciplinary projects offered through Area Health Education Center for students in schools of Dentistry, Medicine, Nursing, Pharmacy, Social Work and Community Planning.

Degrees Conferred: 377 *baccalaureate:* health professions and related sciences; 582 *master's:* health professions and related sciences; 103 *doctorate:* health professions and related sciences; 684 *first-professional:* dentistry, pharmacy, law, medicine.

Fees and Other Expenses: *Full-time tuition per academic year 2004–05:* Contact the university for tuition/costs for undergraduate, graduate, and professional programs.

Financial Aid: Aid from institutionally generated funds is provided on the basis of academic merit, financial need. Institution has a Program Participation Agreement with the U.S. Department of Education for eligible students to receive Pell Grants and other federal aid.

Departments and Teaching Staff: *Total instructional faculty:* 1,094. Degrees held by full-time faculty: doctorate 48%, master's 6%, baccalaureate 4%, professional 42%. 94% hold terminal degrees.

Enrollment: Total enrollment 5,602. Undergraduate 946 (12.2% men, 87.8% women).

Characteristics of Student Body: *Ethnic/racial makeup (undergraduate):* Black non-Hispanic: 26.3%; American Indian or Alaska Native: .7%; Asian or Pacific Islander: Hispanic: 3.5%; White non-Hispanic: 56.7%; unknown: .5%.

International Students: 25 undergraduate nonresident aliens enrolled fall 2004. No programs available to aid students whose native language is not English. No financial aid specifically designated for international students.

Student Life: On-campus residence halls house 9% of student body. *Special regulations:* Cars restricted by availability of space. *Special services:* medical services. *Student publications: The Voice,* campus newspaper. *Surrounding community:* Baltimore metropolitan area population over 3 million. Served by mass transit bus system, airport 120 miles from campus, passenger rail service 1 mile from campus.

Publications: *Maryland in Baltimore* is a university magazine, produced twice yearly.

Library Collections: 575,000 volumes. 300,000 microforms; 10,000 audiovisual materials; 6,775 current periodical subscriptions. Online catalog. Students have access to online information retrieval services and the Internet.

Buildings and Grounds: The campus is an urban institution located in downtown Baltimore; occupies 32 acres and comprised of 37 buildings.

Chief Executive Officer: Dr. David J. Ramsay, President.

Address admission inquiries to Director of Admissions.

Baltimore College of Dental Surgery

Degree Programs Offered: *Baccalaureate* in dental hygiene; *first-professional*.

Admission: *For baccalaureate program:* 2 years from accredited college or university with preprofessional curriculum. Standardized allied health profession test. Personal interview. Recommend 2.2 GPA. *For first-professional degree:* 90 semester hours from accredited college or university with 6 units English, 8 biology, 8 inorganic chemistry, 8 organic chemistry, 8 physics. ASD-SAS. Recommend DAT. For in-state residents recommend 2.6 GPA; for out-of-state students 3.2 GPA.

Degree Requirements: *For baccalaureate degree:* 125 credit hours; 2.5 GPA; last 30 hours in residence. *For first-professional degree:* 237 credit hours; 2.0 GPA; 1,852 clinical clock hours. *For all degrees:* Prescribed curriculum.

Distinctive Educational Programs: Postdoctoral study in endodontics, oral and maxillofacial surgery, oral pathology, orthodontics, periodontics, prosthodontics. Continuing professional education.

School of Medicine

Degree Programs Offered: *Baccalaureate* in medical technology, physical therapy, radiologic technology; *first-professional*.

Admission: *For baccalaureate programs:* 2 years from accredited university or college with preprofessional curriculum. Standardized allied health profession test. 2.0–2.5 GPA. *For first-professional program:* 90 semester hours from accredited university or college with 6 units English, 8 biology or zoology, 8 inorganic chemistry, 8 physics, 6 organic chemistry. MCAT.

Degree Requirements: *For baccalaureate degree:* 2.0 GPA; prescribed curriculum; clinical clerkships. *For first-professional degree:* Prescribed curriculum first 2 years; 72 weeks clinical clerkships last 2 years.

Distinctive Educational Programs: Joint M.D.-Ph.D. programs in microbiology, pharmacology and experimental therapeutics, pathology, physiology. Continuing professional education.

School of Nursing

Degree Programs Offered: *Baccalaureate*.

Admission: 2 years from accredited college or university; standardized allied health professions test.

Degree Requirements: 120–122 credit hours; 2.0 GPA; final year in residence; prescribed curriculum.

Distinctive Educational Programs: Baccalaureate completion program for registered nurses. Continuing professional education.

School of Pharmacy

Degree Programs Offered: *First-professional, doctorate*.

Admission: 2 years from accredited college or university with 6 hours English, 8-10 organic chemistry, 8 general chemistry, 8 physics, 6–7 mathematics (precalculus and calculus), 4 biology or zoology, 17–20 from among humanities, social sciences, academic electives. PCAT. Minimum 2.25 GPA; recommended 3.0 GPA.

Degree Requirements: *For first-professional degree:* 100 credit hours; 6 months professional experience.

School of Law

Degree Programs Offered: *First-professional*.

Admission: Graduation from accredited college or university. LSAT. LSDAS.

Degree Requirements: 84 credit hours; 2.0 GPA; 3 years in residence.

Distinctive Educational Programs: Joint J.D.-master's program in cooperation with School of Social Work and Community Planning.

School of Social Work and Community Planning

Degree Programs Offered: *Master's*.

Distinctive Educational Programs: Cooperative baccalaureate program in liberal arts and social work with University of Maryland at Baltimore County. Dual-degree program with Baltimore Hebrew College. Joint J.D.-master's program in cooperation with Baltimore Hebrew College. Continuing education.

Graduate School

Degree Programs Offered: *Master's* in institutional pharmacy, nursing, oral surgery; *doctorate* in social welfare; *master's, doctorate* in anatomy, biochemistry, biological chemistry, biophysics, legal medicine, medicinal chemistry, medical pathology, microbiology, oral pathology, pharmaceutics, pharmacognosy, pharmacology and physiology.

University of Maryland Baltimore County

1000 Hilltop Circle
Baltimore, Maryland 21250
Tel: (410) 455-2291   **E-mail:** admissions@umbc.edu
Fax: (410) 455-1094   **Internet:** www.umbc.edu

Institution Description: *Enrollment: 11,852. Degrees awarded:* Baccalaureate, master's, doctorate.

Accreditation: *Regional:* MSA. *Professional:* clinical psychology, computer science, diagnostic medical sonography, EMT-paramedic, psychology internship, public administration, social work, teacher education

History: Established 1963; offered first instruction at postsecondary level 1966; awarded first degree (baccalaureate) 1969.

Institutional Structure: *Composition of institution:* Executives/administrators/other staff 1,046. Academic affairs headed by vice president for academic affairs and provost. Management/business/finances directed by vice president for administrative affairs. Full-time instructional faculty 456. Academic governance body, Faculty Senate, meets an average of 7 times per year.

Calendar: Semesters (4-1-4 plan). Academic year Sept. to May. Freshmen admitted Sept., Jan., Feb., June, July. Degrees conferred June, Aug., Jan. Formal commencement Dec., June. Summer session June to Aug.

Characteristics of Freshmen: 70% of applicants admitted. 37% of applicants admitted and enrolled.

98.2% (1,398 students) submitted SAT scores; 10.3% (147 students) submitted ACT scores. *25th percentile:* SAT Verbal 540, SAT Math 580; ACT Composite 22, ACT English 21, ACT Math 23. *75th percentile:* SAT Verbal 650, SAT Math 670; ACT Composite 28, ACT English 28, ACT Math 28.

48% of entering freshmen expected to graduate within 6 years. 85% of freshmen from Maryland.

Admission: Periodic admissions points (3 times per year). For fall acceptance, apply as early as fall of senior year of secondary school, but no later than July 1 of year of enrollment. Early acceptance available.

College credit and advanced placement for postsecondary level work completed in secondary school. Tutoring available. Noncredit developmental-remedial courses offered in summer session and regular academic year.

Degree Requirements: 120 semester hours; 2.0 GPA; last 30 hours in residence; 2 physical education courses; general education requirements. Must complete with a grade of C or better: English 100 (or equivalent course taken at another institution).

Fulfillment of some degree requirements and exemption from some beginning courses possible by passing College Board CLEP, AP. *Grading system:* A–F.

Distinctive Educational Programs: Joint baccalaureate/first professional programs in dentistry, law, medicine with University of Maryland at Baltimore. Baccalaureate and graduate programs in computer science and engineering; applied molecular biology. Emergency Health Services in cooperation with Maryland Institute for Emergency Medical Services Systems. Meyerhoff Program in the sciences and engineering, a baccalaureate program for academically excellent students. Public affairs, artist, and humanities programs. Cooperative education. Weekend and evening classes. Special facilities for using telecommunications in the classroom. Interdisciplinary programs in American studies, African-American studies, ancient studies, biochemistry, and others. Programs and facilities for independent research, including honors programs, individual majors, and tutorials. Study abroad programs in England, Germany, Italy, Mexico.

ROTC: Army available at cooperating host institutions.

Degrees Conferred: 1,708 *baccalaureate* (B), 400 *master's* (M); 65 *doctorate* (D): area and ethnic studies 47 (B); biological/life sciences 187 (B), 14 (M), 7 (D); business/marketing 4 (M); computer and information sciences 480 (B), 152 (M), 6 (D); education 137 (M); engineering and engineering technologies 80 (B), 24 (M), 12 (D); English 71 (B); foreign languages and literature 26 (B); health professions and related sciences 51 (B), 6 (M); interdisciplinary studies 35 (B), 13 (M), 5 (D); mathematics 20 (B), 8 (M), 4 (D); philosophy/religion/theology 7 (B), 5 (M); physical sciences 6 (B), 14 (M), 9 (D); protective services/public administration 70 (B), 6 (M), 11 (D); psychology 186 (B), 8 (M), 11 (D); social sciences and history 279 (B), 24 (M); visual and performing arts 158 (B), 5 (M); other 3 (B).

Fees and Other Expenses: *Full-time tuition per academic year 2005–06:* undergraduate resident $6,484 plus $2,036, nonresident $14,560 plus $2,036; graduate resident $395 per credit hour, out-of-state $652 per credit hour. *Room and board per academic year:* $8,090.

Financial Aid: Aid from institutionally generated funds is provided on the basis of academic merit, financial need, athletic ability, other criteria. Institution has a Program Participation Agreement with the U.S. Department of Education for eligible students to receive Pell Grants and other federal aid.

Financial aid to full-time, first-time undergraduate students: need-based scholarships/grants totaling $11,022,320, self-help $12,235,082; non-need-based scholarships/grants totaling $14,273,969, self-help $10,515,736, parent loans $6,450,646, tuition waivers $808,102, athletic awards $3,001,345.

Departments and Teaching Staff: Full-time *professors* 126, *associate professors* 141, *assistant professors* 124, *instructors* 20 *part-time faculty* 275.

Total instructional faculty: 731 (full-time 456, part-time 275; women 290, men 441; members of minority groups 112). Total faculty with doctorate, first-professional, or other terminal degrees: 495. Student-to-faculty ratio: 18.2:1. Degrees held by full-time faculty: doctorate 81%, master's 16%, baccalaureate 3%. 87% hold terminal degrees.

Enrollment: Total enrollment 11,852. Undergraduate full-time 4,380 men / 3,782 women, part-time 791m / 715w; graduate full-time 388m / 459w, part-time 636m / 701w. *Transfer students:* 1,094.

Characteristics of Student Body: *Ethnic/racial makeup:* number of Black non-Hispanic: 1,400; American Indian or Alaska Native: 34; Asian or Pacific Islander: 1,405; Hispanic: 315; White non-Hispanic: 3,448; unknown: 147. *Age distribution:* number under 18: 55; 18–19: 2,731; 20–21: 2,994; 22–24: 2,235; 25–29: 890; 30–34: 321; 35–39: 161; 40–49: 192; 50–64: 71; 65 and over: 12; unknown: 6.

International Students: 818 nonresident aliens enrolled fall 2004. Programs available to aid students whose native language is not English: English as a Second Language Program. No financial aid specifically designated for international students.

Student Life: On-campus residence halls house 26.9% of student body. *Intercollegiate athletics:* men only: baseball, basketball, golf, lacrosse, soccer, tennis, indoor and outdoor track, cross-country, swimming; women only: basketball, lacrosse, soccer, softball, tennis, indoor and outdoor track, cross-country, swimming, volleyball. *Special services:* Learning Resources Center, medical services. *Student publications, radio:* A weekly newspaper, an annual literary magazine. Radio station WUMD. *Surrounding community:* Baltimore is served by mass transit bus system, airport 8 miles from campus, passenger rail service 10 miles from campus.

Library Collections: 951,781 volumes including bound books, serial backfiles, electronic documents, and government documents not in separate collections. Online catalog. Current serial subscriptions: paper 4,170, microform 1,100,926. 19,263 recordings; 3,092 compact discs; 2,024 CD-ROMs. Students have access to the Internet at no charge. Total budget for books, periodicals, audiovisual materials, microforms 2004–05: $2,939,786.

Most important special holdings include photographic collections; American Society for Microbiology Archives; Rosenfeld Science Fiction Research Collection.

Buildings and Grounds: Campus area 544 acres. *New buildings:* The Commons; Public Policy Building; Physics Building; Walker Avenue Apartments.

Chief Executive Officer: Dr. Freeman A. Hrabowski, President.

Undergraduates address admission inquiries to Office of Undergraduate Admissions; graduate inquiries to Graduate School.

University of Maryland College Park

College Park, Maryland 20742

Tel: (301) 405-1000   **E-mail:** admit@umd.edu
Fax: (301) 314-9560   **Internet:** www.maryland.edu

Institution Description: The University of Maryland College Park is a state institution. *Enrollment:* 34,933. *Degrees awarded:* Baccalaureate, master's, first-professional, doctorate. Certificates also awarded.

Accreditation: *Regional:* MSA. *Professional:* business, clinical psychology, counseling, psychology internship, engineering, journalism, landscape architecture, librarianship, marriage and family therapy, music, planning, public health, rehabilitation counseling, school psychology, speech-language pathology, teacher education, theatre

History: Established as Maryland Agricultural College 1856; offered first instruction at postsecondary level 1859; awarded first degree 1862; changed name to Maryland State College of Agriculture 1916; adopted present name 1920; reorganized to college system 1986.

Institutional Structure: *Composition of institution:* Administrators 120 men / 101 women. Academic affairs headed by vice president for academic affairs and provost. Management/business/finances directed by vice president for administrative affairs. Full-time instructional faculty 1,389. Academic governance body, Faculty Senate.

Calendar: Semesters. Academic year Sept. to May. Freshmen admitted Aug., Jan., May, June. Degrees conferred and formal commencements June, Aug., Dec. Summer session of 2 terms from mid-May to early Aug.

Characteristics of Freshmen: 22,292 applicants (10,496 men, 11796 women. 61.6% of applicants admitted. 36.3% of admitted students enrolled full-time.

99% (4,141 students) submitted SAT scores; 42 students) submitted ACT scores. *25th percentile:* SAT I Verbal 560, SAT I Math 590. *75th percentile:* SAT I Verbal 670, SAT I Math 700.

58% of entering freshmen expected to graduate within 5 years. 66% of freshmen from Maryland. Freshmen from 46 states and 62 foreign countries.

Admission: Modified rolling admissions plan. Freshmen not rolling; transfers admitted on a rolling basis. Applications by Dec. 1 yield Feb. 1 decision. General application deadline Feb. 15 for Apr. 1 decision notification.

Degree Requirements: 120 semester hours; 2.0 GPA; last 30 hours in residence; 2 physical education courses; distribution requirements. Fulfillment of some degree requirements and exemption from some beginning courses possible by passing departmental examinations, College Board CLEP, APP. *Grading system:* A–F; pass-fail.

Distinctive Educational Programs: Cooperative education in engineering. Interdisciplinary programs. Preprofessional programs, including allied health sciences, dentistry, law, medicine, veterinary medicine. Study abroad in Brazil, Denmark, England, France, Germany, Israel, Italy, Mexico, Spain. Living/learning programs: College Park Scholars and University Honors. World courses. First Year Focus cluster courses.

ROTC: Air Force, Army.

Degrees Conferred: 5,959 *baccalaureate*; 1,990 *master's*; 482 *doctorate* (D). Bachelor's degrees awarded in top five disciplines: social sciences 1,177; business, management, marketing, and related support services 907; engineering 585; biological and biomedical sciences 460; computer and information sciences and support 443.

Fees and Other Expenses: *Full-time tuition per academic year 2004–05:* undergraduate resident $7,410, out-of-state student $18,710. Contact the university for current graduate tuition, fees, and other costs. *Room and board per academic year:* $7,791.

Financial Aid: Aid from institutionally generated funds is provided on the basis of academic merit, financial need, athletic ability. Institution has a Program Participation Agreement with the U.S. Department of Education for eligible students to receive Pell Grants and other federal aid.

Financial aid to full-time, first-time undergraduate students: 13% received federal grants averaging $3,252; 25% state/local grants averaging $2,872; 44% institutional grants averaging $4,212; 36% received loans averaging $4,249.

Departments and Teaching Staff: *Professors* 618, *associate professors* 383, *assistant professors* 254, *instructors* 39, *lecturers* 534, *other* 44.

Total instructional faculty: 1,918. Student-to-faculty ratio: 14:1. Degrees held by full-time faculty: doctorate 83.9%, master's 12.2%, baccalaureate 3.2%, professional .3%. 88.8% hold terminal degrees.

Enrollment: Total enrollment 34,953. Undergraduate 25,140 (51.% men, 48.9% women).

Characteristics of Student Body: *Ethnic/racial makeup:* Black non-Hispanic: 12.1%; American Indian or Alaska Native: .3%; Asian or Pacific Islander: 13.7%; Hispanic: 5.5%; White non-Hispanic: 58.2%; unknown: 7.8%.

International Students: 603 undergraduate nonresident aliens enrolled fall 2004. Students from Europe, Asia, Central and South America, Africa, Canada, Australia, New Zealand. Programs available to aid students whose native language is not English: social. English as a Second Language Program. No financial aid specifically designated for international students.

Student Life: On-campus residence halls house 33% of student body. Some men join and live in fraternities; some women join and live in sororities. *Intercollegiate athletics:* men only: baseball, basketball, cross-country, fencing, football, golf, lacrosse, soccer, swimming, tennis, track, wrestling; women only: basketball, cross-country, field hockey, golf, gymnastics, lacrosse, swimming, tennis, track, volleyball. *Special regulations:* Registered cars permitted in designated areas. *Special services:* Medical services, shuttle bus service. *Student publications, radio:* The Diamondback, a daily newspaper; yearbook. Radio station WMUC. *Surrounding community:* College Park population 24,000. Campus is 9 miles from center of Washington DC. Served by mass transit rail/bus system, airport 30 miles from campus, passenger rail service 12 miles from campus.

Library Collections: 3,017,000 volumes. 745,000 government documents; 5,542,000 microforms; 245,000 audiovisual materials; 34,100 periodicals. Online catalog. Access to online information retrieval services and the Internet.

Most important special holdings include Gordon W. Prange Collection of Japanese Language Publications and unpublished materials from the Allied Occupation of Japan 1945–1949; International Piano Music Archives at Maryland (IPAM).

Buildings and Grounds: Campus area 1,250 acres.

Chief Executive Officer: Dr. C.D. Mote, Jr., President.

Address admission inquiries to Barbara A. Gill, Director of Undergraduate Admissions; graduate inquiries to Graduate Admissions Director.

University of Maryland Eastern Shore

Backbone Road
Princess Anne, Maryland 21853-1299
Tel: (410) 651-2200   **E-mail:** admissions@umes.edu
Fax: (410) 651-6105   **Internet:** /www.umes.edu

Institution Description: *Enrollment: 3,775. Degrees awarded:* Baccalaureate, master's, doctorate.

Accreditation: *Regional:* MSA. *Professional:* construction education, physical therapy

History: Established as Princess Anne of the Delaware Conference Academy 1886; became division of University of maryland and changed name to Maryland State College 1948; adopted present name 1970.

Institutional Structure: *Composition of institution:* Administrators 16 men / 2 women. Academic affairs headed by vice chancellor for academic affairs. Management/business/finances directed by vice chancellor for administrative affairs. Full-time instructional faculty 81. Academic governance body, Faculty Senate, meets an average of 9 times per year.

Calendar: Semesters. Academic year Aug. to May. Freshmen admitted Aug., Jan., June. Degrees conferred and formal commencement May. Summer session from early June to Aug.

Characteristics of Freshmen: 2,838 applicants (1,032 men, 1,806 women). 76.3% of applicants admitted. 45.3% of admitted students enrolled full-time.

100% (1,057 students) submitted SAT scores. *25th percentile*: SAT I Verbal 370, SAT I Math 360. *75th percentile*: SAT I Verbal 470, SAT I Math 460.

33% of entering freshmen expected to graduate within 5 years. 78% of freshmen from Maryland. Freshmen from 16 states and 15 foreign countries.

Admission: Rolling admissions plan. For fall acceptance, apply as early as 1 year prior to enrollment, but not later than day of registration. Early acceptance available.

Degree Requirements: *For undergraduate degrees:* 122 semester hours; 2.0 GPA; last 30 hours in residence; 2 physical education courses; general education requirements. *Grading system:* A–F.

Distinctive Educational Programs: Cooperative education. Weekend and evening classes. Interdisciplinary programs. Facilities and programs for independent research, including honors programs, independent study.

Degrees Conferred: 374 *baccalaureate*; 77 *master's*. Bachelor's degrees awarded in top five disciplines: business, management, marketing, and related support services 88; security and protective services 43; biological and biomedical sciences 38; health professions and related clinical sciences 31; computer and information sciences and support services 30.

Fees and Other Expenses: *Full-time tuition per academic year 2004–05:* undergraduate resident $5,568, out-of-state student $11,421. Contact the university for graduate study tuition and fees. *Room and board per academic year:* $5,880. *Books and supplies:* $1,200 (undergraduate).

Financial Aid: Aid from institutionally generated funds is provided on the basis of academic merit, financial need, athletic ability, major field. Institution has a Program Participation Agreement with the U.S. Department of Education for eligible students to receive Pell Grants and other federal aid.

Financial aid to full-time, first-time undergraduate students: 73% received federal grants averaging $2,203; 46% state/local grants averaging $2,823; 41% institutional grants averaging $2,474; 82% received loans averaging $2,914.

Departments and Teaching Staff: *Professors 8, associate professors 23, professors 36, instructors 34, part-time faculty 30.*

Total instructional faculty: 111. Degrees held by full-time faculty: doctorate 63.7%, master's 26.7%, baccalaureate 9.9%. 66.3% hold terminal degrees.

Enrollment: Total enrollment 3,775. Undergraduate 3,346 (41.1% men, 58.9% women).

Characteristics of Student Body: *Ethnic/racial makeup (undergraduate):* Black non-Hispanic: 75%; American Indian or Alaska Native: .4%; Asian or Pacific Islander: .8%; Hispanic: .9%; White non-Hispanic: 9.7%; unknown: .4%.

International Students: 224 undergraduate nonresident aliens enrolled fall 2004. No programs available to aid students whose native language is not English. No financial aid specifically designated for international students.

Student Life: On-campus residence halls house 55% of student body. Residence halls for men constitute 50% of such space, for women 50%. *Intercollegiate athletics:* men only: baseball, basketball, tennis, track; women only: basketball, tennis, track, volleyball. *Special regulations:* Registered cars permitted. *Special services:* Medical services. *Student publications:* A newspaper pub-

lished irregularly; a yearbook. *Surrounding community:* Princess Anne population 1,500. Baltimore, 130 miles from campus, is nearest metropolitan area. Served by airport 12 miles from campus.

Library Collections: 150,000 titles. 24,000 government documents; 97,000 microforms; 18,077 audiovisual materials; 1,260 current periodical subscriptions. Online catalog. Students have access to online information retrieval services.

Buildings and Grounds: Campus area 7000 acres.

Chief Executive Officer: Dr. Thelma B. Thompson, President.

Address admission inquiries to Edwina Morse, Director of Admissions.

University of Maryland University College

3501 University Boulevard East
College Park, Maryland 20783-8010
Tel: (301) 985-7000   **E-mail:** umucinfo@umuc.edu
Fax: (301) 985-7678   **Internet:** www.umuc.edu

Institution Description: The University of Maryland University College is primarily for adults who prefer to pursue part-time study. Instruction is offered at more than 30 sites in Maryland and the D.C. metropolitan area for Statewide Programs division. Instruction is also offered by the European Division in 20 countries (more than 100 sites) and by the Asian Division in 8 countries (more than 50 sites). *Enrollment: 28,374. Degrees awarded:* Baccalaureate, master's, doctorate. Associate degree awarded to military personnel on active duty.

Accreditation: *Regional:* MSA.

History: Established as College of Special Continuation Studies and offered first instruction at postsecondary level 1947; awarded first degree (baccalaureate) 1948; adopted present name 1970.

Institutional Structure: *Composition of institution:* Executives 75 men / 52 women. Academic affairs headed by vice president for academic affairs. Management/business/finance managed by executive vice president.

Calendar: Semesters. Academic year Aug. to May. Degrees conferred May, Aug., Dec. Formal commencement May. Summer session of 2 terms from June to Aug.

Admission: Apply no later than registration period. Early acceptance available.

Degree Requirements: *For all associate degrees:* 60 semester hours; 15 hours in residence; additional requirements vary by program. *For all baccalaureate degrees:* 120 hours; 30 hours in residence; general education requirements. *For all degrees:* 2.0 GPA.

Fulfillment of some degree requirements and exemption from some beginning courses possible by taking College Board AP, other standardized tests. *Grading system:* A–F; withdraw (carries time limit).

Distinctive Educational Programs: Cooperative education; weekend and evening classes. Baccalaureate-granting Open University offers programs in behavioral and social sciences, humanities, technology, and guided study management and incorporates courses from England's Open University. College credit for USAFI/DANTES and for extrainstitutional learning (life experience) on basis of ACE *2006 Guide to the Evaluation of Educational Experiences in the Armed Services*, portfolio, faculty assessment, personal interview, and completion of 3-credit course in experiential learning. Graduate programs in general administration, computer systems management, technology management, international management, engineering management, telecommunications management, executive programs. *Other distinctive programs:* Servicemembers Opportunity College. Noncredit training and enrichment programs. Tutoring available.

Degrees Conferred: 107 *associate*; 2,405 *baccalaureate*; 1,362 *master's*; 6 *doctorate*. Bachelor's degrees awarded in top five disciplines: multidisciplinary studies 1,040; computer and information sciences and support services 648; business, management, marketing, and related support services 455; psychology 77; legal professions and studies 74.

Fees and Other Expenses: *Tuition per academic year 2004–05:* undergraduate resident $5,424, out-of-state $9,888. Contact the university for current tuition/fees for graduate level study.

Financial Aid: Aid from institutionally generated funds is provided on the basis of academic merit, financial need. Institution has a Program Participation Agreement with the U.S. Department of Education for eligible students to receive Pell Grants and other federal aid.

Financial aid to full-time, first-time undergraduate students: 45% received federal grants averaging $2,430; 23% state/local grants averaging $2,725; 10% institutional grants; 63% received loans averaging $4,430.

Departments and Teaching Staff: *Total instructional faculty:* 718. Student-to-faculty ratio: 22:1.

Enrollment: Total enrollment 28,374. Undergraduate 19,857 (42.3% men, 57.7% women).

Characteristics of Student Body: *Ethnic/racial makeup (undergraduate):* Black non-Hispanic: 31.9%; American Indian or Alaska Native: .8%; Asian or Pacific Islander: 5.3%; Hispanic: 5%; White non-Hispanic: 46.5%; unknown: 8.9%. *Age distribution:* 17–21: 4.5%; 22–24: 10.6%; 25–29: 21%; 30–34: 19.5%; 35–39: 17.5%; 40–49: 20.6%; 60–and over: 6%.

International Students: 318 nonresident aliens enrolled fall 2004. No programs available to aid student whose native language is not English. No financial aid specifically designated for international students.

Student Life: No on-campus housing. *Special regulations:* Cars with decals permitted in designated areas during designated times. *Special services:* Academic Support Center; computer labs.

Library Collections: Students have access to the resources of all state-supported, four-year academic University of Maryland System libraries.

Buildings and Grounds: Campus area 13 acres.

Chief Executive Officer: Dr. Gerald Heeger, President.

Address undergraduate admission inquiries to Director of Admissions; graduate inquiries to Office of Graduate Admissions and Advising.

Villa Julie College

1525 Green Spring Valley Road
Stevenson, Maryland 21153
Tel: (410) 486-7000   **E-mail:** admissions@vjc.edu
Fax: (410) 486-3552   **Internet:** www.vjc.edu

Institution Description: Villa Julie College is a private, independent, nonprofit institution. *Enrollment:* 2,740. *Degrees awarded:* Associate, baccalaureate, master's.

Accreditation: *Regional:* MSA. *Professional:* clinical lab technology, nursing

History: Founded 1947 by Sisters of Notre Dame de Namur; officially approved as a two-year college 1954; first accreditation by MSA 1962; became independent institution 1967; became a four-year college 1988; began graduate division 1996.

Institutional Structure: *Governing board:* Villa Julie College Board of Trustees. *Extrainstitutional representation:* 19 trustees. *Institutional representation:* president of the college, vice president/dean of the college. *Composition of institution:* Administrators 13 men / 27 women. Academic affairs headed by vice president/dean of the college. Management/business/finances directed by chief business officer. Total instructional faculty 290.

Calendar: Semesters. Academic year Aug. to May. Freshmen admitted Aug., Jan. Degrees conferred May, Aug., Dec. Formal commencement May, Dec. May term. Summer session.

Characteristics of Freshmen: 71% of applicants admitted. 36% of applicants admitted and enrolled.

99% (563 students) submitted SAT scores. *25th percentile:* SAT Verbal 450, SAT Math 450. *75th percentile:* SAT Verbal 570, SAT Math 570.

54% of entering freshmen expected to graduate within 5 years. 98% of freshmen from Maryland. Freshmen from 13 states and 8 foreign countries.

Admission: Rolling admissions plan. Early application encouraged. Preferred application date Feb. 15 prior to Sept. enrollment. Admissions process for freshmen requires application, essay, two recommendations, high school transcript, SAT or ACT scores. Interview recommended but not required. Recommendations and standardized test scores waived for transfer students.

Degree Requirements: *For all associate degrees:* minimum of 60 credit hours; 30 credits including the final 15 must be earned at Villa Julie College. *For all baccalaureate degrees:* minimum 120 credit hours (must include 45 credits of upper level work); final 30 credits at Villa Julie College. *For all undergraduate degrees:* 2.0 GPA; .5 credit physical education; general college requirements. Fulfillment of some degree requirements and exemption from some beginning courses possible by passing College Board CLEP, APP, other standardized tests. *Grading system:* A–F, pass-fail; withdraw; incomplete (carries time limit).

Distinctive Educational Programs: Work-experience programs. Weekend and evening classes. Liberal Arts and Technology interdisciplinary programs. Internships and cooperative education available. Master's degree in advanced information technologies. Master's program in forensic science and forensic studies.

ROTC: Army in cooperation with Johns Hopkins University.

Degrees Conferred: 49 *associate;* 455 *baccalaureate:* biological/life sciences 22; business/marketing 59; computer and information sciences 101; education 34; English 10; health professions and related sciences 82; home economics and vocational home economics 9; interdisciplinary studies 47; law/legal studies 31; mathematics 1; physical sciences 1; psychology 16; visual and performing ars 23. 23 *master's:* business/marketing 12; computer and information sciences 11.

Fees and Other Expenses: *Full-time tuition per academic year 2004–05:* $13,715. *Required fees:* $938. *Room and board per academic year:* $6,250.

Financial Aid: Aid from institutionally generated funds is provided on the basis of academic merit, financial need, other considerations. Institution has a Program Participation Agreement with the U.S. Department of Education for eligible students to receive Pell Grants and other federal aid.

Financial aid to full-time, first-time undergraduate students: need-based scholarships/grants totaling $7,450,164, self-help $3,870.590; non-need-based scholarships/grants totaling $4,841,576, self-help $4,259,181, parent loans $11,537,447, tuition waivers $507,176.

Departments and Teaching Staff: *Professors 19, associate professors 32, assistant professors 34, instructors 6, part-time faculty 199.*

Total instructional faculty: 290 (full-time 91, part-time 199; women 161, men 129; members of minority groups 25). Total faculty with doctorate, first-professional, or other terminal degree: 137. Student-to-faculty ratio: 13:1. *Faculty development:* 2 faculty members awarded sabbaticals 2004–05.

Enrollment: *Total enrollment,* 2,740. Undergraduate full-time 608 men / 1,520 women, part-time 90m / 441w; graduate part-time 37m / 44w. *Transfer students:* in-state 159; from out-of-state 40.

Characteristics of Student Body: *Ethnic/racial makeup:* number of Black non-Hispanic: 345; American Indian or Alaska Native: 8; Asian or Pacific Islander: 72; Hispanic: 35; White non-Hispanic: 2,078; unknown: 111. *Age distribution:* number under 18: 17; 18–19: 956; 20–21: 855; 22–24: 310; 25–29: 12; 30–34: 80; 35–39: 83; 40–49: 115; 50–64: 115; 65 and over: 2.

International Students: 10 nonresident aliens enrolled fall 2004. 1 student from Europe, 5 Central and South America, 2 Africa, 2 other. No programs available to aid students whose native language is not English. No financial aid specifically designated for international students.

Student Life: Campus-owned student housing is located at complex in nearby Owings Mills. *Athletics:* NCAA Division II, Intercollegiate, intramural, and club sports for men and women. *Student activities:* Student government association; student clubs; honor societies; lecture series; drama productions; chorus. *Special services:* Learning Resources Center, Communication Skills Laboratory, computer laboratories; counseling services; services for adult students. *Student publications: The Villager,* monthly newspaper; *FYI,* weekly newsletter; *The Evening News,* biweekly newsletter; *Spectrum,* annual literary magazine. *Surrounding community:* Baltimore is nearest metropolitan area. Served by mass transit bus system.

Library Collections: 641,930 volumes. Online catalog. Current serial subscriptions: paper 565, microform 329, via electronic access 14,609. 2,800 audiovisual materials. Access to online information retrieval services and the Internet.

Buildings and Grounds: Campus area 60 acres. *new buildings:* Residential apartment-style housing complex for 500 students completed 2004.

Chief Executive Officer: Dr. Kevin J. Manning, President.

Address admission inquiries to Mark S. Hergan, Director of Admissions.

Washington Bible College - Capital Bible Seminary

6511 Princess Garden Parkway
Lanham, Maryland 20706-3599
Tel: (301) 552-1400   **E-mail:** admissions@bible.edu
Fax: (301) 552-2775   **Internet:** www.bible.edu

Institution Description: Washington Bible College - Capital Bible Seminary is a private interdenominational institution emphasizing professional Bible training. *Enrollment:* 649. *Degrees awarded:* Associate, baccalaureate, master's, first-professional.

Accreditation: *Regional:* MSA. *National:* ABHE.

History: Established 1938.

Calendar: Semesters. Academic year Aug. to May.

Characteristics of Freshmen: 104 applicants (48 men, 56 women). 59.6% of admitted students enrolled. 67.7% of admitted students enrolled full-time.

22% (4 students) submitted SAT scores; 3% (4 students) submitted ACT scores.

Admission: *Requirements:* Graduation from secondary school or equivalent. *Entrance tests:* ACT.

Degree Requirements: Completion of prescribed courses; Bible curriculum.

Degrees Conferred: 40 *baccalaureate:* theology/ministerial studies; 15 *master's:* theology/ministerial studies; 14 *first-professional:* master of divinity.

Fees and Other Expenses: *Full-time tuition per academic year 2004–05:* $8,890. *Books and supplies:* $600. *Room and board per academic year:* $5,410.

Financial Aid: Aid from institutionally generated funds is provided on the basis of academic merit, financial need, other criteria. Institution has a Program

Participation Agreement with the U.S. Department of Education for eligible students to receive Pell Grants and other federal aid.

Financial aid to full-time, first-time undergraduate students: 32% received federal grants; 14% state/local grants; 79% institutional grants; 50% received loans.

Departments and Teaching Staff: *Total instructional faculty:* 44 (full-time 14, part-time 30). Degrees held by full-time faculty: doctorate 50%, master's 50%.

Enrollment: Total enrollment 649. Undergraduate 309 (55.7% men, 44.3% women).

Characteristics of Student Body: *Ethnic/racial makeup (undergraduate):* Black non-Hispanic: 42.1%; American Indian or Alaska Native: .3%; Asian or Pacific Islander: 2.9%; Hispanic: $3.2%; White non-Hispanic: 46.9%; unknown: 1.6%.

International Students: 9 undergraduate nonresident aliens enrolled fall 2004. No programs to aid students whose native language is not English. No financial aid specifically designated for international students.

Student Life: Residence facilities available on campus.

Library Collections: 77,000 volumes. 250 current periodical subscriptions.

Buildings and Grounds: Campus area 63 acres.

Chief Executive Officer: Dr. Homer Heater, Jr., President.

Address admission inquiries to Shea Kaurin, Director of Admissions.

Washington College

300 Washington Avenue

Chestertown, Maryland 21620-1197

Tel: (410) 778-2800   **E-mail:** adm.off@washcoll.edu

Fax: (410) 778-7850   **Internet:** www.washcoll.edu

Institution Description: Washington College is a private, independent, non-profit college. *Enrollment:* 1,426. *Degrees awarded:* Baccalaureate, master's.

Accreditation: *Regional:* MSA.

History: Established as Kent County School early in the eighteenth century; chartered, offered first instruction at postsecondary level, and adopted present name 1782; awarded first degree (baccalaureate) 1783. *See* Frederick W. Dumschott, *Washington College* (Baltimore: Johns Hopkins University Press, 1980) for further information.

Institutional Structure: *Governing board:* The Visitors and Governors of Washington College. Representation: 37 trustees, including 20 alumni and 4 administrators. 1 ex officio. 36 voting. *Composition of institution:* Administrators 15 men / 16 women. Academic affairs headed by dean of the college. Management/business/finances directed by vice president for finance. Full-time instructional faculty 85. Academic governance body, The Academic Council, meets an averaged of 30 times per year.

Calendar: Semesters. Academic year Aug. to May. Freshmen admitted Aug. and Jan. Degrees conferred and formal commencement May.

Characteristics of Freshmen: 85% of applicants accepted. 22% of accepted applicants enrolled.

90% (271 students) submitted SAT scores; 9% (26 students) submitted ACT scores. *25th percentile:* SAT Verbal 520, SAT Math 520; ACT Composite 20. *75th percentile:* SAT Verbal 630, SAT Math 610; ACT Composite 25.

63% of entering freshmen expected to graduate within 5 years. 46% of freshmen from Maryland. Freshmen from 26 states and 11 foreign countries.

Admission: Rolling admissions plan. For fall acceptance, application deadline Feb. 28; 5 decision dates Jan. 30 to Mar. 30; early decision Nov. 15, students notified by Dec. 15. Early acceptance available. *Requirements:* Either graduation from accredited secondary school or GED. 16 college preparatory units including 4 English, 2 in a foreign language, 3 mathematics, 3 science, and 5 electives recommended. Minimum 2.5 GPA. *Entrance tests:* College Board SAT or ACT composite. For foreign students TOEFL. *For transfer students:* 2.0 minimum GPA; from 4-year accredited institution 96 hours maximum transfer credit; from 2-year accredited institution 64 hours; correspondence/extension students minimum GPA and maximum transfer credit determined by registrar.

College credit and advanced placement for postsecondary-level work completed in secondary school.

Degree Requirements: 128 credit hours (32 courses); no more than 10 grades of 1.0 or lower; final year in residence; comprehensives in individual fields of study. Fulfillment of some degree requirements possible by passing College Board CLEP, APP, and departmental examinations. *Grading system:* A–F; pass-fail; withdraw (deadline after which pass-fail is appended to withdraw); incomplete.

Distinctive Educational Programs: *For all undergraduates:* Interdisciplinary programs in American studies, behavioral neuroscience, humanities, multicultural studies, and international studies. Individual majors. Study abroad at Manchester College in Oxford, England, and various other locations. Work-study psychology practicum with Cambridge Hospital (MD). Washington (DC) semester in cooperation with American University. Internships in business management, drama, mathematics, and political science. *For graduate students:* Evening classes. Interdisciplinary master's program in English, history, social science and psychology. *Available to all students:* Facilities and programs for independent research. *Other distinctive programs:* Creative writing, academic computing; environmental studies.

Degrees Conferred: 315 *baccalaureate*; 17 *master's*. Bachelor's degrees awarded in top five disciplines: social sciences 83; business, management, marketing, and related support services 42; English language and literature/letters 33; psychology 32; biological and biomedical sciences: 28.

Fees and Other Expenses: *Full-time tuition per academic year 2004–05:* $25,990. *Required fees:* $660. *Room and board per academic year:* $6,000.

Financial Aid: Aid from institutionally generated funds is provided on the basis of academic merit, financial need. Institution has a Program Participation Agreement with the U.S. Department of Education for eligible students to receive Pell Grants and other federal aid.

Financial aid to full-time, first-time undergraduate students: need-based scholarships/grants totaling $8,099,022, self-help $2,484,295; non-need-based scholarships/grants totaling $6,950,233, self-help $2,075,259, parent loans $4,341,015, tuition waivers $1,526,349.

Departments and Teaching Staff: *Total instructional faculty:* 142 (full-time 90, part-time 52; women 59, men 83; members of minority groups 26). Student-to-faculty ratio: 12:1. Total faculty with doctorate, first-professional, or other terminal degree: 92.

Enrollment: Total enrollment 1,426. Undergraduate full-time 504 men / 804 women, part-time 15m / 26w; graduate full-time 7m / 3w, part-time 24m / 33w.

Characteristics of Student Body: *Ethnic/racial makeup:* number of Black non-Hispanic: 50; American Indian or Alaska Native: 2; Asian or Pacific Islander: 25; Hispanic: 13; White non-Hispanic: 1,100; unknown: 101.

International Students: 58 nonresident aliens enrolled fall 2004. Students from Europe, Asia, Central and South America, Africa, Canada, Australia. Programs available to aid students whose native language is not English: English as a Second Language. Financial aid available for international students: scholarships available to qualifying students.

Student Life: On-campus residence halls house 80% of student body. Residence halls for men constitute 40% of such space, for women only 45%, for both sexes 15%. 18% of men join fraternities; 17% of women join sororities. *Intercollegiate athletics:* men only: baseball, basketball, crew, cross-country, lacrosse, soccer, tennis; women only: crew, field hockey, lacrosse, softball, swimming, tennis, volleyball. *Special regulations:* Cars permitted without restriction. *Special services:* Learning Resources Center for writing, medical services. *Student publications: Elm,* a weekly newspaper; *Pegasus,* a yearbook; *W.C. Review,* a monthly literary magazine; *Washington College Collegian,* a monthly publication. *Surrounding community:* Chestertown population 3,500. Baltimore, 70 miles from campus, is nearest metropolitan area.

Library Collections: 243,600 volumes. 250,600 microforms; 6,350 audiovisual materials; 865 current periodical subscriptions. Access to online information retrieval services and the Internet.

Most important special holdings include Washington Collegiana; College Archives, federal government documents; Chesapeake Bay Collection.

Buildings and Grounds: Campus area 104 acres.

Chief Executive Officer: Dr. Baird Tipson, President.

Address admission inquiries to Kevin Coveney, Vice President for Admissions.

Massachusetts

American International College

1000 State Street

Springfield, Massachusetts 01109

Tel: (413) 737-7000   **E-mail:** admissions@aic.edu

Fax: (413) 205-3943   **Internet:** www.aic.edu

Institution Description: American International College is a private, independent, nonprofit college. *Enrollment:* 1,621. *Degrees awarded:* Associate, baccalaureate, master's. Certificates of advanced graduate studies also awarded.

Member of Cooperating Colleges of Greater Springfield.

Accreditation: *Regional:* NEASC. *Professional:* nursing, occupational therapy, physical therapy, teacher education

History: Established in Lowell, chartered as French-Protestant College, and offered first instruction at postsecondary level 1885; moved to present location 1888; changed name to French-American College 1889; first degree (baccalaureate) awarded 1894; adopted present name 1904.

Institutional Structure: *Governing board:* The Board of Trustees of American International College, Inc. Extrainstitutional representation: 32 trustees; including 4 alumni; institutional representation: 1 administrator. 1 ex officio. 32 voting. *Composition of institution:* Administrators 12 men / 4 women. Academic affairs headed by vice president for academic affairs and dean of the College. Management/business/finances directed by comptroller. Full-time instructional faculty 82. Academic governance body, the faculty, meets an average of 5 times per year.

Calendar: Semesters. Academic year Sept. to May. Freshmen admitted Sept., Jan., June, July. Degrees conferred and formal commencement May. Summer session from early June to late Aug.

Characteristics of Freshmen: 1,274 applicants (men 624, women 550). 85.4% of applicants admitted. 27.5% of admitted students enrolled full-time.

93% (279 students) submitted SAT scores. *25th percentile:* SAT I Verbal 430, SAT I Math 430. *75th percentile:* SAT I Verbal 520, SAT I Math 580.

64% of entering freshmen expected to graduate within 5 years. 50% of freshmen from Massachusetts. Freshmen from 14 states and 22 foreign countries.

Admission: Rolling admissions plan. Apply by Nov. 1 for early decision; need not limit application to American International. Early acceptance available. *Requirements:* Either graduation from accredited secondary school with 16 units which should include 4 English, 2 mathematics, 1 science, 1 social studies, 8 electives in languages or other academic disciplines; or GED. Minimum GPA 2.0. Lowest acceptable secondary school class standing 65th percentile. *Entrance tests:* College Board SAT. *For transfer students:* 2.0 minimum GPA; from 2-year institution 60–75 hours maximum transfer credit; from 4-year institution 90 hours credit.

College credit and advanced placement for extrainstitutional learning on basis of ACE *2006 Guide to the Evaluation of Educational Experiences in the Armed Services.* College credit on basis of postsecondary-level work completed in secondary school. Tutoring available.

Degree Requirements: *For all degrees:* 2.0 GPA on 4.0 scale; 30 hours in residence. *For all baccalaureate degrees:* 120 hours; 4 semesters physical education. *For all associate degrees:* 60 hours. Fulfillment of some degree requirements and exemption from some beginning courses possible by passing College Board CLEP or other standardized tests. *Grading system:* A–F; pass-fail; withdraw (carries penalty and time limit; deadline after which pass-fail is appended to withdraw); incomplete.

Distinctive Educational Programs: *Available to all students:* Flexible meeting places and schedules. Evening classes. Accelerated degree programs. Facilities for independent research, including honors programs and individual majors. Training in special education through Curtis Blake Child Development Center. Oral History Center for training history majors in technique of data collection and evaluation. Special training for human technology majors through Center for Human Relations and Community Affairs. *For undergraduates:* Work-experience programs. Study abroad in conjunction with other institutions (schools and countries vary). Assistance for learning disabled students through Curtis Blake Center. Economic Education Center for specialized teacher training. Strong emphasis on internships in all majors. *For graduate students:* Off-campus courses at various locations for education majors.

ROTC: Army and Air Force offered in cooperation with Western New England College.

Degrees Conferred: 3 *associate;* 230 *baccalaureate;* 184 *master's;* 3 *doctorate.* Bachelor's degrees awarded in top five disciplines: business, management, marketing, and related support services 69; health professions and related clinical sciences 31; multidisciplinary studies 25; security and protective services 23; social sciences 16.

Fees and Other Expenses: *Full-time tuition per academic year 2004–05:* undergraduate $18,000; contact the college for current graduate tuition/fees. *Room and board per academic year:* $8,510.

Financial Aid: Aid from institutionally generated funds is provided on the basis of academic merit, financial need, athletic ability. Institution has a Program Participation Agreement with the U.S. Department of Education for eligible students to receive Pell Grants and other federal aid.

Financial aid to full-time, first-time undergraduate students: 44% received federal grants averaging $2,828; 24% state/local grants averaging $1,497; 94% institutional grants averaging $5,745; 76% received loans averaging $2,186.

Departments and Teaching Staff: *Total instructional faculty:* 91. Student-to-faculty ratio: 18:1. Degrees held by full-time faculty: doctorate 65%, master's 100%. 70% hold terminal degrees.

Enrollment: Total enrollment 1,621. Undergraduate 1,273 (40.5% men, 59.5% women).

Characteristics of Student Body: *Ethnic/racial makeup (undergraduate):* Black non-Hispanic: 24%; American Indian or Alaska Native: .3%; Asian or Pacific Islander: 2.8%; Hispanic: 7.6%; White non-Hispanic: 54.8%; unknown: 7.6%. *Age distribution:* 17–21: 36%; 22–24: 21%; 25–29: 13%; 30–34: 11%; 35–39: 5%; 40–49: 9%; 50–59: 2%; 60–and over: 1%. 22% of total student body attend summer sessions.

International Students: 37 undergraduate nonresident aliens enrolled fall 2004. Students from Europe, Asia, Central and South America, Africa, Canada. Programs available to aid students whose native language is not English: social, cultural. English as a Second Language Program. No financial aid specifically designated for international students.

Student Life: On-campus residence halls house 44% of student body. Residence halls for men constitute 30% of such space, for women only 10%, for both sexes 60%. 6% of men join and 2% live in fraternities. *Intercollegiate athletics:* men only: baseball, basketball, football, golf, hockey, soccer, tennis; women only: basketball, softball, volleyball. *Special regulations:* Cars permitted without restrictions. *Special services:* Learning Resources Center, medical services, shuttle van service between campus segments. *Student publications, radio:* Criterion, an annual literary magazine; *Taper,* a yearbook; *Yellow Jacket,* a weekly newspaper. Radio station WAIC broadcasts 120 hours per week. *Surrounding community:* Springfield population 155,000. Served by mass transit bus and rail systems; airport 10 miles from campus; passenger rail service 3 miles from campus.

Library Collections: 120,000 volumes. 84,000 microforms; 425 current periodical subscriptions; Computer work stations available. Students have access to online information retrieval services and the Internet.

Most important holdings include Rare Book Collection (French, German, English); Oral History Collection of Southern New England.

Buildings and Grounds: Campus area 58 acres.

Chief Executive Officer: Dr. Harry J. Courniotes, President.

Address admission inquiries to Peter J. Miller, Dean of Admissions.

Amherst College

100 Boltwood Avenue
Amherst, Massachusetts 01002-5000
Tel: (413) 542-2000   **E-mail:** admission@amherst.edu
Fax: (413) 542-2040   **Internet:** www.amherst.edu

Institution Description: Amherst College is a private, independent, non-profit college. *Enrollment:* 1,638. *Degrees awarded:* Baccalaureate.

Member of Consortium on Financing Higher Education, Five Colleges, Inc.

Accreditation: *Regional:* NEASC.

History: Established as a college for men and offered first instruction at post-secondary level 1821; awarded first degree (baccalaureate) 1822; chartered 1825; admitted women as transfer student 1975; admitted women as freshmen 1976. *See* Claude M. Fuess, *Amherst, the Story of a New England College* (Boston: Little, Brown, and Co., 1935) for further information.

Institutional Structure: *Governing board:* The Trustees of Amherst College. Extrainstitutional representation: 14 term trustees; institutional representation: 6 alumni. 1 ex officio. 21 voting. *Composition of institution:* Administrators 56 men / 63 women (14% are members of minority groups, 56% are women). Academic affairs headed by dean of faculty. Management/business/finances directed by treasurer. Full-time instructional faculty 159. Academic governance body, faculty and Committee on Educational Policy, meet an average of 6 and 18 times per year, respectively.

Calendar: Semesters. Academic year Sept. to May. Freshmen admitted Apr. Degrees conferred and formal commencement May.

Characteristics of Freshmen: 20.7% of applicants admitted. 37.8% of applicants admitted and enrolled.

89% (388 students) submitted SAT scores; 11% (47 students) submitted ACT scores. *25th percentile:* SAT Verbal 680,SAT Math 680; ACT Composite 30. *75th percentile:* SAT Verbal 770, SAT Math 780; ACT Composite 33.

95% of entering freshmen expected to graduate within 5 years. 16% of freshmen from Massachusetts. Freshmen from 41 states 14 countries.

Admission: For fall acceptance, apply as early as Sept. 1 of previous year, but not later than Jan. 1. Students are notified of acceptance Apr. Apply by Nov. 15 for early decision; may not limit apply to any other college or university's early decision program concurrently; must withdraw any other applications if accepted. *Requirements:* Recommend 4 years English, 3–4 in a foreign language, 3 or more mathematics (through pre-calculus), 2 history and social science, 3 natural science (including 1 year of a laboratory science), additional academic units in areas of interest; personal interview when possible. GED accepted. *Entrance tests:* College Board SAT of ACT, plus 3 SAT II's (a subject test in English is recommended). *For transfer students:* 64 hours maximum transfer credit. Tutoring available.

Degree Requirements: 128 credit hours; GPA 6 on 14-point scale; 2 years in residence; comprehensive evaluations in individual fields of study. *Grading system:* A–F; pass-fail; withdraw (deadline after which pass-fail is appended to withdraw).

Distinctive Educational Programs: Interdisciplinary programs, including African, American, Asian, Black, European, Latin American, and Russian studies; natural sciences; neuroscience. Facilities and programs for independent research including honors programs, individual majors, tutorials. Study abroad in Japan through Associated Kyoto Program; elsewhere through programs offered by other colleges or institutions. Off-campus study for semester or academic year through Twelve College Exchange Program. Noncredit field study of 1 or 2 semesters by individual arrangement. Through Five Colleges, Inc., cross-registration and other comprehensive programs with Hampshire, Mount Holyoke, and Smith Colleges, and the University of Massachusetts at Amherst, including cooperative doctorate with degree awarded by University of Massachusetts. The recently added Department of Law, Jurisprudence, and Social Thought places the study of law within the context of liberal arts education.

ROTC: Air Force and Army in cooperation with University of Massachusetts.

Degrees Conferred: 430 *baccalaureate:* area and ethnic studies 21; biological/life sciences 21; computer and information sciences 18; English 59; foreign languages and literature 32; interdisciplinary studies 10; law/legal studies 38; mathematics 7; philosophy/religion/theology 12; physical sciences 26; psychology 36; social sciences and history 132; visual and performing arts 18. *Honorary degrees awarded 2004–05:* Doctor of Humane Letters 4, Doctor of Law 1, Doctor of Science 1.

Fees and Other Expenses: *Full-time tuition per academic year 2005–06:* $30,780. *Other fees:* $584. *Room and board per academic year:* $8,160.

Financial Aid: Amherst College offers a direct lending program. Aid from institutionally generated funds is provided on the basis of financial need.

Financial aid to full-time, first-time undergraduate students: need-based scholarships/grants totaling $20,318,807, self-help $2,627,650; non-need-based scholarships/grants totaling $1,266,176, self-help $772,527, parent loans $3,168,465.

Departments and Teaching Staff: *Total instructional faculty:* 218 (full-time 190, part-time 28; women 93, men 125; members of minority groups 34). Total faculty with doctorate, first-professional, or other terminal degree: 205. Student-to-faculty ratio: 8:1. Degrees held by full-time faculty: baccalaureate 100%, master's 98%, doctorate 88%, professional 3%. 90% hold terminal degrees. *Faculty development:* $924,500 in grants for research. 33 faculty members awarded sabbaticals 2004–05.

Enrollment: Total enrollment 1,638. Undergraduate full-time 850 men / 788 women/

Characteristics of Student Body: *Ethnic/racial makeup:* number of Black non-Hispanic: 148; American Indian or Alaska Native: 4; Asian or Pacific Islander: 212; Hispanic: 116; White non-Hispanic: 758; unknown: 299.

International Students: 101 nonresident aliens enrolled fall 2004. Students from Europe, Asia, Central and South America, Africa, Canada. Programs available to aid students whose native language is not English: English as as Second Language Program. Financial aid specifically designated for international students: 15 scholarships for undergraduates available annually.

Student Life: 98% of students live on campus in co-ed dormitories. *Intercollegiate athletics:* men: baseball, basketball, crew, cross-country, football, golf, hockey, lacrosse, skiing, soccer, squash, swimming, tennis, track; women: basketball, crew, cross country, field hockey, golf, lacrosse, skiing, soccer, squash, swimming, tennis, track. *Special regulations:* Freshmen are not permitted to have cars on campus. *Special services:* Medical services. *Student publications, radio:* The Amherst Student, a biweekly newspaper; *Scrutiny,* a semiannual evaluation of courses by students. Radio station WAMH broadcasts approximately 20 hours per day. *Surrounding community:* Amherst population 35,000. Boston, 80 miles from campus, is nearest metropolitan area. Served by mass transit bus system.

Library Collections: 1,003,887 volumes. Online catalog. Current serial subscriptions: 5,630 paper, 100 microform, 5,002 via electronic access. 14,498 recordings; 14,303 compact discs; 491 CD-ROMs. 110 computer work stations. Students have access to online information retrieval services and the Internet. Total 2004–05 budget for books and materials: $1,800,000.

Most important special holdings include Emily Dickinson Collection; Robert Frost Collection; John J. McCloy Papers.

Buildings and Grounds: Campus area 100 acres. *New buildings:* Geology Building and Museum completed 2005.

Chief Executive Officer: Dr. Anthony W. Marx, President.

Address admission inquiries to Dean of Admission and Financial Aid.

Andover Newton Theological School

210 Herrick Road
Newton Centre, Massachusetts 02459-2243
Tel: (617) 964-1100   **E-mail:** admissions@ants.edu
Fax: (617) 965-9756   **Internet:** www.ants.edu

Institution Description: Andover Newton Theological School is a private, independent, nonprofit institution with an historical relation to the United Church of Christ and the American Baptist Churches of the United States. *Enrollment:* 513. *Degrees awarded:* First-professional (master of divinity), master's, doctorate.

Member of Boston Theological Institute.

Accreditation: *Regional:* NEASC. *National:* ATS. *Professional:* theology

History: Andover Theological Seminary established and incorporated 1807; offered first instruction at postsecondary level 1808; first certificate awarded 1811; Newton Theological Institution founded 1825; 2 institutions affiliated and adopted present name 1931; merged 1965. *See* Leonard Woods, *History of Andover Theological Seminary* (Boston: J.R. Osgood, 1885) and Henry K. Rowe, *History of Andover Theological Seminary* (Newton: Andover Newton, 1933) for further information.

Institutional Structure: *Governing board:* Board of Trustees. Extrainstitutional representation: 23 trustees; institutional representation: 1 administrator, 1 ex officio. 24 voting (12.5% are members of minority groups; 29% are women). *Composition of institution:* senior administrators 3 men / 2 women. Academic affairs headed by dean. Management/business/finances directed by vice president for finance and management. Full-time instructional faculty 22. Academic governance body, the faculty, meets an average of 10 times per year.

Calendar: Semesters. Academic year Sept. to June. Degrees conferred and formal commencement May. Summer session of 1 term in June. Summer school Clinical Pastoral Education June–August.

Admission: For fall acceptance, apply as early as possible in year preceding enrollment, but not later than July 1. *Requirements:* Graduation with baccalaureate or equivalent degree from regionally accredited postsecondary institution. Master of divinity, ordination, other requirements for some programs. Broadly based liberal arts and undergraduate background recommended. *Entrance tests:* M.Div. candidates participate in personality assessment program early in the semester. MAT or GRE are encouraged and may be requested.

Degree Requirements: *For all degrees:* Half of required course credits in residence. *For master of divinity:* 90 course credits (3 years); 2.0 GPA. *For master of arts:* 48 course credits (2 years); 3.0 GPA; thesis. *For master of sacred theology:* 24 course credits (2 semesters); 3.0 GPA master of divinity; thesis. *For doctor of ministry* in department of psychology and clinical studies, or in general studies: 32 course credits (1 calendar year); 3.3 GPA master of divinity or equivalent; ordination (in most cases); and other requirements. *Grading system:* A–F; withdraw and incomplete (may carry penalty); satisfactory and pass (not available to Ph.D. candidates).

Distinctive Educational Programs: Evening classes. Joint doctoral program in theological studies with Boston College, which confers the degree. Television studio. Study abroad in England, Scotland, India, Germany, Puerto Rico, Central and South America. Multicultural studies (Orlando E. Costas Hispanic and Latin American and Kelsey-Owens Black Ministries programs), rural and urban ministries.

Degrees Conferred: 17 *master of arts;* 9 *doctor of ministry;* 56 *first-professional:* master of divinity.

Fees and Other Expenses: *Full-time tuition per academic year 2004–05:* $398 per credit hour. Contact the seminary for current information.

Financial Aid: Aid from institutionally generated funds is provided on the basis of academic merit, financial need, other criteria. Institution has a Program Participation Agreement with the U.S. Department of Education for eligible students to receive Pell Grants and other federal aid. *Graduate aid:* 124 students received $1,302,456 in federal and state-funded loans (ranging from $5,000 to $10,500); 136 fellowships/grants totaling $501,088 (ranging from $600 to $6,200); 12 students held teaching assistantships totaling $11,144 (ranging from $398 to $1,592).

Departments and Teaching Staff: *Professors* 9, *associate professors* 2, *assistant professors* 5, *part-time faculty* 36.
Total instructional faculty: 52 (full-time 16, part-time 36; women 22, men 30; members of minority groups 9). Total faculty with doctorate, first-professional, or other terminal degree: 44.

Enrollment: Total enrollment 513.

Characteristics of Student Body: *Ethnic/racial makeup:* number of Black non-Hispanic: 36; American Indian or Native Alaskan: 1; Asian or Pacific Islander: 8; Hispanic: 15; White non-Hispanic: 403.

International Students: 14 nonresident aliens enrolled fall 2004. No programs available to aid students whose native language is not English. Financial aid specifically designated for international students: scholarships available annually.

Student Life: On-campus residence halls house 35% of student body. Housing available for married students. *Special regulations:* Cars permitted without restrictions. *Surrounding community:* Newton Centre population 84,000. Boston, 8 miles from campus, is nearest metropolitan area. Served by mass transit systems; airport 10 miles from campus; passenger rail service 8 miles from campus.

Publications: *Today's Ministry* (triennially) first published in 1950s; *Andover Newton Review* (annually).

Library Collections: 230,000 volumes. 10,300 microforms; 500 current periodical subscriptions. Students have access to online information retrieval services.

Most important special holdings include Isaac Backus Manuscripts; Jonathan Edwards Manuscripts; New England Baptist Library.

Buildings and Grounds: Campus area 87 acres.

Chief Executive Officer: Dr. Nick Carter, President.

Address admission inquiries to Margaret Carroll, Director of Enrollment.

Anna Maria College

Sunset Lane
Paxton, Massachusetts 01612-1198
Tel: (508) 849-3360   **E-mail:** admission@annamaria.edu
Fax: (508) 849-3362   **Internet:** www.annamaria.edu

Institution Description: Anna Maria College (Anna Maria College for Women until 1973) is a private, independent, nonprofit college affiliated with the Roman Catholic Church. *Enrollment:* 1,108. *Degrees awarded:* Associate, baccalaureate, master's.

Member of Worcester Consortium for Higher Education.

Accreditation: *Regional:* NEASC. *Professional:* music, nursing, social work.

History: Established, chartered, and offered first instruction at postsecondary level 1946; awarded first degree 1949; men admitted 1973.

Institutional Structure: *Governing board:* Anna Maria College Board of Trustees. Extrainstitutional representation: 26 trustees; institutional representation: 1 administrator, 10 alumni, 2 ex officio. 26 voting. *Composition of institution:* Administrators 2 men / 3 women. Academic affairs headed by dean of the college. Management/business/finances directed by chief business officer. Full-time instructional faculty 36. Academic governance body, the Faculty Assembly, meets 10 times per year.

Calendar: Semesters. Academic year Sept. to May. Freshmen admitted Sept., Jan. Degrees conferred May. Formal commencement May. Summer session of 2 terms from late May to mid-June (1st term), mid-June to early Aug. (2nd term).

Characteristics of Freshmen: Ave Maria does not place qualification on rank as not all secondary schools provide ranking information. SAT range 850 to 1000. 74% of freshmen from Massachusetts. Freshmen from 11 states and 5 foreign countries.

Admission: Rolling admissions plan. For fall acceptance, apply no later than July 15. Apply by Nov. 1 for early decision; need not limit application to Anna Maria. *Requirements:* Either 16 secondary school units including 4 English 3 units in math, 2 units in social science, and 1 unit in laboratory science or GED. Additional college preparatory courses recommended. *Entrance tests:* College Board SAT or ACT. *For transfer students:* 2.0 minimum GPA; 60 hours maximum transfer credit.

Advanced placement for postsecondary-level work completed in secondary school accepted upon receipt of completed AP test results. College credit for extrainstitutional learning on basis of ACE *2006 Guide to the Evaluation of Educational Experiences in the Armed Services*; portfolio and faculty assessment; personal interview.

Degree Requirements: *For all associate degrees:* 60 credit hours. *For all baccalaureate degrees:* 40 3-credit courses. *For all undergraduate degrees:* 2.0 minimum GPA. Some undergraduate degree requirements (up to 50%) can be fulfilled by taking achievement tests. Exemption from elementary and intermediate language courses, general biology, and mathematics possible by passing College Board CLEP offered before matriculation. *Grading system:* A–F; pass-fail (elective courses only); withdraw (deadline after which pass-fail is appended to withdrawal).

Distinctive Educational Programs: *For undergraduates:* Interdisciplinary programs in business/art, business/music, business/management information systems, education/human growth and development. Senior honors program. Study in Europe. *Available to all students:* off-campus sites for criminal justice program (bachelor's and master's), business administration (bachelor's and master's), and and fire science (bachelor's and master's). Evening classes. Special facilities for using telecommunications in the classroom. Study abroad in Quebec, Canada, and Spain. *For graduate students:* Weekend classes. Accelerated degree programs.

ROTC: Army offered in cooperation with Worcester Polytechnic Institute; Air Force in cooperation with College of the Holy Cross.

Degrees Conferred: 2 *associate;* 207 *baccalaureate* (B), 170 *master's:* biological/life sciences 2 (B); business/marketing 29 (B), 35 (M); education 12 (B), 38 (M); English 3 (B); health professions and related sciences 19 (B); law/legal studies 4 (B); liberal arts/general studies 17 (B); natural resources/environmental science 4 (B), 2 (M); protective services/public administration 91 (B), 15 (M); psychology 10 (B), 13 (M); visual and performing arts 12 (B); other 4 (B), 7 (M). *Honorary degrees awarded 2004–05:* Doctor of Humane Letters 3. Humane Letters 1.

Fees and Other Expenses: *Full-time tuition per academic year 2005–06:* $19,900 undergraduate, graduate $1,150 per 3-credit course. *Required fees:* $1,780. *Room and board per academic year:* $8,035.

Financial Aid: Aid from institutionally generated funds is provided on the basis of academic merit, financial need. Institution has a Program Participation Agreement with the U.S. Department of Education for eligible students to receive Pell Grants and other federal aid.

Financial aid to full-time, first-time undergraduate students: need-based scholarships/grants totaling $4,660,614, self-help $2,888,270, parent loans $517,537, tuition waivers $88,343; non-need-based scholarships/grants totaling $569,454, self-help $1,167,840, parent loans $445,332, tuition waivers 104,522. *Graduate aid:* 128 students received federal and state-funded loans totaling $726,797 (ranging from $100 to $18,500).

Departments and Teaching Staff: *Total instructional faculty:* 152 (full-time 33, part-time 119; women 73, men 83). Total faculty with doctorate, first-professional, or other terminal degree 22. Student-to-faculty ratio: 13:1.

Enrollment: Total enrollment 1,108. Undergraduate full-time 196 men / 356 women, part-time 85m / 107w; graduate full-time 25m / 61w, part-time 97m / 181w. *Transfer students:* in-state 17; from out-of-state 5.

Characteristics of Student Body: *Ethnic/racial makeup:* number of Black non-Hispanic: 18; American Indian or Alaska Native: 3; Asian or Pacific Islander: 8; Hispanic: 19; White non-Hispanic: 534; unknown: 757. *Age distri-*

bution: number under 18: 1; 18–19: 275; 20–21: 211; 22–24: 77; 25–29: 27; 30–34: 221 35–39: 33; 40–49: 60;50–64: 26.

International Students: 11 nonresident aliens enrolled fall 2004. 3 students from Europe, 2 Asia, 1 Central and South America, Africa 4, 1 Canada. Programs available to aid students whose native language is not English: English as a Second Language Program. No financial aid specifically designated for international students.

Student Life: On-campus coed residence halls house 346 full-time undergraduate students. *Intercollegiate athletics:* men only: baseball; women only: field hockey, softball, volleyball; both sexes: basketball, cross-country, golf, soccer. *Special regulations:* Residence visitation Sun.-Thurs. 8am to 11pm, Fri.-Sat. 8am to 1am. *Special services:* Medical services; two 12-passenger vans operate 7:30am to 7:30pm Mon.–Fri. *Surrounding community:* Worcester population 162,000. Boston, 41 miles from campus, is nearest metropolitan area. Served by mass transit system; airport 4 miles from campus.

Library Collections: 76,000 volumes. Online catalog. 1,525 microform titles; 285 current periodical subscriptions; 3,500 recordings/tapes. 57 computer work stations. Students have access to online information retrieval services and the Internet.

Buildings and Grounds: Campus area 180 acres. *New buildings:* addition to the Miriam Arts Building.

Chief Executive Officer: Dr. William McGarry, President.

Address admission inquiries to Julie Mitchell, Director of Admission.

Assumption College

500 Salisbury Street
Worcester, Massachusetts 01609-0005

Tel: (508) 767-7000   **E-mail:** admiss@assumption.edu
Fax: (508) 756-1780   **Internet:** www.assumption.edu

Institution Description: Assumption College is a private college affiliated with the Augustinians of the Assumption (Roman Catholic Church). *Enrollment:* 2,452. *Degrees awarded:* Baccalaureate, master's. Post-master's (certificate of advanced graduate study) awarded. Associate awarded through center for continuing and professional education.

Member of Worcester Consortium for Higher Education, Inc.

Accreditation: *Regional:* NEASC. *Professional:* rehabilitation counseling

History: Established and incorporated as Trustees of Assumption College, a men's institution, 1904; offered first instruction at postsecondary level 1911; chartered 1917; awarded first degree (baccalaureate) 1918; adopted graduate program 1950; adopted present name 1968; became coeducational 1969.

Institutional Structure: *Governing board:* Board of Trustees. Extrainstitutional representation: 32 trustees; 11 representatives of the Augustinians of the Assumption (including provincial of the North American Province); institutional representation: president of the college, 1 member of the Augustinians of the Assumption. 2 ex officio. All voting. *Composition of institution:* Administrators 140 full-time, 14 part-time. Academic affairs headed by provost. Management/business/finances directed by vice president for administration and finance. Full-time instructional faculty 116. Academic governance body, Faculty Representative Senate, meets an average of 10 times per year.

Calendar: Semesters. Academic year Aug to May. Freshmen admitted Aug., Jan. Degrees conferred and formal commencement May. Summer session.

Characteristics of Freshmen: 74% of applicants accepted. 30.5% of accepted applicants enrolled.

99% (632 students) submitted SAT scores; 19% (120 students) submitted ACT scores. *25th percentile:* SAT Verbal 490, SAT Math 500; ACT Composite 19, ACT English 18, ACT Math 19. *75th percentile:* SAT Verbal 590, SAT Math 590; ACT Composite 25, ACT English 24, ACT Math 26.

69% of entering freshmen expected to graduate within 5 years. 17% of freshmen from Massachusetts. Freshmen from 20 states and 9 foreign countries.

Admission: Rolling admissions plan. For fall acceptance, apply as early as Sept. 1 of previous year, but not later than Mar. 1 of year of enrollment. Apply by Nov. 1 for early decision; must limit application to Assumption College Early acceptance available. *Requirements:* Either graduation from accredited secondary school with 17 academic units or GED. Recommend 4 units English, 2 in a foreign language, 2 mathematics, 2 history, 2 science, 5 academic electives. *Entrance tests:* College Board SAT or ACT composite. *For transfer students:* From 4-year accredited institution 2.5 minimum GPA; from 2-year accredited institution 2.75 minimum GPA; 60 semester hours maximum transfer credit; correspondence/extension students 30 hours.

College credit and advanced placement for postsecondary-level work completed in secondary school and for USAFI/DANTES. Tutoring available. Noncredit remedial courses offered during regular academic year.

Degree Requirements: *For all baccalaureate degrees:* 120 semester hours; 2.0 GPA; 30 hours in residence; distribution requirements; 4 courses in philosophy and religious studies. Fulfillment of some degree requirements possible by passing departmental examinations, ACT, APP. Exemption from some beginning courses possible by passing International Baccalaureate. *Grading system:* A–F; pass-fail; withdraw (carries time limit); incomplete.

Distinctive Educational Programs: Internships. Evening classes. Accelerated degree programs. Dual-degree program in engineering with Worcester Polytechnic Institute. Cooperative baccalaureate in medical technology with approved hospitals. Interdisciplinary programs in community studies, foundations of western civilizations, Native American studies, developing countries studies, Latin American studies, women's studies. Facilities and programs for independent research, including individual majors, directed study. Study abroad in Australia, Austria, Czechoslovakia, England, France, Greece, Ireland, Italy, Netherlands, Spain. Cross-registration through consortium. *Other distinctive programs:* Certificate, degree, and nondegree programs available through Center for Continuing and Professional Education. Ecumenical Institute of Religious Studies.

ROTC: Air Force in cooperation with Worcester Polytechnic Institute.

Degrees Conferred: 11 *associate;* 437 *baccalaureate* (B), 104 *master's* (M): biological sciences 17 (B); business and management 104 (B), 30 (M); communications 27 (B); computer and information sciences 9 (B); education 23 (M); English 25 (B); foreign languages and literature 9 (B); health professions 48 (M); mathematics 8 (B); philosophy 4, physical sciences 7 (B); psychology 38 (B); social sciences and history 123 (B); theology 2 (B); other 6 (B), 3 (M).

Fees and Other Expenses: *Full-time tuition per academic year 2004–05:* $23,930. *Required fees:* $415. *Room and board per academic year:* $8,780.

Financial Aid: Aid from institutionally generated funds is provided on the basis of academic merit, financial need, athletic ability, other criteria.

Financial aid to full-time, first-time undergraduate students: need-based scholarships/grants totaling $16,304,447, self-help $8,665,130, parent loans 2,102,000, tuition waivers $355,136, athletic awards $58,253; non-need-based scholarships/grants totaling $3,643,245, self-help $3,289,121, parent loans $4,101,434, tuition waivers $482,704, athletic awards $430,549.

Departments and Teaching Staff: *Total instructional faculty:* 217 (full-time 132, part-time 85; women 93, men 124; members of minority groups 9). Total faculty with doctorate, first-professional, or other terminal degree: 167. Student-to-faculty ratio: 13:1. Degrees held by full-time faculty: doctorate 80%, master's 20%. 92% hold terminal degrees.

Enrollment: Total enrollment 2,452. Undergraduate full-time 860 men / 1,305 women, part-time 11m / 8w; graduate full-time 12m / 89w, part-time 44m / 123w.

Characteristics of Student Body: *Ethnic/racial makeup:* number of Black non-Hispanic: 22; American Indian or Alaska Native: 1; Asian or Pacific Islander: 27; Hispanic: 40; White non-Hispanic: 1,840; unknown: 234.

International Students: Programs available to aid students whose native language is not English: social, cultural. No financial aid specifically designated for international students.

Student Life: On-campus residence halls house 89% of student body. Residence hall for men constitute 41%, for women 59%. *Intercollegiate athletics:* men only: baseball, basketball, crew, cross-country, football, golf, hockey, lacrosse, soccer, tennis, track; women only: basketball, crew, cross-country, field hockey, soccer, softball, lacrosse, tennis, track, volleyball. *Special regulations:* Freshmen not permitted cars on campus. Quiet hours set by residents in individual halls. *Special services:* Learning Resources Center, medical services, shuttle bus sponsored by consortium. *Student publications: The Heights,* a yearbook; *The Phoenix,* a biannual literary publication; *Le Provocateur,* a newspaper published 7 times per year. *Surrounding community:* Worcester population 165,000. Boston, 45 miles from campus, is nearest metropolitan area. Served by mass transit system; airport 4 miles from campus.

Library Collections: 185,000 volumes. 8,250 microforms; 1,120 current periodical subscriptions; 48 microform subscriptions. 220 compact discs. Online catalog. Computer work stations available. Students have access to online information retrieval services and the Internet.

Most important special holdings include Ecumenical Institute of Religious Studies; French Literature.

Buildings and Grounds: Campus area 175 acres. *New buildings:* West Hall (residence) completed 2001; Information Technology Building 2002; Testa Science Building 2003.

Chief Executive Officer: Dr. Thomas R. Plough, President.

Address admission inquiries to Kathleen Murphy, Dean of Enrollment; graduate inquiries to Adrian M. Dumas, Director of Graduate Enrollment Management and Services.

Atlantic Union College

338 Main Street
P.O. Box 1000
South Lancaster, Massachusetts 01561-1000
Tel: (978) 368-2000   **E-mail:** enroll@atlanticuc.edu
Fax: (978) 368-2015   **Internet:** www.atlanticuc.edu

Institution Description: Atlantic Union College is a private college affiliated with the Seventh-day Adventist Church. *Enrollment:* 486. *Degrees awarded:* Associate, baccalaureate, master's.

Accreditation: *Regional:* NEASC. *Professional:* music, nursing, social work, teacher education

History: Established as That New England School 1882; incorporated as South Lancaster Academy 1883; offered first instruction at postsecondary level and changed name to Lancaster Junior College 1918; adopted present name 1922; awarded first degree (baccalaureate) 1923. *See* Rowena Purdon, *That New England School,* (Lancaster: The College Press, 1956) and Myron F. Wehtje, *And There Was Light* (South Lancaster: Atlantic Press, 1962) for further information.

Institutional Structure: *Governing board:* Atlantic Union College Board of Trustees. Extrainstitutional representation: 30 trustees, including president of Atlantic Union Conference of Seventh-day Adventists, 16 denominational representatives, 7 alumni; institutional representation: president of the college, 2 ex officio. All voting. *Composition of institution:* Administrators 3 men / 2 women. Academic affairs headed by Vice President of Academic Affairs. Management/business/finances directed by Vice President of Finance. Full-time instructional faculty 40. Academic governance body, Academic Affairs Committee, meets an average of 18 times per year.

Calendar: Semesters. Academic year early Aug. to May. Freshmen admitted Aug., Jan., June. Degrees conferred at formal commencements May, July, Jan. Summer session of 3 terms from mid-May to mid-Aug.

Characteristics of Freshmen: Mean ACT composite score 21. Freshmen from 22 states and 9 foreign countries.

Admission: Rolling admissions plan. For fall acceptance, apply as early as 9 months, but not later than 1 month, prior to registration. Early acceptance available. *Requirements:* Either graduation from secondary school or GED. College preparatory curriculum recommended. Minimum 2.0 GPA. *Entrance tests:* ACT composite. For foreign students TOEFL. *For transfer students:* From 4-year accredited institution maximum transfer credit limited only by residence requirement; from 2-year accredited institution 72 hours; correspondence/extension students 12 hours.

College credit and advanced placement for postsecondary-level work completed in secondary school. College credit for extrainstitutional learning on basis of ACE *2006 Guide to the Evaluation of Educational Experiences in the Armed Services*; portfolio and faculty assessments through Adult Degree Program. Tutoring available. Remedial courses offered during regular academic year.

Degree Requirements: *For all associate degrees:* 64 credit hours. *For all baccalaureate degrees:* 128 credit hours; distribution requirements. *For Master of Education degree:* 33 credit hours; distribution requirements, 2.0 GPA. *For master's degrees:* 3.0 GPA. *For all degrees:* 2.0 GPA; 2 terms in residence; weekly chapel attendance; 3 physical education courses.

Fulfillment of some degree requirements and exemption from some beginning courses possible by passing departmental examinations, College Board CLEP, APP (score of 3), International Baccalaureate (score of 4). *Grading system:* A–F; pass-fail; withdraw (carries time limit); incomplete (carries time limit).

Distinctive Educational Programs: Evening classes. Honors programs. Summer Advantage programs. Study abroad in Austria, France, Spain, through Adventist Colleges Abroad. *Other distinctive programs:* English Language Institute. Certificate, degree, accelerated and non-degree programs through the Center for Continuing Education including baccalaureate programs for registered nurses. Adult Degree Program combines self-directed study at home with 2 weeks on campus each semester for students 25 years of age or over. Work-experience programs, including field activities and internships. The Preparatory School of Music at Thayer Conservatory.

Degrees Conferred: 21 *associate*; 106 *baccalaureate*; 17 *master's*. Bachelor's degrees awarded in top five disciplines: health professions and related clinical sciences 17; psychology 13; business, management, marketing, and related support services 12; liberal arts and sciences, general studies, and humanities 12; philosophy and religious studies 11.

Fees and Other Expenses: *Full-time tuition per academic year 2004–05:* $12,780. *Books and supplies:* $1,000. *Room and board per academic year:* $4,700.

Financial Aid: Aid from institutionally generated funds is provided on the basis of academic merit, financial need, athletic ability, other criteria. Institution

has a Program Participation Agreement with the U.S. Department of Education for eligible students to receive Pell Grants and other federal aid.

Financial aid to full-time, first-time undergraduate students: 68% received federal grants averaging $2,870; 18% state/local grants averaging $1,000; 79% institutional grants averaging $1,575; 57% received loans averaging $1,955.

Departments and Teaching Staff: *Professors* 17, *associate professors* 11, *assistant professors* 11, *instructors* 1, *part-time faculty:* 24. *Total instructional faculty:* 64. Degrees held by full-time faculty: 60% hold terminal degrees.

Enrollment: Total enrollment 486. Undergraduate 468 (40% men, 60% women).

Characteristics of Student Body: *Ethnic/racial makeup* Black non-Hispanic: 40.8%; Asian or Pacific Islander: 1.7%; Hispanic: 17.3%; White non-Hispanic: 13.9%; unknown: 14.3%.

International Students: Programs available to aid students whose native language is not English: social, cultural, financial. English as a Second Language Program.

Student Life: On-campus residence halls house 50% of student body. Residence halls for men constitute 40% of such space, for women only 60%. Housing available for married students. 75% of married students request institutional housing; 40% are so housed. 62% of students live on campus. *Special regulations:* Cars must be registered. *Special services:* Learning Resources Center, medical services. *Student publications: Campus Clatter*, a student and faculty directory; *The Lancastrian*, a monthly newspaper; *The Minuteman*, a yearbook. *Surrounding community:* South Lancaster, unincorporated, located in Worcester County, population 650,000. Boston, 40 miles from campus, is nearest metropolitan area.

Library Collections: 173,000 volumes including bound books, serial backfiles, electronic documents, and government documents not in separate collections. Online catalog. Current serial subscriptions: 585 paper, 2 microform. 15,000 microform units; 4,500 audiovisual materials. 15 computer work stations. Students have access to the Internet at no charge.

Most important special holdings include Ottilie Stafford Poetry Collection of 20th Century American and British poets; 700 titles in the African Studies Collection; 3,000 titles by or about Seventh-day Adventists.

Buildings and Grounds: Campus area 135 acres.

Chief Executive Officer: Dr. George P. Babcock, President.

Address admission inquiries to Rosita E. Ashley, Director of Admissions.

Babson College

231 Forest Street
Babson Park
Wellesley, Massachusetts 02157-0310
Tel: (781) 239-5522   **E-mail:** ugradadmission@babson.edu
Fax: (781) 239-4006   **Internet:** www.babson.edu

Institution Description: Babson College is a private, independent institution. *Enrollment:* 3,352. *Degrees awarded:* Baccalaureate, master's.
Member of Wellesley-Lexington Cooperating Libraries.

Accreditation: *Regional:* NEASC. *Professional:* business

History: Established as Babson Institute and offered first instruction 1919; incorporated 1923; awarded first degree (baccalaureate) 1947; became coeducational 1968; changed name to Babson College 1969.

Institutional Structure: *Governing board:* Babson Members of the Corporation and Trustees. Extrainstitutional representation: 29 trustees, 71 members of the corporation. 8 ex officio. *Composition of institution:* Administrators 9 men / 2 women. Academic affairs headed by vice president for academic affairs. Management/business/finances directed by vice president for business and financial affairs. Full-time instructional faculty 159. Academic governance body, the faculty and trustees, meet an average of 7 times per year.

Calendar: Semesters. Academic year early Sept. to early May. Freshmen admitted Sept., Jan. Degrees conferred May, Sept., Dec. Formal commencement May. Summer session from mid-May to mid-Aug.

Characteristics of Freshmen: 3,064 applicants (3,064 men, 2,051 women). 36.7% of applicants admitted. 37.9% of admitted students enrolled full-time.

96% (410 students) submitted SAT scores. *25th percentile:* SAT I Verbal 520, SAT I Math 570. *75th percentile:* SAT I Verbal 620, SAT I Math 680.

81% of entering freshmen expected to graduate within 5 years. 34% of freshmen from Massachusetts. Freshmen from 30 states and 41 foreign countries.

Admission: Application for undergraduate admission must be filed before Feb. 1 of the candidate's final year of secondary school. Students are notified of acceptance on Apr. 1. Early decision plan is available and all required credentials for early decision must be received by the Undergraduate Admission Office before Dec. 1. *Requirements:* Either graduation from accredited secondary school with 16 units which must include 4 English, 3 in mathematics, (algebra I, algebra II, and geometry), 2 in social studies, and 1 in laboratory science; or GED. Strongly recommend a 4th year of mathematics and remaining electives in additional science courses, languages, and other college preparatory courses. *For transfer students:* From 4-year and junior community colleges, 64 hours maximum transfer credit.

College credit and advanced placement for Advanced Placement (AP) of the College Board, and CLEP. Advanced placement for work/life experience on basis of faculty assessment. Tutoring available.

Degree Requirements: *For all baccalaureate degrees:* 128 credit hours with 64 in liberal arts; 2.0 GPA; last 32 hours must be taken in residence. Fulfillment of some degree requirements (up to 64 hours) and exemption from beginning English, mathematics, and science courses possible by passing departmental exams and CLEP. *Grading system:* A–F; withdraw.

Distinctive Educational Programs: *Available to all students:* Work-experience programs. Special facilities for using telecommunications equipment in the classroom. Interdepartmental/interdisciplinary programs in entrepreneurial studies. Study abroad programs in Argentina, Australia, Austria, Chile, Czech Republic, England, France, Ireland, Italy, Japan, Monaco, The Netherlands, New Zealand, Russia, Scotland, South Africa, Spain. Semester at Sea Program. Tutorials. Cluster courses. All first-year students participate in starting and running a business; self-designed concentrations. *Available to graduate students:* Evening courses. Facilities and programs for independent research in international business. Concentration in international studies.

Degrees Conferred: 469 *baccalaureate;* 572 *master's.* Bachelor's degrees awarded: business, management, marketing, and related support services.

Fees and Other Expenses: *Full-time tuition per academic year 2004–05:* $28,832. *Room and board per academic year:* $10,376.

Financial Aid: Aid from institutionally generated funds is provided on the basis of academic merit, financial need. Institution has a Program Participation Agreement with the U.S. Department of Education for eligible students to receive Pell Grants and other federal aid.

Financial aid to full-time, first-time undergraduate students: 12% received federal grants averaging $4,032; 17% state/local grants averaging $1,649; 46% institutional grants averaging $16,667; 42% received loans averaging $4,980.

Departments and Teaching Staff: Accounting/law *professors* 4, *associate professors* 10, *assistant professors* 4, *instructors* 1, *part-time teachers* 1; arts and humanities 5, 4, 3, 0, 13; economics 2, 5, 5, 1, 5; entrepreneurship 2, 2, 4, 1, 7; finance 1, 4, 9, 2, 3; finance 1, 4, 9, 2, 3; history and society 3, 5, 7, 0, 7; management 5, 11, 9, 5, 6; marketing 4, 5, 6, 3, 4; mathematics/science 5, 11, 5, 3, 9.

Total instructional faculty: 174.33 FTE. Student-to-faculty ratio: 11:1. Degrees held by full-time faculty: doctorate 88%, master's 8%, professional 4%. 92% hold terminal degrees.

Enrollment: Total enrollment 3,352. Undergraduate 1,028 men / 689 women; graduate full-time 1,168m / 467w.

Characteristics of Student Body: *Ethnic/racial makeup:* number of Black non-Hispanic: 59; American Indian or Native Alaskan: 7; Asian or Pacific Islander: 191; Hispanic: 95; White non-Hispanic 1,781. *Age distribution:* 17–21: 47%; 228+24: 3%; 25–29: 26%; 30–34: 16%; 35–39: 5%; 40–49: 3%.

International Students: 483 nonresident aliens enrolled fall 2004. Students from Europe, Asia, Central and South America, Africa, Canada, Australia. No programs available to aid students whose native language is not English. No financial aid specifically designated for international students.

Student Life: On-campus residence halls house 85% of student body. Residence halls for men constitute 21% of such space, for women 9%, for both sexes 70%. College-controlled rental apartments house 5% of the student body (graduate students). 15% of student body live off-campus. Housing available for married students. *Intercollegiate athletics:* men only: baseball, basketball, golf, ice hockey, squash; women only: field hockey, softball, volleyball; both sexes: basketball, cross-country running, lacrosse, skiing, soccer, swimming, tennis. *Special regulations:* Cars permitted with parking stickers. *Special services:* Learning Resources Center, counseling and medical services, van service to off-campus housing. *Student publications: Babson Bulletin* a quarterly alumni magazine; *Babson Free Press,* a weekly student newspaper; *Babsonian,* the yearbook. *Surrounding community:* Nearby Wellesley population 27,000. Boston, 10 miles from campus, is the nearest metropolitan area. Served by subway, bus, trolley systems. Airport is 10 miles from campus; passenger rail service available.

Library Collections: 132,500 volumes. 346,950 microforms; 4,650 audiovisual materials; 510 periodicals. Computer work stations available. Students have access to online information retrieval services and the Internet.

Most important special holdings include Isaac Newton Collection; Roger Babson Collection.

Buildings and Grounds: Campus area 450 acres.

Chief Executive Officer: Brian M. Barefoot, President.

Address admission inquiries to Admissions Office.

Bay Path College

588 Longmeadow Street
Longmeadow, Massachusetts 01106
Tel: (413) 565-1000   **E-mail:** admiss@baypath.edu
Fax: (413) 567-0501   **Internet:** www.baypath.edu

Institution Description: Bay Path College is an independent four-year college for women. *Enrollment:* 1,417. *Degrees awarded:* Associate, baccalaureate.

Accreditation: *Regional:* NEASC. *Professional:* occupational therapy

History: Founded 1897 as Bay Path Institute in Springfield; moved to present campus 1945; chartered as Bay Path Junior College and present name adopted 1988.

Institutional Structure: *Governing board:* Extrainstitutional representation: 28 trustees; institutional representation: 3 administrators. *Composition of institution:* Administrators 6 men / 18 women. Academic affairs headed by academic dean. Management/business/finances directed by treasurer. Full-time instructional faculty 21. Academic governance body, the Faculty, meets 9 times per year.

Calendar: Semesters. Academic year early Sept. to early May. Freshmen admitted Sept., Jan. Degrees conferred Jan., May. Formal commencement May. Two summer sessions of six-weeks each.

Characteristics of Freshmen: Average secondary school rank 73rd percentile. Mean SAT score 480 verbal,455 mathematical.

77% of applicants accepted. 37% of accepted applicants enrolled.

61% of entering freshmen expected to graduate within five years. 43% of freshmen from Massachusetts. Freshmen from 7 states and 7 foreign countries.

Admission: *Requirements:* For Sept. enrollment, Dec. 1 is application deadline for early decision consideration, with notification by Dec. 15 and candidate's reply by May 1. Standard admission deadline Mar. 15 for application, Apr. 1 for notification, and May 1 for candidate's reply. After Mar. 15, applications accepted on a rolling admission basis. Entrance recommendations for bachelor's degree: present a minimum of 4 academic courses each year; courses include 4 years English, 2 foreign language, 3 mathematics (algebra I and II, geometry), and 2 or more years of laboratory science, and 2 or more of social studies. SAT or ACT.

College credit and advanced placement for postsecondary-level work completed in secondary school and for extrainstitutional learning on basis of ACE *2006 Guide to the Evaluation of Educational Experiences in the Armed Services.* Developmental/remedial courses offered in summer session and regular academic year; credit given.

Degree Requirements: *For all associate degrees:* minimum of 60 credits. *For all undergraduate degrees:* minimum of 120 credits. *Grading system:* A-F; passfail; withdrawal prior to the date designated in the calendar for that particular semester.

Distinctive Educational Programs: Academic Development Center; Assessment Activities; Bay Path Scholars Program; Capitals of the World; Career Exploration Semester; Career Workshop; College Preschool; Community Service credit; computer laboratories; cross-registration with the Cooperating Colleges of Greater Springfield; Directed Study; English and Mathematics Remediation; English as a Second Language Program.

Degrees Conferred: 89 *associate;* 187 *baccalaureate:* business/marketing 101; computer and information sciences 4; health professions and related sciences 7; law/legal studies 11; liberal arts/general studies 41; psychology 23. 49 *master's:* communication/communication technologies 44 (M); health professions and related clinical sciences 5.

Fees and Other Expenses: *Full-time tuition per academic year 2004–05:* $19,440 undergraduate, $18,288 graduate. *Room and board per academic year:* $18,260.

Financial Aid: Aid from institutionally generated funds is provided on the basis of academic merit, financial need.

Financial aid to full-time, first-time undergraduate students: need-based scholarships/grants totaling $6,556,248, self-help $6,107,605, parent loans $905,020, tuition waivers $47,575; non-need-based scholarships/grants totaling $715,201, self-help $2,426,457, parent loans $583,915, tuition waivers $15,745. *Graduate aid:* 58 students received federal and state-funded loans totaling $609,383 (ranging from $3,048 to $18,500).

Departments and Teaching Staff: *Professors* 12, *associate professors* 6, *assistant professors* 13, *instructors* 3, *part-time faculty* 150.

Total instructional faculty: 187 (full-time 34, part-time 153; women 114, men 73; members of minority groups 7). Total faculty with doctorate, first-professional, or other terminal degree: 65. Student-to-faculty ratio: 8:1.

Enrollment: Total enrollment 1,417. Undergraduate full-time 11,00 women, part-time 247 women; graduate full-time 10m / 48w, part-time 2m / 10w.

Characteristics of Student Body: *Ethnic/racial makeup:* number of Black non-Hispanic: 149; American Indian or Alaska Native: 6; Asian or Pacific Islander: 14; Hispanic: 96; White non-Hispanic: 1,067. *Age distribution:* number under 18: 14; 18–19: 257; 20–21: 211; 22–24: 130; 25–29: 185; 30–34: 163; 35–39: 142; 40–49: 200; 50–64: 45.

International Students: 16 nonresident aliens enrolled fall 2004. 7 students from Asia, 2 Africa, 7 other. Programs available to aid students whose native language is not English: English as a Second Language Program.

Student Life: 23 Social organizations open to all students. Student Government, Theatre Club, Golden Z Service Club, Phi Beta Lambda, Law Club. 24-hour emergency response devices and patrols; late-night transport-escort service; controlled dormitory access. Freshmen guaranteed college housing. *Intercollegiate athletics:* basketball, golf, soccer, softball, tennis. Intramural bowling, equestrian sports, field hockey, golf, lacrosse, skiing, soccer, softball, swimming and diving, ping-pong, tennis, volleyball.

Library Collections: 54,929 volumes. 3,100 microforms; 2,540 audiovisual materials; 118 periodical subscriptions. Students have access to online information retrieval services and the Internet. Total 2004–05 budget for materials and operations: $94,494.

Most important special holdings include business, psychology, legal studies.

Buildings and Grounds: Campus area 32 acres.

Chief Executive Officer: Dr. Carol A. Leary, President.

Address admissions inquiries to Lisa Casassa, Director of Admissions; graduate inquiries to Diane Ronald, Dean of Graduate and Continuing Education.

Bentley College

175 Forest Street

Waltham, Massachusetts 02154-4705

Tel: (781) 891-2000   **E-mail:** ugadmission@bentley.edu
Fax: (781) 891-2569   **Internet:** www.bentley.edu

Institution Description: Bentley College is a private, independent, nonprofit institution. *Enrollment:* 5,554. *Degrees awarded:* Baccalaureate, master's.

Accreditation: *Regional:* NEASC. *Professional:* business

History: Established in Boston as Bentley School of Accounting and Finance 1917; offered first instruction at postsecondary level 1917; incorporated 1948; changed name to Bentley College of Accounting and Finance 1961; awarded first degree (baccalaureate) 1964; moved to Waltham 1968; adopted present name 1971.

Institutional Structure: *Governing board:* Board of Trustees. Extrainstitutional representation: 34 trustees. All voting. *Composition of institution:* Administrators President, academic vice president/provost, vice president for administration and finance, vice president for student affairs, vice president for institutional advancement, vice president for information services. 3 academic deans, 16 academic department chairs. Full-time instructional faculty 224. Senate meets an average of 18 times per year.

Calendar: Semesters. Academic year Sept. to May. Freshmen admitted Jan., May, June, Sept. Degrees conferred May, Oct., Feb. Formal commencement May. Summer session of 2 terms from mid-May to mid-Aug.

Characteristics of Freshmen: 45% of applicants admitted. 16% of applicants admitted and enrolled.

92% (850 students) submitted SAT scores; 15% (144 students) submitted ACT scores. *25th percentile:* SAT Verbal 540, SAT Math 580; ACT Composite 23. *75th percentile:* SAT Verbal 620, SAT Math 660; ACT Composite 27.

75% of freshmen expected to graduate within 5 years. 46% of freshmen from Massachusetts. Freshmen from 24 states and 29 foreign countries.

Admission: For fall acceptance, apply as early as Sept. 1, but not later than Mar. 10. Students are notified of acceptance by Apr. 1. Apply by Dec. 1 for early decision; must limit application to Bentley. Early acceptance available. *Requirements:* Either 16 secondary school units which must include 4 English, 3 mathematics (including 2 algebra and 1 geometry), 2 social studies, 1 laboratory science, and 6 electives; or GED. Lowest acceptable secondary school class standing 40th percentile. *Entrance tests:* College Board SAT or ACT composite. *For transfer students:* 75 hours maximum transfer credit.

Advanced standing available through CLEP and Advanced Placement tests. Tutoring available. Noncredit developmental courses offered during regular academic year.

Degree Requirements: *For all baccalaureate degrees:* 120 credit hours; 2.0 GPA; 1 year physical education for freshmen and matriculants. *For all undergraduate degrees:* 2 terms in residence.

Fulfillment of some degree requirements possible by passing College Board CLEP. *Grading system:* 1.0–4.0; pass-fail (for noncredit courses only); withdraw (deadline after which pass-fail is appended to withdraw).

Distinctive Educational Programs: *For undergraduates:* Day or evening classes. Work-experience internship programs. Interdepartmental/interdisciplinary majors in liberal arts. Dual-degree programs: BA/MSA, BS/MSAIS, BS/MSA. Service Learning Center. Extensive integration of computer use into all curricula; all full-time students assigned individual portable microcomputers. Individually arranged study abroad in several European and Far Eastern universities. The Office of International Programs offers study abroad programs in Australia, Austria, Bahrain, Belgium, England, Estonia, France, Germany, Hungary, Italy, Jamaica, Japan, Mexico, The Netherlands, Spain. Academic Learning Center. *For all students:* Special facilities for computer access. Supervised open learning laboratories for English/writing, mathematics/statistics, accounting, foreign languages, economics/finance. Facilities and programs for independent research, individual majors. Tutorials. Laptop computers required through Bentley Mobile Computing Program.

ROTC: Air Force offered in cooperation with Boston University.

Degrees Conferred: 11 *associate;* 1,037 *baccalaureate:* business/marketing 911; communications/communication technologies computer and information sciences 85; English 2; interdisciplinary studies 18; law/legal studies 8; liberal arts/general studies 5; mathematics 2; philosophy/religion/theology 1; social sciences and history 5. 447 *master's:* business/marketing 409; computer and information sciences 36.

Fees and Other Expenses: *Full-time tuition per academic year 2005–06:* $28,390. undergraduate, $21,864 graduate. *Required fees:* $224. *Room and board per academic year:* $10,170.

Financial Aid: Aid from institutionally generated funds is provided on the basis of academic merit, financial need, athletic ability. Institution has a Program Participation Agreement with the U.S. Department of Education for eligible students to receive Pell Grants and other federal aid.

Financial aid to full-time, first-time undergraduate students: need-based scholarships/grants totaling $31,001,412, self-help $12,951,975, parent loans $1,421,225; non-need-based scholarships/grants totaling $5,260,308, self-help $7,389,350, parent loans $7,207,569.

Departments and Teaching Staff: *Total instructional faculty:* 453 (full-time 265, part-time 188; women 168, men 285; members of minority groups 52). Total faculty with doctorate, first-professional, or other terminal degree: 287. Student-to-faculty ratio: 13:1. Degrees held by full-time faculty: doctorate 81.7%.

Enrollment: Total enrollment 5,554. Undergraduate full-time 2,303 men / 1,596 women, part-time 173m / 165w; graduate full-time 203m / 106w, part-time 518m / 410w. *Transfer students:* in-state 113; from out-of-state 72.

Characteristics of Student Body: *Ethnic/racial makeup:* number of Black non-Hispanic: 150; American Indian or Alaska Native: 5; Asian or Pacific Islander: 306; Hispanic: 170; White non-Hispanic: 2,946; unknown: 326. *Age distribution:* number under 18: 3; 18–19: 1,579; 20–21: 1,843; 22–24: 524; 25–29: 122; 30–34: 61; 35–39: 39; 40–49: 62; 50–64: 20.

International Students: 514 nonresident aliens enrolled fall 2004. Programs available to aid students whose native language is not English: social. English as a Second Language Program. No financial programs specifically designated for international students.

Student Life: On-campus residence halls house 74% of full-time undergraduates; half in dormitories and half in apartments. Some graduate apartments available to full-time students. *Intercollegiate athletics:* men only: baseball, basketball, football, golf, hockey, soccer, track; women only: basketball, field hockey, softball, volleyball; both sexes: cross-country. *Special services:* Learning Resources Center, medical services. *Student publications:* Vanguard, a weekly newspaper; *Vale,* a yearbook. *Student-operated radio:* Station WBTV. *Surrounding community:* Waltham population 58,000. Boston, 10 miles from campus, is nearest metropolitan area. Served by mass transit bus systems; airport 12 miles from campus; passenger rail service 2 miles from campus.

Publications: *Business Ethics Proceedings* (annually) first published 1978.

Library Collections: 136,094 volumes including bound books, serial backfiles, electronic documents, and government documents not in separate collections. Online catalog. Current serial subscriptions: 1,744 microform, Computer work stations available. Students have access to the Internet at no charge.

Most important special collections include Historical Accounting, Business History; Business Ethics.

Buildings and Grounds: Campus area 163 acres.

Chief Executive Officer: Dr. Joseph G. Morone, President.

Address undergraduate admission inquiries to Kenton W. Rinehart, Director of Undergraduate Admission; graduate admission inquiries to Sharon Hill, Director of Graduate Admissions.

Berklee College of Music

1140 Boylston Street
Boston, Massachusetts 02215-3693

Tel: (617) 266-1400   **E-mail:** admissions@berklee.edu
Fax: (617) 747-2047   **Internet:** www.berklee.edu

Institution Description: Berklee College of Music is a private institution. *Enrollment:* 3,882. *Degrees awarded:* Baccalaureate. Certificates and diplomas also awarded.

Accreditation: *Regional:* NEASC.

History: Established as Berklee School of Music 1945; offered first instruction at postsecondary level 1963; awarded first degree (baccalaureate) 1966; adopted present name 1970.

Institutional Structure: *Governing board:* Board of Trustees. Extrainstitutional representation: 13 trustees; institutional representation: president of the college. 1 ex officio. *Composition of institution:* Administrators 15 men / 4 women. Academic affairs headed by dean of the college. Management/business/finances directed by business officer. Full-time instructional faculty 145.

Calendar: Semesters. Academic year early Sept. to early May. Formal commencement May. Summer sessions: 5-week and 12-week sessions.

Characteristics of Freshmen: 70% of applicants accepted. 50% of accepted applicants enrolled.

22% of freshmen from Massachusetts. Freshmen from 50 states and 32 foreign countries.

Admission: *Requirements:* Graduation from accredited secondary school or preparatory school. Minimum of 2 years formal music study or significant musical experience, as well as basic theory knowledge. GED accepted. *Entrance tests:* College Board SAT or ACT composite. *For transfer students:* C-average; maximum transfer credit limited only by residence requirement.

Degree Requirements: 120–123 semester hours; 4 semesters in residence; core curriculum. Fulfillment of some degree requirements and exemption from some beginning courses possible by passing College Board CLEP. Exemption from courses also possible by passing institutional examinations. *Grading system:* A–F; no credit; withdraw.

Distinctive Educational Programs: 12-week Accelerated Summer Program. 5-week Performance Program (geared toward high school and college students). College is divided into 4 divisions: Performance, Writing (including arranging, composition and songwriting), General Education, and Technology (including music production and engineering, music synthesis and film scoring). International Jazz Program encourages worldwide information exchange about jazz. Community Services Ensemble Program performs free concerts for various community organizations. 4-year professional diploma or 2-year certificate programs available.

Degrees Conferred: 580 *baccalaureate:* visual and performing arts.

Fees and Other Expenses: *Full-time tuition per academic year 2004–05:* $20,450. *Room and board per academic year:* $10,900.

Financial Aid: Aid from institutionally generated funds is provided on the basis of academic merit, financial need, other criteria. Institution has a Program Participation Agreement with the U.S. Department of Education for eligible students to receive Pell Grants and other federal aid.

Financial aid to full-time, first-time undergraduate students: need-based scholarships/grants totaling $3,266,428, self-help $32,959,606; non-need-based scholarships/grants totaling $11,614,218, self-help $277,301, parent loans $12,780,316, tuition waivers $314,207.

Departments and Teaching Staff: *Total instructional faculty:* 482 (full-time 205, part-time 277; women 106, men 364; members of minority groups 73). Total faculty with doctorate, first-professional, or other terminal degree: 40. Degrees held by full-time faculty: 16% hold terminal degrees.

Enrollment: Total enrollment 3,882. Undergraduate full-time 2,673 men / 884 women, part-time 225m / 100w.

Characteristics of Student Body: *Ethnic/racial makeup:* number of Black non-Hispanic: 189; American Indian or Alaska Native: 18; Asian or Pacific Islander: 149; Hispanic: 191; White non-Hispanic: 2,141; unknown: 287. *Age distribution:* number under 18: 52, 18–19: 1,116, 20–21: 1,264; 22–24: 813; 25–29: 445; 30–34: 130; 35–39: 32; 40–49: 20; 50–64: 10.

International Students: 916 nonresident aliens enrolled fall 2004. Students from Europe, Asia, Central and South America, Africa, Canada, Australia, New Zealand. America, Africa, Canada, Australia, New Zealand. Programs available to aid students whose native language is not English: English as a Second Language Program. Some financial aid available for international students.

Student Life: 3 on-campus residence halls available. Freshmen under 21 usually recommended to live in a residence hall unless commuting from their own homes. *Surrounding community:* Boston metropolitan population over 3 million.

Served by mass transit bus and rail systems; airport 3 miles from campus; passenger rail service 1 mile from campus.

Library Collections: 41,739 volumes, primarily in the field of music. 18,000 scores, 8,000 jazz and pop recordings, 400 videos, 2,000 recordings of Berklee concerts and recitals; 153 current periodical subscriptions. Online catalog. Students have access to online information retrieval services and the Internet. Total 2004–05 budget for materials and operations $124,251.

Special holdings include an extensive lead sheet collection.

Chief Executive Officer: Roger H. Brown, President.

Address admission inquiries to Office of Admissions.

Blessed John XXIII National Seminary

558 South Avenue
Weston, Massachusetts 02493-2699

Tel: (781) 899-5500   **E-mail:** seminary@blessedjohnxxiii.edu
Fax: (781) 899-9057   **Internet:** www.blessedjohnxxiii.edu

Institution Description: Blessed John XXIII National Seminary, formerly named Pope John XXIII National Seminary, is a private institution of the Roman Catholic Church offering professional graduate study only. *Enrollment:* 70. *Degrees awarded:* First-professional, master's.

Accreditation: *National:* ATS. *Professional:* theology

Calendar: Semesters. Academic year Aug. to May.

Admission: *Requirements:* Bachelor's degree from an accredited college or university.

Degree Requirements: Completion of prescribed curriculum.

Degrees Conferred: 17 *first-professional:* master of divinity.

Fees and Other Expenses: *Full-time tuition per academic year:* Contact the seminary for current tuition and fees.

Financial Aid: Financial assistance is available in the form of Pell Grants, Veterans Administration Benefits, Supplemental Education Opportunity Grants (SEOG), Stafford Loans.

Enrollment: Total enrollment 70 (full-time 70).

Chief Executive Officer: Fr. Peter S. Uglietto, Rector/President.

Address admission inquiries to Admissions Office.

Boston Architectural Center

320 Newbury Street
Boston, Massachusetts 02115-2703

Tel: (617) 262-5000   **E-mail:** admissions@the-bac.edu
Fax: (617) 585-0111   **Internet:** www.the-bac.edu

Institution Description: The Boston Architectural Center is a private, independent, nonprofit institution whose principal purpose is to conduct schools of architecture and interior design offering baccalaureate and master's programs. Both programs consist of a unique concurrent curriculum comprised of practices and academic requirements. *Enrollment:* 1,048.

Accreditation: *Regional:* NEASC. *Professional:* architecture

History: Founded 1889; accredited 1971; awarded first degree 1978.

Institutional Structure: *Governing board:* The BAC Board of Directors approves policy and philosophy and employs the president who is the chief administrative officer. *Composition of institution:* Administrators 25 (responsible to the director of administration and the director of education).

Calendar: Semesters. Academic year early Sept. to mid-May. Summer session for makeup, acceleration, and for the interested public.

Characteristics of Freshmen: 95% of applicants accepted. 55% of accepted applicants enrolled. 53% of freshmen from Massachusetts. Freshmen from 21 states.

Admission: Open admission policy.

Degree Requirements: 123 academic credits; 54 work credits; 6-semester residency requirement; completed thesis; 2.5 GPA.

Distinctive Educational Programs: Summer program for high school students in architecture; full range of other continuing education courses.

Degrees Conferred: 27 *baccalaureate:* architecture and related services; 16 *master's:* environmental design.

Fees and Other Expenses: *Full-time tuition per academic year 2004–05:* $8,220 undergraduate; contact the center for current graduate tuition/fees. *Off-campus room and board:* $9,838 (varies depending on accommodations).

Financial Aid: Aid from institutionally generated funds is provided on the basis of financial need. Institution has a Program Participation Agreement with the U.S. Department of Education for eligible students to receive Pell Grants and other federal aid.

Departments and Teaching Staff: *Instructors* 275 (all part-time). *Total instructional faculty:* 275. Degrees held by faculty: doctorate 80%.

Enrollment: Total enrollment 1,048. Undergraduate 644 (56.1% men, 43.9% women).

Characteristics of Student Body: *Ethnic/racial makeup (undergraduate):* Black non-Hispanic: 1.2%; American Indian or Alaska Native: .2%; Asian or Pacific Islander: 2.2%; Hispanic: 2.2%; White non-Hispanic: 20.2%; unknown: .2%. *Age distribution:* 17–21: 7%; 22–24: 19%; 25–29: 38%; 30–34: 19%; 35–39: 9%' 40–49: 6%. 28% of total student body attend summer sessions.

International Students: No programs available to aid students whose native language is not English. No financial aid specifically designated for international students.

Student Life: There is no campus at the Boston Architectural Center. There is a student council (ATELIER) which is active and holds social functions. Students are invited to participate on all advisory committees of the School of Architecture.

Library Collections: 25,000 volumes. 140 current periodical subscriptions. Students have access to online information retrieval services and the Internet.

Buildings and Grounds: Campus area one 6-story building in the city of Boston.

Chief Executive Officer: Dr. Theodore Landsmark, President.

Address admission inquiries to William Dunfey, Director of Admissions.

Boston College

140 Commonwealth Avenue
Chestnut Hill, Massachusetts 02467
Tel: (617) 552-800   **E-mail:** ugadmis@bc.edu
Fax: (617) 552-8828   **Internet:** www.bc.edu

Institution Description: Boston College is a private, independent, nonprofit institution affiliated with the Society of Jesus, Roman Catholic Church. *Enrollment:* 14,561. *Degrees awarded:* Baccalaureate, first-professional (law), master's, doctorate. Certificate of Advanced Educational Specialization and of Advanced Graduate Studies also awarded.

Member of the consortium Boston Theological Institute.

Accreditation: *Regional:* NEASC. *Professional:* business, counseling psychology, law, nursing, nursing education, social work, teacher education

History: Established and chartered 1863; offered first instruction at postsecondary level 1864; awarded first degree (baccalaureate) 1877. *See* Rev. C.F. Donovan, S.J., Rev. D.R. Dunigan, S.J., and Rev. P.A. Fitzgerald, S.J., *History of Boston College: From the Beginnings to 1900* (Chestnut Hill: University Press of Boston College, 1990) for further information.

Institutional Structure: *Governing board:* Board of Trustees of Boston College. Extrainstitutional representation: 44 trustees, including 36 alumni; institutional representation: president of the college. 1 ex officio. All voting. *Composition of institution:* Administrators 28. Academic affairs headed by academic vice president and dean of faculties. Management/business/finances directed by vice president for financial and business affairs. Full-time instructional faculty 591. Academic governance body, Council of Deans, meets an average of 9 times per year.

Calendar: Semesters. Academic year early Sept. to early May. Freshmen admitted Sept., Jan. Degrees conferred May, Sept., Jan. Formal commencement May.

Characteristics of Freshmen: 22,451 applicants (9,491 men, 12,960 women). 32% of applicants admitted. 32.2% of admitted students enrolled full-time.

97% (2,227 students) submitted SAT scores. *25th percentile*: SAT I Verbal 610, SAT I Math 630. *75th percentile*: SAT I Verbal 700, SAT I Math 710.

84% of entering freshmen expected to graduate within 5 years. 29% of freshmen from Massachusetts. Freshmen from 43 states and 38 foreign countries.

Admission: For fall acceptance, apply as early as Sept. of the previous year, but not later than Jan. 10 of year of enrollment for preliminary application, Jan. 25 for final completed application. Students are notified of acceptance Apr. Apply by Nov. 1 for early action; notified of decision by Dec. 15. Early acceptance available. *Requirements:* Either graduation from accredited secondary school or GED. Recommend 4 units English, 4 in a foreign language, 4 mathematics, 3 laboratory science. 2 units in laboratory science, including 1 chemistry, required for nursing program. Applicants to the Carroll School of Management are strongly encouraged to take 4 years of college preparatory mathematics. *Entrance tests:* College Board SAT or ACT, 3 Achievements. *For transfer students:* 2.5 minimum GPA; from 4-year and 2-year accredited institutions 60 hours maximum transfer credit.

College credit and advanced placement for postsecondary-level work completed in secondary school. Tutoring available. Noncredit remedial courses offered in summer session.

Degree Requirements: *For all baccalaureate degrees:* completion with satisfactory cumulative average (at least 1.5, with the exception of the College of Arts and Sciences which requires a minimum average of 1.667) of at least 38 three-credit courses or their equivalent distributed over 8 semesters of full-time academic work; 2 years residency required; all undergraduates must fulfill core requirements. *Grading system:* A–F.

Distinctive Educational Programs: Cross-registration with Boston University, Brandeis University, Hebrew College, Pine Manor College, Regis College, and Tufts University. Program for the Study of Faith, Peace, and Justice. American studies; Asian studies; Biblical studies; Black studies; church history; cognitive science; computer science; faith, peace and justice; film studies; general education; German studies; international studies; Irish studies; Italian studies; medieval studies; Middle Eastern studies; modern Greek studies; Russian and East European studies; secondary education; women's studies minors. Irish studies, Immersion Program in French and Spanish, Perspective Programs in Philosophy and Theology. Study abroad program: University is a member of the Institute for European Studies. Students may participate in a variety of programs principally in Western Europe and also in Eastern Europe, Australia, Southeast Asia, and Latin America. In addition, the University administers a program in Irish Studies at University College, Cork.

ROTC: Army in cooperation with Northeastern University; Navy, Air Force with Boston University.

Degrees Conferred: 2,223 *baccalaureate*; 1,178 *master's*; 122 *doctorate*; 275 *first-professional:* (law). Bachelor's degrees awarded in top five disciplines: business, management, marketing, and related support services; social sciences 353; English language and literature/letters 210; communication, journalism, and related programs 200; education 195.

Fees and Other Expenses: *Full-time tuition per academic year 2004–05:* undergraduate $28,940; contact the college for current information regarding graduate and first-professional study tuition and fees. *Room and board per academic year:* $9,620.

Financial Aid: Aid from institutionally generated funds is provided on the basis of academic merit, financial need, athletic ability. Institution has a Program Participation Agreement with the U.S. Department of Education for eligible students to receive Pell Grants and other federal aid.

Financial aid to full-time, first-time undergraduate students: 13% received federal grants averaging $3,483; 5% state/local grants averaging $2,557; 46% institutional grants averaging $18,159; 50% received loans averaging $3,195.

Departments and Teaching Staff: Arts and sciences *professors* 106, *associate professors* 158, *assistant professors* 74, *instructors* 9, *part-time faculty* 193; education 12, 20, 14, 1, 41; law 16, 9, 19, 0, 40; management 14, 24, 34, 9, 34; nursing 6, 22, 11, 7, 2; social work 3, 5, 6, 0, 50. *Total instructional faculty:* 982 (full-time 591, part-time 391). Degrees held by full-time faculty: 95% hold terminal degrees.

Enrollment: Total enrollment 14,561. Undergraduate 9,786 (47.4% men, 52.6% women).

Characteristics of Student Body: *Ethnic/racial makeup:* Black non-Hispanic: 5.7%; American Indian or Alaska Native: .3%; Asian or Pacific Islander: 8.5%; Hispanic: 7.1%; White non-Hispanic: 71.7%; unknown: 4.8%. *Age distribution:* 17–21: 68%; 22–24: 31%; 25–29: 1%.

International Students: 470 undergraduate nonresident aliens enrolled fall 2004. Programs available to aid students whose native language is not English: social, cultural. No financial aid specifically designated for international students.

Student Life: On-campus residence halls house 62% of the undergraduate student body. Residence halls include traditional double rooms, suites, townhouses and apartments. *Intercollegiate athletics:* men only: baseball, basketball, cross-country, diving, fencing, football, golf, ice hockey, lacrosse, sailing, skiing, soccer, swimming, tennis, track (indoor and outdoor), water polo, wrestling; women only: basketball, cross-country, fencing, field hockey, golf, lacrosse, sailing, skiing, soccer, softball, swimming and diving, tennis, track (indoor and outdoor), volleyball. *Special regulations:* All resident students are required to subscribe to University Health Services. Dining service meal plans are mandatory except for residents in apartment style units. *Special services:* Orientation program, academic advisement, personal/psychological and career counseling, leadership training, commuter center, physically challenged assistance, medical services, off-campus housing assistance, summer housing services, intercultural programs, theater arts programs, liturgies, programs fostering faith, justice and community, women's resource center, honor societies, Phi Beta Kappa, Sigma Xi, continuous bus service between two campuses. *Student publications, radio:* *The Heights*, a weekly student newspaper; the *UGBC Newsletter* (student government); *Eagle's Eye*, a monthly calendar; *Stylus*, a triennial literary magazine; *Sub Turri*, a yearbook. Radio station WZBC-FM broadcasts throughout the week. *Surrounding community:* Situated in Chestnut Hill, a scenic suburb 7 miles from downtown Boston. Served by mass transit bus and subway system; airport 10 miles from campus; passenger rail service 7 miles from campus.

Publications: *Boston College Law Review* (5 times per year) first published 1959, *Boston College Studies in Philosophy* (irregularly) first published 1968, *Environmental Affairs Law Review* (quarterly) first published 1972, *International and Comparative Law Review* (biannually) first published 1978, *Uniform Commercial Code Reporter-Digest* (quarterly) first published 1974, *Third World Law Review,* first published 1980; *Sui Juris,* first published 1980; *Studies in Soviet Thought,* first published 1961.

Library Collections: 1,738,000 volumes. 3,250,000 microforms; 20,910 periodicals; 118,000 audiovisual materials. Online catalog. Students have access to online information retrieval services and the Internet.

Most important special holdings include Francis Thompson Collection; Thomas P. O'Neill, Jr. Collection; Hilaire Belloc Collection.

Buildings and Grounds: Campus area 240 acres.

Chief Executive Officer: Rev. William P. Leahy, S.J., President.

Address admission inquiries to John L. Mahoney, Jr., Director of Admissions; graduate inquiries to Graduate Arts and Sciences Admission Director; law students to Law School Director.

College of Arts and Sciences

Degree Programs Offered: *Baccalaureate* in art history, biochemistry, biology, chemistry, classical civilization, classics, communication, computer science, economics, English, environmental geosciences, geology, geology/geophysics, geophysics, Germanic studies, Greek, history, independent, Latin, linguistics, mathematics, music, philosophy, physics, political science, psychology, French, Italian, Spanish, Russian, Slavic studies, sociology, studio art, theater, theology, unclassified.

Distinctive Educational Programs: Minors in American studies; Asian studies; Biblical studies; Black studies; church history; cognitive science; computer science; faith, peace and justice; film studies; general education; German studies; international studies; Irish studies; Italian studies; medieval studies; Middle Eastern studies; modern Greek studies; Russian and East European studies; secondary education; women's studies. Other programs include predental; pre-medical; pre-law; Honors Program; Department Honors; Scholar of the College; BA/MSW; BA/MA; Center for East Europe, Russia and Asia; environmental studies; Greycliff French and Spanish; language houses; Immersion Program in French and Spanish; PULSE; Capstone Courses. Exchange and special study programs include Abbey Theatre (Ireland); European Experience (Belgium); University College (Cork, Ireland); Sophia University (Japan); American University; Junior Year Abroad.

Boston College Law School

Degree Programs Offered: *First-professional.*
Admission: Baccalaureate from accredited college or university, LSAT.
Degree Requirements: 85 credit hours, 2.0 GPA, 27 months in residence.

Evening College of Arts, Sciences, and Business Administration

Degree Programs Offered: *Baccalaureate.*

School of Education

Degree Programs Offered: *Baccalaureate* education majors include special needs, early childhood, elementary education, human development, secondary education, special needs teacher, intensive special needs; arts and science majors include biology, chemistry, geology, physics, English, history, mathematics, French, Spanish, and theology. All students in certification programs must complete two majors. Human development majors must complete a major and a minor. *Master's* in counseling children and adolescents; counseling adolescents and adults; human development and ed. psych.; early childhood specialist; higher education; secondary teaching. *Doctorate* in counseling psychology; developmental and ed. psych.; early childhood education; ed. research, measurement and evaluation; higher education; school administration and supervision; curriculum and instruction; prof. school administrator; visually handicapped studies; special education and rehabilitation. Certificates of Advanced Educational Specialization offered in human development and ed. psych; early childhood teacher; school administration and supervision; curriculum and instruction; Catholic school leadership; multihandicapped and deaf/blind; special ed. administration.

Distinctive Educational Programs: Interdisciplinary majors include child in society; math/computer science; human development; American heritage; Hispanic experience. Honors Program. Five-year BA/MA programs in elementary or secondary education; moderate special needs; severe special needs; visu-

ally handicapped studies; human development. BA/MSW in human development/social work.

School of Management

Degree Programs Offered: *Baccalaureate* in accounting, computer science, economics, finance, information systems, general management, human resource management, marketing, operations and strategic management, managerial economics and operations research. *MBA* in management. *MS, Ph.D.* in finance. *Ph.D.* in organizational studies.

Distinctive Educational Programs: Minor in international studies. Honors Program.

School of Nursing

Degree Programs Offered: *Baccalaureate* in nursing; *master's* in adult health, community health, maternal child health, medical-surgical nursing and psychiatric-mental health nursing. *Ph.D.* (clinical research focus) in ethics, ethical judgment and decision making, nursing diagnosis and diagnostic/therapeutic judgment, life processes/selected human response patterns.

Distinctive Educational Programs: Ph.D. program in nursing. BS/MS Articulation Program.

Graduate School of Arts and Sciences

Degree Programs Offered: *Master's* in chemistry, economics, English, French, geology, geophysics, Greek, history, Italian, Latin, Latin and Greek, linguistics, mathematics, nursing, philosophy, physics, political science, Russian language and literature, sociology, Spanish, theology, American studies, Biblical studies, medieval studies, Slavic studies, religious education, pastoral ministry; *doctorate* in biology, chemistry, economics, English, French, history, nursing, philosophy, physics, political science, psychology, romance literatures, sociology, Spanish, theology, medieval studies, religion and education. Certificates of Advanced Graduate Studies in English and in religious education are also given.

Departments and Teaching Staff: *See* College of Arts and Sciences.

Graduate School of Social Work

Degree Programs Offered: *Master's, doctorate.*
Distinctive Educational Programs: Selected first year courses of the master's program also offered at off-campus sites in Worcester, Plymouth, and Portland (ME). *See* College of Arts and Sciences, School of Management, Law School for cooperative programs.

The Boston Conservatory

8 The Fenway
Boston, Massachusetts 02215

Tel: (617) 536-6340   **E-mail:** info@bostonconservatory.edu
Fax: (617) 912-9101   **Internet:** www.bostonconservatory.edu

Institution Description: The Boston Conservatory, formerly known as the Boston Conservatory of Music, is a private, independent, nonprofit institution. *Enrollment:* 547. *Degrees awarded:* Baccalaureate, master's. Diplomas also awarded.

Accreditation: *Regional:* NEASC. *Professional*: dance, music

History: Established 1867; incorporated 1896; offered first instruction at postsecondary level 1933; awarded first degree (baccalaureate) 1938.

Institutional Structure: *Governing board:* Board of Trustees. Extrainstitutional representation: 13 trustees, 1 trustee emeritus; institutional representation: president of the college. 1 ex officio. *Composition of institution:* Administrators 8. Academic affairs headed by dean. Full-time instructional faculty 64.

Calendar: Semesters. Academic year Sept. to May. Formal commencement May. Summer session.

Characteristics of Freshmen: 865 applicants (266 men, 599 women). 43.7% of applicants admitted. 32.3% of admitted students enrolled full-time.

Mean SAT scores 472 verbal, 454 mathematical.

25% of freshmen from Massachusetts. Freshmen from 39 states and 13 foreign countries.

Admission: *Requirements:* GED accepted. Graduation from accredited secondary school (specific academic program not required); audition. *Entrance tests:* Not required. For foreign students TOEFL. *For transfer students:* 2.0 GPA.

Degree Requirements: *For undergraduate degree:* No more than 12 credits below C-; prescribed curriculum. For applied music and music education majors, recitals; for composition majors, examination of folio of original composition; for dance and theater majors, original choreographies and directed pieces.

Fulfillment of some degree requirements possible by passing College Board AP. *Grading system:* A–E; withdraw (carries time limit); no credit; incomplete.

Distinctive Educational Programs: Practicums.

Degrees Conferred: 58 *baccalaureate:* visual and performing arts; 41 *master's:* visual and performing arts.

Fees and Other Expenses: *Full-time tuition per academic year:* $24,750. *Other fees:* $835. *Room and board per academic year:* $11,600.

Financial Aid: Aid from institutionally generated funds is provided on the basis of artistic talent. Institution has a Program Participation Agreement with the U.S. Department of Education for eligible students to receive Pell Grants and, depending upon the agreement, other federal aid.

Financial aid to full-time, first-time undergraduate students: 11% received federal grants averaging $4,217; 4% state/local grants; 39% institutional grants averaging $8,074; 42% received loans averaging $2,797.

Departments and Teaching Staff: Total instructional faculty: 139 (64 full-time, 75 part-time).

Enrollment: Total enrollment 547. Undergraduate 409 (37.7% men, 62.3% women).

Characteristics of Student Body: *Ethnic/racial makeup:* Black non-Hispanic: 6.8%; American Indian or Alaska Native: .2%; Asian or Pacific Islander: 2.9%; Hispanic: 6.1%; White non-Hispanic: 13.1%; unknown: 3.7%. *Age distribution:* 17–21: 65%; 22–24: 18%; 25–29: 13%; 30–34: 3%; 35–39: 1%.

International Students: 29 undergraduate nonresident aliens enrolled fall 2004. Students from Europe, Asia, Central and South America, Canada, Australia. Programs available to aid students whose native language is not English: social, cultural. English as a Second Language Program. No financial aid specifically designated for international students.

Student Life: On-campus housing available. *Surrounding community:* Boston population over 700,000.

Library Collections: 40,000 volumes. Online and card catalogs. 8,500 recordings/tapes; 120 current periodical subscriptions. 18 computer work stations. Students have access to online information retrieval services and the Internet.

Most important special holdings include Jan Veen-Katrine Armory Hooper Memorial Collection (rare and foreign books on dance with special items on dance notations); music education library; tapes of Boston Conservatory of Music performances from 1966 to present and selected lectures, recitals and video tapings.

Chief Executive Officer: Richard Ortner, President.

Address admission inquiries to Zargoza Guerra, Director of Admissions.

Boston University

One Dearborn Street
Boston, Massachusetts 02215-1700
Tel: (617) 353-2300   **E-mail:** admissions@bu.edu
Fax: (617) 353-9695   **Internet:** www.bu.edu

Institution Description: Boston University is an independent, nonprofit institution. *Enrollment:* 29,596. *Degrees awarded:* Associate, baccalaureate, first-professional (dentistry, divinity, law, medicine), master's, doctorate. Certificates of advanced graduate study also awarded.

Accreditation: *Regional:* NEASC. *Professional:* athletic training, audiology, business, clinical psychology, dentistry, dietetics, endodontics, engineering, English language education, health services administration, law, medicine, music, nursing-midwifery, occupational therapy, pediatric dentistry, periodontics, physical therapy, psychology internship, public health, rehabilitation counseling, social work, speech-language pathology

History: Established in Newbury, Vermont, as Methodist General Biblical Institute 1839; moved to Boston, and changed name to Boston Theological Seminary 1867; chartered and adopted present name 1869; offered first instruction at postsecondary level and awarded first degree (baccalaureate) 1871.

Institutional Structure: *Governing board:* Board of Trustees. Extrainstitutional representation: 46 trustees, including 2 administrators. *Composition of institution:* Administrators 38 men / 8 women. Academic affairs headed by provost. Management/business/finances directed by executive vice president. Full-time instructional faculty 2,046. Academic governance body, Faculty Council, meets an average of 18 times per year.

Calendar: Semesters. Academic year early Sept. to mid-May. Freshmen admitted Sept., Jan. Degrees conferred Sept., May, Jan. Formal commencement May. Summer session of 2 terms from mid-May to mid-Aug.

Characteristics of Freshmen: 55% of applicants accepted. 27% of accepted applicants enrolled.

Average secondary school rank men 87th percentile, women 89th percentile, class 88th percentile. Mean SAT scores 636 verbal, 640 mathematical. Mean ACT composite score 28.

66% of entering freshmen expected to graduate within 5 years. 18% of freshmen from Massachusetts. Freshmen from 47 states and 60 foreign countries.

Admission: For fall acceptance, apply as early as Sept. of previous year, but not later than Jan. 1 for fall admissions. Students are notified of acceptance mid-March through mid-Apr. Apply by Nov. 1 for early decision; only available for high school seniors applying for Sept. admission. Early admission available. *Requirements:* Either graduation from accredited secondary school with 4 units English, 3 history, 3 mathematics, 3 science, 3 lab science, 2 foreign language (4 recommended), 1 social studies; or GED. Additional requirements for some programs. Minimum GPA varies. *Entrance tests:* College Board SAT or ACT composite accepted. For foreign students TOEFL. *For transfer students:* minimum GPA varies by program; maximum transfer credit varies by program.

College credit for extrainstitutional learning on basis of ACE *2006 Guide to the Evaluation of Educational Experiences in the Armed Services.* Tutoring available. Developmental courses offered during regular academic year.

Degree Requirements: *For all baccalaureate degrees:* 128 credit hours; 1.7–2.7 GPA. *For all undergraduate degrees:* 32 hours in residence for some programs.

Fulfillment of some degree requirements and exemption from some beginning courses possible by passing College Board AP. *Grading system:* A–F; pass-fail; withdraw (carries time limit).

Distinctive Educational Programs: Numerous interdisciplinary programs. The breadth and depth of more than 250 combinations of majors/minors with 5,500 course offerings create the flexibility of curricular design that serves as a hallmark of the Boston University experience. Cross registration among colleges as well as dual degree enrollment through the Boston University Collaborative Degree Program (BUCOP) continue the possibilities. Facilities and programs for independent research, including honors programs, individual majors, tutorials. Research centers and institutes include African Studies Center, Center for Asian Developmental Studies, Afro-American Studies Center, Center for Applied Social Science, Institute on Employment Policy, Center for Energy-Environmental Studies, Center for Latin American Development Studies, Institute for Literacy and Language, Center for Philosophy and History of Science, Institute for Philosophy and Religion, Center for Polymer Studies. Honors programs are offered by the College of Arts and Sciences and the School of Management. 5-year B.S>/M.S. programs in physical and occupational therapy area available in Sargent College. Study abroad in Africa, Australia, Belize, China, Ecuador, England, France, Germany, Ireland, Israel, Italy, Japan, Russia, Scotland, Spain. Multidisciplinary baccalaureate, master's, and doctoral programs for exceptionally qualified students. Summer program at Marine Biological Laboratory, Woods Hole Institute.

ROTC: Army, Navy, Air Force.

Degrees Conferred: 3,815 *baccalaureate* (B); 3,053 *master's:* (M): 287 *doctorate* (D): architecture 6 (M); area and ethnic studies 17 (B), 1 (M), 6 (D); biological and life sciences 212 (B), 61 (M), 45 (D); business and management 575 (B), 708 (M), 9 (D); communications 582 (B), 158 (M); computer and information sciences 76 (B), 169 (M), 3 (D); education 187 (B), 307 (M), 32 (D); engineering/engineering technologies 256 (B), 86 (M), 15 (D); English 128 (B), 30 (M), 10 (D); foreign languages and literature 50 (B), 2 (M), 4 (D); health professions 344 (B), 619 (M), 21 (D); law 12 (B), 179 (M); mathematics 40 (B), 17 (M), 8 (D); physical sciences 39 (B), 30 (M), 30 (D); protective services/public administration 280 (B), 39 (M), 28 (D); social sciences and history 749 (B), 240 (M), 49 (D); visual and performing arts 199 (B), 133 (M), 18 (D); other 69 (B), 15 (M), 9 (D). 613 *first-professional:* dentistry 127, law 332, medicine 154.

Fees and Other Expenses: *Full-time tuition per academic year 2004–05:* undergraduate $31,350. Tuition varies among graduate and professional schools. Contact the school of interest for current rates. *Fees:* $436; exact amounts vary by program. *Room and board per academic year:* $10,080.

Financial Aid: Aid from institutionally generated funds is provided on the basis of academic merit, financial need, athletic ability, other criteria. Institution has a Program Participation Agreement with the U.S. Department of Education for eligible students to receive Pell Grants and depending upon the agreement, other federal aid.

Financial aid to full-time, first-time undergraduate students: need-based scholarships/grants totaling $137,269,541, self-help $46,654,997, parent loans $13,332,662, tuition waivers $2,250,216, athletic awards $1,370,037; non-need-based scholarships/grants totaling $27,513,549, self-help $19,391,617, parent loans $30,679,049, tuition waivers $3,411,394, athletic awards $6,608,148.

Graduate aid: 1,832 students received scholarships/grants totaling $8,029,193 (ranging from $40 to $50,000); 4,192 received $89,842,435 in federal and state-funded loans; 1,174 students held teaching and research assistantships totaling $13,660,869 (ranging from $308 to $22,750).

Departments and Teaching Staff: *Total instructional faculty:* 3,326 (full-time 2,241, part-time 1,085). Degrees held by full-time faculty: 80% hold terminal degrees.

Enrollment: Total enrollment 29,596. Undergraduate full-time 6,252 men / 9,357 women, part-time 182m / 162w; first-professional full-time 1,031m / 988w, part-time 14m / 12w; graduate full-time 2,640m / 3,191w, part-time 1,841m / 2m139w.

Characteristics of Student Body: *Ethnic/racial makeup:* Black non-Hispanic: 274 men / 504 women; American Indian or Naive Alaskan: 33m / 42w; Asian or Pacific Islander: 1,278m / 1,635w; Hispanic: 462m / 727w; White non-Hispanic: 6,458m / 9,432w; other: 1,958m / 2,016w. *Age distribution:* number under 18: less than 1%; 18–19: 20%; 20–21: 48%; 22–24: 28%; 25–29: 1%; 30–34: 2%; 35–39: 1%; 40–49: less than 15; 50–64: less than 1%.

International Students: 3,671 nonresident aliens enrolled. Programs available to aid students whose native language is not English: social, cultural. English as a Second Language Program. No financial aid specifically designated for international students.

Student Life: On-campus residence halls and apartments available. Cooperative facilities also offer residence space. Housing available for married students. *Intercollegiate athletics:* men only: basketball, golf, crew, cross-country, frisbee, gymnastics, hockey, inline skating, karate, kung fu, ski racing, lacrosse, rugby, soccer, ski racing, snow boarding, swimming, tae kwan do, tennis, track; volleyball; women only: basketball, cheerleading, crew, cross-country, dance theatre, equestrian, fencing, field hockey, lacrosse, swimming, tennis, track, *Special services:* University Resource Center, campus shuttle bus, and evening escort service. *Student publications, radio: Free Press,* a daily newspaper. Radio station WTBU is a student-run radio station. WBUR, a member of National Public Radio, is a leader in news, classical music, and jazz programming. *Surrounding community:* Boston population over 500,000. Served by mass transit bus and train systems; airport less than 6 miles from campus; passenger rail service less than 3 miles from campus.

Library Collections: 2,36,194 volumes. 4,464,136 microform items, 72,153 audio/video tapes/discs; 30,067 periodicals; 1,142 CD-ROMs. 22 commercial online, Internet, and computer network services. Online and card catalogs. Students have access to online services and the Internet at no charge. Total 2004–05 budget for books and materials: $4,216,000.

Most important special holdings include the papers of Martin Luther King, Jr.; variety of letters and manuscripts of George Bernard Shaw; the papers of H.G. Wells; Robert Frost Collection; Theodore Roosevelt Collection.

Buildings and Grounds: Campus area 133 acres.

Chief Executive Officer: Dr. Aram Chobanian, President.

Undergraduates address admission inquiries to Director, Office of Undergraduate Admissions; other inquiries contact individual school/college.

College of Arts and Sciences/The Graduate School

Degree Programs Offered: *Baccalaureate, master's, doctorate* in various fields.

Distinctive Educational Programs: Accelerated baccalaureate-master's programs. Directed study. Undergraduate minor in management. Study abroad in France, Spain, Italy, England. Washington Legislative Internships provide semester field experience in the United States Congress. Joint baccalaureate-first-professional degree programs with Law School, School of Medicine and Henry M. Goldman School of Graduate Dentistry. Modular Medical Integrated Curriculum admits a limited number of qualified students to School of Medicine after 2 years of liberal arts undergraduate study.

Sargent College of Health and Rehabilitation Sciences

Degree Programs Offered: *Baccalaureate* in athletic training, clinical exercise physiology, health studies, human physiology, communication disorders, occupational therapy, rehabilitation services, *master's* in applied anatomy and physiology, nutrition, 5-year baccalaureate/master's program in occupational therapy, rehabilitation counseling, speech pathology; *doctorate* in applied anatomy and physiology, rehabilitation sciences, 6-year baccalaureate/doctor of physical therapy, speech pathology, audiology. Certificates of advanced graduate study in occupational therapy, rehabilitation counseling, speech pathology. 5-year combined baccalaureate/master's program in physical therapy.

School for the Arts

Degree Programs Offered: *Baccalaureate, master's* in art, music, theater; *doctorate* in music. Artist diploma in music.

Admission: Candidates for admission are required to submit a portfolio.

School of Education

Degree Programs Offered: *Baccalaureate, master's, doctorate.* Certificates of advanced graduate study also awarded.

College of Engineering

Degree Programs Offered: *Baccalaureate, master's, doctorate.* Ph.D. offered through the Graduate School.

Distinctive Educational Programs: Combined Master of Engineering in manufacturing engineering and M.B.A. Interdisciplinary study in various fields.

School of Management

Degree Programs Offered: *Baccalaureate, master's, doctorate.*

Distinctive Educational Programs: BSBA, MBA, MS in investment management, MS information systems, doctor of business administration; various dual degree options.

College of Communication

Degree Programs Offered: *Baccalaureate* in television and film, journalism, mass communications, public relations, and advertising; *master's* in film, photo journalism, science journalism, television broadcasting, television management, mass communication, public relations, business and economic journalism.

Henry M. Goldman School of Dental Medicine

Degree Programs Offered: *Baccalaureate* in dental technology; *first-professional* in dental medicine; *master's* in dental public health, nutritional sciences. Certificates of advanced graduate study in dental assisting, endodontics, operative dentistry, oral surgery, orthodontics, pedodontics, periodontology, prosthodontics, public health dentistry.

Admission: *For first-professional degree:* Baccalaureate degree, DAT.

Degree Requirements: *For first-professional degree:* Successful completion of prescribed curriculum, 40 months in residence.

Distinctive Educational Programs: Cooperative baccalaureate program in dental technology and associate program in dental assisting with Metropolitan College of Boston University. *See also* College of Liberal Arts.

School of Law

Degree Programs Offered: *First-professional, master's* in taxation; *master's* in banking law studies; American law and intellectual property law. Dual degree programs in law with public management, with philosophy, with preservation studies; management, public health, health care management, mass communications, international relations, social work.

Admission: *For first-professional degree:* Baccalaureate from accredited college or university, LSAT.

Degree Requirements: *For first-professional degree:* 84 semester hours, 3 year program with required courses, 2 years in residence.

School of Medicine

Degree Programs Offered: *First-professional. Certificate* in dermatology, educational media and technology, medical science, ophthalmic technology. *Master's* degree in anatomy and neurobiology, biochemistry, clinical investigation, genetic counseling, medical sciences, mental health and behavioral medicine, pharmacology, physiology and biophysics. *Doctorate* in anatomy and neurobiology, biochemist, cell and molecular biology, immunology, microbiology, molecular medicine, oral biology, pathology and laboratory medicine, pharmacology and experimental therapeutics.

Admission: *For first-professional degrees:* Normally baccalaureate from approved college of arts and sciences, or engineering with 1 year general chemistry with laboratory, 1 English composition or literature, 1 organic chemistry with laboratory, 1 humanities, 1 biology with laboratory, 1 physics. MCAT.

Degree Requirements: *For first-professional degree:* 4-year prescribed curriculum; 3–4 years in residence.

School of Theology

Degree Programs Offered: *First-professional; master's* in divinity, sacred music, theological studies; *second professional* in sacred theology; *doctorate* in ministry, theology.

Admission: *For first-professional degree:* Graduation from accredited college; proficiency in Greek or Hebrew and in French, German, Latin, or Spanish desirable; broad understanding of social sciences, humanities; competence in natural sciences; general knowledge of theological subjects; ability to write and speak English with clarity; normally should be candidate for Christian ministry.

Degree Requirements: *For first-professional degree:* 2.0 GPA, 12 months in residence. Master of Theological Studies, 64 credit hours; Master of Sacred Music, 60 credit hours; Master of Divinity, 96 credit hours.

Distinctive Educational Programs: Dual degrees with School of Social Work.

School of Social Work

Degree Programs Offered: *Master's* in social work.

Admission: Baccalaureate from accredited college or university with courses in the social, behavioral, and biological sciences; 3.0 GPA, MAT.

Degree Requirements: 65 credit hours, 3.0 GPA.

Distinctive Educational Programs: Dual degrees with School of Theology and School of Public Health. Interdisciplinary Ph.D. program in Sociology and Social Work. Part-time satellite programs on the campuses of the University of Lowell and Southeastern Massachusetts University.

Enrollment: *Total enrollment:* 490.

Metropolitan College

Degree Programs Offered: *Baccalaureate* in art history, biology, biomedical and clinical sciences, computer science, economics, English, history, interdisciplinary studies, management studies in business administration, information systems, electronic commerce, financial management, innovation and technology management, marketing management,mathematics, philosophy, psychology, sociology, urban affairs; *master's*in actuarial studies, economic development and tourism management, electronic commerce, financial economics, advertising, arts administration, business administration, city planning, computer information security systems, computer science security, criminal justice, gastronomy, insurance management online, interdisciplinary studies, telecommunication, urban affairs.

Distinctive Educational Programs: Program for adults unable to attend full-day schedule of classes.

College of General Studies

Departments and Teaching Staff: Science and mathematics *professors* 1, *associate professors* 6, *assistant professors* 11, *instructors* 0; humanities and rhetoric 1, 5, 17, 0; social science 2, 1, 9, 1.

University Professors Program

Degree Programs Offered: *Baccalaureate, master's, doctorate:* independent (interdisciplinary) concentration.

Admission: English, foreign language, and math achievement tests required; additional essay required.

School of Public Health

Degree Programs Offered: *Master of Public Health* with concentrations in environmental health, epidemiology and biostatistics, health law, health services, international health; maternal and child health; and health behavior, health promotion, and disease prevention. *Doctor of Science* in environmental health, epidemiology. Certificate in financing health care in developing countries; management methods for international health; financing health care in developing countries.

Brandeis University

415 South Street
P.O. Box 9110
Waltham, Massachusetts 02454-9110

Tel: (781) 736-2000   **E-mail:** sendinfo@brandeis.edu
Fax: (781) 736-3536   **Internet:** www.brandeis.edu

Institution Description: Brandeis University is a private, independent, non-profit institution founded by the American Jewish Community. *Enrollment:* 5,072. *Degrees awarded:* Baccalaureate, master's, doctorate.

Accreditation: *Regional:* NEASC. *Professional:* social work, teacher education.

History: Established 1947; chartered and offered first instruction at postsecondary level 1948; incorporated 1949; awarded first degree (baccalaureate) 1952. See Abram L. Sachar, *A Host at Last* (Boston: Little, Brown, and Co., 1976) for further information.

Institutional Structure: *Governing board:* Board of Trustees of Brandeis University. Extrainstitutional representation: 42 trustees, 5 of whom serve as Alumni Term Trustees. Institutional representation: president of the university. All voting. *Composition of institution:* Academic affairs headed by Provost and Senior Vice President for Academic Affairs. Management/business/finances directed by Executive Vice President for and Chief Operating Officer. Full-time instructional faculty 333. Academic governance body, the faculty, meets an average of 7 times per year.

Calendar: Semesters. Academic year Aug. to May. Freshmen admitted Sept., Jan. Degrees conferred May, Dec. Formal commencement May. Summer session.

Characteristics of Freshmen: 52% of applicants accepted. 26.5% of accepted applicants enrolled.

82% (628 students) submitted SAT scores; 18% (students) submitted ACT scores. *25th percentile:* SAT Verbal 630, SAT I Math 630; ACT Composite 28, ACT English 28, ACT Math 27. *75th percentile:* SAT I Verbal 720, SAT I Math 720; ACT Composite 33, ACT English 33, ACT Math 32.

79% of entering freshmen expected to graduate within 5 years. 26.4% of freshmen from Massachusetts. Freshmen from 37 states and 25 foreign countries.

Admission: For fall acceptance, apply as early as early as Sept. 1 of previous year, but not later than Jan. 31 of year of enrollment. Students are notified of acceptance by Apr. 15. Apply by Jan. 1 for early decision; need not limit application to Brandeis. *Requirements:* Either graduation from accredited secondary school with 4 units English, 3 in a foreign language, 3 college preparatory mathematics, 1 history, 1 laboratory science, 4 college preparatory electives. *Entrance tests:* SAT I and 3 SAT II or ACT. 3 Achievements or ACT. *For transfer students:* 3.0 minimum GPA; 2 years maximum transfer credit.

College credit and advanced placement for postsecondary-level work completed in secondary school. Advanced placement for extrainstitutional learning (life experience) on basis of faculty assessment. Tutoring available.

Degree Requirements: *For undergraduate degrees:* 32 semester courses; C average in field of concentration; 4 semesters of 16 semester courses in residence; 2 semesters of physical activity; university-wide requirements. Exemption from some beginning courses possible by passing departmental examinations, College Board AP. *Grading system:* A–E; pass-fail.

Distinctive Educational Programs: Liberal arts program of study. Research university environment enables undergraduate students to participate in frontier research programs. Double major programs. Career experience programs including internships, field study, practice teaching. Interdisciplinary programs in African and Afro-American Studies, American Studies, East Asian Studies, European Cultural Studies, Film Studies, Health Law and Society, History of Ideas, Islamic and Middle Eastern Studies, Italian Studies, International Studies, Journalism, Latin American Studies, Legal Studies, Medieval Studies, Near Eastern and Judaic Studies, Neuroscience, Peace Studies, Russian Studies, Women's Studies. Preprofessional programs in dentistry, religious studies, medicine. Honors programs. Minors in all creative arts and humanities departments and selected science and social-science departments (e.g. international business). Honors programs. Study abroad in over 30 countries in Asia, Europe, Latin America, and Middle East.

ROTC: Air Force and Army in cooperation with Boston University.

Degrees Conferred: 816 *baccalaureate;* 459 *master's;* 82 *doctorate.* Bachelor's degrees offered in top five disciplines: social sciences 314; biological and biomedical sciences 90; psychology 72; area, ethnic, cultural, and gender studies 88; English language and literature/letters 56.

Fees and Other Expenses: *Full-time tuition per academic year 2004–05:* $30,160. *Required fees:* 912. *Room and board per academic year:* $9,656.

Financial Aid: Brandeis University offers a direct lending program. Aid from institutionally generated funds is provided on the basis of academic merit, financial need. Institution has a Program Participation Agreement with the U.S. Department of Education for eligible students to receive Pell Grants and other federal aid.

Financial aid to full-time, first-time undergraduate students: need-based scholarships/grants totaling $26,905,494, self-help $8,872,704, parent loans $1,744,265, tuition waivers $134,778; non-need-based scholarships/grants totaling $9,431,358, self-help $4,260,660, parent loans $3,881,168, tuition waivers $283,692.

Departments and Teaching Staff: *Total instructional faculty:* 475 (full-time 333, part-time 192; women 184, men 291; members of minority groups 44). Student-to-faculty ratio: 8.5:1. Degrees held by full-time faculty: doctorate 86.34%, master's 11.05%, baccalaureate 1.45%, professional 1.16%. 97% hold terminal degrees.

Enrollment: Total enrollment 5,072. Undergraduate full-time 1,395 men / 1,771 women, part-time 14m / 10w; graduate full-time 623m / 750w, part-time 302m / 197w.

Characteristics of Student Body: *Ethnic/racial makeup (undergraduate):* number of Black non-Hispanic: 88; American Indian or Alaska Native: 4; Asian or Pacific Islander: 293; Hispanic: 94; White non-Hispanic: 2,137; unknown: 416.

International Students: 218 undergraduate nonresident aliens enrolled fall 2004. Programs available to aid students whose native language is not English: social, cultural, financial. English as a Second Language Program. No financial aid specifically designated for international students.

Student Life: On-campus residence halls house 85% of undergraduate student body. Residence halls for men and women constitute 100% of such space. 10% of graduate students housed in apartments. Housing available for married students. *Varsity athletics:* men only: baseball, basketball, cross-country, fencing, golf, soccer, swimming and diving, tennis, indoor and outdoor track and field; women only: basketball, cross-country, fencing, soccer, softball, swimming and diving, tennis, indoor and outdoor track and field, volleyball; both sexes: sailing. Club sports: ice hockey, lacrosse, frisbee, rugby, wrestling, karate, bowling, cycling, skiing, water polo, crew. *Special regulations:* Registered cars permitted. *Special services:* Medical services, psychological counseling, career services, intercultural center, morning and evening campus shuttle bus. *Student publications, radio: Justice,* a weekly newspaper; *Louis,* a magazine; *Watch,* a monthly magazine; *Gravity,* a humor magazine; *Kalam,* a magazine of Judaic, Islamic, and Middle Eastern Studies; *Laurel Moon,* a poetry magazine; *Steal This Paper,* a political magazine; *Where the Children Play,* a literary magazine. Radio station WBRS-FM. *Surrounding community:* Waltham population 58,300. Boston, 12 miles from campus. Served by mass transit bus, subway systems; airport 15 miles from campus; passenger rail service to campus.

Publications: *The Brandeis Review* (4 times per year) first published in 1980; *Brandeis Reporter* (9 times per year). Member of University Press of New England.

Library Collections: 1,100,800 volumes. Online catalog. 16,119 serial publications; 30,620 recording. 162,400 government documents; 849,000 microforms; 23,500 audiovisual materials. 158 computer work stations. Students have access to online information retrieval services and the Internet.

Most important special holdings include Spanish Civil War Collection; American Judaica; Sakharov Archives; Trustman Collection of Honore Daumier Lithographs.

Buildings and Grounds: Campus area 250 acres. *New buildings:* Carl and Ruth Shapiro Campus Center; Lois Foster Eing addition to the Rose Art Museum; The Village (residential complex); Lemberg Academic Center at the Brandeis International Business School.

Chief Executive Officer: Dr. Jehuda Reinharz, President.

Address admission inquiries to Deana Whitfield, Dean of Enrollment.

Bridgewater State College

Bridgewater, Massachusetts 02325

Tel: (508) 697-1200   **E-mail:** admission @bridgew.edu
Fax: (508) 697-1707   **Internet:** www.bridgew.edu

Institution Description: Bridgewater State College is a public institution. *Enrollment:* 9,731. *Degrees awarded:* Baccalaureate, master's. Joint doctoral program with the University of Massachusetts Lowell. Certificates also awarded.

Academic offerings subject to approval by statewide coordinating bodies. Budget subject to approval by state governing boards. Member of the consortium Southeastern Association for Cooperation in Higher Education in Massachusetts.

Accreditation: *Regional:* NEASC. *Professional:* athletic training, social work, teacher education

History: Established as Bridgewater Normal School and offered first instruction at postsecondary level 1840; awarded first degree (baccalaureate) 1921; changed name to Bridgewater State Teachers College 1932, to State College at Bridgewater 1960; adopted present name 1968.

Institutional Structure: *Governing board:* Board of Higher Education: 11 members. All voting. Board of Trustees (appointed for Bridgewater State College). 10 members. All voting. *Composition of institution:* Academic affairs headed by vice president for academic affairs. Management/business/finances directed by vice president for administration and finance. Full-time instructional faculty 256. *Faculty representation:* Faculty served by collective bargaining agent affiliated with NEA and Massachusetts Teachers Association.

Calendar: Semesters. Academic year early Sept. to late May. Freshmen admitted Sept., Jan. Degrees conferred May, Aug., Jan. Formal commencement May, Jan. Summer session from June through Aug.

Characteristics of Freshmen: 5,924 applicants (2,557 men, 3,367 women). 78% of applicants admitted. 27.1% of admitted students enrolled full-time.

93% (1,210 students) submitted SAT scores; 3% (44 students) submitted ACT scores.

25th percentile: SAT I Verbal 460, SAT I Math 460; ACT Composite 19. *75th percentile:* SAT I Verbal 550, SAT I Math 550, ACT Composite 23.

95% of freshmen from Massachusetts. Freshmen from 16 states and 5 foreign countries.

Admission: Application deadline Mar. 1. *Requirements:* Graduation from accredited secondary school or GED; 20college preparatory academic units. *Entrance tests:* College Board SAT. For foreign students TOEFL. *For transfer students:* 2.0 minimum GPA; from 4-year accredited institution 90 semester hours maximum transfer credit; from 2-year accredited institution 69 semester hours maximum.

College credit and advanced placement for postsecondary-level work completed in secondary school. Tutoring available. Developmental courses offered in summer session and regular academic year; credit given.

Degree Requirements: 120 semester hours; 2.0 GPA; 30 hours in residence; general education requirements, including course in U.S. and Massachusetts constitutions; demonstrated proficiency in English composition. Fulfillment of some degree requirements and exemption from some beginning courses possible by passing College Board CLEP, AP. *Grading system:* A–F; withdraw (carries time limit); incomplete (carries time limit).

Distinctive Educational Programs: Work-experience programs, including field experience, internships, practicums. Interdisciplinary programs in American studies, Canadian studies, chemistry-geology, dance, health resources management, public history, radio and television operation, women's studies, Russian and East European studies, scientific and technical illustration, urban affairs; also oceanography in cooperation with Woods Hole Oceanographic Institute. Facilities and programs for independent research, including honors programs, independent study. Study abroad in various locations in cooperation with other Massachusetts state colleges through consortium. *Other distinctive programs:* Collaborative Doctorate of Education Program with the University of Massachusetts Lowell. Program for Recruitment and Retention of Special Students providing academic and other support services to educationally and economically disadvantaged students. Outreach program offering support services to working adults, veterans, and other nontraditional students. Degree-granting and nondegree continuing education available on campus and at various off-campus centers. Aviation Science major; Academic Advising Center; Children's Physical Developmental Clinic; and Human Performance Laboratory also available. Study abroad at Acadia University (Nova Scotia), Manchester Metro (England), Shanxi University (China), Lavall University and McGill University (Canada), and University of Oldenburg (Germany).

Degrees Conferred: 1,232 *baccalaureate;* 246 *master's.* Bachelor's degrees awarded in top five disciplines: business, management, marketing, and related support services 192; education 156; psychology 137; communication, journalism, and related programs 114; social sciences 88.

Fees and Other Expenses: *Full-time tuition per academic year 2004–05:* $5,248 resident, $11,388 out-of-state student. *Room and board per academic year:* $6,512.

Financial Aid: Aid from institutionally generated funds is provided on the basis of academic merit, financial need. Institution has a Program Participation Agreement with the U.S. Department of Education for eligible students to receive Pell Grants and, depending upon the agreement, other federal aid.

Financial aid to full-time, first-time undergraduate students: 20% received federal grants averaging $2,272; 42 % state/local grants averaging $1,563; 34% institutional grants averaging $503; 61% received loans averaging $2,787.

Departments and Teaching Staff: *Professors* 138, *associate professors* 48, *assistant professors* 55, *instructors* 15, *part-time faculty* 221. *Total instructional faculty:* 329 FTE. Student-to-faculty ratio: 22:1. Degrees held by full-time faculty: doctorate 75%, master's 100%, baccalaureate 100%. 77% hold terminal degrees.

Enrollment: Total enrollment 9,731. Undergraduate 7,753 (39.8% men, 60.2% women).

Characteristics of Student Body: *Ethnic/racial makeup (undergraduate):* Black non-Hispanic: 3.6%; American Indian or Alaska Native: .3%; Asian or Pacific Islander: 1.1%; Hispanic: 1.5%; White non-Hispanic: 68.7%; unknown: 22.8%.

International Students: 155 undergraduate nonresident aliens enrolled fall 2004. Students from Europe, Asia, Central and South America, Africa, Canada. Programs available to aid students whose native language is not English: social, cultural, financial.

Student Life: On-campus residence halls and apartments house 26% of student body. *Intercollegiate athletics:* men only: baseball, basketball, cross-country, football, soccer, swimming, tennis, track, wrestling; women only: basketball, cross country, lacrosse, softball, swimming, tennis, track, volleyball. *Special regulations:* Registered cars permitted in designated areas for commuters, and upperclass and graduate residents. Quiet hours. *Special services:* Medical services; mathematics, reading, and writing laboratory. Bus service runs throughout campus until 11pm. *Student publications, radio:* Weekly newspaper; yearbook. Radio station WBIM-FM broadcasts 105 hours per week. *Surrounding commu-*

nity: Bridgewater population 17,000. Boston, 30 miles from campus, is nearest metropolitan area. Served by mass transit system; airport and passenger rail service each 30 miles from campus.

Publications: *Alumni News*, athletic brochure, *Bridgewater Review*, *Bridgewater Today*, college catalog, departmental brochures, financial aid brochure, honor's brochure, minority brochure, program of graduate and continuing education brochure.

Library Collections: 290,500 volumes. 11,0-00 audiovisual materials; 4,000 microfilms; 1,065 current periodical subscriptions. Online catalog. Students have access to online information retrieval services.

Most important special holdings include collections on Abraham Lincoln, Charles Dickens, and early children's literature and textbooks.

Buildings and Grounds: Campus area 235 acres.

Chief Executive Officer: Dr. Dan Mohler-Faria, President.

Address admission inquiries to Greg Meyer, Director of Admissions.

Cambridge College

1000 Massachusetts Avenue
Cambridge, Massachusetts 02138-5304
Tel: (617) 868-1000   **E-mail:** enroll@cambridgecollege.edu
Fax: (617) 349-3545   **Internet:** www.cambridgecollege.edu

Institution Description: Cambridge College offers graduate programs in counseling psychology, education, integrated studies and management specifically for the adult working professional. Classes are held in the evenings and on weekends, and courses are taught so that students can immediately apply what they learn in class to what they are doing at work. Nearly all of the college's graduate programs can be completed within two years.

Because the College places a premium on the value of learning through life and work experience, it admits a number of students each year who have not yet completed an undergraduate degree. Through the college's Graduate Studies Preparation Program (GSPP), these students can prepare for the rigors of graduate study at the college and then be admitted as graduate students.

Enrollment: 3.487. *Degrees awarded:* Baccalaureate, master's.

Accreditation: *Regional:* NEASC.

Calendar: Semesters. Academic year Sept. to Aug.

Admission: Cambridge College admits students in Sept., Feb., and June. Every applicant has an assigned Admissions Representative who answers questions and helps guide the applicant through every phase of the admissions process. There are no standardized tests required for admission. Instead, the College has designed its own reading comprehension and writing assessment tools. *For Master of Education:* An undergraduate degree and 5 years of work experience or successful completion of the College's GSPP. *For Master's Degree Completion Program:* Acceptance into the MEd program plus up to 16 graduate credits earned with a B or better in courses from an accredited institution. *For Master of Management:* An undergraduate degree and 5 years of work experience, plus prerequisite courses in math and statistical methods, economics, and computer literacy or successful performance on College-administered waiver exams in these areas OR a minimum of 60 undergraduate credits plus successful completion of the College's three-semester GSPP. *For Graduate Studies Preparation Program (GSPP):* 10 years of work experience beyond high school, some post-high school technical or professional training, or college credits, plus acceptance by the college's Faculty Admissions Committee.

Degree Requirements: Completion of prescribed curriculum.

Degrees Conferred: 106 *baccalaureate*; 1,284 *master's*. Bachelor's degrees awarded: psychology 66; liberal arts and sciences, general studies, and humanities 32; business, management, marketing, and related support services 8.

Financial Aid: Institution has a Program Participation Agreement with the U.S. Department of Education for eligible students to receive Pell Grants and other federal aid.

Financial aid to full-time, first-time undergraduate students: 44% received federal grants averaging $2,543; 13% state/local grants; 14% institutional grants; 44% received loans averaging $5,268.

Enrollment: Total enrollment 3,487. Undergraduate 345 (35.1% men, 64.9% women).

Characteristics of Student Body: *Ethnic/racial makeup:* Black non-Hispanic: 24.6%; American Indian or Alaska Native: 1.7%; Asian or Pacific Islander: 1.4%; Hispanic: 21.7%; White non-Hispanic: 20%; unknown: 27.5%. *Age distribution:* 22–24: .5%, 25–29: 11%; 30–34: 15%; 35–39: 24%; 40–49: 37%; 50–59: 12%; 60–and over: .5%.

International Students: 10 undergraduate nonresident aliens enrolled fall 2004. Students from Europe, Asia, Central and South America, Africa. No programs available to aid students whose native language is not English. No financial aid specifically designated for international students.

Buildings and Grounds: Urban campus.

Chief Executive Officer: Mahesh C. Sharma, President.

Address admission inquiries to Joy King, Director of Admissions.

Clark University

950 Main Street
Worcester, Massachusetts 01610-1477
Tel: (508) 793-7711   **E-mail:** admissions@clarku.edu
Fax: (508) 793-7780   **Internet:** www.clarku.edu

Institution Description: Clark University is a private, independent, nonprofit institution. *Enrollment:* 3,115. *Degrees awarded:* Baccalaureate, master's, doctorate.

Member of the Colleges of Worcester Consortium.

Accreditation: *Regional:* NEASC. *Professional:* business, clinical psychology

History: Established and chartered as a graduate institution for men 1887; offered first instruction at postsecondary level 1889; awarded first degree (doctorate) 1892; established undergraduate college 1902; established women's college 1942. *See* William Koelsch, "Distinguished Traditions, New Beginnings," *Clark Now*, No. 4 (winter 1981) for further information.

Institutional Structure: *Governing board:* Trustees of Clark University. Extrainstitutional representation: 30 trustees, including 6 alumni and 6 honorary members (nonvoting); 30 voting. *Composition of institution:* Administrators 16 men / 8 women. Academic affairs headed by president. Management/business/finances directed by vice president for business and finance. Full-time instructional faculty 150. Academic governance body, Faculty Assembly, meets an average of 7 times per year.

Calendar: Semesters. Academic year Aug. to May. Freshmen admitted Sept., Jan. Degrees conferred and formal commencement May.

Characteristics of Freshmen: 62% of applicants admitted. 20% of applicants admitted and enrolled.

96% (509 students) submitted SAT scores; 20% (107 students) submitted ACT scores. *25th percentile:* SAT Verbal 540, SAT I Math 540; ACT Composite 22. *75th percentile:* SAT Verbal 660, SAT Math 645; ACT Composite 28.

68% of entering freshmen expected to graduate within 5 years. 39% of freshmen from Massachusetts. Students from 32 states and 33 foreign countries.

Admission: For fall acceptance, apply as early as Sept. of previous year, but not later than Feb. 1 of year of enrollment. Students are notified of acceptance Apr. Apply by Dec. 1 for early decision; need not limit application to Clark. Early acceptance available. *Requirements:* Recommend 16 secondary school units typically including 4 English, 2 or more foreign language (preferably 1 language), 2 or more mathematics (3 for science and mathematics majors), 1 social studies, 1 natural science (more lab work for prospective science majors). GED accepted. *Entrance tests:* College Board SAT, 3 Achievements (including English composition). For foreign students TOEFL. *See* College of Professional and Continuing Education for different requirements. *For transfer students:* 50% of Clark's BA and major requirements maximum transfer credit.

College credit and advanced placement for postsecondary-level work completed in secondary school. Noncredit developmental courses offered during regular academic year.

Degree Requirements: 32 courses, minimum 2.0 grade point average; 24 courses with grade of C- or better; 2 years or 16 courses in residence; completion of institutional, major departmental, and Program in Liberal Studies requirements. *Grading system:* A–F; pass-no record option; withdraw; incomplete; credit-no credit.

Distinctive Educational Programs: *For undergraduates:* Accelerated degree programs. Cooperative doctorate in biomedical science with Worcester Polytechnic Institute. Fifth-year free program if student maintains a 3.25 GPA. International Studies Stream: students can earn a liberal arts degree with a global perspective through courses, guest speakers, internships, and study-abroad opportunities. Center for Holocaust Studies. Interdepartmental/interdisciplinary program in women's studies. Facilities for independent research, including honors programs, tutorials. Institutionally sponsored study abroad during junior year at: London School of Economics, University of East Anglia, and University of Sussex, England; University of Bourgogne, Dijon, France; University of Trier, Germany; Centro Tandem, Madrid, and University of Seville, Spain; Intercollegiate Center for Classical Studies, Rome; Kansai Gaidai, Osaka, and Sophia University, Tokyo, Japan; Development Studies Center, Rehovot, Israel (environmental studies internship); May-term at Clark Center in Luxembourg; and others. Off-campus study and internships through Washington Semester Program at American University in Washington, D.C., and the Washington Center for Internships and Academic Seminars. *Special Institutes/Centers:* The Jacob Hiatt Center for Urban Education, a partnership between private philanthropy, public schools and higher education, designed to serve as a national model for public school reform. The George Perkins Marsh Institute, the first university research institute devoted primarily to the human causes of and responses to global environmental change. *Available to all students:* Evening classes.

ROTC: Air Force and Navy offered in cooperation with Worcester Polytechnic Institute; Army with College of Holy Cross.

Degrees Conferred: 504 *baccalaureate* (B), 316 *master's* (M), 26 *doctorate* (D): biological/life sciences 90 (B), 10 (M), 4 (D); business/marketing 26 (B), 118 (M); communications/communication technologies 36 (B), 37 (M); computer and information sciences 26 (B), 18 (M); education 21 (M); English 31 (B), 15 (M); foreign languages and literature 13 (B); interdisciplinary studies 7 (B), 2 (L); liberal arts/general studies 3 (M); mathematics 8 (B); natural resources/environmental science 14 (B), 14 (M); philosophy/religion/theology 7 (B); physical sciences 8 (B), 1 (M), 3 (D); protective services/public administration 4 (B), 20 (M); psychology 86 (B), 5 (M), 3 (D); social sciences and history 160 (B), 52 (B), 16 (D); visual and performing arts 38 (B).

Fees and Other Expenses: *Full-time tuition per academic year 2005–06:* $23,900. *Other fees:* $265. *Room and board per academic year:* $5,600.

Financial Aid: Aid from institutionally generated funds is provided on the basis of academic merit, financial need. Institution has a Program Participation Agreement with the U.S. Department of Education for eligible students to receive Pell Grants and other federal aid.

Financial aid to full-time, first-time undergraduate students: need-based scholarships/grants totaling $16,835,284, self-help $6,970,493, parent loans $226,164; non-need-based scholarships/grants totaling $6,169,682, self-help $2,365,676, parent loans $3,127,625, tuition waivers $447,300.

Departments and Teaching Staff: *Professors* 70, *associate professors* 49, *assistant professors* 50, *part-time faculty* 99. *Total instructional faculty:* 276 (full-time 169, part-time 107; women 60, men 109; members of minority groups 23). Total faculty with doctorate, first-professional, or other terminal degree: 167. Student-to-faculty ratio: 10:1. *Faculty development:* 25 faculty members awarded sabbaticals 2004–05.

Enrollment: Total enrollment 3,115. Undergraduate full-time 798 men / 1,242 women, part-time 80m / 87w; graduate full-time 262m / 339w, part-time 158m / 157w.

Characteristics of Student Body: *Ethnic/racial makeup (undergraduate):* number of Black non-Hispanic: 61; American Indian or Alaska Native: 5; Asian or Pacific Islander: 83; Hispanic: 67; White non-Hispanic: 1,390; unknown: 510. *Age distribution:* number under 18: 55; 18–19: 957; 20–21: 853; 22–24: 182; 25–29: 28; 30–34: 30; 35–39: 29; 40–49: 39; 50–64: 17.

International Students: 453 nonresident aliens enrolled fall 2004. 15 students from Europe, 253 Asia, 41 Central and South America, 53 Africa, 9 Canada, 1 Australia, 31 other. Programs available to aid students whose native language is not English: social, cultural. English as a Second Language Program. Financial aid specifically designated for international students: scholarships awarded annually to qualifying students.

Student Life: On-campus residence halls house 77% of undergraduate student body. Residence halls for women only constitute 10% of such space, for both sexes 90%. 8% of student body live off-campus in institutionally owned houses. *Intercollegiate athletics:* men only: baseball, basketball, crew, cross-country, lacrosse, soccer, swimming and diving, tennis, track and field; women only: basketball, crew, cross-country, field hockey, soccer, softball, swimming and diving, tennis, track and field, volleyball. *Special regulations:* Registered cars permitted. *Special services:* Escort service, medical services, EMT squad. *Student publications: The Journal of Arts,* an annual literary magazine; *Pasticcio,* a yearbook; *The Scarlet,* a weekly newspaper; *Wheatbread,* an alternative newspaper/magazine. *Surrounding community:* Worcester population 175,000. Boston, 45 miles from campus, is nearest metropolitan area. Served by mass transit system; airport 3 miles from campus; passenger rail service 3 miles from campus.

Publications: *Academic publications: Economic Geography* (quarterly) first published in 1926; *Idealistic Studies* (three times per year) first published 1971. *University publications: Clark News,* quarterly tabloid; *Clark Week,* weekly campus news and calendar; university academic catalog; Graduate School of Management newsletter, admissions brochures, departmental brochures. *Publisher:* Clark University Press.

Library Collections: 603,262 volumes. Online catalog. Current serial subscriptions: 1,385 paper, 18 microform; 4605 electronic. 68 recordings; 177 compace discs; 222 CD-ROMs. 28 computer work stations. Students have access to online information retrieval services and the Internet.

Most important special holdings include papers of Robert H. Goddard (national repository); Hanna Collection of social fiction (4,000 volumes of 1901–1950 economic, political and social history); World War I collection of journals, books, and posters collected by Louis Napoleon Wilson.

Buildings and Grounds: Campus area 45 acres with 38 buildings including 8 residence halls and 11 residence houses.

Chief Executive Officer: Dr. John Bassett, President.

Address admission inquiries to Office of Admissions.

College of the Holy Cross

1 College Street
Worcester, Massachusetts 01610-2395
Tel: (508) 793-2011   **E-mail:** admission@holycross.edu
Fax: (508) 793-3888   **Internet:** www.holycross.edu

Institution Description: College of the Holy Cross is a private, independent, nonprofit college affiliated with the Society of Jesus, Roman Catholic Church. *Enrollment:* 2,789. *Degrees awarded:* Baccalaureate.

Member of Worcester Consortium for Higher Education, Inc.

Accreditation: *Regional:* NEASC. *Professional:* theatre

History: Established as men's college and offered first instruction at postsecondary level 1843; awarded first degree (baccalaureate) 1849; incorporated 1865; became coeducational 1972. *See* Walter J. Meagher and William J. Grattan, *The Spires of Fenwick: History of the College of the Holy Cross 1843–1963* (New York: Vantage Press, 1966) for further information.

Institutional Structure: *Governing board:* Trustees of the College of the Holy Cross. Extrainstitutional representation: 31 trustees (21 alumni); institutional representation: president of the college. All voting. *Composition of institution:* Administrators 116 men / 84 women. Academic affairs headed by provost. Management/business/finances directed by vice president for business affairs and treasurer. Full-time instructional faculty 135 men / 73 women. Academic governance body, the Faculty Assembly, meets an average of 4 times per year.

Calendar: Semesters. Academic year early Sept. to early May. Freshmen admitted Sept., Jan. Degrees conferred May, Oct. Formal commencement May. No summer session.

Characteristics of Freshmen: 4,969 applicants (2,460 men, 2,509 women). 44.5% of applicants admitted. 31.9% of admitted students enrolled full-time.

97% (683 students) submitted SAT scores. *25th percentile:* SAT I Verbal 580, SAT I Math 580. *75th percentile:* SAT I Verbal 670, SAT I Math 680.

98% entering freshmen expected to graduate within 5 years. 33% of freshmen from Massachusetts. Freshmen from 32 states and 6 foreign countries.

Admission: Rolling admissions plan. For fall acceptance, apply as early as Sept. 15 of previous year, but not later than Jan. 15 of year of enrollment. Students are notified of acceptance early Apr. Apply by Dec. 15 of previous year for early decision; must limit application to College of the Holy Cross. Early acceptance available. *Requirements:* Either graduation from accredited secondary school or GED. Recommend 4 units English, 3–4 foreign language (preferably 3 in 1 language, or 2 in 2 languages), 3 college preparatory mathematics (4 for science, mathematics majors), 2 history or social studies, 2 laboratory science. *Entrance tests:* 3 College Board Achievements (including English) and SAT or ACT composite. *For transfer students:* 3.0 minimum GPA; 16 courses maximum transfer credit; personal interview.

College credit and advanced placement for postsecondary-level work completed in secondary school. Tutoring available.

Degree Requirements: 32 courses; 2.0 GPA; 4 semesters, including last 2, in residence. Fulfillment of some degree requirements and exemption from some beginning courses possible by passing College Board APP. *Grading system:* A–F; pass-no pass; withdraw (carries time limit); incomplete (carries time limit).

Distinctive Educational Programs: *For undergraduates:* Concentrations offered in International Studies, Peace and Conflict Studies, African-American Studies, Women's Studies, Biochemistry, and Biopsychology. 3-2 Engineering program with Columbia, Dartmouth, and Washington University (St. Louis). 5-year MBA with Clark University. Special facilities for using telecommunications in the classroom. Interdepartmental/interdisciplinary programs in European literature, humanities, religious studies, Russian studies, urban studies. Preprofessional programs in dentistry, medicine. Teacher education Program leading to state certification. Facilities and programs for independent research, including honors programs, individual majors, tutorials. Full-integrated study abroad programs in Australia, England, France. Gerontology studies in cooperation with consortium institutions. Off-campus study by individual arrangement. Summer research grants. Fenwick Scholar Program for outstanding senior.

ROTC: Navy.

Degrees Conferred: 615 *baccalaureate.* Bachelor's degrees awarded in top five disciplines: social sciences 212; English language and literature/letters 90; psychology 88; history 75; philosophy and religious studies 50.

Fees and Other Expenses: *Full-time tuition per academic year 2004–05:* $29,686. *Room and board per academic year:* $8,860. Other mandatory fees required.

Financial Aid: Aid from institutionally generated funds is provided on the basis of academic merit, financial need, athletic ability. Institution has a Program Participation Agreement with the U.S. Department of Education for eligible students to receive Pell Grants and other federal aid.

Financial aid to full-time, first-time undergraduate students: 10% received federal grants averaging $5,475; 8% state/local grants averaging $3,327; 50 % institutional grants averaging $16,670; 50% received loans averaging $4,811.

Departments and Teaching Staff: Biology *professors* 4, *associate professors* 4, *assistant professors* 3, *instructors* 0, *part-time teachers* 3; interdisciplinary studies 1, 0, 0, 0, 12; chemistry 2, 3, 5, 0, 1; classics 2, 4, 3, 0, 2; economics 3, 8, 4, 0, 1; education 0, 1, 0, 0, 2; English 10, 8, 3, 3, 2; history 7, 6, 3, 1, 1; mathematics 2, 6, 6, 0, 0; modern language 3, 9, 7, 3, 11; music 1, 1, 3, 0, 4; philosophy 2, 4, 4, 0,0; physics 3, 3, 1, 0, 1; political science 1, 6, 6, 1, 1; psychology 1, 5, 5, 2, 1; religious studies 2, 6, 4, 2, 0; sociology 4, 3, 3, 0, 2; theatre 0, 3, 1, 0, 4; visual arts 1, 3, 3, 0, 3.

Total instructional faculty: 234.4 FTE. Degrees held by full-time faculty: Baccalaureate 100%, master's 100%, doctorate 93% .

Enrollment: Total enrollment 2,745 (45.9% men, 54.1% women).

Characteristics of Student Body: *Ethnic/racial makeup:* Black non-Hispanic: 3.3%; American Indian or Alaska Native: .3%; Asian or Pacific Islander: 4.4%; Hispanic: 4.7%; White non-Hispanic: 75.9%; unknown: 10.3%. *Age distribution:* 17–21: 75%; 22–24: 25%.

International Students: 27 nonresident aliens enrolled fall 2004. Students from Europe, Asia, Central and South America, Canada. No programs available to aid students whose native language is not English. No financial aid specifically designated for international students.

Student Life: On-campus residence halls house 82% of student body. Residence halls for both sexes constitute 100% of such space. *Intercollegiate athletics:* men only: baseball, basketball, crew, football, golf, ice hockey, lacrosse, soccer, swimming, tennis, track; women only: basketball, crew, field hockey, lacrosse, soccer, softball, swimming, tennis, track, volleyball. *Club sports:* men and women: rugby; women only: ice hockey, water polo. *Special regulations:* Cars permitted for juniors and seniors only. *Special services:* Learning Resources Center, Counseling Center and Career Planning Office, Health Services, Office of Student Alcohol and Other Drug Education. *Student publications, radio: The Crusader,* a weekly newspaper; *The Purple,* an annual literary journal; *Purple Patcher,* a yearbook. Radio station WCHC broadcasts 112 hours per week. *Surrounding community:* Worcester population 170,000. Boston, 39 miles from campus.

Library Collections: 594,000 volumes. 16,000 microforms; 25,700 audiovisual materials; 1,810 current periodical subscriptions. Online catalog. Students have access to online information retrieval services and the Internet.

Most important special collections include Jesuitana, Americana Treasure, Holocaust.

Buildings and Grounds: Campus area 74 acres.

Chief Executive Officer: Rev. Michael McFarland, S.J. President.

Address admission inquiries to Ann B. McDermott, Director of Admissions.

College of Our Lady of the Elms

291 Springfield Street
Chicopee, Massachusetts 01013-2839
Tel: (413) 594-2761   **E-mail:** admissions@elms.edu
Fax: (413) 592-4871   **Internet:** www.elms.edu

Institution Description: College of Our Lady of the Elms is a private coeducational college affiliated with the Roman Catholic Church. *Enrollment:* 963. *Degrees awarded:* Associate (paralegal studies), baccalaureate, master's.

Member of the consortium Cooperating Colleges of Greater Springfield; Sisters of St. Joseph College Consortium.

Accreditation: *Regional:* NEASC. *Professional:* nursing, social work

History: Established, chartered, and offered first instruction at postsecondary level 1928; awarded first degree (baccalaureate) 1932.

Institutional Structure: *Governing board:* Board of Trustees. Extrainstitutional representation: 32 trustees; institutional representation: 2 administrators, 2 full-time instructional faculty members; 9 alumnae. 5 ex officio. 27 voting. *Composition of institution:* Administrators 1 man / 5 women. Academic affairs headed by academic dean. Management/business/finances directed by treasurer. Full-time instructional faculty 44. Academic governance body, the faculty, meets 5 times per year.

Calendar: Semesters. Academic year early Sept. to mid-May. Freshmen and transfer students admitted Sept., Jan. Degrees conferred and formal commencement May. Summer session of 2 terms from late May to late Aug.

Characteristics of Freshmen: 90% of applicants admitted. 90% of applicants admitted and enrolled. 97% (122 students) submitted SAT scores; 2% (3

students) submitted ACT scores. *25th percentile:* SAT Verbal 420, SAT Math 430; ACT Composite 16, ACT English 16, ACT Math 10. *75th percentile:* SAT Verbal 550, SAT Math 540, ACT Composite 21, ACT English 21, ACT Math 30.

55% of entering freshmen expected to graduate within 5 years. 85% of freshmen from Massachusetts. Freshmen from 6 states and 4 foreign countries.

Admission: Rolling admissions plan. Apply as early as summer following junior year, but not later than summer of year of enrollment. Applications for early decision by Dec. 15; decision made by Jan. 1. *Requirements:* Either graduation from accredited secondary school with 10 units which must include 4 English, 2 in a foreign language, 2 mathematics, 1 laboratory science, 1 social studies; or GED. 6 additional units recommended. Minimum 2.35 GPA. Lowest acceptable secondary school class standing 25th percentile. *Entrance tests:* College Board SAT. *For transfer students:* 2.0 minimum GPA; 75 hours maximum transfer credit.

College credit and advanced placement for postsecondary-level work completed in secondary school and for extrainstitutional learning (life experience) on basis of faculty assessment. Tutoring available. Noncredit remedial courses offered during regular academic year.

Degree Requirements: *For all associate degrees:* 60 credit hours; 2.0 Quality Point average. *For all baccalaureate degrees:* 120 credit hours; 2.0 Quality Point Average. Fulfillment of some degree requirements and exemption from some beginning courses possible by passing departmental examinations, College Board CLEP, APP. *Grading system:* A–F; pass-fail; withdraw (carries penalty, time limit); incomplete (carries penalty, time limit).

Distinctive Educational Programs: Evening classes. Interdepartmental programs in American studies and international studies; programs may also be student-designed. Individual majors. Weekend College Degree Program and Prior Learning Assessment (PLA). Institutionally sponsored study abroad in France and Spain; study abroad available for qualified juniors through programs offered by other institutions.

Degrees Conferred: 3 *associate:* 133 *baccalaureate* (B), 25 *master's* (M): biological/life sciences 6 (B); business/marketing 23 (B); communications/communication technologies 3 (B); computer and information sciences 1 (B); education 7 (B), 18 (M); English 1 (B); health professions and related sciences 27 (B); interdisciplinary studies 5 (B); law/legal studies 4 (B); liberal arts/general studies 8 (B), 1 (M); mathematics 1 (B); philosophy/religion/theology 2 (B); psychology 15 (B); social sciences and history 24 (B); visual and performing arts 3 (B).

Fees and Other Expenses: *Full-time tuition per academic year 2004–05:* $19,250 undergraduate; $8,820 graduate. *Other fees:* $720. *Room and board per academic year:* $7,750.

Financial Aid: Aid from institutionally generated funds is provided on the basis of academic merit, financial need. Institution has a Program Participation Agreement with the U.S. Department of Education for eligible students to receive Pell Grants and other federal aid.

Departments and Teaching Staff: *Total instructional faculty:* 67 (full-time 63, part-time 4; women 48, men 18; members of minority groups 3). Total faculty with doctorate, first-professional, or other terminal degree: 43. Student-to-faculty ratio: 10:1. *Faculty development:* 4 faculty members awarded sabbaticals 2004–05.

Enrollment: Total enrollment 963. Undergraduate full-time 135men / 473 women, part-time 30m / 185w; graduate full-time 2m / 7w, part-time 15m / 116w. *Transfer students:* in-state 124.

Characteristics of Student Body: *Ethnic/racial makeup (undergraduate):* number of Black non-Hispanic: 38; American Indian or Alaska Native: 1; Asian or Pacific Islander: 9; Hispanic: 30; White non-Hispanic: 568; unknown: 148. *Age distribution:* number under 18: 2; 18–19: 235; 20–21: 223; 22–24: 103; 25–29: 43; 30–34: 55; 35–39: 66; 40–49: 49; 50–64: 14.

International Students: 1 nonresident alien from Africa enrolled fall 2004. Programs available to aid students whose native language is not English: social, cultural, financial. English as a Second Language Program.

Student Life: On-campus residence halls house 50% of student body. *Intercollegiate athletics:* field hockey, soccer, basketball, lacrosse, softball, equestrian. *Special regulations:* Cars permitted in designated areas. Resident hall visitation from 2pm to 2am Fri. and Sat.; 1pm to 11pm Sun. *Special services:* Medical services, van service for social and academic affairs. *Student publications, Elmata,* a yearbook; *Elmscript,* a student newspaper. *Surrounding community:* Chicopee population 55,000. Springfield, 2 miles from campus, is nearest metropolitan area. Served by mass transit bus system, airport 20 miles from campus; passenger mail service 2 miles from campus.

Publications: *The Elms Today.*

Library Collections: 178,538 volumes. Online and card catalogs. 38,000 government documents; 13,200 audiovisual materials; 818 current periodical subscriptions. 126,796 microforms; 1,306 recordings; 194 compact discs; 63 CUD-ROMs. 7 computer work stations. Students have access to online information retrieval services and the Internet.

Most important special holdings include Illuminated Manuscripts from Third Century BC to 15th Century AD; rare books, tracts, and treatises (1485 through the 1800s in the humanities); Irish Studies; film and video collection; Ecclesiology Collection.

Buildings and Grounds: Campus area 25 acres.

Chief Executive Officer: Dr. James Mullen, Jr. President.

Address admission inquiries to Joseph Wagner, Director of Admissions.

Curry College

1071 Blue Hill Avenue
Milton, Massachusetts 02186-2395

Tel: (617) 333-0500   **E-mail:** admissions@curry.edu
Fax: (617) 333-6860   **Internet:** www.curry.edu

Institution Description: Curry College is a private, independent, nonprofit college. *Enrollment:* 2,877. *Degrees awarded:* Baccalaureate, master's.

Academic offerings subject to approval by statewide coordinating bodies.

Accreditation: *Regional:* NEASC. *Professional:* nursing

History: Established 1879; incorporated as School of Expression 1888; offered first instruction at postsecondary level 1938; awarded first degree (baccalaureate) 1939; adopted present name 1943; became liberal arts college 1955; discontinued associate program 1980.

Institutional Structure: *Governing board:* Curry College Board of Trustees and Corporation. Extrainstitutional representation: 20 trustees, including 3 alumni representatives; institutional representation: president of the college, ex officio. *Composition of institution:* Administrators 17 men / 20 women. Academic affairs headed by academic vice president and dean of the college. Management/business/finances directed by chief executive officer. Full-time instructional faculty 101. Academic governance body, Curry College Faculty, meets an average of 8 times per year. *Faculty representation:* Faculty served by collective bargaining agent affiliated with AAUP.

Calendar: Semesters. Academic year Sept. to May. Freshmen admitted Sept., Jan. Degrees conferred May, Aug., Dec. Formal commencement May. Summer session from mid-May to late Aug. with several different options for scheduling available within that time frame.

Characteristics of Freshmen: 71% of applicants admitted. 32% of applicants admitted and enrolled.

75% (495 students) submitted SAT scores. *25th percentile:* SAT Verbal 470, SAT Math 450. *75th percentile:* SAT Verbal 550, SAT Math 500.

48% of entering freshmen expected to graduate within 5 years. 745 of freshmen from Massachusetts. Freshmen from 21 states and 7 foreign countries.

Admission: Modified rolling admissions plan. For fall acceptance, apply as early as August of previous year, but not later than Apr. 1 of year of enrollment. LD students must apply prior to March 1. Students are notified of acceptance beginning Jan. 1. Apply by Dec. 1 for early decision; must limit application to Curry. Early acceptance available. *Requirements:* Graduation from accredited secondary school with 16 units which should include 4 years English, 2 mathematics, 2 science, 2 social studies. Recommend 2 years foreign language. Minimum 2.0 GPA. *Entrance tests:* College Board SAT or ACT composite. For foreign students TOEFL. *For transfer students:* 2.0 minimum GPA; from 4-year accredited institution 90 hours maximum transfer credit; from 2-year accredited institution 66 hours; correspondence/extension students 30 hours.

College credit and advanced placement for postsecondary-level work completed in secondary school. For extrainstitutional learning, college credit and advanced placement on basis of ACE *2006 Guide to the Evaluation of Educational Experiences in the Armed Services,* portfolio assessment, personal interviews, and faculty assessment.

Tutoring available. Developmental courses offered in summer session and regular academic year; credit given for most.

Degree Requirements: *For all baccalaureate degrees:* 120 credit hours; general education requirements. . *For all undergraduate degrees:* 2.0 GPA.

Fulfillment of some degree requirements and exemption from some beginning courses possible by passing departmental examinations, College Board CLEP. *Grading system:* A–F; pass-fail; pass; withdraw (carries time limit).

Distinctive Educational Programs: Program for Advancement of Learning (PAL) Honors Program. Work-experience programs. Evening classes. Accelerated degree programs. Facilities and programs for independent research, including individual majors, tutorials. Study abroad through programs offered by other institutions. *Other distinctive programs:* Continuing education.

Degrees Conferred: 494 *baccalaureate:* biological/life sciences 1; business/marketing 107; communications/communication technologies 44; education 10; English 5; health professions and related sciences 68; natural resources/environmental science 1; protective services/public administration 194; psychology 22;

social sciences and history 23; visual and performing arts 9. 36 *master's:* education 14; protective services/public administration 22.

Fees and Other Expenses: *Full-time tuition per academic year 2004–05:* $20,860. undergraduate, graduate tuition $365 to $385 per credit (varies by major). *Other fees:* $810. *Room and board per academic year:* $8,930.

Financial Aid: Aid from institutionally generated funds is provided on the basis of academic merit, financial need. Institution has a Program Participation Agreement with the U.S. Department of Education for eligible students to receive Pell Grants and, depending upon the agreement, other federal aid.

Financial aid to full-time, first-time undergraduate students: need-based scholarships/grants totaling $11,854,095, self-help $5,894,071, tuition waivers $457,605; non-need-based scholarships/grants totaling $671,416, self-help $7,346,103, parent loans $5,707,143, tuition waivers $175,099. *Graduate aid:* 48 students received federal and state-funded loans totaling $579,542 (ranging from $1,000 to $17,809).

Departments and Teaching Staff: *Total instructional faculty:* 367 (101 full-time, 266 part-time; women 196, men 171; members of minority groups 19). Total faculty with doctorate, first-professional, or other terminal degree: 53. Student-to-faculty ratio: 12:1.

Enrollment: Total enrollment 2,877. Undergraduate full-time 867 men / 1,006 women, part-time 286m / 536w; graduate full-time 4m / 2w, part-time 82m / 94w.

Characteristics of Student Body: *Ethnic/racial makeup:* number of Black non-Hispanic: 179; American Indian or Alaska Native: 5; Asian or Pacific Islander: 37; Hispanic: 65; White non-Hispanic: 1,494; unknown: 88. *Age distribution:* number under 18: 31; 18–19: 782; 20–21: 687; 22–24: 245; 25–29: 176; 30–34: 164; 35–39: 42; 40–49: 259; 50–64: 103; 65 and over: 2. 42% of student body attend summer sessions.

International Students: 29 nonresident aliens enrolled fall 2004. 2 students from Europe, 7 Asia, 4 Central and South America, 1 Africa, 2 Canada, 10 other. Programs available to aid students whose native language is not English: social, cultural. English as a Second Language Program. No financial aid specifically designated for international students.

Student Life: On-campus residence halls house 73% of student body. *Intercollegiate athletics:* men only: baseball, basketball, football, hockey, soccer, tennis; women only: basketball, soccer, softball, tennis. *Special regulations:* Cars permitted without restrictions. *Special services:* Learning Resources Center, medical services, campus transportation. *Student publications, radio:* The Currier-Times, a bimonthly newspaper; Curry Arts Journal, a biannual literary magazine; The Amethyst, a yearbook. Radio stations WMLN-AM, WMLN-FM broadcast 134 hours per week each. *Surrounding community:* Milton is located within the Boston metropolitan area. Served by mass transit bus system; airport 12 miles from campus; passenger rail service 7 miles from campus.

Library Collections: 91,350 Online catalog. Current periodical subscriptions: 400 paper; 92 microform; 117 via electronic access. 146 recordings; 7 compact discs, 80 CD-ROMs. 35 computer work stations. Students have access to online information retrieval services and the Internet.

Buildings and Grounds: Campus area 137 acres. *New buildings:* ARC Alumni Recreation Center/Dance Studio; 3 residence halls completed.

Chief Executive Officer: Kenneth K. Quigley, Jr., President.

Address admission inquiries to Jane Fidler, Director of Admission; graduate inquires to Judith Stoessel, Dean of Continuing Education and Graduate Studies.

Eastern Nazarene College

23 East Elm Avenue
Quincy, Massachusetts 02170

Tel: (617) 773-6350   **E-mail:** admissions@enc.edu
Fax: (617) 745-3915   **Internet:** www.enc.edu

Institution Description: Eastern Nazarene College is a private Christian liberal arts college. *Enrollment:* 1,193. *Degrees awarded:* Associate, baccalaureate, master's.

Accreditation: *Regional:* NEASC. *Professional:* social work, teacher education

History: Established and incorporated 1918; offered first instruction at postsecondary level 1919; chartered 1920; awarded first degree (baccalaureate) 1930; master's program authorized by Commonwealth of Massachusetts 1964. *See* James R. Cameron, *The First Fifty Years* (Kansas City, MO: Nazarene Publishing House, 1968) for further information.

Institutional Structure: *Governing board:* Board of Trustees. Representation: 40 trustees, including president of the college, 2 alumni. 1 ex officio. All voting. *Composition of institution:* Administrators 5 men / 1 woman. Academic affairs headed by academic dean and vice president. Management/business/finances directed by director of financial affairs. Full-time instructional faculty

100. Academic governance body, Faculty of Eastern Nazarene College, meets an average of 8 times per year.

Calendar: Semesters (4-1-4 plan). Academic year early Sept. to late May. Freshmen matriculate Sept. Degrees conferred in Feb., May, Aug. Formal commencements Feb., May. Summer session from mid-May to mid-June.

Characteristics of Freshmen: 85% of applicants accepted. 62% of accepted applicants enrolled. Mean SAT scores men 540 verbal, 552 mathematical; women 513 verbal, 487 mathematical .

49% of entering freshmen expected to graduate within 5 years. Freshmen from 18 states and 3 foreign countries.

Admission: Rolling admissions plan. For fall acceptance, apply as early as Sept. 15 of previous year, but not later than Aug. 15 of year of enrollment. Early acceptance available. *Requirements:* graduation from an approved secondary school with 16 college preparatory credits: English 4, history 1-2, language 2-4, mathematics 2-4, social science 1-2, natural sciences 2-4. *Entrance tests:* College Board SAT or ACT; For foreign students TOEFL.

College credit and advanced placement for postsecondary-level work completed in secondary school.

Degree Requirements: *For all associate degrees:* 66 semester hours; cumulative quality point average of 1.8 or better; completion of specified curriculum. *For all baccalaureate degrees:* 123 semester hours; 2.0 GPA; 3 semesters and half the credit hours toward major in residence; core curriculum; comprehensives in individual fields of study. *For all undergraduate degrees:* Chapel attendance 3 times per week; 2 hours physical education.

Fulfillment of some degree requirements and exemption from some beginning courses possible by passing College Board AP. *Grading system:* A–F; pass-fail.

Distinctive Educational Programs: *For undergraduates:* Accelerated degree programs. Cooperative baccalaureate programs in pharmacy with Massachusetts College of Pharmacy. Opportunities for independent research in biology, chemistry, physics. Individually arranged study abroad in various countries. Council of Christian Colleges and Universities Program (Russian Studies, Latin American Studies, Los Angeles Film Studies, Oxford Summer School). *For graduate students:* Work-experience programs, including internships in family counseling and practicums in education.

Degrees Conferred: 101 *associate;* 232 *baccalaureate* (B); 50 *master's* (M): biological/life sciences 10 (B); business/marketing 109 (B), 16 (M); communications/communication technologies 8 (B); computer and information sciences 3 (B); education 13 (B), 28 (M); engineering and engineering technologies 2 (B); English 7 (B); health professions and related sciences 5 (B); liberal arts/general studies 16 (B); mathematics 2 (B); parks and recreation 4 (B); philosophy/religion/theology 12 (B); physical sciences 1 (B); protective services/public administration 2 (B); psychology 20 (B); social sciences and history 14 (B), 6 (M); visual and performing arts 4 (B). *Honorary degrees awarded 2003–04:* Doctor of Science 1, Doctor of Divinity 2.

Fees and Other Expenses: *Full-time tuition per academic year 2004–05:* $16,854; contact the college for current graduate tuition/fees. *Required fees:* $580. *Student fees* $776. Various rates for room and board per academic year: contact the college for current information.

Financial Aid: Aid from institutionally generated funds is provided on the basis of academic merit, financial need, other criteria. Institution has a Program Participation Agreement with the U.S. Department of Education for eligible students to receive Pell Grants and, depending on the agreement, other federal aid.

Departments and Teaching Staff: *Professors* 21, *associate professors* 14, *assistant professors* 19, *instructors* 6, *part-time teachers* 46.

Total instructional faculty: 146. Student-to-faculty ratio: 10.2:1. Degrees held by full-time faculty: doctorate 65%, master's 35%. 65% hold terminal degrees.

Enrollment: Total enrollment 1,193. Undergraduate full-time 395 men / 658 women, part-time 4m / 81w; graduate full-time 27m / 45w, part-time 8m / 48w. *Transfer students:* in-state 22; from out-of-state 16.

Characteristics of Student Body: *Ethnic/racial makeup:* number of Black non-Hispanic: 134; American Indian or Alaska Native: 7; Asian or Pacific Islander: 26; Hispanic: 51; White non-Hispanic: 771; unknown: 62.

International Students: 16 nonresident aliens enrolled fall 2004. 3 students from Europe, 2 Asia, 1 Central America, 5 Africa, 2 other. Programs available to aid students whose native language is not English: social, cultural. English as a Second Language Program. Financial aid specifically designated for international students: 3 scholarships available annually.

Student Life: On-campus resident halls house 85% of student body. Housing available for married students. *Intercollegiate athletics:* men: baseball, basketball, cross-country, soccer, tennis; women: basketball, cross-country, soccer, softball, tennis, volleyball; club sports: men's volleyball, lacrosse. *Special regulations:* Curfews for freshmen. Quiet hours Residence hall visitation in lounge areas. *Special services:* Center for Academic Services, Supplemental Instruction; tutoring; security; escort; medical services. *Student publications, radio:* *Campus Camera,* a bimonthly newspaper; *Nautilus,* a yearbook; Radio station WENC. *Surrounding community:* Quincy, population 85,000, is located in Boston metropolitan area. Served by mass transit bus and rail systems, airport 15 miles from campus, passenger rail service 10 miles from campus.

Library Collections: 125,842 volumes including bound books, serial backfiles, electronic documents, and government documents not in separate collections. Online catalog. Current serial subscriptions: 466 paper, 177 microform, 6,714 electronic. 440 recordings; 775 compact discs; 154 CD-ROMs. 44 computer work stations. Students have access to the Internet at no charge.

Most important special holdings include Gould Collection (religion).

Buildings and Grounds: Campus area 16 acres.

Chief Executive Officer: Dr. J. David McClung, President.

Address admission inquiries to Doris Webb, Vice President for Admissions and Financial Aid; graduate inquiries to Anderson Mar, Coordinator for Graduate Enrollment.

Emerson College

120 Boylston Street
Boston, Massachusetts 02116-1596
Tel: (617) 824-8600   **E-mail:** admission@emerson.edu
Fax: (617) 824-8609   **Internet:** www.emerson.edu

Institution Description: Emerson College is a private, independent, nonprofit college specializing in communication and the arts. *Enrollment:* 3,816. *Degrees awarded:* Baccalaureate, master's, doctorate.

Member of Fenway Library Consortium, Professional Arts Consortium.

Accreditation: *Regional:* NEASC. *Professional:* speech-language pathology

History: Established and chartered as Boston Conservatory of Oratory and offered first instruction at postsecondary level 1880; changed name to Monroe College of Oratory 1881, to Emerson College of Oratory 1890; awarded first degree (baccalaureate) 1919; adopted present name 1939.

Institutional Structure: *Governing board:* Board of Trustees, including president of the college, 1 full-time faculty member, 1 student representative, 1 alumnus/alumni. *Composition of institution:* Graduate division and schools for the arts, communication, management and public policy, and communication sciences and disorders headed by deans. Academic affairs, administration and finance, enrollment and student affairs, information technology, and public relations headed b vice presidents. *Academic governance:* faculty assembly. Full-time instructional faculty 109.

Calendar: Semesters. Academic year early Sept. to early May. Freshmen admitted Sept., Jan. Degrees conferred May, Aug., Dec. Formal commencement May. Summer session of 2 terms from late May to early Aug.

Characteristics of Freshmen: 48% of applicants admitted. 32% of applicants admitted and enrolled.

93.8% (660 students) submitted SAT scores; 17.5% (123 students) submitted ACT scores. *25th percentile:* SAT Verbal 580, SAT Math 540; ACT Composite 24, ACT English 25, ACT Math 23. *75th percentile:* SAT Verbal 670, SAT Math 640; ACT Composite 28, ACT English 31, ACT Math 27. 22% of freshmen from Massachusetts. Freshmen from 41 states and 25 foreign countries.

Admission: Fall application deadline Jan.; ; spring deadline Nov. 15. Early action deadline Nov. 1. Transfer application priority deadline Mar 1 (fall), Nov. 15 (spring). Audition required for acting, dance, and musical theatre candidates. *Requirements:* College preparatory program including 4 years of English, 3 years each of mathematics, science, social science, and foreign language, and 4 units of academic electives. *Entrance tests:* SAT or ACT. TOEFL for non-native speakers. *For transfer students:* 3.0 GPA. Credits accepted from both two- and four-year accredited colleges/universities. Advanced standing credit granted for successful AP, CLEP exams and select international credentials, i.e. IB, Abitur, GCE A-levels.

Degree Requirements: 128 credit hours; 2.0 GPA; 32 hours in residence; general education requirements. Fulfillment of some degree requirements and exemption from some beginning courses possible by passing College Board CLEP, AP. *Grading system:* A–F; pass-fail; withdraw.

Distinctive Educational Programs: Institute for Liberal Arts and Interdisciplinary Studies sponsors Honors Program, Freshman Academic Studies Program, individually designed study, and interdisciplinary minors. Internships and hands-on experience available throughout the curriculum. Semester program in Los Angeles. Course cross-registration with 6-member Boston ProArts Consortium. Dual-degree B.A./M.A. with Wheaton College; joint M.A. in health communication with Tufts University. Study abroad in Czech Republic and The Netherlands.

Degrees Conferred: 811 *baccalaureate;* 476 *master's.*

Fees and Other Expenses: *Full-time tuition per academic year 2004–05:* $22,976: undergraduate, graduate $718 per credit. *Required fees:* $579. *Room and board per academic year:* $10,118.

Financial Aid: Aid from institutionally generated funds is provided on the basis of academic merit, financial need.

Financial aid to full-time, first-time undergraduate students: need-based scholarships/grants totaling $13,303,822, self-help $13,036,874, parent loans $2,699,386, tuition waivers $173,863; non-need-based scholarships/grants totaling $1,236,834, self-help $6,734,358, parent loans $4,333,246, tuition waivers $125,081. *Graduate aid:* 620 students received federal and state-funded loans totaling $10,312,252 (ranging from $100 to $1,000); 195 held college-assigned jobs worth $1,055,716 (ranging from $500 to $14,000).

Departments and Teaching Staff: *Professors* 14, *associate professors* 44, *assistant professors* 38, *instructors* 37, *part-time faculty* 201.

Total instructional faculty: 359 (full-time 138, part-time 201; women 148, men 192; members of minority groups 42). Total faculty with doctorate, first-professional, or other terminal degree: 182. Student-to-faculty ratio: 15:1. Degrees held by full-time faculty: doctorate 57%, master's 37%, baccalaureate 5%. 78% hold terminal degrees.

Enrollment: Total enrollment 4,398. Undergraduate full-time 1,277 men / 1,743 women, part-time 117; graduate full-time 167m / 629w, part-time 50m / 134w. *Transfer students:* 224.

Characteristics of Student Body: *Ethnic/racial makeup (undergraduate):* number of Black non-Hispanic: 76; American Indian or Alaska Native: 13; Asian or Pacific Islander: 127; Hispanic: 153; White non-Hispanic: 2,346; unknown: 268. *Age distribution:* number under 18: 45; 18–19: 1,317; 20–21: 1,332; 22–24: 798; 25–29: 60; 30–34: 21; 35–39: 12; 40–49: 8; 50–64: 3.

International Students: 384 nonresident aliens enrolled fall 2004. Students from Europe, Asia, Central and South America, Africa, Canada, Australia. No programs available to aid students whose native language is not English. No financial aid specifically designated for international students.

Student Life: More than 60 student organizations, performance groups, honor societies, and NCAA intercollegiate teams: baseball (men), basketball (men, women), volleyball (women). Club sport in lacrosse (men) and intramural program for aerobics, tag football, volleyball, weight training, and basketball. *Student services:* Offices for academic advising and counseling, Center for Spiritual Life, health clinic, shuttle bus service, offices for career planning, international student affairs, off-campus services. *Student publications: Berkeley-Beacon,* a student newspaper; *Emerson Review,* a literary magazine; *Plowshares,* journal for new creative writing; *Surrounding community:* Boston is a major metropolitan area. Served by mass public transit bus and rail system within blocks of the campus; airport 3 miles from campus; passenger bus and rail service within 1 mile of campus.

Library Collections: 174,782 volumes. 11,000 microforms; 7,395 audiovisual materials; 1,000 current periodical subscriptions. Online and card catalogs. 1,622 recordings; 1,024 compact discs; 200 CD-ROMs. Computer work stations available. Students have access to online information retrieval services and the Internet. Total 2004–05 budget for books and materials: $2,789,016.

Most important special holdings include speech communication; mass communication; communication disorders; performing arts.

Buildings and Grounds: Campus area includes more than a dozen buildings in Boston's Theatre District and nearby historic Back Bay neighborhood. *New buildings:* Cutler Majestic Theatre restoration completed 2004; Tufte Performance and Production Center 2005.

Chief Executive Officer: Jacqueline Weis Liebergott, President.

Address admission inquiries to Sara S. Ramirez, Director of Admissions.

Emmanuel College

400 The Fenway
Boston, Massachusetts 02115
Tel: (617) 735-9715   **E-mail:** enroll@emmanuel.edu
Fax: (617) 735-9801   **Internet:** www.emmanuel.edu

Institution Description: Emmanuel College is a private women's college affiliated with the Roman Catholic Church. *Enrollment:* 2,165. *Degrees awarded:* Baccalaureate, master's.

Member of Fenway Library Consortium.

Accreditation: *Regional:* NEASC. *Professional:* nursing

History: Established and offered first instruction at postsecondary level 1919; incorporated 1921; awarded first degree (baccalaureate) 1923.

Institutional Structure: Emmanuel College Governance is a 2-tier structure. The name of the corporation is the Trustees of Emmanuel College which delegates management of the college to the Board of Trustees comprised of 22 members with diverse expertise. Reporting to the president of the college are the vice president for academic affairs, vice president for finance and administration, vice president for student affairs, vice president for development and alumnae relations.

Calendar: Semesters. Academic year Aug. to May. Freshmen admitted Aug., Jan., June, July. Degrees conferred and formal commencement May. Summer session from late May to mid-Aug.

Characteristics of Freshmen: 78% of applicants accepted. 33% of accepted applicants enrolled. 97% (435 students) submitted SAT scores; 4% (69 students) submitted ACT scores. *25th percentile:* SAT Verbal 580, SAT Math 570. *75th percentile:* SAT Verbal 480, SAT Math 460.

62% of freshman from Massachusetts. Freshmen from 23 states and 16 foreign countries.

Admission: Rolling admissions plan. For fall acceptance, apply as early as Sept. of senior year, but not later than 1 month prior to enrollment. Apply by Nov. 1 for early decision; must limit application to Emmanuel. Early acceptance available. *Requirements:* 16 units including the following courses: 4 years English; 2 years social science; 3 years mathematics; 3 years foreign language; 2 years laboratory science. *Entrance tests:* College Board SAT or ACT. *For transfer students:* 2.0 minimum GPA. Students must complete 16 courses at Emmanuel. Tutoring available.

Degree Requirements: *For all baccalaureate degrees:* 128 credit hours, 4 terms in residence. *For all undergraduate degrees:* 2.0 minimum GPA. *For adult learner students only:* Fulfillment of some degree requirements and exemption from some English composition, first-year language, biology, and chemistry possible by taking achievement tests. Maximum credit of 64 hours toward baccalaureate by passing College Board CLEP or APP. *Grading system:* A–F; pass-fail; withdraw.

Distinctive Educational Programs: *For undergraduates:* Internship programs. Off-campus centers. Accelerated degree programs. Dual-degree program in engineering with Northeastern University. Facilities and programs for independent research. Study abroad available. Honors program available. Students can take courses at other four colleges of the Fenway: Simmons, Wheelock, Wentworth, Massachusetts College of Pharmacy. Individual majors.

Degrees Conferred: 256 *baccalaureate:* area and ethnic studies 2; biological/life sciences 18; business/marketing 102; communications/communication technologies 6; education 14; English 37; interdisciplinary studies 8; mathematics 5; physical sciences 6; psychology 30; social sciences and history 16; visual and performing arts 6. 65 *master's:* business/marketing 30; education 35.

Fees and Other Expenses: *Full-time tuition per academic year 2004–05:* $20,100. *Books and supplies:* $750. *Room and board per academic year:* $9,000.

Financial Aid: Aid from institutionally generated funds is provided on the basis of academic merit, financial need.

Financial aid to full-time, first-time undergraduate students: need-based scholarships/grants totaling $11,501,253, self-help $4,290,470, parent loans $1,927,425; non-need-based scholarships/grants totaling $1,689,351, self-help $4,075,231, parent loans $1,565,277, tuition waivers $150,750.

Departments and Teaching Staff: *Total instructional faculty:* 183 (full-time 57, part-time 126; women 97, men 86; members of minority groups 11). Student-to-faculty ratio: 16:1. Degrees held by full-time faculty: doctorate 67%, master's 100%, professional 9%.

Enrollment: Total enrollment 2,165. Undergraduate full-time 362 men / 962 women, part-time 119m / 504w; graduate full-time 5m / 19w, part-time 49m / 145w.

Characteristics of Student Body: *Ethnic/racial makeup:* number of Black non-Hispanic: 153; American Indian or Alaska Native: 4; Asian or Pacific Islander: 72; Hispanic: 82; White non-Hispanic: 1,219; unknown: 361. *Age distribution:* number under 11; 18: 934; 18–19: 512; 20–21: 512; 22–24: 125; 25–29: 109; 30–34: 112; 35–39: 101; 40–49: 168; 50–64: 63.

International Students: 56 nonresident aliens enrolled fall 2004. 7 students from Europe, 31 Asia, 5 Central and South America, 3 Africa, 9 other. Programs available to aid students whose native language is not English: English as a Second Language Program. No financial aid specifically designated for international students.

Student Life: On-campus residence halls house 65% of full-time student body. *Intercollegiate athletics:* women only: basketball, soccer, softball, tennis, volleyball. *Special regulations:* No alcohol allowed on campus; residence hall quiet hours. *Special services:* Academic Resource Center, commuter shuttle service provided to nearby colleges of the Fenway and to other academic and vocational attractions; extensive new student orientation programs. *Student publications: Epilogue,* a yearbook; *Emmanuel College Times,* a newspaper; *Bang!,* a literary magazine. *Surrounding community:* Boston area population 3,000,000. Served by mass transit bus, trolley and subway systems; airport 20 minutes from campus; passenger rail service 15 minutes from campus.

Publications: Continuing Education brochures and *Admissions Viewbook* new editions.

Library Collections: 97,627 volumes. 594 current periodical subscriptions. 2,128 microform titles. 115 computer work stations campus-wide. Students have access to the Internet at no charge.

Most important special collections include religious studies (Catholicism); women's studies; art therapy; nursing.

Buildings and Grounds: Campus area 17 acres. *New buildings:* John Yawkey Center completed 2000.

Chief Executive Officer: Sr. Janet Eisner, SND, President.

Address admission inquiries to Sandra Robbins, Dean for Enrollment; graduate inquiries to Ellen Sweeney, Director of Graduate Programs.

Endicott College

376 Hale Street
Beverly, Massachusetts 01915
Tel: (978) 927-0585   **E-mail:** admissions@endicott.edu
Fax: (978) 927-0084   **Internet:** www.endicott.edu

Institution Description: Endicott College is an independent college linking classroom and off-campus work experience through required internships. *Enrollment:* 2,390. *Degrees awarded:* Associate, baccalaureate, master's.

Accreditation: *Regional:* NEASC. *Professional:* athletic training, interior design, nursing, physical therapy

Calendar: Semesters. Academic year Aug. to May.

Characteristics of Freshmen: 2,818 applicants (974 men, 1,844 women). 44.2% of applicants admitted. 33.9% of admitted students enrolled full-time.

94% (396 students) submitted SAT scores; 10% (40 students) submitted ACT scores. *25th percentile:* SAT I Verbal 490, SAT I Math 500; ACT Composite 20. *75th percentile:* SAT I Verbal 570, SAT I Math 580; ACT Composite 24.

Admission: Graduation from an accredited secondary school.

Degree Requirements: *For baccalaureate degree:* Completion of prescribed curriculum.

Degrees Conferred: 2 *associate*; 352 *baccalaureate*; 230 *master's*. Bachelor's degrees awarded in top five disciplines: business, management, marketing, and related support services 107; visual and performing arts 49; communication, journalism, and related programs 40; liberal arts and sciences, general studies, and humanities 30; psychology 29.

Fees and Other Expenses: *Full-time tuition per academic year 2004–05:* $15,572. *Room and board per academic year:* $9,300. *Books and supplies:* $600.

Financial Aid: Aid from institutionally generated funds is provided on the basis of academic merit, financial need, athletic ability. Institution has a Program Participation Agreement with the U.S. Department of Education for eligible students to receive Pell Grants and other federal aid.

Departments and Teaching Staff: *Total instructional faculty:* 57. 40% of hold doctorate degrees. Student-to-faculty ratio: 27:1.

Enrollment: Total enrollment 2,390. Undergraduate 1,796 (39.3% men, 60.7% women).

Characteristics of Student Body: *Ethnic/racial makeup:* number of Black non-Hispanic: 1.7%; American Indian or Alaska Native: .2%; Asian or Pacific Islander: .8%; Hispanic: 1.7%; White non-Hispanic: 82.7%; unknown: 8.6%.

International Students: 83 undergraduate nonresident aliens enrolled fall 2004. No programs available to aid students whose native language is not English. No financial aid specifically designated for international students.

Library Collections: 114,000 volumes. Online catalog. Current periodical subscriptions: 4,000. 23,500 microforms; 50 audiovisual materials. Computer work stations available. Students have access to the Internet at no charge.

Buildings and Grounds: Campus area 240 acres.

Chief Executive Officer: Richard E. Wylie, President.

Address admission inquiries to Director of Admissions.

Episcopal Divinity School

99 Brattle Street
Cambridge, Massachusetts 02138-3494
Tel: (617) 868-3450   **E-mail:** info@eds.edu
Fax: (617) 864-5385   **Internet:** www.eds.edu

Institution Description: Episcopal Divinity School is a private professional theological school affiliated with the Boston Theological Institute, a consortium of nine theological schools in the Boston area. *Enrollment:* 80. *Degrees awarded:* First-professional, master's, doctorate.

Accreditation: *National:* ATS. *Professional:* theology

History: Formed 1974 by merger of the Philadelphia Divinity School (founded 1857) and the Episcopal Theological School (founded 1867).

Calendar: Semesters. Academic year from early Sept. to late May.

Admission: *Requirements:* Bachelor's degree from an accredited college or university.

Degree Requirements: Completion of prescribed curriculum.

Degrees Conferred: 5 *master's:* theology; 3 *doctorate:* theology; 16 *first-professional:* master of divinity.

Fees and Other Expenses: *Full-time tuition per academic year:* Contact the school for current, tuition, fees, and living costs.

Financial Aid: Aid from institutionally generated funds is provided on the basis of academic merit, financial need. Institution has a Program Participation Agreement with the U.S. Department of Education for eligible students to receive Pell Grants and other federal aid.

Departments and Teaching Staff: Theology *professors* 5, *associate professors* 7, *assistant professors* 1, *part-time teachers* 17.

Total instructional faculty: 30. Student-to-faculty ratio: 5:1. Degrees held by full-time faculty: doctorate 100%, professional 92%. 100% hold terminal degrees.

Enrollment: Total enrollment 80 (35% men, 65% women).

Characteristics of Student Body: *Ethnic/racial makeup:* Black non-Hispanic: 75%; American Indian or Alaska Native: 1.3%; Asian or Pacific Islander: 2.5%; Hispanic: 2.5%; White non-Hispanic: 75%; unknown: 2.5%. *Age distribution:* 22–24: 8%; 25–29: 9%; 30–34: 5%; 35–39: 10%; 40–49: 28%; 50–59: 36%; 60–and over: 3%.

International Students: 6 nonresident aliens enrolled fall 2004. Programs available to aid students whose native language is not English: social, cultural, financial. 2 scholarships available annually to international graduate students.

Student Life: Housing available on campus.

Library Collections: 226,000 volumes. Online catalog. 6,200 current periodical subscriptions (paper, microform, electronic). Computer work stations available. Students have access to the Internet at no charge.

Chief Executive Officer: Rev. Susan Charleston, President and Dean.

Address admission inquiries to Christopher J. Medeiros, Director of Admissions.

Fisher College

118 Beacon Street
Boston, Massachusetts 02116-1500
Tel: (617) 236-8800   **E-mail:** admissions@fisher.edu
Fax: (617) 236-8858   **Internet:** www.fisher.edu

Institution Description: Fisher College is an independent four-year urban college offering career and transfer programs combined with a liberal arts and sciences general education component. *Enrollment:* 458. *Degrees awarded:* Associate, baccalaureate. Certificates also awarded.

Accreditation: *Regional:* NEASC. *Professional:* health information technician, physical therapy

History: Fisher College began in 1903 as a two-year institution known as the Winter Hill Business School and in 1952 became Fisher Junior College; changed name to Fisher College in 1999.

Institutional Structure: *Governing board:* Board of Trustees of 9 members. Senior administration consists of 5 vice-presidents for academic affairs, finance, co-curricular life, enrollment management, and continuing and distance education operations.

Calendar: Semesters. Weekend college operates on three fifteen-week trimesters.

Admission: *Requirements:* Either graduation from accredited secondary school with a minimum GPA of 2.5. Recommends completion of 4 units English, 3 math, 3 history, social science, or behavioral sciences, and 2 units of science.

Degree Requirements: *For baccalaureate degree:* 121 credits; minimum 2.0 GPA; final 30 credits at Fisher College. *For all associate degrees:* 60 credits; complete at least 50% of required credit hours in coursework at Fisher College; 24 of final 30 credits at Fisher College.

Distinctive Educational Programs: Through distance education, it is possible for students to earn the majority of certificate and degree programs offered.

Degrees Conferred: 74 *associate*; 87 *baccalaureate*.

Fees and Other Expenses: *Full-time tuition per academic year 2005–06:* undergraduate $16,775. *Required fees:* $1,675. *Room and board per academic year:* $10,475.

Financial Aid: Aid from institutionally generated funds is provided on the basis of academic merit, financial need, athletic ability. Institution has a Program Participation Agreement with the U.S. Department of Education for eligible students to receive Pell Grants and other federal aid.

Financial aid to full-time, first-time undergraduate students: need-based scholarships/grants totaling $3,674,583, self-help $2,348,240, parent loans

$649,477; non-need-based scholarships/grants totaling $293,500, self-help $364,914, parent loans $264,232.

Departments and Teaching Staff: *Total instructional faculty:* 22 (women 15, men 7). Student-to-faculty ratio: 21:1.

Enrollment: Total enrollment 458. Undergraduate 149 men / 291 women; part-time 5m / 13w.

Characteristics of Student Body: *Ethnic/racial makeup:* number of Black non-Hispanic: 95; American Indian or Alaska Native: 1; Asian or Pacific Islander: 31; Hispanic: 70; White non-Hispanic: 206; unknown: 15. *Age distribution:* number under 18: 1; 18–19: 211; 20–21: 151; 22–24: 78; 25–29: 12; 30–34: 3; 35–39: 1; 40–49: 1.

International Students: 36 nonresident aliens enrolled fall 2004. Students from Europe, Asia, Central and South America, Africa. Programs available to aid students whose native language is not English: English as a Second Language Program. No financial aid specifically designated for international students.

Student Life: College provides housing and food service for 260 students and offers a variety of co-curricular programs for all students.

Library Collections: 31,295 volumes. Online catalog. 14,270 full-text titles via electronic access. 105 journal subscriptions. 8 computer work stations. Students have access to the Internet at no charge.

Buildings and Grounds: The college operates within 11 turn-of-the century town houses.

Chief Executive Officer: Dr. Charles C. Perkins, President.

Address admission inquiries to Robert McLaragni, Director of Admissions.

Framingham State College

100 State Street
P.O. Box 9101
Framingham, Massachusetts 01701-9101
Tel: (508) 620-1220   **E-mail:** admiss@framingham.edu
Fax: (508) 626-4592   **Internet:** www.framingham.edu

Institution Description: Framingham State College is a member of Massachusetts Board of of Higher Education. *Enrollment:* 6,016. *Degrees awarded:* Baccalaureate, master's.

Academic offerings subject to approval by statewide coordinating bodies. Budget subject to approval by state governing boards.

Accreditation: *Regional:* NEASC. *Professional:* dietetics, family and consumer science, nursing

History: Established and chartered in Lexington as State Normal School, a women's institution, and offered first instruction at postsecondary level 1839; moved to West Newton 1844; moved to present location 1853; awarded first degree (baccalaureate) 1923; changed name to Framingham State Teachers College 1935; changed name to State College at Framingham 1960; added graduate curriculum 1961; became coeducational 1964; adopted present name 1968. *See* Framingham State College Alumni Association, *First State Normal School in America* (Framingham, Mass.: Alumni Association, 1959) for further information.

Institutional Structure: *Governing board:* Massachusetts Board of Higher Education. Representation: 15 regents. All voting. Board of Trustees (appointed for Framingham State College) 8 members. All voting. *Composition of institution:* Administrators 28 men / 16 women. Academic affairs headed by vice president, academic affairs. Management/business/finances directed by vice president for administration and finance. Total instructional faculty 175. Academic governance body, All College Council, meets an average of 20 times per year. *Faculty representation:* Faculty served by collective bargaining agent affiliated with NEA and Massachusetts Teachers Association.

Calendar: Semesters. Academic year Sept. to May. Freshmen admitted Sept., Jan. Degrees conferred and formal commencement May. Summer session from early June to mid-Aug.

Characteristics of Freshmen: 3,803 applicants (1,372 men, 2,431 women). 62.5% of applicants admitted. 27% of admitted students enrolled full-time.

97% (632 students) submitted SAT scores. *25th percentile:* SAT I Verbal 480, SAT I Math 470. *75th percentile:* SAT I Verbal 570, SAT I Math 580.

90% of freshmen from Massachusetts. Freshmen from 15 states and 5 foreign countries.

Admission: Rolling admissions plan. For fall acceptance, apply as early as Oct. 15 of previous year, but not later than Mar. 15 of year of enrollment. Students are notified of acceptance beginning Jan. Early acceptance available. *Requirements:* Either graduation from accredited secondary school or GED. Recommend 4 units English, 2 foreign language, 3 mathematics, 2 history, and 3 science; additional units foreign language, mathematics, and science also rec-

ommended. Minimum GPA 2.5. Lowest acceptable secondary school class standing 50th percentile. *Entrance tests:* College Board SAT; recommend 3 Achievements, including English and mathematics. *For transfer students:* 2.0 minimum GPA; from 4-year accredited institution 24 courses maximum transfer credit; from 2-year accredited institution 16 courses.

College credit and advanced placement for postsecondary-level work completed in secondary school. For External Degree Program students, college credit and advanced placement for extrainstitutional learning on basis of ACE *2006 Guide to the Evaluation of Educational Experiences in the Armed Services* and faculty assessment. Tutoring available. Noncredit developmental courses offered during regular academic year.

Degree Requirements: 32 courses; 2.0 GPA; 2 terms in residence; distribution requirements, including course in national and state constitutions. Fulfillment of some degree requirements and exemption from some beginning courses possible by passing departmental examinations, College Board CLEP, APP, other standardized tests. *Grading system:* A–F; pass-fail; withdraw (carries time limit); incomplete (carries time limit).

Distinctive Educational Programs: *For undergraduates:* Interdepartmental/interdisciplinary programs in American, environmental, and liberal studies. Honors programs and unstructured independent research. Preprofessional program in medicine. Study abroad available. Cross-registration at other Massachusetts state colleges through Center for Academic Program Sharing. Alternative for Individual Development program provides academic, career and personal assistance and counseling for disadvantaged students. *For graduate students:* Evening classes. Facilities and programs for independent research. *Available to all students:* Special facilities for using telecommunications in the classroom.

Degrees Conferred: 588 *baccalaureate;* 651 *master's.* Bachelor's degrees awarded in top five disciplines: business, management, marketing, and related support services 100; social sciences 84; psychology 74; family and consumer sciences/human sciences 65; communication technologies/technicians, and support services 47.

Fees and Other Expenses: *Full-time tuition per academic year 2004–05:* $4,654 resident, $10,734 out-of-state students. *Books and supplies:* $700. Contact the university for current information regarding graduate tuition and fees. *Room and board per academic year:* $5,548.

Financial Aid: Aid from institutionally generated funds is provided on the basis of academic merit, financial need. Institution has a Program Participation Agreement with the U.S. Department of Education for eligible students to receive Pell Grants and other federal aid.

Financial aid to full-time, first-time undergraduate students: 18% received federal grants averaging $2,573; 36% state/local grants averaging $2,840; 14% institutional grants averaging $1,707; 60% received loans averaging $4,218.

Departments and Teaching Staff: *Professors* 87, *associate professors* 33, *assistant professors* 42, *instructors* 7, *part-time teachers* 71.

Total instructional faculty: 192.60 FTE. Degrees held by full-time faculty: doctorate 72%, master's 28%. 75% hold terminal degrees.

Enrollment: Total enrollment 6,016 Undergraduate 5,873 (33.3% men, 66.7% women).

Characteristics of Student Body: *Ethnic/racial makeup (undergraduate):* Black non-Hispanic: 3%, American Indian or Alaska Native: .5%; Asian or Pacific Islander: 2.5%; Hispanic: 3.4%; White non-Hispanic: 80.2%; unknown: 8.7%.

International Students: 66 undergraduate nonresident aliens enrolled fall 2004. Students from Europe, Asia, Central and South America, Africa, Australia. Programs available to aid students whose native language is not English: social, cultural. Some financial aid available annually for qualifying undergraduate international students.

Student Life: On-campus residence halls house 40% of student body. Residence halls for women only constitute 20% of such space, for both sexes 80%. *Intercollegiate athletics:* men only: baseball, basketball, football, hockey, soccer; women only: basketball, field hockey, softball, volleyball. *Special regulations:* Cars permitted for commuters and resident students with medical excuse or off-campus employment. *Special services:* Medical services. *Student publications, radio: Dial,* a yearbook; *Gatepost,* a weekly newspaper; *Onyx,* a biannual literary magazine. Radio station WDJM-FM broadcasts 108 hours per week. *Surrounding community:* Framingham population 65,000. Boston, 20 miles from campus, is nearest metropolitan area. Served by airport 20 miles from campus; passenger rail service 3 miles from campus.

Library Collections: 202,500 volumes. 659,000 microforms; 3,320 audiovisual materials; 470 current periodical subscriptions. Online catalog. Students have access to online information retrieval services and the Internet.

Most important special collections include Callahan Collection of Local History; O'Connor Collection of Poetry; Curriculum Library Materials.

Buildings and Grounds: Campus area 73 acres.

Chief Executive Officer: Dr. Helen L. Heineman, President.

Address admission inquiries to Philip M. Dooher, Dean of Admissions.

Gordon College

255 Grapevine Road
Wenham, Massachusetts 01984
Tel: (978) 927-2300   **E-mail:** admissions@gordon.edu
Fax: (978) 524-3704   **Internet:** www.gordon.edu

Institution Description: Gordon College is a private, independent, nonprofit, Christian college. *Enrollment:* 3,285. *Degrees awarded:* Baccalaureate, master's.

Member of Christian College Consortium and Northeast Consortium of Colleges and Universities in Massachusetts.

Accreditation: *Regional:* NEASC. *Professional*: music, social work

History: Established as the Boston Missionary Training Institute and offered first instruction at postsecondary level 1889; chartered 1914; changed name to Gordon Bible College 1916; awarded first degree (baccalaureate) 1919; changed name to Gordon College of Theology and Missions 1921, to Gordon College and Gordon Divinity School 1962; adopted present name 1970; Barrington College of Rhode Island merged with Gordon College 1985.

Institutional Structure: *Governing board:* Board of Trustees. Representation: 36 trustees. All voting. *Composition of institution:* Administrators 6 men / 2 women. Academic affairs headed by provost. Management/business/finances directed by vice president for finance. Full-time instructional faculty 83. Academic governance body, the faculty, meets an average of 8 times per year.

Calendar: Semester. Academic year late Aug. to mid-May. Students may enter Aug., Jan. No summer term.

Characteristics of Freshmen: 78% of applicants admitted. 40% of applicants admitted and enrolled.

93% (397students) submitted SAT scores; 9% (10 students) submitted ACT scores. *25th percentile:* SAT Verbal 560, SAT I Math 550; ACT Composite 24. *75th percentile*: SAT Verbal 670, SAT Math 640; ACT Composite 30.

67% of entering freshmen expected to graduate within 5 years. 24% of freshmen from Massachusetts. Freshmen from 40 states and 21 foreign countries.

Admission: Rolling admissions plan. Apply no later than the day of registration. Apply by Dec. 1 for early decision. Early acceptance available. *Requirements:* Either graduation from accredited secondary school or GED. Recommend 4 English, 3 foreign language, 2 mathematics, 2 science, 2 social studies, 2 academic electives. *Entrance tests:* College Board SAT or ACT composite. For foreign students TOEFL. *For transfer students:* 2.0 minimum GPA; from 2-year or 4-year accredited institution 96 semester hours maximum transfer credit.

College credit and advanced placement for postsecondary-level work completed in secondary school. Tutoring available. Developmental courses offered during regular academic year; credit given.

Degree Requirements: 124 semester hours; core curriculum; 32 of final 40 semester hour in residence; 2 physical education and outdoor education program; 2.0 GPA. *For master of education degree:* Track I - 33 semester hours (for students with provisional with advanced standing certificate or equivalent); Track II: 45 semester hours.

Fulfillment of some degree requirements and exemption from some beginning courses possible by passing College Board CLEP. *Grading system:* A–F; pass-fail; withdraw (carries time limit).

Distinctive Educational Programs: Work-experience programs, including cooperative education. Interdepartmental programs in American studies, social services, special education, youth services, international affairs, pre-law, health professions. Study abroad in China, Kenya, England, France, Israel, Costa Rica, Egypt, Italy, Russia. Domestic study in Washington (DC), Los Angeles (CA), and San Francisco (CA).

ROTC: Offered In cooperation with Boston University and University of Massachusetts-Lowell.

Degrees Conferred: 388 *baccalaureate:* area and ethnic studies 3; biological/life sciences 37; business/marketing 35; communications/communication technologies 34; computer and information sciences 7; education 13; English 48; foreign languages and literature 10; mathematics 8; parks and recreation 8; philosophy/religion/theology 47; physical sciences 6; protective services/public administration 30; psychology 26; social sciences and history 59; visual and performing arts 27. 18 *master's*: education 18.

Fees and Other Expenses: *Full-time tuition per academic year 2004–05:* $21,930 undergraduate; contact the college for current graduate tuition/fees. *Other fees:* $994. *Room and board per academic year:* $6,270.

Financial Aid: Aid from institutionally generated funds is provided on the basis of academic merit, financial need, other criteria.

Financial aid to full-time, first-time undergraduate students: need-based scholarships/grants totaling $10,573,025, self-help $1,434,509, parent loans $746,480; non-need-based scholarships/grants totaling $3,855,910; self-help $3,086,452, parent loans $958,847.

Departments and Teaching Staff: *Total instructional faculty:* 146 (full-time 93, part-time 53; women 51, men 95; members of minority groups 12). Total faculty with doctorate, first-professional, or other terminal degree: 71. Student-to-faculty ratio: 14:1.

Enrollment: Total enrollment 3,285. Undergraduate full-time 563 men / 1,039 women, part-time 17m / 21w; graduate part-time 6m / 37w. *Transfer students:* 70.

Characteristics of Student Body: *Ethnic/racial makeup:* number of Black non-Hispanic: 21; American Indian or Alaska Native: 3; Asian or Pacific Islander: 35; Hispanic: 25; White non-Hispanic: 1,492; unknown: 32.

International Students: 39 nonresident aliens enrolled fall 2004. Students from Europe, Asia, Central and South America, Africa, Canada, Australia. No programs available to aid students whose native language is not English. No financial aid specifically designated for international students.

Student Life: On-campus residence halls house 84% of student body. Students must live in on-campus housing unless they are married, living with family, or have college approval to live off-campus. *Intercollegiate athletics:* men only: basketball, hockey, soccer, tennis; women only: basketball, field hockey, softball, tennis, volleyball. *Special regulations:* Cars permitted without restrictions. *Special services:* Learning Resources Center, medical services. *Student publications: Hypernikon,* a yearbook; *The Tartan,* a bimonthly newspaper; *Stillpoint,* a quarterly publication, *The Idiom,* a student literary publication. *Surrounding community:* Boston, 25 miles from campus, is nearest metropolitan area. Served by airport 25 miles from campus, passenger rail service 5 miles from campus.

Library Collections: 186,224 volumes. 87,000 government documents; 19,400 microforms; 4,543 audiovisual materials; 536 current periodical subscriptions. Online catalog. Computer work stations available. Students have access to online information retrieval services and the Internet.

Most important special holdings include Vining Rare Book Collection (8,063 volumes); William Wilberforce Papers; rare Shakespeare Folios.

Buildings and Grounds: Campus area 800 acres. *New buildings:* Chase Resident Hall completed 2004.

Chief Executive Officer: Dr. R. Judson Carlberg, President.

Address admission inquiries to Silvio Vazquez, Dean of Admissions.

Gordon-Conwell Theological Seminary

130 Essex Street
South Hamilton, Massachusetts 01982
Tel: (978) 468-7111   **E-mail:** adminfo@gordonconwell.edu
Fax: (978) 468-6591   **Internet:** www.gordonconwell.edu

Institution Description: Gordon-Conwell Theological Seminary is a private, independent and multidenominational graduate theological seminary. *Enrollment:* 2,011. *Degrees awarded:* First-professional (master of divinity), master's, doctorate.

Member of Boston Theological Institute, a consortium of 9 schools involved with theological education.

Accreditation: *Regional:* NEASC. *National:* ATS. *Professional*: theology

History: Gordon-Conwell traces its roots to Conwell School of Theology founded 1884 and Gordon Divinity School founded 1889; merger of the two institutions occurred 1969; present name adopted 1970.

Institutional Structure: *Governing board:* Extrainstitutional representation: 31 trustees; institutional representation: 1 administrator. All voting. *Composition of institution:* Administrators 6 men. Academic affairs headed by vice president for academic affairs. Management/business/finances directed by vice president for fiscal affairs. Alumni/church relations/public relations directed by vice president for resource management. Full-time instructional faculty 38. Academic governance body, the faculty, meets an average of 9 times per year.

Calendar: Semesters (4-1-4 plan). Academic year mid-Sept. to mid-May. Students admitted Sept., Feb. Degrees conferred and formal commencement May. Summer session June to Aug.

Admission: Rolling admission. International students must apply by May 1 for fall entrance. *Requirements:* Baccalaureate degree from accredited college or university. Master of Divinity a prerequisite for master of theology and doctorate.

Distinctive Educational Programs: Member of Boston Theological Institute, a consortium of 9 theological schools.

Degrees Conferred: 158 *master's:* theology; 73 *doctorate:* theology; 92 *first-professional:* master of divinity.

Fees and Other Expenses: *Full-time tuition per academic year 2004–05:* Contact the seminary for current information regarding tuition, fees, and housing.

Financial Aid: Aid from institutionally generated funds is provided on the basis of academic merit, financial need. Institution has a Program Participation

Agreement with the U.S. Department of Education for eligible students to receive Pell Grants and other federal aid.

Departments and Teaching Staff: New Testament *professors* 4, *associate professors* 1, *assistant professors* 1, *instructors* 1, *part-time teachers* 0; Old Testament 3, 2, 0, 1, 0; church history 1, 0, 1, 1, 0; theology 3, 1, 0, 0, 0; missions 1, 0, 0, 1, 0; preaching 1, 1, 0, 1, 0; Christian education 0, 1, 0, 2, 0; evangelism 1, 0, 0, 0, 0; ministry 2, 0, 1, 1, 3; pastoral psychology 2, 0, 0, 1, 0; youth ministry 1, 0, 0, 0, 0; social ethics 1, 0, 0, 0, 0.

Total instructional faculty: 41. Degrees held by full-time faculty: doctorate 100%.

Enrollment: Total enrollment 2,011 (65.6% men, 33.4% women).

Characteristics of Student Body: *Ethnic/racial makeup:* Black non-Hispanic: 135; American Indian or Alaska Native: .2%; Asian or Pacific Islander: 9.3%; Hispanic: 4%; White non-Hispanic: 68.6%; unknown: 1%.

International Students: 38 nonresident aliens enrolled fall 2004. No programs available to aid students whose native language is not English. Financial aid specifically designated for international students: scholarships available annually.

Student Life: On-campus residence halls house 63% of single and married student body. *Special regulations:* Quiet hours set by members of each residence hall. *Special services:* Medical services. *Surrounding community:* Campus is 2.5 miles from mass transit train service. Campus is located 25 miles north of Boston.

Library Collections: 220,000 volumes. 42,000 microforms; 1,000 current periodicals. Students have access to online information retrieval services.

Most important special holdings include Babson Bible Collection; Edward Payson Vining Collection of rare bibles, manuscripts, and linguistic studies.

Buildings and Grounds: Campus area 118 acres.

Chief Executive Officer: Dr. Walter C. Kaiser, Jr., President.

Address admission inquiries to John D. Standrige, Director of Admissions.

Hampshire College

893 West Street
Amherst, Massachusetts 01002
Tel: (413) 559-3000   **E-mail:** admissions@hampshire.edu
Fax: (413) 559-5631   **Internet:** www.hampshire.edu

Institution Description: Hampshire College is a private, independent, non-profit college. *Enrollment:* 1,352. *Degrees awarded:* Baccalaureate.

Member of the consortium Five Colleges, Inc.

Accreditation: *Regional:* NEASC.

History: Established as an experimental college under sponsorship of Amherst, Mount Holyoke, and Smith Colleges and the University of Massachusetts, and incorporated 1965; offered first instruction at postsecondary level 1970; first degree (baccalaureate) awarded 1971. *See* Franklin Patterson and Charles Longsworth, *The Making of a College* (Cambridge, Mass.: The MIT Press, 1975) for further information.

Institutional Structure: *Governing board:* The Trustees of Hampshire College. Extrainstitutional representation: 24 trustees; institutional representation: president of college, 1 full-time instructional faculty member, 1 student; 10 alumni. 1 ex officio. All voting. *Composition of institution:* Administrators 40 men / 88 women (17% are members of minority groups; at dean's level and above, 40% are women; 2 women deans are members of minority groups). Academic affairs headed by dean of faculty. Management/business/finances directed by treasurer. Full-time instructional faculty 103. Academic governance body, College Senate, meets an average of 12 times per year.

Calendar: Semesters (4-1-4 plan). Academic year early Sept. to early May. Freshmen admitted Sept., Feb. Degrees conferred and formal commencement May. No summer session.

Characteristics of Freshmen: 59% of applicants admitted. 26% of applicants admitted and enrolled.

88% (315 students) submitted SAT scores; 21% (75 students) submitted ACT scores. *25th percentile:* SAT Verbal 610, SAT Math 550; ACT Composite 25. *75th percentile:* SAT Verbal 700, SAT Math 660; ACT Composite 29.

60% of entering freshmen expected to graduate within 5 years. 14% of freshmen from Massachusetts. Freshmen from 47 states and 10 foreign countries.

Admission: For fall acceptance, apply no later than Feb. 1. Students are notified of acceptance Apr. 1. Apply by Nov. 15 for early decision; must commit to attend Hampshire College and must withdraw applications to other institutions if accepted. Apply by Jan. 1 for Jan. 21 notification. Early acceptance available

to qualified high school juniors. *Entrance tests:* College Board SAT and ACT composite not required but scores considered if submitted. *For transfer students:* Transfer examination committees may pass students in up to 3 out of 4 Division I examinations.

Degree Requirements: Students complete a full-time program composed of three levels of study (Basic Studies, Concentration, Advanced Studies). Additional requirements include community service and consideration of one's work from a non-Western perspective. *Grading system:* Narrative evaluations.

Distinctive Educational Programs: Students are given major responsibility for planning and directing individual courses of study. Three divisions replace freshman-to-senior year sequence; five multidisciplinary schools replace usual academic departments. Work-experience programs. Most programs are interdisciplinary. Programs for independent research including individual majors; tutorials. Facilities for independent research, including open science and computer laboratories; special farm center; television, film, and photography studios. Over 100 study abroad programs available to Hampshire students, as well as individually arranged overseas experiences. Cross-registration through consortium. Third World Advising Center. Women's Center. Civil Liberties and Public Policy Program. Multicultural Center. Student Advising Center. Jointly sponsored academic programs available through consortium.

ROTC: Army in cooperation with University of Massachusetts-Amherst.

Degrees Conferred: 261 *baccalaureate:* agriculture 6; architecture 4; area and ethnic studies 20; biological/life sciences 34; communications/communication technologies 4; computer and information sciences 6; education 10; English 28; liberal arts/general studies 1; mathematics 1; philosophy/religion/theology 16; psychology 2; social sciences and history 37; visual and performing arts 92.

Fees and Other Expenses: *Full-time tuition per academic year 2004–05:* $30,418. *Required fees:* $560. *Room and board per academic year:* $8,113.

Financial Aid: Aid from institutionally generated funds is provided on the basis of academic merit and financial need.

Financial aid to full-time, first-time undergraduate students: need-based scholarships/grants totaling $14,581,095, self-help $4,032,910, parent loans $3,182,700; non-need-based scholarships/grants totaling $330,400, self-help $383,675, parent loans $1,587,770.

Departments and Teaching Staff: *Professors* 35, *associate professors* 18, *assistant professors* 41, *part-time faculty:* 45. *Total instructional faculty:* 140 (full-time 95, part-time 45; women 68, men 71; members of minority groups 23). Student-to-faculty ratio: 12:1. Degrees held by full-time faculty: baccalaureate 4%, master's 10%, doctorate 86%. 86% hold terminal degrees.

Enrollment: Total enrollment 1,352. Undergraduate full-time 573 men / 779 women. *Transfer students:* in-state 12; from out-of-state 40.

Characteristics of Student Body: *Ethnic/racial makeup:* number of Black non-Hispanic: 42; American Indian or Alaska Native: 5; Asian or Pacific Islander: 49; Hispanic: 67; White non-Hispanic: 971; unknown: 178. *Age distribution:* number under 18: 9; 18–19: 563; 20–21: 549; 22–24: 214; 25–29: 9; 30–34: 3; 35–39: 2.

International Students: 43 nonresident aliens enrolled fall 2004. 8 students from Europe, 16 Asia, 3 Central and South America, 5 Africa, Australia, 10 other. Programs available to aid students whose native language is not English: social, cultural, financial. Scholarships available annually for qualifying undergraduate international students.

Student Life: On-campus residence halls and institutionally controlled cooperative facilities house 95% of student body. Residence halls for both sexes constitute 100% of such space. *Special regulations:* Cars permitted; registration fee charged. *Special services:* Quantitative Skills Program, Disabilities Support Services, Student Advising Centers (STAR), Women's Center, International Studies Office, Office of Multicultural Affairs, Writing and Reading Program and Laboratory, Health Services, Career Options Resource Center, Five College bus service, Counselor Advocates. *Student publications: The Phoenix,* an irregularly published newspaper; *Race and Women, The Logo, Reckoning, Student Action Bulletin, The Reader, Detritus, The Ground. Surrounding community:* Amherst population 33,500. Boston, 89 miles from campus, is nearest metropolitan area. Served by mass transit system; airport 40 miles from campus; passenger rail service 20 miles from campus.

Library Collections: 136,326 volumes. Online catalog. 2,288 current periodical subscriptions. 39,135 audiovisual items. 186 computer work stations. Students have access to information retrieval services and the Internet. Total 2004–05 budget for books and materials: $258,000.

Most important special holdings include collections on non-Western science; environmental studies; film/photography.

Buildings and Grounds: Campus area 800 acres.

Chief Executive Officer: Dr. Gregory Prince, President.

Address admission inquiries to Karen Parker, Director of Admissions.

Harvard University

8 Garden Street
Cambridge, Massachusetts 02138-3800
Tel: (617) 495-1551   **E-mail:** college@harvard.edu
Fax: (617) 495-8821   **Internet:** www.harvard.edu

Institution Description: Harvard University is a private, independent, non-profit institution. The undergraduate program is Harvard Colleges. *University enrollment:* 19,201. . *Degrees awarded:* Associate, baccalaureate, first-professional (architecture, dentistry, law, medicine, theology), master's, doctorate. Certificates in education also awarded.

Accreditation: *Regional:* NEASC. *Professional:* applied science, architecture, business, dentistry, engineering, landscape architecture, law, medicine, pediatric dentistry, psychology internship, planning, public health, teacher education, theology

History: Established 1636; offered first instruction at postsecondary level 1638; awarded first degree (baccalaureate) 1642; added School of Medicine 1792, Divinity 1816, Law 1817, Dental Medicine 1867, Graduate School of Arts and Sciences 1872, Business Administration 1908, Education 1920, Public Health 1922, Graduate School of Design 1935, Public Administration 1938. *See* Samuel Eliot Morrison, *Three Centuries of Harvard* (Cambridge: Harvard University Press, n.d.) for further information.

Institutional Structure: *Governing boards:* The President and Fellows of Harvard College. Extrainstitutional representation: 5 fellows; institutional representation: president and treasurer of the university. All voting. The Board of Overseers. Extrainstitutional representation: 30 overseers; institutional representation: president and treasurer of the university. 2 ex officio. 30 voting. *Composition of institution:* Academic affairs headed by president. Management/business/finances directed by financial vice president and chief financial officer.

Calendar: Semesters. Academic year Sept. to May. Freshmen admitted Sept. Degrees conferred June, Nov., Mar. Formal commencement June.

Characteristics of Freshmen: 10% of applicants admitted. 77% of applicants admitted and enrolled.

99% of applicants submitted SAT scores; 17% submitted ACT scores. *25th percentile:* SAT Verbal 700, SAT Math 700; ACT Composite 31. *75th percentile:* SAT Verbal 790, SAT Math 790; ACT Composite 34,

96% of entering freshmen expected to graduate within 5 years. 13% of freshmen from Massachusetts. Freshmen from 50 states and 47 foreign countries.

Admission: Apply before Nov. 1 for early action; (Oct. 15 is recommended filing date). Apply before Jan. 1 for regular action (Dec. 15 is recommended filing date). Early acceptance occasionally available. *Requirements:* Recommended: 4 years English with intensive composition, 4 years mathematics or study through calculus, 4 years laboratory science, 3 years history, 4 years study of 1 foreign language. *Entrance tests:* College Board SAT I or ACT; 3 SAT II subject tests. *For transfer students:* Maximum transfer credit limited by 2-year residence requirement.

Degree Requirements: 16 full-year courses; minimum grade of C- in 10.5 courses; 4 terms in residence; core curriculum; writing requirements; demonstrated knowledge of a foreign language.

Fulfillment of some degree requirements and exemption from some beginning courses possible by passing institutional examinations, College Board AP exams and some international credentials. *Grading system:* A–F; pass-fail; satisfactory-unsatisfactory; credit-no credit; withdraw (carries time limit).

Distinctive Educational Programs: Interdisciplinary programs. Facilities and programs for independent research, including honors programs, individual majors, tutorials. Study abroad. Associate, baccalaureate, and master's degrees awarded through extension program. Nieman Foundation program for mid-career journalists. Harvard-Yenching Institute for Advancement of Education in East and Southeast Asia. Center for Hellenic Studies in Washington, D.C. William E. B. DuBois Institute for Afro-American Research. Villa I Tatti in Florence, Italy for study of the Italian Renaissance. Dumbarton Oaks Museum and Research Center for Byzantine, Pre-Columbian, and Medieval Cultures in Washington, D.C. Undergraduate teacher education program. Special facilities for using telecommunications in the classroom.

ROTC: Army, Navy, Air Force in cooperation with Massachusetts Institute of Technology. 6 Army, 2 Navy, and 2 Air Force commissions awarded 2004.

Degrees Conferred: 19 *associate;* 1,750 *baccalaureate* (B); 3,159 *master's* (M); 576 *doctorate:* architecture 242 (M), 13 (D); area and ethnic studies 42 (B), 69 (M), 24 (D); biological/life sciences 166 (B), 38 (M), 132 (D); business/marketing 906 (M), 14 (D); computer and information sciences 55 (B), 20 (M), 6 (D); education 603 (M), 60 (D); engineering and engineering technologies 25 (B), 21 (M), 11 (D); English 130 (B), 4 (M), 9 (D); foreign languages and literature 63 (B), 27 (M), 24 (D); health professions and related sciences 355 (M), 62 (D); law/legal studies 8 (D); liberal arts/general studies 10 (B); mathematics 89

(B), 36 (M), 18 (D); natural resources/environmental science 29 (B); philosophy/religion/theology 49 (B), 111 (M), 12 (D); physical sciences 99 (B), 69 (M), 60 (D); protective services/public administration 515 (M), 7 (D); psychology 116 (B), 32 (M), 13 (D); social sciences and history 809 (B), 87 (M), 87 (D); visual and performing arts 68 (B), 24 (M), 16 (D). 805 *first-professional:* dentistry 33; law 551; medicine 177. *Honorary degrees awarded 2004–05:* Doctor of Laws 4, Doctor of Letters 2, Doctor of Science 2, Doctor of Arts 1.

Fees and Other Expenses: *Full-time tuition per academic year 2004–05:* $27,448. Tuition varies for various graduate and professional schools. *Other fees:* $3,172 (undergraduate). *Room and board per academic year:* $9,260.

Financial Aid: Harvard University offers a direct lending program. Aid from institutionally generated funds is provided on the basis of financial need.

Financial aid to full-time, first-time undergraduate students: need-based scholarships/grants totaling $85,817,215, self-help $9,352,236; non-need-based scholarships/grants totaling $5,841,851, self-help $3,460,638, parent loans $14,988,429.

Departments and Teaching Staff: *Total instructional faculty* 1,959 (full-time 1,555, part-time 404; women 604, men 1,355; members of minority groups 231). Student-to-faculty ratio: 7:1.

Enrollment: Total enrollment 19,201. Undergraduate full-time 3,386 men / 3,176 women, first-professional full-time 1,438m / 1,242w, part-time 3m / 18w; graduate full-time 4,884m / 4,327w, part-time 308m / 419w.

Characteristics of Student Body: *Ethnic/racial makeup (undergraduate):* number of Black non-Hispanic: 499; American Indian or Alaska Native: 58; Asian or Pacific Islander: 1,141; Hispanic: 512; White non-Hispanic: 3,155; unknown: 612. *Age distribution:* number under 18: 171; 18–19: 2,861; 20–21: 2,997; 22–24: 511; 25–29: 14; 30–34: 6; 40–49: 1; 50–64: 1.

International Students: 3,619 nonresident aliens enrolled fall 2004. 1,018 students from Europe, 1,267 Asia, 769 Central and South America, 148 Africa, 467 Canada, 67 Australia, 15 New Zealand, 295 other. Programs available to aid students whose native language is not English: social and cultural. English as a Second Language. No financial aid is specifically designated for international students; need-based aid available for international students.

Student Life: On-campus residence halls house 96.5% of student body. Residence halls for men and women constitute 100% of such space. Cooperative facilities and married student housing available. *Intercollegiate athletics:* Harvard/Radcliffe supports 41 intercollegiate sports teams including men's baseball, basketball, crew, cross country, fencing, football, golf, ice hockey, lacrosse, sailing, skiing, soccer, squash, swimming, tennis, track (indoor and outdoor), volleyball, water polo, wrestling; women's crew, cross country, fencing, field hockey, golf, ice hockey, lacrosse, sailing, skiing, soccer, softball, squash, swimming, tennis, track (indoor and outdoor), volleyball, water polo. Various club sport organizations. *Special regulations:* Cars permitted without restrictions. *Special services:* Learning Resources Center, medical services, shuttle buses. *Student publications, radio:* The Advocate, a literary magazine; *Harvard Crimson,* daily newspaper; *Harvard Independent,* weekly newspaper; *Harvard Lampoon,* humor magazine; *Harvard Political Review; Harvard Yearbook.* Radio station WHRB broadcasts 168 hours per week. *Surrounding community:* Boston population over 500,000. Served by mass transit bus; rail systems; airport 5 miles from campus; passenger rail service 3 miles from campus.

Library Collections: 15,391,906 volumes. Online catalog. 7 million microforms; 100,000 periodicals. Students have access to online information retrieval services and the Internet. Total 2004–05 library expenditures: $28,000,000.

Most important special holdings include Houghton Library Rare Books Collection; Harvard-Yenching Library of works in Far Eastern Languages; Tozzer Library of volumes relating to the Peabody Museum of Archaeology and Ethnology.

Buildings and Grounds: *New buildings:* Graduate Student Housing (One Western Avenue) completed 2003; Dental Research Building 2004; Harkness Commons 2004; Science Center addition 2005.

Chief Executive Officer: Dr. Lawrence H. Summers, President.

Address admission inquiries to Director of Admissions.

Divinity School

Degree Programs Offered: *First-professional, master's, doctorate.*

Admission: *For first-professional:* Baccalaureate or equivalent from accredited institution.

Degree Requirements: *For first-professional:* 3 years full-time study or equivalent, reading knowledge of 1 language of theological scholarship, 2 years field education, senior paper.

Fees and Other Expenses: Contact the school for current information.

Distinctive Educational Programs: Center for Study of World Religions. Summer language program. Cross-registration with Boston Theological Institute schools. Women's Studies in Religion Program. Merrill Fellow program for parish ministers. *See also* Faculty of Arts and Sciences.

Graduate School of Arts and Sciences

Degree Programs Offered: *Baccalaureate, master's, doctorate* in various fields.

Distinctive Educational Programs: Cooperative doctorate in study of religion; in Near Eastern languages and civilizations with Divinity School.

Graduate School of Education

Degree Programs Offered: *Master's* in various fields; *doctorate* in administration, planning, social policy; teaching, curriculum, and learning environments; human development, reading, counseling and consulting psychology. Specialist certificates also awarded.

Distinctive Educational Programs: Institute for Educational Management. Institution for Management of Lifelong Education. Institute for Evaluating School Program Effectiveness.

Harvard Business School

Degree Programs Offered: *Master's, doctorate.*

Distinctive Educational Programs: Joint M.B.A.-Master of Public Policy degree with Kennedy School of Government. Executive education programs.

Harvard Design School

Degree Programs Offered: *First-professional, master's* in architecture, landscape architecture, urban planning and design, and design studies; *doctorate* in design.

Distinctive Educational Programs: Early entry program for qualified Harvard and Radcliffe undergraduates. Joint center for Urban Studies with Massachusetts Institute of Technology. Carpenter Center for Visual Arts offers programs in visual and environmental studies. Laboratory for Computer Graphics and Spatial Analysis Research and Development Program. Student exchange program with Cambridge University (England).

John F. Kennedy School of Government

Degree Programs Offered: *Master's* public policy, public administration, urban planning, international development; *doctorate* in public policy, political economy and government, health policy, social policy and government.

Distinctive Educational Programs: Center for Science and International Affairs, Energy and Environmental Policy Center, Business and Government Center, Center for Press, Politics and Public Policy, Center for Health Policy and Management, Program in Criminal Justice, Policy and Management, Institute of Politics, Executive Training Programs, Training Programs for Newly Elected Officials, MPA Summer Program.

Law School

Degree Programs Offered: *Associate, baccalaureate, master's, doctorate.*

Admission: *For first-professional:* Baccalaureate from accredited institution. Liberal college education recommended. LSAT. LSDAS.

Degree Requirements: *For first-professional:* 3 years full-time study, 2 years in residence, professional responsibility and written work requirements.

Fees and Other Expenses: Contact the school for current information.

Distinctive Educational Programs: Joint J.D.-master of public policy degree with Kennedy School of Government. Center for Criminal Justice. International legal studies program. International tax program. East Asian legal studies program. Liberal arts fellowship in law.

Medical School

Degree Programs Offered: *First-professional, doctorate.*

Fees and Other Expenses: Contact the school for current information.

Distinctive Educational Programs: Joint M.D.-Ph.D. with Faculty of Arts and Sciences, M.D.-Master of public health and M.D.-M.S. with School of Public Health, M.D.-Master in public policy with Kennedy School of Government. Joint M.D.-Ph.D. and cross-registration with Massachusetts Institute of Technology.

School of Dental Medicine

Degree Programs Offered: *First-professional.*

Admission: Recommend 1 year college level English (preferably writing), 8 semester hours biology (including laboratory), 16 organic and inorganic chemistry, 8 physics, 1 year calculus (unless taken in secondary school), 2 or 3 advanced science courses, additional social and behavioral sciences and humanities courses. DAT. AADAS.

Degree Requirements: 4-year prescribed curriculum, research thesis, externship.

Fees and Other Expenses: Contact the school for current information.

School of Public Health

Degree Programs Offered: *Master's, doctorate* in various fields related to public health management, policy, and research.

Distinctive Educational Programs: Joint MD/MPH program with any medical school. Joint JD/MPH with Harvard Law School. Summer programs in clinical effectiveness and quantitative methods for physicians. Cross-registration with Massachusetts Institute of Technology and Tufts University. Interdisciplinary program in environmental health management. Center for Population Studies. Center for Prevention of Infectious Diseases. Kresge Center for Environmental Health. Educational Resource Center for Occupational Safety and Health. Office of Health Policy Information. Office of International Health Programs. Community Health Improvement Program. Continuing Education in Environmental Health. Executive Programs in Health Policy and Management.

Hebrew College

160 Herrick Road
Newton Centre, Massachusetts 02459

Tel: (617) 559-8600   **E-mail:** admissions@hebrewcollege.edu
Fax: (617) 559-8601   **Internet:** www.hebrewcollege.edu

Institution Description: Hebrew College was founded in 1921 and is a private, independent, nonprofit institution. Classes are conducted in Hebrew and English. *Enrollment:* 6. *Degrees awarded:* Baccalaureate, master's.

Member of Fenway Library Consortium.

Accreditation: *Regional:* NEASC.

History: Established as Hebrew Teachers College and offered first instruction at postsecondary level 1921; chartered and awarded first baccalaureate 1925; adopted present name 1969.

Institutional Structure: *Governing board:* Board of Trustees. *Composition of institution:* Administrators 11. Academic affairs headed by provost. Full-time instructional faculty 7 men / 2 women.

Calendar: Semesters. Academic year early Aug. to May. Formal commencement May. Summer session of 1 term.

Admission: Certificate of graduation from Hebrew High School (maintained by the College) or its equivalent. Students must have reached senior year or its equivalent in general high school studies. Proficiency in Hebrew.

Degree Requirements: 120 credit hours (including 78 credits in Jewish Studies and 42 in liberal arts subjects from approved colleges); 2.0 GPA; half of program in residence; core courses; distribution requirements. *Grading system:* A–F; pass-fail.

Distinctive Educational Programs: Off-campus center (at Hartford, CT). Cross-registration and dual-degree programs with Boston University, Simmons College; cross-registration with Boston College, Northeastern University, University of Massachusetts at Boston. Reciprocal borrowing privileges at Boston University library and at libraries of consortium members. Interdisciplinary programs in Jewish literature, history, and thought. Junior year in Israel. *Other distinctive programs:* Transitional program prepares high school seniors for Hebrew College.

Degrees Conferred: 3 *baccalaureate:* education; 11*master's:* education.

Fees and Other Expenses: *Full-time tuition per academic year 2004–05:* $660 per credit hour. *Required fees:* $95.

Financial Aid: Aid from institutionally generated funds is provided on the basis of financial need, other considerations. Contact Marilyn Jay (617) 559-8642 for financial aid information.

Departments and Teaching Staff: Total instructional faculty: 52 (full-time 19, part-time 23; women 14, men 28). *Degrees held by full-time faculty:* doctorate 100%.

Enrollment: Total enrollment: full-time 4 women, part-time 1m / 1w.

Characteristics of Student Body: *Ethnic/racial makeup:* White non-Hispanic: 4; unknown: 2.

International Students: 2 nonresident aliens enrolled fall 2004. 1 student from South America, 1 Middle East.

Library Collections: 114,285 volumes. 2,000 microforms; 1,450 audiovisual materials; 180 current periodical subscriptions. Total 2004–05 budget for materials and operations: $79,500.

Most important special holdings include Dr. Harry A. and Beatrice C. Savitz Medical History Collection; John S. and Florence G. Lawrence Microfilm Collection; Hebrew College Women's Association Women's Studies Collection.

Chief Executive Officer: Dr. David M. Gordis, President.

Address admission inquiries to Ina Regosin, Dean of Students.

Hellenic College/Holy Cross Greek Orthodox School of Theology

50 Goddard Avenue

Brookline, Massachusetts 02146-7496

Tel: (617) 731-3500   **E-mail:** admission@hchc.edu
Fax: (617) 850-1464   **Internet:** www.hchc.edu

Institution Description: Hellenic College-Holy Cross Greek Orthodox School of Theology is a private college affiliated with the Greek Orthodox Church. *Enrollment:* 255. *Degrees awarded:* Baccalaureate, first-professional (master of divinity), master's.

Accreditation: *Regional:* NEASC. *National:* ATS. *Professional:* theology

History: Established as Holy Cross Greek Orthodox Theological School 1937; offered first instruction at postsecondary level 1963; awarded first degree (baccalaureate) and adopted present name 1968.

Institutional Structure: *Governing board:* Board of Trustees. Representation: 81 trustees. 28 voting. Academic affairs headed by president. Management/business/finances directed by business manager. Full-time instructional faculty 12. Academic governance by dean of the School of Theology and dean of the College.

Calendar: Semesters. Academic year Sept. to May. Freshmen admitted Sept., Jan. Degrees conferred and formal commencement May. Summer session from early June to mid-July.

Admission: Rolling admissions plan. Apply no later than May 1. *Requirements:* Graduation from accredited secondary school or GED. *Entrance tests:* College Board SAT or ACT composite. *For transfer students:* 2.0 minimum GPA, 62 hours maximum transfer credit.

College credit and advanced placement for postsecondary-level work completed in secondary school.

Degree Requirements: 125 credit hours; 2.0 GPA; 2 years in residence; daily chapel attendance; 4 semesters physical education; core curriculum.

Fulfillment of some degree requirements and exemption from some beginning courses possible by passing College Board CLEP, AP. *Grading system:* A–F; withdraw.

Distinctive Educational Programs: Work-experience programs. Summer study abroad in Greece.

Degrees Conferred: 27 *baccalaureate*; 30 *master's*; 18 *first-professional*. Bachelor's degrees awarded: area ethnic, cultural, and gender studies 16; philosophy and religious studies 10; education 1.

Fees and Other Expenses: *Full-time tuition per academic year 2004–05:* $14,700. *Books and supplies:* $1,000. *Room and board per academic year:* $8,820.

Departments and Teaching Staff: *Total instructional faculty:* 16 (full-time 12, part-time 4). Degrees held by full-time faculty: 100% hold terminal degrees.

Enrollment: Total enrollment 255. Undergraduate 35 (48.6% men, 51.4% women).

Characteristics of Student Body: *Ethnic/racial makeup (undergraduate):* Black non-Hispanic: 2.9%; Hispanic: 2.9%; White non-Hispanic: 80%.

International Students: 5 undergraduate nonresident aliens enrolled fall 2004. Programs available to aid students whose native language is not English: social, cultural. No financial aid specifically designated for international students.

Student Life: On-campus residence halls available. *Intercollegiate athletics:* men only: basketball, soccer; women only: basketball. *Surrounding community:* Brookline population 55,000.

Library Collections: 117,000 volumes. 2,500 microform titles; 755 serial subscriptions. 3,200 audiovisual materials. Online catalog. Students have access to online information retrieval services and the Internet.

Buildings and Grounds: Campus area 52 acres.

Chief Executive Officer: Rev. Nicholas C. Triantafilou, President.

Address admission inquiries to Rev. James Katinas, Director of Admissions.

Hult International Business School

One Education Street

Cambridge, Massachusetts 02141

Tel: (617) 746-1990   **E-mail:** admissions@hult.edu
Fax: (617) 746-1991   **Internet:** www.hult.edu

Institution Description: Hult International Business School, formerly known as Arthur D. Little School of Management, is a nonprofit school. *Enrollment:* 65 in each annual master's degree program. *Degrees awarded:* Master's.

Accreditation: *Regional:* NEASC.

History: The Master of Science in Management Program began as an agro-industrial management development training program in 1963. The institute was chartered in 1971 and began awarding the master's degree in 1972.

Institutional Structure: *Governing board:* Education Board of Trustees. Extrainstitutional representation: 1 administrator, 1 EF member. 8 voting. *Composition of institution:* President, dean, controller, director of corporate relations and career services. Full-time instructional faculty 3. Academic governance body and full faculty meet an average of 6 times per year.

Calendar: 4 phases. Academic year Aug. to July. Students admitted Aug. Degrees conferred and formal commencement July. Summer tutorial program.

Admission: *Requirements:* Baccalaureate degree from an accredited college or university. Most participants have between four and eight years of work experience.

Degree Requirements: 62 credit hours; student must maintain stipulated minimum GPA. As a result of its strategic alliance with Boston College's (BC) Carroll School of Management, the program is housed on BC's 148-acre Chestnut Hill campus and at ADLSOM headquarters in Cambridge.

Distinctive Educational Programs: Management consulting projects. Elective courses with business practitioners in global franchise management, international negotiations and entrepreneurship.

Degrees Conferred: 441 *master's:* business and management.

Fees and Other Expenses: *Tuition 2004–05:* $36,500.

Financial Aid: *Graduate aid:* 33 students received fellowships and grants totaling $338,600 (ranging from $3,500 to $20,000).

Departments and Teaching Staff: *Total instructional faculty:* 29 (3 full-time, 26 part-time). Total faculty with doctorate, first-professional, or other terminal degree: 17. Student-to-faculty ratio: 1.5:1.

Enrollment: Total enrollment 50 (38 men / 12 women).

International Students: 46 nonresident aliens enrolled fall 2004. 8 students from Europe, 20 Asia, 18 Central and South America. Programs available to aid students whose native language is not English: English as a Second Language Program. No financial aid specifically designated for international students.

Student Life: No on-campus housing. School assists students in locating housing suitable to personal and family needs. *Special regulations:* Registered cars permitted. *Special services:* Medical services. *Surrounding community:* Cambridge population 95,000, is within Boston metropolitan area. Served by mass transit systems, airport 2 miles from campus, passenger rail service .5 miles from campus.

Publications: *Management Notes* and *Alumni Update*, both periodicals.

Library Collections: While at Hult International Business School, participants have complete access to the academic, library, and athletic facilities of Boston College.

Most important special holdings include MEI Library; Management Library; Thomas P. O'Neill Collection; Research Library.

Buildings and Grounds: Classes are held in a state-of-the-art classroom within the Hult International Business School which is housed in the North American headquarters of EF Education.

Chief Executive Officer: Dr. Lynne H. Rosansky, President.

Address admission inquiries to Susan Adler, Director of Worldwide Recruiting.

Lasell College

1844 Commonwealth Avenue

Newton, Massachusetts 02466-2716

Tel: (617) 243-2225   **E-mail:** info@lasell.edu
Fax: (617) 243-2880   **Internet:** www.lasell.edu

Institution Description: Lasell College is a private institution with an emphasis on teaching and lifelong learning. Lasell's philosophy of education offers students "connected learning," that allows students to apply the skills they are learning in the classroom to work experience. *Enrollment:* 1,196. *Degrees offered:* Baccalaureate, master's.

Accreditation: *Regional:* NEASC. *Professional:* athletic training, physical therapy

History: Founded by Edward Lasell in 1851 as a school for the advanced education of women.

Calendar: Semesters. Academic year Sept. to May. Formal commencement May.

Characteristics of Freshmen: 75% of applicants admitted. 24% of applicants admitted and enrolled.

90% (348 students) submitted SAT scores; 10% (38 students) submitted ACT scores. *25th percentile:* SAT Verbal 430, SAT Math 420; ACT Composite 20. *75th percentile:* SAT Verbal 520, SAT Math 510; ACT Composite 21.

42% of entering students expected to graduate within 5 years. 51% of freshmen from Massachusetts. Freshmen from 15 states and 4 foreign countries.

Admission: Rolling admissions. Applicants are evaluated on the basis of their academic achievement and overall initiative. SAT I or ACT required for all students and nursing applicants. *Requirements:* High school transcript and letter of recommendation. *For transfer students:* Applicants to a baccalaureate program must submit an official college transcript in addition to the other required materials listed above.

Degree Requirements: *For baccalaureate degrees:* 120 to 124 semester hours. *For master's degrees:* 36 semester hours.

Distinctive Educational Programs: Lasell College Institute for Fashion Technology, Center for Research on Aging and Intergenerational Studies, Lasell Village. Academic support is offered through the Learning Center with study skills, additional academic monitoring, and a writing lab.

Degrees Conferred: 192 *baccalaureate:* business/marketing 80; communications/communication technologies 3; education 29; health professions and related sciences 7; law/legal studies 3; liberal arts/general studies 10; protective services/public administration 6; psychology 9; social sciences and history 13; visual and performing arts 25. 2 *master's:* business/marketing.

Fees and Other Expenses: *Full-time tuition per academic year 2005–06:* $18,700. *Other fees:* $1,000. *Room and board per academic year:* $8,800.

Financial Aid: Aid from institutionally generated funds is provided on the basis of financial need.

Financial aid to full-time, first-time undergraduate students: need-based scholarships/grants totaling $10,844,181, self-help $4,860,379, parent loans $1,346,197; non-need-based scholarships/grants totaling $903,995, self-help $2,693,116, parent loans $1,927,079, tuition waivers $17,500.

Departments and Teaching Staff: *Total instructional faculty:* 150 (full-time 49, part-time 101; women 92, men 58; members of minority groups 11). Total faculty with doctorate, first-professional, or other terminal degree: 30. Student-to-faculty ratio: 14.4:1.

Enrollment: Total enrollment 1,196. Full-time 328 men / 810 women, part-time 11m / 21w; graduate full-time 2w, part-time 1m / 23w.

Characteristics of Student Body: *Ethnic/racial makeup:* number of Black non-Hispanic: 75; American Indian or Alaska Native: 5; Asian or Pacific Islander: 45; Hispanic: 66; White non-Hispanic: 870; unknown: 45. *Age distribution:* number under 18: 25; 18–19: 597; 20–21: 375; 22–24: 132; 25–29: 18; 30–34: 4; 35–39: 1; 40–49: 2; 65 and over: 1.

International Students: 50 nonresident aliens enrolled fall 2004. 7 students from Europe, 32, Asia, 6 Central and South America, 3 Africa. Programs available to aid students whose native language is not English: English as a Second Language program. No financial aid specifically designated for international students.

Student Life: Lasell College is a predominately residential college. Students are encouraged to participate in any of the 20 campus clubs and organizations. Sports activities for men include: basketball, cross-country, lacrosse, soccer, volleyball; for women: basketball, soccer, softball, volleyball. Student government elects representatives in the fall and spring. Lasell students publish *The Campus Crier* monthly.

Library Collections: 60,250 volumes. Online catalog. 474 current periodical subscriptions. 50,083 microforms. 125 computer work stations. Students have access to online information retrieval services and the Internet.

Most important special holdings include Altina Mead Collection; Lasell Archives.

Chief Executive Officer: Dr. Thomas J, DeWitt, President.

Address admissions inquiries to James M. Tweed, Director of Admissions.

Lesley College

29 Everett Street
Cambridge, Massachusetts 02138-2790
Tel: (617) 349-8800   **E-mail:** ugadm@lesley.edu
Fax: (617) 349-8150   **Internet:** www.lesley.edu

Institution Description: Lesley College is a private, independent, nonprofit college offering programs in education, human services, liberal studies, and management. *Enrollment:* 7,046. Undergraduate Women's College is for women only; all other programs are coeducational. *Degrees awarded:* Associate (Liberal Studies and Adult Learning Division only), baccalaureate, master's, doctorate. Certificate of advance graduate study also awarded.

Accreditation: *Regional:* NEASC. *Professional:* teacher education

History: Established as Lesley Normal School and offered first instruction at postsecondary level 1909; awarded first degree (associate) 1911; incorporated 1941; adopted present name 1943; initiated master's program 1934. Ph.D. program approved 1986.

Institutional Structure: *Governing board:* Lesley College Board of Trustees. Extrainstitutional representation: 30 trustees; institutional representation: president of the college, 5 administrators, 2 full-time instructional faculty members, 2 students; 2 alumni. 6 ex officio. 20 voting. *Composition of institution:* Administrators 10 men / 10 women. Academic affairs headed by provost. Management/business/finances directed by vice president. Full-time instructional faculty 75. Academic governance body, Faculty Assembly, the School of Management faculty, and the Graduate School faculty, each meets an average of 9 times per year.

Calendar: Semesters. Accelerated and weekend options for off-campus students. Academic year early Sept. to early May. Freshmen admitted Sept., Jan. Degrees conferred Nov., May; formal commencement May. Summer session of 1 term June to Aug.

Characteristics of Freshmen: 349 applicants (all women). 50.8% of applicants admitted. 39.4% of admitted students enrolled full-time.

93% (106 students) submitted SAT scores. *25th percentile:* SAT I Verbal 450, SAT I Math 430. *75th percentile:* SAT I Verbal 570, SAT I Math 530.

60% of entering freshmen expected to graduate within 5 years. 65% of freshmen from Massachusetts. Freshmen from 20 states and 7 foreign countries.

Admission: Rolling admissions plan. Apply no later than Mar. 15. Decisions roll after Jan. 15. *Requirements:* College preparatory program including 4 years of English, at least 2 years of mathematics, 2 of science, at least 1 being a laboratory course, 1 U.S. history. *Entrance tests:* College Board SAT I or ACT. TOEFL for foreign students. *For transfer students:* 2.0 minimum GPA; 65 credit hours maximum transfer credit.

College credit for postsecondary-level work completed in secondary school. Tutoring available. Developmental courses offered during regular academic year; credit given.

Degree Requirements: A student who satisfactorily meets the following requirements is awarded a degree of Bachelor of Science with a major in Human Services, Management Studies, or Liberal Studies; minimum 128 credit hours with cumulative GPA of no less than 2.0. In designing their 4-year baccalaureate program, Undergraduate School students select courses from 3 areas: General Education, Liberal Arts Programs, and Professional Programs. All students must complete the General Education component of the curriculum.

Distinctive Educational Programs: *Undergraduate School:* Programs combining professional and liberal arts study with practical field experience beginning in the freshman year. Students combine a professional program of their choice (Education, Human Services, or Management) with either an interdisciplinary liberal arts major or a liberal arts minor. Internships and placement in local schools, community centers, courts; private, public, and not-for-profit organizations; day care centers, and other community programs are available. Special academic programs include Student Exchange Program (STEP) with study abroad opportunity in England; the American University Justice Semester in Washington D.C.; the Spring, Texas Partnership Program (for Education); the New England Kindergarten Conference and the Computer Conference for Educators are held on campus annually. *Graduate School:* Unique adult bachelor degree programs; bachelor's and master's degree programs in Environmental Education with Audubon Expedition Institute, independent study, Expressive Therapies, and Intercultural Relations. Many programs offered at off-campus sites throughout New England and the mid-West and West in intensive weekend format. "Say Yes to Education" affiliate institution. *School of Management:* Master's in Training and Development; accelerated bachelor's and master's programs in management. Education with Audubon Expedition Institute, independent study, Expressive Therapies, and Intercultural Relations. Many programs offered at off-campus sites throughout New England and the mid-West and West in intensive weekend format. "Say Yes to Education" affiliate institution. *School* *of Management:* Master's in Training and Development; accelerated bachelor's and master's programs in management.

Degrees Conferred: 2 *associate;* 391 *baccalaureate;* 2,875 *master's;* 6 *doctorate.* Bachelor's degrees awarded in top five disciplines: business and management 101, education 69, health professions and related sciences 68, liberal arts/general studies 107; 2,145 *master's:* various disciplines; 4 *doctorate:* education.

Fees and Other Expenses: *Full-time tuition per academic year 2004–05:* $21,125. *Books and supplies:* $700. *Room and board per academic year:* $9,570.

Financial Aid: Aid from institutionally generated funds is provided on the basis of academic merit, financial need, other criteria. Institution has a Program Participation Agreement with the U.S. Department of Education for eligible students to receive Pell Grants and other federal aid.

Financial aid to full-time, first-time undergraduate students: 32% received federal grants averaging $3,767; 24% state/local grants averaging $1,963; 81% institutional grants averaging $11,326; 81% received loans averaging $3,639.

Departments and Teaching Staff: *Professors* 27, *associate professors* 37, *assistant professors* 36, *instructors* 6, *part-time teachers* 36.

Total instructional faculty: 150. Degrees held by full-time faculty: 70% hold terminal degrees.

Enrollment: Total enrollment 7,046. Undergraduate 1,253 (7.2% men, 92.8% women).

Characteristics of Student Body: *Ethnic/racial makeup (undergraduate):* Black non-Hispanic: 8.2% American Indian or Alaska Native: .2%; Asian or Pacific Islander: 2.6%; Hispanic: 2.9%; White non-Hispanic: 36%; unknown: 50.5%. *Age distribution:* 17–21: 5%; 22–24: 6%; 25–29: 22%; 30–34: 16%; 35–39: 13%; 40–49: 27%.

International Students: 18 undergraduate nonresident aliens enrolled fall 2004. Students from Europe, Asia, Central and South America, Canada, Israel, Saudi Arabia. Programs available to aid students whose native language is not English: social, cultural. English as a Second Language Program. No financial aid specifically designated for international students.

Student Life: On-campus residence halls house 70% of Women's College student body. *Special services:* The Learning Center. *Student publications:* Literary magazine; yearbook. *Surrounding community:* Cambridge population 96,000. Served by mass transit bus, subway, and rail system; passenger rail and subway service is less than a mile from campus; airport is 15 miles from campus. Boston is 7 miles from campus.

Library Collections: 120,200 volumes. 685 current periodical subscriptions. 55,800 audiovisual materials. 878,000 microforms. Online catalog. Students have access to online information retrieval services.

Most important holdings include teaching resource materials; Expressive Therapies materials; computer software; juvenile literature collection of 17,500 titles.

Buildings and Grounds: Campus area 5 acres.

Chief Executive Officer: Dr. Margaret A. McKenna, President.

Address admission inquiries James A Raley, Director of Undergraduate Admissions; graduate inquiries to Dean of Graduate Admissions.

Massachusetts College of Art

621 Huntington Avenue
Boston, Massachusetts 02115-5882
Tel: (617) 232-1555   **E-mail:** admissions@massart.edu
Fax: (617) 232-0050   **Internet:** www.massart.edu

Institution Description: Massachusetts College of Art is a member of Massachusetts Board of Regents of Higher Education. *Enrollment:* 2,049. *Degrees awarded:* Baccalaureate, master's. Certificates also awarded.

Budget subject to approval by state governing boards. Member of Boston Six, Consortium of East Coast Art Schools, College Academic Program Sharing (CAPS).

Accreditation: *Regional:* NEASC. *Professional:* art

History: Established as Massachusetts Normal Art School, chartered, and offered first instruction at postsecondary level 1924; awarded first degree (baccalaureate) 1924; changed name to Massachusetts School of Art 1926; adopted present name 1959; initiated master's program 1971.

Institutional Structure: *Governing board:* Massachusetts Board of Regents of Higher Education (statewide policy-making body). Extrainstitutional representation: 16 regents. All voting. Board of Trustees (appointed for Massachusetts College of Art). 11 members, including 1 student trustee. *Composition of institution:* Administrators 16 men / 9 women. Academic affairs headed by senior vice president for academic affairs. Management/business/finances directed by vice president for administration and finance. Full-time instructional faculty 72. Academic governance body, All College Committee, meets an average of 8 times per year. *Faculty representation:* Faculty served by collective bargaining agent affiliated with NEA and Massachusetts Teachers Association.

Calendar: Semesters. Academic year early Sept. to late May. Freshmen admitted Sept. Degrees conferred and formal commencement May. Summer session from late June to late Aug.

Characteristics of Freshmen: 56% of applicants admitted. 43% of applicants admitted and enrolled.

100% of students submitted SAT scores. *25th percentile:* SAT Verbal 520, SAT I Math 480. *75th percentile:* SAT Verbal 630, SAT Math 580.

55% of entering freshmen expected to graduate within 5 years. 66% of freshmen from Massachusetts. Freshmen from 23 states and 48 foreign countries.

Admission: Transfers with a minimum of 12 semester credits in studio art and 6 semester credits in liberal arts including English composition are eligible for January admission; completion deadline is November 15. First-time freshmen and all transfers eligible for fall admission. Deadline for completion of application is June 1; early completion is strongly encouraged. *Requirements:* Board of Regents' Admissions Standards require college preparatory program in high school with the following years of study: English 4, mathematics 3, science (laboratory courses) 2, social sciences 2 (including 1 year of U.S. history/government), 2 years of one foreign language. Portfolio of art work, high school transcript, SAT score report, written statement of purpose required. Transfers also send transcripts from each college attended. 78 hours maximum transfer credit (45 maximum in studio, 33 in liberal arts). AP grades of 4 or 5 earn credit. Tutoring and remedial courses available.

Degree Requirements: 132 credit hours; 4 terms in residence; portfolio review by faculty twice a year for all but freshmen; 42 credits in critical studies. Fulfillment of some degree requirements possible by passing College Board CLEP, AP. *Grading system:* Pass-fail.

Distinctive Educational Programs: Cross-registration through Pro-Arts Consortium, College Academic Program Sharing (all state colleges in Massachusetts), and with other public colleges in the Boston area. Guest student programs with the Consortium of East Coast Art Colleges. Individualized majors, internships, tutorials available to all students. Cooperative programs for selected students in some department. Study abroad programs in China, England, France, Germany, Greece, Ireland, Italy, Mexico, Spain.

Degrees Conferred: 297 *baccalaureate:* education 18; visual and performing arts 271. 25 *master's:* education 5; visual and performing arts 20.

Fees and Other Expenses: *Full-time tuition per academic year 2005–06:* $6,850 resident undergraduate, $19,200 out-of-state student. *Room and board per academic year:* $9,800.

Financial Aid: The college offers a direct lending program. Aid from institutionally generated funds is provided on the basis of financial need.

Financial aid to full-time, first-time undergraduate students: need-based scholarships/grants totaling $2,550,988, self-help $3,772,599; non-need-based scholarships/grants totaling $288,822, self-help $1,991,968, parent loans $4,632,682, tuition waivers $73,993.

Departments and Teaching Staff: *Total instructional faculty:* 98 (full-time 14, part-time 24; women 48, men 50; members of minority groups 18). Student-to-faculty ratio: 13:1. Degrees held by full-time faculty: doctorate 25%, master's 67%, baccalaureate 6%. 71% hold terminal degrees.

Enrollment: Total enrollment 2,049. Undergraduate full-time 496 men / 851 women, part-time 199m / 371w; graduate full-time 27m / 41w, part-time 19m / 45w. *Transfer students:* 182.

Characteristics of Student Body: *Ethnic/racial makeup (undergraduate):* number of Black non-Hispanic: 48; American Indian or Alaska Native: 1; Asian or Pacific Islander: 65; Hispanic: 65; White non-Hispanic: 1,065; unknown: 214. *Age distribution:* number under 18: 6; 18–19: 382; 20–21: 447; 22–24: 326; 25–29: 207; 30–34: 69; 35–39: 26; 40–49: 17; 50–64: 30; 65 and over: 2.

International Students: 75 nonresident aliens enrolled fall 2004. No programs available to aid students whose native language is not English. No financial aid specifically designated for international students.

Student Life: Smith Hall residence houses 116 students in suites of four. An additional 120 students are housed in nearby Simmons College resident hall. *Special regulations:* Registered cars permitted in designated areas. *Special services:* Learning Resources Center, medical services. *Student publications:* A monthly newspaper. *Surrounding community:* Boston area population over 3 million. Served by mass transit bus and rail system; airport 5 miles from campus; passenger rail service 2 miles from campus.

Library Collections: 249,999 volumes. 8,700 microforms; 125,000 audiovisual materials; 757 current periodical subscriptions. Online catalog. Students have access to online information retrieval services and the Internet.

Most important special holdings include collections on early art education in the United States, history of the college, and artist's books.

Buildings and Grounds: Campus area 5 buildings in Back Bay section of Boston.

Chief Executive Officer: Katherine Sloan, President.

Address admission inquiries to Kay Ransdell, Dean of Admissions and Enrollment Management.

Massachusetts College of Liberal Arts

375 Church Street

North Adams, Massachusetts 01247-4100

Tel: (413) 662-5000   **E-mail:** admissions@mcla.edu
Fax: (413) 662-5179   **Internet:** www.mcla.edu

Institution Description: Massachusetts College of Liberal Arts, formerly known as North Adams State College, is a public institution. *Enrollment:* 1,831. *Degrees awarded:* Baccalaureate, master's.

Accreditation: *Regional:* NEASC. *Professional:* teacher education

History: Established and chartered as State Normal School 1894; offered first instruction at postsecondary level 1897; changed name to State Teachers College at North Adams, added upper division curriculum, and awarded first degree (baccalaureate) 1932; added graduate program 1937; changed name to State College at North Adams 1960; adopted present name 1968.

Institutional Structure: *Governing board:* Massachusetts Higher Education Coordinating Council. Extrainstitutional representation: 11 regents. All voting. Board of Trustees (appointed for North Adams State College) 11 members, all voting. *Composition of institution:* Administrators 38 men / 29 women. Academic affairs headed by vice president for academic affairs. Management/business/finances directed by vice president for administration and finance. Student Affairs headed by Vice President for Student Affairs. Full-time instructional faculty 64 men / 28 women. Academic governance body, All College Committee, meets an average of 9 times per year. *Faculty representation:* Faculty is represented by collective bargaining agent, North Adams State College Association, affiliated with NEA and Massachusetts Teachers Association.

Calendar: Semesters. Academic year early Sept. to late May. Summer session June to Aug. Freshmen admitted Sept., Jan. Degrees conferred and formal commencement May.

Characteristics of Freshmen: 1,206 applicants (488 men, 118 women). 66.7% of applicants admitted. 30.6% of admitted students enrolled full-time.

93% (233 students) submitted SAT scores. *25th percentile:* SAT I Verbal 480, SAT I Math 450. *75th percentile:* SAT I Verbal 500, SAT I Math 560.

58% of entering freshmen expected to graduate within 5 years. 82% of freshmen from Massachusetts. Freshmen from 7 states and 2 foreign countries.

Admission: Rolling admissions plan. For fall acceptance, apply as early as Nov. 1 of previous year. Apply by Dec. 1 for early decision; need not limit application to North Adams. Early acceptance available. *Requirements:* Either graduation from accredited secondary school or GED. *Entrance tests:* College Board SAT or ACT composite. *For transfer students:* 2.0 minimum GPA; from 4-year accredited institution 90 hours maximum transfer credit; from 2-year accredited institution 60 hours; correspondence/extension students 60 hours.

College credit and advanced placement for postsecondary-level work completed in secondary school. College credit for extrainstitutional learning (life experience) on basis of portfolio and faculty assessments; ACE *2006 Guide to the Evaluation of Educational Experiences in the Armed Services.* Tutoring available. Noncredit developmental/remedial courses offered in summer session and regular academic year.

Degree Requirements: 120 credit hours; 2.0 GPA; 30 credits in residence; 2 hours physical education; general education requirements.

Fulfillment of some degree requirements and exemption from some beginning courses possible by passing departmental examinations, College Board CLEP or APP. *Grading system:* A–F; I (incomplete); pass-fail; pass; U (unsatisfactory); withdraw (carries time limit); WX (withdrawn from institution).

Distinctive Educational Programs: *For undergraduates:* Internships. January Interim encourages off-campus study in U.S. and abroad. North Adams State College is a member of the College Consortium for International Studies (CCIS). Variety of programs in the United Kingdom, Europe, Mideast and South America.

Degrees Conferred: 271 *baccalaureate*; *master's.* Bachelor's degrees awarded in top five disciplines: business, management, marketing, and related support services include biological and life sciences 62, business, management, marketing, and related support services 62; English language and literature/letters 55; social sciences 53; psychology 23; visual and performing arts 22.

Fees and Other Expenses: *Full-time tuition per academic year 2004–05:* $5,417 resident, $14,362 out-of-state student. *Books and supplies:* $750. *Room and board per academic year:* $6,174.

Financial Aid: Aid from institutionally generated funds is provided on the basis of financial need. Institution has a Program Participation Agreement with the U.S. Department of Education for eligible students to receive Pell Grants and other federal aid.

Financial aid to full-time, first-time undergraduate students: 27% received federal grants averaging $2,895, 36% state/local grants averaging $2,435; 42% institutional grants averaging $2,413; 69% received loans averaging $2,817.

Departments and Teaching Staff: Biology *professors* 36, *associate professors* 36, *assistant professors* 17, *instructors* 1, *part-time teachers* 33.

Total instructional faculty: 123. Degrees held by full-time faculty: master's 84%, doctorate 64%. 74% hold terminal degrees.

Enrollment: Total enrollment 1,831. Undergraduate 1,426 (39.1% men; 60.9% women).

Characteristics of Student Body: *Ethnic/racial makeup (undergraduate):* Black non-Hispanic: 3/7%; American Indian or Alaska Native: .2%; Asian or Pacific Islander: 1/2%; Hispanic: 2.1%; White non-Hispanic: 90.9%; unknown: 1.6%. *Age distribution:* 17–21: 50%; 22–24: 29%; 25–29: 11%; 30–34: 7%; 35–39: 3%.

International Students: 4 nonresident aliens enrolled fall 2004. Students from Europe, Asia. No programs available to aid students whose native language is not English. No financial aid specifically designated for international students.

Student Life: On-campus residence halls house 60% of student body. All residence halls are co-ed. *Intercollegiate athletics:* men only: baseball, basketball, cross-country, hockey, soccer; women only: basketball, cross-country, soccer, softball, tennis, *Special regulations:* Cars permitted with campus registration for all but freshmen. *Special services:* Learning Resources Center, medical services. *Student publications, radio: The Beacon,* a weekly newspaper; *Kaleidoscope,* a biannual literary magazine. Radio station WJJW broadcasts 140 hours per week. *Surrounding community:* North Adams population 15,000. Albany (NY), 45 miles from campus, is nearest metropolitan area.

Library Collections: 182,000 volumes. 200,000 microforms; 5,000 audiovisual materials; 540 current periodical subscriptions. Online catalog. Students have access to online information retrieval services and the Internet.

Most important special holdings include Northern Berkshire area materials; business and economics, education.

Buildings and Grounds: Campus area 80 acres.

Chief Executive Officer: Dr. Katharine Sloan, President.

Undergraduates address admission inquiries to Kay Randell, Director of Admissions. graduate inquiries to Graduate Studies, Education Department.

Massachusetts College of Pharmacy and Health Sciences

179 Longwood Avenue

Boston, Massachusetts 02115-5896

Tel: (800) 225-5506   **E-mail:** admissions@mcp.edu
Fax: (617) 732-2801   **Internet:** www.mcp.edu

Institution Description: Massachusetts College of Pharmacy and Health Sciences is a private, independent, nonprofit college. *Enrollment:* 2,587. *Degrees awarded:* Baccalaureate, first-professional (pharmacy), master's, doctorate. Post-baccalaureate certificates (dental hygiene, nuclear medicine technician, radiation therapy, radiography) also awarded.

Academic offerings subject to approval by statewide coordinating bodies.

Accreditation: *Regional:* NEASC. *Professional:* dental hygiene, nuclear medicine technology, pharmacy, physician assisting, surgeon assisting, radiation therapy

History: Established as Massachusetts College of Pharmacy 1823; incorporated 1852; offered first instruction at postsecondary level 1867; awarded first degree (baccalaureate) 1869; adopted present name 1998. Westchester campus opened 2000; Manchester (NH) campus 2002.

Institutional Structure: *Governing board:* Board of Trustees. Extrainstitutional representation: 21 trustees; institutional representation: president of the college. All voting. *Composition of institution:* Administrators 18 men / 15 women. Academic affairs headed by vice president/provost. Management/business/finances directed by vice president for finance/administration; vice president for institutional advancement. Academic governance bodies, Academic Council and Faculty Council, meet 12 times per year.

Calendar: Semesters. Academic year Aug. to May. Degrees conferred Sept., Jan., May/June; formal commencements Dec./Jan., May. Summer sessions from late May to early Aug.

Characteristics of Freshmen: 72% of applicants admitted. 49% of applicants admitted and enrolled.

98% (310 students) submitted SAT scores; 11% (36 students) submitted ACT scores. *25th percentile:* SAT Verbal 490, SAT Math 520; ACT Composite 18. *75th percentile:* SAT Verbal 560, SAT Math 620; ACT Composite 25.

63% of entering freshmen expected to graduate within 5 years. 59% of freshmen from Massachusetts. Freshmen from 17 states and 4 foreign countries.

Admission: Priority application deadlines: Nov. 1 for early decision; freshman deadline Jan. 15. Transfers and graduate admissions: Feb. 1. *Requirements:* Either graduation from accredited secondary school with 4 units English, 3 mathematics, 2 laboratory science (biology and chemistry), 6 college preparatory electives; or GED. Recommend additional units in advanced mathematics and chemistry. Minimum 2.5 GPA. Lowest acceptable secondary school class standing 35th percentile. *Entrance tests:* College Board SAT or ACT composite. For foreign students TOEFL. *For transfer students:* 2.5 minimum GPA; maximum transfer credit subject to residence requirement depending on degree program. Advanced placement credit accepted with a score of 3 or better.

Degree Requirements: Completion of core and professional curriculum; supervised professional practice experience; 2.0 GPA; all professional coursework and one half of electives must be completed while in residence. *Grading system:* A–F, satisfactory/unsatisfactory; withdraw/incomplete (time limit).

Distinctive Educational Programs: *For undergraduates/first-professional degree students:* Accelerated Pharm.D. program (Worcester and Manchester); accelerated BSN; dual degree programs; premedical options; cross-registration with Colleges of the Fenway for additional elective courses. *For graduate students:* evening/weekend classes; nontraditional Doctor of Pharmacy; Drug Regulatory Affairs and Health Policy; Drug Discovery and Development; Pharmacy Systems Administration.

Degrees Conferred: 61 *baccalaureate;* 89 *master's;* 2 *doctorate:* health professions and related sciences. 400 *first-professional:* pharmacy 400. *Honorary degrees awarded 2004–05:* Doctor of Health Science 1; Doctor of Science in Pharmacy 2.

Fees and Other Expenses: *Full-time tuition per academic year 2004–05:* $19,600 undergraduate, $25,000 graduate. *Other fees:* $620. *Room and board per academic year:* $10,500.

Financial Aid: Aid from institutionally generated funds is provided on the basis of academic merit, financial need.

Financial aid to full-time, first-time undergraduate students: need-based scholarships/grants totaling $7,384,955, self-help $22,726,153, parent loans $696,492; non-need-based scholarships/grants totaling $336,314, self-help $4,395,355,parent loans $570,438.

Departments and Teaching Staff: *Professors* 15, *associate professors* 32, *assistant professors* 81, *instructors* 13, *part-time faculty* 9. *Total instructional faculty:* 150 (full-time 141, part-time 9; women 90, men 60). Total faculty with doctorate, first-professional, or other terminal degree: 120. Student-to-faculty ratio: 17:1. *Faculty development:* 2 faculty members awarded sabbaticals 2004–05.

Enrollment: Total enrollment 2,587. Undergraduate full-time 448 men / 1,069 women, part-time 42m / 73w; first-professional full-time 238m / 425w; graduate full-time 26m / 97w, part-time 59m / 110w.

Characteristics of Student Body: *Ethnic/racial makeup (undergraduate):* Black non-Hispanic: 85; American Indian or Alaska Native: 6; Asian or Pacific Islander: 563; Hispanic: 32; White non-Hispanic: 791; unknown: 111.

International Students: 99 nonresident aliens enrolled fall 2004. Students from Europe, Asia, Africa, Canada. Programs available to aid students whose native language is not English: social, cultural. No financial aid specifically designated for international students.

Student Life: On-campus housing for 470 students. No daytime parking; free evening/weekend parking. Intramural program and fitness center. *Special services:* Counseling and Career Services, Academic Support Services, Health Services, Activities. Member of the Colleges of Fenway Consortium (5 neighboring colleges). *Student publications: The Dispenser,* a monthly newspaper. *Surrounding community:* Boston area population 3,000,000. Served by mass transit bus and rail system; airport 7 miles from campus; passenger rail service 6 miles from campus.

Library Collections: 34,000 volumes. Online catalog. Access to 2.8 million holdings through consortium. 80,000 microforms; 650 current periodical subscriptions via electronic access. 250 computer work stations. Students have access to online information retrieval services and the Internet.

Most important special holdings include Sheppard Collection of U.S. pharmacopeias.

Buildings and Grounds: Campus area (Boston Campus) 3 acres. *New buildings:* Academic Student Center completed 2004.

Chief Executive Officer: Charles F. Monahan, Jr., President.

Address admission inquiries to William Dunfey, Director of Admissions.

Massachusetts Institute of Technology

77 Massachusetts Avenue
Cambridge, Massachusetts 02139

Tel: (617) 253-1000   **E-mail:** admissions@mit.edu
Fax: (617) 258-8000   **Internet:** www.mit.edu

Institution Description: Massachusetts Institute of Technology is a private, independent, nonprofit institution. *Enrollment:* 10,320. *Degrees awarded:* Baccalaureate, master's, doctorate.

Research alliances: Alliance for Global Sustainability, Broad Institute, Charles Stark Draper Laboratory; Howard Hughes Medical Institute, Northeast Radio Observatory Corporation; Whitehead Institute for Biomedical Research, World Wide Web Consortium.

Accreditation: *Regional:* NEASC. *Professional:* architecture, business, engineering, planning

History: Established and chartered 1861; offered first instruction at postsecondary level 1865; awarded first degree (baccalaureate) 1868. *See* Francis E. Wiley, *MIT in Perspective: A Pictorial History* (Boston: Little, Brown, Inc., 1975) for further information.

Institutional Structure: *Governing board:* The Corporation, Massachusetts Institute of Technology. Extrainstitutional representation: 67 members, including 21 life members, 23 term members, 19 alumni term members, 4 ex officio members (Governor of Massachusetts, Chief Justice of the Supreme Judicial Court, Commissioner of Education; President of the alumni Association). *Composition of institution:* Administrators 545 men / 430 women. Academic affairs headed by provost. Management/business/finances directed by vice president of operations. Full-time instructional faculty 1,290. Academic governance body, the Faculty, meets an average of 10 times per year.

Calendar: Semesters (4-1-4 plan). Academic year early Sept. to mid-May. Freshmen admitted Sept. Degrees conferred Sept., Feb., Jun. Formal commencement May or June. Summer session from early June to mid-Aug.

Characteristics of Freshmen: 16% of applicants accepted. 65% OF accepted applicants enrolled.

98% (1,060 students) submitted SAT scores; 24% (255 students) submitted ACT scores. *25th percentile:* SAT Verbal 680, SAT Math 730; ACT Composite 31. *75th percentile:* SAT Verbal 760, SAT Math 800; ACT Composite 34.

90% of entering freshmen expected to graduate within 5 years. 9% of freshmen from Massachusetts. Freshmen from 50 states and 45 foreign countries.

Admission: Apply by Jan. 1 for fall acceptance. Students are notified of acceptance Mar. Apply by Nov. 1 for early action. *Requirements:* Either graduation from accredited secondary school with 4 units English, 4 mathematics, 4 science, 2 foreign language, 2 social studies. *Entrance tests:* College Board SAT or ACT, and 3 SAT Subject Tests. *For transfer students:* 5 semesters maximum transfer credit.

Degree Requirements: 17 General Institute Requirements (GIRs) plus at least 180 departmental program units beyond the GIRs. GIRs include requirements in science, laboratory, restricted electives in science and technology, humanities, arts and social sciences, physical education, and communication requirements.

Fulfillment of some degree requirements and exemption from some beginning courses possible by passing departmental examinations, College Board AP. *Grading system:* A–F; pass-fail (freshman year); withdraw (carries time limit); incomplete (carries time limit).

Distinctive Educational Programs: *For undergraduates:* Interdepartmental programs in biomedical engineering, environmental studies, law-related studies, mineral resource studies. Individual majors. Study abroad through programs offered by other institutions and by individual arrangement. *For graduate students:* Dual-degree program in engineering and oceanography with Woods Hole Oceanographic Institute; in health sciences and technology with Harvard University. Cooperative doctoral program in medical engineering and physics, and in medical radiological physics with Harvard University. Cooperative doctoral program in medical engineering and physics, and in medical radiological physics with Harvard University. Interdepartmental programs in acoustics, communications policy, polymeric materials, statistics. Cross-registration with Boston University, Brandeis University, Tufts University, Woods Hole Oceanographic Institute. *Available to all students:* Internships. Evening classes. Tutorials. Cross-registration with Harvard University and Wellesley College.

ROTC: Army, Navy, Air Force offered in cooperation with Harvard University and Tufts University.

Degrees Conferred: 1,194 *baccalaureate;* 1,640 *master's;* 467 *doctorate.* Bachelor's degrees awarded in top five disciplines: biological and biomedical sciences 103; business/marketing 108; computer and information sciences and support services 142; engineering 503; physical sciences 95.

Fees and Other Expenses: *Full-time tuition per academic year 2005–06:* $32,100. *Required fee:* $200. *Room and board per academic year:* $9,500. *Books and supplies:* $1,100.

Financial Aid: Aid from institutionally generated funds is provided on the basis of financial need.

Financial aid to full-time, first-time undergraduate students: need-based scholarships/grants totaling $63,584,572, self-help $12,690,446; non-need-based scholarships/grants totaling $695,311, self-help $1,986,899, parent loans $7,614,516. *Graduate aid:* 829 students received $15,385,436 in federal and state-funded fellowships/grants (ranging from $840 to $24,500); 90 received $435,497 in federal and state-funded loans (ranging from $432 to $6,900); 1,069 teaching assistantships awarded totaling $25,791,917 (ranging from $225 to $54,510); 3,087 research assistantships were awarded totaling $119,384,406 (ranging from $450 to $51,840).

Departments and Teaching Staff: *Full-time instructional faculty:* 1,669 (full-time 1,298, part-time 371; women 342, men 1,327; members of minority groups 185). Total faculty with doctorate, first-professional, or other terminal degree: 1,561. Student-to-faculty ratio: 7:1. Degrees held by full-time faculty: 99% hold terminal degrees.

Enrollment: Total enrollment 10,320. Undergraduate full-time 2,331 men / 1,747 women, part-time 40m / 18w; graduate full-time 4,159m / 1,748w, part-time 189m / 88w.

Characteristics of Student Body: *Ethnic/racial makeup (undergraduate):* number of Black non-Hispanic: 248; American Indian or Alaska Native: 66; Asian or Pacific Islander: 1,149; Hispanic: 476; White non-Hispanic: 1,457; unknown: 433. *Age distribution:* number under 18: 206; 18–19: 1,974; 20–21: 1,687; 22–24: 240; 25–29: 22; 30–34: 5; 35–39: 1; 40–49: 1.

International Students: 2,485 nonresident aliens enrolled fall 2004. Programs available to aid students whose native language is not English: social, cultural. English as a Second Language program. No financial aid specifically designated for international students.

Student Life: On-campus residence halls house 55% of student body. Residence halls for men constitute 14% of such space, for women 9%, for both sexes 77%. 2% of student body housed on campus in cooperative facilities. 26% of men join and live in fraternities. Some women join and live in coed fraternities. *Intercollegiate athletics:* men only: baseball, basketball, crew, cross-country, fencing, football, golf, gymnastics, lacrosse, pistol, rifle, sailing, skiing, squash, soccer, swimming-diving, tennis, indoor track, outdoor track, volleyball, water polo, wrestling; women only: basketball, crew, cross-country, fencing, field hockey, gymnastics, sailing, soccer, softball, swimming-diving, tennis, volleyball. *Special regulations:* Registered cars permitted. *Special services:* Medical services, shuttle bus between MIT and Wellesley College. *Student publications, radio: The Graduate*, a monthly newspaper; *Rune*, an annual literary magazine; *The Tech*, a semiweekly newspaper; *Technique*, a yearbook. Radio station WMBR broadcasts 133 hours per week. *Surrounding community:* Cambridge, population 95,000, is located in Boston metropolitan area. Served by mass transit bus and subway system, airport 5 miles from campus, passenger rail service 2 miles from campus.

Publications: Information is available online about a wide range of publications from MIT academic programs, research laboratories and centers, and administrative offices (www.mit.edu/offices/category/publications).

Library Collections: 2,769,667 volumes. Current serial subscriptions: 14,054 paper, 1,936 microforms; 6,280 via electronic access. 27,334 audio recordings; 4,212 film/video. Online catalog. Students have access to online information retrieval services and the Internet. 131 computer work stations.

Most important special holdings include Vail Collection of the History of Aero and Electrical Engineering; Roman Jacobson Collection on Linguistics; History of Architecture.

Buildings and Grounds: Campus area 157 acres. *New buildings:* Albert and Barrie Zesiger Sports and Fitness Center completed 2002; Sidney-Pacific Street Residence Hall 2002; Simmons Hall 2002; Ray and Maria Stata Center for Computer, Information, and Intelligence Sciences 2004.

Chief Executive Officer: Dr. Susan Hockfield, President.

Address admission inquiries to Marilee Jones, Dean of Admissions.

Massachusetts Maritime Academy

101 Academy Drive
Buzzards Bay, Massachusetts 02532-1803

Tel: (508) 830-5000   **E-mail:** mmaadmit@maritime.edu
Fax: (508) 830-5077   **Internet:** www.maritime.edu

Institution Description: Massachusetts Maritime Academy is a member of Massachusetts Board of Regents of Higher Education. *Enrollment:* 953. *Degrees awarded:* Baccalaureate.

Academic offerings subject to approval by statewide coordinating bodies. Budget subject to approval by state governing boards.

Accreditation: *Regional:* NEASC.

History: Established as Massachusetts Nautical Training School, incorporated, and offered first instruction at postsecondary level 1891; awarded first degree (baccalaureate) and adopted present name 1946.

Institutional Structure: *Governing board:* Board of Trustees (appointed for Massachusetts Maritime Academy). Extrainstitutional representation: 10 trustees. All voting. *Composition of institution:* Administrators 30 men / 6 women. Academic affairs headed by vice president of academic affairs. Administration/finances directed by vice president of administration and finance. Vice president of student services and maritime training in charge of student affairs and maritime training. Full-time instructional faculty 59. Academic governance body, All-college committee, meets biweekly. *Faculty representation:* Faculty served by collective bargaining agent affiliated with NEA and Massachusetts Teachers Association.

Calendar: Quarters. Academic year early Sept. to late June. Freshmen admitted Aug. Degrees conferred and formal commencement June.

Characteristics of Freshmen: 681 applicants (592 men, 89 women). 64.5% of applicants admitted. 54% of admitted students enrolled full-time.

98% (232 students) submitted SAT scores; 7% (18 students) submitted ACT scores. *25th percentile:* SAT I Verbal 470, SAT I Math 480, ACT Composite 20. *75th percentile:* SAT I Verbal 570, SAT I Math 590, ACT Composite 24.

Freshmen from 8 states and 2 foreign countries.

Admission: Rolling admissions plan. For fall acceptance, apply as early as Nov. of previous year, but not later than Feb. of year of enrollment. *Requirements:* Either graduation from accredited secondary school with 4 units English, 2 algebra, 2 science (biology, chemistry, or physics), 1 geometry, 7 academic electives; or GED. Additional units in mathematics recommended. *Entrance tests:* College Board SAT and physical examination. *For transfer students:* Transfer credit accepted.

College credit and advanced placement for postsecondary-level work completed in secondary school. Tutoring available. Noncredit developmental/remedial courses offered during regular academic year.

Degree Requirements: 164 credit hours; 2.0 GPA; 6 terms in residence; 2 physical education courses; core curriculum; 6 months at sea on training vessel; introductory computer science course. Fulfillment of some degree requirements and exemption from some beginning courses possible by passing College Board CLEP, AP. *Grading system:* A–F.

Distinctive Educational Programs: Internships. Concentrations in mechanical engineering, business management, marine fisheries. *Other distinctive programs:* Credit and noncredit continuing education courses offered in cooperation with Bridgewater State College.

ROTC: Navy.

Degrees Conferred: 155 *baccalaureate.* Bachelor's degrees awarded: engineering 80; natural resources and conservation 36; transportation and materials moving 23; business, management, marketing, and related support services 16.

Fees and Other Expenses: *Full-time tuition per academic year 2004–05:* resident $4,963, out-of-state $15,443. *Books and supplies:* $700. *Room and board per academic year:* $6,157.

Financial Aid: Aid from institutionally generated funds is provided on the basis of academic merit, financial need, other criteria. Institution has a Program Participation Agreement with the U.S. Department of Education for eligible students to receive Pell Grants and other federal aid.

Financial aid to full-time, first-time undergraduate students: 16% received federal grants averaging $2,643; 29% state/local grants averaging $1,744; institutional grants averaging $995; 57% received loans averaging $2,630.

Departments and Teaching Staff: *Professors 27, associate professors 19, assistant professors 12, instructors 1, part-time teachers 1.*

Total instructional faculty: 59. *Degrees held by full-time faculty:* doctorate 19%, master's 20%, baccalaureate 15%. 3% hold terminal degrees.

Enrollment: Total enrollment 953 (88.3% men, 11.7% women).

Characteristics of Student Body: *Ethnic/racial makeup:* number of Black non-Hispanic: .7%; American Indian or Alaska Native: .3%; Asian or Pacific Islander: 1.8%; Hispanic: .9%; White non-Hispanic: 95.6%; unknown: .3%. *Age distribution:* 17–21: 62%; 22–24: 35%; 25–29: 2%.

International Students: 4 nonresident aliens enrolled fall 2004. Programs available to aid students whose native language is not English: English as a Second Language Program. No financial aid specifically designated for international students.

Student Life: On-campus residence halls for men and women house 100% of student body. *Intercollegiate athletics:* men only: baseball, football, lacrosse, soccer, tennis; women only: volleyball, softball; both sexes: sailing, cross-country. Sport clubs include weight lifting, boxing, hockey, rugby. *Special regulations:* Cars permitted without restrictions. Cadets wear military uniforms at all times. Curfews. *Special services:* Learning Resources Center, medical services.

Student publications: The Compass, a monthly newspaper; *Muster*, a yearbook. *Surrounding community:* Buzzards Bay population 3,500. Boston, 55 miles from campus, is nearest metropolitan area.

Library Collections: 45,000 volumes. 22,000 microforms; 855 audiovisual materials; 505 current periodical subscriptions. Students have access to online information retrieval services and the Internet.

Most important special holdings include Maritime Collection; archives of the Massachusetts Maritime Academy.

Buildings and Grounds: Campus area 59 acres.

Chief Executive Officer: Rr. Adm. M.J. Bresnahan, President.

Address admission inquiries to Col. Francis X. McDonald, Director of Enrollment.

Merrimack College

315 Turnpike Street
North Andover, Massachusetts 01845-5800

Tel: (978) 837-5000   **E-mail:** admission@merrimack.edu
Fax: (978) 837-5222   **Internet:** www.merrimack.edu

Institution Description: Merrimack College is a private college affiliated with the Order of Saint Augustine, Roman Catholic Church. *Enrollment:* 2,324. *Degrees awarded:* Associate, baccalaureate, master's.

Member of Association of Independent Colleges and Universities in Massachusetts.

Accreditation: *Regional:* NEASC.*Professional*: business, engineering, teacher education

History: Established and chartered as Augustinian College of the Merrimack Valley, a college for men, and offered first instruction at postsecondary level 1947; awarded first degree (baccalaureate) and first women admitted 1951; present name adopted 1969. *See* Edward G. Roddy, Jr., *Merrimack College: Genesis and Growth 1947–1972* (Boston: Crawley and Co., 1972) for further information.

Institutional Structure: *Governing board:* Merrimack College Board of Trustees. Extrainstitutional representation: 28 trustees; institutional representation: president of the college. 1 ex officio. All voting. *Composition of institution:* Administrators 5 men / 5 women. Academic affairs headed by provost. Management/business/finances directed by vice president for fiscal affairs. Full-time instructional faculty 139. Academic governance body, Merrimack College Faculty Senate, meets an average of 8 times per year.

Calendar: Semesters. Academic year Aug. to May. Freshmen admitted Sept., Jan. Degrees conferred and formal commencement May. Summer session of 2 terms May to Aug.

Characteristics of Freshmen: 64% of applicants admitted. 29% of applicants admitted and enrolled.

97% (3,443 students) submitted SAT scores; 3% (101 students) submitted ACT scores. *25th percentile*: SAT Verbal 500, SAT Math 500; ACT Composite 20. *75th percentile*: SAT Verbal 590, SAT Math 590, ACT Composite 23.

63% of entering freshmen expected to graduate within 5 years. 78% of freshmen from Massachusetts. Freshmen from 23 states and 15 foreign countries.

Admission: Rolling admissions plan. For fall acceptance, apply as early as beginning of senior year in secondary school, but not later than Feb. 1. Apply by Nov. 30 for early action; need not limit application to Merrimack. *Requirements:* Graduation from accredited secondary school with 4 units in English or GED. For liberal arts and business students, 4 social studies, 3 college preparatory mathematics, 2 science, 6 academic electives. For engineering, mathematics, and science students, 4 college preparatory mathematics, 3 science, 2 social studies, 3 academic electives. *Entrance tests:* College Board SAT required. *For transfer students:* 2.0 minimum GPA; 75 hours maximum transfer credit.

Advanced placement for postsecondary-level work completed in secondary school and for extrainstitutional learning on basis of ACE *2006 Guide to the Evaluation of Educational Experiences in the Armed Services*; portfolio and faculty assessments. Tutoring available.

Degree Requirements: *For all associate degrees:* 60–72 credit hours; 8 courses in residence. *For all baccalaureate degrees:* 120 credit hours; 15 courses in residence; distribution requirements. *For all undergraduate degrees:* 2.0 GPA.

Fulfillment of some degree requirements and exemption from some beginning courses possible by passing College Board CLEP or AP. *Grading system:* A–F; pass-fail; withdraw (carries time limit).

Distinctive Educational Programs: Internships, cooperative education program. Evening classes. Interdisciplinary program in humanities. Individual majors. Double-degree program. Study abroad in Austria, England, China, France, Germany, Italy, and Spain; elsewhere by individual arrangement. Evening, summer, and daytime programs for adult students.

ROTC: Air Force offered in cooperation with University of Massachusetts-Lowell.

Degrees Conferred: 17 *associate;* 503 *baccalaureate:* biological sciences 8; business/marketing 210; communications/communication technologies 29; computer and information sciences 21; engineering and engineering technologies 30; English 75; foreign languages and literature 7; health professions and related sciences 14; law/legal studies 1; liberal arts/general studies 7; mathematics 9; natural resources/environmental science 2; philosophy/religion/theology 4; physical sciences 7; psychology 67; social sciences and history 64; visual and performing arts 8. *Master's:* education 4.

Fees and Other Expenses: *Full-time tuition per academic year:* $23,000 undergraduate; $350 per credit for graduate study. *Room and board per academic year:* $9,200.

Financial Aid: Aid from institutionally generated funds is provided on the basis of academic merit, financial need.

Financial aid to full-time, first-time undergraduate students: need-based scholarships/grants totaling $10,724,792, self-help $4,413,833; non-need-based scholarships/grants totaling $1,935,449, self-help $6,146,256, parent loans $6,033,252, tuition waivers $584,488, athletic awards $2,501,406.

Departments and Teaching Staff: *Professors* 31, *associate professors* 71, *assistant professors* 37, *part-time faculty* 69. *Total instructional faculty:* 208 (full-time 139, part-time 69; women 56, men 83; members of minority groups 11). Total faculty with doctorate, first-professional, or other terminal degree: 105. Student-to-faculty ratio: 12:1. *Faculty development:* 14 faculty members awarded sabbaticals 2004–05.

Enrollment: Total enrollment 2,324. Undergraduate full-time 943 men / 1,084 women, part-time 134m / 143w; graduate part-time 2m / 18w.

Characteristics of Student Body: *Ethnic/racial makeup:* number of Black non-Hispanic: 13; American Indian or Alaska Native: 3; Asian or Pacific Islander: 33; Hispanic: 44; White non-Hispanic: 1,328; unknown: 378. *Age distribution:* number under 18: 29; 18–19: 946; 20–21: 830; 22–24: 188; 25–29: 17; 30–34: 7; 35–39: 3; 40–49: 6; 50–64: 1.

International Students: 31 nonresident aliens enrolled fall 2004. No programs available to aid students whose native language is not English. No financial aid specifically designated for international students.

Student Life: On-campus residence halls house 55% of student body. Apartment, townhouse, and traditional-style halls for both sexes constitute 100% of such space. *Intercollegiate athletics:* men only: baseball, basketball, ice hockey, lacrosse, cross-country, soccer, tennis, golf; women only: basketball, cross-country, tennis, volleyball, softball, golf. *Special services:* Health services, career development and placement. *Student publications: Merrimackan*, a yearbook; *Argus*, a student newspaper; *The Alternative Voice*, a student literary magazine. 50 clubs and organizations including cocurricular, student government, fraternities and sororities, creative and performing arts, special interest groups. *Surrounding community:* North Andover population 20,000. Boston, 25 miles from campus, is nearest metropolitan area.

Library Collections: 115,639 volumes. Online catalog. 7,200 microforms; 900 periodicals; 4,000 recordings and tapes. Students have access to online information retrieval services and the Internet.

Buildings and Grounds: Campus area 220 acres. *New buildings:* Santagati Hall (student residence) completed 2003.

Chief Executive Officer: Dr. Richard I. Santagati, President.

Address admission inquiries to Mary Lou Betelle, Dean of Admissions.

MGH Institute of Health Professions

36 First Avenue
Boston, Massachusetts 02129-4557

Tel: (617) 726-2947   **E-mail:** admission@mghihp.edu
Fax: (617) 726-8010   **Internet:** www.mghihp.edu

Institution Description: The MGH Institute of Health Professions is a graduate-level academic institution whose mission is to prepare health care leaders and clinical specialists in the fields of dietetics, nursing, physical therapy, social work, and speech-language pathology. The institute is an affiliate of Massachusetts General Hospital (MGH). *Enrollment:* 671. *Degrees awarded:* Master's, doctorate. Post-baccalaureate certificates also awarded

Accreditation: *Regional:* NEACS. *Professional*: nursing, clinical lab scientist, physical therapy, speech-language pathology

History: The MGH Institute of Health Professions was created in 1977 when the Commonwealth of Massachusetts awarded degree-granting authority to Massachusetts General Hospital. The MGH Institute became a separate corporation in 1985 though it remains an MGH affiliate.

Institutional Structure: Board of Trustees. Full-time faculty 48.

Calendar: Semesters. Academic year Sept. to Aug.

Admission: Rolling admissions. *Requirements:* Graduate of baccalaureate program with 3.0 GPA; verbal and quantitative test of the GRE exam taken within the last five years; three letters of recommendation. January application deadlines.

Degree Requirements: Credits required to complete graduate degrees vary with program; may require one or a combination of: completion of a scholarly project; research thesis or comprehensive examination.

Distinctive Educational Programs: Individualized learning programs; clinical and research experiences. Evening and summer classes available.

Degrees Conferred: 111 *master's* and 99 *doctorate:* health professions and related sciences.

Fees and Other Expenses: *Tuition and fees per academic year 2004–05:* $707 per credit hour; $354 per audit credit hour. *Fees:* General student fee (per term) $400 for 12 or more credit hours. Other fees may apply.

Financial Aid: Aid from institutionally generated funds is provided on the basis of academic merit, financial need.

Graduate aid: 20 students received $120,073 in federal and state-funded fellowships/grants (ranging from $6,000 to $6,705); 360 received $8,000,000 in federal and state-funded loans; (ranging from $1,000 to $18,500); 28 received $77,000 for other teaching/research assistantships.

Departments and Teaching Staff: *Professors* 5, *associate professors* 10, *assistant professors* 25, *instructors* 8, *part-time faculty* 18. *Total instructional faculty:* 66. Student-to-faculty ratio: 7:1. Degrees held by full-time faculty: doctorate 72%, master's 28%. 72% hold terminal degrees.

Enrollment: *Total enrollment:* 674 (full-time 36 men / 310 women, part-time 68m / 260w).

Characteristics of Student Body: *Age distribution:* 22–24: 43; 25–29: 175; 30–34: 78; 35–39: 61; 40–49: 10; 50–64: 7.

International Students: 11 nonresident aliens enrolled fall 2004. No programs available for students whose native language is not English. No financial aid specifically designated for international students.

Library Collections: MGH Treadwill Library serves as the institute's library while also addressing the library resource needs of health care professionals within the library and Partners Health-Care System's Information System Division. 737 journal subscriptions; 721 E-journals; 31,843 journal volumes; 13,000 books. Students have access to online information retrieval services and the Internet.

Chief Executive Officer: Dr. Ann W. Caldwell, President.

Address admission inquiries to Office of Admissions.

Montserrat College of Art

23 Essex Street
P.O. Box 26
Beverly, Massachusetts 01915-4508
Tel: (978) 921-4142   **E-mail:** admiss@montserrat.edu
Fax: (978) 922-4268   **Internet:** www.montserrat.edu

Institution Description: Montserrat College of Visual Art is a private, independent, nonprofit college. *Enrollment:* 332. *Degrees awarded:* Baccalaureate. Four-year professional diploma also awarded.

Accreditation: *Regional:* NEASC (diploma program). *National:* NASAD. *Professional:* art

History: Established, chartered, offered first instruction at postsecondary level, and awarded first diploma (3-year) 1970.

Institutional Structure: *Governing board:* Board of Trustees. Representation: 19 trustees. All voting. *Composition of institution:* Administrators 2 men / 2 women. Academic affairs headed by dean of faculty. Management/business/finances directed by vice president for administration and finance. Full-time instructional faculty 19. Academic governance body, the faculty, meets an average of 9 times per year.

Calendar: Semesters. Academic year Aug. to May. Freshmen admitted Sept., Jan. Degrees conferred and formal commencement May. Summer terms in June and July.

Characteristics of Freshmen: 85% of applicants accepted. 35% of accepted applicants enrolled.

49% (62 students) submitted SAT scores; 10% (7 students) submitted ACT scores. Mean SAT class scores 513 verbal, 480 mathematical.

48% of entering freshmen expected to graduate within 5 years. 40% of freshmen from Massachusetts. Freshmen from 13 states.

Admission: Rolling admissions plan. Sept. and Jan. admissions. Priority filing date of Mar. 1 for financial aid. Notification of admissions is by letter. *Requirements:* Application, previous school record, portfolio, 2 letters of recommendation and SAT, ACT or TOEFL. Transfer students accepted.

Advanced placement for postsecondary-level work completed in secondary school and extrainstitutional learning on basis of ACE *2006 Guide to the Evaluation of Educational Experiences in the Armed Services,* portfolio, faculty assessments, personal interview.

Degree Requirements: 120 credits; 78 credits in studio; 42 credits in art history and liberal arts. *Grading system:* Letter grades with individual evaluation of studio work.

Distinctive Educational Programs: Each student's work is evaluated and discussed with the entire faculty twice each year. Internships are available in the senior year. Sister school Niigata Design College, Japan. Summer program in Italy and Ireland. Independent study. Cross-registration at 10 local colleges. Semester exchanges through Alliance of Independent Colleges of Art and Design.

Degrees Conferred: 68 *baccalaureate:* fine and applied arts.

Fees and Other Expenses: *Full-time tuition per academic year 2004–05:* $18,500. *Required fees:* $710. *Room and board per academic year:* $5,050.

Financial Aid: Aid from institutionally generated funds is provided on the basis of academic merit, financial need.

Financial aid to full-time, first-time undergraduate students: need-based scholarships/grants totaling $1,650,324, self-help $1,117,175, parent loans $1,188,182; non-need-based scholarships/grants totaling $1,461,463, self-help $1,461,483, tuition waivers $27,750.

Departments and Teaching Staff: *Total instructional faculty:* 63 (full-time 30, part-time 33; women 55, men 28; members of minority groups 4). Total faculty with doctorate, first-professional, or other terminal degree: 24. Student-to-faculty ratio: 11:1. *Faculty development:* 7 faculty members awarded sabbaticals 2004–05.

Enrollment: Total enrollment 332. Full-time 122 men / 191 women, part-time 6m / 13w; *Transfer students:* in-state 13; from out-of-state 5.

Characteristics of Student Body: *Ethnic/racial makeup:* number of Black non-Hispanic: 2; American Indian or Alaska Native: 1; Asian or Pacific Islander: 8; Hispanic: 4; White non-Hispanic: 256;unknown: 59. *Age distribution:* number under 18: 1; 18–19: 122; 20–21: 111; 22–24: 74; 25–29: 14; 30–34: 3; 35–39: 5; 50–64: 2.

International Students: 3 nonresident aliens enrolled fall 2004. No programs available to aid students whose native language is not English. No financial aid specifically designated for international students.

Student Life: Off-campus housing. *Special services:* Students have access to college studios at all hours. Activities include gallery openings, visiting artists' events, and informally organized social occasions in the college. *Surrounding community:* Beverly, population 37,000, a seaside community 24 miles from downtown Boston. Served by public bus and trains.

Publications: Catalog is published biennially; student handbook annually; other information pieces irregularly.

Library Collections: 12,025 volumes. 50,000 slides. 76 current periodical subscriptions. 12 CD-ROMs. 12 computer work stations. Students have access to online information retrieval services and the Internet. Total 2004–05 budget for books and materials: $18,200.

Most important special holdings include collections of art books; Paul M. Scott Papers.

Buildings and Grounds: Campus area 24 acres.

Chief Executive Officer: Stan Archer, President.

Address admission inquiries to Jodie Lane, Director of Admissions and Enrollment Management.

Mount Ida College

777 Dedham Street
Newton Centre, Massachusetts 02159
Tel: (617) 928-4500   **E-mail:** admissions@mountida.edu
Fax: (617) 928-4706   **Internet:** www.mountida.edu

Institution Description: Mount Ida College is a private, independent, coeducational college. *Enrollment:* 1,293. *Degrees awarded:* Associate, baccalaureate.

Accreditation: *Regional:* NEASC.

History: Founded as junior college 1899; became Mount Ida College 1982.

Institutional Structure: 29 trustees; 17 overseers. *Administration:* executive offices 7, academic offices 11, student services 15, business office 9, administrative offices 9, admissions office 15, Learning Resource Center 11, institutional advancement 6, Health Center 7.

Calendar: Semesters (4-2-4 plan). Academic year early Sept. to late May.

Characteristics of Freshmen: 1,635 applicants. 84.2% of applicants admitted. 27.3% of admitted students enrolled. 20% of accepted applicants enrolled.

89% (379 students) submitted SAT scores. *25th percentile*: SAT I Verbal 390, SAT I Math 380. *75th percentile*: SAT I Verbal 500, SAT I Math 480.

60% of freshmen from Massachusetts. Freshmen from 34 states and 51 foreign countries.

Admission: Rolling admissions plan. Applications will be considered as long as space in a desired program is available. *Requirements:* High school graduation or GED; on-campus interview recommended. *Entrance tests:* SAT preferred.

Degree Requirements: *For all associate degrees:* 64 credit hours (communications and veterinary technology require 96 credits). *For all baccalaureate degrees:* 128 credit hours. *For all degrees:* core program.

Distinctive Educational Programs: Bachelor of Liberal Studies will guarantee full junior year status from any completed associate degree at any junior college. Study abroad at Regents College, London.

Degrees Conferred: 54 *associate*; 101 *baccalaureate*. Bachelor's degrees awarded in top five disciplines: visual and performing arts 31; business, management, marketing, and related support services 22; health professions and related clinical sciences 21; liberal arts and sciences, general studies, and humanities 12; security and protective services 8.

Fees and Other Expenses: *Full-time tuition per academic year 2004–05:* $17,075. *Room and board per academic year:* $9,400. *Books and supplies:* $800.

Financial Aid: Aid from institutionally generated funds is provided on the basis of academic merit, financial need, other criteria. Institution has a Program Participation Agreement with the U.S. Department of Education for eligible students to receive Pell Grants and other federal aid.

Financial aid to full-time, first-time undergraduate students: 38% received federal grants averaging $3,031; 23% state/local grants averaging $1,578; 89% institutional grants averaging $5,503; 79% received loans averaging $6,690.

Departments and Teaching Staff: Animal science *professors* 0, *associate professors* 1, *assistant professors* 3, *instructors* 1, *part-time teachers* 5; business 1, 3, 3, 1, 15; design and merchandising 2, 3, 8, 1, 25; education 0, 2, 0, 0, 4; electricity 0, 1, 1, 0, 5; liberal arts 2, 10, 3, 0, 30; funeral service 0, 1, 1, 0, 9; science and allied health 1, 2, 5, 2, 19.

Total instructional faculty: 170. Degrees held by full-time faculty: doctorate 21%, master's 53%, baccalaureate 19%, professional 9%.

Enrollment: Total enrollment 1,293 (30.8% men, 69.2% women).

Characteristics of Student Body: *Ethnic/racial makeup:* Black non-Hispanic: 12.2%; American Indian or Alaska Native: .1%; Asian or Pacific Islander: 2.9%; Hispanic: 6%; White non-Hispanic: 58.9%; unknown: 11.7%. *Age distribution:* 17–21: 75%; 22–24: 20%; 25–29: 2%; 30–34: 2%; 35–39 1%.

International Students: 105 nonresident aliens enrolled fall 2004. Programs available to aid students whose native language is not English: English as a Second Language Program. No financial aid specifically designated for international students.

Student Life: Five residence halls house 930 students. A staff of 9 residence directors and 24 resident assistants oversee these facilities under the supervision of the Director of Residence Life. The staff also provides social and life skills programming. The student government takes an active role in campus life. A Programming Committee plans all activities including coffee house, comic night, and "spring fling" and winter weekends. The Mount Ida yearbook staff is also part of student government. *The Voice*, a college student newspaper, publishes twice a month. Preprofessional student organizations prepare students for the challenges and benefits of their chosen careers. *Surrounding community:* Mt. Ida College is located within a residential section of Newton (MA), population 90,000. Boston is 8 miles away from campus and accessible by rapid transit from Mt. Ida.

Library Collections: 62,500 volumes. 4,500 microforms; 2,000 audiovisual materials; 530 periodicals. Students have access to online information retrieval services and the Internet.

Most important special collections include the National Center for Death Education-Thanatology Collection; literary criticism; graphic and interior design.

Buildings and Grounds: Campus area 85 acres, a former country estate, within a residential section of Newton.

Chief Executive Officer: Dr. Carol Masterson, President.

Address admission inquiries to Elizabeth Storinge, Dean of Admissions.

New England Conservatory of Music

290 Huntington Avenue
Boston, Massachusetts 02115-5018
Tel: (617) 585-1100   **E-mail:** admissions@ndconservatory.edu
Fax: (617) 262-0500   **Internet:** www.neconservatory.edu

Institution Description: New England Conservatory of Music is a private, independent, nonprofit institution. *Enrollment:* 792. *Degrees awarded:* Baccalaureate, master's, doctorate. Artist diploma, undergraduate diploma, graduate diploma also awarded.

Accreditation: *Regional:* NEASC. *Professional:* music

History: Established and chartered 1867; offered first instruction at postsecondary level 1879; awarded first degree (baccalaureate) 1926.

Institutional Structure: *Governing board:* Board of Trustees. Extrainstitutional representation: 21 trustees; institutional representation: president of the conservatory, ex officio. All voting. Board of Overseers 100 members. *Composition of institution:* Administrators 13 men / 14 women. Academic affairs headed by provost. Management/business/finances directed by vice president for administration and finance. Full-time instructional faculty 77. Academic governance body, Faculty Council, meets an average of 12 times per year.

Calendar: Semesters. Academic year early Sept. to May. Freshmen admitted Sept., Jan. Degrees conferred May, Dec. Formal commencement May. No summer session.

Characteristics of Freshmen: 2,086 applicants. 41.6% of applicants admitted. 37% of admitted students enrolled full-time.

74% (239 students) submitted SAT scores; 14% (45 students) submitted ACT scores. *25th percentile*: SAT I Verbal 799, SAT I Math 799, *75th percentile*: SAT I Verbal 800, SAT I Math 800.

6% of freshmen from Massachusetts. Freshmen from 27 states and 5 foreign countries.

Admission: For fall acceptance, apply by Dec. 1 of year prior to enrollment. *Requirements:* Graduation from accredited secondary, performance audition on major instrument; for composition majors 3–4 original compositions. *Entrance tests:* College Board SAT or ACT. For foreign students TOEFL. *For transfer students:* 2.0 minimum GPA; transfer credit evaluated individually.

Advanced placement for postsecondary-level work completed in secondary school. Baccalaureate degree required for master's candidates; Master of Music for doctoral candidates.

Degree Requirements: *For baccalaureate degree:* 120 credit hours; 2.0 cumulative GPA; 8 semesters of studio instruction in residence; core curriculum. *For master's degree:* 36 credit hours. *For doctorate:* 60 credit hours.

Exemption from some beginning courses possible by passing departmental examinations. *Grading system:* A–F; pass-unsatisfactory; withdraw.

Distinctive Educational Programs: All programs include one hour private lesson per week with major teacher (except ½ hour for music history, musicology, and graduate music education). Five-year dual-degree program with Tufts University leads to bachelor of arts or sciences from Tufts and bachelor of music from the conservatory. Cross-registration with Northeastern University, Simmons College, Tufts University. Academic and music computing facility. Electronic music studio. Independent study. *Other distinctive programs:* one-year piano technology course. Extension Division offers preparatory program to precollege students. Third Stream Certificate program; continuing education; community services outreach.

Degrees Conferred: 82 *baccalaureate:* performing arts; 160 *master's:* performing arts; 7 *doctorate:* fine and applied arts.

Fees and Other Expenses: *Full-time tuition per academic year 2004–05:* $26,000. *Room and board per academic year:* $10,650.

Financial Aid: Aid from institutionally generated funds is provided on the basis of academic merit, financial need, other considerations. Institution has a Program Participation Agreement with the U.S. Department of Education for eligible students to receive Pell Grants and, depending on the agreement, other federal aid.

Financial aid to full-time, first-time undergraduate students: 22% received federal grants averaging $4,031; 7% state/local grants; 77% institutional grants averaging $8,572; 62% received loans averaging $7,374.

Departments and Teaching Staff: *Professors* 77; *part-time faculty:* 139. *Total instructional faculty:* 216. Student-to-faculty ratio: 4:1.

Enrollment: Total enrollment 792. Undergraduate 406 (54.4% men, 45.6% women).

Characteristics of Student Body: *Ethnic/racial makeup (undergraduate):* Black non-Hispanic: 2.7%; American Indian or Alaska Native: .5%; Asian or Pacific Islander: 6.7%; Hispanic: 4.7%; White non-Hispanic: 58.4%; unknown: 9.6%. *Age distribution:* 17–21: 36%; 22–24: 35%; 25–29: 20%; 30–34: 6%; 35–39: 1%; 40–49: 1%; 50–59: 1%.

International Students: 71 undergraduate nonresident aliens enrolled fall 2004. Students from Europe, Asia, Central and South America, Africa, Canada, Australia, New Zealand. Programs available to aid students whose native language is not English: social and cultural. English as a Second Language Program. No financial aid specifically designated for international students.

Student Life: On-campus residence hall available. *Special services:* Peer advising; international student advising; counseling center. Student groups include student government, musical sorority and fraternity, gay and lesbian alliance, and others. Career planning office; community outreach. *Surrounding community:* Boston is a major metropolitan area. Campus served by mass transit bus and subway system; airport and passenger rail service each 1 mile from campus.

Library Collections: 120,000 volumes. Online catalog. 1,000 microforms; 20,000 audiovisual materials; 275 current periodical subscriptions; 30,000 recordings/tapes. Students have access to online information retrieval services and the Internet.

Most important special holdings include manuscripts and early editions of Boston composers; "Voice of Firestone" kinescopes; New England Conservatory Concert tapes.

Buildings and Grounds: Campus area less than one square block (includes 2 instructional buildings, 3 concert halls, library, residence hall).

Chief Executive Officer: Daniel Steiner, President.

Address admission inquiries to Dean of Enrollment Services.

New England College of Optometry

424 Beacon Street
Boston, Massachusetts 02115-1129
Tel: (617) 236-2030   **E-mail:** admissions@neco.edu
Fax: (617) 424-9202   **Internet:** www.neco.edu

Institution Description: The New England College of Optometry (Massachusetts College of Optometry until 1976) is a private, independent, nonprofit college. *Enrollment:* 430. *Degrees awarded:* Baccalaureate, first-professional (optometry).

Accreditation: *Regional:* NEASC. *Professional:* optometry

History: Established as the Klein School of Optics 1894; incorporated and chartered as the Massachusetts School of Optometry in 1946. awarded first degree (first-professional) 1951; adopted present name 1976.

Institutional Structure: *Governing board:* Board of Trustees. 44 voting members.

Calendar: Trimesters. Academic year Aug. to May. Degrees conferred Aug., Nov., May. Formal commencement May.

Admission: Rolling admissions for fall acceptance only: apply as early as Aug. 1 of previous year, but not later than Mar. 31. *Requirements:* 90 semester hours (or 135 credit hours) from accredited college or university, with 2 semesters or 3 quarters of chemistry with lab; 1 semester or 1 quarter organic chemistry with lab; 2 semesters or 3 quarters biology with lab; 1 semester or 1 quarter microbiology; 2 semesters or 3 quarters physics with lab; 2 semesters or 3 quarters mathematics including calculus (1 semester or 1 quarter statistics strongly recommended); 1 semester or 1 quarter psychology.

Degree Requirements: *For first-professional degree:* curriculum (didactic and clinical) satisfactorily completed; 2.00 cumulative GPA with no outstanding grades of F, remedial, or incomplete registered for 2 academic years preceding graduation. *For baccalaureate degree:* No previous bachelor's degree; successfully complete 12 semester hours of undergraduate coursework in social sciences and in humanities; first 2 years of curriculum satisfactorily completed; 2.00 cumulative GPA.

Distinctive Educational Programs: Accelerated degree program. Advanced standing program: program for graduates from foreign optometry school who have at least 2 years of full-time practice.

Degrees Conferred: 5 *baccalaureate:* health professions; 111 *first-professional* optometry 111.

Fees and Other Expenses: *Full-time tuition per academic year 2004–05:* $26,405. *Required fees:* $480.

Financial Aid: Aid from institutionally generated funds is provided on the basis of financial need. Contact Carol Rubel (617) 236-6275 for information.

Departments and Teaching Staff: Optometry *professors* 14, *associate professors* 10, *assistant professors* 9, *part-time faculty* 48. *Total instructional faculty:* 81. Degrees held by full-time faculty: doctorate 97%, master's 12%, baccalaureate 100%, professional 76%. 97% hold terminal degrees.

Enrollment: Total enrollment 430. First-professional full-time 170 men / 260 women.

Characteristics of Student Body: *Ethnic/racial makeup:* number of Black non-Hispanic: 21; Asian or Pacific Islander: 116; Hispanic: 15; White non-Hispanic: 212.

International Students: 66 nonresident aliens enrolled fall 2004. No programs available to aid students whose native language is not English. No financial aid specifically designated for international students.

Student Life: Boston is a metropolitan area served by mass transit bus and subway systems, as well as passenger rail service near the college which connects the city to the surrounding suburbs. The airport is accessible to the campus by public transportation or taxi.

Library Collections: 15,000 volumes. 260 audiovisual materials; 229 current periodical subscriptions. Students have access to online information retrieval services and the Internet.

Buildings and Grounds: Campus consists of five buildings located in Back Bay (Boston) and an off-campus clinical facility.

Chief Executive Officer: Alan Lewis, President.

Address admission inquiries to Lawrence Shattuck, Director of Admissions.

Nichols College

Center Road
Dudley, Massachusetts 01571
Tel: (508) 943-1560   **E-mail:** admissions@nichols.edu
Fax: (508) 943-9885   **Internet:** www.nichols.edu

Institution Description: Nichols College is a private, independent, nonprofit college. *Enrollment:* 1,792. *Degrees awarded:* Associate, baccalaureate, master's.

Accreditation: *Regional:* NEASC.

History: Established as Nichols Academy 1815; closed 1909; reorganized as Nichols Junior College and offered first instruction at postsecondary level 1931; incorporated and awarded first degree 1932; changed name to Nichols College of Business Administration and added upper division curriculum 1958; adopted present name, became coeducational, and added liberal arts program 1971; added graduate curriculum 1975. See Darcy C. Coyle, *Nichols College: A Brief History* (New York: The Newcomen Society in North America, 1975) for further information.

Institutional Structure: *Governing board:* Board of Trustees. Representation: 20 trustees, including 1 alumnus, college president. 1 ex officio. All voting. *Composition of institution:* Administrators 8 men / 1 woman. Academic affairs headed by president. Management/business/finances directed by directed by bursar. Full-time instructional faculty 33. Academic governance body, Academic Policy Committee, meets an average of 4 times per year.

Calendar: Semesters. Academic year Aug. to May. Freshmen admitted Sept. Degrees conferred and formal commencement May. Summer session of two terms from June to Aug.

Characteristics of Freshmen: 84% of applicants admitted. 26% of applicants admitted and enrolled 98% (311 students) submitted SAT scores; 1% (2 students) submitted ACT scores. *25th percentile:* SAT Verbal 410, SAT Math 420. *75th percentile:* SAT Verbal 500, SAT Math 510.

48% of entering freshmen expected to graduate within 5 years. 57% of freshmen from Massachusetts. Freshmen from 20 states.

Admission: Rolling admissions plan. For fall acceptance, apply as early as Sept. 15 of previous year, but not later than Sept. 1 of year of enrollment. Apply by Nov. 1 for early decision; need not limit application to Nichols. Early acceptance available. *Requirements:* Either graduation from accredited secondary school with 16 units which must include 4 English, 3 college preparatory mathematics, 2 laboratory science, 2 social studies, 5 academic electives; or GED. Minimum 2.0 GPA. *Entrance tests:* College Board SAT or ACT. *For transfer students:* 2.0 minimum GPA; maximum transfer credit limited only by residence requirement. Correspondence/extension students credit evaluated individually.

College credit and advanced placement for postsecondary-level work completed in secondary school and for extrainstitutional learning on basis of ACE *2006 Guide to the Evaluation of Educational Experiences in the Armed Services* and faculty assessment. Tutoring available. Noncredit remedial courses offered in summer session and regular academic year.

Degree Requirements: *For all associate degrees:* 61 credit hours. *For all baccalaureate degrees:* 122 credit hours. *For all undergraduate degrees:* 2.0 GPA; 30 hours in residence.

Fulfillment of some degree requirements possible by passing departmental examinations, College Board CLEP or APP, or other standardized tests. *Grading system:* A–F; pass; withdraw (deadline after which pass-fail is appended to withdraw).

Distinctive Educational Programs: *For undergraduates:* Work-experience programs. Independent study. Public administration internships in Washington

(DC), Massachusetts, and Rhode Island. *Available to all students:* Evening classes. Study abroad at Regents' College, London, England.

ROTC: Army offered in cooperation with Worcester Polytechnic Institute.

Degrees Conferred: 18 *associate;* 176 *baccalaureate:* business/marketing 168; English 4; mathematics 2; social sciences and history 2. *Master's* business/marketing 119.

Fees and Other Expenses: *Full-time tuition per academic year 2004–05:* $20,560. *Required fees:* $250. *Other fees:* 150. *Room and board per academic year:* $8,052.

Financial Aid: Nichols College offers a direct lending program. Aid from institutionally generated funds is provided on the basis of academic merit, financial need.

Financial aid to full-time, first-time undergraduate students: need-based scholarships/grants totaling $4,871,036, self-help $3,903,392, parent loans $844,060, tuition waivers $98,956; non-need-based scholarships/grants totaling $1,273,666, self-help $1,488,119, parent loans $1,118,853, tuition waivers $198,354.

Departments and Teaching Staff: *Professors* 13, *associate professors* 9, *assistant professors* 11, *part-time faculty* 42. *Total instructional faculty:* 75 (full-time 33, part-time 42; women 29, men 46). Total faculty with doctorate, first-professional, or other terminal degree: 23. Student-to-faculty ratio: 22:1. Degrees held by full-time faculty: doctorate 64%, master's 36%. 64% hold terminal degrees.

Enrollment: Total enrollment 1,792. Undergraduate full-time 612 men / 326 women, part-time 222m / 272w; graduate full-time 27m / 21, part-time 179m / 133w.

Characteristics of Student Body: *Ethnic/racial makeup (undergraduate):* number of Black non-Hispanic: 101; American Indian or Alaska Native: 4; Asian or Pacific Islander: 24; Hispanic: 52; White non-Hispanic: 1,249; unknown: 2. *Age distribution:* number under 18: 44; 18–19: 661; 20–21: 209; 22–24: 100; 25–29: 94; 30–34: 77; 35–39: 84; 40–49: 136; 50–64: 24; 65 and over: 1.

International Students: 5 nonresident aliens enrolled fall 2004. No programs available to aid students whose native language is not English. No financial aid specifically designated for international students.

Student Life: On-campus residence halls house 78% of student body. Dormitories for men only constitute 69% of such space, for women only 31%. *Intercollegiate athletics:* men only: baseball, basketball, football, golf, hockey, lacrosse, soccer, tennis; women only: basketball, field hockey, soccer, softball; both sexes: track. *Special regulations:* Cars permitted without restrictions. Quiet hours from 8pm to 10pm weekdays. *Special services:* Learning Resources Center, medical services. *Student publications, radio: Bison,* a newspaper published 10 times a year. Radio station WNRC broadcasts approximately 25 hours per week. *Surrounding community:* Dudley population 8,800. Worcester, 20 miles from campus, is nearest metropolitan area. Served by airport 25 miles from campus.

Library Collections: 54,000 volumes. 3,800,000 microforms; 2,200 audiovisual materials; 214 current periodical subscriptions. Online catalog. 3,499 recordings. 351 compact discs. 15 DVDs. 22 computer work stations. Students have access to the Internet and online information retrieval services.

Most important special holdings include Nichols Academy and Nichols College archival records.

Buildings and Grounds: Campus area 210 acres.

Chief Executive Officer: Dr. Debra M. Murphy, President.

Undergraduates address admission inquiries to Joseph Bellavance, Dean of Admissions; graduate inquiries to Joanne Williams, Dean of Graduate and Professional Studies.

Northeastern University

360 Huntington Avenue
Boston, Massachusetts 02115-0195

Tel: (617) 373-2000   **E-mail:** admissions@neu.edu
Fax: (617) 373-5506   **Internet:** www.neu.edu

Institution Description: Northeastern University is a private, independent, nonprofit institution with branch campuses at Burlington, Dedham and Nahant *Enrollment:* 18,979. *Degrees awarded:* Baccalaureate, first-professional (law, pharmacy), master's, doctorate.

Member of Boston Library Consortium.

Accreditation: *Regional:* NEASC. *Professional:* athletic training, audiology, business, clinical lab scientist, clinical lab technology, computer science, engineering, engineering technology, health information administration, law, nurse anesthesia education, nursing, pharmacy, physical therapy, physician assisting,

surgeon assisting, public administration, radiography, rehabilitation counseling, respiratory therapy, speech-language pathology

History: Established as Northeastern College of the Boston Young Men's Christian Association and offered first instruction at postsecondary level 1898; awarded first degree (baccalaureate) 1904; changed name to Northeastern University of the Boston Young Men's Christian Association 1922; incorporated and adopted present name 1936; merged with New England College of Pharmacy 1962; merged with Bouve-Boston School (established 1914) 1964. *See* Everett C. Marston, *Origin and Development of Northeastern University 1898–1960* (Boston: Northeastern University, 1961) and Antoinette Frederick, *Northeastern University An Emerging Giant: 1959–1975* (Boston, MA: Northeastern University, 1982) for further information.

Institutional Structure: *Governing board:* Northeastern University Board of Trustees. Extrainstitutional representation: 42 trustees, 4 honorary trustees, 25 lifetime trustees emeriti (non-voting). *Composition of institution:* Administrators and professional staff 445 men / 483 women. Provost and Senior Vice President for Academic Affairs, Senior Vice Presidents direct: academic affairs, treasury, government and community affairs, development. Vice Presidents direct: cooperative education, business, student affairs, alumni development. Full-time instructional faculty 751. Academic governance body, Faculty Senate, meets an average of 20 times per year.

Calendar: Quarters. Academic year Sept. to June. Freshmen admitted Sept., Jan., June. Degrees conferred and formal commencements June, Sept. Summer session of 1 term from mid-June to mid-Sept.

Characteristics of Freshmen: 62% of applicants accepted. 24% of accepted applicants enrolled.

93% (2,579 students) submitted SAT scores; 17% (462 students) submitted ACT scores. *25th percentile:* SAT Verbal 550, SAT Math 570; ACT Composite 24. *75th percentile:* SAT Verbal 650, SAT Math 660; ACT Composite 28.

43% of freshmen from Massachusetts. Freshmen from 50 states and 120 foreign countries.

Admission: Rolling admissions plan. For fall acceptance, apply as early as spring of junior year in secondary school. Early acceptance available. *Requirements:* Either graduation from accredited secondary school with courses in English, foreign language, mathematics, laboratory science, history; or GED. Additional requirements vary with program. *Entrance tests:* College Board SAT or ACT required. *For foreign students:* TOEFL. *For transfer students:* from 4-year accredited institution 120 quarter hours (90 semester hours) maximum transfer credit; from 2-year accredited institution 80 quarter hours (60 semester hours). Transfer hours vary among colleges within the university.

College credit and advanced placement for postsecondary-level work completed in secondary school. Tutoring available. Developmental courses offered during regular academic year; credit given for some courses.

Degree Requirements: *For all baccalaureate degrees:* 176 quarter hours; 3–4 quarters in residence. *For all degrees:* 2.0 GPA. Additional requirements vary with program. *Grading system:* A–F; pass-fail.

Distinctive Educational Programs: International leader in practice-oriented education, fusing academic rigor with workplace experience. Structured program of cooperative education that gives students paid professional experience. Double/dual majors and interdisciplinary majors/minors available. Many research opportunities. Participation in co-op is required of all full-time undergraduate students except those in the College of Arts and Sciences. Accelerated degree programs leading to baccalaureate and master's degrees in electrical engineering, industrial engineering, mechanical engineering, and nursing, in 5 years. Cooperative baccalaureate in allied health professions with affiliated hospitals. Special facilities for using telecommunications in the classroom. An 8-year joint Bachelor of Arts or Bachelor of Science/Juris Doctor Degree Program. Interdisciplinary minor programs offered by the College of Arts and Sciences include Asian studies, business, cinema studies, linguistics, marine studies, media studies, urban studies, international affairs, Jewish studies; Latino, Latin American, and Caribbean studies; technical communication, and women's studies. Facilities and programs for independent research, including honors programs, individual majors, tutorials. International Cooperative Education in Great Britain, the Netherlands, Sweden, Ireland, Australia, Spain, and the French and German speaking countries of Europe. Study abroad in Spain, Egypt, Ireland, Italy, Australia, Ghana, England, Belgium, France, Czech Republic, Mexico, Israel, and Canada. *Other distinctive programs:* University College offers degree and nondegree programs for adults and an Alternative Freshmen Year program for students lacking college preparation.

ROTC: Army, Air Force and Navy; classes conducted at Boston University campus.

Degrees Conferred: 2,818 *baccalaureate*; 1,366 *master's*; 93 *doctorate*. Bachelor's degrees awarded in top five disciplines: business, management, marketing, and related support services 944; health professions and related clinical sciences 253; engineering 250; security and protective services 202; communication, journalism, and related programs 200. 247 *first-professional:* pharmacy 51; law 196.

Fees and Other Expenses: *Full-time tuition per academic year 2004–05:* $26,750. *Books and supplies:* $900. *Room per academic year:* $5,440. *Board per academic year:* $4,740.

Financial Aid: Aid from institutionally generated funds is provided on the basis of academic merit, financial need, athletic ability.

Financial aid to full-time, first-time undergraduate students: need-based scholarships/grants totaling $100,883,433, self-help $71,703,901, parent loans $8,811,401; non-need-based scholarships/grants totaling $20,012,743, self-help $26,534,901, parent loans $12,499,290.

Departments and Teaching Staff: *Total instructional faculty:* 1,174 (full-time 839, part-time 335; women 478, men 696; member of minority groups 132). Total faculty with doctorate, first-professional, or other terminal degree: 791. Student-to-faculty ratio: 16:1. Degrees held by full-time faculty: 80% hold terminal degrees.

Enrollment: Total enrollment 18,979. Undergraduate full-time 7,186 men / 7,432 women; first-professional full-time 235m / 364w; graduate full-time 1,098m / 1,108w, part-time 827m / 729w.

Characteristics of Student Body: *Ethnic/racial makeup (undergraduate):* number of Black non-Hispanic: 686; American Indian or Alaska Native: 57; Asian or Pacific Islander: 1,082; Hispanic: 719; White non-Hispanic: 9,739; unknown: 1,492.

International Students: 686 undergraduate nonresident aliens enrolled fall 2004. Programs available to aid students whose native language is not English: social, cultural. English as a Second Language Program. Financial aid specifically designated for international students: scholarships available annually for undergraduate students.

Student Life: On-campus residence halls house 65% of full-time undergraduates. 1% of men belong to fraternities; 1% of women belong to sororities. *Intercollegiate athletics:* men only: baseball, basketball, crew, cross country, football, ice hockey, track and field, soccer, swimming and diving; women only: basketball, crew, cross-country, field hockey, ice hockey, soccer, track and field, volleyball. *Special regulations:* Registered cars with validation stickers permitted. Quiet hours determined by individual residence halls. *Special services:* Learning Resources Center, medical services, an academic support program designed to assist minority students to develop their academic skills with counseling services, peer mentors, tutorials, a reading and study skills course, and educational workshops; escort service to locations on and off campus. *Student publications, radio: Cauldron,* senior-class annual; *The Northeastern News,* weekly student newspaper; *Onyx/Informer,* minority student newspaper, *Spectrum,* a literary magazine. Radio station WRBB-FM. *Surrounding community:* Boston population over 500,000. University is served by mass transit bus and rail system, airport 3 miles from campus.

Publications: *The New England Quarterly; Scriblerian; Studies in American Fiction; Journal of Reality Therapy, Quantitative Journal of Criminology.*

Library Collections: 896,000 volumes. 168,797 government documents; 2,108,893 microforms; 21,799 audiovisual materials; 8,585 periodicals (including 473 electronic). Online catalog. Computer work stations available. Students have access to online information retrieval services and the Internet.

Most important special records of Freedom House, a community-based social agency in Roxbury, and the papers of its founders, Otto P. and Muriel S. Snowden; records of La Alianza Hispana; administrative and historical records of the Massachusetts AIDS Action Committee; records of the Elma Lewis School of Fine Arts and the National Center of Afro-American Artists; Glen Gray Collection and original scores of the Casa Loma swing orchestra.

Buildings and Grounds: Main campus area 65 acres in Boston's Back Bay and consisting of 44 academic and administrative service buildings.

Chief Executive Officer: Dr. Richard M. Freeland, President.

Undergraduates address admission inquiries Director of Admissions; graduate inquiries directed to various graduate schools.

Pine Manor College

400 Heath Street
Chestnut Hill, Massachusetts 02167
Tel: (617) 731-7000   **E-mail:** admissions@pmc.edu
Fax: (617) 731-7199   **Internet:** www.pmc.edu

Institution Description: Pine Manor College (Pine Manor Junior College until 1977) is a private, independent, nonprofit college for women. *Enrollment:* 478. *Degrees awarded:* Associate, baccalaureate.

Accreditation: *Regional:* NEASC.

History: Established in Wellesley as Pine Manor Junior College and offered first instruction at postsecondary level for Dana Hall, a secondary school, 1911; became junior college 1916; incorporated as nonprofit college 1938; created sep-

arate Board of Trustees 1960; separated from Dana Hall 1962; moved to present location 1965; adopted present name 1977.

Institutional Structure: *Governing board:* Board of Trustees. Extrainstitutional representation: 32 trustees; institutional representation: president of the college. 1 ex officio. All voting. *Composition of institution:* Administrators 12. Academic affairs headed by academic dean. Management/business/finances directed by comptroller. Full-time instructional faculty 30. Academic governance body, the faculty, meets an average of 10 times per year.

Calendar: Semesters. Academic year early Sept. to May. Freshmen admitted Sept., Jan., June, July. Degrees conferred and formal commencement May. Summer session of 2 terms from May to Aug.

Characteristics of Freshmen: 478 applicants (478 women). 74.9% of applicants admitted. 41.9% of admitted students enrolled full-time.

87% (130 students) submitted SAT scores; 9% (14 students) submitted ACT scores. *25th percentile:* SAT I Verbal 360, SAT I Math 340; ACT Composite 15m ACT English 14, ACT Math 14. *75th percentile:* SAT I Verbal 480, SAT I Math 450; ACT Composite 30, ACT English 22, ACT Math 10.

60% of entering freshmen expected to graduate within 5 years. 20% of freshmen from Massachusetts. Freshmen from 30 states and 14 foreign countries.

Admission: Rolling admissions plan. For fall acceptance, apply no later than day of registration. *Requirements:* Graduation from accredited secondary school. *Entrance tests:* College Board SAT preferred; ACT composite accepted. For foreign students TOEFL. *For transfer students:* 2.0 minimum GPA; maximum transfer credit limited only by residence requirement.

Tutoring available. Remedial courses offered during regular academic year; credit given.

Degree Requirements: *For all associate degrees:* 64 credit hours. *For all baccalaureate degrees:* 128 credit hours. *For all undergraduate degrees:* 2.0 GPA; 2 years in residence; core curriculum.

Fulfillment of some degree requirements and exemption from some beginning courses possible by passing departmental examinations. *Grading system:* A–F; pass-fail; withdraw (carries time limit).

Distinctive Educational Programs: Work-experience programs. Evening classes. Interdisciplinary programs. Facilities and programs for independent research, including honors (national honor society) programs, individual majors, tutorials, independent study. Study abroad in France, Switzerland in cooperation with Consortium of Colleges Abroad. American University semester in Washington (DC). Cross-registration with Babson College and Boston College. *Other distinctive programs:* Degree-granting continuing education program. International Language Institute. Interior Design Program; collaboration with Wentworth Institute of Tech. and the Boston Architectural Center; Marine Studies Consortium (at MIT); teacher certification, K–3 and 1–6.

Degrees Conferred: 12 *associate;* 85 *baccalaureate.* Bachelor's degrees awarded in top five disciplines: business, management, marketing, and related support services 23; communication, journalism, and related programs 18; psychology 12; biological and biomedical sciences 10; visual and performing arts 9.

Fees and Other Expenses: *Full-time tuition per academic year 2004–05:* $14,544. *Room and board per academic year:* $9,000.

Financial Aid: Aid from institutionally generated funds is provided on the basis of academic merit, financial need. Institution has a Program Participation Agreement with the U.S. Department of Education for eligible students to receive Pell Grants and, depending upon the agreement, other federal aid.

Financial aid to full-time, first-time undergraduate students: 52% received federal grants averaging $3,614; 42% state/local grants averaging $1,958; 76% institutional grants averaging $7,234; 75% received loans averaging $6,472.

Departments and Teaching Staff: *Total instructional faculty:* 71 (30 full-time). Degrees held by full-time faculty: 56% hold terminal degrees.

Enrollment: Total enrollment 478 (100% women).

Characteristics of Student Body: *Ethnic/racial makeup:* Black non-Hispanic: 42.5%; American Indian or Alaska Native: .4%; Asian or Pacific Islander: 4.2%; Hispanic: 11.1%; White non-Hispanic: 24.5%; unknown: 9.2%. *Age distribution:* 17–21: 79%; 22–24: 16%; 25–29: 5%.

International Students: 39 nonresident aliens enrolled fall 2004. No programs available to aid students whose native language is not English: No financial aid specifically designated for international students.

Student Life: On-campus residence halls house 95% of student body. Residence halls for women only constitute 100% of such space. *Intercollegiate athletics:* women only: basketball, field hockey, lacrosse, soccer, tennis, volleyball. *Special regulations:* Cars permitted in designated areas only; fee charged. *Special services:* Learning Resources Center, medical services, van service to and from Babson and Boston Colleges. *Student publications:* A monthly newspaper; a yearbook. *Surrounding community:* Newton population 85,000. Boston is nearest metropolitan area. Served by mass transit bus, subway systems; airport and passenger rail service, each 5 miles from campus.

Library Collections: 65,000 volumes. 57,300 microforms; 1,835 audiovisual materials; 275 current periodical subscriptions; 3,000 recordings/tapes. Online catalog. Students have access to online information retrieval services and the Internet.

Most important special collections include first edition American women authors.

Buildings and Grounds: Campus area 60 acres.

Chief Executive Officer: Dr. Gloria Nemerowicz, President.

Address admission inquiries to William Nichols, Dean of Admissions.

Regis College

235 Wellesley Street
Weston, Massachusetts 02493-1571

Tel: (781) 768-7000   **E-mail:** admission@regiscollege.edu
Fax: (781) 768-8339   **Internet:** www.regiscollege.edu

Institution Description: Regis College is a private, independent, nonprofit college for women and is affiliated with the Roman Catholic Church. *Enrollment:* 1,271. *Degrees awarded:* Associate, baccalaureate, master's. Certificates also awarded.

Accreditation: *Regional:* NEASC. *Professional:* nursing, social work

History: Established and chartered as Regis College for Women, and offered first instruction at postsecondary level 1927; awarded first degree (baccalaureate) 1931; adopted present name 1971.

Institutional Structure: *Governing board:* Board of Trustees of Regis College. Extrainstitutional representation: 27; institutional representation: president; 26 voting. *Composition of institution:* Administrators 2 man / 4 women. Academic affairs headed by vice president for academic affairs. Management/business/finances directed by vice president of finance and business. Full-time instructional faculty 54. Academic governance body, Faculty Meeting, meets an average of 8 times per year.

Calendar: Semesters (4-1-4 plan). Academic year Sept. to May. Freshmen admitted Sept., Jan. Degrees conferred May, Aug., Dec. Formal commencement May. Summer session of 2 terms from May to July.

Characteristics of Freshmen: 81% of applicants admitted. 32% of applicants admitted and enrolled.

99% (456 students) submitted SAT scores; 1% (1 student) submitted ACT scores. *25th percentile*: SAT Verbal 410, SAT Math 420. *75th percentile*: SAT Verbal 520, SAT Math 510.

65% of entering freshmen expected to graduate within 5 years. 83% of freshmen from Massachusetts. Freshmen from 10 states and 2 foreign countries.

Admission: Rolling admissions plan. Apply at any time. *Requirements:* Either 15–16 secondary school units, which should include 4 English, 2 foreign language, 3 mathematics, 2 natural science, 3–4 additional academic; or GED. Minimum 2.0 GPA. *Entrance tests:* College Board SAT or ACT. *For transfer students:* 2.0 minimum GPA; 20 courses (3–4 credits each) maximum transfer credit.

College credit and advanced placement for postsecondary-level work completed in secondary school. Tutoring available.

Degree Requirements: 36 courses; 2.0 GPA. Degree requirements may be met by passing College Board Advanced Placement tests with scores of 3, 4, or 5. *Grading system:* A–F; pass-fail; withdraw.

Distinctive Educational Programs: *For undergraduates:* 5-year dual-degree program with Worcester Polytechnic Institute leading to baccalaureates in 2 major fields at both colleges or, if fields coincide, to Regis baccalaureate and Worcester Polytechnic master's. Cross-registration with Babson, Bentley, and Boston Colleges for upper division. Interdisciplinary programs in American studies, communications, Greek studies, and women's studies. Facilities and programs for independent research. Honors programs. Individual majors. Tutorials. Internship office. Study abroad in England, France, Greece, Spain. Nondegree programs in art therapy, legal studies, and management studies. *Available to all students:* Evening classes.

ROTC: Students may join the Army ROTC through affiliation with the Boston College Campus.

Degrees Conferred: 156 *baccalaureate* (B); 68 *master's*: biological/life sciences 10 (B); business/marketing 10 (B), 9 (M); communications/communication technologies 23 (B); computer and information sciences 2 (B); education 5 (M); English 15 (B), foreign languages and literature 1 (B); health professions and related sciences 38 (B), 50 (M); interdisciplinary studies 6 (B); mathematics 2 (B); philosophy/religion/theology 4 (M); protective services/public administration 9 (M); psychology 8 (M); social sciences and history 24 (B); visual and performing arts 8 (B).

Fees and Other Expenses: *Full-time tuition per academic year 2004–05:* $20,500. *Room and board per academic year:* $9,360.

Financial Aid: Aid from institutionally generated funds is provided on the basis of academic merit, financial need, other considerations.

Financial aid to full-time, first-time undergraduate students: need-based scholarships/grants totaling $6,419,557, self-help $3,577,520, parent loans $1,323,160; non-need-based scholarships/grants totaling $760,150, self-help $51,395, tuition waivers $224,901. *Graduate aid:* 129 students received federal and state-funded loans totaling $2,692,373 (ranging from $2,100 to $48,500); 12 received fellowships and grants totaling $42,500 (ranging from $2,500 to $5,000).

Departments and Teaching Staff: *Professors 8, associate professors 31, assistant professors 9, instructors 6, part-time faculty 62. Total instructional faculty:* 116 (full-time 54, part-time 62; women 88, men 28; members of minority groups 4). Total faculty with doctorate, first-professional, or other terminal degree: 62. Student-to-faculty ratio: 12:1. *Faculty development:* 5 faculty members awarded sabbaticals 2004–05.

Enrollment: Total enrollment 1,211. Undergraduate full-time 645 women, part-time 24m / 228w; graduate full-time 11m / 135w, part-time 18m / 210w. *Transfer students:* in-state 42; from out-of-state 5.

Characteristics of Student Body: *Ethnic/racial makeup:* number of Black non-Hispanic: 101; American Indian or Alaska Native: 2; Asian or Pacific Islander: 48; Hispanic: 77; White non-Hispanic: 360; unknown: 299. *Age distribution:* number under 18: 3; 18–19: 239; 20–21: 259; 22–24: 111; 25–29: 36; 30–34: 15; 35–39: 12; 40–49: 24; 50–64: 9; unknown: 189.

International Students: 10 nonresident aliens enrolled 2004. 3 students from Europe, 5 Asia, 1 Central America, 1 Africa. No programs available to aid students whose native language is not English. No financial aid designated for international students.

Student Life: On-campus residence halls for women only house 65% of student body. *Intercollegiate athletics:* women only: basketball, crew, cross-country, field hockey, indoor and outdoor track, soccer, swimming and diving, softball, tennis, volleyball. *Special regulations:* Quiet hours set by each residence hall. Visitation from 10am to 12 midnight weekdays, 10am to 2am Fri. and Sat. *Special services:* Academic Resources Center, medical services. Campus bus connects with local transit system. *Student publications: Hemetera,* an annual literary magazine; *Mount Regis,* a yearbook; *Regis Today,* a college magazine; *Tower Trumpet,* a weekly newsletter of activities. *Surrounding community:* Weston population 12,000. Boston, 12 miles from campus, is nearest metropolitan area. Served by mass transit system; airport 15 miles from campus.

Library Collections: 139,837 volumes including bound books, serial backfiles, electronic documents, and government documents not in separate collections. Online catalog. Current serial subscriptions: 334 paper, 253 microform, 9,242 via electronic access. 2,474 recordings; 767 compact discs; 381 CD-ROMs. 44 computer work stations. Students have access to the Internet at no charge.

Most important special holdings include Newman Collection (works by and about Cardinal Newman); Madeleine Doran Collection; Regis College Archives.

Buildings and Grounds: Campus area 131 acres.

Chief Executive Officer: Dr. Mary Jane England, President.

Address admission inquiries to Emily Kelly, Director of Admissions; graduate inquiries to Sarah Barrett, Director of Graduate Admissions.

Saint John's Seminary

127 Lake Street
Brighton, Massachusetts 02135-3898

Tel: (617) 254-2610   **E-mail:** admissions@sjs.edu
Fax: (617) 787-2336   **Internet:** www.sjs.edu

Institution Description: Saint John's Seminary is a school of theology affiliated with the Archdiocese of Boston, Roman Catholic Church. The seminary trains men for the priesthood. *Enrollment:* 125 men. *Degrees awarded:* First-professional (master of divinity), master's.

Member of the consortium Boston Theological Union.

Accreditation: *Regional:* NEASC. *National:* ATS. *Professional:* theology

History: Established and chartered as Boston Ecclesiastical Seminary 1883; offered first instruction at postsecondary level 1884; established undergraduate program and adopted present name 1941; merged with Cardinal O'Connell Seminary 1968. *See* John Sexton and Daniel Riley, *History of Saint John's Seminary* (Boston: Archdiocese of Boston, 1945) for further information.

Institutional Structure: *Governing board:* Board of Trustees. Representation: 5 members of the corporation, including cardinal of archdiocese, chancellor of diocese, rector of seminary; 14 members of the board. All voting. *Composition of institution:* Administrators 4 men. Academic affairs headed by academic dean. Management/business/finances directed by business manager. Full-time instructional faculty 36. Academic governance body, Academic Policy Committee, meets an average of 8 times per year.

Calendar: Semesters. Academic year Sept. to May. Freshmen admitted Sept., Jan. Degrees conferred and formal commencement May.

Admission: Rolling admissions plan. For fall acceptance, apply as early as 1 year prior to enrollment, but not later than 1 week prior to beginning of semester.

Degree Requirements: Completion of prescribed curriculum.

Distinctive Educational Programs: *For first-professional students:* Fourth-year candidates may participate in Diaconal Internship Program or in special education program. *Available to all students:* Field education program. Interdepartmental/interdisciplinary programs.

Degrees Conferred: 16 *master's:* theology.

Fees and Other Expenses: Contact the seminary for current tuition/fees and other costs.

Financial Aid: Aid from institutionally generated funds is provided on the basis of special considerations.

Departments and Teaching Staff: *Total instructional faculty:* 36. Degrees held by full-time faculty: doctorate 86.7%, master's 100%. 86.7% hold terminal degrees.

Enrollment: Total enrollment 125.

Characteristics of Student Body: *Ethnic/racial makeup:* Asian or Pacific Islander: 7; Hispanic: 10; White non-Hispanic: 108.

International Students: 3 nonresident aliens enrolled. Programs available to aid students whose native language is not English: social, cultural, financial. English as a Second Language Program.

Student Life: On-campus residence halls house 100% of student body. *Special regulations:* Registered cars permitted; parking spaces assigned. Clerical dress required at all times. Curfews begin midnight. Residence hall visitation in public rooms only. *Special services:* Medical services. *Surrounding community:* Brighton is located within the Boston metropolitan area. Served by mass transit bus system; airport 10 miles from campus; passenger rail service 8 miles from campus.

Library Collections: 120,000 volumes. 345 current periodical subscriptions.

Buildings and Grounds: Campus area 40 acres.

Chief Executive Officer: Rev. John A. Farren, OP, Rector.

Address admission inquiries to Rector's Office.

Salem State College

352 Lafayette Street
Salem, Massachusetts 01970-5353

Tel: (978) 542-6000   **E-mail:** admissions@salem.mass.edu
Fax: (978) 542-6970   **Internet:** www.salem.mass.edu

Institution Description: Salem State College (within the Massachusetts State College System until 1981) is a member of Massachusetts Board of Regents of Higher Education. *Enrollment:* 9,347. *Degrees awarded:* Baccalaureate, master's. Academic offerings subject to approval by statewide coordinating bodies. Budget subject to approval by state governing boards. Member of Northeast Consortium of Colleges and Universities in Massachusetts.

Accreditation: *Regional:* NEASC. *Professional:* art, athletic training, nuclear medicine technology, nursing, nursing education, occupational therapy, social work, teacher education

History: Established as Salem Normal School, chartered, and offered first instruction at postsecondary level 1854; awarded first degree (baccalaureate) 1929; changed name to Salem State Teachers College 1932, State Teachers College at Salem 1960; adopted present name 1963.

Institutional Structure: *Governing board:* Massachusetts Board of Regents of Higher Education (statewide policy making body). Extrainstitutional representation: 15 regents. All voting. Board of Trustees (appointed for Salem State) 8 members. All voting. *Composition of institution:* Administrators 34 men / 16 women. Academic affairs headed by vice president for academic affairs. Management/business/finances directed by vice president for administration and finance. Full-time instructional faculty 301. Academic governance: president, advised by academic vice president and faculty committee, determines academic policy. *Faculty representation:* Faculty served by collective bargaining agent affiliated with NEA, Massachusetts Teacher Association, and Salem chapter of Massachusetts State College Association.

Calendar: Semesters. Academic year early Sept. to early May. Freshmen admitted Sept., Feb. Degrees conferred and formal commencement June. Summer session from early July to mid-Aug.

Characteristics of Freshmen: 3,954 applicants (1,388 men, 2,566 women). 84.8% of applicants admitted. 30.1% of admitted students enrolled full-time. 93% (971 students) submitted SAT scores; 2% (28 students) submitted ACT scores. *25th percentile:* SAT I Verbal 410, SAT I Math 410; ACT Composite 18,

ACT English 16, ACT Math 16. *75th percentile*: SAT I Verbal 530, SAT I Math 520; ACT Composite 23, ACT English 23, ACT Math 22.

60% of entering freshmen expected to graduate within 5 years. 98% of freshmen from Massachusetts. Freshmen from 9 states.

Admission: Rolling admissions plan. For fall acceptance, apply as early as Nov. 1 of previous year, but not later than Mar. 1 of year of enrollment. Students are notified of acceptance beginning in Jan. Early acceptance available. *Requirements:* Either graduation from accredited secondary school or GED. Recommend 16 units which normally include 4 English, 2 history and social studies, 2 mathematics, 1 laboratory science. 2 additional units foreign language for bachelor of arts candidates, units in biology and chemistry for nursing students. *Entrance tests:* College Board SAT. For foreign students TOEFL. *For transfer students:* 2.0 minimum GPA; from 4-year accredited institution 90 semester hours maximum transfer credit; from 2-year accredited institution 60 semester hours.

College credit for postsecondary-level work completed in secondary school and for extrainstitutional learning on basis of ACE *2006 Guide to the Evaluation of Educational Experiences in the Armed Services.* Tutoring available. Developmental courses offered in summer session and regular academic year; credit given.

Degree Requirements: 122–137 semester hours; 2.0 GPA; 1 year in residence; 4 courses physical education; general education and distribution requirements; exit competency examination in writing.

Fulfillment of some degree requirements possible by passing departmental examinations, College Board CLEP, AP. *Grading system:* A–F; pass-fail; withdraw (deadline after which fail is appended to withdraw).

Distinctive Educational Programs: Work-experience programs including internships, cooperative education. Evening classes. Special facilities for using telecommunications in the classroom. Interdisciplinary programs in Afro-American studies, general studies, marine studies, women's studies. Facilities and programs for independent research, including honors programs, individual majors. Institutionally sponsored study abroad in England and Spain; other study abroad through cooperating institutions. Baccalaureate completion program for registered nurses. *Other distinctive programs:* Continuing education.

ROTC: Army.

Degrees Conferred: 830 *baccalaureate;* 468 *master's.* Bachelor's degrees awarded in top five disciplines: business, management, marketing, and related support services 192; education 105; security and protective services 81; health professions and related clinical sciences 77; social sciences 69.

Fees and Other Expenses: *Full-time tuition per academic year 2004–05:* undergraduate resident $5,454, out-of-state student $11,594. Contact the college for current tuition and fees for graduate study. *Room and board per academic year:* $7,237. Books and supplies: $800.

Financial Aid: Aid from institutionally generated funds is provided on the basis of academic merit, financial need, other criteria. Institution has a Program Participation Agreement with the U.S. Department of Education for eligible students to receive Pell Grants and depending on the agreement, other federal aid.

Financial aid to full-time, first-time undergraduate students: 32% received federal grants averaging $3,005; 39% state/local grants averaging $2,032; 5% institutional grants averaging $1,285; 46% received loans averaging $2,798.

Departments and Teaching Staff: *Total instructional faculty:* 409. Student-to-faculty ratio: 20:1. Degrees held by full-time faculty: 70% hold terminal degrees.

Enrollment: Total enrollment 9,347 (36.8% men, 53.2% women).

Characteristics of Student Body: *Ethnic/racial makeup (undergraduate):* Black non-Hispanic: 5%; American Indian or Alaska Native: .4%; Asian or Pacific Islander: 2.1%; Hispanic: 4.8%; White non-Hispanic: 78.6%; unknown: 4.2%.

International Students: 339 undergraduate nonresident aliens enrolled fall 2004. Programs available to aid students whose native language is not English: English as a Second Language Program; tutoring, counseling. No financial aid specifically designated for international students.

Student Life: On-campus residence halls house 12% of student body. Dormitories for women only constitute 54% of such space, for both sexes 46%. *Intercollegiate athletics:* men only: baseball, basketball, cross-country, hockey, soccer, tennis, track, volleyball; women only: basketball, field hockey, gymnastics, swimming, tennis, volleyball. *Special regulations:* Registered cars with decals permitted on campus in designated areas. *Special services:* Learning Resources Center, medical services, shuttle bus. *Student publications, radio:* The Log, a weekly newspaper; *Soundings East,* a biannual literary magazine. Radio station WMWM-FM broadcasts 133 hours per week. *Surrounding community:* Salem population 39,000. Boston, 18 miles from campus, is nearest metropolitan area. Served by mass transit bus system; airport 18 miles from campus; passenger rail service 1 mile from campus.

Library Collections: 302,000 volumes. 566,500 microforms; 70,000 audiovisual materials; 1,145 periodicals. Access to online information retrieval systems.

Most important holdings include 19th-century textbook collection; Bates archive papers; papers of Representative Michael Harrington.

Buildings and Grounds: Campus area 62 acres.

Chief Executive Officer: Dr. Nancy D. Harrington, President.

Address admission inquiries to Nate Bryant, Director of Admissions.

School of the Museum of Fine Arts, Boston

230 The Fenway
Boston, Massachusetts 02115-9975
Tel: (617) 267-6100   **E-mail:** admissions@smfa.edu
Fax: (617) 424-6271   **Internet:** www.smfa.edu

Institution Description: The mission of the School of the Museum of Fine Arts is to provide an education in the fine arts for undergraduate and graduate artists that is interdisciplinary, self-directed, and evolving. *Enrollment:* 1,527. *Degrees awarded:* Baccalaureate, master's. Certificates and diplomas also awarded.

Accreditation: *National:* NASAD. *Professional:* : art

History: Chartered 1870; awarded first degree (MFAA) 1876; adopted present name in 1926.

Institutional Structure: Overseen by a Board of Governors, delegated by and reporting to the school's trustees.

Calendar: Semesters. Academic year early Sept. to mid-May.

Characteristics of Freshmen: 79% (129 students) submitted SAT scores; 16% (26 students) submitted ACT scores. *25th percentile:* SAT Verbal 510, SAT Math 480; ACT Composite 20, ACT English 19, ACT Math 17. *75th percentile:* SAT Verbal 620, SAT Math 590; ACT Composite 23, ACT English 23; ACT Math 21.

Freshmen from 26 states and 21 foreign countries.

Degrees Conferred: 157 *baccalaureate:* visual and performing arts; 26 *master's:* visual and performing arts.

Fees and Other Expenses: *Full-time tuition per academic year :* $22,490. *Required fees:* $1,185.

Financial Aid: Aid from institutionally generated funds is provided on the basis of financial need, other considerations.

Financial aid to full-time, first-time undergraduate students: need-based scholarships/grants totaling $4,018,675, self-help $3,510,961, parent loans $2,445,105, tuition waivers $67,470; non-need-based scholarships/grants totaling $453,300.

Departments and Teaching Staff: *Total instructional faculty:* 158 (full-time 51, part-time 107; women 87, men 71; members of minority groups 14). Total faculty with doctorate, first-professional, or other terminal degree: 74. Student-to-faculty ratio: 10:1. Degrees held by full-time faculty: baccalaureate 58%, master's 42%.

Enrollment: Total enrollment 780. Undergraduate 211 men / 383 women, part-time 15m / 55w; graduate full-time 34m / 82w. *Transfer students:* 89.

Characteristics of Student Body: *Ethnic/racial makeup:* number of Black non-Hispanic: 19; American Indian or Alaska Native: 4; Asian or Pacific Islander: 18; Hispanic: 31; White non-Hispanic: 542; unknown: 14. *Age distribution:* number under 18: 16; 18–19: 229; 20–21: 171; 22–24: 125; 25–29: 64; 30–34: 17; 35–39: 5; 40–49: 17; 50–64: 17; 65 and over: 3.

International Students: 36 nonresident aliens enrolled fall 2004. Programs available to aid students whose native language is not English: financial.

Library Collections: 19,000 volumes. 670 current periodical subscriptions; 80,000 recordings/tapes. Online catalog. Students have access to online information retrieval services.

Most important special collections include contemporary art books, rare art books, artists' books.

Buildings and Grounds: Campus area 14 acres.

Chief Executive Officer: Deborah H. Dluhy, Dean and Deputy Director.

Address admission inquiries to Dean of Admissions.

Simmons College

300 The Fenway
Boston, Massachusetts 02115-5898
Tel: (617) 521-2000   **E-mail:** ugadm@simmons.edu
Fax: (617) 521-3190   **Internet:** www.simmons.edu

Institution Description: Simmons College is a private, independent, non-profit college for women. *Enrollment:* 4,537. Men are admitted to graduate programs. *Degrees awarded:* Baccalaureate, master's, doctorate. Certificates also awarded.

Accreditation: *Regional:* NEASC. *Professional:* business, dietetics, health services administration, librarianship, nursing, physical therapy, social work

History: Chartered as Simmons Female College 1899; offered first instruction at postsecondary level 1902; awarded first degree (baccalaureate) 1906; adopted present name 1915. *See* Kenneth L. Mark, *Delayed by Fire: Being the Early History of Simmons College* (Concord, N.H.: Rumford Press, 1945).

Institutional Structure: *Governing board:* Simmons College Corporation. Extrainstitutional representation: 24 trustees, including 10 alumnae; institutional representation: president of the college (president serves as ex officio member of each of the Simmons College Corporation Standing Committees). All voting. *Composition of institution:* Administrators 20 men / 42 women. Academic affairs headed by president. Management/business/finances directed by treasurer. Full-time instructional faculty 189. Academic governance body, the faculty, meets an average of 9 times per year.

Calendar: Semesters. Academic year early Sept. to mid-May. Freshmen admitted Sept., Jan. Degrees conferred Jan., May, Aug., Oct. Formal commencement May. Summer session of 2 terms.

Characteristics of Freshmen: 2,041 applicants (2,041 women). 67.3% of applicants admitted. 30.3% of admitted students enrolled full-time.

94% (392 students) submitted SAT scores. *25th percentile:* SAT I Verbal 510, SAT I Math 500; ACT Composite 21. *75th percentile:* SAT I Verbal 610, SAT I Math 590; ACT Composite 25.

67% of entering freshmen expected to graduate within 5 years. 45% of freshmen from Massachusetts. Freshmen from 25 states and 9 foreign countries.

Admission: For fall acceptance, apply as early as Sept. 1 of previous year, but not later than Feb. 1 of year of enrollment. Students are notified of acceptance no later than early April. Early action plan: apply by Dec. 1 with notification by Jan. 20. *Requirements:* Graduation from accredited secondary school or GED; essay and 2 recommendations. *Entrance tests:* College Board SAT or ACT composite. TOEFL for foreign students. *For transfer students:* 80 hours maximum transfer credit.

College credit and advanced placement available for postsecondary-level work completed in secondary school.

Degree Requirements: 128 credit hours; competence in math skills; proficiency in a foreign language; independent learning; multidisciplinary core courses MCC 101 and 102. One course from each of the following categories of study: creative and performing arts; language, literature, and culture; quantitative analysis; scientific inquiry; social and historical perspectives; and psychological and ethical development.

Fulfillment of some degree requirements and exemption from some beginning courses possible by passing departmental examinations, College Board CLEP, AP. *Grading system:* A–F; high pass/pass-fail; withdraw (carries time limit).

Distinctive Educational Programs: Internships, field work, and independent study. Domestic exchange with Mills College, Spelman College, or Fisk University. Washington semester at American University. Inter-college registration with Emmanuel College, Wentworth Institute of Technology, New England Conservatory, Hebrew College, Wheelock College. OPEN Program available for students who would like to plan an individualized concentration. Various study abroad programs arranged through the Institute of European Studies. Freshman Honors Program. Dual degree program in chemistry and pharmacy with Massachusetts College of Pharmacy and Allied Health Sciences.

ROTC: Army in cooperation with Northeastern University, Boston (MA).

Degrees Conferred: 290 *baccalaureate*; 966 *master's*; 3 *doctorate.* Bachelor's degrees awarded in top five disciplines: social sciences 58; health professions and related clinical sciences 51; communication, journalism, and related programs 31; visual and performing arts 27; psychology 25.

Fees and Other Expenses: *Full-time tuition per academic year 2004–05:* undergraduate $24,490. Contact the college for current graduate tuition/fees. *Books and supplies:* $800. *Room and board per academic year:* $9,820.

Financial Aid: Aid from institutionally generated funds is provided on the basis of academic merit, financial need. Institution has a Program Participation Agreement with the U.S. Department of Education for eligible students to receive Pell Grants and other federal aid.

Financial aid to full-time, first-time undergraduate students: 27% received federal grants averaging $4,366; 19% state/local grants averaging $1,376; 93% institutional grants averaging $10,630; 89% received loans averaging $3,690.

Departments and Teaching Staff: *Professors* 56, *associate professors* 47, *assistant professors* 81, *instructors* 5, *part-time teachers* 173.

Total instructional faculty: 362. Student-to-faculty ratio: 10:1. Degrees held by full-time faculty: baccalaureate 100%, master's 100%, doctorate 62%. 78% hold terminal degrees.

Enrollment: Total enrollment 5,537. Undergraduate 1,874 (1.5% men, 98.5% women).

Characteristics of Student Body: *Ethnic/racial makeup (undergraduate):* Black non-Hispanic: 5.5%; American Indian or Alaska Native: .3%; Asian or Pacific Islander: 7.3%; Hispanic: 3.1%; White non-Hispanic: 78.1%; unknown: 2.9%. *Age distribution:* 17–21: 29%; 22–24: 26%; 25–29: 19%; 30–34: 8%; 35–39: 6%; 40–49: 10%; 50–59: 1%; 60–and over: 1%. 20% of total student body attend summer sessions.

International Students: 34 undergraduate nonresident aliens enrolled fall 2004. Students from Europe, Asia, Central and South America, Africa, Canada. Programs available to aid students whose native language is not English: social, cultural. No financial aid specifically designated for international students.

Student Life: On-campus residence halls house 65% of student body. Residence halls for women only constitute 100% of such space. *Intercollegiate athletics:* basketball, crew, cross-country, field hockey, sailing, soccer, softball, swimming, tennis, track, volleyball. *Special facilities:* Career Resource and Placement Center, microcomputer labs, media center, sports center. Quadside Cafe located on residence campus serves food, non-alcoholic beverages. *Student publications: Simmons News* , a weekly newspaper; *Microcosm,* a senior yearbook; *Sidelines* , a biannual literary newsletter. *Surrounding community:* Boston population over 500,000. Served by mass transit bus, subway, trolley systems; airport 6 miles from campus; passenger rail service 3 miles from campus.

Publications: *Essays and Studies* (biannually) first published in 1943; *Simmons Review,* a quarterly Alumnae magazine; *Simmons Now,* a quarterly newsletter to alumnae, faculty, staff, and friends of Simmons College.

Library Collections: 275,000 volumes. 1,900 periodicals. 11,200 microform units. Online catalog. Computer work stations available. Students have access to online information retrieval services and the Internet.

Most important special holdings include Simmons College Archives and manuscript collections; Historical Social Welfare Collection; Knapp Collection of Early Children's Books.

Buildings and Grounds: Campus area 12 acres.

Chief Executive Officer: Dr. Daniel S. Cheever, Jr., President.

Address undergraduate admission to Director of Admissions; graduate inquiries to Admission Officer of individual graduate schools.

Graduate School of Library and Information Science

Degree Programs Offered: *Master's, doctorate.*

Graduate School of Management

Degree Programs Offered: *Master's* in business administration.

Distinctive Educational Programs: Middle Management Program, an intensive, company-sponsored, 10-week residential program, prepares qualified women for middle management positions.

School of Social Work

Degree Programs Offered: *Master's, doctorate.*

Admission: Graduation from an accredited college; 3.0 GPA in last 2 years of undergraduate work; evidence of personal qualifications: maturity, stability, desire to help; experience in the field through paid, volunteer, or coursework.

Degree Requirements: 60 academic credits for 2-year programs; 2 days in classes each year; 3 days in field placement each year.

Graduate Studies

Degree Programs Offered: *Master's* in children's literature, communications management, English, French, liberal studies, philosophy, special needs inclusion specialist, teaching ESL, history, Spanish, teaching, moderate special needs.

Degree Requirements: 32–44 credits depending on program; some programs have a thesis requirement.

Departments and Teaching Staff: Faculty drawn from various departments of the college.

Simon's Rock College of Bard

84 Alford Road
Great Barrington, Massachusetts 01230-9702
Tel: (413) 528-0771   **E-mail:** admit@simons-rock.edu
Fax: (413) 528-7365   **Internet:** www.simons-rock.edu

Institution Description: Simon's Rock College of Bard is a private, independent, nonprofit college that admits students after the 10th or 11th grade. *Enrollment:* 386. *Degrees awarded:* Associate, baccalaureate.

Accreditation: *Regional:* NEASC.

History: Established and incorporated as Simon's Rock Early College 1964; offered first instruction at postsecondary level 1966; awarded first degree (associate) 1970; authorized to grant B.A. degree 1974; became part of Bard College 1979; adopted present name 1990.

Institutional Structure: *Governing boards:* Board of Trustees of Bard College and Board of Overseers of Simon's Rock College of Bard. Representation: 30 trustees and 20 overseers, including president of the college. 1 ex officio. All voting. *Composition of institution:* Administrators 5 men / 4 woman. Academic affairs headed by dean of of academic affairs. Campus directed by vice president and dean of the college. Management/business/finances directed by executive vice president of the college. Full-time instructional faculty 35. Academic governance body, Academic Senate, meets an average of 9 times per year.

Calendar: Semesters. Academic year Aug. to May. Freshmen admitted Aug., Jan. Degrees conferred and formal commencement May. No summer session.

Characteristics of Freshmen: 247 applicants (98 men, 149 women). 78.9% of applicants admitted. 71,8% of admitted students enrolled full-time. 38% (53 students) submitted SAT scores; 6% (9 students) submitted ACT scores. *25th percentile:* SAT I Verbal 600, SAT I Math 570; ACT Composite 24. *75th percentile:* SAT I Verbal 700, SAT I Math 680; ACT Composite 30.

91% of entering freshmen expected to graduate within 5 years. 19% of freshmen from Massachusetts. Freshmen from 39 states and 4 foreign countries.

Admission: Rolling admissions plan. For fall acceptance, apply as early as 1 year prior to enrollment, but not later than June 30 for fall semester and Nov. 30 for spring semester. Early acceptance available. *Requirements:* Minimum 2.0 GPA; essays, recommendations, interview. *Entrance tests:* College Board SAT, ACT composite, TOEFL, or other standardized test. *For transfer students:* 2.0 minimum GPA; 10 hours maximum transfer credit for associate degree program, 60 hours for baccalaureate program.

College credit and advanced placement for postsecondary-level work completed in secondary school.

Degree Requirements: *For all associate degrees:* 60 credit hours; 4 semesters in residence. *For all baccalaureate degrees:* 120 credit hours; 4 semesters in residence; senior thesis. *For all degrees:* 2.0 GPA; 4 units physical education; core and distribution requirements; demonstrated proficiency in mathematics, foreign language. All students must complete a Writing and Thinking Workshop, a 2-semester Freshmen Seminary, a Sophomore Seminary, and a Cultural Perspectives Seminary. The core curriculum includes distribution requirements in the arts, mathematics, natural sciences, foreign languages, and a physical education requirement.

Exemption from some beginning courses possible by passing institutional examinations. *Grading system:* A–F; pass-fail; withdraw (carries time limit), faculty comments with grades.

Distinctive Educational Programs: There are 36 concentrations available. A major involves students selecting two concentrations from the list, one of which may be self-designed. Options also offered are independent study, internships in many fields, study abroad, cooperative program with Bard College, and choice of pass/fail options.

Degrees Conferred: 118 *associate;* 51 *baccalaureate.* Bachelor's degrees awarded in top five disciplines: visual and performing arts 11; English language and literature/letters 7; psychology 6; area, ethnic, cultural, and gender studies 6; social sciences 5.

Fees and Other Expenses: *Full-time tuition per academic year 2004–05:* $30,687. *Room and board per academic year:* $8,088.

Financial Aid: Aid from institutionally generated funds is provided on the basis of academic merit, financial need. Institution has a Program Participation Agreement with the U.S. Department of Education for eligible students to receive Pell Grants and, depending upon the agreement, other federal aid.

Financial aid to full-time, first-time undergraduate students: 34% received federal grants averaging $2,725; 12% state/local grants averaging $1,213; 78% institutional grants averaging $14,779; 65% received loans averaging $3,417.

Departments and Teaching Staff: Arts *professors* 8, *part-time faculty* 3; languages and literature 9, 3; natural sciences/mathematics 9, 2; social studies 9, 3. *Total instructional faculty:* 46. Student-to-faculty ratio: 9:1. Degrees held by full-time faculty: 97% hold terminal degrees.

Enrollment: Total enrollment 386 (42.5% men, 57.5% women).

Characteristics of Student Body: *Ethnic/racial makeup:* Black non-Hispanic: 4.1%; American Indian or Alaska Native: 1.35; Asian or Pacific Islander: 5.4%; Hispanic: 4.1%; White non-Hispanic: 68.4%; unknown: 16.1%. *Age distribution:* 17–21: 88%; 22–24: 12%.

International Students: 2 nonresident aliens enrolled fall 2004. 1 student from Europe, 1 Africa. No programs available to aid students whose native language is not English. No financial aid specifically designated for international students.

Student Life: On-campus residences house 94% of student body. *Special regulations:* Cars permitted except first semester freshmen. Parking available at no additional cost. Quiet hours. Residence hall visitation until 12pm. *Special ser-*

vices: Medical services, counseling, study skills, transportation to/from airport/train, food co-op, career development, substance abuse prevention, harassment committee, governance by Community Council. *Student publications:* annual literary magazine; weekly newspaper; yearbook. *Surrounding community:* Great Barrington population 8,000. Springfield, 45 miles from campus, is nearest metropolitan area. Served by airport 50 miles from campus; passenger rail service 30 miles from campus.

Library Collections: 72,000 volumes. 9,000 microforms; 3,000 audiovisual materials; 360 current periodical subscriptions. 9,800 microform units. 1,200 recordings. 672 compact discs. Online catalog. 25 computer work stations. Students have access to online information retrieval services and the Internet.

Most important special holdings include W.E.B. Dubois Collection (books related to the Black experience); Krainis Collection (scores of early chamber music, many for the recorder); Adolf A. Berle Collection (books from the personal library of a scholar and public servant).

Buildings and Grounds: Campus area 275 acres.

Chief Executive Officer: Dr. Leon Botstein, President.

Address admission inquiries to Leslie Davidson, Director of Admissions.

Smith College

Elm Street
Northampton, Massachusetts 01063-0001
Tel: (413) 585-2500　**E-mail:** admission@smith.edu
Fax: (413) 585-2527　**Internet:** www.smith.edu

Institution Description: Smith College is a private, independent, nonprofit college for women. *Enrollment:* 2,682 women. Men are admitted to graduate programs and on a non-degree basis to undergraduate courses through Five College exchange and the Twelve College Exchange Program. *Degrees awarded:* Baccalaureate, master's, doctorate.

Member of Five Colleges, Inc.

Accreditation: *Regional:* NEASC. *Professional:* social work

History: Established and chartered 1871; offered first instruction at postsecondary level 1875; awarded first degree (baccalaureate) 1879; added master's program ca. 1900; opened School for Social Work 1918; added doctoral program 1971. *See* L. Clark Seelye, *The Early History of Smith College 1871–1910* (Cambridge: The Riverside Press, 1923) for further information.

Institutional Structure: *Governing board:* Board of Trustees. Representation: 25 trustees, including 17 alumnae, president of the college, 2 former student government presidents. All voting. *Composition of institution:* Academic affairs headed by the dean of faculty/provost. Management/business/finances directed by chief financial officer. Full-time instructional faculty 276. Academic governance body, the faculty, meets an average of 8 times per year.

Calendar: Semesters. Academic year early Sept. to early May. Freshmen admitted Sept., Jan. Degrees conferred and formal commencement May.

Characteristics of Freshmen: 57% of applicants admitted. 41% of applicants admitted and enrolled.

95% (659 students) submitted SAT scores; 31% (213 students) submitted ACT scores. *25th percentile:* SAT Verbal 590, SAT Math 570; ACT Composite 25, ACT English 25, ACT Math 23. *75th percentile:* SAT Verbal 700, SAT Math 670; ACT Composite 30, ACT English 31, ACT Math 28.

83% of entering freshmen expected to graduate within 5 years. 22% of freshmen from Massachusetts. Freshmen from 50 states and 29 foreign countries.

Admission: For fall acceptance, apply as early as Sept. of previous year, but not later than Jan. 15 of year of enrollment. Students are notified of acceptance in April. Early decision deadlines are Nov. 15. and Jan 1; need not limit application to Smith, but must withdraw other applications if accepted. Early acceptance available. *Requirements:* Recommend 4 years of English, 3 years in a foreign language (or 2 years each in 2 foreign languages), 3 mathematics, 3 science, 2 history. Personal interview recommended. *Entrance tests:* College Board SAT I or ACT required. SAT II exams recommended (writing and two others). Course credit given for score of 4 or 5 on the College Board AP examination. *For transfer students:* 64 hours maximum transfer credit.

Degree Requirements: *For baccalaureate degree:* completion to a specified standard of 128 credit of academic work. 36–48 of these credits must be chosen to satisfy the requirements of the major field; 64 credits must be chosen from outside the major department. For graduation the minimum standard of performance is a cumulative average of 2.0 on all academic work and a minimum average of 2.0 in the senior year. Candidates for the degree must complete at least 2 years of academic work, a minimum of 64 credits, in residence at Smith College in Northampton; 1 of these years must be either the junior or senior year. Advanced placement credit or summer school credit may be used to supplement a minimum 12-credit program or to make up a shortage of hours.

Distinctive Educational Programs: Guaranteed internship for every Smith student. Accelerated degree programs. Cooperative doctoral programs through consortium. Dual-degree programs leading to a baccalaureate or master's in engineering in cooperation with the University of Massachusetts at Amherst. Interdepartmental majors are offered in American studies, ancient studies, biochemistry, comparative literature, women studies, and medieval studies, Latin American studies. Facilities for independent research, including honors programs, individual majors, and Smith Scholars program. Junior year abroad through Smith College programs in France, Italy, Switzerland, and Germany. Other foreign study on affiliated programs in England, Italy, India, Spain, Japan, China, and Russia; independent study elsewhere may be individually arranged. Off-campus study in the U.S. includes a year at one of the following predominantly Black institutions: Howard University (DC), North Carolina Central University, Spelman College (GA), and Tougaloo College (MS), and with Smithsonian. Off-campus study for semester or year through Twelve College Exchange Program.

ROTC: Army in cooperation with University of Massachusetts.

Degrees Conferred: 688 *baccalaureate* (B), 107 *master's* (M), 9 *doctorate* (D): architecture 15 (B); area and ethnic studies 54 (B); biological/life sciences 48 (B), 4 (M); computer and information sciences 14 (B); education 22 (B), 30 (M); engineering and engineering technologies 19 (B); English 14 (B); foreign languages and literature 49 (B); interdisciplinary studies 14 (B); mathematics (14); parks and recreation 9 (M); philosophy/religion/theology 20 (B); physical sciences 32 (B); protective services/public administration 105 (M), 9 (D); psychology 61 (B); social sciences and history 211 (B); visual and performing arts 71 (B), 9 (M).

Fees and Other Expenses: *Full-time tuition per academic year 2005–06:* $30,250. . *Other fees:* $234. *Room and board per academic year:* $10,270.

Financial Aid: Smith College offers a direct lending program. Aid from institutionally generated funds is awarded on the basis of academic merit, financial need.

Financial aid to full-time, first-time undergraduate students: need-based scholarships/grants totaling $39,780,172, self-help $9,777,546, parent loans $7,344,219; non-need-based scholarships/grants totaling $1,108,473.*Graduate aid:* 41 students received $508,725 in federal and state-funded fellowships/grants (ranging from $2,500 to $18,500); 55 students held teaching assistantships totaling $633,305 (ranging from $7,240 to $28,930).

Departments and Teaching Staff: *Professors* 127, *associate professors* 73, *assistant professors* 74, *instructors* 2, *part-time faculty* 26. *Total instructional faculty:* 302 (full-time 276, part-time 26; women 153, men 149; members of minority groups 42). Total faculty with doctorate, first-professional, or other terminal degree: 290. Student-to-faculty ratio: 9:1. Degrees held by full-time faculty: master's 3%, doctorate 97%. *Faculty development:* $4,025,261 total grants for research. 60 faculty members awarded sabbaticals 2004–05.

Enrollment: Total enrollment 3,095. Undergraduate full-time 2,655 women, part-time 37w; graduate full-time 48m / 382w, part-time 6m / 37w.

Characteristics of Student Body: *Ethnic/racial makeup:* number of Black non-Hispanic: 153; American Indian or Alaska Native: 28; Asian or Pacific Islander: 264; Hispanic: 160; White non-Hispanic: 1,457; unknown: 450. *Age distribution:* number under 18: 66; 18–19: 1,178; 20–21: 1,078; 22–24: 167; 25–29: 63; 30–34: 39; 35–39: 45; 40–49: 52; 50–64: 41.

International Students: 180 nonresident aliens enrolled fall 2004. 36 students from Europe, 99 Asia, 20 Central and South America, 19 Africa, 20 Canada, 2 Australia, 10 other. Programs available to aid students whose native language is not English: social, cultural, financial. Financial aid specifically designated for international students: variable number of scholarships available annually.

Student Life: 90% of students are housed in 36 residence buildings that can accommodate from 16–98 women students. *Intercollegiate athletics:* women only: basketball, crew, diving, field hockey, lacrosse, riding, soccer, softball, squash, swimming, tennis, track, volleyball, cross-country, and skiing. *Special regulations:* Cars permitted for upperclassmen. *Special services:* Medical services, campus shuttle bus service. Consortium intercampus bus. *Student publications: New Current*, a quarterly magazine; *The Sophian*, a weekly newspaper; *Grecourt Review*, an annual publication of poetry; *Green Age Literary Review*, an annual publication of original literary works. *Surrounding community:* Hartford (CT), 50 miles from campus, and Boston, 100 miles from campus, are the nearest metropolitan areas. Served by mass transit bus system; airport 40 miles from campus.

Publications: *Smith College Studies in Social Work* (quarterly), first published 1930; *Smith College Studies in History* (triennially), first published 1915; *Meridians*, a scholarly journal by and about women of color, published jointly by Smith College and Wesleyan University (first published in 2000).

Library Collections: 1,596,174 volumes. 205,786 microforms; 60,135 audiovisual materials; 8,441 serial subscriptions. Online and card catalogs. Computer work stations available. Students have access to online information retrieval services and the Internet.

Most important special holdings include Rare Book Room (Sylvia Plath, Virginia Woolf, early lithography); Sophia Smith Collection (Margaret Sanger, Garrison Family); College Archives (student letters and diaries, photographs of college life); Bloomfield Collection.

Buildings and Grounds: Campus area 125 acres with 105 academic, administrative, residence and maintenance buildings.

Chief Executive Officer: Dr. Carol Christ, President.

Address admission inquiries to Debra Shaver, Director of Admissions; graduate inquiries to Debbie Cotrell, Director of Graduate Programs.

School for Social Work

Degree Programs Offered: *Master's, doctorate.* Third-year diploma also awarded.

Admission: Requirements vary with program and level.

Degree Requirements: Requirements vary.

Distinctive Educational Programs: Block Plan organization for all degree programs, with field work concentrated in winter sessions and academic work in summer sessions. Four-track system emphasizes clinical casework and provides study in treatment methods, human behavior, social policy, and research. Continuing Education program offers advanced training and supervision for social work practitioners.

Southern New England School of Law

333 Faunce Corner Road
North Dartmouth, Massachusetts 02747-1252
Tel: (508) 998-9600   **E-mail:** admissions@snesl.edu
Fax: (508) 998-9561   **Internet:** www.snesl.edu

Institution Description: The Southern New England School of Law is an independent, nonprofit, educational institution approved by the Commonwealth of Massachusetts to award the Juris Doctor degree. *Enrollment:* 274.

Accreditation: *Regional:* NEASC. *Professional:* law

History: Founded in 1981; degree-granting authority awarded 1988; first class graduated 1989.

Institutional Structure: *Governing board:* Representation: Southern New England School of Law Board of Trustees: 11 trustees. The Dean is the chief academic and executive officer of the school and reports directly to the Board of Trustees. *Composition of institution:* Four divisions, all of which report tot he Dean (Academic Administration, Business Administration, Library, Faculty).

Calendar: Semesters. Academic year late Aug. to Aug. First year students admitted Sept. Degrees conferred and formal commencement June. Summer session.

Admission: Applicants must have a baccalaureate degree from an accredited college or university. Southern New England School of Law Committee on Admissions considers applications as they are submitted. The LSAT and registration with LSDAS also required.

Degree Requirements: *For all Juris Doctor degrees:* 70 credits in required coursework, 19 elective credits for a total degree requirement of 89 credits.

Distinctive Educational Programs: Six-year (three-plus-three) program leading to a baccalaureate degree granted from University of Massachusetts Dartmouth and a juris doctor degree granted from Southern New England School of Law; joint JD/MBA program with University of Massachusetts Dartmouth.

Degrees Conferred: 41 *first-professional:* law.

Fees and Other Expenses: *Full-time tuition per academic year 2004–05:* $18,286. *Required fees:* $145.

Financial Aid: Aid from institutionally generated funds is provided on the basis of financial need. Contact Sandra Silva at (508) 998-9600 for details.

Departments and Teaching Staff: *Total instructional faculty:* 36 (full-time 14, part-time 22). Total tenured faculty: 4. Degrees held by full-time faculty: doctorate 26%, master's 33%, baccalaureate 100%, professional 100%.

Enrollment: Total enrollment 274. *First-professional:* full-time 81 men / 82 women, part-time 45m / 66 w.

Characteristics of Student Body: *Ethnic/racial makeup:* number of Black non-Hispanic: 46; American Indian or Alaska Native: 2; Asian or Pacific Islander: 16; Hispanic: 12; White non-Hispanic: 184; unknown: 13. *Age distribution:* number 22–24: 44; 25–29: 98; 30–34: 43; 35–39: 27; 40–49: 43; 50–64: 19.

International Students: 1 nonresident alien enrolled fall 2004. No programs available to aid students whose native language is not English. No financial aid specifically designated for international students.

Student Life: The Law School is about 1 hour from Boston and Worcester and 30 minutes from Cape Cod and Providence, Rhode Island. Career Develop-

ment and Placement. Extracurricular activities include Student Bar Association, local chapters of the Black Law Student's Association, International Law Student's Association, Criminal Justice Society. *Student publications: Restatement, The Brief,* and the *Law Library Newsletter.*

Library Collections: 114,000 volumes. Online and card catalogs. 240,000 microforms; 50 audiovisual materials; 400 current periodical subscriptions. Students have access to online information retrieval services.

Most important special holdings include congressional publications.

Chief Executive Officer: Robert V. Ward, Jr., Dean.

Address admissions inquiries to Nancy Fitzsimmons Hebert, Director of Admissions.

Springfield College

263 Alden Street
Springfield, Massachusetts 011090-3788
Tel: (413) 748-5000   **E-mail:** admissions@spfldcol.edu
Fax: (413) 748-3764   **Internet:** www.spfldcol.edu

Institution Description: Springfield College is a private, independent, non-profit institution. *Enrollment:* 5,062. *Degrees awarded:* Baccalaureate, master's, doctorate.

Member of the consortium Cooperating Colleges of Greater Springfield.

Accreditation: *Regional:* NEASC. *Professional:* athletic training, occupational therapy, physical therapy, physician assisting, surgeon assisting, radiation therapy, radiography, surgical technology

History: Established and chartered as A School for Christian Workers, and offered first instruction at postsecondary level 1885; awarded first degree (baccalaureate) 1888; adopted present name 1953. *See* Dr. Laurence Locke Doggett, *A Man and a School* (New York: Association Press, 1943) for further information.

Institutional Structure: *Governing board:* Springfield College Corporation and Board of Trustees. Representation: 100 members, including a Board of Trustees with 44 members (including president of the college, 1 student, 5 alumni). All voting. *Composition of institution:* Administrators 100. Vice president for academic affairs, vice president for finance/administration, dean of students, vice president for institutional advancement. Full-time instructional faculty 174. Academic governance body, Senate, meets bimonthly.

Calendar: Semesters. Academic year Sept. to May. Freshmen admitted Sept., Jan. Degrees conferred and formal commencement May. Summer session of 2 terms from June to Aug.

Characteristics of Freshmen: 61% of applicants accepted. 39% of accepted applicants enrolled. Average secondary school rank men upper 35th percentile, women 41st percentile, class 38th percentile. Mean SAT scores 420 verbal, 480 mathematical.

38% of freshmen from Massachusetts. Freshmen from 25 states and 4 foreign countries.

Admission: Rolling admissions plan. For fall acceptance, apply as early as summer following junior year of secondary school, but not later than Apr. 1 of year of enrollment. Early application deadlines for physical therapy and athletic training candidates is Jan. 15. Early acceptance available. *Requirements:* Either graduation from accredited secondary school with college preparatory program which must include 10 units from among English, mathematics, science, social studies, 6 academic electives; or GED. Recommend additional units in laboratory science, mathematics for some programs. *Entrance tests:* College Board SAT. *For transfer students:* 2.0 minimum GPA; from 4-year accredited institution 72 hours maximum transfer credit; from 2-year accredited institution 66 hours.

College credit for postsecondary-level work completed in secondary school. Advanced placement for extrainstitutional learning (life experience) on basis of faculty assessment. Tutoring available.

Degree Requirements: 130 semester hours; 2.0 GPA; 48 semester hours in residence; 4 semester hours physical education; general education requirements. Additional requirements for some programs.

Fulfillment of some degree requirements possible by passing departmental examinations, College Board CLEP, AP. *Grading system:* A–F; pass-fail; withdraw (carries time limit).

Distinctive Educational Programs: Focus upon allied health sciences. Community service and cooperative education. International programs. Graduate program in occupational therapy.

ROTC: Army in cooperation with Western New England College.

Degrees Conferred: 597 *baccalaureate:* degrees awarded in top five disciplines include biological and live sciences 21, health professions and related sciences 132, parks and recreation 97, psychology 25, public administration and services 258; 339 *master's:* various disciplines; 6 *doctorate.*

Fees and Other Expenses: *Full-time tuition per academic year 2004–05:* $19,410. *Room and board per academic year:* $7,520.

Financial Aid: Aid from institutionally generated funds is provided on the basis of financial need. Institution has a Program Participation Agreement with the U.S. Department of Education for eligible students to receive Pell Grants and other federal aid.

Financial aid to full-time, first-time undergraduate students: federal scholarships and grants 22% (average $3,061); state/local scholarships and grants 14% (average $1,023); institutional fellowships 75% (average $7,365); loans 80% (average $3,124).

Departments and Teaching Staff: *Professors* 39, *associate professors* 43, *assistant professors* 61, *instructors* 16, *part-time teachers* 123. *Total instructional faculty:* 232. Total tenured faculty: 85. Student-to-faculty ratio: 15:1. Degrees held by full-time faculty: 58% hold terminal degrees.

Enrollment: Total enrollment 5,062. Undergraduate 2,953.

Characteristics of Student Body: *Ethnic/racial makeup:* Black non-Hispanic: 11.5%; American Indian or Native Alaskan: .6%; Asian or Pacific Islander: 1.2%; Hispanic: 7%; White non-Hispanic: 71.5%; unknown: 6.5%.

International Students: 65 nonresident aliens enrolled. Programs available to aid students whose native language is not English: social, cultural.

Student Life: On-campus residence halls house 73% of student body. Residence halls for men constitute 30% of such space, for women only 30%, for both sexes 40%. 25% of married students request institutional housing. *Intercollegiate athletics:* men only: baseball, basketball, football, golf, gymnastics, lacrosse, soccer, swimming, tennis, track, volleyball, wrestling; women only: basketball, field hockey, golf, gymnastics, lacrosse, soccer, softball, swimming, tennis, track, volleyball. *Special regulations:* Registered cars permitted. *Special services:* Learning Resources Center, medical services. *Student publications, radio:* The Inkling, a literary magazine; The Student, a weekly newspaper. Radio station WSCB. *Surrounding community:* Springfield metropolitan area population 530,000. Served by airport 25 miles from campus; passenger rail service 5 miles from campus.

Library Collections: 168,400 volumes. 736,000 microforms; 3,200 audiovisual materials; 830 current periodical subscriptions. Students have access to online information retrieval services.

Most important holdings include collections on health, physical education, and recreation; 19th- and 20th-century sports and physical education literature; Joseph F. Marks III Dance Collection.

Buildings and Grounds: Campus area 165 acres.

Chief Executive Officer: Dr. Richard Flynn, President.

Address admission inquiries to Director of Admissions.

Stonehill College

320 Washington Street
North Easton, Massachusetts 02357-6110
Tel: (508) 565-1000   **E-mail:** admissions@stonehill.edu
Fax: (508) 565-1444   **Internet:** www.stonehill.edu

Institution Description: Stonehill College is a private, independent, nonprofit college affiliated with the Roman Catholic Church. *Enrollment:* 2,490. *Degrees awarded:* Baccalaureate, master's.

Member of the consortium Southeastern Association for Cooperation in Higher Education in Massachusetts.

Accreditation: *Regional:* NEASC. *Professional:* teacher education

History: Established as a men's college, chartered, and offered first instruction at postsecondary level 1948; admitted women 1951; awarded first degree (baccalaureate) 1952; offered Evening College degree programs 1970.

Institutional Structure: *Governing board:* Board of Trustees. Representation: 37 trustees, including representative of the Holy Cross Fathers, representative of the President's Council, president of the college, executive vice president of the college. All voting. *Composition of institution:* Administrators 81 men / 86 women. Academic affairs headed by academic vice president. Management/business/finances directed by financial vice president. Full-time instructional faculty 89 men / 44 women. Academic governance body, Academic Committee, meets biweekly.

Calendar: Semesters. Academic year Sept. to mid-May. Freshmen admitted Sept., Jan. Degrees conferred and formal commencement May. Summer session of 2 terms from mid-May to mid-Aug.

Characteristics of Freshmen: 57% of applicants admitted. 23% of applicants admitted and enrolled.

98% (602 students) submitted SAT scores; 19% (102 students) submitted ACT scores. *25th percentile:* SAT Verbal 550, SAT Math 550; ACT Composite 23. *75th percentile:* SAT Verbal 630, SAT Math 630; ACT Composite 27.

82% of entering freshmen expected to graduate within 5 years. 55% of freshmen from Massachusetts. Freshmen from 17 states and 2 foreign countries.

Admission: Application deadline for fall acceptance Jan. 15 of senior year in secondary school. Early decision application deadline Nov. 1. Transfer application deadline Apr. 1. Spring application deadline Nov. 1. Early acceptance and deferred admissions available. *Requirements:* Graduation from secondary school with 4 units English, 2 of same foreign language, 2 algebra, 1 geometry, 3 combined units history/political science/social science, 2 science, and 3 academic electives. Additional units in foreign language, science, mathematics recommended. GED accepted. Official high school transcripts required. *Entrance tests:* SAT I with writing or ACT with writing required. TOEFL for foreign students. *For transfer students:* from 2-year and 4-year accredited institutions, 3.0 GPA preferred. Transfer students must attend the Stonehill College for at least 2 years, including the senior year, to qualify for a Stonehill degree.

College credit and advanced placement for postsecondary-level work completed in secondary school on basis of departmental review. Peer tutoring and summer session available.

Degree Requirements: *For all baccalaureate degrees:* 40 courses; 20 courses in residence; 2.0 GPA; distribution requirements. Fulfillment of some degree requirements and exemption from some beginning courses possible by passing College Board CLEP, AP. *Grading system:* A–F; pass-fail; withdraw (requires dean's permission, carries time limit).

Distinctive Educational Programs: Cross-registration with 8 area institutions. Preprofessional programs in dentistry, medicine, veterinary science, and theology. Evening classes for continuing education students. Medical technology program and computer engineering program with the University of Notre Dame (IN). Washington internship program. Stonehill Undergraduate Research Experience (SURE) summer program. Student-designed majors, double majors, independent study, Honors Program, internships, field study. Foreign studies program; semester in Irish Studies at University College Dublin, Stonehill-Quebec exchange, joint program in England, French Studies with the University of Nice. Full-time international internships in London, Brussels, Dublin, Paris, Montreal, and Madrid.

ROTC: Army offered in cooperation with Boston University. 3 commissions awarded 2004.

Degrees Conferred: 732 *baccalaureate:* area and ethnic studies 3; biological/life sciences 42; business/marketing 169; communications/communication technologies 54; computer and information sciences 14; education 37; English 39; foreign languages and literature 32; health professions and related sciences 17; interdisciplinary studies 33; liberal arts/general studies 5; mathematics 29; philosophy/religion/theology 16l physical sciences 4; protective services/public administration 5; psychology 70; social sciences and history 142; visual and performing arts 21. *Honorary degrees awarded 2004:* Doctor of Humanities 1, Doctor of Laws 1, Doctor of Business Administration 1.

Fees and Other Expenses: *Full-time tuition per academic year 2005–06:* undergraduate $25,540, graduate $25,780. *Room and board per academic year:* $10,564.

Financial Aid: Stonehill College offers a direct lending program. Aid from institutionally generated funds is provided on the basis of academic merit, financial need, athletic ability, other criteria.

Financial aid to full-time, first-time undergraduate students: need-based scholarships/grants totaling $16,642,026, self-help $8,699,179, tuition waivers $214,176, athletic awards $760,461; non-need-based scholarships/grants totaling $2,614,156, self-help $3,592,818, parent loans $359,287, tuition waivers $359,287; athletic awards $549,640.

Departments and Teaching Staff: *Professors* 31, *associate professors* 55, *assistant professors* 40, *instructors* 7, *part-time faculty* 117. *Total instructional faculty:* 250 (full-time 133, part-time 117; women 101, men 149; members of minority groups 22). Total faculty with doctorate, first-professional, or other terminal degree: 153. Student-to-faculty ratio: 14:1. Degrees held by full-time faculty: master's 14%, doctorate 86%. *Faculty development:* $311,072 total grants for research. 9 faculty members awarded sabbatical 2004–05.

Enrollment: Total enrollment 2,490. Undergraduate full-time 927 men / 1,301 women, part-time 70m / 168w; graduate full-time 7m / 12w, part-time 3m / 21w.

Characteristics of Student Body: *Ethnic/racial makeup:* number of Black non-Hispanic: 72; American Indian or Alaska Native: 8; Asian or Pacific Islander: 70; Hispanic: 73; White non-Hispanic: 2,223; unknown: 5. *Age distribution:* number under 18: 33; 18–19: 1,091; 20–21: 1,011; 22–24: 130; 25–29: 29; 30–34: 27; 35–39: 36; 40–49: 70; 50–64: 33; 65 and over: 4.

International Students: 9 nonresident aliens enrolled fall 2004. 5 students from Europe, 4 Asia, 3 Central and South Latin America, 1 other. Programs available to aid students whose native language is not English: social, cultural. No financial aid specifically designated for international students.

Student Life: On-campus residence halls house 82% of student body. Residence halls for women only constitute 24% of such space, for coed halls 66%. *Intercollegiate athletics:* men only: baseball, basketball, cross-country, equestrian, football, ice hockey, sailing, soccer, tennis, track; women only: basketball, cross-country, equestrian, field hockey, sailing, soccer, softball, tennis, track, volleyball. *Special regulations:* First-year students must apply for permission to have a car on campus. *Special services:* Academic and career counseling, health and disabled services; weekend transportation to Boston subway system. *Student publications, radio: Acres,* a yearbook; *Cairn,* a student literary magazine; *Summit,* a weekly newspaper. Radio station WSHL broadcasts 24 hours per day. Over 70 student clubs and organizations. *Surrounding community:* Easton population 23,000. Boston, 22 miles from campus, is nearest metropolitan area. Served by mass transit system; airport 22 miles from campus; passenger rail service 5 miles from campus.

Library Collections: 226,581 volumes. 305,255 government documents; 61,305 microforms; 3,603 audiovisual materials; 1,280 current periodical subscriptions. Online catalog. 73 computer work stations. 2,783 compact discs. 1,100 CD-ROMS. Students have access to online information retrieval services and the Internet. Total 2004–05 budget for books and materials: $542,000.

Most important special holdings include Joseph Martin Papers, Michael Novak Papers, Tofias Industrial Archives.

Buildings and Grounds: Campus area 375 acres. *New buildings:* Corr Residence Hall completed 2001.

Chief Executive Officer: Rev. Mark T. Cregan, C.S.C., President.

Address admission inquiries to Brian P. Murphy, Dean of Admissions and Enrollment.

Suffolk University

8 Ashburton Place

Boston, Massachusetts 02108-2770

Tel: (617) 573-8460   **E-mail:** admission@suffolk.edu
Fax: (617) 742-4291   **Internet:** www.suffolk.edu

Institution Description: Suffolk University is a private, independent, nonprofit institution. *Enrollment:* 8,188. *Degrees awarded:* Associate, baccalaureate, first-professional (law), master's, doctorate. Certificates in counseling also awarded.

Accreditation: *Regional:* NEASC. *Professional:* accounting, business, law, psychology internship, public administration

History: Established as Suffolk Law School and offered first instruction at postsecondary level 1906; awarded first degree (first-professional) 1909; chartered 1914; established college of liberal arts 1934; established school of management, merged law school and colleges, and incorporated new entity as Suffolk University 1937; opened campus in Madrid, Spain 1995; acquired the New England School of Art and Design 1996. *See* David L. Robbins, *The Heritage Series* (Boston: Suffolk University, 1979, 1980) for further information.

Institutional Structure: *Governing board:* Suffolk University Board of Trustees. Representation: 19 trustees (including 1 alumnus), 1 administrator, president of the college. 2 ex officio. All voting. *Composition of institution:* Administrators 50 men / 58 women. Academic affairs headed by president. Management/business/finances directed by vice president and treasurer. Full-time instructional faculty 272. Academic governance body, Faculty Council, meets an average of 5 times per year.

Calendar: Semesters. Academic year Sept. to May. Freshmen admitted Sept., Jan., May, July. Degrees conferred June, Sept., Jan. Formal commencement May. Summer session of 2 terms.

Characteristics of Freshmen: 85% of applicants admitted. 24% of applicants admitted and enrolled.

94% (966 students) submitted SAT scores; 9% (89 students) submitted ACT scores. *25th percentile:* SAT Verbal 450, SAT Math 460; ACT Composite 17. *75th percentile:* SAT Verbal 550, SAT I 550; ACT Composite 22.

51% of entering freshmen expected to graduate within 5 years. 70% of freshmen from Massachusetts. Freshmen from 18 states and 39 foreign countries.

Admission: Rolling admissions plan. For fall acceptance, apply by March 1. Apply by Dec. 1 for early acceptance. *Requirements:* 15–16 college preparatory units earned at accredited secondary school; GED accepted. Minimum recommended GPA 3.0. *Entrance tests:* College Board SAT; recommend score in mid 500s. For foreign students TOEFL. *For transfer students:* 2.0 minimum GPA; from 4-year accredited institution 90 hours maximum transfer credit; from 2-year accredited institution 80 hours.

College credit and advanced placement for postsecondary-level work completed in secondary school. College credit for extrainstitutional learning on basis of ACE *2006 Guide to the Evaluation of Educational Experiences in the Armed Services.*

Degree Requirements: *For all associate degrees:* 62 credit hours. *For all baccalaureate degrees:* 122 credit hours. *For all undergraduate degrees:* 2.0 GPA; last 30 hours in residence.

Fulfillment of some degree requirements possible by passing College Board CLEP, AP. *Grading system:* A–F; pass-fail; withdraw (carries time limit).

Distinctive Educational Programs: *For undergraduates:* Cooperative education and internship programs. Saturday and evening classes. Extensive study abroad opportunities; campuses in Madrid, Spain and Dakar, Senegal. 6-year program leading to baccalaureate and first-professional degree in law. Marine biology laboratory in Cobstock Bay, Maine. Fine Arts, Graphic Design, and Interior Design at the New England School of Art and Design at Suffolk University. *For graduate students:* combined programs leading to MBA/JD, MPA/JD, MS (International Economics)/JD, MPA/MA (Counseling), MSF/JD. *Available to all students:* Facilities and programs for independent research.

ROTC: Army offered in cooperation with Northeastern University.

Degrees Conferred: 744 *baccalaureate* (B), 763 *master's* (M): 5 *doctorate:* biological/life sciences 13 (B); business/marketing 340 (B), 482 (M); communications/communication technologies 97 (B), 34 (M); computer and information sciences 3 (B), 16 (M); education 44 (M); engineering and engineering technologies 9 (B); English 25 (B); foreign languages and literature 1 (B); health professions and related sciences 43 (M); home economics and vocational home economics 16 (B); interdisciplinary studies 2 (M); philosophy/religion/theology 11 (B); physical sciences 2 (B); protective services/public administration 6 (B), 96 (M); psychology 46 (B), 15 (M), 5 (D); social sciences and history 122 (B), 20 (M); visual and performing arts 48 (B), 14 (M). *First-professional:* law 417.

Fees and Other Expenses: *Full-time tuition and per academic year 2004–05:* $21,140 undergraduate; graduate tuition varies by degree program. *Other fees:* $80. *Room and board per academic year:* $11,940.

Financial Aid: Suffolk University offers a direct lending program. Aid from institutionally generated funds is provided on the basis of academic merit, financial need. Institution has a Program Participation Agreement with the U.S. Department of Education for eligible students to receive Pell Grants and other federal aid.

Departments and Teaching Staff: *Total instructional faculty:* 687 (full-time 269, part-time 415; women 277, men 407; members of minority groups 54). Student-to-faculty ratio: 12:1. Degrees held by full-time faculty: 95% hold terminal degrees.

Enrollment: Total enrollment 8,188. Undergraduate full-time 1,582 men / 2,134 women, part-time 269m / 442m; first-professional full-time 500 m / 564w, part-time 327m / 277w; graduate full-time 103m / 261w, part-time 735m / 884w. *Transfer students:* in-state 229; from out-of-state 90.

Characteristics of Student Body: *Ethnic/racial makeup (undergraduate):* number of Black non-Hispanic: 146; American Indian or Alaska Native: 16; Asian or Pacific Islander: 281; Hispanic: 201; White non-Hispanic: 2,613; unknown: 786. *Age distribution:* number under 18: 77; 18–19: 1,693; 20–21: 1211; 22–24: 675; 25–29: 223; 30–34: 108; 35–39: 82; 40–49: 1,112; 50–64: 44; 65 and over: 14.

International Students: 491 nonresident aliens enrolled fall 2004. 154 students from Europe, 187 Asia, 104 Central and South America, 72 Africa, 14, Canada, 20 other. Programs available to aid students whose native language is not English: social, cultural. English as a Second Language Program. No financial aid specifically designated for international students.

Student Life: On-campus housing available in a newly renovated state-of-the-art facility. *Intercollegiate athletics:* men: baseball, basketball, hockey, tennis, cross country, golf; women only: basketball, tennis, cross-country. *Special services:* Learning Center, medical services. *Student publications, radio, television: The Beacon,* a yearbook; *Dicta,* a law school quarterly; *Suffolk Evening Voice,* a biweekly newspaper for evening students; *Suffolk Journal,* a weekly newspaper; *Venture,* a biannual literary magazine. Radio station WSFR broadcasts 40 hours per week. TV station WSUB. *Surrounding community:* Boston population over 500,000. Mass transit bus and subway system; airport 5 miles from campus; passenger rail service less than 1 mile from campus.

Publications: *Suffolk Law Review* (5 times per year) first published in 1967.

Library Collections: 117,000 volumes. 184,000 microforms; 895 current periodicals. Online catalog. Students have access to online information retrieval services and the Internet.

Most important special holdings include Business Reference section; collection of Afro-American literature; social sciences.

Buildings and Grounds: Campus area less than 1 square mile.

Chief Executive Officer: Dr. David J. Sargent, President.

Undergraduates address admission inquiries to John Hamel, Director of Undergraduate Admissions; graduate inquiries to Director of Graduate Admissions.

Tufts University

Medford, Massachusetts 02155

Tel: (617) 628-5000   **E-mail:** admissions@tufts.edu
Fax: (617) 627-3860   **Internet:** www.tufts.edu

Institution Description: Tufts University is a private, independent, nonprofit institution. *Enrollment:* 9,602. *Degrees awarded:* Baccalaureate, first-professional (dentistry, medicine, veterinary medicine), master's, doctorate. Postgraduate certificates also awarded.

Member of Boston Library Consortium, Marine Studies Consortium.

Accreditation: *Regional:* NEASC. *Professional:* chemistry, dentistry, engineering, medicine, occupational therapy, veterinary medicine

History: Established and chartered as Tufts College under control of Universalist Church of American 1852; offered first instruction at postsecondary level 1854; awarded first degree (baccalaureate) 1857; adopted present name 1955. *See* Russell E. Miller, *Light on the Hill,* (Boston: Beacon Press, 1966) for further information.

Institutional Structure: *Governing board:* Board of Trustees of Tufts University. Extrainstitutional representation: 25 charter trustees, 10 alumni trustees, and 1 ex officio trustee; institutional representation: President of the University. All voting. Academic affairs headed by senior vice president-provost. Management/business/finances directed by executive vice president. Full-time instructional faculty 739. Academic governance bodies, the faculty of each school, meet an average of no less than 9 times per year.

Calendar: Semesters. Academic year Aug. to May. Freshmen admitted Aug., Jan. Degrees conferred May. Formal commencement May. Summer session of 2 terms from late May to early July, early July to mid-Aug.

Characteristics of Freshmen: 27% of applicants accepted. 32% of accepted applicants enrolled.

Average secondary school rank of freshmen 95th in class. Middle 50% range class 640–730 verbal, 650–740 mathematical.

23% of freshmen from Massachusetts.

Admission: For fall acceptance, apply no later than Jan. 10 of year of enrollment. Students are notified of acceptance Apr. 1. A binding early decision programs exists; round 1 deadline Nov. 15, notification Dec. 15; round 2 deadline Jan. 1, notification Feb. 7. *Requirements:* Grades since the first year of high school; other requirements given on the application (http://apply.tufts.edu). *Entrance tests:* Applicants should submit the SAT I and 3 SAT II subject tests, or the ACT. *For transfer students:* maximum transfer credit limited only by residence requirement.

College credit and advanced placement for postsecondary-level work completed in secondary school. TOEFL for students whose native language is not English. Tutoring available. Accommodations for students with disabilities.

Degree Requirements: *College of Liberal Arts:* 34 courses; 1.67 GPA; *College of Engineering:* 38 courses, 1.67 GPA. 8 semesters in residence. Fulfillment of some degree requirements and exemption from some beginning courses possible by passing departmental examinations, College Board AP. *Grading system:* A–F; pass-fail; withdraw (carries time limit).

Distinctive Educational Programs: Evening classes. Combined degrees programs with New England Conservatory of Music, School of the Museum of Fine Arts and the combined 5-year liberal arts-engineering program, the combined B.A./M.A. Arts and Sciences-Fletcher School of Law and Diplomacy program, the combined DVM/MA with Fletcher School of Law and Diplomacy, the Graduate Special Student Program, the Resumed Education for Adult Learners (REAL), EPIIC (Education for Public Inquiry and International Citizenship), and CMS (Communications and Media Studies), the Experimental College, the combined bachelor's and master's degrees program, the arts and sciences thesis honors program, prearchitectural programs, prelaw programs, predental, premedical, preveterinary programs, freshmen exploration program, perspectives program. Interdisciplinary programs include Africa and the New World, American studies, Asian Studies, communication and media studies, community health, environmental studies, international relations, Middle Eastern studies, peace and justice studies, urban planning and environmental policy, women's studies, world civilization, writing across the curriculum. Interdepartmental minors include African and new world studies, Latin American studies, science, technology and society, linguistics, women's studies. Special facilities for using telecommunications in the classroom. Global classroom project. Facilities and programs for independent research, including honors programs, individual majors, tutorials. Institutionally sponsored study abroad in Chile, Ghana, England, France, Japan, Germany, Russia, Spain. Tufts European Center is an international conference and educational facility in the French Alps. Cross-registration with Boston College, Boston University, Brandeis University. Center for Environmental Management, USDA Human Nutrition Research Center on Aging. Biotechnology Engineering Center, Center for Cognitive Studies, Center on Hunger, Poverty, and Nutrition Policy, Curricula Software Studio, Electro-

Optics Technology Center, Lincoln-Filene Center for Public Policy, Center for Science and Mathematics Teaching, Center for South Asian and Indian Ocean Studies, Manufacturing Resource Center, Nuclear Age History and Humanities Center, Center for Applied Child Development.

ROTC: Army, Air Force and navy in cooperation with Massachusetts Institute of Technology.

Degrees Conferred: 1,274 *baccalaureate*; 916 *master's*; 100 *doctorate*. 406 *first-professional:* dentistry 162, veterinary medicine 78, medicine 166. *Honorary degrees awarded 2004:* Doctor of Business Administration 1, Doctor of Humane Letters 1, Doctor of Science 1, Doctor of Laws 1, Doctor of Engineering 1, Doctor of Fine Arts 1.

Fees and Other Expenses: *Full-time tuition per academic year 2004–05:* $30,203 undergraduate, $19,894 to $41,360 graduate. *Other fees:* $766 (undergraduate). *Undergraduate room per academic year:* $4,640. *Undergraduate board per academic year:* $4,389.

Financial Aid: Aid from institutionally generated funds is provided on the basis of academic merit, financial need. 2,460 undergraduate students received financial aid 2003–04; average award $26,706. Total aid granted $63.2 million to undergraduates. Aid granted included university scholarships $34.7 million; $2.8 million federal scholarships; $1.1 million state scholarships; $1.6 million private scholarships; $2.5 million work-study jobs; $20.5 million long term loans. *Graduate aid:* 94% of graduate students received financial aid totaling $88.3 million.

Departments and Teaching Staff: *Total instructional faculty:* 1,141. *Total tenured faculty:* 356. Student-to-faculty ratio: 12:1. Degrees held by full-time faculty: 99% hold terminal degrees.

Enrollment: Total enrollment 9,602. Undergraduate full-time 2,257 men / 2,586 women, part-time 45m/w; unclassified 425m/w; first-professional full-time 763m / 903w; graduate full-time 762m / 1,234w, part-time 546m/w.

Characteristics of Student Body: *Ethnic/racial makeup:* number of Black non-Hispanic: 447; American Indian or Native Alaskan: 30; Asian or Pacific Islander: 1,120; Hispanic: 513; White non-Hispanic: 4,561; unknown: 947. *Age distribution:* 17–21: 48%; 22–24: 16%; 25–29: 22%; 30–34: 8%; 35–39: 3%; 40–49: 2%; 50–and over: less than 1%.

International Students: 878 nonresident aliens enrolled fall 2004. Programs available to aid students whose native language is not English: social, cultural. English as a Second Language Program. No financial aid specifically designated for international students.

Student Life: On-campus co-ed undergraduate residence halls house 68% of student body. All residence halls are co-ed (except for 1 single-sex residence for women, which houses 1.5% of women in the student body), with some single sex floors and halls within the residences. 12 special interest houses for sophomores, juniors, and seniors. *Intercollegiate athletics:* men only: baseball, basketball, crew, football, ice hockey, lacrosse, soccer, squash, swimming and diving, tennis, track and field; women only: basketball, crew, fencing, field hockey, golf, lacrosse, sailing, soccer, softball, squash, swimming, tennis, track and field, volleyball; co-ed: sailing. *Special regulations:* Cars permitted for all but resident freshmen. *Special services:* Learning Resources Center, medical and counseling services, career placement, international students center, center for all faiths, academic resource center, students with disabilities, African-American center, Asian-American center, women's center, computer services, foreign language and culture media center, shuttle bus to and from Boston and intracampus shuttle on Medford/Somerville campuses. *Student publications, radio: The Observer,* a weekly magazine; *Tufts Daily,* a daily newspaper; *Portfolio ,* annually; *Politica, Sportspectrum, Queenshead* and *Artichokes, Proteus, Continuum, Zamboni, Outbreath,* a literary magazine, *Radix; S.A.L.A.A.M* (South Asian Literary and Art Magazine); *Tuftscope,* the interdisciplinary journal of health ethics, and policy. Annual publications include a yearbook, *Hemispheres, Onyx,* and *Voices.* Radio station WMFO. Student theatre groups include *Pen, Paint and Pretzels, Torn Ticket,* and *Black Theater Company. Surrounding community:* Medford population 76,493. Boston, 5 miles from the Medford-Somerville campus, is nearest metropolitan area. Served by mass transit system.

Publications: *Tufts Magazine,* published 4 times a year by the Trustees of Tufts College, distributed without charge to alumni, alumnae, parents, and other members of the Tufts community; *Tufts Journal,* published monthly Sept. through May, distributed without charge to faculty, staff, and other members of the Tufts community; *International Journal of Middle East Studies,* the journal of the Middle East Studies Association, edited by Professor Leila Fawaz, Department of History; *Tufts Diet and Nutrition Letter,* nationally renowned subscription newsletter on nutrition, edited by Dr. Stanley Gershoff, Dean, School of Nutrition; *Nutrition Reviews,* edited by Dr. Irwin Rosenberg, Director, USDA Human Nutrition Research Center on Aging, Tufts University; *Tufts Medicine,* a magazine reporting on the latest medical research at Tufts, published 3 times annually, distributed to medical school alumni/ae. Member of University Press of New England.

Library Collections: 1,134,519 volumes. Library collections - units (includes books, serial backfiles, government documents, microforms, cartographic units, graphic materials, sound recordings, film and video units, computer file units, and other library materials units) 2,108,806. 5,861 current serials subscriptions. Students have access to online information retrieval services and the Internet.

Most important collections include Edward R. Murrow Collection; Dameshek Library of Hematology; Berliner Periodontal Collection.

Buildings and Grounds: Campus area includes 4 campuses: Medford/Somerville 150 acres; Boston (Health Sciences) 2.5 acres; Grafton (veterinary school) 585 acres; Talloires (France) 3 acres.

Chief Executive Officer: Dr. Lawrence S. Bacow, President.

Address admission inquiries to Dean of Admissions; first-professional inquiries to appropriate school; graduate inquiries to appropriate graduate school.

College of Arts and Sciences

Degree Programs Offered: *Baccalaureate* in American studies, anthropology, applied physics, archaeology, art history, Asian studies, astrophysics, biology, bio-psychology, chemical physics, chemical engineering, chemistry, child study, civil engineering, classics, computer science, drama, economics, electrical engineering, engineering physics, engineering science, engineering psychology, English, environmental studies, French, geology, German, German area studies, Greek and Latin studies, Greek or Latin, history, international relations, mathematics, mechanical engineering, music, philosophy, physics, political science, psychology, psychology/clinical, quantitative economics, religion, Russian, social psychology, sociology, Soviet and Eastern European area studies, Spanish; *master's* in civil engineering, chemistry, physics, classics education, fine arts, French, German, history, music, occupational therapy, philosophy, political science, urban and environmental policy; *master's, doctorate* in biology, chemical engineering, chemistry, child study, drama, electrical engineering, electrical design, English, mathematics, mechanical engineering, physics, psychology, interdisciplinary programs. *Interdisciplinary doctorate degree, dual master's in sustainable development* with Fletcher School of Law and Diplomacy.

Departments and Teaching Staff: *Total instructional faculty:* 530 (full-time 328, part-time 202).

Cummings School of Veterinary Medicine

Degree Programs Offered: *First-professional.*

Admission: 90 semester hours accredited college-level coursework with 2 units English, 2 biology, 2 inorganic chemistry, 2 organic chemistry, 2 physics, 2 mathematics (including 1 calculus), 2 social and behavioral sciences, 2 humanities and fine arts, 1 genetics, 1 biochemistry; GRE.

Degree Requirements: 4 years and 1 summer in residence.

Departments and Teaching Staff: *Total instructional faculty:* 88 (full-time 75, part-time 13).

Distinctive Educational Programs: Signature programs: Ethics and Values in Veterinary Medicine, International Veterinary Medicine, Wildlife Medicine, Issam M. Fares Equine Sports Medicine, Biotechnology and Veterinary Medicine.

School of Dental Medicine

Degree Programs Offered: *First-professional.* Postgraduate certificates also given in endodontics, general practice, oral and maxillofacial surgery, pediatric dentistry, orthodontics, periodontology, prosthodontics.

Admission: 60 semester hours, 2 years college-level coursework with 2 units English, 2 biological science, 2 inorganic chemistry, 2 physics, 1 organic chemistry; DAT.

Degree Requirements: Prescribed curriculum; 2.0 GPA; 45 months in residence.

Departments and Teaching Staff: *Total instructional faculty:* 180 (full-time 68, part-time 92).

Distinctive Educational Programs: Cooperative clinical programs with area hospitals, externship sites, geriatrics, dentistry for handicapped, implant and cosmetic dentistry.

School of Engineering

Degree Programs Offered: *See* http://engineering.tufts.edu/

Degree Requirements: 38 credits (one class is one credit). Introductory credits required for all engineers: 4 mathematics, 1-2 credits physics, 1-2 credits chemistry, 1 introductory physics, 1 English, 1 science elective. Students must complete the requirements of an engineering major.

Departments and Teaching Staff: *Total instructional faculty* 88 (full-time 64, part-time 24).

School of Medicine

Degree Programs Offered: *First-professional:* MD, MD/PhD, MD/MPH.

Admission: MCAT and 3 years of college are required. College credits must include 1 year biology with lab; 1 year inorganic chemistry with lab; 1 year organic chemistry with lab; 1 year physics with lab. Facility in English speech and composition.

Degree Requirements: Prescribed curriculum.

Departments and Teaching Staff: *Total instructional faculty:* Basic Sciences 99 (full-time 94, part-time 5); Clinical Departments 58 (full-time 37. part-time 21).

Distinctive Educational Programs: Strong emphasis on Problem Based Learning. 4 year MD/MPH Program. 7 year combined MD/PhD program with Sackler School of Graduate Biomedical Sciences.

Sackler School of Graduate Biomedical Sciences

Degree Programs Offered: *Doctorate* in biochemistry; cell, molecular, and developmental biology; cellular and molecular physiology; immunology; molecular biology and microbiology; neuroscience.

Admission: Strong background in the biological sciences. Course work in inorganic and organic chemistry, physics and mathematics. GRE.

Degree Requirements: Minimum of 3 years in residence, preparation and defense of dissertation.

Departments and Teaching Staff: Faculty members are drawn from schools of medicine and veterinary medicine.

The Fletcher School of Law and Diplomacy

Degree Programs Offered: *Master's, doctorate* in diplomatic history and international political relations, international economic relations, international law and organization, political institutions and systems, and international business.

Departments and Teaching Staff: *Total instructional faculty:* 42 (full-time 30, part-time 12).

Distinctive Educational Programs: Joint J.D.-M.A. in law and diplomacy with Harvard Law School and University of California at Berkeley, Boalt Hall School of Law. Exchange program with the Graduate School of International Studies in Geneva. Ford Foundation program in public international law. Combined degree programs with Tufts University's Faculty of Arts and Sciences, School of Veterinary Medicine, and Department of Urban and Environmental Policy. Course cross-registration in graduate departments and professional schools of Harvard University and Tufts University. Use of Harvard's Widener Library.

Gerald J. and Dorothy R. Friedman School of Nutrition Science and Policy

Degree Programs Offered: *Master's, doctorate, combined master's/doctorate*

Admission: *For all degrees:* Baccalaureate degree from accredited college or university, GRE-General Tests; TOEFL for non-English speaking students. For human nutrition sciences program, course preparation in chemistry, biological sciences, physics, mathematics, biochemistry. *Program in social sciences of food policy and applied nutrition:* training in the social sciences.

Degree Requirements: Prescribed curriculum, comprehensive written and oral examination, thesis for doctorate; prescribed curriculum for master's.

Departments and Teaching Staff: *Total instructional faculty:* 24 (full-time 16, part-time 8).

Distinctive Educational Programs: The only graduate school of nutrition in the United States. Ph.D. program in clinical nutrition for physicians with the USDA Human Nutrition Research Center on Aging at Tufts. Coordinated Dietetic Internship with the Frances Stern Nutrition Center.

University of Massachusetts Amherst

Amherst, Massachusetts 01003-9313

Tel: (413) 545-0941   **E-mail:** admissions@umass.edu
Fax: (413) 545-3010   **Internet:** www.umass.edu

Institution Description: University of Massachusetts Amherst is a Research I public land-grant institution. *Enrollment:* 24,646. *Degrees awarded:* Associate, baccalaureate, master's, doctorate. Specialist certificates in education also awarded.

Academic offerings subject to approval by statewide coordinating bodies. Budget subject to approval by state governing boards. Member of the consortium Five-Colleges, Inc.

Accreditation: *Regional:* NEASC. *Professional:* accounting, audiology, chemistry, clinical psychology, counseling psychology, engineering, forestry, interior design, landscape architecture, music, nursing, nursing education, psychology internship, public health, planning, speech-language pathology, teacher education

History: Established as Massachusetts Agricultural College 1863; offered first instruction at postsecondary level 1867; awarded first degree (baccalaureate) 1871; authorized to grant graduate degrees 1892; changed name to Massachusetts State College 1931; adopted present name 1947. *See* Harold W. Cary, *University of Massachusetts: A History of 100 Years* (Amherst: University of Massachusetts Press, 1962) for further information.

Institutional Structure: *Governing board:* Primarily governed by a Board of Trustees with governance responsibility in some areas (e.g., tuition rates) shared with the statewide Board of Higher Education. *Composition of institution:* Full-time instructional faculty 1,100. Academic governance body, Faculty Senate, meets an average of 14 times per year. *Faculty representation:* Faculty served by collective bargaining agent, Massachusetts Teachers Association, affiliated with NEA.

Calendar: Semesters. Academic year early Sept. to mid-May. Freshmen admitted Sept., Jan. Degrees conferred May, Sept., Feb. Formal commencement May. Winter session in January. Summer session of 2 terms from early June to mid-Aug.

Characteristics of Freshmen: 69% of applicants accepted. 30% of accepted applicants enrolled.

99% (4,172 students) submitted SAT scores. *25th percentile*: SAT Verbal 510, SAT Math 520. *75th percentile*: SAT Verbal 610, SAT Math 630.

60% of entering freshmen expected to graduate within 5 years. 75% of freshmen from Massachusetts. Freshmen from 50 states and 60 foreign countries.

Admission: Rolling admissions plan. For fall acceptance, apply as early as Oct. of previous year, but not later than Feb. 1 of year of enrollment. Students are notified of acceptance no later than Apr. 15. *Requirements:* Recommend graduation from accredited secondary school with 4 units English, 2 foreign language, 3 college preparatory mathematics (2 algebra, 1 plane geometry preferred), 2 natural science (with 2 labs), 2 social science. GED accepted. 2 additional units also recommended. *Entrance tests:* College Board SAT or ACT. For foreign students TOEFL. *For transfer students:* Recommend 2.5 minimum GPA for in-state residents, 2.70 for out-of-state students; from 2-year and 4-year accredited institutions maximum transfer credit limited to 75 credits.

College credit and advanced placement on CLEP exams, CEEB exams, military experience, and relevant life experience. Academic Support Programs and Learning Resource Center available.

Degree Requirements: *For all associate degrees:* 60 credit hours; 30 hours in residence; 2.0 GPA overall and in the major, with at least 2 courses having a diversity component; core requirements. *For all baccalaureate degrees:* 120 credit hours (for engineering program 128–136 credit hours); 45 hours in residence. *For all undergraduate degrees:* 2.0 GPA; core requirements.

Fulfillment of some degree requirements and exemption from some beginning courses possible by passing College Board CLEP, AP. *Grading system:* A–F; pass-fail; withdraw.

Distinctive Educational Programs: Opened in 1999, the Commonwealth College (an honors college) offers a dynamic curriculum such as interdisciplinary seminars, enriched honors courses, and opportunities to link academics and community outreach. Residential Academic Programs. Accelerated degree programs. Cooperative baccalaureate programs in astronomy and dance, and doctorate programs in various fields through Five College Consortium with Smith, Amherst, Mount Holyoke and Hampshire Colleges. Interdisciplinary programs in classics and philosophy, Near Eastern studies, science, social thought and political economy, Russian and East European studies, or one of student's choice. Facilities for independent research, including honors programs, individual majors, tutorials. Academic opportunities include national and international student exchange programs. Cross-registration through Five College Consortium. Study at other state institutions in New England through regional student program or others throughout the U.S. through the National Student Exchange. University Without Walls program for nontraditional students. Committee for the Collegiate Education of Black and Other Minority Students, an academic support program. Bilingual Collegiate Program for Hispanic and Bilingual students.

ROTC: Army, Air Force.

Degrees Conferred: 67 *associate;* 3,919 *baccalaureate* (B), 1,086 *master's* (M), 274 *doctorate* (D): agriculture 105 (B), 11 (M), 9 (D); architecture 52 (B), 34 (M), 2 (D); biological/life sciences 234 (B), 28 (M), 18 (D); business/marketing 551 (B), 171 (M), 9 (D); communications/communication technologies 332 (B), 2 (M), 7 (D); computer and information sciences 84 (B), 40 (M), 12 (D);

education 1 (B), 262 (M), 55 (D); engineering and engineering technologies 174 (B), 107 (M), 33 (D); English 170 (B), 28 (M), 12 (D); foreign languages and literature 114 (B), 26 (M), 13 (D); health professions and related sciences 182 (B), 108 (M), 7 (D); home economics and vocational home economics 15 (B); interdisciplinary studies 85 (B), 10 (M), 3 (D); law/legal studies 83 (B); liberal arts/general studies 102 (B); mathematics 32 (B), 20 (M), 3 (D); natural resources/environmental science 122 (B), 20 (M); parks and recreation 165 (B), 27 (M), 4 (D); philosophy/religion/theology 35 (B), 3 (M), 5 (D); physical sciences 68 (B), 63 (M), 35 (D); protective services/public administration 20 (M); psychology 280 (B), 10 (M), 19 (D); social sciences and history 771 (B), 46 (M), 26 (D); visual and performing arts 144 (B), 95 (M).

Fees and Other Expenses: *Full-time tuition per academic year 2005–06:* undergraduate resident $2,640, nonresident $9,937. *Required fees:* $7,564 undergraduate resident, $6,917 nonresident. *Room and board per academic year:* $6,417. Contact the university for graduate tuition and fees which vary by program.

Financial Aid: Aid from institutionally generated funds is provided on the basis of academic merit, financial need, athletic ability, other criteria. Institution has a Program Participation Agreement with the U.S. Department of Education for eligible students to receive Pell Grants and other federal aid.

Financial aid to full-time, first-time undergraduate students: need-based scholarships/grants totaling $41,457,429, self-help $43,427,354, parent loans $2,680,723, tuition waivers $5,614,529, athletic awards $1,345,796; non-need-based scholarships/grants totaling $4,620,516, self-help $21,334,275, parent loans $2,680,723, tuition waivers $5,614,529, athletic awards $2,664,336.

Departments and Teaching Staff: *Total instructional faculty:* 1,316 (full-time 1,100, part-time 216; women 457, men 859; members of minority groups 165). Total faculty with doctorate, first-professional, or other terminal degree: 125. Student-to-faculty ratio: 17:1. Degrees held by full-time faculty: baccalaureate 2%, master's 10%, doctorate 86%, professional 2%. 92% hold terminal degrees.

Enrollment: Total enrollment 24,646. Undergraduate full-time 8,846 men / 8,717 women, part-time 621m / 182w; graduate full-time 1,007m / 1,134w, part-time 1,802m / 1,737w.

Characteristics of Student Body: *Ethnic/racial makeup (undergraduate):* number of Black non-Hispanic: 773; American Indian or Alaska Native: 58; Asian or Pacific Islander: 1,311; Hispanic: 589; White non-Hispanic: 13,795; unknown: 1,319. *Age distribution:* number under 18: 332; 18–19: 1,495; 20–21: 7,171; 22–24: 2,469; 25–29: 239; 30–34: 246; 35–39: 198; 40–49: 291; 50–64: 113; 65 and over: 6.

International Students: 294 undergraduate nonresident aliens enrolled fall 2004. Programs available to aid students whose native language is not English: social, cultural. English as a Second Language Program. No financial aid specifically designated for international students.

Student Life: On-campus residence halls house 61% of undergraduates. 92% of residence halls are coeducational, 1% are all male, 7% all-female. 6% of men join and 3% live in fraternities; 4% of women join and 3% live in sororities. Housing available for married students. *Intercollegiate athletics:* men: baseball, basketball, cross-country, football, gymnastics, ice hockey, lacrosse, skiing, soccer, swimming and diving, tennis, track and field, water polo; women: basketball, crew, cross-country, field hockey, gymnastics, lacrosse, skiing, soccer, softball, swimming and diving, tennis, track and field, volleyball, water polo. *Special regulations:* Registered cars with decals permitted. Quiet hours. *Special services:* Medical services; academic support services; career counseling; housing placement; employment assistance; legal and child care services; services for disabled and learning disabled; campus bus service. *Student publications, radio:* Collegian, a daily newspaper; Radio station WMUA broadcasts 24 hours per day. *Surrounding community:* Amherst population 35,500. Nearby metropolitan areas include Springfield, Hartford and Boston. Served by mass transit bus system; airport 45 miles from campus; passenger rail service 10 miles from campus.

Publications: University of Massachusetts Press has over 900 titles in print.

Library Collections: 3,158,359 volumes. 645,000 government documents; 2,200,000 microforms; 15,500 periodicals; 22,781 audiovisual materials. 14,000 recordings. Online catalog. Students have access to online information retrieval services and the Internet.

Most important special holdings include W.E.B. DuBois Papers; Russel K. Alspoch - Yeats Collection; Anti-Slavery Pamphlet.

Buildings and Grounds: Campus area 1,463 acres. *New buildings:* Computer Science Building; Animal Care Facility; Engineering Research Center.

Chief Executive Officer: Dr. John V. Lombardi, Chancellor.

Undergraduates address admission inquiries to Joseph C. Marshall, Dean of Enrollment Services; graduate inquiries to Patricia Stowell, Director of Graduate Admission.

University of Massachusetts Boston

100 Morrissey Boulevard
Boston, Massachusetts 02125-3393
Tel: (617) 287-5000   **E-mail:** enrollment.info@umb.edu
Fax: (617) 265-7173   **Internet:** www.umb.edu

Institution Description: *Enrollment:* 13,778. *Degrees awarded:* Baccalaureate, master's, doctorate. Certificates, at both the undergraduate and graduate levels, as well as Certificates of Advanced Graduate Study (CAGS) are also awarded.

Member of Boston Library Consortium.

Accreditation: *Regional:* NEASC. *Professional:* business, clinical psychology, marriage and family therapy, nursing, nursing education, rehabilitation counseling, psychology internship, teacher education

History: Founded as a coeducational institution in 1964. Enrolled first class in 1965. Awarded first degree (baccalaureate) 1969. Former Boston State College merged with the university 1982.

Institutional Structure: *Governing board:* University Board of Trustees (17 appointed; 5 student trustees, 1 from each of the 5 institutions in the system). *Composition of institution:* The campus is administered by a Chancellor; senior administrative officials: Vice Chancellor for Academic Affairs and Provost (the Deans of the College of Arts and Sciences, College of Management, College of Public and Community Service, College of Nursing, Graduate College of Education, and Graduate Studies and Research and Vice Provost for Academic Support report to the Vice Chancellor for Academic Affairs and Provost; Vice Chancellor for Administration and Finance; Dean of Student Affairs; Vice Chancellor for External Relations. Directors of the Institute for Learning and Teaching, and Physical Education report to the Vice chancellor for Academic Affairs and Provost. Administrators: 10 men / 2 women. Full-time instructional faculty 437. Academic governance body, Faculty Council, meets an average of 10 times a year. Faculty served by collective bargaining agent, Massachusetts Teachers Association (MTA), affiliated with NEA.

Calendar: Semesters. Academic year early Sept. to mid-May. Freshmen admitted Sept., Jan. Degrees conferred May (or June), Sept., Dec. Formal commencement May (or June). 2 summer sessions of 6 weeks each from late May to late Aug. Winter intersession in Jan.

Characteristics of Freshmen: 53% of applicants admitted. 19% of applicants admitted and enrolled.

89% (503 students) submitted SAT scores. *25th percentile*: SAT Verbal 460, SAT Math 470. *75th percentile*: SAT Verbal 570, SAT Math 570.

28% of entering freshmen expected to graduate within 5 years. 85% of freshmen from Massachusetts.

Admission: Applicants for freshman status have usually taken the standard college preparatory program in high school: 4 years English, 3 college preparatory mathematics, 2 social science (1 being U.S. history), 2 years of a foreign language, and 3 science courses with at least 2 involving laboratory work, plus 2 electives in the above academic areas or in computer science, humanities, or the arts. *Entrance tests:* College Board SAT. *Transfer students:* The university is a member of the Massachusetts Transfer Compact which facilitates admissions for graduates of public two-year colleges in the state. College credit and advanced placement for postsecondary-level work completed in secondary school and for extrainstitutional learning (life experience) on basis of portfolio and faculty assessments, personal interviews. Tutoring available. Developmental courses offered in summer session and regular academic year; credit given.

Degree Requirements: 120 credit hours; 2.0 GPA; 30 credits in residence; general education requirements. Fulfillment of some degree requirements and exemption from some beginning courses possible by passing departmental examinations, College Board CLEP, AP; fulfillment of some degree requirements possible by passing College Board CLEP. *Grading system:* A–F.

Distinctive Educational Programs: Extended day program. Honors program, individual majors; services and equipment available for handicapped students. Study abroad in Canada, France, Germany, Ireland. Cooperative education and internship opportunities. Competency-based degree program in College of Public and Community Service.

Degrees Conferred: 1,543 *baccalaureate;* 656 *master's;* 36 *doctorate.*

Fees and Other Expenses: *Full-time tuition per academic year 2004–05:* undergraduate resident $1,714, nonresident $9,758; graduate resident $2,590, nonresident $9,758. *Required fees:* $6,310 resident, $8,998 nonresident.

Financial Aid: Aid from institutionally generated funds is provided on the basis of financial need. Institution has a Program Participation Agreement with the U.S. Department of Education for eligible students to receive Pell Grants and other federal aid.

Financial aid to full-time, first-time undergraduate students: need-based scholarships/grants totaling $16,542,598, self-help $3,933,264, parent loans $319,646, tuition waivers $3,153,575; non-need-based scholarships/grants total-

ing $246,470, self-help $7,079,540, parent loans $460,216, tuition waivers $152,930.

Departments and Teaching Staff: *Total instructional faculty:* 821 (full-time 437, part-time 384; women 412, men 409; members of minority groups 129). Total faculty with doctorate, first-professional, or other terminal degree: 539. Student-to-faculty ratio: 14:1. Degrees held by full-time faculty: baccalaureate 1%, master's 10%, doctorate 87%, professional 2%. 90% hold terminal degrees.

Enrollment: Total enrollment 11,682. Undergraduate full-time 2,328 men / 3,174 women, part-time 1,510m / 1,820w; graduate full-time 228m / 578w, part-time 620m / 1,484w.

Characteristics of Student Body: *Ethnic/racial makeup:* number of Black non-Hispanic: 1,348; American Indian or Alaska Native: 49; Asian or Pacific Islander: 1,005; Hispanic: 606; White non-Hispanic: 5,576; unknown: 2,542. *Age distribution:* number under 18: 70; 18–19: 1,020; 20–21: 1,511; 22–24: 2,006; 25–29: 583; 30–34: 622; 35–39: 80; 40–49: 441; 50–64: 184; 65 and over: 16; unknown: 1,094.

International Students: 556 nonresident aliens enrolled fall 2004. Programs available to aid students whose native language is not English: social, cultural. English as a Second Language Program. No financial aid specifically designated for international students.

Student Life: Commuter campus. *Intercollegiate athletics:* men only: baseball, basketball, cross-country, football, ice hockey, indoor/outdoor track, lacrosse, soccer, tennis; women only: basketball, cross-country, indoor/outdoor track, softball, soccer, tennis, volleyball; intramural: aqua aerobics, basketball, tag football, ice and floor hockey, horseshoes, racquetball, sailing, soccer, softball, squash, table tennis, tennis, volleyball, wallyball, weight lifting. Classes in aerobics, dancercise, ice skating, nautilus training, and wellness. Athletic and fitness centers available. *Student activities:* Student government; a variety of campus organizations are available for student participation. *Student services:* Personal counseling; academic advising; career services and counseling; cooperative education/internship program; student national and international exchange programs; health services; veterans affairs and counseling; child care; disabled student center; ACCESS program; project REACH; adaptive computer laboratory; student supported centers: Advocacy, Black students, women students, etc. Art gallery; 52 recognized student organizations/clubs (Accounting and Finance Academy, Anthropology Society, Asian American Society, Ballroom Dance, Music Society, Student Nurses Association, Political Science Forum, etc.).; child care; disabled student center; campus ministry. *Student publications, radio:* Mass Media, a weekly newspaper; *Howth Castle,* a literary magazine; radio station WUMB-91.9 FM. *Surrounding community:* Boston population over 500,000. Served by mass transit bus, subway systems; airport 5 miles from campus; passenger rail service 2 miles from campus.

Library Collections: 584,015 volumes. Online catalog. 795,552 microforms; 2,770 serial subscriptions. 1,865 recordings; 13 CD-ROMs. 300 computer work stations. Students have access to information retrieval services.

Most important special holdings include German Bauhaus movement; antiwar material of Vietnam era; 19th century Boston settlement houses; Judge W. Arthur Garrity Papers (Boston schools desegregation case); reports of 19th century child welfare agencies.

Buildings and Grounds: Harbor Campus area 177 acres.

Chief Executive Officer: Dr. J. Keith Motley, Chancellor.

Address admission inquiries to Office of Admissions.

University of Massachusetts Dartmouth

285 Old Westport Road
North Dartmouth, Massachusetts 02747-2300
Tel: (508) 999-8000   **E-mail:** admissions@umassd.edu
Fax: (508) 999-8183   **Internet:** www.umassd.edu

Institution Description: University of Massachusetts Dartmouth is a public institution. *Enrollment:* 8,319. *Degrees awarded:* Baccalaureate, master's, doctorate.

Accreditation: *Regional:* NEASC. *Professional:* business, clinical lab scientist, computer science, engineering, nursing

History: Established in 1964 as Southeastern Massachusetts Technology Institute as a result of merger of New Bedford Textile School (established 1895; incorporated 1897; offered first instruction at postsecondary level 1945; changed name to New Bedford Textile Institute 1950; awarded first degree (baccalaureate) 1951; changed name to New Bedford Institute of Textiles and Technology 1955; changed name to New Bedford Institute of Technology 1957) and Bradford Durfee Textile School (established 1895; incorporated 1899; offered first instruction at postsecondary level 1945; changed name to Bradford Durfee Technical Institute 1946; awarded first baccalaureate 1948; changed name to Bradford Durfee College of Technology 1955); changed name to Southeastern Massachusetts University 1969; adopted present name August 31, 1991, joining the University of Massachusetts system with campuses in Amherst, Lowell, Boston, and Worcester, Massachusetts.

Institutional Structure: *Governing board:* A single Board of Trustees governs the entire University of Massachusetts system; UMass Dartmouth has 3 appointed voting representatives. Chief administrative officer on campus is the chancellor. *Composition of institution:* Administrators 27 men / 13 women. Academic affairs headed by vice chancellor, advised by council of academic deans and directors. Business/finances directed by a vice chancellor. Full-time instructional faculty 340. Academic governance body, Council of Academic Deans, meets weekly. *Faculty representation:* Faculty represented by collective bargaining agent, Massachusetts Federation of Teachers, affiliated with American Federation of Teachers.

Calendar: Semesters. Academic year Sept. to May. Freshmen admitted Sept., Jan. Degrees conferred June, Sept., Jan. Formal commencement June. Summer session of 4 terms from mid-May to mid-Aug.

Characteristics of Freshmen: 68% of applicants admitted. 83% of applicants admitted and enrolled. 98.8% (1,314 students) submitted SAT scores; 3.5% (97 students) submitted ACT scores. *25th percentile*: SAT Verbal 470, SAT Math 490; ACT Composite 19. *75th percentile*: SAT Verbal 570, SAT Math 480; ACT Composite 23. 45.5% of entering freshmen expected to graduate within 5 years. 94.2% of freshmen from Massachusetts. Freshmen from 13 states and 6 foreign countries.

Admission: Rolling admissions plan. Early decision/acceptance available. *Requirements:* Either graduation from accredited secondary school with minimum 2.0 GPA and with 16 units that must include 4 English, 2 in the same foreign language, 3 mathematics, 2 social studies (including 1 U.S. history), 3 science, 2 academic electives; or GED. *Entrance tests:* College Board SAT. For foreign students also TOEFL. *For transfer students:* credits from accredited institution; maximum transfer credit limited only by residence requirement.

College credit and advanced placement for postsecondary-level work completed in secondary school and for extrainstitutional learning (life experience) on basis of portfolio and faculty assessments.

Degree Requirements: 120 credit hours minimum; 2.0 GPA; 4 semesters in residence; general education requirements.

Fulfillment of some degree requirements and exemption from some beginning courses possible by passing departmental examinations, College Board CLEP, AP. *Grading system:* A–F; withdraw (carries time limit).

Distinctive Educational Programs: Special audiovisual and computing facilities available in classrooms and small labs. Computer mainframe port in each dormitory room and classroom. Internships, study-related work opportunities through contract learning, and facilities for independent research, including honors programs. Interdisciplinary minors in African-American studies, gerontology, Judaic studies, labor studies, women's studies. Certificate program in international marketing/French. Pre-medical and pre-law advisory programs. Various study abroad programs in England, France, Germany, Portugal, Nova Scotia. Multidisciplinary majors. Evening and summer courses. Tutoring available.

ROTC: Army in cooperation with Providence College.

Degrees Conferred: 1,063 *baccalaureate*: biological/life sciences 41; business/marketing 297; computer and information sciences 28; education 9; engineering and engineering technologies 91; English 63; foreign languages and literature 16; health professions and related sciences 92; interdisciplinary studies 8; mathematics 12; physical sciences 5; psychology 99; social sciences and history 144; visual and performing arts 108.

Fees and Other Expenses: *Full-time tuition per academic year 2004–05:* undergraduate resident $1,417, nonresident $8,099; graduate resident $2,071, nonresident $8099. *Required fees:* $6,385 to $9,203. *Room and board per academic year:* $7,634.

Financial Aid: Aid from institutionally generated funds is provided on the basis of financial need, other criteria. Institution has a Program Participation Agreement with the U.S. Department of Education for eligible students to receive Pell Grants and other federal aid.

Departments and Teaching Staff: *Total instructional faculty:* 543 (full-time 340, part-time 203; women 323, men 220; members of minority groups 78). Total faculty with doctorate, first-professional, or other terminal degree: 252. Student-to-faculty ratio: 16:1.

Enrollment: Total enrollment 8,319. Undergraduate full-time 3,078 men / 3,073 women, part-time 448m / 691w; graduate full-time 164m / 148w, part-time 290m / 407w. *Transfer students:* in-state 462; from out-of-state 39.

Characteristics of Student Body: *Ethnic/racial makeup (undergraduate):* number of Black non-Hispanic: 447; American Indian or Alaska Native: 39; Asian or Pacific Islander: 179; Hispanic: 165; White non-Hispanic: 5,614; unknown: 797. *Age distribution:* number under 18: 38; 18–19: 2,237; 20–21: 2,408; 22–24: 1,505; 25–29: 433; 30–34: 198; 35–39: 142; 40–49: 203; 50–64: 87; 65 and over: 29.

International Students: 299 nonresident aliens enrolled fall 2004. Students from Europe, Asia, Central and South America, Africa. Programs available to aid students whose native language is not English: social, cultural. No financial aid specifically designated for international students.

Student Life: On-campus residence halls house 39% of student body. *Intercollegiate athletics:* men only: baseball, basketball, cross-country, football, hockey, golf, soccer, swimming and diving, tennis, track; women only: basketball, cross-country, field hockey, softball, soccer, swimming and diving, tennis, track, volleyball. *Special regulations:* Cars permitted without restrictions. *Special services:* Academic Advising Center, career counseling, disabled student services, Learning Resources Center, minority student office. *Student publications, radio, television: The Scrimshaw,* a yearbook; *Torch,* a weekly newspaper; *Siren,* magazine of the Women's Center; *Temper,* student literary magazine. Radio station WSMU broadcasts 140 hours per week. Closed-circuit TV station. *Surrounding community:* North Dartmouth. Boston, 62 miles from campus, and Providence, RI, are nearest metropolitan areas. Served by mass transit system; nearest airport 40 miles (Warwick, RI) from campus.

Library Collections: 1,500,000 volumes. Online catalog. 13,835 audiovisual materials; 43,000 government documents; 2,957 periodicals. Computer work stations available.students have access to online information retrieval services and the Internet.

Most important special holdings include Robert F. Kennedy Assassination Archive; Diario de Noticias, Portuguese Newspaper; Regional Textile Industry History.

Buildings and Grounds: North Dartmouth campus area 710 acres. *New buildings:* Charleton College of Business Administrative Building completed 2004; 400-bed residence hall completed 2005.

Chief Executive Officer: Dr. Jean F. MacCormack, Chancellor.

Undergraduates address admission inquiries to Director of Admissions; graduate inquiries to Graduate Admissions.

University of Massachusetts Lowell

One University Avenue
Lowell, Massachusetts 01854-9985

Tel: (978) 934-4000   **E-mail:** admissions@uml.edu
Fax: (978) 934-3000   **Internet:** www.uml.edu

Institution Description: University of Massachusetts Lowell, formerly known as the University of Lowell, is a public institution. *Enrollment:* 11,089. *Degrees awarded:* Associate, baccalaureate, master's, doctorate.

Academic offerings subject to approval by statewide coordinating bodies. Budget subject to approval by state governing boards. Member of Northeast Consortium for Colleges and Universities in Massachusetts.

Accreditation: *Regional:* NEASC. *Professional*: art, business, clinical lab scientist, engineering, engineering technology, medical laboratory technology, music, nursing, nursing education, physical therapy, teacher education

History: Formed 1975 by a merger of Lowell State College (chartered 1894; established as Massachusetts State Normal School at Lowell 1897; offered first instruction at postsecondary level, awarded first degree (baccalaureate); and changed name to State Teachers College at Lowell 1932; changed name to Massachusetts State College at Lowell 1960, to Lowell State College 1968) and Lowell Technological Institute (established as Lowell Textile School 1895; offered first instruction at postsecondary level 1913; awarded first baccalaureate 1915; changed name to Lowell Technical Institute 1928, to Lowell Technological Institute 1953, to present name 1975).

Institutional Structure: *Governing board:* Massachusetts Board of Higher Education (statewide policy-making body). Extrainstitutional representation: Board of Trustees (appointed for University of Lowell). 11 members, including 1 student. All voting. *Composition of institution:* Administrators 20 men / 10 women. Academic affairs headed by provost. Management/business/finances directed by vice president for fiscal affairs. Full-time instructional faculty 361. Academic governance body, University Council, meets an average of 12 times per year. *Faculty representation:* Faculty served by collective bargaining agent affiliated with NEA and Massachusetts Teachers Association.

Calendar: Semesters. Academic year Sept. to May. Freshmen admitted Aug., Jan. Degrees conferred June, Oct., Mar. Formal commencement May. Summer session from late May to mid-Aug.

Characteristics of Freshmen: 66% of applicants admitted. 39% of applicants admitted and enrolled.

99% (1,008 students) submitted SAT scores. *25th percentile*: SAT Verbal 490, SAT Math 500. *75th percentile*: SAT Verbal 580, SAT Math 610.

41% of entering freshmen expected to graduate within 5 years. 90% of freshmen from Massachusetts. Freshmen from 25 states and 4 foreign countries.

Admission: Rolling admissions plan. For fall acceptance, apply as early as Sept. 15 of previous year, but not later than June 1 of year of enrollment. *Requirements:* Either graduation from accredited secondary school with 16 units which must include 4 English, 2 American history and social studies, 2 college-preparatory mathematics, 1 laboratory science; or GED. Additional requirements for some programs. *Entrance tests:* College Board SAT. *For transfer students:* 2.0 minimum GPA (2.5 preferred); from 4-year accredited institution 90 hours maximum transfer credit; from 2-year accredited institution 60 hours.

College credit and advanced placement for postsecondary-level work completed in secondary school and for extrainstitutional learning on basis of ACE *2006 Guide to the Evaluation of Educational Experiences in the Armed Services*; faculty assessment. Tutoring available. Noncredit developmental/remedial courses offered.

Degree Requirements: *For all associate degrees:* 60 credit hours; 24 credit hours in residence. *For all baccalaureate degrees:* 120 credit hours; 1 year in residence. *For all undergraduate degrees:* 2.0 GPA; core requirements. Additional requirements for some programs.

Fulfillment of some degree requirements and exemption from some beginning courses possible by passing departmental examinations, College Board CLEP, APP. *Grading system:* A–F; pass-fail; withdraw.

Distinctive Educational Programs: *For undergraduates:* Work-experience programs, including internships, cooperative education. Dual-degree program in engineering with St. Anselm's College (NH). Facilities for independent research, including honors programs, individual majors, tutorials. Study abroad available through programs offered by other institutions. *Available to all students:* Evening classes. Special facilities for using telecommunications in the classroom. *Other distinctive programs:* Credit and noncredit continuing education courses offered during afternoons and evenings. Part-time Second Chance Program allows adults with high school diploma or GED to begin or continue postsecondary-level training.

ROTC: Air Force offered in cooperation with Bentley College, Daniel Webster College (NH), Middlesex Community College, New Hampshire College, Northern Essex Community College, Notre Dame College (NH), Rivier College (NH), Saint Anselm's College (NH).

Degrees Conferred: 48 *associate;* 1,248 *baccalaureate* (B); 589 *master's* (M); 96 *doctorate:* area and ethnic studies 2 (B); biological/life sciences 20 (B), 21 (M); business/marketing 273 (B), 68 (M); computer and information sciences 154 (B), 55 (M), 4 (D); education 19 (B), 112 (M), 9 (D); engineering and engineering technologies 191 (B), 195 (M), 6 (D); English 20 (B); foreign languages and literature 2 (B); health professions and related sciences 104 (B), 25 (M), 63 (D); liberal arts/general studies 66 (B); mathematics 10 (B), 12 (M); philosophy/religion/theology 8 (B); physical sciences 16 (B), 16 (M), 14 (D); protective services/public administration 104 (B), 50 (M); psychology 71 (B), 13 (M); social sciences and history 68 (B), 20 (M); visual and performing arts 100 (B), 2 (M).

Fees and Other Expenses: *Full-time tuition per academic year 2005–06:* resident undergraduate $1,454, graduate $1,637; out-of-state undergraduate $8,567, graduate $6,425. *Required fees:* $6,437. *Room and board per academic year:* $6,011.

Financial Aid: Financial aid packages comprised of institutional, state, and federal funds are available to qualified applicants.

Financial aid to full-time, first-time undergraduate students: need-based scholarships/grants totaling $7,642,904, self-help $10,015,886, tuition waivers $1,363,279; non-need-based scholarships/grants totaling $2,698,542, self-help $10,382,020, parent loans $2,764,320, tuition waivers $689,445, athletic awards $1,003,152.

Departments and Teaching Staff: *Total instructional faculty:* 591 (full-time 361, part-time 230; women 236, men 355; members of minority groups 73). Total faculty with doctorate, first-professional, or other terminal degree: 341. Student-to-faculty ratio: 14:1. *Faculty development:* $14,950,000 in grants for research.

Enrollment: Total enrollment 12,038. Undergraduate full-time 3,395 men / 2,420 women, part-time 1,780m / 1,077; graduate full-time 397m / 323w, part-time 897m / 810w. *Transfer students:* in-state 607; from out-of-state 166.

Characteristics of Student Body: *Ethnic/racial makeup (undergraduate):* number of Black non-Hispanic: 266; American Indian or Alaska Native: 21; Asian or Pacific Islander: 524; Hispanic: 335; White non-Hispanic: 4,401; unknown: 3,005. *Age distribution:* number under 18: 98; 18–19: 1,957; 20–21: 1,964; 22–24: $1,446; 25–29: 467; 30–34: 145; 35–39: 96; 40–49: 127; 50–64: 16.

International Students: 400 nonresident aliens enrolled fall 2004. No programs available to aid students whose native language is not English. No financial aid specifically designated for international students.

Student Life: On-campus residence halls house available. *Intercollegiate athletics:* men only: baseball, basketball, football, ice hockey, tennis, track; women only: basketball, field hockey, tennis, volleyball. Both sexes: soccer. *Special regulations:* Registered cars permitted in designated parking areas. *Special services:* Learning Resources Center, medical services, intercampus buses. *Student*

publications, radio: The Connector, a weekly newspaper; *The Moonstone,* a biannual literary magazine; *The Sojourn,* a yearbook. Radio station WJUL broadcasts 113 hours per week. *Surrounding community:* Lowell population 93,000. Boston, 30 miles from campus, is nearest metropolitan area. Served by mass transit bus system; airport 30 miles from campus; passenger rail service 1 mile from campus.

Library Collections: 397,652 titles. 1,639,771 microform units. 955,720 government documents; 534 periodicals. Online catalog. Students have access to online information retrieval services and the Internet. Total 2004–05 budget for books and materials: $1,497,216.

Most important holdings include Paul. E. Tsongas Papers; Boston and Maine Railroad Collection; Lowell Historical Society Collection.

Buildings and Grounds: Campus area 103 acres. *New buildings:* Recreation Center.

Chief Executive Officer: Dr. William T. Hogan, Chancellor.

Address admission inquiries to Office of Admissions.

University of Massachusetts Medical School

55 Lake Avenue North
Worcester, Massachusetts 01655
Tel: (508) 856-1542   **E-mail:** admission@umassmed.edu
Fax: (508) 856-3797   **Internet:** www.umassmed.edu

Institution Description: *Enrollment:* 871. *Degrees awarded:* First-professional, master's, doctorate.

Academic offerings subject to approval by statewide coordinating bodies.

Accreditation: *Regional:* NEASC. *Professional:* medicine, nursing

History: The University of Massachusetts Medical School was founded in 1962 to meet the health care needs of the residents of the commonwealth. Its basic mission is to serve the people of the commonwealth through national distinction in health sciences education, research, public service, and clinical care.

Calendar: Academic year mid-Aug. to mid-June.

Admission: *For first-professional degree:* Resident of Massachusetts with undergraduate study which includes 1 year each of English, biology, inorganic chemistry, organic chemistry, physics; MCAT; AMCAS. *For graduate school of biomedical sciences:* baccalaureate in one of the physical or biological sciences and superior performance in undergraduate studies. *For graduate school of nursing:* RN with a baccalaureate degree from a program accredited by a nationally recognized accrediting agency.

Degree Requirements: *For all degrees:* Completion of prescribed curricula.

Degrees Conferred: 26 *master's:* biomedical sciences; 95 *first-professional:* medicine; 8 *doctorate:* medicine.

Fees and Other Expenses: *Full-time tuition per academic year:* Contact the Medical School for appropriate tuition and fees.

Financial Aid: Aid from institutionally generated funds is provided on the basis of financial need, other criteria. Institution has a Program Participation Agreement with the U.S. Department of Education for eligible students to receive Pell Grants and other federal aid.

Departments and Teaching Staff: Anesthesiology *professors* 4, *associate professors* 3, *assistant professors* 23, *associate etc.* 0; *instructors* 8, *adjunct* 0; biochemistry and molecular biology 10, 4, 5, 1, 3, 8; cell biology 20, 0, 7, 0, 4, 1; emergency medicine 1, 5, 21, 0, 47, 0; family medicine and community health 10, 17, 79, 58, 13, 2; medicine 63, 67, 220, 38, 116, 7; molecular genetics and microbiology 19, 8, 8, 0, 0, 6; neurology 12, 11, 15, 0, 1, 2; obstetrics and gynecology 10, 7, 20, 11, 4, 0; orthodontics and physical rehabilitation 8, 3, 24, 11, 8, 1; otolaryngology 1, 1, 4, 13, 0, 0; pathology 24, 13, 18, 2, 5, 6; pediatrics 17, 20, 50, 81, 16, 1; pharmacology and molecular toxicology 14, 2, 10, 0, 4, 3; physiology 20, 10, 6, 0, 3, 4; psychiatry 11, 26, 62, 22, 3, 9; radiology 19, 20, 21, 3, 4, 3; radiology 19, 20, 21, 3, 4, 3; surgery 34, 24, 65, 36, 12, 8.

Total instructional faculty: 1,871. Degrees held by full-time faculty: doctorate 99%, master's 29%, baccalaureate 92%.

Enrollment: Total enrollment 871 (40.5% men, 59.4% women).

Characteristics of Student Body: *Ethnic/racial makeup:* Black non-Hispanic: 1.7%; American Indian or Alaska Native: .5%; Asian or Pacific Islander: 9.3%; Hispanic: 1.1%; White non-Hispanic: 71.8%; unknown: 15. *Age distribution:* 17–21: .1%; 22–24: 28.6%; 25–29: 43%; 30–34: 11.6%; 35–39: 5%; 40–49: 7.5%; 50–59: 1.3%; unknown: 2.9%.

International Students: 126 nonresident aliens enrolled fall 2004. Students from Europe, Asia, Central and South America. Programs available to aid students whose native language is not English: English as a Second Language Program. No financial aid specifically designated for international students.

Library Collections: 275,000 volumes. 43,000 government documents; 27,500 microforms; 4,000 audiovisual materials; 2,108 periodicals. Online catalog. Computer work stations available. Students have access to online information retrieval services and the Internet.

Most important special holdings include collections on medicine, biological sciences, Worcester Historical Medical Materials.

Chief Executive Officer: Aaron Lazare, M.D., Dean of the Medical School. Address admission inquiries to Dean for Admissions.

Wellesley College

106 Central Street
Wellesley, Massachusetts 02181-8203
Tel: (781) 283-1000   **E-mail:** admission@wellesley.edu
Fax: (781) 283-3639   **Internet:** www.wellesley.edu

Institution Description: Wellesley College is a private, independent, non-profit college for women. *Enrollment:* 2,289. *Degrees awarded:* Baccalaureate.

Member of Twelve College Exchange and the Consortium on Financing Higher Education.

Accreditation: *Regional:* NEASC.

History: Established as Wellesley Female Seminary, chartered, and incorporated 1870; adopted present name 1872; offered first instruction at postsecondary level 1875; awarded first degree (baccalaureate) 1879. *See* Jean Glasscock, ed., *Wellesley College, 1875–1975: A Century of Women* (Wellesley: Wellesley College, 1975) for further information.

Institutional Structure: *Governing board:* Board of Trustees. Extrainstitutional representation: 34 trustees; institutional representation: president and treasurer of the college, 26 alumnae (including president of the association). 2 ex officio. All voting. *Composition of institution:* Administrators 4 men / 7 women. Academic affairs headed by dean of the college. Management/business/finances directed by vice president for finance and administration. Full-time instructional faculty 333. Academic governance body, Academic Council, meets an average of 14 times per year.

Calendar: Semesters. Academic year early Sept. to mid-May. First-year students admitted Sept. Degrees conferred May, Oct. Formal commencement May. No summer session.

Characteristics of Freshmen: 4,094 applicants (4,094 women). 36.1% of applicants admitted. 36.1% of admitted students enrolled full-time.

95% (585 students) submitted SAT scores; 28% (172 students) submitted ACT scores. *25th percentile*: SAT I Verbal 640, SAT I Math 640, ACT Composite 27. *75th percentile*: SAT I Verbal 740, SAT I Math 720; ACT Composite 31.

13% of freshmen from Massachusetts. Freshmen from 42 states and 20 foreign countries.

Admission: For fall admissions, first-year students may apply through one of three decision plans: Early Decision, deadline Nov. 1, for those students who know Wellesley is their first choice; if accepted these students will withdraw applications from all other schools; Early Evaluation, deadline Jan. 1, students receive an evaluation of chances for admission in mid-February; Regular Decision, deadline Feb. 1, admission decision sent early April. *Requirements:* No specific program of study in secondary school is required. Most accepted students will have had 4 years of college preparatory study, typically including 4 years of foreign language, 4 of mathematics, 2 of laboratory science, and ample work in writing, literature, and history. Students considering Wellesley should enroll in all advanced high school courses available. An interview is highly recommended. *Entrance tests:* The College Board SAT is required. Class standing: 95% of first-year students rank in the top 20% of their graduating class. TOEFL required for students whose first language is not English. *For transfer students:* Students who transfer to Wellesley must complete 16 units of coursework at Wellesley (1 unit equals 4 credits). An interview is required of all transfer applicants.

College credit and advanced placement for postsecondary-level work completed in secondary school. Tutoring available. Noncredit developmental courses offered during regular academic year.

Degree Requirements: 32 units; 2.0 GPA; 16 units in residence; 8 credit points physical education; distribution requirements; demonstrated competency in a foreign language; 1 unit first-year writing course required; 1 unit multicultural course; 1 unit quantitative reasoning course.

Fulfillment of some degree requirements and exemption from some beginning courses possible by passing departmental examinations, College Board AP. *Grading system:* A–F; credit/noncredit; withdraw.

Distinctive Educational Programs: 31 departmental majors, 17 interdepartmental majors: American studies, architecture, biological chemistry, Chinese studies, classical civilization, classical and Near Easter archeology, cognitive science, French studies, German studies, Italian culture, Japanese studies, Jewish studies, language studies, medieval/renaissance studies, psychobiology, Soviet studies, and women's studies; or individual major. Interdisciplinary and experimental courses. Interdisciplinary First-Year Cluster Program. First-year and sophomore colloquia. Facilities and program for independent research, including honors programs. Cross-registration with Massachusetts Institute of Technology; cooperative program with Brandeis University and Babson College. 5-year double degree program with M.IT. Study abroad: Wellesley programs in Aix-en-Provence, France; Konstanz, Germany; Cordoba, Spain (sponsored in cooperation with several institutions); exchange programs with Soviet Union and Japan Women's University (Tokyo); study in various countries through established programs. Off-campus study in U.S. including exchange program with Spelman College (GA), Mills College (CA), and member institutions of Twelve College Exchange; Williams Mystic Seaport (CT) program in maritime studies and National Theater Institute (CT). Non-credit summer internships in Washington, DC, and Los Angeles. Elisabeth Kaiser Davis Degree Program: flexible degree program for women beyond traditional college age; Post-baccalaureate Study Program (non-degree).

ROTC: Air Force and Army programs offered at MIT are open to Wellesley students as part of cross-registration program.

Degrees Conferred: 603 *baccalaureate.* Bachelor's degrees awarded in top five disciplines: social sciences and history 185; psychology 52; English 52; multidisciplinary studies 49; foreign languages and literature 46.

Fees and Other Expenses: *Full-time tuition per academic year 2004–05:* $29,796. *Room and board per academic year:* $9,202.

Financial Aid: Aid from institutionally generated funds is provided on the basis of financial need. Institution has a Program Participation Agreement with the U.S. Department of Education for eligible students to receive Pell Grants and, depending upon the agreement, other federal aid.

Financial aid to full-time, first-time undergraduate students: 17% received federal grants averaging $4,513; 5% state/local grants averaging $2,233; 53% institutional grants averaging $21,354; 41% received loans averaging $2,507.

Departments and Teaching Staff: Africana studies *professors* 3, *associate professors* 1, *assistant professors* 2, *instructors/lecturers* 0; American studies 1, 0, 0, 0; anthropology 2, 2, 2, 0; architecture 3, 0, 0, 0; art 10, 4, 10, 6; astronomy 2, 2, 0, 1; biological chemistry 1, 0, 0, 0; biological sciences 5, 5, 9, 8; chemistry 6, 3, 6, 7; Chinese 1, 1, 2, 3; Chinese studies 2, 0, 0, 0; classical civilization 1, 0, 0, 0; classical and Near Eastern archaeology 1, 0, 0, 0; cognitive science 0, 1, 0, 0; computer science 1, 1, 3, 2; economics 7, 3, 7, 1; English 8, 3, 9, 0; French 6, 1, 6, 1; French studies 0, 0, 1, 0; geology 2, 1, 0, 2; German language and literature 2, 1, 3, 0; Greek and Latin 4, 2, 2, 1; history 6, 4, 6, 2; international relations 1, 1, 0, 0; Italian 1, 2, 1, 0; Italian culture 0, 1, 0, 0; Japanese 0, 1, 1, 3; Japanese studies 1, 1, 0, 0; Jewish studies 1, 0, 0, 0; language studies 1, 0, 0, 0; Latin American studies 1, 0, 0, 0; mathematics 7, 1, 6, 0; medieval/renaissance studies 2, 0, 0, 0; music 2, 2, 2, 41; peace studies 1, 0, 0, 0; philosophy 8, 1, 1, 0; physics 2, 3, 2, 3; political science 9, 1, 4, 2; psychobiology 1, 0, 1, 0; psychology 8, 6, 6, 1; religion 4, 4, 2, 0; Russian 2, 0, 0, 2; Russian area studies 1, 0, 0, 0; sociology 4, 1, 1, 2; Spanish 4, 1, 4, 3; theatre studies 0, 0, 0, 2; women's studies 2, 1, 2, 0; education 2, 13, 1, 1; physical education 3, 1, 9, 19; writing 0, 0, 2, 2.

Total instructional faculty: 333. Student-to-faculty ratio: 10:1. Degrees held by full-time faculty: 96.3% hold terminal degrees.

Enrollment: Total enrollment 2,289 (1.7% men, 98.3% women).

Characteristics of Student Body: *Ethnic/racial makeup:* Black non-Hispanic: 5.9%; American Indian or Alaska Native: .4%; Asian or Pacific Islander: 27.1%; Hispanic: 6.4%; White non-Hispanic: 42.3%; unknown: 9.8%. *Age distribution:* 17–21: 93%; 22–24: 3%; 25–and over: 4%.

International Students: 185 nonresident aliens enrolled fall 2004. Programs available to aid students whose native language is not English: social and cultural. Some financial aid designated for qualifying international students.

Student Life: On-campus residence halls house 95% of student body. 1% of student body housed on campus in cooperative facilities. *Intercollegiate athletics:* women only: basketball, crew, cross country, fencing, field hockey, lacrosse, soccer, squash, swimming/diving, tennis, volleyball. *Special regulations:* Registered cars permitted for sophomores, juniors, and seniors. *Special services:* Learning and Teaching Center, medical and counseling services, bus service to and from Massachusetts Institute of Technology, Cambridge, and Boston. *Student publications: Legenda,* a yearbook; *Wellesley News,* weekly newspaper; *Counterpoint,* a Wellesley/MIT monthly journal; WZLY, student-run college radio station. *Surrounding community:* Wellesley, population 27,000 is located in Boston metropolitan area. Served by mass transit bus system, airport 15 miles from campus, passenger rail service .5 mile from campus.

Publications: *The Wellesley College Illuminator,* monthly newsletter; *Wellesley College Calendar,* weekly events listing; *Wellesley Alumnae Magazine.*

Library Collections: 1,300,000 volumes. 165,342 government documents; 389,742 microforms; 19,521 audiovisual materials; 2,562 current periodical subscriptions. Online and card catalogs. Computer work stations available. Students have access to online information retrieval services and the Internet.

Most important special holdings include English poetry collection (including Robert and Elizabeth Barrett Browning); Book Arts Collection; Plimpton Collection (15th and 16th century Italian literature).

Buildings and Grounds: Campus area 500 acres.

Chief Executive Officer: Dr. Diana Chapman Walsh, President.

Address admission inquiries to Jennifer Desjarlais, Director of Admissions.

Wentworth Institute of Technology

550 Huntington Avenue
Boston, Massachusetts 02115

Tel: (617) 989-4000   **E-mail:** admissions@wit.edu
Fax: (617) 989-4010   **Internet:** www.wit.edu

Institution Description: Wentworth Institute of Technology is a private, independent, nonprofit institution. *Enrollment:* 3,597. *Degrees awarded:* Associate, baccalaureate. Certificates also awarded.

Member of Fenway Library Consortium and Fenway Libraries Online.

Accreditation: *Regional:* NEASC. *Professional:* construction education, engineering, interior design

History: Formed in 1977 as Wentworth Institute of Technology by a merger of Wentworth Institute (established 1904) and Wentworth College of Technology (established and offered first instruction as upper-division institution 1970, awarded first baccalaureate degree 1972).

Institutional Structure: *Governing board:* Wentworth Institute of Technology Board of Trustees. Representation: 20 trustees, including president of the institution. 1 ex officio. All voting. *Composition of institution:* Administrators 38 men / 8 women. Academic affairs headed by provost. Management/business/finances directed by vice president of business and finance. Full-time instructional faculty 119 men / 15 women. Academic governance body, Academic Council, meets 6 times per year. *Faculty representation:* Faculty served by collective bargaining agent, Wentworth Faculty Federation, affiliated with AFT.

Calendar: Semesters. Academic year Aug. to May. Freshmen admitted Sept. Degrees conferred and formal commencement May, Sept. Summer session of 1 term from early May to mid-Aug.

Characteristics of Freshmen: 83% of applicants accepted. 35% of accepted applicants enrolled. Mean SAT scores 492 verbal, 515 mathematical.

59% of freshmen from Massachusetts. Freshmen from 27 states and 58 foreign countries.

Admission: Rolling admissions plan. For fall acceptance, apply as early as beginning of senior year, but not later than Aug. 1 of year of enrollment. *Requirements:* Graduation from accredited secondary school with 4 units of English, 3 units of mathematics including algebra II; or GED. *Entrance tests:* College Board ACT or SAT required. For foreign students TOEFL score 525 or minimum University of Michigan Language Institute Test score 85 or higher. *For transfer students:* C average from an accredited institution and a minimum of 50% of program completed in residence.

Advanced placement for postsecondary-level work completed in secondary school. Tutoring available. Developmental courses offered in summer session.

Degree Requirements: *For all associate degrees:* 72–80 credit hours. *For all baccalaureate degrees:* 128–172 hours. *For all undergraduate degrees:* 2.0 GPA; 30% of program in residence, satisfactory completion of 2 terms cooperative education; successful completion of all coursework with no outstanding failing grades.

Fulfillment of some degree requirements possible by passing College Board CLEP or AP. *Grading system:* A–F; S-U (satisfactory-unsatisfactory, for cooperative education); withdraw (carries time limit).

Distinctive Educational Programs: Cross-registration with Colleges of the Fenway, a consortium of 5 distinctive colleges in the Fenway area of Boston. Junior year abroad option in Montpelier, France for students in Architecture Department.

ROTC: ROTC available through Northeastern University.

Degrees Conferred: 253 *associate;* 484 *baccalaureate.* Bachelor's degrees awarded in top five disciplines: engineering 256; business, management, marketing, and related support services 74; computer and information sciences 56; visual and performing arts 56; architecture and related sciences 39.

Fees and Other Expenses: *Full-time tuition per academic year 2004–05:* $15,700. *Books and supplies:* $1,000. *Room and board per academic year:* $8,600.

Financial Aid: Wentworth Institute of Technology offers a direct lending program. Aid from institutionally generated funds is provided on the basis of academic merit, financial need. Institution has a Program Participation Agreement with the U.S. Department of Education for eligible students to receive Pell Grants and, depending upon agreement, other federal aid. 47% received federal grants averaging $1,905; 24% state/local grants averaging $1,324; 84% institutional grants averaging $5,877; 70% received loans averaging $3.055.

Departments and Teaching Staff: Computer science *professors* 0, *associate professors* 5, *assistant professors* 0, *instructors* 0; humanities/social sciences 9,

8, 1, 0; management science 0, 1, 1, 0; mathematics 3, 11, 1, 0; physics 1, 11, 0, 0; architecture 3, 6, 12, 0; construction sciences 2, 5, 2, 0; interior design/fashion merchandising 0, 2, 2, 0; aeronautics 1, 1, 0, 0; civil engineering technology 1, 6, 0, 0; electricity/electronics 4, 12, 1, 0; mechanical/manufacturing 3, 13, 2, 0. *Total instructional faculty:* 169. Student-to-faculty ratio: 24:1. Degrees held by full-time faculty: 22% hold terminal degrees.

Enrollment: Total enrollment 3,597 (81.3% men, 18.7% women).

Characteristics of Student Body: *Ethnic/racial makeup:* Black non-Hispanic: 4.1$; American Indian or Alaska Native: .1%; Asian or Pacific Islander: .7%; Hispanic: 3.4%; White non-Hispanic: 4.1%; unknown: 9.2%. *Age distribution:* 17–21: 63%; 22–24: 21%; 25–29: 12%; 30–34: 3%; 35–39: 1%.

International Students: 108 nonresident aliens enrolled fall 2004. Programs available to aid students whose native language is not English: social, cultural. English as a Second Language Program. No financial aid specifically designated for international students.

Student Life: On-campus residence halls house 47% of student body. Residence halls for men only constitute 44% of such space, for both sexes 56%. Housing available for married students. *Intercollegiate athletics:* men: baseball, basketball, golf, hockey, lacrosse, riflery, soccer, tennis, volleyball; for women: basketball, riflery, soccer, softball, tennis, volleyball. *Special regulations:* Quiet hours from 11pm to 7am Mon.–Sun.; 24 hours on some floors. *Special services:* Medical services. *Student publications: Texton,* a yearbook; *Spectrum,* a monthly newspaper. *Surrounding community:* Boston are population over 3 million. Served by mass transit bus and rail systems; airport 5 miles from campus; passenger rail service approximately 2 miles from campus.

Library Collections: 77,788 volumes. 13,332 microforms; 950 audiovisual materials; 525 current periodical subscriptions. Online and card catalogs. Students have access to online information retrieval services and the Internet.

Most important special holdings include Kingman Trust of electronics and electrical books; Lufkin Trust of technical books; history of technology.

Buildings and Grounds: Campus area 35 acres.

Chief Executive Officer: Dr. John F. Van Domelen, President.

Address admission inquiries to Dr. Kathleen Lynch, Director of Admissions.

Western New England College

1215 Wilbraham Road
Springfield, Massachusetts 01119-2684

Tel: (413) 782-3111   **E-mail:** admissions@wnec.edu
Fax: (413) 782-1746   **Internet:** www.wnec.edu

Institution Description: Western New England College is a private, independent, nonprofit college. *Enrollment:* 4,025. *Degrees awarded:* Associate, baccalaureate, first-professional (law), master's.

Member of the consortium Cooperating Colleges of Greater Springfield.

Accreditation: *Regional:* NEASC. *Professional:* engineering, law, social work

History: Established as Northeastern University, Springfield Division and offered first instruction at postsecondary level 1919; awarded first degree (baccalaureate) 1922; chartered and adopted present name 1951.

Institutional Structure: *Governing board:* Board of Trustees of Western New England College. Extrainstitutional representation: 35 trustees; institutional representation: president of the college (ex officio). *Composition of institution:* Administrators 8 men / 2 women. Academic affairs headed by academic vice president. Management/business/finances directed by vice president for finance and vice president for administration and planning. Student services and undergraduate admissions directed by vice president for student affairs and dean of students. Full-time instructional faculty 139. Academic governance body, Faculty Senate, meets an average of 7 times per year.

Calendar: Semesters. Academic year early Sept. to mid-May. Freshmen admitted Sept., Jan., May, June. Degrees conferred May, Oct., Feb. Summer session.

Characteristics of Freshmen: 4,427 applicants (2,554 men, 1,873 women). 78.7% of applicants admitted. 23.1% of admitted students enrolled full-time.

98% (students) submitted SAT scores. *25th percentile:* SAT I Verbal 470, SAT I Math 490. *75th percentile:* SAT I Verbal 560, SAT I Math 590.

52% of entering freshmen expected to graduate within 5 years. 50% of freshmen from Massachusetts. Freshmen from 16 states and 7 foreign countries.

Admission: Rolling admissions plan. Early acceptance available. *Requirements:* Either graduation from accredited secondary school with 4 units in English, 2 mathematics, 1 laboratory science, 1 U.S. history; or GED. Additional requirements for chemistry, mathematics, computer science, engineering, and pharmacy programs. *Entrance tests:* College Board SAT. For foreign students TOEFL. *For transfer students:* From 4-year accredited institutions 90 hours maximum transfer credit; from 2-year accredited institutions 70 hours.

College credit and advanced placement for postsecondary-level work completed in secondary school. College credit for extrainstitutional learning on basis of ACE 2006 *Guide to the Evaluation of Educational Experiences in the Armed Services*. Tutoring available.

Degree Requirements: *For all associate degrees:* 60 credit hours. *For most baccalaureate degrees:* 120 credit hours (engineering 128 credit hours); 2 semesters physical education; distribution requirements. *For all undergraduate degrees:* 2.0 GPA; 2 terms in residence.

Fulfillment of some degree requirements possible by passing College Board APP (score of 3). Exemption from some beginning courses by passing College Board CLEP. *Grading system:* A–F; pass-fail; withdraw.

Distinctive Educational Programs: *For undergraduates:* Work-experience programs. Interdisciplinary programs in business, engineering, liberal arts. Cooperative baccalaureate in pharmacy with degree offered by Massachusetts College of Pharmacy and Allied Health Sciences. Preprofessional programs in dentistry and medicine. Study abroad through Center for International Education in Europe, South America; by individual arrangement. Washington (DC) semester at American University and London Seminar through American University. *Available to all students:* Flexible meeting places and schedules, including degree-granting off-campus centers (at Hanscom Air Force Base, 75 miles away from main institution; Fort Devens, 85 miles away; Otis Air Force Base, 130 miles away; North Truro Air Force Station, 180 miles away; Portsmouth Naval Shipyard, 135 miles away and Chelsea, MA, 97 miles away). Weekend and evening classes. Facilities and programs for independent research. Cross-registration through consortium. *Other distinctive programs:* Degree-granting continuing education program. New programs in social work, criminal justice, criminal justice administration, and management information systems.

ROTC: Army and Air Force offered in cooperation with the University of Massachusetts.

Degrees Conferred: 2 *associate;* 750 *baccalaureate;* 508 *master's;* 128 *first-professional:* law. Bachelor's degrees awarded in top five disciplines: security and protective services 315; business, management, marketing, and related support services 198; engineering 54; psychology 43; history 19.

Fees and Other Expenses: *Full-time tuition per academic year:* $17,434. *Room and board per academic year:* $8,254.

Financial Aid: Western New England College offers a direct lending program. Aid from institutionally generated funds is provided on the basis of academic merit, financial need. Institution has a Program Participation Agreement with the U.S. Department of Education for eligible students to receive Pell Grants and, depending upon the agreement, other federal aid.

Financial aid to full-time, first-time undergraduate students: 19% received federal grants averaging $2,874; 14% state/local grants averaging $1,271; 83% institutional grants averaging $7,444; 87% received loans averaging $5,593.

Departments and Teaching Staff: *Professors* 58, *associate professors* 35, *assistant professors* 32, *instructors* 14, *part-time faculty* 14.

Total instructional faculty: 153. Student-to-faculty ratio: 17:1. Degrees held by full-time faculty: 69% hold terminal degrees.

Enrollment: Total enrollment 4,025. Undergraduate 3,038 (62.8% men, 37.2% women).

Characteristics of Student Body: *Ethnic/racial makeup (undergraduate):* Black non-Hispanic: 3%; American Indian or Alaska Native: .3%; Asian or Pacific Islander: 2.2%; Hispanic: 3.2%; White non-Hispanic: 84.6%; unknown: 6.6%.

International Students: 29 nonresident aliens enrolled fall 2004. Students from Europe, Asia, Africa. No programs available to aid students whose native language is not English. No financial aid specifically designated for international students.

Student Life: On-campus residence halls house 60% of student body. Residence halls for men constitute 24% of such space, for women only 14%, for both sexes 62%. *Intercollegiate athletics:* The college offers a Varsity intercollegiate program for both men and women in several sports. Currently, Varsity teams are fielded in soccer, tennis, basketball, wrestling, volleyball, football, bowling, skiing, field hockey, ice hockey, baseball, softball, and lacrosse. Active member of NCAA Division III, ECAC, and CAC. *Special regulations:* Registered cars permitted without restrictions. *Special services:* Medical services available on campus. The college also has a strong wholistic student development system contributing to special tutoring, advising, summer and fall orientation, and co-curricular student assistance programs. *Student publications, radio: Cupola,* a yearbook; *The Review,* an annual literary magazine; *Lex Brevis,* a biweekly newspaper for law students; *The Westerner,* a biweekly newspaper. Radio station WNEK-FM broadcasts an average of 100 hours per week. *Surrounding community:* Springfield population 150,000. Boston, 90 miles from campus, is nearest metropolitan area; Hartford 35 miles from campus. Served by mass transit bus system, airport 25 miles from campus, passenger rail service 4 miles from campus.

Library Collections: 123,475 volumes. 36,000 microforms; 6,000 audiovisual materials; 176 periodical subscriptions. Students have access to online information retrieval services and the Internet.

Most important special holdings include Saex Judaica Collection; Business Collection; J.F. Kennedy Assassination materials.

Buildings and Grounds: Campus area 215 acres.

Chief Executive Officer: Dr. Anthony S. Caprio, President.

Address admission inquiries to Dean of Enrollment Management.

Westfield State College

57 Western Avenue
Westfield, Massachusetts 01086-1630
Tel: (413) 572-5300   **E-mail:** admission@wsc.mass.edu
Fax: (413) 562-3613   **Internet:** www.wsc.mass.edu

Institution Description: Westfield State College is a public institution and member of Massachusetts Board of Higher Education. *Enrollment:* 4,914. *Degrees awarded:* Baccalaureate, master's.

Academic offerings subject to approval by statewide coordinating bodies. Budget subject to approval by state governing boards.

Accreditation: *Regional:* NEASC. *Professional:* teacher education

History: Established as Barre Normal School 1838; offered first instruction at postsecondary level 1839; changed name to Westfield Normal School 1844, to State Teachers College at Westfield 1932; awarded first degree (baccalaureate) 1933; changed name to State College at Westfield 1960; adopted present name 1968; celebrated 150th anniversary 1987.

Institutional Structure: *Governing board:* Massachusetts Board of Regents of Higher Education (statewide policymaking body). Extrainstitutional representation: 15 regents. All voting. Board of Trustees (appointed for Westfield State College). Representation: 9 members. All voting. *Composition of institution:* Administrators 30. Academic affairs headed by vice president for academic affairs. Management/business/finances directed by vice president for administration and finance. Full-time instructional faculty 168. Academic governance body, All-College Committee, meets an average of 18 times per year. *Faculty representation:* Faculty served by collective bargaining agent affiliated with NEA and Massachusetts Teachers Association.

Calendar: Semesters. Academic year early Sept. to mid-May. Freshmen admitted Sept., Jan. Degrees conferred May, Aug. Formal commencement May. Summer session from early June to mid-Aug.

Characteristics of Freshmen: 3,570 applicants (1,634 men, 1936 women). 69% of applicants admitted. 34.9% of admitted students enrolled full-time.

87% (751 students) submitted SAT scores; 2% (23 students) submitted ACT scores. *25th percentile:* SAT I Verbal 460, SAT I Math 460; ACT Composite 18. *75th percentile:* SAT I Verbal 560, SAT I Math 560; ACT Composite 21.

60% of entering freshmen expected to graduate within 5 years. 94% of freshmen from Massachusetts. Freshmen from 14 states.

Admission: Rolling admissions plan. Early acceptance available. *Requirements:* Either graduation from accredited secondary school with 16 units including 4 English, 3 mathematics, 2 foreign language, 3 natural and physical science, 2 social sciences, 2 electives from specific group of subjects; or GED. *Entrance tests:* College Board SAT. For foreign students TOEFL. *For transfer students:* 2.0 minimum GPA; from regionally accredited institutions 67 hours maximum transfer credit.

College credit and advanced placement for postsecondary-level work completed in secondary school. Tutoring available. Noncredit developmental courses offered in summer session and regular academic year.

Degree Requirements: 120 credit hours; 2.0 GPA; 30 semester hours in residence; general education requirements. Fulfillment of some degree requirements and exemption from some beginning courses possible by passing College Board CLEP, AP. *Grading system:* A–F; pass-fail; withdraw (carries time limit).

Distinctive Educational Programs: Internships. Evening classes. Special facilities for using telecommunications in the classroom. Facilities and programs for independent research, including honors programs, individual majors, tutorials. Institutional study abroad in England, France, Greece, Italy, Mexico, Spain. *Other distinctive programs:* Applied chemistry; media communication; regional and urban planning; management information systems.

ROTC: Army in cooperation with University of Massachusetts at Amherst.

Degrees Conferred: 876 *baccalaureate;* 113 *master's.* Bachelor's degrees awarded in top five disciplines: security and protective services 154; education 126; business, management, marketing, and related support services 108; communication, journalism, and related programs regional planning 88; psychology 81.

Fees and Other Expenses: *Full-time tuition per academic year 2004–05:* in-state $4,557, out-of-state $10,637. *Room and board per academic year:* $5,730.

Financial Aid: Aid from institutionally generated funds is provided on the basis of financial aid. Institution has a Program Participation Agreement with the U.S. Department of Education for eligible students to receive Pell Grants and, depending upon the agreement, other federal aid.

Financial aid to full-time, first-time undergraduate students: 19% received federal grants averaging $3,017; 31% state/local grants averaging $3,820; 26% institutional grants averaging $1,884; 65% received loans averaging $2,568.

Departments and Teaching Staff: Art *professors* 5, *associate professors* 2, *assistant professors* 1, *instructors* 0, *part-time teachers* 6; biology 7, 1, 2, 1, 0; communication 2, 2, 5, 0, 4; computer science 2, 2, 1, 0, 0; criminal justice 2, 3, 4, 0, 6; economics and business management 6, 5, 5, 0, 3; education 6, 6, 3, 0, 3; English 9, 0, 7, 0, 18; foreign languages 4, 1, 0, 0, 2; geography/regional planning 4, 3, 0, 0, 1; history 8, 1, 0, 0, 1; mathematics 5, 1, 3, 0, 2; movement science 1, 3, 6, 0, 5; music 4, 2, 1, 0, 16; philosophy 4, 0, 0, 0, 1; physical sciences 2, 1, 2, 0, 3; political science 4, 1, 0, 0, 0; psychology 6, 4, 4, 0, 4; sociology 1, 1, 2, 0, 5; women's studies 0, 0, 0, 0, 2.

Total instructional faculty: 248. Degrees held by full-time faculty: doctorate 75%, master's 24%, baccalaureate less than 1%, professional less than 1%. 81% hold terminal degrees.

Enrollment: Total enrollment 4,914. Undergraduate 4,299 (44.5% men, 55.5% women).

Characteristics of Student Body: *Ethnic/racial makeup:* Black non-Hispanic: 3%; American Indian or Alaska Native: .4%; Asian or Pacific Islander: .9%; Hispanic: 2.6%; White non-Hispanic: 82.2%; unknown: 10.8%. *Age distribution:* 17–21: 82%; 22–24: 13%; 25–29: 3%; 30–34: 1%; 35–59: less than 1%.

International Students: 8 nonresident aliens enrolled fall 2004. Programs available to aid students whose native language is not English: English as a Second Language Program. No financial aid specifically designated for international students.

Student Life: On-campus residence halls house 57% of student body. Residence halls for men constitute 21% of such space, for women 56%, for both sexes 23%. *Intercollegiate athletics:* men only: baseball, basketball, football, golf, gymnastics, hockey, soccer, tennis, track, volleyball; women only: basketball, field hockey, golf, gymnastics, soccer, softball, tennis, track, volleyball. *Special regulations:* Cars permitted for seniors and commuters only. *Special services:* Learning Resources Center, medical services. *Student publications, radio:* WKSB broadcasts 140 hours per week. *Surrounding community:* Westfield population 36,500. Boston, 100 miles from campus, is nearest metropolitan area. Served by mass transit bus system; airport 25 miles from campus; passenger rail service 12 miles from campus.

Library Collections: 130,000 volumes. Book, serial, and government titles accessible through the library's catalog. 971 current serial title subscriptions. 533,355 microform units; 1,519 audio/video units. Students have access to online information retrieval services and the Internet.

Buildings and Grounds: Campus area 261 acres.

Chief Executive Officer: Dr. William H. Lopes, President.

Address admission inquiries to Director of Admissions; graduate inquiries to Dean of Graduate Studies.

Weston Jesuit School of Theology

3 Phillips Place
Cambridge, Massachusetts 02138
Tel: (617) 492-1960   **E-mail:** admissionsinfo@wjst.edu
Fax: (617) 492-5833   **Internet:** www.wjst.edu

Institution Description: Weston Jesuit School of Theology, formerly known as Weston School of Theology, is a private seminary conducted by the Jesuit Order of the Roman Catholic Church. *Enrollment:* 191. *Degrees awarded:* First-professional, master's.

Accreditation: *National:* ATS. *Professional:* theology

Calendar: Semesters. Academic year early Sept. to mid-May.

Admission: *Requirements:* Bachelor's degree from an accredited college or university; letters of recommendation, essay, and some special requirements for STL and STD. *Entrance tests:* GRE or MAT.

Degree Requirements: Completion of prescribed curriculum.

Degrees Conferred: 27 *master's:* theology; 15 *first-professional:* master of divinity.

Fees and Other Expenses: *Full-time tuition per academic year:* $14,954. *Room per academic year:* $6,000.

Financial Aid: Aid from institutionally generated funds is provided on the basis of academic merit, financial need. Institution has a Program Participation Agreement with the U.S. Department of Education for eligible students to receive Pell Grants and, depending upon the agreement, other federal aid.

Departments and Teaching Staff: Biblical studies *professors* 3, *associate professors* 0, *assistant professors* 1, *part-time teachers* 0; church history 2, 0, 1, 0; historical and systematic theology 2, 1, 2, 0; word and worship 1, 1, 0, 0; moral theology 2, 0, 1, 0; pastoral studies 0, 2, 0, 1.

Total instructional faculty: 20. Student-to-faculty ratio: 10:1. Degrees held by full-time faculty: doctorate 100%.

Enrollment: Total enrollment 191 (64.9% men, 35.1% women).

Characteristics of Student Body: *Ethnic/racial makeup:* Black non-Hispanic: 2.6%; Asian or Pacific Islander: 2.1%; Hispanic: 1.6%; White non-Hispanic: 75.4%. *Age distribution:* 22–24: 3%; 25–29: 11%; 30–34: 21%; 35–39: 18%; 40–49: 23%; 50–59: 15%; 60–and over: 9%.

International Students: Programs available to aid students whose native language is not English. Financial aid available for international students.

Library Collections: 250,000 volumes. 1,100 current periodicals. Online catalog. Students have access to online information retrieval services and the Internet.

Most important special collections include New Testament Abstracts; Anson Phelps Stokes Collection of Historical Bibles and Books of Common Prayer; John Wallace Suter Collection of Books of Common Prayer.

Chief Executive Officer: Robert E. Manning, S.J., President.

Address admission inquiries to Karen A. McLennan, Director of Admissions.

Wheaton College

28 East Main Street
Norton, Massachusetts 02766-2322
Tel: (508) 286-8251   **E-mail:** admission@wheatoncollege.edu
Fax: (508) 286-8271   **Internet:** www.wheatoncollege.edu

Institution Description: Wheaton College is a private, independent, non-profit college. *Enrollment:* 1,538. *Degrees awarded:* Baccalaureate.

Accreditation: *Regional:* NEASC.

History: Established as Wheaton Female Seminary, a college preparatory and junior college 1834; incorporated as Norton Female Seminary 1837; readopted original name 1839; offered first instruction at postsecondary level 1898; changed name to Wheaton College and became 4-year college 1912; awarded first degree (baccalaureate) 1914; coeducational 1988. *See* Carolyn M. Clewes, *Wheaton Through the Years: 1835–1960* (Norton, Mass.: Wheaton College, 1960) for further information.

Institutional Structure: *Governing board:* Wheaton College Board of Trustees. Extrainstitutional representation: 10 trustees; institutional representation: president of the college; 19 alumnae, president of the alumnae association, 1 alumna trustee. 2 ex officio. 28 voting. *Composition of institution:* Academic affairs headed by headed by provost. Management/business/finances directed by vice president for finance and operations. Full-time instructional faculty 122. Academic governance body, the faculty, meets an average of 8 times per year.

Calendar: Semesters. Academic year Sept. to May. Freshmen admitted Sept. Degrees conferred May, Oct., Feb. Formal commencement May. No summer session.

Characteristics of Freshmen: 45% of applicants admitted. 28% of applicants admitted and enrolled.

39% (171 students) submitted SAT scores; 7% (31 students) submitted ACT scores. *25th percentile:* SAT Verbal 560, SAT Math 580; ACT Composite 24. *75th percentile:* SAT Verbal 650, SAT Math 650; ACT Composite 30.

77% entering freshmen expected to graduate within 5 years. 27% of freshmen from Massachusetts. Freshmen from 38 states and 28 foreign countries.

Admission: For fall acceptance, apply as early as Sept. 1 of previous year, but not later than Feb. 1 of year of enrollment. Students are notified of acceptance Apr. Apply by Nov. 1 for early decision 1; by Jan. 15 for early decision 2. *Recommended program:* Graduation from accredited secondary school, 4 units English, 3–4 foreign language, 3–4 mathematics, 3 social studies, 2–3 laboratory science. Honors or advanced level placement course and personal interview expected. *Entrance tests:* Optional for admission, College Board English Composition Achievement (with or without essay) or ACT required for English placement upon enrollment. For foreign students TOEFL. *For transfer students:* 3.0 minimum GPA; 64 hours maximum transfer credit from accredited institution.

College credit and advanced placement for postsecondary-level work completed in secondary school and for International Baccalaureate. College credit for College Board CLEP in Continuing Education only. Tutoring available.

Degree Requirements: 128 semester hours; 2.0 GPA on 4.0 scale; 4 semesters in residence; General Education Curriculum; major.

Fulfillment of freshman writing requirement and degree credit possible through CEEB Advanced Placement Program scores, International Baccalaureate, A-levels. *Grading system:* A–F; pass-fail; withdraw (carries time limit).

Distinctive Educational Programs: *For all undergraduates:* Career Exploration Internship program. Field work in anthropology, sociology, urban studies (in Boston and Providence). Semester at Marine Biological Laboratory at Woods Hole (MA). Semester at SALT Center for Documentary Field Studies at Portland (ME). Dual-degree programs with Emerson College, Clark University, Dartmouth's Thayer School of Engineering; George Washington University, Worcester Polytechnic Institute, Andover-Newton Theological School; New England School of Optometry, School of the Museum of Fine Arts. Students may experience Junior Year Abroad in as many as 25 countries. Facilities and programs for independent research, including honors programs, individual majors, tutorials, and independent study. Member of Twelve College Exchange Program. Cross-registration with Stonehill College, Brown University (RI). Washington (DC) semester at American University; semester at Williams College/Mystic Seaport Program in American Maritime Studies (CT). Semester at the Eugene O'Neill Theater Center (CT).

ROTC: Army in cooperation with Stonehill College.

Degrees Conferred: 296 *baccalaureate:* area studies 21, biological sciences 17, computer and information science 3, English 29, foreign languages and literature 9, mathematics 2, philosophy/religion 7, physical sciences 15, psychology 59, social sciences and history 93, visual and performing arts 41.

Fees and Other Expenses: *Full-time tuition per academic year 2005–06:* $32,115. *Other fees:* $235. *Room and board per academic year:* $7,830.

Financial Aid: Aid from institutionally generated funds is provided on the basis of academic merit, financial need. Institution has a Program Participation Agreement with the U.S. Department of Education for eligible students to receive Pell Grants and other federal aid.

Financial aid to full-time, first-time undergraduate students: need-based scholarships/grants totaling $16,127,226, self-help $5,045,045, tuition waivers $274,685; non-need-based scholarships/grants totaling $2,068,486, self-help $1,811,637, parent loans $4,540,800, tuition waivers $514,095.

Departments and Teaching Staff: *Professors 42, associate professors 34, assistant professors 39, instructors 7, part-time faculty 41.*

Total instructional faculty: 163 (full-time 122, part-time 41; women 72, men 91; members of minority groups 31). Total faculty with doctorate, first-professional, or other terminal degree 147. Student-to-faculty ratio: 11:1. Degrees held by full-time faculty: baccalaureate 100%, master's 11%. 96% hold terminal degrees. *Faculty development:* $1,714,634 total grants for research. 17 faculty members awarded sabbaticals 2004–05.

Enrollment: Total enrollment 1,538. Undergraduate full-time 561 men / 960 women, part-time 5m / 12w. *Transfer students:* in-state 15.

Characteristics of Student Body: *Ethnic/racial makeup:* number of Black non-Hispanic: 47; American Indian or Alaska Native: 5; Asian or Pacific Islander: 47; Hispanic: 58; White non-Hispanic: 1,206; unknown: 133. *Age distribution:* number under 18: 5; 18–19: 656; 20–21: 669; 22–24: 297; 25–29: 3; 30–34: 1; 35–39: 2; 40–49: 1; 50–64: 3; unknown: 1.

International Students: 42 nonresident aliens enrolled fall 2004. Students from Europe, Asia, Central and South America, Africa, Canada. No programs available to aid students whose native language is not English. No financial aid specifically designated for international students.

Student Life: On-campus residence halls house 98% of student body. *Intercollegiate athletics:* NCAA Div. III; men only: cross-country, soccer, lacrosse, basketball, tennis, swimming; women only: cross-country, basketball, soccer, field hockey, volleyball, lacrosse, tennis, swimming, synchronized swimming. *Special regulations:* Registered cars permitted for all. Quiet hours set by individual residence halls. *Special services:* Medical services, shuttle van service to and from nearby passenger rail service. *Student publications, radio:* Nike, a yearbook; *Rushlight,* an annual literary magazine; *Wheaton Wire,* a weekly newspaper. Radio station WCCS broadcasts on a regular schedule. *Surrounding community:* Norton population 18,036. Providence (RI), 18 miles from campus, is nearest metropolitan area; Boston (MA) 35 miles. Served by mass transit system, airport 25 miles from campus, passenger rail service 5 miles from campus.

Library Collections: 372,322 volumes. Current serial subscriptions: paper 1,525, microform 85,105, 3,726 via electronic access. 285 computer work stations. Online catalog. Students have access to online information retrieval services and the Internet. Total 2004–05 budget for books, periodicals, audiovisual materials, microforms: $1,033,363.

Most important special holdings include rare books, Wheaton Collection, Historical Collection on Women.

Buildings and Grounds: Campus area 385 acres.

Chief Executive Officer: Dr. Ronald A. Crutcher, President.

Address admission inquiries to Gail Berson, Dean of Admission and Student Aid.

Wheelock College

200 The Riverway
Boston, Massachusetts 02215-4176
Tel: (617) 879-2206   **E-mail:** undergrad@wheelock.edu
Fax: (617) 879-2449   **Internet:** www.wheelock.edu

Institution Description: Wheelock College is a private, independent, nonprofit college. *Enrollment:* 1,021. *Degrees awarded:* Baccalaureate, master's. Certificates also awarded.

Accreditation: *Regional:* NEASC. *Professional:* social work, teacher education

History: Established as Wheelock School and offered first instruction at postsecondary level 1888; chartered 1939; became 4-year institution and adopted present name 1941; awarded first degree (baccalaureate) 1943; first admitted men 1968. *See* Winifred E. Bain, *Leadership in Childhood Education (1888–1964)* (Boston: Wheelock College, 1964) for further information.

Institutional Structure: *Governing board:* Board of Trustees. Extrainstitutional representation: 25 trustees; institutional representation: 2 students; 3 alumni. 26 voting. *Composition of institution:* Administrators 8 men / 22 women. Academic affairs headed by academic dean. Management/business/finances directed by vice president for administration. Full-time instructional faculty 68. Academic governance body, Faculty Senate, meets an average of 30 times per year.

Calendar: Semesters. Academic year Sept. to May. Freshmen admitted Sept., Jan. Degrees conferred May, Aug., Dec. Formal commencement May. Summer session from late June to early Aug.

Characteristics of Freshmen: 78% of applicants admitted. 38% of applicants admitted and enrolled.

100% of applicants submitted SAT scores. *25th percentile*: SAT Verbal 480, SAT Math 450. *75th percentile*: SAT Verbal 590, SAT Math 550.

65% of entering freshmen expected to graduate within 5 years. 48% of freshmen from Massachusetts. Freshmen from 17 states and 1 foreign country.

Admission: Rolling admissions plan. Apply by Dec. 1 for early decision; must limit application to Wheelock. Early acceptance available. *Requirements:* Either graduation from accredited secondary school or GED. Commitment to field of early childhood. *Entrance tests:* College Board SAT or ACT. For foreign students TOEFL minimum score 500. *For transfer students:* 2.0 minimum GPA; 64 semester hours maximum transfer credit.

College credit and advanced placement for postsecondary-level work completed in secondary school.

Degree Requirements: *For all baccalaureate degrees:* 134 total credits and cumulative GPA of 2.0; 4 terms in residence. *For all undergraduate degrees:* distribution requirements.

Fulfillment of some degree requirements and exemption from some beginning courses possible by passing College Board CLEP, AP. *Grading system:* A–F; pass-fail; withdraw (carries time limit).

Distinctive Educational Programs: *For undergraduates:* Independent study. *Available to all students:* Early childhood education programs with specialties in teaching children, children in health care settings, and social services for children. Off-campus domestic study or study abroad by individual arrangement. Social work offered; juvenile justice and youth advocacy; teaching grades 1-6. *Other distinctive programs:* Continuing Education programs, including graduate level courses at the Center for Parenting Studies. All students participate in field work/internships for their four years. Combined degree program for BS/MS is available.

Degrees Conferred: 166 *baccalaureate:* education 96, health professions and related sciences 27, home economics 12, protective services/public administration 31; 227 *master's.*

Fees and Other Expenses: *Full-time tuition per academic year 2004–05:* $23,100 undergraduate; $745 per credit hour for graduate study. *Room and board per academic year:* $9,975.

Financial Aid: Aid from institutionally generated funds is provided on the basis of academic merit, financial need.

Financial aid to full-time, first-time undergraduate students: need-based scholarships/grants totaling $5,169,805, self-help $2,408,411; non-need-based scholarships/grants totaling $2,517,373, self-help $48,816, parent loans $1,584,947. *Graduate aid:* 289 students received federal and state-funded loans totaling $4,317,328 (ranging from $500 to $18,500).

Departments and Teaching Staff: *Professors 10, associate professors 25, assistant professors 16, instructors 5, part-time faculty 110. Total instructional faculty:* 166 (full-time 56, part-time 110; women 44, men 22; members of minority groups 24). Total faculty with doctorate, first-professional, or other terminal degree: 64. Degrees held by full-time faculty: 66% hold terminal degrees. *Fac-*

ulty development: $176,900 in grants for research. 3 faculty members awarded sabbaticals 2004–05.

Enrollment: Total enrollment 1,021. Undergraduate full-time 30 men / 363 women, part-time 2m / 22w; graduate full-time 5m / 165w, part-time 14m / 220w.

Characteristics of Student Body: *Ethnic/racial makeup (undergraduate):* number of Black non-Hispanic: 47; American Indian or Alaska Native: 5; Asian or Pacific Islander: 1; Hispanic: 26; White non-Hispanic: 961; unknown: 84. *Age distribution:* number under 18: 9; 18–19: 258; 20–21: 214; 22–24: 63; 25–29: 13; 30–34: 5; 35–39: 7; 40–49: 15; 50–64: 4.

International Students: 14 nonresident aliens enrolled fall 2004. No programs available to aid students whose native language is not English. No financial aid specifically designated for international students.

Student Life: On-campus residence halls house 69% of student body. Three all-women residence halls and two co-ed residence halls. *Division III athletics:* basketball, cross-country, field hockey, softball, swimming/diving. *Special regulations:* Cars not permitted on campus. Quiet hours vary according to residence hall. *Special services:* Medical services. *Student publications: The Wheel,* a yearbook. *Surrounding community:* Boston area population 3 million. Served by mass transit subway, bus, and train system; airport 3 miles from campus; passenger rail service 1 mile from campus.

Library Collections: 93,534 volumes. 355,000 microforms; 3,500 audiovisual materials; 526 current periodical subscriptions; 2,400 recordings/tapes. Online catalog. Students have access to online information retrieval services and the Internet.

Most important special holdings include collections of historical and contemporary children's literature; manuscript and print material by and about founder Lucy Wheelock; historical materials detailing kindergarten movement in U.S.

Buildings and Grounds: Campus area 5.5 acres.

Chief Executive Officer: Janice Jenkins-Scott, President.

Address admission inquiries to Lynne Harding, Dean of Admissions.

Williams College

880 Main Street
Williamstown, Massachusetts 01267
Tel: (413) 597-3131   **E-mail:** admission@williams.edu
Fax: (413) 597-4015   **Internet:** www.williams.edu

Institution Description: Williams College is a private, independent, nonprofit college. *Enrollment:* 2,050. *Degrees awarded:* Baccalaureate, master's.

Accreditation: *Regional:* NEASC.

History: Established, chartered, and offered first instruction at postsecondary level 1793; awarded first degree (baccalaureate) 1795. *See* Leverett Wilson Spring, *A History of Williams College* (Boston: Houghton Mifflin Company, 1955) for further information.

Institutional Structure: *Governing board:* The president and trustees of Williams College. Representation: President plus 21 trustees. All voting. *Composition of institution:* Academic affairs headed by dean of the faculty. Management/business/finances directed by vice president for administration and treasurer. Budgeting headed by provost. Alumni relations and development headed by vice president for alumni relations and development. Full-time instructional faculty 221. Academic governance body, The Faculty of Williams College, meets an average of 8 times per year.

Calendar: Semesters (4-1-4 plan). Academic year early Sept. to May. Freshmen admitted Sept. Degrees conferred and formal commencement June. No summer session.

Characteristics of Freshmen: 19% of applicants accepted. 49% of accepted applicants enrolled.

99% (527 students) submitted SAT scores. *25th percentile*: SAT Verbal 660, SAT I Math 670. *75th percentile*: SAT Verbal 760, SAT Math 760.

94% of entering freshmen expected to graduate within 5 years. 16% of freshmen from Massachusetts. Freshmen from 41 states and 14 foreign countries.

Admission: For fall acceptance, apply no earlier than Jan. 1 of year of enrollment. Apply by Nov. 10 for early decision. *Requirements:* Carnegie units are recommended: 4 English, 4 mathematics, 4 foreign language, 3 social studies, 3 laboratory science. *Entrance tests:* College Board SAT I or ACT, as well as three SAT II subject tests. For foreign students TOEFL. *For transfer students:* 3.5 minimum GPA; maximum transfer credit limited only by residence requirement. Consideration will be given students with GPA below 3.5.

Advanced placement for postsecondary-level work completed in secondary school and for extrainstitutional learning (life experience) on basis of portfolio and faculty assessment. Tutoring available.

Degree Requirements: Completion of coursework in each of three basic areas: arts and humanities, social studies, and math and science. Students must

also satisfy a one-course Peoples and Cultures requirement, a one-course Quantitative/Formal Reasoning requirement, and a two-course Intensive Writing requirement. *Grading system:* A–E; pass-fail.

Distinctive Educational Programs: *For undergraduates:* Interdisciplinary programs in Afro-American studies, American studies, area studies, environmental studies, history of science, political economy. Facilities and programs for independent research, including honors programs, contract majors, independent study, double majors, student-initiated courses. Coordinate programs offered in African and Middle Eastern studies; biochemistry and molecular biology; neuroscience; Russian, Soviet, and East European studies; environmental studies; women's studies. Study abroad at Oxford University in cooperation with Exeter College, Oxford; in Madrid (in cooperation with Hamilton, Mount Holyoke and Swarthmore Colleges); in Cairo (in cooperation with the American University in Cairo); in the Russia (through the Tbilisi exchange and also in cooperation with the American Collegiate Consortium); in Sweden (in cooperation with twelve other colleges and the University of Stockholm); in Denmark (with the University of Copenhagen Danish International Studies); and in Kyoto (the Associated Kyoto Program, run by a group of 11 colleges). Williams students may also receive credit for approved programs at a wide variety of other institutions, or for work done directly in a foreign university if acceptable evaluation is possible. The Twelve College Exchange Program includes Amherst, Bowdoin, Connecticut College, Dartmouth, Mount Holyoke, Smith, Trinity, Vassar, Wellesley, Wesleyan, Wheaton, and, for a semester program, the National Theatre Institute, in Waterford, Connecticut. In addition, the College maintains an exchange with California Institute of Technology, with Howard University, with Fisk University, with the Thayer School of Engineering at Dartmouth, and with Rensselaer Polytechnic Institute.

Degrees Conferred: 500 *baccalaureate* (B), 27 *master's* (M): area and ethnic studies 15 (B); biological and life sciences 35 (B); computer and information science 10 (B); English 55 (B); foreign languages and literature 20 (B); interdisciplinary studies 5 (B); mathematics 25 (B); philosophy//religion/theology 10 (B); physical sciences 40 (B); psychology 60 (B); social sciences and history 175 (B), 29 (M); visual and performing arts 50 (B), 11 (M). *Honorary degrees awarded 2004–05:* Doctor of Humane Letters 3, Doctor of Science 1, Doctor of Fine Arts 11, Doctor of Letters 2.

Fees and Other Expenses: *Full-time tuition per academic year 2004–05:* $29,786 undergraduate; graduate study varies by program. *Required fees:* $204. *Room and board per academic year:* $8,110.

Financial Aid: Williams College offers a direct lending program. Aid from institutionally generated funds is provided on the basis of financial need.

Financial aid to full-time, first-time undergraduate students: need-based scholarships/grants totaling $19,619,195, self-help $2,920,155; non-need-based scholarships/grants totaling $960,636, self-help $466,315, parent loans $4,212,243.

Departments and Teaching Staff: *Total instructional faculty:* 291 (full-time 247, part-time 44; women 117, men 174; members of minority groups 41). Total faculty with doctorate, first-professional, or other terminal degree: 276. Student-to-faculty ratio: 7.5:1. Degrees held by full-time faculty: 96% hold terminal degrees.

Enrollment: Total enrollment 2,050. Undergraduate full-time 964 men / 989 women, part-time 11m / 27w; graduate full-time 23m / 26w.

Characteristics of Student Body: *Ethnic/racial makeup:* number of Black non-Hispanic: 191; American Indian or Alaska Native: 4; Asian or Pacific Islander: 178; Hispanic: 148; White non-Hispanic: 1,302.

International Students: 112 nonresident aliens enrolled fall 2004. No programs available to aid students whose native language is not English. No financial aid specifically designated for international students.

Student Life: On-campus residence halls house 96% of student body. Residence halls for both sexes constitute 100% of such space. *Intercollegiate athletics:* men only: baseball, basketball, crew, cross-country, football, ice hockey, lacrosse, soccer, squash, swimming, tennis, track, water polo, wrestling; women only: basketball, crew, cross-country, field hockey, ice hockey, lacrosse, soccer, softball, squash, swimming, tennis, track, volleyball. *Special regulations:* Cars permitted. *Special services:* Medical services. Radio station WMS-WCFM broadcasts 119 hours per week. *Surrounding community:* Williamstown population 5,000. Albany (N.Y.), 40 miles from campus, and Boston, 120 miles from campus, are nearest metropolitan areas.

Publications: *Comics Coalition; Culture Counter; Daily Advisor; Dissonance; Gharial; Gulielmensian; Medcow; People's Native Tongues; The Record; Unbound; Williams Free Press; Williams Literary Review.*

Library Collections: 862,940 volumes. 32,729 recordings/tapes; 407,698 government documents; 484,405 microtext items; 22,000 audiovisual materials. Current serial subscriptions: paper 1,686; via electronic access 10,377. Online catalog. 30 computer work stations. Students have access to online information retrieval services and the Internet.

Most important special holdings include Chapin Library of Rare Books (35,000 volumes including incunabula); Shaker Collection (1,300 volumes including 18th century rare books, diaries, letters); original copies of the 4 founding documents of the U.S. (the Constitution, Bill of Rights, Declaration of Independence, Articles of Confederation).

Buildings and Grounds: Campus area 450 acres.

Chief Executive Officer: Dr. Morton Owen Schapiro, President.

Address admission inquiries to Richard Nesbitt, Director of Admissions.

Worcester Polytechnic Institute

100 Institute Road
Worcester, Massachusetts 01609-2280

Tel: (508) 831-5000   **E-mail:** admissions@wpi.edu
Fax: (508) 831-5931   **Internet:** www.wpi.edu

Institution Description: Worcester Polytechnic Institute is a private, independent, nonprofit institution. *Enrollment:* 3,817. *Degrees awarded:* Baccalaureate, master's, doctorate.

Member of Worcester Consortium for Higher Education.

Accreditation: *Regional:* NEASC. *Professional:* business, computer science, engineering

History: Established and incorporated as Worcester County Free Institute of Industrial Science, a men's institution, 1865; offered first instruction at postsecondary level 1868; awarded first degree (baccalaureate) 1871; adopted present name 1887; became coeducational 1968. *See* Mildred M. Tymeson, *Two Towers* (Worcester: Barre Publishing Company, 1965) for further information.

Institutional Structure: *Governing board:* The Board of Trustees of the Worcester Polytechnic Institute consisting of not less than 12 members including: Ex-Officio Trustee, the President; At-large Trustees, not limited in number; Alumni Trustees, not to exceed 15 in number; Emeriti Trustees, not limited in number. *Composition of institution:* Academic Affairs headed by provost and vice president academic affairs. Management/business/finances directed by vice president of business affairs. Full-time instructional faculty 189 men / 25 women. Academic governance body, the faculty, meets an average of 10 times per year.

Calendar: Four 7-week terms. Academic year late Aug. to early May. Formal commencement May. Summer session late May to mid-July.

Characteristics of Freshmen: 2,783 applicants admitted. 746 applicants admitted and enrolled.

97% (725 students) submitted SAT scores; 29% (217 students) submitted ACT scores. *25th percentile:* SAT Verbal 570, SAT Math 630; ACT Composite 24. *75th percentile:* SAT Verbal 670, SAT Math 720; ACT Composite 29.

72% of entering freshmen expected to graduate within 5 years. 52% of freshmen from Massachusetts. Freshmen from 33 states and 32 foreign countries.

Admission: For fall acceptance, apply as early as Sept. of previous year, but not later than Feb. 15 of year of enrollment. Students are notified of acceptance Apr. 1. Apply by Dec. 1 for early decision. Early acceptance available. *Requirements:* Either graduation from accredited secondary school with 4 units in English, 4 mathematics (including pre-calculus), 2 lab sciences (including physics and chemistry). *Entrance tests:* College Board SAT-1 and 3 SAT-2s (writing, mathematics 1 or 1C or 2C). ACT composite also accepted. *For transfer students:* 60 credit hours maximum transfer credit. Applications via the Internet accepted on WPI's Home page (www.wpi.edu) or by diskette. Fee waived for electronic application. Common Application and applications submitted through College View, CollegeLink, and ExPan also accepted.

College credit and advanced placement for postsecondary-level work completed in secondary school. Tutoring available.

Degree Requirements: Minimum academic credit to equal 45 credit hours. 2 years in residence; humanities minor; 2 qualifying projects: 1 in major field, 1 relating technology to society; distribution requirements in most majors; 2 courses in social sciences; 4 courses in physical education.

Fulfillment of some degree requirements and exemption from some beginning courses possible by passing College Board AP. *Grading system:* A-B-C-No record.

Distinctive Educational Programs: International Scholars Program, Project Centers in Washington (D.C.), London, Puerto Rico, San Francisco (CA), Bangkok, Hong Kong, Venice, Mexico, France, Copenhagen, and Holland. Exchange programs with universities in Canada, England, Germany, Ireland, Mexico, Switzerland, Sweden. Flexible class scheduling and course selection within distributions. Facilities and programs for independent research, including interdisciplinary and individually developed majors. Cross-registration with other Worcester colleges through consortium. 3-2 program with College of the Holy Cross, Tufts Veterinary School, and other colleges. Cooperative educational available.

ROTC: Army, Air Force. Navy offered in cooperation with College of the Holy Cross. 4 Air Force, 4 Navy, and 5 Navy commissions awarded 2004.

Degrees Conferred: 605 *baccalaureate:* degrees awarded in top five disciplines include biological and life sciences 71, computer and information science 63, engineering 406, mathematics 14, physical sciences 20; 293 *master's:* various disciplines; 17 *doctorate.*

Fees and Other Expenses: *Full-time tuition per academic year 2004–05:* $29,530. *Room and board per academic year:* $9,164.

Financial Aid: Aid from institutionally generated funds is provided on the basis of academic merit, financial need.

Financial aid to full-time, first-time undergraduate students: need-based scholarships/grants totaling $32,910,310, self-help $11,555,444; non-need-based scholarships/grants totaling $6,564,795, self-help $8,101,543, parent loans $5,334,645.

Departments and Teaching Staff: *Professors* 95, *associate professors* 74, *assistant professors* 50, *instructors* 16, *part-time faculty* 119. *Total instructional faculty:* 354 (full-time 235, part-time 119; women 72, men 282; members of minority groups 44). Total faculty with doctorate, first-professional, or other terminal degree: 299. Student-to-faculty ratio: 12.5:1. Degrees held by full-time faculty: 97% hold terminal degrees. *Faculty development:* $13.7 million in grants for research. 17 faculty members awarded sabbaticals in 2204-05.

Enrollment: Total enrollment 3,817. Undergraduate full-time 2,088, part-time 676, part-time 83m / 21w; graduate full-time 304m / 127w, part-time 407m / 111w. *Transfer students:* in-state 24; from out-of-state 13.

Characteristics of Student Body: *Ethnic/racial makeup (undergraduate):* number of Black non-Hispanic: 50; American Indian or Alaska Native: 16; Asian or Pacific Islander: 180; Hispanic: 96; White non-Hispanic: 2,324; unknown: 70. *Age distribution:* number under 18: 72; 18–19: 1,274; 20–21: 1,212, 22–24: 241; 25–29: 37; 30–34: 9; 35–39: 5; 40–49: 10.

International Students: 416 nonresident aliens enrolled fall 2004. Programs available to aid students whose native language is not English: social, cultural. English as a Second Language Program. Financial aid specifically designated for undergraduate international students: scholarships available annually to qualifying students.

Student Life: On-campus residence halls house 48% of student body. Students are housed in traditional residence halls, on-campus apartments and suites. 32% of male students join fraternities with 60% of them living in fraternity housing. 39% of female students join sororities. *Varsity athletics:* men only: baseball, basketball, crew, football, golf, lacrosse, soccer, swimming, tennis, track, wrestling, cross-country; women only: basketball, crew, field hockey, soccer, softball, tennis, volleyball, track, golf, cross-country, swimming, lacrosse. *Club athletics:* men only: hockey, volleyball, rugby, fencing, sailing, frisbee; women: crew, fencing, skiing, bowling, soccer, sailing, rugby, frisbee. *Special regulations:* Cars permitted in designated areas for all but freshmen. *Special services:* Learning Resources Center, medical services, shuttle bus to consortium member institutions. *Student publications: Tech News,* a weekly student newspaper. *Surrounding community:* Worcester population 170,000. Boston, 45 miles from campus, is nearest metropolitan area. Served by mass transit bus system, airport 4 miles from campus, passenger rail service 2 miles from campus.

Library Collections: 267,554 volumes. Online catalog. 445 serials. 80,903 microforms; 92,627 audiovisual materials. Students have access to online information retrieval services and the Internet.

Most important special holdings include collection of diaries (1890–1977) of Theo Brown, an alumnus of Worcester Polytechnic Institute and a major designer of agricultural machinery; correspondence and research papers (1900–1950) of Charles Allen, developer of the Alden Hydraulic Laboratory; Fellman Dickens Collection (first editions, unique manuscripts—original and rare, illustrations); a variety of art objects and secondary sources.

Buildings and Grounds: Campus area 80 acres. *New buildings:* Campus Center completed 2001.

Chief Executive Officer: Dr. Dennis D. Berkey, President.

Address undergraduate admission inquiries to Director of Admissions; graduate inquiries to Director, Graduate Admissions.

Worcester State College

486 Chandler Street
Worcester, Massachusetts 01602-2597

Tel: (508) 929-8000   **E-mail:** admissions@worcester.edu
Fax: (508) 929-8185   **Internet:** www.worcester.edu

Institution Description: Worcester State College is a state institution. *Enrollment:* 5,404. *Degrees awarded:* Baccalaureate, master's.

Academic offerings subject to approval by statewide coordinating bodies. Budget subject to approval by state governing boards. Member of Worcester Consortium for Higher Education.

Accreditation: *Regional:* NEASC. *Professional*: nursing, occupational therapy, speech-language pathology

History: Established and chartered as Worcester Normal School and offered first instruction at postsecondary level 1874; awarded first degree (baccalaureate) 1932; adopted present name 1960. *See* Herb Taylor, *The First 100 Years* (Worcester: Worcester State College Office of Community Services, 1974) for further information.

Institutional Structure: *Governing board:* Board of Higher Education of the Commonwealth of Massachusetts. 11 members. Board of Trustees (appointed for Worcester State College) 9 members, all voting. *Composition of institution:* Academic Affairs headed by Vice President for academic affairs. Management/business/finances directed by Vice President for administration and finance. Full-time instructional faculty 166. Academic governance body, All College Committee, meets an average of 9 times per year. *Faculty representation:* Faculty served by bargaining agent affiliated with NEA and Massachusetts Teachers Association.

Calendar: Semesters. Academic year Sept. to May. Freshmen admitted Sept., Jan. Degrees conferred Aug., Dec., May; formal commencement May. Summer session of 2 terms from late May to mid Aug.

Characteristics of Freshmen: 56% of applicants accepted. 38% of accepted applicants enrolled.

95% (597 students) submitted SAT scores; 10% (65 students) submitted ACT scores. *25th percentile*: SAT Verbal 450, SAT Math 460; ACT Composite 18. *75th percentile*: SAT Verbal 540, SAT Math 550; ACT Composite 23.

37% of entering freshmen expected to graduate within 5 years. 88% of freshmen from Massachusetts. Freshmen from 10 states and 20 foreign countries.

Admission: Rolling admissions plan. For fall acceptance, apply as early as December, but not later than June 1. *Requirements:* Either graduation from accredited secondary school or GED. *Entrance tests:* College Board SAT or ACT. *For transfer students:* From 2-year accredited institutions 2.0 minimum GPA, 60 hours maximum transfer credit; in-state residents, out-of-state students, and students from 4-year accredited institutions 2.0 minimum GPA, 90 hours maximum transfer credit.

Tutoring available. Noncredit remedial courses offered during regular academic year.

Degree Requirements: *For all baccalaureate degrees:* 120 hours; 2.0 minimum GPA; 2 semesters in residence; general education requirements including course in U.S. and Massachusetts constitutions. Some degree requirements can be met through CLEP. *For all graduate degrees:* students may have no more than 3 grades of C+ or lower. *Grading system:* A–E; pass-fail; withdraw; incomplete (deadline after which grade is changed to E). *For graduate degree programs:* minimum 33 semester hours of credit; minimum 2.75 GPA.

Distinctive Educational Programs: *For undergraduates:* Joint program in nuclear medicine technology with University of Massachusetts Medical School. Interdepartmental/interdisciplinary program in gerontology, labor studies/labor relations, natural science, women's studies. Engineering Science Transfer Program in cooperation with U. Mass., Dartmouth, U. Mass, Lowell, and Worcester Polytechnic Institute. Cross-registration with other institutions in the Worcester Consortium for Higher Education. Joint baccalaureate and master's degree programs in communications with Clark University. Student and faculty exchange programs with Worcester College in England. Work-experience programs, including internships, field work, practica. Weekend and evening classes.

ROTC: Army in cooperation with Worcester Polytechnic Institute; Navy with the College of the Holy Cross.

Degrees Conferred: 697 *baccalaureate* (B), 160 *master's* (M): biological/life sciences 29 (B), 5 (M); business/marketing 162 (B); communications/communication technologies 52 (B); computer and information sciences 24 (B); education 57 (B), 113 (M); English 36 (B); foreign languages and literature 7 (B); health professions and related sciences 127 (B), 35 (M); interdisciplinary studies 16 (B); mathematics 12 (B); physical sciences 10 (B); protective services/public

administration 8 (B), 7 (M); psychology 107 (B); social sciences and history 70 (B).

Fees and Other Expenses: *Full-time tuition per academic year 2004–05:* undergraduate resident $970, out-of-state $7,050; graduate resident $2,300, out-of-state $2,700. *Required fees:* $3,609. *Room and board per academic year:* $6,896.

Financial Aid: Aid from institutionally generated funds is provided on the basis of academic merit, financial need.

Financial aid to full-time, first-time undergraduate students: need-based scholarships/grants totaling $3,746,794, self-help $1,658,874, tuition waivers $500,214; non-need-based scholarships/grants totaling $1,426,093, self-help 1,447,546, tuition waivers $272,892.

Departments and Teaching Staff: *Professors* 43, *associate professors* 62, *assistant professors* 52, *instructors* 9, *part-time faculty* 95. *Total instructional faculty:* 1261 (full-time 166, part-time 95; women 125, men 136; members of minority groups 28). Total faculty with doctorate, first-professional, or other terminal degree: 130. Student-to-faculty ratio: 17:1. Degrees held by full-time faculty: doctorate 64%, master's 35%, professional 1%. 71% hold terminal degrees. *Faculty development:* 11 faculty members awarded sabbaticals 2004–05.

Enrollment: Total enrollment 5,404. Undergraduate full-time 1,291 men / 1,818 women, part-time 522m / 923w; graduate full-time 8m / 62w, part-time 189m / 593w.

Characteristics of Student Body: *Ethnic/racial makeup (undergraduate):* number of Black non-Hispanic: 170; American Indian or Alaska Native: 14; Asian or Pacific Islander: 130; Hispanic: 157; White non-Hispanic: 3,512; unknown: 348. *Age distribution:* number under 18: 8; 18–19: 1,021; 20–21: 1,139; 22–24: 1,051; 25–29: 473; 30–34: 225; 35–39: 176; 40–49: 247; 50–64: 85; 65 and over: 56.

International Students: 234 nonresident aliens enrolled fall 2004. 58 students from Europe, 52 Asia, 24 Central and South America, 96 other. Programs available to aid students whose native language is not English: social, cultural. English as a Second Language Program. No financial aid specifically designated for international students.

Student Life: On-campus residence halls house 31% of full-time undergraduates. *Intercollegiate athletics:* men only: baseball, basketball, football, golf, ice hockey, rugby; women only: equestrian, field hockey, softball, volleyball; men and women: basketball, crew, cross-country, soccer, tennis, track and field. Hiking, camping, boating, swimming, and skiing available in local area. *Special regulations:* Cars with decals permitted on campus in designated areas only. *Special services:* Learning Resources Center, medical services, shuttle bus to Consortium colleges. *Student publications, radio: The Student Voice*, a weekly newspaper. Radio station WSCW. Student television organization, cable channel to residence halls and student center. *Surrounding community:* Worcester population 170,000. Providence (RI) 45 miles from campus. Served by mass transit bus system; airport 2 miles from campus; passenger rail service 3 miles from campus.

Publications: *Worcester Statement*, alumni publications; college catalog, departmental brochures, financial aid brochure, admissions brochures, evening undergraduate and graduate brochures.

Library Collections: 163,461 volumes. Online catalog. 15,344 microform items; 1,614 current paper and microform serial subscriptions. 9,300 audiovisual materials. 15 computer work stations. Students have access to online information retrieval services and the Internet. Total 2004–05 budget for books and materials: $223,374.

Most important special collections include education resources (K–12 textbooks, instructional materials, tests, curriculum guides); juvenile collection (preschool–8, fiction/nonfiction, reference).

Buildings and Grounds: Campus area 58 acres. *New buildings:* Wesleyan Hall completed 2004.

Chief Executive Officer: Dr. Janelle C. Ashley, President.

Address admission inquiries to Jay Tierney, Director of Admissions.

Michigan

Adrian College

110 South Madison Street
Adrian, Michigan 49221-2575

Tel: (517) 265-5161   **E-mail:** admissions@adrian.edu
Fax: (517) 264-3331   **Internet:** www.adrian.edu

Institution Description: Adrian College is a private college affiliated with the United Methodist Church. *Enrollment:* 1,007. *Degrees awarded:* Associate, baccalaureate.

Accreditation: *Regional:* NCA. *Professional:* teacher education

History: Established, chartered, and offered first instruction at postsecondary level 1859; awarded first degree (baccalaureate) 1863; assimilated West Lafayette College (OH) 1916. *See* Fanny A. Hay, Ruth E. Cargo, and Harlan L. Freeman, *The Story of a Noble Devotion* (Adrian, Mich.: Adrian College Press, 1945) for further information.

Institutional Structure: *Governing board:* Board of Trustees. Representation: 17 trustees-at-large, 6 members of clergy, 6 laypersons, 6 alumni. 2 ex officio (president of the college and 1 church official). 35 voting. *Composition of institution:* Administrators 16 men / 21 women. Academic affairs headed by vice president and dean for academic affairs. Management/business/finances directed by vice president for business affairs. Full-time instructional faculty 69. Academic governance body, College Assembly, meets an average of 9 times per year.

Calendar: Semesters. Academic year Aug. to May. Freshmen admitted Aug., Jan., June. Degrees conferred Apr., Aug., Dec. Formal commencement May. Summer session from May to July.

Characteristics of Freshmen: 1,209 applicants (547 men, 662 women). 84% of applicants admitted. 28.9% of admitted students enrolled full-time. 5% (14 students) submitted SAT scores; 97% (284 students) submitted ACT scores. *25th percentile:* ACT Composite 17, ACT English 15, ACT Math 16. *75th percentile:* ACT Composite 24, ACT English 23, ACT Math 24.

49% of entering freshmen expected to graduate within 5 years. 80.5% of freshmen from Michigan. Freshmen from 11 states.

Admission: Rolling admissions plan. For fall acceptance, apply not later than Apr. 1 of year of enrollment. *Requirements:* Either graduation from accredited secondary school or GED. Recommend 15 units, including 3 English, 2 in a foreign language, 3 college preparatory mathematics, 1 laboratory science, 1 social studies, academic electives. *Entrance tests:* College Board SAT or ACT. *For transfer students:* 2.0 minimum GPA; from 4-year accredited institution 90 semester hours maximum transfer credit; from 2-year accredited institution 60 hours.

College credit and advanced placement for postsecondary-level work completed in secondary school. College credit for extrainstitutional learning on basis of ACE *2006 Guide to the Evaluation of Educational Experiences in the Armed Services;* personal interview; portfolio; and committee assessments.

Tutoring available. Developmental courses offered during regular academic year; credit given.

Degree Requirements: *For all associate degrees:* 62 credit hours; 17 hours in residence. *For all baccalaureate degrees:* 124 credit hours; 34 hours in residence. *For all degrees:* 2.0 GPA; 40 hours distribution requirements plus basic educational proficiency in communication skills, linguistic skills and physical development skills.

Fulfillment of some degree requirements and exemption from some beginning courses possible by passing College Board CLEP, APP, other standardized tests. *Grading system:* A–F; withdraw (carries time limit); incomplete (carries time limit).

Distinctive Educational Programs: Internships. Dual-degree program in engineering. Cooperative baccalaureate program in medical technology with approved hospitals. Special facilities for using telecommunications in the classroom. Interdisciplinary programs, including bilingually sponsored study abroad in England; interior design and fashion merchandising at The American College, London, England; liberal arts studies at Harlaxton College, Grantham, England. Other study abroad and intercultural opportunities in the U.S. through Association for Sharing in International Studies. Honors Program in international business. Off-campus study in the U.S. includes Appalachian semester at Union College (KY); semester or year at Fashion Institute of Technology (NY); urban life study in Chicago (IL); semester or year at the Washington Center (DC); semester in Washington (DC) at American University; Philadelphia Urban Semester.

Degrees Conferred: 1 *associate;* 183 *baccalaureate.* Bachelor's degrees awarded in top five disciplines: business, management, marketing, and related support services 41; visual and performing arts 23; English language and literature/letters 21; parks, recreation, leisure, and fitness studies 12; education 10.

Fees and Other Expenses: *Full-time tuition per academic year 2004–05:* $17,600. *Books and supplies:* $540. *Room and board per academic year:* $5,776.

Financial Aid: Aid from institutionally generated funds is provided on the basis of academic merit, financial need, other considerations. Institution has a Program Participation Agreement with the U.S. Department of Education for eligible students to receive Pell Grants, and, depending upon the agreement, other federal aid.

Financial aid to full-time, first-time undergraduate students: 36% received federal grants averaging $2,738; 72% state/local grants averaging $2,294; 96% institutional grants averaging $9,318; 77% received loans averaging $3,844.

Departments and Teaching Staff: *Professors* 30.5, *associate professors* 15, *assistant professors* 20.5, *instructors* 3, *part-time teachers* 50.

Total instructional faculty: 85.66 FTE. Student-to-faculty ratio: 12:1. Degrees held by full-time faculty: doctorate 74%, master's 8%, professional 18%. 92% hold terminal degrees.

Enrollment: Total enrollment 1,007 (46% men, 54% women).

Characteristics of Student Body: *Ethnic/racial makeup:* Black non-Hispanic: 8.2%; American Indian or Alaska Native: .4%; Asian or Pacific Islander: .7%; Hispanic: 1.5%; White non-Hispanic: 73.8%; unknown: 16.2%.

International Students: 10 nonresident aliens enrolled fall 2004. Programs available to aid students whose native language is not English: cultural, financial. English as a Second Language Program. Financial aid specifically designated for international students: unlimited number of scholarships available annually.

Student Life: On-campus residence halls, sororities, and fraternities house 71% of student body. Coed residence halls constitute 82% of such space. 25% of men join and 13% live in on-campus fraternities; 25% of women join and 17% live in on-campus sororities. *Intercollegiate athletics:* men only: baseball, basketball, cross-country, football, golf, soccer, softball, tennis, track; women only: basketball, cross-country, golf, soccer, softball, tennis, track, volleyball. *Special regulations:* Registered cars permitted. Half of residence halls feature 24-hour visitation. Other host visitation from 10am to midnight Sun.–Thurs, 10am to 2am Fri. and Sat. *Special services:* Learning Resources Center, Health Center, Writing Center, counseling services. *Student publications, radio, television: The College World,* a weekly newspaper; senior memory book, annual student literary publication. Radio station WVAC-FM broadcasts in stereo. *Surrounding community:* Adrian population 22,000. Toledo (OH), 35 miles from campus, is nearest metropolitan area. Served by airport 30 miles from campus.

Library Collections: 146,200 volumes. Online catalog. 475,000 microforms; 1,500 audiovisual materials; 600 current periodical subscriptions. Computer work stations available. Students have access to online information retrieval services and the Internet.

Most important special collections include Methodist Conference Historical Collection; Lincoln Collection; World Food Supply Collection.

Buildings and Grounds: Campus area 100 acres.

Chief Executive Officer: Dr. Stanley P. Caine, President.

Address admission inquiries to Janel A. Sutkus, Director of Admissions.

Albion College

611 East Porter Street
Albion, Michigan 49224
Tel: (517) 629-1000   **E-mail:** admissions@albion.edu
Fax: (517) 629-0581   **Internet:** www.albion.edu

Institution Description: Albion College is a private college affiliated with the United Methodist Church. *Enrollment:* 1,867. *Degrees awarded:* Baccalaureate.

Member of the consortium Great Lakes College Association.

Accreditation: *Regional:* NCA. *Professional:* music

History: Established and chartered as Spring Arbor Seminary 1835; changed name to The Wesleyan Seminary at Albion 1939; offered first instruction at postsecondary level 1843; merged with Albion Female Collegiate Institute and changed name to The Wesleyan Seminary and Female College at Albion 1857; adopted present name and awarded first degree (baccalaureate) 1861. *See* Robert Gildart, *Albion College 1835–1960* (Chicago: The Lakeside Press, 1961) and Keith J. Fennimore, *The Albion College Sesquicentennial History: 1835–1985* for further information.

Institutional Structure: *Governing board:* Board of Trustees. Extrainstitutional representation: 19 trustees, 6 church representatives; 6 alumni. All voting. *Composition of institution:* Administrators 5 men / 1 women. Academic affairs headed by provost. Management/business/finances directed vice president for finance and management. Full-time instructional faculty 131. Academic governance body, Albion College Faculty, meets an average of 8 times per year.

Calendar: Semesters. Academic year late Aug. to early May. Freshmen admitted Aug., Jan., May. Degrees conferred May, Dec. Formal commencement May. Summer session of 1 term from mid-May to early July.

Characteristics of Freshmen: 86% of applicants admitted. 36% of applicants admitted and enrolled.

18% (98 students) submitted SAT scores; 93% (519 students) submitted ACT scores. *25th percentile:* SAT Verbal 512, SAT Math 520; ACT Composite 22, ACT English 21, ACT Math 21. *75th percentile:* SAT Verbal 640, SAT Math 660; ACT Composite 27, ACT English 28, ACT Math 27.

88% of entering g freshmen expected to graduate within 5 years. 88% of freshmen from Michigan. Freshmen from 17 states and 3 foreign countries.

Admission: Rolling admissions plan. For fall acceptance, apply as early as Sept. 1 of previous year, but not later than Apr. 1 of year of enrollment. Early acceptance available. *Requirements:* Either graduation from accredited secondary school with 15 units or GED. Recommend strong background in English, mathematics, social science, science, foreign language. Personal interview encouraged. Minimum 2.0 GPA in academic subjects. Lowest acceptable secondary school class standing 50th percentile. *Entrance tests:* College Board SAT or ACT Composite. *For transfer students:* From 4-year accredited institution 2.0 GPA, 76 hours maximum transfer credit; from 2-year accredited institution 2.0 minimum GPA, 64 hours; correspondence/extension students 8 hours.

College credit and advanced placement for postsecondary-level work completed in secondary school.

Degree Requirements: 128 semester hours; 2.0 GPA; 3 terms in residence; distribution requirements; exit competency examination in writing.

Fulfillment of some degree requirements and exemption from some beginning courses possible by passing College Board CLEP, AP. *Grading system:* A–F; 4.0-0.0; withdraw; credit-no credit; incomplete.

Distinctive Educational Programs: Internships provided through concentrated programs in economics and management (through liberal arts program in professional management), human services, mass communication, public service (through the Gerald R. Ford Institute), and women's studies. Full- and part-time internships may also be individually arranged. Evening classes. Dual-degree programs in engineering with Columbia University (NY), University of Michigan, Washington University (MO); fisheries, forestry and wildlife management with University of Michigan; Cooperative programs in medical technology with local hospitals. Interdepartmental majors in American studies, mathematics/physics, urban studies. Facilities and programs for independent research, including honors programs, individual majors, tutorials, student-designed programs. Institutionally sponsored study abroad in United Kingdom (London School of Economics, University of Sussex, and Stirling University); Scotland (University of Aberdeen) sponsored by GLCA consortium; Spain (Seville); France (Grenoble); Germany (Goethe Institute, University of Augsburg, University of Munster); Yugoslavia (Zagreb, sponsored by GLCA/ACM); Mexico (Guadalajara at the Instituto Nueva Galicia); Colombia (Centro de Estudios University Colombo-Americana, sponsored by GLCA); Costa Rica (San Jose, sponsored by ACM); Soviet Union (Krasnodar, a joint ACM/GLCA program); Africa (Ghana, Kenya, Liberia, Nigeria, Sierra Leone, University of Dakar, Senegal sponsored by GLCA); Jerusalem (sponsored by GLCA); Hong Kong (sponsored jointly by ACM/GLCA); India (University of Poona, sponsored by ACM/GLCA); Japan (Waseda University in Tokyo, sponsored by GLCA); China (Beijing, Shanghai, and Nanjing).

Off-campus study opportunities in the U.S. include programs at American University in Washington, D.C., in political science and American studies; the New York City Arts Program which offers an apprenticeship and seminar on performing, visual and communication arts; GLCA's Philadelphia Center which gives students the opportunity to develop their understanding of urban settings; Oak Ridge, Tennessee science research program for junior and senior Albion students in the social, biological, engineering, mathematical, and physical sciences. Chicago's Newberry Library Program in the humanities open to students and faculty. Through the consortium, Albion College offers students instruction in the following foreign languages and related area studies: Arabic, Chinese, Hindi, and Japanese. In addition, students may study a variety of non-Western languages in summer intensive language training at Beloit College and the University of Michigan through the Program for Inter-Institutional Collaboration in Area Studies (PICAS). Fellowships that include full tuition and fees plus a stipend are available through PICAs for this summer language study.

Degrees Conferred: 309 *baccalaureate:* area and ethnic studies 3; biological/life sciences 31; business/marketing 27; communications/communication technologies 30; computer and information sciences 3; education 34; English 30; foreign languages and literature 14; health professions and related sciences 2; interdisciplinary studies 1; liberal arts/general studies 1; mathematics 9; philosophy/religion/theology 15; physical sciences 29; protective services/public administration 1; psychology 39; social sciences and history 103; visual and performing arts 24. 4 *honorary degrees awarded 2004:* Doctor of Humane Letters.

Fees and Other Expenses: *Full-time tuition per academic year 2005–06:* $24,012. *Room per academic year:* $3,358. *Board per academic year:* $3,540.

Financial Aid: Aid from institutionally generated funds is provided on the basis of academic merit, financial need, other considerations.

Financial aid to full-time, first-time undergraduate students: need-based scholarships/grants totaling $18,885,353, self-help $4,643,357, tuition waivers $366,624; non-need-based scholarships/grants totaling $7,224,841, self-help $3,825,914, parent loans $1,709,746, tuition waivers $157,322.

Departments and Teaching Staff: *Professors* 46, *associate professors* 26, *assistant professors* 51, *instructors* 8, *part-time faculty* 38.

Total instructional faculty: 169 (full-time 131, part-time 35; women65, men 104; members of minority groups 15). Total faculty with doctorate, first-professional, or other terminal degree: 128. Student-to-faculty ratio: 13:1. Degrees held by full-time faculty: doctorate 85%, master's 100%, baccalaureate 100%. 92% hold terminal degrees. *Faculty development:* $120,128 total grants for research. 10 faculty members awarded sabbaticals 2004–05.

Enrollment: Total enrollment 1,867. Undergraduate full-time 828 men / 1,024 women, part-time 5m / 10w.

Characteristics of Student Body: *Ethnic/racial makeup:* number of Black non-Hispanic: 67; American Indian or Alaska Native: 8; Asian or Pacific Islander: 37; Hispanic: 18; White non-Hispanic: 1,640; unknown: 73. *Age distribution:* number under 18: 75, 18–19: 937; 20–21: 763; 22–24: 75; 25–29: 4; 35–39: 1; 40–49: 1; 50–64: 1.

International Students: 24 nonresident aliens enrolled fall 2004. 10 students from Europe, 4 Asia, 5 Central and South America, 3 Africa, 1 Canada, 1 other. No programs available to aid students whose native language is not English. Variable number of scholarships available to international students each year.

Student Life: On-campus residence halls house 94% of student body. All residence halls contain both men and women, with each individual floor section being assigned to one sex. 1.4% of student body housed on campus in cooperative women's residence; 3% housed on campus in small residential units of 5–8 students each.33.8% of men belong to fraternities; 31.6% live in fraternity houses. Most married students who request housing can be accommodated in college-owned apartments. *Intercollegiate athletics:* men only: baseball, basketball, cross-country, football, golf, soccer, swimming, tennis, track; women only: archery, basketball, cross-country, field hockey, softball, swimming, tennis, track, volleyball. *Special regulations:* Cars permitted for sophomores, juniors, and seniors; freshmen by permission only; $50 fee. *Special services:* Learning Resources Center, medical services. *Student publications: Albion Review,* an annual magazine; *Pleiad,* a weekly newspaper. *Surrounding community:* Albion population 11,000. Detroit, 100 miles from campus, is nearest metropolitan area. Served by passenger rail service 1 mile from campus.

Library Collections: 320,000 volumes. Online catalog. 245,000 government documents; 21,000 microforms; 4,600 audiovisual materials; 865 current periodical subscriptions. 500 computer work stations campus-wide. Students have access to online information retrieval services and the Internet.

Most important holdings include West Michigan Conference of United Methodist Church Archives; Albion Americana Collection; Bible Collection.

Buildings and Grounds: Campus area 225 acres.

Chief Executive Officer: Dr. Peter T. Mitchell, President.

Address admission inquiries to Doug Kellar, Associate Vice President for Enrollment.

Alma College

614 West Superior Street
Alma, Michigan 48801-1599
Tel: (989) 463-7111   **E-mail:** admissions@alma.edu
Fax: (989) 463-7037   **Internet:** www.alma.edu

Institution Description: Alma College is a private, independent, nonprofit college associated with the Presbyterian Church (U.S.A.) *Enrollment:* 1,268. *Degrees awarded:* Baccalaureate.

Member of Consortium of Liberal Arts Colleges; Midwest Consortium for Study Abroad.

Accreditation: *Regional:* NEASC. *Professional:* chemistry, music, teacher education

History: Established 1886; incorporated and offered first instruction at postsecondary level 1887; awarded first degree (baccalaureate) 1891. *See* Donna S. Bollinger, *Pines, Prayers, and Perseverance: The Evolution of Alma College* (Traverse City, Mich.: Village Press, 1976) for further information.

Institutional Structure: *Governing board:* Alma College Board of Trustees. Extrainstitutional representation: No more than 36 and no less than 25 trustees. Institutional representation: 2 administrators, 8 full-time instructional faculty members, 6 students, 20 ex officio. 27 voting. *Composition of institution:* Administrators 38 men / 27 women. Academic affairs headed by provost and vice president for academic affairs. Management/business/finances directed by vice president for finance. Full-time instructional faculty 62. Academic governance body, the faculty, meets an average of 8 times per year.

Calendar: Semesters (4-4-1 plan). Academic year early Sept. to late May. Freshmen admitted Aug., Sept., Jan., Apr. Degrees conferred Aug., Dec., Apr., May. Formal commencement Apr.

Characteristics of Freshmen: 84% of applicants admitted. 30% of applicants admitted and enrolled.

12% (39 students) submitted SAT scores; 98% (517 students) submitted ACT scores. *25th percentile:* SAT Verbal 510, SAT Math 490; ACT Composite 21, ACT English 20, ACT Math 20. *75th percentile:* SAT Verbal 620, SAT Math 620, ACT Composite 27, ACT English 27, ACT Math 26. 70% of entering freshmen expected to graduate within 5 years. 96% of freshmen from Michigan. Freshmen from 9 states and 7 foreign countries.

Admission: Rolling admissions plan. For fall acceptance, apply as early as end of junior year in secondary school. Early action on basis of 5 semesters work. *Requirements:* Either graduation from accredited secondary school with 16 units which must include 4 English, 3 mathematics, 3 science, 3 social studies; 2 units of a foreign language required. Minimum 3.0 GPA. *Entrance tests:* ACT composite preferred; College Board SAT accepted. *For transfer students:* 3.0 minimum GPA; 68 credits maximum transfer credit.

College credit and advanced placement for postsecondary-level work completed in secondary school. Tutoring available. Developmental courses offered during regular academic year; nondegree credit given.

Degree Requirements: 136 hours; 2.0 GPA; senior year in residence; proficiency requirement in English composition; comprehensive evaluation in major field. Fulfillment of some degree requirements and exemption from some beginning courses possible by passing departmental examinations, College Board CLEP or APP. *Grading system:* A–F; pass-fail.

Distinctive Educational Programs: Work-experience programs. Dual-degree programs in engineering with University of Michigan, Michigan Technological University, and occupational therapy with Washington University (MO). Interdepartmental/interdisciplinary programs in electronics and computer engineering, environmental studies, foreign service, new media studies, public affairs, public health, and women's studies. Facilities and programs for independent research, including individual majors and tutorials. Study abroad through Alma College programs in Austria, Bolivia, Ecuador, England, France, Scotland, Spain, Germany, Mexico, and through programs offered by other institutions. Other off-campus study opportunities are available with the New York Arts Program, the Philadelphia Center Internship Program, the Urban Life Center in Chicago, and the Washington (DC) Semester Program. Spring Term courses take advantage of the unique format of Spring Term and cross-geographical, cultural, or disciplinary boundaries.

ROTC: Army offered in cooperation with Central University.

Degrees Conferred: 302 *baccalaureate:* biological/life sciences 24; business/marketing 38; communications/communication technologies 12; computer and information sciences 3; education 21; English 15; foreign languages and literature 6; health professions and related sciences 21; mathematics 12; philoso-phy/religion/theology 3; physical sciences 18; psychology 24, social sciences and history 46, visual and performing arts 33.

Fees and Other Expenses: *Full-time tuition per academic year 2005–06:* $20,934. *Room and board per academic year:* $7,410. *Required fees:* $200.

Financial Aid: Aid from institutionally generated funds is provided on the basis of academic merit, financial need, other criteria. Institution has a Program Participation Agreement with the U.S. Department of Education for eligible students to receive Pell Grants and other federal aid.

Financial aid to full-time, first-time undergraduate students: need-based scholarships/grants totaling $16,702,828, self-help $4,378,646, parent loans $570,175, tuition waivers $5,076,000; non-need-based scholarships/grants totaling $2,956,298, self-help $1,776,412, parent loans $1,377,771, tuition waivers $1,257,619.

Departments and Teaching Staff: *Professors 35, associate professors 25, assistant professors 18, instructors 4, part-time faculty 43.*

Total instructional faculty: 125 (full-time 82, part-time 43; women 47, men 78; members of minority groups 6). Total faculty with doctorate, first-professional, or other terminal degree: 83. Student-to-faculty ratio: 12.8:1. Degrees held by full-time faculty: doctorate 86%, master's 13%, 1% baccalaureate. 86% hold terminal degrees. *Faculty development:* $233,443 total grants for research. 6 faculty members awarded sabbaticals 2004–05.

Enrollment: Total enrollment 1,217. Full-time 502 men / 715 women, part-time 16m / 35w. *Transfer students:* in-state 28; from out-of-state 4.

Characteristics of Student Body: *Ethnic/racial makeup:* number of Black non-Hispanic: 27; American Indian or Alaska Native: 6; Asian or Pacific Islander: 17; Hispanic: 19; White non-Hispanic: 1,181; unknown: 1. *Age distribution:* number under 18: 22; 18–19: 513; 20–21: 331; 22–24: 174; 25–29: 17; 30–34: 2; 35–39: 5; 40–49: 4; 50–64: 2.

International Students: 17 nonresident aliens enrolled fall 2004. 4 students from Europe, 8 Asia, 1 Central America, 1 Africa, 3 Canada. No programs available to aid students whose native language is not English. Financial aid specifically designated for international students: variable number of scholarships available annually.

Student Life: On-campus residence halls house 84% of student body. *Intercollegiate athletics:* baseball, basketball, cross country, football, golf, soccer, swimming, tennis, track, volleyball. *Special regulations:* Cars permitted with campus registration. *Special services:* Medical services. *Student publications, radio, television: Almanian,* a weekly newspaper; *Pine River Anthology,* an annual art and literary magazine; *the Scot,* a yearbook. Radio station WQAC broadcasts 42–50 hours per week. TV station Cable 2 broadcasts irregularly. *Surrounding community:* Alma population 9,000. Detroit, 125 miles from campus.

Library Collections: 261,400 volumes. Online catalog. 34,200 microforms; 2,900 audiovisual materials; 1,823 periodicals. Students have access to 4 online information retrieval services. Total 2004–05 budget for materials and operations: $452,465.

Most important special collections include Alma College Archives; U.S. Documents Depository; Holocaust Collection.

Buildings and Grounds: Campus area 125 acres. *New buildings:* Alma J. Stone Center for Recreation completed 2001; Wright Hall (residence) 2005.

Chief Executive Officer: Dr. Sandra J. Tracey, President.

Address admission inquiries to Dr. Anne Monroe, Director of Admissions.

Andrews University

US 31 North
Berrien Springs, Michigan 49104-1500
Tel: (800) 253-2874   **E-mail:** enroll@andrews.edu
Fax: (269) 471-2670   **Internet:** www.andrews.edu

Institution Description: Andrews University is a private institution affiliated with the Seventh-day Adventist Church. *Enrollment:* 3,017. *Degrees awarded:* Associate, baccalaureate, first-professional (master of divinity), master's, doctorate. Certificates also awarded.

Member of the consortium Adventist Colleges Abroad.

Accreditation: *Regional:* NCA. *Professional:* clinical lab scientist, counseling, music, nursing, physical therapy, social work, teacher education

History: Established as Battle Creek College, incorporated and offered first instruction at postsecondary level 1874; awarded first degree (baccalaureate) 1979; moved to Berrien Springs and changed name to Emmanuel Missionary College 1901; merged with Seventh-day Adventist Theological Seminary (established 1934) and Potomac University (established 1958) and adopted present name 1960. *See* Emmett K. VandeVere, *The Wisdom Seekers* (Nashville: Southern Publishing Association, 1972) for further information.

Institutional Structure: *Governing board:* Andrews University Board of Trustees. Representation: 42 trustees, including president of the University, 17 alumni. 1 ex officio. All voting. *Composition of institution:* Administrators 30 men / 14 women. Academic affairs headed by vice president for academic administration. Management/business/finances directed by vice president for financial administration. Full-time instructional faculty 219. Academic governance body, General Faculty, meets an average of 10 times per year.

Calendar: Semesters. Academic year Aug. to May. Freshmen admitted Sept., Jan., Mar, June. Degrees conferred and formal commencements June, Aug. Summer session mid-June to mid-Aug.

Characteristics of Freshmen: 43.4% of applicants admitted. 25.1% of applicants admitted and enrolled. 18.2% (148 students) submitted SAT scores; 70.7% (217 students) submitted ACT scores. *25th percentile:* SAT Verbal 470, SAT Math 450; ACT Composite 20, ACT English 14; ACT Math 18. *75th percentile:* SAT Verbal 590, SAT Math 580; ACT Composite 26, ACT English 26, ACT Math 24.

76.2% of entering freshmen expected to graduate within 5 years. 38% of freshmen from Michigan. Freshmen from 35 states and 12 foreign countries.

Admission: Rolling admissions plan. For fall acceptance, apply no later than Aug. 15. *Requirements:* Either graduation from approved secondary school with 13 (15 recommended) units from among English, foreign language, mathematics, science, social studies; or GED. Minimum 2.0 GPA. *Entrance tests:* ACT composite. For foreign students TOEFL or standardized examination of University of Michigan English Language Institute. *For transfer students:* 2.0 minimum GPA; from four-year institution 90 semester hours maximum transfer credit; from two-year institution 70 semester hours.

College credit and advanced placement for postsecondary-level work completed in secondary school. For extrainstitutional learning (life experience), college credit on basis of faculty assessment. Tutoring available. Developmental courses offered in summer session and regular academic year; credit given.

Degree Requirements: *For all associate degrees:* 62 semester hours. *For all baccalaureate degrees:* 124 semester hours. 3 hours physical education; tests of Undergraduate Assessment Program. Additional requirements for some programs. *For all undergraduate degrees:* 2.0 GPA; weekly chapel attendance; general education requirements.

Fulfillment of some degree requirements and exemption from some beginning courses possible by passing departmental examinations, College Board CLEP, APP. *Grading system:* A–F; withdraw (carries time limit).

Distinctive Educational Programs: *For undergraduates:* Cooperative education programs. Accelerated degree program. Qualified seniors may enroll in master's programs in business administration or divinity while completing baccalaureate requirements. BS in Engineering program; Doctor of Physical Therapy program. Honors programs. Study abroad through consortium in Austria, France, Spain. *For graduate students:* Work-experience programs. Study abroad through American Schools of Oriental Research in Jerusalem and Amman, Jordan. *Available to all students:* Evening classes. Off-campus study in U.S. for marine biology students on Fidalgo Island (WA) with Walla Walla College. *Other distinctive programs:* Off-campus centers offering baccalaureate degree programs (at Adventist Seminary of West Africa, Nigeria; Helderburg College, South Africa); master's programs (at Oakwood College, AL; Columbia Union College, MD; Atlantic Union College, MA; Avondale College, Australia; West Indies College, Jamaica; Montemorelos University, Mexico; Antillian College, Puerto Rico). Seventh-day Adventist Institute of World Missions for training missionaries to developing countries.

Degrees Conferred: 271 *baccalaureate;* 196 *master's;* 44 *first-professional;* 77 master of divinity. Bachelor's degrees awarded in top five disciplines: health professions and related clinical sciences 44; visual and performing arts 30; business, management, marketing, and related support services 22; biological/life sciences 21; architecture 18.

Fees and Other Expenses: *Full-time tuition per academic year 2005–06:* $16,030 undergraduate; $15,890 graduate. *Required fees:* $476. *Room and board per academic year:* $5,280.

Financial Aid: Aid from institutionally generated funds is provided on the basis of academic merit. Institution has a Program Participation Agreement with the U.U. Department of Education for eligible students to receive Pell Grants and other federal aid.

Financial aid to full-time, first-time undergraduate students: need-based scholarships/grants totaling $5,145,331, self-help $4,618,557; non-need-based scholarships/grants totaling $8,060,437, self-help $6,764,503, parent loans $7,081,922, tuition waivers $1,124,201. *Graduate aid:* 44 students received $83,850 in federal and state-funded fellowships/grants (ranging from $100 to $2,000); 365 received $9,074,992 in federal and state-funded loans (ranging from $2,000 to $16,550); 107 received $145,575 for college-assigned jobs; 490 received $1,614,218 other college-assigned jobs (nonteaching, nonresearch) totaling $1,614,218 (ranging from $590 to $13,400); 278 other fellowships and grants totaling $962,892 (ranging from $148 to $29,231).

Departments and Teaching Staff: *Total instructional faculty:* 302 (full-time 220, part-time 82; women 97, men 205; members of minority groups 70). Total faculty with doctorate, first-professional, or other terminal degree: 190. Student-to-faculty ratio: 10:1.

Enrollment: Total enrollment 3,017. Undergraduate full-time 681 men / 827 women, part-time 112m / 110w; graduate full-time 118m / 114w, part-time 334m / 240w; first-professional full-time 203m / 36w, part-time 77m / 15w. *Transfer students:* 157 (undergraduate).

Characteristics of Student Body: *Ethnic/racial makeup:* number of Black non-Hispanic: 329; American Indian or Alaska Native: 7; Asian or Pacific Islander: 150; Hispanic: 181; White non-Hispanic: 864: *Age distribution:* number under 18: 103; 18–19: 517; 20–21: 530; 22–24: 322; 25–29: 107; 30–34: 63; 35–39: 76; 40–49: 46; 50–64: 18.

International Students: 566 nonresident aliens enrolled fall 2004. Programs available to aid students whose native language is not English: social, cultural. English as a Second Language Program. No financial aid specifically designated for international students.

Student Life: On-campus residence halls house 66% of student body. Residence halls for men only constitute 47% of such space, for women only 53%. 4% of student body housed on campus in married student housing. 90% of married students request institutional housing; 85% are so housed. *Special regulations:* Cars permitted for all but first quarter freshmen; parking in designated areas only. Dress code. Curfew from 10pm to 6am. Quiet hours 7:30pm to 9:30pm. Residence hall visitation in lounge areas. *Special services:* Learning Resources Center, medical services. *Student publications, radio:* Cardinal, a yearbook; *Cast* an annual student directory; *Student Movement,* a biweekly newspaper. Radio station WAUS broadcasts 126 hours per week, offers fine arts programming. *Surrounding community:* Berrien Springs population 2,000. Chicago, 105 miles from campus, is nearest metropolitan area. Served by mass transit bus system; airport 15 miles from campus; passenger rail service 15 miles from campus.

Publications: Sources of information about Andrews University include *Focus,* the university magazine. *Andrews University Seminary Studies* (biannually) first published 1963.

Library Collections: 70,591 volumes. Current serial subscriptions: paper 2,400; 759,400 microform; electronic access to 9,000. 12,405 recordings; 100 compact discs. Online catalog. 35 computer work stations. Students have access to online information retrieval services and the Internet.

Most important special holdings include Heritage Room (Seventh-Day Adventist archive and research center); Teaching Materials Center; Music Material Center.

Buildings and Grounds: Campus area 1,300 acres. *New buildings:* Howard Performing Arts Center completed 2003.

Chief Executive Officer: Dr. Niels-Eric Andreasen, President.

Address admission inquiries Charlotte Coy, Supervisor of Undergraduate Admissions; graduate inquiries to Carolyn Hurst, Supervisor of Graduate Admissions.

Aquinas College

1607 Robinson Road, S.E.
Grand Rapids, Michigan 49506-1799

Tel: (616) 662-2900   **E-mail:** admissions@aquinas.edu
Fax: (616) 732-4469   **Internet:** www.aquinas.edu

Institution Description: Aquinas College is a private college affiliated with the Roman Catholic Church. *Enrollment:* 2,695. *Degrees awarded:* Associate, baccalaureate, master's.

Accreditation: *Regional:* NCA.

History: Established and incorporated as Sacred Heart College and offered first instruction at postsecondary level early 1922; changed name to Marywood College late 1922; became coeducational and changed name to Catholic Junior College 1931; became 4-year college and adopted present name 1940; awarded first degree (baccalaureate) 1942.

Institutional Structure: *Governing board:* Aquinas College Board of Trustees. Representation: 38 trustees, including 4 alumni. 4 ex officio. All voting. *Composition of institution:* Administrators 7 men / 3 women. Academic affairs headed by academic vice president. Management/business/finances directed by vice president for business and finance. Full-time instructional faculty 83. Academic governance body, Aquinas College Council, meets an average of 9 times per year.

Calendar: Semesters. Academic year late Sept. to early May. Freshmen admitted Aug., Jan., June. Degrees conferred May, Aug., Dec. Formal commencements May, Dec. Summer session from mid-May to early Aug.

Characteristics of Freshmen: 92% of applicants admitted. 28% of applicants admitted and enrolled.

6% (20 students) submitted SAT scores; 94% (295 students) submitted ACT scores. *25th percentile*: ACT Composite 20, ACT English 20, ACT Math 18. *75th percentile*: ACT Composite 26, ACT English 25, ACT Math 26. 50% of entering freshmen expected to graduate within 5 years. 93% of freshmen from Michigan. Freshmen from 13 states.

Admission: Rolling admissions plan. For fall acceptance, apply as early as Sept. 1 of previous year, but not later than July 1 of year of enrollment. Early acceptance available. *Requirements:* Either graduation from accredited secondary school with 15 academic units or GED. Distribution of units should represent a reasonable coverage of the areas usually considered in a college preparatory curriculum. Minimum GPA in college preparatory courses 2.5. *Entrance tests:* ACT composite preferred: College Board SAT accepted (for either test, minimum score above 50th percentile). For foreign students minimum TOEFL score 550. *For transfer students:* 2.0 minimum GPA; from 4-year accredited institution hours maximum transfer credit limited only by residence requirement; from 2-year accredited institution 64 hours maximum transfer credit.

College credit and advanced placement for postsecondary-level work completed in secondary school. College credit for extrainstitutional learning on basis of ACE 2006 *Guide to the Evaluation of Educational Experiences in the Armed Services* and portfolio and faculty assessments. Peer tutoring available.

Degree Requirements: *For all associate degrees:* 64 credit hours. *For all baccalaureate degrees:* 124 credit hours. *For all undergraduate degrees:* 2.0 GPA; 28 hours in residence; distribution requirements.

Fulfillment of some degree requirements and exemption from some beginning courses possible by passing College Board CLEP, AP (score of 3). *Grading system:* A-B-C-D minus-no credit; credit-no credit; withdraw (carries time limit); incomplete (carries time limit).

Distinctive Educational Programs: *For undergraduates:* Work-experience programs. Cooperative baccalaureate program with Kendall School of Design. Credit transfer agreement with Grand Valley State Colleges and Calvin College. Interdepartmental program in environmental studies. Facilities and programs for independent research, including tutorials, independent study courses. Study abroad in Costa Rica, France, Germany, Ireland, Japan, Spain. Campus interchange with Barry College of San Rafael (CA), St. Mary's Dominican (LA), and St. Thomas Aquinas (NY) Colleges. *Available to all students:* Flexible meeting places and schedules, including off-campus centers (at Holland, Muskegon, and Lansing, 30, 40, and 50 miles away, respectively, from main institution), weekend and evening classes.

Degrees Conferred: 9 *associate;* 348 *baccalaureate;* 155 *master's.* Degrees awarded in top five disciplines: business/marketing 70; social sciences and history 38; communication, journalism, and related programs 23; psychology 24; liberal arts and sciences, general studies, and humanities 19.

Fees and Other Expenses: *Full-time tuition per academic year 2005–06:* $17,926. *Room and board per academic year:* $5,824.

Financial Aid: Aid from institutionally generated funds is provided on the basis of academic merit, financial need, athletic ability. Institution has a Program Participation Agreement with the U.S. Department of Education for eligible students to receive Pell Grants and other federal aid.

Financial aid to full-time, first-time undergraduate students: need-based scholarships/grants totaling $10,618,828, self-help $2,448,238; tuition waivers $67,595; athletic awards $498,112; non-need-based scholarships/grants totaling $2,384,558, self-help $1,270,156, parent loans $537,698, tuition waivers $113,378, athletic awards $101,888.

Departments and Teaching Staff: *Total instructional faculty:* 221 (full-time 95, part-time 126; women 105, men 116; members of minority groups 11). Total faculty with doctorate, first-professional, or other terminal degree: 89. Student-to-faculty ratio: 14:1. Degrees held by full-time faculty: doctorate 57%, master's 40%, baccalaureate 1%, professional 2%.

Enrollment: Total enrollment 2,695. Undergraduate full-time 506 men / 940 women, part-time 81m / 206w; graduate full-time 42m / 95w, part-time 89m / 196w. *Transfer students:* in-state 79.

Characteristics of Student Body: *Ethnic/racial makeup (undergraduate):* number of Black non-Hispanic: 77; American Indian or Alaska Native: 5; Asian or Pacific Islander: 27; Hispanic: 69; White non-Hispanic: 1,613, unknown: 11.

International Students: 11 nonresident aliens enrolled fall 2004. Students from Europe, Asia, Central and South America. No programs available to aid students whose native language is not English. No financial aid specifically designated for international students.

Student Life: On-campus residence halls house 30% of student body. Residence halls for both sexes constitute 100% of such space. *Intercollegiate athletics:* men only: baseball, basketball, cross-country, golf, soccer, tennis, track; women only: basketball, softball, tennis, cross-country, track, volleyball. *Special regulations:* Cars with decals permitted on campus in designated areas only. Quiet hours from 7pm to 7am Sun.–Thurs., midnight to noon Fri. and Sat., 24 hours per day before and during examination period. Residence hall visitation from 9:30am to midnight Sun.–Thurs., 9:30am to 4am Fri. and Sat. *Special services:* Academic Achievement Center, Learning Resources Center, medical ser-

vices. *Student publications: The Saint,* a student newspaper; *AQuinas,* the alumni magazine. *Surrounding community:* Grand Rapids population 182,000. Detroit, 150 miles from campus, is nearest metropolitan area. Served by mass transit bus system, airport 10 miles from campus.

Library Collections: 158,641 volumes. 215,019 microforms; 6,200 audiovisual materials; 845 current periodical subscriptions. Online catalog. Students have access to online information retrieval services and the Internet. Total 2004–05 budget for materials and operations: $140,000.

Most important holdings include Mother Goose Collection (including foreign language and early editions); works pertaining to religion, mainly Catholicism; business collection modeled after Harvard Business School Library.

Buildings and Grounds: Campus area 104 acres.

Chief Executive Officer: Dr. Harry J. Knopke, President.

Address admission inquiries to Thomas Mikowski, Director of Admissions; graduate inquiries to Dean of Graduate Studies.

Calvin College

3201 Burton S.E.
Grand Rapids, Michigan 49546
Tel: (616) 526-6106　　**E-mail:** admissions@calvin.edu
Fax: (616) 526-6777　　**Internet:** www.calvin.edu

Institution Description: Calvin College is a Christian, four-year liberal arts college owned and operated by the Christian Reformed Church in North America. *Enrollment:* 4,180. *Degrees awarded:* Baccalaureate, master's.

Accreditation: *Regional:* NCA. *Professional:* engineering, music, nursing, nursing education, social work, teacher education

History: Established as Theological School and offered first instruction at postsecondary level 1876; changed name to John Calvin Junior College 1906; changed name to Calvin College Seminary and became 4-year college 1908; awarded first degree (baccalaureate) and adopted present name 1921.

Institutional Structure: *Governing board:* Board of Trustees. Extrainstitutional representation: 31 trustees. All voting. *Composition of institution:* Administrators 58 men / 52 women. Academic affairs headed by provost. Management/business/finances directed by vice president for business administration,, finance, and information services. Full-time instructional faculty 282. Academic governance body, the faculty senate, is a representative body of the faculty and meets an average of 7 times per year.

Calendar: Semesters (4-1-4 plan). Academic year Sept. to May. Freshmen admitted Sept., Feb. Degrees conferred May, Aug., Dec. Formal commencement May. Summer session of 3 terms from late May to mid-Aug.

Characteristics of Freshmen: 98% of applicants admitted. 52.4% of applicants admitted and enrolled.

36% (328 students) submitted SAT scores; 81% (326 students) submitted ACT scores. *25th percentile*: SAT Verbal 540, SAT Math 540; ACT Composite 23, ACT English 22, ACT Math 22. *75th percentile*: SAT Verbal 670, SAT Math 670; ACT Composite 29, ACT English 29, ACT Math 28.

74.1% entering freshmen expected to graduate within 5 years. 52.8% of freshmen from Michigan. Freshmen from 50 states and 45 foreign countries.

Admission: Rolling admissions plan. For fall acceptance, apply as early as Sept. of previous year but not later than Aug. 1 of year of enrollment. *Requirements:* Either graduation from accredited secondary school with 15 units which must include one 3-unit sequence in English. Recommendation of educator. 4 additional units of mathematics recommended. Minimum 2.5 GPA. *Entrance tests:* College Board SAT or ACT. Additional requirements for foreign students. *For transfer students:* 2.5 minimum GPA; from 4-year accredited institution 94.5 semester hours maximum transfer credit; from 2-year accredited institution 70 hours; correspondence/extension students 9 hours.

College credit and advanced placement for postsecondary-level work completed in secondary school. Noncredit developmental/remedial courses offered during regular academic year.

Degree Requirements: 124 semester hours; 2.0 GPA; 2 terms in residence; 3 semester hours physical education; distribution requirements; 3 interim courses. Fulfillment of some degree requirements and exemption from some beginning courses possible by passing departmental examinations, College Board CLEP, APP. *Grading system:* A–F; withdraw (deadline after which pass-fail is appended to withdraw); incomplete (carries time limit); honors-pass-fail (for courses taken during interim).

Distinctive Educational Programs: *For undergraduates:* Honors programs. Off-Campus Study Programs in 30 locations both in the US. and abroad. Interdisciplinary courses in bilingual education, religion, science. Professional degree programs including accounting, engineering, nursing, recreation, fine arts, and social work. American Studies program (Washington, D.C.); AuSable Institute of Environmental Studies (AuSable, MI); Central College (France, Germany, Austria, Netherlands, Spain); Chicago Metropolitan Program; Latin American Studies Program (Costa Rica); Los Angeles Film Studies; Semester in Britain, China, Nigeria, or Spain.

Degrees Conferred: 952 *baccalaureate:* biological/life sciences 63; business/marketing 126; communications/communication technologies 25; computer and information sciences 29; education 81; engineering and engineering technologies 66; English 64; foreign languages and literature 61; interdisciplinary studies 29; mathematics 22; natural resources/environmental science 11 parks and recreation 27; philosophy/religion/theology 38; physical sciences 12; protective services/public administration 45; psychology 54; social sciences and history 89; visual and performing arts 59. *Master's:* education 6.

Fees and Other Expenses: *Full-time tuition per academic year 2005–06:* $18,925, undergraduate, $420 per credit hour for graduate study. *Room and board per academic year:* $6,585.

Financial Aid: Aid from institutionally generated funds is provided on the basis of academic merit, financial need, other criteria. Institution has a Program Participation Agreement with the U.S. Department of Education for eligible students to receive Pell Grants and other federal aid.

Financial aid to full-time, first-time undergraduate students: need-based scholarships/grants totaling $20,328,112, self-help $15,040,454, parent loans $259,406, tuition waivers $705,663; non-need-based scholarships/grants totaling $4,422,747; self-help $6,095,773, parent loans $779,521 tuition waivers $837,792.

Departments and Teaching Staff: *Total instructional faculty* 397 (full-time 307, part-time 90; women 135, men 262; members of minority groups 26). Total faculty with doctorate, first-professional, or other terminal degree: 266. Student-to-faculty ratio: 12:1. *Faculty development:* $2,160,000 in grants for research. 22 faculty members awarded sabbaticals 2004–05.

Enrollment: Total enrollment 4,180. Undergraduate full-time 1,791 / 2,161 women; part-time 94m / 81w; graduate full-time 1m, part-time 11m / 41w. *Transfer students:* in-state 131; from out-of-state 155.

Characteristics of Student Body: *Ethnic/racial makeup:* number of Black non-Hispanic: 48; American Indian or Alaska Native: 15; Asian or Pacific Islander: 18; Hispanic: 45; White non-Hispanic: 3,471; unknown: 100. *Age distribution:* number under 18: 10; 18–19: 1,493; 20–21: 1,776; 22–24: 665; 25–29: 41; 30–34: 10; 35–39: 3; 40–49: 6.

International Students: 330 nonresident aliens enrolled fall 2004. 11 students from Europe, 98 Asia, 13 Central and South America, 48 Africa, 175 Canada. Programs available to aid students whose native language is not English: social and cultural. English as a Second Language Program. Financial aid specifically designated for international students: variable number of scholarships awarded annually.

Student Life: On-campus residence halls house 58% of student body. Residence halls for men only constitute 45% of such space, for women only 55%. *Intercollegiate athletics:* men only: baseball, basketball, cross-country, golf, soccer, swimming, tennis, track; women only: basketball, cross-country, soccer, softball, swimming, tennis, track, volleyball. *Special regulations:* Registered cars permitted in designated areas. Quiet hours from 10:30pm to 6:30am daily. *Special services:* Learning Resources Center, medical services. *Student publications, radio: Chimes,* a weekly newspaper; *Dialogue,* a monthly literary magazine; *Prism,* a yearbook. Radio station WCAL (closed-circuit) broadcasts 25 hours per week. *Surrounding community:* Grand Rapids metropolitan population 650,000. Served by mass transit bus system; airport 5 miles from campus.

Library Collections: 760,493 volumes. Online catalog. Current serial subscriptions: 2,621 paper, 15,008 via electronic access. 22,109 recordings; 1,039 compact discs. Students have access to online services and the Internet. Total 2004–05 budget for books, periodicals, audiovisual materials, microforms: $1,105,875.

Most important special collections include John Calvin and Calvinism; the Reformation; Archives of the Christian Reformed Church.

Buildings and Grounds: Campus area 365 acres. *New buildings:* DeVos Communication Center completed 2002; Prince Conference Center 2002; Vincent and Helen Bunker Interpretive Center 2004.

Chief Executive Officer: Dr. Gaylen J. Byker, President.

Address admission inquiries to Dale Kuiper, Director of Admissions.

Calvin Theological Seminary

3233 Burton Street, S.E.
Grand Rapids, Michigan 49546-4387

Tel: (616) 957-6036   **E-mail:** admissions@calvinseminary.edu
Fax: (616) 957-8621   **Internet:** www.calvinseminary.edu

Institution Description: Calvin Theological Seminary is an institution of the Christian Reformed Church in North America. *Enrollment:* 304. *Degrees awarded:* Master's, first-professional, doctorate.

Accreditation: *Regional:* NCA. *National:* ATS. *Professional:* theology

History: Established 1876 as part of Calvin College.

Institutional Structure: Full-time instructional faculty 24.

Calendar: Quarters. Academic year Sept. to May. Degrees conferred and formal commencement May. Summer session May to Aug.

Admission: *Requirements:* Student should meet all regular college requirements for a bachelor's degree as well as the specific course requirements of the seminary for the specific programs; GPA of 2.67 or higher.

Degree Requirements: *For master of divinity degree:* 139 quarter hours. *For master of arts in educational ministry:* 88 quarter hours. *For master of arts in missions and church growth:* 87 quarter hours. *For master of theological studies:* 94 quarter hours. *Grading system:* A–F; incomplete; withdrawal.

Distinctive Educational Programs: *Other distinctive programs:* Master of Theology (generally considered to be a post-Master of Divinity program); Doctor of Philosophy program.

Degrees Conferred: 33 *master's:* theology; 3 *doctorate:* theology; 25 *first-professional:* master of divinity.

Fees and Other Expenses: *Tuition per academic year 2004–05:* Contact the seminary for current information regarding tuition, fees, and housing.

Financial Aid: Aid from institutionally generated funds is provided on the basis of academic merit, financial need. Institution has a Program Participation Agreement with the U.S. Department of Education for eligible students to receive Pell Grants and other federal aid.

Departments and Teaching Staff: Theology *professors* 10, *associate professors* 5, *assistant professors* 3, *instructors* 6.
Total instructional faculty: 24. Degrees held by full-time faculty: doctorate 90%.

Enrollment: Total full-time enrollment 304 (79.9% men, 20.1% women).

Characteristics of Student Body: *Ethnic/racial makeup:* Black non-Hispanic: 1.6%; Asian or Pacific Islander: 3.6%; Hispanic: .7%; White non-Hispanic: 54.6%.

International Students: 90 nonresident aliens enrolled fall 2004.

Student Life: *See:* Calvin College, Grand Rapids, Michigan.

Library Collections: Calvin College library houses 385,000 volumes. 2,475 periodicals.

Most important special holdings include Calvin Research Collection; Calvin Rare Book Collection; H. Henry Meeter Center for Calvin Studies.

Buildings and Grounds: Campus area 165 acres. The Seminary shares the campus of Calvin College.

Chief Executive Officer: Dr. Cornelius A. Plantinga, Jr., President.

Address admission inquiries to the Registrar.

Central Michigan University

106 Warriner Hall
Mount Pleasant, Michigan 48859

Tel: (989) 774-4000   **E-mail:** cmuadmit@cmich.edu
Fax: (989) 774-7267   **Internet:** www.cmich.edu

Institution Description: Central Michigan University is a state institution. *Enrollment:* 27.883. *Degrees awarded:* Baccalaureate, master's, doctorate. Certificates also awarded.

Academic offerings subject to approval by statewide coordinating bodies. Budget subject to approval by state governing boards.

Accreditation: *Regional:* NCA. *Professional:* accounting, athletic training, business, chemistry, clinical psychology, dietetics, journalism, music, physical therapy, physician assisting, recreation and leisure services, social work, speech-language pathology, teacher education

History: Established and incorporated as Center Michigan Normal School and Business Institute, and offered first instruction at postsecondary level 1892; changed name to Central Michigan Normal School 1895; awarded first degree (baccalaureate) 1919; changed name to Central State Teachers College 1927, to

Central Michigan College of Education 1941, to Central Michigan College 1955; adopted present name 1959.

Institutional Structure: *Governing board:* Central Michigan University Board of Trustees. Extrainstitutional representation: 8 trustees (appointed by governor of Michigan); institutional representation: president of the university, vice president for business and finance. 2 ex officio. 8 voting. *Composition of institution:* Administrators 64 men / 63 women. Academic affairs headed by provost. Management/business/finances directed by vice president for finance and administrative services. Full-time instructional faculty 692. Academic governance body, Academic Senate, meets an average of 20 times per year. *Faculty representation:* Faculty served by collective bargaining agent affiliated with NEA.

Calendar: Semesters. Academic year Aug. to May. Freshmen admitted Aug., Jan., June. Degrees conferred May, Aug., Dec. Formal commencement May, Dec. Summer session from mid-May to late July.

Characteristics of Freshmen: 74% of applicants admitted. 37% of applicants admitted and enrolled.

4.7% (75 students) submitted SAT scores; 95.9% (3,586 students) submitted ACT scores. *25th percentile:* SAT Verbal 470, SAT Math 460; ACT Composite 19. *75th percentile:* SAT Verbal 580, SAT Math 590; ACT Composite 24.

46% of entering freshmen expected to graduate within 5 years. 97% of freshmen from Michigan. Freshmen from 24 states and 22 foreign countries.

Admission: Rolling admissions plan. For fall acceptance, apply as early as 1 year, but not later than 4 months prior to enrollment. Early acceptance available. *Requirements:* Either graduation from accredited secondary school with 4 units in English, 2 foreign language, 4 mathematics, 3 science, 1 or 2 social studies; or GED. *Entrance tests:* ACT Composite required; SAT accepted. For foreign students TOEFL. *For transfer students:* 2.0 minimum GPA; from 4-year accredited institution no maximum on transfer credit; from 2-year accredited institution 62 hours.

College credit for postsecondary-level work completed in secondary school. Tutoring available. Developmental courses offered during regular academic year; credit given.

Degree Requirements: 124 credit hours; 2.0 GPA; 30 hours, including last 10, in residence; demonstrated proficiency in writing, mathematics, oral communications; general education requirements.

Fulfillment of some degree requirements and exemption from some beginning courses possible by passing departmental examinations, College Board CLEP, AP, and credit for experiential learning. *Grading system:* A–E; credit-no credit; withdraw (carries time limit).

Distinctive Educational Programs: Off-campus center in Midland, 25 miles away from main institution. Evening classes. Special facilities for using telecommunications in the classroom. Interdepartmental/interdisciplinary programs include international study, humanities, and women's studies. Preprofessional programs in dentistry, engineering, forestry, medicine, nursing, occupational therapy, optometry, osteopathy, pharmacy, physical therapy, veterinary medicine. Study abroad in England, The Netherlands; other countries by individual arrangement. Double majors. Special services and facilities for handicapped students. Minority Student Development Office sponsors social and cultural programs. *Other distinctive programs:* School of Continuing Education credit; noncredit courses also available. Institute for Personal and Career Development offers individualized external degree and nondegree programs in 15 states and 2 foreign countries.

ROTC: Army.

Degrees Conferred: 3,549 *baccalaureate* (B); 2,616 *master's:* 53 *doctorate:* architecture 24 (B); biological/life sciences 76 (B), 12 (M); business/marketing 973 (B), 220 (M); communications/communication technologies 185 (B), 6 (M); computer and information sciences 67 (B), 36 (M); education 402 (B), 656 (M), 9 (D); engineering and engineering technologies 153 (B), 10 (M); English 160 (B), 19 (D); foreign languages and literature 24 (B), 16 (M); health professions and related sciences 244 (B), 390 (M), 35 (D); home economics and vocational home economics 145 (B), 2 (M); interdisciplinary studies 6 (B); liberal arts/general studies 42 (M); mathematics 61 (B), 4 (M); natural resources/environmental science 30 (B); parks and recreation 145 (B), 6 (M); philosophy/religion/theology 22 (B); physical sciences 69 (B), 3 (M); protective services/public administration 179 (B), 97 (M); psychology 169 (B), 22 (M), 9 (D); social sciences and history 317 (B), 34 (M); visual and performing arts 98 (B), 21 (M). *Honorary degrees awarded 2004–05:* Doctor of Commercial Science 3, Doctor of Public Service 2, Doctor of Journalism 1, Doctor of Humane Letters 1.

Fees and Other Expenses: *Full-time tuition per academic year 2004–05:* undergraduate resident $4,610, nonresident $11,712; graduate resident $3,702, nonresident $7,354. *Required fees:* $755. *Room and board per academic year:* $6,160.

Financial Aid: Aid from institutionally generated funds is provided on the basis of academic merit, financial need, athletic ability, other criteria.

Financial aid to full-time, first-time undergraduate students: need-based scholarships/grants totaling $16,971,207, self-help $46,322,810, parent loans $1,874,569, tuition waivers $1,068,510, athletic awards $1,098,962; non-need-based scholarships/grants totaling $10,845,051, self-help $26,748,556; parent loans $7,116,645, tuition waivers $3,495,210, athletic awards $1,953,901.

Departments and Teaching Staff: *Professors* 250 *associate professors* 167. *assistant professors* 205, *instructors* 70, *part-time faculty* 370. *Total instructional faculty:* 1,062 (full-time 692, part-time 370; women 411, men 651; members of minority groups 134).Total faculty with doctorate, first-professional, or other terminal degree: 660. Student-to-faculty ratio: 23:1. *Faculty development:* $12,016,303 in grants for research. 41 faculty members awarded sabbaticals 2004–05.

Enrollment: Total enrollment 22,656. Undergraduate full-time 7,378 men / 10,122 women, part-time 1,032m / 1,394w; graduate full-time 771m / 2,282w, part-time 2,11m / 3,603w. *Transfer students:* in-state 727; from out-of-state 24.

Characteristics of Student Body: *Ethnic/racial makeup:* number of Black non-Hispanic: 1,239; American Indian or Alaska Native: 150; Asian or Pacific Islander: 242; Hispanic: 367; White non-Hispanic: 16,645; unknown: 1,125. *Age distribution:* number under 18: 2,697; 18–19: 3,393; 20–21: 6,213; 22–24: 4,626; 25–29: 1,007; 30–34: 571; 35–39: 457; 40–49: 703; 50–64: 235; 65 and over: 14.

International Students: 488 nonresident aliens enrolled fall 2004. 48 students from Europe, 280 Asia, 11 Central and South America, 58 Africa, 36 Canada, 1 New Zealand, 14 other. Programs available to aid students whose native language is not English: English as a Second Language Program. Financial aid available for qualifying international students. 29 scholarships for undergraduates were awarded in 2004–05 totaling $357,571.

Student Life: On-campus residence halls house 35% of student body. Residence halls for men constitute 10% of such space, for women 10%, for both sexes 80%. *Intercollegiate athletics:* men only: baseball, basketball, football, golf, gymnastics, soccer, swimming, tennis, track, wrestling; women only: basketball, field hockey, golf, gymnastics, softball, swimming, tennis, track, volleyball. *Special regulations:* Registered cars permitted on campus for all but freshmen; fee charged. *Special services:* Learning Resources Center, medical services. *Student publications, radio, television:* Central Michigan Life, a newspaper published 3 times per week; *Chippewa,* a yearbook; *Framework,* a quarterly creative arts magazine. Radio stations WCHP, WRFX, and WMHM-FM each broadcast 168 hours per week. TV station MHTV broadcasts 7 hours per week. *Surrounding community:* Mt. Pleasant population 25,000. Lansing, 70 miles from campus, is nearest metropolitan area. Served by airport 50 miles from campus; passenger rail service 70 miles from campus.

Library Collections: 1,009,746 volumes. 1,131,437 microforms; 3,300 current periodicals. 23,400 audiovisual materials. Online catalog. 350 computer work stations. Students have access to online information retrieval services and the Internet. Total 2004–05 budget for materials and operations: $8.3 million.

Most important holdings include Lucille Clark Memorial Children's Library; Native American Collection; University Archives; Wilbert Wright Collection of Africana and Afro-Americana.

Buildings and Grounds: Campus area 854 acres. *New buildings:* Charles V. Park Library completed 2002; Campbell, Kesseler, Kalhavi Residence Halls 2003; Health Professions Building 2004.

Chief Executive Officer: Dr. Michael Rao,President.

Address admission inquiries to Betty Wagner, Director of Admissions; graduate inquiries to Judy Prince, Director of Graduate Admissions.

Cleary University

3601 Plymouth Road
Ann Arbor, Michigan 48105-2659
Tel: (734) 332-4477   **E-mail:** admissions@cleary.edu
Fax: (734) 332-4646   **Internet:** cleary.edu

Institution Description: Cleary University is a private, independent, nonprofit institution offering programs in business with campuses in Ann Arbor and Howell, Michigan. *Enrollment:* 623. *Degrees awarded:* Associate, baccalaureate., master's.

Accreditation: *Regional:* NCA.

History: Established and offered first instruction at postsecondary level 1883; awarded first degree (baccalaureate) 1885; chartered 1891; incorporated and adopted present name 1933.

Institutional Structure: *Governing board:* Cleary College Board of Trustees. Representation: 32 trustees (including 2 alumni). All voting. *Composition of institution:* Administrators 5 men / 5 women. Academic affairs headed by vice president for academic affairs. Management/business/finances directed by executive vice president. Full-time instructional faculty 26. Academic governance body, Department of Academic Affairs, meets an average of 6 times per year.

Calendar: Quarters. Academic year Sept. to June. Degrees conferred and formal commencement June. Summer session from late June to late Aug.

Characteristics of Freshmen: 16 applicants (6 men, 10 women). 56.3% of applicants admitted. 77.8% of admitted students enrolled full—time. 6 students submitted ACT scores;. *25th percentile:* ACT Composite 22, ACT English 19, ACT Math 22. *75th percentile:* ACT Composite 22, ACT English 19, ACT Math 22.

Admission: Rolling admissions plan. For fall acceptance, apply no later than 30 days prior to beginning of classes. Early acceptance available. *Requirements:* Either graduation from accredited secondary or GED. *For transfer students:* 2.0 minimum GPA; from 4-year accredited institution 135 credit hours maximum transfer credit; from 2-year accredited institution 90 hours; correspondence/ extension students 24 hours.

College credit for postsecondary-level work completed in secondary school and for extrainstitutional learning (life experience) on basis of ACE *2006 Guide to the Evaluation of Educational Experiences in the Armed Services;* portfolio and faculty assessments; personal interview. Developmental courses offered in summer session and regular academic year.

Degree Requirements: *For all associate degrees:* 90 credit hours; 2 quarters plus 24 hours in residence. *For all baccalaureate degrees:* 180 credit hours; 3 quarters plus 45 hours in residence. *For all undergraduate degrees:* 2.0 GPA.

Fulfillment of some degree requirements and exemption from some beginning courses possible by passing College Board CLEP. *Grading system:* A–F; pass-fail; withdraw (carries time limit).

Distinctive Educational Programs: Direct Degree Programs in management, quality management, marketing, finance, and management of information technology. Students entering with two years of college and three years of work experience complete their BBA in one year of accelerated study. Students not quite meeting entry requirements can enroll in Gateway program, six month preparation for the one-year BBA completion program.

Degrees Conferred: 43 *associate;* 311 *baccalaureate:* business/marketing 311.

Fees and Other Expenses: *Full-time tuition per academic year 2004–05:* $11,760. *Room and board per academic year:* $6,646.

Financial Aid: Institution has a Program Participation Agreement with the U.S. Department of Education for eligible students to receive Pell Grants and other federal aid.

Financial aid to full-time, first-time undergraduate students: 38% received federal grants averaging $2,173; 49% state/local grants averaging $1,584; 3% institutional grants; 74% received loans averaging $4,961.

Departments and Teaching Staff: *Total instructional faculty:* 111. 5% hold terminal degrees. Student-to-faculty ratio: 25:1.

Enrollment: Total enrollment 623. Undergraduate 582 (39.7% men, 60.3% women).

Characteristics of Student Body: *Ethnic/racial makeup:* Black non-Hispanic: 10.3%; American Indian or Native Alaskan: 1.2%; Asian or Pacific Islander: .9%; White non-Hispanic: 73.2%; unknown: 12%.

Student Life: Counseling and information services available.

Library Collections: 8,000 volumes. 175 audiovisual materials; 30 current periodical subscriptions. Students have access to online information retrieval services and the Internet.

Buildings and Grounds: Campus area 27 acres.

Chief Executive Officer: Thomas P. Sullivan, President and CEO.

Address admission inquiries to Carrie B. Bonofiglio, Director of Admissions.

College for Creative Studies

201 East Kirby
Detroit, Michigan 48202
Tel: (313) 664-7400   **E-mail:** info@ccscad.edu
Fax: (313) 8377   **Internet:** www.ccscad.edu

Institution Description: The College for Creative Studies educates visual artists and designers who understand the social, cultural, and international dimensions of the arts. Through community service, the college promotes appreciation of and participation in the visual arts and opens pathways of career opportunity to talented youth.

Accreditation: *Regional:* NCA. *National:* NASAD. *Professional:* art

History: The college was established in 1906.

Calendar: Semesters (4-4-1 plan). Academic year early Sept. to late May.

Characteristics of Freshmen: 426 applicants (273 men, 153 women). 49.1% of admitted students enrolled full-time.

83% of study body from Michigan. Students from 35 states and 18 foreign countries.

Admission: Rolling admissions plan. Graduation from an accredited secondary school or GED. Application deadline Aug. 1.

Degree Requirements: 128 hours; 2.0 GPA.

Degrees Conferred: 188 *baccalaureate:* visual and performing arts 153; communication, journalism, and related programs 35.

Fees and Other Expenses: *Full-time tuition per academic year 2004–05:* $21,379. *Books and supplies:* $2,000. *Room and board per academic year:* $5,500.

Financial Aid: Aid from institutionally generated funds is provided on the basis of academic merit, financial need, other criteria. Institution has a Program Participation Agreement with the U.S. Department of Education for eligible students to receive Pell Grants, and, depending upon the agreement, other federal aid.

Financial aid to full-time, first-time undergraduate students: 31% received federal grants averaging $3,362; 64% state/local grants averaging $1,492; 94% institutional grants averaging $4,280; 75% received loans averaging $2,934.

Departments and Teaching Staff: *Total instructional faculty:* 43. 78% of faculty hold terminal degrees. Student-to-faculty ratio: 24:1.

Enrollment: Total enrollment 1,265 (59.3% men, 40.7% women).

Characteristics of Student Body: *Ethnic/racial makeup:* Black non-Hispanic: 6.2%; American Indian or Alaska Native: .4%; Asian or Pacific Islander: 5.6%; Hispanic: 4.2%; White non-Hispanic: 67%; unknown: 11.2%.

International Students: 68 nonresident aliens enrolled fall 2004.

Student Life: 265 students can be accommodated in campus housing. No sports or fraternity/sorority activity.

Library Collections: 21,000 volumes. 100 periodical subscriptions. Students have access to online retrieval systems and the Internet.

Buildings and Grounds: Campus area 11 acres.

Chief Executive Officer: Richard L. Rogers, President.

Address admission inquiries to Director of Admissions.

Concordia University, Ann Arbor

4090 Geddes Road
Ann Arbor, Michigan 48105
Tel: (734) 995-7322   **E-mail:** admissions@cuaa.edu
Fax: (734) 995-4610   **Internet:** www.cuaa.edu

Institution Description: Concordia University, Ann Arbor (formerly Concordia College that was Concordia Lutheran Junior College until 1976) is a private institution affiliated with The Lutheran Church-Missouri Synod. *Enrollment:* 557. *Degrees awarded:* Associate, baccalaureate, master's.

Accreditation: *Regional:* NCA.

History: Established as Concordia Lutheran Junior College and chartered 1962; offered first instruction at postsecondary level 1963; awarded first degree (associate) 1965; awarded first baccalaureate degree 1978; first master's degree 2002. The present name was adopted 2001.

Institutional Structure: *Governing board:* Board of Regents. Extrainstitutional representation: 11 regents. All voting. *Composition of institution:* 4 vice presidents and 4 deans. Full-time instructional faculty 21 men / 15 women. Academic governance body, the faculty, meets an average of 6–8 times per year.

Calendar: Semesters. Academic year Sept. to May. Freshmen admitted Sept. and Jan. Degrees conferred once per month. Formal commencement May. 15-week semesters plus accelerated courses with varying calendars

Characteristics of Freshmen: 74% of applicants accepted. 32% of accepted applicants enrolled.

Mean ACT composite class score 21.8.

38% of entering freshmen expected to graduate within 5 years. 77% of freshmen from Michigan. Freshmen from 8 states and 1 foreign country.

Admission: Rolling admissions plan. For fall acceptance, apply after second semester of junior year of secondary school, but not later than Aug. of year of enrollment. *Requirements:* Either graduation from accredited secondary school or GFED; recommend 13 units including 3 English, 2 in a foreign language, 1 mathematics, 1 science, 1 social studies. *Entrance tests:* ACT Composite or SAT. *For transfer students:* From 4-year accredited institution 2.0 minimum GPA. from 2-year accredited institution 2.0 minimum GPA.

College credit and advanced placement for postsecondary-level work completed in secondary school. College credit for extrainstitutional learning on basis of ACE *2006 Guide to the Evaluation of Educational Experiences in the Armed Services* and faculty assessment. Tutoring available for all courses. Special services available for some students with special needs.

Degree Requirements: *For all associate degrees:* 60 credit hours. *For all baccalaureate degrees:* 128 credit hours. *For all degrees:* 2.0 GPA; 30 credits from Concordia with some specific requirements.

Fulfillment of some degree requirements and exemption from some beginning courses possible by passing departmental examinations, College Board CLEP and AP. *Grading system:* A–F; pass-fail; withdraw.

Distinctive Educational Programs: Internships. Interdisciplinary curriculum. Evening classes. Semester abroad in European cultural history at Oak Hill College, London. Study abroad through programs in Austria, England, Italy, Mexico, Spain. Visiting Student Program and distance learning courses in cooperation with nine other campuses of the Concordia University System.

Degrees Conferred: 125 *baccalaureate:* biological/life sciences 2; business/marketing 36; communications/communication technologies 5; education 26; English 2; health professions and related sciences 7; home economics 7; parks and recreation 4; philosophy/religion/theology 2; protective services/public administration 21; psychology 7; social sciences and history 2; trade and industry 1; visual and performing arts 3. *Master's:* business/marketing 20. *Honorary degrees awarded 2004–05:* Doctor of Laws 1, Doctor of Letters 1.

Fees and Other Expenses: *Full-time tuition per academic year 2004–05:* $17,595 undergraduate, $370 per credit hour for graduate study. *Room and board per academic year:* $6,745.

Financial Aid: Aid from institutionally generated funds is provided on the basis of academic merit, financial need, athletic ability.

Financial aid to full-time, first-time undergraduate students: need-based scholarships/grants totaling $2,708.043, self-help $1,778,501, parent loans $110,616, tuition waivers $49,916; athletic awards $605,923; non-need-based scholarships/grants totaling $387,468, self-help $813,881, parent loans $294,358, tuition waivers $77,106, athletic awards $171,926. *Graduate aid:* 9 students received $14,750 in federal and state-funded fellowships/grants (ranging from $1,000 to $2,000); 18 received $198,937 in federal and state-funded loans (ranging from $3,000 to $16,563).

Departments and Teaching Staff: *Professors* 12, *associate professors* 6, *assistant professors* 8, *part-time faculty* 76.

Total instructional faculty: 102 (full-time 26, part-time 76; women 52, men 50; members of minority groups 13). Total faculty with doctorate, first-professional, or other terminal degree: 31. Student-to-faculty ratio: 10:1. Degrees held by full-time faculty: doctorate 48%, master's 100%.

Enrollment: Total enrollment 557. Undergraduate full-time 208 men / 269 women, part-time 25m / 28w; graduate full-time 10m / 16w, part-time 1w.

Characteristics of Student Body: *Ethnic/racial makeup:* number of Black non-Hispanic: 54; American Indian or Alaska Native: 8; Asian or Pacific Islander: 5; Hispanic: 14; White non-Hispanic: 446. *Age distribution:* number under 18: 13; 18–19: 182; 20–21: 135; 22–24: 56; 25–29: 30; 30–34: 21; 35–39: 32; 40–49: 42; 50–64: 18.

International Students: 3 nonresident aliens enrolled fall 2004. 1 student from Europe, 2 Canada. Programs available to aid students whose native language is not English: social, cultural. No financial aid specifically designated for international students.

Student Life: On-campus residence halls house 56% of traditional students. Residence halls for men constitute 40% of such space, for women 60%. Housing available for married students. *Intercollegiate athletics:* men baseball, basketball, cross-country, golf, soccer, women: basketball, cross-county, golf, soccer, softball, volleyball. *Special regulations:* Cars permitted for $30 fee. *Special services:* Medical services; van service to Ann Arbor and to University of Michigan campus. *Student publications:* irregularly published newspaper. *Surrounding community:* Ann Arbor population 110,000. Detroit, 35 miles from campus, is nearest metropolitan area. Served by airport 20 miles from campus; passenger rail service 3 miles from campus.

Library Collections: 120,000 volumes. 300,000 microforms. 10,500 audiovisual titles; 3,950 current periodical subscriptions. Online catalog. 65 computer work stations. Students have access to online information retrieval services and the Internet.

Most important special collections include Religion (22,000 titles); Language and Literature (22,000 titles); Periodicals in Microfilm (1,638 titles).

Buildings and Grounds: Campus area 200 acres.

Chief Executive Officer: Rev. Dr. Thomas A. Ahlersmeyer, President.

Address admission inquiries Gary Newman, Director of Admissions.

Cornerstone University

1001 East Beltline N.E.
Grand Rapids, Michigan 49525-5897

Tel: (616) 949-5300   **E-mail:** admissions@cornerstone.edu
Fax: (616) 222-1540   **Internet:** www.cornerstone.edu

Institution Description: Cornerstone University, formerly Cornerstone College, is a private, independent, nonprofit institution. *Enrollment:* 2,412. *Degrees*

awarded: Associate, baccalaureate, first-professional (master of divinity), master's, doctorate.

Accreditation: *Regional: NCA.*

History: Established as Baptist Bible Institute of Grand Rapids, chartered, incorporated, and offered first instruction at postsecondary level 1941; changed name to Grand Rapids Baptist Theological Seminary and Bible Institute 1947; awarded first degree (first-professional) 1950; changed name to Grand Rapids Baptist Bible College and Seminary 1963; adopted present name 1972.

Institutional Structure: *Governing board:* Board of Trustees. Extrainstitutional representation: 34 trustees; institutional representation: president of the college. 1 ex officio. 34 voting. *Composition of institution:* Administrators 5 men. Academic affairs headed by academic dean. Management/business/finances directed by business manager and director of business affairs. Full-time instructional faculty 56. Academic governance body, Educational Policy Committee, meets an average of 9 times per year.

Calendar: Semesters. Academic year Aug. to May. Freshmen admitted Aug., Jan. Degrees conferred May, Dec. Formal commencement May. Summer session of 2 terms in College, 5 terms in Seminary from May to Aug.

Characteristics of Freshmen: 1,418 applicants (551 men, 867 women). 70.6% of applicants accepted. 27.85 of admitted students enrolled full-time.

3% (30 students) submitted SAT scores; 97% (248 students) submitted ACT scores. *25th percentile:* SAT I Verbal 500, SAT I Math 510; ACT Composite 20. *75th percentile:* SAT I Verbal 610, SAT I Math 630; ACT Composite 26.

79% of undergraduates from Michigan. Undergraduates from 27 states and 9 foreign countries.

Admission: Rolling admissions plan. Early acceptance available. *Requirements:* Graduation from accredited secondary school or GED. Recommend 4 units in English, 3 mathematics, 2 science, academic electives. Minimum 2.25 GPA. *Entrance tests:* ACT. *For transfer students:* 2.0 minimum GPA; college credit given to transfers from accredited institutions, including correspondence courses. Credit given on basis of ACE *2006 Guide to the Evaluation of Educational Experiences in the Armed Services.*

College credit and placement for CLEP subject exams and Advanced Placement Tests. Learning Centre offers tutoring and remedial coursework.

Degree Requirements: *For all associate degrees:* 64 credit hours; 32 hours in residence including final semester. *For all bachelor of arts degrees:* 129 credit hours; 32 hours including final semester in residence; 12 hours of major must be taken in residence. *For all bachelor of science degrees:* 120 credit hours; 32 hours including final semester in residence; 12 hours of major must be taken in residence. *For all undergraduate degrees:* 2.0 GPA; 2.5 GPA in major; chapel attendance; general education requirements; student ministry.

Grading system: A–F; pass-fail; withdraw (carries time limit).

Distinctive Educational Programs: Required internships in most majors. State certified elementary and secondary education programs. Institutional European and Middle East Study Abroad programs. International and domestic study programs through Christian College Coalition. Environmental studies at Au Sable Trails Environmental Institute; also institutionally sponsored study at varying locations. Military science minor through Army ROTC at Western Michigan University. Summer School. Some evening programs.

ROTC: Army in conjunction with Western Michigan University.

Degrees Conferred: 11 *associate;* 371 *baccalaureate;* 73 *master's.* Bachelor's degrees awarded in top five disciplines: business, management, marketing, and related support services 175; education 78; theology and ministerial studies 22; communication, journalism, and related programs 15. *First-professional:* theology 13.

Fees and Other Expenses: *Full-time tuition per academic year 2004–05:* $14,700. *Books and supplies:* $950. *Room and board per academic year:* $5,520.

Financial Aid: Aid from institutionally generated funds is provided on the basis of academic merit, financial need, athletic ability. Institution has a Program Participation Agreement with the U.S. Department of Education for eligible students to receive Pell Grants and, depending upon the agreement, other federal aid.

Financial aid to full-time, first-time undergraduate students: 31% received federal grants averaging $2,693; 69% state/local grants averaging $2,503; 92% institutional grants averaging $4,035; 74% received loans averaging $6,393.

Departments and Teaching Staff: *Professors* 12, *associate professors* 20, *assistant professors* 12, *instructors* 3.

Total instructional faculty: 56. Student-to-faculty ratio: 15:1. Degrees held by full-time faculty: doctorate 52%, master's 36%, baccalaureate 3%, professional 9%. 60% hold terminal degrees.

Enrollment: Total enrollment 2,412. Undergraduate 2,085 (38.1% men, 61.9% women).

Characteristics of Student Body: *Ethnic/racial makeup:* Black non-Hispanic: 18.6%; American Indian or Alaska Native: .4%; Asian or Pacific Islander: 1.1%; Hispanic: 2%; White non-Hispanic: 77.1%. *Age distribution:* 17–21:

81%; 22–24: 14%; 25–29: 2%; 30–34: 1%; 35–39: 1%; 40–49: 1%; 50–59: 1%; 60–and over: 1%.

International Students: 21 nonresident aliens enrolled fall 2004. Students from Europe, Asia, Central and South America, Canada. No programs available to aid students whose native language is not English. Financial aid specifically designated for international students: unlimited scholarships available annually to qualifying students.

Student Life: On-campus residence halls house 60% of student body. Residence halls for men only constitute 40% of such space, for women only 60%. *Intercollegiate athletics:* men only: basketball, golf, soccer, tennis; women only: basketball, softball, volleyball; co-ed: cross-country, track and field. *Special regulations:* Cars permitted without restrictions. Dress must be neat and in accordance with Christian modesty. Curfews and quiet hours. *Special services:* Learning Centre, medical services. *Student publications, radio:* A newspaper published weekly; a yearbook. Radio station WCSG broadcasts 168 hours weekly. *Surrounding community:* Grand Rapids area population 600,000. Served by mass transit bus system; airport 5 miles from campus.

Library Collections: 125,000 volumes. 282,751 microforms; 7,396 audiovisual materials; 866 current periodical subscriptions. Online catalog. Students have access to online information retrieval services and the Internet.

Most important special collections include the Baptist Collection; personal papers of R. Ketcham; Leon Wood Archives.

Buildings and Grounds: Campus area 132 acres.

Chief Executive Officer: Dr. Rex M. Rogers, President.

Address admission inquiries to Brent Rudin, Director of Enrollment Management.

Davenport University

415 East Fulton
Grand Rapids, Michigan 49503-4498
Tel: (616) 451-3511   **E-mail:** admissions@davenport.edu
Fax: (616) 732-1167   **Internet:** www.davenport.edu

Institution Description: Davenport University, formerly Davenport College, is a private, independent, nonprofit college with branch campuses in Alma, Holland, Kalamzaoo, Lansing, Battle Creek, Michigan and Merrillville and South Bend/Mishawka, Indiana. *Enrollment:* 13,124 (all campuses). *Degrees awarded:* Associate, baccalaureate.

Accreditation: *Regional:* NCA. *Professional:* health information administration, medical assisting, physical therapy

History: Davenport University and its antecedents have a history dating back to 1866. In 1997, Davenport Educational System, Inc., was establish for the overall management and strategy of the total system.

Institutional Structure: *Governing board:* Davenport University Board of Trustees. *Extrainstitutional representation:* 23 trustees. *Institutional representation:* president of the college. All voting. *Composition of institution:* Administrators 17 men / 11 women. Academic affairs headed by vice president for academic affairs. Management/business/finances directed by vice president for administrative and business affairs. Full-time instructional faculty 20 men / 17 women. Academic governance body, Academic Council.

Calendar: Quarters. Academic year Sept. to June. Freshmen admitted Sept., Jan., Mar., June. Degrees conferred Dec., Mar., June, Aug. Formal commencement June. Summer session from mid-June to mid-Aug.

Characteristics of Freshmen: 100% of applicants accepted. 51% of accepted applicants enrolled.

Mean ACT Composite score 18.7.

40% of entering freshmen expected to graduate within 5 years. 99% of freshmen from Michigan.

Admission: Rolling admissions; open enrollment. *Requirements:* High school graduation or GED. Tutoring available. Developmental courses offered during academic year; credit given.

Degree Requirements: *For associate degree:* 90 credit hours. *For baccalaureate degree:* 184.5 credit hours. *For MBA degree:* 54 credit hours. Residency requirements vary with program. Associate and baccalaureate degrees require 2.0 GPA in major field and 2.0 cumulative GPA. MBA requires 3.00 cumulative GPA.

Fulfillment of some degree requirements and exemption from some beginning courses possible by passing departmental examinations and College Board CLEP. *Grading system:* A–D, no credit; incomplete (carries time limit); credit-no credit.

Distinctive Educational Programs: Evening and weekend classes; numerous off-site classrooms; business and industry classroom sites; Adult Accelerated Career Education (AACE); prior learning credit; cooperative education and

internships; study abroad through American Institute of Foreign Studies; lifetime job placement assistance to all graduates.

Degrees Conferred: 515 *certificate/diploma;* 813 *associate;* 1,172 *baccalaureate;* 168 *master's.* Bachelor's degrees awarded in top five disciplines: business, management, marketing, and related support services business 884; computer and information sciences and support services 148; health professions and related clinical sciences 72; legal professions and studies 16; multi/interdisciplinary studies 9.

Fees and Other Expenses: *Full-time tuition per academic year 2004–05:* $8,576. Contact the university for current graduate costs which vary by program. *Room and board per academic year:* $3,400.

Financial Aid: Aid from institutionally generated funds is provided on the basis of academic merit, financial need.Institution has a Program Participation Agreement with the U.S. Department of Education for eligible students to receive Pell Grants and other federal aid.

Financial aid to full-time, first-time undergraduate students: need-based scholarships/grants totaling $32,702,936, self-help $51,975,949, parent loans $729,826; non-need-based scholarships/grants totaling $330,876, self-help $353,214, athletic awards $62,737.

Departments and Teaching Staff: *Total instructional faculty:* 1,082 (full-time 129, part-time 953; women 556, men 526; members of minority groups 127). Total faculty with doctorate, first-professional, or other terminal degree: 88. Student-to-faculty ratio: 16:1. Degrees held by full-time faculty: doctorate 32%, master's 54%, baccalaureate 8%.

Enrollment: *Total enrollment* 13,134. Undergraduate full-time 1,031 men / 2,322 women, part-time 2,025m / 6,945w; graduate full-time 214m / 371w, part-time 83m / 123w.

Characteristics of Student Body: *Ethnic/racial makeup:* number of Black non-Hispanic: 3,023; American Indian or Alaska Native: 52; Asian or Pacific Islander: 200; Hispanic: 451; White non-Hispanic: 7,045; unknown: 1,516.

International Students: 36 nonresident aliens enrolled fall 2004. Programs available to aid students whose native language is not English: English as a Second Language Program. No financial aid specifically for international students.

Student Life: On-campus housing available. Cars with decals permitted on campus in designated areas. Student business-related organizations both co-curricular and extra-curricular. Grand Rapids metropolitan area population 600,000.

Library Collections: 127,500 volumes. 500 government documents; 44,000 microforms; 1,915 current periodical subscriptions. Online catalog. 13,500 audiovisual materials. Computer work stations available. Students have access to online information retrieval services and the Internet.

Special holdings include marketing, business periodicals, and annual reports.

Chief Executive Officer: Dr. Randolph K. Flechsig, President.

Address admission inquiries to Director of Admissions.

Eastern Michigan University

Ypsilanti, Michigan 48197
Tel: (734) 487-1849   **E-mail:** admissions@emich.edu
Fax: (734) 481-1095   **Internet:** www.emich.edu

Institution Description: Eastern Michigan University is a state institution. *Enrollment:* 23,593. *Degrees awarded:* Baccalaureate, master's, doctorate. Specialist certificates also awarded.

Accreditation: *Regional:* NCA. *Professional:* athletic training, aviation technology, business, clinical lab scientist, construction education, counseling, dietetics, industrial technology, interior design, manufacturing technology, music, nursing, nursing education, occupational therapy, planning, public administration, recreation and leisure services, social work, speech-language pathology, teacher education

History: Established as Michigan State Normal School 1849; offered first instruction at postsecondary level 1851; awarded first degree (baccalaureate) 1890; changed name to Michigan State Normal College 1899, Eastern Michigan College 1956; adopted present name 1959. *See* Egbert R. Isbell, *A History of Eastern Michigan University 1849–1965* (Ypsilanti: Eastern Michigan University Press, 1971) for further information.

Institutional Structure: *Governing board:* Board of Regents. Representation: 8 regents. All voting. *Composition of institution:* Administrators 143 men / 91 women (including coaches). Academic affairs headed by provost and vice president for academic affairs. Management/business/finances directed by vice president for business and finance and treasurer to the board. Full-time instructional faculty 767. Academic governance body, Dean's Advisory Council, meets an average of 15 times per year. *Faculty representation:* Faculty served by collective bargaining agent, affiliated with AAUP.

Calendar: Semesters. Academic year Sept. to April. Freshmen admitted Sept., Jan., Apr., June. Degrees conferred Apr., June, Aug., Dec. Formal commencement Apr., Dec. Spring and summer sessions run May through Aug.

Characteristics of Freshmen: 78% of applicants admitted. 36% of applicants admitted and enrolled.

14% (328 students) submitted SAT scores; 94% (2,220 students) submitted ACT scores. *25th percentile*: SAT Verbal 440, SAT Math 440; ACT Composite 18, ACT English 17, ACT Math 17. *75th percentile*: SAT Verbal 570, SAT Math 570; ACT Composite 23, ACT English 23, ACT Math 23.

30% of entering freshmen expected to graduate within 5 years. 90% of freshmen from Michigan. Freshmen from 27 states and 11 foreign countries.

Admission: Rolling admissions plan. For fall acceptance, apply as early as completion of junior year of secondary school, but not later than Aug. 1 of year of enrollment. Admission decisions are made within 4 weeks of receipt of all required documents. *Requirements:* Either graduation from accredited secondary school or GED. Recommend 4 years in English, 3 sciences, 3 social studies, 2 mathematics. *Entrance tests:* College Board SAT or ACT composite. For foreign students TOEFL. *For transfer students:* 2.0 minimum GPA; 90 semester hours maximum transfer credit; correspondence/extension students 15 hours.

College Level Entrance Placement exams available with credit up to 15 hours. College credit and advanced placement for postsecondary-level work completed in secondary school. Credit for prior learning assessment also available. Tutoring available.

Degree Requirements: 124 semester hours; 2.0 GPA; 30 semester hours in residence; 2 semester hours physical education; basic studies courses. Additional requirements for some majors.

Fulfillment of some degree requirements and exemption from some beginning courses possible by passing departmental examinations, College Board CLEP, AP. *Grading system:* A–F; pass-fail; credit-no credit; withdraw (carries time limit); incomplete.

Distinctive Educational Programs: *For undergraduates:* Work-experience programs. Dual-degree program in forestry with University of Michigan. Interdisciplinary programs in labor studies, literature and drama for the young, religious studies, women's studies, languages and international trade. Preprofessional programs in architecture, dentistry, engineering, forestry, medicine, mortuary science, osteopathic medicine, pharmacy, religious careers. Honors programs. Individual majors. *Available to all students:* Flexible meeting places and schedules, including off-campus centers (at Jackson, 40 miles away; Flint, 60 miles away; Mayfield, 70 miles away), weekend and evening classes. Accelerated degree programs. Special facilities for using telecommunications in the classroom. Facilities and programs for independent research. Study abroad in Austria, Canada, Egypt, England, Estonia, France, Germany, Greece, Holland, Israel, Italy, Japan, The Netherlands, Poland, Russia, South Africa, Sweden, Mexico. *Other distinctive programs:* Continuing education. Institution for Community and Regional Development. Institute for the Study of Children and Families. Michigan Consumer Education Center.

ROTC: Army, Navy, Air Force in cooperation with University of Michigan, Ann Arbor. 3 Air Force, 14 Army, and 3 Navy commissions awarded 2004.

Degrees Conferred: 2,884 *baccalaureate* (B), 1,234 *master's* (M), 11 *doctorate* (D): area and ethnic studies9 (B); biological/life sciences 54 (B), 12 (M); business/marketing 560 (B), 330 (M); communications/communication technologies 107 (B); computer and information sciences 86 (B), 33 (M); education 770 (B), 362 (M), 11 (D); engineering and engineering technologies 69 (B), 52 (M); English 175 (B), 29 (M); foreign languages and literature 19 (B), 1 (M); health professions and related sciences 197 (B), 36 (M); home economics and vocational home economics 12 (M); interdisciplinary studies 73 (B), 83 (M); law/legal studies 18 (B); liberal arts/general studies 31 (M); mathematics 11 (B), 23 (M); parks and recreation 10 (B), 1 (M); philosophy/religion/theology 3 (B); physical sciences 29 (B), 7 (M); protective services/public administration 113 (B), 86 (M); psychology 136 (B), 42 (M); social sciences and history 264 (B), 43 (M); trade and industry 17 (B), 4 (M); visual and performing arts 153 (B), 26 (M).

Fees and Other Expenses: *Full-time tuition per academic year 2004–05:* undergraduate resident $4,707, nonresident $14,713; graduate resident $6,821, nonresident $13,808. *Fees:* program fees vary by program; other fees may apply. *Room and board per academic year:* $6,082.

Financial Aid: Aid from institutionally generated funds is provided on the basis of academic merit, athletic ability, financial need.

Financial aid to full-time, first-time undergraduate students: need-based scholarships/grants totaling $14,997,425, self-help $29,840,488; non-need-based scholarships/grants totaling $14,320,554, self-help $32,040,864, parent loans $7,864,676, tuition waivers $505,351, athletic awards $4,214,219. *Graduate aid:* 1,082 students received $12,985,870 in federal and state-funded fellowships/grants; 275 received $2,253,319 for college-assigned job (nonteaching, nonresearch); 433 other fellowships and grants totaling $481,189.

Departments and Teaching Staff: *Professors* 294, *associate professors* 149, *assistant professors* 180, *instructors* 8, *part-time faculty* 376.

Total instructional faculty: 1,11 (735 full-time, 376 part-time; women 568, men 543; members of minority groups 160). Total faculty with doctorate, first-professional, or other terminal degree: 510. Student-to-faculty ratio: 20:1. *Faculty development:* $6,167,719 in grants for research. 16 faculty members awarded sabbaticals 2004–05.

Enrollment: Total enrollment 23,593. Undergraduate full-time 5,145 men / 7,849 women, part-time 2,413m / 3,461w; graduate full-time 309m / 526w, part-time 1,324m / 2,566.

Characteristics of Student Body: *Ethnic/racial makeup:* number of Black non-Hispanic: 3,276; American Indian or Alaska Native: 104; Asian or Pacific Islander: 392; Hispanic: 405; White non-Hispanic: 13,294; unknown: 1,117. *Age distribution:* number under 18: 238; 18–19: 4,217; 20–21: 1,574; 22–24: 4,896; 25–29: 2,436; 30–34: 1,043; 35–39: 607; 40–49: 749; 50–64: 195; 65 and over: 16.

International Students: 742 nonresident aliens enrolled fall 2004. 67 students from Europe, 439 Asia, 29 Central and South Latin America, 26 Africa, 27 Canada, 1 Australia, 153 other. Programs available to aid students whose native language is not English: English as a Second Program. No financial aid specifically designated for international students.

Student Life: On-campus residence halls house 19% of student body. Some students housed on campus in apartments. Housing available for married students. *Intercollegiate athletics:* men only: baseball, basketball, football, golf, gymnastics, hockey, soccer, swimming, tennis, track; women only: basketball, field hockey, gymnastics, softball, swimming, tennis, track, volleyball. *Special regulations:* Cars permitted in designated areas. *Special services:* Learning Resources Center, medical services, evening van service. *Student publications, radio: Eastern Echo*, a newspaper published 3 times per week; *Spectrum*, a biannual magazine. Radio station WEMU broadcasts 24 hours per week. *Surrounding community:* Ypsilanti population 25,000. Detroit, 35 miles from campus, is nearest metropolitan area. Served by mass transit bus system; airport 20 miles from campus; passenger rail service 10 miles from campus.

Publications: *Journal of Narrative Technique* (triennially) first published 1971.

Library Collections: 964,929 volumes including bound books, serial backfiles, electronic documents, and government documents not in separate collections. Online catalog. Current serial subscriptions: 3,700 paper, 751 microform, 13,919 via electronic access. 1,337 recordings; 3,819 compact discs. 400 computer work stations. Students have access to the Internet at no charge.

Most important special holdings include education monograph collection; children's literature collection; African American monographs.

Buildings and Grounds: Campus area 275 acres. *New buildings:* College of Health Human Services Building; University House.

Chief Executive Officer: Dr. Craig D. Willis, President.

Address admission inquiries to Judy Benfield Tatum, Director of Admissions.

Ferris State University

901 South State Street
Big Rapids, Michigan 49307
Tel: (231) 591-2000   **E-mail:** admissions@ferris.edu
Fax: (231) 591-3944   **Internet:** www.ferris.edu

Institution Description: Ferris State University, formerly Ferris State College, is a state institution. *Enrollment:* 11,803. *Degrees awarded:* Associate, baccalaureate, master's, first-professional (optometry, pharmacy). Certificates also awarded.

Academic offerings subject to approval by statewide coordinating bodies.

Accreditation: *Regional:* NCA. *Professional:* clinical lab scientist, construction education, dental hygiene, engineering technology, environmental health, health information technician, nuclear medicine technology, nursing, pharmacy, radiography, recreation and leisure services, respiratory therapy, social work

History: Established as Big Rapids Industrial School, chartered, incorporated, and offered first instruction at postsecondary level 1884; changed name to Ferris Industrial School 1885, to Ferris Institute 1899; awarded first degree (baccalaureate) 1910; became Ferris State College 1963; adopted present name 1987.

Institutional Structure: *Governing board:* Board of Trustees. Extrainstitutional representation: 7 trustees. All voting. *Composition of institution:* Academic affairs headed by vice president for academic affairs. Management/business/finances directed by vice president for business affairs. Total instructional faculty 818. Academic governance body, Representative Faculty Advisory Council, meets an average of 9 times per year. *Faculty representation:* Faculty served by collective bargaining agent, Ferris Faculty Association, affiliated with NEA.

Calendar: Semesters. Academic year Aug. to May.

Characteristics of Freshmen: 49% of applicants admitted. 18% of applicants admitted and enrolled.

91.4% (1,893 students) submitted ACT scores. *25th percentile*: ACT Composite 18, ACT English 16, ACT Math 17. *75th percentile*: ACT Composite 23, ACT English 22, ACT Math 24.

39% of entering freshmen expected to graduate within 5 years. 92% of freshmen from Michigan. Freshmen from 22 states and 17 foreign countries.

Admission: Rolling admissions plan. For fall acceptance, apply up to Aug. 5 for fall admission. Early acceptance available. *Requirements:* Either graduation from accredited secondary school or GED. Minimum 2.35 GPA. *For transfer students:* 2.0 minimum GPA; 3 years maximum transfer credit.

Tutoring available. Developmental courses offered in summer session and regular academic year; credit given.

Degree Requirements: *Associate degrees:* 63 semester hours; 2 years in residence. *Baccalaureate degrees:* 124 semester hours; final year in residence. *Undergraduate degrees:* 2.0 GPA; general education requirements. *Grading system:* A–F; high pass-pass-fail; pass-fail; withdraw (carries time limit).

Distinctive Educational Programs: Work-experience programs, including field experience, internships. Evening classes. External degree programs in allied health/ Facilities and programs for independent research, including honors programs, individual majors, tutorials. *Other distinctive programs:* Professional tennis management.

Degrees Conferred: 1,425 *baccalaureate* (B), 148 *master's* (M): biological/life sciences 31 (B); business/marketing 310 (B), 2 (M); communications/communication technologies 45 (B); computer and information sciences 75 (B), 58 (M); education 122 (B), 60 (M); engineering and engineering technologies 264 (B); English 24 (B); health professions and related sciences 136 (B); mathematics 11 (B); parks and recreation 9 (B); physical sciences 1 (B); protective services/public administration 128 (B), 23 (M); psychology 10 (B); social sciences and history 2 (B); trade and industry 24 (B); visual and performing arts 173 (B), 5 (M). 121 *first-professional:* optometry 32; pharmacy 89.

Fees and Other Expenses: *Full-time tuition per academic year 2004–05:* undergraduate resident $6,190, nonresident $12,380; resident graduate $316 per credit hour, nonresident $632 per credit hour. *Required fees:* $142. *Room and board per academic year:* $6,522.

Financial Aid: Aid from institutionally generated funds is provided on the basis of academic merit, financial need, other criteria.

Financial aid to full-time, first-time undergraduate students: need-based scholarships/grants totaling $13,303,634, self-help $26,990,470; non-need-based scholarships/grants totaling $7,904,281, self-help $20,857,826, parent loans $3,993,980, tuition waivers $979,802, athletic awards $1,315,012.

Departments and Teaching Staff: *Total instructional faculty:* 818 (full-time 521, part-time 297; women 334, men 484; members of minority groups 56). Total faculty with doctorate, first-professional, or other terminal degree: 257. Student-to-faculty ratio: 15:1. *Faculty development:* $143,000 in grants for research. 8 faculty members awarded sabbaticals 2004–05. Degrees held by full-time faculty: doctorate 39%, master's 52%, baccalaureate 9%.

Enrollment: Total enrollment 11,803. Undergraduate full-time 4,670 men / 3,800 women, part-time 1,037m / 3,800w; first-professional full-time 200m / 47w, part-time 2m / 8w; graduate full-time 67m / 63w, part-time 147m / 228w.

Characteristics of Student Body: *Ethnic/racial makeup:* number of Black non-Hispanic: 155; American Indian or Alaska Native: 98; Asian or Pacific Islander: 203; Hispanic: 150; White non-Hispanic: 9,156; unknown: 1,202. *Age distribution:* number under 18: 146; 18–19: 1,191; 20–21: 1,939, 22–24: 2,283; 25–29: 844; 30–34: 422; 35–39: 306; 40–49: 431; 50–64: 136.

International Students: 240 nonresident aliens enrolled fall 2004. Programs available to aid students whose native language is not English: social, cultural. English as a Second Language program. No financial aid specifically designated for international students.

Student Life: On-campus residence halls house 38% of student body. 4% of men join fraternities; 4% of women join sororities. Intercollegiate athletics, intramural and club sports: cross-country, football, golf, handball, ice hockey, lacrosse, racquetball, rugby, skiing, soccer, softball, swimming, table tennis, tennis, track and field, volleyball, water polo, weightlifting. *Special services:* Academic Skills Center, medical services. *Student publications, radio:* Torch, a newspaper. *Surrounding community:* Big Rapids population 15,000. Grand Rapids, 50 miles from campus, is nearest metropolitan area. Served by airport 3 miles from campus.

Library Collections: 344,496 volumes. Online catalog. 1,002 periodicals. 139 computer work stations. Students have access to online information retrieval services and the Internet.

Most important special collections include Michigan Regional and Local Studies Collection; Woodbridge N. Ferris Collection; government documents: Michigan, federal, patents, trademarks.

Buildings and Grounds: Campus area 810 acres. *New buildings:* Ferris Library for Information Technology and Education completed 2001.

Chief Executive Officer: Dr. David L. Eisler, President.

Address admission inquiries to Craig Westman, Director of Admissions.

Grace Bible College

1011 Aldon Street, S.W.
P.O. Box 910
Grand Rapids, Michigan 49509-0190

Tel: (616) 538-2330   **E-mail:** kgilliam@gbcol.edu
Fax: (616) 538-0599   **Internet:** www.gbcol.edu

Institution Description: Grace Bible College is a private institution of the Grace Gospel Fellowship. *Enrollment:* 172. *Degrees awarded:* Associate, baccalaureate.

Accreditation: *Regional:* NCA. *National:* ABHE.

Calendar: Semesters. Academic year Aug. to May.

Characteristics of Freshmen: 57% of applicants admitted. 27% of applicants admitted and enrolled. 13% (5 students) submitted SAT scores; 87% (40 students) submitted ACT scores. *25th percentile*: SAT Verbal 400, SAT Math 420; ACT Composite 18, ACT English 17, ACT Math 17. *75th percentile*: SAT Verbal 660, SAT Math 640; ACT Composite 24, ACT English 23, ACT Math 22.

40% of entering freshmen expected to graduate within 5 years. 82% of freshmen from Michigan. Freshmen from 6 states.

Admission: High school graduation with prescribed distribution requirements. TOEFL required for international students. Credit given for CLEP subject exams and advanced placement tests.

Degree Requirements: Completion of prescribed curriculum.

Distinctive Educational Programs: Bachelor of Christian Music Industry. Dual degree in business with Davenport College and in education with Cornerstone University.

Degrees Conferred: 27 *baccalaureate*: education 6; interdisciplinary studies 4; philosophy/religion/theology 7; protective services/public administration 3; visual and performing arts 7.

Fees and Other Expenses: *Full-time tuition per academic year 2004–05:* $9,950. *Required fees:* $470. *Room and board per academic year:* $6,490.

Financial Aid: Aid from institutionally generated funds is provided on the basis of academic merit, financial need.

Financial aid to full-time, first-time undergraduate students: need-based scholarships/grants totaling $471,619, self-help $372,443, parent loans $21,349, tuition waivers $47,819; non-need-based scholarships/grants totaling $56,837, self-help $119,410, parent loans $14,336, tuition waivers $11,765.

Departments and Teaching Staff: *Associate professors* 3, *assistant professors* 5, *part-time faculty* 33. *Total instructional faculty:* 41 (full-time 8, part-time 33; women 15, men 26; members of minority groups 2). Student-to-faculty ratio: 17:1. Degrees held by full-time instructional faculty: doctorate 14%, master's 86%. 30% hold terminal degrees.

Enrollment: Total enrollment 172. Undergraduate full-time 72 men / 85 women, part-time 10m / 5w; *Transfer students:* in-state 7; from out-of-state 5.

Characteristics of Student Body: *Ethnic/racial makeup:* number of Black non-Hispanic: 2; American Indian or Alaska Native: 1; Asian or Pacific Islander: 2; Hispanic: 1; White non-Hispanic: 164; unknown: 1. *Age distribution:* number 18–19: 59; 20–21: 57; 22–24: 41; 25–29: 5; 30–34: 4; 40–49: 6.

International Students: 1 nonresident alien from Africa enrolled fall 2004. No programs to aid students whose native language is not English. No financial aid specifically designated for international students.

Student Life: Opportunities are available for students to be involved in vocal and instrumental music, drama, intramural and intercollegiate athletics, and student leadership. Missions teams.

Publications: The college publishes *Journey* (quarterly) which contains articles of educational thought, college news, and alumni activities.

Library Collections: 39,079 volumes. 530 microform titles; 1,305 audiovisual materials; 183 current periodical subscriptions. Online catalog. 25 computer work stations. Students have access to online information retrieval services and the Internet. Total 2004–05 budget for books and materials: $65,315.

Most important special collections include Bible books; theology books; institutional archives.

Buildings and Grounds: *New buildings:* Library/Student Center.

Chief Executive Officer: Dr. Kenneth B. Kemper, President.

Address admission inquiries to Kevin Gilliam, Director of Enrollment.

Grand Valley State University

1 Campus Drive
Allendale, Michigan 49401
Tel: (616) 331-2025   **E-mail:** go2gvsu@gvsu.edu
Fax: (616) 331-2000   **Internet:** www.gvsu.edu

Institution Description: Grand Valley State University, formerly Grand Valley State College, is a state institution offering liberal arts and professional programs. *Enrollment:* 22,063. *Degrees awarded:* Baccalaureate, master's.
Member of University Consortium Center.

Accreditation: *Regional:* NCA. *Professional:* accounting, art, athletic training, business, engineering, music, nursing, nursing education, occupational therapy, physical therapy, physician assisting, psychology internship, public administration, social work, surgeon assisting, teacher education

History: Chartered 1960; established as Grand Valley State College and offered first instruction at postsecondary level 1963; changed name to Grand Valley State University in 1987; awarded first degree (baccalaureate) 1967; added master's level 1973. *See* James H. Zumberge, *Grand Valley State College - Its Developing Years* (Allendale: Grand Valley State College, 1969) for further information.

Institutional Structure: *Governing board:* Board of Control, Grand Valley State University. Representation: 8 trustees. All voting. *Composition of institution:* Administrators 25 men / 10 women. Academic affairs headed by provost and vice president for academic affairs. Business and finances directed by vice president for finance and administration. Full-time instructional faculty 598. Academic governance body, University Academic Senate, meets an average of 4 times per year.

Calendar: Semesters. Academic year Aug. to May. Freshmen admitted Aug., Jan., May, July. Degrees conferred Dec., May, Aug. Formal commencement May, Dec. Summer session of 2 terms from May to Aug.

Characteristics of Freshmen: 76% of applicants accepted. 31% of accepted applicants enrolled.
Average secondary school rank of freshmen men 70th percentile, women 75th percentile, class 72nd percentile. Mean ACT composite score 23.
46% of entering freshmen expected to graduate within 5 years. 95% of freshmen from Michigan. Freshmen from 42 states and 24 foreign countries.

Admission: Rolling admissions plan. For fall acceptance, apply in the fall of senior year. Priority application deadline Feb 1. Application closing date May 1. *Requirements:* Either graduation from accredited secondary school with 20 academic units (4 English, 4 science, 4 mathematics, 2 science lab, 2 foreign language, 3 social studies, 1 elective). Minimum 2.7 GPA. *Entrance tests:* ACT composite. For foreign students TOEFL. *For transfer students:* 2.5 minimum GPA; maximum transfer credit 30 semester hours.
College credit and advanced placement for postsecondary-level work completed in secondary school. Tutoring available. Developmental courses offered in summer session and regular academic year; credit given.

Degree Requirements: 120 credit hours; 2.0 GPA; 30 credit hours in residence; general education requirements; exit competency examinations in writing and mathematics. Fulfillment of some degree requirements and exemption from some beginning courses possible by passing departmental examinations, College Board CLEP. *Grading system:* A–F; pass-fail, withdraw (carries time limit).

Distinctive Educational Programs: Internships. Off-campus centers (at Grand Rapids, Holland, Muskegon, Traverse City). Evening classes. Special facilities for using telecommunications in the classroom. Facilities and programs for independent research, including honors programs, tutorials. Study abroad in China, Costa Rica, England, Japan, Poland, Mexico, Germany, Taiwan, Spain, Russia, France. *Other distinctive programs:* 5-year BS/MS in physical therapy, occupational therapy, physician assistant.

Degrees Conferred: 1,822 *baccalaureate* (B), 657 *master's* (M): area and ethnic studies 2 (B); biological and life sciences 64 (B); business 297 (B), 91 (M); communications/communication technologies 111 (B), 10 (M); computer and information science 49 (B), 14 (M); education 136 (B), 293 (M); engineering/engineering technologies 58 (B); English 135 (B); foreign languages and literature 28 (B); health professions and related sciences 305 (B), 136 (M); law/legal studies 20 (B); liberal arts/general studies 36 (B); mathematics 32 (B); natural resources and environmental science 10 (B); physical sciences 12 (B); protective services/public administration 172 (B), 24 (M); psychology 118 (B); social sciences and history 106, visual and performing arts 86 (B); other 45 (B), 89 (M).

Fees and Other Expenses: *Full-time tuition per academic year 2004–05:* resident undergraduate $5,782, out-of-state $12,510; resident graduate $6,664, out-of-state $14,400. *Room and board per academic year:* $6,160.

Financial Aid: Grand Valley State University offers a direct lending program. Aid from institutionally generated funds is provided on the basis of academic merit, financial need, athletic ability.

Financial aid to full-time, first-time undergraduate students: need-based scholarships/grants totaling $28,534,447, self-help $50,480,632; non-need-based scholarships/grants totaling $11,726,018, self-help $19,668,618, tuition waivers $904,003, athletic awards $1,865,085.

Departments and Teaching Staff: *Total instructional faculty:* 1,321 (full-time 874, part-time 447; women 620, men 701). Total faculty with doctorate, first-professional, or other terminal degree: 620. Student-to-faculty ratio: 18:1. Degrees held by full-time faculty: doctorate 84%.

Enrollment: Total enrollment 22,063. Undergraduate full-time 6,233 men / 9,504 women, part-time 1,018m / 1,638w; graduate full-time 230m / 577w, part-time 960m / 1,903w.

Characteristics of Student Body: *Ethnic/racial makeup:* number of Black non-Hispanic: 870; American Indian or Alaska Native: 115; Asian or Pacific Islander: 433; Hispanic: 516; White non-Hispanic: 16,138; unknown: 223.

International Students: 98 undergraduate nonresident aliens enrolled fall 2004. No programs available to aid students whose native language is not English. No financial aid specifically designated for international students.

Student Life: On-campus residence halls house 15% of student body. 3% of student body live on campus in college-controlled single student apartments. *Intercollegiate athletics:* men only: baseball, basketball, football, golf, swimming, tennis, track; women only: basketball, golf, tennis, track, soccer, swimming, volleyball. *Special regulations:* Cars permitted without restrictions. *Special services:* Learning Resources Center, medical services. *Student publications, radio:* Lanthorn, a weekly newspaper; a yearbook. Radio station WGVU-FM. *Surrounding community:* Allendale is 14 miles from Grand Rapids, the nearest metropolitan area. Served by mass transit bus system; airport 20 miles from campus.

Library Collections: 610,000 volumes. 118,500 government documents; 200,314 microforms; 1,400 audiovisual materials; 3,019 periodicals. Online catalog. Students have access to online information retrieval services and the Internet.
Most important special holdings include Lemmen Collection on Abraham Lincoln and the U.S. Civil War; Regional Affairs Resources Collection; Michigan Literature Collection; William Seidman Papers (his tenure as head of FDIC).

Buildings and Grounds: Allendale campus area 900 acres and Grand Rapids campus area 14 acres.

Chief Executive Officer: Dr. Mark A. Murray, President.
Address admission inquiries to Jodi Chycinski, Director of Admissions.

Great Lakes Christian College

6211 West Willow Highway
Lansing, Michigan 48917
Tel: (517) 321-0242   **E-mail:** admissions@glcc.edu
Fax: (517) 321-5902   **Internet:** www.glcc.edu

Institution Description: Great Lakes Christian College, formally known as Great Lakes Bible College, prepares men and women for Christian vocations and is affiliated with the Christian Churches and Churches of Christ. *Enrollment:* 193. *Degrees awarded:* Associate, baccalaureate.

Accreditation: *National:* ABHE.

History: Established in Vestaburg 1949; moved to present campus 1972; adopted present name 1996.

Institutional Structure: Full-time instructional faculty 9.

Calendar: Semesters. Academic year Aug. to May. Freshmen admitted Aug. and Jan.

Characteristics of Freshmen: 84% of applicants accepted. 80% of accepted applicants enrolled.
Average secondary school rank of freshmen men 47th percentile, women 40th percentile, class 43.5 percentile. Mean ACT Composite score 21.
33% of entering freshmen expected to graduate within 5 years. 81% of freshmen from Michigan. Freshmen from 5 states and 1 foreign country.

Admission: Rolling admissions plan; open enrollment. *Requirements:* High school graduation or GED. *Entrance tests:* ACT required.

Degree Requirements: *For all associate degrees:* 64 credit hours. *For all baccalaureate degrees:* 128 credit hours.

Distinctive Educational Programs: *For undergraduates:* Associate and bachelor of religious education degree programs. *Other distinctive programs:* Off-campus adult continuing education classes taught in churches. Cooperative programs in education (including teacher certification) and other areas with Michigan State University, Spring Arbor College, and Milligan College. Cooperative programs in business with Davenport College of Business.

Degrees Conferred: 18 *associate;* 10 *baccalaureate:* theology.

Fees and Other Expenses: *Full-time tuition per academic year 2004–05:* $8,756. *Other expenses:* $1,600. *Room and board per academic year:* $7,050.

Financial Aid: Aid from institutionally generated funds is provided on the basis of academic merit, financial need. Institution has a Program Participation Agreement with the U.S. Department of Education for eligible students to receive Pell Grants and, depending upon the agreement, other federal aid.

Departments and Teaching Staff: *Total instructional faculty:* 16. Student-to-faculty ratio: 10:1. Degrees held by full-time faculty: doctorate 56%, master's 34%.

Enrollment: Total enrollment 193. Undergraduate full-time 86 men / 77 women, part-time 14m / 13w.

Characteristics of Student Body: *Ethnic/racial makeup:* Black non-Hispanic: 8; Asian or Pacific Islander: 2; White non-Hispanic: 175. *Age distribution:* 17–21: 73%; 22–24: 9%; 25–29: 5%; 30–34: 4%; 35–39: 3%; 40–49: 6%.

International Students: 3 nonresident aliens enrolled. 2 students from Europe, 1 Africa. No programs available to aid students whose native language is not English. No financial aid specifically designated for international students.

Student Life: On-campus residence halls available. Married student's apartments available. *Special regulations:* Chapel service twice weekly. *Surrounding community:* Lansing is located 70 miles west of Detroit in the south central portion of Michigan.

Library Collections: 46,395 volumes. 980 microform titles; 245 current periodical subscriptions. Card catalog. 21 computer work stations. Students have access to online information retrieval services and the Internet.

Most important special holdings include Christian Standard (microfilm) 1866–1966, hardcopy thereafter; Library of Religion in America (beginnings to 1914 on microbook); Restoration History (Church of Christ/Christian Churches) publications; Bible collection; C.S. Lewis Collection.

Buildings and Grounds: Campus area 50 acres.

Chief Executive Officer: Lawrence L. Carter, President.

Address admission inquiries to Michael L. Klauka, Director of Admissions.

Hillsdale College

33 East College Avenue
Hillsdale, Michigan 49242

Tel: (517) 437-7341   **E-mail:** admissions@hillsdale.edu
Fax: (517) 437-0190   **Internet:** www.hillsdale.edu

Institution Description: Hillsdale College is a private, independent, nonprofit college. *Enrollment:* 1,250. *Degrees awarded:* Baccalaureate.

Accreditation: *Regional:* NCA.

History: Established by Free Will Baptists as Michigan Central College, incorporated, and offered first instruction at postsecondary level 1844; awarded first degree (baccalaureate) 1851; adopted present name 1853. The College charter was the first in the United States to prohibit discrimination because of race, sex, or religion. *See* John Chamberlain, *Freedom and Independence: The Hillsdale Story* (Hillsdale: Hillsdale College Press, 1979) for further information.

Institutional Structure: *Governing board:* Hillsdale College Board of Trustees. Extrainstitutional representation: 35 trustees; institutional representation: president of the college. 1 ex officio. All voting. *Composition of institution:* Administrators 19 men / 14 women. Academic affairs headed by provost. Management directed by vice president for administration. Business/finances directed by vice president for finance. Full-time instructional faculty 83. Academic governance body, the faculty, meets an average of 10 times per year.

Calendar: Semesters. Academic year late Aug. to mid-May. Freshmen admitted Aug., Jan., June. Degrees conferred May, Aug., Dec. Formal commencement May. Summer session of 2 terms from mid-May to mid-June.

Characteristics of Freshmen: 81% of applicants accepted. 43 of accepted applicants enrolled.

Average secondary school rank men 80th percentile, women 85th percentile, class 84th percentile. Mean SAT scores 610 verbal, 590 mathematical. Mean ACT Composite scores 26.

73% of entering freshmen expected to graduate within 5 years. 44% of freshmen from Michigan. Freshmen from 37 states and 8 foreign countries.

Admission: Rolling admissions plan. For fall acceptance, apply as early as July 1 of previous year, but not later than July 15 of year of enrollment. Early acceptance available. *Requirements:* Either graduation from accredited secondary school or GED. Recommend 4 units English, 3 foreign language, 4 mathematics, 3 science, 3 social studies. Minimum GPA approximately 3.0. Lowest acceptable secondary school class standing approximately 50th percentile. *Entrance tests:* College Board SAT or ACT composite. Achievements, including

English, recommended. For foreign students TOEFL. *For transfer students:* 3.0 minimum GPA.

College credit and advanced placement for postsecondary-level work completed in secondary school and for USAFI.

Degree Requirements: 124 credit hours; 2.0 GPA; senior year in residence; 2 physical education courses; general education requirements; 2 semesters English, 1 semester American heritage; 1 semester Western heritage; additional requirements for specific programs.

Fulfillment of some degree requirements and exemption from some beginning courses possible by passing College Board CLEP, APP. *Grading system:* A–F; withdraw (deadline after which pass-fail is appended to withdraw).

Distinctive Educational Programs: Accelerated degree programs. Dual-degree programs in engineering with Northwestern University (IL), Tri-State University (IN). Interdisciplinary programs in American studies, communication arts, comparative literature, environmental studies, European studies, international business, political economy. Preprofessional programs in dentistry, forestry, medical technology, medicine, nursing, optometry, osteopathy, pharmacy, theology. Honors programs. Study abroad in Austria, Colombia, England, France, Guatemala, Mexico, Spain, Switzerland, Germany. Semester internships in U.S. congressional offices in Washington (DC). Randall Preschool Laboratory for early childhood education majors. *Other distinctive programs:* Symposia with visiting scholars for students and others through The Center for Constructive Alternatives.

Degrees Conferred: 202 *baccalaureate:* biological sciences 30, business and management 61, education 14, fine and applied arts 30, foreign languages 10, mathematics 7, psychology 7, social sciences 35, theology 2, interdisciplinary studies 3.

Fees and Other Expenses: *Full-time tuition per academic year 2004–05:* $16,150.

Financial Aid: Aid from institutionally generated funds is provided on the basis of academic merit, financial need, athletic ability, other criteria. Institution has a Program Participation Agreement with the U.S. Department of Education for eligible students to receive Pell Grants and other federal aid.

Departments and Teaching Staff: Biology *professors* 4, *associate professors* 0, *assistant professors* 1, *instructors* 0, *part-time teachers* 0; chemistry 1, 1, 1, 0, 0; /mathematics/computer science 1, 1, 3, 0, 0; physics 1, 2, 0, 0, 0; TAS 0, 1, 1, 0, 3; religion/philosophy 3, 1, 1, 0, 0; English 4, 3, 3, 0, 3; art 1, 0, 2, 0, 2; modern languages 1, 5, 2, 0, 1; classical studies 0, 1, 1, 0, 0; music 1, 2, 1, 0, 2; psychology/sociology 1, 2, 1, 0,3; history/political science 4, 3, 5, 0, 1; EBA 2, 5, 2, 0, 4; education 0, 1, 3, 3, 0; health/physical education 0, 0, 4, 2, 2.

Total instructional faculty: 89. Student-to-faculty ratio: 12:1. Degrees held by full-time faculty: doctorate 76%, master's 23%. 82% hold terminal degrees.

Enrollment: Total enrollment 1,250. Full-time 585 men / 630 women, part-time 11m / 24w.

Characteristics of Student Body: *Age distribution:* 17–21: 85%; 22–24: 12%; 35–39: 1%; 40–49: 1%; 50–59: 1%.

International Students: 16 nonresident aliens enrolled. Students from Europe, Asia, Central and South America, Canada. Financial aid specifically designated for undergraduate international students: scholarships available annually.

Student Life: On-campus residence halls house 70% of student body. Residence halls for men constitute 46% of such space, for women 54%. 30% of men join and 45% live in fraternity houses; 54% of women join, 43% live in sorority houses. *Intercollegiate athletics:* men only: baseball, basketball, football, golf, tennis, track; women only: basketball, softball, swimming, tennis, track, volleyball. Club sports include soccer, equestrian, and hockey. *Special regulations:* Cars permitted; parking in designated areas only. Quiet hours. Residence hall visitation at specifically stated hours. *Special services:* Mossey Library; medical services. *Student publications: The Collegian,* a weekly newspaper; *Tower Light,* a literary magazine; *The Winona,* a yearbook. *Surrounding community:* Hillsdale population 8,000. Detroit, 100 miles from campus, is nearest metropolitan area.

Publications: *Imprimis,* a monthly newsletter first published 1972, circulates to national readership of 700,000; *Hillsdale Magazine,* 20,000. Hillsdale College Press publishes 1–2 titles annually.

Library Collections: 300,000 volumes. 61,000 microforms; 8,000 audiovisual materials; 1,600 current periodical subscriptions. Online catalog. Students have access to online information retrieval services.

Most important special holdings include personal library of economist Ludwig von Mises (5,000 volumes); Manion Forum Tape Collection (World War II era tapes); Wilber J. Carr Collection (materials on international relations from former assistant secretary of state); Richard Weaver Library.

Buildings and Grounds: Campus area 250 acres.

Chief Executive Officer: Dr. Larry P Arnn, III, President.

Address admission inquiries to Jeffrey S. Lantis, Director of Admissions.

Hope College

141 East 12th Street
P.O. Box 9000
Holland, Michigan 49422-9000
Tel: (616) 395-7000   **E-mail:** admissions@hope.edu
Fax: (616) 395-7922   **Internet:** www.hope.edu

Institution Description: Hope College is a private, independent, nonprofit college affiliated with the Reformed Church in America. *Enrollment:* 3,112. *Degrees awarded:* Baccalaureate.

Member of the consortium Great Lakes College Association (GLCA).

Accreditation: *Regional:* NCA. *Professional:* art, athletic training, dance, engineering, social work, teacher education

History: Established and offered first instruction at postsecondary level 1862; chartered and awarded first degree (baccalaureate) 1866. *See* Wynand Wichers, *Century of Hope* (Grand Rapids: William B. Eerdmans, 1968) for further information.

Institutional Structure: *Governing board:* Hope College Board of Trustees. Extrainstitutional representation: 11 trustees. 15 other members. Institutional representation: president of the college, 2 full-time instructional faculty members; 3 alumni. 1 ex officio (president). 32 voting. *Composition of institution:* Administrators 55 men / 44 women. Academic affairs headed by provost. Management/business/finances directed by vice president for business and finance. Full-time instructional faculty 204. Academic governance body, Academic Affairs Board, meets an average of 12 times per year.

Calendar: Semesters. Academic year Aug. to May. Freshmen admitted Aug., Jan., May, June, July. Degrees conferred May, Aug., Dec. Formal commencement May. Summer session of 3 terms from May to July.

Characteristics of Freshmen: 79% of applicants admitted. 37.3% of applicants admitted and enrolled.

33% (249 students) submitted SAT scores; 91% (695 students) submitted ACT scores. *25th percentile:* SAT Verbal 530, SAT Math 530; ACT Composite 23, ACT English 22, ACT Math 23. *75th percentile:* SAT Verbal 650, SAT Math 660; ACT Composite 28, ACT English 29, ACT Math 28.

74% of entering freshmen expected to graduate within 5 years. 67% freshmen from Michigan. Freshmen from 23 states and 9 foreign countries.

Admission: Rolling admissions plan. For fall acceptance, apply as early as completion of junior year of secondary school. *Requirements:* Either graduation from accredited secondary school with 16 units which normally include 4 English, 2 in a foreign language, 2 mathematics, 2 social sciences, 1 laboratory science, 5 academic electives; or GED. An interview is strongly encouraged. Preferred minimum 2.5 GPA. Preferred secondary school class standing 50th percentile. *Entrance tests:* ACT composite preferred; College Board SAT accepted. For foreign students TOEFL. *For transfer students:* 2.0 minimum GPA; from 4-year accredited institution 96 hours maximum transfer credit; from 2-year accredited institution 65 hours; correspondence/extension students 32 hours.

College credit and advanced placement for postsecondary-level work completed in secondary school. College credit for College Board CLEP, departmental examinations. College credit for extrainstitutional learning on basis of ACE *2006 Guide to the Evaluation of Educational Experiences in the Armed Services*; college credit and advanced placement on the basis of faculty assessment; advanced placement on basis of personal interview. Tutoring available.

Degree Requirements: 126 semester hours; 2.0 GPA; final 2 terms in residence; 2 physical education credits; 2.0 GPA in major field; distribution requirements. Fulfillment of some degree requirements and exemption from some beginning courses possible by passing departmental examinations, College Board CLEP, APP. *Grading system:* A–F; pass-fail; withdraw (carries time limit); incomplete (carries time limit).

Distinctive Educational Programs: Work-experience programs. Evening classes. Dual-degree programs in engineering science with Michigan State University, University of Michigan, Washington University (MO); Special facilities for using telecommunications in the classroom. Facilities for independent research, including honors programs, individual majors, tutorials, composite majors from existing courses, independent off-campus programs, Institutionally sponsored study abroad in Vienna (Austria); Institute of European Studies programs in Vienna (Austria), Adelaide (Australia), Kiev (Soviet Union), Milan (Italy), Nantes and Paris (France), Freiburg (Germany), Durham and London (England), Madrid (Spain). Through Associated Colleges of the Midwest and GLCA, programs in Hong Kong (China), India, Yugoslavia. Through GLCA, programs in comparative urban studies in England, Netherlands, Yugoslavia; also programs in Africa, Bogota (Columbia), at Waseda University in Tokyo (Japan); Aberdeen, Scotland; Costa Rica. Through GLCA, domestic foreign language programs in Arabic, Chinese, Hindi, Japanese, Portuguese. Institutionally sponsored off-campus study in the U.S. includes program in government and politics in Washington, (DC); in urban studies in Chicago (IL). Urban studies in Philadelphia (PA) sponsored by Hope and GLCA. Through GLCA, programs in the sciences in Oak Ridge (TN), arts in New York, humanities at the Newberry Library in Chicago. Through CIEE: study abroad in Czechoslovakia; Dominican Republic; Indonesia; Vietnam; Jerusalem. *Other distinctive programs:* Trustee Scholars program offers extended educational opportunities for gifted students. Upward Bound Program offers educational assistance for low-income secondary school students with potential for college education.

Degrees Conferred: 638 *baccalaureate:* area and ethnic studies 4; biological/life sciences 30; business/marketing 54; communications/communication technologies 35; computer and information sciences 13; education 138; engineering and engineering technologies 8; English 40; foreign languages and literature 30; health professions and related sciences 23; interdisciplinary studies 10; mathematics 110; parks and recreation 9; philosophy/religion/theology 22; physical sciences 26; protective services/public administration 32; psychology 35; social sciences and history 60; visual and performing arts 19.

Fees and Other Expenses: *Full-time tuition per academic year 2004–05:* $20,300. *Required fees:* $120. *Room and board and per academic year:* $6,318.

Financial Aid: Hope College offers a direct lending program. Aid from institutionally generated funds is provided on the basis of academic merit.

Financial aid to full-time, first-time undergraduate students: need-based scholarships/grants totaling $15,694,778, self-help $8,030,497, tuition waivers $660,324; non-need-based scholarships/grants totaling $8,118,389, self-help $4,527,531, tuition waivers $640,364.

Departments and Teaching Staff: *Professors* 75, *associate professors* 67, *assistant professors* 71, *instructors* 2, *part-time faculty* 93.

Total instructional faculty: 307 (full-time 217, part-time 90; women 136, men 171; members of minority groups 26). Total faculty with doctorate, first-professional, or other terminal degree: 192. Student-to-faculty ratio: 13:1. Degrees held by full-time faculty: 77% hold terminal degrees. *Faculty development:* $5 million in grants for research. 15 faculty members awarded sabbaticals 2004–05.

Enrollment: Total enrollment 3,112. Undergraduate full-time 1,145 men / 1,858 women, part-time 149m / 59w. *Transfer students:* 60.

Characteristics of Student Body: *Ethnic/racial makeup:* number of Black non-Hispanic: 47; American Indian or Alaska Native: 7; Asian or Pacific Islander: 64; Hispanic: 59; White non-Hispanic: 2,866; unknown: 21. *Age distribution:* number under 18: 47; 18–19: 1,416; 20–21: 1,287; 22–24: 296; 25–29: 22; 30–34: 11; 35–39: 16; 40–49: 11; 50–64: 5; 65 and over: 1.

International Students: 48 nonresident aliens enrolled fall 2004. 11 students from Europe, 19 Asia, 5 Central and South Latin America, 6 Africa, 2 Canada. Programs available to aid students whose native language is not English: social and cultural. English as a Second Language Program. Financial aid specifically designated for international students: scholarships available annually.

Student Life: A variety of housing options are available through residence halls, apartments, and college-owned houses. Nearly 80% of degree-seeking students reside on campus. Freshmen live in traditional residence halls. Some seniors live off campus. *Intercollegiate athletics:* men only: baseball, basketball, cross-country, football, golf, soccer, swimming, tennis, track; women only: basketball, cross-country, golf, soccer, softball, swimming, tennis, track, volleyball. *Special regulations:* Residence hall visitation from 11am to midnight. *Special services:* Learning Resources Center, counseling (career and personal), medical services, special advising for physically handicapped. *Student publications, radio:* Anchor, a weekly newspaper; *Milestone*, a yearbook; *Opus*, a quarterly literary and fine arts magazine. Radio station WTHS-FM is an open-air FM station with a broadcast range of approximately 10 miles; station is staffed by students. *Surrounding community:* Holland population 35,000. Grand Rapids, 25 miles from campus, is nearest metropolitan area. Served by airport 30 miles from campus; passenger rail service (AMTRAK) from Holland to Chicago; bus service (Greyhound).

Library Collections: 355,998 volumes including bound books, serial backfiles, electronic documents, and government documents not in separate collections. Online catalog. Current serial subscriptions: 1,218 paper, 614 microform, 1,676 electronic. 6,412 recordings. 45 computer work stations. Students have access to the Internet at no charge. Total budget for books, periodicals, audiovisual materials, microforms 2004–05: $823,700.

Most important special collections include Richard P. Wunder Art History Collection; Reformed Church in America Collection; Dutch in America Collection; rare science books.

Buildings and Grounds: Campus area 64 acres. *New buildings:* Science Center completed 2004; Martha Miller Center for Global Communications 2005.

Chief Executive Officer: Dr. James E. Bultman, President.

Address admission inquiries to Dr. James R. Bekkering, Vice President for Admissions.

Kalamazoo College

1200 Academy Street
Kalamazoo, Michigan 49006-3295
Tel: (269) 337-7166   **E-mail:** admission@kzoo.edu
Fax: (269) 337-7390   **Internet:** www.kzoo.edu

Institution Description: Kalamazoo College is a private, independent, non-profit college historically affiliated with the American Baptist Convention. *Enrollment:* 1,234. *Degrees awarded:* Baccalaureate.

Member of the consortium Great Lakes Colleges Association (GLCA); Kalamazoo Consortium for Higher Education (KCHE).

Accreditation: *Regional:* NCA.

History: Established as Michigan and Huron Institute and offered first instruction at postsecondary level 1883; changed name to Kalamzaoo Literary Institute 1837; merged with local branch of University of Michigan and became Kalamazoo Branch of University of Michigan 1840; readopted name Kalamazoo Literary Institute 1850; awarded first degree (baccalaureate) 1851; adopted present name 1855. *See* Arnold Mulder, *Kalamazoo College Story* (Kalamazoo: Kalamazoo College, 1958) for further information.

Institutional Structure: *Governing board:* Kalamazoo College Board of Trustees. Representation: 33 trustees (including 5 alumni), 29 emeriti. 33 voting. *Composition of institution:* Administrators 10 men / 8 women. Academic affairs headed by president. Management/business/finances directed by vice president for business and finance. Full-time instructional faculty 89. Academic governance body, the faculty, meets an average of 12 times per year.

Calendar: Quarters. Academic year Sept. to June. Freshmen admitted Sept., Jan., Mar., June. Degrees conferred and formal commencement June. Summer session of 1 term from late June to late Aug.

Characteristics of Freshmen: 61% of applicants admitted. 27% of applicants admitted and enrolled.

58% (181 students) submitted SAT scores; 87% (270 students) submitted ACT scores. *25th percentile*: SAT Verbal 600, SAT Math 600; ACT Composite 26, ACT English 25, ACT Math 25. *75th percentile*: SAT Verbal 710, SAT Math 680; ACT Composite 31, ACT English 31, ACT Math 30.

70% of freshmen from Michigan. Freshmen from 35 states and 12 foreign countries.

Admission: Rolling admissions plan. Students are notified of acceptance within 4 to 6 weeks of application. *Requirements:* Recommend 16 units which include English, fine arts, a foreign language, mathematics, natural science, social studies. Campus visit strongly encouraged. *Entrance tests:* College Board SAT or ACT composite. *For transfer students:* 135 quarter hours maximum transfer credit.

College credit for college courses completed in secondary school. Tutoring available.

Degree Requirements: *For undergraduate degrees:* 35 courses with grade of C or better; 5 physical education courses; senior project; portfolio; major comprehensive examination; liberal arts colloquium credit consisting of 25 activities.

Fulfillment of some degree requirements and exemption from some beginning courses possible by passing College Board APP. *Grading system:* A–F; pass-fail; withdraw (carries time limit).

Distinctive Educational Programs: Historically, 85% of all graduates have completed study abroad as part of their educational program. Institutionally-sponsored study abroad in China, Ecuador, France, Germany, Japan, Kenya, Mexico, Senegal, Sierra Leone, and Zimbabwe. Additional programs available through the GLCA, as well as other consortial or affiliated agreements.

ROTC: Army in cooperation with Western Michigan University.

Degrees Conferred: 277 *baccalaureate:* area and ethnic studies 6; biological/life sciences 34; computer and information sciences 10; English 32; foreign languages and literature 10; health professions and related sciences 11; mathematics 8; philosophy/religion/theology 5; psychology 35; social sciences and history 84; visual and performing 4.

Fees and Other Expenses: *Full-time tuition per academic year 2005–06:* Contact the college for current tuition/fees and other costs.

Financial Aid: Aid from institutionally generated funds is provided on the basis of academic merit, financial need, other considerations.

Financial aid to full-time, first-time undergraduate students: need-based scholarships/grants totaling $6,013,983, self-help $2,672,465; non-need-based scholarships/grants totaling $8,857,307, self-help $1,941,638, parent loans $1,070,995, tuition waivers $347,243.

Departments and Teaching Staff: *Professors* 23, *associate professors* 31, *assistant professors* 37, *instructors* 9, *part-time faculty* 14.

Total instructional faculty: 114 (full-time 100, part-time 14; women 58, men 56; members of minority groups 18). Total faculty with doctorate, first-professional, or other terminal degree: 95. Student-to-faculty ratio: 12:1. Degrees held

by full-time faculty: doctorate 83%, master's 13%, baccalaureate 3%, professional 1%. *Faculty development:* $648,268 in grants for research. 4 faculty members awarded sabbaticals 2004–05.

Enrollment: Total enrollment 1,234. Undergraduate men 519, women 715. *Transfer students:* in-state 10.

Characteristics of Student Body: *Ethnic/racial makeup:* number of Black non-Hispanic: •30; American Indian or Alaska Native: 1; Asian or Pacific Islander: 56; Hispanic: 25; White non-Hispanic: 968; unknown: 134.

International Students: 20 nonresident aliens enrolled fall 2004. Students from Europe, Asia, Central and South America, Africa, Canada, Australia, Middle East. Programs available for students whose native language is not English: social, cultural, financial.

Student Life: On-campus residence halls house 90% of student body. Students may live in special interest houses (language, clubs, organizations). *Intercollegiate athletics:* men only: baseball, basketball, cross-country, football, golf, soccer, swimming, tennis; women only: basketball, cross-country, golf, soccer, softball, swimming, tennis, volleyball. *Student organizations:* Student Commission, Inter-house Association, Asian Student Organization; College Union Board, Black Student Organization, Intramural, Environmental Organization, Film Society, International Student Organization, Guild of Change Ringers, Ski Club, Ultimate Frisbee Society, Women's Equity Coalition, Religious organizations (Catacombs, Chaverim, Christian Fellowship). *Special regulations:* Freshmen not permitted to have cars on campus. *Special services:* Health counseling and academic advising services. Weekly non-denominational Chapel Service. *Student publications: Boiling Pot,* a yearbook; *Cauldron,* a literary magazine; *Index,* a weekly newspaper. Radio station WJMD broadcasts to college community. *Surrounding community:* Kalamazoo area population 100,000. Kalamazoo is about 2½ hours west of Detroit and 2½ hours east of Chicago. It is served by mass transit bus service, major airlines and Amtrak.

Library Collections: 319,000 volumes. 18,748 microforms; 15,100 audiovisual materials; 1,300 current periodical subscriptions. Online catalog. Students have access to online information retrieval services and the Internet.

Most important special holdings include collections on history of books and printing; history of science; illustrated bird books.

Buildings and Grounds: Campus area 60 acres.

Chief Executive Officer: Dr. Eileen Wilson, Oyelaran, President.

Address admission inquiries to Andrew Strickler, Director of Admissions.

Kettering University

1700 West Third Avenue
Flint, Michigan 48504-4898
Tel: (810) 762-9500   **E-mail:** admissions@kettering.edu
Fax: (810) 762-9837   **Internet:** www.kettering.edu

Institution Description: Kettering University, formerly known as GMI Engineering and Management Institute, is a private, independent, nonprofit institution whose 5-year undergraduate program includes alternating 12-week periods of on-campus study and work experience with one of over 700 corporations and agencies that employ students for closely coupled cooperative work experiences that typically begin in the freshman year. *Enrollment:* 2,992. *Degrees awarded:* Baccalaureate, master's.

Accreditation: *Regional:* NCA. *Professional:* business, engineering

History: Established as Industrial Fellowships League 1919; changed name to School of Automotive Trades 1920; changed name to Flint Institute of Technology 1923; offered first instruction at postsecondary level 1924; changed name to General Motors Institute of Technology 1926; chartered 1927; became General Motors Institute 1932; awarded first degree (baccalaureate) 1946; changed name to GMI Engineering and Management Institute 1982; adopted present name 1998.

Institutional Structure: *Governing board:* Trustees. All voting. *Composition of institution:* Academic affairs headed by vice president and provost of academic affairs. Management/business/finances directed by vice president of finance. Academic governance body, Faculty Senate, meets an average of 36 times per year.

Calendar: Semesters consisting of one 12-week academic term and one 12-week cooperative work experience term. Academic year July to June. Freshmen admitted July, Oct., Jan., Apr. Degrees conferred June, Sept., Dec.

Characteristics of Freshmen: 70% of applicants admitted. 33% of applicants admitted and enrolled.

31% (177 students) submitted SAT scores; 84% (473 students) submitted ACT scores. *25th percentile*: SAT Verbal 540, SAT Math 600; ACT Composite 24, ACT English 22, ACT Math 25. *75th percentile*: SAT Verbal 650, SAT Math 690; ACT Composite 28, ACT English 27, ACT Math 30.

60% of entering freshmen expected to graduate within 5 years. 65% of freshmen from Michigan. Freshmen from 50 states and 29 foreign countries.

Admission: Rolling admissions plan. For fall acceptance, apply as early as Sept. of previous year. Students are notified of acceptance on a rolling basis. *Requirements:* Graduation from accredited secondary school; required coursework for all applicants: 3 English, 2 algebra, 2 laboratory science (1 of which must be chemistry or physics), 1 geometry, 1 trigonometry, calculus or pre-calc recommended. *Entrance tests:* College Board SAT or ACT. *For transfer students:* high school transcript and official college or university transcripts must be submitted.

Degree Requirements: 160 credit hours; 80 GPA on a scale of 70 to 100; 5 semesters in residence; evaluation reports for work-experience semesters; thesis. Fulfillment of some degree requirements and exemption from some beginning courses possible on basis of departmental assessment. *Grading system:* Numerical scale 70 to 100; withdraw (carries time limit).

Distinctive Educational Programs: All undergraduate students participate in paid cooperative education (co-op) work experience that typically begins in the freshman year. Students generally stay with the same employer throughout the five-year program (alternate 12-week terms of study on campus in Michigan with 12-week terms of progressively responsible work experience at employer's location). Over 524 companies and agencies in over 785 locations in 42 states and 4 foreign countries have employed students. In addition, 14 study abroad programs are offered in Australia, Canada, Denmark, England, France, Germany, Mexico, Scotland, Spain, and Sweden.

Degrees Conferred: 417 *baccalaureate* (B), 220 *master's* (M): business/marketing 22 (B), 197 (M); computer and information sciences 16 (B); engineering and engineering technologies 372 (B), 23 (M); mathematics 1 (B); physical sciences 6 (B).

Fees and Other Expenses: *Full-time tuition per academic year 2004–05:* $22,240. *Required fees:* $356. *Room and board per academic year:* $5,230.

Financial Aid: Aid from institutionally generated funds is provided on the basis of academic merit, financial need, other criteria. Institution has a Program Participation Agreement with the U.S. Department of Education for eligible students to receive Pell Grants and other federal aid.

Financial aid to full-time, first-time undergraduate students: need-based scholarships/grants totaling $12,773,150, self-help $17,769,314, parent loans $1,333,272, tuition waivers $186,773; non-need-based scholarships/grants totaling $3,567,552, self-help $3,693,222, parent loans $174,274, tuition waivers $151,993. *Graduate aid:* 3 students received $5,618 in federal and state-funded fellowships/grants; 20 received $251,948 in federal and state-funded loans (ranging from $2,605 to $10,000); 7 teaching assistantships were awarded totaling $122,578 (ranging from $3,000 to $17,784); 23 research assistantships totaling $240,449 (ranging from $1,215 to $22,480).

Departments and Teaching Staff: *Professors* 45, *associate professors* 61, *assistant professors* 27, *instructors* 7, *part-time faculty* 13.

Total instructional faculty: 153 (full-time 140, part-time 13; women 29, men 124; members of minority groups 31). Student-to-faculty ratio: 11:1. 75% hold terminal degrees.

Enrollment: Total enrollment 2,992. Undergraduate full-time 2,115 men, 397 women; graduate full-time 7m / 1w, part-time 358m / 114w.

Characteristics of Student Body: *Ethnic/racial makeup:* number of Black non-Hispanic: 150; American Indian or Alaska Native: 7; Asian or Pacific Islander: 133; Hispanic: 55; White non-Hispanic: 1,850; unknown: 226. *Age distribution:* number under 18: 84; 18–19: 964; 20–21: 850; 22–24: 541; 25–29: 52; 30–34: 16; 35–39: 3; 40–49: 2.

International Students: 99 nonresident aliens enrolled fall 2004. Programs available to aid students whose native language is not English: cultural. No financial aid specifically designated for international students.

Student Life: On-campus residence halls house 40% of student body. 40% of students join and 35% live in fraternity and sorority housing. *Special regulations:* Registered cars permitted without restriction. *Special services:* Academic Resources Center, medical services. *Student publications, radio: Technician,* a weekly newspaper; *Reflector,* a yearbook;. Radio station WKF is Kettering's low power radio station broadcasting 24 hours a day. *Surrounding community:* Flint population 140,000. Detroit, 60 miles from campus, is nearest metropolitan area. Served by airport 5 miles from campus; passenger rail service 3 miles from campus.

Library Collections: 83,046 volumes including government documents. Online catalog. Current serial subscriptions: paper 540; microform 4; via electronic access 1,236. 265 compact discs. 514 CD-ROMs. 12 computer work stations. Students have access to online information retrieval services and the Internet. Total 2004–05 budget for books and materials: $374,759.

Most important special collections include all ground vehicle papers of the Society of Automotive engineers; all papers of the Society of Manufacturing Engineers; all papers and transaction series from the American Society of Mechanical Engineers.

Buildings and Grounds: Campus area 45 acres.

Chief Executive Officer: Dr. Stanley R. Liberty, President.

Address undergraduate admission inquiries to Barbara Sosin, Director of Admissions; graduate inquiries to Jill Osman, Graduate Admissions.

Lake Superior State University

650 West Easterday Avenue
Sault Ste. Marie, Michigan 49783-1699

Tel: (906) 632-6841   **E-mail:** admissions@lssu.edu
Fax: (906) 635-2111   **Internet:** www.lssu.edu

Institution Description: Lake Superior State University, formerly Lake Superior State College, is a state institution. *Enrollment:* 2,888. *Degrees awarded:* Associate, baccalaureate, master's. Certificates also awarded.

Accreditation: *Regional:* NCA. *Professional:* nursing, recreation and leisure services

History: Established as Sault Ste. Marie Branch of Michigan Technological University, chartered, and offered first instruction at postsecondary level 1946; became 4-year autonomous college 1960; awarded first degree (baccalaureate) 1963; became Lake Superior State College 1970; adopted present name 1987.

Institutional Structure: *Governing board:* Board of Regents of Lake Superior State University. Extrainstitutional representation: 8 board members; institutional representation: president of the college. 1 ex officio. 8 voting. *Composition of institution:* Administrators 14 men / 2 women. Academic affairs headed by vice president. Management/business/finances directed by vice president for administration. Full-time instructional faculty 116. Academic governance body, Academic Affairs Council meets an average of 38 times per year. *Faculty representation:* Faculty served by collective bargaining agent, Lake Superior State University Faculty Association, affiliated with NEA.

Calendar: Semesters. Academic year late Aug. to early May. Freshmen admitted Aug., Dec., Mar., June, July. Formal commencement May. Summer session of 2 terms from May to Aug.

Characteristics of Freshmen: 79% of applicants accepted. 47% of accepted applicants enrolled.

86% of freshmen from Michigan. Freshmen from 12 states and 1 foreign country.

Admission: Rolling admissions plan. For fall acceptance, apply as early as Oct. 1 of previous year, but not later than 2 weeks before enrollment. Students are notified of acceptance within 2 weeks. Early acceptance on a part-time basis available. *Requirements:* Either graduation from accredited secondary school with 15 units which must include 3 English, 1 biology, 1 chemistry, 1 history, 1 physics, 1 social studies, and 7 from among a foreign language, mathematics, other academic areas; or GED. Additional mathematics and science units recommended for science and technology programs. Minimum 2.0 GPA. *Entrance tests:* ACT composite. For foreign students TOEFL. *For transfer students:* 2.0 minimum GPA; maximum transfer credit limited only by residence requirement.

College credit for extrainstitutional learning on basis of ACE *2006 Guide to the Evaluation of Educational Experiences in the Armed Services.* Tutoring available. Developmental/remedial courses offered in summer session and regular academic year; credit given.

Degree Requirements: *For all associate degrees:* 62 semester credits, 16 of last 20 hours in residence. *For all baccalaureate degrees:* 124 semester hours; 32 of last 40 hours and at least 50% of their departmental required 300/400 level classes in residence; 3 quarter hours of physical education. *For all undergraduate degrees:* 2.0 GPA; distribution requirements.

Fulfillment of some degree requirements and exemption from some beginning courses possible by passing College Board CLEP, APP, and departmental examinations. *Grading system:* A–F; pass-fail; withdraw (carries time limit).

Distinctive Educational Programs: Work-experience programs. Evening classes. Interdisciplinary course in environmental science. Facilities for independent research including honors programs.

Degrees Conferred: 91 *associate;* 511 *baccalaureate;* 6 *master's.* Bachelor's degrees awarded in top five disciplines: business, management, marketing, and related support services 99; security and protective services 91; education 48; engineering 42; health professions and related clinical sciences 36.

Fees and Other Expenses: *Full-time tuition per academic year 2004–05:* Michigan residents $5,736, nonresidents $11,154. *books and supplies:* $735. *Room and board per academic year:* $6,228.

Financial Aid: Aid from institutionally generated funds is provided on the basis of academic merit, financial need, athletic ability. Institution has a Program Participation Agreement with the U.S. Department of Education for eligible students to receive Pell Grants and, depending on agreement, other federal aid.

Departments and Teaching Staff: Arts/letters *professors* 7, *associate professors* 6, *assistant professors* 5, *instructors* 2, *part-time teachers* 6; biology/chemistry 7, 3, 5, 0, 1; business/economics 1. 10, 0, 2, 2; computer science/geology/mathematics 7, 2, 3, 2, 12; counseling and testing center 0, 0, 1, 2, 0; engineering technology 0, 6, 8, 0, 3; health sciences 1, 2, 7, 0, 6; social sciences 6, 6, 7, 4, 21; library 0, 0, 2, 2, 0.

Total instructional faculty: 114. Student-to-faculty ratio: 22:1. Degrees held by full-time faculty: doctorate 49%, master's 52%, baccalaureate 2%.

Enrollment: Total enrollment 2,888 (49.4% men, 50.6% women).

Characteristics of Student Body: *Ethnic/racial makeup:* Black non-Hispanic: .4%; American Indian or Native Alaskan: 7.2%; Asian or Pacific Islander: .5%; Hispanic: .5%; White non-Hispanic: 76.1%.

International Students: 521 nonresident aliens enrolled. Students from Europe, Asia, Central and South America, Canada. No programs available to aid students whose native language is not English. No financial aid specifically designated for international students.

Student Life: On-campus residence halls house 29% of student body. Residence halls for men constitute 25% of such space, for women 24%; for both sexes 51%. 2% of men join and 1% live in fraternities; 2% of women join sororities. Housing available for married students. *Intercollegiate athletics:* men only: basketball, cross-country, hockey, tennis, track (indoor and outdoor), wrestling; women only: basketball, cross-country, softball, tennis, track (indoor and outdoor), volleyball. *Special regulations:* Cars permitted on campus for $40 fee. Quiet hours from 8pm to 11am Sun.–Thurs. Residence hall visitation from 11am to midnight Sun.–Thurs. and 11am to 2am Fri. and Sat. *Special services:* Learning Resources Center, medical services. *Student publications: The Compass,* a weekly newspaper. *Surrounding community:* Sault Ste. Marie population 15,000. Detroit, 339 miles from campus, is nearest metropolitan area. Served by airport 15 miles from campus.

Library Collections: 154,500 volumes. Federal depository for government documents since 1982; 950 current periodical subscriptions. Online catalog. Students have access to online information retrieval services and the Internet.

Most important special holdings include Michigan Collection about the Upper Peninsula, Hiawatha legend, Sault Ste. Marie, and Indians; Marine Collection (historical texts, scrapbooks about the Great Lakes); Osborn Materials (documents from Governor Osborn dating from the early 1900s).

Buildings and Grounds: Campus area 120 acres.

Chief Executive Officer: Dr. Betty J. Youngblood, President.

Address admission inquiries to Leisa A. Mansfield, Director of Admissions.

Lawrence Technological University

21000 West Ten Mile Road
Southfield, Michigan 48075-1058
Tel: (248) 204-4000   **E-mail:** admissions@ltu.edu
Fax: (248) 204-3727   **Internet:** www.ltu.edu

Institution Description: Lawrence Technological University (formerly Lawrence Institute of Technology) is a private, independent, nonprofit institution. *Enrollment:* 4,148. *Degrees awarded:* Associate, baccalaureate, master's.

Accreditation: *Regional:* NCA. *Professional:* architecture, art, business, engineering, interior design

History: Established, chartered, incorporated, and offered first instruction at postsecondary level 1932; awarded first degree (baccalaureate) 1933.

Institutional Structure: *Governing Board:* Board of Trustees. Extrainstitutional representation: 12 trustees; institutional representation: 1 administrator. All voting. *Composition of institution:* Administrators 24 men / 16 women. Academic affairs and management/business/finances headed by executive vice president and provost. Full-time instructional faculty 105.

Calendar: Semesters. Academic year Aug. to May.

Characteristics of Freshmen: 69.3% of applicants admitted. 24.2% of applicants admitted and enrolled. 12% (44 students) submitted SAT scores; 85.3% (319 students) submitted ACT scores. *25th percentile:* SAT Verbal 470, SAT Math 525; ACT Composite 20, ACT English 17, ACT Math 19. *75th percentile:* SAT Verbal 610, SAT Math 640; ACT Composite 26, ACT English $24, ACT Math 27.

43% of entering freshmen expected to graduate within 5 years. 96% of freshmen from Michigan. Freshmen from 7 states.

Admission: Rolling admissions plan. *Requirements:* Either graduation from secondary school or GED. Minimum 2.0 GPA. *Entrance tests:* Required ACT Composite or SAT exam.

Degree Requirements: *For all associate degrees:* 60–69 semester hours; 24 hours in residence. *For all baccalaureate degrees:* 130–133 semester hours; 28 hours in residence. *For all degrees:* 2.0 GPA; general education requirements.

Distinctive Educational Programs: Detroit Studio and Paris Summer Study Abroad for architecture. Cooperative education programs available for selected majors in the College of Arts and Sciences and the College of Engineering. Internships available for selected majors within all colleges.

Degrees Conferred: 28 *associate;* 432 *baccalaureate,* 531 *master's* (M): architecture 102 (B), 42 (M); business/marketing 14 (B), 245 (M); communications/communication technologies 5 (B), 2 (M); computer and information science 24 (B), 172 (M); education 17 (M); engineering/engineering technologies 263 (B), 53 (M); interdisciplinary studies 3 (B); liberal arts and sciences, general studies, and humanities 3 (B); physical sciences 8 (B); psychology 1 (B); visual and performing arts 4 (B).

Fees and Other Expenses: *Full-time tuition per academic year 2004–05:* undergraduate $17,978, graduate $8,770. *Required fees* $250. *Room and board per academic year:* $7,227

Financial Aid: Lawrence Technological University offers a direct lending program. Aid from institutionally generated funds is provided on the basis of academic merit, financial need.

Financial aid to full-time, first-time undergraduate students: need-based scholarships/grants totaling $7,093,339, self-help $7,896,859, parent loans $2,456,947, tuition waivers $60,549; non-need-based scholarships/grants totaling $2,440,076, self-help $852,378, parent loans $612,378, tuition waivers $379,093. *Graduate aid:* 124 students received $171,212 in federal and state-funded fellowships/grants (ranging from $100 to $2,000); 311 received $2,871,225 in federal and state-funded loans (ranging from $500 to $18,500).

Departments and Teaching Staff: *Professors 28, associate professors 38, assistant professors 21, instructors 25, part-time faculty 297.*

Total instructional faculty: 409 (full-time 112, part-time 297). Student-to-faculty ratio: 12:1. Degrees held by full-time faculty: doctorate 49%, master's 100% 62% hold terminal degrees.

Enrollment: Total enrollment 4,148. Undergraduate full-time 1,210 men / 390 women, part-time 1,037m / 267w; graduate full-time 15m / 8w, part-time 809m / 412

Characteristics of Student Body: *Ethnic/racial makeup:* number of Black non-Hispanic: 323, American Indian or Alaska Native: 9; Asian or Pacific Islander: 117; Hispanic: 45; White non-Hispanic: 1,799; unknown: 506. *Age distribution:* number under 18: 4; 18–19: 296; 20–21: 105; 22–24: 261; 25–29: 251; 30–34: 151; 35–39: 102; 40–49: 137; 50–64: 23.

International Students: 101 nonresident aliens enrolled fall 2004. No programs available to aid students whose native language is not English. No financial aid specifically designated for international students.

Student Life: More than 30 student clubs, groups, and organizations. Intramural and club sports; student government.*Tech News,* a monthly campus newspaper; quarterly alumni magazine; *Prism,* an annual student creative and literary publication.

Library Collections: 84,411 volumes including bound books, serial backfiles, electronic documents, and government documents not in separate collections. Online catalog. Current serial subscriptions: 1,070 paper, 28,000 microform, 12,000 via electronic access. 10 computer work stations. Students have access to the Internet at no charge. Total budget for books, periodicals, audiovisual materials, microforms 2004–05: $227,147.

Most important special holdings include the Albert Kahn Library (personal architectural collection; cataloged); SAE Papers (1965–).

Buildings and Grounds: Suburban campus area 120 acres.

Chief Executive Officer: Dr. Charles M. Chambers, President.

Address admission inquiries to Lisa Kujawa, Director of Admissions.

Madonna University

36600 Schoolcraft Road
Livonia, Michigan 48150
Tel: (734) 432-5339   **E-mail:** admiss@madonna.edu
Fax: (734) 432-5393   **Internet:** www.madonna.edu

Institution Description: Madonna University, formerly Madonna College, is a private, independent, nonprofit college sponsored by the Felician Sisters, Roman Catholic Church. *Enrollment:* 4,047. *Degrees awarded:* Associate, baccalaureate, master's.

Member of Detroit Area Consortium of Catholic Colleges.

Accreditation: *Regional:* NCA. *Professional:* nursing, social work, teacher education

History: Established as Presentation Junior College, chartered, and offered first instruction at postsecondary level 1937; became 4-year college and adopted present name 1947; awarded first degree (baccalaureate) 1948. *See* Sister Rose Marie Kujawa, *Madonna College - Its History of Higher Education 1937–1977* (Detroit: Wayne State University, 1979) for further information.

Institutional Structure: *Governing board:* Board of Trustees. Institutional representation: 24 trustees, including president of the college, 12 Felician Sisters. 1 ex officio. 23 voting. *Composition of institution:* Administrators 6 men / 11 women (at dean's level and above, 65% are women). Academic affairs headed by academic dean. Management/business/finances directed by business manager. Full-time instructional faculty 106. Academic governance body, the faculty, meets an average of 9 times per year.

Calendar: Semesters. Academic year July to June. Freshmen admitted Sept., Jan., May. Degrees conferred Apr., July, Dec. Formal commencement May. Summer session of 1 term from May to July.

Characteristics of Freshmen: 80% of applicants admitted. 54% of applicants admitted and enrolled.

3 students submitted SAT scores; 97 students submitted ACT scores. *25th percentile:* ACT Composite 22, ACT English 23, ACT Math 22. *75th percentile:* ACT Composite 26, ACT English 27, ACT Math 26.

96% of freshmen from Michigan. Freshmen from 5 states and 2 foreign countries.

Admission: Rolling admissions plan. For fall acceptance, apply as early as Sept. of previous year. Early acceptance available. *Requirements:* Either graduation from accredited secondary school with 15 units or GED. Minimum 2.75 GPA. *Entrance tests:* ACT composite required for all current high school students and recent high school graduates. For foreign students TOEFL. *For transfer students:* 2.75 minimum GPA; maximum transfer credit limited only by residence requirements.

College credit and advanced placement for postsecondary-level work completed in secondary school. College credit for extrainstitutional learning (life experience) on basis of faculty assessment, ACE *2006 Guide to the Evaluation of Educational Experiences in the Armed Services* and portfolio assessment; advanced placement on basis of personal interview.

Tutoring available. Developmental/remedial courses offered in summer session and regular academic year; credit given.

Degree Requirements: *For all associate degrees:* 60 credit hours; 15 hours in residence. *For all baccalaureate degrees:* 120 credit hours; 30 hours in residence. *For all undergraduate degrees:* General education requirements; comprehensives in individual fields of study; writing requirement in some departments. *For master of science in administration degree:* 36 credit hours.

Fulfillment of some degree requirements and exemption from some beginning courses possible by passing College Board CLEP, AP. *Grading system:* A–F; pass-fail; withdraw (carries time limit; deadline after which pass-fail is appended to withdraw); incomplete (deadline after which grade of no credit given).

Distinctive Educational Programs: Cooperative education; internship programs. Flexible meeting places and schedules, including weekend and evening classes. Dual-degree program in engineering with University of Detroit. Credit transfer agreements with American Institute of Banking, Control Data Institute, and Michigan Paraprofessional Training Institute. Special facilities for using telecommunications in the classroom. Interdisciplinary program in the humanities. Independent study. Center for International Studies; Japanese studies. Study abroad at Landsdowne College (London, England); Edge Hill College (Ormskirk, England); Jagiellonian University Summer Institute of Polish Language and Culture (Krakow, Poland); Katholieke Industriele Hogeschool der Kempen (Belgium); comparative cultures study program through summer travel. Cross-registration through consortium. *Other distinctive programs:* Continuing education. Sign language studies; gerontology; hospice.

Degrees Conferred: 13 *associate;* 554 *baccalaureate* (B); 212 *master's* (M): area and ethnic studies 1 (B); biological/life sciences 18 (B); business/marketing 109 (B), 121 (M); communications/communication technologies 28; computer and information sciences 2 (B); education 29 (B), 42 (M); engineering and engineering technologies 3 (B); English 45 (B); foreign languages and literature 21 (B); health professions and related sciences 72 (B), 16 (M); home economics and vocational home economics 30 (B); interdisciplinary studies 3 (B); law/legal studies 8 (B); mathematics 6 (B); natural resources/environmental science 2 (B); philosophy/religion/theology 5 (B), 6 (M); physical sciences 5 (B); protective services/public administration 72 (B), 4 (M); psychology 35 (B), 23 (M); social sciences and history 31 (B); visual and performing arts 13 (B).

Fees and Other Expenses: *Tuition per academic year 2004–05:* undergraduate $320 per credit hour, graduate $368 per credit hour. *Room and board per academic year:* $5,612.

Financial Aid: Aid from institutionally generated funds is provided on the basis of academic merit, financial need, athletic ability.

Financial aid to full-time, first-time undergraduate students: need-based scholarships/grants totaling $5,177,751, self-help $7,437,986, parent loans $345,950, tuition waivers $38,410, athletic awards $111,728; non-need-based scholarships/grants totaling $639,419, self-help $2,725,021, parent loans $777,836, tuition waivers $46,674, athletic awards $137,000.

Departments and Teaching Staff: *Professors* 40, *associate professors* 32, *assistant professors* 33, *instructors* 5, *part-time faculty* 215.

Total instructional faculty: 325 (full-time 110, part-time 215; women 166, men 159; members of minority groups 43). Total faculty with doctorate, first-professional, or other terminal degree: 144. Degrees held by full-time faculty: doctorate 55%, master's 43%, professional 2%. 56% hold terminal degrees.

Enrollment: Total enrollment 4,047. Undergraduate full-time 433 men / 1,15 women, part-time 423m / 1,207w; graduate full-time 43m / 61w, part-time 190m / 495w.

Characteristics of Student Body: *Ethnic/racial makeup:* number of Black non-Hispanic: 402; American Indian or Alaska Native: 7; Asian or Pacific Islander: 46; Hispanic: 89; White non-Hispanic: 2,478; unknown: 133. *Age distribution:* number under 18: 31; 18–19: 197; 20–21: 471; 22–24: 709; 25–29: 574; 30–34: 311; 35–39: 289; 40–49: 487; 50–64: 203; 65 and over: 6.

International Students: 94 nonresident aliens enrolled fall 2004. Programs available to aid students whose native language is not English: social, cultural. English as a Second Language Program. Some financial aid designated for qualifying international students.

Student Life: On-campus residence halls house 6% of student body. Residence halls for men only constitute 10% of such space, for women only 90%. *Intercollegiate athletics:* men only: baseball, basketball; women only: basketball, tennis, volleyball. *Special regulations:* Cars permitted without restrictions. Curfews begin midnight Sun.–Thurs., 3am Fri. and Sat. Quiet hours from 10:30pm to noon. *Special services:* Learning Resources Center, medical services. *Student publications: Phoenix Quarterly,* a newspaper. *Surrounding community:* Livonia population 105,000. Detroit, 20 miles from campus, is nearest metropolitan area. Served by mass transit bus system; airport 15 miles from campus; passenger rail service 20 miles from campus.

Library Collections: 140,143 volumes. 5,662 government documents; 18,609 microforms; 5,648 audiovisual materials; 658 current periodical subscriptions. Access to online information retrieval services and the Internet. Total 2004–05 budget for books and materials: $213,000.

Most important special collections: Holocaust Collection; Leininger Collection.

Buildings and Grounds: Campus area 49 acres.

Chief Executive Officer: Sr. Rose Marie Kujawa, President.

Address admission inquiries to Frank Hribar, Director of Enrollment Management; graduate inquiries to Dr. Edith Raleigh, Dean of Graduate Studies.

Marygrove College

8425 West McNichols Road
Detroit, Michigan 48221-2599

Tel: (313) 927-1200   **E-mail:** admissions@marygrove.edu
Fax: (313) 927-1345   **Internet:** www.marygrove.edu

Institution Description: Marygrove College is a private college affiliated with the Sisters, Servants of the Immaculate Heart of Mary, Roman Catholic Church. *Enrollment:* 4,610. *Degrees awarded:* Associate, baccalaureate, master's.

Member of Detroit Area Consortium of Catholic Colleges.

Accreditation: *Regional:* NCA. *Professional:* radiography, respiratory therapy, social work, teacher education

History: Established in Monroe as St. Mary College 1905; chartered and offered first instruction at postsecondary level 1910; awarded first degree (baccalaureate) 1914; adopted present name 1925; moved to Detroit 1927.

Institutional Structure: *Governing board:* Marygrove College Board of Trustees. Extrainstitutional representation: 36 trustees; institutional representation: president of the college; 1 alumnus. 1 ex officio. All voting. *Composition of institution:* Administrators 7 men / 10 women. Academic affairs headed by vice president. Management/business/finances directed by directed by chief financial officer. Full-time instructional faculty 52. Academic governance body, Academic Council, meets an average of 9 times per year.

Calendar: Semesters. Academic year Sept. to May. Freshmen admitted Sept., Jan. Degrees conferred May, Aug., Dec. Formal commencement May. Summer session from May to Aug.

Characteristics of Freshmen: 40% of applicants admitted. 14% of applicants admitted and enrolled.

57% (24 students) submitted ACT scores. *25th percentile:* ACT Composite 16, ACT English 14, ACT Math 15. *75th percentile:* ACT Composite 21, ACT English 21, ACT Math 19.

93% of freshmen from Michigan. Freshmen 2 states and 1 foreign country.

Admission: Rolling admissions plan. For fall acceptance, apply as early as 1 year, but not later than 2 weeks prior to enrollment. Early acceptance available. *Requirements:* Graduation from accredited secondary school with 16 units recommended; or GED. Additional requirements for some programs. Minimum 2.7 GPA. *Entrance tests:* College Board SAT or ACT composite. For foreign students TOEFL. *For transfer students:* 2.0 minimum GPA; from 4-year accredited institution hours maximum transfer credit limited only by residence requirement; from 2-year accredited institution 64 hours.

College credit and advanced placement for postsecondary-level work completed in secondary school. College credit for extrainstitutional learning (life experience) on basis of ACE *2006 Guide to the Evaluation of Educational Experiences in the Armed Services*; portfolio and faculty assessments; advanced placement on basis of personal interviews.

Tutoring available. Developmental courses offered in summer session and regular academic year; credit given.

Degree Requirements: *For all associate degrees:* 64 credit hours; 15 hours in residence. *For all baccalaureate degrees:* 128 credit hours; 30 hours in residence. *For all degrees:* 2.0 GPA; distribution requirements.

Fulfillment of some degree requirements and exemption from some beginning courses possible by passing departmental examinations, College Board CLEP, AP, other standardized tests. *Grading system:* A–E.

Distinctive Educational Programs: *For undergraduates:* Cooperative education, internships, honors programs, individualized majors, tutorials. Institutionally sponsored study abroad in England, France. Cross-registration through consortium. *For graduate students:* Master's degree in the Art of Teaching, a distance learning program. *Available to all students:* Accelerated degree programs.

Degrees Conferred: 21 *associate;* 102 *baccalaureate:* biological life/sciences 1, business/marketing 11; computer and information sciences 10; education 12; English 9; foreign languages and literature 5; health professions and related clinical sciences 4; home economics and vocational home economics 3; liberal arts 1; mathematics 6; philosophy/religion/theology 3; physical sciences 1; protective services/public administration 11; social sciences and history 13; visual and performing arts 12. 3,158 *master's:* business 8, education 3,144, philosophy/religion/theology 6.

Fees and Other Expenses: *Full-time tuition per academic year 2005–06:* $12,800 undergraduate, $6,012 graduate. *Room and board per academic year:* $6,200. *Other fees:* $250.

Financial Aid: Aid from institutionally generated funds is provided on the basis of financial need.

Financial aid to full-time, first-time undergraduate students: need-based scholarships/grants totaling $2,160,31, self-help $2,618,855, parent $29,160.

Departments and Teaching Staff: *Total instructional faculty:* 71 (full-time 65, part-time 6; women 45, men 26). Total faculty with doctorate, first-professional, or other terminal degree: 44. Student-to-faculty ratio: 15.7:1. Degrees held by full-time faculty: doctorate 61%, master's 39%. 74% hold terminal degrees. *Faculty development:* 3 faculty members awarded sabbaticals 2004–05.

Enrollment: Total enrollment 4,610. Undergraduate full-time 84 men / 270 women, part-time 725m / 312w; graduate full-time 825m / 2,922w, part-time 48m / 77w.

Characteristics of Student Body: *Ethnic/racial makeup:* number of Black non-Hispanic: 601; Asian or Pacific Islander: 1; Hispanic: 10; White non-Hispanic: 47; unknown: 170. *Age distribution:* number under 18: 5; 18–19: 52; 20–21: 65; 22–24: 105; 25–29: 108; 30–34: 108; 35–39: 77; 40–49: 139; 50–64: 75; 65 and over: 4.

International Students: 24 nonresident aliens enrolled fall 2004. 6 students from Europe, 8 Asia, 1 Central and South America, 6 Africa. No programs available to aid students whose native language is not English. No financial aid specifically designated for international students.

Student Life: On-campus residence halls house 5% of student body. Residence halls are coed. *Special regulations:* Cars permitted without restrictions. *Special services:* Learning Resources Center, medical services, consortium intercampus bus. *Student publications: The Marygrove News,* a quarterly paper. *Surrounding community:* Detroit area population over 1 million. Served by mass transit bus system, airport 26 miles from campus, passenger rail service 10 miles from campus.

Publications: *Marygrove Matters* published bimonthly.

Library Collections: 83,483 volumes. Partial depository for government documents; 23,301 microforms; 550 current periodical subscriptions. Online catalog. Students have access to the Internet at no charge.

Most important special holdings include Vatican Collection; fine arts; Rare Book Room Collection of signed (alumni and faculty) publications.

Buildings and Grounds: Campus area 50 acres.

Chief Executive Officer: Dr. Glenda Price, President.

Address admission inquiries to Sally Janecek, Admissions Director; graduate inquiries to Dr. Pamela Loyd, Graduate Admissions Director.

Michigan State University

East Lansing, Michigan 48824

Tel: (517) 355-1855   **E-mail:** admis@msu.edu
Fax: (517) 353-1647   **Internet:** www.msu.edu

Institution Description: Michigan State University is a state institution and the nation's pioneer land-grant college. *Enrollment:* 44,836. *Degrees awarded:* Baccalaureate, first-professional (medicine, osteopathic medicine, veterinary medicine), master's, doctorate. Specialist certificates also awarded.

Accreditation: *Regional:* NCA. *Professional:* accounting, audiology, business, clinical lab scientist, clinical psychology, engineering, English language education, forestry, interior design, journalism, landscape architecture, marriage and family therapy, medicine, music, nursing, nursing education, osteopathy, planning, psychology internship, public administration, recreation and leisure services, rehabilitation counseling, school psychology, social work, speech-language pathology, teacher education, veterinary medicine, veterinary technology

History: Established by state legislature as Agricultural College of State of Michigan 1855; chartered and offered first instruction at postsecondary level 1857; changed name to State Agricultural College and awarded first degree (baccalaureate) 1861; changed name to Michigan Agricultural College 1909, to Michigan State College of Agriculture and Applied Science 1925, to Michigan State University of Agriculture and Applied Science 1955; adopted present name 1964. *See* Madison Kuhn, *Michigan State: The First 100 Years 1855–1955* (East Lansing: Michigan State University Press, 1955) for further information.

Institutional Structure: *Governing board:* Board of Trustees. Extrainstitutional representation: 8 trustees; institutional representation: president of the university, 2 officers of the board. 1 ex officio. 8 voting. *Composition of institution:* Academic affairs headed by provost/vice president for academic affairs. Management/business/finances directed by vice president for finance, operations, treasurer. Full-time instructional faculty 1,716 men / 955 women. Academic governance body, Academic Council, meets an average of 8 times per year.

Calendar: Semesters. Academic year Aug. to May. Freshmen admitted Sept., Jan., May. Formal commencement Dec., May. Summer session of 2 terms from mid-May to mid-Aug.

Characteristics of Freshmen: 79% of applicants admitted. 43.9% of applicants admitted and enrolled.

25% (1,869 students) submitted SAT scores; 91% (6,951 students) submitted ACT scores. Mean SAT scores 547 verbal, 563 mathematical. Mean ACT composite score 24.

65% of entering freshmen expected to graduate within 5 years. 89% of freshmen from Michigan. Freshmen from 50 states and 75 foreign countries.

Admission: Students admitted for entering class must demonstrate completion of the following: (1) four years of college preparatory composition and literature courses; 3 years of college preparatory mathematics, including 2 years of algebra and 1 year of geometry; 2 years of college preparatory science courses from the areas of biology, chemistry, physics, and earth science; 3 years in history and the social sciences with at least1 year of history and 1 year of social sciences from such areas as anthropology, economics, geography, government, political science, psychology, or sociology. *Entrance tests:* College Board SAT or ACT composite. For foreign students TOEFL or other standardized test of English. *For transfer students:* in-state residents, 2.0 minimum GPA, out-of-state students 3.0; from 2-year accredited institution 60 semester credits (90 quarter hours) maximum transfer credit; correspondence/extension students 45 hours.

College credit and advanced placement for postsecondary-level work completed in secondary school. Tutoring available. Developmental and remedial courses offered in summer session and regular academic year; credit given.

Degree Requirements: 120–140 credit hours; 2.0 GPA; 1 year (at least 30 credit hours) in residence; 20 credit hours in the major; 26 credit hours in general education courses or approved substitutes.

Fulfillment of some degree requirements and exemption from some beginning courses possible by passing institutional examinations, College Board CLEP, AP. *Grading system:* Numerical (4.0-0-0); pass-no grade; credit-no credit.

Distinctive Educational Programs: Off-campus centers. Dual undergraduate-graduate enrollment for qualified seniors. Special facilities for using telecommunications in the classroom. Interdisciplinary programs in film studies, Jewish studies, women's studies. Preprofessional programs in dentistry, law, medicine, optometry, osteopathy, theology, veterinary medicine. Facilities and programs for independent research, including honors programs, individual majors, tutorials. Study abroad programs in Australia, Bahamas, Baltics, Belgium, Brazil, Canada, China, Costa Rica, Denmark, Dominican Republic, Ecuador, England, France, Germany, Guyana, Hawaii, Hungary, Ireland, Israel, Italy, Japan, Kenya, Lesotho, Malaysia, Mexico, Nepal, New Zealand, Norway, Russia, Scotland, Singapore, South Africa, South Korea, Spain, Surinam, Swaziland, Sweden, Switzerland, Taiwan, The Netherlands, Trinidad, Tobago, Ukraine, Virgin Islands, West Indies, Zimbabwe. *Other distinctive programs:* Lifelong Education Programs, including credit and noncredit courses; external courses at various off-campus locations throughout Michigan and through a television network; courses also offered overseas. College admissions for educationally disadvantaged students through College Achievement Admissions Program.

ROTC: Army, Air Force.

Degrees Conferred: 165 *associate;* 7,783 *baccalaureate* (B), 2,091 *master's* (M), 430 *doctorate* (D): agriculture 482 (B), 97 (M), 34 (D); architecture 45 (B), 8 (M); area and ethnic studies 9 (B), 5 (M), 11 (D); biological/life sciences 548 (B), 52 (M), 53 (D); business/marketing 1,452 (B), 455 (M), 8 (D); communications/communication technologies 1,039 (B), 112 (M), 11 (D); computer and information sciences 89 (B), 41 (M), 7 (D); education 287 (B), 556 (M), 47 (D); engineering and engineering technologies 591 (B), 121 (M), 36 (D); English 216 (B), 5 (M), 13 (D); foreign languages and literature 126 (B), 22 (M), 13 (D); home economics and vocational home economics 186 (B), 53 (M), 12 (D); interdisciplinary studies 100 (B), 15 (M), 1 (D); law/legal studies 16 (B); liberal arts/general studies 64 (B), 3 (D); mathematics 60 (B), 39 (M), 9 (D); natural resources/environmental science 90 (B), 23 (M), 15 (D); parks and recreation 190 (B), 30 (M), 13 (D); philosophy/religion/theology 26 (B), 2 (M), 5 (D); physical sciences 97 (B), 54 (M), 36 (D); protective services/public administration 229 (B), 60 (M), 6 (D); psychology 363 (B), 25 (M), 22 (D); social sciences and history 881 (B), 62 (M), 39 (D); visual and performing arts 247 (B), 72 (M), 29 (D); other 290 (B), 179 (M), 9 (D). 344 *first-professional:* medicine 121; osteopathic medicine 134; veterinary medicine 89.

Fees and Other Expenses: *Full-time tuition per academic year 2004–05:* undergraduate resident $20,625, nonresident $567.75 per credit hour; graduate resident $304 per credit hour, nonresident $632 per credit hour. *Required fees:* $812. *Room and board per academic year:* $5,458.

Financial Aid: Michigan State University offers a direct lending program. Aid from institutionally generated funds is provided on the basis of academic merit, financial need, athletic ability.

Financial aid to full-time, first-time undergraduate students: need-based scholarships/grants totaling $34,990,380, self-help $57,408,667, parent loans $3,974,950, tuition waivers $863,217, athletic awards $1,681,336; non-need-based scholarships/grants totaling $60,972,748, self-help $43,960,303, parent loans $34,935,933, tuition waivers $1,548,896, athletic awards $4,916,621.

Departments and Teaching Staff: *Total instructional faculty:* 2,671 (full-time 2,311, part-time 360; women 955, men 161; members of minority groups 481). Total faculty with doctorate, first-professional, or other terminal degree: 2,406. Student-to-faculty ratio: 18:1. Degrees held by full-time faculty: baccalaureate .4%, master's 4.9%, doctorate 83.5%. 94.6% hold terminal degrees. *Faculty development:* $208,983,765 total grants for research.

Enrollment: Total enrollment 44,836. Undergraduate full-time 14,785 men / 16,913 women, part-time 1,827m / 1,883w; first-professional full-time 500m / 861w, part-time 11m / 16w; graduate full-time 2,672m / 2,826w, part-time 878m / 1,664w. *Transfer students:* 1,682 undergraduate.

Characteristics of Student Body: *Ethnic/racial makeup:* number of Black non-Hispanic: 2,954; American Indian or Alaska Native: 237; Asian or Pacific Islander: 1,931; Hispanic: 982; White non-Hispanic: 2,785; unknown: 301.

International Students: 3,315 nonresident aliens enrolled fall 2004. Programs available to aid students whose native language is not English: social, cultural. English as a Second Language Program. No financial aid specifically designated for international students.

Student Life: On-campus residence halls house 43% of student body. Residence halls for both men and women constitute 86% of such space. 7% of men join and 53% of members live in fraternities; 7% of women join and 57% of members live in sororities. Cooperative houses and special interest houses also offer residence space. Married student housing is readily available on campus. 48% of students live in University housing. *Intercollegiate athletics:* men only: baseball, basketball, cross-country, fencing, football, golf, gymnastics, ice hockey, soccer, swimming, tennis, track, wrestling; women only: basketball, crew, cross-country, field hockey, golf, gymnastics, soccer, softball, swimming, tennis, track, volleyball. *Special regulations:* Cars permitted in commuter parking lots only 7am to 6pm, Mon.–Fri. Quiet hours and residence hall visitation determined by residents; some quiet floors are predetermined. *Special services:* Learning Resources Center, Counseling Center, Service-Learning Center, Career Services and Placement, Minority Programs Office, Student Employment Office, Handicapped Programs Office, Army and Air Force ROTC, medical services, bus service to and from commuter parking lots. *Student publications, radio and television: The State News,* a newspaper; *Red Cedar Log,* a yearbook. Radio stations WDBM-FM, WFIX, WKAR-AM and FM. Television station WKAR-TV. *Surrounding community:* East Lansing population 50,000. Detroit, 85 miles from campus, is nearest metropolitan area. Served by mass transit bus system; airport 10 miles from campus; passenger rail service on campus.

Publications: *African Rural and Urban Studies* (triennially), *African Studies Center Newsletter* (semiannually); *Tuesday Bulletin of the African Studies Center* (weekly); *The Centennial Review* (triennially); *Futures* (Agricultural Experiment Station) published quarterly; *Journal of South Asian Literature* (semiannually).

Library Collections: 4,694,966 volumes. Current serial subscriptions: 37,880 paper; 6,486,127 microforms; 22,591 via electronic access. 6,990 recordings. Online catalog. Computer work stations available. Students have access to online information retrieval services and the Internet.

Most important special holdings include collections on veterinary medicine, French monarchy, and popular culture; modern literary papers of Michigan State University graduates.

Buildings and Grounds: Campus area 5,192 acres (including experimental farms, research facilities, and natural areas).

Chief Executive Officer: Dr. Lou Anna K. Simon, President.

Address admission inquiries to Pamela Horne, Director of Admissions.

College of Arts and Letters

Degree Programs Offered: *Baccalaureate* in ancient studies, art education, composition and music theory, East Asian languages and cultures, humanities, humanities-prelaw, instrumental music education, Latin, music, music theory and composition, musical theater, religious studies, school music-choral, school music-instrumental, school music-stringed instrument teaching; *baccalaureate* and *master's* in French, German, history of art, music therapy, Russian, Spanish, studio art; *baccalaureate, master's,* and *doctorate* in applied music, English, history, linguistics, philosophy, theater; *master's* in art education, American studies, English-community college teaching, English-creative writing, English-secondary school teaching, English-teaching of English to speakers of other languages, French-secondary school teaching, history-secondary school teaching, Spanish-secondary school teaching; *master's* and *doctorate* in history-urban studies, music composition, music education, music theory, musicology; *doctorate* in art education, French-language and literature, German-language and literature, Russian-language and literature, Spanish-language and literature.

College of Agriculture and Natural Resources

Degree Programs Offered: *Baccalaureate* in agribusiness and natural resources education, agriculture and natural resources communications, biochemistry-agriculture, food systems economics and management, natural resources and environmental education, public affairs management; *baccalaureate, master's* in building construction management, packaging; *baccalaureate, master's, doctorate* in agricultural engineering technology, animal science, crop and soil sciences, fisheries and wildlife, food science, forestry, horticulture, park and recreation resources, resource development; *master's* in recreation; *master's, doctorate* in agricultural extension education, agricultural economics, agricultural economics-urban studies, agricultural engineering, biochemistry, park and recreation resources-urban studies, plant breeding and genetics-crop and soil sciences, plant breeding and genetics-forestry, plant breeding and genetics-horticulture, resource development-urban studies.

Distinctive Educational Programs: Joint baccalaureate program in agricultural engineering with College of Engineering. Interdepartmental graduate programs in plant breeding and genetics and urban studies. Interdepartmental graduate specialization in resource economics. Cooperative extension service offers off-campus educational and public service programs. Facilities include agricultural experiment station, biological station, center for remote sensing, plant research laboratory, pesticide research center, Institute of International Agriculture, Institute of Nutrition, Institute of Water Research.

Eli Broad College of Business

Degree Programs Offered: *Baccalaureate* in food industry management, general business administration, general business administration-prelaw, hotel and restaurant management, personnel administration, travel and tourism management; *baccalaureate, master's* in food systems economics and management, materials and logistics management-operations management, materials and logistics management-purchasing management, materials and logistics management-transportation/physical distribution management, professional accounting; *baccalaureate, master's, doctorate* in economics, marketing; *baccalaureate, doctorate* in accounting; *master's* in business administration, hotel/restaurant/institutional management, management science, operations in finance; *doctorate* in management policy and strategy, organizational behavior-personnel, production and operations management, transportation distribution.

Distinctive Educational Programs: 5-year baccalaureate-master's in business administration program in professional accounting. Interdepartmental graduate specializations in resource economics.

College of Communication Arts and Sciences

Degree Programs Offered: *Baccalaureate, master's* in advertising, journalism, telecommunication; *baccalaureate, master's, doctorate* in audiology and speech sciences, communication; *master's* in communication-urban studies, public relations; *doctorate* in audiology and speech sciences-mass media, audiology and speech sciences-urban studies.

Distinctive Educational Programs: Secondary school teacher preparation in cooperation with College of Education. Dual-major programs with College of Agriculture and Natural Resources, College of Engineering, James Madison College. Interdepartmental programs in urban studies.

College of Education

Degree Programs Offered: *Baccalaureate* in education; *baccalaureate, master's, doctorate* in physical education and exercise science, special education; *master's, doctorate* in adult and continuing education, college and university administration, counseling, counseling psychology, curriculum and teaching, educational psychology, educational systems development, k–12 educational administration, measurement, evaluation, and research design.

Distinctive Educational Programs: Facilities include Center for the Study of Human Performance, Institute for Research on Teaching, Michigan Vocational Education Resource Center, Office for International Networks in Education, Research and Development Center in Teacher Education, University Center for International Rehabilitation, and Youth Sports Institute.

College of Engineering

Degree Programs Offered: *Baccalaureate* in biosystems engineering, computer engineering, engineering arts, materials science and engineering; *baccalaureate, master's, doctorate* in chemical engineering, civil engineering, computer science, electrical engineering, mechanical engineering, mechanics; *master's* in civil engineering-urban studies, environmental engineering-urban studies; *master's, doctorate* in environmental engineering, materials science, metallurgy.

Distinctive Educational Programs: 5-year joint baccalaureate program in engineering for international service with College of Arts and Letters or College of Social Science. Cooperative Engineering Education program.

College of Human Ecology

Degree Programs Offered: *Baccalaureate* in apparel design, dietetics, family and consumer resources, family community services, foods: technology and management, nutrition, human environment and design, interior design, merchandising management, nutritional sciences; *baccalaureate, master's* in clothing and textiles, home economics education; *master's* in child development, community services, family economics and management, family studies, human shelter and interior design, institution administration; *master's, doctorate* in foods, human nutrition; *doctorate* in family ecology.

Distinctive Educational Programs: Qualifying programs for teaching home economics in secondary schools and for teaching in nursery schools, kindergarten, primary and elementary grades, all in cooperation with College of Education. Facilities include Institute of Nutrition.

College of Natural Science

Degree Programs Offered: *Baccalaureate* in astrophysics, biology, botany, chemistry-teaching, computer science, earth science, environmental science, medical technology, physical science, science and technology studies; *baccalaureate, master's* in clinical laboratory sciences, computational mathematics, microbiology; *baccalaureate, master's, intermediate, doctorate* in chemistry, geology, mathematics, physics; *baccalaureate, master's, doctorate* in biochemistry, chemical physics, chemistry, entomology, geology, mathematics, physics, physiology, statistics, zoology; *master's* in operations research-statistics; *master's, intermediate, doctorate* in botany and plant pathology; *master's, doctorate* in entomology-urban studies; doctorate in genetics, mathematics education, microbiology and public health.

Distinctive Educational Programs: Lyman Briggs residential school. Interdepartmental majors in biological science, earth science, general science, genetics, physical science. Secondary school mathematics and science teacher preparation programs with College of Education. Facilities include biological station, center for electron optics, pesticide research center, planetarium, plant research laboratory.

College of Social Science

Degree Programs Offered: *Baccalaureate* in landscape architecture, political science-prelaw, social science interdisciplinary program, social work; *bac-*

calaureate, master's in criminal justice, public administration, urban planning; *baccalaureate, master's, doctorate* in anthropology, geography, political science, psychology, social science, sociology; *master's* in administration and program evaluation, administration and program evaluation-urban studies, clinical social work, clinical social work-urban studies, criminal justice-urban studies, geography-urban studies, labor and industrial relations, labor and industrial relations-urban studies; *master's, doctorate* in sociology-urban studies; *doctorate* in political science-urban studies, psychology-urban studies, social science-labor and industrial relations, social science-social work, social science-urban planning, social science-teaching.

Distinctive Educational Programs: Multidisciplinary curriculum. Preprofessional programs in law. Social science residence-program for undergraduates. Undergraduate international development specialization. Cooperative program in secondary school teaching with College of Education. Interdepartmental graduate programs in urban studies. Facilities include Social Science Research Bureau.

College of Nursing

Degree Programs Offered: *Baccalaureate, master's.*

James Madison College

Degree Programs Offered: *Baccalaureate* in social science.

Distinctive Educational Programs: James Madison College is a small residential college that examines how major policy decisions are made in society. Senior or junior year Field Experience Internships.

College of Human Medicine

Degree Programs Offered: *Master's* in epidemiology, surgery; *master's, doctorate* in anatomy, biochemistry, microbiology, pathology, pharmacology and toxicology, physiology; *first-professional* in human medicine; dual degree medical scientist training program in human medicine.

Admission: *For first-professional degree:* 90 undergraduate semester hours which must include 6 hours in English, 8 chemistry (organic and inorganic, both with laboratory), 6 biology with laboratory, 6 physics with laboratory, 6 social science, 18 additional hours in non-science subjects; MCAT; applications through American Medical College Application Service (AAM-CAS) by November 15 of year preceding entrance.

Degree Requirements: Prescribed curriculum; successful completion of Part I of the National Board of Medical Examiners (NBME).

College of Veterinary Medicine

Degree Programs Offered: *Baccalaureate, first-professional* in veterinary medicine; *master's* in microbiology, small animal clinical sciences; *master's, doctorate* in anatomy, large animal clinical sciences, pathology, pharmacology, physiology; *doctorate* in microbiology and public health.

Admission: *For first-professional degree:* 14 undergraduate semester credits in chemistry with laboratory, 8 general physics with laboratory, 6 general biology, 4 algebra and trigonometry, 8 arts and humanities, 8 social science, 6 English; MCAT or GRE; applications by first working Monday of the January preceding anticipated matriculation date.

Degree Requirements: *For first-professional:* Prescribed curriculum.

Distinctive Educational Programs: Preprofessional veterinary program. Interdepartmental doctoral programs in environmental toxicology. Facilities include animal health diagnostic laboratory and veterinary clinical center.

College of Osteopathic Medicine

Degree Programs Offered: *Master's, doctorate* in anatomy, biochemistry, microbiology, pathology, pharmacology and toxicology, physiology; *doctorate* in environmental toxicology-anatomy, environmental toxicology-pharmacology and toxicology, neuroscience interdepartmental program; *first-professional* in osteopathic medicine, dual degree medical scientist training program in osteopathic medicine.

Admission: *For first-professional degree:* 90 undergraduate semester hours from an accredited college or university, including 6 each of English and psycho-social-behavioral sciences and 8 of biology, inorganic chemistry, organic chemistry, physics. No required course grade below 2.0; 2.5 minimum GPA, overall and in all science courses; MCAT. Applications through American Association of Colleges of Osteopathic Medicine Application Service by November 1 of the year prior to entrance.

Degree Requirements: *For first-professional:* Prescribed curriculum; endorsement of the Committee on Student Evaluation and an affirmative vote from college faculty.

Michigan Technological University

1400 Townsend Drive
Houghton, Michigan 49931-1295
Tel: (906) 487-1885   **E-mail:** mtu4u@mtu.edu
Fax: (906) 487-2125   **Internet:** www.mtu.edu

Institution Description: Michigan Technological University is a state institution. *Enrollment:* 6,527. *Degrees awarded:* Associate, baccalaureate, master's, doctorate. Certificates also awarded.

Budget subject to approval by state governing boards.

Accreditation: *Regional:* NCA. *Professional:* applied science, business, engineering, engineering technology, forestry

History: Established and chartered as Michigan Mining School 1885; offered first instruction at postsecondary level 1886; awarded first degree (baccalaureate) 1888; changed name to Michigan College of Mines 1897, to Michigan College of Mining and Technology 1927; adopted present name 1964.

Institutional Structure: *Governing board:* Board of Control. Extrainstitutional representation: president of the university, 1 ex officio. 8 voting. *Composition of institution:* Academic affairs/student affairs headed by provost and senior vice president for academic affairs. General administration/finance/auxiliary/retail services and facilities directed by vice president for finance and administration. Other areas headed by vice presidents. Full-time instructional faculty 311 men / 66 women. Academic governance body, University Senate, meets an average of 16 times per year.

Calendar: Quarters. Academic year early Sept. to mid-May. Freshmen admitted Sept., Dec. Mar., June. Degrees conferred May, Aug., Nov., Feb. Formal commencements May, Nov. Summer session from early June to mid-Aug.

Characteristics of Freshmen: 94.5% of applicants accepted. 43% of accepted applicants enrolled.

Average secondary school rank of freshmen men 74th percentile, women 82nd percentile, class 76th percentile. Mean SAT class score 579.3 verbal, 617.4 mathematical. Mean ACT composite class 25.2.

58% of entering freshmen expected to graduate within 5 years. 79% of freshmen from Michigan. Freshmen from 21 states and 16 foreign countries.

Admission: Rolling admissions plan. For fall acceptance, apply as early as Oct. 1 of previous year, but not later than 30 days prior to beginning of quarter. *Requirements:* Either graduation from accredited secondary school with 15 academic units; or GED. For engineering, forestry, and science programs, 3 units English, 3 mathematics, 1 chemistry or physics recommended. Lowest recommended secondary school class standing 50th percentile. Rank in top third of class preferred for applicants to engineering programs. *For transfer students:* 2.0 minimum GPA; maximum transfer credit from accredited institutions determined by departmental guidelines.

College credit and advanced placement for postsecondary-level work completed in secondary school. College credit for extrainstitutional learning on basis of ACE *2006 Guide to the Evaluation of Educational Experiences in the Armed Services;* faculty assessment. Tutoring available. Remedial courses offered during regular academic year; nondegree credit given.

Degree Requirements: *For all associate degrees:* 96–103 credit hours. *For all baccalaureate degrees:* 186–208 credit hours; general education requirements include specific number of credits in communications, quantitative knowledge, science, humanities, social sciences, physical education, and upper division thematic studies. *For all undergraduate degrees:* 2.0 GPA; final 3 quarters in residence.

Fulfillment of some degree requirements and exemption from some beginning courses possible by passing departmental examinations, College Board CLEP, AP. *Grading system:* A–F; pass-fail.

Distinctive Educational Programs: Undergraduate and graduate research programs. Work-experience and cooperative programs. Flexible meeting places and schedules, including off-campus centers (at Ford Forestry Center, 42 miles from main institution). Double degrees in business administration, surveying, and other disciplines. Clinical internships in clinical laboratory science with approved hospitals. Interdisciplinary programs in bioengineering, environmental reclamation, geo-environmental engineering, and manufacturing engineering. Facilities and programs for independent research, individual majors, tutorials. Community college plan offers counseling to students at state community colleges who plan to transfer to Michigan Tech. *Other distinctive programs:* Institute of Materials Processing. Institute of Wood Research. A.E. Seaman Mineralogical Museum. Keweenaw Research Center. Ford Forestry Center. National Center for Clean Industrial and Treatment Technologies. Biological Sciences Research Groups. Environmental Engineering Center. Center for Manufacturing Research. Remote Sensing and Environmental Monitoring Institute. Institute of Snow Research. Center for Experimental Computation. Academic-year exchange programs, summer programs, or work internships in 23 countries including China, England, Finland, France, Germany, Japan.

ROTC: Army, Air Force.

Degrees Conferred: 71 *associate;* 1,042 *baccalaureate.* Bachelor's degrees awarded in top five disciplines: Engineering 634; business, management, marketing, and related support services 118; engineering technologies 69; computer and information sciences 55; biological/biomedical sciences 53.

Fees and Other Expenses: *Full-time tuition per academic year 2004=05:* undergraduate resident $7,610, nonresident $18,782. Contact the university for graduate tuition/fees. *Room and board per academic year:* $5,795.

Financial Aid: Aid from institutionally generated funds is provided on the basis of academic merit, financial need, athletic ability, other criteria. Institution has a Program Participation Agreement with the U.S. Department of Education for eligible students to receive Pell Grants and, depending upon agreement, other federal aid.

Departments and Teaching Staff: *Professors* 117, *associate professors* 152, *assistant professors* 70, *instructors* 64, *part-time teachers* 29.

Total instructional faculty: 374. Student-to-faculty ratio: 14:1. Degrees held by full-time faculty: doctorate 87%, master's 10%, baccalaureate 2%. 88% hold terminal degrees.

Enrollment: Total enrollment 6,527. Undergraduate 5,696 (71.5% men, 22.5% women).

Characteristics of Student Body: *Ethnic/racial makeup:* Black non-Hispanic: 77; American Indian or Alaska Native: 57; Asian or Pacific Islander: 65; Hispanic: 48; White non-Hispanic: 5,362. *Age distribution:* 17–21: 63%; 22–24: 22%; 25–29: 8%; 30–34: 3%; 35–39: 2%; 40–49: 2%; 50–59: less than .5%; 60–and over: less than .5%.

International Students: 532 nonresident aliens enrolled. Students from Europe, Asia, Central and South America, Africa, Canada. Programs available to aid students whose native language is not English: social, cultural, financial. English as a Second Language Program. Financial aid specifically designated for undergraduate international students: competitive scholarships available annually.

Student Life: On-campus residence halls house 43% of student body. All residence halls are co-ed. Institutionally controlled apartments house 7% of student body. 8% of all men join and 5% live in fraternities; 13% of women join and 5% live in sororities. *Intercollegiate athletics:* men: basketball, cross-country, football, hockey, Nordic skiing, tennis, track and field; women: basketball, cross-country, Nordic skiing, tennis, track and field, volleyball. *Special regulations:* Registered cars permitted. *Special services:* Learning Resources Center, medical services. *Student publications, radio:* Weekly newspaper. Radio station WMTU broadcasts 168 hours per week. *Surrounding community:* Houghton population 8,000. Milwaukee (WI), 325 miles from campus, is nearest metropolitan area. Served by mass transit bus system; airport 8 miles from campus.

Library Collections: 940,065 volumes. 446,700 government documents. 542,200 microforms. 5,114 periodical titles. 5,000 audiovisual materials. Online catalog. 1,636 compact discs; 364 floppy discs. Computer work stations available. Students have access to the Internet at no charge.

Most important special holdings include Upper Peninsula/Keweenaw and University Historical Archives; Calumet and Hecla Mining Companies Collections; Quincy Mining Company Collections; U.S. Congressional Serial Set: Senate and House Reports and Documents from 1817 to the present.

Buildings and Grounds: Main campus area 200 acres.

Chief Executive Officer: Dr. Glenn D. Mroz, President.

Address admission inquiries to Nancy Rehling, Director of Undergraduate Admissions; graduate inquiries to Jill Oliver, Coordinator, Graduate Admissions.

Northern Michigan University

1401 Presque Isle Avenue
Marquette, Michigan 49855
Tel: (906) 227-2650   **E-mail:** admiss@nmu.edu
Fax: (906) 227-1747   **Internet:** www.nmu.edu

Institution Description: Northern Michigan University is a state institution. *Enrollment:* 9,331. *Degrees awarded:* Associate, baccalaureate, master's. Specialist certificates in education and other certificates also awarded.

Academic offerings subject to approval by statewide coordinating bodies.

Accreditation: *Regional:* NCA. *Professional:* business, culinary education, dental assisting, medical assisting

History: Established and chartered as Northern Michigan Normal School 1899; offered first instruction at postsecondary level 1918; awarded first degree (baccalaureate) 1920; adopted present name 1963. *See* Miriam Hilton, *Northern Michigan University: The First 75 Years* (Marquette: Northern Michigan University Press, 1975) for further information.

Institutional Structure: *Governing board:* Northern Michigan University Board of Control Extrainstitutional representation: 8 members; institutional representation: president of the university. 1 ex officio. 8 voting. *Composition of institution:* Administrators 65 men / 7 women. Academic affairs headed by vice president for academic affairs. Management/business/finances directed by vice president for finance and administration. Full-time instructional faculty 294. Academic governance body, Academic Senate, meets an average of 15 times per year. *Faculty representation:* Faculty served by collective bargaining agent affiliated with AAUP.

Calendar: Semesters. Academic year Sept. to May. Freshmen admitted Aug., Jan., June. Degrees conferred Formal commencement May, Aug., Dec.

Characteristics of Freshmen: 89% of applicants accepted. 38% of accepted applicants enrolled.

Mean ACT Composite score 20

40% of entering freshmen expected to graduate within 5 years. 95% of freshmen from Michigan. Freshmen from 19 states and 9 foreign countries.

Admission: Rolling admissions plan. For fall acceptance, apply as early as Sept. 1 of previous year, but not later than Aug. 15 of year of enrollment. *Requirements:* Recommend 4 units in English, 3 college preparatory mathematics, 2 physical and natural sciences. Additional requirements for some programs. *Entrance tests:* ACT composite score of 19, and recomputed high school GPA of 2.25 (academic subjects only) are both required for regular admission in good standing. *For transfer students:* From 4-year accredited institution no maximum transfer credit; from 2-year accredited institution 64 academic hours, 4 physical education; correspondence/extension students 16 hours.

College credit and advanced placement for postsecondary-level work completed in secondary school. College credit for extrainstitutional learning on basis of ACE 2006 *Guide to the Evaluation of Educational Experiences in the Armed Services;* portfolio and faculty assessments. Tutoring available. Developmental courses offered during regular academic year; credit given.

Degree Requirements: *For all associate degrees:* 62–89 credit hours; 1 term in residence; 2 hours physical education. *For all baccalaureate degrees:* 124–132 credit hours; 2 terms in residence; 4 hours physical education; liberal studies requirement; exit competency examination in writing. *For all degrees:* 2.0 GPA.

Fulfillment of some degree requirements and exemption from some beginning courses possible by passing departmental examination, College Board CLEP, AP. *Grading system:* A–F; pass-fail; withdraw (carries time limit).

Distinctive Educational Programs: Weekend and evening classes. Accelerated degree programs. Individualized majors. Facilities and programs for independent research. Study abroad at approved universities. *Other distinctive programs:* Credit and noncredit continuing education. Labor education program for upper Michigan labor organizations. School of Banking offers programs to bank professionals. The Glenn T. Seaborg Center for Teaching and Learning Science and Mathematics; Small Business Development Center; Center for Educational Development; Northern Economic Initiatives Center; Sports Training Center (in conjunction with the United States Olympic Committee).

ROTC: Army.

Degrees Conferred: 130 *associate;* 1,101 *baccalaureate;* 207 *master's.* Bachelor's degrees awarded in top five disciplines: education 198; business, management, marketing, and related support services 163; visual and performing arts 993; health professions and related clinical sciences 89; social sciences 83.

Fees and Other Expenses: *Full-time tuition per academic year 2004–05:* resident $5,334, nonresident $8,742. *Room and board per academic year:* $5,724.

Financial Aid: Northern Michigan University offers a direct lending program. Aid from institutionally generated funds is provided on the basis of academic merit, financial need, athletic ability, other criteria. Institution has a Program Participation Agreement with the U.S. Department of Education for eligible students to receive Pell Grants and, depending on agreement, other federal aid.

Departments and Teaching Staff: *Total instructional faculty:* 338 (full-time 294, part-time 44). Student-to-faculty ratio: 20:1. 80% hold terminal degrees.

Enrollment: Total enrollment 9,331. Undergraduate 8,603 (47.8% men, 53.2% women).

Characteristics of Student Body: *Ethnic/racial makeup:* Black non-Hispanic: 68; American Indian or Native Alaskan: 149; Asian or Pacific Islander: 33; Hispanic: 54; White non-Hispanic: 6,662; unknown: 196. *Age distribution:* 17–21: 49%; 22–24: 17%; 25–29: 12%; 30–34: 8%; 35–39: 6%; 40–49: 4%; 50–59: 1%; 60–and over: 2%.

International Students: 82 nonresident aliens enrolled. Programs available to aid students whose native language is not English: English as a Second Language Program. Financial aid specifically designated for international students: scholarships awarded annually to qualified students.

Student Life: On-campus residence halls house 29% of student body. Some students live in college-operated apartments. Housing available for married students. *Intercollegiate athletics:* men only: basketball, cross-country skiing, football, hockey; women only: basketball, skiing, swimming, tennis, volleyball. *Special regulations:* Cars must be registered. Quiet hours available. *Special services:* Learning Resources Center, medical services. *Student publications, radio, television: North Wind,* a weekly newspaper; Radio stations: WBKX broadcasts 168 hours per week; WNMU-FM. Television station WNMU-TV. *Surrounding community:* Marquette population 24,000. Milwaukee (WI), 300 miles southwest from campus, is nearest metropolitan area. Served by mass transit bus system; airport 30 miles from campus.

Publications: *Publisher:* Northern Michigan University Press.

Library Collections: 592,700 volumes. 830,200 microforms; 7,300 audiovisual materials. 2,485 periodicals; 30,000 maps; 9,000 recordings/tapes. Online catalog. Students have access to online information retrieval services and the Internet.

Most important holdings include Moses Coit Tyler Collection; Finnish-American Collection; Holocaust Collection; Curriculum Media Center; Archives Collection.

Buildings and Grounds: Campus area 320 acres.

Chief Executive Officer: Dr. Leslie E. Wong, President.

Address admission inquiries to Gerri L. Daniels, Director of Admissions.

School of Arts and Science

Degree Programs Offered: *Associate* in crafts, media illustration, industrial media, *baccalaureate* in art and design, biology, chemistry, economics, English, foreign languages, geography, history, mathematics and computer science, military science, music, philosophy, physics, political science, speech; *master's* in administrative services, biology, chemistry, English, geography, history, music education.

Distinctive Educational Programs: Interdisciplinary programs in general science, biochemistry, social studies, water science, special studies. Preprofessional programs in architecture, health science, engineering. Individually designed programs. 160-acre Longyear Tract provides experimental facilities for botany and conservation courses.

College of Professional Studies

Degree Programs Offered: *Associate* in clinical laboratory science; *baccalaureate, master's* in clinical science, cytotechnology, medical technology, nursing, communication disorders, applied sociology, athletic training, corrections, criminal justice, dietetics, elementary education, health, health education, management of health and fitness, nursing, outdoor recreation leadership and management, physical education, psychology, secondary education, social science/sociology, social work, sociology, special education, sports science.

Distinctive Educational Programs: Four-year generic, BSN completion, and MSN programs in nursing. Two- and four-year medical technology programs, four-year clinical science and cytotechnology programs and one-year clinical assistant program. Department of communication disorders has speech and hearing clinic and computer lab for research.

The Walker L. Cisler College of Business

Degree Programs Offered: *Associate* in legal secretary, medical secretary, secretarial, general office, general business and computer information systems; *baccalaureate* in accounting, accounting/computer information systems, finance, management, marketing, computer information systems, office administration and business education; *master's* in business education, business administration.

Distinctive Educational Programs: Computer information systems program requiring CIS core and the business core. A joint major in accounting/CIS requiring the business core, the CIS and the accounting core. Ski area business management. Entrepreneurship.

College of Technology and Applied Sciences

Degree Programs Offered: Construction management, carpentry, wood technology, building technology, refrigeration, air conditioning and heating, cabinetry and furniture, manufacturing technology, CAD graphics and systems, automated systems/robotics, materials testing and inspection, welding, machine tool, metals, automotive service technician, transportation parts management, auto body technician, heavy duty truck service, restaurant and food service management, culinary arts, meat science, electronics engineering technology, electronics technology, consumer electronics, broadcasting technology, biomedical equipment technology, computer maintenance technology, electromechanical technology, electrical maintenance technology.

Distinctive Educational Programs: Internship programs in all departments. 2+2+2 articulation between matriculating programs. 2+2 articulation for transfers from community colleges and appropriate postsecondary institutions. All baccalaureate programs emphasize technology systems and management strategies.

Northwood University

4000 Whiting Drive
Midland, Michigan 48640
Tel: (989) 837-4200   **E-mail:** admissions@northwood.edu
Fax: (989) 837-4111   **Internet:** www.northwood.edu

Institution Description: Northwood University, formerly known as Northwood Institute, is a private institution with branch campuses in West Palm Beach, Florida, and Cedar Hill, Texas. *Enrollment:* 3,748. *Degrees awarded:* Associate, baccalaureate. Certificates also awarded.

Accreditation: *Regional:* NCA.

History: Established 1959.

Institutional Structure: *Governing board:* Northwood Institute Board of Trustees. Extrainstitutional representation: 30 trustees, 9 honorary trustees; institutional representation: 2 administrators. *Composition of institution:* Management/business/finances directed by business manager. Full-time instructional faculty 35.

Calendar: Quarters. Academic year early Sept. to mid-May. Three 10-week terms with mini-sessions between terms and summer sessions. Formal commencement May.

Characteristics of Freshmen: 49% of applicants accepted. 47% of accepted applicants enrolled.

Average secondary school rank of freshmen 71st percentile. Mean SAT score 475 verbal, 480 mathematical. Mean ACT Composite score 21.

39.5% of entering freshmen expected to graduate within 5 years. 79.9% of freshmen from Michigan.

Admission: Rolling admissions plan. *Requirements:* Either graduation from secondary school or GED. Minimum 2.0 GPA. *Entrance tests:* College Board SAT or ACT composite. *For transfer students:* Good academic and social standing at institution previously attended.

College credit and advanced placement for postsecondary-level work completed in secondary school.

Degree Requirements: *For all associate degrees:* 90 credit hours; general education requirements. *For all baccalaureate degrees:* 180 credit hours; prescribed major curriculum; minor requirement. *For all degrees:* 2.0 GPA.

Fulfillment of some degree requirements and exemption from some beginning courses possible by passing departmental, College Board examinations. *Grading system:* A–F; withdraw (carries time limit); incomplete (carries time limit).

Distinctive Educational Programs: Externships. University College emphasizes experiential learning and offers individualized home study as well as directed study at various off-campus centers. Term-in-Europe with study in France, Germany, Czech Republic, Italy, Greece, The Netherlands. *Other distinctive programs:* Credit and noncredit continuing education.

Degrees Conferred: 341 *associate;* 1,036 *baccalaureate;* 120 *master's.* Bachelor's degrees awarded in top four disciplines: business, management, marketing, and related support services 993; parks and recreation 17; computer and information sciences 12; communication, journalism, and related programs 12.

Fees and Other Expenses: *Full-time tuition per academic year 2004–05:* $14,529. *Books and supplies:* $1,265. *Room and board per academic year:* $6,507.

Financial Aid: Aid from institutionally generated funds is provided on the basis of academic merit, financial need, other criteria. Institution has a Program Participation Agreement with the U.S. Department of Education for eligible students to receive Pell Grants and, depending upon the agreement, other federal aid.

Departments and Teaching Staff: *Total instructional faculty:* 57. Student-to-faculty ratio: 26:1. Degrees held by full-time faculty: 30% hold terminal degrees.

Enrollment: Total enrollment 3,748. Undergraduate 3,432 (56.3% men, 43.7% women).

Characteristics of Student Body: *Ethnic/racial makeup:* Black non-Hispanic: .1%; American Indian or Alaska Native: .3%; Asian or Pacific Islander: .7%; Hispanic: 1.6%; White non-Hispanic: 81.7%; unknown: .7%.

International Students: 132 nonresident aliens enrolled. No programs available to aid students whose native language is not English. No financial aid specifically designated for international students.

Student Life: On-campus residence halls and apartments available. *Intercollegiate athletics:* baseball, basketball, cross-country, football, golf, tennis, track.

Special services: Medical services. *Student publications:* newspaper; yearbook. *Surrounding community:* Midland population 37,500. Flint is nearest metropolitan area. Served by airport.

Buildings and Grounds: Campus area 268 acres.

Chief Executive Officer: Dr. David E. Fry, President.

Address admission inquiries to Daniel F. Toland, Director of Admissions; graduate inquiries to Dean, Executive MBA Program.

Oakland University

Rochester, Michigan 48309-4401
Tel: (248) 370-2100   **E-mail:** ouinfo@oakland.edu
Fax: (248) 370-4462   **Internet:** www.oakland.edu

Institution Description: Oakland University is a state institution. *Enrollment:* 16,901. *Degrees awarded:* Baccalaureate, master's, doctorate. Specialist certificates also awarded.

Accreditation: *Regional:* NCA. *Professional:* accounting, business, computer science, counseling, dance, engineering, music, nurse anesthesia education, nursing, nursing education, physical therapy, public administration, teacher education, theatre

History: Established as Michigan State University at Oakland, a branch of Michigan State University 1957; offered first instruction at postsecondary level 1959; adopted present name and awarded first degree (baccalaureate) 1963; became independent institution 1970.

Institutional Structure: *Governing board:* Board of Trustees of Oakland University. Extrainstitutional representation: 8 trustees appointed by the governor of Michigan. All voting. *Composition of institution:* Administrators 31 men / 24 women. Academic affairs headed by senior vice president for academic affairs and provost. Management/business/finances directed by vice president for finance and administration. Full-time instructional faculty 434. Academic governance body, University Senate, meets an average of 12 times per year. *Faculty representation:* Faculty is served by a collective bargaining agent affiliated with AAUP.

Calendar: Semesters. Academic year Sept. to Apr. Freshmen admitted Sept., Jan., Apr., June. Degrees conferred June, Aug., Dec., Apr. Formal commencements June, Sept. Summer session of 2 terms from late Apr. to late Aug.

Characteristics of Freshmen: 81% of applicants admitted. 33% of applicants admitted and enrolled.

91% (1,878 students) submitted ACT scores. *25th percentile:* ACT Composite 18, ACT English 17, ACT Math 17. *75th percentile:* ACT Composite 24, ACT English 24, ACT Math 24.

35% of entering freshmen expected to graduate within 5 years. 97% of freshmen from Michigan. Freshmen from 15 states and '18 foreign countries.

Admission: Rolling admissions plan. For fall acceptance, apply as early as end of junior year of secondary school, but not later than Aug. 1 of year of enrollment. Early acceptance available. *Requirements:* Either graduation from accredited secondary school with 12 academic units, including work in English; or GED. Alternate requirements for students whose education has been interrupted for 3 years or more. Additional requirements for some programs. Recommended 2.8–4.0 GPA. *Entrance tests:* ACT composite. For foreign students TOEFL. *For transfer students:* 2.0 minimum GPA; from 4-year accredited institution 92 semester hours maximum transfer credit; from 2-year accredited institution 62 hours.

College credit and advanced placement for postsecondary-level work completed in secondary school. Tutoring available.

Degree Requirements: 124–138 hours; 2.0 GPA; 32 hours, including final 8, in residence; demonstrated proficiency in writing; general education requirements. Additional requirements for some programs.

Fulfillment of some degree requirements and exemption from some beginning courses possible by passing departmental examinations, College Board CLEP, AP. *Grading system:* A 32-point system of numerical grades from 1.0 to 4.0 by tenths; pass-fail; withdraw; audit.

Distinctive Educational Programs: Work-experience programs. Off-campus centers. Evening classes. Special facilities for using telecommunications in the classroom. Interdepartmental/interdisciplinary programs in international studies, engineering chemistry, engineering physics, environmental health, industrial health and safety. Five-year program for secondary teacher education in specific subjects includes a baccalaureate in the College of Arts and Sciences and one additional year of internship and professional education credits in the School of Education and Human Services. Honors College program; Bachelor of General Studies, and independent major offered. Facilities for independent research. Study abroad programs in Austria, England, France, Italy, Japan. *Other distinctive programs:* Evening classes, some courses and programs at extension sites, and interdisciplinary programs. Collaborative programs with business and industry. Noncredit paraprofessional programs, continuing professional education courses, workshops for personal, career, and professional development, and day and evening programs for union members available.

ROTC: Air Force in cooperation with University of Michigan - Ann Arbor.

Degrees Conferred: 2,028 *baccalaureate* (B), 955 *master's* (M), 28 *doctorate* (D): area studies 2 (B); biological/life sciences 100 (B), 2 (M), 1 (D); business/marketing 453 (B), 193 (M); communications/communication technologies 190 (B); computer and information sciences 39 (B), 63 (M); education 299 (B), 602 (M), 10 (D); engineering and engineering technologies 166 (B), 171 (M), 12 (D); English 76 (B), 10 (M); foreign languages and literature 20 (B), 1 (M); health professions and related sciences 162 (B), 80 (M); liberal arts/general studies 104 (B); mathematics 11 (B), 6 (M), 2 (D); parks and recreation 7 (M); philosophy/religion/theology 11 (B); physical sciences 19 (B), 5 (M), 3 (D); protective services/public administration 6 (B), 10 (M); psychology 117 (B); social sciences and history 224 (B), 1 (M); visual and performing arts 29 (B), 4 (M).

Fees and Other Expenses: *Full-time tuition per academic year 2004–05:* $4,868 resident undergraduate, $11,468 nonresident; graduate resident $7,290, nonresident $12,804. *Required fees:* $486. *Room and board per academic year:* $5,820.

Financial Aid: Aid from institutionally generated funds is provided on the basis of academic merit, financial need, athletic ability, other criteria.

Financial aid to full-time, first-time undergraduate students: need-based scholarships/grants totaling $7,368,138, self-help $10,715,744, parent loans $1,277,375; non-need-based scholarships/grants totaling $7,327,005, self-help $12,898,670, athletic awards $1,429,907.

Departments and Teaching Staff: College of Arts and Sciences *professors* 72, *associate professors* 81, *assistant professors* 48, *instructors* 23, *part-time faculty* 245; School of Business Administration 18, 18, 19, 2, 32; School of Engineering 17, 15, 12, 1, 16; School of Education 11, 27, 31, 3, 90; School of Nursing 1, 7, 4, 3, 10; School of Health Sciences 2, 6, 7, 5, 12.

Total instructional faculty: 839 (full-time 434, part-time 405; women 347, men 442; members of minority groups 160). Total faculty with doctorate, first-professional, or other terminal degree: 529. Student-to-faculty ratio: 22:1. *Faculty development:* 37 faculty members awarded sabbaticals 2004–05.

Enrollment: *Total enrollment:* 16,901. Undergraduate full-time 3,441 men / 5,890 women, part-time 1,456m / 2,327w; graduate full-time 376m / 725w, part-time 986m / 1,700w. Transfer students: in-state 1,252; from out-of-state 33.

Characteristics of Student Body: *Ethnic/racial makeup:* number of Black non-Hispanic: 1,206; American Indian or Alaska Native: 61; Asian or Pacific Islander: 453; Hispanic: 215; White non-Hispanic: 10,143; unknown: 930. *Age distribution:* number under 18: 353; 18–19: 3,562; 20–21: 3,376; 22–24: 3,022; 25–29: 1,271; 30–34: 535; 35–39: 325; 40–49: 492; 50–64: 137; 65 and over: 10.

International Students: 411 nonresident aliens enrolled fall 2004. 43 students from Europe, 145 Asia, 11 Central and South America, 8 Africa, 39 Canada, 23 other. Programs available to aid students whose native language is not English: English as a Second Language Program. No financial aid specifically designated for international students.

Student Life: On-campus residence halls house 12% of student body. Optional Wellness Hall and Scholars Tower; all residence halls are coeducational. Housing available for married students. 126 registered student organizations. *Intercollegiate athletics:* men only: baseball, basketball, cross-country, diving, golf, soccer, swimming; women only: basketball, cross-country, diving, golf, soccer, softball, swimming, tennis, volleyball. *Special regulations:* Cars permitted without restrictions. *Special services:* Medical services. *Student publications, radio:* Oakland Post, student newspaper. Radio station WOUX-FM broadcasts 42 hours per week. *Surrounding community:* Rochester area (cities of Rochester Hills, Rochester, Auburn Hills) population 86,000, located in Detroit metropolitan area. Served by limited public transportation; airport is 40 miles from campus.

Publications: *Oakland University Magazine,* published quarterly and mailed to all alumni; *Oakland University Journal.*

Library Collections: 2,058,769 volumes. Current serial subscriptions: 11,896 (paper, microform, via electronic access). 18,767 recordings. Online catalog. Students have access to online information retrieval services and the Internet. Total 2004–05 budget for books and materials: $1,517,000.

Most important special collections include Hicks Collection of Women in Literature; James Collection (550 folklore monographs including some rare items); William Springer Collection of Lincolniana and Civil War materials; Bingham Historical Children's Literature Collection.

Buildings and Grounds: Campus area 1,500 acres. *New buildings:* Elliott Hall(School of Business Administration); Pawley Hall (School of Education); Oakland Center (extension and upgrade).

Chief Executive Officer: Dr. Gary D. Russi, President.

Undergraduates address admission inquiries to Peter Nact, Vice President for Enrollment Services; graduate inquiries to Christina J. Grabowski, Director of Graduate Study/Lifelong Learning.

College of Arts and Sciences

Degree Programs Offered: *Baccalaureate* in anthropology, art history, biology, chemistry, communication arts, economics, English, history, international studies, journalism, linguistics, mathematics, modern languages and literature, music, philosophy, physics, political science, psychology, sociology, applied statistics, biochemistry, engineering chemistry, environmental health, engineering physics, medical physics, public administration and public policy; *master's* in biology, chemistry, English, history, linguistics, mathematics, industrial applied mathematics, applied statistics, music, physics, public administration; *doctorate* in applied mathematics, biomedical sciences (cellular biology of aging, health and environmental chemistry, medical physics). Graduate certificate program in statistical methods also offered.

Admission: *See* general requirements. Specific programs impose special requirements for admission.

Degree Requirements: *See* general requirements. 124 credits required for B.A.; 128 for B.Music and B.S. programs; complete a major, the college distribution, general education, and writing proficiency.

Departments and Teaching Staff: *See* Departments and Teaching Staff above.

Distinctive Educational Programs: Interdepartmental program in biochemistry. Certificate program in foreign language translation. Internships in physics and public policy. Preprofessional programs in dentistry, medicine, optometry. Independent study.

School of Business Administration

Degree Programs Offered: *Baccalaureate* in accounting, economics, finance, general management, human resources management, management information systems, marketing; *master's* in accounting business administration. Post-master's certificates in accounting, economics, finance, human resource management, management information systems, marketing.

Admission: *See* general requirements. In addition, minimum GPA of 2.80 for all courses, and minimum grade of 2.0 in specific prescore courses; completion of prescore requirements.

Degree Requirements: Completion of 128 credits; general education requirements; prescore, core, and major requirements. See also general requirements.

Departments and Teaching Staff: *See* Departments and Teaching Staff above.

School of Education and Human Services

Degree Programs Offered: *Baccalaureate* in elementary education, human resource development; *master's* in counseling, curriculum, instruction and leadership, early childhood education, special education, reading and language arts; *doctorate* in reading. Education Specialist certificate in microcomputer applications in education.

Admission: *See* general requirements. Additional for elementary education candidacy: 2.70 GPA including minimum 2.0 in all courses; minimum score of 174 on preprofessional skills tests (PPST); completion of writing requirement. Additional requirements for admission to elementary education major.

Degree Requirements: Elementary education: see general requirements. In addition, completion of a major or two minor concentrations, some specific courses, 60 credits of professional education coursework, minimum grade of 2.0 in each noneducation course and 2.8 in preprofessional and professional courses; cumulative GPA of 2.70; 124 credits minimum.

Departments and Teaching Staff: *See* Departments and Teaching Staff above.

Distinctive Educational Programs: Specialization in Youth and Adult Services, in cooperation with agency and industry employers in the community, prepares students for employment in human service occupations.

School of Engineering

Degree Programs Offered: *Baccalaureate* in computer engineering, computer science, electrical engineering, systems engineering, mechanical engineering, engineering chemistry, engineering physics; *master's* in electrical and computer engineering, mechanical engineering, systems engineering, computer science and engineering; *doctorate* in systems engineering. Cooperative programs in engineering and computer science offered.

Admission: *See* general requirements. 3.00 (B average) normally required. Background in English composition essential; coursework in chemistry and physics recommended.

Degree Requirements: *See* general requirements. Completion of 128 credits, core curricula, major, general education, and institutional requirements.

Departments and Teaching Staff: *See* Departments and Teaching Staff above.

School of Health Sciences

Degree Programs Offered: *Baccalaureate* in health sciences (leads to MPT), industrial health and safety, medical laboratory sciences; *master's* in exercise science, physical therapy. Nondegree programs in exercise science and health behavioral science at undergraduate level.

Admission: *See* general requirements.

Degree Requirements: Core curriculum; major; general education and institutional requirements.

Departments and Teaching Staff: *See* Departments and Teaching Staff above.

School of Nursing

Degree Programs Offered: *Baccalaureate* in nursing; *master's* in adult health, nursing, nursing administration. anesthesia.

Admission: *See* general requirements. In addition, completion of required prenursing courses with GPA 3.00 and earn minimum grade of 2.0 in each prenursing course; physical examination and health history; obtain malpractice insurance; completion of an approve Heartsaver or BCL/BLS within the past year.

Degree Requirements: *See* general requirements. *For baccalaureate in nursing:* 125 credits required; maintain a cumulative GPA of at least 2.50 in all nursing courses.

Departments and Teaching Staff: *See* Departments and Teaching Staff above.

Olivet College

320 South Main Street
Olivet, Michigan 49076

Tel: (269) 749-7000   **E-mail:** admissions@olivetcollege.edu
Fax: (269) 749-7148   **Internet:** www.olivetcollege.edu

Institution Description: Olivet College is a private college affiliated with the Congregational and United Church of Christ Churches. *Enrollment:* 1,021. *Degrees awarded:* Baccalaureate.

Accreditation: *Regional:* NCA.

History: Established as Olivet College and offered first instruction at postsecondary level 1844; changed name to Olivet Institute 1847; chartered as Olivet College 1859; awarded first degree (baccalaureate) 1861.

Institutional Structure: *Governing board:* Board of Trustees. Representation: 30 trustees. All voting. *Composition of institution:* Academic affairs headed by vice president and dean for academic affairs. Management/business/finances directed by vice president and chief financial officer. *Total instructional faculty:* 76.

Calendar: Semesters. Academic year Aug. to May.

Characteristics of Freshmen: 83% of applicants accepted. 54% of accepted applicants enrolled.

9% (108 students) submitted SAT scores; 89% (1,068 students) submitted ACT scores. *25th percentile:* ACT Composite 15.3. *75th percentile:* ACT Composite 17.8.

36% of entering freshmen expected to graduate within 5 years. 80% of freshmen from Michigan. Freshmen from 20 states and 10 foreign countries.

Admission: Rolling admissions plan. *Requirements:* Either graduation from accredited secondary school or GED; minimum 2.6 GPA. *Entrance tests:* College Board SAT score 870 minimum or ACT Composite 18 minimum.

Degree Requirements: 120 semester hours; 2.0 GPA; 58 hours in residence; general education requirements. Master of Arts in Teaching 36 semester hours. *Grading system:* A–F; pass-fail; withdraw (deadline after which pass-fail is appended to withdraw).

Distinctive Educational Programs: The college encourages students to pursue work or study in a foreign country. Olivet College belongs to the International Association for the Exchange of Students for Technical Experience. Master of Arts in Teaching. Teacher Certification Program.

Degrees Conferred: 151 *baccalaureate:* biological/life sciences 10; business/marketing 24; communications/communication technologies 12; computer and information sciences 3; English 12; health professions and related sciences 14; law/legal studies 8; liberal arts/general studies 4; mathematics 3; natural resources/environmental science 3; physical sciences 3; social sciences and history 38; visual and performing arts 8; other 2. *Master's:* education 6.

Fees and Other Expenses: *Tuition per academic year 2004–05:* $15,500 undergraduate, $3,120 graduate. *required fees:* $494. *Room and board per academic year:* $5,330.

Financial Aid: Aid from institutionally generated funds is provided on the basis of academic merit, financial need.

Financial aid to full-time, first-time undergraduate students: need-based scholarships/grants totaling $10,121,523, self-help $6,109,269; non-need-based scholarships/grants totaling $205,265, parent loans $399,799, tuition waivers $455,933. *Graduate aid:* 10 students received $16,785 in federal and state-funded fellowships/grants (ranging from $1,000 to $2,000); 26 received $158,476 in federal and state-funded loans (ranging $530 to $10,000).

Departments and Teaching Staff: *Total instructional faculty:* 93 (full-time 35, part-time 58; women 40, men 53; members of minority groups 11). Total faculty with doctorate, first-professional, or other terminal degree: 36. Student-to-faculty ratio: 19:1. degrees held by full-time faculty: doctorate 18%, master's 27%, professional 1%.

Enrollment: Total enrollment 1,072. Undergraduate full-time 552 men / 402 women, part-time 26m / 43w; graduate full-time 9m / 23w, part-time 5m / 9w. *Transfer students:* in-state 292; from out-of-state 15.

Characteristics of Student Body: *Ethnic/racial makeup:* number of Black non-Hispanic: 747; American Indian or Alaska Native: 11; Asian or Pacific Islander: 3; Hispanic: 20; White non-Hispanic: 761; unknown: 6. *Age distribution:* number under 18: 9; 18–19: 295; 20–21: 329; 22–24: 226; 25–29: 84; 30–34: 25; 35–39: 19; 40–49: 33; 50–64: 3.

International Students: 37 nonresident aliens enrolled fall 2004. 4 students from Europe, 5 Asia, 4 Central and South America, 6 Africa, 16 Canada, 2 other. Programs available for students whose native language is not English: social, cultural, financial.

Student Life: On-campus residence halls and apartments available. Housing available for married students. *Special services:* Student Employment Program provides funds and work experience for all students. *Student publications: The Echo,* a monthly newspaper; *Garfield Lake Review,* an annual literary magazine; *The Oaks,* a student yearbook. *Surrounding community:* Olivet population 2,000. 30 miles from campus, is nearest metropolitan area.

Library Collections: 110,256 volumes. Current serial subscriptions: 234 paper; 3 microform; 180 via electronic access. 619 recordings; 84 compact discs. Online and card catalogs. Students have access to online information retrieval services and the Internet. Total 2004–05 budget for books and materials: $59,622.

Most important special holdings: Arctic Exploration Collection (monographs).

Buildings and Grounds: *New buildings/construction:* Cutler Athletic Complex completed 2000.

Chief Executive Officer: Dr. Donald Tuski, President.

Address admission inquiries to Tom Shaw, Vice President for Enrollment Management.

Reformed Bible College

3333 East Beltline, N.E.
Grand Rapids, Michigan 49505-9749

Tel: (616) 222-3000   **E-mail:** admissions@reformed.edu
Fax: (616) 222-3045   **Internet:** www.reformed.edu

Institution Description: Reformed Bible College is a private, interdenominational Calvinistic institution serving Presbyterian and Reformed churches throughout the world. *Enrollment:* 289. *Degrees awarded:* Associate, baccalaureate.

Accreditation: *Regional:* NCA. *National:* ABHE.

History: Chartered as Reformed Bible Institute with a 3-year instruction program 1939; changed to a 4-year program and adopted present name 1970.

Institutional Structure: *Governing board:* Board of Trustees elected by the contributors for 3-year terms. *Full-time instructional faculty:* 10.

Calendar: Semesters (4-1-4 plan). Academic year early Aug. to May. Freshmen admitted Sept., Jan. Commencement May. Nine-week field training program each summer held off-campus.

Characteristics of Freshmen: 99% of applicants accepted. 64% of accepted applicants enrolled.

10% (4 students) submitted SAT scores; 93% (39 students) submitted ACT scores. *25th percentile:* SAT Verbal 520, SAT Math 490; ACT Composite 20. *75th percentile:* SAT Verbal 540, SAT Math 530; ACT Composite 26.

36% of entering freshmen expected to graduate within 5 years. 81% of freshmen from Michigan. Freshmen from 7 states and 1 foreign country.

Admission: *Requirements:* Graduation from accredited secondary school with a minimum 2.5 GPA; in college preparatory courses and a minimum ACT score of 18 or SAT score of 920.

Degree Requirements: *For all associate degrees:* 66 semester credits; 2.0 GPA. *For all baccalaureate degrees:* 128 semester credits; 2.0 GPA. *For all degrees:* Certain required subjects of the course chosen must be fulfilled.

Distinctive Educational Programs: Mexico Summer Training Session is a nine-week field training program from mid-June to Mid-August. Day and evening classes for degree or nondegree continuing education. EXCEL degree completion program.

Degrees Conferred: 4 *associate;* 38 *baccalaureate:* theology.

Fees and Other Expenses: *Full-time tuition per academic year 2005–06:* $10,400. *Required fees:* $520. *Room and board per academic year:* $5,300.

Financial Aid: Aid from institutionally generated funds is provided on the basis of academic merit, financial need, other criteria.

Financial aid to full-time, first-time undergraduate students: need-based scholarships/grants totaling $892,171, self-help $769,550, parent loans $37,950, tuition waivers $16,475; non-need-based scholarships/grants totaling $47,235, self-help $338,147, parent loans $20,450, tuition waivers $24,750.

Departments and Teaching Staff: *Total instructional faculty:* 32 (full-time 17, part-time 15; women 9, men 23; member of minority group 1). Total faculty with doctorate, first-professional, or other terminal degree: 11. Student-to-faculty ratio: 14:1.

Enrollment: Total enrollment 289. Undergraduate full-time 103 men / 134 women, part-time 31m / 18w; graduate full-time 2w, part-time 1m. *Transfer students:* in-state 109; from out-of-state 25.

Characteristics of Student Body: *Ethnic/racial makeup:* number of Black non-Hispanic: 9; Asian or Pacific Islander: 11; Hispanic: 5; White non-Hispanic: 266; unknown: 1. *Age distribution:* number under 18: 1; 18–19: 72; 20–21: 100; 22–24: 55; 25–29: 30; 30–34: 5; 35–39: 10; 40–49: 12; 50–64: 4.

International Students: 24 nonresident aliens enrolled fall 2004. 2 students from Europe, 1 Asia, 5 Central and South America, 5 Africa, 10 Canada, 1 Australia. Programs available to aid students whose native language is not English: English as a Second Language Program. Financial aid for undergraduate international students: scholarships available to qualified students.

Student Life: On-campus residence halls and homes house approximately 150 students. *Intercollegiate athletics:* Basketball and ice hockey; soccer also available. *Student publications: Reflector,* newspaper published throughout the academic year; *Echo,* an annual yearbook published in April. *Surrounding community:* Campus is located in a metropolitan area of single-family homes.

Publications: *Newsletter,* published quarterly for supporters. 57,313 volumes including bound books, serial backfiles, electronic documents, and government documents not in separate collections. Online catalog. Current serial subscriptions: 245 paper, 4,706 microform. 3,482 recordings; 16 CD-ROMs. 15 computer work stations. Students have access to the Internet at no charge. Total budget for books, periodicals, audiovisual materials, microforms 2004–05: $33,500.

Most important special collections include Calvinism/Reformed doctrine; missions; Christian education/youth ministry.

Buildings and Grounds: Campus area 26 acres.

Chief Executive Officer: Nickolas V. Kroeze, President.

Address admission inquiries to David DeBoer, Director of Admissions.

Rochester College

800 West Avon Road
Rochester Hills, Michigan 48307
Tel: (248) 218-2000   **E-mail:** admissions@rc.edu
Fax: (248) 218-2005   **Internet:** www.rc.edu

Institution Description: Rochester College, formerly named Michigan Christian University, is a private, independent, nonprofit institution affiliated with Churches of Christ. *Enrollment:* 992. *Degrees awarded:* Associate, baccalaureate.

Accreditation: *Regional:* NCA.

History: Incorporated 1959; established as North Central Christian College and offered first instruction at postsecondary level 1959; awarded first degree (associate) and changed name to Michigan Christian Junior College 1961; became Michigan Christian College 1978; became Michigan Christian University 1995; adopted present name 1997.

Institutional Structure: *Governing board:* Board of Trustees of Rochester College. Representation: 32 trustees, 6 alumni. All voting. *Composition of institution:* Administrators 6 men / 1 women. Academic affairs headed by vice president for academic affairs. Management/business/finances directed by Business Service Manager. Full-time instructional faculty 28. Academic governance body, Organization of Academic Personnel, meets an average of 10 times per year.

Calendar: Semesters. Academic year early Aug. to early May. Freshmen admitted Sept., Jan. Degrees conferred and formal commencement May. May term from early to late May.

Characteristics of Freshmen: 55% of accepted applicants enrolled. 78% of freshmen from Michigan. Freshmen from 15 states and 2 foreign countries.

Admission: Rolling admissions plan. For fall acceptance, apply as early as 1 year prior to enrollment, but not later than Sept. 1. Early acceptance available. *Requirements:* Either graduation from accredited secondary school or GED. *Entrance tests:* ACT composite. For foreign students TOEFL. *For transfer students:* 2.0 minimum GPA (less than 2.0 admitted on alert); from 4-year accredited institutions 96 hours maximum transfer credit.

Advanced placement for postsecondary-level work completed in secondary school. College credit for extrainstitutional learning on basis of ACE *2006 Guide to the Evaluation of Educational Experiences in the Armed Services;* advanced placement on basis of portfolio and faculty assessments, personal interviews. Tutoring available. Developmental/remedial courses offered during regular academic year; credit given.

Degree Requirements: *For all associate degrees:* 64 credit hours; 2 activity courses; general education requirements. *For all baccalaureate degrees:* 128 credit hours; 2 activity courses; general education requirements. *For all degrees:* 2.0 GPA; 30 hours in residence; daily assembly attendance.

Fulfillment of some degree requirements and exemption from some beginning courses possible by passing institutional examinations, College Board CLEP. *Grading system:* A–F; pass-fail; withdraw (carries time limit).

Distinctive Educational Programs: Internships. Evening classes.

Degrees Conferred: 45 *associate;* 279 *baccalaureate.* Bachelor's degrees awarded in top five disciplines: business, management, marketing, and related support services 134; psychology 54; family and marriage therapy 48; liberal arts and sciences, general studies, and humanities 11; theology 9.

Fees and Other Expenses: *Full-time tuition per academic year 2004–05:* $10,580. *Other expenses:* $684. *Room and board per academic year:* $6,316.

Financial Aid: Aid from institutionally generated funds is provided on the basis of academic merit, financial need, athletic ability, other considerations Financial assistance is available in the form of Pell Grants, College Work-Study, Veterans Administration Benefits, National Direct Student Loans, Supplemental Education Opportunity Grants (SEOG), Higher Education Assistance Loans (HEAL), Stafford Loans, other federal aid programs.

Departments and Teaching Staff: *Total instructional faculty:* 66 (full-time 28, part-time 38). Degrees held by full-time faculty: doctorate 29%, master's 71%. 29% of faculty hold terminal degrees.

Enrollment: Total enrollment 992 (38.8% men, 61.2% women).

Characteristics of Student Body: *Ethnic/racial makeup:* Black non-Hispanic: 71; American Indian or Alaska Native: 1; Asian or Pacific Islander: 5; Hispanic: 8; White non-Hispanic: 553.

International Students: 29 nonresident aliens enrolled. Students from Europe, Asia, Central and South America, Africa, Canada. No programs available to aid students whose native language is not English. Financial aid in the form of scholarships available for Canadian students only.

Student Life: On-campus residence halls house 63% of student body. Residence halls for men constitute 42% of such space, for women only 58%. *Intercollegiate athletics:* men only: basketball, baseball, soccer; women only: basketball, softball, volleyball; both sexes: cross-country, track. *Special regulations:* Cars permitted without restrictions. Curfews. Quiet hours. *Special services:* Learning Resources Center. *Surrounding community:* Rochester population 7,100 and Rochester Hills population 61,500. Detroit, 25 miles from campus, is nearest metropolitan area.

Library Collections: 69,000 volumes. 17,000 microforms. 640 periodical subscriptions. 950 audiovisual items. Computer work stations available. Students have access to online information retrieval services and the Internet.

Most important special collection: Library of American Civilization (microbooks).

Buildings and Grounds: Campus area 83 acres.

Chief Executive Officer: Dr. Michael W. Westerfield, President.

Address admission inquiries to Eric Campbell, Dean of Enrollment.

Sacred Heart Major Seminary

2701 Chicago Boulevard
Detroit, Michigan 48206
Tel: (313) 883-8500
Fax: (313) 868-6440

Institution Description: Sacred Heart Major Seminary and Theologate (formerly Sacred Heart Seminary College) is a private institution affiliated with the Roman Catholic Archdiocese of Detroit. The mission of Sacred Heart Major Seminary is to prepare leaders for the ministerial service within the Church. It accomplishes this mission primarily through the education and formation of candidates for the Roman Catholic priesthood. It further implements this mission through professional preparation of individuals for the diaconate, diverse lay ministries, and other leadership roles within the Church. The seminary also welcomes qualified persons seeking continuing education. *Enrollment:* 305. Women are admitted as full-time students in the associate program and part-time in the baccalaureate. *Degrees awarded:* Associate, baccalaureate.

Accreditation: *Regional:* NCA. *National:* ATS. *Professional*: theology

History: Established 1919; chartered as Sacred Heart High School and College 1921; offered first instruction at postsecondary level 1922; awarded first degree (baccalaureate) 1926; changed name to Sacred Heart Seminary High School and College, Inc. 1959; became Sacred Heart Seminary College 1970; adopted present name and opened a graduate school of theology 1988. *See* Bruce M. Forintos, ed.; *Sacred Heart Seminary, 50th Anniversary* (Birmingham, Mich.: Midwest Yearbook Company, 1969) for further information.

Institutional Structure: *Governing board:* Sacred Heart Major Seminary Board of Trustees. Extrainstitutional representation: 13 trustees; institutional representation: 2 administrators, including rector-president of the college. 4 ex officio. All voting. *Composition of institution:* Administrators 8 men / 1 woman. Academic affairs headed by dean of studies. Management/business/finances directed by building administrator. Full-time instructional faculty 16. Academic governance body, Administration Committee, meets an average of 8 times per year.

Calendar: Semesters. Academic year early Sept. to mid-June. Freshmen admitted Sept., Jan. Degrees conferred and formal commencement May. 6 week spring semester. No summer session.

Characteristics of Freshmen: 100% of freshmen from Michigan.

Admission: Rolling admissions plan. For fall acceptance, apply as early as Dec., but not later than Aug. *Requirements:* Recommend 16 units in college preparatory subjects, including religious studies. Minimum 2.0 GPA. *Entrance tests:* College Board SAT. *For transfer students:* 2.0 minimum GPA; from 4-year accredited institution 96 hours maximum transfer credit; from 2-year accredited institution 64 hours. *See* college catalog for graduate admission requirements.

College credit and advanced placement for postsecondary-level work completed in secondary school. For adult education and associate degree programs, college credit and advanced placement for extrainstitutional learning (life experience) on basis of portfolio and faculty assessments.

Degree Requirements: *For all associate degrees:* 62 credit hours. *For all baccalaureate degrees:* 128 credit hours; 2 terms in residence. *For all degrees:* 2.0 GPA; chapel attendance. *Graduate program:* completion of prescribed curriculum.

Fulfillment of some degree requirements possible by passing College Board CLEP. *Grading system:* A–F; withdraw (carries time limit); incomplete (carries penalty and time limit).

Distinctive Educational Programs: Weekend and evening classes. Interdisciplinary programs. Tutorials. Cross-registration through consortium. Adult education program for lay deacons.

Degrees Conferred: 3 *associate;* 12 *baccalaureate:* theology; 26 *master's* theology.

Fees and Other Expenses: *Full-time tuition per academic year 2004–05:* $9,412 undergraduate; $12,938 graduate. *Required fees:* $60. *Room and board per academic year:* $6,040.

Financial Aid: Aid from institutionally generated funds is provided on the basis of financial need. Institution has a Program Participation Agreement with the U.S. Department of Education for eligible students to receive Pell Grants and other federal aid.

Departments and Teaching Staff: *Total instructional faculty:* 35 (full-time 21, part-time 14; women 8, men 27; member of minority group 1). Total faculty with doctorate, first-professional, or other terminal degree: 24.

Enrollment: Total enrollment 305.

Characteristics of Student Body: *Ethnic/racial makeup:* number of Black non-Hispanic: 18; Asian or Pacific Islander: 4; Hispanic: 11; White non-Hispanic: 118; unknown: 9. *Age distribution:* number under 18: 1; 18–19: 2; 20–21: 4; 22–24: 14; 25–29: 18; 30–34: 17; 35–39: 24; 40–49: 37; 50–64: 32; 65 and over: 12.

International Students: 4 nonresident aliens enrolled fall 2004. Programs available to aid students whose native language is not English: English as a Second Language Program. No financial aid specifically designated for international students.

Student Life: Seminarians live on campus in residence halls. Students may have their own cars. *Student publication: Gothic,* an annual literary magazine. *Surrounding community:* Detroit population over 1 million. Served by mass transit bus system; airport 25 miles from campus; passenger rail service 5 miles from campus.

Library Collections: 138,000 volumes. 6,200 microforms; 2,950 audiovisual materials; 513 periodical subscriptions. Students have access to online information retrieval services.

Most important special holdings include collections on the Church in Michigan; Monsigneur Canfield Collection of early editions; Cardinal Mooney Collection of papers relating to church and state relations and the institutional church; Gabriel Richard Rare Book Collection.

Buildings and Grounds: Campus area 20 acres.

Chief Executive Officer: Rev. Steven Boguslawski, Rector/President.

Address admission inquiries to Rev. Michael Byrnes, Vice Rector.

Saginaw Valley State University

7400 Bay Road
University Center, Michigan 48710-0001
Tel: (989) 964-4000   **E-mail:** admissions@.svsu.edu
Fax: (989) 790-0180   **Internet:** www.svsu.edu

Institution Description: Saginaw Valley State University (Saginaw Valley College until 1975) is a state institution. *Enrollment:* 9,448. *Degrees awarded:* Baccalaureate, master's.

Accreditation: *Regional:* NCA. *Professional*: business, engineering, nursing, occupational therapy, social work, teacher education

History: Established and chartered as Saginaw Valley College 1963; offered first instruction at postsecondary level 1964; awarded first degree (baccalaureate) 1965; changed name to Saginaw Valley State College 1975; adopted present name 1987.

Institutional Structure: *Governing board:* Board of Control of Saginaw Valley State College. Extrainstitutional representation: 8 members; institutional representation: 1 administrator, 1 student. 2 ex officio. 8 voting. *Composition of institution:* Administrators 28 men / 16 women. Academic affairs headed by vice president for academic affairs. Management/business/finances directed by vice president for business affairs. Student services/enrollment management directed by vice president for student services and enrollment management. Full-time instructional faculty 188. Academic governance body, Council of Deans and Directors, meets an average of 48 times per year. *Faculty representation:* Faculty served by collective bargaining agent, Michigan Education Association, affiliated with NEA.

Calendar: Trimesters. Academic year Aug. to Apr. Freshmen admitted Sept., Jan., May, July. Degrees conferred Apr., Aug., Dec. Formal commencement Apr., Dec.

Characteristics of Freshmen: 89.5% of applicants admitted. 36.1% of applicants admitted and enrolled.

98.1% (1,216 students) submitted ACT scores; *25th percentile*: ACT Composite 18, ACT English 16, ACT Math 17. *75th percentile*: ACT Composite 24, ACT English 23, ACT Math 24.

18.4% of entering freshmen expected to graduate within 5 years. 97.5% of freshmen from Michigan. Freshmen from 9 states and 8 foreign countries.

Admission: Rolling admissions plan. For fall acceptance, apply as early as Sept. of previous year, but not later than Aug. of year of enrollment. Early acceptance available. *Requirements:* Either graduation from accredited secondary school with recommended academic units to include 4 years English, 4 years mathematics, 3 years science, 3 years social science, 2 years foreign language, 2 years fine arts, and computer literacy. Minimum 2.0 GPA. *Entrance tests:* ACT composite preferred; College Board SAT accepted. *For transfer students:* 2.0 minimum GPA; from 4-year accredited institution 93 trimester hours maximum transfer credit; from 2-year accredited institution 62 hours.

College credit and advanced placement for postsecondary-level work completed in secondary school. College credit for extrainstitutional learning on basis of ACE *2006 Guide to the Evaluation of Educational Experiences in the Armed Services.* Tutoring available. Developmental courses offered in summer session and regular academic year; credit given.

Degree Requirements: 124 trimester hours; 2.0 GPA; 2 terms in residence; general education requirements; distribution requirements; demonstrated proficiency in reading and writing.

Fulfillment of some degree requirements and exemption from some beginning courses possible by passing departmental examinations, College Board CLEP, AP, other standardized tests. *Grading system:* A–F; pass-fail; pass-no grade; withdraw (deadline after which pass-fail is appended to withdraw).

Distinctive Educational Programs: Cooperative education. Honors program. Flexible meeting places and schedules, including off-campus centers and evening classes. Accelerated degree programs. Facilities for using telecommunications in the classroom. Interdisciplinary programs in applied science-engineering technology, biochemistry, business-chemistry, chemical physics, computer physics, construction technology, criminal justice, electrical engineering technology, ethnic studies, mathematics-economics, mechanical engineering technology, medical technology, nursing, social work, and environmental studies. Institutionally sponsored study abroad in Austria, England, Italy, Japan, Poland, Taiwan. *Other distinctive programs:* Institute of Polish studies offering courses in Polish and Slavic language and culture.

ROTC: Available on cooperative basis through Central Michigan University.

Degrees Conferred: 1,086 *baccalaureate* (B); 487 *master's* (M): biological/life sciences 24 (B); business/marketing 163 (B), 39 (M); communications/communication technologies 36 (B), 39 (M); computer and information sciences 60 (B); education 328 (B), 378 (M); engineering and engineering technologies 54 (B), 10 (M); English 23 (B); foreign languages and literature 8 (B); health professions and related sciences 59 (B), 11 (M); interdisciplinary studies 6 (B); mathematics 16 (B); parks and recreation 1 (B); physical sciences 16 (B); protective services/public administration 136 (B), 20 (M); psychology 37 (B); social sciences and history 73 (B); visual and performing arts 46 (B).

Fees and Other Expenses: *Full-time tuition per academic year 2004–05:* undergraduate resident $4,270.50, nonresident $10,377. Contact the university for graduate costs. *Required fees:* $642.*Room and board per academic year:* $5,850.

Financial Aid: Aid from institutionally generated funds is provided on the basis of academic merit, financial need, athletic ability, other criteria.

Financial aid to full-time, first-time undergraduate students: need-based scholarships/grants totaling 6,261,898, self-help $9,446,165; non-need-based scholarships/grants totaling $6,952,981, self-help $11,872,673, tuition waivers $248,172, athletic awards $800,743. *Graduate aid:* 258 students received $2,365,304 in federal and state-funded loans (ranging from $1,800 to $18,500); 127 students received fellowships/grants totaling $102,777 (ranging from $590 to $4,664).

Departments and Teaching Staff: *Professors* 105, *associate professors* 62, *assistant professors* 48, *instructors* 28, *part-time faculty* 4.

Total instructional faculty: 247 (full-time 243, part-time 4; women 97, men 150). Student-to-faculty ration: 29:1. Degrees held by full-time faculty: master's 17%, doctorate 78.5%, professional 4.5%. 83% hold terminal degrees.

Enrollment: Total enrollment 9,448. Undergraduate full-time 2,331 men / 3,503 women, part-time 774m / 1,181w; graduate full-time 44m / 79w, part-time 381m / 1,155w. *Transfer students:* in-state 588, out-of-state 36.

Characteristics of Student Body: *Ethnic/racial makeup:* number of Black non-Hispanic: 455; American Indian or Alaska Native: 25; Asian or Pacific Islander: 65; Hispanic: 170; White non-Hispanic: 6,452; unknown: 331. *Age distribution:* number under 18: 53; 18–19: 1,073; 20–21: 1,765; 22–24: 1,864; 25–29: 925; 30–34: 442; 35–39: 311; 40–49: 407; 50–64: 126; 65 and over: 3.

International Students: 311 nonresident aliens enrolled fall 2004. 17 students from Europe, 152 Asia, 9 Central and South America, 60 Africa, 69 Canada, 1 Australia, 3 other. Programs available to aid students whose native language is not English: social, cultural, financial. English as a Second Language Program.

Student Life: On-campus residence halls house 8% of student body. Residence halls for men and women constitute 72% of such space; apartments constitute 28%. *Intercollegiate athletics:* men only: baseball, basketball, bowling, cross-country, football, golf, soccer, indoor and outdoor track; women only: basketball, cheerleading, cross-country, soccer, tennis, volleyball, indoor and outdoor track. *Special regulations:* Cars permitted without restrictions. Quiet hours in 2 residence halls. *Special services:* Academic Achievement Center; medical services. *Surrounding community:* Saginaw population 108,000. Detroit, 90 miles from campus, is nearest metropolitan area. Served by mass transit bus system; airport 5 miles from campus.

Publications: *Business and Economic Review* (quarterly) first published 1979.

Library Collections: 226,952 volumes. Current serial subscriptions: 850 paper; 101 microform; 10,542 via electronic access. 4,462 recordings; 783 compact discs; 234 CD-ROMs. Online catalog. 98 computer work stations. Students have access to online information retrieval services and the Internet. Total 2004–05 budget for materials and operations: $649,165.

Most important special holdings include oral history of tri-city area; Calvin Ennes Collection (Northern Michigan history); Crampton Jazz Collection.

Buildings and Grounds: Campus area 782 acres.

Chief Executive Officer: Dr. Eric R. Gilbertson, President.

Address admission inquiries to James Dwyer, Director of Admissions; MBA program inquiries to School of Business and Management; MAT/EDL program inquiries to Dean, School of Education; MA–CJ/PS program inquiries to Dean, School of Arts and Behavioral Sciences.

Siena Heights University

1247 East Siena Heights Drive
Adrian, Michigan 49221
Tel: (517) 263-0731   **E-mail:** admissions@sienahts.edu
Fax: (517) 265-3380   **Internet:** www.sienahts.edu

Institution Description: Siena Heights University, is a Catholic, liberal arts institution with a tradition of academic excellence. *Enrollment:* 2,161. *Degrees awarded:* Associate, baccalaureate, master's.

Accreditation: *Regional:* NCA. *National:* NASAD. *Professional:* art

History: Established as St. Joseph Academy 1893; chartered as St. Joseph College and offered first instruction for women only at postsecondary level 1919; awarded first degree (baccalaureate) 1924; adopted present name 1939; became coeducational late 1960s. *See* Mary Philip Ryan, *Amid the Alien Corn* (St. Charles, Ill.: Jones Wood Press, 1967) for further information.

Institutional Structure: *Governing board:* Board of Trustees. Extrainstitutional representation: 35 trustees. All voting. *Composition of institution:* Administrators 15 men / 19 women. Academic affairs headed by dean of the college and provost. Management/business/finance directed by business manager/treasurer. Full-time instructional faculty 70. Academic governance body, Teaching Faculty Assembly, meets an average of 9 times per year.

Calendar: Semesters. Academic year early Sept. to late Apr. Freshmen admitted Sept., Jan., May, June. Degrees conferred Aug., Dec., May. Formal commencement May. Summer session mid-June to late July.

Characteristics of Freshmen: 85% of applicants accepted. 46% of accepted applicants enrolled.

Mean ACT Composite score 20.

40% of entering freshmen expected to graduate within 5 years. 87% of freshmen from Michigan. Freshmen from 12 states.

Admission: Rolling admissions plan. For fall acceptance, apply as early as Sept. of senior year in secondary school, but not later than Aug. Early acceptance available. *Requirements:* Either graduation from accredited secondary school, or GED. *Entrance tests:* College Board SAT or ACT composite. *For transfer students:* 2.0 minimum GPA; from 4-year accredited institution 96 hours maximum transfer credit; from 2-year accredited institution 48 hours.

College credit and advanced placement for postsecondary-level work completed in secondary school. College credit for extrainstitutional learning on basis of ACE *2006 Guide to the Evaluation of Educational Experiences in the Armed Services;* departmental evaluations. Tutoring available. Developmental courses offered in summer session and regular academic year; credit given.

Degree Requirements: *For all associate degrees:* 60 credit hours; 12 hours in residence. *For all baccalaureate degrees:* 120 credit hours; 24 credits in residence; additional requirements for some programs. *For all undergraduate degrees:* 2.0 GPA; exit competency examinations in reading, writing, and mathematics; general education requirements.

Fulfillment of some degree requirements by passing College Board CLEP, AP. *Grading system:* A–F; pass-fail; withdraw.

Distinctive Educational Programs: *Available to all students:* Work-experience programs, including cooperative education, internships. Weekend and evening classes. Classrooms equipped for TV reception; videotape recording and playback facilities available; fully equipped color TV studio in arts center. Facilities and programs for independent research. Contract majors allow students to design and execute own programs. *For undergraduates:* Accelerated degree programs. Cooperative program with Lourdes College (OH) allows business administration students who have completed Lourdes associate degree to earn Siena Heights baccalaureate through courses offered by Siena Heights faculty on Lourdes campus. Siena Heights external degree program in Southfield serves working adults who wish to complete degree programs. Interdisciplinary studies in American studies and social sciences. Honors programs. Study abroad one semester in Florence Italy.

Degrees Conferred: 22 *associate;* 639 *baccalaureate.* Bachelor's degrees awarded in top five disciplines: business, management, marketing, and related support services 162; engineering technologies 63; public administration 56; health professions and related clinical sciences 51; liberal arts and sciences, general studies, and humanities 45.

Fees and Other Expenses: *Full-time tuition per academic year 2004–05:* $15,520. *Books and supplies:* $677. *Room and board per academic year:* $5,455.

Financial Aid: Aid from institutionally generated funds is provided on the basis of academic merit, financial need, athletic ability. Institution has a Program Participation Agreement with the U.S. Department of Education for eligible students to receive Pell Grants and, depending upon agreement, other federal aid.

Departments and Teaching Staff: Art *professors* 0, *associate professors* 5, *assistant professors* 1, *instructors* 0, *part-time teachers* 2; computing/mathematics/sciences 0, 3, 7, 0, 0; general studies 0, 1, 3, 3, 0; graduate studies 0, 0, 0, 1, 12; human services 0, 4, 3, 0, 10; humanities 2, 5, 6, 0, 12; management 0, 3, 6, 0, 3; performing arts and education 0, 4, 4, 0, 10.

Total instructional faculty: 110. Student-to-faculty ratio: 10:1. Degrees held by full-time faculty: 65% hold terminal degrees.

Enrollment: Total enrollment 2,161. Undergraduate 1,889 (38.6% men, 61.4% women).

Characteristics of Student Body: *Ethnic/racial makeup:* Black non-Hispanic: .2%; American Indian or Native Alaskan: .3%; Asian or Pacific Islander: .5%; Hispanic: 2.2%; White non-Hispanic: 82.9%; unknown: 5.9%.

International Students: 2 nonresident aliens enrolled fall 2004. Programs available to aid students whose native language is not English: cultural. No financial aid specifically designated for international students.

Student Life: On-campus residence halls house 35% of student body. Residence halls for men only constitute 40% of such space, for women only 60%. *Intercollegiate athletics:* men only: baseball, basketball, soccer, tennis, track, wrestling, cross-country; women only: basketball, tennis, track, volleyball, soccer. *Special regulations:* Cars permitted without restriction. Quiet hours from 11pm to 10am. Residence hall visitation noon to midnight Sun.–Thurs., noon to 2am Fri. and Sat. *Special services:* Learning Resources Center, Student Leadership Program. *Student publications: Spectra,* student newspaper; *Eclipse,* literary yearly publication. *Surrounding community:* Adrian population 21,500. Detroit, 65 miles from campus, is nearest metropolitan area. Served by mass transit system.

Publications: *Reflection,* the Alumni magazine of the college, is published 3 times per year.

Library Collections: 120,500 volumes. 25,000 microforms; 5,500 recordings/tapes; 450 current periodical subscriptions. Students have access to online information retrieval services.

Most important special holdings include collections on art, religion, and philosophy.

Buildings and Grounds: Campus area 140 acres.

Chief Executive Officer: Dr. Richard B. Artman, President.

Address admission inquiries to Kevin Kucera, Director of Admissions.

Spring Arbor University

106 East Main
Spring Arbor, Michigan 49283-9799
Tel: (517) 750-1200   **E-mail:** admissions@arbor.edu
Fax: (517) 750-6620   **Internet:** www.arbor.edu

Institution Description: Spring Arbor University is a private 4-year college affiliated with the Free Methodist Church. *Enrollment:* 3,511. *Degrees awarded:* Associate, baccalaureate, master's.

Member of Council of Christian Colleges and Universities (CCCU), Association of Free Methodist Educational Institutions (AFMEI); Wesleyan Urban Coalition; Association of Independent Colleges and Universities of Michigan (AICUM); Michigan Colleges Foundation (MCF).

Accreditation: *Regional:* NCA. *Professional:* nursing, nursing education, social work, teacher education

History: Established and incorporated as Spring Arbor Seminary 1873; added junior college, changed name to Spring Arbor Seminary and Junior College, and offered first instruction at postsecondary level 1928; awarded first degree (associate) 1930; adopted present name 1979. *See* Howard A. Snyder, *100 Years at Spring Arbor* (Spring Arbor, Mich.: Spring Arbor College, 1973) for further information.

Institutional Structure: *Governing board:* Spring Arbor College Board of Trustees. Extrainstitutional representation: 35 trustees; institutional representation: president of the college. 1 ex officio. All voting. *Composition of institution:* Administrators 20 men / 15 women. Academic affairs headed by vice president for academic affairs. Management/business/finances directed by vice president for business affairs. Full-time instructional faculty 76. Academic governance body, Academic Affairs Committee, meets an average of 30 times per year.

Calendar: Semesters (4-1-4 plan). Academic year Sept. to May. Freshmen admitted Sept., Jan., Feb., June. Degrees conferred May, Feb., Aug. Formal commencement May, Feb. Summer session of 2 terms May and June. Adult Studies graduations held June, Oct., Feb.

Characteristics of Freshmen: Average secondary school rank of freshmen 68th percentile.

11.7% (35 students) submitted SAT scores; 94.6% (282 students) submitted ACT scores. *25th percentile:* ACT Composite 19, ACT English 19, ACT Math 18. *75th percentile:* ACT Composite 25, ACT English 26, ACT Math 22. >p<45% of entering freshmen expected to graduate within 5 years. 88% of freshmen from Michigan. Freshmen from 6 states and 3 foreign countries.

Admission: Rolling admissions plan. For fall acceptance, apply as early as completion of junior year of secondary school, but not later than Aug. of year of enrollment. Early acceptance available. *Requirements:* Graduation from accredited secondary school recommended; GED accepted. Minimum 2.6 GPA or Enhanced ACT composite score of 20 recommended. *Entrance tests:* Enhanced ACT composite *For transfer students:* 2.0 GPA; from 4-year accredited institution 94 hours maximum transfer credit; from 2-year accredited institution 68 hours; correspondence/extension students 30 hours.

Tutoring available. Developmental courses offered during regular academic year; credit given.

Degree Requirements: *For all associate degrees:* 62 credit hours; required courses in writing, oral communication, Christian faith. *For all baccalaureate degrees:* 124 credit hours; core requirements; competency in writing shown through examination or courses; competency in speech shown through examination, course, or evidence of public speaking experience; Christian perspective; physical fitness. *For all undergraduate degrees:* 2.0 GPA (2.2 in major courses); 30 hours in residence; chapel attendance twice weekly; distribution requirements.

Fulfillment of some degree requirements and exemption from some beginning courses possible by passing College Board CLEP, APP. *Grading system:* A–D; pass-fail; withdraw (deadline after which pass-fail is appended to withdraw); satisfactory-unsatisfactory; incomplete (work in progress); incomplete.

Distinctive Educational Programs: Work-experience programs. Evening classes. Dual-degree program in engineering with University of Michigan, Michigan State University, and Tri-State University. Cooperative program in medical technology with accredited training institutions. Facilities and programs for independent research, including honors programs, individual majors, tutorials. Study abroad through CCCU or by individual arrangement. Off-campus study through Chicago Urban Life Center, Washington (DC) Semester, Latin America Studies, Middle East, Russia, China, Los Angeles Film Studies. Major programs in Christian lay ministries, sacred music, and supporting church ministries. Degree completion programs are offered at centers in Flint, Grand Rapids, Jackson, Lansing, and Metro-Detroit. Majors offered at off-campus centers: family life education; management of health services; organizational development; prison education program.

Degrees Conferred: 1 *associate,* 781 *baccalaureate;* 324 *master's.* Bachelor's degrees awarded in top five disciplines: business, management, marketing, and related support services 290; family and consumer sciences 199; education 66; health professions and related clinical sciences 41; English language and literature/letters 34.

Fees and Other Expenses: *Full-time tuition per academic year 2004–05:* $15,700. *Room and board per academic year:* $5,610. *Required fees:* $396.

Financial Aid: Aid from institutionally generated funds is provided on the basis of academic merit, financial need, athletic ability, other criteria. Institution has a Program Participation Agreement with the U.S. Department of Education for eligible students to receive Pell Grants and other federal aid.

Financial aid to full-time, first-time undergraduate students: need-based scholarships/grants totaling $10,336,599, self-help $6,578,338, parent loans $1,107,890, tuition waivers $912,609, athletic awards $367,635; non-need-based scholarships/grants totaling $838,581, self-help $6,599,857.

Departments and Teaching Staff: *Total instructional faculty:* 143 (full-time 77, part-time 66; women 68, men 75; members of minority groups 7). Total faculty with doctorate, first-professional, or other terminal degree: 50. Student-to-faculty ratio: 14.8:1. Degrees held by full-time faculty: master's 48%, doctorate 50%, professional 2%.

Enrollment: Total enrollment 3,511. Undergraduate full-time 682 men / 1,324 women, part-time 130m / 374w; graduate full-time 194m / 442w, part-time 107m / 258w.

Characteristics of Student Body: *Ethnic/racial makeup:* number of Black non-Hispanic: 51; American Indian or Alaska Native: 2; Asian or Pacific Islander: 19; Hispanic: 28; White non-Hispanic: 1,550; unknown: 3.

International Students: 22 nonresident aliens enrolled fall 2004. Some scholarships specifically designated for international undergraduate students.

Student Life: On-campus residence halls and apartments house 63% of campus student body. Housing is available for married students. *Intercollegiate athletics:* men only: baseball, basketball, cross-country, soccer, tennis, track, golf; women only: basketball, cross-country, softball, track, volleyball. *Special regulations:* Cars permitted for all but freshmen. Residence halls locked from 11:30pm to 7am. Quiet hours from 11pm to 8am. Residence hall visitation from 2pm to 5pm and 8pm to 11pm on Tue. for women; from 2pm to 5pm and 8pm to 11pm on Thurs. for men; Sunday from 7pm to 10pm for all. *Special services:* Learning Resources Center, medical services, Non-Traditional/Minority Student services. *Student publications, radio: Crusader,* a weekly newspaper. Radio stations WSAE-FM and KTGG-AM broadcast 90 hours per week. *Surrounding community:* Spring Arbor population 7,000. Detroit, 75 miles from campus, is nearest metropolitan area.

Library Collections: 98,000 volumes. 333,100 microforms; 5,207 audiovisual materials; 665 current periodical subscriptions. Online catalog. Students have access to online information retrieval services and the Internet.

Most important special collections include religious studies; current management.

Buildings and Grounds: Campus area 70 acres.

Chief Executive Officer: Dr. Gayle Beebe, President.

Address admission inquiries to Randall Comfort, Director of Admissions.

Thomas M. Cooley Law School

300 South Capitol Avenue
Lansing, Michigan 48901
Tel: (517) 371-5140   **E-mail:** cooleyadm@cooley.edu
Fax: (517) 334-5718   **Internet:** www.cooley.edu

Institution Description: The Thomas M. Cooley Law School is a private professional school. *Enrollment:* 2,868. *Degrees awarded:* Juris Doctor.

Accreditation: *Regional:* NCA. *Professional:* law

Calendar: Semesters.

Admission: 39 nonresident aliens enrolled. No programs available to aid students whose native language is not English. No financial aid specifically designated for international students.

Degree Requirements: Completion of prescribed curriculum.

Distinctive Educational Programs: Weekend College of Law is offered.

Degrees Conferred: 256 *first-professional:* law.

Fees and Other Expenses: *Tuition:* Contact the school for current information.

Financial Aid: Aid from institutionally generated funds is provided on the basis of academic merit. Institution has a Program Participation Agreement with the U.S. Department of Education for eligible students to receive Pell Grants and other federal aid.

Departments and Teaching Staff: *Professors* 30, *associate professors* 13, *assistant professors* 8, *visiting professors* 5, *part-time teachers* 100. *Total instructional faculty:* 156. Degrees held by full-time faculty: professional 100%.

Enrollment: Total enrollment 2,868 (51.2% men, 48.8% women).

Characteristics of Student Body: *Ethnic/racial makeup:* Black non-Hispanic: 16.3%; American Indian or Native Alaskan: 1.2%; Asian or Pacific Islander: 4%; Hispanic: 4.7%; White non-Hispanic: 71.5%; unknown: .1%.

Library Collections: 345,000 volumes. 5,400 periodicals. Students have access to online information retrieval services.

Most important special collections include complete and up-to-date Michigan legal materials; 5,000+ serials publications; U.S. Government Depository Library.

Chief Executive Officer: Don Leduc, President.

Address admission inquiries to Stephanie Gregg, Director of Admissions.

University of Detroit Mercy

4001 West McNichols Road
Detroit, Michigan 48221
Tel: (313) 993-1000   **E-mail:** admissions@udmercy.edu
Fax: (313) 993-3326   **Internet:** www.udmercy.edu

Institution Description: The University of Detroit Mercy is a private, independent, nonprofit institution affiliated with the Jesuit order and Sisters of Mercy of the Roman Catholic Church. *Enrollment:* 5,521. *Degrees awarded:* Associate, baccalaureate, first-professional (dentistry, law), master's, doctorate. Certificates also given.

Member of the Detroit Area Consortium of Catholic Colleges.

Accreditation: *Regional:* NCA. *Professional* business, clinical psychology, counseling, dental hygiene, dentistry, endodontics, engineering, law, nurse anesthesia education, nursing, physician assisting, social work, surgeon assisting

History: Established as Detroit College 1877; offered first instruction at postsecondary level 1878; awarded first degree (baccalaureate) 1881; adopted present name 1911; became University of Detroit Mercy upon the merger with Mercy College of Detroit in 1990. *See* Herman J. Muller, S.J., *The University of Detroit 1877–1977: A Centennial History* (Detroit: University of Detroit Press, 1976) for further information.

Institutional Structure: *Governing board:* University of Detroit Mercy Board of Trustees - 33 lay/religious representation. Extrainstitutional representation: 23 directors, including 6 alumni; institutional representation: president of

the university. 1 ex officio. All voting. *Composition of institution:* Administrators 34 men / 7 women. Academic affairs headed by vice president for academic affairs. Management/business/finances directed by vice president for finance. Full-time instructional faculty 283. Academic governance body, Academic Leadership Team, meets an average of 20 times per year. *Faculty representation:* Faculty served by collective bargaining agent affiliated with NEA.

Calendar: Semesters. Academic year early Sept. to early May. Freshmen admitted Sept., Jan., June. Degrees conferred May, Aug., Dec. Formal commencement May. Summer session of 2 terms from mid-May to mid-Aug.

Characteristics of Freshmen: 76% of applicants accepted. 41% of accepted applicants enrolled.

Mean ACT Composite score 23.

75% of entering freshmen expected to graduate within 5 years. 83% of freshmen from Michigan. Freshmen from 15 states and 7 foreign countries.

Admission: Rolling admissions plan. Early acceptance available. *Requirements:* Graduation from secondary school with 4 units in English, 3 mathematics, 3 social science, 2 sciences, 3 electives or language. Recommend additional units in language, mathematics, science. Minimum 2.0 GPA. *Entrance tests:* College Board SAT or ACT composite. *For transfer students:* 2.0 minimum GPA; from 4-year accredited institution 96 hours maximum transfer credit; from 2-year accredited institution 64 hours.

College credit and advanced placement for postsecondary-level work Tutoring available. Noncredit developmental courses offered in summer session and regular academic year.

Degree Requirements: 126 credit hours; 2.0 GPA; 2 terms in residence; core requirements. Fulfillment of some degree requirements possible by passing departmental examinations, College Board CLEP, AP. Exemption from some beginning courses possible by passing College Board AP. *Grading system:* A–F (plus and minus); pass-fail; withdraw.

Distinctive Educational Programs: Work-experience programs. Evening classes. Accelerated degree programs. Cooperative baccalaureate in art, music with Marygrove College; medical technology, nuclear medicine technology, cytotechnology, and master's degree in nurse anesthesiology. Cooperative baccalaureate-first professional degree in liberal arts with school of dentistry. Interdisciplinary programs in Asian studies, chemistry-business, engineering-biology. Facilities and programs for independent research, including honors programs, individual majors, tutorials. Study abroad in England, Ireland, Poland. *Other distinctive programs:* Small Business Institute, Entrepreneurial Institute, and Kellstadt Consumer Research Center. Professional development continuing education program. International Management Institute.

Degrees Conferred: 576 *baccalaureate;* 486 *master's;* 11 *doctorate.* Bachelor's degrees awarded in top five disciplines: health professions and related clinical sciences 124; engineering 72; biological/biomedical sciences 58; security and protective services 37; education 36. 193 *first-professional:* dentistry 73; law 120.

Fees and Other Expenses: *Full-time tuition per academic year:* $20,970. *Books and supplies:* $1,300. Contact the university for graduate and first-professional tuition and fees. *Room and board per academic year:* $6,880.

Financial Aid: Aid from institutionally generated funds is provided on the basis of academic merit, financial need, athletic ability, other criteria. Institution has a Program Participation Agreement with the U.S. Department of Education for eligible students to receive Pell Grants and, depending upon agreement, other federal aid.

Departments and Teaching Staff: *Total instructional faculty:* 566 (full-time 283). *Student-to-faculty ratio:* 15:1. Degrees held by full-time faculty: 81% hold terminal degrees.

Enrollment: Total enrollment 5,521. Undergraduate 3,311 (33.4% men, 66.6% women).

Characteristics of Student Body: *Ethnic/racial makeup:* Black non-Hispanic: 36.7%; American Indian or Native Alaskan: .5%; Asian or Pacific Islander: 2.3%; Hispanic: 2.6%; White non-Hispanic: 47,9%; unknown: 7.3%. *Age distribution:* 17–21: 20%; 22–24: 20%; 25–29: 18%; 30–34: 13%; 35–39: 11%; 40–49: 14%; 50–59: 3%; 60–up: 1%.

International Students: 172 nonresident aliens enrolled. Programs available to aid students whose native language is not English: social, cultural. English as a Second Language Program. No financial aid specifically designated for international students.

Student Life: On-campus residence halls. Housing available for married students. *Intercollegiate athletics:* men: baseball, basketball, cross-country, fencing, golf, indoor track, riflery, soccer, tennis; women: basketball, softball, cross-country, indoor and outdoor track, fencing. *Special regulations:* Cars permitted without restrictions. Quiet hours. *Special services:* Learning Resources Center, medical services, shuttle bus to consortium schools. *Student publications, radio:* Dichotomy, annual architecture journal; *Herison,* a monthly newspaper; *In Brief,* a monthly law school student newspaper; *The Tower,* a yearbook; *Varsity News,* a weekly newspaper. Radio station WVOD broadcasts 50 hours per week. *Surrounding community:* Detroit population over 1 million. Served by mass transit bus system; airport 15 miles from campus; passenger rail service 5 miles from campus.

Publications: *Publisher:* University of Detroit Press.

Library Collections: 650,000 volumes. 88,500 microforms; 5,500 periodicals; 13,000 recordings and tapes. Online catalog. Students have access to online information retrieval services and the Internet.

Most important special holdings include collections on American and English literature of the 18th and 19th centuries; theology/philosophy; London (England) Law Collection.

Buildings and Grounds: Campus area ½ square mile.

Chief Executive Officer: Dr. Gerard Stockhausen, S.J., President.

Address admission inquiries to Denise Williams, Dean of Admissions.

University of Michigan - Ann Arbor

Ann Arbor, Michigan 48109
Tel: (734) 764-1817   **E-mail:** ugadmiss@umich.edu
Fax: (734) 936-0740   **Internet:** www.umich.edu

Institution Description: The University of Michigan is a state institution with branch campuses at Dearborn and Flint. *Enrollment:* 39,533. *Degrees awarded:* Baccalaureate, first-professional (dentistry, law, medicine, pharmacy), master's, doctorate. Certificates also awarded.

Member of the following consortia: Committee on Institutional Cooperation (CIC), Consortium for International Earth Science Information Network (CIESIN), EDUCOM, Inter-University Consortium for Political and Social Research (ICPSR), Michigan Aquatic Sciences Consortium, Organization of Tropical Studies, Inc. (OTS), Pacific Asian Consortium for International Business Education and Research.

Accreditation: *Regional:* NCA. *Professional:* architecture, art, business, chemistry, dental hygiene, dentistry, engineering, forestry, health services administration, landscape architecture, law, librarianship, medicine, music, nursing, pharmacy, psychology internship, public health, radiation therapy, social work, teacher education

History: Chartered and established as Catholepistemiad, or University of Michigania, a classical and common school in Detroit; adopted present name 1821; organized as state-supported institution and moved to Ann Arbor 1837; offered first instruction at postsecondary level 1841; awarded first degree (baccalaureate) 1845. *See* Wilfred B. Shaw, ed., *The University of Michigan: An Encyclopedic Survey* (Ann Arbor: University of Michigan Press, 1942) for further information.

Institutional Structure: *Governing board:* The Board of Regents of The University of Michigan. Representation: 8 regents elected by statewide popular vote, president of the university. 1 ex officio. 8 voting. *Composition of institution:* Academic affairs headed by provost and vice president for academic affairs. Management/business/finances directed by vice president and chief financial officer. Other executive officers: vice president for government relation, vice president for development, vice president for research, vice president for student affairs, vice president and secretary of the university, vice president for communications. Full-time instructional faculty 2,177 men / 954 women. Academic governance bodies, University Senate and The Senate Assembly, meet 2 and 10 times per year, respectively.

Calendar: Trimesters. Academic year Sept. to May. Freshmen admitted Sept., Jan., May, July. Degrees conferred May, Aug., Dec. Formal commencements Dec., May. Summer session of 1 full term running concurrently with 2 half-terms from early May to mid-Aug.

Characteristics of Freshmen: 21,293 applicants (10,954 men, 10,339 women). 62.5% of applicants admitted. 45.2% of admitted students enrolled full-time.

58% (3,474 students) submitted SAT scores; 67% (4,026 students) submitted ACT scores. *25th percentile:* SAT I Verbal 580, SAT I Math 630; ACT Composite 26, ACT English 25, ACT Math 26. *75th percentile:* SAT I Verbal 700, SAT I Math 740; ACT Composite 31, ACT English 31, ACT Math 30.

80% of entering freshmen expected to graduate within 5 years. 59% of freshmen from Michigan. Undergraduates from 52 states and U.S. territories and 44 foreign countries.

Admission: Rolling admissions plan. For fall acceptance, apply as early as Sept. 1 of previous year, but not later than Feb. 1 of year of enrollment. All applicants must be aware that some schools and colleges may close admissions before the equal consideration date of Feb. 1. *Requirements:* Either graduation from accredited secondary school or a suggested 20 units of credit or GED. *Entrance tests:* College Board SAT or ACT. *For transfer students:* suggested 3.0 minimum GPA; from 4-year accredited institution 60 semester hours maximum transfer credit for most units; from 2-year accredited institution 30 hours.

College credit for postsecondary-level work completed in secondary school. Tutoring available.

Degree Requirements: *For undergraduate degrees:* 120–128 credit hours; 2.0 GPA; distribution requirements. Fulfillment of some degree requirements possible by passing College Board CLEP, APP, and IB. *Grading system:* A–F; pass-fail; credit-no credit; satisfactory-unsatisfactory; withdraw; unofficial withdraw.

Distinctive Educational Programs: Washington semester; cross-registration with Big Ten institutions and the University of Chicago; several programs offer a small-scale learning environment within a large university; liberal arts and career combination programs in cooperation with numerous 4-year liberal arts colleges; combined bachelor's/graduate degree programs leading to an M.D., D.D.S., M.A. (journalism), M.P.P. (public policy), or other graduate degrees. Study abroad in over 15 countries including Egypt, England, France, Germany, India, Israel, Italy, Japan, Mexico, Spain, Sweden, Scotland, Greece, and Africa.

ROTC: Army, Navy, Air Force.

Degrees Conferred: 5,923 *baccalaureate;* 3,446 *master's;* 660 *doctorate.* Bachelor's degrees awarded in top five disciplines: engineering 1,046; social sciences 930; psychology 632; business, management, marketing, and related support services 385; Visual and performing arts 381. 611 *first-professional: first-professional:* dentistry 92, law 334, medicine 127, pharmacy 58.

Fees and Other Expenses: *Full-time tuition per academic year 2004–05:* undergraduate resident $8,201, nonresident $28,027. Contact the university for current graduate tuition/fees. Professional program tuition varies by program. *Books and supplies:* $956. *Room and board per academic year:* $7,030.

Financial Aid: University of Michigan offers a direct lending program. Aid from institutionally generated funds is provided on the basis of academic merit, financial need, athletic ability, other criteria. Institution has a Program Participation Agreement with the U.S. Department of Education for eligible students to receive Pell Grants and, depending upon agreement, other federal aid.

Financial aid to full-time, first-time undergraduate students: 14% received federal grants averaging $3,972; 55% state/local grants averaging $1,570; 39% institutional grants averaging $6,077; 38% received loans averaging $6,117.

Departments and Teaching Staff: *Total instructional faculty:* 3,925. Student-to-faculty ratio: 9:1. Degrees held by full-time faculty: 94% hold doctorates or the highest degree in their field.

Enrollment: Total enrollment 39,533. Undergraduate 24,828 (49.2% men, 50.8% women).

Characteristics of Student Body: *Ethnic/racial makeup:* number of Black non-Hispanic: 64%; American Indian or Alaska Native: .9%; Asian or Pacific Islander: 12.2%; Hispanic: 4.6%; White non-Hispanic: 64%; unknown: 5.8%. *Age distribution:* 17–21: 58%; 22–24: 15%; 25–29: 16%; 30–34: 7%; 35–39: 2%; 40–49: 2%; 50–59: less than 1%, 60–and over: less than 1%.

International Students: 1,216 undergraduate nonresident aliens enrolled fall 2004. Students from Europe, Central and South America, Africa, Canada, Australia, New Zealand. Programs available to aid students whose native language is not English: social, cultural. English as a Second Language Program. No financial aid specifically designated for international students.

Student Life: On-campus residence halls house 39% of student body. Residence halls for men constitute 1% of such space, for women only 7%, for both sexes 92%. 18% of undergraduates join and 10% live in fraternities and sororities on campus. Housing available for married students and families. *Intercollegiate athletics:* men only: baseball, basketball, cross-country, diving, football, golf, gymnastics, ice hockey, soccer, swimming, tennis, track, wrestling; women only: basketball, crew, cross-country, diving, field hockey, golf, gymnastics, soccer, softball, swimming, tennis, track, volleyball, water polo. *Special regulations:* Cars permitted without restrictions. *Special services:* Medical services, campus bus system, Adaptive Technology Computing site, Career Planning and Placement, Center for the Child and Family, Center for the Education of Women, Comprehensive Studies Program, Computing Resource Center, Counseling Services, International Center, Lesbian-Gay Male Programs, Minority Student Services, Office of Ethics and Religion, Reading and Learning Skills Center, Services for Students with Disabilities, Sexual Assault Prevention and Awareness Center, Student Legal Services. *Student publications, radio: Gargoyle,* an irregularly published humor magazine; *Michigan Daily,* a newspaper published 5 days per week; *Michigan Ensian,* a yearbook. Radio station WCBN-FM. *Surrounding community:* Ann Arbor population 110,000. Detroit, 50 miles from campus, is nearest metropolitan area. Served by mass transit bus system; airport 35 miles from campus; passenger rail service 1 mile from campus.

Publications: *The American Magazine and Historical Chronicle, Anchor Bible Dictionary, Anthropological Papers, Ars Orientalis, Bulletin of Chemical Thermodynamics, Bulletin of the Museum of Art and Archaeology, Comparative Studies in Society and History, Health Education Quarterly, Journal of Law Reform, Journal of Polymer Science, Journal of the American Chemical Society, Mathematical Reviews, Michigan Academician, Michigan Botanist, Michigan Journal of International Law, Michigan Journalist, Michigan Law Review, Michigan Mathematical Journal, Michigan Papers in Japanese Studies, Michigan Papers on South and Southeast Asia, Michigan Postgraduate Review, Michigan Quarterly Review, Michigan Slavic Publications, Middle English Dictio-*

nary, Public Opinion Quarterly, Research News, Systematic Botany Monographs, U-M Occasional Papers in Women's Studies.

Library Collections: 7,350,000 volumes including bound books, serial backfiles, electronic documents, and government documents not in separate collections. Online catalog. 6,040,000 microforms. 56,500 audiovisual materials. Current serial subscriptions: 68,800 in paper, microform, and electronic form. Computer work stations available. Students have access to the Internet at no charge.

Most important special holdings include Papyri collection (chiefly Greek and Latin texts, and the scholarly literature supporting their study); Bentley Historical Library (collection of Michigan/University of Michigan); Gerald R. Ford Presidential Library.

Buildings and Grounds: The Ann Arbor campus consists of 3,129 acres and 214 major buildings.

Chief Executive Officer: Dr. Mary Sue Coleman, President.

Undergraduates address admission inquiries to Theodore Spencer, Director of Undergraduate Admissions; first-professional students to the school or college of choice; graduate students to the Admissions Office, Rackham School of Graduate Studies.

College of Literature, Science, and the Arts

Degree Programs Offered: *Baccalaureate* in Afro-American and African studies, American culture, ancient and biblical studies, anthropology, Arabic, Asian studies, astronomy, biology, botany (cultural concentration program/professional concentration program), cellular and molecular biology, biophysics, chemistry, Chinese, classical archaeology, classical languages and literature, communication, comparative literature, computer science, economics, English, film and video studies, French, geological sciences, German, Greek, Hebrew, history, history of art, Iranian, Islamic studies, Italian, Japanese, Judaic studies, Latin, Latin American and Caribbean studies, Latino or Hispanic-American studies, linguistics, mathematics (pure mathematics, actuarial mathematics, mathematical sciences), medieval and renaissance studies, microbiology, Middle Eastern and North African studies, music, oceanography, philosophy, physics, political science, psychology, studies in religion, Romance linguistics, Russian language, Russian and East European studies, Scandinavian studies, social anthropology, sociology, Spanish, statistics, theatre and drama, Turkish, women's studies. *Master's, doctorate* administered by the School of Graduate Studies.

Distinctive Educational Programs: Bachelor in General Studies. Individualized concentration programs. Joint degree programs in liberal arts and architecture, engineering, dentistry, medicine, public policy studies, and landscape architecture. The Concurrent Undergraduate-Graduate Studies Program enables students to enroll simultaneously in the College of L.S.&A. and the Rackham Graduate School. Living-learning communities offered through the Pilot Program (multidisciplinary, academic/residential program for first- and second-year students) and the Residential College (four-year, degree-granting unit offering a combined academic/residential educational experience). The Residential College offers courses and concentrations of its own. The curriculum includes multidisciplinary approaches to the humanities, natural sciences, and social sciences, as well as courses in fine arts, music, and languages. College of L.S.&A. operates study abroad programs in Britain, France, Italy, Spain, Sweden, and Germany, and also participates with other universities in programs in many other countries. Preferred admissions available to Business, Dentistry, Natural Resources, and Pharmacy Schools.

A. Alfred Taubman College of Architecture and Urban Planning

Degree Programs Offered: *Baccalaureate, master's* in architecture. Degrees administered by the School of Graduate Studies: *master's* in urban planning; *doctorate* in architecture, urban planning.

Distinctive Educational Programs: Dual degree programs between: architecture and business administration, architecture and civil engineering, architecture and urban planning, urban planning and social work. 3+ program in architecture for students with degrees in other fields. Study abroad programs in Vienna (Austria), Copenhagen (Denmark), Florence (Italy), and Prague (Czech Republic). Building Technology Laboratory. Computer Laboratory. *See* College of Literature, Science, and the Arts.

School of Art and Design

Degree Programs Offered: *Baccalaureate* in art education, ceramics, design, fibers, general studies, graphic design, industrial design, interior design, metalwork and jewelry design, mixed media, painting, photography, printmaking, sculpture, scientific illustration, weaving and textile design. *master's* in all fields administered by the School of Graduate Studies.

Distinctive Educational Programs: Interdepartmental master's program in medical and biological illustration in cooperation with the Medical School.

School of Business Administration

Degree Programs Offered: *Baccalaureate* in business administration; *master's* in business administration, accounting; *doctorate* in business administration.

Distinctive Educational Programs: Executive Education Program offers continuing education for managers and executives. Evening M.B.A. program available on the Ann Arbor campus and in Dearborn.

School of Education

Degree Programs Offered: *Baccalaureate, master's* in education (elementary, secondary, special). *Doctorate* in education.

Distinctive Educational Programs: Master of Arts plus teaching certificate (MA/C). Peace Corps Fellowships/USA Program. Interdepartmental graduate programs in education and psychology, education and English, and science for teachers in cooperation with the School of Graduate Studies.

College of Engineering

Degree Programs Offered: *Baccalaureate, master's, doctorate* in aerospace engineering; atmospheric, oceanic, and space sciences; chemical engineering; civil and environmental engineering; computer engineering; electrical engineering; engineering; engineering physics; industrial and operations engineering; materials science and engineering; mechanical engineering; naval architecture and marine engineering; nuclear engineering.

Distinctive Educational Programs: Optional Co-op and summer internship work experience opportunities. Interdisciplinary programs in macromolecular science and engineering, applied physics, and intelligent highways and vehicle systems. Dual graduate degrees between engineering and the M.B.A. program in the School of Business Administration. Undergraduate dual degree programs with the College of Literature, Science, and the Arts; the School of Music; and other units. Graduate programs in construction engineering and management, bioengineering, applied mechanics, public works administration, environmental engineering, health services management and industrial engineering, technical information design and management, nuclear science, aerospace science, atmospheric science, and oceanic science in addition to expected programs within departments. Major research laboratories housing graduate research programs include Artificial Intelligence Laboratory, Automotive Research Center, Automotive Structural Durability Simulation, Biomechanics Laboratory, Center for Ergonomics, Center for Nanomaterials Science, Center for Neural Communication Technology, Center for Parallel Computing, Center for Ultrafast Optical Science, Electron Microbeam Analysis Laboratory, Engineering Research Center for Reconfigurable Machining, Financial Engineering Laboratory, Fraunhofer Resource Center, Institute for Environmental Sciences/Engineering/Technology, Integrated Devices and Circuits Research Group, Intelligent Transportation Systems Lab, Laboratory for Scientific Computation, Laboratory for Turbulence and Combustion, W.M. Keck Foundation Computational Fluid Dynamics Laboratory.

School of Music

Degree Programs Offered: *Baccalaureate, master's* in composition, dance, harp, jazz studies, music and technology, music education, music history, music theory, musical theater, organ and church music, piano, string instruments, voice, wind and percussion instruments; *doctorate* in composition and music theory, music education, musicology, music composition, music conducting, music performance, music theory, theatre.

Admission: All students must complete a separate 'Request for Audition' in addition to standard University Application Forms.

Distinctive Educational Programs: Stearns Collection of Musical Instruments. Electronic music studio and recording facilities. Dual degree programs with the College of Engineering and the College of Literature, Science, and the Arts. Joint M.M./M.B.A. in Arts Administration with the School of Business Administration.

School of Natural Resources and Environment

Degree Programs Offered: *Baccalaureate, master's* in environmental policy and behavior, landscape design and planning, and resource ecology and management; aquatic resources, conservation biology and ecosystem management, environmental advocacy, environmental behavior, environmental education, fisheries, forestry, landscape architecture, planning, remote sensing, resource economics, resource policy, and wildlife; *doctorate* in natural resources, landscape architecture, natural resources economics.

Distinctive Educational Programs: Undergraduate and graduate programs integrate biological/ecological sciences, social sciences, and environmental design/planning. Summer residency field training available at the University's Biological Station. Joint master's degree programs with the School of Business Administration (M. Forestry/M.B.A.) and Law School (M.S. in Natural Resources/J.D.). Joint Ph.D. in Natural Resources Economics with the Department of Economics in the College of Literature, Science, and the Arts.

School of Nursing

Degree Programs Offered: *Baccalaureate, master's, doctorate* in administration of nursing and patient care services, community health nursing, gerontological nursing, medical-surgical nursing, nursing, parent-child nursing, and psychiatric-mental health nursing.

Distinctive Educational Programs: Baccalaureate completion program for registered nurses. Joint master's degree program in nursing administration with the School of Business Administration (M.S./M.B.A.). Individually-designed concentration in clinical management available to master's students. Center for Nursing Research provides research consultation and facilities such as a microcomputer site and a behavioral research laboratory.

College of Pharmacy

Degree Programs Offered: *First-professional* (Pharm. D.). *Master's, doctorate* in medicinal chemistry, pharmaceutical chemistry, pharmaceutics, pharmacognosy, pharmacy.

Admission: *For first-professional degree:* 2 years of college study, including 60 hours prepharmacy curriculum.

Degree Requirements: *For first-professional degree:* 128 credit hours beyond prepharmacy work.

Distinctive Educational Programs: Undergraduate programs leading to a B.S. in Medicinal Chemistry or B.S. in Pharmaceutical Sciences. Joint Pharm.D./Ph.D. in pharmaceutics; joint Pharm.D./Ph.D. in pharmacognosoy.

School of Dentistry

Degree Programs Offered: *Baccalaureate* in dental hygiene; *first-professional* (D.D.S.) in dentistry; *master's* in biomaterials, dental hygiene, dental public health, endodontics, oral and maxillofacial surgery, oral pathology and diagnosis, orthodontics, pediatric dentistry, periodontics, prosthodontics, and restorative dentistry (occlusion/operative dentistry); *doctorate* in oral biology and in interdepartmental programs combining biomaterials with materials and metallurgical engineering, pharmaceutical chemistry, mechanical engineering and applied mechanics, oral biology or macromolecular science.

Admission: *For first-professional in dentistry:* 60 semester hours from accredited college or university which must include courses in English, biology, chemistry, physics; DAT.

Degree Requirements: *For first-professional in dentistry:* 200 credit hours, 2.0 GPA, entire program (with few exceptions) in residence.

Distinctive Educational Programs: Joint degree program in liberal arts (bachelor's from the College of Literature, Science, and the Arts) and dentistry (D.D.S.). Joint and dual graduate degree programs in dental public health with School of Public Health.

Law School

Degree Programs Offered: *First-professional* (J.D.); *master's* in comparative law, law; *doctorate* in science of law.

Admission: Baccalaureate from accredited institution; LSAT.

Degree Requirements: 52 credit hours beyond prescribed first-year curriculum.

Distinctive Educational Programs: Joint degree program with School of Business Administration: J.D./M.B.A. Joint degree programs in cooperation with the School of Graduate Studies: J.D./Ph.D. in economics; J.D./Master of Public Policy; J.D./M.A. in Russian and East European studies; J.D./M.A. in Near Eastern and North African studies; J.D./M.A. in world politics. *See* School of Natural Resources.

Medical School

Degree Programs Offered: *First-professional* (M.D.); *master's, doctorate* in anatomy and cell biology, biological chemistry, human genetics, microbiology, neurology, neuroscience, ophthalmology, pharmacology, physiology, radiology.

Admission: Per Admissions Office.

Degree Requirements: 4 year prescribed curriculum.

Distinctive Educational Programs: Joint M.D./Ph.D. in medical scientist training with School of Graduate Studies.

Horace H. Rackham School of Graduate Studies

Degree Programs Offered: *Master's, doctorate.*

Departments and Teaching Staff: Graduate faculty are connected to colleges and schools within the university.

Distinctive Educational Programs: Interdepartmental graduate degree programs in American culture, anthropology and history, Asian studies, bioengineering, biophysics, cellular and molecular biology, classical art and archaeology, clinical research design and statistics analysis, communication, comparative literature, education and psychology, English and education, health services organization and policy, health services management and industrial engineering, macromolecular science and engineering, manufacturing systems engineering, medicinal chemistry, modern Middle Eastern and North African studies, natural resource economics, neuroscience, Russian and East European studies, social work and social science. Individual interdepartmental degree programs. *See* other schools and colleges for additional programs.

School of Information

Degree Programs Offered: *Master's* in archives and records management, human computer interaction, information, information and library studies, information economics/management/policy, library and information services, library science; *doctorate* in information, information and library studies.

Distinctive Educational Programs: History Archival Program.

School of Public Health

Degree Programs Offered: *Master's* in biostatistics, dental public health, health, environmental and industrial health, epidemiology, health behavior and health education, health services management and policy, human nutrition, population planning and international health, and public health policy and administration; *doctorate* in biostatistics, health behavior and health education, health services organization and policy, population planning and international health, human nutrition, industrial health, laboratory practice epidemiology, long term care, medical care administration, medical care organization, occupational health, public health, public health administration, public health genetics, public health policy and administration, radiological health, toxicology.

Distinctive Educational Programs: Laboratory facilities for studies in virology, bacteriology, immunology, parasitology, epidemiology, public health engineering, industrial health, toxicology, and radiological health. Extensive computer facilities available. On Job/On Campus weekend programs for master's degrees in health services management and policy, dental public health administration, occupational medicine, clinical research design and statistical analysis, industrial hygiene, and public health policy and administration. On Job/On Campus program for doctoral degree in health policy. Dual degree programs involving the Master of Public Health (M.P.H.) or the Master of Health Services Administration (M.H.S.A.): M.P.H./M.S. in pedodontics; M.P.H./M.D.; M.P.H. or M.H.S.A./M.A. in applied economics; M.P.H./M.A. in Near Eastern and North African studies; M.H.S.A./M.B.A.; M.P.H./M.S.W.; M.P.H. or M.H.S.A./Master in Public Policy; M.P.H. or M.H.S.A./Bachelor or Arts, Science, or General Studies. Also M.S. in Health Services Management and Policy/Industrial Operations Engineering.

School of Social Work

Degree Programs Offered: *Master's* in administration, adults and elderly in families in society, children and youth in families in society, community and social systems, community organization, evaluation, health, interpersonal practice, management of human services, mental health, research, research and evaluation, social policy and evaluation, social policy and planning.

Distinctive Educational Programs: Continuing education M.S.W. certificate program in administration. Dual degree programs with: School of Public Health (M.S.W./M.P.H.); School of Business Administration (M.S.W./M.B.A.); College of Architecture and Urban Planning (M.S.W./M.U.P.).

Gerald R. Ford School of Public Policy

Degree Programs Offered: *Master's* in public policy, public administration; *doctorate* in public policy.

Distinctive Educational Programs: The Institute of Public Policy Studies offers degree programs that are designed to prepare students for policymaking, general administration, and consulting in the public sector. This graduate study provides a professional education that may serve as an alternative or a supplement to law school or business school. The curriculum is interdisciplinary in nature with a strong emphasis on the development of analytical skills. Joint degree programs are available with Law, Business Administration, Public Health, Natural Resources, and area centers.

Division of Kinesiology

Degree Programs Offered: *Baccalaureate* in athletic training, kinesiology, movement science, physical education, sports management and communications, teacher education; *master's, doctorate* in kinesiology, physical education: kinesiology.

Distinctive Educational Programs: Research projects include: Exercise Adherence Lab, Fitness for Youth Program, Health Management Research Center, Center for Human Motor Research, Center for Motor Behavior in Down Syndrome, Media Research Lab, Sports Marketing Research Lab, Paul Robeson Research Center for Academic and Athletic Prowess, Exercise Endorcrinology Laboratory, Laboratory of Molecular Kinesiology.

University of Michigan - Dearborn

4901 Evergreen Road
Dearborn, Michigan 48128-1491

Tel: (313) 593-5000   **E-mail:** admissions@umd.umich.edu
Fax: (313) 436-9167   **Internet:** www.umd.umich.edu

Institution Description: *Enrollment:* 8,631. *Degrees awarded:* Baccalaureate, master's.

Accreditation: *Regional:* NCA. *Professional:* business, computer science, engineering

History: Established and chartered as upper division branch campus of University of Michigan and offered first instruction at postsecondary level 1959; awarded first degree (baccalaureate) 1961; became 4-year institution 1971.

Institutional Structure: *Composition of institution:* Administrators 25 men / 4 women. Academic affairs headed by vice chancellor for academic affairs. Management/business/finances directed by vice chancellor for business and finance. Full-time instructional faculty 219. Academic governance body, Faculty Congress, meets an average of 3 times per year.

Calendar: Semester. Academic year Sept. to Aug. Freshmen admitted Sept., Jan., June, July. Degrees conferred and formal commencement May, Aug., Dec. Summer session of 3 terms from early May to late Aug.

Characteristics of Freshmen: 70% of applicants accepted. 66% of accepted applicants enrolled.

94% (653 students) submitted ACT scores. *25th percentile:* ACT Composite 21, ACT English 20, ACT Math 20. *75th percentile:* ACT Composite 25, ACT English 26, ACT Math 26.

99% of freshmen from Michigan. Freshmen from 1 state and 2 foreign countries.

Admission: Rolling admissions plan. For fall acceptance, apply as early as 1 year prior to enrollment. Early acceptance available. *Requirements:* Either graduation from accredited secondary school with 15 units which must include 3 English, concentration from among mathematics, laboratory sciences, social studies, or in a foreign language; or GED. Recommend 1 additional unit English, 2 years college preparatory mathematics. Additional requirements for engineering program. *Entrance tests:* College Board SAT or ACT composite. *For transfer students:* 2.0 minimum GPA; from 4-year accredited institution 72 hours maximum transfer credit; from 2-year accredited institution 62 hours.

College credit and advanced placement for postsecondary-level work completed in secondary school. College credit for extrainstitutional learning on basis of ACE *2006 Guide to the Evaluation of Educational Experiences in the Armed Services*; personal interviews; faculty assessment.

Tutoring available. Noncredit remedial offered in summer session.

Degree Requirements: 120–128 credit hours; 2.0 GPA; 45 credit hours in residence; distribution requirements. Fulfillment of some degree requirements and exemption from some beginning courses possible by passing departmental examinations, College Board CLEP. *Grading system:* A–F; pass-fail; withdraw.

Distinctive Educational Programs: Internships. Evening classes. Accelerated degree programs. Special facilities for using telecommunications in the classroom. Interdisciplinary programs in computer information systems, environmental studies, public administration, urban and regional studies. Facilities and programs for independent research, including honors programs, tutorials. Study abroad in England, Sweden.

ROTC: Army, Navy, Air Force in cooperation with University of Michigan - Ann Arbor.

Degrees Conferred: 1.060 *baccalaureate;* 627 *master's.* Bachelor's degrees awarded in top five disciplines: business, management, marketing, and related support services 236; engineering 225; education 130; psychology 89; computer and information sciences and support services 84.

Fees and Other Expenses: *Full-time tuition per academic year 2004–05:* undergraduate resident $5,426, nonresident $10,582; graduate resident $6,228, nonresident $9,342.

Financial Aid: Aid from institutionally generated funds is provided on the basis of academic merit, financial need, athletic ability, other criteria.

Financial aid to full-time, first-time undergraduate students: need-based scholarships/grants totaling $5,929,001, self-help $10,126,664; non-need-based scholarships/grants totaling $4,661,470, self-help $8,085,323, parent loans $265,098, tuition waivers $106,539, athletic awards $65,000.

Departments and Teaching Staff: *Total instructional faculty:* 517 (full-time 277, part-time 240; women 185, men 332; members of minority groups 105). Total faculty with doctorate, first-professional, or other terminal degree: 346. Student-to-faculty ratio: 16:1.

Enrollment: Total enrollment 8m631. Undergraduate full-time 1,902 men / 2,035 women, part-time 1,156m / 1,356w; graduate full-time 1,101m / 102w, part-time 1,041m / 938w.

Characteristics of Student Body: *Ethnic/racial makeup:* number of Black non-Hispanic: 506; American Indian or Alaska Native: 29; 2Asian or Pacific Islander: 416; Hispanic: 181; White non-Hispanic: 4,597; unknown: 606.

International Students: 114 nonresident aliens enrolled fall 2004. No programs available to aid students whose native language is not English. No financial aid specifically designated for international students.

Student Life: No on-campus housing. *Intercollegiate athletics:* men only: basketball; women only: basketball; both sexes: fencing. *Special regulations:* Registered cars permitted in designated areas. *Special services:* Learning Resources Center, medical services. *Student publications, radio:* Literary Arts *Journal,* published annually; *Michigan Journal,* a weekly newspaper. Radio station WUMP. *Surrounding community:* Dearborn population 91,000. Detroit, 1 mile from campus, is nearest metropolitan area. Served by mass transit bus system; airport 10 miles from campus; passenger rail service 1 mile from campus.

Library Collections: 334,800 volumes. 548,000 microforms; 4,600 audiovisual materials. 1,100 current periodical subscriptions. Online catalog. Students have access to online information retrieval services.

Most important special collections include Liberal Arts; Management; Engineering.

Buildings and Grounds: Campus area 200 acres.

Chief Executive Officer: Dr. Daniel Little, Chancellor.

Address admission inquiries to Director of Admissions.

University of Michigan - Flint

Flint, Michigan 48502-1950
Tel: (810) 762-3000   **E-mail:** admissions@umflint.edu
Fax: (810) 762-3141   **Internet:** www.umflint.edu

Institution Description: *Enrollment:* 6,188. *Degrees awarded:* Baccalaureate, master's.

Accreditation: *Regional:* NCA. *Professional:* business, music, nurse anesthesia education, nursing, nursing education, physical therapy, radiation therapy, social work

History: Established as Flint College of The University of Michigan and offered first instruction at postsecondary level 1956; awarded first degree (baccalaureate) 1958; adopted present name 1971.

Institutional Structure: *Composition of institution:* Administrators 1 man / 5 women. Academic affairs headed by provost and vice-chancellor for academic affairs. Administration headed by vice chancellor for administration. Full-time instructional faculty 202. Academic governance body, Faculty Council, meets an average of 18 times per year.

Calendar: Semesters. Academic year July to June. Freshmen admitted Sept., Jan., Apr., June. Degrees conferred Aug., Dec.; formal commencements Dec. and May. Summer session from late June to mid-Aug; spring sessions from early May to late June.

Characteristics of Freshmen: 87% of applicants admitted. 44% applicants admitted and enrolled.

3% (21 students) submitted SAT scores; 97% (336 students) submitted ACT scores. *25th percentile:* SAT Verbal 460, SAT Math 440; ACT Composite 19, ACT English 17, ACT Math 17. *75th percentile:* SAT Verbal 560, SAT Math 610; ACT Composite 24, ACT English 24, ACT Math 24.

18% of entering freshmen expected to graduate within 5 years. 97% of freshmen from Michigan. Freshmen from 5 states and 2 foreign countries.

Admission: Rolling admissions plan. For fall acceptance, apply as early as senior year of secondary school; recommended priority deadline for freshmen is May 1st of year of enrollment. Early acceptance available. *Requirements:* Either graduation from accredited secondary school or GED. Recommend 4 years English, 4 years math, 3 years science, 3 years social studies, 2 years foreign language. GPA 2.7. *Entrance tests:* College board SAT or ACT composite. For foreign students TOEFL. *For transfer students:* 2.0 minimum GPA; from 4-year accredited institution 75 hours maximum transfer credit; from 2-year accredited institution 62 hours.

College credit and advanced placement for postsecondary-level work completed in secondary school. Up to 4 physical education credits for military service.

Degree Requirements: *For undergraduate degrees:* minimum 120 credit hours; minimum 2.0 GPA; 45 credit hours in residence; other requirements depending on program.

Exemption from some beginning courses possible by passing College Board, AP. *Grading system:* A–E; pass-fail; withdraw (carries penalty); incomplete.

Distinctive Educational Programs: Internships. Evening and Saturday classes. Preprofessional programs in business, dentistry, engineering, law, medicinal chemistry, medicine, pharmacy, pharmaceutical sciences, physical therapy, veterinary medicine, actuarial mathematics. Interdisciplinary programs. Facilities and programs for independent research, including honors programs, individual majors, tutorials.

Degrees Conferred: 869 *baccalaureate* (B); 171 *master's* (M): area and ethnic studies 1 (B); biological/life sciences 34 (B), 2 (M); business/marketing 118 (B), 59 (M); communications/communication technologies 31 (B); computer and information sciences 23 (B); education 270 (B), 42 (M); engineering and engineering technologies 7 (B); English 29 (B); foreign languages and literature 8 (B); health professions and related sciences 110 (B), 41 (M); interdisciplinary studies 34 (B); law/legal studies 4 (M); mathematics 3 (B); natural resources/environmental science 9 (B); philosophy/religion/theology 4 (B); physical sciences 9 (B); protective services/public administration 68 (B), 23 (M); psychology 40 (B); social sciences and history 53 (B); visual and performing arts 18 (B).

Fees and Other Expenses: *Full-time tuition per academic year 2004–05:* $5,426 undergraduate resident, $10,582 nonresident; $6,228 graduate resident, $9,342 nonresident. *Required fees:* $296.

Financial Aid: The university offers a direct lending program. Aid from institutionally generated funds is provided on the basis of academic merit, financial need.

Financial aid to full-time, first-time undergraduate students: need-based scholarships/grants totaling $7,218,661, self-help $9,614,302; non-need-based scholarships/grants totaling $613,950, self-help $8,895,588, parent loans $190,350.

Departments and Teaching Staff: *Professors* 36, *associate professors* 56, *assistant professors* 3, *instructors/lecturers* 36, *part-time faculty* 202.

Total instructional faculty: 393 (full-time 191, part-time 202; women 195, men 198; members of minority groups 68); Total faculty with doctorate, first-professional, or other terminal degree: 205. Student-to-faculty ratio: 16:1. Degrees held by full-time faculty: doctorate 71%, master's 28%. *Faculty development:* $3,021,905 in grants for research. 2 faculty members awarded sabbaticals 2004–05.

Enrollment: Total enrollment 6,188. Undergraduate full-time 1,237 men / 2,113 women, part-time 789m / 1,481w; graduate full-time 32m / 83w, part-time 176m / 277w. *Transfer students:* in-state 638; from out-of-state 70.

Characteristics of Student Body: *Ethnic/racial makeup:* number of Black non-Hispanic: 579; American Indian or Alaska Native: 43; Asian or Pacific Islander: 86; Hispanic: 120; White non-Hispanic: 4,357; unknown: 387. *Age distribution:* number under 18: 148; 18–19: 910; 20–21: 1,971; 22–24: 1,297; 25–29: 897; 30–34: 537; 35–39: 293; 40–49: 430; 50–64: 126; 65 and over: 9. 25% of student body attend summer sessions.

International Students: 55 nonresident aliens enrolled fall 2004. 3 students from Europe, 12 Asia, 2 Central and South America, 21 Canada, 13 other. No programs available to aid students whose native language is not English. No financial aid specifically designated for international students.

Student Life: No on-campus housing. *Special regulations:* Cars permitted without restrictions. *Special services:* Learning Resources Center. *Student publications:* Biannual literary magazine, bimonthly student newspaper. *Surrounding community:* Flint population 141,000. Detroit, 55 miles from campus, is nearest metropolitan area. Served by airport 5 miles from campus; passenger rail service 2 miles from campus.

Library Collections: 253,182 volumes including bound books, serial backfiles, electronic documents, and government documents not in separate collections. Online catalog. Current serial subscriptions: 877 paper, 23 microform, over 6,000 via electronic access. 1,577 recordings; 1,434 compact discs; 596 CD-ROMs. 38 computer work stations. Students have access to the Internet at no charge. Total budget for books, periodicals, audiovisual materials, microforms 2004–05: $4818,050.

Most important special collections include the Genesee Historical Collection; Foundation Center Collection; U.S. Government Documents Collection.

Buildings and Grounds: Campus area 47 acres. *New buildings:* William S. White Building completed 2002.

Chief Executive Officer: Dr. Juan E. Mestas, Chancellor.

Address admission inquiries to Kimberly Buster-Williams, Director of Admissions.

Walsh College of Accountancy and Business Administration

3838 Livernois Road
Troy, Michigan 48007-7006

Tel: (248) 689-8282   **E-mail:** admission@walshcollege.edu
Fax: (248) 689-9066   **Internet:** www.walshcollege.edu

Institution Description: Walsh College of Accountancy and Business Administration is a private, independent, nonprofit college providing upper division and graduate study only. *Enrollment:* 3,105. *Degrees awarded:* Baccalaureate, master's.

Accreditation: *Regional:* NCA.

History: Established as Walsh Institute of Accountancy 1922; adopted present name, incorporated, and offered first instruction at postsecondary level 1968; awarded first degree (baccalaureate) 1970; awarded first master's degree 1976.

Institutional Structure: *Governing board:* Board of Trustees. Extrainstitutional representation: 25 trustees; institutional representation: president of the college. 1 ex officio. All voting. *Composition of institution:* Administrators 8 men / 11 women. Academic affairs headed by dean. Management/business/finances directed by treasurer. Full-time instructional faculty 15. Academic governance body, Academic Committee, meets an average of 5 times per year.

Calendar: Semesters. Academic year early Sept. to Aug. Entering students admitted Sept., Jan., May. Degrees conferred Apr., Aug., Dec. Formal commencement Jan., June. Summer session from mid-May to early Aug.

Admission: Rolling admissions plan. *Requirements:* Either associate degree or 60 semester hours (including 30 hours liberal arts) from an accredited institution. Recommend 2 courses accounting, 2 economics, 2 mathematics, 1 business communications, 1 English composition, 1 data processing, 1 management, 1 marketing. Minimum 2.0 GPA. *Entrance tests:* For foreign students TOEFL. *For transfer students:* 2.0 minimum GPA; 91 hours maximum transfer credit.

College credit and advanced placement for postsecondary-level work completed in secondary school. Tutoring available.

Degree Requirements: 127 credit hours (including transfer credit); 2.0 GPA; last 45 hours in residence; core curriculum. *For graduate students:* minimum 2.75 GPA and professional work experience. *Grading system:* A–F; withdraw; incomplete (carries time limit).

Degrees Conferred: 387 *baccalaureate:* business and management; 611 *master's:* business and management.

Fees and Other Expenses: *Full-time tuition per academic year 2004–05:* $8,964. *Required fees:* $345.

Financial Aid: Aid from institutionally generated funds is provided on the basis of academic merit, financial need.

Financial aid to full-time, first-time undergraduate students: need-based scholarships/grants totaling $57,130; self-help $218,211; non-need-based scholarships/grants totaling $210,000; self-help $87,000, parent loans $8,100.

Departments and Teaching Staff: *Total instructional faculty:* 130 (full-time 16, part-time 114; women 30, men 100; members of minority groups 5). Total faculty with doctorate, first-professional, or other terminal degree: 37. Student-to-faculty ratio: 25:1. Degrees held by full-time faculty: doctorate 14%, master's 86%, baccalaureate 100%.

Enrollment: Total enrollment 3,105. Undergraduate full-time 80 men / 65 women, part-time 306m / 458w; graduate full-time 58m / 53w, part-time 1,049m / 1,036w.

Characteristics of Student Body: *Ethnic/racial makeup:* number of Black 49; non-Hispanic: American Indian or Alaska Native: 1; Asian or Pacific Islander: 24; Hispanic: 12; White non-Hispanic: 378; unknown: 159. *Age distribution:* number 20–21: 29; 22–24: 75; 25–29: 30–34: 35; 35–39: 7; 40–49: 1; 50–64: 1.

International Students: 171 nonresident aliens enrolled fall 2004. No programs available to aid students whose native language is not English. No financial aid specifically designated for international students.

Student Life: No on-campus housing. *Student organizations:* Student government, accounting club, student chapter of Data Processing Association; business club. *Student publication: Insight,* student newsletter published 10 times per year. *Surrounding community:* Troy population 75,000, is located within Detroit metropolitan area.

Library Collections: 26,300 volumes. 10,000 microforms; 300 current periodical subscriptions. Students have access to online information retrieval services and the Internet.

Most important special collections include taxation, accounting, management.

Buildings and Grounds: Campus area 44,000 square feet (1 building).

Chief Executive Officer: Keith A. Pretty, President.

Address admission inquiries to Victoria Scavone, Enrollment and Student Services.

Wayne State University

658 West Kirby
Detroit, Michigan 48202

Tel: (313) 577-2424   **E-mail:** admissions@wayne.edu
Fax: (313) 577-3200   **Internet:** www.wayne.edu

Institution Description: Wayne State University is a state institution. *Enrollment:* 33,314. *Degrees awarded:* Baccalaureate, first-professional (law, medicine, pharmacy), master's, doctorate.

Budget subject to approval by state governing boards. Member of the consortia City University Institute for Continuing Legal Education, Institute for Labor and Industrial relations, and Urban 13 Conference.

Accreditation: *Regional:* NCA. *Professional:* business, clinical lab scientist, clinical psychology, counseling, dance, dietetics, engineering, funeral service education, law, librarianship, medicine, music, nurse anesthesia education, nursing, nursing education, occupational therapy, pharmacy, physical therapy, physician assisting, physical therapy, planning, psychology internship, public administration, radiation therapy, rehabilitation counseling, social work, speech-language pathology, surgeon assisting, teacher education, theatre

History: Established 1933 as the Colleges of the City of Detroit through merger of The Detroit Medical College (established 1868), Detroit Teachers College (established as Detroit Normal Training School 1881), and the College of the City of Detroit (established as a Detroit Junior College 1917); became municipal institution and changed name to Wayne University 1934; authorized first doctoral programs 1945; became state institution and adopted present name 1956. *See* Leslie L. Hanawalt, *A Place of Light* (Detroit: Wayne State Press, 1968) for further information.

Institutional Structure: *Governing board:* Wayne State Board of Governors. Extrainstitutional representation: 8 governors; institutional representation: president of the university. 1 ex officio. 8 voting. *Composition of institution:* Administrators 31 men / 12 women. Academic affairs headed by provost and senior vice president for academic affairs. Management directed by senior vice president for finance and administration. Full-time instructional faculty 475 men / 235 women (excludes lectures/faculty members from the School of Medicine). Academic governance body, Academic Senate, meets an average of 10 times per year. *Faculty representation:* Faculty served by collective bargaining agent affiliated with AAUP.

Calendar: Semesters. Academic year Aug. to May. Freshmen admitted Aug., Jan., May. Degrees conferred and formal commencements May and Dec. Summer session of 3 terms from mid-May to late Aug.

Characteristics of Freshmen: 63% of applicants admitted. 32% of applicants admitted and enrolled.

73% (2,282 students) submitted ACT scores. *25th percentile:* ACT Composite 16, ACT English 15, ACT Math 15. *75th percentile:* ACT Composite 24, ACT English 24, ACT Math 25.

15% of entering freshmen expected to graduate within 5 years. 95% of freshmen from Michigan. Freshmen from 4 states.

Admission: Rolling admissions plan. For fall acceptance, apply as early as Sept. 1 of previous year, but not later than Aug. 1 of year of enrollment. *Requirements:* Either graduation from accredited secondary school or GED. Minimum 2.75 GPA. For students with GPA less than 2.75 but greater than 2.0, ACT composite score of 21 or SAT total of 950. *For transfer students:* 2.0 minimum GPA; from 2-year accredited institution 64 hours maximum transfer credit.

College credit for extrainstitutional learning (life experience). Tutoring available. Noncredit developmental courses offered.

Degree Requirements: 120 credit hours; 2.0 GPA; 30 hours in residence; university-wide general education requirements apply to all undergraduate students seeking a bachelor's degree.

Fulfillment of some degree requirements possible by passing College Board CLEP. *Grading system:* A–F; pass-fail; withdraw (carries penalty and time limit).

Distinctive Educational Programs: Work-experience programs. Flexible meeting places and schedules, including off-campus centers (at Farmington Hills, Harper Woods, Detroit, Madison Heights, Clinton Township, Eastpointe);

weekend and evening classes. Cooperative programs with Macomb Community College. Courses over the Internet and via interactive video. Interdisciplinary programs include Weekend College Program and other programs in Africana studies, business-music, Chicano-Boriqua studies, environmental studies, urban planning, urban studies, women's studies. Facilities and programs for independent research, including honors programs, individual majors, tutorials. Numerous study abroad programs (Africa, West Africa, Caribbean Basin, Canada, Cuba, Ecuador, England, Finland, France, Germany, Greece, Italy, Japan, Mexico, The Netherlands) and area programs in the Middle East, Latin America, West Africa, the Caribbean, and Eastern Europe.

ROTC: Air Force in cooperation with the University of Michigan.

Degrees Conferred: 2,380 *baccalaureate* (B), 2,468 *master's* (M), 194 *doctorate* (D): architecture 4 (M); area and ethnic studies 6 (B); biological/life sciences 117 (B), 48 (M), 25 (D); business/marketing 390 (B), 451 (M); communications/communication technologies 89 (B), 33 (M), 5 (D); computer and information sciences 64 (B), 64 (M), 3 (D); education 382 (B), 502 (M), 35 (D); engineering and engineering technologies 180 (B); 475 (M), 27 (D); English 50 (B), 14 (M), 6 (D); foreign languages and literature 26 (B), 13 (M), 4 (D); health professions and related sciences 297 (B), 202 (M), 17 (D); home economics and vocational home economics 37 (B), 15 (M), 5 (D); interdisciplinary studies 61 (B), 18 (M); law/legal studies 19 (M); library science 196 (M); mathematics 20 (B), 9 (M), 4 (D); parks and recreation 31 (M); personal and miscellaneous services 21 (B); philosophy/religion/theology 4 (B), 2 (M), 3 (D); physical sciences 41 (B), 15 (M), 16 (D); protective services/public administration 170 (B), 235 (M); psychology 144 (B), 38 (M), 25 (D); social sciences and history 134 (B), 50 (M), 17 (D); visual and performing arts 147 (B), 34 (M), 2 (D); 507 *first-professional:* law 220; medicine 245; pharmacy 42.

Fees and Other Expenses: *Full-time tuition per academic year 2004–05:* undergraduate resident $4,773, nonresident $10,941; graduate resident $6,838, nonresident $15,098. *Required fees:* $626. *Room and board per academic year:* $6,700.

Financial Aid: Wayne State University offers a direct lending program. Aid from institutionally generated funds is provided on the basis of academic merit, financial need, athletic ability.

Financial aid to full-time, first-time undergraduate students: need-based scholarships/grants totaling $22,106,120, self-help $45,562,644, parent loans $111,461; non-need-based scholarships/grants totaling $14,773,722, self-help $2,453,493, tuition waivers $92,536, athletic awards $1,848,467. *Graduate aid:* 12 students received $644,220 in federal and state-funded fellowships/grants; 49 received $718,632 for college-assigned jobs; 433 teaching assistantships awarded totaling $5,905,010 (ranging from $11,347 to $16,647); 472 research assistantships were awarded totaling $7,589,054 (ranging from $9,000 to $35,000).

Departments and Teaching Staff: *Professors* 322, *associate professors* 267, *assistant professors* 232, *instructors* 37, *part-time faculty* 912.

Total instructional faculty: 1,925 (full-time 1,001, part-time 924; women 853, men 1,072; members of minority groups 484). Total faculty with doctorate, first-professional, or other terminal degree: 757. Student-to-faculty ratio: 17:1. 85% hold terminal degrees. *Faculty development:* $176,714,877 total grants for research. 36 faculty members awarded sabbaticals 2004–05.

Enrollment: Total enrollment 33,314. Undergraduate full-time 4,752 men / 6,856 women, part-time 3,612m / 5,492w; first-professional full-time 1,479m / 1,285w, part-time 95 / 114; graduate full-time 1,675m / 2, 4322w, part-time 2,168m / 3,354w. *Transfer students:* 1,719.

Characteristics of Student Body: *Ethnic/racial makeup:* number of Black non-Hispanic: 6,880; American Indian or Alaska Native: 97; Asian or Pacific Islander: 1,096; Hispanic: 538; White non-Hispanic: 9,850; unknown: 1,553. *Age distribution:* number under 18: 511; 18–19: 4,787; 20–21: 3,950; 22–24: 4,504; 25–29: 3,071; 30–34: 1,523; 35–39: 866; 40–49: 1,010; 50–64: 461; 65 and over: 29.

International Students: 2,597 nonresident aliens enrolled fall 2004. Students from Europe, Asia, Central and South America, Africa, Canada, Australia. Programs available to aid students whose native language is not English: social, cultural. English as a Second Language Program. No financial aid specifically designated for international students.

Student Life: On-campus residence halls house 5% of student body. Less than 1% in fraternity houses. Housing available for married students. *Intercollegiate athletics:* NCAA Division I: men and women's hockey. NCAA Division II men only: baseball, basketball, fencing, football, golf, tennis; women only: basketball, fencing, softball, tennis, volleyball. Coeducational sports: cross-country, swimming. *Special services:* Reading and Study Skills Center, Minority Resource Center, Women's Resource Center, Career and Personal Counseling Services; Life/Career Development Laboratory, Veterans' Educational Opportunity Program, medical services, Educational Accessibility Services. *Student publications, radio: South End,* the daily student newspaper. Radio station: WDET-FM. *Surrounding community:* Detroit population approximately

1,000,000. Served by mass transit bus system; airports 10 and 20 miles from campus; passenger rail service 1 mile from campus.

Publications: University press published 36 titles in 2003–04.

Library Collections: 3,348,242 volumes including bound books, serial back-files, electronic documents, and government documents not in separate collections. Online catalog. 20,940 current serial subscriptions. 46,122 recordings, compact discs, CD-ROMs. Online and card catalogs. 1,200 computer work stations campus-wide. Students have access to the Internet at no charge. Total budget for books, periodicals, audiovisual materials, microforms 2004–05: $7,200,000.

Most important special holdings include Walter Reuther Archives; Ramsey Collection of Children's Literature; collection of classical music scores; Leonard Simons Collection (rare Michigan history texts).

Buildings and Grounds: Campus area 203 acres. *New buildings:* Welcome Center; Wayne State Books Store; North and South Residence Halls; Eugene Applebaum College of Pharmacy and Health Sciences.

Chief Executive Officer: Dr. Irvin D. Reid, President.

Address undergraduate admission inquiries to Susan Ewieg, Director of Undergraduate Admissions; graduate inquiries to Graduate School; Medical School; Law School.

College of Liberal Arts and Sciences

Degree Programs Offered: *Baccalaureate, master's, doctorate.* Joint JD/MA in political science; JD/MA in history.

School of Business Administration

Degree Programs Offered: *Baccalaureate, master's;* Joint JD/MBA.

Admission: Minimum 2.5 GPA required in 64 semester credits (lower division).

College of Education

Degree Programs Offered: *Baccalaureate, master's, doctorate.* Graduate certificate in college and university teaching; education specialist in various program.s

Admission: Minimum 2.5 GPA.

College of Engineering

Degree Programs Offered: *Baccalaureate, master's, doctorate.* Graduate certificates in environmental auditing, hazardous waste control, hazardous materials management on public lands, polymer engineering.

College of Nursing

Degree Programs Offered: *Baccalaureate, master's, doctorate.* Graduate certificate in nursing education.

College of Pharmacy and Allied Health

Degree Programs Offered: *Baccalaureate* in medical technology, occupational therapy, physical therapy, radiation technology; *first-professional* in pharmacy; *master's* in environmental health; *master's, doctorate* in various fields. Certificate program in mortuary science.

Distinctive Educational Programs: Baccalaureate program in anesthesia for registered nurses.

Law School

Degree Programs Offered: *First-professional, master's.*

Admission: *For first-professional degree:* Baccalaureate from accredited college or university; LSAT.

Degree Requirements: 86 credit hours, 2.0 GPA, 3 years in residence and completion within 5 years.

Fees and Other Expenses: Contact the school for current tuition.

School of Medicine

Degree Programs Offered: *First-professional, master's, doctorate.*

Admission: *For first-professional degree:* Baccalaureate or 3 years of study, including 1 year in English, 12 general biology or zoology with laboratory, 1 each inorganic chemistry, both with laboratory; 3.0–3.5 GPA; MCAT.

Fees and Other Expenses: Contact the school for current tuition.

Distinctive Educational Programs: Combined first-professional/doctorate program in medicine. Community health medicine. Continuing medical education.

Graduate School

Degree Programs Offered: *Master's* in industrial relations and library science.

Admission: Baccalaureate degree with minimum 2.6 GPA.

Degree Requirements: 32 semester hours in MAIR; 36 hours in library science.

Library and Information Science Program

Degree Programs Offered: *Master's.*

Admission: Baccalaureate from accredited college; minimum 2.75 GPA.

Degree Requirements: 36 semester hours; certain courses require 86 credit hours. Completion within 5 years.

College of Fine, Performing, and Communication Arts

Degree Programs Offered: Established 1986. *Baccalaureate* and *master's* in art and art history, music, theatre and dance; *doctorate* with majors in communication, theatre. Graduate certificate in Orchestral Studies.

College of Science

Degree Programs Offered: *Baccalaureate, master's, doctorate.*

School of Social Work

Degree Programs Offered: *Baccalaureate, master's.* Graduate certificate in social work practice with families and couples.

College of Urban, Labor and Metropolitan Affairs

Degree Programs Offered: *Baccalaureate, master's, doctorate.* Joint JD/MA in dispute resolution. Graduate certificates in dispute resolution; economic development.

Western Theological Seminary

101 East 13th Street
Holland, Michigan 49423
Tel: (616) 392-8555   **E-mail:** admissions@westernsem.org
Fax: (616) 392-7717   **Internet:** www.westernsem.org

Institution Description: Western Theological Seminary is a private seminary of the Reformed Church in America. *Enrollment:* 216. *Degrees awarded:* First-professional, master's, doctorate.

Accreditation: *Regional:* NCA. *National:* ATS. *Professional:* theology

History: Founded 1866.

Calendar: Quarters. Academic year Aug. to May.

Admission: *Requirements:* Baccalaureate degree from an accredited college or university with a balanced liberal arts program.

Degree Requirements: Completion of prescribed curriculum; requirements vary with program.

Degrees Conferred: *Doctorate:* 4 ministerial; 32 *first-professional:* master of divinity.

Fees and Other Expenses: *Full-time tuition per academic year 2004–05:* 8,320.

Financial Aid: *Institutional funding for graduate students:* 78 fellowships and grants totaling $185,000 (ranging from $500 to $4,000).

Departments and Teaching Staff: *Total instructional faculty:* 21. Degrees held by full-time faculty: doctorate 100%.

Enrollment: Total enrollment 216. Full-time first-professional 105 men / 59 women; graduate full-time 41m / 11w.

Characteristics of Student Body: *Ethnic/racial makeup:* White non-Hispanic 99%. *Average age:* 24.

International Students: 11 nonresident aliens enrolled fall 2004. 3 students from Europe, 3 Asia, 1 South America, 2 Africa, 2 Canada. No programs available to aid students whose native language is not English. Financial aid specifically designated for international students: 6 scholarships awarded annually.

Student Life: Town houses available; students are responsible for making their own housing arrangements.

Library Collections: 111,000 volumes including bound books, serial backfiles, electronic documents, and government documents not in separate collections. Online catalog. Current serial subscriptions: 442 paper, 4,432 microform. 4 computer work stations. Students have access to the Internet at no charge.

Most important special collections include the history and life of the Reformed Church in America, Henry Bast Preaching Resources Center, and the Islam and Christianity collection.

Chief Executive Officer: Rev. Dennis Voskuil, President.

Address admission inquiries to Mark Poppin, Admissions Director.

William Tyndale College

35700 West Twelve Mile Road

Farmington Hills, Michigan 48331

Tel: (248) 553-7200   **E-mail:** admissions@williamtyndale.edu

Fax: (248) 553-5963   **Internet:** www.williamtyndale.edu

Institution Description: William Tyndale College is a private interdenominational Christian, liberal arts college offering programs of study in three divisions: Arts and Sciences, Professional Studies, and Christian Studies. *Enrollment:* 290. *Degrees awarded:* Associate, baccalaureate.

Accreditation: *Regional:* NCA.

History: Founded as Detroit Bible Institute 1945; became Detroit Bible College 1960 when four-year curriculum was offered; new campus established in Farmington Hills 1978; adopted present name 1981.

Calendar: Semesters. Academic year Sept. to Aug.

Characteristics of Freshmen: 82% of applicants accepted. 67% of accepted applicants enrolled.

Mean ACT composite score 21.5.

99% of freshmen from Michigan. Freshmen from 2 states.

Admission: *Requirements:* Graduation from accredited secondary school with rank in upper half of class; 2.25 GPA on a 4.0 scale or GED 50 or above; commendable Christian character. *Entrance tests:* ACT 18 composite score.

Degree Requirements: Completion of prescribed curriculum.

Distinctive Educational Programs: Accelerated degree program that allows adult learners to complete a bachelor of arts degree, with a major in business administration, in 19 months by attending 1 4-hour class per week.

Degrees Conferred: 29 *associate;* 120 *baccalaureate:* business and management 74, fine and applied arts 3, psychology 19, social sciences 13, theology 11.

Fees and Other Expenses: *Full-time tuition per academic year 2004–05:* $8,650. *Room and board per academic year:* $3,520.

Financial Aid: Aid from institutionally generated funds is provided on the basis of academic merit, other criteria. Financial assistance is available in the form of Pell Grants, College Work-Study, Veterans Administration Benefits, National Direct Student Loans, Supplemental Education Opportunity Grants (SEOG), Higher Education Assistance Loans (HEAL), Stafford Loans, other federal aid programs.

Departments and Teaching Staff: Arts and Humanities *professors* 3, *part-time faculty:* 37; Christian studies 2, 33; natural sciences 2, 0. *Total instructional faculty:* 77. Student-to-faculty ratio: 20:1. Degrees held by full-time faculty: doctorate 40%, master's 60%. 87% hold terminal degrees.

Enrollment: Total enrollment 290. Full-time 62 men / 59 women, part-time 94m / 75w.

Characteristics of Student Body: *Age distribution:* 17–21: 22%; 22–24: 7%; 25–29: 12%; 30–34: 13%; 35–39: 14%; 40–49: 23%; 50–59: 7%; 60–up: 2%.

International Students: Students from Europe, Asia, Canada. No programs available to aid students whose native language is not English. Some financial aid specifically designated for international undergraduate students.

Student Life: College-wide activities include an all-college retreat, Staley Distinguished Christian Scholar Lectureship, chapel services, concerts, and recitals. Extracurricular activities include intercollegiate soccer, intramural volleyball and basketball, honor's societies: Alpha Chi and Alpha Sigma Lambda; class social activities.

Publications: *Tyndale Today,* a quarterly magazine for supporters of William Tyndale College.

Library Collections: 65,000 volumes. 2,125 microforms; 95 audiovisual materials; 235 current periodical subscriptions. Computer work stations available. Students have access to online information retrieval services and the Internet.

Buildings and Grounds: Campus area 28 acres.

Chief Executive Officer: Dr. Robert E. Hagerty, President. Address admission inquiries to Fred A. Schebor, Dean of Admissions.

Minnesota

Augsburg College

2211 Riverside Avenue
Minneapolis, Minnesota 55454

Tel: (612) 330-1000   **E-mail:** admissions@augsburg.edu
Fax: (612) 330-1590   **Internet:** www.augsburg.edu

Institution Description: Augsburg College is a private college affiliated with the Evangelical Lutheran Church in America. *Enrollment:* 3,375. *Degrees awarded:* Baccalaureate, master's. Certificates also awarded.

Member of the consortia Associated Colleges of the Twin Cities; Higher Education Consortium for Urban Affairs, Inc.

Accreditation: *Regional:* NCA. *Professional:* nursing, physician assisting, social work, surgeon assisting, social work, teacher education

History: Established in Wisconsin as Augsburg Seminary 1869; moved to present location 1872; offered first instruction at postsecondary level 1874; awarded first degree 1879; changed name to Augsburg College and Seminary 1942; adopted present name 1963. *See* Carl Chrislock, *From Fjord to Freeway* (St. Paul, MN: North Central Publishing Company, 1969) for further information.

Institutional Structure: *Governing board:* Board of Regents. Representation: 33 regents. *Composition of institution:* Academic affairs headed by provost and dean of the college. Management/business/finances directed by vice president for finance and administration. Full-time instructional faculty 157. Academic governance body, the faculty, meets bimonthly.

Calendar: Semesters (4-1-4 plan). (Graduate programs and weekend college on trimester basis). Academic year Sept. to May. Freshmen admitted Sept., Jan., June. Degrees conferred May, Aug. Dec. Formal commencement May. Summer sessions from June to Aug.

Characteristics of Freshmen: 79% of applicants accepted. 38% of accepted applicants enrolled.

12% (42 students) submitted SAT scores; 48% (337 students) submitted ACT scores. *25th percentile:* SAT Verbal 490, SAT Math 485; ACT Composite 20l, ACT English 19, ACT Math 18. *75th percentile:* SAT Verbal 610, SAT Math 605; ACT Composite 25, ACT English 25, ACT Math 25.

47.5% of entering freshmen expected to graduate within 5 years. 81% of freshmen from Minnesota. Freshmen from 17 states and 4 foreign countries.

Admission: Rolling admissions plan. For fall acceptance, apply as early as Nov. 1 of senior year in secondary school, but not later than Aug. 15 of year of enrollment. Apply by Dec. 15 for early decision; need not limit application to Augsburg. Early decision available. *Requirements:* Either graduation from accredited secondary school or GED; 2.5 GPA. Lowest acceptable secondary school class standing 50th percentile. *Entrance tests:* ACT preferred. College Board SAT or PSAT accepted. *For transfer students:* from 4-year accredited institution 2.2 minimum GPA; from 2-year accredited institution 2.0 minimum GPA.

Tutoring available. Developmental/remedial courses offered during regular academic year; credit given.

Degree Requirements: 33 courses; 11 upper division courses; 2.0 GPA (for nursing 2.5); completion of major; final year in residence; 2 activities courses or demonstrated proficiency in physical education; demonstrated proficiency in writing; general education requirements.

Fulfillment of some degree requirements and exemption from some beginning courses possible by passing College Board CLEP, AP. *Grading system:* 4.0–0.0; pass-no credit.

Distinctive Educational Programs: Weekend College. M.A. program in leadership. Dual-degree programs in engineering with University of Minnesota and Michigan Tech University. Interdepartmental/interdisciplinary programs. Preprofessional programs in dentistry, medicine, pharmacy, theology, veterinary medicine. M.S.W. program in social work; M.S. program in physician assistant studies. Information technology certificate program. M.B.A. program. Multicul-tural support programs for American Indian, Pan-Afrikan, Hispanic/Latino, and Pan-Asian students. Study abroad through institutionally sponsored programs in Mexico and other locations; also available through programs at other institutions. Cross-registration through consortium. M.A. program in community health nursing with transcultural nursing focus. Intercultural Center offers support services and programs for American Indians, Blacks. Step-Up programs for students in recovery; strong service-learning and internships.

ROTC: Air Force in cooperation with University of St. Thomas; Army and Navy in cooperation with University of Minnesota.

Degrees Conferred: 477 *baccalaureate:* biological/life sciences 10; business/marketing 153; communications/communication technologies 24; computer and information sciences 24; education 57; English 19; foreign languages and literature 5; health professions and related sciences 29; liberal arts/general studies 5; mathematics 10; philosophy/religion/theology 19; physical sciences 10; protective services/public administration 10; psychology 24; social sciences and history 62; visual and performing arts 19. 69 *master's:* education 11; health professions and related clinical sciences 27; social sciences and history 31.

Fees and Other Expenses: *Full-time tuition per academic year 2004–05:* undergraduate $20,260; contact the university for graduate tuition/fees. *Required fees:* $498. *Room and board per academic year:* $6,080.

Financial Aid: Aid from institutionally generated funds is provided on the basis of academic merit, financial need.

Financial aid to full-time, first-time undergraduate students: need-based scholarships/grants totaling $13,729,158, self-help $12,269,529, parent loans $242,311; non-need-based scholarships/grants totaling $2,367,354, self-help $5,588,633, parent loans $1,047,799.

Departments and Teaching Staff: *Professors* 33, *associate professors* 456 *assistant professors* 60, *instructors* 8, *part-time faculty* 158.

Total instructional faculty: 315 (full-time 157, part-time 158; women 163, men 152; members of minority groups 24). Student-to-faculty ratio: 14.8:1. *Faculty development:* 5 faculty members awarded sabbaticals 2004–05.

Enrollment: Total enrollment 3,375. Undergraduate full-time 1,033 men / 1,321 women, part-time 192m / 370w; graduate full-time 82m / 229w, part-time 31m / 117w. *Transfer students:* 318.

Characteristics of Student Body: *Ethnic/racial makeup:* number of Black non-Hispanic: 150; American Indian or Alaska Native: 32; Asian or Pacific Islander: 88; Hispanic: 42; White non-Hispanic: 1,941; unknown: 612.

International Students: 55 nonresident aliens enrolled fall 2004. Programs available to aid students whose native language is not English: social, cultural. English as a Second Language Program. Financial aid specifically designated for international students: unlimited scholarships available annually; 123 totaling $517,536 were awarded 2004–05.

Student Life: On-campus residence halls house 54% of traditional student body. *Intercollegiate athletics:* men only: baseball, basketball, cross country, football, golf, hockey, soccer, track, wrestling; women only: basketball, golf, gymnastics, hockey, softball, tennis, track, volleyball. *Special regulations:* Cars permitted without restrictions. *Special services:* Learning Resources Center, medical services, bus service between campuses of consortium members. *Student publications:* Augsburg Echo, a weekly newspaper; *Augsburgian,* a yearbook. *Surrounding community:* Minneapolis population 382,000. Served by bus system; airport 7 miles from campus; light rail service 3 blocks from campus.

Library Collections: 184,701 volumes including bound books, serial backfiles, electronic documents, and government documents not in separate collections. Online catalog. Current serial subscriptions: 984 paper, 23,341 microform, 14,241 51 electronic. 500 recordings; 2,100 compact discs; 2,100 CD-ROMs. 250 computer work stations. Students have access to the Internet at no charge.

Most important special collections include Meridel LeSueur Library; Scandinavian Music Collection; Anishanabe (American Indian) Collection.

Buildings and Grounds: Campus area 23 acres.

Chief Executive Officer: Dr. William V. Frame, President.

Address admission inquiries to Director of Admissions.

Bemidji State University

1500 Birchmont Drive N.E.
Bemidji, Minnesota 56601-2699

Tel: (218) 755-2040   **E-mail:** admissions@bemidji.edu
Fax: (218) 755-4048   **Internet:** www.bemidji.edu

Institution Description: Bemidji State University is a public institution. *Enrollment:* 4,348. *Degrees awarded:* Associate, baccalaureate, master's.

Accreditation: *Regional:* NCA. *Professional* social work, teacher education

History: Established as Bemidji State Normal School 1913; chartered and offered first instruction at postsecondary level 1919; changed name to Bemidji State Teachers College 1921; awarded first degree (baccalaureate) 1928; changed name to Bemidji State College 1957; adopted present name 1976. *See* Arthur Lee, *College in the Pines* (Minneapolis: Dillon Press, 1970) for further information.

Institutional Structure: *Composition of institution:* Administrators 24 men / 4 women. Academic affairs headed by vice president for academic affairs. Management/business/finances directed by vice president for administrative affairs. Full-time instructional faculty 154 men / 58 women. Academic governance body, Faculty Senate, meets an average of 12 times per year.

Calendar: Quarters. Academic year early Sept. to mid-May. Freshmen admitted Sept., Nov., Mar., Feb. Formal commencement May. Summer sessions of 2 terms from early June to mid-Aug.

Characteristics of Freshmen: 685 of applicants accepted. 72% of accepted applicants enrolled.

Average secondary school rank of freshmen men 57th percentile, women 69th percentile, class 64th percentile. Mean ACT Composite scores men 22.7, women 22.2, class 22.4.

32% of entering freshmen expected to graduate within 5 years. 93% of freshmen from Minnesota. Freshmen from 17 states and 20 foreign countries.

Admission: Rolling admissions plan. Apply no later than 4 weeks prior to enrollment. Early acceptance available. *Requirements:* Either graduation from accredited secondary school or GED. Lowest acceptable secondary school class standing: in-state residents 50th percentile, out-of-state students 60th percentile. *Entrance tests:* College Board SAT, ACT Composite or other standardized test. For foreign students TOEFL. *For transfer students:* 2.0 minimum GPA; from 4-year and 2-year accredited institutions maximum transfer credit limited only by residence requirement; correspondence students 15 credit hours.

College credit and advanced placement for postsecondary-level work completed in secondary school. Developmental/remedial courses offered during regular academic year; credit given.

Degree Requirements: *For all associate degrees:* 96 credit hours; 32 hours in residence. *For all baccalaureate degrees:* 192 credit hours; 45 hours in residence; general education requirements. *For all undergraduate degrees:* 2.0 GPA overall; 2.25 GPA in major; 2.0 GPA in minor.

Fulfillment of some degree requirements and exemption from some beginning courses possible by passing departmental examinations, College Board CLEP, APP. *Grading system:* A–F; pass-fail; pass-no pass; withdraw (carries time limit); incomplete (carries time limit).

Distinctive Educational Programs: *For undergraduates:* Work-experience programs. Interdisciplinary program in Indian studies. Preprofessional programs in agricultural economics and business, architecture, chiropractic, dentistry, engineering, fisheries and wildlife management, forestry, home economics, law, medicine, mortuary science, nursing, occupational therapy, optometry, pharmacy, physical therapy, speech pathology and speech correction, veterinary medicine. Honors programs. Institutionally sponsored study abroad at the Center for Medieval and Renaissance Studies in Oxford, England, at the Goethe Institute in Germany, at the University of Leningrad in the USSR, work-study programs in France and Switzerland; summer study at the Universidad Ibero-Americanos in Mexico. Summer Russian language study at Putney College (VT) followed by study abroad in the Russia. Eurospring (study at Oxford University, England). *Available to all students:* Flexible meeting places and schedules, including off-campus centers in north central Minnesota and evening classes. Interdisciplinary program in environmental studies. Institutionally sponsored summer study tours to Europe and other locations. *Other distinctive programs:* Educational Development Center offers instruction and counseling for disadvantaged students. Upward Bound programs help prepare low-income secondary school students for college or vocational study. Continuing education. North Central Minnesota Historical Center for Research.

Degrees Conferred: 41 *associate;* 554 *baccalaureate* degrees awarded in top five disciplines include business and management 89, education 159, engineering 36, protective services 33, visual and performing arts 41; 23 *master's:* various disciplines.

Fees and Other Expenses: *Tuition per academic year 2004–05:* undergraduate resident $5,049, nonresident $9,935; graduate resident $4,660, nonresident $7,288. *Books and supplies:* $600. *Room and board per academic year:* $4054.

Financial Aid: Aid from institutionally generated funds is generated on the basis of academic merit, athletic ability. Financial assistance is available in the form of Pell Grants, College Work-Study, Veterans Administration Benefits, National Direct Student Loans, Supplemental Education Opportunity Grants (SEOG), Stafford Loans, other federal aid programs.

Departments and Teaching Staff: *Professors* 86, *associate professors* 45, *assistant professors* 50, *instructors* 6, *part-time teachers* 6.

Total instructional faculty: 190. Degrees held by full-time faculty: doctorate 64%, master's 25%, baccalaureate 2%, professional 9%. 68% hold terminal degrees.

Enrollment: Total enrollment 4,348. Undergraduate 4,136.

Characteristics of Student Body: *Ethnic/racial makeup:* Black non-Hispanic: .5%; American Indian or Alaska Native: 4.1%; Asian or Pacific Islander; .4%; Hispanic: .5%; White non-Hispanic: 74.7%; unknown: 15.7%. *Age distribution:* 17–21: 51%; 22–24: 20%; 25–29: 10%; 30–34: 4%; 35–39: 5%; 40–49 8%; 50–59: 2%; 60–up: 1%.

International Students: 183 nonresident aliens enrolled. Students from Europe, Asia, Latin America, Africa, Canada, New Zealand. *Programs available to aid students whose native language is not English:* Social, cultural. English as a Second Language Program. No financial aid specifically designated for international students.

Student Life: On-campus residence halls house 33% of student body. Residence halls for both sexes only constitute 100% of such space. *Intercollegiate athletics:* men only: baseball, basketball, cross-country, football, golf, hockey, track; women only: basketball, field hockey, gymnastics, swimming, tennis, track, volleyball. *Special regulations:* Cars permitted without restrictions. *Special services:* Medical services. *Student publications, radio, television: Northern Student,* a weekly newspaper. Radio station KBSB broadcasts 126 hours per week. TV station KBSU broadcasts 28 hours per week. *Surrounding community:* Bemidji population 11,000. Minneapolis-St. Paul, 225 miles from campus, is nearest metropolitan area. Served by mass transit bus system; airport 5 miles from campus.

Library Collections: 205,000 volumes. 756,300 microforms; 925 current periodical subscriptions. Online catalog. Students have access to online information retrieval services and the Internet.

Most important special collection is the National Indian Education Collection.

Buildings and Grounds: Campus area 83 acres.

Chief Executive Officer: Dr. Jon E. Quistgaard, President.

Address undergraduate admission inquiries to Paul D. Muller, Director of Admissions; graduate inquiries to Director of Graduate School.

Bethany Lutheran College

700 Luther Drive
Mankato, Minnesota 56001

Tel: (507) 344-7300   **E-mail:** admis@blc.edu
Fax: (507) 344-7376   **Internet:** www.blc.edu

Institution Description: Bethany Lutheran College is a private, residential, Christian, coeducational, liberal arts college. *Enrollment:* 566. *Degrees awarded:* Baccalaureate.

Accreditation: *Regional:* NCA.

History: Established 1927, owned and operated by Evangelical Lutheran Synod.

Institutional Structure: *Composition of institution:* Board of Regents with 12 members. Academic affairs headed by academic vice president. Full-time instructional faculty 38.

Calendar: Semesters. Academic year Aug. to May. Freshmen admitted and degrees conferred Aug., Jan., June, July. Formal commencement June. Summer sessions of 2 terms from mid-June to mid-Aug.

Characteristics of Freshmen: 66% of freshmen expected to graduate within 5 years. Freshmen from 28 states and 10 foreign countries.

Admission: Admission is based on academic records, test scores, class rank, and recommendations.

Degree Requirements: 128 credit hours; 2.0 GPA; pass a total of 14 Religious Studies credits; senior year in residence. Fulfillment of some degree requirements and exemption from some beginning courses possible by passing CLEP. *Grading system:* A, B, C, D, no credit; satisfactory-no credit.

Distinctive Educational Programs: Travel abroad and travel opportunities.

ROTC: Air Force and Army in cooperation with Minnesota State University, Mankato.

Degrees Conferred: 48 *baccalaureate*: biological/life science 4; business administration 19; education 4; English 1; liberal arts/general studies 7; psychology 1; social sciences and history 1; visual and performing arts 4.

Fees and Other Expenses: *Full-time tuition per academic year:* Contact the college for current tuition, fees, and housing costs.

Financial Aid: Aid from institutionally generated funds is provided on the basis of academic merit, financial need. Institution has a Program Participation Agreement with the U.S. Department of Education for eligible students to receive Pell Grants and, depending upon the agreement, other federal aid.

Departments and Teaching Staff: *Total instructional faculty:* 78 (full-time 38, part-time 40; women 26, men 32). Total faculty with doctorate, first-professional, or other terminal degree: 15. Student-to-faculty ratio: 7:1.

Enrollment: Total enrollment 566. Undergraduate full-time 230 men / 303 women, part-time 19m / 14w.

Characteristics of Student Body: *Ethnic/racial makeup:* number of Black non-Hispanic: 15; American Indian or Alaska Native: 3; Asian or Pacific Islander: 3; Hispanic: 4; White non-Hispanic: 479; unknown: 38. *Age distribution:* number under 18: 3; 18–19: 267; 20–21: 189; 22–24: 76; 25–29: 13; 30–34: 6; 35–39: 5; 40–49: 4; unknown: 2.

International Students: 26 nonresident aliens enrolled. 10 students form Europe, 5 Asia, 3 Central and South America, 6 Africa. Programs available to aid students whose native language is not English: English as a Second Language Program. Financial aid specifically designated for international students: one scholarship available annually.

Student Life: On-campus residence halls house 89% of student body. A variety of art, music, theatre, and radio/tv broadcasting provide opportunities for student expression and growth. *Intercollegiate athletics:* men's and women's cross-country, golf, soccer, basketball, tennis. *Student publications: Bethany Scroll*, campus newspaper; *The Fideles*, yearbook, and a literary magazine showcasing student writing, art work, and photography. newspaper.

Library Collections: 76,780 volumes. Online catalog. Current serial subscriptions: paper 475; via electronic access 17,175. 3,082 recordings; 1,100 compact discs; 127 CD-ROMs. 12 computer work stations. Students have access to online information retrieval services and the Internet. Total 2004–05 budget for books and materials: $56,650.

Most important special holdings include the Robert Preus Rare Bible and Hymnal Collection.

Buildings and Grounds: Campus area 700 acres.

Chief Executive Officer: Dr. Dan Bruss, President.

Address admission inquiries to Don Westphal, Dean of Admissions.

Bethel University

3900 Bethel Drive
St. Paul, Minnesota 55112
Tel: (651) 638-6400   **E-mail:** admissions@bethel.edu
Fax: (651) 635-1490   **Internet:** www.bethel.edu

Institution Description: Bethel University is a private institution affiliated with the Baptist General Conference. *Enrollment:* 3,605. *Degrees awarded:* Associate, baccalaureate, master's. Center for Graduate and Continuing Studies awards master of education, master of arts in communication, nursing, organizational leadership, counseling, psychology. Bethel Theological Seminary offers first-professional (master of divinity, master of arts in Christian education), master's, intermediate in cooperation with Luther Northwestern Seminaries and the United Theological Seminary in the Twin City Area, and doctoral awards.

Member of Upper Midwest Association for Intercultural Education (UMAIE), Christian College Consortium, Institute of Holy Land Studies, AuSable Trails Institute of Environmental Studies, Christian College Consortium, Christian College Coalition, Libraries in Consort (CLIC).

Accreditation: *Regional:* NCA. *Professional:* social work, nursing, teacher education

History: Established as Scandinavian Department of Baptist Union Theological Seminary of the University of Chicago 1871; became independent and changed name to Bethel Academy and Seminary 1914, to Bethel Institute 1920; became junior college and offered first instruction at postsecondary level 1931; adopted present name 1947; became 4-year college and awarded first degree (baccalaureate) 1949. In June 2004, Bethel College and Seminary became Bethel University.

Institutional Structure: *Governing board:* Board of Trustees, Baptist General Conference. *Composition of institution:* president of Bethel University is the chief executive officer of the corporation and the official advisor to and executive agent of the Board of Trustees. Academic affairs headed by provost. Finances directed by executive vice president for business affairs.

Calendar: Semesters (4-1-4 plan). Academic year early Aug. to May. Freshmen admitted Aug., Jan., Feb. Degrees conferred and formal commencement May. Summer session of 2 terms from May to Aug.

Characteristics of Freshmen: 81% of applicants accepted. 42% of accepted applicants enrolled.

13% (36 students) submitted SAT scores; 94% (642 students) submitted ACT scores. *25th percentile:* SAT Verbal 540, SAT Math 540; ACT Composite 22, ACT English 21, ACT Math 20. *75th percentile:* SAT Verbal 650, SAT Math 650; ACT Composite 27, ACT English 28, ACT Math 27.

53% of freshmen expected to graduate within 5 years. 745 of freshmen from Minnesota. Freshmen from 27 states and 2 foreign countries.

Admission: Early action plan. For fall acceptance in undergraduate day program, apply by Apr. 1. *Requirements:* Either graduation from accredited secondary school or GED. Recommend 4 units English, 4 social studies, 3 mathematics, 3 science, additional units in foreign language. Lowest acceptable secondary school class standing 50th percentile. Written evidence of personal Christian commitment and willingness to live by Bethel's lifestyle standards. *Entrance tests:* College Board SAT, ACT composite, or PSAT. *For transfer students:* 2.5 minimum GPA; maximum transfer credit determined on individual basis and limited only by residence requirement.

College credit and advanced placement for postsecondary-level work completed in secondary school. Tutoring available.

Degree Requirements: *For all associate degrees:* 61 semester credit hours; 1 interim course. *For all baccalaureate degrees:* 122 semester credit hours; 3 interim courses; minimum 37 credits at upper level; 2.25 GPA in major. *For all degrees:* 2.0 GPA minimum; final 28 semester credits in residence; 51 credits of core requirements developmentally structured throughout the four years. Additional requirements for some baccalaureate programs. *For all graduate programs:* completion of program credits (32 to 61 hours, depending on program); 3.00 GPA in major; at least 80 percent of the credits used to meet the requirements of the major must meet residency requirements. In each major, certain courses are required to be taken in residence.

Fulfillment of some degree requirements and exemption from some beginning courses possible with qualifying score on AP or CEEB, CLEP subject or national standardized credit-bearing (DANTES) examinations. Exemption from some courses possible by passing departmental examinations. *Grading system:* A–no credit; withdraw (carries time limit, may carry penalty); incomplete (carries time limit, may carry penalty); pass/no credit (for some courses); satisfactory/unsatisfactory (for some courses).

Distinctive Educational Programs: Dual-degree program in engineering with Washington University (MO), Case Western Reserve, and University of Minnesota. Study abroad in Ecuador, England, Guatemala, Israel, The Netherlands, Vietnam, and other countries through institutionally sponsored programs; in Costa Rica, Middle East, Russia, China, Kenya through program of the Council of Christian Colleges and Universities (CCCU); during interim in various countries. Off-campus study through American Studies Program (Washington DC), Los Angeles Film Studies Program, Oregon Extension, and AuSable Environment Institute (MI). Individualized majors. Directed Study. Internships. Entire campus (classrooms, residences wired for Internet access).

ROTC: Air Force through the University of St. Thomas; Army through University of Minnesota.

Degrees Conferred: 2 *associate;* 694 *baccalaureate* (B), 140 *master's* (M): biological/life sciences 28 (B); business/marketing 176 (B), 9 (M); communications/communication technologies 42 (B), 10 (M); computer and information sciences 14 (B); education 96 (B), 72 (M); engineering and engineering technologies 3 (B); English 11 (B); health professions and related sciences 96 (B), 14 (M); interdisciplinary studies 12 (B), 21 (M); mathematics 4 (B); natural resources/environmental science 1 (B); parks and recreation 4 (B); philosophy/religion/theology 58 (B); physical sciences 13 (B); protective services/public administration 20 (B); psychology 20 (B), 14 (M); social sciences and history 58 (B); visual and performing arts 20 (B).

Fees and Other Expenses: *Full-time tuition per academic year 2005–06:* undergraduate $21,190. Contact the university for current graduate tuition/fees. *Required fees:* $110. *Room and board per academic year:* $6,800.

Financial Aid: Aid from institutionally generated funds is provided on the basis of academic merit, financial need, other criteria.

Financial aid to full-time, first-time undergraduate students: need-based scholarships/grants totaling $15,620,000, self-help $12,650,000, tuition waivers $1,29,000; non-need-based scholarships/grants totaling $2,4 10,000; athletic awards $1,293,000. *Graduate aid:* 480 students received $3,900,000 in federal and state-funded fellowships/grants (ranging from $1,000 to $18,500).

Departments and Teaching Staff: Anthropology/sociology *professors* 2, *associate professors* 0, *assistant professors* 1, *instructors* 0, *part-time teachers* 0; art 4, 2, 0, 0, 3; biology 4, 4, 0, 1, 1; Biblical and theological 5, 1, 4, 0, 3; chemistry 4, 0, 1, 0, 1; college writing 0, 0, 0, 1, 0; computer science/mathematics 2, 3, 2, 1, 4; communications 2, 0,3, 0, 1; education 5, 4, 3, 1, 11; English 3, 1, 2, 0, 0; general studies 0, 0, 3, 0, 6; history 3, 1, 0, 1, 1; health and physical education 2, 3, 2, 2, 2; music 2, 3, 1, 0, 5; modern world languages 0, 1, 1, 1, 3; nursing 3, 6, 8, 0, 4; organ studies 0, 0, 1, 0, 0; philosophy 3, 0, 1, 0, 2; physics 3, 0, 0, 0, 2; political science 2, 0, 0, 2, 0; psychology 7, 4, 1, 0, 0; science education 0, 1, 0, 0, 0; social work 2, 2, 0, 0, 1; theatre arts 0, 1, 2, 0, 1; writing 1, 0, 0, 0, 0.

Total instructional faculty: 284 (full-time 173, part-time 111; women 141, men 143; members of minority groups 4). Total faculty with doctorate, first-professional, or other terminal degree: 157. Student-to-faculty ratio: 14:1. Degrees held by full-time faculty: baccalaureate 1%, master's 37%, doctorate 62%. 72% hold terminal degrees. *Faculty development:* 16 faculty members awarded sabbaticals 2004–05.

Enrollment: Total enrollment 3,605. Undergraduate full-time 1,119 men / 1,660 women, part-time 74m / 198w; graduate full-time 91m / 224w, part-time 70m / 169w. *Transfer students:* in-state 128; from out-of-state 17.

Characteristics of Student Body: *Ethnic/racial makeup:* number of Black non-Hispanic: 60; American Indian or Alaska Native: 8; Asian or Pacific Islander: 85; Hispanic: 41; White non-Hispanic: 2,842. *Age distribution:* number under 18: 10; 18–19: 1,051; 20–21: 1,181; 22–24: 431; 25–29: 94; 30–34: 61; 35–39: 52; 40–49: 114; 50–64: 34; 65 and over: 1.

International Students: 21 nonresident aliens enrolled fall 2004. Programs available to aid students whose native language is not English: social, cultural, financial. Financial aid specifically designated for international students: variable number of scholarships available annually.

Student Life: Bethel participates in NCAA Division III intercollegiate sports. There are approximately 300 student to be involved in one of three choirs, a wind ensemble, chamber orchestra, jazz ensemble, symphonic band, or music ministry teams. Residence life activities take place in nine residence halls or off-campus apartments. Bethel is 10 minutes away from both Minneapolis and St. Paul.

Publications: Sources of information about Bethel include *Focus*, a quarterly magazine.

Library Collections: 512,000 volumes including bound books, serial backfiles, electronic documents, and government documents not in separate collections. Online catalog. Current serial subscriptions: 866 paper, 19,950 microform; 18,000 electronic. 25,300 audiovisual materials. 24 computer work stations. Students have access to the Internet at no charge. Total budget for books, periodicals, audiovisual materials, microforms 2004–05: $1,120,000.

Most important special collections include Biblical and theological studies; education; anthropology.

Buildings and Grounds: Campus area 252 acres. *New buildings:* Orth Athletic Complex completed 2002; Sophomore Residence Hall 2005.

Chief Executive Officer: Dr. George K. Brushaber, President.

Address undergraduate admission inquiries to Jay Fedje, Director of Admissions; graduate or first-professional inquiries to Carl Poldina, Dean of Continuing and Professional Studies.

Carleton College

One North College Street
Northfield, Minnesota 55057

Tel: (507) 646-4190   **E-mail:** admissions@carleton.edu
Fax: (507) 646-4426   **Internet:** www.carleton.edu

Institution Description: Carleton College is a private, independent, nonprofit college. *Enrollment:* 1,951. *Degrees awarded:* Baccalaureate.

Member of Associated Colleges of the Midwest (ACM); Consortium on Financing Higher Education; Higher Education Data Sharing Consortium.

Accreditation: *Regional:* NCA. *Professional:* teacher education

History: Incorporated and established as Northfield College by Minnesota Conference of the Congregational Churches 1866; offered first instruction at postsecondary level 1870; adopted present name 1871; awarded first degree (baccalaureate) 1874. *See* Leal Headley and Merrill Jarchow, *Carleton: The First Century* (St. Paul: North Central Publishing Co., 1966) for further information.

Institutional Structure: *Governing board:* Carleton College Council: 1 trustee, 1 alumnus, 5 students, 5 faculty, 4 administrators, 2 staff. 2 ex officio. 18 voting. *Composition of institution:* Administrators 12 men / 12 women (at dean's level and above, 29% are women). Academic affairs headed by dean. Management/business/finances directed by vice president and treasurer. Regular continuing faculty appointments 114 men / 53 women. Academic governance body, Education and Curriculum Committee, meets an average of 25 times per year.

Calendar: Trimesters. Academic year mid-Sept. to mid-June. Freshmen admitted Sept. Degrees conferred and formal commencement June. No summer sessions.

Characteristics of Freshmen: 46% of applicants accepted. 31.8% of accepted applicants enrolled.

80% (389 students) submitted SAT scores; 55% (270 students) submitted ACT scores. *25th percentile:* SAT Verbal 650, SAT Math 650; ACT Composite 28. *75th percentile:* SAT Verbal 750, SAT Math 730; ACT Composite 32. ACT 88.1% of entering freshmen expected to graduate within 5 years. 25.8% of freshmen from Minnesota. Freshmen from 46 states and 9 foreign countries.

Admission: For fall acceptance, apply up to Jan. 15. Students are notified of acceptance by Apr. 15. Apply before Nov. 15 or Jan. 15. Early acceptance available. *Requirements:* College preparatory program with 3 years of English, 3 mathematics (2 years of algebra, 1 year of geometry), 3 years of social science, 3 years of science (1 year must be of laboratory science), 2 years of foreign language unless not offered in school. Most Carleton students go well beyond this minimum. *Entrance tests:* College Board SAT or ACT. *For transfer students:* 3.0 minimum GPA; 102 Carleton credits maximum transfer credit.

College credit and advanced placement for postsecondary-level work completed in secondary school. Tutoring available.

Degree Requirements: 210 credits; 2.0 GPA minimum; 6 terms in residence; 4 terms physical education; general education requirements; demonstrated proficiency in writing English and reading a foreign language; recognition and affirmation of difference requirement (1 course). Students must also complete an integrative exercise in their major field to graduate. Exemption from some beginning courses possible by passing departmental tests. *Grading system:* A–F; satisfactory, credit, no credit; withdraw (carries time limit).

Distinctive Educational Programs: Work-experience programs. Dual-degree programs in engineering with Columbia University (NY) and Washington University (MO), in law with Columbia University, and in nursing with Rush University (IL). Interdepartmental/interdisciplinary programs in African/African American Studies, Asian Studies, Classical Studies, Educational Studies, Environmental and Technology Studies, French Studies, Judaic Studies, Latin American Studies, Media Studies, Russian Studies, Women's Studies, Studies in Theater Arts. Facilities and programs for independent research, including honors programs and individual majors. 67% of students study on off-campus programs. ACM Urban Studies, Chicago Arts, Newberry Library, and Urban Education in Chicago. ACM Oak Ridge Science Semester, HECUA (in Minneapolis-St. Paul) MUST, and City Arts. Sea Education Association, Marine Biological Laboratories in Woods Hole, and Eugene O'Neill National Theater Institute. Study abroad programs throughout Asia, India, Central and South America, Africa, Europe, the Middle East, Russia, Australia, New Zealand, United Kingdom, Ireland. *Other distinctive programs:* Carleton in Washington program (full ten-week term); Visions of California (American Studies Seminar).

Degrees Conferred: 455 *baccalaureate.* Bachelor's degrees awarded in top five disciplines: social sciences 404; physical sciences 58; visual and performing arts 48; biological and biomedical sciences 48; English language and literature/letters 44.

Fees and Other Expenses: *Full-time tuition per academic year 2005–06:* $32,460. *Fees:* $189. *Room per academic year:* $3,738. *Board per academic year:* $4,080.

Financial Aid: Aid from institutionally generated funds is provided on the basis of financial need.

Financial aid to full-time, first-time undergraduate students: need-based scholarships/grants totaling $18,670,760, self-help $5,404,218; non-need-based scholarships/grants totaling $1,085,366, self-help $671,601, parent loans $1,651,116.

Departments and Teaching Staff: Total instructional faculty 208 (full-time 186, part-time 22; women 90, men 118; members of minority groups 42). Total faculty with doctorate, first-professional, or other terminal degree: 194. Student-to-faculty ratio: 10:1.

Enrollment: Total enrollment 1,951. Undergraduate full-time 924 men / 1,013 women, part-time 5m / 9w.

Characteristics of Student Body: *Ethnic/racial makeup:* number of Black non-Hispanic: 109; American Indian or Alaska Native: 11; Asian or Pacific Islander: 183; Hispanic: 86; White non-Hispanic: 1,465.

International Students: 95 nonresident aliens enrolled fall 2004. 3 students from Europe, 74 Asia, 6 Central and South America, 5 Africa, 4 Canada, 1 Australia. Programs available to aid students whose native language is not English: social, cultural, financial. English as a Second Language Program. No financial aid specifically designated for international students.

Student Life: On-campus residence halls house 75.8% of student body; 13.5% in off-campus college-owned houses; 10.7% in private rental housing. *Intercollegiate athletics:* men only: baseball, basketball, cross country and track, football, golf, skiing, soccer, swimming, tennis, wrestling; women only: basketball, skiing, soccer, softball, swimming, tennis, track, volleyball. *Special regulations:* Cars not permitted for students living in college housing except under special circumstances. No student cars may be driven on campus. *Special services:* Medical services. College-sponsored buses to Minneapolis-St. Paul. Shuttle vans to St. Olaf College. *Computing facilities for student use:* 247 computers and work stations dedicated to student use in 32 networked labs. *Student publications, radio: The Observer*, a quarterly opinion magazine; *Carletonian*, a weekly newspaper. Radio station KRLX broadcasts 118 24 hours per day during the term. *Surrounding community:* Northfield population 16,000. Minneapolis-St. Paul, 50 miles from campus, is nearest metropolitan area.

Library Collections: 987,000 volumes including bound books, serial backfiles, electronic documents, government documents. Current serial subscriptions: 500 paper; 14,000 via electronic access. 62 computer work stations. Students have access to online information retrieval services and the Internet. Total 2004–05 budget for books, periodicals, audiovisual materials, microforms: $1,600,000.

Most important special collections include Donald Beaty Bloch Collection of Western Americana; Gould Collection of Arctic and Antarctic materials; Thorstein Veblen's personal library.

Buildings and Grounds: Campus area 1,040 acres.

Chief Executive Officer: Dr. Robert A. Olden, Jr., President.

Address admission inquiries to Paul Thiboutot, Dean of Admissions.

College of Saint Benedict

37 South College Avenue
St. Joseph, Minnesota 56374

Tel: (320) 363-2196   **E-mail:** admissions@csbsju.edu
Fax: (320) 363-2750   **Internet:** www.csbsju.edu

Institution Description: College of St. Benedict is a private college affiliated with the Sisters of the Order of St. Benedict, Roman Catholic Church. The school has had a jointly coordinated academic program with St. John's University, a nearby institution for men, since 1963. *Enrollment:* 2,033. *Degrees awarded:* Baccalaureate.

Accreditation: *Regional:* NCA. *Professional*: dietetics, music, nursing, nursing education, social work, teacher education

History: Chartered as St. Benedict's College and Academy in 1887; offered first instruction at postsecondary level 1913; first degree (baccalaureate) awarded 1917; present name adopted 1927; incorporated 1961.

Institutional Structure: *Governing board:* Board of Trustees, College of St. Benedict. Extrainstitutional representation: 36 trustees; institutional representation: 4 ex officio (nonvoting). 25 voting. Academic affairs headed by provost for academic affairs. Management/finances under chief financial and administrative officer. Full-time instructional faculty 53 men / 74 women. Academic governance body, Faculty Governance Coordinating Committee, meets approximately every monthly.

Calendar: Semesters. Academic year Sept. to May. Freshmen admitted Aug., Jan. Degrees conferred Sept., Dec., Jan., May. Formal commencement May. No summer session.

Characteristics of Freshmen: 85% of applicants admitted. 43% of admitted students enrolled.

14% (69 students) submitted SAT scores; 16% (466 students) submitted ACT scores. *25th percentile*: SAT Verbal 535, SAT Math 540; ACT Composite 23, ACT English 22, ACT Math 22. *75th percentile*: SAT Verbal 650, SAT Math 660; ACT Composite 27, ACT English 28, ACT Math 27.

81% of entering freshmen expected to graduate within 5 years. 86% of freshmen from Minnesota. Freshmen from 16 states and 8 foreign countries.

Admission: Rolling admissions plan. Midyear admission and advanced placement plans available. For fall acceptance apply as early as Sept. 1 of previous year. Priority deadline Dec. 1. Students who have completed the application process by Dec. 1 will receive scholarship award notification Dec. 20. *Requirements:* Graduation from accredited secondary school with a program that includes 4 units English, 3 mathematics, 2 laboratory science, and a foreign language recommended. Minimum 3.0 or higher GPA. High school rank of 50% or higher; ACT composite of 21 or higher; SAT combined 1000 or higher. *Entrance tests:* College Board SAT or ACT Composite. *For transfer students:* 2.75 minimum GPA. Maximum transfer credit limited only by residency requirement.

College credit and advanced placement for postsecondary-level work completed in secondary school. Tutoring available.

Degree Requirements: *For all baccalaureate degrees:* 124 semester hours; 2 units physical education or dance; 4 credits senior seminar; completion of core curriculum. *For all undergraduate degrees:* 2.0 GPA; final academic year in residence; demonstrated competence in basic skills (writing, interpersonal communications) and other specified areas.

Fulfillment of some degree requirements and exemption from some beginning courses possible by passing College Board CLEP or APP, international baccalaureate. *Grading system:* A–F; pass-fail; withdraw.

Distinctive Educational Programs: The Center for International Education provides intercultural education experiences for undergraduate students on the

following programs each year: Australia Program, Austrian Program, British Program, Central American Program, Chinese Program, French Program, Irish Program, South American Program, Spanish Program. The office also coordinates an exchange of students with Sophia University in Tokyo, Keele University in Staffordshire, England, and University of Malta. Each program is generally limited to 25–30 participants. Work-experience programs. Evening classes. Interdisciplinary programs in humanities, liberal studies, medieval studies, interdisciplinary honor seminars. Preprofessional programs in dentistry, engineering, forestry, law, medicine, occupational therapy, pharmacy, veterinary medicine. Facilities and programs for independent research, including honors programs, individual majors. Cross-registration with St. Cloud State University and St. John's University. 3–2 program in occupational therapy with Washington University in St. Louis.

ROTC: Army offered in cooperation with St. John's University. 25 commissions awarded 2004.

Degrees Conferred: 475 *baccalaureate:* biological/life sciences 37; business/marketing 54; education 47; English 92; foreign languages and literature 11; health professions and related sciences 56; interdisciplinary studies 15; liberal arts/general studies 9; mathematics 5; natural resources/environmental science 1; philosophy/religion/theology 11; physical sciences 2; protective services/public administration 15; psychology 45; social sciences and history 54; visual and performing arts 21.

Fees and Other Expenses: *Full-time tuition per academic year 2005–06:* $23,064. *Required fees:* $390. *Room per academic year:* $3,419. *Board per academic year:* $3,218.

Financial Aid: Aid from institutionally generated funds is provided on the basis of academic merit, financial need.

Financial aid to full-time, first-time undergraduate students: need-based scholarships/grants totaling $14,440,651, self-help $10,419,514, parent loans $1,479,777, tuition waivers $869,362; non-need-based scholarships/grants totaling $5,225,776, self-help $1,215,019, parent loans $393,146, tuition waivers $550,998.

Departments and Teaching Staff: *Professors 38, associate professors 39, assistant professors 51, instructors 20, part-time faculty 24.*

Total instructional faculty: 172 (full-time 148, part-time 24; women 98, men 74; members of minority groups 13). Total faculty with doctorate, first-professional, or other terminal degree: 132. Student-to-faculty ratio: 13:1. Degrees held by full-time faculty: doctorate 76%, master's 20%, baccalaureate 1%, professional 3%. 86% hold terminal degrees. *Faculty development:* $75,000 in grants for research. 6 faculty members awarded sabbaticals 2004–05.

Enrollment: Total enrollment 2,033. Undergraduate full-time 1,973 women, part-time 60 women. *Transfer students:* 39.

Characteristics of Student Body: *Ethnic/racial makeup:* number of Black non-Hispanic: Asian or Pacific Islander: 44; Hispanic: 20; White non-Hispanic: 1,880. *Age distribution:* number under 18: 22; 18–19: 792; 20–21: 429; 22–24: 251; 25–29: 9; 30–34: 6; 35–39: 4; 40–49: 13; 50–64: 4.

International Students: 78 nonresident aliens enrolled fall 2004. 12 students from Europe, 24 Asia, 8 Africa, 2 Canada, 32 Caribbean. Programs available to aid students whose native language is not English: social, cultural. English as a Second Language Program. Financial aid specifically designated for international students: variable number of scholarships available annually.

Student Life: On-campus residence halls for women, including 3 apartment complexes, house 74% of student body. *Intercollegiate athletics:* women only: basketball, cross-country, diving, golf, ice hockey, Nordic skiing, soccer, softball, swimming, tennis, track and field, volleyball. *Special regulations:* Cars permitted without restrictions. *Special services:* Academic advising and tutoring, medical services, shuttle buses to and from St. John's University and the town of St. Cloud. *Student publications, radio: Studio One*, an annual literary magazine; *Diotima*, a fine arts periodical; *The Saint,* the student newspaper. Radio station KJNB has 50–60 hours per week of student broadcasting; TV station C6TV (in cooperation with St. John's University). *Surrounding community:* St. Joseph population 4,500. Minneapolis-St. Paul, 75 miles from campus, is nearest metropolitan area. Served by airport 80 miles from campus.

Library Collections: 465,410 volumes including bound books, serial backfiles, electronic documents, and government documents not in separate collections. Online catalog. Current serial subscriptions: 1,030 paper; 14,464 microform. 33,471 audiovisual materials. 34 computer work stations. Students have access to the Internet at no charge. Total 2004–05 budget for books and materials: $2,655,718.

Most important special collections include Benedicta Arts Center Music Library; Rare Book Collection; Theology Collection; Women's Studies.

Buildings and Grounds: Campus area 700 acres.

Chief Executive Officer: Dr. MaryAnn Beenninger, President.

Address admission inquiries to Mary Milbert, Dean of Admissions.

College of St. Catherine

2004 Randolph Avenue
St. Paul, Minnesota 55105
Tel: (651) 690-6000   **E-mail:** admissions@stkate.edu
Fax: (651) 690-6024   **Internet:** www.stkate.edu

Institution Description: College of St. Catherine is a private women's college affiliated with the Sisters of St. Joseph of Carondelet, Roman Catholic Church. *Enrollment:* 4,009. Men are admitted to continuing education and graduate programs. *Degrees awarded:* Baccalaureate, master's. Certificates also awarded.

Member of the consortia Associated Colleges of the Twin Cities (ACTC) and National Federation of Carondolet Colleges (NFCC).

Accreditation: *Regional:* NCA. *Professional::* nursing, occupational therapy, social work, teacher education

History: Established, incorporated, and offered first instruction at postsecondary level 1905; awarded first degree (baccalaureate) 1913.

Institutional Structure: *Governing board:* Board of Trustees. Extrainstitutional representation: 38 trustees; institutional representation: president of the college; 1 alumna. 2 ex officio. 38 voting. *Composition of institution:* Administrators 1 man / 15 women. Academic affairs headed by vice president and 3 academic deans. Management/business/finances directed by business manager. Administrators 1 man / 6 women. Full-time instructional faculty 182. Academic governance body, the faculty, meets an average of 9 times per year.

Calendar: Semesters (4-1-4 plan). Academic year Sept. to May. Freshmen admitted Sept., Feb. Degrees conferred and formal commencement May, Dec. Summer session of 3 terms from May to Aug. Trimester plan for weekend college students.

Characteristics of Freshmen: 38% of applicants admitted. 32% of applicants admitted and enrolled.

10% (26 students) submitted SAT scores; 93% (291 students) submitted ACT scores. *25th percentile:* SAT Verbal 565, SAT Math 515; ACT Composite 21, ACT English 21, ACT Math 19. *75th percentile:* SAT Verbal 695, SAT Math 610; ACT Composite 27, ACT English 27, ACT Math 26.

57% of entering freshmen expected to graduate within 5 years. 84% of freshmen from Minnesota. Freshmen from 13 states and 5 foreign countries.

Admission: Rolling admissions plan. For fall acceptance, apply as early as Mar. of previous year, but not later than day of enrollment. Early acceptance available. *Requirements:* Either graduation from accredited secondary school or GED. Recommend 4 units English, 2 in a foreign language, 2 mathematics, 2 natural science, 2 social studies. Lowest acceptable secondary school class standing 67th percentile. Foreign students should apply through the Institute of International Education (NY). *Entrance tests:* College Board SAT, PSAT, or ACT composite. *For transfer students:* 2.0 minimum GPA; 64 semester hours maximum transfer credit.

College credit and advanced placement for postsecondary-level work completed in secondary school and for extrainstitutional learning (life experience) on basis of written narrative. Tutoring available.

Degree Requirements: 130 semester hours; 2.0 GPA; 16 courses in residence (including last 8, 4 in major and 1 interim term); 2 physical education courses; distribution requirements; demonstrated proficiency in writing.

Fulfillment of some degree requirements and exemption from some beginning courses possible by passing departmental examinations, College Board CLEP, APP. *Grading system:* A–F; satisfactory-unsatisfactory; withdraw (carries time limit); incomplete (carries time limit).

Distinctive Educational Programs: Internships. Weekend and evening classes. Dual-degree program in engineering with Washington University (MO). Interdisciplinary programs in humanities, social studies; interdisciplinary majors through ACTC. Programs for independent research, including individual majors and independent study courses. Exchange programs with Nanzan University, Japan; Ewka Women's University, Korea; St. Mary's College, Strawberry Hill, England. No study abroad programs sponsored by the college; students may enroll in study abroad programs that are offered by other institutions. Off-campus study in U.S. through NFCC. *Other distinctive programs:* Degree-granting weekend college. Continuing education credit and enrichment programs. Credit and audit programs available (tuition-free for parents of enrolled students, at reduced tuition for alumnae).

ROTC: Air Force offered in cooperation with University of St. Thomas.

Degrees Conferred: 577 *baccalaureate:* area and ethnic studies 3; biological/life sciences 19; business/marketing 101; communications/communication technologies 28; computer and information sciences 18; education 65; English 40; foreign languages and literature 7; health professions and related sciences 128; home economics and vocational home economics 13; interdisciplinary studies 5; mathematics 4; parks and recreation 16; philosophy/religion/theology 10; physical sciences 4; protective services/public administration 43; psychology 23;

social sciences and history 30; visual and performing arts 20. 350 *master's:* business/marketing 34; education 161; health professions and related clinical sciences 67; philosophy/religion 6; protective services/public administration 82.

Fees and Other Expenses: *Full-time tuition per academic year 2005–06:* $22,464 undergraduate; variable costs for graduate study. *Room nd board per academic year:* $6,120.

Financial Aid: Aid from institutionally generated funds is provided on the basis of academic merit, financial need.

Financial aid to full-time, first-time undergraduate students: need-based scholarships/grants totaling $10,940,297, self-help $8,147,423; non-need-based scholarships/grants totaling $7,293,718, self-help $11,017,015, parent loans $1,285,450, tuition waivers $636,571.

Departments and Teaching Staff: *Professors* 38, *associate professors* 68, *assistant professors* 103, *instructors* 34, *part-time faculty* 200.

Total instructional faculty: 443 (full-time 243, part-time 200; women 355, men 88; members of minority groups 26). Student-to-faculty ratio: 11:1.

Enrollment: Total enrollment 4,009. Undergraduate full-time 21 men / 2,341 women, part-time 71m / 1,149w; graduate full-time 101m / 558w, part-time 50m / 518w.

Characteristics of Student Body: *Ethnic/racial makeup:* number of Black non-Hispanic: 241; American Indian or Alaska Native: 22; Asian or Pacific Islander: 201;Hispanic: 83; White non-Hispanic: 2,688; unknown: 273. *Age distribution:* number under 18: 241; 18–19: 383; 20–21: 665; 22–24: 570; 25–29: 514; 30–34: 343; 35–39: 250; 40–49: 369; 50–64: 137; 65 and over: 6.

International Students: 85 nonresident aliens enrolled fall 2004. Programs available to aid students whose native language is not English: social, cultural. English as a Second Language Program. Financial aid specifically designated for international students: variable number of scholarships available annually for undergraduate students.

Student Life: 78% of freshmen live on-campus. Residence halls for women constitute 100% of such space. 12% of student body housed in institutionally controlled apartments. *Intercollegiate athletics:* women only: basketball, ice hockey, soccer, swimming, tennis, track, volleyball. *Special regulations:* Registered cars permitted without restrictions. Quiet hours set by residents in individual halls. Residence hall visitation from 6pm to 12:45am Fri., 1pm to 12:45am Sat., 1pm to 10:45pm Sun. *Special services:* Learning Resources Center, medical services. *Student publications: Ariston*, an annual literary magazine; *The Wheel*, a biweekly newspaper. *Surrounding community:* Minneapolis-St. Paul population over 2 million. Served by mass transit bus system; airport 6 miles from campus; passenger rail service 2 miles from campus.

Library Collections: 252,107 volumes including bound books, serial backfiles, electronic documents, and government documents not in separate collections. Online and card catalogs. Current serial subscriptions: 14,516 paper, 185,616 microform. 10,706 recordings. Students have access to the Internet at no charge. Total 2004–05 budget for books and materials: $1,595,358.

Most important holdings include performing Ade Bethune Collection; Slade Collection (19th Century signed authors); Mullerleice Collection (fine printing).

Buildings and Grounds: Campus area 110 acres.

Chief Executive Officer: Dr. Andrea J. Lee, President.

Address admission inquiries to Marlene Mohs, Senior Associate Dean of Admissions.

College of St. Scholastica

1200 Kenwood Avenue
Duluth, Minnesota 55811
Tel: (218) 723-6000   **E-mail:** admissions@css.edu
Fax: (218) 723-6290   **Internet:** www.css.edu

Institution Description: The College of St. Scholastica is a private, independent, nonprofit college sponsored by the Duluth Benedictine Sisters (Roman Catholic). *Enrollment:* 2,334. *Degrees awarded:* Baccalaureate, master's, first-professional.

Member of Lake Superior Association of Colleges and Universities.

Accreditation: *Regional:* NCA. *Professional:* clinical lab scientist, health information administration, nursing, occupational therapy, physical therapy, social work

History: First instruction at postsecondary level 1911; established 1912; became 4-year college and adopted present name 1924; first degree (baccalaureate) awarded 1925; graduate program established 1973. *See* Merrill E. Jarchow, *Private Liberal Arts Colleges in Minnesota* (St. Paul: Minnesota Historical Society, 1973) for further information.

Institutional Structure: *Governing board:* Board of Trustees of the College of St. Scholastica, Inc. 32 trustees, including president of the college, president of the Benedictine Sisters Benevolent Association, president of the alumni Association, president of the student senate, the vice-chair of the faculty assembly, and a representative of the staff of the college. *Composition of institution:* 10 senior administrators (6 men / 4 women). Academic affairs headed by senior vice president for academic affairs/dean of faculty. Management/business/finances directed by vice president for finance. Full-time instructional faculty 136. Academic governance body, the faculty, meets an average of 6 times per year.

Calendar: Semesters. Academic year Sept. to May. Degrees conferred and formal commencement Dec., May.

Characteristics of Freshmen: 89% of applicants admitted. 37% of applicants admitted and enrolled.

6% (27 students) submitted SAT scores; 95% (416 students) submitted ACT scores. *25th percentile:* SAT Verbal 490, SAT Math 480; ACT Composite 21, ACT English 20, ACT Math 20. *75th percentile:* SAT Verbal 560, SAT Math 600; ACT Composite 26, ACT English 26, ACT Math 26.

64% of entering freshmen expected to graduate within 5 years. 89% of freshmen from Minnesota. Freshmen from 17 states and 14 foreign countries.

Admission: Rolling admissions plan. For fall acceptance, apply as early as completion of junior year of secondary school, but not later than first day of classes. Early admission of high school students; deferred admission available. *Requirements:* Secondary school transcript showing GPA and class rank or GED transcript, plus a qualified ACT or SAT test score. *Entrance tests:* College Board ACT or SAT Reasoning, . *For transfer students:* 2.0 minimum GPA; 96 semester credits maximum transferable towards a degree.

College credit for postsecondary-level work completed in secondary school and for College Board CLEP. College credit and advanced placement for extrainstitutional learning on basis of ACE *2006 Guide to the Evaluation of Educational Experiences in the Armed Services;* faculty assessment of portfolio prepared in required course.

Tutoring available. Developmental courses offered during regular academic year; credit given.

Degree Requirements: Satisfactorily completed minimum of 128 semester credits with a 2.0 GPA. 52 credits of general education courses are required, including areas of English composition, social science, natural science, foreign language, communication, literature, history, fine arts, philosophy, religious studies, mathematics, and cultural diversity. The hours required in the major area vary.

Fulfillment of some degree requirements and exemption from some beginning courses possible by passing College Board CLEP, APP, departmental examinations. *Grading system:* A–F; pass-fail; withdraw (carries time limit and deadline after which pass-fail is appended to withdraw).

Distinctive Educational Programs: *For undergraduates:* Ojibwe Bilingual/ Bicultural Educational program, gerontology. Preprofessional programs in dietetics, law, medicine, engineering, pharmacy, and veterinary medicine. Individual majors. Tutorials. Study at St. Scholastica's Center in Ireland and elsewhere through programs offered by other institutions. Unlimited cross-registration with University of Minnesota-Duluth; limited cross-registration with University of Wisconsin-Superior available to junior and senior students. *For graduate students:* flexible meeting places and schedules. *Available to all students:* evening classes. Special facilities for using telecommunications in the classroom. Facilities and programs for independent research.

ROTC: Air Force and Army in cooperation with University of Minnesota-Duluth.

Degrees Conferred: 444 *baccalaureate:* biological/life sciences 24; business/marketing 119; communications/communication technologies 14; computer and information sciences 44; education 36; English 11; health professions and related sciences 131; liberal arts/general studies 2; mathematics 3; parks and recreation 14; philosophy/religion/theology 2; physical sciences 2; protective services/public administration 13; psychology 6; social sciences and history 22; visual and performing arts 1. 232 *master's:* business/marketing 87; education 69; health professions and related sciences 56; parks and recreation 20.

Fees and Other Expenses: *Full-time tuition per academic year 2005–06:* $22,110. Graduate tuition varies by program. *Room and board per academic year:* $6,216.

Financial Aid: Aid from institutionally generated funds is provided on the basis of academic merit, financial need.

Financial aid to full-time, first-time undergraduate students: need-based scholarships/grants totaling $8,026,745, self-help $5,524,776; non-need-based scholarships/grants totaling $11,650,457, self-help $6,591,929, parent loans $1,684,312, tuition waivers $979,847. *Graduate aid:* 26 students received $75,252 in federal and state-funded fellowships/grants; 264 received $3.464.436 in federal and state-funded loans; 38 other fellowships and grants totaling $151,455; 12 teaching assistantships awarded totaling $20,409.

Departments and Teaching Staff: *Professors* 22, *associate professors* 30, *assistant professors* 63, *instructors* 17, *part-time faculty* 86.

Total instructional faculty: 222 (full-time 136, part-time 86; women 39, men 83; members of minority groups 13). Total faculty with doctorate, first-profes-

sional, or other terminal degree: 146. Student-to-faculty ratio: 13:1. *Faculty development:* 2 faculty members awarded sabbaticals 2004–05.

Enrollment: Total enrollment 334. Undergraduate full-time 496 men / 270 women, part-time 29m / 87w; graduate full-time 54m / 221w, part-time 36m / 136w; first-professional: full-time 3m / 2w. *Transfer students:* in-state 128; from out-of-state 44.

Characteristics of Student Body: *Ethnic/racial makeup:* number of Black non-Hispanic: 18; American Indian or Alaska Native: 17; Asian or Pacific Islander: 27; Hispanic: 12; White non-Hispanic: 1,662; unknown: 97. *Age distribution:* number under 18: 16; 18–19: 714; 20–21: 672; 22–24: 240; 25–29: 96; 30–34: 39; 35–39: 38; 40–49: 52; 50–64: 15.

International Students: 53 nonresident aliens enrolled fall 2004. 4 students from Europe, 20 Asia, 7 Central and South America, 9 Africa, 13 Canada. Programs available to aid students whose native language is not English: social, cultural, financial. Financial aid specifically designated for international students: variable number of scholarships available annually.

Student Life: On-campus residence halls house 49% of student body. Residence halls for men constitute 25% of such space, for women 75%. *Intercollegiate athletics:* men only: baseball, basketball, cross-country, hockey, soccer, tennis; women only: basketball, cross-country, soccer, softball, tennis, volleyball. *Special regulations:* Cars permitted without restrictions. Residence hall visitation from 8am to midnight Sun.–Thurs., 8am to 2am Fri. and Sat. *Special services:* Learning Resources Center, medical services, Career Counseling Center, Student Development Center. *Student publications: The Cable,* a weekly newspaper; *Out of Words,* a literary and artistic journal. *Surrounding community:* Duluth population 87,000. Minneapolis-St. Paul, 150 miles from campus, is nearest metropolitan area. Duluth services mass transit bus system; airport 3 miles from campus.

Library Collections: 127,328 volumes. Current serial subscriptions: paper 614; microform 86; via electronic access 3,874. 13,185 recordings; 1,153 compact discs; 366 CD-ROMs. Online catalog. 18 computer work stations. Students have access to the Internet. Total 2004–05 budget for books and materials: $280,000.

Most important special holdings include American Indian Studies Collection; Children and Young Adult Collection; Curriculum Materials Collection.

Buildings and Grounds: Campus area 186 acres. *New buildings:* Cedar Hall (residence) completed 2003; Wellness Center 2004.

Chief Executive Officer: Dr. Larry Goodwin, President.

Address admission inquiries to Brian Dalton, Vice President for Enrollment Management.

College of Visual Arts

344 Summit Avenue
St. Paul, Minnesota 551020-2199
Tel: (651) 224-3416 **E-mail:** info@cva.edu
Fax: (651) 224-8854 **Internet:** www.cva.edu

Institution Description: The College of Visual Arts is a private, four-year college of art and design located in the historic residential Summit Hill area of St. Paul. *Enrollment:* 199. *Degrees awarded:* Baccalaureate. Certificates also awarded.

Accreditation: *Regional:* NCA. *National:* ACCSCT.

History: Founded as the School of Associated Arts 1924.

Institutional Structure: *Governing board:* Board of Directors. Instructional faculty 60.

Calendar: Semesters. Academic year early Sept. to mid-May. Degrees conferred and formal commencement May.

Characteristics of Freshmen: 5% (3 students) submitted SAT scores; 45% (55 students) submitted ACT scores. 35% of entering freshmen are expected to graduate within 5 years. 79% of freshmen from Minnesota. Freshmen from 5 states.

Admission: *Requirements:* Either graduation from accredited secondary school or GED; personal essay stating intent; ACT or SAT; interview; portfolio review. Transfer students must also submit transcripts from all postsecondary institutions attended.

Degree Requirements: Completion of major curriculum; 126 semester credits consisting of 48 liberal arts credits and 78 credits of studio art.

Distinctive Educational Programs: Internship and independent study opportunities. Teaching Artist Program. Summer study abroad. German Exchange Program.

Degrees Conferred: 31 *baccalaureate:* fine and applied arts.

Fees and Other Expenses: *Full-time tuition per academic year 2004–05:* $17,000. *Required fees:* $530. No on-campus housing.

Financial Aid: Aid from institutionally generated funds is provided on the basis of academic merit, financial need.

Financial aid to full-time, first-time undergraduate students: need-based scholarships/grants totaling $491,900, self-help $1,371,139, parent loans $109,831; non-need-based scholarships/grants totaling $60,150, self-help $418,097, parent loans $77,184.

Departments and Teaching Staff: *Total instructional faculty:* 46 (full-time 8, part-time 38; women 19, men 27). Total faculty with doctorate, first-professional, or other terminal degree: 20. Student-to-faculty ratio: 8:1.

Enrollment: Total enrollment 199. Undergraduate full-time 79 men / 94 women, Part-time 9m / 17w. *Transfer students:* in-state 15; from out-of-state 3.

Characteristics of Student Body: *Ethnic/racial makeup:* number of Black non-Hispanic: 1; American Indian or Alaska Native: 3; Asian or Pacific Islander: 5; Hispanic: 2; White non-Hispanic: 183; unknown: 5. *Age distribution:* number 18–19: 45; 20–21: 99; 22–24: 64; 25–29: 26; 30–34: 7; 35–39: 1; 40–49: 4; 50–64: 2; 65 and over: 1.

International Students: 4 nonresident aliens enrolled fall 2004. 3 students from Europe, 1 Asia. No programs available to aid students whose native language is not English. No financial aid specifically designated for international students.

Student Life: CVA offers a variety of exhibition opportunities, multidisciplinary performances and presentation, guest lecturers, and group rates to a number of cultural events and museum shows. Students also organize their own group shows and art teams for different Twin Cities venues.

Library Collections: 10,989 volumes. Online catalog. 30,000 slides; 150 videos; 29 current periodical subscriptions. 8 computer work stations.

Most important special holdings include art reference materials; slide collections; private art collection.

Buildings and Grounds: The campus consists of 5 facilities: Summit Avenue mansion housing printmaking, photography, and sculpture facilities plus computer labs, classroom space, and administrative offices; 2 buildings dedicated primarily to studio courses and the college's gallery; a new library building completed in 1997; residence apartments.

Chief Executive Officer: Joseph Culligan, President.

Address admission inquiries to Jane Nordhorn, Director of Admissions.

Concordia College - Moorhead

901 South Eighth Street
Moorhead, Minnesota 56562
Tel: (218) 299-4000   **E-mail:** admissions@cord.edu
Fax: (218) 299-3947   **Internet:** www.cord.edu

Institution Description: Concordia College is a private liberal arts college affiliated with the Evangelical Lutheran Church of America. *Enrollment:* 2,814. *Degrees awarded:* Baccalaureate.

Member of Tri-College University.

Accreditation: *Regional:* NCA. *Professional:* dietetics, music, nursing, nursing education, social work, teacher education

History: Established and incorporated 1891; offered first instruction at postsecondary level 1913; offered first baccalaureate degrees 1917; For further information, see Carroll Engelhardt, *On Firm Foundation Grounded: The First Century of Concordia College 1891-1991* (Moorhead, MN: Concordia College, 1991).

Institutional Structure: *Governing board:* Concordia College Board of Regents. Extrainstitutional representation: 26 regents (including 1 alumnus). All voting. *Composition of institution:* Administrators 37 men / 58 women. Academic affairs headed by vice president for academic affairs. Management/business/finances directed by vice president/treasurer for financial affairs. Full-time instructional faculty 200. Academic governance body, Faculty Senate, meets an average of 10 times per year.

Calendar: Semesters. Academic year late Aug. to early May. Freshmen admitted Aug., Jan., May, June. Degrees conferred and formal commencements May, Dec. Summer session of 2 terms from early May to early July.

Characteristics of Freshmen: 85.8% of applicants admitted. 35.4% of applicants admitted and enrolled.

13.4% (102 students) submitted SAT scores; 96.8% (737 students) submitted ACT scores. *25th percentile:* SAT Verbal 530, SAT Math 520; ACT Composite 22, ACT English 22, ACT Math 20. *75th percentile:* SAT Verbal 660, SAT Math 660; ACT Composite 27, ACT English 28, ACT Math 27.

61% of entering freshmen expected to graduate within 5 years. 66% of freshmen from Minnesota. Freshmen from 25 states and 19 foreign countries.

Admission: Rolling admissions plan. For fall acceptance, apply as early as end of junior year (preferably before Jan. of senior year), but not later than Aug. the first day of fall semester. Early acceptance available. *Requirements:* Gradu-

ation from accredited secondary school or GED. *Entrance tests:* College Board SAT, or ACT. *For transfer students:* 2.0 minimum GPA; maximum transfer credit limited only by residence requirement.

Advanced placement for postsecondary-level work completed in secondary school. Tutoring available. Noncredit developmental courses offered during regular academic year.

Degree Requirements: 31.5 course credits; cumulative GPA of 2.0 or higher; minimum of two resident semesters on campus; ten courses at 300 level or higher; mathematics proficiency and proficiency in a world language at second semester distribution requirements; 2 semesters physical education.

Fulfillment of some degree requirements possible by passing departmental examinations, Board CLEP or AP. *Grading system:* A–F; withdraw (carries time limit).

Distinctive Educational Programs: Work-experience programs. Evening classes. Accelerated degree programs. Special facilities for using telecommunications in the classroom. Interdepartmental/interdisciplinary programs in environmental, ethnic, or women's studies. Interdisciplinary honors seminars and department honors programs. Study abroad in various countries through Concordia's May Seminars program. Academic year in: Jera, Germany; Pamploma, Spain; Oslo, Norway; semester programs: India, Malta, Scandinavia, Crete; programs at the University of Oslo and Hamar Teacher's College; Norway's International Business internships in Germany, France, Spain, and Mexico. 2- to 4-month practicum in France. Through consortium, special programs and cross-registration with Moorhead State and North Dakota State Universities. Urban studies program in Chicago and Washington semester in cooperation with American University. Archeological expeditions abroad. Biology field studies.

ROTC: Air Force offered in cooperation with North Dakota State University.

Degrees Conferred: 569 *baccalaureate*: area and ethnic studies 12; biological/life sciences 45; business/marketing 69; communications/communication technologies 36; computer and information sciences 9; education 107; engineering and engineering technologies 1; English 6; foreign languages and literature 42; health professions and related sciences 17; home economics and vocational home economics 14; liberal arts/general studies 1; mathematics 17; natural resources/environmental science 4; parks and recreation 7; philosophy/religion/theology 15; physical sciences 5; protective services/public administration 7; psychology 31; social sciences and history 78; visual and performing arts 36.

Fees and Other Expenses: *Full-time tuition per academic year 2004–05:* $19,366. *Required fees:* $154. *Room and board per academic year:* $4,990.

Financial Aid: Aid from institutionally generated funds is provided on the basis of academic merit, financial need.

Financial aid to full-time, first-time undergraduate students: need-based scholarships/grants totaling $20,127,223, self-help $10,070,913, tuition waivers $595,447; non-need-based scholarships/grants totaling $8,261,552, self-help $6,359,418, parent loans $1,474,888, tuition waivers $710,709.

Departments and Teaching Staff: *Professors* 40, *associate professors* 56, *assistant professors* 64, *instructors* 30, *lecturers* 3; *part-time faculty* 67.

Total instructional faculty: 260 (full-time 174, part-time 86; women 130, men 130; members of minority groups 13). Total faculty with doctorate, first-professional, or other terminal degree: 147. Student-to-faculty ratio: 14.7:1. Degrees held by full-time faculty: doctorate 64%, master's 32%, baccalaureate 4%. 64% hold terminal degrees. *Faculty development:* $645,000 in grants for research. 9 faculty members awarded sabbaticals 2004–05.

Enrollment: Total enrollment 2,814. Undergraduate full-time 1,006 men / 1,723 women, part-time 31m / 52w; graduate full-time 2w.

Characteristics of Student Body: *Ethnic/racial makeup:* number of Black non-Hispanic: 20; American Indian or Alaska Native: 10; Asian or Pacific Islander: 44; Hispanic: 24; White non-Hispanic: 2,553, unknown: 25. *Age distribution:* number under 18: 26; 18–19: 1,123; 20–21: 1,192; 22–24: 418; 25–29: 22; 30–34: 8; 35–39: 2; 40–49: 14; 50–64: 7.

International Students: 136 nonresident aliens enrolled fall 2004. 24 students from Europe, 32 Asia, 9 Central and South America, 65 Africa, 5 Canada, 1 Australia. Programs available to aid students whose native language is not English: special assistance in beginning English sections. Financial aid specifically designated for international students: variable number of scholarships available annually.

Student Life: On-campus residence halls and apartments house 63% of student body. Residence halls for men constitute 35% of such space, for women 65%. *Intercollegiate athletics:* men only: baseball, basketball, soccer, cross country, football, golf, hockey, tennis, track, wrestling; women only: basketball, cross-country, soccer, golf, gymnastics, swimming, tennis, track, volleyball. *Special regulations:* Cars permitted for all. *Special services:* Placement office, medical services, reading-writing center, College supports free weekend and evening bus service to and from business and entertainment centers. *Student publications, radio: Concordian*, a weekly newspaper; *Intercom*, a weekly listing of campus events; *New Voices*, a collection of nonfiction writing from across the curriculum; *After Work*, a literary magazine featuring short stories, poetry, and art; *C'Monologue*, May Seminars office newsletter; *Cobber*, a yearbook;

The New Student Directory, a photo collection of all new freshmen. KORD student-run radio station. *Concordia On-Air*, a student-run television program. *Surrounding community:* Fargo-Moorhead metropolitan area population 170,000. Minneapolis-St. Paul, 235 miles from campus, is nearest metropolitan area. Served by mass transit bus system; airport 3 miles from campus; passenger rail service 1½ miles from campus.

Library Collections: 321,000 volumes. 22,000 audiovisual materials; 1,200 print periodical subscriptions and access to over 24,000 full-text serial titles. Students have access to online information retrieval services and the Internet.

Most important special holdings include Lutheran Church history; Norwegian-Americana (history and literature; history of religions).

Buildings and Grounds: Campus area 120 acres.

Chief Executive Officer: Dr. Pamela Jolicoeur, President.

Address admission inquiries to Director of Admissions.

Concordia University St. Paul

275 North Syndicate Street
St. Paul, Minnesota 55104-5494

Tel: (651) 641-8278   **E-mail:** admiss@csp.edu
Fax: (651) 659-0207   **Internet:** www.csp.edu

Institution Description: Concordia University at St. Paul is a private college affiliated with the Lutheran Church-Missouri Synod. *Enrollment:* 2,217. *Degrees awarded:* Associate, baccalaureate, master's.

Member of Cooperating Libraries in Consortium, Higher Education Consortium for Urban Affairs, Inc. (HECUA).

Accreditation: *Regional:* NCA. *Professional:* teacher education

History: Established 1893; offered first instruction at postsecondary level 1905; awarded first degree (associate) 1907; added upper division 1962. *See* O.B. Overn, *History of Concordia College* (St. Paul: Concordia College, 1967) for further information.

Institutional Structure: *Governing board:* Board of Regents. Extrainstitutional representation: 11 board members; institutional representation: president of the college. 1 ex officio. 8 voting. *Composition of institution:* Administrative governance by president and cabinet comprised of vice presidents and other key leaders. Representative Faculty Senate meets monthly August through May. Full faculty meets semiannually.

Calendar: Semesters. Academic year Aug. to May. Freshmen admitted Aug. Jan. May. Formal commencement May. Four 3-week summer sessions May to Aug.

Characteristics of Freshmen: 63% of applicants admitted. 25% of applicants admitted and enrolled.

11% (20 students) submitted SAT scores; 91% (160 students) submitted ACT scores. *25th percentile:* SAT Verbal 470, SAT Math 510; ACT Composite 18; ACT English 17, ACT Math 17. *75th percentile:* SAT Verbal 620, SAT Math 640; ACT Composite 24, ACT English 25, ACT Math 24.

42% of entering freshmen expected to graduate within 5 years. 69% of freshmen from Minnesota. Freshmen from 13 states.

Admission: Rolling admissions plan. For fall acceptance, apply up to Aug. 1. Early acceptance available. *Requirements:* Graduation from accredited secondary school with 4 units English, 2 mathematics, 2 science, 2 history/social studies, 1 fine arts, 1 health/physical education; or GED. Minimum 2.0 GPA. *Entrance tests:* ACT Composite score of 19. *For transfer students:* at least 2.minimum GPA from previous institution.

College credit and advanced placement for postsecondary-level work completed in secondary school. College credit for extrainstitutional learning on basis of ACE *2006 Guide to the Evaluation of Educational Experiences in the Armed Services;* portfolio and faculty assessments; personal interview. Tutoring available. Developmental courses offered in summer session and regular academic year; transfer credit given.

Degree Requirements: *For all associate degrees:* 64 credit hours. *For all baccalaureate degrees:* 128 credit hours. Students complete at least one major or two minors. *Grading system:* A–F; pass-fail; withdraw (carries time limit).

Distinctive Educational Programs: Degree completion programs in a variety of majors for adult learners; programs are short-based and are offered in both face-to-face and distance education formats. Study abroad programs in England, China, India, and Mexico. Urban study programs available through HECUA.

ROTC: Army and Navy offered in cooperation with University of Minnesota; Air Force with University of St. Thomas.

Degrees Conferred: 5 *associate;* 477 *baccalaureate:* biological/life sciences 1; business/marketing 308; communications/communication technologies 16; education 50; English 3; home economics and vocational home economics 25; interdisciplinary studies 5; liberal arts/general studies 4; parks and recreation 5; philosophy/religion/theology 16; protective services/public administration 20;

psychology 11; social sciences and history 2; visual and performing arts 11. 151 *master's:* business/marketing 62; education 32; home economics 15; philosophy/religion/theology 5; protect services/public administration 28; social sciences and history 9.

Fees and Other Expenses: *Full-time tuition per academic year 2005–06:* $21,312. Graduate tuition $395 per credit hour. *Room and board per academic year:* $6,464.

Financial Aid: Aid from institutionally generated funds is provided on the basis of academic need, financial need, other considerations.

Financial aid to full-time, first-time undergraduate students: need-based scholarships/grants totaling $7,530,559, self-help $7,944,610, parent loans $838,552, athletic awards $825,900; non-need-based scholarships/grants totaling $784,288, self-help $1,088,674, parent loans $1,088,674, athletic awards $181,310. *Graduate aid:* 2 students received $5,190 in federal and state-funded fellowships/grants; 208 received $2,214,782 in federal and state-funded loans.

Departments and Teaching Staff: *Total instructional faculty:* 466 (full-time 81, part-time 355; women 209, men 256; members of minority groups 28). Total full-time faculty with doctorate, first-professional, or other terminal degree: 54. Student-to-faculty ratio: 12:1. Degrees held by full-time faculty: doctorate 77.3%, master's 22.7%. 77.3% hold terminal degrees.

Enrollment: Total enrollment 2,217. Undergraduate full-time 652 men / 936 women, part-time 82m / 155w; graduate full-time 107m / 241w, part-time 11m / 23w.

Characteristics of Student Body: *Ethnic/racial makeup:* number of Black non-Hispanic: 114; American Indian or Alaska Native: 9; Asian or Pacific Islander: 52; Hispanic: 25; White non-Hispanic: 1,214; unknown: 380. *Age distribution:* number under 18: 48; 18–19: 297; 20–21: 1,296; 22–24: 224; 25–29: 217; 30–34: 228; 35–39: 176; 40–49: 258; 50–64: 79; 65 and over: 2; unclassified: 10.

International Students: 13 nonresident aliens enrolled fall 2004. No programs available to aid students whose native language is not English. No financial aid specifically designated for international students.

Student Life: On-campus residence halls house 50% of student body. In general, students not living with parents or close relatives must live in college residence halls. Housing available for married students. *Intercollegiate athletics:* men only: baseball, basketball, football, soccer, tennis; women only: basketball, soccer, softball, tennis, volleyball; both sexes: cross-country. *Special regulations:* Cars permitted. Quiet hours set by residence halls. Residence hall visitation hours Sun.–Thurs. noon to 11pm, Fri.–Sat. noon to 1am. *Special services:* Academic Development Program, Learning Resources Center, Career Resource Center, medical services. *Student publications: Sword*, weekly newspaper. *Surrounding community:* St. Paul, population 270,500, is within Minneapolis/St. Paul metropolitan area. Served by mass transit bus system; airport 5 miles from campus.

Library Collections: 136,216 volumes. 10,266 microforms; 6,000 audiovisual materials; 1,400 current serial subscriptions. Online catalog. All full-time students on traditional programs have laptop computers. Students have access to online information retrieval services and the Internet.

Most important special holdings include hymnbook collection; historical textbook collection; Lutheran and Reformation-related materials.

Buildings and Grounds: Campus area 37 acres. *New buildings:* Library Technology Center completed 2003.

Chief Executive Officer: Dr. Robert Holst, President.

Address admission inquiries to Robert DeWerft, Director of Admissions.

Crossroads College

920 Maywood Road, S.W.
Rochester, Minnesota 559022382

Tel: (507) 288-4563   **E-mail:** admit@crossroadscollege.edu
Fax: (507) 288-9046   **Internet:** www.crossroadscollege.edu

Institution Description: Crossroads College, formerly named Minnesota Bible College, is a private institution operated under the auspices of the Christian Churches/Churches of Christ. *Enrollment:* 149. *Degrees awarded:* Associate, baccalaureate.

Accreditation: *National:* ABHE.

History: Originally established in 1913 in Minneapolis for the purpose of educating immigrants to return to their homelands as missionaries. Campus was moved to Rochester in 1971; adopted present name 2001.

Institutional Structure: Headed by 18-member Board of Trustees.

Calendar: Semesters. Academic year Sept. to May.

Characteristics of Freshmen: 50 applicants (27 men, 23 women). 100% of applicants admitted. 84% of admitted students enrolled full-time.

3% (1 student) submitted SAT scores; 77% (27 students) submitted ACT scores. *25th percentile*: ACT Composite 18, ACT English 17, ACT Math 16. *75th percentile*: ACT Composite 24, ACT English 25, ACT Math 23.

46% of freshmen from Minnesota. Freshmen from 7 states and 1 foreign country.

Admission: *Requirements:* Graduation from secondary school; GED acceptable under certain circumstances. *Entrance tests:* SAT or ACT.

Degree Requirements: Completion of prescribed curriculum.

Distinctive Educational Programs: Associated school relationship with Jerusalem University College. Cooperative programs in nursing with Rochester Community and Technical College and Winona State University; in education with Winona State University; also in several other areas of interest to students.

Degrees Conferred: 12 *associate;* 18 *baccalaureate:* philosophy/religion and theology 10; psychology 8.

Fees and Other Expenses: *Full-time tuition per academic year 2004–05:* $8,660. *Books and supplies:* $500. *Room and board per academic year:* $6,405.

Financial Aid: Aid from institutionally generated funds is provided on the basis of academic merit, financial need, other criteria. Institution has a Program Participation Agreement with the U.S. Department of Education for eligible students to receive Pell Grants and, depending on agreement, other federal aid.

Departments and Teaching Staff: Theology *professors* 4, *part-time teachers* 3; education 1, 0; music 1, 0; arts and science 2, 7. *Total instructional faculty:* 19. Student-to-faculty ratio: 10:1. Degrees held by full-time faculty: doctorate 67%, master's 33%. 67% hold terminal degrees.

Enrollment: Total enrollment 149 (55.7% men, 44.3% women).

Characteristics of Student Body: *Ethnic/racial makeup:* Black non-Hispanic: 4.7%, Asian or Pacific Islander: 2.7%; White non-Hispanic: 88.6%; unknown: .7%.

International Students: 5 nonresident aliens enrolled fall 2004. Students from Europe, Asia, Haiti, Africa. No programs available to aid students whose native language is not English. No financial aid specifically designated for international students.

Student Life: Students live in town-house units that house up to 7 students. Several apartments are available for older students and/or married students. Students have the opportunity to participate in choral groups, sports, mission trips, and community service as a regular part of their educational experience.

Library Collections: 35,000 volumes. 1,129 microforms; 179 current periodical subscriptions. Online adn card catalogs. 750 recordings. 7 computer work stations. Students have access online information retrieval services and the Internet.

Most important special collections include historical collection on history of Christianity and of Resurrection Churches; papers of Dean G.H. Cashiaras on the history of the college; Classic and Contemporary Biblical Commentary Collection.

Buildings and Grounds: Campus area 38 acres.

Chief Executive Officer: Robert W. Cash, President.

Address admission inquiries to Alan W. Wager, Director of Admissions.

Crown College

8700 College View Drive
St. Bonifacius, Minnesota 55375-9002
Tel: (952) 446-4100   **E-mail:** info@crown.edu
Fax: (952) 446-4149   **Internet:** www.crown.edu

Institution Description: Crown College, formerly known as St. Paul Bible College, is a private college affiliated with The Christian and Missionary Alliance. *Enrollment:* 1,106. *Degrees awarded:* Associate, baccalaureate, master's. Certificates also awarded.

Accreditation: *Regional:* NCA. *National:* ABHE.

History: Established, chartered, and offered first instruction at postsecondary level 1916; awarded first degree (baccalaureate) 1948.

Institutional Structure: *Governing board:* College Board of Trustees. Extrainstitutional representation: 29 trustees; institutional representation: president of the college. 9 ex officio. All voting. *Composition of institution:* Administrators 26 men / 3 women. Academic affairs headed by academic dean. Management/business/finances directed by executive vice president. Full-time instructional faculty 36. Academic governance body, Plenary Faculty, meets an average of 15 times per year.

Calendar: Semesters. Academic year Aug. to May. Freshmen admitted Aug., Jan., May, June. Degrees conferred and formal commencement May. Summer session from mid-May to early July.

Characteristics of Freshmen: 93% of applicants accepted. 53% of accepted applicants enrolled.

Average secondary school rank men 59.04 percentile, women 68.62 percentile, class 65.15 percentile. Mean ACT composite score 22.1.

51% of entering freshmen expected to graduate within 5 years. Freshmen from 221 states and 3 foreign countries.

Admission: Rolling admissions plan. Apply as early as 1 year prior to enrollment, but not later than 6 days after beginning of classes. *Requirements:* Either graduation from secondary school or GED. Minimum 2.0 GPA. Lowest acceptable secondary school class standing 25th percentile. *Entrance tests:* College Board SAT, ACT composite, or other standardized tests. *For transfer students:* 2.0 minimum GPA; from 4-year accredited institution and for correspondence/extension students, 95 semester hours maximum transfer credit; from 2-year accredited institution 64 hours.

College credit and advanced placement for postsecondary-level work completed in secondary school. College credit for extrainstitutional learning on basis of ACE *2006 Guide to the Evaluation of Educational Experiences in the Armed Services;* advanced placement on basis of faculty assessment.

Tutoring available. Developmental courses offered during regular academic year; credit given.

Degree Requirements: *For all associate degrees:* 66 semester hours. *For all baccalaureate degrees:* 125 semester hours; student ministries requirement. *For all degrees:* 2.0 GPA; 2 semesters in residence; daily chapel attendance; 2 credit hours physical education.

Fulfillment of some degree requirements and exemption from some beginning courses possible by passing College Board CLEP, AP. *Grading system:* A–F; pass-fail; satisfactory-unsatisfactory; withdraw; incomplete.

Distinctive Educational Programs: Evening and weekend classes. Summer week-long intensive classes. Study abroad in China, Indonesia, Latin America, Middle East. *Other distinctive programs:* Missionary education program for nurses.

Degrees Conferred: 42 *associate;* 182 *baccalaureate:* education 29; business 34; English 7; music 6; natural science e4; history 7; liberal arts 4; psychology 9; ministry 103; missiology 15. 5 *master's:* missiology 1; ministry 4.

Fees and Other Expenses: *Tuition per academic year 2005–06:* $14,354. *Room per academic year:* $2,600. *Board per academic year:* $3,144.

Financial Aid: Aid from institutionally generated funds is provided on the basis of academic merit, financial need. Institution has a Program Participation Agreement with the U.S. Department of Education for eligible students to receive Pell Grants and other federal aid. *Institutional funding for undergraduates:* 520 scholarships and grants totaling $1,489,148. *State funding for undergraduates:* 487 scholarships and grants totaling $1,754,277. 783 loans totaling $3,865,112.

Departments and Teaching Staff: *Professors* 27, *part-time faculty* 25. *Total instructional faculty:* 52. Student-to-faculty ratio: 14:1. Degrees held by full-time faculty: doctorate 26%, master's 27%, baccalaureate 100%. 50% hold terminal degrees.

Enrollment: Total enrollment 1,106. Full-time 341 men / 445 women, part-time 358m / 25w; graduate full-time 39 / 17w, part-time 2m / 1w.

Characteristics of Student Body: *Ethnic/racial makeup:* Black non-Hispanic: 5; American Indian or Alaska Native: 1; Asian or Pacific Islander:49; Hispanic: 16; White non-Hispanic: 584.

International Students: 8 nonresident aliens enrolled fall 2004. Programs available to aid students whose native language is not English: social, cultural. English as a Second Language. No financial aid specifically designated for international students.

Student Life: On-campus residence halls house 79% of student body. Housing available for married students. *Intercollegiate athletics:* men only: baseball, football; women only: softball, volleyball; both sexes: basketball, cross-country, golf, soccer. *Special regulations:* Cars permitted in designated areas. Curfews. Quiet hours. *Special services:* Learning Resources Center, computer lab, medical services. *Student publications* bimonthly newspaper; yearbook. *Surrounding community:* Minneapolis-St. Paul, 35 miles from campus, is nearest metropolitan area. Served by airport 35 miles from campus.

Library Collections: 79,386 volumes. 70,000 microforms; 19,000 full-text periodicals; over 70 online subscription databases. 500 audiovisual materials; Students have access to online information retrieval services and the Internet. Total 2004–05 budget for books and materials: $316,003.

Most important special holdings include 9,500 children's books in a curriculum library for student teachers; 1,500 children's AV items in a curriculum nonprint library for student teachers; archives material about St. Paul Bible College and The Christian and Missionary Alliance; Howard Jones Evangelism Collection.

Buildings and Grounds: Campus area 193 acres.

Chief Executive Officer: Dr. Gary Benedict, President.

Address undergraduate admission inquiries to Mitch Fisk, Director of Admissions; graduate inquiries to Director of Graduate School.

Gustavus Adolphus College

800 West College Avenue
St. Peter, Minnesota 56082
Tel: (507) 933-7676   **E-mail:** admission@gustavus.edu
Fax: (507) 933-7474   **Internet:** www.gustavus.edu

Institution Description: Gustavus Adolphus College is a private college affiliated with the Evangelical Lutheran Church in America. *Enrollment:* 2,577. *Degrees awarded:* Baccalaureate.

Accreditation: *Regional:* NCA. *Professional:* athletic training, music, nursing, nursing education, teacher education

History: Established as Minnesota Preparatory School in Red Wing 1862; moved to East Union and changed name to St. Ansgar's Academy 1963; chartered, offered first instruction at postsecondary level, moved to present location, and adopted present name 1876; awarded first degree (baccalaureate) 1890. *See* Doniver A. Lund, *A Centennial History—1862–1962* (St. Peter, Minn.: Gustavus Adolphus College Press, 1963) for further information.

Institutional Structure: *Governing board:* Board of Trustees. Extrainstitutional representation: 36 trustees, including 2 church officials; institutional representation: president of the college. 3 ex officio. All voting. *Composition of institution:* Administrators 60 men / 48 women. Academic affairs headed by Dean of College. Management/business/finances directed by vice president for business affairs. Full-time instructional faculty 170. Academic governance body, Faculty Senate, meets an average of 12 times per year.

Calendar: Semesters (4-1-4 plan). Academic year Sept. to May. Freshmen admitted Sept., Jan., Feb., June. Degrees conferred and formal commencement May.

Characteristics of Freshmen: 77 % of applicants admitted. 32% of applicants admitted and enrolled.

22% (143 students) submitted SAT scores; 98% (644 students) submitted ACT scores. *25th percentile*: SAT Verbal 550, SAT Math 560; ACT Composite 23, ACT English 22, ACT Math 23. *75th percentile*: SAT Verbal 670, SAT Math 670; ACT Composite 28, ACT English 29, ACT Math 28.

79% of entering freshmen expected to graduate within 5 years. 80% of freshmen from Minnesota. Freshmen from 31 states and 3 foreign countries.

Admission: Rolling decisions begin on Nov. 20 for applicants who have completed their file by Nov. 1, Process continues each month through April. CSS profile is used for those who wish an early financial aid decision. No application fee. All admitted students must respond by May 1. *Requirements:* Either graduation from accredited secondary school with 12 units which must include 3 English, 3 mathematics, 3 social studies, 2 natural science; or GED. 2 additional units in a foreign language recommended. *Entrance tests:* College Board SAT or ACT composite. *For transfer students:* 2.4 minimum GPA.

College credit and advanced placement for postsecondary-level work completed in secondary school. Tutoring available.

Degree Requirements: 32 courses plus at least 2 January term courses. 2.0 GPA; 2 years in residence, including the senior year; 3 course writing requirement; general education requirements by one of two curricula.

Fulfillment of some degree requirements and exemption from some beginning courses possible by passing departmental examinations; or College Board APP (score of 4). *Grading system:* A–F; pass-fail; incomplete.

Distinctive Educational Programs: Curriculum II, an integrated studies approach to general education open to 10% of students. Cooperative education. Dual-degree program in engineering with Minnesota State University and University of Minnesota. Cooperative baccalaureate program in nursing with St. Olaf College. Interdepartmental/interdisciplinary programs in Japanese studies, classics, criminal justice, Latin American studies, Russian studies, Scandinavian studies. Preprofessional programs in dentistry, engineering, medicine, ministry, pharmacy, physical therapy, veterinary medicine. Individual majors. Academic assistantships. Study abroad includes institutionally arranged programs in England at Exeter University; Japan at Kansai University of Foreign Studies, Sweden at Vaxjo University College, Mora, Boras, and Upsala Universities, Germany at University of Tubingen. Also available through Beaver College (PA) program in England; through American University of Rome in Rome; through Saint Louis University (MO) in Madrid; through Millersville State College (PA) in Marburg, Germany; through Wayne State University (MI) in Munich. Also through Institute of European Studies; through Associated Colleges of the Midwest at the University of Poona, India; the University of Zagreb, Yugoslavia; and in Israel in cooperation with the University of Haifa. Scandinavian seminars in Denmark, Finland, Norway, Sweden. Foreign study may be individually arranged. Cross-registration with Mankato State University.

ROTC: Army in cooperation with Minnesota State University.

Degrees Conferred: 588 *baccalaureate:* area and ethnic studies 9; biological/life sciences 59; business/marketing 83; communications/communication technologies 15; computer and information sciences 12; education 56; English 28; foreign languages and literature 28; health professions and related sciences 24; mathematics 20; natural resources/environmental science 16; parks and recreation 10; philosophy/religion/theology 19; physical sciences 38; protective services/public administration 13; psychology 60; social sciences and history 147; visual and performing arts 42.

Fees and Other Expenses: *Full-time tuition per academic year 2004–05:* $22.590. *Fees:* $365. *Room and board per academic year:* $5,810.

Financial Aid: Gustavus Adolphus College offers a direct lending program. Aid from institutionally generated funds is provided on the basis of academic merit, financial need, other considerations.

Financial aid to full-time, first-time undergraduate students: need-based scholarships/grants totaling $18,392,079, self-help $8,696,139, parent loans $212,719; non-need-based scholarships/grants totaling $4,726,608, self-help $5,660,633, parent loans $1,632,470.

Departments and Teaching Staff: *Professors 59, associate professors 62, assistant professors 51, instructors 24, part-time faculty 65.*

Total instructional faculty: 235 (full-time 182, part-time 53; women 92, men 143; members of minority groups 18). Total faculty with doctorate, first-professional, or other terminal degree: 161. Student-to-faculty ratio: 13:1. *Faculty development:* $450,000 in grants for research. 16 faculty members awarded sabbaticals 2004–05.

Enrollment: Total enrollment 2,577. Undergraduate full-time 1,093 men / 1,449 women, part-time 15m / 20w. *Transfer students:* in-state 28; from out-of-state 9.

Characteristics of Student Body: *Ethnic/racial makeup:* number of Black non-Hispanic: 26; American Indian or Alaska Native: 7; Asian or Pacific Islander: 104; Hispanic: 34; White non-Hispanic: 2,335; unknown: 7.

International Students: 31 nonresident aliens enrolled fall 2004. 7 students from Europe, 14 Asia, 2 Central and South America, 6 Africa, 2 Canada. Programs available to aid students whose native language is not English: social, cultural, financial. English as a Second Language Program. Financial aid specifically designated for international students: scholarships available annually to qualifying students.

Student Life: On-campus residence halls house 90% of student body. All residence halls are coed. *Intercollegiate athletics:* men only: baseball, basketball, football, golf, hockey, soccer, swimming, tennis, track, women only: basketball, golf, gymnastics, soccer, softball, swimming, tennis, track, volleyball. *Special regulations:* Cars permitted for all but freshmen. Residence hall visitation from 10:30am to 1am daily. *Special services:* Medical services, shuttle service to Minneapolis-St. Paul. *Student publications, radio:* Firethorn, a quarterly literary magazine; *Gustavian Weekly*, a newspaper; *Gustavian Yearbook*. Radio station KGSM broadcasts only on campus 105 hours per week. *Surrounding community:* St. Peter population 10,000. Minneapolis-St. Paul, 65 miles from campus, is nearest metropolitan area. Served by airport 6 miles from campus.

Library Collections: 288,695 volumes including bound books, serial backfiles, electronic documents, and government documents not in separate collections. Online catalog. Current serial subscriptions: 996 paper; 35,480 microform units. 16,623 recordings. 25 computer work stations. Students have fee-based access to online services; access to the

Most important special holdings include Lutheran Church Collection; Mettetal music; college archives.

Buildings and Grounds: Campus area 330 acres. *New buildings:* Mattson Hall completed 2005; residence hall for 190 students completed 2005.

Chief Executive Officer: Dr. James L. Peterson, President.

Address admission inquiries to Mark Anderson, Dean of Admissions.

Hamline University

1536 Hewitt Avenue
St. Paul, Minnesota 55104-1285
Tel: (612) 523-2800   **E-mail:** admis@hamline.edu
Fax: (651) 523-2458   **Internet:** www.hamline.edu

Institution Description: Hamline University is a private, nonprofit university affiliated with the United Methodist Church. *Enrollment:* 4,487. *Degrees awarded:* Baccalaureate, master's, doctorate, first-professional (law).

Member of Association of American Colleges, American Council on Education, Associated Colleges of the Twin Cities (ACTC), Minnesota Private College Council (MPCC), Higher Education Consortium for Urban Affairs, Inc. (HECUA), Upper Midwest Association for Intercultural Education.

Accreditation: *Regional:* NCA.*Professional:* law, music, teacher education

History: Established, chartered, and offered first instruction at postsecondary level 1854; awarded first degree (baccalaureate) 1859; established School of Law 1972; Graduate School (Master of Arts) established 1980. *See* David

Johnson, *Hamline University, A History* (St. Paul: North Central Publishing Co., 1980) for further information.

Institutional Structure: *Governing board:* The Trustees of Hamline University. Extrainstitutional representation: 40 trustees, bishop of Minnesota area of the United Methodist Church; institutional representation: president of the university. 40 voting. *Composition of institution:* Academic affairs headed by vice president for academic affairs. Management/business/finances directed by vice president for finance/administration. Full-time instructional faculty 85 men / 95 women. Academic governance bodies, CLA and Law faculties, meet an average of 8 times per year.

Calendar: Semesters (4-1-4 plan). Academic year Sept. to May. Freshmen may enter fall or spring. Degrees conferred at formal commencement May. Summer session of 4 terms from early June to late July.

Characteristics of Freshmen: 78% of applicants admitted. 25% of applicants admitted and enrolled.

18% (82 students) submitted SAT scores; 94% (421 students) submitted ACT scores. *25th percentile:* SAT Verbal 540, SAT Math 500; ACT Composite 21, ACT English 20, ACT Math 19. *75th percentile:* SAT Verbal 635, SAT Math 630; ACT Composite 27, ACT English 28, ACT Math 27.

67% of entering freshmen expected to graduate within 5 years. 84% of freshmen from Minnesota. Freshmen from 24 states and 28 foreign countries.

Admission: Rolling admissions plan. Priority deadline for regular decision is March 1. Applications accepted after March 1. Early action available. *Requirements:* Recommend graduation from accredited secondary school with 16 units which should include 4 English, 2 in a foreign language, 3 mathematics, 4 social studies, 3 laboratory science; GED accepted. *Entrance tests:* College Board SAT or ACT composite. For foreign students TOEFL. *For transfer students:* 2.0 minimum GPA; from 4-year accredited institution maximum transfer credit limited only by residence requirement; from 2-year accredited institution 96 quarter hours (64 semester hours) maximum transfer credit.

College credit and advanced placement for postsecondary-level work completed in secondary school.

Degree Requirements: 32 courses; 2.0 GPA; 2 years in residence; core course requirements. *Grading system:* A - F; withdraw (carries time limit).

Distinctive Educational Programs: Work-experience programs, including internships and field experience. Evening classes. Accelerated degree programs leading to baccalaureate and first-professional degrees, in cooperation with School of Law. Dual-degree program in engineering with University of Minnesota. Interdisciplinary undergraduate programs in East Asian studies, environmental studies, Latin American studies, Russian area studies, urban studies; graduate program in liberal arts. Facilities for independent research, including honors programs, individual majors, tutorials, independent study. Preprofessional programs in dentistry, medicine. Institutionally sponsored study abroad in Brazil, England, France, Germany, Japan, China, Spain, Columbia, Ecuador, Brazil, Jamaica, Kenya, India. Overseas student teaching assignments primarily for education majors. Study abroad in various countries through HECUA or by individual arrangement. Cross-registration through ACTC. *Other distinctive programs:* Continuing education for credit and enrichment. English as a Second Language through on-campus English Language Service.

ROTC: Air Force in cooperation with University of St. Thomas.

Degrees Conferred: 504 *baccalaureate*; 321 *master's*; 4 *doctorate*. Bachelor's degrees awarded in top five disciplines: social sciences and history 129; business/marketing 56; psychology 56; English 36; protective services/public administration 32. *First-professional:* law 160.

Fees and Other Expenses: *Full-time tuition per academic year 2004–05:* undergraduate $21,820; graduate tuition/fees vary by program. *Room and board per academic year:* $6,536.

Financial Aid: Aid from institutionally generated funds is provided on the basis of academic merit, financial need.

Financial aid to full-time, first-time undergraduate students: need-based scholarships/grants totaling $10,059,670; self-help $5,477,655; non-need-based scholarships/grants totaling $9,032,491, self-help $5,588,952, parent loans $1,133,075.

Departments and Teaching Staff: *Total instructional faculty:* 433 (full-time 150, part-time 253; women 239, men 94; members of minority groups 37). Total full-time faculty with doctorate, first-professional, or other terminal degree: 153. Student-to-faculty ratio: 14:1.

Enrollment: Total enrollment 4,487. Undergraduate full-time 721 men / 1,186 women, part-time 28m / 58w; first-professional full-time 217, / 295w, part-time 93m / 106w; graduate full-time 174m / 299w, part-time 259m / 1,051w.

Characteristics of Student Body: *Ethnic/racial makeup:* number of Black non-Hispanic: 82; American Indian or Alaska Native: 12; Asian or Pacific Islander: 119; Hispanic: 37; White non-Hispanic: 1,523, unknown: 62.

International Students: 208 nonresident aliens enrolled fall 2004. Programs available to aid students whose native language is not English: social, cultural.

English as a Second Language Program. No financial aid specifically designated for international students.

Student Life: On-campus residence halls and selected residential properties house nearly 50% of the student body. Housing accommodations are coeducational and include undergraduates, fraternities, sororities, graduate and law students. *Intercollegiate athletics:* men only: baseball, basketball, cross-country, football, hockey, soccer, swimming, tennis, track, wrestling; women only: basketball, cross-country, gymnastics, soccer, softball, swimming, tennis, track, volleyball. *Special regulations:* Cars permitted without restrictions. *Special services:* Study Resource Center, medical services, intercampus bus between member schools of ACTC. *Student publications: The Oracle,* student newspaper (first published in 1888); *The Liner,* student yearbook; annual literary magazine. *Student organizations:* undergraduate student council, A capella choir, mixed chorus, jazz band, orchestra, Oratorio Society, intercollegiate debate, PIRG, athletic clubs, departmental groups, service groups, special-interest organizations, honor societies. *Surrounding community:* Minneapolis-St. Paul population over 2 million. Served by mass transit bus system; airport 10 miles from campus; passenger rail service 2 miles from campus.

Publications: *Hamline Law Review* (biannually) first published 1976; *Hamline Review* (annually) first published 1968; *Hamline Journal of Public Law and Policy* (biannually); *Journal of Law and Religion* (biannually).

Library Collections: 556,450 volumes. Access to 3,858 periodicals. Online catalog. 2,612 recordings. 130 computer work stations. Students have access to online information retrieval services and the Internet.

Most important special holdings include Burke Library South Asia Collection; Upper Midwest Jewish Historical Society; Brass Rubbings Collection.

Buildings and Grounds: Campus area 44 acres.

Chief Executive Officer: Dr. Larry G. Osnes, President.

Undergraduates address admission inquiries to Steve Bjork, Director of Admission; first-professional students to Director, Law Admissions; graduate inquiries student to Dean of Graduate and Continuing Studies.

School of Law

Degree Programs Offered: *First-professional.*

Admission: Graduation from accredited college or university; LSAT; LSDAS.

Degree Requirements: 88 credit hours; 2.0 GPA.

Departments and Teaching Staff: *Professors 16, associate professors 8, assistant professors 1, instructors 7, part-time faculty 23. Total instructional faculty:* 55. *Degrees held by full-time faculty:* 32 professional degrees.

Distinctive Educational Programs: Federal district court internships. Flexible schedules. Special facilities for using telecommunications in the classroom. Independent study. *Other distinctive programs:* Instruction to secondary school students in practical applications of law through community law program. JD/MAPA dual degree. JD/MBA exchange program.

Luther Seminary

2481 Como Avenue
Saint Paul, Minnesota 55108-1496

Tel: (651) 641-3456   **E-mail:** admissions@luthersem.edu
Fax: (651) 641-3425   **Internet:** www.luthersem.edu

Institution Description: Luther Seminary, formerly known as Luther Northwestern Theological Seminary, is a private institution affiliated with the Evangelical Lutheran Church in America. *Enrollment:* 804. Member of Minnesota Consortium of Theological Schools. *Degrees awarded:* First-professional (master of divinity), master of arts, master of sacred music, master of theology, doctorate (professional), doctor of ministry, doctor of philosophy.

Accreditation: *Regional:* NCA. *National:* ATS. *Professional"* theology

History: Luther Theological Seminary established and offered first instruction at postsecondary level 1869; Northwestern Lutheran Theological Seminary established and offered first instruction at postsecondary level 1920; Luther Theological Seminary and Northwestern Lutheran Seminary merged 1982; present name adopted 1994.

Institutional Structure: *Governing board:* Board of Directors. Representation: 31 directors. *Composition of institution:* Administrators 19 men / 5 women. Academic affairs headed by dean of academic affairs. Finance headed by vice president for finance. Administration headed by vice president for administration. Seminary relations headed by vice president for seminary relations and vice president for advancement. Student services head by dean of students. Full-time instructional faculty 39 men / 9 women. Academic governance body, faculty, meets an average of 10 times a year.

Calendar: Semesters. Academic year Sept. to May. First-professional students admitted Sept., Nov., Mar. Degrees conferred and formal commencement May. Summer session of 2 terms from June to Aug.

Admission: Rolling admissions plan. For fall acceptance, apply no later than May 1. *Requirements:* Graduation from accredited college or university with English, history, social sciences, natural sciences, philosophy, 4 semester hours or 6 quarter hours Greek; Minimum 2.8 GPA. *For transfer students:* Consideration given on an individual basis.

Degree Requirements: *For all first-professional degree:* 30 courses; no more than 3 marginal grades overall, senior year in residence; core curriculum. *Grading system:* A–F; Pass-marginal-fail.

Distinctive Educational Programs: Work-experience programs. Evening classes. Online courses. Study abroad in Germany, Hong Kong, India, Korea, Mexico, Norway, Pakistan, Zimbabwe. Islamic Studies; Christian Lay Ministry; Cross-cultural Christian Education; Youth and Family Ministry; Ministry with the Aged; M.S.M. degree with St. Olaf College; Ph.D. degree in bible, history/theology, pastoral care/counseling. Credit and noncredit continuing education. Lay School of theology.

Degrees Conferred: 74 *first-professional:* master of divinity; 37 *master's:* theology; 8 *doctorate:* ministerial studies/theology.

Fees and Other Expenses: *Full-time tuition per academic year 2004–05:* Contact the seminary for current tuition/fees/housing costs.

Financial Aid: Institutional funding is based on academic merit, financial need. Institution has a Program Participation Agreement with the U.S. Department of Education for eligible students to receive Pell Grants and, depending upon agreement, other federal aid.

Departments and Teaching Staff: Bible *professors* 12, *associate professors* 2, *assistant professors* 1, *instructors* 0; Church history 4, 1, 0, 0; systematic theology 4, 4, 0, 1; leadership (pastoral care, Christian education, homiletics, worship) 7, 2, 0, 0.

Total instructional faculty: 38. Degrees held by full-time faculty: doctorate 93%, master's 100%, professional 91%. 95% hold terminal degrees.

Enrollment: Total enrollment 804 (52.6% men, 47.4% women).

Characteristics of Student Body: *Ethnic/racial makeup:* Black non-Hispanic: 1.4%; Asian or Pacific Islander: .4%; Hispanic: .4%; White non-Hispanic: 51.6%; unknown: 43.3%.

International Students: 24 nonresident aliens enrolled fall 2004. Students from Europe, Asia, Central and South America, Africa, Canada. Programs available to aid students whose native language is not English: social, cultural, financial. English as a Second Language Program. Financial aid specifically designated for international students: variable number of scholarships available annually.

Student Life: On-campus residence halls for single students. On-campus apartments for married students with families. 50% of student body lives on campus. *Surrounding community:* Minneapolis-St. Paul area population 2.5 million. Served by airport 10 miles from campus; rail service 3 miles from campus.

Publications: *The Concord*, a biweekly newspaper; *The Luther Seminary Story*, magazine published periodically; *Word & World*, a quarterly theological journal.

Library Collections: 230,000 volumes. Online catalog. Current serial subscriptions: 778 paper. 101,000 microforms; 2,940 recordings; 21 compact discs; 3 CD-ROMS. 11 computer work stations. Students have access to online information retrieval services and the Internet.

Most important special holdings include Doving Hymnal Collection; Tanner Catechism Collection; Early Lutherana; Lutheran Brotherhood Reformation Research Library (16th-century imprints).

Buildings and Grounds: Campus area 50 acres.

Chief Executive Officer: David L. Tiede, President.

Address admission inquiries to Ronald Olson, Director of Admissions.

Macalester College

1600 Grand Avenue
St. Paul, Minnesota 55105-1899
Tel: (651) 696-6000   **E-mail:** admissions@macalester.edu
Fax: (651) 696-6689   **Internet:** www.macalester.edu

Institution Description: Macalester College is a private college affiliated with the Presbyterian Church (U.S.A.). *Enrollment:* 1,900. *Degrees awarded:* Baccalaureate.

Member of Associated Colleges of the Midwest (ACM), Associated Colleges of the Twin Cities (ACTC).

Accreditation: *Regional:* NCA. *Professional:* music

History: Incorporated as Baldwin School 1853; changed name to Baldwin University 1864; adopted present name 1874; offered first instruction at postsecondary level 1885; awarded first degree (baccalaureate) 1889; admitted women 1893.

Institutional Structure: *Governing board:* Macalester College Board of Trustees. Extrainstitutional representation: 28 trustees, 24 of whom are Alumni Trustees; 22 Honorary members. Institutional representation: 1 administrator. 28 voting. *Composition of institution:* Administrators 9 men / 1 woman. Academic affairs headed by dean of faculty and provost. Management/business/finance directed by treasurer. Full-time instructional faculty 147. Academic governance body, the faculty, meets an average of 8 times per year.

Calendar: Semesters. Academic year Sept. to May. Freshmen admitted Sept. Degrees conferred May. Formal commencement May. No summer session.

Characteristics of Freshmen: 39% of applicants admitted. 28% of applicants admitted and enrolled.

83% (403 students) submitted SAT scores; 52% (255 students) submitted ACT scores. *25th percentile:* SAT Verbal 640, SAT Math 620; ACT Composite 28. *75th percentile:* SAT Verbal 740, SAT Math 710; ACT Composite 32.

77% of entering freshmen expected to graduate within 5 years. 18% of freshmen from Minnesota. Freshmen from 43 states and 43 foreign countries.

Admission: For fall acceptance, apply by Jan. 15. Apply by Nov. 15 and Jan. 13 for early decision; need not limit application to Macalester. Early acceptance available. *Requirements:* Graduation from accredited secondary school. Recommend 4 units in English, 3 in a foreign language, 3 history or social studies, 3 mathematics, and 3 laboratory science, some honors or advanced secondary school courses where available. *Entrance tests:* College Board SAT or ACT composite. *For transfer students:* Minimum GPA varies depending on institution and course of study; 16 courses maximum transfer credit; from accredited 2-year institutions 3.0 minimum GPA.

Macalester College credit for college-level coursework completed prior to high school graduation may be granted if the course was not offered toward the partial fulfillment of the requirements for the high school diploma. Tutoring available.

Degree Requirements: 128 credit hours; 2.0 cumulative GPA, 4 semesters in residence, distribution requirements.

Distinctive Educational Programs: Women's and Gender Studies. Dual-degree programs in engineering with Washington University (St. Louis) and the University of Minnesota, nursing with Rush University (Chicago), architecture with Washington University (St. Louis). Interdisciplinary programs in East Asian studies, Japan studies, law and society, Soviet and East European studies, urban studies. Preprofessional programs in law, medicine; may be individually arranged. Facilities and programs for independent research, including honors programs, individual majors, tutorials, preceptorships. Study abroad through Macalester program in Germany; in cooperation with Miyagi University; Tubingen, Germany, in cooperation with Eberhard-Karls University; Prague, Czech Republic, in cooperation with Charles University; Scotland in cooperation with Stirling University, Edinburgh University and Glasgow University; and in Germany and in Vienna, Austria, in cooperation with ACTC; immunology study at the University of Munich, Germany; business studies in Japan (CIEE) and Denmark (DIS). Foreign study programs available through ACM, including Arts programs in Florence, Italy, and in London, England; Chinese studies in Hong Kong; Tropical Field Research in Costa Rica; Japan studies in Tokyo at Waseda University; studies in Zimbabwe. Urban studies abroad available through HECUA's Scandinavian Urban Studies Program and South American Urban Semester. Study-travel in varying countries through Student Project for Amity Among Nations. Interterm travel through ACM, including geology in the Rocky Mountains (CO); humanities program at the Newberry Library in Chicago (IL); Oak Ridge (TN) science semester; urban studies and education, and arts programs in Chicago; summer program Wilderness Field Station (MN). Programs available through HECUA in the Twin Cities area. Cross-registration with Minneapolis College of Art and Design and with other member institutions of the Associated Colleges of the Twin Cities (ACTC). First-year classes of 16 or fewer students with teacher serving as advisor to students.

ROTC: Air Force in cooperation with University of St. Thomas; Army and Navy in cooperation with University of Minnesota.

Degrees Conferred: 428 *baccalaureate:* area and ethnic studies 16; biological/life sciences 35; communications/communication technologies 10; computer and information sciences 23; English 27; foreign languages and literature 30; interdisciplinary studies 27; liberal arts/general studies 3; mathematics 14; natural resources/environmental science 9; philosophy/religion/theology 23; physical sciences 23; psychology 47; social sciences and history 112; visual and performing arts 29.

Fees and Other Expenses: *Full-time tuition per academic year 2005–06:* $28,474. *Fees:* $168. *Room per academic year:* $4,084. *Board per academic year:* $3,774.

Financial Aid: Aid from institutionally generated funds is provided on the basis of academic merit, financial need.

Financial aid to full-time, first-time undergraduate students: need-based scholarships/grants totaling $23,415,342, self-help $6,765,241; non-need-based scholarships/grants totaling $838,927, self-help $1,387,031, parent loans $1,622,795.

Departments and Teaching Staff: *Total instructional faculty:* 216 (full-time 151, part-time 65; women 102, men 114; members of minority groups 44). Total faculty with doctorate, first-professional, or other terminal degree: 181. Student-to-faculty ratio: 11:1. Degrees held by full-time faculty: doctorate 88%, master's 11%, baccalaureate 1%. 93% hold terminal degrees. *Faculty development:* $1,212,491 in grants for research. 27 faculty members awarded sabbaticals 2004–05.

Enrollment: Total enrollment 1,900. Undergraduate full-time 810 men / 1,037 women, part-time 22m / 31w. *Transfer students:* in-state 6; from out-of-state 9.

Characteristics of Student Body: *Ethnic/racial makeup:* number of Black non-Hispanic: 63; American Indian or Alaska Native: 17; Asian or Pacific Islander: 120; Hispanic: 53; White non-Hispanic: 1,358. *Age distribution:* number under 18: 50; 18–19: 859; 20–21: 835; 22–24: 141; 25–29: 9; 30–34: 3; 35–39: 2; 40–49: 1.

International Students: 258 nonresident aliens enrolled fall 2004. Students from Europe, Asia, Central and South America, Africa, Canada, Australia, New Zealand. No programs available to aid students whose native language is not English. Some financial aid available for qualifying international students.

Student Life: On-campus residence halls for both sexes house 66% of student body. 2% housed in language and cultural houses. *Intercollegiate athletics:* men only: baseball, basketball, cross-country, football, golf, soccer, swimming, tennis, track; women only: basketball, soccer, cross-country, softball, swimming, tennis, track, volleyball; cross-country skiing for both men and women. *Special services:* Learning Center, counseling and medical services. *Student publications, radio: Chanter,* a biannual literary magazine; *Focal Point,* a biannual political magazine; *MacWeekly,* a newspaper; *Include,* an international journal; *Happy Friendly Flower,* humorous journal; *Query,* issues journal; *Muse,* feminist journal; *JaMaa,* minority concerns opinion journal. Radio station WMCN broadcasts 148 hours per week. *Surrounding community:* St. Paul population 2.5 million. Served by mass transit system; airport 5 miles from campus; passenger rail service 4 miles from campus.

Library Collections: 389,262 volumes including bound books, serial backfiles, electronic documents, and government documents not in separate collections. Online catalog. Current serial subscriptions: 971 paper and microform; 763 via electronic access. 50 computer work stations. Students have access to the Internet at no charge. Total 2004–05 budget for books and materials: $1,000,000.

Most important special holdings include Sinclair Lewis Collection; Edward D. Neill Collection; Robert Frost Collection.

Buildings and Grounds: Campus area 50 acres. *New buildings:* Campus Center completed 2001.

Chief Executive Officer: Dr. Brian C. Rosenberg, President.

Address admission inquiries to Office of Admissions.

Metropolitan State University

700 East Seventh Street
St. Paul, Minnesota 55106-5000

Tel: (651) 793-1212   **E-mail:** admissions@metrostate.edu
Fax: (651) 793-1310   **Internet:** www.metrostate.edu

Institution Description: Metropolitan State University is a four-year university offering baccalaureate degrees in over 30 majors. Master's programs are offered in business administration, management, nursing, and technical communications. *Enrollment:* 6,516. *Degrees awarded:* Baccalaureate, master's.

Accreditation: *Regional:* NCA.

History: Established and chartered 1971; offered first instruction at postsecondary level 1972; awarded first degree (baccalaureate) 1973; adopted present name 1975; offered first baccalaureate nursing instruction 1982; first B.A.N. degree awarded 1983; first graduate instruction offered 1985; first master's degree awarded 1985.

Institutional Structure: *Composition of institution:* Administrators 7 men / 5 women. Academic affairs headed by provost; student affairs headed by vice president; administrative affairs headed by vice president; public affairs headed by assistant vice president. Four colleges: College of Arts and Science, College of Professional and Community Studies, College of Management, First College. Two schools: Law Enforcement and Nursing. Academic governance though VP Council, faculty, staff, and professional administrator organizations.

Calendar: Semesters. Academic year July 1 to June 30. Summer session. Formal commencements Jan., June.

Admission: Rolling admissions, students admitted daily. For freshmen: high school graduation or GED; rank in the upper one-half of the graduating class or score above the national median on any one of the standardized admission tests (ACT preferred). For transfer students: completed 24 acceptable quarter credits or 16 semester credits at an accredited college or university.

College credit awarded for postsecondary work completed in secondary school, CLEP, other standardized tests; military credit based on ACE *2006 Guide to the Evaluation of Educational Experiences in the Armed Services.* Requirements for the Master of Management and Administration are that applicants have a baccalaureate degree in any field, have equivalent knowledge through courses, independent study, or experience in macroeconomics, microeconomics, financial accounting I and II, and statistics. The GMAT is required. Admission to the Collaborative Master of Science in Nursing requires submission of all graduate and undergraduate transcripts, verification of a baccalaureate degree from a regionally-accredited college or university. GRE scores or MAT scores and information required of international students, if appropriate.

Degree Requirements: 120–124 semester credits. At least 40 credits must be completed at the upper division level and at least 30 credits must be completed through Metropolitan State. Distribution requirements in the major and in personal education/liberal studies must be met.

Distinctive Educational Programs: Each student in First College designs own plan, identifying educational goals, competencies to be acquired and learning strategies to be used (courses, independent study, internships, or evaluation of experiential learning). Social Work students complete two internships. One must be completed in a multicultural setting. The Bachelor of Science in Nursing is designed for registered nurses from associate degree and diploma programs who are interested in pursuing a bachelor's in nursing.

Degrees Conferred: 1,008 *baccalaureate:* area and ethnic studies 4; biological/life sciences 14; business/marketing 334; communications/communication technologies 26; computer and information sciences 84; education 14; English 56; health professions and related sciences 41; interdisciplinary studies 69; liberal arts/general studies 10; mathematics 4; philosophy/religion/theology 31 protective services/public administration 134; psychology 70; social sciences and history 29; trade and industry 10; visual and performing arts 6. 141 *master's:* business/marketing 105; English 12; health professions and related clinical sciences 2; protective services/public administration 21; psychology 1.

Fees and Other Expenses: *Full-time tuition per academic year 2004–05:* undergraduate resident $4,140, nonresident $8,280; graduate resident $4,180, nonresident $4,348. *Other fees:* $252. No campus housing.

Financial Aid: Aid from institutionally generated funds is provided on the basis of academic merit, financial need.

Financial aid to full-time, first-time undergraduate students: need-based scholarships/grants totaling $4,971,335, self-help $18,171,916, parent loans $15,727; tuition waivers $101,574.

Departments and Teaching Staff: *Professors 33, associate professors 41, assistant professors 39, part-time faculty 304.*

Total instructional faculty: 422 (full-time 118, part-time 304; women 199, men 223; members of minority groups 65). Student-to-faculty ratio: 17:1. Degrees held by full-time faculty: doctorate 69%, master's 27%, baccalaureate 1%, professional 3%. 74% hold terminal degrees.

Enrollment: Total enrollment 6,516. Undergraduate full-time 796 men / 1,152 women, part-time 1,526m / 2,427w; graduate full-time 105m / 129w, part-time 168m / 213w.

Characteristics of Student Body: *Ethnic/racial makeup:* number of Black non-Hispanic: 519; American Indian or Alaska Native: 60; Asian or Pacific Islander: 410; Hispanic: 99; White non-Hispanic: 3,176; 1,524 unknown: *Age distribution:* number under 18: 26; 18–19: 126; 20–21: 363; 22–24: 954; 25–29: 1,171; 30–34: 772; 35–39: 502; 40–49: 808; 50–64: 300; 65 and over: 8.

International Students: 138 nonresident aliens enrolled fall 2004. Programs available to aid students whose native language is not English: English as a Second Language Program. No financial aid specifically designated for international students.

Student Life: No on-campus housing. *Surrounding community:* Minneapolis-St. Paul population 2,300,000. Area served by mass transit, scheduled airlines, rail, and bus.

Library Collections: Students use the libraries of other schools in the state university and community college systems and of the University of Minnesota.

Buildings and Grounds: The university administration is housed in 2 centers (St. Paul and Minneapolis). Classes held throughout Twin Cities area.

Chief Executive Officer: Dr. Wilson Bradshan, President.

Address admission inquiries to Rosa Rodriguez, Director of Admissions.

Minneapolis College of Art and Design

2501 Stevens Avenue South
Minneapolis, Minnesota 55404
Tel: (612) 874-3700   **E-mail:** admissions@mcad.edu
Fax: (612) 874-3704   **Internet:** www.mcad.edu

Institution Description: Minneapolis College of Art and Design is a private, independent, nonprofit college. *Enrollment:* 694. *Degrees awarded:* Baccalaureate, master's.
Member of the consortium Union of Independent Colleges of Art.

Accreditation: *Regional:* NCA. *Professional:* art

History: Chartered 1883; established as Minneapolis School of Art and offered first instruction at postsecondary level 1886; awarded first degree (baccalaureate) 1950; adopted present name 1966.

Institutional Structure: Extrainstitutional representation: 60 trustees. 14 ex officio. 60 voting. *Composition of institution:* Administrators 4 men / 3 women. Academic affairs headed by dean of faculty. Management directed by president, vice president of administration, dean of faculty. Full-time instructional faculty 48. Academic governance body, College Assembly, meets an average of 10 times per year.

Calendar: Semesters. Academic year early Sept. to mid-May. Freshmen admitted Aug., Jan., June. Degrees conferred May, Dec. Formal commencement May. Summer session from mid-June to mid-July.

Characteristics of Freshmen: 316 applicants (153 men, 163 women). 76% of applicants admitted. 40% of admitted students enrolled full-time.

45% of entering freshmen expected to graduate within 5 years. 56% of freshmen from Minnesota. Freshmen from 17 states and 12 foreign countries.

Admission: Rolling admissions plan. For fall acceptance, apply no later than July 31. *Requirements:* Either graduation from accredited secondary school or GED. Recommend 2 or more units in art, related subjects; personal interview. Portfolio strongly recommended. Minimum 2.0 GPA. Lowest acceptable secondary school class standing 50th percentile. *Entrance tests:* College Board SAT or ACT composite. For foreign students TOEFL. *For transfer students:* 2.0 minimum GPA; from 4-year accredited institution 102 hours maximum transfer credit; from 2-year accredited institution 66 hours. Transfer of studio credits based on portfolio assessment.

College credit for postsecondary-level work completed in secondary school. College credit and advanced placement for extrainstitutional learning (life experience) on basis of portfolio assessment. Noncredit developmental courses offered during regular academic year.

Degree Requirements: 120 credit hours; 2.0 GPA; senior year in residence; distribution requirements; portfolio review; internship requirement. *Grading system:* A–F; withdraw (carries time limit).

Distinctive Educational Programs: Internships. Evening classes. Special facilities for using telecommunications in the classroom. Interdisciplinary programs in fine arts, design. Facilities and programs for independent research, including individual majors, independent study. Study abroad by individual arrangement. Cross-registration through consortium. Student exchange program with Macalester College; Nova Scotia College of Art and Design (Canada); Philadelphia College of Art. *Other distinctive programs:* Student-at-large program for nonmatriculating students.

Degrees Conferred: 11 *baccalaureate:* visual and performing arts; 15 *master's:* visual and performing arts.

Fees and Other Expenses: *Full-time tuition per academic year 2004–05:* $23,910. *Books and supplies:* $1,800. *Room and board per academic year:* $5,500.

Financial Aid: Aid from institutionally generated funds is provided on the basis of academic merit, financial need. Financial assistance is available in the form of Pell Grants, College Work-Study, Veterans Administration Benefits, National Direct Student Loans, Supplemental Education Opportunity Grants (SEOG), Stafford Loans, other federal aid programs.

Departments and Teaching Staff: *Total instructional faculty:* 83. Student-to-faculty ratio: 11:1. Degrees held by full-time faculty: doctorate 6%, master's 59%, baccalaureate 35%. 75% hold terminal degrees.

Enrollment: Total enrollment 694. Undergraduate 638 (52.4% men, 47.6% women).

Characteristics of Student Body: *Ethnic/racial makeup:* Black non-Hispanic: 2.2%; American Indian or Alaska Native: 1.1%; Asian or Pacific Islander: 3.1%; Hispanic: 2.5%; White non-Hispanic: 70.5%; unknown: 20.5%. *Age distribution:* 17–21: 47%; 22–24: 28%; 25–29: 15%; 30–34: 6%; 35–39: 2%; 40–49: 1%.

International Students: 8 nonresident aliens enrolled fall 2004. No programs available to aid students whose native language is not English. No financial aid specifically designated for international students.

Student Life: On-campus residence halls house 27% of student body. Residence halls for both sexes constitute 100% of such space. Housing available for married students. *Special regulations:* Cars permitted without restrictions. *Special services:* Learning Resources Center, medical services. *Surrounding community:* Minneapolis-Saint Paul metropolitan area population over 2 million. Served by mass transit bus system, airport 12 miles from campus, passenger rail service 8 miles from campus.

Library Collections: 62,500 volumes. 850 microforms; 2,100 audiovisual materials; 180 current periodical subscriptions. Online catalog. Students have access to online information retrieval services and the Internet.

Most important special holdings include collections of art books, slide library of art.

Buildings and Grounds: Campus area 7 acres.

Chief Executive Officer: Dr. Michael O'Keefe, President.

Address admission inquiries to William Mullen, Director of Admissions.

Minnesota State University, Mankato

228 Weiking Center
Mankato, Minnesota 56001
Tel: (800) 722-0544   **E-mail:** admissions@mnsu.edu
Fax: (507) 389-2227   **Internet:** www.mnsu.edu

Institution Description: Minnesota State University, Mankato was formerly named Mankato State University. *Enrollment:* 8,319. *Degrees awarded:* Associate, baccalaureate, master's. Specialist certificates also awarded.

Accreditation: *Regional:* NCA. *Professional:* art, athletic training, business, counseling, dental hygiene, engineering, music, nursing, recreation and leisure services, rehabilitation counseling, social work, speech-language pathology, teacher education

History: Established as Mankato State Normal School 1868; offered first instruction at postsecondary level 1917; changed name to Mankato State Teachers College 1921; awarded first degree (baccalaureate) 1927; changed name to Mankato State College 1957; became Mankato State University 1975; adopted present name 1998. *See* Donald B. Youel, *Mankato State College: An Interpretive Essay* (Mankato: Mankato State University, 1968) for further information.

Institutional Structure: *Composition of institution:* Administrators 39. Academic affairs headed by vice president for academic affairs. Management/business/finances directed by vice-president for fiscal affairs. Full-time instructional faculty 485. Academic governance body, faculty and administration, meets an average of 10 times per year.

Calendar: Semesters. Academic year Aug. to May. Degrees conferred Dec., Nay, July. Formal commencement Dec., May.

Characteristics of Freshmen: 87% of applicants accepted. 51% of accepted applicants enrolled.

1% (25 students) submitted SAT scores; 94% (2,044 students) submitted ACT scores. *25th percentile:* SAT Verbal 480, SAT Math 500; ACT Composite 19, ACT English 18, ACT Math 18. *75th percentile:* SAT Verbal 560, SAT Math 600; ACT Composite 23, ACT English 23, ACT Math 24.

51% of entering freshmen expected to graduate within 5 years. 86% of freshmen from Minnesota. Freshmen from 22 states and 1 foreign country.

Admission: Rolling admissions plan. For fall acceptance, apply as early as end of junior year of secondary school, but not later than first day of classes. Early acceptance available. *Requirements:* Either graduation from accredited secondary school or GED. In most cases, secondary school class rank is in top 50%. *Entrance tests:* ACT required. For foreign students TOEFL. *For transfer students:* 2.0 minimum GPA; from 4-year institution 162 quarter hours maximum transfer credit; from 2-year institution 96 quarter hours; correspondence/extension students 15 hours.

College credit and advanced placement for postsecondary-level work completed in secondary school. College credit for extrainstitutional learning on basis of ACE *2006 Guide to the Evaluation of Educational Experiences in the Armed Services.* Tutoring available.

Degree Requirements: *For all associate degrees:* 60 semester hours; 30 of last hours in residence. *For all baccalaureate degrees:* 124 semester hours; 60 hours of last 2 years in residence; 4 physical education courses. *For all undergraduate degrees:* 2.0 GPA; general education requirements.

Fulfillment of some degree requirements and exemption from some beginning courses possible by passing departmental examinations, College Board CLEP, international baccalaureate. *Grading system:* A–F; pass-fail; withdraw (carries penalty, time limit).

Distinctive Educational Programs: *For undergraduates:* Interdisciplinary programs in environmental studies, gerontological studies, ethnic studies, Scandinavian studies, urban studies, women's studies. Preprofessional programs in agriculture, dentistry, engineering, forestry, medicine, mortuary science, pharmacy, veterinary medicine. Honors programs. Study abroad in England, France, Japan, Mexico. *Available to all students:* 25 off-campus centers from 25 to 115 miles away from main institution, including Bloomington, Burnsville, Fairmont, New Ulm, Faribault, and Owatonna. Special facilities for using telecommunications in the classroom. Individual majors. Cross-registration with the Gustavus Adolphus College. *Other distinctive programs:* Continuing education; growing number of Internet courses. Tuition waiver for senior citizens.

ROTC: Army.

Degrees Conferred: 68 *associate;* 1,927 *baccalaureate;* (B); 414 *master's* (M); 55 *post-master's certificates.* Degrees awarded: area and ethnic studies 4 (B), 8 (M); biological and life sciences 36 (B), 6 (M); business 303 (B), 25 (M); communications/communication technologies 38 (B), computer and information science 107 (B), 5 (M); education 279 (B), 304 (M); engineering/engineering technologies 85 (B), 4 (M); English 55 (B), 38 (M); foreign languages and literature 14 (B), 2 (M); health professions and related sciences 132 (B), 37 (M); home economics 37 (B), 1 (M); law/legal studies 10 (B), liberal arts/general studies 7 (B); mathematics 6 (B), 4 (M); natural resources/environmental science 10 (B), 2 (M); parks and recreation 67 (B); physical sciences 10 (B); protective services/public administration 164 (B), 37 (M); psychology 43 (B), 21 (M); social sciences and history 115 (B), 28 (M); trade and industry 31 (B); visual and performing arts 29 (B), 7 (M); other 34 (B), 33 (M).

Fees and Other Expenses: *Full-time tuition per academic year: 2004–05:* undergraduate resident $4,376, nonresident $9,286. Contact the university for graduate tuition/fees. *Required fees:* $712. *Room and board per academic year:* $4,716.

Financial Aid: Aid from institutionally generated funds is provided on the basis of academic merit, financial need, athletic ability, other criteria.

Financial aid to full-time, first-time undergraduate students: need-based scholarships/grants totaling $14,471,469; self-help $28,007,125; non-need-based scholarships/grants totaling $3,091,632, self-help $21,643,133, parent loans $2,082,072, athletic awards $659,536.

Departments and Teaching Staff: *Total instructional faculty:* 696 (full-time 485, part-time 211; women 310, men 386; members of minority groups 37). Student-to-faculty ratio: 23:1. Degrees held by full-time faculty: master's 30%, doctorate 66%, baccalaureate 3%. 59% hold terminal degrees.

Enrollment: Total enrollment 14 153. Undergraduate full-time 5,305 men / 5,926 women, part-time 539m / 696w; graduate full-time 231m / 386w, part-time 410m / 660w.

Characteristics of Student Body: *Ethnic/racial makeup:* number of Black non-Hispanic: 201; American Indian or Alaska Native: 37; Asian or Pacific Islander: 196; Hispanic: 75; White non-Hispanic: 8,033; unknown: 3,218.

International Students: 371 nonresident aliens enrolled fall 2004. Programs available to aid students whose native language is not English: social, cultural, financial. English as a Second Language Program.

Student Life: There are 13 on-campus residence halls and all are coeducational. *Intercollegiate athletics:* men only: baseball, basketball, cross country, football, golf, hockey, swimming, tennis, track and field, wrestling; women only: softball, basketball, cross country, dance team, golf, soccer, swimming, tennis, track and field, volleyball. *Special regulations:* Cars permitted without restrictions; permit required. *Special services:* Learning Resources Center, medical services. *Student publications, radio: Reporter,* a biweekly newspaper; *Minnesota River Review,* the campus literary publication. Radio station KMSU broadcasts 24 hours a day; KRNR broadcasts 116 hours per week. *Surrounding community:* Mankato population 32,000. Minneapolis-St. Paul, 90 miles from campus, is nearest metropolitan area. Served by mass transit bus systems; airport 10 miles from campus.

Library Collections: 1,100,000 volumes. 182,000 government documents; 230,000 microforms units. 26,000 audiovisual materials; 2,500 periodicals. 44,000 recordings. Computer work stations available. Students have access to online information retrieval services and the Internet.

Most important special holdings include Center for Minnesota Studies; music collection; children's literature; map collection.

Buildings and Grounds: Campus area 360 acres. *New buildings:* Andreas Theatre completed 2000; Taylor Center 2000; Indoor Track 2000.

Chief Executive Officer: Richard R. Rush, President.

Undergraduates address admission inquiries to Walt Wolff, Director of Admissions; graduate inquiries to Anthony Filipovitch, Dean of Graduate Studies and Research.

Minnesota State University, Moorhead

1104 7th Avenue South
Moorhead, Minnesota 56563

Tel: (218) 477-2011   **E-mail:** admissions@mstate.edu
Fax: (218) 477-4374   **Internet:** www.mstate.edu

Institution Description: Minnesota State University Moorhead was formerly named Moorhead State University. *Enrollment:* 7,642. *Degrees awarded:* Associate, baccalaureate, master's.

Accreditation: *Regional:* NCA. *Professional:* art, business, construction education, construction technology, industrial technology, music, nursing, nursing education, social work, speech-language pathology, teacher education

History: Established as Moorhead Normal School and chartered 1885; offered first instruction at postsecondary level 1887; awarded first degree (associate) 1890; became 4-year institution and changed name to Moorhead State Teachers College 1921; initiated master's program 1953; changed name to Moorhead State College 1957; changed name to Moorhead State University 1975; adopted present name 2000. *See* Dr. Joseph Kise, *History of Moorhead State College* (Moorhead: Moorhead State College, 1961) for further information.

Institutional Structure: *Composition of institution:* Administrators 14. 15 excluded managers (excluded by bargaining units); 41 mid-managers. Academic affairs headed by vice president for academic affairs. Management/business/finances directed by vice president for administrative affairs. Admissions/counseling/financial aid directed by vice president for student services. Fund-raising/community relations/volunteer leadership headed by vice president for public affairs. Full-time instructional faculty 324. Academic governance body, Academic Policy Advising Committee, meets an average of 15 times per year.

Calendar: Semesters. Academic year Aug. to May. Freshmen admitted Sept., Dec., Mar., June, July. Degrees conferred May, Aug., Nov., Feb. Formal commencement May, Aug. Summer session of 2 terms from June to Aug.

Characteristics of Freshmen: 80% of applicants accepted. 53% of accepted applicants enrolled.

Average secondary school rank men 65th percentile, women 78th percentile, class 75th percentile. Mean ACT composite scores 22.

37% of entering freshmen expected to graduate within 5 years. 35% of freshmen from Minnesota. Freshmen from 35 states.

Admission: Rolling admissions plan. Apply no later than Aug. 7. Early acceptance available. *Requirements:* Either graduation from secondary school or GED. Secondary school rank in top half of class, minimum ACT composite score 21, PSAT of 90, or SAT combined score of 900. Completion of high school preparation standards required. *Entrance tests:* For foreign students TOEFL with score of 500. *For transfer students:* 2.0 minimum GPA; 96 quarter hours maximum transfer credit; vocational-technical students 48 hours; correspondence/extension students 15 hours.

College credit and advanced placement for postsecondary-level work completed in secondary school. College credit for extrainstitutional learning on basis of ACE *2006 Guide to the Evaluation of Educational Experiences in the Armed Services.* Tutoring available. Noncredit remedial courses offered during regular academic year.

Degree Requirements: *For all associate degrees:* 64 semester hours; 32 hours, including 8 of last 12, in residence. *For all baccalaureate degrees:* 128 semester hours; 45 hours, including 8 of last 12, in residence. *For all undergraduate degrees:* 2.0 GPA; general studies requirements. Additional requirements for some programs. Fulfillment of some degree requirements and exemption from some beginning courses possible by passing institutional examinations, College Board CLEP, AP. *Grading system:* A–F; pass-fail; pass-no credit; withdraw (carries time limit).

Distinctive Educational Programs: *For undergraduates:* Work-experience programs. Cooperative preprofessional programs in agriculture, architecture, engineering, geology, home economics, pharmacy leading to degrees awarded by North Dakota State University. Facilities and programs for independent research, including honors programs, individual majors. Institutionally sponsored study abroad in Africa, Asia, Australia, China, Europe, India, South America. EUROSPRING-Oxford Program (one year at Oxford University, England). Off-campus study in U.S. for sophomores and juniors through National Student Exchange Program. *Available to all students:* Cluster colleges. Flexible meeting places and schedules, including off-campus centers, weekend and evening classes. Special facilities for using telecommunications in the classroom. Facilities and programs for independent research, including tutorials, independent study. Cross-registration through consortium. *Other distinctive programs:* Individualized external degree program primarily for adults. New Center for Multidisciplinary Studies offers career-oriented associate degree programs in nontraditional setting. Regional Science Center. Students may pay MSU tuition rates and take courses at Concordia College and North Dakota State University through Tri-College agreement.

ROTC: Army, Air Force in cooperation with North Dakota State University.

Degrees Conferred: 39 *associate;* 979 *baccalaureate:* degrees awarded in top five disciplines include business and management 164, communications 74, education 210, social sciences and history 63, public administration and services 66; 95 *master's:* various disciplines.

Fees and Other Expenses: *Full-time tuition per academic year 2004–05:* undergraduate resident $4,254, nonresident $9,935; graduate resident $4,660, nonresident $7.288. *Room and board per academic year:* $4,340.

Financial Aid: Aid from institutionally generated funds is provided on the basis of academic merit, financial need, athletic ability, other criteria. Institution has a Program Participation Agreement with the U.S. Department of Education for eligible students to receive Pell Grants and, depending upon agreement, other federal aid.

Departments and Teaching Staff: *Professors* 114, *associate professors* 66, *assistant professors* 93, *instructors* 29, *part-time faculty* 151.

Total instructional faculty: 302. Student-to-faculty ratio: 18:1. Degrees held by full-time faculty: baccalaureate 1%, master's 23%, doctorate 70%, professional 1%. 75% hold terminal degrees.

Enrollment: Total enrollment 7,642. Undergraduate 7,211.

Characteristics of Student Body: *Ethnic/racial makeup:* Black non-Hispanic: 42; American Indian Alaska Native 68; Asian or Pacific Islander 45; Hispanic 76; White non-Hispanic 5,838. *Age distribution:* 17–21: 58.2%; 22–24: 20%; 25–29: 8.8%; 30–34: 3.9%; 35–39: 3.6%; 40–49: 4.3%; 50–64: 1%; 65 and over: .2%.

International Students: 96 nonresident aliens enrolled. Students from Europe, Asia, Latin America, Africa, Canada. Programs available to aid students whose native language is not English: social, cultural. No financial aid specifically designated for international students.

Student Life: *Intercollegiate athletics:* men: basketball, cross-country, football, track, wrestling; women: basketball, cross-country, soccer, softball, tennis, track, volleyball. *Special regulations:* Cars must be registered; parking permit required. Residence hall visitation from 8am to 2am. *Special services:* Learning Resources Center, medical services, disabled student services. *Student publications, radio: Advocate,* a weekly newspaper; *Social Science Journal,* an annual scholarly magazine; Radio station KMSC broadcasts 94 hours per week. *Surrounding community:* Moorhead population 35,000. Minneapolis-St. Paul 240 miles from campus, is nearest metropolitan area. Served by mass transit bus system; airport 5 miles from campus; passenger rail service 2 miles from campus.

Library Collections: 370,500 volumes. 174,064 government documents; 51,047 microforms; 1,540 current periodicals. Online catalog. Students have access to online information retrieval services and the Internet.

Buildings and Grounds: Campus area 112 acres. *New buildings:* Science Lab completed 2004.

Chief Executive Officer: Dr. Roland Barden, President.

Address admission inquiries to Director of Admissions.

North Central University

910 Elliott Avenue South
Minneapolis, Minnesota 55404

Tel: (612) 343-4400   **E-mail:** info@northcentral.edu
Fax: (612) 343-4778   **Internet:** www.northcentral.edu

Institution Description: North Central University, formerly named North Central Bible College, is owned and operated by the Minnesota District Council of the Assemblies of God. *Enrollment:* 1,223. *Degrees awarded:* Associate, baccalaureate.

Accreditation: *Regional:* NCA. *National:* ABHE.

History: Established as North Central Bible Institute 1930; became four-year institution 1955; became North Central Bible College 1957; adopted present name 1997.

Calendar: Semesters. Academic year from mid-Sept. to mid-May.

Characteristics of Freshmen: 433 applicants (151 men, 283 women). 85.9% of applicants admitted. 65.9% of admitted students enrolled full-time.

14% (37 students) submitted SAT scores; 89% (222 students) submitted ACT scores. *25th percentile:* SAT I Verbal 480, SAT I Math 450; ACT Composite 19, ACT English 19, ACT Math 18. *75th percentile:* SAT I Verbal 570, SAT I Math 570; ACT Composite 25, ACT English 25, ACT Math 25.

Admission: *Requirements:* Graduation from accredited secondary school. *Entrance tests:* College Board SAT or ACT.

Degree Requirements: 126 credits including 30-credit Biblical Studies core and a 44-credit general education core; internships required; minimum 2.0 GPA.

Degrees Conferred: 3 *associate;* 205 *baccalaureate.* Bachelor's degrees awarded in top five disciplines: theology and ministerial studies 57; education 33; area and ethnic studies 21, business, management, marketing, and related support services 20; multidisciplinary studies 20.

Fees and Other Expenses: *Full-time tuition per academic year 2004–05:* $11,284. *Books and supplies:* $900. *Room and board per academic year:* $4,350.

Financial Aid: Institution has a Program Participation Agreement with the U.S. Department of Education for eligible students to receive Pell Grants and other federal aid. Financial aid to full-time, first-time undergraduate students: 38% received federal grants averaging $2,652; 29% state/local grants averaging $3,193; 96% institutional grants averaging $2,754; 78% received loans averaging $5,447.

Departments and Teaching Staff: *Total instructional faculty:* 64 (35 full-time). 20% hold terminal degrees.

Enrollment: Total enrollment 1,223 (43.1% men, 56.9% women).

Characteristics of Student Body: *Ethnic/racial makeup:* Black non-Hispanic: 4.1%; American Indian or Alaska Native: .4%; Asian or Pacific Islander: 2.5%; Hispanic: 2.1%; White non-Hispanic: 82.3%; unknown: 8.15.

International Students: 48 nonresident aliens enrolled fall 2004.

Library Collections: 72,000 volumes. 40 microform titles; 3,000 recordings/tapes. 385 current periodical subscriptions. Students have access to online information retrieval services and the Internet.

Chief Executive Officer: Dr. Gordon L. Anderson, President.

Address admission inquiries to James Hubert, Director of Admissions.

Northwestern College

3003 Snelling Avenue North
St. Paul, Minnesota 55113-1598

Tel: (651) 631-5100   **E-mail:** admissions@nwc.edu
Fax: (651) 631-5269   **Internet:** www.nwc.edu

Institution Description: Northwestern College is a private, independent, nonprofit Christian college. *Enrollment:* 2,734. *Degrees awarded:* Associate, baccalaureate. Certificates in Bible also awarded.

Member of Council for Christian Colleges and Universities, and Council of Independent Colleges.

Accreditation: *Regional:* NCA.

History: Established as Northwestern Bible and Missionary Training School and offered first instruction at postsecondary level 1902; chartered 1904; changed name to Northwestern Theological Seminary and Training School 1942, to Northwestern Schools-Bible School, College of Liberal Arts, Theological Seminary 1946; awarded first degree (baccalaureate) 1948; changed name to Northwestern Schools-Bible College, College of Liberal Arts, Theological Seminary 1952, to Northwestern College-Bible College, College of Liberal Arts, Theological Seminary 1955; adopted present name 1959.

Institutional Structure: *Governing board:* Northwestern College Board of Trustees. Extrainstitutional representation: 20 trustees; institutional representation: president. 1 ex officio. 21 voting. *Composition of institution:* Administrators 23 men / 11 women. Academic affairs, student services, and computing services headed by provost/vice president for academic affairs. Business/finances, auxiliary services, plant management, and human resources overseen by vice president for business and finance. Full-time instructional faculty 60 men / 30 women. Academic governance body, Academic Policies Committee, meets an average of 9 times per year.

Calendar: Semesters. Academic year Aug. to May. Freshmen admitted Aug., Jan., May. Degrees conferred May, Aug., Dec. Formal commencements May, Dec. Summer session from May to June.

Characteristics of Freshmen: 98% of applicants admitted. 38% of applicants admitted and enrolled.

13% (52 students) submitted SAT scores; 95% (386 students) submitted ACT scores. *25th percentile:* SAT Verbal 530, SAT Math 510; ACT Composite 21; ACT English 20; ACT Math 18. *75th percentile:* SAT Verbal 670, SAT Math 670; ACT Composite 26, ACT English 28, ACT Math 26.

55% of entering freshmen expected to graduate within 5 years. 69% of freshmen from Minnesota. Freshmen from 18 states and 3 foreign countries.

Admission: Rolling admissions plan. Early acceptance available. *Requirements:* Either graduation from accredited secondary school or GED. *Entrance tests:* ACT Composite or SAT I (ACT preferred).

College credit and advanced placement for postsecondary-level work completed in secondary school. College credit for extrainstitutional learning on basis of ACE *2006 Guide to the Evaluation of Educational Experiences in the Armed Services.* Developmental courses offered during regular academic year.

Degree Requirements: *For all associate degrees:* 60 semester hours. *For all baccalaureate degrees:* 125 or more semester hours. *For all degrees:* 2.0 GPA; last 30 semester hours in residence; daily chapel attendance; 1 semester hour physical education; distribution requirements.

Fulfillment of some degree requirements and exemption from some beginning courses possible by passing CLEP, AP, DANTES, and International Baccalaureate Examination. *Grading system:* A–F; withdraw (carries time limit).

Distinctive Educational Programs: Five-year mathematics/engineering dual-degree program in cooperation with University of Minnesota-Twin Cities. Cooperative agreement with William Mitchell College of Law, St. Paul, for summer partnership in law. *Other distinctive programs:* Distance Education Program with Intercultural Ministries major and Bible certificate. Northwestern owns and operates 15 radio stations and a satellite programming service that broadcast programs of an inspirational, educational, and religious nature nationwide. Participates in Council for Christian Colleges and Universities Off-Campus and Study-Abroad Programs: American Studies; China, Latin American, Russian, Middle East Studies Programs; Los Angeles Film Studies Center; Oxford Honors Program. Other study-abroad opportunities available through Jerusalem University College. Summer School.

Degrees Conferred: 13 *associate;* 492 *baccalaureate:* biological/life sciences 14; business/marketing 113; communications/communication technologies 34; education 17; English 15; foreign languages and literature 2; mathematics 4; parks and recreation 2; philosophy/religion/theology 76; psychology 78; social sciences and history 27; visual and performing arts 30.

Fees and Other Expenses: *Full-time tuition per academic year 2004–05:* $18,370. *Room and board per academic year:* $4,020.

Financial Aid: Aid from institutionally generated funds is provided on the basis of academic merit, financial need, musical ability, leadership.

Financial aid to full-time, first-time undergraduate students: need-based scholarships/grants totaling $8,899,038, self-help $6,799,472; non-need-based scholarships/grants totaling $5,611,139, self-help $4,714,673, parent loans $1,683,714.

Departments and Teaching Staff: *Professors* 24, *associate professors* 34, *assistant professors* 28, *instructors* 4, *part-time faculty* 77.

Total instructional faculty: 167 (full-time 90, part-time 77; women 68, men 99; members of minority groups 14). Student-to-faculty ratio: 14:1. Degrees held by full-time faculty: doctorate 67%, master's 26%, baccalaureate 2%, professional 5. 72% hold terminal degrees. *Faculty development:* 8 faculty members awarded sabbaticals 2004–05.

Enrollment: Total enrollment 2,734. Undergraduate full-time 755 men / 1,237 women, part-time 298m / 444w.

Characteristics of Student Body: *Ethnic/racial makeup:* number of Black non-Hispanic: 80; American Indian or Alaska Native: 10; Asian or Pacific Islander: 67; Hispanic: 39; White non-Hispanic: 2,481; 48 unknown: *Age distribution:* number under 18: 350; 18–19: 782; 20–21: 729; 22–24: 294; 25–29: 138; 30–34: 86; 35–39: 90; 40–49: 196; 50–64: 67; 65 and over: 1; unknown: 1.

International Students: 9 nonresident aliens enrolled fall 2004. 2 students from Europe, 2 Asia, 2 Central and South America, 1 Africa. Programs available to aid students whose native language is not English: English as a Second Language. Financial aid specifically designated for undergraduate international students: variable number of scholarships available annually; 8 totaling $64,053 awarded 2004–05.

Student Life: On-campus residence halls house 57% of traditional undergraduate student body. Residence halls for men constitute 36% of such space, for women 64%.*Intercollegiate athletics:* men only: baseball, basketball, cross-country, football, golf, soccer, tennis, indoor and outdoor track; women only: basketball, cross-country, soccer, softball, tennis, indoor and outdoor track, volleyball; coed: golf. *Special regulations:* Freshmen living in college housing are not permitted to have vehicles on campus. Commuters and non-freshmen resident students with vehicle permits may drive and park on campus. Students are asked to exercise discernment about appropriate attire, reflecting consideration for others and personal modesty. Quiet hours from 11pm to 8am. Residence hall visitation from 5pm to 9pm Tues. and Thurs., 5pm to 11pm Fri., 12pm to 11pm Sat., and 12am to 9pm Sun. *Special services:* Academic learning assistance center, career development center, disabilities services office, counseling services, medical services, vans available for transportation to and from school activities. *Student publications, radio: The Column,* a newspaper published biweekly; *Pipeline,* a weekly online information newsletter; *The Scroll,* a yearbook. Radio station WVOE broadcasts by carrier current 30 hours per week. *Surrounding community:* Roseville population 33,69036,000. Served by mass transit bus system; airport 13 miles from campus; passenger rail service 7 miles from campus.

Library Collections: 112,394 volumes. Online catalog. Current serial subscriptions: paper 501; via electronic access 464. 4,334 recordings; 2,102 compact discs; 25 CD-ROMs. 48 computer work stations. Access to online information retrieval services. Total budget for books and materials 2004–05: $178,000.

Most important special collections include archives collection by/about Dr. W.B. Riley and other institutional leaders; circulating religion and theology collection.

Buildings and Grounds: Campus area 102.5 acres. *New buildings:* Mel Johnson Media Center completed 2003.

Chief Executive Officer: Dr. Alan S. Cureton, President.

Address admission inquiries to Kenneth Faffler, Director of Admissions.

Northwestern Health Sciences University

2501 West 84th Street
Bloomington, Minnesota 55431
Tel: (952) 888-4777   **E-mail:** admit@nwhealth.edu
Fax: (952) 888-6713   **Internet:** www.nwhealth.ecu

Institution Description: Northwestern Health Sciences University, formerly known as Northwestern College of Chiropractic, is a private institution. *Enrollment:* 850. *Degrees awarded:* Baccalaureate, first-professional (chiropractic).

Accreditation: *Regional:* NCA. *Professional:* acupuncture, chiropractic education

History: Founded 1941; organized as a nonprofit corporation 1949; moved to present location 1983.

Institutional Structure: *Governing board:* Board of Trustees. Institutional representation: president's cabinet. *Composition of institution:* vice presidents of administrative services, academic affairs, institutional advancement.

Calendar: Trimesters (fall, winter, summer). Academic year Sept. to Aug. Entering students admitted Sept., Jan., Apr.

Admission: Applications due mid-May for Sept. enrollment, mid-Aug. for Jan., mid-Jan. for Apr. enrollment. Transfer students admitted Jan., Apr., Sept. All candidates must meet NWCC and CCE standards: graduation from accredited high school or GED; completion of two academic years (60 semester hours or 90 quarter hours) of college credit toward B.A./B.S. degree. No more than 20 semester hours accepted through CLEP exams. Cumulative overall GPA of at least 2.5; 2.0 GPA in science courses is minimum accepted average. Specific science courses at college level completed (6 semester hours each in biology or zoology with lab; general/inorganic chemistry with lab; organic chemistry with lab; physics with lab; English/communications skills and 15 semester hours in humanities or social sciences and 3 semester hours in psychology. All courses cited must be passed with C or better). Strong, well-rounded liberal arts background recommended. Recent years average acceptance of students with 3.0 GPA or better.

Degree Requirements: *Doctor of Chiropractic degree:* Satisfactory completion of a minimum of 10 trimesters of educational and clinical experience beyond entrance requirements and who are recommended for that degree by college faculty; must complete required course of study, internship and clinical experience, financial obligations to the college; minimum 2.0 GPA; passing grade in every course in curriculum. *For Bachelor of Science in Human Biology degree:* Completion of 134.5 semester (trimester) credits by following certain requirements including enrollment in the NWCC undergraduate curriculum; official transcript with 60 semester hours or 90 quarter hours; minimum 2.0 GPA; (these requirements not conclusive).

Distinctive Educational Programs: Postgraduate Office coordinates academic and educational symposia year-round, including first-time programs on pediatric and geriatric care, institutional (work-place) care, and others. Research groups, including student Research Club. Department of Occupational and Community Health.

Degrees Conferred: 34 *baccalaureate:* biological/life sciences; 29 *master's:* oriental massage 21; acupuncture/massage therapy 8. 151 *first-professional:* chiropractic.

Fees and Other Expenses: *Full-time tuition per academic year 2004–05:* $15,351. *Other fees:* $800.

Financial Aid: Aid from institutionally generated funds is provided on the basis of academic merit, financial need, other considerations. Institution has a Program Participation Agreement with the U.S. Department of Education for eligible students to receive Pell Grants and other federal aid.

Departments and Teaching Staff: *Professors* 13, *associate professors* 27, *assistant professors* 22, *instructors* 7, *part-time faculty* 54.

Total instructional faculty: 123 (full-time 69, part-time 54; women 67, men 56; members of minority groups 123). Total faculty with doctorate, first-professional, or other terminal degree: 82. Student-to-faculty ratio: 7:1. Degrees held by full-time faculty: doctorate 11%, master's 9%, professional 80%. 91% hold terminal degrees.

Enrollment: Total enrollment 843. Undergraduate full-time 5 men / 53 women, part-time 2w; first-professional full-time 376m / 265w, part-time 19m / 18w; graduate full-time 21m / 78w, part-time 2m / 4w.

Characteristics of Student Body: *Ethnic/racial makeup:* number of Black non-Hispanic: 13; American Indian or Alaska Native: 7; Asian or Pacific Islander: 16; Hispanic: 6; White non-Hispanic: 764; unknown: 1. *Age distribution:* number 18–19: 16; 20–21: 34; 22–24: 360; 25–29: 288; 30–34: 53; 35–39: 30; 40–49: 48; 50–64: 14.

International Students: 39 nonresident aliens enrolled fall 2004. 2 students from Europe, 1 Central America, 35 Canada. No programs available to aid students whose native language is not English. No financial aid specifically designated for international students.

Student Life: No on-campus housing; a listing service for housing is available through the admissions office. *Special services:* Health service; social, educational, athletic and individual counseling programs are available for students and their immediate families; graduate placement aid. *Surrounding community:* Campus is located in Bloomington (MN), a suburb of Twin Cities (Minneapolis/St. Paul).

Publications: *Northwestern Today, Northwestern Weekly, Northwestern Naturally, In Touch, Synapse, University Update.*

Library Collections: 16,605 volumes. Online catalog. 348 current journal subscriptions. 1,014 recordings; 47 CD-ROMs. 26 computer work stations. Students have access to online information retrieval services and the Internet.

Most important special holdings include collections on chiropractic, other conservative therapies, and radiology.

Buildings and Grounds: Campus area consists of one building of 190,000 square feet situated on 25 acres.

Chief Executive Officer: Dr. Alfred Traina, President.

Address admission inquiries to William Kuehl, Director of Admissions.

Oak Hills Christian College

1600 Oak Hills Road S.W.
Bemidji, Minnesota 56601-8834
Tel: (218) 751-8670　　**E-mail:** admissions@oakhills.edu
Fax: (218) 751-8825　　**Internet:** www.oakhills.edu

Institution Description: Oak Hills Christian College, formerly known as Oak Hills Bible College, is a nondenominational college. *Enrollment:* 171. *Degrees awarded:* Associate, baccalaureate.

Accreditation: *Regional:* NCA. *National:* ABHE.

History: Established as Oak Hills Christian Training School 1946; became Oak Hills Bible Institute 1959 and Oak Hills Bible College 1985; adopted present name 1997.

Institutional Structure: *Governing board:* Oak Hills Christian College Board of Trustees. Academic affairs headed by dean of education. Student life headed by dean of students.

Calendar: Semesters. Academic year Sept. to May.

Characteristics of Freshmen: 75 applicants (31 men, 44 women). 88% of applicants admitted. 90.9% of admitted students enrolled full-time.

80% (36 students) submitted ACT scores. *25th percentile:* ACT Composite 17. *75th percentile:* ACT Composite 24.

83% of freshmen from Minnesota. Freshmen from 4 states and 4 foreign countries.

Admission: *Requirements:* Application; two references (pastor, friend); health form; application fee; high school transcript or GED equivalent; transcripts from other postsecondary institutions.

College credit and advanced placement for postsecondary-level work completed in secondary school and for extrainstitutional learning (life experience) on basis of ACE *2006 Guide to the Evaluation of Educational Experiences in the Armed Services.*

Degree Requirements: *For all associate degrees:* 60 minimum semester hours. *For all undergraduate degrees:* 120 minimum semester hours.

Distinctive Educational Programs: Internships; outreach ministry requirements.

Degrees Conferred: 10 *associate*; 29 *baccalaureate:* theology/religious vocations.

Fees and Other Expenses: *Full-time tuition per academic year 2004–05:* $10,800. *Books and supplies:* $6,710. *Room and board per academic year:* $4,030.

Financial Aid: Aid from institutionally generated funds is provided on the basis of academic merit, financial need. Institution has a Program Participation Agreement with the U.S. Department of Education for eligible students to receive Pell Grants and, depending upon the agreement, other federal aid.

Departments and Teaching Staff: *Instructors* 9, *part-time teachers* 10.

Total instructional faculty: 19. Degrees held by full-time faculty: doctorate 22%, master's 100%.

Enrollment: Total enrollment 171 (49.1% men, 50l9% women).

Characteristics of Student Body: *Ethnic/racial makeup:* Black non-Hispanic: 2.3%; American Indian or Alaska Native: 6.4%; Asian or Pacific Islander: 1.2%; White non-Hispanic: 89.5%.

International Students: 1 nonresident alien enrolled fall 2004.

Student Life: On campus housing includes men's residence hall, women's residence hall, apartment building for upperclass women, apartment buildings for families. *Surrounding community:* Campus is located 5 miles from Bemidji, population 11,000.

Library Collections: 25,000 volumes. 1,266 audiovisual materials; 150 current periodical subscriptions. Online catalog. Students have access to online information retrieval services and the Internet.

Most important special holdings include theological resources; Native American resources.

Buildings and Grounds: Campus area 180 acres.

Chief Executive Officer: Dr. Daniel G. Clausen, President.

Address admissions inquiries to Dan Hovestol, Director of Admissions.

St. Cloud State University

720 Fourth Avenue South
St. Cloud, Minnesota 56379-4498
Tel: (320) 308-2111　　**E-mail:** SCSU4U@stcloudstate.edu
Fax: (320) 308-2059　　**Internet:** www.stcloudstate.edu

Institution Description: *Enrollment:* 15,607. *Degrees awarded:* Associate, baccalaureate, master's. Specialist certificates also awarded.

Accreditation: *Regional:* NCA. *Professional:* business, computer science, counseling, engineering, journalism, music, rehabilitation counseling, social work, speech-language pathology, teacher education, theatre

History: Established as Third State Normal School and offered first instruction at postsecondary level 1869; changed name to St. Cloud State Normal School 1869, St. Cloud State Teachers College 1921; awarded first degree (baccalaureate) 1928; changed name to St. Cloud State College 1957; adopted present name 1975. *See* Edwin Cates, *A Centennial History of St. Cloud State College* (Minneapolis: Dillon Press, 1968) for further information.

Institutional Structure: *Composition of institution:* Administrators 50 men / 28 women. Academic affairs headed by vice president for academic affairs. Management/business/finances directed by vice president for administrative affairs. Full-time instructional faculty 650. Academic governance body, University Curriculum Council, meets an average of 18 times per year.

Calendar: Semesters. Academic year Sept. to May. Freshmen admitted Sept., Dec., Mar., June, July. Degrees conferred and formal commencements May, Aug., Nov., Mar. Summer session of 2 terms from June to Aug.

Characteristics of Freshmen: 74% of applicants admitted. 37% of applicants admitted and enrolled.

97% (1,997 students) submitted ACT scores. *25th percentile:* ACT Composite 19, ACT English 18, ACT Math 18. *75th percentile:* ACT Composite 24, ACT English 23, ACT Math 25.

36% of entering freshmen expected to graduate within 5 years. Freshmen from 25 states and 32 foreign countries.

Admission: Rolling admissions plan. For fall acceptance, apply no later than Aug. 15. Early acceptance available. *Requirements:* Either graduation from accredited secondary school or GED. Additional requirements for some programs. Lowest acceptable secondary school class standing top two thirds. *Entrance tests:* College Board PSAT, SAT, or ACT composite. For foreign students TOEFL or other proof of English proficiency. *For transfer students:* 2.0 minimum GPA; from 4-year accredited institution maximum transfer credit limited only by residence requirement; from 2-year accredited institution 96 quarter hours; correspondence/extension students 15 hours.

College credit and advanced placement for postsecondary-level work completed in secondary school. College credit for extrainstitutional learning on basis of ACE *2006 Guide to the Evaluation of Educational Experiences in the Armed Services.* Tutoring available.

Degree Requirements: *For all associate degrees:* 60 semester hours; 15 hours in residence. *For all baccalaureate degrees:* 124 semester hours; 30 hours in residence; distribution requirements; core requirements for some majors. *For all undergraduate degrees:* 2.0 GPA; 2 hours physical education; general education requirements.

Fulfillment of some degree requirements and exemption from some beginning courses possible by passing College Board CLEP, AP. *Grading system:* A–F; pass-fail; withdraw.

Distinctive Educational Programs: *For undergraduates:* Honors program, internships, Division of General Studies. Interdepartmental programs in American studies, East Asian studies, environmental studies, futures studies, gerontology, international relations, Latin American studies, local and urban affairs, medical technology, Middle East studies, minority studies, nuclear medical technology, physical therapy, public administration, religious studies, rhetoric, social science, social studies, speech interdepartmental, women's studies. Preprofessional programs in agriculture, allied health fields, dentistry, engineering, fisheries management, forestry, home economics, horticulture, law, medical records administration, medicine, mortuary science, nursing, occupational therapy, optometry, pharmacy, physical therapy, veterinary medicine, wildlife management. Institutionally arranged study abroad in China, Costa Rica, England, France, Germany, Japan. Cross-registration with College of Saint Benedict and Saint John's University. *For graduate students:* Interdepartmental programs in social science. *Available to all students:* Evening classes. Independent study. *Other distinctive programs:* Continuing education.

Degrees Conferred: 91 *associate;* 2,526 *baccalaureate* (B), 305 *masters:* (M): biological/life sciences 99 (B), 3 (M); business/marketing 620 (B), 19 (M); communications/communication technologies 159 (B), 12 (M); computer and information sciences 41 (B), 8 (M); education 478 (B), 100 (M); engineering and engineering technologies 48 (B), 25 (M); English 128 (B), 25 (M); foreign languages and literature 31 (B); health professions and related sciences 67 (B), 14 (M); home economics and vocational home economics 1 (B); interdisciplinary studies 10 (B), 7 (M); liberal arts/general studies 129 (B), 16 (M); mathematics 35 (B); natural resources/environmental science 12 (B), parks and recreation 57 (B), 7 (M); philosophy/religion/theology 9 (B); physical sciences 12 (B); protective services/public administration 153(B), 17 (M); psychology 117 (B), 48 (M); social sciences and history 278 (B), 5 (M); trade and industry 50 (B); visual and performing arts 53 (B), 1 (M).

Fees and Other Expenses: *Full-time tuition per academic year 2004–05:* undergraduate resident $4,577, nonresident $9,935; graduate resident $4,660, nonresident $7,288. *Required fees:* $599. *Room and board per academic year:* $4,088.

Financial Aid: Aid from institutionally generated funds is provided on the basis of academic merit, financial need, athletic ability, other criteria.

Financial aid to full-time, first-time undergraduate students: need-based scholarships/grants totaling $16,075,239, self-help $31,561,770, parent loans $64,083, tuition waivers $103,011, athletic awards $225,598; non-need-based scholarships/grants totaling $2,927,383, self-help $35,177,787, parent loans $1,052,895, tuition waivers $244,894, athletic awards $699,894.

Departments and Teaching Staff: *Total instructional faculty:* 842 (full-time 642, part-time 200; women 374, men 468; members of minority groups 121). Total faculty with doctorate, first-professional, or other terminal degree: 566. Student-to-faculty ratio: 19:1.

Enrollment: Total enrollment 15,607. Undergraduate full-time 5,430 men / 6,375 women, part-time 1,015m / 1,389w; graduate full-time 196m / 304w, part-time 329m / 571486w.

Characteristics of Student Body: *Ethnic/racial makeup:* number of Black non-Hispanic: 242; American Indian or Alaska Native: 94; Asian or Pacific Islander: 263; Hispanic: 90; White non-Hispanic: 10,842; unknown: 2,037.

International Students: 827 nonresident aliens enrolled fall 2004. Programs available to aid students whose native language is not English: social, cultural. English as a Second Language Program. No financial aid specifically designated for international students.

Student Life: On-campus residence halls house 25% of student body. Residence halls for men constitute 7% of such space, for women 16%, for both sexes 79%. *Intercollegiate athletics:* men only: baseball, basketball, cross-country, football, golf, hockey, swimming, tennis, track; women only: basketball, cross-country, golf, softball, swimming, tennis, track, volleyball. *Special regulations:* Cars permitted in designated areas only. Quiet hours. Dormitory visitation varies. *Special services:* Learning Resources Center, medical services. *Student publications, radio: Chronicle,* a biweekly newspaper. Radio station KVSC-FM broadcasts 133 hours per week. *Surrounding community:* St. Cloud population 45,000. Minneapolis-St. Paul, 70 miles from campus, is nearest metropolitan area. Served by mass transit bus system; airport 70 miles from campus; passenger rail service 5 miles from campus.

Library Collections: 620,000 books. Online catalog. 1,310 current periodical subscriptions; 8,140 electronic journal subscriptions. 1,230,362 federal and 56,289 state government documents; 497,878 microform units. 61,381 maps/atlases. 26,970 audio/video units.

Most important special collections include rare books; manuscripts of Minnesota authors; children's collections; papers and letters of Sinclair Lewis.

Buildings and Grounds: Campus area 964 acres.

Chief Executive Officer: Dr. Roy H. Saigo, President.

Undergraduates address admission inquiries to Office of Admissions; graduate inquiries to School of Graduate Studies.

Saint John's University

Collegeville, Minnesota 56321

Tel: (320) 363-2196   **E-mail:** admissions@csbsju.edu
Fax: (320) 363-2750   **Internet:** www.csbsju.edu

Institution Description: Saint John's University is a private liberal arts college for men conducted by the Benedictine monks of Saint John's Abbey. Since 1963, academic and social programs have been jointly coordinated with the College of St. Benedict, a Catholic liberal arts college for women. *Enrollment:* 2,015. *Degrees awarded:* Baccalaureate. Saint John's University School of Theology, which admits women, offers first-professional and master's degrees.

Accreditation: *Regional:* NCA. *Professional:* nursing, social work

History: Chartered 1856; established and offered first instruction at postsecondary level 1857; awarded first degree (baccalaureate) 1870. *See* Colman Barry, *Worship and Work* (Collegeville, MN: Liturgical Press, 1956) for further information.

Institutional Structure: *Governing board:* Board of Regents: 12 members form monastic community, 1 student, 1 faculty member, 30 additional members. All voting. *Composition of institution:* Administrators 100 men / 33 women. Academic affairs headed by provost. Management/business/finances directed by vice president of finance and administration. Full-time instructional faculty 108 men / 46 women. Faculty governance: joint faculty assembly meets an monthly.

Calendar: Semesters (4-1-4 plan). Academic year Sept. to May. Freshmen admitted Sept., Feb. Degrees conferred May, Dec. Formal commencement May. Summer session for graduate School of Theology.

Characteristics of Freshmen: 86% of applicants admitted. 51% of applicants admitted and enrolled.

18% (92 students) submitted SAT scores; 13% (478 students) submitted ACT scores. *25th percentile:* SAT Verbal 520, SAT Math 560; ACT Composite 23, ACT English 21, ACT Math 23. *75th percentile:* SAT Verbal 640, SAT Math 660; ACT Composite 28, ACT English 27, ACT Math 28.

81% of entering freshmen expected to graduate within 5 years. 82% of freshmen from Minnesota. Freshmen from 22 states and 9 foreign countries.

Admission: Rolling admissions beginning Oct. 1. Priority deadline Dec. 1. Students who have completed application process by Dec. 1 will receive scholarship award notification on Dec. 20. *Requirements:* Accredited high school graduation or equivalent; completion of 17 units including 4 English, 3 mathematics, 2 laboratory science, 2 social studies, 6 academic electives; study of a foreign language is recommended; high school rank of 50% or higher; ACT composite of 21 or higher; SAT combined 1000 or higher.

College credit and advanced placement for postsecondary-level work completed in secondary school. For transfer students: 2.5 GPA and transfer student evaluation form required with college transcript. Maximum transfer credit limited only by residency requirement. Tutoring available.

Degree Requirements: 124 credit hours; 2.0 GPA; 2 terms in residence; 1 physical education course; completion of core curriculum.

Fulfillment of some degree requirements and exemption from some beginning courses possible by passing College Board APP or International Baccalaureate. *Grading system:* A–F; high pass-pass-fail; pass-fail; withdraw (carries time limit).

Distinctive Educational Programs: *For undergraduates:* Dual-degree program in engineering with the University of Minnesota. Cross-registration with St. Cloud State University. Preprofessional programs in dentistry, engineering, forestry, law, medicine, pharmacy, physical therapy, veterinary medicine. Interdepartmental/interdisciplinary programs in humanities, medieval studies, Christian humanism. Facilities for independent research, including honors seminars, individual majors, and tutorials. The Center for International Education provides intercultural education experiences for undergraduate students in Australia, Austria, England, Granada, China, France, Greece, Ireland, South Africa, Spain. Exchange programs with Sophia University in Tokyo, Japan; Keele University in Staffordshire, England; University of Malta. *For graduate students:* Facilities and programs for independent research. Study abroad in Jerusalem. *Available to all students:* Work-experience programs. Evening classes.

ROTC: Army in cooperation with College of St. Benedict. 25 commissions awarded 2004–05.

Degrees Conferred: 494 *baccalaureate:* biological/life sciences 35; business/marketing 121; computer and information sciences 23; education 9; English 55; foreign languages and literature 10; health professions and related sciences 5; home economics and vocational home economics 3; interdisciplinary studies 25; liberal arts/general studies 7; mathematics 12; natural resources/environmental science 2; philosophy/religion/theology 12; physical sciences 11; psychology 33; social sciences and history 115; visual and performing arts 16. 32 *master's:* philosophy/religion/theology.4 *first-professional:* master of divinity. *Honorary degrees awarded 2004–05:* Doctor of Laws 1, Doctor of Humane Letters 2.

Fees and Other Expenses: *Full-time tuition per academic year 005–06:* $23,064. *Fees:* $410. *Room per academic year:* $3,151. *Board per academic year:* $3,124.

Financial Aid: Aid from institutionally generated funds is provided on the basis of academic merit, financial need, other criteria.

Financial aid to full-time, first-time undergraduate students: need-based scholarships/grants totaling $12,600,929, self-help $7,156,796, parent loans $998,729, tuition waivers $701,358; non-need-based scholarships/grants totaling $4,979,155, self-help $1,246,659, parent loans $573,282, tuition waivers $693,373.

Departments and Teaching Staff: *Professors 50, associate professors 42, assistant professors 40, instructors 12, part-time faculty 25.*

Total instructional faculty: 169 (full-time 144, part-time 25; women 52, men 117; members of minority groups 14). Total faculty with doctorate, first-professional, or other terminal degree: 137. Student-to-faculty ratio: 13:1. *Faculty development:* $75,000 in grants for research. 14 faculty members awarded sabbaticals 2004–05.

Enrollment: Total enrollment 2,015. Undergraduate full-time 1,845 men; part-time 30m; first-professional full-time 1m, part-time 1m; graduate full-time 26m / 20w, part-time 26m / 46w. *Transfer students:* in-state 38.

Characteristics of Student Body: *Ethnic/racial makeup:* number of Black non-Hispanic: 14; American Indian or Alaska Native: 5; Asian or Pacific Islander: 42; Hispanic: 21; White non-Hispanic: 1,752. *Age distribution:* number under 18: 155; 18–19: 778; 20–21: 869; 22–24: 271; 25–29: 13; 30–34: 1; 35–39: 3; 40–49: 3; 50–64: 2.

International Students: 61 nonresident aliens enrolled fall 2004. 11 students from Europe, 16 Asia, 4 Central and South America, 9 Africa, 1 Canada, 20 Caribbean. Programs available to aid students whose native language is not English: social, cultural. English as a Second Language Program. No financial aid specifically designated for international students. e\260 On-campus residence halls house 77% of student body. Residence halls for men constitute 89% of such space, for women only 1%, apartments for men 10%. *Intercollegiate athletics:* men only: baseball, basketball, cross country, football, golf, hockey, Nordic skiing, soccer, swimming and diving, tennis, track and field, and wrestling. *Special regulations:* Cars permitted with campus registration; fee charged. Each residence hall has the option of establishing its own open house hours not to exceed Sun.-Thurs. 11am to 12 midnight; Fri. and Sat. 11 to 2am. Medical services, campus shuttle bus service to and from College of St. Benedict and the city of St. Cloud. *Student publications, radio: Record,* a biweekly newspaper; *Saints,* a yearbook. Radio station KJMB has 50–60 hours per week of student broadcasting. *Surrounding community:* Collegeville township population 3,200. Minneapolis-St. Paul, 75 miles from campus, is nearest metropolitan area. Served by airport 90 miles from campus; passenger rail service 15 miles from campus.

Library Collections: 833,908 volumes including bound books, serial backfiles, electronic documents, and government documents not in separate collections. Online catalog. 33,471 audiovisual materials. Current serial subscriptions: 1,030 paper; 44,464 microform. 34 computer work stations. Students have access to the Internet and online information retrieval services. Total2004–05 budget for books and materials: $2,655,718.

Most important special collections include Hill Monastic Manuscript Microfilm Library; Kacmarcik Liturgical Design Collection; Theology and History Collection.

Buildings and Grounds: Campus area 2,400 acres.

Chief Executive Officer: Brother Dietrich Reinhart, O.S.B., President.

Undergraduates address admission inquiries to Mary Milbert, Dean of Admissions; School of Theology inquiries to Brandon Duffy, Director of Enrollment.

Saint Mary's University of Minnesota

700 Terrace Heights
Winona, Minnesota 55987-1399
Tel: (507) 457-1700   **E-mail:** admissions@smumn.edu
Fax: (507) 457-1722   **Internet:** www.smumn.edu

Institution Description: Saint Mary's University of Minnesota is a private, nonprofit institution operated by the Christian Brothers and affiliated with the Roman Catholic church. *Enrollment:* 4,996. *Degrees awarded:* Baccalaureate, master's, doctorate.

Academic offerings subject to approval by Minnesota Higher Education Coordinating Board. Saint Mary's is affiliated with more than 24 professional organizations.

Accreditation: *Regional:* NCA.

History: Established and incorporated as a men's college 1912; offered first instruction at postsecondary level 1913; awarded first degree (baccalaureate) 1915; added graduate program 1955; became coeducational 1969.

Institutional Structure: *Governing board:* Saint Mary's University Board of Trustees. Extrainstitutional representation: 42 trustees, including alumni; 3 emeritus (ex officio); institutional representation: president of the university. *Composition of institution:* Cabinet composed of president, 8 vice presidents, 4 deans (9 men / 5 women). Academic affairs headed by Vice President for Academic Affairs. Full-time instructional faculty 59. Academic governance body, Faculty Body, meets an average of 5 times per year.

Calendar: Semesters. Academic year Aug. to May. Freshmen admitted Aug., Jan. Degrees conferred May, Dec. Formal commencement May.

Characteristics of Freshmen: 1,267 applicants (544 men, 723 women). 73.2% of applicants admitted. 36.9% of admitted students enrolled full-time.

9% (32 students) submitted SAT scores; 95% (339 students) submitted ACT scores. *25th percentile:* SAT I Verbal 435, SAT I Math 420; ACT Composite 19, ACT English 18, ACT Math 17. *75th percentile:* SAT I Verbal 600, SAT I Math 570; ACT Composite 25, ACT English 25, ACT Math 25.

55% of freshmen from Minnesota. Freshmen from 21 states and 17 foreign countries.

Admission: Rolling admissions plan. For fall acceptance, apply as early as Nov. 1 of previous year, but not later than Aug. 1 of year of enrollment. *Requirements:* Either graduation from accredited secondary school with 16 units which should include 4 English, 3 mathematics, 2 natural science, 2 social sciences, 7 in academic electives; or GED. Minimum composite ACT score of 18; rank in top 50% of secondary school class and minimum of 2.2 GPA recommended. Aquinas Program for students not normally admissible. *Entrance tests:* ACT composite preferred. College Board SAT accepted. For foreign students TOEFL. *For transfer students:* From accredited institution 2.0 GPA; 62 hours maximum transfer credit.

College credit and advanced placement for postsecondary-level work completed in secondary school. College credit for extrainstitutional learning on basis of ACE *2006 Guide to the Evaluation of Educational Experiences in the Armed Services;* portfolio and faculty assessments. Tutoring available. Developmental courses offered during regular academic year; credit given.

Degree Requirements: Earn at least 122 semester credits; 2.0 GPA; complete minimum of 45 credits in 300 courses or above; complete general education program minimum of 1 major program; earn a minimum of 60 credits in residence; spend final year in residence unless enrolled in an approved off-campus program; apply no more than 4 semester hours of music ensemble toward the minimum of 122 credits; complete 2 half-semester (no credit) sport activity courses; complete E120 English Composition with a minimum of a C grade or earn a passing grade in E220 Argumentative and Research Writing; demonstrate a mathematical competency at the intermediate algebra level.

Fulfillment of some degree requirements and exemption from some beginning courses on basis of College Board APP and CLEP subject examinations. *Grading system:* A–F; pass-no credit; withdraw (carries time limit).

Distinctive Educational Programs: *For undergraduate students:* Minors offered in most majors. Self-designed majors. Double majors. Independent study. Accelerated study. Pass/fail grading options. Internships. Pre-professional programs in dentistry, engineering, law, medicine, physical therapy, theology and veterinary science. 3-2 programs in engineering at University of Minnesota and Illinois Institute of Technology, 3-1 program in medical technology; 3-1 program in cytotechnology at Mayo School of Health Related Sciences, Rochester, MN. Cross-registration at Winona State University. B.S. completion programs in telecommunications, health care management, business, industrial technology, psychology. Ed.D. program in leadership. Graduate studies in nurse anesthesia, telecommunications, resource analysis, management, educational administration, counseling and psychological services, human and health services administration, human development, art administration, developmental disabilities, education, philanthropy and development, pastoral ministries, instruction, international business; double majors/degrees; master of education in teaching and learning. Post-master certification in marriage/family therapy; child psychopathology; educational administration/licenser; geographic information. Overseas programs: M.A. in African studies at Maryknoll Institute of African Studies; B.S. in education at Christian Brothers Institute for Education in Nairobi, Kenya.

Degrees Conferred: 336 *baccalaureate.* 1,397 *master's;* 21 *doctorate.* Bachelor's degrees awarded in top five disciplines: business, management, marketing, and related support services 88; visual and performing arts 36; engineering technologies/technicians 22; education 22; computer and information sciences and support services 21.

Fees and Other Expenses: *Full-time tuition per academic year 2004–05:* $18,704. *Required fees:* $445. *Room and board per academic year:* $5,720.

Financial Aid: Aid from institutionally generated funds is provided on the basis of academic merit, financial need. Institution has a Program Participation Agreement with the U.S. Department of Education for eligible students to receive Pell Grants and, depending upon agreement, other federal aid.

Financial aid to full-time, first-time undergraduate students: 19% received federal grants averaging $2,763; 26% state/local grants averaging $3,279; 85% institutional grants averaging $5,848; 65% received loans averaging $6,240.

Departments and Teaching Staff: Art *professors* 0, *associate professors* 1, *assistant professors* 1, *instructors* 0, *part-time faculty* 0; biology 4, 1, 3, 0, 1; business 3, e, 2, 0, 0; chemistry 2, 0, 1, 0, 3; computer science 0, 0, 3, 0, 1; education 0, 3, 5, 1, 3; English 1, 1, 3, 2, 3; history 1, 2, 1, 0, 0; interdisciplinary studies 0, 0, 3, 4, 5; languages 2, 0, 1, 0, 3; mathematics 2, 2, 1, 3, 0; media communications 0, 0, 2, 0, 0; music 1, 0, 3, 0, 14; philosophy 0, 3, 1, 0, 0; physics 1, 0, 1, 0, 0; political science 2, 0, 1, 0, 0; psychology 4, 0, 2, 0, 0; sociology 1, 1, 1, 1, 2; theatre 1, 0, 4, 0, 1; theology 0, 3, 1, 0, 1; School of Graduate Programs and Special Programs 0, 2, 1, 0, 0.

Total instructional faculty: 255.7 FTE. *Student-to-faculty ratio:* 14:1. Degrees held by full-time faculty: master's 31%, doctorate 69%. 86% hold terminal degrees.

Enrollment: Total enrollment 4,996. Undergraduate full-time 4,704 (45% men, 55% women).

Characteristics of Student Body: *Ethnic/racial makeup:* Black non-Hispanic: 2.7%; American Indian or Alaska Native: .5%; Asian or Pacific Islander: 1.5%; Hispanic: 2.2%; White non-Hispanic: $75.4%; unknown: 16.9%.

International Students: 14 undergraduate nonresident aliens enrolled fall 2004. Students from Europe, Asia, Central and South America. Programs available to aid students whose native language is not English: social, cultural. English as a Second Language Program. No financial aid specifically designated for international students.

Student Life: On-campus residence halls provide housing for 85% of student body. Residence halls for men constitute 10% of such space, for women 12%, co-ed 78%. *Intercollegiate athletics:* men only: baseball, basketball, cross-country, golf, hockey, indoor track, soccer, swimming/diving, tennis, track; women only: basketball, cross-country, Nordic skiing, golf, indoor track, soccer, softball, swimming/diving, volleyball. *Special regulations:* Cars permitted with campus registration. Quiet and visiting hours determined by individual dormitories. *Special services:* Study Skills Center, medical services. *Student publications, radio:* Cardinal, a monthly newspaper; *Troll*, a daily newsletter. Radio station KSMR-FM broadcasts 133 hours per week. *Surrounding community:* Winona population 26,000. Minneapolis-St. Paul, 110 miles from campus, is nearest metropolitan area. Served by mass transit bus system; airport 25 miles from campus; passenger rail service 3 miles from campus.

Library Collections: 170,449 volumes. 35 microform titles; 1,843 audiovisual materials; 715 current periodical subscriptions. Online catalog. Students have access to online information services and the Internet.

Most important special holdings include curriculum library; extensive materials in biology, theology and business administration; University Archives; Rare Book Room.

Buildings and Grounds: Campus area 350 acres.

Chief Executive Officer: Brother Louis Dethomasis, F.S.C., President.

Undergraduates address admission inquiries to Tony Piscitiello, Vice President for Admissions; graduate inquiries to James Bedktke, Associate Provost and Vice President of Graduate and Special Programs.

St. Olaf College

1520 St. Olaf Avenue
Northfield, Minnesota 55057

Tel: (507) 646-222 **E-mail:** admissions@stolaf.edu
Fax: (507) 646-3549 **Internet:** www.stolaf.edu

Institution Description: St. Olaf College is a private liberal arts college affiliated with Evangelical Lutheran Church in America. Students at St. Olaf may propose self-designed, integrative majors through the Center for Integrative Studies. *Enrollment:* 3,046. *Degrees awarded:* Baccalaureate.

Member of Associated Colleges of the Midwest (ACM), Higher Education Consortium for Urban Affairs (HECUA), American Association of Colleges of Nursing, American Council on Education, Association of American Colleges, Lutheran Educational Council of North America, National Council of Social Workers Education; National League for Nursing, Minnesota Intercollegiate Athletic Conference, National Collegiate Athletic Association (Division III), Minnesota Association of Colleges of Nursing, Minnesota Private College Council, National Association of Independent Colleges and Universities, Phi Beta Kappa.

Accreditation: *Regional:* NCA. *Professional:* dance, music, nursing, social work, teacher education, theatre

History: Established and incorporated as St. Olaf's School 1874; offered first instruction at postsecondary level 1886; adopted present name 1889; awarded first degree 1890. *See* Joseph M. Shaw, *History of St. Olaf College, 1874–1974* (Northfield, Minn.: 1974) for further information.

Institutional Structure: *Governing board:* St. Olaf College Board of Regents. 30 regents plus the president. *Composition of institution:* Administra-

tors 58 men / 40 women (at vice presidential level, 2 women). Academic affairs headed by provost and dean of the college. Management/business/finances directed by vice president and treasurer. Full-time instructional faculty 82 men / 113 women. Academic governance body, St. Olaf College Faculty, meets an average of 8 times per year.

Calendar: Semesters (4-1-4 plan). Academic year Sept. to May. Freshmen admitted June, Sept., Jan., Feb. Degrees conferred and formal commencement May. Summer session of 2 terms from early June to mid-Aug.

Characteristics of Freshmen: 64.4% of applicants accepted. 38.4% of accepted applicants enrolled.

48% (576 students) submitted SAT scores; 86% (666 students) submitted ACT scores. *25th percentile:* SAT Verbal 710, SAT Math 700; ACT Composite 30, ACT English 31, ACT Math 29. *75th percentile:* SAT Verbal 600,SAT Math 590; ACT Composite 25, ACT English 25, ACT Math 24.

84% of entering freshmen expected to graduate within 5 years. 56% of freshmen from Minnesota. Freshmen from 39 states and 5 foreign countries.

Admission: Rolling admissions beginning Feb. 15. Apply by Nov. 1 of previous year for early decision. *Requirements:* Graduation from accredited secondary school with rank in upper 25%; completion of 15 units including 3–4 English, 2–3 mathematics, 2–3 science (including 1 lab course), 1 foreign languages and academic electives. *Entrance tests:* College Board SAT. or ACT required. *For transfer students:* 2.0 minimum GPA; up to 18 courses maximum transfer credit.

College credit and advanced placement for postsecondary-level work completed in secondary school.

Degree Requirements: 35 courses; 2.0 GPA; 17 St. Olaf courses minimum; 2 one-quarter physical education courses, general education; distribution and interim (4-week period of intensive study in Jan.) requirements; minimum 24 graded courses, maximum 6 S/U (satisfactory/unsatisfactory).

Fulfillment of some degree requirements and exemption from some beginning courses possible by passing College Board AP and institutional examinations. *Grading system:* A–F; pass/no pass; satisfactory/ unsatisfactory.

Distinctive Educational Programs: Work-experience programs. Dual-degree programs in engineering with Washington University (MO). Interdepartmental and interdisciplinary programs in American Racial and Multicultural studies, American studies, ancient studies, Asian studies, environmental studies, family studies, fine arts, Hispanic studies, medieval studies, Russian studies, women's studies. Facilities and programs for independent research, including individual majors and tutorials. January interims, full year and terms abroad in varying locations. Five-month faculty accompanied study-travel programs include the Global Semester concentrating on Egypt, India, South Korea, and Hong Kong; the Terms in Asia (Indonesia, Hong Kong, China, and Thailand), Term in Middle East (Turkey, Morocco, Egypt, Israel), and the Term in Germany. Additional programs offered in China, Japan, Germany, Scotland, Ireland, Latin America, India, and England. Study-service abroad in Indonesia, Korea, and Germany. Study abroad is also available through ACM (London and Florence arts program; University of Puna, India; Waseda University, Japan; University of Zagreb, Yugoslavia); through HECUA Scandinavian Urban Studies and South American Urban Studies terms; through Council of International Educational Exchange in St. Petersburg. Off-campus programs in the U.S. through ACM biology program at Wilderness Field Station in boundary waters, Oak Ridge science semester, humanities program at Newberry Library, Chicago; through HECUA urban studies programs including Metro in Minneapolis/St. Paul. Washington (DC) semester in cooperation with American University. Cross-registration with Carleton College. Center for Integrative Studies provides support for students who seek to design integrative majors through a sequence of courses, seminars, independent studies, or experiential learning.

Degrees Conferred: 708 *baccalaureate*. Bachelor's degrees awarded in top five disciplines: social sciences 125; visual and performing arts 109; biological and biomedical sciences 67; English language and literature/letters 67; psychology 56.

Fees and Other Expenses: *Total fees per academic year 2005–06:* $26,500. *Room and board per academic year:* $6,300.

Financial Aid: Aid from institutionally generated funds is provided on the basis of academic merit, financial need. Institution has a Program Participation Agreement with the U.S. Department of Education for eligible students to receive Pell Grants and other federal aid.

Financial aid to full-time, first-time undergraduate students: need-based scholarships/grants totaling $26,340,106, self-help $10,960,051, tuition waivers $709,626; non-need-based scholarships/grants totaling $4,278,505, self-help $5,300,323, parent loans $8,135,316, tuition waivers $491,068.

Departments and Teaching Staff: *Professors* 64, *associate professors* 63, *assistant professors* 54, *instructors* 11, *other* 3. *part-time faculty* 132.

Total instructional faculty: 327 (full-time 195, part-time 132; women 144, men 183; members of minority groups 16). Total faculty with doctorate, first-professional, or other terminal degree: 257. Student-to-faculty ratio: 12.5:1. *Fac-

ulty development: $310,110 in grants for research. 17 faculty members awarded sabbaticals 2004–05.

Enrollment: Total enrollment 3,046. Undergraduate full-time 1,232 men / 1,741 women, part-time 34m / 395w. *Transfer students:* in-state 20; from out-of-state 15.

Characteristics of Student Body: *Ethnic/racial makeup:* number of Black non-Hispanic: 34; American Indian or Alaska Native: 6; Asian or Pacific Islander: 127; Hispanic: 48; White non-Hispanic: 2,561; unknown: 236. *Age distribution:* number under 18: 23; 18–19: 1,338; 20–21: 1,381; 22–24: 224; 25–29: 5; 40–49: 2.

International Students: 34 nonresident aliens enrolled fall 2004. 17 students from Europe, 14 Asia, 2 Central and South, 1 Africa. Programs available to aid students whose native language is not English: social, cultural. English as a Second language. Financial aid available for international undergraduate students: variable number of scholarship available annually; 18 totaling $196,738 awarded 2004–05.

Student Life: On-campus residence halls house 98% of student body. All residence halls for both sexes. 2% of student body live off-campus in non-college-owned houses and apartments. *Intercollegiate athletics:* men only: baseball, basketball, cross-country, football, golf, hockey, skiing, soccer, swimming, tennis, track, wrestling; women only: basketball, cross-country, golf, skiing, softball, swimming, tennis, track, volleyball. *Special regulations:* Residence hall visitation 10am to midnight Sun.–Thurs., 10am to 1am Fri. and Sat. *Special services:* Learning Resources Center, medical services. St. Olaf, in association with Carleton College, operates minibus service between campuses and to Minneapolis-St. Paul. *Student publications, radio: Literary Arts Magazine,* an annual literary publication; *Manitou Messenger,* a weekly newspaper; *Viking,* a yearbook. KSTO student radio station. *Surrounding community:* Northfield population 15,000. Minneapolis/St. Paul, 40 miles north of campus, is nearest metropolitan area.

Library Collections: 697,516 volumes. 158,000 government documents; 56,488 microforms; 12,672 recordings; 7,193 compact discs; 5,582 CD-ROMs. Current periodical subscriptions: 2,149 paper; 11,317 microform. Online catalog. Computer work stations available. Students have access to online information retrieval services and the Internet. Total 2004–05 budget for books and materials: $1,073,456.

Most important holdings include materials of the Norwegian-American Historical Society; Kierkegaard Special Collection; Rare Books Collection.

Buildings and Grounds: Campus area 300 acres with 51 buildings. *New buildings:* Dittmann Center completed 2002.

Chief Executive Officer: Dr. Christopher M. Thomforde, President.

Address admission inquiries Jennifer Krengel Olsen, Director of Admissions.

Southwest State University

1501 State Street
Marshall, Minnesota 56258

Tel: (507) 537-7021   **E-mail:** admissions@southweststate.edu
Fax: (507) 537-7154   **Internet:** www.southweststate.edu

Institution Description: *Enrollment:* 5,977. *Degrees awarded:* Associate, baccalaureate.

Accreditation: *Regional:* NCA. *Professional:* music, social work, teacher education

History: Established as Southwest Minnesota State College 1963; chartered and offered first instruction at postsecondary level 1967; awarded first degree (associate) 1969; adopted present name 1976.

Institutional Structure: *Composition of institution:* Administrators 48; excluded management 14. Academic affairs headed by vice president of university. Management/business/finances directed by vice president of student and administrative services. Full-time instructional faculty 79 men / 35 women. Academic governance through the union.

Calendar: Semesters. Academic year Sept. to May. Freshmen admitted at the beginning of any quarter. Degrees conferred and formal commencement June. Summer session of 2 sessions from June to Aug.

Characteristics of Freshmen: 1,359 applicants (594 men, 755 women). 81.2% of applicants admitted. 49% of admitted students enrolled full-time.

4% (19 students) submitted SAT scores; 81% (435 students) submitted ACT scores. *25th percentile:* ACT Composite 17, ACT English 17, ACT Math 17. *75th percentile:* ACT Composite 24, ACT English 24, ACT Math 24.

77% of freshmen from Minnesota. Freshmen from 11 states and 12 foreign countries.

Admission: Rolling admissions plan. For fall acceptance, apply as early as Oct. 1 of senior year of secondary school, but not later than 10 days after begin-

ning of classes. Early acceptance available. *Requirements:* Either graduation from accredited secondary school or GED. Lowest acceptable secondary school class standing 33rd percentile. *Entrance tests:* College Board SAT or ACT composite. For foreign students TOEFL. *For transfer students:* 2.0 minimum GPA.

College credit and advanced placement for postsecondary-level work completed in secondary school. College credit for extrainstitutional learning on basis of ACE *2006 Guide to the Evaluation of Educational Experiences in the Armed Services,* faculty assessment, personal interviews.

Tutoring available. Remedial courses offered in summer session and regular academic year; credit given.

Degree Requirements: *For all associate degrees:* 96 credit hours. *For all baccalaureate degrees:* 192 credit hours. *For all degrees:* 2.0 GPA; 1 year in residence; basic study requirement. Fulfillment of some degree requirements and exemption from some beginning courses possible by passing departmental examinations, College Board CLEP. *Grading system:* A–F; high pass-pass-fail; withdraw.

Distinctive Educational Programs: Internships. Evening classes. Preprofessional programs in agriculture, chiropractic, dentistry, engineering, fishery and wildlife management, forestry, law, medicine, ministry, mortuary science, nursing, occupational therapy, optometry, pharmacy, physical therapy, veterinary medicine. Interdisciplinary programs, including rural studies. Facilities and programs for independent study, including honors programs, individual majors, tutorials. Study abroad in various countries throughout the world. *Other distinctive programs:* Community Academic Program (CAP) at Willmar Community College providing junior and senior level courses for business administration degree. Certificate programs in business and administration and engineering administration. Common market program - ability to transfer courses and programs between 7 state universities. Fully integrated interactive TV facilities and networks. On and off-campus continuing education. Graduate-level courses for educators in southwest Minnesota are offered in cooperation with Mankato State University, St. Cloud State University.

Degrees Conferred: 12 *associate;* 425 *baccalaureate;* 98 *master's.* Bachelor's degrees awarded in top five disciplines: business, management, marketing, and related support services 126; education 97; parks and recreation 23; social sciences 22; security and protective services 21.

Fees and Other Expenses: *Full-time tuition per academic year 2004–05:* $5,294. *Room and board per academic year:* $4,806.

Financial Aid: Aid from institutionally generated funds is provided on the basis of academic merit, financial need, athletic ability, other criteria. Institution has a Program Participation Agreement with the U.S. Department of Education for eligible students to receive Pell Grants and, depending upon agreement, other federal aid.

Departments and Teaching Staff: *Professors* 43, *associate professors* 36, *assistant professors* 38, *instructors* 7.

Total instructional faculty: 124. Degrees held by full-time faculty: 77% hold terminal degrees.

Enrollment: Total enrollment 5,977. Undergraduate 5,370 (41.1% men, 58.9% women).

Characteristics of Student Body: *Ethnic/racial makeup:* Black non-Hispanic: 82.4%; American Indian or Alaska Native: .3%; Asian or Pacific Islander: 1.25; Hispanic: 1%; White non-Hispanic: 82.4%; unknown: 10.5%.

International Students: 105 nonresident aliens enrolled fall 2004. Programs available to aid students whose native language is not English: English as a Second Language Program. Financial aid specifically designated for international students: scholarships available for qualifying undergraduate international students.

Student Life: On-campus residence halls house 60% of student body. *Intercollegiate athletics:* men only: baseball, basketball, football, wrestling; women only: soccer, softball, tennis. *Special services:* Learning Resources Center, medical services, physically handicapped resource center. *Student publications, radio, television:* Biweekly newspaper; annual literary magazine. Radio station KSSU broadcasts 10 hours per week. Cable television broadcasts 10 hours per week. *Surrounding community:* Marshall population 14,000. Minneapolis-St. Paul, 150 miles from campus, is nearest metropolitan area; served by airport 3 miles from campus.

Library Collections: 165,000 volumes. 37,000 microforms; 12,000 audiovisual materials; 800 current periodical subscriptions. Online catalog. Students have access to online information retrieval services and the Internet.

Most important special holdings include collections in literature, arts and humanities.

Buildings and Grounds: Campus area 216 acres.

Chief Executive Officer: Dr. Donald C. Danahar, President.

Address admission inquiries to Richard Shearer, Director of Enrollment Services.

United Theological Seminary of the Twin Cities

3000 Fifth Street, N.W.
New Brighton, Minnesota 55112
Tel: (937) 278-5817   **E-mail:** admissions@united.edu
Fax: (937) 278-1218   **Internet:** www.united.edu

Institution Description: United Theological Seminary of the Twin Cities is a private institution affiliated with the United Church of Christ. *Enrollment:* 352. *Degrees awarded:* First-professional (master of divinity), master's, doctorate. Member of The Minnesota Consortium of Theological Schools.

Accreditation: *Regional:* NCA. *National:* ATS. *Professional:* theology

History: Established and incorporated 1960; offered first instruction at post-secondary level 1962; awarded first degree (baccalaureate) 1963.

Institutional Structure: *Governing board:* Board of Trustees. Extrainstitutional representation: 25 trustees; institutional representation: 2 full-time instructional faculty members, 2 students. All voting. *Composition of institution:* Administrators 5 men / 3 women. Academic affairs headed by dean of the seminary. Management/business/finances directed by director of financial affairs. Student services directed by vice president for enrollment management. Full-time instructional faculty 15. Academic governance body, Faculty Senate, meets an average of 11 times per year.

Calendar: Semesters (4-1-4 plan). Academic year Sept. to May. Entering students admitted Sept., Jan., Feb. Degrees conferred and formal commencement May. Summer session early June.

Admission: Rolling admissions plan. For fall acceptance, apply as early as 1 year prior to enrollment, but not later than 1 week prior to beginning of term. *Requirements:* Baccalaureate from accredited institution; minimum 2.75 GPA. *For transfer students:* 2.75 minimum GPA; maximum transfer credit determined by evaluation.

Degree Requirements: *For all first-professional degrees:* 30 courses; required curriculum; yearly integrative examinations. *For all master's degrees:* 18 courses; oral comprehensive examination. *For first-professional and master's degrees:* 1 year in residence.

Distinctive Educational Programs: Internships. Evening classes. Special facilities for using telecommunications in the classroom. Honors programs. Cross-registration through consortium.

Degrees Conferred: 5 *master's:* theology; 62 *doctorate:* theology; 26 *first-professional:* master of divinity.

Fees and Other Expenses: *Full-time tuition per academic year 2004–05:* $8,544. *Required fees:* $660. Contact the seminary for housing costs.

Financial Aid: Aid from institutionally generated funds is provided on the basis of academic merit, financial need.

Departments and Teaching Staff: Theology *professors* 7, *associate professors* 4, *assistant professors* 1, *part-time faculty* 13.
Total instructional faculty: 25. Student-to-faculty ratio: 17:1. Degrees held by full-time faculty: doctorate 100%.

Enrollment: Total enrollment 352. First-professional full-time 50 men / 18 women, part-time 10m / 5w; graduate full-time 122m / 89w, part-time 14m / 14w.

Characteristics of Student Body: *Ethnic/racial makeup:* Black non-Hispanic: 8; American Indian or Native Alaskan: 1; Asian or Pacific Islander: 1; Hispanic: 1; White non-Hispanic: 64; unknown: 152. *Age distribution:* 22–24: 1%, 25–29: 6%; 30–34: 10%; 35–39: 11%; 40–49: 35%; 50–59: 33%; 60–up: 4%.

International Students: 14 nonresident aliens enrolled fall 2004. 2 students from Europe, 5 Asia, 1 South America, 5 Africa, 1 Canada. Programs available to aid students whose native language is not English: social, cultural. No financial aid specifically designated for international students.

Student Life: On-campus residence halls available. *Special regulations:* Cars permitted without restrictions. *Surrounding community:* New Brighton population 25,000. Minneapolis, 8 miles from campus, is nearest metropolitan area. Served by airport 20 miles from campus; mass bus transport.

Library Collections: 81,500 volumes. 700 microforms; 2,000 audiovisual materials; 292 current periodical subscriptions. Online catalog. 14 computer work stations. Students have access to online information retrieval services and the Internet.

Most important special holdings include Theology Collection; Women and Religion Collection; Evangelical and Reformed Church History; faculty writings.

Buildings and Grounds: Campus area 11 acres.

Chief Executive Officer: Dr. Wilson Yates, President.

Address admission inquiries to Director of Admissions.

University of Minnesota - Crookston

2900 University Avenue
Crookston, Minnesota 56716
Tel: (218) 281-8343   **E-mail:** admissions@crk.umn.edu
Fax: (218) 281-8050   **Internet:** www.crk.umn.edu

Institution Description: The University of Minnesota - Crookston provides teaching, research, and service of selected baccalaureate degrees, with a focus on applied undergraduate instruction in agriculture, business, environmental sciences, human resource development, and appropriate interdisciplinary studies. *Enrollment:* 2,320 *Degrees awarded:* Associate, baccalaureate.

Accreditation: *Regional:* NCA.

History: Established 1895 as the Northwest Experimental Station; Northwest School of Agriculture established and graduated first class in 1909; University of Minnesota Technical College began classes on the campus 1966; renamed University of Minnesota - Crookston 1988.

Institutional Structure: *Governing board:* One of four campuses within the University of Minnesota system.

Calendar: Semesters. Academic year Aug. to May.

Characteristics of Freshmen: Average secondary school rank of freshmen 52nd percentile. Mean ACT composite score 21.2.

Admission: *Requirements:* All graduates of accredited or approved high schools or persons with equivalent educational background (GED) are eligible for admission. Students are encouraged to complete the ACT assessment and submit test results before attending.

College credit and advanced placement for postsecondary-level work completed in secondary school and for extrainstitutional learning on basis of ACE *2006 Guide to the Evaluation of Educational Experiences in the Armed Services.* Developmental/remedial courses offered in summer session and regular academic year; credit given.

Degree Requirements: 120 credits required for graduation.

Distinctive Educational Programs: UMC is the original notebook university. UMC offers a distinctive educational opportunity to every full-time student with a "notebook" computer. Computer technology is incorporated in all courses. This is part of an intense strategic planning process to ensure that students receive a high quality education that connects with people, technology, and student careers. IBM named the campus a charter member of the IBM Global Campus.

Degrees Conferred: 55 *associate;* 203 *baccalaureate.* Bachelor's degrees awarded in top five disciplines: business, management, marketing, and related support services 70; agriculture, agriculture operations and related sciences 38; multidisciplinary studies 19; natural resources and conservation 18; parks and recreation, leisure and fitness studies.

Fees and Other Expenses: *Full-time tuition per academic year 2004–5:* $7,607. *Other expenses:* $1,600. *Books and supplies:* $700. *Room and board per academic year:* $4,800.

Financial Aid: Aid from institutionally generated funds is provided on the basis of academic merit, financial need. Institution has a Program Participation Agreement with the U.S. Department of Education for eligible students to receive Pell Grants and other federal aid.

Financial aid to full-time, first-time undergraduate students: 33% received federal grants averaging $2,983; 36% state/local grants averaging $2,344; 74% institutional grants averaging $2,365; 67% received loans averaging $4,986.

Departments and Teaching Staff: Agricultural management *professors* 3, *associate professors* 7, *assistant professors* 6; management 0, 0, 9; technical studies 1, 0, 17; part-time faculty 57.
Total instructional faculty: 100. Total tenured faculty: 47. Degrees held by full-time faculty: doctorate 38%, master's 60%, baccalaureate 2%. 38% hold terminal degrees.

Enrollment: *Total enrollment:* 2,320 (48.5% men, 51.5% women).

Characteristics of Student Body: *Ethnic/racial makeup:* Black non-Hispanic: 1.5%; American Indian or Alaska Native: .8%; Asian or Pacific Islander: Hispanic: 1.2%; White non-Hispanic: 75.1%; unknown: 18.8%. *Age distribution:* 17–21: 69%; 22–24: 10%; 25–29: 6%; 30–34: 3%; 35–39: 3%; 40–and over: 5%.

International Students: 37 nonresident aliens enrolled fall 2003. Programs available to aid students whose native language is not English: social, cultural. No financial aid specifically designated for international students.

Student Life: More than 20 student clubs and organizations plan events and activities and provide professional development and leadership opportunities. UMC is a member of the National Association of Intercollegiate Athletics (NCIA) Division II and competes in the North Dakota College Athletic Conference (NDCAC).

Library Collections: 32,000 volumes. 25,150 microforms; 2,200 audiovisual materials; 770 current periodical subscriptions. Online catalog. 32 computer work stations. Students have access to the Internet at no charge.

Most important special holdings include agriculture; hospitality industry; management.

Buildings and Grounds: Campus area 237 acres.

Chief Executive Officer: Dr. Velmer S. Burton, Chancellor.

Address admissions inquiries to James Mootz, Director of Enrollment Management.

University of Minnesota - Duluth

10 University Drive
Duluth, Minnesota 55812
Tel: (218) 726-8000 **E-mail:** umadmis@d.umn.edu
Fax: (218) 726-6254 **Internet:** www.d-umn.edu

Institution Description: *Enrollment:* 10,366. *Degrees awarded:* Baccalaureate, master's.
Member of the consortium Lake Superior Association of Colleges and Universities.

Accreditation: *Regional:* NCA. *Professional:* business, chemistry, computer science, counseling, engineering, medicine, music, social work, speech-language pathology, teacher education

History: Chartered as State Normal School 1895; changed name to Duluth State Normal School 1905; changed name to Duluth State Teachers College and awarded first degree (baccalaureate) 1927; joined university system and adopted present name 1947; added graduate programs 1964.

Institutional Structure: *Composition of institution:* Administrators 62 men / 35 women. Academic affairs headed by vice chancellor for academic administration. Student affairs headed by vice chancellor for academic support and student life. Finance and operations headed by vice chancellor for finance and operations. Full-time instructional faculty 241 men / 124 women. *Faculty representation:* Faculty served by collective bargaining agent, University Education Association, affiliated with NEA.

Calendar: Semesters. Academic year early Sept. to mid-May. Freshmen admitted Sept., Jan. Undergraduate degrees conferred Jan., May, Aug.. Graduate degrees conferred monthly. Formal commencement May. Intersession mid-May to early June. Summer term early June to early Aug.

Characteristics of Freshmen: 6,726 applicants (3,208 men, 3,518 women). 79.5% of applicants admitted. 41.9% of admitted students enrolled full-time.
4% (94 students) submitted SAT scores; 98% (2,222 students) submitted ACT scores. *25th percentile:* SAT I Verbal 490, SAT I Math 527; ACT Composite 21, ACT English 19, ACT Math 20. *75th percentile:* SAT I Verbal 512, SAT I Math 630; ACT Composite 25, ACT English 25, ACT Math 26.

Admission: Rolling admissions plan. Feb. 1 priority deadline for fall semester. *Requirements:* Open admission for students in top 35 percent of secondary school class who meet all course preparation requirements; others, including those with GED, selectively admitted based upon entrance exam scores and academic preparation. *Entrance tests:* ACT or SAT. *For transfer students:* 2.0 minimum GPA and 75 percent completion ratio of all college work attempted.
Skills development courses offered during regular academic year for credit.

Degree Requirements: *For all baccalaureate degrees:* 120 semester hours. *For all undergraduate degrees:* 2.0 GPA; 30 degree credits in residence; distribution requirements.
Fulfillment of some degree requirements possible by passing departmental examinations, College Board CLEP. *Grading system:* A–F; pass; withdraw (deadline after which pass-fail is appended to withdraw).

Distinctive Educational Programs: Evening classes. Special facilities for using telecommunications in the classroom. Interdisciplinary programs. Facilities for independent research, including honors programs, individual majors. Study abroad in England, Sweden, Finland. Cross-registration with College of St. Scholastica and University of Wisconsin. *Other distinctive programs:* Continuing education.

ROTC: Air Force in cooperation with College of St. Scholastica and University of Wisconsin, Superior.

Degrees Conferred: 1,562 *baccalaureate*; 185 *master's*. Bachelor's degrees awarded in top five disciplines: business, management, marketing, and related support services 327; education 221; social sciences 186; psychology 128; biological/biomedical sciences 126.

Fees and Other Expenses: *Tuition per academic year 2004–05:* resident undergraduate $7,934, nonresident $19,039. Contact the university for current graduate tuition/fees. *Room and board per academic year:* $5,500.

Financial Aid: University of Minnesota - Duluth offers a direct lending program. Aid from institutionally generated funds is provided on the basis of academic merit, financial need, athletic ability, other criteria. Institution has a Program Participation Agreement with the U.S. Department of Education for eligible students to receive Pell Grants and other federal aid.

Departments and Teaching Staff: Accounting *professors* 2, *associate professors* 3, *assistant professors* 2, *instructors* 1, *part-time faculty* 3; economics 6, 1, 0, 1, 1; finance and management information systems 3, 1, 3, 1, 0; management studies 4, 2, 3, 0, 4; art 5, 4, 3, 2, 11; music 4, 1, 8, 1, 6; theatre 0, 7, 1, 0, 4; communication sciences and disorders 0, 3, 0, 1, 6; education 4, 9, 3, 5, 28; health/physical education/recreation 1, 4, 3, 1, 12; psychology 4, 7, 4, 0, 1; social work 1, 2, 2, 2, 6; American Indian studies 2, 0, 1, 0, 2; communication 1, 4, 0, 6, 2; composition 1, 3, 3, 7, 3; English 2, 5, 5, 1, 0; foreign languages and literature 2, 3, 0, 3, 0; geography 1, 1, 3, 1, 1; history 1, 1, 3, 0, 1; philosophy 2, 3, 0, 1, 2; political science 2, 3, 2, 2, 1; sociology and anthropology 8, 2, 3, 2, 3; women's studies 1, 0, 1, 0, 0; chemical engineering 1, 1, 2, 1, 3; chemistry 8, 1, 5, 1, 0; electrical and computer engineering 3, 3, 2, 0, 0; computer science 1, 4, 4, 1, 0; geological sciences 3, 4, 0, 0, 4; industrial engineering 4, 1, 3, 0, 6; mathematics and statistics 5, 7, 5, 1, 4; physics 3, 1, 3, 1, 0; School of Medicine 12, 16, 8, 0, 2.
Total instructional faculty: 463. Student-to-faculty ratio: 18:1. Degrees held by full-time faculty: doctorate 75%, master's 21%, baccalaureate 2%, professional 2%. 81% hold terminal degrees.

Enrollment: Total enrollment 10,366. Undergraduate 9,441 (51.1% men, 48.9% women).

Characteristics of Student Body: *Ethnic/racial makeup:* Black non-Hispanic: 1.3%; American Indian or Alaska Native: .7%; Asian or Pacific Islander: 2.6%; Hispanic: .8%; White non-Hispanic: 89.5%; unknown: 3.6%.

International Students: 142 undergraduate nonresident aliens enrolled fall 2004. Students from Europe, Asia, Central and South America, Africa, Canada. Programs are available to aid students whose native language is not English: social, cultural. English as a Second Language Program. No financial aid specifically designated for international students.

Student Life: On-campus residence halls house and apartments house 34% of student body. *Intercollegiate sports:* 8 men's and 9 women's programs. Intramural sports, life fitness sports, and club sports for the entire university community. *Special services:* Medical services, student organizations, student equity programs. *Student publications, radio:* UMD Statesman, a weekly newspaper. Radio station KUMD provides opportunities for experience as on-air hosts for for-credit interns in news, public affairs, or marketing. *Surrounding community:* Duluth population 85,000. Minneapolis-St. Paul, 150 miles from campus, is nearest metropolitan area. Served by mass transit bus system; airport 5 miles from campus; passenger rail service 3 miles from campus.

Library Collections: 705,000 volumes. 2,740 periodicals. 7,500,000 microforms. 14,000 audiovisual materials. Computer work stations available. Online catalog. Students have access to online information retrieval services and the Internet.
Most important special holdings include Voyageur Collection (northeastern Minnesota history); Ramseyer-Northern Bible Society museum collection.

Buildings and Grounds: Campus area 244 acres.

Chief Executive Officer: Dr. Kathryn A. Martin, Chancellor.
Address admission inquiries to Beth Esselstrom, Director of Admissions.

University of Minnesota - Morris

600 East 4 Street
Morris, Minnesota 56267
Tel: (320) 589-2211 **E-mail:** admisfa@morris.umn.edu
Fax: (320) 589-6399 **Internet:** www.mrs.umn.edu

Institution Description: *Enrollment:* 1,859. *Degrees awarded:* Baccalaureate.

Accreditation: *Regional:* NCA. *Professional:* teacher education

History: Established 1959; chartered and offered first instruction at postsecondary level 1960; awarded first degree (baccalaureate) 1964.

Institutional Structure: *Composition of institution:* Academic affairs headed by vice chancellor and dean. Management/business/finances directed by senor administrative director for finance and administration. Full-time instructional faculty 125. Academic governance body, Morris Campus Assembly, meets an average of 5 times per year.

Calendar: Semesters. Academic year Aug. to May. Freshmen admitted and degrees conferred Aug., Jan., June, July. Formal commencement June. Summer sessions of 2 terms from mid-June to mid-Aug.

Characteristics of Freshmen: 78% of applicants accepted. 45% of accepted applicants enrolled.
11% (45 students) submitted SAT scores; 89% (366 students) submitted ACT scores. *25th percentile:* SAT Verbal 520, SAT Math 495; ACT Composite 23,

ACT English 21, ACT Math 22. *75th percentile*: SAT Verbal 640, SAT Math 655; ACT Composite 28, ACT English 28, ACT Math 27. 8 National Merit Scholars.

55% of entering freshmen expected to graduate within 5 years. 86% of freshmen from Minnesota. Freshmen from 17 states and 3 foreign countries.

Admission: Admission is selective and decisions are based on a combination of high school record, ACT/SAT scores, letters of recommendation, leadership activities, special talents, and ability to add to the diversity of the campus student body. Approximately 80% of students were in the top 20% of their high school class; nearly 35% graduated in the top 10%. The SAT combined average is 1200; ACT Composite average is 25. Early action deadline Dec 1.; final deadline Mar. 15.

Degree Requirements: 120 credit hours; 2.0 GPA; 2 terms in residence; distribution requirements; major. fulfillment of some degree requirements and exemption from some beginning courses possible by passing CLEP. *Grading system:* A, B, C, D, no credit; satisfactory-no credit.

Distinctive Educational Programs: Interdisciplinary programs in Latin American and European area studies, women's studies. Facilities and programs for independent research, including individual majors, tutorials. Study abroad in various countries on all continents. *Other distinctive programs:* service learning and undergraduate research.

Degrees Conferred: 345 *baccalaureate*: majors in area and ethnic studies 3; biological/life sciences 38; business/marketing 36; communications/communication technologies 12; computer and information sciences 18; education 36; English 21; foreign languages and literature 19; interdisciplinary studies 16; liberal arts/general studies 25; mathematics 24; philosophy/religion/theology 3; physical sciences 23; psychology 20; social sciences and history 95; visual and performing arts 31.

Fees and Other Expenses: *Full-time tuition per academic year 2004–05:* $7,668. *Required fees:* $1,388. *Room and board per academic year:* $5,250.

Financial Aid: Aid from institutionally generated funds is provided on the basis of academic merit, financial need.

Financial aid to full-time, first-time undergraduate students: need-based scholarships/grants totaling $5,588,806, self-help $6,976,423; non-need-based scholarships/grants totaling $940,129, self-help $1,882,275, parent loans $249,664, tuition waivers $1,045,916, athletic awards $15,400.

Departments and Teaching Staff: *Professors* 22, *associate professors* 42, *assistant professors* 51, *instructors* 4; *part-time faculty* 44.

Total instructional faculty: 163 (full-time 119, part-time 44; women 67, men 96; members of minority groups 22). Student-to-faculty ratio: 13.5:1. *Faculty development:* $533,414 in grants for research. 5 faculty members awarded sabbaticals 2004–05.

Enrollment: Total enrollment 1,859. Undergraduate full-time 671 men / 995 women, part-time 54m / 116w. *Transfer students:* in-state 46; from out-of-state 17.

Characteristics of Student Body: *Ethnic/racial makeup:* number of Black non-Hispanic: 41; American Indian or Alaska Native: 143; Asian or Pacific Islander: 57; Hispanic: 28; White non-Hispanic: 1,459; unknown: 89. *Age distribution:* number under 18: 82; 18–19: 680; 20–21: 723; 22–24: 253; 25–29: 43; 30–34: 17; 35–39: 15; 40–49: 21; 50–64: 4; 65 and over: 1. 25% of student body attend summer sessions. Distance education courses available.

International Students: 22 nonresident aliens enrolled. 2 students form Europe, 7 Asia, 3 Central and South America, 8 Africa, 2 other. No programs available to aid students whose native language is not English. No financial aid specifically designated for international students.

Student Life: On-campus residence halls house 50% of student body. Residence halls for both sexes constitute 100% of such space. *Intercollegiate athletics:* men only: baseball, basketball, football, golf, tennis, track; woman only: basketball, cross-country, soccer, softball, swimming/diving, tennis, track, volleyball. Cars permitted without restrictions. *Special services:* social justice programs, medical services, academic assistance center, writing room. *Student publications, radio:* Weekly newspaper. Radio station KUMM broadcasts 24 hours/day during academic year. *Surrounding community:* Morris population 6,000. Minneapolis-St. Paul, 150 miles from campus, is nearest metropolitan area.

Publications: *Midwest Studies in Philosophy* (annual) first published 1976.

Library Collections: 203,651 volumes. Online catalog. Current serial subscriptions: paper 663; microform 1; via electronic access 17,000. 3,300 video recordings; 900 compact discs; 214 CD-ROMs. Students have access to online information retrieval services and the Internet. Total 2004–05 budget for materials and operations: $356,730.

Most important special holdings include government documents collection.

Buildings and Grounds: Campus area 152 acres. *New buildings:* Regional Fitness Center completed 1999; Science Building 2000; Social Science Building renovation2006.

Chief Executive Officer: Dr. Samuel Schuman, Chancellor.

Address admission inquiries to James Morales, Associate Vice Chancellor for Enrollment.

University of Minnesota - Twin Cities

100 Church Street S.E.
Minneapolis, Minnesota 55455
Tel: (612) 625-5000   **E-mail:** admissions@1umn.edu/tc
Fax: (612) 624-6369   **Internet:** www.1umn.edu/tc

Institution Description: University of Minnesota - Twin Cities is a state institution. *Enrollment:* 50,954. *Degrees awarded:* Baccalaureate, first-professional (dentistry, law, medicine, pharmacy, veterinary medicine), master's, doctorate. Specialist certificates also awarded.

Academic offerings subject to approval by statewide coordinating bodies. Member of the Consortia Committee on Institutional Cooperation and the University of Middle America.

Accreditation: *Regional:* NCA. *Professional:* accounting, applied science, audiology, clinical lab scientist, clinical psychology, dance, dental hygiene, dentistry, dietetics, endodontics, engineering, forestry, funeral service education, health services administration, interior design, journalism, landscape architecture, law, marriage and family therapy, medicine, music, nurse anesthesia education, occupational therapy, pediatric dentistry, perfusion, periodontics, pharmacy, physical therapy, planning, psychology internship, public health, radiation therapy, radiography, recreation and leisure services, school psychology, social work, speech-language pathology, teacher education, theatre, veterinary medicine

History: Established and chartered 1851; offered instruction at postsecondary level 1869; awarded first degree (baccalaureate) 1873. *See* James Gray, *The University of Minnesota, 1851–1951* (Minneapolis: University of Minnesota Press, 1951) for further information.

Institutional Structure: *Governing board:* Regents of the University of Minnesota. Representation: 12 regents. All voting. President serves ex officio. *Composition of institution:* Administrators 67 men / 26 women. Academic affairs headed by executive vice president and provost. Management/business/finance directed by associate vice president for budget and finance. Full-time instructional faculty 2,538 (tenured). Academic governance body is University Senate.

Calendar: Semesters. Academic year Sept. to May. Freshmen admitted Sept. and Jan. Degrees conferred and formal commencements May, Aug., Dec. One 8-week summer session.

Characteristics of Freshmen: 18,537 applicants (8,442 men, 10,995 women). 73.9% of applicants admitted. 40.6% of admitted students enrolled full-time.

17% (999 students) submitted SAT scores; 95% (5,337 students) submitted ACT scores. *25th percentile*: SAT I Verbal 540, SAT I Math 560; ACT Composite 23, ACT English 21, ACT Math 22. *75th percentile*: SAT I Verbal 660,SAT I Math 680; ACT Composite 28, ACT English 28, ACT Math 28.

42.5% of entering freshmen expected to graduate within 5 years. 59% of freshmen from Minnesota.

Admission: Rolling admissions plan. For fall acceptance, apply as early as Oct. 1 of year prior to planned enrollment; apply by Dec. 15 for priority consideration; after that applications considered on a space available basis by program. *Requirements:* Either graduation from accredited secondary school or GED. High school course requirements include 4 years English, 3 years math (one each of elementary algebra, geometry, and intermediate algebra), 3 years science with some lab including 1 biological science and 1 physical science, 2 years social studies (one must be U.S. history and 1 must be geographic studies), 2 years of one foreign language, 1 year visual or performing arts (including history and interpretation). Additional math and/or science courses, portfolio, audition, or high school activities required for some programs. *Entrance tests:* SAT I or ACT required (no preference). TOEFL required for international students. *For transfer students:* 2.5 minimum GPA for preferred consideration, 2.2 to 2.49 GPA for special review.

Credit and placement may be granted through CEEB AP exams for scores of 4 or higher; scores of 3 may be considered. Credit may be granted through CLEP subject exams, CLEP general exams, and DANTES exams. Credit and placement may be granted through challenge exams. Credit may be granted for military experience.

Tutoring available. Developmental courses offered in summer session and regular academic year; credit given.

Degree Requirements: *For all baccalaureate degrees:* 120 semester credit hours; minimum GPA of 2.0; minimum GPA in major of 2.0; C- or better in each course in the major; of lest 30 semester credit hours in residence; liberal education requirement; writing requirement.

Fulfillment of some degree requirements and exemption from some beginning courses possible by passing College Board CLEP, AP. *Grading system:* A–F; S–N (satisfactory, no credit).

Distinctive Educational Programs: Work-experience programs, including field experience, internships, practicums. Weekend and evening classes. Special facilities for using telecommunications in the classroom. Interdisciplinary programs in area, ethnic and culture studies, literature and fine arts, natural science and technology, social science, urban studies. Facilities and programs for independent research, including honors programs, individual designed majors, tutorials. Study abroad in Argentina, Australia, Austria, Belgium, Brazil, Bulgaria, Chile, China (People's Republic), Colombia, Costa Rica, Cyprus, Czechoslovakia, Denmark, Dominican (Republic), Ecuador, England, Estonia, Finland, France, Germany, Hong Kong, Hungary, Indonesia, Italy, Jamaica, Japan, Kenya, Malta, Mexico, Morocco, Netherlands, Nigeria, Northern Ireland, Norway, Philippines, Poland, Russia, Scotland, Senegal, Singapore, South Korea, Spain, Sweden, Switzerland, Taiwan, Tanzania, Thailand, Uruguay, Venezuela, Wales, Zambia. *Other distinctive programs:* Continuing education.

ROTC: Air Force, Army, Navy.

Degrees Conferred: 6,049 *baccalaureate*; 2,677 *master's*; 592 *doctorate*. Bachelor's degrees awarded in top five disciplines: social sciences 748; engineering/engineering technologies 587; business, management, marketing, and related support services 541; psychology 427; English language/letters 425. *First-professional:* 715 (law, medicine, pharmacy).

Fees and Other Expenses: *Full-time tuition per academic year 2004–05:* undergraduate resident $8,230, out-of-state students $19,860. Contact the university for current graduate/first-professional tuition and fees; rates vary by program. *Room and board per academic year:* $6,458.

Financial Aid: University of Minnesota - Twin Cities offers a direct lending program. Aid from institutionally generated funds is provided on the basis of academic merit, financial need, athletic ability, other criteria. Institution has a Program Participation Agreement with the U.S. Department of Education for eligible students to receive Pell Grants and depending upon the agreement, other federal aid.

Departments and Teaching Staff: *Total full-time instructional faculty:* 1,461. *Degrees held by full-time faculty:* 92.1% hold terminal degrees.

Enrollment: Total enrollment undergraduate 50,954. Undergraduate 32,716 (46.8% men, 53.2% women).

Characteristics of Student Body: *Ethnic/racial makeup:* Black non-Hispanic: 4.3%; American Indian or Alaska Native: .6%; Asian or Pacific Islander: 8.9%; Hispanic: 2%; White non-Hispanic: 76.5%; unknown: 5.6% *Age distribution:* 17–21: 43%; 22–24: 19.7%; 25–29: 17.8%; 30–34: 8.2%; 35–39: 4.3%; 40–49: 4.9%; 50–59: 1.2%; 60–up: 3%.

International Students: 622 undergraduate nonresident aliens enrolled fall 2004. Programs available to aid students whose native language is not English: social, cultural. English as a Second Language Program. No financial aid specifically designated for international students.

Student Life: On-campus residence halls house 19% of student body. Residence halls for both sexes constitute 100% of such space. Housing for married students also available. *Intercollegiate athletics:* men only: baseball, basketball, football, golf, hockey, gymnastics, swimming and diving, tennis, track, cross-country, wrestling; women only: basketball, golf, gymnastics, hockey, softball, swimming and diving, tennis, track, cross country, volleyball. *Special regulations:* Cars permitted without restrictions. *Special services:* Learning Resources Center, medical services, campus bus system. *Student publications, radio:* A daily newspaper. Radio station KUOM broadcasts 88 hours per week. *Surrounding community:* Minneapolis-St. Paul population 650,000. Served by mass transit bus system; airport 12 miles from campus; passenger rail service 4 miles from campus.

Library Collections: 5,613,176 volumes including bound books, serial backfiles, electronic documents, and government documents not in separate collections. Online and card catalogs. Current serial subscriptions: 48,105 paper, 5,582,760 microforms. 1,185,373 recordings. Students have access to online information retrieval services and the Internet.

Most important holdings include James Ford Bell Library on European expansion before 1800; Ames Collection of books about South Asia; Wangensteen Historical Library of Biology and Medicine.

Buildings and Grounds: Campus area 2,000 acres.

Chief Executive Officer: Dr. Robert H. Bruininks, President.

Address admission inquiries to Dr. Wayne Sigler, Director of Admissions; graduate school inquiries to Andrea Scott, Director of Graduate School Admissions.

College of Liberal Arts

Degree Programs Offered: *Baccalaureate* in Afro-American studies, American Indian studies, American studies, ancient Near Eastern studies, anthropology, art history, astronomy, biometry, Chicano studies, child psychology, Chinese, dance, East Asian studies, economics, English, film studies, Finnish, French, French area studies, geography, German, Greek, Hebrew, history, humanities, international relations, Italian, Japanese, Jewish studies, journalism and mass communication, Latin, linguistics, Middle Eastern studies, music, music education, music therapy, philosophy, physiology, political science, psychology, religious studies, Russian, Russian area studies, Scandinavian languages, sociology, Spanish, speech and hearing science, speech-communication, statistics, studio art, theatre arts, urban studies, women's studies; *master's, doctorate* offered through the Graduate School.

College of Agriculture, Food, and Environmental Sciences

Degree Programs Offered: *Baccalaureate* in agricultural business management (jointly with the Carlson School of Management), agricultural education (jointly with College of Education), agricultural industries and marketing, animal and plant systems, applied economics, food science, natural resources and environmental studies (jointly with College of Natural Resources), nutrition, science in agriculture, scientific and technical communication; *master of agriculture; other master's, and doctorate* offered through the Graduate School.

College of Biological Sciences

Degree Programs Offered: *Baccalaureate* in biochemistry, biology, botany, ecology evolution and behavior, genetics and cell biology, microbiology; *master's, doctorate* offered through the Graduate School.

College of Education and Human Development

Degree Programs Offered: *Baccalaureate* in business and industry education, child psychology, early childhood education; kinesiology; recreation, park and leisure studies; music education; *postbaccalaureate* in art education, elementary education, secondary education, physical education, agricultural education, business education, home economics education, industrial education; *master of education* in various fields; *master of arts* and *doctorate* offered through the Graduate School.

College of Natural Resources

Degree Programs Offered: *Baccalaureate* in fisheries and wildlife, forest products, forest resources, natural resources and environmental studies, recreation resource management, and urban forestry; *master of forestry, master of science* and *doctorate* offered through the Graduate School.

College of Human Ecology

Degree Programs Offered: *Baccalaureate* in apparel science and design, applied design, clothing design, costume design, food science, home economics, graphic design, housing, housing studies, human ecology, human relations, family and youth services, interior design, retail merchandising, textiles and clothing; *master's, doctorate* offered through the Graduate School.

Curtis L. Carlson School of Management

Degree Programs Offered: *Baccalaureate* in accounting, general management (areas of specialization in actuarial science, banking, finance, small business management and entrepreneurship, marketing, logistics management, operations management, general management studies); *master of business taxation; master's* and *doctorate* offered through the Graduate School.

School of Nursing

Degree Programs Offered: *Baccalaureate* in nursing; *master's, doctorate* offered through the Graduate School.

Admission: Admission as juniors after completion of 2 years of liberal arts studies at any regionally accredited college or university, including community and junior colleges; 2.8 GPA.

Degree Requirements: 200 credits; 2.0 GPA.

College of Pharmacy

Degree Programs Offered: *First-professional; master's, doctorate* offered through the Graduate School.

Admission: 2 semesters English, 2 calculus, 2 economics, 2 general biology (including zoology), 2 general chemistry, 2 organic chemistry, 2 physics, 1 psychology, 1 sociology.

Degree Requirements: 300 credit hours; 2.0 GPA; 9 months in residence.

Institute of Technology

Degree Programs Offered: *Baccalaureate* in aerospace engineering, astrophysics, chemistry, computer science, geology, geophysics, mathematics, physics, statistics, agricultural engineering, chemical engineering, civil engineering, electrical engineering, geoengineering, mechanical engineering, materials science and engineering; *master's, doctorate* offered through the Graduate School.

School of Dentistry

Degree Programs Offered: *Baccalaureate* in dental hygiene, dental hygiene public health, dentistry; *first-professional; master's, doctorate* offered through the Graduate School.

Admission: 130 quarter or 87 semester credits from accredited liberal arts college or university in the U.S. or Canada. Minimum overall GPA 2.5.

Degree Requirements: 2.0 GPA; 4 years in residence.

Law School

Degree Programs Offered: *First-professional.*

Admission: Baccalaureate of arts degree or equivalent; LSAT.

Degree Requirements: 88 semester course credits; 6 semesters in residence.

Medical School

Degree Programs Offered: *First-professional; master's, doctorate* offered through the Graduate School.

Admission: Baccalaureate degree from accredited college or university with the following minimum course and credit requirements: 1 year English and literature, 27 credits social and behavioral sciences and humanities; 20 credits chemistry (general or inorganic, organic; must include laboratory), 12 credits physics, 10 credits general biology or zoology; MCAT.

Degree Requirements: 4 years in residence.

College of Veterinary Medicine

Degree Programs Offered: *Baccalaureate* in veterinary science (BSVS); *first-professional; master's, doctorate* offered through the Graduate School.

Admission: Preprofessional program at accredited college or university including 9 credit hours English composition, 30 chemistry, 10 introductory biology, 10 physics, 5 mathematics, 5 microbiology, 4 genetics, 16–20 designated liberal arts. Chemistry, physics and biology must include laboratory.

Degree Requirements: 274 credit hours; 2.0 GPA; 13 quarters in residence.

Graduate School

Degree Programs Offered: *Master's* and *doctorate* in aerospace engineering, agricultural and applied economics, agricultural engineering, agronomy, American studies, anatomy, ancient studies, animal physiology, animal science, anthropology, art history, astrophysics, biochemistry, biomedical engineering, biophysical sciences, biostatistics, business administration, cell and developmental biology, chemical engineering, chemical physics, chemistry, child psychology, Chinese, civil engineering, classical studies, classics, communication disorders, comparative literature, comparative studies in discourse and society, computer and information sciences, conservation biology, design/housing and apparel, ecology, economics, education, educational administration, educational psychology, electrical engineering, English, entomology, environmental health, epidemiology, family social science, fisheries, fluid mechanics, food science, geology, geophysics, German, Germanic philosophy, Greek, health informatics, history, history of medicine and biological sciences, history of science and technology, horticulture, industrial engineering, industrial relations, Japanese, kinesiology, Latin, linguistics, mass communication, materials science and engineering, mathematics, mechanical engineering, mechanics, medicinal chemistry, microbiology, mineral engineering, neurosurgery, nursing, nutrition, oral biology, otolaryngology, pharmaceutics, pharmacology, philosophy, physical medicine and rehabilitation, physics, physiology, plant biological sciences, plant breeding, plant pathology, political science, psychology, Scandinavian studies, social and administrative pharmacy, social work, sociology, soil science, South Asian languages, speech-communication, statistics, surgery, theatre arts, therigenology, toxicology, veterinary biology, veterinary medicine, veterinary microbiology, veterinary parasitology, veterinary pathology, veterinary surgery/radiology/anesthesiology, wildlife conservation, zoology; *master's* only in agriculture education, American legal institutions; Arabic, architecture, art education, business education, business taxation, clinical laboratory science, dentistry, East Asian studies, elementary education, English as a second language, experimental surgery, family practice and community health, health services research and policy, Hispanic linguistics, Hispanic literature, home economics education, hospital pharmacy, industrial education, Italian, landscape architecture, Luso-Brazilian literature, management of technology, marketing

education, mathematics education, microbial engineering, music education, obstetrics and gynecology, physical therapy, planning, public affairs, public health, recreation/park and leisure studies, religious studies, Russian area studies, scientific and technical communication, social and philosophical foundations of education, studio arts; *doctorate* only in biomedical science, control science and dynamical systems, health services research/policy/administration, Hispanic and Luso-Brazilian literature/linguistics, neuroscience, pathobiology, vocational education.

Departments and Teaching Staff: Faculty are drawn from other colleges within the university.

General College

Degree Programs Offered: The General College does not grant degrees. The mission of the college since 1991–92 has been the preparation for transfer unit a the University of Minnesota. As such, it admits both underprepared and underqualified students who have less than 39 college-level credits.

Hubert H. Humphrey Institute of Public Affairs

Degree Programs Offered: *Master's* in planning, public affairs, public policy; other *master's* programs offered through the Graduate School.

School of Public Health

Degree Programs Offered: *Master of Public Health* in biostatistics, community health education, environmental health, epidemiology, health services administration, maternal and child health, public health administration, public health nutrition; *Master of Healthcare Administration* in hospital and healthcare administration; other *master's, doctorate* offered through the Graduate School.

Admission: Baccalaureate from accredited college or university with major in a relevant field; minimum 3.0 GPA or minimum 1500 GRE or 500 GMAT.

Degree Requirements: 3.0 GPA; completion of major requirements with a minimum 45 credits; 2 quarters in residence.

College of Architecture and Landscape Architecture

Degree Programs Offered: *Baccalaureate* in architecture, environmental design, landscape architecture; *master of architecture* and *master of landscape architecture* offered through the Graduate School.

University of St. Thomas

2115 Summit Avenue
St. Paul, Minnesota 55105-1078

Tel: (651) 962-5000   **E-mail:** admissions@stthomas.edu
Fax: (651) 962-6160   **Internet:** www.admissions@stthomas,edu

Institution Description: The University of St. Thomas is a private college affiliated with the Archdiocese of St. Paul and Minneapolis, Roman Catholic Church. *Enrollment:* 10,474. *Degrees awarded:* Baccalaureate, master's, first-professional, doctorate.

Member of the consortia Associated Colleges of the Twin Cities (ACTC); Higher Education Consortium for Urban Affairs, Inc. (HECUA); and Upper Midwest Association for Intercultural Education (UMAIE).

Accreditation: *Regional:* NCA. *Professional:* music, social work, teacher education, theology

History: Established, chartered, and offered first instruction at postsecondary level 1885; became College of St. Thomas 1894; awarded first degree (baccalaureate) 1910; added master's programs 1950, intermediate program 1968; women admitted to undergraduate program 1977; adopted present name 1989.

Institutional Structure: *Governing board:* University of St. Thomas Board of Trustees. Representation: 37 trustees, including 16 alumni; 1 administrator. 3 ex officio. All voting. *Composition of institution:* Administrators 36 men / 9 women. Academic affairs headed by vice president for academic affairs. Management/business/finances directed by vice president for administration. Full-time instructional faculty 223 men / 125 women. Academic governance body, the faculty, meets an average of 8 times per year.

Calendar: Semesters (4-1-4 plan). Academic year Sept. to May. Freshmen admitted Sept., Feb. Degrees conferred and formal commencement

Characteristics of Freshmen: 4,249 applicants (1,812 men, 2,437 women).

18% (208 students) submitted SAT scores; 97% (1,124 students) submitted ACT scores. *25th percentile:* SAT I Verbal 520, SAT I Math 528; ACT Composite 22, ACT English 22, ACT Math 22. *75th percentile:* SAT I 620, Verbal SAT I Math 640; ACT Composite 27, ACT English 27, ACT Math 27.

64% of entering freshmen expected to graduate within 5 years. 78% of freshmen from Minnesota. Freshmen from 45 states and 36 foreign countries.

Admission: Rolling admissions plan. For fall acceptance, apply as early as Sept. 1 of previous year, but not later than Jan. 1 of year of enrollment. *Requirements:* Either graduation from accredited secondary school or GED. Recommend 4 units English, 4 foreign language, 2 history or social science, 4 mathematics, 2 natural science. Lowest acceptable secondary school class standing 60th percentile. *Entrance tests:* College Board SAT, ACT composite, or PSAT. For foreign students TOEFL. *For transfer students:* 2.3 minimum GPA; maximum transfer credit limited only by residence requirement.

College credit and advanced placement for postsecondary-level work completed in secondary school. College credit for extrainstitutional learning on basis of ACE 2006 *Guide to the Evaluation of Educational Experiences in the Armed Services* and departmental examinations. Tutoring available. Developmental courses offered in fall term; credit given.

Degree Requirements: 132 semester hours; 2.0 GPA; final 2 terms in residence; 1 unit physical education; general requirements.

Fulfillment of some degree requirements possible by passing departmental examinations, College Board CLEP, APP (score of 3), and PEP. *Grading system:* A–R (failure to earn credit); satisfactory-poor-failure; satisfactory-failure; incomplete (carries time limit).

Distinctive Educational Programs: *For undergraduates:* Cooperative education. Dual-degree programs in engineering with Washington University (MO) and University of Notre Dame (IN). Cooperative interdisciplinary majors in Russian area studies and East Asian studies through ACTC. Interdepartmental majors in foreign language-business administration and international studies. Preprofessional programs in engineering, law, and medicine. Institutionally sponsored year or semester abroad in Vienna, Paris, Rome, Tokyo, Mexico, Madrid, London, Wales. HECUA terms in Oslo, Norway and Bogota, Colombia. UMAIE January abroad in Africa, Asia, Europe, South America, Hawaii. Individually arranged semester, year, or summer abroad. Financial aid available for study abroad programs. Student Program for Amity Among Nations. Cross-registration and additional degree programs through ACTC. Free tuition for parents. Special programs in reading, writing, and mathematics skills. *For graduate students:* External master's degree in curriculum and instruction at varying locations in Minnesota. *Available to all students:* Flexible meeting places and schedules, including weekend and evening classes. Special facilities for using telecommunications in the classroom.

ROTC: Air Force.

Degrees Conferred: 1,075 *baccalaureate*; 1,319 *master's*; 34 *doctorate*. Bachelor's degrees awarded in top five disciplines: business, management, marketing, and related support services 468; social sciences 101; communication, journalism, and related programs 84; biological/biomedical sciences 56; psychology 48. *First-professional:* 117.

Fees and Other Expenses: *Full-time tuition per academic year 2004–05:* $21,828. *Books and supplies:* $750. *Room and board per academic year:* $6,838.

Financial Aid: Aid from institutionally generated funds is provided on the basis of academic merit, financial need. Institution has a Program Participation Agreement with the U.S. Department of Education for eligible students to receive Pell Grants and other federal aid.

Departments and Teaching Staff: *Professors* 70, *associate professors* 129, *assistant professors* 126, *instructors* 22, *part-time faculty* 397.

Total instructional faculty: 745. Student-to-faculty ratio: 14:1. Degrees held by full-time faculty: doctorate 82%, master's 14%, baccalaureate 4%. 82% hold terminal degrees.

Enrollment: Total enrollment 10,474. Undergraduate 5,302 (49.5% men, 50.5% women).

Characteristics of Student Body: *Ethnic/racial makeup:* Black non-Hispanic: 2.8%; American Indian or Alaska Native: .5%; Asian or Pacific Islander: 4.9%; Hispanic: 1.8%; White non-Hispanic: 85.2%; unknown: 3.7%. *Age distribution:* 17–21: 73%; 22–24: 14%; 25–29: 5%; 30–34: 3%; 35–39: 2%; 40–49: 3%; 50–64: less than 1%.

International Students: 64 undergraduate nonresident aliens enrolled fall 2004. Students from Europe, Asia, Central and South America, Africa. Programs available to aid students whose native language is not English: social, cultural. English as a Second Language. No financial aid specifically designated for international students.

Student Life: On-campus residence halls house 40% of student body. Halls for men only constitute 58% of such space, for women only 42%. 2% of student body live off-campus in college-owned houses. *Intercollegiate athletics:* men only: baseball, basketball, cross-country, football, golf, hockey, ice hockey, soccer, swimming, tennis, track, wrestling; women only: basketball, cross-country, golf, soccer, softball, swimming, tennis, track, volleyball. *Special regulations:* Registered cars permitted in specified parking areas. Hall visitation from 10am to 11pm Sun.–Thurs., from 10am to 2:30am. Fri. and Sat. *Special services:* Learning Resources Center, medical services, ACTC intercampus bus. *Student*

publications: The Aquin, a biweekly newspaper; *Aquinas,* a yearbook; *Summit Avenue Express,* an annual literary magazine. *Surrounding community:* Minneapolis-St. Paul 1990 population 2,200,000. Served by airport 9 miles from campus; passenger rail service 1.5 miles from campus.

Publications: *Catholic Digest* (monthly) first published 1936.

Library Collections: 541,500 volumes. 481,000 microforms; 5,200 audiovisual materials; 5,750 periodicals. Online catalog. Students have access to online information retrieval services and the Internet.

Most important special holdings include Celtic Collection (6,000 titles, some in Gaelic, including literature, political science); collection of 18th- and 19th-century pre-Revolutionary French literature and history, including rare editions and diaries (500 titles); rare book collection (1,000 titles, including first editions and autographed copies).

Buildings and Grounds: Campus area 78 acres.

Chief Executive Officer: Rev. Dennis J. Dease, Ph.D., President.

Address admission inquiries to Kris Getling, Director of Enrollment Management; inquiries for graduate programs to Miriam Williams, Associate Vice President for Academic Affairs.

Walden University

155 South Fifth Avenue
Minneapolis, Minnesota 55401

Tel: (800) 925-3368	**E-mail:** apply@waldenu.edu
Fax: (612) 338-5092	**Internet:** www.waldenu.edu

Institution Description: Walden University is a comprehensive, private university offering undergraduate and graduate degrees. The university combines the highest academic standards of an accredited university with the flexibility and convenience of distance learning making it possible for busy professionals balancing work, family and education to pursue and educational experience *Enrollment:* 16,000. *Degrees awarded:* Baccalaureate, master's, doctorate.

Accreditation: *Regional:* NCA.

History: Established 1969; first degree (doctorate) awarded 1971. Walden University is owned by Laureate Education Inc.

Institutional Structure: *Composition of institution:* Governing board: Board of Directors with 9 members.

Calendar: Quarter-based and semester-based programs are offered.

Admission: Admission to the bachelor degree completion program requires an associate of arts degree or its equivalent; admission to master's programs requires a baccalaureate degree; admissions to doctoral programs require a master's degree. All degrees must have been earned from a regionally accredited institution or its equivalent. Some programs have additional requirements.

Degree Requirements: Varies by school and degree level. For baccalaureate programs, 181 quarter credits required; master degree programs require 54 to 68 quarter or 30 to 41 semester credits; doctorate programs require 134 to 136 quarter credits.

Distinctive Educational Programs: Dual degree programs; residency program for doctoral students; programs leading to professional licensure in psychology and social work; professionally accredited programs in nursing and public health; programs that focus on applying theory to practice.

Degrees Conferred: 1 *baccalaureate*: business/marketing1; 1,989 *master's*: business/marketing 18; education 1,939; health professions and related clinical sciences 5; psychology 27; 108 *doctorate*: business/marketing 24; education 25; health professions and related clinical sciences 10; psychology 36; social sciences and history 13.

Fees and Other Expenses: *Full-time tuition per academic year 2004–05:* $8,280. *Required fees:* $771.

Financial Aid: Aid from institutionally generated funds is provided on the basis of academic merit, financial need. Institution has a Program Participation Agreement with the U.S. Department of Education for eligible students to receive Pell Grants and other federal aid. Pell grant awards $224,624. Student loans totaling $145,803,256; parent loans $51,115.

Departments and Teaching Staff: *Professors* 40, *part-time faculty* 748. *Total instructional faculty:* 788 (women 422, men 366; members of minority groups 788). Student-to-faculty ratio: 22:1.

Enrollment: Total enrollment 13,553. Undergraduate full-time 72 men / 112 women, part-time 86m / 124w.

Characteristics of Student Body: *Ethnic/racial makeup (undergraduate):* number of Black non-Hispanic: 27; American Indian or Alaska Native: 3; Asian or Pacific Islander: 4; Hispanic: 3; White non-Hispanic: 41; unknown: 316.

International Students: 163 nonresident aliens enrolled. 21 students form Europe, 45 Asia, 3 Central and South America, 8 Africa, 66 Canada, 1 Australia,

19 other. No programs available to aid students whose native language is not English. No financial aid specifically designated for international students.

Student Life: Walden's virtual online environment provides students with 24/7 access to a suite of electronic services, including technical support, library services, Writing Center, Research Center, registration, and bursar information. Students have individual "portals" to access all these services as well as their online classrooms and for communication with faculty and support staff. *Student publications: The Walden Ponder* is the school newsletter for students, alumni, faculty, and staff. the university also publishes the *International Journal of Applied Management and Technology.*

Library Collections: The Walden University Library is located at Indiana University in Bloomington. Two librarians and their part-time reference assistants provide instruction to faculty and students in identifying, locating, and obtaining scholarly materials. Walden University provides a number of electronic scholarly databases for faculty and students.

Chief Executive Officer: Dr. Paula Peinovich, President and Provost.

Address admission inquiries to Larry Fishman, Director of Admissions.

William Mitchell College of Law

875 Summit Avenue
St. Paul, Minnesota 55105-3706
Tel: (651) 290-6476   **E-mail:** admissions@wmitchell.edu
Fax: (651) 290-6414   **Internet:** www.wmitchell.edu

Institution Description: The William Mitchell College of Law is a private, professional school. *Enrollment:* 1,078. *Degrees awarded:* First-professional (law).

Accreditation: *Professional:* law

History: Incorporated 1900; current organization formed by merger of the Minneapolis-Minnesota College of Law and the St. Paul College of Law 1956.

Calendar: Semesters. Academic year Aug. to May.

Admission: *Requirements:* Baccalaureate degree from an accredited college or university. *Entrance tests:* LSAT.

Degree Requirements: Completion of prescribed curriculum.

Distinctive Educational Programs: Joint degree programs: JD/MS in Health; JD/MA in Public Administration; JD/MS in Women's Studies.

Degrees Conferred: 309 *first-professional:* law.

Fees and Other Expenses: *Full-time tuition per academic year 2005–06:* $25,950.

Financial Aid: 340 students received federal and state-funded fellowships and grants totaling $168,981.

Departments and Teaching Staff: *Total instructional faculty:* 237 (full-time 34, part-time 203; women 100, men 136; members of minority groups 44). Degrees held by full-time faculty: professional 100%. Total faculty with doctorate, first-professional, or other terminal degree: 237. Student-to-faculty ratio: 22:1.

Enrollment: Total enrollment 1,078. Full-time 325 men / 328 women, part-time 212m / 213w. .

International Students: 21 nonresident aliens enrolled fall 2004. No programs available to aid students whose native language is not English.

Student Life: *Student publication: William Mitchell Law Review,* student-edited and student-published periodical.

Library Collections: 331,340 volumes. Current serial subscriptions: 4,118 paper; 17,029 microform. 240 computer work stations. Students have access to online information retrieval services and the Internet.

Buildings and Grounds: Urban campus.

Chief Executive Officer: Maureen Warren, Chief Administrative Officer.

Address admission inquiries to Kendra Dane, Director of Admission.

Winona State University

8th and Johnson Streets
Winona, Minnesota 55987-5838
Tel: (507) 457-5000   **E-mail:** admissions@winona.msus.edu
Fax: (507) 457-5620   **Internet:** www.winona.msus.edu

Institution Description: *Enrollment:* 8,076. *Degrees awarded:* Associate, baccalaureate, master's. Specialist and sixth-year certificates in education also awarded.

Accreditation: *Regional:* NCA. *Professional:* athletic training, business, engineering, music, nursing, nursing education, social work, teacher education

History: Established as First State Normal School at Winona 1860; offered first instruction at postsecondary level 1877; changed name to Winona State Normal School 1905, to Winona State Teachers College 1921; awarded first degree (baccalaureate) 1926; changed name to Winona State College 1956; adopted present name 1976.

Institutional Structure: *Composition of institution:* President, cabinet consisting of vice president of academic affairs, vice president of university relations, dean of students, comptroller. Five academic colleges: Business, Education, Liberal Arts, Nursing and Health Sciences, Science and Engineering. Full-time instructional faculty 146 men / 51 women. Academic governance body, Faculty Senate, meets an average of 9 times per year.

Calendar: Semesters. Academic year Sept. to May. Freshmen admitted year round. Formal commencement May. Summer session from mid-June to mid-Aug.

Characteristics of Freshmen: 5,183 applicants (1,830 men, 3,353 women). 79.4% of applicants admitted. 38.5% of admitted students enrolled full-time.

2% (38 students) submitted SAT scores; 98% (1,537 students) submitted ACT scores. *25th percentile:* SAT I Verbal 460, SAT I Math 500; ACT Composite 21, ACT English 19, ACT Math 19. *75th percentile:* SAT I Verbal 580, SAT I Math 610; ACT Composite 24, ACT English 24, ACT Math 25.

48% of entering freshmen expected to graduate within 5 years. 55% of freshmen from Minnesota. Freshmen from 14 states and 40 foreign countries.

Admission: Rolling admissions plan. Apply no later than 1 month prior to registration. Early acceptance available. *Requirements:* Either graduation from secondary school or GED. Recommend college preparatory academic units, including 4 units English, 3 mathematics, 3 science, 3 social studies, 2 foreign language, 1 elective. Lowest acceptable secondary school class standing 50th percentile. *Entrance tests:* SAT or ACT. For foreign students minimum TOEFL score 550. *For transfer students:* 2.40 minimum GPA and 36 credits for automatic admission, 2.00 –2.39 requires an interview.

Advanced placement for postsecondary-level work completed in secondary school. College credit for extrainstitutional learning (life experience) on basis of ACE *Military Guide,* portfolio, and faculty assessments. Tutoring available. Remedial courses offered during regular academic year; credit given.

Degree Requirements: *For all associate degrees:* 60 semester hours; 24 hours in residence. *For all baccalaureate degrees:* 124 hours; 48 hours in residence. *For all undergraduate degrees:* 2.0 GPA; general education requirements. For education degree, additional requirements.

Fulfillment of some degree requirements and exemption from some beginning courses possible by passing College Board CLEP. Fulfillment of requirements also possible by passing departmental examinations. Exemption from some courses also possible by passing College Board AP. *Grading system:* A–F; pass; withdraw (carries time limit).

Distinctive Educational Programs: Internships. Mentorships. Honors Program, Capstone Experiences, individualized study program. Residential College, Electronic Portfolio, Study abroad in England, Norway, Denmark, China, Japan and other countries through programs sponsored by other MSU institutions. Cross-registration with Saint Mary's University.

ROTC: Army.

Degrees Conferred: 53 *associate;* 1,348 *baccalaureate;* 266 *master's.* Bachelor's degrees awarded in top five disciplines: education 309; business, management, marketing, and related support services 254; health professions and related clinical sciences 145; communication, journalism, and related programs 81; parks and recreation 68.

Fees and Other Expenses: *Full-time tuition per academic year 2004–05:* undergraduate resident $6,324, nonresident $10,270. *Books and supplies* $980. *Room and board per academic year:* $5,630.

Financial Aid: Aid from institutionally generated funds is provided on the basis of academic merit, talent. Institution has a Program Participation Agreement with the U.S. Department of Education for eligible students to receive Pell Grants and, depending upon agreement, other federal aid.

Departments and Teaching Staff: Liberal arts *professors* 44, *associate professors* 24, *assistant professors* 26, *instructors* 10; education 19, 8, 20, 4; business 27, 10, 2, 0; science and engineering 33, 14, 18, 3; nursing 5, 12, 8, 0; non-instructional 5, 4, 6, 0.

Total instructional faculty: 302. Student-to-faculty ratio: 21:1. Degrees held by full-time faculty: master's 32%, doctorate 68%. 73% hold terminal degrees.

Enrollment: Total enrollment 8,076. Undergraduate 7,427 (37.8% men, 62.2% women).

Characteristics of Student Body: *Ethnic/racial makeup:* Black non-Hispanic: .7%; American Indian or Alaska Native: .3%; Asian or Pacific Islander: 1.7%; Hispanic: .8%; White non-Hispanic: 69.2%; unknown: 24.1%.

International Students: 230 undergraduate nonresident aliens enrolled. Students from Europe, Asia, Central and South America, Africa, Canada, Australia. Programs available to aid students whose native language is not English: social, cultural. English as a Second Language Program. Financial aid specifically designated for international students: variable number of scholarships available annually.

Student Life: On-campus residence halls house 1,800 students. Residence halls consist of co-ed, male, and female. *Intercollegiate athletics:* men only: baseball, basketball, football, golf, tennis, women only: basketball, cross-country, golf, gymnastics, soccer, softball, tennis, track, volleyball. *Special regulations:* Cars permitted without restrictions. *Special services:* Learning Resources Center, medical services. *Student publications, radio, television: Winonan,* a weekly newspaper. Radio station KQAL and WECC TV. *Surrounding community:* Winona population 30,000. Minneapolis-St. Paul, 180 miles from campus, is nearest metropolitan area. Nearest airport in LaCrosse, 25 miles from campus. Rail and and bus services close to campus.

Library Collections: 245,000 volumes. 894,000 microforms; 41,000 government documents; 6,700 audiovisual materials; 1,950 periodicals. Online catalog. Students have access to online information retrieval services and the Internet.

Most important special holdings include Education; Nursing; Paralegal.

Buildings and Grounds: Campus area 40 acres.

Chief Executive Officer: Dr. Darrell W. Krueger, President.

Address admission inquiries to Carl Stange, Director of Admissions.

Mississippi

Alcorn State University

Lorman, Mississippi 39096-7500
Tel: (601) 877-6100   **E-mail:** admissions@alcorn.edu
Fax: (601) 877-2975   **Internet:** www.alcorn.edu

Institution Description: Alcorn State University is a state institution and land-grant college. *Enrollment:* 3,443. *Degrees awarded:* Associate, baccalaureate, master's.

Accreditation: *Regional:* SACS. *Professional:* teacher education

History: Chartered as Alcorn University; offered first instruction at postsecondary level and changed name to Alcorn Agricultural and Mechanical College 1878; awarded first degree (baccalaureate) 1882; adopted present name 1974.

Institutional Structure: *Governing board:* Board of Trustees, State Institutions of Higher Learning. Representation: 13 trustees. All voting. *Composition of institution:* Administrators 11 men / 3 women. Academic affairs headed by dean of academic affairs. Management/business/finances directed by business manager. Full-time instructional faculty 184.

Calendar: Semesters. Academic year late Aug. to early May. Freshmen admitted Aug., Jan., June. Degrees conferred and formal commencement May. Summer session of 2 terms from early June to early Aug.

Characteristics of Freshmen: 6,802 applicants (2,631 men, 4,171 women). 35.2% of applicants admitted. 23% of admitted students enrolled full-time.

12% (63 students) submitted SAT scores; 88% (447 students) submitted ACT scores. *25th percentile:* ACT Composite 16, ACT English 15, ACT Math 15. *75th percentile:* ACT Composite 20, ACT English 18, ACT Math 18.

48% of freshmen from Mississippi. Freshmen from 29 states and 2 foreign countries.

Admission: *Requirements:* Either graduation from accredited secondary school with 15 units or GED (if over 21 years of age). Minimum 2.0 GPA. *Entrance tests:* ACT composite. For foreign students TOEFL. *For transfer students:* 2.0 minimum GPA; maximum transfer credit limited only by residence requirement.

Advanced placement for postsecondary-level work completed in secondary school.

Degree Requirements: *For all associate degrees:* 67 credit hours. *For all baccalaureate degrees:* 124 credit hours; exit competency examinations in writing; comprehensives or written project in major fields of study. *For all undergraduate degrees:* 2.0 GPA; 30 hours in residence; general education requirements.

Fulfillment of some degree requirements and exemption from some beginning courses possible by passing departmental examinations, other standardized tests. *Grading system:* A–F; withdraw (deadline after which pass-fail is appended to withdraw).

Distinctive Educational Programs: Cooperative education. Interdisciplinary programs. Preprofessional programs in engineering, forestry, and veterinary medicine. Honors programs.

ROTC: Army.

Degrees Conferred: 32 *associate;* 340 *baccalaureate;* 168 *master's.* Bachelor's degrees awarded in top five disciplines: liberal arts and sciences, general studies, and humanities 56; business, management, marketing, and related support services 41; health professions and related clinical sciences 40; education 33; biological/biomedical sciences 31.

Fees and Other Expenses: *Full-time tuition per academic year 2004–05:* in-state $3,732, out-of-state $8,463. Contact the university for graduate tuition. *Books and supplies:* $1,320. *Room and board per academic year:* $4,012.

Financial Aid: Aid from institutionally generated funds is provided on the basis of academic merit, financial need, athletic ability, other criteria. Financial assistance is available in the form of Pell Grants, College Work-Study, Veterans Administration Benefits, Supplemental Education Opportunity Grants (SEOG), Higher Education Assistance Loans (HEAL), Stafford Loans.

Departments and Teaching Staff: Agriculture *professors* 3, *associate professors* 5, *assistant professors* 4, *instructors* 0; biology 2, 1, 3, 6; education 2, 5, 1, 7; English 3, 2, 0, 12; communications 1, 0, 1, 2; social science 4, 3, 1, 7; industrial technology 1, 0, 4, 4; nursing 2, 2, 4, 2; business 0, 3, 1, 9; fine arts 1, 3, 4, 7; mathematics 0, 3, 2, 9; chemistry/physics 0, 8, 3, 1; home economics 0, 0, 3, 1; library 1, 1, 3, 2; health, physical education, and recreation 0, 2, 1, 0.

Total instructional faculty: 206. Student-to-faculty ratio: 13:1. Degrees held by full-time faculty: 48% hold terminal degrees.

Enrollment: Total enrollment 3,443. Undergraduate 2,832 (37.1% men, 62.9% women).

Characteristics of Student Body: *Ethnic/racial makeup (undergraduate):* Black non-Hispanic: 90.7%; Asian or Pacific Islander: 2%; Hispanic: .3%; White non-Hispanic: 6.6%. *Age distribution:* 17–21: 72%; 22–24: 14%; 25–29: 4.4%; 30–34: 3%; 35–39: 2%; 40–49: 2.3%; 50–59: .5%; 60–up: .6%.

International Students: 59 undergraduate nonresident aliens enrolled fall 2004. No programs available to aid students whose native language is not English. No financial aid specifically designated for international students.

Student Life: On-campus housing available. *Special regulations:* Cars must be registered. *Special services:* Learning Resources Center, medical services. *Student publications: The Alcornite,* a yearbook; *The Biweekly Bulletin,* a newspaper; *The Greater Alcorn Herald,* an annual literary magazine. *Surrounding community:* Lorman. Jackson, 90 miles from campus, is nearest metropolitan area. Served by airport 35 miles from campus; passenger rail service 90 miles from campus.

Library Collections: 220,000 volumes. 544,000 microforms; 1,045 periodicals; 6,300 audiovisual materials. Online catalog. Students have access to online information retrieval services and the Internet.

Buildings and Grounds: Campus area 1,700 acres.

Chief Executive Officer: Dr. Clinton Bristow, Jr., President.

Address admission inquiries to Emmanuel Barnes, Director of Admissions.

Belhaven College

1500 Peachtree Street
Jackson, Mississippi 39202
Tel: (601) 968-5928   **E-mail:** admissions@belhaven.edu
Fax: (601) 968-9998   **Internet:** www.belhaven.edu

Institution Description: Belhaven College is a private institution affiliated with the Presbyterian Church (USA). *Enrollment:* 2,493. *Degrees awarded:* Associate, baccalaureate, master's.

Accreditation: *Regional:* SACS. *Professional:* art, music

History: Established as independent college for women and offered first instruction at postsecondary level 1883; chartered 1893; awarded first degree (baccalaureate) 1894; reorganized as senior college for women under control of Presbyteries of Mississippi and Central Mississippi and merged with McComb Female Institute 1910; merged with Mississippi Synodical College of Holly Springs, a 2-year college, 1939; became coeducational 1954.

Institutional Structure: *Governing board:* Belhaven College Board of Trustees. Representation: 33 trustees. All voting. *Composition of institution:* Administrators 16 men / 17 women. Academic affairs headed by vice president for academic affairs. Management/business/finances directed by vice president for business affairs. Full-time instructional faculty 65. Academic governance body, the faculty, meets an average of 9 times per year.

Calendar: Semesters. Academic year late Aug. to early May. Degrees conferred May, Aug., Dec. Formal commencements May, Dec. Summer session from early June to early Aug.

Characteristics of Freshmen: 55% of applicants admitted. 41% of applicants admitted and enrolled.

35% (64 students) submitted SAT scores; 67% (122 students) submitted ACT scores. *25th percentile:* SAT Verbal 520, SAT Math 510; ACT Composite 21, ACT English 21, ACT Math 19. *75th percentile:* SAT Verbal 660, SAT Math 610; ACT Composite 27, ACT English 28, ACT Math 25.

39% of entering freshmen expected to graduate within 5 years. 33% of freshmen from Mississippi. Freshmen form 29 states and 12 foreign countries.

Admission: Rolling admissions plan. For fall acceptance, apply no later than 2 weeks after start of semester. *Requirements:* Graduation from accredited secondary school with minimum of 16 units, including 4 English, 2 math, 1 history, 1 natural sciences. *Entrance tests:* ACT or ACT. *For transfer students:* 2.0 minimum GPA; from 4-year accredited institution 94 hours maximum transfer credit; from 2-year accredited institution 62 hours; correspondence/extension students 6 hours.

College credit and advanced placement for postsecondary level work completed in secondary school. College credit for extrainstitutional learning on basis of ACE *2006 Guide to the Evaluation of Educational Experiences in the Armed Services.*

Degree Requirements: 124 credit hours; 2.0 GPA; 34 hours in residence; weekly chapel attendance.

Fulfillment of some degree requirements and exemption from some beginning courses possible by passing College Board CLEP. *Grading system:* A–F (plus/minus grading system is used); pass-fail; withdraw (carries time limit).

Distinctive Educational Programs: Adult Studies Program. Evening classes. Facilities and programs for independent research, honors programs, individual majors, internships.

Degrees Conferred: 330 *baccalaureate:* biological/life sciences 14; business/marketing 211; communications/communication technologies 6; computer and information sciences 13; education 24; English 12; liberal arts and sciences, general studies, and humanities 8; mathematics 7; philosophy/religion/theology 11; psychology 24. 121 *master's:* business/marketing 96; education 25.

Fees and Other Expenses: *Full-time tuition per academic year 2004–05:* $12,800. *Required fees:* $610. *Room and board per academic year:* $5,240.

Financial Aid: Aid from institutionally generated funds is provided on the basis of academic merit, athletic ability, other criteria.

Financial aid to full-time, first-time undergraduate students: need-based scholarships/grants totaling $2,748,478, self-help $6,829,376; non-need-based scholarships/grants totaling $3,643,095, self-help $6,648,363, parent loans $694,469, tuition waivers $141,515, athletic awards $141,515.

Departments and Teaching Staff: *Professors 16, associate professors 22, assistant professors 5, part-time faculty 198.*

Total instructional faculty: 263 (full-time 65, part-time 198; women 96, men 167). Student-to-faculty ratio: 18.6:1. Degrees held by full-time faculty: doctorate 70%, master's 28%. 80% hold terminal degrees.

Enrollment: Total enrollment 2,493. Undergraduate full-time 650 men / 1,402 women, part-time 32m / 61w; graduate full-time 75m / 228w, part-time 6m / 39w.

Characteristics of Student Body: *Ethnic/racial makeup (undergraduate):* number of Black non-Hispanic: 825; American Indian or Alaska Native: 13; Asian or Pacific Islander: 8; Hispanic: 35; White non-Hispanic: 1,077; unknown: 157. *Age distribution:* number under 18: 12; 18–19: 225; 20–21: 274; 22–24: 317; 25–29: 320; 30–34: 312; 35–39: 240; 40–49: 330; 50–64: 98; 65 and over: 1.

International Students: 30 nonresident aliens enrolled fall 2004. 6 students from Europe, 12 Asia, 2 Central and South America, 6 Africa, 4 other. Programs available to aid students whose native language is not English: English as a Second Language Program. No financial aid specifically designated for international students.

Student Life: On-campus residence halls house 19% of student body. Residence halls for men constitute 41% of such space, for women 59%. *Intercollegiate athletics:* men: baseball, basketball, cheerleading, cross-country, golf, soccer, tennis; women: basketball, cheerleading, cross-country, soccer, softball, tennis, volleyball. *Special regulations:* Cars permitted without restriction. Quiet hours. *Student publications:* An annual literary magazine, a quarterly newspaper, an annual yearbook. *Surrounding community:* Jackson population 350,000. Memphis (TN) and New Orleans (LA) are nearest metropolitan areas located 200 miles away. Served by mass transit bus system, airport, and passenger rail service, each 10 miles from campus.

Library Collections: 99,765 volumes. Current serial subscriptions: paper 167; microform 11,271; via electronic access 3,546. Online catalog. Students have access to online information retrieval services and the Internet. Total 2004–05 budget for books and materials: $125,783.

Most important special holdings include Presbyterianism (history and records); Belhaven College Archives; art.

Buildings and Grounds: Campus area 42 acres. *New buildings:* Student Center completed 2001; Bitsy Irby Visual Arts and Dance Center 2005.

Chief Executive Officer: Dr. Roger Parrott, President.

Address admission inquiries to Suzanne Sullivan, Director of Admissions.

Blue Mountain College

201 West Main
P.O. Box 160
Blue Mountain, Mississippi 38610-0160
Tel: (662) 685-4771 **E-mail:** admissions@bmc.edu
Fax: (662) 685-4776 **Internet:** www.bmc.edu

Institution Description: Blue Mountain College is a private college affiliated with the Southern Baptist Convention. *Enrollment:* 388. Men preparing for Christian vocations are admitted under special arrangement. *Degrees awarded:* Baccalaureate.

Accreditation: *Regional:* SACS.

History: Established and chartered as Blue Mountain Female Institute and offered first instruction at postsecondary level 1873; changed name to Blue Mountain Female College 1877; awarded first degree (baccalaureate) 1901; adopted present name 1907. *See* Robbie Neal Sumrall, *A Light on a Hill* (Nashville, TN: Benson Printing Company, 1947) for further information.

Institutional Structure: *Governing board:* Board of Trustees. Extrainstitutional representation: 10 trustees; institutional representation: president of the college; 8 alumni. 1 ex officio. 18 voting. *Composition of institution:* Administrators 1 man / 3 women. Academic affairs headed by vice president for academic affairs. Management/business/finances directed by business manager. Full-time instructional faculty 23. Academic governance body, Academic Dean's Council, meets monthly.

Calendar: Semesters. Academic year late Aug. to early May. Freshmen admitted Aug., Jan., June, July. Degrees conferred May and Aug. Formal commencement May. Summer session from late May to early Aug.

Characteristics of Freshmen: 47% of applicants accepted. 26% of accepted applicants enrolled.

89% (47 students) submitted ACT scores. *25th percentile:* ACT Composite 17, ACT English 17, ACT Math 16. *75th percentile:* ACT Composite 22, ACT English 24, ACT Math 20.

40% of entering freshmen expected to graduate within 5 years. 83% of freshmen from Mississippi. Freshmen from 5 states.

Admission: Rolling admissions plan. For fall acceptance, apply up to Aug. 15. Early acceptance available. *Requirements:* Either graduation from accredited secondary school or GED. *Entrance tests:* College Board SAT or ACT composite required. *For transfer students:* 2.0 minimum GPA; from 4-year accredited institution maximum transfer credit limited only by residence requirements; from 2-year accredited institution 64 semester hours; correspondence students 12 hours.

Degree Requirements: 120 semester hours; 2.0 GPA; minimum residence of 32 weeks; 25% of the total hours required for a degree must be earned in residence; chapel attendance 3 times weekly; 2 hours physical education; core requirements, English and mathematics proficiency requirement.

Fulfillment of some degree requirements and exemption from some beginning courses possible by passing departmental examinations, College Board CLEP. *Grading system:* A–F; pass-fail; withdraw (deadline after which pass-fail is appended to withdraw).

Distinctive Educational Programs: Internships. Weekend and evening classes. Accelerated degree program. Honors program. *Other distinctive programs:* Continuing education program. Summer enrichment program for exceptional students with a B average who have completed junior year of high school. Teacher Assistants Bachelor of Education degree program.

Degrees Conferred: 111 *baccalaureate:* biological/life sciences 6; business/marketing 5; communications/communication technologies 1; education 73; English 2; mathematics 1; philosophy/religion/theology 11; psychology 12.

Fees and Other Expenses: *Full-time tuition per academic year 2004–05:* $6,300. *Required fees:* $520. *Room and board per academic year:* $3,766.

Financial Aid: Aid from institutionally generated funds is provided on the basis of academic merit, financial need, athletic ability.

Financial aid to full-time, first-time undergraduate students: need-based scholarships/grants totaling $587,221, self-help $1,014,096; non-need-based scholarships/grants totaling $669,301, self-help $145,925, parent loans $78,565, tuition waivers $22,963, athletic awards $137,783.

Departments and Teaching Staff: *Total instructional faculty:* 35 (full-time 23, part-time 12; women 21, men 14; members of minority groups 1). Student-to-faculty ratio: 11:1. Degrees held by full-time faculty: doctorate 36%, master's 63%, professional 1%. 36% hold terminal degrees.

Enrollment: Total enrollment 388. Full-time 76 men / 223 women, part-time 9m / 80w. *Transfer students:* in-state 192; from out-of-state 21.

Characteristics of Student Body: *Ethnic/racial makeup:* number of Black non-Hispanic: 51; American Indian or Alaska Native: 1; White non-Hispanic:

334. *Age distribution:* number under 18: 1; 18–19: 74; 20–21: 27; 2–24: 73; 25–29: 39; 30–34: 41; 35–39: 27; 40–49: 28; 50–64: 9.

International Students: 2 nonresident aliens from Asia enrolled fall 2004. No programs available to aid students whose native language is not English. No financial aid specifically designated for international students.

Student Life: On-campus residence halls house 42% of student body. Residence halls for women only constitute 100% of such space. Some students live in college-owned houses off campus. *Intercollegiate athletics:* women only: basketball, tennis. *Special regulations:* Cars with decals permitted; fee charged. Dress regulations apply criteria of appropriateness and good taste. Curfews from 12pm to 6am. Quiet hours from 10pm to 8am Mon.–Thurs. *Special services:* Medical services. *Student publications: The Mountaineer,* a yearbook; *The Mountain Breeze,* a semiannual literary journal. *Surrounding community:* Blue Mountain population 700. Memphis (TN), 72 miles from campus, is nearest metropolitan area. Served by mass transit bus system; airport 40 miles from campus.

Library Collections: 52,915 volumes including bound books, serial backfiles, electronic documents, and government documents not in separate collections. Online catalog. Current serial subscriptions: 185 paper. 628 recordings; 214 CD-ROMs. 14 computer work stations. Students have access to the Internet at no charge. Total 2004–05 budget for books and materials: $40,000.

Most important special collection is the *Southern Reporter* (law books).

Buildings and Grounds: Campus area 44 acres.

Chief Executive Officer: Dr. Bettye R. Coward, President.

Address admission inquiries to Tim Barkley, Director of Admissions.

Delta State University

Highway 8 West

Cleveland, Mississippi 38733

Tel: (662) 846-3000   **E-mail:** dheslep@deltast.edu
Fax: (662) 846-4684   **Internet:** www.deltast.edu

Institution Description: Delta State University is a state institution. *Enrollment:* 3,863. *Degrees awarded:* Baccalaureate, master's, doctorate. Specialist certificates also awarded.

Academic offerings subject to approval by statewide coordinating bodies. Budget subject to approval by state governing boards.

Accreditation: *Regional:* SACS. *Professional:* art, business, counseling, family and consumer science, music, nursing, nursing education, social work, teacher education

History: Established as Delta State Teachers College 1924; offered first instruction as postsecondary level 1925; awarded first degree (baccalaureate) 1928; changed name to Delta State College 1955; adopted present name 1974. *See* Jack W. Grunn, *A Pictorial History of Delta State University* (Jackson, MS: University Press, 1980) for further information.

Institutional Structure: *Governing board:* Board of Trustees, State Institutions of Higher Learning. Representation: 13 trustees. All voting. *Composition of institution:* Administrators 31 men / 11 women. Academic affairs headed by dean of university. Management/business/finances directed by business manager. Full-time instructional faculty 201. Academic governance body, Academic Council, meets an average of 40 times per year.

Calendar: Semesters. Academic year late Aug. to early May. Freshmen admitted Aug., Jan., June, July. Degrees conferred May, Aug., Dec. Formal commencement May. Summer session of 2 terms from early June to early Aug.

Characteristics of Freshmen: 94% of applicants accepted. 97% of accepted applicants enrolled.

Mean ACT composite score men 20.19, women 19.32, class 19.67.

39% of entering freshmen expected to graduate within 5 years. 92% of freshmen from Mississippi. Freshmen from 17 states and 2 foreign countries.

Admission: Rolling admissions plan. For fall acceptance, apply as early as 1 year prior to enrollment, but not later than 20 days prior to enrollment. Early acceptance available. *Requirements:* Either graduation from accredited secondary school with 15 units which must include 3 English, 3 mathematics, 2 social studies; or GED. Minimum GPA 2.0. *Entrance tests:* College Board SAT; ACT composite (minimum score 15). *For transfer students:* 2.0 minimum GPA; from 4-year accredited institution 98 hours maximum transfer credit; from 2-year accredited institution 64 hours; correspondence/extension students 24 hours.

College credit and advanced placement for postsecondary-level work completed in secondary school. Tutoring available. Developmental courses offered during regular academic year; credit given.

Degree Requirements: 128–132 credit hours; 2.0 GPA; 24 of last 30 hours in residence; 2 physical education courses; general education requirements; demonstrated proficiency in writing; exit competency examination for English proficiency. Additional requirements for some programs.

Fulfillment of some degree requirements and exemption from some beginning courses possible by passing College Board CLEP, AP, other standardized tests. *Grading system:* A–F; pass-fail; withdraw (deadline after which pass-fail is appended to withdraw).

Distinctive Educational Programs: Cooperative education. Off-campus centers (at Clarksdale and Greenville, both 35 miles from main institution). Evening classes. Distance learning courses. Cooperative baccalaureate in medical technology with approved hospitals. Interdisciplinary majors in general studies, science. Preprofessional programs in dentistry, engineering, medicine, occupational and physical therapy, pharmacy, veterinary science. Honors programs. Child Development Center provides student laboratory experience and community service. *Other distinctive programs:* On- and off-campus continuing education. Commercial aviation program offers degree in flight management. Performing Arts Center.

ROTC: Air Force in cooperation with Mississippi Valley State University.

Degrees Conferred: 620 *baccalaureate* (B), 173 *master's* (M), 6 *doctorate*(D): biological/life sciences 29 (B); business/marketing 196 (B), 52 (M); communications/communication technologies 1 (B); education 151 (B), 76 (M), 6 (D); English 8 (B); foreign languages and literature 1 (B); health professions and related sciences 33 (B), 5 (M); home economics and vocational home economics 28 (B); interdisciplinary studies 3 (B), 10 (M); mathematics 1 (B); physical sciences 11 (B); protective services/public administration 49 (B), 19 (M); psychology 19 (B); social sciences and history 27 (B); trade and industry 26 (B), 11 (M); visual and performing arts 36 (B).

Fees and Other Expenses: *Full-time tuition per academic year 2004–05:* resident undergraduate/graduate $3,582, nonresident $8,522. *Required fees:* $490. *Room and board per academic year:* $3,734.

Financial Aid: Aid from institutionally generated funds is provided on the basis of academic merit, athletic ability, other considerations.

Financial aid to full-time, first-time undergraduate students: need-based scholarships/grants totaling $4,191,000, self-help $788,000; non-need-based scholarships/grants totaling $4,191,000, self-help $7,880,000; non-need-based scholarships/grants totaling $4,803,302, self-help $3,417,972, parent loans $356,488, tuition waivers $86,456, athletic awards $1,114,102.

Departments and Teaching Staff: *Total instructional faculty:* 281 (full-time 164, par-time 117; women 127, men 154; members of minority groups 32). Student-to-faculty ratio: 14:1. Degrees held by full-time faculty: doctorate 56%, master's 39%, baccalaureate 2%, professional 1%. 57% hold terminal degrees.

Enrollment: Total enrollment 3,863. Undergraduate full-time 1,096 men / 1,574 women, part-time 138m / 340w; graduate full-time 102m / 143w, part-time 116m / 346w. *Transfer students:* in-state 602; from out-of-state 6.

Characteristics of Student Body: *Ethnic/racial makeup (undergraduate):* number of Black non-Hispanic: 1,154; American Indian or Alaska Native: 6; Asian or Pacific Islander: 11; Hispanic: 22; White non-Hispanic: 1,955. *Age distribution:* number under 18: 14; 18–19: 654; 20–21: 961; 22–24: 758; 25–29: 277; 30–34: 138; 35–39: 82; 40–49: 102; 50–64: 73; 65 and over: 89.

International Students: 51 nonresident aliens enrolled fall 2004. Students from Europe, Africa, Canada. No programs available to aid students whose native language is not English. No financial aid specifically designated for international students.

Student Life: On-campus residence halls house 27% of student body. Housing available for married students. *Intercollegiate athletics:* men only: baseball, basketball, football, golf, swimming and diving, tennis, track; women only: basketball, softball, swimming and diving, tennis, track. *Special regulations:* Cars permitted without restrictions. *Special services:* Learning Resources Center, medical services. *Student publications: Broom,* a yearbook; *Confidante,* a biannual literary magazine; *Delta Statement,* a weekly newspaper. *Surrounding community:* Cleveland population 15,600. Memphis, 110 miles from campus, is nearest metropolitan area. Served by airport 1 mile from campus.

Library Collections: 295,694 volumes. 102,000 government documents; 828,979 microforms; 15,524 audiovisual materials. 298 computer work stations. Students have access to the Internet at no charge.

Most important special holdings include Dr. Blanche Cotton Williams Collection; Gilberr-Knolton-Lytle Family Papers; Walter Sillers, Jr. papers; Boyd-Walters-Bobo Family Papers.

Buildings and Grounds: Campus area 274 acres.

Chief Executive Officer: Dr. John Hilpert, President.

Address admission inquiries to Debbie Heslep, Coordinator of Admissions.

Jackson State University

1400 John R. Lynch Street
Jackson, Mississippi 39217
Tel: (601) 968-2121   **E-mail:** admissions@.jsums.edu
Fax: (601) 968-2358   **Internet:** www.jsums.edu

Institution Description: Jackson State University (Jackson State College until 1974) is a state institution. *Enrollment:* 8,351. *Degrees awarded:* Baccalaureate, master's, doctorate. Specialist in Education degree also awarded.

Academic offerings subject to approval by statewide coordinating bodies. Budget subject to approval by state governing boards. Member of the consortium National Student Exchange.

Accreditation: *Regional:* SACS. *Professional:* art, business, computer science, industrial technology, journalism, music, public administration, rehabilitation counseling, social work, speech-language pathology, teacher education

History: Established by American Baptist Home Mission Society 1877; offered first instruction at postsecondary level 1921; awarded first degree (baccalaureate) 1924; changed name to Mississippi Negro Training School and became 2-year state college 1940; changed name to Jackson College for Negro Teachers and added upper-division program 1944; adopted present name 1974. *See* Lelia Gaston Rhodes, *Jackson State University: The First Hundred Years, 1877–1977* (Jackson: University Press of Mississippi, 1979) for further information.

Institutional Structure: *Governing board:* Board of Trustees, State Institutions of Higher Learning. Representation: 13 trustees. All voting. *Composition of institution:* Administrators 53 men / 10 women. Academic affairs headed by vice president of academic affairs. Management/business/finances directed by vice president for fiscal affairs. Full-time instructional faculty 308. Academic governance body, Faculty Senate, meets an average of 3 times per year.

Calendar: Semesters. Academic year Sept. to May. Freshmen admitted Aug., Jan., June, July. Degrees conferred May, Aug., Dec. Formal commencement May, Aug. Summer session of 1 term.

Characteristics of Freshmen: 5,966 applicants (2,315 men, 3,641 women). 42.4% of applicants admitted. 36.7% of admitted students enrolled full-time.

78% (141 students) submitted ACT scores. *25th percentile:* ACT Composite 16, ACT English 15, ACT Math 15. *75th percentile:* ACT Composite 20, ACT English 21, ACT Math 18.

3% of entering freshmen expected to graduate within 5 years. 68% of freshmen from Mississippi.

Admission: Rolling admissions plan. For fall acceptance, apply as early as 1 year prior to enrollment, but not later than Aug. 15 of year of enrollment. Early acceptance available. *Requirements:* Either graduation from accredited secondary school with 16–17 units; or GED with minimum average score of 45, or score of 40 on each section. Minimum 2.0 GPA. *Entrance tests:* College Board SAT or ACT composite. For foreign students TOEFL. *For transfer students:* 2.0 minimum GPA; from 4-year accredited institutions 95 hours maximum transfer credit; from 2-year accredited institution 65 hours.

College credit and advanced placement for postsecondary-level work completed in secondary school. For extrainstitutional learning on basis of ACE *2006 Guide to the Evaluation of Educational Experiences in the Armed Services.* Tutoring available. Remedial courses offered in summer session and regular academic year; credit given.

Degree Requirements: 128 credit hours; 2.0 GPA; 2 terms in residence; 2–4 hours physical education; general education requirements; core requirements; exit competency examination in English.

Fulfillment of some degree requirements and exemption from some beginning courses possible by passing College Board CLEP. *Grading system:* A–F; withdraw.

Distinctive Educational Programs: Cooperative education programs. Special facilities for using telecommunications in the classroom. Interdisciplinary program in urban affairs. Facilities and programs for independent research, including honors programs, tutorials.

ROTC: Army.

Degrees Conferred: 780 *baccalaureate;* 275 *master's;* 39 *doctorate.* Bachelor's degrees awarded in top five disciplines: business, management, marketing, and related support services 163; education 169; engineering/engineering technologies 84; biological/biomedical sciences 59; public administration 51.

Fees and Other Expenses: *Full-time tuition per academic year 2004–05:* instate $3,842; out-of-state $8,570. *Books and supplies:* $1,600. *Room and board per academic year:* $4,974.

Financial Aid: Aid from institutionally generated funds is provided on the basis of academic merit, financial need, athletic ability. Institution has a Program Participation Agreement with the U.S. Department of Education for eligible stu-

dents to receive Pell Grants and, depending upon the agreement, other federal aid.

Departments and Teaching Staff: *Professors* 77, *associate professors* 82, *assistant professors* 98, *instructors* 51, *part-time teachers* 71.

Total instructional faculty: 324 FTE. Degrees held by full-time faculty: doctorate 73%, master's 26%, professional 1%. 73% hold terminal degrees.

Enrollment: Total enrollment 8,351. Undergraduate 6,605 (37.7% men, 62.3% women).

Characteristics of Student Body: *Ethnic/racial makeup (undergraduate):* Black non-Hispanic: 96.7%; American Indian or Alaska Native: .1%; Asian or Pacific Islander: .3%; Hispanic: .2%; White non-Hispanic: 1.4%.

International Students: 86 nonresident aliens enrolled fall 2004. No programs available to aid students whose native language is not English. No financial aid specifically designated for international students.

Student Life: On-campus residence halls house 32% of student body. Residence halls for men only constitute 36% of such space, for women only 64%. *Intercollegiate athletics:* men only: baseball, basketball, football, golf, tennis, track; women only: basketball, tennis, track, volleyball. *Special regulations:* Registered cars with decals permitted in designated parking areas. Quiet hours. Residence hall visitation from 6pm to 10pm. *Special services:* Learning Resources Center, medical services. *Student publications, radio: Black and White Flash,* a weekly newspaper; *Jacksonian,* a yearbook. Radio station WJSU broadcasts 126 hours per week. *Surrounding community:* Jackson metropolitan area population 322,000. Served by mass transit bus system; airport 8 miles from campus; passenger rail service 2 miles from campus.

Publications: Member of University Press of Mississippi.

Library Collections: 486,500 volumes. 675,000 microforms; 2,200 audiovisual materials; 1,740 current periodical subscriptions. Online catalog. Students have access to online information retrieval services and the Internet.

Most important holdings include Bibbs-Green Collection; Beadle Collection of Photographs; Mississippi Big 8 Conference Records.

Buildings and Grounds: Campus area 120 acres.

Chief Executive Officer: Dr. Ronald Mason, President.

Address admission inquiries to Director of Admissions.

School of Liberal Studies

Degree Programs Offered: *Baccalaureate* in criminal justice and correctional services; mass communications; music; psychology; social work; speech communications and theater arts; *master's* in alcohol and drug abuse; linguistics; music education; public policy and administration; *baccalaureate, master's* in art; English; history; modern foreign languages; political science; social science; education and geography; sociology. Education Specialist degrees also awarded.

Distinctive Educational Programs: Dual-degree programs in engineering with Auburn University (AL), California Institute of Technology, Mississippi State University. Preprofessional programs in medicine, pharmacy. Research Institute. Academic Skills Center.

School of Business

Degree Programs Offered: *Baccalaureate* in finance and general business, management, marketing; *baccalaureate, master's* in accountancy, business administration, business education and administrative services, economics. Specialist degree in education also given.

Distinctive Educational Programs: Cooperative education. Assistance to businessmen through Small Business Institute.

School of Education

Degree Programs Offered: *Baccalaureate* in elementary education; health, physical education, and recreation; secondary education; special education; *master's* in adult education; early childhood; educational administration and supervision; educational technology; elementary education; guidance; health education; health, physical education, and recreation; reading; secondary education; special education. Specialist certificates in early childhood education; educational administration and supervision; elementary education; guidance and counseling; health, physical education; reading; recreation; secondary education; special education.

Distinctive Educational Programs: Cooperative baccalaureate program in health with State Department of Health.

School of Science and Technology

Degree Programs Offered: *Baccalaureate, master's.* Education Specialist degrees also awarded.

Magnolia Bible College

822 South Huntington

Kosciusko, Mississippi 39090-1109

Tel: (662) 289-2896   **E-mail:** admissions@magnolia.edu

Fax: (662) 289-7904   **Internet:** www.magnolia.edu

Institution Description: Magnolia Bible College is a private institution affiliated with the Churches of Christ. *Enrollment:* 51. *Degrees awarded:* Baccalaureate.

Accreditation: *Regional:* SACS.

History: Classes began in the fall of 1976 with 9 students.

Calendar: Semesters. Academic year late Aug. to early May. Freshmen admitted Aug., Jan., June. Degrees conferred May, Dec. Formal commencement May. Summer sessions from May to Aug.

Characteristics of Freshmen: 90% of applicants accepted. 60% of accepted applicants enrolled. 60% of entering freshmen expected to graduate within 5 years.

Admission: Rolling admissions. *Requirements:* Graduation from an accredited secondary school or GED.ACT or SAT. Transfer credit accepted from accredited institutions and unaccredited schools of preaching; 2.0 minimum course GPA.

Degree Requirements: *For all baccalaureate degrees:* 128 semester hours; 32 semester hours in residence; 49 hours in residence required for the bachelor of theology degree; demonstrated proficiency in writing; 2 weeks of documented campaign participation.

Distinctive Educational Programs: *Available to all students:* Bachelor of Theology program allows students who already have a baccalaureate degree in any subject to complete a bachelor's degree in biblical studies in two years of full-time study.

Degrees Conferred: 6 *baccalaureate:* theology.

Fees and Other Expenses: *Full-time tuition per academic year 2004–05:* $4,890. *Room and board per academic year:* $4,890. *Other fees:* $40.

Financial Aid: Aid from institutionally generated funds is provided on the basis of academic merit, financial need, other criteria.

Financial aid to full-time, first-time undergraduate students: need-based scholarships/grants totaling $91,684, self-help $8,162, tuition waivers $400; non-need-based scholarships/grants totaling $26,935, self-help $626, tuition waivers $4,390.

Departments and Teaching Staff: *Total instructional faculty:* 10 (full-time 4, part-time 6; women 2, men 4). Total faculty with doctorate, first-professional, or other terminal degree: 4. Student-to-faculty ratio: 5:1.

Enrollment: Total enrollment 41. Undergraduate full-time 22 men / 3 women, part-time 11m / 7w. *Transfer students:* in-state 5; from out-of-state 1.

Characteristics of Student Body: *Ethnic/racial makeup:* Black non-Hispanic: 9; Hispanic: 1; White non-HispanicL 39. *Age distribution:* 17–21: 50%; 25–29: 305; 30–34: 19%; 35–39: 1%. 5% of total student body attend summer sessions.

International Students: 1 nonresident alien enrolled fall 2004. No programs available to aid students whose native language is not English. No financial aid specifically designated for international students.

Student Life: On-campus housing for men and married students. Cars permitted without restrictions. *Intermural sports:* basketball, football, golf, pool tournaments. Many opportunities for service in established local ministries.

Library Collections: 36,500 volumes including bound books, serial backfiles, electronic documents, and govern documents not in separate collections. Card catalog. Current serial subscriptions in paper, microform, and electronic form. 3 computer work stations. Students have access to online information retrieval services and the Internet.

Most important special collections include Restoration history (books and artifacts).

Buildings and Grounds: J.B. Hayes Activity Center houses administrative offices, meeting rooms, and gymnasium.

Chief Executive Officer: Dr. Leslie E. Ferguson, President.

Address admission inquiries to Allen Coker, Director of Admissions.

Millsaps College

1701 North State Street

Jackson, Mississippi 39210-0001

Tel: (601) 974-1000   **E-mail:** admissions@millsaps.edu

Fax: (601) 974-1059   **Internet:** www.millsaps.edu

Institution Description: Millsaps College is a private college affiliated with the United Methodist Church. *Enrollment:* 1,146. *Degrees awarded:* Baccalaureate, master's.

Accreditation: *Regional:* SACS. *Professional:* business, teacher education

History: Established and chartered 1890; offered first instruction at postsecondary level 1892; awarded first degree (baccalaureate) 1895.

Institutional Structure: *Governing board:* Board of Trustees of Millsaps College. Extrainstitutional representation: 39 voting trustees and an additional 12 life trustees. *Composition of institution:* Administrators 8 men / 4 women. Academic affairs headed by senior vice president and dean of the college. Management/business/finances directed by vice president for finance and the vice president for campus services. Full-time instructional faculty 92. Academic governance body, the faculty, meets an average of 10 times per year.

Calendar: Semesters. Academic year Aug. to May. Degrees conferred and formal commencement May. Summer session from early June to late July.

Characteristics of Freshmen: 85% of applicants admitted. 28% of applicants admitted and enrolled.

41% (115 students) submitted SAT scores; 87% (244 students) submitted ACT scores. *25th percentile:* SAT Verbal 520, SAT Math 540; ACT Composite 23, ACT English 23, ACT Math 21. *75th percentile:* SAT Verbal 660, SAT Math 640; ACT Composite 29, ACT English 31, ACT Math 28.

68% of entering freshmen expected to graduate within 5 years. 48% of freshmen from Mississippi. Freshmen from 19 states and 6 foreign countries.

Admission: Notification dates Dec. 20 and on a rolling basis thereafter. *Requirements:* Graduation from accredited secondary school with 14 academic units including 4 English, 3 math, 3 science (1 with lab), 2 social studies, 2 history. Recommended: 4 math, 4 science, 2 foreign language. Minimum 2.75 to 3.0 GPA. *Entrance tests:* College Board SAT or ACT Composite scores. *For transfer students:* 2.5 minimum GPA; maximum transfer credit 64 hours.

Advanced placement available for postsecondary-level work completed in secondary school.

Degree Requirements: 128 semester hours; 2.0 GPA; 32 of last 40 hours in residence as a degree-seeking student; core and distribution requirements; writing proficiency portfolio by junior year; comprehensives in individual fields of study. Additional requirements for some programs.

Fulfillment of some degree requirements and exemption from some beginning courses possible by passing departmental examinations, College Board CLEP Subject Examinations. *Grading system:* A–F; withdraw (permission required).

Distinctive Educational Programs: Internships. Evening classes. Adult Degree Program. Dual-degree program in engineering with Auburn University (AL), Columbia University (NY), Vanderbilt University (TN), Washington University (MO). Interdisciplinary humanities course for freshmen. Ford Fellows Program. Honors Program. Washington (DC) semester at American University. Public Administration Internship. School of Management Internship Program. Study abroad: Semester Program in Central Europe; Summer Program in London, Munich, and Prague; Summer Program in Costa Rica; British Studies at Oxford. Millsaps Institute of Central American Studies offers hands-on research, anthropology, archaeology, culture, environment, geology, and marine science. Fieldwork in Yellowstone.

ROTC: Army in cooperation with Jackson State University.

Degrees Conferred: 249 *baccalaureate;* 47 *master's.*

Fees and Other Expenses: *Full-time tuition per academic year 2005–06:* $19,490 undergraduate; $18,480 graduate. *Other fees:* $1,200 (undergraduate). *Room and board per academic year:* $7,566.

Financial Aid: Aid from institutionally generated funds is provided on the basis of academic merit, financial need, other criteria.

Financial aid to full-time, first-time undergraduate students: need-based scholarships/grants totaling $8,068,624, self-help $2,924,011, parent loans $215,085, tuition waivers $42,137; non-need-based scholarships/grants totaling $5,027,662, self-help $1,513,611, parent loans $1,172,763, tuition waivers $148,907. *Graduate aid:* 31 students received $386,590 in federal and state-funded fellowships/grants; 49 received $127,651 in federal and state-funded loans; 14 held research assistantships totaling $60,000 (ranging from $2,000 to $6,000 per year).

Departments and Teaching Staff: *Professors* 17, *associate professors* 39, *assistant professors* 33, *instructors* 3, *part-time faculty* 5.

Total instructional faculty: 97 (full-time 92, part-time 5; women 42, men 55; members of minority groups 8). Total faculty with doctorate, first-professional, or other terminal degree: 91. Student-to-faculty ratio: 12:1. *Faculty development:* $208,347 in grants for research. 5 faculty members awarded sabbaticals 2004–05.

Enrollment: Total enrollment 1,146. Undergraduate full-time 502 men / 551 women, part-time 13m / 20-w; graduate full-time 14m / 9w, part-time 15m / 22w. *Transfer students:* in-state 72; from out-of-state 68.

Characteristics of Student Body: *Ethnic/racial makeup:* number of Black non-Hispanic: 121; American Indian or Alaska Native: 4; Asian or Pacific Islander: 38; Hispanic: 16; White non-Hispanic: 884; unknown: 19. *Age distribution:* number under 18: 22; 18–19: 482; 20–21: 459; 22–24: 78; 25–29: 23; 30–34: 7; 35–39: 2; 40–49: 8; 50–64: 5.

International Students: 27 nonresident aliens enrolled fall 2004. No programs available to aid students whose native language is not English. No financial aid specifically designated for international students.

Student Life: On-campus residence halls house 82% of student body. Coed housing; freshmen women's dormitory. 54% of men join fraternities; 56% of women join sororities. *Intercollegiate athletics:* men only: baseball, basketball, cross-country, football, tennis, soccer, golf; women only: basketball, cross-country, golf, soccer, softball, tennis, volleyball. *Special regulations:* Residence hall visitation for freshmen according to firm schedule; second semester same as upperclassmen's schedule. *Special services:* Wesson Health Center, Guidance and Career Planning Center, Chaplain. *Student publications: The Purple and White,* a weekly newspaper; *Stylus,* a literary magazine; *Bobashela,* college annual. *Surrounding community:* Jackson metro-area population 425,000. New Orleans (LA), 150 miles from campus; Memphis (TN), 200 miles. Served by mass transit bus system, airport 7 miles from campus, passenger rail service 2 miles from campus.

Library Collections: 219,520 volumes. Online catalog. Current serial subscriptions: 517 paper; 8,697 via electronic access. 6,052 recordings; 798 compact discs; 114 CD-ROMs. 49 computer work stations. Students have access to online information retrieval services and the Internet.

Most important special holdings include College and Mississippi United Methodist Archives; Eudora Welty Collection; Johnson Military History Collection.

Buildings and Grounds: Campus area 100 acres. *New buildings:* Campbell College Center; Hall Activities Center; Student Plaza.

Chief Executive Officer: Dr. Frances Lucas-Tauchar, President.

Address undergraduate admission inquiries to Ann Hendrick, Dean of Admissions and Financial Aid; graduate inquiries to Melanie McCubbin, Director of Graduate Admissions.

Mississippi College

200 West College Street
Clinton, Mississippi 39058
Tel: (601) 925-3000   **E-mail:** enrollment-services@mc.edu
Fax: (601) 925-3276   **Internet:** www.mc.edu

Institution Description: Mississippi College is a private college affiliated with the Mississippi Baptist Convention (Southern Baptist). *Enrollment:* 3,588 *Degrees awarded:* Baccalaureate, first-professional (law), master's, doctorate. Education specialist degrees in education and counseling also awarded.

Accreditation: *Regional:* SACS. *Professional:* business, counseling, law, music, nursing, social work, teacher education

History: Established as Hampstead Academy, a coeducational institution, chartered, and offered first instruction at postsecondary level 1826; changed name to Mississippi Academy 1827; awarded first degree (baccalaureate) 1833; adopted present name 1830; became men's institution 1850; absorbed Hillman College, a women's institution and became coeducational again 1942; added graduate program 1950. *See* Richard A. McLemore and Nancy Pitts McLemore, *The History of Mississippi College* (Jackson, MS: Hederman Brothers, 1979) for further information.

Institutional Structure: *Governing board:* Board of Trustees of Mississippi College. Representation: 24 trustees. All voting. *Composition of institution:* Administrators 11 men / 3 women. Academic affairs headed by vice president for academic affairs. Management/business/finances directed by senior vice president for administration and chief executive officer. Full-time instructional faculty 162. Academic governance body, The general Faculty, meets an average of 8 times per year.

Calendar: Semesters. Academic year mid-Aug. to mid-May. Freshmen admitted Aug., Jan., June. Degrees conferred and formal commencement May, Aug.. Dec. Summer session from late May to early Aug.

Characteristics of Freshmen: 54% of applicants accepted. 39 of accepted applicants enrolled.

2% (30 students) submitted SAT scores; 95% (374 students) submitted ACT scores. *25th percentile:* SAT Verbal 527, SAT Math 510; ACT Composite 20, ACT English 21, ACT Math 18. *75th percentile:* SAT Verbal 660, SAT Math 607; ACT Composite 27, ACT English 29, ACT Math 25.

79% of freshmen expected to graduate in 5 years. 74% of freshmen from Mississippi. Freshmen from 14 states and 7 foreign countries.

Admission: Rolling admissions plan. Early acceptance available. *Requirements:* Either graduation from accredited secondary school with 15 units; or GED. *Entrance tests:* ACT Composite (minimum score 18) preferred; College Board SAT accepted. For foreign students TOEFL. *For transfer students:* 2.0 minimum GPA; from 4-year accredited institution 100 hours maximum transfer credit; from 2-year accredited institution 65 hours.

College credit and advanced placement for postsecondary-level work completed in secondary school and for extrainstitutional learning on basis of ACE *2006 Guide to the Evaluation of Educational Experiences in the Armed Services;* faculty assessment.

Degree Requirements: 130 credit hours; 2.0 GPA; 2 semesters in residence; weekly chapel attendance; 3 hours physical education; core curriculum; English proficiency examination.

Fulfillment of some degree requirements and exemption from some beginning courses possible by passing departmental examinations, College Board CLEP, AP. *Grading system:* A–F; withdraw (deadline after which pass-fail is appended to withdraw); incomplete (carries time limit).

Distinctive Educational Programs: *For undergraduates:* Work-experience programs, including cooperative education, internships. Cooperative baccalaureate program in medical technology in cooperation with approved schools. Preprofessional program in agriculture leading to baccalaureate awarded by Mississippi State University; other preprofessional programs in dentistry, law, medicine, pharmacy. Honors programs. Exchange program with University of Mainz in Germany. London Semester; Coalition of Christian College Study in Morocco; Australian/British Summer Study in Vienna/London; Salzburg College; French Study in Tours, France. Dual-degree programs in engineering in cooperation with Auburn University (AL) and University of Mississippi; in dentistry and medicine in cooperation with University of Mississippi. *Available to all students:* Evening classes. Special facilities for using telecommunications in the classroom.

ROTC: Army in cooperation with Jackson State University.

Degrees Conferred: 498 *baccalaureate* (B); 146 *master's* (M): biological/life sciences 17 (B), 1 (M); business/marketing 95 (B), 33 (M); communications/communication technologies 28 (B), 5 (M); computer and information sciences 12 (B), 1 (M); education 99 (B), 57 (M); English 14 (B), 4 (M); foreign languages and literature 11 (B); health professions and related sciences 66 (B), 20 (M); home economics and vocational home economics 1 (B); law/legal studies 7 (B); mathematics 10 (B), 3 (M); philosophy/religion/theology 23 (B); physical sciences 3 (B), 2 (M); protective services/public administration 25 (B), 4 (M); psychology 30 (B); social sciences and history 29 (B), 7 (M); visual and performing arts 28 (B), 9 (M). 121 *first-professional:* law.

Fees and Other Expenses: *Full-time tuition per academic year 2005–06:* undergraduate $11,400, graduate $7,074. Contact the college for law school tuition and fees. *Required fees:* $658. *Room and board per academic year:* $5,694.

Financial Aid: Aid from institutionally generated funds is provided on the basis of academic merit, financial need, other criteria.

Financial aid to full-time, first-time undergraduate students: need-based scholarships/grants totaling $7,962,327, self-help $7,461,407; non-need-based scholarships/grants totaling $10,018,742, self-help $1,765,168, parent loans $754,958, tuition waivers $860,303. *Graduate aid:* 82 students received $208,425 in federal and state-funded fellowships/grants; 527 received $5,781,969 in federal and state-funded loans; 6 received $11,499 for college-assigned jobs; 55 received other fellowships/grants totaling $140,483; 12 teaching assistantships awarded totaling $32,990.

Departments and Teaching Staff: *Professors* 53, *associate professors* 33, *assistant professors* 48, *instructors* 31, *part-time faculty* 127.

Total instructional faculty: 290 (full-time 163, part-time 127; women 133, men 157; members of minority groups 12). Total faculty with doctorate, first-professional, or other terminal degree: 174. Student-to-faculty ratio: 12:1.

Enrollment: Total enrollment 3,695. Undergraduate full-time 879 men / 1,278 women, part-time 87m / 178w; graduate full-time 40m / 107w, part-time 172m / 372w; first-professional full-time 287m / 157w, part-time 7m / 4w. *Transfer students:* 349.

Characteristics of Student Body: *Ethnic/racial makeup (undergraduate):* number of Black non-Hispanic: 429; American Indian or Alaska Native: 6; Asian or Pacific Islander: 20; Hispanic: 10; White non-Hispanic: 1,931, unknown: 12. *Age distribution:* number under 18: 8; 18–19: 685; 20–21: 833; 22–24: 460; 25–29: 184; 30–34: 106; 35–39: 62; 40–49: 69; 50–64: 14.

International Students: 16 nonresident aliens enrolled fall 2004. Students from Europe, Asia, Central and South America, Canada. Programs available to aid students whose native language is not English: social, cultural, financial. English as a Second Language Program.

Student Life: On-campus residence halls house 41% of student body. Residence halls for men constitute 50% of such space, for women 50%. *Intercollegiate athletics:* men only: baseball, basketball, football, track; women only: basketball, track. *Special regulations:* Registered cars permitted on campus in designated areas; fee charged. *Special services:* Learning Resources Center, medical services. *Student publications, radio: The Arrowhead,* a quarterly literary magazine; *The Mississippi Collegian,* a weekly newspaper; *The Tribesman,* a yearbook. Radio station WHJT-FM broadcasts 126 hours per week. *Surrounding community:* Clinton, population 15,000, is located in Jackson metropolitan area. Served by airport 20 miles from campus; passenger rail service 10 miles from campus.

Library Collections: 248,322 volumes. 205,054 microforms; 5,000 government documents; 13,000 audiovisual materials; 579 current periodical subscriptions. Online catalog. Students have access to online information retrieval services and the Internet.

Most important special holdings include Mississippi Baptist Historical Collection; Osborn Collection (Woodrow Wilson materials); alumni publications; Mississippi College Archives.

Buildings and Grounds: Campus area 75 acres.

Chief Executive Officer: Dr. Lee G. Royce, President.

Address admission inquiries to Chad Phillips, Director of Admissions; graduate inquiries to Dr. Debbie C. Norris, Graduate Dean.

Mississippi State University

P.O. Box 6305
Mississippi State, Mississippi 39762
Tel: (662) 325-2323   **E-mail:** admissions@msstate.edu
Fax: (661) 325-7360   **Internet:** www.msstate.edu

Institution Description: Mississippi State University is a state institution and land-grant college. *Enrollment:* 15,934. *Degrees awarded:* Baccalaureate, first-professional (veterinary medicine), master's, doctorate. Education specialist certificate also awarded.

Academic offerings subject to approval by statewide coordinating bodies. Budget subject to approval by state governing boards. Member of Gulf Coast Research Corporation, Mississippi-Alabama Sea Grant Consortium, Oak Ridge Associated Universities.

Accreditation: *Regional:* SACS. *Professional:* accounting, art, business, computer science, counseling, dietetics, engineering, family and consumer science, forestry, interior design, landscape architecture, music, public administration, rehabilitation counseling, school psychology, social work, teacher education, veterinary medicine

History: Established as Mississippi Agricultural and Mechanical College 1878; chartered and offered first instruction at postsecondary level 1880; awarded first degree (baccalaureate) 1883; changed name to Mississippi State College 1932; adopted present name 1958. *See* John Bettersworth, *the People's University: The Centennial History of Mississippi State* (Jackson, MS: University of Mississippi, 1980) for further information.

Institutional Structure: *Governing board:* Board of Trustees, State Institutions of Higher Learning. Representation: 13 trustees. All voting. *Composition of institution:* Administrators 169 men / 17 women. Academic affairs headed by president. Management/business/finances directed by vice president for business affairs. Full-time instructional faculty 800. Academic governance body, Faculty Council, meets an average of 9 times per year.

Calendar: Semesters. Academic year Aug. to May. Freshmen admitted Aug., Jan., June, July. Degrees conferred May, Aug., Dec. Formal commencement May, Aug., Dec. Summer sessions from June to Aug.

Characteristics of Freshmen: 68% of applicants admitted. 49% of applicants admitted and enrolled.

100% (1,753 students) submitted ACT scores. *25th percentile:* ACT Composite 20, ACT English 20, ACT Math 18. *75th percentile:* ACT Composite 27, ACT English 29, ACT Math 26.

51% of entering freshmen expected to graduate within 5 years. 74% of freshmen from Mississippi. Freshmen from 43 states and 14 foreign countries.

Admission: Apply as early as 20 days prior to the date of registration. *Requirements:* Graduation from an approved secondary school with 4 units English, 3 mathematics (algebra I and II and geometry), 3 science (1 must be laboratory-based), 2½ social science (must include U.S. history and American government), 1 required elective (from among foreign languages, mathematics, or science), 1½ free electives. *Entrance tests:* ACT score of 15; nonresident applicants may submit SAT score of 720 in lieu of ACT. *For transfer students:* 2.0 minimum GPA (architecture program 2.5); from 4-year accredited institution up

to 75% of degree requirement may be transferred; from 2-year accredited institution up to 50%.

Tutoring available. Remedial courses offered in summer session and regular academic year; credit given.

Degree Requirements: Minimum of 128 semester hours; 2.0 GPA; core curriculum; 1 year in residence.

Fulfillment of some degree requirements possible by passing departmental examinations, College Board CLEP. *Grading system:* A–F; withdraw.

Distinctive Educational Programs: Work-experience programs. Flexible meeting places and schedules, including off-campus centers (at Meridian, 90 miles away from main institution; Jackson, 125 miles away; Vicksburg, 150 miles away); evening classes. Interdisciplinary program in genetics. Facilities and programs for independent research, including honors programs, individual majors, tutorials. Study abroad programs in 15 countries.

ROTC: Army, Air Force. 14 Air Force and 12 Army commissions awarded 2004.

Degrees Conferred: 2,715 *baccalaureate* (B), 841 *master's* (M), 85 *doctorate* (D): agriculture 129 (B), 28 (M), 9 (D); architecture 53 (B), 9, (M); biological/life sciences 103(B), 20 (M), 7 (D); communications/communication technologies 123 (B); computer and information sciences 39 (B), 58 (M), 2 (D); education 427 (B), 245 (M), 30 (D); engineering/engineering technologies 388 (B), 112 (M), 10 (D); English 25 (B), 9 (M); foreign languages and literature 44 (B), 10 (M); health professions and related sciences 5 (B), 9 (M), 1(D); home economics 74 (B); interdisciplinary studies 109 (B), 11 (M); liberal arts/general studies 6 (B); mathematics 14 (B), 9 (M), 1 (D); natural resources/environmental science 53 (B), 21 (M), 8 (D); philosophy/religion/theology 7 (B); physical sciences 55 (B), 125 (M), 1 (D); protective services/public administration 34 (B), 19 (M), 1 (D); psychology 163(B), 14 (M), 3 (D); social sciences and history 110 (B), 12 (M), 7 (D); visual and performing arts 33 (B), 3 (M); 51 *first-professional:* veterinary medicine.

Fees and Other Expenses: *Full-time tuition per academic year 2004–05:* resident $3,874, nonresident $8,780. *Room per academic year:* $5,269.

Financial Aid: Aid from institutionally generated funds is provided on the basis of academic merit, financial need, athletic ability, other criteria.

Financial aid to full-time, first-time undergraduate students: need-based scholarships/grants totaling $20,215,242, self-help $31,510,775, parent loans $933,192; non-need-based scholarships/grants totaling $8,237,675, self-help $3,515,426, parent loans $2,356,203, tuition waivers $7,337,049, athletic awards $2,580,808. *Graduate aid:* 2,043 received $14,468,627 in federal and state-funded loans; 53 received $234,462 for work-study jobs; 1,159 received $7,849,575 for college-assigned jobs; 38 received other fellowships/grants totaling $227,696; 1,051 teaching assistantships awarded totaling $5,556,053; 1,203 research assistantships were awarded totaling $7,752,399.

Departments and Teaching Staff: *Professors* 326, *associate professors* 203, *assistant professors* 275, *instructors* 76, *part-time faculty* 259.

Total instructional faculty: 1,139 (full-time 1,005, part-time 134; women 388, men 751; members of minority groups 146). Total faculty with doctorate, first-professional, or other terminal degree: 972. Student-to-faculty ratio: 13:1. *Faculty development:* $167,789,559 in grants for research. 11 faculty members awarded sabbaticals 2004–o5.

Enrollment: Total enrollment 15,934. Undergraduate full-time 5,848 men / 5,136 women, part-time 770m / 741w; first-professional full-time 80m / 143w, part-time 2m / 6w; graduate full-time 822m / 694w, part-time 750m / 942w. *Transfer students:* in-state 1,334; from out-of-state 184.

Characteristics of Student Body: *Ethnic/racial makeup (undergraduate):* number of Black non-Hispanic: 2,469; American Indian or Alaska Native: 69; Asian or Pacific Islander: 164; Hispanic: 106; White non-Hispanic: 9,571. *Age distribution:* number under 18: 16; 18–19: 2,731; 20–21: 4,176; 22–24: 3,600; 25–29: 945; 30–34: 384; 35–39: 37; 40–49: 288; 50–64: 110; 65 and over: 8. 525 of student body attend summer sessions. Correspondence courses offered for credit.

International Students: 597 nonresident aliens enrolled fall 2004. Programs available to aid students whose native language is not English: social, cultural. English as a Second Language Program. No financial aid specifically designated for international students.

Student Life: On-campus residence halls house 21% of student body. Housing available for married students. Honor students are housed in an Honor Dorm. *Intercollegiate athletics:* men: baseball, basketball, cross country, football, golf, soccer, tennis, track; women: basketball, cross country, golf, soccer, softball, tennis, track, volleyball. *Special regulations:* Cars with decals permitted in designated areas only. *Special services:* Learning Resources Center; medical services; Student Support Services. *Student publications; radio: Reflector,* a biweekly newspaper; *Reveille,* an annual. Radio station student operated. *Adjacent community:* Starkville population 25,000. Memphis (TN), 135 miles from campus, is nearest metropolitan area. Served by airport approximately 15 miles from campus.

Library Collections: 2,451,640 volumes. Online catalog. 2,018,135 microforms; 41,500 government documents; 18,104 8,310 periodicals via electronic access. 137,000 audiovisual materials. 115 computer work stations. Students have access to online information retrieval services and the Internet.

Most important special holdings include John C. Stennis Collection; B.V. "Sonny" Montgomery Collection; Hodding Carter Papers; Mass Communications Collection; Mississippi Cooperative Extension Service and the Mississippi Agricultural and Forestry Experiment Station Records.

Buildings and Grounds: Campus area 4,960,794 square feet. *New buildings:* Hunter Henry Center completed 2003; Franklin Center 2004; Coastal research and Extension Center2004; Capps Entrepreneurial Center 2004; Roy Ruby Residence Hall 2005.

Chief Executive Officer: Dr. Charles Lee, President.

Address undergraduate admission inquiries to Diane Wolfe, Director of Admissions; graduate inquiries to Director, Graduate School.

College of Agriculture and Life Sciences

Degree Programs Offered: *Baccalaureate, master's, doctorate* in various fields.

Distinctive Educational Programs: Inter-American Elective allows students to spend their junior year in Central or South America. Double-degree program with College of Business and Industry. Nondegree programs in agriculture. Preprofessional programs in veterinary medicine. Interdisciplinary in agricommunication, animal physiology, food science and technology, genetics, nutrition, turf grass management. *See* College of Arts and Sciences.

School of Architecture

Degree Programs Offered: *Baccalaureate, master's* in architecture/applied visualization.

Distinctive Educational Programs: Accelerated degree program.

College of Arts and Sciences

Degree Programs Offered: *Baccalaureate, masters, doctorate.*

Distinctive Educational Programs: Preprofessional programs in dentistry, medicine, nursing, optometry, physical therapy. Cooperative baccalaureate in medical technology with approved hospitals. Field work in social work through the Health-Related Child and Family Services Program in Starkville. Double-degree program with College of Engineering and College of Agriculture and Home Economics.

College of Business and Industry

Degree Programs Offered: *Baccalaureate* in accounting, business statistics and data processing, economics, finance, general business administration, marketing, secretarial science; *master's, doctorate* in business administration.

Distinctive Educational Programs: Double-degree programs with other colleges of the university. Division of Business Services provides training and other services to the business community and governmental agencies. Division of Business Research sponsors research on state economic issues. 5-year baccalaureate-master's in engineering and business administration with College of Engineering.

College of Education

Degree Programs Offered: *Baccalaureate, master's,* and *doctorate* in various fields. Specialist certificate also given.

College of Engineering

Degree Programs Offered: *Baccalaureate, master's, doctorate* in aerospace engineering, agricultural engineering, biological engineering, chemical engineering, civil engineering, electrical engineering, industrial engineering, mechanical engineering, nuclear engineering, petroleum engineering;

Distinctive Educational Programs: Special facilities for using telecommunications in the classroom. Distance education master's degrees are offered in civil, chemical, electrical, computer, industrial, mechanical engineering and in computer science.

School of Forest Resources

Degree Programs Offered: *Baccalaureate* in forestry, fishery management, wood science and technology; *master's* in forestry, wildlife and fisheries science, forest products; and *doctorate* in forest resources.

Distinctive Educational Programs: Research opportunities through Mississippi Agricultural and Forestry Experiment Station and Mississippi Forest Products Utilization Laboratory.

College of Veterinary Medicine

Degree Programs Offered: *First-professional.*

Admission: Preveterinary curriculum including 6 English composition, 3 oral communication, 6 mathematics, 14 biological science, 18 physical science, 3–5 nutrition, 6 humanities, 3 fine arts, 6 social/behavior science; 3.0 GPA. Preference given to Mississippi residents.

Degree Requirements: 180 credit hours.

Mississippi University for Women

1100 College Street
Columbus, Mississippi 39701-5800

Tel: (662) 329-8543   **E-mail:** admissions@muw.edu
Fax: (662) 329-7263   **Internet:** www.muw.edu

Institution Description: Mississippi University for Women is a state institution. *Enrollment:* 2,415. *Degrees awarded:* Associate, baccalaureate, master's.

Academic offerings subject to approval by statewide coordinating bodies. Budget subject to approval by state governing boards.

Accreditation: *Regional:* SACS. *Professional:* art, business, music, nursing, speech-language pathology, teacher education

History: Established and chartered as Industrial Institute and College 1884; offered first instruction at postsecondary level 1885; awarded first degree (baccalaureate) 1889; changed name to Mississippi State College for Women 1920; adopted present name 1974.

Institutional Structure: *Governing board:* Board of Trustees, State Institutions of Higher Learning. Extrainstitutional representation: 13 trustees. All voting. *Composition of institution:* Administrators 14 men / 8 women. Academic affairs headed by provost. Management/business/finances directed by chief financial officer. Full-time instructional faculty 83 men / 50 women. Academic governance body, Academic Council, meets an average of 12 times per year.

Calendar: Semesters. Academic year July to June. Freshmen admitted Aug., Jan., June, July. Degrees conferred and formal commencement May. Summer and evening session from early May to mid-Aug.

Characteristics of Freshmen: 85% of applicants accepted. 62% of accepted applicants enrolled.

49% (11 students) submitted SAT scores; 94% (232 students) submitted ACT scores. *25th percentile:* ACT Composite 18, ACT English 18, ACT Math 17. *75th percentile:* ACT Composite 24, ACT English 25, ACT Math 22.

35% of entering freshmen expected to graduate within 5 years. 85% of freshmen from Mississippi. Freshmen from 12 states and 13 foreign countries.

Admission: Rolling admissions plan. For fall acceptance, apply as early as junior year of secondary school, but not later than Aug. of year of enrollment. Early acceptance available. *Requirements:* Either graduation from accredited secondary school with 15.5 units which must include 4 English, 2 mathematics, 3 social studies, 3 science; or GED. *Entrance tests:* ACT minimum composite 16. *For transfer students:* From 4-year accredited institution 98 semester hours maximum transfer credit; from 2-year accredited institution 60 semester hours; good standing at institution previously attended.

College credit for postsecondary-level work completed in secondary school. Tutoring available. Noncredit remedial courses offered during regular academic year.

Degree Requirements: *For all associate degrees:* 72 credit hours. *For all baccalaureate degrees:* 128–133 credit hours; 2 hours physical education. *For all undergraduate degrees:* 2.0 GPA; 25% of courses must be taken in residence.

Fulfillment of some degree requirements and exemption from some beginning courses possible by passing departmental examinations, College Board CLEP, APP. *Grading system:* A–F; pass-fail; withdraw (deadline after which pass-fail is appended to withdraw).

Distinctive Educational Programs: *For undergraduates:* Dual-degree programs in engineering with Auburn University (AL), Mississippi State University. Honors programs. Summer study in biological sciences at Gulf Coast Research Laboratory. *Available to all students:* Weekend and evening classes. Accelerated degree programs. Individual majors.

ROTC: Air Force and Army in cooperation with Mississippi State University.

Degrees Conferred: 45 *associate;* 345 *baccalaureate:* biological/life sciences 11; business/marketing 11; communications/communication technologies 15; education 57; English 23; foreign languages and literature 1; health professions and related sciences 71; home economics and vocational home economics 31; law/legal studies 13; mathematics 6; parks and recreation 8; personal and miscellaneous services 9; physical sciences 3; psychology 20; social sciences and history 10; visual and performing arts 25; 58 *master's*: education 25; health professions and related clinical sciences 33.

Fees and Other Expenses: *Full-time tuition per academic year 2004–05:* $3,495. *Room and board per academic year:* $3,778.

Financial Aid: Aid from institutionally generated funds is provided on the basis of academic merit, athletic ability.

Financial aid to full-time, first-time undergraduate students: need-based scholarships/grants totaling $3,217,783, self-help $3,575,345; non-need-based scholarships/grants totaling $3,628,796, self-help $3,229,500, parent loans $88,766; tuition waivers $106,878.

Departments and Teaching Staff: *Total instructional faculty:* 179 (full-time 134, part-time 45; women 114, men 65; members of minority groups 179). Total faculty with doctorate, first-professional, or other terminal degree: 92. Student-to-faculty ratio: 12.2:1. Degrees held by full-time faculty: doctorate 54.1%, master's 44.3%, baccalaureate 1.6%. 59.1% hold terminal degrees.

Enrollment: Total enrollment 2,415. Undergraduate full-time 225 men / 1,384 women, part-time 99m / 357w; graduate full-time 6m / 65w, part-time 11m / 86w.

Characteristics of Student Body: *Ethnic/racial makeup:* number of Black non-Hispanic: 709; American Indian or Alaska Native: 11; Asian or Pacific Islander: 30; Hispanic: 15; White non-Hispanic: 1,436. *Age distribution:* number under 18: 59; 18–19: 350; 20–21: 303; 22–24: 468; 25–29: 312; 30–34: 188; 35–39: 118; 40–49: 163; 50–64: 64; 65 and over: 6.

International Students: 30 nonresident aliens enrolled fall 2004. Students form Europe, Asia, Central and South America, Africa, Canada. No programs available to aid students whose native language is not English. No financial aid specifically designated for international students.

Student Life: On-campus residence halls house 29% of student body. Housing available for married students. Over 70 student organizations representing divers student population. Concerts each semester. *Special regulations:* Cars with parking permits allowed in designated parking areas; fee charged. *Special services:* Academic Support Computer Lab; medical services. *Student publications: Dilletanti,* an annual literary magazine; *Meh Lady,* a yearbook; *Spectator,* a weekly newspaper. *Surrounding community:* Columbus population 30,000. Birmingham (AL), 120 miles from campus, is nearest metropolitan area. Served by airport 9 miles from campus.

Publications: *Publisher:* Member of State of Mississippi University Press.

Library Collections: 242.593 volumes. Current periodical subscriptions: 2,236 paper; 770.979 microform. Online catalog. 21 computer work stations. Students have access to online information retrieval services. Total 2004–05 budget for books and materials: $299,705.

Most important special holdings include Mississippiania (books by and about local authors). Library is a depository for U.S. government documents.

Buildings and Grounds: Campus area 104 acres.

Chief Executive Officer: Dr. Claudia A. Limbert, President.

Address admission inquiries to Dr. Bucky Wesley, Vice President of Student Services.

Mississippi Valley State University

14000 Highway 82 West
Itta Bena, Mississippi 38941-1400
Tel: (662) 254-9041   **E-mail:** admissions@mvsu.edu
Fax: (662) 254-3717   **Internet:** www.mvsu.edu

Institution Description: Mississippi Valley State University (Mississippi Valley State College until 1974) is a state institution. *Enrollment:* 3,244. *Degrees awarded:* Baccalaureate, master's. Certificates also awarded.

Academic offerings subject to approval by statewide coordinating bodies. Budget subject to approval by state governing boards.

Accreditation: *Regional:* SACS. *Professional:* art, business, environmental health, industrial technology, music, social work, teacher education

History: Established and chartered as Mississippi Vocational College 1946; awarded first degree (baccalaureate) 1953; changed name to Mississippi Valley State College 1964; adopted present name 1974.

Institutional Structure: *Governing board:* Board of Trustees, State Institutions of Higher Learning. Representation: 13 trustees. All voting. *Composition of institution:* Administrators 16 men / 6 women. Academic affairs headed by dean of instruction. Management/business/finances directed by business manager. Full-time instructional faculty 112. Academic governance body, Academic Policy Committee, meets an average of 10 times per year.

Calendar: Semesters. Academic year Aug. to May. Freshmen admitted Aug., Sept., Dec., Jan., June, July. Degrees conferred and formal commencement May. Summer session from late May to early Aug.

Characteristics of Freshmen: 25% of applicants admitted. 9% of applicants admitted and enrolled.

83% (321 students) submitted ACT scores. *25th percentile:* ACT Composite 15. *75th percentile:* ACT Composite 19.

35% of entering freshmen expected to graduate within 5 years. 78% of freshmen from Mississippi. Freshmen from 19 states and 2 foreign countries.

Admission: Rolling admissions plan. For fall acceptance, apply no later than 20 days prior to registration. *Requirements:* Either graduation from accredited secondary school with 4 units in English, 2 mathematics, 2 social studies, 1 science, 7 electives; or GED. Additional requirements for some programs. Minimum 2.0 GPA. *Entrance tests:* College Board SAT or ACT composite. For foreign students TOEFL. *For transfer students:* 2.0 minimum GPA; from 4-year accredited institution maximum transfer credit limited only by residence requirement; from 2-year accredited institution 64 semester hours; correspondence/extension 6 hours.

Tutoring available. Noncredit developmental/remedial courses offered in summer session and regular academic year.

Degree Requirements: *For all associate degrees:* 54–60 credit hours. *For all baccalaureate degrees:* 124 credit hours; general core curriculum; exit competency examination in writing. *For all undergraduate degrees:* 2.0 GPA; last 30 hours in residence; 2 hours physical education. Additional requirements for some programs.

Exemption from some beginning courses possible by passing standardized tests. *Grading system:* A–F; pass-fail; withdraw (deadline after which pass-fail is appended to withdraw).

Distinctive Educational Programs: Work-experience programs. Evening classes. Cooperative program in oceanography with the Gulf Coast Research Laboratory. Special facilities for using telecommunications in the classroom. Preprofessional programs in dental hygiene, medicine, nursing, physical therapy. Facilities and programs for independent research, including honors programs, individual majors, tutorials. Study abroad in Italy. *Other distinctive programs:* Continuing education for adult community residents.

ROTC: Army in cooperation with Delta State University; Air Force.

Degrees Conferred: 310 *baccalaureate:* (B); 90 *master's* (M): biological/life sciences 15 (B); business/marketing 43 (B); communications/communication technologies 11 (B); computer and information sciences 19; education 63 (B), 43 (M); engineering and engineering technologies 9 (B); English 12 (B); health professions and related sciences 1 (B), 2 (M); mathematics 5 (B); physical sciences 1 (B); protective services/public administration 82 (B), 45 (M); social sciences and history 45 (B); visual and performing arts 4 (B).

Fees and Other Expenses: *Full-time tuition per academic year 2004–05:* resident undergraduate $3,832, nonresident $8,840; resident graduate $3,932, nonresident $10,123. *Room and board per academic year:* $3,506.

Financial Aid: Institution has a Program Participation Agreement with the U.S. Department of Education for eligible students to receive Pell Grants and other federal aid.

Departments and Teaching Staff: *Professors* 16, *associate professors* 22, *assistant professors* 58; *instructors* 19. *Total instructional faculty:* 115 (women 48, men 67; members of minority groups 101). Total faculty with doctorate, first-professional, or other terminal degree: 69. Student-to-faculty ratio: 13:1.

Enrollment: Total enrollment 3,244. Undergraduate full-time 842 men / 1,870 women, part-time 70m / 307w; graduate full-time 16m / 48w, part-time 69m /399w.

Characteristics of Student Body: *Ethnic/racial makeup:* number of Black non-Hispanic: 2,903; American Indian or Alaska Native: 1; Asian or Pacific Islander: 2; Hispanic: 6; White non-Hispanic: 88; unknown: 89. *Age distribution:* number under 18: 1; 18–19: 475; 20–21: 548; 22–24: 690; 25–29: 434; 30–34: 291; 35–39: 229; 40–49: 296; 50–64: 122; 65 and over: 3.

International Students: 19 nonresident aliens enrolled fall 2004. No programs available to aid students whose native language is not English. No financial aid specifically designated for international students.

Student Life: On-campus residence halls house 83% of student body. Residence halls for men only constitute 50% of such space, for women only 50%. *Intercollegiate athletics:* men only: baseball, basketball, football, golf, tennis; women only: basketball; both sexes: track. *Special regulations:* Cars permitted without restrictions. *Special services:* Learning Resources Center, medical services, bus service to Greenville. *Student publications: Delvian Gazette,* a monthly newspaper. *Surrounding community:* Itta Bena population 3,000. Memphis, 135 miles from campus, is nearest metropolitan area. Served by airport 17 miles from campus.

Publications: Member of University Press of Mississippi.

Library Collections: 148,000 volumes. 14,000 microforms; 750 periodical subscriptions; 8,500 recordings/tapes. Online catalog. Students have access to online information retrieval services and the Internet.

Buildings and Grounds: Campus area 450 acres.

Chief Executive Officer: Dr. Lester C. Newman, President.

Address undergraduate admission inquiries to Mark Green, Director of Admissions; graduate inquiries to Dr. Rickey Hill, Dean, Graduate School.

Reformed Theological Seminary

5422 Clinton Boulevard
Jackson, Mississippi 39209-3099
Tel: (601) 923-1600   **E-mail:** rts.jackson@rts.edu
Fax: (601) 923-1654   **Internet:** www.rts.edu

Institution Description: Reformed Theological Seminary is a private, nonprofit, independent *Enrollment:* 216. *Degrees awarded:* First-professional (divinity), master's, doctorate. Diplomas (certificates) also awarded.

Accreditation: *Regional:* SACS. *National:* ATS. *Professional:* marriage and family therapy, theology

History: Established and chartered as a Bible institute 1964; offered first instruction at postsecondary level and adopted present name 1966; awarded first degree (first-professional) 1968.

Institutional Structure: *Governing board:* Board of Trustees of Reformed Theological Seminary. Extrainstitutional representation: 21 trustees. All voting. *Composition of institution:* Administrators 8 men / 2 women. Academic affairs headed by vice president for academic affairs. Management/business/finances directed by vice president for administration. Full-time instructional faculty 20. Academic governance body, the faculty, meets an average of 10 times per year.

Calendar: Semesters (4-1-4 plan). Academic year late Aug. to mid-May. Entering students admitted Aug., Feb., June. Degrees conferred May, Aug., Dec. Formal commencement May. Summer session of 2 terms from early June to early Aug.

Admission: For fall/spring acceptance, apply no later than 3 months prior to enrollment. *Requirements:* Baccalaureate from accredited college or university with 2.6 minimum GPA. Recommend strong liberal arts education, including work in Greek, philosophy, and modern languages. *Entrance tests:* For international students TOEFL. For Marriage and Family Therapy students GRE. *For transfer students:* 2.0 minimum GPA.

College credit for extrainstitutional learning (life experience) on basis of portfolio and faculty assessments.

Degree Requirements: *For first-professional (master of divinity) degree:* 105 semester credit hours; 3 years in residence. *For MA/M&FT, MA/Missions, MA/Christian Education, MA/Biblical Studies degrees:* MA/Theological Studies 66 semester hours; 2 years in residence. *For Th.M. degree:* 30 hours; 1 year in residence. *For Doctor of Ministry degree:* 30 semester hours. *For Doctor of Missiology degree:* 60 semester hours. *For M.Div., MA/CE, MA/BS, MA/TS:* comprehensive exam in Biblical content; Westminster Shorter Catechism exam. *For M.Div. and MA/CE degrees:* supervised field education. *For D.Min. and D.Miss. degrees:* required dissertation and final 3.00 GPA. *For master's degrees:* 2.00 GPA. *For all degrees:* required courses. *Grading system:* A–F; incomplete; satisfactory-unsatisfactory; withdrawn passing; L (language deficiency).

Distinctive Educational Programs: Work-experience programs, including field experience, internships. Evening classes. Interdisciplinary programs. Directed study. Study abroad in Israel and Europe.

Degrees Conferred: 44 *master's:* theology; 9 *doctorate:* theology; 29 *first-professional:* master of divinity.

Fees and Other Expenses: *Full-time tuition per academic year:* Contact the seminary for current tuition, fees, and housing costs.

Financial Aid: Aid from institutionally generated funds is provided on the basis of academic merit, financial need. Institution has a Program Participation Agreement with the U.S. Department of Education for eligible students to receive Pell Grants and other federal aid.

Departments and Teaching Staff: New Testament *professors* 1, *associate professors* 0, *assistant professors* 1, *instructors* 0; Old Testament 1, 1, 0, 1; marriage and family therapy 2, 0, 0, 0; practical theology 0, 1,0, 0; Christian education 1, 0, 1, 0; missions 1, 3, 1, 0; Church history 2, 0, 0, 0; systematic theology 1, 1, 1, 0.

Total instructional faculty: 20. *Degrees held by full-time faculty:* Doctorate 90%, master's 100%. 90% hold terminal degrees.

Enrollment: Total enrollment 216. Unclassified full-time 3 men, part-time 4m; first-professional full-time 68m, part-time 19m; graduate full-time 56m / 20w, part-time 25m / 21w.

Characteristics of Student Body: *Ethnic/racial makeup:* Black non-Hispanic 9, Asian or Pacific Islander 3, Hispanic 1, White non-Hispanic 163.

International Students: 32 nonresident aliens enrolled. Programs available to aid students whose native language is not English: social, cultural, financial. English as a Second Language Program.

Student Life: On-campus married and single student housing available. Off-campus institutionally controlled student housing also available. *Special regulations:* Cars permitted without restrictions. *Surrounding community:* Jackson metropolitan area population 400,000. Served by airport 20 miles from campus; passenger rail service 5 miles from campus.

Publications: *Reformed Quarterly.*

Library Collections: 150,000 volumes. 49,000 microforms; 9,000 audiovisual materials; 700 current periodical subscriptions. Students have access to online information retrieval services and the Internet.

Most important special holdings include Blackburn Collection; Special Collection (books older than 1830); Southern Collection (Southern Presbyterian History, Authors); John L. Girardeau Papers.

Chief Executive Officer: Dr. Robert C. Cannada, Jr., President.

Address admission inquiries to C. Brian Gault, Director of Admissions.

Rust College

150 East Rust Avenue
Holly Springs, Mississippi 38635
Tel: (662) 252-8000   **E-mail:** admissions@rustcollege.edu
Fax: (662) 252-1607   **Internet:** www.rustcollege.edu

Institution Description: Rust College is a private college affiliated with the United Methodist Church. *Enrollment:* 1,001. *Degrees awarded:* Associate, baccalaureate.

Accreditation: *Regional:* SACS.

History: Established as Shaw School 1866; changed name to Shaw University, chartered, and offered first instruction at postsecondary level 1870; awarded first degree (baccalaureate) 1878; adopted present name 1915.

Institutional Structure: *Governing board:* Board of Trustees of Rust College. Extrainstitutional representation: 28 trustees; institutional representation: president of the college, 4 student representatives, 10 alumni. 11 ex officio. 36 voting. *Composition of institution:* Administrators 7 men / 14 women. Academic affairs headed by academic dean. Business/finances directed by business manager. Full-time instructional faculty 44. Academic governance body, Academic Policy Committee, meets an average of 4 times per year.

Calendar: Semesters. Academic year Aug. to Apr. Degrees conferred and formal commencement Apr. Summer session from late Apr. to late May.

Characteristics of Freshmen: 38% of applicants accepted. 24% of accepted applicants enrolled.

25th percentile: ACT Composite 14. *75th percentile:* ACT Composite 18.

26% of entering freshmen expected to graduate within 5 years. 46% o freshmen from Mississippi. Freshmen from 18 states and 4 foreign countries.

Admission: Rolling admissions plan. *Requirements:* Either graduation from accredited secondary school with 4 units English, 3 mathematics, 3 natural science, 3 social studies, 6 electives; or GED. Minimum 2.0 GPA. *Entrance tests:* ACT composite. *For transfer students:* 2.0 minimum GPA.

College credit and advanced placement for postsecondary level work completed in secondary school. Tutoring available. Noncredit developmental courses offered in summer session and regular academic year.

Degree Requirements: *For all associate degrees:* 66 credit hours. *For all baccalaureate degrees:* 124 minimum credit hours; physical education; academic enrichment. *For all degrees:* 2.0 GPA; distribution requirements.

Fulfillment of some degree requirements and exemption from some beginning courses possible by passing departmental examinations. *Grading system:* A–F.

Distinctive Educational Programs: Work-experience programs. Evening classes. Accelerated degree programs. Dual-degree programs. Dual-degree programs in engineering with Georgia Institute of Technology, University of Memphis (TN), Mississippi State University and in medical technology with Meharry Medical School/Tennessee State University. Special facilities for using telecommunications in the classroom. Facilities for independent research, including honors programs, tutorials.

Degrees Conferred: 4 *associate;* 93 *baccalaureate:* biological/life sciences 10; business/marketing 19; communications/communication technologies 4; computer and information sciences 20; education 3; English 7; home economics and vocational home economics 3; parks and recreation 3; physical sciences 1; protective services/public administration 5; social sciences and history 17; visual and performing arts 1.

Fees and Other Expenses: *Full-time tuition per academic year 2004–05:* $6,000. *Required fees:* $60. *Room and board per academic year:* $2,600.

Financial Aid: Aid from institutionally generated funds is provided on the basis of academic merit, financial need, other criteria.

Financial aid to full-time, first-time undergraduate students: need-based scholarships/grants totaling $3,172,213, self-help $1,849,053; non-need-based scholarships/grants totaling $640,901, self-help $311,436, parent loans $23,787, tuition waivers $32,697.

Departments and Teaching Staff: Business *professors* 1, *associate professors* 2, *assistant professors* 1, *instructors* 1, *part-time faculty* 3; education 0, 1, 2, 0, 4; humanities 0, 2, 5, 11, 3; science and mathematics 2, 2, 3, 5, 6; social science 3, 2, 2, 5, 1.

Total instructional faculty: 67 (full-time 50, part-time 17; women 10, men 20; members of minority groups 30). Student-to-faculty ratio: 15:1. Degrees held by full-time faculty: doctorate 52%, master's 48%. 54.5% hold terminal degrees.

Enrollment: Total enrollment 1,001. Undergraduate full-time 293 men / 546 women, part-time 58m / 104w.

Characteristics of Student Body: *Ethnic/racial makeup:* number of Black non-Hispanic: 927; White non-Hispanic: 9; nonresident aliens 64. *Age distribution:* number under 18: 3; 18–19: 292l 20–21: 267; 22–24: 149; 25–29: 54; 30–34: 24; 35–39: 14; 40–49: 9; 50–64: 6.

International Students: 64 nonresident aliens enrolled fall 2004. Student from Europe, Central and South America, Africa. No programs available to aid students whose native language is not English. No financial aid designated for international students.

Student Life: On-campus residence halls house 65% of student body. Residence halls for men only constitute 40% of such space, for women only 60%. *Intercollegiate athletics:* men only: baseball, basketball, cross-country, tennis, track; women only: basketball, cross-country, tennis, track, volleyball. *Special regulations:* Registered cars permitted. Curfews. Quiet hours. Residence hall visitation from 1pm to midnight. *Special services:* Counseling; Outreach; Problem-Solving for Excellence Center. Van and bus transportation available for student groups. *Student publications: Rustorian,* a monthly publication; *Campus News Briefs,* weekly newsletter; *The Sentinel. Surrounding community:* Holly Springs population 10,000. Memphis (TN), 45 miles from campus, is nearest metropolitan area.

Library Collections: 124,055 volumes including bound books, serial backfiles, electronic documents, and government documents not in separate collections. Online and card catalogs. Current serial subscriptions: 361 paper, 211 microform, 2 electronic. 95 recordings; 95 CD-ROMs. Computer work stations available. Students have access to the Internet at no charge. Total 2004–05 budget for books, periodicals, audiovisual materials, microforms: $164,000.

Most important special holdings include the Pendergrass Collection (books); Roy Wilkins Collection (books, plaques, degrees, citations); West Africa Ethnic Culture Collections; Dr. Martin Luther King Tape Collection.

Buildings and Grounds: Campus area 125 acres. *New buildings:* Conference/Community Service Building; James Elam Chapel; John Davis Physical Plant.

Chief Executive Officer: Dr. David L. Beckley, President.

Address admission inquiries to Johnny McDonald, Director of Enrollment Services.

Southeastern Baptist College

4229 Highway 15 North
Laurel, Mississippi 39440-9989

Tel: (601) 426-6346   **E-mail:** info@southeasternbaptist.edu
Fax: (601) 426-6347   **Internet:** www.southeasternbaptist.edu

Institution Description: Southeastern Baptist College is a four-year, private, Bible college affiliated with the Baptist Missionary Association of Mississippi. *Enrollment:* 97. *Degrees awarded:* Associate, baccalaureate.

Accreditation: *National:* ABHE.

History: Established 1948.

Calendar: Semesters. Academic year Aug. to July.

Characteristics of Freshmen: 100% of applicants accepted. 83% of accepted applicants enrolled. 43% of entering freshmen expected to graduate within 5 years. 90% of freshmen from Mississippi. Freshmen from 3 states and 1 foreign country.

Admission: High school diploma or GED.

Degree Requirements: *For associate degree:* 66 semester hours; 2.0 GPA. *For baccalaureate degree:* 129 semester hours; 2.0 GPA.

Degrees Conferred: 7 *associate;* 3 *baccalaureate:* theology.

Fees and Other Expenses: *Full-time tuition per academic year 2004–05:* $3,750. *Other expenses:* $800. *Room and board per academic year:* $1,000.

Financial Aid: Aid from institutionally generated funds is provided on the basis of academic merit, financial need. Institution has a Program Participation Agreement with the U.S. Department of Education for eligible students to receive Pell Grants and, depending on the agreement, other federal aid.

Departments and Teaching Staff: *Professors* 8, *part-time teachers* 7. *Total instructional faculty:* 15. *Degrees held by full-time faculty:* 25% hold terminal degrees.

Enrollment: *Total enrollment:* 97 (60.8% men, 39.2% women).

Characteristics of Student Body: *Ethnic/racial makeup:* Black non-Hispanic: 38.1%; American Indian or Alaska Native: 1%; Hispanic: 1%; White non-Hispanic: 59.8%. *Age distribution:* 17–21: 35%; 22–24: 3%; 25–29: 4%; 30–34: 17%; 35–39: 8%; 40–49: 17%; 50–59: 5%; 60–up: 1%.

International Students: 1 nonresident alien enrolled fall 2004. No programs available to aid students whose native language is not English. No financial aid specifically designated for international students.

Library Collections: 25,000 volumes. 3,000 microforms; 285 current periodical subscriptions.

Buildings and Grounds: Campus area 23 acres.

Chief Executive Officer: Dr. Jentry Bond, President.

Address admission inquiries to Emma Bond, Director of Admissions.

Tougaloo College

500 West County Line Road
Tougaloo, Mississippi 39174

Tel: (601) 977-7700   **E-mail:** admissions@tougaloo.edu
Fax: (601) 977-7824   **Internet:** www.tougaloo.edu

Institution Description: Tougaloo College is a private college affiliated with the United Church of Christ and the Christian Church (Disciples of Christ). *Enrollment:* 971. *Degrees awarded:* Associate, baccalaureate.

Accreditation: *Regional:* SACS.

History: Established 1869; chartered as Tougaloo University 1871; offered first instruction at postsecondary level 1897; awarded first degree (baccalaureate) 1901; adopted present name 1916; merged with Southern Christian Institute to become Tougaloo Christian College 1954; readopted present name 1963. *See* Clarice Campbell and Oscar Allen Rogers, Jr., *Mississippi: The View from Tougaloo* (Jackson: University Press of Mississippi, 1979) for further information.

Institutional Structure: *Governing board:* Board of Trustees. Representation: 36 trustees. All voting. *Composition of institution:* Administrators 13 men / 9 women. Academic affairs headed by vice president for academic affairs. Management/business/finances directed by business manager. Full-time instructional faculty 68. Academic governance body, Academic Standing Committee, meets an average of 10 times per year.

Calendar: Semesters. Academic year Aug. to May. Freshmen admitted Aug., Jan. Degrees conferred and formal commencement May. No summer session.

Characteristics of Freshmen: 1,021 applicants (356 men, 665 women). 98% of applicants admitted. 27.9% of admitted students enrolled full-time.

10% (27 students) submitted SAT scores; 91% (253 students) submitted ACT scores. *25th percentile:* SAT I Verbal 270, SAT I Math 330; ACT Composite 15, ACT English 15, ACT Math 15. *75th percentile:* SAT I Verbal 430, SAT I Math 420; ACT Composite 20, ACT English 22, ACT Math 18.

38% of entering freshmen expected to graduate within 5 years. 86% of freshmen from Mississippi. Freshmen from 24 states and 2 foreign countries.

Admission: Rolling admissions plan. Early acceptance available. *Requirements:* Either graduation from state-approved secondary school with 16 units which must include 3 English, 2 history and social studies, 2 mathematics, 2 science; or GED. Minimum 2.0 GPA. *Entrance tests:* College Board SAT or ACT composite. For foreign students TOEFL. *For transfer students:* 2.0 minimum GPA; from 4-year accredited institution 90 hours maximum transfer credit; from 2-year accredited institution 34 hours; correspondence/extension students 12 hours.

College credit and advanced placement for postsecondary-level work completed in secondary school. Tutoring available. Remedial courses offered during regular academic year; credit given.

Degree Requirements: *For all associate degrees:* 64 credit hours. *For all baccalaureate degrees:* 124 credit hours. *For all undergraduate degrees:* 2.0 GPA; 2 terms in residence; 2 semesters physical education; distribution requirements; demonstrated proficiency in English and writing, mathematics. *Grading system:* A–F; pass-fail; withdraw (carries time limit).

Distinctive Educational Programs: Work-experience programs including cooperative education and internships. Evening classes. Accelerated degree programs. Dual-degree programs in engineering with Brown University (RI), Georgia Institute of Technology, Howard University (DC), Tuskegee Institute (AL), University of Mississippi, University of Wisconsin-Madison. Interdisciplinary program in Afro-American studies. Facilities for independent research, including honors programs and tutorials. Washington (DC) semester at American University. Cooperative academic program with Brown University (RI), including student exchange program. Student exchange programs also with Bowdoin College (ME) and Meharry Medical College (TN). Cross-registration with Millsaps College.

ROTC: Army offered in cooperation with Jackson State University.

Degrees Conferred: 21 *associate;* 147 *baccalaureate.* Bachelor's degrees awarded in top five disciplines: social sciences 32; psychology 23; English 23; biological and biomedical sciences 14; physical sciences 12/

Fees and Other Expenses: *Full-time tuition per academic year:* $8,860. *Books and supplies:* $1,300. *Room and board per academic year:* $5,080.

Financial Aid: The college offers a direct lending program. Aid from institutionally generated funds is provided on the basis of financial need, academic need, athletic ability, other criteria. Institution has a Program Participation Agreement with the U.S. Department of Education for eligible students to receive Pell Grants and, depending upon the agreement, other federal aid.

Departments and Teaching Staff: Art *professors* 1, *associate professors* 1, *assistant professors* 0, *instructors* 1, *part-time teachers* 0, biology 2, 2, 0, 1, 0; chemistry 2, 1,2, 1, 0; economics 0, 0, 3, 0, 1; education 3, 2, 1, 1, 0; English 4, 2, 3, 4, 9; health and physical education 0, 1, 1, 2, 0; history 0, 1, 1, 0, 0; information and computer sciences 0, 1, 1, 1, 0; library 0, 0, 4, 0, 0; mathematics 0, 4, 1, 1, 6; music 1, 2, 1, 1, 0; physics 0, 1, 1, 0, 0; physical science 1, 0, 1, 0, 0; psychology 0, 0, 1, 1, 2; sociology 0, 1, 1, 1, 3.

Total instructional faculty: 91. Student-to-faculty ratio: 16:1. Degrees held by full-time faculty: doctorate 57%, master's 43%. 63% hold terminal degrees.

Enrollment: Total enrollment 971 (31.6% men, 68.4% women).

Characteristics of Student Body: *Ethnic/racial makeup:* Black non-Hispanic: 99.3%; White non-Hispanic: .1%.

International Students: 6 nonresident aliens enrolled fall 2004. No programs available for students whose native language is not English. No financial aid specifically designated for international students.

Student Life: On-campus residence halls house 69% of student body. Residence halls for men only constitute 35% of such space, for women only 65%. *Intercollegiate athletics:* men only: basketball, soccer, tennis, track; women only: basketball. *Special regulations:* Cars permitted without restrictions. Residence hall visitation from 8am to midnight. *Special services:* Medical services. *Student publications: The Eagle,* a yearbook; *Harambee,* a biweekly newspaper. *Surrounding community:* Tougaloo, unincorporated, located in Jackson metropolitan area, population 321,00. Served by airport 20 miles from campus.

Library Collections: 117,000 volumes. 7,200 microforms; 4,300 recordings/ tapes; 370 current periodical subscriptions. Computer work stations available. Students have access to online information retrieval services and the Internet.

Most important special holdings include African American Collection; legal papers of the Civil Rights Movement; Tracy Sugarmon Collection of Original Prints in Mississippi.

Buildings and Grounds: Campus area 509 acres.

Chief Executive Officer: Dr. Beverly W. Hogan, President.

Address admission inquiries to Junoesque Jacobs, Director of Admissions.

University of Mississippi

P.O. Box 1848
University, Mississippi 38677-1848
Tel: (662) 915-7226   **E-mail:** admissions@olemiss.edu
Fax: (662) 915-5869   **Internet:** www.olemiss.edu

Institution Description: University of Mississippi is a state institution. *Enrollment:* 12,747. *Degrees awarded:* Baccalaureate, master's, doctorate, first-professional (law).

Academic offerings subject to approval by statewide coordinating bodies. Budget subject to approval by state governing boards. Member of Mississippi-Alabama Sea Grant Consortium and Oak Ridge Associated Universities.

Accreditation: *Regional:* SACS. *Professional:* accounting, art, audiology, business, clinical psychology, computer science, counseling, engineering, family and consumer science, journalism, law, music, nursing, pharmacy, psychology internship, social work, speech-language pathology, teacher education

History: Established and chartered 1844; offered first instruction at postsecondary level 1848; awarded first degree (baccalaureate) 1851. *See* Allen Cabaniss, *The University of Mississippi: Its First Hundred Years* (Hattiesburg: University and College Press of Mississippi, 1971) for further information.

Institutional Structure: *Governing board:* Board of Trustees of State Institutions of Higher Learning. Representation: 12 trustees. All voting. Academic affairs headed by provost. Management/business/finances directed by vice chancellor for administration and finance. Full-time instructional faculty 698. Academic governance body, Faculty Senate, meets an average of 6 times per year.

Calendar: Semesters. Academic year Aug. to May. Freshmen admitted Aug., Jan., June, July. Degrees conferred May, Aug., Dec. Formal commencement May. Summer session of 2 terms from late May to early Aug.

Characteristics of Freshmen: 43% of applicants admitted and enrolled. 22% (516 students) submitted SAT scores; 77% (1,834 students) submitted ACT scores. *25th percentile:* ACT Composite 20, ACT English 20, ACT Math 18. *75th percentile:* ACT Composite 26, ACT English 28, ACT Math 25.

52% of freshmen expected to graduate within 5 years. 52% of freshmen from Mississippi. Freshmen from 43 states.

Admission: Rolling admissions plan. Apply as early as 1 year, but not later than 20 days prior to registration. Provisional admission based on 6-semester transcript and a record of senior year courses in progress with minimum composite score of 18 of ACT or 840 SAT. By high school graduation must have completed at least 15½ units including 4 in English, 3 in mathematics (algebra I, geometry, algebra II or above), 3 in science (physical, biology, chemistry), 3 units social science (1 unit U.S. history, ½ unit government, and economics or geography), and ½ unit computer applications. *Entrance tests:* ACT or SAT. Early admission with 3.5GPA, 15 approved units, and a 25 composite ACT (1120 SAT). *For transfer students:* Transfer students who meet above requirements may transfer at any time with a 2.0 GPA. Those who would not have met freshman requirements must have 24 semester hours of 2.0 work at an accredited college with a 2.0 average. That transfer work must include 6 hours English composition, 3 hours college algebra or higher, 6 semester hours of laboratory science, and 9 additional transferable electives.

CLEP and AP credit acceptable as well as limited military experience and/or coursework based upon the ACE *Military Guide.* Tutoring available. Developmental and study skills programs offered.

Degree Requirements: 126–164 credit hours; 2.0 GPA; 2 semesters in residence; course requirements. Additional requirements for some programs.

Fulfillment of some degree requirements and exemption from some beginning courses possible by passing departmental examinations, College Board CLEP, AP. *Grading system:* A–F; pass-fail; withdraw (carries time limit).

Distinctive Educational Programs: Flexible meeting places and schedules, including off-campus centers, weekend and evening classes. Special facilities for using telecommunications in the classroom. Interdisciplinary programs in Black studies, interdisciplinary science, gender studies. McDonnell-Barksdale Honors College. Crost Institute for International Studies. Facilities and programs for independent research, including honors programs, individual majors, tutorials. Center for the Study of Southern Culture, Mississippi Law Research Institute, Mississippi Mineral Resources Institute, Research Institute of Pharmaceutical Sciences. Center for the Study of Southern Culture, Mississippi Law Research Institute, Mississippi Mineral Resources Institute, Research Institute of Pharmaceutical Sciences, Jamie Whitten National Center for Physical Acoustics, National Food Service Management Institute, National Center for the Technological Development of Natural Products, Marine Minerals Technology Center. Trent Lott Leadership Institute. Study abroad in England, Germany, Russia, Mexico, Spain, Japan, The Netherlands, Australia, Hong Kong, Scotland. The International Student Exchange Program offers possible exchanges to 35 countries.

ROTC: Army, Navy, Air Force. 3 Air Force, 15 Army, and 6 Navy commissions awarded 2004.

Degrees Conferred: 1,989 *baccalaureate* (B), 716 *master's* (M), 73 *doctorate* (D): area and ethnic studies 3 (B), 7 (M); biological/life sciences 73 (B), 6 (M); business/marketing 588 (B), 129 (M); 7 (D); communications/communication technologies 89 (B), 9 (M); computer and information sciences 20 (B); education 223 (B), 167 (M), 18 (D); engineering and engineering technologies 64 (B) 60 (M), 8 (D); English 102 (B), 9 (M), 8 (D); foreign languages and literature 19 (B), 4 (M); health professions and related sciences 108 (B), 90 (M), 7 (D); home economics and vocational home economics 101 (B); law/legal studies 10 (B), 142 (M); liberal arts/general studies 14 (B); mathematics 12 (B), 6 (M), 1 (D); parks and recreation 57 (B), 13 (M); philosophy/religion/theology 6 (B), 2 (M); physical sciences 24 (B), 7 (M), 8 (D); protective services/public administration 44 (B); psychology 119 (B), 26 (M), 7 (D); social sciences and history 208 (B), 21 (M), 6 (D); visual and performing arts 85 (B), 15 (M), 3 (D). 218 *first-professional:*law 142; pharmacy 76.

Fees and Other Expenses: *Full-time tuition per academic year 2004–05:* undergraduate and graduate resident $4,100; nonresident $9,264. Professional schools vary; contact the school of interest for current information. *Room and board per academic year:* $5,610.

Financial Aid: Aid from institutionally generated funds is provided on the basis of academic merit, financial need, athletic ability.

Financial aid to full-time, first-time undergraduate students: need-based scholarships/grants totaling $9,577,017, self-help $12,435,073; non-need-based scholarships/grants totaling $19,734,173, self-help $12,788,683, parent loans $5,168,350, tuition waivers $933,412, athletic awards $3,506,963. *Graduate aid:* 1,421 students received $7,329,204 in federal and state-funded fellowships/grants; 1,115 received $14,959,175 in federal and state-funded loans; 4 received $6,400 for work-study jobs; 434 received other fellowships/grants totaling $850,625.

Departments and Teaching Staff: Liberal arts *professors* 85, *associate professors* 73, *assistant professors* 110, *instructors* 57, *part-time faculty* 83; accountancy 4, 4, 3, 1, 1; applied science 4, 15, 14, 8, 26; business 7, 18, 18, 1, 19; education 4, 14, 14, 9, 21; engineering 21, 22, 16, 2, 16; law 13, 4, 14, 1, 18; pharmacy 22, 18, 37, 20, 96; graduate school 0, 2, 0, 0, 0; provost funded 2, 6, 25, 10, 10.

Total instructional faculty: 988 (women 366, men 622; members of minority groups 116). Student-to-faculty ratio: 21:1.

Enrollment: Total enrollment 14,497. Undergraduate full-time 5,172 men / 5,693 women, part-time 392m / 563w; first-professional full-time 375m / 357w, part-time 3m / 1w; graduate full-time 554m / 591w, part-time 238m / 558w.

Characteristics of Student Body: *Ethnic/racial makeup (undergraduate):* number of Black non-Hispanic: 1,547; American Indian or Alaska Native: 27; Asian or Pacific Islander: 121; Hispanic: 96; White non-Hispanic: 9,780; unknown: 143. *Age distribution:* number under 18: 70; 18–19: 4,155; 20–21: 4,248; 22–24: 2,033; 25–29: 596; 30–34: 271; 35–39: 167; 40–49: 187; 50–64: 71; 65 and over: 11.

International Students: 423 nonresident aliens enrolled fall 2004. 39 students from Europe, 295 Asia, 26 Central and South America, 37 Africa, 4 Canada, 1 Australia, 21 other. Programs available to aid students whose native language is not English: social, cultural, financial. English as a Second Language Program. Financial aid specifically designated for international students: variable number of scholarships available annually.

Student Life: On-campus residence halls house 35% of student body. 27% of men join and 10% live in fraternities; 34% of women join and 10% live in sororities. Housing available for married students. *Intercollegiate athletics:* men only: baseball, basketball, cross-country, football, golf, tennis, track and field; women only: basketball, cross-country, tennis, track and field, riflery, soccer, softball, volleyball. *Special regulations:* Cars permitted without restrictions. Residence hall visitation hours have restrictions. *Special services:* University Teaching and Learning Center, medical services. *Student publications, radio, television: Daily Mississippian*, a student-run newspaper; *The OLE MISS Yearbook*. Radio station WUMS-FM student-run broadcasts 24 hours per day; Channel 12 Newswatch, student-produced news and specialty programs. *Surrounding community:* Memphis (TN), 80 miles from campus, is nearest metropolitan area. Passenger rail service 30 miles from campus; shuttle service available to Memphis airport.

Library Collections: 1,512,900 volumes including bound books, serial backfiles, electronic documents, and government documents not in separate collections. Online catalog. Current serial subscriptions: 8,471. Students have access to the Internet at no charge.

Most important special holdings include Faulkner Collection of books and manuscripts; 20th Century Mississippi Literature Collection; Seymour Lawrence Collection.

Buildings and Grounds: Campus area 2,500 acres. *New buildings:* Ford Center for Performing Arts.

Chief Executive Officer: Dr. Robert C. Khayat, Chancellor.

Undergraduates address admission inquiries to Dr. Charlotte Fant, Director of Admissions; graduate inquiries to Dr. Tyrus McCarty; law inquiries to Barbara Vinson; pharmacy inquiries to Dr. Mavin Wilson.

University of Mississippi Medical Center

2500 North State Street
Jackson, Mississippi 39216-4505
Tel: (601) 984-1000 **E-mail:** registrar@umsmed.edu
Fax: (601) 984-1079 **Internet:** www.umsmed.edu

Institution Description: The University of Mississippi Medical Center provides *baccalaureate* (upper division study only), *first-professional* (dentistry, medicine, physical therapy), *master's, doctorate* programs. Certificates also awarded. *Enrollment:* 2,003.

Accreditation: *Regional:* SACS. *Professional:* dentistry, medicine, nursing, physical therapy, psychology internship

History: The University of Mississippi Medical Center in Jackson is the health sciences campus of the university. The School of Medicine opened in 1955, the School of Nursing in 1958, the School of Related Professions in 1971, and the School Dentistry in 1974. The Medical Center functions a separately funded semi-autonomous unit of the University of Mississippi.

Calendar: Semesters. Academic year Aug. to May.

Admission: *For first-professional degree in medicine:* 90 credit hours from accredited college or university which must include 1 year each in English, organic chemistry, inorganic chemistry, mathematics, physics, and advanced science; MCAT. Recommend baccalaureate. *For first-professional degree in dentistry:* 90 hours from accredited college or university which must include 12 semester hours in English (6 must be in composition), 8 each in organic chem-

istry, physics, biology or zoology; 4 hours in advanced chemistry or biology, 6 in mathematics (algebra or trigonometry), and 6 in behavioral sciences; DAT. Baccalaureate recommended.

Degree Requirements: *For first-professional in medicine:* 3-year prescribed curriculum, 1 year electives. *For first-professional in dentistry:* 4-year prescribed curriculum.

Degrees Conferred: 193 *baccalaureate:* health professions and related sciences 192; biological/biomedical sciences 1; 51 *master's:* health professions and related sciences; 15 *doctorate:* health professions and related sciences; 126 *first-professional:* dentistry 30, medicine 96.

Fees and Other Expenses: *Full-time tuition per academic year 2004–05:* Contact the university for current tuition and fees; rates vary by program.

Financial Aid: Aid from institutionally generated funds is provided on the basis of academic merit, financial need. Institution has a Program Participation Agreement with the U.S. Department of Education for eligible students to receive Pell Grants and other federal aid.

Departments and Teaching Staff: School of Medicine *professors* 120, *associate professors* 117, *assistant professors* 137, *instructors* 30; *part-time faculty* 954; School of Nursing 9, 7, 11, 11, 67; School of Health Related Professions 3, 26, 11, 5, 537; School of Dentistry 19, 12, 9, 1, 181.

Total instructional faculty: 1,107 FTE. Degrees held by full-time faculty: doctorate 31%, master's 11%, baccalaureate 5%, professional 53%. 100% hold terminal degrees.

Enrollment: Total enrollment 2,003. Undergraduate 620 (20.6% men, 79.4% women).

Characteristics of Student Body: *Ethnic/racial makeup (undergraduate):* Black non-Hispanic: 19.4%; Asian or Pacific Islander: .6%; Hispanic: .3%; White non-Hispanic: 79.7%. *Age distribution:* 17–21: 10%; 22–24: 28%; 25–29: 35%; 30–34: 15%; 35–39: 7%; 40–49: 5%; 50–up: 1%.

International Students: 106 nonresident aliens enrolled fall 2004. Students from Europe, Asia, Central and South America, Africa, Canada, Australia. No programs available to aid students whose native language is not English. No financial aid specifically designated for international students.

Library Collections: 265,000 volumes including bound books, serial backfiles, electronic documents, and government documents not in separate collections. Online catalog. Current serial subscriptions: 2,524 paper, 165 microform, 47 electronic. Computer work stations available. Students have access to the Internet at no charge.

Chief Executive Officer: Daniel W. Jones, M.D., Vice Chancellor.

Address admission inquiries to Dr. Billy M. Bishop, Director of Student Services and Records.

University of Southern Mississippi

2701 Hardy Street
Hattiesburg, Mississippi 39406-0001
Tel: (601) 266-5000 **E-mail:** admissions@usm.edu
Fax: (601) 266-5148 **Internet:** www.usm.edu

Institution Description: The University of Southern Mississippi is a state institution with a branch campus in Long Beach. *Enrollment:* 15,257. *Degrees awarded:* Baccalaureate, master's, doctorate.

Academic offerings subject to approval by statewide coordinating bodies. Budget subject to approval by state governing boards.

Accreditation: *Regional:* SACS. *Professional:* accounting, art, athletic training, audiology, business, clinical lab scientist, clinical psychology, computer science, construction education, counseling, counseling, psychology internship, dance, dietetics, engineering technology, English language education, family and consumer science, interior design, journalism, librarianship, marriage and family therapy, music, nursing, nursing education, psychology internship, public health, recreation and leisure services, school psychology, social work, speech-language pathology, teacher education, theatre

History: Chartered as Mississippi Normal College 1910; offered first instruction at postsecondary level 1922; awarded first degree (baccalaureate) 1923; changed name to State Teachers College 1924, to Mississippi Southern College 1940; adopted present name 1962. *See* Alma Hickman, *Southern as I Saw It: Personal Remembrances of an Era, 1912–1954* (Hattiesburg: University of Southern Mississippi Press, 1966). *See* Chester Morgan, *Dearly Bought Deeply Treasured* (Hattiesburg: University of Southern Mississippi, 1987) for further information.

Institutional Structure: *Governing board:* Board of Trustees, State Institutions of Higher Learning. Representation: 13 trustees. All voting. *Composition of institution:* Administrators 29 men / 17 women. Academic affairs headed by vice president for academic affairs. Management/business/finances directed by vice president for business and finance. Full-time instructional faculty 390 men

/ 208 women. Academic governance bodies, Academic Council, Graduate Council, each meet an average of 12 times per year.

Calendar: Semesters. Academic year July to June. Freshmen admitted Aug., Dec., May. Degrees conferred and formal commencement May, Aug. Summer session from late May to mid-Aug.

Characteristics of Freshmen: 19.4% of applicants admitted. 9.7% of applicants admitted and enrolled.

9% (143 students) submitted SAT scores; 91% (1,433 students) submitted ACT scores. *25th percentile*: SAT Verbal 450, SAT Math 440; ACT Composite 18, ACT English 18, ACT Math 16. *75th percentile*: SAT Verbal 570, SAT Math 570; ACT Composite 24, ACT English 25, ACT Math 24.

46% of freshmen expected to graduate within 5 years. 70% freshmen from Mississippi. Freshmen from 22 states and 21 foreign countries.

Admission: Rolling admissions plan. For fall acceptance, apply no later than 20 days prior to registration. Early acceptance available. *Requirements:* Graduation from high school with 4 units English, 3 mathematics (algebra I, geometry, and algebra II), 3 sciences, 3 social studies, 2 advanced electives, ½ unit in computer applications. Recommend 2 units of foreign language, 1 unit of mathematics and a computer science course during senior year, and a level of typing proficiency. *Entrance tests:* ACT composite, minimum score 15 required; any student with ACT 24 or above is exempt from high school units requirement. *For transfer students:* 2.0 minimum GPA; from 4-year accredited institution hours maximum transfer credit limited only by residence requirement; from 2-year accredited institution 64 semester hours maximum transfer credit.

College credit and advanced placement for postsecondary level work completed in secondary school and for USAFI/DANTES. College credit for extrainstitutional learning on basis of ACE *2006 Guide to the Evaluation of Educational Experiences in the Armed Services.* Tutoring available. Developmental-remedial courses offered in summer session and regular academic year; credit given.

Degree Requirements: 128 semester hours; 2.0 GPA; 2 terms in residence; 1 hour concepts of physical fitness, 1 hour nutrition for living; core requirements.

Fulfillment of some degree requirements and exemption from some beginning courses possible by passing departmental examinations, College Board CLEP Subject Examinations, AP; for students who have been out of secondary school at least 3 years, CLEP General Examination (score of 500). *Grading system:* A–F; pass-fail; withdraw.

Distinctive Educational Programs: *For undergraduates:* Cooperative education. Interdisciplinary honors program and programs in polymer science, music. Preprofessional programs in dentistry, dental hygiene, engineering, medicine, optometry, pharmacy, physical therapy, veterinary medicine, pre-cytotechnology, pre-health information management, pre-occupational therapy. Individual majors. *Available to all students:* Flexible meeting places and schedule, including off-campus centers (at Keesler Air Force Base, 90 miles away from main institution; Jackson, Gautier, Picayune, 100, 80, and 60 miles away, respectively), and evening classes. Special facilities for using telecommunications in the classroom. Interdisciplinary program in area studies. Study abroad in Australia, Austria, Canada, Caribbean, England, France, Germany, Israel, Japan, Mexico, United Kingdom, Ireland. *American studies* offers faculty and student exchanges with British universities and annual summer term programs at the Universities of London and Essex. *Other distinctive programs:* Continuing education and public service programs. Institute of Environmental Science, Mississippi Polymer Institute, and Gulf Coast Research Lab offer educational research programs for students and provide services to the community. English Language Institute offers intensive language training for nonmatriculated foreign students.

ROTC: Army in cooperation with William Carey College. Air Force in cooperation with William Carey College and Jones Junior College. 2 Air Force and 3 Army commissions awarded 2004.

Degrees Conferred: 2,165 *baccalaureate* (B); 750 *master's* (M); 120 *doctorate* (D): architecture 22 (B); area and ethnic studies 6 (B); biological/life sciences 10 (B), 2 (M); 1 (D); business/marketing 584 (B), 92 (M); communications/communication technologies 94 (B), 18 (M), 9 (D); computer and information sciences 94 (B), 12 (M), 4 (D); education 367 (B), 236 (M), 60 (D); engineering and engineering technologies 48 (B), 40 (M), 14 (D); English 76 (B), 10 (M), 5 (D); foreign languages and literature 18 (B); health professions and related sciences 238 (B), 10 (M); home economics and vocational home economics 64 (B), 6 (M), 2 (D); interdisciplinary studies 4 (B), 3 (M); law/legal studies 26 (B); library science 9 (B), 45 (M); mathematics 19 (B), 3 (M); parks and recreation 156 (B), 34 (M); philosophy/religion/theology 4 (B), 4 (M); physical sciences 35 (B), 18 (M), 5 (D); protective services/public administration 111 (B), 62 (M), 4 (D); psychology 13 (B), 5 (M), 5 (D); social sciences and history 128 (B), 26 (M), 7 (D); visual and performing arts 52 (B), 16 (M), 4 (D).

Fees and Other Expenses: *Full-time tuition per academic year 2004–05:* undergraduate and graduate resident $4,106, nonresident $9,276. *Room and board per academic year:* $4,190.

Financial Aid: Aid from institutionally generated funds is provided on the basis of academic merit, financial need, athletic ability, other criteria.

Financial aid to full-time, first-time undergraduate students: need-based scholarships/grants totaling $161,572,036, self-help $28,385,953, parent loans $475,166, athletic awards $1,071,020; non-need-based scholarships/grants totaling $8,801,180, self-help $14,873,457, parent loans $1,908,369, athletic awards $1,822,626. *Graduate aid:* 131 students received $275,450 for college-assigned jobs; 325 received other fellowships/grants totaling $5,041,500; 287 teaching assistantships awarded totaling $2,012,605; 191 research assistantships were awarded totaling $777,181.

Departments and Teaching Staff: *Total instructional faculty:* 808 (full-time 659, part-time149; women 564, men 444; members of minority groups 77). Total faculty with doctorate, first-professional, or other terminal degree: 534. Student-to-faculty ratio: 17:1. Degrees held by full-time faculty: doctorate 78%, master's 21%, baccalaureate 1%. 90% hold terminal degrees. *Faculty development:* $69,004,140 in grants for research.

Enrollment: Total enrollment 15,257. Undergraduate full-time 4,256 men / 6,425 women, part-time 713m / 1,126w; graduate full-time 585m / 856w, part-time 480m / 812w. *Transfer students:* in-state 1,761; from out-of-state 108.

Characteristics of Student Body: *Ethnic/racial makeup (undergraduate):* number of Black non-Hispanic: 3,483; American Indian or Alaska Native: 54; Asian or Pacific Islander: 155; Hispanic: 129; White non-Hispanic: 8,418; unknown: 150. *Age distribution:* number under 18: 18; 18–19: 958; 20–21: 9,033; 22–24: 882; 25–29: 644; 30–34: 364; 35–39: 219; 40–49: 248; 50–64: 100; 65 and over: 11.

International Students: 345 nonresident aliens enrolled fall 2004. Programs available to aid students whose native language is not English: social, cultural. English as a Second Language Program. No financial aid specifically designated for international students.

Student Life: On-campus residence halls house 26% of student body. Residence halls for men constitute 39% of such space, for women 61%. 21% of men join and 6% live in fraternities. 12% of married students live in married student housing. *Intercollegiate athletics:* men: baseball, basketball, cross-country, football, golf, tennis, track; women: basketball, cross-country, soccer, tennis, track, volleyball. *Special regulations:* Registered cars permitted without restrictions. *Special services:* Learning Resources Center, medical services, bus service to and from outer limits of campus. *Student publications, radio: Product,* an annual literary magazine; *The Southerner,* a yearbook; *The Student Printz,* a biweekly newspaper. Radio station WUSM. *Surrounding community:* Hattiesburg 2-county population 104,000. New Orleans (LA), 110 miles from campus, is nearest metropolitan area. Served by mass transit bus system; airport 13 miles from campus; passenger rail service 3 miles from campus.

Publications: *Explorations in Renaissance Culture* (annually) first published in 1978, *Journal of Mississippi History* (quarterly) first published 1939, *Mississippi Review* (biannually) first published 1972, *Southern Quarterly* first published 1962.

Library Collections: 1,077,401 volumes. 972,529 government documents; 2,415,228 microforms; 9,507 audiovisual materials; electronic access to 15,231 periodicals. Online catalog. Students have access to online information retrieval services and the Internet. Total 2004–05 budget for books and materials: $2,211,519.

Most important special holdings include de Grummond Collection of Children's Literature; papers of Congressman William M. Colmer and U.S. Senator Theodore G. Bilbo; Cleanth Brooks Collection.

Buildings and Grounds: Campus area 1,090 acres. *New buildings:* International Center completed 2005; University Union 2006.

Chief Executive Officer: Dr. Shelby Thames, President.

Address undergraduate admission inquiries to Matthew Cox, Director of Admissions; graduate inquiries to Office of Graduate Studies.

Wesley College

111 Wesley Circle
P.O. Box 1070
Florence, Mississippi 39208-0070

Tel: (601) 845-2265   **E-mail:** admissions@wesleycollege.edu
Fax: (601) 845-2266   **Internet:** www.wesleycollege.edu

Institution Description: Wesley College is a private, independent, nonprofit institution affiliated with the Congregational Methodist Church. *Enrollment:* 80. *Degrees awarded:* Baccalaureate.

Accreditation: *National:* ABHE.

History: Established 1944 in Dallas, Texas; ; offered first instruction at postsecondary level 1944; moved to Tehuacana, Texas 1953 and changed name to Westminster College and Bible Institute; moved to Florence, Mississippi 1972; adopted present name 1975.

Institutional Structure: *Governing board:* Extrainstitutional representation: 9 directors; institutional representation: 1 administrator (ex officio - not voting); all others voting. *Composition of institution:* Administrators 3 men 1 woman. Academic affairs headed by Academic dean. Business/finances directed by business manager. Total instructional faculty 17. Faculty meets weekly.

Calendar: Semesters. Academic year Aug. to May. Freshmen admitted Aug., Jan. Degrees conferred and formal commencement May.

Characteristics of Freshmen: 100% of applicants admitted. 86% of applicants admitted and enrolled.

38% of applicants submitted SAT scores; 46% submitted ACT scores. *25th percentile*: SAT Verbal 410, SAT Math 440; ACT Composite 14. *75th percentile*: SAT Verbal 470, SAT I Math 440; ACT Composite 14.

33% of entering freshmen expected to graduate within 5 years. 61% of freshmen from Mississippi. Freshmen from 8 states and 2 foreign countries.

Admission: Rolling admissions plan. For fall acceptance, apply as early as end of junior year of secondary school, but not later than 1 month prior to beginning of term. Apply by December 1 for early decision; must limit application to Wesley. Early acceptance available. *Requirements:* Either graduation from accredited secondary school with 15 units normally including 4 English, 2 mathematics, 2 science, 2 social studies; or GED. *Entrance tests:* College Board SAT1 or ACT. *For transfer students:* 2.0 minimum GPA; from 4-year accredited institution 96 hours maximum transfer credit; from 2-year accredited institution 64 hours.

Degree Requirements: *For all baccalaureate degrees:* 125 credit hours; 2.0 GPA; 2 semesters in residence; general education requirements.

Fulfillment of some degree requirements and exemption from some beginning courses possible by passing College Board CLEP, AP (score of 3). *Grading system:* A–F; pass-fail; withdraw (deadline after which pass-fail is appended to withdraw).

Degrees Conferred: 15 *baccalaureate:* philosophy/religion/theology.

Fees and Other Expenses: *Full-time tuition per academic year 2005–06:* $6,000. *Room and board per academic year:* $2,960. *Required fees:* $620.

Financial Aid: Aid from institutionally generated funds is provided on the basis of academic merit, financial need, other considerations. Institution has a Program Participation Agreement with the U.S. Department of Education for eligible students to receive Pell Grants and, depending upon agreement, other federal aid.

Financial aid to full-time, first-time undergraduate students: need-based scholarships/grants totaling $126,627, self-help $209,637, parent loans $38,500.

Departments and Teaching Staff: *Total instructional faculty:* 17 (full-time 4, part-time 13; women 4, men 13; member of minority group 1). Total faculty with doctorate, first-professional, or other terminal degree: 14. Student-to-faculty ratio: 9.34:1. Degrees held by full-time faculty: doctorate 18%, master's 80%, baccalaureate 2%. 18% hold terminal degrees.

Enrollment: Total enrollment 80. Full-time 34 men / 26 women, part-time 12m / 8w. *Transfer students:* in-state 5; from out-of-state 4.

Characteristics of Student Body: *Ethnic/racial makeup:* number of Black non-Hispanic: 35; Asian or Pacific Islander: 1; Hispanic: 3; White non-Hispanic: 35. *Age distribution:* number under 18: 2; 18–19: 13; 20–21: 15; 22–24: 13; 25–29: 11; 30–34: 7; 35–39: 6; 40–49: 10; 50–64: 3.

International Students: 2 nonresident aliens enrolled fall 2004. 1 student from Asia, 1 Africa. Programs available to aid students whose native language is not English: social, cultural. No financial aid specifically designated for international student.s

Student Life: On-campus residence halls house all dependent students unless married or living with their parents or guardians. *Special regulations:* All students are expected to conduct themselves as a respected member of Christian society and to behave in an orderly, respectful, and courteous manner; campus dress and appearance code; required attendance at regularly scheduled chapel services. *Special services:* Counseling program. *Student publications: The Beacon*, college pictorial annual. *Surrounding community:* Florence has a population of 1,100 and is located 12 miles south of Jackson, Mississippi (population 300,000). Jackson is served by rail and air transportation.

Library Collections: 25,357 volumes. Online catalog. 250 microforms; 35 audiovisual materials; 143 current periodical subscriptions. 3 computer work stations.

Special collections in Holiness; Cults; Classical Literature; Congregational Methodist Church papers.

Buildings and Grounds: Campus area 40 acres.

Chief Executive Officer: Dr. S. Lance Sherer, President.

Address admission inquiries to Sander Bruce, Director of Admissions.

William Carey College

498 Tuscan Avenue
Hattiesburg, Mississippi 39401-5499
Tel: (601) 582-5051   **E-mail:** admiss@mail.wmcarey.edu
Fax: (601) 582-6454   **Internet:** www.wmcarey.edu

Institution Description: William Carey College is a private college affiliated with the Mississippi Baptist Convention (Southern Baptist). The school has branch campuses in Gulfport and New Orleans. *Enrollment:* 2,758. *Degrees awarded:* Baccalaureate, master's.

Accreditation: *Regional:* SACS. *Professional:* music, nursing

History: Established as South Mississippi College, a coeducational institution, and offered first instruction at postsecondary level 1906; chartered and became Mississippi Woman's College 1911; awarded first degree (baccalaureate) 1914; became coeducational 1953; adopted present name 1954.

Institutional Structure: *Governing board:* Board of Trustees of William Carey College. Representation: 24 trustees. *Composition of institution:* Administrators 17 men / 7 women. Academic affairs headed by academic vice president. Management/business/finances directed by controller. Full-time instructional faculty 109. Academic governance body, Academic Council, meets an average of 2 times per year.

Calendar: Trimesters. Academic year Aug. to May. Freshmen admitted Aug., Nov., Feb., June. Degrees conferred and formal commencement May, Aug. Summer session of 2 five-week terms plus regular 10-week term from late May to mid-Aug.

Characteristics of Freshmen: 907 applicants (259 men, 648 women). 87.1% of applicants accepted. 15.4% of accepted applicants enrolled full-time.

8% (10 students) submitted SAT scores; 92% (110 students) submitted ACT scores. *25th percentile*: SAT I 450, Verbal SAT I 470; Math ACT Composite 18, ACT English 19, ACT Math 17. *75th percentile*: SAT I Verbal 530, SAT I Math 530; ACT Composite 24, ACT English 25, ACT Math 21.

28% of entering freshmen expected to graduate within 5 years. 65% of freshmen from Mississippi. Freshmen from 15 states and 8 foreign countries.

Admission: Rolling admissions plan. For fall acceptance, apply as early as summer of previous year, but not later than Aug. 1 of year of enrollment. Early acceptance available. *Requirements:* Graduation from secondary school with 16 units or GED. Minimum 2.0 GPA. *For transfer students:* from 4-year accredited institution 1.4–2.0 minimum GPA (minimum GPA determined by hours attempted), 98 hours maximum transfer credit; from 2-year accredited institution 1.7 minimum GPA, 64 hours maximum transfer credit.

College credit and advanced placement for postsecondary-level work completed in secondary school and credit on basis of ACE *2006 Guide to the Evaluation of Educational Experiences in the Armed Services.* Tutoring available. Developmental courses offered during regular academic year; credit given.

Degree Requirements: Minimum 128 credit hours; 2.0 GPA; 1 year in residence; weekly chapel attendance; 2 semesters physical education; core curricula; demonstrated proficiency in English.

Fulfillment of some degree requirements and exemption from some beginning courses possible by College Board CLEP, other standardized tests. *Grading system:* A–F; credit-no credit.

Distinctive Educational Programs: *For undergraduates:* Work-experience programs. Accelerated degree programs. Affiliated with Hattiesburg School of Radiologic Technology through Forrest General and Methodist Hospitals. Interdisciplinary programs in medical technology, music therapy, and radiologic technology. Preprofessional programs including dentistry, engineering, medicine, optometry, pharmacy, veterinary medicine. *Available to all students:* Evening classes. Tutorials.

ROTC: Army, Air Force in cooperation with University of Southern Mississippi.

Degrees Conferred: 409 *baccalaureate*; 405 *master's.* Bachelor's degrees awarded in top five disciplines: health professions and related clinical sciences 80; education 69; liberal arts and sciences, general studies, and humanities 63; psychology 52; business, management, marketing, and related support services 44.

Fees and Other Expenses: *Full-time tuition per academic year 2004–05:* undergraduate $8,115. *Books and supplies:* $1,410. *Room and board per academic year:* $4,266.

Financial Aid: Aid from institutionally generated funds is provided on the basis of academic merit, athletic ability, other criteria. Institution has a Program Participation Agreement with the U.S. Department of Education for eligible students to receive Pell Grants and, depending upon the agreement, other federal aid.

Departments and Teaching Staff: Arts, Humanities, and Sciences *professors* 14, *associate professors* 4, *assistant professors* 8, *instructors* 3, *part-time*

faculty 36; Business 5, 1, 3, 3, 18; Education and Psychology 10, 7, 5, 7, 20; Missions and Biblical Studies 3, 1, 2, 1, 1; Music 4, 3, 2, 2, 6; Nursing 1, 3, 14, 3, 3.

Total instructional faculty: 125. Degrees held by full-time faculty: doctorate 70%, master's 99%, baccalaureate 100%. 70% hold terminal degrees.

Enrollment: Total enrollment 2,758. Undergraduate 1,853 (26.9% men, 73.1% women).

Characteristics of Student Body: *Ethnic/racial makeup:* Black non-Hispanic: 34%; American Indian or Alaska Native: .5%; Asian or Pacific Islander: .9%; Hispanic: 2.1%; White non-Hispanic: 60.1%; unknown: .6%. *Age distribution:* 17–21: 26%; 22–24: 19%; 25–29: 19%; 30–34: 9%; 35–39: 10%; 40–49: 14%; 50–59: 2%; 60–up: 1%.

International Students: 33 nonresident aliens enrolled fall 2004. Students from Europe, Asia, Latin America, Africa, Canada. No programs available for students whose native language is not English. No financial aid specifically designated for international students.

Student Life: On-campus residence halls house 24% of student body. Residence halls for men constitute 47% of such space, for women 53%. Housing available for married students. *Intercollegiate athletics:* men only: baseball; both sexes: basketball soccer, tennis. *Special regulations:* Cars with decals permitted in designated areas. Quiet hours. *Special services:* Student support services. *Student publications: The Cobbler,* a weekly newspaper; *The Crusader,* a yearbook; *Indigo,* an annual literary magazine. *Surrounding community:* Hattiesburg population 46,000. New Orleans (LA), 105 miles from campus, is nearest metropolitan area. Served by mass transit bus system, airport 10 miles from campus, passenger rail service 2 miles from campus.

Library Collections: 135,000 volumes. 31,000 microforms; 3,000 audiovisual materials; 600 current periodical subscriptions. Students have access to online information retrieval services and the Internet.

Most important holdings include the Dickinson Sacred Music Collection (5,500 items, including books, scores, manuscripts, microforms, phonodiscs, tapes, paintings and memorabilia); Library of American Civilization.

Buildings and Grounds: Campus area 128 acres.

Chief Executive Officer: Dr. Larry Kennedy, President. Undergraduates address admission inquiries to William N. Curry, Director of Admissions; graduate inquiries to: Director, M.Ed. Program; Director, MBA Program.

Missouri

A.T. Still University of Health Science/ Kirksville College of Osteopathic Medicine

800 West Jefferson Street
Kirksville, Missouri 63501-1497
Tel: (866) 626-2878   **E-mail:** admissions@atsu.edu
Fax: (660) 626-2926   **Internet:** www.atsu.edu

Institution Description: A.T. Still University of Health Sciences/Kirksville College of Osteopathic Medicine is a private professional institution. *Enrollment:* 649. *Degrees awarded:* First-professional.

Accreditation: *Regional:* NCA. *Professional:* osteopathy

History: First accredited 1901.

Institutional Structure: *Governing board:* Board of Trustees. Full-time instructional faculty 83.

Calendar: Quarters. Academic year Aug. to Aug.

Admission: Applicants applying with a baccalaureate degree prior to matriculation must have achieved a minimum 2.5 cumulative GPA. Applicants applying with 90 credit hours must have a cumulative and science GPA of 3.5 minimum and a composite MCAT score of at least 28. Applicants must have completed one full academic year or the equivalent (8 semester or 12 quarter hours) in each of the following: biology, physics, general chemistry, organic chemistry, English (6 semester or 8 quarter hours).

Degree Requirements: Completion of prescribed curriculum.

Degrees Conferred: 140 *first-professional:* osteopathic medicine.

Fees and Other Expenses: *Full-time tuition per academic year 2004*05:* $31,700. *required fees:* $690.

Financial Aid: Aid from institutionally generated funds is provided on the basis of academic merit, financial need. Institution has a Program Participation Agreement with the U.S. Department of Education for eligible students to receive Pell Grants and, depending on the agreement, other federal aid.

Departments and Teaching Staff: Anatomy *professors* 3, *associate professors* 0, *assistant professors* 3, *instructors* 0; *part-time faculty:* 0; anesthesiology 0, 2, 3, 0, 0; biochemistry 1, 4, 0, 1, 0; community health education 1, 0, 3, 3, 3; dermatology 1, 0, 0, 0, 0; general practice/family medicine 0, 4, 3, 0, 1; internal medicine 1, 4, 5 0, 0; medical education 0, 1, 3, 0, 0; microbiology/immunology 1, 3, 0, 0, 0; obstetrics/gynecology 0, 1, 1, 0, 0; osteopathic theory and methods 5, 5, 0, 0, 0; pathology 1, 1, 0, 0, 0; pediatrics 0, 0, 1, 0, 0; pharmacology 1, 3, 1, 0, 0; physiology 1, 4, 0, 0, 0; radiology 2, 1, 0, 0, 0; surgery 0, 7, 5, 0, 0.

Total instructional faculty: 89 (full-time 80, part-time 9; women 22, men 67; members of minority groups 7). Total faculty with doctorate, first-professional, or other terminal degree: 81. Student-to-faculty ratio: 7:1. *Faculty development:* $1,269,378 total grants for research.

Enrollment: Total enrollment 649. First-professional full-time 394 men / 255 women.

International Students: 6 nonresident aliens enrolled fall 2004. 3 students from Asia, 1 Africa, 2 Canada. No programs available to aid students whose native language is not English. No financial aid specifically designated for international students.

Library Collections: 88,000 volumes. 8,105 audiovisual materials; 450 current periodical subscriptions. 4,304 recordings. 30 computer work stations. Online catalog. Students have access to online information retrieval services (fee-based) and the Internet (no charge). Total 2004–05 budget for books and materials: $575,000.

Most important special holdings include osteopathic medicine collection; A.T. Still Manuscript Collection; college archives.

Buildings and Grounds: *New buildings:* Connell Information Technologies Center planned for completion 2006.

Chief Executive Officer: Dr. James J. McGovern, President.

Address admission inquiries to Lori Haxton, Director of Admissions.

Aquinas Institute of Theology

3642 Lindell Boulevard
St. Louis, Missouri 63108-3396
Tel: (314) 977-3882   **E-mail:** aquinas@slu.edu
Fax: (314) 977-7225   **Internet:** www.op.org/aquinas

Institution Description: Aquinas Institute of Theology is a private graduate school of theology affiliated with the Dominican Friars of the Province of St. Albert the Great, Roman Catholic Church. *Enrollment:* 300. *Degrees awarded:* First-professional (master of divinity), master's, doctorate.

Accreditation: *Regional:* NCA. *National:* ATS. *Professional* theology

History: Established as College of St. Thomas Aquinas in River Forest, Illinois, and offered first instruction 1939; awarded first degree (baccalaureate) 1941; incorporated as the Dominican College of St. Rose of Lima 1950; School of Theology separated from School of Philosophy and moved to Dubuque, Iowa 1951; first degrees (master's, doctorate) awarded 1952; branches reorganized as Aquinas Institute of Philosophy and Theology 1961; joined Dubuque campus and changed name to Aquinas Institute of Theology 1970; moved to campus of St. Louis University 1981.

Institutional Structure: *Governing board:* Aquinas Institute of Theology Board of Trustees. Extrainstitutional representation: 16 trustees, 2 ex officio; institutional representation: president. All voting. *Composition of institution:* Administrators 3 men / 1 women. Academic affairs headed by academic dean. Business and finances directed by business manager. Full-time instructional faculty 8 men / 6 women. Overall administrator is the president.

Calendar: Semesters (4-1-4 plan). Academic year Sept. to May. Students admitted Sept., Jan. Degrees conferred Dec., May. Formal commencement May. Summer session.

Admission: *Requirements:* Baccalaureate degree, or its equivalent, from recognized institution. Additional requirements for some programs. *Entrance tests:* Miller Analogies.

Degree Requirements: *For first-professional degree:* 90 semester hours, 3 years in residence, major written project. *For master's degree:* 36–48 hours, 2 years in residence, major paper or thesis; *For Master of Divinity:* 90 hours; 3 years in residence. *For doctor's degree (doctor of ministry in preaching):* 30 hours, 1 year in residence, thesis/project. *For all degrees:* B average, supervised ministry experience. *Grading system:* A–F; pass.

Distinctive Educational Programs: Evening and late afternoon classes. Cross-registration with Saint Louis University and other local schools. Distance learning master's degree program in Oklahoma City. Unique doctoral degree in preaching.

Degrees Conferred: 53 *first-professional:* master of divinity; 6 *doctorate.*

Fees and Other Expenses: *Full-time tuition per academic year 2005–06:* $13,464. Contact the institute for current information regarding housing costs.

Financial Aid: Aid from institutionally generated funds is provided on the basis of academic merit, financial need, other criteria. *Graduate aid:* 32 students received $327,315 in federal and state-funded loans; 42 received fellowships/ grants totaling $300,760.

Departments and Teaching Staff: Theology *professors* 1, *associate professors* 7, *assistant professors* 7, *part-time faculty* 9.

Total instructional faculty: 24 (full-time 15, part-time 9; women 9, men 15). Total faculty with doctorate, first-professional, or other terminal degree: 23. Student-to-faculty ratio: 8:1. *Faculty development:* 2 faculty members awarded sabbaticals 2004–05.

Enrollment: Total enrollment 292. First-professional full-time 22 men / 15 women, part-time 34m / 70w; graduate full-time 45m / 14w, part-time 37m / 55w.

Characteristics of Student Body: *Ethnic/racial makeup:* Black non-Hispanic: 7%; Asian or Pacific Islander: 2.6%; Hispanic: 4.8%; White non-Hispanic: 83.9%.

International Students: 11 nonresident aliens enrolled fall 2004. Students from Central and South America, Africa, Canada. No programs available to aid students whose native language is not English. *Financial aid specifically designated for international students:* 1 scholarship available annually.

Student Life: Students must find housing off campus. *Surrounding community:* St. Louis population 455,000. Served by mass transit bus system; airport 7 miles from campus; passenger rail service 2 miles from campus.

Library Collections: 105,000 volumes. 255,000 government documents; 513,648 microforms; 4,370 audiovisual materials; 6,097 periodicals (access to St. Louis University Pius XII and Divinity Library). Students have access to online information retrieval services and the Internet.

Special collection of Dominican materials.

Buildings and Grounds: Campus area 2 city blocks. The building, containing classrooms, offices, lounge, meditation room, and library, is on the campus of St. Louis University.

Chief Executive Officer: Charles E. Bouchard, O.P., President.

Address admission inquiries Jared Ainsewort-Bryson, Director of Admissions.

Assemblies of God Theological Seminary

1435 North Glenstone
Springfield, Missouri 65802-2131
Tel: (417) 268-1000   **E-mail:** agts@agseminary.edu
Fax: (417) 268-1001   **Internet:** www.agts.edu

Institution Description: Assemblies of God Theological Seminary is a private institution affiliated with the Assemblies of God. *Enrollment:* 496. *Degrees awarded:* First-professional (master of divinity), master's, doctorate.

Accreditation: *Regional:* NCA. *National:* ATS. *Professional:* theology

History: Established, incorporated, and offered first instruction at postsecondary level 1972; awarded first degree (master's) 1974.

Institutional Structure: *Governing board:* Assemblies of God Theological Seminary Board of Directors. Representation: 15 directors, 1 administrator. 3 ex officio (Seminary president, general superintendent of denomination, national director of Christian Education of denomination). All voting. *Composition of institution:* Administrators 8 men / 1 woman. Academic affairs headed by academic dean. Management/business/finances directed by business manager. Full-time instructional faculty 10 men / 1 woman. Academic governance body, Academic Affairs Committee, meets an average of 10 times per year.

Calendar: Semesters. Academic year Sept. to July. Degrees conferred Dec., Apr., Aug. Summer session of 3 terms from May to Aug.

Characteristics of Freshmen: 61% of applicants accepted. 63% of accepted applicants enrolled. Students from 47 states and 25 foreign countries.

Admission: Rolling admissions plan. For fall acceptance, apply as early as 1 year prior to enrollment, but not later than Aug. 15. *Requirements:* Baccalaureate degree or equivalent from acceptable 4-year institution. Minimum GPA 2.5 for master's, 3.0 for doctorate. *Entrance tests:* For foreign students TOEFL. *For transfer students:* Maximum transfer credit limited to half of academic program.

Degree Requirements: *For first-professional degrees:* 90 credit hours; distribution requirements. *For master's degrees:* 36–60 credit hours; 2.0 GPA for M.Div; 2.5 GPA for M.A. *For core requirements:* comprehensives in individual fields of study or thesis; approval of Academic Affairs Committee. *For doctoral degrees:* 30 credit hours; 3.0 GPA; core requirements; doctor project; approval of Academic Affairs Committee.

Grading system: A–F; withdraw (passing-failing appended to withdraw).

Distinctive Educational Programs: Practicums. Flexible meeting places and schedules, including off-campus centers (at Assemblies of God undergraduate colleges throughout the U.S.) and evening classes. Special facilities for using telecommunications in the classroom. Individually arranged directed study.

Degrees Conferred: 86 *master's:* theology 67; counseling 19; 16 *doctorate:* theology; 26 *first-professional:* master of divinity.

Fees and Other Expenses: *Tuition per academic year 2005–06:* $8,544. *Required fees:* $300.

Financial Aid: Aid from institutionally generated funds is provided on the basis of academic merit, financial need. *Graduate aid:* 226 students received $2,030,240 in federal and state-funded loans (ranging from $350 to $9,500); 18 received $65,780 for work-study jobs (ranging from $2,100 to $4,200).

Departments and Teaching Staff: Bible/theology *professors* 5, *associate professors* 0, *assistant professors* 0, *instructors* 0, *part-time faculty* 2; practical theology 2, 1, 2, 0, 7; global missions 1, 0, 0, 0, 7.

Total instructional faculty: 27 (full-time 11, part-time 16; women 5, men 22; member of minority group 1). Total faculty with doctorate, first-professional, or other terminal degree: 26. Student-to-faculty ratio: 12:1.

Enrollment: Total enrollment 496. First-professional full-time 71 men / 17 women, part-time 25m / 12w; graduate full-time 87m / 53w, part-time 174m / 57w.

Characteristics of Student Body: *Ethnic/racial makeup:* number of Black non-Hispanic: 13; American Indian or Alaska Native: 3; Asian or Pacific Islander: 11; Hispanic: 17; White non-Hispanic: 417; unknown: 21.

International Students: 14 nonresident aliens enrolled fall 2004. Students from Europe, Asia, Central and South America, Africa, Canada. No programs available to aid students whose native language is not English. No financial aid

Student Life: No on-campus housing. *Special regulations:* Registered cars permitted. *Surrounding community:* Springfield population 156,335. St. Louis, 200 miles from campus, is nearest metropolitan area. Served by airport 10 miles from campus.

Library Collections: 89,853 volumes. 63,792 microforms; 3,994 audiovisual materials; 421 current periodical subscriptions. Online catalog. 23 computer work stations. Students have access to online information retrieval services and the Internet. Total 2004–05 budget for books and materials: $77,600.

Most important special holdings include materials on theology, missions, and Pentecostal studies.

Buildings and Grounds: Seminary facility with 2-floor library, 5 classrooms, 2 lecture halls, chapel, administration and faculty office suites.

Chief Executive Officer: Dr. Byron D. Klaus, President.

Address admissions inquiries to Mario H. Guerreiro, Director of Enrollment Management.

Avila College

11901 Wornall Road
Kansas City, Missouri 64145
Tel: (816) 942-8400   **E-mail:** admissions@avila.edu
Fax: (816) 942-3362   **Internet:** www.avila.edu

Institution Description: Avila College is a private college affiliated with the Roman Catholic Church. *Enrollment:* 2,104. *Degrees awarded:* Baccalaureate, master's.

Member of the Sisters of Saint Joseph College consortium.

Accreditation: *Regional:* NCA. *Professional:* nursing, nursing education, radiography, social work

History: Established as College of St. Teresa, a women's college, chartered and offered first instruction at postsecondary level 1916; awarded first degree (associate) 1918; adopted present name 1963; became coeducational 1969.

Institutional Structure: *Governing board:* Avila College Board of Trustees. Extrainstitutional representation: 24 trustees including 8 Sisters of Saint Joseph, 1 emeritus; institutional representation: president of the college. 1 ex officio. All voting. *Composition of institution:* President and 4 vice presidents; academic areas organized into 6 departments. Full-time instructional faculty 56. Academic governance body meets an average of 9 times per year.

Calendar: Semesters (trimesters for MBA program). Academic year Aug. to July. Freshmen admitted Aug., June, Jan. Degrees conferred May, Aug., Jan. Formal commencement May. Summer session of 1 term from early June to late July.

Characteristics of Freshmen: 832 applicants (366 men, 446 women).

9% (12 students) submitted SAT scores; 84% (109 students) submitted ACT scores. *25th percentile:* SAT I Verbal 430, SAT I Math 440; ACT Composite 19, ACT English 19, ACT Math 17. *75th percentile:* SAT I Verbal 550, SAT I Math 550; ACT Composite 24, ACT English 25, ACT Math 24.

40% of entering freshmen expected to graduate within 5 years. 79% of freshmen from Missouri. Freshmen from 11 states and 2 foreign countries.

Admission: Rolling admissions plan. Early acceptance available. *Requirements:* Either graduation from accredited secondary school with 16 units which must include 4 English, 2 mathematics, 2 natural science; or GED. Minimum GPA 2.5. *Entrance tests:* College Board SAT or ACT composite. For foreign students TOEFL. *For transfer students:* 2.0 minimum GPA; from 2-year accredited institution 64 hours maximum transfer credit; correspondence/extension students 9 hours.

College credit and advanced placement for postsecondary-level work completed in secondary school, International Baccalaureate Program, CLEP. College credit for extrainstitutional learning (life experience) on basis of faculty assessments. Tutoring available. Noncredit developmental courses offered in summer session and regular academic year.

Degree Requirements: *For all baccalaureate degrees:* 128 semester hours; 30 hours in residence; comprehensives or exit competency examinations in individual fields of study. *For all undergraduate degrees:* 2.0 GPA; core and distribution requirements.

Fulfillment of some degree requirements and exemption from some beginning courses possible by passing departmental examinations, College Board CLEP, AP, experiential learning. *Grading system:* A–F; credit/noncredit; withdraw; audit.

Distinctive Educational Programs: *For undergraduates:* Interdisciplinary programs and gerontological studies, women's studies. Preprofessional program in medicine, baccalaureate degree in radiologic technology. *Available to all students:* Weekend and evening classes. Off-campus study through consortia.

Degrees Conferred: 201 *baccalaureate:* business, management, marketing, and related support services 55; psychology 33; health professions and related clinical sciences 33l; education 19; and performing arts 14. 55 *naster's:* business 26, education 20,psychology 9.

Fees and Other Expenses: *Full-time tuition per academic year 2004–05:* $15,500 undergraduate; graduate study charged per credit hour; contact the university for current information. *Books and supplies:* $800. *Room and board per academic year:* $6,300.

Financial Aid: Aid from institutionally generated funds provided on the basis of academic merit, financial need, athletic ability. Institution has a Program Participation Agreement with the U.S. Department of Education for eligible students to receive Pell Grants and other federal aid.

Departments and Teaching Staff: Business *professors* 2; *associate professors* 3, *assistant professors* 2, *instructors* 1, *part-time teachers* 11; education/psychology 4, 2, 2, 1, 23; humanities 1, 4, 6, 1, 25; nursing 0, 1, 4, 2, 0; social science 1, 2, 4, 0, 4.

Total instructional faculty: 80 FTE. Student-to-faculty ratio: 11:1. Degrees held by full-time faculty: doctorate 70%, master's 25%. 75% hold terminal degrees.

Enrollment: Total enrollment 2,104. Undergraduate 1,579 (men 52.1%, women 47.9%).

Characteristics of Student Body: *Ethnic/racial makeup (undergraduate):* number of Black non-Hispanic: 17%; American Indian or Alaska Native: .8%; Asian or Pacific Islander: 1.8%; White non-Hispanic: 71.6%; unknown: 2.7%. *Age distribution:* 17–21: 21%; 22–24: 26%; 25–29: 15%; 30–34: 11%; 35–39: 9%; 40–49: 13%; 50–59: 4%; 60–up: 1%.

International Students: 54 undergraduate nonresident aliens enrolled fall 2004. Students from Europe, Asia, Latin America, Africa, Canada. Programs available to aid students whose native language is not English: social, cultural, financial. English as a Second Language Program.

Student Life: On-campus residence halls available. *Special regulations:* Cars permitted without restrictions. *Special services:* Learning Resources Center. *Student publication: Avila Talon,* a bimonthly newspaper. *Surrounding community:* Kansas City population 500,000. Served by mass transit bus system; airport 40 miles from campus; passenger rail service 10 miles from campus.

Library Collections: 73,000 volumes. 1,200 government documents; 442,080 microforms; 11,390 audiovisual materials; 495 current periodical subscriptions. Online catalog. Computer work stations available. Students have access to online information retrieval services and the Internet.

Most important holdings include collections on business, nursing, special education; Women Religious Collection.

Buildings and Grounds: Campus area 49 acres.

Chief Executive Officer: Thomas F. Gordon, President.

Address admission inquiries to Paige Illum, Director of Admissions.

Calvary Bible College and Theological Seminary

15800 Calvary Road
Kansas City, Missouri 64147-1341

Tel: (816) 322-0110   **E-mail:** admissions@calvary.edu
Fax: (816) 331-4474   **Internet:** www.calvary.edu

Institution Description: Calvary Bible College is a private, independent, nonprofit, nondenominational institution. *Enrollment:* 320. *Degrees awarded:* Associate, baccalaureate, master's.

Accreditation: *Regional:* NCA. *National:* ABHE.

History: Created by merger in 1961 of Kansas City Bible College (founded 1932) and Midwest Bible College (founded 1938).

Institutional Structure: *Governing board:* Board of Trustees. Representation: 19 trustees. All voting. *Composition of institution:* Administrators 5, president of the college.

Calendar: Semesters (4-1-4 plan). Academic year late Aug. to May. Degrees conferred May.

Characteristics of Freshmen: 90% of applicants accepted. 74% of accepted applicants enrolled.

11% of students submitted SAT scores; 89% submitted ACT scores. *25th percentile*: SAT Verbal 550, SAT Math 460; ACT Composite 19. *75th percentile*: SAT Verbal 730, SAT Math 620; ACT Composite 26.

32% of freshmen from Missouri.

Admission: All prospective students must testify that they have trusted the Lord Jesus Christ as their personal Savior and give evidence of commendable Christian character. A limited number of students who were in the lower 50% of their high school class and had a grade average below C may be accepted on probation.

Degree Requirements: 132–160 credit hours; 2.0 GPA; 2 semesters in residence.

Distinctive Educational Programs: Teacher education program that allows those interested in missionary work to student teach overseas. Christian broadcasting major taught through college-owned and operated radio station KLJC.

Degrees Conferred: 3 *associate* ; 37 *baccalaureate:* business/marketing 11; education 3; religion/theology 22; social sciences 1; 4 *master's:* religion/theology.

Fees and Other Expenses: *Full-time tuition per academic year 2004–05:* $6,187. *Required fees:* $432. *Room and board per academic year:* $3,700.

Financial Aid: Aid from institutionally generated funds is provided on the basis of academic merit, financial need. Institution has a Program Participation Agreement with the U.S. Department of Education for eligible students to receive Pell Grants and, depending upon the agreement, other federal aid.

Financial aid to full-time, first-time undergraduate students: need-based scholarships/grants totaling $356,910, self-help $54,173, parent loans $47,442; non-need-based scholarships/grants totaling $48,717, self-help $261,020, tuition waivers $49,611.

Departments and Teaching Staff: *Total instructional faculty:* 34 (full-time 14, part-time 20; women 10, men 24; member of minority group 1). Total faculty with doctorate, first-professional, or other terminal degree: 9. Student-to-faculty ratio: 12:1. Degrees held by full-time faculty: doctorate 20%, master's 40%, baccalaureate 40%.

Enrollment: Total enrollment 320. Undergraduate full-time 101 men / 93 women, part-time 40m / 28w; first-professional full-time 8m, part-time 6m; graduate full-time 1m / 6w, part-time 26m / 11w.

Characteristics of Student Body: *Ethnic/racial makeup:* number of Black non-Hispanic: 12; Asian or Pacific Islander: 5; Hispanic: 5; White non-Hispanic: 236.

International Students: 4 nonresident aliens enrolled. No programs available to aid students whose native language is not English.

Student Life: On-campus residence halls house 60% of student body. 46% are used by men only, 54% women only. *Intercollegiate athletics:* men only: soccer, basketball; women only: basketball, volleyball; both sexes: golf, tennis. *Student publications, radio: Calvary Review,* a quarterly magazine; *The Crown,* a yearbook. Radio station KLJC broadcasts 24 hours per day.

Library Collections: 56,000 volumes. Online and card catalogs. 2,700 microforms; 249 current periodical subscriptions. 16 computer work stations. Students have access to online information retrieval services and the Internet.

Most important holdings are in the field of theology.

Buildings and Grounds: Campus area 55 acres.

Chief Executive Officer: Dr. Elwood H. Chipchase, President.

Address admission inquiries to Robert Reinsch, Director of Admissions.

Central Bible College

3000 North Grant Avenue
Springfield, Missouri 65803-1033

Tel: (417) 833-2551   **E-mail:** admissions@cbcag.edu
Fax: (417) 833-5141   **Internet:** www.cbcag.edu

Institution Description: Central Bible College is owned and controlled by the General Council of the Assemblies of God, Springfield, Missouri. *Enrollment:* 777. *Degrees awarded:* Associate, baccalaureate.

Accreditation: *National:* ABHE.

History: Established 1922; expanded by merger with Bethel Bible Training Institute 1929, South Central Bible College 1953, and Great Lakes Bible Institute 1954.

Institutional Structure: *Governing board:* Board of Directors. 14 members. *Composition of institution:* Board of administration, divisional chairmen. Academic affairs headed by dean. Management/business/finances directed by business manager. Full-time instructional faculty 34.

Calendar: Semesters. Academic year early Sept. to late Apr. 3 summer sessions.

Characteristics of Freshmen: 83% of applicants accepted. 65% of applicants accepted and enrolled.

17% (25 students) submitted SAT scores; 53% (77 students) submitted ACT scores. *25th percentile*: SAT I Verbal 440, SAT I Math 440; ACT Composite 20,

ACT English 20, ACT Math 17. *75th percentile*: SAT I Verbal 610, SAT I Math 590; ACT Composite 25, ACT English 26, ACT Math 24.

37% of freshmen expected to graduate within 5 years. 15% of freshmen from Missouri. Freshmen from 27 states and 2 foreign countries.

Admission: *Requirements:* High school graduation in upper 60% of class or *Entrance tests:* College Board SAT or ACT.

Degree Requirements: *For all associate degrees:* 64 semester hours. *For all baccalaureate degrees:* 128 semester hours; prescribed courses; general education requirements.

Distinctive Educational Programs: Diploma programs are offered in Bible and Missions and require completion of 95 semester hours.

Degrees Conferred: 6 *associate;* 124 *baccalaureate:* theology/ministerial studies.

Fees and Other Expenses: *Full-time tuition per academic year 2004–05:* $8,505. *Room and board per academic year:* $4,344. *Books and supplies:* $750.

Financial Aid: Aid from institutionally generated funds is provided on the basis of academic merit, financial need, other criteria. Institution has a Program Participation Agreement with the U.S. Department of Education for eligible students to receive Pell Grants and, depending upon the agreement, other federal aid.

Departments and Teaching Staff: Biblical literature *professors* 2, *associate professors* 4, *assistant professors* 1, *instructors* 0, *part-time teachers* 1; church ministries 3, 3, 0, 2, 7; general education 1, 2, 7, 3, 7; music 0, 4, 2, 1, 4.

Total instructional faculty: 66. Student-to-faculty ratio: 21:1. Degrees held by full-time faculty: doctorate 31%, master's 66%, baccalaureate 3%. 29% hold terminal degrees.

Enrollment: Total enrollment 777 (66.1% men, 43.9% women).

Characteristics of Student Body: *Ethnic/racial makeup:* number of Black non-Hispanic: 2.6%; American Indian or Alaska Native: 1.0%; Asian or Pacific Islander: 1.8%; Hispanic: 2.2%; White non-Hispanic: 91,1%; unknown: .1%. *Age distribution:* 17–21: 61%; 22–24: 18%; 25–29: 11%; 30–34: 5%; 35–39: 4%; 40–49: 1%; 50–59: .03%.

International Students: 7 nonresident aliens enrolled fall 2004. No program available to aid students whose native language is not English. No financial aid specifically designated for international students.

Library Collections: 110,000 volumes. 28,000 microforms; 6,000 recordings/tapes; 540 current periodical subscriptions. Students have access to online information retrieval services and the Internet.

Most important special holdings include collections on the Bible, theology, and missions; Assemblies of God Collection.

Chief Executive Officer: Dr. R. Wayne Benson, President.

Address admission inquiries to Scott Lindner, Director of Enrollment Management.

Central Christian College of the Bible

911 Urbandale Drive East
Moberly, Missouri 65270
Tel: (660) 263-3900   **E-mail:** iwant2be@cccb.edu
Fax: (660) 263-3936   **Internet:** www.cccb.edu

Institution Description: Central Christian College of the Bible is a private, church-related Bible college. *Enrollment:* 466. *Degrees awarded:* Associate, baccalaureate.

Accreditation: *National:* ABHE.

History: Established 1957.

Institutional Structure: *Governing board:* Independent external Board comprised of 18 directors. *Composition of institution:* 4 administrators report to the president (academic dean, business manager, dean of students, development director). Full-time instructional faculty 18.

Calendar: Semesters. Academic year late Aug. to mid-May. Formal commencement May. Summer classes are offered.

Characteristics of Freshmen: 89% of applicants accepted. 91% of accepted applicants enrolled. 24% of entering freshmen expected to graduate within 5 years. 45% of freshmen from Missouri. Freshmen from 45 states and 2 foreign countries.

Admission: Rolling admissions plan. Earlybird grant for those completing application by Apr. 1. *Requirements:* High school graduation or GED. Modified open admissions with required references on moral character. No mandatory entrance tests.

Degree Requirements: 133 credit hours; 2.0 GPA; 2 semesters in residence; core curriculum. *Grading system:* A–F; 4-point system.

Distinctive Educational Programs: Classes offered Monday afternoon through Friday afternoon. Cooperative programs with Moberly Area Community College, Hannibal-LaGrange College, and Columbia College.

Degrees Conferred: 8 *baccalaureate:* religion 7; psychology 1.

Fees and Other Expenses: *Full-time tuition per academic year 2004–05:* $210 per credit hour. *Incidental fee:* $250. *Room and board per semester:* $2,250.

Financial Aid: Aid from institutionally generated funds is provided on the basis of academic merit, financial need, other considerations. The college offers all full-time students a full-tuition scholarship.

Departments and Teaching Staff: *Professors* 7, *associate professors* 2, *assistant professors* 2, *instructors* 2, *part-time faculty* 14.

Total instructional faculty: 27. Student-to-faculty ratio: 25:1. Degrees held by full-time faculty: doctorate 22%, baccalaureate 100%, master's 89%, professional 56%. 22% hold terminal degrees.

Enrollment: Total enrollment 466. Undergraduate full-time 247 men / 203 women, part-time 10m / 6w.

Characteristics of Student Body: *Ethnic/racial makeup:* number of Black non-Hispanic: 31; American Indian or Alaska Native: 3; Asian or Pacific Islander: 16; Hispanic: 8; White non-Hispanic: 295; unknown: 7. *Age distribution:* 17–21: 73%; 22–24: 13%; 25–29: 1%; 30–34: 3%; 35–39: 4%; 40–49 2%; 50–59: 3%; 60–up: 1%.

International Students: 10 nonresident aliens enrolled fall 2004. 3 students from Asia, 4 Central and South America, 3 Africa. No programs available to aid students whose native language is not English. No financial aid specifically designated for international students.

Student Life: Students taking 8 hours or more live in residence halls. *Intercollegiate athletics:* men only: basketball; women only: volleyball. *Special regulations:* Christian lifestyle expected. Alcohol and tobacco are forbidden on campus. *Student publications: Scroll,* a student newspaper; *The Torchbearer,* a student yearbook.

Publications: *The Sentinel,* a newsletter for donors; *Looking Ahead,* a recruitment newsletter.

Library Collections: 71,000 volumes. Online catalog. 90 microform titles; 2,000 audiovisual materials; 196 current periodical subscriptions. 30 computer work stations. Students have access to online information retrieval services and the Internet.

Most important special holdings include ancient Biblical texts; Walter Coble Collection (missionary files); John Hall charts.

Buildings and Grounds: Campus is located at the edge of Moberly (MO) on 40 acres. *New buildings:* Library completed 2000.

Chief Executive Officer: Dr. Russell James, President.

Address admission inquiries to Tracy Roach, Admissions Director.

Central Methodist University

411 Central Methodist Square
Fayette, Missouri 65248
Tel: (660) 248-3391   **E-mail:** admissions@centralmethodist.edu
Fax: (660) 248-2287   **Internet:** www.centralmethodist.edu

Institution Description: Central Methodist University, formerly Central Methodist College, is a private institution affiliated with the United Methodist Church. *Enrollment:* 781. *Degrees awarded:* Associate, baccalaureate, master's.

Accreditation: *Regional:* NCA. *Professional:* music

History: Established as Central College 1853; chartered 1854; incorporated 1855; offered first instruction at postsecondary level 1857; awarded first degree (baccalaureate) 1859; merged with Howard-Payne College, Central College for Women, Scarrit-Morrisville, and Marvin Colleges 1922–25; adopted present name 1961. *See* Frank C. Tucker, *Central Methodist College: One Hundred and Ten Years* (Nashville: Parthenon Press, 1967) for further information.

Institutional Structure: *Governing board:* Central Methodist College Board of Curators. Extrainstitutional representation: 30 curators, bishop of Missouri area; institutional representation: president of the college. 2 ex officio. 30 voting. *Composition of institution:* Administrators 3 men / 7 women. Academic affairs headed by dean of the college. Management/business/finances directed by comptroller. Full-time instructional faculty 54. Academic governance bodies, faculty and Academic Affairs Committee, each meet an average of 9 times per year.

Calendar: Semesters. Academic year Aug. to mid-May. Freshmen admitted Aug., Jan., June. Degrees conferred and formal commencement May. Summer session from early June to mid-July.

Characteristics of Freshmen: 669 students applied; 281 of applicants accepted and enrolled.

3% (6 students) submitted SAT scores; 96% (186 students) submitted ACT scores. *25th percentile*: SAT Verbal 457.5, SAT Math 415; ACT Composite 19, ACT English 18, ACT Math 17. *75th percentile*: SAT Verbal 515, SAT Math 458; ACT Composite 24, ACT English 24, ACT Math 23.

96% of freshmen from Missouri. Freshmen from 7 states.

Admission: Rolling admissions plan. For fall acceptance, apply as early as May of previous year, but not later than Sept. of year of enrollment. Early acceptance available. *Requirements:* Either graduation from accredited secondary school or GED. Recommend 4 units English, 3 mathematics, 2 humanities, 2 science, 4 electives. Lowest acceptable secondary school class standing in upper two-thirds. *Entrance tests:* ACT composite. For foreign students TOEFL score 550. *For transfer students:* 2.0 minimum GPA; maximum transfer credit limited only by residence requirement.

College credit and advanced placement for postsecondary-level work completed in secondary school. College credit for extrainstitutional learning on basis of ACE *2006 Guide to the Evaluation of Educational Experiences in the Armed Services*.

Tutoring available. Developmental/remedial courses offered during regular academic year; nondegree credit given.

Degree Requirements: *For all associate degrees:* 62 semester hours; 24 hours in residence. *For all baccalaureate degrees:* 124–133 semester hours; 30 hours in residence. *For all degrees:* 2.0 GPA; 2 hours physical education; distribution requirements; demonstrated proficiency in English. Higher GPA for some programs.

Fulfillment of some degree requirements and exemption from some beginning courses possible by passing departmental examinations, College Board CLEP, AP subject examinations. *Grading system:* A–F; pass-fail; withdraw (deadline after which pass-fail is appended to withdraw).

Distinctive Educational Programs: Dual-degree program in engineering with Stanford University (CA), University of Missouri (at Columbia and at Rolla); in law with University of Missouri (at Columbia and at Kansas City). Cooperative baccalaureate in medical technology with approved schools of medical technology; in physical therapy with approved schools of physical therapy. Special facilities for using telecommunications in the classroom. Preprofessional programs in engineering awarded by University of Missouri at Rolla. Interdisciplinary programs. Facilities and programs for independent research, including honors programs, individual majors, tutorials. Off-campus study available during January interim.

ROTC: Army in cooperation with Kemper Military School and College.

Degrees Conferred: 2 *associate;* 323 *baccalaureate*: biological/life sciences 19; business/marketing 56; communications/communication technologies 3; computer and information sciences 3; education 132; English 4; foreign languages and literature 2; health professions and related sciences 29; interdisciplinary studies 10; mathematics 2; parks and recreation 1; philosophy/religion/theology 6; protective services/public administration 8; psychology 26; social sciences and history 9; other 2. 24 *master's*: education.

Fees and Other Expenses: *Full-time tuition per academic year 2004–05:* $14,490. *Required fees:* $710. *Room and board per academic year:* $5,360.

Financial Aid: Aid from institutionally generated funds is provided on the basis of academic merit, financial need, athletic ability, other criteria.

Financial aid to full-time, first-time undergraduate students: need-based scholarships/grants totaling $1,768,391, self-help $1,910,845; non-need-based scholarships/grants totaling $3,187,202, self-help $1,700,431, parent loans $1,284,068, tuition waivers $289,974, athletic awards $2,415,465.

Departments and Teaching Staff: Business and economics *professors* 0, *associate professors* 3, *assistant professors* 1, *instructors* 0, *part-time teachers* 1; education 1, 1, 1, 1, 0; English, communication/theatre arts/foreign languages/art 2, 1, 7, 0, 2; music 2, 2, 2, 0, 11; nursing 1, 2, 1, 2, 2; philosophy/religion 2, 0, 1, 0, 0; physical education 0, 2, 2, 0, 7; science 4, 1, 2, 1, 4.

Total instructional faculty: 63 (full-time 54, part-time 9; women 25, men 38; member of minority group 1). Student-to-faculty ratio: 14:1. Degrees held by full-time faculty: doctorate 54.5%, master's 43.6%, baccalaureate 1.8%. 45.8% hold terminal degrees.

Enrollment: Total enrollment 781. Undergraduate full-time 373 men / 378 women, part-time 10m / 20w.

Characteristics of Student Body: *Ethnic/racial makeup:* number of Black non-Hispanic: 71; American Indian or Alaska Native: 4; Asian or Pacific Islander: 4; Hispanic: 13; White non-Hispanic: 657; unknown: 13.

International Students: 18 nonresident aliens enrolled fall 2004. Students from Europe, Asia, Central and South America, Africa. No programs available to aid students whose native language is not English. Financial aid specifically designated for international students: some scholarships available annually to qualifying international students.

Student Life: On-campus residence halls house 66% of student body. Residence halls for men constitute 56% of such space, for women 44%. Off-campus housing available for married students. *Intercollegiate athletics:* men only: baseball, basketball, football, soccer, tennis, track; women only: basketball, softball,

tennis, track, volleyball. *Special regulations:* Registered cars permitted in designated areas. Quiet hours. Residence hall visitation from noon to midnight. *Special services:* Learning Resources Center, medical services. *Student publications: The Central Collegian*, a weekly newspaper; *Enscape*, a biannual literary magazine; *Ragout*, a yearbook. *Surrounding community:* Fayette population 3,000. Kansas City, 100 miles from campus, is nearest metropolitan area. Served by airport 35 miles from campus.

Library Collections: 998,920 volumes. 50,000 government documents. 82,100 microforms; 70 audiovisual materials; 241 serial subscriptions. Online catalog. Students have access to online information retrieval services and the Internet. Total 2004–05 budget for materials and operations: $58,322.

Most important special holdings include Official Archives of Missouri West Conference; Methodist Church; History of Methodism; CMC Archives.

Buildings and Grounds: Campus area 52 acres. *New buildings:* Student Union completed 2005.

Chief Executive Officer: Dr. Marianne Inman, President.

Address admission inquiries to Vice President for Enrollment Management.

Central Missouri State University

Warrensburg, Missouri 64093

Tel: (660) 543-4290   **E-mail:** admit@cmsu1.cmsu.edu
Fax: (660) 543-8517   **Internet:** www.cmsu.edu

Institution Description: Central Missouri State University is a state institution. *Enrollment:* 17,458. *Degrees awarded:* Associate, baccalaureate, master's. Specialist certificates in education also awarded. Ed.D and Ph.D. offered in cooperation with the University of Missouri-Columbia and the University of Indiana.

Academic offerings subject to approval by statewide coordinating bodies.

Accreditation: *Regional:* NCA. *Professional:* accounting, applied science, art, audiology, business, construction education, electronic technology, industrial technology, music, nursing, nursing education, social work, speech-language pathology, teacher education

History: Established and chartered as State Normal School for Second National District of Missouri, and offered first instruction at postsecondary level 1871; awarded first degree (baccalaureate) 1875; changed name to Central Missouri State Teachers College 1919, to Central Missouri State College 1946; adopted present name 1972. *See* Leslie Anders, *Education for Service* (Warrensburg: Central Missouri State University, 1971) for further information.

Institutional Structure: *Governing board:* Board of Governors of Central Missouri State University. Representation: 8 voting members including 1 nonvoting student governor and the Missouri commissions of elementary and secondary education. *Composition of institution:* Administrators 16 men / 8 women. The university is divided into 3 major units headed by the vice president for academic affairs, vice president for finance and administration, and vice president for student and alumni affairs. Full-time instructional faculty 430. Academic governance body, Faculty Senate, meets an average of 16 times per year.

Calendar: Semesters. Academic year Aug. to May. Freshmen admitted Aug., Jan., May, June. Degrees conferred Aug., Dec., May. Formal commencement Dec., May. Summer sessions of two 6-week and one 8-week sessions from mid-May to mid-Aug.

Characteristics of Freshmen: 86% of applicants admitted. 45% of applicants admitted and enrolled.

91% (1,372 students) submitted ACT scores. *25th percentile*: ACT Composite 19, ACT English 18, ACT Math 17. *75th percentile*: ACT Composite 24, ACT English 24, ACT Math 24.

51% of entering freshmen expected to graduate within 6 years. 95% of freshmen from Missouri. Freshmen from 44 states and 51 foreign countries.

Admission: Central Missouri State University admits students from accredited high schools who rank in the upper two-thirds of their graduating class, achieve 20 or above on the ACT, and complete the high school core curriculum. Rolling admissions plan. Early acceptance available. For foreign students TOEFL required. *For transfer students:* 2.0 minimum GPA; from 4-year accredited institution 94 hours maximum transfer credit, the final 30 of which must be completed at Central; from 2-year accredited institution 64 hours; correspondence/extension students 30 hours.

College credit and advanced placement for postsecondary-level work completed in secondary school and for extrainstitutional learning (life experience) on basis of ACE *Military Guide*, portfolio assessment. Tutoring available. Remedial courses offered in summer session and regular academic year; credit given.

Degree Requirements: *For all associate degrees:* 60 semester hours; 20 credits in residence. *For all baccalaureate degrees:* 124 hours; 30 credits in residence; distribution requirements; exit competency examinations required for selected academic programs. *For all undergraduate degrees:* 2.0 GPA; general education requirements.

Fulfillment of some degree requirements and exemption from some beginning courses possible by passing College Board CLEP, AP. *Grading system:* A–F; pass-fail; unfinished; withdraw, IB.

Distinctive Educational Programs: Programs in industrial hygiene, safety management, graphics, aviation nursing, actuarial science, speech pathology and audiology, criminal justice, photography, and individualized majors. Study abroad in England, Sweden, Hungary, France, Spain, Germany, Japan, The Netherlands, Denmark, Scotland, Finland, Ghana, Mexico, Wales, Australia.

ROTC: Army.

Degrees Conferred: 36 *associate;* 1,732 *baccalaureate* (B), 326 *master's* (M): agriculture and natural resources 14 (B); architecture 14 (B); area and ethnic studies 1 (B); biological/life sciences 35 (B); business/marketing 339 (B); communications/communication technologies 79 (B), 13 (M); computer and information sciences 75 (B); education 349 (B), 151 (M); engineering and engineering technologies 151 (B), 21 (M); English 21 (B), 4 (M); foreign languages and literature 21 (B), 11 (M); health professions and related sciences 42 (B), 34 (M); home economics and vocational home economics 41 (B); interdisciplinary studies 1 (B); liberal arts/general studies 48 (B); library science 1 (B), 3 (M); mathematics 2 (B), 5 (M); parks and recreation 13 (B); philosophy/religion/theology 1 (B); physical sciences 9 (B); protective services/public administration 178 (B), 23 (M); psychology 49 (B), 19 (M); social sciences and history 67 (B), 15 (M); trade and industry 67 (B); visual and performing arts 114 (B), 7 (M).

Fees and Other Expenses: *Tuition per academic year 2004–05:* undergraduate resident $5,340, nonresident $10,260; graduate resident $5,328, nonresident $10,320. *Required fees:* $14 per credit hour. *Room and board per academic year:* $4,988.

Financial Aid: Aid from institutionally generated funds provided on the basis of academic merit, financial need, athletic ability, other criteria.

Financial aid to full-time, first-time undergraduate students: need-based scholarships/grants totaling $8,662,692, self-help $14,683,489; non-need-based scholarships/grants totaling $8,186,903, self-help $11,246,719, parent loans $6,581,094, tuition waivers $1,121,881, athletic awards $1,484,031.

Departments and Teaching Staff: *Total instructional faculty:* 573 (full-time 430, part-time 143; women 251, men 322; members of minority groups 157). Total faculty with doctorate, first-professional, or other terminal degree: 471. Student-to-faculty ratio: 18:1. *Faculty development:* $8.3 million in grants for research. 9 faculty members awarded sabbaticals 2004–05.

Enrollment: Total enrollment 17,458. Undergraduate full-time 3,203 men / 3,520 women, part-time 531m / 7494w; graduate full-time 174m / 210w, part-time 451m / 913w. *Transfer students:* in-state 830.

Characteristics of Student Body: *Ethnic/racial makeup (undergraduate):* number of Black non-Hispanic: 468; American Indian or Alaska Native: 46; Asian or Pacific Islander: 83; Hispanic: 154; White non-Hispanic: 6,959; unknown: 349. *Age distribution:* number under 18: 51; 18–19: 2,286; 20–21: 2,632; 22–24: 1,866; 25–29: 581; 30–34: 252; 35–39: 171; 40–49: 747; 50–64: 66. 46% of student body attend summer sessions.

International Students: 350 nonresident aliens enrolled fall 2004. Students from Europe, Asia, Central and South America, Africa, Canada, Australia. Programs available to aid students whose native language is not English: social, cultural. English as a Second Language Program. Some financial aid specifically designated for international students. 20 scholarships are available annually to qualifying students.

Student Life: On-campus residence halls accommodate 3,737 students. 19 residence halls (2 for women only, 1 for men only, 15 are co-ed). Housing is available for students with family. *Intercollegiate athletics:* men only: baseball, basketball, cross-country, football, golf, track, wrestling; women only: basketball, cross-country, soccer, softball, track, volleyball. *Special regulations:* Registered cars with university issued permits allowed in designated areas. Quiet hours set by individual residence halls. Residence hall visitation policy for first-year students from 7am to midnight Mon.–Thurs., unlimited on Fri. and Sat.; for second year students and beyond visitation is allowed 24 hours 7 days a week not to exceed 3 consecutive days. *Special services:* Learning Resources Center, medical services. *Student radio, television:* Radio station KCMW-FM broadcasts 168 hours per week. TV station KMOS-TV broadcasts 121 hours per week. *Surrounding community:* Warrensburg population 18,500. Kansas City, 60 miles from campus, is nearest metropolitan area. Served by passenger rail service less than 1 mile from campus.

Publications: *The Muleskinner,* school newspaper; *The Rhetor,* school yearbook; *Pleiades,* literary journal published by the Department of English.

Library Collections: 2,088,896 volumes. Online and card catalogs. 664,421 government documents; 690,836 microforms; 14,699 audiovisual materials; 2,705 current periodical subscriptions. 300 computer work stations. Access to online information retrieval services and the Internet. Online catalog. Total 2004–05 budget for books, periodicals, audiovisual materials, microforms: $1,346,383.

Most important special holdings include Historical Children's Literature Collection; Missouri Collection; Civil War Collection.

Buildings and Grounds: Campus area 1,561 acres.

Chief Executive Officer: Dr. Bobby R. Patton, President.

Address undergraduate admission inquiries to Paul Orseheln, Chief Admissions Officer; graduate inquiries to Terry Sigler, Coordinator, Graduate Studies.

Cleveland Chiropractic College

6401 Rockhill Road
Kansas City, Missouri 64131-1181

Tel: (816) 501-0100   **E-mail:** admis@cleveland.edu
Fax: (816) 361-0272   **Internet:** www.cleveland.edu

Institution Description: Cleveland Chiropractic College is a private, independent, nonprofit college. *Enrollment:* 621. *Degrees awarded:* First-professional (chiropractic).

Accreditation: *Regional:* NCA. *Professional:* chiropractic education

History: Established as Central College of Chiropractic, chartered, incorporated, and offered first instruction at postsecondary level 1922; awarded first degree (first-professional) 1923; adopted present name 1924.

Institutional Structure: *Governing board:* Multi-campus Board of Trustees. Representation: 13 trustees, including 10 alumni. All voting. *Composition of institution:* 14 officers of administration (8 men / 6 women). Academic affairs under the direction of vice president for academic and student services. Management/business/finances directed by director of vice president for administrative and financial services. Full-time instructional faculty 45. Academic governance body, President's Council, meets and average of 48 times per year.

Calendar: Trimesters. Academic year Sept. to Aug. Entering students admitted Sept., Jan., May. Degrees conferred and formal commencement Apr., Aug., Dec. Summer session May through Aug.

Characteristics of Freshmen: 54% of applicants accepted. 41% of accepted applicants enrolled.

Admission: Rolling admissions plan. Applications for enrollment should be 9 months to 1 year in advance. *Requirements:* 60 semester hours from accredited college or university which must include 6 hours English or other communications courses, 6 laboratory biology (other than botany), 6 inorganic and 6 organic laboratory chemistry, 6 physics, 3 psychology, and an additional 15 hours in humanities/social science. A 2.5 GPA is required for full acceptance. Tutoring available.

Degree Requirements: 4,410 clock hours; 2.25 GPA; last 12 months in residence; core curriculum; 8-month internship; clinical competency examination. *Grading system:* A–F.

Distinctive Educational Programs: Choice of a nine- or twelve-trimester curriculum. Radiologic learning laboratory provides over 4,000 films for study. Practical experience gained treating patients in public clinic. *Other distinctive programs:* Nationwide preceptorship program for interns. Residency program in chiropractic roentgenology. Postgraduate and related education for area doctors.

Degrees Conferred: 25 *baccalaureate:* biological/life sciences; 98 *first-professional:* chiropractic.

Fees and Other Expenses: *Full-time tuition per academic year 2004–05:* undergraduate $5,976; contact the college for first-professional tuition.

Financial Aid: Aid from institutionally generated funds is provided on the basis of academic merit, financial need. Institution has a Program Participation Agreement with the U.S. Department of Education for eligible students to receive Pell Grants and, depending upon the agreement, other federal aid.

Departments and Teaching Staff: Basic science *professors* 2, *associate professors* 0, *assistant professors* 7, *instructors* 0, *part-time teachers* 1; diagnostic science 1, 2, 4, 2, 6; chiropractic science 3, 0, 5, 2, 0; library 0, 1, 0, 0, 0; clinical science 2, 0, 9, 0, 0; undergraduate 1, 0, 2, 2, 0.

Total instructional faculty: 54. Student-to-faculty ratio: 13.4:1. Degrees held by full-time faculty: doctorate 24%, master's 16%, professional 71%. 94% hold terminal degrees.

Enrollment: Total enrollment 621. Undergraduate full-time 47 men and women, part-time 11 m/w; first-professional 552m/w, part-time 11m/w.

Characteristics of Student Body: *Ethnic/racial makeup:* Black non-Hispanic: 14; American Indian or Native Alaskan: 1; Asian or Pacific Islander: 25; Hispanic: 10; White non-Hispanic: 497. *Age distribution:* 17–21: 5%; 22–24: 27%; 25–29: 41%; 30–34: 13%; 35–39: 7%; 40–49: 6%; 50–59: 1%.

International Students: 37 nonresident aliens enrolled fall 2004. No programs available to aid students whose native language is not English. No financial aid specifically designated for international students.

Student Life: No on-campus housing. *Special regulations:* Registered cars permitted. Clinical attire required last 2 trimesters. *Special services:* Professional counseling; health services. *Student publications: Intouch,* campus newsletter. *Surrounding community:* Greater Kansas City population 2 million.

Served by mass transit bus system; airport 35 miles from campus; passenger rail service 7 miles from campus.

Publications: *Clevelander* , alumni magazine.

Library Collections: 14,000 volumes. 28,000 microforms; 10,500 audiovisual materials; 245 current periodical subscriptions. Students have access to online information retrieval services and the Internet.

Most important special holdings include collections on chiropractic practice and principles, radiology, orthopedics.

Buildings and Grounds: Campus area 10 acres.

Chief Executive Officer: Dr. Carl S. Cleveland III, President.

Address admission inquiries to Melissa Denton, Director of Admissions.

College of the Ozarks

P.O. Box 17
Point Lookout, Missouri 65726
Tel: (414) 334-6411   **E-mail:** admiss4@cofo.edu
Fax: (414) 335-2618   **Internet:** www.cofo.edu

Institution Description: The College of the Ozarks, formerly School of the Ozarks, is a private, independent, nonprofit college related by covenant to the Presbyterian Church (U.S.A.). *Enrollment:* 1,348. *Degrees awarded:* Baccalaureate.

Accreditation: *Regional:* NCA. *Professional:* music, teacher education

History: Established, chartered, and incorporated 1906; offered first instruction at postsecondary level 1956; became a 4-year institution 1965; awarded first degree (baccalaureate) 1967.

Institutional Structure: *Governing board:* Board of Trustees. Extrainstitutional representation: 21 trustees, including 8 alumni; institutional representation: 2 administrators present but non-voting. *Composition of institution:* Administrators 15 men / 4 women. Academic affairs headed by Dean of College. Management/business/finances directed by vice president and business manager. Full-time instructional faculty 71. Academic governance body, Academic Council, meets an average of 8 times per year.

Calendar: Semesters. Academic year Aug. to May. Freshmen admitted Aug., Jan. Degrees conferred and formal commencement May. No summer session.

Characteristics of Freshmen: 13% of applicants admitted. 12$ of applicants admitted and enrolled.
25th percentile: ACT Composite 20, ACT English 19, ACT Math 24. *75th percentile*: ACT Composite 24, ACT English 25, ACT Math 24.

47% of entering freshmen expected to graduate within 5 years. 63% of freshmen from Missouri. Freshmen from 36 states and 1 foreign country.

Admission: Rolling admissions plan. For fall acceptance, apply as early as Oct. of previous year, but not later than Feb. Priority consideration date Feb. 15; secondary consideration date Mar. 15. Early acceptance available. *Requirements:* Either graduation from accredited secondary school or GED; homeschooled students also admitted. Student should have an ACT of 19 or better and in top half of graduating class. Minimum 3.0 GPA. *Entrance tests:* ACT. For foreign students minimum TOEFL score 550. *For transfer students:* Maximum transfer credit limited only by residence institution hours.

College credit for postsecondary-level work completed in secondary school and for extrainstitutional learning (life experience) on basis of ACE *2006 Guide to the Evaluation of Educational Experiences in the Armed Services.* Tutoring available.

Degree Requirements: 125 semester hours (excluding Freshmen Orientation); 2.0 GPA (2.5 for teacher education students); 45 hours in residence (including last 30 hours); chapel attendance 2 times per month for all residents except seniors; 3 physical education courses; distribution requirements; participation in work program 15 hours per week plus two 40-hour work weeks for all full-time students.

Fulfillment of some degree requirements and exemption from some beginning courses possible by passing departmental examinations, College Board CLEP, and AP. *Grading system:* A–F; pass-fail; withdraw (deadline after which A–F is appended to withdraw).

Distinctive Educational Programs: Some evening classes. Dual-degree program in engineering with cooperating institutions: University of Missouri at Rolla; nursing with St. John's. Preprofessional programs in medicine, pharmacy, veterinary medicine. Facilities and programs for independent research, individual majors, tutorials. Study abroad exchange program with Christellijke Hogeschool Noord-Netherland, Leeuwarden Tethus, Rotterdam, The Netherlands.

ROTC: Army. 5 commissions awarded 2004.

Degrees Conferred: 304 *baccalaureate:* agriculture 37; biological/life sciences 2; business/marketing 54; communications/communication technologies 30; computer and information sciences 10; education 52; English 7; foreign languages and literature 7; health professions and related sciences 3; home econom-

ics and vocational home economics 7; interdisciplinary studies 1; mathematics 1; natural resources/environmental science 2; parks and recreation 4; philosophy/religion/theology 7; physical sciences 2; protective services/public administration 21; psychology 24; social sciences and history 12; trade and industry 6; visual and performing arts 21.

Fees and Other Expenses: *Tuition per academic year 2005–06:* All tuition is covered by work study, Pell, and scholarship combination. *Required fees:* $280. *Room and board per academic year:* $3,850.

Financial Aid: Aid from institutionally generated funds is provided on the basis of academic merit, financial need, athletic ability.

Financial aid to full-time, first-time undergraduate students: need-based scholarships/grants totaling $12,065,440, self-help $2,698,427; non-need-based scholarships/grants totaling $2,201,293, self-help $1,697,818, athletic awards $164,000.

Departments and Teaching Staff: *Total instructional faculty:* 115 (full-time 71, part-time 44; women 33, men 82; members of minority groups 2). Total faculty with doctorate, first-professional, or other terminal degree: 52. Student-to-faculty ratio: 16:1. Degrees held by full-time faculty: doctorate 54%, master's 33%, baccalaureate 4%, professional 9%. 61% hold terminal degrees.

Enrollment: Total enrollment 1,1,348. Undergraduate full-time 585 men / 719 women, part-time 18m / 26w.

Characteristics of Student Body: *Ethnic/racial makeup:* number of Black non-Hispanic: 9; American Indian or Alaska Native: 10; Asian or Pacific Islander: 7; Hispanic: 14; White non-Hispanic: 1,268; unknown: 9. *Age distribution:* number under 18: 5; 18–19: 385, 20–21: 54; 22–24: 36; 25–29: 41; 30–34: 11; 35–39: 8; 40–49: 6; 50–64: 1.

International Students: 31 nonresident aliens enrolled fall 2004. 5 students from Europe, 4 Asia, 8 Central and South America, 3 Africa. No programs available to aid students whose native language is not English. No financial aid specifically designated for international students.

Student Life: On-campus residence halls house 67% of student body. Residence halls for men constitute 46% of such space, for women 54%. *Intercollegiate athletics:* men only: baseball, basketball; women only: basketball, volleyball. *Special regulations:* Cars permitted on campus in nine designated areas. Curfews from 1am to 6am. Quiet hours from 9pm to 9am. *Special services:* Learning Resources Center, medical services; bus service to town. *Student publications, radio: Gordian Knot,* an annual literary magazine; *Outlook,* a weekly newspaper; *Phoenix,* a yearbook. Radio station KCOZ broadcasts 140 hours per week. *Surrounding community:* Taney County population 25,500. Kansas City-St. Louis, 200 miles from campus, is nearest metropolitan area. Served by airport on campus.

Publications: Sources of information about College of the Ozarks include *Ozark Visitor,* a magazine published 4 times per year.

Library Collections: 157,364 volumes including bound books, serial backfiles, electronic documents, and government documents not in separate collections. Online catalog. Current serial subscriptions: 444 paper. 5,370 recordings; 5,063 compact discs; 75 CD-ROMs. 15 computer work stations. Students have access to the Internet at no charge. Total budget for books, periodicals, audiovisual materials, microforms 2004–05: $168,000.

Most import special collection: Ozarkiana Collection (materials relating to the Missouri and Arkansas Ozarks); Taney County Newspapers (1860-current).

Buildings and Grounds: Campus area 930 acres. *New buildings:* Gittinger Music Building completed 2003; Campus Ministries Building (remodel/renovation) 2004.

Chief Executive Officer: Dr. Jerry C. Davis, President.

Address admission inquiries to Marci Linson, Director of Admissions.

Columbia College

1001 Rogers Street
Columbia, Missouri 65216
Tel: (573) 875-8700   **E-mail:** admissions@email.ccis.edu
Fax: (573) 875-7506   **Internet:** www.ccis.edu

Institution Description: Columbia College is a private, independent, nonprofit college affiliated with the Christian Church (Disciples of Christ). *Enrollment:* 1,088. *Degrees awarded:* Associate, baccalaureate, master's.

Member of the consortium Mid-Missouri Associated Colleges and Universities.

Accreditation: *Regional:* NCA.

History: Established and chartered as Christian Female College, a 4-year institution, and offered first instruction at postsecondary level 1851; awarded first degree (baccalaureate) 1855; reorganized as junior college 1913; changed name to Christian College 1929; adopted present name and admitted men 1969;

reorganized as 4-year college 1973. *See* Allean Lemmon Hale, *Petticoat Pioneer* (Saint Paul, MN.: North Central Publishing Co., c. 1968).

Institutional Structure: *Governing board:* Board of Trustees. Representation: 36 trustees, including 2 full-time instructional faculty members, all voting. *Composition of institution:* Administrative council 6 men / 2 women; at dean's level and above, 20% are women. Academic affairs headed by vice-president for academic affairs and dean of faculties. Finances directed by chief executive officer. Full-time instructional faculty 55. Academic governance body, the faculty, meets an average of 9 times per year.

Calendar: Semesters. Academic year late Aug. to July. Freshmen admitted Aug., Jan., June. Degrees conferred May, Dec. Formal commencement Dec., May. Summer session of 1 term from June to July.

Characteristics of Freshmen: 60% of applicants admitted. 22% of applicants admitted and enrolled.

5% (9 students) submitted SAT scores; 86% (157 students) submitted ACT scores. *25th percentile*: SAT Verbal 510, SAT Math 440; ACT Composite 19, ACT English 18, ACT Math 17. *75th percentile*: SAT Verbal 580, SAT Math 580; ACT Composite 25, ACT English 26, ACT Math 24.

44% of entering freshmen expected to graduate within 5 years. 67% of freshmen from Missouri. Freshmen from 11 states and 4 foreign countries.

Admission: Rolling admissions plan. For fall acceptance, apply as early as junior year of secondary school, but not later than Aug. of year of enrollment. Apply during second half of junior year for early decision, need not limit application to Columbia. Early acceptance available. *Requirements:* Either graduation from accredited secondary school with 15 academic units, including 3–4 in English, 2 history or social science, 1 mathematics, 1 science, and 8 electives; minimum 2.0 GPA; rank in top 50% of high school class; ACT or SAT in 50th percentile; or GED. *For transfer students:* 96 hours maximum transfer credit; correspondence/extension students 60 hours.

College credit for postsecondary-level work completed in secondary school and for extrainstitutional learning on basis of ACE *2006 Guide to the Evaluation of Educational Experiences in the Armed Services* and portfolio assessment. Tutoring available. Developmental courses offered during regular academic year.

Degree Requirements: *For all associate degrees:* 60 credit hours; 1 term in residence. *For all baccalaureate degrees:* 120 credit hours; 2 terms in residence; distribution requirements. *For all degrees:* 2.0 GPA; 2 terms English composition.

Fulfillment of some degree requirements and exemption from some beginning courses possible by passing departmental examinations, PEP, College Board CLEP or AP. *Grading system:* A–F; pass-fail; withdraw (carries time limit).

Distinctive Educational Programs: Internships. Evening classes. Online program. Facilities and programs for independent research, including honors programs and individual studies majors. Cross-registration through consortium. Associate and baccalaureate degree programs at 30 off-campus sites in 11 states and Cuba; master's programs available at 3 locations. Study abroad at University of Bradford (England) and Kanagawa University (Japan).

ROTC: Army, Navy, and Air Force in cooperation with University of Missouri-Columbia.

Degrees Conferred: 83 *associate;* 229 *baccalaureate:* biological/life sciences 8; business/marketing 87; computer and information sciences 4; education 28; English 9; interdisciplinary studies 14; liberal arts/general studies 20; natural resources/environmental science 1; philosophy/religion/theology 1; protective services/public administration 24; psychology 14; social sciences and history 8l visual and performing arts 11.

Fees and Other Expenses: *Full-time tuition per academic year 2004–05:* $11,588 undergraduate; $235 per credit hour for graduate courses. *Room and board per academic year:* $4,810.

Financial Aid: Aid from institutionally generated funds is provided on the basis of academic merit, financial need, athletic ability, other criteria.

Financial aid to full-time, first-time undergraduate students: need-based scholarships/grants totaling $1,301,037, self-help $1,624,829; non-need-based scholarships/grants totaling $3,287,075, self-help $1,793,586, parent loans $970,875, athletic awards $742,667. *Graduate aid:* 108 students received $1,076,215 in federal and state-funded loans (ranging from $1,800 to $18,500); 28 other fellowships and grants totaling $43,024.

Departments and Teaching Staff: *Professors* 9, *associate professors* 11, *assistant professors* 27, *instructors* 9, *part-time faculty* 38.

Total instructional faculty: 94 (full-time 56, part-time 38; women 45, men 49; members of minority groups 4). Total faculty with doctorate, first-professional, or other terminal degree: 50. Student-to-faculty ratio: 12:1. Degrees held by full-time faculty: doctorate 75%, master's 25%. 89% hold terminal degrees. *Faculty development:* 2 faculty members awarded sabbaticals 2004–05.

Enrollment: Total enrollment 1,088. Undergraduate full-time 283 men / 459 women, part-time 93m / 128w; graduate full-time 51m / 97w, part-time 1m / 6w. *Transfer students:* in-state 77.

Characteristics of Student Body: *Ethnic/racial makeup:* number of Black non-Hispanic: 49; American Indian or Alaska Native: 4; Asian or Pacific Islander: 16; Hispanic: 17; White non-Hispanic: 758; unknown: 55. *Age distribution:* number under 18: 9; 18–19: 273; 20–21: 266; 22–24: 189; 25–29: 100; 30–34: 50; 35–39: 25; 40–49: 30; 50–64: 7; 65 and over: 4.

International Students: 56 nonresident aliens enrolled fall 2004. 6 students from Europe, 25 Asia, 6 Central and South America, 5 Africa, 3 Canada, 1 Australia, 2 other. Programs available to aid students whose native language is not English: social, cultural; English as a Second Language Program. Financial aid specifically designated for international students: variable number of scholarships awarded to qualifying students.

Student Life: On-campus residence halls house 40% of student body. Dormitories for men only constitute 30% of such space, for women only 70%. *Intercollegiate athletics:* men only: basketball, soccer; women only: softball, volleyball. *Special regulations:* Cars permitted without restrictions. *Special services:* Academic Enrichment Center, math and writing centers, tutoring services, counseling services, health services. *Student publications: Columbian,* a student newspaper; literary magazine; alumni magazine. *Surrounding community:* Columbia population 95,000. St. Louis and Kansas City, each 125 miles from campus. Columbia served by mass transit bus system; airport 15 miles from campus.

Library Collections: 62,348 volumes. Online catalog. Current serial subscriptions: paper 10,706; microform 2,860; via electronic access 7,642. 1,128 recordings; 384 compact discs; 176 CD-ROMs. 16 computer work stations. Students have access to online information retrieval services and the Internet. total 2004–05 budget for books and materials: $103,870.

Most important special holdings include 19,000 volumes in the Library of American Civilization; Jane Froman Archive (documents, recordings, photographs, and other artifacts).

Buildings and Grounds: Campus area 21 acres. *New buildings:* Atkins-Holman Student Commons completed 2003.

Chief Executive Officer: Dr. Gerald Brouder, President.

Address admission inquiries to Regina Morin, Director of Admissions.

Conception Seminary College

317174 State Highway V V
Conception, Missouri 64433-0502

Tel: (660) 944-2218   **E-mail:** admissions@conceptionabbey.edu
Fax: (660) 944-2829   **Internet:** www.conceptionabbey.edu

Institution Description: Conception Seminary College (Immaculate Conception Seminary until 1972), a private college owned and conducted by the Benedictine monks of Conception Abbey, Roman Catholic Church, trains men for the priesthood. Sisters from area convents are also admitted. *Enrollment:* 102. *Degrees awarded:* Baccalaureate.

Accreditation: *Regional:* NCA.

History: Established as New Engelberg College 1873; chartered 1882; offered first instruction at postsecondary level 1886; changed name to Conception College 1891; awarded first degree (baccalaureate) 1899; changed name to Conception Seminary 1942, Immaculate Conception Seminary 1958; adopted present name 1972. *See* Edward E. Malone, O.S.B., *Conception* (Omaha: Interstate Printing Co., 1971) for further information.

Institutional Structure: *Governing board:* The Council of Conception Abbey, Inc. Representation: 6 councillors, abbot. 1 ex officio. 6 voting. *Composition of institution:* Administrators 8 men. Academic affairs headed by dean of studies. Management/business/finances directed by business manager. Full-time instructional faculty 11. Academic governance body, the faculty, meets an average of 9 times per year.

Calendar: Semesters. Academic year late Aug. to mid-May. Freshmen admitted Aug., Jan. Degrees conferred May, Dec. Formal commencement May. No summer session.

Characteristics of Freshmen: 11 applicants. 100% of applicants admitted. 100% of admitted students enrolled full-time.

61% (11 students) submitted ACT scores. *25th percentile*: ACT Composite 20, ACT English 16, ACT Math 19. *75th percentile*: ACT Composite 24, ACT English 25, ACT Math 25.

64% of entering freshmen expected to graduate within 5 years. 64% of freshmen from Missouri. Freshmen from 5 states.

Admission: Rolling admissions plan. For fall acceptance, apply no later than July 31. *Requirements:* Either graduation from accredited secondary school with 16 college preparatory units or GED. Recommendation from secondary school official, pastor's appraisal, certificates of baptism and confirmation. Minimum 2.0 GPA. *Entrance tests:* ACT composite. For foreign students TOEFL. *For* *transfer students:* 2.0 minimum GPA; maximum transfer credit limited only by residence requirement.

College credit and advanced placement for postsecondary-level work completed in secondary school and for extrainstitutional learning on basis of ACE *2006 Guide to the Evaluation of Educational Experiences in the Armed Services* and faculty assessment. Tutoring available. Developmental courses offered during regular academic year.

Degree Requirements: 126 credit hours; 2.0 GPA; last 2 terms in residence; chapel attendance 3 times daily; 4-year physical activity program; comprehensives in individual fields of study.

Fulfillment of some degree requirements and exemption from some beginning courses possible by passing College Board CLEP, AP (score of 3). *Grading system:* A–F; pass-fail; withdraw (deadline after which pass-fail is appended to withdraw).

Distinctive Educational Programs: Directed independent study. Study by individual arrangement. Cross-registration with Northwest Missouri State University.

Degrees Conferred: 16 *baccalaureate:* liberal arts/general studies 11, religion/philosophy 5.

Fees and Other Expenses: *Full-time tuition per academic year 2004–05:* $11,432. *Room and board per academic year:* $6,794. *Books and supplies:* $550.

Financial Aid: Aid from institutionally generated funds is provided on the basis of academic merit, financial need, other considerations. Institution has a Program Participation Agreement with the U.S. Department of Education for eligible students to receive Pell Grants and, depending upon the agreement, other federal aid.

Departments and Teaching Staff: Art *professors* 1, *part-time teachers* 0; English 1, 0; language 2, 1; health/physical education 1, 0; history 2, 0; humanities 2, 0; mathematics 2, 0; natural science 2, 0; music 3, 0; philosophy 3, 0; psychology 2, 2; religion 3, 3; sociology 1, 0.

Total instructional faculty: 22. Student-to-faculty ratio: 3:1. Degrees held by full-time faculty: doctorate 55%, master's 18%. 70% hold terminal degrees.

Enrollment: Total enrollment 102. Undergraduate 93 (97.8% men, 2.25 women).

Characteristics of Student Body: *Ethnic/racial makeup:* number of Asian or Pacific Islander: 5.4%; Hispanic: 6.5%; White non-Hispanic: 73.1%. *Age distribution:* 17–21: 37%; 22–24: 34%; 25–29: 17%; 30–34: 8%; 35–39: 3%; 40–49: .1%.

International Students: No programs available to aid students whose native language is not English. No financial aid specifically designated for international students.

Student Life: On-campus residence halls house 94% of student body. Residence halls for men only constitute 100% of such space. *Special regulations:* Cars permitted for $5. *Special services:* Medical services. *Student publications: The Spirit,* a monthly newspaper. *Surrounding community:* Conception population 250. Kansas City, 100 miles from campus, is nearest metropolitan area. Served by airport 80 miles from campus.

Library Collections: 132,000 volumes. 1,290 microforms; 18,393 audiovisual materials; 342 current periodical subscriptions.

Most important special holdings include collections on Monastic history and theology, primary sources in history of philosophy, art history in slides.

Buildings and Grounds: Campus area 30 acres.

Chief Executive Officer: Rev. Benedict T. Neenan, Rector-President.

Address admission inquiries to Vince Casper, Director of Admissions.

Concordia Seminary

801 Seminary Place
St. Louis, Missouri 63105-3199
Tel: (314) 505-7000   **E-mail:** admissions@csl.edu
Fax: (314) 505-7001   **Internet:** www.csl.edu

Institution Description: Concordia Seminary is a private institution affiliated with the Lutheran Church-Missouri Synod. *Enrollment:* 828. *Degrees awarded:* First-professional (master of divinity), master's, doctorate.

Accreditation: *Regional:* NCA. *National:* ATS. *Professional:* theology

History: Established and offered first instruction at postsecondary level 1839; awarded first degree (baccalaureate) 1923. See Carl S. Meyer, *Log Cabin to Luther Tower* (St. Louis: Concordia Publishing House, 1965) for further information.

Institutional Structure: *Governing board:* Board of Regents. Representation: 9 regents. 2 ex officio. All voting. *Composition of institution:* 6 general and division administrators. Management/business/finances directed by business

manager. Full-time instructional faculty 35. Academic governance body, the faculty, meets an average of 9 times per year.

Calendar: Quarters. Academic year Sept. to May. Degrees conferred and formal commencement May. Summer session of 6 terms from June to July.

Admission: Rolling admissions plan. Early acceptance available. *Requirements:* Baccalaureate from accredited college or university. For first-professional degree, liberal arts background which must include courses in Greek or Hebrew; 2.0 GPA. For master's degrees, 30 hours religion; 3.0 GPA. *Entrance tests:* GRE. For foreign students TOEFL. Developmental/remedial courses offered in summer session and regular academic year; nondegree credit given.

Degree Requirements: *For first-professional degrees:* 137 quarter hours; 2.0 GPA; 119 hours in residence; field education; internship. *For all master's degrees:* 36–48 hours; 3.0 GPA; 30–42 hours in residence; exit competency examinations-comprehensives in individual fields of study. *Grading system:* A–F; withdraw (carries time limit).

Distinctive Educational Programs: Special facilities for using telecommunications in the classroom. Tutorials. Exchange programs in Brazil, England, Germany, Korea.

Degrees Conferred: 103 *first-professional:* master of divinity; 19 *master's:* theology/ministerial studies; 3 *doctorate:* theology.

Fees and Other Expenses: *Full-time tuition per academic year 2004–05:* $17,400.

Financial Aid: Aid from institutionally generated funds is provided on the basis of financial need, other considerations. Institution has a Program Participation Agreement with the U.S. Department of Education for eligible students to receive Grants and, depending upon the agreement, other federal aid.

Departments and Teaching Staff: *Professors* 12, *associate professors* 12, *assistant professors* 10, *instructors* 1.

Total instructional faculty: 35. Degrees held by full-time faculty: doctorate 69%, master's 31%, baccalaureate 100%, professional 97%. 69% hold terminal degrees.

Enrollment: Total enrollment 828 (men 94.8%; women 5.2%).

Characteristics of Student Body: *Ethnic/racial makeup:* number of Black non-Hispanic: 6.3%; American Indian or Alaska Native: .4%; Asian or Pacific Islander: 2.9%; Hispanic: 3.5%; White non-Hispanic: 83.9%.

International Students: 16 nonresident aliens enrolled fall 2004. Students from Europe, Asia, Latin America, Africa. No programs available to aid students whose native language is not English. No financial aid specifically designated for international students.

Student Life: On-campus residence halls for men only house 31% of student body. 23% of student body live in institutionally controlled married student housing. *Intercollegiate athletics:* men only: basketball, tennis. *Special regulations:* Registered cars permitted with no restrictions. *Special services:* Medical services. *Student publications: Spectrum,* a weekly newspaper; *Concordia Student Journal,* a quarterly theological journal. *Surrounding community:* St. Louis metropolitan population 2.5 million. Served by mass transit bus system; airport 15 miles from campus; passenger rail service 6 miles from campus.

Library Collections: 225,000 volumes including bound books, serial backfiles, electronic documents, and government documents not in separate collections. Online catalog. Current serial subscriptions: 1,028 paper; 47,890 microforms; 16 electronic journals. 65 recordings. 27 computer work stations. Students have access to the Internet at no charge.

Most important special holdings include Maier Collection of Medieval and Reformation publications; Haffenreffer Collection of works by or about Johannes Brenz; incunabula; Luther and the Lutheran Reformation Collection.

Buildings and Grounds: Campus area 72 acres.

Chief Executive Officer: John F. Johnson, President.

Address first-professional admission inquiries to Rev. Jeff Moore, Director of Ministerial Recruitment; graduate inquiries to Dr. James W. Voelz, Director of Graduate Studies.

Covenant Theological Seminary

12330 Conway Road
St. Louis, Missouri 63141-8697
Tel: (314) 434-4044   **E-mail:** admissions@covenant.edu
Fax: (314) 434-4819   **Internet:** www.covenant.edu

Institution Description: Covenant Theological Seminary is a private institution affiliated with the Presbyterian Church in America. *Enrollment:* 879. *Degrees awarded:* First-professional (master of divinity), master's, doctorate.

Accreditation: *Regional:* NCA. *National:* ATS. *Professional:* theology

History: Established, incorporated, and offered first instruction at postsecondary level 1956; awarded first degree (first-professional) 1957.

Institutional Structure: *Governing board:* 24 voting trustees elected by the PCA General Assembly. *Composition of institution:* Administrators 7 men. Academic affairs headed by vice president for academic affairs and dean of faculty. Management/business/finances directed by vice president for business and finance. Full-time instructional faculty 16 men. Academic governance body, the Faculty, meet an average of 24 times per year.

Calendar: Semesters (4-1-4 plan). Academic year Sept. to May. Entering students admitted July, Sept., Jan. Degrees conferred and formal commencement May. Summer session of 3 terms from late May to late Aug.

Admission: Rolling admissions plan. *Requirements:* Baccalaureate degree from accredited institution, or equivalent. Master of Divinity and Master of Arts require baccalaureate degree from accredited institution or equivalent; Master of Theology and Doctor of Ministry require Master of Divinity from accredited institution. *Entrance tests:* TOEFL for students whose first language is not English.

Degree Requirements: *For first-professional degree:* 103 credit hours; 24 hours in residence. *For master of arts degree:* 60 credit hours; thesis (exegetical theology), practicum (counseling), optional ministry project (general theological Studies). *For both degrees:* 1.25 GPA on 3.0 scale; completion of prescribed curriculum. *Grading system:* A–F.

Distinctive Educational Programs: Master of Divinity majors in church planting; theology; Biblical studies; counseling, Christianity and contemporary culture. Master of Arts programs days and evenings. Extension classes offered. Study abroad in Israel, Jordan.

Degrees Conferred: 76 *master's:* Bible/biblical studies; 8 *doctorate:* theology. 58 *first-professional:* master of divinity.

Fees and Other Expenses: *Full-time tuition per academic year 2004–05:* Contact the seminary for current information regarding tuition, fees, and housing costs.

Financial Aid: Aid from institutionally generated funds is provided on the basis of academic merit, financial need, other criteria. Institution has a Program Participation Agreement with the U.S. Department of Education for eligible students to receive Pell Grants and, depending upon the agreement, other federal aid.

Departments and Teaching Staff: *Total instructional faculty:* 22 FTE. Degrees held by full-time faculty: doctorate 81%, professional 100%. 81% hold terminal degrees.

Enrollment: Total enrollment 879 (men 72.4%; women 27.6%).

Characteristics of Student Body: *Ethnic/racial makeup:* number of Black non-Hispanic: 4.7%; American Indian or Alaska Native: .1%; Asian or Pacific Islander: 4.2%; Hispanic: .9%; White non-Hispanic: 87.4%; unknown: .6%.

International Students: 19 nonresident aliens enrolled fall 2004. Students from Europe, Asia, Latin America, Africa, Canada. Programs available to aid students whose native language is not English: social, cultural. Financial aid specifically designated for international students: scholarships available annually to qualifying international students.

Student Life: On-campus residence halls house 20% of student body. Residence halls and apartments house single students and married students with families. Assistance is provided in locating housing. *Special regulations:* Cars permitted; fee charged. Quiet hours. *Special services:* medical services. *Surrounding community:* St. Louis metropolitan area population 2.5 million. Served by mass transit bus system; airport 12 miles from campus; passenger train service 15 miles from campus.

Publications: *Presbyterion: The Covenant Seminary Review* (biannually) first published 1975.

Library Collections: 72,000 volumes. 2,300 microforms; 1,620 audiovisual materials; 320 current periodical subscriptions.

Most important holdings include Puritan and rare book collection.

Buildings and Grounds: Campus area 22 acres.

Chief Executive Officer: Dr. Bryan Chapell, President.

Address admission inquiries to Eric Richards, Director of Admissions.

Culver-Stockton College

One College Hill
Canton, Missouri 63435
Tel: (573) 288-6000   **E-mail:** enrollment@culver.edu
Fax: (573) 288-6611   **Internet:** www.culver.edu

Institution Description: Culver-Stockton College is a private college affiliated with the Christian Church (Disciples of Christ). *Enrollment:* 855. *Degrees awarded:* Baccalaureate.

Member of Quincy Area Education Consortium.

Accreditation: *Regional:* NCA.

History: Established, chartered, and incorporated as Christian University and offered first instruction at postsecondary level 1853; awarded first degree (baccalaureate) 1860; adopted present name 1918. *See* George L. Peters, *Dreams Come True* (St. Louis: Bethany Press, 1941) for further information.

Institutional Structure: *Governing board:* Board of Trustees of Culver-Stockton College. Extrainstitutional representation: 36 trustees, 3 representatives of the Christian Church (Disciples of Christ); institutional representation: president of the college; 1 student; 1 alumnus, 1 faculty, 2 ex officio. 37 voting. *Composition of institution:* Administrators 8 men / 2 women. Academic affairs headed by vice president for academic affairs. Business/finance headed by chief financial officer and treasurer. Full-time instructional faculty 54. Academic governance body, Faculty Assembly, meets an average of 8 times per year.

Calendar: Semesters. Academic year Aug. to May. Freshmen admitted Aug., Jan., June, July. Degrees conferred May, Aug., Dec. Formal commencement May. Summer session of 2 terms from mid-May through mid-July.

Characteristics of Freshmen: 92% of applicants accepted. 44% of accepted applicants enrolled.

97% (177 students) submitted ACT scores. *25th percentile*: ACT Composite 23, ACT English 23, ACT Math 23. *75th percentile*: ACT Composite 26, ACT English 27, ACT Math 26.

48% of entering freshmen expected to graduate within 5 years. 71% of freshmen from Missouri. Freshmen from 10 states and 6 foreign countries.

Admission: Rolling admissions plan. For fall acceptance, apply as early as junior year of secondary school, but not later than Apr. of year of enrollment. Apply by Dec. of junior year of secondary school for early decision; must limit application to Culver-Stockton. Early acceptance available. *Requirements:* Either graduation from accredited secondary school or GED. Recommend 4 units English, 3 social studies, 2 mathematics, 2–4 sciences, additional units. Minimum 2.0 GPA. *Entrance tests:* College Board SAT or ACT composite. *For transfer students:* 2.0 minimum GPA; from 4-year accredited institution 94 hours maximum transfer credit; from 2-year accredited institution 64 hours; correspondence/extension students 30 hours.

College credit for extrainstitutional learning on basis of ACE *2006 Guide to the Evaluation of Educational Experiences in the Armed Services*; advanced placement on basis of faculty assessment, portfolio assessment, personal interview. Tutoring available. Remedial courses offered during regular academic year; credit given.

Degree Requirements: *For all baccalaureate degrees:* 124 credit hours; distribution requirements. *For all degrees:* 2.0 minimum GPA; 45 of the last 60 hours in residence; general education requirements.

Fulfillment of some degree requirements and exemption from some beginning courses possible by passing College Board CLEP or AP exam. *Grading system:* A–F; pass-fail; withdraw (carries time limit after which F is assigned); incomplete (carries time limit).

Distinctive Educational Programs: Evening classes. Dual-degree program in engineering with Washington University and University of Missouri. Cooperative baccalaureate in medical technology with approved schools or hospitals. Facilities and programs for independent research, including honors programs, individual majors, tutorials. Joint Program (B.S.N.) with Blessing-Rieman College of Nursing.

Degrees Conferred: 150 *baccalaureate.* Bachelor's degrees awarded in top five disciplines: business, management, marketing, and related support services 34; health professions and related clinical sciences 21; education 21; psychology 19; communication, journalism, and related programs 15.

Fees and Other Expenses: *Full-time tuition per academic year 2004–05:* $13,200. *Books and supplies:* $700. Contact the college for current housing costs.

Financial Aid: Culver-Stockton College offers a direct lending program. Aid from institutionally generated funds is provided on the basis of academic merit, financial need, athletic ability, other criteria.

Financial aid to full-time, first-time undergraduate students: need-based scholarships/grants totaling $4,801,254, self-help $3,184,453; non-need-based scholarships/grants totaling $738,321, self-help $1,244,584, parent loans $838,444, tuition waivers $78,704, athletic awards $203,106.

Departments and Teaching Staff: *Total instructional faculty:* 79 (full-time 50, part-time 29; women 30, men 49; member of minority group 1). Total faculty with doctorate, first-professional, or other terminal degree: 41. Student-to-faculty ratio: 13:1. Degrees held by full-time faculty: master's 43%, doctorate 57%. 70% hold terminal degrees.

Enrollment: Total enrollment 855. Full-time 340 men / 445 women, part-time 23m / 47.

Characteristics of Student Body: *Ethnic/racial makeup:* number of Black non-Hispanic: 58; American Indian or Alaska Native: 2; Asian or Pacific Islander: 4; Hispanic: 23; White non-Hispanic: 760,

International Students: 8 nonresident aliens enrolled fall 2004. Students from Europe, Asia, Africa, Canada. Programs available to aid students whose native language is not English: social, financial.

Student Life: 74% of student body live in on-campus. *Intercollegiate athletics:* men only: football, basketball, baseball, soccer, golf; women only: basketball, golf, soccer, softball, volleyball. *Student publications: Harmony,* a literary magazine; *The Megaphone,* a biweekly student newspaper. *Surrounding community:* Canton population 2,500. St. Louis, 150 miles from campus, is nearest metropolitan area. Served by airport 35 miles from campus; passenger rail service 20 miles from campus.

Library Collections: 151,000 volumes. 5,500 microforms; 1,530 audiovisual materials; 920 current periodical subscriptions. Online catalog. Students have access to online information retrieval services and the Internet.

Most important special holdings include Johann Midwest Americana Collection; Sverdrup Performing Arts Collection; Disciples of Christ Historical Collection.

Buildings and Grounds: Campus area 140 acres. *New buildings:* Science Center completed 2002.

Chief Executive Officer: Dr. William L. Fox, President.

Address admission inquiries to Jim Jennette, Assistant Director of Admissions.

Eden Theological Seminary

475 East Lockwood Avenue
St. Louis, Missouri 63119
Tel: (314) 961-3627   **E-mail:** dwindler@eden.edu
Fax: (314) 918-2640   **Internet:** www.eden.edu

Institution Description: Eden Theological Seminary is a private institution affiliated with the United Church of Christ. *Enrollment:* 222. *Degrees awarded:* First-professional (master of divinity), master's, doctorate.

Accreditation: *Regional:* NCA. *National:* ATS. *Professional:* theology

History: Established as German Evangelical Missouri College and offered first instruction at postsecondary level 1850; chartered 1855; awarded first degree (first-professional) 1928; adopted present name 1962.

Institutional Structure: *Governing board:* Board of Directors of Eden Theological Seminary. Extrainstitutional representation: 30 directors; institutional representation: president of the seminary. 1 ex officio. 30 voting. *Composition of institution:* Administrators 5. Academic affairs headed by dean of academic affairs. Management/business/finances directed by business manager. Full-time instructional faculty 10. Academic governance body, the faculty, meets an average of 9 times per year.

Calendar: Semesters (4-1-4 plan). Academic year early Sept. to May. Entering students admitted Sept., Feb. Degrees conferred and formal commencement May.

Admission: Rolling admissions plan. *Requirements:* Baccalaureate degree from accredited college or university; autobiographical essay; 4 letters of reference. *For transfer students:* maximum transfer credit limited by residence requirement of one year.

Degree Requirements: *For first-professional degree:* 81 semester hours and 7 field education units; B average; 3 years in residence; core requirements; oral evaluations. *For master's degree:* 54 hours; 3.0 GPA; 2 years in residence; 24 hours in area of concentration; thesis examination. *Grading system:* A–F or pass-fail (student option).

Distinctive Educational Programs: Internships. Directed study programs. Cross-registration with 3 local seminaries. Off-campus center for students in doctoral program in Avon Park, Florida. *Other distinctive programs:* Education for Black Urban Ministries program. Continuing education for ministers and directors of Christian education. Credit-noncredit courses available to local students. Master of Arts in Pastoral Studies degree program.

Degrees Conferred: 27 *first-professional:* master of divinity; 32 *master's:* theology; 1 *doctorate:* theology. *Honorary degrees awarded 2003–04:* Doctor of Divinity 1; Doctor of Human Letters 1.

Fees and Other Expenses: *Tuition for academic year 2004–05:* $8,500. *Required fees:* $165. Contact the seminary for housing arrangements.

Financial Aid: Aid from institutionally generated funds is provided on the basis of academic merit, financial need, other considerations. *Graduate aid:* 83 students received $997,151 in federal and state-funded loans.

Departments and Teaching Staff: Scripture Studies *professors* 3, *associate professors* 1, *part-time faculty* 0; theological studies 1, 0, 3; historical studies 0, 1, 1; studies in ministry 4, 0, 0.

Total instructional faculty: 13 (full-time 12, part-time 1; women 5, men 8; members of minority groups 3). Student-to-faculty ratio: 17:1. Degrees held by full-time faculty: baccalaureate 100%, master's 100%, doctorate 80%. 80% hold terminal degrees.

Enrollment: Total enrollment 222. First-professional full-time 67 men / 75 women; graduate full-time 27m / 20w, part-time 12m / 21w.

Characteristics of Student Body: *Ethnic/racial makeup:* number of Black non-Hispanic: 32; Hispanic: 10; White non-Hispanic: 181. *Age distribution:* number 22–24: 16; 25–29: 23; 30–34: 20; 35–39: 33; 40–49: 74; 50–64: 55.

International Students: 6 nonresident aliens enrolled fall 2004. 2 students from Asia, 4 Africa. Programs available to aid students whose native language is not English: social, cultural, financial.

Student Life: On-campus residence halls house 50% of student body. *Special regulations:* Cars must have parking permits. *Special services:* medical services. *Surrounding community:* St. Louis metropolitan area population 2.5 million. Served by mass transit bus system; airport 13 miles from campus.

Publications: *Eden Events* published twice a year.

Library Collections: 299,339 volumes. Current serial subscriptions: 1,644 paper; 137,062 microforms. 17,355 recordings. 5 computer work stations. Online catalog. Students have access to the Internet and online information retrieval services.

Most important holdings include the James I. Good Collection (5,000 items, including catechisms, liturgies, other materials, some rare, of the Reformed Church of the U.S.); the Evangelical Synod Archives (records, correspondence, and files from the Evangelical Synod of North America, a denomination which existed from 1850 until it merged with the Reformed Church in 1934).

Buildings and Grounds: Campus area 20 acres.

Chief Executive Officer: Dr. David M. Greenhaw, President. Address admission inquiries to Rev. Diane Windler, Director of Admissions.

Evangel University

1111 North Glenstone Avenue
Springfield, Missouri 65802
Tel: (417) 865-2515   **E-mail:** admissions@evangel.edu
Fax: (417) 865-9599   **Internet:** evangel.edu

Institution Description: Evangel University is a private school of arts and sciences affiliated with the Assemblies of God. *Enrollment:* 1,987. *Degrees awarded:* Associate, baccalaureate, master's

Accreditation: *Regional:* NCA. *Professional:* music, social work, teacher education

History: Established, chartered, and offered first instruction at postsecondary level 1955; awarded first degree (baccalaureate) 1959.

Institutional Structure: *Governing board:* Board of Directors of Evangel University. Extrainstitutional representation: 14 directors, including 2 church representatives, 3 alumni; institutional representation: president of the college. 3 ex officio. All voting. *Composition of institution:* Administrators 5 men. Academic affairs headed by academic dean. Management/business/finances directed by business manager. Full-time instructional faculty 84. Academic governance body, Academic Council, meets an average of 10 times per year.

Calendar: Semesters. Academic year from early September to early May. Freshmen admitted Sept., Jan., May, June. Degrees conferred May, July, Dec. Formal commencement May. Summer session from mid-May to mid-July.

Characteristics of Freshmen: 98% of applicants admitted. 50% of applicants admitted and enrolled.

15% (63 students) submitted SAT scores; 80% (339 students) submitted ACT scores. *25th percentile:* ACT Composite 19, ACT English 19, ACT Math 17. *75th percentile:* ACT Composite 24, ACT English 25, ACT Math 24.

53% of entering freshmen expected to graduate within 5 years. 47% of freshmen from Missouri. Freshmen from 47 states and 4 foreign countries.

Admission: Rolling admissions plan. For fall acceptance, apply as early as Sept. of previous year, but not later than Aug. 15 of year of enrollment. Early acceptance available. *Requirements:* Either graduation from accredited secondary school with 3 units English, 2 mathematics, 2 social studies, 1 laboratory science, or GED. Minimum GPA 2.0. Lowest acceptable secondary school class standing 40th percentile. *Entrance tests:* ACT composite. For foreign students TOEFL. *For transfer students:* 2.0 minimum GPA; from 4-year accredited institution 90 hours maximum transfer credit; from 2-year accredited institution 30 hours.

College credit and advanced placement for postsecondary-level work completed in secondary school. College credit for extrainstitutional learning on basis of ACE *2006 Guide to the Evaluation of Educational Experiences in the Armed Services.* Developmental/remedial courses offered during regular academic year; credit given.

Degree Requirements: *For all associate degrees:* 60 credit hours; 1 physical education course. *For all baccalaureate degrees:* 124 hours; 2 physical education courses. *For all degrees:* 2.0 GPA; 2 terms in residence; daily chapel attendance; general education courses; exit competency examinations in writing and mathematics.

Fulfillment of some degree requirements and exemption from some beginning courses possible by passing departmental examinations, College Board CLEP, AP. *Grading system:* A–F; withdraw (deadline after which pass-fail is appended to withdraw).

Distinctive Educational Programs: Evening classes. Interdisciplinary programs in humanities, mental health, public administration. Preprofessional program in engineering. Directed study and independent research for seniors only.

ROTC: Army.

Degrees Conferred: 2 *associate;* 314 *baccalaureate:* biological/life sciences 14; business/marketing 36; communications/communication technologies 91 computer and information sciences 3; education 46; English 11; foreign languages and literature 7; mathematics 3; philosophy/religion/theology 28; protective services/public administration 2; psychology 24; social sciences and history 17; visual and performing arts 4; other 10. 16 *master's:* education 9; psychology 7.

Fees and Other Expenses: *Full-time tuition per academic year 2004–05:* $4,200 undergraduate; $250 per credit hour for graduate courses. *Required fees:* $710. *Room and board per academic year:* $2,260.

Financial Aid: Aid from institutionally generated funds is provided on the basis of academic merit, financial need, athletic ability, other criteria.

Financial aid to full-time, first-time undergraduate students: need-based scholarships/grants totaling $13,316,664; self-help $298,320, parent loans $142,784, athletic awards $1,260,938. *Graduate aid:* 58 students received federal and state-funded loans totaling $311,247.

Departments and Teaching Staff: Behavioral sciences *professors:* 4, *associate professors* 2, *assistant professors* 5, *instructors* 1, *part-time faculty* 2; Biblical studies 0, 0, 8, 0, 6; business and economics 0, 0, 5, 0, 4; communications 0, 1, 2, 2, 2; education 0, 2, 4, 0, 1; health, physical education, and recreation 1, 1, 9, 1, 2; humanities 2, 2, 6, 4, 8; music 3, 4, 3, 4, 14; science and technology 6, 1, 4, 0, 1; social sciences 2, 0, 2, 0, 2.

Total instructional faculty: 128 (full-time 96, part-time 32; women 52, men 76; members of minority groups 3). Total faculty with doctorate, first-professional, or other terminal degree: 48. Student-to-faculty ratio: 18:1. Degrees held by full-time faculty: doctorate 40%, master's 56%, baccalaureates 4%. 76% hold terminal degrees.

Enrollment: Total enrollment 1,987. Undergraduate full-time 107m / 1,075 women, part-time 41m / 84w; graduate full-time 11m / 15w, part-time 16m / 38w. *Transfer students:* 49.

Characteristics of Student Body: *Ethnic/racial makeup:* number of Black non-Hispanic: 49; American Indian or Alaska Native: 21; Asian or Pacific Islander: 27; Hispanic: 62; White non-Hispanic: 1,822; unknown: 2. *Age distribution:* number under 18: 1; 18–19: 790; 20–21: 672; 22–24: 332; 25–29: 68; 30–34: 43; 35–39: 49; 40–49: 26; 50–64: 6.

International Students: 5 nonresident aliens enrolled fall 2004. Students from Europe, Asia, Central and South America, Africa. No programs available to aid students whose native language is not English. No financial aid specifically designated for international students.

Student Life: On-campus residence halls house 80% of student body. Residence halls for men constitute 30% of such space, for women 30%, for both sexes 40%. 3% of student body housed on campus in apartments and mobile homes for married students. *Intercollegiate athletics:* men only: baseball, basketball, cross-country, football, tennis; women only: basketball, tennis, volleyball. *Special regulations:* Registered cars permitted without restrictions. Curfews. Specified quiet hours. Residence hall visitation during open house. *Special services:* Learning Resources Center, medical services. *Student publications, radio:* Epiphany, a bimonthly literary publication; *The Excalibur*, a yearbook; *The Lance*, a weekly newspaper. Radio station KECC broadcasts 100 hours per week. *Surrounding community:* Springfield population 135,000. Kansas City (MO), 190 miles from campus, is nearest metropolitan area. Served by mass transit bus system; airport 12 miles from campus.

Library Collections: 127,000 volumes. 23,000 microforms; 3,300 audiovisual materials; 670 current periodical subscriptions. Online catalog. Students have access to online information retrieval services and the Internet.

Special collections include Library of American Civilization (19,000 volumes on microfiche).

Buildings and Grounds: Campus area 80 acres.

Chief Executive Officer: Robert H. Spence, President.

Address admission inquiries to Charity Fahlstrom, Director of Admissions.

Fontbonne University

6800 Wydown Boulevard
St. Louis, Missouri 63105
Tel: (314) 862-3456   **E-mail:** pmusen@fontbonne.edu
Fax: (314) 889-1451   **Internet:** www.fontbonne.edu

Institution Description: Fontbonne College, formerly Fontbonne College, is a private, independent, nonprofit college sponsored by the Sisters of St. Joseph of Carondelet, Roman Catholic Church. *Enrollment:* 2,827. *Degrees awarded:* Baccalaureate, master's.

Accreditation: *Regional:* NCA. *Professional:* dietetics, speech-language pathology, teacher education

History: Established and chartered 1917; offered first instruction at postsecondary level 1923; awarded first degree (baccalaureate) 1927; became coeducational 1975; added branch campus in O'Fallon, Missouri 1985; became Fontbonne University 2002.

Institutional Structure: *Governing board:* Board of Trustees. Extrainstitutional representation: 33 trustees, including 12 trustees emeriti; institutional representation: president of the college. 1 ex officio. 14 voting. *Composition of institution:* Administrators 5 men / 3 women. Academic affairs headed by vice president and dean of academic affairs. Management/business/finances directed by vice president for administration and business. Full-time instructional faculty 65. Academic governance body, Faculty General Assembly, meets an average of 15 times per year.

Calendar: Semesters. Academic year Aug. to May. Freshmen admitted Aug., Jan., May. Degrees conferred and formal commencement May. Summer session early June to late July.

Characteristics of Freshmen: 87% of applicants accepted. 42% of accepted applicants enrolled.

98% (186 students) submitted ACT scores. *25th percentile:* ACT Composite 19, ACT English 19, ACT Math 18. *75th percentile:* ACT Composite 24, ACT English 25, ACT Math 23.

24% of entering freshmen expected to graduate within 5 years. 84% of freshmen from Missouri. Freshmen from 5 states and 2 foreign countries.

Admission: Rolling admissions plan. For fall acceptance, apply as early as summer following junior year of secondary school, but not later than Aug. 1 of year of enrollment. Early acceptance available. *Requirements:* Either graduation from accredited secondary school with 16 units which must include 4 English, 3 mathematics, 3 science including 1 lab, 3 units core electives including foreign language, 1 visual and performing arts. *Entrance tests:* College Board SAT or ACT composite. For foreign students TOEFL. *For transfer students:* 2.0 minimum GPA; from 4-year accredited institution maximum transfer credit limited by residence requirement; from community college 72 hour maximum transfer credit.

College credit and advanced placement for postsecondary-level work completed in secondary school. College credit for extrainstitutional learning (life experience) on basis of portfolio and faculty Tutoring available. Developmental/remedial courses offered during regular academic year; credit given.

Degree Requirements: *For all baccalaureate degrees:* 128 credit hours. *For all undergraduate degrees:* 2.0 GPA; 32 semester hours in residence; distribution requirements; exit competency examinations in some fields of study.

Fulfillment of some degree requirements and exemption from some beginning courses possible by passing College Board CLEP, AP. *Grading system:* A–F; pass-fail; withdraw (carries time limit); incomplete (carries time limit).

Distinctive Educational Programs: *For undergraduates:* Work-experience programs with business, industry, social, and governmental agencies. Dual-degree program in social work with Washington University (MO). Interdisciplinary program in human services. Individual majors. Cross-registration with several area colleges. *For graduate students:* Paid practicums. *Available to all students:* Weekend and evening classes. Tutorials. *Other distinctive programs:* Continuing education. Program for Adult College Education assists mature students wishing to complete or begin earning degrees.

Degrees Conferred: 339 *baccalaureate:* biological/life sciences 3; business/marketing 169; communications/communication technologies 14; computer and information sciences 2; education 30; English 4; health professions and related clinical sciences 17; home economics and vocational home economics 7; law/legal studies 2; liberal arts/general studies 5; mathematics 6; personal and miscellaneous services 6; protective services/public administration; psychology 6; social sciences and history 1; visual and performing arts 17. 248 *master's:* business/marketing 119; education 85; health professions 22; visual and performing arts 22.

Fees and Other Expenses: *Full-time tuition per academic year 2004–05:* $115,100 undergraduate; $8,136 graduate. *Required fees:* $320. *Room and board per academic year:* $6,988.

Financial Aid: Aid from institutionally generated funds is provided on the basis of academic merit, financial need.

Financial aid to full-time, first-time undergraduate students: need-based scholarships/grants totaling $5,405,529, self-help $3,477,110, parent loans $544,509; non-need-based scholarships/grants totaling $3,508,652, self-help $5,177,568. *Graduate aid:* 914 students received $5,197,921 in federal and state-funded loans (ranging from $500 to $18,500); 24 students received $4,555 for other fellowships/grants (ranging from $500 to $12,000).

Departments and Teaching Staff: *Professors* 11, *associate professors* 18, *assistant professors* 23, *instructors* 13. *Total instructional faculty:* 345 (full-time 65, part-time 280; women 226, men 119; members of minority groups 10). Total faculty with doctorate, first-professional, or other terminal degree: 97. Student-to-faculty ratio: 12:1. Degrees held by full-time faculty: doctorate 57%, master's 38%, professional 5%. 72% hold terminal degrees.

Enrollment: Total enrollment 2,827. Undergraduate full-time 378 men / 1,135 women, part-time 131m / 372w; graduate full-time 118m / 271w, part-time 95m / 327w.

Characteristics of Student Body: *Ethnic/racial makeup:* number of Black non-Hispanic: 647; American Indian or Alaska Native: 9; Asian or Pacific Islander: 16; Hispanic: 26; White non-Hispanic: 1,269; unknown: 33. *Age distribution:* number under 18: 14; 18–19: 325; 20–21: 346; 22–24: 294; 25–29: 304; 30–34: 238; 35–39: 182; 40–49: 239; 50–64: 65; 65 and over: 5.

International Students: 68 nonresident aliens enrolled fall 2004. Students from Europe, Asia, Central and South America, Africa, Canada. Programs available to aid students whose native language is not English: social, cultural. English as a Second Language Program. No financial aid specifically designated for international students.

Student Life: On-campus residence halls house 15% of student body. Residence halls for men constitute 37% of such space, for women 63%. *Special regulations:* Cars must have parking permits; fee charged. Quiet hours beginning at 10pm. Residence hall visitation until 9pm to midnight Sun.–Thurs., until 2am Fri. and Sat. *Special services:* Learning Resources Center, medical services. *Student publications: Chiasma,* an annual literary magazine; *Frontrunner,* monthly newspaper. *Surrounding community:* Clayton, population 15,000 is located within the St. Louis metropolitan area. Served by mass transit bus system; airport and passenger rail service 10 miles from campus.

Library Collections: 104,000 volumes including bound books, serial backfiles, electronic documents, and government documents not in separate collections. Online and card catalogs. Current serial subscriptions: 496 paper, 2 microform, over 1,500 electronic. 10,198 recordings; 438 compact discs. Computer work stations available. Students have access to the Internet at no charge.

Most important special collections include Mark Twain Collection (465 volumes, including some first editions); Father St. Cyr collection (rare religious books, written in French, and dating from the late 17th- and early 18th-centuries); Clarkson Tax Library.

Buildings and Grounds: Campus area 13 acres.

Chief Executive Officer: Dr. Dennis C. Golden, President.

Address admission inquiries to Peggy Musen, Associate Vice President for Enrollment Management.

Hannibal-LaGrange College

2800 Palmyra Road
Hannibal, Missouri 63401-1999
Tel: (573) 221-3675   **E-mail:** rcarty@hlg.edu
Fax: (573) 221-6594   **Internet:** www.hlg.edu

Institution Description: Hannibal-LaGrange College is a private institution affiliated with the Missouri Baptist Convention (Southern Baptist). *Enrollment:* 1,067. *Degrees awarded:* Associate, baccalaureate. Certificates and diplomas also awarded.

Accreditation: *Regional:* NCA.

History: Established 1858 as LaGrange College in La Grange; moved to Hannibal and merged with a Baptist college, adopted present name 1928; came under control of Missouri Baptist Convention 1957; consolidated with Missouri Baptist College of St. Louis 1967; became separate college 1973; assumed full senior college status 1981.

Institutional Structure: *Governing board:* Board of Trustees. Representation: 30 trustees. *Composition of institution:* Academic affairs headed by vice president-dean of academic affairs. Management/business/finances directed by dean of business affairs. Full-time instructional faculty 65.

Calendar: Semesters. Academic year Aug. to May.

Characteristics of Freshmen: 96% of applicants admitted. 47% of applicants admitted and enrolled.

1% (2 students) submitted SAT scores; 99% (160 students) submitted ACT scores. *25th percentile:* SAT Verbal 520, SAT Math 510; ACT Composite 20, ACT English 19, ACT Math 18. *75th percentile:* SAT Verbal 560, SAT Math 640; ACT Composite 25, ACT English 27, ACT Math 24.

65% of freshmen from Missouri. Freshmen from 11 states and 6 foreign countries.

Admission: Early acceptance available. *Requirements:* Either graduation from accredited secondary school or GED. *Entrance tests:* College Board SAT or ACT composite. For foreign students TOEFL. *For transfer students:* From 2-year accredited institutions maximum transfer credit 64 hours.

College credit for extrainstitutional learning on basis of ACE *2006 Guide to the Evaluation of Educational Experiences in the Armed Services;* faculty assessment.

Degree Requirements: *For all associate degrees:* 64 credit hours. *For all baccalaureate degrees:* 124–130 credit hours. *For all degrees:* 2.0 GPA; last 32 hours in residence; regular chapel attendance; general education requirements.

Fulfillment of some degree requirements and exemption from some beginning courses possible by passing institutional examinations, College Board CLEP. *Grading system:* A–F; pass-fail; withdraw; incomplete.

Distinctive Educational Programs: Evening classes. Independent study. Honors programs. Continuing education. Advance Program (18 months degree completion program).

Degrees Conferred: 165 *baccalaureate:* biological/life sciences 1; business/marketing 56; communications/communication technologies 5; computer and information sciences 9; education 33; English 6; Liberal arts/general studies 7; philosophy/religion/theology 12; protective services/public administration 26; psychology 5; social sciences and history 3; visual and performing arts 2.

Fees and Other Expenses: *Full-time tuition per academic year 2004–05:* $10,530. *Room and board per academic year:* $4,050. *Required fees:* $350.

Financial Aid: Aid from institutionally generated funds is provided on the basis of academic merit, athletic ability, other criteria.

Financial aid to full-time, first-time undergraduate students: need-based scholarships/grants totaling $962,721, self-help $1,844,915; non-need-based scholarships/grants totaling $1,334,209, self-help $1,583,449, parent loans $821,146, tuition waivers $9,875, athletic awards $475,000.

Departments and Teaching Staff: *Total instructional faculty:* 110 (full-time 59, part-time 51; women 56, men 54; members of minority groups 4). Total faculty with doctorate, first-professional, or other terminal degree: 28. Student-to-faculty ratio: 12:1. Degrees held by full-time faculty: doctorate 32%, master's 66%, baccalaureate 2%. 34% hold terminal degrees.

Enrollment: Total enrollment 1,067. Full-time 269 men / 482 women, part-time 111m / 205w.

Characteristics of Student Body: *Ethnic/racial makeup:* number of Black non-Hispanic: 20; American Indian or Alaska Native: 4; Asian or Pacific Islander: 2; Hispanic: 10; White non-Hispanic: 1,018; unknown: 3.

International Students: 10 nonresident aliens enrolled fall 2004. 2 students from Europe, 1 Asia, 5 Central and South America, 2 Africa. No programs available to students whose native language is not English. No financial aid specifically designated for international students.

Student Life: *Special regulations:* Registered cars permitted. *Student publications: Campus Horizons,* a student newspaper; *Trojan,* a yearbook. *Surrounding community:* Hannibal population 19,000. St. Louis, 95 miles from campus, is nearest metropolitan area.

Library Collections: 234,408 volumes. Current serial subscriptions: 6,451 paper; 21,376 microform; 66 via electronic access. 200 CD-ROMs. Online catalog. 11 computer work stations. Students have access to the Internet at no charge.

Most important special holdings include Missouri Collection; College Archives; Rare Book Collection.

Buildings and Grounds: Campus area 110 acres. *New buildings:* Pearl Bonner Prince Home and Mary Wiehe House (residential housing); Carroll Mission Center; Poland Fine Arts Center.

Chief Executive Officer: Dr. Woodrow W. Burt, President.

Address admission inquiries to Raymond W. Carty, Vice President for Enrollment Management.

Harris-Stowe State College

3026 Laclede Avenue
St. Louis, Missouri 63103-2136
Tel: (314) 340-3366   **E-mail:** admissions@hssc.edu
Fax: (314) 340-3355   **Internet:** www.hssc.edu

Institution Description: Harris-Stowe State College is a 4-year state institution. *Enrollment:* 1,605. *Degrees awarded:* Baccalaureate.

Academic offerings subject to approval by statewide coordinating bodies. Budget subject to state higher education budgeting process.

Accreditation: *Regional:* NCA. *Professional:* business, teacher education

History: Established as St. Louis Normal School, a women's institution, and offered first instruction at postsecondary level 1857; changed name to Teachers College 1904, Harris Teachers College 1910; became a 4-year institution 1919; awarded first degree (baccalaureate) 1924; became coeducational 1940; merged with Stowe Teachers College 1954; changed name to Harris-Stowe College 1977, Harris-Stowe State College 1979. *See* Ruth M. Harris, *Stowe Teachers College and Her Predecessors* (Boston: Christopher Publishing House, 1967) for further information.

Institutional Structure: *Governing board:* Board of Regents of Harris-Stowe State College. Representation: 6 regents (voting) and 1 student member (nonvoting). *Composition of institution:* Administrators 10 men / 12 women, includes the president, vice presidents for administration, academic affairs, student affairs, business/financial affairs. Full-time instructional faculty 46.

Calendar: Semesters. Academic year Aug. to May. Freshmen admitted May, Aug., Jan. Degrees conferred May, Dec. Formal commencement May. Two summer sessions (1 five-week session and 1 eight-week session).

Characteristics of Freshmen: 857 applicants (276 men, 581 women). 47.8% of applicants admitted; 47.8% of admitted students enrolled full-time.

49% (129 students) submitted ACT scores. *25th percentile*: ACT Composite 15, ACT English 13, ACT Math 15. *75th percentile*: ACT Composite 19, ACT English 20, ACT Math 18.

97% of freshmen from Missouri. Freshmen from 3 states and 12 foreign countries.

Admission: Rolling admissions plan. For fall acceptance, apply no later than Aug. 10. Early acceptance available. *Requirements:* Either graduation from accredited secondary school with 11 units from among English, mathematics, social studies, as well as 1 laboratory science and 6 academic electives; or GED. ACT composite score 20 or higher. *For transfer students:* 2.0 minimum GPA; from 4-year accredited institution 90 hours maximum transfer credit; from 2-year accredited institution 64 hours.

College credit for postsecondary-level work completed at Harris-Stowe while in secondary school. Tutoring available. Developmental courses offered in summer session and regular academic year.

Degree Requirements: 120–128 credit hours depending on degree program; 2.5 GPA; last 30 hours in residence; distribution requirements. Different requirements for urban education program.

Grading system: A–F; withdraw; incomplete.

Distinctive Educational Programs: Internships in professional programs. Saturday and evening classes. Interdisciplinary program in urban education. New degree programs in business administration, criminal justice, information sciences and computer technology, secondary education. Professional interdisciplinary studies; health care management.

ROTC: Army and Air Force in cooperation with Park College, Washington University, and University of Missouri-St. Louis.

Degrees Conferred: 125 *baccalaureate.* Bachelor's degrees awarded in top five disciplines: education 38; business, management, marketing, and related support services 36; multidisciplinary studies 31; computer and information sciences 13; protective/security services 5.

Fees and Other Expenses: *Full-time tuition per academic year 2004–05:* in-state $3,436, out-of-state $6,306. *Books and supplies:* $900. *Room and board per academic year:* $6,252.

Financial Aid: Aid from institutionally generated funds is provided on the basis of academic merit, financial need, athletic ability. Institution has a Program Participation Agreement with the U.S. Department of Education for eligible students to receive Pell Grants and, depending upon the agreement, other federal aid.

Financial aid to full-time, first-time undergraduate students: 57% received federal grants averaging $2,955; 4% state/local grants; 57% institutional grants averaging $2,102; 32% received loans averaging $2,010.

Departments and Teaching Staff: Business administration *professors:* 0, *associate professors* 1, *assistant professors* 2, *instructors* 4, *part-time teachers* 16; arts and sciences 8, 1, 3, 6, 30; education 4, 0, 7, 3, 36; urban specializations 2, 2, 1, 2, 3; academic support 0, 0, 0, 0, 5.

Total instructional faculty: 76 FTE. Student-to-faculty ratio: 11:1. Degrees held by full-time faculty: doctorate 54%, master's 100%. 54% hold terminal degrees.

Enrollment: Total enrollment 1,605 (men 29.7%, women 70.3%).

Characteristics of Student Body: *Ethnic/racial makeup:* number of Black non-Hispanic: 93,8%; American Indian or Alaska Native: .2%; Asian or Pacific Islander: .1%; Hispanic: .1%; White non-Hispanic: 13.5%; unknown: .7%. *Age distribution:* 17–21: 29%; 22–24: 17%; 25–29: 18%; 30–34: 10%; 35–39: 9%; 40–49: 13%; 50–59: 4%.

International Students: 17 nonresident aliens enrolled fall 2004. Students from Europe, Asia, Latin America, Africa, Canada, Australia. No programs available to aid students whose native language is not English. No financial aid specifically designated for international students.

Student Life: No on-campus housing. *Intercollegiate athletics:* men only: baseball, basketball, soccer; women only: basketball, softball, track, volleyball. *Special regulations:* Cars permitted without restrictions. *Special services:* Learning Resources Center, medical services. *Student publications: Hornets Nest,* a monthly newspaper; *Torch,* a yearbook. *Surrounding community:* St. Louis metropolitan population 2.5 million. Served by mass transit bus system; airport 18 miles from campus.

Library Collections: 90,000 volumes. 6,400 microforms; 347 current periodical subscriptions. Online catalog. Computer work stations available campus-wide. Students have access to online information retrieval services and the Internet.

Most important special collections include Proceedings and Reports of the St. Louis Public Schools (1851–Present); civil rights; African American studies.

Buildings and Grounds: Campus area 9 acres.

Chief Executive Officer: Dr. Henry Givens, Jr., President.

Address admission inquiries to LaShanda Boone, Director of Admissions.

Kansas City Art Institute

4415 Warwick Boulevard
Kansas City, Missouri 64111
Tel: (816) 472-4852   **E-mail:** admissions@kcai.edu
Fax: (816) 802-3439   **Internet:** www.kcai.edu

Institution Description: Kansas City Art Institute is a private, independent, nonprofit institution. *Enrollment:* 592. *Degrees awarded:* Baccalaureate.

Member of Association of Independent Colleges of Art and Design.

Accreditation: *Regional:* NCA. *Professional:* art

History: Established as a sketch club 1885; chartered and incorporated as Kansas City Art Institute and School of Design 1887; changed name to Fine Arts Institute of Kansas City 1907, Kansas City Art Institute and School of Design 1945; awarded first degree (baccalaureate) 1947; readopted present name 1966.

Institutional Structure: *Governing board:* Board of Governors. Extrainstitutional representation: 33 trustees. 1 ex officio. 33 voting. *Composition of institution:* President, presidents for academic affairs, advancement, enrollment management; executive vice president for administration. *Full-time instructional faculty:* 43. Academic governance body, Faculty Assembly, meets an average of 4 times per year.

Calendar: Semesters. Academic year Aug. to May. Freshmen admitted Aug., Jan. Degrees conferred May, Aug., Dec. Formal commencement May.

Characteristics of Freshmen: 83% of applicants admitted. 32% of applicants admitted and enrolled.

29% (119 students) submitted SAT scores; 71% (288 students) submitted ACT scores. *25th percentile*: SAT Verbal 490, SAT Math 460; ACT Composite 18, ACT English 18, ACT Math 16. *75th percentile*: SAT Verbal 630, SAT Math 590; ACT Composite 25, ACT English 27, ACT Math 23.

56% of entering freshmen expected to graduate within 5 years. 31% of freshmen from Missouri. Freshmen from 22 states.

Admission: Rolling admissions plan. Priority application/scholarship deadlines Jan. 15, Feb. 15, Mar 1. Early acceptance available. *Requirements:* Either graduation from accredited secondary school or GED; and portfolio including at least 15–20 slide samples of work. Interview strongly recommended. *Entrance tests:* College Board SAT or ACT composite. For foreign students TOEFL. *For transfer students:* portfolio.

College credit and advanced placement for postsecondary-level work completed in secondary school. Developmental courses offered during regular academic year; credit given.

Degree Requirements: 129 credit hours; 2.0 GPA; 4 terms in residence; 45 liberal arts hours, 81 studio hours, 3 hours of open electives.

Fulfillment of some degree requirements and exemption from some beginning courses possible by passing College Board CLEP, AP. *Grading system:* A–F; withdraw (carries time limit).

Distinctive Educational Programs: Internships in design and photo. Evening classes. Extensive continuing education program for adults and high school students. Part-time program offering up to 18 graduate credits. Study abroad at Instituto di Italiani, Florence, Italy; Brighton Polytechnic, United Kingdom; Victorian College, Melbourne, Australia; Nova Scotia College of Art and Design, Canada. Credit transfer agreement and off-campus study through AICA. Cross-registration through K-Case. Individual and group art projects conducted by students and faculty members for civic and private organizations. New York Studio Program. Skowhegan Residency Program.

Degrees Conferred: 111 *baccalaureate:* visual and performing arts. 2 *honorary degree awarded 2004:* Doctor of Fine Arts.

Fees and Other Expenses: *Full-time tuition per academic year 2005–06:* $21,446. *Room and board per academic year:* $7,150. *Required fees:* $946.

Financial Aid: Aid from institutionally generated funds is provided on the basis of academic merit, financial need.

Financial aid to full-time, first-time undergraduate students: need-based scholarships/grants totaling $4,806,274, self-help $3,758,482, parent loans $1,199,126, tuition waivers $100,129; non-need-based scholarships/grants totaling $926,305, self-help $673,071, parent loans $1,237,380, tuition waivers $31,131.

Departments and Teaching Staff: Fine arts *professors* 19 *associate professors* 6, *assistant professors* 14, *instructors* 4, *part-time faculty* 38.

Total instructional faculty: 81 (full-time 43, part-time 38; women 7, men 44; members of minority groups 2). Total faculty with doctorate, first-professional, or other terminal degree: 6. Student-to-faculty ratio: 8:1. 3 faculty members awarded sabbaticals 2004–05.

Enrollment: Total enrollment 592. Undergraduate full-time 261 men / 329 women, part-time 2w. *Transfer students:* in-state 27; from out-of-state 37.

Characteristics of Student Body: *Ethnic/racial makeup:* number of Black non-Hispanic: 19; American Indian or Alaska Native: 9; Asian or Pacific Islander: 22; Hispanic: 40; White non-Hispanic: 490; unknown: 6. *Age distribution:* number under 18: 5; 18–19: 227; 20–21: 224; 22–24: 81; 25–29: 26; 30–34: 14; 35–39: 3; 40–49: 6; 50–64: 3.

International Students: 6 nonresident aliens enrolled fall 2004. 4 students from Asia, 1 Canada, 1 New Zealand. No programs available to aid students whose native language is not English. No financial aid specifically designated for international students.

Student Life: On-campus residence halls house 41 men / 62 women. *Special regulations:* Cars permitted in designated areas. Quiet hours. *Surrounding community:* Kansas City metropolitan population 1,657,000. Served by mass transit bus system; airport 28 miles from campus.

Publications: *Magazine,* published by Public Relations Department; *Tute Newsletter,* published weekly.

Library Collections: 31,879 volumes. 105,000 slides; 100 current periodical subscriptions. 5 computer work stations. Students have access to online information services and the Internet. Total 2004–05 budget for books, periodicals, audiovisual materials, microforms: $12,845.

Most important special holdings include the slide library (a teaching collection containing 100,000 slides).

Buildings and Grounds: Campus area 18 acres.

Chief Executive Officer: Kathleen Collins, President.

Address admission inquiries to Larry Stone, Vice President for Enrollment Management.

Kansas City University of Medicine and Biosciences

1750 Independence Boulevard
Kansas City, Missouri 64106-1453
Tel: (816) 283-2000   **E-mail:** admissions@kcumb.edu
Fax: (816) 283-2484   **Internet:** www.kcumb.edu

Institution Description: Kansas City University of Medicine and Biosciences, formerly named University of Health Sciences College of Osteopathic Medicine, is a private, four-year, osteopathic medical school. *Enrollment:* 926. *Degrees awarded:* First-professional.

Accreditation: *Regional:* NCA. *Professional:* biomedical, osteopathy

History: in July 2004, the University of Health Sciences assumed its present name.

Calendar: Semesters. Academic year Aug. to July.

Characteristics of Freshmen: 13% of applicants accepted. 7% of accepted applicants enrolled.

Degree Requirements: Completion of prescribed curriculum and passing score on the National Board of Osteopathic Medicine examination.

Degrees Conferred: 214 *first-professional:* osteopathic medicine.

Fees and Other Expenses: *Full-time tuition per academic year:* $35,055. *Required fees:* $60.

Financial Aid: Aid from institutionally generated funds is provided on the basis of academic merit, financial need. *Graduate aid:* 809 students received $30,095,176 in federal and state-funded loans (ranging from $500 to $5,000); 56 students received fellowships and grants totaling $71,000 (ranging from $700 to $2,000).

Departments and Teaching Staff: *Professors* 16, *associate professors* 20, *assistant professors* 10, *instructors* 7, *part-time faculty* 1.

Total instructional faculty: 54 (full-time 53, part-time 1; women 18, men 36; members of minority groups 10). Total faculty with doctorate, first-professional, or other terminal degree: 50. Student-to-faculty ratio: 8.7:1. Degrees held by full-time faculty: doctorate 50%, master's 32%, baccalaureate 97%. 50% hold terminal degrees. *Faculty development:* $390,834 total grants for research.

Enrollment: Total enrollment 926. First-professional full-time 493 men / 433 women.

Characteristics of Student Body: *Ethnic/racial makeup:* Black non-Hispanic: 29; American Indian or Native Alaskan: 7; Asian or Pacific Islander: 97; Hispanic: 16; White non-Hispanic: 756; unknown: 21.

International Students: 8 nonresident aliens enrolled fall 2004. No programs available to aid students whose native language is not English. No financial aid specifically designated for international students.

Library Collections: 54,347 volumes including bound books, serial backfiles, electronic documents, and government documents not in separate collections. Online catalog. Current serial subscriptions: 90 paper, 265 electronic. 159 recordings; 1,090 compact discs; 2,209 CD-ROMs. 26 computer work stations. Students have access to the Internet at no charge. Total budget for books, periodicals, audiovisual materials, microforms 2004–05: $425,172.

Most important special collections include Osteopathic Collection; Alternative/Complementary Medicine Collection; Evidence-Based Medicine.

Buildings and Grounds: Urban campus. *New buildings:* Mary Butterworth Alumni Center completed 2000; Dybedal Life Sciences Center 2005.

Chief Executive Officer: Karen L. Platz, M.D., President.

Address admission inquiries to Phil Byrne, Director, Recruitment Activities.

Kenrick-Glennon Seminary

5200 Glennon Drive
St. Louis, Missouri 63119
Tel: (314) 792-6100   **E-mail:** richard@kenrick.edu
Fax: (314) 792-6500   **Internet:** www.kenrick.edu

Institution Description: Kenrick-Glennon Seminary is a private institution affiliated with the Roman Catholic Church. *Enrollment:* 58 men. Women admitted through cross-registration agreements with other institutions. *Degrees awarded:* First-professional (master of divinity), master of arts.

Accreditation: *Regional:* NCA. *National:* ATS. *Professional:* theology

History: Incorporated as St. Louis Roman Catholic Theological Seminary 1969; adopted present name 1893.

Institutional Structure: *Governing board:* Board of Directors. Representation: 5 members, Archbishop of St. Louis. Full-time instructional faculty 16.

Calendar: Semesters. Academic year Aug. to May.

Admission: For fall acceptance, apply no later than June 1. *Requirements:* Baccalaureate from accredited college or its equivalent; prerequisite philosophy and theology courses; transcript of credits of the applicant from all colleges or seminaries attended; Miller Analogies Test.

Degree Requirements: *For first-professional degree:* 87 required credit hours, 20 elective hours, 34 hours of practicum work; 2.0 GPA. *For master's degree:* 30 credit hours; 3.0 GPA. *Grading system:* A–F; pass-fail; withdraw; incomplete.

Degrees Conferred: 9 *first-professional:* master of divinity.

Fees and Other Expenses: *Full-time tuition per academic year 2004–05:* $14,200. *Room and board per academic year:* $4,500. *Required fees:* $185.

Financial Aid: Aid from institutionally generated funds is provided on the basis of financial need. Institution has a Program Participation Agreement with the U.S. Department of Education for eligible students to receive Pell Grants and, depending upon the agreement, other federal aid.

Departments and Teaching Staff: *Total instructional faculty:* 14.

Enrollment: *Total enrollment* 58. First-professional full-time 58 men.

Characteristics of Student Body: *Ethnic/racial makeup:* number of Black non-Hispanic: 3; White non-Hispanic: 55. *Age distribution:* number 22–24: 11; 25–29: 17; 30–34: 11; 35–39: 6; 40–49: 9; 50–64: 2.

International Students: No programs available to aid students whose native language is not English. No financial aid specifically designated for international students.

Student Life: On-campus residence halls available. *Surrounding community:* St. Louis population 455,000.

Publications: *Spirit Newsletter;* yearly catalog; *The Harold,* published twice yearly.

Library Collections: 76,000 volumes. 300 current periodical subscriptions. Online and card catalogs. Students have access to the Internet.

Most important special collections include writings of Thomas Merton, religious collection (including Bibles, church histories, Catholic yearbooks), cuneiform tablets, rare books (including 1495 Bible).

Chief Executive Officer: Msgr. Ted L. Wojcicki, President-Rector.

Address admission inquiries to Fr. Edward Richard, Vice/Rector and Dean of Students.

Lincoln University

820 Chestnut Street
Jefferson City, Missouri 65101
Tel: (573) 681-5000   **E-mail:** enroll@lincoln.edu
Fax: (573) 881-5566   **Internet:** www.lincoln.edu

Institution Description: Lincoln University is a state institution. *Enrollment:* 3,275. *Degrees awarded:* Baccalaureate, master's.

Academic offerings subject to approval by statewide coordinating bodies.

Accreditation: *Regional:* NCA. *Professional:* business, music, nursing, teacher education

History: Established as Lincoln Institute, a private institution, 1866; offered first instruction at postsecondary level 1877; incorporated and became a state institution 1879; became a land-grant institution 1890; awarded first degree (baccalaureate) 1891; adopted present name 1921.

Institutional Structure: *Governing board:* Board of Curators. Representation: 9 curators. All voting. *Composition of institution:* Administrators 9 men / 4 women. Academic Affairs headed by vice president. Business and Finance headed by vice president. Student Affairs headed by vice president. Full-time instructional faculty 129. Academic governance body, Faculty Senate, meets an average of 6 times per year.

Calendar: Semesters. Academic year Aug. to Aug. Freshmen admitted Aug., Jan., June. Degrees conferred and formal commencement May, Dec. Summer session includes 4- and 8=week terms.

Characteristics of Freshmen: 99% of applicants accepted. 59% of accepted applicants enrolled.

Mean ACT composite score 18.

26% of entering freshmen expected to graduate within 5 years. 74% of freshmen from Missouri, Freshmen from 33 states and 27 foreign countries.

Admission: Rolling admissions plan. For fall acceptance, apply no later than July 15. *Requirements:* Either graduation from accredited secondary school or GED. *Entrance tests:* ACT composite required. For foreign students TOEFL or MELAB. *For transfer students:* maximum transfer credit limited: 90 hours for 4-year program, 64 hours for 2-year program; 2.0 GPA. Good standing at institution previously attended.

College credit and advanced placement for postsecondary-level work completed in secondary school. Tutoring available. Noncredit developmental courses offered in summer session and regular academic year.

Degree Requirements: *For undergraduate degree:* 124 credit hours; 2.0 GPA; 30 hours in residence; general education requirements.

Fulfillment of some degree requirements and exemption from some beginning courses possible by passing College Board CLEP. *Grading system:* A–F; withdraw (carries time limit).

Distinctive Educational Programs: Work-experience programs, including cooperative education, internships. Weekend and evening classes. Special facilities for using telecommunications in the classroom. Facilities and programs for independent research, honors programs, tutorials. Programs in business administration, accounting, nursing, and computer science.

ROTC: Air Force and Navy in cooperation with University of Missouri - Columbia. 8 Army commissions awarded 2004.

Degrees Conferred: 54 *associate;* 389 *baccalaureate:* agriculture 1; biological/life sciences 4; business/marketing 115; communications/communication technologies 15; computer and information sciences 64; education 41; engineering and engineering technologies 8; English 4; foreign languages and literature 2; liberal arts/general studies 24; mathematics 6; philosophy/religion/theology 4; physical sciences 2; protective services/public administration 47; psychology 19; social sciences and history 27; visual and performing arts 8; other 9. 85 *master's:* business/marketing 32; education 41; social sciences and history 12.

Fees and Other Expenses: *Full-time tuition per academic year 2005–06:* resident $4,412; nonresident $8,059. *Room and board per academic year:* $3,190. *Required fees:* $672.

Financial Aid: Aid from institutionally generated funds is provided on the basis of academic merit, financial need, athletic ability. Institution has a Program Participation Agreement with the U.S. Department of Education for eligible students to receive Pell Grants and, depending upon the agreement, other federal aid.

Departments and Teaching Staff: *Professors* 30, *associate professors* 24, *assistant professors* 62, *instructors* 13, *part-time faculty* 5.

Total instructional faculty: 134 (full-time 129, part-time 5; women 61, men 73; members of minority groups 43). Total faculty with doctorate, first-professional, or other terminal degree: 81. Student-to-faculty ratio: 18:1. Degrees held by full-time faculty: master's 58%, doctorate 45%.

Enrollment: Total enrollment 3,275. Full-time undergraduate 904 men / 1,152 women, part-time 331m / 1,154w; graduate full-time 23m / 46w, part-time 54m / 111w. *Transfer students:* in-state 109; from out-of-state: 87.

Characteristics of Student Body: *Ethnic/racial makeup:* number of Black non-Hispanic: 1,111; American Indian or Alaska Native: 13; Asian or Pacific Islander: 28; Hispanic: 40; White non-Hispanic: 1,671; unknown: 46. *Age distribution:* number under 18: 336; 18–19: 896; 20–21: 102; 22–24: 534; 25–29: 286; 30–34: 149; 35–39: 92; 40–49: 113; 50–64: 26; 65 and over: 4. 30% of student body attend summer sessions.

International Students: 155 nonresident aliens enrolled fall 2004. No programs available to aid students whose native language is not English. No financial aid specifically designated for international students.

Student Life: On-campus residence halls house 27% of student body. Residence halls for men only constitute 50% of such space, for women only 50%. *Intercollegiate athletics:* men only: baseball, basketball, golf, football, cross-country, track; women only: basketball, cross-country, softball, tennis, track, volleyball. *Special regulations:* Cars permitted in designated areas. Visitation hours vary according to residence hall. *Special services:* Medical services, comprehensive counseling center, career planning and placement center. *Student publications, radio, television:* Archives, a yearbook; The Clarion, a weekly newspaper. Radio station KLUM-FM broadcasts 112 hours per week. Public access television station JCTV. *Surrounding community:* Jefferson City population 39,000. Served by mass transit bus system; airport 25 miles from campus; passenger rail service 1 mile from campus.

Library Collections: 187,456 volumes. 79,905 microforms. 772 current periodical subscriptions. 1,655 recordings; 43 compact discs; 145 CD-ROMs. Online catalog. 48 computer work stations. Students have access to online information retrieval services and the Internet.

Most important special holdings include African Americans Collection; Lincoln Collection (University and staff items); juvenile collection.

Buildings and Grounds: Main campus area 152 acres.

Chief Executive Officer: Dr. Carolyn R. Mahoney, President.

Undergraduates address admission inquiries to Debra Cooper, Associate Director of Admissions; graduate inquiries to Dr. Linda Bickel, Dean, School of Graduate Studies and Continuing Education.

Lindenwood University

209 South Kings Highway
St. Charles, Missouri 63301-1695
Tel: (636) 949-2000   **E-mail:** admissions@lindenwood.edu
Fax: (636) 949-4910   **Internet:** www.lindenwood.edu

Institution Description: Lindenwood University, formerly Lindenwood College, offers a coeducational-liberal arts program, an evening division, and a college for individualized education. The institution is a private, independent, nonprofit college informally affiliated with The Presbyterian Church (U.S.A.). *Enrollment:* 8,613. *Degrees awarded:* Baccalaureate, master's.

Accreditation: *Regional:* NCA. *Professional:* teacher education

History: Established as Linden Wood, a women's institution 1827; offered first instruction at postsecondary level 1828; awarded first degree (baccalaureate) 1832; incorporated as Linden Wood Female College 1853; changed name to Lindenwood College 1870; established Lindenwood College II, a men's institution, and added graduate program 1969; adopted the name The Lindenwood Colleges 1970; changed name to Lindenwood College 1983 and became Lindenwood University in 1997. *See* L.D. Templin, *Reminiscences of Lindenwood College 1827–1920* (St. Charles: Lindenwood College, 1920) for further information.

Institutional Structure: *Governing board:* Board of Directors and Board of Overseers. Representation: 40 directors; 7 life members; 2 overseers. All voting. *Composition of institution:* Administrators 10 men / 6 women. Academic affairs headed by dean of faculty. Management/business/finances directed by chief business officer. Full-time instructional faculty 57. Academic governance body, Educational Governance Committee, meets an average of once a month.

Calendar: Residential and Evening College on semester calendar; College for Individualized Education and Saturday Campus on trimester calendar; Satellite centers on quarter calendar. Degrees conferred May, June, Sept., Dec. Formal commencement May.

Characteristics of Freshmen: 2,494 applicants (1,266 men, 1,208 women). 47.2% of applicants admitted. 77.8% of admitted students enrolled full-time.

7% (62 students) submitted SAT scores; 82% (754 students) submitted ACT scores. *25th percentile*: ACT Composite 19, ACT English 19, ACT Math 18. *75th percentile*: ACT Composite 26, ACT English 26, ACT Math 25.

89% of freshmen from Missouri. Freshmen from 19 states and 2 foreign countries.

Admission: Rolling admissions plan. For fall acceptance, apply as early as junior year of secondary school, but not later than Aug. 1 of year of enrollment. Early acceptance available. *Requirements:* Either graduation from accredited secondary school or GED. Recommend 16 academic units, including 4 in English. Minimum 2.5 GPA. *Entrance tests:* College Board SAT or ACT composite. *For transfer students:* 2.0 minimum GPA; from 4-year accredited institution maximum transfer credit limited only by residence requirement; from 2-year accredited institution 65 hours; correspondence students 6 hours.

College credit and advanced placement for postsecondary-level work completed in secondary school.

College credit for extrainstitutional learning on basis of ACE *2006 Guide to the Evaluation of Educational Experiences in the Armed Services*; portfolio and faculty assessments.

Degree Requirements: *For all baccalaureate degrees:* 126 credit hours; 1 year in residence; distribution requirements. For bachelor of arts, 6 hours foreign language or culture. *For all undergraduate degrees:* 2.0 GPA.

Fulfillment of some degree requirements and exemption from some beginning courses possible by passing College Board CLEP, APP. *Grading system:* A–F; pass-fail; withdraw; incomplete.

Distinctive Educational Programs: *For undergraduates:* Dual-degree programs in engineering with Washington University (MO); social work with Washington University (MO). Interdisciplinary program in international studies. Individually designed independent study terms for academically qualified upper division students. Study abroad by individual arrangement. Cross-registration with Fontbonne, Maryville, and Webster Colleges. Washington (DC) semester at The American University. *For graduate students:* Interdisciplinary program in international business. *Available to all students:* Work-experience programs, including field study internships. Flexible meeting places and schedules, including off-campus centers, evening and weekend classes. Accelerated degree programs. Facilities and programs for independent research, including individual majors, tutorials. *Other distinctive programs:* Degree-granting evening college primarily for adults. College for Individualized Education provides accelerated degree programs. Satellite educational centers. Continuing education.

Degrees Conferred: 853 *baccalaureate*; 942 *master's*. Bachelor's degrees awarded in top five disciplines: business, management, marketing, and related support services 338; education 137; communication, journalism, and related programs 59; visual and performing arts 30; 53; social sciences and history 51.

Fees and Other Expenses: *Full-time tuition for academic year 2004–05:* $11,200. *Books and supplies:* $2,600. *Room and board per academic year:* $5,600.

Financial Aid: Aid from institutionally generated funds is provided on the basis of academic merit, financial need, athletic ability, talent, other criteria. Institution has a Program Participation Agreement with the U.S. Department of Education for eligible students to receive Pell Grants and, depending upon the agreement, other federal aid.

Departments and Teaching Staff: *Professors* 7, *associate professors* 14, *assistant professors* 36.

Total instructional faculty: 57. Student-to-faculty ratio: 17:1. Degrees held by full-time faculty: doctorate 55%, master's 100%. 55% hold terminal degrees.

Enrollment: Total enrollment 8,613. Undergraduate 5,512 (men 42.9%, women 57.1%).

Characteristics of Student Body: *Ethnic/racial makeup:* number of Black non-Hispanic: 10.3%; American Indian or Alaska Native: .4%; Asian or Pacific Islander: .5%; Hispanic: 1.6%; White non-Hispanic: 27.1%; unknown: 13.8%. *Age distribution:* 17–21: 42%; 22–24: 16%; 25–29: 13%; 30–34: 8%; 35–39: 7%; 40–49: 11%; 50–59: 3%.

International Students: 347 undergraduate nonresident aliens enrolled fall 2004. Programs available to aid students whose native language is not English: social, cultural, financial. English as a Second Language Program.

Student Life: On-campus residence halls house 50% of full-time students. Two halls are coeducational, representing 55% of occupancy limits; two halls are for women only. *Intercollegiate athletics:* men only: basketball, soccer; women only: basketball, soccer. *Special regulations:* Cars permitted without restrictions. Quiet hours. *Student publications, radio: The Griffin*, an annual literary magazine; *Linden Leaves*, a yearbook; *The Linden World*, a biweekly newspaper. Radio station KCLC-FM broadcasts 126 hours per week. *Surrounding community:* St. Charles, population 37,500, is located in the metropolitan St. Louis area, 10 miles northwest of the international airport.

Library Collections: 171,000 volumes. 28,008 government documents; 26,100 microforms; 1,740 audiovisual materials; 598 current periodical subscriptions. Students have access to online information retrieval services and the Internet.

Most important special holdings include partial U.S. Government Documents depository.

Buildings and Grounds: Campus area 420 acres.

Chief Executive Officer: Dr. Dennis C. Spellmann, President.

Address admission inquiries to Director of Admissions.

Logan College of Chiropractic

1851 Schoettler Road
Chesterfield, Missouri 63006-1065

Tel: (636) 221-2100   **E-mail:** loganadm@logan.edu
Fax: (636) 207-2431   **Internet:** www.logan.edu

Institution Description: Logan College of Chiropractic is a private professional school. *Enrollment:* 1,045. *Degrees awarded:* Baccalaureate, first-professional.

Accreditation: *Regional:* NCA. *Professional:* chiropractic education

History: Established 1935.

Calendar: Semesters. Academic year Sept. to Apr.

Characteristics of Freshmen: 100% of applicants accepted. 56% of applicants accepted and enrolled.

Average secondary school rank of freshmen men 67.7 percentile, women 32.3 percentile, class 11th percentile.

98% of entering freshmen expected to graduate within 5 years. 19% of freshmen from Missouri. Freshmen from 25 states and 1 foreign country.

Admission: 90 semester hour of preprofessional liberal arts studies at an accredited college or university. *Entrance tests:* ACT.

Degree Requirements: Completion of prescribed curriculum.

Degrees Conferred: 195 *baccalaureate:* health professions and related sciences; 301 *first-professional:* chiropractic.

Fees and Other Expenses: *Full-time tuition per academic year 2005–06:* undergraduate $95 per credit hour; graduate $18,435.

Financial Aid: Aid from institutionally generated funds is provided on the basis of academic merit, financial need.

Financial aid to full-time, first-time undergraduate students: need-based scholarships/grants totaling $76,649; self-help $130,000; non-need-based self-help $30,000, parent loans $20,000. *Graduate aid:* 20 students received $51,221 in federal and state-funded fellowships/grants (ranging from $5,000 to $15,000); 800 received $33,921,735 in federal and state-funded loans (ranging from $8,000 to $39,000); 100 students held work-study jobs totaling $450,000.

Departments and Teaching Staff: *Professors* 5, *associate professors* 11, *assistant professors* 10, *instructors* 12, *part-time faculty:* 37.

Total instructional faculty: 75 (full-time 38, part-time 37; women 26, men 49; members of minority groups 3). Total faculty with doctorate, first-professional, or other terminal degree: 75.

Enrollment: Total enrollment 1,045. Undergraduate full-time 36 men / 30 women, part-time 15m / 15w; first-professional full-time 610m / 314w, part-time 14m / 11w.

Characteristics of Student Body: *Ethnic/racial makeup (undergraduate):* number of Black non-Hispanic: 5; American Indian or Alaska Native: 1; Asian or Pacific Islander: 4; Hispanic: 3; White non-Hispanic: 78. *Age distribution:* number 18–19: 3; 20–21: 19; 22–24: 36; 25–29: 27; 30–34: 6; 35–39: 3; 40–49: 2.

International Students: 67 nonresident aliens enrolled fall 2004. 2 students from Europe, 2 Asia, 7 Central and South America, 56 Canada. No programs available to aid students whose native language is not English. No financial aid specifically designated for international students.

Library Collections: 11,000 volumes. Online catalog. 225 periodical subscriptions. 1,972 recordings; 50 compact discs. 75 computer work stations. Students have access to online information retrieval services and the Internet. Total 2004–05 budget for books and materials: $85,000.

Most important special holdings include anatomical models; alternative/complementary medicine; chiropractic reference materials.

Buildings and Grounds: Campus area 103 acres. *New buildings:* William M. Harris Sports and Wellness Complex completed 2000.

Chief Executive Officer: Dr. George A. Goodman, President.

Address admission inquiries to Dean of Admissions; post graduate inquiries to Dean, Post Graduate Education.

Maryville University of Saint Louis

13550 Conway Road
St. Louis, Missouri 63141-7299

Tel: (314) 529-9300   **E-mail:** admissions@maryville.edu
Fax: (314) 542-9085   **Internet:** www.maryville.edu

Institution Description: Maryville University of Saint Louis is a private, independent, nonprofit college. *Enrollment:* 3,140. *Degrees awarded:* Baccalaureate, master's.

Accreditation: *Regional:* NCA. *Professional:* art, interior design, music, nursing, nursing education, occupational therapy, physical therapy, rehabilitation counseling, teacher education

History: Established by the Society of the Sacred Heart as Maryville Academy, an institution for women, chartered, and offered first instruction at postsecondary level 1872; became junior college 1919; became 4-year college 1923; awarded first degree (baccalaureate) 1925; became coeducational 1969; incorporated Mercy Junior College 1970; transferred to independent control 1972; adopted present name 1991.

Institutional Structure: *Governing board:* Board of Trustees. Representation: 33 trustees, including 6 alumni. All voting. *Composition of institution:* Administrators 5 men / 8 women. Academic affairs headed by vice president for academic and student affairs. Business/finances directed by vice president for administration and finance. Full-time instructional faculty 91. Academic governance body, Faculty Senate, meets an average of 5 times per year.

Calendar: Semesters. Academic year Aug. to May. Freshmen admitted Aug., Jan., May. Degrees conferred May. Formal commencement May. Summer sessions.

Characteristics of Freshmen: 1,230 applicants (273 men, 957 women). 73.2% of applicants admitted. 34.9% of admitted students enrolled full-time.

5% (24 students) submitted SAT scores; 97% (305 students) submitted ACT scores. *25th percentile:* SAT I Verbal 480, SAT I Math 500; ACT Composite 21, ACT English 20, ACT Math 19. *75th percentile:* SAT I Verbal 630, SAT I Math 640; ACT Composite 26, ACT English 27, ACT Math 26.

52% of entering freshmen expected to graduate within 5 years. 84% of freshmen from Missouri. Freshmen from 9 states and 2 foreign countries.

Admission: Rolling admissions plan. For fall acceptance, apply as early as end of junior year of secondary school. Early acceptance available. *Requirements:* Either graduation from accredited secondary school with minimum of 22 units or GED. Recommend 4 units English, 3 mathematics, 2 science, 2 social science plus 3 units from any of the areas. Minimum 2.5 GPA. *Entrance tests:* SAT or ACT composite. Admission requirements vary for certain programs. For foreign students TOEFL. *For transfer students:* 2.0 minimum GPA; from 4-year accredited institution maximum transfer credit limited only by residence requirement; from 2-year accredited institution 68 hours.

College credit and advanced placement for postsecondary-level work completed in secondary school. For extrainstitutional learning (life experience) on basis of DANTES; faculty assessment; advanced placement on basis of portfolio assessment. Tutoring available.

Degree Requirements: *For all baccalaureate degrees:* minimum of 128 semester hours. *For all degrees:* 2.0 GPA; last 30 hours in residence; distribution requirements.

Fulfillment of some degree requirements and exemption from some beginning courses possible by passing departmental examinations, College Board CLEP, AP, other standardized tests. *Grading system:* A–F; pass-fail; withdraw (pass-fail or, after deadline).

Distinctive Educational Programs: Day, evening, and weekend formats. Programs in actuarial science, business, accounting information systems, e-marketing, education, interior design, graphic design, liberal studies, occupational therapy, physical therapy. Cooperative education opportunities. Weekend College in 14 fields of study. Study abroad in a number of countries throughout the world. Honors programs, cross-registration with four other St. Louis area colleges; credit and noncredit continuing education courses; corporate education programs and seminars; courses for credit for qualified high school seniors.

ROTC: Army offered in cooperation with Washington University.

Degrees Conferred: 545 *baccalaureate;* 210 *master's.* Bachelor's degrees awarded in top five disciplines: business, management, marketing, and related support services 215; health professions and related clinical sciences 115; psychology 51; visual and performing arts 49; education 20.

Fees and Other Expenses: *Full-time tuition per academic year 2004–05:* $16,000. *Books and supplies:* $950. *Room and board per academic year:* $7,000.

Financial Aid: Aid from institutionally generated funds is provided on the basis of academic merit, financial need, other considerations. Institution has a Program Participation Agreement with the U.S. Department of Education for eligible students to receive Pell Grants and, depending upon the agreement, other federal aid.

Financial aid to full-time, first-time undergraduate students: 39% received federal grants averaging $3,338; 54% state/local grants averaging $1,771; 95% institutional grants averaging $7,056; 62% received loans averaging $4,751.

Departments and Teaching Staff: *Professors* 25, *associate professors* 18, *assistant professors* 42, *instructors* 113 *part-time faculty* 187.

Total instructional faculty: 158 FTE. Student-to-faculty ratio: 19:1. Degrees held by full-time faculty: baccalaureate 100%, master's 45%, doctorate 52%. 63% hold terminal degrees.

Enrollment: Total enrollment 3,140. Undergraduate 2,584 (men 24.1%, women 75.9%).

Characteristics of Student Body: *Ethnic/racial makeup:* number of Black non-Hispanic: 6.3%; American Indian or Alaska Native: .3%; Asian or Pacific Islander: .5%; Hispanic: 1.4%; White non-Hispanic: 75.6%; unknown: 13.5%. *Age distribution:* 17–21: 30%; 22–24: 13%; 25–29: 15%; 30–34: 12%; 35–39: 11%.; 40–49: 15%; 50–59: 4%.

International Students: 34 undergraduate nonresident aliens enrolled fall 2004. Students from Europe, Asia, Latin America, Africa, Canada, Middle East. Programs available to aid students whose native language is not English: social, cultural. English as a Second Language Program. No financial aid specifically designated for international students.

Student Life: Two on-campus air-conditioned residence halls accommodate 350. *Intercollegiate athletics:* men only: baseball; women only: softball, volleyball; both sexes: basketball, golf, soccer, cross-country, tennis. *Special regulations:* Cars permitted for all students. Visitation and quiet hours. Other regulations are listed in the Student Handbook and Residence Hall Handbook. *Special services:* Advising Learning Center, Health Center, Career Management Office (includes information on internships, cooperative education, and other opportunities), Campus Ministry. *Student publications:* A literary magazine published periodically; student newsletter published 4–5 issues per year. *Surrounding community:* St. Louis County. Airport 20 miles from campus.

Publications: Alumni magazine published 2 times per year.

Library Collections: 205,500 volumes including bound books, serial backfiles, electronic documents, and government documents not in separate collections. Online catalog. Current serial subscriptions: 9,000. 488,000 microforms; 10,000 audiovisual materials. Computer work stations available. Students have access to the Internet at no charge.

Most important special holdings include Father Edward Dowling Papers; Teaching Materials Center; Pepper Coil Curriculum Collection; Music Therapy Collection; art books.

Buildings and Grounds: Campus area 130 acres.

Chief Executive Officer: Dr. Keith Lovin, President.

Address undergraduate admission inquiries to Lynn Jackson, Director of Admissions.

Midwestern Baptist Theological Seminary

5001 North Oak Street
Kansas City, Missouri 64118-4697

Tel: (816) 414-3700   **E-mail:** admissions@mbts.edu
Fax: (816) 414-3799   **Internet:** www.mbts.edu

Institution Description: Midwestern Baptist Theological Seminary is a private institution affiliated with the Southern Baptist Convention. *Enrollment:* 586. *Degrees awarded:* First-professional (master of divinity), master's, doctorate. Diplomas also awarded.

Accreditation: *Regional:* NCA. *National:* ATS. *Professional:* theology

History: Chartered 1957; offered first instruction at postsecondary level 1958; awarded first degree 1961.

Institutional Structure: *Governing board:* Board of Trustees. Representation: 35 trustees. *Composition of institution:* Administrators 5 men. Academic affairs headed by academic dean. Full-time instructional faculty 14.

Calendar: Semesters. Academic year late Aug. to mid-July.

Admission: *Requirements:* Graduation from accredited college or university.

Degree Requirements: *For first-professional degree:* 89 credit hours; 2.0 GPA; last 20 hours in residence; prescribed curriculum. *Grading system:* A-F; withdraw.

Distinctive Educational Programs: Work-experience programs.

Degrees Conferred: 5 *master's:* religious education; 36 *first-professional:* master of divinity; 13 *doctorate:* theology.

Fees and Other Expenses: *Tuition per academic year:* varies depending upon program. *Room per academic year:* $1,648.

Financial Aid: Aid from institutionally generated funds is provided on the basis of academic merit, financial need. Institution has a Program Participation Agreement with the U.S. Department of Education for eligible students to receive Pell Grants and other federal aid.

Departments and Teaching Staff: *Total instructional faculty:* 32 (full-time 14, part-time 18). Degrees held by full-time faculty: doctorate 84%, master's 100%, professional 8%. 84% hold terminal degrees.

Enrollment: Total enrollment 542 (full-time 163, part-time 379).

Characteristics of Student Body: *Ethnic/racial makeup:* Black non-Hispanic 4%, American Indian or Native Alaskan .7%, Asian or Pacific Islander .7%, Hispanic .7%, White non-Hispanic 91.9%, unknown .7%. *Age distribution:* 22–24: 7%; 25–29: 20%; 30–34: 16%; 35–39: 22%; 40–49: 28%; 50–59: 6%; 60–up: 1%.

International Students: 6 nonresident aliens enrolled. No programs available to aid students whose native language is not English. No financial aid specifically designated for international students.

Student Life: On-campus residence halls for single students. Housing available for married students. *Surrounding community:* Kansas City metropolitan area population 1.6 million. Served by mass transit bus system, airport, and rail service.

Library Collections: 94,464 volumes. 943 microforms; 3,218 audiovisual materials; 371 current periodical subscriptions. 13 computer work stations. Students have access to online information retrieval services and the Internet. Total 2004–05 budget for books and materials: $68,751.

Buildings and Grounds: Campus area 205 acres.

Chief Executive Officer: Dr. Philip Roberts, President.

Address admissions inquiries to Jensen Peterson, Director of Student Enlistment.

Missouri Baptist University

One College Park Drive
St. Louis, Missouri 63141-8698
Tel: (314) 434-1115   **E-mail:** admissions@mobap.edu
Fax: (314) 434-7596   **Internet:** www.mobap.edu

Institution Description: Missouri Baptist University is a private institution affiliated with the Missouri Baptist Convention (Southern Baptist). *Enrollment:* 1,645. *Degrees awarded:* Associate, baccalaureate.

Accreditation: *Regional:* NCA.

History: Established as extension center of Hannibal-LaGrange College and offered first instruction at postsecondary level 1957; chartered as Missouri Baptist College of St. Louis, a 2-year institution, 1963; merged with Hannibal-LaGrange College and adopted name of Missouri Baptist College 1967; awarded first degree (associate) 1970; became 4-year institution 1972; became separate institution 1973; achieved university status 2002.

Institutional Structure: *Governing board:* Board of Trustees of Missouri Baptist University. Representation: 25 trustees. All voting. *Composition of institution:* Academic affairs headed by academic dean. Management/business/finances directed by business manager. Full-time instructional faculty 39. Academic governance body, the faculty, meets an average of 10 times per year.

Calendar: Semesters. Academic year Aug. to Apr. Freshmen admitted Aug., Jan., June, July. Degrees conferred and formal commencement May. Summer session of 2 terms from May to Aug.

Characteristics of Freshmen: 391 applicants. 61.1% of applicants admitted. 89.5% of admitted students enrolled full-time.

8% (17 students) submitted SAT scores; 65% (145 students) submitted ACT scores. *25th percentile:* SAT I Verbal 390, SAT I Math 420; ACT Composite 18, ACT English 16, ACT Math 16. *75th percentile:* SAT I Verbal 550, SAT I Math 550; ACT Composite 24, ACT English 24. ACT Math 23.

38% of entering freshmen expected to graduate within 5 years. 54% of freshmen from Missouri. Freshmen from 6 states and 6 foreign countries.

Admission: Rolling admissions plan. For fall acceptance, apply as early as Nov. of previous year but not later than Aug. of year of enrollment. Early acceptance available. *Requirements:* Either graduation from accredited secondary school with 22 units: 4 units English, 2 social science, 3 mathematics, 2 science, 1 fine arts, 3 academic electives; or GED. Minimum ACT of 18. *Entrance tests:* ACT composite. For foreign students TOEFL. *For transfer students:* 2.0 minimum GPA; from 4-year accredited institution 104 hours maximum transfer credit; from 2-year accredited institution 64 hours; correspondence/extension students 30 hours.

College credit and advanced placement for postsecondary-level work completed in secondary school. Developmental courses offered in summer session and regular academic year; credit given.

Degree Requirements: *For all associate degrees:* 68 credit hours. *For all baccalaureate degrees:* 128 credit hours; GRE; exit competency examination in writing. *For all undergraduate degrees:* 2.0 GPA; 24 of last 30 hours in residence; chapel attendance 5 times per month; 2 units physical activity; general education requirements.

Fulfillment of some degree requirements and exemption from some beginning courses possible by passing College Board CLEP, APP. *Grading system:* A–F; withdraw (carries time limit).

Distinctive Educational Programs: Internships. Evening classes. Accelerated degree programs. Special facilities for using telecommunications in the classroom. Interdepartmental programs in biblical history. Facilities and programs for independent research, including honors programs, individual majors, independent study. Study abroad in Brazil, England, France, Hong Kong, Scotland, Sweden. *Other distinctive programs:* Program in Bible and Christian training for area churches.

Degrees Conferred: 2 *associate*; 201 *baccalaureate*; 136 *master's*. Bachelor's degrees awarded in top five disciplines: education 62; business, management, marketing, and related support services 43; communication, journalism, and related programs 22; psychology 14; parks and recreation 10.

Fees and Other Expenses: *Full-time tuition per academic year 2004–05:* $13,030. *Books and supplies:* $1,825. *Room and board per academic year:* $5,800.

Financial Aid: Aid from institutionally generated funds is provided on the basis of academic merit, financial need, athletic ability, other criteria. Institution has a Program Participation Agreement with the U.S. Department of Education for eligible students to receive Pell Grants and, depending upon the agreement, other federal aid.

Financial aid to full-time, first-time undergraduate students: 27% received federal grants averaging $2,694; 20% state/local grants averaging $1,848; 82% institutional grants averaging $6,558; 49% received loans averaging $5,758.

Departments and Teaching Staff: *Professors* 5, *associate professors* 7, *assistant professors* 16, *instructors* 11, *part-time faculty* 64.

Total instructional faculty: 60 FTE. Student-to-faculty ratio: 151. Degrees held by full-time faculty: doctorate 53%, master's 100%. 53% hold terminal degrees.

Enrollment: Total enrollment 4,058. Undergraduate 3,336 (men 40.1%, women 59.9%).

Characteristics of Student Body: *Ethnic/racial makeup (undergraduate):* number of Black non-Hispanic: 6%; American Indian or Alaska Native: .2% Asian or Pacific Islander: 1.1%; Hispanic: .8%; White non-Hispanic: 78%; unknown: 11.8%. *Age distribution:* 17–21: 77%; 22–24: 7%; 25–29: 4%; 30–34: 3%; 35–39: 3%; 40–49: 4%; 50–59: 1%; 60–up: 1%.

International Students: 73 undergraduate nonresident aliens enrolled fall 2004. Programs available to aid students whose native language is not English: English as a Second Language Program. No financial aid specifically designated for international students.

Student Life: On-campus residence halls house 20% of student body. Residence halls for men constitute 38% of such space, for women 62%. *Intercollegiate athletics:* men only: baseball, basketball, golf, soccer; women only basketball, soccer, softball, volleyball. *Special regulations:* Cars permitted without restrictions. Curfews. *Student publications: Images,* a yearbook; *Courier,* published biannually; *Cantos,* a literary publication. *Surrounding community:* St. Louis population 500,000. Served by airport and passenger rail service, each 12 miles from campus.

Library Collections: 104,000 volumes. 52,200 microforms; 450 current periodicals. 460 recordings; 174 compact discs. Computer work stations available. Students have access to online information retrieval services and the Internet.

Buildings and Grounds: Campus area 65 acres.

Chief Executive Officer: Dr. R. Alton Lacey, President.

Address admission inquiries to Jon Hessel, Director of Admissions.

Missouri Southern State University

3950 East Newman Road
Joplin, Missouri 64801-1595
Tel: (417) 625-9300   **E-mail:** admissions@mssc.edu
Fax: (417) 659-4429   **Internet:** www.mssc.edu

Institution Description: Missouri Southern State University is a public institution. *Enrollment:* 5,256. *Degrees awarded:* Associate, baccalaureate, master's.

Academic offerings subject to approval by statewide coordinating bodies. Budget subject to by state governing boards.

Accreditation: *Regional:* NCA. *Professional:* business, dental hygiene, engineering technology, environmental health, nursing, radiography, respiratory therapy, teacher education

History: Established as Joplin Junior College, chartered, and offered first instruction at postsecondary level 1937; awarded first degree (associate) 1938; changed name to Jasper County Junior College 1964; chartered under present name 1965; began upper division curriculum 1967; became Missouri Southern State University 2003.

Institutional Structure: *Governing board:* Board of Missouri Southern State College. Representation: 7 Board of Governors members. All voting. *Composition of institution:* Administrators 35 men / 24 women. Academic affairs headed by vice president for academic affairs. Management/business/finances directed by vice president for business affairs. Full-time instructional faculty 204. Academic governance body, Faculty Senate, meets an average of 16 times per year.

Calendar: Semesters. Academic year Aug. to July. Freshmen admitted Aug., Jan., May. Degrees conferred and formal commencement May, Dec.

Characteristics of Freshmen: 99% of applicants admitted. 35% of applicants admitted and enrolled.

82% (639 students) submitted ACT scores. *25th percentile*: ACT Composite 19, ACT English 18, ACT Math 17. *75th percentile*: ACT Composite 25, ACT English 25, ACT Math 24.

27% of entering freshmen expected to graduate within 5 years. 83% of freshmen from Missouri. Freshmen from 10 states.

Admission: Students with a composite score of 21 or above and rank in the upper one-half of high school graduating class or a 3.5 GPA shall be granted regular admission. Recommend 4 units English, 3 mathematics, 3 sciences, 2 social sciences, 1 fine arts, 3 additional units selected from foreign languages, mathematics, physical or biological science, or social science. *For transfer students:* 2.0 minimum GPA; from 4-year accredited institution maximum transfer credit limited only by residence requirement; from 2-year accredited institution 64 semester hours; correspondence/extension students 12 hours.

College credit and advanced placement for postsecondary-level work completed in secondary school. Remedial courses offered in summer session and regular academic year; credit given.

Degree Requirements: *For all associate degrees:* 64 semester hours; 15 hours in residence. *For all baccalaureate degrees:* 124 semester hours; 30 hours in residence. *For all degrees:* 2.0 GPA; general education and core requirements. *Grading system:* A–F; withdraw (deadline after which pass-fail is appended to withdraw).

Distinctive Educational Programs: Evening classes. Cooperative baccalaureate program in medical technology with affiliated schools. Cooperative associate program in radiologic technology with St. John's Medical Center. Individual majors. *Other distinctive programs:* Continuing education. Emphasis on international mission offers great study abroad opportunities in more than 100 countries. Weekend college. Online degree programs offered in General Studies, Business and Law Enforcement.

Degrees Conferred: 160 *associate;* 734 *baccalaureate:* biological/life sciences 27; business/marketing 148; communications/communication technologies 46; computer and information sciences 32; education 149; engineering and engineering technologies 2; English 23; foreign languages and literature 15; health professions and related sciences 40; mathematics 7; parks and recreation 10; physical sciences 4; protective services/public administration 65; psychology 29; social sciences and history 46; visual and performing arts 21.

Fees and Other Expenses: *Tuition per academic year 2004–05:* resident $3,810, nonresident $7,620. *Required fees:* $166. *Room and board per academic year:* $4,700.

Financial Aid: Aid from institutionally generated funds is provided on the basis of academic merit, financial need, athletic ability, other criteria.

Financial aid to full-time, first-time undergraduate students: need-based scholarships/grants totaling $6,121,899, self-help $8,024,761; non-need-based scholarships/grants totaling $2,164,797, self-help $7,352,272, parent loans $196,411, tuition waivers $248,800, athletic awards $953,045.

Departments and Teaching Staff: *Professors* 61, *associate professors* 59 *assistant professors* 57, *instructors* 23, *part-time faculty* 84.

Total instructional faculty: 284 (full-time 200, part-time 84; women 115, men 169; members of minority groups 16). Total faculty with doctorate, first-professional, or other terminal degree: 138. Student-to-faculty ratio: 18:1. Degrees held by full-time faculty: baccalaureate 1%, master's 36%, doctorate 59%, professional 1%. 62% hold terminal degrees.

Enrollment: Total enrollment 5,256. Undergraduate full-time 1,525 men / 2,096 women, part-time 560m / 1,075w. *Transfer students:* in-state 194; from 179.

Characteristics of Student Body: *Ethnic/racial makeup:* number of Black non-Hispanic: 125; American Indian or Alaska Native: 125; Asian or Pacific Islander: 61; Hispanic: 101; White non-Hispanic: 4,707. *Age distribution:* number under 18: 108; 18–19: 913; 20–21: 1,047; 22–24: 1,123; 25–29: 739; 30–34: 457; 35–39: 330; 40–49: 370; 50–64: 150; 65 and over: 15. 335 of student body attend summer sessions.

International Students: 144 nonresident aliens enrolled fall 2004. 21 students from Europe, 14 Asia, 79 Central and South America, 27 Africa, 1 Canada,

2 other. Programs available to aid students whose native language is not English: English as a Second Language Program. No financial aid specifically designated for international students.

Student Life: On-campus residence halls house 10% of student body. Residence halls for men only constitute 28% of such space, for women only 15%; for both sexes 57%. *Intercollegiate athletics:* men only: baseball, basketball, cross-country, football, golf, soccer, track and field; women only: basketball, cross-country, soccer, softball, tennis, track and field, volleyball. *Special regulations:* Cars permitted without restrictions. Residence hall visitation 6pm to 11pm. *Special services:* Learning Resources Center, health services, public safety, disability services, project stay, student activites, campus wellness and recreation program, career services, new student programs. *Student publications: The Chart*, a weekly newspaper; *Crossroads, The Magazine. Surrounding community:* Joplin metropolitan area population 149,500. Tulsa (OK), 110 miles from campus. Served by airport 6 miles from campus.

Library Collections: 235,497 volumes including bound books, serial backfiles, electronic documents, and government documents not in separate collections. Online catalog. Current serial subscriptions: 560 paper; 751,274 microform; 26 electronic. 4,713 recordings; 348 computer discs; 1,215 CD-ROMs. 55 computer work stations. Students have access to the Internet at no charge.

Most important special holdings include Gene Taylor Papers; Tri-State Mineral Maps; Arell Gibson Papers.

Buildings and Grounds: Campus area 365 acres.

Chief Executive Officer: Dr. Julio Leon, President.

Address admission inquiries to Derek Skaggs, Director of Enrollment Services.

Missouri Valley College

500 East College Street
Marshall, Missouri 65340

Tel: (660) 831-4000   **E-mail:** admissions@moval.edu
Fax: (660) 831-4039   **Internet:** www.moval.edu

Institution Description: Missouri Valley College is a private college affiliated with the Presbyterian Church (U.S.A.). *Enrollment:* 1,645. *Degrees awarded:* Associate, baccalaureate.

Member of the consortium Kansas City Regional Council for Higher Education.

Accreditation: *Regional:* NCA.

History: Established 1888; chartered and offered first instruction at postsecondary level 1889; awarded first degree (baccalaureate) 1890.

Institutional Structure: *Governing board:* Board of Trustees. Representation: 42 trustees. All voting. *Composition of institution:* Administrators 6 men / 3 women. Academic affairs headed by academic dean. Management/business/finances directed by business manager. Full-time instructional faculty 54. Academic governance body, the faculty, meets an average of 8 times per year.

Calendar: Semesters. Academic year early Aug. to May. Freshmen admitted Aug., Jan, spring, summer. Degrees conferred May, Aug., Dec. Formal commencement May. Summer session of 2 terms from May to July.

Characteristics of Freshmen: 1,478 applicants (1,008 men, 470 women).

21% (80 students) submitted SAT scores; 70% (262 students) submitted ACT scores. *25th percentile*: SAT I Verbal 372, SAT I Math 435; ACT Composite 18, ACT English 16, ACT Math 17. *75th percentile*: SAT I Verbal 650, SAT I Math 663; ACT Composite 32, ACT English 30, ACT Math 30.

20% of entering freshmen expected to graduate within 5 years. 65% of freshmen from Missouri. Freshmen from 33 states and 10 foreign countries.

Admission: Rolling admissions plan. For fall acceptance, apply as early as end of junior year in secondary school, but not later than day of registration. Early acceptance available. *Requirements:* Either graduation from secondary school or GED. Recommend college preparatory program, including 4 years in English, 2 foreign language, 2 history, 2 mathematics, 2 science, 2 social studies. Minimum 2.0 GPA. Lowest acceptable secondary school class standing 33rd percentile. *Entrance tests:* College Board SAT or ACT composite. *For transfer students:* 2.0 GPA.

College credit and advanced placement for postsecondary-level work completed in secondary school. College credit for extrainstitutional learning on basis of ACE *2006 Guide to the Evaluation of Educational Experiences in the Armed Services.*

Developmental/remedial courses offered during regular academic year; credit given.

Degree Requirements: *For all associate degrees:* 64 credit hours. *For all baccalaureate degrees:* 128 credit hours. *For all undergraduate degrees:* 2.0 GPA; last 2 terms in residence; core curriculum.

Fulfillment of some degree requirements and exemption from some beginning courses possible by passing College Board CLEP. *Grading system:* A–F; pass-fail; withdraw (carries time limit).

Distinctive Educational Programs: Work-experience programs, including field experience, internships. Evening classes. Interdepartmental major in science. Facilities and programs for independent research, including honor programs, individual majors, tutorials.

Degrees Conferred: 3 *associate;* 203 *baccalaureate.* Bachelor's degrees awarded in top five disciplines: business, management, marketing, and related support services 63; education 32; protective and security services 24; parks and recreation 16; biomedical/biosciences 14.

Fees and Other Expenses: *Full-time tuition per academic year 2004–05:* $13,400. *Books and supplies:* $1,500. *Room and board per academic year:* $10,250.

Financial Aid: Aid from institutionally generated funds is provided on the basis of financial need. Institution has a Program Participation Agreement with the U.S. Department of Education for eligible students to receive Pell Grants and, depending upon the agreement, other federal aid.

Financial aid to full-time, first-time undergraduate students: 47% received federal grants averaging $3,040; 30% state/local grants averaging $1,437; 100% institutional grants averaging $9,222; 79% received loans averaging $3,078.

Departments and Teaching Staff: *Professors* 12, *associate professors* 16, *assistant professors* 20, *instructors* 6, *part-time faculty* 2.

Total instructional faculty: 56. Student-to-faculty ratio: 24:1. Degrees held by full-time faculty: master's 59%, doctorate 41%. 41% hold terminal degrees.

Enrollment: Total enrollment 1,645 (men 53.7%, women 43.3%).

Characteristics of Student Body: *Ethnic/racial makeup:* number of Black non-Hispanic: 11.7%; American Indian or Alaska Native: .4%; Asian or Pacific Islander: 4.1%; Hispanic: 3.7%; White non-Hispanic: 71.4%. *Age distribution:* 17–21: 79%; 22–24: 35%; 25–29: 3%; 30–34: 1%; 35–39: 1%; 40–49: 1%; 50–59: 1%; 60–up: .5%.

International Students: 145 nonresident aliens enrolled fall 2004. Programs available to aid students whose native language is not English: English as a Second Language Program. No financial aid specifically designated for international students.

Student Life: On-campus residence halls house 70% of student body. Residence halls for men only constitute 64% of such space, for women only 36%. 30% of men join and live in college-owned fraternities. *Intercollegiate athletics:* men: baseball, basketball, football, wrestling; women: basketball, softball, volleyball; men and women: cheerleading, cross-country, golf, rodeo, soccer, track. both sexes: tennis. *Special regulations:* Cars permitted without restrictions. Quiet hours. *Special services:* Learning Resources Center, medical services. *Student publications, radio:* Monthly newspaper; yearbook. Radio Station KNOS-FM. Cable television station broadcasts 10 hours per week. *Surrounding community:* Marshall population 13,000. Kansas City, 80 miles from campus, is nearest metropolitan area.

Library Collections: 71,000 volumes. 430 current periodical subscriptions. 1,700 microforms; 11,000 audiovisual materials. Computer work stations available. Students have access to online information retrieval services and the Internet.

Most important special holdings include art collection; children's collection; fiction section.

Buildings and Grounds: Campus area 140 acres.

Chief Executive Officer: Dr. Chadwick B. Freeman, President.

Address admission inquiries to Jamie Gold-Naylor, Director of Admissions.

Missouri Western State College

4525 Downs Drive
St. Joseph, Missouri 64507-2294
Tel: (816) 271-4200   **E-mail:** admissn@.mwsc.edu
Fax: (816) 271-4525   **Internet:** www.mwsc.edu

Institution Description: Missouri Western State College is a state institution. *Enrollment:* 5,065. *Degrees awarded:* Associate, baccalaureate. Certificates also awarded.

Academic offerings subject to approval by statewide coordinating bodies. Budget subject to approval by state governing boards.

Accreditation: *Regional:* NCA. *Professional:* engineering technology, health information technician, music, nursing, nursing education, physical therapy, social work, teacher education

History: Established 1915 as St. Joseph Junior College; transformed into a 4-year college 1969; became full member of the state of Missouri system 1977.

Institutional Structure: *Governing board:* Board of Regents for Missouri Western State College. Extrainstitutional representation: 6 regents. All voting.

Composition of institution: Administrators 17 men / 8 women. Academic and student affairs headed by vice president of academics. Management/business/finances directed by vice president of business affairs. Full-time instructional faculty 178. Academic governance body, Faculty Senate, meets an average of 12 times per year.

Calendar: Semesters. Academic year Aug. to May. Freshmen admitted Aug., Jan., June. Degrees conferred Dec., May, July. Formal commencement May. Summer session early June to late July.

Characteristics of Freshmen: 100% of applicants admitted.

98% (1,003 students) submitted ACT scores. *25th percentile:* ACT Composite 16, ACT English 15, ACT Math 15. *75th percentile:* ACT Composite 22, ACT English 22, ACT Math 20.

32% of entering freshmen expected to graduate within 5 years. 93% of freshmen from Missouri. Freshmen students from 17 states.

Admission: Rolling admissions plan. Early acceptance available. *Requirements:* Either graduation from accredited secondary school with 3 units social sciences, 4 English, 3 mathematics (algebra I, II, and geometry); 2 science (at least 1 with lab), 1 visual/performing arts, 3 electives (recommend 2 in foreign language); or GED. *Entrance tests:* ACT composite. For foreign students minimum TOEFL score 500. *For transfer students:* From 4-year accredited institution 94 hours maximum transfer credit; from 2-year accredited institution 64 hours; for correspondence/extension students 30 hours.

College credit for postsecondary-level work completed in secondary school. College credit for extrainstitutional learning on basis of ACE *2006 Guide to the Evaluation of Educational Experiences in the Armed Services.* Tutoring available. Developmental courses offered in summer session and regular academic year; credit given.

Degree Requirements: *For all associate degrees:* 62 credit hours; last 15 credits in residence; 3 credits physical education. *For all baccalaureate degrees:* 124 hours; 30 credits of the last 45 in residence; 4 credits physical education; exit competency examinations—Graduate Record Examination, or appropriate substitute selected by department. *For all undergraduate degrees:* 2.0 GPA.

Fulfillment of some degree requirements and exemption from some beginning courses possible by passing College Board CLEP and departmental examinations. *Grading system:* A–F; pass-fail, withdraw (carries time limit).

Distinctive Educational Programs: Evening/weekend classes. Dual-degree program in law in cooperation with University of Missouri at Kansas City. Dual credit enrollment for high school students; distance learning classes. Honors programs available in most majors. Individually arranged independent study for seniors. Bachelor of Interdisciplinary Studies.

ROTC: Army. 2 commissions awarded 2004.

Degrees Conferred: 82 *associate;* 672 *baccalaureate:* biological/life sciences 32; business/marketing 140; computer and information sciences 25; education 66; engineering 18; English 52; foreign languages 11; health professions 70; interdisciplinary studies 12, mathematics 8; parks and recreation 56; physical sciences 11; protective services/public administration 88; psychology 29; social sciences and and history 37; visual and performing arts 17.

Fees and Other Expenses: *Full-time tuition per academic year 2004–05:* undergraduate resident $4,380, out-of-state resident $8,010. *Room per academic year:* $2,544. *Board per academic year:* $1,852. *Required fees:* $396.

Financial Aid: Aid from institutionally generated funds is provided on the basis of academic merit, financial need, athletic ability, other criteria. Institution has a Program Participation Agreement with the U.S. Department of Education for eligible students to receive Pell Grants and, depending upon the agreement, other federal aid.

Departments and Teaching Staff: *Professors* 35, *associate professors* 57, *assistant professors* 63, *instructors* 25, *part-time faculty* 143.

Total instructional faculty: 323 (full-time 180, part-time 143; women 155, men 168; members of minority groups 8). Total faculty with doctorate, first-professional, or other terminal degree: 133. Student-to-faculty ratio: 17:1. degrees held by full-time faculty: 71% hold terminal degrees. *Faculty development:* 2 faculty members awarded sabbaticals 2004–05.

Enrollment: Total enrollment 5,065. Undergraduate full-time 1,546 men / 2,213 women, part-time 487m / 819w. *Transfer students:* 286.

Characteristics of Student Body: *Ethnic/racial makeup:* number of Black non-Hispanic: 540; American Indian or Alaska Native: 41; Asian or Pacific Islander: 37; Hispanic: 109; White non-Hispanic: 4,327. *Age distribution:* number under 18: 273; 18–19: 1,482; 20–21: 1,370; 22–24: 829; 25–29: 394; 30–34: 239; 35–39: 150; 40–49: 243; 50–64: 75; 65 and over: 10.

International Students: 11 nonresident aliens enrolled fall 2004. No programs available to aid students whose native language is not English. No financial aid specifically designated for international students.

Student Life: On-campus residence halls house 20% of student body. Residence halls for men constitute 50% of such space, for women 50%. 6% of men join and 1% live in fraternities. On-campus apartment-style dormitory for upperclass students. *Intercollegiate athletics:* men only: baseball, basketball, football, golf, tennis; women only: basketball, golf, soccer, softball, tennis, volleyball. *Special regulations:* Cars permitted without restrictions. *Special services:* Learning Resources Center, medical services, shuttle bus to student apartments. *Student publications: Griffon News*, a weekly newspaper; *Griffon Yearbook; Icarus*, annual literary publication. *Surrounding community:* St. Joseph population 77.000. Kansas City, 50 miles from campus, is nearest metropolitan area.

Library Collections: 460,000 volumes. 105,887 microforms; 13,075 audio-visual materials; 1,182 current periodical subscriptions. 20 computer work stations. Online catalog. Students have access to online information retrieval services and the Internet.

Buildings and Grounds: Campus area 744 acres. *New buildings:* Fulkerson Conference Center completed 2005.

Chief Executive Officer: Dr. James Scanlon, President.

Address admission inquiries to Howard McCauley, Director of Admissions.

Nazarene Theological Seminary

1700 East Meyer Boulevard
Kansas City, Missouri 64131-1246

Tel: (816) 333-6254   **E-mail:** enroll@nts.edu
Fax: (816) 333-6271   **Internet:** www.nts.edu

Institution Description: Nazarene Theological Seminary is a graduate school of theology affiliated with the Church of the Nazarene. *Enrollment:* 396. *Degrees awarded:* master's, first-professional, doctorate.

Accreditation: *National:* ATS. *Professional:* theology

History: Established 1945.

Institutional Structure: *Governing board:* Board of Trustees.

Calendar: Semesters. Academic year Aug. to May. Summer term.

Admission: *Requirements:* Baccalaureate degree from accredited institution or equivalent; minimum 2.5 GPA; references.

Degree Requirements: *Master of Divinity:* 75 hours of prescribed courses and 15 hours of electives. *Master Arts in Missiology:* 45 hours of prescribed courses and 3 hours of electives. *Master of Arts (Theological Studies)* includes two tracks: (a) general academic- 27 hours of prescribed courses and 24 hours of electives, and (b) research. The research track includes two majors: (1) biblical studies - 36 hours of prescribed courses and 12 hours of electives, and (b) Christian though and history - 33 hours of prescribed courses and 15 hours of electives. *Doctor of Ministry:* 4 residential seminars offered consecutively each January and Jane, culminating with a Pastoral Research Project and Symposium.

Degrees Conferred: 46 *first-professional:* master of divinity; 8 *doctorate* theology.

Fees and Other Expenses: *Full-time tuition per academic year 2004–05:* $310 per credit hour.

Financial Aid: Aid from institutionally generated funds is provided on the basis of academic merit, financial need. *Graduate aid:* 127 students received $872,426 in federal and state-funded loans (ranging from $2,000 to $18,500).

Departments and Teaching Staff: Theology *professors* 15, *associate professors* 1, *assistant professors* 2, *part-time faculty* 14.

Total instructional faculty: 32 (full-time 18, part-time 14; women 4, men 28; member of minority group 1). Total faculty with doctorate, first-professional, or other terminal degree: 89%. Student-to-faculty ratio: 14:1.

Enrollment: Total enrollment 396. First-professional full-time 125 men / 19 women, part-time 55m / 22w; graduate full-time 33m / 26w, part-time 58m / 38w.

International Students: 10 nonresident aliens enrolled fall 2004. 1 student from Europe, 3 Asia, 29 Central and South America, 3 Africa, 6 Canada, 4 other. No programs available to aid students whose native language is not English. No financial aid specifically designated for international students.

Student Life: All general offices of the Church of the Nazarene are located in Kansas City, population over 1 million.

Library Collections: 119,954 volumes including bound books, serial backfiles, electronic documents, and government documents not in separate collections. Online catalog. Current serial subscriptions: 542. 10 computer work stations. Students have access to the Internet at no charge.

Most important special collections include history of the Church of the Nazarene; Wesleyan-Methodism; Arminanism.

Chief Executive Officer: Dr. Don Benefiel, President.

Address admission inquiries to Cindy R. Wright, Director of Admissions.

Northwest Missouri State University

800 University Drive
Maryville, Missouri 64468-6001

Tel: (816) 562-1212   **E-mail:** admissions@nwmissouri.edu
Fax: (816) 562-1900   **Internet:** www.nwmissouri.edu

Institution Description: Northwest Missouri State University is a state institution. *Enrollment:* 6,230. *Degrees awarded:* Baccalaureate, master's. Education specialist certificates also awarded.

Accreditation: *Regional:* NCA. *Professional:* business, chemistry, family and consumer science, music, teacher education

History: Established and chartered as Fifth Normal School District and offered first instruction at postsecondary level 1905; awarded first degree (baccalaureate) 1917; changed name to Northwest Missouri State Teachers College 1919, to Northwest Missouri State College 1949; adopted present name and added graduate program 1972. *See* Mattie Dykes, *Behind the Birches: A History of Northwest Missouri State College* (Maryville: Rush Printing, 1955) and Virgil and Delores Albertini, *The Towers in the Northwest: A History of Northwest Missouri State University, 1956–1980* (Maryville: Rush Printing, 1980) for further information.

Institutional Structure: *Governing board:* Board of Regents of Northwest Missouri State University. Extrainstitutional representation: 6 regents (all voting), 1 student regent (non-voting), commissioner of elementary and secondary education (voting in case of tie). 1 ex officio. *Composition of institution:* Intra-university committees (president's cabinet composed of vice president for academic affairs, dean of students, vice president and director of Center for Applied Research, vice president for finance, public relations officer, director of development/alumni and executive assistant to the president). Other committees: Faculty Senate, Graduate Council, Student Senate, Council on Teacher Education, Vice President's Advisory Council, Administrative Council.

Calendar: Semesters. Academic year mid-Aug. to mid-May. Freshmen admitted Aug., Jan., June, July. Degrees conferred May, Dec., Aug. Formal commencement May, Aug. Summer session of 2 terms from early June to early Aug.

Characteristics of Freshmen: 2,780 applicants (1,234 men, 1,546 women). 87.2% of applicants admitted. 49.6% of admitted students enrolled full-time.

3% (44 students) submitted SAT scores; 96% (1,214 students) submitted ACT scores. *25th percentile:* SAT I Verbal 477, SAT I Math 480; ACT Composite 19, ACT English 19, ACT Math 18. *75th percentile:* SAT I Verbal 572, SAT I Math 627; ACT Composite 24, ACT English 25, ACT Math 24.

45% of entering freshmen expected to graduate within 5 years. 58% of freshmen from Missouri. Freshmen from 22 states and 20 foreign countries.

Admission: Rolling admissions plan. For fall acceptance, apply as early as Sept. 1 of previous year. *Requirements:* Either graduation from accredited secondary school or GED. Lowest recommended secondary school class standing 34th percentile for in-state residents, 50th percentile for out-of-state students. *Entrance tests:* ACT composite recommended (minimum score 20 for in-state residents, 21 for out-of-state students). For foreign students TOEFL (minimum score 500 for undergraduates, 550 for graduates). *For transfer students:* 2.0 minimum GPA; from 4-year accredited institution 64 hours maximum transfer credit.

College credit and advanced placement for postsecondary-level work completed in secondary school. College credit for USAFI, for one year military service, and for military training on basis of ACE *2006 Guide to the Evaluation of Educational Experiences in the Armed Services.*

Tutoring available. Developmental courses offered during regular academic year; credit given.

Degree Requirements: 124 credit hours; 2.0–2.5 GPA; general education requirements: 9 hours English/speech, 3–4 hours mathematics, 8 lab science, 12 social and cultural studies, 3 behavioral science, 9 humanities, 3 computer literacy, 4 physical education, 1 freshman seminary plus specific degree requirements, advanced standing requirements; exit competency examinations; comprehensives in some individual fields of study.

Fulfillment of some degree requirements and exemption from some beginning courses possible by passing departmental examinations. *Grading system:* A–F; pass-fail; withdraw; no credit.

Distinctive Educational Programs: Internships on- and off-campus. Off-campus graduate center at St. Joseph, 40 miles south of the University. Weekend and evening classes. Accelerated degree programs. Dual-degree programs in engineering with University of Missouri-Columbia and University of Missouri-Rolla. Interdepartmental programs in agribusiness, art, computer science, international marketing, journalism-business, music. ESL Program. Preprofessional programs in architecture, dentistry, engineering, nursing, physical therapy, pharmacy, optometry. Institutionally sponsored study abroad. Cross-registration with Conception Seminary College for juniors and seniors.

ROTC: Army.

Degrees Conferred: 37 *associate*; 1,039 *baccalaureate*; 172 *master's*. Bachelor's degrees awarded in top five disciplines: business, management, marketing, and related support services 241; education 236; communication, journalism, and related programs 117; psychology 83; agriculture 67.

Fees and Other Expenses: *Full-time tuition per academic year 2004–05:* undergraduate resident $5,325, nonresident $9,180. Contact the university for current graduate tuition/fees. *Books and supplies:* $450. *Room and board per academic year:* $6,080.

Financial Aid: Aid from institutionally generated funds is provided on the basis of academic merit, athletic ability. Institution has a Program Participation Agreement with the U.S. Department of Education for eligible students to receive Pell Grants and, depending upon the agreement, other federal aid.

Financial aid to full-time, first-time undergraduate students: 28% received federal grants averaging $2,520; 48% state/local grants averaging $1,438; 58% institutional grants averaging $1,403; 57% received loans averaging $2,022.

Departments and Teaching Staff: *Total instructional faculty:* 274. Degrees held by full-time faculty: master's 43%, doctorate 60%.

Enrollment: Total enrollment 6,230. Undergraduate 5,218 (44.2% men, 56.8% women).

Characteristics of Student Body: *Ethnic/racial makeup:* number of Black non-Hispanic: 2.5%; American Indian or Alaska Native: .4%; Asian or Pacific Islander: 1.1%; Hispanic: 1.7%; White non-Hispanic: 87.7%; unknown: 3.7%. *Age distribution:* 17–21: 67%; 22–24: 16%; 25–29: 5%; 30–34: 4%; 35–39: 4%; 40–49: 3%; 50–64: 1%.

International Students: 141 nonresident aliens enrolled fall 2004. Students from Europe, Asia, Latin America, Africa, Canada. Programs available to aid students whose native language is not English: social, cultural. English as a Second Language Program. No financial aid specifically designated for international students.

Student Life: On-campus residence halls house 46% of student body. Two co-ed halls. Some women join and live in sorority housing. *Intercollegiate athletics:* men only: baseball, basketball, cross-country, football, tennis, track and field; women only: baseball, basketball, cross-country, tennis, track, volleyball. Intramural competition for all. *Special services:* Talent Development Center, Student Support Services, health services, counseling center, electronic campus (computer terminal and RECAL automated library network, and telephone link including voice mail capabilities in each residence hall room). *Student publications, radio, television:* New Wine, an annual poetry publication; *Northwest Missourian*, a weekly newspaper; *The Tower*, a yearbook; *Heartland Review*, a magazine. Radio stations KXCV and KDLX broadcast 131 and 125 hours per week respectively. Television station KNWT broadcasts 168 hours per week. *Surrounding community:* Maryville population 11,000. Omaha (NE), 120 miles from campus, Kansas City 90 miles from campus, St. Joseph, 50 miles from campus, are nearest metropolitan areas. A municipal airport, 2 miles from campus, serves business and general aviation needs.

Publications: *Laurel Review* (quarterly); *Regional Business Review* (quarterly).

Library Collections: 286,500 volumes. 16,000 microforms; 2,000 audiovisual materials; 3,400 current periodical subscriptions. Online catalog. Students have access to online information retrieval services and the Internet.

Most important special holdings include Missouriana Collection; University Archives; Morehouse Collection and Willa Cather Collection.

Buildings and Grounds: Campus area 240 acres.

Chief Executive Officer: Dr. Dean L. Hubbard, President.

Address admission inquiries to Beverly S.Schenkel, Director of Enrollment Management.

Ozark Christian College

1111 North Main Street
Joplin, Missouri 64801-4804
Tel: (417) 624-2518   **E-mail:** occadmin@occ.edu
Fax: (417) 624-0090   **Internet:** www.occ.edu

Institution Description: Ozark Christian College is a private institution affiliated with the Christian Churches/Churches of Christ. *Enrollment:* 841. *Degrees awarded:* Associate, baccalaureate.

Accreditation: *National:* ABHE.

Calendar: Semesters. Academic year Aug. to May.

Characteristics of Freshmen: 100% of applicants accepted. 68% of accepted applicants enrolled.

68% of freshmen from Missouri. Freshmen from 21 states and 13 foreign countries.

Admission: Open enrollment. High school graduate or equivalent; completion of 15 units include 3 English, 2 mathematics, 1 history, 2 science.

Degree Requirements: Completion of prescribed curriculum (major area and general education requirements).

Degrees Conferred: 11 *associate;* 88 *baccalaureate:* theology.

Fees and Other Expenses: *Full-time tuition per academic year 2005–06:* $220 per credit hour. *Required fees:* $440. *Room and board per academic year:* $4,050.

Financial Aid: Aid from institutionally generated funds is provided on the basis of academic merit, financial need, other criteria.

Financial aid to full-time, first-time undergraduate students: need-based scholarships/grants totaling $911,111, self-help $1,033,465; non-need-based self-help $555,002, parent loans $220,142.

Departments and Teaching Staff: *Instructors* 33, *part-time faculty* 39. *Total instructional faculty:* 72 (full-time 33, part-time 39; women 12, men 60). Total faculty with doctorate, first-professional, or other terminal degree: 8. Student-to-faculty ratio: 18:1. Degrees held by full-time faculty: 70% hold terminal degrees.

Enrollment: Total enrollment 841. Full-time 405 men / 322 women, part-time 47m / 67w.

Characteristics of Student Body: *Ethnic/racial makeup:* number of Black non-Hispanic: 11; American Indian or Alaska Native: 12; Asian or Pacific Islander: 5; Hispanic: 22; White non-Hispanic: 773.

International Students: 18 nonresident aliens enrolled fall 2004. 1 student from Europe, 4 Asia, 5 Central and South America, 6 Africa, 2 other. No programs available to aid students whose native language is not English. Financial aid specifically designated for international students: 7 scholarships available annually; 7 totaling $6,240 awarded 2004–5.

Student Life: Unmarried students not living with parents are required to live in college residence halls. Intramural athletic program.

Publications: *Compass*, published quarterly for alumni and constituency; *Reachout News*, published 3 times per year for youth.

Library Collections: 64,000 volumes. 182 microform titles; 18,824 audiovisual materials; 385 current periodical subscriptions. 20,0000 recordings; 302 CD-ROMs. Online catalog. Students have access to the Internet at no charge. Total 2004–05 budget for books and materials: $39,000.

Most important special collections include the Restoration Movement (Christianity); Creationism; Hermeneutics.

Chief Executive Officer: Dr. Kenneth Idleman, President.

Address admission inquiries to Troy Nelson, Executive Director of Admissions.

Park University

8700 NW River Park Drive
Parkville, Missouri 64152-3795
Tel: (816) 741-2000   **E-mail:** admissions@park.edu
Fax: (816) 746-6423   **Internet:** www.park.edu

Institution Description: Park University is a private institution affiliated with the Reorganized Church of Jesus Christ of Latter Day Saints. *Enrollment:* 12,548. *Degrees awarded:* Associate, baccalaureate, master's.

Member of the consortium Kansas City Regional Council for Higher Education and Kansas City Professional Development Council.

Accreditation: *Regional:* NCA. *Professional:* music, nursing, teacher education

History: Established, chartered, and offered first instruction at postsecondary level 1875; awarded first degree (baccalaureate) 1879. *See* Kenneth Eggleston, *Centennial Sketches* (Parkville: Park College, 1975) for further information.

Institutional Structure: *Governing board:* Board of Trustees of Park University. Extrainstitutional representation: 23 trustees; institutional representation: 1 administrator; 1 alumnus. All voting. *Composition of institution:* Administrators 14 men / 12 women. Academic affairs headed by vice president for academic affairs. Management/business/finances directed by vice president for business affairs. Full-time instructional faculty 32 men / 20 women. Academic governance body, Academic Council, meets an average of 12 times per year. *Faculty representation:* Faculty served by collective bargaining agent, Missouri Federation of Teachers, affiliated with AFT.

Calendar: Semesters. Academic year late Aug. to early May. Freshmen admitted Aug., Oct., Jan., Mar., June. Degrees conferred and formal commencement May. Summer session from early June to early Aug.

Characteristics of Freshmen: 409 applicants (176 men, 233 women). 78% of applicants admitted. 78% of applicants admitted and enrolled full-time.

67% (85 students) submitted ACT scores. *25th percentile*: ACT Composite 18, ACT English 16, ACT Math 17. *75th percentile*: ACT Composite 24, ACT English 24, ACT Math 22.

43% of entering freshmen expected to graduate within 5 years. 57% of freshmen from Missouri. Freshmen from 17 states.

Admission: Rolling admissions plan. For fall acceptance, apply no later than registration week. Early acceptance available. *Requirements:* Either graduation from accredited secondary school or GED. Minimum GPA 2.0 plus ACT 20 and upper 50% of graduating class. *Entrance tests:* College Board SAT or ACT composite. *For transfer students:* 2.0 minimum GPA; from 4-year accredited institution 96 semester hours maximum transfer credit; from 2-year accredited institution 75 hours.

College credit and advanced placement for postsecondary-level work completed in secondary school. College credit for extrainstitutional learning on basis of ACE *2006 Guide to the Evaluation of Educational Experiences in the Armed Services*; portfolio assessment. Advanced placement on basis of faculty assessment.

Tutoring available. Developmental courses offered during regular academic year; credit given.

Degree Requirements: *For all associate degrees:* 60 semester hours; 15 hours in residence. *For all baccalaureate degrees:* 120 semester hours; 24 hours in residence. *For all degrees:* 2.0 GPA; distribution requirements. Fulfillment of some degree requirements and exemption from some beginning courses possible by passing College Board CLEP. *Grading system:* A–F; pass-fail; withdraw (carries time limit); incomplete (carries time limit).

Distinctive Educational Programs: Internships. Flexible meeting places and schedules, including off-campus centers for evening division students at 5 locations within Kansas City metropolitan area, weekend and evening classes. Accelerated degree program. Interdisciplinary programs in liberal arts, liberal studies, and social studies. Facilities and programs for independent research, including individual majors, tutorials. Cross-registration through consortium. *Other distinctive programs:* School for Distance Learning offers degree programs for adult learners at over 30 locations nationwide.

ROTC: Army.

Degrees Conferred: 47 *associate;* 2,489 *baccalaureate;* 80 *master's.* Bachelor's degrees awarded in top five disciplines: business, management, marketing, and related support services 1,558; psychology 378; security and protective services 209; computer and information sciences 122; education 51.

Fees and Other Expenses: *Full-time tuition per academic year 2004–05:* undergraduate $6,048; contact the university for current graduate tuition/fees. *Room and board per academic year:* $6,300. *Books and supplies:* $1,200.

Financial Aid: Aid from institutionally generated funds is provided on the basis of academic merit, financial need, athletic ability, other criteria. Institution has a Program Participation Agreement with the U.S. Department of Education for eligible students to receive Pell Grants and, depending upon the agreement, other federal aid.

Departments and Teaching Staff: Accounting *professors* 0, *associate professors* 1, *assistant professors* 0, *part-time teachers* 1; art 0, 1, 0, 3; athletic training 0, 0, 0, 5; biology 2, 0, 1, 1; business administration 1, 1, 1, 3; chemistry 0, 0, 3, 2; communication arts 0 3, 0, 0; computer science 0, 0, 2, 2; criminal justice 0, 1, 0, 0; economics 0, 1, 0, 0; education 1, 2, 4, 6; English 1, 1, 2, 3; foreign language 0, 0, 1, 2; history 1, 0, 0, 1; human services 1, 0, 0, 2; mathematics 1, 0, 1, 0; music 0, 0, 0, 3; nursing 0, 0, 6, 2; philosophy/religion 0, 0, 1, 0; physical education 0, 0, 0, 3; political science 1, 0, 0, 1; psychology 1, 0, 1, 3; theatre 0, 1, 0, 1.

Total instructional faculty: 61 FTE. Degrees held by full-time faculty: doctorate 40%, master's 77%, professional 1%, baccalaureate 100%. 60% hold terminal degrees.

Enrollment: Total enrollment 12,548. Undergraduate 12,077 (33.3% men, 46.7% women).

Characteristics of Student Body: *Ethnic/racial makeup:* number of Black non-Hispanic: 214; American Indian or Alaska Native: .6%; Asian or Pacific Islander: 2.6%; Hispanic: 15.75%; White non-Hispanic: 58.3%. *Age distribution:* 17–21: 7%; 22–24: 10%; 25–29: 14%; 30–34: 14%; 35–39: 14%; 40–49: 15%; 50–59: 1%; 60–up: less than 1%.

International Students: 193 nonresident aliens enrolled fall 2004. Students from Europe, Asia, Latin America, Africa, Canada. Programs available to aid students whose native language is not English: social and cultural. English as a Second Language Program. No financial aid specifically designated for international students.

Student Life: On-campus residence halls house 14% of home campus student body. All residence halls are co-ed. *Intercollegiate athletics:* men only: baseball, basketball, cross-country, golf, soccer, track; women only: basketball, cross-country, track, volleyball. *Special regulations:* Cars permitted without restrictions. Quiet hours from 10pm to noon. *Student publications, radio: Narva,* a yearbook; *The Journal,* an annual art and literary magazine; *Stylus,* a newspaper. Radio station KGSP broadcasts 45 hours per week. *Surrounding community:* Parkville population 2,000. Kansas City, 12 miles from campus, is nearest metropolitan area. Served by airport and passenger rail service, each 12 miles from campus.

Publications: *Midwest Review of Public Administration,* a quarterly.

Library Collections: 142,000 volumes. 145,500 microforms; 670 audiovisual materials; 775 current periodical subscriptions. Online catalog. Students have access to online information retrieval services and the Internet.

Most important special holdings include Archives of Park University; photograph collection of Park University and Parkville.

Buildings and Grounds: Campus area 800 acres.

Chief Executive Officer: Dr. Beverley Byers-Pevitts, President.

Address admission inquiries to Director of Admissions.

Research College of Nursing

2300 East Meyer Boulevard
Kansas City, Missouri 64132
Tel: (816) 276-4729   **E-mail:** admissions@rockhurst.edu
Fax: (816) 276-3526   **Internet:** www.researchcollege.edu

Institution Description: Research College of Nursing is an independent college of nursing in partnership with Rockhurst University. *Enrollment:* 225. *Degrees awarded:* Baccalaureate, master's.

Accreditation: *Regional:* NCA. *Professional:* nursing

History: Established 1980.

Calendar: Semesters.

Characteristics of Freshmen: 85% of applicants accepted.

Admission: Graduation from accredited secondary school or GED. *Entrance tests:* ACT required.

Degree Requirements: 69 semester hours in liberal arts and sciences; 59 semester hours in nursing major; 2.0 GPA.

Distinctive Educational Programs: Honors Program.

Degrees Conferred: 35 *baccalaureate:* health professions and related sciences; 3 *master's.*

Fees and Other Expenses: *Tuition per academic year 2005–06:* $18,900. *Required fees:* $640. *Room and board per academic year:* $5,900.

Financial Aid: Financial assistance is available in the form of Pell Grants, College Work-Study, Veterans Administration Benefits, National Direct Student Loans, Supplemental Education Opportunity Grants (SEOG), Stafford Loans, other federal aid programs.

Financial aid to full-time, first-time undergraduate students: need-based scholarships/grants totaling $357,504, self-help $291,773; non-need-based scholarships/grants totaling $1,541,596, self-help $364,292. *Graduate aid:* 7 students recevued $51,400 in federal and state-funded loans (ranging from $3,000 to $19,500).

Departments and Teaching Staff: *Total instructional faculty:* 53 (full-time 28, part-time 5; women 33; member of minority groups 1). Total faculty with doctorate, first-professional, or other terminal degree: 6. Student-to-faculty ratio: 7:1.

Enrollment: *Total enrollment:* 211. Undergraduate full-time 12m / 173 women; graduate full-time 1m / 1w, part-time 3m / 21w.

Characteristics of Student Body: *Ethnic/racial makeup:* number of Black non-Hispanic: 13; Asian or Pacific Islander: 6; Hispanic: 10; White non-Hispanic: 147; unknown: 9. *Age distribution:* number under 20–21: 36; 22–24: 46; 25–29: 2; 30–34: 26.

Student Life: Housing available on Rockhurst College campus.

Library Collections: 100,000 volumes. 450 microform titles; 675 current periodical subscriptions. Access to online information retrieval systems. Students have access to the holdings of the Rockhurst College library as well as the Research Medical Center.

Buildings and Grounds: Dr. Nancy O. Debasio, R.N., President/Dean.

Address admission inquiries to Mrs. Leslie Mendenhall, Director of Transfer and Graduate Recruitment.

Rockhurst University

1100 Rockhurst Road
Kansas City, Missouri 64110-2561
Tel: (816) 501-4000   **E-mail:** admission@.rockhurst.edu
Fax: (816) 501-4588   **Internet:** www.rockhurst.edu

Institution Description: Rockhurst University is a private, independent, non-profit Jesuit college affiliated with the Roman Catholic Church. *Enrollment:* 2,764. *Degrees awarded:* Baccalaureate, master's, doctorate.

Accreditation: *Regional:* NCA. *Professional:* occupational therapy, physical therapy

History: One of the 28 Jesuit Colleges and Universities in the United States, Rockhurst was founded by the Society of Jesus (Jesuits). It was established and chartered by the State of Missouri in 1910; offered its first instruction at post-secondary level in 1917; became coeducational in 1969; and added its first graduate program in 1976; became Rockhurst University 1998; first doctoral program offered 2004. *See* Hugh M. Owens, *History of Rockhurst College* (Kansas City MO.: Rockhurst College, 1953) and *Rockhurst College: 75 Years of Jesuit Education in Kansas City* (Kansas City, MO: Rockhurst College, 1985) for further information.

Institutional Structure: *Governing board:* Board of Trustees of Rockhurst University. Extrainstitutional representation: 30, including 10 alumni and 5 ex officio member. *Composition of institution:* Administrators 3 men / 5 women. Academic affairs headed by Dean's Team. Management/business/finances directed by vice president for business and finance. Full-time instructional faculty 115. Academic governance body, Faculty Senate, meets monthly.

Calendar: Semesters. Academic year Aug. to May. Freshmen admitted Aug., Jan., June, July. Degrees conferred May, Aug., Dec. Formal commencement Dec., May. Summer session early June to mid-Aug.

Characteristics of Freshmen: 72% of applicants admitted. 22% of applicants admitted and enrolled.

12% (88 students) submitted SAT scores; 97% (296 students) submitted ACT scores. *25th percentile:* SAT Verbal 500, SAT Math 460; ACT Composite 21, ACT English 21, ACT Math 19. *75th percentile:* SAT Verbal 610, SAT Math 620; ACT Composite 27, ACT English 28, ACT Math 27.

60% of entering freshmen expected to graduate within 5 years. 60% of freshmen from Missouri. Freshmen from 18 states and 2 foreign countries.

Admission: Rolling admission plan. For fall acceptance, apply no later than June 30. *Requirements:* Either graduation from accredited secondary school or GED. Recommend 16 secondary school units including 4 English, 3 mathematics, 3 history/social science, 2–3 science (1 must include laboratory), 4–5 academic electives (at least 2 units of a foreign language recommended). Top 50th percentile of high school graduating class required. *Entrance tests:* All applicants must submit either an ACT or SAT result. *For transfer students:* unlimited transfer credits from a regionally accredited 4-year institution. Minimum 2.25 GPA required.

Degree Requirements: *For all baccalaureate degrees:* Minimum 128 credit hours. Some majors require a final comprehensive examination. *For all undergraduate degrees:* 2.0 GPA; half of coursework for major concentration and last 30 hours earned in residence; completion of core curriculum; minimum of C grades in last 30 hours of courses required for major concentration.

Fulfillment of some degree requirements and exemption from some beginning courses possible by passing College Board CLEP, Advanced Placement. *Grading system:* A–F; withdrawal and incomplete (carries time limit).

Distinctive Educational Programs: Rockhurst has a variety of programs with local schools which gives college students first-hand experience working as tutors and mentors to local school children. Other undergraduate experiences include a cooperative education program; joint degree programs with Research College of Nursing (BSN, Accelerated BSN); cooperative baccalaureate programs in clinical laboratory sciences with area hospitals; preprofessional programs in dentistry, engineering, medicine, optometry, pharmacy, veterinary medicine; institutionally sponsored foreign study in China, England, France, Germany, Greece, Israel, Italy, Mexico. Programs for independent research including college honors program, tutorials; Human Services Agencies program offered in conjunction with American Humanics, Inc.; Global studies program; and cross-registration with 20 area colleges and universities through a consortium. Graduate programs in occupational therapy, physical therapy, business administration. Complete degree programs in some undergraduate majors and MBA also offered evenings and weekends. Non-credit programs offered through Rockhurst University Continuing Education Center; national and international training programs offered through National Seminars Group, a wholly owned subsidiary of the Rockhurst University Continuing Education Center; and the Small Business Center.

ROTC: Army offered in cooperation with University of Missouri-Kansas City.

Degrees Conferred: 367 *baccalaureate:* biological/life sciences 24; business and management 98; communications 8; computer and information sciences 7; education 18; English 21; foreign languages 5; health professions 97; interdisciplinary studies 1; mathematics 3, philosophy/religion 7, physical sciences 16; protective services/public administration 1; psychology 29; social sciences and history 32. 268 *masters:* business and management 182; education 43; health professions 43.

Fees and Other Expenses: *Full-time tuition per academic year 2005–06:* undergraduate $18,900; graduate $460 per credit hour. *Required fees:* $640. *Room and board per academic year:* $5,900.

Financial Aid: Aid from institutionally generated funds is provided on the basis of academic merit, financial need, athletic ability, other criteria.

Financial aid to full-time, first-time undergraduate students: need-based scholarships/grants totaling $7,171,121, self-help $3,240,795, tuition waivers $675,849, athletic awards $575,897; non-need-based scholarships/grants totaling $2,401,575, self-help $1,979,375, tuition waivers $405,947, athletic awards $1,074,623. *Graduate aid:* 302 students received $5,886,259 in federal and state-funded loans; 10 received $32,641 in other fellowships/grants; 17 research assistantships awarded totaling $27,900.

Departments and Teaching Staff: *Professors* 34, *associate professors* 41, *assistant professors* 47, *instructors* 2, *part-time faculty* 55.

Total instructional faculty: 203 (full-time 128, part-time 75; women 89, men 114; members of minority groups 9). Student-to-faculty ratio: 12:1. Degrees held by full-time faculty: baccalaureate 2%, master's 17%, doctorate 81%. 84% hold terminal degrees. *Faculty development:* $32,000 in grants for research. 5 faculty members awarded sabbaticals 2004–05.

Enrollment: Total enrollment 2,764. Undergraduate full-time 551 men / 584 women, part-time 324m / 503w; graduate full-time 105m / 176w, part-time 239m / 202w. *Transfer students:* in-state 85; from out-of-state 68.

Characteristics of Student Body: *Ethnic/racial makeup:* Black non-Hispanic: 152; American Indian or Native Alaskan 11; Asian or Pacific Islander: 49; Hispanic: 80; White non-Hispanic 1,520; unknown: 128. *Age distribution:* under 18: 460; 18–19: 612; 20–21: 451; 22–24: 202; 25–29: 79; 30–34: 43; 35–39: 26; 40–49: 66; 50–64: 19; 65 and over: 4. 34% of student body attend summer sessions.

International Students: 25 nonresident aliens enrolled fall 2004. No programs available to aid students whose native language is not English. No financial aid specifically designated for international students.

Student Life: On-campus residence halls house 50% of the full-time undergraduate student body. Three dormitories, 1 men, 1 women, 1 co-educational. Quiet hours set by dormitory residents. Some designated quiet floors by students choice. Theme houses for students with special interests, e.g. math/science/computer in college-owned neighborhood properties. *Intercollegiate athletics:* men only: baseball, basketball, soccer; women only: basketball, soccer, softball, volleyball; men and women: cross-country, golf, tennis. *Special regulations:* Cars permitted without restrictions. *Special services:* Learning Resources Center, Career Center with vocational counseling and placement, medical services, Counseling Center, Campus Ministry; fraternities; service fraternity; Rockhurst Organization of Collegiate Women (ROCW); Black Student Union; opportunities for community outreach such as Christmas in October; Appalachian service (one week each spring); tutoring in local schools; clubs sponsored by academic departments. Student Activity fee allocated by Student Activities Board. Subsidized tickets to Season of the Arts available to full-time undergraduate students. *Student publications, radio:* The Sentinel, a newspaper; The Rock, a yearbook; The BSN News, a nursing student newspaper. *Surrounding community:* Kansas City, population over 1.5 million. Mass transit bus system stops on campus; airport 30 miles from campus; passenger rail service 4 miles from campus; walking distance to nationally known Country Club Plaza shopping and entertainment district.

Publications: Publications by and for faculty and staff include *Bibliography of Papers, Presentation, and Publications* (annual), and *The Rockhurst Community* (bimonthly). Publications by and for faculty, staff, and students include *Rockhurst Occasional Papers* (1 or 2 per year); *The Rockhurst Review,* a literary magazine published annually; and *The Rockhurst Daily News* (daily). Publications for faculty, staff, students, alumni, and constituents include *The Rockhurst Magazine* (2 or 3 per year) and *The Rockhurst Report* (4 per year).

Library Collections: 306,200 volumes. Online catalog. Current serial subscriptions: 600 paper; 550 microform; 15,000 via electronic access. 33 computer work stations. Students have access to online information retrieval services and the Internet. Total 2004–05 budget for books, periodicals, audiovisual materials, microforms: $315,000.

Library houses the Van Ackeren Gallery holding a collection of medieval religious art. Nationally known private science library, Linda Hall Library, within walking distance.

Buildings and Grounds: Campus area 55 acres.

Chief Executive Officer: Rev. E. Edward Kinerk, S.J., President.

Undergraduates address admission inquiries to Phil Gebauer, Director of Undergraduate Admissions; graduate inquiries to Directors of Graduate Recruitment.

St. Louis Christian College

1360 Grandview Drive
Florissant, Missouri 63033-6499
Tel: (314) 837-6777   **E-mail:** admissions@slcc4ministry.edu
Fax: (314) 837-8291   **Internet:** www.slcc4ministry.edu

Institution Description: St. Louis Christian College is Bible college affiliated with the Christian Churches/Churches of Christ. *Enrollment:* 193. *Degrees awarded:* Associate, baccalaureate.

Accreditation: *National:* ABHE.

Calendar: Semesters. Academic year late Aug. to early May.

Characteristics of Freshmen: 82 applicants (49 men, 33 women). 46.4% of admitted students enrolled full-time.

96% (25 students) submitted ACT scores. *25th percentile:* ACT Composite 19, ACT English 12, ACT Math 11. *75th percentile:* ACT Composite 26, ACT English 25, ACT Math 21.

64% of freshmen from Missouri. Freshmen from 24 states and 1 foreign country.

Admission: *Requirements:* Graduation from accredited secondary school or GED.

Degree Requirements: Completion of prescribed curriculum.

Degrees Conferred: 13 *associate;* 26 *baccalaureate:* theology/ministerial studies.

Fees and Other Expenses: *Full-time tuition per academic year 2004–05:* $7,280. *Room and board per academic year:* $6,180. *Books and supplies:* $650.

Financial Aid: Aid from institutionally generated funds is provided on the basis of academic merit, financial need. Institution has a Program Participation Agreement with the U.S. Department of Education for eligible students to receive Pell Grants and, depending upon the agreement, other federal aid.

Departments and Teaching Staff: Bible/theology *professors* 7, *part-time teachers* 15.

Total instructional faculty: 22. Degrees held by full-time faculty: doctorate 14%, master's 86%.

Enrollment: Total enrollment 193 (56.5% men, 43.5% women).

Characteristics of Student Body: *Ethnic/racial makeup:* number of Black non-Hispanic: 21.2%; American Indian or Alaska Native: 1.6%; Hispanic: 1.6%; White non-Hispanic: 75.6%. *Age distribution:* 17–21: 42%; 22–24: 11%; 25–29: 15%; 30–34: 6%; 35–39: 8%; 40–49: 13%; 50–59: 4%; 60–up: 1%.

International Students: 2 nonresident aliens enrolled fall 2004. No programs to aid students whose native language is not English. No financial aid specifically designated for international students.

Student Life: Housing available on campus for both single and married students.

Library Collections: 42,000 volumes. 15,900 microforms; 2,580 audiovisual materials; 145 current periodical subscriptions. Students have access to online information retrieval services and the Internet.

Most important special collections include Bible; Theology; Church History.

Chief Executive Officer: Dr. Thomas W. McGee. President.

Address admission inquiries to Richard A. Fordyce, Dean of Enrollment Growth.

St. Louis College of Pharmacy

4588 Parkview Place
St. Louis, Missouri 63110
Tel: (314) 367-8700   **E-mail:** admissions@stlcop.edu
Fax: (314) 446-8310   **Internet:** www.stlcop.edu

Institution Description: St. Louis College of Pharmacy is a private, independent, nonprofit college. *Enrollment:* 991. *Degrees awarded:* Master's, first-professional.

Accreditation: *Regional:* NCA. *Professional:* pharmacy

History: Established as St. Louis College of Pharmacy 1864; offered first instruction at postsecondary level 1865; incorporated 1866; awarded first degree (baccalaureate) 1936; changed name to St. Louis College of Pharmacy and Allied Sciences 1946; present name readopted 1962. *See* John P. Winkelmann, *History of the St. Louis College of Pharmacy* (St. Louis; privately published, 1964) for further information.

Institutional Structure: *Governing board:* Board of Trustees. Representation: 20 trustees, 4 alumni. All voting. *Composition of institution:* Academic affairs headed by dean. Management/business/finances directed vice president of finance and administration. Full-time instructional faculty 64. Academic governance body, the faculty, meets an average of 9 times per year.

Calendar: Semesters. Academic year Aug. to May. Freshmen admitted Aug. Degrees conferred and formal commencement May. Summer session May to July.

Characteristics of Freshmen: 62% of applicants accepted. 85% of accepted applicants enrolled.

100% (252 students) submitted ACT scores. *25th percentile:* ACT Composite 24. *75th percentile:* ACT Composite 25.

52% of freshmen from Missouri. Freshmen from 11 states.

Admission: Rolling admissions plan. For fall acceptance, apply as early as Sept. 1 of previous year, but not later than Aug. 1 of year of enrollment. *Requirements:* Either graduation from accredited secondary school with 16 units which normally include 4 English, 2 from among chemistry, physics, or biology, 2 algebra, 1 geometry; or GED. Minimum 2.5 GPA. *Entrance tests:* ACT composite (minimum score 23; math score 21). For foreign students TOEFL. *For transfer students:* 2.0 minimum GPA. Preference will be given to transfer students with cumulative GPAs of 3.0 or higher on a 4.0 scale.

College credit and advanced placement for postsecondary-level work completed in secondary school. Tutoring available. Noncredit developmental courses offered during regular academic year.

Degree Requirements: *Pharm.D. degree:* 203 credit hours. Fulfillment of some degree requirements and exemption from some beginning courses possible by passing College Board CLEP, AP. *Grading system:* A–F; pass-fail; withdraw (deadline after which pass-fail is appended to withdraw).

Distinctive Educational Programs: Special facilities for using telecommunications in the classroom. *Other distinctive programs:* Continuing education for professional development; Bachelor of Science in Pharmaceutical Sciences.

Degrees Conferred: 156 *baccalaureate:* health professions; 2 *master's:* health professions; 41 *first-professional:* pharmacy.

Fees and Other Expenses: *Full-time tuition per academic year 2004–05:* undergraduate $17,000, graduate $17,700. *Required fees:* $135. *Room and board per academic year:* $6,202.

Financial Aid: Aid from institutionally generated funds is provided on the basis of academic merit, financial need.

Financial aid to full-time, first-time undergraduate students: need-based scholarships/grants totaling $585,543, self-help $5,164,508; non-need-based scholarships/grants totaling $3,430,183, self-help $7,410,410, parent loans $2,509,008, tuition waivers $39,926.

Departments and Teaching Staff: Pharmacy *professors* 15, *associate professors* 15, *assistant professors* 35, *instructors* 1, *part-time faculty* 43.

Total instructional faculty: 109 (full-time 66, part-time 43; women 61, men 48). Total faculty with doctorate, first-professional, or other terminal degree: 109. Student-to-faculty ratio: 15:1. Degrees held by full-time faculty: doctorate 43%, master's 9%, professional 48%. 94% hold terminal degrees.

Enrollment: Total enrollment 991. Undergraduate full-time 1 woman; first-professional full-time 357m / 625w, part-time 1m / 3w; graduate part-time 3m / 1w. *Transfer students:* in-state 23; from out-of-state 7.

Characteristics of Student Body: *Ethnic/racial makeup:* number of Black non-Hispanic: 28; American Indian or Alaska Native: 2; Asian or Pacific Islander: 108; Hispanic: 7; White non-Hispanic: 828; unknown: 3. *Age distribution:* number 18–19: 368; 20–21: 272; 22–24: 235; 25–29: 68; 30–34: 26; 35–39: 81 40–49: 4; 50–64: 1.

International Students: 6 nonresident aliens enrolled fall 2004. 4 students from Asia, 1 Africa. No programs available to aid students whose native language is not English. No financial aid specifically designated for international students.

Student Life: On-campus residence halls house 33% of student body. Residence halls for both sexes constitute 100% of such space. 20% of men join and 3% live in fraternities; 17% of women join sororities (no sorority houses available). Housing available for married students. *Intercollegiate athletics:* men: basketball, cross-country; women: cross-country, volleyball. *Special regulations:* Cars permitted without restrictions. Residence hall visitation from noon to 11pm Mon.–Thurs., noon to midnight Fri.–Sun. *Student publications: The Pharmakon,* a newspaper published 2 times per semester; *Prescripto,* a yearbook. *Surrounding community:* St. Louis metropolitan population over 2.5 million. Served by mass transit bus system and MetroLink Light Rail System; airport 20 miles from campus.

Publications: *News Capsule* (twice a year); *Script Magazine* (four times a year); *Annual Report* (once a year); *Phamrakon* a quarterly; *Inverstor's Link,* (4 times a year).

Library Collections: 68,187 volumes. 308 microform titles; 802 audiovisual materials; 400 current periodical subscriptions. Computer work stations available. Students have access to online information retrieval services and the Internet.

Most important special holdings include Drug Information Collection; pharmaceutical literature; Materia Medica.

Buildings and Grounds: Campus area 5 acres.

Chief Executive Officer: Dr. Thomas F. Patton, President.

Address admission inquiries to Penny Myers Bryant, Director of Admissions.

Saint Louis University

221 North Grand Boulevard
St. Louis, Missouri 63103-2097

Tel: (314) 977-3678   **E-mail:** admitme@slu.edu
Fax: (314) 977-7136   **Internet:** www.slu.edu

Institution Description: Saint Louis University is a private institution affiliated with the Society of Jesus, Roman Catholic Church. *Enrollment:* 11,422. *Degrees awarded:* Associate, baccalaureate, first-professional (law, medicine), master's, doctorate. Specialist certificates in education and other graduate certificates also awarded.

Academic offerings subject to approval by statewide coordinating bodies. Member of the consortium Higher Education Center of St. Louis.

Accreditation: *Regional:* NCA. *Professional:* business, clinical lab scientist, clinical pastoral education, clinical psychology, dietetics, endodontics, engineering, health information administration, health services administration, law, medicine, nuclear medicine technology, nursing, occupational therapy, periodontics, physical therapy, physician assisting, public administration, public health, social work, speech-language pathology, surgeon assisting, teacher education

History: Established as Saint Louis Academy 1818; offered first instruction at postsecondary level and changed name to Saint Louis College 1820; chartered and adopted present name 1832; awarded first degree (baccalaureate) 1834. *See* Rev. William B. Faherty, *Better the Dream* (St. Louis: Saint Louis University, 1968) for further information.

Institutional Structure: *Governing board:* Board of Trustees of Saint Louis University. Extrainstitutional representation: 48 trustees, including 19 alumni; institutional representation: 1 administrator - ex officio. All voting. Governing Board meets an average of 4 times a year. *Composition of institution:* Academic affairs headed by provost. Management/business division directed by vice president for business and finance. Full-time instructional faculty 1,150. Academic governance body, Faculty Senate, meets an average of 5 times a year in addition to committee meetings.

Calendar: Semesters. Academic year July to June. Freshmen admitted Aug., Jan., June. Degrees conferred May, Aug., Jan. Formal commencement May. 8-week summer session; two 6-week summer sessions.

Characteristics of Freshmen: 80% of applicants admitted. 27% of applicants admitted and enrolled.

44% (633 students) submitted SAT scores; 91% (1,314 students) submitted ACT scores. *25th percentile:* SAT Verbal 540, SAT Math 540; ACT Composite 23, ACT English 23, ACT Math 22. *75th percentile:* SAT Verbal 645, SAT Math 660; ACT Composite 29, ACT English 29, ACT Math 28.

72% of entering freshmen expected to graduate within 5 years. 40% freshmen from Missouri. Freshmen from 41 states and 5 foreign countries.

Admission: Applications for fall accepted early in senior year of high school. No priority based on application date, but enrollment in School of Allied Health Professions is limited; Dec. 1 deadline for physical therapy applicants. Students are notified of decisions regarding admission within 3 weeks after completion of their file of supporting credentials. *Requirements:* Freshman candidate must present a transcript of courses from an accredited secondary school. Strongly recommend 4 units English, 3 college preparatory mathematics, 2 units classical or modern foreign language, 2 units social science, 2 units science (natural science) 3 additional units of academic electives. School of Nursing and School of Allied Health Professions require a course in chemistry (high school or junior college level). Department of Medical Record Administration requires typing ability to be acquired prior to or within first 2 years of enrollment in program. Department of Medical Technology requires course in biology. *For transfer students:* At least a C average for both overall college level work and work taken at an accredited college or university in the semester immediately preceding enrollment at SLU. If applying for admission into programs in nursing and accounting, student must have attained at least 2.5 credit point average in previous college work.

Tutoring available. Noncredit developmental courses offered in summer session and regular academic year.

Degree Requirements: *For all baccalaureate degrees:* 120 credit hours; 2 semesters in residence. *For all undergraduate degrees:* 2.0 GPA; general education requirements. Additional requirements for some programs.

Fulfillment of some degree requirements and exemption from some beginning courses possible by passing departmental examinations, College Board CLEP Subject Examination. *Grading system:* A–F; pass-fail; satisfactory-unsatisfactory; pass; withdraw (carries time limit); deferred grade (N).

Distinctive Educational Programs: *Other distinctive programs:* African American Studies Program; Saint Louis University - Madrid, Spain Campus; Micah House Program; Honors Program; Manresa Program in the College of Arts and Sciences.

ROTC: Army and Air Force in cooperation with Washington University. Air Force awarded 18 commissions 2004.

Degrees Conferred: 1,806 *baccalaureate* (B), 593 *master's* (M), 155 *doctorate* (D): architecture 3 (M); area and ethnic studies 4 (B), 4 (M), 2 (D); biological/life sciences 81 (B), 8 (M), 20 (D); business/marketing 491 (B), 82 (M), 4 (D); communications/communication technologies 124 (B), 15 (M); computer and information sciences 57 (B); education 62 (B), 41 (M), 66 (D); engineering and engineering technologies 86 (B), 7 (D); English 49 (B), 10 (M), 5 (D); foreign languages and literature 46 (B), 21 (M); health professions and related sciences 257 (B), 219 (M), 27 (D); home economics and vocational home economics 13 (B), 5 (M); law/legal studies 3 (D); mathematics 15 (B), 5 (M); natural resources/environmental science 2 (B); philosophy/religion/theology 46 (B), 11 (M), 7 (D); physical sciences 51 (B), 15 (M), 3 (D); protective services/public administration 57 (B), 120 (M), 4 (D); psychology 143 (B), 6 (M), 2 (D); social sciences and history 143 (B), 6 (M), 2 (D); trade and industry 67 (B); visual and performing arts 21 (B). 363 *first-professional:* law 213; medicine 140.

Fees and Other Expenses: *Full-time tuition per academic year 2005–06:* undergraduate $24,760; graduate $760 per credit hour. *Required fees:* $198. Tuition and fees for professional schools vary; contact the specific school of interest for current rates. *Room and board per academic year:* $8,200.

Financial Aid: Aid from institutionally generated funds is provided on the basis of academic merit, financial need, athletic ability, other criteria.

Financial aid to full-time, first-time undergraduate students: need-based scholarships/grants totaling $51,114,017, self-help $35,114,489, parent loans $7,079,559, tuition waivers $6,172,646, athletic awards $1,101,657; non-need-based scholarships/grants totaling $12,041,212, self-help $5,012,821, parent loans $5,437,459, tuition waivers $4,268,712, athletic awards $2,052,862.

Departments and Teaching Staff: *Total instructional faculty:* 1,002 (full-time 620, part-time 382; women 422, men 580; members of minority groups 93). Total faculty with doctorate, first-professional, or other terminal degree: 735. Student-to-faculty ratio: 12:1. Degrees held by full-time faculty: 95% hold terminal degrees. *Faculty development:* $74,635,013 total grants for research. 33 faculty members awarded sabbaticals 2004–05.

Enrollment: Total enrollment 11,422. Undergraduate full-time 2,898 men / 3,623 women, part-time 216m / 349w; first-professional full-time 641m / 617w, part-time 127m / 115w; graduate full-time 494m / 860w, part-time 564m / 918w. *Transfer students:* in-state 318; from out-of-state 257.

Characteristics of Student Body: *Ethnic/racial makeup (undergraduate):* number of Black non-Hispanic: 531; American Indian or Alaska Native: 26; Asian or Pacific Islander: 325; Hispanic: 163; White non-Hispanic: 4,963;; unknown: 663. *Age distribution:* number under 18: 57; 18–19: 2,728; 20–21: 2,728; 22–24: 807; 25–29: 282; 30–34: 149; 35–39: 117; 40–49: 159; 50–64: 41.

International Students: 321 nonresident aliens enrolled fall 2004. 95 students from Europe, 172 Asia, 26 Central and South America, 14 Africa, 11 Canada. Programs available to aid students whose native language is not English: social, cultural. English as a Second Language Program. No financial aid specifically designated for international students.

Student Life: 53.4% of full-time, day undergraduates live in college dorms or apartments; 46.6% live off campus. *Intercollegiate athletics:* men only: basketball, cross-country, field hockey, golf, tennis, soccer, softball, swimming/diving, volleyball; women only: basketball, cross-country, field hockey, golf, tennis, soccer, softball, swimming/diving, volleyball. softball. *Special regulations:* Cars with permits allowed. *Special services:* Learning Resources Center, medical services, shuttle bus service; co-curricular transcript, counseling services, Career Center, Community Volunteer Center. *Student publications, radio: University News,* a weekly newspaper; *Archive,* yearbook. Radio station KSLU broadcasts 70 hours per week through tv-cable lines. *Surrounding community:* St. Louis metropolitan population over 2.5 million. Served by mass transit bus system; airport 15 miles from campus; passenger rail service 1 mile from campus.

Publications: *Universitas* (published quarterly); *International Legal Education Newsletter, Law Journal, Manuscripta, The Modern Schoolman, Review for Religious/Theology Digest, Studies in the Spirituality of Jesus,* all published quarterly.

Library Collections: 1,878,213 volumes. Online catalog. 317,073 units of government documents; 1,370,633 microforms; 5,697 audiovisual materials; 14,309 periodicals. 178 computer work stations. Students have access to online information retrieval services and the Internet. Total 2004–05 budget for books and materials: $4,591,335.

Most important special holdings include Vatican Film Library; Smurfit Irish Law Collection; Western Americana; Jesuitica.

Buildings and Grounds: Campus area 279 acres.

Chief Executive Officer: Dr. Lawrence Biondi, S.J., President.

Undergraduates address admission inquiries to Admissions Staff; first-professional inquiries to appropriate school; graduate inquiries to Graduate Admissions Staff.

College of Arts and Sciences

Degree Programs Offered: *Baccalaureate* in American studies, biology, chemistry, chemistry/engineering, classical language and culture, communication, communication disorders, computer science, contract major, criminal justice, economics, education, English, fine and performing arts (art history, studio art, music, theatre), French, geology, geophysics, German studies, Greek, history, honors, Latin, mathematics, mathematics/engineering, meteorology, philosophy, physics, physics/engineering, political science, psychology, sociology, theological studies.

Distinctive Educational Programs: Dual-degree program in chemistry, mathematics, or physics/engineering with Washington University and Parks College; preprofessional programs in the health professions, law, and honors; Premedical and Prelaw Scholars programs, Honors Program, evening division for adult learners, Reis Biological Field Station, Orientation-USA for foreign students, established overseas programs in Madrid, Spain, and Lyon, France, 13 certificate/degree programs.

School of Allied Health Professions

Degree Programs Offered: *Baccalaureate* in health information management, medical record administration, medical technology, nuclear medicine technology, occupational therapy, perfusion (cardiovascular) technology, physical therapy, physical assistant; *master's* in dietetics, physical therapy (awarded through the Graduate School). Certificate in nuclear medicine technology, physician assistant, health information management. Internship in dietetics.

School of Business and Administration

Degree Programs Offered: *Baccalaureate* in accounting, economics, finance, information systems management, international business, management and decision sciences, marketing, personnel and industrial relations; *master's* in accounting, business administration, economics, finance, management and decision sciences. Joint M.H.A./M.B.A.; J.D./M.B.A.; M.S.N./M.B.A. Certificates also given.

Distinctive Educational Programs: Joint M.H.A.-M.B.A. with School of Allied Health Professions; joint J.D.-M.B.A. with School of Law.

School of Nursing

Degree Programs Offered: *Baccalaureate. Master's, doctorate* awarded through Graduate School.

College of Philosophy and Letters

Degree Programs Offered: *Baccalaureate* in philosophy.

School of Social Service

Degree Programs Offered: *Baccalaureate, master's.*
Admission: Baccalaureate degree required for M.S.W. admission.
Degree Requirements: *For baccalaureate degree:* 120 credit hours. *For master's degree:* 57 credit hours.
Distinctive Educational Programs: Joint M.P.H./M.S.W. degree.

School of Law

Degree Programs Offered: *First-professional:* J.D.; LL.M. in health law; LL.M. for foreign lawyers; J.D./M.H.A.; J.D./M.B.A.; J.D./U.A.
Admission: Baccalaureate degree; LSAT.
Degree Requirements: 88 credit hours; 2.0 GPA; 6 semesters in residence.

School of Medicine

Degree Programs Offered: *First-professional.* M.D. degree, M.D./Ph.D. degree.
Admission: 8 hours general biology or zoology, 8 hours inorganic chemistry, 8 hours organic chemistry, 8 hours physics, 6 hours English, 12 hours other humanities and behavioral sciences.

Degree Requirements: Satisfactory completion of prescribed curriculum; successful completion of Parts I and II of the examinations of the National Board of Medical Examiners.

Graduate School

Degree Programs Offered: *Master's* in aerospace engineering, allied health administration, chemistry, communication, communication disorders, community health, dietetics, French, hospital and health care administration, nursing, orthodontics, physical therapy, public administration, religious studies, Spanish, and urban affairs; *doctorate* in biochemistry, business administration, cell and molecular biology, health services research, microbiology, neurobiology, nursing, public policy analysis and administration; *master's, doctorate* in American studies, anatomy, biology, economics, education, English, geophysics, historical theology, mathematics, meteorology, pathology, pharmacology, philosophy, physiology, and psychology.

Distinctive Educational Programs: Interdisciplinary degree programs in American studies, community health, health services research, public administration, public policy, analysis and administration; individual interdisciplinary option. Joint first-professional-master's programs with School of Law in hospital administration, public administration, urban affairs. Joint first-professional-doctorate programs with School of Medicine in anatomy, biochemistry, microbiology, pathology, pharmacology, physiology; also in interdepartmental areas of cellular and molecular biology, molecular virology.

School of Public Health

Degree Programs Offered: *Master's* in health administration, public health; *doctorate* in health services research. *Joint M.H.A./M.B.A.* with School of Business Administration; *joint M.H.A./J.D.* with School of Law; *joint M.P.H./M.S.W.* with School of Social Services; *joint M.P.H./M.S.N.* with School of Nursing.

Admission: The prerequisite for admission to any of the School's degree programs is a baccalaureate degree from a recognized college or university in this country or abroad. Applicants for the 36-hour Generalist M.P.H. program or any of the joint degree programs must satisfy additional admission requirements as outlined in the School *Bulletin.*

Institute for Leadership

Degree Programs Offered: *Master's, doctorate.*

School for Professional Studies

Degree Programs Offered: *Master's, doctorate.*

Saint Luke's College

8320 Ward Parkway
Kansas City, Missouri 81102
Tel: (816) 932-2367   **E-mail:** slc-admissions@saint-lukes.org
Fax: (816) 932-9064   **Internet:** www.saintlukescollege.edu

Institution Description: Saint Luke's College is a private, independent, non-profit college offering a four-year program in which the general education courses are completed a the regionally accredited school of the student's choice and all nursing courses are completed at Saint Lukes College. The college is affiliated with the Saint Luke's Hospitals of Kansas City. *Enrollment:* 112. *Degrees awarded:* Baccalaureate.

Accreditation: *Regional:* NCA. *Professional:* nursing

History: In 1885 the All Saints Hospital was opened and the training school for nurses was established in 1887; In 1991, Saint Luke's College admitted their first class for baccalaureate nursing education.

Calendar: Semesters. Academic year from Aug. to May. Summer sessions from May to July.

Admission: Admissions criteria include: graduation from high school or the equivalent (GED); completion of a minimum of 29 semester hours of general education college coursework, including two required science courses; minimum grade of C and a minimum GPA average of 2.7 in prerequisite coursework. Applicants are considered for admission based on the potential to complete the program, their possession of necessary functional abilities, and their ability to meet the standards to apply for nursing licensure.

Degree Requirements: For Bachelor of Science in Nursing degree: completion of 124 hours; 60 hours of nursing coursework within four years of enrollment at Saint Luke's College; cumulative GPA of 2.0 with no grade below C counting towards graduation; final 38 hours of nursing coursework must be completed at Saint Luke's College.

Degrees Conferred: 1 *baccalaureate:* health professions and related sciences.

Fees and Other Expenses: *Full-time tuition per academic year 2005–06:* $295 per credit hour. *Required fees:* $670.

Financial Aid: Aid from institutionally generated funds is provided on the basis of academic merit, financial need. Institution has a Program Participation Agreement with the U.S. Department of Education for eligible students to receive Pell Grants and, depending upon the agreement, other federal aid.

Departments and Teaching Staff: *Total instructional faculty:* 17 (women 15, men 2; members of minority groups 2).

Enrollment: Total enrollment 112. Undergraduate full-time 9 men and 90 women, part-time 13w.

Characteristics of Student Body: *Ethnic/racial makeup:* Black non-Hispanic: 9; Asian or Pacific Islander: 5; Hispanic: 1; White non-Hispanic: 97.

International Students: No programs available to aid students whose native language is not English. No financial aid specifically designated for international students.

Student Life: *Special services:* Professional counseling; health services. *Student publications: Intouch,* campus newsletter. *Surrounding community:* Saint Luke's College is situated in the Kansas City metropolitan area. Student Nurses Association is active on campus.

Library Collections: Students have access to online information retrieval services and the Internet.

Chief Executive Officer: Dr. Helen Jepson, Dean, Chief Education Officer.

Address admission inquiries to Lindsey Borgett, Assistant Director of Admissions.

Saint Paul School of Theology

5123 Truman Road
Kansas City, Missouri 64127

Tel: (816) 483-9600   **E-mail:** admiss@spst.edu
Fax: (816) 483-9605   **Internet:** www.spst.edu

Institution Description: Saint Paul School of Theology is a private college affiliated with The United Methodist Church. *Enrollment:* 322. *Degrees awarded:* First-professional (master of divinity), master's, doctorate.

Accreditation: *Regional:* NCA. *National:* ATS. *Professional:* theology

History: Established and chartered as National Methodist Theological Seminary 1958; offered first instruction at postsecondary level 1959; became Saint Paul School of Theology Methodist, 1961; awarded first degree (first-professional) 1962; adopted present name 1986.

Institutional Structure: *Governing board:* Saint Paul School of Theology Board of Trustees. Extrainstitutional representation: 35 trustees including 1 student, 1 faculty, 1 staff, 1 alumnus; institutional representation: 2 administrators, 2 full-time instructional faculty members, 2 students, 2 staff members; 2 alumni. 1 ex officio. *Composition of institution:* Administrators 4 men / 3 women. Academic affairs headed by academic dean. Management/business/finances directed by comptroller. Full-time instructional faculty 17. Academic governance body, Faculty Council, meets an average of 12 times per year.

Calendar: Semesters; January 4-week interterm. Academic year Sept. to May. Entering students admitted Sept., Jan., Feb. Degrees conferred and formal commencement May. Summer session from mid-June to mid-July consisting of 1- and 2-week concentrated courses.

Admission: Rolling admissions plan. *Requirements:* Baccalaureate from accredited institution; minimum 2.8 GPA.

Degree Requirements: *For first-professional degree:* 90 semester hours for Master of Divinity; 60 semester hours for Master of Arts in Theological Studies and Master of Arts in Specialized Ministry. 30 semester hours for Doctor of Ministry. All terms in residence; 4 hours field education; distribution requirements. *Grading system:* Excellent, good, satisfactory, marginal, unsatisfactory.

Distinctive Educational Programs: Internships. Evening classes. Special facilities for using telecommunications in the classroom. Facilities and programs for independent research, including directed study, tutorials. Individually arranged study abroad. Specializations in Black Church Ministries, Town and Country Ministries, Christian Religious Education, Evangelism. *Other distinctive programs:* Diaconal ministry program for lay persons. Summer school program for unordained ministers. Continuing education program for clergy and lay persons.

Degrees Conferred: 3 *master's* theology; 4 *doctorate:* theology; 28 *first-professional:* master of divinity.

Fees and Other Expenses: *Full-time tuition per academic year 2005–06:* $400 per semester hour. *Required fees:* $750 per academic year.

Financial Aid: Aid from institutionally generated funds is provided on the basis of financial need, other criteria (leadership ability and promise for ministry). *Graduate aid:* 101 students received $755,000 in federal and state-funded loans (ranging from $1,000 to $10,000).

Departments and Teaching Staff: *Professors* 7, *associate professors* 3, *assistant professors* 8, *part-time faculty* 11.

Total instructional faculty: 29 (full-time 18, part-time 11; women 10, men 18; members of minority groups 6). Total faculty with doctorate, first-professional, or other terminal degree: 21. Degrees held by full-time faculty: baccalaureate 100%, master's 100%, doctorate 70%, professional 100%. 70% hold terminal degrees.

Enrollment: Total enrollment 322. First-professional full-time 65 men / 74 women; graduate full-time 13m / 14w, part-time 33m / 46w.

Characteristics of Student Body: *Ethnic/racial makeup:* number of Black non-Hispanic: 38; Asian or Pacific Islander: 12; Hispanic: 1; White non-Hispanic: 263; unknown: 8. *Age distribution:* number under 22–24: 15; 25–29: 41; 30–34: 39; 35–39: 38; 40–49: 91; 50–64: 93; 65 and over: 3.

International Students: 12 nonresident aliens enrolled fall 2004. 12 students from Asia. No programs available to aid students whose native language is not English. No financial aid specifically designated for international students.

Student Life: On-campus residence halls for both men and women house 50% of student body. Housing available for married students. *Special regulations:* Registered cars permitted without restrictions. *Surrounding community:* Kansas City population 500,000. Served by mass transit bus system, airport 20 miles from campus; passenger rail service 6 miles from campus.

Library Collections: 88,705 volumes. 650 current periodical subscriptions. Online catalog. 16 computer work stations. Students have access to online information retrieval services and the Internet. Total 2004–05 budget for books and materials: $949,000.

Most important special holdings include Wesleyan-Methodist Collection; religion and theology collection; Wilder Collection.

Buildings and Grounds: Campus area 15 acres.

Chief Executive Officer: Dr. Myron F. McCoy, President.

Graduate students address admission inquiries to Alan Herndon, Director of Admissions and External Relations.

Southeast Missouri State University

1 University Plaza
Cape Girardeau, Missouri 63701

Tel: (573) 651-2000   **E-mail:** admissions@semo.edu
Fax: (573) 651-5061   **Internet:** www.semo.edu

Institution Description: Southeast Missouri State University is a public institution. *Enrollment:* 9,618. *Degrees awarded:* Associate, baccalaureate, master's. Specialist certificates also awarded.

Academic offerings subject to approval by statewide coordinating bodies.

Accreditation: *Regional:* NCA. *Professional:* athletic training, business, dietetics, engineering, industrial technology, music, nursing, recreation and leisure services, social work, speech-language pathology, teacher education

History: Established as the Southeast Missouri Normal School and offered first instruction at postsecondary level 1873; awarded first degree (baccalaureate) 1908; changed name to Southeast Missouri State Teachers College 1919; changed name to Southeast Missouri State College 1946; adopted present name 1972. *See* Arthur Mattingly, *Normal to University* (Cape Girardeau: Missourian Litho and Printing Company, 1979) for further information.

Institutional Structure: *Governing board:* Board of Regents of Southeast Missouri State University. Representation: 6 regents, commissioner of elementary and secondary education. 1 ex officio. 6 voting. *Composition of institution:* Administrators 57. Academic services headed by provost. Financial services and university advancement headed by vice president-finance, administration and enrollment management headed by vice president-administration and enrollment management. Full-time instructional faculty 408. Academic governance body, Faculty Senate, meets an average of 17 times per year; University Academic meets 9 times per year.

Calendar: Semesters. Academic year late Aug. to mid-May. Freshmen admitted anytime. Degrees conferred and formal commencements May, Aug., Dec. Summer sessions mid-May to early Aug.

Characteristics of Freshmen: 91% of applicants admitted. 42 % of applicants admitted and enrolled.

92% (1,385 students) submitted ACT scores. *25th percentile:* ACT Composite 19, ACT English 19, ACT Math 17. *75th percentile:* ACT Composite 26, ACT English 26, ACT Math 25.

46% of entering freshmen expected to graduate within 5 years. 86% of freshmen from Missouri. Freshmen from 14 states and 11 foreign countries.

Admission: Rolling admissions plan. For fall acceptance, apply no later than Aug. 1. Early acceptance available. *Requirements:* Either graduation from accredited secondary school or GED. *Entrance tests:* ACT. For foreign students TOEFL. *For transfer students:* must have 24 credit hours and minimum GPA 2.0. From a 4-year accredited institution 90 hours maximum transfer credit; from 2-year accredited institutions 68 hours maximum transfer credit.

College credit for postsecondary-level work completed in secondary school and for extrainstitutional learning on basis of ACE *2006 Guide to the Evaluation of Educational Experiences in the Armed Services.* Tutoring available. Developmental courses offered in summer session and regular academic year; credit given.

Degree Requirements: *For all associate degrees:* 64 credit hours; minimum of 20 hours and last term in residence; 2.0 GPA. *For all baccalaureate degrees:* 124 credit hours; 2.0 GPA; 30 hours in residence including 12 of final 18 hours general education requirements.

Fulfillment of some degree requirements and exemption from some beginning courses possible by passing College Board CLEP. *Grading system:* A–F; pass-fail; withdraw (carries time limit).

Distinctive Educational Programs: University Studies Program. Preprofessional curricula in architecture, chiropractic medicine, dentistry, engineering, law, medicine, optometry, pharmacy, physical therapy, veterinary medicine. Internship Honors program. Articulation agreements with public college and universities in Missouri as well as various colleges in Arkansas, Illinois, Kentucky, and Tennessee. *Other distinctive programs:* Study abroad in London and in Maastricht, The Netherlands. Numerous opportunities for independent study.

ROTC: Air Force. 6 commissions awarded 2004.

Degrees Conferred: 62 *associate;* 1,429 *baccalaureate* (B), 228 *master's* (M): agriculture and natural resources 38 (B); biological sciences 43 (B); business and management 262 (B); communications 94 (B); 60 (B); computer and information sciences 25 (B); education 265 (B), 116 (M); engineering and engineering technologies 25 (B); English 29 (B), 20 (M); foreign languages 16 (B); health professions 75 (B), 20 (M); mathematics 9 (B); natural resources 7 (B); parks and recreation 80 (B); philosophy/religion 1 (B); physical sciences 20 (B); protective services/public administration 105 (B), 5 (M); psychology 34 (B); social sciences and history 55 (B), 8 (M); visual and performing arts 22 (B).

Fees and Other Expenses: *Full-time tuition per academic year 2004–05:* undergraduate resident $4,554, nonresident $8,139; graduate resident $3,190, nonresident $5,780. *Required fees:* $321. *Room and board per academic year:* $5,187.

Financial Aid: Aid from institutionally generated funds is provided on the basis of academic merit, financial need, athletic ability.

Financial aid to full-time, first-time undergraduate students: need-based scholarships/grants totaling $10,096,331, self-help $14,947,500, parent loans $1,054,053, tuition waivers $58,737, athletic awards $702,990; non-need-based scholarships/grants totaling $4,182,091, self-help $11,127,908, parent loans $4,999,796, tuition waivers $166,165, athletic awards $1,226,314. *Graduate aid:* 37 students received $74,218 in federal and state-funded fellowships/grants; 215 received $1,883,238 in federal and state-funded loans; 6 received $7,603 for work-study jobs; 55 received $55,128 for college assigned jobs; 30 other fellowships/grants totaling $27,915; 63 teaching assistantships awarded totaling $350,750; 121 research assistantships awarded totaling $610,000.

Departments and Teaching Staff: *Professors* 117, *associate professors* 94, *assistant professors* 87, *instructors* 90, *part-time faculty* 129.

Total instructional faculty: 517 (full-time 388, part-time 129; women 250, men 266; members of minority groups 53). Total faculty with doctorate, first-professional, or other terminal degree: 333. Student-to-faculty ratio: 18:1. Degrees held by full-time faculty: baccalaureate 100%, master's 100%, doctorate 81%. 91% hold terminal degrees. *Faculty development:* $114,234 in grants for research.

Enrollment: Total enrollment 9,618. Undergraduate full-time 2,716 men / 3,750 women, part-time 757m / 1,237w; graduate full-time 62m / 119w, part-time 212m / 765w. *Transfer students:* in-state 489; from out-of-state 75.

Characteristics of Student Body: *Ethnic/racial makeup:* number of Black non-Hispanic: 627; American Indian or Alaska Native: 43; Asian or Pacific Islander: 52; Hispanic: 78; White non-Hispanic: 7,506. *Age distribution:* number under 18: 481; 18–19: 2,318; 20–21: 2,553; 22–24: 1,604; 25–29: 593; 30–34: 322; 35–39: 228; 40–49: 275; 50–64: 81.

International Students: 191 nonresident aliens enrolled fall 2004. Programs available to aid students whose native language is not English: social, cultural. English as a Second Language Program. Some financial aid specifically designated for qualifying international students.

Student Life: On-campus residence halls house 28% of student body. Residence halls for men constitute 43% of such space, for women 57%. *Intercollegiate athletics:* men only: baseball, basketball, cross-country, football, track, volleyball; women only: basketball, cross-country, gymnastics, soccer, softball,

track, volleyball. *Special regulations:* Cars permitted on campus in designated areas only; fee charged. Quiet hours. *Special services:* Medical services. *Student publications, radio, television: The Capaha Arrow,* a biweekly newspaper; a calendar. Radio station KRCU broadcasts 24 hours per day. *Surrounding community:* Cape Girardeau population 37,000. St. Louis, 120 miles from campus, is nearest metropolitan area. Campus served by airport 6 miles away.

Publications: *Cape Rock Journal* (biannually) first published in 1964; *Discoveries,* a publication of conference-length papers, book reviews, news and notes; *Big Muddy,* a semiannual journal of the Mississippi River Valley; *Helix,* undergraduate and graduate research publication; *Journey,* a student literary magazine.

Library Collections: 320,151 volumes. 281,858 government documents. Current serial subscriptions: paper 2,510; microform 76; via electronic access 14,654. CD-ROMs 953. Online catalog. Students have access to information retrieval services. Total 2004–05 budget for books and materials: $1,329,281.

Most important special collections are the Charles L. Harrison Collection of Rare Books and the Brodsky Collection of William Faulkner Manuscripts.

Buildings and Grounds: Campus area 325 acres.

Chief Executive Officer: Dr. Kenneth W. Dobbins, President.

Address undergraduate admission inquiries to Debbie Below, Director of Admissions; graduate inquiries to Fred Janzow, Dean, School of Graduate and University Studies.

Southwest Baptist University

1600 University Avenue
Bolivar, Missouri 65613-2496
Tel: (417) 328-5281   **E-mail:** dcrowder@sbuniv.edu
Fax: (417) 328-1514   **Internet:** www.sbuniv.edu

Institution Description: Southwest Baptist University (Southwest Baptist College until 1981) is a private institution supported by the Missouri Baptist Convention (Southern Baptist). *Enrollment:* 3,445. *Degrees awarded:* Associate, baccalaureate, master's, doctorate. Certificates also awarded.

Accreditation: *Regional:* NCA. *Professional:* business, music, nursing, teacher education

History: Established as Southwest Baptist College and offered first instruction at postsecondary level 1878; chartered 1879; awarded first degree (baccalaureate) 1882; became Southwest Academy, a secondary school, under direction of William Jewell College 1908; suspended operations 1910; reestablished as Southwest Baptist College, a junior college, 1913; became 4-year college 1965; adopted present name 1981.

Institutional Structure: *Governing board:* Board of Trustees. Representation: 25 trustees. All voting. *Composition of institution:* Administrators 6. Academic affairs headed by provost. Management/business/finances directed by vice president of administration. Full-time instructional faculty 106. Academic governance body, Faculty Senate, meets an average of 8 times per year.

Calendar: Semesters Academic year Aug. to July. Freshmen admitted Aug., Jan., Feb., June, July. Degrees conferred and formal commencement May, July, Dec. Summer session of 2 terms from early June to late July.

Characteristics of Freshmen: 73% of applicants accepted. 71% of accepted applicants enrolled.

12% (50 students) submitted SAT scores; 82% (845 students) submitted ACT scores. *25th percentile:* SAT Verbal 420, SAT Math 410; ACT Composite 26, ACT English 28, ACT Math 25. *75th percentile:* SAT Verbal 570, SAT Math 540; ACT Composite 26, ACT English 28, ACT Math 25. 49% of entering freshmen expected to graduate within 5 years. 69% of freshmen from Missouri. Freshmen from 21 states and 13 foreign countries.

Admission: Rolling admissions plan. *Requirements:* Either graduation from accredited secondary school or GED; composite score of 19 or above on ACT or composite score of 880 or above on SAT for unconditional admission. Students who do not meet his qualification may be provisionally admitted. *Entrance tests:* College Board SAT or ACT composite. *For transfer students:* From 4-year accredited institution 94 hours maximum transfer credit; from 2-year accredited institution 64 hours; correspondence/extension students 30 hours.

College credit and advanced placement for postsecondary-level work completed in secondary school. College credit for extrainstitutional learning on basis of ACE *2006 Guide to the Evaluation of Educational Experiences in the Armed Services.* Tutoring available. Developmental/remedial courses offered in summer session and regular academic year.

Degree Requirements: *For all associate degrees:* 64 credit hours; 1 term in residence. *For all baccalaureate degrees:* 128 credit hours: 2.0 GPA in major field of study; 2 terms in residence. *For all undergraduate degrees:* 2.0 GPA; weekly chapel attendance; 2 credit hours physical education; general education requirements; 5 Bible courses.

Fulfillment of some degree requirements and exemption from some beginning courses possible by passing College Board CLEP, APP, other standardized tests. *Grading system:* A–F; pass-fail; withdraw (carries penalty, carries time limit).

Distinctive Educational Programs: Cooperative baccalaureate in engineering with University of Missouri-Rolla. BSN program with St. John's Regional Health Center. Independent study. Study abroad in Costa Rica, England, France, Hong Kong, Russia, Spain, Scotland.

Degrees Conferred: 17 *associate;* 430 *baccalaureate:* biological/life sciences 8; business/marketing 70; communications/communication technologies 17; computer and information sciences 8; education 80; English 15; foreign languages and literature 3; health professions and related sciences 28; mathematics 12; parks and recreation 21; philosophy/religion/theology 54; physical sciences 2; protective services/public administration 11; psychology 60; social sciences and history 28; visual and performing arts 13. 347 *master's:* business/marketing 14; education 315; health professions 18.

Fees and Other Expenses: *Full-time tuition per academic year 2005–06:* undergraduate $12,450; graduate tuition varies by degree program. *Required fees:* $800. *Room and board per academic year:* $5,950.

Financial Aid: Aid from institutionally generated funds is provided on the basis of academic merit, financial need, athletic ability, other criteria.

Financial aid to full-time, first-time undergraduate students: need-based scholarships/grants totaling $5,033,040, self-help $5,558,281; non-need-based scholarships/grants totaling $6,621,924, self-help $3,593,120, parent loans $942,017, tuition waivers $421,545, athletic awards $1,521,525.

Departments and Teaching Staff: Arts *professors* 0, *associate professors* 1, *assistant professors* 0, *instructors* 0, *part-time teachers* 2; accounting 1, 0, 0, 2, 2; behavioral sciences 0, 1, 4, 3, 15; biology 3, 0, 1, 1, 5; business administration 1, 1, 3, 3, 10; chemistry and physics 3, 1, 0, 0, 3; communication arts 1, 1, 0, 2, 6; computer and information science 1, 1, 1, 0, 2; education 1, 3, 4, 3, 5; health/physical education/recreation 3, 0, 2, 2, 6; history and political science 1, 2, 0, 0, 8; language and literature 1, 0, 1, 3, 12; mathematics 1, 3, 0, 1, 6; music 4, 4, 2, 1, 10; nursing 0, 1, 4, 15, 1; physical therapy 1, 2, 2, 0, 0; University Learning Center 0, 0, 1, 0, 1; Christian ministries 2, 2, 1, 0, 7; religious studies 2, 2, 0, 0, 3, 1; library services 1, 1, 4, 0, 0.

Total instructional faculty: 281 (full-time 106, part-time 175; women 128, men 153; members of minority groups 2). Total faculty with doctorate, first-professional, or other terminal degree: 109. Student-to-faculty ratio: 15:1. Degrees held by full-time faculty: doctorate 54%. 54% hold terminal degrees.

Enrollment: Total enrollment 3,445. Undergraduate full-time 709 men / 1,120 women, part-time 212m / 705w; graduate full-time 30m / 75w, part-time 140m / 454w

Characteristics of Student Body: *Ethnic/racial makeup:* number of Black non-Hispanic: 61; American Indian or Alaska Native: 13; Asian or Pacific Islander: 19; Hispanic: 22; White non-Hispanic: 2,597; unknown: 716. *Age distribution:* number under 18: 157; 18–19: 665; 20–21: 736; 22–24: 124; 25–29: 249; 30–34: 157; 35–39: 114; 40–49: 166; 50–64: 65; 65 and over: 9.

International Students: 17 nonresident aliens enrolled fall 2004. 5 students from Europe, 3 Asia, 4 Latin America, 3 Africa, 1 Australia, 3 New Zealand. No programs available to aid students whose native language is not English. No financial aid specifically designated for international students.

Student Life: On-campus residence halls house 64% of student body. *Intercollegiate athletics:* men only: baseball, basketball, cross country, football, tennis, track and field; women only: basketball, cross country, soccer, softball, tennis, track and field, volleyball. *Special regulations:* Registered cars permitted without restrictions. Curfew 12pm to 6am Sun.-Thurs.; 1am to 6am Fri.–Sat. Quiet hours 8:30pm to 8:30am. *Special services:* Learning Resources Center, medical services, Career Planning and Placement Center. *Student publications: The Mozarkian,* a yearbook; *The Omnibus,* a weekly newspaper. *Surrounding community:* Bolivar population approximately 10,000. Springfield, 28 miles from campus, is nearest metropolitan area. Served by airport 1 mile from campus.

Publications: *Kwik Chek,* weekly news sheet produced by the office of public relations; *SBU Life,* official publication of the university.

Library Collections: 193,821 volumes including bound books, serial backfiles, electronic documents, and government documents not in separate collections. Online catalog. Current serial subscriptions: 924 paper, 5 microform, 2,631 electronic. 480 recordings; 129 compact discs. Students have access to the Internet at no charge.

Most important special holdings include Missouri State documents; University Archives; Butler Baptist History and Heritage Collection; R. Earl Allen Model Pastor's Library.

Buildings and Grounds: Campus area 123 acres. *New buildings:* Moyer Sports and Wellness Center.

Chief Executive Officer: Dr. C. Pat Taylor, President.

Undergraduates address admission inquiries to Darren Crowder, Director of Admissions; graduate inquiries to area of interest.

Southwest Missouri State University

901 South National Avenue
Springfield, Missouri 65804
Tel: (417) 836-5000   **E-mail:** smsuinfo@smsu.edu
Fax: (417) 836-6583   **Internet:** www.smsu.edu

Institution Description: Southwest Missouri State University is a state-assisted multipurpose university with a branch campus at West Plains and a research campus in Mountain Grove, Missouri. *Enrollment:* 18,390. *Degrees awarded:* Associate, baccalaureate, master's. Specialist certificate in education also awarded.

Academic offerings subject to approval by statewide coordinating bodies. Budget subject to approval by state governing bodies.

Accreditation: *Regional:* NCA. *Professional:* accounting, athletic training, business, computer science, construction education, family and consumer science, industrial technology, music, nursing, physical therapy, physician assisting, public administration, recreation and leisure services, social work, speech-language pathology, surgeon assisting, teacher education, theatre

History: Established as State Normal School 1905; offered first instruction at postsecondary level 1906; awarded first degree (baccalaureate) 1915; changed name to Southwest Missouri State Teachers College 1919, to Southwest Missouri State College 1945; adopted present name 1972. *See* Roy Ellis, *Shrine of the Ozarks: A History of Southwest Missouri State College, 1905–1965* (Columbia, MO: American Press, Incorporated) for further information.

Institutional Structure: *Governing board:* Southwest Missouri State Board of Governors. Representation: 10 governors. All voting. 1 ex officio and 1 student, nonvoting. *Composition of institution:* Administrators 66 men / 15 women. Academic affairs headed by vice president for academic affairs. Management/business/finances directed by vice president for financial services. Full-time instructional faculty 609. Academic governance body, Faculty Senate, meets an average of 9 times per year.

Calendar: Semesters. Academic year late Aug. to mid-May. Freshmen admitted Aug., Jan., June. Degrees conferred and formal commencements May, Aug., Dec. Summer session of one 8-week term from early June to late July.

Characteristics of Freshmen: 75% of applicants accepted. 60% of applicants accepted and enrolled.

Average secondary school rank of freshmen 66th percentile. Mean ACT score 22.4.

32% of freshmen expected to graduate within 5 years. 93% of freshmen from Missouri. Freshmen from 44 states and 67 foreign countries.

Admission: Rolling admissions plan. Early acceptance available. *Requirements:* Either graduation from accredited secondary school or GED. Missouri residents must rank in upper two-thirds of graduating class or above 60th percentile on tests; out-of-state students must rank in upper one-half or above 60th percentile. Minimum 2.0 GPA. *For transfer students:* 2.0 minimum GPA; from 4-year accredited institution maximum transfer credit limited only by residence requirement; from 2-year accredited institution 64 hours maximum transfer credit.

College credit and advanced placement for postsecondary-level work completed in secondary school and for extrainstitutional learning on basis of ACE *2006 Guide to the Evaluation of Educational Experiences in the Armed Services.* Developmental/remedial courses offered in summer session and regular academic year; credit given.

Degree Requirements: *For all associate degrees:* 62 semester hours. *For all baccalaureate degrees:* 125 hours, of which 40 hours must be in upper division work; minimum 2.00 GPA on all work attempted at SMSU and 2.00 GPA on all college work (SMSU and transfer combined); minimum 2.00 GPA on all coursework required in the major; some programs require higher GPAs; coursework on U.S. and Missouri constitutions. 30 hours in residence; general education requirements. General Education Assessment examination required. *Grading system:* A–F; pass-fail; withdraw (carries time limit).

Distinctive Educational Programs: Work-experience programs. Evening classes. Special facilities for using telecommunications in the classroom. Interdisciplinary programs and courses in antiquities, minorities studies, career-life planning. Individual majors. Study abroad through Missouri London Program in Harrington Gardens in central London, England.

ROTC: Army.

Degrees Conferred: 2,411 *baccalaureate;* 823 *master's.* Bachelor's degrees awarded in top five disciplines: business, management, marketing, and related support services 807; education 384; communication, journalism, and related programs 183; psychology 124; visual and performing arts 113.

Fees and Other Expenses: *Tuition per academic year 2004–05:* in-state $5,128, out-of-state $9,748. *Room and board per academic year:* $5,050. *Books and supplies:* $800.

Financial Aid: Aid from institutionally generated funds is provided on the basis of academic merit, financial need, athletic ability, other criteria. Institution has a Program Participation Agreement with the U.S. Department of Education for eligible students to receive Pell Grants and, depending upon the agreement, other federal aid.

Financial aid to full-time, first-time undergraduate students: 27% received federal grants averaging $2,540; 4% state/local grants averaging $1,869; 32% institutional grants averaging $2,904; 56% received loans averaging $4,839.

Departments and Teaching Staff: *Professors* 245, *associate professors* 183, *assistant professors* 168, *instructors* 65, *part-time teachers* 160.

Total full-time faculty: 714. Degrees held by full-time faculty: baccalaureate 1%, master's 20%, doctorate 78%, professional 1%. 85% hold terminal degrees.

Enrollment: Total enrollment 18,930. Undergraduate 15,771 (44.2% men, 55.8% women).

Characteristics of Student Body: *Ethnic/racial makeup (undergraduate):* number of Black non-Hispanic: 2.3%; American Indian or Alaska Native: .9%; Asian or Pacific Islander: 1.3%; Hispanic: 1.4%; White non-Hispanic: 87.5%; unknown: 4.9%.

International Students: 268 undergraduate nonresident aliens enrolled fall 2003. No programs available to aid students whose native language is not English. No financial aid specifically designated for international students.

Student Life: On-campus residence halls house 21% of student body. Residence halls for women only constitute 37% of such space, for both sexes 47%. 15% of student body lives in on-campus, college-controlled apartments. 10.5% of men join and 3.5% live in fraternities; 6% of women join and 2% live in sororities. *Intercollegiate athletics:* men only: baseball, basketball, cross country, football, golf, soccer, swimming, tennis, track, wrestling; women only: basketball, cross country, field hockey, golf, softball, tennis, track, volleyball. *Special regulations:* Registered cars permitted on campus; fee charged. Quiet hours. Residence hall visitation typically from 10am to 1am. *Special services:* Medical services. *Student publications, radio: The Standard,* a weekly newspaper. Radio station KSMU broadcasts 146 hours per week. *Surrounding community:* Springfield population 134,000. Kansas City, 170 miles from campus, is nearest metropolitan area. Served by airport 10 miles from campus.

Library Collections: 675,000 volumes. 835,000 government documents; 900,000 microforms; 30,000 audiovisual materials; 5,000 current periodical subscriptions. Online catalog. Students have access to online information retrieval services and the Internet.

Most important special holdings include William J. Jones Collection of French poet Jean Arthur Rimbaud (1854-91), 1,818 items; William J. Jones Collection of French novelist Michel Butor, 994 items; map collection (500,000 maps).

Buildings and Grounds: Campus area 225 acres.

Chief Executive Officer: Dr. John H. Keiser, President.

Address admission inquiries to Jill M. Duncan, Assistant Director of Admissions.

Stephens College

1200 East Broadway
Columbia, Missouri 65215
Tel: (573) 442-2211   **E-mail:** apply@stephens.edu
Fax: (573) 876-7248   **Internet:** www.stephens.edu

Institution Description: Stephens College is the second-oldest women's college in the United States. Stephens is a private, independent, nonprofit college. *Enrollment:* 705. Men are admitted through scholarship in the performing arts and through the School of Continuing Education. *Degrees awarded:* Associate, baccalaureate.

Accreditation: *Regional:* NCA. *Professional:* music, theatre

History: Established 1833 as Columbia Female Academy; chartered and offered first instruction at postsecondary level 1857; awarded first degree (baccalaureate) 1859; changed name to Stephens Female College 1870; adopted present name 1917. *See* John C. Crighton, *Stephens: A Story of Educational Innovation* (Columbia, MO: American Press, 1970) for further information.

Institutional Structure: *Governing board:* Board of Trustees. Extrainstitutional representation: 20 trustees. 16 voting. *Composition of institution:* Administrators 2 women / 3 men. Academic affairs headed by vice president for academic and student affairs. Management/business/finances directed by vice president for administration and finance. Full-time instructional faculty 32 women / 22 men. Academic governance: Faculty Executive council and governing committees. Faculty meets monthly as does the Faculty Executive Council. Council.

Calendar: Semesters. Academic year Aug. to May.

Characteristics of Freshmen: 80% of applicants admitted. 48% of applicants admitted and enrolled.

15% (44students) submitted SAT scores; 85% (134 students) submitted ACT scores. *25th percentile:* SAT Verbal 540, SAT Math 480; ACT Composite 21. *75th percentile:* SAT Verbal 610, SAT Math 580; ACT Composite 26.

51% of entering freshmen expected to graduate within 5 years. 56% of freshmen from Missouri. Freshmen from 30 states and 2 foreign countries.

Admission: Rolling admissions plan. For fall acceptance, apply as early as 1 year prior to enrollment, but not later than Aug. 15. Early acceptance available. *Requirements:* Either graduation from accredited secondary school with 12-15 units; or GED. *Entrance tests:* College Board SAT or ACT composite. *For transfer students:* 2.0 minimum GPA; maximum transfer credit limited only by residence requirement.

College credit and advanced placement for postsecondary-level work completed in secondary school. College credit for extrainstitutional learning on basis of ACE *2006 Guide to the Evaluation of Educational Experiences in the Armed Services* and portfolio assessment. Tutoring available. Developmental courses offered in summer session and regular academic year; credit given.

Degree Requirements: *For all associate degrees:* 20.0 course credits; freshman composition; general education requirement; basic math skills; 2 sessions physical education; 2.0 cumulative GPA; 4 semesters residency. *For all baccalaureate degrees:* 40.0 course credits; freshman composition; lower and upper division general education requirement; basic math skills; 4 sessions physical education; 2.0 cumulative GPA; 7 semesters residency. Three-year BA degree program available.

Fulfillment of some degree requirements and exemption from some beginning courses possible by passing College Board CLEP, APP, or departmental examination. *Grading system:* A–F; pass-fail; incomplete.

Distinctive Educational Programs: Work-experience programs. Flexible meeting places and schedules. Off-campus center (at Okoboji Summer Theater in Iowa). Fashion, theater, and business field trips to New York and Europe. Evening classes. Accelerated degree programs. Equestrian business management major; American public policy major; East Asian studies major. Public Leadership Education Network. Dual-degree programs in animal science with the University of Missouri - Columbia, and in engineering with Washington University (St. Louis, MO), Georgia Institute of Technology, and Auburn University. External degree program through Stephens College Without Walls for men and women aged 23 and older. Interdepartmental/interdisciplinary programs in fashion merchandising, business. Facilities and programs for independent research. Individual majors. Tutorials. Internships.

ROTC: Available at the University of Missouri through the Mid-Missouri Associated Colleges and Universities consortium.

Degrees Conferred: 6 *associate;* 112 *baccalaureate:* agriculture 1; biological sciences 3; 10, business/marketing 4; communications 4; education 4; English 4; health professions 10; interdisciplinary studies 9; law/legal studies 3; natural resources/environmental science 1; psychology 3; visual and performing arts 41. 26 *master's:* business/marketing 5; education 21.

Fees and Other Expenses: *Full-time tuition per academic year 2005–06:* $19,300. *Room and board per academic year:* $7,630.

Financial Aid: Aid from institutionally generated funds is provided on the basis of academic merit, financial need, other criteria.

Financial aid to full-time, first-time undergraduate students: need-based scholarships/grants totaling $3,840,753, self-help $1,191,392, parent loans $273,687, tuition waivers $64,053, athletic awards $38,000; non-need-based scholarships/grants totaling $1,281,487, self-help $879,229, parent loans $780,097, tuition waivers $38,296, athletic awards $19,900. *Graduate aid:* 34 students received $217,870 in federal and state-funded loans (ranging from $2,540 to $10,539); 7 students received fellowships and grants totaling $27,010 (ranging from $1,460 to $5,840).

Departments and Teaching Staff: *Professors* 4, *associate professors* 14, *assistant professors* 23, *instructors* 5, *part-time faculty* 26.

Total instructional faculty: 72 (full-time 45, part-time 27; women 48, men 24). Total faculty with doctorate, first-professional, or other terminal degree: 36. Student-to-faculty ratio: 10:1. Degrees held by full-time faculty: baccalaureate 15%, master's 35%, doctorate 50%. 61% hold terminal degrees.

Enrollment: Total enrollment 705. Undergraduate 17 men / 475 women, part-time 9m / 132w; graduate full-time 1m / 34w, part-time 6m / 31w. *Transfer students:* in-state 56; from out-of-state 93.

Characteristics of Student Body: *Ethnic/racial makeup:* number of Black non-Hispanic: 58; American Indian or Alaska Native: 3; Asian or Pacific Islander: 13; Hispanic: 16; White non-Hispanic: 532; unknown: 9. *Age distribution:* number under 18: 5; 18–19: 210; 20–21: 212; 22–24: 60; 25–29: 21; 30–34: 23; 35–39: 19; 40–49: 61; 50–64: 21; 65 and over: 1.

International Students: 2 nonresident aliens from Asia enrolled fall 2004. No programs available to aid students whose native language is not English. No financial aid specifically designated for international students.

Student Life: On-campus residence halls house 90% of student body. Athletic teams, women only: basketball, swimming, volleyball, tennis. *Special services:* Medical services, counseling services. *Student publications: Harbinger,* an annual literary magazine, *Stephens Life,* award-winning student newspaper; chapbooks published by bachelor of fine arts seniors in English. Radio station KWWC broadcasts 116 hours per week. *Surrounding community:* Columbia population 79,000. St. Louis, 126 miles from campus, and Kansas City, 125 miles from campus, are nearest metropolitan areas. Served by airport 8 miles from campus.

Library Collections: 129,126 volumes. 10,722 microforms; 105 audiovisual materials; 166 current periodical subscriptions. 22 computer work stations. Students have access to online information retrieval services.

Most important special holdings include Women's Studies; Political Science; Educational Resources (children's literature); literature.

Buildings and Grounds: Campus area 240 acres.

Chief Executive Officer: Dr. Wendy B. Libby, President.

Address admission inquiries to Director of Admissions.

Truman State University

100 East Normal
Kirksville, Missouri 63501-4221
Tel: (660) 785-4114   **E-mail:** admissions@truman.edu
Fax: (660) 785-7456   **Internet:** www.truman.edu

Institution Description: Formerly named Northeast Missouri State University, Truman State University is the premier liberal arts and sciences institution for the state of Missouri. *Enrollment:* 5,862. *Degrees awarded:* Baccalaureate, master's.

Academic offerings subject to approval by statewide coordinating bodies. Budget subject to approval by state governing boards.

Accreditation: *Regional:* NCA. *Professional:* accounting, business, counseling, music, nursing, nursing education, speech-language pathology, teacher education

History: Established as North Missouri Normal School and Commercial College, chartered, and offered first instruction at postsecondary level 1867; changed name to First District Normal School and awarded first degree (baccalaureate) 1870; changed name to Northeast Missouri State Teachers College 1919, to Northeast Missouri State College 1968, to Northeast Missouri State University 1972, to Truman State University 1996; designated the official statewide public liberal arts and sciences university by the Missouri legislature in 1986. *See* Dr. Walter H. Ryle, *Centennial History of the Northeast Missouri State Teachers College* (Kirksville: Northeast Missouri State University 1972) for further information.

Institutional Structure: *Governing board:* Board of Governors of Truman State University. Representation: 7 governors from Missouri (all voting), 2 governors from out-of-state (non-voting), 1 student representative (non-voting), 1 ex officio member. *Composition of institution:* Academic affairs headed by Vice President for Academic Affairs. Management/business/finances headed by controller. Full-time instructional faculty total 347. Academic governance body, Faculty Senate, meets an average of 12 times per year.

Calendar: Semesters. Academic year Aug. to May. Freshmen admitted Aug., Jan., June. Degrees conferred and formal commencement May, Aug., Dec. Summer sessions June to Aug.

Characteristics of Freshmen: 84% of applicants admitted. 39% of applicants admitted and enrolled.

19% (284 students) submitted SAT scores; 97% (1,431 students) submitted ACT scores. *25th percentile:* SAT Verbal 25, SAT Math 25; ACT Composite 24, ACT English 25, ACT Math 24. *75th percentile:* SAT Verbal 670, SAT Math 670; ACT Composite 30, ACT English 31, ACT Math 29.

63% of entering freshmen expected to graduate within 5 years. 76% of freshmen from Missouri. Freshmen from 23 states and 24 foreign countries.

Admission: Early admission plan available to students ranking in the top 20% of their high school graduating classes and scoring at the 80th percentile on the college entrance exam. Application deadline Nov. 15. General application deadline is March 1. GED accepted only if acceptable college entrance exam score is furnished. Additional requirements for some programs. Truman will accept ACT or SAT. Foreign students must receive a minimum 550 TOEFL score. Transfer student positions are limited to 250 per year; must have a 2.0 minimum college GPA.

Degree Requirements: Minimum 124 credit hours; 2.0 GPA; 45 hours in residence; 63 credit hours of liberal arts and sciences courses required for each major; comprehensive assessment program of testing and surveying measures student growth in and satisfaction with education in liberal arts and sciences core and major area of study.

Distinctive Educational Programs: Honors programs available in liberal arts and sciences as well as in the discipline. Study abroad programs in Japan, Germany, France, Quebec, Costa Rica, England, Spain, and other countries. Residential colleges provide students with a living-learning residential environment. A senior faculty member called a College Rector leads each hall, and numerous Faculty Fellows teach liberal arts and sciences courses within the halls and interact with residents on a daily basis. Freshmen and undeclared students receive professional residentially-based academic advising and all residents are supported by upper-class student advisors. Facilities and programs for undergraduate research are available and encouraged.

ROTC: Army. 11 commissions awarded 2004.

Degrees Conferred: 1,114 *baccalaureate* (B), 165 *master's* (M): agriculture 13 (B); biological/life sciences 105 (B), 5 (M); business/marketing 186 (B); ; communications/communication technologies 57 (B); computer and information sciences 38 (B); education 95 (M); English 100 (B), 13 (M); foreign languages and literature 27 (B); health professions and related sciences 97 (B), 30 (M); mathematics 15 (B); parks and recreation 66 (B); philosophy/religion/theology 15 (B); physical sciences 29 (B); protective services/public administration 38 (B); psychology 111 (B); social sciences and history 93 (B); visual and performing arts 73 (B), 7 (M); other 51 (B), 15 (M).

Fees and Other Expenses: *Full-time tuition per academic year:* resident undergraduate $5,740, nonresident $9,920. *Required fees:* $222. *Room and board per academic year:* $5,455.

Financial Aid: Aid from institutionally generated funds is provided on the basis of academic merit, financial need, athletic ability, other criteria.

Financial aid to full-time, first-time undergraduate students: need-based scholarships/grants totaling $2,617,979, self-help $5,896,371; non-need-based scholarships/grants totaling $18,134,356, self-help $6,477,366, parent loans $1,283,285, tuition waivers $647,948, athletic awards $1,076,455. *Graduate aid:* 2 students received $5,057 in federal and state-funded fellowships/grants; 103 received $1,000,462 in federal and state-funded loans (ranging from $600 to $4,457); 2 received $498 for college-assigned jobs; 210 received other fellowships/grants totaling $194,955; 5353 teaching assistantships awarded totaling $521,800.

Departments and Teaching Staff: *Professors* 123, *associate professors* 120, *assistant professors* 80, *instructors* 24, *part-time faculty* 34.

Total instructional faculty: 381 (full-time 347, part-time 34; women 154, men 227; members of minority groups 31). Total faculty with doctorate, first-professional, or other terminal degree: 300. Student-to-faculty ratio: 15:1. Degrees held by full-time faculty: baccalaureate less than 1%, master's 19%, doctorate 81%, professional less than 1%. 82% hold terminal degrees. *Faculty development:* $2,193,349 total grants for research.

Enrollment: Total enrollment 5,862. Undergraduate full-time 2,255 men / 3,231 women, part-time 66m / 64w; graduate full-time 58m / 130w, part-time 15m / 43w. *Transfer students:* in-state 87; from out-of-state 17.

Characteristics of Student Body: *Ethnic/racial makeup:* number of Black non-Hispanic: 201; American Indian or Alaska Native: 28; Asian or Pacific Islander: 116; Hispanic: 100; White non-Hispanic: 4,788; unknown: 158. *Age distribution:* number under 18: 12; 18–19: 961; 20–21: 2,356; 22–24: 870; 25–29: 47; 30–34: 7; 35–39: 7; 40–49: 6; 50–64: 2; 65 and over: 18. 25% of student body attend summer sessions.

International Students: 240 nonresident aliens enrolled fall 2004. 40 students from Europe, 130 Asia, 6 Central and South America, 53 Africa, 2 Australia, 1 other. Programs available to aid students whose native language is not English: social, cultural. Financial aid specifically designated for international students: variable number of scholarships available annually for undergraduate international students; 216 totaling $540,000 awarded 2004–05.

Student Life: On-campus residence halls house 48% of student body. Residence halls for women constitute 11% of such space; remaining space accommodates both men and women in gender-specific suites or wings. 7% of student body live in college-owned apartments. Housing available for married students. *Intercollegiate athletics:* men: baseball, basketball, football, golf, soccer, swimming, tennis, track and cross-country, wrestling; women: basketball, cross-country, golf, soccer, softball, swimming, tennis, track, volleyball. *Special regulations:* Registered cars permitted with designated parking. Quiet hours in residence halls; entrances monitored 10:30pm to 6am. *Special services:* Medical, mental health counseling and disability services are available. *Student publications, radio:* Windfall, a literary magazine; *Index*, a weekly newspaper; *Paintbrush, Synthesis* and *Northeast Writers; Detours,* quarterly magazine; *Echo,* a yearbook. Radio station KTRM broadcasts 124 hours per week. *Surrounding community:* Kirksville population 18,000. Kansas City, 140 miles from campus, is nearest metropolitan area. Served by airport 6 miles from campus; passenger rail service 12 miles from campus.

Publications: Truman State University Press publishes *Detours, 16th Century Journal, and The Green Lantern Literary Review* are published on campus. *National Association of College Wind and Percussions Instructor Journal* and *Journal of Political Science Education* are edited on campus.

Library Collections: 445,971 volumes including bound books, serial back-files, electronic documents, and government documents not in separate collections. Online catalog. Current serial subscriptions: 2,580 paper, 153 microform; 670 via electronic access. 18,944 recordings. 5,768 computer discs; 100 CD-ROMs. 804 computer work stations campus-wide. Students have access to the Internet at no charge. Total budget for books, periodicals, audiovisual materials, microforms 2004–05: $1133,245.

Most important special collections include Missouriana Collection; John J. Audobon's *Birds of North America*; Rare Books Collection; Laughlin Collection; Abraham Lincoln Collection.

Buildings and Grounds: The Truman campus consists of 140 acres and 39 buildings with Georgian style architecture.

Chief Executive Officer: Dr. Barbara Dixon, President.

Undergraduates address admission inquiries to Brad Chamnbers, Co-Director of Admission; graduate graduate inquires to Maria DiStefano, Dean of Graduate Studies.

University of Missouri - Columbia

105 Jesse Hall
Columbia, Missouri 65211
Tel: (573) 882-2121 **E-mail:** MU4U@missouri.edu
Fax: (573) 882-7786 **Internet:** www.missouri.edu

Institution Description: *Enrollment:* 27,003. *Degrees awarded:* Baccalaureate, first-professional (law, medicine, veterinary medicine), master's, doctorate. Certificates also awarded.

Member of the consortium Mid-Missouri Associated Colleges and Universities.

Accreditation: *Regional:* NCA. *Professional:* accounting, business, clinical psychology, dietetics, engineering, health services administration, interior design, journalism, law, librarianship, medicine, nursing, nursing education, occupational therapy, physical therapy, psychology internship, public administration, radiography, recreation and leisure services, rehabilitation counseling, respiratory therapy, school psychology, social work, speech-language pathology, veterinary medicine

History: Established and chartered 1839; awarded first degree (baccalaureate) 1843.

Institutional Structure: *Composition of institution:* Academic affairs headed by chancellor. Management/business/finances directed by vice chancellor, administrative services. Full-time instructional faculty 2,028. Academic governance body, Faculty Council, meets an average of 16 times per year.

Calendar: Semesters. Academic year Aug. to May. Freshmen admitted Aug., Jan., June. Degrees conferred and formal commencements May, Dec. Summer session of 2 terms from mid-June to early Aug.

Characteristics of Freshmen: 89.3% of applicants admitted. 47% of applicants admitted and enrolled.

18% (824 students) submitted SAT scores; 96% (4,393 students) submitted ACT scores. *25th percentile:* ACT Composite 23, ACT English 23, ACT Math 22. *75th percentile:* ACT Composite 28, ACT English 29, ACT Math 28. 110 National Merit Scholars.

64.5% of entering freshmen expected to graduate within 5 years. 86% of freshmen from Missouri. Freshmen from 43 states and 35 foreign countries.

Admission: Admission is determined by a combination of class rank and test score as well as completion of the following minimum high school coursework of 17 units to include 4 units English (2 must be composition or writing); 4 units mathematics (including algebra I or higher); 3 units each in science and social science; 1 unit fine arts; 2 units of foreign language.

College credit for postsecondary-level work completed in secondary school.

Degree Requirements: 120–128 semester hours; 2.0 GPA; final 30 credit hours in residence; general education requirements; some requirements may vary by division.

Fulfillment of some degree requirements and exemption from some beginning courses possible by passing College Board CLEP, AP, International Baccalaureate. *Grading system:* A–F; pass-fail; withdraw (carries time limit).

Distinctive Educational Programs: Accelerated degree programs. Special facilities for using telecommunications in the classroom. Facilities and programs for independent research, including honors programs, individual majors, tutorials. Honors College, National Student Exchange. Freshmen interest groups. Study abroad in Japan, Mexico, London, Denmark, Germany, Russia, Taiwan, Manchester, Australia.

ROTC: Army, Air Force, Marines, Navy. 23 Air Force, 17 Army and 15 Marine/Navy commissions awarded 2004.

Degrees Conferred: 4,086 *baccalaureate* (B), 1,291 *master's* (M), 251 *doctorate* (D): agriculture 199 (B), 27 (M); area and ethnic studies 55 (B); biologi-cal/life sciences 238 (B), 11 (M), 23 (D); business/marketing 701 (B), 258 (M), 8 (D); communications/communication technologies 471 (B), 64 (M), 18 (D); computer and information sciences 109 (B), 64 (M), 18 (D); education 247 (B), 421 (M), 70 (D); engineering and engineering technologies 299 (B), 69 (M), 13 (D); English 126 (B), 10 (M), 14 (D); foreign languages and literature 59 (B), 11 (M), 7 (D); health professions and related sciences 230 (B), 18 (M), 4 (D); home economics and vocational home economics 233 (B), 13 (M), 6 (D); interdisciplinary studies 159 (B), 2 (D); law/legal studies 12 (M); liberal arts/general studies 67 (B); library science 1 (M); mathematics 40 (B), 21 (M), 7 (D); natural resources/environmental science 49 (B), 12 (M), 2 (D); parks and recreation 38 (B), 5 (M); philosophy/religion/theology 35 (B), 1 (M); physical sciences 58 (B), 22 (M), 18 (D); protective services/public administration 32 (B), 141 (M); psychology 219 (B), 12 (M), 8 (D); social sciences and history 354 (B), 41 (M), 31 (D); visual and performing arts 78 (B), 13 (M), 2 (D). 331 *first-professional:* law 175; medicine 92; veterinary medicine 64. 4 honorary degrees awarded 2004: Doctor of Humane Letters.

Fees and Other Expenses: *Full-time tuition per academic year 2004–05:* undergraduate resident $5,858, nonresident $14,675; graduate resident $5,086, nonresident $13,134. Professional school tuition varies. *Required fees:* $804. *Room and board per academic year:* $6,220.

Financial Aid: University of Missouri offers a direct lending program. Aid from institutionally generated funds is provided on the basis of academic merit, financial need, athletic ability.

Financial aid to full-time, first-time undergraduate students: need-based scholarships/grants totaling $36,615,774, self-help $32,127,171, parent loans $11,900,505, tuition waivers $776,890, athletic awards $1,634,253; non-need-based scholarships/grants totaling $20,572,826, self-help $17,750,046, parent loans $16,903,944, tuition waivers $2,593,764, athletic awards $3,124,141. *Graduate aid:* 100 students received $983,950 in federal and state-funded fellowships/grants (ranging $100 to $10,000); 3,000 received $40,564,236,in federal and state-funded loans ($100 to $38,500); 76 students held work-study jobs earning $160,039 (ranging from $1,000 to $5,000); 4,000 received $27,234,198 for other fellowships/grants (ranging from $500 to $20,000); 112 teaching assistantships awarded totaling $12,437,720 (ranging from $8,900 to $16,500); 1,138 research assistantships were awarded totaling $12,417,856 (ranging from $8,900 to $16,500).

Departments and Teaching Staff: Agriculture, Food and Natural Resources *professors* 68, *associate professors* 67, *assistant professors* 72, *instructors* 5, *part-time faculty* 19; Arts and Science 168, 139, 173, 17, 62; Business 20, 12, 20, 0, 10; Education 24, 32, 29, 8, 10; Engineering 24, 43, 30, 2, 3; Graduate School 6, 6, 2, 0, 5; Health Professions 6, 12, 14, 6, 12; Human Environmental Sciences 11, 14, 27, 35, 19; Journalism 18, 18, 30, 6, 13; Law 16, 13, 1, 0, 7; Medicine 77, 101, 174, 23, 92; Sinclair School of Nursing 4, 6, 13, 19, 6; Veterinary Medicine 22, 41, 44, 8, 12;

Total instructional faculty: 1,364 (full-time 1,255, part-time 109; women 493, men 721; members of minority groups 210). Student-to-faculty ratio: 18:1. Degrees held by full-time faculty: baccalaureate 1%, master's 11.5%, doctorate 62%, professional 26%. *Faculty development:* $12.9 million in grants for research.

Enrollment: Total enrollment 23,055. Undergraduate full-time 9,489 men / 10,044 women, part-time 633m / 717w, first-professional full-time 996m / 512w, part-time 18m / 43w; graduate full-time 1,177m / 1,337w, part-time 1,041m / 1,496w. *Transfer students:* in-state 1,114; from out-of-state 222.

Characteristics of Student Body: *Ethnic/racial makeup (undergraduate):* number of Black non-Hispanic: 1,161; American Indian or Alaska Native: 134; Asian or Pacific Islander: 576; Hispanic: 343; White non-Hispanic: 17,657; unknown: 695. *Age distribution:* number under 18: 120; 18–19: 8,253; 20–21: 8,175; 22–24: 3,278; 25–29: 598; 30–34: 180; 35–39: 107; 40–49: 148; 50–64: 59; 65 and over: 2.

International Students: 1,400 nonresident aliens enrolled fall 2004. Students from Europe, Asia, Latin America, Africa, Canada, Australia, New Zealand. Programs available to aid students whose native language is not English: English as a Second Language Program. Financial aid specifically designated for qualifying international students: variable number of scholarship available annually.

Student Life: On-campus residence halls house 28% of student body. 47% of undergraduates live in campus-owned or operated facilities. No private residence halls. *Intercollegiate athletics:* men only: baseball, basketball, football, golf, swimming, tennis, track, wrestling; women only: basketball, golf, gymnastics, soccer, softball, swimming, tennis, track, volleyball. *Special regulations:* Registered cars permitted without restrictions. Quiet hours in selected residence halls. *Special services:* Learning Center, medical services, weekday shuttle bus service between campus and remote parking areas. *Student publications, radio, television:* Maneater, a twice weekly newspaper; Missourian, a daily newspaper. Radio station KBIA broadcasts 168 hours per week; radio station KCOU broadcasts 168 hours weekly. TV station KOMU (NBC affiliate) broadcasts 138 hours per week. *Surrounding community:* Columbia population 79,802. St. Louis and

Kansas City, both 120 miles from campus, are nearest metropolitan areas. Served by mass transit bus system; airport 7 miles from campus; passenger rail service 30 miles from campus.

Library Collections: 4,861,015 volumes including bound books, serial backfiles, electronic documents, and government documents not in separate collection. Online catalog. Current serial subscriptions: 26,886 paper; 6,872,209 microform and via electronic access. Computer work stations available. Students have access to online information retrieval services and the Internet. Total 2004–05 budget for books and materials: $5,141,759.

Most important special holdings include Library of the State Historical Society; special collections area (English, political and religious history); Western Historical Manuscripts.

Buildings and Grounds: Campus area 1,348 acres. *New buildings:* Life Sciences Center completed 2004; Virginia Housing and Dining Facility 2004; Mizzou Sports Arena 2004.

Chief Executive Officer: Dr. Brady Deaton, Chancellor.

Undergraduates address admission inquiries to Barbara Rupo, Director of Admissions; graduate inquiries to professional school of interest.

College of Arts and Sciences

Degree Programs Offered: *Baccalaureate* in anthropology, art, art history and archaeology, biological sciences, chemistry, classics, communication, economics, English, French, general studies, geography, German, history, interdisciplinary studies, international studies, linguistics, mathematics, microbiology, music, philosophy, physics, political science, psychology, religious studies, Russian, sociology, Spanish, statistics, theatre; *master's* and *doctorate* in most of these fields.

Distinctive Educational Programs: Internships. Joint B.A.–B.S. degree with College of Engineering. Joint B.A.-M.D. degree with School of Medicine. Joint B.A.-J.D. degree with School of Law. Preprofessional programs in business and public administration, journalism, law, veterinary medicine. Interdepartmental programs in Latin American studies, linguistics, microbiology, Russian area studies, South Asian studies.

College of Agriculture, Food and Natural Resources

Degree Programs Offered: *Baccalaureate* in agricultural economics, agricultural education, agricultural journalism, agricultural systems management, agribusiness management, animal science, atmospheric science, biochemistry, food science and nutrition, fisheries and wildlife, forestry, hotel and restaurant management, plant sciences, soil and atmospheric sciences, parks/recreation/tourism; *master's, doctorate* in various fields.

Distinctive Educational Programs: Interdepartmental programs in general agriculture and pest management.

College of Business

Degree Programs Offered: *Baccalaureate* in accountancy, business administration with emphasis areas administration, management, economics, international business, finance and banking, real estate, marketing, human resource management, operations management; *master's, doctorate.*

Admission: Baccalaureate degree from accredited institution; must meet admission standards of the Graduate School.

Distinctive Educational Programs: Internships. Interdepartmental programs in economics, general business, secretarial science. Administrative Behavior and Survey Research Laboratory. B.S. and M.S. in accountancy have been merged into an integrated 150-hour curriculum and both degrees are awarded on completion of the program.

Graduate School of Public Affairs

Degree Programs Offered: *Master's* in public administration.

Admission: Baccalaureate degree from accredited institution; must meet admission standards of the Graduate School.

Degree Requirements: 24 hours of public administration core; 9 hours electives or area of specialization; 6 hours internship.

College of Education

Degree Programs Offered: *Baccalaureate* in early childhood education, educational studies, elementary education, middle school education, secondary education; *master's, doctorate* in curriculum and instruction, educational and counseling psychology, educational leadership and policy analysis, information science and learning technology, special education, practical arts and vocational-technical education; *doctorate* in educational leadership. Education specialist certificates also given.

Distinctive Educational Programs: Interdepartmental program in educational studies.

College of Engineering

Degree Programs Offered: *Baccalaureate* in biological engineering, chemical engineering, civil engineering, computer engineering, computer science, electrical engineering, industrial engineering, mechanical engineering; *master's* computer science; *master's, doctorate* in all fields, plus computer science/computer engineering, nuclear engineering, mechanical and aerospace engineering.

School of Health Related Professions

Degree Programs Offered: *Baccalaureate* in clinical laboratory sciences/cytotechnology, clinical laboratory sciences/medical technology, radiologic sciences/nuclear medicine technology, radiologic sciences/radiography, respiratory therapy, radiologic sciences/radiation therapy technology, communication science, occupational therapy, pre-physical therapy; *master's* in physical therapy, communication science and disorders/audiology, communication science and disorders/speech-language pathology.

Admission: Individual requirements for each professional program (in addition to general University requirements).

College of Human Environmental Sciences

Degree Programs Offered: *Baccalaureate* in environmental design, consumer and family economics, human development and family studies, human nutrition and foods, textile and apparel management; *master's, doctorate* in exercise physiology and each department listed. Also BSW and MSW in social work.

Distinctive Educational Programs: Undergraduate interdepartmental program in home economics-journalism; graduate interdepartmental program in home economics-communication.

School of Journalism

Degree Programs Offered: *Baccalaureate* in journalism/ advertising, journalism/broadcast news, journalism/magazine, journalism/news editorial, journalism/photo journalism; *master's, doctorate.*

Admission: In addition to general university requirements, 60 semester hours in a prejournalism program (3.0 GPA to assure admission).

Charles and Josie Smith Sinclair School of Nursing

Degree Programs Offered: *Baccalaureate, master's, doctorate.*

Admission: 30–33 graded semester hours in prenursing courses with a 2.50 GPA, satisfactory score on the SCAT Form 1C Test.

Fees and Other Expenses: M.S. level clinical nursing courses require additional $113.10 per credit hour.

School of Law

Degree Programs Offered: *First-professional; master's* in dispute resolution.

Admission: Baccalaureate, LSAT.

Degree Requirements: 88 semester hours, 70 average GPA on 100-point scale, 2 years in residence.

School of Medicine

Degree Programs Offered: *First-professional; master's* in health administration, public health, pathology; *master's, doctorate* in microbiology, pharmacology, physiology.

Admission: *For first-professional students:* 90 semester hours from recognized college or university with 2 semesters English composition and literature, 2 biology (with laboratory), 2 inorganic chemistry (with laboratory), 2 organic chemistry (with laboratory), 2 general physics (with laboratory), 2 mathematics, 1 general biology or zoology.

Degree Requirements: *For first-professional degree:* 173 semester hours, entire program in residence.

College of Veterinary Medicine

Degree Programs Offered: *First-professional, master's* in biomedical sciences; *doctorate:* in pathobiology.

Admission: *For first-professional students:* 64 semester hours preprofessional courses from accredited college or university.

Degree Requirements: *For first-professional degree:* 3.0 GPA, 4-year curriculum.

University of Missouri - Kansas City

5100 Rockhill Road
Kansas City, Missouri 64110-2499
Tel: (816) 235-1000   **E-mail:** admit@umkc.edu
Fax: (816) 235-1717   **Internet:** www.umkc.edu

Institution Description: *Enrollment:* 7,955. *Degrees awarded:* Baccalaureate, first-professional (dentistry, law, medicine, pharmacy), master's, doctorate. Specialist certificates in education also awarded.

Member of the consortium Kansas City Regional Council for Higher Education.

Accreditation: *Regional:* NCA. *Professional:* business, counseling psychology, dental hygiene, dentistry, law, medicine, music, nursing, nursing education, pediatric dentistry, pharmacy, psychology internship, public administration, social work, teacher education

History: Established and chartered as University of Kansas City 1929; offered first instruction at postsecondary level 1933; awarded first degree (baccalaureate) 1936; became part of University of Missouri system and adopted present name 1963. *See* Carleton F. Scofield, *History of the University of Kansas City: Prologue to a Public University* (Kansas City: Lowell Press, 1976) for further information.

Institutional Structure: *Composition of institution:* Headed by chancellor who reports to University of Missouri System president. Academic affairs headed by provost/vice chancellor for academic affairs. Management/business/ finances directed by vice chancellor for administrative affairs. Full-time instructional faculty 523. Academic governance body, Faculty Senate, meets an average of 7 times per year.

Calendar: Semesters. Academic year late Aug. to early May. Freshmen admitted Aug., Jan., June. Degrees conferred May, July, Dec. Formal commencements Dec., May. Summer session of 1 term from mid-May to late July.

Characteristics of Freshmen: 69% of applicants admitted. 52% of applicants admitted and enrolled.

6% (55 students) submitted SAT scores; 41% (829 students) submitted ACT scores. *25th percentile:* SAT Verbal 510, SAT Math 500; ACT Composite 20, ACT English 19, ACT Math 19. *75th percentile:* SAT Verbal 650, SAT Math 700; ACT Composite 27, ACT English 28, ACT Math 27.

30% of entering freshmen expected to graduate within 5 years. 76% of freshmen from Missouri. Freshmen from 28 states and 16 foreign countries.

Admission: Overall admissions requirements are: high school courses 4 English, 3 social studies, 2 science, 1 science with lab, 4 math, 2 foreign language, 1 fine arts. High school diploma or GED. *See* individual academic units below.

Degree Requirements: *See individual academic units below. Grading system:* A–F; pass-fail; withdraw.

Distinctive Educational Programs: School offers college credit and advanced placement for postsecondary-level work completed in secondary school. Developmental courses offered in summer session and regular academic year. Evening classes. Special facilities for using telecommunications in the classroom. Facilities and programs for independent research, including honors programs, independent study. Student exchange programs with Kansas State University, University of Kansas, University of Nebraska. *Other distinctive programs:* Continuing education, PACE (Program of Adult College Education). Interdisciplinary Ph.D. programs; Master of Fine Arts in Theatre; Executive MBA.

Degrees Conferred: 1,232 *baccalaureate* (B); 156 *master's* (M); 60 *doctorate* (D): area and ethnic studies 1 (B); biological/life sciences 45 (B), 13 (M); business/marketing 141 (B), 189 (M); communications/communication technologies 70 (b); computer and information sciences 92 (B), 51 (M); education 122 (B), 18 (M), 4 (D); engineering and engineering technologies 45 (B), 21 (M); English 40 (B), 10 (M); foreign languages and literature 18 (B), 1 (M); health professions and related sciences 45 (B)< 66 (M), 1 (D); interdisciplinary studies 9 (B), 28 (D); law/legal studies 21 (M); liberal arts/general studies 255 (B), 8 (m); mathematics 8 (B); philosophy/religion/theology 3 (B); physical sciences 35 (B), 4 (M); protective services/public administration 31 (B), 87 (M); psychology 80 (B), 4 (M), 10 (D); social sciences and history 103 (B), 17 (M); visual and performing arts 89 (B), 46 (M), 17 (D). 365 *first-professional:* dentistry 70; law 152; medicine 85; pharmacy 70.

Fees and Other Expenses: *Full-time tuition per academic year 2004–05:* undergraduate resident $6,276, nonresident $15,723; contact the university for current graduate and first-professional tuition and fees. *Required fees:* $899. *Room and board per academic year:* $6,435.

Financial Aid: Aid from institutionally generated funds is provided on the basis of academic merit, financial need, athletic ability, other criteria.

Financial aid to full-time, first-time undergraduate students: need-based scholarships/grants totaling $11,283,143, self-help $29,369,180, parent loans $186,412, athletic awards $321,115; non-need-based scholarships/grants totaling $5,657,487, self-help $10,512,780, parent loans $1,272,036, athletic awards $1,443,063. *Graduate aid:* 67 students received $311,650 in federal and state-funded fellowships/grants; 72 students held teaching assistantships totaling $204,148; 69 students held research assistantships totaling $69,718.

Departments and Teaching Staff: *Professors* 145, *associate professors* 191, *assistant professors* 198, *instructors* 65, *part-time faculty* 389.

Total instructional faculty: 993 (full-time 602, part-time 391; women 433, men 560; members of minority groups 150). Student-to-faculty ratio: 14:1. Degrees held by full-time faculty: baccalaureate 2%, master's 17%, doctorate 66%, professional 13%. 80% hold terminal degrees.

Enrollment: Total enrollment 7,955. Undergraduate full-time 2,151 men / 3,270 women, part-time 1,623m / 2,349w; first-professional full-time 709m / 738w, part-time 22m / 25w; graduate full-time 459m / 628w, part-time 371m / 1,411w. *Transfer students:* in-state 609; from out-of-state 450.

Characteristics of Student Body: *Ethnic/racial makeup (undergraduate):* number of Black non-Hispanic: 969; American Indian or Alaska Native: 53; Asian or Pacific Islander: 368; Hispanic: 295; White non-Hispanic: 4,459; unknown: 707. *Age distribution:* number under 18: 40; 18–19: 1,462; 20–21: 1,677; 22–24: 1,736; 25–29: 1,033; 30–34: 460; 35–39: 223; 40–49: 323; 50–64: 114; 65 and over: 6. 40% of student body attend summer sessions.

International Students: 785 nonresident aliens enrolled fall 2004. Students from Europe, Asia, Latin America, Africa, Canada. Programs available to aid students whose native language is not English: English as a Second Language Program.

Student Life: On-campus co-ed residence halls house 13% of student body. *Intercollegiate athletics:* basketball, golf, tennis, riflery, cross-country, track and field; men only: soccer; women only: cheerleading, softball, volleyball. volleyball, softball, cross-country, tennis, track and field, golf. *Special regulations:* Registered cars permitted. *Special services:* Student learning center, counseling center, career services, women's center, child care center, Minority Student Affairs, International Student Affairs; academic computing. *Student radio:* KCUR-FM broadcasts 132 hours per week. *Surrounding community:* Kansas City metropolitan area population 1.4 million. Served by mass transit bus system; airport 20 miles from campus; passenger rail service 3 miles from campus.

Publications: *New Letters* first published in 1934; *U-News*, student newspaper; *Perspectives* (official university news magazine); *UMKC Community*, newsletter for faculty and staff.

Library Collections: 1,301,267 volumes. 769,870 government documents. Current serial serial subscriptions: paper 5,816; microform 169; 8,192 via electronic access. 331,408 recording; 10,810 compact discs; 750 CD-ROMs. Online catalog. 295 computer work stations. Students have access to online information retrieval services and the Internet. Total 2004–05 budget for materials and operations: $2,479,576.

Most important special holdings include Marr Sound Recordings; American Popular Sheet Music Collection; Snyder Collection of Americana; Congressman Richard Bolling's Papers.

Buildings and Grounds: Campus area 191 acres *New buildings:* Robert H. Flarsheim Science and Technology Hall; Health Sciences Building.

Chief Executive Officer: Dr. Martha W. Gilliland, Chancellor.

Address admission inquiries to Jennifer DeHaemers, Director of Admissions.

College of Arts and Sciences

Degree Programs Offered: *Baccalaureate* in American Studies, art, art history, architecture, chemistry, communication studies, criminal justice and criminology, economics, English, environmental studies, French, geography, geology, German, history, liberal arts, mathematics and statistics, philosophy, physics, political science, psychology, sociology, Spanish, studio art, theater, urban planning and design, affairs; *master's, doctorate* in various fields.

Admission: 17 specified high school units; ACT or SAT I; minimum score based on combined high school percentile rank and test percentile rank.

Degree Requirements: 120 credit hours; 2.0 GPA; course requirements.

Henry W. Bloch School of Business and Public Administration

Degree Programs Offered: *Baccalaureate* in accounting, business administration; *master's* in accounting, business administration, public administration.

Admission: Completion of 60 hours of specified college work with a cumulative GPA of 2.75; requirements vary by program.

School of Education

Degree Programs Offered: *Baccalaureate* in early childhood education, elementary education, middle school education, secondary education; *master's, specialists, doctorate* in various fields.

Admission: Cumulative GPA of 2.5 in previous college work; completion of 65 hours of prerequisites; passing scores on College Basic Academic Subjects Examination; special application. Graduate admission: 2.75 undergraduate GPA, 3.0 graduate GPA, GRE for some students.

Degree Requirements: Requirements vary by program.

School of Computing and Engineering

Degree Programs Offered: *Baccalaureate* in civil engineering, electrical and computer engineering, mechanical engineering; computer science, information technology; *master's* in civil engineering, mechanical engineering, electrical engineering computer science; *doctorate* in interdisciplinary engineering, computing, engineering.

Admission: *For undergraduate degree:* same as general rules for undergraduate admission; *for graduate degree:* GPA of 3.0 for the last 60 credit hours of undergraduate study; acceptance of advisement in the departments is based on a 3.0 or higher GPA in undergraduate study in an engineering degree; GRE with a quantitative percentile of at least 80; (TOEFL score of at least 550 for international students); recommendation letters; written statement of purpose.

Degree Requirements: Completion of prescribed program for the degree program pursued.

Conservatory of Music

Degree Programs Offered: *Baccalaureate* in dance, music, music composition, music education, music, music history and literature, music theory; *master's* in music education, music, music history and literature, music theory; *master's, doctorate* in music composition, music conducting, music education, performance.

Admission: Ten minutes audition on sight (in cases of extreme distance or scheduling problems, a taped audition must be submitted).

Degree Requirements: Requirements vary by program.

School of Pharmacy

Degree Programs Offered: *Bachelor's* and *master's* in pharmaceutical sciences; *first-professional* in pharmaceutical sciences, pharmacology.

Admission: *For first-professional degree:* Baccalaureate in pharmacy or senior status at University of Missouri - Kansas City School of Pharmacy; 2.5 GPA; Pharmacy College Admission Test; interview.

Degree Requirements: *For first-professional:* 210 credit hours; 3.0 GPA in all work applicable to a graduate degree.

School of Dentistry

Degree Programs Offered: *Baccalaureate* in dental hygiene; *first-professional* in dentistry; *master's* in dental hygiene education, oral biology. Certificates also awarded.

Admission: *For first-professional degree:* 90 semester hours in predental courses; satisfactory DAT scores and GPA; interview.

Degree Requirements: *For first-professional:* 155 credit hours, 2.5 GPA.

School of Law

Degree Programs Offered: *Master's joint degrees:* JD/MBA, JDMPA, LLM/MPA. *First-professional:* JD, LLM (laws, taxation, urban affairs), joint degree JD/LLM.

Admission: *For first-professional degree:* Graduation from accredited college or university; acceptable index score which is a function of undergraduate GPA and LSAT score or acceptance based on additional factors indicating qualification.

Degree Requirements: *For first-professional:* Completion of 91 credit hours, 80 of which must be classroom credits; cumulative GPA of 2.0; six semesters in residence carrying not less than 10 classroom credit hours each semester; satisfactory completion of all required course work. *Graduate degree:* Completion of 24 credit hours, 18 of which must be taken from the list of required and elective courses provided for each program; cumulative GPA of at least 3.0 for the General LL.M. and 2.70 for the Taxation LL.M; completion of all required courses.

School of Medicine

Degree Programs Offered: *First-professional.* Program, in collaboration with the College of Arts and Sciences and the School of Biological Sciences, offers a six-year integrated program leading to the baccalaureate and doctor of medicine degrees.

Admission: The program is primarily designed for high school graduates who are entering college. Applicant's high school curriculum must include specific courses. Applicant must meet a minimum academic screen based on ACT composite score and rank in high school class. Qualified applicants are invited for a required interview.

Degree Requirements: 2.5–4.0 GPA in basic science/social science/humanities classes; satisfactory completion of requirements for baccalaureate degree; 38 months medical curriculum credit; minimum 48 months enrollment in School of Medicine years 3–6; passage of Steps I and II of United States Medical Licensing Examination; docent certification in clinical competency.

School of Biological Sciences

Degree Programs Offered: *Baccalaureate* in biology, medical technology; *master's* in biology, cellular and molecular biology; *doctorate* in molecular biology, molecular and biochemistry, biochemistry, cell biology and biophysics.

Admission: *For baccalaureate degree:* transfer admission requires 2.0 GPA of all college coursework attempted and an overall 2.0 science and math GPA; *for graduate degree:* baccalaureate degree; 3.0 GPA, 1500 GRE.

Degree Requirements: *For baccalaureate degree:* 120 credit hours; 2.0 biology and UM GPA; *for graduate degree:* 36 to 44 hours in approved courses and research; 3.0 GPA.

School of Nursing

Degree Programs Offered: *Baccalaureate, master's, doctorate.*

Admission: BSN 2.5 GPA; MSN 3.0 GPA and California Critical Thinking Skills Test; Ph.D. 3.0 GPA and GRE test.

Degree Requirements: BSN 121 semester hours and 2.5 GPA; MSN 36–43 semester hours and 3.0 GPA; Ph.D. 75 post-baccalaureate credit hours; comprehensive examination; dissertation.

School of Graduate Studies

Degree Programs Offered: *Interdisciplinary Ph.D. Program:* Students select 2 or more areas in which to take classes and conduct research. The areas that are participating are art history, cell biology and biophysics, chemistry, computing, economics, education, English, engineering, geoscience, health psychology, history, mathematics, molecular biology and biochemistry, music education, oral biology, pharmaceutical science, pharmacology, philosophy, physics, political science, psychology, public affairs and administration, religious studies, social sciences consortium (economics, political science, sociology), Urban Leadership and Policy Studies in Education, sociology.

Admission: GRE combined raw score of at least 1500. Previous GPA of at least 2.75 on a 4.00 scale. Admission by at least 2 participating disciplines.

Degree Requirements: Coursework, comprehensive examination, written dissertation and oral defense of significant research.

University of Missouri - Rolla

1870 Miner Circle
Rolla, Missouri 65409-0910

Tel: (573) 341-4114   **E-mail:** umrolla@umr.edu
Fax: (573) 341-6306   **Internet:** www.umr.edu

Institution Description: *Enrollment:* 5,404. *Degrees awarded:* Baccalaureate, master's, doctorate.

Member of consortium Oak Ridge Associated Universities; Universities of Mid-America.

Accreditation: *Regional:* NCA. *Professional:* chemistry, computer science, engineering

History: Established as University of Missouri School of Mines and Metallurgy 1870; offered first instruction at postsecondary level 1871; awarded first degree (baccalaureate) 1874; became part of University of Missouri system, added master's and doctoral programs, and adopted present name 1964. *See* Bonita H. Mann and Clair V. Mann, *The History of the Missouri School of Mines and Metallurgy* (Rolla: Phelps Country Historical Society, 1941) and also Lawrence O. Christensen and Jack B. Ridley, *UM - Rolla: A History of MSM/UMR,* (University of Missouri Printing Services, 1983) for further information.

Institutional Structure: *Composition of institution:* Administrators 8 men. Three academic deans: School of Engineering, School of Mines and Metallurgy, College of Arts and Sciences. Academic affairs headed by vice chancellor of academic affairs. Physical facilities/business/finances directed by vice chancellor of administrative services. Student academic and social enhancement are under the management of vice-chancellor of student affairs. Full-time instructional faculty 337. Academic governance body, Academic Council, meets an average of 10 per year.

Calendar: Semesters. Academic year Aug. to May. Freshmen admitted Aug., Jan., May. Degrees conferred May, July, Dec. Formal commencement May, Dec. 2 summer sessions of variable lengths.

Characteristics of Freshmen: 1,918 applicants (1,497 men, 421 women). 93% of applicants admitted and enrolled full-time.

95% (793 students) submitted ACT scores. *25th percentile*: ACT Composite 24, ACT English 23, ACT Math 25. *75th percentile*: ACT Composite 30, ACT English 30, ACT Math 31.

40% of entering freshmen expected to graduate within 6 years. 74% of freshmen from Missouri. Freshmen from 28 states and 4 foreign countries.

Admission: Applications for fall semester should be submitted by July 1, for the winter semester by Dec. 1, and for summer school by May 1. All new applicants pay an admissions application fee: $20. An application, high school transcript, and 1 appropriate test score (SAT, ACT, SCAT) must be submitted.

Advanced placement for postsecondary-level work completed in secondary school. College credit and advanced placement for extrainstitutional learning on the basis of ACE *2006 Guide to the Evaluation of Educational Experiences in the Armed Services.*

Degree Requirements: 120 to 132 semester hours depending on program. 2.0 minimum GPA. General education requirements.

Fulfillment of some degree requirements possible by passing College Board CLEP Subject Examinations, Advanced Placement Program (subject examinations only), UMR Placement Testing Program, International Baccalaureate Program and departmental examinations. *Grading system:* A–F; pass-fail; withdraw (carries no penalty).

Distinctive Educational Programs: Freshman Engineering Program provides advising, career counseling, and a set of specified courses with the goal of the student making an informed decision regarding an engineering major. Work-experience programs. Evening classes. Interdepartmental program in management systems. Honors programs. Study abroad in Australia, Belgium, Chile, Finland, Germany, Ireland, Mexico, the Netherlands, Republic of George, South Africa, Turkey. *Other distinctive programs:* Continuing education. Statewide Master's Degree in Engineering Management. Distance Learning Program in Engineering Management.

ROTC: Army, Air Force.

Degrees Conferred: 756 *baccalaureate;* 502 *master's;* 61 *doctorate.* Bachelor's degrees awarded in top five disciplines: engineering 542; computer and information sciences 85; physical sciences 27; biological/biomedical sciences 19; English language and literature 16.

Fees and Other Expenses: *Full-time tuition per academic year 2004–05:* undergraduate resident $7,238, nonresident $16,055. Contact the university for current graduate tuition/fees. *Books and supplies:* $875. *Room and board per academic year:* $5,646.

Financial Aid: Aid from institutionally generated funds is provided on the basis of academic merit, financial need, athletic ability. Institution has a Program Participation Agreement with the U.S. Department of Education for eligible students to receive Pell Grants and, depending upon the agreement, other federal aid.

Financial aid to full-time, first-time undergraduate students: 30% received federal grants averaging $2,524; 33% state/local grants averaging $2,100; 67% institutional grants averaging $4,071; 44% received loans averaging $2,705.

Departments and Teaching Staff: Mining engineering *professors* 5, *associate professors* 2, *assistant professors* 1, *instructors* 0, *part-time teachers* 1; geology and petro. 6, 3, 2, 0, 1; ceramic engineering 6, 1, 0, 0, 1; geology and geophysics 5, 1, 1, 0, 1; metallurgical engineering 5, 4, 1, 0, 2; nuclear engineering 3, 3, 0, 0, 0; basic engineering 1, 4, 2, 0, 5; civil engineering 8, 6, 3, 0, 8; electrical engineering 15, 11, 4, 0, 8; engineering management 6, 3, 8, 0, 6; M.A. aerospace 2, 4, 0, 0, 0; M.A. mechanical 15, 8, 1, 0, 4; M.A. EM-engineering mechanical 3, 2, 1, 0, 0; English 3, 4, 2, 1, 8; philosophy and liberal arts 3, 3, 3, 3, 9; history and political science 5, 2, 2, 1, 1; psychology 4, 2, 1, 0, 3; economics 1, 3, 0, 0, 1; chemistry 10, 5, 3, 0, 4; life sciences 2, 2, 0, 0, 4; mathematics and statistics 6, 7, 8, 1, 6; physics 11, 6, 2, 0, 4; physical education and recreation 0, 0, 2, 6, 0.

Total instructional faculty: 399. Student-to-faculty ratio: 12:1. Degrees held by full-time faculty: master's 2%, doctorate 98%. 98% hold terminal degrees.

Enrollment: Total enrollment 5,404. Undergraduate 4,119 (77.5% men, 22.5% women).

Characteristics of Student Body: *Ethnic/racial makeup (undergraduate):* number of Black non-Hispanic: 4.2%; American Indian or Alaska Native: .5%; Hispanic: 3.6%; White non-Hispanic: 83.3%; unknown: 5%. *Age distribution (undergraduate):* 17–21: 56%; 22–24: 25%; 25–29: 11%; 30–34: 4%; 35–39: 2%; 40–49: 2%.

International Students: 99 undergraduate nonresident aliens enrolled fall 2004. Programs available to aid students whose native language is not English: English as a Second Language Program. No financial aid specifically designated for international students.

Student Life: On-campus residence halls house 26% of student body. 28% of on-campus undergraduate men join a fraternity. 22% of on-campus undergraduate women join a sorority. Housing available for married students. Apartments available for both single and married students. *Intercollegiate athletics:* men only: baseball, basketball, cross-country, football, golf, rifle, soccer, swimming, tennis, track, wrestling; women only: basketball, cross-country, soccer, softball, tennis. *Special regulations:* Freshmen and sophomore students required to live in residence halls. Registered cars permitted. *Special services:* Computer Learning Center, Learning Resource Center, medical services. *Student radio:* Radio station KMNR broadcasts 24 hours a day, 7 days a week, for a total of 168 hours per week. *Surrounding community:* Rolla population 16,000. St. Louis, 110 miles from campus, is nearest metropolitan area. Served by airport 2 miles from campus.

Library Collections: 455,000 volumes including bound books, serial backfiles, electronic documents, and government documents not in separate collections. Online catalog. Current serial subscriptions: 1,580. 51,500 microforms; 6,300 audiovisual materials. Over 800 computer work stations campus-wide. Students have access to the Internet at no charge.

Most important special holdings include IEEE; U.S. Geological Survey; Dougherty Collection (mines and mining).

Buildings and Grounds: Campus area 284 acres.

Chief Executive Officer: Dr. Gary Thomas, Chancellor.

Address admission inquiries to Jay W. Goff, Dean of Enrollment Management.

College of Arts and Sciences

Degree Programs Offered: *Baccalaureate* in biological sciences management systems, economics, English, history, life sciences, philosophy and psychology; *baccalaureate, master's, doctorate* in chemistry, computer science, mathematics and physics.

Degree Requirements: *For Bachelor of Arts degree:* minimum of 120 credit hours. *For Bachelor of Science degree:* minimum 130 credit hours.

Distinctive Educational Programs: Cooperative program in teacher education with University of Missouri - Columbia.

School of Engineering

Degree Programs Offered: *Baccalaureate, master's, doctorate* in chemical engineering, civil engineering, computer engineering, electrical engineering, aerospace engineering, mechanical engineering, engineering management; *master's* in environmental and planning engineering.

Degree Requirements: *For Bachelor of Science degree:* minimum of 132 credit hours.

Distinctive Educational Programs: Professional development program for students with baccalaureate in engineering.

School of Mines and Metallurgy

Degree Programs Offered: *Baccalaureate, master's, doctorate* in ceramic engineering, geology/geophysics, metallurgical engineering, mining engineering, nuclear engineering, petroleum engineering.

Degree Requirements: *For bachelor of science degree:* minimum of 132 credit hours.

Distinctive Educational Programs: Professional development program for students with baccalaureate in engineering.

University of Missouri - St. Louis

One University Boulevard
St. Louis, Missouri 63121-4100
Tel: (314) 516-5451   **E-mail:** admissions@umsl.edu
Fax: (314) 516-5378   **Internet:** www.umsl.edu

Institution Description: The University of Missouri - St. Louis is a public, state-supported institution. *Enrollment:* 15,512. *Degrees awarded:* Baccalaureate, first-professional (optometry), master's, doctorate. Certificates also awarded.

Accreditation: *Regional:* NCA. *Professional:* accounting, business, clinical psychology, music, nursing, nursing education, optometry, public administration, social work, teacher education

History: Established as Normandy Residence Center of the University of Missouri 1960; offered first instruction at postsecondary level 1961; chartered, became 4-year institution, and adopted present name 1963; awarded first degree (baccalaureate) 1967.

Institutional Structure: *Composition of institution:* Administrators 32 men / 28 women. Campus headed by chancellor, vice chancellors for academic affairs, administrative services, managerial and technological services, university relations; vice provosts for research, student affairs. Two governance bodies, Faculty Senate and University Assembly, meet an average 8 and 4 tunes one year respectively.

Calendar: Semesters. Academic year Aug. to May. Freshmen admitted Aug., Jan., June. Degrees conferred and formal commencement May, Aug., Jan. Summer session of 1 term from mid-June to early Aug.

Characteristics of Freshmen: 38.8% of applicants admitted. 50.2% of applicants admitted and enrolled.

8% (37 students) submitted SAT scores; 90% (401 students) submitted ACT scores. *25th percentile*: SAT Verbal 480, SAT Math 500; ACT Composite 21, ACT English 20, ACT Math 19. *75th percentile*: SAT Verbal 640, SAT Math 650; ACT Composite 26, ACT English 26, ACT Math 26.

18% of entering freshmen expected to graduate within 5 years. 87% of freshmen from Missouri. Freshmen from 16 states and 13 foreign countries.

Admission: Combination of class rank and test score from ACT SAT in addition to 17 academic units which must include 4 units of English (2 emphasizing writing; 1 may be in speech/debate); 4 units mathematics (algebra 1 or higher); 3 units of science (1 must have a lab and not including general units of science); 3 units of social science; 1 unit of fine arts; 2 units of the same foreign language.

College credit and advanced placement for postsecondary-level work completed in secondary school. College credit for extrainstitutional learning (life experience) on basis of ACE *2006 Guide to the Evaluation of Educational Experiences in the Armed Services*; portfolio and faculty assessments; personal interviews. Tutoring available. Noncredit developmental and remedial courses offered in summer session and regular academic year.

Degree Requirements: 120 credit hours; 2.0 GPA; 1 year in residence; general education requirements.

Fulfillment of some degree requirements and exemption from some beginning courses possible by passing College Board CLEP. *Grading system:* A–F; passfail; withdraw.

Distinctive Educational Programs: Internships. Flexible meeting places and schedules, including weekend and evening classes. Interdisciplinary program in general studies. Facilities and programs for independent research, including tutorials, independent study. Study abroad programs include International Exchange in over 30 locations including Australia, England, France, Germany, Northern Ireland, Sweden, Switzerland. *Other distinctive programs:* Continuing education.

ROTC: Air Force in cooperation with St. Louis University; Army in cooperation with Washington University.

Degrees Conferred: 1,932 *baccalaureate* (B), 675 *master's* (M), 40 *doctorate* (D): biological/life sciences 57 (B), 15 (M), 7 (D); business/marketing 612 (B), 117 (M); communications/communication technologies 123 (B), 2 (M); computer and information sciences 51 (B); 37 (D); education 292 (B), 272 (M), 15 (D); engineering and engineering technologies 42 (B); English 47 (B), 20 (M); foreign languages and literature 21 (B); health professions and related sciences 123 (B), 65 (M), 2 (D); interdisciplinary studies 6 (M); liberal arts/general studies 48 (B); mathematics 7 (B), 5 (M); philosophy/religion 9 (B), 4 (M); physical sciences 20 (B), 9 (M), 6 (D); protective services/public administration 67 (B), 62 (M); psychology 136 (B), 9 (M); 6 (D); social sciences and history 226 (B), 52 (M), 4 (D); visual and performing arts 51 (B). 35 *first-professional:* optometry.

Fees and Other Expenses: *Full-time tuition per academic year 2005–06:* undergraduate resident $6,495, nonresident $6,317; graduate resident $16,272; nonresident $16,313. *Required fees:* $1,123. *Room and board per academic year:* $6,428.

Financial Aid: Aid from institutionally generated funds is provided on the basis of academic merit, financial need, athletic ability.

Financial aid to full-time, first-time undergraduate students: need-based scholarships/grants totaling $10,567,256, self-help $29,954,652, parent loans $2,283,098, athletic awards $288,515; non-need-based scholarships/grants totaling $2,558,029, self-help $4,356,716, parent loans $1,018,491, athletic awards $262,067. *Graduate aid:* 45 students received $409,931 in federal and state-funded fellowships/grants; 1,056 received $15,568,650 in federal and state-funded loans; 1,229 received other fellowships/grants totaling $3,226,162; 304 teaching and research assistantships awarded totaling $2,348,730.

Departments and Teaching Staff: *Professors* 99, *associate professors* 102, *assistant professors* 93, *instructors* 74, *part-time faculty* 381. *Total instructional faculty:* 749 (full-time 368, part-time 381; women 381, men 358; members of minority groups 108). Total faculty with doctorate, first-professional, or other terminal degree: 382. Student-to-faculty ratio: 18.9:1. Degrees held by full-time faculty: doctorate 72%, master's 24%, baccalaureate 3%. 51% hold terminal degrees. *Faculty development:* $6,933,727 total grants for research. 2 faculty members awarded sabbaticals 2004–05.

Enrollment: Total enrollment 15,512. Undergraduate full-time 2,242 men / 3,327 women, part-time 2,632m / 4,385w; first-professional full-time 64m / 101w; graduate full-time 206m / 347w, part-time 769m / 1,439w. *Transfer students:* in-state 1,482; from out-of-state 237.

Characteristics of Student Body: *Ethnic/racial makeup (undergraduate):* number of Black non-Hispanic: 1,570; American Indian or Alaska Native: 33; Asian or Pacific Islander: 360; Hispanic: 209; White non-Hispanic: 9,374; unknown: 806. *Age distribution:* number under 18: 3,053; 18–19: 1,262; 20–21: 1,988; 22–24: 2,743; 25–29: 1,650; 30–34: 749; 40–49: 532; 50–64: 177; 65 and over: 19. 35.4% of student body attend summer sessions.

International Students: 430 nonresident aliens enrolled fall 2004. 92 students from Europe, 238 Asia, 62 Latin America, 19 Africa, 8 Canada, 11 other. Programs available to aid students whose native language is not English: social, cultural. English as a Second Language Program. No financial aid specifically designated for international students.

Student Life: Housing units for 1,200 students. *Intercollegiate athletics:* men only: baseball, basketball, golf, soccer, tennis; women only: softball, basketball, soccer, tennis, volleyball. *Special regulations:* Registered cars permitted in designated areas only. *Special services:* Learning Resources Center, health services. *Student radio:* KWMU-FM National Public Radio affiliate. *Surrounding community:* St. Louis metropolitan statistical area population over 2.5 million. Served by mass transit bus system; airport 3 miles from campus; passenger rail service 12 miles from campus. Light rail system from east St. Louis and downtown St. Louis to Lambert International Airport with 2 stops on campus.

Library Collections: 1,105,983 volumes. Online catalog. Current serial subscriptions: 8,579 (paper and microform). 35 public access work stations. Students have access to online information retrieval services and the Internet.

Most important special holdings include Mercantile Library (American History and Westward Expansion); Pott Collection (Inland Waterways); Barriger Collection (Railroads).

Buildings and Grounds: Campus area 232 acres. *New buildings:* Student Union completed 2000; Performing Arts Center 2003.

Chief Executive Officer: Dr. Thomas F. George, Chancellor.

Undergraduates address admission inquiries to Melissa Hattman, Director of Admissions; first-professional degree inquiries to Chairperson, Admissions Committee, College of Optometry.

College of Arts and Sciences

Degree Programs Offered: *Baccalaureate* in anthropology, art and art history, studio art, computer science, French, German, Spanish, music education, philosophy, social work, communication; *baccalaureate, master's* in criminology and criminal justice, economics, English, history, mathematics, music, sociology; *master's* in public policy administration; *baccalaureate, master's, doctorate* in biology, chemistry, psychology, physics, and political science.

Admission: Applicants must meet university admission requirements.

Degree Requirements: Non-Euro-American course requirement; requirements of chosen degree program and department; 2.0 GPA, minimum 120 semester hours.

Distinctive Educational Programs: Interdisciplinary master's program in public policy administration in cooperation with School of Business Administration. Preprofessional programs in engineering, medical science, pharmacy.

Enrollment: *Total enrollment:* 7,468.

College of Business Administration

Degree Programs Offered: *Baccalaureate, master's* in business administration (areas of accounting, finance, management, marketing, and quantitative management science); *master's* in accounting, management information systems.

Admission: 2.0 GPA for all qualifying work. Completion of both the University's and the School's general education requirements.

Degree Requirements: 48 credit hours minimum in business administration and a minimum of 72 hours in business administration and approved electives combined and a total of 120 hours; minimum 2.0 GPA overall and 2.0 GPA in all business courses.

Departments and Teaching Staff: *Total instructional faculty:* 77.

Distinctive Educational Programs: The school offers an 18-hour Graduate Certificate programs in Human Resources Management, Business Administration, Taxation, Marketing Management, Electronic Commerce, Telecommunications Management, Information Resource Management, and Information Systems Development. The school also offers an MBA online program.

Enrollment: *Total enrollment:* 2,818.

College of Education

Degree Programs Offered: *Baccalaureate* in early childhood education, physical education; *master's* in educational administration, counseling; *doctorate* in learning-instructional processes, behavioral-developmental processes; *baccalaureate, master's* in elementary education, secondary education, and special education.

Admission: Score of 20 on the ACT composite; 235 in each area on the C-BASE; completed 60 semester hours of college or university courses; cumulative GPA 2.75; vision and hearing screening; affidavit of moral character; course prerequisites fulfilled.

Degree Requirements: Prescribed courses for area of specialization.

Departments and Teaching Staff: *Total instructional faculty:* 100.

Enrollment: *Total enrollment:* 2,465.

College of Fine Arts and Communication

Degree Programs Offered: *Baccalaureate* in art history; studio art with emphasis in drawing, painting, photography, printmaking, and art education; *baccalaureate, master's* in music, music education, communication with undergraduate emphasis in theatre.

Admission: Applications must meet university admission requirements.

Degree Requirements: Math proficiency; state requirement; junior level writing course; non-Euro-America course requirements plus requirements of chosen degree program and department; 2.0GPA; minimum 120 semester hours.

Departments and Teaching Staff: *Total instructional faculty:* 90.

Enrollment: *Total enrollment:* 989.

College of Nursing

Degree Programs Offered: *Baccalaureate, master's, doctorate.*

Admission: Meet University admission criteria; cumulative GPA of 2.5 or better; upper third of high school class; ACT score 21. *BSN completion:* Meet University admission criteria; cumulative GPA of 2.5 or better; graduate of accredited diploma or associate nursing program; current Missouri professional nurse licensure; minimum 30 college credits applicable to a degree. *Master of Science:* BSN from accredit program; minimum GPA of 3.0; current Missouri professional nurse licensure; undergraduate statistics; undergraduate health assessment; two years clinical experience within past five years for nurse practitioner option. *Doctor of philosophy:* BSN with minimum GPA of 3.2 or MSN with minimum GPA of 3.5; GRE with composite of 1500 of better desires; three letters of reference; essay; interview by invitation.

Degree Requirements: *Basic baccalaureate:* 120 credit hours; *BSN completion* 120 credit hours; *Master of science:* 36 credit hours for nonpractitioner options, 43 credit hours for nurse practitioner option; *Doctor of philosophy:* minimum 60 graduate credits beyond BSN.

Departments and Teaching Staff: *Total instructional faculty:* 6.

Distinctive Educational Programs: Accelerated track of the college's BSN program designed for students who have earned a degree in a discipline other than nursing, and for outstanding transfer students who have completed a minimum of 62 hours; full-time, 15 months over a period of two regular semesters and two summer sessions.

Enrollment: *Total enrollment:* 695.

College of Optometry

Degree Programs Offered: *First-professional. Master's* and *doctorate* in physiological optics.

Admission: 90 semester hours or equivalent from college or university. At least 30 of the 90 must have been completed at a 4-year institution. Optometry Admissions Test Program (OATP). Recommend baccalaureate. 98% of the entering class has completed the baccalaureate prior to entry.

Degree Requirements: Complete 4-year program of professional study, beyond the undergraduate curriculum, 168 semester hours, 2.0 GPA.

Fees and Other Expenses: *Full-time tuition per academic year 2004–05:* resident $16,157, nonresident $32,211. *Student fees:* $562.

Departments and Teaching Staff: *Total instructional faculty:* 10.

Enrollment: *Total enrollment:* 1169.

School of Social Welfare

Degree Programs Offered: *Baccalaureate* in social work.

Admission: Applicants must meet university admission requirements as well as a school admissions requirement.

Degree Requirements: Math proficiency; state requirement; junior level writing course; Non-Euro-American course requirement plus requirements of chosen degree program and department; 2.0 GPA; minimum 120 semester hours.

Departments and Teaching Staff: *Total instructional faculty:* 12.

Enrollment: *Total enrollment:* 351.

Washington University in St. Louis

One Brooking Drive
Campus Box 1089
St. Louis, Missouri 63130-4899

Tel: (314) 935-6000   **E-mail:** admission@wustl.edu
Fax: (314) 935-4290   **Internet:** www.wustl.edu

Institution Description: Washington University is a private, independent, nonprofit institution. *Enrollment:* 12,088. *Degrees awarded:* Baccalaureate, first-professional (medicine, law), master's, doctorate.

Accreditation: *Regional:* NCA. *Professional:* art, audiology, clinical psychology, engineering, health services administration, law, medicine, occupational therapy, physical therapy, social work, teacher education

History: Established and chartered 1853; offered first instruction at postsecondary level 1854; adopted present name 1857; awarded first degree (baccalaureate) 1862.

Institutional Structure: *Governing board:* Board of Trustees of the Washington University in St. Louis. Representation: 55 trustees, including chancellor of the university who is an ex officio member and the only nonvoting trustee. *Composition of institution:* Administrators 35 men / 15 women. Academic affairs headed by executive vice chancellor. Management/business/finances directed by vice chancellor for finance. Full-time instructional faculty 2,299. Academic governance body, Faculty Senate, meets an average of 2 times per year.

Calendar: Semesters. Academic year Aug. to May. Freshmen admitted Apr. for fall semester. Degrees conferred May, Jan. Formal commencement May. Summer sessions.

Characteristics of Freshmen: 22% of applicants admitted. 33% of applicants admitted and enrolled.

86% (1,250 students) submitted SAT scores; 48% (697 students) submitted ACT scores. *25th percentile:* SAT Verbal 660, SAT Math 690; ACT Composite 30, ACT English 30, ACT Math 29. *75th percentile:* SAT Verbal 740, SAT Math 780, ACT Composite 33, ACT English 34, ACT Math 34.

91% of entering freshmen expected to graduate within 5 years. 11% of freshmen from Missouri. Freshmen from 49 states and 18 foreign countries.

Admission: Application deadline is Jan. 15 with notification by Apr. 1. Admitted students are asked to reply by May 1. Early decision plan is binding. Early decision deadlines are Nov. 15 with notification by Dec. 15 and Jan. 1 with notification by Jan. 15. *Requirements:* no specific requirements; GED accepted. *Entrance tests:* College Board SAT or ACT required. Tutoring available.

Degree Requirements: Vary by academic area.

Distinctive Educational Programs: Accelerated program, cooperative (work-study plan) program, cross-registration, double major, dual enrollment, English as a Second Language, exchange student program, independent study, internships, liberal arts/career combination, student-design major, teacher certification, university scholars program. Study abroad in Australia, Chile, China, England, France, Germany, Greece, Hungary, Ireland, Israel, Italy, Japan, Kenya, Korea, Netherlands, Russia, South Africa, Spain, Taiwan.

ROTC: Army. Air Force in cooperation with St. Louis University.

Degrees Conferred: 1,634 *baccalaureate;* 1,275 *master's;* 241 *doctorate;* 358 *first-professional.*

Fees and Other Expenses: *Full-time tuition per academic year 2005–06:* $31,000. Professional school tuition varies. *Required fees:* $942. *Room and board per academic year:* $10,064.

Financial Aid: Washington University offers a direct lending plan. Aid from institutionally generated funds is provided on the basis of academic merit, financial need.

Financial aid to full-time, first-time undergraduate students: need-based scholarships/grants totaling $14,087,818; self-help $16,406,093; parent loans $2,710,579; tuition waivers $4,848,755; non-need-based scholarships/grants totaling $5,970,674, self-help $957,497, parent loans $1,939,806, tuition waivers $347,835.

Departments and Teaching Staff: College of Arts and Sciences *professors* 187, *associate professors* 83, *assistant professors* 95, *instructors* 158, *part-time faculty* 121; School of Architecture 5, 7, 8, 2, 44; School of Engineering and Applied Science 40, 22, 34, 2, 102; Olin School of Business 18, 11, 30, 7, 17; 15; School of Art 7, 6, 7, 12, 124; School of Law 30, 9, 0, 9, 67; School of Medicine 336, 338, 466, 335, 115; School of Social Work 10, 9, 12, 1, 41; University College 0, 0, 0, 3, 125. *Total instructional faculty:* 2,455. Student-to-faculty ratio: 7:1. 99% hold terminal degrees.

Enrollment: Total enrollment 10,642. Undergraduate full-time 2,977 men / 3,052 women, part-time 516m / 805w; first-professional full-time 670 men / 540 women, part-time 3m / 2w; graduate full-time 1,743m / 1,660w, part-time 712m / 530w. *Transfer students:* 124 undergraduate.

Characteristics of Student Body: *Ethnic/racial makeup:* number of Black non-Hispanic: 691; American Indian or Alaska Native: 18; Asian or Pacific Islander: 685; Hispanic: 223; White non-Hispanic: 4,711; unknown: 667. *Age distribution (undergraduate):* number under 18: 88; 18–19: 2,628; 20–21: 2,850; 22–24: 769; 25–29: 281; 30–34: 224; 35–39: 144; 40–49: 250; 50–64: 110; 65 and over: 5.

International Students: 1,470 nonresident aliens enrolled fall 2004. Programs available for students whose native language is not English: English as a Second Language Program. No financial aid specifically designated for international students.

Student Life: On-campus residence halls house 70% of undergraduate students. On-campus housing includes coed dorms, apartments for single students, special interest suites, upper-class housing, single sex floors in coed buildings, and fraternity and sorority housing. 25% of undergraduate men join fraternities and 25% of women join sororities. *Intercollegiate athletics:* men only: baseball, basketball, cross-country, football, soccer, swimming/diving, tennis, track, wrestling; women only: basketball, cross-country, softball, swimming/diving, tennis, track, volleyball. *Special regulations:* Cars with decals permitted without restrictions for all but freshmen. *Special services:* Learning Resources Center, medical services, shuttle bus. *Student publications: Cadenza,* quarterly; *Hatchet Yearbook,* an annual; *Law Quarterly, Student Life,* published weekly; *Eliot Review, Washington Ripple Magazine. Surrounding community:* St. Louis population over 2.6 million. Served by mass transit bus system; airport 12 miles from campus; passenger rail service 8 miles from campus.

Library Collections: 3,647,457 volumes including bound books, serial backfiles, electronic documents, and government documents not in separate collections. Online catalog. Current serial subscriptions: 47,266 print and electronic. 32,838 recordings; 5,446 compact discs; 5,212 CD-ROMs. 192 computer work stations. Students have access to the Internet at no charge.

Most important holdings include Modern Literary Manuscripts Collection; Arnold Semiology Collection; Holly Hall Book Arts Collection; Triple Crown and Eric Gill Collection.

Buildings and Grounds: Campus area 228 acres. *New buildings:* Charles F. Knight Executive Education Center; Laboratory Sciences Building; Uncas A. Whitaker Hall for biomedical Engineering; Earth and Planetary Sciences Building.

Chief Executive Officer: Dr. Mark S. Wrighton, Chancellor.

Address admission inquiries to Nanette H. Tarbouni, Director of Admissions; graduate inquiries to Graduate School.

College of Arts and Sciences

Degree Programs Offered: *Baccalaureate, master's, doctorate.*

Distinctive Educational Programs: Interdisciplinary programs in Asian studies; African American Studies, Germanic studies, Jewish studies; history and technology; international development; Latin American studies; law, liberty, and justice; linguistic studies; literature and history; religious studies; women's studies. Scholars program in medicine provides provisional admission. Focus program provides year long seminars for freshmen. Off-campus study in Washington (DC) semester.

John H. Olin School of Business

Degree Programs Offered: *Baccalaureate, master's, doctorate.*

Distinctive Educational Programs: Joint M.B.A.-baccalaureate program with School of Engineering, College of Arts and Sciences; M.B.A.-master's program with School of Architecture, School of Social Work; M.B.A.-first-professional program with Law School.

School of Engineering and Applied Science

Degree Programs Offered: *Baccalaureate, master's, doctorate.*

Distinctive Educational Programs: Interdisciplinary programs in biomedical engineering, materials science, economics and systems science, technology and human affairs. Joint M.B.A.-baccalaureate program with John M. Olin School of Business.

School of Art

Degree Programs Offered: *Baccalaureate, master's, doctorate.*

Distinctive Educational Programs: Programs include ceramics, fashion design, graphic communications, painting, photography, printmaking, and sculpture.

School of Architecture

Degree Programs Offered: *Baccalaureate, master's.*

Distinctive Educational Programs: Joint degree program- master of Architecture with Bachelor of Science from the School of engineering and Applied Science. 4+2 curriculum - Bachelors degree and professional master's degree in six years.

Webster University

470 East Lockwood Avenue
St. Louis, Missouri 63119-3194

Tel: (314) 968-2660   **E-mail:** admit@webster.edu
Fax: (314) 968-7120   **Internet:** www.webster.edu

Institution Description: Webster University is a private, independent, multi-campus, nonprofit institution. *Enrollment:* 19,038. *Degrees awarded:* Baccalaureate, master's, doctorate.

Accreditation: *Regional:* NCA. *Professional:* music, nursing

History: Established as Loretto College by the Sisters of Loretto, Roman Catholic Church and offered first instruction at postsecondary level 1915; incorporated 1916; awarded first degree (baccalaureate) 1919; became legally secular 1967; became a University in 1983 to reflect the scope and range of academic programs, growth of student populations, and commitment to internationalism.

Institutional Structure: *Governing board:* Board of Trustees. Extrainstitutional representation: 36 trustees; institutional representation: 4 administrators; 1 alumnus. 1 ex officio. 36 voting. *Composition of institution:* Administrators 4 men / 2 women. Academic affairs headed by vice president for academic affairs. Business/finance directed by vice president for finance and administration. Full-time instructional faculty 56 men / 53 women. Academic governance body, Faculty Senate, meets an average of 4 times per year.

Calendar: Semesters. Academic year Aug. to May.

Characteristics of Freshmen: 1,434 applicants. 673% of applicants admitted and enrolled. 55.8% of admitted students enrolled full-time.

22% of applicants submitted SAT scores; 67% submitted ACT scores. *25th percentile:* SAT I Verbal 520, SAT I Math 500, ACT Composite 22. *75th percentile:* SAT I Verbal 650, SAT I Math 610; ACT Composite 27.

31% freshmen from Missouri. Freshmen from 47 states 25 foreign countries.

Admission: Rolling admissions plan. Freshmen admission: applicants considered for admission based upon 6 semesters of high school work; qualified candidates considered for early admissions; deferred admission available. *Requirements:* Graduation from accredited secondary school or GED. *Entrance tests:* SAT or ACT. College credit may be awarded for advanced placement, international baccalaureate, and postsecondary-level work completed while in high school. *For transfer students:* Official transcripts required from each postsecondary institution previously attended; applicants who have completed less than 30 semester credit hours of college-level work must also submit a high school transcript. Maximum transfer credit 98 semester hours; maximum from a community college 64 hours.

College credit for acceptable scores on CLEP; USAFI; GED, COLLEGE LEVEL; and ACT-PEP. Institutional credit by examination available. Prior experiential learning can be evaluated for the possibility of college credit as part of a degree program. Additional transfer credit options on basis of *2006 Guide to the Evaluation of Educational Experiences in the Armed Services.*

Degree Requirements: 128 semester credit hours; satisfactory completion of major requirements; successful completion of at least 30 credit hours registered for and earned directly from Webster University; 2.0 cumulative GPA on Webster University coursework. *Grading system:* A/B/C/D/NC or CR/NC.

Distinctive Educational Programs: Career experience: undergraduate internships and practica provide valuable experience in selected areas of study. Programs of distinction include business/management, media communications and fine arts (theatre, music, art). Pre-professional programs in engineering, architecture, medicine, and law. Freshmen seminars provide academic orientation for new students. Extended campuses serving adult learners at 44 locations throughout the United States. These campuses feature evening and weekend classes. Four European locations for study abroad offer undergraduate and graduate programs: Geneva, Switzerland; Leiden, The Netherlands; Vienna, Austria; London, England; Bangkok, Thailand; Graduate MBA program at campus in Shanghai, China.

Degrees Conferred: 1,170 *baccalaureate;* 5,407 *master's;* 14 *doctorate.* Bachelor's degrees awarded in top five disciplines: business, management, marketing, and related support services 424; communication, journalism, and related programs 168; computer and information sciences 120; visual and performing arts 117; social sciences and history 81.

Fees and Other Expenses: *Full-time tuition per academic year 2004–05:* $16,250 undergraduate; contact the university for graduate tuition/fees. *Books and supplies:* $1,500. *Room and board per academic year:* $9,364.

Financial Aid: Aid from institutionally generated funds is provided on the basis of academic merit, financial need. Institution has a Program Participation Agreement with the U.S. Department of Education for eligible students to receive Pell Grants, and, depending upon the agreement, other federal aid.

Financial aid to full-time, first-time undergraduate students: 24% received federal grants averaging $3,073; 32% state/local grants averaging $1,637; 90% institutional grants averaging $7,165; 72% received loans averaging $3,144.

Departments and Teaching Staff: Art *professors* 2, *associate professors* 3, *assistant professors* 4, *instructors* 0, *part-time teachers* 31; behavioral and social sciences 3, 4, 1, 0, 11; business 4, 1, 1, 0, 64; management 2, 2, 3, 0, 120; education 6, 5, 4, 0, 46; foreign languages 2, 1, 1, 0, 12; history/politics/law 4, 1, 5, 0, 24; literature 2, 1, 2, 0, 18; mathematics/computer science 2, 3, 1, 0, 51; media 6, 1, 5, 3, 100; music 5, 3, 2, 1, 55; nursing 1, 3, 3, 0, 5; philosophy 1, 1, 1, 0, 6; religion 1, 0, 1, 0, 12; science 2, 3, 1, 0, 17; theatre/dance 3, 4, 7, 0, 37.

Total instructional faculty: 341 FTE. Student-to-faculty ratio: 15:1. Degrees held by full-time faculty: baccalaureate 100%, master's 22%, doctorate 76%, professional 76%. 76% hold terminal degrees.

Enrollment: Total enrollment 19,038. Undergraduate 3,899 (men 37.2%, women 62.8%).

Characteristics of Student Body: *Ethnic/racial makeup (undergraduate):* number of Black non-Hispanic: 13.2%; American Indian or Alaska Native: .3%; Asian or Pacific Islander: 1.4%; Hispanic: 2.5%; White non-Hispanic: 70.9%; unknown: 8.9%. *Age distribution:* 17–21: 1%; 22–24: 5%; 25–29: 18%; 30–34: 21%; 35–39: 19%; 40–49: 30%; 50–59: 6%; 60–up: less than 1%.

International Students: 109 undergraduate nonresident aliens enrolled fall 2004. Programs available to aid students whose native language is not English: social, cultural. English as a Second Language Program. No financial aid specifically designated for international students.

Student Life: On-campus residence halls house 10% of undergraduate student body. Residence halls for both single-sex and coed floors. *Special regulations:* Cars permitted. *Special services:* Academic Support Center, medical services. *Student publications: The Journal,* a weekly newspaper; *The Green Fuse,* annual literary magazine. *Surrounding community:* St. Louis metropolitan area population 2.5 million. Served by airport 20 miles from campus.

Publications: *Accent; Webster World; Media Resource Directory and Speakers Bureau.*

Library Collections: 290,000 volumes. 137,000 microforms; 15,00 audiovisual materials; Access to 14,500 periodicals (paper, microform, electronic). Online catalog. Students have access to online information retrieval services and the Internet.

Most important special holdings include collections on international business, education, and liberal arts.

Buildings and Grounds: Campus area 45 acres.

Chief Executive Officer: Dr. Richard S. Meyers, President.

Address admission inquiries to Director of Admissions.

Westminster College

501 Westminster Avenue
Fulton, Missouri 6525-12991

Tel: (573) 642-3361   **E-mail:** admissions@westminster-mo.edu
Fax: (573) 592-5255   **Internet:** www.westminster-mo.edu

Institution Description: Westminster College is a private, independent, non-profit college. *Enrollment:* 837. *Degrees awarded:* Baccalaureate.

Accreditation: *Regional:* NCA.

History: Established as Fulton College and offered first instruction at postsecondary level 1851; chartered and adopted present name 1853; awarded first degree (baccalaureate) 1855; admitted women as full-time students 1979. *See* William E. Parrish, *Westminster College: An Informed History, 1851–1969* (Fulton: Ovid Bell Press, 1971) for further information.

Institutional Structure: *Governing board:* Westminster College Board of Trustees. Representation: 70 trustees (including 42 active, 24 life, 4 honorary). 31 ex officio. 42 voting. *Composition of institution:* Administrators 7 men / 1 woman. Academic affairs headed by dean of faculty. Management/business/finances directed by business manager. Full-time instructional faculty 35 men / 17 women. Academic governance body, the faculty, meets an average of 9 times per year.

Calendar: Semesters. Academic year Aug. to May. Freshmen admitted Aug., Jan. Degrees conferred May, Sept. Formal commencement May. Summer session from May to June.

Characteristics of Freshmen: 66% of applicants admitted. 33% of applicants admitted and enrolled.

23% (54 students) submitted SAT scores; 41% (210 students) submitted ACT scores. *25th percentile:* SAT Verbal 540, SAT Math 500; ACT Composite 22,

ACT English 22, ACT Math 20. *75th percentile:* SAT Verbal 640, SAT Math 620; ACT Composite 27, ACT English 29, ACT Math 27.

70% of entering freshmen expected to graduate within 5 years. 66% of freshmen from Missouri. Freshmen from 10 states and 26 foreign countries.

Admission: Rolling admissions plan. For fall acceptance, apply as early as end of junior year of secondary school, but not later than Aug. 1 of year of enrollment. *Requirements:* Either graduation from accredited secondary school or GED. Recommend 4 units English, 2 laboratory science, 2 mathematics, 2 social studies, 2 academic elective, 3 foreign language. Lowest acceptable secondary school class standing 40th percentile. *Entrance tests:* College Board SAT or ACT composite. *For transfer students:* 2.0 minimum GPA; from 4-year accredited institution and for correspondence/extension students maximum transfer credit limited only by residence requirement; from 2-year institution 62 hours.

College credit and advanced placement for postsecondary-level work completed in secondary school.

Tutoring available. Developmental courses offered during regular academic year; credit given.

Degree Requirements: 122 credit hours; 2.0 GPA; senior year in residence; 1 semester of physical education; distribution requirements.

Fulfillment of some degree requirements and exemption from some beginning courses possible by passing departmental examinations, College Board CLEP, APP. *Grading system:* A–F; credit-no credit; withdraw passing (carries time limit); withdraw failing (carries time limit).

Distinctive Educational Programs: Internships. Dual-degree program in engineering with Washington University (MO). Facilities and programs for independent research, including individual majors, tutorials. Study abroad through the Institute of European Studies in Vienna; in England at Durham and London; in France at Nantes and Paris; in Spain at Madrid; in Germany at Freiburg. Off-campus study in the U.S. includes Washington (DC) semester in cooperation with American University, United Nations semester in cooperation with Drew University (NJ). Learning Disabilities Program provides individualized instruction and support for students clinically diagnosed as learning disabled. Chicago Urban Semester, United Nations Semester, International Student Exchange Programs.

ROTC: Air Force, Army, Navy available through University of Missouri-Columbia.

Degrees Conferred: 185 *baccalaureate:* biological/life sciences 12; business/marketing 61; communications 5; computer and information sciences 8; education 20; English 14; foreign languages and literatures 10; health professions 2; liberal arts/general studies 3; mathematics 7; philosophy/religion/theology 3; physical sciences 1; psychology 11; social sciences and history 16.

Fees and Other Expenses: *Full-time tuition per academic year 2005–06:* $13,750. *Required fees:* $420. *Room and board per academic year:* $5,870.

Financial Aid: Aid from institutionally generated funds is provided on the basis of academic merit, financial need.

Financial aid to full-time, first-time undergraduate students: need-based scholarships/grants totaling $8,189,857, self-help $1,149,790, tuition waivers $121,610; non-need-based self-help $1,109,893, parent loans $1,084,763.

Departments and Teaching Staff: *Professors* 17, *associate professors* 16, *assistant professors* 17, *instructors* 3, *part-time faculty:* 25.

Total instructional faculty: 78 (full-time 53, part-time 25; women 38, men 50; members of minority groups 5). Student-to-faculty ratio: 14:1. Degrees held by full-time faculty: doctorate 73%, master's 100%, baccalaureate 100%. 75% hold terminal degrees. *Faculty development:* 4 faculty members awarded sabbaticals 2004–05.

Enrollment: Total enrollment 861. Undergraduate full-time 486 men / 358 women, part-time 2m / 15w. *Transfer students:* 95.

Characteristics of Student Body: *Ethnic/racial makeup:* number of Black non-Hispanic: 36; American Indian or Alaska Native: 17; Asian or Pacific Islander: 11; Hispanic: 12; White non-Hispanic: 723; unknown: 9. *Age distribution:* number under 18: 2; 18–19: 366; 20–21: 348; 22–24: 103; 25–29: 12; 35–39: 1; 40–49: 2.

International Students: 73 nonresident aliens enrolled fall 2004. 20 students from Europe, 30 Asia, 3 Central and South America, 18 Africa, 2 other. Programs available to aid students whose native language is not English: social, cultural. No financial aid specifically designated for international students.

Student Life: Freshman students live in freshmen quadrangle. 80% of all students live on campus in residence halls and social fraternity houses. 58% of men and 50% of women join national social fraternities. *Intercollegiate athletics:* men only: baseball, football, rifle, basketball, cross-country, golf, soccer, tennis; women only: cross-country, tennis, volleyball, golf, basketball, soccer, rifle, softball. *Student publications: The Bluejay,* a yearbook; *The Columns,* a bimonthly newspaper; *Janus,* an annual literary magazine. *Surrounding community:* Fulton population 11,500. St. Louis, 110 miles from campus, and Kansas City, 150 miles from campus, are nearest metropolitan areas.

Library Collections: 123,515 volumes including bound books, serial backfiles, electronic documents, and government documents not in separate collections. Online catalog. Current serial subscriptions: 415 paper, 5 microform, 2,523 electronic. 76 recordings; 15 compact discs; 61 CD-ROMs. 92 computer work stations campus-wide. Students have access to the Internet at no charge. Total budget for books, periodicals, audiovisual materials, microforms 2004–05: $105,599.

Most important special holdings include Winston Churchill Memorial and Library (Sir Winston Churchill and Anglo-American relations); *New York Times* on microfilm, 1851–to date.

Buildings and Grounds: Campus area 55 acres. *New buildings:* Coulter Science Center completed 2204.

Chief Executive Officer: Dr. Fletcher M. Lamkin, President.

Address admission inquiries to Kelle Silvey; Director of Admissions.

William Jewell College

500 College Hill
Liberty, Missouri 64068
Tel: (816) 781-7700   **E-mail:** admission@william.jewell.edu
Fax: (816) 415-5040   **Internet:** www.jewell.edu

Institution Description: William Jewell College is a private college affiliated with the Baptist Church. *Enrollment:* 1,310. *Degrees awarded:* Baccalaureate.

Accreditation: *Regional:* NCA. *Professional:* music, nursing, nursing education

History: Established as a men's college and chartered 1849; offered first instruction at postsecondary level 1851; awarded first degree (baccalaureate) 1855; became coeducational 1921. *See* H.I. Hester, *Jewell Is Her Name* (Liberty: Nowell Press, 1967) for further information.

Institutional Structure: *Governing board:* Board of Trustees of William Jewell College. 24 trustees. All voting. *Composition of institution:* Administrators 6 men / 1 women. Academic affairs headed by dean and provost of the college. Management/business/finances directed by vice president. Full-time instructional faculty 87. Academic governance body, the Faculty of William Jewell, meets an average of 20 times per year.

Calendar: Semesters. Academic year Aug. to May. Freshmen admitted Aug., Jan., June. Degrees conferred and formal commencement May. Summer session from early June to late July.

Characteristics of Freshmen: 86% of applicants accepted. 45% of accepted applicants enrolled.

16% (53 students) submitted SAT scores; 97% (313 students) submitted ACT scores. *25th percentile:* SAT Verbal 550, SAT Math 540; ACT Composite 22, ACT English 22, ACT Math 20. *75th percentile:* SAT Verbal 700, SAT Math 670; ACT Composite 27, ACT English 29, ACT Math 27.

62% of entering freshmen expected to graduate within 5 years. 78% of freshmen from Missouri. Freshmen from 17 states and 3 foreign countries.

Admission: Modified rolling admissions plan. Apply as early as end of junior year of secondary school. Early acceptance available. *Requirements:* Either graduation from accredited secondary school with 20 units which must include 4 English, 2 foreign language, 3 mathematics, 3 science; or GED. *Entrance tests:* ACT composite or SAT I. *For transfer students:* 2.0 minimum GPA; from 2-year accredited institution 64 hours.

College credit and advanced placement for postsecondary-level work completed in secondary school. Tutoring available. Developmental courses offered regular academic year; credit given.

Degree Requirements: 124 credit hours; 2.0 GPA; 30 hours in residence; 2 hours physical education courses; general education requirements.

Fulfillment of some degree requirements and exemption from some beginning courses possible by passing College Board CLEP, AP. *Grading system:* A–F; pass-fail; withdraw (carries time limit).

Distinctive Educational Programs: Internships. Evening classes. Accelerated degree programs. Innovative curricula. Oxbridge Alternative for tutorial majors; interdisciplinary core courses. Dual-degree programs in engineering with Columbia University (NY), Washington University (MO), University of Kansas, University of Missouri-Columbia, University of Missouri-Rolla; in forestry with Duke University (NC). Baccalaureate program in medical technology in cooperation with area hospitals. Preprofessional programs in dentistry, journalism, law, medical technology, medicine, ministry, occupational therapy. Facilities and programs for independent research, including honors programs, individual majors, tutorials. Study abroad in Australia, Austria, China, England, France, Germany, Italy, Japan, Spain.

Degrees Conferred: 270 *baccalaureate:* biological/life sciences 16, business/marketing 69; computer and information sciences 8; education 32; English 27; fine and applied arts 5; foreign languages 24; mathematics 5; physical sciences 8; psychology 40; social sciences and history 19; visual and performing arts 51; other 12.

Fees and Other Expenses: *Full-time tuition per academic year 2004–05:* $18,500. *Room and board per academic year:* $5,350.

Financial Aid: The college offers a direct lending program. Aid from institutionally generated funds is provided on the basis of academic merit, financial need, athletic ability, other criteria.

Financial aid to full-time, first-time undergraduate students: need-based scholarships/grants totaling $7,744,738, self-help $5,905,359, parent loans $1,882,859, tuition waivers $317,610, athletic awards $1,176,584; non-need-based scholarships/grants totaling $2,845,612, self-help $683,039, parent loans $768,758, tuition waivers $474,841, athletic awards $699,725.

Departments and Teaching Staff: *Total instructional faculty:* 150 (full-time 75, part-time 75; women 83, men 67; members of minority groups 11). Student-to-faculty ration: 13:1. Degrees held by full-time faculty: doctorate 80%, master's 15%, professional 5%. 85% hold terminal degrees.

Enrollment: Total enrollment 1,310. Undergraduate full-time 516 men / 748 women, part-time 18m / 28w.

Characteristics of Student Body: *Ethnic/racial makeup:* Black non-Hispanic: 49; American Indian or Native Alaskan: 9; Asian or Pacific Islander: 10; Hispanic: 30; White non-Hispanic 1,179; unknown: 23.

International Students: 11 undergraduate nonresident aliens enrolled fall 2004. No programs available to aid students whose native language is not English. Financial aid specifically designated for international students: unlimited scholarships available annually.

Student Life: On-campus residence halls house 88% of student body. 37% of women join sororities; 58% of men join fraternities. 60% of married students request institutional housing; 50% are so housed. 63% of students live on campus. *Intercollegiate athletics:* men only: baseball, basketball, cross country, football, golf, soccer, tennis, track; women only: basketball, cross country, softball, tennis, track, volleyball. *Special regulations:* Cars with decals permitted. Residence hall visitation varies. *Special services:* Learning Resources Center, Writing Center, medical services. *Student publications, radio: The Hilltop Monitor,* a weekly newspaper; *The Tatler,* a yearbook. Radio station KWJC. *Surrounding community:* Liberty population 25,000. Kansas City, 18 miles from campus, is nearest metropolitan area. Served by mass transit bus system; airport and passenger rail service, both 20 miles from campus.

Library Collections: 272,000 volumes. 219,500 microforms; 29,500 audiovisual materials; 780 current periodical subscriptions. 5,075 recordings. Computer work stations available. Online catalog. Students have access to online information retrieval services and the Internet.

Most important special holdings include Spurgeon Collection (the private library, including letters, papers, books, manuscripts, of Charles H. Spurgeon, an English preacher, and a collection of old hymnals and material written by early Puritans); Settle Collection (western Americana including a collection of historical and contemporary works on Missouri, and material on the pony express and other aspects of settling of the West); Mertins Collection (first editions, silhouettes, signatures); Doherty Collection of Shakespeare.

Buildings and Grounds: Campus area 200 acres.

Chief Executive Officer: Dr. David L. Sallee, President.

Address admission inquiries to John Olsen, Dean of Enrollment Management.

William Woods University

One University Avenue
Fulton, Missouri 65251-2388
Tel: (573) 642-2251   **E-mail:** admissions@wmwoods.edu
Fax: (573) 592-1136   **Internet:** www.wmwoods.edu

Institution Description: William Woods University is an independent, coeducational institution offering both undergraduate and graduate degree opportunities in a variety of academic and professional disciplines. *Enrollment:* 2,453. *Degrees awarded:* Baccalaureate, master's. Specialist certificates also awarded.

Accreditation: *Regional:* NCA. *Professional:* art, social work, teacher education, theatre

History: Chartered in northwestern Missouri as Female Orphans School of the Christian Church of Missouri 1870; moved to Fulton 1890; changed name to Daughter's College of the Christian Church of Missouri and offered first instruction at postsecondary level 1900; adopted present name 1901; became a four-year institution 1962; awarded first degree (baccalaureate) 1964; College of Graduate and Adult Studies created 1992; achieved university status 1993; became coeducational 1996.

Institutional Structure: *Governing board:* Board of Trustees. Representation: 27 trustees. *Composition of institution:* Administrators 3 men / 3 women. Academic affairs headed by vice president and dean of academic affairs. Management/business/finances directed by vice president for fiscal affairs. Admissions/financial aid/athletics/student development directed by vice president and dean of students. Full-time instructional faculty 56.

Calendar: Semesters. Academic year Aug. to May.

Characteristics of Freshmen: 39% of applicants admitted. 30% of applicants admitted and enrolled.

15% (37 students) submitted SAT scores; 64% (161 students) submitted ACT scores. *25th percentile*: SAT Verbal 460, SAT Math 420; ACT Composite 18. *75th percentile*: SAT Verbal 540, SAT Math 550; ACT 21.

48% of entering freshmen expected to graduate within 5 years. 59% of freshmen from Missouri. Freshmen from 35 states and 6 foreign countries.

Admission: Rolling admissions plan. Apply by senior year of secondary school for early decision. Early acceptance available. *Requirements:* Graduation from accredited secondary school with 16 units, including 11 from among English, foreign languages, mathematics, natural sciences, social studies. *Entrance tests:* College Board SAT or ACT composite. *For transfer students:* 2.0 minimum GPA.

College credit and advanced placement for postsecondary-level work completed in secondary school.

Degree Requirements: 122 credit hours; 2.0 GPA; last year in residence; general education requirements.

Fulfillment of some degree requirements through College Board CLEP, AP. *Grading system:* A–F; withdraw (carries time limit); incomplete.

Distinctive Educational Programs: Accelerated undergraduate/graduate degree programs. Year-round scheduling. Work-experience programs, including internships, practicums. Study abroad in Austria, Ecuador, France, Germany, Italy, Japan, Mexico, Spain, Switzerland.

Degrees Conferred: 240 *baccalaureate:* biological/life sciences 3, business/marketing 101; communications 10; 3, computer and information sciences 27; education 12; English 1; equestrian studies 19; foreign languages 2; health professions 3; law/legal studies 2; liberal arts/general studies 32; protective services/public administration 4; psychology 5; social sciences and history 7; visual and performing arts 10. 672 *master's:* business/marketing 137; education 335.

Fees and Other Expenses: *Full-time tuition per academic year 2005–06:* $14,700 undergraduate; graduate tuition/fees vary by program. *Required fees:* $425. *Room and board per academic year:* $5,900.

Financial Aid: Aid from institutionally generated funds is provided on the basis of academic merit, financial need, athletic ability, other criteria.

Financial aid to full-time, first-time undergraduate students: need-based scholarships/grants totaling $1,402,037, self-help $2,117,123; non-need-based scholarships/grants totaling $4,850,207, self-help $1,695,497, parent loans $645,695, tuition waivers $415,848, athletic awards $1,047,715. *Graduate aid:* 2,008 students received $4,279,945 in federal and state-funded loans (ranging from $1,000 to $11,500).

Departments and Teaching Staff: *Total instructional faculty:* 56 (full-time 55, part-time 1; women 28, men 28; members of minority groups 2). Total faculty with doctorate, first-professional, or other terminal degree: 30. Student-to-faculty ratio: 13:1. Degrees held by full-time faculty: doctorate 50%, master's 50%. 66% hold terminal degrees.

Enrollment: Total enrollment 2,191. Undergraduate full-time 185 men / 589 women, part-time 65m / 173w; graduate full-time 1390m / 240w, part-time 315m / 485w. *Transfer students:* in-state 181; from out-of-state 34.

Characteristics of Student Body: *Ethnic/racial makeup:* number of Black non-Hispanic: 33; American Indian or Alaska Native: 4; Asian or Pacific Islander: 4; Hispanic: 13; White non-Hispanic: 890; unknown: 33. *Age distribution:* number under 18: 8; 18–19: 298; 20–21: 271; 22–24: 122; 25–29: 711 30–34: 69; 35–39: 69; 40–49: 77; 50–64: 27.

International Students: 88 nonresident aliens enrolled fall 2004. Students from Europe, Asia, Africa, Canada, Australia. No programs available for students whose native language is not English. No financial aid specifically designated for international students.

Student Life: 13 on-campus residence halls. *Intercollegiate athletics:* men: baseball, golf, soccer, volleyball; women: basketball, golf, soccer, softball, tennis, volleyball. *Special services:* Student Diversity, counseling, Co-curricular Developmental Transcript Program, Women's Leadership. *Student publications: The Green Owl*, newspaper; *Ideas and Trends*, literary publication. *Surrounding community:* Fulton population 12,000. St. Louis, 100 miles and Kansas City 150 miles from campus, are nearest metropolitan areas.

Library Collections: 131,820 volumes including bound books, serial backfiles, electronic documents, and government documents not in separate collections. Online catalog. Current serial subscriptions: 2,380 paper; 11,060 microform; 4,084 electronic. 28,443 audiovisual materials. 15 computer work stations. Students have access to the Internet at no charge.

Most important special holdings include Educational Materials Collection; Equestrian Science Collection; law collection; music scores and discs (11,935 items not counted above).

Buildings and Grounds: *New buildings:* Kemper Arts Center; Stone-Campbell Apartments; Center for Human Performance.

Chief Executive Officer: Jahnae H. Barnett, President.

Address admission inquiries to Jimmy Clay, Vice President of Admissions and Recruitment Services.

Montana

Carroll College

1601 North Benton Avenue
Helena, Montana 59625
Tel: (406) 447-4384   **E-mail:** enroll@carroll.edu
Fax: (406) 447-4533   **Internet:** www.carroll.edu

Institution Description: Carroll College is an independent liberal arts college affiliated with the Diocese of Helena, Roman Catholic Church. *Enrollment:* 1,441. *Degrees awarded:* Associate, baccalaureate.

Accreditation: *Regional:* NWCCU. *Professional:* engineering, nursing, social work

History: Established as Mount St. Charles College, chartered, and offered first instruction at postsecondary level 1909; awarded first degree (baccalaureate) 1916; adopted present name 1932.

Institutional Structure: *Governing board:* Carroll College Board of Trustees. Extrainstitutional representation: 10 trustees, bishop of Helena; institutional representation: president of the college. 2 ex officio. All voting. *Composition of institution:* Administrators 11 men / 10 women. Academic affairs headed by vice president for academic affairs. Management/business/finances directed by vice president for financial affairs. Full-time instructional faculty 77. Academic governance body, Board of Educational Policy and Practice, meets an average of 15 times per year.

Calendar: Semesters. Academic year Aug. to May. Freshmen admitted Aug., Jan., June. Degrees conferred May, Aug., Dec. Formal commencement May. Summer session from mid-June to end of July.

Characteristics of Freshmen: 80% of applicants admitted. 43% of applicants admitted and enrolled.

65% (231 students) submitted SAT scores; 68% (244 students) submitted ACT scores. *25th percentile:* SAT Verbal 490, SAT Math 490; ACT Composite 21, ACT English 20, ACT Math 20. *75th percentile:* SAT Verbal 620, SAT Math 610; ACT Composite 27, ACT English 26, ACT Math 27.

55% of entering freshmen expected to graduate within 5 years. 47% of freshmen from Montana. Freshmen from 21 states and 1 foreign country.

Admission: Rolling admissions plan. For fall acceptance, apply as early as Nov. 1 of previous year, but not later than June 1 of year of enrollment. *Requirements:* Either graduation from accredited secondary school with 15 units which normally include 4 English, 2 in a foreign language, 3 mathematics/laboratory science, 1 American history/government, 5 academic electives; or GED. Minimum GPA 2.5. *Entrance tests:* College Board SAT, ACT composite. For foreign students TOEFL. *For transfer students:* 2.5 minimum GPA, 60 semester hours maximum lower division transfer credit.

College credit and advanced placement for postsecondary-level work completed in secondary school and for extrainstitutional learning (life experience) on basis of ACE *Military Guide* and *National Guide* (American Institute of Banking and National Secretaries Association programs only).

Tutoring available.

Degree Requirements: *For all associate degrees:* 66 credit hours. *For all baccalaureate degrees:* 122 credit hours; comprehensives in individual fields of study. *For all degrees:* 2.0 GPA; 30 semester hours in residence; distribution requirements.

Fulfillment of some degree requirements and exemption from some beginning courses possible by passing departmental examinations, College Board APP. *Grading system:* A–F; pass-fail; withdraw (carries time limit); incomplete (carries time limit).

Distinctive Educational Programs: Preprofessional programs in medicine, law, and ministry. Graduate school placement. Dual-degree programs in engineering with 6 affiliated engineering schools. Public relations programs. Internships to students in every major at the state capital, local health facilities, and community businesses. Facilities and programs are available for independent research, including honors programs, tutorials, and independent study. Study abroad by individual arrangement.

ROTC: Army.

Degrees Conferred: 11*associate;* 248 *baccalaureate:* biological/life sciences 32; business/marketing 33; communications/communication technologies 12; computer and information sciences 9; education 31; engineering and engineering technologies 4; English 3; foreign languages and literature 2; health professions and related sciences 25; interdisciplinary studies 2; natural resources/environmental science 1; parks and recreation 11; philosophy/religion/theology 5; physical sciences 11; protective services/public administration 1; psychology 27; social sciences and history 35; trade and industry 4.

Fees and Other Expenses: *Full-time tuition per academic year 2005–06:* $16,778. *Room and board per academic year:* $6,246. *Required fees:* $200.

Financial Aid: Aid from institutionally generated funds is provided on the basis of academic merit, financial need, athletic ability.

Financial aid to full-time, first-time undergraduate students: need-based scholarships/grants totaling $6,771,445, self-help $3,934,936, parent loans $48,331, tuition waivers $205,444, athletic awards $545,259; non-need-based scholarships/grants totaling $2,943,219, self-help $3,228,437, parent loans $785,873, tuition waivers $419,639, athletic awards $656,835.

Departments and Teaching Staff: *Total instructional faculty:* 142 (full-time 77, part-time 65; women 61, men 81; members of minority groups 5). Total faculty with doctorate, first-professional, or other terminal degree: 64. Student-to-faculty ratio: 14:1. Degrees held by full-time faculty: doctorate 59%, master's 36%, baccalaureate 1%, professional 4%. 63% hold terminal degrees.

Enrollment: Total enrollment 1,441. Full-time 527 men / 724 women, part-time 69m / 121w.

Characteristics of Student Body: *Ethnic/racial makeup:* number of Black non-Hispanic: 5; American Indian or Alaska Native: 10; Asian or Pacific Islander: 12; Hispanic: 20; White non-Hispanic: 1,009; unknown: 362.

International Students: 23 nonresident aliens enrolled fall 2004. Students from Europe, Asia, Latin America, Canada. Programs available available to aid students whose native language is not English: social, cultural. English as a Second Language Program. Financial aid specifically designated for international undergraduate students: scholarships available annually.

Student Life: On-campus residence halls house 58% of student body. Residence halls for men constitute 50% of such space, for women 50%. *Intercollegiate athletics:* men only: basketball, football, golf; women only: basketball, golf, soccer, volleyball. *Special regulations:* Cars permitted without restrictions. Residence hall visitation 11am to 1am school days, 11am to 2am weekends. *Special services:* Academic Resources Center, Wellness Center, Student Development Center. *Student publications, radio, television:* Colours, an annual literary magazine; *Hilltopper,* a yearbook; *Prospector,* a weekly newspaper. *Surrounding community:* Helena population 48,000. Spokane (WA), 300 miles from campus, is nearest metropolitan area. Served by airport 2 miles from campus.

Library Collections: 97,995 volumes. 10,000 government documents; 16,160 microforms; 2,800 audiovisual materials; 640 current periodical subscriptions. 15 computer work stations. Students have access to the Internet at no charge.

Most important special collections include Dante Collection; Health Sciences; Carroll College Archives.

Buildings and Grounds: Campus area 64 acres. *New buildings:* Nelson Stadium; Trinity Hall.

Chief Executive Officer: Dr. Thomas Trebon, President.

Address admission inquiries to Cynthia Thornquist, Director of Admissions.

Montana State University - Billings

1500 North 30th Street
Billings, Montana 59101-0298
Tel: (406) 657-2158   **E-mail:** admissions@msubillings.edu
Fax: (406) 657-2202   **Internet:** www.msubillings.edu

Institution Description: Montana State University - Billings, formerly known as Eastern Montana College, is a public institution. *Enrollment:* 4,700. *Degrees awarded:* Associate, baccalaureate, master's.

Academic offerings subject to approval by statewide coordinating bodies. Budget subject to approval by state governing boards. Member of The Northern Rockies Consortium for Higher Education.

Accreditation: *Regional:* NWCCU. *Professional:* art, business, music, rehabilitation counseling, teacher education

History: Established and chartered as Eastern Montana State Normal School 1927; offered first instruction at postsecondary level 1928; changed name to Eastern Montana College of Education and awarded first degree (baccalaureate) 1949; became Eastern Montana College 1965; adopted present name 1994.

Institutional Structure: *Governing board:* Board of Regents of Higher Education for the Montana University System. Representation: 7 regents, including 1 student; governor of Montana; superintendent of public instruction; commissioner of higher education. 3 ex officio. 7 voting. *Composition of institution:* Administrators 15 men / 16 women. Academic affairs headed by provost/vice chancellor. Management/business/finances directed by administrative vice chancellor. Student affairs headed by vice chancellor. Full-time instructional faculty 99 men / 59 women. Academic governance body, Faculty Senate, meets an average of 20 times per year. *Faculty representation:* Faculty served by collective bargaining agent, AFT/MFA.

Calendar: Semesters. Academic year Sept. to May. Freshmen admitted Aug., Jan., May. Degrees conferred and formal commencement May. Summer session of 2 six-week terms from mid-May to late July.

Characteristics of Freshmen: 96% of applicants admitted. 66% of applicants admitted and enrolled.

15% (81 students) submitted SAT scores; 65% (359 students) submitted ACT scores. *25th percentile:* SAT Verbal 460, SAT Math 440; ACT Composite 19, ACT English 17, ACT Math 18. *75th percentile:* SAT Verbal 560, SAT Math 550; ACT Composite 23, ACT English 23, ACT Math 24.

36% of entering freshmen expected to graduate within 5 years. 93% of freshmen from Montana. Freshmen from 39 states and 13 foreign countries.

Admission: Rolling admissions plan. For fall acceptance, apply as early as summer following junior year of secondary school. Early acceptance available. *Requirements:* high school GPA 2.5 or composite score of 22 on the ACT or combined score of 1030 on the SAT; or rank in the upper half of high school graduating class; must have 4 years English; 3 mathematics (algebra I, II, and geometry); 3 social studies, 2 laboratory science, 2 years of foreign language, computer science, visual and performing arts, or vocational education. *For transfer students:* in-state and out-of-state applicants must meet admission and/or college preparatory requirements unless out of high school 3 or more years.

College credit and advanced placement for postsecondary-level work completed in secondary school. Tutoring available. Noncredit developmental/remedial courses offered during summer session and regular academic year.

Degree Requirements: *For all associate degrees:* 60 credit hours; 20 credits earned in residence. *For all baccalaureate degrees:* 120 credit hours; 30 credits earned in residence. For education degree, additional requirements. *For all undergraduate degrees:* 2.0 GPA minimum; additional requirements for education and human services degrees.

Fulfillment of some degree requirements and exemption from some beginning courses possible by passing departmental examinations, College Board CLEP. *Grading system:* A–F; pass-withdraw; incomplete (deadline after which A–F assigned).

Distinctive Educational Programs: *For undergraduates:* Interdisciplinary programs in human services, Native American Studies, special education, health administration. *For graduates:* Health administration, sport management, education. *Available to all students:* Work-experience programs. Evening classes. Tutorials. *Other distinctive programs:* Online courses.

Degrees Conferred: 96 *associate;* 517 *baccalaureate:* biological/life sciences 11; business/marketing 96; communications 31; education 149; English 9; foreign languages 5; health professions 9; interdisciplinary studies 13; liberal arts 79; mathematics 5; natural resources/environmental science 5; parks and recreation 5; psychology 61; social sciences and history 26; visual and performing arts 11. 136 *master's:* business/marketing 4; communications 14; education 91; health professions 19; parks and recreation 5; psychology 3.

Fees and Other Expenses: *Full-time tuition per academic year 2004–2005:* undergraduate resident $4,550, nonresident $12,830; graduate resident $5,258, nonresident $13,540. *Room and board per academic year:* $4,200.

Financial Aid: Aid from institutionally generated funds is provided on the basis of academic merit, financial need, athletic ability.

Financial aid to full-time, first-time undergraduate students: need-based scholarships/grants totaling $6,324,038, self-help $8,977,870, tuition waivers $661,208, athletic awards $714,874; non-need-based scholarships/grants totaling $289,437, self-help $6,174,467, parent loans $241,438, tuition waivers $304,217, athletic awards $26,974.

Departments and Teaching Staff: *Professors* 53, *associate professors* 31, *assistant professors* 26, *instructors* 22, *part-time faculty* 117.

Total instructional faculty: 279 (full-time 163, part-time 117; women 125, men 154; members of minority groups 4). Total faculty with doctorate, first-professional, or other terminal degree: 118. Student-to-faculty ratio: 19:1. Degrees held by full-time faculty: doctorate 70%, master's 19%, baccalaureate 2%. 81% hold terminal degrees. *Faculty development:* 4 faculty members awarded sabbaticals 2004–05.

Enrollment: Total enrollment 4,702. Undergraduate full-time 490 men / 2,009 women, part-time 311m / 720w; graduate full-time 65m / 128w, part-time 80m / 199w. *Transfer students:* in-state 182; from out-of-state 152.

Characteristics of Student Body: *Ethnic/racial makeup:* number of Black non-Hispanic: 27; American Indian or Alaska Native: 235; Asian or Pacific Islander: 50; Hispanic: 121; White non-Hispanic: 3,567; unknown: 192. *Age distribution:* number under 18: 34; 18–19: 876; 20–21: 911; 22–24: 849; 25–29: 601; 30–34: 305; 35–39: 207; 40–49: 227; 50–64: 114; 65 and over: 6.

International Students: 28 nonresident aliens enrolled fall 2004. 6 students from Europe, 10 Asia, 1 Latin America, 8 Canada, 3 Australia. Programs available to aid students whose native language is not English: social, cultural. English as a Second Language Program. Financial aid specifically designated for international students: variable number of scholarships available annually.

Student Life: On-campus residence halls house 15% of student body. *Intercollegiate athletics:* men only: baseball, basketball, cross-country, golf, soccer, tennis; women only: basketball, cross-country, golf, soccer, softball, tennis, volleyball. *Special regulations:* Cars permitted without restrictions. *Special services:* Disability Support Services; Student Opportunity Services, Upward Bound, Multicultural Student Services, medical services. *Student publications:* The Retort, a weekly newspaper. *Surrounding community:* Billings population 125,000. Denver, 600 miles from campus, is nearest metropolitan area. Served by mass transit bus system; airport 2 miles from campus.

Publications: Sources of information about the college include *MSU-Billings General Bulletin.*

Library Collections: 523,131 volumes including bound books, serial backfiles, electronic documents, and government documents not in separate collections. Online catalog. 870 current periodical subscriptions. Students have access to the Internet at no charge.

Most important holdings include Elizabeth B. Custer Collection (memorabilia, letters of General George Armstrong Custer covering his career from West Point to Little Big Horn, integrated with material on the Indian wars and the 7th Cavalry collection); Dora White Memorial Collection (2,000 volumes, prints, photographs of the early West, including material on travel and exploration, fur trade, homestead period, Indian frontier and Indian culture); Barstow Collection of Indian Drawings (includes drawings by Medicine Crow recording his trip to Washington, DC in 1880).

Buildings and Grounds: Campus area 112 acres.

Chief Executive Officer: Dr. Ronald P. Sexton, Chancellor.

Address admission inquiries to Shelley Anderson, Director of New Student Services.

Montana State University - Bozeman

Bozeman, Montana 59717-2000

Tel: (406) 994-0211   **E-mail:** admissions@montana.edu
Fax: (406) 994-1923   **Internet:** www.montana.edu

Institution Description: Montana State University is a public institution and land-grant college. *Enrollment:* 12,003. *Degrees awarded:* Baccalaureate, master's, doctorate.

Accreditation: *Regional:* NWCCU. *Professional* art, computer science, counseling, engineering, engineering technology, family and consumer science, music, nursing, nursing education, psychology internship, teacher education

History: Chartered as Agricultural College of the State of Montana at Bozeman and offered first instruction at postsecondary level 1893; awarded first degree (baccalaureate) 1895; changed name to College of Agriculture and Mechanic Arts 1913, to Montana State College 1935; became Montana State University 1965; adopted present name 1996.

Institutional Structure: *Governing board:* Board of Regents of Higher Education for the Montana University System. Extrainstitutional representation: 7 regents (including 1 student), governor of Montana, superintendent of public education, commissioner of higher education. 3 ex officio. All voting.

Calendar: Semesters. Academic year Aug. to May. Freshmen admitted Aug., Jan., May. Degrees conferred Aug., Dec., May. One commencement in May.

Characteristics of Freshmen: 77% of applicants admitted. 58% of applicants admitted and enrolled.

47% (1,030 students) submitted SAT scores; 72% (1,566 students) submitted ACT scores. *25th percentile:* SAT Verbal 490, SAT Math 500; ACT Composite 20, ACT English 19, ACT Math 19. *75th percentile:* SAT Verbal 610, SAT Math 630; ACT Composite 26, ACT English 26, ACT Math 26.

67% of freshmen from Montana. Freshmen from 45 states and 6 foreign countries.

Admission: Rolling admissions plan. For fall acceptance, apply 6–8 months prior to enrollment, but not later than Mar. 1 of year of enrollment for students seeking financial aid. *Requirements:* Either graduation from accredited secondary school or GED; 2.5 GPA or ACT enhanced composite score of 20, or SAT combined verbal/math score of 1030, or rank in the upper half of the graduation class; successful completion of college preparatory curriculum: 4 years of English, 3 years of mathematics, 3 years social studies, 2 years laboratory science. *For transfer students:* 2.0 minimum GPA; students with less than 45 quarter credits or 30 semester credits must submit SAT or ACT scores and secondary school transcript; in-state residents must be in good standing at last college or university attended.

College credit and advanced placement for postsecondary-level work completed in secondary school on basis of College Board AP.

Degree Requirements: 120 semester hours. Core curriculum requirement.

Fulfillment of some degree requirements possible by passing College Board CLEP. *Grading system:* A–F; pass-fail up to 12 hours for students with 30 hours and 2.5 minimum GPA.

Distinctive Educational Programs: The Office of International Programs offers students the opportunity to study at 220 universities in 50 countries.

ROTC: Army; Air Force.

Degrees Conferred: 1,821 *baccalaureate* (B); 375 *master's* (M), 42 *doctorate* (D): agriculture 94 (B), 12 (M), 1 (D); architecture 68 (B), 47 (M); area and ethnic studies1 (M); biological/life sciences 125 (B), 16(M), 7 (D); business/ marketing 221 (B), 16 (M), 7 (D); communications 1 (B); computer and information sciences 44 (B), 10 (M); education 170 (B), 97 (M), 9 (D); engineering 272 (B), 46 (M), 1 (D); English 61 (B), 11 (M); foreign languages and literature 27 (B); health professions and related sciences 125 (B), 6 (M); interdisciplinary studies 2 (B); mathematics 20 (B), 20 (M), 1 (D); natural resources and environmental science 15 (B), 19 (M), 1 (D); parks and recreation 8 (B); philosophy/religion 11 (B); physical sciences 78 (B), 15 (M), 14 (D); protective services/public administration 7 (M); psychology 59 (B), 2 (M); social sciences and history 141 (B), 9 (M); visual and performing arts 150 (B)m6 (M); other 19 (B).

Fees and Other Expenses: *Full-time tuition per academic year 2004–05:* resident $4,327, nonresident $14,327. *Room and board per academic year:* $5,746.

Financial Aid: The university offers a direct lending program. Aid from institutionally generated funds is provided on the basis of academic merit, financial need, athletic ability.

Financial aid to full-time, first-time undergraduate students: need-based scholarships/grants totaling $14,395,879, self-help $19,375,596, parent loans $714,970, tuition waivers $1,234,160, athletic awards $3,441,166; non-need-based scholarships/grants totaling $5,987,277, self-help $13,867,716, parent loans $849,243, tuition waivers $1,234,160, athletic awards $2,441,166.

Departments and Teaching Staff: *Total instructional faculty:* 816 (full-time 534, part-time 282; women 342, men 474; members of minority groups 21). Total faculty with doctorate, first-professional, or other terminal degree: 563. Student-to-faculty ratio: 17:1. Degrees held by full-time faculty: doctorate 74%, master's 24%, baccalaureate 2%. 79% hold terminal degrees. *Faculty development:* $87,964,958 in grants for research. 10 faculty members awarded sabbaticals 2004–05.

Enrollment: Total enrollment 12,003. Undergraduate full-time 5,031 men / 4,136 women, part-time 744m / 757w; graduate full-time 260m / 231w, part-time 431m / 413w.

Characteristics of Student Body: *Ethnic/racial makeup (undergraduate):* number of Black non-Hispanic: 57; American Indian or Alaska Native: 226; Asian or Pacific Islander: 130; Hispanic: 130; White non-Hispanic: 9,506; unknown: 459.

International Students: 298 nonresident aliens enrolled fall 2004. 59 students from Europe, 126 Asia, 11 Latin America, 23 Africa, 19 Canada, 2 Australia, 50 other. Programs available to aid students whose native language is not English: social. English as a Second Language Program. No financial aid specifically designated for international students.

Student Life: On-campus residence halls house 23% of student body. 9 fraternities and 4 sororities. Housing available for married students. *Intercollegiate athletics:* NCAA Division 1 Big Sky Athletic Conference competition in basketball, football, indoor and outdoor track, cross-country, tennis for men; competition in basketball, cross-country, golf, indoor and outdoor track, skiing, tennis, volleyball for women. Rodeo competition for men and women is conducted through the Big Sky Region of the National Intercollegiate Rodeo Association. *Surrounding community:* Bozeman population 35,000. Billings, 140 miles from campus, is nearest metropolitan area.

Library Collections: 675,000 volumes including bound books, serial backfiles, electronic documents, and government documents not in separate collections. Online and card catalogs. Current serial subscriptions: 6,643 paper. 2,107,544 microform. 4,101 recordings; 1,285 compact discs. 125 computer

work stations. Students have access to the Internet at no charge. Total 2004–05 budget for books and materials: $5,264,007.

Most important holdings include collections on Yellowstone National Park; Montana History; Montana Architectural Drawings.

Buildings and Grounds: Campus area 1,170 acres on main campus.

Chief Executive Officer: Dr. Geoff Gamble, President.

Address undergraduate admission inquiries to Director of Admissions and New Student Services; graduate inquiries to Bruce McLeod, Dean, College of Graduate Studies.

Montana State University - Northern

300 West 11th Street
Havre, Montana 59501
Tel: (406) 265-3700   **E-mail:** msunadmit@msun.edu
Fax: (406) 265-3777   **Internet:** www.msun.edu

Institution Description: Montana State University - Northern, formerly known as Northern Montana College, is a public institution. *Enrollment:* 1,421. *Degrees awarded:* Associate, baccalaureate, master's. Certificates also awarded.

Academic offerings subject to approval by statewide coordinating bodies. Budget subject to approval by state governing boards.

Accreditation: *Regional:* NWCCU.

History: Established as Northern Montana Agriculture and Manual Training School 1913; chartered, changed name to Northern Montana School and offered first instruction at postsecondary level 1929; adopted present name 1931; awarded first degree (baccalaureate) 1955.

Institutional Structure: *Governing board:* Board of Regents of Higher Education for the Montana University System. Representation: 7 regents (including 1 student), governor of Montana, superintendent of public education, commissioner of higher education. 3 ex officio. All voting. *Composition of institution:* Administrators 16 men / 13 women. Academic affairs headed by vice president for academic affairs. Management/business/finances directed by director of fiscal affairs. Full-time instructional faculty 73. Academic governance body, Faculty Senate, meets an average of 12 times per year. *Faculty representation:* Faculty served by collective bargaining agent, Northern Montana College Federation of Teachers, affiliated with AFT.

Calendar: Semesters. Academic year Aug. to May. Freshmen admitted Aug., Jan., Mar., June. Degrees conferred and formal commencement June. Summer session from mid-June to mid-Sept.

Characteristics of Freshmen: 278 applicants (194 men, 84 women). 72.7% of applicants admitted. 86.1% of admitted students enrolled full-time.

14% (27 students) submitted SAT scores; 77% (161 students) submitted ACT scores. *25th percentile:* SAT I Verbal 415, SAT I 400; Math ACT Composite 16, ACT English 15, ACT Math 16. *75th percentile:* SAT I Verbal 510, SAT I Math 500; ACT Composite 21, ACT English 20, ACT Math 21.

21% of entering freshmen expected to graduate within 5 years. 97% of freshmen from Montana. Freshmen from 8 states and 3 foreign countries.

Admission: Rolling admissions plan. For fall acceptance, apply no later than Oct. 6 of year of enrollment. Early acceptance available. *Requirements:* Either graduation from accredited secondary school or GED. Out-of-state applicants must rank in upper half of secondary school class or provide other evidence of ability to do college work. *Entrance tests:* ACT composite. For foreign students TOEFL. *For transfer students:* 2.0 minimum GPA; 151 hours maximum transfer credit; for correspondence-extension students transfer credit allowance varies.

Tutoring available. Developmental and remedial courses offered in summer session and regular academic year; credit given for developmental courses.

Degree Requirements: *For all associate degrees:* 60–72 semester credit hours. *For all baccalaureate degrees:* 120–128 semester credit hours. *For all undergraduate degrees:* 2.0 GPA; 30 credits in residence; distribution requirements.

Fulfillment of some degree requirements possible by passing departmental examinations. *Grading system:* A–F; pass-fail; withdraw (carries time limit).

Distinctive Educational Programs: *For undergraduates:* Cooperative education. Interdisciplinary programs in Native American studies. Preprofessional programs in dentistry, medicine, physical therapy, veterinary medicine. *For graduate students:* Internships. *Available to all students:* Flexible meeting places and schedules, including off-campus center at Montana State University College of Technology in Great Falls; evening classes.

Degrees Conferred: 141 *associate;* 226 *baccalaureate;* 56 *master's.* Bachelor's degrees awarded in top five disciplines: education 62; engineering/engineering technologies 31; mechanical/repair technologies 26; health professions and related clinical sciences 15.

Fees and Other Expenses: *Full-time tuition per academic year 2004–05:* undergraduate resident $4,167, nonresident $12,961. Contact the university for current graduate tuition/fees. *Books and supplies:* 1,000. *Room and board per academic year:* $5,500.

Financial Aid: Aid from institutionally generated funds is provided on the basis of academic merit, financial need, athletic ability, other criteria. Institution has a Program Participation Agreement with the U.S. Department of Education for eligible students to receive Pell Grants and, depending upon the agreement, other federal aid.

Financial aid to full-time, first-time undergraduate students: 50% received federal grants averaging $3,250; 34% state/local grants averaging $1,995; 37% institutional grants averaging $2,219; 64% received loans averaging $ 3,040.

Departments and Teaching Staff: Nursing *professors* 0, *associate professors* 3, *assistant professors* 1, *instructors* 5, *part-time teachers* 4; business 1, 2, 1, 4, 3; education 6, 2, 1, 2, 2; science and math 6, 3, 2, 1, 3; social science and humanities 4, 4, 5, 6, 5; technology 1, 5, 5, 7, 2; vocational 0, 2, 2, 10, 0.

Total instructional faculty: 111. 43% hold terminal degrees.

Enrollment: Total enrollment 1,421. Undergraduate 1,306 (men 42.7%, women 52.8%).

Characteristics of Student Body: *Ethnic/racial makeup (undergraduate):* number of Black non-Hispanic: 1.1%; American Indian or Alaska Native: 12.6%l Asian or Pacific Islander: .5%; Hispanic: 1.2%; White non-Hispanic: 74.7%; unknown: 8.3%.

International Students: 21 undergraduate nonresident aliens enrolled fall 2004. Programs available to aid students whose native language is not English: social, cultural, English as a Second Language. No financial aid specifically designated for international students.

Student Life: On-campus residence halls house 30% of student body. Residence halls for men constitute 60% of such space, for women 40%. Housing available for married students. *Intercollegiate athletics:* men only: basketball, track, wrestling; women only: basketball, track, volleyball. *Special regulations:* Cars permitted without restrictions. Quiet hours from 7am to 7pm. Residence hall visitation from 10pm to midnight. *Special services:* Learning Resources Center. *Student publications, radio: NoMoCo,* a weekly newspaper; *Northerner,* a yearbook. Radio station KNOG broadcasts 99 hours per week. *Surrounding community:* Havre population 11,000. Calgary (Canada), 334 miles from campus, is nearest metropolitan area. Served by airport 3 miles from campus; passenger rail service 1 mile from campus.

Library Collections: 125,000 volumes. 600,000 microforms; 3,000 audiovisual materials; 750 current periodical subscriptions. Students have access to online information retrieval services and the Internet.

Most important special holdings include Western Americana (books on the history of Montana, the Western states, and western Canada, with emphasis on Western art and literature and Indian art, culture, and history); Lucke photograph collection (pictures showing the history and development of Havre from the 19th century); Harrison Lane Collection.

Buildings and Grounds: Campus area 105 acres.

Chief Executive Officer: Dr. Alex Capdeville, Chancellor.

Address admission inquiries to James Potter, Director of Admissions.

Montana Tech of the University of Montana

1300 West Park Street
Butte, Montana 59701-8997

Tel: (406) 496-4178   **E-mail:** admissions@mtech.edu
Fax: (406) 496-4710   **Internet:** www.mtech.edu

Institution Description: Montana Tech of the University of Montana, formerly known as Montana College of Mineral Science and Technology is a public institution. *Enrollment:* 1,869. *Degrees awarded:* Associate, baccalaureate, master's.

Academic offerings subject to approval by statewide coordinating bodies. Budget subject to approval by state governing boards. Member of Northern Rockies Consortium for Higher Education.

Accreditation: *Regional:* NWCCU. *Professional:* engineering

History: Established as Montana School of Mines 1893; offered first instruction at postsecondary level 1900; awarded first degree (engineer of mines) 1903; adopted present name 1965.

Institutional Structure: *Governing board:* Board of Regents of Higher Education for the Montana University System. Representation: 7 regents (including 1 student), governor of Montana, superintendent of public instruction, commissioner of higher education. 3 ex officio. 7 voting. *Composition of institution:* Administrators 14 men / 1 woman. Academic affairs headed by vice president for academic affairs. Management/business/finances directed by vice president for administrative and student services. Full-time instructional faculty 110. Academic governance body, Faculty Senate, meets an average of 9 times per year.

Calendar: Semesters. Academic year Aug. to May. Freshmen admitted Aug., Jan., May. Degrees conferred and formal commencement May. Summer session of 1 term.

Characteristics of Freshmen: 97% of applicants accepted. 75% of accepted applicants enrolled.

25th percentile: SAT Verbal 460, SAT Math 510; ACT Composite 21, ACT English 17, ACT Math 18. *75th percentile:* SAT Verbal 580, SAT Math 620; ACT Composite 27, ACT English 23, ACT Math 26.

86% of freshmen from Montana. Freshmen from 34 states and 17 foreign countries.

Admission: Rolling admissions plan. For fall acceptance, apply no later than close of registration. Early acceptance available. *Requirements:* Either graduation from secondary school or GED. Freshmen applicants must satisfy one of the following 3 admission standards: ACT score of 22 or recentered SAT score of 1030; or 2.5 GPA or above (on a 4.0 scale); or rank in upper half of graduating class. Applicants must complete the full college preparatory requirements: 4 years of English, 3 mathematics (minimum of algebra I, geometry, and algebra II); 3 social studies; 2 laboratory science; 2 electives (foreign language, computer science, visual and performing arts, vocational education units). International students are admissible by Director's decision (AS and CP are not used). Nonresident first-time full-time freshmen must meet their own state's or Montana's College Prep program. Those students who reside in a state that does not have a college prep program must meet two of the three admission standards listed above to be admissible.

College credit and advanced placement for postsecondary-level work completed in secondary school. College credit for extrainstitutional learning on the basis of ACE *2006 Guide to the Evaluation of Educational Experiences in the Armed Services.*

Degree Requirements: *For all associate degrees:* 60 credit hours. *For all baccalaureate degrees:* 128–146 credit hours. *For all undergraduate degrees:* 2.0 GPA, 2 terms in residence.

Fulfillment of some degree requirements and exemption from some beginning courses possible by passing departmental examinations, College Board APP. Fulfillment of some requirements also possible by passing College Board CLEP subject examinations. *Grading system:* A–F; pass-fail; withdraw (deadline after which fail may be appended to withdraw); incomplete (carries time limit).

Distinctive Educational Programs: *For undergraduates:* Program in human values, public policy, communication and organizational management. Work-experience programs. Evening classes. *For graduate students:* Facilities for independent research.

Degrees Conferred: 45 *associate;* 235 *baccalaureate:* biological/life sciences 8; business/marketing 42; computer and information sciences 17, engineering 93; English 5; health professions 53; liberal arts 7; mathematics 5; physical science 5. 28 *master's:* engineering 15; English 4; health professors 3; physical sciences 6.

Fees and Other Expenses: *Full-time tuition per academic year 2004–05:* resident $3,743, nonresident $12,935. *Required fees:* $1,136. *Room and board per academic year:* $4,918.

Financial Aid: Aid from institutionally generated funds is provided on the basis of academic merit, financial need.

Financial aid to full-time, first-time undergraduate students: need-based scholarships/grants totaling $2,710,000, self-help $3,350,000; non-need-based scholarships/grants totaling $2,000,000, self-help $2,500,000, parent loans $165,000; tuition waivers $700,000, athletic awards $400,000. *Graduate aid:* 80 students received $700,000 in federal and state-funded loans (ranging from $1,000 to $10,000); 47 teaching and 32 research assistantships were awarded.

Departments and Teaching Staff: *Professors* 46, *associate professors* 17, *assistant professors* 27, *instructors* 20, *part-time faculty* 87.

Total instructional faculty: 147 (full-time 110, part-time 87; women 72, men 125). Total faculty with doctorate, first-professional, or other terminal degree: 73. Student-to-faculty ratio: 15:1. *Faculty development:* $6,891,162 in grants for research. 2 faculty members awarded sabbaticals 2004–05.

Enrollment: Total enrollment 1,869. Undergraduate full-time 875 men / 598 women, part-time 109m / 183w; graduate full-time 28m / 23w, part-time 29m / 19w. *Transfer students:* in-state 58; from out-of-state 40.

Characteristics of Student Body: *Ethnic/racial makeup:* number of Black non-Hispanic: 5; American Indian or Alaska Native: 23; Asian or Pacific Islander: 12; Hispanic: 26; White non-Hispanic: 1,612; unknown: 151. *Age distribution:* number under 18: 88; 18–19: 414; 20–21: 402; 22–24: 339; 25–29: 30–34: 58; 35–39: 54; 40–49: 104; 50–64: 23.

International Students: 47 nonresident aliens enrolled fall 2004. 2 students from Europe, 9 Asia, 1 Latin America, 2 Africa, 28 Canada, 20 other. No programs available to aid students whose native language is not English.

Student Life: On-campus residence halls house 11% of student body. One residence hall for both sexes constitutes 100% of such space. Institutionally controlled off-campus apartments also offer residence space. Housing available for married students. *Intercollegiate athletics:* men only: basketball, football;

women only: basketball, volleyball. *Special regulations:* Cars permitted for a fee. *Student publications, radio: Magma,* a yearbook; *Technocrat,* a monthly newspaper. Radio station KMSM-FM. *Surrounding community:* Butte population 35,000. Spokane (WA), 330 miles from campus, is nearest metropolitan area. Served by mass transit bus system; airport 5 miles from campus.

Publications: Sources of information about Montana College include *M-News,* an alumni newsletter; *Admissions Yearbook.*

Library Collections: 171,203 volumes. Online catalog. Current serial subscriptions: 441 paper; 21,644 via electronic access. 19 computer work stations. Students have access to the Internet at no charge. Total budget for books, periodicals, audiovisual materials, microforms 2004–05: $179,102.

Most important holdings include geology collection (volumes dating from 1830; international and state geological documents); mining engineering collection (volumes dating from 1846 on all aspects of mining and metallurgy); materials on early Montana history, including diaries, letters, journals. Library is partial depository for U.S. government documents; patent and trademark depository.

Buildings and Grounds: Campus area 60 acres.

Chief Executive Officer: Dr. W. Franklin Gilmore, Chancellor.

Address admission inquiries Tony Campeau, Associate Director of Admissions.

Rocky Mountain College

1511 Poly Drive
Billings, Montana 59102-1796
Tel: (406) 657-1000   **E-mail:** admissions@rocky.edu
Fax: (406) 259-9751   **Internet:** www.rocky.edu

Institution Description: Rocky Mountain College is a private college affiliated with the United Church of Christ, the United Methodist Church, and the United Presbyterian Church in the United States of America. *Enrollment:* 988. *Degrees awarded:* Associate, baccalaureate.

Accreditation: *Regional:* NWCCU. *Professional:* business, physician assisting

History: Established as Montana Collegiate Institute 1878; offered first instruction at postsecondary level 1882; taken over by the Presbyterian Church, chartered as College of Montana, and awarded first degree (baccalaureate) 1883; merged with Montana Wesleyan University (founded as Montana University 1889) and changed name to Intermountain University 1923; affiliated with Billings Polytechnic Institute (founded 1908) 1936; merged with Billings Polytechnic Institute and adopted present name 1947. *See* Marjorie Buhl, *History of Higher Education in Montana* (Billings, MT: Rocky Mountain College, 1959) for further information.

Institutional Structure: *Governing board:* Board of Trustees. Extrainstitutional representation: 34 trustees, including 5 alumni and 8 church officials. 3 ex officio. All voting. *Composition of institution:* Administrators 5 men / 1 woman. Academic affairs headed by vice president for academic affairs and dean of the college. Management/business/finances directed by vice president for finance. Full-time instructional faculty 52. Academic governance body, the faculty, meets an average of 9 times per year.

Calendar: Semesters. Academic year late Aug. to early May. Freshmen admitted Aug., Jan., May. Degrees conferred May, Dec. Formal commencement May. Summer session of 3 terms from mid-May to mid-July.

Characteristics of Freshmen: 81% of applicants admitted. 35% of applicants admitted and enrolled.

31.4% (72 students) submitted SAT scores; 73.5% (173 students) submitted ACT scores. *25th percentile:* SAT Verbal 440, SAT Math 470; ACT Composite 18, ACT English 17, ACT Math 17. *75th percentile:* SAT Verbal 580, SAT Math 590; ACT Composite 25, ACT English 25, ACT Math 25.

39% of entering freshmen expected to graduate within 5 years. 64% of freshmen from Montana. Freshmen from 20 states and 6 foreign countries.

Admission: Rolling admissions plan. For fall acceptance, apply as early as summer following junior year in secondary school, but not later than 1 week prior to registration. Early acceptance available. *Requirements:* Either graduation from accredited secondary school with 13 units which must include 4 English, 2 mathematics, 2 science (1 with lab), 1 foreign language, 2 social studies; or GED. Minimum GPA 2.0. *Entrance tests:* ACT preferred; SAT accepted. *For transfer students:* 2.0 minimum GPA; from 4-year accredited institution 94 semester hours maximum transfer credit; from 2-year institution 64 hours.

College credit and advanced placement for postsecondary-level work completed in secondary school. For extrainstitutional learning college credit on basis of ACE *2006 Guide to the Evaluation of Educational Experiences in the Armed Services* and faculty assessment.

Tutoring available. Remedial courses offered during regular academic year.

Degree Requirements: *For all associate degrees:* 62 credit hours. *For all baccalaureate degrees:* 124 credit hours. *For all undergraduate degrees:* 2.0 GPA, 2.5 GPA in major; last 2 terms in residence; distribution requirements.

Fulfillment of some degree requirements and exemption from some beginning courses possible by passing College Board CLEP or APP. Fulfillment of requirements also possible by passing departmental examinations and other standardized tests. *Grading system:* A–F; pass-fail; withdraw (carries time limit); incomplete (carries time limit).

Distinctive Educational Programs: Work-experience programs. Interdepartmental/interdisciplinary programs in history of ideas, mathematics, natural science. Physician Assistant Program. Facilities for independent research, including individual majors, tutorials, directed reading courses. Study abroad by individual arrangement. Off-campus study in U.S. also available. Expanded set of offerings available via distance learning through the Internet.

Degrees Conferred: 1 *associate;* 190 *baccalaureate:* agriculture 11; biological/life sciences 17; business/marketing 41; communications/communication technologies 4; computer and information sciences 14; education 14; English 4; health professions and related sciences 22; interdisciplinary studies 1; natural resources/environmental science 3; parks and recreation 5; philosophy/religion/theology 3; physical sciences 2; psychology 16; social sciences and history 12; trade and industry 13; visual and performing arts 6.

Fees and Other Expenses: *Full-time tuition per academic year 2004–05:* $14,500 undergraduate. Contact the college for current graduate tuition/fees. *Required fees:* $215. *Room and board per academic year:* $5,480.

Financial Aid: Aid from institutionally generated funds is provided on the basis of academic merit, financial need, athletic ability.

Financial aid to full-time, first-time undergraduate students: need-based scholarships/grants totaling $5,385,224, self-help $3,076,667, parent loans $598,564, tuition waivers $164,756, athletic awards $716,986; non-need-based scholarships/grants totaling $1,636,024, self-help $288,432, parent loans $148,192, tuition waivers $212,238, athletic awards $567,033. *Graduate aid:* 40 students received $729,000 in federal and state-funded loans.

Departments and Teaching Staff: *Total instructional faculty:* 120 (full-time 52, part-time 68; women 52, men 68; member of minority groups 4). Total faculty with doctorate, first-professional, or other terminal degree: 47. Student-to-faculty ratio: 12:1. Degrees held by full-time faculty: doctorate 67%, master's 29%, baccalaureate 4%. *Faculty development:* 4 faculty members were awarded sabbaticals 2004–05.

Enrollment: Total enrollment 988. Undergraduate full-time 396 men / 485 women, part-time 33m / 32w; graduate full-time 17m / 25w. *Transfer students:* 74.

Characteristics of Student Body: *Ethnic/racial makeup:* number of Black non-Hispanic: 10; American Indian or Alaska Native: 79; Asian or Pacific Islander: 13; Hispanic: 25; White non-Hispanic: 752. *Age distribution:* number under 18: 23; 18–19: 545; 20–21: 266; 22–24: 153; 25–29: 52; 30–34: 32; 35–39: 22; 40–49: 41; 50–64: 9; 65 and over: 1. 24% of student body attend summer sessions.

International Students: 67 nonresident aliens enrolled fall 2004. Students from Europe, Asia, Latin America, Canada. Programs available to aid students whose native language is not English: social, cultural. English as a Second Language Program. Financial aid specifically designated for international students: variable number of scholarships available annually.

Student Life: On-campus residence halls house 30% of student body. *Intercollegiate athletics:* men only: basketball, football, golf, skiing; women only: basketball, golf, skiing, soccer, volleyball. *Special regulations:* Cars permitted in designated areas only. Quiet hours 10pm to 9am Sun.–Fri.; 12am to 9am Fri.-Sat. Residence hall visitation 9am to 12am Sun.–Thurs., 9am to 4am Fri.–Sat. *Special services:* medical services. *Student publications: Top of the Rock,* a monthly student publication; *Rocky Today,* a tabloid quarterly newsletter for alumni, trustees, and other friends of the college; *Soliloquy,* an annual art magazine. *Surrounding community:* Billings and surrounding area population 120,000. Denver (CO), 560 miles from campus, is nearest metropolitan area. Campus on route of Billings city mass transit bus system; airport 3 miles from campus.

Library Collections: 55,340 volumes including bound books, serial backfiles, electronic documents, and government documents not in separate collections. Online catalog. 324 current periodical subscriptions. 1,613 recordings. Computer work stations available. Students have access to the Internet at no charge.

Most important holdings include Geology Collection (5,000 items with emphasis on oil); Religion Collection (3,000 items with emphasis on Christianity and Protestantism); American Indian Collection (3,500 items).

Buildings and Grounds: Campus area 60 acres. *New buildings/construction:* Prescott Hall renovation and expansion completed 2001; Flight Training Operations 2002; Rimview Hall (residence) 2004.

Chief Executive Officer: Dr. Thomas R. Oates, President.

Address admission inquiries to Bonnie Knapp, Director of Admissions.

University of Great Falls

1301 20th Street South
Great Falls, Montana 59405-4996
Tel: (406) 791-5200   **E-mail:** adminrec@ugf.edu
Fax: (406) 791-5209   **Internet:** www.ugf.edu

Institution Description: University of Great Falls, formerly named College of Great Falls, is a private college affiliated with the Sisters of Providence, Roman Catholic Church. *Enrollment:* 764. *Degrees awarded:* Associate, baccalaureate, master's.

Accreditation: *Regional:* NWCCU.

History: Established as Great Falls Normal College, chartered, and offered first instruction at postsecondary level 1932; became 4-year college 1936; first degree (baccalaureate) awarded 1939; changed name to Great Falls College of Education 1949; adopted present name 1952.

Institutional Structure: *Governing board:* College of Great Falls Board of Trustees. Extrainstitutional representation: 17 trustees, 1 church official; institutional representation: president of the college, 1 full-time instructional faculty member, 1 student. 2 ex officio. All voting. *Composition of institution:* Administrators 5 men / 1 woman. Academic affairs headed by academic vice president. Management/business/finances directed by director of business and finance. Full-time instructional faculty 64 men / 43 women. Academic governance body, General Faculty, meets an average of 8 times per year.

Calendar: Semesters. Academic year late Aug. to early May. Freshmen admitted Aug., June, July. Degrees conferred May, Dec. Formal commencement May. Summer session of 3 terms from mid-May to mid-Aug.

Characteristics of Freshmen: Average secondary school rank of freshmen men 32nd percentile, women 68th percentile, class 49th percentile. 2 National Merit Scholars.

Admission: Rolling admissions plan. For fall acceptance, apply as early as Jan. of previous year, but not later than mid-Aug. of year of enrollment. Early acceptance available. *Requirements:* Either graduation from accredited secondary or GED. *Entrance tests:* Placement test required of all undergraduate students. *For foreign students:* TOEFL score 500. *For transfer students:* From accredited institution 2.0 minimum GPA, 98 hours maximum transfer credit.

College credit and advanced placement for postsecondary-level work completed in secondary school. Advanced placement for College Board CLEP. Tutoring available. Developmental courses offered in summer and regular academic year; credit given.

Degree Requirements: *For all associate degrees:* 64 semester hours; 2.0 GPA; 15 semester credits in residence. *For all baccalaureate degrees:* 128 semester hours; 30 semester credits in residence. Additional requirements for some majors. *For all undergraduates:* 2.0 GPA; must complete core curriculum. business, management, marketing, and related support services 15; legal/professional studies 13.

Fulfillment of some degree requirements and exemption from some beginning courses possible by passing departmental examinations; CLEP. *Grading system:* A–F; pass-fail; withdraw (pass-fail appended to withdraw); incomplete (carries time limit).

Distinctive Educational Programs: *For undergraduates:* Work-experience programs, including cooperative education and internships. Telecom, combining videotaped instruction with telephonic discussion for nontraditional students living in outlying areas of Montana. Interdisciplinary programs in history and political science, liberal arts, Native American studies, public administration, social science. Independent study and research projects. *For graduate students:* Weekend classes. Master's degree in Human Services with various emphases. *Available to all students:* Evening classes. Special facilities for use of computers and telecommunications in the classroom.

Degrees Conferred: 11 *associate;* 155 *baccalaureate;* 50 *master's.* Bachelor's degrees awarded in top five disciplines: education 60; security and protective services 21; psychology 21; protective services 30, psychology 22, public administration and services 27; 25 *master's:* various disciplines.

Fees and Other Expenses: *Full-time tuition per academic year 2004–05:* undergraduate $12,908. Contact the university for graduate tuition/fees. *Books and supplies:* $750. *Room and board and board per academic year:* $5,100.

Financial Aid: Aid from institutionally generated funds is provided on the basis of academic merit, financial need. Institution has a Program Participation Agreement with the U.S. Department of Education for eligible students to receive Pell Grants, and depending upon the agreement, other federal aid.

Financial aid to full-time, first-time undergraduate students: 59% received federal grants averaging $3,491; 8% state/local grants; 73% institutional grants averaging $3,922; 68% received loans averaging $6,134.

Departments and Teaching Staff: *Total instructional faculty:* 41. Student-to-faculty ratio: 12:1.

Enrollment: *Total enrollment:* 764. Undergraduate 671 (men 33.8%, women 66.2%).

Characteristics of Student Body: *Ethnic/racial makeup:* number of Black non-Hispanic: 3.3%; American Indian or Alaska Native: 5.2%; Asian or Pacific Islander: 1.6%; Hispanic: 3%; White non-Hispanic: 78.5%; unknown: 8.9%. *Age distribution:* 17–21: 16%; 22–24: 3%; 25–29: 18%; 30–34: 14%; 35–39: 13%; 40–49: 21%; 50–59: 4%; 60–up: 1%.

International Students: 10 undergraduate nonresident aliens enrolled fall 2004. Students from Europe, Canada. No programs available to aid students whose native language is not English. Some financial aid specifically designated for international students; variable number of scholarships available for both undergraduate and graduate international students.

Student Life: 54 campus-leased and campus-operated apartments are available to students. *Special regulations:* Cars permitted without restrictions. *Special services:* Learning Resources Center, Placement Office, study skills opportunities. *Student publications: Impact,* a weekly newspaper; *Scribe,* an annual literary magazine; *Caritas,* a yearbook. *Surrounding community:* Great Falls population 60,000. Seattle (WA), 600 miles from campus, is nearest metropolitan area. Served by airport 4 miles from campus.

Library Collections: 106,200 volumes. 125,000 microforms; 3,900 audiovisual materials; 590 current periodical subscriptions. Students have access to online information retrieval services and the Internet.

Most important special holdings include collections on philosophy, religious studies, Native American studies, elementary education with emphasis on science education, and U.S. law.

Buildings and Grounds: Campus area 64 acres.

Chief Executive Officer: Dr. Eugene McAllister, President.

Address admission inquiries to Director of Admissions and Records.

University of Montana - Missoula

Missoula, Montana 59812
Tel: (406) 243-0211   **E-mail:** admiss@umt.edu
Fax: (406) 243-2797   **Internet:** www.umt.edu

Institution Description: University of Montana is a state institution. *Enrollment:* 12,18,558. *Degrees awarded:* Associate, baccalaureate, first-professional (law), master's, doctorate.

Academic offerings subject to approval by statewide coordinating bodies. Budget subject to approval by state governing boards. Member of the Northern Rockies Consortium for Higher Education.

Accreditation: *Regional:* NWCCU. *Professional:* accounting, art, business, clinical psychology, computer science, forestry, journalism, law, music, pharmacy, physical therapy, recreation and leisure services, social work, teacher education, theatre

History: Established and chartered as University of Montana 1893; offered first instruction at postsecondary level 1895; awarded first degree (baccalaureate) 1989; changed name to State University of Montana 1913, to Montana State University 1935; readopted present name 1965. *See* H. G. Merriam, *The University of Montana, A History* (Missoula: University of Montana Press, 1970) for further information.

Institutional Structure: *Governing board:* Board of Regents of Higher Education for the Montana University System. Representation: 7 regents (including 1 student), governor of Montana, superintendent of public education, commissioner of higher education. 3 ex officio. All voting. *Composition of institution:* Administrators 30 men / 12 women. Academic affairs headed by provost and vice president for academic affairs. Fiscal affairs headed by the vice president for administration and finance. Full-time instructional faculty 479. Academic governance body, University of Montana Faculty Senate, meets an average of 10 times per year.

Calendar: Semesters. Academic year Aug. to May. Freshmen admitted Aug., Jan. Degrees conferred Dec., May, Aug. Formal commencement May. Summer session of 2 five-week terms from May to July.

Characteristics of Freshmen: 4,452 applicants (2,114 men, 2,33 women). 92.8% of applicants admitted; 48.5% of admitted students enrolled full-time.

38% (726 students) submitted SAT scores; 76% (1,459 students) submitted ACT scores. *25th percentile:* SAT I Verbal 515, SAT I Math 491; ACT Composite 20, ACT English 19, ACT Math 28. *75th percentile:* SAT I Verbal 562, SAT I Math 562; ACT Composite 25, ACT English 25, ACT Math 25.

34% of entering freshmen expected to graduate within 5 years. 73% of freshmen from Montana. Freshmen from 43 states and 16 foreign countries.

Admission: Rolling admissions plan. For fall acceptance, apply as early as 6 months prior to enrollment, but not later than July 1 of year of enrollment. *Requirements:* State residents must have cumulative 2.50 GPA (on a 0–4 scale) or a 22 composite on the Enhanced ACT or 1030 combined verbal/math on SAT (test dates after April 1995) or upper half of graduating class. College prep courses (4 years English, 3 mathematics, 3 social studies, 2 laboratory science, 2 electives). Out-of-state students must have the same as state residents unless not meeting requirements. *Entrance tests:* College Board SAT or ACT composite. For foreign students TOEFL. *For transfer students:* 2.0 minimum GPA; from 4- and 2-year accredited institutions 150 quarter hours maximum transfer credit; correspondence/extension students 30 hours.

College credit and advanced placement for postsecondary-level work completed in secondary school; college credit for extrainstitutional learning (life experience) on basis of faculty assessment. Tutoring available. Remedial courses offered during regular academic year; credit given.

Degree Requirements: *For all associate degrees:* 60 semester hours. *For all baccalaureate degrees:* 130 semester hours. *For all undergraduate degrees:* 2.0 GPA; 30 hours in residence; distribution requirements. Additional requirements for some programs.

Fulfillment of some degree requirements and exemption from some beginning courses possible by passing departmental examinations, College Board CLEP, AP. *Grading system:* A–F; pass-fail.

Distinctive Educational Programs: Integrated Program Agreement with Western Montana College which permits students to begin programs in biology, pharmacy, history, political science, forestry, French, journalism, and computer science at Western Montana College and later transfer to the University of Montana. *Other distinctive programs:* Honors College; The Mansfield Center, which honors the public life of Mike Mansfield, offers programs in ethics in public affairs and modern Asian affairs. Activities in both programs include courses, conferences, special lectures, internships, foreign exchange, and research projects.

ROTC: Army.

Degrees Conferred: 207 *associate;* 1,808 *baccalaureate;* 468 *master's;* 38 *doctorate.* Bachelor's degrees awarded in top five disciplines: business, management, marketing, and related support services 405; social sciences and history 218; communication, journalism, and related programs 136; natural science and environmental studies 130; psychology 122. 134 *first-professional:* law 85; pharmacy 49.

Fees and Other Expenses: *Full-time tuition per academic year 2004–05:* resident undergraduate $4,377, nonresident $12,368. Contact the university for current graduate and professional school tuition/fees that vary by program. *Books and supplies:* $800. *Room and board per academic year:* $5,292.

Financial Aid: Aid from institutionally generated funds is provided on the basis of academic merit, financial need, athletic ability, other criteria. Institution has a Program Participation Agreement with the U.S. Department of Education for eligible students to receive Pell Grants and, depending upon the agreement, other federal aid.

Financial aid to full-time, first-time undergraduate students: 32% received federal grants averaging $2,931; 26% state/local grants averaging $2,053; 32% institutional grants averaging $1,840; 55% received loans averaging $3,575.

Departments and Teaching Staff: *Professors* 190, *associate professors* 116, *assistant professors* 108, *instructors* 65, *part-time faculty* 193.

Total instructional faculty: 672. Student-to-faculty ratio: 20.2:1. Degrees held by full-time faculty: doctorate 65.9%, master's 22.5%, baccalaureate 3.6%, professional 6.7%. 78.3% hold terminal degrees.

Enrollment: Total enrollment 18,558. Undergraduate 11,280 (men 46.7%, women 53.3%).

Characteristics of Student Body: *Ethnic/racial makeup (undergraduate):* number of Black non-Hispanic: .6%; American Indian or Alaska Native: 3.8%; Asian or Pacific Islander: 1.1%; Hispanic: 1.5%; White non-Hispanic: 83.8%; unknown: 7.4%. *Age distribution:* 17–21: 49%; 22–24: 20.8%; 25–29: 14.1%; 30–34: 5.3%; 35–39: 4%; 40–49: 3.3%; 50–59: 1.2%; 60–up: .3%.

International Students: 214 undergraduate nonresident aliens enrolled fall 2004. Students from Europe, Asia, Latin America, Africa, Canada, New Zealand. Programs available to students whose native language is not English: social, cultural, financial. English as a Second Language Program. No financial aid specifically designated for international students.

Student Life: On-campus residence halls house 19% of student body; of these, 5% live in men only residence halls, 5% in women-only residence halls; 90% live co-ed residence halls. 295 live in smoke-free residence halls. *Intercollegiate athletics:* men only: basketball, cross country, football, indoor and outdoor track, tennis; women only: basketball, cross country, golf, indoor and outdoor track, soccer, tennis, volleyball. *Special regulations:* Registered cars permitted without restrictions. *Special services:* Medical services. *Student publications, radio: Montana Kaimin,* a newspaper published 4 days per week. Radio station KUFM. *Surrounding community:* Missoula population 79,000. Spokane (WA), 207 miles from campus, is nearest metropolitan area. Served by mass transit bus system (free to students, staff, and faculty); airport 12 miles from campus.

Publications: *Montanan,* the official magazine of the University, is published 3 time a year and mailed to approximately 45,000 alumni and friends; *Vision,* a research magazine is published every other year; *Montana Business Quarterly,* first published in 1962; *Montana Journalism Review* (annually) first published 1957; *The Barrister,* publication of the School of Law, is produced biannually; *The University of Montana Annual Report.*

Library Collections: 929,000 volumes including bound books, serial backfiles, electronic documents, and government documents not in separate collections. Online catalog. Current serial subscriptions: 4,700 paper and microform, 70 electronic. 27,500 audiovisual materials. Computer work stations available. Students have access to the Internet at no charge.

Most important holdings include the Mansfield Papers; Montana Collections; Girard Papers.

Buildings and Grounds: Campus area 220 acres.

Chief Executive Officer: Dr. George M. Dennison, President. Undergraduates address admission inquiries to Dr. Frank Matule, Director, Admissions and New Student Services; law school inquiries to Dr. Edwin Eck, Dean of Law; graduate inquiries to Dr. David Strobel, Associate Dean of the Graduate School; pharmacy and allied health services inquiries to Dr. David Forbes, Dean of Pharmacy and Allied Health Services.

College of Arts and Sciences

Degree Programs Offered: *Associate* in general studies; *baccalaureate* in anthropology, biology, chemistry, classics, communication studies, computer science, computer science-physics, economics, economics-philosophy, economics-political science, English, French, geography, geology, German, history, history-political science, Latin, liberal studies, mathematics, medical technology, microbiology, philosophy, physics and astronomy, physics-computer science, political science, political science-history, psychology, Russian, social work, sociology, Spanish; *master's* and *doctorate* in various fields.

Distinctive Educational Programs: Preprofessional programs in agriculture-horticulture, engineering. Institutionally sponsored study abroad in Austria, France, Mexico, Spain.

School of Business Administration

Degree Programs Offered: *Baccalaureate* in business administration; *master's* in business administration, accountancy.

School of Education

Degree Programs Offered: *Baccalaureate* in education, elementary education, health and human performance, secondary education (business education); *master's* in guidance and counseling, education, education specialist, health and human performance; *master's, doctorate* in education.

Admission: To be considered for admission to teacher education a student must have a cumulative GPA of 2.50 or higher and must have passed the Communication Skills and General Knowledge portions of the National Teacher's Examination.

School of Fine Arts

Degree Programs Offered: *Baccalaureate* in art, dance, drama, music, music education, music performance or composition; *master's* in art, drama, music performance or composition, music education, music history and literature.

School of Forestry

Degree Programs Offered: *Baccalaureate, master's* in forestry, recreation management, resource conservation, wildlife biology; *doctorate* in forestry.

School of Journalism

Degree Programs Offered: *Baccalaureate* in journalism, radio-television; *master's* in journalism.

School of Pharmacy and Allied Health

Degree Programs Offered: *Baccalaureate* in pharmacy, physical therapy; *master's* in microbiology, pharmacy; *first-professional* in pharmacy; *doctorate* in microbiology.

Admission: *For first-professional:* 2 years of prepharmacy curriculum with 2.3 GPA at time of admission. Applications for the professional curriculum must be submitted no later than April 15 preceding the autumn quarter of the year for which admission is requested.

Distinctive Educational Programs: Preprofessional programs in dentistry, medicine, nursing, osteopathy, podiatry, veterinary medicine. Cooperative master's program with School of Business Administration.

School of Law

Degree Programs Offered: *First-professional.*

Admission: Baccalaureate from accredited institution, LSAT.

Degree Requirements: 90 semester hours, 2.0 GPA. Must complete 6 semesters in residence at a law school approved by the American Bar Association, with 60 semester hours successfully completed at the University of Montana School of Law.

College of Technology

Degree Programs Offered: *Associate* in accounting technology, building maintenance engineering, diesel equipment technology, electronics technology, food service management, legal assisting, legal secretarial technology, business management, medical assisting, medical laboratory assisting, medical office technology, medical transcription, microcomputing technology, surgical technology, welding technology. *Certificates* also awarded in various occupational fields.

University of Montana - Western

710 South Atlantic Street
Dillon, Montana 59725-3598

Tel: (406) 683-7011   **E-mail:** admissions@wmwestern.edu
Fax: (406) 683-7493   **Internet:** www.wmwestern.edu

Institution Description: University of Montana - Western, formerly named Western Montana College is a state land-grant college. *Enrollment:* 1,146. *Degrees awarded:* Associate, baccalaureate.

Academic offerings subject to approval by statewide coordinating bodies. Budget subject to approval by state governing boards.

Accreditation: *Regional:* NWCCU.

History: Established as State Normal School 1893; chartered and offered first instruction at postsecondary level 1897; changed name to State Normal College 1903; awarded first degree (baccalaureate) 1932; changed name to Western Montana College of Education 1949; became Western Montana College 1965; merged administratively with the University of Montana to become a 4-year branch campus and adopted present name 1988.

Institutional Structure: *Governing board:* Board of Regents of Higher Education of the Montana University System. Representation: 7 regents, including 1 student; governor of Montana; superintendent of public instruction; commissioner of higher education. 3 ex officio. 7 voting. *Composition of institution:* Academic affairs headed by dean of faculty. Management/business/finances directed by director of fiscal affairs. Full-time instructional faculty 32 men / 17 women. Academic governance body, Academic Council, meets an average of 10 times per year. *Faculty representation:* Faculty served by collective bargaining agent, Montana Education Association, affiliated with NEA.

Calendar: Semesters. Academic year late Aug. to early May. Freshmen admitted Sept., Jan., June. Degrees conferred May, Aug., Dec. Formal commencement May. Summer session from mid-June to mid-Aug.

Characteristics of Freshmen: 805 of applicants accepted. 60% of accepted applicants enrolled.

ACT composite score men 19.2, women 19.4, class 19.3.

90% of freshmen from Montana. Freshmen from 20 states and 3 foreign countries.

Admission: Rolling admissions plan. For fall acceptance, apply no later than month of enrollment. Early acceptance available. *Requirements:* Either graduation from accredited secondary school or GED; out-of-state students must also either rank in upper half of secondary school class or have acceptable scores on College Board SAT or ACT composite. *For transfer students:* Good standing at institution previously attended, correspondence/extension students 2.0 minimum GPA.

Degree Requirements: *For all associate degrees:* 64 credit hours; 1 semester in residence. *For all baccalaureate degrees:* 120–128 credit hours; 2 semesters in residence. *For all undergraduate degrees:* 2.0 GPA; distribution requirements.

Fulfillment of some degree requirements possible by passing CLEP and AP. *Grading system:* A–F; pass-withdraw (carries time limit); incomplete (carries time limit).

Distinctive Educational Programs: *For undergraduates:* Cooperative education programs; Service Learning Program; Honors Program; interdisciplinary B.L.S. programs with internships and undergraduate research education programs with extensive pre-student teaching field experiences; Professional Guide Institute Certification Program; Child Development Associate Program. Facilities and programs for independent research. Weekend and evening classes. *Other distinctive programs:* Servicemembers Opportunity College. Western Montana also participates in Operation Bootstrap and Project Ahead programs for members of armed services. Continuing education and Elderhostel programs.

Degrees Conferred: 34 *associate;* 131 *baccalaureate.* Bachelor's degrees awarded in top disciplines: education 75; liberal arts and sciences, general studies, and humanities 46; 9; multidisciplinary studies 1.

Fees and Other Expenses: *Full-time tuition per academic year 2004–05:* resident $3,730, nonresident $11,570. *Books and supplies:* 700. *Room and board per academic year:* $4,530.

Financial Aid: Aid from institutionally generated funds is provided on the basis of academic merit, financial need, athletic ability. Institution has a Program Participation Agreement with the U.S. Department of Education for eligible students to receive Pell Grants and, depending upon the agreement, other federal aid.

Financial aid to full-time, first-time undergraduate students: 43% received federal grants averaging $3,139; 36% state/local grants averaging $843; 29% institutional grants averaging $500; 58% received loans averaging $2,371.

Departments and Teaching Staff: English *professors* 1, *associate professors* 3, *assistant professors* 2, *instructors* 1, *part-time teachers* 5; physical education 0, 1, 3.5, 0, 1; art 1, 1, 1, 1, 0; history 0, 0, 2.5, 0, 1; music 2, 0, 0, 0, 0; anthropology/psychology 1, 0, 1, 0, 0; business 1, 1, 5, 0, 0; science 0, 3, 1.75, 0, 0; industrial arts 0, 0, 0, 2.0, 0; education .5, 2, 2.5, 1.0, 5; mathematics 0, 0, 3.0, 0, 1.

Total instructional faculty: 49. Degrees held by full-time faculty: doctorate 43.5%, master's 47.8%, baccalaureate 8.7%. 45.7% hold terminal degrees.

Enrollment: Total enrollment 1,146 (men 42%, women 58%).

Characteristics of Student Body: *Ethnic/racial makeup:* number of Black non-Hispanic: .3%; American Indian or Alaska Native: 3.6%; Asian or Pacific Islander: 1.9%; Hispanic: 1.7%; White non-Hispanic: 83%; unknown: 9.4%. *Age distribution:* 17–21: 46%; 22–24: 22%; 25–29: 10%; 30*-34: 6%; 35–39: 55; 40–49: 5%; 40–49: 7%; 60–up: 4%.

International Students: 5 nonresident aliens enrolled fall 2004. Students from Europe, Asia, Canada. No programs to aid students whose native language is not English. Variable number of scholarships available annually to undergraduate international students.

Student Life: On-campus residence halls house 35% of student body. Residence halls for men constitute 45% of such space, for women 40%, for both sexes 15%. 3% of student body housed on campus in married student housing. *Intercollegiate athletics:* men only: basketball, football; women only: basketball, volleyball. *Special regulations:* Cars permitted without restrictions. *Special services:* Medical services. *Student publications: Chinook,* a yearbook; *Wescolite,* a weekly newspaper. *Surrounding community:* Dillon population 5,000. Salt Lake City, 350 miles from campus, is nearest metropolitan area.

Library Collections: 65,000 volumes. 5,800 microforms; 1,200 audiovisual materials; 565 current periodical subscriptions. Students have access to online information retrieval services and the Internet.

Most important holdings include Montana Room collection (1,500 books by Montana authors or about Montana); Emerick Art Collection.

Buildings and Grounds: Campus area 34 acres.

Chief Executive Officer: Dr. Richard D. Storey, Chancellor.

Address admission inquiries to Arlene Williams, Director of Admissions.

Nebraska

Bellevue University

1000 Galvin Road South
Bellevue, Nebraska 68005
Tel: (800) 736-7920 **E-mail:** info@bellevue.edu
Fax: (402) 293-2020 **Internet:** www.bellevue.edu

Institution Description: Bellevue University, formerly Bellevue College, is a private, independent, nonprofit institution. *Enrollment:* 5,524. *Degrees awarded:* Baccalaureate, master's.

Accreditation: *Regional:* NCA.

History: Established, chartered, and offered first instruction at postsecondary level 1966; awarded first degree (baccalaureate) 1967.

Institutional Structure: *Governing board:* Board of Directors. Representation: 20 directors, 19 voting, 1 non-voting. *Composition of institution:* Administrators 18 men / 9 women. Full-time instructional faculty 78. Academic governance body, Faculty Meeting, meets an average of 9 times a year.

Calendar: Semesters. Academic year late Aug. to late May. Freshmen admitted at the start of any day or evening session. Degrees conferred and formal commencement June, Jan. Summer session from June to Aug.

Characteristics of Freshmen: 88% of applicants accepted. 64% of accepted applicants enrolled.

54% of entering freshmen expected to graduate within 5 years. 86% of freshmen from Nebraska. Freshmen from 6 states and 7 foreign countries.

Admission: Rolling admissions plan. Early acceptance available. *Requirements:* Either graduation from secondary school or GED. Minimum 2.0 GPA. Lowest acceptable secondary school class standing 33rd percentile. *Entrance tests:* College Board SAT or ACT composite required for recent secondary school graduates. For international students TOEFL. *For transfer students:* 2.0 minimum GPA; maximum transfer credit limited only by residence requirement.

College credit and advanced placement for postsecondary-level work completed in secondary school. College credit for extrainstitutional learning on basis of ACE *2006 Guide to the Evaluation of Educational Experiences in the Armed Services*; portfolio assessment.

Tutoring available. Developmental courses offered.

Degree Requirements: 127 credit hours; 2.0 GPA (2.5 in major field); 30 hours in residence, including at least 12 hours in upper division coursework in major field; distribution requirements. Fulfillment of some degree requirements and exemption from some beginning courses possible through AP/CLEP/DANTES examinations. *Grading system:* A-F; withdraw (carries time limit).

Distinctive Educational Programs: Degree-granting evening division operating under trimester plan. Interdepartmental programs in social sciences, urban studies. Courses offered at 10 off-campus locations.

ROTC: Army in cooperation with Creighton University; Air Force in cooperation with University of Nebraska-Lincoln.

Degrees Conferred: 1,369 *baccalaureate*: biological/life sciences 14; business/marketing 849; computer and information sciences 123; education 13; English 27; health professions and related sciences 96; mathematics 13; philosophy/religion/theology 14; psychology 14; social sciences and history 192; visual and performing arts 14. 421 *master's:* various disciplines.

Fees and Other Expenses: *Full-time tuition per academic year 2005–06:* undergraduate $4,950, graduate $7,800. *Required fees:* $75.

Financial Aid: Aid from institutionally generated funds is provided on the basis of academic merit, financial need, athletic ability, other criteria.

Financial aid to full-time, first-time undergraduate students: need-based scholarships/grants totaling $2,732,038, self-help $16,888,583, parent loans $519,212; non-need-based scholarships/grants totaling $1,058,757, athletic awards $175,240.

Departments and Teaching Staff: *Total instructional faculty:* 361 (full-time 78, part-time 383; women 121, men 230; members of minority groups 21). Total faculty with doctorate, first-professional, or other terminal degree: 83. Student-to-faculty ratio: 16:1. Degrees held by full-time faculty: doctorate 61%, master's 74%, baccalaureate 100%, professional 34%. 60% hold terminal degrees.

Enrollment: Total enrollment 5,524.

Characteristics of Student Body: *Ethnic/racial makeup:* number of Black non-Hispanic: 403; American Indian or Alaska Native: 23; Asian or Pacific Islander: 88; Hispanic: 264; White non-Hispanic: 2,819; unknown: 30.

International Students: 425 nonresident aliens enrolled fall 2004. Programs available to aid students whose native language is not English: social, cultural. English as a Second Language Program. No financial aid specifically designated for international students.

Student Life: No on-campus housing. *Intercollegiate athletics:* men only: baseball, basketball; women only: softball, volleyball; men and women: soccer. . *Special regulations:* Cars permitted without restrictions. *Special services:* Learning Center, Career Counseling Center. *Student publications: The Belweather,* an annual literary magazine. *Surrounding community:* Bellevue, population 50,000, is located in Omaha metropolitan area.

Library Collections: 130,000 volumes. 29,000 microforms; 1,507 audiovisual materials; 667 current periodical subscriptions. Online catalog. Students have access to online information retrieval services and the Internet.

Most important special holdings include Human Relations Area File (on microfiche, 5,234 volumes); New York Times plus indices 1899–1919 and 1945–1974 (on microfilm); the Barbara Miller Memorial Collection (economics) consisting of 250 volumes.

Buildings and Grounds: Campus area 35 acres.

Chief Executive Officer: Dr. John B. Muller, President.

Address undergraduate admission inquiries to Roberta Mersch, Director of Admissions; graduate inquiries to Richard Preston, Director of Graduate Enrollment.

Chadron State College

1000 Main Street
Chadron, Nebraska 69337-2690
Tel: (308) 432-6000 **E-mail:** inquire@csc.edu
Fax: (308) 432-6464 **Internet:** www.csc.edu

Institution Description: Chadron State College is a state institution. *Enrollment:* 2,629. *Degrees awarded:* Baccalaureate, master's. Specialist certificates also awarded.

Academic offerings subject to approval by statewide coordinating bodies. Budget subject to approval by state governing boards. Member of the consortium NETCHE, Inc. (formerly Nebraska Educational Television Council for Higher Education).

Accreditation: *Regional:* NCA. *Professional:* business, social work, teacher education

History: Chartered 1910; established as Nebraska State Normal College and offered first instruction at postsecondary level 1911; awarded first degree (baccalaureate) 1918; changed name to Nebraska State Teachers College 1943; adopted present name 1960. *See* Conrad Marshall, *A Mini History of Chadron State College* (Chadron: Chadron State College, 1971) for further information.

Institutional Structure: *Governing board:* Board of Trustees of the Nebraska State Colleges. Representation: commissioner of education, 6 trustees and 3 students (appointed by the governor of Nebraska). 1 ex officio. 7 voting. *Composition of institution:* Administrators 11 men / 6 women. Academic affairs headed by vice president. Management/business/finances directed by director of financial affairs. Full-time instructional faculty 104. Academic governance body, Academic Affairs Committee, meets an average of 30 times per year.

Calendar: Semesters. Academic year Aug. to May. Freshmen admitted Aug., Jan., June, July. Degrees conferred May, Aug., Dec. Formal commencements May, Aug. Summer session from mid-May to mid-Aug.

Characteristics of Freshmen: 100% of applicants accepted. 54% of accepted applicants enrolled.

2% (7 students) submitted SAT scores; 94% (308 students) submitted ACT scores. *25th percentile*: ACT Composite 18, ACT English 17, ACT Math 17. *75th percentile*: ACT Composite 25, ACT English 24, ACT Math 25.

42% of entering freshmen expected to graduate within 5 years. 66% of freshmen from Nebraska. Freshmen from 15 states,

Admission: Rolling admissions plan. Apply as early as 1 year prior to, but not later than, registration day. Early acceptance available. *Requirements:* Either graduation from accredited secondary school or GED; health form. Requirements the same for out-of-state students. *Entrance tests:* ACT composite. *For transfer students:* 2.0 minimum GPA; maximum 66 hours may transfer from any accredited institution.

College credit for postsecondary-level work completed in secondary school and for extrainstitutional learning on basis of ACE *2006 Guide to the Evaluation of Educational Experiences in the Armed Services*; portfolio assessment.

Tutoring available. Remedial courses offered during regular academic year; credit given.

Degree Requirements: *For undergraduate degrees:* 125 credit hours; 2.0 GPA for BA, 2.5 for BS; 2 terms in residence; 2 hours physical education; distribution requirements; core curriculum.

Fulfillment of some degree requirements possible by passing College Board CLEP. *Grading system:* A–F; pass-fail; withdraw.

Distinctive Educational Programs: Study abroad in Mexico (Spanish) and England (criminal justice).

Degrees Conferred: 506 *baccalaureate* (B), 74 *master's* (M): agriculture 9 (B); biological/life sciences 26 (B); business/marketing 92 (B); computer and information sciences 5 (B); education 135 (B), 36 (M); engineering and engineering technologies 8 (B); English 3 (B);

Fees and Other Expenses: *Full-time tuition per academic year 2004–05:* undergraduate resident $2,280, nonresident $4,560; graduate resident $2,165, nonresident $4,329. *Required fees:* $548. *Room and board per academic year:* $3,986.

Financial Aid: Aid from institutionally generated funds is provided on the basis of financial need, financial need, athletic ability, other. Institution has a Program Participation Agreement with the U.S. Department of Education for eligible students to receive Pell Grants and, depending upon the agreement, other federal aid.

Departments and Teaching Staff: *Professors* 25, *associate professors* 22, *assistant professors* 30, *instructors* 16, *part-time faculty* 22.

Total instructional faculty: 115 (full-time 93, part-time 22; women 45, men 70; members of minority groups 6). Degrees held by full-time faculty: master's 33%, doctorate 65%, baccalaureate 2%. 67% hold terminal degrees.

Enrollment: Total enrollment 2,629. Undergraduate full-time 784 men / 993 women, part-time 159m / 294w; graduate full-time 18m / 27w, part-time 82m / 212w.

Characteristics of Student Body: *Ethnic/racial makeup:* number of Black non-Hispanic: 34; American Indian or Alaska Native: 65; Asian or Pacific Islander: 24; Hispanic: 66; White non-Hispanic: 2,212; unknown: 211. *Age distribution:* number under 18: 26; 18–19: 617; 20–21: 657; 22–24: 471; 25–29: 159; 30–34: 77; 35–39: 71; 40–49: 98; 50–64: 49; 65 and over: 2.

International Students: 34 nonresident aliens enrolled fall 2004. Students from Europe, Asia, Africa, Canada. No programs available to aid students whose native language is not English. Some financial aid available for undergraduate international students.

Student Life: On-campus residence halls house 40% of student body. Residence halls for men only constitute 45% of such space, for women only 45%, for both sexes 10%. Housing available for married students. 5% of married students request institutional housing; 3% are so housed. 43% of students live on campus. *Intercollegiate athletics:* men only: basketball, football, track, wrestling; women only: basketball, track, volleyball. *Special regulations:* Registered cars permitted without restrictions. Quiet hours from 7pm to 7am. Residence hall visitation from noon to midnight. *Special services:* Learning Resources Center, medical services. *Student publications:* The Eagle, a biweekly newspaper. *Surrounding community:* Chadron population 6,000. Denver (CO), 300 miles from campus, is nearest metropolitan area. Served by airport 7 miles from campus.

Library Collections: 131,000 volumes including bound books, serial backfiles, electronic documents, and government documents not in separate collections. Online catalog. Current serial subscriptions (paper, microform, electronic) 112,500; 325,063 microforms; 5,596 audiovisual materials. 120 computer work stations. Students have access to the Internet at no charge.

Most important special holdings include photographic collection; Mari Sandoz Heritage Society Collection.

Buildings and Grounds: Campus area 281 acres.

Chief Executive Officer: Dr. Thomas L. Krepel, President.

Address undergraduate inquiries to Tena Gould, Director of Admissions; graduate inquiries to Mary Burke, Graduate School.

Clarkson College

101 South 42nd Street
Omaha, Nebraska 68131-2739
Tel: (402) 552-3100   **E-mail:** admiss@clarksoncollege.edu
Fax: (402) 552-2369   **Internet:** www.clarksoncollege.edu

Institution Description: Clarkson College is a private, professional institution affiliated with the Episcopal Church. *Enrollment: 666. Degrees awarded:* Associate, baccalaureate, master's.

Accreditation: *Regional:* NCA. *Professional:* nursing, occupational therapy, physical therapy, radiation therapy

History: Clarkson College was established as Bishop Clarkson College in 1888; adopted present name 1994.

Calendar: Semesters. Academic year Sept. to Aug. Summer session.

Characteristics of Freshmen: 544 applicants (68 men, 476 women). 54% of applicants admitted. 21.4% of admitted students enrolled full-time.

100% (75 students) submitted ACT scores. *25th percentile:* ACT Composite 21, ACT English 21, ACT Math 21. *75th percentile:* ACT Composite 24, ACT English 24, ACT Math 24.

85% of entering freshmen expected to graduate within 5 years. 70% of freshmen from Nebraska. Freshmen from 25 states and 3 foreign countries.

Admission: Rolling admissions. *Requirements:* High school graduation or GED; upper 50% of class; minimum 2.0 GPA and 2.5 GPA in math and science. ACT 19 or above. TOEFL minimum score 600 for international students.

Degree Requirements: *For baccalaureate degree:* 128 semester hours. *For associate degree:* 70 semester hours.

Distinctive Educational Programs: Distance education is available for students studying in business, radial imagery, RN to BSN, and the master's degree program anywhere in the U.S. Material is delivered to students using the Internet and other media. Study abroad at Chester College in England.

ROTC: Available through Creighton University and the University of Nebraska at Omaha.

Degrees Conferred: 36 *associate;* 58 *baccalaureate;* 25 *master's.* Bachelor's degrees awarded in top disciplines: health professions and related clinical sciences 56; business, management, marketing, and related support services 2.

Fees and Other Expenses: Full-time tuition per academic year 2004–05: $8,310 undergraduate. Contact the college for current graduate tuition/fees. *Books and supplies:* $1,200. *Room and board per academic year:* $5,600.

Financial Aid: Aid from institutionally generated funds is provided on the basis of academic merit, financial need. Institution has a Program Participation Agreement with the U.S. Department of Education for eligible students to receive Pell Grants and, depending upon the agreement, other federal aid.

Financial aid to full-time, first-time undergraduate students: 31% received federal grants averaging $2,986; 13% state/local grants; 82% institutional grants averaging $3,959; 76% received loans averaging $7,250.

Departments and Teaching Staff: Full-time nursing 25, radiography/medical imaging 3, physical therapist assistant 3, occupational therapist assistant 3, health services management and business 2, liberal arts/general education 5.

Total instructional faculty 41. Student-to-faculty ratio: 10:1. Degrees held by full-time faculty: doctorate 22%, master's 96%, professional 2%. 37% hold terminal degrees.

Enrollment: Total enrollment 666. Undergraduate 565 (7.8% men, 92.2% women).

Characteristics of Student Body: *Ethnic/racial makeup:* number of Black non-Hispanic: 6.4%; American Indian or Alaska Native: 1.1%; Asian or Pacific Islander: .9%; Hispanic: 1.9%; White non-Hispanic: 88.7%; unknown: 1.1%.

International Students: No programs available to aid students whose native language is not English. No financial aid specifically designated for international students.

Student Life: 75 students can be housed in college housing. Campus housing is coed. *Student activities:* Professional and social organizations; student government.

Library Collections: 8,100 volumes including bound books, serial backfiles, electronic documents, and government documents not in separate collections. Online catalog. Current serial subscriptions: 300. 115 microform titles. 560 audiovisual units. Computer work stations available. Students have access to the Internet at no charge.

Buildings and Grounds: 30-acre campus shared with Clarkson Regional Health Services.

Chief Executive Officer: Dr. J.W. Upright, President.

Address admission inquiries to Jeff Beals, Director of Enrollment Management.

College of Saint Mary

1901 South 72nd Street
Omaha, Nebraska 68124
Tel: (402) 399-2400   **E-mail:** enroll@csm.edu
Fax: (402) 399-2342   **Internet:** www.csm.edu

Institution Description: College of Saint Mary is a private, independent, nonprofit women's college founded by the Sisters of Mercy, Roman Catholic Church. *Enrollment:* 994. Men are admitted to continuing education division. *Degrees awarded:* Associate, baccalaureate.

Accreditation: *Regional:* NCA. *Professional:* dental hygiene, health information administration, health information technician, nursing, occupational therapy, radiation therapy

History: Established and chartered as normal training academy 1873; adopted present name and offered first instruction at postsecondary level 1923; awarded first degree (associate) 1924; became 4-year institution 1955; awarded first baccalaureate 1957.

Institutional Structure: *Governing board:* College of Saint Mary Board of Directors. Extrainstitutional representation: 20 directors, including 4 alumni; institutional representation: president of the college. 1 ex officio. *Composition of institution:* Cabinet 1 man / 4 women. Academic affairs headed by vice president for academic affairs. Management/business/finances directed by vice president for finance and administrative services. Full-time instructional faculty 56. Academic governance body, the Faculty Assembly, meets an average of 9 times per year.

Calendar: Semesters. Academic year Aug. to May. Freshmen admitted Aug., Jan., June. Degrees conferred May, July, Dec. Formal commencement May. Summer session of 3 terms from early May to late July.

Characteristics of Freshmen: 1,393 applicants (all women). 48.7% of applicants admitted. 14.9% of admitted students enrolled full-time.

68% (69 students) submitted ACT scores. *25th percentile:* ACT Composite 18, ACT English 18, ACT Math 17. *75th percentile:* ACT Composite 23, ACT English 23, ACT Math 23.

51% of entering freshmen expected to graduate in five years.

Admission: Rolling admissions plan. For fall acceptance, apply as early as Aug. of previous year, but not later than Aug. of year of enrollment. *Requirements:* Either graduation from accredited secondary school with 16 units or GED. Recommended 4 units English, 2 mathematics, 2 science, 2 social studies. Additional requirements for some programs. Minimum 2.0 GPA. Lowest acceptable secondary school standing 50th percentile. *Entrance tests:* ACT composite preferred; College Board SAT accepted. For foreign students TOEFL. *For transfer students:* 2.0 minimum GPA; 98 hours maximum transfer credit.

College credit and advanced placement for postsecondary-level work completed in secondary school.

Tutoring available. Developmental courses offered during regular academic year; credit given.

Degree Requirements: *For all associate degrees:* 64–72 credit hours; 30 hours in residence. *For all baccalaureate degrees:* 128 credit hours; 30 hours in residence; 2 hours physical education; 47 semester hours general education requirement. *For all degrees:* 2.0 GPA; distribution requirements; demonstrated proficiency in writing and mathematics; comprehensives in some fields of study. Additional requirements for some majors.

Fulfillment of some degree requirements and exemption from some beginning courses possible by passing departmental examinations, College Board CLEP, APP. *Grading system:* A–F; pass-fail; withdraw (on approval of registrar); incomplete (carries time limit).

Distinctive Educational Programs: Flexible meeting schedules. Weekend and evening classes. Research projects; independent study. *Other distinctive programs:* Degree-granting continuing education; Bachelor General Studies; Health Information Management; Paralegal Studies; Associate Nursing degree. Study abroad in Austria, China, England, France, Mexico, Wales.

ROTC: Army offered in cooperation with Creighton University; Air Force with University of Nebraska at Omaha.

Degrees Conferred: 60 *associate;* 93 *baccalaureate.* Bachelor's degrees awarded in top five disciplines: business, management, marketing, and related support services 24; health professions and related sciences 24; education 16; public administration 8; legal professions 5.

Fees and Other Expenses: *Full-time tuition per academic year:* $18,928. *Book and supplies:* $600. *Room and board per academic year:* $5,700.

Financial Aid: Aid from institutionally generated funds is provided on the basis of academic merit, financial need, athletic ability. Institution has a Program Participation Agreement with the U.S. Department of Education for eligible students to receive Pell Grants and, depending upon the agreement, other federal aid.

Financial aid to full-time, first-time undergraduate students: 59% received federal grants averaging $4,030; 32% state/local grants averaging $940; 94% institutional grants averaging $6,308; 94% received loans averaging $6,180.

Departments and Teaching Staff: Accounting *professors* 0, *associate professors* 1, *assistant professors* 0, *instructors* 0, *part-time teachers* 4; art/computer graphics 0, 1, 0, 0, 4; business 0, 0, 2, 0, 7; biology 0, 1, 1, 0, 4; chemistry 1, 0, 1, 0, 2; computer science 0, 0, 2, 0, 12; creative arts 0, 1, 0, 0, 1; education 1, 0, 1, 0, 4; English 0, 1, 0, 0, 6; health information management 0, 1, 0, 1, 7; history 0, 1, 0, 0, 0; human services/psychology 1, 0, 1, 0, 8; law 0, 2, 0, 0, 8; mathematics 0, 0, 1, 0, 4; music 0, 1, 0, 0, 1; nursing 2, 5, 3, 1, 12; physical education 0, 0, 0, 0, 5; philosophy 0, 0, 0, 0, 3; sociology 1, 0, 0, 0, 0; theology 0, 0, 1, 0, 3; occupational therapy 0, 0, 1, 0, 3.

Total instructional faculty: 70. Student-to-faculty ratio: 15:1. Degrees held by full-time faculty: baccalaureate 3%, master's 64%, doctorate 33%. 33% hold terminal degrees.

Enrollment: Total enrollment 994. Undergraduate 969 (men .2%, women 99.8%).

Characteristics of Student Body: *Ethnic/racial makeup:* number of Black non-Hispanic: 6.5%; American Indian or Alaska Native: .8%; Asian or Pacific Islander: 1%; Hispanic: 5.2%; White non-Hispanic: 85.4%. *Age distribution:* 17–2: 31%; 22–24: 11%; 25–29: 14%; 30–34: 10%; 35–39: 11%; 40–49: 18%; 50–59: 4%; 60–up: less than 1%.

International Students: 9 nonresident aliens enrolled fall 2004. Students from Europe, Asia, Australia. No programs available to aid students whose native language is not English. No financial aid specifically designated for international students.

Student Life: On-campus residence halls house approximately 20% of the student body. Residence halls for women only constitute 100% of such space. *Intercollegiate athletics:* women only: golf, soccer, softball, tennis, volleyball. *Special regulations:* Cars with decals permitted on campus in designated areas only. Residence hall visitation in public lounge areas permitted 24 hours per day. *Special services:* Campus Ministry, a volunteer program for community service and involvement through a student-run Mertz Outreach] Center; Career Development; Health Services; Student Senate; Women's Initiative Program provides opportunities to study women's issues, book reviews about women and written by women; Leadership Seminar Program; Learning Support Center and Writing Lab; opportunities through the Convocations Committee to attend cultural events on campus and within the Omaha community. *Students publications: Around CSM,* a weekly newsletter; *Campus Connections,* newspaper. *Surrounding community:* Omaha metropolitan area population 325,000. Served by mass transit bus system; airport 13 miles from campus; passenger rail service 9 miles from campus.

Library Collections: 85,000 volumes including bound books, serial backfiles, electronic documents, and government documents not in separate collections. Online catalog. Current serial subscriptions: 401 paper, 10 microform, 2,000 electronic. 2,371 audiovisual materials. Computer work stations available. Students have access to the Internet at no charge.

Most important special holdings include collection on women's studies.

Buildings and Grounds: Campus area 25 acres.

Chief Executive Officer: Dr. Maryanne Stevens, R.S.M., President.

Address admission inquiries to Sue Kropf, Director of Admissions.

Concordia University

800 North Columbia Avenue
Seward, Nebraska 68434
Tel: (402) 643-3651   **E-mail:** admiss@cune.edu
Fax: (402) 643-4073   **Internet:** www.cune.edu

Institution Description: Concordia University is a private institution affiliated with the Lutheran Church-Missouri Synod. *Enrollment:* 1,379. *Degrees awarded:* Baccalaureate, master's.

Accreditation: *Regional:* NCA. *Professional:* teacher education

History: Established as The Lutheran Seminary, a preparatory school, 1894; became secondary school and 2-year college and offered first instruction at postsecondary level 1905; chartered 1918; renamed Concordia College 1924; became 4-year college 1939; awarded first degree (baccalaureate) 1940; added graduate program 1966; renamed Concordia University 1998.

Institutional Structure: *Governing board:* The Board of Regents. Extrainstitutional representation: 11 trustees; institutional representation: 1 administrator. 1 ex officio. 11 voting. *Composition of institution:* Administrators 13 men / 6 women. Academic services headed by vice president for academic services. Business/finances directed by vice president for administrative services. Full-time instructional faculty 65. Academic governance body, the faculty, meets an average of 10 times per year.

Calendar: Semesters. Academic year late Aug. to May. Freshmen admitted on a rolling basis. Degrees conferred May, Aug., Dec. Formal commencement May. May Term from mid-May to late May. Summer session of 3 terms from mid-June to late July.

Characteristics of Freshmen: 745 applicants (376 men / 369 women). 86.4% of applicants admitted. 43.3% of admitted students enrolled full-time.

20% (57 students) submitted SAT scores; 90% (252 students) submitted ACT scores. *25th percentile*: SAT I Verbal 480, SAT I Math 480; ACT Composite 21, ACT English 20, ACT Math 19. *75th percentile*: SAT I Verbal 590, SAT I Math 610; ACT Composite 27, ACT English 27, ACT Math 26.

65% of entering freshmen expected to graduate within 5 years. 61% of freshmen from Nebraska. Freshmen from 28 states and 2 foreign countries.

Admission: Rolling admissions plan. For fall acceptance, apply as early as Sept. of previous year, but not later than beginning of term. Early acceptance available. *Requirements:* Graduation from accredited secondary school with 16 units. GED accepted. Minimum 2.0 GPA. *Entrance tests:* ACT or SAT. *For transfer students:* 2.0 minimum GPA; from 2-year accredited institution 64 hours maximum transfer credit.

College credit and advanced placement for postsecondary-level work completed in secondary school and for extrainstitutional learning (life experience) on basis of faculty assessment.

Degree Requirements: 128 credit hours; 2.0 GPA; 30 hours in residence, 12 of which must be upper level and 15 of which must be in student's major if there is room or opportunity; 3 hours physical education; distribution requirements.

Fulfillment of some degree requirements and exemption from some beginning courses possible by passing departmental examinations, College Board CLEP, and Advanced Placement. *Grading system:* A–F; pass-fail; withdraw (carries time limit).

Distinctive Educational Programs: *For undergraduates:* Internships. Cooperative baccalaureate programs in business education, industrial arts, and home economics with the University of Nebraska - Lincoln and medical technology with Nebraska Wesleyan University. Preprofessional programs in clinical medical technology, medicine; preseminary pastoral program also available. Facilities for independent research, including honors programs, individual majors, tutorials. Institutionally-sponsored study abroad in Belize, Canada, China, England, Germany, Hong Kong, Israel, Mexico, Soviet Union, and Taiwan. Degree completion program for working professionals. *Available to all students:* Evening classes. Special facilities for using telecommunications in the classroom.

Degrees Conferred: 298 *baccalaureate*; 51 *master's*. Bachelor's degrees awarded in top five disciplines: business, management, marketing, and related support services 100; theology/ministerial studies 70; liberal arts/general studies 59; visual and performing arts 14; biological/life sciences 9.

Fees and Other Expenses: *Full-time tuition per academic year 2004–05:* $16,880. *Books and supplies:* $700. *Room and board per academic year:* $4,580.

Financial Aid: Aid from institutionally generated funds is provided on the basis of academic merit, financial need, athletic ability, other criteria. Institution has a Program Participation Agreement with the U.S. Department of Education for eligible students to receive Pell Grants and, depending upon the agreement, other federal aid.

Financial aid to full-time, first-time undergraduate students: 13% received federal grants averaging $2,724; 5% state/local grants averaging $845; 75% institutional grants averaging $4,038; 52% received loans averaging $2,478.

Departments and Teaching Staff: Education *professors* 7, *associate professors* 1, *assistant professors* 9, *instructors* 0; health/physical education 1, 2, 2, 0; English 2, 3, 1, 1; art 3, 1, 1, 0; science 4, 0, 4, 0; mathematics/computer science 1, 2, 2, 0; business administration 1, 1, 0, 0; theology 2, 2, 2, 0; music 2, 0, 3, 0; social science 4, 0, 1, 0.

Total full-time instructional faculty: 65; part-time professors: 53. Student-to-faculty ratio: 13:1. Degrees held by full-time faculty: master's 29%, doctorate 63%, baccalaureate 1%. 59% hold terminal degrees.

Enrollment: Total enrollment 1,379. Undergraduate 1,179 (43.7% men, 56.3% women).

Characteristics of Student Body: *Ethnic/racial makeup:* number of Black non-Hispanic: 1.1%; American Indian or Alaska Native: .2%; Asian or Pacific Islander: .8%; Hispanic: 1%; White non-Hispanic: 84.8%; unknown: 12%.

International Students: 21 nonresident aliens enrolled 2004. Students from Europe, Asia, Latin America, Africa. No programs available to aid students whose native language is not English. No financial aid specifically designated for international students.

Student Life: On-campus residence halls house 80% of student body. Residence halls for men constitute 43% of such space, for women 57%. Housing available for married students. *Intercollegiate athletics:* men only: baseball, basketball, cross-country, football, golf, soccer, tennis, track; women only: basketball, cross country, soccer, softball, tennis, track, volleyball. *Special regulations:* Cars permitted without restrictions. Quiet hours coincide with the end of visita-

tion hours. Residence hall visitation from noon to 10:30pm Mon.–Thurs., noon to midnight Fri. and Sat., noon to 10:30pm Sun. Use of alcohol not permitted on campus. *Special services:* Academic support services, medical services, campus transportation to and from airport, railroad, bus depots. *Student publications:* *The Sower*, student newspaper; *Tower*, a yearbook. *Surrounding community:* Seward. Lincoln, 25 miles from campus, is nearest metropolitan area; Omaha, 80 miles from campus. Served by airport and passenger rail service, both 25 miles from campus.

Publications: Sources of information about Concordia College include *Broadcaster*, a tabloid distributed to 40,000 people; *Issues in Christian Education* (triennially) first published in 1966. *Publisher:* Service Press, Henderson, NE.

Library Collections: 210,000 volumes including bound books, serial backfiles, electronic documents, and government documents not in separate collections. Online catalog. Current serial subscriptions: 576 paper, 12 microform, 4,450 electronic. 6,692 recordings; 137 compact discs; 10 CD-ROMs. Computer work stations available. Students have access to the Internet at no charge.

Most important special holdings include curriculum materials for teacher education program; theology materials for pre-seminary program; extensive teacher education collection; Koschmann Memorial Children's Collection.

Buildings and Grounds: Campus area 120 acres.

Chief Executive Officer: Dr. Brian L. Friedrich, President.

Address admission inquiries to Don Vos, Director of Admissions.

Creighton University

2500 California Plaza
Omaha, Nebraska 68178

Tel: (402) 280-2701   **E-mail:** admissions@creighton.edu
Fax: (402) 280-2527   **Internet:** www.creighton.edu

Institution Description: Creighton University is a private, independent, nonprofit institution. *Enrollment:* 6,723. *Degrees awarded:* Associate, baccalaureate, first-professional (dentistry, medicine, pharmacy, law), master's, doctorate.

Accreditation: *Regional:* NCA. *Professional:* business, dentistry, law, medicine, nursing, occupational therapy, pharmacy, physical therapy, social work, teacher education

History: Established as Creighton College 1878; incorporated as The Creighton University 1879; offered first instruction at postsecondary level 1888; awarded first degree (baccalaureate) 1891.

Institutional Structure: *Governing board:* University Board of Directors. 35 members: 28 lay members and 7 Jesuits (includes the President of the University). All voting. *Composition of institution:* 7 Vice Presidents, 9 Deans and 53 Directors (36 men / 18 women). Academic affairs under jurisdiction of the Vice President for Academic Affairs and the Vice President for Health Sciences. Management of business and finances directed by the vice president of administration and finance and treasurer of the university. Full-time instructional faculty 724. Academic governance body, Academic Council, meets an average of 9 times per year.

Calendar: Semesters. Academic year Aug. to May. Freshmen admitted Aug., Jan., June, July. Degrees conferred May, Aug., Dec. Formal commencements Dec. and May. Summer session of 3 terms from mid-May to mid-Aug.

Characteristics of Freshmen: 86% of applicants admitted. 28% of applicants admitted and enrolled.

32% (309 students) submitted SAT scores; 92% (891 students) submitted ACT scores. *25th percentile*: ACT Composite 23, ACT English 22, ACT Math 22. *75th percentile*: ACT Composite 28, ACT English 29, ACT Math 27.

69% of entering freshmen expected to graduate within 5 years. 38% of freshmen from Nebraska. Freshmen from 34 states and 5 foreign countries.

Admission: Rolling admissions plan. For fall acceptance, apply as early as completion of junior year of secondary school, but not later than 1 month prior to beginning of classes. *Requirements:* Either graduation from accredited secondary school with 3 English, 2 mathematics (including 1 algebra), 6 academic electives; or GED. 1 additional unit in English, 2 foreign language, 2 natural science, 2 social science highly recommended. Preference for admission given to students with a 2.5 GPA and class ranking in the top 50th percentile. *Entrance tests:* ACT or SAT accepted. *For transfer students:* Residency requirement to earn a Creighton degree: Arts and Sciences, 48 hours; Business Administration, 64 hours; Nursing, 48 hours.

College credit and advanced placement for postsecondary level work completed in secondary school. College credit for extrainstitutional learning (life experience) on basis of portfolio and faculty assessments, personal interviews.

Developmental courses offered in summer session and regular academic year.

Degree Requirements: *For all associate degrees:* 64 semester hours; 32 semester hours in residence. *For all baccalaureate degrees:* 128 semester hours;

48 semester hours in residence; general education requirements. *For all undergraduate degrees:* 2.0 GPA.

Fulfillment of some degree requirements and exemption from some beginning courses possible by passing departmental examinations, College Board CLEP, AP. *Grading system:* A–F; pass-fail; withdraw (carries time limit).

Distinctive Educational Programs: Interdisciplinary programs for undergraduates in American studies, Black studies, Justice and Peach Studies, and Native American Studies; graduate programs in International Relation, Information Technology Management, Christian Spirituality, and Theology; first-professional web-based Doctor of Pharmacy degree program. Creighton offers its students faculty-led and independent study abroad programs in nearly 40 countries. Programs vary in length, content, format, and cost. Creighton students are offered the opportunity to participate in Spring Break service trips to serve those with greater needs than their own. Cooperative 4/3 program with Creighton Preparatory School.

ROTC: Army. Air Force in cooperation with University of Nebraska at Omaha. 8 commissions awarded 2004.

Degrees Conferred: 3 *associate;* 814 *baccalaureate* (B), 181 *master's* (M), 108 *doctorate* (D): area and ethnic studies 2 (B); biological/life sciences 56 (B), 8 (M), 8 (D); business/marketing 157 (B), 74 (M); communications/communication technologies 42 (B); computer and information sciences 13 (B), 6 (M); education 25 (B), 18 (M); English 34 (B), 5 (M); foreign languages and literature 12 (B); health professions and related sciences 206 (B), 32 (M), 100 (D); interdisciplinary studies 10 (B); law/legal studies 8 (B); library science 4 (M); mathematics 11 (B); natural resources/environmental science 9 (B); parks and recreation 24 (B); philosophy/religion/theology 24 (B), 36 (M); physical sciences 31 (B), 5 (M); protective services/public administration 7 (B); psychology 80 (B); social sciences and history 39 (B), 3 (D); visual and performing arts 24 (B). 467 *first-professional:* : dentistry 82; law 168; medicine 108; pharmacy 109.

Fees and Other Expenses: *Full-time tuition per academic year 2004–05:* undergraduate $20,354. Graduate study costs vary by program; contact the university for current rates. *Required fees:* $724. *Room and board per academic year:* $7,200.

Financial Aid: Aid from institutionally generated funds is provided on the basis of academic merit, financial need, athletic ability.

Financial aid to full-time, first-time undergraduate students: need-based scholarships/grants totaling $21,283,999, self-help $14,664,120, tuition waivers $2,082,279, athletic awards $954,448; non-need-based scholarships/grants totaling $8,876,529, self-help $1,115,447, parent loans $4,519,158, tuition waivers $2,896,974, athletic awards $1,695,743. *Graduate aid:* 132 students received $3,103,538 in federal and state-funded fellowships/grants (ranging from $1,000 to $49,000); $49,603,705 awarded in federal and state-funded loans; 39 students received other fellowships/grants totaling $283,674.

Departments and Teaching Staff: College of Arts and Sciences *professors* 36, *associate professors* 75, *assistant professors* 82, *instructors* 25, *part-time faculty* 16; College of Business Administration 9, 13, 6, 2, 2; School of Dentistry 8, 25, 13, 8, 3; School of Law 16, 3, 3, 8, 5; School of Medicine 49, 74, 109, 28, 9; School of Nursing 0, 5, 25, 15, 9; School of Pharmacy and Health Professions 9, 29, 44, 10, 8.

Total instructional faculty: 783 (full-time 724, part-time 59; women 205, men 498; members of minority groups 119). Total faculty with doctorate, first-professional, or other terminal degree: 699. Student-to-faculty ratio: 13:1. *Faculty development:* $32,679,217 total grants for research.

Enrollment: Total enrollment 6,723. Undergraduate full-time 1,423 men / 2,122 women, part-time 116m / 227w; first-professional full-time 186m / 1,124w, part-time 75m / 117w; graduate full-time 97m / 92w, part-time 146m / 198w. *Transfer students:* in-state 171; from out-of-state 63.

Characteristics of Student Body: *Ethnic/racial makeup (undergraduate):* number of Black non-Hispanic: 136; American Indian or Alaska Native: 55; Asian or Pacific Islander: 267; Hispanic: 129; White non-Hispanic: 3,211; unknown: 35. *Age distribution:* number under 18: 7; 18–19: 1,492;20–21: 1,576; 22–24: 612; 25–29: 136; 30–34: 52; 35–39: 49; 40–49: 66; 50–64: 46; 65 and over: 3. 30% of student body attend summer sessions.

International Students: 159 nonresident aliens enrolled fall 2004. 14 students from Europe, 93 Asia, 9 Latin America, 27 Africa, 14 Canada, 2 Australia. Programs available to aid students whose native language is not English: social, cultural. Financial aid specifically designated for international students: scholarships available annually for qualifying students.

Student Life: On-campus residence halls available. *Intercollegiate athletics:* men only: baseball, basketball, cross-country, golf, soccer, tennis; women only: basketball, crew, cross-country, golf, soccer, softball, tennis. *Special regulations:* Registered cars permitted; fee charged. Quiet hours. Resident hall visitation from noon to 1am Sun.–Thurs., noon to 2am Fri. and Sat. *Special services:* Learning Resources Center, medical services, special residential living options, shuttle bus between campus housing and other university buildings. *Student publications: The Bluejay,* a yearbook; *Creightonian,* a weekly newspaper; *The Creighton Law Review,* published quarterly; *Shadows,* a biannual literary mag-

azine. *Surrounding community:* Omaha metropolitan area population 720,000. Served by mass transit bus system; airport 5 miles from campus; passenger rail service 3 miles from campus.

Library Collections: 1,896,607 volumes. Online catalog. Current serial subscriptions: 6,253 paper; 234 microform; 16,476 via electronic access. 145 computer work stations. Students have access to the Internet at no charge. Total budget for books, periodicals, audiovisual materials, microforms 2004–05: $3,196,866.

Most important special holdings include Theology Collection; personal papers of author Ron Hansen; Biomedical Sciences Collection; Sir Joseph Gold International Monetary Fund Collection; Carlson Fable Collection; Law Collection.

Buildings and Grounds: Campus area 86 acres. *New buildings:* Hixon Lied Science Building; Davis Square Town Homes; Cardiac Center.

Chief Executive Officer: Rev. John P. Schlegel, S.J., President.

Address undergraduate admission inquiries to Mary Chase, Director of Admissions; graduate and professional school inquiries to Graduate School, School of Pharmacy and Health Professions, School of Medicine, School of Dentistry, School of Law.

College of Arts and Sciences

Degree Programs Offered: *Baccalaureate* in area studies, biology, communications, computer and information science, education, environmental science, exercise science, fine and applied arts, foreign languages, letters, mathematics, philosophy, physical sciences, psychology, public affairs and services, social sciences, theology.

Distinctive Educational Programs: Interdisciplinary programs for undergraduates in American studies and Black studies; for graduate students in international relations.

Enrollment: *Total enrollment:* 2,410.

College of Business Administration

Degree Programs Offered: *Baccalaureate* in accounting, economics, finance, international business, management, management information systems, marketing, prelaw-business.

Distinctive Educational Programs: *See* School of Law.

Enrollment: *Total enrollment:* 665.

School of Law

Degree Programs Offered: *First-professional.*

Admission: Baccalaureate degree from accredited college or university. Exceptions can be made for students who have completed at least 90 hours of credit and can show exceptional performance or conditions making them qualified to successfully study law, LSAT.

Degree Requirements: Students must successfully complete first year curriculum plus 60 semester hours. Cumulative grade point average must be 65 or higher.

Distinctive Educational Programs: Joint bachelor of science-law degree. Joint bachelor of science-master's in business administration-law degree.

Enrollment: *Total enrollment:* 480.

School of Nursing

Degree Programs Offered: *Baccalaureate.*

Distinctive Educational Programs: Accelerated nursing curriculum for students with baccalaureate or higher degree.

Enrollment: *Total enrollment:* 459.

School of Pharmacy and Health Professions

Degree Programs Offered: *Baccalaureate* in occupational therapy; *first-professional* in occupational therapy, pharmacy, physical therapy.

Admission: Completion of 63 hours in pre-professional curriculum for pharmacy, 60 hours for occupational therapy, 90 hours for doctor of physical therapy.

Degree Requirements: Completion of all courses in the prescribed curriculum and a cumulative grade point average not less than 2.0 on all work attempted while enrolled in the program. Candidate must be determined by the faculty to be of good moral character and fit for the practice of the profession.

Enrollment: *Total enrollment:* 1,018.

Graduate School

Degree Programs Offered: *Master's* in atmospheric sciences, biomedical sciences, business administration, Christian spirituality, clinical anatomy, counseling, elementary school administration, English, health services administration, information technology management, international relations, liberal studies, medical microbiology, ministry, nursing, pharmaceutical science, pharmacology, physics, secondary school administration, secondary teaching, theology; *doctorate* in biomedical sciences, medical microbiology, pharmacology.

Admission: Baccalaureate or its equivalent from accredited institution; GRE or GMAT.

Degree Requirements: Requirements vary with program.

Enrollment: *Total enrollment: 533.*

School of Dentistry

Degree Programs Offered: *First-professional.*

Admission: 2 years of work in an accredited college of arts and sciences with 64 semester hours in academic subjects. DAT and 3 letters of recommendation.

Degree Requirements: Candidates bear a good moral character, must have finished satisfactorily the prescribed courses, passed the examinations therein, and complied with technical, laboratory and clinical requirements.

Enrollment: *Total enrollment: 338.*

School of Medicine

Degree Programs Offered: *First-professional.*

Admission: Three years of study in an approved college of Arts and Sciences with a minimum of 90 semester hours in academic courses including required pre-medical courses, MCAT.

Degree Requirements: Students must complete a prescribed curriculum during the first two years and prescribed offerings during the second one and one-half years. The fourth year must be completed before a degree is awarded but subjects studied are chosen by the student with the guidance of the faculty advisor.

Enrollment: *Total enrollment: 457.*

University College

Degree Programs Offered: *Associate, baccalaureate.*

Admission: Admission requirements are flexible. No entrance examinations are required. Final acceptance decisions are based on student's motivation and maturity, as well as prior college-level academic performance.

Enrollment: *Total enrollment: 347.*

Dana College

2848 College Drive
Blair, Nebraska 68008-1099
Tel: (402) 426-9000   **E-mail:** admissions@dana.edu
Fax: (402) 426-7332   **Internet:** www.dana.edu

Institution Description: Dana College is a private college affiliated with the Evangelical Lutheran Church in America. *Enrollment:* 639. *Degrees awarded:* Baccalaureate.

Member of the consortium NETCHE (formerly Nebraska Television Council for Higher Education).

Accreditation: *Regional:* NCA. *Professional:* social work, teacher education

History: Established as Trinity Seminary 1884; incorporated 1885 as Trinity Seminary and Blair College, and offered first instruction at postsecondary level 1899; changed name to Dana College and Trinity Seminary 1903; separated from Trinity Seminary and adopted present name 1960.

Institutional Structure: *Governing board:* Board of Regents. Representation: 17 regents, including 8 regents emeriti. *Composition of institution:* Administrators 6 men / 1 woman. Academic affairs headed by vice president for academic affairs. Management/business/finances directed by vice president for business affairs. Full-time instructional faculty 42.

Calendar: Semesters (4-1-4 plan). Academic year late Aug. to mid-May. Formal commencement May. Summer session of 1 three-week term in May.

Characteristics of Freshmen: 677 applicants (389 men, 308 women). 96.6% of applicants admitted. 31.3% of admitted students enrolled full-time.

6% (13 students) submitted SAT scores; 95% (196 students) submitted ACT scores. *25th percentile:* SAT I Verbal 400, SAT I Math 420; ACT Composite 19, ACT English 18, ACT Math 18. *75th percentile:* SAT I Verbal 490, SAT I Math 500; ACT Composite 24, ACT English 24, ACT Math 24.

38% of entering freshmen expected to graduate within 5 years. 56% of freshmen from Nebraska. Freshmen from 13 states and 3 foreign countries.

Admission: Rolling admissions plan. Apply as early as senior year of secondary school. *Requirements:* Either graduation from accredited secondary school

or GED. Multiple measures used in making final admission decision. *Entrance tests:* ACT composite preferred; SAT accepted. TOEFL required of international students. *For transfer students:* 2.0 minimum GPA; maximum transfer credit limited only by residence requirement.

Degree Requirements: 128 semester hours; 2.0 GPA on a 4-point scale; senior year in residence; 2 hours physical education; general education requirements; demonstrated proficiency in mathematics, writing, speech, and a foreign or computer language. Credit may be granted for qualified military training and portfolio of previous learning experiences.

Fulfillment of some degree requirements and exemption from some beginning courses possible by passing College Board CLEP, AP. *Grading system:* A-F; pass; withdraw (may carry penalty).

Distinctive Educational Programs: Interdisciplinary program in environmental studies. Study abroad in Denmark, Egypt, Hong Kong, Germany, Israel, Japan, Jordan, Korea, Spain. Internships, exchange programs, experimental courses offered during interim. Liberal Arts Reading Program discusses classical literature. Foundations of Lifelong Learning; Liberal Arts Senior Seminar; Honors Program affiliated with the National Honors Council.

Degrees Conferred: 115 *baccalaureate.* Bachelor's degrees awarded in top five disciplines: 47; education 29; communication, journalism, and related programs 8; public administration 7; psychology 6.

Fees and Other Expenses: *Full-time tuition per academic year 2004–05:* $16,800. *Room and board per academic year:* $5,060. *Books and supplies:* $600.

Financial Aid: Aid from institutionally generated funds is provided on the basis of academic merit, financial need, athletic ability, other criteria. Institution has a Program Participation Agreement with the U.S. Department of Education for eligible students to receive Pell Grants and, depending upon the agreement, other federal aid.

Departments and Teaching Staff: Art *professors* 1, *associate professors* 2, *assistant professors* 0, *instructors* 0, *part-time faculty* 2; biology 1, 1, 1, 0, 0; business 1, 1, 3, 0, 1; chemistry, 0, 0, 1, 0, 1; foreign language 0, 2, 0, 0, 1; geography 0, 0, 0, 0, 1; history 1, 1, 0, 0, 1; music 1, 0, 3, 0, 9; physical education 0, 0, 1, 6, 2; education 2, 0, 1, 0, 2; religion 1, 1, 0, 0, 1; speech/theater 0, 0, 1, 0, 0; communication 0, 0, 1, 0, 1; English 2, 0, 1, 0, 3; mathematics 0, 1, 1, 0, 1; social work/sociology 0, 2, 1, 0, 6; computer science 0, 0, 1, 0, 0; physics 0, 0, 0, 1.

Total instructional faculty: 76. Student-to-faculty ratio: 12:1. Degrees held by full-time faculty: doctorate 51%, master's 49%. 51% hold terminal degrees.

Enrollment: Total enrollment 639 (men 55.6%, women 49.4%).

Characteristics of Student Body: *Ethnic/racial makeup:* number of Black non-Hispanic: 4.9%; American Indian or Alaska Native: .3%; Asian or Pacific Islander: .6%; Hispanic: 3.9%; White non-Hispanic: 90%.

International Students: 19 nonresident aliens enrolled. Students from Europe, Asia, Latin America, Africa, Canada. Programs to aid students whose native language is not English: social, financial. English as a Second Language Program. Financial aid specifically designated for international students: variable number of scholarships available annually.

Student Life: On-campus residence halls. Full-time students required to live on campus; exemptions granted. *Intercollegiate athletics:* men: baseball, basketball, football, track, wrestling; women: basketball, soccer track, volleyball. *Student publications: Danian,* a yearbook; *Hermes,* a newspaper; *Sower,* a literary magazine. *Surrounding community:* Blair population 7,000. Omaha, 15 miles from campus, is nearest metropolitan area.

Library Collections: 195,000 volumes. 3,800 audiovisual materials; 1,480 serial subscriptions. Online catalog. Students have access to online information retrieval services.

Most important special collections include Danish literature and history; Lauritz Melchoir personal papers, music, and scores; papers of Sophus Keith Winther; religion collection.

Buildings and Grounds: Campus area 150 acres.

Chief Executive Officer: Dr. Myrvin Christopherson, President.

Address admission inquiries to Director of Admissions.

Doane College

1014 Boswell Avenue
Crete, Nebraska 68333
Tel: (402) 826-8200   **E-mail:** admission@doane.edu
Fax: (402) 826-8600   **Internet:** www.doane.edu

Institution Description: Doane College is a private, independent, nonprofit, liberal arts college affiliated with the United Church of Christ. The home campus is located in Crete (NE) and a campus for nontraditional students in Lincoln (NE). *Enrollment:* 774. *Degrees awarded:* Baccalaureate, master's.

Member of the consortium NETCHE, Inc. (formerly Nebraska Educational Television Council for Higher Education).

Accreditation: *Regional:* NCA. *Professional:* teacher education

History: Established in Fontenelle as Nebraska University 1858; moved to Crete, adopted present name, and incorporated 1872; first instruction at postsecondary level 1873; awarded first degree (baccalaureate) 1877.

Institutional Structure: *Governing board:* Board of Trustees of Doane College. Extrainstitutional representation: 38 trustees; institutional representation: President of the College, 1 ex officio. 40 voting. *Composition of institution:* Top administrators 7 men. Academic affairs headed by vice president for academic affairs. Management/business/finances directed by vice president for financial affairs. Advancement/alumni directed by vice president for advancement. Full-time instructional faculty 38 men / 24 women. Academic governance body, the faculty, meets an average of 9 times per year.

Calendar: Semesters (4-1-4 plan). Academic year Aug. to May. Freshmen admitted Sept., Jan. Degrees conferred May, Aug., Dec., Jan. Formal commencement May.

Characteristics of Freshmen: 89% of applicants accepted. 30% of accepted applicants enrolled.

98% (299 students) submitted ACT scores. *25th percentile:* ACT Composite 19, ACT English 18, ACT Math 19. *75th percentile:* ACT Composite 26, ACT English 27, ACT Math 26.

68% of entering freshmen expected to graduate within 5 years. 80% of freshmen from Nebraska.

Admission: Rolling admissions plan. For fall acceptance, apply as early as Sept. of previous year, but not later than Aug. 15 of year of enrollment. Early acceptance available. *Requirements:* Either graduation from accredited secondary school or GED. Multiple measures used in making final admission decisions. *Entrance tests:* College Board SAT or ACT composite. For foreign students TOEFL. *For transfer students:* 2.0 minimum GPA; maximum transfer credit limited only by residence requirement.

College credit and advanced placement for postsecondary-level work completed in secondary school. College credit for extrainstitutional learning (life experience).

Developmental courses offered during regular academic year; credit given.

Degree Requirements: 132 credit hours, including participation in interterm; 2.0 GPA; 2 terms in residence; 2 physical education courses; distribution requirements; demonstrated proficiency in writing.

Fulfillment of some degree requirements and exemption from some beginning courses possible by passing departmental examinations, College Board CLEP, AP, ACT PEP. (Adult education students who are qualified military personnel may also earn credit through DANTES). *Grading system:* A–F; pass-fail; withdraw (carries time limit).

Distinctive Educational Programs: Academic offerings in the liberal arts and professional fields (business, teacher education, and communication studies). Particularly strong programs in the social sciences, natural sciences and mathematics have been enhanced with a state-of-the-art computer system and laboratories. The teacher education program, which warranties its graduates, has been nationally recognized. Dual-degree programs in engineering with Columbia University (NY) and Washington University (MO); in forestry with Duke University (NC). Cooperative baccalaureate program with accredited schools of medical technology. The College offers a comprehensive array of international opportunities from courses on the home campus to study abroad through ISEP, CIEE, Central College, a special arrangement with the University of Copenhagen, and the Goethe Institut, and Jumamoto YMCA College. Through an innovative program, junior and senior students receive $700 from the College for study tours abroad, primarily during the January term. The College also offers students a comprehensive leadership development curriculum starting with a required freshman course focused on community service. The Talent and Leadership Curriculum results in the development of a co-curricular transcript. In addition to internship opportunities for all students, an alumni network assists graduates in making connections leading to career placement.

ROTC: Army, Air Force.

Degrees Conferred: 178 *baccalaureate:* biological/life sciences 16; business and management 25; communications 13; computer and information science 8; education 37; English 9; fine and applied arts 9; foreign language 6; mathematics 6; natural science 1; philosophy 3; physical sciences 3; psychology 15; public affairs and services 1; social sciences 28; visual and performing arts 4; other 1.

Fees and Other Expenses: *Full-time tuition per academic year 2005–06:* $17,186. *Required fees:* $350. *Room and board per academic year:* $4,922.

Financial Aid: Aid from institutionally generated funds is provided on the basis of academic merit, financial need, athletic ability.

Financial aid to full-time, first-time undergraduate students: need-based scholarships/grants totaling $3,595,866, self-help $2,936,544, tuition waivers $388,657, athletic awards $955,588; non-need-based scholarships/grants totaling $3,759,024, self-help $991,593, parent loans $3,670,415, tuition waivers $177,060, athletic awards $162,637.

Departments and Teaching Staff: *Total instructional faculty:* 80 (women 32, men 48; members of minority groups 2). Total faculty with doctorate, first-professional, or other terminal degree: 51. Student-to-faculty ratio: 12.5:1. Degrees held by full-time faculty: master's 30%, doctorate 68%.

Enrollment: Total enrollment 774. Undergraduate full-time 1,408 men and women, part-time 247 m/w.

Characteristics of Student Body: *Ethnic/racial makeup:* Black non-Hispanic: 3%; Asian or Pacific Islander: .4%; Hispanic: 2%; White non-Hispanic: 94%. *Age distribution:* Average age of freshmen 18, class 20.

International Students: Programs available to aid students whose native language is not English: English as a Second Language Program. No financial specifically designated for international students.

Student Life: 80% of the student body lives on campus in co-ed, male, and female residence halls. Alternative on-campus apartments are also available to students. Married student housing and a special Honors Residence are available. *Intercollegiate athletics:* baseball, basketball, cross-country, football, golf, softball, tennis, track and field, volleyball. *Special regulations:* Cars permitted without restrictions. *Special services:* Doane features a fall orientation program which directly involves all new students with a faculty mentor, an upper-class peer advisor and a small peer group. An involved student body supports nearly 50 clubs and organizations, including a Greek system, Student Congress, Student Activities Council, Council of Presidents, and class officers. A variety of other extracurricular activities are available for all students. TLC, the Talent Leadership Curriculum, showcases a progressive, integrated student leadership development component, bridging classroom learning with outside experiences. The IRS, Intramural and Recreational Services, offers a wide variety of sports leagues and competitive athletic tourneys. *Student publications, television: Owl,* a weekly student newspaper; *Tiger,* a yearbook; *Xanadu,* an annual literary magazine. BBTV, 24-hour TV announcements; DCBS, cable TV, broadcasts 25 hours per week. *Surrounding community:* Crete population 5,000. The state capital, Lincoln, is 25 miles northeast of the campus. Served by public air and passenger rail service 25 miles from campus.

Library Collections: 86,221 volumes. Online catalog; 2,100 audiovisual materials. Current periodical subscriptions: 939 paper; 6,588 microform. Computer work stations available. Students have access to online information retrieval services and the Internet. Total 2004–05 budget for books and materials: $510,844.

Most important special holdings include United Church of Christ - Southeast Nebraska history; strength in English/American literature; Doane College Archives.

Buildings and Grounds: Campus area 300 acres.

Chief Executive Officer: Dr. Frederic D. Brown, President.

Undergraduates address admission inquiries to Dean of Admissions; graduate inquiries to Dean of Graduate School.

Grace University

1311 South Ninth Street
Omaha, Nebraska 68108-3629

Tel: (402) 449-2831   **E-mail:** admissions@graceu.edu
Fax: (402) 341-9587   **Internet:** www.graceu.edu

Institution Description: Grace University, formerly known as Grace College of the Bible, is a coeducational, evangelical, and interdenominational college. *Enrollment:* 540. *Degrees awarded:* Associate, baccalaureate, master's.

Accreditation: *Regional:* NCA. *National:* ABHE.

History: Established 1943.

Institutional Structure: *Governing board:* Board of Directors. 15 directors from U.S. and Canada. *Composition of institution:* President, vice presidents overseeing academic affairs, public relations, business affairs, and student affairs. Full-time instructional faculty 26.

Calendar: Semesters. Academic year Aug. to May. Summer session of 2 terms from May to June.

Characteristics of Freshmen: 20% of applicants admitted. 20% of applicants admitted and enrolled.

2% (7 students) submitted SAT scores; 69% (64 students) submitted ACT scores. *25th percentile:* SAT Verbal 540, SAT Math 460; ACT Composite 19, ACT English 19, ACT Math 17. *75th percentile:* SAT Verbal 580, SAT Math 560; ACT Composite 26, ACT English 27, ACT Math 26.

68% of freshmen from Nebraska. Freshmen from 27 states and 5 foreign countries.

Admission: Rolling admissions plan. *Requirements:* High school graduation with college preparatory courses recommended; Christian character verified by references. *Entrance tests:* ACT.

CLEP exams accepted in certain subjects; college credit allowed for advanced placement program.

Degree Requirements: *For all associate degrees:* 63 to 90 hours. *For all baccalaureate degrees:* 124 to 167 hours; requirements in Bible, general education, and professional areas; character, doctrine, and Christian ministry are further requirements.

Distinctive Educational Programs: Professional church ministries, Christian camping, Christian counseling. International studies; urban ministries.

Degrees Conferred: 21 *associate;* 71 *baccalaureate:* business /marketing 18; computer and information sciences 1; education 19; health professions 1; liberal arts/general studies 9; psychology 9; social sciences and history 14. 14 *master's:* philosophy/religion/theology 8; psychology 6.

Fees and Other Expenses: *Full-time tuition per academic year 2004–05:* $11,100 undergraduate, $10,500 graduate. *Room and board per academic year:* $3,850.

Financial Aid: Aid from institutionally generated funds is provided on the basis of academic merit, financial need, other considerations.

Financial aid to full-time, first-time undergraduate students: need-based scholarships/grants totaling $1,189,819, self-help $1,832,723, parent loans $367,485, tuition waivers $65,866; non-need-based scholarships/grants totaling $143,546, self-help $262,764,parent loans $242,678, tuition waivers $26,713. *Graduate aid:* 59 students received $698,349 in federal and state-funded loans; 5 students received $14,130 for college-assigned jobs.

Departments and Teaching Staff: Christian education *professors* 0, *associate professors* 1, *assistant professors* 0, *instructors* 0, *part-time teachers* 2; general education 2, 2, 0, 0, 4; pastoral ministries 0, 1, 0, 0, 0; cross-cultural studies 0, 0, 1, 0, 0; music 0, 0, 2, 0, 5; communications 0, 0, 1, 0, 1; management 0, 1, 0, 0, 5; counseling 0, 1, 1, 0, 2; bible 1, 1, 0, 1, 4.

Total instructional faculty: 23. Student-to-faculty ratio: 14:1. Degrees held by full-time faculty: doctorate 55%, master's 91%. 55% hold terminal degrees.

Enrollment: Total enrollment 540. Undergraduate full-time 144 men / 196 women, part-time 38m / 62w; graduate full-time 8m / 29w, part-time 33m / 30w.

Characteristics of Student Body: *Ethnic/racial makeup:* number of Black non-Hispanic: 28; American Indian or Alaska Native: 7; Asian or Pacific Islander: 1; Hispanic: 6; White non-Hispanic: 496; unknown: 2.

International Students: No programs available to aid students whose native language is not English. Some financial aid specifically designated for qualifying international students.

Student Life: On-campus residence halls. *Intercollegiate athletics:* men only: basketball, soccer; women only: volleyball.

Publications: *Grace Tidings*, published quarterly.

Library Collections: 57,000 volumes. Online catalog. Current serial subscriptions: 230 paper; 3,300 via electronic access. 2,980 audiovisual materials. Students have access to online information retrieval services and the Internet.

Most important special holdings include teacher education resources; Biblical studies materials.

Buildings and Grounds: Campus located in residential area of Omaha.

Chief Executive Officer: James E. Eckman, President.

Address admission inquiries to Director of Admissions.

Hastings College

710 North Turner Avenue
Hastings, Nebraska 68901-7621

Tel: (402) 463-2402   **E-mail:** admissions@hastings.edu
Fax: (402) 461-7490   **Internet:** www.hastings.edu

Institution Description: Hastings College is a private, nonprofit college affiliated with the Presbyterian Church (USA). *Enrollment:* 1,153. *Degrees awarded:* Baccalaureate, master's.

Member of the consortia Association of Nebraska Interterm Colleges and NETCHE, Inc.

Accreditation: *Regional:* NCA. *Professional:* music, teacher education

History: Established, incorporated, and offered first instruction at postsecondary level 1882; first degree (baccalaureate) awarded 1886. *See* Frank E. Weyer, *Hastings College: 75 Years in Retrospect 1882–1957* (Hastings, NE: Hastings College Anniversary Committee, 1957) for further information.

Institutional Structure: *Governing board:* Board of Trustees. Extrainstitutional representation: 33 trustees. *Composition of institution:* Administrators 20 men / 15 women. Academic affairs headed by dean of the college. Management/business/finances directed by treasurer. Full-time instructional faculty 81. Academic governance body, the Faculty Senate, meets monthly during the academic year.

Calendar: Semesters (4-1-4 plan). Academic year Aug. to May. Freshmen admitted Aug., Jan., Feb., June. Degrees conferred and formal commencement May. Summer session of 1 term from early June to mid-July.

Characteristics of Freshmen: 80% of applicants admitted. 25% of admitted students enrolled.

8% (27 students) submitted SAT scores; 95% (325 students) submitted ACT scores. *25th percentile:* SAT Verbal 460, SAT Math 490; ACT Composite 20, ACT English 20, ACT Math 20. *75th percentile:* SAT Verbal 600, SAT Math 590; ACT Composite 26, ACT English 26, ACT Math 27.

61% of entering freshmen expected to graduate within 5 years. 80% freshmen from Nebraska. Freshmen from 10 states and 5 foreign countries.

Admission: Rolling admissions plan. For fall acceptance, apply as early as June 1 of junior year of secondary school, but not later than Aug. 1 of year of enrollment. *Requirements:* Either 9 secondary school units which must include 4 English, 2 mathematics, 2 social studies, and 1 laboratory science; or GED. Counselor's report and 2 units in a foreign language recommended. Lowest acceptable secondary school class standing 50th percentile. *Entrance tests:* College Board SAT or ACT composite. *For transfer students:* 2.0 minimum GPA; from 4-year institution 97 hours maximum transfer credit; from 2-year institution 70 hours; correspondence/extension students 20 hours.

College credit and advanced placement for postsecondary-level work completed in secondary school and for extrainstitutional learning (life experience) on basis of faculty assessment. Advanced placement on basis of personal interviews.

Tutoring available. Developmental courses offered during regular academic year; credit given.

Degree Requirements: 127 credit hours; 2.0 GPA; final 2 terms in residence; 2 hours physical activity; distribution requirements.

Fulfillment of some degree requirements and exemption from some beginning courses possible by passing College Board CLEP and other achievement examinations. *Grading system:* A–F; pass-fail; withdraw (carries time limit and deadline after which pass-fail is appended to withdraw).

Distinctive Educational Programs: Work-experience programs. Evening classes. Dual-degree agreements in engineering with Columbia University (NY), Georgia Institute of Technology, and Washington University (MO). Special facilities for using telecommunications in the classroom. Interdisciplinary programs in communication arts, health promotion management, human services administration, information science. Facilities and programs for independent research, individual majors, tutorials, and contract majors. International exchange agreements with University of Muenster (Germany); Letterkenny Institute of Technology (Ireland); University of Leicester (England); Pyatigorsk Federal Linguistics University (Russia); University of Salamanca (Spain).

Degrees Conferred: 259 *baccalaureate:* biological/life sciences 21; business/marketing 23; communications 20; computer and information sciences 7; education 47; English 12; foreign language 5; health professions 13; interdisciplinary studies 10; mathematics 1; parks and recreation 5; philosophy/religion 2; physical sciences 5; psychology 27; social sciences and history 35; visual and performing arts 16. 17 *master's:* education 17.

Fees and Other Expenses: *Full-time tuition per academic year 2004–05:* $15,640. *Required fees:* $650. *Room per academic year:* $2,034. *Board per academic year:* $2,726.

Financial Aid: Aid from institutionally generated funds is provided on the basis of academic merit, financial need, athletic ability, other criteria.

Financial aid to full-time, first-time undergraduate students: need-based scholarships/grants totaling $3,406,735, self-help $3,160,793, parent loans $856,411, tuition waivers $110,172, athletic awards $1,608,579; non-need-based scholarships/grants totaling $2,098,121, self-help $1,158,039, parent loans $1,205,583, tuition waivers $286,456, athletic awards $631,031.

Departments and Teaching Staff: *Professors* 27, *associate professors* 20, *assistant professors* 21, *instructors* 9, *part-time faculty* 30.

Total instructional faculty: 115 (full-time 81, part-time 34; women 43, men 72; member of minority group 1). Total faculty with doctorate, first-professional, or other terminal degree: 66. Student-to-faculty ratio: 13:1. Degrees held by full-time faculty: doctorate 68.1%, master's 30.4%, baccalaureate 1.4%. *Faculty development:* 4 faculty members awarded sabbaticals 2004–05.

Enrollment: Total enrollment 1,253. Undergraduate full-time 354 men / 536 women, part-time 3m / 12w; graduate full-time 11m / 19w, part-time 7m / 11w.

Characteristics of Student Body: *Ethnic/racial makeup:* number of Black non-Hispanic: 29; American Indian or Alaska Native: 2; Asian or Pacific Islander: 10; Hispanic: 17; White non-Hispanic: 1,018; unknown: 6. *Age distribution:* number under 18: 2; 18–19: 484; 20–21: 426; 22–24: 144; 25–29: 19; 30–34: 8; 35–39: 1; 40–49: 5; 50–64: 2.

International Students: 11 nonresident aliens enrolled fall 2004. 7 students from Europe, 3 Latin America, 1 Canada. No programs available to aid students whose native language is not English. No financial aid specifically designated for international students.

Student Life: On-campus residence halls house 67% of student body. Residence halls for men only constitute 30% of such space, for women only 30%, for both genders 30%. *Intercollegiate athletics:* men: basketball, cross country, football, golf, tennis, track; women: basketball, cross country, golf, tennis, track, volleyball. *Special regulations:* Cars permitted without restrictions. Residence hall visitation from 10am to midnight Sun.–Thurs., 10am to 2am Fri. and Sat. *Special services:* Learning Resources Center, counseling services, medical services. *Student publications: Bronco,* an annual publication; *Collegian,* a weekly newspaper; *Spectrum,* an annual literary magazine; online news at HCworldnews.com. *Surrounding community:* Hastings population 24,000. Lincoln, 100 miles from campus, is nearest metropolitan area. Served by airport 30 miles from campus; passenger rail service 1 mile from campus.

Library Collections: 125,000 volumes. 100,497 microforms; 1,341 audiovisual materials; 636 current periodical subscriptions. Online catalog. Computer work stations available. Students have access to online information retrieval services and the Internet.

Most important special holdings include Brown Western Americana Collection; Hastings College Archives; Hymnal Collection; Holcomb Lewis & Clark Collection.

Buildings and Grounds: Campus area 109 acres. *New buildings:* Sachtleben Observatory 2000; Fleharty Educational Center/Farrell Arena 2002; Barrett Alumni Center 2002; Bronco Village Apartments 2004.

Chief Executive Officer: Dr. Phillip Dudley, Jr., President.

Address admission inquiries to Mary Mollliconi, Director of Admissions.

Midland Lutheran College

900 North Clarkson
Fremont, Nebraska 68025

Tel: (402) 721-5480   **E-mail:** admissions@mlc.edu
Fax: (402) 721-0250   **Internet:** www.mlc.edu

Institution Description: Midland Lutheran College is a private college affiliated with the Nebraska and Rocky Mountain Synods of the Evangelical Lutheran Church in America. *Enrollment:* 947. *Degrees awarded:* Associate, baccalaureate.

Member of consortium NETCHE, Inc. (formerly Nebraska Educational Television Council for Higher Education).

Accreditation: *Regional:* NCA. *Professional:* nursing, teacher education

History: Established and chartered in Atchison, Kansas, as Midland College and offered first instruction at postsecondary level 1887; awarded first degree (baccalaureate) 1891; merged with Fremont College (established 1888) and moved to present location 1919; merged with Luther Junior College (chartered 1883) and adopted present name 1962.

Institutional Structure: *Governing board:* Board of Trustees. Representation: 38 trustees, including 18 elected by the church, 16 members at large, 4 alumni. 2 ex officio. All voting. *Composition of institution:* Administrators 6 men. Academic affairs headed by vice president for academic affairs and academic dean. Management/business/finances directed by vice president for finance and treasurer. Full-time instructional faculty 55. Academic governance body, the faculty, meets an average of 10 times per year.

Calendar: Semesters (4-1-4 plan). Academic year Sept. to May. Freshmen admitted Sept., Jan., Feb., June. Degrees conferred and formal commencement May. Summer session of 3 terms from May Aug. One-month interterm in January.

Characteristics of Freshmen: 950 applicants (422 men, 538 women). 83.7% of applicants admitted. 31.4% of admitted students enrolled full-time.

7% (17 students) submitted SAT scores; 93% (242 students) submitted ACT scores. *25th percentile:* SAT I Verbal 380, SAT I Math 340; ACT Composite 19, ACT English 18, ACT Math 18. *75th percentile:* SAT I Verbal 490, SAT I Math 560; ACT Composite 24, ACT English 24, ACT Math 24.

55% of freshmen expected to graduate within 5 years. 77% of freshmen from Nebraska. Freshmen from 15 states and 3 foreign countries.

Admission: Rolling admissions plan. For fall acceptance, apply as early as junior year of secondary school, but not later than Sept. 1 of year of enrollment. *Requirements:* Either graduation from secondary school or GED. Recommend 3 units in English, 2 mathematics. *Entrance tests:* ACT composite. *For transfer students:* 2.0 minimum GPA; from 4-year accredited institution 96 hours maximum transfer credit; from 2-year accredited institution 64 hours; correspondence/extension students 32 hours.

College credit and advanced placement for postsecondary-level work completed in secondary school and for extrainstitutional learning on basis of ACE *2006 Guide to the Evaluation of Educational Experiences in the Armed Services*; portfolio and faculty assessments; personal interviews.

Tutoring available. Developmental courses offered during regular academic year; credit given.

Degree Requirements: *For all associate degrees:* 64 credit hours. *For all baccalaureate degrees:* 128 credit hours. *For all degrees:* 2.25 GPA; 2 terms in residence; distribution requirements.

Fulfillment of some degree requirements and exemption from some beginning courses possible by passing departmental examinations, College Board CLEP, other standardized tests. *Grading system:* A–F; pass-fail; withdraw (deadline after which fail is appended to withdraw).

Distinctive Educational Programs: Internships. Evening classes. Interdisciplinary programs offered during interim. Preprofessional programs in 17 allied health fields, architecture, criminal justice, engineering, environmental studies, fisheries and wildlife biology, forestry, home economics, library science, mortuary science, music therapy, social work. Facilities and programs for independent research, including honors programs, individual majors, tutorials. African study program at Cuttington University College in Liberia; Latin American study program with Institute Allende of San Miguel de Allende in Guanajuato, Mexico. Study abroad in affiliation with Central College, Pella, Iowa program.

ROTC: Army available in cooperation with Creighton University.

Degrees Conferred: 184 *baccalaureate.* Bachelor's degrees awarded in top five disciplines:business, management, marketing, and related support services 66; education 29; health professions and related clinical sciences 20; social sciences and history 15; parks and recreation 11.

Fees and Other Expenses: *Full-time tuition per academic year 2004–05:* $17,210. *Room and board per academic year:* $4,450. *Books and supplies:* $600.

Financial Aid: Aid from institutionally generated funds is provided on the basis of academic merit, financial need, athletic ability, other criteria. Institution has a Program Participation Agreement with the U.S. Department of Education for eligible students to receive Pell Grants and, depending upon the agreement, other federal aid.

Financial aid to full-time, first-time undergraduate students: 53% received federal grants averaging $2,871; 28% state/local grants averaging $948; 99 % institutional grants averaging $7,844; 86 % received loans averaging $4,262.

Departments and Teaching Staff: Art *professors* 1, *associate professors* 0, *assistant professors* 1, *instructors* 0, *part-time teachers* 0; biology 1, 0, 1, 0, 0; business/economics 1, 0, 5, 0, 2; chemistry 1, 0, 1, 0, 1; education 0, 0, 3, 0, 2; English 1, 0, 3, 0, 1; history 0, 0, 1, 0, 1; journalism 0, 0, 1, 2, 0; mathematics/computer science 0, 1, 3, 0, 0; music 2, 0, 1, 0, 6; nursing 1, 0, 8, 0, 3; philosophy/religion 1, 0, 2, 0, 0; physical education 0, 0, 5, 2, 20; psychology 2, 0, 0, 0, 0; sociology 0, 0, 1, 1, 1; speech/theatre 0, 0, 1, 1, 0.

Total instructional faculty: 62.3 FTE. Student-to-faculty ratio: 16:1. Degrees held by full-time faculty: doctorate 50%, master's 50%. 50% hold terminal degrees.

Enrollment: Total enrollment 947 (40.5% men, 59.5% women).

Characteristics of Student Body: *Ethnic/racial makeup:* number of Black non-Hispanic: 2.7%; American Indian or Alaska Native: .1%; Asian or Pacific Islander: .7%; Hispanic: .6%; White non-Hispanic: 86.9%; unknown: 8.9%. *Age distribution:* 17–21: 73%; 22–24: 12%; 25–29: 3%; 30–34: 2%; 35–39: 3%; 40–49: 6%; 50–59: 1%.

International Students: Programs available to aid students whose native language is not English: social, cultural, financial. Financial aid specifically designated for international students: variable number of scholarships available annually for undergraduate students.

Student Life: On-campus residence halls house 60% of student body. Residence halls for men constitute 41% of such space, for women 59%, for both sexes 34%. *Intercollegiate athletics:* men only: basketball, cross-country, football, tennis, track; women only: basketball, cross-country, tennis, track, volleyball. *Special regulations:* Cars permitted without restrictions. Residence hall visitation from 11:30am to 2am Mon.–Sun. *Special services:* Learning Resources Center, medical services, career resource center. *Student publications: Bits of Flint,* an annual literary magazine; *The Midland,* a weekly newspaper; *The Warrior,* a yearbook. *Surrounding community:* Fremont population 24,000. Omaha, 35 miles from campus, is nearest metropolitan area. Served by mass transit bus system; airport 5 miles from campus; passenger rail service 2 miles from campus.

Library Collections: 112,000 volumes. 6,100 government documents; 12,500 microforms; 5,200 audiovisual materials; 900 current periodical subscriptions. Online catalog. Students have access to online information retrieval services and the Internet.

Most important special holdings include the Library of Biblical Literature (2,000 volumes including various versions of the Bible, works on biblical interpretation and on the Bible as literature); Archives of Nebraska Synod of Lutheran Church in America.

Buildings and Grounds: Campus area 30 acres.

Chief Executive Officer: Dr. Steven E. Titus, President.

Address admission inquiries to Douglas G. Watson, Vice President for Enrollment Services.

Nebraska Christian College

1800 Syracuse Avenue
Norfolk, Nebraska 68701-2458
Tel: (402) 379-5000   **E-mail:** admissions@nechristian.edu
Fax: (402) 379-5100   **Internet:** www.nechristian.edu

Institution Description: Nebraska Christian College is an independent, four-year, coeducational institution affiliated with the Christian Church/Churches of Christ. *Degrees offered:* Baccalaureate. *Enrollment:* 155.

Accreditation: *National:* ABHE.

History: The college was founded in 1944.

Calendar: Semesters. Academic year Aug. to May.

Characteristics of Freshmen: Average secondary school rank of freshmen men 39.4 percentile, women 56.9 percentile, class 45.1 percentile. Mean ACT composite score men 19.6, women 21.3, class 20.7.

28% of freshmen from Nebraska. Freshmen from 16 states and 1 foreign country.

Admission: *Requirements:* Essay; high school transcript; two recommendations; ACT; transcripts of any college work must also be submitted.

Degree Requirements: *For all associate degrees:* 64 credit hours. *For all undergraduate degrees:* 130 credit hours; bachelor of theology degree requires completion of 160 credit hours. *Grading system:* A–F.

Degrees Conferred: 19 *associate;* 21 *baccalaureate:* theology/ministerial studies.

Fees and Other Expenses: *Full-time tuition per academic year 2004–05:* $6,144. *Room and board per academic year:* $4,600. *Books and supplies:* $750.

Financial Aid: Aid from institutionally generated funds is provided on the basis of academic merit, financial need. Institution has a Program Participation Agreement with the U.S. Department of Education for eligible students to receive Pell Grants and, depending upon the agreement, other federal aid.

Financial aid to full-time, first-time undergraduate students: 49% received federal grants averaging $2,614; 19% state/local grants; 98% institutional grants averaging $1,678; 72% received loans averaging $2,991.

Departments and Teaching Staff: *Professors* 12, *part-time professors and instructors* 6.

Total instructional faculty: 18. Student-to-faculty ratio: 16:1. Degrees held by full-time faculty: doctorate 20%, master's 80%. 20% hold terminal degrees.

Enrollment: Total enrollment 155 (57.4% men, 42.6% women).

Characteristics of Student Body: *Ethnic/racial makeup:* number of Black non-Hispanic: .6%; American Indian or Alaska Native: .6%; Asian or Pacific Islander: 1.9%; Hispanic: 3.2%; White non-Hispanic: 91.6%; unknown: 1.9%.

International Students: No programs to aid students whose native language is not English. No financial aid specifically designated for international students.

Student Life: *Surrounding community:* Norfolk, population 22,000, is located in northeastern Nebraska, 100 miles northwest of Omaha.

Library Collections: 250,000 volumes including bound books, serial backfiles, electronic documents, and government documents not in separate collections. 150 serial subscriptions. Students have access to the Internet and online information retrieval services.

Chief Executive Officer: Richard Milliken, President.

Address admissions inquiries to Jason Epperson, Director of Admissions.

Nebraska Wesleyan University

5000 St. Paul Avenue
Lincoln, Nebraska 68504-2796
Tel: (402) 466-2237   **E-mail:** admissions@nebrwesleyan.edu
Fax: (402) 465-2565   **Internet:** www.nebrwesleyan.edu

Institution Description: Nebraska Wesleyan University is a private, liberal arts institution affiliated with the United Methodist Church. *Enrollment:* 1,953. *Degrees awarded:* Baccalaureate.

Accreditation: *Regional:* NCA. *Professional:* business, chemistry, music, nursing, social work, teacher education

History: Established through merger of 3 Methodist colleges and chartered 1887; offered first instruction at postsecondary level 1888; awarded first degree (baccalaureate) 1890.

Institutional Structure: *Governing board:* Board of Governors. Extrainstitutional representation: 25 members; institutional representation: president of the university, 2 faculty members, 2 students, the president of the Alumni Association, and the Bishop of the Nebraska Annual Conference of the United Methodist Church. *Composition of institution:* Academic affairs headed by provost. Enrollment and marketing headed by vice president for university enrollment and marketing. Business affairs directed by vice president for administration. Student affairs headed by vice president for student affairs; university advancement headed by vice president for university advancement. Full-time instructional faculty 92. Academic governance body, the faculty, meets an average of 8 times per year.

Calendar: Semesters. Academic year late Aug. to May. Freshmen admitted Aug., Jan., May. Degrees conferred and formal commencement May. Summer session of 4 terms from May to Aug.

Characteristics of Freshmen: 94.2% of applicants accepted. 32.5% of accepted applicants enrolled.

8% (33 students) submitted SAT scores; 99% (424 students) submitted ACT scores. *25th percentile:* ACT Composite 22, ACT English 20, ACT Math 21. *75th percentile:* ACT Composite 27, ACT English 27, ACT Math 27.

66% of freshmen expected to graduate within 5 years. 95.3% of freshmen from Nebraska. Freshmen from 10 states.

Admission: Rolling admissions plan. For fall acceptance, apply as early as Sept. of previous year, but not later than Aug. of year of enrollment. Early acceptance available. *Requirements:* Either graduation from accredited secondary school or GED. Lowest acceptable secondary school class standing 50th percentile. *Entrance tests:* Enhanced ACT composite (minimum score of 20). For foreign students TOEFL. *For transfer students:* 2.0 minimum GPA; from 4-year accredited institution and for correspondence/extension students maximum transfer credit limited only by residence requirement; from 2-year accredited institution 64 hours. Consideration will be given students with GPA below 2.0.

College credit and advanced placement for postsecondary-level work completed in secondary school. Tutoring available.

Degree Requirements: *For all baccalaureate degrees:* 126 credit hours (with at least 18 upper-level credits); GPA of 2.0 on a 4.0 scale; major of at least 30 credit hours; senior comprehensive; at least 30 credit hours in residence. All courses that satisfy major requirement must be completed with a C (2.0) grade or higher. General education curriculum of minimum of 39 credit hours; first-year seminary, composition, speech, literature, mathematics, physical education, global perspectives (including modern language), religious traditions, U.S. culture, fine arts, natural sciences, social sciences.

Fulfillment of some degree requirements and exemption from some beginning courses possible by passing departmental examinations, College Board CLEP, APP. *Grading system:* A–F; pass-fail; withdraw (carries time limit).

Distinctive Educational Programs: Work-experience programs. Evening classes. Dual-degree program in engineering with Columbia University (NY) and Washington University (MO). Special facilities for using telecommunications in the classroom. Interdisciplinary programs in biochemistry, biopsychology, business-psychology, business-sociology, global studies, music-theatre, political science-communication, information systems, biochemistry and molecular biology, international business/language, communication studies. Facilities for independent research, including honors programs, individual majors, tutorials, independent study. Student exchange program with Kansai University (Japan). Affiliation with Central College (IA) for a variety of overseas study programs. Off-campus study in the U.S. includes summer drama program at Brownville Village Theatre, inner-city teacher education internship in Kansas City (MO), Washington (DC) Semester at American University, United Nations semester through Drew University (NJ). *Other distinctive programs:* Art gallery management laboratory.

ROTC: Army, Air Force in cooperation with University of Nebraska (Lincoln campus).

Degrees Conferred: 359 *baccalaureate.* Bachelor's degrees awarded in top five disciplines: business, management, marketing, and related support services 64; biological and biomedical sciences 38, education 35; health professions and related clinical sciences 32; psychology 31.

Fees and Other Expenses: *Full-time tuition per academic year 2005–06:* $18,100. *Room and board per academic year:* $5,015. *Books and supplies:* $900.

Financial Aid: Aid from institutionally generated funds is provided on the basis of academic merit, financial need, and other considerations.

Financial aid to full-time, first-time undergraduate students: need-based scholarships/grants totaling $9,251,467, self-help $4,968,759, parent loans $1,284,584; non-need-based scholarships/grants totaling $2,097,215, self-help $1,188,842, parent loans $2,092,985.

Departments and Teaching Staff: *Total instructional faculty:* 190 (full-time 98, part-time 92; women 96, men 94; members of minority groups 6). Total faculty with doctorate, first-professional, or other terminal degree: 81. Student-to-faculty ratio: 14:1. Degrees held by full-time faculty: doctorate 77%, master's 21.70%, baccalaureate .01%. 81% hold terminal degrees.

Enrollment: Total enrollment 1,953. Undergraduate full-time 702 men / 884 women, part-time 66m / 145w; graduate full-time 4m / 3w, part-time 20m / 129w.

Characteristics of Student Body: *Ethnic/racial makeup (undergraduate):* number of Black non-Hispanic: 22; American Indian or Alaska Native: 6; Asian or Pacific Islander: 25; Hispanic: 29; White non-Hispanic: 1,676; unknown: 18.

International Students: 21 undergraduate nonresident aliens enrolled fall 2004: Programs available to aid students whose native language is not English: social, cultural. No financial aid specifically designated for international students.

Student Life: On-campus residence halls house 52% of student body. 42% of men join fraternities; 34% of women join sororities. *Athletics:* 25% of the student population participates in intercollegiate athletics. Men's sports: baseball, basketball, cross-country, football, golf, soccer, tennis, indoor and outdoor track. Women's sports: basketball, cross-country, golf, soccer, softball, tennis, volleyball, indoor and outdoor track. 60% of the student body participates in intramural sports. *Special services:* Medical and counseling services; ADA accommodations; health and fitness center. *Student publications: The Plainsman,* a yearbook; *The Reveille,* a weekly newspaper; *Flintlock,* a literary magazine; *The Coyote* (arts, entertainment). *Surrounding community:* Lincoln population 225,000. Omaha, 50 miles from campus, is nearest metropolitan area. Served by mass transit bus system; airport 10 miles from campus; passenger rail service 7 miles from campus.

Library Collections: 195,000 volumes including bound books, serial backfiles, electronic documents, and government documents not in separate collections. Online catalog. Current serial subscriptions: 722 paper, 10 microform, 1,585 electronic. 3,934 recordings; 1,119 compact discs; 18 CD-ROMs. 85 computer work stations campus-wide. Students have access to the Internet and online information retrieval services.

Most important special collection is the Mignon Eberhart Collection; Nebraska Wesleyan University Archives.

Buildings and Grounds: Campus area 50 acres.

Chief Executive Officer: Dr. Jeanie Watson, President.

Address admission inquiries to Patty F. Karthauser, Vice President for University Enrollment and Marketing.

Peru State College

P.O. Box 10
Peru, Nebraska 68421-9751
Tel: (402) 872-3815   **E-mail:** admissions@peru.edu
Fax: (402) 872-2296   **Internet:** www.peru.edu

Institution Description: Peru State College is a state institution. *Enrollment:* 1,683. *Degrees awarded:* Baccalaureate, master's.

Academic offering subject to approval by statewide coordinating bodies. Budget subject to approval by Board of Trustees of Nebraska State Colleges and by state legislature. Member of NETCHE, Inc. (formerly Nebraska Educational Television Council for Higher Education).

Accreditation: *Regional:* NCA. *Professional:* teacher education

History: Established as Mount Vernon College 1865; chartered as Nebraska State Normal College and offered first instruction at postsecondary level 1867; awarded first degree (baccalaureate) and changed name to Nebraska State Teachers College - Peru 1921; changed name to Peru State Teachers College 1949; adopted present name 1963. *See* Ernest Longfellow, *The Normal on the Hill* (Grand Island, NE: Augustine Co., 1967) for further information.

Institutional Structure: *Governing board:* Board of Trustees of Nebraska State Colleges. Representation: Commissioner of Education, 6 trustees and 4 students (appointed by governor); students nonvoting. *Composition of institution:* Administrators 18 men / 6 women. Academic affairs headed by vice president. Management/business/finances directed by vice president of administration and finance. Full-time instructional faculty 29 men / 11 women. Academic governance body, Faculty Senate, meets an average of 39 times per year. *Faculty representation:* Faculty served by collective bargaining agent, Nebraska State College Education Association, affiliated with NEA.

Calendar: Semesters. Academic year late Aug. to mid-May. Freshmen admitted Aug., Jan., June, July. Degrees conferred May, Aug., Dec. Formal commencement May. Summer session from early June to early Aug.

Characteristics of Freshmen: 67% of applicants accepted. 40% of accepted applicants enrolled.

93 (175 students) submitted ACT scores. *25th percentile:* ACT Composite 17. *75th percentile:* ACT Composite 22.

35% of entering freshmen expected to graduate within 5 years. 78% of freshmen from Nebraska. Freshmen from 16 states.

Admission: Open admissions plan. *Requirements:* Either graduation from accredited secondary school or GED. Recommend 16 college preparatory units. Home schooled students with an 18 ACT accepted. *Entrance tests:* ACT composite or College Board SAT. *For transfer students:* Must be in good standing with previous institution; transfer credits that apply to curriculum will be accepted from 2- and 4-year accredited institutions.

College credit and advanced placement for postsecondary-level work completed in secondary school. College credit for extrainstitutional learning on basis of ACE *2006 Guide to the Evaluation of Educational Experiences in the Armed Services.*

Tutoring available. Developmental courses offered during regular academic year; credit given.

Degree Requirements: *For all baccalaureate degrees:* 125 credit hours. *For all undergraduate degrees:* 2.0 GPA on 4.0 scale; 30 hours in residence; 1 hour physical education; distribution requirements for all bachelor degree candidates.

Fulfillment of some degree requirements and exemption from some beginning courses possible by passing departmental examinations, College Board CLEP. *Grading system:* 4.0-point scale; withdraw; incomplete (carries time limit).

Distinctive Educational Programs: Honors program (must meet specific entrance criteria). Internships. Independent study. Flexible meeting places and schedules, including off-campus centers at varying locations. Evening classes on- and off-campus. Cooperative baccalaureate in medical technology with approved schools. External degree programs in business administration. Preprofessional programs in agriculture, dentistry, engineering, forestry, law, medicine, mortuary science, nursing, optometry, pharmacy, physical therapy, x-ray technology, veterinary science. Agricultural transfer program with University of Nebraska - Lincoln. Master of science in education program with emphasis on rural education.

Degrees Conferred: 330 *baccalaureate:* business/marketing 127; computer and information sciences 4; education 155; natural resources/environmental science 13; protective services/public administration 12; psychology 19. 55 *master's:* education 55.

Fees and Other Expenses: *Full-time tuition per academic year 2005–06:* Contact the college for current resident/nonresident undergraduate/graduate tuition, housing costs, and other fees.

Financial Aid: Aid from institutionally generated funds is provided on the basis of academic merit, financial need, athletic ability, other criteria.

Financial aid to full-time, first-time undergraduate students: need-based scholarships/grants totaling $1,368,366, self-help $11,842,423, tuition waivers $19,675; non-need-based scholarships/grants totaling $1,273,630, self-help $1,409,664, parent loans $142,693, tuition waivers $370,576, athletic awards $217,691. *Graduate aid:* 74 students received $305,969 in federal and state-funded loans (ranging from $500 to $10,500).

Departments and Teaching Staff: *Professors* 17, *associate professors* 4, *assistant professors* 16, *instructors* 3, *part-time faculty* 61.

Total instructional faculty: 101. Student-to-faculty ratio: 20:1. Total faculty with doctorate, first-professional, or other terminal degree: 34. Degrees held by full-time faculty: doctorate 51%, master's 49%. 51% hold terminal degrees.

Enrollment: Total enrollment 1,683. Undergraduate full-time 435 men / 547 women; part-time 253m / 258w; graduate full-time 1m / 7w, part-time 55m / 127w.

Characteristics of Student Body: *Ethnic/racial makeup:* number of Black non-Hispanic: 61; American Indian or Alaska Native: 7; Hispanic: 29; White non-Hispanic: 1,292; unknown: 91. *Age distribution:* number under 18: 133; 18–19: 324; 20–21: 274; 22–24: 267; 25–29: 148; 30–34: 90; 35–39: 89; 40–49: 133; 50–64: 25; 65 and over: 3. 25% of student body attend summer sessions.

International Students: 9 nonresident aliens enrolled fall 2004. 3 students from Europe, 1 Asia, 1 Africa, 4 Canada. No programs available to aid students whose native language is not English. No financial aid specifically designated for international students.

Student Life: On-campus residence halls house 33% of student body. Residence halls for men only constitute 24% of such space, for women only 25%, for both sexes 51%. *Intercollegiate athletics:* men only: baseball, basketball, cross-country, football, volleyball; women only: basketball, cross-country, golf, softball, volleyball. *Special regulations:* Registered cars permitted without restrictions. Residence hall quiet hours from 9pm to 9am. Men's residence hall visitation from noon to midnight Sun.–Thurs., noon to 2am Fri. and Sat. Women's residence hall visitation from noon to 10pm Sun.–Thurs., noon to 1am Fri. and Sat. *Special services:* Communication Skills Center, medical services, human performance laboratory. *Student publications: Perusal,* a weekly online newsletter; *Student Support Services,* a newsletter published twice each semester; *Redline,* a weekly publication; *Peru State Times,* a student newspaper published 5 times per semester; *The Three-point Club,* booster newsletter for PSC women's basketball and golf, published monthly September to May. *Surrounding commu-*

nity: Peru population 1,000. Nearby metropolitan areas include Kansas City (MO), 120 miles from campus; Omaha (NE), 65 miles; Lincoln (NE), 75 miles.

Library Collections: 111,852 volumes. Online catalog. Current periodical subscriptions; 240 paper; 16 microform; 5,697 via electronic access. 7,947 recordings; 224 compact discs. 45 computer work stations. Students have access to online information retrieval services and the Internet. Total 2004–05 budget for books and materials: $72,000.

Most important special holdings include collections on Southeastern Nebraska; Marion Marsh Brown Collection.

Buildings and Grounds: Campus area 103 acres. *New buildings:* Hoyt Science Building completed 2002; Campus Services Building 2002; Library completed 2003; Academic Resource Center 2004.

Chief Executive Officer: Dr. Ben Johnson, President.

Address admission inquiries to Janelle Moran, Director of Admissions.

Union College

3800 South 48th Street
Lincoln, Nebraska 68506
Tel: (402) 486-2331   **E-mail:** ucenroll@ucollege.edu
Fax: (402) 486-2895   **Internet:** www.ucollege.edu

Institution Description: Union College is a private liberal arts college affiliated with the Seventh-day Adventist Church. *Enrollment: 936. Degrees awarded:* Associate, baccalaureate.

Member of the consortia Adventist Colleges Abroad (ACA).

Accreditation: *Regional:* NCA. *Professional:* nursing, social work, teacher education

History: Established and offered first instruction at postsecondary level 1891; awarded first degree (baccalaureate) 1894. *See* Everett Dick, *Union, College of the Golden Chords* (Lincoln: Union College Press, 1967) for further information.

Institutional Structure: *Governing board:* Board of Trustees. Representation: 39 trustees, including president of the college. All voting. *Composition of institution:* Academic affairs headed by vice president for academic affairs. Management/business/finances directed by vice president for finance. Full-time instructional faculty 47. Academic governance body, Academic Council, meets an average of 20 times per year.

Calendar: Semesters. Academic year mid-Aug. to mid-May. Freshmen admitted Aug., Jan., May. Degrees conferred Aug., Dec., May. formal commencement May. Summer session of 4 terms from early May to early July.

Characteristics of Freshmen: 622 applicants (274 men, 348 women). 51% of applicants admitted. 58% of admitted students enrolled full-time.

92% (175 students) submitted ACT scores. *25th percentile*: ACT Composite 20, ACT English 19, ACT Math 17. *75th percentile*: ACT Composite 26, ACT English 26, ACT Math 26.

37% of entering freshmen expected to graduate within 5 years. 24% of freshmen from Nebraska. Freshmen from 35 states and 29 foreign countries.

Admission: Rolling admissions plan. For fall acceptance, apply as early as 1 year prior to enrollment, but not later than 2 weeks after beginning of semester. Early acceptance available. *Requirements:* Either graduation from accredited secondary school with 3 units in English, 1 history, 1 mathematics, 1 natural science (with laboratory), 3 academic electives; or GED. Minimum 2.0 GPA. *Entrance tests:* ACT composite. For foreign students TOEFL or other standardized English language test. *For transfer students:* 2.0 minimum GPA; from 4-year accredited institution 94 hours maximum transfer credit. Transfer credit accepted from 2-year accredited institution and correspondence/extension programs.

College credit and advanced placement for postsecondary-level work completed in secondary school, for student missionary work abroad, and for Missionary Volunteer Taskforce work in the United States. Tutoring available. Developmental courses offered during regular academic year; some credit given.

Degree Requirements: *For all associate degrees:* 62 credit hours; 24 hours in residence. *For all baccalaureate degrees:* 128 credit hours; 30 hours in residence; 4 hours physical education. ACT College Outcome Measures Program examination required for baccalaureate degree. Advanced placement credit is also accepted along with CLEP credit.

Fulfillment of some degree requirements and exemption from some beginning courses possible by passing institutional examination, College Board CLEP. *Grading system:* A–F; credit-no credit; withdraw (carries time limit).

Distinctive Educational Programs: Off-campus centers include Canadian Union College in Alberta. Dual-degree program in dental hygiene, occupational therapy, physical therapy, public health, respiratory therapy, and radiologic technology with Loma Linda University (CA). Cooperative programs with Nebraska Wesleyan University, Southeast Community College-Lincoln campus, and the

University of Nebraska-Lincoln. Individual majors. Study abroad through consortium (Austria, France, Germany, Spain).

Degrees Conferred: 16 *associate;* 164 *baccalaureate.* Bachelor's degrees awarded in top five disciplines: health professions and related clinical sciences 39; education 23; business, management, marketing, and related support services 16; visual and performing arts 12; psychology 11.

Fees and Other Expenses: *Full-time tuition per academic year 2004–05:* $13,380. *Room and board per academic year:* $3,774. *Books and supplies:* $900.

Financial Aid: Union College offers a direct lending program. Aid from institutionally generated funds is provided on the basis of academic merit, financial need. Institution has a Program Participation Agreement with the U.S. Department of Education for eligible students to receive Pell Grants and, depending upon the agreement, other federal aid.

Financial aid to full-time, first-time undergraduate students: 30% received federal grants averaging $2,965; 2% state/local grants; 96% institutional grants averaging $4,383; 56% received loans averaging $5,800.

Departments and Teaching Staff: *Professors* 18; *associate professors* 21; *assistant professors* 5, *part-time teachers* 42.

Total instructional faculty: 87. Degrees held by full-time faculty: 98% hold terminal degrees.

Enrollment: Total enrollment 936. Undergraduate 912 (44.5% men, 56.5% women).

Characteristics of Student Body: *Ethnic/racial makeup:* number of Black non-Hispanic: 2.5%; American Indian or Alaska Native: 1.1%; Asian or Pacific Islander: 2.4%; Hispanic: 5.8%; White non-Hispanic: 67.5%; unknown: 10.6%.

International Students: Programs available to aid students whose native language is not English: social, cultural. English as a Second Language Program. No financial aid specifically designated for international students.

Student Life: On-campus residence halls house 76% of student body. Dormitories for men only constitute 55% of such space, for women only 45%. Off-campus housing available for married students. *Special regulations:* Registered cars permitted for all but first semester freshmen, who may use them only for weekend home leave. Students must adhere to required standards of dress and appearance as indicated in the student handbook. Curfews. Quiet hours. Residence hall visitation (limited to public areas) from 6am to 10pm. *Special services:* Learning Resources Center, medical services. *Student publications: Clocktower,* a biweekly newspaper; *Golden Cords,* a yearbook. *Surrounding community:* Lincoln population 250,000. Omaha, 60 miles from campus, is nearest metropolitan area. Served by mass transit bus system; airport 10 miles from campus; passenger rail service 6 miles from campus.

Library Collections: 130,000 volumes. 1,025 microform titles; 3,100 audiovisual materials; 515 current periodical subscriptions. Students have access to online information retrieval services and the Internet.

Most important special holdings include Union College Archives; Seventh-Day Adventist history and theology; frontier history monographs.

Buildings and Grounds: Campus area 40 acres.

Chief Executive Officer: Dr. David E. Smith, President.

Address admission inquiries to Rob Weaver, Vice President of Enrollment Services.

University of Nebraska - Lincoln

Fourteenth and R Streets
Lincoln, Nebraska 68588-0419
Tel: (402) 472-7211   **E-mail:** nuhusker@unl.edu
Fax: (402) 472-6670   **Internet:** www.unl.edu

Institution Description: *Enrollment:* 21,792. *Degrees awarded:* Associate, baccalaureate, first-professional (law), master's, doctorate. Certificates also awarded.

Budget subject to approval by state governing boards. Member of the consortia NETCHE, Inc.

Accreditation: *Regional:* NCA. *Professional:* accounting, architecture, art, audiology, business, construction education, counseling psychology, dental hygiene, dentistry, dietetics, orthodontic and dentofacial orthopedics, engineering, family and consumer science, interior design, journalism, law, marriage and family therapy, music, oral and maxillofacial surgery, pediatric dentistry, periodontics, planning, psychology internship, school psychology, speech-language pathology, teacher education, theatre

History: Established and chartered 1869; offered first instruction at postsecondary level 1871; awarded first degree (baccalaureate) 1873. *See* R.N. Manley, *Centennial History of the University of Nebraska, Part I, Frontier University 1869-1919* (Lincoln: University of Nebraska Press, 1969) and R.M. Sawyer,

Centennial History of the University of Nebraska, Part II, The Modern History 1920–1969 (Lincoln: Centennial Press, 1973) for further information.

Institutional Structure: *Composition of institution:* Administrators 94 men / 57 women. Academic affairs headed by senior vice chancellor for academic affairs. Management/business/finances directed by vice chancellor for business and finance. Institute of Agriculture and natural Resources directed by vice chancellor. Research and Graduate Studies directed by vice chancellor. Full-time instructional faculty 1,159. Academic governance body, Faculty Senate, meets an average of 9 times per year.

Calendar: Semesters. Academic year Aug. to May. Freshmen admitted Aug., Jan., May, June, July. Degrees conferred May, Aug., Dec. Formal commencements Aug., Dec., May. Summer session from mid-May to mid-Aug.

Characteristics of Freshmen: 74% of applicants admitted. 64% of applicants admitted and enrolled.

17% (543 students) submitted SAT scores; 97% (345 students) submitted ACT scores. *25th percentile*: SAT Verbal 510, SAT Math 530; ACT Composite 22, ACT English 21, ACT Math 21. *75th percentile*: SAT Verbal 640, SAT Math 660; ACT Composite 28, ACT English 28, ACT Math 28.

32% of entering freshmen expected to graduate within 5 years. 82% of freshmen from Nebraska. Freshmen from 43 states and 22 foreign countries.

Admission: Rolling admissions plan. For fall acceptance, apply as early as Sept. 1 of previous year, but not later than Aug. 15 of year of enrollment. Early acceptance available. *Requirements:* Graduation from accredited secondary school and meet one of the following conditions: (1) applicants must complete 4 units English, 2 units of one foreign language, 4 units mathematics (must include algebra I and II, geometry), 3 units natural science (1 lab course), 3 units social science. Student must present scores on the ACT or SAT; recommend elective courses in foreign language (at least a 2-year sequence), fine arts, and/or the humanities; or (2) applicants must rank in the upper one-half of their graduating class; or (3) applicants must present an ACT score of 20 (enhanced) or a combined SAT score of 850 or above or (4) applicants at least 18 years of age who complete equivalent academic training such as GED plus ACT or SAT scores; or (5) applicants may be admitted providing they show good promise of success in university work. Some colleges have additional requirements. *Entrance tests:* SAT or ACT composite. *For transfer students:* 2.0 minimum GPA; from 4-year accredited institution 95 hours maximum transfer credit; from 2-year accredited institution 66 hours.

College credit and advanced placement for postsecondary level work completed in secondary school. College credit for extrainstitutional learning on basis of ACE *2006 Guide to the Evaluation of Educational Experiences in the Armed Services*; faculty assessment.

Degree Requirements: 125–134 credit hours; 2.0 GPA; 30 of last 36 hours in residence.

Fulfillment of some degree requirements possible by passing College Board CLEP, AP, other standardized tests. *Grading system:* A–F; pass-fail; withdraw (carries time limit).

Distinctive Educational Programs: Honors program offers learning experience to students with the ability and desire to pursue high levels of academic achievement. University Foundations Program consists of two courses designed to help entering freshmen learn more about themselves and resources at the university. Experiential education includes internships, field work, or cooperative placements. Continuing Studies offers evening courses and approximately 70 college courses by correspondence. ADAPT is a program for freshmen to help develop thought processes essential to success in advanced subjects and university study. As a member of International Student Exchange Program, UNL is able to place it students in over 90 universities around the world.

ROTC: Air Force, Army, Navy. 27 Air Force, 17 Army, and 8 Navy commissions awarded 2004.

Degrees Conferred: 6 *associate;* 3,119 *baccalaureate* (B), 837 *master's* (M); 236 *doctorate* (D): agriculture 200 (B), 47 (M), 27 (D); architecture 59 (B), 48 (M); area and ethnic studies 5 (B); biological/life sciences 143 (B), 21 (M), 9 (D); business/marketing 703 (B), 116 (M), 15 (D); communications/communication technologies 280 (B), 18 (M), 9 (D); computer and information sciences 50 (B), 44 (M), 2 (D); education 324 (B); engineering and engineering technologies 398 (B), 120 (M), 21 (D); English 80 (B), 13 (M), 15 (D); foreign languages and literature 32 (B), 6 (M), 4 (D); health professions and related sciences 73 (B), 23 (M); home economics and vocational home economics 164 (B), 24 (M), 3 (D); interdisciplinary studies 13 (M), 3 (D); law/legal studies 2 (M); liberal arts/general studies 3 (B); mathematics 23 (B), 40 (M), 2 (D); natural resources/environmental science 33 (B), 5 (M), 2 (D); parks and recreation 34 (B); philosophy/religion/theology 8 (B), 4 (M), 5 (D); physical sciences 28 (B), 20 (M), 21 (D); psychology 167 (B), 16 (M), 32 (D); social sciences and history 204 (B), 25 (M), 15 (D); visual and performing arts 108 (B), 34 (M), 5 (D). 131 *first-professional:* law 131. *Honorary degrees awarded 2004–05:* Doctor of Humane Letters 2; Doctor of Science 3.

Fees and Other Expenses: *Full-time tuition per academic year 2004–05:* undergraduate resident $4,313, nonresident $12,803; graduate resident $8,664,

nonresident $12,288. *Required fees:* $955. *Room and board per academic year:* $5,555.

Financial Aid: The university offers a direct lending program. Aid from institutionally generated funds is provided on the basis of academic merit, financial need, athletic ability.

Financial aid to full-time, first-time undergraduate students: need-based scholarships/grants totaling $22,610,364, self-help $29,757,123, parent loans $7,954,046; non-need-based scholarships/grants totaling $15,353,379, self-help $14,649,528, parent loans $9,446,832, athletic awards $4,634,890. *Graduate aid:* 70 students received $62,000 in federal and state-funded fellowships/grants; 1,308 received $14,813,311 in federal and state-funded loans (ranging from $200 to $19,700).

Departments and Teaching Staff: *Professors* 489, *associate professors* 340, *assistant professors* 193, *part-time faculty* 21.

Total instructional faculty: 1,043 (full-time 1,022, part-time 21; women 269, men 774; members of minority groups 132). Total faculty with doctorate, first-professional, or other terminal degree: 1,008. Student-to-faculty ratio: 18.9:1. Degrees held by full-time faculty: baccalaureate 5%, master's 17%, doctorate 70%, professional 32%. 79% hold terminal degrees. *Faculty development:* $151,390,630 total grants for research. 41 faculty members awarded sabbaticals 2004–05.

Enrollment: Total enrollment 21,792. Undergraduate full-time 8,278 men / 7,406 women, part-time 824m / 629w; first-professional full-time 220m / 85w, part-time 3m / 1w; graduate full-time 1,094m / 999w, part-time 970m / 1,183w. *Transfer students:* in-state 732; from out-of-state 145.

Characteristics of Student Body: *Ethnic/racial makeup (undergraduate):* number of Black non-Hispanic: 359; American Indian or Alaska Native: 89; Asian or Pacific Islander: 421; Hispanic: 401; White non-Hispanic: 14,713; unknown: 671. *Age distribution:* number under 18: 173; 18–19: 5,982; 20–21: 6,042; 22–24: 3,607; 25–29: 815; 30–34: 252; 35–39: 102; 40–49: 120; 50–64: 44. 39% of student body attend summer sessions.

International Students: 1,566 nonresident aliens enrolled fall 2004. 220 students from Europe, 977 Asia, 156 Latin America, 79 Africa, 48 Canada, 2 Australia, 1 New Zealand, 102 other. Programs available to aid students whose native language is not English: social, cultural. English as a Second Language Program. Financial aid specifically designated for international students: variable number of scholarships available annually for both undergraduate and graduate international students.

Student Life: Eleven on-campus residence halls are available for the housing of 5,558. These halls house the following: 30% single-sex male; 30% single-sex female, and 40% co-ed. 16% of men join and 12% live in fraternities; 15% of women join and 6% live in sororities. Housing is available for married students. 24% of undergraduate student body lives off campus. *Intercollegiate athletics:* men only: baseball, basketball, football, golf, gymnastics, swimming, tennis, track and cross country, wrestling; women only: basketball, golf, gymnastics, soccer, softball, swimming, tennis, track and cross country, volleyball. *Special regulations:* Cars permitted on campus; parking in designated areas only. *Special services:* Student Center (academic success, advising, counseling, and multicultural affairs consolidates services to make the transition to university life), International Educational Services, AA/EEO and Handicapped Services, Career Planning and Placement, Adult Learning Services, student health services and campus bus service in cooperation with City of Lincoln. *Student publications: Daily Nebraskan*, a newspaper; *The Journalist*, a newspaper; papers and magazines from the various colleges. *Surrounding community:* Lincoln population 225,000. Omaha, 50 miles from campus, is nearest metropolitan area. Served by mass transit bus system; airport 5 miles from campus; passenger rail service 1/2 mile from campus.

Library Collections: 3,357,028 volumes including bound books, serial backfiles, electronic documents, and government documents not in separate collections. Online catalog. Current serial subscriptions: 31,571 paper, microform, and electronic. 21,326 recordings. 4,237 compact discs. 62 CD-ROMs. 174 computer work stations. Students have access to the Internet and online information retrieval services (fee-based). Total budget for books, periodicals, audiovisual materials, microforms 2004–05: $5,758,469.

Most important special holdings include Benjamin Botkin Collection (folklore monographs); Charles Bessey Collection (botany professional papers); Mari Sandoz Collection (personal working library); Bernice Slote Collection (Willa Cather Research); Alvin Johnson Papers (Social Science Research).

Buildings and Grounds: City and east campus area 616 acres.

Chief Executive Officer: Dr. Harvey Perlman, Chancellor.

Undergraduates address admission inquiries to Alan Cervany, Dean of Admissions; graduate inquiries to Director of Graduate Studies.

College of Agricultural Sciences and Natural Resources

Degree Programs Offered: *Baccalaureate* in agribusiness, agricultural economics, agricultural education, agricultural honors, agricultural journalism, agricultural sciences, agronomy, animal science, crop protection (entomology, plant pathology or week science options), food science and technology, general agriculture, horticulture, mechanized agriculture, natural resources, soil science; *master's* in agricultural biochemistry; agricultural economics; agricultural education; agronomy; animal science; entomology; food science and technology; forestry, fisheries, and wildlife; horticulture; mechanized agriculture; plant pathology; veterinary science; interdepartmental area of nutrition; *doctorate* in agricultural biochemistry, agricultural economics, agronomy, animal science, entomology, food science and technology, horticulture and forestry, plant pathology, interdepartmental area of nutrition.

Admission: 16 high school units (1 unit equals a full year of high school work): 3 units English, 3 units mathematics (elementary algebra, geometry, and advanced algebra or trigonometry); 3 additional academic units (English, foreign language, mathematics, natural science, social science); and 7 units electives.

Distinctive Educational Programs: Combined 6-year program in agriculture and law. Dual major in agriculture and journalism. Interdisciplinary major in crop protection (entomology, plant pathology, weed science). Interdepartmental program in natural resources. Major in agricultural honors. Minor in agriculture and minor in agricultural economics for students in colleges other than Agriculture. Joint agribusiness major with College of Business Administration. Staff members in the Biometrics and Information Systems Center provide offering of courses in biometry. The School of Technical Agriculture in Curtis offers a 2-year program to prepare students for employment in technical jobs related to agriculture. Nebraska Agricultural Experiment Station has stations at Scottsbluff, North Platte, Concord, Clay Center, and Lincoln; the station operates a field laboratory at Mead and several laboratory farms throughout the state. Agricultural Extension Service in cooperation with U.S. Department of Agriculture.

College of Architecture

Degree Programs Offered: *Baccalaureate* in architectural studies; *master's* in architecture, and community and regional planning.

Distinctive Educational Programs: Study abroad in England, Mexico, China, and Germany. Internships in architecture and planning. Community Design Center. Hyde Lecture and Critics program.

College of Arts and Sciences

Degree Programs Offered: *Baccalaureate* in anthropology, art, art history, astronomy, chemistry, classics, computer science, dance, economics, English, environmental studies, French, geography, geology, German, Greek, history, integrated studies, international affairs, Latin American studies, biological sciences, mathematics, music, philosophy, physics, political science, psychology, recreation, Russian, sociology, Spanish, speech communication, speech pathology and audiology, theater arts, women's studies; *master's* in most departments.

Distinctive Educational Programs: Preprofessional programs in dental hygiene, medicine, physical therapy, radiologic technology, social work. Interdisciplinary programs in dance, international affairs, recreation, women's studies, ethnic studies, Slavic and East European studies, actuarial science, African studies, Asian studies, film studies, medieval and Renaissance studies, policy analysis, religious studies, Great Plains studies. Cooperative baccalaureate program in medical technology with University of Nebraska Medical Center. Accelerated baccalaureate-J.D. and J.D.-M.A. in economics, joint J.D.-Ph.D. in psychology, all with College of Law. Integrated studies and university studies programs for individualized or nontraditional majors.

College of Business Administration

Degree Programs Offered: *Baccalaureate* in accounting, actuarial science, agribusiness, economics, finance, international business, management, marketing; *master's* in professional accountancy; *master's* and *doctorate* in business administration. Joint master's program in MBA-law.

Degree Requirements: International course requirement (in addition to basic requirements).

Distinctive Educational Programs: Bureau of Business Research offers training and research programs for advanced students. Center for Economic Education in cooperation with Teachers College provides pre-service and in-service training for economics teachers. Center for Study of the American Business System. Executive-in-Residence Program encourages communication between successful business practitioners and students of management. Visiting Scholars Program. E. J. Faulkner Lecture Series. Nebraska Business Development Center. Nebraska Center for Productivity and Entrepreneurship. International Center for Franchise Studies.

College of Engineering and Technology

Degree Programs Offered: *Baccalaureate* in agricultural engineering, biological systems engineering, chemical engineering, civil engineering, electrical engineering, industrial engineering, mechanical engineering, computer science, construction management, construction engineering technology, drafting and design engineering technology, electronics engineering technology industrial technology, manufacturing engineering technology; *master's* in agricultural engineering, chemical engineering, civil engineering, electrical engineering, industrial engineering, mechanical engineering, computer science; *doctorate* in agricultural engineering, chemical engineering, civil engineering, electrical engineering, engineering mechanics, industrial engineering, mechanical engineering, computer science.

Distinctive Educational Programs: Cooperative education program. Interdisciplinary engineering programs. Engineering Research Centers. Some programs offered at the University of Nebraska-Omaha.

College of Human Resources and Family Science

Degree Programs Offered: *Baccalaureate* in community services, consumer science, home economics education, home economics and journalism, home economics and communication, child development/early childhood education, family science, dietetics, foods, hospital management, nutritional sciences, fashion merchandising, fashion and textile design, interior design; *master's* in human development and the family, nutritional science and hospital management, textiles/clothing/design; *doctorate* in home economics, interdisciplinary nutrition.

Distinctive Educational Programs: Cooperative programs with School of Journalism. Double majors in human development and elementary or secondary education in cooperation with Teachers College. Individualized program in human development and the family. Tours of New York, London and Paris relative to markets for study of fashions and Interior Design.

College of Journalism

Degree Programs Offered: *Baccalaureate* and *master's* in journalism.

Distinctive Educational Programs: The News-Editorial Department publishes a laboratory newspaper, *The Journalist,* each semester. Students are used as reporters, editors, and photographers. Students also publish a depth report on a chosen subject. Broadcasting students get hands-on experience with KRNU radio station. Advertising students do an advertising idea book.

College of Law

Degree Programs Offered: *First-professional.*

Admission: Baccalaureate from accredited college or university, LSAT, application through LSDAS.

Degree Requirements: 96 credit hours, 4.0 on a 9.0 scale, first-year curriculum, course or seminar in professional responsibility, course in constitutional law, seminar with a major writing requirement, moot court competition.

Distinctive Educational Programs: Accelerated joint degree programs with psychology (J.D./Ph.D.; J.D./M.A.); educational administration (J.D./Ph.D.); and College of Business (J.D./M.B.A.). Potential ad hoc joint degree programs with agricultural economics, journalism, and other disciplines. Joint course in professional responsibility with College of Medicine.

Teachers College

Degree Programs Offered: *Baccalaureate* in art education, music education, elementary education, middle school education, special education, and various secondary school fields. *Master's* in business education, educational administration, educational psychology and measurements, elementary education, health-physical education and recreation, secondary education, special education, speech pathology and audiology, adult education, and vocational education. *Specialist degrees* in educational administration, educational psychology and measurement, curriculum and instruction, and vocational and adult education. *Doctorate* in administration-curriculum-instruction, community and human resources, and psychological and cultural studies.

Distinctive Educational Programs: Nonteaching degree programs in administrative office management, athletic training, community health services, and recreation. Specialized programs in community services, Latin American studies, minority and multicultural education, and special field based programs in elementary education, junior high/middle school teacher education, and a special alternative certification program for persons with degrees and experience in other fields.

Graduate Studies

Degree Programs Offered: *Master's* in accountancy; actuarial science; agricultural economics; agricultural education; agronomy; animal science; anthropology; architecture; art; biological sciences; biometry, business; chemistry; classics; community and regional planning; computer science; economics; adult education and social foundations; Center for Business and Vocational Teacher Ed.; business education; vocational education; curriculum and instruction; educational administration; educational psychology; health, physical education and recreation; special education; speech pathology and audiology; agricultural engineering; chemical engineering; civil engineering; electrical engineering; engineering mechanics; industrial and management systems engineering; manufacturing systems engineering; mechanical engineering; English; entomology; food science and technology; forestry, fisheries and wildlife; geography; geology; history; home economics; horticulture; human development and family; human nutrition and food service management; journalism; legal studies; mathematics and statistics; mechanized agriculture; modern languages and literatures; music; nutrition; philosophy; physics and astronomy; political science; psychology; sociology; speech and dramatic art; textiles, clothing, and design; theatre arts and dance; veterinary science; *doctorate* in agricultural economics; agronomy; animal science; biological sciences; business; chemistry; computer science; economics; education (administration, curriculum and instruction; community and human resources; psychological and cultural studies); engineering; English; entomology; food sciences and technology; geography; geology; history; home economics, horticulture and forestry; mathematics and statistics; modern languages and literatures; music; nutrition; philosophy; physics and astronomy; political science; psychology; sociology; speech and dramatic art. Six-year Certificate of Specialization in Administration and Supervision.

Degree Requirements: Requirements vary with program and degree.

Departments and Teaching Staff: Faculty is drawn from individual colleges.

University of Nebraska at Kearney

905 West 25th Street
Kearney, Nebraska 68849-1212

Tel: (308) 865-8441   **E-mail:** admissions@unk.edu
Fax: (308) 865-8157   **Internet:** www.unk.edu

Institution Description: The University of Nebraska at Kearney (formerly Kearney State College) is a state institution. *Enrollment:* 6,382. *Degrees awarded:* Baccalaureate, master's. Specialist degrees also awarded.

Academic offers subject to approval by statewide coordinating bodies. Budget subject to approval by state governing boards.

Accreditation: *Regional:* NCA. *Professional:* chemistry, dietetics, music, school psychology, social work, speech-language pathology, teacher education

History: Established as Nebraska State Normal School at Kearney 1903; offered first instruction at postsecondary level 1905; first degree (associate) awarded 1906; changed name to Nebraska State Teachers College at Kearney 1921; became Kearney State College 1963; became University of Nebraska at Kearney 1991. *See* Philip Holmgren, *Kearney State College 1905–1980* (Kearney, NE: Kearney State College Press, 1980) for further information.

Institutional Structure: *Governing board:* Board of Regents of University of Nebraska. Extrainstitutional representation: 8 regents; institutional representation: 4 students. 8 voting. *Composition of institution:* Administrators 23 men / 18 women. Academic affairs headed by vice chancellor for academic affairs. Management/business/finances directed by vice chancellor for business and finance. Full-time instructional faculty 321. Academic governance body, Faculty Senate, meets an average of 12 times per year. *Faculty representation:* Faculty served by collective bargaining agent, NEA.

Calendar: Semesters. Academic year Aug. to May. Freshmen admitted Aug., Oct., Jan., Feb., May, June, July. Degrees conferred and formal commencement May, Dec. Summer session of 2 terms from mid-May to early Aug.

Characteristics of Freshmen: 2,676 applicants (1,115 men, 1,561 women). 84% of applicants admitted. 46.9% of admitted students enrolled full-time.

3% (36 students) submitted SAT scores; 84% (941 students) submitted ACT scores. *25th percentile*: SAT I Verbal 450, SAT I Math 460; ACT Composite 19, ACT English 18, ACT Math 17. *75th percentile*: SAT I Verbal 600, SAT I Math 600; ACT Composite 24, ACT English 24, ACT Math 24.

35% of entering freshmen expected to graduate within 5 years. 91% of freshmen from Nebraska.

Admission: Rolling admissions plan. For fall acceptance, apply as early as end of junior year in secondary school, but not later than 30 days prior to beginning of term. Early acceptance available. *Requirements:* Graduation from accredited secondary school with 16 units which must include courses in English, mathematics, natural science, social studies. GED accepted. Rank in

upper one-half of graduating class. *Entrance tests:* ACT composite recommended; College Board SAT accepted. *For transfer students:* 2.0 minimum GPA; 93 hours maximum transfer credit; from 2-year accredited institution 66 hours; correspondence/extension students 10 hours.

Advanced placement for postsecondary-level work completed in secondary school. College credit and advanced placement for extrainstitutional learning (life experience) on basis of departmental assessment; college credit on basis of ACE *2006 Guide to the Evaluation of Educational Experiences in the Armed Services.*

Tutoring available. Developmental/remedial courses offered during regular academic year; credit given.

Degree Requirements: *For all baccalaureate degrees:* 125 credit hours of which 40 hours must be 300 and 400 level courses; 2.0 GPA; 32 hours in residence; core curriculum; proficiency requirements in English composition and speech, cultural diversity.

Fulfillment of some degree requirements and exemption from some beginning courses possible by passing departmental examinations, College Board CLEP or APP. *Grading system:* A–F; credit-no credit; withdraw (carries time limit).

Distinctive Educational Programs: *For undergraduates:* Cooperative baccalaureate degree program for registered nurses with University of Nebraska College of Nursing; cooperative baccalaureate programs in medical technology, radiography, respiratory therapy with approved institutions.

Degrees Conferred: 874 *baccalaureate*; 190 *master's*. Bachelor's degrees awarded in top 5 disciplines: business, management, marketing, and related support services 262; education 133; visual and performing arts 48; parks and recreation 45; English language/literature 45.

Fees and Other Expenses: *Full-time tuition per academic year 2004–05:* undergraduate resident $4,618, nonresident $8,514. Contact the university for current graduate tuition/fees. *Books and supplies:* $764. *Room and board per academic year:* $4,402.

Financial Aid: Aid from institutionally generated funds is provided on the basis of academic merit, financial need, athletic ability, other criteria. Institution has a Program Participation Agreement with the U.S. Department of Education for eligible students to receive Pell Grants and, depending upon the agreement, other federal aid.

Financial aid to full-time, first-time undergraduate students: 32% received federal grants averaging $2,661; 15% state/local grants averaging $926; 58% institutional grants averaging $2,390; 58% received loans averaging $2,767.

Departments and Teaching Staff: Art *professors* 6, *associate professors* 2, *assistant professors* 4, *instructors* 0; *part-time teachers* 6; biology 11,2, 0, 0, 3; business 4, 13, 7, 4, 33; chemistry 7, 1, 0, 0, 0; computer science 0, 2, 4, 1, 4; criminal justice 1, 2, 1, 0, 0; counseling and psychology 4, 2, 4, 0, 2; economics 2, 3, 2, 2, 3; educational media 0, 0, 0, 0, 1; educational administration 1, 3, 0, 0, 1; elementary education 4, 1, 4, 0, 0; English 6, 5, 9, 1, 13; family and consumer 0, 3, 1, 5, 1; foreign languages 1, 2, 2, 1, 5; geography 1, 3, 2, 0, 1; history 3, 2, 5, 0, 0; health and science 0, 1, 0, 0, 0; health/physical education/recreation 5, 1, 8, 17, 2; industrial technology 3, 1, 2, 1, 0; journalism and mass communication 0, 1, 4, 3, 0; learning skills 0, 1, 0, 1, 0; mathematics and statistics 4, 3, 3, 3, 1; music 6, 3, 0, 5, 2; nursing 0, 1, 8, 3, 4; philosophy 0, 1, 1, 0, 0; physics 4, 3, 0, 0, 2; political science 2, 0, 3, 1, 0; psychology 2, 2, 2, 1, 1; teacher education 2, 0, 6, 1, 5; safety education 0, 2, 1, 0, 0; sociology 0, 4, 1, 0, 0; social work 0, 0, 3, 0, 3; speech/theatre 2, 0, 9, 0, 10; special education 0, 4, 3, 3, 2; vocational education 2, 1, 1, 0, 0.

Total instructional faculty: 321. Student-to-faculty ratio: 18:1. Degrees held by full-time faculty: doctorate 72%, master's 27%, baccalaureate 1%.

Enrollment: Total enrollment 6,342. Undergraduate 5,380 (45.6% men, 54.4% women).

Characteristics of Student Body: *Ethnic/racial makeup (undergraduate):* number of Black non-Hispanic: 8.8%; American Indian or Alaska Native: .2%; Asian or Pacific Islander: .7%; Hispanic: 3.8%; White non-Hispanic: 83.4%; unknown: 5.3%. *Age distribution:* 17–21: 58%; 22–24: 19%; 25–29: 8%; 30–34: 4%; 35–39: 3%; 40–49: 6; 50–up: 2%.

International Students: 366 undergraduate nonresident aliens enrolled fall 2004. Program to aid students whose native language is not English: English as a Second Language Program. No financial aid specifically designated for international students.

Student Life: On-campus residence halls house 26% of student body. Residence halls for men men only constitute 14% of such space, for women only 23%. Housing available for married students. 2% of student body so housed. *Intercollegiate athletics:* men only: baseball, basketball, football, golf, tennis, track, cross-country, wrestling; women only: basketball, cross-country, golf, softball, swimming, tennis, track, volleyball. *Special regulations:* Cars permitted on campus in designated areas only; fee charged. *Special services:* Learning Resources Center, medical services. *Student publications, radio, television: Antelope,* a weekly newspaper. Radio station KOVF broadcasts 148 hours per week. Closed-circuit TV station KSTV broadcasts local news and information 24 hours per week. *Surrounding community:* Kearney population 25,000. Denver (CO), 350 miles from campus, is nearest metropolitan area. Served by airport 5 miles from campus.

Publications: *Platte Valley Review* (annually) first published in 1973.

Library Collections: 287,000 volumes. 182,000 government documents; 935,000 microforms; 1,300 audiovisual titles; 1,650 current periodical subscriptions. Online catalog. Students have access to online information retrieval services and the Internet.

Most important special holdings include KSC archives. Library is a selective depository for federal government documents, full depository for documents from the State of Nebraska.

Buildings and Grounds: Campus area 235 acres.

Chief Executive Officer: Dr. Douglas A. Kristensen, Chancellor.

Address admission inquiries to Dusty Newton, Director of Admissions.

University of Nebraska at Omaha

60th and Dodge Street
Omaha, Nebraska 681820-0108

Tel: (402) 554-2800   **E-mail:** unoadm@unomaha.edu
Fax: (402) 554-2873   **Internet:** www.unomaha.edu

Institution Description: *Enrollment:* 14,667. *Degrees awarded:* Baccalaureate, master's, doctorate. Specialist certificates in education also awarded.

Budget subject to approval by state governing boards.

Accreditation: *Regional:* NCA. *Professional:* art, athletic training, aviation, business, chemistry, computer science, counseling, engineering, engineering technology, music, public administration, social work, speech-language pathology, teacher education

History: Established as University of Omaha 1908; offered first instruction at postsecondary level 1909; awarded first degree (baccalaureate) 1912; became campus of University of Nebraska and adopted present name 1968.

Institutional Structure: *Composition of institution:* Administrators 23 men / 8 women. Campus led by chancellor, vice chancellor for academic, vice chancellor for administration. Full-time instructional faculty 470. Academic governance body, Faculty Senate. *Faculty representation:* Faculty served by collective bargaining agent affiliated with AAUP.

Calendar: Semesters. Academic year Aug. to May. Freshmen admitted Aug., Jan., and beginning of any summer session. Degrees conferred and formal commencements May, Aug., Dec. Summer session from May to Aug.

Characteristics of Freshmen: 87% of applicants admitted. 52% of applicants admitted and enrolled.

8% (134 students) submitted SAT scores; 95% (1,565 students) submitted ACT scores. *25th percentile:* SAT Verbal 480, SAT Math 478; ACT Composite 20, ACT English 19, ACT Math 18. *75th percentile:* SAT Verbal 620, SAT Math 603; ACT Composite 25, ACT English 25, ACT Math 25.

27% of entering freshmen expected to graduate within 5 years. 92% of freshmen from Nebraska. Freshmen from 25 states and 33 foreign countries.

Admission: Rolling admissions plan. For fall acceptance, apply as early as Jan. 1, but not later than day of registration. Early acceptance available. *Requirements:* Either graduation from accredited secondary school or GED. Exceptions possible. *Entrance tests:* Recommend College Board SAT or ACT composite. For foreign students minimum TOEFL score 500. *For transfer students:* From 4-year accredited institution hours maximum transfer credit limited only by residence requirement; from 2-year accredited institution 64–66 hours maximum transfer credit. Good standing at institution previously attended.

College credit and advanced placement for postsecondary-level work completed in secondary school. Tutoring available. Noncredit developmental/remedial courses offered during regular academic year.

Degree Requirements: 125–134 semester hours; 2.0 GPA; 30 of last 36 hours in residence; distribution requirements.

Fulfillment of some degree requirements and exemption from some beginning courses possible by passing departmental examinations, College Board CLEP, AP. *Grading system:* A–F; pass-fail; withdraw (deadline after which pass-fail is appended to withdraw).

Distinctive Educational Programs: Cooperative education. Flexible meeting places and schedules, including off-campus centers (at varying locations throughout the community), weekend and evening classes. Facilities for independent research, including honors programs, individual majors, tutorials. The Goodrich Program provides supportive services for students with substantial financial need and offers a core sequence of interdisciplinary courses. College of Home Economics offers intercampus programs in consumer affairs, home economics, vocational education, human development and the family, and interior, fashion, or textile design. *Other distinctive programs:* Division of Continuing Studies offers baccalaureate programs primarily for adults, emphasizing flexible

course selection and credit for life experience. Study abroad programs in Austria, China, Czech Republic, Germany, Japan, Philippines, Romania.

ROTC: Air Force 14 commissions awarded 2004.

Degrees Conferred: 1,597 *baccalaureate* (B), 709 *master's* (M), 15 *doctorate* (D): area and ethnic studies 4 (B), biological/life sciences 100 (B), 12 (M); business/marketing 414 (B), 143 (M); communications/communication technologies 128 (B), 14 (M); computer and information sciences 145 (B), 81 (M); education foreign languages and literature 19 (B); health professions and related sciences 2 (B), 2 (M); interdisciplinary studies 48 (B); library science 2 (B); mathematics 18 (B), 8 (M); parks and recreation 25 (B), 24 (M); philosophy/religion/theology 9 (B); physical sciences 8 (B); protective services/public administration 142 (B), 133 (M), 6 (D); psychology 58 (B), 13 (M); social sciences and history 87 (B), 9 (M); trade and industry 32 (B); visual and performing arts 57 (B), 11 (M).

Fees and Other Expenses: *Full-time tuition per academic year 2004–05:* resident undergraduate $3,938, nonresident $21,603; graduate resident $3,924, nonresident $10,320. *Required fees:* $595. *Room and board per academic year:* $5,960.

Financial Aid: Aid from institutionally generated funds is provided on the basis of academic merit, financial need, athletic ability, other criteria.

Financial aid to full-time, first-time undergraduate students: need-based scholarships/grants totaling $10,633,181, self-help $15,817,086; non-need-based scholarships/grants totaling $10,481,938, self-help $14,930,451, parent loans $853,754, athletic awards $582,804.

Departments and Teaching Staff: *Professors* 159, *associate professors* 139, *assistant professors* 125, *instructors* 47, *part-time faculty* 342.

Total instructional faculty: 812 (full-time 470, part-time 342; women 349, men 463; members of minority groups 119). Total faculty with doctorate, first-professional, or other terminal degree: 498. Student-to-faculty ratio: 18:1. Degrees held by full-time faculty: doctorate 86%, master's 11%, other 3%. 87% hold terminal degrees. *Faculty development:* $15 million in grants for research. 18 faculty members awarded sabbaticals 2004–05.

Enrollment: Total enrollment 14,667. Undergraduate full-time 4,325 men / 4,461 women, part-time 1,574m / 1,524w; graduate full-time 280m / 378w, part-time 812m / 1,313w.

Characteristics of Student Body: *Ethnic/racial makeup (undergraduate):* number of Black non-Hispanic: 624; American Indian or Alaska Native: 58; Asian or Pacific Islander: 324; Hispanic: 351; White non-Hispanic: 9,851; unknown: 374. *Age distribution:* number under 18: 130; 18–19: 3,145; 20–21: 3,261; 22–24: 2,723; 25–29: 1,333; 30–34: 482; 35–39: 291; 40–49: 377; 50–64: 142.

International Students: 755 nonresident aliens enrolled fall 2004. Programs to aid students whose native language is not English: social, cultural, financial. English as a Second Language Program. Scholarship available annually for qualifying international students.

Student Life: On-campus housing available. *Intercollegiate athletics:* men only: baseball, basketball, cross-country, football, track, wrestling; women only: basketball, soccer, softball, swimming, track, volleyball. *Special regulations:* Cars permitted without restrictions. *Special services:* Learning Resources Center, medical services, shuttle bus service to parking areas. *Student publications:* Gateway, a biweekly newspaper. *Surrounding community:* Greater Omaha population 800,000. Served by mass transit bus system; airport 6 miles from campus; passenger rail service 4 miles from campus.

Library Collections: 3,056,595 volumes including bound books, serial backfiles, electronic documents, and government documents not in separate collections. Online catalog. Current serial subscriptions: 2,807 paper; 177 microform; 23,357 via electronic access. 6,630 video recordings; 3,372 compact discs; 1,781 CD-ROMs. 200 computer work stations. Students have access to the Internet at no charge. Total 2004–05 budget for books and materials: $1,859,650.

Most important special holdings include Afghanistan Collection; Mary L. Richmond Cummington Press Collection; Nebraska authors and history collection.

Buildings and Grounds: Campus areas (2) 159 acres.

Chief Executive Officer: Dr. Nancy Belck, Chancellor.

Address undergraduate admission inquiries to Joline Adams, Director of Admissions; graduate inquiries inquiries to Dean, Graduate Studies.

College of Arts and Sciences

Degree Programs Offered: *Baccalaureate* in area studies, biology, communications, interdisciplinary studies, letters, mathematics, physical sciences, psychology, social sciences; *master's* in biology, communications, English, geography, history, mathematics, political science, psychology, sociology.

Degree Requirements: *See* general requirements. *For baccalaureate degree:* In addition to general requirements, demonstrated proficiency in English. For bachelor of arts degree, 2 years college work in a foreign language or equivalent. Graduate requirements vary.

Distinctive Educational Programs: Preprofessional programs in dentistry, dental hygiene, medical technology, medicine, nuclear medicine technology, optometry, pharmacy, physical therapy, physician's assistant, radiologic technology. Interdisciplinary programs in black studies, general science, international studies, liberal studies.

College of Business Administration

Degree Programs Offered: *Baccalaureate* in business administration; *master's* in business administration, economics.

Admission: In addition to general requirements, 1 unit algebra. Graduate requirements vary according to program.

Degree Requirements: In addition to general requirements, demonstrated proficiency in English; core curriculum. Graduate requirements vary.

Distinctive Educational Programs: Business-prelaw program.

College of Education

Degree Programs Offered: *Baccalaureate. Master's* in counseling and guidance, educational administration, elementary education, secondary education, special education, urban education.

Degree Requirements: *See* general requirements. *For baccalaureate degree:* In addition to general requirements, demonstrated proficiency in audiovisual media, English, speech, hearing, mathematics, and library usage. Professional education sequence. Graduate requirements vary.

College of Fine Arts

Degree Programs Offered: *Baccalaureate* in art history, dramatic arts, fine arts, music; *master's* in dramatic arts.

Admission: *See* general requirements. *For master's degree:* Baccalaureate from accredited college or university with 15 semester hours in dramatic arts beyond the introductory course.

Degree Requirements: *For baccalaureate degree:* In addition to general requirements, demonstrated proficiency in English, 2.5-3.0 in major field. *For master's degree:* 30–36 hours, including thesis or final project; research methods course, comprehensive examination.

College of Public Affairs and Community Service

Degree Programs Offered: *Baccalaureate* and *master's* in criminal justice, public administration, social work, urban studies.

Degree Requirements: *See* general requirements. *For baccalaureate degree:* In addition to general requirements, demonstrated proficiency in English. For all but criminal justice majors, urban studies requirement. Graduate requirements vary.

Distinctive Educational Programs: Center for Applied Urban Research.

University of Nebraska Medical Center

600 South 42nd Street
Omaha, Nebraska 68198-7020

Tel: (402) 559-6648   **E-mail:** admissions@unmc.edu
Fax: (402) 559-6796   **Internet:** unmc.edu

Institution Description: *Enrollment:* 2,896. *Degrees awarded:* Baccalaureate, first-professional (dentistry, medicine, pharmacy), master's, doctorate. Certificates also awarded.

Accreditation: *Regional:* NCA. *Professional:* clinical lab scientist, cytotechnology, diagnostic medical sonography, dietetics, medicine, nuclear medicine technology, nursing, nursing education, perfusion, pharmacy, physical therapy, physician assisting, radiation therapy, radiation therapy technology, radiography, surgeon assisting

History: Established by the state legislature 1869; chartered as Omaha Medical College and offered first instruction at postsecondary level 1881; awarded first degree (first-professional) 1883; became part of the University of Nebraska system 1902; adopted present name 1968.

Institutional Structure: *Composition of institution:* Academic affairs headed by vice chancellor. Management/business/finances directed by vice chancellor for business and finance. Full-time instructional faculty 627. Academic governance body, Faculty Senate, meets an average of 10 times per year.

Calendar: Semesters. Academic year late Aug. to early May. Entering students admitted Aug. Degrees conferred May, Aug., Dec. Formal commencements May, Dec.

Admission: Rolling admissions plan. For fall acceptance, apply as early as July 1 of previous year, but not later than Mar. 1 of year of enrollment. Students are notified of acceptance monthly, beginning in Dec. *For transfer students:* Maximum transfer credit varies.

Tutoring available.

Degree Requirements: *For all baccalaureate degrees:* 120–148 hours; 2.0–2.5 GPA. For nursing degree, general education core curriculum. *For all undergraduate degrees:* Last 30 hours in residence; comprehensives in individual fields of study.

Fulfillment of some degree requirements and exemption from some beginning courses possible by passing departmental examinations (in College of Nursing), College Board CLEP, other standardized tests. *Grading system:* A–F; pass-fail; withdraw (pass-fail appended upon withdrawal).

Distinctive Educational Programs: Special facilities for using telecommunications in the classroom. Facilities and programs for independent research, including individual majors, tutorials.

Degrees Conferred: 442 *baccalaureate:* health professions and related sciences; 675 *masters:* biological/life sciences 6; health professions and related sciences 669; 238 *doctorate:* biological/life sciences 11; health professions and related sciences 227. *First-professional:* dentistry 44, pharmacy 59, medicine 110.

Fees and Other Expenses: *Full-time tuition per academic year 2004–05:* Undergraduate resident $6,468, nonresident 19,203; graduate resident $5,130, nonresident $13,824. *Required fees:* $182.

Financial Aid: Aid from institutionally generated funds is provided on the basis of academic merit, financial need.

Financial aid to full-time, first-time undergraduate students: need-based scholarships/grants totaling $2,135,310, self-help $5,953,757, parent loans $736,927. *Graduate aid:* 90 students received $311,469 in federal and state-funded fellowships/grants (ranging from $1,000 to $9,500); 213 received $1,641,712 in federal and state-funded loans (ranging from $8,500 to $18,500); 10 students received other fellowships/grants totaling $35,073 (ranging from $500 to $10,000).

Departments and Teaching Staff: Dentistry *professors* 13, *associate professors* 17, *assistant professors* 15, *instructors* 1, *part-time faculty* 17; medicine 126, 137, 175, 39, 86; nursing 4, 30, 35, 19, 23; pharmacy 5, 8, 6, 0, 0; allied health professions 1, 6, 18, 5, 4.

Total instructional faculty: 825 (full-time 695, part-time 130; women 271, men 447; members of minority groups 93). Total faculty with doctorate, first-professional, or other terminal degree: 626. Degrees held by full-time faculty: baccalaureate 1.9%, master's 10.7%, doctorate 87.4%. 90% hold terminal degrees. *Faculty development:* $68 million in grants for research. 4 faculty members awarded sabbaticals 2004–05.

Enrollment: Total enrollment 2,896. Undergraduate full-time 54 men / 653 women, part-time 5m / 59w; first-professional full-time 446m / 459w, part-time 2; graduate full-time 412m / 473w, part-time 58m / 275w.

Characteristics of Student Body: *Ethnic/racial makeup (undergraduate):* number of Black non-Hispanic: 16; American Indian or Alaska Native: 4; Asian or Pacific Islander: 6; Hispanic: 721; White non-Hispanic: 721; unknown: 3. *Age distribution:* number 18–19: 3; 20–21: 265; 22–24: 286; 25–29: 85; 30–34: 66; 35–39: 21; 40–49: 38; 50–64: 14; 65 and over: 1.

International Students: 97 nonresident aliens enrolled fall 2004. No programs available to aid students whose native language is not English. No financial aid specifically designated for international students.

Student Life: Campus apartments available. *Special regulations:* Cars with decals permitted in designated areas only; fee charged. *Special services:* Learning Resources Center, medical services. *Surrounding community:* Greater Omaha population 800,000. Served by mass transit bus system, airport 6 miles from campus, passenger rail service 4 miles from campus.

Library Collections: 975,830 volumes. Online and card catalogs. Current serial subscriptions: 1,138 paper; 3,533 via electronic access. 3,636 recordings. 69 computer work stations. Students have access to online information retrieval services and the Internet. Total 2004–05 budget for books and materials: $2,842,728.

Most important special collections include Consumer Health Information Resource Services Collection; Moon Collection (obstetrics and gynecology); History of Medicine.

Buildings and Grounds: Campus area 50 acres.

Chief Executive Officer: Harold Maurer, M.D., Chancellor.

Address admission inquiries to Tymaree Tonjes, Associate Director of Admissions; graduate inquiries to Graduate Studies, College of Medicine, College of Dentistry, College of Pharmacy.

College of Nursing

Degree Programs Offered: *Baccalaureate* in nursing; *master's* in community health, maternal-child, medical-surgical, and psychiatric-mental health nursing; *doctor of philosophy, post-master's certificate.*

Admission: Pre-requisite courses: English composition, psychology, sociology, human anatomy, introduction to psychology, introduction to sociology, human development and chemistry. 2.0 college GPA.

Departments and Teaching Staff: *See* Departments and Teaching Staff above.

Distinctive Educational Programs: Part-time, off-campus baccalaureate program offered in cooperation with several local community and state colleges. Dual-degree school nurse-health educator program in cooperation with the University of Nebraska at Omaha.

College of Dentistry

Degree Programs Offered: *Baccalaureate* in dental hygiene; *first-professional* in dentistry; *master's* in dentistry, endodontics, orthodontics, pedodontics, periodontics; *doctorate* in dental surgery, medical sciences.

Admission: *For first-professional degree:* 64 semester hours (89 hours preferred) of predental study which must include 2 semesters each of English composition, inorganic chemistry, biology or zoology, organic chemistry, and physics; DAT; AADAS.

Degree Requirements: *See* general requirements. *For first-professional degree:* 178 credit hours; 2.0 GPA; 36 months in residence.

Departments and Teaching Staff: *See* Departments and Teaching Staff above.

Distinctive Educational Programs: Work-experience programs. Research programs by individual arrangement. Optional B.A. or B.S. for dental students after completion of prescribed curriculum of first-year study. *Other distinctive programs:* Continuing education for practicing professionals.

College of Medicine

Degree Programs Offered: *Baccalaureate* in physical therapy, nurse anesthetist, nuclear medicine, radiologic technology, diagnostic medical sonography, radiation science technology, cytotechnology; *first-professional* in medicine; *master's* in clinical perfusion, physician assistant, physical therapy, anatomy, biochemistry, medical microbiology, pathology, physiology, and biophysics. *Graduate certificate* in clinical perfusion, biomedical communications education, cytotechnology, medical nutrition education.

Admission: *For first-professional degree:* 90 semester hours from an accredited college with 1 year in English, 1 year each biology, inorganic chemistry, organic chemistry, physics, introductory calculus or statistics; MCAT; AMCAS.

Degree Requirements: *For first-professional degree:* 2 years of basic science; 2.0 GPA; 2 years clinical experience.

Departments and Teaching Staff: *See* Departments and Teaching Staff above.

Distinctive Educational Programs: Cooperative master's and doctorates in medical sciences with College of Pharmacy. *Other distinctive programs:* Continuing education courses for health workers via closed circuit system with participating hospitals.

College of Pharmacy

Degree Programs Offered: *First-professional; master's* in biomedical chemistry, pharmaceutics, pharmacodynamics, toxicology; *doctorate* in pharmaceutical sciences.

Admission: *For first-professional degree:* 60 semester hours of undergraduate study which must include 24 hours of chemical and biological sciences; 6 hours of oral and written communication; 10 hours analytical sciences; 6 hours administrative sciences; 6 hours behavioral and social sciences; 6 general education; 2.0 college GPA.

Degree Requirements: *For first-professional degree:* 225 semester hours; 2.0 GPA; 36 hours in residence.

Departments and Teaching Staff: *See* Departments and Teaching Staff above.

Distinctive Educational Programs: Joint D.Pharm.-M.S. degree in cooperation with the University of Nebraska at Omaha. *See also* College of Medicine.

York College

1125 East 8th Street
York, Nebraska 68467-2699
Tel: (402) 363-5600   **E-mail:** enroll@yc.ne.edu
Fax: (402) 363-5623   **Internet:** www.yc.ne.edu

Institution Description: York College is a private liberal arts college affiliated with the Churches of Christ. *Enrollment:* 444. *Degrees awarded:* Associate, baccalaureate.

Member of the Nebraska Independent Colleges Foundation.

Accreditation: *Regional:* NCA. *Professional:* teacher education

History: Established 1890 by a syndicate of local visionaries, administration of York College was initially entrusted to the untied Brethren Church. A Board of Trustees composed of members of Churches of Christ acquired the original corporate charter 1956; membership in NCA achieved 1970; awarding of baccalaureate degrees resumed 1991.

Institutional Structure: *Governing board:* Representation: York College Board of Trustees. Extrainstitutional representation: 28 trustees. All voting. *Composition of institution:* Administrators 4 men. Academic affairs headed by vice president for academic affairs/dean of the college. Finances/business operations directed by vice president for finance and operations. Development/external relations directed by vice president for institutional advancement. Full-time instructional faculty 35, part-time 18. Academic governance bodies: York College faculty, meets 8 to 10 times per year; York Academic Council meets 16 to 24 times per year.

Calendar: Semesters. Academic year Aug. to May. Freshmen admitted Aug., Jan., May. Formal commencement May. Summer session of 3 terms from May to Aug.

Characteristics of Freshmen: Average secondary school rank of freshmen class top 50%. 97% of applicants accepted. 40% of accepted applicants enrolled.

66% of entering freshmen expected to graduate within five years. 34% of freshmen from Nebraska. Freshmen from 19 states and 4 foreign countries.

Admission: Rolling admissions plan. For fall acceptance, apply as early as middle of junior year in secondary school. Early acceptance available. *Requirements for regular acceptance:* incoming freshmen need two of the following three criteria—2.00 cumulative GPA; ranked in top half of graduating class, and/or 18 ACT of 860 SAT. *For transfer students:* 2.00 GPA; 68 semester hours maximum from junior/community colleges, 98 semester hours maximum from all other institutions.

Degree Requirements: *For all associate degrees:* At least 64 semester hours; 2.00 GPA. *For all undergraduate degrees:* At least 128 semester hours of which at least 44 must be upper division, distributive requirements; last 30 hours in residence. *For all undergraduate degrees:* 2.00 GPA, at least 30 semester hours in residence.

Fulfillment of some degree requirements and exemption from some beginning courses possible by passing CLEP or AP with a score of 3 or higher. *Grading system:* A–F with pluses; pass-fail; incomplete (carries time limit).

Distinctive Educational Programs: Internships. Interdisciplinary program in liberal arts. Program in biopsychology.

ROTC: Air Force, Army, and Navy offered in cooperation with University of Nebraska - Lincoln.

Degrees Conferred: 67 *baccalaureate:* business 13; communications 5; education 21; English 3; liberal arts 9; philosophy/religion 4; science 7; psychology 5.

Fees and Other Expenses: *Full-time tuition per academic year 2005–06:* $10,900. *Other fees:* $1,030. *Room per academic year:* $1,500. *Board per academic year:* $2,300.

Financial Aid: Aid from institutionally generated funds is provided on the basis of academic merit, financial need, athletic ability.

Financial aid to full-time, first-time undergraduate students: need-based scholarships/grants totaling $1,287,933, self-help $1,439,213; non-need-based self-help $863,705, parent loans $542,013, tuition waivers $192,360, athletic awards $765,138.

Departments and Teaching Staff: *Total instructional faculty:* 53 (full-time 35, part-time 18; women 21, men 32). Total faculty with doctorate, first-professional, or other terminal degree: 17. Student-to-faculty ratio: 12:1. Degrees held by full-time faculty: doctorate 32%, master's 68%. 32% hold terminal degrees.

Enrollment: Total enrollment 444. Undergraduate full-time 220 men / 204 women, part-time 5m / 15w. *Transfer students:* in-state 10; from out-of-state 33.

Characteristics of Student Body: *Ethnic/racial makeup:* number of Black non-Hispanic: 15; American Indian or Alaska Native: 2; Asian or Pacific Islander: 11; Hispanic: 13; White non-Hispanic: 385; unknown: 4. *Age distribution:* number under 18: 9; 18–19: 69; 20–21: 153; 22–24: 96; 25–29: 7; 30–34: 2; 35–39: 2; 40–49: 3.

International Students: 22 nonresident aliens enrolled fall 2004. 4 students from Europe, 5 Asia, 7 Latin America, 1 Africa, 5 Canada. No programs available to aid students whose native language is not English. No financial aid specifically designated for international students.

Student Life: On-campus resident halls house 60% of student body. All full-time students required to live in residence halls unless married, living with family, or over 20 years of age. *Intercollegiate athletics:* men only: baseball, basketball cross country, golf, soccer. tennis, track, wrestling; women only: basketball, cross country, golf, softball, tennis, track, soccer, volleyball. *Special regulations:* All students required to attend daily Chapel. Alcohol and tobacco are not allowed on campus. Cars permitted except in reserved spaces. *Special services:* Career development and placement. Local coordinated social/service clubs; student government; music performance groups. *Student publications, radio: Spokesman Panther Press*, a student newspaper; *Crusader*, a yearbook; *Sower Heritage*, an alumni and public relations newspaper magazine. *Surrounding community:* York has a population of 8,000.

Library Collections: 106,994 volumes including bound books, serial backfiles, electronic documents, and government documents not in separate collections. Card catalog. Current serial subscriptions: 338 paper. 2,514 recordings; 152 compact discs; 58 CD-ROMs. 57 computer work stations. Students have access to the Internet at no charge. Total budget for books, periodicals, audiovisual materials, microforms 2004–05: $49,700.

Most important special collections include Yorkana; Restoration; and E.A. Levitt Personal Papers.

Buildings and Grounds: Campus area 40 acres.

Chief Executive Officer: Dr. Wayne Baker, President.

Address admissions inquiries to Todd Martin, Director of Admissions.

Wayne State College

1111 Main Street

Wayne, Nebraska 68787-1923

Tel: (402) 375-7000   **E-mail:** admit1@wsc.edu
Fax: (402) 375-7204   **Internet:** www.wsc.edu

Institution Description: Wayne State College is a unit of the Nebraska State College System. *Enrollment:* 3,400. *Degrees awarded:* Baccalaureate, master's. Education Specialist degree also awarded.

Academic offers subject to approval by statewide coordinating bodies. Budget subject to approval by state governing boards.

Accreditation: *Regional:* NCA. *Professional:* teacher education

History: Established 1909; chartered as Nebraska State Normal School, and offered first instruction at postsecondary level 1910; changed name to Nebraska State Normal School and Teachers College 1921; changed name to Nebraska State Teachers College 1949; adopted present name 1963.

Institutional Structure: *Governing board:* Board of Trustees of the Nebraska State Colleges. Extrainstitutional representation: commissioner of education, 6 trustees and 4 students (appointed by governor of Nebraska). 1 ex officio. 7 voting. *Composition of institution:* Academic affairs headed by vice president of academic affairs. Management/business/finances directed by vice president of administration and finance. Full-time instructional faculty 142. Academic governance body, Faculty Senate, meets an average of 16 times per year. *Faculty representation:* Faculty served by collective bargaining agent, Nebraska State College Education Association, affiliated with NEA.

Calendar: Semesters. Academic year Aug. to May. Freshmen admitted Aug., Jan. Degrees conferred May, Aug., Dec. Formal commencements May, Dec. Summer session of 3 terms from May to Aug.

Characteristics of Freshmen: 100% of applicants admitted. 39% of admitted students enrolled full-time.

96% (544 students) submitted ACT scores. *25th percentile:* ACT Composite 18, ACT English 16, ACT Math 17. *75th percentile:* ACT Composite 23, ACT English 23, ACT Math 23.

47% of entering freshmen expected to graduate within 5 years. 84% of freshmen from Nebraska. Freshmen from 11 states.

Admission: Rolling admissions plan. For fall acceptance, apply as early as end of junior year of secondary school, but not later than 1 week after beginning of term. Early acceptance available. *Requirements:* Either graduation from accredited secondary school with 20 units (recommended) with 4 in English, 3 mathematics, 3 science, 2 foreign language, 3 social studies, 2 electives; or GED. Open admission for Nebraska secondary school graduates. *Entrance tests:* College Board SAT or ACT composite. *For transfer students:* 2.0 minimum GPA; from 4-year accredited institution 85 semester hours maximum transfer credit; from 2-year accredited institution 66 hours; correspondence/extension students 16 hours.

College credit and advanced placement for postsecondary-level work completed in secondary school. College credit for extrainstitutional learning on basis of ACE *2006 Guide to the Evaluation of Educational Experiences in the Armed Services.*

Tutoring available.

Degree Requirements: 125 semester hours; 2.0 GPA (2.5 for teacher education degree); 24 of last 30 hours in residence; 3 hours physical education; general education and distribution requirements.

Fulfillment of some degree requirements possible by passing departmental examinations, College Board CLEP, APP. *Grading system:* A–F; pass-fail; withdraw (carries time limit).

Distinctive Educational Programs: *For undergraduates:* Internships. Interdisciplinary majors in American studies, international commerce, public relations, sports journalism, technical theater; interdisciplinary majors and interdisciplinary courses offered. Facilities and programs for independent research, including honors programs, tutorials. *Available to all students:* Flexible meeting places and schedules, including off-campus centers (throughout northeast Nebraska), online courses, weekend and evening classes. Special facilities for using telecommunications in the classroom. Institutionally sponsored study abroad each spring semester to a country in Europe.

ROTC: Army in cooperation with University of South Dakota.

Degrees Conferred: 519 *baccalaureate:* biological/life sciences 12; business/marketing 114; communications/communication technologies 21; computer and information sciences 19; education 122; engineering and engineering technologies 15; English 6; foreign languages and literature 2; health professions and related sciences 3; interdisciplinary studies 1; mathematics 2; parks and recreation 91; physical sciences 15; protective services/public administration 31; psychology 35; social sciences and history 31; visual and performing arts 16. 105 *master's:* business/marketing 16; education 89.

Fees and Other Expenses: *Full-time tuition per academic year 2004–05:* undergraduate resident $2,850, nonresident $5,700; graduate resident $2,886, nonresident $5,772. *Required fees:* $822. *Room and board per academic year:* $4,120.

Financial Aid: Aid from institutionally generated funds is provided on the basis of academic merit, financial need, other criteria.

Financial aid to full-time, first-time undergraduate students: need-based scholarships/grants totaling $3,591,852, self-help $5,485,578; non-need-based scholarships/grants totaling $1,214,448, self-help $3,180,642, parent loans $676,563, tuition waivers $802,232, athletic awards $529,914. *Graduate aid:* 64 students received $89,214 in federal and state-funded fellowships/grants; 236 received $1,449,673 in federal and state-funded loans; 30 students held teaching assistantships worth $112,000 plus tuition (ranging from $2000 to $4,000).

Departments and Teaching Staff: *Professors* 51, *associate professors* 37, *assistant professors* 20, *instructors* 20, *part-time faculty* 76.

Total instructional faculty: 205 (full-time 127, part-time 78; women 113, men 92; members of minority groups 8). Total faculty with doctorate, first-professional, or other terminal degree: 109. Student-to-faculty ratio: 19:1. Degrees held by full-time faculty: baccalaureate 1%, master's 30%, doctorate 69%. 74% hold terminal degrees. *Faculty development:* $31,375 in grants for research. 6 faculty members awarded sabbaticals 2004–05.

Enrollment: Total enrollment 3,398. Undergraduate full-time 1,144 men / 1,392 women, part-time 154m / 456w; graduate 15m / 23w, part-time 154m / 456m. *Transfer students:* in-state 197; from out-of-state 39.

Characteristics of Student Body: *Ethnic/racial makeup:* number of Black non-Hispanic: 87; American Indian or Alaska Native: 30; Asian or Pacific Islander: 13; Hispanic: 71; White non-Hispanic: 2,439; unknown: 96. *Age distribution:* number under 18: 19; 18–19: 922; 20–21: 937; 22–24: 540; 25–29: 127; 30–34: 60; 35–39: 37; 40–49: 88; 50–64: 20.

International Students: 18 nonresident aliens enrolled fall 2004. 2 students from Europe, 5 Asia, 6 Latin America, 4 Africa, 1 other. No programs available to aid students whose native language is not English. No financial aid specifically designated for international students.

Student Life: On-campus residence halls available. 42% of undergraduate students live on campus. *Intercollegiate athletics:* men: baseball, basketball, cross-country, football, golf, track; women: basketball, cross-country, golf, soccer, softball, track, volleyball. *Special regulations:* Cars permitted without restrictions. Quiet hours and dormitory visitation hours vary according to residence hall. *Special services:* Learning Resources Center; medical services; STRIDE Program. *Student publications, radio, television: Wayne Stater*, a weekly newspaper. Radio station KWSC; KWSC-TV. *Surrounding community:* Wayne population 5,500. Omaha, 90 miles from campus, is nearest metropolitan area.

Library Collections: 243,848 volumes. 180,000 government documents; 565,000 microforms; 13,029 audiovisual materials; 652 current periodical subscriptions. Online catalog. Students have access to online information retrieval services and the Internet.

Buildings and Grounds: Campus area 128 acres.

Chief Executive Officer: Dr. Richard Collings, President.

Address admissions inquiries to R. Lincoln Morris, Dean of Admissions.

Nevada

Morrison University

10315 Professional Circle
Reno, Nevada 89521
Tel: (775) 850-0700   **E-mail:** admissions@morrison.edu
Fax: (775) 850-0711   **Internet:** www.morrison.edu

Institution Description: Morrison University is a private college offering programs in business administration, accounting, computer information systems, travel and tourism, and office administration. *Enrollment:* 125. *Degrees offered:* Associate, baccalaureate. Certificates and diplomas also awarded.

Accreditation: *Professional:* ACICS.

History: Founded as the Reno Business College in 1902, the college became a senior college in 1987 and adopted the present name 2002.

Institutional Structure: *Governing board:* Morrison College is owned by Northface Learning, Inc. Board of Directors include president, vice president, and secretary/treasurer. Full-time instructional faculty 12.

Calendar: Quarters. Academic year Sept. to Sept. .

Admission: *Requirements:* High school diploma or GED equivalency.

Degree Requirements: *For all associate degrees:* 90 credits (27 credit of general education and 63 credits of core courses and electives). *For all baccalaureate degrees:* 180 credits (63 general education credits and 117 core courses, electives, and specialty area).

Distinctive Educational Programs: Accounting Information Systems; Computer Information Systems; Paralegal/Legal Assistant; Electronic Gaming Equipment Technology.

Degrees Conferred: 5 *associate;* 15 *baccalaureate:* business and management; 4 *master's:* business, management, marketing, and related support services.

Fees and Other Expenses: *Full-time tuition per academic year 2004–05:* $9,600. *Books and supplies:* $1,250. *Room and board per academic year:* $5,000.

Financial Aid: Aid from institutionally generated funds is provided on the basis of academic merit, financial need. Institution has a Program Participation Agreement with the U.S. Department of Education for eligible students to receive Pell Grants and, depending upon the agreement, other federal aid. .

Financial aid to full-time, first-time undergraduate students: 35% received federal grants averaging $2,654; 8% state/local grants; 51% received loans averaging $2,500.

Departments and Teaching Staff: Business administration *professors* 0, *instructors* 0, *part-time teachers:* 5; accounting 1, 0, 3; computer information systems 3, 0, 4; office administration 2, 0, 0; medical administration 1, 0, 0; general education 1, 0, 2; English 1, 0, 0; travel and tourism 0, 0, 1; paralegal 0, 0, 4; electronics 0, 2, 0; gaming 0, 1, 1.

Total instructional faculty: 32. Student-to-faculty ratio: 10:1. Degrees held by full-time faculty: doctorate 15%, master's 77%, baccalaureate 100%. 41% hold terminal degrees.

Enrollment: Total enrollment 125.

Characteristics of Student Body: *Ethnic/racial makeup:* number of Black non-Hispanic: 6.6%; American Indian or Alaska Native: 9.8%; Asian or Pacific Islander: 8.2%; Hispanic: 16.4%; White non-Hispanic: 52.5%; unknown: 4.9%. *Age distribution:* 17–21:13%; 22–24: 13%; 25–29: 19%; 30–34: 14%; 35–39: 16%; 40–49: 17%; 50–59: 6%; 60–up: 2%.

International Students: 4 nonresident aliens from Asia enrolled. Programs available to aid students whose native language is not English: English as a Second Language Program. No financial aid specifically designated for international students.

Library Collections: 6,000 volumes. 500 microforms; 82 audiovisual materials. 55 current periodical subscriptions. The university has access to 40,000 online volumes and 20,000 online journals.

Most important special holdings include law (925); travel (125); Nevada (95).

Chief Executive Officer: Graham Doxey, President.

Address admissions inquiries to Director of Admissions.

Sierra Nevada College

999 Tahoe Boulevard
Incline Village, Nevada 89450-4269
Tel: (775) 831-1314   **E-mail:** admissions@sierranevada.edu
Fax: (775) 831-1347   **Internet:** www.sierranevada.edu

Institution Description: Sierra Nevada College is a private, independent, nonprofit college. *Enrollment:* 1,542. *Degrees awarded:* Baccalaureate, master's.

Accreditation: *Regional:* NWCCU.

History: Established, chartered, and offered first instruction at postsecondary level 1969; awarded first degree (baccalaureate) 1971.

Institutional Structure: *Governing board:* Board of Trustees. 30 trustees. Extrainstitutional representation: 5 administrators, 1 full-time instructional faculty member, 1 student. All voting. *Composition of institution:* The president supervises the dean of faculty, dean of enrollment, chief financial officer, and director of institutional advancement. Five academic chairs. The president chairs the college council, 15 faculty and staff members responsible for strategic planning and policy development.

Calendar: Semesters. Academic year Aug. to May. Freshmen admitted Aug., Jan., Apr., July. Degrees conferred June, May, Aug., Dec. Formal commencement June. Summer session of 1 term from early June to early Aug.

Characteristics of Freshmen: 85% of applicants admitted. 36% of applicants admitted and enrolled.

58% (38 students) submitted SAT scores; 20% (13 students) submitted ACT scores. *25th percentile*: SAT Verbal 440, SAT Math 430; ACT Composite 18, ACT English 18, ACT Math 17. *75th percentile*: SAT Verbal 630, SAT Math 600; ACT Composite 26, ACT English 28, ACT Math 27.

30% of entering freshmen expected to graduate within 5 years. 26% of freshmen from Nevada. Freshmen from 21 states and 4 foreign countries.

Admission: Rolling admissions plan. For fall acceptance, apply no later than 2 weeks prior to beginning of class. Early acceptance available. *Requirements:* Either graduation from accredited secondary school or GED; minimum GPA 2.0; 2 letters of recommendation. *Entrance tests:* College Board SAT or ACT. For foreign students TOEFL. *For transfer students:* 2.0 minimum GPA; credits subject to review.

College credit for postsecondary-level work completed in secondary school and for extrainstitutional learning (life experience) on basis of portfolio and faculty assessments.

Tutoring available. Developmental courses offered during regular academic year; credit given.

Degree Requirements: 120 semester hours; 45 upper division hours; 2.0 GPA; 45 credits in residence; general education requirements.

Fulfillment of some degree requirements and exemption from some beginning courses possible by passing College Board CLEP. *Grading system:* A–F; pass-fail; withdraw (carries penalty, carries time limit); descriptive reports.

Distinctive Educational Programs: Work-experience programs. Evening classes. Accelerated degree programs. Interdisciplinary programs. Facilities and programs for independent research, including individual majors, tutorials. Master of Arts in Teaching program with first class graduating spring 2006. certification program.

Degrees Conferred: 46 *baccalaureate:* business/marketing 17; computer and information sciences 3; natural resources/environmental science 2; psychology 12; social sciences and history 3; visual and performing arts 9.

Fees and Other Expenses: *Full-time tuition per academic year: 2004–05:* $19,500 undergraduate; $350 per credit for graduate study. *Required fees:* $150. *Room and board per academic year:* $7,450.

Financial Aid: Aid from institutionally generated funds is provided on the basis of academic merit, financial need, athletic ability. Institution has a Program Participation Agreement with the U.S. Department of Education for eligible students to receive Pell Grants and, depending upon the agreement, other federal aid.

Financial aid to full-time, first-time undergraduate students: need-based scholarships/grants totaling $3,311,699, self-help $3,190,841; non-need-based scholarships/grants totaling $80,800, athletic awards $156,000.

Departments and Teaching Staff: Fine arts *professors* 0, *associate professors* 3, *assistant professors* 2, *instructors* 0, *part-time faculty* 4; humanities 2, 2, 0, 0, 6; management 2, 0, 1, 1, 8; science and technology 2, 0, 2, 0, 5; teacher education 0, 1, 1, 0, 26.

Total instructional faculty: 68 (full-time 19, part-tine 49; women 38, men 30; members of minority groups 4). Total faculty with doctorate, first-professional, or other terminal degree: 23. Student-to-faculty ratio: 12:1. Degrees held by full-time faculty: doctorate 47%, master's 47%, baccalaureate 6%. 74% hold terminal degrees.

Enrollment: Total enrollment 1,542. Undergraduate full-time 148 men / 139 women, part-time 21m / 21w; graduate full-time 62m / 88w, part-time 10m / 16w.

Characteristics of Student Body: *Ethnic/racial makeup:* number of Black non-Hispanic: 5; American Indian or Alaska Native: 5; Asian or Pacific Islander: 4; Hispanic: 5; White non-Hispanic: 145; unknown: 157. *Age distribution:* number under 18: 1; 18–19: 64; 20–21: 97; 22–24: 71; 25–29: 37; 30–34: 9; 35–39: 3; 40–49: 3; 50–64: 2.

International Students: 8 nonresident aliens enrolled fall 2004. 6 students from Europe, 1 Latin America, 1 Canada. No programs available to aid students whose native language is not English. No financial aid specifically designated for international students.

Student Life: On-campus housing available. *Intercollegiate athletics:* men's and women's skiing. *Special regulations:* Cars permitted without restrictions. *Student publications:* Eagle's Eye, a monthly newspaper. *Surrounding community:* Lake Tahoe, Incline Village, and Reno, 35 miles from campus, is nearest metropolitan area. Served by airport 35 miles from campus; passenger rail service 25 miles from campus.

Library Collections: 25,000 volumes. 170 current periodical subscriptions. Online catalog. Students have access to online information retrieval services and the Internet.

Most important special holdings include collections on teacher education; Lake Tahoe; hotel, restaurant, ski resort management.

Buildings and Grounds: Campus area 3 acres. *New buildings:* Prim-Schultz Hall (104-bed residence facility) completed 2000; Prim Library 2004; Tahoe Center for Environmental Science 2006.

Chief Executive Officer: Dr. Paul Ranslow, President.

Address admission inquiries to Charles Timinsky, Director of Admissions; graduate inquiries to Mary Maringello, Teacher Education Graduate Admission.

University of Nevada, Las Vegas

4505 Maryland Parkway
Las Vegas, Nevada 89154

Tel: (702) 895-3443   **E-mail:** admission@ccmail.nevada.edu
Fax: (702) 895-1118   **Internet:** www.unlv.edu

Institution Description: *Enrollment:* 27,344. *Degrees awarded:* Associate, baccalaureate, master's, doctorate. Education specialist also awarded.

Member of National Park Internship Service Program; WICHE.

Accreditation: *Regional:* NWCCU. *Professional:* accounting, art, athletic training, business, clinical lab scientist, computer science, construction education, counseling, dentistry, engineering, interior design, kinesiotherapy, landscape architecture, law, music, nuclear medicine technology, nursing, physical therapy, public administration, radiography, social work, teacher education, theatre

History: Established as Southern Regional Branch of the University of Nevada and offered first instruction at postsecondary level 1951; became division 1957; chartered and awarded first degree (baccalaureate) 1964; changed name to Nevada Southern University 1965; became autonomous 1968; adopted present name 1969. *See* James W. Hulse, *University of Nevada: A Centennial History* (Reno, Nevada: University of Nevada Press, 1974) for further information.

Institutional Structure: *Composition of institution:* President, academic vice president/provost, vice president business affairs, vice president for student affairs, enrollment management. College of: Business, Education, Engineering, Extended Studies, Fine Arts, Graduate, Health Sciences, Hotel Administration, Liberal Arts, Sciences, Urban Affairs. Academic governance: Faculty Senate.

Calendar: Semesters. Academic year early Aug. to May. Freshmen admitted on rolling admissions basis. Degrees conferred May, Aug., Dec. Formal commencement May. Summer session early June to mid-Aug.

Characteristics of Freshmen: 81% of applicants accepted. 61% of accepted applicants enrolled.

48% (1,905 students) submitted SAT scores; 44% (1,428 students) submitted ACT scores. *25th percentile:* SAT Verbal 440, SAT Math 450; ACT Composite 18, ACT English 17, ACT Math 17. *75th percentile:* SAT Verbal 560, SAT Math 580; ACT Composite 24, ACT English 23, ACT Math 24.

35% of entering freshmen expected to graduate within 5 years. 80% of freshmen from Nevada. Freshmen from 43 states and 42 foreign countries.

Admission: Rolling admissions plan. For fall acceptance, apply as early as preceding semester. Priority application date is May 1. Early acceptance available. *Requirements:* Graduation from accredited high school; minimum 2.50 GPA and completion of core requirements: English 4 units, mathematics 3 units at algebra level or higher, social science 3 units, natural science 3 units, computer literacy one half unit. Some exceptions possible through admission by Alternative Criteria Program. *Entrance tests:* College Board SAT or ACT composite. For foreign students TOEFL. *For transfer students:* Minimum of 2.00 GPA.

College credit and advanced placement for postsecondary-level work completed in secondary school. Tutoring available. Noncredit remedial courses offered during regular academic year.

Degree Requirements: Minimum 124 credits; minimum 2.00 GPA; core requirements; English 9 credits; U.S. and Nevada constitution; logic 3 credits; mathematics 3 credits; computer science or statistics 3 credits; social science 9 credits; science 6–8 credits; fine arts 3 credits; humanities 6 credits; 3 credit multicultural requirement; 3 credit international requirements. Last 30 credits earned in residence. Minimum credits and minimum GPA may vary by college.

Fulfillment of some degree requirements and exemption from some beginning courses possible by passing College Board CLEP, AP. *Grading system:* A–F; pass-fail; withdraw (deadline after which pass-fail is appended to withdraw).

Distinctive Educational Programs: Weekend and evening classes. Special facilities for using telecommunications in the classroom. Tutorials. Study abroad by individual arrangement; Australia, England, Costa Rica, Chile, France, Germany, Greece, Ireland, Italy, Mexico, New Zealand, Norway, Spain, Switzerland, Thailand. Honors program. *Other distinctive programs:* Continuing education.

ROTC: Army.

Degrees Conferred: 2,913 *baccalaureate* (B), 902 *master's* (M), 166 *doctorate* (D): architecture 30 (B), 11 (M); area and ethnic studies 7 (B); biological/life sciences 76 (B), 5 (M), 3 (D); business/marketing 975 (B), 108 (M), 6 (D); communications/communication technologies 208 (B), 6 (M); computer and information sciences 43 (B), 18 (M); education 432 (B), 468 (M), 21 (D); engineering and engineering technologies 76 (B), 53 (M), 21 (D); English 50 (B), 11 (M), 4 (D); foreign languages and literature 16 (B); health professions and related sciences 111 (B), 25 (M); interdisciplinary studies 8 (B); law/legal studies 118 (D); mathematics 10 (B), 6 (M); natural resources/environmental science 14 (B), 4 (M); parks and recreation 109 (B), 13 (M); personal and miscellaneous services 13 (B); philosophy/religion/theology 7 (B); physical sciences 17 (B), 17 (M), 2 (D); protective services/public administration 193 (B), 67 (M); psychology 166 (B), 29 (M); social sciences and history 201 (B), 20 (M), 4 (D); visual and performing arts 151 (B), 41 (M), 1 (D). 118 *first-professional:* law.

Fees and Other Expenses: *Full-time tuition per academic year 2004–05:* resident $3,060, nonresident $12,527. *Required fees:* $472. Contact the university for current graduate and first-professional tuition/fees. *Room and board per academic year:* $8,326. *Books and supplies:* $850.

Financial Aid: Aid from institutionally generated funds is provided on the basis of academic merit, financial need, athletic ability, other criteria. Institution has a Program Participation Agreement with the U.S. Department of Education for eligible students to receive Pell Grants and, depending upon the agreement, other federal aid.

Financial aid to full-time, first-time undergraduate students: need-based scholarships/grants totaling $17,100,000, self-help $41,500,000, parent loans $7,200,000, tuition waivers $300,000; non-need-based scholarships/grants totaling $26,90,000, self-help $29,000,000, parent loans $2,400,000, tuition waivers $2,100,000, athletic awards $5,500,000.

Departments and Teaching Staff: *Total instructional faculty:* 1,542 (full-time 810, part-time 732; women 267, men 543; members of minority groups 142). Total faculty with doctorate, first-professional, or other terminal degree: 717. Student-to-faculty ratio: 20:1. Degrees held by full-time faculty: doctorate 84.6%, master's 14.5%, baccalaureate .9%. 91.4% hold terminal degrees.

Enrollment: Total enrollment 27,344. Undergraduate full-time 6,782, part-time 8,788; first-professional full-time 317m / 209w, part-time 95m / 83w; graduate full-time 668m / 935w, part-time 1,275m / 1,979w.

Characteristics of Student Body: *Ethnic/racial makeup (undergraduate):* number of Black non-Hispanic: 1,780; American Indian or Alaska Native: 207; Asian or Pacific Islander: 2,992; Hispanic: 2,336; White non-Hispanic: 11,595; unknown: 2,108.

International Students: 1,153 nonresident aliens enrolled fall 2004. 91 students from Europe, 953 Asia, 29 Latin America, 20 Africa, 50 Canada, 7 Australia, 3 New Zealand. Programs available to aid students whose native language is not English: social, cultural. English as a Second Language Program. Some financial aid specifically designated for international students.

Student Life: On-campus residence halls house 8.5% of student body. Residence halls for both sexes constitute 100% of such space. *Intercollegiate athletics:* men only: baseball, cross-country, football, soccer, tennis, track; women only: basketball, cross-country, softball, swimming, tennis, track, volleyball. *Special regulations:* Cars permitted in designated areas only. Dormitory visitation from 9am to 11pm. *Special services:* Learning Resources Center, medical services; Office of International Programs (assists foreign students in all aspects of educational life); Academic Resource Center provides academic and career counseling, testing, and tutoring. *Student publications, radio:* The Yell, a weekly newspaper. Radio station KUNV broadcasts 96 hours per week. *Surrounding community:* Las Vegas population 1,200,000. Served by mass transit bus system, airport 2 miles from campus.

Library Collections: 1,007,638 volumes including bound books, serial backfiles, electronic documents, and government documents not in separate collections. Online catalog. Current serial subscriptions: 2,700 paper, 12,300 via electronic access. 350 computer work stations. Students have access to the Internet at no charge. Total budget for books, periodicals, audiovisual materials, microforms 2003–04: $4,600,586.

Most important special holdings include collections include Gaming Research Collections; Urban and Regional Historical Collections; Architectural Drawings.

Buildings and Grounds: Campus area 335 acres. *New buildings:* Student Union; Science and Technology.

Chief Executive Officer: Dr. Carol H. Harter, President.

Address undergraduate admission inquiries to Pamela Hicks, Director of Admissions; graduate inquiries to Gale Sinatra, Dean, Graduate College; law inquiries to Frank Durand, Law School; Christine c. Ancajas, Dental School.

College of Liberal Arts

Degree Programs Offered: *Baccalaureate, master's* in communications, fine and applied arts, foreign languages, letters, psychology, social sciences.

Admission: *See* general requirements. Graduate requirements vary with program and level.

Degree Requirements: *See* general requirements. Graduate requirements vary.

Distinctive Educational Programs: Interdisciplinary programs in Asian studies, ethnic studies, film studies, Latin American studies, social science studies, women's studies. Individual majors.

Enrollment: *Total enrollment:* 3,058.

College of Allied Health Professions

Degree Programs Offered: *Associate, baccalaureate, master's* in nursing; *associate, baccalaureate* in radiologic technology.

Admission: *See* general requirements. Nursing students 2.75 GPA, radiologic technology 2.5 GPA and standardized test.

Degree Requirements: *See* general requirements. For baccalaureate of nursing students exit competency examination—State Board Examination; 2.75 GPA.

Distinctive Educational Programs: Baccalaureate completion program.

Enrollment: *Total enrollment:* 1,107.

College of Business

Degree Programs Offered: *Baccalaureate* in business administration, economics; *master's* in accounting, business administration, economics, public administration.

Admission: *See* general requirements. Graduate requirements vary with program and level.

Degree Requirements: *See* general requirements. Graduate requirements vary.

Enrollment: *Total enrollment:* 4,271.

College of Education

Degree Programs Offered: *Baccalaureate, master's, doctorate* in education. Specialist certificates also awarded.

Admission: *See* general requirements. Graduate requirements vary with program and level.

Degree Requirements: *See* general requirements. For elementary education majors 2.5 GPA in professional education courses; for secondary education majors 2.3 GPA in professional education courses, and in two courses teaching fields.

Enrollment: *Total enrollment:* 3,068.

College of Hotel Administration

Degree Programs Offered: *Baccalaureate* in hotel administration.

Admission: *See* general requirements.

Degree Requirements: *See* general requirements. 800 hours of gainful employment in the hotel industry.

Enrollment: *Total enrollment:* 2,183.

College of Sciences

Degree Programs Offered: *Baccalaureate* in biological sciences, chemistry, computer science, engineering, earth sciences, geology, mathematical sciences; *master's* in biological sciences, mathematical sciences.

Admission: *See* general requirements. Graduate requirements vary with program and level.

Degree Requirements: *See* general requirements. 2.0 GPA in major field. Graduate requirements vary.

Distinctive Educational Programs: Independent study and research.

Enrollment: *Total enrollment:* 1,672.

University of Nevada, Reno

9th and North Virginia Streets
Reno, Nevada 89557-0002

Tel: (702) 784-1110   **E-mail:** asknevada@unr.edu
Fax: (702) 784-4283   **Internet:** www.unr.edu

Institution Description: *Enrollment:* 15,950. *Degrees awarded:* Baccalaureate, first-professional (medicine), master's, doctorate. Education specialist also awarded.

Accreditation: *Regional:* NWCCU. *Professional:* accounting, business, clinical psychology, computer science, counseling, dietetics, engineering, journalism, medicine, music, nuclear medicine technology, nursing, nursing education, social work, speech-language pathology, teacher education

History: Chartered as a preparatory school 1864; established as Nevada State University in Elko 1874; moved to Reno and changed name to University of Nevada 1885; offered first instruction at postsecondary level 1887; awarded first degree (baccalaureate) 1891; adopted present name 1969. *See* James W. Hulse, *University of Nevada: A Centennial History* (Reno: University of Nevada Press, 1974) for further information.

Institutional Structure: *Composition of institution:* Administrators 332 men / 211 women. Academic affairs headed by vice president, academic affairs. Business/finances directed by vice president, administration and finance. Full-time instructional faculty 717. Academic governance bodies: Faculty Senate meets an average of 10 times per year.

Calendar: Semesters. Academic year Aug. to May. Freshmen admitted Aug., Jan., June, July. Degrees conferred May, Aug., Dec. Formal commencement May. Summer session of 2 terms from to Aug. (includes miniterm).

Characteristics of Freshmen: 87% of applicants accepted. 59% of accepted applicants enrolled.

69% (1,502 students) submitted SAT scores; 58% (1,265 students) submitted ACT scores. *25th percentile:* SAT Verbal 460, SAT Math 470; ACT Composite 20,ACT English 18, ACT Math 19. *75th percentile:* SAT Verbal 580, SAT Math 590; ACT Composite 25, ACT English 25, ACT Math 25.

36% of entering freshmen expected to graduate within 5 years. 87% of freshmen from Nevada. Freshmen from 46 states and 82 foreign countries.

Admission: Rolling admissions plan. For fall acceptance, apply as early as completion of junior year of secondary school, preferably Mar. 1 of year of enrollment. Early acceptance available. *Requirements:* Graduation from accredited secondary school. College preparatory curriculum strongly recommended; 13.5 units of specific coursework required. Minimum 2.75 GPA. *Entrance tests:* College Board SAT or ACT composite. For foreign students TOEFL. *For transfer students:* 2.0 minimum GPA; from 4-year accredited institution 96 hours maximum transfer credit; from 2-year accredited institution 64 hours; correspondence/extension students 60 hours.

College credit and advanced placement for postsecondary level work completed in secondary school and for extrainstitutional learning on basis of *2006 Guide to the Evaluation of Educational Experiences in the Armed Services.*

Tutoring available. Remedial courses offered during regular academic year; nondegree credit given.

Degree Requirements: *For all baccalaureate degrees:* 124–137 credit hours. *For all undergraduate degrees:* 2.0 GPA; 32 credit hours in residence; courses in English and in Nevada and U.S. constitutions.

Fulfillment of some degree requirements and exemption from some beginning courses possible by passing College Board CLEP, APP, ACT, departmental examinations, other standardized tests. *Grading system:* A–F; satisfactory/

unsatisfactory; withdraw (deadline after which pass-fail is appended to withdraw); incomplete (carries time limit).

Distinctive Educational Programs: Flexible meeting places and schedules, including weekend and evening classes. Special facilities for using telecommunications in the classroom. Interdisciplinary programs. Honors programs. Study abroad through University Studies Abroad Consortium (England, France, Germany, Italy, Spain, Chile, Costa Rica, Thailand, Australia). *Other distinctive programs:* Continuing education and extension programs provide postsecondary educational opportunities to Nevada residents.

ROTC: Army. 16 commissions awarded 2004.

Degrees Conferred: 1,786 *baccalaureate* (B), 464 *master's* (M), 77 *doctorate* (D): agriculture 24 (B), 19 (M); area and ethnic studies 2 (B); biological/life sciences 126 (B), 11 (M); 12 (D); business/marketing 265 (B), 50 (M); communications/communication technologies 88 (B), 10 (M); computer and information sciences 100 (B), 16 (M); education 183 (B), 111 (M), 10 (D); engineering and engineering technologies 147 (B), 66 (M), 10 (D); English 58 (B), 20 (M), 2 (D); foreign languages and literature 44 (B), 5 (M); health professions and related sciences 126 (B), 31 (M), 1 (D); home economics and vocational home economics 68 (B), 5 (M); law/legal studies 4 (M); liberal arts/general studies 95 (B); mathematics 12 (B), 11 (M); natural resources/environmental science 25 (B); philosophy/religion/theology 6 (B), 3 (M); physical sciences 25 (B), 17 (M), 12 (D); protective services/public administration 32 (B), 19 (M); psychology 107 (B), 39 (M), 21 (D); social sciences and history 196 (B), 19 (M), 9 (D); visual and performing arts 57 (B), 8 (M). 50 *first-professional:* medicine.

Fees and Other Expenses: *Full-time tuition per academic year 2004–05:* undergraduate resident $2,850, nonresident $11,726. Contact the university for current graduate/first-professional tuition and fees. *Room and board academic year:* $7,385. *Required fees:* $160.

Financial Aid: Aid from institutionally generated funds is provided on the basis of academic merit, financial need, athletic ability, other criteria. Institution has a Program Participation Agreement with the U.S. Department of Education for eligible students to receive Pell Grants and, depending upon the agreement, other federal aid.

Financial aid to full-time, first-time undergraduate students: need-based scholarships/grants totaling $11,184,205, self-help $14,218,013, parent loans $1,277,932; non-need-based scholarships/grants totaling $12,758,334, self-help $2,640,442, parent loans $447,258, tuition waivers $767,587. *Graduate aid:* 581 students received $1,064,301 in federal and state-funded fellowships/grants; 448 received $5,500,413 in federal and state-funded loans; 363 teaching assistantships awarded totaling $4,105,396; 670 research assistantships were awarded totaling $6,916,220.

Departments and Teaching Staff: *Total instructional faculty:* 1,144 (full-time 697, part-time 447; women 466, men 678; members of minority groups 161). Total faculty with doctorate, first-professional, or other terminal degree: 775. Student-to-faculty ratio: 16:1.

Enrollment: Total enrollment 15,950. Undergraduate full-time 4,429 men / 5,409 women, part-time 1,259m / 1,427w; first-professional full-time 113m / 104w; graduate full-time 492m / 667w, part-time 829m / 1,321w.

Characteristics of Student Body: *Ethnic/racial makeup (undergraduate):* number of Black non-Hispanic: 288; American Indian or Alaska Native: 157; Asian or Pacific Islander: 853; Hispanic: 867; White non-Hispanic: 8,877; unknown: 1,102.

International Students: 380 undergraduate nonresident aliens enrolled fall 2004. Students from Europe, Asia, Latin America, Africa, Canada, Australia. Programs available to aid students whose native language is not English: social, cultural. English as a Second Language Program. Financial aid specifically designated for international students: scholarships available annually for undergraduates.

Student Life: On-campus residence halls house 11% of student body. Halls for men only constitute 7% of such space, for women only 10%, for both sexes 83%. 9% of men join and 5% live in fraternities; 8% of women join and 3% live in sororities. Housing available for married students. *Intercollegiate athletics:* men only: baseball, basketball, football, golf, rifle, skiing, tennis; women only: basketball, cross-country, golf, rifle, skiing, softball, swimming, tennis, track and field, volleyball. *Special regulations:* Cars permitted with parking stickers. *Special services:* Learning Resources Center, medical services. *Student publications, radio:* Sagebrush, a student newspaper; Brushfire, a literary magazine. Radio station KUNR-FM. *Surrounding community:* Reno population 106,000. Sacramento (CA), 138 miles from campus, is nearest metropolitan area. Served by airport 4 miles from campus; passenger rail service ½ mile from campus.

Publications: *Silver and Blue*, an alumni magazine;

Library Collections: 1,128,944 volumes including bound books, serial backfiles, electronic documents, and government documents not in separate collections. Online catalog. Current serial subscriptions: 2,746 paper; 16,000 via electronic access. 62,392 recordings; 6,274 CD-ROMs. 120 computer work stations. Students have access to the Internet at no charge. Total budget for books, periodicals, audiovisual materials, microforms 2004–05: $4,163,231.

Most important special holdings include Basque Studies Collection; collections on Nevada history and the Great Basin Indians; Women in the West Collection.

Buildings and Grounds: Campus area 200 acres.

Chief Executive Officer: Dr. John N. Lilley, President.

Address admission inquiries to Dr. Melisa Choroszy, Associate Vice President for Enrollment Services. Contact the appropriate departments for graduate programs.

College of Agriculture, Biotechnology, and Natural Resources

Degree Programs Offered: *Baccalaureate* in agricultural economics, agricultural education, animal science, biochemistry, plant science and resource management; *master's* in agricultural economics, animal science, biochemistry, integrated pest management, plant science and resource management. Students with an interest in agricultural education may register in a foregoing program (except biochemistry) and supplement with courses from the College of Education. A *doctorate* is offered in biochemistry. Students may also obtain interdisciplinary degree in hydrology and hydrogeology, land use planning and cellular and molecular biology.

Departments and Teaching Staff: *Total instructional faculty:* 50.

Distinctive Educational Programs: Three-year preprofessional program in veterinary medicine.

Enrollment: *Total enrollment:* 865.

College of Liberal Arts and Science

Degree Programs Offered: *Baccalaureate* in anthropology, art, biology, chemistry, criminal justice, English, foreign languages and literature, geography, history, mathematics, music, philosophy, physics, political science, psychology, sociology, speech communication, Spanish, theatre, women's studies; *master's* and *doctorate*.

Departments and Teaching Staff: *Total instructional faculty:* 180.

Distinctive Educational Programs: Special an/or minor programs also in Army ROTC; Basque studies; environmental literature; historic preservation; holocaust, genocide, and peace studies; Italian studies; Japanese studies; Latin American studies; medieval and renaissance studies; museoology; pre-law; religious studies.

Enrollment: *Total enrollment:* 4,947.

College of Business Administration

Degree Programs Offered: *Baccalaureate* in accounting, computer information systems, economics, finance, gaming management, international business, logistics, management, marketing; *master's* in business administration, economics.

Departments and Teaching Staff: *Total instructional faculty:* 53.

Enrollment: *Total enrollment:* 1,889.

College of Education

Degree Programs Offered: *Baccalaureate* in elementary/special education and secondary education; *master's* and *doctorate* in education.

Departments and Teaching Staff: *Total instructional faculty:* 47.

Enrollment: *Total enrollment:* 1,989.

College of Engineering

Degree Programs Offered: *Baccalaureate* in computer science, chemical engineering, civil engineering, electrical engineering, engineering physics, materials science, mechanical engineering; *master's, doctorate* in engineering.

Admission: In addition to university requirements, the College of Engineering recommends 3 units of mathematics (1.5 in algebra, 1 in geometry, and .5 in trigonometry), plus 1 unit of science.

Departments and Teaching Staff: *Total instructional faculty:* 57.

Distinctive Educational Programs: Summer work-experience programs.

Enrollment: *Total enrollment:* 1,582.

College of Human and Community Sciences

Degree Programs Offered: *Baccalaureate* in child and family studies, consumer sciences, criminal justice, housing and interior design, fashion merchandising, nursing; *master's* in home economics, nursing with clinical and administrative options.

Departments and Teaching Staff: *Total instructional faculty:* 58.

Enrollment: *Total enrollment:* 1,721.

College of Science

Degree Programs Offered: *Baccalaureate* in chemical engineering, geology, geological engineering, geophysics, metallurgical engineering, mining engineering; *master's* and *doctorate* in mining engineering.

Departments and Teaching Staff: *Total instructional faculty:* 164.

Distinctive Educational Programs: Post-master's professional degrees in geological engineering, metallurgical engineering, engineer of mines.

Enrollment: *Total enrollment:* 1,320.

Donald W. Reynolds School of Journalism

Degree Programs Offered: *Baccalaureate* in journalism, with emphases in print journalism, broadcast journalism, advertising and public relations; *master's* in journalism with individualized plans of study.

Admission: Undergraduate admission to the journalism major requires a 2.5 GPA during the first 2 years of undergraduate study.

Degree Requirements: *Undergraduate:* A GPA of at least 2.5, completion of 32 credits in journalism and at least 90 credits outside journalism, including 65 in the liberal arts. *Graduate:* A GPA of at least 3.0, completion of 30 credits including a thesis or professional research project. A fourth semester course in a foreign language.

Departments and Teaching Staff: *Total instructional faculty:* 10.

Enrollment: *Total enrollment:* 536.

School of Medicine

Degree Programs Offered: *Baccalaureate* in biochemistry, speech pathology or audiology; *master's* in speech pathology and audiology and biochemistry; *doctorate* in biochemistry and pharmacology. M.D. degree. M.D./Ph.D. degree in pharmacology.

Admission: The new Medical College Aptitude Test (MCAT) is required of all applicants. The admission committee strongly recommends completion of a baccalaureate degree, 16 credits of chemistry, 8 credits of biology, 8 credits of physics and 9 credits of behavioral sciences (3 credits of which must be upper division). In addition, a demonstrated proficiency in English composition and expression is required. Students should take courses that deal with the psychological stages of the life cycle (i.e., human growth and development, adolescence, aging, human sexuality, abnormal psychology, family dynamics, or medical oriented sociology). Recommended but not required: calculus, biochemistry, genetics and embryology.

Degree Requirements: Year one and two, basic sciences: 94 credits; third and fourth year required clerkships (including a four-week rural preceptorship): 56 credits; passing score on parts I and II of the National Board of Medical Examiners examination.

Departments and Teaching Staff: *Total instructional faculty:* 155.

Distinctive Educational Programs: Preprofessional program in pharmacy, leading to baccalaureate awarded by approved schools of pharmacy.

Enrollment: *Total enrollment:* 389.

New Hampshire

Colby-Sawyer College

541 Main Street
New London, New Hampshire 03257-7835
Tel: (603) 526-3000   **E-mail:** csadmiss@colby-sawyer.edu
Fax: (603) 526-3452   **Internet:** www.colby-sawyer.edu

Institution Description: Colby-Sawyer College (Colby Junior College until 1975) is a private, independent, nonprofit, coeducational college. *Enrollment:* 964. *Degrees awarded:* Associate, baccalaureate.

Member of New Hampshire College and University Council (NHCUC).

Accreditation: *Regional:* NEASC. *Professional:* athletic training, nursing

History: Established and incorporated as New London Academy 1837; offered first instruction at postsecondary level 1928; awarded first degree (associate) in 1930; adopted present name 1975. *See* Henry K. Rowe, *A Centennial History 1837–1937 Colby Academy-Colby Junior College* (Cambridge, Mass.: Harvard University Press, 1937) for further information.

Institutional Structure: *Governing board:* Colby-Sawyer College Board of Trustees of not more than 30 trustees, including the president (ex officio) and 3 alumni (29 voting), Non-member institutional representatives: 1 full-time faculty member, 1 student. *Composition of institution:* Administrators 4 men / 2 women. Academic affairs headed by provost and dean of faculty. Management directed by vice president for administration. Business/finances headed by treasurer. Full-time instructional faculty: 59. Academic governance body, the faculty, meets an average of 9 times per year.

Calendar: Semesters. Academic year Sept. to May. Freshmen admitted Sept., Jan. Degrees conferred and formal commencement May. No summer session.

Characteristics of Freshmen: 82% of applicants admitted. 19% of applicants admitted and enrolled.

97% (259 students) submitted SAT scores; 16% (42 students) submitted ACT scores. *25th percentile:* SAT Verbal 460, SAT Math 460; ACT Composite 17. *75th percentile:* SAT Verbal 540, SAT Math 560; ACT Composite 22.

59% entering freshmen expected to graduate within 5 years. 30% of freshmen from New Hampshire. Freshmen from 23 states and 5 foreign countries.

Admission: Rolling admissions plan. For fall acceptance, apply as early as Sept. 1 of previous year. Students are notified of acceptance beginning Dec. 15; Apply by Dec. 15 for early notification. Early acceptance available. *Requirements:* Either graduation from accredited secondary school with 15 units or GED. Recommend 4 units English, 3 mathematics, 2 of the same foreign language, 3 or more social studies, 2 or more laboratory science, academic electives. For nursing program, 3 years of college preparatory laboratory science, including biology and chemistry, are recommended. Minimum recommended GPA 2.0. Lowest recommended secondary school class standing 50th percentile. *Entrance tests:* College Board SAT or ACT composite. *For transfer students:* At least one half of the prescribed courses for a particular degree program, including the final 30 credit hours, must be Colby-Sawyer sponsored.

College credit and advanced placement for postsecondary-level work completed in secondary school. For extrainstitutional learning college credit and advanced placement on basis of ACE *2006 Guide to the Evaluation of Educational Experiences in the Armed Services;* faculty and dean's assessments.

Tutoring available.

Degree Requirements: (Courses measured in credit hours). *For all associate degrees:* 60 credit hours; last 30 credit hours in residence. *For all baccalaureate degrees:* 120 credit hours; final 30 credit hours must be Colby-Sawyer sponsored. *For all degrees:* 2.00 GPA; distribution requirements (core curriculum).

Fulfillment of some degree requirements and exemption from some beginning courses possible by passing departmental examinations, College Board CLEP, or APP. *Grading system:* A–F; pass-fail; withdraw (carries time limit); incomplete.

Distinctive Educational Programs: Integration of liberal arts and sciences with career preparation. Internships recommended for all students (required by some majors). Honors programs. Study abroad strongly encouraged; experiences tailored to individual needs and interests. Off-campus programs in U.S. include Washington Semester at American University. Cross-registration and off-campus study through New Hampshire College and University Council membership.

ROTC: Air Force and Navy in cooperation with University of New Hampshire.

Degrees Conferred: 10 *associate;* 197 *baccalaureate:* biological/life sciences 5; business/marketing 30; communications/communication technologies 18; education 5; health professions and related sciences 14; natural resources/environmental science 4; parks and recreation 28; psychology 42; social sciences and history 7; visual and performing arts 25.

Fees and Other Expenses: *Full-time tuition per academic year 2004–05:* $24,700. *Room and board per academic year:* $8,490.

Financial Aid: Aid from institutionally generated funds is provided on the basis of academic merit, financial need, other considerations.

Financial aid to full-time, first-time undergraduate students: need-based scholarships/grants totaling $6,613,856, self-help $2,793,076, non-need-based scholarships/grants totaling $2,165,165, self-help $2,004,731, parent loans $2,967,507.

Departments and Teaching Staff: Business *professors* 0, *associate professors* 2, *assistant professors* 2, *instructors* 1, *part-time faculty* 6; community and environment 0, 0, 1, 0, 1; exercise and sport sciences 1, 1, 3, 0, 8; fine and performing arts 3, 3, 2, 0, 11; humanities 4, 6, 4, 0, 12; natural sciences 1, 2, 6, 1, 5; nursing 0, 1, 5, 0, 1; social sciences and education 1, 3, 5, 0, 11.

Total instructional faculty: 114 (full-time 59, part-time 55; women 66, men 48). Total faculty with doctorate, first-professional, or other terminal degree: 63. Student-to-faculty ratio: 12:1. Degrees held by full-time faculty: doctorate 61%, master's 100%. 75% hold terminal degrees. *Faculty development:* 3 faculty members awarded sabbaticals 2004–05.

Enrollment: Total enrollment 989. Full-time 327 men / 612 women, part-time 9m / 16w. *Transfer students:* in-state 18; from out-of-state 19.

Characteristics of Student Body: *Ethnic/racial makeup:* number of Black non-Hispanic: 5; American Indian or Alaska Native: 1; Asian or Pacific Islander: 14; Hispanic: 2; White non-Hispanic: 892; unknown: 38. *Age distribution:* number under 18: 23; 18–19: 448; 20–21: 384; 22–24: 78; 25–29: 6; 30–34: 6; 35–39: 5; 40–49: 50–64: 7.

International Students: 12 nonresident aliens enrolled fall 2004. 3 students from Europe, 7 Asia, 2 other. Programs available to aid students whose native language is not English: social, cultural, financial. English as a Second Language Program. No financial aid specifically designated for international students.

Student Life: On-campus residence halls house 87% of student body. 10 residence halls of which 9 are coed, 1 women only; 1 is substance free. *Intercollegiate athletics:* men: baseball, basketball, soccer, swimming/diving, tennis, track and field, alpine ski racing; women: basketball, lacrosse, soccer, swimming/diving, tennis, track and field, alpine ski racing, volleyball; coed: equestrian. NCAA Division III, Commonwealth Coast Conference. *Special regulations:* Cars permitted; $50 fee charged. Quiet hours set by individual residence halls. *Special services:* Medical services. *Student publications: The Informer,* a literary magazine; *Colbyan,* an annual yearbook; *Colby-Sawyer Courier,* a campus newspaper. *Surrounding community:* New London population 3,000. Boston (MA), 100 miles from campus, is nearest metropolitan area. Served by airport 30 miles from campus; passenger rail service 33 miles from campus.

Library Collections: 90,055 volumes. 203,532 microform units. Current periodical subscriptions: paper 514; microform 349; via electronic access 12,253. 1,900 audiovisual materials. 189 computer work stations campus-wide. Students have access to online information retrieval services and the Internet.

Most important special holdings include the Cleveland family papers.

Buildings and Grounds: Campus area 200 acres.

Chief Executive Officer: Dr. Anne Ponder, President.

Address admission inquiries to Admissions Office.

College for Lifelong Learning

125 North State Street
Concord, New Hampshire 03301-6430
Tel: (603) 228-3000   **E-mail:** info@cll.edu
Fax: (603) 229-0964   **Internet:** www/cll.edu

Institution Description: The College for Lifelong Learning, formerly named School for Lifelong Learning, is the nonresidential state college for adults offering individualized degree study in eleven regional offices of the state. It is one of four institutions in the University System of New Hampshire. *Enrollment:* 2,697. *Degrees awarded:* Associate, baccalaureate.

Budget subject to approval by state governing boards. Member of the consortium New Hampshire College and University Council.

Accreditation: *Regional:* NEASC.

History: Established as School of Continuing Studies and offered first instruction at postsecondary level 1972; awarded first degree (baccalaureate) 1974; adopted name School for Lifelong Learning 1979; adopted present name 1992.

Institutional Structure: *Governing board:* Board of Trustees, University System of New Hampshire. Representation: 11 trustees (appointed by governor of New Hampshire); 4 University of New Hampshire alumni, Keene State College alumnus, 1 Plymouth State College alumnus (all elected by alumni of their respective schools); 1 student (elected on a rotating basis); governor of New Hampshire; commissioners of agriculture, education; presidents of the University of New Hampshire, Keene State, and Plymouth State; chancellor of University System of New Hampshire. 7 ex officio. All voting. *Composition of institution:* Administrators 2 men / 2 women. Academic affairs headed by vice president for academic affairs. Management/business/finances directed by associate dean of administration. Admissions/student services directed by vice president for learner services. Academic governance body, Curriculum Committee, meets monthly.

Calendar: Semesters. Academic year July to June. Degrees conferred June, Sept., Dec. Formal commencement June. Summer sessions vary.

Characteristics of Freshmen: 74 applicants (26 men, 49 women). 93.2% of applicants admitted. 20.3% of admitted students enrolled full-time.

Admission: Rolling admissions plan. *Requirements:* Graduation from secondary school, GED, or other demonstrated ability to do college work. Applicants to baccalaureate program must be adults who have not pursued full-time study for at least 2 years since secondary school. *For transfer students:* From 4-year accredited institution 94 hours maximum transfer credit; from 2-year accredited institution 64 hours.

College credit for USAFI-DANTES, CLEP, and for extrainstitutional learning on basis of ACE *2006 Guide to the Evaluation of Educational Experiences in the Armed Services*; portfolio assessment.

Degree Requirements: *For all associate degrees:* 64 credit hours; 16 hours in residence. *For all baccalaureate degrees:* 124 credit hours; 30 hours in residence. *For all degrees:* 2.0 GPA; general education requirements.

Fulfillment of some degree requirements and exemption from some beginning courses possible by passing institutional examinations, College Board CLEP, other standardized tests. *Grading system:* A–F; pass; withdraw.

Distinctive Educational Programs: Flexible meeting places and schedules with courses at various locations throughout the state; weekend and evening classes. Accelerated degree programs. Facilities and programs for independent research, including individual majors and degree plans, tutorials. Learners are offered assessment of prior learning as a credit course to prepare portfolio on prior learning credits.

Degrees Conferred: 151 *associate;* 237 *baccalaureate.* Bachelor's degrees awarded in top five disciplines: liberal arts and sciences, general studies, and humanities 125; business, management, marketing, and related support services 54; multidisciplinary studies 50; security and protective services 4; computer and information sciences

Fees and Other Expenses: *Full-time tuition per academic year 2004–05:* resident $4,563, nonresident $5,043.

Financial Aid: Aid from institutionally generated funds is provided on the basis of financial need.

Financial aid to full-time, first-time undergraduate students: 50% received federal grants averaging $3,075; 18% state/local grants; 53% received loans averaging $4,058.

Departments and Teaching Staff: All faculty members are part-time. 33% are drawn from institutions in the University System of New Hampshire. School-wide: 700.

Enrollment: Total enrollment 1,627 (men 21%, women 79%).

Characteristics of Student Body: *Ethnic/racial makeup:* number of Black non-Hispanic: .7%; American Indian or Alaska Native: .4%; Asian or Pacific

Islander: .4%; Hispanic: .6%; White non-Hispanic: 84.8%; unknown: 13%. *Age distribution:* 17–21: 5%; 22–24: 6; 25–29: 10%; 30–34: 12%; 35–39: 15%; 40–49: 31%; 50–64: 10%; 65–up: .7%, unknown: 10.3%.

International Students: 2 nonresident aliens enrolled fall 2004. No programs available to aid students whose native language is not English. No financial aid specifically designated for international students.

Student Life: Students attend the College for Lifelong Learning on a regional basis, often after work or on weekends. *Special services:* Career assistance program. *Student publications: ACCESS,* a quarterly newsletter.

Library Collections: Regional public and private libraries are used in conjunction with institutional libraries of the university system.

Chief Executive Officer: Dr. Karol Lacroix, President.

Address admission inquiries to Karen R. King, Registrar.

Daniel Webster College

20 University Drive
Nashua, New Hampshire 03063-1300
Tel: (603) 577-6000   **E-mail:** admissions@dwc.edu
Fax: (603) 577-6001   **Internet:** www.dwc.edu

Institution Description: Daniel Webster College is a private, independent, nonprofit college. *Enrollment:* 1,051. *Degrees awarded:* Associate, baccalaureate.

Accreditation: *Regional:* NEASC.

History: Established 1965.

Institutional Structure: *Governing board:* Board of Trustees. Extrainstitutional representation: 12 trustees. All voting. *Composition of institution:* Administrators 4 men / 4 women. Academic affairs headed by vice president. Management/business/finances directed by vice president. Full-time instructional faculty 23.

Calendar: Semesters. Academic year Sept. to May.

Characteristics of Freshmen: 782 applicants (782 men, 160 women). 74.2% of applicants admitted. 28.6% of admitted students enrolled full-time.

92% (163 students) submitted SAT scores; 15% (25 students) submitted ACT scores. *25th percentile:* SAT I 450, Verbal SAT I Math 480; ACT Composite 18. *75th percentile:* SAT I 590, Verbal SAT I Math 590; ACT Composite 25.

43% of entering freshmen expected to graduate within 5 years. 27% of freshmen from New Hampshire. Freshmen from 20 states and 2 foreign countries.

Admission: Rolling admissions plan. *Requirements:* Either graduation from secondary school or GED. *Entrance tests:* College Board SAT or ACT composite. For foreign students TOEFL.

Degree Requirements: *For all associate degrees:* 60 credit hours. *For all baccalaureate degrees:* 120 credit hours. *For all degrees:* 2.0 GPA; last 30 hours in residence; general education requirements. *Grading system:* A–F;

Distinctive Educational Programs: Bachelor and associate degree programs in accounting, aviation management, aviation management/flight operations, air traffic control, business management, information sciences, computer science, sport management. Associate degree programs in aeronautical engineering, engineering science, management and organizational studies, general studies.

ROTC: Air Force.

Degrees Conferred: 24 *associate;* 212 *baccalaureate.* Bachelor's degrees awarded in top five disciplines: transportation/materials moving 69; business, management, marketing, and related support services 68; computer and information sciences 65; parks and recreation 8; social sciences and history 2.

Fees and Other Expenses: *Full-time tuition per academic year 2004–05:* $21,380. *Room and board per academic year:* $8,170. *Books and supplies:* $800.

Financial Aid: Aid from institutionally generated funds is provided on the basis of academic merit, financial need. Institution has a Program Participation Agreement with the U.S. Department of Education for eligible students to receive Pell Grants and, depending upon the agreement, other federal aid. Financial aid to full-time, first-time undergraduate students: 33% received federal grants averaging $3,645; 6% state/local grants; 78% institutional grants averaging $9,009; 69% received loans averaging $2,781.

Departments and Teaching Staff: *Professors* 23; *part-time teachers* 49. *Total instructional faculty:* 72. Degrees held by full-time faculty: doctorate 45%, master's 52%, baccalaureate 3%.

Enrollment: Total enrollment 1,051. Undergraduate 973 (74.1% men, 25.9% women).

Characteristics of Student Body: *Ethnic/racial makeup:* number of Black non-Hispanic: 2.1%; American Indian or Alaska Native: .7%; Asian or Pacific Islander: .2%; Hispanic: 1%; White non-Hispanic: 56.1%; unknown: 39.6%.

International Students: 3 nonresident aliens enrolled fall 2004. No programs available to aid students whose native language is not English. No financial aid specifically designated for international students.

Library Collections: 35,000 volumes. 55,300 microforms; 1,500 audiovisual materials; 390 current periodical subscriptions. Online catalog. Students have access to online information retrieval services and the Internet.

Most important special holdings include collections on aviation, business, and computer science.

Buildings and Grounds: Campus area 55 acres.

Chief Executive Officer: Dr. Hannah M. McCarthy, President.

Address admission inquiries to Sean Ryan, Director of Admissions.

Dartmouth College

Hanover, New Hampshire 03755-4030

Tel: (603) 646-1110 **E-mail:** admissions.office@dartmouth.edu
Fax: (603) 646-1216 **Internet:** www.dartmouth.edu

Institution Description: Dartmouth College is a private, independent, non-profit college. *Enrollment:* 5,704. *Degrees awarded:* Baccalaureate, first-professional (medicine), master's, doctorate.

Accreditation: *Regional:* NEASC. *Professional:* business, engineering, engineering technology, medicine

History: Established as a school for men, chartered and offered first instruction at postsecondary level 1769; awarded first degree (baccalaureate) 1771; became coeducational 1972. *See* Leon Burr Richardson, *History of Dartmouth College,* 2 vols. (Hanover: Dartmouth College Publications, 1932) for further information.

Institutional Structure: *Governing board:* Board of Trustees of Dartmouth College. President, Governor of New Hampshire, ex officio; 7 charter trustees nominated and elected by the Board; 7 alumni trustees, nominated by alumni and elected by the Board. All voting. *Composition of institution:* Administrators 340 men / 363 women. Academic affairs headed by president. Vice Presidential level officers: Provost, Dean of Faculty, Dean of College, Vice President of Development and Alumni Affairs, Vice President and Treasurer.

Calendar: Quarters. Academic year Sept. to June. One summer term required. Freshmen admitted in September. Degrees conferred and formal commencement in June.

Characteristics of Freshmen: 23% of applicants admitted. 9.2% of applicants admitted and enrolled.

90% (968 students) submitted SAT scores; 10% (110 students) submitted ACT scores. *25th percentile:* SAT Verbal 670, SAT Math 690; ACT Composite 28. *75th percentile:* SAT Verbal 770, SAT Math 780; ACT Composite 34.

94.6% of freshmen expected to graduate within 5 years. 29% of freshmen from New Hampshire. Freshmen from 47 states and 24 foreign countries.

Admission: For undergraduate admission, apply by Jan. 1 of the calendar year in which the candidate expects to enter college. New students are enrolled only in the fall term; selection takes place during the preceding spring and notification concerning admission is usually issued in mid-April. *Entrance tests:* 3 SAT II: Subject Tests of the College Board and either the SAT I of the College Board or the ACT of the American College Testing Program.

Degree Requirements: 35 courses and 12 terms (including one summer term) in residence. Students must also take a First-Year Seminar, and demonstrate proficiency in both English composition and a foreign language. Distributive requirements; multidisciplinary or interdisciplinary course; three World Culture courses; ten courses distributed across eight intellectual fields: the arts; literature; either philosophy, religion, or history; international or comparative studies; social analysis (two courses); natural sciences (two courses, one of which must be a laboratory, field, or experimental course); quantitative or deductive science; technology or applied science. Students must complete at least one major.

Distinctive Educational Programs: Study abroad in Argentina, Brazil, China, Costa Rica, Czech Republic, England, France, Germany, Greece, Ireland, Italy, Jamaica, Japan, Mexico, Morocco, Russia, Scotland, Spain, Trinidad, Zimbabwe. Additional programs in various countries. Exchange programs also available with various institutions and through the Twelve College Exchange.

ROTC: Army in cooperation with Norwich University.

Degrees Conferred: 1,281 *baccalaureate* (B), 417 *master's* (M), 56 *doctorate* (D): area and ethnic studies 27 (B); biological/life sciences 81 (B), 5 (M), 34 (D); business/marketing 241 (M); computer and information sciences 31 (B), 8 (M), 7 (D); engineering and engineering technologies 119 (B), 48 (M), 4 (D); English 96 (B); foreign languages and literature 88 (B), 8 (M); health professions and related sciences 52 (M), 1 (D); interdisciplinary studies 9 (B), 1 (D); liberal arts/general studies 37 (M); mathematics 38 (B), 7 (M), 2 (D); natural resources/environmental science 27 (B); philosophy/religion/theology 64 (B); physical

sciences 61 (B), 6 (M), 4 (D); psychology 88 (B), 2 (M), 3 (D); social sciences and history 485 (B); visual and performing arts 67 (B), 3 (M). 49 *first professional:* medicine. *Honorary degrees awarded 2004–05:* Doctor of Laws 3, Doctor of Science 1, Doctor of Arts 3, Doctor of Humane Letters 2.

Fees and Other Expenses: *Full-time tuition per academic year 2004–05:* $30,279. *Fees:* $296 (1st year); $186 (2nd year and on). *Room and board per academic year:* $9,124.

Financial Aid: Aid from institutionally generated funds is provided on the basis of financial need. Institution has a Program Participation Agreement with the U.S. Department of Education for eligible students to receive Pell Grants and, depending upon the agreement, other federal aid.

Financial aid to full-time, first-time undergraduate students: need-based scholarships/grants totaling $40,934,017, self-help $11,700,523; non-need-based scholarships/grants totaling $679,089, self-help $3,286,129, parent loans $6,678,471. *Graduate aid:* 17 students received $327,648 in federal and state-funded fellowships/grants; total of $1,468,396 in federal and state-funded loans; 130 students received $2,346,201 for other fellowships/grants; 35 teaching assistantships awarded totaling $699,032; 245 research assistantships were awarded totaling $4,130,725.

Departments and Teaching Staff: *Total instructional faculty:* 600 (485 full-time, 115 part-time; women 211, men 389; members of minority groups 60). Total faculty with doctorate, first-professional, or other terminal degree: 524. Student-to-faculty ratio: 8.5:1. Degrees held by full-time faculty: doctorate 93.6%, master's 2.3%, baccalaureate 1.5%, professional 2.6%. 95.9% hold terminal degrees. Faculty development: 45 faculty members awarded sabbaticals 2004–05.

Enrollment: Total enrollment 5,704. Undergraduate full-time 2,024 men / 2,002 women, part-time 22m / 30w; first-professional full-time 147m / 151w, part-time 5m; graduate full-time 818m / 419w, part-time 42m / 43w. *Transfer students:* in-state 13.

Characteristics of Student Body: *Ethnic/racial makeup:* number of Black non-Hispanic: 274; American Indian or Alaska Native: 140; Asian or Pacific Islander: 540; Hispanic: 258; White non-Hispanic: 2,316; unknown: 332. *Age distribution:* number under 18: 131; 18–19: 1,877; 20–21: 1,787; 22–24: 269; 25–29: 7; 30–34: 2.

International Students: 595 nonresident aliens enrolled fall 2004. Students from Europe, Asia, Latin America, Africa, Canada, Australia. Programs available to aid students whose native language is not English: social, cultural. English as a Second Language Program. No financial aid specifically designated for international students.

Student Life: On-campus residence halls house 72% of student body in 10 clusters, 3 independent residence halls, 4 academic affinity houses, 3 special interest houses, and 3 language apartments. All residence halls are coed by room or floor. 55% of eligible men are members of a fraternity or coed organization; 50% of eligible women are members of a sorority or coed organization; 14% of students live in fraternity/sorority/coed houses. Some students live in married student housing 1.5 miles from campus. *Intercollegiate athletics:* men only: baseball, basketball, cross-country, football, golf, gymnastics, hockey, lacrosse, rowing, skiing, soccer, squash, swimming, tennis, track and field; women only: basketball, cross-country, field hockey, golf, hockey, lacrosse, rowing, skiing, soccer, squash, swimming, tennis, track and field; both sexes: sailing. Club sports and intramural programs are also offered. *Special regulations:* Cars permitted in designated parking areas for all but freshmen. *Special services:* Academic Skills Center, Career Services, International Office, Women's Resource Center, Native American Program, Advisor to Latino/Hispanic Students, Advisor to Gay/Lesbian and Bisexual Students, Coordinator of the Sexual Abuse Awareness Program, Student Disabilities Coordinator, Administrative Liaison to the African-American Society, College Health Services, Asian Pacific American Programming Liaison. *Student publications, radio:* The Aegis, a yearbook; *Black Praexis,* a special-interest group quarterly; *Aporia,* a journal of philosophy; *Black Praxis,* a special-interest group quarterly; *BLD,* a journal focusing on political, religious, and social issues; *Cahiers du Dartma,* a quarterly journal devoted to intellectual thought on film; *Disquisitions,* quarterly undergraduate academic journal; *The Beacon,* a conservative journal and news magazine; *The Dartmouth,* a daily campus newspaper; *Forum,* a journal to foster open debate on various issues; *Freehand Publications,* creative journal of original ideas and artistic expression; *Jack O'Lantern,* a humorous literary quarterly; *Rice Magazine,* a journal of facts, folklore tales, etc. of Asian countries; *Snapshots of Color,* a literary magazine to voice issues relating to race and ethnicity; *Sports Weekly,* a weekly newspaper on Dartmouth intercollegiate and club sports; *Stoneface Review,* a semiannual creative writing journal; *Uncommon Threads,* a journal focused on racial, ethnic, religious, and sexual issues; *World Outlook,* journal of international affairs. Commercially licensed radio stations WDCR and WFRD (FM) each broadcast 24 hours per day. *Surrounding community:* Hanover population 9,500. Boston, 135 miles from campus, is nearest metropolitan area. Served by mass transit bus system; airport 5 miles from campus; passenger rail service 5 miles from campus.

Publications: *General Information Bulletin, College Directory, Freshman Book, Student Term Directory, VOX of Dartmouth,* a biweekly publication of campus events; *Alumni Magazine, Dartmouth Life, Faculty Handbook, Organization of the Faculty of Dartmouth College, Dartmouth College Library Bulletin* (biannually) first published in 1960; *Faculty Research and Publications and Abstracts of Student Theses* (annually) first published in 1972; *Journal of Neurosurgery* (monthly) first published in 1944. *Publisher:* Member of University Press of New England.

Library Collections: 5,755,552 volumes. Online catalog. Current serial subscriptions: 16,786 paper; 960 microform; 20,147 via electronic access. 10,460 recordings; 33,763 compact discs; 9,014 CD-ROMs. 298 computer work stations. Students have access to online information retrieval services and the Internet. Total 2004–05 budget for books and materials: $7,532,071.

Most important special holdings include Robert Frost Collection (1,300 printed items, 39 feet of manuscripts); Vilhjalmur Stefansson Collection (5,000 books, 440 feet of manuscripts, and artifacts pertaining to the arctic explorer); Daniel Webster Collection; Shakespearean Collection of Allerton Wheelock.

Buildings and Grounds: Campus area 200 acres. *New buildings:* Berry Library and Kiewitt Computation Center; Moore Hall; Ross Tennis Center and Gordon Pavilion.

Chief Executive Officer: Dr. Barry P. Sherr, Provost.

Undergraduates address admission inquiries to Maria Laskaris, Director of Admissions; graduate inquiries to Director of Graduate Studies; Medical School inquiries to Andrew G. Welch, Director of Admissions, Dartmouth Medical School.

Arts and Sciences Graduate Program

Degree Programs Offered: *Master's* in comparative literature, computer sciences, liberal studies; *doctorate* in biochemistry, biological sciences, chemistry, cognitive neuroscience, computer science, earth science, evaluative clinical science, mathematics, pharmacology/toxicology, physics/astronomy, physiology, psychology.

Admission: Admission requirements vary with department.

Degree Requirements: Degree requirements vary with department.

Distinctive Educational Programs: All Ph.D. programs designed to train teacher/scholars. M.D./Ph.D. dual-degree program with Dartmouth Medical School. Joint ownership with Michigan and MIT of Observatory on Kitt Peak, Arizona. Interdisciplinary programs in Cell and Molecular Biology, Cognitive Neuroscience, and Comparative Literature.

Dartmouth Medical School

Degree Programs Offered: *First-professional* in medicine.

Admission: *For first-professional degree:* At least 3 years of college-level work at a U.S. or Canadian college or university including 1 year biology, 1 general chemistry, 1 organic chemistry, 1 physics, 1 semester calculus. Proficiency in written and spoken English. MCAT.

Degree Requirements: Prescribed curriculum; must pass all courses.

Distinctive Educational Programs: Combined first-professional and doctoral programs in cooperation with science departments of Dartmouth School of Arts and Sciences, or in cooperation with Brown University (RI). Hitchcock Medical Center Teaching Hospitals offer fellowships and other training programs in 20 medical specialties. Training in primary and preventive health care available at outreach facilities in Maine, New Hampshire, Vermont. Interact television network programming provides consultations, training programs, and other services for Dartmouth Medical School, University of Vermont Medical School, and 3 community hospitals. The C. Everett Koop Institute at Dartmouth contributes to national initiatives that examine medical education issues.

Thayer School of Engineering

Degree Programs Offered: *First-professional* in engineering, engineering management; *master's, doctorate* in biomedical engineering, biotechnical and biochemical engineering, electrical and computer engineering, environmental science and engineering, materials science and engineering, mechanical engineering.

Admission: Graduate requirements vary with programs and levels.

Degree Requirements: Graduate requirements vary.

Distinctive Educational Programs: Interdisciplinary emphasis without departmental divisions. Dual-degree program with the Amos Tuck School of Business Administration. M.D./Ph.D. Program in conjunction with the Dartmouth Medical School. Cook Engineering Design Center attracts the industrial contract research carried on by students for their required projects.

Tuck School of Business

Degree Programs Offered: *Master's* in business administration.

Admission: Baccalaureate degree from accredited institution. Demonstrated scholastic achievement and potential to achieve leadership in management. Prior work experience desirable. GMAT required; TOEFL for foreign nationals.

Distinctive Educational Programs: Dual-degree programs with Thayer School of Engineering, Dartmouth Medical School, Fletcher School at Tufts University.

Franklin Pierce College

College Road
Rindge, New Hampshire 03461-0060
Tel: (603) 899-4000   **E-mail:** admissions@fpc.edu
Fax: (603) 899-4050   **Internet:** www.fpc.edu

Institution Description: Franklin Pierce College is a private, independent, nonprofit college. *Enrollment:* 1,608. *Degrees awarded:* Baccalaureate.

Member of the consortium New Hampshire College and University Council

Accreditation: *Regional:* NEASC.

History: Established, chartered, and incorporated 1962; offered first instruction at postsecondary level 1963; awarded first degree 1966.

Institutional Structure: *Governing board:* Board of Trustees. 27 voting members, including 4 alumni and president of the college. *Composition of institution:* Administrators and staff 206, including a dean and vice president of academic affairs, vice president for student affairs, senior executive vice president. Full-time instructional faculty 156. Academic governance bodies include the Pierce Council, comprised of faculty and administration representatives, and the Rindge Faculty Federation, a collective bargaining agent affiliated with AFT.

Calendar: Semesters. Academic year Sept. to May. Freshmen and transfers admitted Sept., Jan., and summer sessions. Degrees conferred and formal commencement May. Summer session from mid-May to mid-Aug.

Characteristics of Freshmen: 4,192 applicants (1,876 men, 2,316 women). 77.2% of applicants admitted. 17.5% of admitted students enrolled full-time.

81% (462 students) submitted SAT scores. *25th percentile:* SAT I Verbal 460, SAT I Math 440. *75th percentile:* SAT I Verbal 550, SAT I Math 530.

43% of entering freshmen expected to graduate within 5 years. 14% of freshmen from New Hampshire. Freshmen from 22 states and 18 foreign countries.

Admission: Rolling admissions plan. For fall acceptance, apply by May 30. Early acceptance available. *Requirements:* Graduation from accredited secondary school with 4 units English, 2 mathematics, 3 science, 2 social studies, 6 electives. GED accepted. *Entrance tests:* College Board SAT or ACT composite. For foreign students TOEFL. *For transfer students:* 2.0 minimum GPA; transfer credit may be awarded for up to 56 credits of coursework in which the student received a grade of C or better from an accredited institution.

College credit and advanced placement for postsecondary-level work completed in secondary school and for extrainstitutional learning. Tutoring available. Noncredit basic skills courses offered in summer session and regular academic year.

Degree Requirements: 120 semester hours of academic credit with a minimum GPA of 2.0 required for graduate. In addition to required courses within a major (generally ranging from 30 to 54 credits), all undergraduate students must take 44 credits in the college's nationally-recognized general core curriculum (The Individual and Community), a sequence of interdisciplinary and term-taught liberal arts courses. *Grading system:* A–F.

Distinctive Educational Programs: Walk in Europe, a 3-month experiential education program; Washington Center for Internships and Academic Seminars; pre-professional programs in medicine, veterinary medicine, and law; Honors program; individually-designed interdisciplinary majors and minors. Institutionally arranged study-travel during intersession in U.S. and abroad. Cross-registration and off-campus study through consortium.

Degrees Conferred: 308 *baccalaureate.* Bachelor's degrees awarded in top five disciplines: communication, journalism, and related programs 50; visual and performing arts 46; business, management, marketing, and related support services 39; psychology 25; security and protective services 23.

Fees and Other Expenses: *Full-time tuition per academic year 2004–05:* $22,510. *Room and board per academic year:* $7,655. *Books and supplies:* $826.

Financial Aid: Aid from institutionally generated funds is provided on the basis of academic merit, financial need, athletic ability. Institution has a Program Participation Agreement with the U.S. Department of Education for eligible students to receive Pell Grants and, depending upon the agreement, other federal aid.

Financial aid to full-time, first-time undergraduate students: 25% received federal grants averaging $2,743; 16% state/local grants averaging $672; 95% institutional grants averaging $9,998; 75% received loans averaging $6,852.

Departments and Teaching Staff: *Professors* 71, *part-time faculty:* 85. *Total instructional faculty:* 156. Student-to-faculty ratio: 14:1. Degrees held by full-time faculty: Doctorate 54%, master's 45%. 74% hold terminal degrees.

Enrollment: Total enrollment 1,608 (men 50.3%, women 49.7%).

Characteristics of Student Body: *Ethnic/racial makeup:* number of Black non-Hispanic: 78.7%; American Indian or Alaska Native: .1%; Asian or Pacific Islander: .9%; Hispanic: 1.8%; White non-Hispanic: 78.7%; unknown: 12.1%. *Age distribution:* 17–21: 78%; 22–24: 19%; 25–29: 3%.

International Students: 47 nonresident aliens enrolled fall 2004. Students from Europe, Asia, Latin America, Africa, Canada. Programs available to aid students whose native language is not English: social, cultural. English as a Second Language Program. Financial aid specifically designated for international students: scholarships available annually to qualifying students.

Student Life: On-campus residence halls house 85% of student body. Residence halls for women only constitute 8%, for both sexes 92%. Apartment-style residence options on and bordering campus. The college sponsors a wide variety of opportunities in the performing arts. Other activities include an on-campus radio station (WFPR), *The Pierce Arrow,* a student newspaper, student government, and over 30 clubs and organizations. Intramural program. NCAA II programs in 18 sports. *Special regulations:* Cars permitted without restrictions. *Special services:* Learning Resources Center, medical services, shuttle bus for long distance transportation and for campus trips. *Surrounding community:* Rindge population 3,500. Boston (MA), 75 miles from campus, is nearest metropolitan area. Served by airport 20 miles from campus, passenger rail service 25 miles from campus.

Library Collections: 115,200 volumes. 26,200 microforms; 240 current periodical subscriptions. Computer work stations available. Students have access to online information retrieval services and the Internet.

Most important special holdings include collections on anthropology (HRAF files); English literature; newspaper collection from the era of the Franklin Pierce Presidency.

Buildings and Grounds: Campus area 1,000 acres.

Chief Executive Officer: Dr. George J. Hagerty, President.

Address admission inquiries to Lucy C. Shonk, Director of Admissions.

Franklin Pierce Law Center

2 White Street
Concord, New Hampshire 03301-4197
Tel: (603) 228-1541   **E-mail:** admissions@piercelaw.edu
Fax: (603) 225-4016   **Internet:** www.piercelaw.edu

Institution Description: Franklin Pierce Law Center is New Hampshire's only law school. It is a private, independent institution approved by the American Bar Association. *Enrollment:* 507. *Degrees awarded:* Master's, juris doctor.

Accreditation: *Professional:* Law.

History: Established 1973 to encourage innovation in education by melding theory and practice-based education and offer a focus on public interest law and law as it relates to science and technology.

Institutional Structure: *Governing board:* Representation: Executive Board of 12 members plus the dean and president of the school.

Calendar: Semesters. Academic year Aug. to Apr. First-year students admitted in Aug., transfer students in Aug, Jan. Summer session June to Aug. Freshmen admitted . Degrees conferred and formal commencement .

Admission: Rolling admissions plan. Apply between Oct. and May. *Requirements:* B.A. or B.S. degree; law school admissions test.

College credit and advanced placement for postsecondary-level work completed in secondary school and for extrainstitutional learning on basis of ACE *2006 Guide to the Evaluation of Educational Experiences in the Armed Services.*

Developmental/remedial courses offered in summer session and regular academic year; credit given.

Degree Requirements: *For juris doctor degree:* 84 credit hours. *For master of intellectual property (MIP) students:* 30 credit hours; *For joint JD/MIP candidates:* 99 credit hours, 30 of which must be in intellectual property topics. *Grading system:* A–F; pass-fail; withdraw (carries time limit).

Distinctive Educational Programs: Externships; real-client clinics; joint juris doctor-master of intellectual property degree; Intellectual Property Summer Institute

Degrees Conferred: 108 *master's:* education 9; legal services 49; business, management, marketing, and related support services 50; 109 *first-professional:* juris doctor 109.

Fees and Other Expenses: *Full-time tuition per academic year 2005–06:* Contact the center for current tuition/fees and other costs.

Financial Aid: Aid from institutionally generated funds is provided on the basis of academic merit, financial need, other criteria. Institution has a Program

Participation Agreement with the U.S. Department of Education for eligible students to receive Pell Grants and, depending upon the agreement, other federal aid.

Departments and Teaching Staff: *Professors* 21, *instructors* 2, *part-time faculty* 58. *Total instructional faculty:* 81. Degrees held by full-time faculty: doctorate 9%, master's 33%, baccalaureate 100%, professional 100%.

Enrollment: Total enrollment 507 (men 57%, women 43%).

Characteristics of Student Body: *Ethnic/racial makeup:* number of Black non-Hispanic: 3.7%; American Indian or Alaska Native: 3.7%; Asian or Pacific Islander: 3.7%; Hispanic: 3.6%; White non-Hispanic: 59.6%; unknown: 9.9%. *Age distribution:* 17–21: 7%, 22–24: 30%; 25–29: 32%; 30–34: 14%; 35–39: 9%; 40–49: 9%.

International Students: 69 nonresident aliens enrolled fall 2004. Programs available to aid students whose native language is not English: social. Financial aid specifically designated for international students: 30 undergraduate scholarships available annually.

Student Life: *Surrounding community:* Located in Concord, the capital city of New Hampshire. Nearest metropolitan area is Boston, one hour away.

Publications: *Risk: Issues of Health and Safety; IDEA: The Journal of Law and Technology; Annual Survey of New Hampshire Law.*

Library Collections: 220,000 volumes. 72,000 microforms; 245 audiovisual titles: cassettes, audio, video. 52 computer work stations. Students have access to online information retrieval services and the Internet. .

Most important special holdings include Intellectual Property Collection; New Hampshire Law Collection; collection of conference materials from U.S. and international patent associations from the past 25 years.

Chief Executive Officer: John T. Hutson, Dean.

Address admissions inquiries to Katie MacDonald, Associate Dean of Admissions.

Keene State College

229 Main Street
Keene, New Hampshire 03435-1506
Tel: (603) 352-1909   **E-mail:** admissions@keene.edu
Fax: (603) 358-2767   **Internet:** www.keene.edu

Institution Description: Keene State College is a state institution and is part of the University System of New Hampshire. *Enrollment:* 4,937. *Degrees awarded:* Associate, baccalaureate, master's.

Academic offerings subject to approval by statewide coordinating bodies. Budget subject to approval by state governing boards. Member of the consortium New Hampshire College and University Council.

Accreditation: *Regional:* NEASC. *Professional:* music, teacher education

History: Established, chartered as Keene Normal School, and offered first instruction at postsecondary level 1909; awarded first degree (baccalaureate) 1928; became 4-year institution and changed name to Keene Teachers College 1939; became division of University System of New Hampshire and adopted present name 1939; changed name to Keene State College 1963.

Institutional Structure: *Governing board:* Board of Trustees of the University System of New Hampshire. Representation: 11 trustees (appointed by the governor of New Hampshire); 4 University of New Hampshire alumni, 1 Keene College alumnus, Plymouth State College alumnus (all elected by alumni of their respective schools); 1 student (elected on a rotating basis); governor of New Hampshire; commissioners of agriculture, education; presidents of University of New Hampshire, Keene State, and Plymouth State; Chancellor of University System of New Hampshire. 7 ex officio. All voting. *Composition of institution:* Administrators 19 men / 23 women. Academic affairs headed by vice president for academic affairs; management/business/finances directed by vice president of finance and planning. Full-time instructional faculty 349. Academic governance body, College Senate, meets an average of 10 times per year. *Faculty representation:* Faculty served by collective bargaining agent, New Hampshire Education Association, affiliated with NEA.

Calendar: Semesters. Academic year Aug. to May. Freshmen admitted Aug., Jan., May, July. Degrees conferred and formal commencement May. Summer session of 2 terms from late May to mid-Aug.

Characteristics of Freshmen: 4,207 applicants (1,766 men, 2,441 women). 71.2% of applicants admitted. 33.2% of admitted students enrolled full-time.

99% (994 students) submitted SAT scores; 6% (60 students) submitted ACT scores. *25th percentile:* SAT I Verbal 460, SAT I Math 450. *75th percentile:* SAT I Verbal 550, SAT I Math 550.

53% of entering freshmen expected to graduate within 5 years. 48% of freshmen from New Hampshire. Freshmen from 16 states and 1 foreign country.

Admission: Rolling admissions plan. For fall acceptance, apply as early as junior year of secondary school, but not later than Apr. 1 of year of enrollment.

Early acceptance available. For transfer students entering in fall, apply no later than May 1. *Requirements:* Either graduation from accredited secondary school with college preparatory program or GED. Minimum 2.0 GPA. Lowest recommended secondary school class standing 50th percentile. *Entrance tests:* College Board SAT. For foreign students TOEFL. *For transfer students:* 2.0 minimum GPA; maximum transfer credit limited only by residence requirement.

College credit and advanced placement for postsecondary-level work completed in secondary school; college credit for USAFI and for extrainstitutional learning on basis of ACE *2006 Guide to the Evaluation of Educational Experiences in the Armed Services*; portfolio and faculty assessments.

Tutoring available. Remedial courses offered during regular academic year; credit given.

Degree Requirements: *For all associate degrees:* 60–62 semester hours. *For all baccalaureate degrees:* 120–126 hours. *For all undergraduate degrees:* 2.0 GPA 24 of last 30 hours in residence; general education requirements. *Grading system:* A–F; pass-fail; withdraw (deadline after which A–F is appended to withdraw).

Distinctive Educational Programs: Evening classes. Some classes available online. Special facilities for using telecommunications in the classroom. Interdisciplinary study in American studies, English-American studies, environmental science and policy, history-American studies, industrial and public safety. Facilities and programs for independent research, including individual majors, tutorials. Study abroad during junior year by individual arrangement; direct exchange programs in Canada, Ecuador, England, France, Ireland, Russia. Institutionally sponsored study-travel in England for education majors. Cross-registration through consortium. *Other distinctive programs:* Upward Bound program provides college preparation for economically and educationally disadvantaged secondary school students.

ROTC: Army offered in cooperation with University of Massachusetts - Lowell.

Degrees Conferred: 63 *associate*; 835 *baccalaureate*: 52 *master's*. Bachelor;'s degrees awarded in top five disciplines: education 176; psychology 95; social sciences and history 94; visual and performing arts 87; business, management, marketing, and related support services 84.

Fees and Other Expenses: *Full-time tuition per academic year 2004–05:* resident $6,900, nonresident $13,340. *Room and board per academic year:* $5,966. *Books and supplies:* $600.

Financial Aid: The college has a direct lending program. Aid from institutionally generated funds is provided on the basis of academic merit, financial need. Institution has a Program Participation Agreement with the U.S. Department of Education for eligible students to receive Pell Grants and, depending upon the agreement, other federal aid.

Financial aid to full-time, first-time undergraduate students: 16% received federal grants averaging $3,120; 26% state/local grants averaging $1,650; 43% institutional grants averaging $2,712; 68% received loans averaging $4,575.

Departments and Teaching Staff: *Total instructional faculty:* 349. Student-to-faculty ratio: 19:1. Degrees held by full-time faculty: doctorate 80%, master's 19%, baccalaureate 1%, professional 4%. 80% hold terminal degrees.

Enrollment: Total enrollment 4,937. Undergraduate 4,797 (men 42.3%, women 67.7%)

Characteristics of Student Body: *Ethnic/racial makeup:* number of Black non-Hispanic: .4%; American Indian or Alaska Native: .2%; Asian or Pacific Islander: .7%; Hispanic: 1%; White non-Hispanic: 91.5%; unknown: 5.5%. *Age distribution:* 17–21: 73%; 22–24: 17%; 25–29: 4%; 30–34: 2%; 35–39: 1%; 40–49: 2%; 50–59: less than 1%.

International Students: 38 nonresident aliens enrolled fall 2004. Students from Europe, Asia, Latin America, Africa. No programs available to aid students whose native language is not English. No financial aid specifically designated for international students.

Student Life: On-campus residence halls house 1,991 students; 53% live in coed residence halls; 5% live in women-only residence halls; 59% of student body live on campus; 1% of student body live in married student housing. Residence hall regulations are dependent upon the wishes of the occupants. *Intercollegiate athletics:* men only: basketball, skiing, soccer, swimming, tennis, track, wrestling; women only: basketball, field hockey, gymnastics, skiing, soccer, softball, swimming, tennis, track, volleyball. *Special regulations:* Registered cars permitted on campus; fee charged. Quiet hours. Residence hall visitation from 7am to 1am. *Special services:* Learning Resources Center, medical services. *Student publications, radio, television:* The Equinox, a weekly newspaper; The Kronicle, a yearbook. Radio station WKNH broadcasts 119 hours per week. *Surrounding community:* Keene population 21,500. Boston (MA), 85 miles from campus, is nearest metropolitan area. Served by airport 2 miles from campus; passenger rail service 20 miles from campus.

Library Collections: 248,000 volumes. 727,000 microforms; 5,200 audiovisual materials; 1,260 periodical titles. Computer work stations available. Students have access to online information retrieval services and the Internet.

Most important special collections include the Preston Collection of New Hampshire publications; Children's Festival Collection; Holocaust Center.

Buildings and Grounds: Campus area 150 acres.

Chief Executive Officer: Dr. Stanley J. Yarosewick, President.

Address admission inquiries to Margaret Richmond, Director of Admissions.

New England College

7 Main Street
Henniker, New Hampshire 03242-3244
Tel: (603) 428-2203   **E-mail:** admission@nec.edu
Fax: (603) 428-2266   **Internet:** www.nec,edu

Institution Description: New England College is a private, independent, nonprofit college. *Enrollment:* 1,329. *Degrees awarded:* Baccalaureate, master's.

Member of the consortium New Hampshire College and University Council.

Accreditation: *Regional:* NEASC.

History: Established 1946; chartered and incorporated 1947; awarded first degree (baccalaureate) 1949; added Arundel Campus 1971.

Institutional Structure: *Governing board:* The Board of Trustees of New England College. Representation: 25 trustees, including the president of the college. 1 ex officio. 24 voting. *Composition of institution:* Administrators 22 men / 18 women. Academic affairs headed by vice president for academic affairs. Management/business/finances directed by director of finance and administration. Full-time instructional faculty 50. Academic governance body, the faculty, meets an average of 15 times per year.

Calendar: Early semester (5-5 plan). Academic year Aug. to May. Freshmen admitted Aug.. Degrees conferred May, Nov. Formal commencement May. Summer session of 1 term from early June to late July.

Characteristics of Freshmen: 82% of applicants admitted. 18% of applicants admitted and enrolled.

74% (31 students) submitted SAT scores. *25th percentile*: SAT Verbal 420, SAT Math 400. *75th percentile*: SAT Verbal 530, SAT I Math 510.

48% of entering freshmen expected to graduate within 5 years. 24% of freshmen from New Hampshire. Freshmen from 28 states and 14 foreign countries.

Admission: Rolling admissions for applications received after Dec. 20. For fall acceptance, apply as early as 1 year prior to enrollment, but not later than Aug. 20. Early notification deadline Dec. 6 (notification Dec. 18). *Requirements:* Recommend 4 units English, 2 foreign language, 2 mathematics, 2 science, 2 social studies. GED accepted. Minimum 2.0 GPA. *Entrance tests:* College Board SAT preferred; ACT composite accepted. For foreign students TOEFL. *For transfer students:* 2.0 minimum GPA; no limit on transfer credits but student must complete 30 credits residence in senior year.

College credit and advanced placement for postsecondary-level work completed in secondary school.

Degree Requirements: 120 credit hours; 2.0 GPA; 60 credits, or senior year in residence; distribution requirements.

Fulfillment of some degree requirements possible by passing College Board AP, CLEP General Examination; exemption from some beginning courses possible by passing CLEP Subject Examinations, AP. *Grading system:* A–F; pass; withdraw (carries time limit).

Distinctive Educational Programs: Internships available in U.S. and some foreign countries. Overseas study opportunities available in England, France, Ireland, Lithuania, Mexico, and Quebec. Students may also study at other consortium institutions. Interdisciplinary programs include American studies, environmental studies, public administration, women's studies. Cross-registration and off-campus study through consortium. External degree programs through School of Graduate and Continuing Education.

ROTC: Air Force and Army in cooperation with University of New Hampshire.

Degrees Conferred: 136 *baccalaureate:* biological sciences 3, business and management 20, communications 15, education 13, English 8, fine and applied arts 12, health professions 1, liberal arts 1, natural resources/environmental sciences 5, psychology 15, social sciences and history 13, visual and performing arts 4, other 26; 45 *master's:* business 211 education 7; English 9; health professions 7.

Fees and Other Expenses: *Full-time tuition per academic year 2004–05:* $21,300 undergraduate; $390 per credit for graduate study. *Required fees:* $640. *Room and board per academic year:* $8,052.

Financial Aid: Aid from institutionally generated funds is provided on the basis of academic merit, financial need, other criteria.Institution has a Program Participation Agreement with the U.S. Department of Education for eligible students to receive Pell Grants and, depending upon the agreement, other federal aid.

Financial aid to full-time, first-time undergraduate students: need-based scholarships/grants totaling $5,223,561, self-help $3,350,096, parent loans $385,038, tuition waivers $187,554; non-need-based scholarships/grants totaling $2,124,694, self-help $2,443,636, parent loans $1,365,137, tuition waivers $203,183. *Graduate aid:* 101 students received $943,305 in federal and state-funded loans; 237 students received other fellowships/grants totaling $316,906.

Departments and Teaching Staff: *Total instructional faculty:* 146 (full-time 51, part-time 95; women 78, men 68; members of minority groups 4). Total faculty with doctorate, first-professional, or other terminal degree: 50. Student-to-faculty ratio: 13:1. Degrees held by full-time faculty: doctorate 47%, master's 47%, baccalaureate 2% 63% hold terminal degrees.

Enrollment: Total enrollment 1,329. Undergraduate full-time 438 men / 439 women, part-time 21m / 38w; graduate full-time 44m / 74w, part-time 83m / 192w. *Transfer students:* in-state 15; from out-of-state 40.

Characteristics of Student Body: *Ethnic/racial makeup:* number of Black non-Hispanic: 16; American Indian or Alaska Native: 2; Asian or Pacific Islander: 6; Hispanic: 80; White non-Hispanic: 919. *Age distribution:* number under 18: 3; 18–19: 378; 20–21: 316; 22–24: 167; 25–29: 23; 30–34: 11; 35–39: 7; 40–49: 9; 50–64: 4; 65 and over: 1.

International Students: 56 nonresident aliens enrolled fall 2004. 15 students from Europe, 23 Asia, 3 Latin America, 2 Africa, 1 Canada. Programs available to aid students whose native language is not English: social, cultural. English as a Second Language Program. Financial aid specifically designated for international undergraduate students: scholarships available annually.

Student Life: On-campus residence halls house 65% of student body. Dormitories for both sexes constitute 100% of such space. *Intercollegiate athletics:* men only: baseball, basketball, alpine and nordic skiing, lacrosse, soccer; women only: basketball, alpine and nordic skiing, field hockey, lacrosse, soccer, softball. *Special regulations:* Parking permitted in designated areas. Quiet hours from 7pm to 7am. *Special services:* Learning Resources Center, medical services. *Student publications, radio: Compass,* an annual student handbook; *Henniker Review,* a biannual literary magazine; *New Englander,* a weekly newspaper. Radio station WNEC-FM broadcasts 140 hours per week. *Surrounding community:* Henniker population 3,500. Boston (MA), 85 miles from campus, is nearest metropolitan area. Served by airport 45 miles from campus; passenger rail service 20 miles from campus.

Library Collections: 105,000 volumes. 3,500 government documents; 38,000 microforms; 3,600 audiovisual materials; 586 current periodical subscriptions. 40 computer work stations. Students have access to online information retrieval services and the Internet. Total 2004–05 budget for books and other materials: $100,000.

Most important special holdings include Styles Bridges Papers; Adams Shakespeare Collection; New Hampshiriana; Vietnam Collection.

Buildings and Grounds: Campus area 212 acres.

Chief Executive Officer: Dr. Steven E. Fritz, President.

Address admission inquiries to Paul Miller, Director of Admissions.

Plymouth State University

17 High Street
Plymouth, New Hampshire 03264-1595
Tel: (603) 535-5000 **E-mail:** psuadmit@plymouth.edu
Fax: (603) 535-2654 **Internet:** www.plymouth.edu

Institution Description: Plymouth State University is a member of the University System of New Hampshire. *Enrollment:* 4,108. *Degrees awarded:* Associate, baccalaureate, master's.

Academic offerings subject to approval by statewide coordinating bodies. Budget subject to approval by state governing boards. Member of the consortium New Hampshire College and University Council.

Accreditation: *Regional:* NEASC. *Professional:* teacher education

History: Established as Plymouth Normal School and offered first instruction at postsecondary level 1871; changed name to Plymouth Teachers College 1928; awarded first degree (baccalaureate) 1931; adopted present name and incorporated 1963. *See* Norton R. Bagley, *One Hundred Years of Service: Plymouth State College* (Plymouth: Plymouth State College, 1971) for further information.

Institutional Structure: *Governing board:* Board of Trustees of the University System of New Hampshire. Representation: 11 trustees (appointed by governor of New Hampshire); 4 University of New Hampshire alumni, 1 Keene State College alumnus, 1 Plymouth State College alumnus (all elected by alumni of respective schools), 1 student (elected on a rotating basis); governor of New Hampshire; commissioners of agriculture, education; president of University of New Hampshire, Keene State, and Plymouth State; chancellor of University System of New Hampshire. 7 ex officio. All voting. *Composition of institution:* Administrators 18 men / 17 women. Academic affairs headed by dean of the col-

lege. Management/business/finances directed by director of business operations. Full-time instructional faculty 170. Academic governance body, the faculty, meets an average of 8 times per year.

Calendar: Semesters. Academic year Sept. to May. Freshmen admitted Sept., Feb. Degrees conferred and formal commencement May. Summer session from late May to mid-Aug.

Characteristics of Freshmen: 77% of applicants accepted. 38% of accepted applicants enrolled.

Average secondary school rank of freshmen 53rd percentile. Mean SAT scores 480 verbal, 490 mathematical.

52% of entering freshmen expected to graduate within 5 years. 52% of freshmen from New Hampshire. Freshmen from 21 states and 10 foreign countries.

Admission: Rolling admissions plan. For fall acceptance, apply as early as Sept. of previous year, but not later than June 1 of year of enrollment. Early acceptance available. *Requirements:* Either graduation from accredited secondary school or GED; essay required; auditions for music majors. *Entrance tests:* College Board SAT. For foreign students TOEFL. *For transfer students:* 2.0 minimum GPA; from 4-year accredited institution maximum transfer credit limited only by residence requirement; from 2-year accredited institution 65 hours.

College credit and advanced placement for postsecondary-level work completed in secondary school. College credit for extrainstitutional learning on basis of ACE *2006 Guide to the Evaluation of Educational Experiences in the Armed Services.*

Tutoring for students with disabilities available.

Degree Requirements: *For all baccalaureate degrees:* 122 credit hours; 2 credits physical education; distribution requirements; demonstrated proficiency in writing, mathematics. For baccalaureate of arts students demonstration of proficiency in a foreign language. *For all undergraduate degrees:* 2.0 GPA; 30 hours in residence.

Fulfillment of some degree requirements and exemption from some beginning courses possible by passing departmental examinations, College Board CLEP. *Grading system:* A–F; pass-fail; withdraw (deadline after which A–F is appended to withdraw).

Distinctive Educational Programs: Work-experience programs. Evening classes. 5-year baccalaureate-master's program in business administration. Interdisciplinary programs in Canadian studies, medieval studies. New Hampshire and Northern New England studies. Facilities and programs for independent research, including honors programs, individual majors, tutorials, independent study. Study abroad in Canada, England, France, Mexico, Spain through programs offered by other institutions; may be individually arranged. Off-campus centers for graduate students (at Tilton, 30 miles away; Keene, 100 miles away). Cross-registration through consortium. Two-summer master's program in education. *Other distinctive programs:* Degree-granting continuing education.

ROTC: Army, Air Force in cooperation with University of New Hampshire.

Degrees Conferred: 599 *baccalaureate:* degrees awarded in top five disciplines: business/marketing 120; education 100; social sciences and history 38; visual and performing arts 62; multi-interdisciplinary studies 20. 203 *master's:* in various disciplines.

Fees and Other Expenses: *Full-time tuition per academic year 2004–05:* undergraduate resident $5,060, nonresident $11,500. *Books and supplies:* $2,000. *Room and board per academic year:* $6,322.

Financial Aid: Aid from institutionally generated funds is provided on the basis of academic merit, financial need, athletic ability, music/theatre talent. Institution has a Program Participation Agreement with the U.S. Department of Education for eligible students to receive Pell Grants and, depending upon the agreement, other federal aid.

Financial aid to full-time, first-time undergraduate students: need-based scholarships/grants totaling $5,760,364, self-help $11,120,976; non-need-based scholarships/grants totaling $1,930,972, self-help $9,744,408, parent loans $5,456,564. *Graduate aid:* 136 students received $1,164,928 in federal and state-funded loans; 15 received $96,000 for college-assigned jobs; 19 teaching teaching assistantships awarded totaling $340,500 (ranging from $2,000 to $13,000).

Departments and Teaching Staff: *Professors 77, associate professors 44, assistant professors 27, instructors 22, part-time faculty 261.*

431 (full-time 170, part-time 261; women 205, men 226; members of minority groups 13). Total faculty with doctorate, first-professional, or other terminal degree: 210. Student-to-faculty ratio: 17:1. Degrees held by full-time faculty: doctorate 85%, master's 15%. 90% hold terminal degrees.

Enrollment: Total enrollment 5,151. Undergraduate full-time 1,916 men / 1,978 women, part-time 117m / 97w; graduate full-time 28m / 41w, part-time 250m / 724w. *Transfer students:* in-state 159; from out-of-state 46.

Characteristics of Student Body: *Ethnic/racial makeup:* number of Black non-Hispanic: 26; American Indian or Alaska Native: 10; Asian or Pacific Islander: 37; Hispanic: 43; White non-Hispanic: 3,691; unknown: 286. *Age distribution:* number under 18: 57; 18–19: 1,704; 20–21: 1,443; 22–24: 701; 25–29:

106; 30–34: 33; 35–39: 13; 40–49: 30; 50–64: 12; 65 and over: 4. 20% of student body attend summer sessions.

International Students: 23 nonresident aliens enrolled fall 2004. No programs available to aid students whose native language is not English. Some financial aid specifically designated for international students after first year.

Student Life: On-campus residence halls house 52% of student body. Residence halls are co-ed by floor or door. Housing available for nontraditional students. 3% of men and women join fraternities/sororities. *Intercollegiate athletics:* men only: baseball, basketball, football, golf, hockey, lacrosse, soccer, skiing, tennis, wrestling; women only: basketball, field hockey, lacrosse, soccer, softball, skiing, tennis. *Special regulations:* Registered cars permitted in designated areas only. Residence hall visitation 7am to 1am Sun.–Thurs., 7am to 2am Fri.and Sat. *Special services:* Writing and Reading Center, medical services. *Student publications, radio: Centripetal*, a literary journal; *The Clock*, a weekly newspaper; *The Conning Tower*, a yearbook. Radio station WPCR-FM broadcasts 133 hours per week. *Surrounding community:* Plymouth population 5,900. Boston (MA), 120 miles from campus, is nearest metropolitan area. Served by airport 60 miles from campus.

Library Collections: 306,314 volumes. 1,043 current periodical subscriptions. Online catalog. Students have access to online information retrieval services and the Internet. Total 2004–05 budget for materials and operations: $524,514.

Most important holdings include George H. Browne Collection of Robert Frost's poetry; Ernest L. Silver Collection of early textbooks; state and local history; Brown Company Collection (photographs).

Buildings and Grounds: Campus area 170 acres.

Chief Executive Officer: Dr. Donald P. Wharton, President.

Address undergraduate admission inquiries to Director of Admissions; graduate inquiries: Education to Director of Graduate Study; M.B.A. Program to Director of M.B.A. Program.

Rivier College

420 South Main Street
Nashua, New Hampshire 03060

Tel: (603) 888-1311   **E-mail:** rivadmit@rivier.edu
Fax: (603) 897-8811   **Internet:** www.rivier.edu

Institution Description: Rivier College is a private, independent, nonprofit college affiliated with the Sisters of the Presentation of Mary, Roman Catholic Church. *Enrollment:* 2,266. *Degrees awarded:* Associate, baccalaureate, master's. Certificates also awarded.

Member of the consortium New Hampshire College and University Council.

Accreditation: *Regional:* NEASC. *Professional:* nursing

History: Established and offered first instruction at postsecondary level 1933; chartered 1935; awarded first degree 1936; approved master's program 1953. *See* Sister Rose Marie, *A Brief History of Rivier College—1933–1953* (Nashua, NH: Rivier College, 1953) for further information.

Institutional Structure: *Governing board:* Rivier College Board of Trustees. Extrainstitutional representation: 2516 trustees; institutional representation: 1 administrator. 1 ex officio. 21 voting. *Composition of institution:* Administrators 10 men / 40 women. Academic affairs headed by vice president for academic affairs. Management/business/finances directed by vice president for finance and operations. Full-time instructional faculty 63. Academic governance body, the faculty, meets an average of 7 times per year.

Calendar: Semesters. Academic year Aug. to May. Freshmen admitted Aug., Jan. Degrees conferred and formal commencement May. Summer session of 2 terms from mid-May to early Aug.

Characteristics of Freshmen: 75% of accepted applicants enrolled. Average secondary school rank top 44th percentile. Mean SAT class scores 500 verbal, 480 mathematical.

75% of accepted applicants enrolled. 53% of entering freshmen expected to graduate within 5 years. 52% of freshmen from New Hampshire. Freshmen from 6 states.

Admission: Rolling admissions plan. For fall acceptance, apply as early as Sept. 1 of previous year. Freshmen are encouraged to apply as early as possible in their senior year of high school. *Requirements:* Either graduation from accredited secondary school with 16 units which must include 4 English, 2 in a modern foreign language (may be waived for some programs), 2 social studies, 1 lab science; or GED. Additional requirements for ART department requires student to submit a portfolio. Minimum GPA approximately 2.5. *Entrance tests:* College

Board SAT for baccalaureate degree applicants. For foreign students SAT or TOEFL. *For transfer students:* 2.0 minimum GPA; 90 hours maximum transfer credit.

College credit and advanced placement for postsecondary-level work completed in secondary school. College credit for extrainstitutional learning on basis of ACE *2006 Guide to the Evaluation of Educational Experiences in the Armed Services.*

Tutoring available. Remedial courses offered during regular academic year; credit given.

Degree Requirements: *For all associate degrees:* 60 credit hours. *For all baccalaureate degrees:* 120 credit hours; 2 terms in residence. *For all undergraduate degrees:* 2.0 GPA; distribution requirements.

Fulfillment of some degree requirements and exemption from some beginning courses possible by passing departmental examinations, College Board CLEP, APP. *Grading system:* A–F; withdraw (carries time limit); incomplete (carries time limit).

Distinctive Educational Programs: *For undergraduates:* Internships. Interdepartmental/interdisciplinary programs. Study abroad may be individually arranged. *Available to all students:* Independent study. Cross-registration through the consortium. *Other distinctive programs:* Nondegree enrichment programs; credit-bearing certificate programs.

ROTC: Air Force in cooperation with University of Massachusetts at Lowell.

Degrees Conferred: 122 *associate;* 203 *baccalaureate:* biological sciences 10, business and management 26, communications 5, computer and information science 2, education 50, English 4, fine and applied arts 6, foreign languages 1, health professions 41, law/legal studies 12, liberal arts 3, philosophy/religion 4, physical sciences 3, psychology 30, social sciences and history 6; 259 *master's:* business 68, computer and information science 29, education 114, English 10, health professions 37, philosophy/religion 1. 2 *honorary degrees awarded 2004–05:* Doctor of Humane Letters, Doctor of Business Administration.

Fees and Other Expenses: *Full-time tuition per academic year 2005–06:* $13,980. *Required fees:* $950. *Room and board per academic year:* $7,564.

Financial Aid: Aid from institutionally generated funds is provided on the basis of academic merit, financial need. Institution has a Program Participation Agreement with the U.S. Department of Education for eligible students to receive Pell Grants and, depending upon the agreement, other federal aid.

Financial aid to full-time, first-time undergraduate students: need-based scholarships/grants totaling $5,330,376, self-help $6,202,670, parent loans $499,294, tuition waivers $176,679; non-need-based scholarships/grants totaling $658,872, self-help $3,591,460, parent loans $430,355, tuition waivers $60,805.

Departments and Teaching Staff: *Professors* 74, *part-time faculty* 106. *Total instructional faculty:* 180 (full-time 74, part-time 106; women 118, men 62). Total faculty with doctorate, first-professional, or other terminal degree: 74. Student-to-faculty ratio: 10:1.

Enrollment: Total enrollment 2,266. Undergraduate full-time 186 men / 641 women, part-time 99m / 321w; graduate full-time 33m / 109w, part-time 144m / 533.

Characteristics of Student Body: *Ethnic/racial makeup:* number of Black non-Hispanic: 32; American Indian or Alaska Native: 5; Asian or Pacific Islander: 39; Hispanic: 60; White non-Hispanic: 1,994; unknown: 105.

International Students: 29 nonresident aliens enrolled fall 2004. Students from Europe, Asia, Latin America, Africa. Programs available to aid students whose native language is not English: English as a Second Language Program. No financial aid specifically designated for international students.

Student Life: On-campus residence halls house 34% of student body. Residence halls are co-ed. *Intercollegiate athletics:* women only: basketball, volleyball, softball. *Special regulations:* Registered cars permitted without restrictions. *Special services:* Career and counseling services, access to 2 hospitals within 2 miles. *Student publications: Perspective*, a monthly newspaper; *Images*, a yearbook. *Surrounding community:* Nashua population 75,000. Boston (MA), 40 miles from campus, is nearest major metropolitan area.

Library Collections: 208,459 volumes. 82,500 microforms; 26,665 audiovisual materials; 512 current serial subscriptions. 1,404 recordings; 20 compact discs. 25 computer work stations. Students have access to online information retrieval services and the Internet.

Most important special holdings include collections on education (early childhood, special education, counseling, general education); paralegal; business; personal papers of Corinne Rocheleau-Rouleau.

Buildings and Grounds: Campus area 46 acres.

Chief Executive Officer: Dr. William J. Farrell, President.

Address admission inquiries David Boisvert, Director of Admissions.

Saint Anselm College

100 Saint Anselm Drive
Manchester, New Hampshire 03102-1310
Tel: (603) 641-7000   **E-mail:** admission@anselm.edu
Fax: (603) 641-7116   **Internet:** /www.anselm.edu

Institution Description: Saint Anselm College (Saint Anselm's College until 1981) is a private college affiliated with the Order of Saint Benedict of New Hampshire, Roman Catholic Church. *Enrollment:* 1,987. *Degrees awarded:* Associate, baccalaureate.

Academic offerings subject to approval by statewide coordinating bodies. Member of the consortium New Hampshire College and University Council.

Accreditation: *Regional:* NEASC. *Professional:* nursing

History: Established as Saint Anselm's College, chartered, and incorporated 1889; offered first instruction at postsecondary level 1893; awarded first degree (baccalaureate) 1895; adopted present name 1981.

Institutional Structure: *Governing board:* Order of Saint Benedict of New Hampshire. Institutional representation: 9 members of the Order of St. Benedict. All voting. Board of Trustees. Representation: 38 trustees, 3 trustee emeritus. *Composition of institution:* Administrators 45 men / 48 women. Academic affairs headed by dean. Management/business/finances directed by treasurer. Full-time instructional faculty 116. Academic governance body, Faculty Senate, meets an average of 9 times per year.

Calendar: Semesters. Academic year Aug. to May. Freshmen admitted March. May. Degrees conferred May, Sept. Formal commencement May. Summer session of 7 terms from mid-May to mid-Aug.

Characteristics of Freshmen: 60% of applicants admitted. 25% of applicants admitted and enrolled.

99% (512 students) submitted SAT scores; 14% (73 students) submitted ACT scores. *25th percentile:* SAT Verbal 520, SAT Math 510; ACT Composite 22. *75th percentile:* SAT Verbal 600, SAT Math 600; ACT Composite 26.

73% of entering freshmen graduating within 5 years. 19% of freshmen from New Hampshire. Freshmen from 24 states and 18 foreign countries.

Admission: Rolling admissions plan. For fall acceptance, apply as early in senior year and not later than Mar. 1. Early decision application must be submitted by Nov. 15. *Requirements:* Graduation from accredited secondary school with 16 units which normally include 4 English, 2 foreign language, 3 mathematics, 3 lab science, 2 social studies, 2 or more electives, 4 academic electives; or GED. *Entrance tests:* College Board SAT or ACT. For foreign students TOEFL. *For transfer students:* 2.5 minimum GPA; 20 courses maximum transfer credit.

College credit and placement for score of 3 or better on College Board Advance Placement Tests; college credit and advanced placement for postsecondary-level work completed in secondary school. Tutoring available.

Degree Requirements: *For all baccalaureate degrees:* 40 courses; 4 terms in residence. *For all undergraduate degrees:* 2.0 GPA in major, core requirements. distribution requirements.

Fulfillment of some degree requirements and exemption from some beginning courses possible by passing College Board CLEP, AP. *Grading system:* A–F; withdraw (deadline after which pass-fail is appended to withdraw).

Distinctive Educational Programs: Internships. Evening classes. Dual-degree programs in engineering with the University of Notre Dame (IN), Catholic University (Washington, DC), University of Massachusetts Lowell, and Manhattan College (NY). Certificate programs in Asian studies, Catholic studies, communications, environmental studies, fine arts, forensics, French, German, Greek, Latin, medieval studies, public policy studies, secondary education, international studies, Latin American studies, Russian area studies, Spanish, and human relations and work. Provision for independent study or research, including individual majors and tutorials. Study abroad may be arranged individually. Cross-registration through consortium.

ROTC: Air Force and Army in cooperation with University of New Hampshire. 2 Army commission awarded 2004.

Degrees Conferred: 1 *associate,* 408 *baccalaureate:* biological sciences 14; business/marketing 90; computer and information sciences 12; engineering/engineering technologies 2; English 35; foreign languages and literature 6; health professions 39; liberal arts/general studies 3; mathematics 3; philosophy/religion/theology 7; physical sciences 22; protective services 55; psychology 29; social sciences 86; visual and performing arts 5.

Fees and Other Expenses: *Full-time tuition per academic year* $22,740. *Required fees:* $650. *Room and board per academic year:* $8,580.

Financial Aid: Aid from institutionally generated funds is provided on the basis of academic merit, financial need, athletic ability.

Financial aid to full-time, first-time undergraduate students: need-based scholarships/grants totaling $17,038,645, self-help $9,448,467, parent loans

$881,079, tuition waivers $672,304, athletic awards $148,299; non-need-based scholarships/grants totaling $1,896,271, self-help $4,314,836, parent loans $3,830,194, tuition waivers $974,942, athletic awards $459,961.

Departments and Teaching Staff: Biology *professors* 3, *associate professors* 4, *assistant professors* 3, *instructors* 0, *part-time faculty* 0; chemistry 1, 4, 0, 0, 0; classics 1, 0, 2, 0, 1; computer science 0, 1, 2, 0, 1; criminal justice 2, 1, 1, 1, 0; economics and business 1, 4, 4, 0, 2; education 0, 1, 0, 0, 2; English 5, 4, 1, 0, 11; fine arts 2, 1, 1, 0, 5; history 1, 2, 4, 0, 1; humanities 1, 0, 0, 0, 6; mathematics 3, 0, 0, 0, 0; modern languages 2, 5, 1, 3, 5; nursing 4, 2, 3, 3, 7; philosophy 6, 2, 2, 2, 1; physics 0, 1, 1, 1, 0; politics 1, 3, 2, 0, 1; psychology 3, 2, 1, 1, 1; sociology 1, 2, 2, 0, 3; theology 4, 2, 4, 1, 1.

Total instructional faculty: 176 (full-time 128, part-time 48; women 70, men 106; members of minority groups 2). Total faculty with doctorate, first-professional, or other terminal degree: 135. Student-to-faculty ratio: 14:1. Degrees held by full-time faculty: doctorate 75.86%, master's 20.68%. 88.79% hold terminal degrees.

Enrollment: Total enrollment 1,987. Full-time students: 827 men / 1,119 women, part-time 17m / 24w. *Transfer students:* in-state 12; from out-of-state 18.

Characteristics of Student Body: *Ethnic/racial makeup:* number of Black non-Hispanic: 10; American Indian or Alaska Native: 1; Asian or Pacific Islander: 15; Hispanic: 22; White non-Hispanic: 1,533; unknown: 383. *Age distribution:* number 18–19: 352; 20–21: 976; 22–24: 614; 25–29: 8; 30–34: 5; 35–39: 1; 40–49: 2; 50–64: 1.

International Students: 23 nonresident aliens enrolled fall 2004. 11 students from Europe, 2 Asia, 7 Latin America, 1 Africa, 1 Canada, 1 other. Programs available to aid students whose native language is not English: social, cultural. Financial aid specifically designated for international students: scholarships available annually to qualifying students.

Student Life: On-campus residence halls house 87% of student body. Residence halls for men constitute 44% of such space, for women 56%. *Intercollegiate athletics:* men only: baseball, soccer, cross-country, tennis, basketball, hockey, skiing, golf; women only: basketball, cross-country, field hockey, golf, ice hockey, soccer, softball, skiing, tennis. *Student publications: Anselmia,* a yearbook; *St. Anselm Crier,* a newspaper. *Surrounding community:* Manchester population 130,000. Boston (MA), 55 miles from campus, served by bus and plane; airport 5 miles from campus.

Library Collections: 235,000 volumes. Online catalog. Current serial subscriptions: 1,813 paper; 69,000 microform; 10,000 via electronic access. 1,750 compact discs. 64 computer work stations. Students have access to the Internet at no charge. Total 2004–05 budget for books and materials: $466,221.

Most important special holdings include New England collection; nursing subject collection; Classics; Catholic theology collections.

Buildings and Grounds: Campus area 450 acres. *New buildings:* New Hampshire Institute of Politics completed 2002; Fr. Bernard Court 2002; Sullivan Ice Arena 2003.

Chief Executive Officer: Rev. Jonathan P. DeFelice, O.S.B., President.

Address admission inquiries to Nancy Davis Griffin, Director of Admissions.

Southern New Hampshire University

2500 North River Road
Manchester, New Hampshire 03106-1045
Tel: (603) 668-2211   **E-mail:** admissions@snhu.edu
Fax: (603) 645-9665   **Internet:** www.snhu.edu

Institution Description: *Enrollment:* 6,352. *Degrees awarded:* Associate, baccalaureate, master's. Certificates also awarded.

Member of consortium New Hampshire College and University Council.

Accreditation: *Regional:* NEASC. *Professional:* business, culinary education

History: Established as the New Hampshire School of Accounting and Secretarial Science 1932; changed name to New Hampshire School of Accounting and Finance 1945, to New Hampshire School of Accounting and Commerce 1947; incorporated as New Hampshire College of Accounting and Commerce, Inc., and offered first instruction at postsecondary level 1961; awarded first degree (baccalaureate) 1966; changed name to New Hampshire College of Accounting and Commerce 1968; became New Hampshire College 1969; achieved university status and adopted the current name 2002.

Institutional Structure: *Governing board:* Trustees of the college. Representation: 20 trustees, president of the university. *Composition of institution:* Academic affairs headed by academic dean. Management/business/finances directed by treasurer. Full-time instructional faculty 88.

Calendar: Semesters. Academic year Sept. to May. Formal commencement May.

Characteristics of Freshmen: 2,250 applicants (906 men, 1,284 women). 86.7% of applicants admitted. 27.8% of admitted students enrolled full-time.

98% (535 students) submitted SAT scores; 1% (5 students) submitted ACT scores. *25th percentile*: SAT I Verbal 448, SAT I 443; Math ACT Composite 21, ACT English 23, ACT Math 17. *75th percentile*: SAT I Verbal 534, SAT I Math 537; ACT Composite 24, ACT English 25, ACT Math 19.

51% of entering freshmen expected to graduate within 5 years. 445 of freshmen from New Hampshire. Freshmen from 23 states and 38 foreign countries.

Admission: Rolling admissions plan. Early action plan. *Requirements:* Either graduation from accredited secondary school or GED; essay; minimum 2.25 GPA. *Entrance tests:* College Board SAT. For foreign students TOEFL.

Degree Requirements: *For all associate degrees:* 60 semester hours. *For all baccalaureate degrees:* 120 semester hours. *For all degrees:* 2.0 GPA; college core; major core; 30 hours in residence.

Fulfillment of some degree requirements and exemption from some beginning courses possible by passing institutional examinations, College Board CLEP, AP, other standardized tests. *Grading system:* A-F; satisfactory-unsatisfactory; withdraw (deadline after which pass-fail is appended to withdraw); incomplete.

Distinctive Educational Programs: Work-experience programs. Off-campus centers at Concord, Laconia, Nashua, Portsmouth, Salem, Brunswick (ME); Ceiba, San Juan (Puerto Rico). Cross-registration through consortium. Study abroad in Canada, Denmark, England, France, Germany. NHC/Landsdown College Program (London, England) and Polytechnic Program (North London, England).

ROTC: Army, Air Force offered in cooperation with University of New Hampshire.

Degrees Conferred: 197 *associate;* 682 *baccalaureate;* 682 *master's.* Bachelor's degrees awarded in top five disciplines: business, management, marketing, and related support services 677; computer and information sciences 53; psychology 51; communication, journalism, and related programs 33; social science and history 23. 682 *master's*: various disciplines.

Fees and Other Expenses: *Full-time tuition per academic year 2004–05:* undergraduate $19,314. Contact the university of graduate study tuition/fees. *Room and board per academic year:* $7,866.

Financial Aid: Aid from institutionally generated funds is provided on the basis of academic merit, financial need, athletic ability, other criteria. Institution has a Program Participation Agreement with the U.S. Department of Education for eligible students to receive Pell Grants and, depending upon the agreement, other federal aid.

Financial aid to full-time, first-time undergraduate students: 19% received federal grants averaging $3,543; 18% state/local grants averaging $749; 86% institutional grants averaging $8,917; 68% received loans averaging $6,001.

Departments and Teaching Staff: *Professors* 39, *associate professors* 35, *assistant professors* 14.

Total instructional faculty: 88. 63% hold terminal degrees.

Enrollment: Total enrollment 6,352. Undergraduate 4,308 (men 41.4%, women 58.6%).

Characteristics of Student Body: *Ethnic/racial makeup:* number of Black non-Hispanic: 1.1%; American Indian or Alaska Native: .2%; Asian or Pacific Islander: .9%; White non-Hispanic: 47.4%; unknown: 47.5%. *Age distribution:* 17–21: 55.7%; 22–24: 15.3%; 25–29: 13.4%; 30–34: 5.1%; 35–39: 3.5%; 40–49: .5; 50–59: .1, 60–up: .05%.

International Students: 90 undergraduate nonresident aliens enrolled fall 2004. Programs available to aid students whose native language is not English: social, cultural. English as a Second Language Program. No financial aid specifically designated for international students.

Student Life: On-campus residence halls, apartments, townhouses, Greek system available. *Intercollegiate athletics:* men only: baseball, basketball, cross-country, ice hockey, lacrosse, soccer; women only: basketball, cross-country, softball, volleyball. *Special services:* Learning Resources Center, medical services, Center for International Exchange, Career Development Center. *Student publications, radio: Daily News,* a daily campus newsletter; *The Observer,* a biweekly newspaper; yearbook. Radio station WHNC. *Surrounding community:* Manchester population 91,000.

Publications: *The Reporter,* a quarterly alumni publication.

Library Collections: 88,000 volumes. 235,000 microforms; 965 current periodical subscriptions. Students have access to online information retrieval services and the Internet.

Most important special holdings include business, teacher education, AMEX and NYSE 10K annual reports; federal and state depository documents.

Buildings and Grounds: *New buildings:* Residence Hall; Hospitality Building; American Language and Cultural Center.

Chief Executive Officer: Dr. Paul LeBlanc, President.

Address admission inquiries to Brad Poznanski, Director of Admissions.

Thomas More College of Liberal Arts

6 Manchester Street
Merrimack, New Hampshire 03054
Tel: (603) 880-8308   **E-mail:** admissions@thomasmorecollege.edu
Fax: (603) 880-9280   **Internet:** www.thomasmorecollege.edu

Institution Description: Thomas More College of Liberal Arts is a four-year, coeducational college affiliated with the Roman Catholic Church. *Enrollment:* 86. *Degrees awarded:* Baccalaureate.

Accreditation: *Regional:* NEASC.

History: The college was founded in 1978.

Calendar: Semesters. Academic year Aug. to May.

Characteristics of Freshmen: Average secondary school GPA 3.1.

Admission: *Requirements:* High school graduation with 4 credits of English, 3 mathematics, 2 foreign language, 2 social studies, 2 science with lab.

Degree Requirements: *For all baccalaureate degrees:* 129 semester credits. 6 credits mathematics, 6 credits biology, 2 years study of classical Latin or Greek, senior project.

Distinctive Educational Programs: Study abroad program available.

Degrees Conferred: 21 *baccalaureate:* English language and literature 9; philosophy/religion/theology 6; social sciences 5; biological/biomedical 1.

Fees and Other Expenses: *Full-time tuition per academic year 2004–05:* $10,450. *Room and board per academic year:* $7,700. *Books and supplies:* $600.

Financial Aid: Aid from institutionally generated funds is provided on the basis of academic merit, financial need. Institution has a Program Participation Agreement with the U.S. Department of Education for eligible students to receive Pell Grants and, depending upon the agreement, other federal aid.

Financial aid to full-time, first-time undergraduate students: 50% received federal grants; 4% state/local grants; 100% institutional grants; 73% received loans.

Departments and Teaching Staff: Literature *professors* 0 *associate professors* 1, *assistant professors* 1, *instructors* 0, *part-time teachers* 0; philosophy 0, 0, 0, 1, 0; political science 1, 0, 0, 0, 0; language 0, 0, 0, 1; science/mathematics 0, 0, 1, 0, 1. *Total instructional faculty:* 7. Student-to-faculty ratio: 10:1. Degrees held by full-time faculty: doctorate 57%, master's 43%. 100% hold terminal degrees.

Enrollment: Total enrollment 86 (men 51.2%, women 48.8%).

Characteristics of Student Body: *Ethnic/racial makeup:* number of American Indian or Alaska Native: 1.2%; Asian or Pacific Islander: 1.2%; Hispanic: 5.8%; White non-Hispanic: 75.6%; unknown: 12.8%. *Age distribution:* 17–21: 80%; 22–24: 13%; 25–29: 6%; 35–39: 1%.

International Students: 3 nonresident aliens enrolled fall 2004. Students from Asia, Canada. No programs available to aid students whose native language is not English. No financial aid specifically designated for international students.

Student Life: On-campus residence required through senior year. Various clubs and organizations available for student participation.

Library Collections: 50,000 volumes including bound books, serial backfiles, electronic documents, and govern documents not in separate collections. 20 current journal subscriptions. Computer work stations available. Students have access to online information retrieval services and the Internet.

Most important special collection include political philosophy, Southern literature, founding of America.

Buildings and Grounds: Campus area 14 acres.

Chief Executive Officer: Dr. Peter V. Sampo, President.

Address admission inquiries to Director of Admissions.

University of New Hampshire

105 Main Street
Durham, New Hampshire 03824-3547
Tel: (603) 862-1234   **E-mail:** admissions@unh.edu
Fax: (603) 862-1360   **Internet:** www.unh.edu

Institution Description: University of New Hampshire is a state institution and land-grant, sea-grant, and space-grant institution. *Enrollment:* 14,370. *Degrees awarded:* Associate, baccalaureate, master's, doctorate. Certificates of Advanced Graduate Study also awarded.

Budget subject to approval by Board of Trustees and Governor. Member of the consortium New Hampshire College and University Council.

Accreditation: *Regional:* NEASC. *Professional:* athletic training, business, chemistry, clinical lab scientist, computer science, dietetics, engineering, engineering technology, forestry, health services administration, marriage and family therapy, music, nursing, nursing education, occupational therapy, psychology internship, recreation and leisure services, social work, speech-language pathology

History: Established and chartered 1866 in Hanover as New Hampshire College of Agriculture and the Mechanic Arts, a division of Dartmouth College; offered first instruction at postsecondary level 1868; awarded first degree (baccalaureate) 1871; moved to present location 1893; rechartered and adopted present name 1923. *See* Everett B. Sackett, *New Hampshire University: Story of a New England Land-Grant College* (Durham: University of New Hampshire Press, 1974) for further information.

Institutional Structure: *Governing board:* 27-member Board of Trustees of the University System of New Hampshire. 11 members appointed by the governor of New Hampshire. 7 ex officio members: governor, commissioners of agriculture and education; chancellor of university system, presidents of University of New Hampshire (UNH), Keene State College (KSC), Plymouth State College (PSC); 2 students enrolled at and elected by student bodies of UNH, KS, PSC; 6 alumni elected by their respective schools (4 UNH, 1 KSC, 1 PSC). All voting. *Composition of institution:* Administrators 20 men / 11 women. Academic affairs headed by provost vice president for academic affairs. Management/business/finances directed by vice president for finance and administration. Academic governance body, Faculty Senate, meets an average of 12 times per year.

Calendar: Semesters. Academic year Aug. to May. Freshmen admitted Aug., Jan. Degrees conferred May, Sept., Dec. Formal commencement May. Summer session of 4 terms from June to Aug.

Characteristics of Freshmen: 12,009 applicants (5,514 men, 6,495 women). 68.5% of applicants admitted. 31.1% of admitted students enrolled full-time.

99% (2,541 students) submitted SAT scores; 6% (167 students) submitted ACT scores. *25th percentile*: SAT I Verbal 510, SAT I Math 520. *75th percentile*: SAT I Verbal 610, SAT I Math 620.

69% of entering freshmen expected to graduate within 5 years. 48% of freshmen from New Hampshire. Freshmen from 35 states and 14 foreign countries.

Admission: For fall admission, freshmen application deadline Feb. 1. Students are notified of acceptance by Apr. 15. Apply by Dec. 1 for early action. program (applicants are not obligated to enroll). Admission based primarily upon successful completion of college-preparatory coursework. Most successful candidates for admission will present: 4 years English, 4 years college preparatory mathematics, 4 years laboratory science, 3 years social science, 3 years of foreign language study. Students interested in studying engineering, science, mathematics, or forestry should present laboratory science coursework in chemistry and physics. Students planning to major in health-related disciplines should present laboratory courses in biology and chemistry. Music applicants must audition. GED accepted. *Entrance tests:* College Board SAT. For foreign students TOEFL. *For transfer students:* From 4-year accredited institution 2.5 minimum GPA, 96 semester hours maximum transfer credit; from 2-year accredited institution 3.0 minimum GPA, 64 semester hours maximum credit transferred from a 2-year degree program.

College credit and advanced placement for postsecondary level work completed in secondary school and College Board Advanced Placement examinations. College credit for extrainstitutional learning on basis of ACE *2006 Guide to the Evaluation of Educational Experiences in the Armed Services* and CEEB College Level Examination Program.

Tutoring available in Academic Resources Center.

Degree Requirements: *For all associate degrees:* 64 credit hours. *For all baccalaureate degrees:* 128 credits (minimum); 2.0 GPA; general education requirements: 8 components. Intensive writing requirement; students admitted as freshmen or as freshmen transfers must complete 4 writing intensive courses including English composition and 3 additional courses from a prescribed list (one course must be in the student's major and one must be an upper level course); last quarter of total credits residence; distribution requirements.

Fulfillment of some degree requirements and exemption from some beginning courses possible by passing College Board CLEP, AP. *Grading system:* A–F; pass-fail; withdraw (deadline after which A-F is appended to withdraw).

Distinctive Educational Programs: Cooperative education programs, including field experience, internships. External degree, evening degree, and summer session programs. Credit and enrichment continuing education programs. Telecommunications in the classroom. Facilities and programs for independent research, including Honors programs, individual majors, tutorials. More than 25 interdisciplinary minors offered. Preprofessional programs. Accelerated program (e.g., bachelor's degree in three years). Combined bachelor's graduate program (e.g., bachelor of arts and master of business administration in five years). Early acceptance in graduate programs for qualified students. Exchange programs with more than 140 colleges and universities nationwide. Through cross-registration with other institutions, international study is available virtually anywhere in the world. Full-time program at Regent's College (London)

available to upperclass students. International Affairs dual major provides the opportunity to combine any major with a second major in International Affairs. Cross-registration through National Student Exchange Program. Undergraduate Research Opportunities Program. Off-campus summer program in marine science at Shoals Marine Laboratory in cooperation with Cornell University.

ROTC: Army, Air Force. 13 Air Force and 28 Army commissions awarded 2004.

Degrees Conferred: 156 *associate*; 2,338 *baccalaureate*; 714 *master's*; 46 *doctorate*. Bachelor's degrees awarded in top five disciplines: business, management, marketing, and related support services 245; social sciences and history 280; health professions and related clinical sciences 209; English language and literature 199; psychology 179.

Fees and Other Expenses: *Full-time tuition per academic year 2005–06:* undergraduate resident $7,710, nonresident $19,430. Surcharge may apply for certain majors; graduate resident $8,010, nonresident $19,730. Contact the university for current graduate/professional schools tuition/fees and other costs. *Room and board per academic year:* $7,032.

Financial Aid: Aid from institutionally generated funds is provided on the basis of academic merit, financial need, athletic ability, other criteria. Institution has a Program Participation Agreement with the U.S. Department of Education for eligible students to receive Pell Grants and, depending upon the agreement, other federal aid.

Financial aid to full-time, first-time undergraduate students: 18% received federal grants averaging $3,999; 14% state/local grants averaging $769; 58% institutional grants averaging $5,403; 68% received loans averaging $4,998.

Departments and Teaching Staff: *Total instructional faculty:* 689 (full-time 607, part-time 82; women 254, men 435; members of minority groups 54). Total faculty with doctorate, first-professional, or other terminal degree: 588. Student-to-faculty ratio: 14:1. Degrees held by full-time faculty: doctorate 92%, master's 7%, baccalaureate 1%. 94% hold terminal degrees. *Faculty development:* $99,500,000 in grants for research. 70 faculty members awarded sabbaticals 2004–05.

Enrollment: Total enrollment 14,370. Undergraduate 11,382 (men 43.6%, women 56.4%).

Characteristics of Student Body: *Ethnic/racial makeup (undergraduate):* number of Black non-Hispanic: 1.2%; American Indian or Alaska Native: .3%; Asian or Pacific Islander: 2.1%; Hispanic: 1.4%; White non-Hispanic: 85.4%; unknown: .6%.

International Students: 102 undergraduate nonresident aliens enrolled fall 2004. Students from Europe, Asia, Latin America, Africa, Canada. Programs available to aid students whose native language is not English: social, cultural, financial. English as a Second Language Program. Financial aid specifically designated for international students: variable number of scholarships available annually for qualifying undergraduate students.

Student Life: On-campus residence halls house 56% of student body. Some men and women join and live in fraternities and sororities. Housing available for married students, students with children and graduate students. Two on-campus apartment complexes available. Of those who commute, 75% live in Durham or the immediately adjoining towns. *Intercollegiate athletics:* men only: basketball, cross-country, football, hockey, lacrosse, skiing, soccer, swimming, tennis, track; women only: basketball, cross-country, field hockey, gymnastics, ice hockey, skiing, soccer, swimming, track, volleyball. . *Special services:* Freshman Transfer, Non-Traditional and International Student Orientation, Full Service University union, Commuter Student Services including a daily bus service to all surrounding communities, over 160 student organizations, Handicapped Student Services, Non-Traditional Student Center, Foreign and Domestic Exchange programs, 24 hour medical services, Health Education Center, Personal Counseling and Testing, Hot Line, Women's Center; Center for Academic Resources; Writing Center. *Student publications, radio: The New Hampshire,* the twice weekly student paper; *Main Street,* a monthly news magazine; *Catalyst* and *Aegis,* fiction and poetry journals, and the *Granite,* a yearbook. Radio station WUNH broadcasts 24 hours/day during academic year. *Surrounding community:* Durham population 12,000. Portsmouth, 12 miles from campus, is an historic seaport with theater, music, dance, art galleries, shopping and cinema. Boston, 60 miles away, is the nearest major metropolitan area. Durham is served by 2 airports; Boston and Manchester (NH), 30 miles away.

Library Collections: 1,771,477 volumes. Online catalog. Current serial subscriptions: 5,136 paper; 267 microform; 35,631 via electronic access. 21,108 recordings; 7,057 compact discs; 10,515 CD-ROMs. audiovisual materials; 21,000 recordings. 94 computer work stations available. Students have access to online information retrieval services and the Internet.

Most important special holdings include New Hampshire Collection; Donald Hall Archives; Milne Angling Collection; Amy Beach Papers.

Buildings and Grounds: Central campus area 200 acres; contiguous campus land area 2,400 acres. *New buildings:* Mills Residence Hall; Holloway Commons.

Chief Executive Officer: Dr. Ann Weaver Hart, President.

Undergraduates address admission inquiries to Robert P.H. McGann, Director of Admissions; graduate inquiries to Graduate Admissions Office.

College of Liberal Arts

Degree Programs Offered: *Baccalaureate* programs in communications, ethnic and cultural studies, foreign languages and literatures, letters, liberal arts and sciences, philosophy, psychology, social sciences and history. *master's, doctorate* in counseling, education, letters, liberal arts and sciences, public administration, social sciences and history, visual and performing arts.

Distinctive Educational Programs: Interdisciplinary programs in justice studies, African American studies, Asian studies, Latin American studies; race, culture, and power; women's studies; Cambridge, London, and Budapest programs.

College of Engineering and Physical Sciences

Degree Programs Offered: *Baccalaureate* in computer and information sciences, engineering, engineering technology, mathematics, physical sciences; *master's, doctorate* in computer and information sciences, engineering, mathematics, physical sciences.

Distinctive Educational Programs: Integrated undergraduate/graduate program culminating in a BS in Engineering and an MBA degree. Interdisciplinary minors in lumination and optical engineering, materials science, ocean engineering, oceanography, hydrology, environmental engineering. Fall semester of junior year program at Technicoa University of Budapest, Hungary. Junior/senior level engineering technology program for accepted associate degree qualified students. Special programs in chemistry and physics teaching, earth science teaching, mathematics teaching.

College of Life Science and Agriculture

Degree Programs Offered: *Baccalaureate* programs in animal sciences, biochemistry, biology, community development, environmental conservation, forestry, general studies, horticulture/agronomy, medical lab science, microbiology, nutritional science/dietetics, plant biology, soil science, tourism/planning/development, water resources management, wildlife management, zoology.

Distinctive Educational Programs: Integrated undergraduate/graduate program leading to a BS in plant biology and an MBA degree. Interdisciplinary minors in integrated pest management. Minor in agribusiness. Intercollege graduate program in genetics. Biotechnology teaching and research. Core curriculum in all biological sciences programs, allowing easy transfer between programs.

School of Health and Human Services

Degree Programs Offered: *Baccalaureate* programs in communication science and disorders, family studies, health management/policy, kinesiology, nursing, occupation therapy, recreation management/policy, social work.

Distinctive Educational Programs: Baccalaureate completion program for registered nurses. Articulation transfer agreements between the Associate Degree programs at the State Technical Colleges in Nursing, Medical Laboratory Science, and Occupational Therapy and with the respective baccalaureate programs at the University. There is also an External Degree Program in Medical Technology and an Executive Master's Program in Health Administration. A Marriage and Family Therapy Center in the Department of Family Studies is the only center in the region which offers graduate training and research in marriage and family therapy. Minors are available to undergraduates in the areas of Health Management, Gerontology, and Health Promotion. Programs in outdoor education, occupational therapy.

Thompson School of Applied Science

Degree Programs Offered: *Associate* degrees offered in applied animal science, applied business management, civil technology, community service and leadership, resources and services, food service management/dietetics, forest technology, general studies, horticulture technology. *Baccalaureate* in applied sciences.

University of New Hampshire at Manchester

Degree Programs Offered: *Associate* programs in business, general studies, studio arts, biological sciences; *baccalaureate* programs in communications, engineering technology, nursing, letters, psychology, sign language and interpretation, social sciences and history.

Admission: Recommended secondary school program of study to include at least 4 years of English, 3 each of foreign language, mathematics and science, and 2 years of social science.

Distinctive Educational Programs: Credit and enrichment continuing education programs. Alternative freshman year program. College opportunity program for high school students. Access to academic programs from other units in the University System.

Whittemore School of Business and Economics

Degree Programs Offered: *Baccalaureate* programs in business administration, economics, hospitality management; *master's, doctorate* programs in business administration, economics.

Distinctive Educational Programs: Five-year B.S.-M.B.A. and five-year B.A.-M.B.A. degree programs for exceptional students. Executive M.B.A. program offers a week-long international residency. Part-time M.B.A. evening program offered. Intensive executive development program each August.

New Jersey

Bloomfield College

467 Franklin Street
Bloomfield, New Jersey 07003
Tel: (973) 748-9000 **E-mail:** admission@bloomfield.edu
Fax: (973) 743-3998 **Internet:** www.bloomfield.edu

Institution Description: Bloomfield College is a private college affiliated with the Presbyterian Church (U.S.A.), through the Synod of the Northeast. *Enrollment:* 2,164. *Degrees awarded:* Baccalaureate. Certificates also awarded.

Accreditation: *Regional:* MSA. *Professional:* nursing

History: Established as a German Theological Seminary in 1868; offered first instruction at postsecondary level 1869; chartered 1871; awarded first degree (baccalaureate) 1874; changed name to Bloomfield Theological Seminary 1913, to Bloomfield College and Seminary 1926; adopted present name 1960.

Institutional Structure: *Governing board:* Board of Trustees. Extrainstitutional representation: 28 trustees plus trustees emeriti, faculty, and student representatives. *Composition of institution:* administrators 15 men/ 20 women. Academic affairs headed by vice president for academic affairs and dean of the college. Management/business/finances directed by vice president for finance and administration. Full-time instructional faculty 66. Academic governance body, the faculty, meets an average of 8 times per year. *Faculty representation:* Faculty served by collective bargaining agent affiliated with AAU.

Calendar: Semesters (4-1-4 plan). Academic year early Sept. to mid-May. Freshmen admitted Sept., Jan., June, July. Degrees conferred and formal commencement May. Summer session from mid-May to late Aug.

Characteristics of Freshmen: 33% of applicants admitted. 19% of applicants admitted and enrolled.

78% (332 students) submitted SAT scores. *25th percentile:* SAT Verbal 370, SAT Math 370. *75th percentile:* SAT I Verbal 450, SAT I Math 460.

32% of entering freshmen expected to graduate within 5 years. 96% of freshmen from New Jersey. Freshmen from 7 states.

Admission: Rolling admissions plan. Priority application deadline Mar. 14 for fall semester. Applications submitted after Mar. 14 are considered on an availability basis. Fall applications will not be considered past Aug. 1. Early action program available. *Requirements:* Either graduation from accredited secondary school, or GED. *Entrance tests:* College Board SAT preferred, ACT accepted. For foreign students TOEFL. *For transfer students:* only courses for which a grade of C or better was earned will be accepted.

College credit and advanced placement for postsecondary-level work completed in secondary school. Credit granted for CLEP examinations up to 16 course units. Tutoring available. Developmental courses offered during regular academic year.

Degree Requirements: 33 course units; at least 16 of these course units must be at an advanced level (200 or above). Includes general education courses.

Distinctive Educational Programs: Weekend and evening classes. Interdisciplinary programs. Preprofessional program in chiropractic medicine. Facilities and programs for independent research, including honors programs, individual majors. *Other distinctive programs:* Women's Program, a nontraditional program for adult women beginning or returning to college. Audit program for senior citizens. Continuing education.] Study abroad through Bloomfield's membership in the College Consortium for International Studies. Teacher certification in elementary and secondary education. Bloomfield College's Institute for Technology and Professional Studies is an umbrella for all noncredit program courses.

ROTC: Army offered in cooperation with Seton Hall University.

Degrees Conferred: 223 *baccalaureate:* biological sciences 17; business/marketing 57; computer and information sciences 6; education 6; English 13; health professions and related sciences 28; liberal arts/general studies 2; mathematics 4; philosophy/religion/theology 1; physical sciences 3; psychology 30; social sciences and history 40; visual and performing arts 16. *Honorary degrees awarded 2004:* Doctor of Fine Arts 2; Doctor of Laws 1.

Fees and Other Expenses: *Full-time tuition per academic year 2005–06:* $14,850. *Room and board per academic year:* $7,400. *Required fees:* $250.

Financial Aid: Aid from institutionally generated funds is provided on the basis of academic merit, financial need, athletic ability. Institution has a Program Participation Agreement with the U.S. Department of Education for eligible students to receive Pell Grants and, depending upon the agreement, other federal aid.

Financial aid to full-time, first-time undergraduate students: need-based scholarships/grants totaling $13,359,324, self-help $6,368,431, parent loans $549,166; non-need-based scholarships/grants totaling $1,001,184, self-help $47,623; tuition waivers $99,171, athletic awards $661,313.

Departments and Teaching Staff: *Professors* 26, *associate professors* 21, *assistant professors* 15, *instructors* 4, *part-time faculty* 138.

Total instructional faculty: 204 (full-time 66, part-time 138; women 98, men 106; members of minority groups 54). Total faculty with doctorate, first-professional, or other terminal degree: 71. Student-to-faculty ratio: 17:1. *Faculty development:* 5 faculty members awarded sabbaticals 2004–05.

Enrollment: Total enrollment 2,164. Full-time 556 men / 1,165 women, part-time 108m / 335w. *Transfer students:* in-state 223; from out-of-state 8.

Characteristics of Student Body: *Ethnic/racial makeup:* number of Black non-Hispanic: 1,165; American Indian or Alaska Native: 5; Asian or Pacific Islander: 72; Hispanic: 490; White non-Hispanic: 314; unknown: 166. *Age distribution:* number under 18: 69; 18–19: 529; 20–21: 423; 22–24: 344; 25–29: 283; 30–34: 162; 35–39: 129; 40–49: 159; 50–64: 61; 65 and over: 7.

International Students: 26 nonresident aliens enrolled fall 2004. Students from Europe, Asia, Latin America, Africa. Programs available to aid students whose native language is not English: English as a Second Language Program available. Some financial aid specifically designated for qualifying international students.

Student Life: On-campus residence halls house 12% of student body; an additional 4% are housed at the local Wellesley Inn. *Special regulations:* Registered cars permitted without restrictions. *Special services:* Center for Academic Development. College has 37 registered student organizations. *Student publications: Collective Voice*, a monthly newspaper; *Common Ground*, a biannual literary magazine; *Saga*, a yearbook. *Surrounding community:* Bloomfield, population 48,000, is located in the Newark metropolitan area. Served by mass transit bus system; airport 7 miles from campus; passenger rail service less than a mile from campus.

Library Collections: 64,700 volumes. Online catalog. Current serial subscriptions: 456 paper; 59 microform; 4,000 via electronic access. 50 compact discs. 100 CD-ROMs. 430 computer work stations campus-wide. Students have access to online information retrieval services and the Internet. Total 2004–05 budget for books and materials: $144,000.

Most important holdings include Administrative Reserve (400 volumes on all aspects of higher education); The Abraham Lincoln collection (150 volumes on Lincoln's life); Black and Urban Studies (200 volumes, multidisciplinary in nature and focusing on the years from 1960 to 1970).

Buildings and Grounds: Campus area 12 acres. *New buildings:* Library (fully wired for network connections); Talbott Hall Technology Learning Center.

Chief Executive Officer: Dr. Richard A. Levao, President.

Address admission inquiries to Mayten Sanchez, Director of Admission.

Caldwell College

9 Ryerson Avenue
Caldwell, New Jersey 07006
Tel: (973) 618-3000 **E-mail:** admissions@caldwell.edu
Fax: (973) 618-3600 **Internet:** www.caldwell.edu

Institution Description: Caldwell College is a private, coeducational, liberal arts college affiliated with the Sisters of Saint Dominic, Roman Catholic Church. *Enrollment:* 2,181. *Degrees awarded:* Baccalaureate, master's. Certificates also awarded.

Accreditation: *Regional:* MSA.

History: Established and chartered as Caldwell College for Women and offered first instruction at postsecondary level 1939; awarded first degree (baccalaureate) 1943; adopted present name 1969; offered bachelor of fine arts degree 1974; external degree program offered 1979; became coeducational 1985; awarded first graduate degree 1994.

Institutional Structure: *Governing board:* Board of Trustees. Extrainstitutional representation: 25 trustees, 4 ex officio, including 2 members of general counsel of Sisters of Saint Dominic; institutional representation: 2 administrators, including president of the college; 1 alumna. All voting. *Composition of institution:* Administrators 10 men / 45 women. Academic affairs headed by academic dean. Management/business/finances directed by treasurer. Full-time instructional faculty 72. Academic governance body, Curriculum Committee, meets an average of 7 times per year.

Calendar: Semesters. Academic year early Aug. to May. Freshmen admitted Aug., Jan. Degrees conferred May, Aug., Dec. Formal commencement May. Summer session of 4 terms begins late May.

Characteristics of Freshmen: 74% of applicants accepted. 25% of accepted applicants enrolled.

Average secondary school rank 49th percentile. Mean SAT scores 452 verbal, 448 mathematical.

52.6% of entering freshmen expected to graduate within 5 years. 91% of freshmen from New Jersey. Freshmen from 3 states and 9 foreign countries.

Admission: Rolling admissions plan. For fall acceptance, apply as early as end of junior year of secondary school, but not later than July 31. of year of enrollment. Apply by Nov. 1 for early decision. *Requirements:* Either graduation from accredited secondary school with 16 units which must include 4 English, 2 in a foreign language, 2 mathematics, 2 science, 1 history; or GED. Minimum GPA 2.5. Lowest acceptable secondary school class standing 50th percentile. *Entrance tests:* College Board SAT or ACT composite. *For transfer students:* 2.0 minimum GPA; from 4-year accredited institution 75 hours maximum transfer credit; from 2-year accredited institution 60 hours.

College credit and advanced placement for postsecondary-level work completed in secondary school and for extrainstitutional learning (life experience) college credit on basis of ACE *2006 Guide to the Evaluation of Educational Experiences in the Armed Services*; portfolio and faculty assessments.

Tutoring available. Noncredit developmental courses offered in summer session and regular academic year.

Degree Requirements: 122 credit hours; 2.0 GPA; distribution requirements; outcomes assessment or comprehensives according to department.

Fulfillment of some degree requirements and exemption from some beginning courses possible by passing College Board CLEP, APP (score of 3). *Grading system:* A–F; withdraw (carries time limit); incomplete (carries time limit).

Distinctive Educational Programs: Internships. Cooperative education. Evening classes. External degree program enables students to complete degree requirements outside the classroom. Special facilities for using telecommunications in the classroom. Interdisciplinary programs in American studies, criminal justice, futures studies, Latin American studies, management/behavioral science, public administration, telecommunications, theater arts, urban studies, women's studies, world concerns and world literature. Programs for independent research, including honors programs, tutorials. Study abroad programs available by individual arrangement. *Other distinctive programs:* Continuing education program offering late afternoon and evening classes.

Degrees Conferred: 376 *baccalaureate:* biological/life sciences 6; business/marketing 82; communications/communication technologies 19; computer and information sciences 18; education 36; English 32; foreign languages and literature 4; interdisciplinary studies 7; mathematics 7; philosophy/religion/theology 5l; physical sciences 3; protective services/public administration 6; psychology 64; social sciences and history 74; visual and performing arts 13. 81 *master's:* business/marketing 5; education 61; liberal arts 1; philosophy/religion/theology 3; psychology 11.

Fees and Other Expenses: *Full-time tuition per academic year 2004–05:* $17,810 undergraduate; $525 per credit hour graduate. *Required fees:* $435. *Room and board per academic year:* $7,350.

Financial Aid: Aid from institutionally generated funds is provided on the basis of academic merit, financial need, athletic ability, other criteria.

Financial aid to full-time, first-time undergraduate students: need-based scholarships/grants totaling $5,192,632, self-help $2,108,784, non-need-based scholarships/grants totaling $182,211, self-help $2,761,479, parent loans $1,390,758, tuition waivers $368,084, athletic awards $471,910. *Graduate aid:* 205 students received $966,422 in federal and state-funded loans; 4 research assistantships awarded totaling $17,622.

Departments and Teaching Staff: Art *professors* 1, *associate professors* 2, *assistant professors* 1, *instructors* 0; *part-time faculty* 4; business 2, 4, 4, 0, 3; education 0, 4, 3, 0, 10; English 3, 0, 3, 0, 9; foreign languages 1, 0, 2, 0, 5; history/political science 1, 0, 3, 0, 4; mathematics/computer science 0, 6, 3, 0, 11; music 0, 2, 0, 0, 6; natural science 2, 3, 1, 0, 2; psychology 2, 1, 2, 0, 9; religion/philosophy 1, 2, 3, 0, 5; sociology 0, 2, 2, 0, 6; communications 0, 0, 2, 0, 2; Learning Center 0, 0, 0, 4, 0.

Total instructional faculty: 152. *Student-to-faculty ratio:* 13:1.

Enrollment: Total enrollment 2,181. Undergraduate full-time 383 men / 666 women, part-time 158m / 505w; graduate full-time 11m / 36w, part-time 89m / 333w. *Transfer students:* in-state 559; from out-of-state 45.

Characteristics of Student Body: *Ethnic/racial makeup:* number of Black non-Hispanic: 268; American Indian or Alaska Native: 3; Asian or Pacific Islander: 24; Hispanic: 183; White non-Hispanic: 1,087; unknown: 81. *Age distribution:* number 18–19: 231; 20–21: 386; 22–24: 332; 25–29: 143; 30–34: 96; 35–39: 30; 40–49: 244; 50–64: 136; 65 and over: 14. 44% of student body attend summer sessions.

International Students: 71 nonresident aliens enrolled fall 2004. 7 students from Europe, 27 Asia, 6 Latin America, 6 Africa, 24 other. Programs available to aid students whose native language is not English: English as a Second Language. Financial aid specifically designated for international students: variable number of scholarships available annually.

Student Life: On-campus residence halls house 45% of student body. *Intercollegiate athletics:* baseball, basketball, soccer, softball, tennis, volleyball, co-ed golf. *Special regulations:* Cars permitted on campus with permit. *Special services:* Learning Resources Center, career and counseling services, medical services. *Student publications: Carillon,* a yearbook; *The Kettle,* a student newspaper; *Paw Prints,* athletic department newsletter; *Calyx,* a poetry publication. *Surrounding community:* Caldwell population 8,000. New York City, 20 miles from campus, is nearest metropolitan area. Served by mass transit bus system; airport and passenger rail service, each 10 from campus.

Library Collections: 126,805 volumes including bound books, serial backfiles, electronic documents, and government documents not in separate collections. Online catalog. Current serial subscriptions: 452 paper, 250 microform, 10 electronic. 600 recordings; 250 compact discs; 20 CD-ROMs. 40 computer work stations. Students have access to the Internet at no charge.

Most important special holdings include women's studies; curriculum materials; Irish historical literature; Caldwell College Archives; juvenile collections.

Buildings and Grounds: Campus area 90 acres.

Chief Executive Officer: Sr. Patrice Werner, O.P., President.

Address admission inquiries to Kathryn Reilley, Director of Admissions.

Centenary College

400 Jefferson Street
Hackettstown, New Jersey 07840
Tel: (908) 852-1400   **E-mail:** admissions@centenarycollege.edu
Fax: (908) 852-4288   **Internet:** www.centenarycollege.edu

Institution Description: Centenary College (Centenary College for Women until 1976) is a private, independent, nonprofit college. *Enrollment:* 2,. *Degrees awarded:* Associate, baccalaureate, master's.

Accreditation: *Regional:* MSA.

History: Established as Centenary Collegiate Institute and chartered as coeducational secondary school and 4-year women's college 1867; offered first instruction at postsecondary level 1874; discontinued college division 1896; ceased coeducation 1910; added junior college program and awarded first degree (associate) 1929; closed secondary school and changed name to Centenary Junior College 1940; became Centenary College for Women 1956; added 4-year baccalaureate program and became Centenary College 1976; added 4-year coeducational Continuing Education Division 1976; became coeducational for full-time students 1988. *See* Leila Roberta Custard, *Through Golden Years* (New York: Lewis Historical Publishing Company, Inc., 1947) for further information.

Institutional Structure: *Governing board:* 25 trustees; institutional representation: president of the college, vice president for academic affairs/dean of the college, vice president for finance, vice president for enrollment management and marketing, vice president for development, dean of students, director of athletics. *Composition of institution:* Administrators 11 men / 30 women. Full-time instructional faculty 40. Academic governance body, the faculty, meets an average of 9 times per year.

Calendar: Semesters. Academic year Sept. to May. Freshmen admitted Sept., Jan. Degrees conferred May, Sept., Dec. Formal commencement May. Summer session of 2 terms: May–July, July–Aug.

Characteristics of Freshmen: 857 applicants (321 men, 536 women). 76.1% of applicants admitted. 36.2% of admitted students enrolled full-time.

92% (217 students) submitted SAT scores; 2% (2 students) submitted ACT scores. *25th percentile:* SAT I Verbal 400, SAT I Math 400; ACT Composite 17, ACT English 13, ACT Math 17. *75th percentile:* SAT I Verbal 510, SAT I Math 520; ACT Composite 20, ACT English 19, ACT Math 22.

73% of freshmen from New Jersey. Freshmen from 10 states and 5 foreign countries.

Admission: Rolling admissions plan. For fall acceptance, apply as early as Sept. of previous year, but not later than Aug. of year of enrollment. Students are notified of acceptance beginning Oct. 1. Early acceptance available. *Requirements:* Graduation from accredited secondary school or GED. Minimum GPA 2.0. Minimum SAT combined score 850. Personal interview for equine students. *Entrance tests:* For foreign students TOEFL, minimum score 500. *For transfer students:* 2.0 minimum GPA; 96 hours maximum transfer credit.

College credit and advanced placement for postsecondary-level work completed in secondary school. College credit for extrainstitutional learning (life learning) on basis of portfolio and faculty assessment. College credit for CLEP exams.

Tutoring available. Developmental courses offered during regular academic year. ESL courses offered during regular academic year for credit.

Degree Requirements: *For all associate degrees:* 64 credit hours; 2.0 minimum GPA. *For all baccalaureate degrees:* 128 credit hours; 2.0 minimum GPA. *For all master's degrees:* residence requirement of 27 graduate credits; completion of minimum of 33 graduate credit hours; successfully pass comprehensive assessment; maintain 3.0 GPA.; complete program within 6 years of initial enrollment in the M.A. program. *For all degrees:* 1 year in residence; demonstrated competency in writing and mathematics.

Fulfillment of some degree requirements and exemption from some beginning courses possible by passing College Board CLEP, APP, other standardized tests. *Grading system:* A–F; pass-fail; withdraw (deadline after which pass-fail is appended to withdraw); incomplete (carries time limit).

Distinctive Educational Programs: Four integrative Centenary College Seminars representing the College's philosophy and mission of success through commitment to self, community, and profession; centerpiece of the College Core Requirements. Award winning Educational Opportunity Fund Program (EOF). Work-experience programs, including internships and practicums. Interdisciplinary programs in fine arts, liberal arts, and performing arts, including programs for independent research, individualized majors, tutorials, and independent study. Study abroad for junior year equine students in England and for other students through the International Studies Division. *Other distinctive programs:* Continuing education, evening division for adults; certification programs in elementary/secondary education, child care administration and teacher of the handicapped; program for the learning disabled.

Degrees Conferred: 59 *associate*; 524 *baccalaureate*; 110 *master's.* Bachelor's degrees awarded in top five disciplines: business, management, marketing, and related support services 171; psychology 31; liberal arts and sciences, general studies, and humanities 30; social science and history 23; English language/literature 23.

Fees and Other Expenses: *Full-time tuition per academic year 2004–05:* $18,450 undergraduate; contact the college for current graduate tuition. *Room and board per academic year:* $7,500. *Books and supplies:* $850.

Financial Aid: Aid from institutionally generated funds is provided on the basis of academic merit, financial need, other criteria. Institution has a Program Participation Agreement with the U.S. Department of Education for eligible students to receive Pell Grants and, depending upon the agreement, other federal aid.

Financial aid to full-time, first-time undergraduate students: 19% received federal grants averaging $3,638; 25% state/local grants averaging $5,452; 62% institutional grants averaging $5,613; 55% received loans averaging $6,566.

Departments and Teaching Staff: Business and fashion *professors* 0, *associate professors* 4, *assistant professors* 1, *instructors* 1, *part-time teachers* 26; education 0, 0, 5, 0, 7; equine 0, 0, 0, 5, 2; humanities 0, 5, 1, 1, 4; literature and communications 1, 1, 4, 0, 8; mathematics and natural science 0, 0, 5, 0, 1; social and behavioral science 1, 1, 4, 0, 9.

Total instructional faculty: 97. Student-to-faculty ratio: 13:1. Degrees held by full-time faculty: baccalaureate 15%, master's 42.5%, doctorate 47.5%. 62% hold terminal degrees.

Enrollment: Total enrollment 2,339. Undergraduate 1,427 (men 33.7%, women 56.3%).

Characteristics of Student Body: *Ethnic/racial makeup (undergraduate):* number of Black non-Hispanic: 3.9%; American Indian or Alaska Native: .5%; Asian or Pacific Islander: 2.5%; Hispanic: 3.8%; White non-Hispanic: 49.5%; unknown: 38.3%. *Age distribution:* 17–21: 31.1%; 22–24: 7.6%; 25–29: 11.2%; 30–34: 11%; 35–39: 10 4%; 40–49: 14.8%; 50–59 3%; 60–up: .4%.

International Students: 32 nonresident aliens enrolled 2004. Students from Europe, Asia. Programs available to aid students whose native language is not English: social, cultural. English as a Second Language Program. No financial aid specifically designated for international students.

Student Life: On-campus residence halls house 66% of student body. Coed dormitories. *Intercollegiate athletics:* women only: cross-country, softball, tennis, volleyball, basketball. *Recreational activities:* volleyball, ping-pong, swimming, aerobics, jogging, basketball, badminton, and weight lifting. *Special regulations:* Cars permitted; parking fee charged. Quiet hours from 9pm to 9am. Visitation hours vary according to residence hall. *Special services:* Learning Resources Center, medical services. Van service to and from equestrian center,

also available for field trips. Campus Ministry. Career Planning and Placement. Counseling Center. Student Assistance Program for counseling in the area of substance abuse and dependence. *Student publications, radio:* HACK, a yearbook; *Prism,* an annual literary magazine; *The Quill,* a biweekly newspaper. Radio station WNTI. *Surrounding community:* Hackettstown population 12,000. New York, 60 miles from campus, is nearest metropolitan area. Served by mass transit bus system; airport and passenger rail service, each 60 miles from campus.

Library Collections: 68,000 volumes. 20,000 microforms; 5,000 audiovisual materials; 875 current periodical subscriptions. Online catalog. Students have access to online information retrieval services and the Internet.

Most important holdings include George Wyckoff Cummins Collection of archaeological and historical books and documents (with some artifacts of North American Indians) dating from late 1700s–early 1900s; William Lewis Lancey, Abraham Lincoln Collection (105 volumes, photographs, busts, a daguerreotype, and *Lincoln Loire Newsletter* 1858–present).

Buildings and Grounds: Campus area 42 acres.

Chief Executive Officer: Dr. Kenneth L. Hoyt, President.

Address undergraduate admission inquiries to Diane P. Fennian, Dean of Enrollment Management; graduate inquiries to Director, Graduate Program.

College of New Jersey

200 Pennington Road
P.O. Box 7718
Ewing, New Jersey 08628-0718
Tel: (609) 771-1855   **E-mail:** admiss@vm.tcnj.edu
Fax: (609) 637-5191   **Internet:** www.tcnj.edu

Institution Description: The College of New Jersey, formerly named Trenton State College, is a public institution. *Enrollment:* 6,812. *Degrees awarded:* Baccalaureate, master's.

Academic offerings subject to approval by statewide coordinating bodies. Budget subject to approval by state governing boards.

Accreditation: *Regional:* MSA. *Professional:* business, computer science, counseling, engineering technology, music, nursing, nursing education, speech-language pathology, teacher education

History: Chartered as New Jersey State Normal and Model Schools and offered first instruction at postsecondary level 1855; awarded first degree (baccalaureate) 1926; changed name to State Teachers College and Normal School 1929, to New Jersey State Teachers College 1937; became Trenton State College 1958; adopted present name 1996.

Institutional Structure: *Governing board:* Board of Trustees. Representation: 15 trustees, including 1 student, voting. President, 2 faculty representatives, DHE representative, non-voting. *Composition of institution:* Executive staff 22 members, 13 men / 9 women. Vice President for College Advancement oversees development, alumni affairs, public relations, admissions, financial aid, registration and bursar. Full-time instructional faculty 335. College Governance Structure with 8 standing committees. 3 advisory councils and 12 advisory committees. Membership includes faculty, staff and students. Academic governance body, Faculty Senate, meets an average of 10 times per year. *Faculty representation:* Faculty served by collective bargaining agent, New Jersey State Federation of Teachers Local 2364, affiliate with AFT.

Calendar: Semesters. Academic year Sept. to May. Freshmen admitted Sept., Jan., June. Degrees conferred and formal commencement May. Summer session of 2-, 5-, and 6-week courses from mid-June to early Aug.

Characteristics of Freshmen: 48% of applicants admitted. 40% of applicants admitted and enrolled.

98% (1,208 students) submitted SAT scores. *25th percentile:* SAT Verbal 575, SAT Math 595. *75th percentile:* SAT Verbal 670, SAT Math 670. 78% of entering freshmen expected to graduate within 5 years. 95% of freshmen from New Jersey. Freshmen from 6 states and 3 foreign countries.

Admission: Admission to the College of New Jersey is very competitive; the academic profiles of entering freshmen are very high. While SAT scores and high school class rank are important considerations, each application is carefully reviewed on an individual basis. For fall admissions: students completing early decision applications by Nov. 1 will be notified Dec. 15; students completing applications by March 1 will notified April 1. *Requirements:* Graduation from approved secondary school with 16 college preparatory units, including 4 English, 2 social studies, 3 mathematics, 2 laboratory science; or GED. *Entrance tests:* College Board SAT. For foreign students TOEFL. *For transfer students:* 2.75 minimum GPA; from 4-year accredited institution maximum transfer credit limited only by residence requirement; from 2-year accredited institution 64 credits.

College credit and advanced placement for postsecondary-level work completed in secondary school. For extrainstitutional learning (life experience) college credit on basis of portfolio assessment.

Tutoring available. Developmental courses offered in summer session and regular academic year.

Degree Requirements: Minimum of 32 course units; 2.0 GPA; at least 12 courses must be taken in residence including the final 8 course units; completion of liberal learning and major requirements. Additional requirements for some programs. *Grading system:* A–F; pass-fail (option); withdraw (carries time limit).

Distinctive Educational Programs: Honors programs. Work-experience programs, including internships. Evening classes. Special facilities for using telecommunications in the classroom. Interdepartmental programs in African-American program, Asian studies, women's studies. More than 180 exchange and study abroad programs in over 50 countries as well as opportunities for student teaching abroad.

ROTC: Army in cooperation with Princeton University; Air Force with Rutgers, The State University of New Jersey. .

Degrees Conferred: 1,496 *baccalaureate:* area and ethnic studies 12; biological/life sciences 91; business/marketing 261; computer and information sciences 43; education 364; engineering and engineering technologies 44; English 182; foreign languages and literature 11; health professions and related sciences 31; mathematics 28; philosophy/religion/theology 7; physical sciences 23; protective services/public administration 76; psychology 127; social sciences and history 112; visual and performing arts 84.

Fees and Other Expenses: *Full-time tuition per academic year 2004–05:* undergraduate resident $6,621, nonresident $11,562; graduate resident $8,219, nonresident $11,502. *Required fees:* $2,497. *Room and board per academic year:* $8,093.

Financial Aid: Aid from institutionally generated funds is provided on the basis of academic merit, financial need, other considerations.

Financial aid to full-time, first-time undergraduate students: need-based scholarships/grants totaling $8,546,315, self-help $8,642,265, parent loans $133,441; non-need-based scholarships/grants totaling $12,709,865, self-help $10,291,873, parent loans $4,240,891, tuition waivers $796,184.

Departments and Teaching Staff: *Professors* 85, *associate professors* 108, *assistant professors* 137, *instructors* 1, *part-time faculty* 354.

Total instructional faculty: 685 (full-time 354; part-time 354; women 324, men 361; members of minority groups 93). Student-to-faculty ratio: 13:1. Degrees held by full-time faculty: master's 12%, doctorate 86%, professional 2%. 88% hold terminal degrees. *Faculty development:* $1,193,187 in grants for research. 6 faculty members awarded sabbaticals 2004–05.

Enrollment: Total enrollment 6,812. Undergraduate full-time 2,350 men / 3,358 women, part-time 82m / 128w; graduate full-time 28m / 83w, part-time 150m / 633w.

Characteristics of Student Body: *Ethnic/racial makeup:* number of Black non-Hispanic: 557; American Indian or Alaska Native: 4; Asian or Pacific Islander: 283; Hispanic: 390; White non-Hispanic: 4,593; unknown: 266. *Age distribution:* number under 18: 1; 18–19: 46; 20–21: 2,520; 22–24: 2,111; 25–29: 165; 30–34: 44; 35–39: 34; 40–49: 68; 50–64: 27; 65 and over: 2.

International Students: 25 nonresident aliens enrolled fall 2004. No programs available to aid students whose native language is not English. No financial aid specifically designated for international students.

Student Life: On-campus residence halls house 61% of full-time undergraduates. Intercollegiate athletics for men and women. *Special regulations:* Cars permitted with restrictions. *Special services:* Learning Resources Center, medical services. *Student publications, radio: The Signal,* a weekly newspaper; *Fire II, Lion's Eye, Utimme Umane,* literary magazines. Radio station WTSR broadcasts 50 hours per week. *Surrounding community:* Ewing Township population 36,000. Philadelphia (PA), 30 miles from campus, is nearest metropolitan area. Served by mass transit bus system; airport 2 miles from campus; passenger rail service 5 miles from campus.

Library Collections: 572,582 volumes including bound books, serial backfiles, electronic documents, and government documents not in separate collections. Online catalog. Current serial subscriptions 1,450 paper; 133 microform; 16,000 via electronic access. 100 computer work stations. Students have access to the Internet at no charge. Total 2004–05 budget for books and materials: $1,376,241.

Most important special holdings include New Jersey materials; historical textbooks; College Archives; Oral History Collection.

Buildings and Grounds: Campus area 255 acres.

Chief Executive Officer: Dr. R. Barbara Gitenstein, President.

Undergraduate address admission inquiries to Lisa Poponiak, Director of Admissions; graduate inquiries to Susan Hydro, Office of Graduate Studies.

College of Saint Elizabeth

2 Convent Road
Morristown, New Jersey 07960-6989

Tel: (973) 290-4000   **E-mail:** apply@cse.edu
Fax: (973) 290-4488   **Internet:** www.cse.edu

Institution Description: College of Saint Elizabeth is a private women's college affiliated with Sisters of Charity of Saint Elizabeth, Roman Catholic Church. *Enrollment:* 1,976. *Degrees awarded:* Baccalaureate, master's.

Accreditation: *Regional:* MSA. *Professional:* nursing

History: Established and offered first instruction at postsecondary level 1899; incorporated 1900; awarded first degree (baccalaureate) 1903. *See* Sister Blanche Marie McEniry, *Three Score and Ten* (Convent Station: College of Saint Elizabeth, 1969) for further information.

Institutional Structure: *Governing board:* Two-tiered system: (1) Corporation of 5 Sisters of Charity; (2) Corporation plus 19 additional Board members. 3 ex officio, 24 voting members. *Composition of institution:* Administrators 3 men / 17 women. Academic affairs headed by dean of studies. Management/business/finances directed by treasurer. Full-time instructional faculty 53. Academic governance body, the faculty, meets an average of 7 times per year.

Calendar: Semesters. Academic year Sept. to May. Freshmen admitted Sept., Jan., June. Degrees conferred May, Oct. Formal commencement May. Summer session of 2 terms from mid-May to early Aug.

Characteristics of Freshmen: 472 applicants (472 women). 78.9% of applicants admitted. 48.2% of admitted students enrolled full-time.

96% (157 students) submitted SAT scores. *25th percentile:* SAT I Verbal 400, SAT I Math 390. *75th percentile:* SAT I Verbal 520, SAT I Math 510.

50% of entering freshmen expected to graduate within 5 years. 90% of freshmen from New Jersey. Freshmen from 2 states and 9 foreign countries.

Admission: Rolling admissions plan. For fall acceptance, apply as early as Sept. 1 of previous year, but not later than Aug. 15 of year of enrollment. Apply by Nov. 15 for early decision; must limit application to College of Saint Elizabeth. Early acceptance available. *Requirements:* Either graduation from accredited secondary school with 3 units English, 2 in a foreign language, 3 college preparatory mathematics and/or science, 1 American history, 7 academic electives; or GED. Lowest acceptable secondary school class standing 50th percentile. *Entrance tests:* College Board SAT. For foreign students TOEFL. *For transfer students:* 2.0 minimum GPA, 64 semester hours maximum transfer credit.

College credit and advanced placement for postsecondary-level work completed in secondary school or the CLEP subject examinations or Thomas Edison College Examination Program that contribute to its degree program.

Tutoring available. Noncredit remedial courses offered in summer session and during regular academic year.

Degree Requirements: 128 semester hours; 2.0 GPA; 64 credit hours in residence; fulfillment of major requirements; cluster requirements; writing competency requirement; fitness/wellness requirement.

Fulfillment of some degree requirements and exemption from some beginning courses possible by passing College Board CLEP, AP. *Grading system:* A–F; pass-fail; withdrew; incomplete (carries time limit); 2 final grade not received.

Distinctive Educational Programs: Work experience programs. Weekend and evening classes. Accelerated degree program. Honors program. Study abroad may be individually arranged during junior year. Cross-registration with Fairleigh Dickinson and Drew Universities. *Other distinctive programs:* Degree-granting weekend college and continuing education program. Hispanic Leadership Program; co-curricular leadership program; master's degree programs.

Degrees Conferred: 212 *baccalaureate*; 77 *master's.* Bachelor's degrees awarded in top five disciplines: business, management, marketing, and related support services 63; education 35; psychology 28; social sciences and history 13; health professions and related clinical sciences 13.

Fees and Other Expenses: *Full-time tuition per academic year:* undergraduate $17,437. Contact the college for current graduate tuition/fees. *Books and supplies:* $1,200. *Room and board per academic year:* $8,618.

Financial Aid: Aid from institutionally generated funds is provided on the basis of academic merit, financial need. Institution has a Program Participation Agreement with the U.S. Department of Education for eligible students to receive Pell Grants and, depending upon the agreement, other federal aid.

Financial aid to full-time, first-time undergraduate students: 92% received federal grants averaging $3,472; 54% state/local grants averaging $6,150; 95% institutional grants averaging $9,599; 81% received loans averaging $3,564.

Departments and Teaching Staff: *Total instructional faculty:* 57. Student-to-faculty ratio: 13:1. Degrees held by full-time faculty: master's 26.4%, doctorate 73.6%. 75.5% hold terminal degrees.

Enrollment: Total enrollment 1,976. Undergraduate 1,327 (men 7.5%, women 92.5%).

Characteristics of Student Body: *Ethnic/racial makeup (undergraduate):* number of Black non-Hispanic: 14.4%; American Indian or Alaska Native: .2%; Asian or Pacific Islander: 4.4%; Hispanic: 15.2%; White non-Hispanic: 51.2%; unknown: 11.8%. *Age distribution:* 17–21: 25.1%; 22–24: 9.6%; 25–29: 14%; 30–34: 12.5%; 35–39: 9.7%; 40–49; 19.5%; 50–64: 8.5%; 65–up: 0.8%; unknown: .3%.

International Students: 57 nonresident aliens enrolled fall 2004. Students from Europe, Asia, Latin America, Africa. Programs available to aid students whose native language is not English: social, cultural, financial. English as a Second Language Program.

Student Life: On-campus residence halls house 65% of full-time student body. *Intercollegiate athletics:* women only: basketball, horseback riding, soccer, softball, swimming, tennis, volleyball. *Special services:* Learning Resources Center, Health Center, Counseling Center, Center for Volunteer Services, Career Services, Student Activities, Campus Ministry. Twenty student clubs/organizations. *Student publications: Elizabethan,* a yearbook; *The Station,* a newspaper; *Sector,* annual literary magazine. *Surrounding community:* Morris County population 422,000. New York City, 25 miles from campus, is nearest metropolitan area. Served by airport 20 miles from campus, passenger rail service with stop on campus.

Library Collections: 110,300 volumes. 105,000 microforms; 1,600 audiovisual materials; 635 serial subscriptions. Online catalog. Students have access to online information retrieval services.

Most important holdings include Florence E. Wall Collection (100 volumes on history of chemistry from 16th to 19th centuries); Henry C. and Ann Fox Wolfe Collection (150 items dating from World War I, including literary first editions, photographs, memorabilia); Doris and Yisrael Mayer Collection (social history of women, late 19th and early 20th centuries).

Buildings and Grounds: Campus area 190 acres.

Chief Executive Officer: Sr. Francis Raftery, President.

Address undergraduate admission inquiries to Donna Tatarka, Dean of Admissions; graduate inquiries to Associate Dean of Graduate Programs.

Drew University

36 Madison Avenue
Madison, New Jersey 07940

Tel: (973) 408-3000   **E-mail:** cadm@drew.edu
Fax: (973) 408-3939   **Internet:** www.drew.edu

Institution Description: Drew University is an independent, nonprofit institution affiliated with the United Methodist Church. *Enrollment:* 2,675. *Degrees awarded:* Baccalaureate, first-professional (master of divinity), master's, doctorate.

Accreditation: *Regional:* MSA. *National:* ATS. *Professional* theology

History: Established as Drew Theological Seminary 1866; offered first instruction at postsecondary level 1867; chartered 1868; awarded first degree (baccalaureate) 1869; established College of Liberal Arts and adopted present name 1928; became coeducational 1943; established Graduate School 1955. *See* John Cunningham, *University in Forest* (Florham Park, N.J.: Afton Publishing Company, 1972) for further information.

Institutional Structure: *Governing board:* Board of Trustees. Representation: 41 voting trustees, president (ex officio), 15 trustee emeriti (non-voting). *Composition of institution:* Administrators 20 men / 19 women. Deans head each of the college, theological school and the graduate school. Management/business/finances and administration each directed by a vice president. Full-time instructional faculty 127. Academic governance body, the faculty, meets an average of 9 times per year.

Calendar: Semesters. Academic year Sep. to May. Freshmen admitted Aug., Jan. Degrees conferred and formal commencements May, Oct. Summer session of 3 terms from early June to late July.

Characteristics of Freshmen: 70% of applicants admitted. 18% of applicants admitted and enrolled.

99% (414 students) submitted SAT scores; 11% (48 students) submitted ACT scores. *25th percentile:* SAT Verbal 560, SAT Math 550; ACT Composite 22, ACT English 22, ACT Math 23. *75th percentile:* SAT Verbal 670, SAT Math 650; ACT Composite 29, ACT English 31, ACT Math 28.

72% of entering freshmen expected to graduate within 5 years. 51% of freshmen from New Jersey. Freshmen from 30 states and 7 foreign countries.

Admission: For fall acceptance, apply as early as Sept. 1 of previous year, but not later than Feb. 15. Students are notified of acceptance Apr. 1. Apply by Dec. 1 for early decision; need not limit application to Drew. Early acceptance available. *Requirements:* Either graduation from accredited secondary school with 16 units which must include 4 English, 2 foreign language, 3 mathematics, 2 laboratory science, 2 social studies; or GED. Lowest acceptable secondary school

class standing 60th percentile. *Entrance tests:* College Board SAT or ACT composite. For foreign students TOEFL. *For transfer students:* 3.0 GPA; from 4-year accredited institution 89 hours maximum transfer credit; from 2-year institution 72 hours.

College credit and advanced placement for postsecondary-level work completed in secondary school. For extrainstitutional learning (life experience), advanced placement on basis of faculty assessment; college credit on basis of ACE *2006 Guide to the Evaluation of Educational Experiences in the Armed Services.*

Tutoring available. Developmental courses offered in summer session; credit given.

Degree Requirements: 128 semester credits; 2.0 GPA; 64 hours in residence; freshman seminar; distribution requirements; demonstrated proficiency in writing.

Fulfillment of some degree requirements and exemption from some beginning courses possible by passing departmental examinations, College Board CLEP, AP. *Grading system:* A–U; pass-fail; withdraw (deadline after which pass-fail is appended to withdraw).

Distinctive Educational Programs: *For undergraduates:* Work-experience programs, including fieldwork and internships. Evening classes. Dual-degree programs in environmental management and in forestry with Duke University (NC); in applied science and technology and in engineering with Georgia Institute of Technology and Washington University (M). Interdepartmental programs in archaeology, behavioral science, linguistics, psychobiology, Russian area studies, women's studies. Facilities and programs for independent research, including honors programs and individual majors. Institutionally sponsored study abroad in Brussels, London, Oxford. Institutionally sponsored art, theatre, Wall Street, and United Nations semester in New York, Washington DC semester; marine biology study with approved schools. Cross-registration with College of Saint Elizabeth and Fairleigh Dickinson/Madison campus. Many off-campus programs, including new program in Africa. Interdepartmental programs in Modern History and Literature and in religion and society. Cooperative liturgical studies program with faculty of 4 other institutions. *Available to all students:* Special facilities for using telecommunications in the classroom. Tutorials. United Nations semester. *Other distinctive programs:* Degree-granting continuing education. Research Institute for Scientists Emeriti appoints recently retired scientists as directors of undergraduate research or as researchers.

Degrees Conferred: 359 *baccalaureate* (B); 70 *master's* (M); 73 *doctorate*: area and ethnic studies 1 (B), 2 (M); biological/life sciences 23 (B); computer and information sciences 8 (B); English 41 (B), 6 (M), 4 (D); foreign languages and literature 10; health professions and related sciences 3 (M), 3 (D); interdisciplinary studies 27 (B), 24 (M), 7 (D); liberal arts/general studies 4 (B); mathematics 4 (B); philosophy/religion/theology 9 (B), 35 (M), 59 (D); physical sciences 4 (B); psychology 51 (B); social sciences and history 137 (B); visual and performing arts 30 (B). 40 *first-professional:* master of divinity. *Honorary degrees awarded 2004–05:* Doctor of Humane Letters 4.

Fees and Other Expenses: *Full-time tuition per academic year 2004–05:* undergraduate $29,000; graduate $27,414. *Required fees:* $546. *Room and board per academic year:* $8,018.

Financial Aid: Aid from institutionally generated funds is provided on the basis of academic merit, financial need.

Financial aid to full-time, first-time undergraduate students: need-based scholarships/grants totaling $11,868,739, self-help $3,407,146, parent loans $1,291,617; non-need-based scholarships/grants totaling $5,597,992, self-help $1,019,947, parent loans $4,271,447. *Graduate aid:* 116 students received $1,470,679 in federal and state-funded loans; 32 received $69,329 for work-study jobs; 296 received other fellowships/grants totaling $2,464,273.

Departments and Teaching Staff: Anthropology *professors* 2, *associate professors* 1, *assistant professors* 2, *instructors* 0, *part-time faculty* 0; art 3, 0, 2, 0, 5; biology 4, 1, 3, 2, 0; chemistry 3, 1, 2, 1, 1; economics 2, 3, 1, 0, 0; English 7, 2, 2, 1, 7; history 4, 0, 4, 0, 7; mathematics/computer science 2, 6, 0, 1, 1; music 3, 0, 0, 0, 4; philosophy 1, 1, 1, 0, 0; physics 2, 1, 1, 0, 1; political science 6, 2, 2, 0, 0; psychology 3, 1, 4, 0, 3; religion 2, 2, 2, 0, 1; sociology 3, 0, 3, 0, 0; theatre arts 3, 2, 1, 0, 7; French/Italian 1, 1, 2, 0, 4; Spanish 3, 0, 2, 0, 3; German/Russian/Chinese 1, 0, 1, 1, 5; classics 0, 2, 0, 0, 1.

Total instructional faculty: 166 (full-time 122, pat-time 44; women 57, men 65; members of minority groups 15). Total faculty with doctorate, first-professional, or other terminal degree: 116. Student-to-faculty ratio: 11.6:1.

Enrollment: Total enrollment 2,675. Undergraduate full-time 638 men / 931 women, part-time 19m / 41w; first-professional full-time 106m / 91w, part-time 15m / 20w; graduate full-time 184m / 136w, part-time 212m / 282w. *Transfer students:* in-state 116; from out-of-state 17.

Characteristics of Student Body: *Ethnic/racial makeup:* number of Black non-Hispanic: 63; American Indian or Alaska Native: 7; Asian or Pacific Islander: 90; Hispanic: 91; White non-Hispanic: 1,020; unknown: 344. *Age distribution:* number under 18: 7; 18–19: 722; 20–21: 700; 22–24: 136; 25–29: 17; 30–34: 9; 35–39: 4; 40–49: 12; 50–64: 10; 65 and over: 1.

International Students: 180 nonresident aliens enrolled fall 2004. Programs available to aid students whose native language is not English: English as a Second Language Program. Financial aid specifically designated for international students: scholarships available annually for undergraduate and graduate students.

Student Life: On-campus residence halls house 60% of total student body (93% of undergraduates). 6% of student body live on campus in apartments for graduate and first-professional students. Housing available for married students. *Intercollegiate athletics:* men only: baseball, basketball, cross-country, fencing, lacrosse, soccer, tennis; women only: basketball, cross-country, fencing, field hockey, lacrosse, tennis; both sexes: horseback riding. *Special services:* Tutoring, counseling, writing center, medical services. *Student publications, radio:* Acorn, a weekly tabloid; Oak Leaves, a yearbook. Radio station WMNJ broadcasts 117 hours per week. *Surrounding community:* Madison population 15,500. New York City, 25 miles from campus, is nearest metropolitan area. Served by mass transit bus and commuter train system; airport 20 miles from campus; passenger rail service 1 mile from campus.

Publications: *Drew Magazine*(trimonthly) first published in 1930.

Library Collections: 558,025 volumes. Online catalog. Current serial subscriptions: 2,263 paper; 350 microform; 1,781 via electronic access. 1,858 recordings. 215 compact discs. 132 CD-ROMs. 26 computer work stations. Students have access to online information retrieval services and the Internet. Total 2004–05 budget for books and materials: $1,148,929.

Most important holdings include the McClintock Collection (2,000 volumes, primarily rare books from the 16th and 17th centuries, concentrating on the English dissenting tradition and the humanistic tradition in Europe); government documents; Methodistical Wesleyana.

Buildings and Grounds: Campus area 186 acres. *New buildings:* Dorothy Young Center for the Arts completed 2003.

Chief Executive Officer: Dr. Thomas H. Kean, President.

Address admission inquiries to Director of Admissions.

Fairleigh Dickinson University

1000 River Road
Teaneck, New Jersey 07666-1996
Tel: (201) 692-2000   **E-mail:** admissions@fdu.edu
Fax: (201) 692-8088   **Internet:** www.fdu.edu

Institution Description: Fairleigh Dickinson University is a private, independent, nonprofit institution with campuses in Madison and Teaneck, New Jersey. *Enrollment:* 7,634. *Degrees awarded:* Associate, baccalaureate, doctorate.

Academic offerings subject to approval by statewide coordinating bodies. Member of New Jersey Marine Sciences Consortium.

Accreditation: *Regional:* MSA. *Professional:* business, clinical psychology, computer science, engineering, nursing education, physical therapy assisting

History: Established as Fairleigh Dickinson Junior College, incorporated, and offered first instruction at postsecondary level 1942; awarded first degree (associate) 1944; acquired second campus in New Jersey (Teaneck) 1954; became 4-year institution and changed name to Fairleigh Dickinson College 1956; adopted present name 1956; acquired third campus in New Jersey 1958; acquired first overseas campus (Wroxton, England) 1965.

Institutional Structure: *Governing board:* Fairleigh Dickinson University Board of Trustees. Representation: 25 trustees, including 14 alumni. All voting. *Composition of institution:* Administrators 29 men / 18 women. Academic affairs headed by Vice President for Academic Affairs. Management/business/finances directed by Executive Vice President. Full-time instructional 256. Academic governance body, University Senate, meets an average of 8 times per year.

Calendar: Semesters. Academic year Sept. to May. Freshmen admitted Sept., Jan., May, June. Degrees conferred May, Feb. Formal commencement May. Summer session of 2 terms (6 weeks each) from late May to mid-Aug.

Characteristics of Freshmen: 3,070 applicants (1,300 men, 1,770 women). 61.8% of applicants admitted. 26.6% of admitted students enrolled full-time. 95% (481 students) submitted SAT scores. *25th percentile:* SAT I Verbal 430, SAT I Math 440. *75th percentile:* SAT I Verbal 570, SAT I Math 580.

69% of freshmen from New Jersey. Freshmen from 12 states and 16 foreign countries.

Admission: Rolling admissions plan. For fall acceptance, apply no later than registration day. Apply by Nov. 1 for early decision; Fairleigh Dickinson must be first choice. Early acceptance available. *Requirements:* Either graduation from accredited secondary school with 4 units in English, 2 history, 2 college preparatory mathematics, 1 laboratory science, 5–7 academic electives; or GED. Recommend 2–3 units in a foreign language, 2 additional laboratory science. Additional requirements in mathematics and laboratory science for allied health, engineering, and science programs. *Entrance tests:* College Board SAT or ACT

composite. For foreign students TOEFL. *For transfer students:* 2.0 minimum GPA; from 4-year accredited institution 96 hours maximum transfer credit; from 2-year accredited institution 64 hours.

College credit and advanced placement for postsecondary-level work completed in secondary school. College credit for extrainstitutional learning on basis of ACE *2006 Guide to the Evaluation of Educational Experiences in the Armed Services.*

Tutoring available. Developmental/remedial courses offered in summer session and regular academic year.

Degree Requirements: *For all associate degrees:* 60–72 credit hours. *For all baccalaureate degrees:* 128 credit hours; for liberal arts and science majors 1 credit physical education. *For most undergraduate degrees:* 2.0 GPA; 32 hours in residence. *For business administration undergraduate degree:* 2.50 GPA in the major.

Fulfillment of some degree requirements and exemption from some beginning courses possible by passing College Board CLEP, APP (score of 3), other standardized tests. *Grading system:* A–F; pass-no credit; withdraw (carries time limit); incomplete (carries time limit); plus and minus grades.

Distinctive Educational Programs: Work experience programs, including cooperative education, internships. Flexible meeting places and schedules, including off-campus centers at varying locations throughout the state; weekend and evening programs. Accelerated degree programs. Cooperative baccalaureate program in medical technology with approved hospitals. Interdepartmental programs in biochemistry, humanities, international studies, marine biology. Honors programs. Independent study. Study abroad at Wroxton College Campus, England, including master's program in English literature; Marine Biology Laboratory experience, Hilo, Hawaii and Shoals Lab, Maine. *Other distinctive programs:* Degree granting Saturday College provides classes for adults. Federally funded educational program in the humanities for law enforcement officials.

ROTC: Army in cooperation with Seton Hall University.

Degrees Conferred: 54 *associate*; 726 *baccalaureate*; 730 *master's*; 19 *doctorate*. Bachelor's degrees awarded in top five disciplines: liberal arts and sciences, general studies, and humanities 160; business, management, marketing, and related support services 101; health professions and related clinical sciences 49; psychology 34; biomedical/biological sciences 31.

Fees and Other Expenses: *Full-time tuition per academic year 2004–05:* undergraduate $21,734. *Books and supplies:* $784. *Room and board per academic year:* $9,056. Contact the university for current graduate tuition/fees and other costs.

Financial Aid: Aid from institutionally generated funds is provided on the basis of academic merit, financial need, athletic ability, other criteria. Institution has a Program Participation Agreement with the U.S. Department of Education for eligible students to receive Pell Grants and, depending upon the agreement, other federal aid.

Financial aid to full-time, first-time undergraduate students: 35% received federal grants averaging $3,775; 32% state/local grants averaging $6,314; 78% institutional grants averaging $10,381; 62% received loans averaging $4,518.

Departments and Teaching Staff: Accounting *professors* 7, *associate professors* 10, *assistant professors* 6, *instructors* 1, *part-time teachers* 18; biology 17, 1, 0, 0, 10; chemistry 11, 3, 0, 0, 15; communications 2, 3, 1, 0, 5; economics and finance 11, 4, 8, 1, 17; education 2, 3, 2, 0, 14; electrical engineering 8, 1, 1, 0, 4; engineering technology 2, 2, 2, 0, 3; English 13, 5, 1, 0, 5; English, communications and philosophy 6, 2, 2, 0, 22; entrepreneurial studies 2, 0, 0, 0, 0; fine arts 10, 3, 1, 0, 5; health and physical education 2, 0, 0, 0, 11; hotel, restaurant and tourism management 0, 0, 2, 3, 0; information systems and science 6, 4, 3, 2, 25; language 3, 4, 2, 0, 7; management and marketing 15, 4, 5, 5, 41; math, computer science and physics 11, 8, 4, 2, 27; nursing 1, 2, 5, 1, 9; philosophy 4, 0, 0, 1, 5; psychology 15, 4, 4, 1, 7; public administration 2, 1, 0, 1, 5; social science 11, 4, 5, 0, 7; sociology and anthropology 4, 0, 1, 0, 2; Edward Williams College (2 year) 7, 8, 6, 17, 32.

Total instructional faculty: 667 (256 full-time, 411 part-time). 79% hold terminal degrees. Student-to-faculty ratio: 12:1.

Enrollment: Total enrollment 7,634. Undergraduate 5,417 (42.6% men, 57.4% women).

Characteristics of Student Body: *Ethnic/racial makeup (undergraduate)* >number of Black non-Hispanic: 12.5%; American Indian or Alaska Native: .2%; Asian or Pacific Islander: 5.2%; Hispanic: 11.2%; White non-Hispanic: 60.3%; unknown: 5.8%. *Age distribution:* 17–21: 28.1%; 22–24: 14.1%; 25–29: 21%; 30–34: 11.2%; 35–39: 6.7%; 40–49: 7%; 50–59: 1.6%; 60–up: 1.2%; unknown: 9.1%.

International Students: 374 nonresident aliens enrolled fall 2004. Programs available to aid students whose native language is not English: social, cultural. English as a Second Language Program. No financial aid specifically designated for international students.

Student Life: On-campus residence halls house 50% of full-time undergraduates and 4% of the graduate and professional students. *Intercollegiate athletics:* men only: (Madison) football, basketball, lacrosse, baseball, golf, soccer, tennis;

(Teaneck, Rutherford) basketball, soccer, baseball, lacrosse, wrestling, tennis, golf, indoor track, outdoor track, cross-country; women only: (Madison) basketball, field hockey, softball, tennis, volleyball; (Teaneck/Rutherford) basketball, volleyball, fencing, tennis, indoor track, outdoor track, cross-country. *Special services:* Learning Resource Center, medical services, shuttlebus between Rutherford and Teaneck. *Student publications, radio:* Weekly newspaper and yearbook at all 3 campuses. Radio station on each campus. *Surrounding community:* Madison population 15,500. New York City is 40 miles from campus. Rutherford and Teaneck located in New York metropolitan area with a population over 7 million. All 3 campuses served by mass transit commuter train system, airport, and passenger rail service.

Publications: *Literary Review* (quarterly) first published in 1957; *FDU, The Magazine of Fairleigh Dickinson University* (biannually); *Alumni News* (biannually); *Family News* (biannually); Fairleigh Dickinson University Press published 30 titles in 1991.

Library Collections: 269,000 volumes. 156,000 government documents; 481,000 microforms; 1,900 audiovisual materials; 1,420 current periodical subscriptions; 6,000 recordings/tapes. Online catalog. Students have access to online information retrieval services and the Internet.

Most important special holdings include Outdoor Advertising Association Archives; William Carlos Williams Personal Collection; selected presidential papers on microfilm.

Buildings and Grounds: Campus area 88 acres.

Chief Executive Officer: Dr. J. Michael Adams, President.

Address admission inquiries to Carol Creekmore, Dean of Enrollment Management.

Felician College

262 South Main Street
Lodi, New Jersey 07644

Tel: (201) 559-6000   **E-mail:** admissions@felician.edu
Fax: (201) 559-6188   **Internet:** www.felician.edu

Institution Description: Felician College is an independent, four-year, coeducational Catholic College sponsored by the Felician Sisters of the Lodi, New Jersey Province. *Enrollment:* 1,699. *Degrees awarded:* Associate, baccalaureate, master's. Certificates also awarded.

Accreditation: *Regional:* MSA. *Professional:* nursing

History: Established by the Felician Sisters of Lodi, New Jersey, as Immaculate Conception Normal School 1923; became teacher training college affiliated with Catholic University of America (DC) and changed name to Immaculate Conception Teachers College 1935; was incorporated under the laws of the State of New Jersey as Immaculate Conception Junior College 1942; first admitted lay women 1964; awarded first degree (associate) 1966; became a 4-year institution and adopted present name 1967; became coeducational 1986.

Institutional Structure: *Governing board:* Felician College Board of Trustees. Extrainstitutional representation: 21 trustees (voting); institutional representation: 5 administrators (non-voting). *Composition of institution:* Senior administrators 3 men / 4 women. Academic affairs headed by vice president and dean for academic affairs. Management/business/finance directed by director of business and finance. Full-time instructional faculty 56. Academic governance body, General Faculty, meets 4 to 6 times per year.

Calendar: Semesters. Academic year Sept. to May. Freshmen admitted Sept., Jan., June. Degrees conferred and formal commencement May. Summer session of 2 terms from mid-May to early Aug.

Characteristics of Freshmen: 1,114 applicants (313 men, 801 women). 76.4% of applicants admitted. 26.9% of admitted students enrolled full-time.

79% (193 students) submitted SAT scores. *25th percentile:* SAT I Verbal 410, SAT I Math 400. *75th percentile:* SAT I Verbal 500, SAT I Math 510.

16% of entering freshmen expected to graduate within 5 years. 95% of freshmen from New Jersey. Freshmen from 3 states and 6 foreign countries.

Admission: Applications should be made during early fall of the senior year. The Committee on Admissions evaluates applicants' credentials on a rolling basis. Applicants to the fall semester are strongly encouraged to apply by Aug. 1. *Requirements:* Applicants must be graduates of an accredited high school and must present 16 academic unit or the high school equivalency certificate, character references, satisfactory SAT or ACT scores, and a physician's certificate of health. *Entrance tests:* College Board SAT or ACT composite. For foreign students TOEFL. *For transfer students:* Students graduating with an associate degree from a recognized junior college are eligible for admission into the upper

division of Felician College. Transfer students may apply up to 75 credits earned elsewhere toward a bachelor's degree. No credit for grades below a C. No more than 15 credits transferable in a major. Admission requirements may be adjusted for adults on the basis of maturity and experience.

College credit and advanced placement for acceptable scores on the College Board Advanced Placement tests and the College-Level Examination Program tests. Superior high school students who have completed their junior year may be granted part- or full-time admission to Felician College upon the recommendation by their high school principal and guidance counselor.

Tutoring available. Developmental courses offered in summer session and regular academic year; credit given.

Degree Requirements: *For all associate degrees:* 64–68 credit hours; 30 hours in residence. *For all baccalaureate degrees:* 120–130 credit hours; minimum of 45 hours in residence. *For all degrees:* 2.0 GPA in most programs; core requirements.

Fulfillment of some degree requirements and exemption from some beginning courses possible by passing College Board CLEP, other standardized tests. *Grading system:* A–F; pass-fail withdraw (carries time limit, pass-fail may be appended); FA (failure due to excessive absence); incomplete (carries time limit).

Distinctive Educational Programs: Work-experience programs. Service learning programs. Evening classes. Weekend College. Honors Program. Transition Year program. International studies. Joint degree with University of Medicine and Dentistry of New Jersey (UMDNJ) in medical technology, toxicology, and cytotechnology.

Degrees Conferred: 43 *associate;* 188 *baccalaureate;* 13 *master's.* Bachelor's degrees awarded in top five disciplines: business, management, marketing, and related support services 79; education 35; psychology 16; social sciences and history 11; English language/literature 11.

Fees and Other Expenses: *Full-time tuition per academic year:* $15,900. *Books and supplies:* $2,140. *Room and board per academic year:* $7,500.

Financial Aid: Aid from institutionally generated funds is provided on the basis of academic merit, athletic ability. Institution has a Program Participation Agreement with the U.S. Department of Education for eligible students to receive Pell Grants and, depending upon the agreement, other federal aid.

Financial aid to full-time, first-time undergraduate students: 48% received federal grants averaging $2,425; 43% state/local grants averaging $3,052; 40% institutional grants averaging $4,075; 73% received loans averaging $4,966.

Departments and Teaching Staff: *Professors* 2, *associate professors* 13, *assistant professors* 27, *instructors* 14, *part-time teachers* 11.

Total instructional faculty: 67. Student-to-faculty ratio: 10:1. Degrees held by full-time faculty: master's 100%, doctorate 46%, professional 3%. 59% hold terminal degrees.

Enrollment: Total enrollment 1,699. Undergraduate 1,483 (men 23.9%, women 76.1%).

Characteristics of Student Body: *Ethnic/racial makeup:* number of Black non-Hispanic: 13.1%; American Indian or Alaska Native: .4%; Asian or Pacific Islander: 5.1%; Hispanic: 14%; White non-Hispanic: 47.7%; unknown: 15.9%. *Age distribution:* 17–21: 34%; 22–24: 19%; 25–29: 13%; 30–34: 8%; 35–39: 7%; 40–49: 12%; 50–59: 5%; 60–up: 1%.

International Students: 56 undergraduate nonresident aliens enrolled fall 2004. Students from Europe, Asia, Latin America, Africa, Canada. No programs available to aid students whose native language is not English. No financial aid specifically designated for international students.

Student Life: No on-campus housing. *Special regulations:* Registered cars with decals permitted in designated parking areas. *Special services:* Learning Resources Center, Child Care Center, Student Health Office. *Student publications: Felicianews,* a monthly newsletter; *Questing,* an annual literary magazine. *Surrounding community:* Lodi population 25,000. New York City, 10 miles from campus, is nearest metropolitan area. Served by airport and passenger rail service, each 10 miles from campus.

Library Collections: 104,000 volumes including bound books, serial backfiles, electronic documents, and government documents not in separate collections. Online catalog. 400 current serial subscriptions. 78,000 microforms. 4,200 audiovisual materials. Computer work stations available. Students have access to the Internet at no charge.

Most important special holdings include arts and sciences, health sciences, education.

Buildings and Grounds: Campus area 32 acres.

Chief Executive Officer: Sr. Theresa M. Martin, C.S.S.F., President.

Address admission inquiries to Cara McCloud, Director of Admissions.

Georgian Court University

900 Lakewood Avenue
Lakewood, New Jersey 08701-2697
Tel: (732) 364-2200 **E-mail:** admissions@georgian.edu
Fax: (732) 987-2000 **Internet:** /www.georgian.edu

Institution Description: Georgian Court University is a private women's school affiliated with and owned by the Sisters of Mercy, Roman Catholic Church. *Enrollment:* 3,065. Men are admitted to the Evening Division and the Graduate School. *Degrees awarded:* Baccalaureate, master's.

Accreditation: *Regional:* MSA. *Professional*: business, social work

History: Incorporated as Mount Saint Mary College 1905; established and offered first instruction at postsecondary level 1908; awarded first degree (baccalaureate) 1912; became Georgia Court College 1924; awarded university status 2004.

Institutional Structure: *Governing board:* Board of Trustees. Extrainstitutional representation: 24 trustees; 2 trustee emeriti. All voting. *Composition of institution:* Administrators 13 men / 38 women. Academic affairs headed by provost. Management/business/finances directed by vice president for finance and administration. Full-time instructional faculty 38 men / 61 women. Academic governance body, the faculty, meets an average of 6 times per year.

Calendar: Semesters. Academic year Aug. to May. Freshmen admitted Sept., Jan., June. Degrees conferred May, Aug., Dec. Formal commencement May.

Characteristics of Freshmen: 79% of applicants admitted. 46% of applicants admitted and enrolled.

94% (186 students) submitted SAT scores. *25th percentile*: SAT Verbal 420, SAT Math 410. *75th percentile*: SAT Verbal 510, SAT Math 510.

57% of entering freshmen expected to graduate within 5 years. 98% of freshmen from New Jersey. Freshmen from 3 states and 2 foreign countries.

Admission: Rolling admissions plan. Apply by Nov. 15 for early decision; need not limit application to Georgian Court. Early acceptance available. *Requirements:* Either graduation from accredited secondary school with 16 units which must include 4 English, 2 in a foreign language, 2 college preparatory mathematics, 1 history, 1 laboratory science, 6 academic electives; or GED. *Entrance tests:* College Board SAT. *For transfer students:* 2.0 minimum GPA, 82 hours maximum transfer credit and no more than 66 credits may be from an accredited two-year institution.

College credit and advanced placement for postsecondary-level work completed in secondary school. Tutoring available. Developmental courses offered in summer session and regular academic year; credit given.

Degree Requirements: 124 credit hours; 2.0 GPA and: 2.5 GPA in major; 18 courses in basic programs of humanities, natural science, mathematics, social sciences, and physical education; 50 credits minimum at Georgian Court University; exit competency examinations vary according to department.

Fulfillment of some degree requirements and exemption from some beginning courses possible by passing departmental examinations, College Board CLEP, APP. *Grading system:* A–F; pass-fail; withdraw; incomplete.

Distinctive Educational Programs: *For undergraduates:* Work-experience programs. Dual degree program (BA/BS in mathematics and engineering through partnership with George Washington University). Interdepartmental/ interdisciplinary programs on American, international, Latin American, and women's studies. Bilingual-bicultural studies for education majors. Students may seek to study abroad in the country of their choice. Baccalaureate completion program for registered nurses. *Available to all students:* Evening classes. Facilities and programs for independent research, including individual majors and independent study. French language and cultural studies in Quebec. Students may seek to study abroad in the country of their choice.

Degrees Conferred: 499 *baccalaureate* (B); 191 *master's* (M): biological/ life sciences 18 (B), 4 (M); business/marketing 58 (B), 46 (M); computer and information sciences 1 (B); education 177 (B), 120 (M); English 35 (B), foreign languages and literature 8 (B); health professions and related sciences 1 (B), 5 (M); liberal arts/general studies 28 (B); mathematics 6 (B), 1 (M); philosophy/ religion/theology 1 (B), 9 (M); physical sciences 3 (B); protective services/public administration 20 (B); psychology 83 (B); social sciences and history 33 (B); visual and performing arts 27 (B).

Fees and Other Expenses: *Full-time tuition per academic year 2004–05:* $17,224 undergraduate; $530 per credit for graduate study. *Required fees:* $700 undergraduate; $350 graduate. *Room and board per academic year:* $7,200.

Financial Aid: Aid from institutionally generated funds is provided on the basis of academic merit, financial need, athletic ability.

Financial aid to full-time, first-time undergraduate students: need-based scholarships/grants totaling $7,994,217, self-help $7,090,076, parent loans $378,896, tuition waivers $18,964, athletic awards $5,000; non-need-based scholarships/grants totaling $981,951, self-help $2,210,325, parent loans $530,329, tuition waivers $7,036.

Departments and Teaching Staff: *Professors* 24, *associate professors* 19, *assistant professors* 56, *part-time faculty* 183.

Total instructional faculty: 282 (full-time 99, part-time 183; women 155, men 127; members of minority groups 20). Total faculty with doctorate, first-professional, or other terminal degree: 129. Student-to-faculty ratio: 14:1. Degrees held by full-time faculty: doctorate 66%, master's 33%, professional 15. 68% hold terminal degrees.

Enrollment: Total enrollment 3,065. Undergraduate full-time 78 men / 1,289 women, part-time 136m / 543w; graduate full-time 18m / 101w, part-time 134m / 766w. *Transfer students:*in-state 267; from out-of-state 1.

Characteristics of Student Body: *Ethnic/racial makeup:* number of Black non-Hispanic: 46; American Indian or Alaska Native: 4; Asian or Pacific Islander: 36; Hispanic: 120; White non-Hispanic: 1,454; unknown: 321. *Age distribution:* number under 18: 180; 18–19: 291; 20–21: 415; 22–24: 414; 25–29: 236; 30–34: 138; 35–39: 104; 40–49: 198; 50–64: 60; 65 and over: 6. 33% of student body attend summer sessions.

International Students: 20 nonresident aliens enrolled fall 2004. 10 students from Europe, 3 Asia, 2 Latin America, 2 Africa, 3 Canada. Programs available to aid students whose native language is not English: English as a Second Language Program. No financial aid specifically designated for international students.

Student Life: On-campus residence halls house 20% of full-time undergraduate student body. Residence halls for women constitute 100% of such space. *Intercollegiate athletics:* women only: volleyball, basketball, karate, cross-country, softball. *Special regulations:* Registered cars permitted without restrictions. *Special services:* Learning Resources Center, Student Health Center. *Student publications: Court Page*, a campus newspaper; *Courtier*, a yearbook; *Fountainspray*, a literary magazine. *Surrounding community:* Lakewood township population 60,552. New York City, 60 miles from campus, and Philadelphia, 57 miles from campus, are nearest metropolitan areas. Served by mass transit bus system; passenger rail service 12 miles from campus.

Library Collections: 842,219 volumes. 520,311 microforms; 2,206 audiovisual materials; 1,076 current periodical subscriptions. Online catalog. Students have access to online information retrieval services and the Internet.

Most important special collections include Education; Religious Studies; New Jersey History.

Buildings and Grounds: Campus area 150 acres.

Chief Executive Officer: Sr. Rosemary Jeffries, R.S.M., President.

Address undergraduate admission inquiries to Director of Admissions; graduate inquiries to Director of Graduate Admissions and Records.

Immaculate Conception Seminary

400 South Orange Avenue
South Orange, New Jersey 07079
Tel: (973) 761-9575 **E-mail:** theology@shu.edu
Fax: (973) 761-9977 **Internet:** www.shu.edu

Institution Description: Immaculate Conception Seminary is a private institution affiliated with the Roman Catholic Church and Seton Hall University. *Enrollment:* 265. *Degrees awarded:* First-professional (theology), master's.

Accreditation: *Regional:* MSA. *National:* ATS. *Professional*: theology

History: Established on the campus of Seton Hall College (South Orange) 1861;.

Institutional Structure: *Governing board:* Board of Trustees. Extrainstitutional representation: 13 trustees, archbishop of Newark; institutional representation: 1 administrator. 2 ex officio. *Composition of institution:* Academic affairs headed by academic dean. Management/business/finances directed by business manager.

Calendar: Semesters. Academic year Sept. to May. Formal commencement May. Summer session of 2 terms early June to early Aug.

Admission: *Requirements:* Baccalaureate with either a major in the humanities, behavioral science, or social sciences; or 12 semester hours in English, 24 philosophy, 12 religious studies, 6 social studies, 3 psychology. Recommend proficiency in French, German, Latin, or Spanish. *Entrance tests:* For M.A. candidates, GRE or MAT. *For transfer students:* 3.0 minimum GPA; 6 hours maximum transfer credit.

Degree Requirements: *For first-professional degree:* 84 credit hours; field education; internships; comprehensive seminar; core curriculum. *For master's degree:* 36 credit hours; reading knowledge of a foreign language (preferably French or German); comprehensives in individual fields of study. *For both degrees:* 3.0 GPA. *Grading system:* A–F; withdraw.

Distinctive Educational Programs: Practicums. Hispanic Institute. *Other distinctive programs:* Continuing education program for ministerial development. Institute for Christian Spirituality.

Degrees Conferred: 10 *master's:* theology; 65 *first-professional:* master of divinity.

Fees and Other Expenses: *Full-time tuition per academic year 2005–06:* Contact the seminary for current tuition, fees, expenses, and housing.

Enrollment: Total enrollment 225.

Library Collections: 70,000 volumes. 650 current periodical subscriptions. Most important holdings include collections on Biblical studies, church history, liturgy; rare book collection.

Buildings and Grounds: Suburban campus location.

Chief Executive Officer: Robert F. Coleman, Rector/Dean.

Address all inquiries to Academic Dean.

Kean University

1000 Morris Avenue
P.O. Box 411
Union, New Jersey 07083-7131
Tel: (908) 737-5326   **E-mail:** admitme@kean.edu
Fax: (908) 737-1105355-5134**Internet:** www.kean.edu

Institution Description: Kean University, formerly known as Kean College of New Jersey, is a state institution. *Enrollment:* 12,897. *Degrees awarded:* Baccalaureate, master's. Diplomas in school psychology also awarded.

Academic offerings subject to approval by statewide coordinating bodies. Budget subject to approval by state governing boards. Member of Consortium of East Jersey.

Accreditation: *Regional:* MSA. *Professional:* industrial technology, music, social work, teacher education

History: Established as Newark Normal School 1855; offered first instruction at postsecondary level 1878; changed name to New Jersey State Normal School at Newark 1913; became 4-year institution 1934; changed name to Newark State Teachers College and awarded first degree (baccalaureate) 1935; changed name to Newark State College 1958; became Kean College of New Jersey 1973; achieved university status 1997. *See* Donald Raichele, *From a Normal Beginning* (Rutherford, NJ: Fairleigh Dickinson Press, 1980) for further information.

Institutional Structure: *Governing board:* Kean University Board of Trustees. Representation: 13 trustees, including president of the college. 1 ex officio. All voting. *Composition of institution:* Administrators 67 men / 76 women. Academic affairs headed by vice president for academic affairs. Management/business/finances directed by vice president for academic affairs. Full-time instructional faculty 353. Academic governance body, Faculty Senate, meets an average of 16 times per year. *Faculty representation:* Faculty served by collective bargaining agent, affiliated with AFT.

Calendar: Semesters (4-1-4 plan). Academic year Sept. to May. Freshmen admitted Sept., Jan., June. Degrees conferred and formal commencement June. Summer session from late June to early Aug.

Characteristics of Freshmen: 90% (1,181 students) submitted SAT scores. *25th percentile:* SAT I Verbal 410, SAT I Math 430. *75th percentile:* SAT I Verbal 510, SAT I Math 520.

96% of freshmen from New Jersey.

Admission: Rolling admissions plan. For fall acceptance, apply no later than June 1. *Requirements:* 16 units from accredited secondary school, including 4 English, 2 college preparatory mathematics, 2 history, 2 laboratory science, 4 additional college preparatory units. Recommended 2 units in a foreign language. GED accepted. *Entrance tests:* College Board SAT or ACT composite. *For transfer students:* 2.0 minimum GPA; from 4-year accredited institution 96 credit hours maximum transfer credit; from 2-year accredited institution 64 hours. Transfer credit also available for correspondence/extension students.

College credit and advanced placement for postsecondary-level work completed in secondary school. Tutoring available. Noncredit developmental courses offered in summer session and regular academic year.

Degree Requirements: *Undergraduate:* 126 semester hours; 2.0 GPA; 2 terms in residence; 2 credits physical or health education; general education requirements.

Fulfillment of some degree requirements and exemption from some beginning courses possible by passing College Board CLEP, AP. *Grading system:* A–F; pass-fail, withdraw (deadline after which pass-fail is appended to withdraw).

Distinctive Educational Programs: *For undergraduates:* Off-campus centers (at varying locations less than 30 miles away from main institution). Interdisciplinary programs in Afro-American studies, environmental studies, geoscience technology, gerontology, marine studies, study of the future, urban studies. Preprofessional program in law. *For graduate students:* Study abroad in Australia, Denmark, England, Israel; study-travel also available in Africa, Asia, Europe. *Available to all students:* Cooperative education. Weekend and evening classes. Special facilities using telecommunications in the classroom. Facilities

and programs for independent research, including honors programs, individual majors. *Other distinctive programs:* Continuing education. Center for Continuing Professional Education and Center for Corporate Education offer credit and noncredit courses. Adult Advisory Center provides counseling, testing, workshops pertaining to education and vocation. Tuition-free courses for senior citizens.

ROTC: Army offered in cooperation with Seton Hall University.

Degrees Conferred: 1,688 *baccalaureate;* 583 *master's.* Bachelor's degrees awarded in top five disciplines: business, management, marketing, and related support services 441; education 335; psychology 140; health professions and related clinical sciences 86; social sciences 78.

Fees and Other Expenses: *Full-time tuition per academic year 2004–05:* undergraduate resident $7,151 (includes required fees). Contact the university for current graduate tuition/fees. *Books and supplies:* $1,040. *Room and board per academic year:* $8,093.

Financial Aid: Aid from institutionally generated funds is provided on the basis of academic merit, financial need, other criteria. Institution has a Program Participation Agreement with the U.S. Department of Education for eligible students to receive Pell Grants and, depending upon the agreement, other federal aid.

Financial aid to full-time, first-time undergraduate students: need-based scholarships/grants totaling $1,019,632, self-help $15,032,782; non-need-based scholarships/grants totaling $79,000, self-help $12,812,398, parent loans $3,350,398, tuition waivers $252,986.

Departments and Teaching Staff: *Professors 147, associate professors 93, assistant professors 109, instructors 4, part-time faculty 13.*

Total instructional faculty: 366. *Student-to-faculty ratio:* 20:1. Degrees held by full-time faculty: master's 21.5%, doctorate 77.9%, baccalaureate .6%. 88.1% hold terminal degrees.

Enrollment: Total enrollment 12,897. Undergraduate full-time 2,797 men / 4,564 women, part-time 721m / 1,865w; graduate full-time 66m / 239w, part-time 232m / 787w.

Characteristics of Student Body: *Ethnic/racial makeup (undergraduate):* number of Black non-Hispanic: 2,032; American Indian or Alaska Native: 26; Asian or Pacific Islander: 591; Hispanic: 1,912; White non-Hispanic: 4,866; unknown: 261.

International Students: 259 undergraduate nonresident aliens enrolled fall 2004. Programs available to aid students whose native language is not English: social, cultural. Financial aid specifically designated for international students: scholarships available annually.

Student Life: On-campus residence halls house 9% of student body. Residence halls for both sexes constitute 100% of such space. *Intercollegiate athletics:* men only: baseball, basketball, football, golf, hockey, lacrosse, soccer, swimming, tennis, wrestling; women only: basketball, field hockey, gymnastics, softball, swimming, tennis, volleyball. *Special regulations:* Registered cars permitted without restrictions. *Special services:* Learning Resources Center, medical services. *Student publications, radio: Expressions,* a newsletter for Third World students; *Grub Street Writer,* an annual literary magazine; *Independent,* a weekly newspaper; *Memorabilia,* a yearbook; *The Night Owl,* a monthly newspaper for evening students. Radio station WKNJ broadcasts 133 hours per week. *Surrounding community:* Union population 56,000. Newark, 4 miles from campus, is nearest metropolitan area. Served by airport and passenger rail service, each 5 miles from campus.

Library Collections: 271,000 volumes. 792,000 microforms; 1,370 current periodical subscriptions. 6,000 audiovisual materials. Online catalog. Students have access to online information retrieval services and the Internet.

Most important holdings include Curriculum Materials Center (resource library of curriculum guides serving tri-state area of New Jersey, New York, and Connecticut); New Jersey Collection (monographs, rare books on history of New Jersey and of Union County); papers and letters of former Congresswoman Florence Dwyer (served 1957–1972); Holocaust Resource Center; Schomburg Collection.

Buildings and Grounds: Campus area 150 acres.

Chief Executive Officer: Dr. Dawed Farahi, President.

Address admission inquiries to Audley Bridges, Director of Admissions.

Monmouth University

400 Cedar Avenue
West Long Branch, New Jersey 07764-1898
Tel: (732) 571-3400   **E-mail:** admission@monmouth.edu
Fax: (732) 571-3629   **Internet:** www.monmouth.edu

Institution Description: Monmouth University, formerly known as Monmouth College, is a private, comprehensive, coeducational university. *Enroll-*

ment: 6,329. *Degrees awarded:* Baccalaureate, master's. Certificates also awarded.

Member of New Jersey Marine Sciences Consortium.

Accreditation: *Regional:* MSA. *Professional:* business, chemistry, nursing, social work

History: Established as Monmouth Junior College and offered first instruction at postsecondary level 1933; became 4-year college 1956; chartered 1957; awarded first degree (baccalaureate) 1958; added graduate programs 1967; designated a teaching university 1995.

Institutional Structure: *Governing board:* Board of Trustees. Representation: 42 trustees. *Composition of institution:* Administrators 45 men / 107 women. Academic affairs headed by provost/senior vice president for academic affairs. Finances and business directed by vice president for finance. Full-time instructional faculty 197. Academic governance body, the Faculty, meets an average of 9 times per year. *Faculty representation:* Faculty served by collective bargaining agent, Faculty Association of Monmouth College, affiliated with AAUP.

Calendar: Semesters. Academic year Sept. to May. Freshmen admitted Sept., Jan. Degrees conferred and formal commencement May. Summer session of 5 terms from May to Aug.

Characteristics of Freshmen: 5,280 applicants (2,266 men, 3,014 women). 65.8% of applicants admitted. 2.3% of admitted students enrolled full-time.

98% (933 students) submitted SAT scores; 2% (18 students) submitted ACT scores. *25th percentile:* SAT I Verbal 480, SAT I Math 490; ACT Composite 21. *75th percentile:* SAT I Verbal 560, SAT I Math 570; ACT Composite 24.

46% of entering freshmen expected to graduate within 5 years. 91% of freshmen from New Jersey. Freshmen from 10 states and 5 foreign countries.

Admission: Rolling admissions plan. The deadline for freshman applications for fall semester is Apr. 1. For spring semester, the deadline for applications is Jan. 1. Applications received after due dates will be considered on a space-available basis. When all necessary materials have been submitted, a decision and notification are made as quickly as possible. *Requirements:* Either graduation from accredited secondary school with 16 Carnegie units in academic subjects, or GED. Minimum GPA 2.0. *Entrance tests:* College Board SAT. For foreign students TOEFL. *For transfer students:* 2.0 minimum GPA; from 4-year accredited institution 96 hours maximum transfer credit; from 2-year accredited institution 72 hours.

College credit and advanced placement for postsecondary level work completed in secondary school.

Tutoring available. Developmental education offered in summer session and regular academic year.

Degree Requirements: *For all baccalaureate degrees:* 128–135 credit hours; 2.0 GPA; 2.1 GPA in major field; last 32 credits in residence; core and distribution requirements.

College credit and advanced placement for postsecondary-level work completed in secondary school. Tutoring available. Developmental education offered in summer session and regular academic year. *Grading system:* A–F; withdraw (carries time limit); I (incomplete, carries time limit).

Distinctive Educational Programs: 25 undergraduate and 18 graduate programs in liberal arts, business, science, education, and engineering. Honors Program. Internships and cooperative education opportunities. Study abroad.

ROTC: Air Force offered through cross-enrollment at Rutgers University.

Degrees Conferred: 5 *associate;* 676 *baccalaureate:* 560 *master's.* Bachelor's degrees awarded in top five disciplines: business, management, marketing, and related support services 205; communication, journalism, and related programs 149; psychology 82; visual and performing arts 74; education 63.

Fees and Other Expenses: *Full-time tuition per academic year 2004–05:* undergraduate $7,332. Contact the university for current graduate tuition/fees. *Room and board per academic year:* $7,911.

Financial Aid: Aid from institutionally generated funds is provided on the basis of academic merit, financial need, athletic ability. Institution has a Program Participation Agreement with the U.S. Department of Education for eligible students to receive Pell Grants and, depending upon the agreement, other federal aid.

Financial aid to full-time, first-time undergraduate students: 18% received federal grants averaging $3,854; 26% state/local grants averaging $5,022; 83% institutional grants averaging $6,171; 69% received loans averaging $8,336.

Departments and Teaching Staff: School of Humanities and Social Sciences *professors* 13, *associate professors* 26, *assistant professors* 37, *instructors* 24; School of Business Administration 3, 12, 11, 1; School of Education 9, 3, 12, 2; School of Science, Technology, and Engineering 18, 15, 7, 6; School of Nursing and Health Studies 0, 0, 5, 1.

Total instructional faculty: 459. Student-to-faculty ratio: 17:1. Degrees held by full-time faculty: 60% hold doctorate, first-profession, or other terminal degree.

Enrollment: Total enrollment 6,329. Undergraduate 4,501 (men 41.3%, women 58.7%).

Characteristics of Student Body: *Ethnic/racial makeup (undergraduate):* number of Black non-Hispanic: 4.7%; American Indian or Alaska Native: 2.4%; Asian or Pacific Islander: 2.2%; Hispanic: 3.9%; White non-Hispanic: 78.3%; unknown: 10.4%.

International Students: 189 nonresident aliens enrolled fall 2004. Programs available to aid students whose native language is not English: social, cultural. English as a Second Language Program. Unlimited financial aid available to international students.

Student Life: On-campus residence halls house 40% of undergraduates. 10 coed halls and 3 coed apartment complexes. *Intercollegiate athletics:* men: baseball, basketball, cross-country, golf, indoor track, track and field, soccer, tennis; women: lacrosse, soccer, softball. *Special regulations:* Cars permitted in designated areas. *Special services:* Medical services, life and career advising center, cooperative education, placement. 7 fraternities and 6 sororities. *Student publications, radio: Monmouth Review,* an annual literary magazine; *The Outlook,* a weekly newspaper; *Shadows,* a yearbook. Radio station WMCX broadcasts continuously. *Surrounding community:* West Long Branch population 7,700. New York, 50 miles from campus, is nearest metropolitan area. Served by mass transit bus and train system, airport 45 miles from campus, passenger rail service 2 miles from campus.

Publications: *Monmouth University Magazine* (quarterly); *Campus Connection* (internal campus newsletter).

Library Collections: 255,700 volumes. 328,775 microforms; 1,344 current periodical subscriptions; 215 audiovisual units. Access to a variety of electronic resources including full-text databases, indexes, and abstracts.

Most important holdings include the New Jersey Collection (over 2,000 books, microforms and miscellaneous items dealing with New Jersey, particularly Monmouth County); depository for U.S. government documents and New Jersey documents; Mumford Collection (books, photos, and memorabilia of Lewis Mumford).

Buildings and Grounds: Campus area 152 acres.

Chief Executive Officer: Dr. Paul G. Gaffney II, President.

Undergraduates address inquiries to Miriam King, Vice President for Enrollment Management; graduate inquiries to Sean Warner, Director of Graduate Admissions and Adult Enrollment Services.

Montclair State University

1 University Avenue
Upper Montclair, New Jersey 07043-1624
Tel: (973) 655-4000   **E-mail:** admissions@montclair.edu
Fax: (973) 655-7700   **Internet:** montclair.edu

Institution Description: Montclair State University, formerly Montclair State College, is a public institution. *Enrollment:* 15,837. *Degrees awarded:* Baccalaureate, master's. Certificates also awarded.

Accreditation: *Regional:* MSA. *Professional:* art, business, computer science, music, recreation and leisure services, speech-language pathology, teacher education

History: Established as New Jersey Normal School at Montclair, chartered and offered first instruction at postsecondary level 1908; became 4-year college and changed name to Montclair State Teachers College 1927; awarded first baccalaureates 1930; authorized to offer the master's degree 1932; became Montclair State College 1958 and a comprehensive multipurpose institution 1966; became Montclair State University 1994.

Institutional Structure: *Governing board:* Representation: 16; 140 voting (including 1 student); 2 non-voting (president of the university, 1 student); 1 faculty representative, 1 alumni/ae representative. *Composition of institution:* Administrators 54 men / 49 women. Academic affairs headed by provost and vice president for academic affairs. Management/business/finances directed by vice president for administration. Full-time instructional faculty 263 men / 202 women. Academic governance body, University Senate, meets an average of 10 times per year. *Faculty representation:* Faculty served by collective bargaining agent, Local 1904, AFT/AFL-CIO.

Calendar: Semesters. Academic year Sept. to May. Freshmen admitted Sept., Jan. (those accepted for September entrance may attend preceding summer session). Degrees conferred May, Aug., Jan. Formal commencement May. Summer session of 4 terms from June to Aug.

Characteristics of Freshmen: 50% of applicants admitted. 20% of admitted applicants enrolled.

98% (1,726 students) submitted SAT scores. *25th percentile:* SAT Verbal 450, SAT I Math 470. *75th percentile:* SAT Verbal 550, SAT Math 560.

50% of entering freshmen expected to graduate within 5 years. 96.4% of freshmen from New Jersey. Freshmen from 10 states and 40 foreign countries.

Admission: Rolling admissions plan. Apply no later than March 1. *Requirements:* Either graduation from accredited secondary school with 4 units in English, 2 in a foreign language, 2 American history, 3 mathematics, 2 science (including 2 laboratory science), 5 academic electives; or GED. Additional requirements for some programs. *Entrance tests:* College Board SAT or ACT. For international students TOEFL. *For transfer students:* 2.0 minimum GPA; maximum transfer credit limited only by residence requirement.

College credit and advanced placement for postsecondary level work completed in secondary school. For extrainstitutional learning (life experience) college credit and advanced placement on basis of ACE *2006 Guide to the Evaluation of Educational Experiences in the Armed Services*; portfolio assessment; faculty assessment.

Tutoring available. Developmental courses offered in summer session and regular academic year; nondegree credit given.

Degree Requirements: *Undergraduate:* 120 credit hours; 2.0 GPA; 32 semester hours in residence; 1 hour physical education; distribution requirements; demonstrated proficiency in reading, speaking, and writing.

Fulfillment of some degree requirements and exemption from some beginning courses possible by passing departmental examinations, College Board CLEP, APP. *Grading system:* A–F; pass; withdraw (carries time limit); AU (audit, no credit); incomplete (no credit).

Distinctive Educational Programs: *For undergraduates:* Cooperative education. Seven-year program offered jointly by MSU and University of Medicine and Dentistry of New Jersey. University Honors Program. Interdisciplinary programs in African-American studies, Asian studies, community psychology, environmental studies, general humanities, Hispanic community affairs, Latin American studies, Russian area studies, urban studies, women's studies. Semester or academic year of study abroad and student exchanges, through the New Jersey State College Council for International Education and the College Consortium for International Studies. Locations include Australia, Denmark, Ecuador, France, United Kingdom, Greece, Ireland, Israel, Italy, Jamaica, Mexico, Spain, Portugal. Programs combine foreign language instruction with comprehensive college courses in English. Financial aid is applicable. All programs are characterized by excellence and affordability. Global Education Center. New Jersey Marine Sciences Consortium Centers at Sandy Hook and Seaville. New Jersey School of Conservation at Stokes State Forest. Evening classes; independent study; computer labs; psychoeducational center. *Other distinctive programs:* Educational Opportunity Fund; Health Careers Program.

Degrees Conferred: 2,176 *baccalaureate* (B), 691 *master's* (M), 4 *doctorate* (D): area and ethnic studies 6 (B); biological/life sciences 137 (B), 19 (M); business/marketing 471 (B), 96 (M); communications/communication technologies 68 (B), 3 (M); computer and information sciences 66 (B), 16 (M); education 96 (B), 372 (M), 4 (D); English 131 (B), 9 (M); foreign languages and literature 59 (B), 10 (M); health professions and related sciences 12 (B), 85 (M); home economics and vocational home economics 191 (B), 8 (M); interdisciplinary studies 107 (B); law/legal studies 8 (M); liberal arts/general studies 32 (B); mathematics 38 (B), 9 (M); natural resources/environmental science 14 (M); parks and recreation 32 (B); philosophy/religion/theology 10 (B); physical sciences 25 (B), 7 (M); psychology 249 (B), 42 (M); social sciences and history 285 (B), 16 (M); visual and performing arts 161 (B), 32 (M).

Fees and Other Expenses: *Full-time tuition per academic year 2004–05:* undergraduate resident $5,168, nonresident $8,836. *Required fees:* $1,858. *Room and board per academic year:* $8,212.

Financial Aid: Aid from institutionally generated funds is provided on the basis of academic merit.

Financial aid to full-time, first-time undergraduate students: need-based scholarships/grants totaling $18,640,766, self-help $17,603,306; non-need-based scholarships/grants totaling $5,021,305, self-help $19,004,945, parent loans $51,299,921, tuition waivers $416,853. *Graduate aid:* 143 students received $609,736 in federal and state-funded fellowships/grants (ranging from $365 to $12,423); 659 received $8,134,455 in federal and state-funded loans (ranging from $424 to $18,500); 305 received $2,303,817 for college-assigned jobs (ranging from $3,770 to $10,578); 49 students received other fellowships/grants totaling $106,775 (ranging from $500 to $8,975).

Departments and Teaching Staff: *Total instructional faculty:* 1,102 (full-time 465, part-time 637; women 532, men 560; members of minority groups 198).Total faculty with doctorate, first-professional, or other terminal degree: 426. Student-to-faculty ratio: 18:1. Degrees held by full-time faculty: baccalaureate 96.4%, master's 90.8%, doctorate 79.3%, professional 2.5%. 84.2% hold terminal degrees. *Faculty development:* $1,172,000 in grants for research. 9 faculty members granted sabbaticals 2004–05.

Enrollment: Total enrollment 15,837. Undergraduate full-time 3,735 men / 5,808 women, part-time 846m / 1,430w; graduate full-time 236m / 598 w, part-time 853m / 2,131w.

Characteristics of Student Body: *Ethnic/racial makeup: number of* Black non-Hispanic: 1,217; American Indian or Alaska Native: 52; Asian or Pacific Islander: 654; Hispanic: 1,862; White non-Hispanic: 6,623; unknown: 935. *Age distribution: number* under 18: 51; 18–19: 2,962; 20–21: 3,436; 22–24: 2,923; 25–29: 1,093; 30–34: 474; 35–39: 318; 40–49: 415; 50–64: 34; 65 and over: 12; unknown: 1.

International Students: 597 nonresident aliens enrolled fall 2004. 156 students from Europe, 238 Asia, 103 Latin America, 99 Africa, 7 Canada, 9 Australia, 15 other. Programs available to aid students whose native language is not English: social, cultural. English as a Second Language Program. No financial aid specifically designated for international students.

Student Life: On-campus residence halls house 20% of student body. Residence halls for men only constitute 5% of such space, for women only 5%, for both sexes 90%. *Intercollegiate athletics:* men only: baseball, basketball, cross-country, football, golf, lacrosse, soccer, swimming and diving, tennis, track and field, wrestling; women only: basketball, cross-country, field hockey, golf, lacrosse, soccer, softball, swimming and diving, tennis, track and field, volleyball. *Special regulations:* Cars with decals permitted (fee charged). *Special services:* Learning Resources Center, medical services. *Student publications, radio: La Campana,* a yearbook; *Montclarion,* a weekly newspaper; *Quarterly,* a literary magazine. Radio station WMSU-FM broadcasts 91 hours per week. *Surrounding community:* Montclair population 38,500. New York, 14 miles from campus, is nearest metropolitan area. Served by mass transit bus system; airport 20 miles from campus; passenger rail service .1 mile from campus.

Library Collections: 477,215 volumes. 22,014 government documents collections; 1,134,242 microforms; 41,264 audiovisual materials; 1,234 periodicals. Online catalog. Students have access to online information retrieval services.

Most important holdings include the Webster Memorial Collection (350 volumes of mostly American 20th century poetry, including first editions, some signed by notable poets); Margaret D. Penick Collection (250 volumes); Sullivan Collection (850 volumes) which consist mostly of American 20th-century poetry, including first editions (some signed by notable poets); William Carlos Williams Collection (50 volumes) of poetry and criticism, including first editions from the library of the 20th-century American poet; the Justus Buchler Collection (325 volumes) of philosophy and related subjects from the library of Justus Buchler, including his notations.

Buildings and Grounds: Campus area 200 acres. *New buildings:* Village at the Falls completed 2003; Children's Center 2005.

Chief Executive Officer: Dr. Susan Cole, President.

Address admission inquiries to Dennis Craig, Director of Admissions.

New Brunswick Theological Seminary

17 Seminary Place
New Brunswick, New Jersey 08901-1196
Tel: (908) 247-5241   **E-mail:** admissions@nbts.edu
Fax: (908) 247-5412   **Internet:** www.nbts.edu

Institution Description: New Brunswick Theological Seminary is a private, nonprofit institution affiliated with the Reformed Church in America. *Enrollment:* 237. *Degrees awarded:* Master's, first-professional.

Accreditation: *National:* ATS. *Professional:* theology

History: Founded 1784 in New York City by the General Synod of the Reformed Church in America; moved to New Brunswick 1810; development of present campus (adjacent to Rutgers University) begun in 1856.

Institutional Structure: *Governing board:* Board of Theological Education. Representation: 26 members. 3 ex officio. *Composition of institution:* Administrative Council of 4 members. Academic affairs headed by Academic Dean. Management/business/finances directed by director of finance and and administration. Full-time instructional faculty 7 men / 3 women. Academic governance body, the faculty, meets an average of 10 times per year.

Admission: *Requirements:* Baccalaureate degree from an accredited institution or its equivalent; 2.5 GPA; requirements for various programs vary.

Degree Requirements: 60–96 credit hours; 3.0 GPA; general education requirements. Fulfillment of some degree requirements and exemption of some courses possible by passing departmental examinations.

Distinctive Educational Programs: Evening classes on campus and also in Queens, New York in cooperation with St. John's University.

Degrees Conferred: 8 *master's:* theology; 22 *first-professional:* master of divinity.

Fees and Other Expenses: *Full-time tuition per academic year 2004–05:* $300 per credit. Contact the seminary for current fees, expenses, and housing.

Departments and Teaching Staff: *Total instructional faculty:* 32 (full-time 10, part-time 22; women 9, men 23; members of minority groups 15). Degrees held by full-time faculty: degrees held by full-time faculty: doctorate 88%, master's 100%.

Enrollment: Total enrollment 237. First-professional full-time 6 men / 21 women, part-time 50m / 33w; graduate full-time 2m / 6w, part-time 24m / 25w.

International Students: 7 nonresident aliens enrolled. No programs available to aid students whose native language is not English. No financial aid specifically designated for international students.

Student Life: On-campus residence halls house both single and married students. *Publication: The Inquisitor,* a Student Society publication. *Surrounding community:* New Brunswick is located in the New York metropolitan area; served by bus, rail, and airport transportation.

Library Collections: 155,000 volumes. 1,000 microforms; 180 audiovisual materials; 315 current periodical subscriptions.

Most important special holdings include Leiby Collection (Colonial Dutch-American, mainly 17th- and 18th-centuries).

Buildings and Grounds: Campus area 8 acres.

Chief Executive Officer: Rev. Dr. Edwin G. Mulder, President.

Address admission inquiries to Director of Admissions.

New Jersey City University

2039 Kennedy Boulevard
Jersey City, New Jersey 07305-1597

Tel: (201) 200-2000   **E-mail:** admissions@@njcu.edu
Fax: (201) 200-2044   **Internet:** www.njcu.edu

Institution Description: New Jersey City University, formerly named Jersey City State College, is a state institution. *Enrollment:* 8,799. *Degrees awarded:* Baccalaureate, master's.

Accreditation: *Regional:* MSA. *Professional:* art, music, nursing, teacher education

History: Established as New Jersey State Normal School 1927; offered first instruction at postsecondary level 1919; awarded first degree (baccalaureate) 1935; changed name to New Jersey State Teachers College 1955; became Jersey City State College 1958; adopted present name 1998.

Institutional Structure: *Governing board:* Board of Trustees. Extrainstitutional representation: 9 trustees; institutional representation: president of the college. 2 ex officio. *Composition of institution:* Administrators 47 men / 21 women. Full-time instructional faculty 153 men / 92 women.

Calendar: Semesters. Academic year Sept. to May.

Characteristics of Freshmen: 84% (462 students) submitted SAT scores. *25th percentile:* SAT Verbal 420, SAT Math 410; *75th percentile:* SAT Verbal 490, SAT Math 510.

10% of entering freshmen expected to graduate within 5 years. 95% of freshmen from New Jersey.

Admission: High school graduation with college preparatory program including 4 unit English, 3 mathematics 2 science with lab, 2 social studies, plus foreign language and electives. *Entrance tests:* SAT required of all full-time freshmen applicants. For foreign students TOEFL. *For transfer students:* 2.0 minimum GPA; from 2-year accredited institution 64 semester hours maximum transfer credit.

Remedial courses offered.

Degree Requirements: 128 semester hours; 2.0 GPA; 32 hours in residence; core curriculum.

Grading system: A–F; pass-fail; withdraw; incomplete.

Distinctive Educational Programs: Cooperative education. Interdepartmental programs, including African-Afro-American studies, environmental studies, multi-ethnic studies, women's studies. Honors programs. *Other distinctive programs:* Continuing education.

ROTC: Army.

Degrees Conferred: 837 *baccalaureate;* 544 *master's.*

Fees and Other Expenses: *Tuition per academic year 2004–05:* undergraduate resident $4,860, out-of-state $9,540. *Required fees:* $1,690. *Room and board per academic year:* $6,958.

Financial Aid: Aid from institutionally generated funds is provided on the basis of financial need. Institution has a Program Participation Agreement with the U.S. Department of Education for eligible students to receive Pell Grants and, depending upon the agreement, other federal aid.

Financial aid to full-time, first-time undergraduate students: need-based scholarships/grants totaling $14,137,201, self-help $8,016,518, parent loans $433,565; non-need-based scholarships/grants totaling $990,707, self-help $5,613,971.

Departments and Teaching Staff: *Total instructional faculty:* 636 (full-time 241, part-time 395; women 240, men 376; members of minority groups 147).

Student-to-faculty ratio: 14:1. degrees held by full-time faculty: doctorate 67%, master's 33%. 74% hold terminal degrees.

Enrollment: Total enrollment 8,799. Undergraduate full-time 1,483 men / 2,433 women, part-time 733m / 1,369w; graduate full-time 32m / 92w, part-time 798m / 1,859.

Characteristics of Student Body: *Ethnic/racial makeup:* number of Black non-Hispanic: 1,178; American Indian or Alaska Native: 10; Asian or Pacific Islander: 538; Hispanic: 1,984; White non-Hispanic: 1,933; unknown: 317. *Age distribution:* 17–21: 86%; 22–24: 4%; 25–29: 4%; 30–34: 3%; 35–39: 3%.

International Students: 54 undergraduate nonresident aliens enrolled fall 2004. Programs available to aid students whose native language is not English: social, cultural. English as a Second Language Program. No financial aid specifically designated for international students.

Student Life: *Surrounding community:* Jersey City metropolitan area population 560,000.

Library Collections: 250,000 volumes. 85,104 government documents; 475,000 microforms; 2,240 audiovisual materials; 1,500 periodicals. Students have access to online information retrieval services and the Internet.

Most important special holdings include Human Relations Area Files; ethnic studies; nursing; special education.

Chief Executive Officer: Dr. Carols Hernandez, President.

Address admission inquiries to Jason Hand, Director of Admissions; graduate inquiries to Director of Graduate Studies.

New Jersey Institute of Technology

Dr. Martin Luther King Boulevard
University Heights
Newark, New Jersey 07102-1982

Tel: (973) 596-3000   **E-mail:** admissions@njit.edu
Fax: (973) 642-4380   **Internet:** www.njit.edu

Institution Description: New Jersey Institute of Technology (Newark College of Engineering until 1975) is a state institution. *Enrollment:* 8,249. *Degrees awarded:* Baccalaureate, master's, doctorate.

Accreditation: *Regional:* MSA. *Professional:* Architecture, computer science, engineering, engineering technology, nursing, public health

History: Established as Newark Technical School 1881; incorporated and offered first instruction at postsecondary level 1884; changed name to Newark College of Engineering 1919; first degree (baccalaureate) awarded 1923; added graduate-level curriculum 1945; opened School of Architecture 1974, College of Liberal Arts 1982, School of Management 1988, Albert Dorman Honors College 1993; College of Computing Science 2001; adopted present name 1975.

Institutional Structure: *Governing board:* Board of Trustees. Extrainstitutional representation: 15 trustees, including governor of New Jersey and mayor of Newark (all voting), 2 ex officio (nonvoting). *Composition of institution:* Administrators 16 men / 4 women. Academic affairs headed by provost and vice president for academic affairs. Management/business/finances directed by treasurer and chief financial officer. Full-time instructional faculty 352 men / 63 women. Academic governance body, the faculty, meets an average of 6 times per year. *Faculty representation:* Faculty represented by independent collective bargaining agent associated with AAUP.

Calendar: Semesters. Academic year Sept. to May. Freshmen admitted Sept., Jan. Degrees conferred Jan., May, Oct. Formal commencement Jan., May. Summer session of 2 terms from early June to mid-Aug.

Characteristics of Freshmen: 58% of applicants accepted. 46% of accepted applicants enrolled.

Average secondary school rank 74th percentile. Mean SAT scores 544 verbal, 608 mathematical.

39% of entering freshmen expected to graduate within 5 years. 91% of freshmen from New Jersey. Freshmen from 15 states and 18 foreign countries.

Admission: Rolling admissions plan. For fall acceptance, apply as early as Sept. 1 of previous year, but no later than Apr. 1 of year of enrollment. Early acceptance available. *Requirements:* Either graduation from accredited secondary school with 16 units which must include 4 English, 4 college preparatory mathematics (including trigonometry), 2 units laboratory science (recommended physics). Recommend units in foreign language and social studies and, for some majors, additional units in mathematics and science. Lowest recommended secondary school class standing 60th percentile. For architecture majors, portfolio. *Entrance tests:* College Board SAT. For all programs, College Board Achievement in mathematics. *For transfer students:* 2.0 minimum GPA; must completed 33 credits at NJIT.

College credit and advanced placement for postsecondary- level work completed in secondary school.

Tutoring available. Remedial courses offered in summer session and regular academic year.

Degree Requirements: *Undergraduate:* 124–143 credit hours (the 5-year architecture program is 164 credits); 2.0 GPA; 2 semesters physical education.

Fulfillment of some degree requirements and exemption from some beginning courses possible by passing departmental examinations, College Board CLEP, AP. *Grading system:* A–F; pass-fail; withdraw (deadline after which pass-fail is appended to withdraw).

Distinctive Educational Programs: *For undergraduates:* The Albert Dorman Honors College offer students individual experience in a science and technology education. Cooperative education facilities and programs for independent research, including honors programs and tutorials. Cross-registration programs with University of Medicine Dentistry of New Jersey and SUNY-New York School of Optometry. Distance learning program. Off-campus programs at 11 locations including NJIT's branch campus named "Technology and Engineering Center." Individual majors. Interdisciplinary majors in biomedical engineering, computer engineering, engineering science, and manufacturing engineering. Study abroad in France, Germany, Italy.

ROTC: Air Force.

Degrees Conferred: 997 *baccalaureate* (B); 891 *master's:* 69 *doctorate*: architecture 70 (B), 28 (M); biological/life 5 (B), 15 (M) 1 (D); business/marketing 105 (B), 131 (M); computer and information sciences 291 (B), 324 (M), 13 (D); engineering and engineering technologies 491 (B), 336 (M), 42 (D); English 6 (B), 5 (M); health professions and related sciences 6 (B); interdisciplinary studies 3 (B); mathematics 16 (B), 13 (M), 3 (D); natural resources/environmental science 24 (M), 3 (D); physical sciences 2 (B), 5 (M), 7 (D); social sciences and history 2 (B), 10 (M).

Fees and Other Expenses: *Full-time tuition per academic year 2004–05:* undergraduate resident $7,118, nonresident $13,716; graduate resident $10,390, nonresident $14,624. *Required fees:* $1,262. *Room and board per academic year:* $8,242.

Financial Aid: Aid from institutionally generated funds is provided on the basis of academic merit, financial need, athletic ability.

Financial aid to full-time, first-time undergraduate students: need-based scholarships/grants totaling $16,236,410, self-help $7,199,525, parent loans $9,290,340, athletic awards $24,519; non-need-based scholarships/grants totaling $4,237,507, self-help $6,583,423, parent loans $6,583,423, athletic awards $442,159.

Departments and Teaching Staff: *Professors* 163, *associate professors* 95, *assistant professors* 66, *instructors* 91, *part-time faculty* 228.

Total instructional faculty: 643 (full-time 415, part-time 228; women 101, men 542; members of minority groups 94). Total faculty with doctorate, first-professional, or other terminal degree: 415. Student-to-faculty ratio: 13:1. Degrees held by full-time faculty: doctorate 89%, master's 10.7%, baccalaureate .3%. 98% hold terminal degrees. *Faculty development:* $75 million in grants for research. 12 faculty members awarded sabbaticals 2004–05.

Enrollment: Total enrollment 8,249. Undergraduate full-time 3,250 men / 819 women, part-time 1,037m / 260w; graduate full-time 800m / 345w, part-time 1,207m / 531w. *Transfer students:* in-state 1,627; from out-of-state 213.

Characteristics of Student Body: *Ethnic/racial makeup:* number of Black non-Hispanic: 563; American Indian or Alaska Native: 12; Asian or Pacific Islander: 1,144; Hispanic: 676; White non-Hispanic: 1,828; unknown: 829. *Age distribution:* number under 18: 49; 18–19: 1,201; 20–21: 1,329; 22–24: 1,447; 25–29: 709; 30–34: 259; 35–39: 174; 40–49: 156; 50–64: 32; 65 and over: 2. 36.5% of student body attend summer sessions.

International Students: 1,384 nonresident aliens enrolled. Students from Europe, Asia, Latin America, Africa, Canada. Programs available to aid students whose native language is not English: social, cultural. English as a Second Language Program. Some financial aid designated for qualifying international students.

Student Life: On-campus residence halls for both sexes house 18% of student body. *Special regulations:* Cars with parking stickers permitted without restrictions. Quiet hours set by dormitory residents. *Special services:* Learning Resources Center, medical services, shuttle bus to local transportation centers. *Student publications, radio: Nucleus,* a yearbook; *Vector,* a weekly newspaper. Radio station WJTB broadcasts 75 hours per week. *Surrounding community:* Newark population 330,000. Served by mass transit bus and rail systems; airport 5 miles from campus, passenger rail service 1 mile from campus.

Publications: Sources of information about New Jersey Institute of Technology include *NJIT Magazine.*

Library Collections: 206,000 volumes. 7,649 microforms; 636 audiovisual materials; 13,693 current periodical subscriptions. Online catalog. Students have access to online information retrieval services and the Internet.

Most important holdings include the Weston Library, Weston Papers, Weston Museum; Gilbreth Collection (memorabilia and books belonging to Frank and Lillian Gilbreth who were partners in developing scientific management).

Buildings and Grounds: Campus area 45 acres.

Chief Executive Officer: Dr. Robert A. Attenkirch, President.

Address admission inquiries to Office of University Admissions.

Princeton Theological Seminary

64 Mercer Street
Princeton, New Jersey 08542-0803

Tel: (609) 921-8300   **E-mail:** matt.spina@ptsem.edu
Fax: (609) 924-2973   **Internet:** www.ptsem.edu

Institution Description: Princeton Theological Seminary is a private institution affiliated with the Presbyterian Church (USA). *Enrollment:* 766. *Degrees awarded:* First-professional (master of divinity), master's, doctorate.

Accreditation: *Regional:* MSA. *National:* ATS. *Professional:* theology

History: Established and offered first instruction at postsecondary level 1812; awarded first degree 1814; chartered 1922; adopted present name 1962.

Institutional Structure: *Governing board:* Board of Trustees of Princeton Theological Seminary. Representation: 40 trustees, including 20 alumni/ae. All voting. *Composition of institution:* Administrators 26 men / 15 women. Academic affairs headed by academic dean. Management/business/finances directed by vice president for financial affairs. Full-time instructional faculty 48. Academic governance body, the faculty, meets an average of 9 times per year.

Calendar: Semesters. Academic year late Sept. to late May. Entering students admitted Sept., Feb., June, July. Degrees conferred and formal commencement May or June. Summer session from early July to mid-Aug.

Admission: Rolling admissions plan. *Requirements:* Baccalaureate degree from approved college or university. For first-professional program, 60 semester hours in liberal arts and some work in natural and social sciences recommended. *Entrance tests:* For foreign students TOEFL. *For transfer students:* For first-professional students 1 year maximum transfer credit from accredited school of theology.

Degree Requirements: *For first-professional degree:* 90 credit hours; 3 years in residence. *For master's degree in Christian education:* 60 credit hours. *For first-professional and master's in Christian education:* distribution requirements and an approved program of field education. *Grading system:* A–F; pass-fail.

Distinctive Educational Programs: Dual-degree program in ministry and social work with Rutgers, The State University of New Jersey (New Brunswick). Tutorials. Cross-registration with Princeton University. *Other distinctive programs:* Continuing education for ministers and lay people. Princeton Institute of Theology offers summer workshops and seminars for ministers, educators, and lay people. Program for Asian-American Theology and Ministry for second generation Asian-American pastors. Summer cross-cultural programs in Africa, India, Middle East.

Degrees Conferred: 60 *master's:* theology; 29 *doctorate:* theology; 127 *first-professional:* master of divinity.

Fees and Other Expenses: *Full-time tuition per academic year 2004–05:* Contact the seminary for current tuition, fees, and housing costs.

Financial Aid: Aid from institutionally generated funds is provided on the basis of both merit and financial need. Institution has a Program Participation Agreement with the U.S. Department of Education for eligible students to receive Pell Grants and, depending upon the agreement, other federal aid.

Departments and Teaching Staff: Bible *professors* 8, *associate professors* 2, *assistant professors* 38, *part-time faculty* 2; history 8, 1, 0, 2; theology 8, 3, 0, 0; practical theology 7, 4, 4, 15.

Total instructional faculty: 72. Degrees held by full-time faculty: doctorate 100%. 100% hold terminal degrees.

Enrollment: Total enrollment 766 (men 58%, women 42%).

Characteristics of Student Body: *Ethnic/racial makeup:* number of Black non-Hispanic: 11.5%; American Indian or Alaska Native: .3%; Asian or Pacific Islander: 6.1%; Hispanic: 2%; White non-Hispanic: 72.2%.

International Students: 65 nonresident aliens enrolled fall 2004. Programs available to aid students whose native language is not English: social, cultural, financial.

Student Life: On-campus residence halls: 298 students are housed in apartments and 244 in residence halls. Housing available for married students. 90% of married students request institutional housing and 100% of these are so housed. *Special regulations:* Cars permitted without restrictions. *Special services:* Medical services. *Student publications: Sitz im Leben,* a monthly newspaper. *Surrounding community:* Princeton population 13,000. New York and Philadelphia, each 50 miles from campus, are nearest metropolitan areas. Served by airport 7 miles from campus; passenger rail service less than one mile from campus.

Publications: Sources of information about Princeton Theological Seminary include quarterly *Alumni/ae News, The Spire,* a quarterly newsletter, the Seminary catalogue, and various brochures for applicants and donors; *The Princeton*

Seminary Bulletin, (triennially) first published in 1907, and *Theology Today* (quarterly) first published 1944.

Library Collections: 549,000 volumes. 34,080 microforms; 3,324 current periodical subscriptions. Access to online information retrieval services and the Internet.

Most important holdings include the Benson Collection of Hymnology (10,000 hymnals and books about hymnology); Puritan Collection; Latin American Theology Collection.

Buildings and Grounds: Main campus area 35 acres.

Chief Executive Officer: Dr. Iain R. Torrence, President.

Address admission inquiries to Matthew R. Spina, Director of Admissions.

Princeton University

Princeton, New Jersey 08544-0015

Tel: (609) 258-3000   **E-mail:** admissions@princeton.edu
Fax: (609) 258-6743   **Internet:** www.princeton.edu

Institution Description: Princeton University is a private, independent, non-profit institution. *Enrollment:* 6,831. *Degrees awarded:* Baccalaureate, master's, doctorate.

Member of Consortium on Financing Higher Education.

Accreditation: *Regional:* MSA. *Professional:* architecture, engineering, public administration

History: Established and chartered as College of New Jersey 1746; and offered first instruction at postsecondary level 1746; awarded first degree (baccalaureate) 1748; adopted present name 1896. *See* Alexander Leitch, *A Princeton Companion* (Princeton: Princeton University Press, 1978) for further information.

Institutional Structure: *Governing board:* The Trustees of Princeton University. Extrainstitutional representation: 37 trustees (including 36 alumni), governor of New Jersey; institutional representation: president of the university. 2 ex officio. 39 voting. *Composition of institution:* Administrators 20 men / 2 women. Academic affairs headed by dean of the faculty. Management/business/finances directed by financial vice president and treasurer. Full-time instructional faculty 799. Academic governance body, University Faculty, meets an average of 10 times per year.

Calendar: Semesters. Academic year Sept. to May. Freshmen admitted Sept. Degrees conferred June, Oct., Jan., Apr. Formal commencement June. No summer session.

Characteristics of Freshmen: 13% of applicants admitted. 68% of applicants admitted and enrolled.

100% of applicants submitted SAT scores. *25th percentile*: SAT Verbal 680, SAT Math 690. *75th percentile*: SAT Verbal 770, SAT Math 790.

78% of entering freshmen expected to graduate within 5 years. 14% of freshmen from New Jersey. Freshmen from 49 states and 42 foreign countries.

Admission: For fall acceptance, apply as early as fall of senior year in secondary school, but not later than Jan. 1 of year of enrollment. Students are notified of acceptance April. Apply by Nov. 1 for early decision; need not limit application to Princeton. *Requirements:* Either graduation from accredited secondary school or GED. Recommend 4 units in English, 4 in a foreign language, 4 college preparatory mathematics, 2 laboratory science, 2 history. Additional units in art, music, and another foreign language also recommended. *Entrance tests:* College Board SAT, 3 Achievements. For foreign students TOEFL.

Advanced placement for postsecondary-level work completed in secondary school. Tutoring available.

Degree Requirements: *Undergraduate:* 30–36 courses; 4 terms in residence; comprehensives in individual fields of study; 2 semesters of physical education courses; distribution requirements.

Grading system: A–F; pass-fail; withdraw (carries time limit).

Distinctive Educational Programs: Evening classes. Accelerated degree programs. Interdepartmental and interdisciplinary programs in African studies, African-American studies, American studies, East Asian studies, energy and environmental studies. European cultural studies, Latin American studies, Near Eastern studies, Russian studies, science in human affairs, transportation, urban studies, women's studies. Facilities and programs for independent research, including individual majors. Directed reading courses. Study abroad available through programs with other U.S. universities. Students may enroll for courses at Rutgers, The State University of New Jersey and Princeton Theological Seminary.

ROTC: Air Force and Army in cooperation with Rutgers, The State University of New Jersey. 4 Army commissions awarded 2004.

Degrees Conferred: 1,115 *baccalaureate*; 404 *master's*; 295 *doctorate*. *Honorary degrees awarded 1998–99:* Doctor of Laws 3, Doctor of Science 1, Doctor of Humane Letters 1.

Fees and Other Expenses: *Full-time tuition per academic year 2004–05:* $29,910. *Room per academic year:* $4,315. *Board per academic year:* $4,072.

Financial Aid: Aid from institutionally generated funds is provided on the basis of financial need.

Institutional funding for undergraduates: 896 scholarships and grants totaling $53,577,000; 225 loans totaling $560,000.

Federal and state funding for undergraduates: 620 scholarships and grants totaling $2,660,000; 344 loans totaling $1,022,000; 850 work-study jobs totaling $1,080,000.

Departments and Teaching Staff: *Professors* 406 *associate professors* 54, *assistant professors* 162, *instructors* 71, *lecturers* 71, *part-time teachers* 238.

Total instructional faculty: 941. Student-to-faculty ratio: 5.7:1. Degrees held by full-time faculty: doctorate 81%, master's 96%, baccalaureate 100%, professional 5%. 94% hold terminal degrees.

Enrollment: Total enrollment 6,324. Full-time 2,405 men / 2,151 women; graduate full-time 1,105m / 663w.

Characteristics of Student Body: *Ethnic/racial makeup:* number of Black non-Hispanic: 385; American Indian or Alaska Native: 34; Asian or Pacific Islander: 609; Hispanic: 316; White non-Hispanic: 2,443. *Age distribution:* number under 18: 51; 18–19: 2,004; 20–21: 2,248; 22–24: 377; 25–29: 6.

International Students: 391 undergraduate nonresident aliens enrolled fall 2004. No programs available to aid students whose native language is not English. Financial aid available for qualifying international students.

Student Life: On-campus residence halls house 98% of student body. Residence halls for men constitute 18% of such space, for women 7%, for both sexes 75%. Less than 1% of student body live in cooperative facilities. Housing available for married students. 25% of married students request institutional housing; 17% are so housed. *Intercollegiate athletics:* men only: baseball, basketball, cricket, football, gymnastics, ice hockey, rugby, soccer, swimming, tennis, track, volleyball, water polo; women only: basketball, crew, cross-country, fencing, field hockey, golf, gymnastics, ice hockey, lacrosse, rugby, soccer, softball, squash, swimming, tennis, track, volleyball; both sexes: archery, badminton, bicycling, equestrianism, frisbee, judo, karate, paddle tennis, rifle, sailing, skiing, table tennis. *Special regulations:* Cars permitted without restrictions. *Special services:* Medical services. *Student publications: The Daily Princetonian,* a daily newspaper; *Forerunner,* a newspaper, published irregularly; *Journal of Arts and Sciences,* a biannual journal; *Kuumba,* an annual literary magazine; *Nassau Literary Review,* a biannual literary publication; *Nassau Weekly,* a weekly newspaper; *Nexus,* an annual (or biannual) literary magazine. *Surrounding community:* Princeton population 13,000. Philadelphia (PA), 55 miles from campus, is nearest metropolitan area. Served by commuter transit bus and train system; airport 5 miles from campus; passenger rail service 1 mile from campus.

Publications: *Annals of Mathematics* (published 6 times annually) first published 1884; *Philosophy and Public Affairs* (quarterly) first published 1970; *Population Index* (quarterly) first published 1935; *World Politics* (quarterly) first published 1948.

Library Collections: 6,968,555 volumes. 44,634 current serial titles; 4,746,602 microform units; 365,139 audiovisual units. 522,790 recordings. Online catalog. Students have access to the Internet and online information retrieval services.

Most important holdings include Gest Oriental Library, Near East collections; rare books department.

Buildings and Grounds: Campus area 548 acres.

Chief Executive Officer: Dr. Shirley M. Tilghman, President.

Address undergraduate admission inquiries to Janet L. Rapelye, Dean of Admissions; graduate inquiries William B. Russel, Dean of the Graduate School.

Ramapo College of New Jersey

505 Ramapo Valley Road
Mahwah, New Jersey 07430-1680

Tel: (201) 684-7500   **E-mail:** admissions@ramapo.edu
Fax: (201) 684-7989   **Internet:** www.ramapo.edu

Institution Description: Ramapo College of New Jersey is a four-year state college. *Enrollment:* 5,617. *Degrees awarded:* Baccalaureate, master's.

Academic offerings subject to approval by statewide coordination board. Budget subject to approval by state coordination board and legislature. Member of College Consortium for International Studies (CCIS) and University Field Staff International.

Accreditation: *Regional:* MSA. *Professional:* chemistry, social work

History: Established and chartered 1969; offered first instruction at postsecondary level 1971; awarded first degree (baccalaureate) 1973. *See* Gerald Grant and David Riesman, *The Perpetual Dream* (Chicago: University of Chicago Press, 1978) for further information.

Institutional Structure: *Governing board:* Ramapo College Board of Trustees. Extrainstitutional representation: 11 trustees appointed by Board of Higher Education with approval of the Governor; Chancellor, ex officio; President, ex officio; Student Trustee with vote; Student Alternate Trustee, with no vote. 2 ex officio. 12 voting. *Composition of institution:* Administrators 34 men / 34 women. Academic affairs headed by provost and vice president of academic affairs. Management/business/finances directed by vice president for administration and finance. Full-time instructional faculty 179. Academic governance body, Faculty Assembly, meets an average of 12 times per year. *Faculty representation:* Faculty served by collective bargaining agent, AFT.

Calendar: Semesters. Academic year Sept. to May. Freshmen admitted Sept., Jan. Degrees conferred June, Aug., Jan. Formal commencement June. Summer session from early June to early Aug. Winter session in Jan.

Characteristics of Freshmen: 47% of applicants accepted. 42% of accepted applicants enrolled.

Average secondary school rank of freshmen men 51st percentile, women 68th percentile, class 61st percentile. Mean SAT scores men 576 verbal, 599 mathematical; women 572 verbal, 575 mathematical; class 574 verbal, 584 mathematical.

93% of freshmen from New Jersey. Freshmen from 7 states and 13 foreign countries.

Admission: Rolling admissions plan. For fall acceptance, apply as early as Sept. of previous year, but not later than March of year of enrollment. Early acceptance available. *Requirements:* Either graduation from accredited secondary school with 18 academic units, or GED. 2 additional units recommended. Minimum GPA 2.0. *Entrance tests:* College Board SAT. *For transfer students:* 2.5 minimum GPA; 83 hours maximum transfer credit.

College credit and advanced placement for postsecondary-level work completed in secondary school and for extrainstitutional learning on basis of ACE *2006 Guide to the Evaluation of Educational Experiences in the Armed Services.*

Tutoring available. Developmental/remedial courses offered in summer session and regular academic year; nondegree credit given.

Degree Requirements: 128 credit hours; cumulative 2.0 GPA, 2.0 GPA in major; last 45 hours in residence; distribution requirements.

Fulfillment of some degree requirements and exemption from some beginning courses possible by passing College Board CLEP, other standardized tests. *Grading system:* A–F; pass-fail; withdraw (carries time limit).

Distinctive Educational Programs: Incorporation of an international, multicultural component throughout the academic curriculum which includes telecommunications, satellite, and computer technology. Thirty-eight traditional and interdisciplinary majors in American and International studies, business, international business, contemporary arts, nursing, information systems, law and society, social science and human services, and theoretical and applied science. Traditional minor programs as well as foreign languages, African-American studies, Latin American studies, women's studies, Judaic studies and substance abuse. Experiential Education programs including domestic and international cooperative education, educational internships, and institutionally sponsored study abroad programs in Australia, China, Costa Rica, Cuba, England, India, Ireland, Italy, Jamaica, Prague, and Quebec. *Other distinctive programs:* Facilities and services for the physically disabled.

ROTC: Air Force in cooperation with New Jersey Institute of Technology.

Degrees Conferred: 1,010 *baccalaureate:* area and ethnic studies 13; biological/life sciences 31; business/marketing 213; communications/communication technologies 146; computer and information sciences 63; foreign languages and literature 47; health professions and related sciences 62; law/legal studies 35; liberal arts/general studies 13; mathematics 4; natural resources/environmental science 24; physical sciences 4; protective services/public administration 30; psychology 176; social sciences and history 81; visual and performing arts 68. 96 *master's:* business/marketing 26; education 61; liberal arts/general studies 9.

Fees and Other Expenses: *Full-time tuition per academic year 2003–04:* undergraduate resident $5,640, nonresident $10,192; graduate resident $386 per credit hour, nonresident $496 per credit hour. *Other fees:* $2,142 (undergraduate only). *Room per academic year:* $5,628. *Board per academic year:* $2,580.

Financial Aid: The college offers a direct lending program. Aid from institutionally generated funds is provided on the basis of academic merit, financial need, other considerations.

Financial aid to full-time, first-time undergraduate students: need-based scholarships/grants totaling $11,707,187, self-help $6,240,187, tuition waivers $160,137; non-need-based scholarships/grants totaling $4,128,309, self-help $9,088,283, tuition waivers $156,442. *Graduate aid:* 17 students received $64,677 in federal and state-funded loans.

Departments and Teaching Staff: *Professors* 65, *associate professors* 55, *assistant professors* 59, *part-time faculty* 209.

Total instructional faculty: 388 (full-time 179, part-time 209; women 74, men 105; members of minority groups 23). Total faculty with doctorate, first-professional, or other terminal degree: 169. Student-to-faculty ratio: 17:1. Degrees held by full-time faculty: master's 26%, doctorate 74%. 97% hold terminal degrees. *Faculty development:* $100,375 total grants for research. 3 faculty members awarded sabbaticals 2004–05.

Enrollment: Total enrollment 5,617. Undergraduate full-time 1,667 men / 2,479 women, part-time 472m / 660w; graduate full-time 3m / 13w, part-time 85m / 238w. *Transfer students:* 491.

Characteristics of Student Body: *Ethnic/racial makeup:* number of Black non-Hispanic: 320; American Indian or Alaska Native: 18; Asian or Pacific Islander: 214; Hispanic: 408; White non-Hispanic: 4,118. *Age distribution:* number under 18: 33; 18–19: 1,402; 20–21: 1,647; 22–24: 1,131; 25–29: 414; 30–34: 162; 35–39: 139; 40–49: 229; 50–64: 84; 65 and over: 37.

International Students: 206 nonresident aliens enrolled fall 2004. 86 students from Europe, 58 Asia, 20 Latin America, 23 Africa, 19 Canada. Programs available to aid students whose native language is not English: social, cultural. English as a Second Language Program. No financial aid specifically designated for international students.

Student Life: On-campus residence halls housed 2,497 students (60% of full-time student body). Campus residences include both residence halls and apartments. Meal plans are required with some of the dormitories. No special housing for married students. *Intercollegiate athletics:* men only: football, soccer, track and field, baseball, basketball, golf, tennis; women only: softball, basketball, volleyball, tennis, track and field. *Special services:* Academic Skills Center, Office of Specialized Service, Career Planning and Placement Office, Advisement Center, counseling services, medical services, experiential learning programs. *Student publications, radio: The Ramapo News,* a weekly newspaper; *Trillium,* a quarterly literary magazine; a yearbook. Radio station WRPR. *Surrounding community:* Ramapo College's barrier-free campus, over 300 acres in size, is located in the foothills of the Ramapo Mountains in Mahwah, New Jersey, just 25 miles from New York City and all of its cultural advantages. Airport 30 miles from campus; passenger rail service 3 miles from campus.

Library Collections: 159,853 volumes. Online catalog. 4,217 video recordings; 642 audio recordings; 33,008 government documents; 567 current periodical subscriptions; access to 49 electronic reference sources and databases. Online catalog. Students have access to online information retrieval services and the Internet. Total 2003–04 budget for books and materials: $1,141,552.

Most important holdings include Bergen County (NJ) government documents; Mahwah Township publications; Holocaust and Genocide Studies Collections. Depository for United States and New Jersey Government Publications.

Buildings and Grounds: Campus area 357 acres.

Chief Executive Officer: Dr. William Stanborn Pfeiffer, President.

Address admission inquiries to Nancy Jaeger, Director of Admissions.

Richard Stockton College of New Jersey

Jimmie Leeds Road
P.O. Box 195
Pomona, New Jersey 08240-0195

Tel: (609) 652-1776   **E-mail:** admissions@stockton.edu
Fax: (609) 652-0275   **Internet:** www.stockton.edu

Institution Description: Richard Stockton State College is a public institution. *Enrollment:* 7,002. *Degrees awarded:* Baccalaureate.

Budget subject to approval by state governing boards.

Accreditation: *Regional:* MSA. *Professional:* chemistry, nursing, physical therapy, social work, teacher education

History: Established 1969; offered first instruction at postsecondary level 1971; awarded first degree 1973.

Institutional Structure: *Governing board:* Board of Trustees. Representation: 9 trustees. 3 Ed officio, 1 trustee Emeritus, 2 student alternate. All voting. *Composition of institution:* Administrators 42 men / 21 women. Academic affairs headed by vice president for academic affairs. Management/business/ finances directed by vice president for administration and finance. Full-time instructional faculty 184. Academic governance body, Faculty Assembly, meets an average of 10 times per year. *Faculty representation:* Faculty served by collective bargaining agent, Stockton Federation of Teachers, affiliated with AFT.

Calendar: Semesters. Academic year Sept. to May. Freshmen admitted Sept., Jan., June. Degrees conferred May, Aug., Dec. Formal commencements May, Jan. Summer session of 1 term from late June to mid-Aug.

Characteristics of Freshmen: 3,767 applicants (1,733 men, 2,034 women). 46.2% of applicants admitted. 47.4% of admitted students enrolled full-time.

94% (767 students) submitted SAT scores; 6% (52 students) submitted ACT scores. *25th percentile:* SAT I Verbal 510, SAT I Math 520; ACT Composite 21, ACT English 20, ACT Math 22. *75th percentile:* SAT I Verbal 590, SAT I Math 610; ACT Composite 26, ACT English 25, ACT Math 27.

46% of entering freshmen expected to graduate within 5 years. 97% of freshmen from New Jersey. Freshmen from 12 states and 22 foreign countries.

Admission: Rolling admissions plan. For fall acceptance, apply as early as Sept. 1 of previous year, but not later than June 1 of year of enrollment. Early acceptance available. *Requirements:* Either graduation from secondary school with 16 units which must include 14 academic; or GED. *Entrance tests:* College Board SAT or ACT composite for students over 21 years of age. For foreign students TOEFL. *For transfer students:* 2.0 minimum GPA; from 4-year accredited institution 96 semester hours maximum transfer credit; from 2-year accredited institution 64 hours.

College credit for postsecondary-level work completed in secondary school and for extrainstitutional learning (life experience) on basis of portfolio assessment, USAFI.

Tutoring available. Developmental courses offered in summer session and regular academic year.

Degree Requirements: 128 semester hours; 2 semesters in residence; demonstrated proficiency in basic skills; general education requirements; distribution requirements.

Fulfillment of some degree requirements possible by passing departmental examinations, college Board CLEP, other standardized tests. *Grading system:* A–F; high pass-pass-fail; withdraw (carries time limit).

Distinctive Educational Programs: Work-experience programs, including cooperative education and internships. Evening classes. Accelerated degree programs. Special facilities for using telecommunications in the classroom. Interdisciplinary programs in gerontology, Jewish studies, teacher education, women's studies. Facilities and programs for independent research, including individual majors, tutorials. Independent study. Washington (D.C.) Internship Program. Governor's School on the Environment. Study English abroad in England, Australia, Germany; Chinese in China; Spanish in Mexico; German in Germany; Hebrew in Israel. *Other distinctive programs:* Special admissions for students with academic potential who require educational or financial support. Continuing education programs.

Degrees Conferred: 1,586 *baccalaureate*; 88 *master's*. Bachelor's degrees awarded in top five disciplines: business, management, marketing, and related support services 266; social sciences 247; psychology 205; biomedical/biological sciences 149; education 147.

Fees and Other Expenses: *Full-time tuition per academic year 2004–05:* resident $7,203, nonresident $10,368. *Books and supplies:* $850. *Room and board per academic year:* $7,308.

Financial Aid: Aid from institutionally generated funds is provided on the basis of academic merit, financial need. Institution has a Program Participation Agreement with the U.S. Department of Education for eligible students to receive Pell Grants and, depending upon the agreement, other federal aid.

Financial aid to full-time, first-time undergraduate students: 24% received federal grants averaging $3,034; 32% state/local grants averaging $3,151; 32% institutional grants averaging $1,463; 61% received loans averaging $4,134.

Departments and Teaching Staff: Arts and humanities *professors* 13, *associate professors* 6, *assistant professors* 14, *instructors* 2, *part-time faculty* 1; general studies 2, 3, 4, 1, 2; natural sciences and mathematics 14, 17, 17, 1, 1; professional studies 8, 13, 17, 8, 5; social/behavioral sciences 13, 17, 11, 0, 1.

Total instructional faculty: 287 (184 full-time, 103 part-time). Student-to-faculty ratio: 17:1. 19% hold terminal degrees.

Enrollment: Total enrollment 7,002. Undergraduate 6,578 (men 41.9%, women 58.1%).

Characteristics of Student Body: *Ethnic/racial makeup (undergraduate):* number of Black non-Hispanic: 7.4%; American Indian or Alaska Native: .4%; Asian or Pacific Islander: 4%;Hispanic: 5.9%; White non-Hispanic: 81.6%. *Age distribution:* 17–21: 42%; 22–24: 34%; 25–29: 10%; 30–34: 5%; 35–39: 3%; 40–49: 2%; 50–59: 1%.

International Students: 49 nonresident aliens enrolled fall 2004. No programs available for students whose native language is not English. No financial aid specifically designated for international students.

Student Life: On-campus residence halls and apartments houses available. *Intercollegiate athletics:* men only: basketball, soccer, track; women only: basketball, softball, volleyball. *Special regulations:* Cars permitted without restrictions. *Special services:* Learning Resources Center, medical services. *Student publications, radio:* Argo, a weekly newspaper; *Stockpot,* an annual literary magazine. Radio station WLFR broadcasts 119 hours per week. SSTV is a closed circuit TV channel broadcasting 24 hours a day. *Surrounding community:* Pomona population 2,500. Philadelphia, 60 miles from campus, is nearest metropolitan area. Served by mass transit system; airport 20 miles from campus.

Library Collections: 575,000 volumes. 703,000 microforms; 14,300 audiovisual materials; 1,335 current periodical subscriptions; 9,500 recordings/tapes. Online catalog. Students have access to online information retrieval services and the Internet.

Most important holdings include a collection on the New Jersey Pine Barrens; the New Jersey Collection. Library is a depository for federal, state, and county documents.

Buildings and Grounds: Campus area 1,600 acres.

Chief Executive Officer: Dr. Herman Saatkamp, Jr., President.

Address admission inquiries to Alison Henry, Assistant Director of Admissions.

Rider University

2083 Lawrenceville Road
Lawrenceville, New Jersey 08648-3099

Tel: (609) 896-5000	**E-mail:** admissions@rider.edu
Fax: (609) 895-5681	**Internet:** www.rider.edu

Institution Description: Rider University, formerly Rider College, is a private, independent, nonprofit college. *Enrollment:* 5,502. *Degrees awarded:* Associate, baccalaureate, master's. Information regarding Westminster Choir College of Rider University can be found on the Rider University website.

Accreditation: *Regional:* MSA. *Professional:* accounting, business, counseling, music, teacher education

History: Established 1865; incorporated as Rider Business College 1897; name changed to Rider-Moore Business College 1898; merged with Stewart School of Business and changed name to Rider-Moore and Stewart School of Business 1901; offered first instruction at postsecondary level 1919; present name adopted 1921; awarded first degree (baccalaureate) 1922; converted to nonprofit status 1937; accredited by MSA 1955; moved from downtown Trenton site to present campus 1964. Announced affiliation and merger process with Westminster Choir College 1991; full merger took place 1992.

Institutional Structure: *Governing board:* Board of Trustees. Extrainstitutional representation: 20 trustees (including 24 alumni); institutional representation: 1 administrator. 1 ex officio. 28 voting. *Composition of institution:* Administrators 74 men / 120 women. Academic affairs headed by vice president for academic affairs and provost. Management/business/finances directed by vice president for business and finance. Full-time instructional faculty 207. Academic governance body, College Academic Policy Committee, meets an average of 18 times per year. *Faculty representation:* Faculty represented by collective bargaining agent affiliated with AAUP.

Calendar: Semesters Academic year Sept. to May. Degrees conferred and formal commencement May. Summer session of 2 terms from mid-May to late Aug.

Characteristics of Freshmen: 88% of applicants accepted. 24% of accepted applicants enrolled.

Mean SAT scores men 512 verbal, 528 mathematical; women 522 verbal, 511 mathematical; class 517 verbal, 519 mathematical.

57% of entering freshmen expected to graduate within 5 years. 79% of freshmen from New Jersey. Freshmen from 17 states and 7 foreign countries.

Admission: Rolling admissions plan; once file is complete, student is notified in approximately 4–6 weeks. Recommend applying by Jan. 1 of senior year of secondary school. Tuition and housing deposits due May 1. Early admission available. *Requirements:* 16 secondary school units which must include 4 English, 3 mathematics up to and including Algebra II, and 9 other academic subjects selected from foreign language, humanities, mathematics, science, and social sciences; or GED. Science, mathematics and business administration programs require 3 units mathematics including algebra II. *For transfer students:* High school transcript required for verification of high school graduation and used for admission decision if less than 30 credits completed at accredited college/university.

College credit and advanced placement for postsecondary-level work completed in secondary school. Tutoring available. Noncredit developmental courses are offered.

Degree Requirements: *For all associate degrees:* At least 63 credit hours. *For all baccalaureate degrees:* At least 120 credit hours. *For all undergraduate degrees:* 2.0 GPA; final 30–45 hours in residence.

Fulfillment of some degree requirements and exemption from some beginning courses possible by passing College Board CLEP. *Grading system:* A–F plus and minus; high pass/pass-fail.

Distinctive Educational Programs: *For undergraduates:* Interdisciplinary programs in entrepreneurial studies, international business concentration, law and justice minor, bilingual/bicultural teacher preparation, and ESL teacher preparation. Honors programs. Individual majors. Study abroad program in Argentina, Austria, Belgium, Chile, China, Costa Rica, Cuba, Czech Republic, England, France, Ireland, Italy, Netherlands, New Zealand, Puerto Rico, Scotland, South Africa, Spain, Wales, and other locations. Partnership for business students at Sanda University, China to complete two semesters at Rider and earn a Rider/Sanda degree in business administration and communications. Resource center for Holocaust and genocide studies. Departmental and baccalaureate honors programs. Writing-Across-the-Curriculum Program.

Degrees Conferred: 4 *associate*; 851 *baccalaureate*; 302 *master's*.

Fees and Other Expenses: *Full-time tuition per academic year 2004–05:* undergraduate $22,910, graduate programs by credit hour (varies by program; contact the university for current rates). *Room per academic year:* $4,940 to $5,940. *Board per academic year:* $3,900. *Other fees:* $250.

Financial Aid: Aid from institutionally generated funds is provided on the basis of academic merit, financial need, athletic ability, other criteria. Institution has a Program Participation Agreement with the U.S. Department of Education for eligible students to receive Pell Grants and, depending upon the agreement, other federal aid.

Financial aid to full-time, first-time undergraduate students: need-based scholarships/grants totaling $25,734,919, self-help $20,230,347, parent loans $1,675,071, tuition waivers $787,029, athletic awards $1,255,364; non-need-based scholarships/grants totaling $5,541,345, self-help $10,478,881, parent loans $3,929,932, tuition waivers $362,407, athletic awards $1,411,408.

Departments and Teaching Staff: *Professors* 91, *associate professors* 91, *assistant professors* 55, *instructors* 2, *part-time faculty* 267. *Total instructional faculty:* 512 (full-time 237, part-time 275; women 237, men 275; members of minority groups 54). Total faculty with doctorate, first-professional, or other terminal degree: 348. Student-to-faculty ratio: 12.56:1. Degrees held by full-time faculty: master's 11.1%, doctorate 87.6%, baccalaureate .4%. 88% hold terminal degrees.

Enrollment: Total enrollment 5,502. Undergraduate full-time 1,470 men / 2,048 women, part-time 255m / 495w; graduate full-time 57m / 230w, part-time 266m / 661w.

International Students: Programs available to aid students whose native language is not English: English as a Second Language Program. No financial aid specifically designated for international students.

Student Life: 41% of student body live in on-campus residence halls, 42% of whom are male and 55% are female in residence halls. *Intercollegiate athletics:* men only: basketball, baseball, tennis, soccer, swimming, wrestling, indoor track, cross country track, track and field, golf; women only: basketball, softball, volleyball, tennis, swimming, field hockey. All men and women compete in NCAA Division I coed rifle team. *Special regulations:* Cars permitted without restrictions. *Special services:* Learning Resources Center, medical services. *Student publications, radio: Rider News*, a weekly newspaper; *Venture*, an annual literary magazine; *The Shadow*, a yearbook. Radio station WRRC. *Surrounding community:* Lawrenceville township population 20,000. Philadelphia (PA), 30 miles from campus, is nearest metropolitan area. Served by mass transit bus system; airport 7 miles from campus; passenger rail service 7 miles from campus.

Library Collections: 486,310 volumes. Online catalog. Current serial subscriptions: 810,783 microform; 69 via electronic access. 9,650 recordings. 5,220 compact discs and CD-ROMs. 35 computer work stations. Students have access to online information retrieval services and the Internet. Total 2004–05 budget for books, periodicals, audiovisual materials, microforms: $949,777.

Most important special holdings include Riderana; Louis A. Lesley Collection of the History of Shorthand; Lloyd Collection of the History of Typewriting; Dr. DeWitt Nasson Research Collection of Organ Music.

Buildings and Grounds: Campus area 340 acres.

Chief Executive Officer: Dr. Mordechai Rozanski, President.

Undergraduates address admission inquiries to Susan C. Christian, Director of Admissions; graduate inquiries to Christine Zelenak, Director of Graduate Admissions.

Rowan University

201 Mullica Hill Road
Glassboro, New Jersey 08028-1701

Tel: (856) 256-4000   **E-mail:** admissions@rowan.edu
Fax: (856) 256-4929   **Internet:** www.rowan.edu

Institution Description: Rowan University, formerly known as Glassboro State College, is a public institution. *Enrollment:* 9,688. *Degrees awarded:* Baccalaureate, master's, doctorate. Educational specialist (post M.A.) also awarded.

Accreditation: *Regional:* MSA.

History: Incorporated as Glassboro State Normal School 1921; established and offered first instruction at postsecondary level 1923; changed name to Glassboro State Teachers College 1935; awarded first degree (baccalaureate) 1937; name changed from Glassboro State College to Rowan College of New Jersey 1992; adopted present name 1997.

Institutional Structure: *Governing board:* Board of Trustees. Representation: 12 trustees. *Composition of institution:* Administrators 8 men / 4 women. Academic affairs headed by executive vice president and provost. Full-time instructional faculty 325.

Calendar: Semesters. Academic year Sept. to May.

Characteristics of Freshmen: 6,175 applicants. 51.8% of applicants admitted. 40.9% of admitted students enrolled full-time.

99% (1,243 students) submitted SAT scores. *25th percentile:* SAT I Verbal 480, SAT I Math 490. *75th percentile:* SAT I Verbal 585, SAT I Math 600.

47% of entering freshmen expected to graduate within 5 years. 98% of freshmen from New Jersey. Freshmen from 8 states and 5 foreign countries.

Admission: Rolling admissions plan. Early acceptance available. *Requirements:* Either graduation from accredited secondary school with 16 units which must include 4 English, 1 laboratory science, 2 mathematics, 2 social studies, and 5 in at least two of the following fields; foreign language (minimum 2 units in one language), history, mathematics, sciences; or GED. *Entrance tests:* College Board SAT or ACT composite.

Degree Requirements: 120 semester hours; 2.0 GPA; general education requirements.

Distinctive Educational Programs: Co-op program. Communications, business, teacher education. Study abroad through affiliation in Australia, England, France, Mexico, Spain.

ROTC: Army.

Degrees Conferred: 1,633 *baccalaureate*; 307 *master's*; 3 *doctorate*. Bachelor's degrees awarded in top five disciplines: education 345; communication, journalism, and related programs 250; business, management, marketing, and related support services 242; social sciences 125; security and protective services 125.

Fees and Other Expenses: *Full-time tuition per academic year 2004–05:* $7,975. Contact the university for current graduate tuition/fees. *Books and supplies:* $1,200. *Room and board per academic year:* $7,902.

Financial Aid: Aid from institutionally generated funds is provided on the basis of academic merit, financial need, other considerations. Institution has a Program Participation Agreement with the U.S. Department of Education for eligible students to receive Pell Grants and, depending upon the agreement, other federal aid.

Financial aid to full-time, first-time undergraduate students: 54% received federal grants averaging $838; 31% state/local grants averaging $1,397; 46% institutional grants averaging $916; 76% received loans averaging $1,209.

Departments and Teaching Staff: *Professors* 84, *associate professors* 93, *assistant professors* 133, *instructors* 15, *part-time teachers* 257.

Total instructional faculty: 582. Student-to-faculty ratio: 16:1. Degrees held by full-time faculty: doctorate 78%, master's 22%. 78% hold terminal degrees.

Enrollment: Total enrollment 9,688. Undergraduate 8,385 (men 44.4%, women 56.6%).

Characteristics of Student Body: *Ethnic/racial makeup:* number of Black non-Hispanic: 78.7%; American Indian or Alaska Native: .3%; Asian or Pacific Islander: 3.4%; Hispanic: 6%; White non-Hispanic: 78.7%; unknown: 2.2%.

International Students: 194 nonresident aliens enrolled fall 2004. Students from Europe, Asia, Latin America, Africa, Canada. Programs available to aid students whose native language is not English: social and cultural. English as a Second Language Program. No financial aid specifically designated for international students.

Student Life: On campus residence halls house 20% of student body. Housing consists of women and coed dormitories and 3 apartment complexes. *Intercollegiate athletics:* men only: football, soccer, cross-country, basketball, wrestling, gymnastics, swimming, indoor track, tennis, baseball, golf, club ice hockey; women: field hockey, volleyball, cross country, tennis, basketball, swimming, softball, lacrosse, track. *Special services:* Career and Academic Planning, medical services; special services office for international students, handicapped, and veterans. *Student publications: The White*, a weekly newspaper; *The Venue*, student opinion magazine; *The Oak*, a yearbook; *Advant*, literary magazine. *Surrounding community:* Glassboro (site of 1967 summit meeting between President Lyndon Johnson and Soviet Premier Aleskei Kosygin), population 15,000, is located 20 miles southeast of Philadelphia and 40 miles west of Atlantic City.

Publications: *Glassboro Today*, a journal for alumni, students, and friends of the college.

Library Collections: 465,000 volumes. 118,000 microforms; 11,800 audiovisual materials; 1,560 periodicals. Online catalog. Students have access to online information retrieval services and the Internet.

Most important special holdings include Stewart Room Manuscript Collection; Rare Book Collection (contains material on New Jersey and Delaware Valley History); Old Text Book Collection (over 100 years old); Children's Collection.

Buildings and Grounds: Campus area 175 acres.

Chief Executive Officer: Dr. Donald J. Farish, President.

Address undergraduate inquiries to Marvin Sills, Director of Admissions; graduate inquiries to Director of Graduate Admissions.

Rutgers, The State University of New Jersey

New Brunswick, New Jersey 08901

Tel: (732) 932-4636   **E-mail:** admissions@rutgers.edu
Fax: (732) 932-9359   **Internet:** www.rutgers.edu

Institution Description: Rutgers, The State University of New Jersey, is a state institution and a land-grant college with campuses in New Brunswick/Piscataway, Newark, and Camden. *Enrollment:* Total University 50,552. *Degrees awarded:* Baccalaureate, first-professional (law, pharmacy), master's, doctorate. Certificates also awarded.

Academic offerings subject to approval by state governing boards: Member of the Alliance for Undergraduate Education, American Association of Colleges for Teacher Education, American Council of Learned Societies, American Council on Education, Association of American Colleges and Universities, Association of American Universities, Middle States Association of Colleges and Schools, National Association of State Universities and Land Grant Colleges.

Academic offerings subject to approval by State Coordinating Board.

Accreditation: *Regional:* MSA. *Professional:* clinical psychology, dance, engineering, landscape architecture, librarianship, music, orthist/prothetist, pharmacy, planning, public health, school psychology, social work

History: Chartered as Queens College 1766; offered first instruction at postsecondary level 1771; awarded first degree (baccalaureate) 1774; changed name to Rutgers College 1825; became a land-grant college 1864; assumed university status 1924; legislative acts in 1945 and 1956 designated all divisions as the State University of New Jersey. *See* Richard P. McCormick, *Rutgers: A Bicentennial History* (New Brunswick: Rutgers University Press, 1966) for further information.

Institutional Structure: *Governing board:* Board of Governors of Rutgers, The State University. Extrainstitutional representation: 11 voting members. The president of the university is an ex officio, nonvoting member. Two faculty and one student are elected by the University Senate as nonvoting representatives. Of the 11 voting members, 6 are appointed by the governor of the state with confirmation by the New Jersey State Senate and 5 are elected by and from the Board of Trustees. Board of Trustees has 59 voting members. *Composition of institution:* Executive administrators 88 men / 60 women; professionals 1,169 men / 1,854 women. Academic affairs headed by university vice president for academic affairs. Management/business/finances directed by executive vice president and chief financial officer. Full-time instructional faculty 1,455 men / 697 women. Academic governance body, University Senate, meets an average of 6 times per year. *Faculty representation:* Full-time faculty represented for collective bargaining purposes by AAUP; part-time faculty by independent agent.

Calendar: Semesters. Academic year Sept. to May. Freshmen admitted Sept., Jan. Degrees conferred May, Oct., Jan. Formal commencement May. Summer session of 3 terms from May to Aug. Winter session Dec. to Jan.

Characteristics of Freshmen: 62.9% of applicants accepted. 33.3% of accepted applicants enrolled.

Average high school rank of freshmen men 77th percentile, women 82nd percentile, class 80th percentile. Mean SAT scores men 571 verbal, 611 mathematical; women 557 verbal, 566 mathematical.

62% of entering freshmen expected to graduate within 5 years. 90% of freshmen from New Jersey. .

Admission: Priority deadline Dec. 15 for first-year students. Students who submit completed application by that date will receive full consideration at college of their choice and receive notification by Feb. 28. Students who apply after Dec. 15 will be considered at the colleges of their choice as long as space is available. Early admission available. *Requirements:* Either graduation from accredited secondary school with 16 academic units which must include 4 English, 3 mathematics; or GED. Additional requirements for some programs. Graduates of nonaccredited secondary schools and non-graduates may also be admitted by examination. *Entrance tests:* College Board SAT or ACT, and, if appropriate, 3 Achievements.

College credit and advanced placement for postsecondary-level work completed in secondary school.

Tutoring available. Developmental courses offered for nondegree credit.

Degree Requirements: *Undergraduate:* 120–180 credit hours; 1.933–2.0 GPA; 30 of last 42 hours in residence; additional requirements for some majors.

Fulfillment of some degree requirements and exemption from some beginning courses possible by passing departmental examinations, College Board CLEP, AP. *Grading system:* A–F; pass-fail; withdraw (carries time limit).

Distinctive Educational Programs: Flexible meeting places and schedules, including off-campus centers at varying locations throughout the state, and evening classes. Special facilities for using telecommunications in the classroom. Facilities and programs for independent research, including honors programs, individual majors. Study abroad in England, Israel, France, Italy, Germany, Spain, Mexico, Ireland; summer programs in Paris and Sussex. Educational opportunity program provides academic and other support services for economically and educationally disadvantaged students. Joint 8-year Bachelor/Medical degree program with UMDNJ-Robert Wood Johnson Medical School. *Other distinctive programs:* Credit and noncredit continuing education programs.

ROTC: Army, Air Force at New Brunswick campus. Army in cooperation with University of Pennsylvania; Air Force with St. Joseph's University (PA) at Camden campus; Air Force with New Jersey Institute of Technology at Newark. 24 commissions awarded 2004.

Degrees Conferred: 7,709 *baccalaureate;* 2,545 *master's;* 438 *doctorate;* 671 *first-professional:* health professions 171, law 500. *Honorary degrees awarded 2004–05:* Doctor of Laws 1, Doctor of Science 1, Doctor of Letters 1, Doctor of Fine Arts 2.

Fees and Other Expenses: *Full-time tuition per academic year 2004–05:* undergraduate resident $6,793, nonresident $13,828; graduate resident $9,668, nonresident $14,174. *Required fees:* $1,171. *Room and board per academic year:* $7,862 to $8,570.

Financial Aid: The university offers a direct lending program. Aid from institutionally generated funds is provided on the basis of academic merit, financial need, other criteria. Institution has a Program Participation Agreement with the U.S. Department of Education for eligible students to receive Pell Grants and, depending upon the agreement, other federal aid.

Financial aid to full-time, first-time undergraduate students: need-based scholarships/grants totaling $102,512,310, self-help $102,819,939, parent loans $7,944,483, tuition waivers $1,013,741, athletic awards $1,929,176; non-need-based scholarships/grants totaling $11,329,383, self-help $22,583,502, parent loans $3,589,178, tuition waivers $2,456,043, athletic awards $2,587,715.

Departments and Teaching Staff: *Professors* 997, *associate professors* 702, *assistant professors* 547, *instructors/lecturers* 399, *part-time faculty* 1,245.

Total instructional faculty: 2,567 FTE. *Total tenured faculty:* 1,445. *Student-to-faculty ratio:* 14:1. Degrees held by full-time faculty: 98% hold terminal degrees. *Faculty development:* $258,607,692 total grants for research. 175 faculty members awarded sabbaticals 2004–05.

Enrollment: Total enrollment 50,552. Undergraduate full-time 15,229 men / 17,282 women, part-time 2,187m / 2,730w; first-professional full-time 775m / 714w, part-time 308m / 174w; graduate full-time 2,927m / 2,563w, part-time 2,711m / 3,852w.

Characteristics of Student Body: *Ethnic/racial makeup (undergraduate):* number of Black non-Hispanic: 4,158; American Indian or Alaska Native: 95; Asian or Pacific Islander: 7,530; Hispanic: 3,661; White non-Hispanic: 19,275; unknown: 2,069.

International Students: 2,876 nonresident aliens enrolled fall 2004. 626 students from Europe, 2,368 Asia, 196 Latin America, 146 Africa, 97 Canada, 11 Australia, 8 New Zealand, 83 other. Programs available to aid students whose native language is not English: social, cultural. English as a Second Language Program. Financial aid specifically designated for international students: scholarships available annually.

Student Life: New Brunswick on-campus residence halls and apartments house 55% of undergraduates. Residence halls for women only constitute 14% of housing space, for both sexes 86%. Camden provides on-campus housing for 252 undergraduates, 248 graduates; Newark, 450 undergraduates, 250 graduates and professionals, plus 20 apartments for family housing. *Intercollegiate athletics:* men only: baseball, basketball, cheerleading, crew, fencing, football, golf, lacrosse, soccer, swimming, tennis, track, cross country, wrestling; women only: basketball, cheerleading, crew, fencing, field hockey, golf, gymnastics, lacrosse, soccer, softball, swimming, tennis, track, cross-country, volleyball. *Special regulations:* Cars not permitted for freshmen or sophomores in certain areas of New Brunswick campuses. *Special services:* Learning Resources Center, medical services, bus transportation to all campus facilities in New Brunswick. *Student publications, radio:* New Brunswick campus, 1 daily and 2 weekly newspapers, 1 monthly, 2 every other month; radio station WRSU-FM broadcasts 168 hours per week, WRLC-FM broadcasts 24 hours per week. Newark campus: WRNU-FM broadcasts 50 hours per week. *Surrounding community:* New Brunswick population 42,000. Newark population 280,000. Camden population 90,000.

Publications: *Journal for International Law; Tramoya: Mickle Street Review; Raritan Review; Journal of the History of Ideas; American Imago; Horn of Africa Journal; The American Book Review; Public Productivity and Management Review; Journal of Research in Crime and Delinquency.*

Library Collections: 6,679,947 volumes including bound books, serial backfiles, electronic documents, and government documents not in separate collections. Online catalog. Current serial subscriptions: 26,648. E-books 131,163.

Audiovisual materials 142,505. Microforms 5,968,614. Computer work stations available. Students have access to the Internet at no charge.

Most important holdings include New Jerseyana; Alcohol Studies Collection; Sinclair New Jersey Collection; Archive of Jazz and Jazz-related Materials.

Buildings and Grounds: Campus area 6,307 acres: New Brunswick 2,847 acres, Newark 38 acres, Camden 27 acres, Experiment Station 1,876, other 1,141.

Chief Executive Officer: Dr. Richard L. McCormick, President.

Address admission inquiries to Diane W. Harris, Associate Director of Admissions.

NEW BRUNSWICK CAMPUS

New Brunswick, New Jersey 08903
Tel: (732) 932-1766

Cook College - New Brunswick

Degree Programs Offered: *Baccalaureate* in bioresource engineering (5 year program); agricultural science; animal science; biochemistry; biological sciences; biotechnology; chemistry; communication; computer science; environmental and business economics; environmental planning and design; environmental policy, institutions, and behavior; environmental sciences; exercise science and sports studies; food science; geography; geological sciences; journalism and mass media; marine sciences, meteorology, natural resource management; nutritional sciences; plant science; professional occupational education; public health, teacher certification.

Degree Requirements: 128 credits; minimum GPA of 2.0; at least 42 credits in residence.

Fees and Other Expenses: Contact the college for current information.

Distinctive Educational Programs: 5-year B.A. or B.S./MBA program in Rutgers Business School. Joint 8-year Bachelor/Medical Degree program with UMDNJ-Robert Wood Johnson Medical School. 5-year BS/BS in bioresource engineering with the College of Engineering.

Douglass College - New Brunswick

Degree Programs Offered: *Baccalaureate* accounting, Africana studies, American studies; anthropology; art history; biological sciences (with numerous specializations); biomathematics; cell biology and neuroscience; chemistry; Chinese; communication; comparative literature; computer science; dance; East Asian languages and area studies; economics; English; evolution anthropology; exercise science and sport studies; finance; French; genetics and microbiology; geological sciences; geography; German; Hebraic studies; history/French; history-political science; Italian; Jewish studies; journal and mass media; labor studies and employment relations; Latin; Latin American studies, linguistic management; management science and information systems; marine sciences; marketing; mathematics; medical technology; medieval studies; Middle Eastern studies; molecular biology and biochemistry; music; philosophy; physics; political science; Portuguese; psychology; public health; Puerto Rican and Hispanic Caribbean studies; religion; Russian, Central, and East European studies; sociology; Spanish; statistics; statistics-mathematics; theater arts; urban studies; visual arts; women's studies. The following baccalaureate degrees are offered through Cook College: biotechnology; environmental policy, institutions, and behavior; food science; meteorology; nutritional sciences.

Admission: Required entrance courses: 4 years English; 2 years of 1 foreign language; 3 years college preparatory mathematics; 2 year science plus 5 other approved academic units for a minimum of 16 units.

Degree Requirements: 120 credits with a minimum GPA 1.951; 30 of last 42 credits earned in residence.

Fees and Other Expenses: Contact the college for current tuition and fees.

Distinctive Educational Programs: 5-year BA/BS in liberal arts and engineering in cooperation with the College of Engineering; 5-year BA/MBA in cooperation with the Graduate School of Management. Alumnae externship program. Language and Cultural House program. Joint 8-year Bachelor/Medical Degree with UMDNJ - Robert Wood Johnson Medical School.

School of Engineering - New Brunswick

Degree Programs Offered: *Baccalaureate* in bioresource engineering, biomedical engineering, applied science in engineering, ceramic engineering, chemical and biochemical engineering, civil and environmental engineering, electrical and computer engineering, industrial engineering, mechanical and aerospace engineering.

Admission: Required entrance units: 4 years English, 4 years college preparatory mathematics; 2 years science including 1 year chemistry, 1 year physics; plus 6 other approved academic units for a minimum of 16 (computer programming recommended).

Degree Requirements: 125 to 135 credits required for graduation from 4-year program; cumulative GPA of 2.0; 30 of last 42 credits in residence.

Fees and Other Expenses: Contact the school for current tuition/fees.

Distinctive Educational Programs: 5-year accelerated baccalaureate-M.B.A. with Graduate School of Management. Bureau of Engineering Research, supported by the university, industry, state and federal government, provides research opportunities for students and faculty. Continuing professional education. Exchange program between College of Engineering and the City University of London for qualified students majoring in civil, electrical, or mechanical engineering. 5-year (BA/BS degree) program in liberal arts and engineering. 5-year (2 BS degrees) program in bioresource engineering and a degree from Cook College.

Livingston College - New Brunswick

Degree Programs Offered: *Baccalaureate* in accounting; administration of justice; Africana studies; American studies; anthropology; art history; biological sciences; biomathematics; cell biology and neuroscience; chemistry; Chinese; classics; classical humanities; communication; comparative literature; computer science; dance; East Asian languages and area studies; evolutionary anthropology; exercise science and sport studies; economics; English; finance; French; genetics and microbiology; geography; geological sciences; history/French; German; Greek (Ancient); Greek and Latin; Hebraic studies; history; history-political science; Italian; Jewish studies; journalism and mass media; labor studies and employment relations; Latin American studies; linguistics; management; management science and information systems; marine sciences; marketing; mathematics; medical technology; medieval studies; Middle Eastern studies; molecular biology and biochemistry; music; philosophy; physics; political science; Portuguese; psychology; public health; Puerto Rican and Hispanic Caribbean studies; religion; Russian; Russian, Central, and East European studies; social work; sociology; Spanish; statistics; statistics-mathematics; theater arts; urban studies; visual arts; women's studies.

Admission: Required entrance courses: 4 years English; 2 years of 1 foreign language; 3 years college preparatory mathematics; 2 year science plus 5 other approved academic units for a minimum of 16 units.

Degree Requirements: 120 credits with a minimum GPA 2.0; 30 of last 42 credits earned in residence.

Fees and Other Expenses: Contact the college for current tuition and fees.

Distinctive Educational Programs: 5-year BA/BS in cooperation with the Graduate School of Management. Joint 8-year Bachelor/Medical Degree Program with UMDNJ - Robert Wood Johnson Medical School.

Mason Gross School of the Arts - New Brunswick

Degree Programs Offered: *Baccalaureate* in dance; *baccalaureate* and *master's* in visual arts, theater arts, music.

Admission: Required entrance courses: 4 years English; 2 years of 1 foreign language; 3 years college preparatory mathematics; plus 9 other approved academic units; audition/portfolio,interview required.

Degree Requirements: *For baccalaureate:* 120–129 credits (depending on major) for graduation; 2.0 GPA; 2 year-residency (visual arts and music), 3-year residency (theater arts and dance).

Fees and Other Expenses: Contact the school for current tuition and fees.

College of Pharmacy - New Brunswick

Degree Programs Offered: *Pharm. D.*

Degree Requirements: *For baccalaureate degree:* completion of the 6-year curriculum for the doctoral degree; cumulative GPA greater than 2.0.

Fees and Other Expenses: Contact the school for current tuition and fees.

Distinctive Educational Programs: Externships programs; industrial experience for all students. Clerkship program.

Rutgers College - New Brunswick

Degree Programs Offered: *Baccalaureate* in accounting; administration of justice; Africana studies; American studies; anthropology; art history; biological sciences; biomathematics; cell biology and neuroscience; chemistry; Chinese; classics; classical humanities; communication; comparative literature; computer science; dance; East Asian languages and area studies; evolutionary anthropology; exercise science and sport studies; economics; English; finance; French; genetics and microbiology; geography; geological sciences; history/French; German; Greek (Ancient); Greek and Latin; Hebraic studies; history; history-political science; Italian; Jewish studies; journalism and mass media; labor studies and employment relations; Latin American studies; linguistics; management; management science and information systems; marine sciences; marketing; mathematics; medical technology; medieval studies; Middle Eastern studies; molecular biology and biochemistry; music; philosophy; physics; political science; Portuguese; psychology; public health; Puerto Rican and Hispanic Caribbean studies; religion; Russian; Russian, Central, and East European Studies; social work; sociology; Spanish; statistics; statistics-mathematics; theater arts; urban studies; visual arts; women's studies.

Admission: Required entrance courses: 4 years English; 2 years of 1 foreign language; 3 years college preparatory mathematics; plus 5 other approved academic units for a minimum of 16.

Degree Requirements: 119.5 credits with a cumulative GPA of 2.0; 30 of last 42 credits earned in residence.

Fees and Other Expenses: Contact the college for current tuition and fees.

Distinctive Educational Programs: 5-year BA/BS program in liberal arts and engineering with the College of Engineering. 5-year BA/MBA program in cooperation with Graduate School of Management. 5-year BA or BS/M.Ed. with the Graduate School of Education. Joint 8-year Bachelor/Medical Degree program with UMDNJ - Robert Wood Johnson Medical School. Interdepartmental programs and certificate programs are available. Study abroad in France, Italy, Germany, Mexico, Israel.

Rutgers Business School - Undergraduate, New Brunswick

Degree Programs Offered: *Baccalaureate* in accounting, finance, management, management science and information systems, marketing. (Degree awarded jointly by School of Business and Undergraduate Liberal Arts College).

Admission: 19 credits in eligibility courses; 31 credits in courses common to all majors; 18 to 24 additional units in areas of specialization.; grade of C or better in all courses.

Fees and Other Expenses: Contact the school for current tuition and fees.

University College - New Brunswick

Degree Programs Offered: *Baccalaureate* (offered in evening) in accounting; administration of justice; biological sciences; chemistry; communication; computer science; economics; English; finance; French; German; history; history/French; history-political science; journalism and mass media; labor studies and employment relations; management; marketing; mathematics; philosophy; political science; psychology; sociology; Spanish; statistics; statistics-mathematics; (additional offered in daytime) Africana studies; American studies; anthropology; art history; biomathematics; cell biology and neuroscience; Chinese; classics; comparative literature; dance; East Asian languages and area studies; evolutionary anthropology; exercise science and sport studies; food science; genetics and microbiology; geography; geological sciences; Hebraic studies; Italian; Jewish studies; journalism and mass media; Latin; Latin American studies; linguistics; management science and information systems; marine sciences; medical technology; medieval studies; Middle Eastern studies; molecular biology and biochemistry; music; nutritional sciences; physics; Portuguese; public health; Puerto Rican and Hispanic Caribbean studies; religion; Russian; Russian, Central, and East European studies; theater arts; urban studies; visual arts; women's studies.

Admission: Required entrance courses: 4 years English; 2 years of 1 foreign language; 3 years college preparatory mathematics; plus 5 other approved academic units for a minimum of 16.

Degree Requirements: 120 credits, including the college liberal arts and sciences distribution requirements; major program of study; proficiency in English, mathematics, and foreign language must be demonstrated; minimum GPA 2.0; 30 of last 42 credits earned in residence.

Fees and Other Expenses: Contact the college for current tuition and fees.

Distinctive Educational Programs: BA/MBA program. Interdisciplinary major.

The Graduate School - New Brunswick

Degree Programs Offered: *Master's* in agricultural economics, animal sciences, anthropology, art history, biochemistry, biomedical engineering, bioscience engineering; cell and developmental biology, cellular and molecular pharmacology; ceramic science and engineering, chemical and biochemical engineering, chemistry, civil and environmental engineering, classics, comparative literature, computer science, economics, electrical and computer engineering, English, entomology, environmental sciences, food science, French, geography, geological sciences, German, history, Italian, labor studies, linguistics, materials science and engineering, mathematics, mechanical and aerospace engineering, mechanics, microbiology and molecular pharmacology; music, nutritional sciences; oceanography; operations research, pharmaceutical science, philosophy, physics and astronomy, physiology and neurobiology, plant biology, political science, psychology, radiation science, sociology, Spanish, statistics, toxicology, urban planning and policy development; women's studies; *doctorate* in animal sciences, anthropology, art history, biochemistry, biomedical engineering, cell and developmental biology, cellular and molecular phar-

macology; ceramic science and engineering, chemical and biochemical engineering, chemistry, civil and environmental engineering, classics, communication/information/library studies, comparative literature, computer science, economics, ecology and evolution, electrical and computer engineering, English, entomology, environmental sciences, food science, French, geography, geological sciences, German, history, industrial and systems engineering, industrial relations and human resources, Italian, linguistics, mathematics, mechanical and aerospace engineering, mechanics, microbiology and molecular genetics, music, nutritional sciences, oceanography, operations research, pharmaceutical science, philosophy, physics and astronomy, physiology and neurobiology, plant biology, political science, psychology, public health (offered jointly with and administered by UMDNJ-RWJMS), social work, sociology, Spanish, statistics, toxicology, urban planning and policy development.

Fees and Other Expenses: Contact the school for current tuition and fees.

Departments and Teaching Staff: Faculty is drawn from other colleges in the university.

Distinctive Educational Programs: Interdisciplinary Ph.D.s may be arranged between formal doctoral programs. Specialized foci in marine and coastal sciences and in packaging science and engineering may be arranged within the context of relevant degree programs. Specific interdisciplinary programs in educational policy and in linguistics. Certificate awarded in conjunction with degrees in alcohol studies, Asian studies, biotechnology, molecular and cell biology, molecular biophysics. Dual degree programs include MCRP/JD (with the Schools of Law-Camden and Newark), Ph.D./JD in jurisprudence, through the philosophy program (with the School of Law-Newark). Joint programs with the University of Medicine and Dentistry of New Jersey: M.P.H., Dr.P.H. and Ph.D. in public health (with Robert Wood Johnson Medical School) and Ph.D. in biochemistry, biomedical engineering, cell and developmental biology, microbiology, pharmacology, physiology and neurobiology, and toxicology (with the Graduate School of Biomedical Sciences).

Graduate School of Applied and Professional Psychology - New Brunswick

Degree Programs Offered: *Doctor of Psychology* (Psy.D.) in Professional Psychology with options in clinical psychology, school psychology or organizational psychology.

Fees and Other Expenses: Contact the school for current tuition and fees.

Distinctive Educational Programs: The Center for Applied Psychology is the research, service, and training organization of the GSAPP. Its purpose is to increase knowledge, to provide the most advanced psychological services, and to contribute to the educational aims of the school. It provides settings in which faculty can demonstrate the skills for which many of them are internationally renowned, and for students to learn the skills of practice and research in collaboration with and under the supervision of faculty. The Center seeks out projects to provide opportunities for diverse research and community service in which faculty, professional psychologists, and students work together. Some examples include: a counselor training program for AT&T Bell Laboratories; a contract with the NJ Division of Youth and Family Services to provide therapy services to children in foster care; and the evaluation of school communities as distant as Florida. The projects provide intervention at the individual, group, and systems level in service delivery and problem solving.

School of Communication, Information, and Library Studies - New Brunswick

Degree Programs Offered: *Baccalaureate* in communication, journalism and mass media; information technology and informatics; *master's* in library service, communication and information studies.

Fees and Other Expenses: Contact the school of current tuition and fees.

Distinctive Educational Programs: (1) Master's Program in Library and Information Studies (MLS) provides professional education for a wide variety of service and management careers in libraries, information agencies, the information industry, and in business, industry, government, research, and similar environments where information is a vital resource. (2) Master's in Communication and Information Studies (MCIS) integrates emphasis on the interrelationships of communication, information technology, and human behavior in complex, contemporary organizations. (3) Ph.D. Program in Communication, Information and Library Studies focuses on the nature and functions of communication and information processes, systems, institutions, and policies, and their impact on individuals, and on social, organizational, national and international affairs.

Graduate School of Education - New Brunswick

Degree Programs Offered: *Master's, Doctor of Education* in educational theory, policy and administration; learning and teaching; educational psychology. *Specialist in Education* in educational theory, policy and administration; learning and teaching.

Fees and Other Expenses: Contact the school for current tuition and fees.

Distinctive Educational Programs: Sponsored/associated centers which provide research and development opportunities to students as well as community and statewide service include: Center for Policy Research in Education, Center for Education Policy Analysis-New Jersey, and the Center for Mathematics, Science and Computer Education.

School of Social Work - New Brunswick

Degree Programs Offered: *Master's.*

Fees and Other Expenses: Contact the school of current tuition and fees.

Distinctive Educational Programs: M.Div/MSW, joint program with Princeton Theological Seminary, New Brunswick Theological Seminary or Drew University Theological Seminary.

Enrollment: *Total enrollment:* 937. Graduate full-time 35 men / 240 women, part-time 101m / 561w.

School of Management and Labor Relations - New Brunswick

Degree Programs Offered: *Baccalaureate* in labor studies and employment relations. *Master's* in human resource management; labor and employment relations.

Fees and Other Expenses: Contact the school of current tuition and fees.

Edward J. S. Bloustein School of Planning and Policy

Degree Programs Offered: *Baccalaureate* in public health; urban studies; *master's* in city and regional planning; city and regional studies; public affairs and politics; public health; *doctorate* in public health.

Fees and Other Expenses: Contact the school for current tuition and fees.

NEWARK CAMPUS

Newark, New Jersey 07102
Tel: (973) 648-1766

Newark College of Arts and Sciences

Degree Programs Offered: *Baccalaureate* in accounting, African-American and African studies, allied health technologies, American studies, ancient Mediterranean civilizations; anthropology, art, biology, botany, chemistry, clinical laboratory science, computer science, criminal justice, economics, English, environmental sciences, finance, French, geology, geoscience engineering; German, history, information systems, interdisciplinary, Italian, journalism, management, marketing, mathematics, mathematics-applied, medical technology, music, philosophy, physics, physics-applied, political science, psychology, Puerto Rican studies, science/technology/society, social work, sociology, Spanish, teacher certification, theater arts and speech, visual arts; women's studies, zoology.

Admission: Required entrance courses: 4 years English; 2 years of 1 foreign language; 3 years college preparatory mathematics; 2 years science; plus 5 other approved academic units.

Degree Requirements: 124 credits with a minimum GPA 2.0; 30 of last 42 credits earned in residence.

Fees and Other Expenses: Contact the college for current tuition and fees.

Distinctive Educational Programs: 5-year baccalaureate-MBA with Graduate School of Management. Cooperative baccalaureate program with College of Engineering (New Brunswick campus). Cooperative baccalaureate in medical technology with affiliated hospitals. Interdisciplinary programs in archaeology, international affairs, legal studies, women's studies.

College of Nursing - Newark

Degree Programs Offered: *Baccalaureate.*

Admission: Required entrance courses: 4 years English; 2 years 1 foreign language; 3 years college preparatory mathematics; 2 years science (1 each of biology and chemistry); plus 7 other approved academic units.

Degree Requirements: 125 credits with a minimum GPA 2.0; 30 of last 42 credits earned in residence; completion of required senior-level and 705 courses at the College of Nursing. Prior to graduation, all seniors must take the NLN comprehensive diagnostic exam.

Fees and Other Expenses: Contact the college for current tuition and fees.

University College - Newark

Degree Programs Offered: *Baccalaureate* in accounting, computer science, criminal justice, economics, English, finance, history, information systems, management, marketing, mathematics, mathematics-applied, philosophy, political science, psychology, social work, sociology.

Admission: Required entrance courses: 4 years English; 2 years of 1 foreign language; 3 years college preparatory mathematics; 2 years science; plus 5 other approved academic units.

Degree Requirements: 124 credits with a minimum GPA 2.0; 30 of last 42 credits earned in residence.

Fees and Other Expenses: Contact the college for current tuition and fees.

Distinctive Educational Programs: Joint baccalaureate-master's programs with the School of Criminal Justice and Graduate School of Management.

The Graduate School - Newark

Degree Programs Offered: *Master's* in accounting, biology, chemistry, economics, English, environmental geology, environmental science, finance, history, international studies, jazz history and research, liberal studies, management, marketing, nursing, political science, physics-applied, psychology, public administration, public health; *doctorate* in behavioral and neural sciences, biology, chemistry, criminal justice, environmental science, management, mathematical sciences, nursing, physics-applied, psychology, public administration.

Fees and Other Expenses: Contact the college for current tuition and fees.

Departments and Teaching Staff: Faculty is drawn from other colleges in the university.

Distinctive Educational Programs: Cooperative doctoral programs in criminal justice with School of Criminal Justice; in management with Graduate School of Management. Cross-registration for graduate courses at the University of Medicine and Dentistry of New Jersey and the New Jersey Institute of Technology.

Rutgers Business School - Newark

Degree Programs Offered: *Baccalaureate* in accounting finance, management and global business; marketing; concentration in management science and information systems; *master's* in accountancy (governmental accounting), business administration-management, business administration-professional accounting.

Fees and Other Expenses: Contact the college for current tuition and fees.

Distinctive Educational Programs: Joint degree programs with Law School (MBA/JD). Ph.D. in Management offered through the Graduate School-Newark. Joint BA/MBA programs with Douglass, Newark College of Arts and Sciences, University College (New Brunswick and Newark). Internships. Continuing Education programs for business executive through University Center for Management Development.

School of Criminal Justice - Newark

Degree Programs Offered: *Master's.*

Fees and Other Expenses: Contact the college for current tuition and fees.

School of Law - Newark

Degree Programs Offered: *First-professional.*

Admission: Baccalaureate from accredited college or university, LSAT.

Degree Requirements: 84 credit hours, 6 semesters in residence.

Fees and Other Expenses: Contact the college for current tuition and fees.

Distinctive Educational Programs: Clinical studies program provides upper division students with opportunity for supervised work on actual cases. Joint J.D.-master's in city and regional planning with Graduate School-New Brunswick. Joint J.D.-master's in criminal justice with School of Criminal Justice. Joint 5-year JD/Ph.D. in philosophy with the Graduate School-New Brunswick. Clinic in Constitutional Litigation; Urban Legal Clinic; Environmental Law Clinic; Women's Rights Litigation Clinic; Animal Rights Clinic. Publications include *Law Review; Women's Rights Law Reporter; Computer and Technology Law Journal.*

CAMDEN CAMPUS

406 Penn Street
Camden, New Jersey 08102
Tel: (856) 757-1766

Camden College of Arts and Sciences

Degree Programs Offered: *Baccalaureate* in accounting, African-American studies, art, biology, biomedical technology, chemistry, computer science, criminal justice, economics, English, finance, French, general science, German, history, management, marketing, mathematics, music, nursing, philosophy, physics, political science, psychology, social work, sociology, Spanish, teacher certification, theater arts, urban studies.

Admission: Required entrance courses: 4 years English; 2 years of 1 foreign language; 3 years college preparatory mathematics; 2 years science; plus 5 other approved academic units.

Degree Requirements: 120 credits with a minimum GPA 2.0; 30 of last 42 credits earned in residence.

Fees and Other Expenses: Contact the college for current tuition and fees.

Distinctive Educational Programs: Cooperative baccalaureate program in engineering with College of Engineering (New Brunswick Campus). Interdisciplinary programs in African-American studies, general science. Cooperative baccalaureate in medical technology with approved hospitals.

University College - Camden

Degree Programs Offered: *Baccalaureate* in accounting, computer science (information systems option only), English, finance, history, liberal studies, management, marketing, physics, political science, psychology.

Admission: Required entrance courses: 4 years English; 2 years of 1 foreign language; 3 years college preparatory mathematics; 2 years science; plus 5 other approved academic units for a minimum of 16.

Degree Requirements: 120 credits with a minimum GPA 2.0; 30 of last 42 credits earned in residence.

Fees and Other Expenses: Contact the college for current tuition and fees.

Departments and Teaching Staff: Faculty of Arts and Sciences-Camden serves University College-Camden.

The Graduate School - Camden

Degree Programs Offered: *Master's* in biology, chemistry, criminal justice, English, history, liberal studies, mathematical sciences, public policy and administration, physical therapy; *Master of Social Work* through the School of Social Work.

Fees and Other Expenses: Contact the college for current tuition and fees.

Departments and Teaching Staff: Faculty is drawn from other colleges in the university.

School of Law - Camden

Degree Programs Offered: *First-professional.*

Admission: Baccalaureate from accredited college or university, LSAT, LSDAS.

Degree Requirements: 84 credit hours, 2.0 GPA, 6 semesters in residence.

Fees and Other Expenses: Contact the college for current tuition and fees.

Distinctive Educational Programs: Clinical Studies program provides third year students with opportunity for supervised work on actual cases. Joint J.D.-master's in city and regional planning with Graduate School-New Brunswick. Joint J.D.-master's in political science in conjunction with the Eagleton Institute of Politics. Joint J.D.-MBA in conjunction with the Graduate School of Management.

School of Business - Camden

Degree Programs Offered: *Baccalaureate* in accounting, finance, management, marketing; *master's* in accounting, business administration.

Admission: Students applying for admission to the undergraduate School of Business must complete 45 college credits and have a minimum GPA of 2.5.

Fees and Other Expenses: Contact the college for current tuition and fees.

Distinctive Educational Programs: Business Forum has speakers from outside sources to help prepare students for careers.

Saint Peter's College

2641 Kennedy Boulevard
Jersey City, New Jersey 07306-5997
Tel: (201) 915-9000   **E-mail:** admissions@spc.edu
Fax: (201) 451-0036   **Internet:** www.spc.edu

Institution Description: Saint Peter's College is a private, nonprofit institution conducted by the Society of Jesus, Roman Catholic Church. The school operates a branch campus at Englewood Cliffs. *Enrollment:* 3,152. *Degrees awarded:* Associate, baccalaureate, master's.

Accreditation: *Regional:* MSA. *Professional:* nursing, nursing education

History: Established, chartered, and incorporated 1872; offered first instruction at postsecondary level 1878; awarded first degree (baccalaureate) 1889; closed 1918 as a result of World War I; reopened 1930; became coeducational 1966; initiated master's program in education 1980. *See* James O'Donnell, *The Young Estate* (Jersey City, N.J.: Saint Peter's College, 1972); Richard J. Cronin, *The Jesuits and the Beginnings of Saint Peter's College,* (S.J. Peacock Publications, Jersey City, N.J., 1983) *The Closing and Reopening of SPC: 1918–1938* (Jersey City, NJ: St. Peter's College, 1989) for further information.

Institutional Structure: *Governing board:* Board of Trustees. Extrainstitutional representation: 33 trustees; institutional representation: president of the college (ex officio). All voting. *Composition of institution:* Administrators 27 men / 32 women. Academic affairs headed by academic vice president. Management/business/finances directed by vice president for finance and administrative services. Full-time instructional faculty 78 men / 40 women. Academic governance bodies: Faculty Senate holds 2 regular meetings annually and calls others as needed; Faculty Senate Committee of the Faculty Senate meets biweekly during the academic year.

Calendar: Semesters. Academic year Aug. to May. Freshmen admitted Aug., Jan., June. Degrees conferred May, Aug. Formal commencement May. Summer session of 3 terms from late May to mid-Aug.

Characteristics of Freshmen: 3,127 applicants (1,401 men, 1,726 women). 83.2% of applicants admitted. 25.8% of admitted students enrolled full-time.

98% (500 students) submitted SAT scores. *25th percentile*: SAT I Verbal 420, SAT I Math 440. *75th percentile*: SAT I Verbal 520, SAT I Math 530.

43% of entering freshmen expected to graduate within 5 years. 86.6% of freshmen from New Jersey. Freshmen from 16 states.

Admission: Rolling admissions plan. For fall acceptance, apply as early as Oct. 1 of previous year. Apply early for residence accommodations. Apply by Nov. 1 for early decision; need not limit application to Saint Peter's. Early acceptance available. *Requirements:* Either graduation from accredited secondary school with 16 units which must include 4 English, 2 foreign language (preferably 1 language), 2 history, 2 college preparatory mathematics, 6 academic electives; or GED. Recommend 1 additional college preparatory mathematics for applicants to mathematics and science programs. *Entrance tests:* College Board SAT. *For transfer students:* 2.5 minimum GPA; from 4-year accredited institution 99 hours maximum transfer credit; from 2-year accredited institution 66 hours; correspondence/extension students 96 hours.

College credit and advanced placement for postsecondary-level work completed in secondary school and for extrainstitutional learning on basis of ACE 2006 *Guide to the Evaluation of Educational Experiences in the Armed Services.* Faculty evaluation and personal interview required; portfolio assessment.

Tutoring available. Developmental courses offered in summer session and regular academic year; credit given for some courses.

Degree Requirements: *For all associate degrees:* 69 credit hours. *For all baccalaureate degrees:* 129 credit hours. *For all undergraduate degrees:* 2.0 GPA; last 30 hours and final academic year in residence; completion of core curriculum.

Fulfillment of some degree requirements and exemption from some beginning courses possible by passing departmental examinations, College Board CLEP, AP. *Grading system:* 4.0–0.0; pass-fail; withdraw (carries time limit; pass, fail, or no grade designation appended to all withdrawals); incomplete (carries time limit).

Distinctive Educational Programs: *For undergraduates:* Work-experience programs including cooperative education and internships. Off-campus centers at Newark Airport and at various area hospitals, all less than 30 miles from main institution. Distance learning facilities with satellite links and television studio. Interdepartmental/interdisciplinary programs and majors in Afro-American studies, biological chemistry, business law, health care management, natural science, urban studies. Bachelor of science in nursing for students possessing a diploma or associated degree as a registered nurse. Honors program requiring interdisciplinary seminars. Preprofessional programs in medicine, dentistry. Individualized majors. Study abroad at various locations may be individually arranged; the College is a charter member of the International Student Exchange Program (ISEP) giving students the opportunity to study at over 40 foreign universities; also Intercultural Relations Program in Hawaii; Italian Cultural Travel Program. Baccalaureate of arts *in curso classico* offered in some majors. Distance learning facilities with satellite links and TV studio; Management Information Services runs Institute for the Advancement of Urban Education in connection with area elementary and secondary schools. *For graduate students:* Interdisciplinary program in education/computer science-data processing. Master's in teaching. *Available to all students:* Weekend and evening classes. Special facilities for using telecommunications in the classroom. Tutorials. *Other distinctive programs:* Degree-granting evening division on a trimester schedule. Continuing education courses. Secondary school scholars' program for sophomores and juniors during the summer, for seniors during the academic year.

ROTC: Army available through Seton Hall University; Air Force through New Jersey Institute of Technology.

Degrees Conferred: 9 *associate;* 401 *baccalaureate*; 279 *master's.* Bachelor's degrees awarded in top five disciplines: business, management, marketing, and related support services 157; computer and information sciences 46; education 41; social sciences and history 33; health professions and related clinical sciences 25.

Fees and Other Expenses: *Full-time tuition per academic year 2004–05:* undergraduate $19,750. Contact the college for graduate tuition/fees. *Books and supplies:* $700. *Room and board per academic year:* $8,430.

Financial Aid: Aid from institutionally generated funds is provided on the basis of academic merit, financial need, athletic ability, other criteria. Institution has a Program Participation Agreement with the U.S. Department of Education for eligible students to receive Pell Grants and, depending upon the agreement, other federal aid.

Financial aid to full-time, first-time undergraduate students: 48% received federal grants averaging $3,804; 50% state/local grants averaging $6,064; 98% institutional grants averaging $9,284; 60% received loans averaging $4,575.

Departments and Teaching Staff: Accounting *professors* 1, *associate professors* 7, *assistant professors* 0, *instructors* 0, *part-time teachers* 13; biology 3, 1, 3, 0, 11; chemistry 3, 1, 0, 0, 1; computer science 1, 4, 0, 1, 11; economics 2, 0, 2, 0, 13; education 2, 1, 2, 0, 35; English 7, 3, 2, 5, 36; fine arts 2, 0, 1, 0, 9; history 4, 1, 2, 0, 7; management/marketing 0, 5, 2, 1, 20; mathematics 6, 2, 1, 2, 15; modern/classical languages 1, 2, 1, 0, 10; nursing 1, 1, 1, 1, 8; physics 2, 0, 0, 0, 0; political science 0, 2, 1, 1, 4; psychology 2, 0, 3, 0, 11; sociology 3, 1, 0, 0, 5; theology 3, 1, 2, 0, 8; urban studies 0, 1, 0, 0, 7.

Total instructional faculty: 353. Student-to-faculty ratio: 20:1. Degrees held by full-time faculty: doctorate 78%, master's 22%. 78% hold terminal degrees.

Enrollment: Total enrollment 3,152. Undergraduate 2,374 (men 46.7%, women 54.3%).

Characteristics of Student Body: *Ethnic/racial makeup:* number of Black non-Hispanic: 19.5%; American Indian or Alaska Native: .3%; Asian or Pacific Islander: 6.8%; Hispanic: 23.8%; White non-Hispanic: 28.7%; unknown: 18.7%.

International Students: 76 nonresident aliens enrolled fall 2004. Programs available for students whose native language is not English: social, cultural, financial. English as a Second Language Program.

Student Life: Residence hall and apartment-style residences available. *Intercollegiate athletics:* men's and women's teams: baseball, soccer, swimming, track/cross-country, tennis; men's teams: baseball, football, golf; women's teams: softball, volleyball. *Special regulations:* Cars permitted for $20 fee per semester. *Special services:* Center for the Advancement of Language and Learning (CALL), computer laboratories. *Student publications, radio: Pauw Wow,* a newspaper; *Pavan,* an annual literary magazine; *Peacock Pie,* a yearbook. Radio station WSPC broadcasts 35 hours per week. *Surrounding community:* Jersey City population 230,000. New York City, 3 miles from campus, is nearest metropolitan area. Served by mass transit bus and commuter train systems; airport 6 miles from campus; passenger rail service 1 mile from campus.

Publications: Sources of information about the college include *Saint Peter's College Magazine,* distributed to the business community and throughout the surrounding area, the *President's Report,* and other periodic newsletters are also published.

Library Collections: 285,000 volumes. 70,000 microforms; 3,800 audiovisual materials; 1,800 current periodical subscriptions. Online catalog. Students have access to online information retrieval services.

Most important holdings include English and American literature; classics; and Latin American literature.

Chief Executive Officer: Rev. James N. Loughran. S.J., President.

Undergraduates address admission inquiries to Guiseppe Giglio, Director of Admissions; graduate inquiries to Graduate Admissions Recruiter.

Seton Hall University

400 South Orange Avenue
South Orange, New Jersey 07079-2697
Tel: (973) 761-9000   **E-mail:** thehall@shu.edu
Fax: (973) 761-9452   **Internet:** www.shu.edu

Institution Description: Seton Hall University is a private institution affiliated with the Archdiocese of Newark, Roman Catholic Church. *Enrollment:* 9,824. *Degrees awarded:* Baccalaureate, first-professional (law), master's, doctorate. Specialist certificates also given. Member of the Consortium of East Jersey.

Accreditation: *Regional:* MSA. *Professional:* business, chemistry, law, nursing, rehabilitation counseling, social work, teacher education

History: Established as Seton Hall College and offered first instruction at postsecondary level 1856; chartered and incorporated 1861; awarded first degree (baccalaureate) 1862; adopted present name 1950.

Institutional Structure: *Governing board:* Board of Regents-Board of Trustees. Extrainstitutional representation: 7 trustees (diocesan representatives), 25 regents; institutional representation: chancellor of the university. All voting. *Composition of institution:* Academic affairs headed by provost. Management/ business/finances directed by executive vice chancellor. Full-time instructional faculty 351. Academic governance body, Faculty Governance Committee, in place. *Faculty representation:* Faculty served by collective bargaining agent, Faculty Council.

Calendar: Semesters. Academic year Sept. to May. Freshmen admitted Sept., Jan.. Degrees conferred May, Aug., Dec. Formal commencement May. Summer session of 2 terms from June to Aug.

Characteristics of Freshmen: 5,151 applicants (2,197 men, 2,954 women). 86.8% of applicants admitted. 27.7% of admitted students enrolled full-time.

99% (1,234 students) submitted SAT scores; 9% (108 students) submitted ACT scores. *25th percentile:* SAT I Verbal 490, SAT I Math 590; ACT Composite 21, ACT English 21, ACT Math 19. *75th percentile:* SAT I Verbal 600, SAT I Math 600; ACT Composite ACT 28, English 29, ACT Math 27.

60% of entering freshmen expected to graduate within 5 years. 85% of freshmen from New Jersey.

Admission: Rolling admissions plan. For fall acceptance, apply as early as Sept. 1 of previous year, but not later than March 1 of year of enrollment. *Requirements:* Either graduation from accredited secondary school with 16 units which normally include 4 English, 2 in a foreign language, 3 mathematics, 2 social studies, 1 laboratory science; or GED. Additional requirements for some programs. Minimum GPA 2.5; 950 or better on combined SAT score. *Entrance tests:* College Board SAT preferred; ACT composite accepted. For foreign students TOEFL. *For transfer students:* 2.5 minimum GPA; from 4-year accredited institution, 30 credits.

College credit and advanced placement for postsecondary-level work completed in secondary school. For extrainstitutional learning college credit on basis of ACE *2006 Guide to the Evaluation of Educational Experiences in the Armed Services;* advanced placement on basis of faculty assessment.

Tutoring available.

Degree Requirements: Approximately 128 credit hours; 2.0 GPA; last 30 credits in residence; core requirements. Fulfillment of some degree requirements and exemption from some beginning courses possible by passing departmental examinations (nursing and business only), College Board CLEP, AP. *Grading system:* A–F; pass-fail; withdraw (carries time limit).

Distinctive Educational Programs: *For undergraduates:* Cooperative baccalaureate in engineering with New Jersey Institute of Technology. Semester in Washington. Interdisciplinary majors. Honors programs. Study abroad in Japan, China, Poland, South America. *Available to all students:* Cooperative education programs, internships. Flexible schedules, including weekend and evening classes. Cross-registration through consortium. *Other distinctive programs:* Continuing education.

ROTC: Army. Air Force offered in cooperation with New Jersey Institute of Technology.

Degrees Conferred: 972 *baccalaureate*; 944 *master's*; 53 *doctorate*; 337 *first-professional.* Bachelor's degrees awarded in top five disciplines: business, management, marketing, and related support services 205; health professions and related clinical sciences 130; communication, journalism, and related programs 119; social sciences and history 83; education 83.

Fees and Other Expenses: *Full-time tuition per academic year 2004–05:* $22,490. *Books and supplies:* $1,200. *Room and board per academic year:* $8,806. Contact the university for current tuition for graduate and first-professional study.

Financial Aid: Aid from institutionally generated funds is provided on the basis of academic merit, financial need, athletic ability. Institution has a Program Participation Agreement with the U.S. Department of Education for eligible students to receive Pell Grants and, depending upon the agreement, other federal aid.

Financial aid to full-time, first-time undergraduate students: 27% received federal grants averaging $3,933; 26% state/local grants averaging $5,285; 76% institutional grants averaging $11,372; 60% received loans averaging $3,269.

Departments and Teaching Staff: Arts and Sciences *professors* 42, *associate professors* 61, *assistant professors* 58, *instructors* 17, *part-time faculty* 209; Business 16, 20, 15, 3, 35; Education 10, 13, 8, 1, 47; Nursing 1, 10, 6, 9, 22; Theology 2, 5, 3, 0, 26.

Total instructional faculty: 781. Student-to-faculty ratio: 18:1. Degrees held by full-time faculty: 89% hold terminal degrees.

Enrollment: *Total enrollment:* 9,824. Undergraduate 5,414 (men 46.9%, women 53.1%).

Characteristics of Student Body: *Ethnic/racial makeup (undergraduate):* number of Black non-Hispanic: 11.6%; American Indian or Alaska Native: .1%;

Asian or Pacific Islander: 7.4%; Hispanic: 9.2%; White non-Hispanic: 50.8%; unknown: 9.2%. *Age distribution:* 17–21: 40%; 22–24: 17%; 25–29: 17%; 30–34: 9%; 35–39: 6%; 40–49: 8%; 50–59: 2%.

International Students: 177 nonresident aliens enrolled fall 2004. Students from Europe, Asia, Latin America, Africa, Canada, New Zealand. No programs available to aid students whose native language is not English. No financial aid specifically designated for international students.

Student Life: On-campus residence halls house 50% of undergraduate student body. Residence halls for men only constitute 23% of such space, for women only 20%, for both sexes 56%. 1% of student body live on campus in other university-controlled accommodations. *Intercollegiate athletics:* men only: baseball, basketball, football, golf, soccer, swimming, tennis, track, wrestling; women only: basketball, softball, swimming, tennis, track, volleyball. *Special regulations:* Cars with decals permitted. *Special services:* Learning Resources Center, medical services, Freshman Studies Program. *Student publications, radio: The Galleon,* a yearbook; *Setonian,* a weekly newspaper. Radio station WSOU-FM broadcasts 24 hours a day. *Surrounding community:* South Orange population 17,000. Newark, less than 1 mile from campus, is nearest metropolitan area. Served by mass transit bus system; airport 6 miles from campus; passenger rail service less than 1 mile from campus.

Publications: *Journal of Business; University Magazine.*

Library Collections: 523,000 volumes. 777,000 microforms; 2,250 audiovisual titles; 1,875 current periodical subscriptions. Online catalog. Students have access to online information retrieval services and the Internet.

Most important holdings include Asian Studies Collection (4,000 volumes on Chinese, Japanese, and Korean history, political science, and literature); materials on the American Civil War; rare books.

Buildings and Grounds: Campus area 58 acres.

Chief Executive Officer: Monsignor Robert Sheeran, S.T.D., President.

Address admission inquiries to Dr. Daryl Jones, Director of Recruitment.

Seton Hall University School of Law

Degree Programs Offered: *First-professional.*

Admission: Baccalaureate from accredited college or university, LSAT.

Degree Requirements: 84 credit hours.

Fees and Other Expenses: Contact the school for current tuition.

Departments and Teaching Staff: *Total instructional faculty:* 60.

Stevens Institute of Technology

Castle Point on the Hudson
Hoboken, New Jersey 07030

Tel: (800) 458-5523   **E-mail:** admissions@stevens-tech.edu
Fax: (201) 216-8348   **Internet:** www.stevens-tech.edu

Institution Description: Stevens Institute of Technology is a private, independent, nonprofit institution. *Enrollment:* 4,647. *Degrees awarded:* Baccalaureate, master's, doctorate.

Accreditation: *Regional:* MSA. *Professional:* computer science, engineering

History: Established as a men's college, incorporated, and offered first instruction at postsecondary level 1870; awarded first degree (baccalaureate) 1873; added master's program 1939, doctoral program 1951; became coeducational 1971.

Institutional Structure: *Governing board:* The Trustees of the Stevens Institute of Technology comprised of 42 voting trustees including 36 charter trustees, 5 alumni trustees, and the president. *Composition of institution:* Administrators 42 men / 34 women. Academic affairs headed by chair of dean's council. Management/business/finances directed by treasurer. Full-time instructional faculty 133. Academic governance body, The Voting Faculty of the Stevens Institute of Technology, meets an average of 5 times per year.

Calendar: Semesters (trimesters for some of the Graduate School programs). Academic year late Aug. to mid-May. Freshmen enrolled Aug. Degrees conferred and formal commencement May. Summer session from May to late July.

Characteristics of Freshmen: 47% of applicants accepted. 41% of accepted applicants enrolled. 93% of applicants submitted SAT scores; 10% ACT scores. *25th percentile:* SAT I Verbal 560, SAT I Math 630; ACT Composite 25. *75th percentile:* SAT I Verbal 670, SAT I Math 720; ACT Composite 30.

Admission: Rolling admissions plan. For fall acceptance, apply as early as Sept. of previous year, but not later than Feb. 15 of year of enrollment. Apply by Nov. 15 for early decision; must limit application to Stevens. *Requirements:* Either graduation from accredited secondary school with 16 units which must include 4 English, 4 college preparatory mathematics (algebra, geometry, pre-calculus/calculus), 3 science (biology, chemistry, physics); or GED. 2 units foreign language recommended. *Entrance tests:* College Board SAT or ACT; 3 SAT

II tests recommended. Personal interview required for all students within a radius of 250 miles. For foreign students TOEFL. *For transfer students:* 3.0 minimum GPA; 76 semester hours maximum transfer credit.

College credit and advanced placement for postsecondary-level work completed in secondary school possible.

Degree Requirements: 151 semester hours; 2.0 GPA; 4 terms in residence; 3 years physical education; distribution requirements. Fulfillment of some degree requirements and exemption from some beginning courses possible by passing departmental examinations, College Board APP. *Grading system:* A–F; withdraw; incomplete (carries time limit).

Distinctive Educational Programs: *For undergraduates:* Scholars Program; Cooperative Education (5-year program); Pre-professional: pre-dental, pre-medicine, pre-law; accelerated (3-year) programs. Institutionally sponsored study abroad in Scotland in cooperation with University of Dundee and University of Sydney, Australia.

ROTC: Air Force offered in cooperation with New Jersey Institute of Technology; Army in cooperation with Seton Hall University.

Degrees Conferred: 373 *baccalaureate* (B); 76 *master's* (M); 27 *doctorate* (D): biological/life sciences 15 (B), 2 (D); business/marketing 24 (B), 460 (M); computer and information sciences 57 (B), 145 (M); engineering and engineering technologies 237 (B), 161 (M), 13 (D); liberal arts/general studies 10 (B); mathematics 4 (B); physical sciences 6 (B), 10 (M), 8 (D).

Fees and Other Expenses: *Full-time tuition per academic year 2004–05:* undergraduate $27,300 (first-year $28,800). graduate programs vary. *Required fees:* $1,200. *Room and board per academic year:* $8,930.

Financial Aid: Aid from institutionally generated funds is provided on the basis of academic merit, financial need. Institution has a Program Participation Agreement with the U.S. Department of Education for eligible students to receive Pell Grants and, depending upon the agreement, other federal aid.

Financial aid to full-time, first-time undergraduate students: need-based scholarships/grants totaling $10,850,000, self-help $5,200,000; non-need-based scholarships/grants totaling $10,110,000, self-help $1,600,000, parent loans $2,800,000, tuition waivers $450,000.

Departments and Teaching Staff: *Total instructional faculty:* 328 (full-time 179, part-time 149; women 46, men 282). Total faculty with doctorate, first-professional, or other terminal degree: 267. Student-to-faculty ratio: 9:1. Degrees held by full-time faculty: doctorate 85%, master's 100%.

Enrollment: Total enrollment 4,647. Undergraduate full-time 1,318 men / 408 women, part-time 4w; graduate full-time 534m / 174w, part-time 1,645m / 551w.

Characteristics of Student Body: *Ethnic/racial makeup (undergraduate):* number of Black non-Hispanic: 69; American Indian or Alaska Native: 2; Asian or Pacific Islander: 268; Hispanic: 162; White non-Hispanic: 922; unknown: 184.

International Students: 123 nonresident aliens enrolled fall 2004. Programs available to aid students whose native language is not English: social, cultural. English as a Second Language Program. No financial aid specifically designated for international students.

Student Life: On-campus residence halls house 80% of student body. Residence halls for men constitute 80% of such space, for women 20%. 30% of men and women join and live fraternity/sorority houses. and 15% live in fraternities. 90% of married students request institutional housing and are so housed. 75% of students live on campus. *Intercollegiate athletics:* men: baseball, basketball, cross-country, fencing, lacrosse, soccer, swimming, tennis, track, volleyball, wrestling; women: basketball, cross-country, equestrian, fencing, field hockey, soccer, swimming, tennis, track volleyball. *Special regulations:* Cars permitted for all but freshmen. *Special services:* Medical services. *Student publications, radio: Link,* a yearbook; *The Suite,* a weekly newspaper, *The Resume Booklet; Observations.* Radio station WCPR broadcasts 40 hours per week; WEXP-TV broadcasts daily. *Surrounding community:* Hoboken population 75,000. New York (NY), 5 miles from campus, is nearest metropolitan area. Served by mass transit bus and train system; airport 10 miles from campus; passenger rail service 1 mile from campus.

Library Collections: 115,234 volumes. Online catalog. Current serial subscriptions: paper 134; microfilm 11,062; via electronic access 20,000. CD-ROMs 2,726. Students have access to online information retrieval services and the Internet. Total 2004-05 budget for books and materials: $97,460 plus $201000 for electronic periodicals.

Most important holdings include The John Lieb Leonardo da Vinci Collection (1,500 volumes, including facsimiles of da Vinci's *Codex Leicester* and other notebooks, prints, and many rare books and first editions dating to 1504); The Frederick Winslow Taylor Collection (the only existing collection of materials on the "father of scientific management," including his private papers totaling 3,000 items and 1,000 volumes with first editions of all of his books); The Colonel John Stevens Family Papers (microfilm copies include those of Edwin Augustus Stevens who founded the Institute, also extensive reference materials on the family, including articles, books, photographs, slides, and genealogy).

Library also has approximately 100 original drawings of U.S.S. Monitor by draftsman Charles MacCord.

Buildings and Grounds: Campus area 55 acres. *New buildings:* Lawrence T. Babbio Center for Technology Management.

Chief Executive Officer: Harold J. Raveche, President.

Address admission inquiries to Daniel Gallagher, Director of Admissions.

Thomas Edison State College

101 West State Street
Trenton, New Jersey 08608-1176

Tel: (609) 984-1100   **E-mail:** admissions@tesc.edu
Fax: (609) 292-9000   **Internet:** www.tesc.edu

Institution Description: Thomas Edison State College is a state institution that offers external degree programs. *Enrollment:* 11,000. *Degrees awarded:* Associate, baccalaureate, master's.

Academic offerings subject to approval by statewide coordinating bodies. Budget subject to approval by Board of Trustees.

Accreditation: *Regional:* MSA. *Professional:* nursing

History: Established as Thomas Edison College 1972; chartered and awarded first degree (associate) 1973; adopted present name 1990.

Institutional Structure: *Governing board:* Thomas Edison State College Board of Trustees. Extrainstitutional representation: 12 trustees, 2 nonvoting, 1 ex officio; institutional representation: president of the college, ex officio, nonvoting. *Composition of institution:* Administrators 31 men / 48 women. Academic affairs headed by vice president of academic affairs. Management/business/finances directed by vice president for administration and finance. External Affairs headed by vice president of public affairs. Academic governance body, Academic Council, meets an average of 4 times per year.

Calendar: Students may apply and enroll at any time during the year. Degrees conferred Mar., Jun., Sept., Dec. Formal commencement Oct.

Admission: Rolling admissions plan. *Requirements:* High school diploma or equivalent; 21 years old. *Entrance tests:* None required. *For transfer students:* From 4-year accredited institution no limit to transfer credit; from 2-year accredited institution 80 hours maximum transfer credit; correspondence/extension students no maximum transfer credit from 4-year institutions.

College credit for postsecondary level-work completed in secondary school, for USAFI/DANTES, and for extrainstitutional learning (life experience) on basis of ACE *2006 Guide to the Evaluation of Educational Experiences in the Armed Services*; portfolio assessment; institutionally approved educational programs, College Credit Recommendation Service, recommendations for CLEP, ACT-PEP, AP and other testing programs.

Degree Requirements: *For all associate degrees:* 60 credit hours. *For all baccalaureate degrees:* 120 credit hours. *For all undergraduate degrees:* 2.0 GPA; liberal arts distribution requirements; demonstrated proficiency in writing.

Fulfillment of some (or all) degree requirements possible by passing institutional examinations, College Board CLEP, AP, other standardized tests.

Distinctive Educational Programs: Most credits earned through independent study, evaluation of learning from work experiences and other extrainstitutional educational activities, and courses at other institutions. Interdisciplinary programs in humanities, human services, natural sciences, social sciences, applied science and technology. Individual majors. *Other distinctive programs:* Bachelor of Science in Nursing, access available world-wide through computer on College's CALL Network. Distance and Independent Adult Learning (DIAL) offers three course delivery modes: guided study, online courses, and e-Pack.

Degrees Conferred: 158 *associate;* 1,540 *baccalaureate:* biological/life sciences 3; business/marketing 135; communications/communication technologies 18; computer and information sciences 34; engineering and engineering technologies 263; English 14; foreign languages and literature 3; health professions and related sciences 66; home economics and vocational home economics 2; interdisciplinary studies 1; law/legal studies 2; liberal arts/general studies 552; mathematics 5; parks and recreation 1; philosophy/religion/theology 3; physical sciences 65; protective services/public administration 37; psychology 97; social sciences and history 122; trade and industry 95; visual and performing arts 2. 48 *master's:* business/marketing 41; interdisciplinary studies 7.

Fees and Other Expenses: *Tuition 2004–05:* Students can choose either the Comprehensive Plan ($3,490 per year for state residents and military personnel, $5,015 for out-of-state) for unlimited tests, portfolios, courses OR the Per Service Plan ($1,050 640 per year for state residents and military personnel, $1,880 out-of-state) for annual enrollment and technology services fee ($85); tests, portfolios, courses, and other fees at additional cost.

Financial Aid: Aid from institutionally generated funds is provided on the basis of financial need. Institution has a Program Participation Agreement with

the U.S. Department of Education for eligible students to receive Pell Grants and, depending upon the agreement, other federal aid.

Financial aid to full-time, first-time undergraduate students: need-based scholarships/grants totaling $1,333,080, self-help $4,432,218.

Departments and Teaching Staff: The college contracts with subject master experts to act as monitors to the academic units of the college. There were 318 subject matter experts during 2004–05.

Enrollment: Total enrollment 11,000. All part-time: undergraduate 5,912 men / 4,838 women; graduate 121m / 129w.

Characteristics of Student Body: *Ethnic/racial makeup:* number of Black non-Hispanic: 1,205; American Indian or Alaska Native: 112; Asian or Pacific Islander: 214; Hispanic: 522; White non-Hispanic: 7,219; unknown: 1,229. *Age distribution:* number under 18: 4; 18–19: 196; 20–21: 467; 22–24: 1,011; 25–29: 1,716; 30–34: 1,756; 35–39: 1,714; 40–49: 2,621; 50–64: 965; 65 and over: 28.

International Students: 245 nonresident aliens enrolled fall 2004. No programs available to students whose native language is not English. No financial aid specifically designated for international students.

Student Life: No on-campus housing. *Surrounding community:* Trenton population 90,000. Served by mass transit bus system; airport 9 miles from campus; passenger rail service 3 miles from campus.

Publications: *Prospectus* for interested adults.

Library Collections: The New Jersey State Library became an affiliate of Thomas Edison State College in July 1996.

Chief Executive Officer: Dr. George A. Pruitt, President.

Address admission inquiries to Renee San Giacomo, Director of Admissions; graduate inquires to Gregory Dye, Director of Graduate Services.

University of Medicine and Dentistry of New Jersey

65 Bergen Street
Newark, New Jersey 07107-3001

Tel: (973) 972-4400   **E-mail:** admissions@umdnj.edu
Fax: (973) 972-4429   **Internet:** www.umdnj.edu

Institution Description: University of Medicine and Dentistry of New Jersey is a public specialized health sciences university located on five campuses (Newark, New Brunswick/Piscataway, Camden, Scotch Plains, and Stratford). Includes eight schools: New Jersey Medical School, Robert Wood Johnson Medical School, School of Osteopathic Medicine, School of Public Health, New Jersey Dental School, Graduate School of Biomedical Sciences, School of Health Related Professions, School of Nursing; University Hospital in Newark; University Behavioral Health Care Centers in Newark and Piscataway. *Enrollment:* 5,329. *Degrees awarded:* Associate, baccalaureate, first-professional (medicine, dentistry, osteopathy), master's, doctorate.

Accreditation: *Regional:* MSA. *Professional:* cytotechnology, dental assisting, dental hygiene, dentistry, diagnostic medical sonography, dietetics, medical laboratory technology, medicine, nuclear medicine technology, nursing, nursing-midwifery, osteopathy, physical therapy, physician assisting, public health, respiratory therapy, surgical technology

History: Established 1970 as the College of Medicine and Dentistry in New Jersey through a merger of New Jersey College of Medicine and Dentistry (established under that name 1965; previously Seton Hall College of Medicine and Dentistry) and Rutgers Medical School (established 1966); granted free-standing university status in 1981.

Institutional Structure: *Governing board:* Trustees of the University of Medicine and Dentistry of New Jersey. Representation: 11 trustees. 1 ex officio. *Composition of institution:* president, senior vice president for academic affairs, senior vice president for administration and finance, various deans. Business/finances directed by vice president. Full-time instructional faculty 2,566. Academic governance body, the faculty. *Faculty representation:* Faculty served by collective bargaining unit affiliated with AAUP, NJEA.

Calendar: Semesters. Academic year varies by school.

Characteristics of Freshmen: 82% of students from New Jersey.

Admission: As a state-supported institution, UMDNJ is committed to meeting the manpower needs in New Jersey; preference is given to state residents.

Degree Requirements: Completion of prescribed curriculum. See individual schools below.

Distinctive Educational Programs: The university offers programs across the spectrum of the health professions.

Degrees Conferred: 98 *associate:* health professions; 101 *baccalaureate:* health professions; 307 *master's:* biological/life sciences 65; health professions 242; 185 *doctorate:* biological/life sciences 75; 110 health professions 5. 1,148 *first-professional:* dentistry 69; medicine 311; osteopathic medicine 77.

Fees and Other Expenses: *Full-time tuition per academic year 2004–05: SEE individual schools below.*

Financial Aid: Aid from institutionally generated funds is provided on the basis of academic merit, financial need.

Financial aid to full-time, first-time undergraduate students: need-based scholarships/grants totaling $1,273,092, self-help $1,283,092; non-need-based scholarships/grants totaling $9,611, self-help $808,357, parent loans $19,641. *Graduate aid:* 432 students received $2,090,488 in federal and state-funded fellowships/grants; 2,253 received $63,726,016 in federal and state-funded loans; 199 received $366,721 for college-assigned jobs; 81 received other fellowships/grants totaling $284,250; 396 received $2,446,242 internal/external scholarships.

Departments and Teaching Staff: New Jersey Medical School *professors* 179, *associate professors* 165, *assistant professors* 314, *associate professors* 29, *part-time faculty* 92; Robert Wood Johnson Medical School 195, 253, 312, 58, 146; School of Osteopathic Medicine 21, 30, 87, 16, 43; School of Health Professions 13, 32, 43, 47, 175; School of Nursing 5, 10, 20, 7, 17; School of Public Health 9, 7, 16, 4, 21.

Total instructional faculty: 2,566 (full-time 1,965, part-time 601; women 1,041, men 1,525; members of minority groups 658).

Enrollment: Total enrollment 4,996. Undergraduate full-time 134 men / 555 women, part-time 37m / 130w; first-professional/graduate full-time 1,014m / 1,068w, part-time 1m / 2w; graduate full-time 505m / 561w, part-time 174m / 545w.

Characteristics of Student Body: *Ethnic/racial makeup:* number of Black non-Hispanic: 712; American Indian or Alaska Native: 10; Asian or Pacific Islander: 1,100; Hispanic: 397; White non-Hispanic: 2,557; unknown: 154. *Age distribution (undergraduate):* number 18–19: 7; 20–21: 89; 22–24: 169; 25–29: 170; 30–34: 119; 35–39: 97; 40–49: 161; 50–64: 43; 65 and over: 1.

International Students: 377 nonresident aliens enrolled fall 2004. Programs available to aid students whose native language is not English: social, cultural. No financial aid specifically designated for international students.

Student Life: Residential apartments for 465 students on the Newark campus. *Special regulations:* Cars permitted with permits. *Special services:* Medical services, shuttle bus service at Newark campus and between Camden and Piscataway campuses. *Student publications:* Newspapers at Newark and Piscataway campuses. *Surrounding community:* Newark population 350,000.

Library Collections: 253,023 volumes including bound books, serial backfiles, electronic documents, and government documents not in separate collections. Online catalog. Current serial subscriptions: 2,368 paper; 2,237 via electronic access. 160 computer work stations. Students have access to online information retrieval services and the Internet.

Most important holdings include the Morris H. Saffron Collection of Books on Historical Medicine; 1,500 rare medical works dating from the sixteenth to nineteenth century, presented by the Academy of Medicine of New Jersey; HIV-AIDS library.

Buildings and Grounds: *New buildings/construction:* numerous facilities at all campuses have been completed since 2000.

Chief Executive Officer: John J. Petillo, President.

Address admission inquiries to individual school for which admission is sought.

School of Health Related Professions

Degree Programs Offered: Certificates, associate, bachelor's, master's, and doctorates awarded as well as joint degrees/certificates in the following areas: biomedical informatics, clinical lab sciences, clinical nutrition, cytotechnology, dental assisting, dental hygiene, dietetic internship, EMT-paramedic, health informatics, health professions education, medical technology, nurse-midwifery, physical therapy, physician's assistant, psychiatric rehabilitation, radiology, respiratory therapy and surgical technology, toxicology, diagnostic medical ultrasonography, radiography, respiratory therapy technician, vascular technology. Also Ed.M. in allied health.

Degree Requirements: Each program determines the course requirements for graduates from its program.

Fees and Other Expenses: Tuition and fees vary by program. Contact the school for current information.

Enrollment: *Total enrollment* 1,139.

New Jersey Dental School

Degree Programs Offered: *First-professional, certificate.*

Admission: At least 3 years of full-time undergraduate study with 6 hours English, 16 chemistry (inorganic with analytic, organic), 8 biology (including zoology), 8 physics; DAT.

Degree Requirements: Satisfactory completion of curricular requirements.

Fees and Other Expenses: *Full-time tuition per academic year 2004–05:* resident $20,567, nonresident $32,185. *Fees:* $3,290. *Instrument costs:* $2,400.

Enrollment: *Total enrollment:* 382.

New Jersey Medical School

Degree Programs Offered: *First-professional.*

Admission: 90 semester hours from accredited college or university with 8 semester hours of biology or zoology (with lab), 8 of inorganic or general chemistry, 8 organic chemistry, 8 general physics (with lab), 6 English; MOAT. Baccalaureate degree recommended.

Degree Requirements: Satisfactory completion of curricular requirements; 4-year curriculum.

Fees and Other Expenses: *Full-time tuition per academic year 2004–05:* resident $20,567, nonresident $32,185. *Fees:* $2,184.

Enrollment: *Total enrollment:* 699.

Graduate School of Biomedical Sciences

Degree Programs Offered: *Master's, doctorate* in biochemistry and molecular biology, bioinformatics, biomedical engineering, biomedical sciences, experimental pathology, microbiology and molecular genetics, molecular biology, molecular genetics, microbiology and immunology, molecular pathology and immunology, neuroscience, pharmacology and physiology, physiology and integrative biology.

Admission: Baccalaureate degree required. Also acceptable: M.D., D.D.S., D.V.M., D.Sc., or D.O. from accredited institutions in U.S. Test of English as a Foreign Language required of foreign students. Graduate Record Examination required.

Degree Requirements: Completion of curricular requirements.

Fees and Other Expenses: *Full-time tuition per academic year 2004–05:* tuition and fees vary by program. Contact the school for current information.

Departments and Teaching Staff: Faculty hold appointments in Medical or Dental Schools.

Enrollment: *Total enrollment:* 1,056.

School of Osteopathic Medicine

Degree Programs Offered: *First-professional.*

Admission: Baccalaureate from accredited college or university, MCAT, applications through American Association of Osteopathic Medicine Application Service. Recommend 6 semester hours in English, 16 biology, 16 chemistry, 8 physics, 6 behavioral science, 6 mathematics. Preference given to New Jersey residents.

Degree Requirements: Satisfactory completion of 4-year curriculum; final 2 years in residence.

Fees and Other Expenses: *Full-time tuition per academic year 2004–05:* resident $20,567, nonresident $32,185. *Fees:* $2,379.

Enrollment: *Total enrollment:* 366.

Robert Wood Johnson Medical School

Degree Programs Offered: *First-professional.*

Admission: 90 semester hours from accredited college or university with 2 semesters of biology or zoology (with lab), inorganic chemistry (with lab), organic chemistry (with lab), physics (with lab), English, 1 semester of college mathematics. MCAT must be taken no later than fall of year of application.

Degree Requirements: Satisfactory completion of 4-year curriculum.

Fees and Other Expenses: *Full-time tuition per academic year 2004–05:* resident $20,567, nonresident $32,185. *Fees:* $2,354.

Enrollment: *Total enrollment:* 632.

School of Public Health

Degree Programs Offered: *Master's, doctorate* in public health.

Admission: Admission requirements vary by program. GRE required. Test of English as a foreign language required of international students.

Degree Requirements: Satisfactory completion of academic requirements.

Fees and Other Expenses: Tuition and fees vary by program. Contact the school for current information.

Enrollment: *Total enrollment:* 372.

School of Nursing

Degree Programs Offered: *Associate, baccalaureate, master's, post master's certificate, doctorate.*

Admission: For master's program, accredited National League for nursing baccalaureate degree; minimum 3.0 GPA for undergraduate nursing content;

basic statistics course; licensure/reciprocity as an RN in New Jersey. Undergraduate admission requirements vary by program.

Degree Requirements: Fulfill curricular requirements of program.

Fees and Other Expenses: Tution and fees vary by program. Contact the school for current information.

Enrollment: *Total enrollment:* 754.

William Paterson University of New Jersey

300 Pompon Road
Wayne, New Jersey 07470
Tel: (973) 720-3115   **E-mail:** admissions@wpunj.edu
Fax: (973) 720-3624   **Internet:** www.wpunj.edu

Institution Description: William Paterson University of New Jersey is a state institution of higher learning. *Enrollment:* 11,409. *Degrees awarded:* Baccalaureate, master's.

Accreditation: *Regional:* MSA. *Professional:* athletic training, business, counseling, music, nursing, nursing education, speech-language pathology, teacher education

History: Established as Paterson Normal School and offered first instruction at postsecondary level 1855; awarded first degree (baccalaureate) in 1936; became New Jersey State Teachers College in 1937, Paterson State College in 1958, William Paterson College in 1970, William Patterson University in 1997. *See* Kenneth B. White, *Paterson State College: A History 1855–1966* (Wayne: privately published, 1967) for further information.

Institutional Structure: *Governing board:* William Paterson University Board of Trustees. Extrainstitutional representation: 9 trustees; institutional representation: 1 administrator (ex officio), 2 students; 11 voting. *Composition of institution:* Administrators 39 men / 19 women. Administrative structure consists of president, provost and executive vice president, vice president for administration and finance, vice president for institutional advancement. Full-time instructional faculty 198 men / 154 women. Academic governance body, Faculty Senate, meets an average of 8 times each semester.

Calendar: Semesters. Academic year early Sept. to May. Degrees conferred May, Aug., Jan. Formal commencement May, Jan. Summer session from mid-May to early Aug.

Characteristics of Freshmen: 49.7% of applicants accepted. 43.2% of accepted applicants enrolled.

98% (1,497 students) submitted SAT scores; *25th percentile:* SAT Verbal 450, SAT Math 450. *75th percentile:* SAT Verbal 530, SAT Math 540.

36% of entering freshmen expected to graduate within 5 years. 97% of freshmen from New Jersey. Freshmen from 13 states and 7 foreign countries.

Admission: Rolling admissions plan. Early acceptance available. *Requirements:* Either graduation from accredited secondary school with 4 units English, 3 college preparatory mathematics, 3 social science, 2 laboratory science, 4–5 other college preparatory units, 2 electives; or GED. Art majors must submit a portfolio for review. Music majors must audition. *Entrance tests:* College Board SAT or ACT accepted. *For transfer students:* 2.0 minimum GPA required, 2.5 GPA for certain majors (nursing, special education, teacher certification programs); maximum transfer credits 70 from a two-year institution; 90 from a four-year college or university.

Advanced placement for postsecondary-level work completed in secondary school. College credit for extrainstitutional learning is granted on basis of ACE *2006 Guide to the Evaluation of Educational Experiences in the Armed Services* and evaluation by the university's admissions office.

Tutoring available. Noncredit Developmental courses offered in summer session and regular academic year.

Degree Requirements: 128 credit hours; 2.0 GPA; Last 30 credits must be completed at William Paterson. Fulfillment of some degree requirements possible by passing College Board CLEP. *Grading system:* A–F; pass-fail.

Distinctive Educational Programs: University honor s programs in biopsychology, cognitive science, humanities, life science and environmental ethics,

music, nursing, and performance studies. Cluster Course program. Preprofessional academic programs in dentistry, engineering, law, medicine, veterinary medicine, and communication. Study abroad in Argentina, Austria, Australia, Brazil, Canada, China, Columbia, Denmark, Ecuador, England, France, Greece, Hungary, Ireland, Israel, Mexico, Spain. *Available to all students:* Evening classes. *Special facilities:* State-of-the art technology centers, computer-intensive classroom with video projection capacity; multimedia labs; fiber-optic network infrastructure with ATM technology connecting entire campus; interactive television classrooms.

Degrees Conferred: 1,556 *baccalaureate*; 296 *master's.*

Fees and Other Expenses: *Full-time tuition per academic year 2004–05:* undergraduate resident $12,890. Contact the university for current graduate tuition. *Room and board per academic year:* $8,340.

Financial Aid: The university offers a direct lending program. Aid from institutionally generated funds is provided on the basis of academic merit. Institution has a Program Participation Agreement with the U.S. Department of Education for eligible students to receive Pell Grants and, depending upon the agreement, other federal aid.

Financial aid to full-time, first-time undergraduate students: need-based scholarships/grants totaling $12,820,000, self-help $12,300,000; non-need-based scholarships/grants totaling $5,870,000, self-help $14,275,000, parent loans $6,000,000; tuition waivers $1,200,000.

Departments and Teaching Staff: *Total instructional faculty:* 1,048 (full-time 371, part-time 677; women 488, men 560; members of minority groups 203). Total faculty with doctorate, first-professional, or other terminal degree: 335. Student-to-faculty ratio: 15.4:1. Degrees held by full-time faculty: doctorate 79.5%, master's 17%, baccalaureate 1%. 84.8% hold terminal degrees.

Enrollment: Total enrollment 11,409. Undergraduate full-time 3,186 / 4,403 women, part-time 677m / 1,152w; graduate full-time 125m / 329w, part-time 340m / 1,197w.

Characteristics of Student Body: *Ethnic/racial makeup (undergraduate):* number of Black non-Hispanic: 155; American Indian or Alaska Native: 24; Asian or Pacific Islander: 469; Hispanic: 1,507; White non-Hispanic:5,704; unknown: 304.

International Students: 148 nonresident aliens enrolled fall 2004. Students from Europe, Asia, Latin America, Africa, Canada, Australia, Caribbean. Programs available to aid students whose native language is not English: social, cultural. English as a Second Language Program. No financial aid specifically designated for international students.

Student Life: On-campus residence halls house 24% of the undergraduate student body. Residence halls for both sexes constitute 100% of such space. *Intercollegiate athletics:* men: baseball, basketball, cross-country, football, ice hockey, soccer, swimming, track; women: basketball, cross-country, field hockey, soccer, softball, swimming, track, volleyball; co-ed: cheerleading, equestrian team. *Special services:* Academic Support Center, Science Enrichment Center, Writing Center, Child Care Center, Disabled Student Services, Student Information and Referral Center, Women's Center, medical services. *Student publications, radio:* The Beacon, a weekly newspaper; *Pioneers,* yearbook; *Essence,* literary magazine. Two radio stations: WPSC and WCRN. *Surrounding community:* Wayne, population 50,000 is located in northern New Jersey, approximately 20 miles from New York City. Served by mass transit bus system; airport 30 miles from campus; passenger rail service 2 miles from campus.

Library Collections: 335,000 volumes including bound books, serial backfiles, electronic documents, and government documents not in separate collections. Online catalog. Current serial subscriptions: 1,600 paper, 900 microform, 200 electronic. 4,200 recordings; 2,500 compact discs; 100 CD-ROMs. Computer work stations available. Students have access to the Internet at no charge.

Most important special collections include William Paterson Papers; first and autographed editions; New Jersey History; Holocaust Collection for Educators.

Buildings and Grounds: Campus area 255 acres.

Chief Executive Officer: Dr. Arnold Speert, President.

Address admission inquiries to Jonathan McCoy, Director of Admissions.

New Mexico

College of Santa Fe

1600 St. Michael's Drive
Santa Fe, New Mexico 87501
Tel: (505) 473-6011   **E-mail:** admissions@csf.edu
Fax: (505) 473-6129   **Internet:** /www.csf.edu

Institution Description: College of Santa Fe is a private, independent college founded by the Christian Brothers, a Catholic teaching order. *Enrollment:* 1,761. *Degrees awarded:* Associate, baccalaureate, master's (business administration, education). Certificates also awarded.

Accreditation: *Regional:* NCA.

History: Established as St. Michael's College, a school for men, 1859; chartered under present official name, College of the Christian Brothers of New Mexico, 1874; offered first instruction at postsecondary level 1947; awarded first degree (baccalaureate) 1950; became coeducational and became known as College of Santa Fe 1966.

Institutional Structure: *Governing board:* Board of Trustees. Extrainstitutional representation: 26 trustees; institutional representation: president of the college; 1 alumnus. 4 ex officio. All voting. Administrators 8. Academic affairs headed by academic dean. Management/business/finances directed by executive vice president. Full-time instructional faculty 60. Academic governance body, Faculty Council, meets an average of 9 times per year.

Calendar: Semesters. Academic year late Aug. to early May. Freshmen admitted Aug., Jan., May, June, July. Degrees conferred May, July, Dec. Formal commencement May. Summer session of 3 terms.

Characteristics of Freshmen: 79% of applicants accepted. 39% of accepted applicants enrolled.

67% (104 students) submitted SAT scores; 41% (64 students) submitted ACT scores. *25th percentile:* SAT Verbal 540, SAT Math 490 ACT Composite 21, ACT English 21, ACT Math 18. *75th percentile*: SAT Verbal 630, SAT Math 610; ACT Composite 26, ACT English 27, ACT Math 24.

18% of freshmen from New Mexico. Freshmen from 32 states and 1 foreign country.

Admission: Rolling admissions plan. For fall acceptance, apply as early as June of previous year, but not later than Mar. 15 of year of enrollment. Early decision available. *Requirements:* Either graduation from accredited secondary school with 16 units which must include 3 English, 2 laboratory science, 2 mathematics, 2 social studies; or GED. Minimum GPA 2.5. *Entrance tests:* College Board SAT or ACT composite. For foreign students TOEFL. *For transfer students:* 2.5 minimum GPA.

College credit and advanced placement for postsecondary-level work completed in secondary school and for extrainstitutional learning on basis of ACE *2006 Guide to the Evaluation of Educational Experiences in the Armed Services*; portfolio and faculty assessments.

Tutoring available. Developmental courses offered in summer session and regular academic year; credit given.

Degree Requirements: *For all associate degrees:* 64 credit hours. *For all baccalaureate degrees:* 128 credit hours; 1 hour physical education. *For all degrees:* 2.0 GPA; last 30 hours in residence; core curriculum; exit competency examinations in reading and writing.

Fulfillment of some degree requirements and exemption from some beginning courses possible by passing College Board CLEP, APP. *Grading system:* A–F; pass-fail; withdraw (carries time limit); incomplete (carries time limit).

Distinctive Educational Programs: Work-experience programs including cooperative education, internships. Flexible meeting places and schedules including off-campus center (at Kirtland Air Force Base), Los Alamos National Laboratories, and correctional facilities in Santa Fe, Los Luna, and Grants. Evening and weekend courses; credit for prior learning and independent study. Interdepartmental/interdisciplinary programs in arts administration, college studies, and public administration. Independent major option. Semester in New York program for visual arts students. Facilities and programs for independent research, tutorials.

Degrees Conferred: 295 *baccalaureate*; 104 *master's*. Bachelor's degrees awarded in top five disciplines include visual and performing arts 88; business, management, marketing, and related support services 48; computer and information sciences and support services 39; education 31; psychology 29.

Fees and Other Expenses: *Full-time tuition per academic year 2004–05:* $21,530. *Books and supplies:* $816. *Room and board per academic year:* $6.702.

Financial Aid: Aid from institutionally generated funds is provided on the basis of academic merit, financial need, other considerations. Institution has a Program Participation Agreement with the U.S. Department of Education for eligible students to receive Pell Grants and, depending upon the agreement, other federal aid.

Financial aid to full-time, first-time undergraduate students: need-based scholarships/grants totaling $5,132,619, self-help $3,316,944; non-need-based scholarships/grants totaling $1,993,834, self-help $2,512,067,parent loans $1,497,161, tuition waivers $297,947, athletic awards $143,071.

Departments and Teaching Staff: *Total instructional faculty:* 268 (full-time 73, part-time 195; women 114, men 154; members of minority groups 40). Total faculty with doctorate, first-professional, or other terminal degree: 63. Student-to-faculty ratio: 8:1. Degrees held by full-time faculty: doctorate 45%, master's 50%, baccalaureate 5%. 73% hold terminal degrees.

Enrollment: Total enrollment 1,769. Undergraduate full-time 298 men / 380 women, part-time 289m / 463w; graduate full-time 49m / 105w, part-time 45m / 140w.

Characteristics of Student Body: *Ethnic/racial makeup:* number of Black non-Hispanic: 29; American Indian or Alaska Native: 43; Asian or Pacific Islander: 24; Hispanic: 317; White non-Hispanic: 741; unknown: 115.

International Students: 10 nonresident aliens enrolled fall 2004. No programs available to aid students whose native language is not English. No financial aid specifically designated for international students.

Student Life: On-campus residence halls house 21% of student body. Residence halls include men's only, women's only, and co-ed. *Intramural athletics:* available in a wide variety of sports. *Special regulations:* Registered cars permitted without restrictions. Quiet hours set by individual residence halls. *Special services:* Learning Resources Center. *Student publications: Guideline,* a weekly newsletter; *Paladin,* a yearbook; *Vistas,* a quarterly alumni paper with campus news. *Surrounding community:* Santa Fe population 49,000. Albuquerque, 50 miles from campus, is nearest metropolitan area. Served by airport 50 miles from campus; passenger rail service 17 miles from campus.

Library Collections: 146,000 volumes. 88,500 microforms; 12,115 audiovisual materials; 415 current periodical subscriptions. Online catalog. Students have access to online information retrieval services and the Internet.

Most important holdings include Southwest Collection (6,000 volumes dating from the 19th century on local culture and folklore, by New Mexican authors); Art; College Archives.

Buildings and Grounds: Campus area 118 acres.

Chief Executive Officer: Dr. James A. Fries, President.

Address admission inquiries to Admissions Director.

College of the Southwest

6610 Lovington Highway
Hobbs, New Mexico 88240
Tel: (505) 392-6561   **E-mail:** admissions@csw.edu
Fax: (505) 392-6006   **Internet:** www.csw.edu

Institution Description: College of the Southwest is a private, independent, nonprofit college. *Enrollment:* 741. *Degrees awarded:* Baccalaureate, master's.

Accreditation: *Regional:* NCA.

History: Established as New Mexico Baptist Junior College; chartered, and offered first instruction at postsecondary level 1956; awarded first degree (baccalaureate) 1961; adopted present name 1965.

Institutional Structure: *Governing board:* Board of Trustees. Extrainstitutional representation: 27 trustees; institutional representation: 1 alumnus. All voting. *Composition of institution:* Administrators 2 men / 1 woman. Academic affairs headed by vice president for academic affairs. Finances directed by vice president for fiscal affairs. Full-time instructional faculty 20. Academic governance body, curriculum committee, meets an average of 8 times per year.

Calendar: Semesters. Academic year Aug. to May. Freshmen admitted Aug., Jan., June, July. Degrees conferred May, July, Aug., Dec. Formal commencement May. Summer session of 2 terms from early June to mid-Aug.

Characteristics of Freshmen: 46% of applicants admitted. 9% of applicants admitted and enrolled.

57% (33students) submitted SAT scores; 64% (49students) submitted ACT scores. *25th percentile:* SAT Verbal 400, SAT Math 410; ACT Composite 16, ACT English 15, ACT Math 16. *75th percentile:* SAT Verbal 570, SAT Math 560; ACT Composite 20, ACT English 20, ACT Math 19.

46% of entering freshmen expected to graduate within 5 years. 58% of freshmen from New Mexico. Freshmen from 7 states and 5 foreign countries.

Admission: Rolling admissions plan. Early acceptance available. *Requirements:* Entering freshmen must meet two of the following 3 requirements: graduation from an accredited high school in top 50% of class; cumulative GPA of 2.0 or higher on a 4.0 scale; ACT composite score 19 or SAT 910. *Entrance tests:* ACT composite. For foreign students TOEFL. *For transfer students:* 2.0 minimum GPA; from 4-year accredited institution 97 hours maximum transfer credit; from 2-year accredited institution 67 hours; correspondence/extension students 6 hours.

College credit and advanced placement for postsecondary-level work completed in secondary school and for extrainstitutional learning (life experience) on basis of ACE *2006 Guide to the Evaluation of Educational Experiences in the Armed Services;* faculty assessment.

Degree Requirements: 128 credit hours; 2.5 GPA; 2 terms in residence; distribution requirements.

Fulfillment of some degree requirements and exemption from some beginning courses possible by passing College Board CLEP, Achievement Test in foreign language, AP. *Grading system:* A–F; withdraw (carries time limit).

Distinctive Educational Programs: Internships in some fields. Weekend and evening classes.

Degrees Conferred: 100 *baccalaureate:* business and management 26; computer and information sciences 1; education 35; English 1; liberal arts and sciences, general studies, and humanities 1; mathematics 2; protective services/public administration 14; psychology 13; social sciences and history 7.

Fees and Other Expenses: *Full-time tuition per academic year 2004–05:* undergraduate $8,000, graduate study $6,288. *Required fees:* $300. *Room and board per academic year:* $4,600.

Financial Aid: Aid from institutionally generated funds is provided on the basis of academic merit, financial need, athletic ability, other criteria.

Financial aid to full-time, first-time undergraduate students: need-based scholarships/grants totaling $1,470,618, self-help $1,718,054; non-need-based scholarships/grants totaling $828,130, self-help $1,042,774, parent loans $16,840, tuition waivers $144,298, athletic awards $386,314. *Graduate aid:* 43 students received $339,919 in federal and state-funded loans; 2 students received $6,000 for work study jobs.

Departments and Teaching Staff: Arts and sciences *professors* 3, *associate professors* 2, *assistant professors* 7, *part-time faculty* 48; business 1, 1, 0, 8; education 0, 4, 7, 25. *Total instructional faculty:* 97 (full-time 29, part-time 68; women 48, men 49; members of minority groups 8). Total faculty with doctorate, first-professional, or other terminal degree: 28. Student-to-faculty ratio: 12:1. Degrees held by full-time faculty: doctorate 38%, master's 62%. 38% hold terminal degrees.

Enrollment: Total enrollment 741. Undergraduate full-time 168 men / 259 women, part-time 62m / 119w; graduate full-time 16m / 39w, part-time 17m / 61w.

Characteristics of Student Body: *Ethnic/racial makeup:* number of Black non-Hispanic: 18; American Indian or Alaska Native: 20; Asian or Pacific Islander: 2; Hispanic: 180; White non-Hispanic: 357l unknown: 4.*Age distribution:* number under 18: 14; 18–19: 105; 20–21: 109; 22–24: 98; 25–29: 86; 30–34: 62; 35–39: 55; 40–49: 56; 50–64: 21; 65 and over: 1. 40% of student body attend summer sessions.

International Students: 28 nonresident alien enrolled fall 2004. 1 student from Europe, 6 Asia, 9 Latin America, 6 Canada, 5 other. No programs available to aid students whose native language is not English. No financial aid specifically designated for international students.

Student Life: On-campus residence halls house 23% of student body. *Special regulations:* Cars permitted without restrictions. Residence hall visitation from noon to 10pm. *Surrounding community:* Hobbs population 30,000. Dallas (TX), 350 miles from campus, is nearest metropolitan area. Served by airport 10 miles from campus.

Library Collections: 76,217 volumes. 17,950 microforms; 1,200 audiovisual materials; 287 current periodical subscriptions. Online catalog. Students have access to online information retrieval services and the Internet. Total budget for books and materials 2004–05: $62,882.

Most important holdings include collection of Southwestern American history and literature; New Mexico State textbook collection.

Buildings and Grounds: Campus area 160 acres. *New buildings:* Mabee Teaching and Learning Center completed 2002.

Chief Executive Officer: Dr. Gary A. Dill, President.

Address admission inquiries to Office of Admissions.

Eastern New Mexico University

Campus Station #1
Portales, New Mexico 88130

Tel: (505) 562-1011   **E-mail:** admissions@enmu.edu
Fax: (505) 562-2118   **Internet:** /www.enmu.edu

Institution Description: Eastern New Mexico University is a state school with branch campuses in Roswell and Ruidoso. *Enrollment:* 3,959. *Degrees awarded:* Associate, baccalaureate, master's. Specialist certificates in education also awarded.

Academic offerings subject to approval by statewide coordinating bodies. Budget subject to approval by state governing boards.

Accreditation: *Regional:* NCA. *Professional:* business, music, teacher education

History: Established and chartered 1927; incorporated 1929; offered first instruction at postsecondary level and named Eastern New Mexico Junior College 1934; changed name to Eastern New Mexico College 1939; awarded first degree (baccalaureate) 1941; adopted present name 1949.

Institutional Structure: *Governing board:* Board of Regents for Eastern New Mexico University. Representation: 5 regents (appointed by governor of New Mexico), governor, superintendent of public instruction. 2 ex officio. 5 voting. *Composition of institution:* Administrators 16 men / 10 women. Academic affairs headed by vice president. Management/business/finances directed by vice president for business affairs. Full-time instructional faculty 141. Academic governance body, Faculty Senate, meets an average of 24 times per year.

Calendar: Semesters. Academic year Aug. to May. Freshmen admitted Aug., Jan., June. Degrees conferred and formal commencements May, Aug., Dec. Summer session of 1 term from early June to late July.

Characteristics of Freshmen: 67% of applicants accepted. 47% of accepted applicants enrolled.

18% (101 students) submitted SAT scores; 94% (544 students) submitted ACT scores. *25th percentile:* SAT Verbal 380, SAT Math 410; ACT Composite 16, ACT English 15, ACT Math 16. *75th percentile:* SAT Verbal 540, SAT Math 510; ACT Composite 22, ACT English 22, ACT Math 20.

23% of entering freshmen expected to graduate within 5 years. 81% of freshmen from New Mexico. Freshmen from 15 states and 16 foreign countries.

Admission: Rolling admissions plan. For fall acceptance, apply as early as end of junior year of secondary school, but not later than 6 weeks prior to enrollment. *Requirements:* Either graduation from accredited secondary school or GED. *Entrance tests:* College Board SAT with 1 Achievement, or ACT composite. For foreign students TOEFL or English Language Service examination. *For transfer students:* 2.0 minimum GPA; maximum transfer credit limited only by residence requirement.

College credit for postsecondary-level work completed in secondary school and for extrainstitutional learning on basis of ACE *2006 Guide to the Evaluation of Educational Experiences in the Armed Services.*

Tutoring available. Developmental courses offered in during regular regular academic year; credit given.

Degree Requirements: *For all associate degrees:* 64 hours; 15 credits in residence. *For all baccalaureate degrees:* 128 hours; 32 credits in residence. *For all undergraduate degrees:* 2.0 GPA; 2 credit hours physical education; general education requirements.

Fulfillment of some degree requirements possible by passing College Board CLEP. *Grading system:* A–F; withdraw (carries time limit).

Distinctive Educational Programs: Work-experience programs. Evening classes. Special facilities for using telecommunications in the classroom. Interdepartmental and interdisciplinary programs in agribusiness, American studies, environmental studies, ethnic studies, industrial technology, Latin American studies, music theater, social studies, women's studies. Preprofessional program in forestry. Communication (emphasis in radio/TV). Facilities and programs for independent research, including honors programs, individual majors, tutorials. Institutionally sponsored study abroad in England. *Other distinctive programs:*

Women's Re-entry Program assists women returning to pursue studies or careers.

Degrees Conferred: 24 *associate;* 591 *baccalaureate;* 70 *master's.* Bachelor's degrees awarded in top five disciplines: business/marketing 138; education 81; liberal arts/general studies 67; social sciences and history 51; protective services/public administration 29.

Fees and Other Expenses: *Full-time tuition per academic year 2004–005:* undergraduate resident $1,878, nonresident $7,434; graduate resident $2,184, nonresident $7,740. *Books and supplies:* $800. *Room and board per academic year:* $4,340.

Financial Aid: Aid from institutionally generated funds is available on the basis of academic merit, financial need, athletic ability, other criteria.

Financial aid to full-time, first-time undergraduate students: need-based scholarships/grants totaling $9,467,654, self-help $13,382,919; non-need-based scholarships/grants totaling $1,326,166, self-help $3,357,578, parent loans $139,689, athletic awards $777.051.

Departments and Teaching Staff: *Total instructional faculty:* 238 (full-time 141, part-time 97; women 112, men 126; members of minority groups 30). Total faculty with doctorate, first-professional, or other terminal degree: 129. Student-to-faculty ratio: 18:1.

Enrollment: Total enrollment 3,939. Undergraduate full-time 1,155 men / 1,364 w, part-time 209m / 432w; graduate full-time 71m / 133w, part-time 144m / 431w.

Characteristics of Student Body: *Ethnic/racial makeup:* number of Black non-Hispanic: 198; American Indian or Alaska Native: 87; Asian or Pacific Islander: 33; Hispanic: 908; White non-Hispanic: 1,826; unknown: 160.

International Students: 49 nonresident aliens enrolled fall 2004. Programs available to aid students whose native language is not English: social. No financial aid specifically designated for international students.

Student Life: On-campus residence halls house 28% of student body. Housing available for married students. *Intercollegiate athletics:* men only: basketball, cross-country, football, soccer, track and field; women only: basketball, cross-country, soccer, softball, tennis, track and field, volleyball. *Special regulations:* Cars permitted without restriction; first-time freshmen required to live on campus for first year. *Special services:* Learning Resources Center, medical services, computer laboratory, van service to and from branch campus. *Student publications, radio, television: The Chase,* a weekly newspaper; *The Magazine,* a biannual literary magazine; *QT3,* a monthly TV magazine; *Silver Pack,* a yearbook. Radio stations KENW-AM and FM broadcast 63 hours and 168 hours per week, respectively. TV station KENW broadcasts 130 hours per week. *Surrounding community:* Portales population 12,000. El Paso (TX), 300 miles from campus, is nearest metropolitan area.

Publications: *Liberal and Fine Arts Review.*

Library Collections: 158,655 volumes. 67,500 microforms; 31,000 recordings/tapes; 1,068 current periodical subscriptions. Online catalog. 43 computer work stations. Students have access to online information retrieval services and the Internet.

Most important holdings include Williamson Library of Science Fiction; Hope Sheridan Collection of Music and Dance; New Mexico History.

Buildings and Grounds: Campus area 240 acres. *New buildings:* Communication Building completed 2005.

Chief Executive Officer: Dr. Steven Gamble, President.

Address admission inquiries to Director of Admissions,

New Mexico Highlands University

University Avenue
Las Vegas, New Mexico 87701

Tel: (505) 425-7511   **E-mail:** admission@nmhu.edu
Fax: (505) 426-2117   **Internet:** www.nmhu.edu

Institution Description: New Mexico Highlands University is a state institution. *Enrollment:* 3,304. *Degrees awarded:* Associate, baccalaureate, master's.

Accreditation: *Regional:* NCA. *Professional:* business, engineering, social work, teacher education

History: Chartered and incorporated as New Mexico Normal College 1893; offered first instruction at postsecondary level and changed name to New Mexico Normal University 1898; awarded first degree (baccalaureate) 1917; adopted present name 1941.

Institutional Structure: *Governing board:* Board of Regents. Representation: 5 regents. 2 ex officio. Academic affairs headed by vice president. Management/business/finances directed by chief finance officer. Full-time instructional faculty 109.

Calendar: Semesters. Academic year Aug. to May.

Characteristics of Freshmen: 90% of applicants accepted. 67% of accepted applicants enrolled.

10% of applicants submitted SAT scores; 72% ACT scores. *25th percentile:* SAT Verbal 380, SAT Math 420; ACT Composite 15, ACT English 14, ACT Math 15. *75th percentile:* SAT Verbal 550, SAT Math 510; ACT Composite 20, ACT English 20, ACT Math 19.

23% of entering freshmen expected to graduate within 5 years. 90% of freshmen from New Mexico. Freshmen from 10 states and 3 foreign countries.

Admission: For fall acceptance, apply no later than July 15. Early acceptance available. *Requirements:* Either graduation from accredited secondary school with 15 units which must include 9 from among English, foreign language, and social studies, with not more than 4 in any one subject; or equivalency certificate. Minimum GPA 2.0. *Entrance tests:* ACT composite preferred; College Board SAT accepted. For foreign students TOEFL.

Degree Requirements: *For all associate degrees:* 64 semester hours. *For all baccalaureate degrees:* 128 hours; 1 year, including final semester, in residence; 2 physical education courses; general education requirements. Additional requirements for some programs.

Exemption from some beginning courses possible by passing College Board CLEP, AP. *Grading system:* A–F; satisfactory.

Distinctive Educational Programs: Independent study.

Degrees Conferred: 2 *associate;* 310 *baccalaureate;* 275 *master's.* Bachelor's degrees awarded in top five disciplines: education 86; business/marketing 75; health professions 66; social sciences and history 19; visual and performing arts 13.

Fees and Other Expenses: *Full-time tuition per academic year 2004–05:* undergraduate resident $2,280, nonresident $9,624; graduate resident $2,424, nonresident $10,248. *Room and board per academic year:* $4,274.

Financial Aid: Aid from institutionally generated funds is provided on the basis of academic merit, financial need, athletic ability, other criteria.

Financial aid to full-time, first-time undergraduate students: need-based scholarships/grants totaling $4,693,922, self-help $6,491,181; non-need-based scholarships/grants totaling $2,594,828, self-help $3,130,180, parent loans $72,051, tuition waivers $119,808, athletic awards $470,862. *Graduate aid:* 15 students received $26,175 in federal and state-funded fellowships/grants; 167 received $4,536,773 in federal and state-funded loans; 5 students received $2,443 for college-assigned jobs; 107 received $607,916 for other fellowships and grants.

Departments and Teaching Staff: *Total instructional faculty:* 117 (full-time 117; women 45, men 72). Total faculty with doctorate, first-professional, or other terminal degree: 88. Student-to-faculty ratio: 20:1.

Enrollment: Total enrollment 3,304. Undergraduate full-time 580 men / 688 women, part-time 129m / 467w; graduate full-time 143m / 313w, part-time 381m / 843w. *Transfer students:* in-state 230; from out-of-state 77.

Characteristics of Student Body: *Ethnic/racial makeup:* number of Black non-Hispanic: 78; American Indian or Alaska Native: 63; Asian or Pacific Islander: 16; Hispanic: 1,022; White non-Hispanic: 478; unknown: 98. *Age distribution:* number under 18: 50; 18–19: 332; 20–21: 316; 22–24: 364; 25–29: 223; 30–34: 178; 35–39: 130; 40–49: 168; 50–64: 83; 65 and over: 30.

International Students: 38 nonresident aliens enrolled fall 2004. 2 students from Europe, 11 Asia; 2 Latin America, 17 Africa; 2 Canada; 4 other. Programs available to aid students whose native language is not English: social, cultural. No financial aid specifically designated for international students.

Student Life: On-campus housing available. *Intercollegiate athletics:* men only: baseball, basketball, cross-country, football; women only: basketball, softball, volleyball. *Student publications: La Mecha,* a weekly newspaper; *Southwest Wind,* a yearbook. *Surrounding community:* Las Vegas population 15,000. Santa Fe, 60 miles from campus, is nearest metropolitan area.

Publications: *Vista de Highlands,* formerly New Mexico Highlands University Magazine.

Library Collections: 613,657 volumes. Online catalog. Current serial subscriptions: 740 paper; 183,913 microform; 17,203 via electronic access. 826 audiovisual materials. Students have access to online information retrieval services and the Internet. Total 2004–05 budget for books and materials: $398,291.

Most important special holdings include Arrott Collection; Schomberg Collection; William Gray Collection.

Chief Executive Officer: Dr. Manny Alagon, President.

Address admission inquiries to Director of Admissions.

New Mexico Institute of Mining and Technology

801 Leroy Place
Socorro, New Mexico 87801
Tel: (800) 428-TECH   **E-mail:** admission@nmt.edu
Fax: (505) 835-5989   **Internet:** www.nmt.edu

Institution Description: New Mexico Institute of Mining and Technology, informally known as New Mexico Tech, is a state institution. *Enrollment:* 1,826. *Degrees awarded:* Associate, baccalaureate, master's, doctorate.

Accreditation: *Regional:* NCA. *Professional:* engineering

History: Established by territorial legislature as New Mexico School of Mines 1889; offered first instruction at postsecondary level 1893; awarded first degree (baccalaureate) 1897; added graduate program 1946; adopted present name 1951. *See* Paige W. Christiansen, *College on the Rio Grande* (Socorro: New Mexico Institute of Mining and Technology, 1989) for further information.

Institutional Structure: *Governing board:* Board of Regents of New Mexico Institute of Mining and Technology. Extrainstitutional representation: 5 regents. All voting. *Composition of institution:* Administrators 17 men / 4 women. Academic affairs headed by vice president for academic affairs. Management/business/finances directed by vice president for administration and finance. Full-time instructional faculty 92 FTE. Academic governance body, Institute Senate, meets an average of 9 times per year.

Calendar: Semesters. Academic year Aug. to May. Freshmen admitted Aug., Jan., June. Degrees conferred May, Dec. Formal commencement May. Summer session 1 term from June to Aug.

Characteristics of Freshmen: 68% of applicants accepted. 30% of accepted applicants enrolled.

Average secondary school rank 79th percentile. Mean ACT composite class score 25.8.

35% of entering freshmen expected to graduate within 5 years. 74% of freshmen from New Mexico. Freshmen from 23 states and 5 foreign countries.

Admission: Rolling admissions plan. For fall acceptance, apply as early as end of junior year of secondary school, but not later than Aug. 15 of year of enrollment. Early acceptance available. *Requirements:* Either graduation from accredited secondary school with 15 units which normally include 4 English, 3 college preparatory mathematics, 2 science, 3 social studies; or GED. Additional units in mathematics and science recommended. Minimum GPA 2.0. *Entrance tests:* ACT minimum composite 21. *For transfer students:* 2.0 minimum GPA; maximum transfer credit limited by residence requirement.

College credit and advanced placement for postsecondary-level work completed in secondary school.

Tutoring available. Remedial courses offered in summer session and regular academic year; credit given.

Degree Requirements: *For all associate degrees:* 65 credit hours. *For all baccalaureate degrees:* Minimum of 130 credit hours. *For all undergraduate degrees:* 2.0 GPA. 30 hours in residence. General education requirements.

Fulfillment of some degree requirements and exemption from some beginning courses possible by passing departmental examinations; College Board AP. *Grading system:* A–F; pass-fail; withdraw; incomplete (carries time limit).

Distinctive Educational Programs: *For undergraduates:* Interdepartmental programs in basic sciences. Honors programs. *For graduate students:* Facilities and programs for independent research. Cooperative doctoral program in computer science with New Mexico State University and University of New Mexico.

Degrees Conferred: 9 *associate;* 179 *baccalaureate;* 108 *master's;* 10 *doctorate.* Bachelor's degrees awarded in top five disciplines: engineering 78; political science 33; computer and information sciences 26; biomedical/biological sciences 12; liberal arts and sciences, general studies, and humanities 9.

Fees and Other Expenses: *Full-time tuition per academic year 2004–05:* undergraduate resident $3,280, nonresident $9,911. Contact the institute for current tuition/fees for graduate study. *Books and supplies:* $800. *Room and board per academic year:* $4,000.

Financial Aid: Aid from institutionally generated funds is provided on the basis of academic merit and financial need. Institution has a Program Participation Agreement with the U.S. Department of Education for eligible students to receive Pell Grants and, depending upon the agreement, other federal aid.

Financial aid to full-time, first-time undergraduate students: 24% received federal grants averaging $3,348; 59% state/local grants averaging $1,619; 82% institutional grants averaging $3,017; 35% received loans averaging $2,682.

Departments and Teaching Staff: Biology *professors* 2, *associate professors* 1, *assistant professors* 2, *part-time faculty* 0; business administration 1, 0, 2, 1; chemistry 4, 1, 4, 0; computer science 1, 3, 2, 1; earth science 7, 6, 4, 0; humanities 4, 3, 3, 1; mathematics 2, 7, 1, 1; physics 6, 5, 2, 1; psychology 1, 0, 0, 0; electrical engineering 0, 4, 1, 0; materials engineering 3, 2, 2, 0; mineral and environmental engineering 2, 5, 2, 0; petroleum and chemical engineering 2, 6, 2, 1. *Total instructional faculty:* 102.375 FTE. Student-to-faculty ratio: 11:1. Degrees held by full-time faculty: baccalaureate 100%, master's 98%, doctorate 95%. 95% hold terminal degrees.

Enrollment: Total enrollment 1,826. Undergraduate 1,357 (70.2% men, 29.8% women).

Characteristics of Student Body: *Ethnic/racial makeup:* number of Black non-Hispanic: 1.3%; American Indian or Alaska Native: 3.9%; Asian or Pacific Islander: 3.1%; Hispanic: 21.2%; White non-Hispanic: 68.2%; unknown: 1.3%. *Age distribution:* 17–21: 47%; 22–24: 17%; 25–29: 14%; 30–34: 6%; 35–39: 5%; 40–49: 7%; 50–59: 4%.

International Students: 26 nonresident aliens enrolled fall 2004. No programs available to aid students whose native language is not English. Some scholarships available for international students.

Student Life: On-campus residence halls house 45% of student body. Residence halls for men only constitute 29% of such space, for women only 17%, for both sexes 54%. Housing available for married students. *Special regulations:* Cars permitted without restrictions. Quiet hours set by residents in individual halls. *Student publications, radio: Paydirt,* a semi-monthly newspaper. *Surrounding community:* Socorro population 10,000. Albuquerque, 75 miles from campus, is nearest metropolitan area. Served by airport 75 miles from campus.

Publications: Bureau of Mines and Mineral Resources bulletins, maps, books.

Library Collections: 125,000 volumes. 315,000 government documents (separate collection). 39,000 microforms; 950 current periodical subscriptions. Online catalog. Students have access to online information retrieval services and the Internet.

Most important special collections include publications of U.S. Geological Survey, U.S. Bureau of Mines, and New Mexico Bureau of Mines.

Buildings and Grounds: Campus area 320 acres.

Chief Executive Officer: Dr. Daniel H. Lopez, President.

Undergraduates address admission inquiries to Michael Kloeppel, Director of Admissions; graduate inquiries to Dr. David B. Johnson, Dean of Graduate Studies.

New Mexico State University

P.O. Box 30001
Las Cruces, New Mexico 88003
Tel: (505) 646-3121   **E-mail:** admissions@nmsu.edu
Fax: (505) 646-6330   **Internet:** www.nmsu.edu

Institution Description: New Mexico State University is a state institution and land-grant college, with 2-year colleges at Alamogordo, Dona Ana, Carlsbad, and Grants. *Enrollment:* 16,428. *Degrees awarded:* Associate, baccalaureate, master's, doctorate. Certificates also awarded.

Budget subject to approval by state governing boards.

Accreditation: *Regional:* NCA. *Professional:* accounting, applied science, business, counseling, counseling psychology, engineering, engineering technology, journalism, music, nursing, nursing education, public administration, public health, social work, speech-language pathology, teacher education

History: Established as Las Cruces College and offered first instruction at postsecondary level 1888; chartered as New Mexico College of Agriculture and Mechanic Arts 1889; awarded first degree (baccalaureate) 1894; changed name to New Mexico State University of Agriculture, Engineering, and Science 1958; adopted present name 1960. *See* Simon F. Kopp, *That All May Learn: New Mexico State University 1888–1964* (Las Cruces: New Mexico State University, 1972) for further information.

Institutional Structure: *Governing board:* Board of Regents. Representation: 5 members (appointed by governor of New Mexico), governor, superintendent of public instruction. 2 ex officio. 5 voting. *Composition of institution:* Academic affairs headed by executive vice president. Management/business/finances directed by vice president, business affairs. Full-time instructional faculty 634. Academic governance body, Faculty Senate, meets an average of 10 times per year.

Calendar: Semesters. Academic year Aug. to Aug. Freshmen admitted Aug., July, Jan., May. Degrees conferred May, June, July, Aug., Jan. Formal commencement May, Dec. Summer session of 2 terms.

Characteristics of Freshmen: 5,109 applicants admitted. 2,111 admitted applicants enrolled.

14% (295 students) submitted SAT scores; 98% (2,080 students) submitted ACT scores. *25th percentile:* ACT Composite 18, ACT English 17, ACT Math 17. *75th percentile:* ACT Composite 24, ACT English 24, ACT Math 23. 33% of entering freshmen expected to graduate within 5 years. 79% of freshmen from New Mexico. Freshmen from 30 states and 5 foreign countries.

Admission: Rolling admissions plan. Apply no later than 1 month prior to registration. Early acceptance available. *Requirements:* Graduation from accredited secondary school with 3 units in English, 2-3 mathematics, 1 laboratory science, 1 social studies, electives from among art, business, communications, English, foreign language, mathematics, natural science, social studies. GED also accepted. Additional requirements for some programs. Minimum GPA 2.0. *Entrance tests:* ACT composite. For foreign students TOEFL or demonstrated proficiency in English. *For transfer students:* 2.0 minimum GPA; from 4-year accredited institution 98 hours maximum transfer credit; from 2-year accredited institution 66 hours.

College credit and advanced placement for postsecondary-level work completed in secondary school and for USAFI/DANTES. College credit for extrainstitutional learning on basis of ACE *2006 Guide to the Evaluation of Educational Experiences in the Armed Services.*

Tutoring available. Noncredit developmental and remedial courses offered in summer session and regular academic year.

Degree Requirements: *For all associate degrees:* 66 credit hours; last 15 credits in residence. *For baccalaureate degrees:* 128–132 credit hours; last 30 credits in residence. *For all undergraduate degrees:* 2.0 GPA; demonstrated proficiency in English and mathematics.

Fulfillment of some degree requirements and exemption from some beginning courses possible by passing departmental examinations, College Board CLEP. ACT exam scores also considered. *Grading system:* A–F; pass-fail; withdraw (carries time limit).

Distinctive Educational Programs: Work-experience programs. Evening classes. Special facilities for using telecommunications in the classroom. Facilities and programs for independent research, including honors programs, individual majors, tutorials, independent study. Student exchange through National Student Exchange program. Servicemembers Opportunity College. 13 research and experiment centers. Study abroad in English, history, journalism, music, philosophy, and theatre taught in London, England.

ROTC: Army, Air Force.

Degrees Conferred: 62 *associate;* 2,012 *baccalaureate* (B), 750 *master's;* 78 *doctorate:* agriculture 35 (B), 4 (M); architecture 4 (B); biological/life sciences 94 (B), 16 (M), 9 (D); business/marketing 330 (B), 73 (M), 3 (D); communications/communication technologies 62 (B); computer and information sciences 93 (B), 17 (M), 1 (D); education 255 (B), 246 (M), 27 (D); engineering and engineering technologies 244 (B), 102 (M), 8 (D); English 59 (B), 32 (M), 6 (D); foreign languages and literature 75 (B), 12 (M); health professions and related sciences 84 (B), 17 (M); liberal arts/general studies 1 (B), 2 (M); mathematics 8 (B), 14 (M), 3 (D); natural resources/environmental science 22 (B), 7 (M); parks and recreation 12 (B); philosophy/religion/theology 9 (B); physical sciences 16 (B), 18 (M), 10 (D); protective services/public administration 147 (B), 86 (M); psychology 50 (B), 9 (M), 4 (D); social sciences and history 112 (B), 37 (M); visual and performing arts 50 (B), 16 (M); other 142 (B), 29 (M), 5 (D).

Fees and Other Expenses: *Full-time tuition per academic year 2004–05:* undergraduate resident $2,628, nonresident $11,172; graduate resident $2,898, nonresident $11,496. *Required fees:* $1,038. *Other fees:* $3,059. *Room and board per academic year:* $5,046.

Financial Aid: Aid from institutionally generated funds is provided on the basis of academic merit, financial need, athletic ability, other criteria.

Financial aid to full-time, first-time undergraduate students: need-based scholarships/grants totaling $26,901,023, self-help $23,383,860, parent loans $324,288, tuition waivers $8,528,141, athletic awards $877,339, non-need-based scholarships/grants totaling $8,647,120, self-help $5,751,599, parent loans $784,105, tuition waivers $2,180,496, athletic awards $1,364,177.

Departments and Teaching Staff: *Professors* 199, *associate professors* 205, *assistant professors* 237, *instructors* 25, *part-time faculty* 968. *Total instructional faculty:* 968 (full-time 666, part-time 302; women 401, men 567; members of minority groups 145). Total faculty with doctorate, first-professional, or other terminal degree: 676. Student-to-faculty ratio: 19:1. Degrees held by faculty: 80% hold terminal degrees.

Enrollment: Total enrollment 16,428. Undergraduate full-time 4,878 men / 5,770 women, part-time 965m / 1,362w; graduate full-time 805m / 813w, part-time 639m / 1,196w.

Characteristics of Student Body: *Ethnic/racial makeup (undergraduate):* number of Black non-Hispanic: 373; American Indian or Alaska Native: 403; Asian or Pacific Islander: 166; Hispanic: 5,883; White non-Hispanic: 6,023.

International Students: 127 nonresident aliens enrolled fall 2004. 73 students from Europe, 320 Asia, 35 Latin America, 45 Africa, 13 Canada, 4 Australia, 219 other.

Student Life: On-campus residence halls house 24% of student body. 8% of men join and 6% live in fraternities; 6% of women join and 2% live in sororities. 5% of married students live in institutional housing. *Intercollegiate athletics:* men only: baseball, basketball, football, golf, swimming, tennis, track; women only: basketball, golf, softball, swimming, tennis, volleyball. *Special regulations:* Cars permitted without restrictions. Residence hall visitation 9am to mid-

night weekdays, 9am to 2am Fri. and Sat. *Special services:* Learning Resources Center, medical services. *Student publications, radio, television: Round Up,* a newspaper published 3 times per week. Radio station KRWG broadcasts 133 hours per week. TV station KRWG broadcasts 75 hours per week. *Surrounding community:* Las Cruces population 45,000. El Paso (TX), 45 miles from campus, is nearest metropolitan area. Served by airport 5 miles from campus.

Library Collections: 1,642,678 volumes. 370,000 government documents. Online catalog. Current serial subscriptions: paper 5,915; microform 1,410,675. 34,345 recordings. Students have access to online information retrieval services and the Internet.

Most important holdings include Rio Grande Historical Collection (personal papers, organizational records, photographs, tape recordings, and other documented material related to New Mexico and the Southwest).

Buildings and Grounds: Campus area 6,250 acres.

Chief Executive Officer: Dr, Michael V. Martin, President.

Address admission inquiries to Director of Admissions.

College of Arts and Sciences

Degree Programs Offered: *Associate* in arts, police science; *baccalaureate* in anthropology, art, biology, chemistry, city and regional planning, computer science, drama, economics, English, fine arts, foreign languages, geography, geological science, geology, government, history, journalism, mass communications, mathematics, medical technology, music, music education, philosophy, physics, police science, psychology, Russian, sociology, speech communication and communicative disorders; *master's, doctorate* in various fields.

Distinctive Educational Programs: Preprofessional programs in dentistry, medicine, nursing, veterinary medicine. Internship in medical technology through cooperating hospitals. Cooperative work phase-study phase program with government agencies and business. Individual majors. Cooperative doctoral program in computer science with New Mexico Institute of Mining and Technology, University of New Mexico.

College of Agriculture and Home Economics

Degree Programs Offered: *Associate* in agricultural machinery and technology; *baccalaureate* in agricultural biology, agricultural business management, agricultural and extension education, animal science, communication, crop science, environmental and resource economics, family and consumer studies, farm and ranch management, fishery science, food and nutrition services, general agriculture, general agronomy, home economics business, home economics education, horticulture, pest management, range science, recreation areas management, soil science, wildlife science; *master's, doctorate* in various fields.

Distinctive Educational Programs: Preprofessional programs in forestry, veterinary medicine. Cooperative programs in agriculture, home economics with county governments.

College of Business Administration and Economics

Degree Programs Offered: *Associate* in business; *baccalaureate* in accountancy, business administration, business systems analysis, economics, finance, management, marketing, real estate; *master's* in business administration, economics.

Distinctive Educational Programs: Cooperative work phase-study phase program with governmental agencies and businesses.

College of Education

Degree Programs Offered: *Associate; baccalaureate* in elementary education, secondary education; *master's* in counseling and guidance, education, educational administration; *doctorate* in counseling and guidance, curriculum and instruction, educational administration. Specialist certificates in counseling and guidance, curriculum and instruction, educational administration, reading also given.

Distinctive Educational Programs: 5-year baccalaureate-master's program in science and teaching.

College of Engineering

Degree Programs Offered: *Associate* in civil technology, electronic technology, electromechanical technology, mechanical technology; *baccalaureate* in agricultural engineering, chemical engineering, civil engineering, electrical engineering, engineering technology, geological engineering, industrial engineering, mechanical engineering; *master's, doctorate* in various fields. Certificate in drafting also given.

Distinctive Educational Programs: Cooperative work phase-study phase program with governmental agencies and businesses.

College of Human and Community Services

Degree Programs Offered: *Associate* in applied science, education paraprofessional, electromechanical technology, medical laboratory technology, nursing, occupational business, radiologic technology, secretarial administration, water utility operation; *baccalaureate* in community health, health science, nursing, social work.

Distinctive Educational Programs: Cooperative 2-year radiologic technology program with local hospitals. Nontraditional, noncredit cultural enrichment program. Newspaper and public television courses offered for credit through continuing education.

St. John's College

1160 Camino Cruz Blanca
Santa Fe, New Mexico 87505-4599
Tel: (800) 331-5232   **E-mail:** admissions@sjcsf.edu
Fax: (505) 984-6162   **Internet:** www.sjcsf.edu

Institution Description: St. John's College is a nonsectarian, private, independent, nonprofit college, with a second campus in Annapolis, Maryland. In addition to its regular program, the school offers a year-round Graduate Institute in Liberal Education. *Enrollment:* 520. *Degrees awarded:* Baccalaureate, master's.

Accreditation: *Regional:* NCA.

History: Founded in 1696; chartered as St. John's College 1784. The Santa Fe campus established and offered first instruction at postsecondary level 1964; awarded first degree (baccalaureate) 1968.

Institutional Structure: *Governing board:* Board of Visitors and Governors. Representation: 51 voting members; 16 ex officio and honorary including governors of New Mexico and Maryland, alumni officers, deans, administrators; *Composition of institution:* Academic affairs headed by dean. Management/business/finances directed by treasurer. Full-time instructional faculty 74. Academic governance body, Instruction Committee, meets an average of 40 times per year.

Calendar: Semesters. Academic year Aug. to May. Freshmen admitted Aug., Jan. Undergraduate degrees conferred May; graduate degrees, Aug. Formal commencements May, Aug. Summer session of 1 term from late June to mid-Aug.

Characteristics of Freshmen: 82% of applicants accepted. 44% of accepted applicants enrolled.

30% (83students) submitted SAT scores; 31% (37 students) submitted ACT scores. *25th percentile:* SAT Verbal 630, SAT Math 560; ACT Composite 25. *75th percentile:* SAT Verbal 740, SAT Math 660; ACT Composite 31.

50% of entering freshmen expected to graduate within 5 years. 9% of freshmen from New Mexico. Freshmen from 35 states and 2 foreign countries.

Admission: Rolling admissions plan. For fall acceptance, recommended Mar. 1 submission. Early acceptance available. *Requirements:* Either graduation from accredited secondary school with 2 years of algebra, 1 geometry, 2 foreign language, 2-3 natural science; or GED. Strong college preparatory background and additional units in foreign language and science recommended; 3 personal essays required which are most important to the decision.

Degree Requirements: 124 credit hours earned of 135 attempted credit hours; 4 years in residence; senior essay and oral examinations. *Grading system:* A–F.

Distinctive Educational Programs: Great Books Program: Students and faculty work together in small discussion classes without lecture courses, written finals, or emphasis on grades.

Degrees Conferred: 90 *baccalaureate:* liberal arts/general studies; 65 *master's:* liberal arts/general studies 40; Eastern classics 25.

Fees and Other Expenses: *Full-time tuition per academic year 2005–06:* undergraduate $32,374; graduate $12,152 liberal arts, $18,104 Eastern classics. *Room and board per academic year:* $7,876.

Financial Aid: Aid from institutionally generated funds is provided on the basis of financial need.

Financial aid to full-time, first-time undergraduate students: need-based scholarships/grants totaling $5,057,078, self-help $1,761,888; non-need-based scholarships/grants totaling $116,674, self-help $893,447, parent loans $1,400,466, tuition waivers $122,180. *Graduate aid:* 86 students received $633,487 in federal and state-funded loans (ranging from $500 to $8,500); 102 students received other fellowships/grants totaling $532,876 (ranging from $1,000 to $12,000).

Departments and Teaching Staff: Faculty members are unranked. *Total instructional faculty:* 70 (full-time 69, part-time 1; women 19, men 51). Total faculty with doctorate, first-professional, or other terminal degree: 54. Student-to-faculty ratio: 7:1. *Total tenured faculty:* 41. Degrees held by full-time faculty: doctorate 72%, master's 18%, baccalaureate 6%. 79% hold terminal degrees. *Faculty development:* 5 faculty members awarded sabbaticals 2004–05.

Enrollment: Total enrollment 520. Undergraduate full-time 219 men / 190 women, part-time 5w; graduate full-time 60m / 40w, part-time 2m / 4w.

Characteristics of Student Body: *Ethnic/racial makeup:* number of Black non-Hispanic: 4; American Indian or Alaska Native: 3; Asian or Pacific Islander: 10; Hispanic: 29; White non-Hispanic: 348; unknown: 5. *Age distribution:* number under 18: 11; 18–19: 150; 20–21: 159; 22–24: 73; 25–29: 13; 30–34: 5; 35–39: 2; 40–49: 2. 13% of student body attend summer sessions.

International Students: 14 nonresident aliens enrolled fall 2004. No programs available to aid students whose native language is not English. Financial aid specifically designated for international students: 15 grants available annually.

Student Life: On-campus residence halls house 75% of student body. Residence halls for both sexes constitute 100% of such space. Many extracurricular activities available. Students and faculty offers a variety of study groups to complement the academic program. *Special regulations:* Cars permitted. *Special services:* Medical services, campus bus service to Santa Fe. *Student publications:* annual literary magazine; weekly newspaper. *Surrounding community:* Santa Fe population 65,000. Albuquerque, 60 miles from campus, is nearest metropolitan area. Served by airport 15 miles from campus, passenger rail service 20 miles from campus.

Publications: *The St. John's Review* (first published as *The College,* 1969) biannually; *Dialogue,* newsletter biannually; *The Letter Home,* newsletter for parents published 3 times per year.

Library Collections: 66,500 volumes. Online and card catalogs. 122 current periodical subscriptions. 2,850 recordings. 1,250 compact discs. 9 computer work stations. Students have access to the Internet at no charge. Total 2004–05 budget for books and materials: $40,227.

Most important special collections include Witter Bynner Collection; Edgar Allan Poe Collection; Music Collection.

Buildings and Grounds: Campus area 287 acres.

Chief Executive Officer: Dr. Michael Peters, President.

Address undergraduate admission inquiries to Larry Clendenin, Director of Admissions; graduate inquiries to Jean-Paul Ruch, Director of the Graduate Institute.

Southwestern College

P.O. Box 4788
Santa Fe, New Mexico 87502-4788
Tel: (877) 471-5756   **E-mail:** admissions@swc.edu
Fax: (505) 471-4071   **Internet:** www.swc.edu

Institution Description: Southwestern College is a private, independent graduate institution with a focus on professional education in the helping professions of art therapy and counseling. The college also offers a post graduate art therapy certificate program and community services programs for professionals. *Enrollment:* 65. *Degrees awarded:* Master's.

Accreditation: *Regional:* NCA.

History: The development of Southwestern College began with the establishment of the Quimby Memorial Library in 1945. The college was dedicated in 1976 and began its programs in 1979. The first class graduated in 1981.

Institutional Structure: *Governing board:* Representation: Board of Trustees. Extrainstitutional representation: 9 trustees; institutional representatives: president of the college (ex officio and nonvoting), faculty representative (nonvoting), and student representative (nonvoting). Administrators: 6. Academic affairs headed by senior vice president and dean of the college. Management/business/finances directed by president. Full-time instructional faculty: 20. Academic governance body, Faculty Council, meets an average of 9 times per year.

Calendar: Quarters. Academic year Sept. to May. Summer session.

Admission: Rolling admissions. *Requirements:* BA degree with minimum 3.0 GPA; application with $50 fee; personal statement; 3 letters of recommendation, official transcripts, and admissions interview. MA program may be completed in 1–6 years, part- of full-time. Psychology prerequisites need: general or introductory psychology, abnormal, developmental, and a psychology elective. Studio art prerequisites required for art therapy are a minimum of one 3-unit semester class in each medium: painting, drawing, ceramics, sculpture, and printmaking.

Degree Requirements: MA degrees require minimum 3.0 GPA for graduation and completion of prescribed curriculum; can be completed in 2 to 6 years. Counseling or Art Therapy Internship requires the completion of 600–700 clock hours.

Distinctive Educational Programs: The college is guided by a transformational approach to education which is holistic, person-centered, reflective, and experiential. Programs focus on a balanced blending of transitional, holistic, and transpersonal methods of counseling and art therapy. Year One classes offered include counseling psychology, group dynamics, applied theories of human development, and psychology of consciousness and lifestyle. Year two classes include: assessment, applied ethics, cross-cultural issues in counseling, and art therapy techniques. Programs conclude with an internship in a mental health setting.

Fees and Other Expenses: Contact the college for current information regarding tuition and fees.

Departments and Teaching Staff: *Total instructional faculty:* full and adjunct faculty: 36.

Library Collections: 20,000 books, journals, audiovisual materials.

Quimby Collection contains rare metaphysical books as well as the professional collection in counseling, art therapy, and grief and loss.

Buildings and Grounds: Campus area 2.5acres.

Chief Executive Officer: Dr. Marylou Butler, President.

Address admissions inquiries to Director of Admissions.

University of New Mexico

Albuquerque, New Mexico 87131-1001

Tel: (505) 277-0111   **E-mail:** apply@unm.edu
Fax: (505) 277-1981   **Internet:** www.unm.edu

Institution Description: University of New Mexico is a state institution with branch campuses at Gallup, Los Alamos, Valencia, and Taos plus graduate centers at Los Alamos and Santa Fe. *Enrollment:* 26,339. *Degrees awarded:* Associate, baccalaureate, first-professional (law, medicine, pharmacy), master's, doctorate.

Budget subject to approval by state governing boards.

Accreditation: *Regional:* NCA. *Professional:* accounting, athletic training, audiology, clinical lab scientist, clinical psychology, computer science, construction education, counseling, dance, dental hygiene, dentistry, dietetics, EMT-paramedic, engineering, journalism, law, medicine, music, nursing-midwifery, nursing, nursing education, occupational therapy, pharmacy, physical therapy, physician assisting, planning, psychology internship, public administration, public health, radiography, speech-language pathology, surgeon assisting, teacher education

History: Established as a normal school and chartered 1889; offered first instruction at postsecondary level 1892; awarded first degree (baccalaureate) 1894; opened as university 1898. *See* Dorothy Hughes, *Pueblo on the Mesa* (Albuquerque: University of New Mexico, 1939) for further information.

Institutional Structure: *Governing board:* University of New Mexico Board of Regents. Representation: 7 regents, governor of New Mexico, state superintendent of public instruction, ex officio. 7 voting. *Composition of institution:* Administrators 72 men / 13 women. Academic affairs/research headed by provost. Management/business/finances directed by vice president. Student affairs headed by vice president. Full-time instructional faculty 871 men / 252 women. Academic governance body, Faculty Senate, meets an average of 9 times per year.

Calendar: Semesters. Academic year Aug. to May. Freshmen admitted Aug., Jan.. Degrees conferred Aug., Dec., May. Formal commencement May, Dec. Summer session of 2 terms from June to Aug.

Characteristics of Freshmen: 74% of applicants accepted. 41% of accepted applicants enrolled.

Average secondary school rank 71st percentile. Mean SAT score 530 verbal, 520 mathematical. Mean ACT composite score 22.

33% of entering freshmen expected to graduate within 6 years. 87% of freshmen from New Mexico. Freshmen from 48 states and 7 foreign countries.

Admission: Rolling admissions plan. For fall acceptance, apply as early as end of first semester of senior year of secondary school, but not later than 1 month prior to beginning of class. Early acceptance available. *Requirements:* Either graduation from accredited secondary school with 4 units English, 3 mathematics, 2 natural science (including 1 biology, chemistry, or physics, with laboratory), 2 social studies (1 U.S. history), 2 foreign language; or GED. Additional requirements for some programs. Minimum GPA 2.0. *Entrance tests:* College Board SAT or ACT. Foreign students TOEFL. *For transfer students:* 2.0 minimum GPA (some departments higher); from 4- and 2-year accredited institutions maximum transfer credit limited only by residence requirement; correspondence/extension students 40 hours (no more than 30 hours correspondence).

College credit for postsecondary-level work completed in secondary school and for formal military coursework on basis of ACE recommendations.

Tutoring available. Developmental courses offered in summer session and regular academic year; credit given.

Degree Requirements: *For all associate degrees:* 60 credit hours; 1 term in residence. *For all baccalaureate degrees:* 128 credit hours; 2 terms in residence. *For all undergraduate degrees:* 2.0 GPA.

Fulfillment of some degree requirements and exemption from some beginning courses possible by passing College Board CLEP, AP, other standardized tests. *Grading system:* A–F; pass-fail; pass; withdraw (carries penalty, carries time limit).

Distinctive Educational Programs: Flexible meeting places and schedules, including off-campus centers (at Los Alamos, 93 miles away from main institution) and evening classes. Study in Mexico, Spain, Colombia, Italy, China, and Russia for credit and noncredit course offerings and adult education through Division of Continuing Education. Audiovisual, technical and graphic support services are provided by Instructional Media Services. Broadcasting mediums are offered by KNME-TV/Channel 5 and KUNM-FM radio station. *Other distinctive programs:* Delivery of live courses via Instructional Television Fixed Service (ITFS) to a variety of work sites. Office of International Technical Cooperation offers technical assistance in the field of international development.

ROTC: 23 Air Force and 13 Navy commissions awarded 2004.

Degrees Conferred: 41 *associate;* 2,790 *baccalaureate;* 1,073 *master's;* 195 *doctorate.* 243 *first-professional::* law 91; medicine 74; pharmacy 81.

Fees and Other Expenses: *Full-time tuition per academic year 2005–06:* undergraduate resident $3,360, nonresident $12,689; graduate resident $3,447, nonresident $13,444. *Required fees:* $574. *Room and board per academic year:* $5,576. Contact the university for tuition and fees for first-professional programs.

Financial Aid: Aid from institutionally generated funds is provided on the basis of academic merit, financial need, athletic ability, other criteria.

Financial aid to full-time, first-time undergraduate students: need-based scholarships/grants totaling $29,857,650, self-help $27,861,813, parent loans $503,210, tuition waivers $4,046,281, athletic awards $632,610; non-need-based scholarships/grants totaling $12,827,168, self-help $3,711,712, parent loans $626,265, tuition waivers $3,309,659, athletic awards $1,289,066. *Graduate aid:* 587 students received federal and state-funded fellowships/grants; 2,120 received federal and state-funded loans; 148 held college-assigned jobs; 766 received other fellowships/grants; 870 teaching assistantships awarded; 734 research assistantships awarded.

Departments and Teaching Staff: *Professors* 333, *associate professors* 233, *assistant professors* 208, *instructors/lecturers* 100, *part-time faculty* 526.

Total instructional faculty: 1,400 (full-time 874, part-time 526; women 614, men 786; members of minority groups 259). Total faculty with doctorate, first-professional, or other terminal degree 980. Student-to-faculty ratio: 19:1. Degrees held by full-time faculty: doctorate 61%, master's 21%, baccalaureate 5%. 88% hold terminal degrees. *Faculty development:* $130 million in grants for research. 59 faculty members awarded sabbaticals 2004–05.

Enrollment: Total enrollment 26,339. Undergraduate 17,289; graduate 9,030.

Characteristics of Student Body: *Ethnic/racial makeup:* number of Black non-Hispanic: 324; American Indian or Alaska Native: 1,193; Asian or Pacific Islander: 592; Hispanic: 6,258; White non-Hispanic: 8,269; unknown: 1,042. *Age distribution:* number under 18: 176; 18–19: 5,384; 20–21: 4,497; 22–24: 3,566; 25–29: 1,859; 30–39: 1,431; 40–49: 729; 50–64: 321; 65 and over: 17. 45% of student body attend summer sessions.

International Students: 906 nonresident aliens enrolled fall 2004. 160 students from Europe, 481 Asia, 135 Latin America, 23 Africa, 19 Canada; 4 Australia, 4 New Zealand, 31 other. Programs available to aid students whose native language is not English: English as a Second Language Program. Financial aid specifically designated for international students: 34 scholarship available annually to qualifying students.

Student Life: On-campus residence halls house 6.7% of student body. Residence halls for men constitute 20.5% of such space, for women 19%, for both sexes 60.5%. 3.5% of men join and 2.2% live in fraternities; 2.1% of women join and 1.4% live in sororities. 2% of married students request institutional housing; 1.5% are so housed. *Intercollegiate athletics:* men only: baseball, basketball, football, golf, skiing, soccer, tennis, track; women only: basketball, golf, gymnastics, skiing, softball, swimming, tennis, track, volleyball. *Special services:* Shuttle bus service from parking areas to main campus, Leisure Services, Wellness Center, Women's Ethic and Cultural Centers, University Skills Center, medical services. *Student publications, radio, television:* Daily newspaper, annual arts journal. Radio station KUNM broadcasts 168 hours per week. Television station KNME broadcasts 124 hours per week. *Surrounding community:* Albuquerque metropolitan area population 480,000. Served by mass transit bus system; airport and passenger rail service, both 2 miles from campus.

Publications: *American Poetry,* (triennially) first published 1983; *Hispanic American Historical Review* (quarterly) first published 1981; *Latin American Research Review* (triennially) first published 1965; *Journal of Anthropological Research* (quarterly) first published 1945, *MASS* (biannually) first published 1983; *Natural Resources Journal* (quarterly) first published 1960; *New America* (triennially) first published 1974; *New Mexico Business* (monthly) first published 1948; *New Mexico Historical Review* (quarterly) first published 1926, *New Mexico Law Review* (biannually) first published 1970; *New Mexico R&D Forum* (monthly) first published 1986; *New Mexico Studies in the Fine Arts* (annually) first published 1976; *Quantum* (biannually) first published 1984; *Southwestern Review of Management and Economics* (biannually) first published 1984; *The Tamarind Papers* (biannually) first published 1974; *American Literary Realism* first published 1967; *Shakespeare Studies* first published 1965.

Library Collections: 2,150,000 volumes (includes Medical and Law Libraries). 6.2 million microforms; 1.7 million audiovisual materials; 17,965 serial subscriptions. Online catalog. Students have access to online information retrieval services and the Internet.

Most important special holdings include New Mexicana and Spanish borderlands materials; John Donald Robb Archive of Southwestern Music; papers of New Mexican congressmen, including Pete Dominici; Doris Duke: Collection of Native American Oral History; John Gaw Meem: Collection of Southwestern Architecture.

Buildings and Grounds: Campus area over 600 acres.

Chief Executive Officer: Dr. Louis Caldera, President.

Address admission inquiries to Terry Babbitt, Director of Recruitment Services.

College of Arts and Sciences

Degree Programs Offered: *Baccalaureate* in American studies, anthropology, art, astrophysics, biology, chemistry, classics, communicative disorders, comparative literature, creative writing, criminal justice, economics, economics-philosophy, English, English-philosophy, family studies, French, geography, geology, German, history, journalism, Latin American studies, linguistics, mathematics, philosophy, physics, political science, Portuguese, psychology, religious studies, Russian studies, sign language interpreting, sociology, Spanish, communication; *master's* in American studies, anthropology, biology, chemistry, communicative disorders, comparative literature, economics, English, French, geography, geology, German studies, history, language sciences, Latin American studies, mathematics, philosophy, physics, political science, Portuguese, psychology, sociology, Spanish, communication; *doctorate* in American studies, anthropology, biology, chemistry, economics, English, geology, history, Ibero-American studies, romance languages, mathematics, optical sciences, philosophy, physics, political science, psychology, sociology.

Admission: Requirements from University College to College of Arts and Sciences: 25 hours of earned credit, 23 of which must be acceptable toward graduation; cumulative GPA of at least 2.0 on hours attempted or a cumulative GPA of 2.0 on last 30 hours; demonstrated competence in the writing of English; any exceptions to the above must be approved by the Dean.

Degree Requirements: Minimum 96 hours of courses taught by Arts and Sciences departments; total of 128 acceptable hours; scholarship index of at least 2.0; 42 hours of courses numbered 300 or above with at least a 2.0 average on all hours attempted; major and minor or a double major; demonstration of competence in the writing of English; subsequent to admissions, one semester of resident enrollment; minimum of 6 semester hours of courses taught by Arts and Sciences departments while enrolled in the College of Arts and Sciences.

Distinctive Educational Programs: Cooperative education. Interdisciplinary programs in Afro-American studies, American studies, Asian studies, Chicano studies, classics, comparative literature, English-philosophy, Ibero-American studies, Latin American studies, native American studies, paleocology, philosophy-education, religious studies, Russian studies, women's studies. Combined curricula with Anderson School of Management, College of Engineering. Caswell Silver Foundation. Institute of Meteorites. Institute of Modern Optics. Office of Contract Archaeology.

College of Education

Degree Programs Offered: *Associate* elementary/preprofessional, secondary preprofessional, elementary/option I, secondary option II, community/teacher aides, special education paraprofessional training; *baccalaureate* in art education, arts in recreation, elementary education, secondary education, family studies education, family studies, child development and family relations, school health education, community health education, physical education, nutrition/dietetics, exercise technology, athletic training, recreation, business education, industrial education, industrial technical education, occupational education; *master's* in adult and community education, art education, elementary school counseling, secondary school counseling, mental health counseling, elementary education, secondary education, educational administration, educational foundations, family studies, health education, physical education, recreation, special education, technological and occupational education; *doctorate* in adult and community education, counseling psychology, counseling, multicultural teacher and childhood education, secondary education, educational administration, psychological foundations, educational linguistics, educational

thought and sociocultural studies, health education, physical education, recreation, special education, technological and occupational education. *Education Specialist certificate programs* in adult and community education, counselor education, elementary education, secondary education, educational administration, health education, physical education, recreation, special education, technological and occupational education.

Admission: Varies by program.

Degree Requirements: Varies by program.

School of Engineering

Degree Programs Offered: *Baccalaureate* in chemical engineering, civil engineering, computer engineering, computer science, construction engineering, construction management, electrical engineering, manufacturing and robotics engineering, mechanical engineering, nuclear engineering; *master's* in chemical engineering, civil engineering, computer science, electrical engineering, hazardous waste engineering, manufacturing engineering, mechanical engineering, nuclear engineering; *doctorate* in computer science, engineering, optical sciences.

Admission: Completion of 26 hours of acceptable credit with 2.2 GPA, or direct admission with acceptable high school record and test scores.

Degree Requirements: Completion of all work outlined in respective curricula; at least a 2.0 GPA.

Distinctive Educational Programs: Extensive television delivery capability throughout New Mexico; graduate instructional programs in manufacturing engineering, waste management, applied mechanics, electro-optics, inorganic materials, signal processing, pulsed power, and other areas. Major research facilities in materials, opto-electronics, space nuclear power, and high power devices and systems. Substantial joint research programs with Sandia National Laboratories, Los Alamos National Laboratory, and the Air Force Research Laboratory. Undergraduate programs for Hispanic, Native American, Black, and women students to increase retention and interest. Undergraduate co-op program.

College of Fine Arts

Degree Programs Offered: *Baccalaureate* in art history, art studio, media arts, music, music education, theatre, dance; *master's* in art history, art studio, music, music education, theatre, dance; *MFA* in art studio, dramatic writing; *doctorate* in art history.

Admission: Completion of 26 hours of earned credit; GPA of at least 2.5; competency in English writing; 12 completed credit hours in coursework in the major area.

Degree Requirements: Minimum 128 hours; GPA of 2.0 or higher; minimum of 12 semesters earned while enrolled in college; core curriculum courses completed with a grade of C or better.

Distinctive Educational Programs: Arts of the Americas Institute, Composers' Symposium, Flamenco dance, Native American art history, photography and photo history, Arts Technology Center, Tamarind Institute printer training program.

The Robert O. Anderson School and Graduate School of Management

Degree Programs Offered: *Baccalaureate* in management; *master's* in accounting, management.

Admission: Minimum requirements for transfer to Anderson School from the University College, degree-granting colleges, nondegree status, and other institutions: 55 hours of earned credit; minimum scholarship index of 2.0 (UNM cumulative); satisfactory competence in written communications.

Degree Requirements: Completion of all pre-admission requirements; completion of minimum of 128 hours (excluding physical education activity courses, management courses for nonmajors, math 120, and university skills courses) with the scholastic index of at least 2.0 on all semester hours attempted at UNM; completion of minimum of 53 hours in management courses and economics; transfer students from other universities must take a minimum of 24 hours in economics and management courses while enrolled at the Anderson School.

Distinctive Educational Programs: Dual-degree programs with other units of the university: MBA/JD; MBA/MA in Latin American studies; MBA program for full-time executives; master of accounting program.

College of Nursing

Degree Programs Offered: *Baccalaureate* in nursing, basic and RN completion; *master's* in nursing with 6 concentrations including Graduate Nurse Practitioner specialty, Certified Nurse Midwifery specialty and BSN/MSN Articulation Program.

Admission: 2.5 GPA.

Degree Requirements: 134 credit hours in basic baccalaureate program; degree completion program for Registered Nurses (upper division). *Master's program has 2 plans: Plan I is 39 credits and includes thesis; Plan II is non-thesis and requires 42 credits.*

Distinctive Educational Programs: Special approval by military for RN completion. Joint master's Latin-American dual-degree program and Public Health/Nursing as a dual-degree program. W.K. Kellogg Health Promotion interdisciplinary program. Practicum offers nursing in ethnically diverse populations, Hispanic and Indian Pueblos, Navajo, in addition to modern hospital tertiary centers.

School of Architecture and Planning

Degree Programs Offered: *Baccalaureate* in architecture, environmental design; *master's* in architecture, community and regional planning, landscape architecture.

Admission: *For first-professional:* 3.0 GPA; for 1- and 2-year programs, baccalaureate in architecture; for 3½-year program, baccalaureate.

Degree Requirements: *For first-professional:* 3.0 GPA; for 1-, 2-, and 3½-year programs, 32, 48, and 64 credit hours respectively.

Distinctive Educational Programs: Interdisciplinary joint degree master's program with the School of Public Administration, the Latin American Institute, the Program in Public Health and Architecture Program. Sophisticated computing laboratories for architectural design, planning, and landscape architecture. Architecture master's degree emphases in history/theory, technology, community-based design and professional practice. Master's degree emphases in community and regional planning in environmental and natural resource planning, and community development. Landscape architecture master's degree emphases in southwestern xeriscape design, natural resources and sustainable development, and cultural landscape history and realism.

School of Law

Degree Programs Offered: *First-professional:* law.

Admission: Baccalaureate from accredited college or university, LSAT.

Degree Requirements: 86 credit hours, 2.0 GPA, full first-year curriculum, professional responsibility course, 6 hours clinical field courses, writing requirement.

Distinctive Educational Programs: Joint master's-J.D. program in public administration. Joint J.D.-M.B.A. programs. Natural resources program. Clinical facilities.

School of Medicine

Degree Programs Offered: *Associate* in human services, radiologic technology, respiratory therapy; *baccalaureate* in medical technology, physical therapy; *master's* in medical sciences; *doctorate* in medical sciences; *first-professional* in medicine.

Admission: Varies by program.

Degree Requirements: Varies by program.

College of Pharmacy

Degree Programs Offered: *Doctor of pharmacy* (Pharm.D), *master's* in pharmacy administration, hospital pharmacy, radiopharmacy, toxicology; *doctorate* in pharmacy administration, toxicology.

Admission: *For first-professional:* Baccalaureate from an accredited college or university.

Distinctive Educational Programs: Certificate and ASHP Approved Residency in radiopharmacy; master's degree in radiopharmacy; certificate in waste management in conjunction with WERC program.

Division of Dental Programs

Degree Programs Offered: *Baccalaureate* in dental hygiene; degree completion program.

Admission: *Baccalaureate:* completion of all courses in the preprofessional curriculum with overall GPA of 2.4 on a 4.0 scale. *Degree completion program:* graduation from an accredited dental hygiene program; 2.5 GPA for all previous college training.

Division of Public Administration

Degree Programs Offered: *Master's* in public administration (MPA).

Admission: Baccalaureate degree from an accredited college or university; GPA of at least 3.0 on a 4.0 scale during last 2 years of undergraduate work, or (MPA) Graduate Record Examination.

Degree Requirements: Completion of a minimum of 42 credit hours thesis or non-thesis options (MPA); 36 credit hours (MWRA) non-thesis.

Distinctive Educational Programs: Concentration in justice administration, health services administration, human resources management, dispute resolution, public management, and public budgeting.

University College

Degree Programs Offered: *Baccalaureate* in University Studies.

Admission: Accredited high school graduation with minimum C average; 4 units English, 3 units mathematics, 2 units foreign language; College Board SAT or ACT composite.

Degree Requirements: Minimum 128 semester hours of earned credit; minimum 50 semester hours earned in upper division level; 2.0 GPA; fulfillment of residence credit requirements.

Distinctive Educational Programs: Individualized program of studies including intercollege and interdepartmental course combinations.

Western New Mexico University

1000 West College Avenue
Silver City, New Mexico 88061
Tel: (505) 538-6106 **E-mail:** admissions@wnmu.edu
Fax: (505) 538-6155 **Internet:** www.wnmu.edu

Institution Description: Western New Mexico University is a state institution. *Enrollment:* 2,751. *Degrees awarded:* Associate, baccalaureate, master's.

Academic offerings subject to approval by statewide coordinating bodies. Budget subject to approval by state governing boards.

Accreditation: *Regional:* NCA. *Professional:* teacher education

History: Established and chartered as Territorial Normal School 1893, offered first instruction at postsecondary level 1894; awarded first degree (baccalaureate) 1924; adopted present name 1963. *See* Donald Overturf, *History of Western New Mexico University* (Lincoln, NE: University of Nebraska, 1960) for further information.

Institutional Structure: *Governing board:* Board of Regents. Representation: 5 regents, state governor, state superintendent of public instruction. 2 ex officio. 1 student. 5 voting. *Composition of institution:* Administrators 14 men / 16 women. Academic affairs headed by vice president for academic affairs. Management/business/finances directed by business manager. Full-time instructional faculty 90. Academic governance body, Faculty Senate, meets an average of 9 times per year.

Calendar: Semesters. Academic year July to June. Freshmen admitted Aug., Jan., June, July. Degrees conferred May, Aug., Dec. Formal commencements May, Dec. Summer session of 2 terms from early June to early Aug.

Characteristics of Freshmen: 100% of applicants accepted. 76% of accepted applicants enrolled.

Mean ACT class score 17.

90% of freshmen from New Mexico. Freshmen from 10 states.

Admission: Rolling admissions plan. For fall acceptance, apply no later than Aug. 15. Early acceptance available. *Requirements:* Either graduation from accredited secondary school or GED. Minimum GPA 2.0. *Entrance tests:* ACT composite. For foreign students minimum TOEFL score 550.

College credit and advanced placement for postsecondary-level work completed in secondary school. College credit for extrainstitutional learning on basis of ACE *2006 Guide to the Evaluation of Educational Experiences in the Armed Services.*

Tutoring available. Developmental courses offered in summer session and regular academic year; credit given.

Degree Requirements: *For all associate degrees:* 64 credit hours. *For all baccalaureate degrees:* 128 credit hours. *For all undergraduate degrees:* 2.0 GPA; 16 credit hours in residence; 4 physical education courses; general education requirements.

Fulfillment of some degree requirements and exemption from some beginning courses possible by passing College Board CLEP, AP. *Grading system:* A–F, withdraw.

Distinctive Educational Programs: Evening classes. Preprofessional programs in engineering, forestry, medicine, pharmacy, veterinary science. Facilities and programs for independent research, including individual majors, tutorials.

Degrees Conferred: 103 *associate;* 141 *baccalaureate;* 128 *master's.* Bachelor's degrees awarded in top five disciplines: education 47; business, management, marketing, and related support services 28; liberal arts and sciences, general studies, and humanities 14; psychology 12; public administration 7.

Fees and Other Expenses: *Full-time tuition per academic year 2004–05:* resident undergraduate $2,557, nonresident $9,565. Contact the university for tuition and fees for graduate study. *Books and supplies:* $1,000. *Room and board per academic year:* $4,466.

Financial Aid: Aid from institutionally generated funds is provided on the basis of academic merit, financial need, other criteria. Institution has Program Participation Agreement with the U.S. Department of Education for eligible students to receive Pell Grants and, depending upon the agreement, other federal aid.

Financial aid to full-time, first-time undergraduate students: 72% received federal grants averaging $2,997; 8% state/local grants averaging $1,600; 23% institutional grants averaging $1,252; 31% received loans averaging $2,917.

Departments and Teaching Staff: *Professors* 22, *associate professors* 29, *assistant professors* 31, *instructors* 7, *part-time faculty* 55. *Total instructional faculty:* 135. Student-to-faculty ratio: 16:1. Degrees held by full-time faculty: doctorate 60%, master's 23%, baccalaureate 5%, professional 12%.

Enrollment: Total enrollment 2,751. Undergraduate 2,176 (men 36.4%, women 63.6%).

Characteristics of Student Body: *Ethnic/racial makeup:* number of Black non-Hispanic: 2.8%; American Indian or Alaska Native: 21%; Asian or Pacific Islander: .8%; Hispanic: 45.7%; White non-Hispanic: 39.8%; unknown: .8%.

International Students: 21 nonresident aliens enrolled fall 2004. No programs available to aid students whose native language is not English. No financial aid specifically designated for international students.

Student Life: On-campus residence halls house 12% of student body. Residence halls for men constitute 44% of such space, for women 56%. 91% of married students request institutional housing and are so housed. *Intercollegiate athletics:* men only: basketball, football, golf, tennis; women only: basketball, golf, tennis, volleyball. *Special regulations:* Cars permitted without restrictions. Quiet hours. Residence hall visitation from 7pm to midnight. *Student publications: Mustang,* a newspaper; *Westerner,* a yearbook. *Surrounding community:* Silver City population 14,000. Paso (TX), 150 miles from campus, is nearest metropolitan area. Served by airport 20 miles from campus.

Library Collections: 246,000 volumes. 2,000 government documents; 528,000 microforms; 7,300 audiovisual materials; 235 current periodical subscriptions. Online catalog. Students have access to online information retrieval services and the Internet.

Most important holdings include Library of American Civilization (19,000 volumes on microform); local newspapers on microfilm (pre-1900 to present day).

Buildings and Grounds: Campus area 307 acres.

Chief Executive Officer: Dr. John E. Counts, President.

Address admission inquiries to Michael Aleckson, Director of Admissions.